G.K. Hall Bibliographic Guide to Psychology

2003

G.K. HALL
An imprint of Thomson Gale, a part of The Thomson Corporation

Detroit • New York • San Francisco • San Diego • New Haven, Conn. • Waterville, Maine • London • Munich

Ref.
Z
7203
.B582
2003

G.K. Hall Bibliographic Guide to Psychology

Product Manager
Peg Bessette

Project Editor
Marie Toft

Product Design
Kate Scheible

Manufacturing
Lori Kessler

© 2004 Thomson Gale, a part of The Thomson Corporation.

Thomson, Star Logo and G.K. Hall are trademarks and Gale is a registered trademark used herein under license.

For more information, contact
G.K. Hall
27500 Drake Rd.
Farmington Hills, MI 48331-3535
Or you can visit our Internet site at
http://www.gale.com

ALL RIGHTS RESERVED
No part of this work covered by the copyright hereon may be reproduced or used in any form or by any means—graphic, electronic or mechanical, including photocopying, recording, taping, Web distribution, or information storage retrieval systems—without the written permission of the publisher.

For permission to use material from this product, submit your request via the Web at http://www.gale-edit.com/permissions, or you may download our Permission Request form and submit your request by fax or mail to:

Permissions
G.K. Hall
27500 Drake Rd.
Farmington Hills, MI 48331-3535
Permissions Hotline:
248-699-8006 or 800-877-4253, ext. 8006
Fax: 248-699-8074 or 800-762-4058

While every effort has been made to ensure the reliability of the information presented in this publication, Thomson Gale does not guarantee the accuracy of the data contained herein. Thomson Gale accepts no payment for listing; and inclusion in the publication of any organization, agency, institution, publication, service, or individual does not imply endorsement of the editors or publisher. Errors brought to the attention of the publisher and verified to the satisfaction of the publisher will be corrected in future editions.

ISBN 0-7838-0481-4
ISSN 0360-277X

Printed in the United States of America
10 9 8 7 6 5 4 3 2 1

Preface

G.K. Hall Bibliographic Guides are comprehensive annual subject bibliographies. They bring together recent publications cataloged by The Research Libraries of The New York Public Library and the Library of Congress for thorough subject coverage. This edition includes selected materials cataloged during the last ten years. Included are works in all languages and all forms—non-book materials as well as books and serials.

G.K. Hall Bibliographic Guides provide complete LC cataloging information for each title, as well as ISBN. Access is by main entry (personal author, corporate body, name of conference, etc.), added entries (co-authors, editors, compilers, etc.), titles, series titles, and subject headings. All entries are integrated into one alphabetical sequence. Filing is on a character-by-character basis in alphanumeric sequence, with numbers preceding letters. Full bibliographic information, including tracings, is given in the main entry, with abbreviated or condensed citations for secondary entries. In certain records, the term *in process* is used to denote titles not yet assigned a call number by the Library of Congress. Subject headings appear in capital letters in boldface type. Cataloging follows the *Anglo-American Cataloging Rules*. The following is a sample entry with full bibliographic information:

(a) Domhoff, G. William. (b) Finding meaning in dreams: **(c)** a quantitative approach / G. William Domhoff. **(d)** New York: **(e)** Plenum Press, **(f)** c1996. **(g)** xiv, 356 p. **(h)** ill. ; 24 cm. **(i)** (Emotions, personality, and psychotherapy) **(j)** Book includes much of Calvin Hall's thinking and unpublished work. Includes bibliographical references (p. 335-346). **(k)** ISBN 0-306-45172-7 **(l)** DDC 154.6/34 **(m)** *1. Hall, Calvin S. - (Calvin Springer), - 1909-1985. - Content analysis of dreams. 2. Dreams. I. Hall, Calvin S. (Calvin Springer), 1909-1985* **(n)** *II. Title. III. Series.* **(o)** *BF1078.D577 1996*

(a) Author's name.

(b) Short, or main, title.

(c) Subtitle and/or other title page information.

(d) Plate of publication.

(e) Publisher.

(f) Date of publication.

(g) Pagination.

(h) Illustration statement.

(i) Series.

(j) Note(s).

(k) ISBN.

(l) DDC number.

PREFACE

(m) Subject heading.

(n) Added entry.

(o) LC Call number.

G.K. Hall Bibliographic Guides offer easy, multiple access to a wealth of material in various subject areas. They serve as authoritative reference sources for librarians and scholars, valuable technical aids for library acquisition and cataloging, and useful research tools for students and library patrons.

G.K. Hall Bibliographic Guides for 2003 are available in nineteen fields:

Anthropology and Archaeology

Art and Architecture

Black Studies

Business and Economics

Conference Publications

Dance

East Asian Studies

Education

Government Publications-Foreign

Government Publications-U.S.

Latin American Studies

Law

Maps and Atlases

Music

North American History

Psychology

Slavic, Baltic, and Eurasian Studies

Technology

Theatre Arts

Introduction

The *G.K. Hall Bibliographic Guide to Psychology* lists recent publications cataloged during the past year by the Library of Congress and The Research Libraries of The New York Public Library. Selection of titles from LC MARC tapes is based on the LC classification *BF*. Entries from NYPL are selected on the following basis: if an NYPL record contains two or more subject headings that correspond to two or more LC subject headings from MARC psychology records, then that NYPL record is included in this *Guide*. LC subject headings from all psychology records in the entire MARC database are scanned to provide comprehensive selection of NYPL psychology titles.

The following major subject areas in psychology are included in the *Guide*:

- Applied psychology
- Child psychology
- Cognition, Perception, Intelligence
- Comparative psychology
- Emotion
- Genetic psychology
- Graphology
- Occult sciences (Including demonology, witchcraft, astrology)
- Parapsychology (including dreams, hypnotism, telepathy, hallucinations, sleep)
- Personality
- Phrenology
- Physiognomy
- Sensation
- Temperament, Character
- Will

10-minute magic spells.
Alexander, Skye. Gloucester, Mass. : Fair Winds Press, 2003.
BF1611 .A43 2003

10-minute tarot.
Alexander, Skye. Gloucester, Mass. : Fair Winds Press, c2003.
BF1879.T2 A445 2003

10 sure signs a movie character is doomed, and other surprising movie lists.
Roeper, Richard, 1959- 1st ed. New York : Hyperion, c2003.
PN1998 .R568 2003

100 thoughts that lead to happiness.
Chetkin, Len. Charlottesville, VA : Hampton Roads Pub., c2002.
BF637.C5 C477 2002

1000 A.D. *See* **ONE THOUSAND, A.D.**

1000 primet pogody.
Turovich, V. (Vasiliĭ) Perm' : Izd-vo "Poligrafist", 1997.
BF1777 .T87 1997

1000 symbols.
Shepherd, Rowena. New York : Thames & Hudson, 2002.
BF458 .S63 2002

10,000 ways to say I love you.
Godek, Gregory J. P., 1955- Naperville, Ill. : Casablanca Press, c1999.
BF575.L8 G63 1999

The 1000s / Brenda Stalcup, book editor. San Diego, Calif. : Greenhaven Press, c2001. 314 p. : ill., maps ; 24 cm. (Headlines in history) Includes bibliographical references (p. 299-303) and index. CONTENTS: Awaiting the Apocalypse -- Rise of feudalism -- Peace of God movement -- Truce of God for the diocese of cologne -- Papal reform -- Investiture controversy -- Limitations of royal authority -- Norman conquest -- William the conqueror's claim to the english throne -- Normans in Italy and Sicily -- Chapter 2 -- Viking discovery of North America -- Relations with the native Americans -- Iceland's conversion to christianity -- Viking rulers of England -- End of the viking age -- Chapter 3 -- Origin of the first crusade -- Pope Urban's call for the first crusade -- Speech at clermont -- Peasants' crusade -- Byzantine's view of the first crusaders -- Victory and atrocities: Conquest of Jerusalem -- Muslim perspective on the first crusade -- Chapter 4 -- Turks' rise to power -- Reign of the mad caliph -- Culture and society of Muslim Spain -- Battles between the spanish christians and muslims -- Terms of surrender: El Cid at valencia -- Muslim dominion in India -- Golden age of the kingdom of Ghana -- Chapter 5 -- Life in China during the early sung dynasty -- Economic reform and trade development -- Importance of the intellectual class -- Proposals for the training and selection of government officials -- Priting's contribution to literacy and education -- Growth of a native culture i Japan -- Murasaki Shikibu's literacy achievement -- Art of storytelling -- Chapter 6 -- Toltecs of Mexico -- Toltec conquest of the maya -- Anasazi culture at its height -- Were the anasazi cannibals -- Mound builders of Cahokia. ISBN 0-7377-0527-2 (pbk. : alk. paper) ISBN 0-7377-0528-0 (lib. : alk. paper) DDC 940.1/46
1. Eleventh century. 2. Civilization, Medieval. 3. Middle Ages - History. 4. Crusades - First, 1096-1099. 5. Indians - History. 6. Asia - History. I. Stalcup, Brenda. II. Title: One thousands III. Series.
CB354.3 .A16 2001

101 ways black women can learn to love themselves.
Walker, Jamie. Washington, D.C. : J.D. Publishing, c2002.

12 Weltanschauungen.
Grünewald, Lars. Zwölf Weltanschauungen. 1. Aufl. Borchen : Ch. Möllmann, 2001.

The 15-second principle.
Secunda, Al. Franklin Lakes, NJ : Career Press, 2004.
BF637.S4 S43 2004

The 1500s / Stephen Currie, book editor. San Diego, Calif : Greenhaven Press, c2001. 304 p. : ill., maps ; 24 cm. (Headlines in history) Includes bibliographical references (p. 293-295) and index. CONTENTS: Chapter 1 -- Elizabeth I and Mary, queen of scots -- Battle of Lepanto: Last crusade -- Huguenots and catholics in France -- Russia and Ivan the terrible -- Freebooters and sea dogs: Pirates of the spanish main -- Henry VIII and Thomas More: Conscience versus politics -- Chapter 2 -- Lost colony: Roanoke -- Singing the King's beard: Exploits of Francis Drake -- Spanish Armada: Less than invincible -- Chapter 3 -- Superstition and the sixteenth-century worldview -- Renaissance city life -- Pre-Shakespearean drama -- Apparel and attire -- Gregorian calendar -- Copernican revolution -- Shakespeare -- Chapter 4 -- Michelangelo -- Renaissance painting -- Science, art, and the renaissance -- Leonardo da Vinci -- Chapter 5 -- Church in 1500 -- Justification by faith: Early lutheran thought -- Luther and the diet of worms -- John Calvin: Philosophy of protestantism -- Counter reformation -- Chapter 6 -- Atlantic slave trade -- North African culture -- Suleyman the magnificent -- Japan and the west -- Mughal empire of India -- Expanding the menu -- Chapter 7 -- Portuguese arrival in Brazil -- Magellan in the pacific -- Northeast passage: Search of the impossible grail -- Maps and atlases -- Chapter 8 -- Massacre and siege -- End of empire -- Fall of the Inca. ISBN 0-7377-0538-8 ISBN 0-7377-0537-X (pbk.) DDC 940.1
1. Civilization, Medieval. 2. Sixteenth century. 3. Europe - Civilization - 16th century. I. Currie, Stephen, 1960- II. Series: Headlines in history (San Diego, Calif.)
CB367 .A165 2001

The 16PF fifth edition administrator's manual.
Russell, Mary T. 3rd ed. Champaign, Ill. : Institute for Personality and Ability Testing, 2002.
BF698.8.S5 A37 2002

1816.
Skeen, Carl Edward. Lexington : University Press of Kentucky, c2003.
E341 .S57 2003

20:21 vision.
Emmott, Bill. London : Allen Lane, 2003.

20 shi ji Chao ren wen hua cui ying cong shu
Luo, Zongqiang. Luo Zongqiang gu dai wen xue si xiang lun ji. Di 1 ban. Shantou Shi : Shantou da xue chu ban she, 1999.
PL2264 .L95 1999

20. vek : metodologicheskie problemy istoricheskogo poznaniĭa.
XX vek. Moskva : INION RAN, 2001-

2000 years and beyond : faith, identity and the 'common era' / edited by Paul Gifford ... [et al.]. London ; New York : Routledge, 2003. ix, 227 p., [1] leaf of plates : ill. ; 22 cm. Includes bibliographical references (p. 191-219) and index. ISBN 0-415-27807-4 (hbk.) ISBN 0-415-27808-2 (pbk.) DDC 200/.9/0511
1. Christianity. 2. Religion. 3. Christianity - Forecasting. 4. Humanism. 5. Capitalism - Religious aspects - Christianity. 6. Postmodernism - Religious aspects - Christianity. I. Gifford, Paul, 1944- II. Title: Two thousand years and beyond
BR53 .T86 2003

2001, año de las Naciones Unidas del diálogo entre civilizaciones. Guatemala : Fundación Casa de la Reconciliación : MINUGUA, 2001. 40 p. ; 21 cm. "Mensaje de Su Santidad Juan Pablo II para la celebración de la Jornada Mundial de la Paz, 1 de enero de 2001"--P. 21-40.
1. United Nations. 2. Peace. I. John Paul II, Pope, 1920- II. Fundación Casa de la Reconciliación. III. Misión de las Naciones Unidas de Verificación de los Derechos Humanos y del Cumplimiento de los Compromisos del Acuerdo Global sobre Derechos Humanos en Guatemala. IV. Title: Año de las Naciones Unidas del diálogo entre civilizaciones
JX1952 .A233 2001

2001 ony shildėg nom
Khurmetbek, Khalikiĭn. Ŭl bichigdmėlŭŭd. Ulaanbaatar : "Monsudar" Khėvlėliĭn Gazar, 2001.
QA465 .K48 2001

The 2030 spike.
Mason, Colin, 1926- London ; Sterling, VA : Earthscan Publications, 2003.
CB161 .M384 2003

The 20th-century muse.
Vezin, Annette. [Egéries dans l'ombre des créateurs. English] New York : Harry N. Abrams, 2003.
N71 .V4913 2003

21. Goldegger Dialoge : Gesundheit ist lernbar : "Grenzen sprengen, Mitte finden" / [Tagungsband mit Beiträgen von Doris Bach ... et al.]. 1. Aufl. Goldegg : Kulturverein Schloss Goldegg, 2002. 164 p. : ill. ; 21 cm. + 1 booklet (1 v. : ill. ; 20 cm.). Includes bibliographical references. Booklet (Seconds / Markus Schinwald) in pocket. ISBN 3-901152-20-2
1. Conformity - Congresses. 2. Social norms - Congresses. 3. Social control - Congresses. 4. Social influence - Congresses. I. Bach, Doris. II. Title: Grenzen sprengen, Mittle finden

21 ideas for managers.
Handy, Charles B. 1st ed. San Francisco : Jossey-Bass, c2000.
HD31 .H31259 2000

21ST CENTURY. *See* **TWENTY-FIRST CENTURY.**

21st century's new chakra healing.
Nudel, Michael. Los Angeles, CA : Bio-Energy System Services, c2000.
BF1999 .N83 2000

25 things to do when grandpa passes away, mom and dad get divorced, or the dog dies.
Kanyer, Laurie A., 1959- Seatte Wash., : Parenting Press, 2004.
BF723.G75 K36 2003

365 glorious nights of love and romance.
Darbo, Patrika. 1st ed. New York : ReganBooks, c2002.
HQ46 .D35 2002

40 years of Philippine psychology.
Forty years of Philippine psychology. Diliman, Quezon City, Philippines : Psychological Association of the Philippines, c2002.
BF108 .F67 2002

5 secrets of teen success.
Mawi Asgedom. The code. New York : Little, Brown, 2003.
BF724.3.S9 M34 2003

500 reasons why you're my best friend.
Bodger, Lorraine. Kansas City, Mo. : Andrews McMeel Pub., c2003.
BF575.F66 B63 2003

52 reflections on the faith we sing.
Hickman, Martha Whitmore, 1925- Wade in the water. Nashville, TN : Abingdon Press, 2003.
BV310 .H53 2003

The 60 second procrastinator.
Davidson, Jeffrey P. Avon, MA : Adams Media Corp., c2003.
BF637.P76 D38 2003

8 best practices of high-performing salespeople.
Trainor, Norm, 1946- The eight best practices of high-performing salespeople. Toronto ; New York : Wiley, c2000.
HF5438.25 .T72 2000

8th International Conference on Motivation.
International Conference on Motivation (8th : 2002 Moscow, Russia) Moscow : Russian State University for Humanities, 2002.
BF501.5 .I58 2002

9-11 in American culture / edited by Norman K. Denzin and Yvonna S. Lincoln. Walnut Creek ; Oxford : AltaMira Press, c2003. xxi, 290 p. : ill. ; 24 cm. Includes bibliographical references. ISBN 0-7591-0349-6 (cloth : alk. paper) ISBN 0-7591-0350-X (pbk. : alk. paper) DDC 973.931
1. September 11 Terrorist Attacks, 2001 - Miscellanea. I. Denzin, Norman K. II. Lincoln, Yvonna S. III. Title: Nine-eleven in American culture
HV6432.7 .A13 2003

9 journeys home.
Mandel, Robert Steven, 1943- Berkeley : Celestial Arts, c2003.
BF575.S4 M36 2003

A che servono i simboli? / a cura di Vincenzo Loriga e Sergio Caruso. Milano : FrancoAngeli, c2002. 223 p. : ill. ; 22 cm. (La ginestra ; 10) Includes bibliographical references. ISBN 88-464-3454-4 DDC 398
1. Symbolism. 2. Signs and symbols. I. Loriga, Vincenzo. II. Caruso, Sergio. III. Series.

A la recherche de l'homme.
Picq, Pascal G. Paris : Nil, c2002.
GN281 .P48 2002

A partes iguales.
Jordan, Denise. [Your fair share. Spanish] Chicago : Heinemann Library, c2004.
BF723.S428 J6718 2003

The A-Z of postmodern life.
Sardar, Ziauddin. London : Vision, c2002.

Aaltio-Marjosola, Iiris.
Gender, identity and the culture of organizations. London ; New York : Routledge, 2002.
HD58.7 .G46 2002

AARS.
Burney, DeAnna McKinnie. Odessa, FL (P.O. Box 998, Odessa, 33556) : Psychological Assessment Resources, c2001.
BF724.3.A55 B87 2001

Abadie, M. J. (Marie-Jeanne) Tarot for teens / M.J. Abadie. Rochester, Vt. : Bindu Books, c2002. vii, 245 p. : ill. ; 23 cm. CONTENTS: Getting to know the tarot -- The art of interpretation -- Preliminaries to reading -- The major arcana and their meanings -- More about the trumps -- Interpreting the major arcana in a reading -- The minor arcana -- Interpreting the minor arcana -- The wands -- The pentacles -- The swords -- The cups -- Spreads for readings. ISBN 0-89281-917-0 DDC 133.3/2424
1. Tarot - Juvenile literature. I. Title.

Abadie, M. J. (Marie-Jeanne)
BF1879.T2 A28 2002
Teen dream power : unlock the meaning of your dreams / M.J. Abadie. Rochester, Vt. : Bindu Books, 2003. xi, 206, [2] p. ; 23 cm. CONTENTS: What dreams can do for you -- Dream explorers around the world -- Interpretation of dreams -- Dreams and everyday life -- Dream recall -- Keeping a dream diary -- Creating your own dream dictionary -- Different states of dreaming -- Dreams and spiritual development. ISBN 0-89281-086-6 DDC 154.6/3/0835
1. Teenagers' dreams. 2. Dream interpretation. 3. Symbolism (Psychology) 4. Teenagers' dreams - Problems, exercises, etc. 5. Dreams. 6. Dream interpretation. I. Title.
BF1099 .T43 2003

ABANDONED CHILDREN. *See* **FOUNDLINGS.**

Abaya, Ma. Concepcion O. (Maria Concepcion O.).
Feminine voices. [Manila?] : NCCA, c2001-

Abbass, Hussein A.
Data mining. Hershey : Idea Group, c2002.
QA76.9.D343 D36 2002

Abbinnett, Ross. Culture and identity : critical theories / Ross Abbinnett. London ; Thousand Oaks, Ca. : SAGE, 2003. vii, 230 p. ; 25 cm. (Politics and culture. A Theory Culture & Society series) Includes bibliographical references (p. [217]-220) and index. ISBN 0-7619-6518-1 ISBN 0-7619-6519-X (PBK.) DDC 306
1. Culture. 2. Group identity. 3. Postmodernism. I. Title. II. Series: Politics and culture (London, England)
HM621 .A23 2003

Abbo of Fleury and Ramsay : commentary on the Calculus of Victorius of Aquitaine / edited by A.M. Peden. Oxford ; New York : Oxford University Press, 2002. liii, 159 p. : ill. ; 24 cm. Includes bibliographical references (p.[143] 148) and indexes. ISBN 0-19-726260-0 DDC 510.902
1. Victorius, - Aquitaine. - Calculus. 2. Abbo, - of Fleury, Saint, - ca. 945-1004. 3. Mathematics, Medieval. 4. Philosophy, Medieval. I. Peden, A. M. II. Series: Auctores Britannici Medii Aevi ; no. 15.

ABBO, OF FLEURY, SAINT, CA. 945-1004.
Abbo of Fleury and Ramsay. Oxford ; New York : Oxford University Press, 2002.

ABBREVIATIONS. *See* **SIGNS AND SYMBOLS.**

The ABCs of full tilt living.
Smith, Maureen (Maureen J.), 1947- Boston, MA : Red Wheel/Weiser, 2003.
BF637.C5 S5449 2003

ABC's of grief.
Adams, Christine A. Amityville, N.Y. : Baywood, c2003.
BF575.G7 A32 2003

Abdel Sayed, Gawdat Gabra.
Be thou there. Cairo ; New York : American University in Cairo Press, c2001.

Abel, Günter.
Neuzeitliches Denken. Berlin ; New York : De Gruyter, 2002.

ABELARD, PETER, 1079-1142.
Zerbi, Piero. "Philosophi" e "logici". Roma : Istituto storico italiano per il Medio Evo ; Milano : Vita e pensiero, 2002.
B765.A24 Z473 2002

ABELARD, PETER, 1079-1142 - CONTRIBUTIONS IN ETHICS.
Gill, Harjeet Singh, 1935- Signification in Buddhist and French traditions. New Delhi : Harman Pub. House, 2001.
BC25 .G55 2001

ABELARD, PETER, 1079-1142 - CONTRIBUTIONS IN THEOLOGY.
Gill, Harjeet Singh, 1935- Signification in Buddhist and French traditions. New Delhi : Harman Pub. House, 2001.
BC25 .G55 2001

Abelhauser, Alain, 1954- Le sexe et le signifiant : suites cliniques / Alain Abelhauser. Paris : Seuil, c2002. 352 p. ; 21 cm. (Champ freudien) Includes bibliographical references (p. [331]-[347]). ISBN 2-02-054001-0
1. Sex (Psychology) 2. Psychoanalysis. I. Title. II. Series.
BF175.5.S48 A24 2002

Abhandlungen zur Philosophie, Psychologie, Soziologie der Religion und Ökumenik
(n.F., Heft 50.) Hoffmann, Monika, 1972- Selbstliebe. Paderborn : Schöningh, c2002.
BF575.S37 H66 2002

ABHORRENCE. *See* **AVERSION.**

Abi-Ḥasira, Jacob ben Masoud, 1808-1880.
[Abir Ya'aḳov. Selections. 2002]
Sefer Penine Avir Ya'aḳov : leḳeṭ peninim, amarot, ḥidushim 'al Shir ha-shirim ... ha-mevusas 'al divre musar ... / mi-kol 12 sifre Ya'aḳov Aviḥatsira ; yotse le-or 'a. y. Shim'on b. ha-g. R. Y. Aviḥatsira. Yerushalayim : Hotsa'at ha-Makhon le-hotsa'at sefarim she-'a. y. Yeshivat Ner Yitshaḳ : Mekhon Avraham : Shim'on Abiḥatsira, 763 [2002] 198 p. ; 22 cm. Cover title: Penine Avir Ya'aḳov 'al Shir ha-shirim. Text and commentary vocalized.
1. Bible. - O.T. - Song of Solomon - Commentaries. 2. Cabala. I. Abiḥatsira, Shim'on ben Y. II. Ṭoledano, Avraham ben Shemu'el. III. Title. IV. Title: Bible. O.T. Song of Solomon. Hebrew. 2002. V. Title: Penine Avir Ya'aḳov 'al Shir ha-shirim
BS1485.X33 A25 2002

Magele tsedek.
Ḥalfon, Eliyahu ben Ḥayim. Shir ha-shirim.
[Israel] : Or tsaḥ hadpasah ve-hafatsah shel sipre Yahadut, [2001]

Abiḥatsira, Shim'on ben Y.
Abi-Ḥasira, Jacob ben Masoud, 1808-1880. [Abir Ya'aḳov. Selections. 2002] Sefer Penine Avir Ya'aḳov. Yerushalayim : Hotsa'at ha-Makhon le-hotsa'at sefarim she-'a. y. Yeshivat Ner Yitshaḳ : Mekhon Avraham : Shim'on Abiḥatsira, 763 [2002]
BS1485.X33 A25 2002

ABILITY. *See also* **CREATIVE ABILITY; EXPERTISE; INTELLECT; LEADERSHIP; MECHANICAL ABILITY; PSYCHIC ABILITY; SPATIAL ABILITY.**
Bryden, Barbara E., 1954- Sundial. Gainesville, FL : Center for Applications of Psychological Type, 2003.
BF698.3 .B79 2003

Shadrikov, V. D. (Vladimir Dmitrievich) Sposobnosti cheloveka. Moskva : In-t prakticheskoĭ psikhologii ; Voronezh : NPO "MODĖK", 1997.
BF431 .S46512 1997

ABILITY, INFLUENCE OF AGE ON. *See* **COGNITION - AGE FACTORS.**

ABILITY, MECHANICAL. *See* **MECHANICAL ABILITY.**

Abimbola, Idowu Hakeem.
Adeosun, Kola A. [Ọrọ ti obi n sọ. English] What the kolanut is saying. Ibadan, Nigeria : Creative Books, 1999.
BF1779.K6 A33 1999

Abitbul, Elisha'.
Abitbul, Yosef Ḥayim, d. 1998. Ma'agar ha-ḥalomot u-fitronam. Kiryat Gat : Elisha' Abitbul, 762 [2002]
BM496.9.D73 A25 2002

Abitbul, Yosef Ḥayim, d. 1998. Ma'agar ha-ḥalomot u-fitronam / Yosef Ḥayim Abitbul. Kiryat Gat : Elisha' Abitbul, 762 [2002] 169 p. : col. ill., ports. ; 25 cm. Includes bibliographical references.
1. Dreams - Religious aspects - Judaism. 2. Dream interpretation. I. Abitbul, Elisha'. II. Title.
BM496.9.D73 A25 2002

Aboab, Isaac, 14th cent.
[Menorat ha-ma'or. Ladino]
Una cala en la literatura religiosa sefardí : La almenara de la luz / Purificación Albarral Albarral. Granada : Universidad de Granada, 2001. 317 p. ; 21 cm. (Monográfica ; 264. Crítica literaria) Includes bibliographical references (p. [299]-313) and indexes. Spanish and romanized Ladino. ISBN 84-338-2779-0
1. Ethics, Jewish. I. Albarral Albarral, Purificación. II. Title. III. Series: Monográfica ; 264. IV. Series: Monográfica. Crítica literaria.
BJ1287.A152 L33 2001

ABOLITION OF SLAVERY. *See* **SLAVERY.**

Aboriginal populations in the mind.
Brickman, Celia. New York : Columbia University Press, c2003.
BF173 .B79 2003

ABORIGINES. *See* **INDIGENOUS PEOPLES.**

ABORIGINES, AMERICAN. *See* **INDIANS.**

About face.
Gray, Richard T. Detroit : Wayne State University Press, c2004.
BF851 .G73 2004

About psychology : essays at the crossroads of history, theory, and philosophy / Darryl B. Hill, Michael J. Kral, editors. Albany : State University of New York Press, c2003. vii, 182 p. ; 23 cm. (SUNY series, alternatives in psychology) Includes bibliographical references and index. ISBN 0-7914-5703-6 ISBN 0-7914-5704-4 (pbk.) DDC 150/.1
1. Psychology - Philosophy. I. Hill, Darryl B., 1963- II. Kral, Michael J., 1956- III. Series.
BF38 .A28 2003

Abraham ben Alexander, of Cologne, 13th cent. Keter Shem Tov.
Sefer 'Amude ha-Ḳabalah. Yerushalayim : Nezer Sheraga, 761 [2001]

ABRAHAM (BIBLICAL PATRIARCH).
Pinter, Leib. Sefer 'Aśarah nisyonot. Brooklyn, N.Y. : E.Y.L. Pinter, c[2002?]

Abraham Ibn Ezra and the rise of medieval Hebrew science.
Sela, Shlomo. Leiden ; Boston, MA : Brill, 2003.
BM538.S3 S45 2003

Abraham Lincoln's daily treasure : moments of faith with America's favorite president / edited by Thomas Freiling. Grand Rapids, Mich. : F.H. Revell, c2002. 272 p. ; 22 cm. ISBN 0-8007-1809-7 (cloth) DDC 973.7/092
1. Lincoln, Abraham, - 1809-1865 - Religion. 2. Lincoln, Abraham, - 1809-1865 - Philosophy. 3. Lincoln, Abraham, - 1809-1865 - Quotations. 4. Conduct of life - Quotations, maxims, etc. 5. Christian life - Quotations, maxims, etc. 6. Presidents - United States - Biography. I. Freiling, Tom.
E457.2 .F787 2002

Abrahamsson, Hans, 1949- Understanding world order and structural change : poverty, conflict and the global arena / Hans Abrahamsson. Basingstoke, Hampshire ; New York : Palgrave Macmillan, 2003. xxiv, 256 p. : ill. ; 23 cm. (International political economy series) Includes bibliographical references (p. 184-246) and index. Publisher description URL: http://www.loc.gov/catdir/description/hol032/2003040546.html ISBN 0-333-77385-3 (cloth) DDC 337
1. International economic relations. 2. Globalization. 3. Poverty. 4. Social conflict. I. Title. II. Series: International political economy series (Palgrave Macmillan (Firm))
HF1359 .A24 2003

Abramowicz, Witold.
Knowledge-based information retrieval and filtering from the Web. Boston : Kluwer Academic Publishers, c2003.
TK5105.888 .K58 2003

Abramson, Paul R., 1949- With pleasure : thoughts on the nature of human sexuality / Paul R. Abramson, Steven D. Pinkerton. Rev. ed. Oxford ; New York : Oxford University Press, 2002. x, 313 p. : ill. ; 24 cm. Includes bibliographical references (p. 229-294) and index. ISBN 0-19-514609-3 (pbk. : acid-free paper) DDC 306.7
1. Sex. 2. Sexual excitement. 3. Pleasure. I. Pinkerton, Steven D. II. Title.
HQ23 .A25 2002

ABRAVANEL, ISAAC, 1437-1508.
Feldman, Seymour. Philosophy in a time of crisis. London ; New York : RoutledgeCurzon, 2003.
BM755.A25 F45 2003

Abréu, Diógenes.
La palabra como cuerpo del delito. Santo Domingo, República Dominicana : Biblioteca Nacional "Dr. Pedro Henríquez Ureña", 2001.

ABSTRACTION. *See also* **CATEGORIZATION (PSYCHOLOGY); MENTAL REPRESENTATION.**
Was kostet den Kopf? Marburg : Tectum Verlag, 2001.

Abstraction planning in real time [microform].
Washington, Richard. Stanford, Calif. : Stanford University, Dept. of Computer Science, [1994] (Springfield, Va. : U.S. Dept. of Commerce, National Technical Information Service).

ABSURD (PHILOSOPHY).
Fotiade, Ramona. Conceptions of the absurd. Oxford : Legenda, 2001.

ABSURD (PHILOSOPHY) IN LITERATURE.
Fotiade, Ramona. Conceptions of the absurd. Oxford : Legenda, 2001.

ABSURDITY (PHILOSOPHY). *See* **ABSURD (PHILOSOPHY).**

The abuse of beauty.
Danto, Arthur Coleman, 1924- Chicago : Open Court, c2003.
BH39 .D3489 2003

ABUSE, SEXUAL. *See* **SEX CRIMES.**

ABUSE, VERBAL. *See* **INVECTIVE.**

ABUSED CHILDREN. *See* **SEXUALLY ABUSED CHILDREN.**

ABUSIVE MEN.
Mills, Linda G. Insult to injury. Princeton, N.J. : Princeton University Press, c2003.
HV6626 .M55 2003

ABUSIVE WOMEN.
Carter, Jay. Nasty women. Chicago : Contemporary Books, c2003.
BF632.5 .C365 2003

Mills, Linda G. Insult to injury. Princeton, N.J. : Princeton University Press, c2003.
HV6626 .M55 2003

Academia Mexicana Correspondiente de la Española.
Beuchot, Mauricio. La filosofía y el lenguaje en la historia. México, D.F. : UNAM, 2000.

ACADEMIC ACHIEVEMENT - UNITED STATES - LONGITUDINAL STUDIES.
Hodges, Carolyn R., 1947- Making schools work. New York : P. Lang, c2003.
LC213.2 .H63 2003
1. Black author.

ACADEMIES (LEARNED SOCIETIES). See **LEARNED INSTITUTIONS AND SOCIETIES.**

Ācārya, Harirāma, 1936-.
Śāstrī, Vinoda, 1959- Jyotisha-vijñāna-nirjharī. Jayapura : Rājasthāna Saṃskṛta Akādamī, [2002?]
BF1714.H5 S288 2002

Ācārya Varāhamihira.
Śāstrī, Girijā Śaṅkara. 1. saṃskaraṇa. Ilāhābāda : Jyotisha, Karmakāṇḍa evaṃ Adhyātma Śodha Saṃsthāna, 2001.
BF1679.8.V37 S27 2001

Ācāryavarāhamihira kā jyotisha meṃ yogadāna.
Dvivedī, Bhojarāja. 1. saṃskaraṇa. Naī Dillī : Rañjana Pablikeśansa, 2002.
BF1679.8.V37 D85 2002

Accidental courage, boundless dreams.
Barzach, Amy Jaffe. 1st ed. West Hartford, CT : Aurora Pub., c2001.
BF575.G7 B375 2001

The accidental manager.
Topchik, Gary S. [1st ed.]. New York : AMACOM, c2004.
HD31 .T6368 2004

ACCIDENTS. See **DISASTERS.**

ACCIDENTS (PHILOSOPHY).
Arthurs, Jane. Crash cultures. Bristol, UK ; Portland, OR : Intellect, 2002.

ACCIDENTS - PSYCHOLOGICAL ASPECTS.
Roads to recovery. St. Leonards, NSW : Allen & Unwin, 1997.
BF698.35.D48 R63 1997

Suicide & risk-taking deaths of children & young people. Surry Hills, NSW : The Commission, c2003.

ACCOMMODATION (PSYCHOLOGY). See **ADJUSTMENT (PSYCHOLOGY).**

ACCULTURATION. See also **ASSIMILATION (SOCIOLOGY).**
Castro, Vanessa Smith, 1969- Acculturation and psychological adaptation. Westport, Conn. : Greenwood Press, 2003.
HM841 .C37 2003

The emerging monoculture. Westport, Conn. : Praeger, 2003.
HM843 .E44 2003

Acculturation and psychological adaptation.
Castro, Vanessa Smith, 1969- Westport, Conn. : Greenwood Press, 2003.
HM841 .C37 2003

Acerca de la mujer.
Margarit i Tayà, Remei. 1. ed. Barcelona : Plaza & Janés, 2002.

ACHES. See **PAIN.**

ACHIEVEMENT, ACADEMIC. See **ACADEMIC ACHIEVEMENT.**

ACHIEVEMENT MOTIVATION.
Fettke, Rich. Extreme success. New York : Fireside Book, c2002.
BF637.S8 F46 2002

Personality and work. 1st ed. San Francisco, CA : Jossey-Bass, c2003.
BF698.9.O3 P47 2003

Tips, Jack. Passion play. 1st ed. Austin, Tex. : Apple-A-Day Press, c2002.
BF503 .T56 2002

ACHIEVEMENT MOTIVATION IN CHILDREN.
Danzig, Robert J., 1932- Every child deserves a champion. Washington, DC : Child & Family Press, c2003.
BF637.E53 D36 2003

The achievement of American liberalism : the New Deal and its legacies / edited by William H. Chafe. New York : Columbia University Press, c2003. xviii, 346 p. ; 24 cm. Includes bibliographical references and index. CONTENTS: New Deal experiments / Alan Brinkley -- High tide : Roosevelt, Truman, and the Democratic party, 1932-1952 / Alonzo L. Hamby -- Roosevelt court / Melvin I. Urofsky -- Voting against the hammer and sickle : Communism as an issue in American politics / Richard M. Fried -- Ethical responsibilities of the scientist : the case of J. Robert Oppenheimer / Richard Polenberg -- Race in America : the ultimate test of liberalism / William H. Chafe -- African Americans, American Jews, and the Holocaust / Harvard Sitkoff -- Race, rock and roll, and the rigged society : the payola scandal and the political culture of the 1950s / Steven F. Lawson -- "A revolution but half accomplished" : the twentieth century's engagement with child-raising, women's work, and feminism / Cynthia Harrison -- Race, class, and gender in southern history : forces that unite, forces that divide / William H. Chafe -- Liberalism after the sixties : a reconnaissance / Otis L. Graham Jr. ISBN 0-231-11212-2 (alk. paper) ISBN 0-231-11213-0 DDC 973.917
1. United States - Politics and government - 1933-1945. 2. New Deal, 1933-1939. 3. World War, 1939-1945 - Social aspects - United States. 4. World War, 1939-1945 - Influence. 5. Liberalism - United States - History - 20th century. 6. Political culture - United States - History - 20th century. 7. United States - Politics and government - 20th century. 8. United States - Social conditions - 20th century. 9. Social movements - United States - History - 20th century. I. Chafe, William Henry.
E806 .M63 2003

ACHIEVEMENT TESTS.
Handbook of psychological and educational assessment of children. 2nd ed. New York, N.Y. : Guilford Press, 2003.
BF722 .H33 2003

Handbook of psychological and educational assessment of children. 2nd ed. New York : Guilford Press, 2003.
BF722 .H33 2003b

ACHIEVERS. See **SUCCESSFUL PEOPLE.**

Achieving abundance.
A guide to getting it. 1st ed. Portland, Or. : Clarity of Vision Pub., 2002.
BF637.S8 G84 2002

Achieving results.
Woodhead, Roy (Roy M.) London : Thomas Telford, 2002.

ACID (DRUG). See **LSD (DRUG).**

Ackeren, Marcel van. Das Wissen vom Guten : Bedeutung und Kontinuität des Tugendwissens in den Dialogen Platons / Marcel van Ackeren. Amsterdam ; Philadelphia : B.R. Gruner, c2003. x, 370 p. ; 24 cm. (Bochumer Studien zur Philosophie, 1384-668X ; Bd. 39) Revision of the author's thesis--Bochum, 2001. Includes bibliographical references (p. 341-361) and indexes. ISBN 90-6032-368-8 DDC 179/.9/092
1. Plato. - Dialogues. 2. Virtue. 3. Ethics. I. Title. II. Series.
B398.V57 A33 2003

Ackerman, Mark S.
Sharing expertise. Cambridge, Mass. : MIT Press, c2003.
HD30.2 .S53 2003

ACOUSTIC VASES. See **VASES, ACOUSTIC.**

ACOUSTICS. See **SOUND.**

ACQUIRED IMMUNE DEFICIENCY SYNDROME. See **AIDS (DISEASE).**

ACQUIRED IMMUNODEFICIENCY SYNDROME. See **AIDS (DISEASE).**

ACQUIRED IMMUNOLOGICAL DEFICIENCY SYNDROME. See **AIDS (DISEASE).**

ACQUISITION, KNOWLEDGE (EXPERT SYSTEMS). See **KNOWLEDGE ACQUISITION (EXPERT SYSTEMS).**

ACQUISITION OF CORPORATIONS. See **CONSOLIDATION AND MERGER OF CORPORATIONS.**

ACQUISITION OF LANGUAGE. See **LANGUAGE ACQUISITION.**

ACQUISITIONS AND MERGERS. See **CONSOLIDATION AND MERGER OF CORPORATIONS.**

ACQUISITIVENESS.
Psychology and consumer culture. 1st ed. Washington, DC : American Psychological Association, c2004.
HC110.C6 P76 2004

Acredolo, Linda P. My first baby signs / [by Linda Acredolo & Susan Goodwyn ; photographs by Penny Gentieu]. [New York] : HarperFestival, c2002. 1 v. (unpaged) : col. ill. ; 18 cm. Publisher description URL: http://www.loc.gov/catdir/description/hc042/2001096647.html ISBN 0-06-009074-X
1. Nonverbal communication in infants. 2. Interpersonal communication in infants. 3. Language acquisition - Parent participation. 4. Sign language. I. Goodwyn, Susan. II. Gentieu, Penny. III. Title.
BF720.C65 A27 2002

ACT (PHILOSOPHY). See also **AGENT (PHILOSOPHY); INTENTIONALITY (PHILOSOPHY).**
Enç, Berent. How we act. Oxford : Clarendon Press ; New York : Oxford University Press, 2003.
B105.A35 E63 2003

Sub"ekt, poznanie, deiatel'nost'. Moskva : Kanon+, 2002.
BD166 .S84 2002

Acta Universitatis Carolinae. Philosophica et historica. Monographia
(156) Machačová, Helena. [Behaviorální prevence stresu. English] Behavioural prevention of stress. 1st ed. Prague : Karolinum Press, 1999.
BF575.S75 M26513 1999

Acta Universitatis Ouluensis. Series B, Humaniora
(no. 42.) Looking at the other. Oulu, Finland : University of Oulu, 2002.

Acta Universitatis Upsaliensis. Studia Anglistica Upsaliensia
(122) Strandberg, Åke. The Orphic voice. Uppsala : Acta Universitatis Upsaliensis, 2002.
PS3509.L43 Z87 2002

Acta Universitatis Upsaliensis. Studia Romanica Upsaliensia
(65) Broth, Matthias, 1965- Agents secrets. Uppsala, Sweden : Uppsala Universitet, c2002.

Acta Universitatis Wratislaviensis
(no 2209) Małyszek, Tomasz, 1971- Ästhetik der Psychoanalyse. Wrocław : Wydawn. Uniwersytetu Wrocławskiego, 2000.

(no 2316.) Paź, Bogusław. Epistemologiczne założenia ontologii Christiana Wolffa. Wrocław : Wydawn. Uniwersytetu Wrocławskiego, 2002.

(no 2420) Szkice psychologiczne. Wrocław : Wydawn. Uniwersytetu Wrocławskiego, 2002.
BF76.5 .S97 2002

Acta Universitatis Wratislaviensis. Filozofia
(39.) Paź, Bogusław. Epistemologiczne założenia ontologii Christiana Wolffa. Wrocław : Wydawn. Uniwersytetu Wrocławskiego, 2002.

L'acte d'être.
Jambet, Christian. [Paris] : Fayard, c2002.

ACTING. See also **DRAMA; EXPRESSION; GESTURE; IMPROVISATION (ACTING); THEATER.**
Tait, Peta, 1953- Performing emotions. Aldershot ; Burlington Vt. : Ashgate, c2002.
PG3458.Z9 D774 2002

Action and its explanation.
Ruben, David-Hillel. 1st ed. Oxford : Clarendon Press, 2003.
BF38 .R83 2003

ACTION, HUMAN. See **HUMAN BEHAVIOR.**

ACTION (PHILOSOPHY). See **ACT (PHILOSOPHY).**

ACTIONS AND DEFENSES. See **EVIDENCE (LAW).**

ACTIVE LEARNING. See **EXPERIENTIAL LEARNING.**

Active vision.
Findlay, John M. (John Malcolm), 1942- Oxford ; New York : Oxford University Press, 2003.
BF241 .F56 2003

ACTIVISTS, POLITICAL. See **POLITICAL ACTIVISTS.**

ACTORS. *See* **MOTION PICTURE ACTORS AND ACTRESSES; THEATER.**

ACTORS - SOCIAL STATUS. *See* **THEATER AND SOCIETY.**

ACTRESSES. *See* **MOTION PICTURE ACTORS AND ACTRESSES.**

ACTRESSES - UNITED STATES - BIOGRAPHY.
Darbo, Patrika. 365 glorious nights of love and romance. 1st ed. New York : ReganBooks, c2002.
HQ46 .D35 2002

ACTS OF TERRORISM. *See* **TERRORISM.**

Actual and the virtual.
Deleuze, Gilles. [Dialogues. English] Dialogues II. 2nd ed. New York : Columbia University Press, 2002.
B2430.D453 D4313 2002

Actual God.
Buxani, Shyam D. Salam. 1st ed. New York : SAU Salam Foundation, c2003.

Acuerdos de paz y seguridad democrática en Guatemala / [coordinadores] Carlos López Chávez, Mónica Ileana de León, Rashid Ricardo Alquijay. 1. ed. [Guatemala] : USAC, DIGI, [2002] vii, 57 p. ; 21 cm. Includes bibliographical references (p. 51-57). ISBN 9992245123 (pbk.)
1. National security - Guatemala. 2. Democracy - Guatemala. 3. Peace. 4. Guatemala - Politics and government - 1945-1985. 5. Guatemala - Politics and government - 1985- 6. Guatemala - Social conditions. I. López Chávez, Carlos. II. León, Monica Ileana de. III. Alquijay, Rashid Ricardo.

ADAGES. *See* **MAXIMS.**

Adair, John Eric, 1934- Not bosses but leaders. 3rd ed. / John Adair with Peter Reed. London ; Sterling, VA : Kogan Page, 2003. 182 p. : ill. ; 22 cm. Previous ed.: i.e. rev. 2nd ed. / James Adair, 1997. Includes bibliographical references. ISBN 0-7494-3899-1 DDC 658.4092
1. Leadership. 2. Management. I. Reed, Peter J. II. Title.

Adam, Barbara.
Making time. Oxford ; New York : Oxford University Press, 2002.
HD69.T54 M34 2002

Adam, of Eynsham, fl. 1196-1232.
[Visio Monachi de Eynsham. English (Middle English) & Latin]
The revelation of the Monk of Eynsham / [Adam of Eynsham] ; edited by Robert Easting. Oxford : Published for the Early English Text Society by the Oxford University Press, 2002. c, 277 p. : ill. ; 22 cm. (Early English Text Society ; no. 318) Includes bibliographical references. Introduction in English; Latin text with parallel Middle English translation. ISBN 0-19-722321-4 DDC 248.29
1. Edmund, - of Eynsham. 2. Private revelations. 3. Purgatory. 4. Paradise. I. Easting, Robert. II. Early English Text Society. III. Title. IV. Series: Early English Text Society (Series) ; no. 318.

Adamovsky, Ezequiel, 1971-.
Historía y sentido. Buenos Aires : Ediciones El Cielo por Asalto, c2001.

Adams, Chris, 1956-.
Neely, A. D. (Andy D.) The performance prism. London ; New York : Financial Times/Prentice Hall, 2002.
HF5549.5.P35 N44 2002

Adams, Christine A. ABC's of grief : a handbook for survivors / Christine A. Adams. Amityville, N.Y. : Baywood, c2003. ix, 181 p. ; 23 cm. Includes bibliographical references (p. 165-168) and index. ISBN 0-89503-243-0 (paper) DDC 155.9/37
1. Grief - Dictionaries. 2. Bereavement - Psychological aspects - Dictionaries. 3. Death - Psychological aspects - Dictionaries. I. Title.
BF575.G7 A32 2003

Adam's curse.
Sykes, Bryan. London ; New York : Bantam, 2003.

Adams, Evangeline Smith, 1872?-1932.
Christino, Karen. Foreseeing the future. Amherst, MA : One Reed Publications, c2002.
BF1679.8.A31 C56 2002

ADAMS, EVANGELINE SMITH, 1872?-1932.
Christino, Karen. Foreseeing the future. Amherst, MA : One Reed Publications, c2002.
BF1679.8.A31 C56 2002

Adams, J. Robert. Prospects for immortality : a sensible search for life after death / J. Robert Adams. Amityville, N.Y. : Baywood Pub., c2003. vi, 170 p. ; 24 cm. (Death, value, and meaning series) Includes bibliographical references (p. 161-164) and index. ISBN 0-89503-228-7 (alk. paper) DDC 129
1. Immortality (Philosophy) 2. Consciousness. I. Title. II. Series.
BD421 .A33 2003

Adams, Jessica.
Astrology for women.
Adams, Jessica. The new astrology for women. [New ed.]. Pymble, Sydney, N.S.W. : HarperCollins, 1998 (2002 printing)

The new astrology for women / Jessica Adams. [New ed.]. Pymble, Sydney, N.S.W. : HarperCollins, 1998 (2002 printing) 538 p. : ill. ; 20 cm. Previous ed.: Astrology for women / Jessica Adams. "Updated to 2005"--Cover. ISBN 0-7322-6433-2 DDC 133.5082
1. Astrology. 2. Women - Miscellanea. I. Adams, Jessica. Astrology for women. II. Title.

Adams, John D., 1942-.
Spencer, Sabina A., 1951- Life changes. New York : Paraview Special Editions, c2002.
BF637.L53 S64 2002

Adams, Michael Vannoy, 1947- The fantasy principle : psychoanalysis of the imagination / Michael Vannoy Adams. New York : Brunner-Routledge, 2004. p. cm. Includes bibliographical references (p.   ) and index. Table of contents URL: http://www.loc.gov/catdir/toc/ecip048/2003018977.html ISBN 1-58391-818-3 (hbk.) ISBN 1-58391-819-1 (pbk.) DDC 150.19/54
1. Jungian psychology. 2. Imagination. I. Title.
BF173.J85 A33 2004

Adamson, Gregory Dale, 1966- Philosophy in the age of science and capital / Gregory Dale Adamson. London ; New York : Continuum, 2002. 169 p. ; 24 cm. (Transversals) Includes bibliographical references (p. 155-164) and index. ISBN 0-8264-6031-3 ISBN 0-8264-6032-1 (pbk.) DDC 190
1. Philosophy, Modern - 20th century. I. Title. II. Series.
B804 .A33 2002

ADAPTABILITY (PSYCHOLOGY). *See also* **ADJUSTMENT (PSYCHOLOGY).**
Borodiuk, N. R. (Nelli Rafkatovna) Dukhovnost' kak faktor uspeshnoĭ sotsial'noĭ adaptatsii cheloveka. Moskva : [s.n.], 2000.
BF335 .B67 2000

Castro, Vanessa Smith, 1969- Acculturation and psychological adaptation. Westport, Conn. : Greenwood Press, 2003.
HM841 .C37 2003

Romm, M. V. (Mark Valerievich) Adaptatsiia lichnosti v sotsiume. Novosibirsk : "Nauka", 2002.
HM696 .R655 2002

ADAPTABILITY (PSYCHOLOGY) - SOCIAL ASPECTS.
Borodiuk, N. R. (Nelli Rafkatovna) Dukhovnost' kak faktor uspeshnoĭ sotsial'noĭ adaptatsii cheloveka. Moskva : [s.n.], 2000.
BF335 .B67 2000

ADAPTATION (BIOLOGY). *See also* **GENETICS; STRESS (PHYSIOLOGY).**
Borodiuk, N. R. (Nelli Rafkatovna) Dukhovnost' kak faktor uspeshnoĭ sotsial'noĭ adaptatsii cheloveka. Moskva : [s.n.], 2000.
BF335 .B67 2000

West-Eberhard, Mary Jane. Developmental plasticity and evolution. Oxford ; New York : Oxford University Press, 2003.
QH546 .W45 2003

Adaptation of a person in a society.
Romm, M. V. (Mark Valerievich) Adaptatsiia lichnosti v sotsiume. Novosibirsk : "Nauka", 2002.
HM696 .R655 2002

ADAPTATION (PHYSIOLOGY) - CONGRESSES.
Adaptivity and learning. New York : Springer, 2003.
BF318 .A33 2003

ADAPTATION, PSYCHOLOGICAL.
Carr, Alan, Dr. Positive psychology. London ; New York : Brunner-Routledge, 2004.
BF121 .C355 2004

McGhee, Paul E. Health, healing and the amuse system. 3rd ed. Dubuque, Iowa : Kendall/Hunt Pub., c1999.
BF575.L3 M38 1999

ADAPTATION (PSYCHOLOGY). *See* **ADAPTABILITY (PSYCHOLOGY); ADJUSTMENT (PSYCHOLOGY).**

Adaptatsiia lichnosti v sotsiume.
Romm, M. V. (Mark Valerievich) Novosibirsk : "Nauka", 2002.
HM696 .R655 2002

ADAPTING BEHAVIOR. *See* **ADJUSTMENT (PSYCHOLOGY).**

Adaptive agents and multi-agent systems : adaptation and multi-agent learning / Eduardo Alonso, Daniel Kudenko, Dimitar Kazakov, eds. Berlin ; New York : Springer, c2003. xiv, 322 p. : ill. ; 24 cm. (Lecture notes in computer science ; 2636. Lecture notes in artificial intelligence) (Hot topics) Includes bibliographical references and index. Also available via the World Wide Web. ISBN 3-540-40068-0 (softcover : alk. paper) DDC 006.3
1. Intelligent agents (Computer software) 2. Artificial intelligence. I. Alonso, Eduardo, 1967- II. Kudenko, Daniel, 1968- III. Kazakov, Dimitar, 1967- IV. Series: Lecture notes in computer science ; 2636. V. Series: Lecture notes in computer science. Lecture notes in artificial intelligence. VI. Series: Hot topics (Berlin, Germany)
QA76.76.I58 A312 2003

ADAPTIVE BEHAVIOR. *See* **ADAPTABILITY (PSYCHOLOGY); ADJUSTMENT (PSYCHOLOGY).**

Adaptivity and learning : an interdisciplinary debate / R. Kühn ... [et al.] (eds.). New York : Springer, 2003. xii, 403 p. : ill. ; 24 cm. Includes bibliographical references. ISBN 3-540-00091-7 (alk. paper) DDC 153.1/53
1. Learning, Psychology of - Congresses. 2. Machine learning - Congresses. 3. Learning - Physiological aspects - Congresses. 4. Adaptation (Physiology) - Congresses 5. Learning - Mathematical models - Congresses. 6. Experiential learning - Congresses. I. Kühn, R. (Reimer), 1955-
BF318 .A33 2003

ADD (CHILD BEHAVIOR DISORDER). *See* **ATTENTION-DEFICIT HYPERACTIVITY DISORDER.**

Addams, Jane, 1860-1935. The long road of woman's memory / Jane Addams ; introduction by Charlene Haddock Seigfried. Urbana : University of Illinois Press, 2002. xxxiv, 84 p. ; 22 cm. Originally published: New York : Macmillan, 1916. Includes bibliographical references and index. ISBN 0-252-02709-4 (Cloth : alk. paper) ISBN 0-252-07024-0 (Paper : alk. paper) DDC 305.4/09
1. Women - Psychology. 2. Women - History. I. Seigfried, Charlene Haddock, 1943- II. Title.
HQ1206 .A25 2002

ADDICTS. *See* **ALCOHOLICS; NARCOTIC ADDICTS.**

ADDRESSES, STREET. *See* **STREET ADDRESSES.**

Adediran, A. A. The problem with the past / by A.A. Adediran. Ile-Ife, Nigeria : Obafemi Awolowo University Press, c2002. 32 p. ; 30 cm. (Inaugural lecture series, 0189-7848 ; 159) Includes bibliographical references (p. 26-32).
1. Yoruba (African people) - Historiography. 2. History - Philosophy. 3. Historiography. 4. Black author. I. Title. II. Series: Inaugural lecture series (Obafemi Awolowo University) ; 159.

Adekanmbi, Joseph. Disabilities : seeking hope and meaning in a dark alley / by Joseph Adekanmbi. Ibadan [Nigeria] : Goalim Publishers, 2001. xii, 211 p. ; 21 cm. Includes index.
1. People with disabilities - Nigeria. 2. Spiritual healing. I. Title.

Adeleke, Veronica I. Concept of gender equality as a paradox in Nigeria's democratic experience / by Veronica I. Adeleke. Ikeja [Nigeria] : Dept. of Political Science and Sociology, Babcock University, 2002. 24 p. ; 20 cm. Includes bibliographical references (p. 22-24). ISBN 978-32041-1-4
1. Feminism. 2. Political science. 3. Nigeria - Politics and government. 4. Black author. I. Title. II. Series: Monograph series (Babcock University. Dept. of Political Science and Sociology) ; no. 3.

Adeleye, Abisola, 1981-.
Adeleye, Modupe, 1980- From our hearts. Rochester, N.Y. : Mo-Biz Publishing Co., 2003.
BF353 .A33 2003

Adeleye, Modupe, 1980- From our hearts : selected essays / by Module and Abisola Adeleye. Rochester, N.Y. : Mo-Biz Publishing Co., 2003. p. cm. Includes bibliographical references and index. ISBN 0-9728673-7-6 (alk. paper) DDC 003
1. Environmental psychology. 2. Chaotic behavior in systems. 3. Speech perception. 4. Attention-deficit hyperactivity disorder. 5. Fictitious characters. 6. Eyre, Jane (Fictitious character) I. Adeleye, Abisola, 1981- II. Title.
BF353 .A33 2003

Adelphi papers.
Boyce, James K. Investing in peace. Oxford : Oxford University Press, 2002.

(no. 344.) Chanaa, Jane. Security sector reform. Oxford ; New York : Oxford University Press for the International Institute for Strategic Studies, 2002.
HV6419 .C52 2002

(no. 351.) Boyce, James K. Investing in peace. Oxford : Oxford University Press, 2002.

Adelsgeschiedenis
(1) Janse, A. Ridderschap in Holland. Hilversum : Verloren, 2001.
DJ152 .J26 2001

Adeniyi, M. O. Yoruba Muslim-Christian understanding / by M.O. Adeniyi and E.O. Babalola. Majiyagbe, Ipaja, Nigeria : Eternal Communications, 2001. 90 p. ; 21 cm. Cover title: Yoruba Muslim-Christian understanding in Nigeria. Includes bibliographical references (p. 83-90). ISBN 978-32757-5-5
1. Yoruba (African people) - Religion. 2. Christianity and other religions - Islam. 3. Islam - Relations - Christianity. 4. Nigeria - Religion. 5. Black author. I. Babalola, E. O. II. Title. III. Title: Yoruba Muslim-Christian understanding in Nigeria

Adeosun, Kola A.
[Ọrọ ti obi n sọ. English]
What the kolanut is saying : the proper use understanding of what the kolanut oracle can tell us / by Kola A. Adeosun ; translated into English by Kayode Idowu Esuleke ; edited by Idowu Hakeem Abimbola and Jare Ajayi ; introduction by Jare Ajayi. Ibadan, Nigeria : Creative Books, 1999. 25 p. ; ill. ; 19 cm. ISBN 978-2866-36-9
1. Divination - Nigeria. 2. Kola nuts - Nigeria. 3. Yoruba (African people) - Religion. I. Esuleke, Kayode Idowu, Chief, Baale Esu of Osogbo. II. Abimbola, Idowu Hakeem. III. Ajayi, Jare. IV. Title.
BF1779.K6 A33 1999

Adesky, Jacques Edgard d'.
Borges, Edson. Racismo, preconceito e intolerancia. [São Paulo, Brazil] : Atual, c2002.

ADHD (CHILD BEHAVIOR DISORDER). *See* **ATTENTION-DEFICIT HYPERACTIVITY DISORDER.**

Adiós a la política, bienvenido la guerra.
Valencia, León. [Bogotá, Colombia?] : Intermedio, c2002.

ADIPOSITY. *See* **OBESITY.**

Adiswarananda, Swami, 1925- Meditation & its practices : a definitive guide to techniques and traditions of meditation in Yoga and Vedanta / Swami Adiswarananda. Woodstock, Vt. : SkyLight Paths Pub., 2003. xvi, 472 p. ; 24 cm. Includes bibliographical references (p. 461-463) and index. CONTENTS: The meaning of meditation -- The meditative state -- The goal of meditation -- The benefits of meditation -- Meditation in the system of yoga -- Meditation in vedanta -- The sacred texts on meditation -- The three key factors in all meditation -- Objects of meditation -- Objects of meditation in yoga and vedanta -- Meditation on a divine form -- Meditation on a divine incarnation -- Meditation on the Lord as inmost self and supreme teacher -- Meditation on Virata Purusha, the cosmic person -- Meditation on the sacred word om -- Meditation on the Gayatri mantra -- Meditation on the great Vedic sayings -- Centers of consciousness -- The centers for meditation -- Dualism, nondualism, and the centers -- Methods of concentration -- Withdrawal and concentration of mind -- Posture -- Time and place, spiritual vibrations, and geographical directions -- Physical condition, eating habits, and exercise -- Self-analysis -- Mystic worship -- Japa, or repetition of a sacred word -- Pranayama, or control of breath -- Progress in meditation -- Milestones of progress -- Mystical experiences and realizations -- The transformation of character -- The sacred texts on progress in meditation -- Obstacles in meditation -- Obstacles in meditation and ways of overcoming them. ISBN 1-89336-183-7 DDC 294.5/435
1. Meditation. I. Title. II. Title: Meditation and its practices
BL627 .A33 2003

ADJUSTMENT (PSYCHOLOGY). *See also* **ADAPTABILITY (PSYCHOLOGY); CONFLICT (PSYCHOLOGY).**
Das äussere und innere Ausland. Wien : WUV, Universitätsverlag, c2000.
BF335 .A9 2000

Beyond coping. Oxford ; New York : Oxford University Press, 2002.
BF335 .B49 2002

Bond, D. Stephenson. The archetype of renewal. Toronto : Inner City Books, c2003.

Bridges, William, 1933- The way of transition. Cambridge, Mass. : Perseus Pub., c2001.
BF335 .B717 2001

Childs-Oroz, Annette. Will you dance? Incline Village, NV : Wandering Feather Press, c2002.
BF637.L53 C45 2002

Ford, Loren. Human relations. 3rd ed. Upper Saddle River, N.J. : Pearson/Prentice Hall, c2004.
BF335 .F67 2004

Gallant, Mary J. Coming of age in the Holocaust. Lanham, Md. : University Press of America, c2002.
D804.3 .G353 2002

Klein, Allen. The healing power of humor. Waterville, Me. : Thorndike Press, 2003.
BF575.L3 K56 2003

Nevid, Jeffrey S. Psychology and the challenges of life. 9th ed. Hoboken, NJ : Wiley, c2005.
BF335 .N475 2005

Spezzano, Charles. Happiness is the best revenge. Townsend, Wiltshire, England : Vision Products Limited, c1997.
BF575.D35 S68 1997

ADJUSTMENT (PSYCHOLOGY) IN ADOLESCENCE.
Beyond coping. Oxford ; New York : Oxford University Press, 2002.
BF335 .B49 2002

Eiguer, Alberto. La famille de l'adolescent. Paris : In press, c2001.

ADJUSTMENT (PSYCHOLOGY) - RELIGIOUS ASPECTS - CHRISTIANITY.
McKinney Hammond, Michelle, 1957- Get over it and on with it!. 1st ed. Colorado Springs, Colo. : WaterBrook Press, 2002.
BV4908.5 .M357 2002
1. Black author.

ADJUSTMENT (PSYCHOLOGY) - UNITED STATES.
Jones, Charisse. Shifting. 1st ed. New York : HarperCollins, c2003.
E185.625 .J657 2003

Adkins, Lisa, 1966- Revisions : gender and sexuality in late modernity / Lisa Adkins. Buckingham [UK] ; Philadelphia : Open University Press, 2002. viii, 152 p. ; 23 cm. Includes bibliographical references (p. [139]-148) and index. ISBN 0-335-20523-2 ISBN 0-335-20522-4 (pbk.) DDC 305.3
1. Sex role. 2. Social mobility. 3. Feminism. 4. Sex role in the work environment. I. Title.
HQ1075 .A24 2002

Adler, Ronald B. (Ronald Brian), 1946- Interplay : the process of interpersonal communication / Ronald B. Adler, Lawrence B. Rosenfeld, Russell F. Proctor II. New York : Oxford University Press, 2004. 9th ed. xiv, 443 p. : ill. (some col.) ; 24 cm. Includes bibliographical references (p. 384-417) and indexes. ISBN 0-19-516707-4 DDC 302.2
1. Interpersonal communication. I. Rosenfeld, Lawrence B. II. Proctor, Russell F. III. Title.
BF637.C45 A33 2004

Adler, William.
Geōrgios, Synkellos, fl. 800. [Ecloga chronographica English] The chronography of George Synkellos. Oxford ; New York : Oxford University Press, 2002.

Adler, Yitshak Eliyahu, ha-Kohen. Sefer Kibud ye-hidur : kol-bo be-hilkhot kibud rabo, talmid hakham ve-zaken be-shanim ; uve-rosho "Sifrenu ha-katsar" : ye-hu tamtsit ha-devarim be-lashon kalah, behirah ve-shavah le-khol nefesh / ne'erakh 'al yede Yitshak Eliyahu ha-Kohen Adler. Ofakim : Y.E. ha-Kohen Adler, 754 [1994] 482 p. ; 25 cm. Includes bibliographical references and indexes.
1. Respect for persons (Jewish law) 2. Rabbis. 3. Jewish scholars. 4. Jewish aged. 5. Ethics, Jewish. 6. Teacher-student relationship - Religious aspects - Judaism. I. Title. II. Title: Kibud ye-hidur

Adlerian, cognitive, and constructivist therapies : an integrative dialogue / Richard E. Watts, editor. New York : Springer Pub., c2003. xi, 145 p. : ill. ; 24 cm. Includes bibliographical references and index. ISBN 0-8261-1984-0 DDC 150.19/53
1. Counseling. 2. Psychotherapy. 3. Adlerian psychology. I. Watts, Richard E.
BF637.C6 A335 2003

ADLERIAN PSYCHOLOGY.
Adlerian, cognitive, and constructivist therapies. New York : Springer Pub., c2003.

BF637.C6 A335 2003

ADMINISTRATION. *See* **ADMINISTRATION OF ESTATES; MANAGEMENT; POLITICAL SCIENCE.**

ADMINISTRATION OF ESTATES - FICTION.
Quindlen, Anna. Blessings. 1st large print ed. New York : Random House Large Print, c2002.
PS3567.U336 B59 2002b

ADMINISTRATION OF JUSTICE. *See* **JUSTICE, ADMINISTRATION OF.**

ADMINISTRATION, PUBLIC. *See* **PUBLIC ADMINISTRATION.**

ADMINISTRATIVE AGENCIES.
Questions and answers [electronic resource]. [Washington, D.C.] : U.S. Equal Employment Opportunity Commission, [2000?]

ADMINISTRATIVE LAW. *See* **CONSTITUTIONAL LAW; PUBLIC ADMINISTRATION.**

ADMINISTRATORS AND EXECUTORS. *See* **EXECUTORS AND ADMINISTRATORS.**

Admur ha-G. ha-Ḳ., Shelita.
['Avodat 'avodah (Torah)]
Sefer 'Avodat 'avodah : dibrot kodesh 'al ha-Torah ... Kiryat Tohsh, Kanada : N. M. Hershkovitsh, 763 [2002 or 2003] 347 p. ; 25 cm. Running title: 'Avodat 'avodah.
1. Bible. - O.T. - Pentateuch - Sermons. 2. Jewish sermons, Hebrew. 3. Ethics, Jewish. 4. Hasidism - Canada - Quebec - Boisbraind (Kiryas Tosh) I. Title. II. Title: 'Avodat 'avodah

ADNEXA OCULI. *See* **EYELIDS.**

Adolescence.
Steinberg, Laurence D., 1952- 7th ed. Boston, Mass. : McGraw-Hill, 2005.
BF724 .S75 2005

ADOLESCENCE.
King, Vera. Die Entstehung des Neuen in der Adoleszenz. Opladen : Leske + Budrich, c2002.

ADOLESCENCE - CONGRESSES.
Seminar "Adoleschencija: kontinuitet i/ili discontinuitet u razvoju" (1997 : Belgrade, Serbia) Adolescencija. Beograd : KBC "Dr Dragiša Mišović", 1997.
BF724 .S399 1997

ADOLESCENCE IN LITERATURE.
Tremblay-Dupré, Thérèse. La mère absente. Monaco : Rocher, 2003.

ADOLESCENCE - ITALY.
Tonolo, Giorgio. Adolescenza e identità. Bologna : Il mulino, c1999.
BF724.I3 T65 1999

ADOLESCENCE - PSYCHOLOGY. *See* **ADOLESCENT PSYCHOLOGY.**

ADOLESCENCE - SOCIAL ASPECTS.
Danesi, Marcel, 1946- Forever young. Toronto : University of Toronto Press, c2003.

Adolescencija.
Seminar "Adoleschencija: kontinuitet i/ili discontinuitet u razvoju" (1997 : Belgrade, Serbia) Beograd : KBC "Dr Dragiša Mišović", 1997.
BF724 .S399 1997

ADOLESCENT ANALYSIS.
The elusive child. London ; New York : Karnac, c2002.

Lhomme-Rigaud, Colette. L'adolescent et ses monstres. Ramonville Saint-Agne : Erès, c2002.

Adolescent anger rating scale.
Burney, DeAnna McKinnie. AARS. Odessa, FL (P.O. Box 998, Odessa, 33556) : Psychological Assessment Resources, c2001.
BF724.3.A55 B87 2001

ADOLESCENT ANGER RATING SCALE.
Burney, DeAnna McKinnie. AARS. Odessa, FL (P.O. Box 998, Odessa, 33556) : Psychological Assessment Resources, c2001.
BF724.3.A55 B87 2001

Adolescent assessment.
Gumbiner, Jann. Hoboken, N.J. : J. Wiley & Sons, c2003.
BF724.25 .G86 2003

Adolescent cultures, school & society
(v. 23) Cornbleth, Catherine. Hearing America's youth. New York : P. Lang, c2003.
BF724.3.I3 .C67 2003

(v. 25.) Cottle, Thomas J. Beyond self-esteem. New York : P. Lang, c2003.
BF697 .C675 2003

(v. 8) Hodges, Carolyn R., 1947- Making schools work. New York : P. Lang, c2003.
LC213.2 .H63 2003

L'adolescent et ses monstres.
Lhomme-Rigaud, Colette. Ramonville Saint-Agne : Erès, c2002.

ADOLESCENT GIRLS. *See* **TEENAGE GIRLS.**

ADOLESCENT PSYCHOLOGY. *See also* **BEREAVEMENT IN ADOLESCENCE; GRIEF IN ADOLESCENCE; IDENTITY (PSYCHOLOGY) IN ADOLESCENCE; INDIVIDUAL DIFFERENCES IN ADOLESCENCE; LOSS (PSYCHOLOGY) IN ADOLESCENCE; PERSONALITY IN ADOLESCENCE; RISK-TAKING (PSYCHOLOGY) IN ADOLESCENCE; STRESS IN ADOLESCENCE; SUCCESS IN ADOLESCENCE.**
Adolescent psychology. Madison, Conn. : International Universities Press, 2003.
BF724 .A274 2003

Davis, Daniel Leifeld. Your angry child. New York : Haworth Press, c2004.
BF723.A4 D38 2004

Dołęga, Zofia. Samotność młodzieży. Wyd. 1. Katowice : Wydawn. Uniwersytetu Śląskiego, 2003.
BF724.3.L64 D65 2003

Eiguer, Alberto. La famille de l'adolescent. Paris : In press, c2001.

King, Vera. Die Entstehung des Neuen in der Adoleszenz. Opladen : Leske + Budrich, c2002.

Lerner, Richard M. Handbook of adolescent psychology. 2nd ed. Hoboken, N.J. : John Wiley & Sons, 2004.
BF724 .L367 2004

Matheus, Tiago Corbisier. Ideais na adolescência. 1a ed. São Paulo, SP : Annablume, 2002.

Psychology of adolescents. Hauppauge, N.Y. : Nova Science, c2003.
BF724 .P783 2003

Tremblay-Dupré, Thérèse. La mère absente. Monaco : Rocher, 2003.

Adolescent psychology : a collection of readings / edited by Deborah L. Browning. Madison, Conn. : International Universities Press, 2003. p. cm. Includes bibliographical references and index. ISBN 0-8236-5769-8 DDC 155.5
1. Adolescent psychology. I. Browning, Deborah L.
BF724 .A274 2003

ADOLESCENT PSYCHOLOGY - CONGRESSES.
Seminar "Adolescencija: kontinuitet i/ili discontinuitet u razvoju" (1997 : Belgrade, Serbia) Adolescencija. Beograd : KBC "Dr Dragiša Mišović", 1997.
BF724 .S399 1997

ADOLESCENT PSYCHOLOGY - RUSSIA (FEDERATION) - CONGRESSES.
Mezhregional'naia Rossiĭskaia nauchno-prakticheskaia konferentsiia "Psikhologicheskie osobennosti preodoleniia ėkstremal'nykh i ėmotsiogennykh situatsiĭ v podrostkovo-iunosheskom vozraste" (2002 : Syktyvkar, Russia) Psikhologicheskie osobennosti preodoleniia ėkstremal'nykh i ėmotsiogennykh situatsiĭ v podrostkovo-iunosheskom vozraste. Syktyvkar : Syktyvkarskiĭ gos. universitet, 2002.
BF724 .M48 2002

ADOLESCENT PSYCHOLOGY - TEXTBOOKS.
Steinberg, Laurence D., 1952- Adolescence. 7th ed. Boston, Mass. : McGraw-Hill, 2005.
BF724 .S75 2005

ADOLESCENT PSYCHOLOGY - UNITED STATES.
Cornbleth, Catherine. Hearing America's youth. New York : P. Lang, c2003.
BF724.3.I3 .C67 2003

ADOLESCENT PSYCHOTHERAPY.
Eiguer, Alberto. La famille de l'adolescent. Paris : In press, c2001.

ADOLESCENTS. *See* **TEENAGERS.**

Adolescenza e identità.
Tonolo, Giorgio. Bologna : Il mulino, c1999.
BF724.3.I3 T65 1999

ADOPTED CHILDREN.
Pierron, Jean-Philippe. On ne choisit pas ses parents. [Paris] : Seuil, c2003.

ADOPTED CHILDREN - COLORADO - PSYCHOLOGY - LONGITUDINAL STUDIES.
Nature, nurture, and the transition to early adolescence. Oxford ; New York : Oxford University Press, 2003.
BF341 .N387 2003

ADOPTED INFANTS. *See* **ADOPTED CHILDREN.**

ADOPTION.
Pierron, Jean-Philippe. On ne choisit pas ses parents. [Paris] : Seuil, c2003.

ADOPTION - PSYCHOLOGICAL ASPECTS.
The elusive child. London ; New York : Karnac, c2002.

ADOPTIVE PARENTS.
Pierron, Jean-Philippe. On ne choisit pas ses parents. [Paris] : Seuil, c2003.

Adorno on popular culture.
Witkin, Robert W. (Robert Winston) London ; New York : Routledge, 2003.
B3199.A34 W58 2003

Adorno, Theodor W., 1903-1969.
[Ob nach Auschwitz noch sich leben lasse. English] Can one live after Auschwitz? : a philosophical reader / Theodor W. Adorno ; edited by Rolf Tiedemann ; translated by Rodney Livingstone and others. Stanford, Calif. : Stanford University Press, 2003. xxvii, 525 p. ; 24 cm. (Cultural memory in the present) Includes bibliographical references and index. ISBN 0-8047-3143-8 ISBN 0-8047-3144-6 DDC 193
1. Philosophy. 2. Holocaust, Jewish (1939-1945) I. Tiedemann, Rolf. II. Title. III. Series.
B3199.A33 O213 2003

ADORNO, THEODOR W., 1903-1969.
Tietz, Udo. Ontologie und Dialektik. Wien : Passagen, c2003.
B3279.H49 T54 2003

Witkin, Robert W. (Robert Winston) Adorno on popular culture. London ; New York : Routledge, 2003.
B3199.A34 W58 2003

La Adquisición de la lengua materna : español, lenguas mayas, euskera / Cecilia Rojas Nieto y Lourdes de León Pasquel, coordinadoras. México : Universidad Nacional Autónoma de México : Centro de Investigaciones y Estudios Superiores en Antropología Social, 2001. 280 p. : ill. ; 23 cm. (Estudios de adquisición y socialización en la lengua materna ; 1) Includes bibliographical references. ISBN 968-36-9861-1 (UNAM) ISBN 968-496-448-X (CIESAS) DDC 401/.93
1. Language acquisition. 2. Spanish language - Acquisition. I. Rojas Nieto, Cecilia. II. León Pasquel, Lourdes de. III. Series.
P118 .A227 2001

ADR (DISPUTE RESOLUTION). *See* **DISPUTE RESOLUTION (LAW).**

Adrift in the technological matrix / edited by David L. Erben. Lewisburg, PA : Bucknell University Press ; London : Associated University Presses, c2003. 157 p. ; 25 cm. (Bucknell review, 0007-2869 ; v. 46, no. 2) Includes bibliographical references. CONTENTS: Introduction : Freedom's absent horizon in the technological world / David L. Erben -- cult@edu.com / Mark C. Taylor -- New media and the natural world : the dialectics of desire / Robert Markley -- Doing what comes generatively : three eras of representation / J. Yellowkees Douglas -- "New world" citizenship in the cyberspatial frontier / Catherine Gouge -- Hegelian Buddhist hypertextual media inhabitation, and criticism in the age of electronic immersion / David Kolb -- Digital hybridity and the question of aesthetic opposition / Johanna Drucker -- The Cyborg and the net : figures of the technological subject / Silvio Gaggi -- Shelf life / Geoffrey Bennington. ISBN 0-8387-5551-8
1. Technology - Aesthetics. 2. Technology - Social aspects. 3. Technology and civilization. 4. Human-computer interaction. I. Erben, David L. II. Series.

ADS. *See* **ADVERTISING.**

Adult age differences in task switching.
Kray, Jutta. Lengerich : Pabst Science Publishers, 2000.
BF724.55.C63 K73 2000

ADULT AND CHILD. *See* **CHILDREN AND ADULTS.**

ADULT CHILD ABUSE VICTIMS. *See* **ADULT CHILD SEXUAL ABUSE VICTIMS.**

ADULT CHILD AND PARENT. *See* **PARENT AND ADULT CHILD.**

ADULT-CHILD RELATIONSHIPS. *See* **CHILDREN AND ADULTS.**

ADULT CHILD SEXUAL ABUSE VICTIMS. *See* **SEXUALLY ABUSED CHILDREN.**

ADULT CHILD SEXUAL ABUSE VICTIMS - MENTAL HEALTH.
Spiegel, Josef. Sexual abuse of males. New York : Brunner-Routledge, 2003.
RC569.5.A28 S65 2003

ADULT CHILD SEXUAL ABUSE VICTIMS - REHABILITATION.
From child sexual abuse to adult sexual risk. 1st ed. Washington, DC : American Psychological Association, c2004.
RC569.5.A28 F76 2004

ADULT CHILD SEXUAL ABUSE VICTIMS - SEXUAL BEHAVIOR.
From child sexual abuse to adult sexual risk. 1st ed. Washington, DC : American Psychological Association, c2004.
RC569.5.A28 F76 2004

ADULT CHILDREN AND PARENTS. *See* **PARENT AND ADULT CHILD.**

ADULT CHILDREN LIVING WITH PARENTS. *See* **PARENT AND ADULT CHILD.**

ADULT EDUCATION - UNITED STATES.
Daniell, Beth, 1947- A communion of friendship. Carbondale : Southern Illinois University Press, c2003.
PE1405.U6 D36 2003

ADULT SURVIVORS OF CHILD SEXUAL ABUSE. *See* **ADULT CHILD SEXUAL ABUSE VICTIMS.**

ADULTERY.
Onken, Julia, 1942- Die Kirschen in Nachbars Garten. Vollständige Taschenbuchausg. München : Goldmann, 1999.

ADULTHOOD. *See also* **AGED; MIDDLE AGE; OLD AGE; YOUNG ADULTS.**
Bee, Helen L., 1939- The journey of adulthood. 5th ed. Upper Saddle River, NJ : Pearson Prentice Hall, c2004.
BF724.5 .B44 2004

ADULTHOOD - PSYCHOLOGICAL ASPECTS.
Bee, Helen L., 1939- The journey of adulthood. 5th ed. Upper Saddle River, NJ : Pearson Prentice Hall, c2004.
BF724.5 .B44 2004

Beutler, Larry E. Integrative assessment of adult personality. 2nd ed. New York : Guilford Press, 2003.
BF698.4 .B42 2003

Bodalev, A. A. Kak stanovíàtsíà velikimi ili vydaiushchimisíà? Moskva : In-t psikhoterapii, 2003.
BF724.5 .B64 2003

The generative society. 1st ed. Washington, DC : American Psychological Association, c2003.
BF724.5 .G45 2003

Problemy obshcheĭ akmeologii. S.-Peterburg : Izd-vo Sankt-Peterburgskogo universiteta, 2000.
BF724.5 .P76 2000

Umberson, Debra. Death of a parent. Cambridge ; New York : Cambridge University Press, 2003.
BF789.D4 U48 2003

ADULTHOOD - PSYCHOLOGICAL ASPECTS - LONGITUDINAL STUDIES.
Schaie, K. Warner (Klaus Warner), 1928- Developmental influences on adult intelligence. [Update]. New York : Oxford University Press, 2004.
BF724.55.C63 S32 2004

ADULTS. *See* **ADULTHOOD.**

ADULTS AND CHILDREN. *See* **CHILDREN AND ADULTS.**

ADULTS, EDUCATION OF. *See* **ADULT EDUCATION.**

ADULTS SEXUALLY ABUSED AS CHILDREN. *See* **ADULT CHILD SEXUAL ABUSE VICTIMS.**

ADVAITA.
Chattopadhyaya, Gauri, 1950- Advaitic ontology and epistemology. 1st ed. Allahabad : Raka Prakashan, 2001.
B132.A3+

Forsthoefel, Thomas A. Knowing beyond knowledge. Alderhot, England ; Burlington, VT. : Ashgate, 2002.
B132.A3 F66 2002

Śaṅkarācārya. [Bhajagovinda. Gujarati & Sanskrit] Mohamudgarastotram. Adyatana āvṛtti. Amadāvāda : Sarasvatī Pustaka Bhaṇḍāra, 1998/99 [i.e. 1999]
B133.S463 B5315 1998

Advaitic ontology and epistemology.
Chattopadhyaya, Gauri, 1950- 1st ed. Allahabad : Raka Prakashan, 2001.
B132.A3+

Advanced lectures on machine learning.
Machine Learning Summer School 2002 (2002 : Canberra, N.C.T.) Berlin ; New York : Springer, 2003.
Q325.5 .M344 2002

Advanced Placement Examination, psychology.
The best test preparation for the Advanced Placement Examination. Piscataway, N.J. : Research & Education Association, c2003.
BF78 .B48 2003

ADVANCED PLACEMENT PROGRAMS (EDUCATION).
The best test preparation for the Advanced Placement Examination. Piscataway, N.J. : Research & Education Association, c2003.
BF78 .B48 2003

Directed self-placement. Cresskill, N.J. : Hampton Press, c2003.
PE1404 .D57 2003

McEntarffer, Robert. Barron's how to prepare for the AP pscyhology advanced placement examination. Hauppauge, N.Y. : Barron's, c2004.
BF78 .M34 2004

Advanced witchcraft.
McCoy, Edain, 1957- 1st ed. St. Paul, Minn. : Llewellyn, 2004.
BF1571 .M45 2004

Advances in applied linguistics
Language acquisition and language socialization. London ; New York : Continuum, 2002.
P118 .L243 2002

Advances in cell aging and gerontology
(v. 15) Recent advances in psychology and aging. Amsterdam ; Boston : Elsevier, 2003.
BF724.8 .R43 2003

Advances in child development within culturally structured environments
Dialogicality in development. Westport, Conn. : Praeger, 2003.
BF713 .D53 2003

Advances in consciousness research
(v. 33) No matter, never mind. Amsterdam ; Philadelphia : John Benjamins Pub. Co., c2002.
QP411 .N598 2002

(v. 34) Consciousness evolving. Amsterdam ; Philadelphia, Pa. : John Benjamins Pub., c2002.
B808.9 .C665 2002

(v. 39) Bartsch, Renate, 1939- Consciousness emerging. Amsterdam ; Philadelphia, Pa. : John Benjamins Pub., 2002.
BF311 .B325 2002

(v. 53) Touching for knowing. Amsterdam ; Philadelphia : John Benjamins Pub., 2003.
BF275 .T69 2003

Advances in gender research
(v. 6) Gendered sexualities. New York : JAI, 2002.
HQ1075.A27 vol. 6

Advances in identity and research / edited by Peter J. Burke ... [et al.]. New York : Kluwer Academic/ Plenum Publishers, c2003. xii, 235 p. : ill. ; 26 cm. Includes bibliographical references. ISBN 0-306-47741-6 (hc) ISBN 0-306-47851-X (pbk.) DDC 155.2
1. Identity (Psychology) - Congresses. I. Burke, Peter J. (Peter James), 1939-
BF697 .A347 2003

Advances in organization studies
(10.) The civilized organization. Amsterdam ; Philadelphia : John Benjamins, c2002.
HD58.7 .C593 2002

Advances in systems theory, complexity, and the human sciences
Burneko, Guy Christian. By the torch of chaos and doubt. Cresskill, N.J. : Hampton Press, c2003.
BD431 .B84 2003

[Nuevos paradigmas. English.] New paradigms, culture, and subjectivity. Cresskill, N.J. : Hampton Press, c2002.
BD161 .N8413 2002

Advances in visual cognition
Perception of faces, objects, and scenes. Oxford ; New York : Oxford University Press, 2003.
BF241 .P434 2003

ADVENTURE AND ADVENTURERS. *See* **FRONTIER AND PIONEER LIFE; SHIPWRECKS.**

ADVERSARIA. *See* **COMMONPLACE-BOOKS.**

ADVERSARY SYSTEM (LAW). *See* **TRIAL PRACTICE.**

ADVERTISEMENTS. *See* **ADVERTISING.**

ADVERTISERS. *See* **ADVERTISING.**

ADVERTISING. *See* **COMMERCIAL ART; SIGNS AND SIGNBOARDS.**

ADVERTISING ART. *See* **COMMERCIAL ART.**

ADVERTISING, ART IN. *See* **COMMERCIAL ART.**

ADVERTISING, CONSUMER. *See* **ADVERTISING.**

ADVERTISING - FASHION.
Lee, Michelle. Fashion victim. 1st ed. New York : Broadway Books, 2003.
GT524 .L44 2003

ADVERTISING, PICTORIAL. *See* **COMMERCIAL ART.**

ADVERTISING, POLITICAL. *See* **PRESS AND POLITICS.**

ADVERTISING - PSYCHOLOGICAL ASPECTS.
McLuhan, Marshall, 1911- The mechanical bride. Corte Madera, CA : Gingko Press, 2002.

Reklama. Moskva : Izd-vo Dom "Bakhrakh-M", 2001.

ADVERTISING - RESEARCH.
Using qualitative research in advertising: strategies, techniques, and applications. Thousand Oaks, Calif. : Sage, c2002.
HF5814 .U78 2002

ADVERTISING, RETAIL. *See* **ADVERTISING.**

ADVERTISING - RETAIL TRADE. *See* **ADVERTISING.**

ADVOCATES. *See* **LAWYERS.**

Aegean Summer School on Cosmology (1st : 2001 : Samos Island, Greece) Cosmological crossroads : an advanced course in mathematical, physical, and string cosmology / S. Cotsakis, E. Papantonopoulos (eds.). Berlin ; New York : Springer, c2002. xvi, 477 p. : ill. ; 25 cm. (Lecture notes in physics, 0075-8450 ; 592) "Edited version of the lectures delivered during the 1st Aegean Summer School on Cosmology, held on Samos island, Greece, in September 21-29, 2001"--P. [v]. Includes bibliographical references. ISBN 3-540-43778-9 (alk. paper) DDC 523.1
1. Cosmology. I. Cotsakis, Spiros, 1963- II. Papantonopoulos, E. (Eleftherios) III. Title. IV. Series.
QB985 .A44 2001

AERA Mook
(no. 76) Gendai tetsugaku ga wakaru. Tōkyō : Asahi Shinbunsha, 2002.
B804 .G43 2002

(no. 83) Heiwagaku ga wakaru. Tōkyō : Asahi Shinbunsha, 2002.
JZ5534 .H44 2002

(no. 89) Shinpan shinrigaku ga wakaru. Tōkyō : Asahi Shinbunsha, 2003.
BF108.J3 S55 2003

Aera (Tokyo, Japan).
Gendai tetsugaku ga wakaru. Tōkyō : Asahi Shinbunsha, 2002.
B804 .G43 2002

Heiwagaku ga wakaru. Tōkyō : Asahi Shinbunsha, 2002.
JZ5534 .H44 2002

Shinpan shinrigaku ga wakaru. Tōkyō : Asahi Shinbunsha, 2003.
BF108.J3 S55 2003

AERIAL STRATEGY. *See* **AIR WARFARE.**

AERIAL TACTICS. *See* **AIR WARFARE.**

AERIAL WARFARE. *See* **AIR WARFARE.**

AERODYNAMICS. *See* **AERONAUTICS.**

AERONAUTICAL ACCIDENTS. *See* **AIRCRAFT ACCIDENTS.**

AERONAUTICAL ENGINEERS - UNITED STATES - BIOGRAPHY.
Eppler, Mark, 1946- The Wright way. New York : AMACOM, c2004.
TL540.W7 E64 2004

AERONAUTICAL RESEARCH. *See* **AERONAUTICS - RESEARCH.**

AERONAUTICS. *See* **AERONAUTICS, COMMERCIAL; ROCKETRY; UNIDENTIFIED FLYING OBJECTS.**

AERONAUTICS - ACCIDENTS. *See* **AIRCRAFT ACCIDENTS.**

AERONAUTICS, COMMERCIAL. *See* **AIRLINES.**

AERONAUTICS, COMMERCIAL - ACCIDENTS. *See* **AIRCRAFT ACCIDENTS.**

AERONAUTICS, COMMERCIAL - SECURITY MEASURES - UNITED STATES.
United States. Congress. House. Committee on Transportation and Infrastructure. Subcommittee on Aviation. The financial condition of the airline industry. Washington : U.S. G.P.O. : For sale by the Supt. of Docs., U.S. G.P.O. [Congressional Sales Office], 2002.

AERONAUTICS, COMMERCIAL - UNITED STATES.
Hecker, JayEtta Z. Commercial aviation [electronic resource]. [Washington, D.C.] : U.S. General Accounting Office, [2002]

United States. Congress. House. Committee on Transportation and Infrastructure. Subcommittee on Aviation. Competition in the U.S. aircraft manufacturing industry. Washington : U.S. G.P.O. : For sale by the Supt. of Docs., U.S. G.P.O., [Congressional Sales Office], 2001.

AERONAUTICS, MILITARY. *See* **AIR WARFARE.**

AERONAUTICS - RESEARCH - UNITED STATES - HISTORY.
Eppler, Mark, 1946- The Wright way. New York : AMACOM, c2004.
TL540.W7 E64 2004

AEROSPACE ENGINEERS. *See* **AERONAUTICAL ENGINEERS.**

AEROSPACE INDUSTRIES. *See* **AIRCRAFT INDUSTRY.**

AEROSTATION. *See* **AERONAUTICS.**

AESTHETIC MOVEMENT (BRITISH ART). *See* **MODERNISM (ART).**

Aesthetic reason.
Singer, Alan, 1948- University Park, Pa. : Pennsylvania State University Press, c2003.
BH91 .S56 2003

AESTHETIC SURGERY. *See* **SURGERY, PLASTIC.**

AESTHETICS. *See also* **ART; CRITICISM; ENVIRONMENT (AESTHETICS); FANTASTIC, THE; FEMININE BEAUTY (AESTHETICS); MODERNISM (AESTHETICS); NATURE (AESTHETICS); ROMANTICISM; VALUES.**
Amašukeli, Elguja. Dro da šemokmedi. T'bilisi : "Merani", 2000.
BF408 .A475 2000

Art and essence. Westport, Conn. ; London : Praeger, 2003.
BH39 .A685 2003

Art and experience. Westport, Conn. ; London : Praeger, 2003.
BH39 .A686 2003

Art and morality. London ; New York : Routledge, 2003.
BH39 .A695 2003

Ästhetik. Hamburg : Kovač, c2002.

Bard, Xavier, 1935- Du plaisir, de la douleur et de quelques autres. Paris, France : Harmattan, c2002.

Baudrillard, Jean. [Objets singuliers. English] The singular objects of architecture. Minneapolis : University of Minnesota Press, c2002.

Aesthetics

NA2500 .B3413 2002
Beguery, Jocelyne. Une esthétique contemporaine de l'album de jeunesse. Paris : Harmattan, c2002.

Bhāvamiśra, 19th cent. [Śṛṅgārasarasī. Hindi & Sanskrit] Śṛṅgārasarasī. Saṃskaraṇa 1. Vṛndāvana : Vṛndāvana Śodha Saṃsthāna, 2001.
PK2916+

Blumenberg, Hans. Ästhetische und metaphorologische Schriften. 1. Aufl. Frankfurt : Suhrkamp, 2001.

Böhme, Gernot. Aisthetik. München : Fink, c2001.
BH39 .B64 2001

Bonesio, Luisa, 1950- Oltre il paesaggio. 1. ed. Casalecchio (Bologna) : Arianna, 2002.

Brock, Bazon, 1936- Der Barbar als Kulturheld. Köln : DuMont, 2002.

Bychkov, V. V. (Viktor Vasil'evich) Ėstetika. Moskva : Gardariki, 2002.

Chang, Zhiqi. Zheng ti lun mei xue guan gang yao. Di 1 ban. Chengdu : Sichuan ren min chu ban she : Sichuan sheng Xin hua shu dian jing xiao, 1994.
BH39 .C435 1994 <Orien China>

Chou, Laixiang. Gu dai de mei, jin dai de mei, xian dai de mei. Di 1 ban. Changchun Shi : Dongbei shi fan da xue chu ban she : Jilin sheng Xin hua shu dian fa xing, 1996.
BH39 .C5455 1996 <Orien China>

The creation of art. New York, NY : Cambridge University Press, 2003.
N71 .C754 2003

Danto, Arthur Coleman, 1924- The abuse of beauty. Chicago : Open Court, c2003.
BH39 .D3489 2003

Deleuze, Gilles. [Dialogues. English] Dialogues II. 2nd ed. New York : Columbia University Press, 2002.
B2430.D453 D4313 2002

Demuth, Volker. Topische Ästhetik. Würzburg : Königshausen & Neumann, c2002.

Desmond, William, 1951- Art, origins, otherness. Albany : State University of New York Press, c2003.
BH39 .D4535 2003

Esteyka czterech żywiołów. Kraków : Universitas, c2002.

Extreme beauty. London ; New York : Continuum, 2002.
BH39 .E98 2002

Fiore, Ann Marie. Understanding aesthetics for the merchandising and design professional. New York : Fairchild, c1997.

Friday, Jonathan. Aesthetics and photography. Aldershot, England ; Burlington, VT : Ashgate, c2002.
TR183 .F75 2002

Glasmeier, Michael, 1951- Extreme 1-8. Köln : Salon, 2001.

Göttner-Abendroth, Heide. Die tanzende Göttin. 6. vollst. überarb. Neuaufl. München : Frauenoffensive, 2001, c1982.

Gučetić, Nikola Vitov, 1549-1610. [Dialogo della bellezza. Serbo-Croatian & Italian] Dijalog o ljepoti = Dvojezično izd. Zagreb : Društvo hrvatskih književnika, 1995.
BH301.L65 G8318 1995

Honegger, Gottfried, 1917- Erfundenes und Erlebtes. München : Chorus, c2002.

Hotho, Heinrich Gustav, 1802-1873. Vorstudien für Leben und Kunst. Stuttgart : Frommann-Holzboog, 2002.

Imagination, philosophy, and the arts. London ; New York : Routledge, 2003.
BH301.I53 I53 2003

Jiang, Kongyang. Jiang Kongyang xue shu wen hua sui bi. Beijing di 1 ban. Beijing : Zhongguo qing nian chu ban she, 2000.
BH39 .J435 2000

Kāviyānī, Shīvā. Farzānagī dar āyinah-i zamān. Tihrān : Nigāh, 2001.

Kemal, Salim. The philosophical poetics of Alfarabi, Avicenna and Averroes. London ; New York : RoutledgeCurzon, 2003.

Krebs, Víctor J., 1957- Del alma y el arte. Caracas, Venezuela : Museo de Bellas Artes, 1997.

N70 .K74 1997
Krollmann, Fritz-Peter, 1963- Ethik und Ästhetik. Essen : Blaue Eule, 2002.

Li, Zehou. Tan xun yu sui. Di 1 ban. Shanghai : Shanghai wen yi chu ban she, 2000.
B126 .L532 2000

Marion, Jean-Luc, 1946- Le phénomène érotique. Paris : Grasset, c2003.
BH301.L65 M37 2003

Martin, Jean-Clet. Parures d'éros. Paris : Kimé, 2003.

Ménasé, Stéphanie. Passivité et création. Paris : Presses universitaires de France, c2003.

Olivetti, Alberto. Gara e bellezza. Fiesole, Firenze : Cadmo, c2002.

Orte des Schönen. Würzburg : Königshausen & Neumann, c2003.
BH23 .O78 2003

Paál, Gábor. Was ist schön? Würzburg : Königshausen & Neumann, c2003.
BH39 .P33 2003

Pan, Zhichang, 1956- Shi yu si di dui hua. Di 1 ban. Shanghai Shi : Shanghai san lian shu dian : Fa xing Xin hua shu dian Shanghai fa xing suo, 1997.
BH39 .P2286 1997<Asian China>

Panorama. New York : Continuum, 2002.
BH39 .P2292 2002

Peinture et musique. Villeneuve-d'Ascq : Presses universitaires du Septentrion, c2002.

Postrel, Virginia I., 1960- The substance of style. 1st ed. New York : HarperCollins, c2003.
BH39 .P6692 2003

Preziosi, Donald, 1941- Brain of the earth's body. Minneapolis : University of Minnesota Press, c2003.
N380 .P67 2003

Qi, Zhixiang. Fo jiao mei xue. Di 1 ban. Shanghai : Shanghai ren min chu ban she : Xin hua shu dian Shanghai fa xing suo jing xiao, 1997.
BQ4570.A72 C45 1997 <Asian China>

Rauschen. Würzburg : Königshausen & Neumann, c2001.

Reck, H. U. Mythos Medienkunst. Köln : König, c2002.

Romero, Pedro G., 1964- En el ojo de la batalla. Valencia : Universitat de València, 2002.

Saldarriaga Roa, Alberto. La Arquitectura como experiencia. 1. ed. Bogotá : Villegas Editores : Universidad Nacional de Colombia, Facultad de Artes, c2002.
NA2765 .S36 2002

Saleev, Vadim Alekseevich. Ėsteticheskoe vospriiatie i detskaia fantaziia. Minsk : Natsional'nyĭ in-t obrazovaniia, 1999.
BF723.P36 S25 1999

Schweppenhäuser, Gerhard. Die Fluchtbahn des Subjekts. Münster : Lit, 2001.

Šik, Miroslav. Altneue Gedanken. Luzern : Quart, c2002.

Simard-Laflamme, Carole. Habit Habitat Habitus. Trois-Rivières, Québec, Canada : Editions d'art Le Sabord, [2002]
TT507 .S653 2002

Singer, Alan, 1948- Aesthetic reason. University Park, Pa. : Pennsylvania State University Press, c2003.
BH91 .S56 2003

Sleinis, E. E. (Edgar Evalt), 1943- Art and freedom. Urbana : University of Illinois Press, c2003.
BH39 .S5518 2003

Solovyov, Vladimir Sergeyevich, 1853-1900. [Essays. English. Selections] The heart of reality. Notre Dame, Ind. : University of Notre Dame Press, c2003.
B4262.A5 W69 2003

Strandberg, Åke. The Orphic voice. Uppsala : Acta Universitatis Upsaliensis, 2002.
PS3509.L43 Z87 2002

Stróżewski, Władysław. Wokół piękna. Kraków : Universitas, c2002.

Sturm, Hermann, 1936- Dinge im Fluss, Fluss der Verzeichnungen. Frankfurt a.M. : Anabas-Verlag, 2002.

Svendsen, Lars Fr. H., 1970- Kunst. Oslo : Universitetsforlaget, c2000.

N6490 .S88499 2000
Tomás Ferré, Facundo. Formas artísticas y sociedad de masas. Madrid : Antonio Machado Libros, c2001.

Tusquets, Oscar, 1941- Más que discutible. 1a. ed. en Fabula. Barcelona : Fabula Tusquets Editores, 2002.

Vom Parergon zum Labyrinth. Wien : Böhlau, c2001.
NK1505 .V65 2001

Wang, Xiaoying, 1957- Xi ju yan chu zhong di jia ding xing. Di 1 ban. Beijing : Zhongguo xi ju chu ban she : Xin hua shu dian zong dian Beijing fa xing suo fa xing, 1995.
PN2039 .W35 1995 <Orien China>

Was kostet den Kopf? Marburg : Tectum Verlag, 2001.

Xiao, Ying. Xing xiang yu sheng cun. Beijing di 1 ban. Beijing : Zuo jia chu ban she : Jing xiao Xin hua shu dian Beijing fa xing suo, 1996.
NX583.A1 H756 1996 <Asian China>

Yan, Xianglin, 1960- Si wang mei xue. Di 1 ban. Shanghai : Xue lin chu ban she, 1998.

Zhang, Fan. Mei xue yu yan xue. Di 1 ban. Beijing : Shou du shi fan da xue chu ban she, 1998.
P121 .Z465 1998

Ziegelmüller, Martin, 1935- Der Maler auf seinem Drehstuhl. [Frauenfeld] : Waldgut, c2001.

Zong, Baihua. Yi jing. Di 2 ban. Beijing : Beijing da xue chu ban she, 1998.
MLCSC 92/01825 (B)

Aesthetics and photography.
Friday, Jonathan. Aldershot, England ; Burlington, VT : Ashgate, c2002.
TR183 .F75 2002

Aesthetics and the philosophy of art
Friday, Jonathan. Aesthetics and photography. Aldershot, England ; Burlington, VT : Ashgate, c2002.
TR183 .F75 2002

AESTHETICS, CHINESE.
Chen, Wei, 1957- Dong fang mei xue dui xi fang de ying xiang = Di 1 ban. Shanghai : Xue lin chu ban she, 1999.
BH221.C6 C444 1999

Chou, Laixiang. Gu dai de mei, jin dai de mei, xian dai de mei. Di 1 ban. Changchun Shi : Dongbei shi fan da xue chu ban she : Jilin sheng Xin hua shu dian fa xing, 1996.
BH39 .C5455 1996 <Orien China>

Jiang, Kongyang. Jiang Kongyang xue shu wen hua sui bi. Beijing di 1 ban. Beijing : Zhongguo qing nian chu ban she, 2000.
BH39 .J435 2000

Zong, Baihua. Yi jing. Di 2 ban. Beijing : Beijing da xue chu ban she, 1998.
MLCSC 92/01825 (B)

AESTHETICS, MODERN - 18TH CENTURY.
Hachet, Pascal. Psychanalyse d'un choc esthétique. Paris, France : Harmattan, c2002.

AESTHETICS, MODERN - 20TH CENTURY.
Lyotard. New York ; London : Routledge, 2002.

Sagnol, Marc, 1956- Tragique et tristesse. Paris : Cerf, 2003.

AESTHETICS - PSYCHOLOGICAL ASPECTS.
Armstrong, Gordon Scott, 1937- Theatre and consciousness. New York ; Oxford : Peter Lang, c2003.
BH301.P78 A75 2003

Evolutionary aesthetics. Berlin ; New York : Springer, c2003.
BH301.P78 E96 2003

Salber, Wilhelm. Psychästhetik. Köln : König, c2002.

AESTHETICS - RELIGIOUS ASPECTS - ORTHODOX EASTERN CHURCH.
Solovyov, Vladimir Sergeyevich, 1853-1900. [Essays. English. Selections] The heart of reality. Notre Dame, Ind. : University of Notre Dame Press, c2003.
B4262.A5 W69 2003

Afanasjev, Valeri, 1963- Russische Geschichtsphilosophie auf dem Prüfstand / Valeri Afanasjev. Münster : Lit, [2002] vi, 185 p. ; 24 cm. (Dokumente und Schriften der Europäischen Akademie Otzenhausen, 0944-7431 ; Bd. 101) Includes bibliographical references. ISBN 3-8258-6124-4 (pbk.)
1. History - Russia - Philosophy. 2. Philosophy, Russian. I. Title. II. Series.

AFFECT (PSYCHOLOGY). *See also* **EMOTIONS.**
Cockcroft, Robert, 1939- Rhetorical affect in early modern writing. New York : Palgrave Macmillan, 2003.
PR428.E56 C63 2003

Handbook of affective sciences. Oxford ; New York : Oxford University Press, 2003.
BF511 .H35 2003

AFFECT (PSYCHOLOGY) - SOCIAL ASPECTS.
Brennan, Teresa, 1952- The transmission of affect. Ithaca : Cornell University Press, 2003.
BF531 .B74 2003

AFFECTION. *See* **FRIENDSHIP; LOVE.**

Affective sciences.
Handbook of affective sciences. Oxford ; New York : Oxford University Press, 2003.
BF511 .H35 2003

AFFIRMATIONS.
Bloch, Douglas, 1949- The power of positive talk. Rev. and updated ed. Minneapolis, Minn. : Free Spirit Pub., 2003.
BF723.S3 B56 2003

Gawain, Shakti, 1948- Creative visualization. [Rev. ed.]. Navato, Calif. : Nataraj Pub./New World Library, c2002.
BF367 .G34 2002

Gawain, Shakti, 1948- Reflections in the light. Rev. ed. Novato, Calif. : Nataraj Pub., c2003.
BF637.S4 G393 2003

Hay, Louise L. I can do it!. Carlsbad, CA : Hay House, c2004.
BF697.5.S47 H388 2004

AFFLICTION. *See* **SUFFERING.**

AFGHANISTAN - POLITICS AND GOVERNMENT - 2001-.
Dupaigne, Bernard. Afghanistan, rêve de paix. Paris : Buchet-Chastel, 2002.

Afghanistan, rêve de paix.
Dupaigne, Bernard. Paris : Buchet-Chastel, 2002.

AFGHANISTAN - SOCIAL CONDITIONS - 20TH CENTURY.
Dupaigne, Bernard. Afghanistan, rêve de paix. Paris : Buchet-Chastel, 2002.

AFICIONADOS. *See* **FANS (PERSONS).**

Afraid.
Nelson, Robin, 1971- Minneapolis, MN : Lerner Publications Co., c2004.
BF723.F4 N45 2004

AFRICA, BLACK. *See* **AFRICA, SUB-SAHARAN.**

AFRICA - CIVILIZATION.
Antinomies of modernity. Durham : Duke University Press, 2003.
CB358 .A59 2003

AFRICA - CIVILIZATION - HISTORIOGRAPHY.
Western historical thinking. New York : Berghahn Books, 2002.
D16.9 .W454 2002

AFRICA - CIVILIZATION - WESTERN INFLUENCES.
Remembering Africa. Portsmouth, NH : Heinemann, c2002.
DT14 .R46 2002

AFRICA - COLONIAL INFLUENCE.
Remembering Africa. Portsmouth, NH : Heinemann, c2002.
DT14 .R46 2002

Africa Community Publishing and Development Trust.
Peace-building. [Harare] : ACPD, 2002.

AFRICA - EMIGRATION AND IMMIGRATION.
Amodélé, Jons. The new Jews. Banjul, The Gambia : Vinasha Publishing, 2000.
1. Black author.

AFRICA - FOREIGN PUBLIC OPINION, FRENCH.
Amougou, Emmanuel. La construction de l'inconscient colonial en Alsace. Paris : L'Harmattan, 2002.
1. Black author.

AFRICA - IN MASS MEDIA.
Remembering Africa. Portsmouth, NH : Heinemann, c2002.
DT14 .R46 2002

AFRICA - LANGUAGES - COLONIAL INFLUENCE.
Language & culture. Lusaka, Zambia : Quest, 1999.

AFRICA - POLITICS AND GOVERNMENT - 1960-.
Kyelem, Apollinaire. L'éventuel et le possible. [Ouagadougou : Presses universitaires de Ouagadougou, 2002]
1. Black author.

AFRICA - SOCIAL CONDITIONS - 1960-.
Kyelem, Apollinaire. L'éventuel et le possible. [Ouagadougou : Presses universitaires de Ouagadougou, 2002]
1. Black author.

AFRICA SOUTH OF THE SAHARA. *See* **AFRICA, SUB-SAHARAN.**

AFRICA, SUB-SAHARAN - RELIGION.
Emtcheu, André. Psychologie et révélation. Yaoundé, Cameroun : Editions SHERPA, c2001.
1. Black author.

AFRICA, SUB-SAHARAN - RELIGIOUS LIFE AND CUSTOMS.
Emtcheu, André. Psychologie et révélation. Yaoundé, Cameroun : Editions SHERPA, c2001.
1. Black author.

AFRICAN AMERICAN CHILDREN - EDUCATION.
Kunjufu, Jawanza. Black students-Middle class teachers. Chicago, Ill. : African American Images, c2002.
1. Black author.

AFRICAN AMERICAN CHILDREN - PSYCHOLOGY.
Ladner, Joyce A. Launching our Black children for success. 1st ed. San Francisco : Jossey-Bass, c2003.
BF723.S77 L33 2003

AFRICAN AMERICAN DANCE - HISTORY.
Gottschild, Brenda Dixon. The Black dancing body. New York : Palgrave Macmillan, 2003.
GV1624.7.A34 G68 2003
1. Black author.

AFRICAN AMERICAN DANCERS.
Gottschild, Brenda Dixon. The Black dancing body. New York : Palgrave Macmillan, 2003.
GV1624.7.A34 G68 2003
1. Black author.

AFRICAN AMERICAN FAMILIES - MENTAL HEALTH.
Boyd-Franklin, Nancy. Black families in therapy. 2nd ed. New York : Guilford Press, c2003.
RC451.5.N4 B69 2003

AFRICAN AMERICAN HIGH SCHOOL STUDENTS - LONGITUDINAL STUDIES.
Hodges, Carolyn R., 1947- Making schools work. New York : P. Lang, c2003.
LC213.2 .H63 2003
1. Black author.

AFRICAN AMERICAN INTELLECTUALS.
Washington, Johnny. Evolution, history and destiny. New York : Peter Lang, c2002.
E185.625 .W37 2002

AFRICAN AMERICAN MAGIC.
McQuillar, Tayannah Lee, 1977- Rootwork. New York : Simon & Schuster, c2003.
BF1622.A34 M37 2003
1. Black author.

AFRICAN AMERICAN MEN - ATTITUDES.
Gardere, Jeffrey Roger. Love prescription. New York : Kensington Pub., c2002.
1. Black author.

AFRICAN AMERICAN MEN - CONDUCT OF LIFE.
From one brother to another. Volume 2. Valley Forge, PA : Judson Press, c2003.

AFRICAN AMERICAN MEN - LIFE SKILLS GUIDES.
Madhubuti, Haki R., 1942- Tough notes. 1st ed. Chicago : Third World Press, c2002.
E185.86 .T68 2002
1. Black author.

AFRICAN AMERICAN MEN - PRAYER-BOOKS AND DEVOTIONS - ENGLISH.
From one brother to another. Volume 2. Valley Forge, PA : Judson Press, c2003.

AFRICAN AMERICAN MEN - PSYCHOLOGY.
Madhubuti, Haki R., 1942- Tough notes. 1st ed. Chicago : Third World Press, c2002.
E185.86 .T68 2002
1. Black author.

AFRICAN AMERICAN MEN - RELIGIOUS LIFE.
From one brother to another. Volume 2. Valley Forge, PA : Judson Press, c2003.

AFRICAN AMERICAN MEN - SOCIAL CONDITIONS.
Madhubuti, Haki R., 1942- Tough notes. 1st ed. Chicago : Third World Press, c2002.
E185.86 .T68 2002
1. Black author.

AFRICAN AMERICAN PHILOSOPHY.
Washington, Johnny. Evolution, history and destiny. New York : Peter Lang, c2002.
E185.625 .W37 2002

AFRICAN AMERICAN PHYSICIANS - BIOGRAPHY.
Davis, Sampson. The pact. Waterville, ME : Thorndike Press, 2002.
1. Black author.

AFRICAN AMERICAN PSYCHOLOGISTS.
Guthrie, Robert V. Even the rat was white a historical view of psychology. Classic ed., 2nd ed. Boston, MA : Allyn and Bacon, 2004.
BF105 .G87 2004

AFRICAN AMERICAN TEENAGERS - PSYCHOLOGY.
Ladner, Joyce A. Launching our Black children for success. 1st ed. San Francisco : Jossey-Bass, c2003.
BF723.S77 L33 2003

AFRICAN AMERICAN WOMEN.
Dyson, Michael Eric. Why I love black women. New York : Basic Civitas Books, c2003.

Walker, Jamie. 101 ways black women can learn to love themselves. Washington, D.C. : J.D. Publishing, c2002.
1. Black author.

AFRICAN AMERICAN WOMEN - ATTITUDES.
Gardere, Jeffrey Roger. Love prescription. New York : Kensington Pub., c2002.
1. Black author.

AFRICAN AMERICAN WOMEN CLERGY - BIOGRAPHY.
Johnson Cook, Suzan D. (Suzan Denise), 1957- Too blessed to be stressed. Nashville, Tenn. : T. Nelson, c1998.
BV4527 .J65 1998
1. Black author.

AFRICAN AMERICAN WOMEN COLLEGE TEACHERS.
Givens, Gretchen Zita. Black women in the field. Cresskill, N.J. : Hampton Press, c2003.
LC2781.5 .G58 2003

AFRICAN AMERICAN WOMEN - INTERVIEWS.
Jones, Charisse. Shifting. 1st ed. New York : HarperCollins, c2003.
E185.625 .J657 2003

Longing to tell. 1st ed. New York : Farrar, Straus and Giroux, 2003.
E185.625 .L66 2003

AFRICAN AMERICAN WOMEN - LIFE SKILLS GUIDES.
Meeks, James T., 1956- Life changing relationships. Chicago, Ill. : Moody Press, c2002.
HQ801 .M515 2002
1. Black author.

AFRICAN AMERICAN WOMEN - PSYCHOLOGY.
Burack, Cynthia, 1958- Healing identities. Ithaca : Cornell University Press, 2004.
BF175.4.F45 B87 2004

Collins, Catherine Fisher. Sources of stress and relief for African American women. Westport, Conn. ; London : Praeger, 2003.
BF575.S75 C57 2003

Jones, Charisse. Shifting. 1st ed. New York : HarperCollins, c2003.
E185.625 .J657 2003

Longing to tell. 1st ed. New York : Farrar, Straus and Giroux, 2003.
E185.625 .L66 2003

AFRICAN AMERICAN WOMEN - RACE IDENTITY.
Givens, Gretchen Zita. Black women in the field. Cresskill, N.J. : Hampton Press, c2003.
LC2781.5 .G58 2003

AFRICAN AMERICAN WOMEN - SEXUAL BEHAVIOR.
Longing to tell. 1st ed. New York : Farrar, Straus and Giroux, 2003.
E185.625 .L66 2003

AFRICAN AMERICAN WOMEN - SOCIAL CONDITIONS.
Jones, Charisse. Shifting. 1st ed. New York : HarperCollins, c2003.
E185.625 .J657 2003

AFRICAN AMERICAN YOUNG MEN - NEW YORK - NEW YORK - SOCIAL CONDITIONS.
Wilkinson, Deanna Lyn, 1968- Guns, violence, and identity among African American and Latino youth. New York : LFB Scholarly Pub., 2003.
HQ799.2.V56 W55 2003

AFRICAN AMERICANS - CIVIL RIGHTS.
Kook, Rebecca B., 1959- The logic of democratic exclusion. Lanham, Md. : Lexington Books, c2002.
E185.615 .K59 2002

AFRICAN AMERICANS - EDUCATION.
Kunjufu, Jawanza. Black students-Middle class teachers. Chicago, Ill. : African American Images, c2002.
1. Black author.

AFRICAN AMERICANS - ETHNIC IDENTITY.
Washington, Johnny. Evolution, history and destiny. New York : Peter Lang, c2002.
E185.625 .W37 2002

AFRICAN AMERICANS - FICTION.
Louise, Kim. True devotion. Washington D.C. : BET Publications, 2002.

AFRICAN AMERICANS - FINANCE, PERSONAL.
Broussard, Cheryl D. What's money got to do with it? Oakland, CA : MetaMedia Pub., [c2002]
1. Black author.

AFRICAN AMERICANS - HISTORY.
Washington, Johnny. Evolution, history and destiny. New York : Peter Lang, c2002.
E185.625 .W37 2002

AFRICAN-AMERICANS - INTELLIGENCE LEVELS.
Jensen, Arthur Robert. Intelligence, race, and genetics. Boulder, Colo. : Westview Press, c2002.
BF431 .J396 2002

AFRICAN AMERICANS - KINSHIP - PENNSYLVANIA.
Daniel, Jack L. (Jack Lee), 1942- We fish. Pittsburgh, Pa. : University of Pittsburgh Press, c2003.
1. Black author.

AFRICAN AMERICANS - PRAYER-BOOKS AND DEVOTIONS - ENGLISH.
Vanzant, Iyanla. Until today!. New York : Simon & Schuster, c2000.
BL625.2 .V369 2000

AFRICAN AMERICANS - RACE IDENTITY.
The afro-asian century. Durham, N.C. : Duke University Press, 2003.

AFRICAN AMERICANS - RELATIONS WITH ASIAN AMERICANS.
The afro-asian century. Durham, N.C. : Duke University Press, 2003.

AFRICAN AMERICANS - RELIGION.
Holmes, Barbara Ann, 1943- Race and the cosmos. Harrisburg, Pa. : Trinity Press International, c2002.
BR563.N4 H654 2002
1. Black author.

What can happen when we pray. Minneapolis : Augsburg Fortress, c2001.

AFRICAN AMERICANS - SOCIAL CONDITIONS.
Boyd-Franklin, Nancy. Black families in therapy. 2nd ed. New York : Guilford Press, c2003.
RC451.5.N4 B69 2003

Corlett, J. Angelo, 1958- Race, racism, & reparations. Ithaca : Cornell University Press, c2003.
HT1523 .C67 2003

Madhubuti, Haki R., 1942- Tough notes. 1st ed. Chicago : Third World Press, c2002.
E185.86 .T68 2002
1. Black author.

Washington, Johnny. Evolution, history and destiny. New York : Peter Lang, c2002.
E185.625 .W37 2002

AFRICAN AMERICANS - SOCIAL CONDITIONS - 1975-.
Hooks, Bell. Rock my soul. New York, NY : Atria Books, c2003.
1. Black author.

AFRICAN AMERICANS - SOCIALIZATION - PENNSYLVANIA.
Daniel, Jack L. (Jack Lee), 1942- We fish. Pittsburgh, Pa. : University of Pittsburgh Press, c2003.
1. Black author.

African cultural revolution of Islam and Christianity in Yoruba land.
Babalola, E. O. Ipaja-Lagos : Eternal Communications, 2002.

African traditional religion.
Kómoláfé, Kóláwolé. Lagos : Ifa-Òrúnmìlà Organisation, 1995.
BL2480.Y6 K65 1995

AFRICAN UNION - EVALUATION.
Imobighe, Thomas A. The OAU (AU) and OAS in regional conflict management. Ibadan : Spectrum Books ; Oxford, UK : USA distributor, African Books Collective, 2003.
JZ6374 .I46 2003

African women and feminism : reflecting on the politics of sisterhood / edited by Oyèrónké Oyěwùmí. Trenton, NJ : Africa World Press, c2003. viii, 273 p. ; 23 cm. Includes bibliographical references and index. ISBN 0-86543-627-4 (hc) ISBN 0865435282 (pbk.) DDC 305.42/096
1. Women - Africa - Social conditions. 2. Feminism. 3. Feminist theory. I. Oyěwùmí, Oyèrónké.
HQ1787 .A372 2003

AFRICANS - FRANCE - SOCIAL LIFE AND CUSTOMS.
Amougou, Emmanuel. La construction de l'inconscient colonial en Alsace. Paris : L'Harmattan, 2002.
1. Black author.

AFRO-AMERICAN ARTS. *See* **HIP-HOP.**

AFRO-AMERICANS - RELATIONS WITH WHITES. *See* **UNITED STATES - RACE RELATIONS.**

The afro-asian century. Durham, N.C. : Duke University Press, 2003. 260 p. : ill. ; 21 cm. Other title: Positions east asia cultures critique. Positions east asia cultures critique, volume 11, no. 1, spring 2003, special issue. Includes bibliographical references. CONTENTS: The shadow of shadows / Brent Hayes Edwards -- Bruce Lee and the anti-imperialism of Kung Fu: a polycultural adventure / Vijay Prashad -- Shanghai savage / William Schaefer -- "Perhaps the Japanese are to be thanked?" Asia, Asian Americans, and the construction of black California / Daniel Widener -- Beyond an alliance of color: the African American impact on modern Japan / Yukiko Koshiro -- Du Bois, Dark Princess, and the Afro-Asian International / Bill V. Mullen -- Writing on water: peripheries, flows, capital, and struggles in the Indian Ocean / François Vergès.
1. African Americans - Relations with Asian Americans. 2. African Americans - Race identity. 3. Asian Americans - Race identity. 4. Asian Americans - Cultural assimilation. 5. Multiculturalism - United States. 6. Social interaction. 7. United States - Race relations. I. Title: Positions (Durham, N.C.) Vol. 11, no. 1, spring 2003. II. Title: Positions east asia cultures critique

AFRO-BRAZILIAN CULTS. *See also* **UMBANDA (CULT).**
Beniste, José. As águas de Oxalá = Rio de Janeiro, RJ, [Brazil] : Editora Bertrand Brasil, c2001 (2002 printing)
BL2592.C35 B46 2001

Salles, Alexandre de. Esù ou Exu? Rio de Jaeiro : Ilú Aiye, 2001.
1. Black author.

Verger, Pierre. Saída de Iaô. Sao Paulo : Fundação Pierre Verger : Axis Mundi Editora, 2002.

After Electra.
Liddelow, Eden. Melbourne : Australian Scholarly, 2002, c2001.

After Lacan.
Apollon, Willy. Albany : State University of New York Press, 2002.
RC506 .A65 2002

After life.
Edward, John (John J.) New York : Princess Books, c2003.
BF1283.E34 A3 2003

After the ice.
Mithen, Steven J. London : Weidenfeld & Nicolson, 2003.

AFTERLIFE. *See* **FUTURE LIFE.**

The afterlife connection.
Greer, Jane, 1951- 1st ed. New York : St. Martin's Press, 2003.
BF1261.2 .G74 2003

AFTERMARKETS. *See* **MARKETING.**

Agacinski, Sylviane.
[Passeur de temps. English]
Time passing : modernity and nostalgia / Sylviane Agacinski ; translated by Jody Gladding. New York : Columbia University Press, c2003. viii, 212 p., [12] p. of plates ill., ports. ; 22 cm. (European perspectives) Includes bibliographical references (p. [193]-196) and index. ISBN 0-231-12514-3 (cloth : alk. paper) ISBN 0-231-12515-1 (pbk. : alk. paper) DDC 304.2/3
1. Time. I. Title. II. Series.
BD638 .A27713 2003

AGADA (TALMUD). *See* **AGGADA.**

AGADAH (TALMUD). *See* **AGGADA.**

Against marriage.
Montpensier, Anne-Marie-Louise d'Orléans, duchesse de, 1627-1693. [Correspondence. English & French] Chicago : University of Chicago Press, 2002.
DC130.M8 A4 2002

Agarwal, G. S., 1936- Dictionary of astrology / G.S. Agarwal, S.K. Duggal, C.M. Bhalla. New Delhi : Sagar Publications, 2002. 338 p. ; 22 cm.
1. Hindu astrology - Dictionaries. I. Duggal, S. K. (Sudarshan Kumar), 1937- II. Bhalla, C. M. (Chander M.) III. Title.
BF1714.H5 A33 2002

AGE. *See* **OLD AGE.**

L'âge des lumières
(17) Ramsay, Chevalier (Andrew Michael), 1686-1743. Les voyages de Cyrus. Paris : Champion, 2002.

AGE DISCRIMINATION IN EMPLOYMENT - UNITED STATES.
Vint/age 2001 conference : [videorecording]. New York, c2001.

AGE FACTORS IN COGNITION. *See* **COGNITION - AGE FACTORS.**

AGE FACTORS IN DISEASE. *See* **AGING.**

AGE GROUPS. *See* **ADULTHOOD; CHILDREN; YOUTH.**

The age of immunology.
Napier, A. David. Chicago : University of Chicago Press, 2003.
GN345 .N36 2003

The age of intimacy.
Clark, Harold A. Laredo, TX : EBookcase.com, c2000.

AGE - PHYSIOLOGICAL EFFECT. *See* **AGING.**

AGE (PSYCHOLOGY). *See* **MATURATION (PSYCHOLOGY).**

AGE REGRESSION, HYPNOTIC. *See* **HYPNOTIC AGE REGRESSION.**

AGED. *See* **OLD AGE.**

AGED ARTISTS.
Lindauer, Martin S. Aging, creativity, and art. New York : Kluwer Academic/Plenum Publishers, c2003.
BF724.85.C73 L56 2003

AGED - CARE.
Promising practies in the field of caregiving [electronic resource]. [Washington, D.C.] : U.S. Dept. of Health and Human Services, Administration on Aging, [2003?]

Velkoff, Victoria Averil. Gender and aging [electronic resource]. [Washington, D.C.] : U.S. Dept. of Commerce, Economics and Statistics Administration, Bureau of the Census, [1998]

Veras, Renato P. (Renato Peixoto) Terceira idade. Rio de Janeiro : UNATI : Relume Dumará, 2002.

With eyes open [electronic resource]. San Francisco : KQED ; [Alexandria, Va.] : PBS
BF789.D4

The young, the old, and the state. Cheltenham, UK ; Northhampton, MA : E. Elgar Pub., c2003.
HQ778.5 .Y69 2003

AGED - CARE AND HYGIENE. *See* **AGED - HEALTH AND HYGIENE.**

AGED - COUNSELING OF.
Counseling diverse populations. 3rd ed. Boston, Mass. : McGraw-Hill, c2004.
BF637.C6 C6372 2004

AGED - FAMILY RELATIONSHIP - EUROPE.
Nashim, zekenim ṿa-taf. Yerushalayim : Merkaz Zalman Shazar le-toldot Yiśra'el, [2001]

AGED - GERMANY - BIOGRAPHY.
Alt möcht ich werden--. 1. Aufl. Berlin : Aufbau-Verlag, c1994.
HQ1064.G3 A72 1994x

AGED - HEALTH AND HYGIENE - BRAZIL.
Veras, Renato P. (Renato Peixoto) Terceira idade. Rio de Janeiro : UNATI : Relume Dumará, 2002.

AGED LESBIANS.
Macdonald, Barbara, 1913- Look me in the eye. New, expanded ed. Denver, CO : Spinsters Ink Books, 2001.

AGED - MEDICAL CARE.
Envejecimiento y cultura. [Madrid] : Instituto de España, c2001.

AGED - MEDICAL CARE - BRAZIL.
Veras, Renato P. (Renato Peixoto) Terceira idade. Rio de Janeiro : UNATI : Relume Dumará, 2002.

AGED - PSYCHOLOGY. *See also* **AGING - PSYCHOLOGICAL ASPECTS.**
Aleksandrova, Nataliĭa. Starite khora. 1. izd. Sofiĭa : Universitetsko izd-vo "Sv. Kliment Okhridski", 2001.
BF724.8 .A42 2001

Alt möcht ich werden--. 1. Aufl. Berlin : Aufbau-Verlag, c1994.
HQ1064.G3 A72 1994x

Envejecimiento y cultura. [Madrid] : Instituto de España, c2001.

Lindauer, Martin S. Aging, creativity, and art. New York : Kluwer Academic/Plenum Publishers, c2003.
BF724.85.C73 L56 2003

Recent advances in psychology and aging. Amsterdam ; Boston : Elsevier, 2003.
BF724.8 .R43 2003

AGED - SOCIAL ASPECTS.
Envejecimiento y cultura. [Madrid] : Instituto de España, c2001.

AGED WOMEN.
Macdonald, Barbara, 1913- Look me in the eye. New, expanded ed. Denver, CO : Spinsters Ink Books, 2001.

AGED WOMEN - PSYCHOLOGY.
Macdonald, Barbara, 1913- Look me in the eye. New, expanded ed. Denver, CO : Spinsters Ink Books, 2001.

McCain, Marian Van Eyk. Elderwoman. Forres : Findhorn Press, 2002.

AGED WOMEN - SOCIAL CONDITIONS.
Macdonald, Barbara, 1913- Look me in the eye. New, expanded ed. Denver, CO : Spinsters Ink Books, 2001.

Ageev, Valentin. Psikhologiĭa transtsendirovaniĭa : vvedenie v problemu : uchebnoe posobie / Valentin Ageev. Almaty: "Qazaq Universitetī", 2002. 375 p. ; 20 cm. Includes bibliographical references. ISBN 9965121540
1. Developmental psychology. I. Āl-Farabi atyndaghy Qazaq memlekettīk ūlttyq universitetī. II. Title.
BF713 .A34 1998

Vvedenie v psikhologiĭu chelovecheskoĭ unikal'nosti / Valentin Ageev. Tomsk : Izd-vo "Peleng", 2002. 428 p. : ill. ; 30 cm. Includes bibliographical references (p. 423-427). ISBN 5886302395
1. Individuality. I. Title.
BF697 .A353 2002

AGEING. *See* **AGING.**

AGEISM.
Macdonald, Barbara, 1913- Look me in the eye. New, expanded ed. Denver, CO : Spinsters Ink Books, 2001.

AGEISM - UNITED STATES.
Vint/age 2001 conference : [videorecording]. New York, c2001.

Agency and self-awareness : issues in philosophy and psychology / edited by Johannes Roessler and Naomi Eilan. Oxford : Clarendon Press ; New York : Oxford University Press, 2003. xi, 415 p. ; 24 cm. (Consciousness and self-consciousness) Includes bibliographical references and indexes. ISBN 0-19-924561-4 (hbk.) ISBN 0-19-924562-2 (pbk.)
1. Agent (Philosophy) 2. Self-perception. 3. Self (Philosophy) 4. Awareness. I. Roessler, Johannes. II. Eilan, Naomi. III. Series.

AGENCY (PHILOSOPHY). *See* **AGENT (PHILOSOPHY).**

Agent Apple.
Monkeywrenching the new world order [sound recording]. Oakland, Calif : AK Press ; San Francisco, CA : Alternative Tentacles Records, 2001.

AGENT (PHILOSOPHY). *See also* **ACT (PHILOSOPHY).**
Agency and self-awareness. Oxford : Clarendon Press ; New York : Oxford University Press, 2003.

Archer, Margaret Scotford. Structure, agency and the internal conversation. Cambridge, U.K. ; New York : Cambridge University Press, 2003.
HM708 .A73 2003

Markell, Patchen, 1969- Bound by recognition. Princeton, N.J. : Princeton University Press, c2003.
JC575 .M37 2003

Mele, Alfred R., 1951- Motivation and agency. Oxford ; New York : Oxford University Press, 2003.
BD450 .M383 2003

AGENTS. *See* **AGENT (PHILOSOPHY).**

AGENTS, INTELLIGENT (COMPUTER SOFTWARE). *See* **INTELLIGENT AGENTS (COMPUTER SOFTWARE).**

AGENTS, LITERARY. *See* **LITERARY AGENTS.**

Agents secrets.
Broth, Matthias, 1965- Uppsala, Sweden : Uppsala Universitet, c2002.

AGGADA.
Golan, Mor Yosef. Sefer ha-Neshamah ba-guf. Itamar : M.Y. Golan, 762 [2001 or 2002]

AGGADA - HISTORY AND CRITICISM - THEORY, ETC.
Neusner, Jacob, 1932- Analysis and argumentation in Rabbinic Judaism. Lanham, Md. : University Press of America, c2003.
BM496.5 .N4775 2003

AGGADAH (TALMUD). *See* **AGGADA.**

AGGRESSION - PSYCHOLOGY.
Rizzuto, Ana-María. The dynamics of human aggression. New York, NY : Brunner-Routledge, 2003.
BF175.5.A36 R59 2003

AGGRESSIVENESS.
Marin, Isabel da Silva Kahn, 1954- Violências. São Paulo : Editora Escuta : FAPESP, 2002.

Rizzuto, Ana-María. The dynamics of human aggression. New York, NY : Brunner-Routledge, 2003.
BF175.5.A36 R59 2003

AGGRESSIVENESS IN ADOLESCENCE.
Elias, Maurice J. Bullying, peer harassment, and victimization in the schools. New York : Haworth Press, 2003.
BF637.B85 E45 2003

Underwood, Marion K. Social aggression among girls. New York ; London : Guilford Press, c2003.
BF723.A35 U53 2003

AGGRESSIVENESS IN CHILDREN.
Elias, Maurice J. Bullying, peer harassment, and victimization in the schools. New York : Haworth Press, 2003.
BF637.B85 E45 2003

Underwood, Marion K. Social aggression among girls. New York ; London : Guilford Press, c2003.
BF723.A35 U53 2003

AGGRESSIVENESS - PREVENTION.
Smith, Shawn T., 1967- Surviving aggressive people. 1st Sentient Publications ed. Boulder, CO : Sentient Publications, 2003.
BF575.A3 S55 2003

AGGRESSIVENESS (PSYCHOLOGY). *See* **BULLYING; FIGHTING (PSYCHOLOGY); HOSTILITY (PSYCHOLOGY); VIOLENCE.**

AGING.
Aging under the microscope [electronic resource]. Bethesda, MD : National Institute on Aging, National Institutes of Health, [2002]

Bee, Helen L., 1939- The journey of adulthood. 5th ed. Upper Saddle River, NJ : Pearson Prentice Hall, c2004.
BF724.5 .B44 2004

Invitation to the life course. Amityville, N.Y. : Baywood Pub. Co., c2003.
HQ1061 .I584 2003

Klarsfeld, André. [Biologie de la mort. English] The biology of death. Ithaca, NY : Comstock Pub. Associates/Cornell University Press, 2004.
QH530 .K5613 2004

Macdonald, Barbara, 1913- Look me in the eye. New, expanded ed. Denver, CO : Spinsters Ink Books, 2001.

Overall, Christine, 1949- Aging, death, and human longevity. Berkeley : University of California Press, c2003.
RA564.8 .O95 2003

Aging, creativity, and art.
Lindauer, Martin S. New York : Kluwer Academic/Plenum Publishers, c2003.
BF724.85.C73 L56 2003

Aging, death, and human longevity.
Overall, Christine, 1949- Berkeley : University of California Press, c2003.
RA564.8 .O95 2003

AGING PERSONS. *See* **AGED.**

AGING - PSYCHOLOGICAL ASPECTS. *See also* **AGEISM.**
Aleksandrova, Nataliĭa. Starite khora. 1. izd. Sofiĭa : Universitetsko izd-vo "Sv. Kliment Okhridski", 2001.
BF724.8 .A42 2001

Bee, Helen L., 1939- The journey of adulthood. 5th ed. Upper Saddle River, NJ : Pearson Prentice Hall, c2004.
BF724.5 .B44 2004

Kirasic, K. C. Midlife in context. Boston : McGraw-Hill, c2004.
BF724.6 .K55 2004

Kray, Jutta. Adult age differences in task switching. Lengerich : Pabst Science Publishers, 2000.
BF724.55.C63 K73 2000

Recent advances in psychology and aging. Amsterdam ; Boston : Elsevier, 2003.
BF724.8 .R43 2003

Vint/age 2001 conference : [videorecording]. New York, c2001.

AGING - PSYCHOLOGICAL ASPECTS - LONGITUDINAL STUDIES.
Schaie, K. Warner (Klaus Warner), 1928- Developmental influences on adult intelligence. [Update]. New York : Oxford University Press, 2004.
BF724.55.C63 S32 2004

Aging under the microscope 48 p.
Aging under the microscope [electronic resource]. Bethesda, MD : National Institute on Aging, National Institutes of Health, [2002]

Aging under the microscope [electronic resource] : a biological quest. Bethesda, MD : National Institute on Aging, National Institutes of Health, [2002] (NIH publication ; no. 02-2756) System requirements: Adobe Acrobat Reader. Mode of access: Internet from the NIA web site. Address as of 4/29/03: http://www.nia.nih.gov/health/pubs/microscope/; current access is available via PURL. Title from title screen (viewed on Apr. 29, 2003). URL: http://purl.access.gpo.gov/GPO/LPS30371 Available in other form: Aging under the microscope 48 p. (OCoLC)52100950.
1. Aging. I. National Institute on Aging. II. Title: Aging under the microscope 48 p. III. Series.

Agiografia, magia, superstizione.
Lozito, Vito. Bari : Levante, [1999]
BF1775 .L69 1999

AGITATION (PSYCHOLOGY).
Tretiack, Philippe. Traité de l'agitation ordinaire. Paris : B. Grasset, c1998.
BF575.A35 T74 1998

AGNATIC DESCENT. *See* **PATRILINEAL KINSHIP.**

AGNATIC KINSHIP. *See* **PATRILINEAL KINSHIP.**

Agora (FLACSO (Organization). Sede Ecuador)
Masculinidades en Ecuador. Quito, Ecuador : FLACSO : [S.l.] : UNFPA, 2001.
BF692.5 .M388 2001

Masculinidades en Ecuador. Quito, Ecuador : FLACSO ; [s.l.] : UNFPA, 2001.
BF692.5 .M37 2001

AGRARIAN QUESTION. *See* **AGRICULTURE - ECONOMIC ASPECTS.**

AGRARIAN TENURE. *See* **LAND TENURE.**

AGRIBUSINESS. *See* **AGRICULTURE - ECONOMIC ASPECTS.**

AGRICULTURAL BIOTECHNOLOGY - RESEARCH.
King, John L. Concentration and technology in agricultural input industries [electronic resource]. [Washington, D.C.] : U.S. Dept of Agriculture, [2001].

AGRICULTURAL ECONOMICS. *See* **AGRICULTURE - ECONOMIC ASPECTS.**

AGRICULTURAL LABORERS. *See* **PEASANTRY.**

AGRICULTURAL PRODUCTION ECONOMICS. *See* **AGRICULTURE - ECONOMIC ASPECTS.**

AGRICULTURE. *See* **LIVESTOCK.**

AGRICULTURE - ECONOMIC ASPECTS - 1945-. *See* **AGRICULTURE - ECONOMIC ASPECTS.**

AGRICULTURE - ECONOMIC ASPECTS - EUROPE - HISTORY.
Duby, Georges. Qu'est-ce que la société féodale? Paris : Flammarion, c2002.

Agriculture information bulletin
(no. 763) King, John L. Concentration and technology in agricultural input industries [electronic resource]. [Washington, D.C.] : U.S. Dept of Agriculture, [2001].

Agua y peña
(16) Velásquez, Andrés, fl. 1553-1615. Libro de la melancholía. Viareggio (Lucca) : M. Baroni, [2002]
BF575.M44 V453 2002

Aguirre Rojas, Carlos Antonio. Ensayos braudelianos : itinerarios intelectuales y aportes historiográficos de Fernand Braudel / Carlos Aguirre Rojas. Rosario, Argentina : Prohistoria : M. Suárez ; México : Asociación Nacional de Profesores de Historia de México, 2000. 240 p. ; 21 cm. (Colección Protextos ; 1) Chiefly a collection of previously published (1993-1997) articles, essays, etc. Includes bibliographical references. ISBN 9879903595
1. Braudel, Fernand. 2. Historiography. 3. Historians - France - Biography. I. Title. II. Series.
D15.B62 A38 2000

Ahammīyat al-rabṭ bayna al-tafkīr al-lughawī 'inda al-'Arab wa- naẓarīyāt al-baḥth al-lughawī al-ḥadīth.
Baḥnasāwī, Ḥusām. al-Qāhirah : Maktabat al-Thaqāfah al-Dīnīyah, 1994.
PJ6106 .B35 1994 <Orien Arab>

Aḥat sha'alti.
Ḳarelits, Ḥayim Sha'ul ben Me'ir. Sefer Aḥat sha'alti. Bene Beraḳ : Mish. Ḳarelits, 762 [2002]

Ahavat 'olam.
Algazi, Solomon ben Abraham, 1610?-ca. 1683. Sefer Ahavat 'olam. Bruḳlin : Sifre Algazi, 760 [2000]

Ahavat shalom.
Hilel, Ya'aḳov Mosheh. Sefer Ahavat shalom. [Hotsa'ah 2], 'im hosafot rabot. Yerushala[y]im : ha-Makhon le-hotsa'at sefarim ve-khitve yad "Ahavat Shalom", 762 [2002]

Ahavat Yiśra'el.
Mosheh ben Ḥayim, Ḳoznitser, d. 1874. Sefer Ahavat Yiśra'el. Yotse le-or me-ḥadash. Yerushalayim : Mekhon Sod yesharim, 760 [2000]

'Ahavat Yisra'el.
Mosheh ben Ḥayim, Ḳoznitser, d. 1874. Sefer 'Ahavat Yiśra'el. Bruḳlin : [Yehoshu'a Pinḥas Bukhinger], 762 [2001]

Ahrendt-Schulte, Ingrid, 1942-.
Geschlecht, Magie und Hexenverfolgung. Bielefeld : Verlag für Regionalgeschichte, 2002.

AHSEN, AKHTER.
Hochman, Judith. Image and word in Ahsen's image psychology. New York : Brandon House, c2000.
BF367 .H63 2000

AI (ARTIFICIAL INTELLIGENCE). *See* **ARTIFICIAL INTELLIGENCE.**

Ai ni, dan bu xiang xin ni / Zan Aizong bian. Di 1 ban. Beijing : Zhongguo hua qiao chu ban she, 2000. ii, 288 p. ; 21 cm. ISBN 7-80120-418-2
1. Chinese essays - 20th century. 2. Love. I. Zan, Aizong.

PL2608.L6 A5 2000

Ai qing de di er zhang mian kong.
Zhang, Hong. Di 1 ban. Jinan : Shandong ren min chu ban she, 2001.

AIDS (DISEASE) - PREVENTION - SOCIAL ASPECTS.
Klitzman, Robert. Mortal secrets. Baltimore : Johns Hopkins University Press, 2003.
RA643.8 .K56 2003

AIDS (DISEASE) - REPORTING.
Privacy and disclosure of HIV in interpersonal relationships. Mahwah, N.J. : Lawrence Erlbaum Associates, 2003.
RA643.8 .P755 2003

AIDS (DISEASE) - SOCIAL ASPECTS.
Califia-Rice, Patrick, 1954- Speaking sex to power. 1st ed. San Francisco : Cleis Press, c2002.
HQ76.25 .C32 2002

Privacy and disclosure of HIV in interpersonal relationships. Mahwah, N.J. : Lawrence Erlbaum Associates, 2003.
RA643.8 .P755 2003

AIDS (DISEASE) - TRANSMISSION.
From child sexual abuse to adult sexual risk. 1st ed. Washington, DC : American Psychological Association, c2004.
RC569.5.A28 F76 2004

[Aids to Sadhana series. Tibetan & Sanskrit. Selections.] Sādhanamālā, Avalokiteśvara section : Sanskrit and Tibetan texts / [edited by] Ruriko Sakuma. Delhi : Adroit Publishers ; New Delhi : Distributors, Akhil Book Distributors, 2002. 279 p. ; 25 cm. (Asian iconography series ; 3) Revision of the author's dissertation (Doctoral--Nagoya University). Includes bibliographical references (p. 277-279). Tibetan and Sanskrit (in roman); introduction and notes in English. ISBN 81-87392-37-1
1. Tantric Buddhism. 2. Avalokiteśvara (Buddhist deity) 3. Art, Tantric. I. Sakuma, Ruriko. II. Title. III. Series.
BQ8915 .S23 2002

Aim first!.
Silber, Lee T. Mission, Kan. : SkillPath Publications, c1999.
BF505.G6 S55 1999

AIMS AND OBJECTIVES OF EDUCATION. *See* **EDUCATION - AIMS AND OBJECTIVES.**

Aiqing de di er zhang miankong.
Zhang, Hong. Ai qing de di er zhang mian kong = Di 1 ban. Jinan : Shandong ren min chu ban she, 2001.

AIR CARRIERS. *See* **AIRLINES.**

AIR CREWS. *See* **FLIGHT CREWS.**

AIR LINES. *See* **AIRLINES.**

AIR NAVIGATION. *See* **AERONAUTICS.**

AIR PILOTS.
Nesbit, Roy Conyers. Missing believed killed. Stroud : Sutton, 2002.

AIR - POLLUTION. *See* **SMOKE.**

AIR POWER. *See* **AIR WARFARE.**

AIR STRATEGY. *See* **AIR WARFARE.**

AIR TACTICS. *See* **AIR WARFARE.**

AIR TRANSPORT. *See* **AERONAUTICS, COMMERCIAL.**

AIR TRANSPORTATION INDUSTRY. *See* **AERONAUTICS, COMMERCIAL; AIRLINES.**

Air University (U.S.). Air Command and Staff College. School of Advanced Airpower Studies.
Givhan, Walter D. The time value of military force in modern warfare [electronic resource]. Maxwell Air Force Base, Ala. : Air University Press, [1996]

Air University (U.S.). Air War College.
Bird, David F. Quality Air Force in an emergency [electronic resource]. Maxwell Air Force Base, Ala. : Air War College, Air University, [1996]

Air University (U.S.). Press.
Givhan, Walter D. The time value of military force in modern warfare [electronic resource]. Maxwell Air Force Base, Ala. : Air University Press, [1996]

Global security concerns [electronic resource]. Maxwell Air Force Base, Ala. : Air University Press, [1996]

Kline, John A. Listening effectively [electronic resource]. Maxwell Air Force Base, Ala. : Air University Press, [1996]

Zentner, John J., 1965- The art of wing leadership and aircrew morale in combat [electronic resource]. Maxwell Air Force Base, Ala. : Air University Press, [2001]

AIR WARFARE.
Givhan, Walter D. The time value of military force in modern warfare [electronic resource]. Maxwell Air Force Base, Ala. : Air University Press, [1996]

AIR WARFARE - CASE STUDIES.
Zentner, John J., 1965- The art of wing leadership and aircrew morale in combat [electronic resource]. Maxwell Air Force Base, Ala. : Air University Press, [2001]

AIRCRAFT ACCIDENT VICTIMS' FAMILIES - PSYCHOLOGY.
Wilkins, David, 1944- United by tragedy. Nampa, Idaho : Pacific Press Pub. Association, c2003.
BF575.G7 W555 2003

AIRCRAFT ACCIDENTS - INVESTIGATION.
Nesbit, Roy Conyers. Missing believed killed. Stroud : Sutton, 2002.

AIRCRAFT CREWS. *See* **FLIGHT CREWS.**

AIRCRAFT INDUSTRY - UNITED STATES.
United States. Congress. House. Committee on Transportation and Infrastructure. Subcommittee on Aviation. Competition in the U.S. aircraft manufacturing industry. Washington : U.S. G.P.O. : For sale by the Supt. of Docs., U.S. G.P.O., [Congressional Sales Office], 2001.

AIRCREWS. *See* **FLIGHT CREWS.**

Airesis
Sermonti, Giuseppe. Il mito della grande madre. Milano : Mimesis, c2002.

AIRLINE CRASHES. *See* **AIRCRAFT ACCIDENTS.**

Airline financial condition.
Hecker, JayEtta Z. Commercial aviation [electronic resource]. [Washington, D.C.] : U.S. General Accounting Office, [2002]

AIRLINE INDUSTRY. *See* **AIRLINES.**

AIRLINES - DEREGULATION - UNITED STATES.
United States. Congress. Senate. Committee on Commerce, Science, and Transportation. Antitrust issues in the airline industry. Washington : U.S. G.P.O. : For sale by the Supt. of Docs., U.S. G.P.O., 2003.

AIRLINES - EMPLOYEES. *See* **FLIGHT CREWS.**

AIRLINES - SECURITY MEASURES - UNITED STATES - FINANCE.
United States. Congress. House. Committee on Transportation and Infrastructure. Subcommittee on Aviation. The financial condition of the airline industry. Washington : U.S. G.P.O. : For sale by the Supt. of Docs., U.S. G.P.O. [Congressional Sales Office], 2002.

AIRLINES - UNITED STATES - COST OF OPERATION.
United States. Congress. House. Committee on Transportation and Infrastructure. Subcommittee on Aviation. The financial condition of the airline industry. Washington : U.S. G.P.O. : For sale by the Supt. of Docs., U.S. G.P.O. [Congressional Sales Office], 2002.

AIRPLANE ACCIDENTS. *See* **AIRCRAFT ACCIDENTS.**

AIRPLANE COLLISIONS. *See* **AIRCRAFT ACCIDENTS.**

AIRPLANE CRASHES. *See* **AIRCRAFT ACCIDENTS.**

AIRPLANE INDUSTRY. *See* **AIRCRAFT INDUSTRY.**

AIRPLANES. *See* **AIRCRAFT INDUSTRY.**

AIRPLANES - ACCIDENTS. *See* **AIRCRAFT ACCIDENTS.**

AIRPLANES - CREWS. *See* **FLIGHT CREWS.**

AIRPLANES, MILITARY. *See* **AIR WARFARE.**

AIRSHIPS. *See* **AERONAUTICS.**

AIRWAYS. *See* **AIRLINES.**

Aisthetik.
Böhme, Gernot. München : Fink, c2001.
BH39 .B64 2001

Aïvanhov, Omraam Mikhaël. L'amour plus grand que la foi / Omraam Mikhaël Aïvanhov. Fréjus : Prosveta, c2000. 230 p. : ill. ; 18 cm. (Collection Izvor ; 239) Includes bibliographical references. ISBN 2-85566-798-4
1. Faith. 2. Love - Religious aspects. 3. Spiritual life. I. Title. II. Series.

"Et il me montra un fleuve d'eau de la vie"-- Apocalypse de saint Jean 22:1 / Omraam Mikhaël Aïvanhov. Fréjus : Prosveta, [2002] 582 p. : ill. (some col.) ; 21 cm. (Collection Synopsis ; 3) Includes bibliographical references and index. ISBN 2-85566-846-8 ISBN 2-85566-851-4
1. Bible. - N.T. - Revelation XX - Miscellanea. 2. Spiritual life. 3. Spiritualism. I. Title.

La foi qui transporte les montagnes / Omraam Mikhaël Aïvanhov. Fréjus : Prosveta, c1999. 219 p. : ill. ; 18 cm. (Collection Izvor ; 238) ISBN 2-85566-793-3
1. Faith. 2. Spiritual life. I. Title. II. Series.

Aizsils, Arvīds, 1904-1940. Latviesu tautas sapņu iztulkosana.
Senie latviešu sapņu skaidrojumi. [Rīga] : Tapals, 2002.
BF1098.L35 S46 2002

Ajayi, Jare.
Adeosun, Kola A. [Ọrọ ti obi n sọ. English] What the kolanut is saying. Ibadan, Nigeria : Creative Books, 1999.
BF1779.K6 A33 1999

Akadēmeia
(7) Piel que habla. Barcelona : Icaria, [2001]
BF697.5.B63 P54 2001

Akhutin, A. V. (Anatoliĭ Valerianovich).
Bibler, V. S. (Vladimir Solomonovich), 1918- Zamysly. Moskva : Rossiĭskiĭ gos. gumanitarnyĭ universitet, 2002.
B99.R9 B53 2002

Akif'ev, A. P. Genetika i sud'by / A.P. Akif'ev. Moskva : TSentrpoligraf, 2001. 317 p. : ill. ; 22 cm. (Rossiía zabytaía i neizvestnaía) ISBN 5227015317
1. Human evolution. 2. Genetics - History. 3. Genetic psychology. I. Title. II. Series.
GN281 . A45 2001

Akopov, G. V. Mentalistika : problemy, resheniía, perspektivy issledovaniĭ : mental'nost' povolzhskogo sotsiuma v nauchnykh proektakh / [nauchnyi redaktor O.M. Buranok ; avtory-sostaviteli G.V. Akopov ... et al.]. Samara : Samarskiĭ gos. pedagog. universitet, 2001. 63 p. ; 21 cm. At head of title: Samarskiĭ nauchnyĭ tsentr RAN. Samarskiĭ gosudarstvennyĭ pedagogicheskiĭ universitet. Includes bibliographical references. ISBN 5934240617
1. Psychology - Russia (Federation) 2. National characteristics, Russian. I. Buranok, O. M. II. Rossiĭskaía akademiía nauk. Samarskiĭ nauchnyĭ tsentr. III. Samarskiĭ gosudarstvennyĭ pedagogicheskiĭ universitet. IV. Title.
BF108.R8 A478 2001

Problema soznaniía v psikhologii : otechestvennaía platforma / G.V. Akopov. Samara : Samarskiĭ gos. pedagog. universitet, 2002. 206 p. ; 21 cm. Includes bibliographical references (p. 177-196). ISBN 5934240706
1. Consciousness. I. Title.
BF311 .A44 2002

Akron, 1948- H.R. Giger tarot / Akron. Köln : Evergreen, c2000. 22 cards : col. ; 17 x 11 cm. + book (223 p. : ill. ; 21 cm.) + poster (52 x 68 cm.). Issued in a container (22 x 16 x 4 cm.). Revised, shortened and translated version of: Baphomet (Neuhausen, Switzerland : Urania AG, 1992). Poster used for spread system. ISBN 3-8228-5850-1
1. Tarot. 2. Tarot cards. 3. Shadow (Psychoanalysis) - Miscellanea. I. Giger, H. R. (Hansruedi), 1940- II. Title.

Aktual'ni problemy psykholohiï. Kyïv : In-tyt psykholohiï im. H.S. Kostiuka, 2001- v. : ill. ; 21 cm. T. 1, ch. 1- . Latest issue consulted: T. 5, ch. 1, published in 2002. Issued in parts.
1. Psychology - Periodicals. I. Instytut psykholohiï im. H.S. Kostiuka.
BF8.U38 A38

Aktual'nye voprosy obshcheĭ, vozrastnoĭ i sotsial'noĭ psikhologii : materialy nauchnoĭ konferentsii fakul'teta psikhologii i sotsial'noĭ raboty ot 27 apreliá 2001 goda, posviashchennoĭ 30-letiiu Tverskogo gosudarstvennogo universiteta / [pod redaktsieĭ A.F Shikuna i B.A. Sazont'eva]. Tver' : Tverskoĭ gos. universitet, 2001. 55 p. : ill. ; 21 cm. Includes bibliographical references.
1. Psychology - Congresses. I. Shikun, A. F. II. Sazont'ev, B. A. III. Tverskoĭ gosudarstvennyĭ universitet.
BF20 .A46 2001

Aktuelle Frauenforschung
Geschlecht und Globalisierung. Königstein : Ulrike Helmer Verlag, c2001.

Weiler, Gerda, 1921- Der enteignete Mythos. Königstein : Helmer, [1996]

Āl-Farabi atyndaghy Qazaq memlekettīk ūlttyq universitetī.
Ageev, Valentin. Psikhologiía transtsendirovaniía. Almaty: "Qazaq Universitetī", 2002.
BF713 .A34 1998

Al oído de Uribe : como iniciar un nuevo proceso de paz en Colombia / Carlos Holmes Trujillo G., editor ; Camilo Gómez A. ... [et al.]. 1a. ed. Bogotá, Colombia : Editorial Oveja Negra, 2002. 182 p. ; 24 cm. "Altos comisionados y consejeros para la paz." ISBN 958-06-1030-4
1. Political violence - Colombia. 2. Negotiation - Colombia. 3. Colombia - Politics and government - 1974- 4. Guerrillas - Colombia. 5. Insurgency - Colombia. 6. Peace. I. Trujillo García, Carlos Holmes. II. Gómez Alzate, Camilo. III. Title: Como iniciar un nuevo proceso de paz en Colombia

Alackapally, Sebastian, 1961- Being and meaning : reality and language in Bhartṛhari and Heidegger / Sebastian Alackapally. 1st ed. Delhi : Motilal Banarsidass Publishers, 2002. xviii, 297 p. ; 23 cm. Includes bibliographical references (p. [269]-291) and index. ISBN 81-208-1803-2
1. Bhartṛhari. - Vākyapadīya. 2. Heidegger, Martin, - 1889-1976. - Sein and Zeit. 3. Sanskrit language - Grammar. 4. Ontology. 5. Space and time. I. Title.
PK541.B48 A43 2002

Alaska Anthropological Association. Meeting (25th : 1998 : Anchorage, Alaska).
Many faces of gender. Boulder : University Press of Colorado ; Calgary, Alta., Canada : University of Calgary Press, c2002.
E98.P95 M35 2002

Albanese, Maria Ausilia.
The Splendors of archaeology. Cairo : American University in Cairo Press, 1998.

ALBANIA - HISTORIOGRAPHY.
Albanian identities. Bloomington : Indiana University Press, 2002.
DR950 .A385 2002

ALBANIA - POLITICS AND GOVERNMENT.
Albanian identities. Bloomington : Indiana University Press, 2002.
DR950 .A385 2002

Albanian identities : myth and history / Stephanie Schwandner-Sievers and Bernd J. Fischer, editors. Bloomington : Indiana University Press, 2002. xvii, 238 p. : ill., map ; 22 cm. Includes bibliographical references and index. Table of contents URL: http://www.loc.gov/catdir/toc/fy033/2002068493.html CONTENTS: Narratives of power : capacities of myth in Albania / Stephanie Schwandner-Sievers -- The nature of myth : some theoretical aspects / George Schöpflin -- Invention of a nationalism : myth and amnesia / Piro Misha -- The role of education in the formation of Albanian identity and its myths / Isa Blumi -- Religion and the politics of 'Albanianism' : Naim Frashëri's Bektashi writings / Ger Duijzings -- Myths of Albanian national identity : some key elements, as expressed in the works of Albanian writers in America in the early twentieth century / Noel Malcolm -- Between the glory of a virtual world and the misery of a real world / Fatos Lubonja -- Ismail Kadare's The H-file and the making of the Homeric verse : variations on the works and lives of Milman Parry and Albert Lord / Galia Valtchinova -- Enver Hoxha's role in the development of socialist Albanian myths / M.J. Alex Standish -- The myth of Ali Pasha and the Bektashis : the construction of an 'Albanian Bektashi national history' / Nathalie Clayer -- Perceptions and reality in twentieth-century Albanian military prowess / Bernd J. Fischer -- Smoke without fire? Albania, SOE and the communist 'conspiracy theory' / Roderick Bailey -- 'Shkolla shqipe' and nationhood : Albanians in pursuit of education in the native language in interwar (1918-41) and post-autonomy (1989-98) Kosovo / Denisa Kostovicova -- The perception of the Albanians in Greece in the 1830s and '40s : the role of the press / Elias Skoulidas -- North American Albanian immigration : narratives on political myths / Annie Lafontaine -- Culture and the reinvention of myths in a border area / Gilles de Rapper -- Myths and new forms of governance in Albania / Mariella Pandolfi -- Youth NGOs in Albania : civil society development, local cultural constructions of democracy, and strategies of survival at work / Nicola Mai -- Conspiracy theories in Albanian politics and media / Fabian Schmidt. ISBN 0-253-34189-2 (cloth : alk. paper) ISBN 0-253-21570-6 (paper : alk. paper) DDC 949.65
1. Nationalism - Albania. 2. Myth. 3. Albania - Historiography. 4. Albania - Politics and government. I. Schwandner-Sievers, Stephanie. II. Fischer, Bernd Jürgen, 1952-

DR950 .A385 2002

Albarral Albarral, Purificación.
Aboab, Isaac, 14th cent. [Menorat ha-ma'or. Ladino] Una cala en la literatura religiosa sefardí. Granada : Universidad de Granada, 2001.
BJ1287.A152 L33 2001

Alber-Reihe Praktische Philosophie
(Bd. 70) Thurnherr, Urs. Vernetzte Ethik. Freiburg : Alber, 2001.

Alberione, James, 1884-1971. La donna associata allo zelo sacerdotale : per il clero e per la donna / Giacomo Alberione. Cinisello Balsamo, Milano : San Paolo, c2001. 302 p. : ill. ; 22 cm. (Opera omnia ; 6) Includes bibliographical references and index. ISBN 88-215-4502-4 DDC 253
1. Women in Christianity. 2. Church work with women - Catholic Church. 3. Women - Religious life. I. Title. II. Series.

Albert, Hans, 1921- Lesebuch : ausgewählte Texte / Hans Albert. Tübingen : Mohr Siebeck, 2001. viii, 398 p. ; 19 cm. (UTB für Wissenschaft. ; 2194) Includes bibliographic references and index. ISBN 3-16-147494-5 (Mohr Siebeck : pbk.) ISBN 3-8252-2194-6 (UTB : pbk.)
1. Philosophy. I. Title. II. Series.

Albert, Michael, 1947-.
Monkeywrenching the new world order [sound recording]. Oakland, Calif : AK Press ; San Francisco, CA : Alternative Tentacles Records, 2001.

Albom ha-Re'iyah Ḳuḳ, zatsal.
Mar'eh Kohen. Yerushalayim : Makhon le-ḥeḳer mishnat ha-Re'iyah Ḳuḳ be-shituf 'im "Bet ha-Rav", c762 [2001 or 2002]

Alborch Bataller, Carmen. Malas : rivalidad y complicidad entre mujeres / Carmen Alborch. 3. ed. [Madrid] : Aguilar, 2002. 343 p. ; 24 cm. Includes bibliographical references (p. 311-342). Filmography: p. 343. ISBN 84-03-09294-6
1. Women - Psychology. 2. Interpersonal relations. I. Title. II. Title: Rivalidad y complicidad entre mujeres

Albrecht, Benno Andres, 1957-.
Metamorfosi della città. Milano : Garzanti / Scheiwiller, 1995 (1996 printing)
HT111 .M472 1995

Alcalá Castro, Marla.
Amar Amar, José Juan. Políticas sociales y modelos de atención integral a la infancia. Barranquilla, Colombia : Ediciones Uninorte, 2001.

Alchemical healing.
Scully, Nicki, 1943- Rochester, Vt. : Bear & Co., 2003.
BF1999 .S369 2003

ALCHEMY. See also MEDICINE, MAGIC, MYSTIC, AND SPAGIRIC.
The alchemy reader. Cambridge, U.K. New York : Cambridge University Press, 2003.
QD26 .A585 2003

Buckland, Raymond. Book of alchemy. 1st ed. St. Paul, Minn. : Llewellyn Publications, 2003.
BF1778.5 .B83 2003

Greenberg, Arthur. The art of chemistry. Hoboken, N.J. : Wiley-Interscience, c2003.
QD11 .G735 2003

Weidner, Jay. The mysteries of the great cross of Hendaye. Rochester, Vt. : Destiny Books, 2003.
BF1999 .W435 2003

ALCHEMY - EUROPE - MANUSCRIPTS - EXHIBITIONS.
Magia, alchimia, scienza dal '400 al '700. Firenze : Centro Di, 2002.
BF1598.H6 M34 2002

ALCHEMY - HISTORY.
Tilton, Hereward. The quest for the phoenix. Berlin ; New York : Walter de Gruyter, 2003.
QD24.M3 T558 2003

ALCHEMY IN LITERATURE - CONGRESSES.
Hermetik. Tübingen : M. Niemeyer Verlag, c2002.
BF1586 .H47 2002

ALCHEMY - ITALY - SIENA - HISTORY - SOURCES.
Maghi, streghe e alchimisti a Siena e nel suo territorio (1458-1571). Monteriggioni (Siena) : Il leccio, c1999.
BF1622.I8 M295 1999

The alchemy of innovation.
Barker, Alan, 1956- London : Spiro Press, 2002.

ALCHEMY - PSYCHOLOGICAL ASPECTS.
Henderson, Joseph L. (Joseph Lewis), 1903-

Transformation of the psyche. New York : Brunner-Routledge, 2003.
BF173 .H4346 2003

The alchemy reader : from Hermes Trismegistus to Isaac Newton / edited by Stanton J. Linden. Cambridge, U.K. New York : Cambridge University Press, 2003. vi, 260 p., 14 p. of plates : ill. ; 26 cm. Includes bibliographical references (p. [250]-253) and index. ISBN 0-521-79234-7 ISBN 0-521-79662-8 (pbk.) DDC 540/.1/12
1. Alchemy. 2. Hermetism. I. Linden, Stanton J., 1935-
QD26 .A585 2003

Alcock, Susan E.
Archaeologies of memory. Malden, MA ; Oxford : Blackwell, 2003.
CC72.4 .A733 2003

ALCOHOLICS - REHABILITATION.
Corley, M. Deborah. Embracing recovery from chemical dependency. Sottsdale, AZ : Gentle Path Press, c2003.
BF632 .C63 2003

ALCOHOLISM - PATIENTS. *See* **ALCOHOLICS.**

Aldama, Arturo J., 1964-.
Violence and the body. Bloomington : Indiana University Press, c2003.
HM1116 .V557 2003

Alefirenko, M. F. Poèticheskai͡a ėnergii͡a slova : sinergetika i͡azyka, soznanii͡a i kul'tury / N.F. Alefirenko. Moskva : Academia, 2002. 391 p. ; 20 cm. "Otdelenie literatury i i͡azyka Rossiĭskoĭ akademii nauk. Obshchestvo li͡ubiteleĭ rossiĭskoĭ slovesnosti. Volgogradskiĭ gosudarstvennyĭ pedagogicheskiĭ universitet." Includes bibliographical references (p. 369-389) ISBN 5874441581
1. Language and culture. 2. Cognition and culture. 3. Semantics. 4. Cognition. 5. Psycholinguistics. 6. Metaphor. I. Rossiĭskai͡a akademii͡a nauk. Otdelenie literatury i iskusstva. II. Obshchestvo li͡ubiteleĭ rossiĭskoĭ slovesnosti. III. Volgogradskiĭ gosudarstvennyĭ pedagogicheskiĭ universitet. IV. Title.
P35 .A544 2002

Aleksander, Igor. How to build a mind : toward machines with imagination / Igor Aleksander. New York : Columbia University Press, 2001. xi, 205 p. ; 24 cm. (Maps of the mind) Includes bibliographical references and index. ISBN 0-231-12012-5 (cloth : alk. paper) DDC 006.3
1. Artificial intelligence. 2. Imagination. I. Title. II. Series.
Q335 .A44225 2001

Aleksandrova, Natalii͡a. Starite khora : lichnostno-psikhologicheski osobenosti / Natalii͡a Aleksandrova. 1. izd. Sofii͡a : Universitetsko izd-vo "Sv. Kliment Okhridski", 2001. 179 p. : ill. ; 20 cm. Includes bibliographical references (p. 158-164). ISBN 9540715601
1. Aged - Psychology. 2. Aging - Psychological aspects. I. Title.
BF724.8 .A42 2001

Alemán, Jorge. Lacan en la razón posmoderna / Jorge Alemán. Málaga : Miguel Gómez Ediciones, c2000. 187 p. ; 21 cm. (Colección Itaca ; 4) Errata sheet inserted. ISBN 84-88326-15-7 DDC 150.19/5/092
1. Lacan, Jacques, - 1901- 2. Philosophy, Modern - 20th century. I. Title. II. Series.
BF109.L28 A44 2000

Alenius, Kari.
Looking at the other. Oulu, Finland : University of Oulu, 2002.

Alexander, Anna, 1956-.
High culture. Albany : State University of New York Press, c2003.
HV4998 .H544 2003

ALEXANDER, F. MATTHIAS (FREDERICK MATTHIAS), 1869-1955.
The Alexander technique [videorecording]. New York, N.Y. : Wellspring Media, c1999.

Alexander, Jane. The smudging and blessings book : inspirational rituals to cleanse and heal / Jane Alexander. New York: Sterling Pub., 2001. 96 p. : col. ill. ; 22 cm. Originally published: New Alresford [England] : Godsfield Press, 1999. Includes index. Publisher description URL: http://www.loc.gov/catdir/description/ste031/2003266714.html ISBN 0-8069-7447-8 (pbk.) DDC 133.3/33
1. Smoke - Miscellanea. 2. Mind and body - Miscellanea. 3. Sacred space - Miscellanea. 4. Spiritual life - Miscellanea. 5. Conduct of life - Miscellanea. 6. Self-care, Health - Miscellanea. I. Title.
BF1999 .A6329 2001

Alexander, Jeffrey C. The meanings of social life : a cultural sociology / Jeffrey C. Alexander. New York : Oxford University Press, 2003. x, 296 p. ; 24 cm. Includes bibliographical references (p. 229-291) and index. CONTENTS: Introduction: The meanings of (social) life : on the origins of a cultural sociology -- 1. The strong program in cultural sociology : elements of a structural hermeneutics / with Philip Smith -- 2. On the social construction of "moral universals" : the "Holocaust" from war crime to trauma drama -- 3. Cultural trauma and collective identity -- 4. A cultural sociology of evil -- 5. The discourse of American civil society / with Philip Smith -- 6. Watergate as democratic ritual -- 7. The sacred and profane information machine -- 8. Modern, anti, post, and neo : how intellectuals explain "our time". ISBN 0-19-516084-3 (cloth) DDC 301
1. Sociology. 2. Prejudices. 3. Culture. 4. Violence. I. Title.
HM585 .A5 2003

Alexander Mitscherlich, 1908-1982.
Hurson, Didier. Paris : Presses de l'Université de Paris-Sorbonne, 2002.

Alexander, Skye. 10-minute magic spells / Skye Alexander. Gloucester, Mass. : Fair Winds Press, 2003. p. cm. Includes bibliographical references. ISBN 1-931412-31-6 (pbk.) DDC 133.4/4
1. Magic. I. Title. II. Title: Ten minute magic spells
BF1611 .A43 2003

10-minute tarot : read the future in an instant / Skye Alexander. Gloucester, Mass. : Fair Winds Press, c2003. iv, 224 p. : ill. ; 16 cm. Includes bibliographical references (p. 223) and index. Table of contents URL: http://www.loc.gov/catdir/toc/ecip048/2003018408.html ISBN 1-59233-018-5 (pbk.) DDC 133.3/2424
1. Tarot. I. Title. II. Title: Ten-minute tarot
BF1879.T2 A445 2003

Magickal astrology : understanding your place in the cosmos / by Skye Alexander. Franklin Lakes, NJ : New Page Books, c2000. 223 p. : ill. ; 21 cm. Includes bibliographical references (p. 211-218) and index. ISBN 1-56414-479-8 (pbk.) DDC 133.4/3
1. Magic. 2. Astrology. I. Title.
BF1611 .A44 2000

Your birthday sign through time. New York : Atria Books, c2002.
BF1728.A2 Y57 2002

ALEXANDER TECHNIQUE.
The Alexander technique [videorecording]. New York, N.Y. : Wellspring Media, c1999.

The Alexander technique [videorecording] / Wellspring Media ; directed by Molly McBride ; conceived and produced by Jane Kosminsky. New York, N.Y. : Wellspring Media, c1999. 1 videodisc (148 min.) : sd., col. ; 4 3/4 in. DVD. The second segment of this recording, Solutions for back trouble, was also released as a videocassette. See: *MGZIA 4-5252 The Alexander technique: solutions for back trouble. Director of photography, Juan Barrera; associate director, Bruce Becker; music, Marianna Rosett; scenic design, Alan Kimmel; costumes, David Zyla; lighting, Mark R. Weaver. DVD production credits: executive producers, Maryann Manelski, Yuri Weber; DVD senior producer, Jeff Stabenau; DVD producer, Michael Veasey. Instructors: Jane Kosminsky, Deborah Caplan. Introduced by William Hurt. CONTENTS: The first lesson (ca. 75 min.) / subtitled An introduction to the Alexander Technique with William Hurt and Jane Kosminsky. Kosminsky provides a brief biography of Frederick Matthias Alexander, the inventor of Alexander Technique, and explains its three-part method (self-observation, inhibition of incorrect habits, direction) and its four concepts of good use. With Hurt as a demonstrator, she presents some basic exercises: chair work, monkey [position], walking, and a self-lesson based on the technique's table work. CONTENTS: Solutions for back trouble (ca. 73 min.) / title given as Solutions for back pain on main menu. Deborah Caplan, a physical therapist and Certified Alexander Technique teacher, explains the Alexander Technique's approach to preventing back pain through correct usage of the body. With the help of demonstrators who have themselves overcome back problems by learning new habits, she describes four basic concepts of good use and their applications at home, in the office and in other everyday activities, and shows how to prevent back attacks. CONTENTS: [Additional features:] Biographies [William Hurt, Jane Kosminsky, Deborah Caplan] [still frames], weblinks. CONTENTS: Weblinks (1 frame). ISBN 1-58350-106-1
1. Alexander, F. Matthias - (Frederick Matthias), - 1869-1955. 2. Alexander technique. 3. Posture. 4. Mind and body. 5. Human mechanics. 6. Back. 7. Backache - Exercise therapy. I. Kosminsky, Jane. II. Caplan, Deborah, 1931- III. Hurt, William. IV. McBride, Molly. V. Barrera, Juan. VI. Rosett, Marianna. VII. Becker, Bruce. VIII. Wellspring Media. IX. Title: Solutions for back trouble [videorecording] X. Title: Solutions for back pain [videorecording]

Alfillé, Helen.
Dilemmas in the consulting room. London ; New York : Karnac, 2002.

Alföldi, Maria R.- Gloria romanorum : Schriften zur Spätantike zum 75. Geburtstag der Verfasserin am 6. Juni 2001 / Maria R.-Alföldi ; herausgegeben von Heinz Bellen und Hans-Markus von Kaenel. Stuttgart : Franz Steiner Verlag, 2001. xi, 381 p. : ill. ; 25 cm. (Historia. Einzelschriften ; Heft 153) ISBN 3-515-07918-1
1. Rome - Civilization. 2. Rome - History. I. Bellen, Heinz. II. Kaenel, Hans-Markus von. III. Title. IV. Series: Historia (Wiesbaden, Germany). Einzelschriften ; Heft 153.
DG78 .A546 2001

Alford, C. Fred. Levinas, the Frankfurt school and psychoanalysis / C. Fred Alford. 1st US ed. Middletown, CT : Wesleyan University Press, c2002. vii, 174 p. ; 24 cm. (Disseminations) Includes bibliographical references (p. [156]-169) and index. ISBN 0-8195-6602-0 (hardcover) ISBN 0-8195-6603-9 (pbk.)
1. Lévinas, Emmanuel. 2. Frankfurt school of sociology. 3. Psychoanalysis. I. Title. II. Series.

Algazi, Gadi.
Negotiating the gift. Göttingen : Vandenhoeck & Ruprecht, c2003.

Algazi, Solomon ben Abraham, 1610?-ca. 1683. Sefer Ahavat 'olam : kolel derushim nifla'im 'al sheloshah ha-'amudim Torah, 'avodah u-gemilut ḥasadim / ḥibro Shelomoh Algazi. Bruḳlin : Sifre Algazi, 760 [2000] 2 v. ; 27 cm. Running title: Ahavat 'olam. CONTENTS: [1] 'Amud Torah. 'Amud 'avodah. ḥ. 1 -- [2] 'Amud 'avodah, ḥ. 2. 'Amud gemilut ḥasadim.
1. Jewish sermons, Hebrew. 2. Ethics, Jewish. I. Title. II. Title: Ahavat 'olam

ALGEBRA, ABSTRACT. *See* **LOGIC, SYMBOLIC AND MATHEMATICAL.**

ALGEBRA OF LOGIC. *See* **LOGIC, SYMBOLIC AND MATHEMATICAL.**

Alger, Janet M., 1937- Cat culture : the social world of a cat shelter / Janet M. Alger, Steven F. Alger. Philadelphia : Temple University Press, 2003. xvi, 239 p. : ill. ; 21 cm. (Animals, culture, and society) Includes bibliographical references (p. 229-234) and index. ISBN 1-56639-997-1 (cloth : alk. paper) ISBN 1-56639-998-X (pbk. : alk. paper) DDC 636.8
1. Cats - Behavior. 2. Cats - Social aspects. 3. Animal shelters. 4. Human-animal relationships. I. Alger, Steven F., 1941- II. Title. III. Series.
SF446.5 .A36 2003

Alger, Steven F., 1941-.
Alger, Janet M., 1937- Cat culture. Philadelphia : Temple University Press, 2003.
SF446.5 .A36 2003

ALGONQUIAN INDIANS. *See* **POWHATAN INDIANS.**

Algorithmic learning theory.
ALT 2002 (2002 : Lübeck, Germany) Berlin ; New York : Springer, c2002.
QA76.9.A43 A48 2002

ALGORITHMS. *See* **COMPUTER ALGORITHMS.**

'ALĪ IBN ABĪ ṬĀLIB, CALIPH, 600 (CA.)-661. JAFR AL-JĀMIʻ WA-AL-NŪR AL-LĀMIʻ.
Dāwūd, Muḥammad 'Īsá. al-Jafr li-Sayyidinā 'Alī. al-Muhandisīn [Giza] : Madbūlī al-Ṣaghīr, [2003]
BF1771+

ALIEN ABDUCTION.
Dennett, Preston E., 1965- Extraterrestrial visitations. 1st ed. St. Paul, Minn. : Llewellyn Publications, 2001.
BF2050 .D46 2001

Evans, Hilary, 1929- From other worlds. Pleasantville, N.Y. : Reader's Digest, c1998.
BF2050 .E93 1998

Hawker, Gloria Ann. Morning glory. Merrimack, NH : Write to Print, c2001.
BF2050 .H373 2001

Herbst, Judith. Aliens. Minneapolis : Lerner Publications, 2005.
BF2050 .H465 2005

ALIEN BEINGS (EXTRATERRESTRIALS). *See* **LIFE ON OTHER PLANETS.**

ALIEN ENCOUNTERS WITH HUMANS. *See* **HUMAN-ALIEN ENCOUNTERS.**

ALIEN LABOR, BRAZILIAN - JAPAN.
Catanio, Percy Antonio Galimbertti. O caminho que o dekassegui sonhou (dekassegui no yumê-ji). São Paulo : EDUC, FAPESP; Londrina : UEL, 2002.

ALIENATION (PHILOSOPHY).
Fremderfahrung und Repräsentation. 1. Aufl. Weilerswist : Velbrück, 2002.

ALIENISTS. *See* **PSYCHIATRISTS.**

ALIENS. *See also* **IMMIGRANTS.**
Herbst, Judith. Minneapolis : Lerner Publications, 2005.

ALIENS (EXTRATERRESTRIALS). See **LIFE ON OTHER PLANETS.**

ALIENS - LEGAL STATUS, LAWS, ETC. See **ALIENS.**

ALIENS - UNITED STATES.
McLaughlin, Bob. [USA immigration & orientation. Spanish] USA inmigración y orientación. 1a. ed. en español. Satellite Beach, Fla. : Wellesworth Pub., c2001.

L'alingua
(176) Tapergi, Fausto, 1909- La filosofia come scienza della vita. 1a ed. Milano : Spirali, 2001.

ALIOTTA, ANTONIO, 1881-1964.
Sava, Gabriella. La psicologia filosofica in Italia. Galatina (Lecce) : Congedo, 2000.
BF38 .S235 2000

Alizade, Alcira Mariam.
Studies on femininity. London ; New York : Karnac, 2003.

ALKABEZ, SOLOMON BEN MOSES, HA-LEVI, CA. 1505-1576.
LEKHA DODI.
Sharir, Avraham Yiśra'el. Pene Shabat neḳablah. Yerushalayim : Avraham Kohen-Erez, 763 [2003]
BM670.L44 S527 2003

Alla ricerca dell'uomo tra Bibbia e modernità.
Altomare, Vincenzo. 1. ed. Cosenza : Progetto 2000, c2000.

Allakhverdov, V. M. (Viktor Mikhaĭlovich).
Fundamental'nye problemy psikhologii. Sankt-Peterburg : Izd-vo S.-Peterburgskogo universiteta, 2002.
BF20 .F86 2002

Allan, Graham, 1948-.
Social relations and the life course. Houndmills, Basingstoke New York : Palgrave Macmillan, 2003.
HM741 .S64 2003

Allard Olmos, Briseida, 1951- Mujer y poder : escritos de sociología política / Briseida Allard O. [Panamá] : Instituto de la Mujer - Universidad de Panamá, 2002. 147 p. ; 24 cm. (Colección Agenda de género del centenario) "Este libro reúne un conjunto de trabajos escritos entre los años 1987 y 1996."--P. 13. Includes bibliographical references. ISBN 9962606233
1. Feminism. 2. Feminism - Latin America. 3. Women in politics. 4. Women in politics - Latin America. I. Title. II. Title: Escritos de sociología política III. Series.
HQ1154 .A62 2002

Allcorn, Seth. The dynamic workplace : present structure and future redesign / Seth Allcorn ; foreword by Michael Diamond. Westport, Conn. ; London : Praeger, 2003. xxi, 185 p. : ill. ; 25 cm. Includes bibliographical references (p. [177]-179) and index. ISBN 1-56720-619-0 (alk. paper) DDC 331.25
1. Office layout. 2. Work environment. 3. Work design. 4. Office management. 5. Organizational behavior. I. Title.
HF5547.2 .A43 2003

Psychoanalysis and management. Heidelberg : Physica-Verlag, c1994.
BF175.4.S65 P777 1994

ALLEGIANCE. See **CITIZENSHIP; PATRIOTISM; SELF-DETERMINATION, NATIONAL.**

ALLEGORY (ART). See **SYMBOLISM IN ART.**

Allen, David, 1945 Dec. 28- Ready for anything : 52 productivity principles for work and life / David Allen. New York : Viking, 2003. p. cm. ISBN 0-670-03250-6 (alk. paper) DDC 646.7
1. Time management. 2. Self-management (Psychology) I. Title.
BF637.T5 A46 2003

Allen, Deborah I.
Bowman, Marjorie A. Women in medicine. 3rd ed. New York ; Berlin : Springer, c2002.
R692 .B69 2002

Allen, Gary L.
Human spatial memory. Mahwah, NJ : Lawrence Erlbaum Associates, 2003.
BF469 .H86 2003

Allen, John, 1951- Lost geographies of power / John Allen. Malden, MA ; Oxford : Blackwell Pub., 2003. ix, 217 p. ; 24 cm. (RGS-IBG book series) Includes bibliographical references (p. [198]-208) and index. ISBN 0-631-20728-7 (hbk. : alk. paper) ISBN 0-631-20729-5 (pbk. : alk. paper) DDC 303.3
1. Human geography. 2. Power (Social sciences) I. Title. II. Series.

Allen, Kathleen R. Time and information management that really works : organization for the '90s / Kathleen R. Allen ; series editor: Peter H. Engel. Los Angeles, Calif : Affinity Pub., c1995. vi, 122 p. : col. ill. ; 26 cm. (Small business solutions) Includes bibliographical references (p. 114) and index. "Recommended by Office Depot." ISBN 0-8442-2998-9
1. Time management. 2. Personal information management. I. Title. II. Series.

Allen, Robert G. Multiple streams of internet income / Robert G. Allen. New York : Wiley, c2001. vi, 279 p. : ill. ; 25 cm. Includes index. ISBN 0-471-41014-4 (cloth : alk. paper) DDC 658.8/4
1. Electronic commerce. 2. Internet. 3. Success in business. 4. Money. 5. Income. I. Title.
HF5548.32 .A45 2001

Allenbaugh, Eric. Deliberate success : realize your vision with purpose, passion, and performance / by Eric Allenbaugh. Franklin Lakes, NJ : Career Press, c2002. 288 p. : ill. ; 24 cm. Includes bibliographical references (p. 279-281) and index. ISBN 1-56414-617-0 (cloth) DDC 650.1
1. Success in business. 2. Success - Psychological aspects. I. Title.
HF5386 .A5434 2002

Aller, Annelies van, 1946- Levenskunst van twee vrouwen : imaginaire dialogen met Anaïs Nin en Simone de Beauvoir / Annelies van Aller. Budel : Damon, c2001. 248 p. ; 24 cm. Added title page title: Art of living of two women. Added t.p. with thesis statement: Levenskunst van twee vrouwen ... Art of living of two women : imaginary dialogues with Anaïs Nin and Simone de Beauvoir. Thesis (doctoral)--Unviversiteit Utrecht, 2001. Includes bibliographical references and index. Summary in English. ISBN 90-5573-168-4 (pbk.)
1. Nin, Anaïs, - 1903-1977. 2. Beauvoir, Simone de, - 1908- 3. Women and literature - United States - History - 20th century. 4. Women and literature - France - History - 20th century. 5. Authors, American - 20th century - Biography. 6. Authors, French - 20th century - Biography. 7. Feminists - France - Biography. 8. Women - Conduct of life. 9. Imaginary conversations. I. Title. II. Title: Art of living of two women
PS3527.I865 Z536 2001

Alley, R. W. (Robert W.).
Jackson, J. S. Bye-bye, bully!. St. Meinrad, IN. : Abbey Press, c2003.
BF637.B85 J33 2003

Mundy, Michaelene. Getting out of a stress mess!. St. Meinrad, IN : One Caring Place, c2000.
BF723.S75 M86 2000

Wigand, Molly. Help is here for facing fear. St. Meinrad, IN : One Caring Place/Abbey Press, c2000.
BF723.F4 W54 2000

ALLIANCES IN BUSINESS. See **STRATEGIC ALLIANCES (BUSINESS).**

Allis, Michael, 1964- Parry's creative process / Michael Allis. Aldershot : Ashgate, 2003. 280 p. : music ; 24 cm. (Music in nineteenth-century Britain) Bibliographical references (p. 243-252) and index. ISBN 1-84014-681-8 DDC 780.92
1. Parry, C. Hubert H. - (Charles Hubert Hastings), - 1848-1918. 2. Creation (Literary, artistic, etc.) 3. Music - Great Britain - 19th century - History and criticism. I. Title. II. Series.

Allman, Dwight D., 1957-.
Cultivating citizens. Lanham : Lexington Books, c2002.
JK1759 .C85 2002

ALLOPATHIC DOCTORS. See **PHYSICIANS.**

All'origine della pretesa cristiana.
Giussani, Luigi. PerCorso. Milano : Rizzoli, c1997-

ALLUSIONS. See **TERMS AND PHRASES.**

Allyn, David (David Smith) I can't believe I just did that : how seemingly small embarrasments can wreak havoc in your life-- and what you can do to put a stop to them / David Allyn. New York : Jeremy P. Tarcher/Penguin, 2004. p. cm. Includes bibliographical references and index. ISBN 1-58542-257-6 (alk. paper) DDC 152.4
1. Embarrassment. 2. Embarrassment - Prevention. 3. Courage. 4. Success - Psychological aspects. I. Title.
BF575.E53 A45 2004

Almeida, Heloísa Buarque de.
Gênero em matizes. Bragança Paulista, SP : EDUSF, [2002]

The almighty dollar.
Lowenkopf, Eugene L. New York : iUniverse, Inc., c2003.

Almontaser, Debbie.
The day our world changed. New York : Harry N. Abrams Inc., 2002.

Alonso, Eduardo, 1967-.
Adaptive agents and multi-agent systems. Berlin ; New York : Springer, c2003.
QA76.76.I58 A312 2003

Alonso, Graciela.
Alonso, Graciela. Hacia una pedagogía de las experiencias de las mujeres. 1. ed. Buenos Aires : Miño y Dávila, 2002.

Hacia una pedagogía de las experiencias de las mujeres / Graciela Alonso, Raúl Díaz ; con la colaboración de: Valeria Flores ... [et al.]. 1. ed. Buenos Aires : Miño y Dávila, 2002. 187 p. : ill. ; 21 cm. (Colección Educación, crítica & debate) Includes bibliographical references (p. [179]-187). ISBN 950-9467-85-5 (pbk.)
1. Women's studies. 2. Feminism. 3. Feminism and education. I. Alonso, Graciela. II. Diaz, Raul. III. Flores, Valeria. IV. Title. V. Series.

Alonso-Nuñez, José Miguel. The idea of universal history in Greece : from Herodotus to the age of Augustus / José Miguel Alonso-Núñez. Amsterdam : J.C. Gieben, 2002. 152 p. : ill., maps ; 25 cm. (Amsterdam classical monographs ; v. 4) "This is an expanded version of the lecture given in the Departments of History and Classics at Harvard University on 26th May 1998"--P. [7]. Includes bibliographical references (p. 141-142) and indexes. DDC 938/.007/2
1. Historiography - Greece - History. 2. World history - Historiography. 3. History, Ancient - Historiography. 4. History - Philosophy. 5. Philosophy, Ancient. I. Title. II. Series.
D13.5.G8 A46 2002

Alper, Gerald. Like a movie : contemporary relationships without the popcorn / Gerald Alper. 1st ed. St. Paul, Minn. : Paragon House, 2004. p. cm. Includes bibliographical references. ISBN 1-55778-833-2 (pbk.) DDC 158.2
1. Control (Psychology) 2. Control (Psychology) in motion pictures. I. Title.
BF632.5 .A44 2004

ALPHABET. See also **RUNES.**
Marchand, Valère-Marie. Les alphabets de l'oubli. Paris : Editions Alternatives, 2002.
P211 .M373 2002

ALPHABET (IN RELIGION, FOLK-LORE, ETC.). See **ALPHABET - RELIGIOUS ASPECTS.**

An alphabet of spells.
Hawke, Elen, 1947- St. Paul, MN : Llewellyn Publications, 2003.
BF1566 .H376 2003

ALPHABET - RELIGIOUS ASPECTS - JUDAISM.
Mantovani, Massimo. Meditazioni sull'albero della cabala. Milano : Xenia, 2002.

ALPHABETS. See **ILLUMINATION OF BOOKS AND MANUSCRIPTS.**

Les alphabets de l'oubli.
Marchand, Valère-Marie. Paris : Editions Alternatives, 2002.
P211 .M373 2002

ALPINE RACE. See **CELTS.**

Alquijay, Rashid Ricardo.
Acuerdos de paz y seguridad democrática en Guatemala. 1. ed. [Guatemala] : USAC, DIGI, [2002]

Alshekh, Moses, 16th cent.
[Torat Mosheh. Selections]
Sefer 'Orot ha-Alshekh : karne hod pene mosheh ... divre musar ... ne'esfu ve-nilketu mi-sef. ha-ḳ. Torat Mosheh 'al ha-Torah / le-rabenu ... Mosheh Alshekh ; ne'erakh ve-nisdar ['a. y.] Menahem Mendel vais. Yerushalayim : [h. mo. l.], 763 [2002 or 2003] 2 v. : facsims. ; 24 cm. Running title: 'Orot ha-Alshekh. On cover: sub-title: Peninim nifla'im be-torah 'avodah ye-yir'at shamayim. CONTENTS: Ḥeleḳ 1. 'Erekh alef - samekh -- Ḥeleḳ 2. 'Erekh 'ayin - tav.
1. Bible. - O.T. - Pentateuch - Commentaries. 2. Ethics, Jewish. 3. Jewish way of life. I. Vais, Menaḥem Mendel. II. Title. III. Title: Torat Mosheh. IV. Title: 'Orot ha-Alshekh

ALT 2002 (2002 : Lübeck, Germany) Algorithmic learning theory : 13th international conference, ALT 2002, Lübeck, Germany, November 24-26, 2002 : proceedings / Nicolò Cesa-Bianchi, Masayuki Numao, Rüdiger Reischuk (eds.). Berlin ; New York : Springer, c2002. xi, 413 p. : ill. ; 24 cm. (Lecture notes in

computer science, 0302-9743 ; 2533. Lecture notes in artificial intelligence) Includes bibliographical references and index. Also available via the World Wide Web. ISBN 3-540-00170-0 (alk. paper) DDC 005.1
1. Computer algorithms - Congresses. 2. Machine learning - Congresses. I. Cesa-Bianchi, Nicolò, 1963- II. Numao, Masayuki, 1961- III. Reischuk, Rüdiger. IV. Title. V. Series: Lecture notes in computer science ; 2533. VI. Series: Lecture notes in computer science. Lecture notes in artificial intelligence.
QA76.9.A43 A48 2002

Alt möcht ich werden-- : fünfzig Frauen und Männer sehen ihr Leben / [herausgegeben von] Christoph Maria Lang. 1. Aufl. Berlin : Aufbau-Verlag, c1994. 239 p. : ill. ; 22 cm. Includes bibliographical references (p. 233-239). ISBN 3-351-02424-X
1. Aged - Germany - Biography. 2. Aged - Psychology. 3. Germany - Biography. I. Lang, Christoph Maria.
HQ1064.G3 A72 1994x

Alt'ai munhwa kihaeng.
Pak, Si-in. Ch'op'an. Sŏul-si : Ch'ŏngnoru, 1995.

Az Általánostól a különösig / szerkesztette Czigler István, Halász László, Marton L. Magda. [Budapest] : Gondolat : MTA Pszichológiai Kutatóintézet, c2002. 465 p. : ill. ; 20 cm. Includes bibliographical references. ISBN 9639450162
1. Psychology. I. Czigler, István. II. Halász, László, 1933- III. Marton, L. Magda.
BF128.H8 A44 2002

Alter, Judah Aryeh Leib, 1847-1905.
[Sefat emet (Torah). Selections]
Sefer Sefat emet : liḳuṭim ; Tiḳune Zohar / me-et Yehudah Ary. Leyb mi-Gur. Yerushalayim : Mir, 762 [2001 or 2002] 2 v. in 1 (390, 44 p.) ; 25 cm. Added title page title: Sefer Sefat emet Tiḳune ha-Zohar. Running title: Sefat emet liḳuṭim.
1. Bible. - O.T. - Pentateuch - Sermons. 2. Tikkunei Zohar - Commentaries. 3. Jewish sermons, Hebrew. 4. Cabala. I. Title. II. Title: Sefer Sefat emet Tikune ha-Zohar III. Title: Sefat emet liḳuṭim IV. Title: Tiḳune ha-Zohar

[Selections. 2000]
Penine Sefat Emet : leḳeṭ amarot mevo'arot 'al pi nos'im / Mosheh Shapira. Ofrah : Mekhon Shovah, [2000?-2003?] 3 v. ; 22 cm. Includes index.
1. Hasidism. 2. Ethics, Jewish. I. Shapira, Mosheh. II. Title.
BM198.2 .A55 2000

Altera
(3) Pieroni, Osvaldo. Pene d'amore. Soveria Mannelli : Rubbettino, c2002.

ALTERED STATES OF CONSCIOUSNESS.
Spotts, Dane. Super brain power. Seattle, Wash. : LifeQuest Pub. Group, c1998.
BF441 .S68 1998

Una alternativa para ser feliz.
Reyes, Arnoldo Juan. Ciudad de La Habana, Cuba : Editorial Científico-Técnica, 2001, c2000.

ALTERNATIVE DISPUTE RESOLUTION. See **DISPUTE RESOLUTION (LAW).**

ALTERNATIVE LIFESTYLES - UNITED STATES.
Life as we know it. 1st Washington Square Press trade pbk. ed. New York : Washington Square Press, 2003.

ALTERNATIVE MEDICINE. See also **MEDICINE, MAGIC, MYSTIC, AND SPAGIRIC; TRADITIONAL MEDICINE.**
Strehlow, Wighard, 1937- Hildegard of Bingen's spiritual remedies. Rochester, Vt. : Healing Arts Press, c2002.
BT732.5 .S87 2002

Alternative religions.
Hunt, Stephen, 1954- Aldershot, Hampshire, England ; Burlington, VT : Ashgate, c2003.
BP603 .H87 2003

ALTHUSSER, LOUIS.
Hong, Joon-kee, 1962- Der Subjektbegriff bei Lacan und Althusser. Frankfurt am Main ; New York : Peter Lang , c2000.
BF109.L28 H66 2000

Read, Jason. The micro-politics of capital. Albany : State University of New York Press, c2003.
HB97.5 .R42 2003

Altmaier, Elizabeth M.
Setting standards in graduate education. 1st ed. Washington, DC : American Psychological Association, c2003.
BF80.7.U6 S48 2003

Altner, Günther.
Soukup, Johannes. Metaphysik der Zeit oder Wirklichkeit und Wissen. Deutsche 1. Ausg. Wien : Passagen Verlag, c1998.

Altneue Gedanken.
Šik, Miroslav. Luzern : Quart, c2002.

Altomare, Vincenzo. Alla ricerca dell'uomo tra Bibbia e modernità / Vincenzo Altomare. 1. ed. Cosenza : Progetto 2000, c2000. 108 p. ; 21 cm. Includes bibliographical references. ISBN 88-8276-038-3 DDC 901
1. History - Philosophy. 2. Civilization, Modern. 3. Postmodernism. I. Title.

Altounian, Janine. L'écriture de Freud : traversée traumatique et traduction / Janine Altounian. Paris : Presses universitaires de France, 2003. 218 p. ; 22 cm. (Bibliothèque de psychanalyse) Includes bibliographical references (p. [213]-218) and index. ISBN 2-13-052974-7 DDC 150
1. Freud, Sigmund, - 1856-1939 - Language. I. Title. II. Series.
BF173.F73 A48 2003

ALTRUISM. See also **HELPING BEHAVIOR; SELF-SACRIFICE.**
Kittredge, William. The nature of generosity. 1st Vintage Departures ed. New York : Vintage, 2001, c2000.
PS3561.I87 Z472 2001

Krieglstein, Werner J., 1941- Compassion. Amsterdam ; New York : Rodopi, c2002.

Nelson, Phillip J., 1929- Signaling goodness. Ann Arbor : University of Michigan Press, c2003.
HV31 .N45 2003

Śliwak, Jacek. Osobowość altruistyczna. Wyd. 1. Lublin : Red. Wydawnictw Katolickiego Uniwersytetu Lubelskiego, 2001.
BF637.H4 S58 2001

Altstein, Howard.
Simon, Rita James. Global perspectives on social issues. Lanham : Lexington Books, c2003.
HQ503 .S56 2003

Aluko, Jonathan O. The spirit of this age : an eyewitness account of a demonic temple / by Jonathan O. Aluko. [[Akure, Nigeria : Christ Liberation Publications, c1996] 72 p. : ill. ; 20 cm. Cover title: Power of darkness revealed : an eye witness of demons in the temple.
1. Demonology. 2. Demoniac possession. 3. Nigeria - Religion. 4. Black author. I. Title. II. Title: Power of darkness revealed : an eye witness of demons in the temple III. Title: Eye witness of demons in the temple
BL480 .A494 1996

Alvarez, Marcelo.
La (indi)gestión cultural. 1. ed. Bs. As., Argentina : Ediciones Ciccus-La Crujía, 2002.
HM621 .I535 2002

Alvrez, Alicia. The ladies' room reader revisited : a curious compendium of fascinating female facts / Alicia Alvrez. Berkeley, Calif. : Conari Press ; [Emeryville, Calif.] : Distributed by Publishers Group West, c2002. iv, 303 p. ; 24 cm. Includes bibliographical references (p. 299-302). ISBN 1-57324-771-5 (pbk.) DDC 305.4
1. Women - Miscellanea. I. Title.
HQ1233 .A68 2002

The ladies' room reader : the ultimate women's trivia book / Alicia Alvrez. Berkeley, Calif. : Conari Press, c2000. iv, 306 p. : ill. ; 24 cm. Includes bibliographical references (p. 302-305). ISBN 1-57324-561-5 ISBN 1-57324-557-7 (pbk.) DDC 305.4
1. Women - Miscellanea. I. Title.
HQ1233 .A68 2000

Always the mountains.
Rothenberg, David, 1962- Athens : University of Georgia Press, c2002.
GF21 .R68 2002

Alzieu, Gérard. Les églises de l'ancien diocèse de Lodève au Moyen-Age / Gérard Alzieu ; préface de Jean-Louis Lignon. Montpellier : Editions P. Clerc, 1998. 170 p. ; 30 cm. Includes bibliographical references and indexes. ISBN 2-904091-06-8
1. Catholic Church. - Diocese of Lodève, France. 2. Church history - Middle Ages, 600-1500. 3. Lodève (France) - Church history. I. Title.
BX1532.L63 A695 1998

Am I a woman?.
Eller, Cynthia (Cynthia Lorraine) Boston : Beacon Press, c2003.
HQ1190 .E424 2003

Amadiume, Ifi, 1947-.
The politics of memory. London ; New York : Zed Books, c2000.

JC571 .P642 2000

AMALGAMATION OF CORPORATIONS. See **CONSOLIDATION AND MERGER OF CORPORATIONS.**

Amar Amar, José Juan. Políticas sociales y modelos de atención integral a la infancia / José Amar Amar, Marla Alcalá Castro. Barranquilla, Colombia : Ediciones Uninorte, 2001. viii, 247 p. : ill. ; 24 cm. Includes bibliographical references (p. 241-247) ISBN 958-813-306-8
1. Social work with children - Latin America. 2. Child development. 3. Latin America - Social policy. I. Alcalá Castro, Marla. II. Title.

Amaral, Rita.
Verger, Pierre. Saída de Iaô. Sao Paulo : Fundação Pierre Verger : Axis Mundi Editora, 2002.

Amašukeli, Elguja. Dro da šemokmedi / Elguja Amašukeli. T'bilisi : "Merani", 2000. 215 p. ; 18 cm. In Georgian. ISBN 9992816848
1. Creative ability. 2. Aesthetics. I. Title.
BF408 .A475 2000

AMATEUR PLAYS. See **PAGEANTS.**

AMATEUR THEATER. See **IMPROVISATION (ACTING).**

Amazing mystic tarot.
McCluskey, John William. 1st ed. East Hampton, N.Y. : Arden Book Co., c2002.
BF1879.T2 M42 2002

Amberstone, Ruth Ann. Tarot tips / Ruth Ann Amberstone & Wald Amberstone ; with foreword by Mary K. Greer. St. Paul, Minn. : Llewellyn, 2003. p. cm. (Special topics in tarot) Includes bibliographical references and index. ISBN 0-7387-0216-1 DDC 133.3/337
1. Tarot - Miscellanea. I. Amberstone, Wald. II. Title. III. Series.
BF1879.T2 A475 2003

Amberstone, Wald.
Amberstone, Ruth Ann. Tarot tips. St. Paul, Minn. : Llewellyn, 2003.
BF1879.T2 A475 2003

Ambiente y democracia
Leff, Enrique. Saber ambiental. 3a ed. correg. y aument. México : PNUMA ; Siglo Veintiuno, 2002.

Ambiguity and choice in public policy.
Zahariadis, Nikolaos, 1961- Washington, D.C. : Georgetown University Press, c2003.
H97 .Z34 2003

AMBITION - HISTORY.
Fernández-Armesto, Felipe. Civilizations. New York : Free Press, c2001.
CB151 .F47 2001

Ambjörnsson, Ronny, 1936- Tankens pilgrimer / Ronny Ambjörnsson. Stockholm : Natur och Kultur, c2002. 387 p. : ill. (some col.) ; 24 cm. (Europas idéhistoria. Medeltiden) Includes bibliographical references (p. 373-380) and index. ISBN 91-27-07923-6
1. Philosophy, Medieval. 2. Philosophy - History. I. Title.

America as second creation.
Nye, David E., 1946- Cambridge : MIT Press, c2003.
E179.5 .N94 2003

America by trial.
Holt, W. V. München : Tuduv, c2001.

America embattled.
Crockatt, Richard. London ; New York : Routledge, 2003.
E902 .C76 2003

America, here I come.
Nwokogba, Isaac, 1957- 2nd ed. Cranston, R.I. : Writers' Collective, c2003.
BF1045.K37 N86 2003

American.
Matthews, Christopher, 1945- New York : Free Press, c2002.
E169.1 .M429 2002

AMERICAN ABORIGINES. See **INDIANS; INDIANS OF NORTH AMERICA.**

American Association for State and Local History book series
Sommer, Barbara W. The oral history manual. Walnut Creek, CA ; Oxford : Altamira Press, c2002.
D16.14 .S69 2002

AMERICAN AUTHORS. See **AUTHORS, AMERICAN.**

American Bar Association. Section of Law Practice Management.
Brenden, Ann E. Persuasive computer presentations. Chicago, Ill. : Law Practice Management Section, American Bar Association, c2001.
KF320.A9 B74 2001

American Botanical Council.
Blumenthal, Mark. Popular herbs in the U.S. market. Austin : American Botanical Council, 1997.

AMERICAN CIVIL WAR, 1861-1865. *See* **UNITED STATES - HISTORY - CIVIL WAR, 1861-1865.**

AMERICAN ENGLISH. *See* **ENGLISH LANGUAGE - UNITED STATES.**

American exceptionalism.
Gutfeld, Arnon. Brighton [England] ; Portland, Or. : Sussex Academic Press, 2002.
E169.1 .G956 2002

AMERICAN FICTION - 20TH CENTURY - HISTORY AND CRITICISM.
D'Cruz, Doreen, 1950- Loving subjects. New York : P. Lang, c2002.
PR888.W6 D39 2002

Gerber, Nancy, 1956- Portrait of the mother-artist. Lanham, Md. : Lexington Books, c2003.
PS374.M547 G47 2003

AMERICAN FICTION - AFRICAN AMERICAN AUTHORS.
Rhodes, Jewell Parker. Douglass' women. New York, NY : Atria Books, c2002.
1. Black author.

AMERICAN FICTION - WOMEN AUTHORS - HISTORY AND CRITICISM.
D'Cruz, Doreen, 1950- Loving subjects. New York : P. Lang, c2002.
PR888.W6 D39 2002

American girl (Middleton, Wis.).
Brian, Sarah Jane. The quiz book 2. Middleton, Wis. : Pleasant Co. , c2001.
BF831 .B75 2001

American governance and public policy.
Zahariadis, Nikolaos, 1961- Ambiguity and choice in public policy. Washington, D.C. : Georgetown University Press, c2003.
H97 .Z34 2003

AMERICAN HISTORY. *See* **UNITED STATES - HISTORY.**

AMERICAN HUMORISTS. *See* **HUMORISTS, AMERICAN.**

AMERICAN INDIANS. *See* **INDIANS; INDIANS OF NORTH AMERICA.**

American intellectual culture
Giberson, Karl. Species of origins. Lanham, Md. : Rowman & Littlefield, c2002.
BL240.3 .G53 2002

AMERICAN LANGUAGE. *See* **ENGLISH LANGUAGE - UNITED STATES.**

AMERICAN LITERATURE. *See* **AMERICAN FICTION; AMERICAN POETRY; AMERICAN PROSE LITERATURE.**

AMERICAN LITERATURE - 20TH CENTURY - HISTORY AND CRITICISM.
Manganaro, Marc, 1955- Culture, 1922. Princeton, N.J. : Princeton University Press, c2002.
PR888.C84 M36 2002

AMERICAN LITERATURE - HISTORY AND CRITICISM.
Marshall, Ian, 1954- Peak experiences. Charlottesville : University of Virginia Press, 2003.
PS163 .M37 2003

American lives
Skloot, Floyd. In the shadow of memory. Lincoln : University of Nebraska Press, c2003.
PS3569.K577 Z47 2003

AMERICAN NOVELISTS. *See* **NOVELISTS, AMERICAN.**

AMERICAN POETRY - AUTHORS, DOMINICAN.
La palabra como cuerpo del delito. Santo Domingo, República Dominicana : Biblioteca Nacional "Dr. Pedro Henríquez Ureña", 2001.

American political thought
Lawson, Melinda, 1954- Patriot fires. Lawrence : University Press of Kansas, c2002.
E468.9 .L39 2002

AMERICAN PROSE LITERATURE - 1783-1850 - HISTORY AND CRITICISM.
Fichtelberg, Joseph. Critical fictions. Athens : University of Georgia Press, c2003.
PS366.S35 F53 2003

AMERICAN PROSE LITERATURE - 19TH CENTURY - HISTORY AND CRITICISM.
Fichtelberg, Joseph. Critical fictions. Athens : University of Georgia Press, c2003.
PS366.S35 F53 2003

American Psychological Association. The directory of ethnic minority professionals in psychology / compiled and edited by the Office of Ethnic Minority Affairs, Sherry T. Wynn, Bertha G. Holliday. 4th ed. Washington, D.C. : American Psychological Association, c2001. xv, 315, 4 p. ; 28 cm. ISBN 1-55798-824-2 (pbk.) DDC 150/.25/73
1. American Psychological Association - Directories. 2. Minority psychologists - United States - Directories. 3. Psychology - United States - Directories. 4. Minority psychologists - Directories. 5. Psychology - Directories. I. Title. II. Title: Ethnic minority professionals in psychology
BF30 .A493 2001

Publication manual of the American Psychological Association. 4th ed. Washington, DC : American Psychological Association, 1994.
BF76.7 .P82 1994

Publication manual of the American Psychological Association. 5th ed. Washington, DC : American Psychological Association, c2001.
BF76.7 .P83 2001

AMERICAN PSYCHOLOGICAL ASSOCIATION - DIRECTORIES.
American Psychological Association. The directory of ethnic minority professionals in psychology. 4th ed. Washington, D.C. : American Psychological Association, c2001.
BF30 .A493 2001

American Psychological Association of Graduate Students.
Internships in psychology. Washington, D.C. : American Psychological Association, c2004.
BF77 .I67 2004

AMERICAN REVOLUTION. *See* **UNITED STATES - HISTORY - REVOLUTION, 1775-1783.**

American shaman.
Kottler, Jeffrey A. New York : Brunner-Routledge, 2004.
BF1598.K43 K68 2004

The American social experience series
McDaniel, Patricia (Patricia A.) Shrinking violets and Caspar Milquetoasts. New York : New York University Press, 2003.
BF575.B3 M34 2003

AMERICAN TELEPHONE AND TELEGRAPH COMPANY.
United States. Congress. Senate. Committee on the Judiciary. Subcommittee on Antitrust, Business Rights, and Competition. Dominance on the ground. Washington : U.S. G.P.O. : For sale by the Supt. of Docs., U.S. G.P.O. [Congressional Sales Office], 2003.

American university studies. Series IV, English language and literature
(v. 195.) D'Cruz, Doreen, 1950- Loving subjects. New York : P. Lang, c2002.
PR888.W6 D39 2002

American university studies. Series IX. History
(v. 191) Harmond, Richard P. A history of Memorial Day. New York : P. Lang, c2002.
E642 .H37 2002

American university studies. Series V. Philosophy
(v. 183) Kovesi, Julius. Values and evaluations. New York ; Bern : P. Lang, c1998.
BD232 .K68 1998

American university studies. Series V, Philosophy
(v. 192.) Essays in honor of Burleigh Wilkins. New York : Peter Lang, c2001.
JA71 .E694 2001

AMERICANISMS. *See also* **ENGLISH LANGUAGE - UNITED STATES.**
Hargraves, Orin. Mighty fine words and smashing expressions. Oxford ; New York : Oxford University Press, 2003.
PE1711 .H37 2003

Spears, Richard A. NTC's dictionary of everyday American English expressions. Lincolnwood, Ill. : National Textbook Co., c1994.
PE2839 .S65 1994

America's political class under fire.
Horowitz, David A. New York ; London : Routledge, 2003.
HN90.S6 H67 2003

Amerika protiv Rossii
Parshev, A. P. (Andreĭ Petrovich) Pochemu Amerika nastupaet. Moskva : AST : Astrel', 2002.
HF1558.2.Z4 P37 2002

Ameriks, Karl, 1947- Interpreting Kant's critiques / Karl Ameriks. Oxford : Clarendon Press ; New York : Oxford University Press, 2003. vii, 351 p. ; 25 cm. Includes bibliographical references and index. ISBN 0-19-924731-5 ISBN 0-19-924732-3 (PBK.) DDC 193
1. Kant, Immanuel, - 1724-1804. - Kritik der reinen Vernunft. 2. Kant, Immanuel, - 1724-1804. - Kritik der praktischen Vernunft. 3. Kant, Immanuel, - 1724-1804. - Kritik der Urteilskraft. 4. Knowledge, Theory of. 5. Causation. 6. Reason. I. Title.
B2779 .A64 2003

AMERINDIANS. *See* **INDIANS.**

AMERINDS. *See* **INDIANS.**

AMIDAH (JEWISH PRAYER).
Armoni, Mosheh Ḥayim. Sefer Ginze Armoni. Yerushalayim : ʻAmutat "Naḥalat-Raḥel", 762 [2002]
BM670.S5 A756 2002

Amidon, Debra M., 1946- The innovation superhighway : harnessing intellectual capital for sustainable collaborative advantage / Debra M. Amidon. Amsterdam ; Boston ; London : Butterworth-Heinemann, c2003. xxx, 379 p. : ill. ; 24 cm. Includes bibliographical references (p. 351-360) and index. ISBN 0-7506-7592-6 (alk. paper) DDC 658.4/063
1. Intellectual capital. 2. Creative ability in business. 3. Management. I. Title.
HD53 .A462 2003

Amitier.
Tiberghien, Gilles A., 1953- Paris : Desclée de Brouwer, c2002.

Ammonius, Hermiae. Commentaria in quinque voces Porphyrii / Ammonius Hermeae ; übersetzt von Pomponius Gauricus. In Aristotelis catgorias : erweiterte Nachschrift des Johannes Philoponus = CAG XIII/i / [Ammonius Hermeae] ; übersetzt von Ioannes Baptista Rasarius ; Neudruck der Ausgaben venedig 1539 und venedig 1562 mit einer Einleitung von Rainer Thiel und Charles Lohr. Stuttgart : Frommann-Holzboog, 2002. xxi, [108] p. : facsims. ; 31 cm. Cover title: In Porphyrium. Includes bibliographical references (p. xix-xxi). Introductory matter in German. ISBN 3-7728-1220-1 (set) ISBN 3-7728-1229-5 (v. 9 : cl.)
1. Aristotle. 2. Aristotle. - Categoriae. 3. Philosophy, Ancient. 4. Categories (Philosophy) I. Ammonius, Hermiae. In Aristotelis categorias commentarius. 2002. II. Gaurico, Pomponio, 1481 or 82-1528. III. Rasario, Giovanni Battista, 1517-1578. IV. Thiel, Rainer. V. Lohr, Charles H. VI. Title. VII. Title: In Porphyrium

Ammonius, Hermiae.
In Aristotelis categorias commentarius. 2002.
Ammonius, Hermiae. Commentaria in quinque voces Porphyrii. Stuttgart : Frommann-Holzboog, 2002.

AMNESTY. *See also* **FORGIVENESS.**
Truth v. justice. Princeton, N.J. : Princeton University Press, c2000.
DT1945 .T78 2000

AMNESTY - SOUTH AFRICA.
Truth v. justice. Princeton, N.J. : Princeton University Press, c2000.
DT1945 .T78 2000

Amodélé, Jons. The new Jews : why africans are fleeing the continent and whatcan be done about it : reflections on the love of power and on the power of love / Amodélé. Banjul, The Gambia : Vinasha Publishing, 2000. 131, xiv p. : ill. ; 21 cm. Running title: The new Jews : reflections on the love of power and on the power of love. Includes as epilogue: The last African : a play to end all illusions. Includes bibliographical references. ISBN 9983990520
1. Africa - Emigration and immigration. 2. Emigration and immigration - Social aspects. 3. Race awareness - Political aspects. 4. Race - Psychological aspects. 5. Blacks - Social conditions. 6. Blacks - Race identity. 7. Black author. I. Title. II. Title: The new Jews : reflections on the love of power and on the power of love

Amor, Daniel.
Hayes-Roth, Frederick, 1947- Radical simplicity. Upper Saddle River, N.J. ; London : Prentice Hall PTR, 2003.

Amores de película : grandes pasiones que han hecho historia / Maruja Torres, Guillermo Cabrera Infante, Terenci Moix ... [et al.]. 1. ed. [Madrid] : Aguilar, 2002. 279 p. : ill. ; 24 cm. ISBN 84-03-09335-7 DDC 791.43/028/0922
1. Motion picture actors and actresses - Biography. 2. Man-woman relationships. I. Torres, Maruja. II. Cabrera Infante, G. (Guillermo), 1929- III. Moix, Terenci, 1943-
PN1998.2 .A46 2002

Amougou, Emmanuel. La construction de l'inconscient colonial en Alsace : un village nègre sous le froid / Emmanuel Amougou ; préface de Pierre Bourdieu. Paris : L'Harmattan, 2002. 217 p. : ill. ; 22 cm. (Logiques sociales) Includes bibliographical references (p. 205-216). ISBN 2-7475-2819-7
1. Exposition coloniale, agricole et industrielle de Strasbourg - (1924) 2. Immigrants - France - Alsace. 3. Africans - France - Social life and customs. 4. Social psychology. 5. France - Ethnic relations. 6. Africa - Foreign public opinion, French. 7. Black author. I. Bourdieu, Pierre. II. Title. III. Series.

L'amour plus grand que la foi.
Aïvanhov, Omraam Mikhaël. Fréjus : Prosveta, c2000.

Amsterdam classical monographs
(v. 4) Alonso-Nuñez, José Miguel. The idea of universal history in Greece. Amsterdam : J.C. Gieben, 2002.
D13.5.G8 A46 2002

'Amude ha-ḳabalah.
Sefer 'Amude ha-Kabalah. Yerushalayim : Nezer Sheraga, 761 [2001]

AMULETS. *See also* **CHARMS; TALISMANS.**
Webster, Richard, 1946- Amulets & talismans for beginners. St. Paul, Minn. : Llewellyn Publications, 2004.
BF1561 .W43 2004

Amulets & talismans for beginners.
Webster, Richard, 1946- St. Paul, Minn. : Llewellyn Publications, 2004.
BF1561 .W43 2004

Amulets and talismans for beginners.
Webster, Richard, 1946- Amulets & talismans for beginners. St. Paul, Minn. : Llewellyn Publications, 2004.
BF1561 .W43 2004

AMULETS - SLAVIC COUNTRIES.
Telúch, Peter. Amulety a talizmany. Bratislava : Print-Servis, 1998.

Amulety a talizmany.
Telúch, Peter. Bratislava : Print-Servis, 1998.

AMUSEMENTS. *See* **CONCERTS; DANCE; FORTUNE-TELLING; GAMES; PLAY.**

An intelligent person's guide to religion.
Haldane, John. London : Duckworth, 2003.

"An jenem Tag im blauen Mond September".
Buschey, Monika. Düsseldorf : Artemis & Winkler, c2000.

An, Lizhi. "Zhen guan zheng yao" yu ling dao yi shu / An Lizhi zhu. Di 1 ban. Shanghai : Shanghai gu ji chu ban she, 1999. 4, 311 p. ; 20 cm. (Li shi de qi shi) Includes bibliographical references. ISBN 7-5325-2550-3 DDC DS749.3.W813
1. Tang Taizong, - Emperor of China, - 597-649. 2. Wu, Jing, - 670-749. - Zhenguan zheng yao. 3. Leadership. 4. China - Politics and government - 581-907. I. Title. II. Title: Zhen guan zheng yao yu ling dao yi shu. III. Series.
DS749.3.W813 A63 1999

Āṇ-peṇ pālpēṭam.
Kōvintaṉ, Ka. Tamiḻt tiraippaṭaṅkaḷil āṇ-peṇ pāl pēṭam. 1. patippu. Ceṉṉai : Kumaraṉ Papḷiṣars, 2001.
BF692.2 .K68 2001

ANA. *See* **ANECDOTES; APHORISMS AND APOTHEGMS; MAXIMS.**

Analecta Cartusiana
(205) Pharmacum carthusiense. Salzburg, Austria : Institut für Anglistik und Amerikanistik, Universität Salzburg, 2002.
BX2435 .P43 2002

Analecta Gregoriana
(v. 285.) Luciani Rivero, Rafael Francisco. El misterio de la diferencia. Roma : Pontificia università gregoriana, 2001.

Analecta Gregoriana. Series Facultatis Theologiae. Sectio B
(n. 101.) Luciani Rivero, Rafael Francisco. El misterio de la diferencia. Roma : Pontificia università gregoriana, 2001.

ANALGESIA. *See* **PAIN.**

La analogía en general.
Gambra, José Miguel. 1. ed. Pamplona : EUNSA, 2002.

ANALOGY.
Gambra, José Miguel. La analogía en general. 1. ed. Pamplona : EUNSA, 2002.

ANALOGY (RELIGION).
Luciani Rivero, Rafael Francisco. El misterio de la diferencia. Roma : Pontificia università gregoriana, 2001.

ANALYSANDS - FRANCE.
Delaisi de Parseval, Geneviève. Le Roman familial d'Isadora D.. Paris : Odile Jacob, c2002.

ANALYSANDS - UNITED STATES - BIOGRAPHY.
Friedman, Bonnie, 1958- The thief of happiness. Boston, Mass. : Beacon Press, 2002.
RC464.F75 A3 2002

Analysis and argumentation in Rabbinic Judaism.
Neusner, Jacob, 1932- Lanham, Md. : University Press of America, c2003.
BM496.5 .N4775 2003

The analysis and interpretation of multivariate data for social scientists / David J. Bartholomew ... [et al.]. Boca Raton, Fla. : Chapman & Hall/CRC, c2002. xi, 263 p. : ill. ; 25 cm. (Texts in statistical science) Includes bibliographical references (p. [253]-256) and index. ISBN 1-58488-295-6 (acid-free paper) DDC 519.5/35
1. Social sciences - Statistical methods. 2. Multivariate analysis. I. Bartholomew, David J. II. Series.
HA29 .A5824 2002

ANALYSIS, DREAM. *See* **DREAM INTERPRETATION.**

ANALYSIS, FACTORIAL. *See* **FACTOR ANALYSIS.**

ANALYSIS, LINGUISTIC (PHILOSOPHY). *See* **ANALYSIS (PHILOSOPHY).**

ANALYSIS, LOGICAL. *See* **ANALYSIS (PHILOSOPHY).**

Analysis of the social and intellectual qualities of good leadership in politics and organizations.
Safari, J. F. The new art of leadership for Africa 2000. Peramiho, Tanzania : Benedictine Publications Ndanda, 1996.
HM1261 S35 1996
1. Black author.

ANALYSIS OF VARIANCE.
Cliff, Norman, 1930- Ordinal measurement in the behavioral sciences. Mahwah, N.J. : Lawrence Erlbaum Associates, 2003.
BF39 .C525 2003

ANALYSIS, PHILOSOPHICAL. *See* **ANALYSIS (PHILOSOPHY).**

ANALYSIS (PHILOSOPHY). *See also* **SEMANTICS (PHILOSOPHY).**
Hüntelmann, Rafael. Existenz und Modalität. Frankfurt a. M. ; New York : Hänsel-Hohenhausen, c2002.
BD331 .H86 2002

Nazarchuk, A. V. (Aleksandr Viktorovich) Ėtika globaliziruiushchegosia obshchestva. Moskva : DirectMediia Pablishing, 2002.
B3199.A634 N39 2002

Salamucha, Jan. [Selections. English. 2003] Knowledge and faith. Amsterdam ; New York, NY : Rodopi, 2003.

ANALYTIC PSYCHOLOGY. *See* **JUNGIAN PSYCHOLOGY.**

ANALYTICAL PHILOSOPHY. *See* **ANALYSIS (PHILOSOPHY).**

ANALYTICAL PSYCHOLOGY. *See* **JUNGIAN PSYCHOLOGY.**

Analyzing Freud : letters of H.D., Bryher, and their circle / edited by Susan Stanford Friedman. New York : New Directions, c2002. lii, 615 p. ; 24 cm. Includes bibliographical references (p. 579-594) and index. ISBN 0-8112-1499-0 (alk. paper) DDC 150.19/52/092
1. Freud, Sigmund, - 1856-1939 - Correspondence. 2. H. D. - (Hilda Doolittle), - 1886-1961 - Correspondence. 3. Bryher, - 1894- - Correspondence. 4. Psychoanalysts - Austria - Correspondence. I. Freud, Sigmund, 1856-1939. II. H. D. (Hilda Doolittle), 1886-1961. III. Bryher, 1894- IV. Friedman, Susan Stanford.
BF109.F74 A845 2002

Analyzing prose.
Lanham, Richard A. 2nd ed. London ; New York : Continuum, 2003.
PE1421 .L295 2003

Analyzing quantitative data.
Blaikie, Norman W. H., 1933- London ; Thousand Oaks, CA : Sage Publications Ltd, 2003.
HA29 .B556 2003

Ānanda, Aruṇā, 1957- Pātañjalayoga evaṃ Jainayoga kā tulanātmaka adhyayana / Aruṇā Ānanda. 1. saṃskaraṇa. Dillī : Motīlāla Banārasīdāsa Pabliśarsa aura Bhogīlāla Leharacanda Bhāratīya Saṃskṛti Saṃsthāna, 2002. xv, 329 p. ; 25 cm. (Bī. Ela. sīrīza ; kra. 15) SUMMARY: Comparative study of the Yoga of Patañjali and Jaina Yoga. Includes bibliographical references (p. [280]-297) and indexes. In Hindi; includes passages in Prakrit and Sanskrit. ISBN 81-208-1787-7
1. Patañjali. - Yogasūtra. 2. Yoga (Jainism) 3. Yoga. I. Bhogilal Leherchand Institute of Indology. II. Title. III. Series: B.L. series ; no. 15.
B132.Y6 A496 2002

Ānandānanda, Swami, 1902-1991.
Smārikā. Jayapura : Yoga Sādhanā Āśrama, 2001.
BL1175.A4955 S62 2001

ĀNANDĀNANDA, SWAMI, 1902-1991.
Smārikā. Jayapura : Yoga Sādhanā Āśrama, 2001.
BL1175.A4955 S62 2001

Anan'ev, Boris Gerasimovich. Psikhologiia chuvstvennogo poznaniia / B.G. Anan'ev. Moskva : "Nauka", 2001. 277 p. : port. ; 25 cm. (Pamiatniki psikhologicheskoĭ mysli) "Nauchnoe izdanie"--Colophon. Includes bibliographical references. ISBN 5020130931
1. Senses and sensation. I. Title. II. Series.
BF233 .A5 2001

ANARCHISM. *See also* **SOCIALISM.**
Quiet rumours. Edinburgh : San Francisco : AK Press/Dark Star, 2002.

ANARCHISTS.
Quiet rumours. Edinburgh : San Francisco : AK Press/Dark Star, 2002.

The anarchy of empire in the making of U.S. culture.
Kaplan, Amy. Cambridge, Mass. : Harvard University Press, 2002.
E661.7 .K37 2002

Anatol, Giselle Liza, 1970-.
Reading Harry Potter. Westport, Conn. ; London : Praeger Publishers, 2003.
PR6068.O93 Z84 2003

ANATOMY. *See* **PHYSIOLOGY.**

Anatomy of success.
Kaufman, Ronald A. Dubuque, Iowa : Kendall/Hunt Pub., c1999.
BF637.S8 .K379 1999

Anaut, Marie.
Matière à symbolisation. Lausanne : Delachaux et Niestlé, c1998.
BF458 .M38 1998

ANAXIMANDER.
Couprie, Dirk, 1940- Anaximander in context. Albany : State University of New York Press, c2003.
B208.Z7 C68 2003

Anaximander in context.
Couprie, Dirk, 1940- Albany : State University of New York Press, c2003.
B208.Z7 C68 2003

ANCHOR MEN. *See* **TELEVISION NEWS ANCHORS.**

ANCHOR PERSONS. *See* **TELEVISION NEWS ANCHORS.**

ANCHORMEN. *See* **TELEVISION NEWS ANCHORS.**

ANCHORPERSONS. *See* **TELEVISION NEWS ANCHORS.**

ANCHORS (TELEVISION JOURNALISM). *See* **TELEVISION NEWS ANCHORS.**

Ancient and medieval philosophy. Series 1
(30) Internationales Eriugena-Colloquium (10th : Maynooth and Dublin : 2002) History and eschatology in John Scottus Eriugena and his time. Leuven : University Press, 2002.

[The ancient commentators on Aristotle]
Simplicius, of Cilicia. [Commentarius in Enchiridion Epicteti. 1-26. English] On Epictetus' "Handbook 1-26". Ithaca, N.Y. : Cornell University Press, 2002.
B561.M523 S5613 2002

ANCIENT HISTORY. *See* **HISTORY, ANCIENT.**

Ancient queens : archaeological explorations / edited by Sarah Milledge Nelson. Walnut Creek, Calif. : Oxford : AltaMira Press, c2003. viii, 200 p. : ill., maps ; 24 cm. (Gender and archaeology series ; v. 5) Includes bibliographical references and index. CONTENTS: Ancient queens : an introduction / Sarah Milledge Nelson -- A reigning queen or the wife of a king--only? gender politics in the Scandinavian Viking age / Elisabeth Arwill-Nordbladh -- Questioning a queen? a gender-informed evaluation of Monte Alban's tomb / Geoffrey G. McCafferty and Sharisse D. McCafferty -- Many wives, one queen in Shang China / Katheryn M. Linduff -- The queens of Silla : power and connections to the spirit world / Sarah Milledge Nelson -- She for whom all is said is done : the ancient Egyptian queen / Lana Troy -- Sacred women in ancient Peru / Melissa A. Vogel -- Ancient queens of the Valley of Mexico / Karen E. Bell -- Katuns : the Mongolian queens of the Genghis Khanite / Jeannine Davis-Kimball -- The divine queens of Minangkabau Lore / Peggy Reeves Sanday. ISBN 0-7591-0345-3 (hbk. : alk. paper) ISBN 0-7591-0346-1 (pbk. : alk. paper) DDC 305.4/09/01
1. Women - History - To 500. 2. Women - Biography - To 500. 3. Queens - Biography. 4. Sex role - History. 5. Power (Social sciences) - History - To 500. 6. Civilization, Ancient. 7. Feminist archaeology. I. Nelson, Sarah M., 1931- II. Series.
HQ1127 .A53 2003

Ancient spellcraft.
Perry, Laura, 1965- Franklin Lakes, NJ : New Page Books, c2002.
BF1591 .P47 2002

Ancis, Julie R.
Culturally responsive interventions. New York : Brunner-Routledge, 2003.
BF637.C6 C777 2003

And a time for hope.
McGovern, James R. Westport, Conn. : Praeger, 2000.
E806 .M45 2000

And the passenger was death.
Daher, Douglas, 1949- Amityville, N.Y. : Baywood Pub., c2003.
BF575.G7 D34 2003

Anders, Martin. Präsenz zu denken-- : die Entgrenzung des Körperbegriffs und Lösungswege von Leibkonzeptionen bei Ernst Mach, Robert Musil und Paul Valéry / Martin Anders. St. Augustin : Gardez!, c2002. 195 p. ; 21 cm. (Philosophie im Kontext ; Bd. 8) Includes bibliographical references (p. 190-195). ISBN 3-89796-084-2
1. Mach, Ernst, - 1838-1916. 2. Musil, Robert, - 1880-1942 - Criticism and interpretation. 3. Valéry, Paul, - 1871-1945 - Criticism and interpretation. 4. Body, Human (Philosophy) I. Title. II. Series.
B3303 .A53 2002

Andersen, Ivory.
Rainieri, Caelum. The Nahualli animal oracle. Rochester, Vt. : Bear & Co., 2003.
BF1773 .R35 2003

Anderson, Cora, 1915-.
Anderson, Victor H. 1917- Etheric anatomy. 1st American pbk. ed. Albany, Calif. : Acorn Guild Press, 2004.
BF1389.A7 A53 2004

Anderson, Harris B.
Kliem, Ralph L. The organizational engineering approach to project management. Boca Raton : St. Lucie Press, c2003.
HD66 .K585 2003

Anderson, Mary Beth, 1952- Good teachers carry on : lessons from the afterlife / Mary Beth Anderson. St. Joseph, Mich. : Cosmic Concepts Press, c2003. p. cm. Table of contents URL: http://www.loc.gov/catdir/toc/ecip047/2003017041.html CONTENTS: Saying good-bye -- My visitor -- The search -- Methods of communication -- Entity of light -- A new association -- Further proof of existence -- Heaven help them -- Life in the 1800's -- The photograph -- Haunting -- Love your life -- Someone is waiting -- Mourning a loss -- The welcoming light -- An emotional reunion -- Conclusive evidence -- Where is the love? -- Where is the love? -- The spiritual realm. ISBN 0-9620507-9-2 DDC 133.9/092
1. Spiritualism. I. Title.
BF1261.2 .A45 2003

Anderson, Rafe. Total palmistry : the love connection / Rafe Anderson. Boston : Red Wheel, 2003. 216 p. : ill. ; 16 cm. ISBN 1-59003-028-1 DDC 133.6
1. Palmistry. 2. Love. I. Title.
BF935.L67 A53 2003

Anderson, Susan, C.S.W. Black swan : the twelve lessons of abandonment recovery : featuring, The allegory of the little girl on the rock / by Susan Anderson. Huntington, N.Y. : Rock Foundations Press, c1999. 111 p. : ill. ; 22 cm. ISBN 0-9673755-1-7
1. Rejection (Psychology) 2. Separation (Psychology) I. Title.
BF575.R35 A52 1999

The journey from heartbreak to connection : a workshop in abandonment recovery / Susan Anderson. Berkley trade pbk. ed. New York : Berkley Books, 2003. xviii, 380 p. ; 24 cm. Includes bibliographical references (p. [361]-370) and index. ISBN 0-425-19020-X (pbk.) DDC 155.9/2
1. Rejection (Psychology) 2. Separation (Psychology) 3. Loss (Psychology) I. Title.
BF575.R35 A533 2003

Anderson, Terry Lee, 1946- Property rights : a practical guide to freedom and prosperity / Terry L. Anderson and Laura E. Huggins. Stanford, Calif. : Hoover Institution Press, c2003. xv, 94 p. ; 23 cm. (Hoover Institution Press publication ; no. 515) Includes bibliographical references (p. [81]-88) and index. ISBN 0-8179-3912-1 (alk. paper) DDC 323.4/6
1. Property. 2. Real property. 3. Right of property. 4. Liberty. 5. Economic development. I. Huggins, Laura E., 1976- II. Title. III. Series: Hoover Institution Press publication ; 515.
HB701 .A44 2003

Anderson, Victor H. 1917- Etheric anatomy : the three selves and astral travel / Victor H. Anderson ; with additional material by Cora Anderson. 1st American pbk. ed. Albany, Calif. : Acorn Guild Press, 2004. p. cm. Includes index. CONTENTS: The etheric anatomy of the human being -- The three selves and etheric sight -- Out-of-body-experiences and astral sex. ISBN 0-9710050-0-1 (pbk. : alk. paper) DDC 133.9/5
1. Astral body. 2. Astral projection. 3. Huna - Miscellanea. I. Anderson, Cora, 1915- II. Title.
BF1389.A7 A53 2004

Anderson, Walt, 1933- The next enlightenment : integrating East and West in a new vision of human evolution / Walter Truett Anderson. 1st ed. New York : St. Martin's Press, 2003. vii, 263 p. ; 25 cm. Includes bibliographical references (p. 245-257) and index. ISBN 0-312-31769-7 DDC 291.4/2
1. Religious awakening. 2. Spirituality - Psychology. 3. Human evolution - Religious aspects. 4. East and West. I. Title.
BL476 .A53 2003

Andrade, Jackie, 1964- Instant notes in cognitive psychology / Jackie Andrade and Jon May. New York, NY : Garland Science/BIOS Scientific Publishers, 2004. p. cm. Includes bibliographical references and index. Table of contents URL: http://www.loc.gov/catdir/toc/ecip048/2003018482.html ISBN 1-85996-223-8 (pbk.) DDC 153
1. Cognitive psychology - Textbooks. I. May, Jon. II. Title.
BF201 .A53 2004

Andrade, X. (Xavier).
Masculinidades en Ecuador. Quito, Ecuador : FLACSO ; [S.l.] : UNFPA, 2001.
BF692.5 .M388 2001

Masculinidades en Ecuador. Quito, Ecuador : FLACSO ; [s.l.] : UNFPA, 2001.
BF692.5 .M37 2001

Andreani, Roland.
Renouvier, Charles, 1815-1903. Sur le peuple, l'église et la république. Paris : Harmattan, c2002.

Andrews, John, 1966- For all those left behind / John Andrews. Edinburgh : Mainstream Pub., c2002. 208 p. : 18 cm. ISBN 1-84018-622-4 DDC 158.1
1. Fathers - Death - Psychological aspects. 2. Loss (Psychology) 3. Fishing - Miscellanea. 4. Andrews, John, - 1966- I. Title.
BF789.D4 A55 2002

ANDREWS, JOHN, 1966-.
Andrews, John, 1966- For all those left behind. Edinburgh : Mainstream Pub., c2002.
BF789.D4 A55 2002

Andrews, Linda Wasmer. Emotional intelligence / Linda Wasmer Andrews. New York : Franklin Watts, 2004. v. cm. (Life balance) Includes bibliographical references and index. Table of contents URL: http://www.loc.gov/catdir/toc/ecip048/2003019772.html CONTENTS: Dealing with feeling -- Name that emotion! -- Understanding yourself -- Handling Your emotions -- Managing relationships -- Glossary -- Further resources. ISBN 0-531-12335-9 DDC 152.4
1. Emotional intelligence - Juvenile literature. 2. Emotional intelligence. 3. Emotions. I. Title. II. Series.
BF576 .A53 2004

Intelligence / Linda Wasmer Andrews. New York : Franklin Watts, c2003. 80 p. : ill. ; 21 cm. (Life balance) Includes bibliographical references (p. 72-75) and index. SUMMARY: Examines various theories and types of intelligence, including a look at historical studies and people who have made significant contributions to the field. CONTENTS: Intelligence: fact and fiction -- Single-minded: the G factor -- New ideas: other intelligences -- Smart question: nature or nurture? -- Testing, testing: the IQ debate. ISBN 0-531-12220-4 DDC 153.9
1. Intellect - Juvenile literature. 2. Intellect. I. Title. II. Series.
BF431 .A576 2003

Meditation / Linda Wasmer Andrews. New York : F. Watts, c2003. p. cm. (Life balance) SUMMARY: Explains popular methods of meditation such as zen, transcendental meditation, and yoga and discusses their effects on stress and general mental health. Includes bibliographical references and index. Table of contents URL: http://www.loc.gov/catdir/toc/ecip042/2003007153.html CONTENTS: Meditation mythbusters -- The relaxation response -- The mind/body/spirit link -- Minding your mindfulness. ISBN 0-531-12219-0 DDC 158.1/2
1. Meditation - Juvenile literature. 2. Meditation. I. Title. II. Series.
BF637.M4 A53 2003

Andrews, Ted, 1952- Magic of believing / by Ted Andrews. 1st ed. Jackson, Tenn. : Dragonhawk Pub., c2000. xi, 246 p. : ill. ; 22 cm. (Young person's school of magic and mystery ; v. 1) Includes bibliographical references (p. 229) and index. ISBN 1-88876-743-X DDC 133.4/3
1. Magic - Juvenile literature. 2. Magic. I. Title. II. Series.
BF1611 .A53 2000

Spirits, ghosts & guardians / by Ted Andrews. 1st ed. Jackson, Tenn. : Dragonhawk Pub., c2002. 255 p. : ill. ; 21 cm. (Young person's school of magic and mystery ; v. 5) Includes bibliographical references (p. 247) and index. ISBN 1-88876-741-3
1. Ghosts - Juvenile literature. 2. Spirits - Juvenile literature. 3. Guardian angels - Juvenile literature. I. Title. II. Title: Spirits, ghosts, and guardians III. Series.
BF1461 .A53 2002

Andrieu, Bernard. L'interprétation des gènes : un exemple de confusion des savoirs / Bernard Andrieu. Paris : Harmattan, 2002. 173 p. ; 22 cm. (Collection "Le Mouvement des savoirs") Includes bibliographical references. ISBN 2-7475-2771-9 DDC 194
1. Bioethics. 2. Genetics. 3. Knowledge, Theory of. I. Title. II. Series: Collection Mouvement des savoirs.

La nouvelle philosophie du corps / Bernard Andrieu. Ramonville Saint-Agne : Erès, 2002. 240 p. ; 19 cm. (Collection "Réponses philosophiques") ISBN 2-7492-0074-1 DDC 194
1. Mind and body. I. Title.

ANDROCENTRISM - COLOMBIA.
Viveros, M. (Mara) De quebradores y cumplidores. 1a ed. [Colombia] : CES Universidad Nacional de Colombia : Fundación Ford : Profamilia Colombia, 2002.

Andrushkiv, Bohdan, 1947- Po toĭ bik bezodni, abo, Mertvi pro vartist' zhyttia ne rozkazhut' : bloknyha / Bohdan Andrushkiv, Petro Soroka. Ternopil' : "Pidruchnyky & posibnyky", 1997. 157 p. : ill. ; 20 cm. Includes bibliographical references (p. 156). ISBN 9665621238 (pbk.)
1. Suicide. I. Soroka, Petro, 1956- II. Title. III. Title: Po toĭ bik bezodni IV. Title: Mertvi pro vartist' Zhyttia ne rozkazhut'
HV6545 .A616 1997

ANECDOTES - HISTORY AND CRITICISM.
Kurganov, E. Anekdot, simvol, mif. Sankt-Peterburg : Izd-vo zhurnala "Zvezda", 2002.

Anejos de Analecta malacitana
(44.) Torre, Francisco Javier de la. Aproximación a las fuentes clásicas latinas de Hannah Arendt. Málaga : Universidad de Málaga, 2002.

Anekdot, simvol, mif.
Kurganov, E. Sankt-Peterburg : Izd-vo zhurnala "Zvezda", 2002.

Les ânes rouges.
Levent, Jean-Marc. Paris : Harmattan, 2003.

Ang, Soon.
Earley, P. Christopher. Cultural intelligence. Stanford, Calif. : Stanford University Press, 2003.
HD57.7 .E237 2003

Angel medicine.
Virtue, Doreen, 1958- Carlsbad, Calif. : Hay House, 2004.
BF1999 .V585 2004

Ángeles, demonios y genios en el mundo Mediterráneo / Aurelio Pérez Jiménez, Gonzalo Cruz Andreotti (eds.). Madrid : Ediciones Clásicas, 2000.
232 p. (Mediterranea ; 7) Includes bibliographical references and index. ISBN 84-7882-457-X DDC 292.215
1. Mediterranean Region - Religion. 2. Angels. 3. Demonology. 4. Spirituality - Mediterranean Region. I. Pérez Jiménez, Aurelio. II. Cruz Andreotti, Gonzalo. III. Series: Mediterránea (Madrid, Spain) ; no. 7.

Angelo Inácio, (Spirit).
Santos, Robson Pinheiro, 1961- Tambores de Angola. Contagem [Brazil] : Casa dos Espíritos, 2002.
1. Black author.

ANGELOLOGY. See **ANGELS.**

ANGELS. See also **GUARDIAN ANGELS.**
Ángeles, demonios y genios en el mundo Mediterráneo. Madrid : Ediciones Clásicas, 2000.

ANGELS - MISCELLANEA.
Virtue, Doreen, 1958- Angel medicine. Carlsbad, Calif. : Hay House, 2004.
BF1999 .V585 2004

Angenendt, Arnold. Grundformen der Frömmigkeit im Mittelalter / von Arnold Angenendt. München : Oldenbourg, 2003. x, 158 p. : ill. ; 23 cm. (Enzyklopädie deutscher Geschichte ; Bd. 68) ISBN 3-486-55704-1 (cl.)
1. Christian life - History - Middle Ages, 600-1500. 2. Church history - Middle Ages, 600-1500. 3. Church history - Middle Ages, 600-1500 - Research. I. Title. II. Series.

Anger.
DeFoore, Bill, 1950- [Rev.]. Deerfield Beach, Fla. : Health Communications, 2004.
BF575.A5 D45 2004

ANGER.
Carter, Les. The anger trap. 1st ed. San Francisco, CA : Jossey-Bass, c2003.
BF575.A5 C37 2003

Childre, Doc Lew, 1945- Transforming anger. Oakland, Calif. : New Harbinger ; London : Hi Marketing, 2003.
BF575.A5 C45 2003

DeFoore, Bill, 1950- Anger. [Rev.]. Deerfield Beach, Fla. : Health Communications, 2004.
BF575.A5 D45 2004

Engel, Beverly. Honor your anger. Hoboken, N.J. : J. Wiley & Sons, 2003.
BF575.A5 E54 2003

Johansen, Heidi Leigh. What I look like when I am angry. 1st ed. New York : PowerStart Press, 2004.
BF723.A4 J63 2004

Johansen, Heidi Leigh. [What I look like when I am angry. Spanish & English] What I look like when I am angry = 1st ed. New York : Rosen PowerKids Press, 2004.
BF723.A4 J6318 2004

Johnston, Marianne. [Dealing with anger. Spanish] Como tratar la ira. New York : PowerKids Press, 2005.
BF575.A5 J6418 2005

Jones, Carol D., 1948- Overcoming anger. Avon, MA : Adams Media, 2004.
BF575.A5 J66 2004

Leonard, Marcia. I feel angry. Nashville, Tenn. : CandyCane Press, 2003.
BF575.A5 L465 2003

Middelton-Moz, Jane, 1947- Good and mad. Deerfield Beach, Fla. : Health Communications Inc., c2003.
BF575.A5 M519 2003

Nay, W. Robert. Taking charge of anger. New York : Guilford Press, c2003.
BF575.A5 N39 2003

Nelson, Robin, 1971- Angry. Minneapolis, MN : Lerner Publications Co., c2004.
BF723.A4 N45 2004

Paleg, Kim. When anger hurts your relationship. Oakland, CA : New Harbinger Publications, c2001.
BF575.A5 P35 2001

Scheunemann, Pam, 1955- Coping with anger. Edina, MN : Abdo Pub., 2004.
BF575.A5 S34 2004

ANGER - CASE STUDIES.
Carter, Les. The anger trap. 1st ed. San Francisco, CA : Jossey-Bass, c2003.
BF575.A5 C37 2003

Eigen, Michael. Rage. Middletown, Conn. : Wesleyan University Press, c2002.
RC569.5.A53 E38 2002

ANGER - HUMOR.
Shulman, Mark, 1962- The voodoo revenge book. New York : Main Street, c2002.
BF637.R48 S55 2002

ANGER IN ADOLESCENCE.
Davis, Daniel Leifeld. Your angry child. New York : Haworth Press, c2004.
BF723.A4 D38 2004

ANGER IN CHILDREN.
Davis, Daniel Leifeld. Your angry child. New York : Haworth Press, c2004.
BF723.A4 D38 2004

Kennedy, Michelle. Tantrums. Hauppauge, N.Y. : Barron's, c2003.
BF723.A4 .K46 2003

McManus, Martha Hansen, 1948- Understanding the angry child. Seattle, Wash. : Parenting Press, 2004.
BF723.A4 M38 2004

Nemeth, Darlyne Gaynor. Helping your angry child. Oakland, Calif. : New Harbinger, c2003.
BF723.A4 N46 2003

ANGER IN CHILDREN - JUVENILE LITERATURE.
Johansen, Heidi Leigh. What I look like when I am angry. 1st ed. New York : PowerStart Press, 2004.
BF723.A4 J63 2004

Johansen, Heidi Leigh. [What I look like when I am angry. Spanish & English] What I look like when I am angry = 1st ed. New York : Rosen PowerKids Press, 2004.
BF723.A4 J6318 2004

Nelson, Robin, 1971- Angry. Minneapolis, MN : Lerner Publications Co., c2004.
BF723.A4 N45 2004

ANGER IN CHILDREN - STUDY AND TEACHING (ELEMENTARY).
Crouch, Roxie J. Anger management. Warminster, PA : Mar*co Products, c2000.
BF723.A4 C76 2000

ANGER - JUVENILE LITERATURE.
Johnston, Marianne. [Dealing with anger. Spanish] Como tratar la ira. New York : PowerKids Press, 2005.
BF575.A5 J6418 2005

Leonard, Marcia. I feel angry. Nashville, Tenn. : CandyCane Press, 2003.
BF575.A5 L465 2003

Scheunemann, Pam, 1955- Coping with anger. Edina, MN : Abdo Pub., 2004.
BF575.A5 S34 2004

Anger management.
Crouch, Roxie J. Warminster, PA : Mar*co Products, c2000.
BF723.A4 C76 2000

ANGER - MISCELLANEA.
Silverman, Stephen M. Envy, anger & sweet revenge. New York : Red Rock Press, c2002.
BF575.E65 S55 2002

ANGER - RELIGIOUS ASPECTS - BUDDHISM.
Thubten Chodron, 1950- Working with anger. Ithaca, NY : Snow Lion Publication, 2001.
BQ4430.A53 T48 2001

The anger trap.
Carter, Les. 1st ed. San Francisco, CA : Jossey-Bass, c2003.
BF575.A5 C37 2003

ANGLING. See **FISHING.**

Angry.
Johansen, Heidi Leigh. What I look like when I am angry. 1st ed. New York : PowerStart Press, 2004.
BF723.A4 J63 2004

Nelson, Robin, 1971- Minneapolis, MN : Lerner Publications Co., c2004.
BF723.A4 N45 2004

ANGST. See **ANXIETY.**

Animal.
Fudge, Erica. London : Reaktion, 2002.
QL85 .F83 2002

ANIMAL BEHAVIOR. See also **PSYCHOLOGY, COMPARATIVE.**
Morris, Desmond. The naked eye. London : Ebury Press, 2000.
QL31.M79 A3 2000

Ziolkowska, Aleksandra. Podróże z moją kotką. Wyd. 1. Warszawa : Wydawn. Nowy Świat, 2002.

ANIMAL BREEDERS. See **DOG BREEDERS.**

ANIMAL COMMUNICATION.
Cimatti, Felice. La mente silenziosa. 1. ed. Roma : Editori riuniti, 2002.

ANIMAL CULTURE. See **LIVESTOCK.**

Animal / editors-in-chief, David Burnie & Don E. Wilson. 1st American ed. New York : DK ; [Washington, D.C.] : Smithsonian Institution, 2001.
624 p. : col. ill., maps ; 32 cm. Subtitle on cover: Definitive visual guide to the world's wildlife. Includes index. Library lacks computer optical disc. CONTENTS: Introduction -- Habitats -- The animal kingdom. Mammals -- Birds -- Reptiles -- Amphibians -- Fishes -- Invertebrates. ISBN 0-7894-7764-5 (alk. paper) ISBN 0-7894-1703-0 DDC 590
1. Animals. 2. Zoology. I. Burnie, David. II. Wilson, Don E. III. Title: Definitive visual guide to the world's wildlife

ANIMAL EVOLUTION. See **EVOLUTION (BIOLOGY).**

ANIMAL-HUMAN RELATIONSHIPS. See **HUMAN-ANIMAL RELATIONSHIPS.**

ANIMAL HUSBANDRY. See **DOMESTIC ANIMALS; LIVESTOCK.**

ANIMAL INDUSTRY. See **LIVESTOCK.**

ANIMAL INTELLIGENCE. See also **LEARNING IN ANIMALS; LEARNING, PSYCHOLOGY OF; PSYCHOLOGY, COMPARATIVE.**
Rumbaugh, Duane M., 1929- Intelligence of apes and other rational beings. New Haven : Yale University Press, c2003.
QL737.P96 R855 2003

ANIMAL LEARNING. See **LEARNING IN ANIMALS.**

Animal life in nature, myth and dreams.
Caspari, Elizabeth, 1926- Wilmette, Ill. : Chiron Publications, c2003.
BF458 .C37 2003

ANIMAL LORE. See **ANIMALS - FOLKLORE.**

ANIMAL-MAN RELATIONSHIPS. See **HUMAN-ANIMAL RELATIONSHIPS.**

ANIMAL OWNERS. See **PET OWNERS.**

Animal patterns.
Reed, Janet (Janet C.) Bloomington, Minn. : Yellow Umbrella Books, c2003.
BF294 .R44 2003

ANIMAL PSYCHOLOGY. See also **PSYCHOLOGY, COMPARATIVE.**
Cimatti, Felice. La mente silenziosa. 1. ed. Roma : Editori riuniti, 2002.

ANIMAL SACRIFICE - EGYPT.
Eyre, Christopher. The cannibal hymn. Liverpool : Liverpool University Press, 2002.

ANIMAL SHELTERS.
Alger, Janet M., 1937- Cat culture. Philadelphia : Temple University Press, 2003.
SF446.5 .A36 2003

Animal spirit.
Telesco, Patricia, 1960- Franklin Lakes, NJ : New Page Books, c2002.
BF1623.A55 T445 2002

Animal voices.
Brunke, Dawn Baumann. Rochester, Vt. : Bear & Co., c2002.
QL776 .B78 2002

ANIMALS. See also **DOMESTIC ANIMALS; HUMAN-ANIMAL RELATIONSHIPS.**
Animal. 1st American ed. New York : DK ; [Washington, D.C.] : Smithsonian Institution, 2001.

Baratay, Eric. Et l'homme créa l'animal. Paris : O. Jacob, c2003.

Keller, Otto, 1838-1920. [Thiere des klassischen Alterthums in kulturgeschichtlicher Beziehung] Tiere des klassischen Altertums in kulturgeschichtlicher Beziehung. Hildesheim : Olms, c2001, 1887.

Reed, Janet (Janet C.) Animal patterns. Bloomington, Minn. : Yellow Umbrella Books, c2003.

BF294 .R44 2003

ANIMALS - ABNORMALITIES. *See* **MONSTERS.**

ANIMALS AND CIVILIZATION.
Baratay, Eric. Et l'homme créa l'animal. Paris : O. Jacob, c2003.

Brüder, Bestien, Automaten. 1. Aufl. Erlangen : H. Fischer, c2000.

ANIMALS AND CIVILIZATION - MIDDLE EAST - HISTORY - TO 1500.
Hyland, Ann. The horse in the ancient world. Stroud : Sutton, 2003.

ANIMALS AND HUMANS. *See* **HUMAN-ANIMAL RELATIONSHIPS.**

Animals, culture, and society
Alger, Janet M., 1937- Cat culture. Philadelphia : Temple University Press, 2003.
SF446.5 .A36 2003

ANIMALS, DOMESTIC. *See* **DOMESTIC ANIMALS.**

ANIMALS - EVOLUTION. *See* **EVOLUTION (BIOLOGY).**

ANIMALS - EXTINCTION. *See* **EXTINCTION (BIOLOGY).**

ANIMALS, FICTITIOUS. *See* **ANIMALS, MYTHICAL.**

ANIMALS - FOLKLORE. *See also* **ANIMALS, MYTHICAL; MONSTERS.**
Barnette, Martha. Dog days and dandelions. 1st ed. New York : St. Martin's Press, 2003.
PE1583 .B37 2003

ANIMALS - FOLKLORE - ENCYCLOPEDIAS.
Caspari, Elizabeth, 1926- Animal life in nature, myth and dreams. Wilmette, Ill. : Chiron Publications, c2003.
BF458 .C37 2003

ANIMALS, IMAGINARY. *See* **ANIMALS, MYTHICAL.**

ANIMALS IN ART.
Fudge, Erica. Animal. London : Reaktion, 2002.
QL85 .F83 2002

ANIMALS IN LITERATURE.
Brüder, Bestien, Automaten. 1. Aufl. Erlangen : H. Fischer, c2000.

Fudge, Erica. Animal. London : Reaktion, 2002.
QL85 .F83 2002

ANIMALS - JUVENILE LITERATURE.
Reed, Janet (Janet C.) Animal patterns. Bloomington, Minn. : Yellow Umbrella Books, c2003.
BF294 .R44 2003

ANIMALS - MISCELLANEA.
Rainieri, Caelum. The Nahualli animal oracle. Rochester, Vt. : Bear & Co., 2003.
BF1773 .R35 2003

Telesco, Patricia, 1960- Animal spirit. Franklin Lakes, NJ : New Page Books, c2002.
BF1623.A55 T445 2002

ANIMALS, MYTHICAL. *See also* **DRAGONS; VAMPIRES; WEREWOLVES.**
Marvels, monsters, and miracles. Kalamazoo, Mich. : Medieval Institute Publications, 2002.
GR825 .M218 2002

Roche, Christian. Le bestiaire des philosophes. [Paris] : Seuil, c2001.

ANIMALS, MYTHICAL - MISCELLANEA.
Conway, D. J. (Deanna J.) Magickal, mystical creatures. 2nd ed. St. Paul, Minn. : Llewellyn Publications, 2003.
BF1623.A55 C67 2003

ANIMALS, MYTHICAL - SCOTLAND.
Fleming, Maurice. Not of this world. Edinburgh : Mercat, 2002.

ANIMALS - MYTHOLOGY. *See* **ANIMALS, MYTHICAL.**

ANIMALS - MYTHOLOGY - ENCYCLOPEDIAS.
Caspari, Elizabeth, 1926- Animal life in nature, myth and dreams. Wilmette, Ill. : Chiron Publications, c2003.
BF458 .C37 2003

ANIMALS - NOMENCLATURE (POPULAR).
Barnette, Martha. Dog days and dandelions. 1st ed. New York : St. Martin's Press, 2003.
PE1583 .B37 2003

ANIMALS (PHILOSOPHY).
Brüder, Bestien, Automaten. 1. Aufl. Erlangen : H. Fischer, c2000.

Roche, Christian. Le bestiaire des philosophes. [Paris] : Seuil, c2001.

ANIMALS - PSYCHOLOGICAL ASPECTS.
Representing animals. Bloomington : Indiana University Press, c2002.
QL85 .R46 2002

ANIMALS - PSYCHOLOGICAL ASPECTS - ENCYCLOPEDIAS.
Caspari, Elizabeth, 1926- Animal life in nature, myth and dreams. Wilmette, Ill. : Chiron Publications, c2003.
BF458 .C37 2003

ANIMALS - RELIGIOUS ASPECTS. *See* **FAMILIARS (SPIRITS).**

ANIMALS - SYMBOLIC ASPECTS - ENCYCLOPEDIAS.
Caspari, Elizabeth, 1926- Animal life in nature, myth and dreams. Wilmette, Ill. : Chiron Publications, c2003.
BF458 .C37 2003

ANIMALS - TERMINOLOGY.
Barnette, Martha. Dog days and dandelions. 1st ed. New York : St. Martin's Press, 2003.
PE1583 .B37 2003

Animated earth.
Statnekov, Daniel K., 1943- 2nd ed. Berkeley Calif. : North Atlantic Books, 2003.
BF1999 .S719 2003

ANIMISM. *See* **MATERIALISM; SOUL; SOUL WORSHIP.**

Ankarloo, Bengt, 1935-.
Cryer, Frederick H. Biblical and pagan societies. Philadelphia : University of Pennsylvania Press, 2001.
BF1567 .C79 2001

Jolly, Karen Louise. The Middle Ages. Philadelphia : University of Pennsylvania Press, 2002, 2001. 12 300 xiv, 280 p. ; 24 cm.
BF1593 .J65 2002

Anna, André d'.
La céramique. Paris : Editions Errance, c2003.

ANNALS. *See* **HISTORY.**

Annals of the New York Academy of Sciences
(v. 1001) The self. New York : New York Academy of Sciences, 2003.
BF697

Année mille An Mil / sous la direction de Claude Carozzi et Huguette Taviani-Carozzi. Aix-en-Provence : Publications de l'université de Provence, 2002. 229 p. : ill. ; 21 cm. (Collection Le temps de l'histoire, 1631-946X) " ... ce volume est le quatrième recueil, édité aux PUP, des actes du séminaire de l'EA SICMA, Sociétés, Idéologies et Croyances au Moyen Age, centre de recherches de l'Université de Provence ... publié entre universitaire 1999-2000"--P. [4] of cover. Includes bibliographical references. ISBN 2-85399-513-5 DDC 900
1. One thousand, A.D. 2. Civilization, Medieval. 3. Europe - Social conditions. I. Carozzi, Claude. II. Taviani-Carozzi, Huguette. III. Université de Provence. IV. Series.

ANNIVERSARIES. *See* **FESTIVALS; HOLIDAYS.**

Año de las Naciones Unidas del diálogo entre civilizaciones.
2001, año de las Naciones Unidas del diálogo entre civilizaciones. Guatemala : Fundación Casa de la Reconciliación : MINUGUA, 2001.
JX1952 .A233 2001

ANOREXIA NERVOSA.
Género, desarrollo psicosocial y trastornos de la imagen corporal. Madrid : Instituto de la Mujer, 2001.

Anschlüsse
(Bd. 4) Zeichen des Todes in der psychoanalytischen Erfahrung. Tübingen : Edition Diskord, c2000.

Anselm Kiefer, Merkaba.
Kiefer, Anselm, 1945- Merkaba. New York : Gagosian Gallery, c2002.
N6888.K43 A4 2002

Anselm, Saint, Archbishop of Canterbury, 1033-1109.
[Dialogues. English. Selections]
Three philosophical dialogues / Anselm ; translated, with introduction and notes, by Thomas Williams. Indianapolis, IN : Hackett Pub., c2002. xiv, 110 p. ; 22 cm. Includes bibliographical references and index.
Translated from the Latin. CONTENTS: On truth -- On freedom of choice -- On the fall of the Devil. ISBN 0-87220-612-2 (cloth : alk. paper) ISBN 0-87220-611-4 (paper : alk. paper) DDC 189/.4
1. Anselm, - Saint, Archbishop of Canterbury, - 1033-1109. 2. Free will and determinism. 3. Truth. 4. Devil - Christianity. 5. Philosophy, Medieval. I. Williams, Thomas, 1967- II. Title.
B765.A81 .A2513 2002

ANSELM, SAINT, ARCHBISHOP OF CANTERBURY, 1033-1109.
Anselm, Saint, Archbishop of Canterbury, 1033-1109. [Dialogues. English. Selections] Three philosophical dialogues. Indianapolis, IN : Hackett Pub., c2002.
B765.A81 .A2513 2002

Anteile.
Günzel, Stephan, 1971- Weimar : Verlag und Datenbank für Geisteswissenschaften, 2002.

ANTHOLOGIES. *See also* **READERS.**
La palabra como cuerpo del delito. Santo Domingo, República Dominicana : Biblioteca Nacional "Dr. Pedro Henríquez Ureña", 2001.

Anthony, Kate.
Technology in counselling and psychotherapy. New York : Palgrave Macmillan, 2003.
BF637.C6 T467 2003

ANTHROPOLOGICAL LINGUISTICS.
Une introduction aux sciences de la culture. 1. ed. Paris : Presses universitaires de France : [Paris] : Institut Ferdinand-de-Saussure, 2002.

Khrolenko, A. T. Lingvokul'turovedenie. Kursk : Izd-vo GUIPP "Kursk", 2000.
P35 .K524 2000

Language evolution. Oxford ; New York : Oxford University Press, 2003.
P140 .L256 2003

Lexique et motivation. Paris : Sterling, Va. : Peeters, c2002.
P326 .L45 2002

Linguistic anthropology of education. Westport, Conn. ; London : Praeger, 2003.
P40.8 .L55 2003

Linguistic evolution through language acquisition. Cambridge : New York : Cambridge University Press, 2002.
P118 .L565 2002

Lurati, Ottavio. Per modo di dire--. Bologna : CLUEB, c2002.

Müller, Klaus E., 1935- Wortzauber. Frankfurt : Lembeck, c2001.
P35 .M945 2001

Razvitie natsional'noĭ, ėtnolingvisticheskoĭ i religioznoĭ identichnosti u deteĭ i podrostkov = Moskva : In-t psikhologii RAN, 2001.
BF723.C5 R39 2001

Une anthropologie des managers.
Flamant, Nicolas. Paris : Presses universitaires de France, c2002.
HD33 .F525 2002

Anthropologie du geste symbolique.
Beauperin, Yves. Paris : Harmattan, c2002.
BL60 .B339 2002

Anthropologie et psychanalyse.
Pulman, Bertrand. Paris : Presses universitaires de France, 2002.
GN502 .P85 2002

ANTHROPOLOGY. *See also* **ARCHAEOLOGY; ASSIMILATION (SOCIOLOGY); ETHNOLOGY; LANGUAGE AND LANGUAGES; PHYSICAL ANTHROPOLOGY.**
Aveni, Anthony F. Conversing with the planets. Rev. ed. Boulder, Colo. : University Press of Colorado, c2002.
QB981 .A99 2002

Pulman, Bertrand. Anthropologie et psychanalyse. Paris : Presses universitaires de France, 2002.
GN502 .P85 2002

ANTHROPOLOGY, CRIMINAL. *See* **CRIMINAL ANTHROPOLOGY.**

ANTHROPOLOGY - MORAL AND ETHICAL ASPECTS.
Logik und Leidenschaft. Berlin : D. Reimer Verlag, c2002.

ANTHROPOLOGY, PHILOSOPHICAL. *See* **PHILOSOPHICAL ANTHROPOLOGY.**

ANTHROPOLOGY - PHILOSOPHY.
Fremderfahrung und Repräsentation. 1. Aufl.
Weilerswist : Velbrück, 2002.

ANTHROPOMETRY. See **CRIMINAL ANTHROPOLOGY.**

ANTHROPOMETRY - HISTORY.
Guthrie, Robert V. Even the rat was white a historical view of psychology. Classic ed., 2nd ed. Boston, MA : Allyn and Bacon, 2004.
BF105 .G87 2004

ANTHROPOSOPHY.
Die Grundsteinmeditation als Schulungsweg. Dornach : Verlag am Goetheanum, c2002.

Steiner, Rudolf, 1861-1925. Reverse ritual. Great Barrington, MA : Anthroposophic Press, c2001.
BP595.S894 R48 2001

ANTI-AMERICANISM.
Crockatt, Richard. America embattled. London ; New York : Routledge, 2003.
E902 .C76 2003

ANTI-APARTHEID MOVEMENTS. See **APARTHEID.**

Anti-discriminatory counselling practice / edited by Colin Lago and Barbara Smith. London ; Thousand Oaks, Calif. : SAGE Publications, 2003. xvi, 154 p. ; 21 cm. (Professional skills for counsellors) Includes bibliographical references and index. Table of contents URL: http://www.loc.gov/catdir/toc/fy041/2002107100.html ISBN 0-7619-6646-3 ISBN 0-7619-6647-1 (pbk.) DDC 158/.3
1. Counseling. 2. Discrimination. I. Lago, Colin, 1944- II. Smith, Barbara, 1955- III. Series.
BF637.C6 A49 2003

ANTI-ENVIRONMENTALISM. See **ENVIRONMENTALISM.**

ANTI-FEMINISM. See also **FEMINISM.**
Schlafly, Phyllis. Feminist fantasies. Dallas : Spence Publishing Co., 2003.
HQ1150 .S34 2003

ANTI-GLOBALIZATION MOVEMENT.
Monkeywrenching the new world order [sound recording]. Oakland, Calif : AK Press ; San Francisco, CA : Alternative Tentacles Records, 2001.

ANTI-IMPERIALIST MOVEMENTS. See **IMPERIALISM.**

ANTICIPATION (PHILOSOPHY). See **EXPECTATION (PHILOSOPHY).**

Anticipatory behavior in adaptive learning systems.
Workshop on Adaptive Behavior in Anticipatory Learning Systems (1st : 2002 : Edinburgh, Scotland) Berlin ; New York : Springer, c2003.
Q325.5 .W65 2003

Antico Gallina, Mariavittoria. I romani : dalla terra all'uomo / Mariavittoria Antico Gallina ; introduzione di Raymond Chevallier. Cinisello Balsamo (Milano) : Silvana, 1998. 141 p. : ill. (chiefly col.), maps, plans ; 32 cm. (Popoli dell'Italia antica) Includes bibliographical references (p. 138-141). ISBN 88-8215-113-1 DDC 937
1. Rome - Civilization. 2. Romans - Italy. 3. Italy - Antiquities, Roman. I. Title. II. Series.

ANTIHEROES. See **HEROES.**

Antike Traumdeutung und moderne Traumforschung.
Walde, Christine, 1960- Düsseldorf : Artemis & Winkler, c2001.

Antike Weisheit und kulturelle Praxis : Hermetismus in der frühen Neuzeit / herausgegeben von Anne-Charlott Trepp und Hartmut Lehmann. Göttingen : Vandenhoeck & Ruprecht, 2001. 475 p. : ill., music ; 25 cm. (Veröffentlichungen des Max-Planck-Instituts für Geschichte ; 171) International conference proceedings held Oct. 28-30, 1999 in Göttingen, Germany. 14 German, 3 English contributions. Includes bibliographical references and index. ISBN 3-525-35374-X (hd.bd.)
1. Hermetism - History - Congresses. 2. Renaissance - Congresses. 3. Occultism - Europe - History - Congresses. I. Trepp, Anne-Charlott. II. Lehmann, Hartmut, 1936- III. Series.
BF1586 .A58 2001

Antinomies of modernity : essays on race, orient, nation / Vasant Kaiwar and Sucheta Mazumdar, editors. Durham : Duke University Press, 2003. viii, 353 p. ; 25 cm. Includes bibliographical references (p. [299]-323) and index. CONTENTS: The Aryan model of history and the oriental renaissance : the politics of identity in an age of revolutions, colonialism, and nationalism / Vasant Kaiwar -- Aryanizing projects, african "collaborators," and colonial transcripts / Andrew E. Barnes -- Orientalism's genesis amnesia / Mohamad Tavakoli-Targhi -- Coining words : language and politics in late colonial Tamilnadu / A. R. Venkatachalapathy -- An anticolonial international? : Indians, India, and Africans in British Central Africa / Michael O. West -- The "moment of manoeuvre" : "race," ethnicity, and nation in postapartheid South Africa / Neville Alexander -- Cultural nationalism and Islamic fundamentalism : the case of Iran / Minoo Moallem -- The politics of religion and national origin : rediscovering Hindu Indian identity in the United States / Sucheta Mazumdar -- Race, orient, nation in the time-space of modernity / Vasant Kaiwar and Sucheta Mazumdar. ISBN 0-8223-3011-3 (alk. paper) ISBN 0-8223-3046-6 (pbk. : alk. paper) DDC 950.4/2
1. Civilization, Modern. 2. Imperialism - History. 3. Capitalism - Social aspects - History. 4. Race relations - History. 5. Orientalism - History. 6. South Asia - Civilization. 7. Middle East - Civilization. 8. Africa - Civilization. 9. East and West. 10. North and south. I. Kaiwar, Vasant, 1950- II. Mazumdar, Sucheta, 1948-
CB358 .A59 2003

ANTINOMY.
Wind, Edgar, 1900- Das Experiment und die Metaphysik. 1. Aufl. Frankfurt am Main : Suhrkamp, 2001.

ANTINUCLEAR MOVEMENT. See **NUCLEAR POWER PLANTS.**

ANTIPATHY. See **AVERSION.**

The antipodes of the mind.
Shanon, Benny. Oxford ; New York : Oxford University Press, 2002.
BF209.A93 S53 2002

ANTIQUITIES. See **ARCHAEOLOGY.**

ANTIQUITIES - MISCELLANEA.
Little, Lora. Secrets of the ancient world. Virginia Beach, Va. : A.R.E. Press, c2003.
BF1045.A74 L58 2003

ANTIQUITIES, PREHISTORIC. See also **MEGALITHIC MONUMENTS; PREHISTORIC PEOPLES.**
Mithen, Steven J. After the ice. London : Weidenfeld & Nicolson, 2003.

Antiquity renewed : late classical and early modern themes / edited by Zweder von Martels and Victor M. Schmidt. Leuven, Netherlands ; Dudley, MA : Peeters, 2003. xii, 262 p. : ill., map ; 25 cm. (Groningen studies in cultural change ; v. 4) Includes bibliographical references (p. [231]-251) and index. ISBN 90-429-1308-8 (alk. paper) DDC 940.2/1
1. Renaissance. 2. Civilization, Medieval - Classical influences. 3. Rome - Civilization - Christian influences. 4. Byzantine Empire - Civilization - To 527. 5. Byzantine Empire - Civilization - 527-1081. 6. Byzantine Empire - Civilization - Classical influences. I. Martels, Z. R. W. M. von. II. Schmidt, Victor Michael. III. Series.
CB365 .A58 2003

ANTISEMITISM.
Ensaios sobre a intolerância. São Paulo, SP, Brasil : Humanitas, FFLCH/USP : FAPESP : LEI-Laboratório de Estudos sobre a Intolerância, 2002.

Kneer, Markus, 1972- Die dunkle Spur im Denken. Paderborn : Schöningh, 2003.
DS145 .K64 2003

ANTISEMITISM - PSYCHOLOGICAL ASPECTS.
Davis, Frederick, 1931- The Jew and deicide. Lanham, Md. : University Press of America, c2003.
BS2555.6.J44 D38 2003

ANTISLAVERY. See **SLAVERY.**

Antitrust issues in the airline industry.
United States. Congress. Senate. Committee on Commerce, Science, and Transportation. Washington : U.S. G.P.O. : For sale by the Supt. of Docs., U.S. G.P.O., 2003.

ANTITRUST LAW.
McAfee, R. Preston. Competitive solutions. Princeton, N.J. : Princeton University Press, c2002.
HD30.28 .M3815 2002

Rahnasto, Ilkka. Intellectual property rights, external effects, and antitrust law. Oxford ; New York : Oxford University Press, 2003.

ANTITRUST LAW - UNITED STATES.
United States. Congress. Senate. Committee on Commerce, Science, and Transportation. Antitrust issues in the airline industry. Washington : U.S. G.P.O. : For sale by the Supt. of Docs., U.S. G.P.O., 2003.

Antologiía : psikhologiíata prez XX vek / velikotŭrnovski izmereniía / [Viacheslav Vasilkivski, sŭstavitel i nauchen redaktor ; Mariana Niagolova, sŭstavitel]. 1. izd. Veliko Tŭrnovo : Izd-vo PAN-VT, 2001. 174 p. : ports. ; 21 cm. (Biblioteka Psikheia) ISBN 954747040x
1. Psychology - Bulgaria - History - 20th century. I. Vasilkivski, Viacheslav. II. Niagolova, Mariana, 1963- III. Series.
BF108.B9 A58 2001

Antonelli, Mauro.
Benussi, V. (Vittorio) [Selections. 2002] Psychologische Schriften. Amsterdam ; New York : Rodopi, 2002.

Antonio Gomes Penna.
Figueiredo, Luís Cláudio M. (Luís Cláudio Mendonça), 1945- Brasília, DF : Conselho Federal de Psicologia ; Rio de Janeiro, RJ : Imago, 2002.

Antonishen, Sherry.
Big Dance [videorecording]. Buffalo, N.Y. : Kineticvideo.com, c1998.

Antropologia culturale
Le figure del padre. Roma : Armando editore, c2001.

Antropologia culturale e sociale. Serie "Studi e ricerche"
(48.) Ferraiuolo, Augusto. "Pro exoneratione sua propria coscientia". Milano : F. Angeli, c2000.
BF1584.I8 F44 2000

Antropología e interpretación / compiladora Cristina Bulacio. Tucumán, Argentina : Instituto de Estudios Antropológicos y Filosofía de la Religión, Facultad de Filosofía y Letras, Universidad Nacional de Tucumán, c2001. 277 p. ; 21 cm. "Programa CIUNT, serie 2." "Programa de investigación CIUNT, serie 4"--Cover. Includes bibliographical references. ISBN 950-554-236-4 DDC 128
1. Philosophical anthropology. 2. Hermeneutics. 3. Humanism. I. Bulacio, Cristina. II. Universidad Nacional de Tucumán. Instituto de Estudios Antropológicos y Filosofía de la Religión.
BD450 .A564 2001

Anttonen, Anneli.
The young, the old, and the state. Cheltenham, UK ; Northhampton, MA : E. Elgar Pub., c2003.
HQ778.5 .Y69 2003

Antunes, Eleonora Haddad.
Psiquiatria, loucura e arte. São Paulo, SP, Brasil : Edusp, c2002.

ANXIETIES. See **ANXIETY.**

ANXIETY. See also **FEAR; PANIC DISORDERS; POST-TRAUMATIC STRESS DISORDER.**
Bourne, Edmund J. Coping with anxiety. Oakland, CA : New Harbinger, c2003.
BF575.A6 B68 2003

Elliott, Charles H., 1948- Overcoming anxiety for dummies. New York : Wiley Pub., c2003.
BF575.A6 E46 2003

Kostina, L. M. (Lïubov' Mikhaĭlovna) Metody diagnostiki trevozhnosti. Sankt-Peterburg : Rech', 2002.
BF575.A6 K65 2002

Mellinger, David. The monster in the cave. 1st ed. New York : Berkley Books, 2003.
BF575.F2 M45 2003

Salecl, Renata, 1962- On anxiety. 1st ed. London ; New York : Routledge, 2004.
BF575.A6 S25 2004

ANXIETY IN CHILDREN.
Foxman, Paul. The worried child. 1st ed. Alameda, CA : Hunter House, c2004.
BF723.A5 F69 2004

Shaw, Mary Ann. Your anxious child. 2nd ed. Irving, Tex. : Tapestry Press, c2003.
BF723.A5 S43 2003

Anxiety of late capitalism.
Bewes, Timothy. Reification, or, The anxiety of late capitalism. London ; New York : Verso, 2002.
HM449 .B49 2002

ANXIETY - PREVENTION.
Mornell, Adina. Lampenfieber und Angst bei ausübenden Musikern. Frankfurt am Main : P. Lang, 2002.
ML3830 .M67 2002

ANXIETY - RELIGIOUS ASPECTS - JUDAISM.
Gross, Esther. You are not alone. Jerusalem, Israel : Nanuet, NY : Feldheim, 2002.

ANXIOUSNESS. See **ANXIETY.**

Anyiam-Fiberesima, Peace.
The search for a holistic approach to human existence and development. [Nigeria?] : Osigwe Anyiam-Osigwe Foundation, [1999?]

B53 .E46 1999

Anyiam-Osigwe, Charles O.
The search for a holistic approach to human existence and development. [Nigeria?] : Osigwe Anyiam-Osigwe Foundation, [1999?]
B53 .E46 1999

ao resgatar debitos mais ou menos pesados, de existencias anteriores, capacitamo-nos para um futuro vitorioso.
Cuin, Joao. A luz de um novo dia. Sao Paulo : DPL, c 2001.

Aoumiel. Grimoire for the green witch : a complete book of shadows / Ann Moura. 1st ed. St. Paul, Minn. : Llewellyn Publications, c2003. x, 347 p. : ill. ; 26 cm. ISBN 0-7387-0287-0 (pbk.) DDC 133.4/3
1. Witchcraft. 2. Herbs - Miscellanea. 3. Magic. 4. Ritual. 5. Charms. I. Title.
BF1572.P43 A583 2003

Origins of modern witchcraft : the evolution of a world religion / Ann Moura. 1st ed. St. Paul, Minn. : Llewellyn Publications, 2000 (2002 printing) xx, 282 p. : ill., maps ; 23 cm. Includes bibliographical references (p. 269-273) and index. ISBN 1-56718-648-3 (pbk : recycled paper) DDC 133.4/3
1. Witchcraft - History. 2. Paganism - History. I. Title.
BF1566 .A56 2000

Tarot for the green witch / Ann Moura. 1st ed,. St. Paul, Minn. : Llewellyn Publications, 2003. xvi, 296 p. : ill. ; 23 cm. ISBN 0-7387-0288-9 DDC 133.3/2424
1. Tarot. 2. Witchcraft. I. Title.
BF1879.T2 A58 2003

AP psychology.
The best test preparation for the Advanced Placement Examination. Piscataway, N.J. : Research & Education Association, c2003.
BF78 .B48 2003

McEntarffer, Robert. Barron's how to prepare for the AP pscyhology advanced placement examination. Hauppauge, N.Y. : Barron's, c2004.
BF78 .M34 2004

APAGS workbook for writing successful applications and finding the right match.
Internships in psychology. Washington, D.C. : American Psychological Association, c2004.
BF77 .I67 2004

APARTHEID - SOUTH AFRICA.
Truth v. justice. Princeton, N.J. : Princeton University Press, c2000.
DT1945 .T78 2000

APATHY. See **EMOTIONS.**

Apel, Karl-Otto. The response of discourse ethics to the moral challenge of the human situation as such and especially today : Mercier lectures, Louvain-la-Neuve, March 1999 / Karl-Otto Apel. Leuven : Peeters, 2001. vii, 118 p. ; 24 cm. (Morality and the meaning of life, 0928-2742 ; 13) Also published in French in the series Bibliothèque Philosophique de Louvain (Peters 2000). Includes bibliographical references and index. ISBN 90-429-0978-1 (pbk.)
1. Ethics. I. Title. II. Series.
BJ1012 .A64 2001

APEL, KARL-OTTO.
Nazarchuk, A. V. (Aleksandr Viktorovich) Ėtika globaliziruiushchegosia obshchestva. Moskva : DirectMedia Publishing, 2002.
B3199.A634 N39 2002

APES - PSYCHOLOGY.
Rumbaugh, Duane M., 1929- Intelligence of apes and other rational beings. New Haven : Yale University Press, c2003.
QL737.P96 R855 2003

APHORISMS AND APOTHEGMS. See also **MAXIMS.**
Morales Villaroel, Oscar. Huellas y relatos. Caracas : [s.n.], 2001.

APHORISMS AND APOTHEGMS - HISTORY AND CRITICISM.
Hoggart, Richard, 1918- Everyday language & everyday life. New Brunswick, N.J. ; London : Transaction Publishers, c2003.
PE1074.8 .H64 2003

APOCALYPTIC LITERATURE.
La fin des temps. Talence : Université Michel de Montaigne, Bordeaux III, L.A.P.R.I.L., 2000-[2001]

Apokalypse oder Umkehr?.
Köhler, Manfred. Marburg : Tectum, 2000.

Apollon, Willy. After Lacan : clinical practice and the subject of the unconscious / Willy Apollon, Danielle Bergeron, and Lucie Cantin ; edited and introduced by Robert Hughes and Kareen Ror Malone. Albany : State University of New York Press, 2002. ix, 197 p. : ill. ; 23 cm. (SUNY series in psychoanalysis and culture) Includes bibliographical references and index. ISBN 0-7914-5480-0 (pbk. : alk. paper) ISBN 0-7914-5479-7 (alk. paper) DDC 616.89/17
1. Lacan, Jacques, - 1901- 2. Psychoanalysis - Practice. 3. Subconsciousness. I. Bergeron, Danielle. II. Cantin, Lucie. III. Hughes, Robert. IV. Malone, Kareen Ror, 1955- V. Title. VI. Series.
RC506 .A65 2002

APOLOGETICS. See also **WITNESS BEARING (CHRISTIANITY).**
Žižek, Slavoj, 1949- [Fragile absolute. Spanish] El frágil absoluto, o, Por qué merece la pena luchar por el legado cristiano? 1. ed. Valencia : Pre-Textos, 2002.
BT1102 .Z58

Apologetika
Karasev, Nikolaĭ, iereĭ. Put' okkul'tizma. Moskva : Izd-vo "Prensa", 2003.
BF1416 .K37 2003

APOTHEGMS. See **APHORISMS AND APOTHEGMS.**

APOTHEOSIS. See **HEROES.**

Apoyo psicosocial en catátrofes colectivas.
Beristain, Carlos M. 1a. ed. Caracas, Venezuela : Asociación Venezolana de Psicología Social-AVESPO : Comisión de Estudios de Posgrado, Facultad de Hunanidades y Educación, Universidad Central de Venezuela, 2000.

APPAREL. See **CLOTHING AND DRESS.**

APPAREL INDUSTRY. See **CLOTHING TRADE.**

APPARITIONS. See also **GHOSTS; POLTERGEISTS.**
Vinokurov, Igor'. Ne smotrite im v glaza!. Moskva : AiF-Print, 2001.
BF1466 .V56 2001

Appel, Dee. Friend to friend : inspirations for lifelong friendships / text by Dee Appel ; paintings by Jack Terry. Sisters, Or. : Multnomah Publishers, c2002. 42 p. : col. ill. ; 22 cm. ISBN 1-57673-932-5 DDC 177/.62
1. Female friendship. 2. Female friendship - Religious aspects - Christianity. I. Terry, Jack, 1952- II. Title.
BF575.F66 A66 2002

APPELLATE PROCEDURE. See **TRIAL PRACTICE.**

APPERCEPTION. See **CONSCIOUSNESS; KNOWLEDGE, THEORY OF; PERCEPTION.**

APPETENCY. See **DESIRE.**

APPETITE DISORDERS. See **EATING DISORDERS.**

Appignanesi, Richard, 1940-.
The end of everything. Cambridge : Icon, 2003.

Applegate, George. The complete book of dowsing : the definitive guide to finding underground water / George Applegate. Shaftesbury, Dorset ; Rockport, Mass. : Element, c1997. xvii 302 p. : ill. ; 25 cm. Includes bibliographical references (p. [285]-287) and index. ISBN 1-86204-142-3 (alk. paper) DDC 133.3/23
1. Dowsing. I. Title.
BF1628 .A67 1997

Applications of political theory
Cultivating citizens. Lanham : Lexington Books, c2002.
JK1759 .C85 2002

Lomax, J. Harvey, 1948- The paradox of philosphical education. Lanham, Md. ; Oxford : Lexington Books, c2003.
B3313.J43 L66 2003

APPLIED ECOLOGY. See **NATURE CONSERVATION.**

APPLIED ETHICS.
The Oxford handbook of practical ethics. Oxford ; New York : Oxford University Press, 2003.
BJ1031 .O94 2003

Applied legal philosophy
Samuel, Geoffrey, 1947- Epistemology and method in law. Aldershot, Hampshire, England : Burlington, VT : Ashgate, c2003.
K213 .S259 2003

Applied metacognition / edited by Timothy J. Perfect, Bennett L. Schwartz. Cambridge, U.K. ; New York : Cambridge University Press, 2002. xi, 297 p. : ill. ; 23 cm. Includes bibliographical references and index. Publisher description URL: http://www.loc.gov/catdir/description/cam022/2002024499.html Table of contents URL: http://www.loc.gov/catdir/toc/cam021/2002024499.html ISBN 0-521-80189-3 ISBN 0-521-00037-8 (pbk.) DDC 153
1. Metacognition - Congresses. I. Perfect, Timothy J. II. Schwartz, Bennett L.
BF311 .A638 2002

APPLIED PSYCHOLOGY. See **PSYCHOLOGY, APPLIED.**

Applied psychology : current issues and new directions / edited by Rowan Bayne and Ian Horton. London ; Thousand Oaks, Calif. : SAGE Publications, 2003. xxi. 264 p. ; 25 cm. Includes bibliographical references (p. [233]-256) and index. ISBN 0-7619-4150-9 (pbk.) ISBN 0-7619-4149-5 DDC 158
1. Psychology, Applied. I. Bayne, Rowan. II. Horton, Ian, 1940-
BF636 .A62 2003

APPLIED SCIENCE. See **TECHNOLOGY.**

Applied social research methods series
(v. 5) Yin, Robert K. Case study research. 3rd ed. Thousand Oaks, Calif. : Sage Publications, c2003.
H62 .Y56 2003

Applying sociolinguistics.
Boxer, Diana, 1948- Amsterdam ; Philadelphia : J. Benjamins Pub., c2002.
P40 .B678 2002

APPRAISAL OF BOOKS. See **CRITICISM; LITERATURE - HISTORY AND CRITICISM.**

Appraisal procedures for counselors and helping professionals.
Drummond, Robert J. 5th ed. Upper Saddle River, N.J. : Merrill/Prentice Hall, 2003.
BF176 .D78 2003

Appraising Lakatos : mathematics, methodology, and the man / edited by George Kampis, Ladislav Kvasz, Michael Stöltzner. Dordrecht ; Boston : Kluwer Academic, c2002. xiv, 382 p. : ill. ; 25 cm. (Vienna Circle Institute library ; 1) ISBN 1402002262 (alk. paper) DDC 501
1. Lakatos, Imre. 2. Lakatos, Imre, - d. 1974. 3. Science - Philosophy. 4. Mathematics - Philosophy. 5. Knowledge, Theory of. I. Kampis, George. II. Kvasz, Ladislav. III. Stöltzner, Michael. IV. Series.
Q175 .A685 2002

APPREHENSION. See also **PERCEPTION.**
Holt, Lynn, 1959- Aldershot, Hants, England ; Burlington, VT : Ashgate, c2002.
BC177 .H655 2002

An apprentice of the heart.
Finley, Guy. Ashland, Ore. : White Cloud Press, 2004.
BF575.L8 F524 2004

Approaches to peacebuilding / edited by Ho-Won Jeong. Houndmills, Basingstoke, Hampshire ; New York : Palgrave Macmillan, 2002. x, 203 p. ; 23 cm. (Global issues series) Includes bibliographical references and index. CONTENTS: Peacebuilding : conceptual and policy issues / Ho-Won Jeong -- Does peacebuilding build peace? / Charles-Philippe David -- Peacekeeping strategies for peacebuilding : multi-functional roles / Ho-Won Jeong -- Negotiation readiness in the development context : adding capacity to ripeness / Bertram I. Spector -- Reconciliation : contexts and consequences / Charles Lerche and Ho-Won Jeong -- Gender in post-conflict reconstruction / Susan McKay -- Peacebuilding design : a synergetic approach / Ho-Won Jeong -- Operational issues for peacebuilding : organisational imperatives / Ho-Won Jeong and David Last. ISBN 0-333-98192-8 ISBN 0-333-79483-4 (SET) DDC 303.6/9
1. Peace. 2. Social engineering. 3. Peacekeeping forces. I. Jeong, Ho-Won. II. Series: Global issues series (Palgrave Macmillan (Firm))
JZ5538 .A675 2002

Apps, Lara. Male witches in early modern Europe / Lara Apps and Andrew Gow. Manchester ; New York : Manchester University Press ; New York : Distributed exclusively in the USA by Palgrave, 2003. ix, 190 p. : ill. ; 23 cm. Includes bibliographical references (p. 167-185) and index. ISBN 0-7190-5708-6 ISBN 0-7190-5709-4 (pbk.) DDC 133.4/081094
1. Witchcraft - Europe - History. 2. Warlocks - Europe - History. I. Gow, Andrew. II. Title.
BF1584.E85 A66 2003

Aproximación a las fuentes clásicas latinas de Hannah Arendt.
Torre, Francisco Javier de la. Málaga : Universidad de Málaga, 2002.

AQUARIAN AGE MOVEMENT. *See* **NEW AGE MOVEMENT.**

AQUATIC ANIMALS. *See* **FISHES.**

AQUATIC BIOLOGY. *See* **AQUATIC ORGANISMS.**

AQUATIC BIOTA. *See* **AQUATIC ORGANISMS.**

AQUATIC ORGANISMS - SYMBOLIC ASPECTS.
Dans l'eau, sous l'eau. [Paris] : Presses de l'Université de Paris-Sorbonne, 2002.
CB353 .D27 2002

AQUATIC SPORTS. *See* **FISHING.**

ARAB ASTROLOGY. *See* **ASTROLOGY, ARAB.**

ARAB ASTRONOMY. *See* **ASTRONOMY, ARAB.**

ARAB COUNTRIES - HISTORY - 20TH CENTURY. *See* **ARAB-ISRAELI CONFLICT.**

ARAB COUTRIES - 21ST CENTURY.
Dāwūd, Muḥammad 'Īsá. al-Jafr li-Sayyidinā 'Alī. al-Muhandisīn [Giza] : Madbūlī al-Ṣaghīr, [2003]
BF1771+

ARAB-ISRAELI CONFLICT. *See* **PROPAGANDA, ZIONIST.**

ARAB-ISRAELI CONFLICT - 1993- - PEACE - BIBLICAL TEACHING.
Glazerson, Matityahu. Migdele ha-te'omim be-diluge otiyot ba-Torah. Yerushalayim : Yerid ha-sefarim, 2002.

ARAB-ISRAELI CONFLICT - 1993- - PEACE - PSYCHOLOGICAL ASPECTS.
Grosbard, Ofer, 1954- Yiśra'el 'al ha-sapah. Tel-Aviv : Yedi'ot aḥaronot : Sifre ḥemed, c2000.

ARAB-ISRAELI CONFLICT - MORAL AND ETHICAL ASPECTS.
Ellis, Marc H. Israel and Palestine out of the ashes. London ; Sterling, Va. : Pluto Press, c2002.
DS119.76 .E56 2002

ARAB-ISRAELI CONFLICT - PEACE - PSYCHOLOGICAL ASPECTS.
Grosbard, Ofer, 1954- [Yiśra'el 'al ha-sapah. English] Israel on the couch. Albany : State University of New York Press, c2003.
DS126.5 .G694 2003

ARAB-ISRAELI CONFLICT - PSYCHOLOGICAL ASPECTS.
Rowland, Robert C., 1954- Shared land/conflicting identity. East lansing : Michigan State University Press, 2002.
DS119.7 .R685 2003

ARAB-ISRAELI PEACE PROCESS. *See* **ARAB-ISRAELI CONFLICT - 1993- - PEACE.**

ARAB NATIONAL CHARACTERISTICS. *See* **NATIONAL CHARACTERISTICS, ARAB.**

ARAB PALESTINIANS. *See* **PALESTINIAN ARABS.**

ARAB PROPAGANDA. *See* **PROPAGANDA, ARAB.**

Arabesque (Series)
Louise, Kim. True devotion. Washington D.C. : BET Publications, 2002.

ARABIAN NIGHTS.
Scholz, Piotr O. Die Sehnsucht nach Tausendundeiner Nacht. Stuttgart : Thorbecke, c2002.

ARABIC LANGUAGE - GRAMMAR - HISTORY.
Bahnasāwī, Ḥusām. Ahammīyat al-rabṭ bayna al-tafkīr al-lughawī 'inda al-'Arab wa- naẓarīyāt al-baḥth al-lughawī al-ḥadīth. al-Qāhirah : Maktabat al-Thaqāfah al-Dīnīyah, 1994.
PJ6106 .B35 1994 <Orien Arab>

ARABIC PHILOSOPHY. *See* **PHILOSOPHY, ISLAMIC.**

ARABS. *See* **PALESTINIAN ARABS.**

ARABS IN PALESTINE. *See* **PALESTINIAN ARABS.**

ARABS - PALESTINE. *See* **PALESTINIAN ARABS.**

Aragão, Gaby de.
Carsalade, Flávio de Lemos. Arquitetura. Belo Horizonte : AP Cultural, 2001.
NA2500 .C37 2001

'Arakhim ye-ḥinukh.
Malkah, Asher. Ḥefaḥ : A. Malkah, [5760 i.e. 2000]

Arana Cañedo-Argüelles, Juan.
El buscador de oro. [Madrid] : Lengua de Trapo Ediciones, c2002.

Aransiola, Moses Olanrewaju. The roots and solutions to peculiar problems (dealing with bad luck, lost opportunities and failure) / Moses Olanrewaju Aransiola. 1st ed. Ibadan, Nigeria : Gethsemane Publications, 2002. (Destiny restoration prayers ; 2)
1. Failure (Psychology) - Religious aspects - Christianity. 2. Suffering - Religious aspects - Christianity. 3. Spiritual warfare. 4. Prayer. 5. Black author. I. Title.

Arantes, Antonio Augusto.
Peixoto, Nelson Brissac. Nelson Brissac, Antonio Augusto Arantes. [São Paulo, SP : Fundação Memorial da América Latina, 1997]

ARANTES, ANTONIO AUGUSTO - INTERVIEWS.
Peixoto, Nelson Brissac. Nelson Brissac, Antonio Augusto Arantes. [São Paulo, SP : Fundação Memorial da América Latina, 1997]

Araujo, Marcelo de. Scepticism, freedom and autonomy : a study of the moral foundations of Descartes' theory of knowledge / by Marcelo de Araujo. Berlin : De Gruyter, 2003. 237 p. ; 24 cm. (Quellen und Studien zur Philosophie ; Bd. 58) Revised thesis (doctoral) - Universität Konstanz, 2002. Includes bibliographical references (p. [207]-234) and index. ISBN 3-11-017538-X (cl.)
1. Descartes, René, - 1596-1650 - Contributions in theory of knowledge. 2. Descartes, René, - 1596-1650 - Ethics. 3. Knowledge, Theory of. 4. Ethics, Modern - 17th century. 5. Skepticism. 6. Autonomy (Philosophy) I. Title. II. Title: Study of the moral foundations of Descartes' theory of knowledge III. Series.

Arbeiten zur Kirchengeschichte
(Bd. 88) Tilton, Hereward. The quest for the phoenix. Berlin ; New York : Walter de Gruyter, 2003.
QD24.M3 T558 2003

Arbeitshefte Führungspsychologie
(Bd. 1) Crisand, Ekkehard. Psychologie der Persönlichkeit. 8., durchgesehene Aufl. Heidelberg : I.H. Sauer-Verlag, 2000.
BF698 .C715 2000

Arbol del Paraíso
(26) Vega, Amador. Ramon Llull y el secreto de la vida. Madrid : Siruela, 2002.

ARBORICULTURE. *See* **TREES.**

ARCA, classical medieval texts, papers, and monographs
(43) Caesar against liberty? Cambridge : Francis Cairns, c2003.

ARCANA, MAJOR (TAROT). *See* **MAJOR ARCANA (TAROT).**

ARCHAEOASTRONOMY.
Aveni, Anthony F. The book of the year. Oxford ; New York : Oxford University Press, 2003.
GT3930 .A94 2003

Aveni, Anthony F. Conversing with the planets. Rev. ed. Boulder, Colo. : University Press of Colorado, c2002.
QB981 .A99 2002

Aveni, Anthony F. Empires of time. Rev. ed. Boulder, Colo. : University Press of Colorado, c2002.
QB209 .A94 2002

Clow, Barbara Hand, 1943- Catastrophobia. Rochester, Vt. : Bear & Company, c2001.
BF1999 .C587 2001

ARCHAEOLOGICAL DIGS. *See* **EXCAVATIONS (ARCHAEOLOGY).**

ARCHAEOLOGICAL EXCAVATIONS. *See* **EXCAVATIONS (ARCHAEOLOGY).**

ARCHAEOLOGICAL SPECIMENS. *See* **ANTIQUITIES.**

Archaeologies of memory / edited by Ruth M. Van Dyke and Susan E. Alcock. Malden, MA ; Oxford : Blackwell, 2003. xiv, 240 p. : ill., maps ; 25 cm. Includes bibliographical references and index. ISBN 0-631-23584-1 (hbk. : alk. paper) ISBN 0-631-23585-X (pbk. : alk. paper) DDC 930.1
1. Social archaeology. 2. Memory - Social aspects. I. Van Dyke, Ruth. II. Alcock, Susan E.
CC72.4 .A733 2003

ARCHAEOLOGISTS - BIOGRAPHY.
Mauerschau. Remshalden-Grunbach : Greiner, 2002.

ARCHAEOLOGY. *See also* **AMULETS; ANTIQUITIES; EXCAVATIONS (ARCHAEOLOGY).**
Archaeology. Oxford : Published for The British Academy by Oxford University Press, c2002.

La céramique. Paris : Editions Errance, c2003.

Mauerschau. Remshalden-Grunbach : Greiner, 2002.

Neubauer, Wolfgang, 1963- Magnetische Prospektion in der Archäologie. Wien : Verlag der Österreichischen Akademie der Wissenschaften, 2001.

Le propre de l'homme. Lausanne : Delachaux et Niestlé, c1998.
BF175 .P69 1998

Smetanka, Z. Archeologické etudy. Praha : [Lidové noviny], 2003.

The Splendors of archaeology. Cairo : American University in Cairo Press, 1998.

Style, function, transmission. Salt Lake City : University of Utah Press, c2003.
CC173 .S79 2003

ARCHAEOLOGY - FIELD WORK.
Theory and practice in late antique archaeology. Leiden ; Boston : Brill, 2003.
CC72.4 .T46 2003

ARCHAEOLOGY IN LITERATURE.
Digging holes in popular culture. Oxford : Oxbow, 2002.
PN3433.6 .D54 2002

ARCHAEOLOGY - LAW AND LEGISLATION. *See* **TREASURE-TROVE.**

ARCHAEOLOGY, MEDIEVAL.
Smetanka, Z. Archeologické etudy. Praha : [Lidové noviny], 2003.

ARCHAEOLOGY - METHODOLOGY.
Mauerschau. Remshalden-Grunbach : Greiner, 2002.

Theory and practice in late antique archaeology. Leiden ; Boston : Brill, 2003.
CC72.4 .T46 2003

ARCHAEOLOGY - PHILOSOPHY.
Theory and practice in late antique archaeology. Leiden ; Boston : Brill, 2003.
CC72.4 .T46 2003

Archaeology : the widening debate / edited by Barry Cunliffe, Wendy Davies, Colin Renfrew. Oxford : Published for The British Academy by Oxford University Press, c2002. viii, 627 p. : ill., maps, port. ; 26 cm. Includes bibliographical references and index. ISBN 0-19-726255-4 DDC 930.1
1. Archaeology. 2. Civilization. I. Cunliffe, Barry W. II. Davies, Wendy, 1942- III. Renfrew, Colin. IV. British Academy.

Archard, David. Children, family, and the state / David William Archard. Aldershot, Hants, England ; Burlington, VT : Ashgate, 2003. xiii, 190 p. ; 22 cm. (Live questions in ethics and moral philosophy) Includes bibliographical references (p. [169]-183) and index. ISBN 0-7546-0554-X (alk. paper) ISBN 0-7546-0555-8 (pbk. : alk. paper) DDC 305.23
1. Children's rights. 2. Family. 3. State, The. I. Title. II. Series.
HQ789 .A695 2003

Archeologické etudy.
Smetanka, Z. Praha : [Lidové noviny], 2003.

ARCHEOLOGY. *See* **ARCHAEOLOGY.**

Archer, Clive.
The Nordic peace. Aldershot, England ; Burlington, VT : Ashgate, c2003.
UA646.7 .N672 2003

Archer, Margaret Scotford. Structure, agency and the internal conversation / Margaret S. Archer. Cambridge, U.K. ; New York : Cambridge University Press, 2003. x, 370 p. : ill. ; 23 cm. Includes bibliographical references and index. Publisher description URL: http://www.loc.gov/catdir/description/cam032/2003043804.html Table of contents URL: http://www.loc.gov/catdir/toc/cam031/2003043804.html ISBN 0-521-82906-2 ISBN 0-521-53597-2 (pbk.) DDC 301
1. Social structure. 2. Agent (Philosophy) 3. Self-knowledge, Theory of. 4. Social perception. 5. Interviews - Great Britain. I. Title.
HM708 .A73 2003

Archetype, attachment, analysis.
Knox, Jean, 1948- Hove, East Sussex ; New York : Brunner-Routledge, 2003.
BF175.5.A72 K68 2003

The archetype of renewal.
Bond, D. Stephenson. Toronto : Inner City Books, c2003.

ARCHETYPE (PSYCHOLOGY).
Balancing the scales. Lanham, Md. ; Oxford : University Press of America, c2003.
HQ1075 .B3417 2003

Davis, Frederick, 1931- The Jew and deicide. Lanham, Md. : University Press of America, c2003.
BS2555.6.J44 D38 2003

Donchenko, E. A. (Elena Andreevna) Arkhetypy sotsial'noho zhyttia i polityka. Kyïv : Lybid', 2001.
JA74.5 .D65 2001

Gilbert, Toni. Messages from the archetypes. Ashland, Or. : White Cloud Press, c2003.
BF1879.T2 G53 2003

Ivanova, E. V. (Elena Vladimirovna) Ved'my. Ekaterinburg : Ural'skiĭ gos. universitet, 2002.
BF1584.R9 I85 2002

Knox, Jean, 1948- Archetype, attachment, analysis. Hove, East Sussex ; New York : Brunner-Routledge, 2003.
BF175.5.A72 K68 2003

McConeghey, Howard. Art and soul. 1st ed. Putnam, CT : Spring Publications, Inc. ; [New York] : Distributed by Continuum, c2003.

Popović, Velimir B. O duši i bogovima. Niš : Prosveta, 2001.
BF175.5.A72 P67 2001

Sciences et archétypes. Paris : Dervy, 2002.

Weiler, Gerda, 1921- Der enteignete Mythos. Königstein : Helmer, [1996]

Wertime, Kent. Building brands & believers. Chichester : Wiley, 2002.

Architect's guide to feng shui.
Bramble, Cate. Amsterdam ; Boston ; London : Architectural Press, 2003.
BF1779.F4 B73 2003

Architectural Association.
Marot, Sébastien, 1961- [Art de la mémoire, la territoire et l'architecture] Sub-urbanism and the art of memory. London : Architectural Association, c2003.

ARCHITECTURAL CRITICISM.
Bruyn, Gerd de. Fisch und Frosch, oder, Die Selbstkritik der Moderne. Gütersloh ; Berlin : Bertelsmann Fachzeitschriften ; Basel ; Boston ; Berlin : Birkhäuser, c2001.

ARCHITECTURAL DESIGN.
Lim, C. J. Realms of impossibility. Ground. Chichester : Wiley-Academy, 2002.

ARCHITECTURAL PERSPECTIVE. See **PERSPECTIVE.**

ARCHITECTURAL SYMBOLISM. See **SYMBOLISM IN ARCHITECTURE.**

ARCHITECTURE. See also **ARCHITECTURE, DOMESTIC; ASTROLOGY AND ARCHITECTURE; BUILDINGS; CHURCH ARCHITECTURE; MONUMENTS; SYMBOLISM IN ARCHITECTURE.**
Carsalade, Flávio de Lemos. Arquitetura. Belo Horizonte : AP Cultural, 2001.
NA2500 .C37 2001

Šik, Miroslav. Altneue Gedanken. Luzern : Quart, c2002.

Sturm, Hermann, 1936- Dinge im Fluss, Fluss der Verzeichnungen. Frankfurt a.M. : Anabas-Verlag, 2002.

ARCHITECTURE - 20TH CENTURY.
Bruyn, Gerd de. Fisch und Frosch, oder, Die Selbstkritik der Moderne. Gütersloh ; Berlin : Bertelsmann Fachzeitschriften ; Basel ; Boston ; Berlin : Birkhäuser, c2001.

ARCHITECTURE AND COSMOLOGY.
Khadiratna, Dayanidhi. Br̥hat śilpaśāstra, bā, Gr̥habandha bijñāna ; Gr̥habandha gaṇanā o śubhastambhāropaṇa bicāra. Kaṭaka : Dharmagrantha Shṭora, [1995?]
TH4809.I4 K48 1995

ARCHITECTURE AND ENERGY CONSERVATION.
Smith, Peter F. (Peter Frederick), 1930- Sustainability at the cutting edge. Oxford ; Boston : Architectural Press, 2003.
NA2542.3 .S65 2003

ARCHITECTURE AND PHILOSOPHY.
Español Llorens, Joaquim. El orden frágil de la arquitectura. Barcelona : Fundación Caja de Arquitectos, c2001.

ARCHITECTURE AND POLITICS. See **ARCHITECTURE AND STATE.**

ARCHITECTURE AND RELIGION. See **CHURCH ARCHITECTURE.**

ARCHITECTURE AND SOCIETY.
Soleri, Paolo, 1919- What if? Berkeley, CA : Berkeley Hills Books, 2002.
NA2543.S6 S637 2002

ARCHITECTURE AND SOCIETY - HISTORY.
Palais et pouvoir. Vincennes : Presses universitaires de Vincennes, c2003.

ARCHITECTURE AND SOCIOLOGY. See **ARCHITECTURE AND SOCIETY.**

ARCHITECTURE AND SPACE. See **SPACE (ARCHITECTURE).**

ARCHITECTURE AND STATE - HISTORY.
Palais et pouvoir. Vincennes : Presses universitaires de Vincennes, c2003.

ARCHITECTURE - BURMA.
'Oṅ' Mraṅ'', 'Aṅ'gyaṅ'nīyā Ū'', 'Im' chok' maṅgalā kyam'". Mantale" : Krī" pvā" re" Cā 'up' Tuik", 2002.
BF1773.A88 O56 2002

San'" Ū", Sutagavesī. Mran' mā' ruī" rā 'im' khraṃ mre nañña'" pañña. Ran' kun' : Rvhe Pu ra puid' Cā pe : Phran'" khyi re", Sa mī" Jotika Cā pe, 2000.
BF1773.2.B93 S26 2000

ARCHITECTURE - COMPOSITION, PROPORTION, ETC. See **SPACE (ARCHITECTURE).**

ARCHITECTURE, DOMESTIC. See **DWELLINGS.**

ARCHITECTURE, DOMESTIC - INDIA.
[Śilpaśāstra. English & Sanskrit.] Vāstu-śāstram. Calcutta : Sanskrit Pustak Bhandar, 2001.
NA7427 .M34 2001

ARCHITECTURE, DOMESTIC - INDIA - DESIGNS AND PLANS.
Khadiratna, Dayanidhi. Br̥hat śilpaśāstra, bā, Gr̥habandha bijñāna ; Gr̥habandha gaṇanā o śubhastambhāropaṇa bicāra. Kaṭaka : Dharmagrantha Shṭora, [1995?]
TH4809.I4 K48 1995

ARCHITECTURE, DUTCH - NETHERLANDS. See **ARCHITECTURE - NETHERLANDS.**

ARCHITECTURE - ENVIRONMENTAL ASPECTS.
Betsky, Aaron. Landscrapers. New York, New York : Thames & Hudson, 2002.

Bramble, Cate. Architect's guide to feng shui. Amsterdam ; Boston ; London : Architectural Press, 2003.
BF1779.F4 B73 2003

Environmentally sustainable buildings. Paris : Organisation for Economic Co-operation and Development, 2003.

Gans, Deborah. The organic approach to architecture. New York ; Chichester : Wiley, 2002.

Smith, Peter F. (Peter Frederick), 1930- Sustainability at the cutting edge. Oxford ; Boston : Architectural Press, 2003.
NA2542.3 .S65 2003

Architecture for the shroud.
Scott, John Beldon, 1946- Chicago : University of Chicago Press, c2003.
NA5621.T823 S36 2003

ARCHITECTURE - FORECASTING.
Soleri, Paolo, 1919- What if? Berkeley, CA : Berkeley Hills Books, 2002.

ARCHITECTURE, GOTHIC. See **CHURCH ARCHITECTURE.**

ARCHITECTURE, HINDU.
Bansal, Ashwinie Kumar. Vastu. Hauppauge, NY : Barron's, 2002.
BF1779.V38 B36 2002

Khadiratna, Dayanidhi. Br̥hat śilpaśāstra, bā, Gr̥habandha bijñāna ; Gr̥habandha gaṇanā o śubhastambhāropaṇa bicāra. Kaṭaka : Dharmagrantha Shṭora, [1995?]

TH4809.I4 K48 1995

Pathy, Dinanath. Art, regional traditions, the Temple of Jagannātha. New Delhi : Sundeep Prakashan, 2001.
NA6002 .P37 2001

[Śilpaśāstra. English & Sanskrit.] Vāstu-śāstram. Calcutta : Sanskrit Pustak Bhandar, 2001.
NA7427 .M34 2001

ARCHITECTURE - HISTORY.
Baumann, Günter, 1962- Meisterwerke der Architektur. Stuttgart : Reclam, c2001.
NA200 .B33 2001

Marmur dziejowy. Poznań : Wydawnictwo Poznańskiego Towarzystwa Przyjaciół Nauk, 2002.

ARCHITECTURE - HUMAN FACTORS. See **ARCHITECTURE AND SOCIETY.**

Architecture landscape urbanism
(8) Marot, Sébastien, 1961- [Art de la mémoire, la territoire et l'architecture] Sub-urbanism and the art of memory. London : Architectural Association, c2003.

ARCHITECTURE, MEDIEVAL - ITALY - PISA.
Gianfaldoni, Paolo. Benvenuto a Pisa. [Fornacette, Pisa] : CLD iniziative speciali, c2000.

ARCHITECTURE, MODERN - 20TH CENTURY.
Betsky, Aaron. Landscrapers. New York, New York : Thames & Hudson, 2002.

ARCHITECTURE - NETHERLANDS - 20TH CENTURY.
Jormakka, Kari. [Olandesi volanti. English] Flying Dutchmen. Basel ; Boston : Birkhäuser, 2002.
NA1148 .J6713 2002

ARCHITECTURE - PHILOSOPHY.
Arkhitekturnoe soznanie XX-XXI vekov. Moskva : Editorial URSS, 2001.
NA712 .A87 2001

Baudrillard, Jean. [Objets singuliers. English] The singular objects of architecture. Minneapolis : University of Minnesota Press, c2002.
NA2500 .B3413 2002

Baumann, Günter, 1962- Meisterwerke der Architektur. Stuttgart : Reclam, c2001.
NA200 .B33 2001

Breitschmid, Markus, 1966- Der bauende Geist. Luzern : Quart, 2001.
B3318.A4 B745 2001

Bruyn, Gerd de. Fisch und Frosch, oder, Die Selbstkritik der Moderne. Gütersloh ; Berlin : Bertelsmann Fachzeitschriften ; Basel ; Boston ; Berlin : Birkhäuser, c2001.

Building gender = Wien : Edition Selene, 2002.

Carsalade, Flávio de Lemos. Arquitetura. Belo Horizonte : AP Cultural, 2001.
NA2500 .C37 2001

Español Llorens, Joaquim. El orden frágil de la arquitectura. Barcelona : Fundación Caja de Arquitectos, c2001.

Inclusive design. London ; New York : Springer, c2003.
TA174 .I464 2003

Jormakka, Kari. [Olandesi volanti. English] Flying Dutchmen. Basel ; Boston : Birkhäuser, 2002.
NA1148 .J6713 2002

Lim, C. J. Realms of impossibility. Ground. Chichester : Wiley-Academy, 2002.

Marot, Sébastien, 1961- [Art de la mémoire, la territoire et l'architecture] Sub-urbanism and the art of memory. London : Architectural Association, c2003.

Mining autonomy. Cambridge, Mass. : London : MIT Press, c2002.

Palumbo, Maria Luisa. [Nuovi ventri. English] New wombs : electronic bodies and architectural disorders. Basel : Birkhäuser, 2000.
NA2765 .P35 2000

Rábago, Jesús. Le sens de bâtir. Lecques : Théétète, c2000.
NA2500 .R29 2000

Revzin, G. I. (Grigoriĭ I.) Ocherki po filosofii arkhitekturnoĭ formy. Moskva : O.G.I., 2002.
NA2500 .R464 2002

Saldarriaga Roa, Alberto. La Arquitectura como experiencia. 1. ed. Bogotá : Villegas Editores : Universidad Nacional de Colombia, Facultad de Artes, c2002.

NA2765 .S36 2002

Soleri, Paolo, 1919- What if? Berkeley, CA : Berkeley Hills Books, 2002.
NA2543.S6 S637 2002

Unschaerferelationen. Wiesbaden : Nelte, c2002.
BF469 .U5 2002

ARCHITECTURE, RURAL. *See* **ARCHITECTURE, DOMESTIC.**

ARCHITECTURE - RUSSIA (FEDERATION) - 20TH CENTURY.
Arkhitekturnoe soznanie XX-XXI vekov. Moskva : Editorial URSS, 2001.
NA712 .A87 2001

ARCHITECTURE - TECHNOLOGICAL INNOVATIONS.
Jormakka, Kari. [Olandesi volanti. English] Flying Dutchmen. Basel ; Boston : Birkhäuser, 2002.
NA1148 .J6713 2002

Architektur und Geschlecht.
Building gender = Wien : Edition Selene, 2002.

Architekturtheorie
Bruyn, Gerd de. Fisch und Frosch, oder, Die Selbstkritik der Moderne. Gütersloh ; Berlin : Bertelsmann Fachzeitschriften ; Basel ; Boston ; Berlin : Birkhäuser, c2001.

An archive of feelings.
Cvetkovich, Ann, 1957- Durham : Duke University Press, 2003.
HQ75.5 .C89 2003

ARCHIVES.
Steedman, Carolyn. Dust. New Brunswick, N.J. : Rutgers University Press, 2002, c2001.
CD947 .S73 2002

ARCHIVES - ADMINISTRATION - CASE STUDIES.
Archives and the public good. Westport, Conn. ; London : Quorum Books, 2002.

Archives and the public good : accountability and records in modern society / edited by Richard J. Cox and David A. Wallace. Westport, Conn. ; London : Quorum Books, 2002. vi, 340 p. ; 24 cm. Includes bibliographical references and index. ISBN 1-56720-469-4 DDC 027
1. Archives - Social aspects. 2. Archives - Administration - Case studies. 3. Records - Management - Case studies. 4. Common good. 5. Public interest. 6. Responsibility. I. Cox, Richard J. II. Wallace, David A.

ARCHIVES - SOCIAL ASPECTS.
Archives and the public good. Westport, Conn. ; London : Quorum Books, 2002.

ARCTIC REGIONS.
Wilkins, George H. (George Hubert), Sir, 1888-1958. Thoughts through space. Charlottesville, VA : Hampton Roads Pub. Co., 2004.
BF1171 .W49 2004

Arden, John Boghosian. Improving your memory for dummies / by John B. Arden. New York : Wiley Pub., c2002. xxii, 312 p. : ill. ; 24 cm. Includes index. Publisher description URL: http://www.loc.gov/catdir/description/wiley038/2002106046.html Table of contents URL: http://www.loc.gov/catdir/toc/wiley023/2002106046.html ISBN 0-7645-5435-2 (pbk.) DDC 153.14
1. Mnemonics. 2. Memory. I. Title.
BF385 .A47 2002

Are you psychic?.
Soskin, Julie. London : Carroll & Brown, 2002.
BF1031 .S674 2002

Are you smarter than you think?.
Gordon, Claire, 1968- New York : Penguin Compass, c2003.
BF432.3 .G67 2003

AREA SPECIALISTS. *See* **HISPANISTS.**

Arenas, Fernando, 1963- Utopias of otherness : nationhood and subjectivity in Portugal and Brazil / Fernando Arenas. Minneapolis : University of Minnesota Press, c2003. xxxii, 179 p. ; 23 cm. Includes bibliographical references (p. 131-173) and index. CONTENTS: Portugal : ideas of empire and nationhood -- Brazilian national identity : intellectual debates and changing cultural realities -- Subjectivities and homoerotic desire in contemporary Brazilian fiction : the nation of Caio Fernando Abreu -- Women's difference in contemporary Portuguese fiction : the case of Maria Isabel Barreno -- Worlds in transition and utopias of otherness. ISBN 0-8166-3816-0 (alk. paper) ISBN 0-8166-3817-9 (pbk. : alk. paper) DDC 869.3/4209353
1. Identity (Psychology) 2. Portuguese fiction - 20th century - Criticism and interpretation. 3. Brazilian fiction - 20th century - Criticism and interpretation. 4. Utopias in literature. 5. Literature and myth. 6. Difference (Psychology) in literature. 7. Portugal - Civilization - 21st century. 8. Brazil - Civilization - 21st century. I. Title.
DP681 .A74 2003

ARENDT, HANNAH.
Torre, Francisco Javier de la. Aproximación a las fuentes clásicas latinas de Hannah Arendt. Málaga : Universidad de Málaga, 2002.

Arethusa books
The Roman gaze. Baltimore : Johns Hopkins University Press, 2002.
BF637.C45 R64 2002

Arfuch, Leonor.
Identidades, sujetos y subjetividades. Buenos Aires : Prometeo Libros, c2002.

ARGENTINA - HISTORIOGRAPHY.
Historiografía y memoria colectiva. 1. ed. Madrid ; Buenos Aires : Miño y Dávila, 2002.

ARGENTINA - LITERATURES. *See* **ARGENTINE LITERATURE.**

ARGENTINE LITERATURE - 20TH CENTURY - HISTORY AND CRITICISM.
Charles, Monique. Borges, ou, L'étrangeté apprivoisée. Paris : Harmattan, c2002.

Argomenti di filosofia
(2.) Cherchi, Gavina, 1957- Tra le immagini. Fiesole (Firenze) : Cadmo ; Siena : Centro Mario Rossi per gli studi filosofici, 2002.

Argüelles, José, 1939- Time and the technosphere : the law of time in human affairs / José Argüelles. Rochester, Vt. : Bear & Co., c2002. xx, 259 p. : ill. (some col.) ; 26 cm. Includes bibliographical references (p. 254-259). ISBN 1-87918-199-1 DDC 001.94
1. Calendar reform - Miscellanea. 2. Social evolution - Miscellanea. 3. Maya chronology - Miscellanea. I. Title.
BF1999 .A6398 2002

ARGUMENTATION. *See* **LOGIC; REASONING; VERBAL SELF-DEFENSE.**

El argumento de la apuesta de Blaise Pascal.
Williams, Jaime Andrés. 1. ed. Pamplona : Ediciones Universidad de Navarra, 2002.

ARI RITE OF JUDAISM. *See* **JUDAISM - ARI RITE.**

Ari'av, Dayid ben Naḥman, ha-Kohen. Le-re'akha kamokha : halakhot u-ve'urim be-mitsyot ... / ḥubar 'a. y. Dayid ben Naḥman ha-Kohen Ari'av. Mahad. 2. Yerushalayim : Dayid ben Naḥman ha-Kohen Ari'av, 760- [2000- v. ; 23 cm. Vol. 2- published: Mekhon Le-re'akha kamokha. Includes responsa by Sh. Y.Ḥ. ben Y.Y. Ḳanevski. Includes bibliographical references. PARTIAL CONTENTS: 1. Lo taḥamod. Lo tit'ayeh. Lo taḥanifu. Isur genevat da'at. Lo teḳalel. Lo tiḳom ye-lo tiṭor -- ḥeleḳ 2. Lo tisna ya-ahavat le-re'akha. Ahavat ha-ger -- ḥeleḳ 3. Ona'at devarim. Hilkhot panim. Ona'at ha-ger.
1. Ethics, Jewish. I. Ḳanevski, Sh. Y. Ḥ. ben Y. Y. (Shemaryahu Yosef Ḥayim ben Y. Y.) II. Title. III. Title: Nir Dayid.

Ariel filosofía
El lenguaje y la mente humana. 1. ed. Barcelona : Ariel Editorial, 2002.

Arien und Lieder [sound recording].
Malaniuk, Ira. [Germany] : Preiser Records, p2000.

'Arindamā, Cha rā krī". Pugguil" thū" myā" nhan" gambhīra lam'" mha phyac' rap' chan'" myā" / Cha rā krī" 'Arindamā. Ran' kun' : Cin' Pan'" Mruin' Cā pe : [Phran'' khyi re''], Cui" Cā pe, 2002- v. <1 > ; 21 cm. In Burmese. SUMMARY: Accounts of spiritualists in Burma, and unusual happenings in their lives; articles.
1. Spiritualists - Burma - Biography. 2. Spiritualism - Burma. I. Title.
BF1281 .A756 2002

Arise, Asia!.
Kamal, Niraj. Delhi : Wordsmiths, 2003.
CB251 .K285 2003

ARISTIDES, AELIUS.
Walde, Christine, 1960- Antike Traumdeutung und moderne Traumforschung. Düsseldorf : Artemis & Winkler, 2001.

ARISTOCRACY (SOCIAL CLASS). *See* **NOBILITY.**

ARISTOTLE.
CATEGORIAE.
Ammonius, Hermiae. Commentaria in quinque voces Porphyrii. Stuttgart : Frommann-Holzboog, 2002.

METAPHYSICS.
Balmès, Marc. Pour un plein accès à l'acte d'être avec Thomas d'Aquin et Aristote. Paris : Harmattan, c2003.

Witt, Charlotte, 1951- Ways of being. Ithaca : Cornell University Press, 2003.
B434 .W59 2003

Yu, Jiyuan. The structure of being in Aristotle's Metaphysics. Dordrecht, Boston : Kluwer Academic, c2003.
B434 .Y8 2003

NICOMACHEAN ETHICS.
Ricot, Jacques. Leçon sur L'éthique à Nicomaque, d'Aristote. 1re ed. Paris : Presses universitaires de France, c2001.
B430 .R536 2001

[**Nicomachean ethics. English**]
Nicomachean ethics / Aristotle ; translated and edited by Roger Crisp. Cambridge, U.K. ; New York : Cambridge University Press, c2002 (2002 printing) xlii, 213 p. ; 24 cm. (Cambridge texts in the history of philosophy) Includes bibliographical references and index. Sample text URL: http://www.loc.gov/catdir/samples/cam032/99036947.html Table of contents URL: http://www.loc.gov/catdir/toc/cam024/99036947.html Publisher description URL: http://www.loc.gov/catdir/description/cam0210/99036947.html ISBN 0-521-63221-8 (hardback) ISBN 0-521-63546-2 (pbk.) DDC 171/.3
1. Ethics. I. Crisp, Roger, 1961- II. Title. III. Series.
B430.A5 C7513 2000

POETICS.
Kemal, Salim. The philosophical poetics of Alfarabi, Avicenna and Averroes. London ; New York : RoutledgeCurzon, 2003.

ARISTOTLE.
Ammonius, Hermiae. Commentaria in quinque voces Porphyrii. Stuttgart : Frommann-Holzboog, 2002.

Schreiber, Scott G. (Scott Gregory), 1952- Aristotle on false reasoning. Albany : State University of New York Press, 2003.
B491.R4 S37 2003

ARISTOTLE, 384-322 B.C.
Fortenbaugh, William W. (William Wale) Aristotle on emotion. 2nd ed. London : Duckworth, 2002.
B491.E7 F67 2002

ARISTOTLE - ETHICS.
Rhonheimer, Martin, 1950- Die Perspektive der Moral. Berlin : Akademie Verlag, c2001.

ARISTOTLE - INFLUENCE.
Cathelineau, Pierre-Christophe, 1961- Lacan, lecteur d'Aristote. 2. éd., rev. et corr. Paris : Éditions de l'Association freudienne internationale, c2001 (2002 printing)

Aristotle on emotion.
Fortenbaugh, William W. (William Wale) 2nd ed. London : Duckworth, 2002.
B491.E7 F67 2002

Aristotle on false reasoning.
Schreiber, Scott G. (Scott Gregory), 1952- Albany : State University of New York Press, 2003.
B491.R4 S37 2003

Arkhetypy sot͡sial'noho z̈hyttï͡a i polityka.
Donchenko, E. A. (Elena Andreevna) Kyïv : Lybid', 2001.
JA74.5 .D65 2001

Arkhitekturnoe soznanie 20.-21. vekov.
Arkhitekturnoe soznanie XX-XXI vekov. Moskva : Editorial URSS, 2001.
NA712 .A87 2001

Arkhitekturnoe soznanie dvadt͡satogo-dvadtsat'pervogo vekov.
Arkhitekturnoe soznanie XX-XXI vekov. Moskva : Editorial URSS, 2001.
NA712 .A87 2001

Arkhitekturnoe soznanie XX-XXI vekov : razlomy i perekhody : sbornik nauchnykh trudov / pod redakt͡sieĭ I.A. Azizi͡an. Moskva : Editorial URSS, 2001. 286 p. ; 20 cm. (Voprosy teorii arkhitektury) Includes bibliographical references. ISBN 5836003513
1. Architecture - Philosophy. 2. Architecture - Russia (Federation) - 20th century. I. Azizi͡an, I. A. (Irina Atykovna) II. NII teorii arkhitektury i gradostroitel'stva (Rossiĭskai͡a akademii͡a arkhitektury i stroitel'nykh nauk) III. Title: Arkhitekturnoe soznanie 20.-21. vekov IV. Title: Arkhitekturnoe soznanie dvadt͡satogo-dvadt͡sat'pervogo vekov V. Series.
NA712 .A87 2001

Arkoun, Mohammed. De Manhattan à Bagdad : au-delà du bien et du mal / Mohammed Arkoun, Joseph Maïla. Paris : Desclée de Brouwer, 2003. 237 p. ; 21 cm. Includes bibliographical references. ISBN 2-220-05122-6
1. Geopolitics. 2. East and West. I. Maila, Joseph. II. Title.
JC319 .A72 2003

ARMED FORCES. *See* **SOLDIERS; VETERANS.**

ARMED FORCES - OFFICERS. *See* **GENERALS.**

ARMED FORCES - OPERATIONS OTHER THAN WAR - CASE STUDIES.
Imobighe, Thomas A. The OAU (AU) and OAS in regional conflict management. Ibadan : Spectrum Books ; Oxford, UK : USA distributor, African Books Collective, 2003.
JZ6374 .I46 2003

ARMED SERVICES. *See* **ARMED FORCES.**

Le armi di Orfeo.
Gervasoni, Marco, 1968- [Scandicci] (Firenze) : La nuova Italia, 2002.
ML3917.E85 G479 2002

Armoni, Mosheh Ḥayim. Sefer Ginze Armoni : u-vo shene sefarim niftaḥim / ḥiber ye-liket Mosheh Ḥayim Armoni. Yerushalayim : ʻAmutat "Naḥalat-Raḥel", 762 [2002] 73, 36, 6 p. ; 31 cm. Running title: Ginze Armoni. Subtitle on cover: Otsar tefilat 18. CONTENTS: ḥelek 1. Bo yevoʻar Tefilat 18 ʻal derekh kavanot ha-Arizal ka-muva be-"Ets ḥayim", "Shaʻar ha-kavanot", "Peri ets ḥayim", "Shaʻar ruaḥ ha-kodesh", kitve ha-Rashash yeha-mefarshim -- ḥelek 2. Derushim ... ʻal derekh ha-pardes ʻal kol berakhah u-verakhah mi-Tefilat 18, mivneh ha-tefilah ye-sidrah.
1. Amidah (Jewish prayer) 2. Kavvanot (Cabala) 3. Cabala. 4. Judaism - Ari rite - Liturgy. 5. Jewish sermons, Hebrew. I. Title. II. Title: Ginze Armoni III. Title: Otsar tefilat 18
BM670.S5 A756 2002

ARMS AID. *See* **MILITARY ASSISTANCE.**

ARMS CONTROL. *See* **CONFIDENCE AND SECURITY BUILDING MEASURES (INTERNATIONAL RELATIONS).**

ARMS TRANSFERS. *See* **MILITARY ASSISTANCE.**

Armstrong, Gordon Scott, 1937- Theatre and consciousness : the nature of bio-evolutionary complexity in the arts / Gordon Scott Armstrong. New York ; Oxford : Peter Lang, c2003. xiv, 177 p. ; 24 cm. (Artists and issues in the theatre ; v. 14) Includes bibliographical references (p. [147]-170) and index. ISBN 0-8204-5773-6 DDC 128
1. Aesthetics - Psychological aspects. 2. Theater - Psychological aspects. 3. Genetic psychology. 4. Brain - Evolution. I. Title. II. Series.
BH301.P78 A75 2003

Army War College (U.S.). Strategic Studies Institute. Why they fight [electronic resource]. Carlisle, PA : Strategic Studies Institute, U.S. Army War College, [2003]
U22

Arnaldez, Roger. Fakhr al-Dîn al-Râzî : commentateur du Coran et philosophe / par Roger Arnaldez. Paris : J. Vrin, 2002. 256 p. ; 24 cm. (Études musulmanes ; 37) Includes bibliographical references. ISBN 2-7116-1571-5 DDC 181
1. Rāzī, Fakhr al-Dīn Muhammad ibn ʻUmar, - 1149 or 50-1210. 2. Philosophy, Islamic. 3. Theologians, Muslim. 4. Philosophy, Medieval. I. Title. II. Title: Commentateur du Coran et philosophe III. Series.

Arnaldi, Girolamo.
Studi sulle società e le culture del Medioevo per Girolamo Arnaldi. [Firenze] : All'insegna del giglio, 2002.
DG443 .S78 2002

ARNALDI, GIROLAMO.
Studi sulle società e le culture del Medioevo per Girolamo Arnaldi. [Firenze] : All'insegna del giglio, 2002.
DG443 .S78 2002

Arnold, Margret. Aspekte einer modernen Neurodidaktik : Emotionen und Kognitionen im Lernprozess / Margret Arnold. München : Ernst Vögel, 2002. 376 p. : ill. (some col.) ; 24 cm. (Schriften der Philosophischen Fakultäten der Universität Augsburg. Philosophisch-erziehungswissenschaftliche Reihe ; Nr. 67) Includes bibliographical references (p. 341-358). ISBN 3-89650-131-3
1. Learning - Physiological aspects. I. Title. II. Series.

AROMATIC PLANT PRODUCTS. *See* **ESSENCES AND ESSENTIAL OILS.**

AROMATIC PLANTS. *See* **ESSENCES AND ESSENTIAL OILS.**

Aron, Arthur.
Handbook of closeness and intimacy. Mahwah, N.J. : Lawrence Erlbaum Associates, 2004.
BF575.I5 H36 2004

AROUSAL, SEXUAL. *See* **SEXUAL EXCITEMENT.**

Arpaly, Nomy. Unprincipled virtue : an inquiry into moral agency / Nomy Arpaly. Oxford ; New York : Oxford University Press, 2003. viii, 203 p. ; 22 cm. Includes bibliographical references (p. 181-196) and index. ISBN 0-19-515204-2 (alk. paper) DDC 170
1. Ethics. 2. Psychology and philosophy. I. Title.
BJ45 .A76 2003

La Arquitectura como experiencia.
Saldarriaga Roa, Alberto. 1. ed. Bogotá : Villegas Editores : Universidad Nacional de Colombia, Facultad de Artes, c2002.
NA2765 .S36 2002

Arquitetura.
Carsalade, Flávio de Lemos. Belo Horizonte : AP Cultural, 2001.
NA2500 .C37 2001

Arquitetura : interfaces.
Carsalade, Flávio de Lemos. Arquitetura. Belo Horizonte : AP Cultural, 2001.
NA2500 .C37 2001

Arrington, Robert L., 1938-.
The world's great philosophers. Malden, MA : Blackwell Pub., 2003.
B29 .W69 2003

Arroyo-Cabrales, Joaquín.
Relaciones hombre-fauna. México, D.F. : CONACULTA, INAH ; Plaza y Valdes, 2002.
QL85 .R453 2002

Arroyo Center.
Leed, Maren. Keeping the warfighting edge. Santa Monica, CA : RAND, 2002.
UB413 .L386 2002

Ars faciendi
(Bd. 10) Kuhn-Wengenmayr, Annemarie. Kompositionsfragen. Frankfurt ; New York : P. Lang, c2001.
N7430 .K826 2001

Arsuaga, Juan Luis de.
[Collar del neandertal. English]
The Neanderthal's necklace : in search of the first thinkers / by Juan Luis Arsuaga ; translated by Andy Klatt ; illustrations by Juan Carlos Sastre. New York : Four Walls Eight Windows, c2002. xv, 334 p. : ill., maps ; 22 cm. Includes bibliographical references (p. 321-326) and index. ISBN 1-56858-187-4 (cloth) DDC 599.93/8
1. Human evolution. 2. Neanderthals. 3. Human ecology. I. Klatt, Andy. II. Sastre, Juan Carlos. III. Title.
GN285 .A7713 2002

ART. *See also* **AESTHETICS; ARCHITECTURE; ARTISTS' PREPARATORY STUDIES; COLLECTORS AND COLLECTING; COMMERCIAL ART; COMPOSITION (ART); CREATION (LITERARY, ARTISTIC, ETC.); DECORATION AND ORNAMENT; DRAWING; EROTIC ART; FOLK ART; GLASS ART; GRAPHIC ARTS; ILLUSTRATION OF BOOKS; MURAL PAINTING AND DECORATION; PARAPSYCHOLOGY AND ART; SPACE (ART); SPIRIT ART; SYMBOLISM IN ART.**
Johnson, Paul, 1928- 1st ed. New York : HarperCollins, c2003.

ART.
Glasmeier, Michael, 1951- Extreme 1-8. Köln : Salon, 2001.

Šik, Miroslav. Altneue Gedanken. Luzern : Quart, c2002.

Sturm, Hermann, 1936- Dinge im Fluss, Fluss der Verzeichnungen. Frankfurt a.M. : Anabas-Verlag, 2002.

Ziegelmüller, Martin, 1935- Der Maler auf seinem Drehstuhl. [Frauenfeld] : Waldgut, c2001.

ART AND ANTHROPOLOGY.
Die Unvermeidlichkeit der Bilder. Tübingen : G. Narr, c2001.
N72.A56 U58 2001x

Art and celebrity.
Walker, John Albert, 1938- London ; Sterling, Va. : Pluto Press, 2003.
NX180.S6 W35 2003

Art and essence / edited by Stephen Davies and Ananta Ch. Sukla. Westport, Conn. ; London : Praeger, 2003. xix, 253 p. ; 25 cm. (Studies in art, culture, and communities) Includes bibliographical references (p. [227]-238) and index. ISBN 0-275-97766-8 (alk. paper) DDC 111/.85
1. Aesthetics. 2. Art - Philosophy. I. Davies, Stephen, 1950- II. Sukla, Ananta Charana, 1942- III. Series.
BH39 .A685 2003

Art and experience / edited by Ananta Ch. Sukla. Westport, Conn. ; London : Praeger, 2003. xxii, 202 p. ; 25 cm. (Studies in art, culture, and communities) Includes bibliographical references (p. [178]-186) and indexes. ISBN 0-275-97394-8 (alk. paper) DDC 111/.85
1. Aesthetics. 2. Art - Philosophy. I. Sukla, Ananta Charana, 1942- II. Series.
BH39 .A686 2003

Art and freedom.
Sleinis, E. E. (Edgar Evalt), 1943- Urbana : University of Illinois Press, c2003.
BH39 .S5518 2003

ART AND INDUSTRY. *See* **COMMERCIAL ART.**

ART AND LITERATURE.
Tomás Ferré, Facundo. Formas artísticas y sociedad de masas. Madrid : Antonio Machado Libros, c2001.

ART AND MENTAL ILLNESS.
Donfrancesco, Francesco. Una poetica dell'analisi. Bergamo : Moretti & Vitali, 2000.

Shoham, S. Giora, 1929- Art, crime, and madness. Brighton [England] ; Portland, Or. : Sussex Academic Press, 2002, c2003.
N71.5 .S53 2003

Shoham, S. Giora, 1929- Ṭeruf, setiyah yi-yetsirah. [Israel] : Miśrad ha-biṭaḥon, [2002]

Wanderley, Lula. O dragão pousou no espaço. Rio de Janerio : Rocco, 2002.

ART AND MENTAL ILLNESS - BRAZIL.
Psiquiatria, loucura e arte. São Paulo, SP, Brasil : Edusp, c2002.

Art and morality / edited by Jose Luis Bermudez and Sebastian Gardner. London ; New York : Routledge, 2003. viii, 303 p. : ill., music ; 25 cm. (International library of philosophy) Includes bibliographical references and index. ISBN 0-415-19252-8 DDC 111/.85
1. Aesthetics. 2. Ethics. 3. Art and morals. I. Bermudez, Jose Luis. II. Gardner, Sebastian. III. Series.
BH39 .A695 2003

ART AND MORALS.
Art and morality. London ; New York : Routledge, 2003.
BH39 .A695 2003

ART AND MUSIC.
Peinture et musique. Villeneuve-d'Ascq : Presses universitaires du Septentrion, c2002.

ART AND NATURE. *See* **NATURE (AESTHETICS).**

ART AND PARAPSYCHOLOGY. *See* **PARAPSYCHOLOGY AND ART.**

ART AND RELIGION.
Stolz, Fritz. Weltbilder der Religionen. Zürich : Pano Verlag, c2001.

Visuality before and beyond the Renaissance. Cambridge, U.K. ; New York, NY, USA : Cambridge University Press, 2000.
N7430.5 .V54 2000

ART AND SCIENCE.
Hayat, Michaël. Dynamique des formes et représentations. Paris : Harmattan, c2002.
B105.R4 H392 2002

ART AND SOCIETY.
Elkins, James, 1955- Visual studies. New York : Routledge, 2003.
N72.S6 E45 2003

Romero, Pedro G., 1964- En el ojo de la batalla. Valencia : Universitat de València, 2002.

Art and soul.
McConeghey, Howard. 1st ed. Putnam, CT : Spring Publications, Inc. ; [New York] : Distributed by Continuum, c2003.

ART BRUT. *See* **ART AND MENTAL ILLNESS.**

ART - CHINESE INFLUENCES.
Chen, Wei, 1957- Dong fang mei xue dui xi fang de ying xiang = Di 1 ban. Shanghai : Xue lin chu ban she, 1999.
BH221.C6 C444 1999

ART COLLECTIONS. *See* **ART MUSEUMS.**

ART, COMMERCIAL. *See* **COMMERCIAL ART.**

ART, COMPARATIVE.
Visuality before and beyond the Renaissance. Cambridge, U.K. ; New York, NY, USA : Cambridge University Press, 2000.
N7430.5 .V54 2000

ART - COMPOSITION. *See* **COMPOSITION (ART).**

Art, crime, and madness.
Shoham, S. Giora, 1929- Brighton [England] ; Portland, Or. : Sussex Academic Press, 2002, c2003.
N71.5 .S53 2003

ART CRITICISM.
Rauschen. Würzburg : Königshausen & Neumann, c2001.

Summers, David, 1941- Real spaces. London : Phaidon, c2003.

ART - CRITICISM AND INTERPRETATION.
Svobodnyĭ vzglí͡ad na literaturu. Moskva : Nauka, 2002.

ART, DECORATIVE. *See* **DECORATION AND ORNAMENT.**

L'art d'éduquer les nobles damoiselles.
Gendt, Anne-Marie Emma Alberta de, 1952- Paris : Champion, 2003.

ART, EROTIC. *See* **EROTIC ART.**

ART - EXHIBITIONS.
Sauerländer, Willibald. Die Luft auf der Spitze des Pinsels. München : Hanser, 2002.

ART, FOLK. *See* **FOLK ART.**

ART GALLERIES. *See* **ART MUSEUMS.**

ART - GALLERIES AND MUSEUMS. *See* **ART MUSEUMS.**

ART, GRAPHIC. *See* **GRAPHIC ARTS.**

ART, HINDU - INDIA.
Kollar, L. Peter (Laszlo Peter), 1926- Symbolism in Hindu architecture as revealed in the Shri Minakshi Sundareswar. New Delhi : Aryan Books International, 2001.
NA6002 .K65 2001

ART - HISTORIOGRAPHY.
Preziosi, Donald, 1941- Brain of the earth's body. Minneapolis : University of Minnesota Press, c2003.
N380 .P67 2003

ART - HISTORY.
Arts en bibliothèques. Paris : Editions du Cercle de la Librairie, c2003.
Z675.A85 A78 2003

Bernshteĭn, Boris Moiseevich. Pigmalion naiznanku. Moskva : I͡Azyki slavi͡anskoĭ kul'tury, 2002.
N5300 .B614 2002

Hornig, Christian. Wollheims Traum. Gauting : Lynx, c2001.

Johnson, Paul, 1928- Art. 1st ed. New York : HarperCollins, c2003.

Klimov, R. B. Teorii͡a stadi͡al'nogo razviti͡a iskusstva i stat'i. Moskva : O.G.I., 2002.
N5300 .K55 2002

Marioni, Tom, 1937- Writings on art. San Francisco, Calif. : Crown Point Press, 2000.

Marmur dziejowy. Poznań : Wydawnictwo Poznańskiego Towarzystwa Przyjaciół Nauk, 2002.

Mörgeli, Christoph. "Über dem Grabe geboren". Bern : Benteli, 2002.

Le propre de l'homme. Lausanne : Delachaux et Niestlé, c1998.
BF175 .P69 1998

Psychische Energien bildender Kunst. 1. Aufl. Köln : DuMont, 2002.

Re-Visionen. Berlin : Akademie Verlag, c2002.

Rosén, Ingrid. Glas i konsten. Stockholm : Carlssons, c2000.

Sauerländer, Willibald. Die Luft auf der Spitze des Pinsels. München : Hanser, 2002.

Summers, David, 1941- Real spaces. London : Phaidon, c2003.

Wentscher, Herbert, 1951- Vor dem Schirm. 1. Aufl. [Freiburg im Breisgau] : Modo, 2002.

ART, IMMORAL. *See* **EROTIC ART.**

ART IN ADVERTISING. *See* **COMMERCIAL ART.**

ART LIBRARIES.
Arts en bibliothèques. Paris : Editions du Cercle de la Librairie, c2003.
Z675.A85 A78 2003

ART LIBRARIES - COLLECTION DEVELOPMENT.
Arts en bibliothèques. Paris : Editions du Cercle de la Librairie, c2003.
Z675.A85 A78 2003

ART LIBRARIES - FRANCE.
Arts en bibliothèques. Paris : Editions du Cercle de la Librairie, c2003.
Z675.A85 A78 2003

ART, MEDIEVAL. *See* **ILLUMINATION OF BOOKS AND MANUSCRIPTS.**

ART, MEDIEVAL - EUROPE.
Jones, Malcolm, 1953- The secret middle ages. Stroud : Sutton, 2002.

ART, MODERN - 20TH CENTURY. *See also* **MODERNISM (ART).**
Grasskamp, Walter. Ist die Moderne eine Epoche? München : C.H. Beck, c2002.

Svendsen, Lars Fr. H., 1970- Kunst. Oslo : Universitetsforlaget, c2000.
N6490 .S88499 2000

ART, MODERN - 20TH CENTURY - HISTORY.
Romero, Pedro G., 1964- En el ojo de la batalla. Valencia : Universitat de València, 2002.

ART, MODERNIST. *See* **MODERNISM (ART).**

ART, MUNICIPAL. *See* **CITY PLANNING.**

ART - MUSEUMS. *See* **ART MUSEUMS.**

Art, museums, and the phantasms of modernity.
Preziosi, Donald, 1941- Brain of the earth's body. Minneapolis : University of Minnesota Press, c2003.
N380 .P67 2003

ART MUSEUMS - PHILOSOPHY.
Preziosi, Donald, 1941- Brain of the earth's body. Minneapolis : University of Minnesota Press, c2003.
N380 .P67 2003

ART, OCCIDENTAL. *See* **ART.**

The art of building people.
Chiodi, Michael. 1st ed. St. Paul, Minn. : Chiberry Press, c2003.
BF637.S4 C497 2003

The art of chemistry.
Greenberg, Arthur. Hoboken, N.J. : Wiley-Interscience, c2003.
QD11 .G735 2003

Art of conversation.
Raam, Gabriel. Omanut ha-śihah. Tel-Aviv : Yedi'ot aharonot : Sifre hemed, c2003.
P95.45 .R33 2003

The art of design.
Cullen, Cheryl Dangel. 1st ed. Cincinnati, OH : How Design Books, c2003.
NC998.4 .C846 2003

The art of happiness at work.
Bstan-'dzin-rgya-mtsho, Dalai Lama XIV, 1935- New York : Riverhead Books, 2003.
BF481 .B76 2003

The art of life.
Holmes, Ernest, 1887-1960. [This thing called life] New York : J.P. Tarcher/Penguin, c2004.
BF645 .H572 2004

Art of living of two women.
Aller, Annelies van, 1946- Levenskunst van twee vrouwen. Budel : Damon, c2001.
PS3527.1865 Z536 2001

The art of predictive astrology.
Rushman, Carol. 1st ed. St. Paul, Minn. : Llewellyn Publications, 2003, c2002.
BF1720.5 .R87 2002

The art of questioning.
Flage, Daniel E., 1951- Upper Saddle River, N.J. : Pearson/Prentice Hall, c2004.

BF441 .F55 2004

The art of the pendulum.
Cohen, Maxi. [Kansas City, Mo.] : Andrews McMeel, [c2002]
BF1779.P45 C64 2002

The art of thinking.
Ruggiero, Vincent Ryan. 7th ed. New York : Pearson/Longman, c2004.
BF441 .R84 2004

The art of waking people up.
Cloke, Ken, 1941- 1st ed. San Francisco : Jossey-Bass, c2003.
HF5385 .C54 2003

The art of wing leadership and aircrew morale in combat [electronic resource].
Zentner, John J., 1965- Maxwell Air Force Base, Ala. : Air University Press, [2001]

Art, origins, otherness.
Desmond, William, 1951- Albany : State University of New York Press, c2003.
BH39 .D4535 2003

ART PATRONAGE.
Vezin, Annette. Egéries dans l'ombre des créateurs. Paris : Martinière, 2002.
NX165 .V49 2002

ART - PHILOSOPHY.
Art and essence. Westport, Conn. ; London : Praeger, 2003.
BH39 .A685 2003

Art and experience. Westport, Conn. ; London : Praeger, 2003.
BH39 .A686 2003

The creation of art. New York, NY : Cambridge University Press, 2003.
N71 .C754 2003

Danto, Arthur Coleman, 1924- The abuse of beauty. Chicago : Open Court, c2003.
BH39 .D3489 2003

Desmond, William, 1951- Art, origins, otherness. Albany : State University of New York Press, c2003.
BH39 .D4535 2003

Greene, Herb. Painting the mental continuum. Berkeley, Calif. : Berkeley Hills Books ; [Berkeley, Calif.] : Distributed by Publishers Group West, c2003.
N71 .G683 2003

Haugen Sørensen, Arne, 1932- Samtaler på en bjergtop. 1. oplag. Højbjerg : Hovedland, c2002.

Honegger, Gottfried, 1917- Erfundenes und Erlebtes. München : Chorus, c2002.

Krebs, Víctor J., 1957- Del alma y el arte. Caracas, Venezuela : Museo de Bellas Artes, 1997.
N70 .K74 1997

Kropotov, S. L. (Sergeĭ Leonidovich) Ėkonomika teksta v neklassicheskoĭ filosofii iskusstva. Ekaterinburg : Gumanitarnyĭ universitet, 1999.
B831.2 .K76 1999

Kuhn-Wengenmayr, Annemarie. Kompositionsfragen. Frankfurt ; New York : P. Lang, c2001.
N7430 .K826 2001

Meo, Oscar. Mondi possibili. Genova : Il melangolo, c2002.
N68.3 .M46 2002

Orte des Schönen. Würzburg : Königshausen & Neumann, c2003.
BH23 .O78 2003

Spoerri, Hubert M. Mensch und Kunst. München : Scaneg, c2002.

Stecker, Robert, 1928- Interpretation and construction. Malden, MA : Blackwell, 2003.
BD241 .S78 2003

Vom Parergon zum Labyrinth. Wien : Böhlau, c2001.
NK1505 .V65 2001

ART - POLITICAL ASPECTS.
Postmodernism and the postsocialist condition. Berkeley : University of California Press, c2003.
N6494.P66 P684 2003

ART, POPULAR. *See* **FOLK ART.**

ART, PRIMITIVE. *See* **FOLK ART.**

ART - PSYCHOLOGICAL ASPECTS.
Salber, Wilhelm. Psychästhetik. Köln : König, c2002.

ART - PSYCHOLOGY. *See also* **ART AND MENTAL ILLNESS.**
Greene, Herb. Painting the mental continuum.

Berkeley, Calif. : Berkeley Hills Books ; [Berkeley, Calif.] : Distributed by Publishers Group West, c2003.
N71 .G683 2003

McConeghey, Howard. Art and soul. 1st ed. Putnam, CT : Spring Publications, Inc. ; [New York] : Distributed by Continuum, c2003.

Psychische Energien bildender Kunst. 1. Aufl. Köln : DuMont, 2002.

Solso, Robert L., 1933- The psychology of art and the evolution of the conscious brain. Cambridge, Mass. : MIT Press, 2003.
BF311 .S652 2003

Spoerri, Hubert M. Mensch und Kunst. München : Scaneg, c2002.

Wanderley, Lula. O dragão pousou no espaço. Rio de Janerio : Rocco, 2002. A.

Art, regional traditions, the Temple of Jagannātha.
Pathy, Dinanath. New Delhi : Sundeep Prakashan, 2001.
NA6002 .P37 2001

ART, RENAISSANCE - ITALY.
Goffen, Rona, 1944- Renaissance rivals. New Haven : University Press, c2002.
N6915 .G54 2002

ART - SOCIAL ASPECTS.
Spoerri, Hubert M. Mensch und Kunst. München : Scaneg, c2002.

Art spirite, mediumnique, visionnaire : messages d'outre-monde : une exposition de la Halle Saint-Pierre du 13 septembre 1999 au 27 février 2000 / [conception du catalogue, Martine Lusardy]. [Paris] : Hoëbeke, c1999. 165 p. : ill. (some col.) : 24 cm. Includes bibliographical references (p. 164-165). ISBN 2-8423-0091-2 DDC 133.9/2
1. Spirit art - Exhibitions. 2. Parapsychology and art - Exhibitions. I. Lusardy, Martine. II. Halle Saint-Pierre (Museum)
BF1313 .A78 1999

ART, TANTRIC.
[Aids to Sadhana series. Tibetan & Sanskrit. Selections.] Sādhanamālā, Avalokiteśvara section. Delhi : Adroit Publishers ; New Delhi : Distributors, Akhil Book Distributors, 2002.
BQ8915 .S23 2002

ART THERAPY.
McConeghey, Howard. Art and soul. 1st ed. Putnam, CT : Spring Publications, Inc. ; [New York] : Distributed by Continuum, c2003.

Wanderley, Lula. O dragão pousou no espaço. Rio de Janerio : Rocco, 2002. A.

ART, VISUAL. See **ART.**

ART, WESTERN. See **ART.**

Artamonov, V. I. (Vladimir Ivanovich) Psikhologiiā ot pervogo litsa : 14 besed s rossiĭskimi uchenymi, B.V. Raushenbakh ... / V.I. Artamonov. Moskva : Academia, 2003. 407 p. : ill. ; 21 cm. ISBN 587444176X
1. Psychologists - Russia (Federation) - Biography. 2. Psychologists - Russia (Federation) - Interviews. 3. Psychology - Russia (Federation) - History - 20th century. I. Raushenbakh, Boris Viktorovich. II. Title.
BF109.A1 A78 2003

Artamonova, E. R. Voprosy vozrastnoĭ i pedagogicheskoĭ psikhologii v tvorchestve P.P. Blonskogo / E.R. Artamonova. Vladimir : Vladimirskiĭ gos. pedagog. universitet, 2001. 149 p. ; 21 cm. Includes bibliographical references. ISBN 5878462583
1. Blonskiĭ, Pavel Petrovich, - 1884-1941. I. Title.
BF109.B59 A78 2001

Artaud, Yvonne.
Medhananda, 1908-1994. [Au fil de l'eternitè avec Medhananda. English. Selections] On the threshold of a new age with Medhananda. 1st ed. Pondicherry : Sri Mira Trust, 2000.
B841 .M4313 2000

Arte. Arquitectura (Sada, Spain)
Pérez-Jofre, Ignacio. Huellas y sombras. Sada, A Coruña : Ediciós do Castro, [2001]
ND195 .P368 2001

Artech House communications law and policy library.
Matsuura, Jeffrey H., 1957- Managing intellectual assets in the digital age. Boston, MA : Artech House, c2003.
K1401 .M378 2003

ARTEFACTS (ANTIQUITIES). See **ANTIQUITIES.**

ARTEMIDORUS, DALDIANUS.
Walde, Christine, 1960- Antike Traumdeutung und moderne Traumforschung. Düsseldorf : Artemis & Winkler, c2001.

Artful making.
Austin, Robert D. (Robert Daniel), 1962- Upper Saddle River, NJ : Financial Times/Prentice Hall, 2003.
HD53 .A96 2003

ARTHUR, KING.
Blake, Steve. Pendragon. London : Rider, 2002.

Snyder, Christopher A. (Christopher Allen), 1966- The Britons. Malden, MA ; Oxford : Blackwell Pub., 2003.
DA140 .S73 2003

Arthur, Richard, 1950-.
Leibniz, Gottfried Wilhelm, Freiherr von, 1646-1716. [Selections. English & Latin. 2001] The labyrinth of the continuum. New Haven : Yale University Press, c2001.
B2558 .A78 2001

Arthurian characters and themes
Perceval = New York : Routledge, 2002.
PN686.P4 P46 2002

Arthurian romance.
Pearsall, Derek Albert. Malden, MA : Blackwell Publishers, 2003.
PN685 .P43 2003

ARTHURIAN ROMANCES. See also **LANCELOT (LEGENDARY CHARACTER); PERCEVAL (LEGENDARY CHARACTER).**
Malory, Thomas, Sir, 15th cent. [Morte d'Arthur] Le morte Darthur, or, The hoole book of Kyng Arthur and of his noble knyghtes of the Rounde Table. 1st ed. New York ; London : Norton, c2004.
PR2041 .M37 2004

ARTHURIAN ROMANCES - HISTORY AND CRITICISM.
Besamusca, Bart. The book of Lancelot. Cambridge : D.S. Brewer, 2003.
PT5568 .B47 2003

Blake, Steve. Pendragon. London : Rider, 2002.

A companion to Gottfried von Strassburg's "Tristan". Rochester, NY : Camden House, 2003.
PT1526 .C66 2003

Durham, Diana. The return of King Arthur. New York : Jeremy P. Tarcher/Penguin, 2004.
BF637.S4 D88 2004

Greene, Virginie Elisabeth, 1959- Le sujet et la mort dans La mort Artu. Saint-Genouph : Nizet, 2002.

Hübner, Gert. Erzählform im höfischen Roman. Tübingen : Francke, 2003.

Malory, Thomas, Sir, 15th cent. [Morte d'Arthur] Le morte Darthur, or, The hoole book of Kyng Arthur and of his noble knyghtes of the Rounde Table. 1st ed. New York ; London : Norton, c2004.
PR2041 .M37 2004

Matthews, Caitlin, 1952- King Arthur and the goddess of the land. 2nd ed. Rochester, Vt. : Inner Traditions, 2002.
PB2273.M33 M36 2002

Matthews, Caitlin, 1952- Mabon and the guardians of Celtic Britain. Rochester, Vt. : Inner Traditions, c2002.
PB2273.M33 M37 2002

Pearsall, Derek Albert. Arthurian romance. Malden, MA : Blackwell Publishers, 2003.
PN685 .P43 2003

Perceval = New York : Routledge, 2002.
PN686.P4 P46 2002

Philologies old and new. Princeton : The Edward C. Armstrong Monographs, 2001.

Radulescu, Raluca, 1974- The gentry context for Malory's Morte Darthur. Cambridge [England] ; Rochester, NY : D.S. Brewer, 2003.
PR2047 .R33 2003

Wickham-Crowley, Kelley M. Writing the future. Cardiff : University of Wales Press, 2002.

Wolfram, von Eschenbach, 12th cent. Titurel. Berlin ; New York : Walter de Gruyter, 2002.

ARTHURIAN ROMANCES - MISCELLANEA.
Phillips, Graham. [Search for the Grail] The chalice of Magdalene. Rochester, Vt. : Bear & Company, 2004.
BF1442.G73 P48 2004

Arthurian studies
(53) Besamusca, Bart. The book of Lancelot. Cambridge : D.S. Brewer, 2003.
PT5568 .B47 2003

(55) Radulescu, Raluca, 1974- The gentry context for Malory's Morte Darthur. Cambridge [England] ; Rochester, NY : D.S. Brewer, 2003.
PR2047 .R33 2003

Arthurs, Jane. Crash cultures : modernity, mediation and the material / edited by Jane Arthurs and Iain Grant. Bristol, UK ; Portland, OR : Intellect, 2002. v, 202 p. : ill. ISBN 1-84150-071-2
1. Philosophy, Modern - 20th century. 2. Accidents (Philosophy) 3. Reality. 4. Technology - Philosophy. 5. Technology and civilization. I. NetLibrary, Inc. II. Title.

ARTIFACTS (ANTIQUITIES). See **ANTIQUITIES.**

ARTIFICIAL INTELLIGENCE. See also **EXPERT SYSTEMS (COMPUTER SCIENCE); KNOWLEDGE REPRESENTATION (INFORMATION THEORY); MACHINE LEARNING; NEURAL NETWORKS (COMPUTER SCIENCE).**
Adaptive agents and multi-agent systems. Berlin ; New York : Springer, c2003.
QA76.76.I58 A312 2003

Aleksander, Igor. How to build a mind. New York : Columbia University Press, 2001.
Q335 .A44225 2001

Boden, Margaret A. The creative mind. 2nd ed. London ; New York : Routledge, 2003.
BF408 .B55 2003

Breazeal, Cynthia L. Designing sociable robots. Cambridge, Mass. : MIT Press, c2002.
TA167 .B74 2002

Caronia, Antonio. Il cyborg. Milano : Shake edizioni underground, c2001.
Q335 .C34 2001

Computationalism. Cambridge, MA : MIT Press, c2002.

Intelligent support systems. Hershey, PA : IRM Press, c2002.
QA76.9.D3 I5495 2002

Kasabov, Nikola K. Evolving connectionist systems. London ; New York : Springer, c2003.
QA76.87 .K39 2003

Knowledge-based information retrieval and filtering from the Web. Boston : Kluwer Academic Publishers, c2003.
TK5105.888 .K58 2003

Levy, Alon Y. (Alon Yitzchak) Irrelevance reasoning in knowledge based systems [miroform]. [Washington, DC : National Aeronautics and Space Administration] ; Springfield, VA : Available from the National Technical Information Service, [1998]

Piscitelli, Alejandro. Meta-cultura. Buenos Aires : La Crujía, 2002.
P96.T42 P575

Roland, Alex, 1944- Strategic computing. Cambridge, Mass. : MIT Press, c2002.
QA76.88 .R65 2002

Rosental, Claude. La trame de l'évidence. 1 éd. Paris : Presses universitaires de France, c2003.

Schmid, U. (Ute) Inductive synthesis of functional programs. Berlin ; New York : Springer, c2003.
QA76.6 .S3855 2003

Wagman, Morton. Logical processes in humans and computers. Westport, Conn. : Praeger, 2003.
BF311 .W26566 2003

Washington, Richard. Abstraction planning in real time [microform]. Stanford, Calif. : Stanford University, Dept. of Computer Science, [1994] (Springfield, Va. : U.S. Dept. of Commerce, National Technical Information Service)

Wood, Gaby. Edison's Eve. 1st American ed. New York : A.A. Knopf, 2002.
TJ211 .W65 2002

ARTIFICIAL INTELLIGENCE - COMPUTER PROGRAMS. See **INTELLIGENT AGENTS (COMPUTER SOFTWARE).**

ARTIFICIAL INTELLIGENCE - DATA PROCESSING - SOCIAL ASPECTS.
Berthier, Denis. Le savoir et l'ordinateur. Paris : Harmattan, c2002.

ARTIFICIAL INTELLIGENCE - PERIODICALS.
Spatial cognition and computation. [Dordrecht], The Netherlands : Kluwer Academic, c1999-
BF469 .S674

ARTIFICIAL INTELLIGENCE - PHILOSOPHY.
Tetens, Holm, 1948- Geist, Gehirn, Maschine. Stuttgart : Reclam, c1994.
BF163 .T48 1994x

ARTIFICIAL INTELLIGENCE - SOCIAL ASPECTS.
Clark, Andy, 1957- Natural-born cyborgs. Oxford ; New York : Oxford University Press, c2003.
T14.5 .C58 2003

ARTIFICIAL NEURAL NETWORKS. *See* **NEURAL NETWORKS (COMPUTER SCIENCE).**

ARTIFICIAL SATELLITES IN TELECOMMUNICATION. *See* **TELEVISION.**

ARTIFICIAL THINKING. *See* **ARTIFICIAL INTELLIGENCE.**

ARTIST COUPLES.
Vezin, Annette. Egéries dans l'ombre des créateurs. Paris : Martinière, 2002.
NX165 .V49 2002

ARTISTS. *See* **AUTHORS; DANCERS; MUSICIANS; PHOTOGRAPHERS.**

Artists and issues in the theatre
(v. 14) Armstrong, Gordon Scott, 1937- Theatre and consciousness. New York ; Oxford : Peter Lang, c2003.
BH301.P78 A75 2003

ARTISTS AND THE THEATER.
Bimont, Bernard. Je veux que l'on soit homme. Brive : Ecritures, [2002]

ARTISTS - BIOGRAPHY.
Brandon, Ruth. The surreal lives. London : Papermac, 2000, c1999.

ARTISTS IN LITERATURE.
Gerber, Nancy, 1956- Portrait of the mother-artist. Lanham, Md. : Lexington Books, c2003.
PS374.M547 G47 2003

ARTISTS - INTERVIEWS.
Tusa, John. On creativity. London : Methuen, 2003.

ARTISTS' MODELS.
Vezin, Annette. Egéries dans l'ombre des créateurs. Paris : Martinière, 2002.
NX165 .V49 2002

ARTISTS' PREPARATORY STUDIES - FRANCE.
Percheron, René. Matisse. Paris : Citadelles & Mazenod, c2002.
N6853.M33 P47 2002

ARTISTS - PSYCHOLOGY.
Shoham, S. Giora, 1929- Art, crime, and madness. Brighton [England] ; Portland, Or. : Sussex Academic Press, 2002, c2003.
N71.S .S53 2003

Shoham, S. Giora, 1929- Ṭeruf, seṭiyah ṿi-yetsirah. [Israel] : Miśrad ha-biṭaḥon, [2002]

Vezin, Annette. [Egéries dans l'ombre des créateurs. English] The 20th-century muse. New York : Harry N. Abrams, 2003.
N71 .V4913 2003

Walker, John Albert, 1938- Art and celebrity. London ; Sterling, Va. : Pluto Press, 2003.
NX180.S6 W35 2003

ARTISTS - RELATIONS WITH WOMEN.
Vezin, Annette. Egéries dans l'ombre des créateurs. Paris : Martinière, 2002.
NX165 .V49 2002

Artman, Lavee. ha-Nisayon ha-yomyomi u-fitron heseḵe tenai ṿa-hakhalah lo-teḵefim / me-et Lavi Artman. [Israel : ḥ. mo. l., 1999?] 1 v. (various pagings) ; 29 cm. Added title page title: Everyday experience and conditional reasoning. Thesis (Ph. D.) -- ha-Universiṭah ha-ʿIvrit bi-Yerushalayim, 1999. Includes bibliographical references (p. 75-81). Abstract also in English.
1. Reasoning (Psychology) 2. Conditionals (Logic) 3. Induction (Logic) 4. Grammar, Comparative and general - Conditionals.
I. Title. II. Title: Everyday experience and conditional reasoning

ARTS. *See also* **ART; SCIENCE AND THE ARTS.**
Brock, Bazon, 1936- Der Barbar als Kulturheld. Köln : DuMont, 2002.

Arts & dreams.
Iskusstvo snovideniĭ = Sankt-Peterburg : Skifiia, 2002.
NX180.D74 I74 2002

ARTS AND CRAFTS MOVEMENT. *See* **DECORATION AND ORNAMENT.**

ARTS AND SCIENCE. *See* **SCIENCE AND THE ARTS.**

ARTS AND SOCIETY.
Randolph, Jeanne, 1943- Why stoics box. Toronto : YYZ Books, 2003.

Walker, John Albert, 1938- Art and celebrity. London ; Sterling, Va. : Pluto Press, 2003.
NX180.S6 W35 2003

ARTS AND SOCIETY - LATIN AMERICA.
García Canclini, Néstor. Culturas híbridas. Nueva edición actualizada. Buenos Aires : Paidós, 2001.

ARTS AND SOCIOLOGY. *See* **ARTS AND SOCIETY.**

ARTS, CHINESE - 20TH CENTURY.
Xiao, Ying. Xing xiang yu sheng cun. Beijing di 1 ban. Beijing : Zuo jia chu ban she ; Jing xiao Xin hua shu dian Beijing fa xing suo, 1996.
NX583.A1 H756 1996 <Asian China>

ARTS, DECORATIVE. *See* **DECORATION AND ORNAMENT.**

Arts en bibliothèques / sous la direction de Nicole Picot ; avec la collaboration de Claire Barbillon ... [et al.] ; préface de Alain Schnapp. Paris : Editions du Cercle de la Librairie, c2003. 270 p. ; col. ill. ; 24 cm. (Collection Bibliothèques) Includes bibliographical references (p. [265]-270). ISBN 2765408505
1. Art libraries. 2. Art libraries - France. 3. Art libraries - Collection development. 4. Art - History. I. Picot, Nicole. II. Barbillon, Claire. III. Schnapp, Alain, 1946- IV. Series.
Z675.A85 A78 2003

ARTS FACILITIES. *See* **ART MUSEUMS.**

ARTS, FINE. *See* **ART; ARTS.**

ARTS, GRAPHIC. *See* **GRAPHIC ARTS.**

ARTS, MODERN. *See* **ART, MODERN; LITERATURE, MODERN.**

ARTS, MODERN - 20TH CENTURY. *See also* **POSTMODERNISM.**
Brandon, Ruth. The surreal lives. London : Papermac, 2000, c1999.

Meyer, Michel. Michel Meyer présente Manifestes du surréalisme d'André Breton. Paris : Gallimard, 2002.
NX600.S9 B735 2002

Powell, Jim, 1946- Postmodernism for beginners. New York : Writers and Readers Pub., c1998.

Vezin, Annette. Egéries dans l'ombre des créateurs. Paris : Martinière, 2002.
NX165 .V49 2002

Walker, John Albert, 1938- Art and celebrity. London ; Sterling, Va. : Pluto Press, 2003.
NX180.S6 W35 2003

ARTS, MODERN - 20TH CENTURY - FRANCE.
La modernité après le post-moderne. Paris : Maisonneuve & Larose, [2002]

ARTS, MODERN - 20TH CENTURY - JAPAN.
La modernité après le post-moderne. Paris : Maisonneuve & Larose, [2002]

ARTS, MODERN - 21ST CENTURY.
Walker, John Albert, 1938- Art and celebrity. London ; Sterling, Va. : Pluto Press, 2003.
NX180.S6 W35 2003

ARTS, OCCIDENTAL. *See* **ARTS.**

ARTS - PHILOSOPHY.
Extreme beauty. London ; New York : Continuum, 2002.
BH39 .E98 2002

Imagination, philosophy, and the arts. London ; New York : Routledge, 2003.
BH301.I53 I53 2003

Sleinis, E. E. (Edgar Evalt), 1943- Art and freedom. Urbana : University of Illinois Press, c2003.
BH39 .S5518 2003

ARTS - SOCIAL ASPECTS. *See* **ARTS AND SOCIETY.**

ARTS, USEFUL. *See* **TECHNOLOGY.**

ARTS, VISUAL. *See* **ART.**

ARTS, WESTERN. *See* **ARTS.**

ArtScroll series
Brezak, Dov. Chinuch in turbulent times. 1st ed. Brooklyn, N.Y. : Mesorah Publications, c2002.

ARYĀVALOKITEŚVARA (BUDDHIST DEITY). *See* **AVALOKITEŚVARA (BUDDHIST DEITY).**

ARYS
(11.) Jornadas de Roles Sexuales y de Género (2nd : 1995 : Madrid, Spain) Mujer, ideología y población. 1. ed. Madrid : Ediciones Clásicas, 1998.
HQ1075 .J67 1995

As luck would have it.
Piven, Joshua. 1st ed. New York : Villard, c2003.
BF1778 .P58 2003

As others see us.
Goldman, Ellen. New York : Brunner-Routledge, 2003.
BF637.N66 G65 2003

ASA research methods in social anthropology (Routledge (Firm))
Edgar, Iain R. Guide to imagework. London ; New York : Routledge, 2004.
BF367 .E34 2004

Asalī prācīna Lāla kitāba.
Śarmā, Kisanalāla. Lāla kitāba. 1. saṃskaraṇa. Dillī : Manoja Pôkeṭa Buksa, [2000?]
BF1714.H5+

Asalī prācīna Vaidika vāstu śāstra / saṅkalana va sampādana, Rājīva Tivārī ; sampādana sahayoga Priyadarśī Prakāśa, Madhusūdana Śarmā. 1. saṃskaraṇa. Dillī : Manoja Pôkeṭa Buksa, [2002?] 174, [1] p. : ill. ; 25 cm. In Hindi; includes passages in Sanskrit. SUMMARY: On Hindu astrology and domestic architecture.
1. Astrology and architecture - India. 2. Domestic architecture - India. 3. Hindu astrology. I. Tivārī, Rājīva. II. Prakāśa, Priyadarśī. III. Śarmā, Madhusūdana. IV. Title: Vaidika vāstu śāstra
BF1729.A7 A83 2002

Asano, Kagyū.
Edo-e kara shomotsu made. Tōkyō : Kyūzansha, 1997.
HQ792.J3 N54 1997 v.19

ʻAśarah nisyonot.
Pinter, Leib. Sefer ʻAśarah nisyonot. Brooklyn, N.Y. : E.Y.L. Pinter, c[2002?]

ASCENDANT (ASTROLOGY).
Lamb, William, 1944 Apr. 22- The secrets of your rising sign. Gloucester, MA : Fair Winds Press, 2004.
BF1717 .L36 2004

ASCETICAL THEOLOGY. *See* **ASCETICISM.**

ASCETICISM - HINDUISM.
Caturvedī, Saccidānanda. Vairāgya. Itanagar : Himālayana Pablīsarsa, 2000.
BL1239.5.A82 C28 2000

ASCETICISM - ORTHODOX EASTERN CHURCH.
Gostev, A. A. (Andreĭ Andreevich) Obraznaia sfera cheloveka v poznanii i perezhivanii dukhovnykh smyslov. Moskva : In-t psikhologii RAN, 2001.
BF367 .G565 2001

ASCETICS. *See* **ASCETICISM.**

Åse, Cecilia.
Myrdal, Alva Reimer, 1902- "Något kan man väl göra. Stockholm : Carlssons, c2002.

Asefat divre ḥakhamim.
Ḥayim Yeroḥam ben Shimshon Meshulam Feybish, mi-Snatin. Sefer Asefat divre ḥakhamim. Yerushalayim : Mekhon Sod yesharim, 761 [2001]

Ashcroft-Nowicki, Dolores. Illuminations : mystical meditations on the Hebrew alphabet : the healing of the soul / Dolores Ashcroft-Nowicki. 1st ed. St. Paul, Minn. : Llewellyn Publications, 2003. xxii, 335 p. : ill. ; 24 cm. Includes bibliographical references (p. 331) and index. ISBN 0-7387-0186-6 DDC 135/.47
1. Cabala. 2. Hebrew language - Alphabet - Miscellanea. I. Title.
BF1623.C2 A84 2003

Asher ben Jehiel, ca. 1250-1327.
Orhot hayim.
He lakhem ḥamishah sefari.. [Brooklyn, NY : Renaissance Hebraica, 2000?]

Ashgate epistemology and mind series
Privileged access. Aldershot ; Burlington, VT : Ashgate, c2003.

Ashgate new critical thinking in philosophy
Gundersen, Lars Bo. Dispositional theories of knowledge. Aldershot, England ; Burlington, VT : Ashgate, c2003.
BD161 .G86 2003

Smith, R. Scott, 1957- Virtue ethics and moral knowledge. Aldershot, England ; Burlington, VT : Ashgate, c2003.
BJ1012 .S5195 2003

Witherall, Arthur, 1966- The problem of existence. Aldershot, England ; Brookfield, VT : Ashgate, c2002.
BD331 .W58 2002

Ashgate new critical thinking in religion, theology, and biblical studies.
Hood, Adam, 1960- Baillie, Oman and Macmurray. Aldershot, England ; Burlington, VT : Ashgate, c2003.
BR110 .H575 2003

Ashgate religion, culture & society series
Herbert, David, 1939- Religion and civil society. Aldershot, Hampshire, England ; Burlington, VT : Ashgate, c2003.
BL60 .H457 2003

Ashgate world philosophies series
Forsthoefel, Thomas A. Knowing beyond knowledge. Alderhot, England ; Burlington, VT. : Ashgate, 2002.
B132.A3 F66 2002

Ashkenazi, Nisim. Ben he-'anan / Nisim Ashkenazi. Tel-Aviv : Gal, 2002. 360 p. ; 21 cm. (Tsemihah ishit u-muda'ut – Otobiyografiyot)
1. Ashkenazi, Nisim. 2. Mysticism. 3. Moral development. 4. Jews - Conduct of life. I. Title.

ASHKENAZI, NISIM.
Ashkenazi, Nisim. Ben he-'anan. Tel-Aviv : Gal, 2002.

Ashley, Leonard R. N. The complete book of sex magic / Leonard R.N. Ashley. Fort Lee, NJ : Barricade Books, 2003. xi, 354 p. : ill. ; 23 cm. Contains text of Carmilla by J.S. Le Fanu. Includes bibliographical references and index. ISBN 1-56980-226-2 (pbk. : alk. paper) DDC 133.4/3
1. Magic. 2. Sex - Miscellanea. I. Le Fanu, Joseph Sheridan, 1814-1873. Carmilla. II. Title.
BF1623.S4 A85 2002

Ashmore, Richard D.
Self, social identity, and physical health. New York : Oxford University Press, 1999.
R726.5 .S46 1999

ASIA. *See* **ASIA, CENTRAL.**

ASIA, CENTRAL - POLITICS AND GOVERNMENT.
Searching for peace in Central and South Asia. Boulder, Colo. : Lynne Rienner Publishers, 2002.
JZ5597 .S43 2002

ASIA - CIVILIZATION - HISTORIOGRAPHY.
Western historical thinking. New York : Berghahn Books, 2002.
D16.9 .W454 2002

ASIA, EAST. *See* **EAST ASIA.**

ASIA, EASTERN. *See* **EAST ASIA.**

ASIA - FOREIGN PUBLIC OPINION, WESTERN.
Gunn, Geoffrey C. First globalization. Lanham, Md. : Rowman & Littlefield, c2003.
CB251 .G87 2003

ASIA - HISTORY.
The 1000s. San Diego, Calif. : Greenhaven Press, c2001.
CB354.3 .A16 2001

ASIA - HISTORY - CHRONOLOGY.
Time matters. Amsterdam : VU University Press, 2001.
BF468 .T555 2001

ASIA - RELATIONS - EUROPE.
Europe and the Asia-Pacific. London ; New York : RoutledgeCurzon, 2003.
D1065.A78 E97 2003

Gunn, Geoffrey C. First globalization. Lanham, Md. : Rowman & Littlefield, c2003.
CB251 .G87 2003

ASIA, SOUTH. *See* **SOUTH ASIA.**

ASIA, SOUTHEASTERN - LANGUAGES.
Collected papers on Southeast Asian and Pacific languages. Canberra, ACT : Pacific Linguistics, Research School of Pacific and Asian Studies, Australian National University, 2002.

ASIA, SOUTHWEST. *See* **MIDDLE EAST.**

ASIA, WESTERN. *See* **MIDDLE EAST.**

Asiáin, Martin, 1962-.
Der Grund, die Not und die Freude des Bewusstseins. Würzburg : Königshausen & Neumann, c2002.
B808.9 .G78 2002

ASIAN AMERICANS - CULTURAL ASSIMILATION.
The afro-asian century. Durham, N.C. : Duke University Press, 2003.

ASIAN AMERICANS - RACE IDENTITY.
The afro-asian century. Durham, N.C. : Duke University Press, 2003.

ASIAN AMERICANS - UNITED STATES. *See* **ASIAN AMERICANS.**

ASIAN AND PACIFIC COUNCIL COUNTRIES. *See* **ASIA.**

Asian face reading.
De Mente, Boye. Boston, MA : Tuttle Pub., 2003.
BF851 .D37 2003

Asian iconography series
(3) [Aids to Sadhana series. Tibetan & Sanskrit. Selections.] Sādhanamālā, Avalokiteśvara section. Delhi : Adroit Publishers ; New Delhi : Distributors, Akhil Book Distributors, 2002.
BQ8915 .S23 2002

ASIANS - CANADA - ETHNIC IDENTITY.
Western eyes [videorecording]. New York, NY : First Run/Icarus Films, 2000.

ASIANS - UNITED STATES. *See* **ASIAN AMERICANS.**

Asiatic mystery.
Hermes, Trismegistus. Divine Pymander. Rev. ed. Quakertown, PA : Philosophical Pub. Co., 2001.
BF1598.H5 E5 2001

ASKÉNAZI, LÉON.
Aviner, Shelomoh Ḥayim, ha-Kohen. Perurim mi-shulḥan gavoah. Yerushalayim : Sifriyat Ḥayah, 762 [2001 or 2002]

Aslan, Madalyn. Madalyn Aslan's Jupiter signs : how to improve your luck, career, health, finances, appearance, and relationships through the new astrology / Madalyn Aslan. New York : Viking Studio, 2003. p. cm. ISBN 0-670-03149-6 (alk. paper) DDC 133.5/36
1. Astrology. 2. Jupiter (Planet) - Miscellanea. I. Title.
BF1724.2.J87 A85 2003

Aslan, Rüstem.
Mauerschau. Remshalden-Grunbach : Greiner, 2002.

ASOCIACIÓN LATINOAMERICANA DE LIBRE COMERCIO COUNTRIES. *See* **LATIN AMERICA.**

Asov, A. I. (Aleksandr Igorevich) Slavi͡anskai͡a astrologii͡a : zvezdomudrie, zvezdochetets, kalendar', obri͡ady / Aleksandr Asov. Moskva : Fair-Press : Grand, 2001. 583 p. : ill. ; 21 cm. ISBN 5818302377
1. Astrology, Slavic. 2. Calendar, Slavic. 3. Slavic countries - Social life and customs. I. Title.
BF1714.S58 A86 2001

Slavi͡anskai͡a astrologii͡a : zvezdomudrie, zvezdochetets, kalendar', obri͡ady / Aleksandr Asov. Moskva : FAIR-PRESS, 2001. 583 p. : ill., music ; 21 cm. ISBN 5818302377
1. Astrology, Slavic. 2. Calendar, Slavic. 3. Slavic countries - Social life and customs. I. Title.

Svi͡ashchennye prarodiny slavi͡an / Aleksandr Asov. Moskva : Veche, 2002. 494 p. : ill. ; 22 cm. (Taĭny zemli russkoĭ) Includes bibliographical references. ISBN 5945380717
1. Mythology, Slavic. 2. Slavs - Religion. 3. Gods, Slavic. 4. Slavs - History. I. Title. II. Series: Taĭny zemli russkoĭ.
BL930 .A863 2002

ASPECT (ASTROLOGY).
Tompkins, Sue. Aspects in astrology. London : Rider, 2001.
BF1717.2 .T65 2001

Aspects in astrology.
Tompkins, Sue. London : Rider, 2001.
BF1717.2 .T65 2001

Aspekte einer modernen Neurodidaktik.
Arnold, Margret. München : Ernst Vögel, 2002.

The assault on truth.
Masson, J. Moussaieff (Jeffrey Moussaieff), 1941- 1st Ballantine Books ed. New York : Ballantine Books, 2003.
BF109.F74 M38 2003

Assessing writing.
Weigle, Sara Cushing. Cambridge ; New York, NY : Cambridge University Press, 2002.
PE1065 .W35 2002

Assessment in counselling.
Milner, Judith, senior lecturer. Houndmills, Basingstoke, Hampshire ; New York : Palgrave Macmillan, 2003.
BF637.C6 M5249 2003

ASSIMILATION (SOCIOLOGY). *See also* **EMIGRATION AND IMMIGRATION; MARGINALITY, SOCIAL; MINORITIES.**
The emerging monoculture. Westport, Conn. : Praeger, 2003.
HM843 .E44 2003

ASSING, OTTILIE - FICTION.
Rhodes, Jewell Parker. Douglass' women. New York, NY : Atria Books, c2002.
1. Black author.

Assink, E., 1944-.
Reading complex words. New York : Kluwer Academic/Plenum Publishers, c2003.
P37.5.R42 R43 2003

ASSISTED CONCEPTION. *See* **HUMAN REPRODUCTIVE TECHNOLOGY.**

ASSISTED HUMAN REPRODUCTION. *See* **HUMAN REPRODUCTIVE TECHNOLOGY.**

Assmann, Aleida.
Identities. New York ; Oxford : Berghahn Books, 2002.
HM716 .I34 2002

Assmann, Jan.
Kontexte und Kulturen des Erinnerns. Konstanz : UVK Verlagsgesellschaft, 2002.
BF378.S65 K65 2002

Association des historiens modernistes des universités (France).
La Renaissance. Paris : Presses de l'université de Paris-Sorbonne, 2003.

ASSOCIATION FOOTBALL. *See* **SOCCER.**

Association for Multicultural Counseling and Development (U.S.).
Multicultural counseling competencies 2003. Alexandria, VA : Association for Multicultural Counseling and Development, 2003.
BF637.C6 M8367 2003

ASSOCIATION FOR RESEARCH AND ENLIGHTENMENT - BIOGRAPHY.
Sugrue, Thomas, 1907- There is a river. Virginia Beach, Va. : A.R.E. Press, c2003.
BF1027.C3 S8 2003

Association for the Psychoanalysis of Culture & Society.
[Journal for the psychoanalysis of culture & society (Online)] Journal for the psychoanalysis of culture and society [electronic resource]. Columbus, Ohio : Ohio State University Press
BF175.4.C84

Association of Local Government Authorities of Kenya.
Conflict management. Nairobi : Friedrich Ebert Stiftung : Centre for Conflict Research : Association of Local Government Authorities of Kenya, 2000.

ASSOCIATIONS, INSTITUTIONS, ETC. *See also* **DANCE COMPANIES; LEARNED INSTITUTIONS AND SOCIETIES.**
Group behaviour and development. Oxford ; New York : Oxford University Press, 2002.
HD58.7 .G76 2002

ASSOCIATIONS, INSTITUTIONS, ETC. - DEVELOPING COUNTRIES.
Group behaviour and development. Oxford ; New York : Oxford University Press, 2002.
HD58.7 .G76 2002

Astartes, Alfa. The magenta gamma / Alfa Astartes. [Philadelphia] : Xlibris, c2002. 220 p. ; 22 cm. ISBN 140104929X ISBN 1401049281 (pbk.) DDC 133.5/925
1. Astrology, Oriental. I. Title.
BF1714.O7 A88 2002

Asteroid goddesses

Asteroid goddesses.
George, Demetra, 1946- Berwick, Me. : Ibis Press, 2003.
BF1724.5 .G46 2003

ASTEROIDS - COLLISIONS WITH EARTH.
Palmer, Trevor, 1944- Perilous planet earth. Cambridge, U.K. ; New York : Cambridge University Press, 2003.
QE506 .P35 2003

ASTEROIDS - MISCELLANEA.
George, Demetra, 1946- Asteroid goddesses. Berwick, Me. : Ibis Press, 2003.
BF1724.5 .G46 2003

Ästhetik der Psychoanalyse.
Małyszek, Tomasz, 1971- Wrocław : Wydawn. Uniwersytetu Wrocławskiego, 2000.

Ästhetik : Ephemeres und Historisches : Beiträge zur Diskussion / Renate Reschke (Hrsg.). Hamburg : Kovač, c2002. 192 p. ; 21 cm. (Schriftenreihe Boethiana ; Bd. 54) Includes bibliographical references and index. ISBN 3-8300-0638-1 (pbk.)
1. Aesthetics. I. Reschke, Renate. II. Series.

Ästhetik und Kulturphilosophie
(Bd. 1) Schweppenhäuser, Gerhard. Die Fluchtbahn des Subjekts. Münster : Lit, 2001.

Ästhetische und metaphorologische Schriften.
Blumenberg, Hans. 1. Aufl. Frankfurt : Suhrkamp, 2001.

Astori, Roberta. Formule magiche : invocazioni, giuramenti, litanie, legature, gesti rituali, filtri, incantesimi, lapidari dall'antichità al Medioevo / Roberta Astori. Milano : Mimesis, c2000. 142 p. ; 21 cm. (Mimesis) Includes bibliographical references (p. 134-142). In Italian and Latin. ISBN 88-87231-74-5
1. Magic, Ancient. 2. Magic in literature. I. Title. II. Series.
BF1591 .A88 2000

Astrakhanskiĭ gosudarstvennyĭ pedagogicheskiĭ universitet.
Romanova, A. P. (Anna Petrovna) Stanovlenie religioznogo kompleksa. Astrakhan : Izd-vo Astrakhanskogo pedagog. universiteta, 1999.
BF51 .R66 1999

ASTRAL BODY.
Anderson, Victor H. 1917- Etheric anatomy. 1st American pbk. ed. Albany, Calif. : Acorn Guild Press, 2004.
BF1389.A7 A53 2004

ASTRAL PROJECTION.
Anderson, Victor H. 1917- Etheric anatomy. 1st American pbk. ed. Albany, Calif. : Acorn Guild Press, 2004.
BF1389.A7 A53 2004

Twitchell, Paul, 1908-1971. [Stranger by the river. Croation] Stranac na rijeci. Minneapolis, MN : ECKANKAR, c1994.

ASTRAUD ANTONIN, 1896-1948.
Shoham, S. Giora, 1929- Teruf, setiyah ṿi-yetsirah. [Israel] : Miśrad ha-biṭaḥon, [2002]

AstroLocality magic.
Cochrane, David. 1st ed. Gainesville, FL : Cosmic Patterns Software, c2002.
BF1729.M68 C63 2002

ASTROLOGERS - INDIA - BIOGRAPHY.
Dvivedī, Bhojarāja. Ācārya Varāhamihira kā jyotisha meṃ yogadāna. 1. saṃskaraṇa. Naī Dillī : Rañjana Pablikeśansa, 2002.
BF1679.8.V37 D85 2002

Śāstrī, Girijā Śaṅkara. Ācārya Varāhamihira. 1. saṃskaraṇa. Ilāhābāda : Jyotisha, Karmakāṇḍa evaṃ Adhyātma Śodha Saṃsthāna, 2001.
BF1679.8.V37 S27 2001

ASTROLOGERS - ITALY - BIOGRAPHY.
Dooley, Brendan Maurice, 1953- Morandi's last prophecy and the end of Renaissance politics. Princeton, N.J. ; Woodstock : Princeton University Press, c2002.
BF1679.8.M59 D66 2002

ASTROLOGERS - PRACTICE.
Mulligan, Bob. Between astrolgers and clients. Naples, Fla. : Astrology Co., c2001.
BF1711 .M85 2001

ASTROLOGERS - UNITED STATES - BIOGRAPHY.
Christino, Karen. Foreseeing the future. Amherst, MA : One Reed Publications, c2002.
BF1679.8.A31 C56 2002

L'astrologia e i miti del mondo antico.
Tamiozzo Villa, Patrizia. 1. ed. Roma : Newton & Compton, 2001.
BF1729.M9 T35 2001

ASTROLOGICAL GEOMANCY - BURMA.
'Oṅ' Mraṅ'', 'Aṅ'gyaṅ'nīyā Ū''. 'Im' chok' maṅgalā kyam'". Mantale" : Krī' pvā' re" Cā 'up' Tuik', 2002.
BF1779.A88 O56 2002

ASTROLOGICAL HOUSES. See **HOUSES (ASTROLOGY).**

Astrologiko hēmerologio 2002.
Papeu, Dēmētrēs, 1947- 3. etos ekd. Leukōsia : Ekdoseis Papeu, [2001]
BF1708.8.G74 P37 2001

ASTROLOGISTS. See **ASTROLOGERS.**

ASTROLOGY. See also **ASCENDANT (ASTROLOGY); ASPECT (ASTROLOGY); DIGNITIES (ASTROLOGY); HINDU ASTROLOGY; JAINA ASTROLOGY; ZODIAC.**
Adams, Jessica. The new astrology for women. [New ed.]. Pymble, Sydney, N.S.W. : HarperCollins, 1998 (2002 printing)

Alexander, Skye. Magickal astrology. Franklin Lakes, NJ : New Page Books, c2000.
BF1611 .A44 2000

Aslan, Madalyn. Madalyn Aslan's Jupiter signs. New York : Viking Studio, 2003.
BF1724.2.J87 A85 2003

Burk, Kevin, 1967- The complete node book. 1st ed. St. Paul, Minn. : Llewellyn Publications, 2003.
BF1723 .B87 2003

Campion, Nicholas. The ultimate astrologer. Carlsbad, Calif. : Astro Room, c2002 (2003 printing)
BF1708.1 .C357 2002

Civilization under attack. 1st ed. St. Paul, Minn. : Llewellyn Publications, 2001.
BF1729.U5 C57 2001

Clement, Stephanie Jean. Mapping your birthchart. 1st ed. St. Paul, Minn. : Llewellyn Publications, 2003.
BF1708.1 .C535 2003

Cochrane, David. AstroLocality magic. 1st ed. Gainesville, FL : Cosmic Patterns Software, c2002.
BF1729.M68 C63 2002

Cochrane, David. Astrology for the 21st century. 1st ed. Gainesville, FL : Cosmic Patterns Software, c2002.
BF1708.1 .C63 2002

Craze, Richard, 1950- Mix & match animal & star signs. 1st ed. Hauppauge, NY : Barron's, 2000.
BF1714.C5 C76 2000

Dixon-Cooper, Hazel, 1947- Love on a rotten day. New York : Simon and Schuster, 2004.
BF1729.L6 D59 2004

Edut, Tali. Astrostyle. New York : Simon & Schuster, c2003.
BF1729.T44 E38 2003

Fenton, Sasha. Astrology for wimps. New York : Sterling Pub., c2003.
BF1708.1 .F453 2003

Garrison, Cal. The old girls' book of dreams. Boston, MA : Red Wheel, 2003.
BF1729.W64 G37 2003

Goldsmith, Martin. The zodiac by degrees. Boston, MA : Weiser Books, 2004.
BF1708.1 .G62 2004

Grigorovich, A. A. (Aleksandr Anatol'evich) Misteriia zvezd. Moskva : MK-Periodika, 2002.
BF1708.6 .G75 2002

Hodges, Jane. Cosmic grooves. San Francisco, Calif. : Chronicle Books, c2001.
BF1726 .H59 2001

Knight, Michele. Good fortune. Kansas City, Mo. : Andrews McMeel Pub., c2002.
BF1726 .K55 2002

Kosarin, Jenni. The everything love signs book. Avon, MA : Adams Media, c2004.
BF1729.L6 K67 2004

Longacre, Celeste B. Love signs. 1st ed. Walpole, NH : Sweet Fern Publications, 2000.
BF1729.L6 L66 2000

Mann, A. T., 1943- A new vision of astrology. New York : Pocket Books, c2002.

BF1708.1 .M355 2002

Mann, A. T., 1943- [Round art] The round art of astrology. London : Vega, c2003.
BF1708.1 .M36 2003

Marriott, Rob. Astrology uncut. 1st trade pbk. ed. New York : One World, 2004.
BF1711 .M45 2004

Papeu, Dēmētrēs, 1947- Astrologiko hēmerologio 2002. 3. etos ekd. Leukōsia : Ekdoseis Papeu, [2001]
BF1708.8.G74 P37 2001

Pharr, Daniel. The moon & everyday living. 2nd ed. St. Paul, Minn. : LLewellyn, 2002.
BF1723 .P48 2002

Roberts, Courtney, 1957- Visions of the Virgin Mary. St. Paul, Minn. : Llewellyn, 2004.
BF1729.R4 R63 2004

Schostak, Sherene. Surviving saturn's return. 1st ed. New York : McGraw-Hill, 2004.
BF1724.2.S3 S36 2004

Shaw, Maria, 1963- Maria Shaw's star gazer. 1st ed. St. Paul, Minn. : Llewellyn Publications, 2003.
BF1411 .S52 2003

Starwoman, Athena. Zodiac. New York : Friedman/Fairfax : Distributed by Sterling Pub., c2000.
BF1708.1 .S695 2000

Stellas, Constance. The astrology gift guide. New York : Signet, c2002.
BF1729.G53 S74 2002

Tamiozzo Villa, Patrizia. L'astrologia e i miti del mondo antico. 1. ed. Roma : Newton & Compton, 2001.
BF1729.M9 T35 2001

Townley, John, 1945- Lunar returns. 1st ed. St. Paul, Minn. : Llewellyn Publications, 2003.
BF1723 .T69 2003

Woolfolk, Joanna Martine. [Only astrology book you'll ever need. Spanish] El unico libro de astrologia que necesitara. Lanham, Md. : Taylor Trade Pub, 2003.
BF1708.1 .W6818 2003

ASTROLOGY AND ARCHITECTURE.
Śukla, Kamalākānta, 1911- Vāstusārasaṅgrahaḥ. 1. saṃskaraṇam. Vārāṇasī : Sampūrṇānanda Saṃskrta Viśvavidyālaye, 2002.
BF1729.A7+

ASTROLOGY AND ARCHITECTURE - INDIA.
Asalī prācīna Vaidika vāstu śāstra. 1. saṃskaraṇa. Dillī : Manoja Pōketa Buksa, [2002?]
BF1729.A7 A83 2002

[Śilpaśāstra. English & Sanskrit.] Vāstu-śāstram. Calcutta : Sanskrit Pustak Bhandar, 2001.
NA7427 .M34 2001

ASTROLOGY AND GEMS.
Bharadwaj, Monisha. The Indian luck book. London : Kyle Cathie, 2001.
BF1778 .B43 2001

ASTROLOGY AND MYTHOLOGY.
George, Demetra, 1946- Asteroid goddesses. Berwick, Me. : Ibis Press, 2003.
BF1724.5 .G46 2003

Astrology and numerology in medieval and early modern Catalonia.
Lucas, John Scott, 1970- Leiden ; Boston : Brill, 2003.
BF1685 .L83 2003

ASTROLOGY AND PERSONAL FINANCE.
Palmer, Lynne. Prosperity. Las Vegas : Star Bright Publishers, [c2001]
BF1729.F48 P35 2001

ASTROLOGY AND PSYCHOLOGY.
George, Demetra, 1946- Asteroid goddesses. Berwick, Me. : Ibis Press, 2003.
BF1724.5 .G46 2003

ASTROLOGY AND SEX.
Knight, Michele. Good sex. Kansas City, Mo. : Andrews McMeel Pub., c2002.
BF1729.S4 .K58 2002

McCormack, Kathleen. Magic for lovers : find your ideal partner through the power of magic. 1st ed. Hauppauge, NY : Barron's, c2003.
BF1623.L6 M38 2003

Omarr, Sydney. [Astrology, love, sex, and you] Sydney Omarr's astrology, love, sex, and you. New York : Signet, c2002.

BF1729.S4 O58 2002

ASTROLOGY, ARAB - EARLY WORKS TO 1800.
Ikhwān al-Ṣafāʾ. [Rasāʾil. 36. French & Arabic] Les révolutions et les cycles . Louvain-la-Neuve : Bruylant-Academia ; Beyrouth : Al-Bouraq Editions, 1996.

ASTROLOGY, ARABIC. *See* **ASTROLOGY, ARAB.**

ASTROLOGY, ASSYRO-BABYLONIAN.
Brown, David, 1968- Mesopotamian planetary astronomy-astrology. Groningen : Styx, 2000.
BF1714.A86 B76 2000

ASTROLOGY, BURMESE.
Mran'' Svan', Ū''. Ca le cha rā krī'' Ū'' Puñña bedan' 'a ho te'' thap' 'a phvan'' kyam'''. Ran' kun' : Khyui Te'' Sam Cā pe : [Phran'' khyi re''], Paññā Rvhe Ton' Cā 'up' Tuik', 2002.
BF1714.B8 M73 2002

ASTROLOGY, CELTIC.
Vega, Phyllis. Celtic astrology. Franklin Lakes, NJ : New Page Books, c2002.
BF1714.C44 V44 2002

ASTROLOGY, CHINESE.
Burns, Debbie. Chinese horoscopes. Sydney : Lansdowne, 2000, c1998.

Craze, Richard, 1950- Mix & match animal & star signs. 1st ed. Hauppauge, NY : Barron's, 2000.
BF1714.C5 C76 2000

Suckling, Nigel. Legends & lore. New York : Friedman/Fairfax Publishers : Distributed by Sterling Pub., c2002.
BF1714.C5 S93 2002

ASTROLOGY - EARLY WORKS TO 1800.
Lucas, John Scott, 1970- Astrology and numerology in medieval and early modern Catalonia. Leiden ; Boston : Brill, 2003.
BF1685 .L83 2003

ASTROLOGY, EGYPTIAN.
Constantine, Storm. Egyptian birth signs. London : Thorsons, 2002.

Vlora, Nedim R., 1943- Le porte del cielo. Bari : M. Adda, c2001.
BF1674 .V56 2001

Astrology for the 21st century.
Cochrane, David. 1st ed. Gainesville, FL : Cosmic Patterns Software, c2002.
BF1708.1 .C63 2002

Astrology for the twenty-first century.
Cochrane, David. Astrology for the 21st century. 1st ed. Gainesville, FL : Cosmic Patterns Software, c2002.
BF1708.1 .C63 2002

Astrology for wimps.
Fenton, Sasha. New York : Sterling Pub., c2003.
BF1708.1 .F453 2003

The astrology gift guide.
Stellas, Constance. New York : Signet, c2002.
BF1729.G53 S74 2002

ASTROLOGY, HINDU. *See* **HINDU ASTROLOGY.**

ASTROLOGY - HISTORY.
Berlinski, David, 1942- The secrets of the vaulted sky. 1st U.S. ed. Orlando, Fla. : Harcourt, c2003.
BF1674 .B47 2003

Pompeo Faracovi, Ornella. Scritto negli astri. Venezia : Marsilio, c1996.
BF1671 .P66 1996x

ASTROLOGY - HISTORY - 17TH CENTURY.
Dooley, Brendan Maurice, 1953- Morandi's last prophecy and the end of Renaissance politics. Princeton, N.J. ; Woodstock : Princeton University Press, c2002.
BF1679.8.M59 D66 2002

ASTROLOGY - HISTORY - 20TH CENTURY.
Christino, Karen. Foreseeing the future. Amherst, MA : One Reed Publications, c2002.
BF1679.8.A31 C56 2002

Astrology, love, sex, and you.
Omarr, Sydney. [Astrology, love, sex, and you] Sydney Omarr's astrology, love, sex, and you. New York : Signet, c2002.
BF1729.S4 O58 2002

ASTROLOGY, ORIENTAL.
Astartes, Alfa. The magenta gamma. [Philadelphia] : Xlibris, c2002.

BF1714.O7 A88 2002

ASTROLOGY - PHILOSOPHY.
Damiani, Anthony, 1922-1984. Astronoesis. Burdett, N.Y. : Published for Wisdom's Goldenrod, Ltd. by Larson Publications, c2000.
BD418.3 .D347 2000

ASTROLOGY, SLAVIC.
Asov, A. I. (Aleksandr Igorevich) Slavi͡anskai͡a astrologii͡a. Moskva : Fair-Press : Grand, 2001.
BF1714.S58 A86 2001

Asov, A. I. (Aleksandr Igorevich) Slavi͡anskai͡a astrologii͡a. Moskva : FAIR-PRESS, 2001.

ASTRONAUTICS. *See* **AERONAUTICS; ROCKETRY; UNIDENTIFIED FLYING OBJECTS.**

ASTRONAUTICS AND CIVILIZATION.
Sandvoss, Ernst. Vom homo sapiens zum homo spaciens. Berlin : Logos, c2002.

T͡Siolkovskiĭ, K. (Konstantin), 1857-1935. Geniĭ sredi li͡udeĭ. Moskva : Mysl', 2002.
TL781.85.T84 A25 2002

ASTRONAUTICS - OPTICAL COMMUNICATION SYSTEMS. *See* **TELEVISION.**

Astronoesis.
Damiani, Anthony, 1922-1984. Burdett, N.Y. : Published for Wisdom's Goldenrod, Ltd. by Larson Publications, c2000.
BD418.3 .D347 2000

ASTRONOMICAL GEOGRAPHY. *See* **SEASONS.**

ASTRONOMY. *See also* **CALENDAR; COSMOLOGY; GALAXIES; SEASONS; ZODIAC.**
On the shoulders of giants. Philadelphia : Running Press, c2002.
QC6.2 .O5 2002

Astronomy and astrophysics library
Börner, G. The early universe. 4th ed. Berlin ; London : Springer, c2003.

ASTRONOMY, ARAB - EARLY WORKS TO 1800.
Ikhwān al-Ṣafāʾ. [Rasāʾil. 36. French & Arabic] Les révolutions et les cycles . Louvain-la-Neuve : Bruylant-Academia ; Beyrouth : Al-Bouraq Editions, 1996.

ASTRONOMY, ARABIC. *See* **ASTRONOMY, ARAB.**

ASTRONOMY, ASSYRO-BABYLONIAN.
Brown, David, 1968- Mesopotamian planetary astronomy-astrology. Groningen : Styx, 2000.
BF1714.A86 B76 2000

ASTRONOMY, EGYPTIAN.
Vlora, Nedim R., 1943- Le porte del cielo. Bari : M. Adda, c2001.
BF1674 .V56 2001

ASTRONOMY - HISTORY - 17TH CENTURY.
Lambert, Ladina Bezzola. Imagining the unimaginable. Amsterdam ; New York, NY : Rodopi, 2002.
QB29 .L35 2002

ASTRONOMY, MEDIEVAL. *See* **ASTROLOGY.**

ASTRONOMY - OBSERVATIONS. *See* **PLANETS - OBSERVATIONS.**

Astrostyle.
Edut, Tali. New York : Simon & Schuster, c2003.
BF1729.T44 E38 2003

Astrum sapientiae.
Gavrilov, D. A. Bogi slavi͡an, i͡azychestvo, traditsii͡a. [Moskva] : Refl-buk, 2002.
BL930 .G38 2002

ASW.
Schutz, Alfred, 1899-1959. Werkausgabe. Konstanz : UVK, Verlagsgesellschaft, 2003-
BD431 .S284916 2003

Aswynn, Freya, 1949-.
Leaves of Yggdrasil.
Aswynn, Freya, 1949- Northern mysteries & magick. 2nd ed. St. Paul, Minn. : Llewellyn Publications, 1998 (2002 printing)
BF1623.R89 A78 1998

Northern mysteries & magick : runes, gods, and feminine powers / Freya Aswynn. 2nd ed. St. Paul, Minn. : Llewellyn Publications, 1998 (2002 printing) xxxi, 251 p. : ill. ; 23 cm. Rev. ed. of: Leaves of Yggdrasil. 1990. "Second edition, fourth printing"--verso t.p. Includes bibliographical references (p. 243-245) and index. Library's copy missing compact disc. CONTENTS: Disc: Nietsche -- Havamal -- Voluspa -- Invocation -- Nithing -- Futhark -- Sigdrifumal -- Wotan -- Ragnarok. ISBN 1-56718-047-5 DDC 133.3/3
1. Runes - Miscellanea. 2. Magic. 3. Fortune-telling by runes. 4. Gods, Norse. I. Aswynn, Freya, 1949- Leaves of Yggdrasil. II. Title. III. Title: Northern mysteries and magick IV. Title: Northern mysteries & magic V. Title: Northern mysteries and magic
BF1623.R89 A78 1998

ASYLUMS. *See* **PSYCHIATRIC HOSPITALS.**

At-Hlan, Spirit. The voice of At-Hlan : channeled information from Atlantis to Sirius / Roger Keenan. Torquay : Pyramid Pub., c1996. 202 p. ; 20 cm. ISBN 0-948694-52-9 (pbk) DDC 133.93
1. Spirit writings. I. Keenan, Roger. II. Title.

At war with ourselves.
Hirsh, Michael, 1957- New York : Oxford University Press, 2003.
E895 .H57 2003

Ataöv, Türkkaya. Discrimination & conflict / Türkkaya Ataöv. Haarlem : SOTA, 2000. 161 p. ; 24 cm. Includes bibliographical references. ISBN 90-804409-3-0
1. Discrimination. 2. Social conflict. 3. Human rights. I. Title. II. Title: Discrimination and conflict

ATHEISM.
Billington, Ray. Religion without God. London ; New York : Routledge, 2002.
BL2747.3 .B55 2002

Athena's sun signs.
Starwoman, Athena. Zodiac. New York : Friedman/Fairfax : Distributed by Sterling Pub., c2000.
BF1708.1 .S695 2000

Athena's sunsigns.
Starwoman, Athena. Zodiac. New York : Friedman/Fairfax : Distributed by Sterling Pub., c2000.
BF1708.1 .S695 2000

Athens, Lonnie H.
Violent acts and violentization. Amsterdam ; Boston : JAI, 2003.

Atherton, Margaret.
Looking into pictures. Cambridge, Mass. : MIT Press, c2003.
BF243 .L66 2003

ATHLETES. *See* **BASEBALL PLAYERS; GLADIATORS.**

ATHLETICS. *See* **SPORTS.**

Athlone contemporary European thinkers
Le Dœuff, Michèle. The philosophical imaginary. London : Continuum, 2002.

Songe-Möller, Vigdis. Philosophy without women. London : Continuum, c2002.

ATHOR (EGYPTIAN DEITY). *See* **HATHOR (EGYPTIAN DEITY).**

ATHYR (EGYPTIAN DEITY). *See* **HATHOR (EGYPTIAN DEITY).**

Atkins, Nancy.
Spotts, Dane. Super brain power. Seattle, Wash. : LifeQuest Pub. Group, c1998.
BF441 .S68 1998

Atkinson & Hilgard's introduction to psychology /
Edward E. Smith ... [et al.]. 14th ed. Australia ; Belmont, CA : Wadworth/Thomson Learning, c2003. 677, [86] p. : col. ill. ; 29 cm. Rev. ed. of: Hilgard's introduction to psychology. 13th ed. c2000. Includes bibliographical references (p. R-1-R-40) and index. ISBN 0-15-505069-9 DDC 150
1. Psychology. I. Smith, Edward E., 1940- II. Atkinson, Rita L. III. Hilgard, Ernest Ropiequet, 1904- IV. Title: Hilgard's introduction to psychology. V. Title: Introduction to psychology
BF121 .I57 2003

Atkinson, Donald R.
Counseling diverse populations. 3rd ed. Boston, Mass. : McGraw-Hill, c2004.
BF637.C6 C6372 2004

Atkinson, Rita L.
Atkinson & Hilgard's introduction to psychology. 14th ed. Australia ; Belmont, CA : Wadworth/Thomson Learning, c2003.
BF121 .I57 2003

Atlantis
Haen, Renate. Du bist die Göttin ; 1. Aufl. Bergish Gladbach : Bastei Lübbe, 1999.

Atmanspacher, Harald.
Between chance and choice. Thorverton, UK ; Charlottesville, VA : Imprint Academic, c2002.

ATOMIC POWER PLANTS. *See* **NUCLEAR POWER PLANTS.**

Atran, Scott, 1952- In gods we trust : the evolutionary landscape of religion / Scott Atran. Oxford ; New York : Oxford University Press, 2002. xvi, 348 p., [24] p. of plates : ill. ; 25 cm. (Evolution and cognition) Includes bibliographical references (p. [281]-336) and index. ISBN 0-19-514930-0 DDC 200/.1/9
1. Psychology, Religious. 2. Genetic psychology. I. Title. II. Series.
BL53 .A88 2002

ATROCITIES. *See also* **PERSECUTION.**
Sontag, Susan, 1933- Regarding the pain of others. 1st ed. New York : Farrar, Straus and Giroux, 2003.
HM554 .S65 2003

ATTACHMENT BEHAVIOR.
Ayers, Mary, 1960- The eyes of shame. 1st ed. Hove, East Sussex ; New York : Brunner-Routledge, 2003.
BF175.5.O24 A94 2003

Knox, Jean, 1948- Archetype, attachment, analysis. Hove, East Sussex ; New York : Brunner-Routledge, 2003.
BF175.5.A72 K68 2003

ATTACHMENT BEHAVIOR IN INFANTS - CROSS-CULTURAL STUDIES.
Regression periods in human infancy. Mahwah, N.J. : Lawrence Erlbaum Associates, 2003.
BF720.R43 R44 2003

ATTACHMENT BEHAVIOR - INDONESIA.
Zevalkink, Dina Johanna, 1962- Attachment in Indonesia. [Netherlands? : s.n.], c1997 (Ridderkerk : Ridderprint)
BF575.A86 Z48 1997

Attachment in Indonesia.
Zevalkink, Dina Johanna, 1962- [Netherlands? : s.n.], c1997 (Ridderkerk : Ridderprint)
BF575.A86 Z48 1997

ATTAR, ḤAYYIM BEN MOSES, 1696-1743. OR HA-ḤAYIM.
Lugasi, Yaʻaḳov Yiśraʼel. Yalḳut Or ha-hayim ha-kadosh. Yerushalayim : [ḥ. mo. l], 762 [2001 or 2002]

ATTENTION. *See also* **BOREDOM; LISTENING.**
Johnson, Addie. Thousand Oaks, Calif. : Sage Publications, c2004.
BF321 .J56 2004

ATTENTION.
Campbell, John, 1956- Reference and consciousness. Oxford : Clarendon Press ; New York : Oxford University Press, 2002.
BF321 .C36 2002

The cognitive and neural bases of spatial neglect. Oxford ; New York : Oxford University Press, 2002.
RC394.N44 C64 2002

Heijden, A. H. C. van der. Attention in vision. 1st ed. New York : Psychology Press, 2003.
BF241 .H42 2003

Johnson, Addie. Attention. Thousand Oaks, Calif. : Sage Publications, c2004.
BF321 .J56 2004

ATTENTION-DEFICIT DISORDER IN ADOLESCENCE.
Attention deficit disorder sourcebook. 1st ed. Detroit, MI : Omnigraphics, c2002.
RJ506.H9 A885 2002

ATTENTION-DEFICIT DISORDER IN ADULTS.
Attention deficit disorder sourcebook. 1st ed. Detroit, MI : Omnigraphics, c2002.
RJ506.H9 A885 2002

Attention deficit disorder sourcebook : basic consumer health information about attention deficit/ hyperactivity disorder in children and adults ... / edited by Dawn D. Matthews. 1st ed. Detroit, MI : Omnigraphics, c2002. xiii, 470 p. ; 24 cm. (Health reference series) Includes bibliographical references and index. Table of contents URL: http://www.loc.gov/catdir/toc/fy034/2002072093.html ISBN 0-7808-0624-7 DDC 616.85/89
1. Attention-deficit hyperactivity disorder. 2. Attention-deficit disorder in adolescence. 3. Attention-deficit disorder in adults. I. Matthews, Dawn D. II. Series.
RJ506.H9 A885 2002

ATTENTION DEFICIT DISORDER WITH HYPERACTIVITY. *See* **ATTENTION-DEFICIT HYPERACTIVITY DISORDER.**

ATTENTION DEFICIT DISORDERS. *See* **ATTENTION-DEFICIT HYPERACTIVITY DISORDER.**

ATTENTION-DEFICIT HYPERACTIVITY DISORDER.
Adeleye, Modupe, 1980- From our hearts. Rochester, N.Y. : Mo-Biz Publishing Co., 2003.
BF353 .A33 2003

Attention deficit disorder sourcebook. 1st ed. Detroit, MI : Omnigraphics, c2002.
RJ506.H9 A885 2002

Köhler, Henning, 1951- War Michel aus Lönneberga aufmerksamkeitsgestört? 2. Aufl. Stuttgart : Freies Geistesleben, 2002.

ATTENTION-DEFICIT HYPERACTIVITY DISORDER - DIAGNOSIS.
Köhler, Henning, 1951- War Michel aus Lönneberga aufmerksamkeitsgestört? 2. Aufl. Stuttgart : Freies Geistesleben, 2002.

Attention in vision.
Heijden, A. H. C. van der. 1st ed. New York : Psychology Press, 2003.
BF241 .H42 2003

ATTENTION, SELECTIVE. *See* **SELECTIVITY (PSYCHOLOGY).**

ATTITUDE CHANGE.
Perloff, Richard M. The dynamics of persuasion. 2nd ed. Mahwah, N.J. : Lawrence Erlbaum Associates, 2003.
BF637.P4 .P39 2003

ATTITUDE CHANGE IN CHILDREN.
Borba, Michele. Don't give me that attitude!. 1st ed. San Francisco : Jossey-Bass, c2004.
BF723.A76 B67 2004

Attitude is everything for success.
Harrell, Keith D. Carlsbad, CA : Hay House, 2004.
BF327 .H373 2004

ATTITUDE (PSYCHOLOGY). *See also* **AGEISM; CONFORMITY; ETHNIC ATTITUDES; PREJUDICES; PUBLIC OPINION; REJECTION (PSYCHOLOGY); SCALE ANALYSIS (PSYCHOLOGY); SEXISM; STEREOTYPE (PSYCHOLOGY); TRUST.**
Grosbard, Ofer, 1954- [Yiśraʼel ʻal ha-sapah. English] Israel on the couch. Albany : State University of New York Press, c2003.
DS126.5 .G694 2003

Grosbard, Ofer, 1954- Yiśraʼel ʻal ha-sapah. Tel-Aviv : Yediʻot aḥaronot : Sifre ḥemed, c2000.

Harrell, Keith D. Attitude is everything for success. Carlsbad, CA : Hay House, 2004.
BF327 .H373 2004

Looking at the other. Oulu, Finland : University of Oulu, 2002.

ATTITUDES (PSYCHOLOGY). *See* **ATTITUDE (PSYCHOLOGY).**

ATTORNEYS. *See* **LAWYERS.**

ATTRITION. *See* **REPENTANCE.**

Attwood, Margaret.
Leading change. Bristol, UK : Policy Press, c2003.

Atwater, P. M. H.
[Children of the new millennium]
The new children and near-death experiences / P.M.H. Atwater ; foreword by Joseph Chilton Pearce. Rochester, Vt. : Bear & Co., 2003. p. cm. Originally published: Children of the new millennium. New York : Three Rivers Press, 1999. Table of contents URL: http://www.loc.gov/catdir/toc/ecip048/2003018534.html CONTENTS: Evolution's nod -- Brain shift/spirit shift -- A new view of near-death states -- Jumbles of good and evil -- The impact of after effects -- Many types, one pattern -- Cases from history -- Evidence for a life continuum -- Alien existences -- A new race aborning -- The promise. DDC 133.9
1. Near-death experiences in children. 2. Human evolution - Miscellanea. I. Title.
BF1045.N42 A88 2003

Au-delà du malaise.
Lévy, Ghyslain. Ramonville Saint-Agne : Erès, c2000.
BF175 .L487 2000

Au-delà du signe.
Jankovic, Zoran. Paris : Harmattan, c2003.

Au fait
Dupaigne, Bernard. Afghanistan, rêve de paix. Paris : Buchet-Chastel, 2002.

Au Maroc avec les Gnawa.
Hell, Bertrand. Le tourbillon des génies. Paris : Flammarion, c2002.

Aucoin, Kevyn. Making faces / Kevyn Aucoin. 1st ed. Boston : Little, Brown, c1997. 159 p. : ill. (some col.) ; 32 cm. ISBN 0-316-28686-9 DDC 646.7/2
1. Beauty, Personal. 2. Cosmetics. 3. Face - Care and hygiene. I. Title.
RA778 .A873 1997

AUCTION BRIDGE. *See* **CONTRACT BRIDGE.**

Auctores Britannici Medii Aevi
(no. 15.) Abbo of Fleury and Ramsay. Oxford ; New York : Oxford University Press, 2002.

The audible past.
Sterne, Jonathan, 1970- Durham : Duke University Press, 2003.
TK7881.4 .S733 2003

AUDING. *See* **LISTENING.**

AUDIO-LINGUAL APPROACH (LANGUAGE TEACHING). *See* **AUDIO-LINGUAL METHOD (LANGUAGE TEACHING).**

AUDIO-LINGUAL METHOD (LANGUAGE TEACHING).
Grundlagen und Modelle für den Hörgerichteten Spracherwerb. Villingen-Schwenningen : Neckar, c1995.

AUDIO RECORDING INDUSTRY. *See* **SOUND RECORDING INDUSTRY.**

AUDIO-VISUAL MATERIALS. *See* **MOTION PICTURES; SOUND RECORDINGS.**

Audiovisuel et communication (Harmattan (Firm))
Beguery, Jocelyne. Une esthétique contemporaine de l'album de jeunesse. Paris : Harmattan, c2002.

Audisio, Gabriel.
Religion et exclusion, XIIe-XVIIIe siècle. Religion et exclusion, douzième-dix-huitième siècle. Aix-en-Provence : Publications de l'Université de Provence, 2001.
BL238 .R448 2001

AUDITORY PERCEPTION.
Eaton, Robert C. The octavolateralis system and Mauthner cell interactions and questions [microform]. [Washington, D.C. : National Aeronautics and Space Administration, 1997]

Moore, Brian C. J. An introduction to the psychology of hearing. 5th ed. Amsterdam ; Boston : Academic Press, c2003.
BF251 .M66 2003

Peinture et musique. Villeneuve-d'Ascq : Presses universitaires du Septentrion, c2002.

AUDITORY PERCEPTION - CONGRESSES.
Oldenburger Symposion zur Psychologischen Akustik (8th : 2000) Contributions to psychological acoustics. 1. ed. Oldenburg : BIS, Bibliotheks- und Informationssystem der Universität Oldenburg, 2000.
BF251 .O44 2000

Audoin-Rouzeau, Stéphane.
Les historiens. Paris : A. Colin, 2003.
D14 .H523 2003

Auerbach, Carl F. Qualitative data : an introduction to coding and analysis / Carl F. Auerbach and Louise B. Silverstein. New York : New York University Press, c2003. ix, 202 p. ; 24 cm. (Qualitative studies in psychology) Includes bibliographical references and index. ISBN 0-8147-0694-0 (cloth : acid-free paper) ISBN 0-8147-0695-9 (paper) DDC 150/.7/23
1. Psychology - Research - Methodology. 2. Qualitative research. I. Silverstein, Louise B. II. Title. III. Series.
BF76.5 .A95 2003

Auf der Suche nach Anerkennung.
Heck, Alexander. Münster : Lit, c2003.

Auffret, Séverine. Des blessures et des jeux : manuel d'imagination libre : essai / Séverine Auffret. Arles : Actes sud, c2003. 213 p. ; 23 cm. Includes bibliographical references and index. ISBN 2-7427-4129-1 DDC 844
1. Play (Philosophy) 2. Imagination (Philosophy) I. Title.

Aufklärungen : Festschrift für Klaus Düsing zum 60. Geburtstag / herausgegeben von Kristina Engelhard. Berlin : Duncker und Humblot, c2002. 212 p. : ill. ; 24 cm. (Philosophische Schriften, 0935-6053 ; Bd. 47) Includes bibliographical references. ISBN 3-428-10772-1 (pbk.)
1. Philosophy. I. Düsing, Klaus. II. Engelhard, Kristina. III. Series.

Aufsätze 1992-2000.
Tugendhat, Ernst. 1. Aufl. Frankfurt : Suhrkamp, 2001.

Augeles, Nikos.
Erkennen und Leben. Hildesheim [Germany] ; New York : Olms, 2002.
BD435 .E75 2002

Auger, Emily E. Tarot and other meditation decks : history, theory, aesthetics, typology / Emily E. Auger. Jefferson, N.C. : McFarland & Co., c2004. p. cm. ISBN 0-7864-1674-2 (softcover : alk. paper) DDC 133.3/2424
1. Tarot - History - 20th century. I. Title.
BF1879.T2 A94 2004

AUGURY. See DIVINATION.

Augustin, Nicole. "Bewegung in Widersprüchen, Widersprüche in Bewegung bringen" : Vorschläge für eine bewegungspädagogische Arbeit mit Mädchen / Nicole Augustin, Karoline Gscheidel. Pfaffenweiler : Centaurus-Verlagsgesellschaft, 1998. 175 p. ; 21 cm. (Betrifft: Geschlecht, 1434-744x ; Bd. 1) "Das vorliegende Buch ist die gekürzte und überarbeitete Version unserer Diplomarbeit."-P. 175. Includes bibliographical references (p. 165-173). Includes interviews with four girls as representative case studies, p. 90-157. CONTENTS: Einleitung -- Bedeutungen von Bewegung für die Identitätsentwicklung und bewegungspädagogische Konsequenzen -- Mädchen zwischen Autonomie und Bindung -- Wie bewegen sich Mädchen? Darstellung, Kritik und pädagogische Konsequenzen -- "Bewegen muss ich mich ja!" Auswertung der Interviews -- Zusammenfassung und Schlussbetrachtung -- Literaturverzeichnis -- Nachwort. ISBN 3-8255-0202-3 ISSN 1434-744x
1. Girls - Education - Germany. 2. Movement education - Germany. 3. Gender identity. I. Gscheidel, Karoline. II. Title. III. Series.
LC2873.G3 A94 1998

Augustine, Saint, Bishop of Hippo. De magistro = Der Lehrer / Augustinus ; zweisprachige Ausgabe unter Mitarbeit von Peter Schulthess und Rudolf Rohrbach ; eingeleitet, kommentiert und herausgegeben von Therese Fuhrer. Paderborn : F. Schöningh, 2002. 223 p. ; 24 cm. (Augustinus. Opera - Werke. B. Philosophische und antipagane Schriften. 1, Philosophische Schriften ; 11. Bd.) Includes bibliographical references (p. 202-208) and indexes. German and Latin. ISBN 3-506-71021-4
1. Language and languages. 2. Teaching - Philosophy. I. Schulthess, Peter, Dr. phil. II. Rohrbach, Rudolf. III. Fuhrer, Therese. IV. Title. V. Title: Lehrer VI. Series: Augustine, Saint, Bishop of Hippo. Works. German & Latin. 2002 ; 11. Bd.
BR65.A5 G4 2002

Works. German & Latin. 2002
(11. Bd.) Augustine, Saint, Bishop of Hippo. De magistro = Paderborn : F. Schöningh, 2002.
BR65.A5 G4 2002

AUGUSTINE, SAINT, BISHOP OF HIPPO.
Eslin, Jean-Claude, 1935- Saint Augustin. Paris : Michalon, c2002.

Aura.
Saraydarian, Torkom. Cave Creek, Ariz. : T.S.G. Pub. Foundation, 1999.
BF1389.A8 S35 1999

AURA.
Larson, Cynthia Sue. Aura advantage. Avon, MA : Adams Media Corp., c2003.
BF1389.A8 L37 2003

Martin, Barbara Y. Change your aura, change your life Sunland, CA : WisdomLight Books, c2003.
BF1389.A8 M37 2003

Musiol, Marie-J. (Marie-Jeanne), 1950- Corps de lumière. Hull, Québec : Axe Néo-7, art contemporain, [2001?]

Saraydarian, Torkom. Aura. Cave Creek, Ariz. : T.S.G. Pub. Foundation, 1999.
BF1389.A8 S35 1999

Aura advantage.
Larson, Cynthia Sue. Avon, MA : Adams Media Corp., c2003.
BF1389.A8 L37 2003

AURAL-ORAL METHOD (LANGUAGE TEACHING). See AUDIO-LINGUAL METHOD (LANGUAGE TEACHING).

Aurotherapy.
Ranchan, Som P., 1932- Delhi : Indian Publishers Distributors, 2001.
BF173.A25 R36 2001

Das äussere und innere Ausland : Fremdes in soziologischer und psychoanalytischer Sicht / Irmgard Eisenbach-Stangl, Wolfgang Stangl (Hg.). Wien : WUV, Universitätsverlag, c2000. 252 p. ; 23 cm. Includes bibliographical references. ISBN 3-85114-481-3 (pbk.)
1. Adjustment (Psychology) I. Eisenbach-Stangl, Irmgard, 1948- II. Stangl, Wolfgang, 1949-
BF335 .A9 2000

Austin, John, 1790-1859.
Mill, John Stuart, 1806-1873. Utilitarianism ; 2nd ed. Malden, MA : Blackwell Pub., 2003.
B1602 .A5 2003

Austin, Linda S., 1951- Heart of the matter : how to find love, how to make it work / Linda Austin. New York : Atria Books, c2003. xx, 261 p. ; 24 cm. Includes index. ISBN 0-7434-3771-3 DDC 306.7
1. Love. 2. Man-woman relationships. 3. Interpersonal relations. 4. Self-actualization (Psychology) I. Title.
BF575.L8 A97 2003

Austin, Robert D. (Robert Daniel), 1962- Artful making : what managers need to know about how artists work / Rob Austin, Lee Devin ; foreword by Eric Schmidt. Upper Saddle River, NJ : Financial Times/Prentice Hall, 2003. xxx, 201 p. ; 24 cm. (Financial Times Prentice Hall) Includes bibliographical references and index. ISBN 0-13-008695-9 (alk. paper) DDC 658.4/001/9
1. Creative ability in business. 2. Creation (Literary, artistic, etc.) I. Devin, Lee, 1938- II. Title. III. Series: Financial Times Prentice Hall books.
HD53 .A96 2003

Australian Broadcasting Corporation.
Little, Graham. The public emotions. Sydney : ABC Books for the Australian Broadcasting Corporation, 1999.
BF531 .L58 1999

AUSTRIA - CIVILIZATION - CONGRESSES.
Philosophie in Aktion. Wien : Turia + Kant, 2000.

AUSTRIA - HISTORY - 20TH CENTURY.
Kraut, Bernhard, 1960- Gefangen, auch im Erinnern. Wien : Edition Selene, c2002.

AUSTRIA - INTELLECTUAL LIFE - 19TH CENTURY.
Le leggi del pensiero tra logica, ontologia e psicologia. Milano : UNICOPLI, 2002.

AUSTRIA - INTELLECTUAL LIFE - 20TH CENTURY.
Le leggi del pensiero tra logica, ontologia e psicologia. Milano : UNICOPLI, 2002.

AUSTRIA - POLITICS AND GOVERNMENT - 1945-.
Philosophie in Aktion. Wien : Turia + Kant, 2000.

AUSTRIA - POLITICS AND GOVERNMENT - 20TH CENTURY.
Kraut, Bernhard, 1960- Gefangen, auch im Erinnern. Wien : Edition Selene, c2002.

AUSTRONESIAN LANGUAGES.
Collected papers on Southeast Asian and Pacific languages. Canberra, ACT : Pacific Linguistics, Research School of Pacific and Asian Studies, Australian National University, 2002.

Auteurs en questions
Jouffroy, Alain, 1928- [Mots et moi] Les mots et moi ; Nantes : Pleins feux, c2002.

AUTHENTICATION. See LEGAL DOCUMENTS.

AUTHENTICITY (PHILOSOPHY).
Hartman, Geoffrey H. Scars of the spirit. New York ; Houndmills, England : Palgrave, 2002.
B105.A8 H37 2002

Miller, William Ian, 1946- Faking it. Cambridge ; New York : Cambridge University Press, 2003.
BF697 .M525 2003

AUTHORITARIANISM. See AUTHORITY; FASCISM; NATIONAL SOCIALISM.

AUTHORITY. See also POWER (PHILOSOPHY).
Norton, Anne. Bloodrites of the post-structuralists. New York : Routledge, 2002.
HM626 .N6785 2002

AUTHORITY (RELIGION). See AUTHORITY - RELIGIOUS ASPECTS.

AUTHORITY - RELIGIOUS ASPECTS.
Lewis, James R. Legitimating new religions. New Brunswick, N.J. : Rutgers University Press, c2003.
BP603 .L49 2003

AUTHORITY - RELIGIOUS ASPECTS - CHRISTIANITY.
Jantzen, Grace. Power, gender, and Christian mysticism. Cambridge ; New York : Cambridge University Press, 1995.
BV5083 .J36 1995

AUTHORS. See JOURNALISTS; LITERATURE; WOMEN AUTHORS.

AUTHORS, AMERICAN - 20TH CENTURY - BIOGRAPHY.
Aller, Annelies van, 1946- Levenskunst van twee vrouwen. Budel : Damon, c2001.
PS3527.1865 Z536 2001

Kingston, Maxine Hong. The fifth book of peace. 1st ed. New York : Alfred A. Knopf, 2003.
PS3561.I52 F44 2003

Kittredge, William. The nature of generosity. 1st Vintage Departures ed. New York : Vintage, 2001, c2000.
PS3561.I87 Z472 2001

Skloot, Floyd. In the shadow of memory. Lincoln : University of Nebraska Press, c2003.
PS3569.K577 Z47 2003

AUTHORS AND PUBLISHERS. See COPYRIGHT; LITERARY AGENTS.

AUTHORS AND READERS - GREAT BRITAIN - HISTORY - 16TH CENTURY.
Cockcroft, Robert, 1939- Rhetorical affect in early modern writing. New York : Palgrave Macmillan, 2003.
PR428.E56 C63 2003

AUTHORS AND READERS - GREAT BRITAIN - HISTORY - 17TH CENTURY.
Cockcroft, Robert, 1939- Rhetorical affect in early modern writing. New York : Palgrave Macmillan, 2003.
PR428.E56 C63 2003

AUTHORS, CHINESE - BIOGRAPHY.
Zhao, Yaotang. Gu dai zuo jia lun. Di 1 ban. Jinan : Shandong you yi chu ban she, 1994.
PL2277 .C355 1994 <Asian China>

AUTHORS - DISEASES.
Ecriture et maladie. Paris : Editions Imago, c2003.

AUTHORS, ENGLISH - 19TH CENTURY - BIOGRAPHY.
Burton, Sarah, 1963- A double life. London : Viking ; New York : Penguin Putnam, 2003.

AUTHORS, FILIPINO - 20TH CENTURY - BIOGRAPHY.
Feminine voices. [Manila?] : NCCA, c2001-

AUTHORS, FRENCH - 20TH CENTURY - BIOGRAPHY.
Aller, Annelies van, 1946- Levenskunst van twee vrouwen. Budel : Damon, c2001.
PS3527.I865 Z536 2001

AUTHORS, ISRAELI.
Me-ayin naḥalti en shiri. Tel Aviv : Yedi‘ot aḥaronot : Sifre ḥemed, c2002.

AUTHORS, LATIN - BIOGRAPHY.
Radford, Robert T. Cicero. Amsterdam ; New York, NY : Rodopi, 2002.
DG260.C5 R33 2002

AUTHORS - MENTAL HEALTH.
Ecriture et maladie. Paris : Editions Imago, c2003.

AUTHORS, PHILIPPINE. See AUTHORS, FILIPINO.

AUTHORS - PSYCHOLOGY.
Esin, Sergeĭ. Poputnye mysli. Moskva : Literaturnyĭ in-t im. A. M. Gor’kogo, 2002.
PN145 .E755 2002

AUTHORS, ROMAN. See AUTHORS, LATIN.

AUTHORS, WOMEN. See WOMEN AUTHORS.

AUTHORSHIP. See also AUTHORS AND READERS; FICTION - TECHNIQUE; HISTORIOGRAPHY; LITERATURE; REPORT WRITING; RHETORIC.
Esin, Sergeĭ. Poputnye mysli. Moskva : Literaturnyĭ in-t im. A. M. Gor’kogo, 2002.
PN145 .E755 2002

Stafford, Kim Robert. The muses among us. Athens : University of Georgia Press, c2003.
PE1408 .S6667 2003

AUTHORSHIP IN LITERATURE.
Esin, Sergeĭ. Poputnye mysli. Moskva : Literaturnyĭ in-t im. A. M. Gor’kogo, 2002.
PN145 .E755 2002

AUTHORSHIP - PSYCHOLOGICAL ASPECTS.
Esin, Sergeĭ. Poputnye mysli. Moskva : Literaturnyĭ in-t im. A. M. Gor’kogo, 2002.
PN145 .E755 2002

AUTISM.
Hobson, R. Peter. The cradle of thought. New York : Oxford University Press, 2004.
BF720.C63 H63 2004

Hobson, R. Peter. The cradle of thought. London : Macmillan, 2002.
BF720.C63 H63 2002

AUTISM IN CHILDREN.
Yankelevich, Héctor, 1946- Du père à la lettre. Ramonville Saint-Agne : Erès, c2003.

AUTOBIOGRAPHICAL FICTION.
Rhodes, Jewell Parker. Douglass' women. New York, NY : Atria Books, c2002.
1. Black author.

AUTOBIOGRAPHICAL MEMORY.
Campbell, Sue, 1956- Relational remembering. Lanham, Md. ; Oxford : Rowman & Littlefield, c2003.
BF378.A87 C36 2003

Kuhn, Annette. Family secrets. New ed. London ; New York : Verso, 2002.
CT274 .K84 2002

McGaugh, James L. Memory and emotion. New York : Columbia University Press, c2003.
BF378.A87 M34 2003

Memory and emotion. Oxford University Press : New York, 2003.
BF378.A87 M46 2003

AUTOBIOGRAPHICAL MEMORY - CONGRESSES.
Narrative and consciousness. Oxford ; New York : Oxford University Press, c2003.
BF311 .N26 2003

Autobiographies.
Darwin, Charles, 1809-1882. London : Penguin, 2002.

AUTOBIOGRAPHIES - HISTORY AND CRITICISM. See **AUTOBIOGRAPHY.**

AUTOBIOGRAPHY.
Schuster, Shlomit C., 1951- The philosopher's autobiography. Westport, Conn. ; London : Praeger, 2003.
B52.7 .S38 2003

AUTOBIOGRAPHY - HISTORY AND CRITICISM. See **AUTOBIOGRAPHY.**

AUTOBIOGRAPHY - MORAL AND ETHICAL ASPECTS.
Couser, G. Thomas. Vulnerable subjects. Ithaca : Cornell University Press, 2004.
CT25 .C698 2004

AUTOBIOGRAPHY - TECHNIQUE. See **AUTOBIOGRAPHY.**

AUTOBIOGRAPHY - THERAPEUTIC USE.
Henehan, Mary Pat. Integrating spirit and psyche. New York ; London : Haworth Pastoral Press, c2003.
RC489.F45 H46 2003

AUTOBIOGRAPHY - WOMEN AUTHORS.
Ingram, Susan. Zarathustra's sisters. Toronto ; Buffalo : University of Toronto Press, c2003.
PN471 .I537 2003

Rishoi, Christy, 1958- From girl to woman. Albany : State University of New York Press, c2003.
HQ1186.A9 R57 2003

AUTOMATA. See **ROBOTS.**

Automated practical reasoning : algebraic approaches / Jochen Pfalzgraf and Dongming Wang, eds. ; with a foreword by Jim Cunningham. Wien ; New York : Springer-Verlag, c1995. xi, 223 p. ; 25 cm. (Texts and monographs in symbolic computation, 0943-853X) Includes bibliographical references and index. ISBN 3-211-82600-9 (Wien : acid-free paper) ISBN 0-387-82600-9 (New York : acid-free paper) DDC 005.13/1
1. Automatic theorem proving. 2. Practical reason. 3. Reasoning. I. Pfalzgraf, Jochen. II. Wang, Dongming. III. Series.
QA76.9.A96 A9 1995

AUTOMATIC COMPUTERS. See **COMPUTERS.**

AUTOMATIC DATA PROCESSORS. See **COMPUTERS.**

AUTOMATIC THEOREM PROVING.
Automated practical reasoning. Wien ; New York : Springer-Verlag, c1995.
QA76.9.A96 A9 1995

AUTOMATONS. See **ROBOTS.**

AUTOMOBILE DEALERS - UNITED STATES.
United States. Congress. Senate. Committee on Commerce, Science, and Transportation. Subcommittee on Consumer Affairs, Foreign Commerce, and Tourism. Customer choice in automotive repair shops. Washington : U.S. G.P.O. : For sale by the Supt. of Docs., U.S. G.P.O., [Congressional Sales Office], 2003.

AUTOMOBILE DEALERSHIPS. See **AUTOMOBILE DEALERS.**

AUTOMOBILE INDUSTRY AND TRADE. See **AUTOMOBILE DEALERS; AUTOMOBILE REPAIR SHOPS.**

AUTOMOBILE REPAIR SHOPS - UNITED STATES.
United States. Congress. Senate. Committee on Commerce, Science, and Transportation. Subcommittee on Consumer Affairs, Foreign Commerce, and Tourism. Customer choice in automotive repair shops. Washington : U.S. G.P.O. : For sale by the Supt. of Docs., U.S. G.P.O., [Congressional Sales Office], 2003.

AUTOMOBILES - MAINTENANCE AND REPAIR. See **AUTOMOBILE REPAIR SHOPS.**

AUTOMOTIVE REPAIR SHOPS. See **AUTOMOBILE REPAIR SHOPS.**

AUTONOMY. See also **SELF-DETERMINATION, NATIONAL.**
McLeod, Carolyn. Self-trust and reproductive autonomy. Cambridge, Mass. : MIT Press, c2002.
RG133.5 .M39 2002

AUTONOMY (PHILOSOPHY).
Araujo, Marcelo de. Scepticism, freedom and autonomy. Berlin : De Gruyter, 2003.

Groarke, Louis. The good rebel. Madison [N.J.] : Fairleigh Dickinson University Press ; London ; Cranbury, NJ : Associated University Presses, c2002.
B808.67 .G76 2002

AUTONOMY (PSYCHOLOGY).
Handbook of self-determination research. Soft cover ed. Rochester, NY : University of Rochester Press, 2004.
BF575.A88 H36 2004

Martin, Jack, 1950- Psychology and the question of agency. Albany : State University of New York Press, c2003.
BF575.A88 M37 2003

AUTOPOIESIS.
Autopoietic organization theory. Oslo, Norway : Abstrakt forlag ; Malmö, Sweden : Liber Ekonomi ; Herndon, VA, USA : Copenhagen Business School Press, c2003.
HD31 .A825 2003

Autopoietic organization theory : drawing on Niklas Luhmann's social systems perspective / Tore Bakken and Tor Hernes (eds.). Oslo, Norway : Abstrakt forlag ; Malmö, Sweden : Liber Ekonomi ; Herndon, VA, USA : Copenhagen Business School Press, c2003. 299 p. : ill. ; 25 cm. "The idea for this book was conceived after a conference organised by the Norwegian School of Management in Oslo in March 2001 on the theme of Niklas Luhmann's autopoietic theory and organization theory. From that conference a special issue was prepared of 'Nordiske Organisasjonsstudier.' Whereas the contributors to that issue were all Scandinavian, other colleagues, notably from Germany and Britain, have since joined us in the effort of producing this edited volume."--Preface, p. 5. Includes bibliographical references. Article by Luhmann (p. 31-52) translated from the German. ISBN 82-7935-022-5 (Norway : pbk.) ISBN 87-630-0103-9 (rest of the world : pbk.)
1. Luhmann, Niklas. 2. Management. 3. Organization. 4. Autopoiesis. 5. Social systems. I. Bakken, Tore. II. Hernes, Tor.
HD31 .A825 2003

Aux frontières des attitudes : entre le politique et le religieux : textes en hommage à Guy Michelat / contributions réunies par Jean-Marie Donegani, Sophie Duchesne & Florence Haegel. Paris, France : Harmattan, c2002. 398 p. : ill. ; 22 cm. (Collection Logiques politiques) Includes bibliographical references. ISBN 2-7475-2789-1 DDC 300
1. Political sociology. 2. Religion and sociology. 3. Sociology - Methodology. 4. Sociology - Research. I. Michelat, Guy. II. Donegani, Jean-Marie. III. Duchesne, Sophie. IV. Haegel, Florence. V. Series.

Aux origines de la sexualité humaine.
Zwang, Gérard. 1re éd. Paris : Presses universitaires de France, 2002.
HQ21 .Z935 2002

Auxier, Randall E., 1961-.
The philosophy of Marjorie Grene. Chicago : Open Court, c2002.
B945.G734 P47 2002

AUXILIARY SCIENCES OF HISTORY. See **ARCHAEOLOGY; ARCHIVES; BIOGRAPHY; CIVILIZATION; HISTORY.**

Auzépy, Marie-France.
Palais et pouvoir. Vincennes : Presses universitaires de Vincennes, c2003.

AVALOKITEŚVARA (BUDDHIST DEITY).
[Aids to Sadhana series. Tibetan & Sanskrit. Selections.] Sādhanamālā, Avalokiteśvara section. Delhi : Adroit Publishers ; New Delhi : Distributors, Akhil Book Distributors, 2002.
BQ8915 .S23 2002

LeBeau, Kara R. Guan yin's chakra meditations. Boulder, Colo. : Mahasimhananda Press, c2001.
BF1442.C53 L43 2001

Xing, Li. Guanyin. Beijing di 2 ban. Beijing : Xue yuan chu ban she, 2001.
BQ4710.A8 X564 2001

AVALOKITEŚVARA (BUDDHIST DEITY) - IN LITERATURE.
Sun, Changwu. Zhongguo wen xue zhong di Weimo yu Guanyin. Di 1 ban. Beijing : Gao deng jiao yu chu ban she : Xin hua shu dian zong dian Beijing fa xing suo fa xing, 1996.
PL2275.B8 S85 1996 <Orien China>

AVANT-GARDE (AESTHETICS). See **POSTMODERNISM.**

Avdeev, V. B. (Vladimir Borisovich) Metafizicheskaia antropologiia / V.B. Avdeev. Moskva : Belye al'vy, 2002. 256 p. : ill. ; 21 cm. (Biblioteka rasovoĭ mysli) ISBN 5761901404
1. Nationalism - Russia (Federation) 2. Racism. 3. Racism in anthropology. I. Title. II. Series: Biblioteka rasovoĭ mysli.
DK510.763 .A93 2002

Russkaia rasovaia teoriia do 1917 goda. Moskva : Feri-V, 2002.

Aveni, Anthony F. Behind the crystal ball : magic, science, and the occult from antiquity through the New Age / Anthony Aveni. Rev. ed. Boulder, Colo. : University Press of Colorado, c2002. xvii, 361 p. : ill. ; 23 cm. Includes bibliographical references (p. 333-346) and index. CONTENTS: Middle East exotica -- The ancient art of hepatoscopy -- The Greek paradox -- Magic in the Roman Empire -- The new outcasts -- Knowledge through number and the Word -- Pathways to knowledge -- Resurrection of the Kabbalah -- Music of the spheres -- Two sides of the coin of Alchemy -- Rise of the Clear Seer -- Medieval astrology -- The devil and the proliferation of good and evil -- It's witchcraft -- Summary: who turned on the lights? -- Rochester rap -- Before Hydesville -- Mr. Sludge -- DDH to HPB -- After the foxes -- My body, my map -- Summary: a light that failed? -- Who's a magician? -- Magic in the twentieth century -- Different time, same channel -- PK wars -- The personalized magic of healing -- You are what you eat -- Come fly with me -- Life after life -- Crystals -- Geomancy -- Summary: on shifting ground -- Is magic a religion? -- Magic and science -- Anthropologists encounter the occult -- Summary: crossing curves in an age of interconnectedness. ISBN 0-87081-671-3 (pbk. : alk. paper) DDC 133.4/3/09
1. Magic - History. 2. Occultism and science. I. Title.
BF1589 .A9 2002

The book of the year : a brief history of our seasonal holidays / Anthony F. Aveni. New York : Oxford University Press, 2003. xiv, 192 p., [16] p. of plates : ill. ; 25 cm. Includes bibliographical references (p. [171]-181) and index. ISBN 0-19-515024-4 (cloth) DDC 394.26
1. Holidays - History. 2. Rites and ceremonies. 3. Archaeoastronomy. 4. Biological rhythms. 5. Chronobiology. I. Title.
GT3930 .A94 2003

Conversing with the planets : how science and myth invented the cosmos / Anthony Aveni. Rev. ed. Boulder, Colo. : University Press of Colorado, c2002. xiv, 243 p. : ill. ; 23 cm. Includes bibliographical references (p. 225-231) and index. ISBN 0-87081-673-X (pbk. : alk. paper) DDC 398/.362
1. Cosmology. 2. Cosmology, Ancient. 3. Cosmology, Babylonian. 4. Archaeoastronomy. 5. Science fiction. 6. Anthropology. I. Title.
QB981 .A99 2002

Empires of time : calendars, clocks, and cultures / Anthony Aveni. Rev. ed. Boulder, Colo. : University Press of Colorado, c2002. xv, 332 p. : ill. ; 23 cm. (Mesoamerican worlds) Includes bibliographical references (p. [305]-320) and index. ISBN 0-87081-672-1 (pbk. : alk. paper)

DDC 529
1. Time. 2. Archaeoastronomy. I. Title. II. Series.
QB209 .A94 2002

Aventuras do sentido : psicanálise e lingüística / Margareth Schäffer (org.) ... [et al.] ; Francisco Franke Settineri ... [et al.]. Porto Alegre : EDIPUCRS, 2002. 264 p. ; 21 cm. Includes bibliographical references. ISBN 85-7430-275-9
1. Psycholinguistics. I. Schäffer, Margareth. II. Settineri, Francisco Franke.

Avenues for success.
Binford, Virgie M. Franklin, Tenn. : Providence House Publishers, c2001.
BF637.S8 B477 2001

AVERROËS, 1126-1198.
Kemal, Salim. The philosophical poetics of Alfarabi, Avicenna and Averroes. London ; New York : RoutledgeCurzon, 2003.

AVERSION. See **HATE.**

AVERSION - CONGRESSES.
Ekel. 1. Aufl. Hürtgenwald : G. Pressler, c2003.
BF575.A886 E34 2003

AVIATION. See **AERONAUTICS.**

AVIATION ACCIDENTS. See **AIRCRAFT ACCIDENTS.**

AVIATION INDUSTRY. See **AIRCRAFT INDUSTRY; AIRLINES.**

AVICENNA, 980-1037.
Kemal, Salim. The philosophical poetics of Alfarabi, Avicenna and Averroes. London ; New York : RoutledgeCurzon, 2003.

Aviner, Shelomoh Ḥayim, ha-Kohen. Be-ahavah uve-emunah / Shelomoh Ḥayim ha-Kohen Aviner. Yerushalayim : [h. mo. l.], 760-762 [1999 or 2000-2001 or 2002] 2 v. ; 22 cm.
1. Judaism - Essence, genius, nature. 2. Judaism - Customs and practices. 3. Ethics, Jewish. 4. Jewish law. I. Title.
BM565 .A93 1999

Perurim mi-shulḥan gavoah : mi-torato shel ha-rav Yehuda Le'on Ashkenazi / Shelomoh Aviner. Yerushalayim : Sifriyat Ḥayah, 762 [2001 or 2002] 63 p. ; 21 cm.
1. Askénazi, Léon. 2. Ethics, Jewish. I. Title.

'Avodat 'avodah.
Admur ha-G. ha-Ḳ., Sheliṭa. ['Avodat 'avodah (Torah)] Sefer 'Avodat 'avodah. Kiryat Ṭohsh, Ḳanada : N. M. Hershḳoviṭsh, 763 [2002 or 2003]

L'avventura del sogno.
Giachery, Emerico. Roma : A. Stango, 2002.

AWAKENING (RELIGION). See **RELIGIOUS AWAKENING.**

AWAKENING, RELIGIOUS. See **RELIGIOUS AWAKENING.**

Awakening to wisdom.
Pike, Diane Kennedy. Scottsdale, AZ : LP Publications, c2003.
BF1999 .P5485 2003

AWARENESS. See also **RACE AWARENESS; SELF-PERCEPTION.**
Agency and self-awareness. Oxford : Clarendon Press ; New York : Oxford University Press, 2003.

Estep, Myrna. A theory of immediate awareness. Dordrecht ; Boston : Kluwer Academic Publishers, 2003.
BF311 .E79 2003

Roehle, Friedrich, 1916-1995. Die Struktur des Bewusstseins. Frankfurt am Main ; New York : Peter Lang, c2001.

Awọn omi Oṣàlá.
Beniste, José. As águas de Oxalá = Rio de Janeiro, RJ, [Brazil] : Editora Bertrand Brasil, c2001 (2002 printing)
BL2592.C35 B46 2001

Axe Néo-7 art contemporain.
Musiol, Marie-J. (Marie-Jeanne), 1950- Corps de lumière. Hull, Québec : Axe Néo-7, art contemporain, [2001?]

AXIOLOGY. See **VALUES.**

AYAHUASCA - PSYCHOTROPIC EFFECTS.
Shanon, Benny. The antipodes of the mind. Oxford ; New York : Oxford University Press, 2002.
BF209.A93 S53 2002

Ayers, Mary, 1960- The eyes of shame / by Mary Ayers. 1st ed. Hove, East Sussex ; New York : Brunner-Routledge, 2003. p. cm. Includes bibliographical references and index. ISBN 1-58391-287-8 (alk. paper) ISBN 1-58391-288-6 (pbk. : alk. paper) DDC 152.4
1. Object relations (Psychoanalysis) 2. Attachment behavior. 3. Gaze - Psychological aspects. 4. Shame. 5. Psychoanalysis. I. Title.
BF175.5.O24 A94 2003

Āyurvedīya mānasaroga cikitsā.
Upādhyāya, Govindaprasāda. 1. saṃskaraṇa. Vārāṇasī : Caukhabā Surabhāratī Prakāśana ; Dillī : Anya Prāptisthāna Caukhambā Saṃskrta Pratishṭhāna, 2000.
R605 .U67 2000

Azbuka Germesa Trismegista.
Dlīasin, G. G. (Gennadiĭ Gennad'vich) Azbuka Germesa Trismegista, ili, Molekuli︠a︡rnai︠a︡ taĭnost' myshlenii︠a︡. Izd. 2-e. Moskva : Izd-vo "Belye al'vy", 2002.
BF1616 .D58 2002

Azbuka Germesa Trismegista, ili, Molekuli︠a︡rnai︠a︡ taĭnost' myshlenii︠a︡.
Dlīasin, G. G. (Gennadiĭ Gennad'vich) Izd. 2-e. Moskva : Izd-vo "Belye al'vy", 2002.
BF1616 .D58 2002

Azizi︠a︡n, I. A. (Irina Atykovna).
Arkhitekturnoe soznanie XX-XXI vekov. Moskva : Ėditorial URSS, 2001.
NA712 .A87 2001

Azoulay, Paul. Uncle Sam : mythes & légendes / Paul Azoulay ; dessins de Anne-Odile Huet-Humeau. Anglet : Atlantica, c2002. 163 p. : col. ill. ; 22 x 24 cm. Includes bibliographical references. ISBN 2-8439-4519-4 DDC 970
1. Uncle Sam (Symbolic character) 2. Folklore - Political aspects - United States. 3. Mythology - Political aspects - United States. 4. National characteristics, American. 5. Signs and symbols - United States. I. Title. II. Title: Uncle Sam : mythes et légendes

Azpeitia Gimeno, Marta.
Piel que habla. Barcelona : Icaria, [2001]
BF697.5.B63 P54 2001

AZTEC INDIANS. See **AZTECS.**

AZTECA INDIANS. See **AZTECS.**

AZTECAN INDIANS. See **AZTECS.**

AZTECS - MISCELLANEA.
Rainieri, Caelum. The Nahualli animal oracle. Rochester, Vt. : Bear & Co., 2003.
BF1773 .R35 2003

Azulai, Tidhar Elon.
['Ets ha-tidhar.] Sidur kavanot 'Ets ha-tidhar. Yerushalayim : Kolel Shemen śaśon, [1998?]
1. Ḳeri'at shema 'al ha-miṭah.

B'a-ok nikib'ij k'ïy ch'ab'äl chwa jun achib'äl.
Morales Tomas, Marco Antonio. Una gráfica dice más que mil palabras = Guatemala : ESEDIR : Editorial Saqil Tzij, 1999.

Babalola, E. O.
Adeniyi, M. O. Yoruba Muslim-Christian understanding. Majiyagbe, Ipaja, Nigeria : Eternal Communications, 2001.
1. Black author.

African cultural revolution of Islam and Christianity in Yoruba land / edited by E. O. Babalola. Ipaja-Lagos : Eternal Communications, 2002. 127 p. ; 20 cm. Includes bibliographical references.
1. Religion and culture - Nigeria. 2. Yoruba (African people) - Religion. 3. Christianity - Nigeria. 4. Islam - Nigeria. 5. Religion and politics - Nigeria. 6. Black author. I. Title.

Studies in the theology and sociology of Yoruba indigenous religion. Lagos, Nigeria : Concept Publications (Nig.), 2002.

Babarinde, A. O. The end of man / by A.O. Babarinde. Lagos, Nigeria : Christ Foundation Baptist Church, 2001. 80 p. ; 19 cm. ISBN 9780520694
1. Death - Religious aspects - Christianity. 2. Man (Christian theology) 3. Future life. 4. Resurrection. 5. Black author. I. Title.

Babel (Arles, France)
(368.) Leibniz, Gottfried Wilhelm, Freiherr von, 1646-1716. Réfutation inédite de Spinoza. Arles [France] : Actes Sud ; [Montréal] : Leméac, 1999.

Babel (Arles, France). Philosophiques.
Leibniz, Gottfried Wilhelm, Freiherr von, 1646-1716. Réfutation inédite de Spinoza. Arles [France] : Actes Sud ; [Montréal] : Leméac, 1999.

Baber, Christopher, 1964- Cognition and tool use : forms of engagement in human and animal use of tools / Christopher Baber. London ; New York : Taylor & Francis, 2003. p. cm. Includes bibliographical references and index. ISBN 0-415-27728-0 (hbk.) ISBN 0-415-27729-9 (pbk.) DDC 152.3/8
1. Cognition and culture. 2. Tools. 3. Tool use in animals. I. Title.
BF311 .B228 2003

Babich, Babette E., 1956-.
Nietzsche and the sciences. Dordrecht ; Boston : Kluwer Academic Publishers, c1999-
B3318.K7 N54 1999

BABIES. See **INFANTS.**

Babin, Pierre. La fabrique du sexe / Pierre Babin ; entretien avec Philippe Petit. Paris : Textuel, [1999] 130 p. ; 21 cm. (Conversations pour demain, 1271-9900 ; no 17) Includes bibliographical references (p. 129-130). ISBN 2-909317-83-8
1. Sex (Psychology) 2. Psychoanalysis. 3. Babin, Pierre - Interviews. 4. Psychoanalysts - France - Interviews. I. Petit, Philippe. II. Title. III. Series.
BF175.5.S48 B23 1999

BABIN, PIERRE - INTERVIEWS.
Babin, Pierre. La fabrique du sexe. Paris : Textuel, [1999]
BF175.5.S48 B23 1999

BABY BOOM GENERATION - UNITED STATES.
McEnroe, Colin. My father's footsteps. New York : Warner Books, c2003.
PS3563.C3615 M9 2003

BABY BOOMERS. See **BABY BOOM GENERATION.**

BACH, CARL PHILIPP EMANUEL, 1714-1788 - CRITICISM AND INTERPRETATION.
Kellner, Herbert Anton. Musicalische Temperatur der Bachsöhne. Darmstadt : Herbert Anton Kellner, c2001.

Bach, Doris.
21. Goldegger Dialoge. 1. Aufl. Goldegg : Kulturverein Schloss Goldegg, 2002.

BACH, WILHELM FRIEDEMANN, 1710-1784 - CRITICISM AND INTERPRETATION.
Kellner, Herbert Anton. Musicalische Temperatur der Bachsöhne. Darmstadt : Herbert Anton Kellner, c2001.

Bachelard critique de Husserl.
Barsotti, Bernard. Paris : Harmattan, c2002.
B2430.B254 B37 2002

Bachelard, Gaston.
[Formation de l'esprit scientifique. English]
The formation of the scientific mind / Gaston Bachelard ; introduced, translated and annotated by Mary McAllester Jones. Manchester : Clinamen, c2002. 258 p. ; 24 cm. (Philosophy of science) Includes bibliographical references and index. Translated from the French. ISBN 1-903083-23-0
1. Knowledge, Theory of. 2. Science - Philosophy. I. Title.

BACHELARD, GASTON, 1884-1962.
Barsotti, Bernard. Bachelard critique de Husserl. Paris : Harmattan, c2002.
B2430.B254 B37 2002

Bachman, Thomas T.
Graham, Douglas, 1950- Ideation. Hoboken, N.J. : John Wiley & Sons, Inc., 2004.
BF408 .G664 2004

BACK.
The Alexander technique [videorecording]. New York, N.Y. : Wellspring Media, c1999.

BACK - DISEASES. See **BACKACHE.**

BACK PAIN. See **BACKACHE.**

BACKACHE - EXERCISE THERAPY.
The Alexander technique [videorecording]. New York, N.Y. : Wellspring Media, c1999.

Backgrounds of early Christianity.
Ferguson, Everett, 1933- 3rd ed. Grand Rapids, Mich. : W.B. Eerdmans, c2003.

Bacon, Terry R. Winning behavior : what the smartest, most successful companies do differently / Terry R. Bacon and David G. Pugh. New York : AMACOM, c2003. xv, 352 p. : ill. ; 24 cm. Includes bibliographical references and index. ISBN 0-8144-7163-3 DDC 658
1. Organizational behavior. 2. Organizational effectiveness. I. Pugh, David G. (David George), 1944- II. Title.
HD58.7 .B3423 2003

Bacques, Marie-Christine.
Pistes didactiques et chemins historiques. Paris : Harmattan, 2003.

Bade, Heide.
Strukturbildung und Lebensstil. München : Ernst Reinhardt, c2002.

Badiou, Alain. L'éthique : essai sur la conscience du mal / Alain Badiou. Caen : Nous, c2003. 120 p. : 20 cm. Includes bibliographical references. ISBN 2-913549-11-X DDC 170
1. Good and evil. 2. Ethics. I. Title.

Zupančič, Alenka. Esthétique du désir, éthique de la jouissance. Lecques : Théétète, c2002.

Badurina, Natka.
Gučetić, Nikola Vitov, 1549-1610. [Dialogo della bellezza. Serbo-Croatian & Italian] Dijalog o ljepoti = Dvojezično izd. Zagreb : Društvo hrvatskih književnika, 1995.
BH301.L65 G8318 1995

Baechler, Günther.
Promoting peace. Berne, Switzerland : Staempfli, 2002.

BAER, DONALD MERLE, 1931 - -CAREER IN PSYCHOLOGY.
A small matter of proof. Reno, NV : Context Press, c2003.
BF121 .S545 2003

Baggett, Byrd. The past doesn't have a future, but you do : achieving the future that's in your hands / Byrd Baggett. Nashville, Tenn. : Cumberland House Pub., c2003. p. cm. Table of contents URL: http://www.loc.gov/catdir/toc/ecip043/2003010620.html CONTENTS: The past doesn't have a future, but you do -- Believe in yourself and in your dreams -- Make the most of every day -- Action will turn your dreams into success -- Look at life through the windshield, not the rear view mirror -- When you stop giving, you stop living -- Live each day with passion, and you'll never have regrets -- Thoughts for your journey. ISBN 1-58182-364-9 (hardcover) DDC 158.1
1. Success - Psychological aspects - Quotations, maxims, etc. I. Title.
BF637.S8 B25 2003

Baggini, Julian. The philosopher's toolkit : a compendium of philosophical concepts and methods / Julian Baggini and Peter S. Fosl. Malden, MA : Blackwell Publishers, 2003. ix, 221 p. : 24 cm. Includes bibliographical references and index. ISBN 0-631-22873-X (alk. paper) ISBN 0-631-22874-8 (pbk. : alk. paper) DDC 101
1. Reasoning. 2. Methodology. I. Fosl, Peter S. II. Title.
BC177 .B19 2003

Bagley, Michael T. Red square & green squigglies : creativity methods handbook / by Michael T. Bagley. Woodcliff Lake, NJ : Green Squiggliess Press, c1996. 122 p. : ill. ; 28 cm.
1. Creative thinking - Problems, exercises, etc. 2. Visualization - Problems, exercises, etc. I. Title. II. Title: Red square and green squigglies
BF408 .B327 1996

Bagnall, Jim.
Koberg, Don, 1930- The universal traveler. 4th ed. Menlo Park, Calif. : Crisp Learning, c2003.
BF441 .K55 2003

BAGRIT͡SKIĬ, ĖDUARD, 1895-1934.
Spivak, M. L. Posmertnai͡a diagnostika genial'nosti. Moskva : Agraf, 2001.
BF416.A1 S68 2001

Bahnasāwī, Ḥusām. Ahammīyat al-rabṭ bayna al-tafkīr al-lughawī 'inda al-'Arab wa- naẓarīyāt al-baḥth al-lughawī al-ḥadīth : fī majālay mafhūm al- lughah wa-al-dirāsāt al-naḥwīyah / ta'līf Ḥusām al-Bahnasāwī. al-Qāhirah : Maktabat al-Thaqāfah al-Dīnīyah, 1994. 64 p. ; 24 cm. Includes bibliographical references (p. 61-64). In Arabic.
1. Arabic language - Grammar - History. 2. Language and languages. I. Title.
PJ6106 .B35 1994 <Orien Arab>

Bahni͡uk, Anatoliĭ. Filosofii͡a : navchal'nyĭ posibnyk dli͡a koledzhiv, tekhnikumiv, uchylyshch / Anatoliĭ Bahni͡uk. Rivne : [s.n.], 1997. v. : ill., ports. ; 20 cm. Authorized for instructional purposes. Includes bibliographical references and index.
1. Philosophy. I. Title.

Bahr, Hans-Dieter. Den Tod denken / Hans-Dieter Bahr. München : Fink, 2002. 164 p. ; 22 cm. Includes bibliographical references (p. [155]-160) and index. ISBN 3-7705-3651-7 (pbk.)
1. Death. I. Title.

Baḥya ben Joseph ibn Paḳuda, 11th cent.
[Hidāyah ilá farā'iḍ al-qulūb]
Torat ḥovat ha-levavot ha-mefo'ar / meha-rav ... Baḥya ... b.R. Yosef ; 'im sheloshah perushim ... Marpe le-nefesh ... Ṭuv ha-levanon ... Pat leḥem. Nyu Yorḳ : Y. Vais : Sṭar Ḳompozishan : [Hotsa'at Aṭeret], 760 [2000] 2 v. ; 25 cm. Cover title: Ḥovat ha-levavot ha-mefo'ar. Includes index.
1. Ethics, Jewish. I. Refa'el ben Zekharyah, mi-ḳ.ḳ. Yampola, 18th cent. Marpe la-nefesh. II. Zamosc, Israel ben Moses, Halevi, ca. 1700-1772. Ṭuv ha-levanon. III. Kats, Ḥayim Avraham ben Aryeh Leyb, 18th/19th cent. Pat leḥem. IV. Title. V. Title: Ḥovat ha-levavot ha-mefo'ar VI. Title: Torat ḥovot ha-levavot ha-mefo'ar

Bai hua wen xue shi.
Hu, Zhi, 1891-1962. Di 1 ban. Beijing : Dong fang chu ban she, 1996.

Baifus, Ya'aḳov Yiśra'el, ha-Kohen.
[Leḳaḥ ṭov (Ḥayim shel Torah)]
Yalḳuṭ Leḳaḥ ṭov : ḥayim shel Torah ... : śiḥot li-vene dorenu ... / devarim she-ne'emru ye-nikhtevu 'al yede Ya'aḳov Yiśra'el ha-Kohen Baifus. Rekhasim : "Tashbar ha-Rav", 760- [1999 or 2000- v. ; 25 cm.
1. Bible. - O.T. - Pentateuch - Sermons. 2. Ethics, Jewish. I. Title.

Bailey, Gordon, 1946- Ideology : structuring identities in contemporary life / Gordon Bailey and Noga Gayle. Peterborough, Ont. : Broadview Press, 2003. vi, 175 p. ; 22 cm. Includes bibliographical references (p. 155-165) and index. ISBN 1-55111-506-9 DDC 303.3/72
1. Ideology. 2. Socialization. I. Gayle, Noga Agnus. II. Title.

Bailey, Helen.
Thomson, Emma. Little book of happiness. 1st ed. London : Hodder Children's, 2001.
BF575.H27 .T56 2001

Bailey, J. Michael. The man who would be queen : the psychology of gender-bending and transsexualism / J. Michael Bailey. Washington, D.C. : Joseph Henry Press, c2003. xii, 233 p. ; 24 cm. Includes bibliographical references (p. 215-219) and index. CONTENTS: The boy who would be princess -- Princess Danny -- Growing pains -- The boy who would not be a girl -- The man he might become -- Gay femininity -- Gay masculinity -- Danny's uncle -- Is homosexuality a recent invention? -- Women who once were boys -- Terese and Cher -- Men trapped in men's bodies -- In search of womanhood and men -- Autogynephilic and homosexual transsexuals : how to tell them apart -- Becoming a woman -- Epilogue. ISBN 0-309-08418-0 (pbk. : alk. paper) DDC 305.38/9664
1. Gay men - United States - Psychology - Case studies. 2. Transsexuals - United States - Psychology - Case studies. 3. Homosexuality, Male - Psychological aspects. 4. Transsexualism - Psychological aspects. 5. Gender identity - Psychological aspects. 6. Sexual orientation - Psychological aspects. 7. Nature and nurture. I. Title.
HQ76.2.U5 B35 2003

Bailey, Michael David, 1971- Battling demons : witchcraft, heresy, and reform in the late Middle Ages / Michael D. Bailey. University Park, Pa. : Pennsylvania State University Press, c2003. xii, 200 p. : ill. ; 25 cm. (The magic in history series) Includes bibliographical references (p. [193]-195) and index. CONTENTS: Introduction: Witchcraft, heresy, and reform in the fifteenth century -- The life of Johannes Nider -- Witchcraft in the writings of Johannes Nider -- The threat of heresy : Hussites, free spirits, and beguines -- Reform of the orders, reform of the religious spirit -- The reform of the Christian world : Johannes Nider's Formicarius -- Witchcraft and reform -- Conclusion: Witchcraft and the world of the late Middle Ages -- Appendix I: Chronology of Nider's life and datable works -- Appendix II: Dating of Nider's major works used in this study -- Appendix III: Manuscript copies of Nider's treatises. ISBN 0-271-02225-6 (alk. paper) ISBN 0-271-02226-4 (pbk. : alk. paper) DDC 133.4/3/09409024
1. Nider, Johannes, - ca. 1380-1438. 2. Witchcraft - History - To 1500. I. Title. II. Series: Magic in history.
BF1569 .B35 2003

Historical dictionary of witchcraft / by Michael D. Bailey. 1st ed. Lanham, Md. : Scarecrow Press, 2003. p. cm. (Historical dictionaries of religions, philosophies, and movements ; no. 47) Includes bibliographical references and index. Table of contents URL: http://www.loc.gov/catdir/toc/ecip044/2003011520.html ISBN 0-8108-4860-0 (alk. paper) DDC 133.4/3/03
1. Witchcraft - History - Dictionaries. I. Title. II. Series.
BF1566 .B25 2003

BAILLIE, JOHN, 1886-1960.
Hood, Adam, 1960- Baillie, Oman and Macmurray. Aldershot, England ; Burlington, VT : Ashgate, c2003.
BR110 .H575 2003

Baillie, Oman and Macmurray.
Hood, Adam, 1960- Aldershot, England ; Burlington, VT : Ashgate, c2003.
BR110 .H575 2003

Bain, Dwight, 1960- Destination success : a map for living out your dreams / Dwight Bain. Grand Rapids, Mich. : F.H. Revell, c2003. 238 p. ; 22 cm. CONTENTS: Secret #1: defining what success means to you -- Envisioning success -- Secret #2: finding success every day -- What to do with the Elvis in you -- Facing your success fears -- Secret #3: building success by mastering yourself -- Self-sabotage : the most dangerous part of you -- Secret #4: developing personal discipline to discover your destiny -- Secret #5: belief : finding your hidden source of inner strength -- Secret #6: opportunity : discovering your success magnet -- Secret #7: excellence : living the life you've always wanted -- Success seekers keep climbing. ISBN 0-8007-5796-3 (pbk.) DDC 158.1
1. Success - Psychological aspects. I. Title.
BF637.S8 B314 2003

Baines, John.
[Hombre estelar. English]
The stellar man / by John Baines ; edited by the editorial staff of the John Baines Institute, Inc. ; [translated from the Spanish by Margaret L. Nuñez]. 2nd ed. New York : John Baines Institute, Inc., 2002. xii, 310 p. : ill. ; 21 cm. (Hermetic philosophy ; bk. 2) ISBN 1-88269-204-7 DDC 135/.45
1. Hermetism. 2. Human beings - Miscellanea. I. Title. II. Series.
BF1621 .B3513 2002

Bair, Deirdre. Jung : a biography / Deirdre Bair. Boston : Little, Brown, 2003. p. cm. Includes bibliographical references and index. ISBN 0-316-07665-1 (alk. paper) DDC 150.19/5/092;
1. Jung, C. G. - (Carl Gustav), - 1875-1961. 2. Psychoanalysts - Switzerland - Biography. I. Title.
BF109.J8 B35 2003

Baker, Alan. The encyclopedia of alien encounters / Alan Baker. London : Virgin, 1999. 272 p., [16] p. of plates : ill., facsim, ports ; 24 cm. Includes bibliographical references. ISBN 1-85227-734-3 DDC 001.94203
1. Human-alien encounters - Encyclopedias. I. Title.

The knight / Alan Baker. Hoboken, N.J. : Wiley, c2003. 217 p. ; 23 cm. Includes bibliographical references (p. 209-212) and index. CONTENTS: Introduction -- The mounted warrior -- From blood to laughter -- The knight's equipment -- Love and war -- Castles and siegecraft -- The fall of Jerusalem -- Warriors of Christ -- Mercenaries -- Conclusion : from lance to firearm. ISBN 0-471-25135-6 (cloth : alk. paper) DDC 940.1/088/355
1. Knights and knighthood - Europe - History. 2. Civilization, Medieval. I. Title.
CR4513 .B32 2003

Baker, David B.
Thick description and fine texture. 1st ed. Akron, Ohio : University of Akron Press, 2003.
BF81 .T47 2003

Baker, Marina. Spells for teenage witches : get your way with magical power / Marina Baker. Berkeley, Calif. : Seastone, c2000. 96 p. : col. ill. ; 19 cm. ISBN 1-56975-244-3 DDC 133.4/4
1. Witchcraft. 2. Charms. 3. Teenagers - Miscellanea. I. Title.
BF1571.5.T44 B34 2000

Baker, Mary.
Vernes, Jean-René. The existence of the external world. Ottawa : University of Ottawa Press, c2000.

Bakken, Tore.
Autopoietic organization theory. Oslo, Norway : Abstrakt forlag ; Malmö, Sweden : Liber Ekonomi ; Herndon, VA, USA : Copenhagen Business School Press, c2003.
HD31 .A825 2003

Balagushḳin, E. G. (Evgeniĭ Gennad'evich)
Netraditsionnye religii v sovremennoĭ Rossii : morfologicheskiĭ analiz / E.G. Balagushkin. Moskva : Rossiĭskai͡a akademii͡a nauk, Institut filosofii, 1999-2002. 2 v. ; 17 cm. "Nauchnoe izdanie"--Colophon. Includes bibliographical references. ISBN 5201020127 (ch. 1) ISBN 5201020941 (ch. 2)
1. Russia (Federation) - Religion. 2. Sects - Russia (Federation) 3. Cults - Russia (Federation) I. Title.
BL980.R8 B35 1999

BALANCE OF NATURE. *See* **ECOLOGY.**

BALANCE OF POWER - HISTORY - 18TH CENTURY.
York, Neil Longley. Turning the world upside down. Westport, Conn. ; London : Praeger, 2003.
E210 .Y67 2003

Balancing the scales : an examination of the manipulation and transformation of symbolic concepts of women / edited by Marie A. Conn, Therese McGuire. Lanham, Md. ; Oxford : University Press of America, c2003. xxx, 134 p. : ill. ; 22 cm. Includes bibliographical references and index. ISBN 0-7618-2513-4 (pbk. : alk. paper) DDC 305.42
1. Sex role. 2. Femininity. 3. Archetype (Psychology) 4. Sexism. 5. Sexism in religion. I. Conn, Marie A., 1944- II. McGuire, Therese.
HQ1075 .B3417 2003

Balashov, N. I. (Nikolaĭ Ivanovich), 1919-.
Svobodnyĭ vzgliad na literaturu. Moskva : Nauka, 2002.

BALASHOV, N. I. (NIKOLAĬ IVANOVICH), 1919-.
Svobodnyĭ vzgliad na literaturu. Moskva : Nauka, 2002.

Baldiserra, Gabriella.
Sentieri della mente. 1. ed. Torino : Bollati Boringhieri, 2001.

Baldock, John, 1948-.
The young, the old, and the state. Cheltenham, UK ; Northampton, MA : E. Elgar Pub., c2003.
HQ778.5 .Y69 2003

Baldriga, Irene. L'occhio della lince : i primi lincei tra arte, scienza e collezionismo : 1603-1630 / Irene Baldriga. Roma : Accademia nazionale dei Lincei, 2002. x, 340 p. : ill. ; 28 cm. (Storia dell'Accademia dei Lincei. Studi ; 3) Includes bibliographical references and index. ISBN 88-218-0867-X DDC 506
1. Lyceums - History - 17th century. 2. Lyceums - Italy - History - 17th century. 3. Learned institutions and societies - Italy - History - 17th century. 4. Learned institutions and societies - History - 17th century. 5. Europe - Intellectual life - 17th century. I. Title. II. Series.

Baldus, Claus, 1947- Weg im Nicht : Wiederkehr eines Lächelns / Claus Baldus. Stuttgart : Hatje, c1994. 34 p. ; 26 cm. Half-title: Weg im Nicht. Includes bibliographical references (p. 25-34). ISBN 3-7757-0532-5
1. Skepticism. 2. Self (Philosophy) 3. Subjectivity. 4. Perspective (Philosophy) I. Title. II. Title: Weg im Nicht

BALDWIN, JAMES MARK, 1861-1934.
Evolution and learning. Cambridge, Mass. : MIT Press, c2003.
BF698.95 .E95 2003

BALINESE DRAMA. *See* **KECAK (DANCE DRAMA).**

BALKAN PENINSULA - LITERATURES. *See* **GREEK LITERATURE.**

Ball, Pamela, 1940- A woman's way to wisdom : through an understanding of her sexuality & relationships / Pamela J. Ball. London ; New York : Quantum, 2002. 318 p. ; 24 cm. Includes bibliographical references and index. ISBN 0-572-02767-2 DDC 158.082
1. Self-actualization (Psychology) 2. Women - Psychology. I. Title.

The ballad of Carl Drega.
Suprynowicz, Vin. Reno, NV : Mountain Media, 2002.

BALLET. *See* **CHOREOGRAPHY.**

BALLET - STUDY AND TEACHING.
The peak performance series. Vol. [4] [videorecording]. Longwood, Fla. : Pamela Bolling Enterprises, c1999.

BALLOONS. *See* **AERONAUTICS.**

BALLS (PARTIES). *See* **DANCE.**

Balmès, Marc. Pour un plein accès à l'acte d'être avec Thomas d'Aquin et Aristote : réenraciner le De ente et essentia, prolonger la Métaphysique / Marc Balmès. Paris : Harmattan, c2003. 191 p. ; 22 cm. (Ouverture philosophique) Includes bibliographical references and index. ISBN 2-7475-3980-6 DDC 180
1. Thomas, - Aquinas, Saint, - 1225?-1274. - De ente et essentia. 2. Aristotle. - Metaphysics. 3. Ontology. I. Title. II. Series: Collection L'ouverture philosophique.

Balota, D. A.
Cognitive psychology. New York : Psychology Press, 2003.
BF201 .C642 2003

Balsa de Medusa (Series)
(121.) Tomás Ferré, Facundo. Formas artísticas y sociedad de masas. Madrid : Antonio Machado Libros, c2001.

BALTHASAR, HANS URS VON, 1905-.
Luciani Rivero, Rafael Francisco. El misterio de la diferencia. Roma : Pontificia università gregoriana, 2001.

Martinelli, Paolo, 1958- Vocazione e stati di vita del cristiano. Roma : Collegio San Lorenzo da Brindisi, 2001.

Bambini, sogni, furori.
Rossi, Paolo, 1923- 1. ed. in "Campi del sapere.". Milano : Feltrinelli, 2001.
BF41 .R67 2001

Bame Bame, Michael. Death and everlasting life / Michael Bame Bame. Nairobi, Kenya : All Africa Conference of Churches, 1994. 102 p. ; 21 cm.
1. Eschatology. 2. Death. 3. Future life - Christianity. I. Title.

Bamnolk̦er, Shimshon ben Eliyahu.
Śiḥot musar Da'at u-tevunah. Ashdod : Sh. ben E. Bamnolk̦er, 761 [2001]
BJ1280 .B34 2001

Bancroft, John.
Sexual development in childhood. Bloomington : Indiana University Press, 2003.
BF723.S4 S47 2003

Bandhold, Hans.
Lindgren, Mats, 1959- Scenario planning. Houndmills [England] ; New York : Palgrave Macmillan, 2002.
HD30.28 .L543 2002

Bands, brands and billions.
Pearlman, Lou. New York : London : McGraw-Hill, 2002.

Bandura, Albert, 1925-.
Qu'est-ce-donc qu'apprendre? Lausanne : Delachaux et Niestlé, 1999.
BF318 .Q84 1999

Banerjee, Manabendu.
[Śilpaśāstra. English & Sanskrit.] Vāstu-śāstram. Calcutta : Sanskrit Pustak Bhandar, 2001.
NA7427 .M34 2001

BANISTERIOPSIS. *See* **AYAHUASCA.**

BANISTERIOPSIS CAAPI. *See* **AYAHUASCA.**

BANISTERIOPSIS INEBRIANS. *See* **AYAHUASCA.**

BANISTERIOPSIS QUITENSIS. *See* **AYAHUASCA.**

Bankart, C. Peter, 1946-.
Psychology and Buddhism. New York : Kluwer Academic/Plenum Publishers, c2003.
BQ4570.P76 P78 2003

Bankes, Steven C.
Lempert, Robert J. Shaping the next one hundred years. Santa Monica, CA : RAND, 2003.
T57.6 .L46 2003

Banks, Amy.
The complete guide to mental health for women. 1st ed. Boston : Beacon Press, c2003.
RC451.4.W6 C65 2003

BANKS AND BANKING. *See* **MONEY.**

Bannister, D. (Donald).
Fransella, Fay. A manual for repertory grid technique. 2nd ed. Hoboken, NJ : Wiley, c2004.
BF698.8.R38 F72 2004

BANQUETS. *See* **DINNERS AND DINING.**

Bansal, Ashwinie Kumar. Vastu / Ashwinie Kumar Bansal. Hauppauge, NY : Barron's, 2002. 144 p. : col. ill. ; 28 cm. Includes bibliographical references (p 141-142) and index. ISBN 0-7641-2106-5 (pbk.) DDC 133.3/33
1. Vāstu. 2. Hindu astrology. 3. Architecture, Hindu. I. Title.
BF1779.V38 B36 2002

Bao, Jialin.
Excursions in Chinese culture. Hong Kong : Chinese University Press, c2002.

BAPTISM - HISTORY.
Keefe, Susan A. Water and the Word. Notre Dame, Ind. : University of Notre Dame Press, c2002.
BR200 .K44 2002

BAR. *See* **LAWYERS.**

Barale, Massimo, 1941-.
Materiali per un lessico della ragione. Pisa : Edizioni ETS, c2001.

Barash, David P. The survival game : how game theory explains the biology of cooperation and competition / David P. Barash. 1st ed. New York : Times Books, 2003. x, 302 p. ; 25 cm. Includes bibliographical references (p. [279]-287) and index. Publisher description URL: http://www.loc.gov/catdir/description/hol032/2003054351.html ISBN 0-8050-7175-X DDC 302
1. Social interaction. 2. Cooperativeness. 3. Competition (Psychology) 4. Choice (Psychology) 5. Game theory. I. Title.

HM1111 .B37 2003

Baratay, Eric. Et l'homme créa l'animal : histoire d'une condition / Eric Baratay. Paris : O. Jacob, c2003. 376 p. ; 24 cm. Includes bibliographical references. ISBN 2-7381-1247-1 DDC 900
1. Human-animal relationships. 2. Animals. 3. Animals and civilization. I. Title.

Barbalet, J. M., 1946-.
Emotions and sociology. Oxford ; Malden, MA : Blackwell Pub./Sociological Review, 2002.

Der Barbar als Kulturheld.
Brock, Bazon, 1936- Köln : DuMont, 2002.

Barbaras, Renaud.
Naturaliser la phénoménologie. Paris : CNRS, c2002.

Barber, Lucy G. (Lucy Grace), 1964- Marching on Washington : the forging of an American political tradition / Lucy G. Barber. Berkeley : University of California Press, c2002. xiv, 323 p. : ill., maps ; 24 cm. Includes bibliographical references and index. CONTENTS: "Without precedent" : Coxey's Army invades Washington, 1894 -- A "national" demonstration : the Woman Suffrage Procession and Pageant, March 3, 1913 -- "A new type of lobbying" : the Veterans' Bonus March of 1932 -- "Pressure, more pressure, and still more pressure" : the Negro March on Washington and its cancellation, 1941 -- "In the great tradition" : the March on Washington for Jobs and Freedom, August 28, 1963 -- The "Spring Offensive" of 1971 : radicals and marches on Washington. ISBN 0-520-22713-1 (alk. paper) DDC 975.3
1. United States - Politics and government - 20th century. 2. United States - Politics and government - 1865-1900. 3. Demonstrations - Washington (D.C.) - History - 20th century. 4. Civil rights movements - United States - History - 20th century. 5. Social movements - United States - History - 20th century. 6. Political participation - United States - History - 20th century. 7. Political culture - United States - History - 20th century. 8. Mall, The (Washington, D.C.) - History - 20th century. 9. Washington (D.C.) - Politics and government - 1878-1967. 10. Washington (D.C.) - Politics and government - 1967-1995. I. Title.
E743 .B338 2002

Barber, Luke.
Weinstein, Matt. Dogs don't bite when a growl will do. 1st ed. New York : Perigee, 2003.
BF637.C5 W445 2003

Barber, Nigel, 1955- The science of romance : secrets of the sexual brain / Nigel Barber. Amherst, N.Y. : Prometheus Books, 2002. 293 p. : ill. ; 24 cm. Includes bibliographical references (p. 269-287) and index. ISBN 1-57392-970-0 (alk. paper) DDC 306.7
1. Sex. 2. Sex (Psychology) 3. Sex differences (Psychology) 4. Man-woman relationships. 5. Genetic psychology. I. Title.
HQ21 .B184 2002

Barbeyrac, Jean, 1674-1744.
Two discourses and a commentary.
Pufendorf, Samuel, Freiherr von, 1632-1694. [De officio hominis et civis. English] The whole duty of man, according to the law of nature. Indianapolis, Ind. : Liberty Fund, c2003.
K457.P8 D4313 2003

Barbiche, Jean-Paul, 1946-.
Des odyssées à travers le temps. Paris : Harmattan, c2002.

Barbieri, Katherine, 1965-.
Globalization and armed conflict. Lanham, Md. : Rowman & Littlefield, c2003.
JZ5538 .G58 2003

The liberal illusion : does trade promote peace? / Katherine Barbieri. Ann Arbor : University of Michigan Press, c2002. xiv, 184 p. ; 24 cm. Includes bibliographical references (p. 163-175) and indexes. CONTENTS: Theories of the trade-conflict relationship -- Investigating the commercial peace -- Interdependence, negotiation, and escalation -- Alternative trends of analysis : the nation-state and the system. ISBN 0-472-11300-3 (acid-free) DDC 303.6/6
1. International trade. 2. International economic relations. 3. Peace. 4. Economic policy. I. Title.
HF1379 .B363 2002

Barbieri, Marcello. The organic codes : an introduction to semantic biology / Marcello Barbieri. Cambridge, UK ; New York : Cambridge University Press, 2003. xiv, 301 p. : ill. ; 24 cm. Includes bibliographical references (p. [279]-293) and index. Publisher description URL: http://www.loc.gov/catdir/description/cam031/2002073767.html Table of contents URL: http://www.loc.gov/catdir/toc/cam031/2002073767.html ISBN 0-521-82414-1 (hbk.) ISBN 0-521-53100-4 (pbk.) DDC 570/.1
1. Biology - Philosophy. 2. Semantics (Philosophy) 3.

Barbillon, Claire.
Evolution (Biology) 4. Developmental biology. 5. Epigenesis - Mathematical models. I. Title.
QH331 .B247 2003

Barbillon, Claire.
Arts en bibliothèques. Paris : Editions du Cercle de la Librairie, c2003.
Z675.A85 A78 2003

Barbosa, Lúcia Helena Siqueira.
Psiquiatria, loucura e arte. São Paulo, SP, Brasil : Edusp, c2002.

Barbre, Claude.
Creative dissent. Westport, Conn. : Praeger Publishers, 2003.
BF173 .C794 2003

Bard, Xavier, 1935- Du plaisir, de la douleur et de quelques autres / Xavier Bard. Paris, France : Harmattan, c2002. 156 p. ; 22 cm. (Ouverture philosophique) ISBN 2-7475-3004-3 DDC 194
1. Pleasure - Philosophy. 2. Pain - Philosophy. 3. Aesthetics. 4. Emotions (Philosophy) I. Title.

Bardah, Asher. Sefer Otsrot av : 'al parashiyot ha-shavu'a : kolel gimatriya'ot, parpera'ot, remazim ye-hidushim meshulavim be-ra'yonot musariyim / ... Asher Bardah. [Bene Berak?] : A. Bardah, 762- [2001 or 2002- v. ; 24 cm. Spine title: Otsrot av. CONTENTS: [1] Be-reshit.
1. Bible. - O.T. - Pentateuch - Sermons. 2. Jewish sermons, Hebrew. 3. Gematria. 4. Ethics, Jewish. I. Title. II. Title: Otsrot av
BS1225.54 .B37 2001

Bardy, Jean. Regard sur "l'évolution créatrice" / Jean Bardy ; préface de François Béal. Paris : Harmattan, c2003. 109 p. ; 22 cm. (Collection Ouverture philosophique) Includes bibliographical references. ISBN 2-7475-3944-X DDC 194
1. Creative ability. 2. Philosophy, Modern - 20th century. I. Béal, François. II. Title. III. Series: Collection L'ouverture philosophique.

Barfod, Werner.
Die Grundsteinmeditation als Schulungsweg. Dornach : Verlag am Goetheanum, c2002.

BARGAINING. *See* **NEGOTIATION.**

Bargh, John A.
The new unconscious. New York : Oxford University Press, 2004.
BF315 .N47 2004

Baritono, Raffaella. La democrazia vissuta : individualismo e pluralismo nel pensiero di Mary Parker Follett / Raffaella Baritono. Torino : La Rosa, c2001. 247 p. ; 21 cm. (Bibliotheca academiae ; 5) Includes bibliographical references (p. 219-248). ISBN 88-7219-047-9 DDC 321
1. Follett, Mary Parker, - 1868-1933. 2. Individualism. 3. Pluralism (Social sciences) 4. Democracy. I. Title. II. Series.

Barkan, Elazar.
Claiming the stones/naming the bones. Los Angeles : Getty Research Institute, c2002.
CC135 .C48 2002

Die Barke der Sonne.
Görg, Manfred. Freiburg im Breisgau : Herder, 2001.
BL2450.R2 G647 2001

Barker, Alan, 1956- The alchemy of innovation : perspectives from the leading edge / Alan Barker. London : Spiro Press, 2002. vii, 224 p. ; 22 cm. Includes bibliographical references (p. [217]-218) and index. ISBN 1-904298-01-X
1. Creative ability in business. 2. Industrial management - Case studies. I. Title.

Barker, Eileen, 1938-.
Challenging religion. London ; New York : Routledge, 2003.
BL60 .C437 2003

Barnard, Frederick M., 1921- Herder on nationality, humanity, and history / F.M. Barnard. Montreal : McGill-Queen's University Press, c2003. xii, 185 p. ; 24 cm. (McGill-Queen's studies in the history of ideas ; 35) Includes bibliographical references and index. ISBN 0-7735-2519-X (bound) ISBN 0-7735-2569-6 (pbk.) DDC 320.01/1
1. Herder, Johann Gottfried, - 1744-1803 - Contributions in political science. 2. Herder, Johann Gottfried, - 1744-1803 - Contributions in philosophy of history. 3. Political science - History - 18th century. 4. History - Philosophy. I. Title. II. Series.

Barnette, Martha. Dog days and dandelions : a lively guide to the animal meanings behind everyday words / Martha Barnette. 1st ed. New York : St. Martin's Press, 2003. xi, 194 p. ; 22 cm. ISBN 0-312-28072-6 DDC 422

1. English language - Etymology - Dictionaries. 2. Animals - Nomenclature (Popular) 3. Animals - Terminology. 4. Animals - Folklore. 5. Figures of speech. I. Title.
PE1583 .B37 2003

Barnhart, Michael, 1956-.
Varieties of ethical reflection. Lanham, Md. ; Oxford : Lexington Books, c2002.
BJ1031 .V37 2002

BARNYARD ANIMALS. *See* **DOMESTIC ANIMALS.**

Baron, Renee. The four temperaments : a fun and practical guide to understanding yourself and the people in your life / Renee Baron. 1st St. Martin's Griffin ed. New York : St. Martin's Griffin, 2004. p. cm. Includes bibliographical references. ISBN 0-312-31578-3 DDC 155.2/6
1. Four temperaments. I. Title.
BF698.3 .B365 2004

Baron Supervielle, Silvia. Le pays de l'écriture / Sylvia Baron Supervielle. Paris : Seuil, c2002. 276 p. ; 19 cm. ISBN 2-02-056568-4 DDC 844
1. Creation (Literary, artistic, etc.) I. Title.

BAROQUE.
Bastl, Beatrix, 1954- Europas Aufbruch in die Neuzeit 1450-1650. Darmstadt : Primus, c2002.
D208 .B37 2002

Barr, Linda R. (Linda Robinson).
Kelly, Brian, 1956- iSearch. Boston, MA : Allyn and Bacon, c2003.
BF76.78 .K45 2003

Barra Ruatta, Abelardo, 1953-.
La tierra nueva. Río Cuarto, Argentina : Universidad Nacional de Río Cuarto, Facultad de Ciencias Humanas, Centro de Estudios y Actividades para una Cultura de la Paz, 2000.

Barrera, Juan.
The Alexander technique [videorecording]. New York, N.Y. : Wellspring Media, c1999.

Barrère, Jean-Jacques.
Roche, Christian. Le bestiaire des philosophes. [Paris] : Seuil, c2001.

Barreto, Rachel.
Carsalade, Flávio de Lemos. Arquitetura. Belo Horizonte : AP Cultural, 2001.
NA2500 .C37 2001

Barrett, Louise. Human evolutionary psychology / Louise Barrett, Robin Dunbar, John Lycett. Princeton, N.J. : Princeton University Press, c2002. xiv, 434 p. : ill. ; 27 cm. Includes bibliographical references (p. [389]-426) and index. Table of contents URL: http://www.loc.gov/catdir/toc/prin031/2001097709.html Publisher description URL: http://www.loc.gov/catdir/desc ription/prin022/2001097709.html ISBN 0-691-09621-X (hardcover : alk. paper) ISBN 0-691-09622-8 (pbk. : alk. paper) DDC 155.7
1. Evolutionary psychology. I. Dunbar, R. I. M. (Robin Ian MacDonald), 1947- II. Lycett, John. III. Title.
BF698.95 .B37 2002

Barrett, Martin.
Razvitie natsional'noĭ, ėtnolingvisticheskoĭ i religioznoĭ identichnosti u deteĭ i podrostkov = Moskva : In-t psikhologii RAN, 2001.
BF723.C5 R39 2001

Barrett, Stanley R. Culture meets power / Stanley R. Barrett. Westport, Conn. ; London : Praeger, 2002. x, 150 p. ; 24 cm. Includes bibliographical references (p. [129]-139) and index. ISBN 0-275-97807-9 (hbk. : alk. paper) ISBN 0-275-97808-7 (pbk. : alk. paper) DDC 303.3
1. Power (Social sciences) 2. Culture. I. Title.
HM1256 .B27 2002

Barrick, Murray R.
Personality and work. 1st ed. San Francisco, CA : Jossey-Bass, c2003.
BF698.9.O3 P47 2003

BARRIER-FREE DESIGN.
Inclusive design. London ; New York : Springer, c2003.
TA174 .I464 2003

Barrios Casares, Manuel.
Metáfora y discurso filosófico. Madrid : Tecnos, 2000.

Barrios, Luis. Josconiando : dimensiones sociales y políticas de la espiritualidad / Luis Barrios ; prólogo de Frei Betto. 1st ed. New York : Editorial Aguiar, 2000. xvii, 340 p. : ill. ; 23 cm. Includes bibliographical references (p. 339-340) and index. ISBN 9993482005
1. Religion and sociology. 2. Capitalism - Religious aspects - Evangelist churches. 3. Religion and state - United States. 4. Religion and politics - United States. I. Title.

Barris, Jeremy. Paradox and the possibility of knowledge : the example of psychoanalysis / Jeremy Barris. Selinsgrove : Susquehanna University Press, c2003. 158 p. ; 24 cm. Includes bibliographical references (p. 149-153) and index. ISBN 1-57591-072-1 DDC 150.19/5/01
1. Psychoanalysis and philosophy. I. Title.
BF175.4.P45 B37 2003

BARRISTERS. *See* **LAWYERS.**

Barron's Educational Series, inc.
Modern mantras. 1st ed. Hauppauge, N.Y. : Barron's Educational Series, 2002.
BF637.C5 M63 2002

Barron's how to prepare for the AP pscyhology advanced placement examination.
McEntarffer, Robert. Hauppauge, N.Y. : Barron's, c2004.
BF78 .M34 2004

Barry, Catherine, 1955-.
Sages paroles du Dalai Lama. English.
Bstan-'dzin-rgya-mtsho, Dalai Lama XIV, 1935- Reflections from the journey of life. Berkeley, Calif. : North Atlantic Books, c2002.
BQ5670 .B76 2002

Bärsch, Claus-Ekkehard. Die politische Religion des Nationalsozialismus : die religiösen Dimensionen der NS-Ideologie in den Schriften von Dietrich Eckart, Joseph Goebbels, Alfred Rosenberg und Adolf Hitler / Claus-Ekkehard Bärsch. 2., vollst. überarb. Aufl. München : W. Fink, c2002. 407 p. : ill. ; 24 cm. Includes bibliographical references (p. [383]-404) and index. ISBN 3-7705-3172-8 (pbk.)
1. Eckart, Dietrich, - 1868-1923. 2. Goebbels, Joseph, - 1897-1945. 3. Rosenberg, Alfred, - 1893-1946. 4. Hitler, Adolf, - 1889-1945. 5. National socialism - Religious aspects. 6. National socialism - History. 7. Germany - Politics and government - 1933-1945. I. Title.

Barsotti, Bernard. Bachelard critique de Husserl : aux racines de la fracture épistémologie, phénoménologie / Bernard Barsotti ; préface de Jean Gayon. Paris : Harmattan, c2002. 188 p. ; 22 cm. (Collection Mouvement des savoirs) Errata slip inserted. Includes bibliographical references (p. 185) and indexes. ISBN 2-7475-1618-0 DDC 194
1. Bachelard, Gaston, - 1884-1962. 2. Husserl, Edmund, - 1859-1938. 3. Phenomenology. 4. Ontology. 5. Knowledge, Theory of. I. Gayon, Jean. II. Title. III. Series.
B2430.B254 B37 2002

Bartel, Pauline C. Spellcasters : witches and witchcraft in history, folklore, and popular culture / Pauline Bartel. Dallas : Taylor Trade Pub., c2000. xiv, 264 p., [8] p. of plates : ill. ; 24 cm. Includes bibliographical references (p. 249-255) and index. CONTENTS: The origins of witches and witchcraft around the world -- The folklore of witches and witchcraft -- The dark days of the great European witch hunt -- "The evil hand is on them" in Salem village -- The Salem witch trials -- Why the peace of Salem was distrubed -- Witches and the craft today -- The basics of witchcraft -- A witches who's who : from historic to contemporary times -- Witches and witchcraft in popular culture. ISBN 0-87833-183-2 (cl.) DDC 133.4/3/09
1. Witchcraft - History. I. Title.
BF1566 .B27 2000

Bartelmus, Peter.
[Wohlstand entschleiern. English] Unveiling wealth. Dordrecht ; Boston : Kluwer, c2002.
HD75.6 .U58 2002

Bartholomew, David J.
The analysis and interpretation of multivariate data for social scientists. Boca Raton, Fla. : Chapman & Hall/CRC, c2002.
HA29 .A5824 2002

Bartholomew, ill.
Leonard, Marcia. I feel angry. Nashville, Tenn. : CandyCane Press, 2003.
BF575.A5 L465 2003

Leonard, Marcia. I feel happy. Nashville, Tenn. : CandyCane Press, 2003.
BF575.H27 L465 2003

Leonard, Marcia. I feel sad. Nashville, Tenn. : CandyCane Press, 2003.
BF575.S23 L46 2003

Leonard, Marcia. I feel scared. Nashville, Tenn. : CandyCane Press, 2003.
BF575.F2 L455 2003

Bartlett, Andy.
Coren, Stanley. The pawprints of history. New York ; London : Free Press, c2002.

Bartlett, Carolyn, 1950- The Enneagram field guide : notes on using the Enneagram in counseling, therapy, and personal growth / Carolyn Bartlett. Portland, OR : Enneagram Consortium, c2003. p. cm. Includes index. CONTENTS: Introduction -- Ones -- Twos -- Threes -- Fours -- Fives -- Sixes -- Sevens -- Eights -- Nines. ISBN 1-932601-01-5 DDC 155.2/6
1. Enneagram. I. Title.
BF698.35.E54 B38 2003

Barton, Bruce B.
Veerman, David. When your father dies. Nashville, Tenn. : Thomas Nelson, c2003.
BF575.G7 V44 2003

Bartos, Joe.
Shulman, Mark, 1962- The voodoo revenge book. New York : Main Street, c2002.
BF637.R48 S55 2002

Bartsch, Renate, 1939- Consciousness emerging : the dynamics of perception, imagination, action, memory, thought, and language / Renate Bartsch. Amsterdam ; Philadelphia, Pa. : John Benjamins Pub., 2002. ix, 256 p. : ill. ; 22 cm. (Advances in consciousness research, 1381-589X ; v. 39) Includes bibliographical references (p. [243]-256 and index. ISBN 1-58811-180-6 (pbk. : alk. paper) ISBN 90-272-5159-2 (Eur.) DDC 153
1. Consciousness. 2. Cognition. I. Title. II. Series.
BF311 .B325 2002

Barylko, Jaime. Los valores y las virtudes / Jaime Barylko. Buenos Aires : Emecé Editoral, c2002. 265 p. ; 23 cm. ISBN 950-04-2368-5
1. Values. 2. Ethics. 3. Conducto of life. I. Title.

Baryshev, Yurij. Discovery of cosmic fractals / Yurij Baryshev, Pekka Teerikorpi. River Edge, N.J. : World Scientific, c2002. xxxi, 373 p. : ill. ; 24 cm. Includes bibliographical references (p. 361) and index. ISBN 981-02-4871-7 ISBN 981-02-4872-5 (pbk.)
1. Cosmology. 2. Fractals. I. Teerikorpi, Pekka, 1948- II. Title.
QB981 .B285 2002

Barzach, Amy Jaffe. Accidental courage, boundless dreams : the true story of one family's search for healing after the death of their young son and how they learned to deal with loss by celebrating life / by Amy Jaffe Barzach and Sandy Tovray Greenberg. 1st ed. West Hartford, CT : Aurora Pub., c2001. iii, 303 p. : ill. ; 23 cm. ISBN 0-9714362-0-7
1. Grief - United States. 2. Bereavement - Psychological aspects - United States. 3. Children - Death - Psychological aspects - United States. 4. Loss (Psychology) - United States. 5. Children with disabilities - United States. 6. Playgrounds - Barrier-free design - United States. I. Tovray, Sandy. II. Title.
BF575.G7 B375 2001

Basch, Reva.
Villamora, Grace Avellana. Super searchers on Madison Avenue. Medford, N.J. : CyberAge Books/ Information Today, c2003.
HF5415.2 .V497 2003

BASEBALL FOR CHILDREN - MANAGERS. See **BASEBALL MANAGERS.**

BASEBALL - MANAGERS. See **BASEBALL MANAGERS.**

BASEBALL MANAGERS - UNITED STATES - BIOGRAPHY.
DeMarco, Michael. Dugout days. New York : AMACOM, c2001.
GV865.M35 D46 2001

BASEBALL PLAYERS - UNITED STATES - ANECDOTES.
Mantle, Mickey, 1931- The quality of courage. Lincoln : University of Nebraska Press, [1999]
GV865.A1 M317 1999

BASEBALL PLAYERS - UNITED STATES - BIOGRAPHY.
Mantle, Mickey, 1931- The quality of courage. Lincoln : University of Nebraska Press, [1999]
GV865.A1 M317 1999

BASHFULNESS - HISTORY.
McDaniel, Patricia (Patricia A.) Shrinking violets and Caspar Milquetoasts. New York : New York University Press, 2003.
BF575.B3 M34 2003

BASHFULNESS IN CHILDREN.
Carducci, Bernardo J. The shyness breakthrough. [Emmaus, Pa.] : Rodale, c2003.
BF723.B3 C37 2003

BASHFULNESS - SOCIAL ASPECTS - UNITED STATES.
McDaniel, Patricia (Patricia A.) Shrinking violets and Caspar Milquetoasts. New York : New York University Press, 2003.
BF575.B3 M34 2003

Basic bioethics
McLeod, Carolyn. Self-trust and reproductive autonomy. Cambridge, Mass. : MIT Press, c2002.
RG133.5 .M39 2002

Basic counselling skills.
Nelson-Jones, Richard. London ; Thousand Oaks, Calif. : SAGE Publications, 2003.
BF637.C6 N433 2003

BASIC NEEDS. See **QUALITY OF LIFE.**

BASIC RIGHTS. See **CIVIL RIGHTS; HUMAN RIGHTS.**

BASIC WRITING (REMEDIAL EDUCATION).
Directed self-placement. Cresskill, N.J. : Hampton Press, c2003.
PE1404 .D57 2003

Basic writings.
Rée, Paul, 1849-1901. [Ursprung der moralischen Empfindungen. English] Urbana : University of Illinois Press, c2003.
B3323.R343 U67 2003

Basiuk, Tomasz.
Odmiany odmieńca. Katowice : "Śląsk", 2002.
HQ23 .O36 2002

Basler Studien zur Philosophie
(13) Majorek, Marek B. Objektivität, ein Erkenntnisideal auf dem Prüfstand. Tübingen : Francke, c2002.

Basler Universitätsreden
(100. Heft) Gäbler, Ulrich. Zeiten des Endes. Basel : Schwabe & Co., c2002.

Basov, R. A. Istoriía drevnegrecheskoĭ filosofii ot Falesa do Aristotelía / R.A. Basov. Moskva : Letopis' XXI, 2002. 415 p. ; 21 cm. Includes bibliographical references (p. 400-411). ISBN 5902007046
1. Philosophy, Ancient. I. Title.
B175.R9 B37 2002

Bast and Sekhmet.
Constantine, Storm. London : R. Hale, c1999.

BAST (EGYPTIAN DEITY).
Constantine, Storm. Bast and Sekhmet. London : R. Hale, c1999.

Basta, Danilo N., 1945-.
Kriza i perspektive filozofije. 1. izd. Beograd : Tersit, 1995.
B99.S462 K75 1995

Bastei-Lübbe-Taschenbuch;
(70136) Haen, Renate. Du bist die Göttin ; 1. Auf. Bergish Gladbach : Bastei Lübbe, 1999.

Bastide, Roger, 1898-1974.
[Eléments de sociologie religieuse. English]
Social origins of religion / Roger Bastide ; translated by Mary Baker ; foreword by James L. Peacock. Minneapolis : University of Minnesota Press, c2003. xxxiii, 221 p. ; 22 cm. Includes bibliographical references (p. 211-216) and index. ISBN 0-8166-3248-0 (alk. paper) ISBN 0-8166-3249-9 (pbk. : alk. paper) DDC 210
1. Religion and sociology. I. Title.
BL60 .B313 2003

BASTING, ANNE DAVIS, 1965-.
Vint/age 2001 conference : [videorecording]. New York, c2001.

Basting, Anne Davis, 1965- panelist.
Vint/age 2001 conference : [videorecording]. New York, c2001.

Bastl, Beatrix, 1954- Europas Aufbruch in die Neuzeit 1450-1650 : eine Kultur- und Mentalitätsgeschichte / Beatrix Bastl. Darmstadt : Primus, c2002. 220 p. : ill. (some col.) ; 28 x 22 cm. (Kultur und Mentalität) Includes bibliographical references (p. 205-211) and indexes. ISBN 3-89678-451-X
1. Europe - History - 1492-1648. 2. Renaissance. 3. Baroque. I. Title. II. Series.
D208 .B37 2002

Bastos, Maria Helena Camara.
Destinos das letras. Passo Fundo : Universidade de Passo Fundo, 2002.
P211 .D47 2002

BATAILLE, GEORGES, 1897-1962.
Kropotov, S. L. (Sergeĭ Leonidovich) Ėkonomika teksta v neklassicheskoĭ filosofii iskusstva. Ekaterinburg : Gumanitarnyĭ universitet, 1999.
B831.2 .K76 1999

BATAILLE, GEORGES, 1897-1962 - CRITICISM AND INTERPRETATION.
Lévesque, Claude, 1927- Par-delà le masculin et le féminin. Paris : Aubier, 2002.

Batarelo, Vice J.
Mir u Hrvatskoj--rezultati istraživanja. Zagreb : Hrvatski Caritas ; Split : Franjevački in-t za kulturu mira, 2001.
HN638.A8 M57 2001

Battle against witchcraft in Malawi.
Soko, Boston. Nchimi chikanga. Blantyre [Malawi] : Christian Literature Association in Malawi, 2002.
1. Black author.

Battling demons.
Bailey, Michael David, 1971- University Park, Pa. : Pennsylvania State University Press, c2003.
BF1569 .B35 2003

Baucum, Don.
Kagan, Jerome. Kagan & Segal's psychology. 9th ed. Belmont, CA : Thomson/Wadsworth, c2004.
BF121 .K22 2004

Baudelot, Christian. Travailler pour être heureux? : le bonheur et le travail en France / Christian Baudelot, Michel Gollac ; avec Céline Bessière ... [et al.]. [Paris] : Fayard, c2003. 351 p. : ill. ; 24 cm. Includes bibliographical references. ISBN 2-213-61505-5 DDC 300
1. Work - Psychological aspects. 2. Happiness. I. Bessière, Céline. II. Gollac, M. (Michel) III. Title.

Baudrillard, Jean.
[Esprit du terrorisme. English]
The spirit of terrorism and requiem for the Twin Towers / Jean Baudrillard ; translated by Chris Turner. London : Verso, 2002. 52 p. ; 21 cm. Translated from the French. ISBN 1-85984-411-1 DDC 973.931
1. Terrorism. 2. Terrorism - Psychological aspects. 3. Symbolism in politics. 4. September 11 Terrorist Attacks, 2001. I. Title.
HV6431 .B38 2002

[Objets singuliers. English]
The singular objects of architecture / Jean Baudrillard and Jean Nouvel ; translated by Robert Bononno ; foreword by K. Michael Hays. Minneapolis : University of Minnesota Press, c2002. xv, 80 p. ; 22 cm. ISBN 0-8166-3912-4 (alk. paper) DDC 720/.1
1. Architecture - Philosophy. 2. Aesthetics. I. Nouvel, Jean, 1945- II. Title.
NA2500 .B3413 2002

Der bauende Geist.
Breitschmid, Markus, 1966- Luzern : Quart, 2001.
B3318.A4 B745 2001

Bauer, Joel, 1960- How to persuade people who don't want to be persuaded : get what you want-every time! / Joel Bauer, Mark Levy. Hoboken, N.J. : John Wiley & Sons, 2004. p. cm. Includes bibliographical references and index. CONTENTS: Draw in the listener (an overview) -- Change the moment -- The transformation mechanism -- The body metaphor -- The paper metaphor -- The quick pitch opening -- The quick pitch body -- The slogan pitch -- Convince with samples -- The power of free -- The magic of gifts -- Solid proof -- Dynamic clarity -- Be distinct -- Overcome resistance -- The look -- The platform pitch -- The mechanism emergency kit. ISBN 0-471-64797-7 (hardcover) DDC 153.8/52
1. Persuasion (Psychology) I. Levy, Mark, 1962- II. Title.
BF637.P4 B32 2004

Bauer, Robert S.
Collected papers on Southeast Asian and Pacific languages. Canberra, ACT : Pacific Linguistics, Research School of Pacific and Asian Studies, Australian National University, 2002.

Baumann, Günter, 1962- Meisterwerke der Architektur : Bilder und Daten / von Günter Baumann. Stuttgart : Reclam, c2001. 332 p. : 152 ill., plans ; 15 cm. (Universal-Bibliothek ; Nr. 18118) Includes bibliographical references (p. 317-319). ISBN 3-15-018118-6 (pbk.)
1. Architecture - History. 2. Historic buildings. 3. Architecture - Philosophy. I. Title. II. Series: Universal-Bibliothek (Stuttgart, Germany) ; Nr. 18118.
NA200 .B33 2001

Baumeister, Roy F.
Handbook of self-regulation. New York : Guilford Press, 2004.
BF632 .H262 2004

Baumel, Judith Tydor, 1959-.
Gender, place, and memory in the modern Jewish experience. London ; Portland, Or. : Vallentine Mitchell, 2003.

DS143 .G36 2003

Baumgartner, Emmanuèle.
Progrès, réaction, décadence dans l'Occident médiéval. Genève : Droz, 2003.
PN681 .P764 2003

Baur, Manfred, 1959- Die Odyssee des Menschen : es begann in Afrika / Manfred Baur, Gudrun Ziegler. München : Ullstein, c2001. 344 p., [8] p. of plates : ill., maps ; 22 cm. Includes bibliographical references and index. ISBN 3-550-07168-X (hd.bd.)
1. Human evolution. 2. Human beings - Origin. I. Ziegler, Gudrun. II. Title.

Bāurī Mahārāṇa.
[Śilpaśāstra. English & Sanskrit.] Vāstu-śāstram. Calcutta : Sanskrit Pustak Bhandar, 2001.
NA7427 .M34 2001

Bauwelt Fundamente
(124) Bruyn, Gerd de. Fisch und Frosch, oder, Die Selbstkritik der Moderne. Gütersloh ; Berlin : Bertelsmann Fachzeitschriften ; Basel ; Boston ; Berlin : Birkhäuser, c2001.

Bayer, Ronald.
Klitzman, Robert. Mortal secrets. Baltimore : Johns Hopkins University Press, 2003.
RA643.8 .K56 2003

Bayers, Peter L., 1966- Imperial ascent : mountaineering, masculinity, and empire / Peter L. Bayers. Boulder, Colo. : University Press of Colorado, c2003. xii, 174 p. : ill. ; 25 cm. Includes bibliographical references (p. 157-166) and index. ISBN 0-87081-716-7 (hardcover : alk. paper) DDC 796.52/2/019
1. Mountaineering - Psychological aspects. 2. Masculinity. 3. Men - Identity. I. Title.
GV200.19.P78 B39 2003

Bayne, Nicholas, 1937-.
The new economic diplomacy. Aldershot, Hampshire, England ; Burlington, VT : Ashgate, c2003.
HF1359 .N4685 2003

Bayne, Rowan.
Applied psychology. London ; Thousand Oaks, Calif. : SAGE Publications, 2003.
BF636 .A62 2003

Baz, Margarita.
Jáidar, Isabel. La psicología. 1. ed. México, D.F. : Universidad Autónoma Metropolitana, Unidad Xochimilco, División de Ciencias Sociales y Humanidades, 2002.

Be-ahavah uve-emunah.
Aviner, Shelomoh Ḥayim, ha-Kohen. Yerushalayim : [h. mo. l.], 760-762 [1999 or 2000-2001 or 2002]
BM565 .A93 1999

Be-ḳarov etslekh.
Gorfine, Yehudit. Petaḥ Tiḳvah : Mar'ot, 2002.

Be-ḳarov etslekha.
Gorfine, Yehudit. Be-ḳarov etslekh. Petaḥ Tiḳvah : Mar'ot, 2002.

Be not afraid, only believe.
Egbunu, Fidelis Eleojo. Enugu, Nigeria : Snaap Press, 2001.

Be-shem omro.
Kuntres Kevod ha-Torah. Bene Beraḳ : ha-Meḥaber, 761 [2000 or 2001]

Be-sod ha-regashot.
Ben-Ze'ev, Aharon. Lod : Zemorah-Bitan, 2001.

Be thou there : the Holy Family's journey in Egypt / edited with an introduction by Gawdat Gabra ; text by William Lyster, Cornelis Hulsman, Stephen J. Davis ; photographs by Norbert Schiller. Cairo ; New York : American University in Cairo Press, c2001. xi, 162 p. : ill. (chiefly col.), map ; 33 cm. Includes bibliographical references (p. 129). "A National Egyptian Heritage Revival Book"--half-title page.
1. Jesus Christ - Flight into Egypt. 2. Jesus Christ - Family. 3. Mary, - Blessed Virgin, Saint - Shrines - Egypt. 4. Coptic Church - Doctrines. 5. Coptic church buildings - Egypt. 6. Christian shrines - Egypt. 7. Egypt - Religion. I. Abdel Sayed, Gawdat Gabra. II. Lyster, William. III. Hulsman, Cornelis. IV. Davis, Stephen J. V. Schiller, Norbert. VI. National Egyptian Heritage Revival Association.

Be your own brand.
McNally, David, 1946- 1st ed. San Francisco, CA : Berrett-Koehler, c2002.
BF697 .M385 2002

Béal, François.
Bardy, Jean. Regard sur "l'évolution créatrice". Paris : Harmattan, c2003.

Beall, Anne E.
The psychology of gender. 2nd ed. New York : Guilford Press, 2004.
BF692.2 .P764 2004

BEAR MARKETS. *See* **STOCK EXCHANGES.**

Beare, John I. (John Isaac), d. 1918 Greek theories of elementary cognition : from Alcmaeon to Aristotle / by John I. Beare. Mansfield Centre, Conn. : Martino Pub., 2004. p. cm. Originally published: Oxford : Clarendon Press, 1906. Includes bibliographical references. ISBN 1-57898-470-X (alk. paper) DDC 128/.3
1. Psychology - History - To 1500. 2. Cognition - History - To 1500. 3. Philosophy, Ancient. I. Title.
BF91 .B3 2004

BEARING WITNESS (CHRISTIANITY). *See* **WITNESS BEARING (CHRISTIANITY).**

BEASTS. *See* **DOMESTIC ANIMALS.**

Beattie, Antonia. Feng shui dictionary : everything you need to know to assess your space, find solutions, and bring harmony to your home : comprehensive explanations of feng shui schools, practices, and tools / Antonia Beattie. San Diego, Calif. : Thunder Bay Press, c2003. p. cm. Includes index. ISBN 1-57145-996-0 DDC 133.3/337
1. Feng shui. I. Title.
BF1779.F4 B43 2003

Fortune teller's dictionary : everything you need to know about the world of fortune-telling : comprehensive explanations of psychic potential, intuition development, and divination practices / Antonia Beattie. San Diego : Thunder Bay, 2003. p. cm. Includes index. ISBN 1-59223-032-6 DDC 133.3
1. Fortune-telling - Dictionaries. I. Title.
BF1861 .B43 2003

Spells dictionary / Antonia Beattie. San Diego, Calif. : Thunder Bay Press, 2003. p. cm. Includes index. ISBN 1-57145-997-9 DDC 133.4/4
1. Magic - Dictionaries. 2. Charms - Dictionaries. I. Title.
BF1611 .B43 2003

Beattie, Geoffrey. Visible thoughts : the new psychology of body language / Geoffrey Beattie. Hove, East Sussex ; New York, NY : Routledge, 2003. p. cm. Includes bibliographical references and index. Table of contents URL: http://www.loc.gov/catdir/toc/ecip045/2003014530.html ISBN 0-415-30809-7 (hardcover) ISBN 0-415-30810-0 (pbk.) DDC 153.6/9
1. Body language. 2. Gesture - Psychological aspects. I. Title.
BF637.N66 B43 2003

Beaty, Michael D.
Cultivating citizens. Lanham : Lexington Books, c2002.
JK1759 .C85 2002

Beauperin, Yves. Anthropologie du geste symbolique / Yves Beauperin. Paris : Harmattan, c2002. 302 p. ; 22 cm. (Collection Religion & sciences humaines) Includes bibliographical references (p. [293]-297). ISBN 2-7475-3086-8 DDC 301
1. Gesture - Religious aspects. 2. Religion and culture. 3. Religion and sociology. 4. Gesture. I. Title. II. Series: Collection Religion et sciences humaines.
BL60 .B339 2002

BEAUTIFUL, THE. *See* **AESTHETICS.**

BEAUTY. *See* **AESTHETICS; BEAUTY, PERSONAL.**

BEAUTY CULTURE. *See* **BEAUTY, PERSONAL.**

BEAUTY, PERSONAL. *See also* **CLOTHING AND DRESS.**
Aucoin, Kevyn. Making faces. 1st ed. Boston : Little, Brown, c1997.
RA778 .A873 1997

Constantine, Susannah. What not to wear. London : Weidenfeld & Nicolson, 2002.

Freedman, Rita Jackaway. Bodylove. Updated ed. Carlsbad, CA : Gürze Books, c2002.
BF697.5.B63 F74 2002

Mustafa, Huda Nura. Practicing beauty. 1997.

Penz, Otto. Metamorphosen der Schönheit. Wien : Turia + Kant, c2001.
GT495 .P459 2001

Weinberg, Norma Pasekoff, 1941- Henna from head to toe!. Pownal, Vt. : Storey Books, c1999.
GT2343 .W45 1999

BEAUTY, PERSONAL - MISCELLANEA.
McCoy, Edain, 1957- [Enchantments. Spanish] Magia y belleza. 1st ed. St. Paul, Minn. : Llewellyn Español, 2002.

BF1623.B43 E6418 2002

Wishart, Catherine, 1965- Teen goddess. 1st ed. St. Paul, Minn. : Llewellyn Publications, c2003.
BF1623.G63 W57 2003

BEAUTY, PERSONAL - PSYCHOLOGICAL ASPECTS.
Western eyes [videorecording]. New York, NY : First Run/Icarus Films, 2000.

BEAUTY SHOPS. *See* **BEAUTY, PERSONAL.**

BEAUVOIR, SIMONE DE, 1908-.
DEUXIÈME SEXE.
Le deuxième sexe. Montréal : Éditions du Remue-ménage, 2001.

DEUXIEME SEXE.
Heinamaa, Sara, 1960- Toward a phenomenology of sexual difference. Lanham, Md. ; Oxford : Rowman & Littlefield Publishers, c2003.
HQ1208 .B3523 2003

BEAUVOIR, SIMONE DE, 1908-.
Aller, Annelies van, 1946- Levenskunst van twee vrouwen. Budel : Damon, c2001.
PS3527.I865 Z536 2001

BEAUVOIR, SIMONE DE, 1908- - CRITICISM AND INTERPRETATION.
Le deuxième sexe. Montréal : Éditions du Remue-ménage, 2001.

BEAUVOIR, SIMONE DE, 1908 - -CRITICISM AND INTERPRETATION.
Heinamaa, Sara, 1960- Toward a phenomenology of sexual difference. Lanham, Md. ; Oxford : Rowman & Littlefield Publishers, c2003.
HQ1208 .B3523 2003

BEAUVOIR, SIMONE DE, 1908- - INFLUENCE.
Le deuxième sexe. Montréal : Éditions du Remue-ménage, 2001.

Beaver, Diana. NLP for lazy learning : how to learn faster and more effectively / Diana Beaver. London : Vega, 2002. xi, 195 p. : ill. ; 22 cm. Includes bibliographical references (p. [185]-189) and index. ISBN 1-84333-049-0
1. Neurolinguistic programming. 2. Learning, Psychology of. I. Title.
BF637.N46 B44 2002

Beavers, Brett. Something worth leaving behind / Brett Beavers & Tom Douglas ; introduction by Lee Ann Womack. Nashville, Tenn. : Rutledge Hill Press, c2002. 63 p. : ill. (some col.) ; 16 cm. + 1 sound disc (digital ; 4 3/4 in.). ISBN 1401600328 DDC 170/.44
1. Success - Psychological aspects. 2. Self-actualization (Psychology) I. Douglas, Tom, 1953- II. Womack, Lee Ann. III. Title.
BF637.S8 B383 2002

Beazley, Hamilton, 1943- No regrets : a ten-step program for living in the present and leaving the past behind / Hamilton Beazley. Hoboken, N.J. : John Wiley & Sons, c2004. p. cm. Includes bibliographical references and index. CONTENTS: Introduction : something remarkable is possible -- Understanding regrets -- Ten steps to letting go -- Using spiritual and psychological tools -- Step one : listing regrets -- Step two : examining regrets -- Step three : changing toxic thought patterns -- Step four : grieving losses -- Step five : making amends -- Step six : identifying lessons and gifts -- Step seven : developing compassion -- Step eight : forgiving others -- Step nine : forgiving ourselves -- Step ten : living free of regret. ISBN 0-471-21295-4 DDC 158.1
1. Regret. I. Title.
BF575.R33 B43 2004

Beck, Kristin.
McKay, Matthew. The self-nourishment companion. Oakland, CA : New Harbinger Publications, c2001.
BF637.S4 M3925 2001

Beck, Robert C. (Robert Clarence), 1931- Motivation : theories and principles / Robert C. Beck. 5th ed. Upper Saddle River, N.J. : Pearson/Prentice Hall, c2004. x, 470 p. : ill. ; 24 cm. Includes bibliographical references (p. [426]-456) and indexes. Table of contents URL: http://www.loc.gov/catdir/toc/ecip043/2003009370.html ISBN 0-13-111445-X DDC 153.8
1. Motivation (Psychology) I. Title.
BF503 .B38 2004

Becker, Bruce.
The Alexander technique [videorecording]. New York, N.Y. : Wellspring Media, c1999.

BECKER, ERNEST.
Death and denial. Westport, Conn. ; London : Praeger, 2002.
BD444 .D377 2002

Becker, Jörg, 1959-.
Process management. Springer-verlag, Berlin, Heidelberg ; New York : Springer, c2003.
HD31 .P756 2003

Becker, Konrad. Tactical reality dictionary : cultural intelligence and social control / Konrad Becker. Vienna : Edition Selene ; [s.l.] : Distribution Canada/ UK/USA by Autonomedia, 2002. 131 p. ; 19 cm. "MMII TRD / WIO PIA." ISBN 3-85266-194-3 (pbk).
1. Persuasion (Psychology) - Dictionaries. 2. Personality and culture - Dictionaries. 3. Social engineering - Dictionaries. 4. Social control - Dictionaries. I. Title.
BF637.P4 B33 2002

Becker, Monika. Familiar dialogues in Englyssh and Frenche : sprachliche Interaktion und ihre Vermittlung in der frühen Neuzeit / Monika Becker. Trier : Wissenschaftlicher Verlag Trier, c2003. 377, xxviii p. : ill. ; 21 cm. (Fokus ; Bd. 26) Includes bibliographical references. ISBN 3-88476-563-9
1. Languages, Modern - Study and teaching - History - 16th century. 2. Languages, Modern - Study and teaching - History - 17th century. 3. Languages, Modern - Conversation and phrase books. 4. Imaginary conversations. I. Title. II. Series.

BECKETT, SAMUEL, 1906- - CRITICISM AND INTERPRETATION.
Keller, John Robert. Samuel Beckett and the primacy of love. Manchester : Manchester University Press, 2002.

Beckford, James A.
Challenging religion. London ; New York : Routledge, 2003.
BL60 .C437 2003

Social theory and religion / James A. Beckford. Cambridge, U.K. ; New York : Cambridge University Press, 2003. ix, 252 p. ; 23 cm. Includes bibliographical references (p. 216-246) and index. ISBN 0-521-77336-9 ISBN 0-521-77431-4 (pbk.) DDC 306.6
1. Religion and sociology. I. Title.
BL60 .B34 2003

Beck'sche Reihe
(1502.) Gelfert, Hans-Dieter, 1937- Typisch amerikanisch. Originalausg. München : Beck, c2002.
E169.1 .G44 2002

Beck'sche Reihe. Wissen.
Haarmann, Harald. Geschichte der Schrift. Originalausg. München : C.H. Beck, c2002.

Become a life balance master.
Giardina, Ric. Hillsboro, Or. : Beyond Words Pub., 2003.
BF637.S4 G486 2003

Becoming a manager.
Hill, Linda A. (Linda Annette), 1956- 2nd ed. Boston, Mass. : Harvard Business School Press, c2003.
HF5384 .H55 2003

Becoming an ally.
Bishop, Anne, 1950- 2nd ed. London ; New York : Zed Books ; Halifax, N.S. : Fernwood Pub. ; New York : Distributed in the USA exclusively by Palgrave, 2002.
HM1256 .B57 2002

Becoming an effective health care manager.
Sperry, Len. Baltimore, Md. : Health Professions Press, c2003.
RA971 .S72 2003

BECOMING (PHILOSOPHY).
Zubiri, Xavier. [Estructura dinámica de la realidad. English] Dynamic structure of reality. Urbana : University of Illinois Press, c2003.
B4568.Z83 E7713 2003

Becoming real.
Saltz, Gail. New York: Riverhead Books, 2004.
BF637.S4 S245 2004

Bederson, Benjamin. The craft of information visualization : readings and reflections / Benjamin B. Bederson, Ben Shneiderman. San Francisco, Calif. : Morgan Kaufmann ; Oxford : Elsevier Science, 2003. 410 p. : ill. ; 28 cm. Includes index. ISBN 1-55860-915-6 DDC 004.019
1. Information visualization. 2. Human-computer interaction. I. Shneiderman, Ben, 1947- II. Title.

Bedi, Ashok. Retire your family karma : decode your family pattern and find your soul path / Ashok Bedi, Boris Matthews. Berwick, Me. : Nicolas-Hays, 2003. p. cm. Includes bibliographical references and index. ISBN 0-89254-081-8 (pbk. : alk. paper) DDC 155.9/24
1. Self-actualization (Psychology) 2. Family - Psychological aspects. 3. Hinduism - Psychology. 4. Karma - Psychology. I. Matthews, Boris. II. Title.

BF637.S4 B423 2003

Bee, Helen L., 1939- The journey of adulthood / Helen L. Bee, Barbara R. Bjorklund. 5th ed. Upper Saddle River, NJ : Pearson Prentice Hall, c2004. xvi, 485 p. : ill. (some col.) ; 26 cm. Includes bibliographical references (p. 419-451) and indexes. ISBN 0-13-097041-7 DDC 155.6
1. Adulthood - Psychological aspects. 2. Aging - Psychological aspects. 3. Adulthood. 4. Aging. I. Bjorklund, Barbara R. II. Title.
BF724.5 .B44 2004

Beebe, Steven A., 1950- Interpersonal communication : relating to others / Steven A. Beebe, Susan J. Beebe, Mark V. Redmond. 4th ed. Boston, MA : Allyn and Bacon, 2004. p. cm. Includes bibliographical references and index. ISBN 0-205-41792-2 DDC 153.6
1. Interpersonal communication - Textbooks. I. Beebe, Susan J. II. Redmond, Mark V., 1949- III. Title.
BF637.C45 B43 2004

Beebe, Susan J.
Beebe, Steven A., 1950- Interpersonal communication. 4th ed. Boston, MA : Allyn and Bacon, 2004.
BF637.C45 B43 2004

Beelmann, Axel. Theoretische Philosophiegeschichte : grundsätzliche Probleme einer philosophischen Geschichte der Philosophie / Axel Beelmann. Basel : Schwabe, c2001. 325 p. ; 23 cm. Includes bibliographical references and index. ISBN 3-7965-1705-6 (Gewebe)
1. Philosophy - Historiography. 2. Philosophy - History. 3. Philosophy. I. Title.

BEELZEBUB. *See* **DEVIL.**
BEELZEBUL. *See* **DEVIL.**

Beem, Ellen Evaline, 1957- Bereavement : physiological and psychological consequences / door Ellen Evaline Beem. [Leiden : Universiteit Leiden, 2000] 139 p. : ill. ; 24 cm. Text in English; summary in Dutch. Thesis (doctoral)--Rijksuniversiteit te Leiden, 2000. Includes bibliographical references. DDC 155.9/37
1. Bereavement - Psychological aspects. 2. Bereavement - Physiological aspects. 3. Grief. 4. Grief - Physiological aspects. 5. Loss (Psychology) I. Title.
BF575.G7 B422 2000

BEER. *See* **BREWING.**

BEER, GILLIAN - BIBLIOGRAPHY.
Literature, science, psychoanalysis, 1830-1970. Oxford ; New York : Oxford University Press, 2003.
PN55 .L58 2003

The Beethoven factor.
Pearsall, Paul. Charlottesville, VA : Hampton Roads Pub. Co., c2003.
BF698.35.R47 P43 2003

Before you cast a spell.
McColman, Carl. Franklin Lakes, NJ : New Page Books, 2004.
BF1611 .M385 2004

Begabung und Selbstkonzept.
Hemming, Jan. Münster : Lit, [2002?]
ML3838 .H46 2002

Begeren en vereren.
Moyaert, Paul, 1952- Amsterdam : SUN, c2002.
BF175.5.S92 M69 2002

Begey, Roger.
Le Fèvre, Jean-Yves. Eloge de la mort. Monaco : Rocher, c2002.

The beginner's guide for the recently deceased.
Staume, David, 1961- 1st ed. St. Paul, Minn. : Llewellyn Publications, 2004.
BF1311.F8 S78 2004

The beginner's guide to quantum psychology.
Wolinsky, Stephen. Capitola, Calif. : S.H. Wolinsky, c2000.
BF38 .W7677 2000

The beginner's guide to self-hypnosis.
Markham, Ursula. London : Vega, 2002.
BF1141 .M36 2002

Beginner's guide to tarot.
Sharman-Burke, Juliet. 1st St. Martin's Griffin ed. New York : St. Martin's Griffin, 2001.
BF1879.T2 S52 2001

The beginner's guide to walking the Buddha's eightfold path.
Smith, Jean, 1938- New York : Bell Tower, 2002.
BQ4320 .S65 2002

BEGINNING. *See also* **CREATION.**
Mircea, Corneliu. Originarul. București : Paideia, 2000.

BD638 .M573 2000

Begriffsgeschichte, Diskursgeschichte, Metapherngeschichte / mit Beiträgen von Mark Bevir ... [et al.] ; herausgegeben von Hans Erich Bödeker. Göttingen : Wallstein, 2002. 421 p. ; 21 cm. (Göttinger Gespräche zur Geschichtswissenschaft ; Bd. 14) Includes bibliographical references. Articles chiefly in German, one in English, one in French. ISBN 3-89244-470-6 (pbk.)
1. Historiography. 2. History - Philosophy. I. Bevir, Mark. II. Bödeker, Hans Erich. III. Series: Göttinger Gespräche zur Geschichtswissenschaft (Series) ; Bd. 14.
D13 .B45 2002

Beguery, Jocelyne. Une esthétique contemporaine de l'album de jeunesse : de grands petits livres / Jocelyne Beguery. Paris : Harmattan, c2002. 256 p. : ill. ; 22 cm. (Collection Audiovisuel et communication) Includes bibliographical references (p. [243]-254). ISBN 2-7475-3261-5 DDC 100
1. Picture books for children - Publishing - France. 2. Children's literature - Publishing - France. 3. Aesthetics. 4. Children's literature, French - France - History and criticism. 5. Picture books for children - France. I. Title. II. Series: Audiovisuel et communication (Harmattan (Firm))

Behari, Bepin. The timing of events / Bepin Behari. 1st ed. Delhi : Motilal Banarsidass Publishers, 2002. xxiv, 187 p. ; 23 cm. Includes index. ISBN 81-208-1887-3
1. Predictive astrology. 2. Planets. I. Title.
BF1720.5+

Behavior analysis and learning.
Pierce, W. David. 3rd ed. Mahwah, N.J. : L. Erlbaum Associates, 2004.
BF199 .P54 2004

BEHAVIOR, ATTACHMENT. *See* **ATTACHMENT BEHAVIOR.**

BEHAVIOR, CHILD. *See* **CHILD PSYCHOLOGY.**

BEHAVIOR, COMPARATIVE. *See* **PSYCHOLOGY, COMPARATIVE.**

BEHAVIOR, CONSUMER. *See* **CONSUMER BEHAVIOR.**

BEHAVIOR DISORDERS IN CHILDREN. *See* **ATTENTION-DEFICIT HYPERACTIVITY DISORDER; PROBLEM CHILDREN.**

BEHAVIOR EVOLUTION.
McFadyen, Ian. Mind wars. St Leonards, N.S.W., Australia : Allen & Unwin, c2000.
BF701 .M38 2000

BEHAVIOR GENETICS.
Behavior genetics principles. Washington, DC : American Psychological Association, 2004.
BF698.9.B5 B44 2004

Behavior genetics principles : perspectives in development, personality, and psychopathology / edited by Lisabeth F. DiLalla. Washington, DC : American Psychological Association, 2004. p. cm. (Decade of behavior) Proceedings of a festschrift conference held in honor of Irving I. Gottesman. Includes bibliographical references and indexes. ISBN 1-59147-083-8 DDC 155.7
1. Personality - Genetic aspects. 2. Behavior genetics. 3. Personality development. 4. Psychology, Pathological. I. DiLalla, Lisabeth F. II. Gottesman, Irving I. III. Series.
BF698.9.B5 B44 2004

BEHAVIOR, HEALTH. *See* **HEALTH BEHAVIOR.**

BEHAVIOR, HELPING. *See* **HELPING BEHAVIOR.**

BEHAVIOR, HUMAN. *See* **HUMAN BEHAVIOR.**

BEHAVIOR IN ORGANIZATIONS. *See* **ORGANIZATIONAL BEHAVIOR.**

BEHAVIOR MODIFICATION. *See also* **BRAINWASHING; HABIT BREAKING.**
Cronin, W. Jean. Going for the gold. Longmont, CO : Sopris West, c2003.
BF637.B4 C76 2003

Harris, Bill, 1950- Thresholds of the mind. Beaverton : Centerpointe Press, c2002.
BF637.B4 H36 2002

Kotler, Philip. Social marketing. 2nd ed. Thousand Oaks, Calif. ; London : Sage Publications, c2002.
HF5414 .K67 2002

Ludwig, Timothy D. Intervening to improve the safety of occupational driving. New York : Haworth Press, 2000.
HE5614 .I586 2000

Pryor, Karen, 1932- On behavior. 1st ed. North Bend, Wash. : Sunshine Books, c1995.

BF637.B4 P68 1995

BEHAVIOR OF CHILDREN. *See* **CHILDREN - CONDUCT OF LIFE.**

BEHAVIOR, SPATIAL. *See* **SPATIAL BEHAVIOR.**

BEHAVIORAL ASSESSMENT OF CHILDREN.
Bierman, Karen L. Peer rejection. New York : Guilford Press, 2004.
BF723.R44 B54 2003

BEHAVIORAL ASSESSMENT OF TEENAGERS.
Gumbiner, Jann. Adolescent assessment. Hoboken, N.J. : J. Wiley & Sons, c2003.
BF724.25 .G86 2003

BEHAVIORAL HEALTH CARE. *See* **MENTAL HEALTH SERVICES.**

BEHAVIORAL MEDICINE. *See* **MEDICINE AND PSYCHOLOGY.**

BEHAVIORAL SCIENCES. *See* **PSYCHOLOGY; SOCIAL SCIENCES.**

BEHAVIORAL SCIENTISTS. *See* **PSYCHOLOGISTS.**

BEHAVIORISM (PSYCHOLOGY).
Foxall, G. R. Context and cognition. 1st ed. Reno, NV : Context Press, 2004.
BF199 .F69 2004

Leslie, Julian C. Essential behaviour analysis. London : Arnold ; New York : Oxford University Press, c2002.
BF199 .L42 2002

Ormrod, Jeanne Ellis. Human learning. 4th ed. Upper Saddle River, N.J. : Merrill, c2004.
BF318 .O76 2004

Pierce, W. David. Behavior analysis and learning. 3rd ed. Mahwah, N.J. : L. Erlbaum Associates, 2004.
BF199 .P54 2004

BEHAVIORISTIC PSYCHOLOGY. *See* **BEHAVIORISM (PSYCHOLOGY).**

Behavioural prevention of stress.
Machačová, Helena. [Behaviorální prevence stresu. English] 1st ed. Prague : Karolinum Press, 1999.
BF575.S75 M26513 1999

Behind the blip.
Fuller, Matthew. Brooklyn, NY, USA : Autonomedia, c2003.
QA76.76.H85 F85 2003

Behind the crystal ball.
Aveni, Anthony F. Rev. ed. Boulder, Colo. : University Press of Colorado, c2002.
BF1589 .A9 2002

Behling, Katja, 1963- Martha Freud : die Frau des Genies / Katja Behling ; mit einem Vorwort von Anton W. Freud. Berlin : Aufbau Taschenbuch Verlag, 2002. 266 p. : ill. ; 19 cm. ISBN 3-7466-1858-4 (pbk.)
1. Freud, Martha, - 1861-1951. 2. Freud, Sigmund, - 1856-1939. I. Title.
BF109.F73 B455 2002

Bei da ming jia ming zhu wen cong
Zong, Baihua. Yi jing. Di 2 ban. Beijing : Beijing da xue chu ban she, 1998.
MLCSC 92/01825 (B)

Being and meaning.
Alackapally, Sebastian, 1961- 1st ed. Delhi : Motilal Banarsidass Publishers, 2002.
PK541.B48 A43 2002

Beins, Bernard. Research methods : a tool for life / Bernard C. Beins. Boston : Pearson/Allyn and Bacon, 2003. p. cm. Includes bibliographical references and indexes. ISBN 0-205-32771-0 DDC 150/.7/2
1. Psychology - Research - Methodology. I. Title.
BF76.5 .B439 2003

Beishan si chuang.
Shi, Zhecun. Di 1 ban. Shanghai : Shanghai wen yi chu ban she : Xin hua shu dian jing xiao, 2000.
PL2272.5 .S543 2000

Beishan sichuang.
Shi, Zhecun. Beishan si chuang. Di 1 ban. Shanghai : Shanghai wen yi chu ban she : Xin hua shu dian jing xiao, 2000.
PL2272.5 .S543 2000

Beiträge zu einer christlichen Kultur
(Bd. 3) Schlosser, Herta. Der Mensch als Wesen der Freiheit. Vallendar-Schönstatt : Patris Verlag, 2002.

Beiträge zur Altertumskunde
(Bd. 173) Zöller, Rainer. Die Vorstellung vom Willen in der Morallehre Senecas. Leipzig : K.G. Saur, 2003.
PA6686 .Z65 2003

Beiträge zur Individualpsychologie
(Bd. 28) Strukturbildung und Lebensstil. München : Ernst Reinhardt, c2002.

Beiträge zur Musikpsychologie
(Bd. 3) Hemming, Jan. Begabung und Selbstkonzept. Münster : Lit, [2002?]
ML3838 .H46 2002

Beiträge zur neueren Literaturgeschichte
(3. Folge, Bd. 166.) Kaus, Rainer J. Psychoanalyse und Sozialpsychologie. Heidelberg : C. Winter, c1999.
BF109.F74 K38 1999

Beiträge zur politischen Wissenschaft
(Bd. 89) Lobkowicz, Nikolaus. Czas kryzysu, czas przełomu. Kraków : Wydawnictwo WAM : Znak, 1996.

Beiträge zur Sexualforschung
(Sonderbd) Verführung, Trauma, Missbrauch. [2. Aufl.]. Giessen : Psychosozial-Verlag, c2002.

BekarovEtzlech.
Gorfine, Yehudit. Be-ḳarov etslekh. Petaḥ Tiḳvah : Marʾot, 2002.

Beli͡aev, G. G. Dukhovnye korni russkogo naroda / Beli͡aev G.G., Torgashev G.A. ; pod redaktsieĭ Chibiri͡aeva S.A. Moskva : Bylina, 2002. 192 p. ; 20 cm. Includes bibliographical references. ISBN 5933840319
1. Russia (Federation) - Civilization. 2. Russia (Federation) - Religion. 3. Russia (Federation) - Intellectual life. 4. National characteristics, Russian. I. Torgashev, G. A. II. Chibiri͡aev, S. A. (Stanislav Arkhipovich) III. Title.
DK32 .B358 2002

BELIEF AND DOUBT. *See also* **TRUTH.**
Devout sceptics. London : Hodder & Stoughton, 2003.

Believe to achieve.
White, Howard, 1950- Hillsboro, Or. : Beyond Words Pub., c2003.
BF637.S8 W453 2003

Bell, Chip R. Managers as mentors : building partnerships for learning / [Chip R. Bell]. 2nd ed., completely rev. and expanded. San Francisco, Calif : Berrett-Koehler Publishers, c2002. xxv, 184 p. ; 24 cm. Includes bibliographical references (p. 173-176) and index. ISBN 1-57675-142-2
1. Mentoring in business. 2. Executives. 3. Employees - Training of. 4. Employees - Counseling of. I. Title.
HF5385 .B45 1996

Bell, Richard.
Fransella, Fay. A manual for repertory grid technique. 2nd ed. Hoboken, NJ : Wiley, c2004.
BF698.8.R38 F72 2004

Bellen, Heinz.
Alföldi, Maria R.- Gloria romanorum. Stuttgart : Franz Steiner Verlag, 2001.
DG78 .A546 2001

BELLES-LETTRES. *See* **LITERATURE.**

Bellman, Kirstie L.
International Conference on Simulation in Engineering Education (2001 : Phoenix, Ariz.) Proceedings of the International Conference on Simulation and Multimedia in Engineering Education & Virtual Worlds and Simulation. San Diego, CA : Society for Computer Simulation International, c2001.

Bellotti, Laura Golden.
Nogales, Ana, 1951- Latina power!. New York : Simon & Schuster, c2003.
BF637.S8 N64 2003

Bellury, Phillip Rob.
Whalen, Charles E., Jr. The gift of renewal. 1st ed. Gainesville, GA : Warren Featherbone Foundation, c2003 (Gainesville, GA : Matthews Print.)
BF637.S4 W47 2003

Belnap, Barbara P.
Hall, L. Michael. The sourcebook of magic. Wales, UK ; Williston, VT : Crown House Pub. Ltd., 2002.
BF637.N46 H36 2002

BELY, ANDREY, 1880-1934.
Spivak, M. L. Posmertnai͡a diagnostika genialʹnosti. Moskva : Agraf, 2001.
BF416.A1 S68 2001

Ben he-ʿanan.
Ashkenazi, Nisim. Tel-Aviv : Gal, 2002.

Ben madaʿ le-filosofyah.
Leibowitz, Yeshayahu, 1903- Yerushalayim : Aḳademon, 762 [2002]

Ben-Porath, Yossef S.
Sherwood, Nancy E. The MMPI-A content component scales. Minneapolis : University of Minnesota Press, c1997.
BF698.8.M5 S54 1997

Ben Ratson-Lahaṭ, Tsiyon. Sefer ha-Nistarot yeha-niglot : ʿal megilat Ester ʿa. pi shiṭat ha-Arizal ... / me-et ha-Tsabar. [Israel? : ḥ. mo. l.], 761 i.e. 2001?] 309 p. ; 24 cm. Includes vocalized text of Megilat Ester.
1. Bible. - O.T. - Esther - Commentaries. 2. Cabala. I. Luria, Isaac ben Solomon, 1534-1572. II. Title.

Ben Torah le-ḥokhmah.
Halbertal, Moshe. Yerushalayim : Hotsaʾat sefarim ʿa. sh. Y. L. Magnes, ha-Universiṭah ha-ʿIvrit, 760, 2000.
BM755.M54 H35 2000

Ben-Zeʾev, Aharon. Be-sod ha-regashot : ʿal ahavah, śinʾah u-mah she-benehen / Aharon Ben-Zeʾev. Lod : Zemorah-Bitan, 2001. 458 p. : ill. ; 21 cm. Title on verso of t.p.: Subtlety of emotions. Includes bibliographical references (p. [433]-446) and index.
1. Emotions. 2. Love. 3. Hate. I. Title. II. Title: Subtlety of emotions

Bencivenga, Ermanno, 1950- Exercises in constructive imagination / Ermanno Bencivenga. Dordrecht ; Boston : Kluwer Academic Publishers, c2001. vii, 211 p. ; 25 cm. (Topoi library ; v. 3) Includes bibliographical references (p. 207-211). ISBN 0-7923-6702-2 (alk. paper) DDC 195
1. Philosophy. I. Title. II. Series.
B3613.B3853 E93 2001

Bender, William N. Haunted Atlanta and beyond : true tales of the supernatural / by William N. Bender. Athens, Ga. : Hill Street Press, 2004. p. cm. Includes bibliographical references. CONTENTS: Civil War ghosts of Atlanta -- An array of Atlanta specters -- Rumors of Atlanta spirits -- Ghosts of Athens and northeast Georgia. ISBN 1-58818-094-8 (alk. paper) DDC 133.1/09758/231
1. Ghosts - Georgia - Atlanta. 2. Ghosts - Georgia. I. Title.
BF1472.U6 B46 2004

Beneath the mask.
Monte, Christopher F. 7th ed. Hoboken, NJ : J. Wiley & Sons, c2003.
BF698 .M64 2003

Benenzon, Rolando O.
Pharmacum carthusiense. Salzburg, Austria : Institut für Anglistik und Amerikanistik, Universität Salzburg, 2002.
BX2435 .P43 2002

Benesch, Friedrich.
Steiner, Rudolf, 1861-1925. Reverse ritual. Great Barrington, MA : Anthroposophic Press, c2001.
BP595.S894 R48 2001

BENEVOLENT INSTITUTIONS. *See* **HOSPITALS; SOCIAL SERVICE.**

Benevolo, Leonardo.
Metamorfosi della città. Milano : Garzanti / Scheiwiller, 1995 (1996 printing)
HT111 .M472 1995

BENIN - RELIGION.
Vallier, Gilles-Félix. La logique de l'éternité. 1998.

Beniste, José. As águas de Oxalá = Awǫn omi Oṣàlá / José Beniste. Rio de Janeiro, RJ, [Brazil] : Editora Bertrand Brasil, c2001 (2002 printing) 335 p. ; 22 cm. Includes bibliographical references (p. 334-335). In Portuguese, with some phrases and texts of songs and ceremonies in both Yoruba and Portuguese. ISBN 85-286-0965-0
1. Candomblé (Religion) 2. Candomblé (Religion) - Rituals. 3. Yoruba (African people) - Religion. 4. Yoruba (African people) - Rites and ceremonies. 5. Afro-Brazilian cults. 6. Gods, Afro-Brazilian. 7. Orishas. I. Title. II. Title: Awǫn omi Oṣàlá
BL2592.C35 B46 2001

Benitez, Juan Carlos. El concepto de poder en Alain Touraine / Juan Carlos Benitez. Buenos Aires : Editorial de Belgrano, 2002. 443 p. ; 23 cm. ISBN 950-577-307-2
1. Touraine, Alain - Political and social views. 2. Power (Social sciences) I. Title.
HM479.T6 B455 2002

Benítez Torres, Milton. Peregrinos y vagabundos : la cultura política de la violencia / Milton Benítez Torres. 1. ed. Quito, Ecuador : Ediciones Abya-Yala,

2002. 216 p. ; 21 cm. Includes bibliographical references.
ISBN 9978222561
1. Violence. 2. Sociology. I. Title.

BENJAMIN, WALTER, 1892-1940.
Sagnol, Marc, 1956- Tragique et tristesse. Paris : Cerf, 2003.

BENJAMIN, WALTER, 1892-1940 - CRITICISM AND INTERPRETATION.
Milmaniene, José E. Clínica del texto. [1. ed.]. Buenos Aires : Editorial Biblos, c2002.

Bennett, Mark, 1956 Dec. 10-.
The development of the social self. 1st ed. London ; New York : Psychology Press, 2003.
BF723.S24 D48 2003

Bennett, Robin Rose. Healing magic : a green witch guidebook / Robin Rose Bennett. New York : Sterling Pub., 2004. p. cm. Includes index. CONTENTS: Reconnecting with the earth -- Engaging mystery -- Moon magic and women's wisdom -- Herbal magic -- The medicine wheel of magic -- Spells -- Rituals -- Epilogue : a final story. ISBN 0-8069-7871-6 DDC 133.4/3
1. Witchcraft. 2. Spiritual healing. 3. Medicine, Magic, mystic, and spagiric. I. Title.
BF1572.S65 B46 2004

Bennis, Warren G. On becoming a leader / Warren Bennis. [Rev. ed.]. Cambridge, MA : Perseus Pub., c2003. xxxv, 218 p. ; 22 cm. "Updated and expanded, with a new introduction"--Cover. Includes bibliographical references (p. 209-212) and index. ISBN 0-7382-0817-5 DDC 158/.4
1. Leadership. 2. Leadership - Case studies. I. Title.
BF637.L4 B37 2003

BenShea, Noah. Dear friend / by Noah BenShea. Naperville, Ill. : Sourcebooks, c2003. p. cm. ISBN 1402201788 (alk. paper) DDC 177/.62
1. Friendship - Miscellanea. I. Title.
BF575.F66 B446 2003

Bentham, Jeremy, 1748-1832.
Mill, John Stuart, 1806-1873. Utilitarianism ; 2nd ed. Malden, MA : Blackwell Pub., 2003.
B1602 .A5 2003

Benussi, V. (Vittorio) [Selections. 2002]
Psychologische Schriften : textkritische Ausgabe in 2 Bänden / Vittorio Benussi ; herausgegeben von Mauro Antonelli. Amsterdam ; New York : Rodopi, 2002. 2 v. : ill. ; 23 cm. (Studien zur österreichischen Philosophie ; Bd. 34-35) Includes bibliographical references and indexes. CONTENTS: Bd. 1. Psychologische Aufsätze (1904-1914) -- Bd. 2. Psychologie der Zeitauffassung (1913). ISBN 90-420-1093-2 (v. 2) ISBN 90-420-1083-5 (v. 1) ISBN 90-420-1073-8 (Bde. 1+2)
1. Psychology. I. Antonelli, Mauro. II. Title. III. Series.

Benvenuto a Pisa.
Gianfaldoni, Paolo. [Fornacette, Pisa] : CLD iniziative speciali, c2000.

Benyon, David.
Designing information spaces. London ; New York : Springer, 2003.
QA76.9.C66 D49 2003

BEQUESTS. See INHERITANCE AND SUCCESSION.

BERDÎAEV, NIKOLAĬ, 1874-1948.
Przesmycki, Piotr, 1965- W stronę Bogoczłowieczeństwa. Łódź : "Ibidem", 2002.
B4238.B44 P79 2002

BEREAVEMENT. See also GRIEF.
Beem, Ellen Evaline, 1957- [Leiden : Universiteit Leiden, 2000]
BF575.G7 B422 2000

BEREAVEMENT.
Edgar, Robin A. In my mother's kitchen. 2nd ed. Charlotte, N.C. : Tree House Enterprises, 2003.
BF378.R44 E34 2003

Moalem, Shuli. Moʻalem, ahuvi. Tel Aviv : Yediʻot aḥaronot : Sifre ḥemed, c2002.

Peacock, Carol Antoinette. Death and dying. New York : Franklin Watts, c2004.
BF575.G7 P3783 2004

Smith, William A. (William Aloysius), 1929- Reflections on death, dying, and bereavement. Amityville, N.Y. : Baywood Pub., c2003.
BD444 .S57 2003

Veerman, David. When your father dies. Nashville, Tenn. : Thomas Nelson, c2003.
BF575.G7 V44 2003

Bereavement and consolation.
Bolitho, Harold. New Haven : Yale University Press, c2003.
DS822.2 .B65 2003

BEREAVEMENT - CASE STUDIES.
Stetson, Brad. Living victims, stolen lives. Amityville, N.Y. : Baywood Pub., c2003.
HV6533.C2 S73 2003

Bereavement dreaming and the individuating soul.
Grubbs, Geri A., 1943- Berwick, Me. : Nicolas-Hays, 2004.
BF1099.D4 G78 2004

BEREAVEMENT - EUROPE - PSYCHOLOGICAL ASPECTS - CASE STUDIES.
Groben, Joseph. Requiem für ein Kind. 2. Aufl. Köln : Dittrich, 2002.
BF575.G7 G76 2002

BEREAVEMENT IN ADOLESCENCE.
Liotta, Alfred J. When students grieve. Horsham, PA : LRP Publications, 2003.
BF724.3.D43 L56 2003

Perschy, Mary Kelly, 1942- Helping teens work through grief. 2nd ed. New York : Brunner-Routledge, 2004.
BF724.3.G73 P47 2004

BEREAVEMENT IN ADOLESCENCE - PSYCHOLOGICAL ASPECTS.
Myers, Edward, 1950- When will I stop hurting? Lanham, Md. : Scarecrow Press, 2004.
BF724.3.G73 M94 2004

BEREAVEMENT IN CHILDREN. See also GRIEF IN CHILDREN.
Fitzgerald, Helen. The grieving child. 2nd ed. New York : Simon & Schuster, 2003.
BF723.D3 F58 2003

Helping kids cope. Minneapolis : Fairview Press, 2003.
BF723.G75 H35 2003

Lewis, Paddy Greenwall, 1945- Helping children cope with the death of a parent. Westport, Conn. : Praeger, 2004.
BF723.G75 L49 2004

Liotta, Alfred J. When students grieve. Horsham, PA : LRP Publications, 2003.
BF724.3.D43 L56 2003

Rathkey, Julia Wilcox. What children need when they grieve. 1st ed. New York : Three Rivers Press, 2004.
BF723.G75 R38 2004

Wakenshaw, Martha. Caring for your grieving child. Oakland, Calif. : New Harbinger ; London : Hi Marketing, 2002.
BF723.G75 W35 2002

BEREAVEMENT IN CHILDREN - JUVENILE LITERATURE.
Dennison, Amy. Our dad died. Minneapolis, MN : Free Spirit Pub., c2003.
BF723.G75 D46 2003

Johnson, Marvin. Where's Jess? Rev. Omaha, NE : Centering Corp. Resource, 2003.
BF723.G75 J645 2003

Stenson, Lila. Daddy, up and down. 1st ed. Snowmass Village, CO : Peaceful Village Pub., 2002.
BF723.G75 S74 2002

BEREAVEMENT IN TEENAGERS. See BEREAVEMENT IN ADOLESCENCE.

BEREAVEMENT - JAPAN.
Bolitho, Harold. Bereavement and consolation. New Haven : Yale University Press, c2003.
DS822.2 .B65 2003

BEREAVEMENT - JUVENILE LITERATURE.
Peacock, Carol Antoinette. Death and dying. New York : Franklin Watts, c2004.
BF575.G7 P3783 2004

BEREAVEMENT - MISCELLANEA.
Kolb, Janice E. M. In corridors of eternal time. Nevada City, Calif. : Blue Dolphin Pub., 2003.
BF1997.K65 A3 2003b

BEREAVEMENT - PHYSIOLOGICAL ASPECTS.
Beem, Ellen Evaline, 1957- Bereavement. [Leiden : Universiteit Leiden, 2000]
BF575.G7 B422 2000

BEREAVEMENT - PSYCHOLOGICAL ASPECTS.
Beem, Ellen Evaline, 1957- Bereavement. [Leiden : Universiteit Leiden, 2000]
BF575.G7 B422 2000

Cornils, Stanley P. Your healing journey through grief. San Francisco, CA : Robert D. Reed Publishers, c2003.
BF575.G7 C677 2003

Daher, Douglas, 1949- And the passenger was death. Amityville, N.Y. : Baywood Pub., c2003.
BF575.G7 D34 2003

Davenport, Donna S. Singing mother home. Denton, Tex. : University of North Texas Press, c2002.
BF575.G7 D365 2002

DeVita, Elizabeth. The empty room. New York : Scribner 2004.
BF575.G7 D48 2004

Feldbaum, Rebecca Bram. If there's anything I can do--. Jerusalem, Israel : Nanuet, NY : Feldheim Publishers, 2003.
BF575.G7 F46 2003

Grubbs, Geri A., 1943- Bereavement dreaming and the individuating soul. Berwick, Me. : Nicolas-Hays, 2004.
BF1099.D4 G78 2004

Hedtke, Lorraine, 1957- Re-membering lives. Amityville, N.Y. : Baywood Pub. Co., 2004.
BF789.D4 H4 2004

Hjelmstad, Lois Tschetter. The last violet. Englewood, Colo. : Mulberry Hill Press, c2002.
BF575.G7 H575 2002

Isaacs, Diane R. Molly & Monet. Seattle, WA : Peanut Butter Pub., c1999.
BF575.G7 I86 1999

Kaufman, Barry Neil. No regrets. Novato, Calif. : HJ Kramer/New World Library, 2003.
BF575.G7 K385 2003

Kuebelbeck, Amy, 1964- Waiting with Gabriel. Chicago, Ill. : Loyola Press, c2003.
BF575.G7 K83 2003

Living beyond loss. 2nd ed. New York : W.W. Norton, 2004.
BF575.D35 L54 2004

Murray, Donald Morison, 1924- The lively shadow. 1st ed. New York : Ballantine Books, 2003.
BF575.G7 M868 2003

Neeld, Elizabeth Harper, 1940- Seven choices. New York : Warner Books, c2003.
BF575.G7 N44 2003

Ricciardi, Alessia. The ends of mourning. Stanford, Calif. : Stanford University Press, 2003.
PN56.D4 R53 2003

Roccatagliata Orsini, Susana. Un hijo no puede morir. 3. ed. Santiago de Chile : Grijalbo, 2000.
BF723.D3 R6 2000

Smith, Alison, 1968- Name all the animals. New York : Scribner, c2004.
BF575.G7 S58 2004

A teen's guide to coping. Minneapolis : Fairview Press, 2003.
BF789.D4 T44 2003

Walter, Carolyn Ambler. The loss of a life partner. New York : Columbia University Press, c2003.
BF575.G7 W3435 2003

White, Sharon. Field notes. Center City, Minn. : Hazelden, 2002.
BF575.G7 W485 2002

Wilkins, David, 1944- United by tragedy. Nampa, Idaho : Pacific Press Pub. Association, c2003.
BF575.G7 W555 2003

With eyes open [electronic resource]. San Francisco : KQED ; [Alexandria, Va.] : PBS
BF789.D4

Wruck, Wilfried, 1938- Zur Ruhe kommst du, Adrian Bruegge, nie. 1. Aufl. Berlin : Frieling, 2000.

BEREAVEMENT - PSYCHOLOGICAL ASPECTS - DICTIONARIES.
Adams, Christine A. ABC's of grief. Amityville, N.Y. : Baywood, c2003.
BF575.G7 A32 2003

BEREAVEMENT - PSYCHOLOGICAL ASPECTS - UNITED STATES.
Barzach, Amy Jaffe. Accidental courage, boundless dreams. 1st ed. West Hartford, CT : Aurora Pub., c2001.
BF575.G7 B375 2001

Bereiter, Carl. Education and mind in the knowledge age / Carl Bereiter. Mahwah, N.J. : L. Erlbaum Associates, 2002. xiii, 526 p. ; 25 cm. Includes bibliographical references (p. 485-506) and indexes. SUMMARY: Bereiter argues that education's conceptual tools are inadequate to address the pressing educational challenges and opportunities of the times. Two things are required: first, to replace the mind-as-container metaphor with one that envisions a mind capable of sustaining knowledgeable, intelligent behavior without actually containing stored beliefs; second, to recognize a fundamental difference between knowledge building and learning--both of which are essential parts of education for the knowledge age. Connectionism in cognitive science addresses the first need; certain developments in post-positivist epistemology address the second. The author explores both the theoretical bases and the practical educational implications of this radical change in viewpoint. The book draws on current new ways of thinking about knowledge and mind, including information processing, cognitive psychology, situated cognition, constructivism, social constructivism, and connectionism, but does not adhere strictly to any "camp." Above all, the author is concerned with developing a way of thinking about the mind that can usher education into the knowledge age. ISBN 0-8058-3942-9 (cloth : alk. paper) ISBN 0-8058-3943-7 (pbk. : alk. paper) DDC 370.15/23
1. Learning, Psychology of. 2. Knowledge, Theory of. 3. Cognition. 4. Educational change. I. Title.
LB1057 .B47 2002

Berezina, T. N. Mnogomernai͡a psikhika : vnutrenniĭ mir lichnosti / T.N. Berezina. Moskva : PER SĖ, 2001. 320 p. : ill. ; 21 cm. Includes bibliographical references (p. 305-317). ISBN 5929200297
1. Time - Psychological aspects. 2. Time perception. I. Title.
BF468 .B47 2001

Berg, Barbara A. How to escape the no-win trap / Barbara A. Berg. New York : McGraw-Hill, c2004. p. cm. Includes bibliographical references and index. Table of contents URL: http://www.loc.gov/catdir/toc/ecip047/2003018142.html CONTENTS: Understanding the world of no-win traps -- The birth of a no-win trap -- Common responses to no-win traps -- How double binded are you? -- Breaking your patterns of dissatisfaction -- Dealing with the no-win trap at work -- Decision points -- Living a trap-free life. ISBN 0-07-142361-3 (alk. paper) DDC 158
1. Decision making. 2. Double bind (Psychology) I. Title.
BF448 .B46 2004

Berg, Henk de, 1963- Freud's theory and its use in literary and cultural studies : an introduction / Henk de Berg. Rochester, NY : Camden House, 2003. xii, 155 p. : ill. ; 24 cm. (Studies in German literature, linguistics, and culture) Includes bibliographical references (p. [143]-149) and index. CONTENTS: 1. The birth of psychoanalysis ; Hysteria ; Conscious, preconscious, and unconscious ; Sexuality ; From polymorphous perversity to adult sexuality ; The normality of perversion -- 2. How to gain access to the unconscious ; The interpretation of dreams I ; The interpretation of dreams II: some problems ; The interpretation of Freudian slips I ; The interpretation of Freudian slips II: applications ; The interpretation of free associations ; The interpretation of resistance and transference -- 3. The unconscious and society ; Id, ego, and superego I ; Id, ego, and superego II: three examples ; The id and society ; The revolutionary nature of psychoanalysis -- 4. The psychoanalysis of literature ; The mystery of Hamlet ; Hamlet and Oedipus ; Hamlet's inner conflict ; The play, the author, the readers ; Psychoanalysis and literary criticism ; Unconscious communication: Heine's "Lore-Ley" ; Snow White, or the meaning and importance of fairy tales -- 5. The psychoanalysis of culture ; Totem and taboo I ; Totem and taboo II: its problems and its influence on literature ; Totem and taboo III: its application to the study of culture ; Man's cultural self-deception ; Two types of psychoanalysis. ISBN 1-57113-254-6 (hardcover : alk. paper) DDC 809/.93353
1. Psychoanalysis and literature. 2. Literature, Modern - History and criticism. 3. Psychoanalysis. I. Title. II. Series.
PN56.P92 B36 2003

Berg, Wendy, 1951- Polarity magic : the secret history of western religion / Wendy Berg and Mike Harris. St. Paul, Minn. : Llewellyn Publications, 2003. xvi, 367 p. : ill. ; 23 cm. Includes bibliographical references (p. 353-355) and index. ISBN 0-7387-0300-1 DDC 133.4/3
1. Magic - History. 2. Mysteries, Religious - History. 3. Mythology - History. 4. Occultism - History. I. Harris, Mike, 1947- II. Title.
BF1589 .B47 2003

Berger, Arthur Asa, 1933- The portable postmodernist / Arthur Asa Berger. Walnut Creek, CA ; Oxford : Altamira Press, c2003. xvii, 119 p. : ill. ; 24 cm. Includes bibliographical references (p. 109-112) and index. ISBN 0-7591-0313-5 (alk. paper) ISBN 0-7591-0314-3 (pbk. : alk. paper) DDC 149/.97
1. Postmodernism. I. Title.
B831.2 .B465 2003

Berger, Helen A., 1949- Voices from the pagan census : a national survey of witches and neo-pagans in the United States / Helen A. Berger, Evan A. Leach, Leigh S. Shaffer. Columbia, S.C. : University of South Carolina Press, c2003. xxii, 279 p. ; 24 cm. (Studies in comparative religion) Includes bibliographical references (p. [259]-266) and index. CONTENTS: The pagan census, neo-paganism, and neo-pagans -- Magic, mysticism, and politics -- Spiritual paths, forms of practice, and regional variations -- Families, children, and sexuality -- Popularization and institutional changes -- Festivals -- Voices of consensus and dissension, voices of concern and joy. ISBN 1-57003-488-5 (alk. paper) DDC 299
1. Witchcraft - United States. 2. Neopaganism - United States. I. Leach, Evan A. II. Shaffer, Leigh S. III. Title. IV. Series: Studies in comparative religion (Columbia, S.C.)
BF1573 .B48 2003

Berger, Kathleen Stassen. The developing person through the life span / Kathleen Stassen Berger. 6th ed. New York : Worth Publishers, 2004. p. cm. Includes bibliographical references and indexes. ISBN 0-7167-5706-0 (pbk.) DDC 155
1. Developmental psychology. I. Title.
BF713 .B463 2004

Berger, Lisa.
Gordon, Barry, M.D. Intelligent memory. New York : Viking, 2003.
BF371 .G66 2003

Bergeret, Jean. La sexualité infantile et ses mythes / Jean Bergeret, Marcel Houser ; avec la collaboration de Josiane Praz. Paris : Dunod, c2001. vii, 279 p. ; 24 cm. (Psychismes) Includes bibliographical references (p. [259]-271) and index. ISBN 2-10-005815-0 DDC 150
1. Children and sex. 2. Child analysis. 3. Children - Sexual behavior. 4. Narcissism in children. 5. Child psychology. 6. Psychoanalysis. I. Houser, Marcel. II. Title. III. Series.

Bergeron, Danielle.
Apollon, Willy. After Lacan. Albany : State University of New York Press, 2002.
RC506 .A65 2002

Bergman, Lars R. Studying individual development in an interindividual context : a person-oriented approach / Lars R. Bergman, David Magnusson, Bassam M. El Khouri. Mahwah, N.J. : L. Erlbaum Associates, 2003. xiv, 218 p. : ill. ; 24 cm. (Paths through life ; v. 4) Includes bibliographical references (p. 199-210) and indexes. ISBN 0-8058-3129-0 (alk. paper) ISBN 0-8058-3130-4 (pbk. : alk. paper) DDC 155
1. Developmental psychology - Social aspects. I. Magnusson, David. II. El-Khouri, Bassam. III. Title. IV. Series.
BF713 .B464 2003

Bergmark, Janet, 1955- In the presence of aliens : a personal experience of dual consciousness / Janet Bergmark. 1st ed. St. Paul, Minn. : Llewellyn Publications, 1997. xi, 209 p. ; 23 cm. Includes bibliographical references (p. 209). ISBN 1-56718-063-9 (pbk.) DDC 001.942
1. Human-alien encounters. I. Title.
BF2050 .B47 1997

BERGSON, HENRI, 1859-1941.
Merleau-Ponty, Maurice, 1908-1961. [Union de l'âme et du corps chez Malebranche, Biran et Bergson. English] The incarnate subject. Amherst, N.Y. : Humanity Books, 2001.
B2430.M379 U513 2001

Beristain, Carlos M. Apoyo psicosocial en catátrofes colectivas : de la prevención a la reconstrucción / Carlos Martín Beristain. 1a. ed. Caracas, Venezuela : Asociación Venezolana de Psicología Social-AVESPO : Comisión de Estudios de Posgrado, Facultad de Hunanidades y Educación, Universidad Central de Venezuela, 2000. 129 p. ; 22 cm. (Colección Temas y autores fundamentales) Includes bibliographical references (p. 127-129). ISBN 980-00-1777-1
1. Disasters - Psychological aspects. 2. Disaster victims - Psychology. 3. Crises intervention (Mental health services) I. Title. II. Series.

Beristáin, Helena.
Filosofía, retórica e interpretación. México, D.F. : Universidad Nacional Autónoma de México, 2000.

Beri'ut ha-'enayim yeha-limud ha-inṭensivi.
Koll, Shmuel, 1938- Sefer Ra'yonot u-mesarim. Yerushalayim : S. Kol, 761- [2001-

The Berkeley Tanner lectures
Raz, Joseph. The practice of value. Oxford ; New York : Oxford University Press, 2003.
BD232 .R255 2003

Berḳovits', Uri'el.
Eyal, Tsevi. Mi she-ṭa'am yayin Hungari. Tel Aviv : Yedi'ot aḥaronot : Sifre ḥemed, c2002.

Berli͡and, I. E. (Irina Efimovna).
Bibler, V. S. (Vladimir Solomonovich), 1918- Zamysly. Moskva : Rossiĭskiĭ gos. gumanitarnyĭ universitet, 2002.
B99.R9 B53 2002

Berlin, Lisa.
Early child development in the 21st century. New York : Teachers College Press, c2003.
LB1115 .E27 2003

Berlin, Naphtali Ẓevi Judah, 1817-1893. [Selections. 2001]
Otsrot ha-Netsiv : peninim, ḥidushim, u-ve'urim, derashot, amarot, 'ovdot ve-hanhagot 'arukh u-mesudar le-fi nośʼim va-'arakhim musariyim ve-hashḳafatiyim / mi-torato shel ... Naftali Tsevi Yehudah Berlin ; meluḳaṭ mi-kol ḥiburav e-k. ḳ. 'al yede Shim'on Vanunu. Yerushalayim : Ben Arzah, 762 [2001 or 2002] 369 p. : ports. ; 25 cm. Cover title: Otsrot ha-Netsiv mi-Voloz'in. Includes bibliographical references.
1. Berlin, Naphtali Ẓevi Judah, - 1817-1893. 2. Ethics, Jewish. 3. Judaism - Doctrines. I. Vanunu, Shim'on. II. Title. III. Title: Otsrot ha-Netsiv mi-Voloz'in
BM755.B52 A25 2001

BERLIN, NAPHTALI ẒEVI JUDAH, 1817-1893.
Berlin, Naphtali Ẓevi Judah, 1817-1893. [Selections. 2001] Otsrot ha-Netsiv. Yerushalayim : Ben Arzah, 762 [2001 or 2002]
BM755.B52 A25 2001

Berliner Theaterwissenschaft
(Bd. 8) Herrschaft des Symbolischen. Berlin : Vistas, c2002.

(Bd. 9) Kalisch, Eleonore. Konfigurationen der Renaissance. Berlin : Vistas, c2002.

Berlinski, David, 1942- The secrets of the vaulted sky : astrology and the art of prediction / David Berlinski. 1st U.S. ed. Orlando, Fla. : Harcourt, c2003. 305 p. : ill. ; 24 cm. Includes bibliographical references (p. [269]-285) and index. Table of contents URL: http://www.loc.gov/catdir/toc/ecip043/2003009789.html Publisher description URL: http://www.loc.gov/catdir/description/har031/2003009789.html ISBN 0-15-100527-3 DDC 133.5
1. Astrology - History. I. Title.
BF1674 .B47 2003

Bermudez, Jose Luis.
Art and morality. London ; New York : Routledge, 2003.
BH39 .A695 2003

Thinking without words / Jose Luis Bermudez. Oxford ; New York : Oxford University Press, 2003. xiii, 225 p. : ill. ; 25 cm. (Philosophy of mind series) Includes bibliographical references (p. [195]-217) and index. ISBN 0-19-515969-1 (alk. paper) DDC 128/.3
1. Philosophy of mind. I. Title. II. Series.
BD418.3 .B47 2003

BERNARD, OF CLAIRVAUX, SAINT, 1090 OR 91-1153.
Zerbi, Piero. "Philosophi" e "logici". Roma : Istituto storico italiano per il Medio Evo ; Milano : Vita e pensiero, 2002.
B765.A24 Z473 2002

Bernardo, Allan B. I.
Forty years of Philippine psychology. Diliman, Quezon City, Philippines : Psychological Association of the Philippines, c2002.
BF108 .F67 2002

Bernasconi, Robert.
Race and racism in continental philosophy. Bloomington : Indiana University Press, c2003.
HT1523 .R2514 2003

Berns, Jörg Jochen.
Seelenmaschinen. Wien : Böhlau Verlag, c2000.
BF381 .S44 2000

Bernshteĭn, Boris Moiseevich. Pigmalion naiznanku : k istorii stanovlenii͡a mira iskusstva / B.M. Bernshteĭn. Moskva : I͡Azyki slavi͡anskoĭ kul'tury, 2002. 219 p. : ill. ; 20 cm. (I͡Azyk, semiotika, kul'tura. Malai͡a serii͡a) Includes bibliographical references (p. [197]-219). ISBN 5944570555
1. Art - History. I. Title. II. Series.
N5300 .B614 2002

Bernstein, Douglas A.
Psychology. 6th ed. Boston : Houghton Mifflin Co., c2003.
BF121 .P794 2003

Bernstein, Frances. Classical living : reconnecting with the rituals of ancient Rome : myths, gods, goddesses, celebrations, and rites for every month of the year / Frances Bernstein. 1st ed. San Francisco : HarperSanFrancisco, 2000. ix, 244 p. : ill. ; 24 cm.

Includes index. ISBN 0-06-251624-8 (hc) ISBN 0-06-251625-6 (paper) DDC 292.3/8
1. Rites and ceremonies - Rome. 2. Religious calendars - Rome. 3. Rome - Religion. 4. Rome - Religious life and customs. 5. Spiritual life. I. Title.
BL808 .B47 2000

Berry, Carmen Renee. When helping you is hurting me : escaping the Messiah trap / Carmen Renee Berry. Revised and updated ed. New York : Crossroad Pub. Co., c2003. 176 p. ; 21 cm. "An 8th Avenue book." Originally published: San Francisco : Harper & Row, c1988. Table of contents URL: http://www.loc.gov/catdir/toc/ecip044/2003010797.html CONTENTS: How I learned about the Messiah trap -- What is the Messiah trap? -- Can there be a hidden trap in a "happy" childhood? -- How Messiahs are trapped through childhood trauma -- What kind of Messiah are you? -- What are the eight Messiah characteristics? -- How the Messiah trap hurts others -- How to escape the Messiah trap -- Take the path to freedom. ISBN 0-8245-2108-0 (alk. paper) DDC 158/.2
1. Self-sacrifice. 2. Child psychology. 3. Self-sacrifice - Case studies. I. Title.
BF637.S42 B47 2003

Berry, Joy Wilt.
Let's talk about.
Berry, Joy Wilt. Let's talk about feeling embarrassed. New York : Scholastic, c2002.
BF723.E44 B47 2002

Berry, Joy Wilt. Let's talk about getting hurt. New York : Scholastic, c2002.
BF723.W67 B475 2002

Berry, Joy Wilt. Saying no. New York : Scholastic, c2001.
BF723.R4 B37 2001

Let's talk about feeling embarrassed / Joy Berry ; illustrated by Maggie Smith. New York : Scholastic, c2002. 1 v. (unpaged) : col. ill. ; 20 cm. (Let's talk about) ISBN 0-439-34164-7
1. Embarrassment in children - Juvenile literature. I. Smith, Maggie, ill. II. Title. III. Title: Feeling embarrassed IV. Series: Berry, Joy Wilt. Let's talk about.
BF723.E44 B47 2002

Let's talk about feeling worried / by Joy Berry ; illustrated by Maggie Smith. New York : Scholastic Inc., c2002. 1 v. (unpaged) : col. ill. ; 20 cm. ISBN 0-439-34158-2
1. Worry in children - Juvenile literature. I. Smith, Maggie, ill. II. Title. III. Title: Feeling worried
BF723.W67 B47 2002

Let's talk about getting hurt / Joy Berry ; illustrated by Maggie Smith. New York : Scholastic, c2002. 1 v. (unpaged) : col. ill. ; 20 cm. (Let's talk about) ISBN 0-439-34165-5
1. Worry in children - Juvenile literature. 2. Children - Wounds and injuries - Juvenile literature. I. Smith, Maggie, ill. II. Title. III. Title: Getting hurt IV. Series: Berry, Joy Wilt. Let's talk about.
BF723.W67 B475 2002

Saying no / by Joy Berry ; illustrated by Maggie Smith. New York : Scholastic, c2001. 1 v. (unpaged) : col. ill. ; 20 cm. (Let's talk about) Spine title: Let's talk about saying no. SUMMARY: Examines, in simple text and illustrations, situations when saying no is an appropriate response and situations when it is the wrong thing to say. ISBN 0-439-34150-7 DDC 158.2
1. Reasoning in children - Juvenile literature. 2. Negation (Logic) in children - Juvenile literature. 3. Decision making. I. Smith, Maggie, ill. II. Title. III. Title: Let's talk about saying no IV. Series: Berry, Joy Wilt. Let's talk about.
BF723.R4 B37 2001

Bersoff, Donald N.
Ethical conflicts in psychology. 3rd ed. Washington, DC : American Psychological Association, c2003.
BF76.4 .E814 2003

Bertelloni, Francisco.
La filosofía medieval. Madrid : Trotta, 2002.
B721 .F47 2002

Bertelsen, Preben. Free will, consciousness, and the self / Preben Bertelsen. New York : Berghahn Books, 2003. p. cm. (Studies in the understanding of the human condition) Includes bibliographical references and index. ISBN 1-57181-661-5 (alk. paper) DDC 150.19/8
1. Free will and determinism. 2. Consciousness. 3. Self. 4. Evolutionary psychology. I. Title. II. Series.
BF621 .B47 2003

Berthier, Denis. Le savoir et l'ordinateur / Denis Berthier. Paris : Harmattan, c2002. 457 p. ; 24 cm. Includes bibliographical references (p. 447-456). ISBN 2-7475-3350-6 DDC 400

1. Artificial intelligence - Data processing - Social aspects. 2. Knowledge, Sociology of. I. Title.

Berto, G. (Graziella) Freud, Heidegger : lo spaesamento / Graziella Berto. Milano : Bompiani, c1998. xiii, 247 p. ; 22 cm. (Studi Bompiani. Filosofia) ISBN 88-452-4199-8
1. Psychoanalysis and philosophy - History. 2. Freud, Sigmund, - 1856-1939. 3. Heidegger, Martin, - 1889-1976. I. Title. II. Series.
BF175.4.P45 B46 1998

Bertram, Georg W., 1967- Hermeneutik und Dekonstruktion : Konturen einer Auseinandersetzung der Gegenwartsphilosophie / Georg W. Bertram. München : Fink, c2002. 234 p. ; 22 cm. Includes bibliographical references (p. [223]-232) and index. ISBN 3-7705-3643-6 (pbk.)
1. Hermeneutics. 2. Deconstruction. I. Title.
BD241 .B47 2002

Holismus in der Philosophie. 1. Aufl. Weilerswist : Velbrück Wissenschaft, c2002.

Bertrand, Jean-Paul.
Le Fèvre, Jean-Yves. Eloge de la mort. Monaco : Rocher, c2002.

Berühmte Frauen.
Müller, Arno, 1930- Wien : Braumüller, 2002.

Besamusca, Bart. The book of Lancelot : the Middle Dutch Lancelot compilation and the medieval tradition of narrative cycles / Bart Besamusca ; translated by Thea Summerfield. Cambridge : D.S. Brewer, 2003. ix, 210 p. : ill. ; 25 cm. (Arthurian studies, 0261-9814 ; 53) Includes bibliographical references (p. [191]-204) and index. ISBN 0-85991-769-X DDC 839.3/11109
1. Lancelot (Prose romance) 2. Dutch literature - To 1500 - History and criticism. 3. Lancelot (Legendary character) - Romances - History and criticism. 4. Arthurian romances - History and criticism. 5. Civilization, Medieval, in literature. 6. Grail - Romances - History and criticism. 7. Knights and knighthood in literature. I. Title. II. Series.
PT5568 .B47 2003

Beskova, I. A. Ėvoliutsiia i soznanie : novyĭ vzgliad / I.A. Beskova. Moskva : "Indrik", 2002. 254 p. : ill. ; 22 cm. "Nauchnoe izdanie"--Colophon. At head of title: Rossiĭskaia akademiia nauk. Institut filosofii. Includes bibliographical references. ISBN 5857591651
1. Consciousness. 2. Human evolution. 3. Symbolism (Psychology) 4. Cognition. I. Title.
B808.9 .B476 2002x

Le besoin de savoir.
Mijolla-Mellor, Sophie de. Paris : Dunod, c2002.
BF723.S4 M556 2002

Bessière, Céline.
Baudelot, Christian. Travailler pour être heureux? [Paris] : Fayard, c2003.

Bessire, Linda M.
Cronin, W. Jean. Going for the gold. Longmont, CO : Sopris West, c2003.
BF637.B4 C76 2003

Bessis, Sophie, 1947-
[Occident et les autres. English]
Western supremacy : triumph of an idea? / Sophie Bessis ; translated by Patrick Camiller. London ; New York : Zed Books, 2003. x, 290 p. ; 24 cm. Original title: L'Occident et les autres: histoire d'une suprematie. Includes bibliographical references (p. 239-280) and index. Publisher description URL: http://www.loc.gov/catdir/description/hol031/2002031119.html ISBN 1-84277-218-X (hbk.) ISBN 1-84277-219-8 (pbk.) DDC 909/.09821
1. Civilization, Western. 2. East and West. 3. North and south. 4. Imperialism - History. 5. Decolonization. 6. Globalization. I. Camiller, Patrick. II. Title.
CB245 .B4613 2003

BEST BOOKS. See CANON (LITERATURE).

Best practice : ideas and insights from the world's foremost business thinkers. Cambridge, MA : Perseus Publishing, c2003. ix, 419 p. ; 23 cm. "With an introduction by Rosabeth Moss Kanter"--Cover. ISBN 0-7382-0822-1
1. Industrial management. 2. Business enterprises. 3. Leadership. I. Title: Ideas and insights from the world's foremost business thinkers

The best test preparation for the Advanced Placement Examination : psychology / staff of Research & Education Association ; M. Fogiel, director. Piscataway, N.J. : Research & Education Association, c2003. xii, 311 p. : ill. ; 26 cm. Spine title: AP psychology. ISBN 0-87891-883-3 DDC 150/.76
1. Psychology - Examinations - Study guides. 2. Psychology - Examinations, questions, etc. 3. Advanced placement programs (Education) I. Fogiel, M. (Max) II. Research and Education

Association. III. Title: Advanced Placement Examination, psychology IV. Title: AP psychology
BF78 .B48 2003

The best test preparation for the CLEP, College-Level Examination Program, human growth & development : featuring the latest on the CLEP computer-based test (CBT) / staff of Research & Education Association, M. Fogiel, director. Piscataway, N.J. : Research & Education Association, c2003. ix, 255 p. : ill. ; 26 cm. Spine title: Best test preparation for the CLEP human growth & development. ISBN 0-87891-902-3 DDC 155/.076
1. Developmental psychology - Examinations, questions, etc. 2. Human growth - Examinations, questions, etc. I. Fogiel, M. (Max) II. Research and Education Association. III. Title: Best test preparation for the CLEP human growth & development
BF713 .B49 2003

Best test preparation for the CLEP human growth & development.
The best test preparation for the CLEP, College-Level Examination Program, human growth & development. Piscataway, N.J. : Research & Education Association, c2003.
BF713 .B49 2003

The best test preparation for the Graduate Record Examination, GRE psychology.
Kellogg, Ronald Thomas. Piscataway, N.J. : Research and Education Association, [2000]
BF78 .K45 2000

Best words, best order.
Dobyns, Stephen, 1941- 2nd ed. New York : Palgrave Macmillan, 2003.

Le bestiaire des philosophes.
Roche, Christian. [Paris] : Seuil, c2001.
BESTIARIES.
Roche, Christian. Le bestiaire des philosophes. [Paris] : Seuil, c2001.

Besuch vom Mittagsdämon.
Decher, Friedhelm. 1. Aufl. Lüneburg : zu Klampen, 2000.
BF575.B67 .D43 2000

Bet ginze.
[Mishnah. Avot. 2001.] Sefer Bet ginze. Yerushalayim : R. M. Lurya, 762 [2001 or 2002]

Bet Raḥel.
Naphtali ben Isaac, ha-Kohen, 1649-1719. Sefer Bet Raḥel. Yerushalayim : Ahavat Shalom, 761 [2001]
BM665 .N257 2001

Beta, Hymenaeus.
[Clavicula Salomonis. English.] The Goetia. York Beach, Me. : Samuel Weiser, 1995.
BF1611 .C5413 1995

Betancourt, Sebastián.
Rosero Garcés, F. (Fernando) Líderes sociales en el siglo XXI. Quito : Ediciones Abya-Yala, 2002.

Betrifft: Geschlecht
(Bd. 1) Augustin, Nicole. "Bewegung in Widersprüchen. Widersprüche in Bewegung bringen". Pfaffenweiler : Centaurus-Verlagsgesellschaft, 1998.
LC2873.G3 A94 1998

BETROTHAL. See COURTSHIP; MARRIAGE; MATE SELECTION.

Betsch, Tilmann.
Etc. frequency processing and cognition. Oxford ; New York : Oxford University Press, c2002.
BF448 .E83 2002

Betsky, Aaron. Landscrapers : building with the land / Aaron Betsky. New York, New York : Thames & Hudson, 2002. 191 p. : ill. ; 24 x 28 cm. Includes index. ISBN 0-500-34188-5 DDC 720.47
1. Architecture - Environmental aspects. 2. Architecture, Modern - 20th century. I. Title.

Better than well.
Elliott, Carl, 1961- 1st ed. New York : W.W. Norton, c2003.
RA418.3.U6 E455 2003

BETTING. See GAMBLING.

Betty.
Driver, Betty, 1920- Large print ed. Long Preston : Magna, 2000.

Betty la fea.
Méndez, José Luis, 1941- El irresistible encanto de Betty la fea. San Juan, P.R. : Ediciones Milenio, 2001.

Between astrolgers and clients.
Mulligan, Bob. Naples, Fla. : Astrology Co., c2001.
BF1711 .M85 2001

Between astrologers & clients.
Mulligan, Bob. Between astrolgers and clients. Naples, Fla. : Astrology Co., c2001.
BF1711 .M85 2001

Between chance and choice : interdisciplinary perspectives on determinism / edited by Harald Atmanspacher and Robert Bishop. Thorverton, UK ; Charlottesville, VA : Imprint Academic, c2002. 527 p. : ill. ; 24 cm. Includes bibliographical references and index. ISBN 0-907845-21-5 DDC 123
1. Free will and determinism. I. Atmanspacher, Harald. II. Bishop, Robert, Dr.
BJ1461 .B48 2002

Between culture and biology : perspectives on ontogenetic development / edited by Heidi Keller, Ype H. Poortinga, Axel Schölmerich. Cambridge, U.K. ; New York : Cambridge University Press, 2002. xxi, 419 p. : ill. ; 23 cm. (Cambridge studies in cognitive and perceptual development) Includes bibliographical references and indexes. Publisher description URL: http://www.loc.gov/catdir/description/cam022/2002020173.html Table of contents URL: http://www.loc.gov/catdir/toc/cam022/2002020173.html ISBN 0-521-79120-0 ISBN 0-521-79452-8 (pbk.) DDC 155
1. Child psychology. 2. Developmental psychology. 3. Child development. I. Keller, Heidi, 1945- II. Poortinga, Ype H., 1939- III. Schölmerich, Axel. IV. Series: Cambridge studies in cognitive perceptual development.
BF721 .B4138 2002

Between femininities.
Gonick, Marnina. Albany : State University of New York Press, c2003.
HQ777 .G65 2003

Between hierarchies & markets.
Thompson, Grahame. Between hierarchies and markets. Oxford ; New York : Oxford University Press, 2003.
HD58.7 .T4786 2003

Between hierarchies and markets.
Thompson, Grahame. Oxford ; New York : Oxford University Press, 2003.
HD58.7 .T4786 2003

Between philosophy and poetry : writing, rhythm, history / edited by Massimo Verdicchio and Robert Burch. New York : Continuum, 2002. vi, 222 p. ; 24 cm. (Textures) Includes bibliographical references (p. [207]-214) and index. ISBN 0-8264-6005-4 ISBN 0-8264-6006-2 (pbk.) DDC 101
1. Philosophy. 2. Poetry. I. Verdicchio, Massimo, 1945- II. Burch, Robert, 1949- III. Series: Textures (New York, N.Y.)
B66 .B48 2002

Between the two World Wars.
Von Mises, Ludwig, 1881-1973. Indianapolis, Ind. : Liberty Fund, c2002.
HB101.V66A25 2002

Between Torah and wisdom : Rabbi Menachem ha-Meiri and the Maimonidean halakhists in Provence.
Halbertal, Moshe. Ben Torah le-hokhmah. Yerushalayim : Hotsa'at sefarim 'a. sh. Y. L. Magnes, ha-Universitah ha-'Ivrit, 760, 2000.
BM755.M54 H35 2000

Between tradition and postmodernity : Polish ethnography at the turn of the millenium / edited by Lech Mróz, Zofia Sokolewicz. Warsaw : Wydawnictwo DiG, 2003. 288 p. ; 25 cm. (Prace Komitetu Nauk Etnologicznych PAN ; v. 11) Includes bibliographical references. At head of title: Committee of Ethnological Sciences, Polish Academy of Science, Institute of Ethnology and Cultural Anthropology of the University of Warsaw. ISBN 83-7181-285-X
1. Ethnology. 2. Ethnology - Philosophy. I. Mróz, Lech. II. Sokolewicz, Zofia. III. Series.

Between worlds.
Chajes, Jeffrey Howard. Philadelphia : University of Pennsylvania Press, c2003.
BM729.D92 C53 2003

Beuchot, Mauricio.
Filosofía, retórica e interpretación. México, D.F. : Universidad Nacional Autónoma de México, 2000.

La filosofía y el lenguaje en la historia : discurso de ingreso a la Academia Mexicana de la Lengua / Mauricio Beuchot ; respuesta / Ramón Xirau. México, D.F. : UNAM, 2000. 51 p. ; 14 cm. Includes bibliographical references. ISBN 968-36-8128-X
1. Language and languages - Philosophy. 2. Historiography. I. Academia Mexicana Correspondiente de la Española. II. Title.

Beutler, Larry E. Integrative assessment of adult personality / by Larry E. Beutler, Gary Groth-Marnat. 2nd ed. New York : Guilford Press, 2003. p. cm. Includes bibliographical references and index. ISBN 1-57230-670-X DDC 155.2/8
1. Personality assessment. 2. Personality tests. 3. Adulthood - Psychological aspects. I. Groth-Marnat, Gary. II. Title.
BF698.4 .B42 2003

BEVERAGES - EUROPE - HISTORY - TO 1500.
Verdon, Jean. Boire au moyen âge. [Paris] : Perrin, c2002.

BEVERAGES - MISCELLANEA.
Telesco, Patricia, 1960- A witch's beverages and brews. Franklin Lakes, NJ : New Page Books, c2001.
BF1572.R4 T447 2001

Beverley-Smith, Huw. Commercial appropriation of personality / Huw Beverley-Smith. Cambridge, UK ; New York : Cambridge University Press, 2002. xxxvi, 364 p. 24 cm. (Cambridge studies in intellectual property rights) Includes bibliographical references (p. 330-348) and index. CONTENTS: Pt. I.A framework. The problem of appropriation of personality -- Pt. II. Economic interests and the law of unfair competition. Introduction ; Statutory and extra-legal remedies ; Goodwill in personality: the tort of passing off in English and Australian law ; unfair competition and the doctrine of misappropriation -- Pt. III. Dignitary interests. Introduction ; Privacy and publicity in the United States ; Privacy interests in English law ; Interests in reputation -- Pt. IV. Pervasive problems. Property in personality ; Justifying a remedy for appropriation of personality -- Pt. V. Conclusions. The autonomy of appropriation of personality. ISBN 0-521-80014-5 (hardback) DDC 346.04/8
1. Personality (Law) 2. Publicity (Law) 3. Intellectual property. I. Title. II. Series.
K627 .B48 2002

Bevir, Mark.
Begriffsgeschichte, Diskursgeschichte, Metapherngeschichte. Göttingen : Wallstein, 2002.
D13 .B45 2002

"Bewegung in Widersprüchen, Widersprüche in Bewegung bringen".
Augustin, Nicole. Pfaffenweiler : Centaurus-Verlagsgesellschaft, 1998.
LC2873.G3 A94 1998

Bewes, Timothy. Reification, or, The anxiety of late capitalism / Timothy Bewes. London ; New York : Verso, 2002. xvii, 334 p. : ill. ; 23 cm. Includes bibliographical references (p. [291]-318) and index. ISBN 1-85984-685-8 (cloth) ISBN 1-85984-456-1 (paper) DDC 301
1. Postmodernism - Social aspects. 2. Civilization, Modern - Philosophy. 3. Reality. 4. Social perception. 5. Philosophy, Modern. I. Title. II. Title: Reification III. Title: Anxiety of late capitalism
HM449 .B49 2002

Bewitching love potions & charms.
Tempest, Raven. London : Cassell Illustrated ; New York, NY : Distributed in the USA by Sterling Pub. Co., c2003.
BF575.L8 .T45 2003

Beyerlein, Michael Martin.
The collaborative work systems fieldbook. San Francisco : Jossey-Bass/Pfeiffer, c2003.
HD66 .C547 2003

Beyond budgeting.
Hope, Jeremy. Boston : Harvard Business School Press, c2003.
HD31 .H635 2003

Beyond coping : meeting goals, visions, and challenges / edited by Erica Frydenberg. Oxford ; New York : Oxford University Press, 2002. xiii, 253 p. : ill. ; 24 cm. Includes bibliographical references and index. ISBN 0-19-850814-X (pbk. : alk. paper) DDC 155.2/4
1. Adjustment (Psychology) 2. Adjustment (Psychology) in adolescence. 3. Success - Psychological aspects. 4. Success in adolescence. I. Frydenberg, Erica, 1943-
BF335 .B49 2002

Beyond death.
Scott, Christopher, 1946- Nevada City, CA : Blue Dolphin Pub., 2001.
BF1261 .S45 2001

Beyond foraging and collecting : evolutionary change in hunter-gatherer settlement systems / edited by Ben Fitzhugh and Junko Habu. New York : Kluwer Academic/Plenum Publishers, c2002. xvii, 442 p. : ill., maps ; 24 cm. (Fundamental issues in archaeology) Includes bibliographical references and index. Table of contents URL: http://www.loc.gov/catdir/toc/fy033/2002066908.html CONTENTS: Introduction, Beyond foraging and collecting : evolutionary change in hunter-gatherer settlement systems / Junko Habu and Ben Fitzhugh -- Going by boat : the forager-collector continuum at sea / Kenneth M. Ames -- Jomon collectors and foragers : regional interactions and long-term changes in settlement systems among prehistoric hunter-gatherers in Japan / Junku Habu -- Logistical organization, social complexity, and the collapse of prehistoric Thule whaling societies in the central Canadian Arctic archipelago / James M. Savelle -- Natufian : a complex society of foragers / Ofer Bar-Yosef -- Mobility, search modes, and food-getting technology : from Magdalenian to Early Mesolithic in the upper Danube basin / Lynn E. Fisher -- Long-term land tenure systems in Central Brazil : evolutionary ecology, risk-management, and social geography / Renato Kipnis. CONTENTS: Central place foraging and prehistoric pinyon utilization in the Great Basin / David W. Zeanah -- Residential and logistical strategies in the evolution of complex hunter-gatherers on the Kodiak archipelago / Ben Fitzhugh -- Sacred power and seasonal settlement on the central northwest coast / Aubrey Cannon -- Long-term change and short-term shifting in the economy of Philippine forager-traders / Laura Lee Junker -- Explaining changes in settlement dynamics across transformations of modes of production : from hunting to herding in the south-central Andes / Mark Aldenderfer -- Afterword, Beyond foraging and collecting : retrospect and prospect / T. Douglas Price. ISBN 0-306-46753-4 DDC 303.4
1. Hunting and gathering societies. 2. Human evolution. 3. Social evolution. 4. Land settlement patterns, Prehistoric. I. Fitzhugh, Ben. II. Habu, Junko, 1959- III. Series.
GN388 .B49 2002

Beyond individual and group differences.
Lamiell, James T. Thousand Oaks, Calif. : Sage Publications, c2003.
BF105 .L36 2003

Beyond integration : challenges of belonging in diaspora and exile / edited by Maja Povrzanović Frykman. Lund, Sweden : Nordic Academic Press, c2001. 224 p. ; 23 cm. Includes bibliographical references. ISBN 91-89116-17-8
1. Emigration and immigration - Social aspects. 2. Refugees. 3. Identity (Philosophical concept) I. Frykman, Maja Povrzanović.
JV6225 .B49 2001

Beyond Keynes / edited by Sheila C. Dow and John Hillard. Cheltenham ; Northampton, Mass. : Edward Elgar, c2002. 2 v. : ill. ; 24 cm. (Post-Keynesian Economics Study Group) "In association with the Post-Keynesian Economics Study Group." Includes bibliographical references and index. CONTENTS: v. 1. Post Keynesian econometrics, microeconomics and the theory of the firm -- v. 2. Keynes, uncertainty and the global economy. ISBN 1-85898-584-6 (v. 1) ISBN 1-85898-797-0 (v. 2)
1. Keynes, John Maynard, - 1883-1946. 2. Econometrics. 3. Microeconomics. 4. Corporations. 5. Macroeconomics. 6. Economic policy. 7. Economic history - 20th century. 8. Economic forecasting. 9. Uncertainty. 10. Competition. 11. Labor economics. 12. International finance. 13. Globalization - Economic aspects. 14. Keynesian economics. I. Dow, Sheila C. II. Hillard, John, 1946- III. Post-Keynesian Economics Study Group. IV. Title: Post Keynesian econometrics, microeconomics and the theory of the firm. V. Title: Keynes, uncertainty and the global economy. VI. Series: Post-Keynesian Economics Study Group (Series)

Beyond knowledge : extracognitive aspects of developing high ability / edited by Larisa V. Shavinina, Eric Sprott, Michel Ferrari. Mahwah, N.J. : L. Erlbaum Associates, 2003. p. cm. (The educational psychology series) Includes bibliographical references and indexes. ISBN 0-8058-3991-7 (cloth : alk. paper) ISBN 0-8058-3992-5 (pbk. : alk. paper) DDC 153.9
1. Genius. 2. Gifted persons. 3. Creative ability. 4. Creative thinking. I. Shavinina, Larisa V. II. Sprott, Eric. III. Ferrari, Michel, Ph. D. IV. Series.
BF412 .B44 2003

Beyond self-esteem.
Cottle, Thomas J. New York : P. Lang, c2003.
BF697 .C675 2003

Beyond sex and gender.
Cealey Harrison, Wendy. London ; Thousand Oaks, Calif. : SAGE, 2002.
HQ1075 .C43 2002

Beyond significance testing: reforming data analysis methods in behavioral research.
Kline, Rex B. 1st ed. Washington, DC : American Psychological Association, c2004.
BF39 .K59 2004

Beyond the breath.
Glickman, Marshall. 1st ed. Boston : Journey Editions ; North Clarendon, VT : Distributed by Tuttle Pub., 2002.
BQ5630.V5 G54 2002

Beyond the century of the child : cultural history and developmental psychology / edited by Willem Koops and Michael Zuckerman. Philadelphia : University of Pennsylvania Press, c2003. xi, 289 p. : ill. ; 24 cm. Includes bibliographical references (p. [249]-274) and index. Table of contents URL: http://www.loc.gov/catdir/toc/fy035/ 2002075057.html ISBN 0-8122-3704-8 (cloth : alk. paper) DDC 305.23/09
1. Children - History. 2. Child development - History. 3. Developmental psychology. I. Koops, W. (Willem) II. Zuckerman, Michael, 1939-
HQ767.87 .B49 2003

Beyond the trauma vortex.
Ross, Gina, 1947- Berkeley, Calif. : North Atlantic Books, c2003.
PN4784.D57 R67 2003

Beyond these four walls.
Occhino, MaryRose. New York : Berkley Books, 2003.
BF1283.O27 A3 2003

Bhalla, C. M. (Chander M.).
Agarwal, G. S., 1936- Dictionary of astrology. New Delhi : Sagar Publications, 2002.
BF1714.H5 A33 2002

Bharadwaj, Monisha. The Indian luck book : how to bring luck into your life / Monisha Bharadwaj. London : Kyle Cathie, 2001. 255 p. : ill. (chiefly col.) ; 25 cm. Includes bibliographical references (p. [254]) and index. ISBN 1-85626-421-1 DDC 158
1. Fortune. 2. Fortune-telling - India. 3. Hindu symbolism. 4. Astrology and gems. I. Title.
BF1778 .B43 2001

Bharateey darshan men dukha aur mukti.
Siṃha, Kīrti Kumāra. Bhāratīya darśana meṃ duḥkha aura mukti. 1. saṃskaraṇa. Ilāhābāda : Śekhara Prakāśana, 2001.
B132.M64 S56 2001

Bhāratīya darśana meṃ duḥkha aura mukti.
Siṃha, Kīrti Kumāra. 1. saṃskaraṇa. Ilāhābāda : Śekhara Prakāśana, 2001.
B132.M64 S56 2001

Bhāratīya darśana paribhāṣhā kośa = Definitional dictionary of Indian philosophy. Naī Dillī : Vaijñānika tathā Takanīkī Śabdāvalī Āyoga, Mānava Saṃsādhana Vikāsa Mantrālaya, Śikṣhā Vibhāga, Bhārata Sarakāra, 1999- v. ; 19 cm. Hindi and English.
1. Philosophy, Indic. I. India. Commission for Scientific and Technical Terminology. II. Title: Definitional dictionary of Indian philosophy
B131 .B498 1999

Bhāratīya Kuṇḍalī-vimarśa.
Śāstrī, Girijā Śaṅkara. 1. saṃskaraṇa. Ilāhābāda : Jyotiṣa Karmakāṇḍa evaṃ Ādhyātma Śodha Saṃsthāna, 2002.
BF1714.H5+

Bhāratīya tattvajñānācā bṛhad itihāsa.
Joṣī, Gajānana Nārāyaṇa. 1. āvṛttī. Puṇe : Marāṭhī Tattvajñāna-Mahākośa Maṇḍala yāñce karitā Śubhadā-Sārasvata Prakāśana, 1994.
B131 .J674 1994

Bhargava, K. K. (Kant Kishore).
South Asia, 2010. Delhi : Konark Publishers, 2002.

BHARTRHARI. VĀKYAPADĪYA.
Alackapally, Sebastian, 1961- Being and meaning. 1st ed. Delhi : Motilal Banarsidass Publishers, 2002.
PK541.B48 A43 2002

Bhattacharyya, Gargi, 1964- Sexuality and society : an introduction / Gargi Bhattacharyya. London ; New York : Routledge, 2002. 193 p. ; cm. Includes bibliographical references (p. [174]-187) and index. ISBN 0-415-22902-2 (HB) ISBN 0-415-22903-0 (pbk.) DDC 306.7
1. Sex. I. Title.
HQ21 .B6185 2002

Bhaṭṭotpala, 12th cent.
Pṛthuyaśas. Ṣaṭpañcāśikā. 1. saṃskaraṇa. Vārāṇasī : Caukhambā Surabhāratī Prakāśana ; Dillī : Caukhambā Saṃskṛta Pratiṣṭhāna, 2002.
BF1714.H5 P7 2002

Vivṛti.
Varāhamihira, 505-587. Bṛhatsaṃhitā. 1. saṃskaraṇam. Vārāṇasī : Sampūrṇānanda Saṃskṛta Viśvavidyālaye, 2002-
BF1714.H5+

Bhāvamiśra, 19th cent.
[Śṛṅgārasarasī. Hindi & Sanskrit]
Śṛṅgārasarasī / Śrīmanbhāvamiśrakṛtā ; anuvādikā evaṃ sampādikā Kamaleśa Pārīka. Saṃskaraṇa 1. Vṛndāvana : Vṛndāvana Śodha Saṃsthāna, 2001. 164 p. : ill. ; 22 cm. Added title page title: Śṛṅgāra sarasī of Bhāva Miśra. SUMMARY: Sanskrit text with Hindi translation on Sanskrit poetics, types of heroines (Nayikā) and aesthetics. Includes bibliographical references (p. [163]-164). Sanskrit and Hindi.
1. Sanskrit poetry - History and criticism. 2. Heroines in literature. 3. Aesthetics. I. Pārīka, Kamaleśa. II. Title. III. Title: Śṛṅgāra sarasī of Bhāva Miśra
PK2916+

Bhavnani, Kum-Kum.
Feminist futures. London : New York : Zed Books ; New York : Distributed in the USA exclusively by Palgrave, c2003.
HQ1161 .F455 2003

Bhogilal Leherchand Institute of Indology.
Ānanda, Aruṇā, 1957- Pātañjalayoga evaṃ Jainayoga kā tulanātmaka adhyayana. 1. saṃskaraṇa. Dillī : Motīlāla Banārasīdāsa Pabliśarsa aura Bhogīlāla Leharacanda Bhāratīya Saṃskṛti Saṃsthāna, 2002.
B132.Y6 A496 2002

Bi-shevile ha-'avodah.
Segal, Yehudah Zeraḥyah, ha-Levi. Sefer Doreshe H.. Tel-Aviv : Talmiday ve-shmom'e likho, 763 [2003]
BJ1287.S43 D66 2003

BĪALO BRATSTVO (BULGARIA).
Dŭnov, Petŭr, 1864-1944. Svetlina na misŭlta. Sofiia : Kulturna asotsiatsiia Beĭnsà Dunò, 1998.
BF641 .D79 1998

Bian fu cong shu
Ma, Changyi. Zhongguo ling hun xin yang. Di 1 ban. Shanghai : Shanghai wen yi chu ban she, 1998.
BL290 .M28 1998

Bianchi, Carlos J. (Carlos Juan) Relatos de la pareja : un delicado equilibrio : (tercera parte) / Carlos J. Bianchi. Buenos Aires : Corregidor, c2001. 157 p. ; 20 cm. ISBN 950-05-1394-3 ISBN 950-05-1074-X
1. Couples - Anecdotes. 2. Interpersonal relations. 3. Marital psychotherapy. 4. Marriage counseling. I. Title.

BIAS. See DISCRIMINATION.

BIAS, JOB. See DISCRIMINATION IN EMPLOYMENT.

BIAS (PSYCHOLOGY). See PREJUDICES.

BIAS, RACIAL. See RACE DISCRIMINATION; RACISM.

BIBLE - CANON.
Brenneman, James E., 1954- Canons in conflict. New York : Oxford University Press, 1997.
BS465 .B74 1997

BIBLE - CHRONOLOGY.
Geōrgios, Synkellos, fl. 800. [Ecloga chronographica English] The chronography of George Synkellos. Oxford ; New York : Oxford University Press, 2002.
Nosovskiĭ, G. V. (Gleb Vladimirovich), 1958- Rekonstruktsiia vseobshcheĭ istorii. Moskva : FID "Delovoĭ ėkspress", 2002.
DK38 .N68 2002

BIBLE - CRITICISM, INTERPRETATION, ETC.
Gruenwald, Ithamar. Rituals and ritual theory in ancient Israel. Leiden ; Boston : Brill, 2003.
BM660 .G78 2003

BIBLE - EVIDENCES, AUTHORITY, ETC.
Brennemen, James E., 1954- Canons in conflict. New York : Oxford University Press, 1997.
BS465 .B74 1997

BIBLE - HERMENEUTICS.
Brenneman, James E., 1954- Canons in conflict. New York : Oxford University Press, 1997.
BS465 .B74 1997

BIBLE - HERMENEUTICS - CONGRESSES.
Internationales Eriugena-Colloquium (10th : Maynooth and Dublin : 2002) History and eschatology in John Scottus Eriugena and his time. Leuven : University Press, 2002.

BIBLE - MISCELLANEA.
Little, Lora. Secrets of the ancient world. Virginia Beach, Va. : A.R.E. Press, c2003.
BF1045.A74 L58 2003

BIBLE. N.T. GOSPELS - CRITICISM, INTERPRETATION, ETC.
Davis, Frederick, 1931- The Jew and deicide. Lanham, Md. : University Press of America, c2003.
BS2555.6.J44 D38 2003

BIBLE. N.T. REVELATION XX - MISCELLANEA.
Aivanhov, Omraam Mikhaël. "Et il me montra un fleuve d'eau de la vie"-- Apocalypse de saint Jean 22:1. Fréjus : Prosveta, [2002]

The Bible on leadership.
Woolfe, Lorin. New York : American Management Association, c2002.
HD57.7 .W666 2002

BIBLE. O.T. - COMMENTARIES.
Vital, Ḥayyim ben Joseph, 1542 or 3-1620. 'Ets ha-da'at tov. Yerushalayim : Hotsa'at Ahavat shalom, 761 [2000 or 2001]

BIBLE. O.T. - CRITICISM, INTERPRETATION, ETC.
Quaglia, Rocco. I sogni della Bibbia. Roma : Borla, c2002.

BIBLE. O.T. ESTHER - COMMENTARIES.
Ben Ratson-Lahaṭ, Tsiyon. Sefer ha-Nistarot vehaniglot. [Israel? : ḥ. mo. l.], 761 i.e. 2001?]

BIBLE. O.T. GENESIS - COMMENTARIES.
Orio de Miguel, Bernardino, 1936- Leibniz y el pensamiento hermético. Valencia : Universidad Politécnica de Valéncia, Editorial U.P.V., [2002]

BIBLE. O.T. GENESIS - COMMENTARIES - HISTORY AND CRITICISM.
Orio de Miguel, Bernardino, 1936- Leibniz y el pensamiento hermético. Valencia : Universidad Politécnica de Valéncia, Editorial U.P.V., [2002]

BIBLE. O.T. GENESIS II-IV - CRITICISM, INTERPRETATION, ETC.
Morgan, Shemu'el. 'Ets ha-da'at. Pedu'el : Sh. Morgan, [1998?]

BIBLE. O.T. LAMENTATIONS - COMMENTARIES.
[Zohar ḥadash. Lamentations. 2000.] Zohar ḥadash Megilat Ekhah. "Hotsa'ah meyuḥedet li-yeme ben ha-metsarim". Yerushalayim : Mekhon Da'at Yosef, 761 [2000 or 2001]
BM525.A6 Z6 2001

BIBLE. O.T. - MISCELLANEA.
Glazerson, Matityahu. Migdele ha-te'omim be-diluge otiyot ba-Torah. Yerushalayim : Yerid ha-sefarim, 2002.

BIBLE. O.T. PENTATEUCH - COMMENTARIES.
Alshekh, Moses, 16th cent. [Torat Mosheh. Selections] Sefer 'Orot ha-Alshekh. Yerushalayim : [ḥ. mo. l.], 763 [2002 or 2003]

Malkah, Asher. 'Arakhim ve-ḥinukh. Ḥefah : A. Malkah, [5760 i.e. 2000]

Milshṭein, Mosheh. Sefer Even shetiyah. Bruklin : [Lee Printing corp.], 758- [1998-

Pinḥasi, Raḥamim. Sefer Ḥesed ve-raḥamim. Yerushalayim : R. Pinḥasi, 762 [2001 or 2002]

Shelomoh ben Ḥayim Haikel. Sefer Liḳuṭe u-ferushe niglot Leshem shevo ve-aḥlamah. Kiryat Sefer : Mosheh Vais, 762 [2002]
BM525 .H4332 2002

Vital, Ḥayyim ben Joseph, 1542 or 3-1620. 'Ets ha-da'at tov. Yerushalayim : Hotsa'at Ahavat shalom, 761 [2000 or 2001]

Yalkuṭ Ṭuv ha-peninim. Yerushala[y]im : P. Y. Liberman, 762 [2001 or 2002]
BS1225.53 .Y35 2001

[Zohar ḥadash.] Sefer Zohar ḥadash. Yerushalayim : Mekhon Da'at Yosef ; Brooklyn, N.Y. (225 Division Ave., Brooklyn 11211) : Le-haśig, B. Daskal, 760- [1999 or 2000-
BM525.A6 Z6+

BIBLE. O.T. PENTATEUCH - MEDITATIONS.
Shooter, Jonathan. The wisdom within. Southfield, MI : Targum Press ; Nanuet, NY : Distributed by Feldheim Publishers, 2002.

BIBLE. O.T. PENTATEUCH - SERMONS.
Admur ha-G. ha-Ḳ., Shelita. ['Avodat 'avodah (Torah)] Sefer 'Avodat 'avodah. Kiryat Ṭohsh, Ḳanada : N. M. Hershḳoviṭsh, 763 [2002 or 2003]

Alter, Judah Aryeh Leib, 1847-1905. [Śefat emet (Torah). Selections] Sefer Śefat emet. Yerushalayim : Mir, 762 [2001 or 2002]

Baifus, Ya'akov Yiśra'el, ha-Kohen. [Lekaḥ ṭov (Ḥayim shel Torah)] Yalḳuṭ Lekaḥ ṭov. Rekhasim : "Tashbar ha-Rav", 760- [1999 or 2000-

Bardah, Asher. Sefer Otsrot av. [Bene Beraḳ?] : A. Bardah, 762- [2001 or 2002-
BS1225.54 .B37 2001

Druḳ, Ya'aḳov ben Zalman. Ohel Ya'aḳov. Yerushala[yi]m : Y. ben Z. Druḳ, 762 [2002]

Bible. O.T. Pentateuch - Sermons.

BS1225.4 .D77 2002
Goldberg, Avraham Yehoshuʻa, 1856-1921. Sefer Kitve paz. Yerushalayim : ha-Mishpaḥah, 763, c2003.

Shemuʼelevits, Ḥayim, 1901-1979. Sefer Śiḥot musar. Mahad. ḥadashah u-metukenet. Yerushalayim : Bene va-ḥatane ha-meḥaber, 762, c2002.
BJ1287.S56 S5 2002

Shooter, Jonathan. The wisdom within. Southfield, MI : Targum Press ; Nanuet, NY : Distributed by Feldheim Publishers, 2002.

Śiḥot musar Daʻat u-tevunah. Ashdod : Sh. ben E. Bamnolker, 761 [2001]
BJ1280 .B34 2001

Vakhṭfoigel, Nathan. Sefer Noʻam ha-musar. Laiḳvud : [h. mo. l.], 762 [2001 or 2002]
BJ1285 .V35 2001

BIBLE. O.T. - PROPHECIES.
Glazerson, Matityahu. Migdele ha-teʻomim be-diluge otiyot ba-Torah. Yerushalayim : Yerid ha-sefarim, 2002.

BIBLE. O.T. PSALMS XXIX, XCII, XCIII, VC-C - COMMENTARIES.
Sharir, Avraham Yiśraʼel. Pene Shabat neḳablah. Yerushalayim : Avraham Kohen-Erez, 763 [2003]
BM670.L44 S527 2003

BIBLE. O.T. RUTH - COMMENTARIES.
[Zohar ḥadash. Lamentations. 2000.] Zohar ḥadash Megilat Ekhah. "Hotsaʼah meyuḥedet li-yeme ben ha-metsarim". Yerushalayim : Mekhon Daʻat Yosef, 761 [2000 or 2001]
BM525.A6 Z6 2001

BIBLE. O.T. SONG OF SOLOMON - COMMENTARIES - HISTORY AND CRITICISM.
Ḥalfon, Eliyahu ben Ḥayim. Shir ha-shirim. [Israel] : Or tsaḥ hadpasah ve-hafatsah shel sipre Yahadut, [2001]

Bible. O.T. Song of Solomon. 2003.
Ḥalfon, Eliyahu ben Ḥayim. Shir ha-shirim. [Israel] : Or tsaḥ hadpasah ve-hafatsah shel sipre Yahadut, [2001]

BIBLE. O.T. SONG OF SOLOMON - COMMENTARIES.
Abi-Ḥasira, Jacob ben Masoud, 1808-1880. [Abir Yaʻaḳov. Selections. 2002] Sefer Penine Avir Yaʻaḳov. Yerushalayim : Hotsaʼat ha-Makhon le-hotsaʼat sefarim she-ʻa. y. Yeshivat Ner Yitsḥaḳ : Mekhon Avraham : Shimʻon Abiḥatsira, 763 [2002]
BS1485.X33 A25 2002

Bible. O.T. Song of Solomon. Hebrew. 2002.
Abi-Ḥasira, Jacob ben Masoud, 1808-1880. [Abir Yaʻaḳov. Selections. 2002] Sefer Penine Avir Yaʻaḳov. Yerushalayim : Hotsaʼat ha-Makhon le-hotsaʼat sefarim she-ʻa. y. Yeshivat Ner Yitsḥaḳ : Mekhon Avraham : Shimʻon Abiḥatsira, 763 [2002]
BS1485.X33 A25 2002

BIBLE - PROPHECIES.
Brenneman, James E., 1954- Canons in conflict. New York : Oxford University Press, 1997.
BS465 .B74 1997

BIBLE - PROPHECIES - END OF THE WORLD.
Van Auken, John. The end times. New York : Signet Book, c2001. [Updated ed.].
BF1791 .V36 2001

Bibler, V. S. (Vladimir Solomonovich), 1918-
Zamysly / Bibler ; otvetstvennyĭ redaktor I.E. Berliand ; sostavlenie, podgotovka teksta, I.E. Berliand pri uchastii A.V. Akhutina. Moskva : Rossiĭskiĭ gos. gumanitarnyĭ universitet, 2002. 2 v. (1113, xxxviii p.) : ill. ; 25 cm. "Nauchnoe izdanie"-- Colophon. Includes bibliographical references (p. 1109-1113). ISBN 5728104096
 1. Philosophy. I. Berliand, I. E. (Irina Efimovna) II. Akhutin, A. V. (Anatoliĭ Valerianovich) III. Title.
B99.R9 B53 2002

Biblical and pagan societies.
Cryer, Frederick H. Philadelphia : University of Pennsylvania Press, 2001.
BF1567 .C79 2001

BIBLICAL COSMOGONY. See CREATION.

BIBLICAL COSMOLOGY. See CREATION.

BIBLICAL LAW. See JEWISH LAW.

Bibliographieverzeichnisse grosser Österreicher in Einzelbänden
Stock, Karl F. Freud-Bibliographien. Graz : Stock & Stock, 1998.

BF109.F73 S76 1998

BIBLIOGRAPHY. See ARCHIVES; BOOKS.

Bibliography on psychology nationally and worldwide.
Psychology, IUPsyS global resource [electronic resource]. Hove, East Sussex, UK : published on behalf of the international Union of Psychological Science by Psychology Press Ltd., 2000-
BF76.5 .P79

BIBLIOMANIA.
Jackson, Holbrook, 1874-1948. [Anatomy of bibliomania. Portuguese. Selections] O tato. São Paulo : Imprensa Oficial do Estado, 2002.
Z992 .J33 2002

Biblioteca Caja de Ahorros de Navarra
(5) Signos de identidad histórica para Navarra. Pamplona : Caja de Ahorros de Navarra, 1996.
DP302.N267 S54 1996

Biblioteca de dialectología y tradiciones populares
(XXXV) Demonio, religión y sociedad entre España y América. Madrid : Consejo Superior de Investigaciones Científicas, 2002.

Biblioteca de filosofía (Buenos Aires, Argentina)
Habitar la tierra. Buenos Aires : Grupo Editor Altamira, 2002.
CB358 .H32 2002

Biblioteca de historia (Córdoba, Argentina)
Tagle Frías de Cuenca, Matilde. Notas sobre historia del libro. Córdoba, República Argentina : Ediciones del Copista, c1997.
Z4

Biblioteca de Psicología, Psiquiatría y Psicoanálisi
Musachi, Graciela. Mujeres en movimiento. Argentina : Fondo de Cultura Económica / Argentina, 2001.

Biblioteca di cultura (Bulzoni editore)
(621.) Erdas, Franco Epifanio. Partecipazione e differenza. Roma : Bulzoni, c2002.

Biblioteca di cultura filosofica (Milan, Italy)
(23.) Le leggi del pensiero tra logica, ontologia e psicologia. Milano : UNICOPLI, 2002.

Biblioteca di studi goriziani
(7) Cumpeta, Silvio. I dialoghi dell'ego. Gorizia : Biblioteca statale isontina, c2001.

Biblioteca Einaudi
(139) Sacerdoti, Gilberto, 1952- Sacrificio e sovranità. Torino : Einaudi, 2002.

 (140) I concetti del male. Torino : Einaudi, c2002.

Biblioteca essenziale Laterza
(41) Marconi, Diego, 1947- Filosofia e scienza cognitiva. 1. ed. Roma-Bari : Editori Laterza, 2001.
BF311 .M36 2001

Biblioteca nazionale marciana.
Magia, alchimia, scienza dal '400 al '700. Firenze : Centro Di, 2002.
BF1598.H6 M34 2002

BIBLIOTECA NAZIONALE MARCIANA - EXHIBITIONS.
Magia, alchimia, scienza dal '400 al '700. Firenze : Centro Di, 2002.
BF1598.H6 M34 2002

Biblioteca Solucion de conflictos
Johnston, Marianne. [Dealing with anger. Spanish] Como tratar la ira. New York : PowerKids Press, 2005.
BF575.A5 J6418 2005

 Johnston, Marianne. [Dealing with bullying. Spanish] Como tratar a los bravucones. New York : PowerKids Press, 2005.
BF637.B85 J6418 2005

 Johnston, Marianne. [Dealing with fighting. Spanish] Como tratar las peleas. New York : PowerKids Press, 2005.
BF637.I48 J6418 2005

 Johnston, Marianne. [Dealing with insults. Spanish] Como tratar los insultos. New York : PowerKids Press, 2005.
BF637.V47 J6418 2005

Biblioteka AZ
Deretić, Jovan. Kratka istorija srpske književnosti. 3., prerađeno i dop. izd. Novi Sad : Svetovi, 2001.

Biblioteka Duša i kultura
Popović, Velimir B. O duši i bogovima. Niš : Prosveta, 2001.

BF175.5.A72 P67 2001

Biblioteka Kulturno naslijedde
Biserje. 3., dop. izd. Sarajevo : Ljiljan, 1998.

Biblioteka Medicina i budućnost
Jovanović, Tihomir. Nepoznati svet snova. Beograd : IPA "Miroslav", 2000.
BF1078 .J69 2000

Biblioteka misao (Tersit (Firm))
Kriza i perspektive filozofije. 1. izd. Beograd : Tersit, 1995.
B99.S462 K75 1995

Biblioteka myśli semiotycznej
(47) Rzepa, Teresa. O interpretowaniu psychologicznym w kręgu szkoły lwowsko-warszawskiej. Warszawa : Polskie Tow. Semiotyczne, 2002.
BF108.P7 R94 2002

Biblioteka NLP
Cherepanova, I. I͡U. (Irina I͡Urʼevna) Dom koldunʼi. Perer., dop. i ispravlennoe izd. Moskva : KSP+, 2001.
BF1156.S8 C53 2001

Biblioteka Povjesnica
Bošković, Hijacint. Filozofski izvori fašizma i nacionalnog socijalizma. 2. izd. Zagreb : Dom i svijet, 2000.
B804 .B66 2000

Biblioteka Psikheĭa
Antologii͡a. 1. izd. Veliko Tŭrnovo : Izd-vo PAN-VT, 2001.
BF108.B9 A58 2001

Biblioteka psikhologa
Ivanov, S. P. (Sergeĭ Petrovich) Psikhologii͡a khudozhestvennogo deĭstvii͡a subʺekta. Moskva : Moskovskiĭ psikhologo-sotsialʼnyĭ institut ; Voronezh : Izd-vo NPO "MODĖK", 2002.
BF408 .I93 2002

Biblioteka rasovoĭ mysli.
Avdeev, V. B. (Vladimir Borisovich) Metafizicheskai͡a antropologii͡a. Moskva : Belye alʼvy, 2002.
DK510.763 .A93 2002

Biblioteka Tragom Slovena
(knj. 15) Petrović, Aleksandar M. Praistorija Srba. Beograd : Pešić i sinovi, 2001.
DR1953 .P48 2001

Biblioteka zhurnala "Ėkologii͡a i zhizn'"
Moiseev, N. N. (Nikita Nikolaevich) Kak daleko do zavtrashnego dni͡a--. Moskva : Taĭdeks Ko, 2002.
DK49 .M64 2002

Bibliotheca academiae
(5) Baritono, Raffaella. La democrazia vissuta. Torino : La Rosa, c2001.

Bibliotheca Germanica
(44) Hübner, Gert. Erzählform im höfischen Roman. Tübingen : Francke, 2003.

Bibliotheca (Lucerne, Switzerland)
(Bd. 2.) Breitschmid, Markus, 1966- Der bauende Geist. Luzern : Quart, 2001.
B3318.A4 B745 2001

 (Bd. 3.) Šik, Miroslav. Altneue Gedanken. Luzern : Quart, c2002.

Bibliotheca Philosophica Hermetica (Amsterdam, Netherlands).
Magia, alchimia, scienza dal '400 al '700. Firenze : Centro Di, 2002.
BF1598.H6 M34 2002

BIBLIOTHECA PHILOSOPHICA HERMETICA (AMSTERDAM, NETHERLANDS) - EXHIBITIONS.
Magia, alchimia, scienza dal '400 al '700. Firenze : Centro Di, 2002.
BF1598.H6 M34 2002

Bibliothèque Albin Michel de l'histoire.
Dumoulin, Olivier. Le rôle social de l'historien. Paris : Albin Michel, 2002, c2003.
D13.2 .D85 2002

La bibliothèque de l'imaginaire
Wunenburger, Jean-Jacques. La vie des images. [Nouvelle édition augmentée]. Grenoble : Presses universitaires de Grenoble, 2002.
BF367 .W85 2002

Bibliothèque de non-philosophie
Del Bufalo, Erik. Deleuze et Laruelle. Paris : Kimé, 2003.

Bibliothèque de psychanalyse
Altounian, Janine. L'écriture de Freud. Paris : Presses universitaires de France, 2003.
BF173.F73 A48 2003

Bibliothèque d'histoire de la philosophie
Dixsaut, Monique. Métamorphoses de la dialectique dans les dialogues de Platon. Paris : Vrin, c2001.
B398.D5 D598 2001

Bichakjian, Bernard H. Language in a Darwinian perspective / Bernard H. Bichakjian. Frankfurt am Main ; New York : Peter Lang, c2002. xxvii, 316 p. : ill. ; 21 cm. (Bochum publications in evolutionary cultural semiotics. New series, 1439-4073 ; v. 3) Includes bibliographical references (p. [279]-295) and index. ISBN 0-8204-5458-3 ISBN 3-631-38882-9 DDC 417/.7
1. Linguistic change. 2. Evolution. 3. Writing - History. 4. Linguistics - History. 5. Language and languages - Origin. I. Title. II. Series: Bochum publications in evolutionary cultural semiotics. New series ; v. 3.
P142 .B53 2002

Bichigdmėlůůd.
Khurmetbek, Khalikiĭn. Ül bichigdmėlůůd. Ulaanbaatar : "Monsudar" Khėvlėliĭn Gazar, 2001.
QA465 .K48 2001

Biddix, Cheryl.
Stenson, Lila. Daddy, up and down. 1st ed. Snowmass Village, CO : Peaceful Village Pub., 2002.
BF723.G75 S74 2002

Bielecki, Jan, OMI.
Psychologia nie tylko dla psychologów. Warszawa : Uniwersytet Kardynała Stefana Wyszyńskiego, 2002.
BF126 .P749 2002

Bierman, Karen L. Peer rejection : developmental processes and intervention strategies / by Karen L. Bierman. New York : Guilford Press, 2004. p. cm. (The Guilford series on social and emotional development) Includes bibliographical references and index. Table of contents URL: http://www.loc.gov/catdir/toc/ecip042/2003007554.html ISBN 1-57230-923-7 (alk. paper) DDC 155.4/18
1. Rejection (Psychology) in children. 2. Social interaction in children. 3. Behavioral assessment of children. 4. Child psychotherapy. I. Title. II. Series.
BF723.R44 B54 2003

BIFURCATION THEORY.
Zhusubaliyev, Zhanybai T. Bifurcations and chaos in piecewise-smooth dynamical systems. River Edge, New Jersey : World Scientific, c2003.

Bifurcations and chaos in piecewise-smooth dynamical systems.
Zhusubaliyev, Zhanybai T. River Edge, New Jersey : World Scientific, c2003.

The big book of business games series
Epstein, Robert, 1953- The big book of creativity games. New York : McGraw-Hill, c2000.
BF408 .E67 2000

The big book of creativity games.
Epstein, Robert, 1953- New York : McGraw-Hill, c2000.
BF408 .E67 2000

The big book of personality tests.
Didato, Salvatore V. New York : Black Dog & Leventhal Publishers, c2003.
BF698.5 .D53 2003

Big Dance (Victoria, B.C.).
Big Dance [videorecording]. Buffalo, N.Y. : Kineticvideo.com, c1998.

Big Dance [videorecording] / produced by The May Street Group Ltd. and Lost Dog Productions Inc. ; directed by Sherry Antonishen ; produced by Hilary Jones-Farrow and Sherry Antonishen. Buffalo, N.Y. : Kineticvideo.com, c1998. 1 videocassette (VHS, NTSC) (48 min.) : sd., col. ; 1/2 in. Written by Sherry Antonishen and Hilary Jones-Farrow; editing, Sherry Antonishen; choreography, Lynda Raino and Connie Cook; produced in association with Women's Television Network. Interviewees: Lynda Raino and members of Big Dance (identified by first names only), Judith Garay, Jan Hanvik, Dr. William Shoichet, others. SUMMARY: Documentary on Big Dance, a modern dance class and company for large women, founded by Lynda Raino in Victoria, British Columbia, Canada. Raino and her dancers discuss the physical, social, and psychological challenges faced by large women in contemporary society, and the role of dance in helping them achieve self-acceptance, a sense of empowerment, and spiritual growth. The company is seen in class, rehearsals, and performances of various works from its repertory, including its pivotal performance at the World Dance Alliance conference in Vancouver.
1. Body image in women. 2. Overweight women. 3. Self-esteem in women. 4. Dance companies - Canada. 5. Dance. 6. Documentaries and factual films and programs. 7. Video. I.

Raino, Lynda. II. Garay, Judith. III. Hanvik, Jan Michael. IV. Antonishen, Sherry. V. Jones-Farrow, Hilary. VI. Big Dance (Victoria, B.C.) VII. Kineticvideo.com (Firm)

The big difference.
Phillips, Nicola. Cambridge, MA : Perseus Pub., c2001.
BF619 .P48 2001

Big five assessment / edited by Boele de Raad, Marco Perugini. Seattle, WA : Hogrefe & Huber Publishers, c2002. x, 491 p. : ill. ; 24 cm. Includes bibliographical references and indexes. ISBN 0-88937-242-X DDC 155.2/8
1. Personality assessment. I. Raad, Boele de. II. Perugini, Marco.
BF698.4 .B52 2002

The big idea.
Duitch, Suri. New York : City Limits Community Information Service, c2002.

Big ideas.
Ceserani, Jonne, 1954- London ; Sterling, VA : Kogan Page Limited, 2002.
HD53 .C46 2002

I big Newton
(65) Tamiozzo Villa, Patrizia. L'astrologia e i miti del mondo antico. 1. ed. Roma : Newton & Compton, 2001.
BF1729.M9 T35 2001

Big - small.
Gordon, Sharon. New York : Benchmark Books, 2003.
BF299.S5 G67 2003

Biggar, Nigel.
Burying the past. Expanded and updated. Washington, D.C. : Georgetown University Press, c2003.
JC578 .B49 2003

Bigideas.
Ceserani, Jonne, 1954- Big ideas. London ; Sterling, VA : Kogan Page Limited, 2002.
HD53 .C46 2002

Biĭskiĭ pedagogicheskiĭ gosudarstvennyĭ universitet im. V.M. Shukshina.
Innovatsii v psikhologii. Biĭsk : Nauchno-izdatel'skiĭ tsentr Biĭskogo pedagog. gos. universiteta, 2001-
BF20 .I45 2001

Bikson, Tora K., 1940-.
New challenges for international leadership. Santa Monica, Calif. : RAND, 2003.
HD57.7 .N488 2003

Bilbeny, Norbert. Por una causa común : ética para la diversidad / Norbert Bilbeny. 1. ed. Barcelona : Gedisa Editorial, c2002. 187 p. ; 24 cm. Includes bibliographical references (p. [181]-187) ISBN 84-7432-975-2
1. Pluralism (Social sciences) 2. Ethics. I. Title.
HM1271 .B553 2002

Bilek, Anita, 1972-.
Kritik der Gewalt. Wien : Promedia, c2002.
D860 .K75 2002

BILINGUAL AUTHORS.
Lives in translation. 1st ed. New York ; Houndmills, England : Palgrave Macmillan, 2003.
P115.25 .L58 2003

Bilingual sentence processing.
Fernández, Eva M. Amsterdam ; Philadelphia : J. Benjamins Pub., 2003.
P115.4 .F47 2003

BILINGUALISM.
Kecskés, István. Situation-bound utterances in L1 and L2. Berlin ; New York : Mouton de Gruyter, 2002.
P95.45 .K4 2002

BILINGUALISM - PSYCHOLOGICAL ASPECTS.
Fernández, Eva M. Bilingual sentence processing. Amsterdam ; Philadelphia : J. Benjamins Pub., 2003.
P115.4 .F47 2003

Lives in translation. 1st ed. New York ; Houndmills, England : Palgrave Macmillan, 2003.
P115.25 .L58 2003

BILINGUALISM - SWITZERLAND.
Büchi, Christophe. "Röstigraben". 2. aufl. Zürich : NZZ, c2001.

BILL-POSTING. See SIGNS AND SIGNBOARDS.

Billington, Ray. Religion without God / Ray Billington. London ; New York : Routledge, 2002. xi, 148 p. ; 25 cm. Includes bibliographical references (p. [140]-143) and index. CONTENTS: Clearing the decks -- Religion -- Images of God -- Why God? -- Mysticism -- Non-dualism in Hinduism -- Buddhism -- Taoism -- Profane religion -- Beyond good and evil -- Substance without form. ISBN 0-415-21785-7

(hbk) ISBN 0-415-21786-5 (pbk.) DDC 200
1. Atheism. 2. Religion. I. Title.
BL2747.3 .B55 2002

Bimont, Bernard. Je veux que l'on soit homme : Pour être comédien, je n'en suis pas moins homme / Bernard Bimont ; préface de Gustave Thibon. Brive : Ecritures, [2002] 308 p. : ill. ; 21 cm. ISBN 2-913506-38-0 DDC 843
1. Artists and the theater. 2. Creation (Literary, artistic, etc.) I. Title.

Binah la-'itim.
He lakhem ḥamishah sefari.. [Brooklyn, NY : Renaissance Hebraica, 2000?]

Binayemotlagh, Saïd. Etre et liberté selon Platon / Saïd Binayemotlagh. Paris : Harmattan, 2002. 291 p. ; 22 cm. Includes bibliographical references and index. ISBN 2-7475-2832-4 DDC 184
1. Plato - Criticism and interpretation. 2. Ontology. 3. Liberty. I. Title.
B395 .B553 2002

BINDING THEORY (LINGUISTICS). See GOVERNMENT-BINDING THEORY (LINGUISTICS).

Binford, Virgie M. Avenues for success : turning adversity into opportunity through strong support systems / Virgie M. Binford. Franklin, Tenn. : Providence House Publishers, c2001. xi, 116 p. ; 24 cm. Includes bibliographical references (p. 113-114). Table of contents URL: http://www.loc.gov/catdir/toc/fy038/00109562.html ISBN 1-57736-218-7 DDC 158
1. Success - Psychological aspects. I. Title.
BF637.S8 B477 2001

Bingaman, Kirk A. Freud and faith : living in the tension / Kirk A. Bingaman. Albany, NY : State University of New York Press, c2003. xi, 167 p. ; 23 cm. Includes bibliographical references (p. 159-164) and index. ISBN 0-7914-5654-4 (pbk. : alk. paper) ISBN 0-7914-5653-6 (alk. paper) DDC 261.5/15
1. Freud, Sigmund, - 1856-1939 - Religion. 2. Psychoanalysis and religion. I. Title.
BF175.4.R44 B56 2003

BINGE-PURGE BEHAVIOR. See BULIMIA.

BIO-BIBLIOGRAPHY. See AUTHORS.

BIOACOUSTICS. See SOUND - PSYCHOLOGICAL ASPECTS.

BIOACTIVE COMPOUNDS. See DRUGS.

BIOENGINEERING. See HUMAN ENGINEERING.

BIOETHICS. See also MEDICAL ETHICS.
Andrieu, Bernard. L'interprétation des gènes. Paris : Harmattan, 2002.

Cotroneo, Girolamo. Le idee del tempo. Soveria Mannelli (Catanzaro) : Rubbettino, c2002.

McLeod, Carolyn. Self-trust and reproductive autonomy. Cambridge, Mass. : MIT Press, c2002.
RG133.5 .M39 2002

Pollard, Irina. Life, love and children. Boston : Kluwer Academic Publishers, c2002.
R725.5 .P655 2002

Biografies i memòries
(52) Cruz, Mariano de la, 1921-1999. Mens sana in corpore insepulto. 1. ed. Barcelona : Edicions 62, 2002.

BIOGRAPHY. See also ANECDOTES.
Deniau, Jean-François, 1928- La gloire à vingt ans. [Paris] : XO editions, c2003.

BIOGRAPHY - 20TH CENTURY.
Karasek, Hellmuth, 1934- Karambolagen. 2. Aufl. München : Ullstein Verlag, c2002.

BIOGRAPHY AS A LITERARY FORM. See AUTOBIOGRAPHY.

BIOGRAPHY - HISTORY.
Hähner, Olaf. Historische Biographik. Frankfurt am Main ; New York : Lang, 1999.

BIOINFORMATICS.
Kasabov, Nikola K. Evolving connectionist systems. London ; New York : Springer, c2003.
QA76.87 .K39 2003

BIOLOGICAL ANTHROPOLOGY. See PHYSICAL ANTHROPOLOGY.

BIOLOGICAL EVOLUTION. See EVOLUTION (BIOLOGY).

Biological rhythms.

BIOLOGICAL RHYTHMS.
Aveni, Anthony F. The book of the year. Oxford ; New York : Oxford University Press, 2003.
GT3930 .A94 2003

Biologische Grundlagen der Psychologie /
herausgegeben von Thomas Elbert und Niels Birbaumer. Göttingen ; Seattle : Hogrefe, 2001. xxvi, 773 p. : ill. ; 25 cm. (Enzyklopädie der Psychologie ; Themenbereich C, Serie I, Bd. 6) ISBN 3-8017-0540-4 (cl.)
1. Psychobiology. 2. Psychology - Physiological aspects. I. Elbert, Thomas. II. Birbaumer, Niels. III. Series.
QP360 .B565 2001

BIOLOGY. See ADAPTATION (BIOLOGY); DEATH (BIOLOGY); ECOLOGY; EVOLUTION (BIOLOGY); EXTINCTION (BIOLOGY); GENETICS; NATURAL HISTORY; PHYSIOLOGY; SEX (BIOLOGY); VARIATION (BIOLOGY).

BIOLOGY - ECOLOGY. See ECOLOGY.

The biology of death.
Klarsfeld, André. [Biologie de la mort. English] Ithaca, NY : Comstock Pub. Associates/Cornell University Press, 2004.
QH530 .K5613 2004

BIOLOGY - PHILOSOPHY.
Barbieri, Marcello. The organic codes. Cambridge, UK ; New York : Cambridge University Press, 2003.
QH331 .B247 2003

Vallejo, Fernando. La tautología darwinista. 1a. ed. México : Universidad Nacional Autónoma de México, 1998.

BIOMASS. See BIOLOGY.

BIOMEDICAL ETHICS. See MEDICAL ETHICS.

BIONICS. See ARTIFICIAL INTELLIGENCE; HUMAN INFORMATION PROCESSING.

BIONOMICS. See ECOLOGY.

Bioprogrammy v prirode i politike.
Khzardzhi︠a︡n, S. M. (Sanatruk M.) Pushchino : ONTI PNTS RAN, 1996.
BF199 .K43 1996

BIOSCIENCES. See LIFE SCIENCES.

BIOTECHNOLOGY. See AGRICULTURAL BIOTECHNOLOGY.

BIOTECHNOLOGY INDUSTRIES.
King, John L. Concentration and technology in agricultural input industries [electronic resource]. [Washington, D.C.] : U.S. Dept of Agriculture, [2001].

BIPEDAL LOCOMOTION. See BIPEDALISM.

BIPEDAL POSTURE. See BIPEDALISM.

BIPEDAL WALKING. See BIPEDALISM.

BIPEDALISM - ORIGIN.
Kingdon, Jonathan. Lowly origin. Princeton : Princeton University Press, c2003.
GN282 .K54 2003

BIPEDALITY. See BIPEDALISM.

BIPEDALIZATION. See BIPEDALISM.

Birbaumer, Niels.
Biologische Grundlagen der Psychologie. Göttingen ; Seattle : Hogrefe, 2001.
QP360 .B565 2001

Bird, David F. Quality Air Force in an emergency [electronic resource] : leadership principles and concepts for emergency response forces / David F. Bird Jr. Maxwell Air Force Base, Ala. : Air War College, Air University, [1996] (Air War College, Maxwell Paper ; No. 2) Mode of access: Internet from the Air University Press web site. Address as of 11/10/03: http://aupress.au.af.mil/Maxwell%5FPapers/Text/mp02.pdf; current access is available via PURL. Title from title screen (viewed on Nov. 10, 2003). "August 1996." Includes bibliographical references. URL: http://purl.access.gpo.gov/GPO/LPS39813 Available in other form: Bird, David F. Quality Air Force in an emergency : leadership principles and concepts for emergency response forces v, 26 p. (OCoLC)35521327.
1. United States. - Air Force - Management. 2. Emergency management. 3. Leadership. I. Air University (U.S.). Air War College. II. Title. III. Title: Bird, David F. Quality Air Force in an emergency : leadership principles and concepts for emergency response forces v, 26 p. IV. Series: Maxwell paper (Air University (U.S.). Air War College) ; no. 2.

Bird, David F. Quality Air Force in an emergency : leadership principles and concepts for emergency response forces v, 26 p.
Bird, David F. Quality Air Force in an emergency [electronic resource]. Maxwell Air Force Base, Ala. : Air War College, Air University, [1996]

Bird, Lise. Human development in Aotearoa : a journey through life / Lise Bird and Wendy Drewery. Sidney ; New York : McGraw-Hill, c2000. ix, 270 p. : ill. ; 25 cm. Includes bibliographical references (p. [245]-260) and index. ISBN 0-07-470720-5 DDC 155/.0993
1. Developmental psychology - New Zealand. I. Drewery, Wendy. II. Title.
BF713 .B57 2000

Birkat Me'ir.
Medan, Barukh. Sefer Birkat Me'ir. Netivot : Barukh Medan, 763 [2002 or 2003]

Birman, Joel.
Femenilidades. Rio de Janeiro : Espaço Brasileiro de Estudos Psicanalíticos : Contra Capa, c2002.

Birner, Betty J.
Spears, Richard A. NTC's dictionary of everyday American English expressions. Lincolnwood, Ill. : National Textbook Co., c1994.
PE2839 .S65 1994

Birtchnell, John. The two of me : the rational outer me and the emotional inner me / John Birtchnell. Hove, East Sussex [England] ; New York : Routledge, 2003. p. cm. Includes bibliographical references and indexes. Table of contents URL: http://www.loc.gov/catdir/toc/ecip042/2003007755.html CONTENTS: The birth of an idea -- The outer me -- The inner me -- Psychodynamic distinctions -- Cognitive distinctions -- Survival -- Reproduction -- Relating -- Sensory input -- Emotion -- Memory -- Motor action -- Communication and language -- Mental activity -- Deception and self-deception -- Delusions and hallucinations -- Dreams -- The arts -- Humour -- Religion. ISBN 1-84169-323-5 DDC 150.19/8
1. Consciousness. 2. Subconsciousness. 3. Interpersonal relations. 4. Philosophy of mind. I. Title.
BF311 .B533 2003

BIRTH ATTENDANTS. See MIDWIVES.

The birth called death.
Jordan, Kathie. 1st ed. Ashland, Or. : RiverWood Books, 2003.
BF1311.F8 B57 2003

The birth of pleasure.
Gilligan, Carol, 1936- 1st ed. New York : A.A. Knopf, 2002.
BF575.L8 G56 2002

The birth of the mind.
Marcus, Gary F. (Gary Fred) New York : Basic Books, 2004.
BF701 .M32 2004

Birthday party murder.
Meier, Leslie. Waterville, Me. : Thorndike Press, 2003.
PS3563.E3455 B57 2003

Biserje : antologija bošnjačke književnosti / odabrao i priredio Alija Isaković ; [ilustracije Safet Zec]. 3., dop. izd. Sarajevo : Ljiljan, 1998. 583 p. : col. ill. ; 25 cm. (Biblioteka Kulturno naslijeđe) Includes bibliographical references. In Serbo-Croatian (roman). ISBN 9958220377
1. Serbian literature - History and criticism. I. Isaković, Alija. II. Zec, Safet. III. Series.

BISEXUAL PERSONS. See BISEXUALS.

BISEXUALITY. See also HOMOSEXUALITY.
Queer counselling and narrative practice. Adelaide : Dulwich Centre Publications, c2002.

BISEXUALS - COUNSELING OF.
Queer counselling and narrative practice. Adelaide : Dulwich Centre Publications, c2002.

Bishop, Anne, 1950- Becoming an ally : breaking the cycle of oppression in people / Anne Bishop. 2nd ed. London ; New York : Zed Books ; Halifax, N.S. : Fernwood Pub. ; New York : Distributed in the USA exclusively by Palgrave, 2002. 188 p. : ill. ; 24 cm. Includes bibliographical references (p. 168-182) and index. ISBN 1-84277-224-4 (cased) ISBN 1-84277-225-2 (limp) ISBN 1-55266-072-9 DDC 302
1. Oppression (Psychology) 2. Social psychology. 3. Social control. I. Title. II. Title: Breaking the cycle of oppression in people
HM1256 .B57 2002

Bishop, Hugh E., 1940- Haunted Lake Superior / by Hugh E. Bishop. 1st ed. Duluth, Minn. : Lake Superior Port Cities, c2003. ix, 182 p. : ill., map ; 22 cm. Includes bibliographical references (p. 172-174) and index. ISBN 0-942235-55-X DDC 133.1/09774/9
1. Ghosts - Superior, Lake, Region. I. Title.
BF1472.U6 B565 2003

Bishop, Robert, Dr.
Between chance and choice. Thorverton, UK ; Charlottesville, VA : Imprint Academic, c2002.
BJ1461 .B48 2002

Bisogno d'amore.
Dacquino, Giacomo, 1930- 1. ed. Milano : Mondadori, 2002.
BF697.5.S43 D33 2002

Bitches, bimbos, and ballbreakers : the Guerrilla Girls' illustrated guide to female stereotypes / by the Guerrilla Girls. New York, N.Y. : Penguin Books, 2003. 95 p. : ill. (chiefly col.) ; 26 cm. Includes bibliographical references. ISBN 0-14-200101-5 DDC 305.4
1. Women - Psychology. 2. Stereotype (Psychology) I. Guerrilla Girls (Group of artists)
HQ1206 .B444 2003

Bittner, Dagmar.
Development of verb inflection in first language acquisition. Berlin ; New York : Mouton de Gruyter, 2003.
P118 .D465 2003

Bittner, Rüdiger, 1945-.
Nietzsche, Friedrich Wilhelm, 1844-1900. [Selections. English. 2003] Writings from the late notebooks. Cambridge, UK ; New York : Cambridge University Press, c2003.
B3312.E5 B58 2003

Bizet, Georges, 1838-1875. Operas. Selections.
Malaniuk, Ira. Arien und Lieder [sound recording]. [Germany] : Preiser Records, p2000.

BJARNI KRISTJÁNSSON, 1953-.
Steinunn Eyjólfsdóttir, 1936- Undir verndarhendi. Reykjavík : Skjaldborg, 1995.
BF1283.B58 S74 1995

Bjelland, Andrew G.
Merleau-Ponty, Maurice, 1908-1961. [Union de l'âme et du corps chez Malebranche, Biran et Bergson. English] The incarnate subject. Amherst, N.Y. : Humanity Books, 2001.
B2430.M379 U513 2001

Bjorklund, Barbara R.
Bee, Helen L., 1939- The journey of adulthood. 5th ed. Upper Saddle River, NJ : Pearson Prentice Hall, c2004.
BF724.5 .B44 2004

Bjornson, Lawrence E. Secrets of power conversation : talk your way to riches, respect & romance / Lawrence E. Bjornson. [S.l.] : L.E. Bjornson, c2002. 220 p. ; 22 cm. ISBN 0-9709719-2-3 DDC 153.6
1. Interpersonal communication. I. Title.
BF637.C45 B575 2002

B.L. series
(no. 15.) Ānanda, Aruṇā, 1957- Pātañjalayoga evaṃ Jainayoga kā tulanātmaka adhyayana. 1. saṃskaraṇa. Dillī : Motīlāla Banārasīdāsa Pablīśarsa aura Bhogīlāla Leharacanda Bhāratīya Saṃskṛti Saṃsthāna, 2002.
B132.Y6 A496 2002

BLACK AFRICA. See AFRICA, SUB-SAHARAN.

BLACK ART (WITCHCRAFT). See WITCHCRAFT.

The Black dancing body.
Gottschild, Brenda Dixon. New York : Palgrave Macmillan, 2003.
GV1624.7.A34 G68 2003

Black families in therapy.
Boyd-Franklin, Nancy. 2nd ed. New York : Guilford Press, c2003.
RC451.5.N4 B69 2003

BLACK MASS. See SATANISM.

Black students-Middle class teachers.
Kunjufu, Jawanza. Chicago, Ill. : African American Images, c2002.

The black sun.
Moon, Peter. New York : Sky Books, c1997.
BF1434.U6 M66 1997

Black swan.
Anderson, Susan, C.S.W. Huntington, N.Y. : Rock Foundations Press, c1999.
BF575.R35 A52 1999

Black women in the field.
Givens, Gretchen Zita. Cresskill, N.J. : Hampton Press, c2003.
LC2781.5 .G58 2003

Blackledge, Paul, 1967-.
Historical materialism and social evolution. New York : Palgrave Macmillan, 2002.
HX523 .H565 2002

Blackmore, Susan J., 1951- Consciousness : an introduction / by Susan Blackmore. New York : Oxford University Press, 2003. p. cm. Includes bibliographical references (p.   ) and index. ISBN 0-19-515342-1 (cloth) ISBN 0-19-515343-X (paper) DDC 153
1. Consciousness. I. Title.
BF311 .B534 2003

BLACKS.
Ephraim, Charles Wm. The pathology of Eurocentrism. Trenton, NJ : Africa World Press, c2003.
HT1581 .E64 2003

BLACKS - PSYCHOLOGY.
Guthrie, Robert V. Even the rat was white a historical view of psychology. Classic ed., 2nd ed. Boston, MA : Allyn and Bacon, 2004.
BF105 .G87 2004

BLACKS - RACE IDENTITY.
Amodélé, Jons. The new Jews. Banjul, The Gambia : Vinasha Publishing, 2000.
1. Black author.

Gibson, Nigel C. Fanon. Cambridge, U.K. : Polity Press in association with Blackwell Pub. ; Malden, MA : Distributed in the USA by Blackwell Pub., 2003.
CT2628.F35 G53 2003

BLACKS - RACE IDENTITY - BRAZIL.
Salles, Alexandre de. Esù ou Exu? Rio de Jaeiro : Ilú Aiye, 2001.
1. Black author.

BLACKS - SOCIAL CONDITIONS.
Amodélé, Jons. The new Jews. Banjul, The Gambia : Vinasha Publishing, 2000.
1. Black author.

BLACKS - UNITED STATES - PERSONAL NARRATIVES.
Davis, Sampson. The pact. Waterville, ME : Thorndike Press, 2002.
1. Black author.

Blackwell brief histories of psychology
(1) Cooper, Cary L. A brief history of stress. 1st ed. Oxford, U.K. ; Malden, MA : Blackwell Pub., 2004.
BF575.S75 C646 2004

The Blackwell companion to sociology of religion / edited by Richard K. Fenn. Oxford, UK ; Malden, Mass. : Blackwell Publishers, 2001. xx, 485 p. ; 25 cm. (Blackwell companions to religion ; 2) Includes bibliographical references and index. CONTENTS: Personal reflections in the mirror of Hal'evy and Weber / David Martin -- Salvation, secularization, and de-moralization / Bryan Wilson -- The Pentecostal gender paradox: a cautionary tale for the sociology of religion / Bernice Martin -- Feminism and the sociology of religion: from gender-blindness to gendered difference / Linda Woodhead -- Melancholia, utopia, and the psychoanalysis of dreams / Donald Capps -- Georg Simmel: American sociology chooses the stone the builders refused / Victoria Lee Erickson -- Transformations of society and the sacred in Durkheim's religious sociology / Donald A. Nielsen -- Classics in the sociology of religion: an ambiguous legacy / Roger O'Toole -- Individualism, the validation of faith, and the social nature of religion in modernity / Danièle Hervieu-L'eger -- The origins of religion / Richard K. Fenn -- Secularization extended: from religious "myth" to cultural commonplace / Nicholas J. Demerath III -- Social movements as free-floating religious phenomena / James A. Beckford -- The social process of secularization / Steve Bruce -- Patterns of religion in Western Europe: an exceptional case / Grace Davie -- The future of religious participation and belief in Britain and beyond / Robin Gill -- Religion as diffusion of values. "Diffused Religion" in the context of a dominant religious institution: the Italian case / Roberto Cipriani -- Spirituality and spiritual practice / Robert Wuthnow -- The Renaissance of community economic development among African-American churches in the 1990s / Katherine Day -- Hell as a residual category: possibilities excluded from the social system / Richard K. Fenn and Marianne Delaporte. CONTENTS: Acting ritually: evidence from the social life of Chinese rites / Catherine Bell -- Moralizing servons, then and now -- Thomas Luckmann -- Health, morality and sacrifice: the sociology of disasters / Douglas J. Davies -- Contemporary social theory as it applies to the understanding of religion in cross-cultural perspective / Peter Beyer -- The return of theology: sociology's distant relative / Kieran Flanagan -- Epilogue: toward a secular view of the individual / Richard K. Fenn. ISBN 0-631-21240-X (hardcover : alk. paper) ISBN 0-631-21241-8 (pbk. : alk. paper) DDC 306.6
1. Religion and sociology. I. Series.
BL60 .B53 2001

Blackwell companions to history
A companion to the worlds of the Renaissance. Malden, MA : Blackwell Publishers, 2002.
CB367 .C65 2002

Blackwell companions to religion
(2) The Blackwell companion to sociology of religion. Oxford, UK ; Malden, Mass. : Blackwell Publishers, 2001.
BL60 .B53 2001

The Blackwell guide to ancient philosophy / edited by Christopher Shields. Malden, MA ; Oxford : Blackwell Pub., 2003. xi, 333 p. ; 25 cm. (Blackwell philosophy guides ; 13) Includes bibliographical references (p. 324-328) and index. ISBN 0-631-22214-6 (hbk. : alk. paper) ISBN 0-631-22215-4 (pbk. : alk. paper) DDC 180
1. Philosophy, Ancient. I. Shields, Christopher John. II. Series.
B171 .B65 2003

The Blackwell guide to philosophy of mind / edited by Stephen P. Stich and Ted A. Warfield. Malden, MA ; Oxford : Blackwell Pub., 2003. xii, 417 p. : ill. ; 26 cm. (Blackwell philosophy guides) Cover title: Philosophy of mind. Includes bibliographical references and index. ISBN 0-631-21774-6 (hbk. : alk. paper) ISBN 0-631-21775-4 (pbk. : alk. paper) DDC 128/.2
1. Philosophy of mind. I. Stich, Stephen P. II. Warfield, Ted A., 1969- III. Title: Philosophy of mind IV. Series.
BD418.3 .B57 2003

Blackwell handbooks of research methods in psychology
Handbook of research methods in experimental psychology. Malden, MA ; Oxford : Blackwell Pub., 2003.
BF76.5 .H35 2003

Blackwell introductions to literature
Pearsall, Derek Albert. Arthurian romance. Malden, MA : Blackwell Publishers, 2003.
PN685 .P43 2003

Blackwell, Judith C., 1944-.
Culture of prejudice. Peterborough, Ont. : Broadview Press, 2003.

Blackwell manifestos
Storey, John, 1950- Inventing popular culture. Malden, MA : Blackwell Pub., 2003.
CB19 .S7455 2003

Ward, Graham. True religion. Malden, MA ; Oxford : Blackwell Pub., 2003.
BL48 .W189 2003

Blackwell philosophy anthologies
(11) Epistemology. Malden, Mass. : Blackwell Publishers, 2000.
BD161 .E615 2000

Blackwell philosophy guides
The Blackwell guide to philosophy of mind. Malden, MA ; Oxford : Blackwell Pub., 2003.
BD418.3 .B57 2003

(13) The Blackwell guide to ancient philosophy. Malden, MA ; Oxford : Blackwell Pub., 2003.
B171 .B65 2003

Blaikie, Norman W. H., 1933- Analyzing quantitative data : from description to explanation / Norman Blaikie. London ; Thousand Oaks, CA : Sage Publications Ltd, 2003. xx, [353] p. : ill. ; 25 cm. Includes bibliographical references (p. [344]-346) and index. ISBN 0-7619-6759-1 ISBN 0-7619-6758-3 DDC 0 1.4/22
1. Social sciences - Statistical methods. 2. Social sciences - Methodology. 3. Mathematical statistics. I. Title.
HA29 .B556 2003

Blake, Steve. Pendragon : the definitive account of the origins of Arthur / Steve Blake and Scott Lloyd. London : Rider, 2002. x, 310 p., [12] p. of plates : ill. (some col.), maps ; 24 cm. Includes bibliographical references and index. ISBN 0-7126-3121-6 DDC 820.9351
1. Arthur, - King. 2. Arthurian romances - History and criticism. I. Lloyd, Scott. II. Title.

Blakely, Mary Louise. Unmasking bullies & victims : revealing their physiological, psychological, and emotional patterns / by Mary Louise Blakely. Tamarac, Fl. : Llumina Press, 2004. p. cm. Includes bibliographical references and index. Table of contents URL: http://www.loc.gov/catdir/toc/ecip044/2003012214.html ISBN 1-932303-60-X (pbk. : alk. paper) DDC 302.3/4
1. Bullying. I. Title. II. Title: Unmasking bullies and victims
BF637.B85 B56 2004

Blanchette, Oliva. Philosophy of being : a reconstructive essay in metaphysics / Oliva Blanchette. Washington, D.C. : Catholic University of America Press, c2003. xxiii, 563 p. ; 24 cm. Includes bibliographical references (p. 557-558) and indexes. ISBN 0-8132-1096-8 (pbk. : alk. paper) ISBN 0-8132-1095-X (alk. paper) DDC 111
1. Ontology. I. Title.
BD331 .B565 2003

BLANCHOT, MAURICE - CRITICISM AND INTERPRETATION.
Lévesque, Claude, 1927- Par-delà le masculin et le féminin. Paris : Aubier, 2002.

Blanco Merlo, Rubén.
Sobre las identidades. Pamplona : Universidad Pública de Navarra, [2001]

The blank slate.
Pinker, Steven, 1954- New York : Viking, 2002.
BF341 .P47 2002

Blanton, Hart, 1967-.
Pelham, Brett W., 1961- Conducting research in psychology. 2nd ed. Australia ; Belmont, CA : Thomson/Wadsworth, c2003.
BF76.5 .P34 2003

Blasi, Augusto.
Moral development, self, and identity. Mahwah, N.J. : Lawrence Erlbaum Associates, 2004.
BF723.M54 M686 2004

Blau, Dick, 1943-.
Gallop, Jane, 1952- Living with his camera. Durham : Duke University Press, 2003.
TR140.B517 G35 2003

BLAU, DICK, 1943-.
Gallop, Jane, 1952- Living with his camera. Durham : Duke University Press, 2003.
TR140.B517 G35 2003

Blaydes, John.
The educator's book of quotes. Thousand Oaks, Calif. : Corwin Press, c2003.
PN6084.E38 E38 2003

BLEPHAROPLASTY.
Western eyes [videorecording]. New York, NY : First Run/Icarus Films, 2000.

Bless, Herbert. Social cognition : how individuals construct social reality / Herbert Bless, Klaus Fiedler, Fritz Strack. Hove, East Sussex, UK ; New York : Psychology Press, 2003. p. cm. (Social psychology, 1368-4574) Includes bibliographical references and index. CONTENTS: Introduction : what is social cognition? -- Memory organizing as a key to understanding social cognition -- Judgmental heuristics in social cognition -- The use of information in judgments -- Testing hypothesis in social interaction - How cognitive processes are constrained by environmental data. ISBN 0-86377-828-3 (hardcover) ISBN 0-86377-829-1 (pbk.) DDC 302
1. Social perception. I. Fiedler, Klaus, 1951- II. Strack, Fritz, 1950- III. Title. IV. Series: Social psychology (Philadelphia, Pa.)
BF323.S63 B55 2003

BLESSING AND CURSING - PSYCHOLOGICAL ASPECTS.
Jay, Timothy. Why we curse. Philadelphia : John Benjamins Publishing Company, c2000.
BF463.I58 J38 2000

Blessings.
Quindlen, Anna. 1st large print ed. New York : Random House Large Print, c2002.
PS3567.U336 B59 2002b

Bleu.
Pastoureau, Michel, 1947- [Paris] : Seuil, c2000.
BF789.C7 P36 2000

Bliesener, Thomas.
Der Brockhaus Psychologie. Mannheim : Brockhaus, c2001.

Blindsight and the nature of consciousness.
Holt, Jason, 1971- Peterborough, Ont. : Broadview Press, c2003.

Bloch, Douglas, 1949-.
George, Demetra, 1946- Asteroid goddesses. Berwick, Me. : Ibis Press, 2003.
BF1724.5 .G46 2003

Positive self talk for children.
Bloch, Douglas, 1949- The power of positive talk. Rev. and updated ed. Minneapolis, Minn. : Free Spirit Pub., 2003.
BF723.S3 B56 2003

**The power of positive talk : words to help every child succeed / by Douglas Bloch with Jon Merritt. Rev. and updated ed. Minneapolis, Minn. : Free Spirit Pub., 2003. p. cm. Rev. ed. of: Positive self-talk for children. c1993. Includes bibliographical references and index. ISBN 1-57542-

127-5 DDC 649/.7
1. Self-esteem in children. 2. Self-talk in children. 3. Affirmations. I. Merritt, Jon. II. Bloch, Douglas, 1949- Positive self-talk for children. III. Title.
BF723.S3 B56 2003

Block, Cathy Collins.
Mangieri, John N. Yale Assessment of Thinking. San Francisco : Jossey-Bass, c2003.
BF442 .M34 2003

Bloechl, Jeffrey, 1966-.
Religious experience and the end of metaphysics. Bloomington, Ind. : Indiana University Press, c2003.
BL53 .R444 2003

Blokh, Avraham Yitshak ben Y. L. (Avraham Yitshak ben Yosef Leyb), d. 1941. Sefer Shi'ure da'at / me-et Avraham Yitshak Blokh. Yerushalayim : Feldhaim ; Wickliffe, Ohio : Peninei Daas Publications, 761 [2001] 230 p. ; 23 cm. Cover title: Shi'ure da'at.
1. Ethics, Jewish. 2. Judaism - Doctrines. 3. Musar movement. I. Title. II. Title: Shi'ure da'at

Blokh, Yosef Zalman. Igeret 'al ha-bitahon : le-va'er ule-laven mahut ha-bitahon be-H. ... / [Yosef Zalman Blokh]. Monsi : [h. mo. l.], 5761 [2000 or 2001] 144 p. ; 24 cm.
1. Trust in God - Judaism. 2. Ethics, Jewish. I. Title.
BM729.T7 .B56 2000

Blondet, Maurizio, 1944-.
Pinotti, Roberto, 1944- Oltre. Firenze : Olimpia, c2002.

BLONSKIĬ, PAVEL PETROVICH, 1884-1941.
Artamonova, E. R. Voprosy vozrastnoĭ i pedagogicheskoĭ psikhologii v tvorchestve P.P. Blonskogo. Vladimir : Vladimirskiĭ gos. pedagog. universitet, 2001.
BF109.B59 A78 2001

The blood of the moon.
Grant, George, 1954- Nashville, Tenn. : Thomas Nelson Publishers, 2002.
DS62 .G73 2002

Bloodrites of the post-structuralists.
Norton, Anne. New York : Routledge, 2002.
HM626 .N6785 2002

Bloody good.
Frantzen, Allen J., 1947- Chicago : University of Chicago Press, 2004.
D523 .F722 2004

Bloom, Harold. Genius : a mosaic of one hundred exemplary creative minds / Harold Bloom. New York : Warner Books, c2002. xviii, 814 p. : ill. ; 25 cm. CONTENTS: I. Keter. William Shakespeare, Miguel de Cervantes, Michel de Montaigne, John Milton, Leo Tolstoy, Lucretius, Vergil, Saint Augustine, Dante Alighieri, Geoffrey Chaucer -- II. Hokmah. The Yahwist, Socrates and Plato, Saint Paul, Muhammad, Dr. Samuel Johnson, James Boswell, Johann Wolfgang von Goethe, Sigmund Freud, Thomas Mann -- III. Binah. Friedrich Nietzsche, Søren Kierkegaard, Franz Kafka, Marcel Proust, Samuel Beckett, Molière, Henrik Ibsen, Anton Chekhov, Oscar Wilde, Luigi Pirandello -- IV. Hesed. John Donne, Alexander Pope, Jonathan Swift, Jane Austen, Lady Murasaki, Nathaniel Hawthorne, Herman Melville, Charlotte Brontë, Emily Jane Brontë, Virginia Woolf -- V. Din. Ralph Waldo Emerson, Emily Dickinson, Robert Frost, Wallace Stevens, T.S. Eliot, William Wordsworth, Percy Bysshe Shelley, John Keats, Giacomo Leopardi, Alfred, Lord Tennyson -- VI. Tiferet. Algernon Charles Swinburne, Dante Gabriel Rossetti, Christina Rossetti, Walter Pater, Hugo von Hofmannsthal, Victor Hugo, Gérard de Nerval, Charles Baudelaire, Arthur Rimbaud, Paul Valéry -- CONTENTS: VII. Nezah. Homer, Luis Vaz de Camões, James Joyce, Alejo Carpentier, Octavio Paz, Stendhal, Mark twain, William Faulkner, Ernest Hemingway, Flannery O'Connor -- VIII. Hod. Walt Whitman, Fernando Pessoa, Hart Crane, Federico García Lorca, Luis Cernuda, George Eliot, Willa Cather, Edith Wharton, F. Scott Fitzgerald, Iris Murdoch -- IX. Yesod. Gustave Flaubert, José Maria Eça de Queiroz, Joaquim Maria Machado de Assis, Jorge Luis Borges, Italo Calvino, William Blake, D.H. Lawrence, Tennessee Williams, Rainer Maria Rilke, Eugenio Montale -- X. Malkhut. Honoré de Balzac, Lewis Carroll, Henry James, Robert Browning, William Butler Yeats, Charles Dickens, Fyodor Dostoevsky, Isaac Babel, Paul Celan, Ralph Ellison. ISBN 0-446-52717-3 DDC 153.9/8
1. Genius. 2. Gifted persons. I. Title.
BF412 .B58 2002

Bloom, Michelle E. Waxworks : a cultural obsession / Michelle E. Bloom. Minneapolis : University of Minnesota Press, c2003. xix, 339 p. ; ill. ; 23 cm. Includes bibliographical references (p. 311-330) and index. Filmography: p. 331. ISBN 0-8166-3930-2 (HC : alk. paper) ISBN 0-8166-3931-0 (PB : alk. paper) DDC 731.4/2
1. Waxworks. 2. Wax-modeling. 3. Popular culture. I. Title.

GV1836 .B56 2003

Bloom, Paul, 1963- Descartes' baby : how the science of child development explains what makes us human / Paul Bloom. New York : Basic Books, 2004. p. cm. Includes bibliographical references and index. CONTENTS: Foundations -- Mindreaders -- The material realm -- Artifacts -- Anxious objects -- The social realm -- Good and evil -- The moral circle -- The body and soul emotion -- The spiritual realm -- Therefore I am -- Gods, souls, and science. ISBN 0-465-00783-X DDC 153
1. Cognition. 2. Child psychology. I. Title.
BF311 .B555 2004

Bloom, Richard W., 1944-.
Evolutionary psychology and violence. Westport, Conn. : Praeger, 2003.
HM1116 .E96 2003

Bloomfield, Andrew, 1960- How to practice Vedic astrology : a beginner's guide to casting your horoscope and predicting your future / Andrew Bloomfield. Rochester, Vt. : Destiny Books, 2003. p. cm. Includes bibliographical references and index. Table of contents URL: http://www.loc.gov/catdir/toc/ecip043/2003010311.html ISBN 0-89281-085-8 DDC 133.5/9445
1. Hindu astrology. I. Title.
BF1714.H5 B585 2003

Blu notte.
Lucarelli, Carlo, 1960- Misteri d'Italia. Torino : Einaudi, c2002.

BLUE.
Pastoureau, Michel, 1947- Bleu. [Paris] : Seuil, c2000.
BF789.C7 P36 2000

BLUE IN ART.
Pastoureau, Michel, 1947- Bleu. [Paris] : Seuil, c2000.
BF789.C7 P36 2000

Bluestone, Sarvananda. The world dream book : use the wisdom of world cultures to uncover your dream power / Sarvananda Bluestone. Rochester, Vt. : Destiny Books, c2002. viii, 256 p. : ill. ; 23 cm. Includes bibliographical references (p. 241-256). CONTENTS: Introduction: Meeting the dreamer : seeing with our eyes shut -- The veil between the worlds : crossing the borders between awake and dream -- Purging the River Lethe : remembering and inducing dreams -- Song and dance, mask and lance : our sleeping artist -- Saddling the night's mare : awakening to our sleeping fears -- On the wings of the night : soul searching and the searching soul -- Dreaming wholeness : shamans, healers, and dreamers -- Remembering the future : dreams, divination, and déjà vu -- Making love to your psyche : understanding dreams. ISBN 0-89281-902-2 (pbk.) DDC 154.6/3
1. Dreams. 2. Dream interpretation. I. Title. II. Title: Dream book
BF1091 .B616 2002

Blum, Deborah Love at Goon Park / Deborah Blum. New York : Berkley Books, 2004. p. cm. Originally published: Cambridge, MA : Perseus Pub., 2002. ISBN 0-425-19405-1 (pbk.) DDC 150/.92
1. Harlow, Harry Frederick, - 1905- I. Title.
BF109.H346 B58 2004

Love at Goon Park : Harry Harlow and the science of affection / Deborah Blum. Cambridge, MA : Perseus Pub., c2002. xvi, 336 p. : ill. ; 24 cm. Includes bibliographical references (p. 309-326) and index. ISBN 0-7382-0278-9 DDC 150/.92
1. Harlow, Harry Frederick, - 1905- I. Title.
BF109.H346 B58 2002

Blum, Paul Richard.
Early studies of Giordano Bruno. Bristol : Thoemmes, 2000.

Blumenberg, Hans. Ästhetische und metaphorologische Schriften / Hans Blumenberg ; Auswahl und Nachwort von Anselm Haverkamp. 1. Aufl. Frankfurt : Suhrkamp, 2001. 461 p. ; 18 cm. (Suhrkamp Taschenbuch Wissenschaft ; 1513) Includes bibliographical references and index. ISBN 3-518-29113-0 (pbk.).
1. Blumenberg, Hans. 2. Aesthetics. 3. Metaphor. I. Haverkamp, Anselm. II. Title. III. Series.

BLUMENBERG, HANS.
Blumenberg, Hans. Ästhetische und metaphorologische Schriften. 1. Aufl. Frankfurt : Suhrkamp, 2001.

Blumenthal, Mark. Popular herbs in the U.S. market / prepared by Mark Blumenthal, Chance W. Riggins. Austin : American Botanical Council, 1997. 68 p. : ill. ; 28 cm. (Therapeutic monographs) Cover title. "Written CE Monograph."
1. Herbs - Therapeutic use. 2. Holistic medicine. 3. Naturopathy. I. Riggins, Chance W. II. American Botanical Council. III. Title. IV. Series.

Bô Yin Râ, 1876-1943.
[Buch vom Menschen. English]
The book on human nature / Bô Yin Râ (J.A. Schneiderfranken) ; translated by B.A. Reichenbach. Berkeley, Calif. : Kober Press, c2000. 167 p. ; 21 cm. ISBN 0-915034-07-7 DDC 128
1. Psychology - Miscellanea. 2. Occultism. I. Title.
BF1999 .B6516713 2000

Bobgan, Deidre, 1935-.
Bobgan, Martin, 1930- Hypnosis. Santa Barbara, Calif. : EastGate Publishers, c2001.
BF1152 .B63 2001

Bobgan, Martin, 1930- Hypnosis : medical, scientific, or occultic? / Martin and Deidre Bobgan. Santa Barbara, Calif. : EastGate Publishers, c2001. 142 p. ; 22 cm. Includes bibliographical references (p. 133-142). ISBN 0-941717-18-6 DDC 154.7
1. Hypnotism. 2. Occultism. I. Bobgan, Deidre, 1935- II. Title.
BF1152 .B63 2001

Bochum publications in evolutionary cultural semiotics. New series
(v. 3.) Bichakjian, Bernard H. Language in a Darwinian perspective. Frankfurt am Main ; New York : Peter Lang, c2002.
P142 .B53 2002

Bochumer Studien zur Philosophie
(Bd. 39) Ackeren, Marcel van. Das Wissen vom Guten. Amsterdam ; Philadelphia : B.R. Gruner, c2003.
B398.V57 A33 2003

Bocock, Robert. Sigmund Freud / Robert Bocock. Rev. ed. London ; New York : Routledge, 2002. xxvii, 14-145 p. ; 21 cm. (Key sociologists) Includes bibliographical references and index. ISBN 0-415-28816-9 ISBN 0-415-28817-7 DDC 150.1952
1. Freud, Sigmund, - 1856-1939. 2. Freud, Sigmund, - 1856-1939 - Political and social views. I. Title. II. Series: Key sociologists (Routledge (Firm))
BF173.F85 B63 2002

Bod Rgya rtsom rig gśib bsdur gyi dpyad brjod / Khri-bsam-gtan sogs kyis brtsams. Par theńs 1. Pe-cin : Mi rigs dpe skrun khań, 2001. 2, 249 p. : col. ill. ; 21 cm. Chinese title on t.p. verso: Zang Han wen xue ming zhu bi jiao yan jiu. SUMMARY: Comparative study between Tibetan and Chinese literature. Includes bibliographical references (p. 248-249). In Tibetan. ISBN 7-105-04115-3
1. Tibetan literature - History and criticism. 2. Chinese literature - History and criticism. 3. Literature, Comparative - Tibetan and Chinese. 4. Literature, Comparative - Chinese and Tibetan. I. Khri-bsam-gtan. II. Title: Zang Han wen xue ming zhu bi jiao yan jiu
PL3705 (P-PZ22)+

Bodalev, A. A. Kak stanovi͡ats͡i͡a velikimi ili vydai͡ushchimis͡i͡a? / A.A. Bodalev, L.A. Rudkevich. Moskva : In-t psikhoterapii, 2003. 285, [1] p. ; 22 cm. (Sovety psikhologa) Includes bibliographical references (p. 282-[286]). ISBN 5899390891
1. Adulthood - Psychological aspects. 2. Personality and creative ability. 3. Creation (Literary, artistic, etc.) - Psychological aspects. I. Rudkevich, L. A. (Lev Aleksandrovich) II. Title. III. Series.
BF724.5 .B64 2003

Bodei, Remo, 1938- Destini personali : l'età della colonizzazione delle coscienze / Remo Bodei. Milano : Feltrinelli, 2002. 421 p. ; 22 cm. (Campi del sapere) Includes bibliographical references (p. 293-402) and name index. ISBN 88-07-10338-9 DDC 128
1. Philosophical anthropology. 2. Civilization - Philosophy. 3. Philosophy. I. Title. II. Series.

Bödeker, Hans Erich.
Begriffsgeschichte, Diskursgeschichte, Metapherngeschichte. Göttingen : Wallstein, 2002.
D13 .B45 2002

Boden, Margaret A. The creative mind : myths and mechanisms / Margaret A. Boden. 2nd ed. London ; New York : Routledge, 2003. p. cm. Includes bibliographical references and index. ISBN 0-415-31453-4 (pbk.) ISBN 0-415-31452-6 DDC 153.3/5
1. Creative ability. 2. Artificial intelligence. I. Title.
BF408 .B55 2003

Bodenhausen, Galen V. (Galen Von), 1961-.
Foundations of social cognition. Mahwah, N.J. : L. Erlbaum, 2003.
BF323.S63 F68 2003

Bodger, Lorraine. 500 reasons why you're my best friend / Lorraine Bodger. Kansas City, Mo. : Andrews McMeel Pub., c2003. 1 v. (unpaged) : ill. ; 16 cm. ISBN 0-7407-3314-1 DDC 302.3/4/082
1. Female friendship - Miscellanea. I. Title. II. Title: Five hundred reasons why you're my best friend

BF575.F66 B63 2003

Bodies of light.
Musiol, Marie-J. (Marie-Jeanne), 1950- Corps de lumière. Hull, Québec : Axe Néo-7, art contemporain, [2001?]

Bodin in Italia.
Valente, Michaela, 1972- Firenze : Centro editoriale toscano, c1999.
BF1602.B633 V35 1999

BODIN, JEAN, 1530-1596 - CENSORSHIP - ITALY.
Valente, Michaela, 1972- Bodin in Italia. Firenze : Centro editoriale toscano, c1999.
BF1602.B633 V35 1999

BODIN, JEAN, 1539-1596. DE LA DÉMONOMANIE DES SORCIERS. ITALIAN.
Valente, Michaela, 1972- Bodin in Italia. Firenze : Centro editoriale toscano, c1999.
BF1602.B633 V35 1999

Bodino, Angela, 1940-.
Racism. Armonk, N.Y. : M.E. Sharpe, c2003.
HT1521 .R323 2003

BODY AND MIND. *See* **MIND AND BODY.**

Body and soul.
Cox, Robert S., 1958- Charlottesville : University of Virginia Press, 2003.
BF1242.U6 C69 2003

BODY AND SOUL (PHILOSOPHY). *See* **MIND AND BODY.**

BODY DYSMORPHIC DISORDER. *See* **BODY IMAGE.**

BODY, HUMAN. *See also* **BODY IMAGE; MIND AND BODY.**
Langford, Elizabeth. Mind and muscle. Leuven : Gafant, 1999.

BODY, HUMAN - GROWTH. *See* **HUMAN GROWTH.**

BODY, HUMAN (IN RELIGION, FOLK-LORE, ETC.). *See* **BODY, HUMAN - RELIGIOUS ASPECTS.**

BODY, HUMAN (PHILOSOPHY).
Anders, Martin. Präsenz zu denken--. St. Augustin : Gardez!, c2002.
B3303 .A53 2002
Cavarero, Adriana. [Corpo in figure. English] Stately bodies. Ann Arbor : University of Michigan Press, c2002.
B105.B64 C3813 2002
Frey, Jean-Marie. Le corps peut-il nous rendre heureux? Nantes : Pleins feux, [2002]
Heinamaa, Sara, 1960- Toward a phenomenology of sexual difference. Lanham, Md. ; Oxford : Rowman & Littlefield Publishers, c2003.
HQ1208 .B3523 2003
Linck, Gudula. Leib und Körper. Frankfurt am Main ; New York : P. Lang, c2001.
B105.B64 L58 2001
Mazis, Glen A., 1951- Earthbodies. Albany, NY : State University of New York Press, 2002.
BJ1695 .M39 2002
Moulding masculinities. Aldershot, Hants, England ; Burlington, VT : Ashgate, c2003.
BF692.5 .M68 2003
Silva, Ana Márcia. Corpo, ciência e mercado. Campinas : Editora da UFSC : Editora Autores Associados, 2001.
GT495 .S55 2001
Tenner, Edward. Our own devices. 1st ed. New York : Alfred A. Knopf, 2003.
T14.5 .T4588 2003
Thinking the limits of the body. Albany : State University of New York Press, c2003.
HM636 .T47 2003

BODY, HUMAN - POLITICAL ASPECTS.
Violence and the body. Bloomington : Indiana University Press, c2003.
HM1116 .V557 2003

BODY, HUMAN - PSYCHOLOGICAL ASPECTS. *See* **MIND AND BODY.**

BODY, HUMAN - RELIGIOUS ASPECTS - JUDAISM.
Tsuri'el, Mosheh Yehi'el. Otsrot ha-musar. Yerushalayim : Yerid ha-sefarim, 763, 2002.

BODY, HUMAN - SOCIAL ASPECTS.
Braidotti, Rosi. [Nomadic subjects. Italian] Soggetto nomade. Roma : Donzelli, 1995.
Discourse, the body, and identity. Basingstoke, Hampshire ; New York : Palgrave Macmillan, 2003.
HM636 .D57 2003
Penz, Otto. Metamorphosen der Schönheit. Wien : Turia + Kant, c2001.
GT495 .P459 2001
Seeing nature through gender. Lawrence : University Press of Kansas, c2003.
GF21 .S44 2003
Silva, Ana Márcia. Corpo, ciência e mercado. Campinas : Editora da UFSC : Editora Autores Associados, 2001.
GT495 .S55 2001
Tenner, Edward. Our own devices. 1st ed. New York : Alfred A. Knopf, 2003.
T14.5 .T4588 2003
Thinking the limits of the body. Albany : State University of New York Press, c2003.
HM636 .T47 2003
Violence and the body. Bloomington : Indiana University Press, c2003.
HM1116 .V557 2003

BODY, HUMAN - SOCIAL ASPECTS - HISTORY.
Cohen, Jeffrey Jerome. Medieval identity machines. Minneapolis : University of Minnesota Press, c2003.
CB353 .C64 2003

BODY, HUMAN - SYMBOLIC ASPECTS - HISTORY.
Cohen, Jeffrey Jerome. Medieval identity machines. Minneapolis : University of Minnesota Press, c2003.
CB353 .C64 2003

BODY IMAGE.
Gottschild, Brenda Dixon. The Black dancing body. New York : Palgrave Macmillan, 2003.
GV1624.7.A34 G68 2003
1. *Black author.*
Guillerault, Gérard. Les deux corps du moi. Paris : Gallimard, c1996.
BF175.5.B64 G86 1996
Mills, Andy, 1979- Shapesville. 1st ed. Carlsbad, CA : Gurze Books, 2003.
BF723.B6 M55 2003

BODY IMAGE IN ADOLESCENCE.
Género, desarrollo psicosocial y trastornos de la imagen corporal. Madrid : Instituto de la Mujer, 2001.

BODY IMAGE IN CHILDREN.
Kater, Kathy. Real kids come in all sizes. New York : Broadway Books, 2004.
BF723.B6 K38 2004

BODY IMAGE IN CHILDREN - JUVENILE LITERATURE.
Mills, Andy, 1979- Shapesville. 1st ed. Carlsbad, CA : Gurze Books, 2003.
BF723.B6 M55 2003

BODY IMAGE IN MEN.
Moulding masculinities. Aldershot, Hants, England ; Burlington, VT : Ashgate, c2003.
BF692.5 .M68 2003

BODY IMAGE IN MEN - AUSTRIA.
Hofstadler, Beate, 1961- KörperNormen, KörperFormen. Wien : Turia + Kant, c2001.
BF692.5 .H64 2001

BODY IMAGE IN WOMEN.
Big Dance [videorecording]. Buffalo, N.Y. : Kineticvideo.com, c1998.
Darbo, Patrika. 365 glorious nights of love and romance. 1st ed. New York : ReganBooks, c2002.
HQ46 .D35 2002
Freedman, Rita Jackaway. Bodylove. Updated ed. Carlsbad, CA : Gürze Books, c2002.
BF697.5.B63 F74 2002
Género, desarrollo psicosocial y trastornos de la imagen corporal. Madrid : Instituto de la Mujer, 2001.
Lee, Michelle. Fashion victim. 1st ed. New York : Broadway Books, 2003.
GT524 .L44 2003
Piel que habla. Barcelona : Icaria, [2001]
BF697.5.B63 P54 2001
Western eyes [videorecording]. New York, NY : First Run/Icarus Films, 2000.

BODY IMAGE - SOCIAL ASPECTS.
Western eyes [videorecording]. New York, NY : First Run/Icarus Films, 2000.

The body in mind.
Rowlands, Mark. Cambridge, U.K. ; New York : Cambridge University Press, 1999.
BD418.3 .R78 1999

The body, in theory
Cavarero, Adriana. [Corpo in figure. English] Stately bodies. Ann Arbor : University of Michigan Press, c2002.
B105.B64 C3813 2002

BODY LANGUAGE. *See also* **FACIAL EXPRESSION; GESTURE.**
Jude, Brian, 1947- Johannesburg : Zebra Press, 1998.
BF637.N66 J83 1998

BODY LANGUAGE.
Beattie, Geoffrey. Visible thoughts. Hove, East Sussex ; New York, NY : Routledge, 2003.
BF637.N66 B43 2003
Chazal, Gérard. Interfaces. Seyssel [France] : Champ Vallon, c2002.
HM1111 .C49 2002
Discourse, the body, and identity. Basingstoke, Hampshire ; New York : Palgrave Macmillan, 2003.
HM636 .D57 2003
Goldman, Ellen. As others see us. New York : Brunner-Routledge, 2003.
BF637.N66 G65 2003
Linson, William. Kinoetics. [United States] : Kinoetics Publishing, c2002.
BF637.N66 L56 2002
Lumsden, Gay. Communicating with credibility and confidence. 2nd ed. Australia ; Belmont, CA : Thomson/Wadsworth, c2003.
BF637.C45 L85 2003
Marshall, Evan, 1956- The eyes have it. New York : Citadel Press, c2003.
BF637.N66 M37 2003
Mindell, Arnold, 1940- The dreambody in relationships. Portland, OR : Lao Tse Press ; Oakland, CA : Distributed to the trade by Words Distributing Co., c2002.
BF637.N66 M56 2002
Nonverbal behavior in clinical settings. Oxford ; New York : Oxford University Press, 2003.
RC489.N65 N66 2003
Richmond, Virginia P., 1949- Nonverbal behavior in interpersonal relations. 5th ed. Boston, Mass. : Pearson, 2004.
BF637.N66 R53 2004

BODY LANGUAGE - PERIODICALS.
[Gesture (Amsterdam, Netherlands)] Gesture. Amsterdam ; Philadelphia : John Benjamins Pub., 2001-
BF637.N66 G47

BODY LANGUAGE - SOUTH AFRICA.
Jude, Brian, 1947- Body language. Johannesburg : Zebra Press, 1998.
BF637.N66 J83 1998

BODY MARKING.
Weinberg, Norma Pasekoff, 1941- Henna from head to toe!. Pownal, Vt. : Storey Books, c1999.
GT2343 .W45 1999

BODY PAINTING.
Weinberg, Norma Pasekoff, 1941- Henna from head to toe!. Pownal, Vt. : Storey Books, c1999.
GT2343 .W45 1999

BODY SIZE. *See* **ANTHROPOMETRY.**

BODY WEIGHT. *See* **OBESITY.**

Bodylove.
Freedman, Rita Jackaway. Bodylove. Updated ed. Carlsbad, CA : Gürze Books, c2002.
BF697.5.B63 F74 2002

BOETHIUS, D. 524. DE CONSOLATIONE PHILOSOPHIAE.
Boethius, d. 524. [De consolatione philosophiae. French] La consolation de philosophie. Paris : Belles lettres, 2002.
Hehle, Christine. Boethius in St. Gallen. Tübingen : Niemeyer, 2002.

[De consolatione philosophiae. English]
Consolation of philosophy / Boethius ; translated, with introduction and notes, by Joel C. Relihan. Indianapolis, IN : Hackett Pub. Co., c2001. xxxiii,

216 p. ; 22 cm. Includes bibliographical references (p. 199-201). ISBN 0-87220-583-5 (pbk.) ISBN 0-87220-584-3 (cloth) DDC 100
1. Philosophy and religion. 2. Happiness. I. Relihan, Joel C. II. Title.
B659.C2 E52 2001

[De consolatione philosophiae. French]
La consolation de philosophie / Boèce ; introduction, traduction et notes par Jean-Yves Guillaumin. Paris : Belles lettres, 2002. 188 p. ; 21 cm. (La roue à livres, 1150-4129 ; 43. v) Translation of: De consolatione philosophiae. Includes bibliographical references (p. [179]-184) and index. ISBN 2-251-33943-4 DDC 871
1. Boethius, - d. 524. - De consolatione philosophiae. 2. Philosophy, Medieval. I. Guillaumin, Jean-Yves. II. Title. III. Series.

Boethius in St. Gallen.
Hehle, Christine. Tübingen : Niemeyer, 2002.

Boff, Leonardo. Espiritualidade : um caminho de transformação / Leonardo Boff. 2a ed. Rio de Janeiro : Sextante, c2001. 94 p. ; 21 cm. + 1 sound disc (4 3/4 in.). ISBN 85-86796-85-9
1. Spirituality. 2. Civilzation, Modern. I. Title.

Ethos mundial : um consenso mínimo entre os humanos / Leonardo Boff. Brasília : Letraviva, 2000. 165 p. : ill. ; 22 cm. Includes bibliographical references (p. 139-145). ISBN 85-87374-19-2
1. Ethics. 2. Ecology. I. Title.

Muraro, Rose Marie. Feminino e masculino. Rio de Janeiro : Sextante, 2002.
HQ801 .M87 2002

Bogdanov, Anatoliĭ Petrovich, 1834-1896. Selections. 2002.
Russkaia rasovaia teoriia do 1917 goda. Moskva : Feri-V, 2002.

Bogdanovic, Nikolai.
Wisdom, Stephen. Gladiators 100 BC-AD 200. Oxford : Osprey, 2001 (2002 printing)

Bogi slavi͡an, i͡azychestvo, tradit͡sii͡a.
Gavrilov, D. A. [Moskva] : Refl-buk, 2002.
BL930 .G38 2002

BOHEMIA. See **BOHEMIA (CZECH REPUBLIC).**

BOHEMIA (CZECH REPUBLIC) - HISTORY - TO 1526.
Člověk českého středověku. Vyd. 1. Praha : Argo, 2002.

BOHEMIA (CZECH REPUBLIC) - SOCIAL LIFE AND CUSTOMS.
Člověk českého středověku. Vyd. 1. Praha : Argo, 2002.

BOHEMIA (CZECHOSLOVAKIA). See **BOHEMIA (CZECH REPUBLIC).**

Bohleber, Werner.
Die Gegenwart der Psychoanalyse, die Psychoanalyse der Gegenwart. 2. Aufl. Stuttgart : Klett-Cotta, 2002.

Böhler, Dietrich.
Philosophieren aus dem Diskurs. Würzburg : Königshausen & Neumann, c2002.

Böhme, Gernot. Aisthetik : Vorlesungen über Ästhetik als allgemeine Wahrnehmungslehre / Gernot Böhme. München : Fink, c2001. 199 p. : ill. ; 22 cm. University lectures. ISBN 3-7705-3600-2 (pbk.)
1. Aesthetics. 2. Perception. I. Title.
BH39 .B64 2001

BÖHMEN (CZECH REPUBLIC). See **BOHEMIA (CZECH REPUBLIC).**

Boire au moyen âge.
Verdon, Jean. [Paris] : Perrin, c2002.

Boix Angelats, Jaume, 1952-.
Cruz, Mariano de la, 1921-1999. Mens sana in corpore insepulto. 1. ed. Barcelona : Edicions 62, 2002.

Boḳer ṭov ʻolam.
Tubali, Shy. [Selections] Tel Aviv : Yediʻot aḥaronot : Sifre ḥemed, c2003.

Bolebrukh, A. G. (Anatoliĭ Grigor'evich).
Istoriohrafichni ta dzhereloznavchi problemy istoriï Ukraïny. Dnipropetrovs'k : Vyd-vo Dnipropetrovs'koho universytetu, 2000.
DK508.46 .I84 2000

Bolich, Gregory G. Psyche's child : the story of psychology / Gregory G. Bolich. Dubuque, Iowa : Kendall/Hunt Pub., c2000. xli, 629 p. : ill. ; 28 cm. Includes bibliographical references (p. 547-602) and index. ISBN 0-7872-6906-9 DDC 150
1. Psychology. I. Title.
BF121 .B57 2000

Bolitho, Harold. Bereavement and consolation : testimonies from Tokugawa Japan / Harold Bolitho. New Haven : Yale University Press, c2003. xv, 226 p. : ill. ; 22 cm. Includes bibliographical references (p. 191-217) and index. ISBN 0-300-09798-0 (alk. paper) DDC 393/.9/095209034
1. Zenjō, - b. 1772. 2. Kobayashi, Issa, - 1763-1827. 3. Hirose, Kyokusō, - 1807-1863. 4. Bereavement - Japan. 5. Consolation. 6. Japan - Civilization - 1600-1868. I. Title.
DS822.2 .B65 2003

BOLLAS, CHRISTOPHER.
The vitality of objects. 1st US ed. Middletown, Conn. : Wesleyan University Press, 2002.
BF173 .V55 2002

Bolle, Kees W. The enticement of religion / Kees W. Bolle. Notre Dame, Ind. : University of Notre Dame Press, c2002. xiii, 330 p. ; 23 cm. Includes bibliographical references and index. CONTENTS: Introduction -- The history of religions -- The ordinariness of religion -- Myth and poetry -- Beginning to understand religions -- From the classics to the Renaissance -- Toward modernity -- The romantic movement -- The nineteenth century -- The painful birth of society : the twentieth century -- Farewell to too much of a system. ISBN 0-268-02764-1 (cloth : alk. paper) ISBN 0-268-02765-X (pbk. : alk. paper) DDC 200
1. Religion. I. Title.
BL48 .B585 2002

The Persistence of religions. Malibu : Undena Publications, 1996.

Bolling, Pamela.
The peak performance series. Vol. [4] [videorecording]. Longwood, Fla. : Pamela Bolling Enterprises, c1999.

BOLSHEVISM. See **COMMUNISM.**

Bolstrom, Brent.
Scales, Peter, 1949- Coming into their own. Minneapolis, MN : Search Institute, c2004.
BF721 .S347 2004

Bolt, Carol, 1963- Mom's book of answers / Carol Bolt. New York : Stewart, Tabori & Chang, 2004. p. cm. ISBN 1-58479-326-0 DDC 133.3
1. Fortune-telling by books. 2. Quotations, English - Miscellanea. I. Title.
BF1891.B66 B649 2004

Bolton, Martha, 1951- The "official" friends book : the who, what, when, where, why, and how of friendship / Martha Bolton ; illustrated by Kristy Caldwell. West Monroe, La : Howard Pub., 2003. p. cm. ISBN 1-58229-307-4 ISBN 1-58229-319-8 (pbk.) DDC 158.2/5
1. Friendship. I. Title.
BF575.F66 B65 2003

Bolzinger, André. La réception de Freud en France : avant 1900 / André Bolzinger. Paris : L'Harmattan, c1999. 189 p. ; 22 cm. (Collection Psychanalyse et civilisations. Série Trouvailles et retrouvailles) Includes bibliographical references (p. [173]-184) and index. ISBN 2-7384-8119-1
1. Freud, Sigmund, - 1856-1939 - Public opinion - France. 2. Psychoanalysis - History - 19th century. 3. Psychoanalysis - France - History. 4. Psychoanalysis and culture - France. I. Title. II. Series: Psychanalyse et civilisations. Série Trouvailles et retrouvailles.
BF175 .B575 1999

BOMBINGS.
Granot, Hayim. Terror bombing. Tel Aviv : Dekel Pub. House, 2002.
HV6431 .G73 2002

BONA VACANTIA. See **TREASURE-TROVE.**

Bonadonna, Angelo.
Burke, Kenneth, 1897- On human nature. Berkeley : University of California Press, c2003.
B945.B771 R84 2003

Bonaiuto, Marino.
Psychological theories for environmental issues. Aldershot, Hants, England ; Burlington, VT : Ashgate, 2003.
BF353 .P774 2003

Bonassi, Fernando, 1962-.
Leonel, Vange, 1963- Grrrls. São Paulo : Edições GLS, c2001.

Boncinelli, Edoardo. Io sono, tu sei : l'identità e la differenza negli uomini e in natura / Edoardo Boncinelli. 1. ed. Milano : Mondadori, 2002. 183 p. ; 23 cm. (Saggi) Includes bibliographical references (p. [173]-176) and index. ISBN 88-04-50437-4 DDC 575
1. Individuality. 2. Variation (Biology) 3. Human beings. 4. Life. I. Title. II. Title: Identità e la differenza negli uomini e in natura

Bond, D. Stephenson. The archetype of renewal : psychological reflections on the aging, death and rebirth of the king / D. Stephenson Bond. Toronto : Inner City Books, c2003. 125 p. : ill. ; 22 cm. (Studies in Jungian psychology by Jungian analysts) Includes bibliographical references and index. ISBN 1-89457-405-2 (pbk.) DDC 155.2
1. Adjustment (Psychology) 2. Jungian psychology. 3. Psychology and religion. I. Title. II. Series.

BOND, JAMES (FICTITIOUS CHARACTER) - MISCELLANEA.
Kyriazi, Paul. The complete live the James Bond lifestyle seminar. Los Angeles, CA : Ronin Books, c2002.
BF637.S8 K97 2002

Bondaletov, V. D.
Russkoe slovo. Penza : Izd-vo PGPU, 1998.
PG2026.B66 R88 1998

BONDS. See **STOCKS.**

Bone, Gavin.
Farrar, Janet. Progressive witchcraft. Franklin Lakes, NJ : New Page Books, 2004.
BF1571 .F346 2004

Bonesio, Luisa, 1950- Oltre il paesaggio : i luoghi tra estetica e geofilosofia / Luisa Bonesio. 1. ed. Casalecchio (Bologna) : Arianna, 2002. 170 p. ; 20 cm. Includes bibliographical references. ISBN 88-87307-26-1 DDC 304
1. Place (Philosophy) 2. Aesthetics. I. Title.

Bonesteel, N. E.
Schrieffer, J. R. (John Robert), 1931- [Papers. Selections] Selected papers of J. Robert Schrieffer. River Edge, NJ : World Scientific, c2002.
QC21.3 .S37 2002

Bonewitz, Ra. Wisdom of the Maya : an oracle of ancient knowledge for today / Ronald L. Bonewitz ; carved ill. by Achim Frederic Kiel. 1st St. Martin's ed. New York : St. Martin's Press, 2000. 144 p. : ill., maps ; 21 cm. Includes bibliographical references (p. 144). ISBN 0-312-26860-2 DDC 133.3/242
1. Fortune-telling by cards. 2. Mayas - Miscellanea. I. Kiel, Achim. II. Title. III. Title: Oracle of ancient knowledge for today
BF1878 .B66 2000

Bongard, Jerry. The near birth experience : a journey to the center of self / Jerry Bongard ; foreword by Hal Zina Bennett. New York : Marlowe & Co. ; [Emeryville, CA?] : Distributed by Publishers Group West, c2000. xvi, 167 p. ; 21 cm. Includes bibliographical references (p. 151-167). ISBN 1-56924-602-5 DDC 133.9/01/35
1. Hypnotic age regression. 2. Pre-existence. 3. Spiritual life - Miscellanea. I. Title.
BF1156.R45 B66 2000

Le bonheur.
Kelen, Jacqueline. Paris : Oxus, c2003.

Bonner, Ronald S.
What can happen when we pray. Minneapolis : Augsburg Fortress, c2001.

Bonnes, Mirilia.
Psychological theories for environmental issues. Aldershot, Hants, England ; Burlington, VT : Ashgate, 2003.
BF353 .P774 2003

Bonnet, Gérard. Défi à la pudeur : quand la pornographie devient l'initiation sexuelle des jeunes / Gérard Bonnet. Paris : Albin Michel, c2003. 229 p. ; 23 cm. Includes bibliographical references. ISBN 2-226-13673-8
1. Children and sex. 2. Pornography. I. Title.
HQ784.S45 .B66 2003

BONS MOTS. See **WIT AND HUMOR.**

Bonvecchio, Claudio. La maschera e l'uomo : simbolismo, comunicazione e politica / Claudio Bonvecchio. Milano : F. Angeli, 2002. 139 p. ; 23 cm. (Il limnisco ; 9) Includes bibliographical references. ISBN 88-464-3767-5 DDC 126
1. Masks - Symbolic aspects. 2. Symbolism. 3. Symbolism in politics. I. Title. II. Series.

Bonz, Jochen. Der Welt-Automat von Malcolm McLaren : Essays zu Pop, Skateboardfahren und Rainald Goetz / Jochen Bonz. Wien : Turia + Kant, [2002] 123 p. : ill. ; 20 cm. Includes bibliographical references. ISBN 3-85132-338-6 (pbk.)
1. Popular culture. 2. Popular music. I. Title.

Boogers and boo-daddies : the best of Blair's ghost stories / edited by the staff of John F. Blair, Publisher. Winston-Salem, N.C. : John F. Blair, Publisher, c2004. p. cm. CONTENTS: "Lady in distress" from legends of the Outer Banks and Tar Heel Tidewater / by Charles Harry Whedbee -- "The hatchet-swinging tire" from ghost tales of the Uwharries / by Fred T. Morgan -- "Sea-born woman" from the flaming ship of Ocracoke & other tales of the Outer Banks / by Charles Harry Whedbee -- "The beckoning hands" from Outer Banks mysteries & seaside stories / by Charles Harry Whedbee -- "The ghost who rang the gatehouse bell" from tales of the South Carolina low country / by Nancy Rhyne -- "Alice, the ghost of the hermitage" from more tales of the South Carolina low country / by Nancy Rhyne -- "The holy ghost shell" from Outer Banks tales to remember / by Charles Harry Whedbee -- "The wicked witch of Nantahala" from mountain ghost stories and curious tales of western North Carolina / by Randy Russell and Janet Barnett -- "Blackbeard's cup" from Blackbeard's cup and stories of the Outer Banks / by Charles Harry Whedbee -- "The ghost who cried for help" from haints, witches, and boogers : tales from Upper East Tennessee / by Charles Edwin Price -- "Stede Bonnet" from Blackbeard and other pirates of the Atlantic Coast / by Nancy Roberts -- "Cleland House" from ghosts of Georgetown / by Elizabeth Robertson Huntsinger -- "The Georgia werewolf" from Georgia ghosts / by Nancy Roberts -- "Pawleys Island terriers" from more ghosts of Georgetown / by Elizabeth Robertson Huntsinger -- "The wagon of death" from the hauntings of Williamsburg, Yorktown, and Jamestown / by Jackie Eileen Behrend -- "Milk and candy" from the granny curse and other ghosts and legends from East Tennessee / by Randy Russell and Janet Barnett -- "Trick or treat" from ghost dogs of the south / by Randy Russell and Janet Barnett -- "The shriek of the banshee" from seaside spectres / by Daniel W. Barefoot -- "Ghostly legacy of the Swamp Fox" from Piedmont phantoms / by Daniel W. Barefoot -- "The evil eye" from haints of the hills / by Daniel W. Barefoot. ISBN 0-89587-296-X DDC 133.1/0975
1. Ghosts - Southern States. I. John F. Blair, Publisher.
BF1472.U6 B66 2004

Book 3 of the Sibylline oracles and its social setting.
Buitenwerf, Rieuwerd. Book III of the Sibylline oracles and its social setting. Leiden ; Boston, MA : Brill, 2003.
BF1769 .B85 2003

BOOK COLLECTING.
Jackson, Holbrook, 1874-1948. [Anatomy of bibliomania. Portuguese. Selections] O tato. São Paulo : Imprensa Oficial do Estado, 2002.
Z992 .J33 2002

Book III of the Sibylline oracles and its social setting.
Buitenwerf, Rieuwerd. Leiden ; Boston, MA : Brill, 2003.
BF1769 .B85 2003

BOOK ILLUSTRATION. *See* **ILLUSTRATION OF BOOKS.**

BOOK INDUSTRIES AND TRADE. *See* **BOOKSELLERS AND BOOKSELLING; PUBLISHERS AND PUBLISHING.**

Book of alchemy.
Buckland, Raymond. 1st ed. St. Paul, Minn. : Llewellyn Publications, 2003.
BF1778.5 .B83 2003

Book of dumb.
Scalzi, John, 1969- Uncle John's presents Book of the dumb. San Diego, CA : Portable Press, 2003.
BF431 .S273 2003

The book of ghosts.
Brandon, Trent. Mineva, Ohio : Zerotime Pub., c2003.
BF1461 .B6949 2003

Book of IQ tests.
Russell, Kenneth, 1928- The Times book of IQ tests. Book 2. London : Milford, CT : Kogan Page, 2002.

The book of Lancelot.
Besamusca, Bart. Cambridge : D.S. Brewer, 2003.
PT5568 .B47 2003

The book of love and happiness.
Howard, Kerry. New York : Ryland Peters & Small, Inc., 2004.
BF575.L8 H69 2004

The book of love and pain.
Nasio, Juan-David. [Livre de la douleur et de l'amour. English] Albany : State University of New York, 2003.
BF515 .N3713 2003

The book of mean people.
Morrison, Toni. 1st ed. New York : Hyperion Books for Children, c2002.

The book of mosts.
Cohl, H. Aaron. 1st ed. New York : St. Martin's Press, 1997.
AG243 .C586 1997

Book of numerology.
King, Richard Andrew. The king's book of numerology. Aptos, Calif. : New Brighton Books, 2003-
BF1729.N85 K56 2003

Book of Pheryllt.
The lost books of Merlyn. 1st ed. St. Paul, Minn : Llewellyn Publications, 1998 (2003 printing)
BF1622.C45 L67 1998

The Book of prayer / compiled & edited by Renuka Narayanan. New Delhi ; New York, USA : Viking, 2001. xiii, 377 p. ; 18 cm. Includes index. ISBN 0-670-91146-1 DDC 291.4/33
1. Prayer. I. Khandekar, Renuka N.
BL560 .B625 2001

The book of risk.
Borge, Dan. New York : Wiley, c2001.
HD61 .B647 2001

The book of runes.
Melville, Francis. 1st ed. Hauppauge, NY : Barrons, c2003.
BF1891.R85 M45 2003

The book of secrets.
Carney, John, 1958- 1st ed. [United States?] : Carney Magic, c2002.
BF1611 .C35 2002

The book of shadows.
Lady Sheba. 1st ed. St. Paul, Minn. : Llewellyn Publications, 2002.

BOOK OF THAT WHICH IS IN THE NETHER WORLD.
Schweizer, Andreas, 1946- Seelenführer durch den verborgenen Raum. München : Kösel, 1994.

[Book of the dead. English.] The Egyptian book of the dead / translated and introduced by E.A. Wallis Budge. London : Cassell, 2001. 96 p. : ill. (some col.) ; 19 cm. "Abridged." ISBN 0-304-35619-0 DDC 299/.31
1. Incantations, Egyptian. 2. Future life. 3. Funeral rites and ceremonies - Egypt. I. Budge, E. A. Wallis (Ernest Alfred Wallis), Sir, 1857-1934. II. Title.
PJ1555.E5 B83 2001

The book of the year.
Aveni, Anthony F. Oxford ; New York : Oxford University Press, 2003.
GT3930 .A94 2003

Book of transformation.
Bstan-'dzin-rgya-mtsho, Dalai Lama XIV, 1935- The Dalai Lama's book of transformation. London : Thorsons, c2000.

The book of wizardry.
Rumstuckle, Cornelius, 1940- 1st ed. St. Paul, Minn. : Llewellyn Publications, 2003.
BF1611 .R85 2003

The book on human nature.
Bô Yin Râ, 1876-1943. [Buch vom Menschen. English] Berkeley, Calif. : Kober Press, 2000.
BF1999 .B6516713 2000

Book on witch trials.
Spee, Friedrich von, 1591-1635. [Cautio criminalis. English] Cautio criminalis, or, A book on witch trials. Charlottesville : University of Virginia Press, 2003.
BF1583.A2 S6813 2003

BOOK PUBLISHING. *See* **PUBLISHERS AND PUBLISHING.**

BOOK REGISTRATION, NATIONAL. *See* **COPYRIGHT.**

BOOK SALES. *See* **BOOKSELLERS AND BOOKSELLING.**

Book three of the Sibylline oracles and its social setting.
Buitenwerf, Rieuwerd. Book III of the Sibylline oracles and its social setting. Leiden ; Boston, MA : Brill, 2003.
BF1769 .B85 2003

BOOKS. *See* **ILLUMINATION OF BOOKS AND MANUSCRIPTS; ILLUSTRATION OF BOOKS.**

BOOKS AND READING.
Jackson, Holbrook, 1874-1948. [Anatomy of bibliomania. Portuguese. Selections] O tato. São Paulo : Imprensa Oficial do Estado, 2002.
Z992 .J33 2002

BOOKS AND READING FOR CHILDREN. *See* **CHILDREN - BOOKS AND READING.**

BOOKS - APPRAISAL. *See* **CRITICISM; LITERATURE - HISTORY AND CRITICISM.**

Books for professionals by professionals
Shea, Linchi. Real world SQL server administration with Perl. [Berkeley, CA] : Apress ; New York : Distributed to the book trade in the U.S. by Springer-Verlag, c2003.
QA76.73.S67 S48 2003

BOOKS - HISTORY.
Tagle Frías de Cuenca, Matilde. Notas sobre historia del libro. Córdoba, República Argentina : Ediciones del Copista, c1997.
Z4

BOOKS, ILLUSTRATED. *See* **ILLUSTRATED BOOKS.**

BOOKS, ILLUSTRATION OF. *See* **ILLUSTRATION OF BOOKS.**

BOOKS OF KNOWLEDGE. *See* **ENCYCLOPEDIAS AND DICTIONARIES.**

BOOKS - PUBLISHING. *See* **PUBLISHERS AND PUBLISHING.**

BOOKSELLERS AND BOOKSELLING. *See* **PUBLISHERS AND PUBLISHING.**

BOOKSELLERS AND BOOKSELLING - UGANDA - PERIODICALS.
Uganda book news. Kampala, Uganda : UPABA, 1996-
Z467.U337 U34

BOOMERS, BABY. *See* **BABY BOOM GENERATION.**

Boose, Lynda E., 1943-.
Shakespeare, the movie, II: popularizing the plays on film, TV, video, and DVD. London ; New York : Routledge, 2003.
PR3093 .S543 2003

Booth, Alan, 1935-.
Children's influence on family dynamics. Mahwah, N.J. : Lawrence Erlbaum Associates, 2003.
HQ518 .C535 2003

Boothman, Nicholas. How to connect in business in 90 seconds or less / Nicholas Boothman. New York : Workman Pub., 2002. v, 250 p. ; 19 cm. ISBN 0-7611-2595-7 ISBN 0-7611-2779-8 (alk. paper) DDC 650.1/3
1. Business networks. 2. Interpersonal communication. 3. Interpersonal relations. I. Title.
HD69.S8 B66 2002

Borba, Michele. Don't give me that attitude! : 24 rude, selfish, insensitive things kids do and how to stop them / Michele Borba. 1st ed. San Francisco : Jossey-Bass, c2004. p. cm. Includes bibliographical references. ISBN 0-7879-7333-5 (alk. paper) DDC 649/.64
1. Attitude change in children. 2. Child rearing. I. Title.
BF723.A76 B67 2004

BORDER LIFE. *See* **FRONTIER AND PIONEER LIFE.**

Bordiugov, G. A. (Gennadiĭ Arkad'evich).
Kul'tura i vlast' v usloviiakh kommunikatsionnoĭ revoliutsii XX veka. Moskva : "AIRO-XX", 2002.
HM621 .K858 2002

BOREDOM - HISTORY.
Decher, Friedhelm. Besuch vom Mittagsdämon. 1. Aufl. Lüneburg : zu Klampen, 2000.
BF575.B67 .D43 2000

BOREDOM - RELIGIOUS ASPECTS - CHRISTIANITY.
Winter, Richard, 1945- Still bored in a culture of entertainment. Downers Grove, Ill. : InterVarsity Press, c2002.
BV4599.5.B67 W56 2002

Borge, Dan. The book of risk / Dan Borge. New York : Wiley, c2001. ix, 244 p. : ill. ; 23 cm. Includes bibliographical references and index. ISBN 0-471-32378-0 (cloth : alk. paper) DDC 658.15/5
1. Risk management. 2. Risk assessment. 3. Risk-taking (Psychology) I. Title.
HD61 .B647 2001

Borges, Edson. Racismo, preconceito e intolerancia / Edson Borges, Carlos Alberto Medeiros, Jacques d'Adesky. [São Paulo, Brazil] : Atual, c2002. 80 p. : ill. (some col.) ; 24 cm. (Espaço & debate) Includes bibliographical references. ISBN 85-357-0248-2
1. Racism. 2. Prejudices. 3. Race relations. 4. Race discrimination. 5. Racism - Brazil. 6. Prejudices - Brazil. 7.

BORGES, JORGE LUIS, 1899- - CRITICISM AND INTERPRETATION.
Charles, Monique. Borges, ou, L'étrangeté apprivoisée. Paris : Harmattan, c2002.

Borges, ou, L'étrangeté apprivoisée.
Charles, Monique. Paris : Harmattan, c2002.

BORN AGAIN CHRISTIANITY. *See* **CONVERSION.**

Born to belonging.
Segrest, Mab, 1949- New Brunswick, NJ : Rutgers University Press, c2002.
HQ75.25 .S44 2002

Börner, G. The early universe / Gerhard Börner. 4th ed. Berlin ; London : Springer, c2003. xvii, 586 p. : ill. (some col.) ; 24 cm. (Astronomy and astrophysics library, 0941-7834) Previous ed.: 1993. Includes bibliographical references and index. ISBN 3-540-44197-2 DDC 523.1
1. Cosmology. 2. Particles (Nuclear physics) 3. Nuclear astrophysics. 4. Dark matter (Astronomy) 5. Galaxies - Evolution. I. Title. II. Series.

Borodiuk, N. R. (Nelli Rafkatovna) Dukhovnost' kak faktor uspeshnoĭ sotsial'noĭ adaptatsii cheloveka : bioenergeticheskie mekhanizmy prisposobitel'nykh reaktsiĭ / N.R. Borodiuk. Moskva : [s.n.], 2000. 118 p. : ill. ; 22 cm. Includes bibliographical references (p. 112-116).
1. Adaptability (Psychology) 2. Adaptation (Biology) 3. Adaptability (Psychology) - Social aspects. I. Title.
BF335 .B67 2000

Borromeo, Federico, 1564-1631. Manifestazioni demoniache / Federico Borromeo ; prefazione di Franco Buzzi ; postfazione di Gabriella Cattaneo ; traduzione e note di Francesco Di Ciaccia. Milano : Terziaria : ASEFI, 2001. 139 p. : ill. ; 22 cm. (Testi ; 7) Includes bibliographical references. ISBN 88-86818-70-X DDC 235
1. Demonology - Early works to 1800. I. Di Ciaccia, Francesco. II. Title. III. Series: Testi (Terziaria (Firm : Milan, Italy)) ; 7.
BF1520 .B67 2001

Borysenko, Joan. Inner peace for busy women : balancing work, family, and your inner life / Joan Borysenko. Carlsbad, Calif. : Hay House, 2003. 179 p. : ill. ; 21 cm. Table of contents URL: http://www.loc.gov/catdir/toc/ecip042/2003007713.html ISBN 1401901220 (hardcover) DDC 158.1/082
1. Peace of mind. 2. Women - Psychology. I. Title.
BF637.P3 B673 2003

Bosco Coletsos, Sandra. La struttura parentale nelle fiabe dei fratelli Grimm / Sandra Bosco Coletsos, Marcella Costa. Alessandria : Edizioni dell'Orso, 2001. 125 p. ; 24 cm. (Cultura tedesca ; 3) Includes bibliographical references. ISBN 88-7694-505-9 DDC 833
1. Grimm, Jacob, - 1785-1863. 2. Grimm, Wilhelm, - 1786-1859. 3. Kinder- und Hausmärchen. 4. Parent and child. 5. Family in literature. 6. Fables, German. I. Costa, Marcella. II. Title. III. Series.

Bošković, Hijacint. Filozofski izvori fašizma i nacionalnog socijalizma / Hijacint Bošković ; priredio Petar Strčić. 2. izd. Zagreb : Dom i svijet, 2000. 104 p. : ill. ; 21 cm. (Biblioteka Povjesnica) Includes bibliographical references (p. 103-104). ISBN 9536491443
1. Bošković, Hijacint. 2. Philosophy, Modern - 20th century. 3. Fascism. 4. National socialism. I. Strčić, Petar. II. Title. III. Series.
B804 .B66 2000

BOŠKOVIĆ, HIJACINT.
Bošković, Hijacint. Filozofski izvori fašizma i nacionalnog socijalizma. 2. izd. Zagreb : Dom i svijet, 2000.
B804 .B66 2000

Bostic, Heidi.
Irigaray, Luce. [Voie de l'amour. English] The way of love. London ; New York : Continuum, 2002.
BF575.L8 I7513 2002

Irigaray, Luce. The way of love. London ; New York : Continuum, 2002.

Boston studies in the philosophy of science
(v. 203-204) Nietzsche and the sciences. Dordrecht ; Boston : Kluwer Academic Publishers, c1999-
B3318.K7 N54 1999

Boston University studies in philosophy and religion
(v. 24) Promise and peril. Notre Dame, Ind. : University of Notre Dame Press, c2003.
BL50 .P65 2003

Boswell, Gwyneth.
Women's minds, women's bodies. Basingstoke ; New York : Palgrave Macmillan, 2003.
RA778 .P724 2003

BOTANY. *See* **TREES.**

Botschaften aus dem Jenseits / Hans Körner (Hrsg.). [Düsseldorf] : Droste, c2002. 213 p. : ill. ; 22 cm. (Studia humaniora ; Bd. 35) Includes bibliographical references. ISBN 3-7700-0843-X (pbk.)
1. Future life. 2. Religious thought - History. I. Körner, Hans, 1951- II. Series.

Botschaften verstehen : Kommunikationstheorie und Zeichenpraxis : Festschrift für Helmut Richter / herausgegeben von Ernest W.B. Hess-Lüttich und H. Walter Schmitz. Frankfurt am Main ; New York : P. Lang, c2000. 298 p. ; 21 cm. List of works by Helmut Richter: p. [15]-26. Includes bibliographical references. ISBN 3-631-36014-2 (pbk.)
1. German philology. 2. Communication. I. Richter, Helmut, 1935- II. Hess-Lüttich, Ernest W. B. III. Schmitz, H. Walter.
P91.25 .B688 2000

Bottenberg, Ernst Heinrich. Seele im Lichtzwang, im Lichtzwang der Seele : eine Assemblage / Ernst Heinrich Bottenberg. 1. Aufl. Sankt Augustin : Academia, 1994. viii, 249 p., 1 leaf of plates : 1 ill. ; 21 cm. Includes bibliographical references (p. 215-249). ISBN 3-88345-426-5
1. Psychology - Philosophy. I. Title.
BF38 .B625 1994

Botturi, Francesco, 1947-.
La persona e i nomi dell'essere. Milano : V&P Università, c2002.
B29 .P414 2002

Bougerol, Jacques Guy.
Jean, de la Rochelle, d. 1245. Summa de anima. Paris : J. Vrin, 1995.
BD420 .J43 1995

Boughton, Harold "Bud" The missing piece : our search for security in an insecure world / Harold "Bud" Boughton. [Lancaster, Ohio] : Lucky Press, c2003. xvii, 182 p. ; 24 cm. ISBN 0-9713318-6-3 (alk. paper) DDC 155.9
1. Security (Psychology) I. Title.
BF575.S35 B68 2003

Bougnoux, Daniel.
Faire face. Paris : Gallimard, [2002]

Bouloumié, Arlette.
Ecriture et maladie. Paris : Editions Imago, c2003.

Boulter, Michael Charles. Extinction : evolution and the end of man / Michael Boulter. New York : Columbia University Press, c2002. xiv, 210 p. : ill., maps ; 22 cm. Includes bibliographical references and index. ISBN 0-231-12836-3 (cloth : alk. paper) DDC 576.8/4
1. Extinction (Biology) 2. Evolution (Biology) 3. Nature - Effect of human beings on. I. Title.
QE721.2.E97 B68 2002

Bound by recognition.
Markell, Patchen, 1969- Princeton, N.J. : Princeton University Press, c2003.
JC575 .M37 2003

Bound by struggle.
Maoz, Zeev. Ann Arbor : University of Michigan Press, c2002.
JZ5595 .M366 2002

BOUNDARIES.
Making and breaking of borders. Helsinki : Finnish Literature Society, 2003.
JC323 .M35 2003

Boundaries of privacy.
Petronio, Sandra Sporbert. Albany : State University of New York Press, c2002.
BF697.5.S427 P48 2002

Bouquet, Simon.
Une introduction aux sciences de la culture. 1. ed. Paris : Presses universitaires de France ; [Paris] : Institut Ferdinand-de-Saussure, 2002.

Bourbon, Fabio.
The Splendors of archaeology. Cairo : American University in Cairo Press, 1998.

Bourdieu, Pierre.
Amougou, Emmanuel. La construction de l'inconscient colonial en Alsace. Paris : L'Harmattan, 2002.
1. Black author.

Bourne, Edmund J. Coping with anxiety : 10 simple ways to relieve anxiety, fear & worry / Edmund Bourne & Lorna Garano. Oakland, CA : New Harbinger, c2003. x, 156, [1] p. ; 19 cm. Includes bibliographical references (p. [157]). ISBN 1-57224-320-1 (pbk.) DDC 152.4/6
1. Anxiety. 2. Fear. 3. Self-help techniques. I. Garano, Lorna. II. Title.
BF575.A6 B68 2003

Bournemouth University. School of Conservation Sciences.
Digging holes in popular culture. Oxford : Oxbow, 2002.
PN3433.6 .D54 2002

Bourque, Susan Carolyn, 1943-.
Women on power. Boston : Northeastern University Press, c2001.
HQ1233 .W597 2001

Bouveresse, Jacques.
Collège de France. Symposium annuel. La vérité dans les sciences. Paris : Jacob, c2003.

Bowden, William.
Theory and practice in late antique archaeology. Leiden ; Boston : Brill, 2003.
CC72.4 .T46 2003

Bowers, Jeffrey S.
Rethinking implicit memory. Oxford ; New York : Oxford University Press, c2003.
RC394.M46 R485 2003

Bowers, Keri. Single pregnancy - single parenting : creating a positive, fulfilling experience / Keri Bowers. Pleasant Hill, CA : Park Alexander Press, c1996. xiv, 297 p. : ill. ; 23 cm. Includes bibliographical references (p. 283-288) and index. ISBN 0-9652441-0-5 DDC 649.1/0243
1. Unmarried mothers. 2. Pregnancy. 3. Child rearing. I. Title.
HQ759.45 .B68 1996

Bowling, Daniel, 1943-.
Bringing peace into the room. 1st ed. San Francisco : Jossey-Bass, 2003.
HM1126 .B75 2003

Bowman, Marjorie A.
Stress and women physicians.
Bowman, Marjorie A. Women in medicine. 3rd ed. New York ; Berlin : Springer, c2002.
R692 .B69 2002

Women in medicine : career and life management / Marjorie A. Bowman, Erica Frank, Deborah I. Allen. 3rd ed. New York ; Berlin : Springer, c2002. xv, 187 p. : ill. ; 24 cm. Rev. ed. of: Stress and women physicians / Marjorie A. Bowman, Deborah I. Allen. 2nd ed. c1990. Includes bibliographical references (p. 147-177) and index. ISBN 0-387-95309-4 (alk. paper) DDC 610.69/52/082
1. Women physicians - Psychology. 2. Stress (Psychology) 3. Women physicians - Mental health. I. Frank, Erica. II. Allen, Deborah I. III. Bowman, Marjorie A. Stress and women physicians. IV. Title.
R692 .B69 2002

Boxer, Diana, 1948- Applying sociolinguistics : domains and face-to-face interaction / Diana Boxer. Amsterdam ; Philadelphia : J. Benjamins Pub., c2002. ix, 244 p. ; 23 cm. (Impact, studies in language and society, 1385-7908 ; v. 15) Includes bibliographical references (p. [227]-239) and index. ISBN 1-58811-197-0 (U.S. : alk. paper) ISBN 1-58811-198-9 (U.S. : pbk. : alk. paper) ISBN 90-272-1850-1 (Europe) ISBN 90-272-1851-X (Europe) DDC 306.44
1. Sociolinguistics. 2. Social interaction. I. Title. II. Series: Impact, studies in language and society ; 15.
P40 .B678 2002

Boyce, James K. Investing in peace : aid and conditionality after civil wars / James K. Boyce. Oxford : Oxford University Press, 2002. 85 p. ; 24 cm. (Adelphi paper ; 351) Includes bibliographical references. CONTENTS: Introduction -- Aid for peace? -- The internal politics of external assistance -- Peace dividends: aid and fiscal policy -- The humanitarian dilemma -- Obstacles to peace conditionality -- Conclusion. ISBN 0-19-851669-X DDC 327.172
1. Peace. 2. Conditionality (International relations) 3. Economic assistance. 4. Civil war. I. Title. II. Title: Adelphi papers. III. Series: Adelphi papers ; no. 351.

Boyd, Denise Roberts.
Wood, Samuel E. Mastering the world of psychology. Boston : Pearson/Allyn and Bacon, c2004.
BF121 .W656 2004

Boyd-Franklin, Nancy. Black families in therapy : understanding the African American experience / Nancy Boyd-Franklin. 2nd ed. New York : Guilford Press, c2003. xiv, 368 p. : ill. ; 25 cm. Includes bibliographical references (p. 335-351) and indexes. CONTENTS: Pt. 1. African American families : the cultural and racial context -- Overview -- Racism, racial identity, and

skin color issues -- Extended family patterns, kinship care, and informal adoption -- Role flexibility and boundary confusion -- African american men and women : socialization and relationships -- Separation, divorce, remarriage, and stepparenting -- Religion and spirituality in African American families -- Additional important topics in African American communities -- Pt. 2. Major treatment theories, issues, and interventions -- The therapist's use of self and value conflicts -- Major family therapy approaches and their relevance to treating African Americans -- The multisystems model -- Public policy issues : a guide for clinicians -- Pt. 3. Socioeconomic class issues and diversity of family structures -- Poor families and the multisystems model -- Single-parent African American families -- Middle-class African American families -- Pt. 4. Implications for supervision, training, and future research -- Implications for training and supervision -- Conclusion and implications for future clinical work and research. ISBN 1-57230-619-X DDC 616.89/156/08996073
1. African American families - Mental health. 2. African Americans - Social conditions. 3. Family psychotherapy. I. Title.
RC451.5.N4 B69 2003

Boyer, J. Patrick.
Leading in an upside-down world. Toronto : Dundurn Group, c2003.
BF637.L4 L425 2003

Leading in an upside-down world. Toronto : Dundurn Group, c2003.

Boyle, Elizabeth, 1961-.
Mezias, Stephen J. Organizational dynamics of creative destruction. Houndmills [England] ; New York : Palgrave Macmillan, 2002.
HB615 .M49 2002

BOYS. See **YOUNG MEN.**

BOYS - EDUCATION - SOCIAL ASPECTS.
Boys, literacies, and schooling. Buckingham [England] ; Philadelphia : Open University Press, 2002.
LC1390 .B69 2002

BOYS - EUROPE - HISTORY - TO 1500.
Karras, Ruth Mazo, 1957- From boys to men. Philadelphia : University of Pennsylvania Press, c2003.
HQ775 .K373 2003

Boys, literacies, and schooling : the dangerous territories of gender-based literacy reform / Leonie Rowan ... [et al.]. Buckingham [England] ; Philadelphia : Open University Press, 2002. xiv, 235 p. ; 24 cm. (Educating boys, learning gender) Includes bibliographical references (p. [212]-230) and index. ISBN 0-335-20757-X (hard) ISBN 0-335-20756-1 (pbk.) DDC 371.823
1. Boys - Education - Social aspects. 2. Masculinity. 3. Sex differences in education - Social aspects. 4. Gender identity. 5. Language arts. I. Rowan, Leonie, 1966- II. Series.
LC1390 .B69 2002

Brace, Nicola. SPSS for psychologists : a guide to data analysis using SPSS for Windows, versions 9, 10 and 11 / Nicola Brace, Richard Kemp, and Rosemary Snelgar. 2nd ed. Mahwah, NJ : Lawrence Erlbaum Associates, 2003. p. cm. Includes bibliographical references and index. ISBN 0-8058-4774-X (pbk. : alk. paper) DDC 150/.7/27
1. Psychology - Statistical methods. 2. Psychometrics. I. Kemp, Richard. II. Snelgar, Rosemary. III. Title.
BF39 .K447 2003

Brachtendorf, Johannes.
Prudentia und Contemplatio. Paderborn : Ferdinand Schöningh, 2002.

Brackert, Helmut.
Wolfram, von Eschenbach, 12th cent. Titurel. Berlin ; New York : Walter de Gruyter, 2002.

Bradford book.
Emotions in humans and artifacts. Cambridge, Mass. : MIT Press, c2002.
BF531 .E517 2002

Bradford, Duncan.
The Ship of thought. London : Karnac, 2002.

Bradler, Christine M.
[Feng Shui Symbole des Ostens. English]
Feng shui symbols : a user's handbook / Christine M. Bradler, Joachim Alfred P. Scheiner ; illustrated by Klaus Holitzka. New York : Sterling Pub., c2001. 272 p. : ill. ; 19 cm. Includes index. Publisher description URL: http://www.loc.gov/catdir/description/ste022/2001042624.html ISBN 0-8069-7153-3 DDC 133.3/337
1. Feng shui. I. Scheiner, Joachim Alfred P. II. Bradler, Christine M. Feng Shui Symbole des Westens. English. III. Title.

BF1779.F4 .B7313 2001

Feng Shui Symbole des Westens. English.
Bradler, Christine M. [Feng Shui Symbole des Ostens. English] Feng shui symbols. New York : Sterling Pub., c2001.
BF1779.F4 .B7313 2001

Bradley, Ian C. The Celtic way / Ian Bradley. [2nd ed.]. London : Darton Longman & Todd, 2003. xvi, 134 p. ; 22 cm. Includes bibliographical references (p. 123-130) and index. ISBN 0-232-52495-5 (pbk.) DDC 274.1
1. Celtic Church - History. 2. Great Britain - Church history - 449-1066. 3. Celts - Religion. I. Title.
BR748 .B73 2003

Bradley, Phil, 1959- Internet power searching : the advanced manual / Phil Bradley. 2nd ed. New York : Neal-Schuman Publishers, c2002. xiii, 258 p. : ill. ; 25 cm. (Neal-Schuman netguide series) Includes index. CONTENTS: An introduction to the Internet -- An introduction to search engines -- Free text search engines -- Index-based search engines -- Multi-search engines -- Natural-language search engines -- Finding images, sounds and multimedia information -- Finding people -- Other available database resources -- Virtual libraries and gateways -- Intelligent agents -- Usenet newsgroups and mailing lists -- The information mix and into the future -- Forty tips and hints for better and quicker searching -- Sources for further help and assistance -- HTML for a search engines home page -- Country codes -- URLs mentioned in the book. ISBN 1-55570-447-6
1. Internet searching. I. Title. II. Series.
ZA4201 .B69 2002

Brady, Mark, 1946-.
The wisdom of listening. Somerville, MA : Wisdom Publications, c2003.
BF323.L5 W57 2003

Bragdon, Allen D.
Gamon, David. Building mental muscle. Rev. and updated ed. New York : Walker & Co., 2003.
BF441 .G35 2003

Use it or lose it! : how to keep your brain fit as it ages / by Allen D. Bragdon and David Gamon. 2nd ed., updated and expanded. New York : Walker & Co., 2004. p. cm. (Brain waves books) Includes bibliographical references and index. ISBN 0-8027-7682-5 (pbk. : alk. paper) DDC 155.67/13
1. Cognition in old age. I. Gamon, David. II. Title. III. Series.
BF724.85.C64 B73 2004

Braham, Barbara J. Finding your purpose : a guide to personal fulfillment / Barbara J. Braham. Rev. ed. Menlo Park, CA : Crisp Publications, c2003. viii, 112 p. : ill. ; 26 cm. (A Fifty-Minute series book) Includes bibliographical references (p. 108). ISBN 1-56052-684-X DDC 158.1/076
1. Self-actualization (Psychology) I. Title. II. Series: Fifty-Minute series.
BF637.S4 B67 2003

BRAHMANISM. See **HINDUISM.**

Braidotti, Rosi.
[Nomadic subjects. Italian]
Soggetto nomade : femminismo e crisi della modernità / Rosi Braidotti ; a cura di Anna Maria Crispino. Roma : Donzelli, 1995. xi, 132 p. ; 22 cm. (Saggi. Scienza e filosofia) Includes bibliographical references. ISBN 88-7989-140-5
1. Feminist theory. 2. Sex differences. 3. Body, Human - Social aspects. I. Title. II. Series.

Braiker, Harriet B., 1948- Who's pulling your strings? : how to break the cycle of manipulation and regain control of your life / Harriet B. Braiker. New York : McGraw-Hill, c2004. xii, 260 p. ; 24 cm. Includes index. Table of contents URL: http://www.loc.gov/catdir/toc/ecip042/2003008602.html Publisher description URL: http://www.loc.gov/catdir/description/mh031/2003008602.html CONTENTS: An overview of manipulation -- Manipulation in five acts -- Are you vulnerable to manipulation? -- Your buttons are showing -- Manipulator's motives -- Who are the manipulators in your life? -- How manipulation works -- What are your hooks? -- The mechanics of manipulation -- Are you in a manipulative relationship? -- The impact of manipulation -- Resistance tactics -- How to make yourself a hardened target -- Final curtain on manipulation in five acts. ISBN 0-07-140278-0 (alk. paper) DDC 158.2
1. Manipulative behavior. 2. Control (Psychology) I. Title.
BF632.5 .B69 2004

BRAIN. See also **MIND AND BODY; PHRENOLOGY.**
Combs, Allan, 1942- The radiance of being. 2nd ed. St. Paul, Minn. : Paragon House, 2002.
BF311 .C575 2002

Dyslexia, fluency, and the brain. Timonium, Md. : York Press, 2001.

RC394.W6 D958 2001

Ornstein, Robert E. (Robert Evan), 1942- Multimind. Cambridge, MA : ISHK, 2003.
BF431 .O68 2003

Understanding the brain. Paris : Organisation for Economic Co-operation and Development, 2002.
QP360.5 .U54 2002

Brain, behavior and evolution. 1995.
Eaton, Robert C. The octavolateralis system and Mauthner cell interactions and questions [microform]. [Washington, D.C. : National Aeronautics and Space Administration, 1997]

BRAIN - COMPUTER SIMULATION.
Kasabov, Nikola K. Evolving connectionist systems. London ; New York : Springer, c2003.
QA76.87 .K39 2003

BRAIN CONTROL. See **BRAINWASHING.**

BRAIN DAMAGE - PATIENTS - BIOGRAPHY.
Skloot, Floyd. In the shadow of memory. Lincoln : University of Nebraska Press, c2003.
PS3569.K577 Z47 2003

BRAIN - DISEASES. See **BRAIN DAMAGE.**

BRAIN - EVOLUTION.
Armstrong, Gordon Scott, 1937- Theatre and consciousness. New York ; Oxford : Peter Lang, c2003.
BH301.P78 A75 2003

Solso, Robert L., 1933- The psychology of art and the evolution of the conscious brain. Cambridge, Mass. : MIT Press, 2003.
BF311 .S652 2003

Sterelny, Kim. Thought in a hostile world. Malden, MA : Blackwell, 2003.
BF698.95 .S74 2003

BRAIN - LOCALIZATION OF FUNCTIONS. See **PHRENOLOGY.**

Brain of the earth's body.
Preziosi, Donald, 1941- Minneapolis : University of Minnesota Press, c2003.
N380 .P67 2003

BRAIN - PHILOSOPHY.
Tetens, Holm, 1948- Geist, Gehirn, Maschine. Stuttgart : Reclam, c1994.
BF163 .T48 1994x

BRAIN - PHYSIOLOGY.
Carter, Rita, 1949- Exploring consciousness. Berkeley : University of California Press, c2002.
BF311 .C289 2002

BRAIN - POPULAR WORKS.
Gamon, David. Building mental muscle. Rev. and updated ed. New York : Walker & Co., 2003.
BF441 .G35 2003

BRAIN - PSYCHOLOGY.
Darlington, Cynthia L. The female brain. London ; New York : Taylor & Francis, c2002.
QP402 .D366 2002

BRAIN - PSYCHOPHYSIOLOGY.
Das Rätsel von Leib und Seele. Herne : Heitkamp, c1997.
BF163 .R28 1997

BRAIN RESEARCH. See **BRAIN - RESEARCH.**

BRAIN - RESEARCH - SOCIAL ASPECTS.
Zigler, Edward, 1930- The first three years & beyond. New Haven : Yale University Press, c2002.
HQ767.9 .Z543 2002

BRAIN - SEX DIFFERENCES.
Darlington, Cynthia L. The female brain. London ; New York : Taylor & Francis, c2002.
QP402 .D366 2002

BRAIN STIMULATION.
Harris, Bill, 1950- Thresholds of the mind. Beaverton : Centerpointe Press, c2002.
BF637.B4 H36 2002

Virtual lesions. Oxford ; New York : Oxford University Press, c2002.
RC350.B72 V57 2002

BRAIN-WASHING. See **BRAINWASHING.**

Brain waves books
Bragdon, Allen D. Use it or lose it!. 2nd ed., updated and expanded. New York : Walker & Co., 2004.
BF724.85.C64 B73 2004

Gamon, David. Building mental muscle. Rev. and updated ed. New York : Walker & Co., 2003.

Brain waves books
BF441 .G35 2003

Brain-wise.
Churchland, Patricia Smith. Cambridge, Mass. : MIT Press, c2002.
RC343 .C486 2002

BRAIN - WOUNDS AND INJURIES. *See* **BRAIN DAMAGE.**

BRAINSTORMING.
Monahan, Tom. The do-it-yourself lobotomy. New York : J. Wiley, c2002.
BF408 .M59 2002

BRAINWASHING. *See also* **WILL.**
Singer, Margaret Thaler. Cults in our midst. Rev. ed. San Francisco : Jossey-Bass, c2003.
BP603 .S56 2003

BRAINWASHING - UNITED STATES.
Constantine, Alex. Virtual government. 1st ed. Venice, CA : Feral House, 1997.
BF633 .C67 1997

Singer, Margaret Thaler. Cults in our midst. Rev. ed. San Francisco : Jossey-Bass, c2003.
BP603 .S56 2003

Bramble, Cate. Architect's guide to feng shui : exploding the myth / by Cate Bramble. Amsterdam ; Boston ; London : Architectural Press, 2003. 206 p. : ill. : 19 cm. Includes bibliographical references (p. [177]-192) and index. ISBN 0-7506-5606-9 DDC 133.3337
1. Feng shui. 2. Architecture - Environmental aspects. I. Title.
BF1779.F4 B73 2003

Brammer, Robert. Diversity in counseling / Robert Brammer. Australia ; Belmont, CA : Thomson : Brooks/Cole, c2004. xii, 404 p. : ill. : 25 cm. Includes bibliographical references (p. 336-377) and indexes. ISBN 0-87581-449-2 DDC 158/.3
1. Cross-cultural counseling. I. Title.
BF637.C6 B677 2004

BRAND CHOICE.
Wertime, Kent. Building brands & believers. Chichester : Wiley, 2002.

Brand driven.
LePla, F. Joseph, 1955- London : Kogan Page, 2003.

BRAND NAME PRODUCTS - MANAGEMENT.
LePla, F. Joseph, 1955- Brand driven. London : Kogan Page, 2003.

BRAND NAME PRODUCTS - MISCELLANEA.
McNally, David, 1946- Be your own brand. 1st ed. San Francisco, CA : Berrett-Koehler, c2002.
BF697 .M385 2002

BRAND NAMES. *See* **BRAND NAME PRODUCTS.**

BRANDED MERCHANDISE. *See* **BRAND NAME PRODUCTS.**

Brandes, Mordekhai.
Zikhron teruah.
He lakhem ḥamishah sefari.. [Brooklyn, NY : Renaissance Hebraica, 2000?]

Brandon, Ruth. The surreal lives : the surrealists, 1917-1945 / Ruth Brandon. London : Papermac, 2000, c1999. 527 p. : ill. : 22 cm. Includes bibliographical references and index. ISBN 0-333-68156-8 DDC 709.04063
1. Surrealism. 2. Artists - Biography. 3. Arts, Modern - 20th century. I. Title. II. Title: Surrealists, 1917-1945

Brandon, Trent. The book of ghosts / written by Trent Brandon. Mineva, Ohio : Zerotime Pub., c2003. 220 p. : ill. : 23 cm. "Information on the characteristics, meanings, and personalities of many different kind of ghots"--P. 6. Includes bibliographical references (p. 219-220). ISBN 0-9703100-7-2 DDC 133.1
1. Ghosts. 2. Parapsychology. 3. Supernatural. I. Title.
BF1461 .B6949 2003

The ghost hunter's Bible / Trent Brandon. Definitive ed. [Ohio?] : Zerotime Paranormal and Supernatural Research, 2002. 175 p. : ill. : 26 cm. Includes bibliographical references (p. 169-171) and an index. ISBN 0-9703100-5-6 (pbk.) DDC 133.1
1. Ghosts. 2. Parapsychology. 3. Supernatural. I. Title.
BF1461 .B695 2002

Brashears, Deya. Challenging biases-- facing our fears : beyond race and culture / DeyaJ. Brashears, Gary J. Kinley. Dubuque, Iowa : Kendall/Hunt Pub., c1999. xv, 255 p. : ill. : 24 cm. Includes bibliographical references (p. 253-255). ISBN 0-7872-5592-0 (pbk.).
1. Prejudices. 2. Stereotype (Psychology) I. Kinley, Gary J. II. Title.
BF575.P9 B735 1999

Bratich, Jack Z., 1969-.
Foucault, cultural studies, and governmentality. Albany : State University of New York Press, c2003.
JC330 .F63 2003

Braud, William. Distant mental influence : its contributions to science, healing, and human interactions / William Braud. Charlottesville, VA : Hampton Roads Pub., c2003. p. : cm. Includes bibliographical references and index. Table of contents URL: http://www.loc.gov/catdir/toc/ecip048/2003019817.html CONTENTS: Transpersonal imagery effects : influencing a distant person's bodily activity using mental imagery -- Calming other persons at a distance -- Mentally protecting human red blood cells at a distance -- Mental interactions with remote biological systems -- Distant mental influence of physiological activity : new experiments and their historical antecedents -- On the use of living target systems in distant mental influence research -- Reactions to an unseen gaze (remote attention) : autonomic staring detection -- Additional studies of bodily detection of remote staring -- Empirical studies of prayer, distant healing, and remote mental influence -- Helping others concentrate using distant mental influence -- Distant mental influence and healing : assessing the evidence -- Health implications of "backward-in-time" direct mental influences. ISBN 1-57174-354-5 (alk. paper) DDC 133.8
1. Parapsychology and science. 2. Parapsychology and medicine. 3. Interpersonal relations - Psychic aspects. 4. Imagery (Psychotherapy) 5. Mental Healing. 6. Mind-Body Relations (Metaphysics) I. Title.
BF1045.S33 B74 2003

Braude, Stephen E., 1945- Immortal remains : the evidence for life after death / Stephen E. Braude. Lanham, Md. ; Oxford : Rowman & Littlefield, c2003. xvi, 328 p. ; 24 cm. Includes bibliographical references (p. 307-321) and index. ISBN 0-7425-1471-4 (hbk. : alk. paper) ISBN 0-7425-1472-2 (pbk. : alk. paper) DDC 133.9/01/3
1. Future life. 2. Spiritualism. I. Title.
BF1311.F8 B73 2003

BRAUDEL, FERNAND.
Aguirre Rojas, Carlos Antonio. Ensayos braudelianos. Rosario, Argentina : Prohistoria ; M. Suárez ; México : Asociación Nacional de Profesores de Historia de México, 2000.
D15.B62 A38 2000

Braudy, Leo. From chivalry to terrorism : war and the changing nature of masculinity / Leo Braudy. New York : Alfred A. Knopf : Distributed by Random House, 2003. xxiv, 613 p., [16] p. of plates : ill. ; 25 cm. Includes bibliographical references (p. 557-590) and index. ISBN 0-679-45035-1 (alk. paper) DDC 305.31
1. Men - Psychology. 2. Masculinity - History. 3. War - History. 4. War - Psychological aspects. 5. Chivalry. 6. Terrorism. I. Title.
HQ1090 .B7 2003

Braun, Edmund. Der Mensch vor seinem eigenen Anspruch : Moral als kritisch-normative Orientierungskraft im Zeitalter der posttraditionalen Gesellschaft / Edmund Braun. Würzburg : Königshausen & Neumann, 2002. 295 p. ; 24 cm. Includes bibliographical references and indexes. ISBN 3-8260-2183-5 (pbk.)
1. Ethics. I. Title.

Braun-Thürmann, Holger. Künstliche Interaktion : wie Technik zur Teilnehmerin sozialer Wirklichkeit wird / Holger Braun-Thürmann. 1. Aufl. Wiesbaden : Westdeutscher Verlag, 2002. 205 p. : ill. ; 21 cm. (Studien zur Sozialwissenschaft) Thesis (Ph. D.)--Technische Universität, Berlin, 2002. Includes bibliographical references. ISBN 3-531-13849-9 (pbk.)
1. Social interaction. 2. Interactive art. I. Title. II. Series: Studien zur Sozialwissenschaft (Westdeutscher Verlag)

Brazier, Caroline. Buddhist psychology : liberate your mind, embrace life / Caroline Brazier. London : Robinson, 2003. 320 p. ; 20 cm. Includes bibliographical references and index. ISBN 1-84119-733-5 DDC 294.3019
1. Buddhism - Psychology. I. Title.

Brazier, Chris. The no-nonsense guide to world history / Chris Brazier. Oxford : New Internationalist Publications ; London : in association with Verso, c2001. 144 p. : ill., maps ; 18 cm. (The no-nonsense guides) Includes bibliographical references (p. 143) and index. ISBN 1-85984-355-7 (pbk.)
1. World history. 2. Civilization - History. I. Title. II. Series: No-nonsense guides (New Internationalist Publications (Firm))
D21 .B78 2001

BRAZIL. *See* **BRAZILIANS.**

BRAZIL - CIVILIZATION.
Cultura e identidade. Rio de Janeiro, RJ, Brasil : DP & A Editores, 2002.

Sampaio, Luiz Sergio Coelho de, 1933- Filosofia da cultura. Rio de Janeiro : Editora Agora da Ilha, 2002.

BRAZIL - CIVILIZATION - 20TH CENTURY.
Psicologia social nos estudos culturais. Petrópolis : Editora Voces, c2003.
HM1033 .P75 2003

BRAZIL - CIVILIZATION - 21ST CENTURY.
Arenas, Fernando, 1963- Utopias of otherness. Minneapolis : University of Minnesota Press, c2003.
DP681 .A74 2003

BRAZIL - ECONOMIC CONDITIONS.
Fonseca, Eduardo Giannetti da, 1957- Nada é tudo. Rio de Janeiro, RJ, Brasil : Editora Campus, c2000.
F2521 .F64 2000

BRAZIL - EMIGRATION AND IMMIGRATION.
Catanio, Percy Antonio Galimbertti. O caminho que o dekassegui sonhou (dekassegui no yumê-ji). São Paulo : EDUC, FAPESP; Londrina : UEL, 2002.

BRAZIL - POLITICS AND GOVERNMENT.
Fonseca, Eduardo Giannetti da, 1957- Nada é tudo. Rio de Janeiro, RJ, Brasil : Editora Campus, c2000.
F2521 .F64 2000

BRAZIL - POPULAR CULTURE - AFRICAN INFLUENCES.
Salles, Alexandre de. Eṣù ou Exu? Rio de Jaeiro : Ilú Aiye, 2001.
1. Black author.

BRAZIL - RACE RELATIONS.
Borges, Edson. Racismo, preconceito e intolerancia. [São Paulo, Brazil] : Atual, c2002.

BRAZIL - RELIGION - AFRICAN INFLUENCES.
Salles, Alexandre de. Eṣù ou Exu? Rio de Jaeiro : Ilú Aiye, 2001.
1. Black author.

Verger, Pierre. Saída de Iaô. Sao Paulo : Fundação Pierre Verger : Axis Mundi Editora, 2002.

BRAZIL - RELIGIOUS LIFE AND CUSTOMS.
Megale, Nilza Botelho. Santos do povo brasileiro. Petrópolis : Editora Vozes, 2002.

Souza, Laura de Mello e. [Diabo e a Terra de Santa Cruz. English] The Devil and the land of the holy cross. 1st University of Texas Press ed. Austin : University of Texas Press : Teresa Lozano Long Institute of Latin American Studies, 2003.
BF1584.B7 S6813 2003

BRAZIL - SOCIAL LIFE AND CUSTOMS - 20TH CENTURY.
Peixoto, Nelson Brissac. Nelson Brissac, Antonio Augusto Arantes. [São Paulo, SP : Fundação Memorial da América Latina, 1997]

BRAZILIAN ALIEN LABOR. *See* **ALIEN LABOR, BRAZILIAN.**

BRAZILIAN FICTION - 20TH CENTURY - CRITICISM AND INTERPRETATION.
Arenas, Fernando, 1963- Utopias of otherness. Minneapolis : University of Minnesota Press, c2003.
DP681 .A74 2003

BRAZILIANS - JAPAN.
Catanio, Percy Antonio Galimbertti. O caminho que o dekassegui sonhou (dekassegui no yumê-ji). São Paulo : EDUC, FAPESP; Londrina : UEL, 2002.

Break through the blocks and win your inner creative battles.
Pressfield, Steven. The war of art. Warner Books ed. New York : Warner Books, c2002, (2003 printing).
BF408 .P69 2003

BREAKING, HABIT. *See* **HABIT BREAKING.**

BREAKING HABITS. *See* **HABIT BREAKING.**

Breaking open the head.
Pinchbeck, Daniel. 1st ed. New York : Broadway Books, 2002.
BF1621 .P56 2002

Breaking out of the box.
Dudgeon, Piers. London : Headline, 2001.
BF109.D39 D83 2001

Breaking the cycle of oppression in people.
Bishop, Anne, 1950- Becoming an ally. 2nd ed. London ; New York : Zed Books ; Halifax, N.S. : Fernwood Pub. ; New York : Distributed in the USA exclusively by Palgrave, 2002.
HM1256 .B57 2002

Breaking the disciplines : reconceptions in knowledge, art, and culture / edited by Martin L. Davies & Marsha Meskimmon. London ; New York : I.B. Tauris, 2003. 248 p. : ill. ; 25 cm. Includes bibliographical references and

index. ISBN 1-86064-917-3 DDC 306.42
1. *Knowledge, Sociology of. I. Davies, Martin L. II. Meskimmon, Marsha.*
BD175 .B74 2003

Breaking the evil blood covenant.
Olorunfemi, Samuel Jimson. Ibadan, Oyo State, Nigeria : Triumphant Faith Publications, 2001.

BREAKING UP (INTERPERSONAL RELATIONS). See **SEPARATION (PSYCHOLOGY).**

Breakthrough techniques to exercise your brain and improve your memory.
Mason, Douglas J. The memory workbook. Oakland, CA : New Harbinger Publications, : c2001. : Distributed in the U.S.A. by Publishers Group West, c2001.
BF724.85.M45 M37 2001

BREAKTHROUGHS, TECHNOLOGICAL. See **TECHNOLOGICAL INNOVATIONS.**

BREAST - CANCER - PSYCHOLOGICAL ASPECTS.
Burch, Wanda Easter, 1947- She who dreams. Novato, Calif. : New World Library, c2003.
BF1099.W65 B87 2003

Breathing spaces : qigong, psychiatry, and healing in China / Nancy N. Chen. New York : Columbia University Press, c2003. xvi, 238 p. : ill. ; 24 cm. Includes bibliographical references (p. [199]-232) and index. CONTENTS: 1. Introduction -- 2. Fever -- 3. Riding the tiger -- 4. Qigong deviation or psychosis -- 5. Chinese psychiatry and the search for order -- 6. Mandate of science -- 7. Transnational qigong -- 8. Suffering and healing. ISBN 0-231-12804-5 (cloth : alk. paper) ISBN 0-231-12805-3 (pbk. : alk. paper) DDC 613.7/1
1. *Qi gong. 2. Qi gong - Political aspects. 3. Qi gong - Social aspects. 4. Exercise therapy. 5. Psychiatry. I. Chen, Nancy N. II. Title: Qigong, psychiatry, and healing in China*
RA781.8 .B73 2003

Breazeal, Cynthia L. Designing sociable robots / Cynthia L. Breazeal. Cambridge, Mass. : MIT Press, c2002. xviii, 263 p. : ill. ; 24 cm. + 1 CD-ROM (4 3/4 in.). (Intelligent robots and autonomous agents) "A Bradford book." ISBN 0-262-02510-8 DDC 006.3
1. *Human-machine systems. 2. Artificial intelligence. 3. Robots - Design and construction. I. Title. II. Series.*
TA167 .B74 2002

Brecher, Erwin. Hocus-pocus : a bridge book with a difference / [Erwin Brecher ; foreword by Zia Mahmood ; edited by Martin Hoffman]. London : Panacea Press, 2001. xii, 202 p. : ill. ; 21 cm. ISBN 0-9539955-0-X DDC 796.41/5
1. *Contract bridge - Problems, exercises, etc. 2. Puzzles. I. Title.*
GV1282.3 .B725 2001

Brecke, Peter.
Long, William J., 1956- War and reconciliation. Cambridge, Mass. : MIT Press, c2003.
JZ5597 .L66 2003

BREEDERS, DOG. See **DOG BREEDERS.**
BREEDERS OF DOGS. See **DOG BREEDERS.**
BREEDING. See **GENETICS.**

Breisach, Ernst. On the future of history : the postmodernist challenge and its aftermath / Ernst Breisach. Chicago : University of Chicago Press, c2003. ix, 243 p. ; 24 cm. Includes bibliographical references and index. ISBN 0-226-07279-7 (cloth : alk. paper) ISBN 0-226-07280-0 (pbk. : alk. paper) DDC 306
1. *Postmodernism - Social aspects. 2. Historiography. I. Title.*
HM449 .B74 2003

Breitschmid, Markus, 1966- Der bauende Geist : Friedrich Nietzsche und die Architektur ; mit einem Textcorpus aus dem philosophischen Werk Friedrich Nietzsches zum Baugedanken / Markus Breitschmid. Luzern : Quart, 2001. 218 p. ; 23 cm. (Bibliotheca ; Bd. 2) Includes bibliographical references and index. ISBN 3-907631-23-4 (pbk.)
1. *Nietzsche, Friedrich Wilhelm, - 1844-1900. 2. Architecture - Philosophy. I. Title. II. Series: Bibliotheca (Lucerne, Switzerland) ; Bd. 2.*
B3318.A4 B745 2001

Bremmer, Jan N.
The metamorphosis of magic from late antiquity to the early modern period. Leuven ; Dudley, MA : Peeters, 2002.
BF1589 .M55 2002

Brenden, Ann E. Persuasive computer presentations : the essential guide for lawyers / Ann E. Brenden and John D. Goodhue. Chicago, Ill. : Law Practice Management Section, American Bar Association, c2001. xv, 225 p. : ill. ; 25 cm. + 1 CD-ROM (4 3/4 in.). Includes index. ISBN 1-57073-952-8
1. *Practice of law - United States - Automation. 2. Trial practice - United States - Automation. 3. Computers - Law and legislation - United States. 4. Persuasion (Psychology) I. Goodhue, John D., 1957- II. American Bar Association. Section of Law Practice Management. III. Title.*
KF320.A9 B74 2001

Brennan, Tad, 1962-.
Simplicius, of Cilicia. [Commentarius in Enchiridion Epicteti. 1-26. English] On Epictetus' "Handbook 1-26". Ithaca, N.Y. : Cornell University Press, 2002.
B561.M523 S5613 2002

Brennan, Teresa, 1952- The transmission of affect / Teresa Brennan. Ithaca : Cornell University Press, 2003. p. cm. Includes bibliographical references and index. Table of contents URL: http://www.loc.gov/catdir/toc/ecip048/2003019730.html ISBN 0-8014-3998-1 (cloth : alk. paper) ISBN 0-8014-8862-1 (pbk. : alk. paper) DDC 152.4
1. *Affect (Psychology) - Social aspects. I. Title.*
BF531 .B74 2003

Brenneman, James E., 1954- Canons in conflict : negotiating texts in true and false prophecy / James E. Brenneman. New York : Oxford University Press, 1997. xvii, 228 p. ; 25 cm. Includes bibliographical references (p. 197-217) and index. ISBN 0-19-510909-0 (cloth : acid-free paper) DDC 220.1/2
1. *Bible - Canon. 2. Bible - Prophecies. 3. Bible - Hermeneutics. 4. Bible - Evidences, authority, etc. 5. Canon (Literature) 6. Prophecy. I. Title.*
BS465 .B74 1997

Brenner, Andreas. Lexikon der Lebenskunst / Andreas Brenner, Jörg Zirfas. Leipzig : Reclam-Verlag, 2002. 375 p. ; 19 cm. (Reclam-Bibliothek ; 20015) Includes bibliographical references. ISBN 3-379-20015-8 (pbk.)
1. *Conduct of life. I. Zirfas, Jörg. II. Title. III. Series.*

Brenot, Philippe. Le sexe et l'amour / Philippe Brenot. Paris : Jacob, c2003. 254 p. ; 22 cm. Includes bibliographical references (p. 249-[251]). ISBN 2-7381-1233-1 DDC 300
1. *Love. 2. Sex. I. Title.*

Breslin, Dawn, 1969- Zest for life : 10 dynamic life-changing solutions for self-empowerment / Dawn Breslin. Carlsbad, Calif. : Hay House, 2004. p. cm. ISBN 1401903312 (pbk.) DDC 158.1
1. *Self-actualization (Psychology) 2. Self-perception. I. Title.*
BF637.S4 B735 2004

BRETON, ANDRÉ, 1896-1966. MANIFESTES DU SURRÉALISME.
Meyer, Michel. Michel Meyer présente Manifestes du surréalisme d'André Breton. Paris : Gallimard, 2002.
NX600.S9 B735 2002

Brett, Jeanne M.
The handbook of negotiation. Stanford, Calif. : Stanford Business Books, c2004.
BF637.N4 H365 2004

Brettschneider, Frank. Spitzenkandidaten und Wahlerfolg : Personalisierung, Kompetenz, Parteien : ein internationaler Vergleich / Frank Brettschneider. 1. Aufl. Wiesbaden : Westdeutscher Verlag, 2002. 256 p. : ill. ; 23 cm. Includes bibliographical references (p. 221-240). ISBN 3-531-13722-0 (pbk.)
1. *Political candidates - Social aspects. 2. Political candidates - Psychology. 3. Political campaigns. 4. Political psychology. I. Title.*

Breuer, Hubertus.
Das Rätsel von Leib und Seele. Herne : Heitkamp, c1997.
BF163 .R28 1997

Breuer, Reinhard A., 1946-.
Das Rätsel von Leib und Seele. Herne : Heitkamp, c1997.
BF163 .R28 1997

Breviario di cinismo ben temperato.
Celli, Pier Luigi. 1. ed. Roma : Fazi, 2002.

Brewer, Marilynn B., 1942-.
Emotion and motivation. Malden, MA : Blackwell Pub., 2004.
BF531 .E4826 2004

Self and social identity. Malden, MA : Blackwell Pub., 2003.
BF697.5.S43 S429 2003

Social cognition. Malden, MA : Blackwell Pub., 2003.
BF316.6 .S65 2003

Brewer, Mary F.
Exclusions in feminist thought. Brighton [England] ; Portland, Or. : Sussex Academic Press, 2002.
HQ1206 .E98 2002

BREWING - MISCELLANEA.
Telesco, Patricia, 1960- A witch's beverages and brews. Franklin Lakes, NJ : New Page Books, c2001.
BF1572.R4 T447 2001

Brezak, Dov. Chinuch in turbulent times : practical strategies for parents and educators / Dov Brezak. 1st ed. Brooklyn, N.Y. : Mesorah Publications, c2002. 420 p. ; 24 cm. (ArtScroll series)
1. *Child rearing - Religious aspects - Judaism. 2. Parent and child. 3. Jewish religious education of children. I. Title. II. Series.*

Brhat śilpaśāstra.
Khadiratna, Dayanidhi. Brhat śilpaśāstra, bā, Grhabandha bijñāna ; Grhabandha gaṇanā o śubhastambhāropaṇa bicāra. Kaṭaka : Dharmagrantha Shtora, [1995?]
TH4809.I4 K48 1995

Brhat śilpaśāstra, bā, Grhabandha bijñāna ; Grhabandha gaṇanā o śubhastambhāropaṇa bicāra.
Khadiratna, Dayanidhi. Kaṭaka : Dharmagrantha Shtora, [1995?]
TH4809.I4 K48 1995

Brhatsaṃhitā.
Varāhamihira, 505-587. 1. saṃskaraṇam. Vārāṇasī : Sampūrṇānanda Saṃskṛta Viśvavidyālaye, 2002-
BF1714.H5+

Bria, Pietro.
L'inconscio antinomico. Milano : F. Angeli, c1999.
BF315 .I56 1999

Brian, Sarah Jane. The quiz book 2 / by Sarah Jane Brian ; illustrated by Debbie Tilley. Middleton, Wis. : Pleasant Co. , c2001. 79 p. : col. ill. ; 21 cm. "American Girl library". SUMMARY: "More secrets revealed!" Ages 8 and up. ISBN 1-58485-285-2
1. *Character tests - Juvenile literature. 2. Questions and answers. I. Tilley, Debbie. II. Title. III. Title: American girl (Middleton, Wis.) IV. Title: Quiz book two*
BF831 .B75 2001

Brickman, Celia. Aboriginal populations in the mind : race and primitivity in psychoanalysis / Celia Brickman. New York : Columbia University Press, c2003. viii, 285 p. ; 24 cm. Includes bibliographical references (p. 255-272) and index. CONTENTS: The figure of the primitive: a brief genealogy -- Psychoanalysis and the colonial imagination: evolutionary thought in Freud's texts -- Race and gender, primitivity and femininity: psychologies of enthrallment -- Historicizing consciousness: time, history, and religion -- Primitivity in the analytic encounter. ISBN 0-231-12582-8 (alk. paper) ISBN 0-231-12583-6 (pbk. : alk. paper) DDC 150.19/5
1. *Freud, Sigmund, - 1856-1939. 2. Psychoanalysis. I. Title.*
BF173 .B79 2003

Bridge (Belgrade, Serbia)
(1955/8.) Gučetić, Nikola Vitov, 1549-1610. [Dialogo della bellezza. Serbo-Croatian & Italian] Dijalog o ljepoti = Dvojezično izd. Zagreb : Društvo hrvatskih književnika, 1995.
BH301.L65 G8318 1995

The bridge between two lifetimes.
Powers, Marilyn. Phoenix, AZ : Sophia Publications, c1999.
BF724.6 .P68 1999

BRIDGE (GAME). See **CONTRACT BRIDGE.**
BRIDGE WHIST. See **CONTRACT BRIDGE.**

Bridgeman, Bruce. Psychology & evolution : the origins of mind / Bruce Bridgeman. Thousand Oaks, Calif. : SAGE Publications, c2003. xvii, 375 p. : ill., maps ; 24 cm. Includes bibliographical references (p. 331-349) and indexes. ISBN 0-7619-2479-5 DDC 155.7
1. *Evolutionary psychology. I. Title. II. Title: Psychology and evolution*
BF698.95 .B75 2003

Bridges, Lillian. Face reading in Chinese medicine / Lillian Bridges. St. Louis, MO : Churchill Livingstone, 2003. p. cm. Includes index. ISBN 0-443-07315-5 (pbk.) DDC 138
1. *Physiognomy. 2. Facial exercises. 3. Facial expression. 4. Face - Care and hygiene. I. Title.*
BF851 .B69 2003

Bridges, Vincent.
Weidner, Jay. The mysteries of the great cross of Hendaye. Rochester, Vt. : Destiny Books, 2003.
BF1999 .W435 2003

Bridges, William, 1933- The way of transition : embracing life's most difficult moments / William Bridges. Cambridge, Mass. : Perseus Pub., c2001. xv, 226 p. ; 21 cm. Includes bibliographical references (p. 223-226). ISBN 0-7382-0529-X ISBN 0-7382-0410-2 (t.p. verso) DDC 155.2/4
1. Adjustment (Psychology) 2. Change (Psychology) 3. Self-actualization (Psychology) 4. Maturation (Psychology) I. Title.
BF335 .B717 2001

Bridging cultural conflicts.
LeBaron, Michelle, 1956- 1st ed. San Francisco, CA : Jossey-Bass, c2003.
BF698.9.C8 L43 2003

Brief an die gottlosen Frauen.
Holl, Adolf, 1930- Wien : Zsolnay, 2002.

A brief history of stress.
Cooper, Cary L. 1st ed. Oxford, U.K. ; Malden, MA : Blackwell Pub., 2004.
BF575.S75 C646 2004

Brill reference library of ancient Judaism
(v. 10) Gruenwald, Ithamar. Rituals and ritual theory in ancient Israel. Leiden ; Boston : Brill, 2003.
BM660 .G78 2003

Brill's Indological library
(v 18) Bühnemann, Gudrun. Mandalas and Yantras in the Hindu traditions. Leiden ; Boston : Brill, 2003.
BL2015.M3 B85 2003

Brill's series in Jewish studies
(v. 32) Sela, Shlomo. Abraham Ibn Ezra and the rise of medieval Hebrew science. Leiden ; Boston, MA : Brill, 2003.
BM538.S3 S45 2003

Brim, Orville Gilbert, 1923-.
How healthy are we? Chicago, Ill. : University of Chicago Press, c2003.
BF724.6 .H69 2003

Brincken, Anna-Dorothee von den. Historische Chronologie des Abendlandes : Kalenderreformen und Jahrtausendrechnungen ; eine Einführung / Anna-Dorothee von den Brincken. Stuttgart : Kohlhammer, 2000. x, 132 p. : ill. ; 23 cm. Includes bibliographical references and index. ISBN 3-17-015156-8
1. Calendar - Europe - History - To 1500. 2. Calendar reform. 3. Civilization, Medieval. I. Title.

Bringing down dreams.
Na'or, Betsal'el. 1st ed. Spring Valley, NY : Orot, c2002.
BF1078 .N28 2002

Bringing peace into the room : how the personal qualities of the mediator impact the process of conflict resolution / Daniel Bowling, David Hoffman, editors. 1st ed. San Francisco : Jossey-Bass, 2003. viii, 310 p. ; 24 cm. Includes bibliographical references (p. 279-281) and index. Table of contents URL: http://www.loc.gov/catdir/toc/ecip044/2003011730.html Publisher description URL: http://www.loc.gov/catdir/desc ription/wiley039/2003011730.html CONTENTS: Introduction : Bringing peace into the room: the personal qualities of the mediator and their impact on the mediation / Daniel Bowling, David A. Hoffman -- What are the personal qualities of the mediator? / Kenneth Cloke -- Unintentional excellence: an exploration of mastery and incompetence / Peter S. Adler -- Managing the natural energy of conflict: mediators, tricksters, and the constructive uses of deception / Robert D. Benjamin -- Trickster, mediator's friend / Michelle LeBaron -- Emotionally intelligent mediation: four key competencies / Marvin E. Johnson, Stewart Levine, Lawrence R. Richard -- Paradoxes of mediation / David A. Hoffman -- Mediation and the culture of healing / Lois Gold -- Creating sacred space: tword a second-generation dispute resolution practice / Sara Cobb -- Personal qualities of the mediator: taking time for reflection and renewal / Jonathan W. Reitman, Esq. -- Style and the family mediator / Donald T. Saposnek -- Tears / David A. Hoffman -- Mindfulness meditation and mediation: where the transcendent meets the familiar / Daniel Bowling ISBN 0-7879-6850-1 (alk. paper) DDC 303.6/9
1. Conflict management. 2. Mediation. I. Bowling, Daniel, 1943- II. Hoffman, David A., 1947-
HM1126 .B75 2003

Brinkerhoff, Shirley. Psychologist / by Shirley Brinkerhoff. Broomall, Pa. : Mason Crest Publishers, c2003. v, 90 p. : ill. (chiefly col.) ; 25 cm. (Careers with character) Includes bibliographical references (p. 86) and index. CONTENTS: Job requirements -- Integrity and trustworthiness -- Respect and compassion -- Justice and fairness -- Responsibility -- Courage -- Self-discipline and diligence -- Citizenship -- Career opportunities. ISBN 1-59084-322-3 DDC 150/.23
1. Psychology - Vocational guidance - Juvenile literature. 2. Psychology - Vocational guidance. 3. Vocational guidance. I. Title. II. Series.
BF76 .B75 2003

Brisard, Frank.
Grounding. Berlin ; Hawthorne, N.Y. : M. de Gruyter, 2002.
P165 .G76 2002

Briscoe, E. J., 1959-.
Linguistic evolution through language acquisition. Cambridge ; New York : Cambridge University Press, 2002.
P118 .L565 2002

British Academy.
Archaeology. Oxford : Published for The British Academy by Oxford University Press, c2002.

History and historians in the twentieth century. Oxford : Published for the British Academy by Oxford University Press, 2002.

British Academy centenary monograph
History and historians in the twentieth century. Oxford : Published for the British Academy by Oxford University Press, 2002.

BRITISH EMPIRE. See **GREAT BRITAIN - COLONIES.**

British idealist studies. Series 3, Green
(1.) Carter, Matt. T.H. Green and the development of ethical socialism. Thorverton : Imprint Academic, 2003.
B1638.E8 C37 2003

British Library.
Clegg, Justin. The medieval Church. London : British Library, 2003.

Frosh, Stephen. Key concepts in psychoanalysis. London : British Library, 2002.
BF173 .F898 2002

BRITISH LITERATURE. See **ENGLISH LITERATURE.**

British moral philosophers
(no. 3) Prichard, H. A. (Harold Arthur), 1871-1947. Moral writings. Oxford : Clarendon Press ; New York : Oxford University Press, 2002.

BRITISH PHILOSOPHY. See **PHILOSOPHY, BRITISH.**

The Britons.
Snyder, Christopher A. (Christopher Allen), 1966- Malden, MA ; Oxford : Blackwell Pub., 2003.
DA140 .S73 2003

BRITONS.
Snyder, Christopher A. (Christopher Allen), 1966- The Britons. Malden, MA ; Oxford : Blackwell Pub., 2003.
DA140 .S73 2003

BRITONS IN LITERATURE.
Wickham-Crowley, Kelley M. Writing the future. Cardiff : University of Wales Press, 2002.

Brittain, Charles.
Simplicius, of Cilicia. [Commentarius in Enchiridion Epicteti. 1-26. English] On Epictetus' "Handbook 1-26". Ithaca, N.Y. : Cornell University Press, 2002.
B561.M523 S5613 2002

BRITTEN, BENJAMIN, 1913-1976. WAR REQUIEM.
Lathan, Mark J., 1961- Emotional progression in sacred choral music. 2001.

Britto García, Luis. Conciencia de América Latina : intelectuales, medios de comunicación y poder / Luis Britto García. 1. ed. Caracas, Venezuela : Editorial Nueva Sociedad, [2002] 208 p. ; 23 cm. Includes bibliographical references. ISBN 980-317-191-7
1. Latin America - Social conditions. 2. Latin America - Intellectual life. 3. Popular culture. I. Title.

Britton, Celia. Race and the unconscious : Freudianism in French Caribbean thought / Celia Britton. Oxford : Legenda, 2002. 115 p. ; 22 cm. (Research monographs in French studies, 1466-8157 ; 12) Published for the Society for French Studies by the European Humanities Research Centre of the University of Oxford. Includes bibliographical references (p. [107]-111) and index. Text in English with passages in French. ISBN 1-900755-68-8
1. Freud, Sigmund, - 1856-1939. 2. Psychoanalysis. 3. Race awareness - Caribbean, French-speaking. I. Society for French Studies (Great Britain) II. University of Oxford. European Humanities Research Centre. III. Title. IV. Series.

Broad, Jacqueline. Women philosophers of the seventeenth century / Jacqueline Broad. Cambridge, UK ; New York : Cambridge University Press, 2002. x, 191 p. ; 24 cm. Includes bibliographical references (p. 168-183) and index. Table of contents URL: http://www.loc.gov/catdir/toc/cam023/2002067376.html Publisher description URL: http://www.loc.gov/catdir/description/cam022/2002067376.html ISBN 0-521-81295-X DDC 190/.82/09032
1. Women philosophers. 2. Philosophy, Modern - 17th century. I. Title.
B105.W6 B76 2002

BROADCAST JOURNALISTS. See **TELEVISION JOURNALISTS.**

Brocas, Isabelle.
The psychology of economic decisions. Oxford [England] ; New York : Oxford University Press, 2003-
HB74.P8 P725 2003

Broch, Henri.
Charpak, Georges. [Devenez sorciers, devenez savants English] Debunked!. Baltimore : Johns Hopkins University Press, 2004.
BF1409.5 .C4313 2004

Brock, Bazon, 1936- Der Barbar als Kulturheld : Ästhetik des Unterlassens : Kritik der Wahrheit : wie man wird, der man nicht ist / Bazon Brock ; herausgeben in Zusammenarbeit mit dem Autor von Anna Zika. Köln : DuMont, 2002. 953 p. : ill. ; 24 cm. "III. Gesammelte Schriften, 1991-2002." ISBN 3-8321-7149-5
1. Aesthetics. 2. Arts. I. Zika, Anna. II. Title.

Der Brockhaus Psychologie : Fühlen, Denken und Verhalten verstehen / herausgegeben von der Lexikonredaktion des Verlags F.A. Brockhaus ; [Autoren, Thomas Bliesener ... et al.]. Mannheim : Brockhaus, c2001. 703 p. : ill. (partly col.) ; 25 cm. Includes bibliographical references and index. ISBN 3-7653-0591-X (hd.bd.)
1. Psychology - Encyclopedias. I. Bliesener, Thomas. II. Title: Psychologie : Fühlen, Denken und Verhalten verstehen

Brodeur, Claude, 1924- Le père : cet étranger / Claude Brodeur. Paris : L'Harmattan, 2001. 264 p. ; 22 cm. (Collection Psychanalyse et civilisations)
1. Fathers. 2. Father and child. 3. Fathers in literature. I. Title. II. Series: Psychanalyse et civilisations. Série Trouvailles et retrouvailles.
HQ756 .B76 2001

Broich, Josef, 1948- Körper- und Bewegungsspiele : über einhundertdreissig Gruppenspiele / Josef Broich. 1. Aufl. 1999. Köln : Maternus, 1999. 159 p. ; 21 cm. Includes index. ISBN 3-88735-017-0
1. Movement education. 2. Role playing. 3. Movement therapy. 4. Games. I. Title.

Brokaw, Tom. A long way from home : growing up in the American heartland / Tom Brokaw. 1st trade ed. New York : Random House, c2002. xii, 233 p. : ill. ; 25 cm. "A leather-bound, signed first edition of this work has been published by The Easton Press"--T.p. verso. ISBN 0-375-50763-9 (acid-free paper) DDC 070/.92
1. Brokaw, Tom. 2. Television news anchors - United States - Biography. 3. Television journalists - United States - Biography. 4. National characteristics, American. 5. United States - Social life and customs - 20th century. I. Title.
PN4874.B717 A3 2002b

BROKAW, TOM.
Brokaw, Tom. A long way from home. 1st trade ed. New York : Random House, c2002.
PN4874.B717 A3 2002b

Broken hegemonies.
Schürmann, Reiner, 1941- [Des hégémonies brisées. English] Bloomington : Indiana University Press, c2003.
BD162 .S48 2003

Bromwich, David, 1951-.
Mill, John Stuart, 1806-1873. On liberty. New Haven : Yale University Press, c2003.
JC585 .M76 2003

Brondwin, C. C., 1945- Clan of the Goddess : Celtic wisdom and ritual for women / by C.C. Brondwin. Franklin Lakes, NJ : New Page Books, c2002. 253 p. : ill. ; 21 cm. Includes bibliographical references (p. 243-244) and index. ISBN 1-56414-604-9 (pbk.) DDC 299/.16
1. Magic. 2. Goddesses - Miscellanea. 3. Women - Miscellanea. 4. Magic, Celtic. 5. Goddess religion. 6. Women - Religious life. I. Title.
BF1623.G63 B76 2002

Bronfen, Elisabeth. Die Diva : eine Geschichte der Bewunderung / Elisabeth Bronfen, Barbara Straumann. München : Schirmer/Mosel, c2002. 223 p. : ill. (some col.) ; 34 cm. ISBN 3-88814-308-X (hd.bd.)
1. Fame - Social aspects. 2. Celebrities. 3. Fame - History. I. Straumann, Barbara. II. Title.
BJ1470.5 .B76 2002

Bronowski, Jacob, 1908-1974. The identity of man / Jacob Bronowski. Amherst, N.Y. : Prometheus Books, 2002. xi, 107 p. ; 22 cm. (Great minds series) Originally published: Garden City, N.Y. : Natural History Press, 1965. ISBN 1-59102-025-5 (alk. paper) DDC 128
1. *Philosophical anthropology.* 2. *Science - Philosophy.* 3. *Self (Philosophy) I. Title. II. Series.*
BD450 .B653 2002

Bronson, Po, 1964- What should I do with my life? / Po Bronson. Waterville, Me. : Thorndike Press, 2003. p. cm. Originally published: New York : Random House, 2002. ISBN 0-7862-5809-8 (lg. print : hc : alk. paper) DDC 170/.44
1. *Self-actualization (Psychology) I. Title.*
BF637.S4 B79 2003

BRONX (NEW YORK, N.Y.) - BIOGRAPHY.
Nuland, Sherwin B. Lost in America. 1st ed. New York : Knopf : Distributed by Random House, 2003.
F128.9.J5 N85 2003

Brood bitch.
Wells, Celia Townsend, 1932- West Lafayette, Ind. : Purdue University Press, c2003.
SF422.82.W44 A3 2003

Brooker, John L., 1923- If heaven is so wonderful--why come here? : how to discover our "whole being" / John L. Brooker. Nevada City, CA : Blue Dolphin, 2004. p. cm. Includes bibliographical references. ISBN 1-57733-143-5 (pbk. : alk. paper) DDC 133.9
1. *Spiritualism. I. Title.*
BF1261.2 .B76 2004

Brookhaven National Laboratory. Energy Sciences and Technology Dept.
Human factors engineering program review model [microform]. Rev. 1. Washington, DC : Division of System Analysis and Regulatory Effectiveness, Office of Nuclear Regulatory Research, U.S. Nuclear Regulatory Commission : Supt. of Docs., U.S. G.P.O. [distributor], 2002.

Brooks-Gunn, Jeanne.
Early child development in the 21st century. New York : Teachers College Press, c2003.
LB1115 .E27 2003

Brooks, Robert B. The power of resilience : achieving balance, confidence, and personal strength in your life / Robert Brooks and Sam Goldstein. Chicago : Contemporary Books, c2004. xii, 320 p. ; 24 cm. Includes bibliographical references (p.303-308) and index. Publisher description http://www.loc.gov/catdir/description/mh031/2003051561.html ISBN 0-07-139104-5 (alk. paper) DDC 155.2/4
1. *Resilience (Personality trait)* 2. *Resilience (Personality trait) - Problems, exercises, etc. I. Goldstein, Sam, 1952- II. Title.*
BF698.35.R47 B76 2004

Broom, Michael F. The infinite organization : celebrating the positive use of power in organizations / Michael F. Broom. 1st ed. Palo Alto, Calif. : Davies-Black, c2002. xiii, 161 p. ; 24 cm. Includes bibliographical references (p. 151-153) and index. ISBN 0-89106-168-1 DDC 658.4/09
1. *Organizational behavior.* 2. *Power (Social sciences) I. Title.*
HD58.7 .B755 2002

Broqueville, Paulette Renée. Unraveling your past to get into the present : a practical guide to personal transformation through the study of soul psychology / Paulette Renée Broqueville. Rev. ed. Costa Mesa, Calif. : Broqueville Pub., c2002- v. <1 > ; 24 cm. ISBN 0-9669024-8-3 (v. 1) DDC 158.1
1. *Subconsciousness.* 2. *Self-realization. I. Title.*
BF315 .B76 2002

Brosman, Catharine Savage, 1934- Finding higher ground : a life of travels : essays / by Catharine Savage Brosman. Reno : University of Nevada Press, c2003. 204 p. ; 24 cm. (Environmental arts and humanities series) ISBN 0-87417-538-0 (hc : alk. paper) DDC 917.904/33
1. *Brosman, Catharine Savage, - 1934- - Childhood and youth.* 2. *Brosman, Catharine Savage, - 1934- - Travel.* 3. *Brosman, Catharine Savage, - 1934- - Homes and haunts.* 4. *Southwest, New - Description and travel.* 5. *Texas, West - Description and travel.* 6. *New Orleans (La.) - Description and travel.* 7. *Europe - Description and travel.* 8. *Identity (Psychology)* 9. *Place (Philosophy)* 10. *Regionalism. I. Title. II. Series.*
F787 .B76 2003

BROSMAN, CATHARINE SAVAGE, 1934- - CHILDHOOD AND YOUTH.
Brosman, Catharine Savage, 1934- Finding higher ground. Reno : University of Nevada Press, c2003.
F787 .B76 2003

BROSMAN, CATHARINE SAVAGE, 1934- - HOMES AND HAUNTS.
Brosman, Catharine Savage, 1934- Finding higher ground. Reno : University of Nevada Press, c2003.
F787 .B76 2003

BROSMAN, CATHARINE SAVAGE, 1934- - TRAVEL.
Brosman, Catharine Savage, 1934- Finding higher ground. Reno : University of Nevada Press, c2003.
F787 .B76 2003

Brossman, Sandra C. The power of oneness : live the life you choose / Sandra Brossman. Boston, MA : Red Wheel, 2003. xiv, 205 p. : ill. ; 22 cm. Table of contents URL: http://www.loc.gov/catdir/toc/ecip042/2003008614.html ISBN 1-59003-040-0 DDC 291.4/4
1. *Self-actualization (Psychology)* 2. *Spiritual life.* 3. *Mind and body. I. Title.*
BF637.S4 B8 2003

Broth, Matthias, 1965- Agents secrets : le public dans la construction interactive de la représentation théâtrale / Matthias Broth. Uppsala, Sweden : Uppsala Universitet, c2002. 176 p. : ill. ; 25 cm. (Acta Universitatis Upsaliensis. Studia Romanica Upsaliensia, 0562-3022 ; 65) Originally presented as the author's thesis (doctoral--Université d'Uppsala, 2001). Includes bibliographical references (p. 169-175). Summary in English. ISBN 91-554-5401-1
1. *Social interaction.* 2. *Sociolinguistics.* 3. *Conversation. I. Title. II. Series.*

BROTHERHOOD. See **BROTHERLINESS**.

Brotherhood of the White Temple.
The emerald tablets of Thoth-the-Atlantean. Sedalia, Colo. : Brotherhood of the White Temple, c2002.
BF1999 .E44 2002

BROTHERLINESS - RELIGIOUS ASPECTS - JUDAISM.
Mermelshtain, Avraham Yitshak Dayid. Kuntres Dover mesharim. Hotsa'ah 2. [Brooklyn] : A.Y.D. Mermelshtain, 762 [2001]

Mosheh ben Hayim, Koznitser, d. 1874. Sefer Ahavat Yiśra'el. Yotse le-or me-ḥadash. Yerushalayim : Mekhon Sod yesharim, 760 [2000]

Mosheh ben Hayim, Koznitser, d. 1874. Sefer 'Ahavat Yiśra'el. Bruklin : [Yehoshu'a Pinḥas Bukhinger], 762 [2001]

BROTHERS AND SISTERS. See also **BROTHERS; SISTERS; TWINS**.
Burton, Sarah, 1963- A double life. London : Viking : New York : Penguin Putnam, 2003.

Mitchell, Juliet, 1940- Siblings. Cambridge, UK : Polity Press, c2003.
BF723.S43 M58 2003

Rufo, Marcel. Frères et soeurs une maladie d'amour. Paris : Fayard, 2002.

Sanders, Robert, 1946- Sibling relationships. New York : Palgrave Macmillan, 2004.
BF723.S43 S159 2004

BROTHERS AND SISTERS - DEATH.
Johnson, Marvin. Where's Jess? Rev. Omaha, NE : Centering Corp. Resource, 2003.
BF723.G75 J645 2003

BROTHERS AND SISTERS - DEATH - PSYCHOLOGICAL ASPECTS.
DeVita, Elizabeth. The empty room. New York : Scribner 2004.
BF575.G7 D48 2004

BROTHERS AND SISTERS - DEATH - PSYCHOLOGICAL ASPECTS - JUVENILE LITERATURE.
Johnson, Marvin. Where's Jess? Rev. Omaha, NE : Centering Corp. Resource, 2003.
BF723.G75 J645 2003

Simon, Jack. This book is for all kids, but especially my sister Libby, Libby died... Kansas City, Mo. : Andrews McMeel Pub., c2002.
BF723.D3 S59 2002

The brothers and sisters learn to write.
Dyson, Anne Haas. New York : Teachers College Press, c2003.
LB1139.L3 D97 2003

BROTHERS - DEATH - PSYCHOLOGICAL ASPECTS.
Smith, Alison, 1968- Name all the animals. New York : Scribner, 2004.
BF575.G7 S58 2004

Brouder, Christian.
Percheron, René. Matisse. Paris : Citadelles & Mazenod, c2002.
N6853.M33 P47 2002

Broussard, Cheryl D. What's money got to do with it? : the ultimate guide on how to make love and money work in your relationship / Cheryl D. Broussard & Michael A. Burns. Oakland, CA : MetaMedia Pub., [c2002] xxiv, 395 p. : ill. ; 24 cm. Includes bibliographical references (p. 381-384) and index. ISBN 0-9720094-1-8
1. *Married people - Finance, Personal.* 2. *African Americans - Finance, Personal.* 3. *Finance, Personal.* 4. *Interpersonal communication.* 5. *Black author. I. Burns, Michael A. II. Title.*

Browitt, Jeff, 1950-.
Milner, Andrew, 1950- Contemporary cultural theory. 3rd ed. Crows Nest, N.S.W. : Allen & Unwin, 2002.

Brown, Alan S. The déjà vu experience / by Alan S. Brown. New York : Psychology Press, 2004. p. cm. (Essays in cognitive psychology) Includes bibliographical references and index. ISBN 1-84169-075-9 (hard : alk. paper) DDC 153.7
1. *Déjà vu. I. Title. II. Series.*
BF378.D45 B76 2004

Brown, Charles H.
Hays, Kate F. You're on!. 1st ed. Washington, DC : American Psychological Association, c2003.
BF637.C6 H366 2003

Brown, David, 1968- Mesopotamian planetary astronomy-astrology / David Brown. Groningen : Styx, 2000. xii, 322 p. : ill. ; 25 cm. (Cuneiform monographs, 0929-0052 ; 18) Includes bibliographical references (p. 287-303) and indexes. ISBN 90-5693-036-2 DDC 133.5/9235
1. *Astrology, Assyro-Babylonian.* 2. *Planets - Observations - History.* 3. *Astronomy, Assyro-Babylonian. I. Title. II. Series.*
BF1714.A86 B76 2000

Brown, Douglas J.
Lord, Robert G. (Robert George), 1946- Leadership processes and follower self-identity. Mahwah, N.J. ; London : Lawrence Erlbaum, 2004.
HM1261 .L67 2004

Brown, Duane. Career choice and development / Duane Brown and associates. 4th ed. San Francisco, CA : Jossey-Bass, c2002. xxii, 534 p. : ill. ; 25 cm. (The Jossey-Bass business & management series) Rev. ed. of: Career choice and development / Duane Brown, Linda Brooks, and associates. 3rd ed. c1996. Includes bibliographical references and indexes. Table of contents URL: http://www.loc.gov/catdir/toc/wiley023/2002005599.html CONTENTS: Part 1: Introduction and cases -- Introduction to theories of career development and choice: origins, evolution, and current efforts / Duane Brown -- Case studies / Duane Brown -- Part 2: Sociological perspective -- Career choice and development from a sociological perspective / Monica Kirkpatrick Johnson, Jeylan T. Mortimer -- Part 3: Developmental and postmodern theories -- Gottfredson's theory of circumscription, compromise, and self-creation / Linda S. Gottfredson -- Career construction: a developmental theory of vocational behavior / Mark L. Savickas -- A contextualist explanation of career / Richard A. Young, Ladislav Valach, Audrey Collin -- Part 4: Career development theories anchored in learning theory -- Social cognitive career theory / Robert W. Lent, Steven D. Brown, Gail Hackett -- A cognitive information processing approach to career problem solving and decision making / Gary W. Peterson, James P. Sampson Jr., Janet G. Lenz, Robert C. Reardon -- Part 5: Trait-factor theories and summation -- Holland's theory of personalities in work environments / Arnold R. Spokane, Erik J. Luchetta, Matthew H. Richwine -- Person-environment-correspondence theory / Rene V. Dawis -- The role of work values and cultural values in occupational choice, satisfaction, and success: a theoretical statement / Duane Brown. ISBN 0-7879-5741-0 (alk. paper) DDC 331.7/02
1. *Career development.* 2. *Vocational guidance. I. Title. II. Series.*
HF5381 .C265143 2002

Brown, Gillian R.
Laland, Kevin N. Sense and nonsense. Oxford ; New York : Oxford University Press, 2002.
BF701 .L34 2002

Brown, H. Jackson, 1940-.
Life's little treasure book.
Brown, H. Jackson, 1940- On friendship. Nashville, Tenn. : Rutledge Hill Press, c1996.
BF575.F66 B76 1996

Brown, H. Jackson, 1940- On things that really matter. Nashville, Tenn. : Rutledge Hill Press, c1999.
BF637.C5 B777 1999

On friendship / H. Jackson Brown, Jr. Nashville, Tenn. : Rutledge Hill Press, c1996. 1 v. (unpaged) ; 16 cm. (Life's treasure book) Spine title: Life's treasure book on

friendship. ISBN 1-55853-802-X
1. Friendship - Miscellanea. I. Title. II. Title: Life's treasure book on friendship III. Series: Brown, H. Jackson, 1940-. Life's little treasure book.
BF575.F66 B76 1996

On things that really matter / H. Jackson Brown, Jr. Nashville, Tenn. : Rutledge Hill Press, c1999. 1 v. (unpaged) ; 16 cm. (Life's treasure book) Spine title: Life's treasure book on things that really matter. ISBN 1-55853-803-8 DDC 170/.44
1. Conduct of life - Miscellanea. I. Title. II. Title: Life's treasure book on things that really matter III. Series: Brown, H. Jackson, 1940-. Life's little treasure book.
BF637.C5 B777 1999

Brown, Michael F. (Michael Fobes), 1950- Who owns native culture? / Michael F. Brown. Cambridge, Mass. : Harvard University Press, 2003. xii, 315 p. : ill. ; 22 cm. Includes bibliographical references (p. [255]-301) and index. ISBN 0-674-01171-6 (alk. paper) DDC 346.04/8
1. Indigenous peoples - Legal status, laws, etc. 2. Intellectual property. 3. Cultural property - Protection. I. Title.
K1401 .B79 2003

Brown, Nina W. Loving the self-absorbed : how to create a more satisfying relationship with a narcissistic partner / Nina W. Brown. Oakland, Calif. : New Harbinger, c2003. vi, 182 p. ; 23 cm. Includes bibliographical references (p. [183]). ISBN 1-57224-354-6 (pbk.) DDC 158.2
1. Narcissism. 2. Man-woman relationships. I. Title.
BF575.N35 B76 2003

Brown, Peter Robert Lamont. The rise of Western Christendom : triumph and diversity, A.D. 200-1000 / Peter Brown. 2nd ed. Malden, MA ; Oxford : Blackwell Publishing, 2003. viii, 625 p. : maps ; 24 cm. (The making of Europe) Includes bibliographical references (p. [554]-598) and index. ISBN 0-631-22137-9 (hbk. : alk. paper) ISBN 0-631-22138-7 (pbk. : alk. paper) DDC 274
1. Church history - Primitive and early church, ca. 30-600. 2. Church history - Middle Ages, 600-1500. 3. Civilization, Medieval. I. Title. II. Series.
BR162.3 .B76 2003

Brown, Robert, medium. We are eternal : what the spirits tell me about life after death / Robert Brown. New York : Warner Books, c2003. xviii, 211 p. ; 22 cm. ISBN 0-446-52845-5 DDC 133.9/1
1. Brown, Robert, - medium. 2. Mediums - Biography. 3. Spiritualism. I. Title.
BF1283.B717 A3 2003

BROWN, ROBERT, MEDIUM.
Brown, Robert, medium. We are eternal. New York : Warner Books, c2003.
BF1283.B717 A3 2003

Browne, Sylvia. Life on the other side : a psychic's tour of the afterlife / Sylvia Browne with Lindsay Harrison. New York : Dutton, c2000. xi, 249 p. : ill. ; 24 cm. ISBN 0-525-94539-3 (alk. paper) DDC 133.9
1. Future life. 2. Spiritualism. I. Harrison, Lindsay. II. Title.
BF1311.F8 B77 2000b

Secrets & mysteries of the world / Sylvia Browne. Carlsbad, Calif. : Hay House, c2005. p. cm. ISBN 1401900852 ISBN 1401904580 DDC 133.9/1
1. Occultism. 2. Parapsychology. I. Title. II. Title: Secrets and mysteries of the world
BF1411 .B78 2005

Visits from the afterlife : the truth about hauntings, spirits, and reunions with lost loved ones / by Sylvia Browne with Lindsay Harrison. New York : Dutton, c2003. p. cm. Table of contents URL: http://www.loc.gov/catdir/toc/ecip045/2003013455.html ISBN 0-525-94756-6 DDC 133.1
1. Ghosts. I. Harrison, Lindsay. II. Title.
BF1461 .B77 2003

Browning, Deborah L.
Adolescent psychology. Madison, Conn. : International Universities Press, 2003.
BF724 .A274 2003

Bruce, Anne, 1952- Discover true north : a 4-week approach to ignite your passion and activate your potential / Anne Bruce. New York : McGraw-Hill, c2004. xxvi, 198 p. : ill. ; 24 cm. Includes bibliographical references (p. 189-192) and index. Table of contents URL: http://www.loc.gov/catdir/toc/ecip044/2003011272.html Publisher description URL: http://www.loc.gov/catdir/description/mh031/2003011272.html CONTENTS: Week 1: Do less of what lessens you. Do more of what magnifies your soul, your gifts, and higher purpose -- If you're going to compromise, compromise up! -- Cultivate people who feed your soul--create a life board of directors -- Self-esteem is intelligence in action -- Week 2: No, you can't be anything you want, but you can be anything you're capable of becoming -- Recognize and activate your inner voice of wisdom and courage -- Cultivating interests before callings -- Pace yourself--life isn't an all-or-nothing proposition -- Week 3: Connecting with your spirit without disconnecting from your brain -- Live your fullest multisensory life -- The four declarations of your authentic power -- Week 4: Romancing your potential--becoming an upgradeable person -- Cornerstones of human potential : focus, service, and gratitude -- Simplicity and the Einstein approach to bringing forth your own genius. ISBN 0-07-140300-0 (pbk. : alk. paper) DDC 158.1
1. Self-actualization (Psychology) 2. Success - Psychological aspects. I. Title.
BF637.S4 B82 2004

Bruce, Barbara. Mental aerobics-- : 75 ways to keep your brain fit / Barbara Bruce. Nashville : Abingdon Press, c2003. p. cm. Includes bibliographical references and index. ISBN 0-687-07322-7 (alk. paper) DDC 153.4/2
1. Mental discipline. 2. Mental efficiency. I. Title.
BF632 .B78 2003

Bruce, Jean K.
Bruce, William C. The dimensional thinker. 1st ed. Tyler, TX : Home Tree Media, 2000.
BF441 .B799 2000

Bruce, Lisa.
Math all around me.
Bruce, Lisa. Math all around me. Chicago, Ill. : Raintree, 2003.
BF294 .B78 2003

Bruce, Lisa. Sizes at school. Chicago, IL : Raintree, c2003.
BF299.S5 B78 2003

Math all around me : patterns in the park / Lisa Bruce. Chicago, Ill. : Raintree, 2003. p. cm. (Math all around me) SUMMARY: Simple text shows patterns made of different shapes that can be found in a park. Includes bibliographical references and index. CONTENTS: Patterns -- Circles -- Curves -- Squares -- Rectangles -- Stripes -- Colors -- Colors and shapes -- Making patterns -- Guess the pattern. ISBN 1410906345 (hardcover) ISBN 1410906604 (pbk.) DDC 152.14/23
1. Pattern perception - Juvenile literature. 2. Pattern perception. 3. Shape. 4. Parks. I. Title. II. Series: Bruce, Lisa. Math all around me.
BF294 .B78 2003

Sizes at school / Lisa Bruce. Chicago, IL : Raintree, c2003. p. cm. (Math all around me) SUMMARY: Simple text shows how different objects in a classroom compare in size. Includes bibliographical references and index. CONTENTS: Size -- Big and small -- How big is your hand? -- Tall and short -- Tallest and shortest -- Long and short -- Longest and shortest -- The same as -- What size? -- All sorts of sizes. ISBN 1410906337 (library bdg. hardcover) ISBN 1410906590 (pbk.) DDC 152.14/2
1. Size perception - Juvenile literature. 2. Size judgment - Juvenile literature. 3. Size. 4. Size perception. 5. Schools. I. Title. II. Series: Bruce, Lisa. Math all around me.
BF299.S5 B78 2003

Bruce, William C. The dimensional thinker : from building a constructivist edge to finding bloom on Mars / William C. Bruce, Jean K. Bruce. 1st ed. Tyler, TX : Home Tree Media, 2000. 308 p. : ill., (some col.) ; 28 cm. Includes bibliographical references (p. 288-299) and index. DDC 153.4/2
1. Thought and thinking. I. Bruce, Jean K. II. Title.
BF441 .B799 2000

Brüder, Bestien, Automaten : das Tier im abendländischen Denken / Manuela Linnemann (Hg.). 1. Aufl. Erlangen : H. Fischer, c2000. 380 p. ; 21 cm. (Tierrechte, Menschenpflichten ; Bd. 3) Anthology. Includes bibliographical references (p.[361]-380). ISBN 3-89131-401-9 (pbk.)
1. Animals (Philosophy) 2. Animals and civilization. 3. Human-animal relationships. 4. Animals in literature. I. Linnemann, Manuela. II. Series.

Brune, François.
Winter, Jean, 1909-1939 (Spirit) Dites-leur que la mort n'existe pas. Chambéry : Exergue, c1997, [1998]
BF1290 .W56 1997

Brune, Jens Peter.
Philosophieren aus dem Diskurs. Würzburg : Königshausen & Neumann, c2002.

Brunero, María Alicia. Etica desde el otro: como el salmón: ensayo de moral profesional para trabajadores sociales, docentes, psicólogos y.../ María Alicia Brunero. Buenos Aires : Grupo Editorial Lumen, c2002. 237 p.; 22 cm.
1. Ethics. I. Title.

BRUNI, LEONARDO, 1369-1444.
Hankins, James. Humanism and platonism in the Italian Renaissance. Roma : Edizioni di storia e letteratura, 2003-

Brunke, Dawn Baumann. Animal voices : telepathic communication in the web of life / Dawn Baumann Brunke. Rochester, Vt. : Bear & Co., c2002. ix, 278 : ill. ; 23 cm. Includes bibliographical references (p. 276-278). ISBN 1-87918-191-6 (pbk.) DDC 133.8/9
1. Human-animal communication. 2. Telepathy. I. Title.
QL776 .B78 2002

Bruno, Frank Joe, 1930- Psychology : a self-teaching guide / Frank J. Bruno. New York : John Wiley & Sons, c2002. x, 276 p. : ill. ; 24 cm. (Self-teaching guides) Includes index. Publisher description URL: http://www.loc.gov/catdir/desc ription/wiley036/2002728446.html Table of contents URL: http://www.loc.gov/catdir/toc/wiley031/2002728446.html ISBN 0-471-44395-6 DDC 150
1. Psychology - Study and teaching. I. Title. II. Series: Self-teaching guide.
BF77 .B78 2002

Bruno, Giordano, 1548-1600. Opere magiche / Giordano Bruno ; edizione diretta da Michele Ciliberto ; a cura di Simonetta Bassi, Elisabetta Scapparone, Nicoletta Tirinnanzi. Milano : Adelphi, 2000. cxlii, 1590 p. ; 23 cm. (Classici ; 67) Text in Latin with facing Italian translation. Includes bibliographical references. CONTENTS: Introduzione / di Michele Ciliberto -- Nota ai testi -- De magia mathematica -- De magia naturali -- Theses de magia -- De vinculis in genere -- De rerum principiis et elementis et causis -- Medicina Lulliana partim ex physicis principiis educta -- Lampas triginta statuarum. ISBN 88-459-1509-3 DDC 133.4/3
1. Magic - Early works to 1800. I. Ciliberto, Michele. II. Title.
BF1600 .B78 2000

BRUNO, GIORDANO, 1548-1600.
Early studies of Giordano Bruno. Bristol : Thoemmes, 2000.

Sacerdoti, Gilberto, 1952- Sacrificio e sovranità. Torino : Einaudi, 2002.

Vecchiotti, Icilio. Introduzione alla filosofia di Giordano Bruno. Urbino : QuattroVenti, c2000.
B783.Z7 V43 2000

Brunschwig, Jacques.
Descartes, René, 1596-1650. [Regulae ad directionem ingenii. French] Règles pour la direction de l'esprit. Paris : Librairie générale française, c2002.

Brunsson, Nils, 1946- The organization of hypocrisy : talk, decisions, and actions in organizations / Nils Brunsson ; translated by Nancy Adler. 2nd ed. Oslo : Abstrakt ; Malmö, Sweden : Liber ; Herndon, VA : [Distributor] Copenhagen Business School Press, c2002. xvii, 242 p. ; 23 cm. Includes bibliographical references and index. ISBN 87-630-0106-3 (Marston : pbk.) ISBN 82-7935-023-3 (Abstrakt : pbk.)
1. Organizational behavior. 2. Organizational change. 3. Corporate culture. 4. Industrial management. I. Title.

Bruschi, Michel Euclides.
Psicologia social nos estudos culturais. Petrópolis : Editora Voces, c2003.
HM1033 .P75 2003

Brush, Lisa Diane. Gender and governance / Lisa D. Brush. Walnut Creek, CA ; Oxford : AltaMira Press, c2003. xiii, 149 p. : ill. ; 24 cm. (The gender lens series) Includes bibliographical references (p. 131-142) and index. ISBN 0-7591-0141-8 (hbk. : alk. paper) ISBN 0-7591-0142-6 (pbk. : alk. paper) DDC 303.3
1. Power (Social sciences) 2. State, The. 3. Feminism. 4. Civil society - United States. 5. Civil society - Europe, Western. 6. United States - Social policy. 7. Europe, Western - Social policy. I. Title. II. Series.
JC330 .B75 2003

Brushlinskiĭ, A. V. (Andreĭ Vladimirovich).
Sovremennai͡a psikhologii͡a. Moskva : In-t psikhologii RAN, 2002.
BF20 .S64 2002

Tvorcheskoe nasledie A.V. Brushlinskogo i O.K. Tikhomirova i sovremennai͡a psikhologii͡a myshlenii͡a (k 70-letii͡u so dni͡a rozhdenii͡a). Moskva : In-t psikhologii RAN, 2003.
BF109.B86 T86 2003

BRUSHLINSKIĬ, A. V. (ANDREĬ VLADIMIROVICH) - CONGRESSES.
Tvorcheskoe nasledie A.V. Brushlinskogo i O.K. Tikhomirova i sovremennai͡a psikhologii͡a myshlenii͡a (k 70-letii͡u so dni͡a rozhdenii͡a). Moskva : In-t psikhologii RAN, 2003.
BF109.B86 T86 2003

Bruun, Ole. Fengshui in China : geomantic divination between state orthodoxy and popular religion / Ole Bruun ; foreword by Stephan Feuchtwang. Honolulu :

University of Hawai'i Press, c2003. xiv, 305 p. : ill. ; 23 cm. Includes bibliographical references (p. 289-300) and index. CONTENTS: Fengshui : a challenge to anthropology -- Fengshui practices and policies, 1850 to 1949 -- Fengshui practices and policies after 1949 -- The fengshui revival : fieldwork in Sichuan -- Another school of fengshui : fieldwork in Jiangsu -- Fengshui applications and possible interpretations -- The construction of a discourse : fengshui as environmental ethics -- Conclusion -- Appendix: On the origin of fengshui and the history of its literature. ISBN 0-8248-2672-8 (alk. paper) DDC 133.3/337/0951
1. Feng shui - China - History. I. Title.
BF1779.F4 B78 2003

Bruun, Ole, 1953- Fengshui in China : geomantic divination between state orthodoxy and popular religion / Ole Bruun ; foreword by Stephan Feuchtwang. Copenhagen, Denmark : NIAS Press, c2003. xiv, 305 p. : ill. ; 23 cm. (Man & nature in Asia ; no. 8) "Simultaneously published in the United States by the University of Hawaii Press"--T.p. verso. Includes bibliographical references (p. 289-300) and index. CONTENTS: Fengshui : a challenge to anthropology -- Fengshui practices and policies, 1850 to 1949 -- Fengshui practices and policies after 1949 -- The fengshui revival : fieldwork in Sichuan -- Another school of fengshui : fieldwork in Jiangsu -- Fengshui applications and possible interpretations -- The construction of a discourse : fengshui as environmental ethics -- Conclusion -- Appendix: On the origin of fengshui and the history of its literature. ISBN 0-7007-1673-4
1. Feng shui - China - History. I. Feuchtwang, Stephan. II. Title. III. Series: Man and nature in Asia ; no. 8.

Bruyn, Gerd de. Fisch und Frosch, oder, Die Selbstkritik der Moderne : ein architekturtheoretischer Essay / Gerd de Bruyn. Gütersloh ; Berlin : Bertelsmann Fachzeitschriften ; Basel ; Boston ; Berlin : Birkhäuser, c2001. 167 p. : ill., facsims., plans ; 19 cm. (Bauwelt Fundamente ; 124) (Architekturtheorie) Includes bibliographical references (p. 161-164). ISBN 3-7643-6497-1 DDC 720.1
1. Architectural criticism. 2. Architecture - 20th century. 3. Architecture - Philosophy. I. Title. II. Title: Selbstkritik der Moderne III. Title: Fisch und Frosch IV. Series. V. Series: Architekturtheorie

Bružis, Miķelis. Pasaules uzskats jeb cilvēks dabā, sabiedrībā un mūžībā Rīga : Jumava, 2002. 708, [1] p. : ill. ; 25 cm. ISBN 9984054616
1. Civilization - History. I. Title.

Bryan, Debra Jordan.
Honey from my heart for you. Nashville, Tenn. : J. Countryman, c2002.
BF575.F66 H66 2002

Bryant, Jennings.
Communication and emotion. Mahwah, N.J. ; London : Lawrence Erlbaum, c2003.
BF637.C45 C6375 2003

Bryden, Barbara E., 1954- Sundial : theoretical relationships between psychological type, talent, and disease / Barbara E. Bryden. Gainesville, FL : Center for Applications of Psychological Type, 2003. p. cm. Includes bibliographical references. ISBN 0-935652-46-9 DDC 155.2/6
1. Typology (Psychology) 2. Mind and body. 3. Ability. 4. Personality - Physiological aspects. 5. Medicine and psychology. 6. Holistic medicine. I. Title.
BF698.3 .B79 2003

Bryher, 1894-.
Analyzing Freud. New York : New Directions, c2002.
BF109.F74 A845 2002

BRYHER, 1894- - CORRESPONDENCE.
Analyzing Freud. New York : New Directions, c2002.
BF109.F74 A845 2002

Brzeziński, Jerzy.
Psychologia w obliczu zachodzących przemian społeczno-kulturowych. Warszawa : Instytut Psychologii PAN, 2002.
BF20 .P79 2002

BSR International series
(1089) Fire in archaeology. Oxford : Archaeopress, 2002.
DA90 .B86 suppl. v.1089

Bstan-'dzin-rgya-mtsho, Dalai Lama XIV, 1935- The art of happiness at work / His Holiness the Dalai Lama and Howard C. Cutler. New York : Riverhead Books, 2003. 212 p. ; 22 cm. ISBN 1-57322-261-5 (alk. paper) DDC 294.3/444
1. Work - Psychological aspects. 2. Work - Religious aspects - Buddhism. 3. Happiness. 4. Happiness - Religious aspects - Buddhism. 5. Buddhism - Doctrines. I. Cutler, Howard C. II. Title.

BF481 .B76 2003
The Dalai Lama's book of transformation. London : Thorsons, c2000. 159 p. ; 13 cm. ISBN 0-00-710097-3 (pbk.)
1. Buddhist meditations. 2. Buddhist literature, Tibetan. I. Title. II. Title: Book of transformation.

Reflections from the journey of life : collected sayings of the Dalai Lama / collected and edited by Catherine Barry ; translated from the French by Joseph Rowe. Berkeley, Calif. : North Atlantic Books, c2002. 195 p. ; 21 cm. ISBN 1-55643-388-3 (pbk. : alk. paper) DDC 294.3/923
1. Spiritual life - Buddhism. 2. Conduct of life. 3. Buddhism - Doctrines. I. Barry, Catherine, 1955- Sages paroles du Dalai Lama. English. II. Title.
BQ5670 .B76 2002

Bu ping ze ming : xuan xie shi ge hao ban fa / Zheng Yanping, Da Lu bian zhu. Di 2 ban. Beijing : Zhongguo cheng shi chu ban she, 2001. 3, 3, 247 p. ; 21 cm. (She jiao jin yao shi cong shu = Shejiao jinyaoshi cong shu) Added title in pinyin Buping ze ming. ISBN 7-5074-1306-3
1. Emotions. 2. Pyschology - Popular works. I. Zheng, Yanping. II. Da, Lu. III. Title: Buping ze ming IV. Series: She jiao jin yao shi cong shu.

Bucay, Jorge, 1949- Hojas de ruta / Jorge Bucay. 1a ed. Buenos Aires : Editorial Sudamericana : Editorial Del nuevo extremo, 2001. 667 p. ; 20 cm. + 1 sound disc (11 min. : digital ; 4 3/4 in.). "Colección completa"--cover. ISBN 950-07-2320-4
1. Self-reliance. 2. Self-confidence. 3. Life skills. I. Title.

Bücher im virtuellen Warenkorb.
Lengen, Haiko van. Berlin : Verlag für Wirtschaftskommunikation, c2001.

Büchi, Christophe. "Röstigraben" : das Verhältnis zwischen deutscher und französischer Schweiz : Geschichte und Perspektiven / Christophe Büchi. 2. aufl. Zürich : NZZ, c2001. 336 p. ; 23 cm. Includes bibliographical references (p. 331-336). ISBN 3-85823-940-2
1. Bilingualism - Switzerland. 2. Language policy - Switzerland. 3. Switzerland - Ethnic relations. 4. National characteristics, German. 5. National characteristics, French. I. Title.

Buchinger, Birgit.
Hofstadler, Beate, 1961- KörperNormen, KörperFormen. Wien : Turia + Kant, c2001.
BF692.5 .H64 2001

BUCKE, RICHARD MAURICE, 1837-1902. COSMIC CONSCIOUSNESS.
Smullyan, Raymond M. Who knows? Bloomington : Indiana University Press, c2003.
BL50 .S59 2003

Buckland, Raymond. Book of alchemy / Raymond Buckland. 1st ed. St. Paul, Minn. : Llewellyn Publications, 2003. xxvii, 209 p. : ill. ; 23 cm. Includes bibliographical references (p. 207-209). ISBN 0-7387-0053-3 DDC 133.3/242
1. Divination cards. 2. Alchemy. I. Title.
BF1778.5 .B83 2003

Buckland's book of spirit communications / Raymond Buckland. 2nd ed., rev. and expanded. St. Paul, Minn. : Llewellyn, 2004. p. cm. Rev. ed. of: Doors to other worlds. 1st ed. 1993. Includes bibliographical references and index. ISBN 0-7387-0399-0 DDC 133.9
1. Spiritualism. I. Buckland, Raymond. Doors to other worlds. II. Title.
BF1261.2 .B78 2004

Coin divination : pocket fortuneteller / Raymond Buckland. 1st ed. St. Paul, Minn. : Llewellyn Publications, 2000. xx, 194 p. : ill. ; 16 cm. Includes bibliographical references (p. 193-194). ISBN 1-56718-089-2 (pbk.) DDC 133.3
1. Divination. 2. Coins - Miscellanea. I. Title.
BF1779.C56 B83 2000

Color magick : unleash your inner powers / Raymond Buckland. 1st ed., rev. St. Paul, Minn. : Llewellyn Publications, 2002. xxi, 191 p. : ill. ; 20 cm. Rev. ed. of: Practical color magick. 1st ed. 1983. Includes bibliographical references (p. 173-182) and index. ISBN 0-7387-0204-8 (pbk.) ISBN 0-87542-047-8 DDC 133.4/3
1. Magic. 2. Occultism. 3. Parapsychology. 4. Meditation. 5. Color - Miscellanea. I. Buckland, Raymond. Practical color magick. II. Title.
BF1623.C6 B83 2002

[Complete book of witchcraft]
Buckland's complete book of witchcraft / Raymond Buckland. 2nd ed., rev. & expanded. St. Paul, Minn. : Llewellyn Publications, 2002. xviii, 346 p. : ill., music ; 28 cm. Includes bibliographical references (p. 335-337) and index. ISBN 0-87542-050-8 DDC 299
1. Witchcraft. I. Title. II. Title: Complete book of witchcraft
BF1566 .B76 2002

Doors to other worlds.
Buckland, Raymond. Buckland's book of spirit communications. 2nd ed., rev. and expanded. St. Paul, Minn. : Llewellyn, 2004.
BF1261.2 .B78 2004

Doors to other worlds : a practical guide to communicating with spirits / Raymond Buckland. 1st ed. St. Paul, Minn. : Llewellyn, 2000. xvii, 250 p. : ill. ; 21 cm. Includes bibliographical references (p. 243-250). ISBN 0-87542-061-3
1. Spiritualism. I. Title.

Gypsy witchcraft & magic / Raymond Buckland ; illustrated by Michelle Dillaire. 1st ed. St. Paul, Minn. : Llewellyn Publications, 2001, c1998. x, 177 p. : ill. ; 25 cm. Includes bibliographical references (p. 169-174) and index. ISBN 1-56718-097-3 (trade paper)
1. Witchcraft. 2. Romanies. I. Title. II. Title: Gypsy witchcraft and magic

Practical color magick.
Buckland, Raymond. Color magick. 1st ed., rev. St. Paul, Minn. : Llewellyn Publications, 2002.
BF1623.C6 B83 2002

Signs, symbols & omens : an illustrated guide to magical & spiritual symbolism / Raymond Buckland. 1st ed. St. Paul, Minn. : Llewellyn Publications, 2003. xiii, 244 p. : ill. ; 23 cm. Includes bibliographical references (p. 235-244). ISBN 0-7387-0234-X DDC 133.3
1. Symbolism. I. Title. II. Title: Signs, symbols, and omens
BF1623.S9 B83 2003

Witchcraft from the inside : origins of the fastest growing religious movement in America / Raymond Buckland. Rev. and enl. 3rd ed. St. Paul, Minn., U.S.A. : Llewellyn Publications, 1995 (2001 printing) xiii, 212 p. : ill. ; 23 cm. (Llewellyn's world religion and magic series) "Third edition, fourth printing"--verso t.p. Includes bibliographical references (p. 199-207) and index. ISBN 1-56718-101-5 DDC 133.4/3
1. Witchcraft. 2. Witchcraft - History. I. Title. II. Series: Llewellyn's world religion & magic series.
BF1566 .B77 1995

Buckland's book of spirit communications.
Buckland, Raymond. 2nd ed., rev. and expanded. St. Paul, Minn. : Llewellyn, 2004.
BF1261.2 .B78 2004

Buckland's complete book of witchcraft.
Buckland, Raymond. [Complete book of witchcraft] 2nd ed., rev. & expanded. St. Paul, Minn. : Llewellyn Publications, 2002.
BF1566 .B76 2002

Buckley, Maureen A., 1964- Mentoring children and adolescents : a guide to the issues / Maureen A. Buckley and Sandra H. Zimmermann. Westport, Conn. : Praeger, 2003. p. cm. (Contemporary youth issues) Includes bibliographical references and index. ISBN 0-275-97975-X (alk. paper) DDC 371.102
1. Children - Counseling of. 2. Teenagers - Counseling of. 3. Mentoring. I. Zimmermann, Sandra Hundley, 1944- II. Title. III. Series.
BF637.C6 B8 2003

Bucknell review
(v. 46, no. 2) Adrift in the technological matrix. Lewisburg, PA : Bucknell University Press ; London : Associated University Presses, c2003.

Budanok, Anastasīi͡a.
Iskusstvo snovidenīĭ = Sankt-Peterburg : Skifīi͡a, 2002.
NX180.D74 I74 2002

Budd, Colin.
The new economic diplomacy. Aldershot, Hampshire, England ; Burlington, VT : Ashgate, c2003.
HF1359 .N4685 2003

Budd, Karen S.
A small matter of proof. Reno, NV : Context Press, c2003.
BF121 .S545 2003

BUDDHA AND BUDDHISM. See BUDDHISM.

The Buddha tarot companion.
Place, Robert Michael. St. Paul, Minn. : Llewellyn, 2004.
BF1879.T2 P547 2004

Buddha vaṅ', mahā vaṅ', rāja vaṅ' myā" nhaṅ'' bisuka kyam'" myā" mha kok' nut' taṅ' pra 'ap' so Mran' mā' rui" rā gehavidhī.
'Oṅ' Mran'', 'Aṅ'gyan'nīyā Ū". 'Im' chok' maṅgalā kyam'". Mantale" : Krī" pvā" re" Cā 'up' Tuik', 2002.

The Buddha's book of daily meditations
BF1779.A88 O56 2002

The Buddha's book of daily meditations : a year of wisdom, compassion, and happiness / edited by Christopher Titmuss. 1st ed. New York : Three Rivers Press, c2001. xxiv, 390 p. ; 16 cm. Includes index. ISBN 0-609-80780-3 (pbk.) DDC 294.3/4432
1. Buddhist devotional calendars. 2. Buddhist meditations. I. Titmuss, Christopher.
BQ5579 .B83 2001

BUDDHISM. *See* **TANTRIC BUDDHISM.**

BUDDHISM AND LITERATURE.
Sun, Changwu. Zhongguo wen xue zhong di Weimo yu Guanyin. Di 1 ban. Beijing : Gao deng jiao yu chu ban she : Xin hua shu dian zong dian Beijing fa xing suo fa xing, 1996.
PL2275.B8 S85 1996 <Orien China>

BUDDHISM AND PSYCHOANALYSIS.
Encountering Buddhism. Albany : State University of New York Press, 2003.
BQ4570.P755 E62 2003

Magid, Barry. Ordinary mind. Boston : Wisdom, c2002.
BQ9286 .M34 2002

Psychoanalysis and Buddhism. 1st ed. Boston : Wisdom Publications, c2003.
BF175.4.R44 P785 2003

BUDDHISM AND THE ARTS.
Qi, Zhixiang. Fo jiao mei xue. Di 1 ban. Shanghai : Shanghai ren min chu ban she : Xin hua shu dian Shanghai fa xing suo jing xiao, 1997.
BQ4570.A72 C45 1997 <Asian China>

BUDDHISM - CHINA.
Xu, Fancheng. Xu Fancheng ji. Di 1 ban. Beijing : Zhongguo she hui ke xue chu ban she, 2001.
PL2262.2 .X84 2001

BUDDHISM - CHINA - HISTORY.
Tang, Yongtong, 1893-1964. [Works. 2000] Tang Yongtong quan ji. Di 1 ban. Shijiazhuang Shi : Hebei ren min chu ban she, 2000.
BQ626 .T37 2000

BUDDHISM - CHINA - TIBET.
Cai, Zhichun. Huo fo zhuan shi. Di 1 ban. Beijing : Hua wen chu ban she : Xin hua shu dian jing xiao, 2000.
BL515 .C345 2000

BUDDHISM - DOCTRINES. *See also* **VIPAŚYANĀ (BUDDHISM).**
Bstan-'dzin-rgya-mtsho, Dalai Lama XIV, 1935- The art of happiness at work. New York : Riverhead Books, 2003.
BF481 .B76 2003

Bstan-'dzin-rgya-mtsho, Dalai Lama XIV, 1935- Reflections from the journey of life. Berkeley, Calif. : North Atlantic Books, c2002.
BQ5670 .B76 2002

Glickman, Marshall. Beyond the breath. 1st ed. Boston : Journey Editions ; North Clarendon, VT : Distributed by Tuttle Pub., 2002.
BQ5630.V5 G54 2002

Hagen, Steve, 1945- Buddhism is not what you think. 1st ed. [San Francisco] : HarperSanFrancisco, c2003.
BQ4570.F7 H34 2003

Nhất Hạnh, Thích. No death, no fear. New York : Riverhead Books, c2002.
BQ4302 .N43 2002

Smith, Jean, 1938- The beginner's guide to walking the Buddha's eightfold path. New York : Bell Tower, 2002.
BQ4320 .S65 2002

Thubten Chodron, 1950- Working with anger. Ithaca, NY : Snow Lion Publication, 2001.
BQ4430.A53 T48 2001

Buddhism is not what you think.
Hagen, Steve, 1945- 1st ed. [San Francisco] : HarperSanFrancisco, c2003.
BQ4570.F7 H34 2003

BUDDHISM - MISCELLANEA.
Place, Robert Michael. The Buddha tarot companion. St. Paul, Minn. : Llewellyn, 2004.
BF1879.T2 P547 2004

BUDDHISM - PSYCHOLOGY.
Brazier, Caroline. Buddhist psychology. London : Robinson, 2003.

Psychoanalysis and Buddhism. 1st ed. Boston : Wisdom Publications, c2003.
BF175.4.R44 P785 2003

Psychology and Buddhism. New York : Kluwer Academic/Plenum Publishers, c2003.
BQ4570.P76 P78 2003

BUDDHISM, TANTRIC. *See* **TANTRIC BUDDHISM.**

BUDDHISM - UNITED STATES - HISTORY - 20TH CENTURY.
Encountering Buddhism. Albany : State University of New York Press, 2003.
BQ4570.P755 E62 2003

BUDDHIST DEVOTIONAL CALENDARS.
The Buddha's book of daily meditations. 1st ed. New York : Three Rivers Press, c2001.
BQ5579 .B83 2001

BUDDHIST LITERATURE, TIBETAN.
Bstan-'dzin-rgya-mtsho, Dalai Lama XIV, 1935- The Dalai Lama's book of transformation. London : Thorsons, c2000.

BUDDHIST LOGIC.
Gill, Harjeet Singh, 1935- Signification in Buddhist and French traditions. New Delhi : Harman Pub. House, 2001.
BC25 .G55 2001

BUDDHIST MEDITATIONS.
Bstan-'dzin-rgya-mtsho, Dalai Lama XIV, 1935- The Dalai Lama's book of transformation. London : Thorsons, c2000.

The Buddha's book of daily meditations. 1st ed. New York : Three Rivers Press, c2001.
BQ5579 .B83 2001

LeBeau, Kara R. Guan yin's chakra meditations. Boulder, Colo. : Mahasimhananda Press, c2001.
BF1442.C53 L43 2001

BUDDHIST PAINTING. *See* **PAINTING, BUDDHIST.**

Buddhist psychology.
Brazier, Caroline. London : Robinson, 2003.

BUDDHIST TANTRISM. *See* **TANTRIC BUDDHISM.**

Budge, E. A. Wallis (Ernest Alfred Wallis), Sir, 1857-1934.
[Book of the dead. English.] The Egyptian book of the dead. London : Cassell, 2001.
PJ1555.E5 B83 2001

Budgeon, Shelley, 1967- Choosing a self : young women and the individualization of identity / Shelley Budgeon. Westport, Conn. : Praeger, 2003. 210 p. ; 25 cm. Includes bibliographical references (p. [199]-208) and index. ISBN 0-275-97637-8 (alk. paper) DDC 155.3/33
1. Young women - Psychology. 2. Women - Identity. 3. Individuality. 4. Femininity. I. Title.
HQ1229 .B83 2003

Budiansky, Stephen. The character of cats : the origins, intelligence, behavior, and stratagems of Felis silvestris catus / Stephen Budiansky. New York, N.Y. : Viking, c2002. x, 227 p., [2] p. of plates : ill. (some col.), maps ; 22 cm. Includes bibliographical references (p. [205]-216) and index. CONTENTS: 1. Cats plot to take over the world, and succeed -- 2. Black cats and tabby cats -- 3. The war between the sexes and other oddities of feline society -- 4. Outta my face, and other useful expressions -- 5. The thinking cat's guide to intelligence -- 6. The cat personality test -- 7. Cats and trouble. ISBN 0-670-03093-7 (alk. paper) DDC 636.8
1. Cats - Behavior. 2. Cats - Psychology. 3. Cats. I. Title.
SF446.5 .B84 2002

Budushchee mira i Rossii.
Tumusov, F. S. (Fedot Semenovich) Moskva : "Mysl'", 2000.
HC340.12.Z7 S2357 2000

Búfalo, Enzo del. Individuo, mercado y utopía : un ensayo genealógico / Enzo del Búfalo. 1. ed. Caracas : Monte Ávila Editores Lationoamericana : Universidad Central de Venezuela, Centro de Investigaciones Post-Doctorales FACES, 1998. 294 p. ; 21 cm. (Estudios. Serie Ideas) Includes bibliographical references p. [289]-294. ISBN 980-01-0980-3 ISBN 980-00-1344-X
1. Subjectivity. 2. Economics - Philosophy. 3. Individualism. 4. Social conflict. I. Title. II. Series: Colección Estudios (Monte Ávila Editores). Serie Ideas.
BD222 .B86 1998

BUFFETT, WARREN.
O'Loughlin, James. The real Warren Buffett. London ; Yarmouth, ME : Nicholas Brealey, 2003.

Bühler, Gerhard, 1959- Postmoderne auf dem Bildschirm, auf der Leinwand : Musikvideos, Werbespots und David Lynchs Wild at heart / Gerhard Bühler. Sankt Augustin : Gardez!, c2002. 412 p. : ill. ; 21 cm. (Filmstudien ; Bd. 24) Thesis (doctoral)--Universität, Heidelberg, 2001. Includes bibliographical references. ISBN 3-89796-034-6 (pbk.)
1. Postmodernism. 2. Television advertising. 3. Music videos - History and criticism. 4. Motion pictures - History. I. Title. II. Series: Filmstudien (Mainz, Rhineland-Palatinate, Germany) ; Bd. 24.

Bühnemann, Gudrun. Maṇḍalas and Yantras in the Hindu traditions / by Gudrun Bühnemann ; with contributions by H. Brunner ... [et al.]. Leiden ; Boston : Brill, 2003. xvii, 303 p., [16] p. of plates : ill. (some col.) ; 25 cm. (Brill's Indological library, 0925-2916 ; v 18) Includes bibliographical references (p. [271]-290) and index. ISBN 90-04-12902-2 (alk. paper) DDC 294.5/37
1. Mandala. 2. Yantras. 3. Hindu symbolism. I. Title. II. Series.
BL2015.M3 B85 2003

Buĭanov, M. I. (Mikhail Ivanovich), vrach. Strakh / Mikhail Buĭanov. Moskva : Rossiĭskoe ob-vo medikov-literatorov, 2002. 168 p. : ill. ; 20 cm. Part of an unnumbered, untitled trilogy. The other separately published titles are: Odin and Zloba. ISBN 5892560112
1. Fear. I. Title.
BF575.F2 B85 2002

Buie, Dan H.
Rizzuto, Ana-María. The dynamics of human aggression. New York, NY : Brunner-Routledge, 2003.
BF175.5.A36 R59 2003

BUILDING. *See* **ARCHITECTURE; CONSTRUCTION INDUSTRY.**

Building brands & believers.
Wertime, Kent. Chichester : Wiley, 2002.

Building brands and believers.
Wertime, Kent. Building brands & believers. Chichester : Wiley, 2002.

BUILDING DESIGN. *See* **ARCHITECTURE.**

Building gender = Architektur und Geschlecht / Dörte Kuhlmann, Kari Jormakka (Hg.). Wien : Edition Selene, 2002. 218 p. : ill. ; 21 cm. Includes bibliographical references (p. 200-207) and index. ISBN 3-85266-181-1 (pbk.)
1. Feminism and architecture. 2. Architecture - Philosophy. I. Kuhlmann, Dörte. II. Jormakka, Kari. III. Title: Architektur und Geschlecht

BUILDING INDUSTRY. *See* **CONSTRUCTION INDUSTRY.**

Building innovative teams.
Harris, Chris. Houndmills [England] ; New York : Palgrave Macmillan, 2003.
HD66 .H3744 2003

Building mental muscle.
Gamon, David. Rev. and updated ed. New York : Walker & Co., 2003.
BF441 .G35 2003

BUILDINGS. *See* **ARCHITECTURE; DWELLINGS.**

BUILDINGS - DESIGN AND CONSTRUCTION. *See* **ARCHITECTURE.**

BUILDINGS - ENVIRONMENTAL ASPECTS.
Environmentally sustainable buildings. Paris : Organisation for Economic Co-operation and Development, 2003.

Buitenwerf, Rieuwerd. Book III of the Sibylline oracles and its social setting / with an introduction, translation and commentary by Rieuwerd Buitenwerf. Leiden ; Boston, MA : Brill, 2003. x, 443 p. ; 25 cm. (Studia in Veteris Testamenti pseudepigrapha, 0929-3523 ; v. 17) Includes bibliographical references (p. [391]-422) and indexes. ISBN 90-04-12861-1 (hc : alk. paper) DDC 888/.01
1. Oracula sibyllina. - Book 3. 2. Oracles, Greek. I. Title. II. Title: Oracula sibyllina. Book 3. English. III. Title: Book 3 of the Sibylline oracles and its social setting IV. Title: Book three of the Sibylline oracles and its social setting V. Series.
BF1769 .B85 2003

Bulacio, Cristina.
Antropología e interpretación. Tucumán, Argentina : Instituto de Estudios Antropológicos y Filosofía de la Religión, Facultad de Filosofía y Letras, Universidad Nacional de Tucumán, c2001.
BD450 .A564 2001

Bulayhid, Muná bint Ṣāliḥ. Tharṭharat muʻallimāt / taʼlīf Muná bint Ṣāliḥ al-Bulayhid. al-Ṭabʻah 1. al-Riyāḍ : Maktabat al-ʻUbaykān, 2001. 230 p. ; 21 cm. In Arabic. ISBN 996020863X
1. Educational psychology. 2. Islamic ethics. I. Title.
BJ1291 .B85 2001

BULIMAREXIA. *See* **BULIMIA.**

BULIMIA.
Cooper, Myra, 1957- The psychology of bulimia nervosa. Oxford ; New York : Oxford University Press, 2003.
RC552.B84 C66 2003

Género, desarrollo psicosocial y trastornos de la imagen corporal. Madrid : Instituto de la Mujer, 2001.

BULIMIA NERVOSA. *See* **BULIMIA.**

BULIMIA - TREATMENT.
Cooper, Myra, 1957- The psychology of bulimia nervosa. Oxford ; New York : Oxford University Press, 2003.
RC552.B84 C66 2003

Bulkeley, Kelly, 1962- Dreams of healing : transforming nightmares into visions of hope / Kelly Bulkeley. New York : Paulist Press, c2003. xvi, 207 p. ; 23 cm. Includes bibliographical references and index. CONTENTS: Post-traumatic stress and nightmares -- Ripple effects -- The fear of new dangers -- Flying and falling -- Disease -- Bad guys -- War and protest -- Anticipations -- Visions of hope. ISBN 0-8091-4153-1 (alk. paper) DDC 155.9/35
1. Nightmares. 2. Dreams. 3. Dream interpretation. 4. Disasters - Psychological aspects. 5. Crisis intervention (Mental health services) 6. Counseling. I. Title.
BF1099.N53 B85 2003

BULL MARKETS. *See* **STOCK EXCHANGES.**

Bulletin (Association des historiens modernistes des universités (France))
(no 28.) La Renaissance. Paris : Presses de l'université de Paris-Sorbonne, 2003.

BULLIES.
Leaney, Cindy. Long walk to school. Vero Beach, Fla. : Rourke Pub., 2003.
BF637.B85 L43 2003

BULLS AND BEARS. *See* **STOCK EXCHANGES.**

BULLS - MYTHOLOGY.
Lombard, René-André. Le nom de l'Europe. Grenoble : Thot, c2001.

BULLYING.
Blakely, Mary Louise. Unmasking bullies & victims. Tamarac, Fl. : Llumina Press, 2004.
BF637.B85 B56 2004

Dellasega, Cheryl. Girl wars. New York : Simon & Schuster, c2003.
BF637.B85 D45 2003

Elias, Maurice J. Bullying, peer harassment, and victimization in the schools. New York : Haworth Press, 2003.
BF637.B85 E45 2003

Hibbert, Adam, 1968- Why do people bully? Chicago, Ill. : Raintree, 2004.
BF637.B85 H53 2004

Johnston, Marianne. [Dealing with bullying. Spanish] Como tratar a los bravucones. New York : PowerKids Press, 2005.
BF637.B85 J6418 2005

Leaney, Cindy. Long walk to school. Vero Beach, Fla. : Rourke Pub., 2003.
BF637.B85 L43 2003

Rennie Peyton, Pauline, 1952- Dignity at work. 1st ed. Hove, East Sussex ; New York : Brunner-Routledge, 2003.
BF637.B85 R46 2003

Scheunemann, Pam, 1955- Dealing with bullies. Edina, MN : Abdo Pub., 2004.
BF637.B85 S37 2004

BULLYING - AUSTRALIA.
Bullying. 2nd ed. Annandale, N.S.W. : The Federation Press 2001.
BF637.B85 B85 2001

The bullying culture.
Hadikin, Ruth. Oxford ; Boston : Books for Midwives, 2000.
BF637.B85 H33 2000

Bullying : from backyard to boardroom / editors: Paul McCarthy ... [et al.]. 2nd ed. Annandale, N.S.W. : The Federation Press 2001. xxx, 146 p. : ill. ; 22 cm. Previously published: Alexandria, N.S.W. : Millennium Books, 1996. Includes bibliographical references and index. ISBN 1-86287-392-5 ISBN 1-86287-392-5
1. Bullying - Australia. 2. Bullying in the workplace - Australia. I. McCarthy, Paul.
BF637.B85 B85 2001

BULLYING IN THE WORKPLACE.
Hadikin, Ruth. The bullying culture. Oxford ; Boston : Books for Midwives, 2000.
BF637.B85 H33 2000

Hearn, Jeff. Gender, sexuality and violence in organizations. London ; Thousand Oaks : SAGE, 2001.

Rennie Peyton, Pauline, 1952- Dignity at work. 1st ed. Hove, East Sussex ; New York : Brunner-Routledge, 2003.
BF637.B85 R46 2003

BULLYING IN THE WORKPLACE - AUSTRALIA.
Bullying. 2nd ed. Annandale, N.S.W. : The Federation Press 2001.
BF637.B85 B85 2001

BULLYING - JUVENILE LITERATURE.
Hibbert, Adam, 1968- Why do people bully? Chicago, Ill. : Raintree, 2004.
BF637.B85 H53 2004

Jackson, J. S. Bye-bye, bully!. St. Meinrad, IN. : Abbey Press, c2003.
BF637.B85 J33 2003

Johnston, Marianne. [Dealing with bullying. Spanish] Como tratar a los bravucones. New York : PowerKids Press, 2005.
BF637.B85 J6418 2005

Leaney, Cindy. Long walk to school. Vero Beach, Fla. : Rourke Pub., 2003.
BF637.B85 L43 2003

Scheunemann, Pam, 1955- Dealing with bullies. Edina, MN : Abdo Pub., 2004.
BF637.B85 S37 2004

Bullying, peer harassment, and victimization in the schools.
Elias, Maurice J. New York : Haworth Press, 2003.
BF637.B85 E45 2003

BULLYISM. *See* **BULLYING.**

Bunning, Joan. Learning tarot reversals / Joan Bunning. Boston, MA : Weiser Books, 2003. p. cm. Table of contents URL: http://www.loc.gov/catdir/toc/ecip046/2003014719.html CONTENTS: Energy and the tarot -- The energy cycle and orientation -- Energy phases -- Repeating cycles -- Mismatches -- Opposing energy pairs -- Energy groups -- Interpretation strategy -- Major Arcana -- Minor Arcana -- Suggestions for exercises -- Card keyword list. ISBN 1-57863-271-4 DDC 133.3/2424
1. Tarot. I. Title.
BF1879.T2 .B834 2003

BUNO, JOHANNES, 1617-1697.
Strasser, Gerhard F. Emblematik und Mnemonik der frühen Neuzeit im Zusammenspiel Johannes Buno und Johann Justus Winckelmann. Wiesbaden : Harrassowitz Wolfenbüttel : Herzog August Bibliothek, c2000.
PN6348.5 .S873 2000

Buping ze ming.
Bu ping ze ming. Di 2 ban. Beijing : Zhongguo cheng shi chu ban she, 2001.

Burack, Cynthia, 1958- Healing identities : Black feminist thought and the politics of groups / Cynthia Burack. Ithaca : Cornell University Press, 2004. p. cm. (Psychoanalysis and social theory) Includes bibliographical references and index. CONTENTS: Psychoanalysis, race, and racism -- From psychoanalysis to political theory -- Reparative group leadership -- Conflict and authenticity -- Bonding and solidarity -- Coalitions and reparative politics. ISBN 0-8014-4146-3 (alk. paper) ISBN 0-8014-8937-7 (pbk. : alk. paper) DDC 150.19/5/082
1. Psychoanalysis and feminism. 2. African American women - Psychology. 3. Group identity. I. Title. II. Series.
BF175.4.F45 B87 2004

Buranok, O. M.
Akopov, G. V. Mentalistika. Samara : Samarskiĭ gos. pedagog. universitet, 2001.
BF108.R8 A478 2001

Burch, Robert, 1949-.
Between philosophy and poetry. New York : Continuum, 2002.
B66 .B48 2002

Burch, Wanda Easter, 1947- She who dreams : a journey into healing through dreamwork / by Wanda Easter Burch. Novato, Calif. : New World Library, c2003. p. cm. Includes bibliographical references and index. Table of contents URL: http://www.loc.gov/catdir/toc/ecip044/2003011375.html CONTENTS: Southern child -- Southern roots : healing in the forest -- Precognitive dreaming : the dance hall of the dead -- The yellow robe -- Packing for twin journeys -- A journey into the sacred forest -- The road to the healing pool -- The healing cocktail -- Turning poison into medicine -- Fields of dreams -- Roller-coaster days -- Angels -- Renegotiating my life contract -- She who dreams -- Bringing dreams to the community -- Healing with dream imagery. ISBN 1-57731-426-3 (pbk. : alk. paper) DDC 135/.3
1. Women's dreams - Case studies. 2. Dream interpretation - Case studies. 3. Dreams - Therapeutic use. 4. Breast - Cancer - Psychological aspects. 5. Burch, Wanda Easter, - 1947- I. Title.
BF1099.W65 B87 2003

BURCH, WANDA EASTER, 1947-.
Burch, Wanda Easter, 1947- She who dreams. Novato, Calif. : New World Library, c2003.
BF1099.W65 B87 2003

Burckhart, Holger.
Philosophieren aus dem Diskurs. Würzburg : Königshausen & Neumann, c2002.

BUREAUCRACY.
Terry, Larry D. Leadership of public bureaucracies. 2nd ed. Armonk, N.Y. : M.E. Sharpe, c2003.
JF1525.L4 .T47 2003

Burger, Jerry M. Personality / Jerry M. Burger. 6th ed. Australia ; Belmont, CA : Thomson/Wadsworth, c2004. xxvii, 586 p. : ill. ; 25 cm. Includes bibliographical references (p. 515-568) and indexes. ISBN 0-534-52796-5 DDC 155.2
1. Personality - Textbooks. I. Title.
BF698 .B84 2004

Burggraf, Jutta. Qué quiere decir género? : en torno a un nuevo modo de hablar / Jutta Burggraf. 1. ed. San Jose, Costa Rica : Promesa, 2001. 39 p. ; 22 cm. (Antropologia ; v. 4) Includes bibliographical references. ISBN 9977-947-99-6
1. Sex (Psychology) 2. Gender identity. I. Title. II. Series: Serie Antropología (San José, Costa Rica)

BURIAL. *See* **FUNERAL RITES AND CEREMONIES.**

BURIDAN, JEAN, 1300-1358.
Reina, Maria Elena. Hoc hic et nunc. [Firenze] : Leo S. Olschki, 2002.

Buridano, Marsilio di Inghen e la conoscenza del singolare.
Reina, Maria Elena. Hoc hic et nunc. [Firenze] : Leo S. Olschki, 2002.

BURIED TREASURE. *See* **TREASURE-TROVE.**

Burity, Joanildo A.
Cultura e identidade. Rio de Janeiro, RJ, Brasil : DP & A Editores, 2002.

Burk, Kevin, 1967- The complete node book : understanding your life's purpose / Kevin Burk. 1st ed. St. Paul, Minn. : Llewellyn Publications, 2003. ix, 224 p. ; 224 cm. ISBN 0-7387-0352-4 DDC 133.5/32
1. Astrology. 2. Moon - Miscellanea. I. Title. II. Title: Node book
BF1723 .B87 2003

Burke, Dan, 1965- Business @ the speed of stupid : building smarter companies after the technology shakeout / Dan Burke and Alan Morrison. Cambridge, MA : Perseus Pub., c2001. viii, 248 p. : ill. 24 cm. Includes bibliographical references (p. 231-234) and index. ISBN 0-7382-0542-7 DDC 658
1. Technological innovations - Management. 2. Industrial management - Communication systems. 3. Customer relations - Technological innovations. 4. Knowledge management. 5. Decision making. 6. Decision support systems. 7. Electronic commerce. 8. Internet. 9. Organizational effectiveness. 10. Total quality management. I. Morrison, Alan, 1946- II. Title. III. Title: Smarter companies after the technology shakeout
HD45 .B7995 2001

Burke, Kenneth, 1897- On human nature : a gathering while everything flows, 1967-1984 / Kenneth Burke ; edited by William H. Rueckert and Angelo Bonadonna ; arranged, and annotated by William H. Rueckert. Berkeley : University of California Press, c2003. xiv, 389 p. ; 24 cm. Includes bibliographical references. CONTENTS: On stress, its seeking, 1967 -- On "creativity", a partial retraction, 1971 -- Towards Helhaven : three stages of a vision, 1971 -- Why satire, with a plan for writing one, 1974 -- Realisms, occidental style, 1982 -- Archetype and entelechy, 1972 -- (Nonsymbolic) motion/ (symbolic) action, 1978 -- Theology and logology, 1979 -- Symbolism as a realistic mode : "de-psychoanalyzing" logologized, 1979 -- A theory of terminology, 1967 -- Towards looking back, 1976 -- Variations on "providence", 1981 -- Eye-crossing, from Brooklyn to Manhattan : an eye-poem for the ear, 1973 -- Counter-gridlock : an interview with Kenneth Burke, 1980-81. ISBN 0-520-21919-8 (alk. paper) DDC 814/.52

1. Philosophy. 2. Criticism. I. Rueckert, William H. (William Howe), 1926- II. Bonadonna, Angelo. III. Title.
B945.B771 R84 2003

Burke, Patrick.
Merleau-Ponty, Maurice, 1908-1961. [Union de l'âme et du corps chez Malebranche, Biran et Bergson. English] The incarnate subject. Amherst, N.Y. : Humanity Books, 2001.
B2430.M379 U513 2001

Burke, Peter, 1937-.
History and historians in the twentieth century. Oxford : Published for the British Academy by Oxford University Press, 2002.

Burke, Peter J. (Peter James), 1939-.
Advances in identity and research. New York : Kluwer Academic/Plenum Publishers, c2003.
BF697 .A347 2003

Burkert, Walter, 1931-
[Wilder Ursprung. English]
Savage energies : lessons of myth and ritual in ancient Greece / Walter Burkert ; translation by Peter Bing. Chicago : University of Chicago Press, c2001. xiv, 110 p. ; 24 cm. Includes bibliographical references. CONTENTS: Greek tragedy and sacrificial ritual -- The legend of Kekrops's daughters and the Arrhephoria: from initiation ritual to Panathenaic festival -- Jason, Hypsipyle, and new fire at Lemnos: a study in myth and ritual -- Buzyges and Palladion: violence and the courts in ancient Greek ritual -- Demaratos, Astrabakos, and Herakles: kingship, myth, and politics at the time of the Persian wars. ISBN 0-226-08085-4 (cloth : alk. paper) DDC 292.08
1. Mythology, Greek. 2. Rites and ceremonies - Greece. I. Title.
BL785 .B8513 2001

Burkhart, Dagmar. Ehre : das symbolische Kapital / Dagmar Burkhart. Originalausg. München : Deutscher Taschenbuch Verlag, c2002. 290 p. : ill. ; 21 cm. (DTV Premium) Bibliographical references (p. 281-286) and index. ISBN 3-423-24293-0 (pbk.)
1. Honor. 2. Social ethics. 3. Conduct of life. I. Title. II. Series.
BJ1533.H8 B87 2002

BURKINA FASO - POLITICS AND GOVERNMENT.
Kyelem, Apollinaire. L'éventuel et le possible. [Ouagadougou : Presses universitaires de Ouagadougou, 2002]
1. Black author.

Burlaeus, Gualterus, 1275-1345?
[De vita et moribus philosophorum. Spanish]
Vida y costumbres de los viejos filósofos : la traducción castellana cuatrocentista del De vita et moribus philosophorum atribuido a Walter Burley / Francisco Crosas (ed.). Madrid : Iberoamericana ; Frankfurt : Vervuert, 2002. 210 p. ; 23 cm. (Medievalia Hispanica ; vol. 7) Includes bibliographical references (p. 195-197). ISBN 84-8489-048-1 (Iberoamericana : pbk.) ISBN 3-89354-476-3 (Vervuert : pbk.)
1. Philosophers, Ancient. 2. Philosophy, Ancient. I. Title. II. Series.

Burlaka, D. K.
Florovsky, Georges, 1893-1979. [Selections. Russian. 2002] Vera i kul'tura. Sankt-Peterburg : Izd-vo Russkogo Khristianskogo gumanitarnogo instituta, 2002.
BX260 .F552 2002

Burlakova, N. S. Proektivnye metody : teoriîa, praktika primeneniîa k issledovaniîu lichnosti rebenka / N.S Burlakova, V.I. Oleshkevich. Moskva : In-t obshchegumanitarnykh issledovaniĭ, 2001. 330, [6] p. ; 24 cm. (Seriîa Uchebniki psikhoterapii ; vyp. 1) Includes bibliographical references (p. [331]-[336]). ISBN 5882300630
1. Projective techniques. I. Oleshkevich, V. I. II. Institut obshchegumanitarnykh issledovaniĭ. III. Title. IV. Series.
BF698.7 .B87 2001

Burlando Bravo, Giannina.
La filosofía medieval. Madrid : Trotta, 2002.
B721 .F47 2002

BURN OUT (PSYCHOLOGY).
Maslach, Christina. [Burnout, the cost of caring] Burnout. Cambridge, MA : ISHK, 2003.
BF481 .M384 2003

Burn this book - .
Hurley, Jessica, 1970- Kansas City, Mo. : Andrews McMeel, c2002.
BF637.S4 H87 2002

Burneko, Guy Christian. By the torch of chaos and doubt : consciousness, culture, poiesis, and religion in the opening global millennium / Guy C. Burneko. Cresskill, N.J. : Hampton Press, c2003. xvii, 254 p. ; 23 cm. (Advances in systems theory, complexity, and the human sciences) Includes bibliographical references and indexes. ISBN 1-57273-281-4 (p) DDC 191
1. Life. I. Title. II. Series.
BD431 .B84 2003

Burnett, Ron, 1947- How images think / Ron Burnett. Cambridge, Mass. : MIT Press, 2004. p. cm. Includes bibliographical references and index. ISBN 0-262-02549-3 (hc. : alk. paper) DDC 153.3/2
1. Visual perception. 2. Imagery (Psychology) 3. Thought and thinking. I. Title.
BF241 .B79 2004

Burney, DeAnna McKinnie. AARS : Adolescent Anger Rating Sale : professional manual / DeAnna McKinnie Burney. Odessa, FL (P.O. Box 998, Odessa, 33556) : Psychological Assessment Resources, c2001. viii, 61 p. ; 28 cm. Includes bibliographical references (p. 41-43). DDC 155.5/1247/0287
1. Adolescent Anger Rating Scale. I. Title. II. Title: Adolescent anger rating scale
BF724.3.A55 B87 2001

Burnie, David.
Animal. 1st American ed. New York : DK ; [Washington, D.C.] : Smithsonian Institution, 2001.

Burnout.
Maslach, Christina. [Burnout, the cost of caring] Cambridge, MA : ISHK, 2003.
BF481 .M384 2003

BURNOUT (PSYCHOLOGY). *See* **BURN OUT (PSYCHOLOGY).**

Burns, Debbie. Chinese horoscopes : an easy guide to the Chinese system of astrology / Debbie Burns. Sydney : Lansdowne, 2000, c1998. 79 p. : col. ill. ; 21 cm. ISBN 1-86302-651-7
1. Astrology, Chinese. I. Title. II. Title: Easy guide to the Chinese system of astrology

Burns, Michael A.
Broussard, Cheryl D. What's money got to do with it? Oakland, CA : MetaMedia Pub., [c2002]
1. Black author.

Burns, William E., 1959- Witch hunts in Europe and America : an encyclopedia / by William E. Burns. Westport, Conn. : Greenwood Press, 2003. p. cm. Includes bibliographical references and index. ISBN 0-313-32142-6 (alk. paper) DDC 133.4/3/09
1. Witchcraft - Europe - History - Encyclopedias. 2. Witchcraft - United States - History - Encyclopedias. 3. Persecution - Europe - History - Encyclopedias. 4. Persecution - United States - History - Encyclopedias. 5. Trials (Witchcraft) - Europe - History - Encyclopedias. 6. Trials (Witchcraft) - United States - History - Encyclopedias. I. Title.
BF1584.E9 B87 2003

Burstein, John.
Math monsters.
Burstein, John. Patterns. Milwaukee, WI : Weekly Reader Early Learning Library, 2003.
BF294 .B87 2003

Patterns : what's on the wall? / by John Burnstein. Milwaukee, WI : Weekly Reader Early Learning Library, 2003. p. cm. (Math monsters) SUMMARY: The four math monsters show how to make different kinds of patterns as they paint their walls. ISBN 0-8368-3816-5 ISBN 0-8368-3831-9 (pbk.) DDC 152.14/23
1. Pattern perception - Juvenile literature. 2. Pattern perception. I. Title. II. Series: Burstein, John. Math monsters.
BF294 .B87 2003

Burt, Richard, 1954-.
Shakespeare, the movie, II: popularizing the plays on film, TV, video, and DVD. London ; New York : Routledge, 2003.
PR3093 .S543 2003

Burt, Robert, 1939- Death is that man taking names : intersections of American medicine, law, and culture / Robert A. Burt. Berkeley : University of California Press ; New York : Milbank Memorial Fund, c2002. xi, 221 p. ; 24 cm. (California/Milbank books on health and the public ; 7) Includes index. Notes: p. 187-218. CONTENTS: Pursuing the good death -- Hidden death -- Death at war -- Judges and death -- Doctors and death -- Choosing death -- The death penalty -- All the days of my life. ISBN 0-520-23282-8 (cloth : alk. paper) DDC 306.9
1. Death. 2. Terminal care - United States. 3. Death - Social aspects - United States. I. Title. II. Series.
R726.8 .B875 2002

Burton, Dan. Magic, mystery, and science : the occult in Western civilization / Dan Burton and David Grandy. Bloomington : Indiana University Press, 2003. p. cm. Includes bibliographical references and index. Table of contents URL: http://www.loc.gov/catdir/toc/ecip044/2003012243.html CONTENTS: Egyptians and the occult -- Magic and miracles -- Numerology, the Cabala, and alchemy -- Astrology : the starry heavens above -- Ancient evil -- Satan, demons, and jinn -- Witches and witch-hunts in the West -- Spirits, science, and pseudo-science in the nineteenth century -- New Age preludes : up the garden path? -- ESP and psi phenomena -- Nazism and ancestral German memories -- UFOs and alien abductions -- Gnosticism, old and new -- NDEs, New Age, and new physics. ISBN 0-253-34372-0 (alk. paper) DDC 133/.09
1. Occultism - History. I. Grandy, David. II. Title.
BF1411 .B885 2003

Burton, Richard Francis, Sir, 1821-1890.
Pinkney, Andrea Marion. [Kāmasūtra. English.] The Kama Sutra illuminated. New York, N.Y. : Abrams, c2002.

Burton, Sarah, 1963- A double life : a biography of Charles and Mary Lamb / Sarah Burton. London : Viking ; New York : Penguin Putnam, 2003. x, 445 p. ; 23 cm. Includes bibliographical references (p. 391-422) and index. ISBN 0-670-89399-4 DDC 823.7
1. Lamb, Charles, - 1775-1834. 2. Lamb, Mary, - 1764-1847. 3. Brothers and sisters. 4. Authors, English - 19th century - Biography. I. Title.

Le Burundi aprés la suspension de l'embargo : aspects internes et régionaux. [Nairobi?] : International Crisis Group, [1999] 33, 4 p. ; 30 cm. (Burundi rapport ; no. 3) "27 avril 1999." Includes bibliographical references.
1. Burundi - Politics and government. 2. Burundi - Economic conditions. 3. Burundi - Ethnic relations - Political aspects. 4. Economic sanctions - Burundi. 5. Conflict management. I. International Crisis Group. II. Series: ICG Burundi report ; no. 3.

BURUNDI - ECONOMIC CONDITIONS.
Le Burundi aprés la suspension de l'embargo. [Nairobi?] : International Crisis Group, [1999]

BURUNDI - ETHNIC RELATIONS - POLITICAL ASPECTS.
Le Burundi aprés la suspension de l'embargo. [Nairobi?] : International Crisis Group, [1999]

BURUNDI - POLITICS AND GOVERNMENT.
Le Burundi aprés la suspension de l'embargo. [Nairobi?] : International Crisis Group, [1999]

Burying the past : making peace and doing justice after civil conflict / Nigel Biggar, editor. Expanded and updated. Washington, D.C. : Georgetown University Press, c2003. xvii, 350 p. ; 23 cm. "Book has its origins in a conference that was held in September 1998 at St. Antony's College, Oxford"--Acknowledgments. Includes bibliographical references and index. CONTENTS: Pt. I. Concepts. Making peace or doing justice: must we choose? / Nigel Biggar -- Where and when in political life is justice served by forgiveness? / Donald W. Shriver -- Politics and forgiveness / Jean Bethke Elshtain -- The philosophy and practice of dealing with the past: some conceptual and normative issues / Tuomas Forsberg -- Pt. II. Dimensions. Innovating responses to the past: human rights institutions / Martha Minow -- National and community reconciliation: competing agendas in South African Truth and Reconciliation Commission / Hugo van der Merwe -- Putting the past in its place: issues of victimhood and reconciliation in Northern Ireland's peace process / Marie Smyth -- Does the truth heal? A psychological perspective on political strategies for dealing with the legacy of political violence / Brandon Hamber -- Pt. III. Cases. Passion, constraint, law, and fortuna: the human rights challenge to Chilean democracy / Alexandra Barahona de Brito -- War, peace, and the politics of memory in Guatemala / Rachel Sieder -- Restorative justice in social context: the South African Truth and Reconciliation Commission / Charles Villa-Vicencio -- Rwanda: dealing with genocide and crimes against humanity in the context of armed conflict and failed political transition / Stef Vandeginste -- Northern Ireland: burying the hatchet, not the past / Terence McCaughey -- Pt. IV. Conclusion / Nigel Biggar -- Epilogue: burying the past after September 11 / Nigel Biggar. ISBN 0-87840-394-9 (pbk. : alk. paper) DDC 303.6/9
1. Restorative justice. 2. Reconciliation. 3. Civil war - Case studies. I. Biggar, Nigel.
JC578 .B49 2003

El buscador de oro : identidad personal en la nueva sociedad / Juan Arana ... [et al.]. [Madrid] : Lengua de Trapo Ediciones, c2002. 234 p. ; 21 cm. (Desórdenes Biblioteca de ensayo ; 2) Includes bibliographical references. ISBN 84-89618-88-7
1. Group identity. 2. Social perception. 3. Self-perception. 4. Perception (Philosophy) I. Arana Cañedo-Argüelles, Juan.

Buschendorf, Bernhard.
Wind, Edgar, 1900- Das Experiment und die Metaphysik. 1. Aufl. Frankfurt am Main : Suhrkamp, 2001.

Buschey, Monika. "An jenem Tag im blauen Mond September" : berühmte Liebespaare / Monika Buschey. Düsseldorf : Artemis & Winkler, c2000. 108 p. : ill. ; 23 cm. Includes bibliographical references. Radio series. ISBN 3-538-07113-6 (hd.bd.)
1. Couples - Biography. 2. Celebrities - Biography. 3. Love. I. Title.

Bush, Ronald.
Claiming the stones/naming the bones. Los Angeles : Getty Research Institute, c2002.
CC135 .C48 2002

BUSHWHACKERS. *See* **GUERRILLAS.**

BUSINESS. *See* **ADVERTISING; BUSINESS ENTERPRISES; CREATIVE ABILITY IN BUSINESS; CUSTOMER RELATIONS; INDUSTRIAL MANAGEMENT; SMALL BUSINESS; SUCCESS IN BUSINESS.**

Business @ the speed of stupid.
Burke, Dan, 1965- Cambridge, MA : Perseus Pub., c2001.
HD45 .B7995 2001

BUSINESS ADMINISTRATION. *See* **INDUSTRIAL MANAGEMENT.**

BUSINESS ALLIANCES, STRATEGIC. *See* **STRATEGIC ALLIANCES (BUSINESS).**

BUSINESS AND POLITICS - MORAL AND ETHICAL ASPECTS.
Garten, Jeffrey E., 1946- The politics of fortune. Boston : Harvard Business School Press, c2002.
HD57.7 .G377 2002

BUSINESS ANTHROPOLOGY. *See* **CORPORATE CULTURE.**

BUSINESS COMBINATIONS. *See* **CONSOLIDATION AND MERGER OF CORPORATIONS.**

BUSINESS COMMUNICATION.
Ceserani, Jonne, 1954- Big ideas. London ; Sterling, VA : Kogan Page Limited, 2002.
HD53 .C46 2002

Huotari, Maija-Leena. Trust in knowledge management and systems in organizations. Hershey, PA ; London : Idea Group Publishing, c2004.
HD30.2 .H865 2004

Plung, Daniel L. Professional communication. Mason, Ohio : Thomson/South-Western, c2004.
HF5718 .P58 2004

BUSINESS CONSULTANTS.
The expansion of management knowledge. Stanford, Calif. : Stanford Business Books, c2002.
HD31 .E873 2002

Holmes, Andrew, 1965- The chameleon consultant. Aldershot ; Burlington, VT : Gower, 2002.

BUSINESS CORPORATIONS. *See* **CORPORATIONS.**

BUSINESS CREATIVITY. *See* **CREATIVE ABILITY IN BUSINESS.**

BUSINESS CYCLES. *See* **BUSINESS FORECASTING; FINANCIAL CRISES.**

BUSINESS EDUCATION.
The expansion of management knowledge. Stanford, Calif. : Stanford Business Books, c2002.
HD31 .E873 2002

BUSINESS ENTERPRISES. *See also* **CORPORATIONS; INTERNATIONAL BUSINESS ENTERPRISES.**
Best practice. Cambridge, MA : Perseus Publishing, c2003.

BUSINESS ENTERPRISES, INTERNATIONAL. *See* **INTERNATIONAL BUSINESS ENTERPRISES.**

BUSINESS ENTERPRISES - MANAGEMENT. *See* **INDUSTRIAL MANAGEMENT.**

BUSINESS ENTERPRISES - TECHNOLOGICAL INNOVATIONS.
Tsai, Hui-Liang. Information technology and business process reengineering. Westport, Conn. : Praeger, 2003.
HD58.87 .T73 2003

BUSINESS ETHICS.
Business, religion, & spirituality. Notre Dame, Ind. : University of Notre Dame Press, c2003.
HF5388 .B87 2003

Celli, Pier Luigi. Breviario di cinismo ben temperato. 1. ed. Roma : Fazi, 2002.

Galford, Robert M., 1952- The trusted leader. New York ; London : Free Press, c2002.
HD57.7 .G33 2002

Garten, Jeffrey E., 1946- The politics of fortune. Boston : Harvard Business School Press, c2002.
HD57.7 .G377 2002

Golin, Al, 1929- Trust or consequences. New York : American Management Association, c2004.
HF5387 .G65 2004

Vardi, Yoav, 1944- Misbehavior in organizations. Mahwah, NJ ; London : Lawrence Erlbaum, 2004.
HD58.7 .V367 2004

Ward, William Aidan. Trust and mistrust. Chichester, England ; Hoboken, NJ : John Wiley & Sons, c2003.
HD69.S8 W37 2003

BUSINESS ETIQUETTE.
Sethi, S. Prakash. Setting global standards. Hoboken, N.J. : J. Wiley, c2003.
HD62.4 .S48 2003

BUSINESS EXECUTIVES. *See* **EXECUTIVES.**

BUSINESS FAILURES. *See also* **SUCCESS IN BUSINESS.**
Finkelstein, Sydney. Why smart executives fail and what you can learn from their mistakes. New York ; London : Portfolio, 2003.
HD38.2 .F56 2003

BUSINESS - FORECASTING. *See* **BUSINESS FORECASTING.**

BUSINESS FORECASTING - MISCELLANEA.
McElroy, Mark, 1964- Putting the tarot to work. 1st ed. St. Paul, Minn. : Llewellyn Publications, 2004.
BF1879.T2 M43 2004

BUSINESS FORECASTS. *See* **BUSINESS FORECASTING.**

BUSINESS MANAGEMENT. *See* **INDUSTRIAL MANAGEMENT.**

BUSINESS MEN. *See* **BUSINESSMEN.**

BUSINESS MERGERS. *See* **CONSOLIDATION AND MERGER OF CORPORATIONS.**

BUSINESS NAMES. *See* **BRAND NAME PRODUCTS.**

BUSINESS NETWORKS. *See also* **STRATEGIC ALLIANCES (BUSINESS).**
Boothman, Nicholas. How to connect in business in 90 seconds or less. New York : Workman Pub., 2002.
HD69.S8 B66 2002

Implementing collaboration technologies in industry. London ; New York : Springer, c2003.
HD30.2 .I38 2003

Thompson, Grahame. Between hierarchies and markets. Oxford ; New York : Oxford University Press, 2003.
HD58.7 .T4786 2003

BUSINESS ORGANIZATIONS. *See* **BUSINESS ENTERPRISES.**

BUSINESS PEOPLE. *See* **BUSINESSPEOPLE.**

BUSINESS PERSONS. *See* **BUSINESSPEOPLE.**

BUSINESS PLANNING. *See also* **STRATEGIC PLANNING.**
Lindgren, Mats, 1959- Scenario planning. Houndmills [England] ; New York : Palgrave Macmillan, 2002.
HD30.28 .L543 2002

McAfee, R. Preston. Competitive solutions. Princeton, N.J. : Princeton University Press, c2002.
HD30.28 .M3815 2002

Business process change.
Harmon, Paul, 1942- Amsterdam ; Boston : Morgan Kaufmann, c2003.
HD58.8 .H37 2003

BUSINESS PROCESS REENGINEERING. *See* **REENGINEERING (MANAGEMENT).**

BUSINESS PSYCHOLOGY. *See* **PSYCHOLOGY, INDUSTRIAL.**

Business, religion, & spirituality : a new synthesis / edited by Oliver F. Williams. Notre Dame, Ind. : University of Notre Dame Press, c2003. vii, 323 p. ; 24 cm. (The John W. Houck Notre Dame series in business ethics) Includes bibliographical references and index. ISBN 0-268-02173-2 (alk. paper) ISBN 0-268-02174-0 (pbk. : alk. paper) DDC 291.1/785
1. Business - Religious aspects. 2. Business ethics. 3. Spiritual life. I. Williams, Oliver F. II. Title: Business, religion, and spirituality III. Series.

HF5388 .B87 2003

Business, religion, and spirituality.
Business, religion, & spirituality. Notre Dame, Ind. : University of Notre Dame Press, c2003.
HF5388 .B87 2003

BUSINESS - RELIGIOUS ASPECTS.
Business, religion, & spirituality. Notre Dame, Ind. : University of Notre Dame Press, c2003.
HF5388 .B87 2003

BUSINESSMEN - GREAT BRITAIN - BIOGRAPHY.
Dudgeon, Piers. Breaking out of the box. London : Headline, 2001.
BF109.D39 D83 2001

Rose, Kenneth, 1924- Elusive Rothschild. London : Weidenfeld & Nicolson, 2003.

BUSINESSPEOPLE. *See* **BUSINESSMEN.**

BUSINESSPEOPLE - CHINA - BIOGRAPHY.
Zhongguo, shui zui fu. Di 1 ban. Beijing : Qi ye guan li chu ban she, 2001.
HC426.5.A2 Z457 2001

BUSINESSPERSONS. *See* **BUSINESSPEOPLE.**

BusinessThink.
Marcum, Dave. New York : Wiley, c2002.
HF5386 .M3087 2002

BUSINESSWOMEN.
Israel-Curley, Marcia. Defying the odds. 1st ed. Woodstock, N.Y. : Overlook Press, 2002.
HB615 .I75 2002

Kazerounian, Nadine. Stepping up. London : McGraw-Hill, c2002.

Buss, David M. The evolution of desire : strategies of human mating / David M. Buss. Rev. ed. New York : BasicBooks, c2003. x, 354 p. Includes bibliographical references (p. [304]-331) and index. ISBN 0-465-00802-X DDC 306.7
1. Sex. 2. Sex (Psychology) 3. Sexual attraction. I. Title.

Evolutionary psychology : the new science of the mind / David M. Buss. 2nd ed. Boston, MA : Allyn and Bacon, 2003. p. cm. Includes bibliographical references and index. ISBN 0-205-37071-3 DDC 155.7
1. Evolutionary psychology. 2. Human evolution. I. Title.
BF698.95 .B87 2003

Butler, Christopher, 1940- Postmodernism : a very short introduction / Christopher Butler. Oxford ; New York : Oxford University Press, 2002. 142 p. : ill. ; 18 cm. (Very short introductions) "First published as a Very Short Introduction 2002"--T.p. verso. Includes bibliographical references (p. 129-131) and index. ISBN 0-19-280239-9 DDC 700/.4113
1. Postmodernism. I. Title. II. Series.
NX456.5.P66 B88 2002

Butt, Trevor, 1947- Understanding people / Trevor Butt. New York : Palgrave Macmillan, 2003. p. cm. Includes bibliographical references and index. ISBN 1403904650 ISBN 1403904669 (pbk.) DDC 155.2
1. Personality. 2. Personal construct theory. 3. Phenomenological psychology. I. Title.
BF698 .B89 2003

Butterfield, Elizabeth.
Laing, Kathleen. Girlfriends' getaway. 1st ed. Colorado Springs, Colo. : WaterBrook Press, 2002.
BF575.F66 L35 2002

Butterfield, Perry M., 1932- Emotional connections : how relationships guide early learning / by Perry Butterfield, Carole A. Martin, Arleen Pratt Prairie. Washington, DC : Zero To Three, 2004. p. cm. Includes bibliographical references and index. Table of contents URL: http://www.loc.gov/catdir/toc/ecip042/2003008724.html ISBN 0-943657-64-4 DDC 649/.1/0248
1. Emotions in infants. 2. Emotions in children. 3. Children and adults. I. Martin, Carole A. II. Prairie, Arleen. III. Title.
BF720.E45 B879 2004

Emotional connections : how relationships guide early learning : instructor's guide / by Perry Butterfield, Carole A. Martin, Arleen Pratt Prairie. 1st ed. Washington, DC : Zero To Three, c2003. p. cm. Includes bibliographical references and index. Table of contents URL: http://www.loc.gov/catdir/toc/ecip042/2003008384.html CONTENTS: Relationships nurture early learning -- The caregiver builds relationships -- Relationships are emotional connections -- Relationships foster a positive sense of self -- Responsive relationships model and promote social skills -- Relationships guide and regulate behavior -- Relationships promote learning and cognition -- Relationships promote language and literacy -- Relationships with families -- Making responsive relationships work in your program. ISBN 0-943657-63-6 DDC 649/.1/0248

1. Emotions in infants - Study and teaching (Higher) 2. Emotions in children - Study and teaching (Higher) 3. Children and adults - Study and teaching (Higher) I. Martin, Carole A. II. Prairie, Arleen. III. Title.
BF720.E45 B88 2003

Butz, Martin V., 1975-.
Workshop on Adaptive Behavior in Anticipatory Learning Systems (1st : 2002 : Edinburgh, Scotland) Anticipatory behavior in adaptive learning systems. Berlin ; New York : Springer, c2003.
Q325.5 .W65 2003

Buxani, Shyam D. Salam : divine revelations from the Actual God / Shyam D. Buxani. 1st ed. New York : SAU Salam Foundation, c2003. 600 p. : ill. ; 24 cm. Includes bibliographical references. ISBN 0-9723955-3-9
1. Spiritual life. 2. Private revelations. 3. God. I. SAU Salam Foundation. II. Title. III. Title: Actual God

BUYER BEHAVIOR. *See* **CONSUMER BEHAVIOR.**

BUYOUTS, CORPORATE. *See* **CONSOLIDATION AND MERGER OF CORPORATIONS.**

By his light.
Ziegler, Reuven. 2nd ed. Jersey City, NJ : KTAV Pub. House ; Alon Shevut, Israel : Yeshivat Har Etzion, 2003.
BM723 .Z54 2003

By the torch of chaos and doubt.
Burneko, Guy Christian. Cresskill, N.J. : Hampton Press, c2003.
BD431 .B84 2003

Bychkov, V. V. (Viktor Vasil'evich) Ėstetika / V.V. Bychkov. Moskva : Gardariki, 2002. 556 p. ; 22 cm. Includes bibliographical references and indexes. Autographed by the author.
1. Aesthetics. I. Title.

Bye-bye, bully!.
Jackson, J. S. St. Meinrad, IN. : Abbey Press, c2003.
BF637.B85 J33 2003

Byington, Carlos Amadeu Botelho, 1933-
[Inveja criativa. English]
Creative envy : the rescue of one of civilization's major forces / Carlos Amadeu Botelho Byington ; translation by Penelope Freeland. 1st American ed. Wilmette, Ill. : Chiron Publications, 2004. p. cm. Includes bibliographical references and index. ISBN 1-88860-230-9 (pbk.) DDC 152.4/8
1. Envy. I. Title.
BF575.E65 B95 2004

Byock, Ira. The four things that matter most : essential wisdom for transforming your relationships and your life / Ira Byock. New York : Free Press, 2004. p. cm. Includes index. ISBN 0-7432-4909-7 DDC 158.2
1. Interpersonal communication. 2. Interpersonal relations. 3. Conduct of life. I. Title.
BF637.C45 B93 2004

Byrd, Da Juana. Ghosts talk / Da Juana Byrd. 1st ed. Cedar Hills, Tex. : Byrd Pub., c2002. 301 p. ; 24 cm. ISBN 0-9702663-2-4 DDC 133.9
1. Psychic ability. 2. Spiritualism. 3. Channeling (Spiritualism) 4. Byrd, Da Juana. I. Title.
BF1031 .B97 2002

BYRD, DA JUANA.
Byrd, Da Juana. Ghosts talk. 1st ed. Cedar Hills, Tex. : Byrd Pub., c2002.
BF1031 .B97 2002

BYZANTINE EMPIRE - CIVILIZATION - 527-1081.
Antiquity renewed. Leuven, Netherlands ; Dudley, MA : Peeters, 2003.
CB365 .A58 2003

BYZANTINE EMPIRE - CIVILIZATION - CLASSICAL INFLUENCES.
Antiquity renewed. Leuven, Netherlands ; Dudley, MA : Peeters, 2003.
CB365 .A58 2003

BYZANTINE EMPIRE - CIVILIZATION - STUDY AND TEACHING.
Speck, Paul. [Selections. English. 1999]
Understanding Byzantium. Aldershot, Great Britain ; Burlington, Vt. : Ashgate/Variorum, c2003.
DF503 .S742513 2003

BYZANTINE EMPIRE - CIVILIZATION - TO 527.
Antiquity renewed. Leuven, Netherlands ; Dudley, MA : Peeters, 2003.
CB365 .A58 2003

BYZANTINE EMPIRE - HISTORY - SOURCES.
Speck, Paul. [Selections. English. 1999]
Understanding Byzantium. Aldershot, Great Britain ; Burlington, Vt. : Ashgate/Variorum, c2003.
DF503 .S742513 2003

BYZANTINE ICONS. *See* **ICONS, BYZANTINE.**

BYZANTINE LITERATURE. *See* **GREEK LITERATURE.**

BYZANTINE LITERATURE - HISTORY AND CRITICISM.
Speck, Paul. [Selections. English. 1999]
Understanding Byzantium. Aldershot, Great Britain ; Burlington, Vt. : Ashgate/Variorum, c2003.
DF503 .S742513 2003

BYZANTINE MURAL PAINTING AND DECORATION. *See* **MURAL PAINTING AND DECORATION, BYZANTINE.**

C CORPORATIONS. *See* **CORPORATIONS.**

Ca dha ba va manomaya.
Hin'" Lat'. Kyok' taṃ tā", [Rangoon] : Yuṃ kraññ' khyak' Cā pe : Pran'' khyi re", Rve Nan'" Mhan' kū Cā 'up' Tuik', 2002.
BF1434.B93 H56 2002

Ca le cha rā krī" Ū" Puññā bedaṅ' 'a ho te" thap' 'a phvaṅ' kyaṃ'".
Mraṅ'' Svaṅ', Ū", Ran' kun' : Khyui Te" Saṃ Cā pe : [Phran'' khyi re"], Paññā Rvhe Toṅ' Cā 'up' Tuik', 2002.
BF1714.B8 M73 2002

CAAPI. *See* **AYAHUASCA.**

CABALA. *See also* **KAVVANOT (CABALA); SEFIROT (CABALA).**
Abi-Ḥasira, Jacob ben Masoud, 1808-1880. [Abir Ya'akov. Selections. 2002] Sefer Penine Avir Ya'akov. Yerushalayim : Hotsa'at ha-Makhon le-hotsa'at sefarim she-'a. y. Yeshivat Ner Yitshak : Mekhon Avraham : Shim'on Abiḥatsira, 763 [2002]
BS1485.X33 A25 2002

Alter, Judah Aryeh Leib, 1847-1905. [Śefat emet (Torah). Selections] Sefer Śefat emet. Yerushalayim : Mir, 762 [2001 or 2002]

Armoni, Mosheh Ḥayim. Sefer Ginze Armoni. Yerushalayim : 'Amutat "Naḥalat-Raḥel", 762 [2002]
BM670.S5 A756 2002

Ashcroft-Nowicki, Dolores. Illuminations. 1st ed. St. Paul, Minn. : Llewellyn Publications, 2003.
BF1623.C2 A84 2003

Ben Ratson-Lahat, Tsiyon. Sefer ha-Nistarot yeha-niglot. [Israel? : ḥ. mo. l.], 761 i.e. 2001?]

Cordovero, Moses ben Jacob, 1522-1570. Sefer Mesilot teshuvah. Bene Berak : Da'at ḳedoshim, 762 [2002]
BM645.R45 C67 2002

Eleazar ben Judah, of Worms, 1176 (ca.)-1238. Sefer Sode razaya .... Bene-Berak : Ḳorah, 759 [1998 or 1999]
BM525 .E432 1999

Elior, Rachel. Ḥerut 'al ha-luḥot. [Tel Aviv] : Miśrad ha-biṭaḥon, [1999]

Eliyahu, Saliman. Sefer Kerem Shelomoh. Yerushala[y]im : Ḥevrat Ahavat shalom, 762 [2001 or 2002]

['Ets ha-tidhar.] Sidur kavanot 'Ets ha-tidhar. Yerushalayim : Kolel Shemen śaśon, [1998?]
1. Keri'at shema 'al ha-mitah.

Ginzburg, Yitshak. Rectifying the state of Israel. 1st ed. Jerusalem : Gal Einai ; Cedarhurst, NY : For information address, Gal Einai Institute, c2002.

Glazerson, Matityahu. Migdele ha-te'omim be-diluge otiyot ba-Torah. Yerushalayim : Yerid ha-sefarim, 2002.

Green, Arthur, 1941- Ehyeh. Woodstock, Vt. : Jewish Lights Publishing, c2003.
BM525 .G84 2003

Ḥalfon, Eliyahu ben Ḥayim. Shir ha-shirim. [Israel] : Or tsaḥ hadpasah ve-hafatsah shel sipre Yahadut, [2001]

Hall, Manly Palmer, 1901- The secret teachings of all ages. Reader's ed. New York : Jeremy P. Tarcher/Putnam, 2003.
BF1411 .H3 2003

Hilel, Ya'akov Mosheh. Sefer Ahavat shalom. [Hotsa'ah 2], 'im hosafot rabot. Yerushala[y]im : ha-Makhon le-hotsa'at sefarim ve-khitve yad "Ahavat Shalom", 762 [2002]

Hilel, Ya'akov Mosheh. Sefer Shorshe ha-Yam. Yerushalayim : ha-Makhon le-hotsa'at sefarim "Ahavat shalom", 759- [1999-
BM525.V532 H5 1999

Hoeller, Stephan A. [Royal road] The fool's pilgrimage. 2nd Quest ed. Wheaton, Ill. : Quest Books/Theosophical Pub. House, 2004.
BF1879.T2 H6 2004

Kanalenstein, Ruben. La palabra. Los rostros. Córdoba, Argentina : Alción, 2000.

Kiefer, Anselm, 1945- Merkaba. New York : Gagosian Gallery, c2002.
N6888.K43 A4 2002

Ḳoraḥ, Shelomoh ben Yaḥya. Netsaḥ ḥayenu. Bene Berak : S. Ḳoraḥ, 762 [2001 or 2002]

Laïtman, Mikhaël'. A guide to the hidden wisdom of kabbalah. Thornhill, Ont. : Laitman Kabbalah Publishers, 2002.

Leibniz, Gottfried Wilhelm, Freiherr von, 1646-1716. Réfutation inédite de Spinoza. Arles [France] : Actes Sud ; [Montréal] : Leméac, 1999.

Luzzatto, Moshe Ḥayyim, 1707-1747. Ḳitsur 138 pitḥe ḥokhmah. Yerushalayim : Mekhon Hadrat Yerushalayim, 761 [2000 or 2001]

Mantovani, Massimo. Meditazioni sull'albero della cabala. Milano : Xenia, 2002.

Milshtein, Mosheh. Sefer Even shetiyah. Bruklin : [Lee Printing corp.], 758- [1998-

Naphtali ben Isaac, ha-Kohen, 1649-1719. Sefer Bet Rahel. Yerushalayim : Ahavat Shalom, 761 [2001]
BM665 .N257 2001

Sack, Bracha, 1933- Shomer ha-pardes. Be'er Sheva' : Universiṭat Ben-Guryon ba-Negev, c2002.

Sasson, Gahl. A wish can change your life. New York : Simon & Schuster, 2003.
BF1623.C2 S27 2003

Sefer 'Amude ha-Ḳabalah. Yerushalayim : Nezer Sheraga, 761 [2001]

Seidman, Richard. The oracle of Kabbalah. 1st ed. New York : St. Martin's Press, 2001.
PJ4589 .S42 2001

Sharir, Avraham Yiśra'el. Pene Shabat neḳablah. Yerushalayim : Avraham Kohen-Erez, 763 [2003]
BM670.L44 S527 2003

Shelomoh ben Hayim Haiḳel. Sefer Liḳuṭe u-ferushe niglot Leshem shevo ve-aḥlamah. Kiryat Sefer : Mosheh Vais, 762 [2002]
BM525 .H4332 2002

Steinsaltz, Adin. [Be'ur Tanya. English] Opening the Tanya. 1st ed. San Francisco : Jossey-Bass, c2003.
BM198.2.S563 S7413 2003

Ta-Shma, Israel M. ha-Nigleh sheba-nistar. Nusaḥ murhav. [Tel Aviv] : ha-Ḳibuts ha-me'uḥad, c2001.

Vainshtoḳ, Bentsiyon Mosheh Ya'ir ben Mordekhai David. Sefer Or ha-da'at. Yerushalayim : ha-Makhon le-hotsa'at sifre ha-g. R. M.Y. Vainshtoḳ, 762 [2001 or 2002]

Vital, Ḥayyim ben Joseph, 1542 or 3-1620. 'Ets ha-da'at tov. Yerushalayim : Hotsa'at Ahavat shalom, 761 [2000 or 2001]

[Zohar ḥadash.] Sefer Zohar ḥadash. Yerushalayim : Mekhon Da'at Yosef ; Brooklyn, N.Y. (225 Division Ave., Brooklyn 11211) : Le-haśig, B. Daskal, 760- [1999 or 2000-
BM525.A6 Z6+

[Zohar ḥadash. Lamentations. 2000.] Zohar ḥadash Megilat Ekhah. "Hotsa'ah meyuḥedet li-yeme ben ha-metsarim". Yerushalayim : Mekhon Da'at Yosef, 761 [2000 or 2001]
BM525.A6 Z6 2001

Caballero, Rufo, 1966- Sedición en la pasarela : cómo narra el cine posmoderno / Rufo Caballero ; prólogo de Julio García Espinosa. La Habana, Cuba : Editorial Arte y Literatura, c2001. 215 p. : ill. ; 21 cm. Includes bibliographical references (p. 203-208) and index. ISBN 9590301576
1. Motion pictures - History. 2. Postmodernism. I. Title. II. Title: Cómo narra el cine posmoderno

CABINET OFFICERS. *See* **PRIME MINISTERS.**

Cabinets of curiosities.
Mauriès, Patrick, 1952- New York : Thames & Hudson, c2002.
AM221 .M38 2002

CABINETS OF CURIOSITIES - EUROPE - HISTORY.
Mauriès, Patrick, 1952- Cabinets of curiosities. New York : Thames & Hudson, c2002.
AM221 .M38 2002

Cable competition and the EchoStar-DIRECTV merger.
United States. Congress. Senate. Committee on the Judiciary. Subcommittee on Antitrust, Business Rights, and Competition. Dominance in the sky. [Washington] : U.S. G.P.O. : For sale by the Supt. of Docs., U.S. G.P.O. [Congressional Sales Office], 2003.

CABLE TELEVISION - LAW AND LEGISLATION - UNITED STATES.
United States. Congress. Senate. Committee on the Judiciary. Subcommittee on Antitrust, Business Rights, and Competition. Dominance on the ground. Washington : U.S. G.P.O. : For sale by the Supt. of Docs., U.S. G.P.O. [Congressional Sales Office], 2003.

CABLE TELEVISION - UNITED STATES.
United States. Congress. House. Committee on the Judiciary. Direct broadcast satellite service in the multichannel video distribution market. Washington : U.S. G.P.O. For sale by the Supt. of Docs., U.S. G.P.O. [Congressional Sales Office], 2003.

United States. Congress. Senate. Committee on the Judiciary. Subcommittee on Antitrust, Business Rights, and Competition. Dominance in the sky. [Washington] : U.S. G.P.O. : For sale by the Supt. of Docs., U.S. G.P.O. [Congressional Sales Office], 2003.

CABLE TV. *See* **CABLE TELEVISION.**

Cabot, Catharine Rush. Jung, my mother and I : the analytic diaries of Catharine Rush Cabot / edited and narrated by Jane Cabot Reid. Einsiedeln : Daimon, 2001. 623 p. : ill., facsims. ; 24 cm. Includes bibliographical references (p. [615]-616) and index. ISBN 3-85630-601-3
1. Cabot, Catharine Rush - Diaries. 2. Jung, C. G. - (Carl Gustav), - 1875-1961. 3. Psychotherapy patients - Switzerland - Zurich - Diaries. 4. Psychotherapist and patient - Switzerland - Zurich. 5. Psychoanalysis. I. Title.

CABOT, CATHARINE RUSH - DIARIES.
Cabot, Catharine Rush. Jung, my mother and I. Einsiedeln : Daimon, 2001.

Cabrera, Derek. Remedial genius : think and learn like a genius with the five principles of knowledge / by Derek Cabrera. 1st ed. Loveland, Colo. : Project N Press, 2001. vii, 161 p. : ill. ; 24 cm. ISBN 0-9708045-0-4
1. Thought and thinking. 2. Meaning (Psychology) 3. Learning, Psychology of. I. Title.
BF441 .C23 2001

Cabrera Infante, G. (Guillermo), 1929-.
Amores de película. 1. ed. [Madrid] : Aguilar, 2002.
PN1998.2 .A46 2002

Cacciatore, Giuseppe, 1945- L'etica dello storicismo / Giuseppe Cacciatore. Lecce : Milella, 2000. 254 p. ; 25 cm. (Collana di cultura filosofica) Includes bibliographical references and index. ISBN 88-7048-362-2 DDC 149
1. History - Philosophy. 2. Ethics. I. Title. II. Series.

CACIQUES (INDIAN LEADERS) - MEXICO - MICHOACÁN DE OCAMPO - HISTORY.
Guerra Manzo, Enrique. Caciquismo y orden público en Michoacán, 1920-1940. 1. ed. México : El Colegio de México, Centro de Estudios Sociológicos, c2002.
F1219.3.P7 G84 2002

Caciquismo y orden público en Michoacán, 1920-1940.
Guerra Manzo, Enrique. 1. ed. México : El Colegio de México, Centro de Estudios Sociológicos, c2002.
F1219.3.P7 G84 2002

Cadernos de psicologia (Belo Horizonte, Brazil : 1993).
Psicologia em revista. Belo Horizonte : Editora PUC Minas, 2000-
BF5 .C24

CADRE paper
(11.) Zentner, John J., 1965- The art of wing leadership and aircrew morale in combat [electronic resource]. Maxwell Air Force Base, Ala. : Air University Press, [2001]

Caesar against liberty? : perspectives on his autocracy / edited by Francis Cairns and Elaine Fantham. Cambridge : Francis Cairns, c2003. xxi, 232 p. ; 22 cm. (ARCA, classical medieval texts, papers and monographs ; 43) (Papers of the Langford Latin Seminar ; 11) Includes bibliographical references (p. 201-220) and indexes. ISBN 0-905205-39-1
1. Caesar, Julius. 2. Rome - History - 53-44 B.C. 3. Liberty. I. Cairns, Francis. II. Fantham, Elaine. III. Series. IV. Series: Papers of the Langford Latin Seminar ; 11

CAESAR, JULIUS.
Caesar against liberty? Cambridge : Francis Cairns, c2003.

CAESARISM. *See* **IMPERIALISM.**

Les cahiers de médiologie
(15) Faire face. Paris : Gallimard, [2002]

Cahiers de philosophie ancienne
(no 18) Collette, Bernard. Dialectique et hénologie chez Plotin. Bruxelles : Ousia, c2002.
B693.Z7 C655 2002

Les cahiers du CEFRESS
Itinéraires de l'imaginaire. Paris : L'Harmattan, c1999.
BF408 .I86 1999

Cahiers du SRED
(no. 7.) Ducret, Jean-Jacques, 1946- Jean Piaget, 1868-1979. Genève, Switzerland : Service de la recherche en éducation, c2000.
BF311 .D813 2000

Cahiers lausannois d'histoire médiévale
(25) Modestin, Georg. Le diable chez l'évêque. Lausanne : Université de Lausanne, Section d'histoire, Faculté des lettres, 1999.
BF1584.S9 M64 1999

Cahill, Ann J.
Continental feminism reader. Lanham, Md. : Rowman & Littlefield Publishers, c2003.
HQ1075 .C668 2003

Cahn, Steven M. Puzzles & perplexities : collected essays / Steven M. Cahn. Lanham, Md. ; Oxford : Rowman & Littlefield, c2002. ix, 137 p. ; 24 cm. Includes bibliographical references (p. 127-131) and index. ISBN 0-7425-1422-6 (hbk. : alk. paper) ISBN 0-7425-1423-4 (pbk. : alk. paper) DDC 191
1. Philosophy. 2. Education - Philosophy. I. Title. II. Title: Puzzles and perplexities
BD41 .C26 2002

Cai, Yuanpei, 1868-1940.
[Selections. 1996]
Cai Yuanpei juan / bian jiao zhe Ouyang Zhesheng. Di 1 ban. Shijiazhuang Shi : Hebei jiao yu chu ban she, 1996. 76, 2, 4, 8, 471 p. ; 22 cm. (Zhongguo xian dai xue shu jing dian) Spine title: Zhongguo xian dai xue shu jing dian. Tai Yuanpei juan. "Cai Yuanpei xian sheng zhu yi yao mu": p. 460-471. Includes bibliographical references. ISBN 7-5434-2843-1
1. Cao, Xueqin, - ca. 1717-1763. - Hong lou meng. 2. Ethics - China - History. 3. Conduct of life. 4. Education - China. I. Ouyang, Zhesheng, 1962- II. Title. III. Title: Zhongguo xian dai xue shu jing dian. Tai Yuanpei juan
BJ117 .T74 1996 <Asian China>

Cai Yuanpei juan.
Cai, Yuanpei, 1868-1940. [Selections. 1996] Di 1 ban. Shijiazhuang Shi : Hebei jiao yu chu ban she, 1996.
BJ117 .T74 1996 <Asian China>

Cai zhi li lian xi lie
Yazi. Qing hua Bei da xue bu dao. Di 1 ban. Beijing : Xin hua chu ban she, 2002.
BJ1618.C5 Y38 2002

Cai, Zhichun. Huo fo zhuan shi / Cai Zhichun, Huang Hao zhu. Di 1 ban. Beijing : Hua wen chu ban she ; Xin hua shu dian jing xiao, 2000. 3, 4, 257 p., [16] p. of plates : ill. ; 21 cm. (Xizang shi dian cong shu) Includes bibliographical references. ISBN 7-5075-0912-5
1. Reincarnation. 2. Buddhism - China - Tibet. 3. Lamas - Biography. I. Huang, Hao. II. Title. III. Series.
BL515 .C345 2000

Caillois, Roger, 1913- The edge of surrealism : a Roger Caillois reader / by Roger Caillois ; edited and with an introduction by Claudine Frank ; translated by Claudine Frank and Camille Naish. Durham : Duke University Press, 2003. 423 p. : ill. ; 25 cm. Includes bibliographical references (p. [401]-413) and index. ISBN 0-8223-3056-3 (cloth : alk. paper) ISBN 0-8223-3068-7 (pbk. : alk. paper) DDC 301/.01
1. Sociology - Philosophy. 2. Religion and sociology. 3. Tales - Themes, motives. 4. Rites and ceremonies. I. Frank, Claudine, 1957- II. Title.
HM590 .C35 2003

CAIN (BIBLICAL FIGURE) - PSYCHOLOGY.
Cannac, Edith. Caïn ou le détournement du sens. [Paris] : Plon, c2002.

CAIN COMPLEX.
Cannac, Edith. Caïn ou le détournement du sens. [Paris] : Plon, c2002.

Caïn ou le détournement du sens.
Cannac, Edith. [Paris] : Plon, c2002.

Cairns, Francis.
Caesar against liberty? Cambridge : Francis Cairns, c2003.

CAIRO (EGYPT) - SOCIAL LIFE AND CUSTOMS.
El-Kholy, Heba Aziz. Defiance and compliance. New York : Berghahn Books, 2002.
HQ1793.Z9 C353 2002

Una cala en la literatura religiosa sefardí.
Aboab, Isaac, 14th cent. [Menorat ha-ma'or. Ladino] Granada : Universidad de Granada, 2001.
BJ1287.A152 L33 2001

Calaba, Jeannine Lemare.
Nelson, Noelle C. The power of appreciation. Hillsboro, Or. : Beyond Words Pub., c2003.
BF575.G68 N45 2003

Calame, Claude.
[Mythe et histoire dans l'antiquité grecque. English]
Myth and history in ancient Greece : the symbolic creation of a colony / Claude Calame ; translated by Daniel W. Berman. Princeton, N.J. : Princeton University Press, c2003. xvii, 178 p. ; 25 cm. Includes bibliographical references (p. [165]-171) and index. ISBN 0-691-11458-7 (alk. paper) DDC 292.1/3
1. Mythology, Greek. 2. Cyrene (Extinct city) I. Title.
BL783 .C3513 2003

Calame-Griaule, Geneviève.
Hurbon, Laënnec. Dieu dans le vaudou haïtien. Nouv. éd. Paris : Maisonneuve et Larose, 2002.
1. Black author.

CALAMITIES. *See* **DISASTERS.**

CALCULATORS. *See* **COMPUTERS.**

Caldwell, George, synthesizer player.
Vint/age 2001 conference : [videorecording]. New York, c2001.

Caldwell, Lesley.
The elusive child. London ; New York : Karnac, c2002.

CALENDAR.
Hardie, Titania. Titania's book of hours. London : Quadrille, 2002.

CALENDAR, CELTIC.
Vega, Phyllis. Celtic astrology. Franklin Lakes, NJ : New Page Books, c2002.
BF1714.C44 V44 2002

CALENDAR - EUROPE - HISTORY - TO 1500.
Brincken, Anna-Dorothee von den. Historische Chronologie des Abendlandes. Stuttgart : Kohlhammer, 2000.

CALENDAR, HINDU.
Śāstrī, Girijā Śaṅkara. Bhāratīya Kuṇḍalī-vimarśa. 1. saṃskaraṇa. Ilāhābāda : Jyotiṣa Karmakāṇḍa evaṃ Adhyātma Śodha Saṃsthāna, 2002.
BF1714.H5+

CALENDAR - REFORM. *See* **CALENDAR REFORM.**

CALENDAR REFORM.
Brincken, Anna-Dorothee von den. Historische Chronologie des Abendlandes. Stuttgart : Kohlhammer, 2000.

CALENDAR REFORM - MISCELLANEA.
Argüelles, José, 1939- Time and the technosphere. Rochester, Vt. : Bear & Co., c2002.
BF1999 .A6398 2002

CALENDAR, RELIGIOUS. *See* **RELIGIOUS CALENDARS.**

CALENDAR, SLAVIC.
Asov, A. I. (Aleksandr Igorevich) Slavi͡anskai͡a astrologii͡a. Moskva : Fair-Press : Grand, 2001.
BF1714.S58 A86 2001

Asov, A. I. (Aleksandr Igorevich) Slavi͡anskai͡a astrologii͡a. Moskva : FAIR-PRESS, 2001.

CALENDARS, RELIGIOUS. *See* **RELIGIOUS CALENDARS.**

Caliandro, Arthur. Lost and found : the 23 things you can do to find personal freedom / Arthur Caliandro with Barry Lenson. 1st ed. New York : McGraw-Hill, 2003. p. cm. Table of contents URL: http://www.loc.gov/catdir/toc/ecip047/2003018132.html ISBN 0-07-140862-2 (hardcover : alk. paper) DDC 158
1. Self-actualization (Psychology) I. Lenson, Barry. II. Title.
BF637.S4 .C32 2003

Califia-Rice, Patrick, 1954- Speaking sex to power : the politics of queer sex / Patrick Califia. 1st ed. San Francisco : Cleis Press, c2002. xxiv, 419 p. ; 22 cm. Includes bibliographical references and index. ISBN 1-57344-132-5 DDC 306.76/6
1. Homosexuality. 2. Transsexualism. 3. Sadomasochism. 4. Gay men. 5. Lesbians. 6. Homophobia. 7. AIDS (Disease) - Social aspects. I. Title.
HQ76.25 .C32 2002

California ghosts.
Dennett, Preston E., 1965- Atglen, PA : Schiffer Pub., 2004.
BF1472.U6 D46 2004

CALIFORNIA - HISTORY.
Didion, Joan. Where I was from. 1st ed. New York : Alfred A. Knopf : Distributed by Random House, 2003.
F861 .D53 2003

CALIFORNIA - IN LITERATURE.
Didion, Joan. Where I was from. 1st ed. New York : Alfred A. Knopf : Distributed by Random House, 2003.
F861 .D53 2003

California/Milbank books on health and the public
(7) Burt, Robert, 1939- Death is that man without names. Berkeley : University of California Press ; New York : Milbank Memorial Fund, c2002.
R726.8 .B875 2002

CALIFORNIA - SOCIAL CONDITIONS.
Didion, Joan. Where I was from. 1st ed. New York : Alfred A. Knopf : Distributed by Random House, 2003.
F861 .D53 2003

Didion, Joan. Where I was from. 1st ed. New York : Alfred A. Knopf : Distributed by Random House, 2003.
F861 .D53 2003

Callahan, Sidney Cornelia. Women who hear voices : the challenge of religious experience / Sidney Callahan. New York : Paulist Press, 2003. 126 p. ; 18 cm. (2003 Madeleva lecture in spirituality) Includes bibliographical references (p. 116-126). ISBN 0-8091-4198-1
1. Private revelations. 2. Experience (Religion) in women. 3. Catholic women - Religious life. I. Title. II. Series: Madeleva lecture in spirituality ; 2003.
BV5091.R4 C35 2003

Callataÿ, Godefroid de.
Ikhwān al-Ṣafā'. [Rasā'il. 36. French & Arabic] Les révolutions et les cycles . Louvain-la-Neuve : Bruylant-Academia ; Beyrouth : Al-Bouraq Editions, 1996.

Calle-Gruber, Mireille, 1945-.
Simone Weil, la passion de la raison. Paris : Harmattan, c2003.
B2430.W474 S55 2003

Callières, Monsieur de (François), 1645-1717. De la manière de négocier avec les souverains : de l'utilité des négociations, du choix des ambassadeurs et des envoyés et des qualités nécessaires pour réussir dans ces emplois (1716) / François de Callières ; édition critique par Alain Pekar Lempereur. Genève : Droz, c2002. 247 p. ; 22 cm. (Les classiques de la pensée politique, 0069-4533 ; 19) Includes bibliographical references (p. [211]-225) and indexes. ISBN 2-600-00685-0 DDC 844
1. Diplomacy. 2. Negotiation. 3. Princes. I. Lempereur, Alain Pekar. II. Title. III. Series.

Calling on extraterrestrials.
Larkins, Lisette. Charlottesville, VA : Hampton Roads Pub., c2003.
BF2050 .L365 2003

CALUMNY. *See* **LIBEL AND SLANDER.**

Calvert, Sandra L.
Children in the digital age. Westport, Conn. : Praeger, 2002.
HQ784.M3 C455 2002

Camarotti, Marco. A linguagem no teatro infantil / Marco Camarotti. 2a edição. [Recife : Editora Universitária UFPE, 2002] 170 p. ; 23 cm. Includes bibliographical references (p. 169-170). ISBN 85-7315-175-7
1. Children's theater - Brazil - History and criticism. 2. Children - Language. I. Title.

Cambier, Alain.
Les dons de l'image. Paris : Harmattan, 2003.

The Cambridge companion to Greek and Roman philosophy / edited by David Sedley. Cambridge, U.K. ; New York : Cambridge University Press, 2003. xiv, 396 p. : maps ; 24 cm. (Cambridge companions) Includes bibliographical references (p. 353-372) and index. ISBN 0-521-77285-0 ISBN 0-521-77503-5 (pbk.) DDC 180
1. Philosophy, Ancient. I. Sedley, D. N. II. Series: Cambridge companions to philosophy.
B111 .C36 2003

The Cambridge companion to medieval Jewish philosophy / edited by Daniel H. Frank and Oliver Leaman. Cambridge, UK ; New York : Cambridge University Press, 2003. xxiv, 483 p. ; 23 cm. (Cambridge companions to philosophy) Includes bibliographical references (p. 446-463) and index. Table of contents URL: http://www.loc.gov/catdir/toc/cam031/2003041200.html Publisher description URL: http://www.loc.gov/catdir/description/cam032/2003041200.html ISBN 0-521-65207-3 (hc.) ISBN 0-521-65574-9 (pbk.) DDC 181/.06
1. Philosophy, Jewish. 2. Philosophy, Medieval. 3. Judaism - History - Medieval and early modern period, 425-1789. I. Frank, Daniel H., 1950- II. Leaman, Oliver, 1950- III. Series.
B755 .C36 2003

The Cambridge companion to medieval philosophy / edited by A.S. McGrade. Cambridge ; New York : Cambridge University Press, 2003. xviii, 405 p. : ill. ; 24 cm. (Cambridge companions) Includes bibliographical references (p. 360-397) and index. ISBN 0-521-80603-8 ISBN 0-521-00063-7 (PBK.) DDC 189
1. Philosophy, Medieval. I. McGrade, Arthur Stephen. II. Series: Cambridge companions to philosophy.
B721 .C36 2003

Cambridge companions to philosophy.
The Cambridge companion to Greek and Roman philosophy. Cambridge, U.K. ; New York : Cambridge University Press, 2003.
B111 .C36 2003

The Cambridge companion to medieval Jewish philosophy. Cambridge, UK ; New York : Cambridge University Press, 2003.
B755 .C36 2003

The Cambridge companion to medieval philosophy. Cambridge ; New York : Cambridge University Press, 2003.
B721 .C36 2003

Cambridge language assessment series
Weigle, Sara Cushing. Assessing writing. Cambridge ; New York, NY : Cambridge University Press, 2002.
PE1065 .W35 2002

Cambridge studies in cognitive perceptual development.
Between culture and biology. Cambridge, U.K. ; New York : Cambridge University Press, 2002.
BF721 .B4138 2002

Cambridge studies in comparative politics
Comparative historical analysis in the social sciences. Cambridge, U.K. ; New York : Cambridge University Press, 2003.
H61 .C524 2003

Cambridge studies in ideology and religion
Davis, Charles, 1923- Religion and the making of society. New York, NY, USA : Cambridge University Press, 1994.
BT738 .D36 1994

(8) Jantzen, Grace. Power, gender, and Christian mysticism. Cambridge ; New York : Cambridge University Press, 1995.
BV5083 .J36 1995

Cambridge studies in intellectual property rights
Beverley-Smith, Huw. Commercial appropriation of personality. Cambridge, UK ; New York : Cambridge University Press, 2002.
K627 .B48 2002

Cambridge studies in medical anthropology
([9]) Moerman, Daniel E. Meaning, medicine, and the "placebo effect". Cambridge ; New York : Cambridge University Press, 2002.
R726.5 .M645 2002

Cambridge studies in new art history and criticism
Visuality before and beyond the Renaissance. Cambridge, U.K. ; New York, NY, USA : Cambridge University Press, 2000.
N7430.5 .V54 2000

Cambridge studies in philosophy
Dretske, Fred I. Perception, knowledge, and belief. Cambridge, U.K. ; New York : Cambridge University Press, 2000.
BD161 .D73 2000

Kvanvig, Jonathan L. The value of knowledge and the pursuit of understanding. Cambridge, U.K. ; New York : Cambridge University Press, 2003.
BD232 .K92 2003

Railton, Peter Albert. Facts, values, and norms. Cambridge, U.K. ; New York : Cambridge University Press, 2003.
BJ1012 .R33 2003

Rowlands, Mark. The body in mind. Cambridge, U.K. ; New York : Cambridge University Press, 1999.
BD418.3 .R78 1999

Cambridge studies in Renaissance literature and culture
(44) West, William. Theatres and encyclopedias in early modern Europe. Cambridge : Cambridge University Press, 2002.

Cambridge studies in the history of psychology
Pandora, Katherine, 1958- Rebels within the ranks. Cambridge ; New York : Cambridge University Press, 1997.
BF105 .P36 1997

Cambridge texts in the history of philosophy
Aristotle. [Nicomachean ethics. English] Nicomachean ethics. Cambridge, U.K. ; New York : Cambridge University Press, c2002 (2002 printing)
B430.A5 C7513 2000

Nietzsche, Friedrich Wilhelm, 1844-1900. [Selections. English. 2003] Writings from the late notebooks. Cambridge, UK ; New York : Cambridge University Press, c2003.
B3312.E5 B58 2003

Schleiermacher, Friedrich, 1768-1834. Lectures on philosophical ethics. Cambridge ; New York : Cambridge University Press, 2002.

CAMEOS. *See* **GEMS.**

CAMERA JOURNALISM. *See* **PHOTOJOURNALISM.**

Cameron, Julia. The sound of paper : starting from scratch / Julia Cameron. New York : Jeremy P. Tarcher, 2004. p. cm. Includes index. ISBN 1-58542-288-6 (alk. paper) DDC 153.3/5
1. Creation (Literary, artistic, etc.) 2. Self-actualization (Psychology) I. Title.
BF408 .C1758 2004

Cameron, Stella. Cold day in July / Stella Cameron. Waterville, Me. : Wheeler Pub. : Bath, England : Chivers Press, 2002. 517 p. (large print) ; 24 cm. ISBN 1-58724-339-3 (U.S. hardcover : Romance series) ISBN 0-7540-1891-1 (U.K. hardcover : Windsor large print) DDC 813/.54
1. Medical examiners (Law) - Fiction. 2. Forensic pathologists - Fiction. 3. Women physicians - Fiction. 4. Louisiana - Fiction. 5. Large type books. I. Title.
PS3553.A4345 C65 2002

Camiller, Patrick.
Bessis, Sophie, 1947- [Occident et les autres. English] Western supremacy. London ; New York : Zed Books, 2003.
CB245 .B4613 2003

Camilleri, Peter James.
Working with men in the human services. Crows Nest, N.S.W. : Allen & Unwin, c2001.

O caminho que o dekassegui sonhou (dekassegui no yumê-ji).
Catanio, Percy Antonio Galimbertti. São Paulo : EDUC, FAPESP; Londrina : UEL, 2002.

Camp, Robert (Robert L.)
[Destiny cards]
Cards of your destiny : what your birthday reveals about you and your past, present & future / by Robert Camp. Naperville, Ill. : Sourcebooks, 2004. p. cm. Originally published: Destiny cards. Naperville, Ill. : Sourcebooks, c1998. Includes index. CONTENTS: Our fascinating playing cards -- Your place among the cards -- The cards of your yearly spreads -- Doing a yearly reading -- Your relationships are in the cards -- How to do the weekly reading -- The art of interpretation -- The life map for your birth and planetary ruling cards -- Articles for advanced study -- The card interpretations -- The yearly spreads -- Hearts -- Clubs -- Diamonds -- Spades. ISBN 1402202482 (alk. paper) DDC 133.3/242
1. Fortune-telling by cards. 2. Fortune-telling by birthday. I. Title.
BF1878 .C265 2004

Campanini, Giorgio, 1930- Le parole dell'etica : il senso della vita quotidiana / Giorgio Campanini. Bologna : EDB, 2002. 171 p. ; 22 cm. (Collana Teologia viva ; 45) Includes bibliographical references (p. 161-163) and index. ISBN 88-10-40957-4 DDC 177
1. Christian life. 2. Christian ethics. I. Title. II. Series.

Campbell, John, 1956- Reference and consciousness / John Campbell. Oxford : Clarendon Press ; New York : Oxford University Press, 2002. vii, 267 p. : ill. ; 24 cm. (Oxford cognitive science series) Includes bibliographical references (p. [255]-263) and index. ISBN 0-19-924380-8 (alk. paper) ISBN 0-19-924381-6 (pbk. : alk. paper) DDC 128/.3
1. Attention. 2. Reference (Linguistics) 3. Consciousness. I. Title. II. Series.
BF321 .C36 2002

Campbell, Kirsten, 1969- Jacques Lacan and feminist epistemology / Kirsten Campbell. New York, NY : Routledge, 2004. p. cm. (Transformations) Includes bibliographical references and index. ISBN 0-415-30087-8 (Hardback) ISBN 0-415-30088-6 (Soft Cover) DDC 305.42
1. Psychoanalysis and feminism. 2. Lacan, Jacques, - 1901- I. Title. II. Series.
BF175.4.F45 .C37 2004

Campbell, Marie L. (Marie Louise), 1936- Mapping social relations : a primer in doing institutional ethnography / Marie Campbell and Frances Gregor. Aurora, Ont. : Garamond Press, c2002. 137 p. ; 23 cm. Includes bibliographical references (p. 129-132) and index. ISBN 1-55193-034-X DDC 361/.007/2
1. Human services - Research - Methodology. 2. Social sciences - Research - Methodology. I. Gregor, Frances Mary. II. Title.

Campbell, Neil, 1967-.
Mental causation and the metaphysics of mind. Peterborough, Ont. : Broadview Press, c2003.

Campbell, Sue, 1956- Relational remembering : rethinking the memory wars / Sue Campbell. Lanham, Md. ; Oxford : Rowman & Littlefield, c2003. x, 227 p. : 24 cm. (Feminist constructions) Includes bibliographical references (p. 203-213) and index. ISBN 0-7425-3280-1 (hbk. : alk. paper) ISBN 0-7425-3281-X (pbk. : alk. paper) DDC 153.1/2
1. Autobiographical memory. 2. Women - Psychology. 3. False memory syndrome. I. Title. II. Series.
BF378.A87 C36 2003

Campi del sapere
Bodei, Remo, 1938- Destini personali. Milano : Feltrinelli, 2002.

Campi del sapere. Filosofia
Rossi, Paolo, 1923- Bambini, sogni, furori. 1. ed. in "Campi del sapere.". Milano : Feltrinelli, 2001.
BF41 .R67 2001

Campion, Nicholas.
  Practical astrologer.
    Campion, Nicholas. The ultimate astrologer. Carlsbad, Calif. : Astro Room, c2002 (2003 printing)
    BF1708.1 .C357 2002

    The ultimate astrologer : a simple guide to calculating and interpreting birth charts for effective application in daily life / Nicholas Campion. Carlsbad, Calif. : Astro Room, c2002 (2003 printing) x, 294 p. : ill. ; 25 cm. Rev. ed. of: The practical astrologer. 1987. Includes bibliographical references (p. 175-178). ISBN 140190081X (pbk.) DDC 133.5
    1. Astrology. I. Campion, Nicholas. Practical astrologer. II. Title.
    BF1708.1 .C357 2002

Campling, Jo.
Lister, Ruth, 1949- Citizenship. 2nd ed. Basingstoke, Hampshire ; New York : Palgrave Macmillan, 2003.
HQ1236 .L57 2003

Milner, Judith, senior lecturer. Assessment in counselling. Houndmills, Basingstoke, Hampshire ; New York : Palgrave Macmillan, 2003.
BF637.C6 M5249 2003

Sanders, Robert, 1946- Sibling relationships. New York : Palgrave Macmillan, 2004.
BF723.S43 S159 2004

Campos, Edemilson Antunes de. A tirania de Narciso : alteridade, narcisismo e política / Edemilson Antunes de Campos. 1. ed. São Paulo, SP, Brasil : Annablume/FAPESP, 2001. 136 p. ; 20 cm. (Selo universidade; v. 156) Originally presented as the author's Dissertação de Mestrado at UNICAMP, in 1998. Includes bibliographical references (p. [133]-136).
1. Rousseau, Jean-Jacques, - 1712-1778. 2. Psychoanalysis. 3. Narcissism. 4. Political participation. 5. Other (Philosophy) I. Title. II. Series.

Campos Hernández, Miguel Angel.
Construcción de conocimiento y educación virtual. 1. ed. Ciudad Universitaria, México, D.F. : Universidad Nacional Autónoma de México, 2000.
LB1060 .C658 2000

Campos, Maria Consuelo Cunha. De Frankenstein ao transgênero : modernidades, trânsitos, gêneros / Maria Consuelo Cunha Campos. Rio de Janeiro : Editora Agora da Ilha, 2001. 111 p. ; 21 cm. Includes bibliographical references (p. [107]-111). ISBN 85-86854-71-9
1. Gender identity. 2. Gender identity in literature. 3. Transsexualism. I. Title.

Campus Historische Studien
(Bd. 32) Maset, Michael. Diskurs, Macht und Geschichte. Frankfurt/Main ; New York : Campus, c2002.
BF24.30.F724 M37 2002

Can one live after Auschwitz?.
Adorno, Theodor W., 1903-1969. [Ob nach Auschwitz noch sich leben lasse. English] Stanford, Calif. : Stanford University Press, 2003.
B3199.A33 O213 2003

CANADA - DESCRIPTION AND TRAVEL.
Frayne, Jill. Starting out in the afternoon. Toronto : Random House Canada, c2002.

CANADA - HISTORY - WAR OF 1812. See **UNITED STATES - HISTORY - WAR OF 1812.**

CANADA - LITERATURES. See **FRENCH-CANADIAN LITERATURE.**

CANADA - SOCIAL CONDITIONS - 1991-.
Helliwell, John F. Globalization and well-being. Vancouver : UBC Press, 2002.
HF1359 .H43 2002

Canadian ghost stories.
Smith, Barbara, 1947- Edmonton, Alta. : Lone Pine Pub., 2001.
BF1472.C3 S533 2001

Canadian journal of philosophy. Supplementary volume
(27) Naturalism, evolution, and intentionality. Calgary, Alta., Canada : University of Calgary Press, c2001.
BD418.3 .N35 2001

Canadian Music Educators' Association.
Creativity and music education. Edmonton, Canada : Canadian Music Educators' Association, c2002.

Canary, Daniel J. Interpersonal communication : a goals-based approach / Daniel J. Canary, Michael J. Cody, Valerie L. Manusov. 3rd ed. Boston : Bedford/St. Martin's, c2003. xv, 558 p. : ill. ; 24 cm. Includes bibliographical references and indexes. ISBN 0-312-25895-X (pbk.) DDC 153.6
1. Interpersonal communication. 2. Interpersonal relations. 3. Interpersonal conflict. I. Cody, Michael J. II. Manusov, Valerie Lynn. III. Title.
BF637.C45 C34 2003

Canault, Nina. Comment le désir de naître vient au foetus : l'inconscient archaïque / Nina Canault. Paris : Desclée de Brouwer, c2001. 171 p. ; 21 cm. (Psychologie) Includes bibliographical references. ISBN 2-220-04617-6 DDC 150
1. Fetus. 2. Fetal behavior. 3. Developmental psychobiology. I. Title. II. Series: Psychologie (Desclée De Brouwer (Firm))

CANDIDATES, POLITICAL. See **POLITICAL CANDIDATES.**

Candido, Antonio. O nobre : contribução para o seu estudo / Antonio Candido. São Paulo : Imprensa Oficial do Estado, 2002. 26 p. ; 19 cm. (Plaquetas da Oficina ; 1) ISBN 85-7060-014-3
1. Nobility of character. 2. Conduct of life. I. Title. II. Series.
BJ1533.N6 C36 2002

Candle therapy.
Riggs-Bergesen, Catherine. Kansas City, Mo. : Andrews McMeel Pub., c2003.
BF1623.C26 R54 2003

CANDLEMAS. See **CANDLES AND LIGHTS.**

CANDLES AND LIGHTS - MISCELLANEA.
Riggs-Bergesen, Catherine. Candle therapy. Kansas City, Mo. : Andrews McMeel Pub., c2003.
BF1623.C26 R54 2003

Telesco, Patricia, 1960- Exploring candle magick. Franklin Lakes, NJ : New Page Books, c2001.
BF1623.C26 T45 2001

CANDLES, LITURGICAL. See **CANDLES AND LIGHTS.**

CANDLES - RELIGIOUS ASPECTS. See **CANDLES AND LIGHTS.**

CANDOMBLÉ (RELIGION).
Beniste, José. As águas de Oxalá = Rio de Janeiro, RJ, [Brazil] : Editora Bertrand Brasil, c2001 (2002 printing)
BL2592.C35 B46 2001

Salles, Alexandre de. Esù ou Exu? Rio de Jaeiro : Ilú Aiye, 2001.
1. Black author.

CANDOMBLÉ (RELIGION) - BRAZIL.
Carvalho, Angela Maria B., 1954- A magia das ervas e seu axé. São Paulo, SP : Madras, 2003.
1. Black author.

CANDOMBLÉ (RELIGION) - RITUALS.
Beniste, José. As águas de Oxalá = Rio de Janeiro, RJ, [Brazil] : Editora Bertrand Brasil, c2001 (2002 printing)
BL2592.C35 B46 2001

Canfield, Jack, 1944-.
Chicken soup for the soul celebrates sisters. Deerfield Beach, Fla. : Health Communications, 2004.
BF723.S43 C43 2004

Canfora, Luciano. Manifesto della libertà / Luciano Canfora. Palermo : Sellerio, c1994. 78 p. : 16 cm. (Il divano ; 85) Includes bibliographical references (p. 75-78). ISBN 88-389-1090-1
1. Liberty. I. Title. II. Series: Divano ; 85.
JC585 .C29 1994

Caniato, Benilde Justo. Um testemunho de mãe / Benilde Justo Caniato. 2a. ed. São Paulo : Lato Senso, 2001. 85 p. : ill. ; 18 cm. ISBN 85-88269-01-5
1. Developmentally disabled children - Brazil - Family relationships. 2. Parents of children with disabilities - Biography. 3. Parent and child. I. Title.
HV901.B6 C36 2001

CANNABIS. See **MARIJUANA.**

Cannac, Edith. Caïn ou le détournement du sens / Edith Cannac. [Paris] : Plon, c2002. 139, [1] p. ; 21 cm. Includes bibliographical references (p. 139-[140]). ISBN 2-259-19478-8 DDC 150
1. Cain - (Biblical figure) - Psychology. 2. Psychoanalysis. 3. Cain complex. I. Title.

Cannadine, David, 1950-.
What is history now? Houndmills [England] ; New York : Palgrave Macmillan, 2002.
D16.8 .W5 2002

The cannibal hymn.
Eyre, Christopher. Liverpool : Liverpool University Press, 2002.

Canning, Joseph.
  [History of medieval political thought, 300-1450. French]
    Histoire de la pensée politique médiévale (300-1450) / Joseph Canning ; traduction par Jacques Ménard. Fribourg, Suisse : Editions universitaires ; Paris : Cerf, [2003] x, 304 p. ; 19 cm. (Vestigia ; 28) Includes bibliographical references. ISBN 2-204-07193-5 (Cerf) ISBN 2-8271-0944-1 (Editions Universitaires) DDC 320
    1. Political science - History. 2. Philosophy, Medieval. I. Title. II. Series: Vestigia (Fribourg, Switzerland) ; 28.

Cannon, Carl M. The pursuit of happiness in times of war / Carl M. Cannon. Lanham, MD ; Oxford : Rowman & Littlefield ; [Lanham, Md.] : Distributed by National Book Network, c2004. xii, 331 p. ; 24 cm. Includes bibliographical references (p. 283-315) and index. ISBN 0-7425-2591-0 (cloth : alk. paper) DDC 973.931
1. United States - Politics and government. 2. United States - Politics and government - Philosophy. 3. United States - History, Military. 4. Iraq War, 2003. 5. National characteristics, American. 6. Civil rights - United States - History. I. Title.
E183 .C25 2004

CANON (LITERATURE).
Brenneman, James E., 1954- Canons in conflict. New York : Oxford University Press, 1997.
BS465 .B74 1997

CANONIZATION. See **CHRISTIAN SAINTS.**

Canons in conflict.
Brenneman, James E., 1954- New York : Oxford University Press, 1997.
BS465 .B74 1997

Can't get through.
Hogan, Kevin. Gretna, La. : Pelican Pub. Co., c2003.
BF637.C45 H635 2003

CANTATAS, SACRED - SCORES.
Lathan, Mark J., 1961- Emotional progression in sacred choral music. 2001.

Cantin, Lucie.
Apollon, Willy. After Lacan. Albany : State University of New York Press, 2002.

RC506 .A65 2002

Canto-Sperber, Monique. Les règles de la liberté / Monique Canto-Sperber. [Paris] : Plon, c2003. 312 p. ; 23 cm. Includes bibliographical references. ISBN 2-259-19839-2 DDC 194
1. Political science - Philosophy. 2. Liberty. 3. Socialism. I. Title.

Cantor, Joanne.
Communication and emotion. Mahwah, N.J. ; London : Lawrence Erlbaum, c2003.
BF637.C45 C6375 2003

Cantril, Hadley, 1906-1969. The psychology of social movements / Hadley Cantril ; with a new introduction by Albert H. Cantril. New Brunswick, [N.J.] : Transaction Publishers, c2002. xxx, 275 p. ; 23 cm. Originally published: New York : J. Wiley, 1941. Includes bibliographical references and index. ISBN 0-7658-0089-6 (alk. paper) DDC 303.48/4
1. Social movements. 2. Crowds. 3. Social psychology. I. Title.
HM881 .C36 2002

CAO, XUEQIN, CA. 1717-1763. HONG LOU MENG.
Cai, Yuanpei, 1868-1940. [Selections. 1996] Cai Yuanpei juan. Di 1 ban. Shijiazhuang Shi : Hebei jiao yu chu ban she, 1996.
BJ117 .T74 1996 <Asian China>

CAPES (COASTS) - NEW YORK (STATE). *See* **MONTAUK POINT (N.Y.).**

CAPITAL. *See* **CAPITALISM.**

CAPITAL SINS. *See* **DEADLY SINS.**

CAPITALISM.
Foley, Duncan K. Unholy trinity. London ; New York : Routledge, 2003.
HB135 .F65 2003

Friedman, Milton, 1912- Capitalism and freedom. 40th anniversary ed. Chicago : University of Chicago Press, 2002.
HB501 .F7 2002

Holt, W. V. America by trial. München : Tuduv, c2001.

Menger, Pierre-Michel. Portrait de l'artiste en travailleur. Paris : Seuil, c2002.

Segrest, Mab, 1949- Born to belonging. New Brunswick, NJ : Rutgers University Press, c2002.
HQ75.25 .S44 2002

Capitalism and freedom.
Friedman, Milton, 1912- 40th anniversary ed. Chicago : University of Chicago Press, 2002.
HB501 .F7 2002

CAPITALISM - MORAL AND ETHICAL ASPECTS.
Markt - Medien - Moral. Bochum : Projekt-Verlag, 2001.

McMurtry, John, 1939- Value wars. London ; Sterling, Va. : Pluto Press, c2002.
HF1359 .M39 2002

CAPITALISM - POLITICAL ASPECTS.
Read, Jason. The micro-politics of capital. Albany : State University of New York Press, c2003.
HB97.5 .R42 2003

CAPITALISM - RELIGIOUS ASPECTS - CHRISTIANITY.
2000 years and beyond. London ; New York : Routledge, 2003.
BR53 .T86 2003

CAPITALISM - RELIGIOUS ASPECTS - EVANGELIST CHURCHES.
Barrios, Luis. Josconiando. 1st ed. New York : Editorial Aguiar, 2000.

CAPITALISM - SOCIAL ASPECTS.
Emmott, Bill. 20:21 vision. London : Allen Lane, 2003.

CAPITALISM - SOCIAL ASPECTS - HISTORY.
Antinomies of modernity. Durham : Duke University Press, 2003.
CB358 .A59 2003

CAPITALISM - UNITED STATES.
Monkeywrenching the new world order [sound recording]. Oakland, Calif : AK Press ; San Francisco, CA : Alternative Tentacles Records, 2001.

Pessanha, Rodolfo Gomes. O irracionalismo--, dos Estados Unidos da América à globalizaçap. Niterói : Muiraquitã, c1998.

Caplan, Deborah, 1931-.
The Alexander technique [videorecording]. New York, N.Y. : Wellspring Media, c1999.

Capp, Ray, 1953- When you mean business about yourself / Ray Capp. Nashville, Tenn. : Rutledge Hill Press, c2002. xiii, 237 p. ; 24 cm. ISBN 1-55853-948-4 DDC 158.1
1. Success - Psychological aspects. 2. Success in business. 3. Role playing. I. Title.
BF637.S8 C37 2002

CAPPELLA DELLA SINDONE (DUOMO DI TORINO).
Scott, John Beldon, 1946- Architecture for the shroud. Chicago : University of Chicago Press, c2003.
NA5621.T823 S36 2003

CAPSULES, TIME. *See* **TIME CAPSULES.**

CARAVAGGIO, MICHELANGELO MERISI DA, 1573-1610.
Shoham, S. Giora, 1929- Ṭeruf, seṭiyah vi-yetsirah. [Israel] : Miśrad ha-biṭaḥon, [2002]

Cardiff papers in qualitative research
Housley, William, 1970- Interaction in multidisciplinary teams. Aldershot, England ; Burlington, VT : Ashgate, c2003.
HV41 .H667 2003

CARDINAL NUMBERS. *See* **NINE (THE NUMBER).**

Cards of your destiny.
Camp, Robert (Robert L.) [Destiny cards] Naperville, Ill. : Sourcebooks, 2004.
BF1878 .C265 2004

Carducci, Bernardo J. The shyness breakthrough : a no-stress plan to help your shy child warm up, open up, and join the fun / Bernardo J. Carducci ; with Lisa Kaiser. [Emmaus, Pa.] : Rodale, c2003. xv, 320 p. ; 23 cm. Includes bibliographical references (p. 305-312) and index. Table of contents URL: http://www.loc.gov/catdir/toc/ecip044/2003011207.html CONTENTS: What shyness is--and isn't -- A breakthrough view of childhood shyness -- Life skills to break out of shyness -- Understanding your family's shyness profile -- Are we born shy? -- The family influence -- Making friends -- Entering school -- The shy student -- Shyness in middle childhood -- Shyness in adolescence -- The successfully shy life. ISBN 1-57954-761-3 (pbk. : alk. paper) DDC 649/.1
1. Bashfulness in children. 2. Child rearing. I. Kaiser, Lisa. II. Title.
BF723.B3 C37 2003

Cardwell, D. S. L. (Donald Stephen Lowell) The development of science and technology in nineteenth-century Britain : the importance of Manchester / Donald Cardwell ; edited by Richard L. Hills. Aldershot, Great Britain ; Burlington, VT : Ashgate/Variorum, c2003. 1 v. (various pagings) : ill. ; 24 cm. (Variorum collected studies series ; 765) Includes bibliographical references and indexes. ISBN 0-86078-908-X (alk. paper) DDC 509.41/09/034
1. Science - Great Britain - History - 19th century. 2. Technology - Great Britain - History - 19th century. 3. Science - England - Manchester - History - 19th century. 4. Technology - England - Manchester - History - 19th century. I. Hills, Richard Leslie, 1936- II. Title. III. Series: Collected studies ; CS765.
Q127.G4 C37 2003

Cardwell, Mike.
Complete A Z psychology handbook.
Cardwell, Mike. Schaum's A-Z psychology. New York : McGraw-Hill, 2003.
BF31 .C29 2003

Schaum's A-Z psychology / Mike Cardwell. New York : McGraw-Hill, 2003. p. cm. (Schaum's A-Z series) Rev. ed. of: The complete A-Z psychology handbook. 2nd ed. 1998. Publisher description URL: http://www.loc.gov/catdir/description/mh031/2003046463.html ISBN 0-07-141938-1 DDC 150/.3
1. Psychology - Dictionaries. I. Cardwell, Mike. Complete A-Z psychology handbook. II. Title. III. Title: Psychology IV. Series.
BF31 .C29 2003

Care and treatment of the mentally ill in North Wales, 1800-2000.
Michael, Pamela. Cardiff : University of Wales Press, 2003.

CARE GIVERS. *See* **CAREGIVERS.**

CARE OF THE SICK. *See also* **SELF-CARE, HEALTH; TERMINAL CARE.**
Dahlin, Olov, 1962- Zvinorwadza. Frankfurt am Main ; New York : P. Lang, c2002.

R726.5 .D34 2002

CAREER CHANGES.
Hill, Linda A. (Linda Annette), 1956- Becoming a manager. 2nd ed. Boston, Mass. : Harvard Business School Press, c2003.
HF5384 .H55 2003

Varner, Don. How to get a really great job!. Toronto : Productive Publications, 1998.

Career choice and development.
Brown, Duane. 4th ed. San Francisco, CA : Jossey-Bass, c2002.
HF5381 .C265143 2002

CAREER COUPLES. *See* **DUAL-CAREER FAMILIES.**

CAREER DEVELOPMENT.
Brown, Duane. Career choice and development. 4th ed. San Francisco, CA : Jossey-Bass, c2002.
HF5381 .C265143 2002

Kazerounian, Nadine. Stepping up. London : McGraw-Hill, c2002.

Salmon, William A. The mid-career tune-up. New York : Amacom, c2000.
HF5381 .S256 2000

Stewardson, John (John E.) Success is the best revenge. Toronto : Productive Publications, c1994.

Varner, Don. How to get a really great job!. Toronto : Productive Publications, 1998.

CAREER PATTERNS. *See* **OCCUPATIONS; PROFESSIONS.**

CAREERS. *See* **OCCUPATIONS; PROFESSIONS.**

Careers in behavioral science.
Clayton, Lawrence, Ph. D. [2nd ed.]. Oklahoma City, Okla. : Transcontinental Pub., 2001.
BF76 .C64 2001

Careers with character
Brinkerhoff, Shirley. Psychologist. Broomall, Pa. : Mason Crest Publishers, c2003.
BF76 .B75 2003

CAREGIVERS.
Promising practies in the field of caregiving [electronic resource]. [Washington, D.C.] : U.S. Dept. of Health and Human Services, Administration on Aging, [2003?]

Velkoff, Victoria Averil. Gender and aging [electronic resource]. [Washington, D.C.] : U.S. Dept. of Commerce, Economics and Statistics Administration, Bureau of the Census, [1998]

CAREGIVERS - FAMILY RELATIONSHIPS.
The subject of care. Lanham, Md. ; Oxford : Rowman & Littlefield Publishers, c2002.
HQ1206 .S9 2002

Caregiving.
Velkoff, Victoria Averil. Gender and aging [electronic resource]. [Washington, D.C.] : U.S. Dept. of Commerce, Economics and Statistics Administration, Bureau of the Census, [1998]

CARERS. *See* **CAREGIVERS.**

Carey, Dennis. How to run a company : lessons from top leaders of the CEO Academy / Dennis Carey and Marie-Caroline von Weichs. 1st ed. New York : Crown Business, c2003. xiii, 289 p. ; 25 cm. Includes index. ISBN 140004927X (hardcover) DDC 658.4/2
1. Chief executive officers. 2. Executive ability. 3. Leadership. 4. Industrial management. 5. Corporate governance. I. Von Weichs, Marie-Caroline. II. CEO Academy. III. Title.
HD38.2 .C374 2003

CARICATURE. *See* **WIT AND HUMOR.**

CARING. *See also* **HELPING BEHAVIOR.**
Krieglstein, Werner J., 1941- Compassion. Amsterdam ; New York : Rodopi, c2002.

Lampert, Khen. Compassionate education. Lanham, Md. : University Press of America, c2003.

Tudor, Steven. Compassion and remorse. Leuven ; Sterling, Va. : Peeters, 2001.
BJ1475 .T84 2001

Caring for your grieving child.
Wakenshaw, Martha. Oakland, Calif. : New Harbinger ; London : Hi Marketing, 2002.
BF723.G75 W35 2002

Carl Beck papers in Russian and East European studies
(no. 1603.) Cherchi, Marcello. Disciplines and nations. Pittsburgh, Pa. : Center for Russian and East European Studies, University Center for

International Studies, University of Pittsburgh, c2002.

Carl Rogers.
Cohen, David, 1946- London : Constable, 1997.
BF109.R63 C64 1997

Carley, Kathleen M.
Lin, Zhiang. Designing stress resistant organizations. Boston : Kluwer Academic Publishers, c2003.
HD58.8 .L58 2003

CARLOVINGIANS. See CAROLINGIANS.

Carlson, Jon.
Kottler, Jeffrey A. American shaman. New York : Brunner-Routledge, 2004.
BF1598.K43 K68 2004

Carlyle, Thomas, 1795-1881. Historical essays / edited by Chris R. Vanden Bossche. Berkeley ; London : University of California Press, c2002. xciii, 1146 p., 9 p. of plates : ill., map ; 24 cm. (The Norman and Charlotte Strouse edition of the writings of Thomas Carlyle ; [3]) Includes bibliographical references (p. 789-808) and index. ISBN 0-520-22061-7 (alk. paper) DDC 940
1. Europe - History. 2. France - History - 18th century. 3. Historiography. I. Vanden Bossche, Chris. II. Title. III. Series: Carlyle, Thomas, 1795-1881. Works. 1993 ; 3.
D208 .C34 2002

Works. 1993
(3.) Carlyle, Thomas, 1795-1881. Historical essays. Berkeley ; London : University of California Press, c2002.
D208 .C34 2002

Carman, Taylor, 1965- Heidegger's analytic : interpretation, discourse, and authenticity in Being and time / Taylor Carman. Cambridge, UK ; New York : Cambridge University Press, 2003. xii, 328 p. ; 24 cm. (Modern European philosophy) Includes bibliographical references (p. 315-324) and index. Publisher description URL: http://www.loc.gov/catdir/description/ cam031/2002067417.html Table of contents URL: http:// www.loc.gov/catdir/toc/cam031/2002067417.html ISBN 0-521-82045-6 DDC 111
1. Heidegger, Martin, - 1889-1976. - Sein und Zeit. 2. Ontology. I. Title. II. Series.
B3279.H48 S459 2003

Carmona Fernández, Fernando. La mentalidad literaria medieval : (siglos XII y XIII) / Fernando Carmona Fernández. 1. ed. Murcia : Universidad de Murcia, Servicio de Publicaciones, 2001. 174 p. ; 20 cm. Includes bibliographical references (p. [163]-174). ISBN 84-8371-286-5
1. Philosophy, Medieval. 2. Literature, Medieval - History and criticism. 3. Philosophy in literature. I. Title.

CARNATIC MUSIC - HISTORY AND CRITICISM.
Padma, N. K., 1956- Navam and the Karṇāṭak group kṛtis. New Delhi : Kanishka Publishers, Distributors, 2002.
ML338 .P197 2002

Carneiro, Maria Luiza Tucci.
Ensaios sobre a intolerância. São Paulo, SP, Brasil : Humanitas, FFLCH/USP : FAPESP : LEI-Laboratório de Estudos sobre a Intolerância, 2002.

Carneiro, Robert L. (Robert Leonard), 1927-
Evolutionism in cultural anthropology : a critical history / Robert L. Carneiro. Boulder, Colo. : Westview Press, 2003. xiii, 322 p. : ill. ; 24 cm. Includes bibliographical references (p. 289-312) and index. ISBN 0-8133-3765-8 (hbk.) ISBN 0-8133-3766-6 (pbk.) DDC 303.4
1. Social evolution. 2. Ethnology - Philosophy. I. Title.
GN360 .C37 2003

Carney, John, 1958- The book of secrets : lessons for progressive conjuring / John Carney. 1st ed. [United States?] : Carney Magic, c2002. 367 p. : ill. ; 24 cm. ISBN 0-9701287-0-3 DDC 793.8
1. Magic. I. Title.
BF1611 .C35 2002

CARNIVAL. See MASKS.

CAROLINGIANS - HISTORY.
Keefe, Susan A. Water and the Word. Notre Dame, Ind. : University of Notre Dame Press, c2002.
BR200 .K44 2002

CAROLINIANS. See CAROLINGIANS.

Carolyn and Ernest Fay series in analytical psychology
(no. 9) Gambini, Roberto, 1944- Soul & culture. 1st ed. College Station : Texas A&M University Press, 2003.
BF698.9.C8 G35 2003

Caronia, Antonio. Il cyborg : saggio sull'uomo artificiale / Antonio Caronia. Milano : Shake edizioni underground, c2001. 130 p. : ill. ; 21 cm. Includes bibliographical references. ISBN 88-86926-99-5
1. Artificial intelligence. 2. Cyborgs. I. Title.
Q335 .C34 2001

Caropreso, Paolo. Von der Dingfrage zur Frage nach Gott : zum eigentlichen Ursprung von Religiosität in Kants Transzendentalphilosophie / Paolo Caropreso. Berlin ; New York : W. de Gruyter, 2003. x, 214 p. ; 24 cm. (Kantstudien. Ergänzungshefte, 0340-6059 ; 143) Includes bibliographical references (p. [213]-214) and index. ISBN 3-11-017942-3
1. Kant, Immanuel, - 1724-1804 - Contributions in concept of faith. 2. Kant, Immanuel, - 1724-1804 - Contributions in concept of God. 3. Kant, Immanuel, - 1724-1804 - Contributions in ontology. 4. Kant, Immanuel, - 1724-1804 - Contributions in ontology. 5. Substance (Philosophy) 6. Transcendence (Philosophy) 7. Ontology. 8. Ding an sich. 9. Knowledge, Theory of. 10. Ethics, Modern - 18th century. I. Title. II. Series.

Carozzi, Claude.
Année mille An Mil. Aix-en-Provence : Publications de l'université de Provence, 2002.

Carpenter, David, 1949-.
Yoga. London ; New York : RoutledgeCurzon, 2003.
BL1238.52 .Y59 2003

Carr, Alan, Dr. Positive psychology / Alan Carr. London ; New York : Brunner-Routledge, 2004. p. ; cm. Includes bibliographical references and index. CONTENTS: Happiness -- Flow -- Hope and optimism -- Emotional intelligence -- Giftedness, creativity, and wisdom -- Positive traits and motives -- Positive self -- Positive relationships -- Positive change. ISBN 1-58391-990-2 (hbk.) ISBN 1-58391-991-0 (pbk.) DDC 150
1. Psychology. 2. Health. 3. Optimism. 4. Happiness. 5. Psychology, Applied - methods. 6. Adaptation, Psychological. I. Title.
BF121 .C355 2004

Carr, David, 1944-.
Spirituality, philosophy and education. London ; New York : RoutledgeFalmer, 2003.
BV4501.3 .S65 2003

Carr, Stuart C. Social psychology : context, communication and culture / Stuart C. Carr. Milton, Qld. : John Wiley & Sons, 2003. xvi, 456 p. : ill. ; 25 cm. Includes index. Bibliography: p. 407-448. ISBN 0-471-34304-8 (pbk.)
1. Social psychology. I. Title.

Carrillo, Juan D.
The psychology of economic decisions. Oxford [England] ; New York : Oxford University Press, 2003-
HB74.P8 P725 2003

Carrington, Victoria. New times : new families / Victoria Carrington. Dordrecht ; Boston : London : Kluwer Academic, c2002. ix, 161 p. ; 25 cm. Includes bibliographical references and index. ISBN 1402004818 DDC 306.85
1. Family. I. Title.
HQ728 .C314 2002

Carroll, John M. HCI models, theories, and frameworks : toward a multidisciplinary science / edited by John M. Carroll. San Francisco, Calif. : Morgan Kaufmann, 2003. xvi, 551 p., [8] p. of plates : ill. (some col.) ; 20 cm. (The Morgan Kaufmann series in interactive technologies) Includes bibliographical references (p. 475-519) and index. ISBN 1-55860-808-7
1. Human-computer interaction. I. Title. II. Series.

Carsalade, Flávio de Lemos. Arquitetura : interfaces / Flávio de Lemos Carsalade ; [coordenação geral, Gaby de Aragão ; revisão, Rachel Barreto]. Belo Horizonte : AP Cultural, 2001. 110 p. : ill. ; 28 cm. Includes bibliographical references (p. 103-104).
1. Architecture. 2. Architecture - Philosophy. I. Aragão, Gaby de. II. Barreto, Rachel. III. Title. IV. Title: Arquitetura : interfaces
NA2500 .C37 2001

Carson, Richard David. Taming your gremlin : a surprisingly simple method for getting out of your own way / Rick Carson. Rev. ed. New York : Quill, 2003. p. cm. Publisher description URL: http://www.loc.gov/ catdir/description/hc042/2002191925.html ISBN 0-06-052022-1 DDC 158.1
1. Happiness. 2. Success - Psychological aspects. 3. Self-perception. 4. Choice (Psychology) I. Title.
BF575.H27 C38 2003

Carter, Jay. Nasty women / Jay Carter. Chicago : Contemporary Books, c2003. xx, 121 p. ; 21 cm. Includes bibliographical references (p. 117-121). Publisher description URL: http://www.loc.gov/catdir/description/mh031/ 2003046055.html ISBN 0-07-141023-6 (acid-free paper) DDC 155.3/33
1. Control (Psychology) 2. Women - Psychology. 3. Abusive women. 4. Interpersonal relations. I. Title.
BF632.5 .C365 2003

Carter, Les. The anger trap : free yourself from the frustrations that sabotage your life / Les Carter ; foreword by Frank Minirth. 1st ed. San Francisco, CA : Jossey-Bass, c2003. xvi, 199 p. ; 24 cm. Publisher description URL: http://www.loc.gov/catdir/desc ription/ wiley039/2003006258.html Table of contents URL: http:// www.loc.gov/catdir/toc/wiley032/2003006258.html ISBN 0-7879-6879-X DDC 152.4/7
1. Anger. 2. Anger - Case studies. I. Title.
BF575.A5 C37 2003

Carter, Matt. T.H. Green and the development of ethical socialism / Matt Carter. Thorverton : Imprint Academic, 2003. x, 223 p. ; 22 cm. (British idealist studies. Series 3, Green) ISBN 0-907845-32-0 DDC 192
1. Green, Thomas Hill, - 1836-1882 - Contributions in ethics. 2. Philosophy, British - 19th century. 3. Ethics. I. Title. II. Series: British idealist studies. Series 3, Green ; 1.
B1638.E8 C37 2003

Carter, Michael, 1950 Aug. 8- Where writing begins : a postmodern reconstruction / Michael Carter. Carbondale : Southern Illinois University Press, c2003. xix, 259 p. ; 24 cm. (Rhetorical philosophy and theory) Includes bibliographical references (p. 235-247) and index. ISBN 0-8093-2520-9 (alk. paper) DDC 808/.001
1. Rhetoric - Philosophy. 2. Rhetoric - Study and teaching. 3. Postmodernism. I. Title. II. Series.
P301 .C29 2003

Carter, Philip J. IQ and psychometric tests : assess your personality, aptitude, and intelligence / Philip Carter. London ; Sterling, VA : Kogan Page Ltd., 2004. p. cm. Includes bibliographical references (p.   ). ISBN 0-7494-4118-6 DDC 153.9/3
1. Intelligence tests. 2. Personality tests. 3. Self-evaluation. I. Title.
BF431.3 .C362 2004

IQ workout series.
Carter, Philip J. Maximize your brainpower. West Sussex, England ; New York : John Wiley & Sons, Ltd, 2002.
BF431.3 .C3647 2002

Carter, Philip J. More IQ testing. Chichester, West Sussex, England ; New York : John Wiley & Sons, Ltd, 2002.
BF431.3 .C367 2002

Maximize your brainpower : 1000 new ways to boost your mental fitness / Philip Carter and Ken Russell. West Sussex, England ; New York : John Wiley & Sons, Ltd, 2002. 232 p. : ill. ; 22 cm. (IQ workout series) Includes bibliographical references (p. 232). Publisher description URL: http://www.loc.gov/catdir/desc ription/ wiley038/2003269057.html Table of contents URL: http:// www.loc.gov/catdir/toc/wiley032/2003269057.html ISBN 0-470-84716-6
1. Intelligence tests. 2. Puzzles. I. Russell, Kenneth A. II. Title. III. Series: Carter, Philip J. IQ workout series.
BF431.3 .C3647 2002

More IQ testing : 250 new ways to release your IQ potential / Philip Carter and Ken Russell. Chichester, West Sussex, England ; New York : John Wiley & Sons, Ltd, 2002. 170 p. : ill. ; 22 cm. (The IQ workout series) Publisher description URL: http://www.loc.gov/catdir/ desc ription/wiley0310/2003267903.html Table of contents URL: http://www.loc.gov/catdir/toc/wiley032/ 2003267903.html ISBN 0-470-84717-4 (pbk. : alk. paper)
1. Intelligence tests. 2. Self-evaluation. I. Russell, Kenneth A. II. Title. III. Series: Carter, Philip J. IQ workout series.
BF431.3 .C367 2002

Russell, Kenneth, 1928- The Times book of IQ tests. Book 1. London : Kogan Page, 2001.

Russell, Kenneth, 1928- The Times book of IQ tests. Book 2. London ; Milford, CT : Kogan Page, 2002.

Russell, Kenneth A. The Times book of IQ tests. Book 3. London ; Sterling, VA : Kogan Page Ltd., 2003.
BF431.3 .R87 2003

Carter, Richard F. (Richard Fremont), 1928-.
Communication, a different kind of horserace. Cresskill, N.J. : Hampton Press, c2003.
P87.3.C37 C66 2003

CARTER, RICHARD F. (RICHARD FREMONT), 1928-.
Communication, a different kind of horserace. Cresskill, N.J. : Hampton Press, c2003.

P87.3.C37 C66 2003

Carter, Rita, 1949- Exploring consciousness / Rita Carter. Berkeley : University of California Press, c2002. 320 p. : ill. (chiefly col.) ; 23 cm. Includes bibliographical references and index. CONTENTS: Pt. 1. A stream of illusion. Vision: the grand illusion / J. Kevin O'Regan ; The higher-order thought model of consciousness / David Rosenthal -- Pt. 2. The hard problem. Facing up to consciousness / David Chalmers ; Facing backwards on the problem of consciousness / Daniel Dennett ; Solving the hard problem- naturally / John Searle ; A quantum description of mind / Andrew Duggins -- Pt. 3. The old steam whistle test. The making of mind / Nicholas Humphrey -- Pt. 4. Making consciousation. -- Pt. 5. Consciousness and the brain. The network mind / John Skoyles -- Pt. 6. The conscious body. What do robots think about? / Igor Aleksander, Rita Carter ; The primordial SELF / Jaak Panksepp -- Pt. 7. The conscious self. Ownership and agency / Chris Frith ; Predicting the present / Jeffrey Gray ; Meme machines and consciousness / Susan Blackmore -- Pt. 8. Fractured consciousness. -- Pt. 9. A conscious universe? Quantum minds / Stuart Hameroff, Alwyn Scott. ISBN 0-520-23737-4 (alk. paper) DDC 153
1. Consciousness. 2. Brain - physiology. 3. Hallucinations and illusions - psychology. 4. Mind-Body Relations (Metaphysics) 5. Neuropsychology. 6. Visual perception. I. Title.
BF311 .C289 2002

CARTOGRAPHY.
Slocum, Terry A. Thematic cartography and visualization. Upper Saddle River, N.J. : Prentice Hall, c1999.
GA108.7 .S58 1999

CARTULARIES. See **ARCHIVES.**

Carubia, Josephine.
Gendered landscapes. University Park, PA : Center for Studies in Landscape History, c2000.

Caruso, Sergio.
A che servono i simboli? Milano : FrancoAngeli, c2002.

Carvalho, Angela Maria B., 1954- A magia das ervas e seu axé / Angela Maria Carvalho e Antonio Navarro Júnior. São Paulo, SP : Madras, 2003. 106 p. ; 21 cm. ISBN 85-7374-551-7
1. Traditional medicine - Brazil. 2. Herbs - Therapeutic use. 3. Materia medica, Vegetable. 4. Medicine, Magic, mystic, and spagiric. 5. Candomblé (Religion) - Brazil. 6. Umbanda (Cult) 7. Black author. I. Navarro Jr., Antonio B., 1963-

Carver, Charles S. Perspectives on personality / Charles S. Carver, Michael F. Scheier. 5th ed. Boston, MA : Allyn and Bacon, 2004. p. cm. Includes bibliographical references and index. ISBN 0-205-37576-6 (alk. paper) DDC 155.2
1. Personality. I. Scheier, Michael. II. Title.
BF698 .C22 2004

Casalla, Mario C.
Habitar la tierra. Buenos Aires : Grupo Editor Altamira, 2002.
CB358 .H32 2002

Cascio, Toni.
Religious organizations in community services. New York : Springer Pub., 2003.
HV530 .R25 2003

Case, Linda P. The cat : its behavior, nutrition & health / by Linda P. Case ; illustrated by Kerry Helms and Bruce MacAllister. Ames, Iowa : Iowa State Press, c2003. xv, 392 p. : ill. ; 27 cm. Includes bibliographical references (p. 363-373) and index. ISBN 0-8138-0331-4 (alk. paper) DDC 636.8
1. Cats. 2. Cats - Behavior. 3. Cats - Nutrition. 4. Cats - Health. I. Title.
SF442 .C37 2003

Case study research.
Yin, Robert K. 3rd ed. Thousand Oaks, Calif. : Sage Publications, c2003.
H62 .Y56 2003

Casoni, Guido, 1561-1642. Della magia d'amore / Guido Casoni ; a cura di Elisabetta Selmi ; introduzione di Pasquale Guaragnella. Torino : Res, 2002. xlix, 169 p. ; 21 cm. (Scrinium ; 20) Includes bibliographical references. ISBN 88-85323-38-3 DDC 858
1. Love - Early works to 1800. I. Selmi, Elisabetta. II. Title. III. Series: Scrinium (San Mauro Torinese, Italy) ; 20.
BF575.L8 C3 2002

Caspari, Elizabeth, 1926- Animal life in nature, myth and dreams / Elizabeth Caspari, with Ken Robbins ; introduction by Ann Belford Ulanov. Wilmette, Ill. : Chiron Publications, c2003. p. cm. Includes bibliographical references. Table of contents URL: http://www.loc.gov/catdir/toc/ecip045/2003014444.html ISBN 1-88860-222-8 (alk. paper) DDC 156/.03
1. Symbolism (Psychology) - Encyclopedias. 2. Animals - Psychological aspects - Encyclopedias. 3. Animals - Symbolic aspects - Encyclopedias. 4. Animals - Mythology - Encyclopedias. 5. Animals - Folklore - Encyclopedias. I. Robbins, Ken, 1945- II. Title.
BF458 .C37 2003

The Cass series in regional and federal studies
The territorial management of ethnic conflict. 2nd rev. and expanded ed. London ; Portland, OR : F. Cass, 2003.
GN496 .T47 2003

Cassagnes-Brouquet, Sophie, 1957-.
Religion et mentalités au Moyen Age. Rennes : Presses universitaires de Rennes, c2003.
BR141 .R45 2003

Cassar, Carmel. Witchcraft, sorcery, and the Inquisition : a study of cultural values in early modern Malta Carmel Cassar. Msida, Malta : Mireva Publications, 1996. 121 p., 32 leaves of plates : col. ill. ; 21 cm. Includes bibliographical references (p. [109]-116) and index. ISBN 1-87057-947-X DDC 133.4/3/094585
1. Witchcraft - Malta - History - 16th century. 2. Inquisition - Malta - History - 16th century. I. Title.
BF1584.M35 C37 1996

CASSIQUES (INDIAN LEADERS). See **CACIQUES (INDIAN LEADERS).**

CASSIRER, ERNST, 1874-1945.
Janz, Nathalie. Globus symbolicus. [Lausanne : Université de Lausanne, 1999]

Castagnino, M. (Mario) Tempo e universo : un approccio filosofico e scientifico / Mario Castagnino, Juan José Sanguineti. Roma : Armando, c2000. 422 p. : ill. ; 22 cm. (Studi di filosofia ; 22) Includes bibliographical references (p. 379-390) and index. ISBN 88-8358-083-4 DDC 115
1. Space and time. 2. Cosmology. 3. Philosophy and science. I. Sanguineti, Juan José. II. Title. III. Series: Studi di filosofia (Rome, Italy) ; 22.
BD632 .C37 2000

CASTE. See **SOCIAL CLASSES.**

Castel, Pierre-Henri. La métamorphose impensable : essai sur le transsexualisme et l'identité personnelle / Pierre-Henri Castel. Paris : Gallimard, c2003. 551 p. ; 24 cm. Includes bibliographical references (p. [511]-534) and index. ISBN 2-07-076898-8
1. Transsexualism. 2. Gender identity. I. Title.
HQ77.9 .C38 2003

Casti, J. L. The one true platonic heaven : a scientific fiction on the limits of knowledge / John L. Casti. Washington, D.C. : Joseph Henry Press, c2003. xviii, 160 p. : ill. ; 20 cm. Table of contents URL: http://www.loc.gov/catdir/toc/fy037/2003002279.html ISBN 0-309-08547-0 DDC 501
1. Science - Philosophy. 2. Knowledge, Theory of. I. Title.
Q175 .C4339 2003

CASTILIAN LANGUAGE. See **SPANISH LANGUAGE.**

Castilla del Pino, Carlos, 1922-.
Cruz, Mariano de la, 1921-1999. Mens sana in corpore insepulto. 1. ed. Barcelona : Edicions 62, 2002.

Castilla y León, siglos 11-13.
Pérez-Embid Wamba, Javier. Hagiología y sociedad en la España medieval. Huelva : Universidad de Huelva, 2002.
BX4659.S8 P47 2002

CASTILLA Y LEÓN (SPAIN) - CHURCH HISTORY.
Pérez-Embid Wamba, Javier. Hagiología y sociedad en la España medieval. Huelva : Universidad de Huelva, 2002.
BX4659.S8 P47 2002

Castillo, Heather. Personality disorder : temperament or trauma? : an account of an emancipatory research study carried out by service users diagnosed with personality disorder / Heather Castillo. London ; Philadelphia : J. Kingsley Pub., 2003. 176 p. : ill. ; 24 cm. (Forensic focus series ; 23) Includes bibliographical references (p. 165-170) and indexes. ISBN 1-84310-053-3 DDC 616.85/8
1. Personality disorders. 2. Temperament. 3. Psychic trauma. I. Title. II. Series: Forensic focus ; 23.
RC554 .C37 2003

Casting the evil eye.
Mishra, Archana, 1962- New Delhi : Namita Gokhale Editions, Roli Books, 2003.
BF1584.A-ZI.Z7 2003+

CASTLES. See **HAUNTED CASTLES.**

Caston, Victor Miles, 1963-.
Presocratic philosophy. Aldershot, Hants, England ; Burlington, VT : Ashgate, 2002.
B187.5 .P743 2002

CASTRATION ANXIETY.
Pieroni, Osvaldo. Pene d'amore. Soveria Mannelli : Rubbettino, c2002.

CASTRATION OF CRIMINALS AND DEFECTIVES. See **STERILIZATION, EUGENIC.**

Castro, Vanessa Smith, 1969- Acculturation and psychological adaptation / Vanessa Smith Castro ; foreword by Ulrich Wagner and Thomas F. Pettigrew. Westport, Conn. : Greenwood Press, 2003. xii, 215 p. : ill. ; 25 cm. (Contributions in psychology, 0736-2714 ; no. 41) Includes bibliographical references (p. [197]-212) and index. ISBN 0-313-32327-5 (alk. paper) DDC 305.8
1. Acculturation. 2. Adaptability (Psychology) 3. Ethnicity. 4. Intergroup relations - Costa Rica. 5. Costa Rica - Ethnic relations. I. Title. II. Series.
HM841 .C37 2003

The cat.
Case, Linda P. Ames, Iowa : Iowa State Press, c2003.
SF442 .C37 2003

Cat culture.
Alger, Janet M., 1937- Philadelphia : Temple University Press, 2003.
SF446.5 .A36 2003

CAT, DOMESTIC. See **CATS.**

CAT OWNERS. See **WOMEN CAT OWNERS.**

Catàbasi e anàstasi.
Zolla, Elémire. Alpignano, [Italy] : Tallone Editore, 2001.

ÇATAL HÜYÜK (TURKEY). See **ÇATAL MOUND (TURKEY).**

ÇATAL MOUND (TURKEY).
Sermonti, Giuseppe. Il mito della grande madre. Milano : Mimesis, c2002.

Català, Natàlia.
El lenguaje y la mente humana. 1. ed. Barcelona : Ariel Editorial, 2002.

CATALOGING. See **BOOKS.**

CATALONIA (SPAIN) - INTELLECTUAL LIFE.
Lucas, John Scott, 1970- Astrology and numerology in medieval and early modern Catalonia. Leiden ; Boston : Brill, 2003.
BF1685 .L83 2003

Catanio, Percy Antonio Galimbertti. O caminho que o dekassegui sonhou (dekassegui no yumê-ji) : cultura e subjetividade no movimento dekassegui / São Paulo : EDUC, FAPESP; Londrina : UEL, 2002. Originalmente apresentado como dissertação de mestrado a PUC-SP, 2000. Includes bibliographical references (p. 209-220).
1. Japanese - Brazil. 2. Brazilians - Japan. 3. Brazil - Emigration and immigration. 4. Group identity. 5. Ethnicity. 6. Alien labor, Brazilian - Japan. I. Title.

CATASTROPHE, JEWISH (1939-1945). See **HOLOCAUST, JEWISH (1939-1945).**

CATASTROPHES. See **DISASTERS.**

CATASTROPHES (GEOLOGY).
Clow, Barbara Hand, 1943- Catastrophobia. Rochester, Vt. : Bear & Company, c2001.
BF1999 .C587 2001

Palmer, Trevor, 1944- Perilous planet earth. Cambridge, U.K. ; New York : Cambridge University Press, 2003.
QE506 .P35 2003

CATASTROPHICAL, THE.
Mason, Colin, 1926- The 2030 spike. London ; Sterling, VA : Earthscan Publications, 2003.
CB161 .M384 2003

Catastrophobia.
Clow, Barbara Hand, 1943- Rochester, Vt. : Bear & Company, c2001.
BF1999 .C587 2001

CATEGORIES (PHILOSOPHY).
Ammonius, Hermiae. Commentaria in quinque voces Porphyrii. Stuttgart : Frommann-Holzboog, 2002.

CATEGORIZATION (PSYCHOLOGY).
Pylyshyn, Zenon W., 1937- Seeing and visualizing. Cambridge, Mass. : MIT Press, 2003.
BF241 .P95 2003

CATERERS AND CATERING. See **DINNERS AND DINING.**

Caterina e il diavolo : una storia di streghe e inquisitori nella campagna pisana del Seicento / [a cura di] Silvia Nannipieri ; con un saggio di Adriano Prosperi. Pisa : ETS, c1999. 165 p. : ill. ; 22 cm. (Muse pisane ; 2) Includes bibliographical references. ISBN 88-467-0129-1 DDC 945
1. Volterrani, Caterina - Trials, litigation, etc. 2. Witchcraft - Italy - Pisa - History. 3. Trials (Witchcraft) - Italy - Pisa - History. 4. Inquisition - Italy - Pisa - History. I. Nannipieri, Silvia. II. Series.
BF1584.I8 C38 1999

Cathelat, Bernard.
La soif d'émotion. Paris : Plon, c1999.
BF531 .S637 1999

Cathelineau, Pierre-Christophe, 1961- Lacan, lecteur d'Aristote : politique, métaphysique, logique / Pierre-Christophe Cathelineau. 2. éd., rev. et corr. Paris : Éditions de l'Association freudienne internationale, c2001 (2002 printing) 405 p. : ill. ; 21 cm. (Discours psychanalytique) Includes bibliographical references. Originally presented as the author's thesis (doctoral)--Université de la Sorbonne-Paris IV, 1993. Includes bibliographical references (p. 393-405). ISBN 2-87612-044-5
1. Lacan, Jacques, - 1901- 2. Aristotle - Influence. 3. Psychoanalysis and philosophy. I. Université de Paris IV: Paris-Sorbonne. II. Title. III. Series.

CATHOLIC CHURCH. DIOCESE OF LAUSANNE (SWITZERLAND) - HISTORY.
Modestin, Georg. Le diable chez l'évêque. Lausanne : Université de Lausanne, Section d'histoire, Faculté des lettres, 1999.
BF1584.S9 M64 1999

CATHOLIC CHURCH. DIOCESE OF LODÈVE, FRANCE.
Alzieu, Gérard. Les églises de l'ancien diocèse de Lodève au Moyen-Age. Montpellier : Editions P. Clerc, 1998.
BX1532.L63 A695 1998

CATHOLIC CHURCH - DOCTRINES.
Chauvet, Louis Marie. [Symbole et sacrement. English] Symbol and sacrament. Collegeville, Minn. : Liturgical Press, c1995.
BV800 .C5213 1995

CATHOLIC CHURCH - FRANCE - PARIS - HISTORY.
Goglin, Jean-Marc. L'enseignement de la théologie dans les ordres mendiants à Paris au XIIIe siècle. Paris : Editions franciscaines, c2002.

CATHOLIC CHURCH - GERMANY - NUREMBERG - HISTORY - TO 1500.
Stark, Heinz. Plecher Kirchengeschichte im Mittelalter. Simmelsdorf : Altnürnberger Landschaft, 2002.

CATHOLIC CHURCH - GERMANY - PLECH - HISTORY - TO 1500.
Stark, Heinz. Plecher Kirchengeschichte im Mittelalter. Simmelsdorf : Altnürnberger Landschaft, 2002.

CATHOLIC CHURCH - LITURGY - HISTORY - MIDDLE AGES, 600-1500.
De Sion exibit lex et verbum domini de Hierusalem. Turnhout, Belgium : Brepols, c2001.

CATHOLIC CHURCH - NIGERIA - DOCTRINES.
Mozia, Michael Ifeanyinachukwu. Holiness & divine mercy (the key to heaven). Ibadan, Oyo State, Nigeria : St. Pauls, 2002.
1. Black author.

CATHOLIC CHURCH - POLAND - CLERGY - HISTORY.
Radzimiński, Andrzej. Życie i obyczajowość średniowiecznego duchowieństwa. Warszawa : Wydawn. DiG, 2002.
BX1565 .R32 2002

CATHOLIC CHURCH - POLAND - HISTORY.
Radzimiński, Andrzej. Życie i obyczajowość średniowiecznego duchowieństwa. Warszawa : Wydawn. DiG, 2002.
BX1565 .R32 2002

CATHOLIC CHURCH - RELATIONS - VOODOOISM.
Hurbon, Laënnec. Dieu dans le vaudou haïtien. Nouv. éd. Paris : Maisonneuve et Larose, 2002.
1. Black author.

CATHOLIC WOMEN - RELIGIOUS LIFE.
Callahan, Sidney Cornelia. Women who hear voices. New York : Paulist Press, 2003.
BV5091.R4 C35 2003

Catrysse, Andrée. Les grecs et la vieillesse : d'Homère à Epicure / Andrée Catrysse. Paris : L'Harmattan, c2003. 241 p. ; 22 cm. (Collection Ouverture philosophique) ISBN 2-7475-4118-5 DDC 180
1. Old age - Greece - History. 2. Old age - Philosophy. 3. Philosophy, Ancient. I. Title. II. Series: Collection L'ouverture philosophique.

CATS.
Budiansky, Stephen. The character of cats. New York, N.Y. : Viking, c2002.
SF446.5 .B84 2002

Case, Linda P. The cat. Ames, Iowa : Iowa State Press, c2003.
SF442 .C37 2003

Kolb, Janice E. M. In corridors of eternal time. Nevada City, Calif. : Blue Dolphin Pub., 2003.
BF1997.K65 A3 2003b

Ziolkowska, Aleksandra. Podróże z moją kotką. Wyd. 1. Warszawa : Wydawn. Nowy Świat, 2002.

CATS - BEHAVIOR.
Alger, Janet M., 1937- Cat culture. Philadelphia : Temple University Press, 2003.
SF446.5 .A36 2003

Budiansky, Stephen. The character of cats. New York, N.Y. : Viking, c2002.
SF446.5 .B84 2002

Case, Linda P. The cat. Ames, Iowa : Iowa State Press, c2003.
SF442 .C37 2003

Ziolkowska, Aleksandra. Podróże z moją kotką. Wyd. 1. Warszawa : Wydawn. Nowy Świat, 2002.

CATS - FICTION.
Marshall, Edison, 1956- Icing Ivy. Waterville, Me. : Thorndike Press, 2003, c2002.
PS3563.A722.36 I27 2003

CATS - HEALTH.
Case, Linda P. The cat. Ames, Iowa : Iowa State Press, c2003.
SF442 .C37 2003

CATS - NUTRITION.
Case, Linda P. The cat. Ames, Iowa : Iowa State Press, c2003.
SF442 .C37 2003

CATS - PSYCHOLOGY.
Budiansky, Stephen. The character of cats. New York, N.Y. : Viking, c2002.
SF446.5 .B84 2002

CATS - RELIGIOUS ASPECTS.
Constantine, Storm. Bast and Sekhmet. London : R. Hale, c1999.

CATS - SOCIAL ASPECTS.
Alger, Janet M., 1937- Cat culture. Philadelphia : Temple University Press, 2003.
SF446.5 .A36 2003

CATTANEO, CARLO, 1801-1869.
Cospito, Giuseppe, 1966- Il "gran Vico". Genova : Name, c2002.

Cattell, Heather Birkett. Essentials of 16PF assessment / Heather Cattell, James M. Schuerger. Hoboken, NJ : John Wiley & Sons, 2003. p. cm. (Essentials of psychological assessment series) Includes bibliographical references and index. Publisher description URL: http://www.loc.gov/catdir/desc ription/wiley039/2003045081.html Table of contents URL: http://www.loc.gov/catdir/toc/wiley032/2003045081.html ISBN 0-471-23424-9 (pbk.) DDC 155.2/83
1. Sixteen Personality Factor Questionnaire. I. Schuerger, James M. II. Title. III. Series.
BF698.8.S5 C265 2003

CATTLE. See **BULLS.**

Caturvedī, Saccidānanda. Vairāgya : eka dārśanika evaṃ tulanātmaka adhyayana / lekhaka, Saccidānanda Caturvedī. Itanagar : Himālayana Pabliśarsa, 2000. 258 p. ; 22 cm. Includes bibliographical references (p. 253-258). Includes passages in Sanskrit. ISBN 81-86393-18-8
1. Asceticism - Hinduism. 2. Renunciation (Philosophy) 3. Philosophy, Indic. 4. Vedic literature - History and criticism. I. Title.
BL1239.5.A82 C28 2000

CATV. See **CABLE TELEVISION.**

CAUCASIAN RACE. See also **WHITES.**
Katz, Judy H., 1950- White awareness. 2nd ed., rev. Norman : University of Oklahoma Press, 2003.
HT1523 .K37 2003

Caukhambā Āyurvijñāna granthamālā
(66) Upādhyāya, Govindaprasāda. Āyurvedīya mānasaroga cikitsā. 1. saṃskaraṇa. Vārāṇasī : Caukhabā Surabhāratī Prakāśana ; Dillī : Anya Prāptisthāna Caukhambā Saṃskṛta Pratiṣṭhāna, 2000.
R605 .U67 2000

Caukhambā Surabhāratī granthamālā
(330) Vaidyanāthadīkṣita, 15th cent. [Jātakapārijāta] Jātakapārijātaḥ. 1. saṃskaraṇa. Vārāṇasī : Caukhambā Surabhāratī Prakāśana ; Dillī : Caukhambā Saṃskṛti Pratiṣṭhāna, 2001.
BF1714.H5 V253 2001

(349) Mantreśvara. Phaladīpikā. 1. saṃskaraṇa. Vārāṇasī : Caukhambā Surabhāratī Prakāśana, 2002.
BF1714.H5+

(350) Pṛthuyaśas. Ṣaṭpañcāśikā. 1. saṃskaraṇa. Vārāṇasī : Caukhambā Surabhāratī Prakāśana ; Dillī : Caukhambā Saṃskṛta Pratiṣṭhāna, 2002.
BF1714.H5 P7 2002

Caulkins, Karinne, ill.
Sanders, Mark D. I hope you dance!. Nashville, Tenn. : Rutledge Hill Press, 2003.
BF410 .S26 2003

CAUSATION.
Ameriks, Karl, 1947- Interpreting Kant's critiques. Oxford : Clarendon Press ; New York : Oxford University Press, 2003.
B2779 .A64 2003

De Muijnck, Wim. Dependencies, connections, and other relations. Dordrecht ; Boston : Kluwer Academic Publishers, c2003.
BD418.3 .D4 2003

Enç, Berent. How we act. Oxford : Clarendon Press ; New York : Oxford University Press, 2003.
B105.A35 E63 2003

Johns, Richard, 1968- A theory of physical probability. Toronto : University of Toronto Press, c2002.

Mental causation and the metaphysics of mind. Peterborough, Ont. : Broadview Press, c2003.

Molnar, George, d. 1999. Powers. Oxford ; New York : Oxford University Press, 2003.
BD541 .M54 2003

Valabrega, Jean-Paul. Les mythes, conteurs de l'inconscient. Paris : Payot, 2001.
BD542 .V353 2001

Cautio criminalis.
Spee, Friedrich von, 1591-1635. [Cautio criminalis. English] Cautio criminalis, or, A book on witch trials. Charlottesville : University of Virginia Press, 2003.
BF1583.A2 S6813 2003

Cautio criminalis, or, A book on witch trials.
Spee, Friedrich von, 1591-1635. [Cautio criminalis. English] Charlottesville : University of Virginia Press, 2003.
BF1583.A2 S6813 2003

Cauville, Sylvie. Le zodiaque d'Osiris / S. Cauville. Leuven : Peeters, 1997. 81 p. : ill. (some col.) ; 20 cm. Includes bibliographical references. ISBN 90-6831-971-X ISBN 2-87723-358-8 (Peeters France)
1. Temple of Hathor (Dandara, Egypt) 2. Zodiac - Religious aspects. 3. Osiris (Egyptian deity) 4. Egypt - Religion. 5. Dandara (Egypt) - Antiquities. I. Title.
BL2450.O7 C399 1997

Cauwelaert, Didier van, 1960-.
Dray, Maryvonne. Karine après la vie. Paris : Albin Michel, c2002.

Cavanaugh, John C.
Kail, Robert V. Human development. 3rd ed. Belmont, CA : Thomson/Wadsworth, c2004.
BF713 .K336 2004

Cavarero, Adriana.
[Corpo in figure. English]
Stately bodies : literature, philosophy, and the question of gender / Adriana Cavarero ; translated by Robert de Lucca and Deanna Shemek. Ann Arbor : University of Michigan Press, c2002. xiv, 220 p. ; 24 cm. (The body, in theory) Includes bibliographical references (p. 209-220). ISBN 0-472-09674-5 (cloth) ISBN 0-472-06674-9 (paper) DDC 128/.6
1. Body, Human (Philosophy) I. Title. II. Series.
B105.B64 C3813 2002

CAYCE, EDGAR, 1877-1945.
EDGAR CAYCE READINGS.
Little, Lora. Secrets of the ancient world. Virginia Beach, Va. : A.R.E. Press, c2003.
BF1045.A74 L58 2003

CAYCE, EDGAR, 1877-1945.
Free, Wynn, 1946- The reincarnation of Edgar Cayce? Berkeley, Calif. : Frog, 2004.
BF1815.W49 F74 2004

Sugrue, Thomas, 1907- There is a river. Virginia Beach, Va. : A.R.E. Press, c2003.
BF1027.C3 S8 2003

Van Auken, John. The end times. New York : Signet Book, c2001. [Updated ed.].
BF1791.V36 2001

Cazenave, Michel.
Sciences et archétypes. Paris : Dervy, 2002.

CBMS (INTERNATIONAL RELATIONS). See **CONFIDENCE AND SECURITY BUILDING MEASURES (INTERNATIONAL RELATIONS).**

Ce que je ne sais pas.
Colloque des Invalides (5th : 2001 : Hôtel des invalides) Tusson, Charente : Du Lérot, [2002?]
PQ145.C65 2001

Cealey Harrison, Wendy. Beyond sex and gender / Wendy Cealey Harrison and John Hood-Williams. London ; Thousand Oaks, Calif. : SAGE, 2002. ix, 258 p. ; 24 cm. Includes bibliographical references and index. ISBN 0-7619-5599-2 ISBN 0-7619-5600-X (pbk) DDC 305.3
1. Sex role. 2. Gender identity. I. Hood-Williams, John. II. Title.
HQ1075.C43 2002

Ceballos Gómez, Diana Luz, 1962- Zauberei und Hexerei : eine Untersuchung magischer Praxen im Neuen Königreich Granada / Diana L. Ceballos Gómez. Frankfurt am Main ; New York : Peter Lang, c2000. xxiv, 259 p. : maps ; 21 cm. (Europäische Hochschulschriften. Reihe III, Geschichte und Hilfswissenschaften, 0531-7320 : Bd. 859= Publications universitaires européennes. Série III, Histoire, sciences auxiliaires de l'histoire ; vol. 859= European university studies. Series III, History and allied studies ; vol. 859) Originally presented as the author's thesis (doctoral)--Tübingen, Universität, 1999. Includes bibliographical references (p. [179]-210). ISBN 3-631-35952-7
1. Witchcraft - Spain - Granada - History. 2. Magic - Spain - Granada - History. I. Title. II. Series: Europäische Hochschulschriften. Reihe III, Geschichte und ihre Hilfswissenschaften ; Bd. 859.
BF1584.S7 C43 2000

ČECHY (CZECH REPUBLIC). See **BOHEMIA (CZECH REPUBLIC).**

CEILINGS, PAINTED. See **MURAL PAINTING AND DECORATION.**

Celebrating Wiccan spirituality.
Sabrina, Lady. Franklin Lakes, NJ : New Page Books, 2003.
BF1572.F37 S23 2003

CELEBRITIES. See also **CHILDREN OF CELEBRITIES.**
Bronfen, Elisabeth. Die Diva. München : Schirmer/Mosel, c2002.
BJ1470.5.B76 2002

Filho, Amilcar Torrão. Tríbades galantes, fanchonos militantes. São Paulo : Edições GLS, 2000.

Karasek, Hellmuth, 1934- Karambolagen. 2. Aufl. München : Ullstein Verlag, c2002.

Surendra Kumar. Legends of Indian cinema. New Delhi : Har-Anand Publications, c2003.
PN1993.5.I4 S87 2003

Veličková, Helena. Grafologie, cesta do hlubin duše. Vyd. 1. Praha : Academia, 2002.
BF896.V45 2002

CELEBRITIES - BIOGRAPHY.
Buschey, Monika. "An jenem Tag im blauen Mond September". Düsseldorf : Artemis & Winkler, c2000.

CELEBRITIES' CHILDREN. See **CHILDREN OF CELEBRITIES.**

CELEBRITIES - DEATH.
Celebrity death certificates. Jefferson, N.C. : McFarland, c2003.

CELEBRITIES - EUROPE - PSYCHOLOGY - CASE STUDIES.
Groben, Joseph. Requiem für ein Kind. 2. Aufl. Köln : Dittrich, 2002.
BF575.G7 G76 2002

CELEBRITIES IN ART.
Walker, John Albert, 1938- Art and celebrity. London ; Sterling, Va. : Pluto Press, 2003.
NX180.S6 W35 2003

CELEBRITIES - PSYCHOLOGY.
Walker, John Albert, 1938- Art and celebrity. London ; Sterling, Va. : Pluto Press, 2003.
NX180.S6 W35 2003

CELEBRITIES - RUSSIA (FEDERATION) - INTERVIEWS.
Maksimov, Andreĭ, 1959- Dialogi li͡ubvi. Moskva : Delovoĭ ėkspress, 1999.
BF575.L8 M336 1999

CELEBRITIES - UNITED STATES.
The right words at the right time. New York : Atria Books, c2002.
BJ1611.2.R52 2002

CELEBRITIES - UNITED STATES - INTERVIEWS.
How we have changed. Gretna, La. : Pelican Pub. Co., 2003.
E169.12.H677 2003

CELEBRITY. See **FAME.**

Celebrity death certificates / [compiled] by M. F. Steen. Jefferson, N.C. : McFarland, c2003. vi, 202 p. : facsim. ; 28 cm. ISBN 0-7864-1641-6 (pbk)
1. Death certificates. 2. Celebrities - Death. 3. Death. I. Steen, M. F.

Célérier, Marie-Claire. Repenser la cure psychanalytique / Marie-Claire Célérier. Paris : Dunod, c2002. vii, 178 p. ; 24 cm. (Collection Psychismes) ISBN 2-10-005889-4 DDC 150
1. Psychoanalysis. I. Title. II. Series: Psychismes.
RC504.C454 2002

CELL DEATH.
Klarsfeld, André. [Biologie de la mort. English] The biology of death. Ithaca, NY : Comstock Pub. Associates/Cornell University Press, 2004.
QH530.K5613 2004

Celli, Pier Luigi. Breviario di cinismo ben temperato / Pier Luigi Celli ; presentazione di Domenico De Masi. 1. ed. Roma : Fazi, 2002. 199 p. ; 20 cm. (Le terre/Scriture ; 42) Suggestions for managers, intellectuals and politicians at the peak of their careers on how to survive ethically in the corrupt world of power. ISBN 88-8112-363-0 DDC 858
1. Ethics. 2. Corruption. 3. Professional ethics. 4. Business ethics. 5. Political ethics. I. Title. II. Series: Terre (Rome, Italy). Scritture ; 42.

CELLULAR TELEPHONES - UNITED STATES.
United States. General Accounting Office. Telecommunications [electronic resource]. [Washington, D.C.] : U.S. General Accounting Office, [2003]

Cellular wisdom.
King, Joan C. Berkeley : Celestial Arts, 2003.
BF637.S4 K548 2003

Celtic astrology.
Vega, Phyllis. Franklin Lakes, NJ : New Page Books, c2002.
BF1714.C44 V44 2002

CELTIC CHURCH - HISTORY.
Bradley, Ian C. The Celtic way. [2nd ed.]. London : Darton Longman & Todd, 2003.
BR748.B73 2003

Snyder, Graydon F. Irish Jesus, Roman Jesus. Harrisburg, Pa. : Trinity Press International, c2002.
BR737.C4 S69 2002

CELTIC CIVILIZATION. See **CIVILIZATION, CELTIC.**

Celtic mysteries in New England.
Imbrogno, Philip J. 1st ed. St. Paul, Minn. : Llewellyn Publications, 2000.
BF2050.I435 2000

Celtic myth and legend.
Squire, Charles. Rev. ed. Franklin Lakes, NJ : New Page Books, c2001.
BL900.S6 2001

CELTIC MYTHOLOGY. See **MYTHOLOGY, CELTIC.**

The Celtic way.
Bradley, Ian C. [2nd ed.]. London : Darton Longman & Todd, 2003.
BR748.B73 2003

CELTS. See **DRUIDS AND DRUIDISM.**

CELTS - CIVILIZATION. See **CIVILIZATION, CELTIC.**

CELTS - FOLKLORE.
Squire, Charles. Celtic myth and legend. Rev. ed. Franklin Lakes, NJ : New Page Books, c2001.
BL900.S6 2001

CELTS - GREAT BRITAIN.
Snyder, Christopher A. (Christopher Allen), 1966- The Britons. Malden, MA ; Oxford : Blackwell Pub., 2003.
DA140.S73 2003

CELTS - RELIGION.
Bradley, Ian C. The Celtic way. [2nd ed.]. London : Darton Longman & Todd, 2003.
BR748.B73 2003

Kelly, Jill. Guardians of the Celtic way. Rochester, Vt. : Bear & Co., c2003.
BF1411.K45 2003

Snyder, Graydon F. Irish Jesus, Roman Jesus. Harrisburg, Pa. : Trinity Press International, c2002.
BR737.C4 S69 2002

Center for Constructive Change (Boise, Idaho).
Constructive change. Boise, Idaho : Center for Constructive Change, c1996-
BF698.9.P47 C66

Center for Emerging Threats and Opportunities (Marine Corps Warfighting Laboratory).
Child soldiers [electronic resource]. Quantico, Va. : Center for Emerging Threats and Opportunities, Marine Corps Warfighting Laboratory, [2002]

Center for Studies in Landscape History.
Gendered landscapes. University Park, PA : Center for Studies in Landscape History, c2000.

CENTRAL ASIA. See **ASIA, CENTRAL.**

CENTRAL NERVOUS SYSTEM. See **BRAIN.**

Centre de recherches en psychopathologie et psychologie clinique.
Matière à symbolisation. Lausanne : Delachaux et Niestlé, c1998.
BF458.M38 1998

Centre for Conflict Research.
Conflict management. Nairobi : Friedrich Ebert Stiftung : Centre for Conflict Research : Association of Local Government Authorities of Kenya, 2000.

Centre for Economic Policy Research (Great Britain).
The psychology of economic decisions. Oxford [England] ; New York : Oxford University Press, 2003-
HB74.P8 P725 2003

Centre for Studies in Civilization (Delhi, India).
Krishna, Daya. Developments in Indian philosophy from Eighteenth century onwards. New Delhi : Project of History of Indian Science, Philosophy, and Culture : Centre for Studies in Civilizations : Distributed by Motilal Banarsidass, 2002.
B131+

The centuries old philosophy and practice of traditional Chinese feng shui and the more advanced Flying Star feng shui.
Lum, Alan S.F. (Alan Sun Fai) Honolulu : Lum Pub., c2002.
BF1779.F4 L86 2002

CEO Academy.
Carey, Dennis. How to run a company. 1st ed. New York : Crown Business, c2003.
HD38.2.C374 2003

CEOS (EXECUTIVES). See **CHIEF EXECUTIVE OFFICERS.**

Ceppari Ridolfi, Maria A.
Maghi, streghe e alchimisti a Siena e nel suo territorio (1458-1571). Monteriggioni (Siena) : Il leccio, c1999.
BF1622.I8 M295 1999

CERAMIC ART. See **POTTERY.**

CERAMICS. See **POTTERY.**

CERAMICS (ART). See **POTTERY.**

La céramique : la poterie du néolithique aux temps modernes / par André d'Anna ... [et al.]. Paris : Editions Errance, c2003. 286 p. : ill., maps ; 25 cm. (Collection "Archéologiques") ISBN 2-87772-243-0 DDC 937
1. Pottery - History. 2. Pottery - Classification. 3. Pottery, Ancient. 4. Pottery, Prehistoric. 5. Archaeology. I. Anna, André d'. II. Series.

CEREBRAL CORTEX.
Virtual lesions. Oxford ; New York : Oxford University Press, c2002.
RC350.B72 V57 2002

CEREBRAL DOMINANCE.
Fagard, Jacqueline. Le développement des habiletés de l'enfant. Paris : CNRS, c2001.
RJ133 .F34 2001

CEREBROVASCULAR DISEASE. See **NEGLECT (NEUROLOGY).**

CEREBRUM. See **BRAIN.**

Cerelia.
Holland, Eileen. A witch's book of answers. York Beach, ME : Weiser Books, 2003.
BF1566 .H647 2003

CEREMONIAL EXCHANGE - EUROPE - MIDDLE AGES, 500-1500.
Negotiating the gift. Göttingen : Vandenhoeck & Ruprecht, c2003.

CEREMONIES. See **RITES AND CEREMONIES.**

Cerezo Manrique, Miguel Ángel. Los comienzos de la psicopedagogía en España, 1882-1936 / Niguel Ángel Cerezo Manrique. Madrid : Biblioteca Nueva, c2001. 317 p., [16] l. of plates : ill. ; 21 cm. (Memoria y crítica de la educación ; 5) Includes bibliographical references (p. [309]-317). ISBN 84-7030-993-5
1. *School psychology - Spain - History.* 2. *Educational psychology.* 3. *Learning, Psychology of.* I. *Title.* II. *Series.*

CERTAINTY. See **TRUTH.**

Le cerveau de Mozart.
Lechevalier, Bernard. Paris : O. Jacob, c2003.
ML3838 .L39 2003

Cesa-Bianchi, Nicolò, 1963-.
ALT 2002 (2002 : Lübeck, Germany) Algorithmic learning theory. Berlin ; New York : Springer, c2002.
QA76.9.A43 A48 2002

Ceserani, Jonne, 1954- Big ideas : putting the zest into creativity & innovation at work / Jonne Ceserani. London ; Sterling, VA : Kogan Page Limited, 2002. x, 197 p. : ill. ; 24 cm. cat 20030331 llb CONTENTS: The structure of this book -- Begin by testing your iq (innovation quotient) -- Some thoughts on how to introduce creativity, innovation and change into a business - describing an ideal -- A perspective about the world we live in from a creativity point of view -- Being - Mission and vision -- Moving towards your goal -- Accessing emotional resources and high-performance states -- Anchoring -- Seeing things from different perspectives -- Reframing: the transformation of meaning -- Speaking another person's language -- Rapport and influencing skills -- Levels of leadership and leadership style -- Doing -- The death of the chairperson -- Metaphors -- Questioning -- the wisdom? -- How lazy we are with language -- Discounting and revenge cycles; how to assume positive intent -- Listening: for ideas and to the meeting in your head -- Speaking for easy listening -- giving ideas or options -- Nine-step creative problem-solving model -- Springboards -- Imaging, metaphor, analogy and excursion -- journeys into absurdity -- Selection of springboards -- Idea development, a process map for using speculation and absurdity in order to generate new ways of working -- Risk taking -- Itemized response -- Best current thinking -- Comfort rating -- Next steps -- Appendix 1. Structures for group working -- Appendix 2. Communication for managing conflict -- Appendix 3. Synectics and its origins -- Appendix 4. What is nlp? -- Appendix 5. CONTENTS: Ground rules for effective meetings -- Appendix 6. The iq-innovation quotient. ISBN 0-7494-3878-9 DDC 658.4/063
1. *Creative ability in business.* 2. *Business communication.* I. *Title.* II. *Title: Bigideas*
HD53 .C46 2002

C.G. Jung and the making of modern psychology.
Shamdasani, Sonu, 1962- Cambridge, UK ; New York : Cambridge University Press, 2003.
BF173 .S485 2003

CGI (COMPUTER NETWORK PROTOCOL).
Fraley, R. Chris. How to conduct behavioral research over the internet. New York : Guilford Press, 2005.
BF76.6.I57 F73 2005

CHABOD, FEDERICO.
Sasso, Gennaro. Il guardiano della storiografia. 2. ed. [Bologna] : Società editrice il Mulino, c2002.

Chacon, Vamireh. O humanismo ibérico : a escolástica progressista e a questão da modernidade / Vamireh Chacon. [Lisboa?] : Imprensa Nacional-Casa da Moeda, [1998] 201 p. ; 24 cm. (Estudos gerais. Série universitária) Includes bibliographical references. ISBN 972-27-0902-X
1. *Humanism - Portugal.* 2. *Philosophy, Portuguese.* 3. *Culture - Philosophy.* I. *Title.* II. *Series.*
B821 .C43 1998

Chafe, William Henry.
The achievement of American liberalism. New York : Columbia University Press, c2003.
E806 .M63 2003

Chaffee, Steven H.
Communication, a different kind of horserace. Cresskill, N.J. : Hampton Press, c2003.
P87.3.C37 C66 2003

Chagas, Arnaldo Sousa das Chagas. O sujeito imaginário no discurso de auto-ajuda / Arnaldo Chagas. Rio Grande do Sul : Editora UNIJUÍ, 2002. 180 p. ; 21 cm. Includes bibliographical references (p. [175]-180). ISBN 85-7429-078-5
1. *Self-help techniques.* 2. *Psychology, Applied.* 3. *Self-perception.* 4. *Semiotics.* I. *Title.*

Chajes, Jeffrey Howard. Between worlds : dybbuks, exorcists, and early modern Judaism / J.H. Chajes. Philadelphia : University of Pennsylvania Press, c2003. 278 p. ; 23 cm. (Jewish culture and contexts) Includes bibliographical references (p. [245]-265) and index. ISBN 0-8122-3724-2 (cloth : alk. paper) DDC 296.3/16
1. *Dybbuk.* 2. *Spirit possession.* 3. *Exorcism.* 4. *Mysticism - Judaism.* 5. *Spiritual life - Judaism.* 6. *Future life - Judaism.* I. *Title.* II. *Series.*
BM729.D92 C53 2003

Chakra power beads.
Davies, Brenda, M.D. Berkeley, Calif. : Ulysses Press, c2001.
BF1442.C53 D36 2001

Chakras.
Ozaniec, Naomi. Rev. ed. Shaftesbury : Element, 2000.

CHAKRAS.
LeBeau, Kara R. Guan yin's chakra meditations. Boulder, Colo. : Mahasimhananda Press, c2001.
BF1442.C53 L43 2001

Nudel, Michael. 21st century's new chakra healing. Los Angeles, CA : Bio-Energy System Services, c2000.
BF1999 .N83 2000

Ozaniec, Naomi. Chakras. Rev. ed. Shaftesbury : Element, 2000.

CHAKRAS - MISCELLANEA.
Davies, Brenda, M.D. Chakra power beads. Berkeley, Calif. : Ulysses Press, c2001.
BF1442.C53 D36 2001

Lee, Ilchi. Healing chakra. Las Vegas, NV : Healing Society, c2002.
BF1442.C53 L44 2002

Lowndes, Florin. [Belebung des Herzchakra. English] Enlivening the chakra of the heart. London : Sophia Books : Rudolf Steiner Press, c1998.
BF1442.C53 L6913 1998

CHALIAPIN, FYODOR IVANOVICH, 1873-1938.
Drankov, V. L. (Vladimir L'vovich) Priroda khudozhestvennogo talanta. Sankt-Peterburg : Sankt-Peterburgskiĭ gos. universitet kul'tury i iskusstv, 2001.
BF408 .D66 2001

CHALIAPIN, FYODOR IVANOVICH, 1873-1938 - CRITICISM AND INTERPRETATION.
Drankov, V. L. (Vladimir L'vovich) Priroda khudozhestvennogo talanta. Sankt-Peterburg : Sankt-Peterburgskiĭ gosudarstvennyĭ universitet kul'tury i iskusstv, 2001.

The chalice of Magdalene.
Phillips, Graham. [Search for the Grail] Rochester, Vt. : Bear & Company, 2004.
BF1442.G73 P48 2004

CHALICES. See **GRAIL.**

The challenges of high command : the British experience / edited by Gary Sheffield and Geoffrey Till. Houndmills, Basingstoke ; New York : Palgrave Macmillan, 2003. xi, 216 p. : ill. ; 23 cm. (Cormorant security studies) Includes bibliographical references and index. ISBN 0-333-80438-4 DDC 355.3/3041/0941
1. *Command of troops - Case studies.* 2. *Leadership - Case studies.* 3. *Great Britain - Armed Forces - History - 20th century.* 4. *Great Britain - History, Military - 20th century - Case studies.* I. *Sheffield, Gary, 1961-* II. *Till, Geoffrey.* III. *Series.*
UB210 .C477 2003

Challenging biases - facing our fears.
Brashears, Deya. Dubuque, Iowa : Kendall/Hunt Pub., c1999.
BF575.P9 B735 1999

Challenging religion : essays in honour of Eileen Barker / edited by James A. Beckford and James T. Richardson. London ; New York : Routledge, 2003. xiii, 267 p. ; 24 cm. In honour of Professor Eileen Barker on the occasion of her retirement for the London School of Economics. Includes 1 pg. erratum. Includes bibliographical references (p. [237]-256) and index. ISBN 0-415-30948-4 (alk. paper) DDC 306.6
1. *Religion and sociology.* 2. *Cults.* I. *Barker, Eileen, 1938-* II. *Beckford, James A.* III. *Richardson, James T., 1941-*
BL60 .C437 2003

The chameleon consultant.
Holmes, Andrew, 1965- Aldershot ; Burlington, VT : Gower, 2002.

Le champ éthique
(no 36) Gilbert, Muriel. L'identité narrative. Genève : Labor et Fides, c2001.

Champ freudien
Abelhauser, Alain, 1954- Le sexe et le signifiant. Paris : Seuil, c2002.
BF175.5.S48 A24 2002

Champion, David R. Narcissism and entitlement : sexual aggression and the college male / David R. Champion. New York : LFB Scholarly Pub. LLC, c2003. x, 164 p. : ill. ; 23 cm. (Criminal justice) Includes bibliographical references (p. 137-154) and index. Table of contents URL: http://www.loc.gov/catdir/toc/fy034/2002010689.html CONTENTS: Sexual aggression as a problem -- Cognitive structures and entitled belief system -- Sexual aggression : an overview -- Machs, narcs, sexual aggressors and the entitled -- Methodology -- Analysis and results -- Discussion and conclusions : the entitled aggressor. ISBN 1-931202-49-4 (alk. paper) DDC 306.7/081
1. *Sexual animosity.* 2. *Entitlement attitudes.* 3. *Narcissism.* 4. *Male college students - United States - Psychology.* I. *Title.* II. *Series: Criminal justice (LFB Scholarly Publishing LLC)*
BF692.15 .C47 2003

Champs psychanalytiques
Matière à symbolisation. Lausanne : Delachaux et Niestlé, c1998.
BF458 .M38 1998

Le propre de l'homme. Lausanne : Delachaux et Niestlé, c1998.
BF175 .P69 1998

Chan, Marie, 1944-.
Excursions in Chinese culture. Hong Kong : Chinese University Press, c2002.

Chanaa, Jane. Security sector reform : issues, challenges and prospects / Jane Chanaa. Oxford ; New York : Oxford University Press for the International Institute for Strategic Studies, 2002. 82 p. ; 24 cm. (Adelphi paper, 0567-932x ; no. 344) Includes bibliographical references (p. [77]-82). ISBN 0-19-851674-6 DDC 327.172
1. *Internal security.* 2. *Conflict management.* 3. *Intervention (International law)* 4. *Institution building.* I. *International Institute for Strategic Studies.* II. *Title.* III. *Series: Adelphi papers ; no. 344.*
HV6419 .C52 2002

CHANCE. See also **COINCIDENCE.**
Gott, Robert. One in a million. Littleton, Mass. : Sundance, c2001.
BF1175 .G68 2001

Johns, Richard, 1968- A theory of physical probability. Toronto : University of Toronto Press, c2002.

Laidler, Keith James, 1916- Energy and the unexpected. Oxford ; New York : Oxford University Press, c2002.
QC72 .L35 2002

CHANCE, GAMES OF. See **GAMBLING.**

CHANCELLORS (PRIME MINISTERS). See **PRIME MINISTERS.**

Chandler, Michael J.
Jean Piaget Society. Meeting (30th : 2000 : Montréal, Québec) Changing conceptions of psychological life. Mahwah, N.J. : L. Erlbaum Associates, 2004.
BF697 .J36 2004

Chang, Edward C. (Edward Chin-Ho).
Virtue, vice, and personality. 1st ed. Washington, D.C. : American Psychological Association, c2003.
BF698 .V57 2003

Chang, Tisa.
Vint/age 2001 conference : [videorecording]. New York, c2001.

CHANG, TISA.
Vint/age 2001 conference : [videorecording]. New York, c2001.

Chang, Zhiqi. Zheng ti lun mei xue guan gang yao / Chang Zhiqi zhu. Di 1 ban. Chengdu : Sichuan ren min chu ban she : Sichuan sheng Xin hua shu dian jing xiao, 1994. 7, 3, 5, 2, 243 p. : ill. ; 21 cm. Includes bibliographical references. ISBN 7-220-02277-8
1. Aesthetics. I. Title.
BH39 .C435 1994 <Orien China>

CHANGE. *See also* **BECOMING (PHILOSOPHY).**
Gelven, Michael. What happens to us when we think. Albany : State University of New York Press, c2003.
BD111 .G45 2003

Napier, A. David. The age of immunology. Chicago : University of Chicago Press, 2003.
GN345 .N36 2003

Change activist.
McConnell, Carmel. Cambridge, MA : Perseus Pub., c2001.
BF481 .M393 2001

CHANGE IN PERSONALITY. *See* **PERSONALITY CHANGE.**

CHANGE OF LIFE. *See* **CLIMACTERIC.**

CHANGE, ORGANIZATIONAL. *See* **ORGANIZATIONAL CHANGE.**

CHANGE (PSYCHOLOGY). *See also* **PERSONALITY CHANGE.**
Bridges, William, 1933- The way of transition. Cambridge, Mass. : Perseus Pub., c2001.
BF335 .B717 2001

Dolnick, Barrie. Instructions for your discontent. New York : Simple Abundance Press/Scribner, c2003.
BF637.C4 D65 2003

Gardner, Howard. Changing minds. Boston, Mass. : Harvard Business School Press, 2004.
BF637.C4 G37 2004

Goodier, Steve. Lessons of the turtle. Divide, CO : Life Support System Pub., c2002.
BF637.C5 G67 2002

Hay, Louise L. I can do it!. Carlsbad, CA : Hay House, c2004.
BF697.5.S47 H388 2004

McConnell, Carmel. Change activist. Cambridge, MA : Perseus Pub., c2001.
BF481 .M393 2001

Mongeau, Pierre, 1954- Survivre. Sainte-Foy : Presses de l'Université du Québec, 2002.
BF122 .M66 2002

Py, Luiz Alberto. Olhar acima do horizonte. Rio de Janeiro : Rocco, 2002.

Sabourin, Teresa Chandler. The contemporary American family. Thousand Oaks, Calif. : Sage Publications, c2003.
HQ536 .S213 2003

Sills, Judith. If the horse is dead, get off!. New York : Viking, 2004.
BF637.S38 S55 2004

Wowisms. 1st ed. New York : Newmarket Press, c2003.
BF637.S8 W7 2003

CHANGE (PSYCHOLOGY) - PROBLEMS, EXERCISES, ETC.
Claiborn, James. The habit change workbook. Oakland, CA : New Harbinger Publications : Distributed in the U.S.A. by Publishers Group West, c2001.
BF337.B74 C57 2001

CHANGE, SOCIAL. *See* **SOCIAL CHANGE.**

Change your aura, change your life.
Martin, Barbara Y. Sunland, CA : WisdomLight Books, c2003.
BF1389.A8 M37 2003

Change your thinking, change your life.
Tracy, Brian. Hoboken, N.J. : J. Wiley & Sons, c2003.
BF637.S8 T634 2003

Changement de perspective.
Dagognet, François. Paris : Table ronde, c2002.

CHANGES, CLIMATIC. *See* **CLIMATIC CHANGES.**

Changeux, Jean-Pierre.
[Ce qui nous fait penser. English]
What makes us think? : a neuroscientist and a philosopher argue about ethics, human nature, and the brain / Jean-Pierre Changeux and Paul Ricœur ; translated by M.B. DeBevoise. Princeton, N.J. : Princeton University Press, c2000. x, 335 p. : ill. ; 23 cm. Includes bibliographical references (p. [313]-326) and index. Translated from the French. Table of contents URL: http://www.loc.gov/catdir/toc/prin031/00024827.html Publisher description URL: http://www.loc.gov/catdir/description/prin022/00024827.html CONTENTS: A necessary encounter -- Body and mind: in search of a common discourse -- The neuronal model and the test of experience -- Consciousness of oneself and of others -- The origins of morality -- Desire and norms -- Ethical universality and cultural conflict. ISBN 0-691-00940-6 (alk. paper) DDC 153
1. Changeux, Jean-Pierre - Interviews. 2. Ricœur, Paul - Interviews. 3. Ethics. 4. Neuropsychology. 5. Neuroscientists - France - Interviews. 6. Philosophers - France - Interviews. 7. Conscience - Interview. 8. Medical ethics - Interview. 9. Mind and body - Interview. I. Ricœur, Paul. II. Title. III. Title: Neuroscientist and a philosopher argue about ethics, human nature, and the brain
BJ45 .C4313 2000

Collège de France. Symposium annuel. La vérité dans les sciences. Paris : Jacob, c2003.

CHANGEUX, JEAN-PIERRE - INTERVIEWS.
Changeux, Jean-Pierre. [Ce qui nous fait penser. English] What makes us think? Princeton, N.J. : Princeton University Press, c2000.
BJ45 .C4313 2000

Changing conceptions of psychological life.
Jean Piaget Society. Meeting (30th : 2000 : Montréal, Québec) Mahwah, N.J. : L. Erlbaum Associates, 2004.
BF697 .J36 2004

Changing mind.
Orsucci, Franco. River Edge, NJ : World Scientific, c2002.
BF161 .O77 2002

Changing minds.
Gardner, Howard. Boston, Mass. : Harvard Business School Press, 2004.
BF637.C4 G37 2004

CHANNELING (SPIRITUALISM).
Byrd, Da Juana. Ghosts talk. 1st ed. Cedar Hills, Tex. : Byrd Pub., c2002.
BF1031 .B97 2002

Wood, Robert S. (Robert Snyder), 1930- Peaceful passing. Sedona, AZ : In Print Pub., c2000.
BF789.D4 W66 2000

CHANNELLING (SPIRITUALISM). *See* **CHANNELING (SPIRITUALISM).**

Chaos and time-series analysis.
Sprott, Julien C. Oxford ; New York : Oxford University Press, 2003.

Chaos control : theory and applications / Guanrong Chen, Xinghuo Yu (eds.). Berlin ; New York : Springer, c2003. x, 369 p. : ill. ; 24 cm. (Lecture notes in control and information sciences, 0170-8643 ; 292) Includes bibliographical references. ISBN 3-540-40405-8 (alk. paper) DDC 629.8
1. Control theory. 2. Chaotic behavior in systems. 3. Systems engineering. 4. Chaotic behavior in systems - Industrial applications. I. Chen, G. (Guanrong) II. Yu, Xing Huo. III. Series.
QA402.3 .C48 2003

CHAOS IN SYSTEMS. *See* **CHAOTIC BEHAVIOR IN SYSTEMS.**

Chaos in Wonderland.
Pickover, Clifford A. 1st ed. New York : St. Martin's Press, 1994.
Q172.5.C45 P53 1994

CHAOTIC BEHAVIOR IN SYSTEMS.
Adeleye, Modupe, 1980- From our hearts. Rochester, N.Y. : Mo-Biz Publishing Co., 2003.
BF353 .A33 2003

Chaos control. Berlin ; New York : Springer, c2003.
QA402.3 .C48 2003

Combs, Allan, 1942- The radiance of being. 2nd ed. St. Paul, Minn. : Paragon House, 2002.
BF311 .C575 2002

Coping with chaos. New York : J. Wiley, c1994.
Q172.5.C45 C67 1994

Dynamics of dissipation. Berlin ; New York : Springer, c2002.
QC174.85 .D96 2002

Laidler, Keith James, 1916- Energy and the unexpected. Oxford ; New York : Oxford University Press, c2002.
QC72 .L35 2002

Pickover, Clifford A. Chaos in Wonderland. 1st ed. New York : St. Martin's Press, 1994.
Q172.5.C45 P53 1994

Sprott, Julien C. Chaos and time-series analysis. Oxford ; New York : Oxford University Press, 2003.

Zhusubaliyev, Zhanybai T. Bifurcations and chaos in piecewise-smooth dynamical systems. River Edge, New Jersey : World Scientific, c2003.

CHAOTIC BEHAVIOR IN SYSTEMS - INDUSTRIAL APPLICATIONS.
Chaos control. Berlin ; New York : Springer, c2003.
QA402.3 .C48 2003

CHAOTIC MOTION IN SYSTEMS. *See* **CHAOTIC BEHAVIOR IN SYSTEMS.**

Chapel of extreme experience.
Geiger, John, 1960- 1st ed. Toronto, Ont. : Gutter Press, c2002.
QP495 .G45 2002

Chapelle, Daniel, 1951- The soul in everyday life / Daniel Chapelle. Albany, NY : State University of New York Press, c2003. xv, 272 p. ; 23 cm. Includes bibliographical references (p. 257-260) and index. ISBN 0-7914-5863-6 (alk. paper) ISBN 0-7914-5864-4 (pbk. : alk. paper) DDC 150.19/5
1. Psychoanalysis and philosophy. 2. Soul - Psychological aspects. 3. Values - Psychological aspects. I. Title.
BF175.4.P45 C48 2003

Chaplin, Nikki. Secrets of a dream catcher / Nikki Chaplin. Hallandale Beach, Fla. : Aglob Pub., 2003. p. cm. Table of contents URL: http://www.loc.gov/catdir/toc/ecip048/2003019093.html ISBN 1-59427-005-8 DDC 158.1
1. Self-actualization (Psychology) I. Title.
BF637.S4 C492 2003

CHARACTER DEVELOPMENT. *See* **PERSONALITY DEVELOPMENT.**

CHARACTER EDUCATION. *See* **MORAL EDUCATION.**

Character education (Raintree (Firm))
Hirschmann, Kris, 1967- Leadership. Chicago, IL : Raintree, 2003.
BF723.L4 H57 2003

CHARACTER FORMATION. *See* **PERSONALITY DEVELOPMENT.**

Character Generators/Video.
Vint/age 2001 conference : [videorecording]. New York, c2001.

CHARACTER - HANDBOOKS, MANUALS, ETC.
Peterson, Christopher, 1950 Feb. 18- Character strengths and virtues. New York : Oxford University Press, 2004.
BF818 .P38 2004

Character in action.
Phillips, Donald T. (Donald Thomas), 1952- Annapolis, Md. : Naval Institute Press, c2003.
VG53 .P49 2003

Character kaleidoscope.
Christesen, Mirka. Port Chester, N.Y. : Dude Pub., c2000.
BF818 .C55 2000

The character of cats.
Budiansky, Stephen. New York, N.Y. : Viking, c2002.
SF446.5 .B84 2002

CHARACTER - POLITICAL ASPECTS - UNITED STATES - HISTORY - 18TH CENTURY.
Trees, Andrew S., 1968- The founding fathers and the politics of character. Princeton, N.J. : Princeton University Press, c2004.
E302.1 .T74 2004

Character strengths and virtues.
Peterson, Christopher, 1950 Feb. 18- New York : Oxford University Press, 2004.
BF818 .P38 2004

CHARACTER - STUDY AND TEACHING (MIDDLE SCHOOL) - UNITED STATES.
Christesen, Mirka. Character kaleidoscope. Port Chester, N.Y. : Dude Pub., c2000.
BF818 .C55 2000

CHARACTER TESTS - JUVENILE LITERATURE.
Brian, Sarah Jane. The quiz book 2. Middleton, Wis. : Pleasant Co. , c2001.
BF831 .B75 2001

CHARACTERS AND CHARACTERISTICS. *See* **PHRENOLOGY; PHYSIOGNOMY; TYPOLOGY (PSYCHOLOGY).**

The characters within.
Clough, Joy. Chicago, IL : ACTA Publications, c1997.

BF531 .C52 1997

CHARITIES. *See also* **INTERNATIONAL RELIEF.**
Nelson, Phillip J., 1929- Signaling goodness. Ann Arbor : University of Michigan Press, c2003.
HV31 .N45 2003

CHARITIES, MEDICAL. *See* **AGED - MEDICAL CARE; HOSPITALS.**

Charlemagne & France.
Morrissey, Robert John, 1947- [Empereur à la barbe fleurie. English] English language ed. Notre Dame, Ind. : University of Notre Dame Press, c2003.
DC73 .M7513 2003

Charlemagne and France.
Morrissey, Robert John, 1947- [Empereur à la barbe fleurie. English] Charlemagne & France. English language ed. Notre Dame, Ind. : University of Notre Dame Press, c2003.
DC73 .M7513 2003

CHARLEMAGNE, EMPEROR, 742-814.
Depreux, Philippe. Charlemagne et les Carolingiens. Paris : Tallandier : Historia, 2002.
DC73 .D38 2002

CHARLEMAGNE, EMPEROR, 742-814 - IN LITERATURE.
Morrissey, Robert John, 1947- [Empereur à la barbe fleurie. English] Charlemagne & France. English language ed. Notre Dame, Ind. : University of Notre Dame Press, c2003.
DC73 .M7513 2003

CHARLEMAGNE, EMPEROR, 742-814 - INFLUENCE.
Morrissey, Robert John, 1947- [Empereur à la barbe fleurie. English] Charlemagne & France. English language ed. Notre Dame, Ind. : University of Notre Dame Press, c2003.
DC73 .M7513 2003

CHARLEMAGNE, EMPEROR, 742-814 - LEGENDS - HISTORY AND CRITICISM.
Morrissey, Robert John, 1947- [Empereur à la barbe fleurie. English] Charlemagne & France. English language ed. Notre Dame, Ind. : University of Notre Dame Press, c2003.
DC73 .M7513 2003

CHARLEMAGNE, EMPEROR, 742-814 - ROMANCES - HISTORY AND CRITICISM.
Morrissey, Robert John, 1947- [Empereur à la barbe fleurie. English] Charlemagne & France. English language ed. Notre Dame, Ind. : University of Notre Dame Press, c2003.
DC73 .M7513 2003

Charlemagne et les Carolingiens.
Depreux, Philippe. Paris : Tallandier : Historia, 2002.
DC73 .D38 2002

Charles, Monique. Borges, ou, L'étrangeté apprivoisée : approche psychanalytique des enjeux, sources et ressources de la création / Monique Charles. Paris : Harmattan, c2002. 316 p. ; 24 cm. (Psychanalyse et civilisations) Includes bibliographical references (p. 295-308) and index. ISBN 2-7475-3105-8 DDC 809
1. Borges, Jorge Luis, - 1899- - Criticism and interpretation. 2. Argentine literature - 20th century - History and criticism. 3. Psychoanalysis and literature. I. Title. II. Title: Etrangeté apprivoisée III. Series.

Charlton-Davis, Mark K. Thoughts from the underworld : the three cycles / Mark K. Charlton-Davis. Los Angeles, Calif. : Amen-Ra Theological Seminary Press, c2001 (Kearney, NE : Morris Pub.) 421 p. : ill. ; 28 cm. Includes bibliographical references (p. 411-413) and index. ISBN 0-9674226-1-2 DDC 133
1. Occultism. 2. Religion - Miscellanea. I. Title.
BF1999 .C5145 2001

CHARMS. *See also* **AMULETS; TALISMANS.**
Aoumiel. Grimoire for the green witch. 1st ed. St. Paul, Minn. : Llewellyn Publications, c2003.
BF1572.P43 A583 2003

Baker, Marina. Spells for teenage witches. Berkeley, Calif. : Seastone, c2000.
BF1571.5.T44 B34 2000

Dunwich, Gerina. Exploring spellcraft. Franklin Lakes, NJ : New Page Books, c2001.
BF1566 .D866 2001

Dunwich, Gerina. The pagan book of Halloween. New York : Penguin/Compass, 2000.
BF1566 .D867 2000

Dunwich, Gerina. A witch's guide to ghosts and the supernatural. Franklin Lakes, NJ : New Page Books, c2002.

BF1471 .D86 2002

Gillotte, Galen, 1952- Sacred stones of the goddess. 1st ed. St. Paul, Minn. : Llewellyn Publications, 2003.
BF1611 .G55 2003

Hawke, Elen, 1947- An alphabet of spells. St. Paul, MN : Llewellyn Publications, 2003.
BF1566 .H376 2003

Madigan, M. A., 1962- Symbols of the craft. 1st ed. St. Paul, Minn. : Llewellyn Publications, 2003.
BF1773 .M29 2003

McQuillar, Tayannah Lee, 1977- Rootwork. New York : Simon & Schuster, c2003.
BF1622.A34 M37 2003
1. Black author.

Richardson, S. Cheryl. Magicka formularia. [Miami, Fla.] : S.C. Richardson, c2001.
BF1611 .R53 2001

Sophia, 1955- The little book of hot love spells. Kansas City, Mo. : Andrews McMeel Pub., c2002.
BF1623.L6 S66 2002

Sophia, 1955- The ultimate guide to goddess empowerment. Kansas City : Andrews McMeel Pub., c2003.
BF1621 .S67 2003

White, Lauren. Spells for a perfect love life. Kansas City, Mo. : Andrews McMeel Pub., 2000.
BF1572.L6 .W45 2000

CHARMS - DICTIONARIES.
Beattie, Antonia. Spells dictionary. San Diego, Calif. : Thunder Bay Press, 2003.
BF1611 .B43 2003

Charodei ponevole.
Vinokurov, Igor' Moskva : AiF-Print, 2003.
BF1288 .V55 2003

Charpak, Georges.
[Devenez sorciers, devenez savants English]
Debunked! : esp, telekinesis, and other pseudoscience / Georges Charpak and Henri Broch ; translated by Bart K. Holland. Baltimore : Johns Hopkins University Press, 2004. v, 208 p. Table of contents URL: http://www.loc.gov/catdir/toc/ecip046/2003015032.html CONTENTS: The first steps in the initiation -- Amazing coincidences -- Let's play detective -- The right to dreams and clarity -- As a new millennium dawn. ISBN 0-8018-7867-5 (hardcover : alk. paper) DDC 130
1. Occultism and science. I. Broch, Henri. II. Title.
BF1409.5 .C4313 2004

CHARTERS. *See* **ARCHIVES.**

Chase, Carol J.
Philologies old and new. Princeton : The Edward C. Armstrong Monographs, 2001.

CHASE, THE. *See* **HUNTING.**

CHASIDISM. *See* **HASIDISM.**

Chassay, Jean-François, 1959-.
Les lieux de l'imaginaire. Montréal : Liber, 2002.

Châtelet, Gilles.
[Enjeux du mobile. English]
Figuring space : philosophy, mathematics, and physics / by Gilles Châtelet (1945-1999) ; translated by Robert Shore and Muriel Zagha. Dordrecht ; Boston : Kluwer, c2000. xxxii, 197 p. : ill. ; 24 cm. (Science and philosophy ; v. 8) Includes bibliographical references. ISBN 0-7923-5880-5 DDC 113
1. Philosophy. 2. Mathematics - Philosophy. 3. Physics - Philosophy. I. Title. II. Series: Science and philosophy ; 8.
B67 .C4313 2000

Chatterjea, Tara, 1937- Knowledge and freedom in Indian philosophy / Tara Chatterjea. Lanham, Md. ; Oxford : Lexington Books, 2002. xvi, 159 p. ; 24 cm. Includes bibliographical references (p. 157-159). ISBN 0-7391-0456-X DDC 181/.4
1. Philosophy, Indic. 2. Knowledge, Theory of. I. Title.
B131 .C518 2002

Chattopadhyaya, Gauri, 1950- Advaitic ontology and epistemology : a critical reassessment / Gauri Chattopadhyaya. 1st ed. Allahabad : Raka Prakashan, 2001. 248 p. ; 23 cm. Includes bibliographical references (p. [239]-248). Includes passages in Sanskrit (Sanskrit in Devanagari and roman).
1. Advaita. 2. Ontology. 3. Knowledge, Theory of. I. Title.
B132.A3+

Chaudhuri, Una, 1951-.
Land/scape/theater. Ann Arbor : University of Michigan, c2002.

PN2020 .L32 2002

Chauvet, Louis Marie.
[Symbole et sacrement. English]
Symbol and sacrament : a sacramental reinterpretation of Christian existence / Louis-Marie Chauvet ; translated by Patrick Madigan and Madeleine Beaumont. Collegeville, Minn. : Liturgical Press, c1995. xvii, 569 p. : ill. ; 23 cm. "A Pueblo book." Includes bibliographical references and indexes. ISBN 0-8146-6124-6 DDC 234/.16
1. Catholic Church - Doctrines. 2. Sacraments - Catholic Church. 3. Symbolism. I. Title.
BV800 .C5213 1995

CHAUVINISM AND JINGOISM. *See* **IMPERIALISM.**

Chayes, Antonia Handler, 1929-.
Imagine coexistence. 1st ed. San Francisco : Jossey-Bass, c2003.
HM1121 .I42 2003

Chazal, Gérard. Interfaces : enquêtes sur les mondes intermédiaires / Gérard Chazal. Seyssel [France] : Champ Vallon, c2002. 275 p. ; 21 cm. (Collection Milieux, 0291-7157) Includes bibliographical references (p. [271]-275). ISBN 2-87673-351-X DDC 194
1. Communication. 2. Social interaction. 3. Communication - Social aspects. 4. Body language. 5. Communication and culture. 6. Language and languages. I. Title.
HM1111 .C49 2002

Chebili, Saïd. La tâche civilisatrice de la psychanalyse selon Freud : le malaise dans la culture à l'épreuve de l'animalité / Saïd Chebili. Paris : L'Harmattan, c2002. 241 p. ; 22 cm. (Ouverture philosophique) Includes bibliographical references (p. [211]-224) and index. ISBN 2-7475-3171-6 DDC 150
1. Freud, Sigmund, - 1856-1939. 2. Psychoanalysis. 3. Human beings - Animal nature. I. Title. II. Series: Collection L'ouverture philosophique.

CHEERFULNESS. *See* **HAPPINESS.**

CHEKHOV, ANTON PAVLOVICH, 1860-1904 - DRAMATIC WORKS.
Tait, Peta, 1953- Performing emotions. Aldershot ; Burlington Vt. : Ashgate, c2002.
PG3458.Z9 D774 2002

Chelovek kak avtor zhizni.
Psikhologiia sub"ektnosti. Kirov : Viatskii gos. pedagog. universitet, 2001.
BF697 .P75 2001

Chelovek kak sub"ekt kul'tury / otv. red. È.V. Saĭko. Moskva : Nauka, 2002. 445 p. ; 22 cm. (Sub"ekt v mire, Mir sub"ekta) Includes bibliographical references. ISBN 5020227536
1. Ethnopsychology. 2. Personality and culture. 3. Subject (Philosophy) 4. Individuality. 5. Ethnicity. 6. Identity (Psychology) 7. Interpersonal communication. I. Saĭko, È. V. (Èdi Viktorovna) II. Series.

CHEMICAL INDUSTRY. *See* **PHARMACEUTICAL INDUSTRY.**

CHEMISTRY. *See* **ALCHEMY; COLOR.**

CHEMISTRY - HISTORY.
Greenberg, Arthur. The art of chemistry. Hoboken, N.J. : Wiley-Interscience, c2003.
QD11 .G735 2003

CHEMOTHERAPY. *See* **DRUGS.**

Chen, Chaomei, 1960-.
Visualizing the semantic Web. London ; [New York] : Springer, c2003.
TK5105.888 .V55 2003

Chen, G. (Guanrong).
Chaos control. Berlin ; New York : Springer, c2003.
QA402.3 .C48 2003

Chen, Huihua.
Feminism/femininity in Chinese literature. Amsterdam ; New York : Rodopi, 2002.

Chen, Nancy N.
Breathing spaces. New York : Columbia University Press, c2003.
RA781.8 .B73 2003

Chen, Wei, 1957- Dong fang mei xue dui xi fang de ying xiang = Dongfang meixue duixifang de yingxiang / Chen Wei, Wang Jie bian zhu. Di 1 ban. Shanghai : Xue lin chu ban she, 1999. 2, 175 p., [8] p. of plates : ill. ; 21 cm. Includes bibliographical references. ISBN 7-80616-685-8
1. Aesthetics, Chinese. 2. Art - Chinese influences. 3. East and West. I. Wang, Jie. II. Title. III. Title: Dongfang meixue duixifang de yingxiang

Chen, William C. C.
Chuckrow, Robert. The tai chi book. Boston : YMAA Publication Center, c1998.
GV504 .C536 1998

Chen, Xinhan. She hui ping jia lun : She hui qun ti wei zhu ti de ping jia huo dong si kao = On social evaluation : the thought of evaluative activities on social group as subject / Ch'en Hsin-han chu. Di 1 ban. Shanghai : Shanghai she hui ke xue yuan chu ban she : Xin hua shu dian Shanghai fa xing suo fa xing, 1997. 7, 11, 5, 8, 400 p. : ill. ; 21 cm. "Ben shu chu ban you shi Makesi zhu yi xue shu zhu zuo chu ban ji jin zi zhu." List of author's works: p.395-398. Includes bibliographical references. Table of contents also in English. ISBN 7-80618-317-5
1. Social groups. 2. Social psychology. I. Title. II. Title: On social evaluation : the thought of evaluative activities on social group as subject
HM131 .C7135 1997 <Asian China>

Chen, Yaoting.
Schipper, Kristofer Marinus. Dao zang suo yin. Di 1 ban. Shanghai : Shanghai shu dian chu ban she : Xin hua shu dian Shanghai fa xing suo fa xing, 1996.
BL1900.T387 S35 1996 <Orien China>

Chen, Yugang. Zhongguo wen xue tong shi / Chen Yugang zhu. Di 1 ban. Beijing Shi : Xi yuan chu ban she : Xin hua shu dian jing xiao, 1996. 2 v. (7, 1313 p.) ; 21 cm. Cover title: Zhong guo wen xue tong shi. In Chinese. ISBN 7-80108-016-5
1. Chinese literature - History and criticism. I. Title. II. Title: Zhong guo wen xue tong shi
PL2264 .C442527 1996 <Orien China>

Chen, Zhimin.
Xie jiao zhen xiang. Di 1 ban. Beijing : Dang dai shi jie chu ban she, 2001.
BT1315.2 .X54 2001

Cheney, Carl D.
Pierce, W. David. Behavior analysis and learning. 3rd ed. Mahwah, N.J. : L. Erlbaum Associates, 2004.
BF199 .P54 2004

Cheng, Qianfan.
[Works. 2000]
Cheng Qianfan quan ji. Di 1 ban. Shijiazhuang Shi : Hebei jiao yu chu ban she, 2000. 15 v. : ill. ; 21 cm. Includes bibliographical references. CONTENTS: v. 1-4. Jiao chou guang yi / Cheng Qianfan, Xu Youfu zhuan -- v. 5. Shi tong jian ji -- v. 6. Wen lun shi jian -- v. 7. Xian tang wen sou -- v. 8. Tang dai jin shi xing juan yu wen xue ; Gu shi kao suo / Cheng Qianfan zhuan -- v. 9. Bei kai tuo de shi shi jie / Cheng Qianfan, Mo Lifeng, Zhang Hongsheng zhuan ; Du shi jing quan pi chao -- v. 10. Gu shi jin xuan -- v. 11. Gu shi jin xuan ; Du Song shi sui bi / Cheng Qianfan zhuan -- v. 12. Cheng shi Han yu wen xue tong shi / Cheng Qianfan, Cheng Zhangcan zhuan -- v. 13. Liang Song wen xue shi / Cheng Qianfan, Wu Xinlei zhuan -- v. 14. Xian tang shi wen he chao / Cheng Qianfan zhuan -- v. 15. Sang yu yi wang / Cheng Qianfan shu ; Zhang Bowei bian. ISBN 7-5434-3979-4
1. Chinese literature - History and criticism. I. Title.
PL2744 .C46 2000

Cheng Qianfan quan ji.
Cheng, Qianfan. [Works. 2000] Di 1 ban. Shijiazhuang Shi : Hebei jiao yu chu ban she, 2000.
PL2744 .C46 2000

Cheng zhang de Zhongguo : dang dai Zhongguo qing nian de guo jia min zu yi shi yan jiu = Chengzhang de Zhongguo / Fang Ning, Wang Bingquan, Ma Lijun deng zhu. Di 1 ban. Beijing : Ren min chu ban she, 2002. 7, 426 p. ; 21 cm. "Guo jia she ke ji jin 'jiu wu' gui hua xiang mu" Includes bibliographical references. ISBN 7-01-003609-8
1. Youth - Political aspects - China. 2. Political psychology. 3. Nationalism - China. I. Fang, Ning. II. Wang, Bingquan. III. Ma, Lijun. IV. Title: Dang dai Zhongguo qing nian de guo jia min zu yi shi yan jiu V. Title: Chengzhang de Zhongguo
HQ799.2.P6 C449 2002

Chengzhang de Zhongguo.
Cheng zhang de Zhongguo. Di 1 ban. Beijing : Ren min chu ban she, 2002.
HQ799.2.P6 C449 2002

Cherchi, Gavina, 1957- Tra le immagini : ricerche di ermeneutica e iconologia / Gavina Cherchi. Fiesole (Firenze) : Cadmo ; Siena : Centro Mario Rossi per gli studi filosofici, 2002. 272 p. : ill. ; 24 cm. (Argomenti di filosofia / Centro Mario Rossi per gli studi filosofici ; 2) Includes bibliographical references (p. 157-255) and index. ISBN 88-7923-275-4 DDC 121
1. Emblems. 2. Hermeneutics. I. Title. II. Series: Argomenti di filosofia ; 2.

Cherchi, Marcello. Disciplines and nations : Niko Marr vs. his Georgian students on Tbilisi State University and the Japhetidology/Caucasology schism / Marcello Cherchi and H. Paul Manning. Pittsburgh, Pa. : Center for Russian and East European Studies, University Center for International Studies, University of Pittsburgh, c2002. 65 p. : ill. ; 21 cm. (The Carl Beck papers in Russian & East European studies, 0889-275X ; no. 1603) "September 2002"--T.p. verso. Includes bibliographical references (p. 56-62).
1. Marr, Nikolaĭ I͡Akovlevich, - 1864-1934. 2. T'bilisis saxelmcip'o universiteti - History. 3. Language and languages. I. Manning, H. Paul. II. Title. III. Series: Carl Beck papers in Russian and East European studies ; no. 1603.

Cherepanova, I. I͡U. (Irina I͡Ur'evna) Dom koldun'i : i͡azyk tvorcheskogo Bessoznatel'nogo / Irina Cherepanova. Perer., dop. i ispravlennoe izd. Moskva : KSP+, 2001. 397 p. ; 21 cm. (Biblioteka NLP) "Nauchno-populi͡arnoe izdanie"--Colophon. Includes bibliographical references (p. [374]-395). ISBN 5896920210
1. Mental suggestion. 2. Therapeutics, Suggestive. 3. Discourse analysis - Psychological aspects. 4. Parapsychology and language. 5. Myth. I. Title. II. Series.
BF1156.S8 C53 2001

CHERUBIM. *See* **ANGELS.**

Chetkin, Len. 100 thoughts that lead to happiness / Len Chetkin. Charlottesville, VA : Hampton Roads Pub., c2002. xv, 143 p. ; 17 cm. Includes bibliographical references (p. 141). ISBN 1-57174-307-3 (pbk. : alk. paper)
1. Conduct of life. 2. Happiness. I. Title. II. Title: One hundred thoughts that lead to happiness
BF637.C5 C477 2002

Chiasmi international
(nouv. sér., 3) Merleau-Ponty. Paris : Vrin ; Milano : Mimesis, 2001.

Chibiri͡aev, S. A. (Stanislav Arkhipovich).
Beli͡aev, G. G. Dukhovnye korni russkogo naroda. Moskva : Bylina, 2002.
DK32 .B358 2002

CHICANERY. *See* **DECEPTION.**

Chicken skin tales.
Grant, Glen. Glen Grant's chicken skin tales. Honolulu, Hawaii : Mutual Pub., c1998.
BF1472.U6 G72 1998

Chicken soup for the soul celebrates sisters : a collection in words and photographs / [compiled] by Jack Canfield & Mark Victor Hansen and Maria Bushkin Stave. Deerfield Beach, Fla. : Health Communications, 2004. p. cm. ISBN 0-7573-0151-7 (tp) DDC 306.875/4
1. Sisters. 2. Sisters - Family relationships. I. Canfield, Jack, 1944- II. Hansen, Mark Victor. III. Stave, Maria Bushkin.
BF723.S43 C43 2004

CHIEF EXECUTIVE OFFICERS.
Carey, Dennis. How to run a company. 1st ed. New York : Crown Business, c2003.
HD38.2 .C374 2003

CHIEF EXECUTIVE OFFICERS - ATTITUDES.
Garten, Jeffrey E., 1946- The politics of fortune. Boston : Harvard Business School Press, c2002.
HD57.7 .G377 2002

CHIEFDOMS - VIRGINIA - JAMES RIVER VALLEY.
Gallivan, Martin D., 1968- James River chiefdoms. Lincoln : University of Nebraska Press, c2003.
E99.P85 G35 2003

CHIEFTAINCIES. *See* **CHIEFDOMS.**

CHIEFTAINSHIPS. *See* **CHIEFDOMS.**

Chihu Amparán, Aquiles, coord.
Sociología de la identidad. México : Miguel Angel Porrúa : Universidad Autónoma Metropolitana, Unidad Iztapalapa, 2002.

CHILD ABUSE. *See also* **CHILD SEXUAL ABUSE.**
López Díaz, Yolanda. Por qué se maltrata al más íntimo? 1. ed. [Bogota] : Universidad Nacional de Colombia, Sede Bogota, 2002.

CHILD-ADULT RELATIONSHIPS. *See* **CHILDREN AND ADULTS.**

CHILD ANALYSIS.
Bergeret, Jean. La sexualité infantile et ses mythes. Paris : Dunod, c2001.

CHILD AND ADULT. *See* **CHILDREN AND ADULTS.**

CHILD AND MOTHER. *See* **MOTHER AND CHILD.**

CHILD AND PARENT. *See* **PARENT AND CHILD.**

CHILD BEHAVIOR. *See* **CHILD PSYCHOLOGY; CHILDREN - CONDUCT OF LIFE.**

CHILD CARE. *See also* **CHILD REARING.**
Dunlap, Linda L. What all children need. Lanham, Md. : University Press of America, c2002.
HQ778.5 .D85 2002

Dziecko w rodzinie i społeczeństwie. Bydgoszsz : Wydawnictwo Uczelniane Akademii Bydgoskiej, 2002.

The young, the old, and the state. Cheltenham, UK ; Northhampton, MA : E. Elgar Pub., c2003.
HQ778.5 .Y69 2003

CHILD DEATH. *See* **CHILDREN - DEATH.**

Child Death Review Team (N.S.W.).
Suicide & risk-taking deaths of children & young people. Surry Hills, NSW : The Commission, c2003.

CHILD DEVELOPMENT. *See also* **CHILD PSYCHOLOGY; CHILD REARING; INFANTS - DEVELOPMENT.**
Amar Amar, José Juan. Políticas sociales y modelos de atención integral a la infancia. Barranquilla, Colombia : Ediciones Uninorte, 2001.

Between culture and biology. Cambridge, U.K. ; New York : Cambridge University Press, 2002.
BF721 .B4138 2002

Children in the digital age. Westport, Conn. : Praeger, 2002.
HQ784.M3 C455 2002

Dunlap, Linda L. What all children need. Lanham, Md. : University Press of America, c2002.
HQ778.5 .D85 2002

Early child development in the 21st century. New York : Teachers College Press, c2003.
LB1115 .E27 2003

Humphrey, James Harry, 1911- Child development through sports. Binghamton, N.Y. ; London : Haworth Press, c2003.
GV709.2 .H845 2003

Ottavi, Dominique. De Darwin à Piaget. Paris : CNRS, c2001.

Pound, Linda. Supporting musical development in the early years. Buckingham ; Philadelphia : Open University Press, 2003.
MT1 .P66 2003

Rogoff, Barbara. The cultural nature of human development. Oxford ; New York : Oxford University Press, 2003.
HM686 .R64 2003

Schaffer, H. Rudolph. Introducing child psychology. Malden, MA : Blackwell Pub. Ltd., 2004.
BF721 .S349 2004

Il "valore" del padre. Torino : UTET libreria, 2001.
BF723.P25 V35 2001

Wallat, Cynthia. Family-institution interaction. New York : P. Lang, c2002.
HQ755.85 .W35 2002

Zigler, Edward, 1930- The first three years & beyond. New Haven : Yale University Press, c2002.
HQ767.9 .Z543 2002

Child development (Cambridge, Mass.)
(3.) Oates, John, 1946- Cognitive and language development in children. Milton Keynes, U.K. : Open University ; Malden, MA : Blackwell Pub., 2004.
BF723.C5 O38 2004

CHILD DEVELOPMENT DEVIATIONS. *See* **DEVELOPMENTALLY DISABLED CHILDREN.**

CHILD DEVELOPMENT - HISTORY.
Beyond the century of the child. Philadelphia : University of Pennsylvania Press, c2003.
HQ767.87 .B49 2003

CHILD DEVELOPMENT - PSYCHOLOGICAL ASPECTS.
The elusive child. London ; New York : Karnac, c2002.

Child development through sports.
Humphrey, James Harry, 1911- Binghamton, N.Y. ; London : Haworth Press, c2003.
GV709.2 .H845 2003

CHILD MOLESTING. *See* **CHILD SEXUAL ABUSE.**

CHILD PLACING. *See* **ADOPTION.**

CHILD PROTECTIVE SERVICES. *See* **CHILD WELFARE.**

CHILD PROTECTIVE SERVICES PERSONNEL. *See* **CHILD WELFARE.**

CHILD PSYCHIATRY. *See* **CHILD PSYCHOLOGY.**

CHILD PSYCHOLOGY. *See also* **ANGER IN CHILDREN; BODY IMAGE IN CHILDREN; CHILD REARING; CHILDREN AND ADULTS; CHILDREN'S DREAMS; EDUCATIONAL PSYCHOLOGY; EMBARRASSMENT IN CHILDREN; EMOTIONS IN CHILDREN; FEAR IN CHILDREN; FRIENDSHIP IN CHILDREN; GRIEF IN CHILDREN; HAPPINESS IN CHILDREN; HELPING BEHAVIOR IN CHILDREN; INDIVIDUALITY IN CHILDREN; INFANT PSYCHOLOGY; INTERPERSONAL COMMUNICATION IN CHILDREN; LEARNING, PSYCHOLOGY OF; LOSS (PSYCHOLOGY) IN CHILDREN; MIND AND BODY IN CHILDREN; MOTIVATION (PSYCHOLOGY) IN CHILDREN; NEGATION (LOGIC) IN CHILDREN; PERSONALITY DEVELOPMENT; PERSONALITY IN CHILDREN; PREJUDICES IN CHILDREN; REASONING IN CHILDREN; RISK-TAKING (PSYCHOLOGY) IN CHILDREN; SHARING IN CHILDREN; STRESS IN CHILDREN; STRESS MANAGEMENT FOR CHILDREN; SURPRISE IN CHILDREN; TERMINALLY ILL CHILDREN - PSYCHOLOGY.**

Bergeret, Jean. La sexualité infantile et ses mythes. Paris : Dunod, c2001.

Berry, Carmen Renee. When helping you is hurting me. Revised and updated ed. New York : Crossroad Pub. Co., c2003.
BF637.S42 B47 2003

Between culture and biology. Cambridge, U.K. ; New York : Cambridge University Press, 2002.
BF721 .B4138 2002

Bloom, Paul, 1963- Descartes' baby. New York : Basic Books, 2004.
BF311 .B555 2004

Davis, Daniel Leifeld. Your angry child. New York : Haworth Press, c2004.
BF723.A4 D38 2004

The day our world changed. New York : Harry N. Abrams Inc., 2002.

Gerő, Zsuzsa. A gyermekrajzok esztétikuma. Budapest : Flaccus Kiadó, 2003.
BF723.D7 G47 2003

Hartley, Ruth E. (Ruth Edith), b.1909 Understanding children's play. London : Routledge, 2000.
BF717 .H3 2000

Korczak, Janusz, 1878-1942. [Works. Hebrew. 1996] Ketavim. [Tel Aviv] : Yad va-shem : ha-Agudah ʻa. sh. Yanush Korts'ak be-Yiśra'el : Bet Lohame ha-geta'ot ʻa. sh. Yitshak Katsenelson : ha-Kibuts ha-meʼuhad, [1996-
LB775.K627 K48 1996 <Hebr>

Montagner, Hubert. L'enfant, la vraie question de l'école. Paris : Jacob, c2002.

Ottavi, Dominique. De Darwin à Piaget. Paris : CNRS, c2001.

Piaget, Jean, 1896- [Développement des quantités chez l'enfant. English] The child's construction of quantities. London ; New York : Routledge, 1997.
BF723.P5 P5 1997

Saleev, Vadim Alekseevich. Esteticheskoe vospriiatie i detskaia fantaziia. Minsk : Natsional'nyĭ in-t obrazovaniia, 1999.
BF723.P36 S25 1999

Scales, Peter, 1949- Coming into their own. Minneapolis, MN : Search Institute, c2004.
BF721 .S347 2004

Schaffer, H. Rudolph. Introducing child psychology. Malden, MA : Blackwell Pub. Ltd., 2004.
BF721 .S349 2004

Xypas, Constantin. Les stades du développement affectif selon Piaget. Paris : Harmattan, c2001.

CHILD PSYCHOLOGY - PHILOSOPHY - HISTORY.

Rossi, Paolo, 1923- Bambini, sogni, furori. 1. ed. in "Campi del sapere.". Milano : Feltrinelli, 2001.
BF41 .R67 2001

CHILD PSYCHOLOGY - RESEARCH - METHODOLOGY.
Pellegrini, Anthony D. Observing children in their natural worlds. 2nd ed. Mahwah, N.J. : L. Erlbaum Associates, 2004.
BF722 .P45 2004

CHILD PSYCHOLOGY - RESEARCH - TEXTBOOKS.
Nadelman, Lorraine, 1924- Research manual in child development. 2nd ed. Mahwah, N.J. : Lawrence Erlbaum Associates, Publishers, 2004.
BF722 .N32 2004

CHILD PSYCHOTHERAPY.
Bierman, Karen L. Peer rejection. New York : Guilford Press, 2004.
BF723.R44 B54 2003

Therapeutic communities for children and young people. London : Jessica Kingsley, 2003.

CHILD RAISING. *See* **CHILD REARING.**

CHILD REARING. *See also* **CHILD DEVELOPMENT; CHILD PSYCHOLOGY; MORAL EDUCATION; PARENTING.**
Borba, Michele. Don't give me that attitude!. 1st ed. San Francisco : Jossey-Bass, c2004.
BF723.A76 B67 2004

Bowers, Keri. Single pregnancy - single parenting. Pleasant Hill, CA : Park Alexander Press, c1996.
HQ759.45 .B68 1996

Carducci, Bernardo J. The shyness breakthrough. [Emmaus, Pa.] : Rodale, c2003.
BF723.B3 C37 2003

Children's influence on family dynamics. Mahwah, N.J. : Lawrence Erlbaum Associates, 2003.
HQ518 .C535 2003

Dowling, Linda Culp. Mentor manager, mentor parent. Burneyville, OK : ComCon Books., c2002.
BF637.C6 D6185 2002

Fitzgerald, Helen. The grieving child. 2nd ed. New York : Simon & Schuster, 2003.
BF723.D3 F58 2003

Gilman, Charlotte Perkins, 1860-1935. Concerning children. A reprint of the 1900 ed. / with an introduction by Michael S. Kimmel. Walnut Creek, CA : Rowman & Littlefield, c2003.
HQ769 .G5 2003

Healy, Jane M. Your child's growing mind. 3rd ed. New York : Broadway Books, 2004.
BF318 .H4 2004

Helping kids cope. Minneapolis : Fairview Press, 2003.
BF723.G75 H35 2003

Humphrey, James Harry, 1911- Childhood stress in contemporary society. New York : Haworth Press, 2004.
BF723.S75 H842 2004

Kater, Kathy. Real kids come in all sizes. New York : Broadway Books, 2004.
BF723.B6 K38 2004

Kennedy, Michelle. Crying. Hauppauge, N.Y. : Barron's, c2003.
BF720.C78 .K46 2003

Kennedy, Michelle. Sleeping. Hauppauge, N.Y. : Barron's, c2003.
BF723.S45 .K46 2003

Kennedy, Michelle. Tantrums. Hauppauge, N.Y. : Barron's, c2003.
BF723.A4 .K46 2003

Korczak, Janusz, 1878-1942. [Works. Hebrew. 1996] Ketavim. [Tel Aviv] : Yad va-shem : ha-Agudah ʻa. sh. Yanush Korts'ak be-Yiśra'el : Bet Lohame ha-geta'ot ʻa. sh. Yitshak Katsenelson : ha-Kibuts ha-meʼuhad, [1996-
LB775.K627 K48 1996 <Hebr>

Ladner, Joyce A. Launching our Black children for success. 1st ed. San Francisco : Jossey-Bass, c2003.
BF723.S77 L33 2003

McManus, Martha Hansen, 1948- Understanding the angry child. Seattle, Wash. : Parenting Press, 2004.
BF723.A4 M38 2004

Nemeth, Darlyne Gaynor. Helping your angry child. Oakland, Calif. : New Harbinger, c2003.

BF723.A4 N46 2003

Rathkey, Julia Wilcox. What children need when they grieve. 1st ed. New York : Three Rivers Press, 2004.
BF723.G75 R38 2004

Rosenberg, Shelley Kapnek. Raising a mensch. 1st ed. Philadelphia : Jewish Publication Society, 2003.
BF723.M54 R68 2003

Shaw, Mary Ann. Your anxious child. 2nd ed. Irving, Tex. : Tapestry Press, c2003.
BF723.A5 S43 2003

Thomas, Pat, 1959- My friends and me. 1st ed. Hauppauge, N.Y. : Barron's Educational Series, c2001.
BF723.F68 T48 2001

Tromellini, Pina. Un corredo per la vita. Milano : Salani editore, c2002.

Wolf, Anthony E. "Mom, Jason's breathing on me!". 1st ed. New York : Ballantine Books, 2003.
BF723.S43 W65 2003

CHILD REARING - RELIGIOUS ASPECTS - JUDAISM.
Brezak, Dov. Chinuch in turbulent times. 1st ed. Brooklyn, N.Y. : Mesorah Publications, c2002.

CHILD SEXUAL ABUSE - HISTORY.
Masson, J. Moussaieff (Jeffrey Moussaieff), 1941- The assault on truth. 1st Ballantine Books ed. New York : Ballantine Books, 2003.
BF109.F74 M38 2003

CHILD SEXUAL ABUSE - LAW AND LEGISLATION. *See* **CHILD SEXUAL ABUSE.**

CHILD SEXUAL ABUSE VICTIMS. *See* **SEXUALLY ABUSED CHILDREN.**

CHILD SEXUAL ABUSE VICTIMS, ADULT. *See* **ADULT CHILD SEXUAL ABUSE VICTIMS.**

CHILD SOLDIERS.
Child soldiers [electronic resource]. Quantico, Va. : Center for Emerging Threats and Opportunities, Marine Corps Warfighting Laboratory, [2002]

Child soldiers [electronic resource] : implications for U.S. forces : seminar report. Quantico, Va. : Center for Emerging Threats and Opportunities, Marine Corps Warfighting Laboratory, [2002] Mode of access: Internet from the Center for Emerging Threats and Opportunities. Address as of 11/14/03: http://www.ceto.quantico.usmc.mil/studies/ChildSoldiersFinal.pdf; current access available via PURL. Title from title screen (viewed on Nov. 14, 2003). "November 2002." URL: http://purl.access.gpo.gov/GPO/LPS39868
1. Child soldiers. 2. Children and war. I. Center for Emerging Threats and Opportunities (Marine Corps Warfighting Laboratory)

CHILD STUDY. *See* **CHILD DEVELOPMENT; CHILD PSYCHOLOGY.**

CHILD SUICIDE. *See* **CHILDREN - SUICIDAL BEHAVIOR.**

CHILD WELFARE - LAW AND LEGISLATION. *See* **CHILDREN - LEGAL STATUS, LAWS, ETC.**

CHILD WELFARE - UNITED STATES.
The subject of care. Lanham, Md. ; Oxford : Rowman & Littlefield Publishers, c2002.
HQ1206 .S9 2002

Zigler, Edward, 1930- The first three years & beyond. New Haven : Yale University Press, c2002.
HQ767.9 .Z543 2002

CHILDHOOD. *See* **CHILDREN.**

CHILDHOOD FRIENDSHIP. *See* **FRIENDSHIP IN CHILDREN.**

Childhood stress in contemporary society.
Humphrey, James Harry, 1911- New York : Haworth Press, 2004.
BF723.S75 H842 2004

Childre, Doc Lew, 1945- Transforming anger : the HeartMath solution for letting go of rage, frustration, and irritation / Doc Childre and Deborah Rozman. Oakland, Calif. : New Harbinger ; London : Hi Marketing, 2003. xvi, 154 p. ; 20 cm. ISBN 1-57224-352-X DDC 152.47
1. Anger. 2. Stress management. I. Rozman, Deborah. II. Title.
BF575.A5 C45 2003

CHILDREN. *See also* **ADOPTED CHILDREN; BOYS; CHILD DEVELOPMENT; GIRLS; HOMELESS CHILDREN; INFANTS; POOR CHILDREN; PRETEENS; PROBLEM CHILDREN; SOCIAL WORK WITH**

CHILDREN; TODDLERS.
Children's influence on family dynamics. Mahwah, N.J. : Lawrence Erlbaum Associates, 2003.
HQ518 .C535 2003

John, Mary. Children's rights and power. London ; New York : Jessica Kingsley Publishers, 2003.
HQ789 .J64 2003

CHILDREN, ADOPTED. *See* **ADOPTED CHILDREN.**

CHILDREN AND ADULTS. *See also* **PARENT AND CHILD.**
Butterfield, Perry M., 1932- Emotional connections. Washington, DC : Zero To Three, 2004.
BF720.E45 B879 2004

The generative society. 1st ed. Washington, DC : American Psychological Association, c2003.
BF724.5 .G45 2003

CHILDREN AND ADULTS - STUDY AND TEACHING (HIGHER).
Butterfield, Perry M., 1932- Emotional connections. 1st ed. Washington, DC : Zero To Three Press, c2003.
BF720.E45 B88 2003

CHILDREN AND ANIMALS.
The world's children and their companion animals. Olney, MD : Association for Childhood Education International, 2004.
BF723.A45 W67 2004

CHILDREN AND DEATH. *See also* **BEREAVEMENT IN CHILDREN.**
Fitzgerald, Helen. The grieving child. 2nd ed. New York : Simon & Schuster, 2003.
BF723.D3 F58 2003

Helping kids cope. Minneapolis : Fairview Press, 2003.
BF723.G75 H35 2003

Liotta, Alfred J. When students grieve. Horsham, PA : LRP Publications, 2003.
BF724.3.D43 L56 2003

CHILDREN AND DEATH - JUVENILE LITERATURE.
Dennison, Amy. Our dad died. Minneapolis, MN : Free Spirit Pub., c2003.
BF723.G75 D46 2003

Johnson, Marvin. Where's Jess? Rev. Omaha, NE : Centering Corp. Resource, 2003.
BF723.G75 J645 2003

Simon, Jack. This book is for all kids, but especially my sister Libby, Libby died.. Kansas City, Mo. : Andrews McMeel Pub., c2002.
BF723.D3 S59 2002

Stalfelt, Pernilla. [Döden boken. English] The death book. Toronto, Ont. : Groundwood Books / Douglas & McIntyrenfrom ; Berkeley, CA : Distrituted by Publishers Group West, c2002.
BF723.D3 S7313 2002

Stenson, Lila. Daddy, up and down. 1st ed. Snowmass Village, CO : Peaceful Village Pub., 2002.
BF723.G75 S74 2002

Children and human rights. Part 1 [videorecording] / produced by Globalvision, Inc. Derry, N.H. : Chip Taylor Communications, 1995. 1 videocassette (26 min.) : sd., col. ; 1/2 in. (Rights and wrongs series) VHS. Jr.Hi.-Adult. Title from cassette label. Cast: Charlayne Hunter-Gault. SUMMARY: First segment: An overview of the conditions of children around the world with a discussion of their intrinsic rights to live, to be free from abuse and forced labor and provided with health care and education. Second segment: Presents a rap video, "What's the right?" written and performed by students at El Puente Academy for Peace and Justice in New York. Third segment: Profiles a 13 year old African-American boy living in Washington, D.C. and a 15 year old girl in India. Fourth segment: Reports on the recent brutality against Brazilian street children. Program concludes with Judy Collins' song, I Dream of Peace, accompanied by drawings and writings of children living with war.
1. Human rights. 2. Children's rights. 3. Children's rights - Brazil. 4. Children - Legal status, laws, etc. 5. Children - Economic conditions. 6. Children - Social conditions. 7. Children - Brazil - Social conditions. 8. Children and war. I. Hunter-Gault, Charlayne. II. Chip Taylor Communications. III. Globalvision, Inc. IV. Series.

CHILDREN AND PARENTS. *See* **PARENT AND CHILD.**

CHILDREN AND SEX. *See also* **CHILDREN - SEXUAL BEHAVIOR.**
Bergeret, Jean. La sexualité infantile et ses mythes. Paris : Dunod, c2001.

Bonnet, Gérard. Défi à la pudeur. Paris : Albin Michel, c2003.
HQ784.S45 .B66 2003

Mijolla-Mellor, Sophie de. Le besoin de savoir. Paris : Dunod, c2002.
BF723.S4 M556 2002

CHILDREN AND VIOLENCE.
Helping children and adolescents cope with violence and disasters [electronic resource]. Bethesda, MD : Office of Communications and Public Liaison, [2001]

CHILDREN AND VIOLENCE - PSYCHOLOGICAL ASPECTS.
Helping children and adolescents cope with violence and disasters [electronic resource]. Bethesda, MD : Office of Communications and Public Liaison, [2001]

CHILDREN AND WAR.
Child soldiers [electronic resource]. Quantico, Va. : Center for Emerging Threats and Opportunities, Marine Corps Warfighting Laboratory, [2002]

Children and human rights. Part 1 [videorecording]. Derry, N.H. : Chip Taylor Communications, 1995.

Children's fears of war and terrorism. Olney, MD : Association for Childhood Education International, c2003.
BF723.W3 C48 2003

CHILDREN - BOOKS AND READING - ENGLISH-SPEAKING COUNTRIES.
Gupta, Suman, 1966- Re-reading Harry Potter. Houndmills, Basingstoke ; New York : Palgrave Macmillan, 2003.
PR6068.O93 Z68 2003

Reading Harry Potter. Westport, Conn. ; London : Praeger Publishers, 2003.
PR6068.O93 Z84 2003

CHILDREN - BRAZIL - SOCIAL CONDITIONS.
Children and human rights. Part 1 [videorecording]. Derry, N.H. : Chip Taylor Communications, 1995.

CHILDREN - CHARITIES. *See* **CHILD WELFARE.**

CHILDREN - CHARITIES, PROTECTION, ETC. *See* **CHILD WELFARE.**

CHILDREN - CIVIL RIGHTS. *See* **CHILDREN'S RIGHTS.**

CHILDREN - CONDUCT OF LIFE - JUVENILE LITERATURE.
Woods, Earl, 1932- Start something. New York : Simon & Schuster, c2000.
BJ1631 .W726 2000

CHILDREN - COUNSELING OF.
Buckley, Maureen A., 1964- Mentoring children and adolescents. Westport, Conn. : Praeger, 2003.
BF637.C6 B8 2003

Kanyer, Laurie A., 1959- 25 things to do when grandpa passes away, mom and dad get divorced, or the dog dies. Seatte Wash., ; Parenting Press, 2004.
BF723.G75 K36 2003

Liotta, Alfred J. When students grieve. Horsham, PA : LRP Publications, 2003.
BF724.3.D43 L56 2003

CHILDREN - CRIMES AGAINST - FICTION.
Cook, Thomas H. The interrogation. Rockland, MA : Wheeler Pub., 2002.
PS3553.O55465 I58 2002

CHILDREN, DEAF. *See* **HEARING IMPAIRED CHILDREN.**

CHILDREN - DEATH. *See also* **TERMINALLY ILL CHILDREN.**
Jarashow, Jonathan. The silent psalms of our son. Jerusalem, Israel : Feldheim Publishers, c2001.

Roccatagliata Orsini, Susana. Un hijo no puede morir. 3. ed. Santiago de Chile : Grijalbo, 2000.
BF723.D3 R6 2000

CHILDREN - DEATH AND FUTURE STATE. *See* **CHILDREN - DEATH.**

CHILDREN - DEATH - PSYCHOLOGICAL ASPECTS.
Daher, Douglas, 1949- And the passenger was death. Amityville, N.Y. : Baywood Pub., c2003.
BF575.G7 D34 2003

Murray, Donald Morison, 1924- The lively shadow. 1st ed. New York : Ballantine Books, 2003.
BF575.G7 M868 2003

CHILDREN - DEATH - PSYCHOLOGICAL ASPECTS - CASE STUDIES.
Polcz, Alaine. Gyermek a halál kapujában. Budapest : PONT, c2001.
BF723.D3 P65 2001

Stetson, Brad. Living victims, stolen lives. Amityville, N.Y. : Baywood Pub., c2003.
HV6533.C2 S73 2003

CHILDREN - DEATH - PSYCHOLOGICAL ASPECTS - UNITED STATES.
Barzach, Amy Jaffe. Accidental courage, boundless dreams. 1st ed. West Hartford, CT : Aurora Pub., c2001.
BF575.G7 B375 2001

CHILDREN - DEVELOPMENT. *See* **CHILD DEVELOPMENT.**

CHILDREN - DEVELOPMENT AND GUIDANCE. *See* **CHILD REARING.**

CHILDREN - ECONOMIC CONDITIONS.
Children and human rights. Part 1 [videorecording]. Derry, N.H. : Chip Taylor Communications, 1995.

CHILDREN - EDUCATION. *See* **EDUCATION.**

CHILDREN - EUROPE.
Nashim, zeḳenim ṿa-taf. Yerushalayim : Merkaz Zalman Shazar le-toldot Yiśra'el, [2001]

Children, family, and the state.
Archard, David. Aldershot, Hants, England ; Burlington, VT : Ashgate, 2003.
HQ789 .A695 2003

CHILDREN - HEALTH AND HYGIENE. *See* **STRESS MANAGEMENT FOR CHILDREN.**

CHILDREN, HEARING IMPAIRED. *See* **HEARING IMPAIRED CHILDREN.**

CHILDREN - HISTORY.
Beyond the century of the child. Philadelphia : University of Pennsylvania Press, c2003.
HQ767.87 .B49 2003

Dziecko w rodzinie i społeczeństwie. Bydgoszsz : Wydawnictwo Uczelniane Akademii Bydgoskiej, 2002.

CHILDREN, HOMELESS. *See* **HOMELESS CHILDREN.**

CHILDREN IN ART.
Dziecko w rodzinie i społeczeństwie. Bydgoszsz : Wydawnictwo Uczelniane Akademii Bydgoskiej, 2002.

Children in charge series
(9) John, Mary. Children's rights and power. London ; New York : Jessica Kingsley Publishers, 2003.
HQ789 .J64 2003

CHILDREN IN LITERATURE.
Dziecko w rodzinie i społeczeństwie. Bydgoszsz : Wydawnictwo Uczelniane Akademii Bydgoskiej, 2002.

Children in the city : home neighbourhood and community / edited by Pia Christensen and Margaret O'Brien. London : Routledge/Falmer, 2003. xvi, 210 p. : ill., map ; 24 cm. (Future of childhood series) Includes bibliographical references and index. ISBN 0-415-25924-X ISBN 0-415-25925-8 (pbk.) DDC 305.235091732
1. City children. 2. City and town life. 3. Urban youth. 4. Neighborhood - Psychological aspects. 5. Spatial behavior. 6. Identity (Psychology) 7. Socialization. 8. Quality of life. I. Christensen, Pia Monrad. II. O'Brien, Margaret, 1954- III. Series.

Children in the digital age : influences of electronic media on development / edited by Sandra L. Calvert, Amy B. Jordan, and Rodney R. Cocking. Westport, Conn. : Praeger, 2002. xv, 260 p. : ill. ; 25 cm. Includes bibliographical references and index. CONTENTS: The impact of computer use on children's and adolescents' development / Kaveri Subrahmanyam ... [et al.] -- American children's use of electronic media in 1997: a national survey / John C. Wright ... [et al.] -- Identity construction on the Internet / Sandra L. Calvert -- Adolescents, the internet, and health: issues of access and content / Dina L.G. Borzekowski ; Vaughn I. Rickert -- Political socialization in the digital age: the "student voices" program / Emory H. Woodard IV ; Kelly L. Schmitt -- Violent video games and aggressive thoughts, feelings, and behaviors / Craig A. Anderson -- "We have these rules inside": the effects of exercising voice in a children's online forum / Justine Cassell -- Developmental implications of commercial broadcasters' educational offerings / Amy B. Jordan ; Kelly L. Schmitt ; Emory H. Woodard IV -- Children's online reports about educational and informational television programs / Sandra L. Calvert ... [et al.] -- The AnimalWatch project:

creating an intelligent computer mathematics tutor / Carole R. Beal ; Ivon Arroyo -- The development of a child into a consumer / Patti M. Valkenburg ; Joanne Cantor -- Family boundaries, commercialism, and the Internet: a framework for research / Joseph Turow -- A family systems approach to examining the role of the internet in the home / Amy B. Jordan. ISBN 0-275-97652-1 (alk. paper) DDC 303.48/34/083
1. Mass media and children. 2. Computers and children. 3. Internet and children. 4. Video games and children. 5. Child development. I. Calvert, Sandra L. II. Jordan, Amy B. (Amy Beth) III. Cocking, Rodney R.
HQ784.M3 C455 2002

CHILDREN - INSTITUTIONAL CARE.
Therapeutic communities for children and young people. London : Jessica Kingsley, 2003.

CHILDREN - INTELLIGENCE TESTING. *See* **WECHSLER INTELLIGENCE SCALE FOR CHILDREN.**

CHILDREN - ISRAEL - BIOGRAPHY.
Jarashow, Jonathan. The silent psalms of our son. Jerusalem, Israel : Feldheim Publishers, c2001.

CHILDREN - JAPAN - HISTORY.
Edo-e kara shomotsu made. Tōkyō : Kyūzansha, 1997.
HQ792.J3 N54 1997 v.19

CHILDREN - LANGUAGE.
Camarotti, Marco. A linguagem no teatro infantil. 2a edição. [Recife : Editora Universitária UFPE, 2002]

Dyson, Anne Haas. The brothers and sisters learn to write. New York : Teachers College Press, c2003.
LB1139.L3 D97 2003

Revealing the inner worlds of young children. New York : Oxford University Press, 2003.
BF723.S74 A37 2003

CHILDREN - LAW. *See* **CHILDREN - LEGAL STATUS, LAWS, ETC.**

CHILDREN - LEGAL STATUS, LAWS, ETC.
Children and human rights. Part 1 [videorecording]. Derry, N.H. : Chip Taylor Communications, 1995.

Dziecko w rodzinie i społeczeństwie. Bydgoszsz : Wydawnictwo Uczelniane Akademii Bydgoskiej, 2002.

CHILDREN - MANAGEMENT. *See* **CHILD REARING.**

CHILDREN OF CELEBRITIES - DEATH - PSYCHOLOGICAL ASPECTS - CASE STUDIES.
Groben, Joseph. Requiem für ein Kind. 2. Aufl. Köln : Dittrich, 2002.
BF575.G7 G76 2002

CHILDREN OF GAY MEN. *See* **CHILDREN OF GAY PARENTS.**

CHILDREN OF GAY PARENTS - PSYCHOLOGY.
Gottlieb, Andrew R. Sons talk about their gay fathers. New York : Harrington Park Press, c2003.
HQ76.13 .G67 2003

CHILDREN OF HOMOSEXUAL PARENTS. *See* **CHILDREN OF GAY PARENTS.**

CHILDREN OF LESBIANS. *See* **CHILDREN OF GAY PARENTS.**

CHILDREN OF THE POOR. *See* **POOR CHILDREN.**

CHILDREN - PHYSIOLOGY. *See* **STRESS IN CHILDREN.**

CHILDREN, POOR. *See* **POOR CHILDREN.**

CHILDREN - PROTECTION. *See* **CHILD WELFARE.**

CHILDREN - PSYCHIC ABILITY.
Virtue, Doreen, 1958- The crystal children. Carlsbad, Calif. : Hay House, c2003.
BF1045.C45 V57 2003

CHILDREN - PSYCHOLOGY. *See* **CHILD PSYCHOLOGY.**

CHILDREN - RECREATION. *See* **GAMES.**

CHILDREN - RELATIONSHIP WITH ADULTS. *See* **CHILDREN AND ADULTS.**

CHILDREN - SEXUAL BEHAVIOR.
Bergeret, Jean. La sexualité infantile et ses mythes. Paris : Dunod, c2001.

CHILDREN - SEXUAL BEHAVIOR - CONGRESSES.
Sexual development in childhood. Bloomington : Indiana University Press, 2003.
BF723.S4 S47 2003

CHILDREN - SLEEP. *See also* **CHILDREN'S DREAMS.**
Kennedy, Michelle. Sleeping. Hauppauge, N.Y. : Barron's, c2003.
BF723.S45 .K46 2003

CHILDREN - SOCIAL CONDITIONS.
Children and human rights. Part 1 [videorecording]. Derry, N.H. : Chip Taylor Communications, 1995.

Dziecko w rodzinie i społeczeństwie. Bydgoszsz : Wydawnictwo Uczelniane Akademii Bydgoskiej, 2002.

Lareau, Annette. Unequal childhoods. Berkeley : University of California Press, c2003.
HQ767.9 .L37 2003

CHILDREN - SUICIDAL BEHAVIOR - AUSTRALIA - NEW SOUTH WALES.
Suicide & risk-taking deaths of children & young people. Surry Hills, NSW : The Commission, c2003.

CHILDREN - TRAINING. *See* **CHILD REARING.**

CHILDREN WITH DISABILITIES - UNITED STATES.
Barzach, Amy Jaffe. Accidental courage, boundless dreams. 1st ed. West Hartford, CT : Aurora Pub., c2001.
BF575.G7 B375 2001

CHILDREN WITH SOCIAL DISABILITIES - EDUCATION (SECONDARY) - UNITED STATES - LONGITUDINAL STUDIES.
Hodges, Carolyn R., 1947- Making schools work. New York : P. Lang, c2003.
LC213.2 .H63 2003
1. Black author.

CHILDREN WITH SOCIAL DISABILITIES - EDUCATION - UNITED STATES.
Lampert, Khen. Compassionate education. Lanham, Md. : University Press of America, c2003.

CHILDREN - WOUNDS AND INJURIES - JUVENILE LITERATURE.
Berry, Joy Wilt. Let's talk about getting hurt. New York : Scholastic, c2002.
BF723.W67 B475 2002

CHILDREN'S ACCIDENTS. *See* **CHILDREN - WOUNDS AND INJURIES.**

CHILDREN'S ART. *See also* **CHILDREN'S DRAWINGS.**
The day our world changed. New York : Harry N. Abrams Inc., 2002.

CHILDREN'S DRAWINGS - PSYCHOLOGICAL ASPECTS.
Gerő, Zsuzsa. A gyermekrajzok esztétikuma. Budapest : Flaccus Kiadó, 2003.
BF723.D7 G47 2003

Golomb, Claire. The child's creation of a pictorial world. 2nd ed. Mahwah, N.J. : L. Erlbaum Associates, 2004.
BF723.D7 G64 2004

Children's dream dictionary.
Cross, Amanda. London : Hamlyn ; New York : Distributed in the U.S. by Sterling Pub., 2002.
BF1099.C55 C76 2002

CHILDREN'S DREAMS - DICTIONARIES.
Cross, Amanda. Children's dream dictionary. London : Hamlyn ; New York : Distributed in the U.S. by Sterling Pub., 2002.
BF1099.C55 C76 2002

CHILDREN'S DREAMS - JUVENILE LITERATURE.
Collier-Thompson, Kristi. The girls' guide to dreams. New York : Sterling Pub., c2003.
BF1099.C55 C65 2003

Kallen, Stuart A., 1955- Dreams. San Diego, Calif. : Lucent Books, 2004.
BF1099.C55 K35 2004

Children's fears of war and terrorism : a resource for teachers and parents / Lisa F. Moses ... [et al.]. Olney, MD : Association for Childhood Education International, c2003. 64 p. ; 26 cm. Includes bibliographical references. Table of contents URL: http://www.loc.gov/catdir/toc/ecip044/2003011040.html ISBN 0-87173-160-6 (pbk.) DDC 155.4/1246
1. Children and war. 2. War - Psychological aspects. 3. Terrorism - Psychological aspects. 4. Fear in children. 5. Emotional problems of children. I. Moses, Lisa F.
BF723.W3 C48 2003

CHILDREN'S GAMES. *See* **GAMES.**

Children's influence on family dynamics : the neglected side of family relationships / edited by Ann C. Crouter, Alan Booth. Mahwah, N.J. : Lawrence Erlbaum Associates, 2003. x, 269 p. : ill. ; 24 cm. Includes bibliographical references and indexes. CONTENTS: pt. 1. What features of children shape family relationships and how? Child effects on family systems : behavioral genetic strategies / David Reiss -- On the meaning of models : a signal amidst the noise / Kathleen McCartney -- Are we finally ready to move beyond "nature vs. nurture"? / Xiaojia Ge, M. Brent Donnellan, and Lawrence Harper -- How to spin straw into gold / J. Richard Udry -- pt. 2. What role does infant and early childhood temperament play in the development of relationship with parents? Infant negative emotionality, caregiving, and family relationships / Susan Crockenberg and Esther Leerkes -- Child effects on the family : an example of the extreme case and a question of methodology / Cynthia A. Stifter -- Sensitivity to infants' cues : as much a mandate for researchers as for parents / James P. McHale, Kathryn C. Kavanaugh, and Julia M. Berkman -- The developmental course from child effects to child effectiveness / Pamela M. Cole -- pt. 3. What roles do adolescents play in actively shaping relationships with parents, siblings, and peers? Parenting of adolescents : action or reaction? / Margaret Kerr and Håkan Stattin -- On the brink : stability and change in parent-child relations in adolescence / Elizabeth G. Menaghan -- Parental monitoring : action and reaction / Gene H. Brody -- Parental monitoring : a person-environment interaction perspective on this key parenting skill / Deborah M. Capaldi -- Straw men, untested assumptions, and bi-directional models : a response to Capaldi and Brody / Margaret Kerr and Håkan Stattin -- pt. 4. How do children affect parents' marriage and other family relationships? The gender of child and parent as factors in family dynamics / Eleanor E. Maccoby -- How do children exert an impact on family life? / Susan M. McHale and Ann C. Crouter -- Eleanor E. Maccoby on the active child : gender differences and family interactions / Håkan Stattin and Margaret Kerr -- Reply to Stattin-Kerr critique / Eleanor E. Maccoby -- A gender-balanced approach to the study of childhood aggression and reciprocal family influences / Nicki R. Crick -- Child effects as family process / Lilly Shanahan and Juliana M. Sobolewski. ISBN 0-8058-4271-3 (alk. paper) DDC 306.85
1. Family. 2. Children. 3. Parent and child. 4. Child rearing. I. Crouter, Ann C. II. Booth, Alan, 1935-
HQ518 .C535 2003

CHILDREN'S LITERATURE, FRENCH - FRANCE - HISTORY AND CRITICISM.
Beguery, Jocelyne. Une esthétique contemporaine de l'album de jeunesse. Paris : Harmattan, c2002.

CHILDREN'S LITERATURE - PUBLISHING - FRANCE.
Beguery, Jocelyne. Une esthétique contemporaine de l'album de jeunesse. Paris : Harmattan, c2002.

CHILDREN'S PICTURE BOOKS. *See* **PICTURE BOOKS FOR CHILDREN.**

CHILDREN'S RIGHTS.
Archard, David. Children, family, and the state. Aldershot, Hants, England ; Burlington, VT : Ashgate, 2003.
HQ789 .A695 2003

Children and human rights. Part 1 [videorecording]. Derry, N.H. : Chip Taylor Communications, 1995.

John, Mary. Children's rights and power. London ; New York : Jessica Kingsley Publishers, 2003.
HQ789 .J64 2003

Children's rights and power.
John, Mary. London ; New York : Jessica Kingsley Publishers, 2003.
HQ789 .J64 2003

CHILDREN'S RIGHTS - BRAZIL.
Children and human rights. Part 1 [videorecording]. Derry, N.H. : Chip Taylor Communications, 1995.

CHILDREN'S STORIES. *See* **FAIRY TALES.**

CHILDREN'S STORIES, ENGLISH - HISTORY AND CRITICISM.
Gupta, Suman, 1966- Re-reading Harry Potter. Houndmills, Basingstoke ; New York : Palgrave Macmillan, 2003.
PR6068.O93 Z68 2003

Harry Potter's world. New York ; London : RoutledgeFalmer, 2003.
PR6068.O93 Z73 2003

The ivory tower and Harry Potter. Columbia : University of Missouri Press, 2002.
PR6068.O93 Z734 2002

Reading Harry Potter. Westport, Conn. ; London : Praeger Publishers, 2003.

Children's stories, English - History and criticism.

PR6068.O93 Z84 2003

CHILDREN'S THEATER - BRAZIL - HISTORY AND CRITICISM.
Camarotti, Marco. A linguagem no teatro infantil. 2a edição. [Recife : Editora Universitária UFPE, 2002]

CHILDREN'S WRITINGS.
Dennison, Amy. Our dad died. Minneapolis, MN : Free Spirit Pub., c2003.
BF723.G75 D46 2003

River of words. Berkeley, Calif. : Heyday Books, c2003.
PS595.W374 R58 2003

Simon, Jack. This book is for all kids, but especially my sister Libby, Libby died.. Kansas City, Mo. : Andrews McMeel Pub., c2002.
BF723.D3 S59 2002

CHILDREN'S WRITINGS, AMERICAN.
River of words. Berkeley, Calif. : Heyday Books, c2003.
PS595.W374 R58 2003

The child's construction of quantities.
Piaget, Jean, 1896- [Développement des quantités chez l'enfant. English] London ; New York : Routledge, 1997.
BF723.P5 P5 1997

The child's creation of a pictorial world.
Golomb, Claire. 2nd ed. Mahwah, N.J. : L. Erlbaum Associates, 2004.
BF723.D7 G64 2004

Childs-Oroz, Annette. Will you dance? / Annette Childs-Oroz ; afterword by Raymond A. Moody, Jr. Incline Village, NV : Wandering Feather Press, c2002. 1 v. (unpaged) : col. ill. ; 19 cm. ISBN 0-9718902-0-X
1. Life change events - Psychological aspects. 2. Adjustment (Psychology) I. Title.
BF637.L53 C45 2002

The child's right to play : a global approach / edited by Rhonda L. Clements and Leah Fiorentino. Westport, Conn. : Praeger, 2003. p. cm. Includes bibliographical references and index. ISBN 0-275-98171-1 (alk. paper) DDC 155.4/18
1. Play - Psychological aspects. I. Clements, Rhonda L. II. Fiorentino, Leah.
BF717 .C44 2003

CHILE - POLITICS AND GOVERNMENT - 1988-.
Loveman, Brian. El espejismo de la reconciliación política. 1. ed. Santiago : LOM Ediciones : DIBAM, 2002.

CHIMENT, MARIE ANNE.
Vint/age 2001 conference : [videorecording]. New York, c2001.

Chiment, Marie Anne, panelist.
Vint/age 2001 conference : [videorecording]. New York, c2001.

CHIMU POTTERY.
Statnekov, Daniel K., 1943- Animated earth. 2nd ed. Berkeley Calif. : North Atlantic Books, 2003.
BF1999 .S719 2003

CHINA.
Dépayser la pensée. Paris : Empêcheurs de penser en rond, 2003.

CHINA - BIBLIOGRAPHY.
Chinese literature. Hauppauge, N.Y. : Nova Science Publishers, c2002.

CHINA - CIVILIZATION.
Huang, Yongnian. [Selections. 2000] Wen shi tan wei. Di 1 ban. Beijing : Zhonghua shu ju, 2000.
DS736 .H795 2000

Tang, Yijie. Xi bu zhi jin. Di 1 ban. Shanghai : Shanghai wen yi chu ban she, 1999.
B126 .T1965 1999

Zhongguo xiang zheng wen hua. Di 1 ban. Shanghai : Shanghai ren min chu ban she : Xin hua shu dian Shanghai fa xing suo jing xiao, 2001.
DS721 .Z4985 2001

CHINA - HISTORIOGRAPHY.
He, Bingsong, 1890-1946. [Works. 1996] He Bingsong wen ji. Di 1 ban. Beijing : Shang wu yin shu guan, 1996.
DS734.7 .H664

Ye, Ying, 1896-1950. Wen shi tong yi jiao zhu. Di 1 ban. Beijing : Zhonghua shu ju : Xin hua shu dian Beijing fa xing suo fa xing, 1994.
DS734.7.C433 Y43 1985 <Orien China>

Zhang, Shunhui. Zhang Shunhui xue shu wen hua sui bi. Beijing di 1 ban. Beijing : Zhongguo qing nian chu ban she, 2001.
PL2272.5 .Z427 2001

CHINA - HISTORY.
Huang, Yongnian. [Selections. 2000] Wen shi tan wei. Di 1 ban. Beijing : Zhonghua shu ju, 2000.
DS736 .H795 2000

CHINA - HISTORY - ANECDOTES.
Sheng yu xiang jie. Di 1 ban. [Peking] : Xian zhuang shu ju, 1995.
BJ117 .S486 1995 <Orien China>

CHINA - HISTORY - SONG DYNASTY, 960-1279.
Shi, Sheng. Fan Zhongyan li shen xing shi jiu jiu fang lüe. Di 1 ban. Beijing : Zhongguo xi ju chu ban she, 2001.
DS751.6.F3 S5 2001

CHINA - LITERATURES. *See* **CHINESE LITERATURE; TIBETAN LITERATURE.**

CHINA - POLITICS AND GOVERNMENT - 581-907.
An, Lizhi. "Zhen guan zheng yao" yu ling dao yi shu. Di 1 ban. Shanghai : Shanghai gu ji chu ban she, 1999.
DS749.3.W813 A63 1999

CHINA - RELIGIOUS LIFE AND CUSTOMS.
Ma, Changyi. Zhongguo ling hun xin yang. Di 1 ban. Shanghai : Shanghai wen yi chu ban she, 1998.
BL290 .M28 1998

CHINA - STUDY AND TEACHING.
Xue lin chun qiu. Di 1 ban. Beijing : Chao hua chu ban she, 1999.
PL2272.5 .X846 1999

CHINAWARE. *See* **POTTERY.**

CHINESE AMERICAN FAMILIES.
Tan, Amy The opposite of fate. New York : Putnam c2003.
PS3570.A48 Z47 2003

CHINESE AMERICANS - BIOGRAPHY.
Tan, Amy The opposite of fate. New York : Putnam c2003.
PS3570.A48 Z47 2003

CHINESE AMERICANS - UNITED STATES. *See* **CHINESE AMERICANS.**

Chinese and western cultural interaction and modern literature.
Guo, Yanli. Zhong xi wen hua peng zhuang yu jin dai wen xue = Di 1 ban. Jinan Shi : Shandong jiao yu chu ban she, 1999.
PL2274 .G86 1999

Chinese art of face reading.
Henning, Hai Lee Yang. Mian xiang. London : Vega, 2001.
BF851 .H46 2001

Henning, Hai Lee Yang. Mian xiang. London : Vega, 2001.
BF851 .H46 2001

CHINESE ARTS. *See* **ARTS, CHINESE.**

CHINESE AUTHORS. *See* **AUTHORS, CHINESE.**

CHINESE CLASSICS - HISTORY AND CRITICISM.
Liang Qichao, Zhang Taiyan jie du Zhonghua wen hua jing dian. Di 1 ban. Shenyang Shi : Liao Hai chu ban she, 2003.
PL2262.2 .L54 2003

Motsch, Monika, 1942- [Mit Bambusrohr und Ahle von Qian Zhongshus Guanzhuibian zu einer Neubetrachtung Du Fus. Chinese] "Guan zhui bian" yu Du Fu xin jie. Di 1 ban. Shijiazhuang Shi : Hebei jiao yu chu ban she, 1997 (2002 printing)
PL2749.C8 Z85 1997

Xu, Wenjing, 1667-1756? Guan cheng shi ji. Di 1 ban. Beijing : Zhonghua shu ju : Xin hua shu dian Beijing fa xing suo fa xing, 1998.
PL2461.Z6 H77 1998

Zhang, Shunhui. Zhang Shunhui xue shu wen hua sui bi. Beijing di 1 ban. Beijing : Zhongguo qing nian chu ban she, 2001.
PL2272.5 .Z427 2001

Zhou, Xunchu. [Selections. 2000] Zhou Xunchu wen ji. Di 1 ban. Nanjing Shi : Jiangsu gu ji chu ban she, 2000.
PL2264 .Z485 2000

CHINESE ESSAYS - 20TH CENTURY.
Ai ni, dan bu xiang xin ni. Di 1 ban. Beijing : Zhongguo hua qiao chu ban she, 2000.

PL2608.L6 A5 2000

CHINESE FOLK LITERATURE. *See* **FOLK LITERATURE, CHINESE.**

Chinese horoscopes.
Burns, Debbie. Sydney : Lansdowne, 2000, c1998.

CHINESE LANGUAGE.
Shi, Yili. Discourse analysis of Chinese referring expressions. Lewiston, N.Y. : E. Mellen Press, c2002.
P325.5.R44 S53 2002

Zhang, Fan. Mei xue yu yan xue. Di 1 ban. Beijing : Shou du shi fan da xue chu ban she, 1998.
P121 .Z465 1998

CHINESE LANGUAGE - HISTORY.
Xue lin chun qiu. Di 1 ban. Beijing : Chao hua chu ban she, 1999.
PL2272.5 .X846 1999

CHINESE LANGUAGE - REFORM.
Ling, Yuanzheng. Xin yu wen jian she shi hua. Di 1 ban. Kaifeng Shi : Henan da xue chu ban she : Henan sheng Xin hua shu dian fa xing, 1995.
PL1175 .L55 1995 <Orien China>

CHINESE LITERATURE. *See also* **CHINESE ESSAYS; CHINESE POETRY; FOLK LITERATURE, CHINESE.**
Shi ji zhi jiao de dui hua. Di 1 ban. Shanghai : Shanghai gu ji chu ban she : Xin hua shu dian Shanghai fa xing suo fa xing, 2000.

CHINESE LITERATURE - 220-589 - HISTORY AND CRITICISM.
Li, Jianzhong, 1955- [Selections. 1999] Li Jianzhong zi xuan ji. Di 1 ban. Wuchang : Hua zhong li gong da xue chu ban she, 1999.
PL2284 .L395 1999

CHINESE LITERATURE - BIBLIOGRAPHY.
Chinese literature. Hauppauge, N.Y. : Nova Science Publishers, c2002.

CHINESE LITERATURE - HISTORY AND CRITICISM.
Bod Rgya rtsom rig gśib bsdur gyi dpyad brjod. Par theńs 1. Pe-cin : Mi rigs dpe skrun khań, 2001.
PL3705 (P-PZ22)+

Chen, Yugang. Zhongguo wen xue tong shi. Di 1 ban. Beijing Shi : Xi yuan chu ban she : Xin hua shu dian jing xiao, 1996.
PL2264 .C442527 1996 <Orien China>

Cheng, Qianfan. [Works. 2000] Cheng Qianfan quan ji. Di 1 ban. Shijiazhuang Shi : Hebei jiao yu chu ban she, 2000.
PL2744 .C46 2000

Chinese literature. Hauppauge, N.Y. : Nova Science Publishers, c2002.

Excursions in Chinese culture. Hong Kong : Chinese University Press, c2002.

Feminism/femininity in Chinese literature. Amsterdam ; New York : Rodopi, 2002.

Hu, Shihou. Hua jia ji. Di 1 ban. Kaifeng Shi : Henan da xue chu ban she, 1998.

Hu, Zhi, 1891-1962. Bai hua wen xue shi. Di 1 ban. Beijing : Dong fang chu ban she, 1996.

Huang, Shizhong. Hun bian, dao de yu wen xue. Di 1 ban. Beijing : Ren min wen xue chu ban she, 2000.

Huang, Yongnian. [Selections. 2000] Wen shi tan wei. Di 1 ban. Beijing : Zhonghua shu ju, 2000.
DS736 .H795 2000

Huo, Songlin. Tang yin ge lun wen ji. [Shijiazhuang Shi] : Hebei jiao yu chu ban she, [2000?]
PL2866.O236 A6 2000 v.1

Huo, Songlin. Tang yin ge sui bi ji. [Shijiazhuang Shi] : Hebei jiao yu chu ban she, [2000?]
PL2866.O236 A6 2000 v.4

Jiang, Yin. Xue shu de nian lun. Di 1 ban. [Beijing] : Zhongguo wen lian chu ban she, 2000.
PL2262 .J536 2000

Li, Jianzhong, 1955- [Selections. 1999] Li Jianzhong zi xuan ji. Di 1 ban. Wuchang : Hua zhong li gong da xue chu ban she, 1999.
PL2284 .L395 1999

Li, Tingba. Li ti wen xue lun. Di 1 ban. Beijing : Guang ming ri bao chu ban she : Xin hua shu dian Beijing fa xing suo jing xiao, 1997.
PL2262 .L47 1997 <Asian China>

Liang Qichao, Zhang Taiyan jie du Zhonghua wen hua jing dian. Di 1 ban. Shenyang Shi : Liao Hai chu ban she, 2003.

PL2262.2 .L54 2003

Lin, Shu, 1852-1924. Tie bi jin zhen. Di 1 ban. Tianjin Shi : Bai hua wen yi chu ban she, 2002.
PL2718.I5 T54 2002

Liu, Zaifu, 1941- Shu yuan si xu. Xianggang : Tian di tu shu you xian gong si, 2002.
PL2879.T653 S58 2002

Luo, Zongqiang. Luo Zongqiang gu dai wen xue si xiang lun ji. Di 1 ban. Shantou Shi : Shantou da xue chu ban she, 1999.
PL2264 .L95 1999

Motsch, Monika, 1942- [Mit Bambusrohr und Ahle von Qian Zhongshus Guanzhuibian zu einer Neubetrachtung Du Fus. Chinese] "Guan zhui bian" yu Du Fu xin jie. Di 1 ban. Shijiazhuang Shi : Hebei jiao yu chu ban she, 1997 (2002 printing)
PL2749.C8 Z85 1997

Santangelo, Paolo. Sentimental education in Chinese history. Leiden ; Boston : Brill, 2003.
BF538.C48 S25 2003

Shi ji zhi jiao de dui hua. Di 1 ban. Shanghai : Shanghai gu ji chu ban she : Xin hua shu dian Shanghai fa xing suo fa xing, 2000.

Shi, Zhecun. Beishan si chuang. Di 1 ban. Shanghai : Shanghai wen yi chu ban she : Xin hua shu dian jing xiao, 2000.
PL2272.5 .S543 2000

Sun, Changwu. Zhongguo wen xue zhong di Weimo yu Guanyin. Di 1 ban. Beijing : Gao deng jiao yu chu ban she : Xin hua shu dian zong dian Beijing fa xing suo fa xing, 1996.
PL2275.B8 S85 1996 <Orien China>

Wang, Bin. Zhongguo wen xue guan nian yan jiu. Beijing : Zhongguo wen lian, 1997.

Wang, Furen. Tu po mang dian. Di 1 ban. Beijing Shi : Zhongguo wen lian chu ban she, 2001.
PL2754.S5 Z89 2001

Wen xue yin lun. Di 1 ban. Ha'erbin Shi : Heilongjiang jiao yu chu ban she, 1999.

Wen, Yiduo, 1899-1946. Wen Yiduo xue shu wen hua sui bi. Beijing di 1 ban. Beijing : Zhongguo qing nian chu ban she, 2001.
PL2272.5 .W46 2001

Writing and materiality in China. Cambridge, Mass. : Published by Harvard University Asia Center for Harvard-Yenching Institute : distributed by Harvard University Press, 2003.
PL2262 .W74 2003

Xu, Fancheng. Xu Fancheng ji. Di 1 ban. Beijing : Zhongguo she hui ke xue chu ban she, 2001.
PL2262.2 .X84 2001

Xu, Wenjing, 1767-1756? Guan cheng shi ji. Di 1 ban. Beijing : Zhonghua shu ju : Xin hua shu dian Beijing fa xing suo fa xing, 1998.
PL2461.Z6 H77 1998

Xue lin chun qiu. Di 1 ban. Beijing : Chao hua chu ban she, 1999.
PL2272.5 .X846 1999

Ye, Ying, 1896-1950. Wen shi tong yi jiao zhu. Di 1 ban. Beijing : Zhonghua shu ju : Xin hua shu dian Beijing fa xing suo fa xing, 1994.
DS734.7.C433 Y43 1985 <Orien China>

Zhang, Shunhui. Zhang Shunhui xue shu wen hua sui bi. Beijing di 1 ban. Beijing : Zhongguo qing nian chu ban she, 2001.
PL2272.5 .Z427 2001

Zhao, Yaotang. Gu dai zuo jia lun. Di 1 ban. Jinan : Shandong you yi chu ban she, 1994.
PL2277 .C355 1994 <Asian China>

Zheng, Chengduo, 1898-1958. Zhongguo su wen xue shi. Di 1 ban. Beijing : Dong fang chu ban she, 1996.
PL2445 .C44 1996

Zhou, Xiuping. Wen xue xin shang yu pi ping. Di 1 ban. Changsha : Zhong nan gong ye da xue chu ban she, 1998.
PL2262 .Z468 1998

Zhou, Xunchu. [Selections. 2000] Zhou Xunchu wen ji. Di 1 ban. Nanjing Shi : Jiangsu gu ji chu ban she, 2000.
PL2264 .Z485 2000

Zhu, Ziqing, 1898-1948. Zhu Ziqing xue shu wen hua sui bi. Beijing di 1 ban. Beijing : Zhongguo qing nian chu ban she, 2000.

Zhuang, Zhongqing. Mao Dun de wen lun li cheng. Di 1 ban. Shanghai : Shanghai wen yi chu ban she : Xin hua shu dian jing xiao, 1996.
PL2801.N2 Z64 1996

CHINESE LITERATURE - HISTORY AND CRITICISM - THEORY, ETC.

Zhou, Xiuping. Wen xue xin shang yu pi ping. Di 1 ban. Changsha : Zhong nan gong ye da xue chu ban she, 1998.
PL2262 .Z468 1998

Chinese literature : overview and bibliography / James L. Claren (editor). Hauppauge, N.Y. : Nova Science Publishers, c2002. 239 p. ; 26 cm. Includes bibliographical references and indexes. ISBN 1-59033-288-1
1. Chinese literature - History and criticism. 2. Chinese literature - Bibliography. 3. China - Bibliography. I. Claren, James L.

CHINESE LITERATURE - QIN AND HAN DYNASTIES, 221 B.C.-220 A.D. - HISTORY AND CRITICISM.

Li, Jianzhong, 1955- [Selections. 1999] Li Jianzhong zi xuan ji. Di 1 ban. Wuchang : Hua zhong li gong da xue chu ban she, 1999.
PL2284 .L395 1999

CHINESE LITERATURE - TO 221 B.C. See CHINESE CLASSICS.

CHINESE LITERATURE - WESTERN INFLUENCES.

Guo, Yanli. Zhong xi wen hua peng zhuang yu jin dai wen xue = Di 1 ban. Jinan Shi : Shandong jiao yu chu ban she, 1999.
PL2274 .G86 1999

CHINESE PHILOSOPHY. See PHILOSOPHY, CHINESE.

CHINESE POETRY - HISTORY AND CRITICISM.

Huo, Songlin. Tang yin ge lun wen ji. [Shijiazhuang Shi] : Hebei jiao yu chu ban she, [2000?]
PL2866.O236 A6 2000 v.1

Huo, Songlin. Tang yin ge sui bi ji. [Shijiazhuang Shi] : Hebei jiao yu chu ban she, [2000?]
PL2866.O236 A6 2000 v.4

CHINESE QUESTION. See CHINA - HISTORY.

Chinese studies
(v. 26) Shi, Yili. Discourse analysis of Chinese referring expressions. Lewiston, N.Y. : E. Mellen Press, c2002.
P325.5.R44 S53 2002

CHINESE - UNITED STATES. See CHINESE AMERICANS.

Chinuch in turbulent times.
Brezak, Dov. 1st ed. Brooklyn, N.Y. : Mesorah Publications, c2002.

Chiodi, Michael. The art of building people : 36 coaching tools for getting more out of work and life / Michael Chiodi. 1st ed. St. Paul, Minn. : Chiberry Press, c2003. 136 p. : ill. ; 19 cm. ISBN 0-9724245-0-4
1. Self-actualization (Psychology) 2. Life skills. 3. Success. I. Title.
BF637.S4 C497 2003

Chip Taylor Communications.
Children and human rights. Part 1 [videorecording]. Derry, N.H. : Chip Taylor Communications, 1995.

Peace and conflict resolution. Part 1 [videorecording]. Derry, N.H. : Chip Taylor Communications, 1996.

Peace and conflict resolution. Part 2 [videorecording]. Derry, N.H. : Chip Taylor Communications, 1997.

Chipere, Ngoni, 1965- Understanding complex sentences : native speaker variation in syntactic competence / Ngoni Chipere. New York : Palgrave Macmillan, 2003. xvi, 248 : ill. ; 24 cm. Includes bibliographical references and index. ISBN 0-333-98639-3 DDC 415
1. Grammar, Comparative and general - Syntax. 2. Psycholinguistics. 3. Language and languages - Variation. I. Title.
P295 .C485 2003

CHIPS (ELECTRONICS). See INTEGRATED CIRCUITS.

CHIROGRAPHY. See WRITING.

CHISTIANITY - 20TH CENTURY.

Sartorio, Ugo. Credere in dialogo. Padova : Edizioni Messaggero, 2002.

Chiurazzi, Gaetano. Modalità ed esistenza : dalla critica della ragion pura alla critica della ragione ermeneutica : Kant, Husserl, Heidegger / Gaetano Chiurazzi. Torino : Trauben, c2001. 283 p. ; 21 cm.

(Estetica & ermeneutica ; 1) Includes bibliographical references (p. 269-283). ISBN 88-88398-01-5 DDC 111
1. Ontology. 2. Modality (Logic) I. Title. II. Series.
BD314 .C458 2001

CHIVALRY. See also CIVILIZATION, MEDIEVAL; CRUSADES; KNIGHTS AND KNIGHTHOOD.

Braudy, Leo. From chivalry to terrorism. New York : Alfred A. Knopf : Distributed by Random House, 2003.
HQ1090 .B7 2003

Frantzen, Allen J., 1947- Bloody good. Chicago : University of Chicago Press, 2004.
D523 .F722 2004

Chiwlean, Eghishē. Patanineru hawatkʻĕ / ashkhatasiretsʻ, Eghishē Chiwlean. Venetik ; Halēp : Mkhitʻarean Hratarakutʻiwn, S. Ghazar, 1998. 55 p. ; 20 cm. In Armenian.
1. Youth - Religious life. 2. Christian life. I. Title.

Chlada, Marvin, 1970- Klangmaschine / Marvin Chlada, Marcus S. Kleiner. 2., überarbeitete und erw. Aufl. Aschaffenburg : Alibri ; [Stuttgart] : Lautsprecher, 2001. 143 p. : ill., music ; 21 cm. German cataloging data indicate that this is the first volume of the trilogy Pop-Analysen. "LSV 099." ISBN 3-932710-37-1 (Alibri : pbk.) ISBN 3-932902-23-8 (Lautsprecher : pbk.)
1. Popular music - History and criticism. 2. Popular culture - History. 3. Postmodernism. I. Kleiner, Marcus S., 1973- II. Title.
ML3470 .C55 2001

Chmykhov, M. O. (Mykola Oleksandrovych) Vid IAĭtsia-raĭtsia do ideĭ Spasytelia / Mykola Chmykhov. Kyïv : "Lybid'", 2001. 428, [1] p. : ill. ; 17 cm. Includes bibliographical references (p. 413-[429]). ISBN 9660601697
1. Cosmology. I. Title.
BD518.U38 C48 2001

Cho, Hyeon-Kweon Stephan, 1962- Heiliger Geist als Lebenskraft in Kirche und Menschheit : die "Qi" (Ki/Ch'i)-Idee als Inkulturationsangebot fernöstlicher Pneumatologie / Hyeon-Kweon Stephan Cho. Frankfurt am Main ; New York : Peter Lang, c2002. 277 p. ; 21 cm. (Regensburger Studien zur Theologie ; Bd. 62) Originally presented as the author's thesis (doctoral)-- Regensburg, Universität, 2001. Includes bibliographical references (p. 251-271) and index. ISBN 3-631-39094-7
1. Holy Spirit. 2. Qi (Chinese philosophy) 3. Vital force. 4. Theology, Doctrinal. I. Title. II. Series.
BT121.3 .C56 2002

CHOCTAW INDIANS - FOLKLORE.

Mould, Tom, 1969- Choctaw prophecy. Tuscaloosa : University of Alabama Press, c2003.
E99.C8 M68 2003

CHOCTAW INDIANS - RELIGION.

Mould, Tom, 1969- Choctaw prophecy. Tuscaloosa : University of Alabama Press, c2003.
E99.C8 M68 2003

Choctaw prophecy.
Mould, Tom, 1969- Tuscaloosa : University of Alabama Press, c2003.
E99.C8 M68 2003

CHOICE - PHILOSOPHY.

Premoli De Marchi, Paola. Etica dell'assenso. Milano : FrancoAngeli, c2002.

CHOICE (PSYCHOLOGY). See also COMMITMENT (PSYCHOLOGY).

Barash, David P. The survival game. 1st ed. New York : Times Books, 2003.
HM1111 .B37 2003

Carson, Richard David. Taming your gremlin. Rev. ed. New York : Quill, 2003.
BF575.H27 C38 2003

Hardin, Russell, 1940- Indeterminacy and society. Princeton, N.J. : Princeton University Press, c2003.
HM1111 .H37 2003

Miller, John G., 1958- QBQ!. Denver, CO : Denver Press, c2001.
BF611 .M55 2001

Pettit, Philip, 1945- Rules, reasons, and norms. Oxford : Oxford University Press ; New York : Clarendon Press, 2002.
B105.T54 P48 2002

Phillips, Nicola. The big difference. Cambridge, MA : Perseus Pub., c2001.
BF619 .P48 2001

Schwartz, Barry, 1946- The tyranny of choice. 1st ed. New York : ECCO, 2004.

BF611 .S38 2004

CHOICE (PSYCHOLOGY) IN CHILDREN - JUVENILE LITERATURE.
Solar, Melanie B. The invisible bag. Greenwell Springs, LA : Solar Pub., 2000.
BF723.C47 S65 2000

CHOICE (PSYCHOLOGY) - MISCELLANEA.
Zukav, Gary. The mind of the soul. New York : Free Press, 2003.
BF611 .Z85 2003

CHOICE (PSYCHOLOGY) - RELIGIOUS ASPECTS - JUDAISM.
Miller, Avigdor. [Lev Avigdor] Sefer Lev Avigdor. Bruklin, N.Y. : S. Miller, 762, c2002.
BM538.P4 .M45 2001

Choices for today's superwoman.
Nicolson, Paula. Having it all? Chichester, West Sussex, England ; Hoboken, NJ : J. Wiley, c2002.
HQ1206 .N645 2002

Chomsky, Noam. Chomsky on democracy & education / Noam Chomsky ; edited by C.P. Otero. New York ; London : RoutledgeFalmer, 2003. xvi, 480 p. ; 24 cm. (Social theory, education, and cultural change) Includes bibliographical references (p. 411-464) and index. ISBN 0-415-92631-9 (hbk.) ISBN 0-415-92632-7 (pbk.) DDC 370.11/5
1. Education - Philosophy. 2. Democracy. 3. Critical pedagogy. 4. Language and languages. I. Otero, Carlos Peregrin, 1930- II. Title. III. Title: Chomsky on democracy and education IV. Series: Social theory, education & cultural change.
LB885.C5215 C46 2003

El lenguaje y la mente humana. 1. ed. Barcelona : Ariel Editorial, 2002.

Monkeywrenching the new world order [sound recording]. Oakland, Calif : AK Press ; San Francisco, CA : Alternative Tentacles Records, 2001.

Chomsky on democracy & education.
Chomsky, Noam. New York ; London : RoutledgeFalmer, 2003.
LB885.C5215 C46 2003

Chomsky on democracy and education.
Chomsky, Noam. Chomsky on democracy & education. New York ; London : RoutledgeFalmer, 2003.
LB885.C5215 C46 2003

Choose peace & happiness.
Reeve, Susyn. Boston, MA : Red Wheel, 2003.
BF637.P3 R44 2003

Choose peace and happiness.
Reeve, Susyn. Choose peace & happiness. Boston, MA : Red Wheel, 2003.
BF637.P3 R44 2003

Choosing a self.
Budgeon, Shelley, 1967- Westport, Conn. : Praeger, 2003.
HQ1229 .B83 2003

Choosing ethnic identity.
Song, Miri, 1964- Cambridge, UK : Polity Press ; Oxford ; Malden, MA : Blackwell Publishing, 2003.
GN495.6 .S65 2003

Choosing truth.
Cole, Harriette. New York : Simon & Schuster, c2003.
BF637.S4 C652 2003

Chopra, Deepak. The spontaneous fulfillment of desire : harnessing the infinite power of coincidence / Deepak Chopra. 1st ed. New York : Harmony Books, c2003. 302 p. ; 25 cm. Includes bibliographical references (p. [269]-273) and index. Table of contents URL: http://www.loc.gov/catdir/toc/ecip041/2003005617.html CONTENTS: Matter, mind, and spirit -- Synchronicity in nature -- The nature of the soul -- Intention -- The role of coincidence -- Desires and archetypes -- Meditation and mantras -- The first principle : you are a ripple in the fabric of the cosmos -- The second principle : through the mirror of relationships I discover my non-local self -- The third principle : master your inner dialogue -- The fourth principle : intent weaves the tapestry of the universe -- The fifth principle : harness your emotional turbulence -- The sixth principle : celebrate the dance of the cosmos -- The seventh principle : accessing the conspiracy of improbabilities -- Living synchrodestiny. ISBN 0-609-60042-7 DDC 128
1. Coincidence. 2. Self-actualization (Psychology) I. Title.
BF1175 .C48 2003

The spontaneous fulfillment of desire : harnessing the infinite power of coincidence / Deepak Chopra. New York : Random House Large Print, 2003. p. cm. ISBN 0-375-43220-5 (large print) DDC 128
1. Coincidence. 2. Self-actualization (Psychology) 3. Large type books. I. Title.
BF1175 .C48 2003b

CHOREOGRAPHY. See **BALLET.**

CHOREOGRAPHY - STUDY AND TEACHING.
Iannitelli, Leda Muhana. Guiding choreography [microform]. 1994.

Chou, Laixiang. Gu dai de mei, jin dai de mei, xian dai de mei / Zhou Laixiang zhu. Di 1 ban. Changchun Shi : Dongbei shi fan da xue chu ban she : Jilin sheng Xin hua shu dian fa xing, 1996. 6, 8, 3, 355 p. ; 21 cm. (Yi shu mei xue cong shu) Colophon title also in pinyin: Gudai de mei, jindai de mei, xiandai de mei. Includes bibliographical references. ISBN 7-5602-1738-9
1. Aesthetics. 2. Aesthetics, Chinese. I. Title. II. Title: Gudai de mei, jindai de mei, xiandai de mei III. Series.
BH39 .C5455 1996 <Orien China>

Chouchena, Emmanuel. L'homme, espoir de dieu : Judaïsme et kabbale pour le monde d'aujourd'hui. Entretiens avec Thomas Sertilanges / Emmanuel Chouchena, Thomas Sertilanges ; préface de Joseph Sitruk. Paris : Trajectoire, 2001. 373 p. ; 25 cm. ISBN 2-8419-7203-8 DDC 296
1. Judaism - Essence, genius, nature. 2. Ethics, Jewish. 3. Spiritual life - Judaism. I. Sertilanges, Thomas. II. Title.

Chouvier, Bernard.
Matière à symbolisation. Lausanne : Delachaux et Niestlé, c1998.
BF458 .M38 1998

Chowdhry, Geeta, 1956-.
Power, postcolonialism, and international relations. London ; New York : Routledge, 2002.
JV51 .P69 2002

CHRESTOMATHIES. See **READERS.**

Christ, Carol P. She who changes : re-imagining the divine in the world / Carol P. Christ. 1st ed. New York ; Houndmills, England : Palgrave Macmillan, 2003. x, 277 p. : maps ; 22 cm. Includes bibliographical references (p. [245]-267) and index. ISBN 1403960836 DDC 146/.7
1. Process philosophy. 2. Feminist theology. 3. Femininity of God. 4. Goddess religion. I. Title.
BD372 .C48 2003

CHRISTENING. See **BAPTISM.**

Christensen, Birgit, 1960-.
Wissen Macht Geschlecht. Zürich : Chronos, c2002.

Christensen, Clayton M. The innovator's solution : creating and sustaining successful growth / Clayton M. Christensen, Michael E. Raynor. Boston, Mass. : Harvard Business School Press, c2003. x, 304 p. : ill. ; 25 cm. Includes bibliographical references and index. ISBN 1-57851-852-0
1. Creative ability in business. 2. Industrial management. 3. Customer services. 4. Success in business. I. Raynor, Michael E. II. Title.

Christensen, Larry B., 1941- Experimental methodology / Larry B. Christensen. 9th ed. Boston, MA : Allyn and Bacon, 2004. p. cm. Includes bibliographical references and index. ISBN 0-205-39369-1 DDC 150/.7/24
1. Psychology, Experimental. 2. Psychology - Experiments. 3. Experimental design. I. Title.
BF181 .C48 2004

Christensen, Pia Monrad.
Children in the city. London : Routledge/Falmer, 2003.

Christesen, Mirka. Character kaleidoscope : a practical, standards-based resource guide for character development / Mirka Christesen with Susan Wasilewski. Port Chester, N.Y. : Dude Pub., c2000. xii, 152 p. : ill. (some col.) ; 28 cm. Includes bibliographical references (p. 139-147). ISBN 1-88794-346-3 DDC 155.2/5
1. Character - Study and teaching (Middle school) - United States. I. Wasilewski, Susan. II. Title.
BF818 .C55 2000

CHRISTIAN ANTIQUITIES. See **FASTS AND FEASTS.**

CHRISTIAN ART AND SYMBOLISM. See **CHURCH ARCHITECTURE; ICONS, BYZANTINE; IMAGE (THEOLOGY).**

CHRISTIAN BIOGRAPHY.
Soku, Leonard. From the coven of witchcraft to Christ. Rev. ed. [Accra, Ghana? : s.n., c2000]
BV4935.S6 F76 2000
1. Black author.

CHRISTIAN CIVILIZATION. See **CIVILIZATION, CHRISTIAN.**

CHRISTIAN CONVERTS - GHANA - BIOGRAPHY.
Soku, Leonard. From the coven of witchcraft to Christ. Rev. ed. [Accra, Ghana? : s.n., c2000]
BV4935.S6 F76 2000
1. Black author.

CHRISTIAN DENOMINATIONS. See **CHRISTIAN SECTS.**

CHRISTIAN DOCTRINES. See **THEOLOGY, DOCTRINAL.**

CHRISTIAN EDUCATION. See **THEOLOGY - STUDY AND TEACHING.**

CHRISTIAN ETHICS.
Campanini, Giorgio, 1930- Le parole dell'etica. Bologna : EDB, 2002.

Gomes, Peter J. The good life. 1st ed. San Francisco : HarperSanFrancisco, c2002.
BJ1581.2 .G575 2002

Noriega, José. "Guiados por el espíritu". Roma : Pontificia università lateranense ; [Milano] : Mursia, 2000.

Salamucha, Jan. [Selections. English. 2003] Knowledge and faith. Amsterdam ; New York, NY : Rodopi, 2003.

CHRISTIAN ETHICS - CATHOLIC AUTHORS.
Simon, Yves René Marie, 1903-1961. [Critique de la connaissance morale. English] A critique of moral knowledge. New York : Fordham University Press, 2002.
BJ1249 .S4513 2002

CHRISTIAN ETHICS - ORTHODOX EASTERN AUTHORS.
Solovyov, Vladimir Sergeyevich, 1853-1900. [Essays. English. Selections] The heart of reality. Notre Dame, Ind. : University of Notre Dame Press, c2003.
B4262.A5 W69 2003

CHRISTIAN HAGIOLOGY - SPAIN - CASTILLA Y LEÓN - HISTORY.
Pérez-Embid Wamba, Javier. Hagiología y sociedad en la España medieval. Huelva : Universidad de Huelva, 2002.
BX4659.S8 P47 2002

CHRISTIAN LIFE. See also **ASCETICISM; CHRISTIAN ETHICS.**
Campanini, Giorgio, 1930- Le parole dell'etica. Bologna : EDB, 2002.

Chiwlean, Eghishē. Patanineru hawatk'ĕ. Venetik ; Halēp : Mkhit'arean Hratarakut'iwn, S. Ghazar, 1998.

Dobson, James C., 1936- Life on the edge. Nashville : Word Pub., c2000.
BF637.L53 D63 2000

Farrington, Debra K. Hearing with the heart. 1st ed. San Francisco : Jossey-Bass, c2003.
BV4509.5 .F37 2003

Gilhooley, James J. Making hope visible. Allahabad : Holy Family International, [2003]

Henry, Michel, 1922- [C'est moi la vérité. English] I am the truth. Stanford, Calif : Stanford University Press, 2003.
BR100 .H39813 2003

Johnson, Kevin Wayne. Give God the glory!. Hillsborough, NJ : Writing for the Lord Ministries, c2001.
1. Black author.

Kuipers, Ronald Alexander. Critical faith. Amsterdam ; New, York, NY : Rodopi, 2002.

Manning, Brennan. A glimpse of Jesus. 1st ed. [San Francisco] : HarperSanFrancisco, c2003.
BV4647.S43 M36 2003

Manning, Brennan. The wisdom of tenderness. 1st ed. New York : HarperCollins, c2002.
BV4520 .M36 2002

Martinelli, Paolo, 1958- Vocazione e stati di vita del cristiano. Roma : Collegio San Lorenzo da Brindisi, 2001.

Mozia, Michael Ifeanyinachukwu. Holiness & divine mercy (the key to heaven). Ibadan, Oyo State, Nigeria : St. Pauls, 2002.
1. Black author.

Noriega, José. "Guiados por el espíritu". Roma : Pontificia università lateranense ; [Milano] : Mursia, 2000.

Ofoegbu, Mike. Exposing satanic manipulations. [Lagos, Nigeria : Holy Ghost Anointed Books Ministries, c1998]
1. Black author.

Ofori Onwona, Samuel. Shadows come to light. Achimota, Ghana : Africa Christian Press, 2000.
BV215 .O46 2000

Smereka, Vira, 1923- Vichnyĭ vohon'. L'viv : Vyd-vo "Spolom", 2000.
PG3949.29.M4 V5 2000

The way of a pilgrim. London : Darton Longman & Todd, 2003, c2001.

Winter, Richard, 1945- Still bored in a culture of entertainment. Downers Grove, Ill. : InterVarsity Press, c2002.
BV4599.5.B67 W56 2002

CHRISTIAN LIFE - CATHOLIC AUTHORS.
Egbunu, Fidelis Eleojo. Be not afraid, only believe. Enugu, Nigeria : Snaap Press, 2001.
1. Black author.

CHRISTIAN LIFE - HISTORY - MIDDLE AGES, 600-1500.
Angenendt, Arnold. Grundformen der Frömmigkeit im Mittelalter. München : Oldenbourg, 2003.

Frömmigkeit im Mittelalter. München : Fink, c2002.

CHRISTIAN LIFE - QUOTATIONS, MAXIMS, ETC.
Abraham Lincoln's daily treasure. Grand Rapids, Mich. : F.H. Revell, c2002.
E457.2 .F787 2002

CHRISTIAN LITERATURE, EARLY - TRANSLATIONS INTO SERBIAN.
Vizantijska filozofija u srednjevekovnoj Srbiji. Beograd : Stubovi kulture, 2002.

CHRISTIAN LITERATURE, ENGLISH - MIDDLE ENGLISH (1100-1500). See **CHRISTIAN LITERATURE, ENGLISH (MIDDLE).**

CHRISTIAN LITERATURE, ENGLISH (MIDDLE) - HISTORY AND CRITICISM.
Thompson, Anne Booth. Everyday saints and the art of narrative in the South English legendary. Aldershot, England : Burlington, Vt. : Ashgate, c2003.
PR2143.S543 T48 2003

CHRISTIAN LITERATURE, MIDDLE ENGLISH. See **CHRISTIAN LITERATURE, ENGLISH (MIDDLE).**

CHRISTIAN PILGRIMS AND PILGRIMAGES. See **CHRISTIAN SHRINES.**

CHRISTIAN SAINTS - BIOGRAPHY.
Megale, Nilza Botelho. Santos do povo brasileiro. Petrópolis : Editora Vozes, 2002.

CHRISTIAN SAINTS - CULT - BRAZIL.
Megale, Nilza Botelho. Santos do povo brasileiro. Petrópolis : Editora Vozes, 2002.

CHRISTIAN SAINTS - CULT - SPAIN - CASTILLA Y LEÓN - HISTORY OF DOCTRINES - MIDDLE AGES, 600-1500.
Pérez-Embid Wamba, Javier. Hagiología y sociedad en la España medieval. Huelva : Universidad de Huelva, 2002.
BX4659.S8 P47 2002

CHRISTIAN SAINTS - INVOCATION. See **CHRISTIAN SAINTS - CULT.**

CHRISTIAN SAINTS - LEGENDS - HISTORY AND CRITICISM.
Thompson, Anne Booth. Everyday saints and the art of narrative in the South English legendary. Aldershot, England : Burlington, Vt. : Ashgate, c2003.
PR2143.S543 T48 2003

CHRISTIAN SAINTS - VENERATION. See **CHRISTIAN SAINTS - CULT.**

CHRISTIAN SAINTS - WORSHIP. See **CHRISTIAN SAINTS - CULT.**

CHRISTIAN SECTS - RUSSIA.
Rozanov, V. V. (Vasiliĭ Vasil'evich), 1856-1919. Vozrozhdaiushchiĭsia Egipet. Moskva : Izd-vo "Respublika", 2002.

CHRISTIAN SHRINES - EGYPT.
Be thou there. Cairo ; New York : American University in Cairo Press, c2001.

CHRISTIAN SOCIOLOGY.
Davis, Charles, 1923- Religion and the making of society. New York, NY, USA : Cambridge University Press, 1994.

BT738 .D36 1994
CHRISTIAN THEOLOGY. See **THEOLOGY.**
CHRISTIAN WOMEN. See **CATHOLIC WOMEN.**

The Christian world of the Middle Ages. Hamilton, Bernard, 1932- Stroud, Glos : Sutton, 2003.

CHRISTIANITY. See also **CHURCH HISTORY; CIVILIZATION, CHRISTIAN; THEOLOGY; WOMEN IN CHRISTIANITY.**
2000 years and beyond. London ; New York : Routledge, 2003.
BR53 .T86 2003

Smullyan, Raymond M. Who knows? Bloomington : Indiana University Press, c2003.
BL50 .S59 2003

CHRISTIANITY - 19TH CENTURY. See **CHRISTIANITY.**

CHRISTIANITY AND ANTISEMITISM.
Davis, Frederick, 1931- The Jew and deicide. Lanham, Md. : University Press of America, c2003.
BS2555.6.J44 D38 2003

CHRISTIANITY AND CULTURE.
Florovsky, Georges, 1893-1979. [Selections. Russian. 2002] Vera i kul'tura. Sankt-Peterburg : Izd-vo Russkogo Khristianskogo gumanitarnogo instituta, 2002.
BX260 .F552 2002

CHRISTIANITY AND CULTURE - AFRICA, SUB-SAHARAN.
Emtcheu, André. Psychologie et révélation. Yaoundé, Cameroun : Editions SHERPA, c2001.
1. Black author.

CHRISTIANITY AND OTHER RELIGIONS.
Hunt, Stephen, 1954- Alternative religions. Aldershot, Hampshire, England ; Burlington, VT : Ashgate, c2003.
BP603 .H87 2003

Medieval cultures in contact. New York : Fordham University Press, 2003.
CB351 .M3922 2003

Ruggiero, Fabio. La follia dei cristiani. Roma : Città nuova, c2002.
BR166 .R84 2002

Tijan Bangura, Abubakar. The truth can be discovered in the Qur'an. [Freetown, Sierra Leone : s.n., 2002]
1. Black author.

CHRISTIANITY AND OTHER RELIGIONS - HINDUISM.
McLaughlin, Michael T. Knowledge, consciousness and religious conversion in Lonergan and Aurobindo. Roma : Editrice Pontificia Universita Gregoriana, 2003.

CHRISTIANITY AND OTHER RELIGIONS - HISTORY. See **CHRISTIANITY AND OTHER RELIGIONS.**

CHRISTIANITY AND OTHER RELIGIONS - ISLAM.
Adeniyi, M. O. Yoruba Muslim-Christian understanding. Majiyagbe, Ipaja, Nigeria : Eternal Communications, 2001.
1. Black author.

Diálogo de civilizaciones Oriente-Occidente. [Madrid] : Biblioteca Nueva ; [Cáceres, España] : Universidad de Extremadura, c2002.

Nuwayhiḍ, Walīd. Min Kābūl ilá Niyūyūrk. al-Ṭab'ah 1. Bayrūt : Dār Ibn Ḥazm, 2002.
BP172+

Van de Weyer, Robert. The shared well. 1st ed. Washington, D.C. : Brassey's, c2002.
BL65.P7 V36 2002

CHRISTIANITY AND OTHER RELIGIONS - JUDAISM. See also **JUDAISM (CHRISTIAN THEOLOGY).**
Diálogo de civilizaciones Oriente-Occidente. [Madrid] : Biblioteca Nueva ; [Cáceres, España] : Universidad de Extremadura, c2002.

Meyuhas Ginio, Alisa, 1937- Ḳerovim u-reḥoḳim. Tel Aviv : Mif'alim Universiṭayim, 760 [1999]

CHRISTIANITY AND OTHER RELIGIONS - NEOPAGANISM.
DiZerega, Gus. Pagans & Christians. 1st ed. St. Paul, Minn. : Llewellyn Publications, 2001.
BF1566 .D59 2001

CHRISTIANITY AND OTHER RELIGIONS - SPAIN.
Diálogo de civilizaciones Oriente-Occidente.

[Madrid] : Biblioteca Nueva ; [Cáceres, España] : Universidad de Extremadura, c2002.

CHRISTIANITY AND SCIENCE. See **RELIGION AND SCIENCE.**

CHRISTIANITY - DOCTRINES. See **THEOLOGY, DOCTRINAL.**

CHRISTIANITY - FORECASTING.
2000 years and beyond. London ; New York : Routledge, 2003.
BR53 .T86 2003

CHRISTIANITY - HISTORY. See **CHURCH HISTORY.**

CHRISTIANITY - MIDDLE AGES, 600-1500. See **CHURCH HISTORY - MIDDLE AGES, 600-1500.**

CHRISTIANITY - MODERN PERIOD, 1500-. See **CHURCH HISTORY - MODERN PERIOD, 1500-.**

CHRISTIANITY - NIGERIA.
Babalola, E. O. African cultural revolution of Islam and Christianity in Yoruba land. Ipaja-Lagos : Eternal Communications, 2002.
1. Black author.

CHRISTIANITY - ORIGIN.
Ferguson, Everett, 1933- Backgrounds of early Christianity. 3rd ed. Grand Rapids, Mich. : W.B. Eerdmans, c2003.

Giussani, Luigi. PerCorso. Milano : Rizzoli, c1997-

CHRISTIANITY - PHILOSOPHY.
Henry, Michel, 1922- [C'est moi la vérité. English] I am the truth. Stanford, Calif : Stanford University Press, 2003.
BR100 .H39813 2003

Kuipers, Ronald Alexander. Critical faith. Amsterdam ; New York, NY : Rodopi, 2002.

Westphal, Merold. Overcoming onto-theology. 1st ed. New York : Fordham University Press, 2001.
BR100 .W47 2001

Christiano, Kevin J. Sociology of religion : contemporary developments / Kevin J. Christiano, William H. Swatos, Jr., Peter Kivisto. Walnut Creek, CA : AltaMira Press, c2002. xiii, 365 p. : ill. ; 25 cm. Includes bibliographical references (p. 327-357) and index. ISBN 0-7591-0035-7 (alk. paper) DDC 306.6
1. Religion and sociology. I. Swatos, William H. II. Kivisto, Peter, 1948- III. Title.
BL60 .C465 2002

CHRISTIANS. See **CLERGY; FRIARS.**
CHRISTIANS - PERSECUTIONS. See **PERSECUTION.**

Christiansen, Morten H., 1963-.
Language evolution. Oxford ; New York : Oxford University Press, 2003.
P140 .L256 2003

Christino, Karen. Foreseeing the future : Evangeline Adams and astrology in America / Karen Christino. Amherst, MA : One Reed Publications, c2002. 217 p. ; 23 cm. Includes bibliography and index. ISBN 9-9628031-6-2
1. Adams, Evangeline Smith, -1872?-1932. 2. Astrologers - United States - Biography. 3. Astrology - History - 20th century. I. Adams, Evangeline Smith, 1872?-1932. II. Title.
BF1679.8.A31 C56 2002

CHRISTMAS.
Die Grundsteinmeditation als Schulungsweg. Dornach : Verlag am Goetheanum, c2002.

Christoff, Joseph A. Issues in implementing international peace operations [electronic resource]. [Washington, D.C.] : U.S. General Accounting Office, [2002] Mode of access: Internet from GPO Access web site. Address as of 10/22/03: http://frwebgate.access.gpo.gov/cgi-bin/getdoc.cgi?dbname=gao&docid=f:d02707r.txt; current access available via PURL. Title from title screen (viewed on Oct. 22, 2003). "24-MAY-02." Paper version available from: General Accounting Office, 441 G St., NW, Rm. LM, Washington, D.C. 20548. Includes bibliographical references. "GAO-02-707R." URL: http://purl.access.gpo.gov/GPO/LPS35462 Available in other form: Issues in implementing international peace operations 21 p. (OCoLC)50192653.
1. Peace. 2. Reconciliation. 3. International relations. 4. Security, International. I. United States. General Accounting Office. II. Title. III. Title: International peace operations IV. Title: Issues in implementing international peace operations 21 p.

CHROMATICS. See **COLOR.**

CHROMOSOME Y. *See* **Y CHROMOSOME.**

CHROMOSOMES. *See* **GENETICS.**

CHRONOBIOLOGY.
Aveni, Anthony F. The book of the year. Oxford ; New York : Oxford University Press, 2003.
GT3930 .A94 2003

The chronography of George Synkellos.
Geōrgios, Synkellos, fl. 800. [Ecloga chronographica English] Oxford ; New York : Oxford University Press, 2002.

CHRONOLOGY. *See* **CALENDAR; MAYA CHRONOLOGY; NIGHT.**

CHRONOLOGY, HISTORICAL. *See also* **CALENDAR.**
Nosovskiĭ, G. V. (Gleb Vladimirovich), 1958- Rekonstruktsiia vseobshcheĭ istorii. Moskva : FID "Delovoĭ ėkspress", 2002.
DK38 .N68 2002

CHRONOLOGY, MAYA. *See* **MAYA CHRONOLOGY.**

CHRONOMETRY, MENTAL. *See* **TIME PERCEPTION.**

Chto posle illiuzii?.
Slutskiĭ, O. I. (Oleg Isaakovich) Moskva : Veche, 2002.
BV4509.R8 S58 2002

Chuckrow, Robert. The tai chi book : refining and enjoying a lifetime of practice : including the teachings of Cheng Man-ch'ing, William C.C. Chen, and Harvey I. Sober / Robert Chuckrow. Boston : YMAA Publication Center, c1998. xiii, 209 p. : ill. ; 24 cm. Rev. ed. of: T'ai chi ch'üan. Includes bibliographical references (p. 204-205) and index. ISBN 1-88696-964-7 DDC 613.7/148
1. Tai chi. 2. Meditation. 3. Exercise. I. Zheng, Manqing. II. Chen, William C. C. III. Sober, Harvey I. IV. Chuckrow, Robert. T'ai chi ch'üan. V. Title.
GV504 .C536 1998

Tai chi chuan.
Chuckrow, Robert. The tai chi book. Boston : YMAA Publication Center, c1998.
GV504 .C536 1998

Tai chi walking : a low-impact path to better health / Robert Chuckrow ; illustrations by the author. Boston, Mass. : YMAA Publication Center, c2002. xii, 138 p. : ill. ; 24 cm. Includes bibliographical references (p. 131-133) and index. ISBN 1-88696-923-X
1. Tai chi. 2. Walking. 3. Meditation. I. Title.

Chudova, N. V.
Virtual'naia real'nost' v psikhologii i iskusstvennom intellekte. Moskva : Rossiĭskaia Assotsiatsiia iskusstvennogo intellekta, 1998.
BF204.5 .V57 1998

Chukwu, Cletus N. Introduction to philosophy in an African perspective / Cletus N. Chukwu. Eldoret, Kenya : Zapf Chancery, 2002. 344 p. ; 21 cm. Spine title: Philosophy in an African perspective. Includes bibliographical references (p. [333]-336) and indexes. ISBN 9966963596
1. Philosophy. 2. Philosophy - Africa. 3. Black author. I. Title. II. Title: Philosophy in an African perspective

Chung, Man Cheung, 1962-.
Psychoanalytic knowledge. New York : Palgrave Macmillan, 2003.
BF173 .P7763 2003

CHURCH. *See also* **SACRAMENTS.**
Giussani, Luigi. PerCorso. Milano : Rizzoli, c1997-

CHURCH AND SOCIAL PROBLEMS - UNITED STATES.
Religious organizations in community services. New York : Springer Pub., 2003.
HV530 .R25 2003

CHURCH ARCHITECTURE - ITALY - TURIN.
Scott, John Beldon, 1946- Architecture for the shroud. Chicago : University of Chicago Press, c2003.
NA5621.T823 S36 2003

CHURCH BUILDINGS. *See* **CHURCH ARCHITECTURE; COPTIC CHURCH BUILDINGS.**

CHURCH CALENDAR. *See* **FASTS AND FEASTS.**

CHURCH CALENDAR - COMPARATIVE STUDIES. *See* **RELIGIOUS CALENDARS.**

CHURCH FESTIVALS. *See* **FASTS AND FEASTS.**

CHURCH HISTORY. *See* **CHRISTIAN SECTS; CHRISTIANITY.**

CHURCH HISTORY IN LITERATURE.
Clegg, Justin. The medieval Church. London : British Library, 2003.

CHURCH HISTORY - MIDDLE AGES, 600-1500. *See also* **CRUSADES.**
Alzieu, Gérard. Les églises de l'ancien diocèse de Lodève au Moyen-Age. Montpellier : Editions P. Clerc, 1998.
BX1532.L63 A695 1998

Angenendt, Arnold. Grundformen der Frömmigkeit im Mittelalter. München : Oldenbourg, 2003.

Brown, Peter Robert Lamont. The rise of Western Christendom. 2nd ed. Malden, MA ; Oxford : Blackwell Publishing, 2003.
BR162.3 .B76 2003

Clegg, Justin. The medieval Church. London : British Library, 2003.

Dawson, Christopher, 1889-1970. The making of Europe. Washington, D.C. : Catholic University of America Press, 2002, 1932.
CB353 .D3 2002

Frömmigkeit im Mittelalter. München : Fink, c2002.

Goglin, Jean-Marc. L'enseignement de la théologie dans les ordres mendiants à Paris au XIIIe siècle. Paris : Editions franciscaines, c2002.

Hamilton, Bernard, 1932- The Christian world of the Middle Ages. Stroud, Glos : Sutton, 2003.

Keefe, Susan A. Water and the Word. Notre Dame, Ind. : University of Notre Dame Press, c2002.
BR200 .K44 2002

Meyuhas Ginio, Alisa, 1937- Ķerovim u-reḥoķim. Tel Aviv : Mif'alim Universiṭayim, 760 [1999]

Modestin, Georg. Le diable chez l'évêque. Lausanne : Université de Lausanne, Section d'histoire, Faculté des lettres, 1999.
BF1584.S9 M64 1999

Peri, Vittorio. Da oriente e da occidente. Roma : Editrice Antenore, 2002.
BR162.3 .P475 2002

Radzimiński, Andrzej. Życie i obyczajowość średniowiecznego duchowieństwa. Warszawa : Wydawn. DiG, 2002.
BX1565 .R32 2002

Religion et mentalités au Moyen Age. Rennes : Presses universitaires de Rennes, c2003.
BR141 .R45 2003

Sankt Georg und sein Bilderzyklus in Neuhaus/ Böhmen (Jindřichův Hradec). Marburg : N.G. Elwert, c2002.
BR1720.G4 S26 2002

Stark, Heinz. Plecher Kirchengeschichte im Mittelalter. Simmelsdorf : Altnürnberger Landschaft, 2002.

CHURCH HISTORY - MIDDLE AGES, 600-1500 - RESEARCH.
Angenendt, Arnold. Grundformen der Frömmigkeit im Mittelalter. München : Oldenbourg, 2003.

CHURCH HISTORY - MIDDLE AGES, 600-1500 - SOURCES.
Clegg, Justin. The medieval Church. London : British Library, 2003.

CHURCH HISTORY - MODERN PERIOD, 1500-.
Peri, Vittorio. Da oriente e da occidente. Roma : Editrice Antenore, 2002.
BR162.3 .P475 2002

CHURCH HISTORY - PRIMITIVE AND EARLY CHURCH, CA. 30-600.
Brown, Peter Robert Lamont. The rise of Western Christendom. 2nd ed. Malden, MA ; Oxford : Blackwell Publishing, 2003.
BR162.3 .B76 2003

Hamilton, Bernard, 1932- The Christian world of the Middle Ages. Stroud, Glos : Sutton, 2003.

Peri, Vittorio. Da oriente e da occidente. Roma : Editrice Antenore, 2002.
BR162.3 .P475 2002

Ruggiero, Fabio. La follia dei cristiani. Roma : Città nuova, c2002.
BR166 .R84 2002

Snyder, Graydon F. Irish Jesus, Roman Jesus. Harrisburg, Pa. : Trinity Press International, c2002.
BR737.C4 S69 2002

CHURCH WORK WITH ADULTS. *See* **CHURCH WORK WITH WOMEN.**

CHURCH WORK WITH WOMEN - CATHOLIC CHURCH.
Alberione, James, 1884-1971. La donna associata allo zelo sacerdotale. Cinisello Balsamo, Milano : San Paolo, c2001.

CHURCHES, COPTIC. *See* **COPTIC CHURCH BUILDINGS.**

Churchill, Ward.
Monkeywrenching the new world order [sound recording]. Oakland, Calif : AK Press ; San Francisco, CA : Alternative Tentacles Records, 2001.

CHURCHILL, WINSTON S. (WINSTON SPENCER), 1874-1965.
Roberts, Andrew, 1963- Hitler and Churchill. London : Weidenfeld & Nicolson, 2003.

CHURCHILL, WINSTON, SIR, 1874-1965.
Sandys, Celia. We shall not fail. New York : Portfolio ; London : Penguin Books, 2003.
DA566.9.C5 S266 2003

CHURCHILL, WINSTON, SIR, 1874-1965 - VIEWS ON LEADERSHIP.
Sandys, Celia. We shall not fail. New York : Portfolio ; London : Penguin Books, 2003.
DA566.9.C5 S266 2003

Churchland, Patricia Smith. Brain-wise : studies in neurophilosophy / Patricia Smith Churchland. Cambridge, Mass. : MIT Press, c2002. xii, 471 p., [4] p. of plates : ill. (some col.) ; 23 cm. "A Bradford book." Includes bibliographical references (p. [421]-450) and index. Table of contents URL: http://www.loc.gov/catdir/toc/fy035/ 2002066024.html ISBN 0-262-03301-1 (hbk.) ISBN 0-262-53200-X (pbk.) DDC 153/.01
1. Neurosciences - Philosophy. 2. Cognitive science - Philosophy. I. Title. II. Title: Studies in neurophilosophy
RC343 .C486 2002

Chvojka, Erhard. Geschichte der Grosselternrollen : vom 16. bis zum 20. Jahrhundert / Erhard Chvojka. Wien : Böhlau, 2003. 378 p., 32 p. of plates : ill. (some col.) ; 22 cm. (Kulturstudien ; Bd. 33) Includes bibliographical references (p. [357]-374). ISBN 3-205-98465-X (cl.)
1. Grandparents. 2. Grandparenting. 3. Grandparent and child. 4. Family. I. Title. II. Series.
HQ759.9 .C45 2003

Cicero.
Radford, Robert T. Amsterdam ; New York, NY : Rodopi, 2002.
DG260.C5 R33 2002

Cicero, Chic, 1936- Creating magical tools : the magician's craft / Chic Cicero, Sandra Tabatha Cicero. 2nd ed. St. Paul, Minn. : Llewellyn Publications, 1999. xxxiii, 343 p. : ill. (some col.) ; 24 cm. Includes bibliographical references (p. 325-328) and index. ISBN 1-56718-142-2 DDC 135/.45
1. Hermetic Order of the Golden Dawn - Rituals. I. Cicero, Sandra Tabatha, 1959- II. Cicero, Chic, 1936- Secrets of a Golden Dawn temple. III. Title.
BF1623.R7 C48 1999b

Guide to the Golden Dawn Enochian skrying tarot. St. Paul, Minn. : Llewellyn, 2004.
BF1623.E55 G65 2004

Secrets of a Golden Dawn temple.
Cicero, Chic, 1936- Creating magical tools. 2nd ed. St. Paul, Minn. : Llewellyn Publications, 1999.
BF1623.R7 C48 1999b

CICERO, MARCUS TULLIUS.
Radford, Robert T. Cicero. Amsterdam ; New York, NY : Rodopi, 2002.
DG260.C5 R33 2002

Cicero, Sandra Tabatha, 1959-.
Cicero, Chic, 1936- Creating magical tools. 2nd ed. St. Paul, Minn. : Llewellyn Publications, 1999.
BF1623.R7 C48 1999b

Ciencia y logica de mundos posibles.
Dufour, Adrian. Bern : Lang, 2001.

Cifali, Mario. Trois rêves freudiens / Mario Cifali. Paris : Eshel, c1999. 124 p. ; 23 cm. (Collection Remise en question) Includes bibliographical references. ISBN 2-906704-70-9
1. Oedipus complex. 2. Dreams - Interpretation. I. Title. II. Series.
BF175.5.O33 C54 1999

Ciliberto, Michele.
Bruno, Giordano, 1548-1600. Opere magiche. Milano : Adelphi, 2000.
BF1600 .B78 2000

Cimatti, Felice. La mente silenziosa : come pensano gli animali non umani / Felice Cimatti. 1. ed. Roma : Editori riuniti, 2002. 239 p. : ill. ; 21 cm. (Futura) Includes bibliographical references (p. 230-239). ISBN 88-359-5160-7 DDC 128
1. Animal psychology. 2. Thought and thinking. 3. Animal communication. 4. Cognition in animals. 5. Psychology, Comparative. I. Title. II. Series.

Cinco ensaios sobre a religiao dos orixás.
Verger, Pierre. Saída de Iaô. Sao Paulo : Fundação Pierre Verger : Axis Mundi Editora, 2002.

CINEMA. *See* **MOTION PICTURES.**

Cioran, E. M. (Emile M.), 1911-
[Histoire et utopie. Romanian]
Istorie şi utopie / Cioran ; traducere din franceză de Emanoil Marcu. Bucureşti : Humanitas, 2002. 162 p. ; 18 cm. Translation of: Histoire et utopie. ISBN 9735002256 (pbk.)
1. Utopias - History. 2. History - Philosophy. I. Marcu, Emanoil. II. Title.

[Précis de décomposition. Romanian]
Tratat de descompunere / Cioran ; traducere din franceză de Irina Mavrodin. Bucureşti : Humanitas, 2002, c1996. 246 p. ; 20 cm. Includes bibliographical references. ISBN 973500223X
1. Human beings. 2. Philosophy. 3. Civilization. I. Mavrodin, Irina. II. Title.

CIPHERS. *See* **WRITING.**

CIPHERS IN THE BIBLE.
Glazerson, Matityahu. Migdele ha-te'omim be-diluge otiyot ba-Torah. Yerushalayim : Yerid ha-sefarim, 2002.

The circle within.
Sylvan, Dianne, 1977- 1st ed. St. Paul, MN : Llewellyn Publications, 2003.
BF1566 .S95 2003

CIRCUITS, INTEGRATED. *See* **INTEGRATED CIRCUITS.**

CIRCUMCISION.
Maciejewski, Franz. Psychoanalytisches Archiv und jüdisches Gedächtnis. 1. Aufl. Wien : Passagen Verlag, 2002.

CIRCUMSTELLAR MATTER. *See* **STARS.**

CIRENE (EXTINCT CITY). *See* **CYRENE (EXTINCT CITY).**

CIT consciousness.
Gupta, Bina, 1947- New Delhi ; New York : Oxford University Press, 2003.
BF311+

CITATION OF ELECTRONIC INFORMATION RESOURCES.
Kelly, Brian, 1956- iSearch. Boston, MA : Allyn and Bacon, c2003.
BF76.78 .K45 2003

Cité des hommes, cité de Dieu : travaux sur la littérature de la Renaissance en l'honneur de Daniel Ménager. Genève : Droz, 2003. 623 p. : ill. ; 26 cm. (Travaux d'humanisme et Renaissance, 0082-6081 ; no 375) Includes bibliographical references and index. ISBN 2-600-00824-1 (cl.) DDC 809
1. Ménager, Daniel - Bibliography. 2. European literature - Renaissance, 1450-1600 - History and criticism. 3. Renaissance. I. Ménager, Daniel. II. Series.
PN723 .C584 2003

La cité des vivants et des morts.
Michelet, Jules, 1798-1874. [Paris] : Belin, c2002.

CITIES AND TOWNS. *See* **COMMUNITY; URBANIZATION.**

CITIES AND TOWNS - EUROPE - GROWTH - HISTORY.
Urban achievement in early modern Europe. Cambridge ; New York : Cambridge University Press, 2001.
HT131 .U688 2001

CITIES AND TOWNS - HISTORY.
Metamorfosi della città. Milano : Garzanti / Scheiwiller, 1995 (1996 printing)
HT111 .M472 1995

CITIES AND TOWNS, MOVEMENT TO. *See* **URBANIZATION.**

CITIES AND TOWNS - PLANNING. *See* **CITY PLANNING.**

CITIES AND TOWNS - PSYCHOLOGICAL ASPECTS.
Huyssen, Andreas. Present pasts. Stanford, Calif. : Stanford University Press, 2003.

BD181.7 .H89 2003

CITIES AND TOWNS - SURVEYING. *See* **SURVEYING.**

CITIZEN PARTICIPATION. *See* **POLITICAL PARTICIPATION.**

Citizens Commission on Human Rights International.
Creating racism. Los Angeles, CA : Citizens Commission on Human Rights, 1995.
RC455.4.E8 C74x 1995

CITIZENSHIP. *See also* **NATURALIZATION.**
Lister, Ruth, 1949- 2nd ed. Basingstoke, Hampshire ; New York : Palgrave Macmillan, 2003.
HQ1236 .L57 2003

CITIZENSHIP.
Cultivating citizens. Lanham : Lexington Books, c2002.
JK1759 .C85 2002

Lister, Ruth, 1949- Citizenship. 2nd ed. Basingstoke, Hampshire ; New York : Palgrave Macmillan, 2003.
HQ1236 .L57 2003

Manville, Brook, 1950- A company of citizens. Boston : Harvard Business School Press, c2003.
HD58.7 .M3714 2003

CITIZENSHIP - SOCIAL ASPECTS - UNITED STATES.
The fractious nation? Berkeley : University of California Press, c2003.
E169.12 .F69 2003

CITY AND TOWN LIFE.
Children in the city. London : Routledge/Falmer, 2003.

CITY CHILDREN.
Children in the city. London : Routledge/Falmer, 2003.

CITY CRIME. *See* **CRIME.**

City Limits Community Information Service.
Duitch, Suri. The big idea. New York : City Limits Community Information Service, c2002.

CITY PLANNING. *See also* **SPACE (ARCHITECTURE).**
Marot, Sébastien, 1961- [Art de la mémoire, la territoire et l'architecture] Sub-urbanism and the art of memory. London : Architectural Association, c2003.

CITY PLANNING - GOVERNMENT POLICY. *See* **CITY PLANNING.**

CITY PLANNING - HISTORY.
Metamorfosi della città. Milano : Garzanti / Scheiwiller, 1995 (1996 printing)
HT111 .M472 1995

CITY SURVEYING. *See* **SURVEYING.**

CIVIC IMPROVEMENT. *See* **CITY PLANNING.**

CIVIC PLANNING. *See* **CITY PLANNING.**

CIVICS. *See also* **CITIZENSHIP.**
Cultivating citizens. Lanham : Lexington Books, c2002.
JK1759 .C85 2002

CIVIL AERONAUTICS. *See* **AERONAUTICS, COMMERCIAL.**

CIVIL AVIATION. *See* **AERONAUTICS, COMMERCIAL.**

CIVIL DEFENSE. *See* **EMERGENCY MANAGEMENT.**

CIVIL GOVERNMENT. *See* **POLITICAL SCIENCE.**

CIVIL LAW. *See* **RECONCILIATION (LAW).**

CIVIL LAW (JEWISH LAW). *See* **JEWISH LAW.**

CIVIL LIBERATION MOVEMENTS. *See* **CIVIL RIGHTS MOVEMENTS.**

CIVIL LIBERTIES. *See* **CIVIL RIGHTS.**

CIVIL LIBERTY. *See* **LIBERTY.**

CIVIL PROCEDURE. *See* **TRIAL PRACTICE.**

CIVIL RIGHTS. *See also* **PRIVACY, RIGHT OF.**
Iadicola, Peter. Violence, inequality, and human freedom. 2nd ed. Lanham, Md. ; Oxford : Rowman & Littlefield Publishers, Inc., c2003.
HM886 .I18 2003

CIVIL RIGHTS - INDIA.
Preventive detention and individual liberty. New Delhi : South Asia Human Rights Documentation Centre, 2000.

KNS4654 .P74 2000

CIVIL RIGHTS (INTERNATIONAL LAW). *See* **HUMAN RIGHTS.**

CIVIL RIGHTS MOVEMENTS - UNITED STATES - HISTORY - 20TH CENTURY.
Barber, Lucy G. (Lucy Grace), 1964- Marching on Washington. Berkeley : University of California Press, c2002.
E743 .B338 2002

CIVIL RIGHTS - UNITED STATES.
Machan, Tibor R. The passion for liberty. Lanham, Md. : Rowman & Littlefield, c2003.
JC599.U5 M263 2003

Suprynowicz, Vin. The ballad of Carl Drega. Reno, NV : Mountain Media, 2002.

CIVIL RIGHTS - UNITED STATES - HISTORY.
Cannon, Carl M. The pursuit of happiness in times of war. Lanham, MD ; Oxford : Rowman & Littlefield ; [Lanham, Md.] : Distributed by National Book Network, c2004.
E183 .C25 2004

CIVIL SOCIETY.
Herbert, David, 1939- Religion and civil society. Aldershot, Hampshire, England ; Burlington, VT : Ashgate, c2003.
BL60 .H457 2003

Infantino, Lorenzo, 1948- [Ignoranza e libertà. English] Ignorance and liberty. London ; New York : Routledge, 2003.
HB95 .I4913 2003

The many faces of individualism. Leuven, Belgium ; Sterling, Va. : Peeters, 2001.
B824 .M354 2001

Turner, Stephen P., 1951- Liberal democracy 3.0. London ; Thousand Oaks, Calif. : SAGE Publications, 2003.
JC423 .T87 2003

CIVIL SOCIETY - EUROPE, WESTERN.
Brush, Lisa Diane. Gender and governance. Walnut Creek, CA ; Oxford : AltaMira Press, c2003.
JC330 .B75 2003

CIVIL SOCIETY - UNITED STATES.
Brush, Lisa Diane. Gender and governance. Walnut Creek, CA ; Oxford : AltaMira Press, c2003.
JC330 .B75 2003

CIVIL WAR. *See also* **INSURGENCY.**
Boyce, James K. Investing in peace. Oxford : Oxford University Press, 2002.

Long, William J., 1956- War and reconciliation. Cambridge, Mass. : MIT Press, c2003.
JZ5597 .L66 2003

CIVIL WAR - CASE STUDIES.
Burying the past. Expanded and updated. Washington, D.C. : Georgetown University Press, c2003.
JC578 .B49 2003

CIVIL WAR - POLITICAL ASPECTS.
Ending civil wars. Boulder, Colo. : Lynne Rienner, 2002.
JZ6368 .E53 2002

CIVIL WAR, U. S., 1861-1865. *See* **UNITED STATES - HISTORY - CIVIL WAR, 1861-1865.**

Civilisation et barbarie : réflexions sur le terrorisme contemporain / sous la direction de Jean-François Mattéi, Denis Rosenfield. 1re éd. Paris : Presses universitaires de France, c2002. 363 p. ; 20 cm. (Intervention philosophique) Includes bibliographical references (p. 351-[362]). ISBN 2-13-053192-X DDC 194
1. Terrorism - Philosophy. 2. Philosophy, Modern - 20th century. I. Mattéi, Jean-François. II. Rosenfield, Denis L. (Denis Lerrer), 1950- III. Series.

CIVILIZATION. *See also* **ANIMALS AND CIVILIZATION; CIVILIZATION, CHRISTIAN; CULTURE; EDUCATION; LEARNING AND SCHOLARSHIP; PERSONALITY AND CULTURE; PROGRESS; RELIGIONS; RENAISSANCE; SOCIAL EVOLUTION; SOCIAL SCIENCES.**
Archaeology. Oxford : Published for The British Academy by Oxford University Press, c2002.

Cioran, E. M. (Emile M.), 1911- [Précis de décomposition. Romanian] Tratat de descompunere. Bucureşti : Humanitas, 2002, c1996.

Tu, Wei-ming. [Selections. 2002] Du Weiming wen ji. Wuhan Shi : Wuhan chu ban she, 2002.

Civilization

B5233.C6 T813 2002

CIVILIZATION - 20TH CENTURY.
Li, Xiaobing. Wo zai, wo si. Di 1 ban. Beijing : Dong fang chu ban she : Xin hua shu dian jing xiao, 1996.
CB425 .L39 1996 <Orien China>

CIVILIZATION, AMERICAN. See **LATIN AMERICA - CIVILIZATION; UNITED STATES - CIVILIZATION.**

CIVILIZATION, ANCIENT.
Ancient queens. Walnut Creek, Calif. ; Oxford : AltaMira Press, c2003.
HQ1127 .A53 2003

Gosden, Chris, 1955- Prehistory. Oxford ; New York : Oxford University Press, 2003.

Mithen, Steven J. After the ice. London : Weidenfeld & Nicolson, 2003.

Rozanov, V. V. (Vasiliĭ Vasil'evich), 1856-1919. Vo dvore i︠a︡zychnikov. Moskva : Izd-vo "Respublika", 1999.
BL96 .R69 1999

Venner, Dominique. Histoire et tradition des Européens. Monaco : Rocher, c2002.
D80 .V46 2002

CIVILIZATION AND ANIMALS. See **ANIMALS AND CIVILIZATION.**

CIVILIZATION AND PERSONALITY. See **PERSONALITY AND CULTURE.**

CIVILIZATION, ARAB. See also **CIVILIZATION, ISLAMIC.**
Ṭahḥān, Aḥmad. Tajā'īd fī wajh al-zaman al-'Arabī. al-Ṭab'ah 1. Bayrūt : Dār al-Fārābī, 2001.

CIVILIZATION, CELTIC - MISCELLANEA.
Imbrogno, Philip J. Celtic mysteries in New England. 1st ed. St. Paul, Minn. : Llewellyn Publications, 2000.
BF2050 I435 2000

CIVILIZATION, CHRISTIAN - HISTORY.
Hamilton, Bernard, 1932- The Christian world of the Middle Ages. Stroud, Glos : Sutton, 2003.

CIVILIZATION, CLASSICAL. See also **ROME - CIVILIZATION.**
Keller, Otto, 1838-1920. [Thiere des klassischen Alterthums in kulturgeschichtlicher Beziehung] Tiere des klassischen Altertums in kulturgeschichtlicher Beziehung. Hildesheim : Olms, c2001, 1887.

CIVILIZATION, EASTERN. See **CIVILIZATION, ORIENTAL.**

CIVILIZATION, ETRUSCAN. See **ETRUSCANS.**

CIVILIZATION - FORECASTING.
Tolsdorf, Samuel, 1926- The theory of reality. Vancouver, B.C. : Leumas Publications, [1998]
BF1999 .T62 1998

CIVILIZATION, GRECO-ROMAN.
Walde, Christine, 1960- Antike Traumdeutung und moderne Traumforschung. Düsseldorf : Artemis & Winkler, c2001.

CIVILIZATION, HISPANIC. See **LATIN AMERICA - CIVILIZATION.**

CIVILIZATION - HISTORY. See also **CIVILIZATION, MEDIEVAL; CIVILIZATION, MODERN.**
Brazier, Chris. The no-nonsense guide to world history. Oxford : New Internationalist Publications ; London : in association with Verso, c2001.
D21 .B78 2001

Bružis, Miķelis. Pasaules uzskats jeb cilvēks dabā, sabiedrībā un mūžībā Rīga : Jumava, 2002.

Des odyssées à travers le temps. Paris : Harmattan, c2002.

Destinos das letras. Passo Fundo : Universidade de Passo Fundo, 2002.
P211 .D47 2002

Fernández-Armesto, Felipe. Civilizations. New York : Free Press, c2001.
CB151 .F47 2001

Fire in archaeology. Oxford : Archaeopress, 2002.
DA90 .B86 suppl. v.1089

Generationswechsel und historischer Wandel. München : Oldenbourg, 2003.

Jarvis, William E., 1945- Time capsules. Jefferson, N.C. : McFarland & Co., c2003.
CB151 .J37 2003

Metamorfosi della città. Milano : Garzanti / Scheiwiller, 1995 (1996 printing)

HT111 .M472 1995

Michalon, Clair. Histoire de différences, différence d'histoires. Saint-Maur : Sépia, c2002.

Murray, Charles A. Human accomplishment. New York : HarperCollins, 2003.
BF416.A1 M87 2003

Neuzeitliches Denken. Berlin ; New York : De Gruyter, 2002.

Romanov, V. N. (Vladimir Nikolaevich) Istoricheskoe razvitie kul'tury. Moskva : Savin, 2003.
CB19 .R65 2003

Schindewolf, Dorrit. Weltbild und Wirklichkeit. [S.l.] : Schindewolf, [1999]
CB88 .S35 1999

Udovik, S. L. (Sergeĭ Leonidovich) Globalizat︠s︡ii︠a︡. [Moscow] : Refl-buk ; [Kiev] : Vakler, 2002.
CB430 .U36 2002

Zwischen Rauschen und Offenbarung. Berlin : Akademie Verlag, c2002.
PN56.V55 Z89 2002

CIVILIZATION, ISLAMIC.
Eidelberg, Paul. Clash of two decadent civilizations. Shaarei Tikva, Israel : ACPR Publications, 2002.
BM537 .E53 2002

Rosen, Lawrence, 1941- The culture of Islam. Chicago : University of Chicago Press, 2002.
DT312 R64 2002

CIVILIZATION, ISLAMIC - WESTERN INFLUENCES.
Van de Weyer, Robert. Islam and the West. Alresford, Hampshire : O Books, c2001.
CB251 .V36 2001

CIVILIZATION - JEWISH INFLUENCES.
Eidelberg, Paul. Clash of two decadent civilizations. Shaarei Tikva, Israel : ACPR Publications, 2002.
BM537 .E53 2002

CIVILIZATION, LATIN. See **ROME - CIVILIZATION.**

CIVILIZATION, MEDIEVAL. See also **MIDDLE AGES; ORDEAL; RENAISSANCE.**
The 1000s. San Diego, Calif. : Greenhaven Press, c2001.
CB354.3 .A16 2001

The 1500s. San Diego, Calif : Greenhaven Press, c2001.
CB367 .A165 2001

Année mille An Mil. Aix-en-Provence : Publications de l'université de Provence, 2002.

Baker, Alan. The knight. Hoboken, N.J. : Wiley, c2003.
CR4513 .B32 2003

Brincken, Anna-Dorothee von den. Historische Chronologie des Abendlandes. Stuttgart : Kohlhammer, 2000.

Brown, Peter Robert Lamont. The rise of Western Christendom. 2nd ed. Malden, MA ; Oxford : Blackwell Publishing, 2003.
BR162.3 .B76 2003

Člověk českého středověku. Vyd. 1. Praha : Argo, 2002.

Cohen, Jeffrey Jerome. Medieval identity machines. Minneapolis : University of Minnesota Press, c2003.
CB353 .C64 2003

The construction of communities in the early Middle Ages. Leiden ; Boston : Brill, 2003.
HN11 .C66 2003

Dans l'eau, sous l'eau. [Paris] : Presses de l'Université de Paris-Sorbonne, 2002.
CB353 .D27 2002

Dawson, Christopher, 1889-1970. The making of Europe. Washington, D.C. : Catholic University of America Press, 2002, 1932.
CB353 .D3 2002

De Sion exibit lex et verbum domini de Hieruselem. Turnhout, Belgium : Brepols, c2001.

Depreux, Philippe. Charlemagne et les Carolingiens. Paris : Tallandier : Historia, 2002.
DC73 .D38 2002

Deutschland und der Westen Europas im Mittelalter. Stuttgart : Thorbecke, 2002.

Duby, Georges. Qu'est-ce que la société féodale? Paris : Flammarion, c2002.

Ducret, Alix. La vie au moyen âge. Courtaboeuf : Didro, c2002.

Effros, Bonnie, 1965- Creating community with food and drink in Merovingian Gaul. 1st ed. New York ; Houndmills, England : Palgrave Macmillan, 2002.
GT2853.F7 E34 2002

Gender and difference in the Middle Ages. Minneapolis : University of Minnesota Press, c2003.
HQ1143 .G44 2003

Gianfaldoni, Paolo. Benvenuto a Pisa. [Fornacette, Pisa] : CLD iniziative speciali, c2000.

Janse, A. Ridderschap in Holland. Hilversum : Verloren, 2001.
DJ152 .J26 2001

Jones, Malcolm, 1953- The secret middle ages. Stroud : Sutton, 2002.

Lucas, John Scott, 1970- Astrology and numerology in medieval and early modern Catalonia. Leiden ; Boston : Brill, 2003.
BF1685 .L83 2003

Marvels, monsters, and miracles. Kalamazoo, Mich. : Medieval Institute Publications, 2002.
GR825 .M218 2002

Medieval cultures in contact. New York : Fordham University Press, 2003.
CB351 .M3922 2003

Medieval Europe, 814-1350. Detroit, MI : Gale Group, c2002.
D102 .M38 2001

Morrissey, Robert John, 1947- [Empereur à la barbe fleurie. English] Charlemagne & France. English language ed. Notre Dame, Ind. : University of Notre Dame Press, c2003.
DC73 .M7513 2003

Nashim, zekenim va-taf. Yerushalayim : Merkaz Zalman Shazar le-toldot Yiśra'el, [2001]

Negotiating the gift. Göttingen : Vandenhoeck & Ruprecht, c2003.

Pleij, Herman. [Dromen van Cocagne. English] Dreaming of Cockaigne. New York : Columbia University Press, c2001.
CB353 .P5413 2001

Scholars and courtiers. Aldershot ; Burlington, Vt. : Ashgate/Variorum, c2002.
AZ183.E8 S36 2002

Studi sulle società e le culture del Medioevo per Girolamo Arnaldi. [Firenze] : All'insegna del giglio, 2002.
DG443 .S78 2002

Theory and practice in late antique archaeology. Leiden ; Boston : Brill, 2003.
CC72.4 .T46 2003

Venner, Dominique. Histoire et tradition des Européens. Monaco : Rocher, c2002.
D80 .V46 2002

Verdon, Jean. Boire au moyen âge. [Paris] : Perrin, c2002.

Verdon, Jean. [Nuit au Moyen Age. English] Night in the Middle Ages. Notre Dame, Ind. : University of Notre Dame Press, c2002.
HM1033 .V4713 2002

CIVILIZATION, MEDIEVAL - CLASSICAL INFLUENCES.
Antiquity renewed. Leuven, Netherlands ; Dudley, MA : Peeters, 2003.
CB365 .A58 2003

CIVILIZATION, MEDIEVAL - HISTORY. See **CIVILIZATION, MEDIEVAL.**

CIVILIZATION, MEDIEVAL, IN ART.
Jones, Malcolm, 1953- The secret middle ages. Stroud : Sutton, 2002.

CIVILIZATION, MEDIEVAL, IN LITERATURE.
Besamusca, Bart. The book of Lancelot. Cambridge : D.S. Brewer, 2003.
PT5568 .B47 2003

Heng, Geraldine. Empire of magic. New York : Columbia University Press, c2003.
PR321 .H46 2003

CIVILIZATION, MEDIEVAL - STUDY AND TEACHING.
Cohen, Jeffrey Jerome. Medieval identity machines. Minneapolis : University of Minnesota Press, c2003.
CB353 .C64 2003

CIVILIZATION, MODERN. *See also* **RENAISSANCE.**
Altomare, Vincenzo. Alla ricerca dell'uomo tra Bibbia e modernità. 1. ed. Cosenza : Progetto 2000, c2000.

Antinomies of modernity. Durham : Duke University Press, 2003.
CB358 .A59 2003

High culture. Albany : State University of New York Press, c2003.
HV4998 .H544 2003

Venner, Dominique. Histoire et tradition des Européens. Monaco : Rocher, c2002.
D80 .V46 2002

CIVILIZATION, MODERN - 1950-.
Globalization and civilizations. London ; New York : Routledge, 2002.
CB430 .G58 2002

Jameson, Fredric. A singular modernity. London ; New York : Verso, 2002.
CB358 .J348 2002

Shayegan, Darius. La lumière vient de l'Occident. [La Tour-d'Aigues] : Éditions de l'Aube, c2001.
CB 430

CIVILIZATION, MODERN - 20TH CENTURY.
Eidelberg, Paul. Clash of two decadent civilizations. Shaarei Tikva, Israel : ACPR Publications, 2002.
BM537 .E53 2002

García Canclini, Néstor. Culturas híbridas. Nueva edición actualizada. Buenos Aires : Paidós, 2001.

Jay, Martin, 1944- Refractions of violence. New York : London : Routledge, 2003.
HM1116 .J39 2003

CIVILIZATION, MODERN - 21ST CENTURY.
Del Moro, Franco. Il dubbio necessario. 1. ed. Murazzano (CN) : Ellin Selae, 2002.

Jannoud, Claude. La crise de l'esprit. Lausanne, Suisse : Age d'homme, c2001.

Melman, Charles, 1931- L'homme sans gravité. Paris : Denoël, c2002.

Sardar, Ziauddin. The A-Z of postmodern life. London : Vision, c2002.

CIVILIZATION, MODERN - PHILOSOPHY.
Bewes, Timothy. Reification, or, The anxiety of late capitalism. London ; New York : Verso, 2002.
HM449 .B49 2002

Habitar la tierra. Buenos Aires : Grupo Editor Altamira, 2002.
CB358 .H32 2002

Jameson, Fredric. A singular modernity. London ; New York : Verso, 2002.
CB358 .J348 2002

CIVILIZATION, MODERN - PSYCHOLOGICAL ASPECTS.
Habitar la tierra. Buenos Aires : Grupo Editor Altamira, 2002.
CB358 .H32 2002

CIVILIZATION, MODERN - RELIGIOUS ASPECTS.
Habitar la tierra. Buenos Aires : Grupo Editor Altamira, 2002.
CB358 .H32 2002

CIVILIZATION, MUSLIM. *See* **CIVILIZATION, ISLAMIC.**

CIVILIZATION, OCCIDENTAL. *See* **CIVILIZATION, WESTERN.**

CIVILIZATION, ORIENTAL - HISTORY.
Diálogo de civilizaciones Oriente-Occidente. [Madrid] : Biblioteca Nueva ; [Cáceres, España] : Universidad de Extremadura, c2002.

CIVILIZATION, ORIENTAL - WESTERN INFLUENCES. *See* **EAST AND WEST.**

CIVILIZATION, PAGAN. *See* **PAGANISM.**

CIVILIZATION - PHILOSOPHY. *See also* **PHILOSOPHICAL ANTHROPOLOGY.**
Bodei, Remo, 1938- Destini personali. Milano : Feltrinelli, 2002.

Crowther, Paul. Philosophy after postmodernism. London ; New York : Routledge, 2003.
B831.2 .C76 2003

Dostovernost' i dokazatel'nost' v issledovaniiakh po teorii i istorii kul'tury. Moskva : RGGU, 2002.
HM621 .D68 2002

Globalization and civilizations. London ; New York : Routledge, 2002.
CB430 .G58 2002

Marías, Julián, 1914- Entre dos siglos. Madrid : Alianza Editorial, c2002.
PQ6663.A72183 E68 2002

Michalon, Clair. Histoire de différences, différence d'histoires. Saint-Maur : Sépia, c2002.

Porus, V. N. Ratsional'nost', nauka, kul'tura. Moskva : Universitet Rossiĭskoĭ akademii obrazovaniia, Kafedra filosofii, 2002.
Q175.32.K45 P678 2002

Romanov, V. N. (Vladimir Nikolaevich) Istoricheskoe razvitie kul'tury. Moskva : Savin, 2003.
CB19 .R65 2003

Sampaio, Luiz Sergio Coelho de, 1933- Filosofia da cultura. Rio de Janeiro : Editora Agora da Ilha, 2002.

Zerubavel, Eviatar. Time maps. Chicago : University of Chicago Press, 2003.
BD638 .Z48 2003

CIVILIZATION - PHILOSOPHY - HISTORY.
Ionov, I. N. (Igor' Nikolaevich) Teoriia tsivilizatsiĭ. Sankt-Peterburg : Aleteiia, 2002.
CB19 .I656 2002

Civilization under attack : September 11, 2001 & beyond : an astrological perspective / edited by Stephanie Jean Clement. 1st ed. St. Paul, Minn. : Llewellyn Publications, 2001. viii, 256 p. : ill., maps ; 20 cm. Includes bibliographical references. CONTENTS: Attack on America / Jonathan Keyes -- The psychology of terrorism / Bernie Ashman -- The George W. Bush chart / Jonathan Keyes -- The United States chart / Robert Hand -- Putting events on the world map / Robert Hand -- "Twin" events / Stephanie Clement -- Structure clashes with beliefs / Robert Hand -- All eyes on Osama bin Laden / Jonathan Keyes -- The targets : hit or missed / Kris Brandt Riske -- Life has changed dramatically / David Crook -- Forecasting with eclipses / David Crook -- Did the perpetrators use astrology / Kris Brandt Riske -- Religion, land, and oil / Jonathan Keyes -- Saturn and slow market periods / Georgia Anna Stathis -- Strategy, spending, and the planet Mars / Georgia Anna Stathis -- A new economy -- The new investment climate / Georgia Anna Stathis -- Meditations on the future / Jonathan Keyes -- Leadership in a time of terror / Kris Brandt Riske -- Where do we go from here / Robert Hand -- The great conjunctions / Robert Hand -- Conclusion / Stephanie Clement. ISBN 0-7387-0247-1 DDC 133.5/8973931
1. Astrology. 2. United States - History - Miscellanea. 3. September 11 Terrorist Attacks, 2001 - Miscellanea. I. Clement, Stephanie Jean.
BF1729.U5 C57 2001

CIVILIZATION, WESTERN.
Bessis, Sophie, 1947- [Occident et les autres. English] Western supremacy. London ; New York : Zed Books, 2003.
CB245 .B4613 2003

Corm, Georges. Orient-Occident, la fracture imaginaire. Paris : Découverte, 2002.

Eidelberg, Paul. Clash of two decadent civilizations. Shaarei Tikva, Israel : ACPR Publications, 2002.
BM537 .E53 2002

La Branche, Stéphane. Mondialisation et terrorisme identitaire, ou, Comment l'Occident tente de transformer le monde. Paris : Harmattan, c2003.
JC330 .L2 2003

Western historical thinking. New York : Berghahn Books, 2002.
D16.9 .W454 2002

CIVILIZATION, WESTERN - 20TH CENTURY.
Limonov, Eduard. Distsiplinarnyĭ sanatoriĭ. Sankt-Peterburg : Amfora, 2002.
CB428 .L556 2002

CIVILIZATION, WESTERN - AFRICAN INFLUENCES.
Remembering Africa. Portsmouth, NH : Heinemann, c2002.
DT14 .R46 2002

CIVILIZATION, WESTERN - CLASSICAL INFLUENCES.
Traverso, Paola. "Psiche è una parola greca--". Genova, Italy : Compagnia dei librai, 2000.
BF109.F74 T73 2000

CIVILIZATION, WESTERN - ORIENTAL INFLUENCES. *See* **EAST AND WEST.**

Civilizations.
Fernández-Armesto, Felipe. New York : Free Press, c2001.
CB151 .F47 2001

The civilized organization : Norbert Elias and the future of organization studies / edited by Ad van Iterson ... [et al.]. Amsterdam ; Philadelphia : John Benjamins, c2002. xxviii, 251 p. : ill. ; 25 cm. (Advances in organization studies, 1566-1075 ; v. 10) Includes bibliographical references and index. ISBN 1-58811-277-2 (US) (hb. : alk. paper) ISBN 1-58811-278-0 (US) (pbk. : alk. paper) DDC 302.3/5
1. Elias, Norbert. 2. Organizational behavior. 3. Organizational sociology. I. Iterson, Ad van, 1952- II. Series: Advances in organization studies ; 10.
HD58.7 .C593 2002

CIVILZATION, MODERN.
Boff, Leonardo. Espiritualidade. 2a ed. Rio de Janeiro : Sextante, c2001.

Civitas europaea
Metamorfosi della città. Milano : Garzanti / Scheiwiller, 1995 (1996 printing)
HT111 .M472 1995

CIXI, EMPRESS DOWAGER OF CHINA, 1835-1908.
Excursions in Chinese culture. Hong Kong : Chinese University Press, c2002.

Cladis, Mark Sydney. Public vision, private lives : Rousseau, religion, and 21st-century democracy / Mark S. Cladis. Oxford ; New York : Oxford University Press, 2003. xvii, 298 p. ; 25 cm. Includes bibliographical references (p. 249-283) and index. ISBN 0-19-512554-1 (alk. paper) DDC 321.8
1. Rousseau, Jean-Jacques, - 1712-1778 - Contributions in political science. 2. Rousseau, Jean-Jacques, - 1712-1778 - Religion. 3. Democracy. 4. Privacy. 5. Public interest. I. Title.
JC179.R9 C53 2003

Claiborn, James. The habit change workbook : how to break bad habits and form good ones / James Claiborn, Cherry Pedrick. Oakland, CA : New Harbinger Publications : Distributed in the U.S.A. by Publishers Group West, c2001. vii, 242 p. : ill. ; 28 cm. Includes bibliographical references (p. [236]-242). ISBN 1-57224-263-9 DDC 153.8/5
1. Habit breaking - Problems, exercises, etc. 2. Change (Psychology) - Problems, exercises, etc. 3. Habit. I. Pedrick, Cherry. II. Title.
BF337.B74 C57 2001

Claiming the stones/naming the bones : cultural property and the negotiation of national and ethnic identity / edited by Elazar Barkan and Ronald Bush. Los Angeles : Getty Research Institute, c2002. ix, 371 p. : ill. ; 26 cm. (Issues & debates) Includes bibliographical references and index. CONTENTS: Amending historical injustices / Elazar Barkan -- Appropriating the stones / Timothy Webb -- Latin America, Native America, and the politics of culture / Clemency Coggins -- Objects and identities / Claire L. Lyons -- Kennewick Man - a kin? Too distant / Douglas W. Owsley and Richard L. Jantz -- Cultural significance and the Kennewick skeleton / Patty Gerstenblith -- Selling grandma / Darrell Addison Posey -- Stones resung / Hélène La Rue -- More than skin deep / Ngahuia Te Awekotuku -- New Negro displayed / Marlon B. Ross -- Birth of whose nation? / Johnathan Arac -- Yeats, group claims, and Irishry / R.F. Foster -- Cultural property and identity politics in Britain / Robert J.C. Young -- Property, schmoperty! / Ronald Bush. ISBN 0-89236-673-7 (alk. paper) DDC 341.7/67
1. Cultural property. 2. Cultural property - Repatriation. 3. Intellectual property. 4. Intellectual property - Moral and ethical aspects. 5. Group identity. 6. Ethnicity. I. Barkan, Elazar. II. Bush, Ronald. III. Series.
CC135 .C48 2002

Clair, André. Sens de l'existence : recherche en philosophie contemporaine / André Clair. Paris : Armand Colin, c2002. 251 p. ; 23 cm. (L'inspiration philosophique) Includes bibliographical references and index. ISBN 2-200-26202-7 DDC 194
1. Ontology. 2. Philosophy, Modern - 20th century. I. Title. II. Series.

Clair, Jean, 1940- Du surréalisme considéré dans ses rapports au totalitarisme et aux tables tournantes : contribution à une histoire de l'insensé / Jean Clair. [Paris] : Mille et une nuits, 2003. 215 p. : ill. ; 20 cm. Includes bibliographical references and index. ISBN 2-8420-5732-5 DDC 809
1. Surrealism (Literature) 2. Surrealism. I. Title.

Clair, Robin Patric.
Expressions of ethnography. Albany, NY : State University of New York Press, c2003.
GN33 .E97 2003

Clairday, Robynn.
Tell me this isn't happening. New York : Scholastic, c1999.
BF723.E44 T45 1999

CLAIRVOYANCE.
Rauscher, William V. The mind readers. Woodbury, N.J. : Mystic Light Press, c2002.
BF1171 .R28 2002

CLAIRVOYANTS - BULGARIA.
Georgiev, Li͡uben, 1933- Sreshti s Vangi͡a. Sofii͡a : Knigo-TSvi͡at, 1996.
BF1283.V33 G46 1996

CLAIRVOYANTS - LATVIA - BIOGRAPHY.
Rīgas gaišregis Eižens Finks. Jauns papildināts izdevums. [Rīga] : Jumava, c2002.
BF1283.F55 R66 2002

Clam, Jean. Was heisst, sich an Differenz statt an Identität orientieren? : zur De-ontologisierung in Philosophie und Sozialwissenschaft / Jean Clam. Konstanz : UVK Verlagsgesellschaft, c2002. 118 p. ; 21 cm. "Wissen und Studium"--P. 4 of cover. Includes bibliographical references (p. 113-118). ISBN 3-89669-796-X (pbk.)
1. Heidegger, Martin, - 1889-1976. 2. Luhmann, Niklas. 3. Difference (Philosophy) 4. Ontology. I. Title.

Clan of the Goddess.
Brondwin, C. C., 1945- Franklin Lakes, NJ : New Page Books, c2002.
BF1623.G63 B76 2002

Claren, James L.
Chinese literature. Hauppauge, N.Y. : Nova Science Publishers, c2002.

Clark, Andy, 1957- Natural-born cyborgs : minds, technologies, and the future of human intelligence / Andy Clark. Oxford ; New York : Oxford University Press, c2003. viii, 229 p. : ill. ; 25 cm. Includes bibliographical references and index. ISBN 0-19-514866-5 (alk. paper) DDC 303.48/34
1. Technology - Social aspects. 2. Neurosciences - Social aspects. 3. Artificial intelligence - Social aspects. 4. Human-computer interaction. 5. Cyborgs. I. Title.
T14.5 .C58 2003

Clark-Carter, David.
Doing quantitative psychological research.
Clark-Carter, David. Quantitative psychological research. 2nd ed. New York, NY : Taylor & Francis, 2004.
BF76.5 .C53 2004

Quantitative psychological research : a student's handbook / David Clark-Carter. 2nd ed. New York, NY : Taylor & Francis, 2004. p. cm. Rev. ed. of: Doing quantitative psychological research. c1997. Includes bibliographical references and indexes. ISBN 1-84169-520-3 ISBN 1-84169-225-5 (pbk.) DDC 150/.72
1. Psychology - Research - Methodology - Textbooks. I. Clark-Carter, David. Doing quantitative psychological research. II. Title.
BF76.5 .C53 2004

Clark, Eve V. First language acquisition / Eve V. Clark. Cambridge, U.K. ; New York : Cambridge University Press, 2003. xvi, 515 p. : ill. ; 23 cm. Includes bibliographical references (p. 441-490) and indexes. Table of contents URL: http://www.loc.gov/catdir/toc/cam031/2002071574.html Publisher description URL: http://www.loc.gov/catdir/description/cam0210/2002071574.html ISBN 0-521-62003-1 ISBN 0-521-62997-7 (pb.) DDC 401/.93
1. Language acquisition. I. Title.
P118 .C547 2003

Clark, Harold A. The age of intimacy : a celebration of life in the new millennium / Harold A. Clark. Laredo, TX : EBookcase.com, c2000. 121 p. ; 21 cm. Includes bibliographical references.
1. Globalization - Social aspects. 2. Internationalism. 3. Intimacy (Psychology) 4. Social sciences and psychoanalysis. 5. World citizenship. 6. Third millennium - Forecasts. I. Title.

Clark, J. C. D. Our shadowed present : modernism, postmodernism and history / Jonathan Clark. London : Atlantic, 2003. xiv, 336 p. ; 24 cm. Includes bibliographical references ans index. ISBN 1-84354-122-X DDC 901
1. History - Philosophy. 2. Historiography. 3. Postmodernism. 4. Ideology. 5. Nationalism - Philosophy. I. Title.

Clark, Jerome. Extraordinary encounters : an encyclopedia of extraterrestrials and otherworldly beings / Jerome Clark. Santa Barbara, Calif. : ABC-CLIO, c2000. xvii, 290 p. : ill., map ; 27 cm. Includes bibliographical references and index. ISBN 1-57607-249-5 (hardcover : alk. paper) ISBN 1-57607-379-3 (e-book) DDC 001.942/03
1. Human-alien encounters - Encyclopedias. I. Title. II. Title: Encyclopedia of extraterrestrials and otherworldly beings

BF2050 .C57 2000

Clark, John, 1946- Stress : a management guide / John Clark. London ; Rollinsford, NH : Spiro Press, 2002. 187 p. ; 24 cm. (Spiro business guides. Business skills) Includes bibliographical references (p. 187). ISBN 1-904298-29-X
1. Job stress. 2. Stress management. I. Title. II. Series.

CLARK, LYGIA, 1920-.
Wanderley, Lula. O dragão pousou no espaço. Rio de Janerio : Rocco, 2002.

Clark, Rosemary, 1948- The sacred magic of ancient Egypt : the spiritual practice restored / Rosemary Clark. 1st ed. St. Paul, Minn. : Llewellyn Publications, 2003. p. cm. Includes bibliographical references and index. ISBN 1-56718-130-9 DDC 133.4/3/09932
1. Magic, Egyptian. I. Title.
BF1591 .C52 2003

Clark, Stuart.
Cryer, Frederick H. Biblical and pagan societies. Philadelphia : University of Pennsylvania Press, 2001.
BF1567 .C79 2001

Jolly, Karen Louise. The Middle Ages. Philadelphia : University of Pennsylvania Press, 2002, 2001. 12 300 xiv, 280 p. ; 24 cm.
BF1593 .J65 2002

Clark, William, 1953-.
The sciences in enlightened Europe. Chicago : University of Chicago Press, 1999.
Q127.E8 S356 1999

Clarke, Desmond M. Descartes's theory of mind / Desmond M. Clarke. Oxford ; New York : Oxford University Press, 2003. viii, 267 p. : ill. ; 24 cm. Includes bibliographical references and index. ISBN 0-19-926123-7 DDC 194
1. Descartes, René, - 1596-1650. 2. Philosophy of mind. 3. Mind and body. 4. Dualism. I. Title.

Clarke, Randolph K. Libertarian accounts of free will / Randolph Clarke. Oxford ; New York : Oxford University Press, c2003. xv, 244 p. ; 25 cm. Includes bibliographical references (p. 223) and index. ISBN 0-19-515987-X DDC 123/.5
1. Free will and determinism. I. Title.
BJ1461 .C53 2003

Clarke, Robert B. The four gold keys : dreams, transformation of the soul, and the western mystery tradition / Robert B. Clarke. Charlottesville, VA : Hampton Roads Pub., c2002. xviii, 397 p. ; 23 cm. Includes bibliographical references (p. 381-383) and index. ISBN 1-57174-313-8 (alk. paper) DDC 154.6/3
1. Dreams. 2. Dream interpretation. 3. Spiritual life. 4. Jungian psychology. 5. Jung, C. G. - (Carl Gustav), - 1875-1961. I. Title.
BF175.5.D74 C58 2002

Clarke, Simon, 1962- Social theory, psychoanalysis, and racism / Simon Clarke. New York : Palgrave Macmillan, 2003. p. cm. Includes bibliographical references and index. ISBN 0-333-96117-X ISBN 0-333-96118-8 (pbk.) DDC 305.8/001/9
1. Psychoanalysis and racism. 2. Race - Psychological aspects. 3. Race awareness. 4. Racism - Psychological aspects. I. Title.
BF175.4.R34 C58 2003

Clarkson, John, 1961-.
Inclusive design. London ; New York : Springer, c2003.
TA174 .I464 2003

Clash of two decadent civilizations.
Eidelberg, Paul. Shaarei Tikva, Israel : ACPR Publications, 2002.
BM537 .E53 2002

CLASS CONFLICT. *See* **SOCIAL CONFLICT.**

CLASS DISTINCTION. *See* **SOCIAL CLASSES.**

CLASS STRUGGLE. *See* **SOCIAL CONFLICT.**

CLASSES, SOCIAL. *See* **SOCIAL CLASSES.**

Classical and Byzantine monographs
(v. 51) Muñoz Llamosas, Virginia. La intervención divina en el hombre a través de la literatura griega de época arcaica y clásica. Amsterdam : Hakkert, 2002.
PA3015.R5 M87 2002

CLASSICAL EDUCATION. *See* **HUMANISM; HUMANITIES.**

CLASSICAL LANGUAGES. *See* **LATIN LANGUAGE.**

CLASSICAL LITERATURE. *See* **CLASSICAL POETRY; GREEK LITERATURE; LATIN LITERATURE.**

CLASSICAL LITERATURE - HISTORY AND CRITICISM.
Gelehrte in der Antike. Köln : Böhlau, c2002.

Classical living.
Bernstein, Frances. 1st ed. San Francisco : HarperSanFrancisco, 2000.
BL808 .B47 2000

CLASSICAL MUSIC. *See* **MUSIC.**

CLASSICAL PHILOLOGY. *See* **GREEK LITERATURE; HUMANISM; LATIN LANGUAGE; LATIN LITERATURE.**

CLASSICAL POETRY - HISTORY AND CRITICISM.
Protopapas-Marneli, Maria. La rhétorique des stoïciens. Paris : Harmattan, c2002.

Classical writings on the Ifa/Yoruba traditional religion
Karade, Akinkugbe. Path to priesthood. Brooklyn, N.Y. : Kânda Mukûtu Books, c2001.
BL2523.I33 K37 2001

Classics in applied mathematics
(22) John, Peter William Meredith. Statistical design and analysis of experiments. Philadelphia : Society for Industrial and Applied Mathematics, c1998.
QA279 .J65 1998

Classics in archetypal psychology
(7) McConeghey, Howard. Art and soul. 1st ed. Putnam, CT : Spring Publications, Inc. ; [New York] : Distributed by Continuum, c2003.

Classics in gender studies
Gilman, Charlotte Perkins, 1860-1935. Concerning children. A reprint of the 1900 ed. / with an introduction by Michael S. Kimmel. Walnut Creek, CA : Rowman & Littlefield, c2003.
HQ769 .G5 2003

CLASSICS, LITERARY. *See* **CANON (LITERATURE).**

CLASSIFICATION.
Khurmetbek, Khaliki͡in. Ūl bichigdmēlūūd. Ulaanbaatar : "Monsudar" Khėvlėli͡in Gazar, 2001.
QA465 .K48 2001

CLASSIFICATION (PSYCHOLOGY). *See* **CATEGORIZATION (PSYCHOLOGY).**

Les classiques de la pensée politique
(19) Callières, Monsieur de (François), 1645-1717. De la manière de négocier avec les souverains. Genève : Droz, c2002.

Classiques de la philosophie
(4672.) Descartes, René, 1596-1650. [Regulae ad directionem ingenii. French] Règles pour la direction de l'esprit. Paris : Librairie générale française, c2002.

CLASSISM - UNITED STATES.
Horowitz, David A. America's political class under fire. New York ; London : Routledge, 2003.
HN90.S6 H67 2003

Claude, Jean.
Texte et théâtralité. Nancy : Presses universitaires de Nancy, 2000.

[Clavicula Salomonis. English.] The Goetia : the lesser key of Solomon the King : Lemegeton--Clavicula Salomonis Regis, book one / translated by Samuel Liddell MacGregor Mathers ; edited, annotated and introduced and enlarged by Aleister Crowley ; illustrated second edition with new annotations by Aleister Crowley ; edited by Hymenaeus Beta. York Beach, Me. : Samuel Weiser, 1995. xxvi, 134 p. : ill. ; 26 cm. ISBN 0-87728-847-X (alk. paper) DDC 133.4/3
1. Magic - Early works to 1800. 2. Magic, Jewish - Early works to 1800. I. Mathers, S. L. MacGregor (Samuel Liddell MacGregor), 1854-1918. II. Crowley, Aleister, 1875-1947. III. Beta, Hymenaeus. IV. Title. V. Title: Lesser key of Solomon the King
BF1611 .C5413 1995

[Clavicula Salomonis. English.] Lemegeton : the complete lesser key of Solomon / edited by Mitch Henson ; illustrated [by] Jeff Wellman. Jacksonville, FL : Metatron Books, 1999. 95 p. ; 23 cm. CONTENTS: Goetia -- Theurgia -- Pauline art -- Almandel. ISBN 0-9672797-0-4
1. Magic, Jewish. I. Henson, Mitch. II. Wellman, Jeff. III. Title. IV. Title: Lesser key of Solomon

Clayton, Charles Walker, 1951- Connections! : change your paradigm and you change your life! / by Charles Walker Clayton. Radcliffe, IA : Ide House Publishers, 2004. p. cm. Includes bibliographical references (p.   ) and

index. ISBN 0-86663-237-9 DDC 153.6
1. Interpersonal communication. 2. Success. I. Title.
BF637.C45 C54 2004

Clayton, Emily. Space clearing : harmonize your home for mind, body & soul / Emily Clayton. San Diego, Calif. : Thunder Bay Press, c2003. 400 p. : ill. (chiefly col.) ; 11 x 15 cm. ISBN 1-57145-957-X DDC 133.3/337
1. Feng shui. I. Title.
BF1779.F4 C58 2003

Clayton, Lawrence, Ph. D. Careers in behavioral science / by Lawrence Clayton. [2nd ed.]. Oklahoma City, Okla. : Transcontinental Pub., 2001. 201 p. ; 22 cm. Rev. ed. of: Careers in psychology. 1992. Includes bibliographical references (p. [199]-200). ISBN 0-9709523-5-X
1. Psychology - Vocational guidance - Juvenile literature. I. Clayton, Lawrence, Ph. D. Careers in psychology. II. Title.
BF76 .C64 2001

Clayton, Lawrence, Ph. D.
Careers in psychology.
Clayton, Lawrence, Ph. D. Careers in behavioral science. [2nd ed.]. Oklahoma City, Okla. : Transcontinental Pub., 2001.
BF76 .C64 2001

Clayton, Susan.
Identity and the natural environment. Cambridge, Mass. : MIT Press, 2004.
BF353 .I34 2004

Cleeremans, Axel.
The unity of consciousness. Oxford ; New York : Oxford University Press, 2003.
BF311 .U55 2003

Clegg, Brian. The professional's guide to mining the Internet : information gathering & research on the Net / Brian Clegg. 2nd ed. London : Kogan Page ; Sterling, VA : Stylus Pub., 2001. ix, 146 p. : ill. ; 22 cm. Includes index. ISBN 0-7494-3655-7 (pbk.) DDC 025.04
1. Internet searching. I. Title.
ZA4230 .C56 2001

Clegg, Justin. The medieval Church : in manuscripts / Justin Clegg. London : British Library, 2003. 64 p. : col. ill. ; 25 cm. Includes bibliographical references and index. ISBN 0-7123-4784-4 DDC 274.03
1. Church history in literature. 2. Church history - Middle Ages, 600-1500. 3. Church history - Middle Ages, 600-1500 - Sources. 4. Manuscripts, Medieval - Europe. 5. Illumination of books and manuscripts - Europe. I. British Library. II. Title.

Cleghorn, Patricia. The secrets of self-esteem : make the changes you want in your life / Patricia Cleghorn. London : Vega, c2002. xii, 171 p. ; 22 cm. Includes index. Publisher description URL: http://www.loc.gov/catdir/description/ste031/2003447867.html ISBN 1-84333-142-X (pbk.) DDC 158.1
1. Self-esteem. 2. Self-actualization (Psychology) 3. Self-help techniques. I. Title.
BF697.5.S46 C55 2002

CLEMENCY. *See* **AMNESTY; FORGIVENESS.**

Clément, Catherine, 1939- Le divan et le grigri / Catherine Clément, Tobie Nathan. Paris : Jacob, c2002. 348 p. ; 22 cm. Dialogue. Includes bibliographical references. ISBN 2-7381-1059-2 DDC 150
1. Psychoanalysis and religion. 2. Religion. 3. Magic. 4. Cultural psychiatry. I. Nathan, Tobie. II. Title.

Clement, Stephanie Jean.
Civilization under attack. 1st ed. St. Paul, Minn. : Llewellyn Publications, 2001.
BF1729.U5 C57 2001

Mapping your birthchart : understanding your needs & potential / Stephanie Jean Clement. 1st ed. St. Paul, Minn. : Llewellyn Publications, 2003. x, 228 p. : ill. ; 24 cm. + 1 CD-ROM (4 3/4 in.). Includes bibliographical references (p. 223-224) and index. ISBN 0-7387-0202-1 DDC 133.5
1. Astrology. I. Title.
BF1708.1 .C535 2003

Clements, Rhonda L.
The child's right to play. Westport, Conn. : Praeger, 2003.
BF717 .C44 2003

CLERGY. *See* **PRIESTS; RABBIS.**

CLERGY - EDUCATION - HISTORY.
Keefe, Susan A. Water and the Word. Notre Dame, Ind. : University of Notre Dame Press, c2002.
BR200 .K44 2002

CLERGY, INDIGENOUS. *See* **CLERGY.**

CLERGY - MAJOR ORDERS. *See* **CLERGY.**

CLERGY, NATIVE. *See* **CLERGY.**

CLIENT-CENTERED PSYCHOTHERAPY.
Cohen, David, 1946- Carl Rogers. London : Constable, 1997.
BF109.R63 C64 1997

Cliff, Norman, 1930- Ordinal measurement in the behavioral sciences / Norman Cliff, John A. Keats. Mahwah, N.J. : Lawrence Erlbaum Associates, 2003. x, 230 p. : ill. ; 24 cm. Includes bibliographical references (p. 212-217) and indexes. ISBN 0-8058-2093-0 (alk. paper) DDC 150/.28/7
1. Psychology - Mathematical models. 2. Social sciences - Statistical methods. 3. Analysis of variance. 4. Psychological tests - Statistical methods. I. Keats, J. A. (John Augustus) II. Title.
BF39 .C525 2003

CLIMACTERIC - PSYCHOLOGICAL ASPECTS.
Marraccini, Eliane Michelini. Encontro de mulheres. São Paulo : Casa do Psicólogo, c2001.

CLIMATE CHANGE. *See* **CLIMATIC CHANGES.**

CLIMATE CHANGES. *See* **CLIMATIC CHANGES.**

CLIMATE VARIATIONS. *See* **CLIMATIC CHANGES.**

CLIMATIC CHANGE. *See* **CLIMATIC CHANGES.**

CLIMATIC CHANGES - MORAL AND ETHICAL ASPECTS.
Singer, Peter, 1946- One world. New Haven, Conn. : London : Yale University Press, 2002.

CLIMATIC FLUCTUATIONS. *See* **CLIMATIC CHANGES.**

CLIMATIC VARIATIONS. *See* **CLIMATIC CHANGES.**

CLIMATOLOGY. *See* **CLIMATIC CHANGES; SEASONS.**

CLIMBING MOUNTAINS. *See* **MOUNTAINEERING.**

Clínica del texto.
Milmaniene, José E. [1. ed.]. Buenos Aires : Editorial Biblos, c2002.

Clinical applications of evidence-based family interventions.
Corcoran, Jacqueline. Cambridge, U.K. ; New York : Oxford University Press, 2003.
HV697 .C67 2003

Clinical counselling in voluntary and community settings / edited by Quentin Stimpson. New York, NY : Brunner-Routledge, 2003. p. cm. Includes bibliographical references and index. Table of contents URL: http://www.loc.gov/catdir/toc/ecip042/2003007347.html ISBN 1-58391-155-3 (alk. paper) ISBN 1-58391-156-1 (pbk. : alk. paper) DDC 361/.06
1. Counseling - Great Britain. I. Stimpson, Quenton.
BF637.C6 C456 2003

CLINICAL HEALTH PSYCHOLOGY.
Women's health and psychiatry. Philadelphia, PA : Lippincott Williams & Wilkins, c2002.
RA564.85 .W6652 2002

Zautra, Alex. Emotions, stress, and health. Oxford ; New York : Oxford University Press, 2003.
R726.7 .Z38 2003

CLINICAL MEDICINE - LABORATORY MANUALS. *See* **DIAGNOSIS, LABORATORY.**

CLINICAL PATHOLOGY. *See* **DIAGNOSIS, LABORATORY.**

CLINICAL PSYCHOLOGY. *See* **PSYCHOLOGICAL TESTS.**

CLINICAL RECORDS. *See* **MEDICAL RECORDS.**

CLINICAL SCIENCES. *See* **MEDICINE.**

CLINICAL SOCIOLOGY. *See* **COUNSELING; PSYCHOTHERAPY.**

Cloke, Ken, 1941- The art of waking people up : cultivating awareness and authenticity at work / Kenneth Cloke, Joan Goldsmith. 1st ed. San Francisco : Jossey-Bass, c2003. xxv, 303 p. : ill. ; 24 cm. (Warren Bennis signature series) Includes index. ISBN 0-7879-6380-1 (alk. paper) DDC 658.3/124
1. Mentoring in business. 2. Incentives in industry. 3. Organizational behavior. I. Goldsmith, Joan. II. Title. III. Series.
HF5385 .C54 2003

Cloninger, Susan C., 1945- Theories of personality : understanding persons / Susan C. Cloninger. 4th ed. Upper Saddle River, N.J. : Pearson/Prentice Hall, c2004. p. cm. Includes bibliographical references (p.   ) and indexes. ISBN 0-13-183204-2 DDC 155.2
1. Personality. 2. Personality - Philosophy. I. Title.
BF698 .C543 2004

CLOSE ENCOUNTERS OF THE FIRST KIND. *See* **UNIDENTIFIED FLYING OBJECTS - SIGHTINGS AND ENCOUNTERS.**

CLOSE ENCOUNTERS OF THE SECOND KIND. *See* **UNIDENTIFIED FLYING OBJECTS - SIGHTINGS AND ENCOUNTERS.**

CLOSE ENCOUNTERS OF THE THIRD KIND. *See* **HUMAN-ALIEN ENCOUNTERS.**

Closing the gap.
Stikker, Allerd, 1928- Amsterdam : Amsterdam University Press : Salomé, c2002.

CLOTHES. *See* **CLOTHING AND DRESS.**

CLOTHIERS. *See* **CLOTHING TRADE.**

CLOTHING. *See* **CLOTHING AND DRESS.**

CLOTHING AND DRESS. *See also* **COSTUME; FASHION.**
Constantine, Susannah. What not to wear. London : Weidenfeld & Nicolson, 2002.

CLOTHING AND DRESS - EROTIC ASPECTS.
Martin, Jean-Clet. Parures d'éros. Paris : Kimé, 2003.

CLOTHING AND DRESS - MARKETING.
Fiore, Ann Marie. Understanding aesthetics for the merchandising and design professional. New York : Fairchild, c1997.

CLOTHING AND DRESS, PRIMITIVE. *See* **COSTUME.**

CLOTHING AND DRESS - PSYCHOLOGICAL ASPECTS.
Fiore, Ann Marie. Understanding aesthetics for the merchandising and design professional. New York : Fairchild, c1997.

Simard-Laflamme, Carole. Habit Habitat Habitus. Trois-Rivières, Québec, Canada : Editions d'art Le Sabord, [2002]
TT507 .S653 2002

CLOTHING AND DRESS - RELIGIOUS ASPECTS - JUDAISM.
Sofer, Mikha'el Uri. Sefer 'Olamot shel tohar. Mahad. 2. Bene Berak : M.U. Sofer, 761 [2000 or 2001]
BM726 .S633 2000

CLOTHING INDUSTRY. *See* **CLOTHING TRADE.**

CLOTHING TRADE.
Fiore, Ann Marie. Understanding aesthetics for the merchandising and design professional. New York : Fairchild, c1997.

CLOTHING TRADE - PSYCHOLOGICAL ASPECTS.
Lee, Michelle. Fashion victim. 1st ed. New York : Broadway Books, 2003.
GT524 .L44 2003

CLOTHING TRADE - SENEGAL - DAKAR.
Mustafa, Huda Nura. Practicing beauty. 1997.

Clough, Joy. The characters within : befriending your deepest emotions / Joy Clough. Chicago, IL : ACTA Publications, c1997. 159 p. ; 22 cm. ISBN 0-87946-165-9 DDC 152.4
1. Emotions. I. Title.
BF531 .C52 1997

Člověk českého středověku / Martin Nodl, František Šmahel (edd.). Vyd. 1. Praha : Argo, 2002. 500 p. : ill. ; 21 cm. (Edice Každodenní život ; sv. 1) Includes bibliographical references and index. ISBN 80-7203-448-0
1. Bohemia (Czech Republic) - Social life and customs. 2. Social classes - Czech Republic - History - To 1500. 3. Bohemia (Czech Republic) - History - To 1526. 4. Civilization, Medieval. I. Nodl, Martin. II. Šmahel, František. III. Series.

Clow, Barbara Hand, 1943- Catastrophobia : the truth behind earth changes in the coming age of light / Barbara Hand Clow ; illustrations by Christopher Cudahy Clow. Rochester, Vt. : Bear & Company, c2001. xix, 299 p. : ill., maps ; 23 cm. Includes bibliographical references (p. 260-290) and index. ISBN 1-87918-162-2 (pbk. : alk. paper) DDC 909
1. Catastrophes (Geology) 2. History, Ancient. 3. Mythology. 4. Archaeoastronomy. 5. Pleiades - Miscellanea. 6. Spiritual life. 7. Cosmology. I. Clow, Christopher Cudahy. II. Title. III. Title: Truth behind earth changes in the coming age of light

BF1999 .C587 2001

Clow, Christopher Cudahy.
Clow, Barbara Hand, 1943- Catastrophobia. Rochester, Vt. : Bear & Company, c2001.
BF1999 .C587 2001

Clutterbuck, David.
The situational mentor. Burlington, VT : Gower, 2004.
BF637.M48 S56 2004

CNRS communication
Naturaliser la phénoménologie. Paris : CNRS, c2002.

CNRS Histoire des sciences
Ottavi, Dominique. De Darwin à Piaget. Paris : CNRS, c2001.

Coakley, John.
The territorial management of ethnic conflict. 2nd rev. and expanded ed. London ; Portland, OR : F. Cass, 2003.
GN496 .T47 2003

Coats, Erik J., 1968-.
Nonverbal behavior in clinical settings. Oxford ; New York : Oxford University Press, 2003.
RC489.N65 N66 2003

Cochrane, David.
AstroLocality magic : advanced astromap features of Kepler / by David Cochrane. 1st ed. Gainesville, FL : Cosmic Patterns Software, c2002. vi, 66 p. : ill. ; 22 cm. ISBN 0-9716952-1-0
1. Astrology. 2. Moving, Household - Miscellanea. I. Title.
BF1729.M68 C63 2002

Astrology for the 21st century / David Cochrane. 1st ed. Gainesville, FL : Cosmic Patterns Software, c2002. vii, 232 p. : ill. ; 23 cm. Includes bibliographical references (p. 231-232). ISBN 0-9716952-0-2 DDC 133.5
1. Astrology. I. Title. II. Title: Astrology for the twenty-first century
BF1708.1 .C63 2002

COCKAIGNE.
Pleij, Herman. [Dromen van Cocagne. English] Dreaming of Cockaigne. New York : Columbia University Press, c2001.
CB353 .P5413 2001

COCKAIGNE IN LITERATURE.
Pleij, Herman. [Dromen van Cocagne. English] Dreaming of Cockaigne. New York : Columbia University Press, c2001.
CB353 .P5413 2001

Cockburn, Alexander.
Monkeywrenching the new world order [sound recording]. Oakland, Calif : AK Press ; San Francisco, CA : Alternative Tentacles Records, 2001.

Cockcroft, Robert, 1939- Rhetorical affect in early modern writing : Renaissance passions reconsidered / Robert Cockcroft. New York : Palgrave Macmillan, 2003. ix, 209 p. ; 23 cm. Includes bibliographical references (p. 197-203) and index. ISBN 0-333-80252-7 DDC 820.9/353
1. English literature - Early modern, 1500-1700 - History and criticism. 2. Emotions in literature. 3. Authors and readers - Great Britain - History - 16th century. 4. Authors and readers - Great Britain - History - 17th century. 5. English language - Early modern, 1500-1700 - Rhetoric. 6. Renaissance - England. 7. Affect (Psychology) I. Title.
PR428.E56 C63 2003

Cocking, Rodney R.
Children in the digital age. Westport, Conn. : Praeger, 2002.
HQ784.M3 C455 2002

Codas, Enrique, 1932- En los caminos de la historia / Enrique Codas. [Asunción, Paraguay] : El Lector, c2002. 369 p. ; 21 cm. Includes bibliographical references. ISBN 9992560150
1. Guairá (Paraguay) - History. 2. Education - Philosophy. 3. History - Philosophy. I. Title.
F2695.G83 C63 2002

The code.
Mawi Asgedom. New York : Little, Brown, 2003.
BF724.3.S9 M34 2003

The code of man.
Newell, Waller Randy. 1st ed. New York : ReganBooks, c2003.
HQ1090 .N49 2003

Coderre, Cécile.
Le deuxième sexe. Montréal : Éditions du Remue-ménage, 2001.

Codices Arabici antiqui
(Bd. 8) Shayzarī, ʻAbd al-Raḥmān ibn Naṣr, 12th cent. Rawdat al-qulūb wa-nuzhat al-muḥibb wa-al-maḥbūb. Wiesbaden : Harrassowitz, 2003.

Cody, Michael J.
Canary, Daniel J. Interpersonal communication. 3rd ed. Boston : Bedford/St. Martin's, c2003.
BF637.C45 C34 2003

COEDUCATION. *See* **EDUCATION; WOMEN - EDUCATION.**

COEXISTENCE. *See* **INTERNATIONAL RELATIONS; PEACE; WORLD POLITICS - 1945-.**

COGAT (PSYCHOLOGY). *See* **COGNITIVE ABILITIES TEST.**

COGNITION. *See also* **METACOGNITION; SCHEMAS (PSYCHOLOGY); SELECTIVITY (PSYCHOLOGY).**
Reed, Stephen K. 6th ed. Australia ; Belmont, CA : Wadsworth/Thomson c2004.
BF311 .R357 2004

Willingham, Daniel T. 2nd ed. Upper Saddle River, NJ : Pearson/Prentice Hall, c2004.
BF201 .W56 2004

COGNITION.
Alefirenko, M. F. Poėticheskaia ėnergiia slova. Moskva : Academia, 2002.
P35 .A544 2002

Bartsch, Renate, 1939- Consciousness emerging. Amsterdam ; Philadelphia, Pa. : John Benjamins Pub., 2002.
BF311 .B325 2002

Bereiter, Carl. Education and mind in the knowledge age. Mahwah, N.J. : L. Erlbaum Associates, 2002.
LB1057 .B47 2002

Beskova, I. A. Ėvoliutsiia i soznanie. Moskva : "Indrik", 2002.
B808.9 .B476 2002x

Bloom, Paul, 1963- Descartes' baby. New York : Basic Books, 2004.
BF311 .B555 2004

Cognitive modeling. Cambridge, Mass. : MIT Press, c2002.
BF311 .C55175 2002

Ducret, Jean-Jacques, 1946- Jean Piaget, 1868-1979. Genève, Switzerland : Service de la recherche en éducation, c2000.
BF311 .D813 2000

Harré, Rom. Cognitive science. London ; Thousand Oaks, Calif. : SAGE Publications, 2002.
BF311 .H347 2002

Jeannerod, Marc. La nature de l'esprit. Paris : Odile Jacob, c2002.
BF311 .J435 2002

Katz, Ruth, 1927- Tuning the mind. New Brunswick, N.J. : Transaction Publishers, c2003.
ML3838 .K28 2003

Language in mind. Cambridge, Mass. : MIT Press, c2003.
P37 .L357 2003

Phonetics, phonology, and cognition. Oxford : Oxford University Press, 2002.
P221 .P475 2002

Reed, Stephen K. Cognition. 6th ed. Australia ; Belmont, CA : Wadsworth/Thomson c2004.
BF311 .R357 2004

Rowlands, Mark. The body in mind. Cambridge, U.K. ; New York : Cambridge University Press, 1999.
BD418.3 .R78 1999

Schmauks, Dagmar. Orientierung im Raum. Tübingen : Stauffenburg, c2002.
QP443 .S363 2002

Solso, Robert L., 1933- The psychology of art and the evolution of the conscious brain. Cambridge, Mass. : MIT Press, 2003.
BF311 .S652 2003

Sterelny, Kim. Thought in a hostile world. Malden, MA : Blackwell, 2003.
BF698.95 .S74 2003

Sub"ekt, poznanie, deiatel'nost'. Moskva : Kanon+, 2002.
BD166 .S84 2002

Trends in cognitive psychology. New York : Nova Science Publishers, c2002.
BF311 .T723 2002

Wagman, Morton. Logical processes in humans and computers. Westport, Conn. : Praeger, 2003.

BF311 .W26566 2003

Weed, Laura E. The structure of thinking. Exeter : Imprint Academic, c2003.

COGNITION - AGE FACTORS.
Kray, Jutta. Adult age differences in task switching. Lengerich : Pabst Science Publishers, 2000.
BF724.55.C63 K73 2000

COGNITION - AGE FACTORS - LONGITUDINAL STUDIES.
Schaie, K. Warner (Klaus Warner), 1928- Developmental influences on adult intelligence. [Update]. New York : Oxford University Press, 2004.
BF724.55.C63 S32 2004

COGNITION AND CULTURE.
Alefirenko, M. F. Poėticheskaia ėnergiia slova. Moskva : Academia, 2002.
P35 .A544 2002

Baber, Christopher, 1964- Cognition and tool use. London ; New York : Taylor & Francis, 2003.
BF311 .B228 2003

Culture and competence. Washington, DC : American Psychological Association, 2004.
BF311 .C845 2004

From girls in their elements to women in science. New York : P. Lang, 2003.
BF378.S65 F76 2003

Göller, Thomas. Kulturverstehen. Würzburg : Königshausen & Neumann, c2000.
BF311 .G586 2000

Lewis, Richard D. The cultural imperative. Yarmouth, Me. : Intercultural Press, c2003.
GN357 .L49 2003

Monteil, Jean-Marc. Social context and cognitive performance. Hove, East Sussex, UK : Psychology Press, c1999.
BF311 .M59 1999

Raĭkov, V. L. (Vladimir Leonidovich), 1934- Soznanie i poznanie III tysiacheletiia. Moskva : [s.n.], 1999.
BF311 .R26 1999

Rogoff, Barbara. The cultural nature of human development. Oxford ; New York : Oxford University Press, 2003.
HM686 .R64 2003

Ross, Norbert. Culture and cognition. Thousand Oaks, CA : Sage Publications, c2004.
BF311 .R6542 2004

Sterelny, Kim. Thought in a hostile world. Malden, MA : Blackwell, 2003.
BF698.95 .S74 2003

Cognition and culture book series
(v. 1) Pyysiäinen, Ilkka. How religion works. Leiden ; Boston : Brill, 2001.
BL53 .P98 2001

Cognition and technology.
International journal of cognition and technology. Amsterdam ; Philadelphia : John Benjamins, c2002-
BF309 .I58

Cognition and tool use.
Baber, Christopher, 1964- London ; New York : Taylor & Francis, 2003.
BF311 .B228 2003

COGNITION DISORDERS. *See* **NEGLECT (NEUROLOGY).**

COGNITION - HISTORY - TO 1500.
Beare, John I. (John Isaac), d. 1918 Greek theories of elementary cognition. Mansfield Centre, Conn. : Martino Pub., 2004.
BF91 .B3 2004

COGNITION IN ADOLESCENCE.
Razvitie natsional'noĭ, ėtnolingvisticheskoĭ i religioznoĭ identichnosti u deteĭ i podrostkov = Moskva : In-t psikhologii RAN, 2001.
BF723.C5 R39 2001

COGNITION IN ANIMALS.
Cimatti, Felice. La mente silenziosa. 1. ed. Roma : Editori riuniti, 2002.

COGNITION IN CHILDREN. *See also* **HUMAN INFORMATION PROCESSING IN CHILDREN; PERCEPTION IN CHILDREN.**
Flavell, John H. Development of children's knowledge about the mind. Worcester, Mass. : Clark University Press, 2003.

BF723.C5 F623 2003
Goldin-Meadow, Susan. Hearing gesture. Cambridge, Mass. : Belknap Press of Harvard University Press, 2003.
P117 .G65 2003
Losquadro-Liddle, Tara. Why motor skills matter. Chicago : Contemporary Books, c2004.
BF723.M6 L67 2004
Oates, John, 1946- Cognitive and language development in children. Milton Keynes, U.K. : Open University ; Malden, MA : Blackwell Pub., 2004.
BF723.C5 O38 2004
Razvitie natsional'noĭ, ėtnolingvisticheskoĭ i religioznoĭ identichnosti u deteĭ i podrostkov = Moskva : In-t psikhologii RAN, 2001.
BF723.C5 R39 2001
Revealing the inner worlds of young children. New York : Oxford University Press, 2003.
BF723.S74 A37 2003
Tomasello, Michael. Constructing a language. Cambridge, Mass. : Harvard University Press, 2003.
P118 .T558 2003

COGNITION IN INFANTS.
Early category and concept development. Oxford ; New York : Oxford University Press, 2003.
BF720.C63 E27 2003

Hobson, R. Peter. The cradle of thought. New York : Oxford University Press, 2004.
BF720.C63 H63 2004

Hobson, R. Peter. The cradle of thought. London : Macmillan, 2002.
BF720.C63 H63 2002

Mandler, Jean Matter. The foundations of mind. Oxford ; New York : Oxford University Press, 2004.
BF720.C63 M36 2004

COGNITION IN OLD AGE.
Bragdon, Allen D. Use it or lose it!. 2nd ed., updated and expanded. New York : Walker & Co., 2004.
BF724.85.C64 B73 2004

COGNITION, SOCIAL. See **SOCIAL PERCEPTION.**

COGNITION - SOCIAL ASPECTS.
The mind as a scientific object. New York : Oxford University Press, c2004.
BF311 .M552 2004

Monteil, Jean-Marc. Social context and cognitive performance. Hove, East Sussex, UK : Psychology Press, c1999.
BF311 .M59 1999

COGNITION - TESTING. See **COGNITIVE ABILITIES TEST.**

COGNITION - TEXTBOOKS.
Oakley, Lisa. Cognitive development. New York : Psychology Press, 2004.
BF311 .O12 2004

COGNITIVE ABILITIES TEST.
Lohman, David F. Interpretive guide for teachers and counselors. Itasca, IL : Riverside Pub., c2001.
BF432.5.C64 L65 2001

Cognitive Abilities Test, form 6, all levels.
Lohman, David F. Chicago (8420 Bryn Mawr, Chicago 60631) : Riverside Pub., c2001.
BF432.5.C64 L64 2001

Cognitive Abilities Test interpretive guide.
Lohman, David F. Interpretive guide for teachers and counselors. Itasca, IL : Riverside Pub., c2001.
BF432.5.C64 L65 2001

COGNITIVE ABILITIES TEST - SCORING - STATISTICS.
Lohman, David F. Cognitive Abilities Test, form 6, all levels. Chicago (8420 Bryn Mawr, Chicago 60631) : Riverside Pub., c2001.
BF432.5.C64 L64 2001

Cognitive and language development in children.
Oates, John, 1946- Milton Keynes, U.K. : Open University ; Malden, MA : Blackwell Pub., 2004.
BF723.C5 O38 2004

The cognitive and neural bases of spatial neglect / edited by Hans-Otto Karnath, A. David Milner, and Giuseppe Vallar. Oxford ; New York : Oxford University Press, 2002. xiv, 401 p. : ill. ; 25 cm. Includes bibliographical references and index. ISBN 0-19-850833-6 (hbk. : alk. paper) DDC 616.8
1. Neglect (Neurology) 2. Space perception. 3. Attention. I. Karnath, H.-O. (Hans-Otto), 1961- II. Milner, A. D. (A. David) III. Vallar, Giuseppe.
RC394.N44 C64 2002

Cognitive development.
Oakley, Lisa. New York : Psychology Press, 2004.
BF311 .O12 2004

COGNITIVE GRAMMAR.
Grounding. Berlin ; Hawthorne, N.Y. : M. de Gruyter, 2002.
P165 .G76 2002

Schröder, Jürgen. Die Sprache des Denkens. Würzburg : Königshausen & Neumann, c2001.

Cognitive linguistics research
(21) Grounding. Berlin ; Hawthorne, N.Y. : M. de Gruyter, 2002.
P165 .G76 2002

Cognitive modeling / edited by Thad A. Polk and Colleen M. Seifert. Cambridge, Mass. : MIT Press, c2002. xxi, 1270 p. : ill. ; 24 cm. "A Bradford book." Includes bibliographical references and index. Table of contents URL: http://www.loc.gov/catdir/toc/fy033/2001018325.html ISBN 0-262-16198-2 (alk. paper) ISBN 0-262-66116-0 (pbk. : alk. paper) DDC 153
1. Cognition. 2. Cognitive science. I. Polk, Thad A. II. Seifert, Colleen M.
BF311 .C55175 2002

COGNITIVE NEUROPSYCHOLOGY. See **COGNITIVE NEUROSCIENCE.**

COGNITIVE NEUROSCIENCE.
Understanding the brain. Paris : Organisation for Economic Co-operation and Development, 2002.
QP360.5 .U54 2002

Virtual lesions. Oxford ; New York : Oxford University Press, c2002.
RC350.B72 V57 2002

COGNITIVE NEUROSCIENCE - TEXTBOOKS.
Medin, Douglas L. Cognitive psychology. 4th ed. Hoboken, NJ : John Wiley & Sons, 2004.
BF201 .M43 2004

Cognitive psychology.
Medin, Douglas L. 4th ed. Hoboken, NJ : John Wiley & Sons, 2004.
BF201 .M43 2004

Robinson-Riegler, Gregory. Boston : Allyn and Bacon, c2004.
BF201 .R63 2004

COGNITIVE PSYCHOLOGY.
Cognitive psychology. New York : Psychology Press, 2003.
BF311 .C642 2003

Harré, Rom. Cognitive science. London ; Thousand Oaks, Calif. : SAGE Publications, 2002.
BF311 .H347 2002

Kommunikation, Kunst und Kultur. Bern ; New York : Peter Lang, c2002.

Perspectives on cognitive psychology. New York : Nova Science, c2002.
BF201 .P48 2002

Qu'est-ce-donc qu'apprendre? Lausanne : Delachaux et Niestlé, 1999.
BF318 .Q84 1999

Raĭkov, V. L. (Vladimir Leonidovich), 1934- Soznanie i poznanie III tysi͡acheletii͡a. Moskva : [s.n.], 1999.
BF311 .R26 1999

Reed, Stephen K. Cognition. 6th ed. Australia ; Belmont, CA : Wadsworth/Thomson c2004.
BF311 .R357 2004

Robinson-Riegler, Gregory. Cognitive psychology. Boston : Allyn and Bacon, c2004.
BF201 .R63 2004

Topics in cognitive psychology. New York : Nova Science Publishers, 2003.
BF201 .T67 2003

Virtual'nai͡a real'nost' v psikhologii i iskusstvennom intellekte. Moskva : Rossiĭskai͡a Assotsiat͡sii͡a iskusstvennogo intellekta, 1998.
BF204.5 .V57 1998

Willingham, Daniel T. Cognition. 2nd ed. Upper Saddle River, NJ : Pearson/Prentice Hall, c2004.
BF201 .W56 2004

Cognitive psychology : key readings / edited by David A. Balota and Elizabeth J. Marsh. New York : Psychology Press, 2003. p. cm. (Key readings in cognition) Includes bibliographical references and index. Table of contents URL: http://www.loc.gov/catdir/toc/ecip043/2003009115.html ISBN 1-84169-064-3 (hardcover) ISBN 1-84169-065-1 (pbk.) DDC 153
1. Cognitive psychology. I. Balota, D. A. II. Marsh, Elizabeth J. III. Series.
BF201 .C642 2003

COGNITIVE PSYCHOLOGY - TEXTBOOKS.
Andrade, Jackie, 1964- Instant notes in cognitive psychology. New York, NY : Garland Science/BIOS Scientific Publishers, 2004.
BF201 .A53 2004

Medin, Douglas L. Cognitive psychology. 4th ed. Hoboken, NJ : John Wiley & Sons, 2004.
BF201 .M43 2004

Readings in cognitive psychology. Boston, Mass. : Pearson Allyn & Bacon, 2003.
BF201 .R425 2003

COGNITIVE SCIENCE. See also **ARTIFICIAL INTELLIGENCE; COGNITIVE NEUROSCIENCE; COGNITIVE PSYCHOLOGY; PHILOSOPHY OF MIND.**
Harré, Rom. London ; Thousand Oaks, Calif. : SAGE Publications, 2002.
BF311 .H347 2002

COGNITIVE SCIENCE.
Cognitive modeling. Cambridge, Mass. : MIT Press, c2002.
BF311 .C55175 2002

Dawson, Michael Robert William, 1959- Minds and machines. Malden, MA : Blackwell Pub., c2003.
BF311 .D345 2003

Estivals, Robert. Théorie générale de la schématisation. Paris : Harmattan, c2002-

Harré, Rom. Cognitive science. London ; Thousand Oaks, Calif. : SAGE Publications, 2002.
BF311 .H347 2002

Hogan, Patrick Colm. Cognitive science, literature, and the arts. New York ; London : Routledge, 2003.
PN56.P93 H64 2003

Une introduction aux sciences de la culture. 1. ed. Paris : Presses universitaires de France ; [Paris] : Institut Ferdinand-de-Saussure, 2002.

Marconi, Diego, 1947- Filosofia e scienza cognitiva. 1. ed. Roma-Bari : Editori Laterza, 2001.
BF311 .M36 2001

Marcus, Gary F. (Gary Fred) The birth of the mind. New York : Basic Books, 2004.
BF701 .M32 2004

The mind as a scientific object. New York : Oxford University Press, c2004.
BF311 .M552 2004

Naturaliser la phénoménologie. Paris : CNRS, c2002.

Orsucci, Franco. Changing mind. River Edge, NJ : World Scientific, c2002.
BF161 .O77 2002

Peterson, Gregory R., 1966- Minding God. Minneapolis, MN : Fortress Press, c2003.
BL53 .P42 2003

Pylyshyn, Zenon W., 1937- Seeing and visualizing. Cambridge, Mass. : MIT Press, 2003.
BF241 .P95 2003

Shultz, Thomas R. Computational developmental psychology. Cambridge, Mass. : MIT Press, c2003.
BF713 .S35 2003

Trends in cognitive psychology. New York : Nova Science Publishers, c2002.
BF311 .T723 2002

Wagman, Morton. Logical processes in humans and computers. Westport, Conn. : Praeger, 2003.
BF311 .W26566 2003

COGNITIVE SCIENCE - DICTIONARIES.
[Vocabulaire de sciences cognitives. English.] Dictionary of cognitive science. New York : Psychology Press, 2003.
BF311 .V56713 2003

Cognitive science, literature, and the arts.
Hogan, Patrick Colm. New York ; London : Routledge, 2003.
PN56.P93 H64 2003

COGNITIVE SCIENCE - PERIODICALS.
International journal of cognition and technology. Amsterdam ; Philadelphia : John Benjamins, c2002-
BF309 .I58

COGNITIVE SCIENCE - PHILOSOPHY.
Churchland, Patricia Smith. Brain-wise. Cambridge, Mass. : MIT Press, c2002.
RC343 .C486 2002

Harré, Rom. Cognitive science. London ; Thousand Oaks, Calif. : SAGE Publications, 2002.
BF311 .H347 2002

Cognitive Technology Society.
International journal of cognition and technology. Amsterdam ; Philadelphia : John Benjamins, c2002-
BF309 .I58

COGNITIVE THERAPY.
Cooper, Myra, 1957- The psychology of bulimia nervosa. Oxford ; New York : Oxford University Press, 2003.
RC552.B84 C66 2003

Trends in cognitive psychology. New York : Nova Science Publishers, c2002.
BF311 .T723 2002

Cohen, Aaron, 1952- Multiple commitments in the workplace : an integrative approach / Aaron Cohen. Mahwah, New Jersey : Lawrence Erlbaum Associates, 2003. xviii, 354 p. : ill. ; 24 cm. (Series in applied psychology) Includes bibliographical references (p. 315-338) and indexes. ISBN 0-8058-4234-9 (cloth) ISBN 0-8058-4368-X (pbk.) DDC 158.7
1. Organizational commitment. 2. Organizational behavior. 3. Employee loyalty. 4. Commitment (Psychology) I. Title. II. Series.
HD58.7 .C6213 2003

Cohen, Allan R. The portable MBA in management / Allan R. Cohen. 2nd ed. New York : J. Wiley, c2002. vi, 402 p. : ill. ; 26 cm. (The portable MBA series) Includes bibliographical references and index. ISBN 0-471-20455-2 (alk. paper) DDC 658.4
1. Industrial management. 2. Personnel management. 3. Teams in the workplace. 4. Management - Employee participation. I. Title. II. Title: MBA in management III. Series.
HD31 .C586 2002

Cohen, David, 1922-.
Mélanges David Cohen. Paris : Maisonneuve et Larose, 2003.

Cohen, David, 1946- Carl Rogers : a critical biography / David Cohen. London : Constable, 1997. 253 p. ; 24 cm. Includes bibliographical references (p. 237-246) and index. ISBN 0-09-477010-7 DDC 150.19/8
1. Rogers, Carl R. : (Carl Ransom), - 1902- 2. Psychologists - United States - Biography. 3. Humanistic psychology. 4. Client-centered psychotherapy. I. Title.
BF109.R63 C64 1997

Cohen, Herb. Negotiate this! : by caring, but not T-H-A-T much / Herb Cohen. New York : Warner Business Books, c2003. xviii, 382 p. ; 24 cm. Includes bibliographical references (p. 370-374) and index. ISBN 0-446-52973-7 DDC 302.3
1. Negotiation. I. Title.
BF637.N4 C545 2003

Cohen, Hermann, 1842-1918.
[Works. 1977. Supplementa]
Werke. Supplementa / Hermann Cohen. Hildesheim : G. Olms, 2000- v. : facsims. ; 20 cm. Vol. 1 issued 2003. Includes bibliographical references and indexes. PARTIAL CONTENTS: Bd. 1. Reflexionen und Notizen / herausgegeben von Hartwig Wiedebach -- Bd. 2. Die Hermann-Cohen-Bibliothek / Hartwig Wiedebach. ISBN 3-487-11695-2 (v. 1) ISBN 3-487-11089-X (v. 2)
1. Philosophy. 2. Religion - Philosophy. 3. Philosophy, Jewish. I. Wiedebach, Hartwig. II. Title.

Cohen, Jeffrey Jerome. Medieval identity machines / Jeffrey J. Cohen. Minneapolis : University of Minnesota Press, c2003. xxix, 336 p. ; 23 cm. (Medieval cultures ; v. 35) Includes bibliographical references (p. 285-322) and index. ISBN 0-8166-4002-5 (alk. paper) ISBN 0-8166-4003-3 (pbk. : alk. paper) DDC 940.1
1. Civilization, Medieval. 2. Social history - Medieval, 500-1500. 3. Philosophy, Medieval. 4. Civilization, Medieval - Study and teaching. 5. Middle Ages - Study and teaching. 6. Medievalism. 7. Body, Human - Social aspects - History. 8. Body, Human - Symbolic aspects - History. 9. Identity (Philosophical concept) 10. Identity (Psychology) I. Title. II. Series.
CB353 .C64 2003

Thinking the limits of the body. Albany : State University of New York Press, c2003.
HM636 .T47 2003

Cohen, Maxi. The art of the pendulum / Maxi Cohen. [Kansas City, Mo.] : Andrews McMeel, [c2002] 1 booklet (vii, 55 p. ; 90 mm.), 1 pendulum, 12 cards ; in container : col. ill. ; 20 cm. Booklet includes bibliographical references (p. 54-55). ISBN 0-7407-3319-2 (kit) DDC 133.3
1. Fortune-telling by pendulum. I. Title.
BF1779.P45 C64 2002

Cohen, Norman H. A step-by-step guide to starting an effective mentoring program / Norman H. Cohen. Amherst, Mass. : HRC Press, c2000. xiii, 74 p. ill. ; 23 cm. DDC 658.3/12404
1. Mentoring in business. I. Title.
HF5385 .C64 2000

Cohen, Norman H. (Norman Harris), 1941- The mentee's guide to mentoring / Norman H. Cohen. Amherst, Mass. : HRD Press, c1999. vi, 73 p. ; 23 cm. ISBN 0-87425-494-9
1. Mentoring in business. 2. Interpersonal relations. 3. Interpersonal communication. I. Title.

Cohen, R. S. (Robert Sonné).
Nietzsche and the sciences. Dordrecht ; Boston : Kluwer Academic Publishers, c1999-
B3318.K7 N54 1999

Cohen, Rhoda, 1933-.
Friends and friendship. Madison, Conn. : Psychosocial Press, 2003.
BF575.F66 F695 2003

Cohen, Robin, 1944-.
Migration, diasporas, and transnationalism. Cheltenham, UK ; Northampton, MA : Edward Elgar, 1999.
JV6032 .M54 1999

Cohen, Tova.
Gender, place, and memory in the modern Jewish experience. London ; Portland, Or. : Vallentine Mitchell, 2003.
DS143 .G36 2003

Cohl, H. Aaron. The book of mosts / H. Aaron Cohl. 1st ed. New York : St. Martin's Press, 1997. ix, 340 p. ; 22 cm. ISBN 0-312-15482-8 DDC 031.02
1. Curiosities and wonders. I. Title.
AG243 .C586 1997

Cohn, Arthur, 1910- Musical puzzlemania : musical quizzical III / by Arthur Cohn. Mew York, NY : Carl Fischer, c1998. 176 p. : ill. ; 23 cm. "110 pazzles, including all the standart designs, such as crosswords and acrostics, word searchers and anagrams, etc., plus many newly created formations..."--p.3. ISBN 0-8258-2242-4 (pbk.) ISBN 0-8258-3368-X (pbk.)
1. Puzzles. 2. Musical games. I. Title. II. Title: Musical quizzical III

Coin divination.
Buckland, Raymond. 1st ed. St. Paul, Minn. : Llewellyn Publications, 2000.
BF1779.C56 B83 2000

COINAGE. *See* **MONEY.**

COINCIDENCE.
Chopra, Deepak. The spontaneous fulfillment of desire. 1st ed. New York : Harmony Books, c2003.
BF1175 .C48 2003

Chopra, Deepak. The spontaneous fulfillment of desire. New York : Random House Large Print, 2003.
BF1175 .C48 2003b

Gott, Robert. One in a million. Littleton, Mass. : Sundance, c2001.
BF1175 .G68 2001

COINCIDENCE IN PSYCHICAL RESEARCH. *See* **COINCIDENCE - PSYCHIC ASPECTS.**

COINCIDENCE - PSYCHIC ASPECTS - JUVENILE LITERATURE.
Gott, Robert. One in a million. Littleton, Mass. : Sundance, c2001.
BF1175 .G68 2001

COINS - MISCELLANEA.
Buckland, Raymond. Coin divination. 1st ed. St. Paul, Minn. : Llewellyn Publications, 2000.
BF1779.C56 B83 2000

Coker, Cheryl A. Motor learning and control for practitioners / Cheryl A. Coker. Boston : McGraw-Hill, c2004. xxi, 247, I-13 p. : ill. ; 24 cm. Includes bibliographical references and indexes. ISBN 0-7674-1645-7 (alk. paper) DDC 152.3/34
1. Motor learning. I. Title.
BF295 .C645 2004

COLA ACUMINATA. *See* **KOLA NUTS.**
COLA-NUT. *See* **KOLA NUTS.**
COLA NUTS. *See* **KOLA NUTS.**

Colantuono, Susan L. Make room for joy : finding magical moments in your everyday life / by Susan L. Colantuono. Charlestown, RI : Interlude Productions, c2000. vii, 133 p. ; 26 cm. ISBN 0-9673129-0-6
1. Joy. 2. Happiness. 3. Life. I. Title.
BF575.H27 C64 2000

Colbert, James G., 1938-.
Dei, Héctor Daniel. The human being in history. Lanham, Md. : Lexington Books, c2003.
BD450 .D395 2003

Cold day in July.
Cameron, Stella. Waterville, Me. : Wheeler Pub. ; Bath, England : Chivers Press, 2002.
PS3553.A4345 C65 2002

Cole, Harriette. Choosing truth : living an authentic life / Harriette Cole. New York : Simon & Schuster, c2003. xviii, 236 p. ; 25 cm. Includes bibliographical references (p. 228) and index. Publisher description URL: http://www.loc.gov/catdir/desc ription/simon034/2002036679.html ISBN 0-684-87311-7 DDC 158.1
1. Self-actualization (Psychology) 2. Black author. I. Title.
BF637.S4 C652 2003

Coleção Comunicação
(22) Sodré, Muniz. Sociedade mídia e violência. Porto Alegre : Editora Sulina : EDIPUCRS, c2002.

Coleção Educação física e esportes
Silva, Ana Márcia. Corpo, ciência e mercado. Campinas : Editora da UFSC : Editora Autores Associados, 2001.
GT495 .S55 2001

Coleção Espaço Brasileiro de Estudos Psicanalíticos
Femenilidades. Rio de Janeiro : Espaço Brasileiro de Estudos Psicanalíticos : Contra Capa, c2002.

(2) Transgressões. Rio de Janeiro, RJ : Espaço Brasileiro de Estudos Psicanalíticos : Contra Capa, 2002.

Coleção Idéias sobre linguagem.
Marcuschi, Luiz Antônio. Investigando a relação oral/escrito e as teorias do letramento. Campinas, SP : Mercado de Letras, 2001.

Coleção Letramento, educação e sociedade
Moita Lopes, Luiz Paulo da. Identidades fragmentadas. Campinas, SP, Brasil : Mercado de Letras, [2002]
HM753 .M65 2002

Coleção Mundo do trabalho (Boitempo Editorial)
Hirata, Helena Sumiko. [División sexual del trabajo. Portuguese] Nova divisão sexual do trabalho? 1a ed. São Paulo : Boitempo, 2002.
HD6060.6 .H5717 2002

Coleção Pioneiros da psicologia brasileira
(9) Figueiredo, Luís Cláudio M. (Luís Cláudio Mendonça), 1945- Antonio Gomes Penna. Brasília, DF : Conselho Federal de Psicologia ; Rio de Janeiro, RJ : Imago, 2002.

Coleção Psicologia social
Psicologia social nos estudos culturais. Petrópolis : Editora Voces, c2003.
HM1033 .P75 2003

Coleção Selo Editorial Letras da Bahia
(66) Pinheiro, José Moura. Mitos atuais. Salvador : Secretaria da Cultura e Turismo : Fundação Cultural do Estado da Bahia : Empresa Gráfoca da Bahia, 2001.

Colección Agenda de género del centenario
Allard Olmos, Briseida, 1951- Mujer y poder. [Panamá] : Instituto de la Mujer - Universidad de Panamá, 2002.
HQ1154 .A62 2002

Colección Arquíthesis
(no. 9) Español Llorens, Joaquim. El orden frágil de la arquitectura. Barcelona : Fundación Caja de Arquitectos, c2001.

Colección Biblionova
Yusty, Miguel. Negociar en medio de la guerra. [Cali, Colombia] : Editorial Universidad Santiago de Cali, 2002.

Colección Ciencias sociales (Universidad Pública de Navarra)
(11.) Sobre las identidades. Pamplona : Universidad Pública de Navarra, [2001]

Colección de la Biblioteca Nacional de la República Dominicana.
La palabra como cuerpo del delito. Santo Domingo, República Dominicana : Biblioteca Nacional "Dr. Pedro Henríquez Ureña", 2001.

Colección de pensamiento medieval y renacentista
(28) Gambra, José Miguel. La analogía en general. 1. ed. Pamplona : EUNSA, 2002.

Colección Educación, crítica & debate
Alonso, Graciela. Hacia una pedagogía de las experiencias de las mujeres. 1. ed. Buenos Aires : Miño y Dávila, 2002.

Colección Estudios (Monte Avila Editores). Serie Ideas.
Búfalo, Enzo del. Individuo, mercado y utopía. 1. ed. Caracas : Monte Ávila Editores Lationoamericana : Universidad Central de Venezuela, Centro de Investigaciones Post-Doctorales FACES, 1998.
BD222 .B86 1998

Colección filosófica (Universidad de Navarra. Facultad de Filosofía y Letras)
(172.) González Ayesta, Cruz. Hombre y verdad. 1. ed. Pamplona : Universidad de Navarra, Ediciones, 2002.

(173.) Williams, Jaime Andrés. El argumento de la apuesta de Blaise Pascal. 1. ed. Pamplona : Ediciones Universidad de Navarra, 2002.

(31.) González, Angel Luis. Ser y participación. 3. ed. revisada y ampliada. Pamplona : Ediciones Universidad de Navarra, c2001.
BX4700.T6 G66 2001

Colección Hermes (Ediciones del Laberinto)
(no. 19.) Goñi Zubieta, Carlos. Futbolsofía. Madrid : Ediciones del Laberinto, [2002]

Colección Inclusiones. Serie Categorías
Piscitelli, Alejandro. Meta-cultura. Buenos Aires : La Crujía, 2002.
P96.T42 P575

Colección Itaca
(4) Alemán, Jorge. Lacan en la razón posmoderna. Málaga : Miguel Gómez Ediciones, c2000.
BF109.L28 A44 2000

Colección La llave (Universidad Autónoma Metropolitana. Unidad Xochimilco. División de Ciencias Sociales y Humanidades)
(24.) Jáidar, Isabel. La psicología. 1. ed. México, D.F. : Universidad Autónoma Metropolitana, Unidad Xochimilco, División de Ciencias Sociales y Humanidades, 2002.

Colección Las ciencias sociales.
Sociología de la identidad. México : Miguel Angel Porrúa : Universidad Autónoma Metropolitana, Unidad Iztapalapa, 2002.

Colección Las Ciencias sociales. Estudios de género.
Serret, Estela. Identidad femenina y proyecto ético. 1. ed. México : UNAM, PUEG : Universidad Autónoma Metropolitana, Azcapotzalco : M.A. Porrúa, 2002.

Colección Leibnizius politechnicus
(no. 3) Orio de Miguel, Bernardino, 1936- Leibniz y el pensamiento hermético. Valencia : Universidad Politécnica de València, Editorial U.P.V., [2002]

Colección Monografías y textos.
Retroprospectivas psicológicas. Santiago : Ediciones UCSH, [2002]
BF75 .R48 2002

Colección popular (Fondo de Cultura Económica (Mexico))
(618.) Cornblit, Oscar. Violencia social, genocidio y terrorismo. 1. ed. México, D.F. : Fondo de Cultura Económica, 2002.
HM886 .C67 2002

Colección Protextos
(1) Aguirre Rojas, Carlos Antonio. Ensayos braudelianos. Rosario, Argentina : Prohistoria : M. Suárez ; México : Asociación Nacional de Profesores de Historia de México, 2000.
D15.B62 A38 2000

Colección Reflexiones
Wagner de Reyna, Alberto. El privilegio de ser latinoamericano. 1. ed. Córdoba, Argentina : Editorial Alejandro Korn, c2002.
F1408.3 .W35 2002

Colección Sabiduría perenne.
Merlo Lillo, Vicente. La fascinación de Oriente. 1. ed. Barcelona : Editorial Kairós, 2002.

Colección Sede
López Díaz, Yolanda. Por qué se maltrata al más íntimo? 1. ed. [Bogota] : Universidad Nacional de Colombia, Sede Bogota, 2002.

Colección Signo (Buenos Aires, Argentina)
La (indi)gestión cultural. 1. ed. Bs. As., Argentina : Ediciones Ciccus-La Crujía, 2002.
HM621 .I535 2002

Colección Temas y autores fundamentales
Beristain, Carlos M. Apoyo psicosocial en catátrofes colectivas. 1a. ed. Caracas, Venezuela : Asociación Venezolana de Psicología Social-AVESPO : Comisión de Estudios de Posgrado, Facultad de Hunanidades y Educación, Universidad Central de Venezuela, 2000.

Colección Ventana abierta.
Metáfora y discurso filosófico. Madrid : Tecnos, 2000.

Colegrave, Nick.
Ruxton, Graeme D. Elementary experimental design for the life sciences. Oxford : Oxford University Press, 2003.

The collaborative work systems fieldbook : strategies, tools, and techniques / Michael M. Beyerlein ... [et al.], editors. San Francisco : Jossey-Bass/Pfeiffer, c2003. xxv, 671 p. : ill. ; 24 cm. (The collaborative work systems series) Includes bibliographical references (p. 617-633) and index. ISBN 0-7879-6375-5 (alk. paper) DDC 658.4/02
1. Teams in the workplace. 2. Leadership. 3. Management. I. Beyerlein, Michael Martin. II. Series.
HD66 .C547 2003

The collaborative work systems series
The collaborative work systems fieldbook. San Francisco : Jossey-Bass/Pfeiffer, c2003.
HD66 .C547 2003

Collana credere oggi
([11].) De Rosa, Giuseppe. Fatica e gioia di credere. Leumann (Torino) : ElleDiCi ; Roma : La civiltà cattolica, c2002.

Collana di astronomia culturale
Vlora, Nedim R., 1943- Le porte del cielo. Bari : M. Adda, c2001.
BF1674 .V56 2001

Collana di cultura filosofica
Cacciatore, Giuseppe, 1945- L'etica dello storicismo. Lecce : Milella, 2000.

Collana di filosofia e storia delle idee.
Vecchiotti, Icilio. Introduzione alla filosofia di Giordano Bruno. Urbino : QuattroVenti, c2000.
B783.Z7 V43 2000

Collana di filosofia (Milan, Italy)
(75.) Premoli De Marchi, Paola. Etica dell'assenso. Milano : FrancoAngeli, c2002.

Collana di psicologia (Turin, Italy)
Il "valore" del padre. Torino : UTET libreria, 2001.
BF723.P25 V35 2001

Collana Dimensioni spirituali
(15) Martinelli, Paolo, 1958- Vocazione e stati di vita del cristiano. Roma : Collegio San Lorenzo da Brindisi, 2001.

Collana Mimesis.
Proto, Antonino, 1925- Ermete Trismegisto. Milano : Mimesis, 2000.
BF1598.H6 P76 2000

Sermonti, Giuseppe. Il mito della grande madre. Milano : Mimesis, c2002.

Collana Teologia viva
(45) Campanini, Giorgio, 1930- Le parole dell'etica. Bologna : EDB, 2002.

The collapse of the fact/value dichotomy and other essays.
Putnam, Hilary. Cambridge, MA : Harvard University Press, 2002.
B945.P873 C65 2002

Collected papers on Southeast Asian and Pacific languages / edited by Robert S. Bauer. Canberra, ACT : Pacific Linguistics, Research School of Pacific and Asian Studies, Australian National University, 2002. xii, 203 p. : ill. ; 25 cm. (Pacific linguistics ; 530) Includes bibliographical references. ISBN 0-85883-528-2
1. Austronesian languages. 2. Asia, Southeastern - Languages. 3. Islands of the Pacific - Languages. 4. Language and languages. 5. Linguistics. I. Bauer, Robert S. II. Series.

Collected studies.
Scholars and courtiers. Aldershot ; Burlington, Vt. : Ashgate/Variorum, c2002.
AZ183.E8 S36 2002

(CS631.) Speck, Paul. [Selections. English. 1999] Understanding Byzantium. Aldershot, Great Britain ; Burlington, Vt. : Ashgate/Variorum, c2003.
DF503 .S742513 2003

(CS765.) Cardwell, D. S. L. (Donald Stephen Lowell) The development of science and technology in nineteenth-century Britain. Aldershot, Great Britain ; Burlington, VT : Ashgate/Variorum, c2003.
Q127.G4 C37 2003

COLLECTIBLES. *See* **COLLECTORS AND COLLECTING.**

COLLECTIBLES - COLLECTORS AND COLLECTING. *See* **COLLECTORS AND COLLECTING.**

COLLECTING. *See* **COLLECTORS AND COLLECTING.**

Collecting and interpreting qualitative materials / editors, Norman K. Denzin, Yvonna S. Lincoln. 2nd ed. Thousand Oaks, Calif. : Sage, c2003. xiii, 682 p. ; 23 cm. Includes bibliographical references and indexes. ISBN 0-7619-2687-9 (pbk.) DDC 300/.7/23
1. Social sciences - Research - Methodology. 2. Qualitative reasoning. I. Denzin, Norman K. II. Lincoln, Yvonna S.
H62 .C566 2003

Collection Actualité de la psychanalyse
Lhomme-Rigaud, Colette. L'adolescent et ses monstres. Ramonville Saint-Agne : Érès, c2002.

COLLECTION AND PRESERVATION. *See* **COLLECTORS AND COLLECTING.**

Collection "Archéologiques"
La céramique. Paris : Editions Errance, c2003.

Collection Bibliothèques
Arts en bibliothèques. Paris : Editions du Cercle de la Librairie, c2003.
Z675.A85 A78 2003

Collection Commentaires philosophiques.
Souchon, Gisèle. Nietzsche. Paris : Harmattan, c2003.

Collection Création/réel
La figure des héros dans la création contemporaine. Paris : Harmattan, c2002.

Collection "Critique"
Green, André. La diachronie en psychanalyse. Paris : Minuit, c2000.
BF468 .G66 2000

Collection DDB
Tiberghien, Gilles A., 1953- Amitier. Paris : Desclée de Brouwer, c2002.

Collection Démons et merveilles
Duplessis, Yvonne, 1912- Surréalisme et paranormal. Agnières : JMG, 2002.
BF1023 .D87 2002

Collection Des lieux et des espaces
Rábago, Jesús. Le sens de bâtir. Lecques : Théétète, c2000.
NA2500 .R29 2000

Collection "des travaux et des jours"
Lévy, Ghyslain. Au-delà du malaise. Ramonville Saint-Agne : Érès, c2000.
BF175 .L487 2000

Collection Deux mondes
Winter, Jean, 1909-1939 (Spirit) Dites-leur que la mort n'existe pas. Chambéry : Exergue, c1997, [1998]
BF1290 .W56 1997

Collection "Essai" (Descartes & Cie)
Flahault, François, 1943- Le sentiment d'exister. Paris : Descartes & Cie, c2002.
BD438.5 .F54 2002

Collection Essais sur le Moyen Age.
(28.) Gendt, Anne-Marie Emma Alberta de, 1952- L'art d'éduquer les nobles damoiselles. Paris : Champion, 2003.

Collection "Ethnologies"
Lioger, Richard. La folie du chaman. Paris : Presses universitaires de France, c2002.

Collection Germod
Mavouangui, David, 1953- Jean-Paul Sartre. Paris : Paari, [2002], c2001.

Collection "Histoire des sciences humaines"
Huteau, Michel. Psychologie, psychiatrie et société sous la troisième république. Paris : Harmattan, c2002.

Collection "Histoire" (Rennes, France)
Religion et mentalités au Moyen Age. Rennes : Presses universitaires de Rennes, c2003.
BR141 .R45 2003

Collection Individu et société
Kaufmann, Jean-Claude. Premier matin. Paris : Colin, 2002.

Collection Izvor
(238) Aïvanhov, Omraam Mikhaël. La foi qui transporte les montagnes. Fréjus : Prosveta, c1999.

(239) Aïvanhov, Omraam Mikhaël. L'amour plus grand que la foi. Fréjus : Prosveta, c2000.

Collection La philosophie en effet (Editions Galilée)
Froment Meurice, Marc. Incitations. Paris : Galilée, c2002.

Collection Le bien commun.
Eslin, Jean-Claude, 1935- Saint Augustin. Paris : Michalon, c2002.

Collection Le temps de l'histoire
Religion et exclusion, XIIe-XVIIIe siècle. Religion et exclusion, douzième-dix-huitième siècle. Aix-en-Provence : Publications de l'Université de Provence, 2001.
BL238 .R448 2001

Collection Les mystères de l'histoire
Ducret, Alix. La vie au moyen âge. Courtaboeuf : Didro, c2002.

Collection L'œuvre et la psyché
Paquette, Didier. La mascarade interculturelle. Paris : Harmattan, c2002.

Vinet, Dominique. Romanesque britannique et psyché. Paris : L'Harmattan, c2003.

Collection Logiques historiques
Pistes didactiques et chemins historiques. Paris : Harmattan, 2003.

Collection Logiques politiques
Aux frontières des attitudes. Paris, France : Harmattan, c2002.

Collection L'ouverture philosophique.
Balmès, Marc. Pour un plein accès à l'acte d'être avec Thomas d'Aquin et Aristote. Paris : Harmattan, c2003.

Bardy, Jean. Regard sur "l'évolution créatrice". Paris : Harmattan, c2003.

Catrysse, Andrée. Les grecs et la vieillesse. Paris : L'Harmattan, c2003.

Chebili, Saïd. La tâche civilisatrice de la psychanalyse selon Freud. Paris : L'Harmattan, c2002.

Hayat, Michaël. Dynamique des formes et représentations. Paris : Harmattan, c2002.
B105.R4 H392 2002

Jankovic, Zoran. Au-delà du signe. Paris : Harmattan, c2003.

Passions du passé. Paris : L'Harmattan, c2000.
BF378.S65 P37 2000

Poitevin, Michel. Georges Dumézil, un naturel comparatiste. Paris : Harmattan, c2002.

Protopapas-Marneli, Maria. La rhétorique des stoïciens. Paris : Harmattan, c2002.

Safty, Essam. La psyché humaine. Paris : Harmattan, c2003.
B528 .S34 2003

Le système et le rêve. Paris : Harmattan, c2002.
BF1078 .S97 2002

Collection Major
Ricot, Jacques. Leçon sur L'éthique à Nicomaque, d'Aristote. 1re ed. Paris : Presses universitaires de France, c2001.
B430 .R536 2001

Collection Mouvement des savoirs
Andrieu, Bernard. L'interprétation des gènes. Paris : Harmattan, 2002.

Barsotti, Bernard. Bachelard critique de Husserl. Paris : Harmattan, c2002.
B2430.B254 B37 2002

Collection of mottos on life from Confucius and Mencius with modern Chinese and English translations.
Confucius. [Selections. Chinese & English. 1998] Kong Meng ren sheng ge yan ji cui. Wuhan : Wuhan gong ye da xue chu ban she, 1998.

Collection Paroles
Nosmas, Alma. La mort élégante. Paris : Horay, c2003.

Collection Philosophica
(no. 54) Vernes, Jean-René. The existence of the external world. Ottawa : University of Ottawa Press, c2000.

Collection "Philosophie en cours"
Martin, Jean-Clet. Parures d'éros. Paris : Kimé, 2003.

Collection Philosophie, épistémologie
Fortitude et servitude. Paris : Kimé, c2003.

Collection Philosophie et connaissance
Nocam. Nostradamus. Champagne-sur-Oise : Kapsos, 1998.
BF1815.N8 A2668 1998

Collection "Pour l'histoire"
Verdon, Jean. Boire au moyen âge. [Paris] : Perrin, c2002.

Collection Psychanalyse et civilisations. Série Trouvailles et retrouvailles
Rhodes, Henry T. F. (Henry Taylor Fowkes), b. 1892. Le génie et le crime. Paris, France : Harmattan, c2002.

Collection Psycho
Nicolas, Serge. Histoire de la psychologie française. Paris : In press, c2002.
BF108.F8 N536 2002

Collection Questions contemporaines
Venne, Jean-François, 1972- Le lien social dans le modèle de l'individualisme privé. Paris : L'Harmattan, c2002.

Collection "Réflexions théologiques du sud"
Oduyoye, Mercy Amba. Les colliers et les perles. Yaoundé : Editions CLE, c2002.

Collection Religion et sciences humaines.
Beauperin, Yves. Anthropologie du geste symbolique. Paris : Harmattan, c2002.
BL60 .B339 2002

Collection Remise en question
Cifali, Mario. Trois rêves freudiens. Paris : Eshel, c1999.
BF175.5.O33 C54 1999

Collection Sciences, modernités, philosophies
Rosental, Claude. La trame de l'évidence. 1 éd. Paris : Presses universitaires de France, c2003.

Collection Tel
Starobinski, Jean. La relation critique. Ed. rev. et augm. [Paris] : Gallimard, c2001.
PN81 .S69 2001

Collection Trait d'union
Simone Weil, la passion de la raison. Paris : Harmattan, c2003.
B2430.W474 S55 2003

COLLECTIVE BEHAVIOR. *See* **DEMONSTRATIONS.**

Collective identities in action : a sociological approach to ethnicity / Klaus Eder ... [et al.]. Aldershot, England ; Burlington, VT : Ashgate, c2002. x, 189 p. : ill. ; 22 cm. Includes bibliographical references (p. [169]-178) and index. ISBN 0-7546-1962-1 (alk. paper) DDC 305.8
1. Ethnicity. 2. Group identity. 3. Ethnic conflict. I. Eder, Klaus, 1946-
GN495.6 .C635 2002

COLLECTIVE IDENTITY. *See* **GROUP IDENTITY.**

COLLECTIVISM. *See* **COMMUNISM; FASCISM; SOCIALISM.**

COLLECTORS AND COLLECTING - EUROPE - HISTORY.
Mauriès, Patrick, 1952- Cabinets of curiosities. New York : Thames & Hudson, c2002.
AM221 .M38 2002

COLLECTORS AND COLLECTING - HISTORY.
Mauriès, Patrick, 1952- Cabinets of curiosities. New York : Thames & Hudson, c2002.
AM221 .M38 2002

COLLÈGE DE FRANCE - CURRICULA.
Foucault au Collège de France. Pessac : Presses universitaires de Bordeaux, c2003.
B2430.F724 F6855 2003

Collège de France. Symposium annuel. La vérité dans les sciences : symposium annuel / Collège de France ; sous la direction de Jean-Pierre Changeux ; avec J. Bouveresse ... [et al.]. Paris : Jacob, c2003. 238 p. ; 22 cm. Includes bibliographical references. ISBN 2-7381-1171-8 DDC 194
1. Truth - Congresses. 2. Knowledge, Theory of - Congresses. 3. Science - Philosophy - Congresses. I. Changeux, Jean-Pierre. II. Bouveresse, Jacques. III. Title.

COLLEGE ENTRANCE ACHIEVEMENT TESTS. *See* **ADVANCED PLACEMENT PROGRAMS (EDUCATION).**

COLLEGE LIFE. *See* **COLLEGE STUDENTS.**

COLLEGE STUDENTS - MISCELLANEA.
Paige, Anthony. Rocking the goddess. New York : Citadel Press, c2002.
BF1571.5.C64 P35 2002

COLLEGE STUDENTS - PERSONALITY. *See* **COLLEGE STUDENTS - PSYCHOLOGY.**

COLLEGE STUDENTS - PSYCHOLOGY - CONGRESSES.
Mezhregional'naiā Rossiĭskaiā nauchno-prakticheskaiā konferentsiiā "Psikhologicheskie osobennosti preodoleniiā ėkstremal'nykh i ėmotsiogennykh situatsiĭ v podrostkovo-iūnosheskom vozraste" (2002 : Syktyvkar, Russia)
Psikhologicheskie osobennosti preodoleniiā ėkstremal'nykh i ėmotsiogennykh situatsiĭ v podrostkovo-iūnosheskom vozraste. Syktyvkar : Syktyvkarskiĭ gos. universitet, 2002.
BF724 .M48 2002

COLLEGES. *See* **UNIVERSITIES AND COLLEGES.**

Collen, Lindsey. Natir imin : Mauritian Creole & English versions / Lindsey Collen. Port Louis, Mauritius : Ledikasyon pu travayer, [2000] 47 p. ; 20 cm. (Public lecture = Konesans pu tu dimunn) Cover title. Mauritian French Creole and English. ISBN 9990333319
1. Ethics. 2. Political science - Philosophy. 3. Philosophical anthropology. 4. Social ethics. I. Title. II. Series: Public lecture series (Ledikasyon pu travayer)

Collenberg-Plotnikov, Bernadette, 1963-.
Hotho, Heinrich Gustav, 1802-1873. Vorstudien für Leben und Kunst. Stuttgart : Frommann-Holzboog, 2002.

Collette, Bernard. Dialectique et hénologie chez Plotin / Bernard Collette. Bruxelles : Ousia, c2002. 223 p. ; 21 cm. (Cahiers de philosophie ancienne ; no 18) ISBN 2-87060-095-X DDC 180
1. Plotinus - Criticism and interpretation. 2. Dialectic. 3. Philosophy of mind. I. Title. II. Series.
B693.Z7 C655 2002

Collier-Thompson, Kristi. The girls' guide to dreams / Kristi Collier-Thompson ; illustrated by Sandie Turchyn. New York : Sterling Pub., c2003. 128 p. : ill. ; 24 cm. SUMMARY: Introduces how to interpret the symbols often found in dreams and to apply what can be learned from them to events in one's waking life, and includes directions for keeping a dream journal. Includes index. Publisher description URL: http://www.loc.gov/catdir/description/ste031/2003001297.html CONTENTS: Introduction -- Alphabetical listings -- Dream exercises. ISBN 1402700326 DDC 154.6/3/08352
1. Children's dreams - Juvenile literature. 2. Dream interpretation - Dictionaries - Juvenile literature. 3. Symbolism (Psychology) - Dictionaries - Juvenile literature. 4. Dreams. 5. Symbolism (Psychology) - Dictionaries. I. Turchyn, Sandie, ill. II. Title.
BF1099.C55 C65 2003

Les colliers et les perles.
Oduyoye, Mercy Amba. Yaoundé : Editions CLE, c2002.

Collin-Smith, Joyce, 1919-.
The occult Webb. Toronto : Colombo & Co., c1999.
BF1408.2.W42 O33 1999

Collingwood and the metaphysics of experience.
D'Oro, Giuseppina, 1964- London ; New York : Routledge, 2002.
B1618.C74 D67 2002

COLLINGWOOD, R. G. (ROBIN GEORGE), 1889-1943 - CONTRIBUTIONS IN METAPHYSICS.
D'Oro, Giuseppina, 1964- Collingwood and the metaphysics of experience. London ; New York : Routledge, 2002.
B1618.C74 D67 2002

Collins, Catherine Fisher. Sources of stress and relief for African American women / Catherine Fisher Collins. Westport, Conn. ; London : Praeger, 2003. xv, 129 p. : ill. ; 25 cm. (Race and ethnicity in psychology) Includes bibliographical references (p. [117]-126) and index. ISBN 0-86569-267-X (alk. paper) DDC 155.9/042/082
1. Stress (Psychology) 2. Stress management for women. 3. African American women - Psychology. I. Title. II. Series.
BF575.S75 C57 2003

COLLINS, STANLEY, 1881-1966.
Dawes, Edwin A. Stanley Collins. Washington, DC : Kaufman and Co., c2002.

Collision of wills.
Gould, Roger V. Chicago : University of Chicago Press, 2003.

COLLISIONS, AIRCRAFT. *See* **AIRCRAFT ACCIDENTS.**

COLLISIONS AT SEA. *See* **SHIPWRECKS.**

COLLISIONS OF COMETS WITH EARTH. *See* **COMETS - COLLISIONS WITH EARTH.**

Collomb, Véronique.
Psychanalyse et décolonisation. Paris : L'Harmattan, c1999.
BF175.4.C84 P76 1999

Colloque de Strasbourg (14th : 1995) Oracles et prophéties dans l'Antiquité : actes du colloque de Strasbourg, 15-17 juin 1995 / édités par Jean-Georges Heintz. Strasbourg : Publications de l'Université de Strasbourg II, 1997. 542 p. : ill. ; 24 cm. (Travaux du Centre de recherche sur le Proche-Orient et la Grèce antiques ; 15) Articles in French, English, and German, with summaries in French and English or French and German. Includes bibliographical references. ISBN 2-911488-01-6
1. Oracles - Congresses. 2. Prophecies - Congresses. I. Heintz, Jean Georges. II. Title. III. Series.
BF1761 .C65 1995

Colloque des Invalides (5th : 2001 : Hôtel des invalides) Ce que je ne sais pas : cinquième Colloque des Invalides, 23 novembre 2001 / textes réunis par Jean-Jacques Lefrère et Michel Pierssens. Tusson, Charente : Du Lérot, [2002?] 143 p. : ill. ; 23 cm. (En marge) "Armand d'Artois, Flaubert, le vicomte Phoebus, Retoqué de Saint-Réac, Philippe Beck, Maupassant, l'affaire Dreyfus, Michel Houellebecq, Les solitaires (vers), tableaux nonymes et anonymes, le parrain de Proust, Raymond Roussel, l'origine des aphorismes, Balzac, Agatha Christie, etc." Includes bibliographical references.
1. Ignorance (Theory of knowledge) in literature - Congresses. 2. First person narrative - Congresses. 3. French literature - History and criticism - Congresses. 4. Fiction - Technique - Congresses. I. Lefrère, Jean-Jacques. II. Pierssens, Michel. III. Hôtel des invalides (France) IV. Title. V. Series.
PQ145 .C65 2001

COLLOQUIAL ENGLISH. *See* **ENGLISH LANGUAGE - SPOKEN ENGLISH.**

COLLOQUIAL LANGUAGE. *See* **CONVERSATION.**

Collste, Göran. Is human life special? : religious and philosophical perspectives on the principle of human dignity / Göran Collste. Bern ; Oxford : Peter Lang, 2002. 233 p. ; 21 cm. Includes bibliographical references and index. ISBN 3-906769-26-7 ISBN 0-8204-5893-7 (New York : pbk.) DDC 128
1. Dignity. 2. Dignity - Religious aspects. 3. Life. 4. Life - Religious aspects. I. Title.

Colombel, Véronique de.
Lexique et motivation. Paris ; Sterling, Va. : Peeters, c2002.
P326 .L45 2002

COLOMBIA - ECONOMIC CONDITIONS - 1970-.
Idrobo Díaz, Hugo, 1954- La joda de la paz en Colombia. 1. ed. Cali, Colombia : [s.n., 2002?]

COLOMBIA - POLITICS AND GOVERNMENT - 1974-.
Al oído de Uribe. 1a. ed. Bogotá, Colombia : Editorial Oveja Negra, 2002.

Giraldo Hurtado, Luis Guillermo, 1944- Del proceso y de la paz. [Colombia? : s.n., 2001] (Manizales : Edigr@ficas)

Idrobo Díaz, Hugo, 1954- La joda de la paz en Colombia. 1. ed. Cali, Colombia : [s.n., 2002?]

Téllez, Edgar. Diario íntimo de un fracaso. 1. ed. Bogotá, D.C., Colombia : Planeta, 2002.

Valencia, León. Adiós a la política, bienvenido la guerra. [Bogotá, Colombia?] : Intermedio, c2002.

Yusty, Miguel. Negociar en medio de la guerra. [Cali, Colombia] : Editorial Universidad Santiago de Cali, 2002.

COLOMBIA - SOCIAL CONDITIONS - 1970-.
Idrobo Díaz, Hugo, 1954- La joda de la paz en Colombia. 1. ed. Cali, Colombia : [s.n., 2002?]

Colombo, John Robert, 1936-.
The occult Webb. Toronto : Colombo & Co., c1999.
BF1408.2.W42 O33 1999

COLONIALISM. *See* **IMPERIALISM; WORLD POLITICS.**

COLONIALISM - HISTORY - CONGRESSES.
Psychanalyse et décolonisation. Paris : L'Harmattan, c1999.
BF175.4.C84 P76 1999

COLONIES. *See also* **DECOLONIZATION; LAND SETTLEMENT.**
Racism. Armonk, N.Y. : M.E. Sharpe, c2003.
HT1521 .R323 2003

COLONIZATION. *See* **DECOLONIZATION; EMIGRATION AND IMMIGRATION; PUBLIC LANDS.**

The color answer book.
Eiseman, Leatrice. Sterling, Va. : Capital Books, c2003.
BF789.C7 E375 2003

COLOR-HEARING. *See* **PERCEPTION.**

COLOR IN ART.
Percheron, René. Matisse. Paris : Citadelles & Mazenod, c2002.
N6853.M33 P47 2002

Pleij, Herman. Van karmijn, purper en blauw. Amsterdam : Prometheus, 2002.

Weber, Jürgen, 1928- The judgement of the eye. Wien ; New York : Springer, c2002.
BF241 .W38 2002

Xizang fo jiao cai hui cai su yi shu. Di 1 ban. Beijing : Zhongguo Zang xue chu ban she : Xin hua shu dian Beijing fa xing suo fa xing, 1997.
ND1489 .X593 1997

Color magick.
Buckland, Raymond. 1st ed., rev. St. Paul, Minn. : Llewellyn Publications, 2002.
BF1623.C6 B83 2002

COLOR - MISCELLANEA.
Buckland, Raymond. Color magick. 1st ed., rev. St. Paul, Minn. : Llewellyn Publications, 2002.
BF1623.C6 B83 2002

COLOR - PSYCHIC ASPECTS.
Larson, Cynthia Sue. Aura advantage. Avon, MA : Adams Media Corp., c2003.
BF1389.A8 L37 2003

Martin, Barbara Y. Change your aura, change your life Sunland, CA : WisdomLight Books, c2003.
BF1389.A8 M37 2003

COLOR - PSYCHOLOGICAL ASPECTS. *See also* **SYMBOLISM OF COLORS.**
Eiseman, Leatrice. The color answer book. Sterling, Va. : Capital Books, c2003.
BF789.C7 E375 2003

Sadka, Dewey. The Dewey color system. 1st ed. New York : Three Rivers Press, 2004.
BF789.C7 S23 2004

Whelan, Bride M. The complete color harmony. Gloucester, Mass. : Rockport Publishers, 2004.
BF789.C7 W47 20041

COLOR - PSYCHOLOGICAL ASPECTS - HISTORY.
Pastoureau, Michel, 1947- Bleu. [Paris] : Seuil, c2000.
BF789.C7 P36 2000

Pleij, Herman. [Van karmijn, purper en blauw. English] Colors demonic and divine. New York : Columbia University Press, 2004.
BF789.C7 P5713 2004

Pleij, Herman. Van karmijn, purper en blauw. Amsterdam : Prometheus, 2002.

COLOR - PSYCHOLOGY. *See* **COLOR - PSYCHOLOGICAL ASPECTS.**

COLOR - SOCIAL ASPECTS - HISTORY.
Pastoureau, Michel, 1947- Bleu. [Paris] : Seuil, c2000.
BF789.C7 P36 2000

COLOR VISION.
Livingstone, Margaret. Vision and art. New York, N.Y. : Harry N. Abrams, c2002.
N7430.5 .L54 2002

COLORADO ADOPTION PROJECT.
Nature, nurture, and the transition to early adolescence. Oxford ; New York : Oxford University Press, 2003.
BF341 .N387 2003

COLORS. *See* **COLOR; SYMBOLISM OF COLORS.**

Colors demonic and divine.
Pleij, Herman. [Van karmijn, purper en blauw. English] New York : Columbia University Press, 2004.
BF789.C7 P5713 2004

The colors of nature : culture, identity, and the natural world / edited by Alison H. Deming and Lauret E. Savoy. 1st ed. Minneapolis, Minn. : Milkweed Editions, 2002. 210 p. ; 23 cm. Includes bibliographical references. CONTENTS: Introduction as conversation / Alison H. Deming and Lauret E. Savoy -- In history / Jamaica Kincaid -- Reclaiming ourselves, reclaiming America / Francisco X. Alarcón -- At the end of Ridge Road : from a nature journal / Joseph Bruchac -- Earthbound : on solid ground / bell hooks -- Sharing breath : some links between land, plants, and people / Enrique Salmon -- Confronting environmental racism in the twenty-first century / Robert D. Bullard -- Dark waters / Yusef Komunyakaa -- Silent parrot blues / Al Young. CONTENTS: Ke Au Lono I Kaho'olawe, Ho'I (the era of Lono at Kaho'olawe, returned) / Pualani Kanaka'ole Kanahele -- Burning the shelter / Louis Owens -- Becoming Métis / Melissa Nelson -- Turning slowly nature / Diane Glancy -- Hazardous cargo / Ray Gonzalez -- Crossing boundaries / Jeanne Wakatsuki Houston -- Writing the diaspora : one black writer's journdy frm cultural isolation to multicultural inclusion / Sandra Jackson-Opoku -- Listening for the ancient tones, watching for sign, tasting for the mountain thyme / Gary Paul Nabhan -- Belonging on the land / David Mas Masumoto. ISBN 1-57131-267-6 (pbk. : alk. paper) DDC 508
1. Nature. 2. Ethnicity. 3. Minorities - United States. I. Deming, Alison Hawthorne, 1946- II. Savoy, Lauret E.
QH81 .C663 2002

COLT/KERNEL 2003.
Conference on Computational Learning Theory (16th : 2003 : Washington, D.C.) Learning theory and Kernel machines. Berlin ; New York : Springer, c2003.
Q325.5 .C654 2003

COLUMNISTS. *See* **JOURNALISTS.**

Colwell, Peter G. Spell success in your life : a road map for achieving your goals and surviving success / Peter Colwell. Germantown, Md. : Dreams Unlimited Press, c2002. xx, 137 p. : ill. ; 23 cm. Includes bibliographical references (p. 133-134). ISBN 0-9717268-0-9 DDC 158.1
1. Success - Psychological aspects. I. Title.
BF637.S8 C57 2002

COMBAT PHOTOGRAPHY. *See* **WAR PHOTOGRAPHY.**

COMBAT - PSYCHOLOGICAL ASPECTS.
Why they fight [electronic resource]. Carlisle, PA : Strategic Studies Institute, U.S. Army War College, [2003]
U22

COMBATIVENESS. *See* **FIGHTING (PSYCHOLOGY).**

COMBE, GEORGE, 1788-1858.
CONSTITUTION OF MAN.
Van Wyhe, John, 1971- Phrenology and the origins of Victorian scientific naturalism. Burlington, VT : Ashgate, c2003.
BF879 .V36 2003

Combrichon, Anny.
Psychanalyse et décolonisation. Paris : L'Harmattan, c1999.
BF175.4.C84 P76 1999

Combs, Allan, 1942- The radiance of being : understanding the grand integral vision : living the integral life / by Allan Combs. 2nd ed. St. Paul, Minn. : Paragon House, 2002. xviii, 380 p. : ill. ; 23 cm. (Omega books) Includes bibliographical references (p. 317-368) and index. ISBN 1-55778-812-X (pbk. : alk. paper) DDC 150.19/8
1. Consciousness. 2. Chaotic behavior in systems. 3. Brain. I. Title. II. Series: Omega book (New York, N.Y.)
BF311 .C575 2002

COMBUSTION. *See* **SMOKE.**

COMCAST CORPORATION.
United States. Congress. Senate. Committee on the Judiciary. Subcommittee on Antitrust, Business Rights, and Competition. Dominance on the ground. Washington : U.S. G.P.O. : For sale by the Supt. of Docs., U.S. G.P.O. [Congressional Sales Office], 2003.

COMEDY. *See* **COMIC, THE.**

Comet of Nostradamus.
Welch, R. W., 1929- 1st ed. St. Paul, Minn. : Llewellyn Publications, 2000 (2001 printing)
BF1815.N8 A269 2000

COMETS - COLLISIONS WITH EARTH - MISCELLANEA.
Welch, R. W., 1929- Comet of Nostradamus. 1st ed. St. Paul, Minn. : Llewellyn Publications, 2000 (2001 printing)

Comfort, Kenneth Jerold.
BF1815.N8 A269 2000

Comfort, Kenneth Jerold. The ego and the social order / by Kenneth Jerold Comfort. Cohoes, N.Y. : Public Administration Institute of New York State, 2000. ii, 351 p. ; 24 cm. Includes bibliographical references (p. 327-332) and index. ISBN 0-9659144-1-0 DDC 155.2
1. Ego (Psychology) 2. Social psychology. 3. Political psychology. I. Title.
BF175.5.E35 C65 2000

Power, politics, and the ego / Kenneth Jerold Comfort. 2nd ed., revised. Cohoes, N.Y. : Public Administration Institute of New York State, 2003. iv, 551 p. ; 24 cm. Includes bibliographical references and index. ISBN 0-9659144-2-9
1. Personality and politics. 2. Political psychology. I. Title.

Comfort secrets for busy women.
Louden, Jennifer. Naperville, Ill. : Sourcebooks, c2003.
BF637.C5 L676 2003

COMIC, THE.
Marmysz, John, 1964- Laughing at nothing. Albany : State University of New York Press, c2003.
B828.3 .M265 2003

Michel-Andino, Andreas, 1961- Kleine Philosophie des Lachens. Koblenz : Fölbach, c2000.
BF575.L3 M53 2000

Oring, Elliott, 1945- Engaging humor. Urbana : University of Illinois Press, c2003.
PN6147 .O74 2003

COMIC, THE - CONGRESSES.
Komik der Renaissance, Renaissance der Komik. Frankfurt am Main ; New York : P. Lang, c2000.
BH301.C7 .K63 2000

Los comienzos de la psicopedagogía en España, 1882-1936.
Cerezo Manrique, Miguel Ángel. Madrid : Biblioteca Nueva, c2001.

Coming in first.
Llewellyn, Jack H. Atlanta : Longstreet Press, c2000.
BF637.S8 L56 2000

Coming into their own.
Scales, Peter, 1949- Minneapolis, MN : Search Institute, c2004.
BF721 .S347 2004

Coming of age in the Holocaust.
Gallant, Mary J. Lanham, Md. : University Press of America, c2002.
D804.3 .G353 2002

COMMAND OF TROOPS. *See* **LEADERSHIP.**

COMMAND OF TROOPS - CASE STUDIES.
The challenges of high command. Houndmills, Basingstoke ; New York : Palgrave Macmillan, 2003.
UB210 .C477 2003

COMMANDMENTS (JUDAISM). *See* **COMMANDMENTS, SIX HUNDRED AND THIRTEEN.**

COMMANDMENTS, SIX HUNDRED AND THIRTEEN - INDEXES.
Globerman, Daniyel Aharon. Yalkut Sefer ha-Ḥinukh. Modi'in 'Ilit : D. A. Globerman, Kolel "Libo ḥafets", 761 [2000 or 2001]
BM520.8.A32 G4 2001

COMMEDIA DELL'ARTE. *See* **IMPROVISATION (ACTING).**

Comment la féminité vient aux femmes.
Godfrind, Jacqueline. Paris : Presses universitaires de France, c2001.
BF175.5.F45 G63 2001

Comment le désir de naître vient au foetus.
Canault, Nina. Paris : Desclée de Brouwer, c2001.

Comment l'occident tente de transformer le monde.
La Branche, Stéphane. Mondialisation et terrorisme identitaire, ou, Comment l'Occident tente de transformer le monde. Paris : Harmattan, c2003.
JC330 .L2 2003

Comment pourquoi.
Jacob, Suzanne. Ecrire comment pourquoi. Paroisse Notre-Dame-des-Neiges, Québec : Éditions Trois-Pistoles, c2002.
PN56.C69 J23 2002

Commentaria in quinque voces Porphyrii.
Ammonius, Hermiae. Stuttgart : Frommann-Holzboog, 2002.

Commentateur du Coran et philosophe.
Arnaldez, Roger. Fakhr al-Dîn al-Râzî. Paris : J. Vrin, 2002.

COMMENTATORS. *See* **JOURNALISTS.**

COMMERCE. *See* **BUSINESS; COMPETITION; ELECTRONIC COMMERCE; INDUSTRIAL PROMOTION; INTERNATIONAL TRADE; RETAIL TRADE.**

COMMERCIAL AERONAUTICS. *See* **AERONAUTICS, COMMERCIAL.**

COMMERCIAL AGENTS. *See* **LITERARY AGENTS.**

Commercial appropriation of personality.
Beverley-Smith, Huw. Cambridge, UK ; New York : Cambridge University Press, 2002.
K627 .B48 2002

COMMERCIAL ART - HISTORY - 20TH CENTURY - THEMES, MOTIVES.
Cullen, Cheryl Dangel. The art of design. 1st ed. Cincinnati, OH : How Design Books, c2003.
NC998.4 .C846 2003

COMMERCIAL AVIATION. *See* **AERONAUTICS, COMMERCIAL.**

Commercial aviation [electronic resource].
Hecker, JayEtta Z. [Washington, D.C.] : U.S. General Accounting Office, [2002]

Commercial aviation : financial condition and industry responses affect competition 16 p.
Hecker, JayEtta Z. Commercial aviation [electronic resource]. [Washington, D.C.] : U.S. General Accounting Office, [2002]

COMMERCIAL CORNERS. *See* **STOCK EXCHANGES.**

COMMERCIAL CRIMES. *See* **ANTITRUST LAW.**

COMMERCIAL DESIGN. *See* **COMMERCIAL ART.**

COMMERCIAL DOCUMENTS. *See* **LEGAL DOCUMENTS.**

COMMERCIAL LAW. *See* **ANTITRUST LAW.**

COMMERCIAL LAW (JEWISH LAW).
Tamari, Meir. Maśa u-matan be-emunah. Yerushalayim : Śimḥonim, [761, 2001]

COMMERCIAL PHOTOGRAPHY. *See* **PHOTOJOURNALISM.**

COMMERCIAL POLICY. *See also* **CONSUMER PROTECTION.**
The new economic diplomacy. Aldershot, Hampshire, England ; Burlington, VT : Ashgate, c2003.
HF1359 .N4685 2003

COMMERCIAL PRODUCTS. *See* **BRAND NAME PRODUCTS; NEW PRODUCTS.**

The commercialization of intimate life.
Hochschild, Arlie Russell, 1940- Berkeley : University of California Press, 2003.
HM1106 .H63 2003

COMMITMENT (PSYCHOLOGY).
Cohen, Aaron, 1952- Multiple commitments in the workplace. Mahwah, New Jersey : Lawrence Erlhaum Associates, 2003.
HD58.7 .C6213 2003

Phillips, Nicola. The big difference. Cambridge, MA : Perseus Pub., c2001.
BF619 .P48 2001

Weinberg, George H. Why men won't commit. New York : Atria Books, c2002.
BF619 .W45 2002

Committed to memory.
Stier, Oren Baruch, 1966- 1st ed. Amherst : University of Massachusetts Press, 2003.
D804.3 .S79 2003

COMMON ACCIDENTS. *See* **ACCIDENTS.**

COMMON GATEWAY INTERFACE (COMPUTER NETWORK PROTOCOL). *See* **CGI (COMPUTER NETWORK PROTOCOL).**

COMMON GOOD.
Archives and the public good. Westport, Conn. ; London : Quorum Books, 2002.

Politique et responsabilité, enjeux partagés. Paris : Harmattan ; Lille : Université des sciences et technologies de Lille, 2003.

COMMON HERITAGE OF MANKIND (INTERNATIONAL LAW). *See* **SOVEREIGNTY.**

COMMON SENSE.
Willaschek, Marcus. Der mentale Zugang zur Welt. Frankfurt am Main : Klostermann, 2003.
B835 .W55 2003

COMMON SHARES. *See* **STOCKS.**

COMMON STOCKS. *See* **STOCKS.**

COMMONPLACE-BOOKS - STUDY AND TEACHING - EUROPE - HISTORY.
Moss, Ann, 1938- Printed commonplace-books and the structuring of Renaissance thought. Oxford : Clarendon Press ; New York : Oxford University Press, 1996.
PA2047 .M67 1996

COMMONS (SOCIAL ORDER). *See* **WORKING CLASS.**

COMMONWEALTH, THE. *See* **POLITICAL SCIENCE.**

COMMUNICABLE DISEASES. *See* **SEXUALLY TRANSMITTED DISEASES.**

Communicating with credibility and confidence.
Lumsden, Gay. 2nd ed. Australia ; Belmont, CA : Thomson/Wadsworth, c2003.
BF637.C45 L85 2003

COMMUNICATION. *See also* **COMMUNICATION AND TRAFFIC; INTERCULTURAL COMMUNICATION; LANGUAGE AND LANGUAGES; ORAL COMMUNICATION; PERSUASION (PSYCHOLOGY); POPULAR CULTURE; TELECOMMUNICATION; VISUAL COMMUNICATION.**
Botschaften verstehen. Frankfurt am Main ; New York : P. Lang, c2000.
P91.25 .B688 2000

Chazal, Gérard. Interfaces. Seyssel [France] : Champ Vallon, c2002.
HM1111 .C49 2002

Communication, a different kind of horserace. Cresskill, N.J. : Hampton Press, c2003.
P87.3.C37 C66 2003

Communication and emotion. Mahwah, N.J. : London : Lawrence Erlbaum, c2003.
BF637.C45 C6375 2003

La comunicazione nei processi sociali e organizzativi. Nuova ed. aggiornata. Milano, Italy : FrancoAngeli, [2001?], c1997.

Dement'ev, V. V. Nepriamaia kommunikatsiia i ee zhanry. Saratov : Izd-vo Saratovskogo universiteta, 2000.
P106 .D4554 2000

Goldin-Meadow, Susan. Hearing gesture. Cambridge, Mass. : Belknap Press of Harvard University Press, 2003.
P117 .G65 2003

Guoron Ajquijay, Pedro. Retomemos la palabra--. Guatemala, Guatemala : Editorial Saqil Tzij, 1995.

Martín Salgado, Lourdes. Marketing político. Barcelona : Paidós, c2002.

McLuhan's wake [videorecording]. [Montreal, Quebec] : Primitive Entertainment/National Film Board of Canada, c2002.

Medien, Texte und Maschinen. 1. Aufl. Wiesbaden : Westdeutscher Verlag, c2001.

Die Politik der Massenmedien. Köln : Halem, 2001.

Reig, Ramón. El éxtasis cibernético. 1. ed. Madrid : Ediciones Libertarias, 2001.

Roelcke, Thorsten. Kommunikative Effizienz. Heidelberg : Winter, c2002.

Stein, Stephan, 1963- Textgliederung. Berlin ; New York : Walter de Gruyter, 2003.

Virtual'naia real'nost' v psikhologii i iskusstvennom intellekte. Moskva : Rossiĭskaia Assotsiatsiia iskusstvennogo intellekta, 1998.
BF204.5 .V57 1998

Communication, a different kind of horse race.
Communication, a different kind of horserace. Cresskill, N.J. : Hampton Press, c2003.
P87.3.C37 C66 2003

Communication, a different kind of horserace :
essays honoring Richard F. Carter / edited by Brenda Dervin, Steven H. Chaffee, with Lois Foreman-

Wernet. Cresskill, N.J. : Hampton Press, c2003. xvi, 393 p. : ill. ; 24 cm. (The Hampton Press communication series. Communication alternatives) Includes bibliographical references and indexes. ISBN 1-57273-502-3 (cloth) ISBN 1-57273-503-1 (paper) DDC 302.2
1. Carter, Richard F. - (Richard Fremont), - 1928- 2. Communication. I. Carter, Richard F. (Richard Fremont), 1928- II. Dervin, Brenda. III. Chaffee, Steven H. IV. Foreman-Wernet, Lois. V. Title: Communication, a different kind of horse race VI. Series.
P87.3.C37 C66 2003

COMMUNICATION AN CULTURE.
Kul'tura i vlast' v usloviiakh kommunikatsionnoĭ revoliutsii XX veka. Moskva : "AIRO-XX", 2002.
HM621 .K858 2002

COMMUNICATION AND CULTURE. See also **COMMUNICATION - SOCIAL ASPECTS.**
Chazal, Gérard. Interfaces. Seyssel [France] : Champ Vallon, c2002.
HM1111 .C49 2002

Elkins, James, 1955- Visual studies. New York : Routledge, 2003.
N72.S6 E45 2003

Kommunikation, Kunst und Kultur. Bern ; New York : Peter Lang, c2002.

Communication and cyberspace : social interaction in an electronic environment / edited by Lance Strate, Ron L. Jacobson, Stephanie B. Gibson. 2nd ed. Creskill, N.J. : Hampton Press, c2003. xiii, 416 p. ; 24 cm. (The Hampton Press communication series. Communication and public space) Includes bibliographical references and indexes. ISBN 1-57273-393-4 (alk. paper) ISBN 1-57273-394-2 (pbk. : alk. paper) DDC 302.2/0285
1. Communication - Data processing. 2. Communication and technology. 3. Computer networks. 4. Cyberspace. 5. Social interaction. 6. Virtual reality. I. Strate, Lance. II. Jacobson, Ronald L., 1956- III. Gibson, Stephanie B. IV. Series.
P96.D36 C66 2003

Communication and emotion : essays in honor of Dolf Zillmann / edited by Jennings Bryant, David Roskos-Ewoldsen, Joanne Cantor. Mahwah, N.J. ; London : Lawrence Erlbaum, c2003. vii, 610 p. : ill. ; 24 cm. (LEA communication series) Includes bibliographical references and indexes. ISBN 0-8058-4032-X (c : alk. paper) DDC 302.2
1. Interpersonal communication. 2. Communication. 3. Emotions. I. Zillmann, Dolf. II. Bryant, Jennings. III. Roskos-Ewoldsen, David R. IV. Cantor, Joanne. V. Series: LEA's communication series.
BF637.C45 C6375 2003

COMMUNICATION AND POLITICS. See **COMMUNICATION - POLITICAL ASPECTS.**

COMMUNICATION AND SEX.
Hopper, Robert. Gendering talk. East Lansing : Michigan State University Press, c2003.
HQ1075 .H67 2003

COMMUNICATION AND TECHNOLOGY.
Communication and cyberspace. 2nd ed. Creskill, N.J. : Hampton Press, c2003.
P96.D36 C66 2003

COMMUNICATION AND THE ARTS.
Kommunikation, Kunst und Kultur. Bern ; New York : Peter Lang, c2002.

COMMUNICATION AND TRAFFIC. See **AERONAUTICS.**

COMMUNICATION AND TRAFFIC - LAW AND LEGISLATION.
Rahnasto, Ilkka. Intellectual property rights, external effects, and antitrust law. Oxford ; New York : Oxford University Press, 2003.

COMMUNICATION - DATA PROCESSING.
Communication and cyberspace. 2nd ed. Creskill, N.J. : Hampton Press, c2003.
P96.D36 C66 2003

Communication et civilisation.
Debras, Sylvie. Lectrices au quotidien. Paris : L'Harmattan, c2003.

COMMUNICATION IN ECONOMIC DEVELOPMENT.
Flores Bedregal, Teresa. Comunicación para el desarrollo sostenible. La Paz : Plural Editores : LIDEMA : Konrad-Adenauer-Stiftung, c2002.

COMMUNICATION IN MANAGEMENT.
Lindgren, Mats, 1959- Scenario planning. Houndmills [England] ; New York : Palgrave Macmillan, 2002.
HD30.28 .L543 2002

Walton, Mark S., 1950- Generating buy-in. New York : American Management Association, c2004.

HD30.3 .W35 2004

COMMUNICATION IN MARKETING. See **ADVERTISING.**

COMMUNICATION IN MARRIAGE.
Gray, John, 1948- [Men are from Mars, women are from Venus. Spanish] Els homes són de Mart, les dones són de Venus. 1. ed. Barcelona : Edicions 62, c2001.

COMMUNICATION IN MEDICINE. See **MEDICAL RECORDS.**

COMMUNICATION IN ORGANIZATIONS.
La comunicazione nei processi sociali e organizzativi. Nuova ed. aggiornata. Milano, Italy : FrancoAngeli, [2001?], c1997.

Implementing collaboration technologies in industry. London ; New York : Springer, c2003.
HD30.2 .I38 2003

Text/work. London ; New York : Routledge, 2003.

COMMUNICATION IN POLITICS. See **MASS MEDIA - POLITICAL ASPECTS.**

COMMUNICATION IN POLITICS - CHINA.
Political communications in greater China. London ; New York : RoutledgeCurzon, 2003.
JF1525.C59 P65 2003

COMMUNICATION IN POLITICS - GERMANY.
Die Politik der Massenmedien. Köln : Halem, 2001.

COMMUNICATION IN POLITICS - HONG KONG (CHINA).
Political communications in greater China. London ; New York : RoutledgeCurzon, 2003.
JF1525.C59 P65 2003

COMMUNICATION IN POLITICS - TAIWAN.
Political communications in greater China. London ; New York : RoutledgeCurzon, 2003.
JF1525.C59 P65 2003

COMMUNICATION IN PSYCHOLOGY - HANDBOOKS, MANUALS, ETC.
Mitchell, Mark L. Writing for psychology. 1st ed. Australia ; Belmont, CA : Wadsworth/Thomson, 2004.
BF76.7 .M58 2004

COMMUNICATION IN THE ENVIRONMENTAL SCIENCES.
Flores Bedregal, Teresa. Comunicación para el desarrollo sostenible. La Paz : Plural Editores : LIDEMA : Konrad-Adenauer-Stiftung, c2002.

COMMUNICATION IN THE FAMILY.
Wallat, Cynthia. Family-institution interaction. New York : P. Lang, c2002.
HQ755.85 .W35 2002

COMMUNICATION, INTERCULTURAL. See **INTERCULTURAL COMMUNICATION.**

COMMUNICATION - PHILOSOPHY.
Comunicação e corporeidades. Brazil : Editora Universitaria : Compas, 2000.

Habermas, Jürgen. Kommunikatives Handeln und detranszendentalisierte Vernunft. Stuttgart : Reclam, c2001.
P91 .H33 2001

Roehle, Friedrich, 1916-1995. Die Struktur des Bewusstseins. Frankfurt am Main ; New York : Peter Lang, c2001.

COMMUNICATION POLICY. See **INFORMATION POLICY; LANGUAGE POLICY.**

COMMUNICATION - POLITICAL ASPECTS - ISRAEL.
Rowland, Robert C., 1954- Shared land/conflicting identity. East lansing : Michigan State University Press, 2002.
DS119.7 .R685 2003

COMMUNICATION, PRIMITIVE. See **COMMUNICATION.**

COMMUNICATION - PSYCHOLOGICAL ASPECTS. See also **INTERPERSONAL COMMUNICATION.**
Lumsden, Gay. Communicating with credibility and confidence. 2nd ed. Australia ; Belmont, CA : Thomson/Wadsworth, c2003.
BF637.C45 L85 2003

Morton, Adam. The importance of being understood. London ; New York : Routledge, 2003.

BF637.C45 M65 2003

Psychologie des Internet. Wien : WUV, Universitätsverlag, 2001.
BF637.C45 P759 2001

Psychology and the Internet. San Diego, Calif. : Academic Press, c1998.
BF637.C45 P79 1998

Tvorogova, N. D. (Nadezhda Tvorogova) Obshchenie. Moskva : Smysl, 2002.
BF637.C45 T88 2002

COMMUNICATION - RELIGIOUS ASPECTS - CHRISTIANITY. See **IMAGE (THEOLOGY).**

COMMUNICATION - SEX DIFFERENCES.
Hopper, Robert. Gendering talk. East Lansing : Michigan State University Press, c2003.
HQ1075 .H67 2003

COMMUNICATION - SOCIAL ASPECTS.
Chazal, Gérard. Interfaces. Seyssel [France] : Champ Vallon, c2002.
HM1111 .C49 2002

Huls, Erica. Dilemma's in menselijke interactie. Utrecht : Lemma, 2001.

Jansen, Sue Curry. Critical communication theory. Lanham, Md. ; Oxford : Rowman & Littlefield, c2002.
HM651 .J36 2002

COMMUNICATION - SOCIAL ASPECTS - GUATEMALA.
Guoron Ajquijay, Pedro. Retomemos la palabra--. Guatemala, Guatemala : Editorial Saqil Tzij, 1995.

COMMUNICATION SYSTEMS, COMPUTER. See **COMPUTER NETWORKS.**

COMMUNICATION WITH THE DEAD. See **SPIRITUALISM.**

COMMUNICATIONS INDUSTRIES. See **COMMUNICATION AND TRAFFIC.**

A communion of friendship.
Daniell, Beth, 1947- Carbondale : Southern Illinois University Press, c2003.
PE1405.U6 D36 2003

COMMUNISM. See also **SOCIALISM.**
Vazeilles, José Gabriel. Platonismo, marxismo y comunicación social. Buenos Aires : Editorial Biblos, c2002.

Žižek, Slavoj, 1949- [Fragile absolute. Spanish] El frágil absoluto, o, Por qué merece la pena luchar por el legado cristiano? 1. ed. Valencia : Pre-Textos, 2002.
BT1102 .Z58

COMMUNISM AND CHRISTIANITY.
Žižek, Slavoj, 1949- [Fragile absolute. Spanish] El frágil absoluto, o, Por qué merece la pena luchar por el legado cristiano? 1. ed. Valencia : Pre-Textos, 2002.
BT1102 .Z58

COMMUNISM AND CULTURE.
Historical materialism and social evolution. New York : Palgrave Macmillan, 2002.
HX523 .H565 2002

COMMUNISM AND PSYCHOLOGY. See **CRITICAL PSYCHOLOGY.**

COMMUNISM AND PSYCHOLOGY - PERIODICALS.
[Critical psychology (Lawrence & Wishart)] Critical psychology. London : Lawrence & Wishart, c2001-
BF39.9 .C75

COMMUNISM AND SOCIETY.
Historical materialism and social evolution. New York : Palgrave Macmillan, 2002.
HX523 .H565 2002

COMMUNISM - HISTORY.
Wilson, Edmund, 1895-1972. To the Finland station. New York : New York Review of Books, 2003.
HX36 .W5 2003

COMMUNIST ETHICS.
Luo, Guojie. [Selections. 2000] Luo Guojie wen ji. Di 1 ban. Baoding Shi : Hebei da xue chu ban she, 2000.
BJ1390 .L892 2000

COMMUNIST MOVEMENTS. See **COMMUNISM.**

COMMUNITY ACTION. See **POLITICAL PARTICIPATION.**

Community and agency counseling.
Gladding, Samuel T. 2nd ed. Upper Saddle River, N.J. : Pearson : Merrill Prentice Hall, c2004.

Community antenna television

BF637.C6 G528 2004

COMMUNITY ANTENNA TELEVISION. *See* **CABLE TELEVISION.**

COMMUNITY CENTERS. *See* **PLAYGROUNDS.**

COMMUNITY - HISTORY - TO 1500.
The construction of communities in the early Middle Ages. Leiden ; Boston : Brill, 2003.
HN11 .C66 2003

COMMUNITY IDENTITY. *See* **GROUP IDENTITY.**

COMMUNITY LIFE. *See* **NEIGHBORHOOD.**

COMMUNITY SURVEYS. *See* **SOCIAL SURVEYS.**

Como iniciar un nuevo proceso de paz en Colombia.
Al oído de Uribe. 1a. ed. Bogotá, Colombia : Editorial Oveja Negra, 2002.

Cómo me veo cuando estoy asustado.
Shepherd, Joanne. [What I look like when I am scared. Spanish & English] What I look like when I am scared = 1st ed. New York : Rosen Pub. Group's PowerKids Press, 2004.
BF723.F4 S5418 2004

Cómo me veo cuando estoy confundido.
Randolph, Joanne. [What I look like when I am confused. Spanish & English] What I look like when I am confused = 1st ed. New York : Rosen Pub. Group's PowerKids Press, 2004.
BF723.I63 R3618 2004

Cómo me veo cuando estoy contento.
Johansen, Heidi Leigh. [What I look like when I am happy. Spanish & English] What I look like when I am happy = 1st ed. New York : Rosen Pub. Group's, 2004.
BF723.H37 J6418 2004

Cómo me veo cuando estoy enojado.
Johansen, Heidi Leigh. [What I look like when I am angry. Spanish & English] What I look like when I am angry = 1st ed. New York : Rosen PowerKids Press, 2004.
BF723.A4 J6318 2004

Cómo me veo cuando estoy triste.
Randolph, Joanne. [What I look like when I am sad. Spanish & English] What I look like when I am sad = 1st ed. New York : Rosen Pub. Group's PowerKids Press, 2004.
BF723.S15 R3618 2004

Cómo narra el cine posmoderno.
Caballero, Rufo, 1966- Sedición en la pasarela. La Habana, Cuba : Editorial Arte y Literatura, c2001.

Como tratar a los bravucones.
Johnstone, Marianne. [Dealing with bullying. Spanish] New York : PowerKids Press, 2005.
BF637.B85 J6418 2005

Como tratar la ira.
Johnstone, Marianne. [Dealing with anger. Spanish] New York : PowerKids Press, 2005.
BF575.A5 J6418 2005

Como tratar las peleas.
Johnstone, Marianne. [Dealing with fighting. Spanish] New York : PowerKids Press, 2005.
BF637.I48 J6418 2005

Como tratar los insultos.
Johnstone, Marianne. [Dealing with insults. Spanish] New York : PowerKids Press, 2005.
BF637.V47 J6418 2005

COMPANIES. *See* **BUSINESS ENTERPRISES.**

Companies are people, too.
Fekete, Sandra. Hoboken, N.J. : John Wiley & Sons, c2003.
HD58.7 .F43 2003

COMPANIES, DANCE. *See* **DANCE COMPANIES.**

COMPANION ANIMALS. *See* **PETS.**

The companion species manifesto.
Haraway, Donna Jeanne. Chicago, Ill. : Prickly Paradigm ; Bristol : University Presses Marketing, 2003.

A companion to Gottfried von Strassburg's "Tristan" / edited by Will Hasty. Rochester, NY : Camden House, 2003. vi, 319 p. : ill. ; 24 cm. (Studies in German literature, linguistics, and culture) Includes bibliographical references and index. CONTENTS: Introduction: the challenge of Gottfried's Tristan / Will Hasty -- Humanism in the high Middle Ages: the case of Gottfried's Tristan / Alois Wolf -- Gottfried's Strasbourg: the city and its people / Michael S. Batts -- Gottfried's adaptation of the story of Riwalin and Blanscheflur / Danielle Buschinger -- This drink will be the death of you: interpreting the love potion in Gottfried's Tristan / Sidney M. Johnson -- God, religion, and ambiguity in Tristan / Nigel Harris -- The female figures in Gottfried's Tristan and Isolde / Ann Marie Rasmussen -- Performances of love: Tristan and Isolde at court / Will Hasty -- Duplicity and duplexity: the Isolde of the white hands sequence / Neil Thomas -- Between epic and lyric poetry: the originality of Gottfried's Tristan / Daniel Rocher -- History, fable and love: Gottfried, Thomas, and the matter of Britain / Adrian Stevens -- The medieval reception of Gottfried's Tristan / Marion E. Gibbs -- The modern conception of Gottfried's Tristan and the Medieval legend of Tristan and Isolde / Ulrich Müller. ISBN 1-57113-203-1 (alk. paper) DDC 831/.21
1. Gottfried, - von Strassburg, - 13th cent. - Tristan. 2. Tristan (Legendary character) - Romances - History and criticism. 3. Arthurian romances - History and criticism. I. Hasty, Will. II. Series: Studies in German literature, linguistics, and culture (Unnumbered)
PT1526 .C66 2003

Companion to the philosophers.
The world's great philosophers. Malden, MA : Blackwell Pub., 2003.
B29 .W69 2003

A companion to the worlds of the Renaissance / edited by Guido Ruggiero. Malden, MA : Blackwell Publishers, 2002. xii, 561 p. ; 26 cm. (Blackwell companions to history) Includes bibliographical references (p. [506]-542) and index. ISBN 0-631-21524-7 (alk. paper) DDC 940.2/1
1. Renaissance. 2. Renaissance - Italy. 3. Power (Social sciences) - Italy. 4. Power (Social sciences) - Europe. 5. Europe - Economic conditions - 16th century. 6. Italy - Civilization - 1268-1559. 7. Europe - Social conditions - 16th century. 8. Italy - Social conditions - 1268-1559. 9. Italy - Intellectual life - 1268-1559. I. Ruggiero, Guido, 1944- II. Series.
CB367 .C65 2002

A companion to Yi jing numerology and cosmology.
Nielsen, Bent. London ; New York : RoutledgeCurzon, 2003.

A company of citizens.
Manville, Brook, 1950- Boston : Harvard Business School Press, c2003.
HD58.7 .M3714 2003

COMPANY OFFICERS. *See* **EXECUTIVES.**

Comparative Asian studies
(21) Time matters. Amsterdam : VU University Press, 2001.
BF468 .T555 2001

COMPARATIVE BEHAVIOR. *See* **PSYCHOLOGY, COMPARATIVE.**

COMPARATIVE GRAMMAR. *See* **GRAMMAR, COMPARATIVE AND GENERAL.**

Comparative historical analysis in the social sciences / edited by James Mahoney, Dietrich Rueschemeyer. Cambridge, U.K. ; New York : Cambridge University Press, 2003. xix, 444 p. : ill. ; 24 cm. (Cambridge studies in comparative politics) Includes bibliographical references and index. CONTENTS: Comparative-historical analysis: achievements and agendas / James Mahoney and Dietrich Rueschemeyer -- Comparative-historical analysis and knowledge accumulation in the study of revolutions / Jack A. Goldstone -- What we know about the development of social policy : comparative and historical research in comparative and historical perspective / Edwin Amenta -- Knowledge accumulation in comparative-historical research : the case of democracy and authoritarianism / James Mahoney -- Big, slow-moving, and ... invisible : macro-social processes in the study of comparative politics / Paul Pierson -- How institutions evolve : insights from comparative historical analysis / Kathleen Thelen -- Uses of network tools in comparative historical research / Roger V. Gould -- Periodization and preferences : reflections on purposive action in comparative historical social science / Ira Katznelson -- Can one or a few cases yield theoretical gains? / Dietrich Rueschemeyer -- Strategies of causal assessment in comparative historical analysis / James Mahoney -- Aligning ontology and methodology in comparative politics / Peter A. Hall -- Doubly engaged social science : the promise of comparative historical analysis / Theda Skocpol. ISBN 0-521-81610-6 ISBN 0-521-01645-2 (pb.) DDC 300/.7/22
1. Social sciences - Research - Methodology. I. Mahoney, James, 1968- II. Rueschemeyer, Dietrich. III. Series.
H61 .C524 2003

COMPARATIVE LITERATURE. *See* **LITERATURE, COMPARATIVE.**

COMPARATIVE PSYCHOLOGY. *See* **PSYCHOLOGY, COMPARATIVE.**

COMPARATIVE RELIGION. *See* **RELIGIONS.**

Compass of the soul.
Giannini, John L., 1921- Gainesville, Fla. : Center for Applications of Psychological Type, 2003.
BF698.3 .G53 2003

Compassion.
Krieglstein, Werner J., 1941- Amsterdam ; New York : Rodopi, c2002.

COMPASSION.
Lampert, Khen. Compassionate education. Lanham, Md. : University Press of America, c2003.

Compassion and remorse.
Tudor, Steven. Leuven ; Sterling, Va. : Peeters, 2001.
BJ1475 .T84 2001

COMPASSION - RELIGIOUS ASPECTS - BUDDHISM.
Thubten Chodron, 1950- Working with anger. Ithaca, NY : Snow Lion Publication, 2001.
BQ4430.A53 T48 2001

A compassionate conservative.
Kenneally, James J. (James Joseph), 1929- Lanham, Md. : Lexington Books, c2003.
E748.M375 K46 2003

Compassionate education.
Lampert, Khen. Lanham, Md. : University Press of America, c2003.

COMPENSATION FOR VICTIMS OF CRIME. *See* **REPARATION.**

COMPENSATION (PHYSIOLOGY). *See* **ADAPTATION (PHYSIOLOGY).**

COMPENSATORY EDUCATION - UNITED STATES - LONGITUDINAL STUDIES.
Hodges, Carolyn R., 1947- Making schools work. New York : P. Lang, c2003.
LC213.2 .H63 2003
1. Black author.

COMPETENCE. *See* **PERFORMANCE.**

COMPETITION.
Beyond Keynes. Cheltenham ; Northampton, Mass. : Edward Elgar, c2002.

Krames, Jeffrey A. The Jack Welch lexicon of leadership. 1st ed. New York : McGraw-Hill, 2001, c2002.
HD57.7 .K726 2001

McAfee, R. Preston. Competitive solutions. Princeton, N.J. : Princeton University Press, c2002.
HD30.28 .M3815 2002

Competition in the U.S. aircraft manufacturing industry.
United States. Congress. House. Committee on Transportation and Infrastructure. Subcommittee on Aviation. Washington : U.S. G.P.O. : For sale by the Supt. of Docs., U.S. G.P.O., [Congressional Sales Office], 2001.

United States. Congress. House. Committee on Transportation and Infrastructure. Subcommittee on Aviation. Competition in the U.S. aircraft manufacturing industry. Washington : U.S. G.P.O. : For sale by the Supt. of Docs., U.S. G.P.O., [Congressional Sales Office], 2001.

COMPETITION, INTERNATIONAL - PSYCHOLOGICAL ASPECTS.
Glendinning, Chellis. Off the map. Gabriola Island, BC : New Society Publishers, c2002.
HF1414 .G553 2002

COMPETITION, INTERNATIONAL - UNITED STATES.
Rosenau, Pauline Vaillancourt. The competition paradigm. Lanham, Md. ; Oxford : Rowman & Littlefield, c2003.
BF637.C47 R67 2003

The competition paradigm.
Rosenau, Pauline Vaillancourt. Lanham, Md. ; Oxford : Rowman & Littlefield, c2003.
BF637.C47 R67 2003

COMPETITION (PSYCHOLOGY).
Barash, David P. The survival game. 1st ed. New York : Times Books, 2003.
HM1111 .B37 2003

Goffen, Rona, 1944- Renaissance rivals. New Haven : University Press, c2002.
N6915 .G54 2002

Reichholf, Josef. Warum wir siegen wollen. München : Deutscher Taschenbuch, c2001.

Rosenau, Pauline Vaillancourt. The competition paradigm. Lanham, Md. ; Oxford : Rowman & Littlefield, c2003.
BF637.C47 R67 2003

COMPETITION - UNITED STATES.
Fisher, Peter S. Industrial incentives. Kalamazoo, Mich. : W.E. Upjohn Institute for Employment Research, 1998.
HF5549.5.I5 F57 1998

Hecker, JayEtta Z. Commercial aviation [electronic resource]. [Washington, D.C.] : U.S. General Accounting Office, [2002]

Jonnes, Jill, 1952- Empires of light. 1st ed. New York : Random House, c2003.
TK18 .J66 2003

Rosenau, Pauline Vaillancourt. The competition paradigm. Lanham, Md. ; Oxford : Rowman & Littlefield, c2003.
BF637.C47 R67 2003

United States. Congress. House. Committee on Energy and Commerce. Subcommittee on Health. Examining issues related to competition in the pharmaceutical marketplace. Washington : U.S. G.P.O. : For sale by the Supt. of Docs., U.S. G.P.O. [Congressional Sales Office], 2002.

United States. Congress. House. Committee on Energy and Commerce. Subcommittee on Telecommunications and the Internet. Health of the telecommunication sector. Washington : U.S. G.P.O. : For sale by the Supt. of Docs., U.S. G.P.O. [Congressional Sales Office], 2003.

United States. Congress. House. Committee on Energy and Commerce. Subcommittee on Telecommunications and the Internet. Health of the telecommunication sector. Washington : U.S. G.P.O. : For sale by the Supt. of Docs., U.S. G.P.O., [Congressional Sales Office], 2003.

United States. Congress. House. Committee on the Judiciary. Direct broadcast satellite service in the multichannel video distribution market. Washington : U.S. G.P.O. For sale by the Supt. of Docs., U.S. G.P.O. [Congressional Sales Office], 2003.

United States. Congress. House. Committee on the Judiciary. Federal Prison Industries Competition in Contracting Act of 2003. [Washington, D.C. : U.S. G.P.O., 2003]

United States. Congress. House. Committee on Transportation and Infrastructure. Subcommittee on Aviation. Competition in the U.S. aircraft manufacturing industry. Washington : U.S. G.P.O. : For sale by the Supt. of Docs., U.S. G.P.O., [Congressional Sales Office], 2001.

United States. Congress. House. Committee on Transportation and Infrastructure. Subcommittee on Aviation. The financial condition of the airline industry. Washington : U.S. G.P.O. : For sale by the Supt. of Docs., U.S. G.P.O. [Congressional Sales Office], 2002.

United States. Congress. Senate. Committee on Commerce, Science, and Transportation. Antitrust issues in the airline industry. Washington : U.S. G.P.O. : For sale by the Supt. of Docs., U.S. G.P.O., 2003.

United States. Congress. Senate. Committee on Commerce, Science, and Transportation. Subcommittee on Consumer Affairs, Foreign Commerce, and Tourism. Customer choice in automotive repair shops. Washington : U.S. G.P.O. : For sale by the Supt. of Docs., U.S. G.P.O., [Congressional Sales Office], 2003.

United States. Congress. Senate. Committee on the Judiciary. Subcommittee on Antitrust, Business Rights, and Competition. Dominance in the sky. [Washington] : U.S. G.P.O. : For sale by the Supt. of Docs., U.S. G.P.O. [Congressional Sales Office], 2003.

United States. Congress. Senate. Committee on the Judiciary. Subcommittee on Antitrust, Business Rights, and Competition. Dominance on the ground. Washington : U.S. G.P.O. : For sale by the Supt. of Docs., U.S. G.P.O. [Congressional Sales Office], 2003.

United States. General Accounting Office. Federal Trade Commission [electronic resource]. [Washington, D.C.] : U.S. General Accounting Office, [2002]

United States. General Accounting Office. Telecommunications [electronic resource].

[Washington, D.C.] : U.S. General Accounting Office, [2003]

United States. General Accounting Office. Telecommunications [electronic resource]. Washington, D.C. : U.S. General Accounting Office, [2002]

COMPETITIVE BEHAVIOR. *See* **COMPETITION (PSYCHOLOGY).**

Competitive solutions.
McAfee, R. Preston. Princeton, N.J. : Princeton University Press, c2002.
HD30.28 .M3815 2002

COMPETITIVENESS (ECONOMICS). *See* **COMPETITION.**

COMPETITIVENESS (PSYCHOLOGY). *See* **COMPETITION (PSYCHOLOGY).**

Complaining, teasing, and other annoying behaviors.
Kowalski, Robin M. New Haven : Yale University Press, c2003.
HM1106 .K69 2003

The complete book of dowsing.
Applegate, George. Shaftesbury, Dorset ; Rockport, Mass. : Element, c1997.
BF1628 .A67 1997

The complete book of sex magic.
Ashley, Leonard R. N. Fort Lee, NJ : Barricade Books, 2003.
BF1623.S4 A85 2002

Complete book of witchcraft.
Buckland, Raymond. [Complete book of witchcraft] Buckland's complete book of witchcraft. 2nd ed., rev. & expanded. St. Paul, Minn. : Llewellyn Publications, 2002.
BF1566 .B76 2002

The complete color harmony.
Whelan, Bride M. Gloucester, Mass. : Rockport Publishers, 2004.
BF789.C7 W47 20041

The complete gods and goddesses of ancient Egypt.
Wilkinson, Richard H. New York : Thames & Hudson, 2003.

A complete guide to divination.
Eason, Cassandra. [Complete book of divination] London : Piatkus, 1998 (2002 [printing])

The complete guide to divination.
Eason, Cassandra. Berkeley, Calif. : Crossing Press, 2003.
BF1751 .E27 2003

The complete guide to mental health for women / edited by Lauren Slater, Jessica Henderson Daniel, and Amy Elizabeth Banks. 1st ed. Boston : Beacon Press, c2003. ix, 403 p. : ill. ; 29 cm. Includes bibliographical references (p. 383-388) and index. Publisher description URL: http://www.loc.gov/catdir/description/hm031/2003010436.html CONTENTS: Late adolescence and early adulthood / Jennifer Coon-Wallman -- Pregnancy as a life passage / Karen Propp -- Living with infertility / Angel Seibring -- Becoming a mother / Bonnie Ohye, Cynthia W. Moore, and Ellen Braaten -- Adoption / Kunya S. Desjardins -- Choosing childlessness / Lisa Dierbeck -- Issues for women in middle age / Janet Shibley Hyde -- The fires of menopause / Nadine Boughton -- Older adulthood / Silvia Sara Canetto -- A guide to grief and bereavement / Laurie Rosenblatt -- How do we define sexual health for women? / Deborah L. Tolman, Meg I. Striepe, and Lucia F. O'Sullivan -- Female sexuality / Audrey Schulman -- Growth in connection / Judith V. Jordan, Amy Elizabeth Banks, and Maureen Walker -- Women of color and relationships / Beverly Greene -- Intimate relationships / Janis V. Sanchez-Hucles -- Adjusting to divorce / Joy K. Rice -- Anger / Lyn Mikel Brown and Dana Crowley Jack -- Women and trauma / Laura S. Brown -- Domestic violence / Carole Sousa, Lisa A. Tieszen, and Janet Yassen -- Sexual abuse and rape / Thema Bryant-Davis -- Child abuse, neglect, and maltreatment / Priscilla Dass-Brailsford -- Terrorism / Nancy Lynn Baker -- The impact of chronic and debilitating illnesses on women's mental health / Dana L. Comstock -- Poverty and women's mental health / Karen Fraser Wyche -- Racism and mental health / Beverly Greene -- Anxiety disorders / Susan Mahler -- Depressive disorders / Susan Mahler -- Bipolar disorder / Nell Casey -- Post-traumatic stress disorder / Amy Elizabeth Banks -- Body image / Susan A. Basow -- Eating disorders and disconnections / Jane MacDonald -- Women and addictions / Kathryn Davis -- Schizophrenia / Susan Mahler -- Marriage and motherhood / Karen Propp -- Postpartum depression / Susan Kushner Resnick -- Menopause and psychiatric illness / Allyson Cherkasky -- Aging and its effects on mood, memory, the brain, and hormones / Mark N. Friedman -- Antidepressants / Susan Mahler -- Antianxiety medications / Susan Mahler --

Mood stabilizers / Martha Brown Martin -- Antipsychotic medications / Martha Brown Martin -- Polypharmacy / Amy Elizabeth Banks -- Medications in pregnancy / Lori Kaplowitz -- Complementary treatments for depression and anxiety / Laura Kramer -- Cognitive behavioral therapy / Susan J. Miller -- Dialectical behavior therapy / Elizabeth B. Simpson -- Eye movement desensitization and reprocessing (EMDR) / Patricia A. Geller -- Insight-oriented psychotherapy / Dale Young -- Group psychotherapy with women / Pratyusha Tummala-Narra and Lauren Slater -- How to find and choose a therapist / Jennifer Coon-Wallman -- What to expect from ethical psychotherapy / Melba J.T. Vasquez -- Questions to ask a psychiatrist / Amy Elizabeth Banks -- The importance of exercise and physical activity for women / Connie S. Chan -- Stress management for women / BraVada Garrett-Akinsanya -- Play / Deb Abramson -- Women and spirituality / G. Rita Dudley-Grant and Jessica Henderson Daniel. ISBN 0-8070-2924-6 (hbk. : alk. paper) ISBN 0-8070-2925-4 (pbk. : alk. paper) DDC 616.89/0082 1. Women - Mental health - United States. 2. Women - Mental health - Social aspects. 3. Feminist psychology. 4. Life cycle, Human. I. Slater, Lauren. II. Daniel, Jessica Henderson. III. Banks, Amy.
RC451.4.W6 C65 2003

The complete guide to psychic development.
Eason, Cassandra. Berkeley, Calif. : Crossing Press, c2003.
BF1031 .E295 2003

The complete idiot's guide to psychology.
Johnston, Joni E., 1960- 2nd ed. Indianapolis, IN : Alpha Books, c2003.
BF121 .J64 2003

The complete idiot's guide to Taoism.
Toropov, Brandon. Indianapolis, IN : Alpha, c2002.
BL1920 .T67 2002

The complete idiot's guide to tarot.
Tognetti, Arlene. 2nd ed. Indianapolis, IN : Alpha, c2003.
BF1879.T2 T64 2003

The complete idiot's guide to wicca and witchcraft.
Zimmermann, Denise. 2nd ed. Indianapolis, IN : Alpha, c2003.
BF1566 .Z55 2003

The complete Infinity walk.
Sunbeck, Deborah. Rochester, N.Y. : Leonardo Foundation Press, c2001-
BF318 .S86 2001

The complete live the James Bond lifestyle seminar.
Kyriazi, Paul. Los Angeles, CA : Ronin Books, c2002.
BF637.S8 K97 2002

The complete node book.
Burk, Kevin, 1967- 1st ed. St. Paul, Minn. : Llewellyn Publications, 2003.
BF1723 .B87 2003

Complex adaptive systems
Imitation in animals and artifacts. Cambridge, Mass. : MIT Press, c2002.
BF357 .I47 2002

Complex systems theory and development practice.
Rihani, Samir, 1938- London ; New York : Zed Books, 2002.
HB71 .R485 2002

COMPLEXION. *See* **BEAUTY, PERSONAL.**

COMPLEXITY (PHILOSOPHY).
Foley, Duncan K. Unholy trinity. London ; New York : Routledge, 2003.
HB135 .F65 2003

Orsucci, Franco. Changing mind. River Edge, NJ : World Scientific, c2002.
BF161 .O77 2002

Rihani, Samir, 1938- Complex systems theory and development practice. London ; New York : Zed Books, 2002.
HB71 .R485 2002

Rysev, Sergeĭ. Vyshe kryshi. Sankt-Peterburg : Gelikon Plius, 2001.
B105.C473 R97 2001

Sornette, D. Why stock markets crash. Princeton, N.J. : Princeton University Press, c2003.
HB3722 .S66 2003

COMPLIANCE. *See* **CONFORMITY.**

COMPLINE - HISTORY.
Verdon, Jean. [Nuit au Moyen Age. English] Night in the Middle Ages. Notre Dame, Ind. : University of Notre Dame Press, c2002.
HM1033 .V4713 2002

COMPOSERS - MENTAL HEALTH.
DiGaetani, John Louis, 1943- Wagner and suicide. Jefferson, N.C. : McFarland, c2003.
ML410.W13 D45 2003

COMPOSITION (ART).
Ivinskaia, A. (Anna) Svet prelomlennogo vremeni v ikonnom prostranstve. Moskva : Khristianskiĭ Vostok, 2002.
N8189.G72 I95 2002

Kuhn-Wengenmayr, Annemarie. Kompositionsfragen. Frankfurt ; New York : P. Lang, c2001.
N7430 .K826 2001

Weber, Jürgen, 1928- The judgement of the eye. Wien ; New York : Springer, c2002.
BF241 .W38 2002

COMPREHENSION. *See also* **LEARNING; LEARNING, PSYCHOLOGY OF; LISTENING; MEMORY.**
Grenzen des Verstehens. Göttingen : Vandenhoeck & Ruprecht, c2002.
BD181.5 .G74 2002

COMPREHENSION (THEORY OF KNOWLEDGE).
Conoscenza e cognizione. 1. ed. Milano : Guerini e associati, 2002.
BJ45.5 .C66 2002

Grenzen des Verstehens. Göttingen : Vandenhoeck & Ruprecht, c2002.
BD181.5 .G74 2002

Merrell, Floyd, 1937- Sensing corporeally. Toronto ; Buffalo : University of Toronto Press, c2003.
P99 .M477 2003

Comprehensive stress management.
Greenberg, Jerrold S. 8th ed. Boston : McGraw-Hill, [2003?]
BF575.S75 G66 2003

COMPULSIVE BEHAVIOR.
Corley, M. Deborah. Embracing recovery from chemical dependency. Sottsdale, AZ : Gentle Path Press, c2003.
BF632 .C63 2003

COMPULSIVE SHOPPING.
Lee, Michelle. Fashion victim. 1st ed. New York : Broadway Books, 2003.
GT524 .L44 2003

COMPULSORY STERILIZATION. *See* **STERILIZATION, EUGENIC.**

Computational developmental psychology.
Shultz, Thomas R. Cambridge, Mass. : MIT Press, c2003.
BF713 .S35 2003

Computationalism : new directions / edited by Matthias Scheutz. Cambridge, MA : MIT Press, c2002. xiii, 209 p. ; 24 cm. (Bradford book) Includes bibliographical references (p. [187]-198) and index. ISBN 0-262-19478-3 DDC 004
1. Computer science. 2. Artificial intelligence. I. Scheutz, Matthias. II. Title.

COMPUTER ALGORITHMS - CONGRESSES.
ALT 2002 (2002 : Lübeck, Germany) Algorithmic learning theory. Berlin ; New York : Springer, c2002.
QA76.9.A43 A48 2002

COMPUTER ART.
Reck, H. U. Mythos Medienkunst. Köln : König, c2002.

COMPUTER-BASED MULTIMEDIA INFORMATION SYSTEMS. *See* **MULTIMEDIA SYSTEMS.**

COMPUTER CHIPS. *See* **INTEGRATED CIRCUITS.**

COMPUTER COMMUNICATION SYSTEMS. *See* **COMPUTER NETWORKS.**

COMPUTER CRIMES. *See* **PRIVACY, RIGHT OF.**

COMPUTER GRAPHICS.
Pickover, Clifford A. Chaos in Wonderland. 1st ed. New York : St. Martin's Press, 1994.
Q172.5.C45 P53 1994

Verbruggen, Martien. Graphics programming with Perl. Greenwich : Manning, c2002.
T385 .V465 2002

Zhou, Xiang Sean. Exploration of visual data. Boston ; London : Kluwer Academic Publishers, c2003.
T385 .Z55 2003

COMPUTER HARDWARE. *See* **COMPUTERS.**
COMPUTER INDUSTRY. *See* **COMPUTERS.**
COMPUTER NETWORK PROTOCOLS. *See* **CGI (COMPUTER NETWORK PROTOCOL).**

COMPUTER NETWORK RESOURCES - EVALUATION.
Kelly, Brian, 1956- iSearch. Boston, MA : Allyn and Bacon, c2003.
BF76.78 .K45 2003

Web of deception. Medford, N.J : CyberAge Books, c2002.
ZA4201 .W43 2002

COMPUTER NETWORKS.
Communication and cyberspace. 2nd ed. Creskill, N.J. : Hampton Press, c2003.
P96.D36 C66 2003

Implementing collaboration technologies in industry. London ; New York : Springer, c2003.
HD30.2 .I38 2003

COMPUTER NETWORKS - PSYCHOLOGICAL ASPECTS.
Psychologie des Internet. Wien : WUV, Universitätsverlag, 2001.
BF637.C45 P759 2001

Psychology and the Internet. San Diego, Calif. : Academic Press, c1998.
BF637.C45 P79 1998

COMPUTER NETWORKS - SOCIAL ASPECTS.
Lovink, Geert. Uncanny networks. Cambridge, Mass. : MIT Press, c2002.
HM851 .L688 2002

COMPUTER PROGRAMMING.
Schmid, U. (Ute) Inductive synthesis of functional programs. Berlin ; New York : Springer, c2003.
QA76.6 .S3855 2003

COMPUTER PROGRAMMING - PSYCHOLOGICAL ASPECTS.
Kaluzniacky, Eugene. Managing psychological factors in information systems work. Hershey PA : Information Science Pub., c2004.
BF576 .K358 2004

COMPUTER SCIENCE.
Computationalism. Cambridge, MA : MIT Press, c2002.

COMPUTER SECURITY.
Schreck, Jorg. Security and privacy in user modeling. Dordrecht ; Boston ; London : Kluwer Academic Publishers, c2003.
QA76.9.A25 S353 2003

COMPUTER SIMULATION. *See* **DIGITAL COMPUTER SIMULATION; VIRTUAL REALITY.**

COMPUTER SOFTWARE. *See* **COMPUTERS.**

COMPUTER SOFTWARE - HUMAN FACTORS.
Fuller, Matthew. Behind the blip. Brooklyn, NY, USA : Autonomedia, c2003.
QA76.76.H85 F85 2003

COMPUTER SOFTWARE PROTECTION. *See* **SOFTWARE PROTECTION.**

Computer supported cooperative work
Crabtree, Andy. Designing collaborative systems. London ; [New York] : Springer, c2003.
QA76.9.S88 C725 2003

Designing information spaces. London ; New York : Springer, 2003.
QA76.9.C66 D49 2003

Implementing collaboration technologies in industry. London ; New York : Springer, c2003.
HD30.2 .I38 2003

Visualizing argumentation. London ; New York : Springer, 2003.
QA76.9.H85 V67 2003

COMPUTER SYSTEMS, VIRTUAL. *See* **VIRTUAL COMPUTER SYSTEMS.**

COMPUTER VISION.
Zhou, Xiang Sean. Exploration of visual data. Boston ; London : Kluwer Academic Publishers, c2003.
T385 .Z55 2003

COMPUTERS. *See also* **COMPUTER SOFTWARE.**
Khurmetbek, Khalikii͡n. Ül bichigdmėlüüd. Ulaanbaatar : "Monsudar" Khėvlėliĭn Gazar, 2001.

QA465 .K48 2001

COMPUTERS - ACCESS CONTROL. *See* **SOFTWARE PROTECTION.**

COMPUTERS AND CHILDREN.
Children in the digital age. Westport, Conn. : Praeger, 2002.
HQ784.M3 C455 2002

COMPUTERS AND CIVILIZATION.
Designing information spaces. London ; New York : Springer, 2003.
QA76.9.C66 D49 2003

Lovink, Geert. Uncanny networks. Cambridge, Mass. : MIT Press, c2002.
HM851 .L688 2002

Malvido Arriaga, Adriana. Por la vereda digital. 1. ed. México : CONACULTA (Consejo Nacional para la Cultura y las Artes), 1999.
QA76.9.C66 M35 1999

Piscitelli, Alejandro. Meta-cultura. Buenos Aires : La Crujía, 2002.
P96.T42 P575

COMPUTERS, ELECTRONIC. *See* **COMPUTERS.**
COMPUTERS - LAW AND LEGISLATION.
Essays for Colin Tapper. London : LexisNexis, 2003.

COMPUTERS - LAW AND LEGISLATION - UNITED STATES.
Brenden, Ann E. Persuasive computer presentations. Chicago, Ill. : Law Practice Management Section, American Bar Association, c2001.
KF320.A9 B74 2001

COMPUTING MACHINES (COMPUTERS). *See* **COMPUTERS.**

COMPUTUS. *See* **CALENDAR.**

Comrey, Andrew Laurence. Revised manual and handbook of interpretations for the Comrey Personality Scales / by Andrew L. Comrey. San Diego, Calif. : EdITS, c1995. vi, 90 p. ; 28 cm. Spine title: Comrey Personality Scales manual and handbook of interpretations. Includes bibliographical references (p. 81-86).
1. Comrey Personality Scales. I. Title. II. Title: Comrey Personality Scales III. Title: Comrey Personality Scales manual and handbook of interpretations
BF698.8.C66 C66 1995

Comrey Personality Scales.
Comrey, Andrew Laurence. Revised manual and handbook of interpretations for the Comrey Personality Scales. San Diego, Calif. : EdITS, c1995.
BF698.8.C66 C66 1995

COMREY PERSONALITY SCALES.
Comrey, Andrew Laurence. Revised manual and handbook of interpretations for the Comrey Personality Scales. San Diego, Calif. : EdITS, c1995.
BF698.8.C66 C66 1995

Comrey Personality Scales manual and handbook of interpretations.
Comrey, Andrew Laurence. Revised manual and handbook of interpretations for the Comrey Personality Scales. San Diego, Calif. : EdITS, c1995.
BF698.8.C66 C66 1995

Comstock, Kani. Journey into love : ten steps to wholeness / Kani Comstock & Marisa Thame. Ashland, OR : Willow Press, c2000. xi, 131 p. ; 22 cm. ISBN 0-9679186-4-2 DDC 177/.7
1. Love. 2. Self-actualization (Psychology) I. Thame, Marisa. II. Title.
BF575.L8 C647 2002

Comte-Sponville, André.
Conche, Marcel. Confession d'un philosophe. Paris : Albin Michel, c2003.
B804 .C66 2003

Comunicação e corporeidades / Antônio Fausto Neto, Antônio Hohlfeldt ... [et al.] (organizadores). Brazil : Editora Universitaria : Compas, 2000. 200 p. ; 21 cm. Includes bibliographical references. ISBN 85-237-0251-2
1. Communication - Philosophy. 2. Knowledge, Sociology of. I. Fausto Neto, Antônio. II. Hohlfeldt, Antônio.

Comunicación, democracia y neototalitarismo a comienzos del siglo XXI.
Reig, Ramón. El éxtasis cibernético. 1. ed. Madrid : Ediciones Libertarias, 2001.

Comunicación para el desarrollo sostenible.
Flores Bedregal, Teresa. La Paz : Plural Editores : LIDEMA : Konrad-Adenauer-Stiftung, c2002.

La comunicazione nei processi sociali e organizzativi / Assunto Quadrio, Lucia Venini (a cura di). Nuova ed. aggiornata. Milano, Italy :

FrancoAngeli, [2001?], c1997. 351 p. : ill. ; 23 cm. (Psicologia ; [136]) First ed. 1997, now updated. Includes bibliographical references. ISBN 88-464-2771-8 DDC 302
1. Communication. 2. Mass media. 3. Communication in organizations. I. Quadrio, Assunto. II. Venini, Lucia. III. Series: Serie di psicologia (Franco Angeli editore) ; 136.

CONATION. *See* **WILL.**

Concentration and technology in agricultural input industries [electronic resource].
King, John L. [Washington, D.C.] : U.S. Dept of Agriculture, [2001].

Concept of gender equality as a paradox in Nigeria's democratic experience.
Adeleke, Veronica I. Ikeja [Nigeria] : Dept. of Political Science and Sociology, Babcock University, 2002.

CONCEPTION - TECHNOLOGICAL INNOVATIONS. *See* **HUMAN REPRODUCTIVE TECHNOLOGY.**

Conceptions of the absurd.
Fotiade, Ramona. Oxford : Legenda, 2001.

El concepto de poder en Alain Touraine.
Benitez, Juan Carlos. Buenos Aires : Editorial de Belgrano, 2002.
HM479.T6 B455 2002

CONCEPTS IN INFANTS.
Mandler, Jean Matter. The foundations of mind. Oxford ; New York : Oxford University Press, 2004.
BF720.C63 M36 2004

Conceptual advances in brain research
(v. 6) Darlington, Cynthia L. The female brain. London ; New York : Taylor & Francis, c2002.
QP402 .D366 2002

Concerning children.
Gilman, Charlotte Perkins, 1860-1935. A reprint of the 1900 ed. / with an introduction by Michael S. Kimmel. Walnut Creek, CA : Rowman & Littlefield, c2003.
HQ769 .G5 2003

CONCERT ETIQUETTE.
Hagberg, Karen A., 1943- Stage presence from head to toe. Lanham, Md. : Scarecrow Press, 2003.
ML3795 .H13 2003

CONCERTS. *See* **MUSIC - PERFORMANCE.**

CONCERTS - HANDBOOKS, MANUALS, ETC.
Hagberg, Karen A., 1943- Stage presence from head to toe. Lanham, Md. : Scarecrow Press, 2003.
ML3795 .H13 2003

I concetti del male / a cura di Pier Paolo Portinaro. Torino : Einaudi, c2002. xxxiii, 388 p. : ill. ; 21 cm. (Biblioteca Einaudi ; 140) Includes bibliographical references and index. ISBN 88-06-13972-X DDC 111
1. Good and evil. 2. Immorality. 3. Suffering. 4. Theodicy. I. Portinaro, Pier Paolo, 1953- II. Series.

I concetti della fisica attraverso il tempo.
Di Silvestre, Ettore. Pisa : ETS, 2000.

Concetto e fondamento della filosofia.
Reinhold, Karl Leonhard, 1757-1823. [Ueber den Begriff der Philosophie. Italian] Roma : Edizioni di storia e letteratura, 2002.

Conche, Marcel. Confession d'un philosophe : réponses à André Comte-Sponville / Marcel Conche. Paris : Albin Michel, c2003. 279, [2] p. ; 23 cm. (Itinéraires du savoir) Includes bibliographical references (p. 279-[281]) and index. ISBN 2-226-13628-2 DDC 194
1. Philosophy, Modern - 20th century. I. Comte-Sponville, André. II. Title. III. Series.
B804 .C66 2003

Conciencia de América Latina.
Britto García, Luis. 1. ed. Caracas, Venezuela : Editorial Nueva Sociedad, [2002]

The concise Corsini encyclopedia of psychology and behavioral science / W. Edward Craighead and Charles B. Nemeroff, editors. 3rd ed. Hoboken, NJ : John Wiley & Sons, 2004. p. cm. Rev. ed. of: Concise encyclopedia of psychology. c1996. Includes bibliographical references and index. ISBN 0-471-22036-1 (cloth) DDC 150/.3
1. Psychology - Encyclopedias. I. Craighead, W. Edward. II. Nemeroff, Charles B. III. Title: Concise encyclopedia of psychology.
BF31 .E52 2004

Concise encyclopedia of psychology.
The concise Corsini encyclopedia of psychology and behavioral science. 3rd ed. Hoboken, NJ : John Wiley & Sons, 2004.
BF31 .E52 2004

CONCRETE INTELLIGENCE. *See* **MECHANICAL ABILITY.**

CONDITIONAL STATEMENTS (LOGIC). *See* **CONDITIONALS (LOGIC).**

CONDITIONALITY (INTERNATIONAL RELATIONS).
Boyce, James K. Investing in peace. Oxford : Oxford University Press, 2002.

CONDITIONALS (LOGIC).
Artman, Lavee. ha-Nisayon ha-yomyomi u-fitron heseḳe tenai ya-hakhalah lo-teḳefim. [Israel : ḥ. mo. l., 1999?]

CONDITIONED RESPONSE. *See also* **REINFORCEMENT (PSYCHOLOGY).**
Pryor, Karen, 1932- On behavior. 1st ed. North Bend, Wash. : Sunshine Books, c1995.
BF637.B4 P68 1995

Condon, Margaret E. Exercises in psychological testing / Margaret E. Condon, Lisa A. Hollis-Sawyer, George C. Thornton, III. Boston : Allyn and Bacon, c2002. viii, 305p. : ill. ; 28 cm. Earlier ed. entered under: Thornton, George C., 1940- ISBN 0-205-33787-2 DDC 150/.28/7
1. Psychological tests - Problems, exercises, etc. I. Hollis-Sawyer, Lisa A., 1963- II. Thornton, George C., 1940- III. Title.
BF176 .T47 2002

CONDUCT OF LIFE. *See also* **BROTHERLINESS; FORGIVENESS; FRIENDSHIP; MODESTY; PATIENCE; SUCCESS.**
Brenner, Andreas. Lexikon der Lebenskunst. Leipzig : Reclam-Verlag, 2002.

Bstan-'dzin-rgya-mtsho, Dalai Lama XIV, 1935- Reflections from the journey of life. Berkeley, Calif. : North Atlantic Books, c2002.
BQ5670 .B76 2002

Burkhart, Dagmar. Ehre. Originalausg. München : Deutscher Taschenbuch Verlag, c2002.
BJ1533.H8 B87 2002

Byock, Ira. The four things that matter most. New York : Free Press, 2004.
BF637.C45 B93 2004

Cai, Yuanpei, 1868-1940. [Selections. 1996] Cai Yuanpei juan. Di 1 ban. Shijiazhuang Shi : Hebei jiao yu chu ban she, 1996.
BJ117 .T74 1996 <Asian China>

Candido, Antonio. O nobre. São Paulo : Imprensa Oficial do Estado, 2002.
BJ1533.N6 C36 2002

Chetkin, Len. 100 thoughts that lead to happiness. Charlottesville, VA : Hampton Roads Pub., c2002.
BF637.C5 C477 2002

Confucius. [Selections. Chinese & English. 1998] Kong Meng ren sheng ge yan ji cui. Wuhan : Wuhan gong ye da xue chu ban she, 1998.

Corrigan, Patricia, 1948- Convertible dreams. 1st ed. St. Louis, MO : Virginia Pub., c2001.
BF637.C5 C675 2001

Dobson, James C., 1936- Life on the edge. Nashville : Word Pub., c2000.
BF637.L53 D63 2000

Dorff, Elliot N. Love your neighbor and yourself. 1st ed. Philadelphia, PA : Jewish Publication Society, 2003.
BJ1285 .D67 2003

Eldershaw, Jane. The little book of moods. Avon, MA : Adams Media, 2004.
BF637.C5 E383 2004

Eyal, Tsevi. Mi she-ta'am yayin Hungari. Tel Aviv : Yedi'ot aharonot : Sifre ḥemed, c2002.

Fabelo Corzo, José Ramón. Los valores y sus desafíos actuales. Puebla : Universidad Autónoma de Puebla, 2001.

Feng, Youlan, 1895- Xin shi xun. Di 1 ban. Beijing : Beijing da xue chu ban she : Jing xiao zhe Xin hua shu dian, 1996.
BJ1588.C5 F42 1996 <Asian China>

Fridman, Aharon (Aharon ben Yehoshu'a) [Gam atah yakhol. Yiddish] Du ḳenst oykh!. Nyu Yorḳ : Lev Yiśroel, 762, 2002.

Gawain, Shakti, 1948- The path of transformation. Rev. ed. Novato, Calif. : Nataraj Pub., 2000.
BJ1581 .G35 2000

Gawain, Shakti, 1948- Reflections in the light. Rev. ed. Novato, Calif. : Nataraj Pub., c2003.

BF637.S4 G393 2003

Gendt, Anne-Marie Emma Alberta de, 1952- L'art d'éduquer les nobles damoiselles. Paris : Champion, 2003.

Gomes, Peter J. The good life. 1st ed. San Francisco : HarperSanFrancisco, c2002.
BJ1581.2 .G575 2002

Goodier, Steve. Lessons of the turtle. Divide, CO : Life Support System Pub., c2002.
BF637.C5 G67 2002

Goodier, Steve. A life that makes a difference. 1st ed. Divide, CO : Life Support System Pub., c2002.
BF637.C5 G68 2002

Heuscher, Julius E. (Julius Ernest), 1918- Psychology, folklore, creativity, and the human dilemma. Springfield, Ill. : Charles C Thomas Publisher, c2003.
BF637.C5 H475 2003

Hong, Zicheng, fl. 1596. [Cai gen tan] Dao jie cai gen tan. Di 1 ban. Beijing Shi : Zong jiao wen hua chu ban she, 1996 (1997 printing)
BJ1558.C5 H85 1996 <Asian China>

Hong, Zicheng, fl. 1596. [Cai gen tan] Ru jie cai gen tan. Di 1 ban. Beijing Shi : Zong jiao wen hua chu ban she, 1996 (1997 printing)
BJ1558.C5 H85 1996b <Asian China>

Kimball, Cheryl. Horse wise. Boston, MA : Conari Press, 2004.
BF637.C5 K55 2004

Kipfer, Barbara Ann. Instant karma. New York : Workman Pub., c2003.
BF637.C5 K56 2003

Kirshenbaum, Mira. Everything happens for a reason. New York : Harmony Books, 2004.
BF637.L53 K57 2004

Leary, Mark R. The curse of the self. New York : Oxford University Press, 2004.
BF697 .L33 2004

Lippe, Toinette, 1939- Nothing left over. New York : J.P. Tarcher/Putnam, c2002.
BJ1496 .L57 2002

Louden, Jennifer. Comfort secrets for busy women. Naperville, Ill. : Sourcebooks, c2003.
BF637.C5 L676 2003

Madhubuti, Haki R., 1942- Tough notes. 1st ed. Chicago : Third World Press, c2002.
E185.86 .T68 2002
1. Black author.

Meiners, Cheri J., 1957- When I feel afraid. Minneapolis, MN : Free Spirit Pub., 2003.
BF723.F4 M45 2003

Merdalor, Jean. Pensées mortelles. Port-au-Prince, Haiti : Editions Choucoune, 1999.
1. Black author.

Murray, Karel, 1954- Straight talk. Portland, Or. : Arnica Pub., c2003.
BF637.C5 M87 2003

Prather, Hugh. Standing on my head. Boston, MA : Conari Press, 2004.
BF637.C5 P82 2004

Reynolds, David K. A handbook for constructive living. Honolulu : University of Hawaii Press, 2002.
RC489.M65 R438 2002

Robinson, Edward Jewitt. Tamil wisdom. New Delhi : Asian Educational Services, 2001.
BJ1571 .R63 2001

Rutledge, Thom. Embracing fear. 1st ed. [San Francisco] : HarperSanFrancisco, c2002.
BF575.F2 R88 2002

Rutlen, Carmen Richardson, 1948- Dancing naked-- in fuzzy red slippers. 1st ed. Fort Bragg, CA : Cypress House, c2003.
BF637.S4 R877 2003

Sardello, Robert J., 1942- Facing the world with soul. 2nd ed. Great Barrington, MA : Lindisfarne Books, c2003.
BF637.C5 S27 2003

Scheunemann, Pam, 1955- Dealing with bullies. Edina, MN : Abdo Pub., 2004.
BF637.B85 S37 2004

The search for a holistic approach to human existence and development. [Nigeria?] : Osigwe Anyiam-Osigwe Foundation, [1999?]

Conduct of life

B53 .E46 1999

Sheng yu xiang jie. Di 1 ban. [Peking] : Xian zhuang shu ju, 1995.
BJ117 .S486 1995 <Orien China>

Shi, Lin. Zhi xin jing. Di 1 ban. Beijing : Zhongguo yan shi chu ban she, 1999.
DS758.23.T74 S522 1999

Shi, Sheng. Fan Zhongyan li shen xing shi jiu jiu fang lüe. Di 1 ban. Beijing : Zhongguo xi ju chu ban she, 2001.
DS751.6.F3 S5 2001

Sima, Lieren. Tong jing. Di 1 ban. Beijing : Zhongguo hua qiao chu ban she, 2002.
DS758.23.T74 S575 2002

Simple joys. Boulder, Colo. : Blue Mountain Arts, Inc., c2003.
BF637.C5 S5443 2003

Simplicius, of Cilicia. [Commentarius in Enchiridion Epicteti. 1-26. English] On Epictetus' "Handbook 1-26". Ithaca, N.Y. : Cornell University Press, 2002.
B561.M523 S5613 2002

Sims, Robert Vincent. Lifting the mind fog. [S.l.] : Garden Rebel Books, c1996.
BF637.C5 S5444 1996

Smith, Maureen (Maureen J.), 1947- The ABCs of full tilt living. Boston, MA : Red Wheel/Weiser, 2003.
BF637.C5 S5449 2003

Tabensky, Pedro Alexis, 1964- Happiness. Aldershot, Hampshire, England ; Burlington, VT : Ashgate, c2003.
BJ1481 .T25 2003

Taofen, 1895-1944. Taofen "Du zhe xin xiang". Di 1 ban. Beijing : Zhongguo cheng shi chu ban she, 1998.

Thurnherr, Urs. Vernetzte Ethik. Freiburg : Alber, 2001.

Tubali, Shy. [Selections] Boḳer ṭov 'olam. Tel Aviv : Yedi'ot aḥaronot : Sifre ḥemed, c2003.

Vieira, Anselmo, 1923- Ser ou não ter. Lisboa : Roma Editora, [2002]-

Weinstein, Matt. Dogs don't bite when a growl will do. 1st ed. New York : Perigee, 2003.
BF637.C5 W445 2003

Woods, Earl, 1932- Start something. New York : Simon & Schuster, c2000.
BJ1631 .W726 2000

Yan, Zhitui, 531-591. Yan shi jia xun zhu ping. Di 1 ban. Beijing Shi : Xue yuan chu ban she, 2000.
BJ117 .Y4 2000

Yazi. Qing hua Bei da xue bu dao. Di 1 ban. Beijing : Xin hua chu ban she, 2002.
BJ1618.C5 Y38 2002

Zeng, Guofan, 1811-1872. Fan jing. Di 1 ban. Beijing : Zhongguo Hua qiao chu ban she, 2001.
BJ1618.C5 H44 2001

Zhuang, Huiming. Yan shi jia xun yi zhu. Di 1 ban. Shanghai : Shanghai gu ji chu ban she : Xin hua shu dian Shanghai fa xing suo fa xing, 1999.

Ziglar, Zig. Zig Ziglar's life lifters. Nashville, Tenn. : Broadman & Holman, c2003.
BF637.C5 Z54 2003

CONDUCT OF LIFE - JUVENILE LITERATURE.
Morrison, Toni. The book of mean people. 1st ed. New York : Hyperion Books for Children, c2002.
1. Black authors.

Scheunemann, Pam, 1955- Coping with anger. Edina, MN : Abdo Pub., 2004.
BF575.A5 S34 2004

Scheunemann, Pam, 1955- Dealing with bullies. Edina, MN : Abdo Pub., 2004.
BF637.B85 S37 2004

CONDUCT OF LIFE - MISCELLANEA.
Alexander, Jane. The smudging and blessings book. New York: Sterling Pub., 2001.
BF1999 .A6329 2001

Brown, H. Jackson, 1940- On things that really matter. Nashville, Tenn. : Rutledge Hill Press, c1999.
BF637.C5 B777 1999

MacGregor, Cynthia. Little indulgences. York Beach, ME : Conari Press, 2003.
BF637.C5 M32 2003

CONDUCT OF LIFE - QUOTATIONS, MAXIMS, ETC.

BIBLIOGRAPHIC GUIDE

Abraham Lincoln's daily treasure. Grand Rapids, Mich. : F.H. Revell, c2002.
E457.2 .F787 2002

The educator's book of quotes. Thousand Oaks, Calif. : Corwin Press, c2003.
PN6084.E38 E38 2003

Jackson, Stonewall, 1824-1863. Stonewall Jackson's book of maxims. Nashville, Tenn. : Cumberland House, 2002.
E467.1.J15 J17 2002

Modern mantras. 1st ed. Hauppauge, N.Y. : Barron's Educational Series, 2002.
BF637.C5 M63 2002

CONDUCTING. See **MUSIC - PERFORMANCE.**

Conducting research in psychology.
Pelham, Brett W., 1961- 2nd ed. Australia ; Belmont, CA : Thomson/Wadsworth, c2003.
BF76.5 .P34 2003

CONDUCTO OF LIFE.
Barylko, Jaime. Los valores y las virtudes. Buenos Aires : Emecé Editoral, c2002.

CONFEDERATE STATES OF AMERICA. See **UNITED STATES - HISTORY - CIVIL WAR, 1861-1865.**

Conference on Computational Learning Theory (16th : 2003 : Washington, D.C.) Learning theory and Kernel machines : 16th Annual Conference on Learning Theory and 7th Kernel Workshop, COLT/Kernel 2003, Washington, DC, USA, August 24-27, 2003 : proceedings / Bernhard Schölkopf, Manfred K. Warmuth (eds.). Berlin ; New York : Springer, c2003 xiv, 746 p. : ill. ; 24 cm. (Lecture notes in computer science. 0302-9743 ; 2777. Lecture notes in artificial intelligence) Spine title: COLT/KERNEL 2003. Includes bibliographical references and index. ISBN 3-540-40720-0 (pbk.)
1. Machine learning - Congresses. 2. Kernel functions - Congresses. I. Schölkopf, Bernhard. II. Warmuth, Manfred. III. Title. IV. Title: COLT/KERNEL 2003. V. Series: Lecture notes in computer science ; 2777. VI. Series: Lecture notes in computer science. Lecture notes in artificial intelligence.
Q325.5 .C654 2003

Confession d'un philosophe.
Conche, Marcel. Paris : Albin Michel, c2003.
B804 .C66 2003

CONFESSION (PRAYER) - JUDAISM.
Tamari, Meir. Maśa u-matan be-emunah. Yerushalayim : Śimḥonim, [761, 2001]

Confessions of a matriarchist.
Longstaff, Bill, 1934- Calgary : Ballot Pub., 2003.

CONFIDENCE. See **SELF-CONFIDENCE.**

CONFIDENCE AND SECURITY BUILDING MEASURES (INTERNATIONAL RELATIONS).
Searching for peace in Central and South Asia. Boulder, Colo. : Lynne Rienner Publishers, 2002.
JZ5597 .S43 2002

Confidence booster workout.
Perry, Martin. San Diego : Thunder Bay Press, 2004.
BF575.S39 P48 2004

CONFIDENCE BUILDING MEASURES (INTERNATIONAL RELATIONS). See **CONFIDENCE AND SECURITY BUILDING MEASURES (INTERNATIONAL RELATIONS).**

Confidence intervals.
Smithson, Michael. Thousand Oaks, Calif. : Sage Publications, c2003.
HA31.2 .S59 2003

CONFIDENCE INTERVALS.
Smithson, Michael. Confidence intervals. Thousand Oaks, Calif. : Sage Publications, c2003.
HA31.2 .S59 2003

CONFIDENTIAL COMMUNICATIONS. See **PRIVACY, RIGHT OF.**

CONFIDENTIAL COMMUNICATIONS - PHYSICIANS. See **MEDICAL RECORDS - ACCESS CONTROL.**

CONFLICT CONTROL. See **CONFLICT MANAGEMENT.**

CONFLICT, INTERGROUP. See **INTERGROUP RELATIONS.**

CONFLICT, INTERPERSONAL. See **INTERPERSONAL CONFLICT.**

CONFLICT MANAGEMENT.
Bringing peace into the room. 1st ed. San Francisco : Jossey-Bass, 2003.
HM1126 .B75 2003

Le Burundi aprés la suspension de l'embargo. [Nairobi?] : International Crisis Group, [1999]

Chanaa, Jane. Security sector reform. Oxford ; New York : Oxford University Press for the International Institute for Strategic Studies, 2002.
HV6419 .C52 2002

Conflict management. Nairobi : Friedrich Ebert Stiftung : Centre for Conflict Research : Association of Local Government Authorities of Kenya, 2000.

Conflict prevention and resolution in water systems. Cheltenham, UK ; Northampton, MA, USA : E. Elgar Pub., c2002.
HD1691 .C664 2002

Conflict resolution for school personnel [electronic resource]. [Washington, D.C.?] : U.S. Dept. of Justice, Office of Justice Programs, National Institute of Justice, c1999.

Efirov, S. A. (Svetozar Aleksandrovich) Sotsial'noe soglasie. Moskva : Izd-vo In-ta sotsiologii RAN, 2002.

Engelhardt, Lisa, 1953- Elf-help for dealing with difficult people. St. Meinrad, IN : One Caring Place/Abbey Press, c2002.
BF637.I48 E54 2002

From promise to practice. Boulder ; London : L. Rienner Publishers, 2003.
JZ6368 .S68 2003

Frost, Peter J. Toxic emotions at work. Boston : Harvard Business School Press, c2003.
HD42 .F76 2003

Gelpi, Christopher, 1966- The power of legitimacy. Princeton, N.J. : Princeton University Press, c2003.
JZ5595.5 .G45 2003

Guttman, Howard M. When goliaths clash. New York ; London : AMACOM, c2003.
HD42 .G88 2003

The handbook of negotiation. Stanford, Calif. : Stanford Business Books, c2004.
BF637.N4 H365 2004

Hart, Lois Borland. The manager's pocket guide to dealing with conflict. Amherst, Mass. : HRD Press, c1999.
BF637.I48 H38 1999

Imagine coexistence. 1st ed. San Francisco : Jossey-Bass, c2003.
HM1121 .I42 2003

Imobighe, Thomas A. The OAU (AU) and OAS in regional conflict management. Ibadan : Spectrum Books ; Oxford, UK : USA distributor, African Books Collective, 2003.
JZ6374 .I46 2003

Křivohlavý, Jaro. Konflikty mezi lidmi. Vyd. 2., přepracované, v Portalu 1. Praha : Portal, 2002.
BF637.I48 K75 2002

LeBaron, Michelle, 1956- Bridging cultural conflicts. 1st ed. San Francisco, CA : Jossey-Bass, c2003.
BF698.9.C8 L43 2003

Lipsky, David B., 1939- Emerging systems for managing workplace conflict. 1st ed. San Francisco : Jossey-Bass, c2003.
HD42 .L564 2003

Peace and conflict resolution. Part 1 [videorecording]. Derry, N.H. : Chip Taylor Communications, 1996.

Peace and conflict resolution. Part 2 [videorecording]. Derry, N.H. : Chip Taylor Communications, 1997.

Peace-building. [Harare] : ACPD, 2002.

Policymaking and peace. Lanham, Md. : Lexington Books, c2003.
JZ5538 .P65 2003

Porter, Norman, 1952- The elusive quest. Belfast : Blackstaff, 2003.

Promoting peace. Berne, Switzerland : Staempfli, 2002.

Regional conflict management. Lanham, Md. : Rowman & Littlefield, c2003.
JZ5330 .R437 2003

Searching for peace in Central and South Asia. Boulder, Colo. : Lynne Rienner Publishers, 2002.

JZ5597 .S43 2002

The territorial management of ethnic conflict. 2nd rev. and expanded ed. London ; Portland, OR : F. Cass, 2003.
GN496 .T47 2003

VanSant, Sondra. Wired for conflict. Gainesville, Fla. : Center for Applications of Psychological Type, c2003.
BF698.3 .V36 2003

Wenger, Andreas. Conflict prevention. Boulder, Colo. ; London : Lynne Rienner Publishers, 2003.
JZ5538 .W46 2003

Conflict management : a handbook for councillors. Nairobi : Friedrich Ebert Stiftung : Centre for Conflict Research : Association of Local Government Authorities of Kenya, 2000. iv, 32 p. : ill. ; 30 cm.
1. Conflict management. I. Friedrich-Ebert-Stiftung. II. Centre for Conflict Research. III. Association of Local Government Authorities of Kenya.

CONFLICT MANAGEMENT - AFRICA.
Kyelem, Apollinaire. L'éventuel et le possible. [Ouagadougou : Presses universitaires de Ouagadougou, 2002]
1. Black author.

CONFLICT MANAGEMENT - CROSS-CULTURAL STUDIES.
The handbook of negotiation. Stanford, Calif. : Stanford Business Books, c2004.
BF637.N4 H365 2004

CONFLICT MANAGEMENT - INTERNATIONAL COOPERATION - CASE STUDIES.
Imobighe, Thomas A. The OAU (AU) and OAS in regional conflict management. Ibadan : Spectrum Books ; Oxford, UK : USA distributor, African Books Collective, 2003.
JZ6374 .I46 2003

CONFLICT MANAGEMENT - ISRAEL.
Grosbard, Ofer, 1954- [Yiśra'el 'al ha-sapah. English] Israel on the couch. Albany : State University of New York Press, c2003.
DS126.5 .G694 2003

Grosbard, Ofer, 1954- Yiśra'el 'al ha-sapah. Tel-Aviv : Yedi'ot aḥaronot : Sifre ḥemed, c2000.

CONFLICT MANAGEMENT - STUDY AND TEACHING.
Peace and conflict resolution. Part 1 [videorecording]. Derry, N.H. : Chip Taylor Communications, 1996.

Peace and conflict resolution. Part 2 [videorecording]. Derry, N.H. : Chip Taylor Communications, 1997.

CONFLICT OF GENERATIONS.
Generationswechsel und historischer Wandel. München : Oldenbourg, 2003.

CONFLICT OF GENERATIONS - CANADA.
Western eyes [videorecording]. New York, NY : First Run/Icarus Films, 2000.

CONFLICT OF GENERATIONS - UNITED STATES.
Fletcher, John Wright. A hermeneutic study of generational music. 2002.

Conflict prevention.
Wenger, Andreas. Boulder, Colo. ; London : Lynne Rienner Publishers, 2003.
JZ5538 .W46 2003

Conflict prevention and resolution in water systems / edited by Aaron T. Wolf. Cheltenham, UK ; Northampton, MA, USA : E. Elgar Pub., c2002. xxiv, 823 p. : ill. ; 25 cm. (The management of water resources) (An Elgar reference collection) Includes bibliographical references and index. ISBN 1-84064-502-4 DDC 333.91
1. Water rights. 2. International rivers. 3. Water rights (International law) 4. Conflict management. I. Wolf, Aaron T. II. Series. III. Series: An Elgar reference collection
HD1691 .C664 2002

CONFLICT (PSYCHOLOGY). See also **COMPETITION (PSYCHOLOGY); INTERPERSONAL CONFLICT.**
Granovskaia, R. M. (Rada Mikhaĭlovna) Konflikt i tvorchestvo v zerkale psikhologii. Moskva : Genezis, 2002.
BF637.I48 G72 2002

Hart, Lois Borland. The manager's pocket guide to dealing with conflict. Amherst, Mass. : HRD Press, c1999.
BF637.I48 H38 1999

Johnston, Marianne. [Dealing with fighting. Spanish] Como tratar las peleas. New York : PowerKids Press, 2005.

BF637.I48 J6418 2005

Křivohlavý, Jaro. Konflikty mezi lidmi. Vyd. 2., přepracované, v Portalu 1. Praha : Portal, 2002.
BF637.I48 K75 2002

Linson, William. Kinoetics. [United States] : Kinoetics Publishing, c2002.
BF637.N66 L56 2002

Little, Graham. The public emotions. Sydney : ABC Books for the Australian Broadcasting Corporation, 1999.
BF531 .L58 1999

CONFLICT RESOLUTION. See **CONFLICT MANAGEMENT; DISPUTE RESOLUTION (LAW).**

Conflict resolution for school personnel [electronic resource] : an interactive school safety training tool. [Washington, D.C.?] : U.S. Dept. of Justice, Office of Justice Programs, National Institute of Justice, c1999. 2 CD-ROMs : sd., col. ; 4 3/4 in. System requirements: a 350 MHz or faster computer with mouse; Microsoft Windows 3.1 or better ; a minimum of 64MB of RAM ; 24x CD-ROM drive, accelerated video card, and sound card with speakers/headphones. Title from disc label. Shipping list no.: 2003-0003-E. "Developed by Materials, Communication & Computer, Inc., under grant number 1999-LT-VX-K015"-- Container insert. SUMMARY: Each module consists of 2 or 3 tutorials and 2 or 3 scenarios. CONTENTS: Disk 1: Installation instructions -- Module 1: Anger -- Module 2: Threats -- Disk 2: Module 1: Attacks with weapons -- Module 2: Suicide -- Module 3: Weapons on Campus.
1. Conflict management. 2. School violence - Prevention. 3. Mediation. 4. School personnel management. I. National Institute of Justice (U.S.) II. MATCOM (Alexandria, Va.)

CONFLICT, SOCIAL. See **SOCIAL CONFLICT.**

Conflicting identity.
Rowland, Robert C., 1954- Shared land/conflicting identity. East lansing : Michigan State University Press, 2002.
DS119.7 .R685 2003

CONFORMITY. See **DEVIANT BEHAVIOR; INFLUENCE (PSYCHOLOGY); PERSUASION (PSYCHOLOGY).**

CONFORMITY - CONGRESSES.
21. Goldegger Dialoge. 1. Aufl. Goldegg : Kulturverein Schloss Goldegg, 2002.

CONFRONTATION, INTERPERSONAL. See **INTERPERSONAL CONFRONTATION.**

Confucius.
[Selections. Chinese & English. 1998]
Kong Meng ren sheng ge yan ji yi : gu wen jin yi, Zhong-Ying dui zhao = A collection of mottos on life from Confucius and Mencius with modern Chinese and English translations / Lu Jinhua bian zhu ; Li Zongjun Ying yi shen ding. Wuhan : Wuhan gong ye da xue chu ban she, 1998. 12, 285 p. : ill. ; 18 cm. ISBN 7-5629-1351-X
1. Conduct of life. I. Mencius. Selections. Chinese & English. 1998. II. Lu, Jinhua. III. Title. IV. Title: Collection of mottos on life from Confucius and Mencius with modern Chinese and English translations

Cong li shi zhe xue xiang jing ji zhe xue de kua yue.
Zhang, Xiong, 1953- Jing ji zhe xue. Di 1 ban. [Kunming] : Yunnan ren min chu ban she, 2002.
D16.8 .Z536 2002

CONGLOMERATE CORPORATIONS. See **COMPETITION.**

CONGO (DEMOCRATIC REPUBLIC) - HISTORY - 1997-.
From Kabila to Kabila. Nairobi ; Brussels : International Crisis Group, 2001.

CONGO (DEMOCRATIC REPUBLIC) - POLITICS AND GOVERNMENT - 1997-.
Le dialogue intercongolais. Bruxelles ; Nairobi : International Crisis Group, [2001]

From Kabila to Kabila. Nairobi ; Brussels : International Crisis Group, 2001.

Masangana Diamaka, Robin, 1962- Dialogue politique. Paris : Editoo.com, 2002.
1. Black author.

Storm clouds over Sun City. Brussels ; Nairobi : International Crisis Group, 2002.

CONGRESSMEN. See **LEGISLATORS - UNITED STATES.**

Conjugal love in India.
Nāgārjuna, Siddha. [Ratiśāstra. English & Sanskrit] Leiden Boston, MA : Brill, 2002.

HQ470.S3 N3413 2002

CONJUGAL VIOLENCE.
Mills, Linda G. Insult to injury. Princeton, N.J. : Princeton University Press, c2003.
HV6626 .M55 2003

CONJURERS. See **MAGICIANS.**

CONJURORS. See **MAGICIANS.**

Conn, Marie A., 1944-.
Balancing the scales. Lanham, Md. ; Oxford : University Press of America, c2003.
HQ1075 .B3417 2003

La connaissance sociologique : contribution à la sociologie de la connaissance / sous la direction de Francis Farrugia : les auteurs Louis Moreau de Bellaing ... [et al.]. Paris : Harmattan, c2002. 216 p. ; 22 cm. (Collection Logiques sociales. Série Sociologie de la connaissance) Includes bibliographical references. ISBN 2-7475-2984-3
1. Knowledge, Sociology of. I. Farrugia, Francis. II. Moreau de Bellaing, Louis. III. Series: Logiques sociales. Sociologie de la connaissance.
HM651 .C65 2002

CONNECTIONISM.
Dawson, Michael Robert William, 1959- Minds and machines. Malden, MA : Blackwell Pub., c2003.
BF311 .D345 2003

Connections!.
Clayton, Charles Walker, 1951- Radcliffe, IA : Ide House Publishers, 2004.
BF637.C45 C54 2004

The connectivity hypothesis.
Laszlo, Ervin, 1932- Albany : State University of New York Press, c2003.
Q175 .L2854 2003

Conner, Floyd, 1951- Hollywood's most wanted : the top 10 book of lucky breaks, prima donnas, box office bombs, and other oddities / Floyd Conner. 1st ed. Washington, D.C. : Brassey's, c2002. xv, 288 p. : ill., ports. ; 21 cm. Includes bibliographical references (p. 273-276) and index. ISBN 1-57488-480-8 DDC 791.43
1. Motion pictures - Miscellanea. I. Title.
PN1998 .C54 2002

Connolly, Kevin J.
Handbook of developmental psychology. London : Thousand Oaks, Calif. : SAGE Publications, 2003.
BF713 .H364 2003

Connolly, William E. Identity/difference : democratic negotiations of political paradox / William E. Connolly. Expanded ed. Minneapolis : University of Minnesota Press, c2002. xxxi, 244 p. ; 23 cm. Originally published: Ithaca : Cornell University Press, 1991. Includes bibliographical references (p. 223-237) and index. ISBN 0-8166-4086-6 (pbk. : alk. paper) DDC 320/.01
1. Political science - Philosophy. 2. Democracy. 3. Difference (Philosophy) 4. Identity (Philosophical concept) 5. Good and evil. I. Title.
JA74 .C659 2002

Neuropolitics : thinking, culture, speed / William E. Connolly. Minneapolis, MN : University of Minnesota Press, c2002. xv, 218 p. ; 26 cm. (Theory out of bounds ; v. 23) Includes bibliographical references and index. ISBN 0-8166-4021-1 ISBN 0-8166-4022-X (pbk.) DDC 128
1. Thought and thinking. 2. Culture - Philosophy. I. Title. II. Series.

Connor, Kerri, 1970- The pocket spell creator : magickal references at your fingertips / by Kerri Connor. Franklin Lakes, N.J. : New Page Books, c2003. p. cm. Includes bibliographical references and index. ISBN 1-56414-715-0 (pbk.) DDC 133.4/4
1. Magic - Handbooks, manuals, etc. I. Title.
BF1611 .C724 2003

Conocimiento, método científico y el proceso de la investigación.
Morales Tomas, Marco Antonio. El que busca encuentra = Guatemala : ESEDIR : Editorial Saqil Tzij, 1999.

Conoscenza e cognizione : tra filosofia e scienza cognitiva / a cura di Paolo Parrini. 1 ed. Milano : Guerini e associati, 2002. 283 p. : ill. ; 23 cm. Includes bibliographical references and index. ISBN 88-8335-293-9 DDC 121
1. Philosophy of mind. 2. Knowledge, Theory of. 3. Comprehension (Theory of knowledge) I. Parrini, Paolo.
BJ45.5 .C66 2002

CONSCIENCE - INTERVIEW.
Changeux, Jean-Pierre. [Ce qui nous fait penser. English] What makes us think? Princeton, N.J. : Princeton University Press, c2000.

BJ45 .C4313 2000

Conscious experience / edited by Thomas Metzinger. Paderborn : Schöningh/Imprint Academic, 1995 (Lawrence, Kan. : Allen Press) xi, 564 p. : ill. ; 24 cm. Includes bibliographical references (p. 507-554). ISBN 0-907845-05-3 (pbk.) ISBN 0-907845-10-X (hardback)
1. Consciousness. 2. Thought and thinking. I. Metzinger, Thomas, 1958-
BF311 .C6443 1995

CONSCIOUSNESS. *See also* **KNOWLEDGE, THEORY OF; PERSONALITY; SELF.**
Blackmore, Susan J., 1951- New York : Oxford University Press, 2003.
BF311 .B534 2003

CONSCIOUSNESS.
Adams, J. Robert. Prospects for immortality. Amityville, N.Y. : Baywood Pub., c2003.
BD421 .A33 2003

Akopov, G. V. Problema soznaniia v psikhologii. Samara : Samarskiĭ gos. pedagog. universitet, 2002.
BF311 .A44 2002

Bartsch, Renate, 1939- Consciousness emerging. Amsterdam ; Philadelphia, Pa. : John Benjamins Pub., 2002.
BF311 .B325 2002

Bertelsen, Preben. Free will, consciousness, and the self. New York : Berghahn Books, 2003.
BF621 .B47 2003

Beskova, I. A. Ėvoliutsiia i soznanie. Moskva : "Indrik", 2002.
B808.9 .B476 2002x

Birtchnell, John. The two of me. Hove, East Sussex [England] ; New York : Routledge, 2003.
BF311 .B533 2003

Blackmore, Susan J., 1951- Consciousness. New York : Oxford University Press, 2003.
BF311 .B534 2003

Campbell, John, 1956- Reference and consciousness. Oxford : Clarendon Press ; New York : Oxford University Press, 2002.
BF321 .C36 2002

Carter, Rita, 1949- Exploring consciousness. Berkeley : University of California Press, c2002.
BF311 .C289 2002

Combs, Allan, 1942- The radiance of being. 2nd ed. St. Paul, Minn. : Paragon House, 2002.
BF311 .C575 2002

Conscious experience. Paderborn : Schöningh/Imprint Academic, 1995 (Lawrence, Kan. : Allen Press)
BF311 .C6443 1995

Consciousness evolving. Amsterdam ; Philadelphia, Pa. : John Benjamins Pub., c2002.
B808.9 .C665 2002

Consciousness. Oxford : Clarendon Press ; New York : Oxford University Press, 2003.
B808.9 .C667 2003

Consenstein, Peter. Literary memory, consciousness, and the group Oulipo. Amsterdam ; New York, NY : Rodopi, 2002.

Demmin, Herbert S., 1959- The ghosts of consciousness. St. Paul, Minn. : Paragon House, c2003.
BF441 .D395 2003

Eisen, Jeffrey S., 1940- Oneness perceived. St. Paul, Minn. : Paragon House, c2003.
BF311 .E39 2003

Hegel's Phenomenology of spirit. Amherst, N.Y. : Humanity Books, 2003.
B2929 .H349 2003

Holt, Jason, 1971- Blindsight and the nature of consciousness. Peterborough, Ont. : Broadview Press, c2003.

Humphrey, Nicholas. How to solve the mind-- body problem. Thorverton, UK ; Bowling Green, OH : Imprint Academic, c2000.
BF698.95 .H86 2000

Humphrey, Nicholas. The inner eye. Oxford ; New York : Oxford University Press, c2002.
BF311 .H778 2002

Humphrey, Nicholas. The mind made flesh. Oxford ; New York : Oxford University Press, 2002.
BF701 .H86 2002

Manzotti, Riccardo. Coscienza e realtà. Bologna : Società editrice il mulino, c2001.

BF311 .M35 2001

Merrell, Floyd, 1937- Sensing corporeally. Toronto ; Buffalo : University of Toronto Press, c2003.
P99 .M477 2003

Models of the self. Thorverton, UK : Imprint Academic, c1999.
BF697 .M568 1999

Mustakova-Possardt, Elena, 1960- Critical consciousness. Westport, Conn. ; London : Praeger, 2003.
BL53 .M98 2003

Raĭkov, V. L. (Vladimir Leonidovich), 1934- Soznanie i poznanie III tysiācheletiia. Moskva : [s.n.], 1999.
BF311 .R26 1999

Redfield, James. God and the evolving universe. New York : Jeremy P. Tarcher/Putnam, c2002.
BD541 .R43 2002

Solso, Robert L., 1933- The psychology of art and the evolution of the conscious brain. Cambridge, Mass. : MIT Press, 2003.
BF311 .S652 2003

Ulybina, E. V. Psikhologiia obydennogo soznaniia. Moskva : Smysl, 2001.
BF311 .U52 2001

The unity of consciousness. Oxford ; New York : Oxford University Press, 2003.
BF311 .U55 2003

The view from within. Thorverton, UK ; Bowling Green, OH : Imprint Academic, 2000.
BF311 .V512 2000

Vrinte, Joseph, 1949- The perennial quest for a psychology with a soul. 1st ed. Delhi : Motilal Banarsidass Publishers, 2002.
BF311+

Wilkens, Sander. Die Konvertibilität des Bewusstseins. 1. Aufl. Würzburg ; Boston : Deutscher Wissenschafts-Verlag (DWV), c2002.
BD163 .E45 2002

Consciousness and self-consciousness
Agency and self-awareness. Oxford : Clarendon Press ; New York : Oxford University Press, 2003.

CONSCIOUSNESS - CONGRESSES.
Der Grund, die Not und die Freude des Bewusstseins. Würzburg : Königshausen & Neumann, c2002.
B808.9 .G78 2002

Narrative and consciousness. Oxford ; New York : Oxford University Press, c2003.
BF311 .N26 2003

Neues Bewusstsein. Wien : Edition Selene, 1999.

No matter, never mind. Amsterdam ; Philadelphia : John Benjamins Pub. Co., c2002.
QP411 .N598 2002

Consciousness emerging.
Bartsch, Renate, 1939- Amsterdam ; Philadelphia, Pa. : John Benjamins Pub., 2002.
BF311 .B325 2002

Consciousness evolving / edited by James H. Fetzer. Amsterdam ; Philadelphia, Pa. : John Benjamins Pub., c2002. xix, 251 p. : ill. ; 22 cm. (Advances in consciousness research, 1381-589X ; v. 34) Includes bibliographical references and indexes. ISBN 1-58811-108-3 (pbk.) ISBN 90-272-5154-1 DDC 126
1. Consciousness. 2. Evolution. 3. Consciousness - Physiological aspects. 4. Evolution (Biology) I. Fetzer, James H., 1940- II. Series.
B808.9 .C665 2002

CONSCIOUSNESS - HISTORY.
Lachman, Gary, 1955- A secret history of consciousness. Great Barrington, MA : Lindisfarne Books, 2003.
BF311 .L19 2003

CONSCIOUSNESS - MISCELLANEA.
Pike, Diane Kennedy. Awakening to wisdom. Scottsdale, AZ : LP Publications, c2003.
BF1999 .P5485 2003

CONSCIOUSNESS, NATIONAL. *See* **NATIONALISM.**

Consciousness : new philosophical perspectives / edited by Quentin Smith and Aleksandar Jokic. Oxford : Clarendon Press ; New York : Oxford University Press, 2003. xii, 532 p. : ill. ; 24 cm. Includes bibliographical references and index. ISBN 0-19-924129-5 (pbk. : alk. paper) ISBN 0-19-924128-7 (hbk : alk. paper) DDC 126

1. Consciousness. I. Smith, Quentin, 1952- II. Jokic, Aleksandar.
B808.9 .C667 2003

CONSCIOUSNESS - PHILOSOPHY.
Hübner, Benno. Sinn in Sinn-loser Zeit. Wien : Passagen, c2002.

CONSCIOUSNESS - PHYSIOLOGICAL ASPECTS.
Consciousness evolving. Amsterdam ; Philadelphia, Pa. : John Benjamins Pub., c2002.
B808.9 .C665 2002

CONSCIOUSNESS - RELIGIOUS ASPECTS.
Cuevas Sosa, Andrés Alejandro, 1939- How do religious figures induce the establishment of sects? 2nd ed. Leicestershire : Upfront Pub., 2002.
BF1272 .C84 2002

CONSCIOUSNESS - RELIGIOUS ASPECTS - CHRISTIANITY.
McLaughlin, Michael T. Knowledge, consciousness and religious conversion in Lonergan and Aurobindo. Roma : Editrice Pontificia Universita Gregoriana, 2003.

CONSCIOUSNESS - RELIGIOUS ASPECTS - HINDUISM.
Gupta, Bina, 1947- CIT consciousness. New Delhi ; New York : Oxford University Press, 2003.
BF311+

McLaughlin, Michael T. Knowledge, consciousness and religious conversion in Lonergan and Aurobindo. Roma : Editrice Pontificia Universita Gregoriana, 2003.

Consejo Superior de Investigaciones Científicas (Spain).
Demonio, religión y sociedad entre España y América. Madrid : Consejo Superior de Investigaciones Científicas, 2002.

Consenstein, Peter. Literary memory, consciousness, and the group Oulipo / Peter Consenstein. Amsterdam ; New York, NY : Rodopi, 2002. 252 p. : ill. ; 23 cm. (Faux titre, 0167-9392 ; no. 220) Includes bibliographical references (p. [239]-247) and index. ISBN 90-420-1438-5 (pbk.) DDC 153.12
1. Oulipo (Association) 2. Memory. 3. Consciousness. I. Title. II. Series.

CONSENSUS (SOCIAL SCIENCES). *See* **AUTHORITY; POWER (SOCIAL SCIENCES).**

CONSERVATION BIOLOGY. *See* **NATURE CONSERVATION.**

CONSERVATION OF ENERGY. *See* **FORCE AND ENERGY.**

CONSERVATION OF NATURAL RESOURCES. *See* **NATURE CONSERVATION.**

CONSERVATION OF NATURE. *See* **NATURE CONSERVATION.**

CONSERVATISM.
Protsenko, Oleh. Konservatyzm. Kyïv : "Smoloskyp", 1998.

CONSERVATISM AND LITERATURE. *See* **POLITICS AND LITERATURE.**

CONSERVATISM - RELIGIOUS ASPECTS - RUSSKAIA PRAVOSLAVNAIA TSERKOV'.
Maler, Arkadiĭ. Strategii sakral'nogo smysla. Moskva : Parad izdatel'skiĭ dom, 2003.

CONSERVATISM - RUSSIA (FEDERATION).
Maler, Arkadiĭ. Strategii sakral'nogo smysla. Moskva : Parad izdatel'skiĭ dom, 2003.

CONSERVATISM - UNITED STATES - HISTORY - 20TH CENTURY.
Kenneally, James J. (James Joseph), 1929- A compassionate conservative. Lanham, Md. : Lexington Books, c2003.
E748.M375 K46 2003

CONSOLATION. *See also* **BEREAVEMENT.**
Bolitho, Harold. Bereavement and consolation. New Haven : Yale University Press, c2003.
DS822.2 .B65 2003

Kaplan, Robbie Miller. How to say it when you don't know what to say. Prentice Hall Press ed. Upper Saddle River, NJ : Prentice Hall Press, 2004.
BF637.C54 K36 2004

La consolation de philosophie.
Boethius, d. 524. [De consolatione philosophiae. French] Paris : Belles lettres, 2002.

Consolation of philosophy.
Boethius, d. 524. [De consolatione philosophiae. English] Indianapolis, IN : Hackett Pub. Co., c2001.

B659.C2 E52 2001

CONSOLIDATION AND MERGER OF CORPORATIONS. *See* **CORPORATE REORGANIZATIONS.**

CONSOLIDATION AND MERGER OF CORPORATIONS - MANAGEMENT.
Lees, Stan. Global acquisitions. Houndmills [England] ; New York : Palgrave Macmillan, 2003.
HD58.8 .L424 2003

CONSOLIDATION AND MERGER OF CORPORATIONS - UNITED STATES.
United States. Congress. Senate. Committee on the Judiciary. Subcommittee on Antitrust, Business Rights, and Competition. Dominance in the sky. [Washington] : U.S. G.P.O. : For sale by the Supt. of Docs., U.S. G.P.O. [Congressional Sales Office], 2003.

United States. Congress. Senate. Committee on the Judiciary. Subcommittee on Antitrust, Business Rights, and Competition. Dominance on the ground. Washington : U.S. G.P.O. : For sale by the Supt. of Docs., U.S. G.P.O. [Congressional Sales Office], 2003.

CONSPIRACY.
Transparency and conspiracy. Durham : Duke University Press, 2003.
JC330 .T73 2003

Constantine, Alex. Virtual government : CIA mind control operations in America / Alex Constantine. 1st ed. Venice, CA : Feral House, 1997. viii, 304 p. : ill. ; 22 cm. Includes bibliographical references. ISBN 0-922915-45-8 (pbk.) DDC 001.9
1. *United States. - Central Intelligence Agency.* 2. *Brainwashing - United States.* 3. *United States - Politics and government - 20th century.* 4. *Cults - United States - History - 20th century.* 5. *Subliminal projection - United States.* I. Title.
BF633 .C67 1997

Constantine, Storm. Bast and Sekhmet : eyes of Ra / Storm Constantine & Eloise Coquio. London : R. Hale, c1999. 320 p. : ill., ports. ; 24 cm. Includes bibliographical references. ISBN 0-7090-6418-7 DDC 291.21140932
1. *Magic, Egyptian.* 2. *Bast (Egyptian deity)* 3. *Sekhmet (Egyptian deity)* 4. *Cats - Religious aspects.* 5. *Egypt - Religion.* I. Coquio, Eloise. II. Title.

Egyptian birth signs : the secrets of the Ancient Egyptian horoscope / Storm Constantine. London : Thorsons, 2002. xv, 235 p. : ill. ; 16 cm. ISBN 0-00-713138-0 DDC 133.59232
1. *Astrology, Egyptian.* 2. *Horoscopes.* I. Title.

Constantine, Susannah. What not to wear / Susannah Constantine and Trinny Woodall ; photography by Robin Matthews. London : Weidenfeld & Nicolson, 2002. 160 p. : col. ill., ports. ; 23 cm. TV tie-in. ISBN 0-297-84331-1 DDC 391.2
1. *Clothing and dress.* 2. *Beauty, Personal.* I. Woodall, Trinny. II. Title.

CONSTELLATIONS. *See* **PLEIADES.**

CONSTITUTIONAL HISTORY, MODERN. *See* **CONSTITUTIONAL HISTORY.**

CONSTITUTIONAL HISTORY - UNITED STATES.
Ryter, Jon Christian. Whatever happened to America? Tampa, FL : Hallberg Pub., 2001, c2000.
E743 .R98 2001

CONSTITUTIONAL LAW. *See* **CIVIL RIGHTS; SOVEREIGNTY.**

CONSTITUTIONAL LAW - HISTORY. *See* **CONSTITUTIONAL HISTORY.**

CONSTITUTIONAL LAW - INDIA.
Preventive detention and individual liberty. New Delhi : South Asia Human Rights Documentation Centre, 2000.
KNS4654 .P74 2000

CONSTITUTIONAL LAW - INTERPRETATION AND CONSTRUCTION. *See* **CONSTITUTIONAL LAW.**

CONSTITUTIONAL LIMITATIONS. *See* **CONSTITUTIONAL LAW.**

CONSTITUTIONAL RIGHTS. *See* **CIVIL RIGHTS.**

CONSTITUTIONS. *See* **CONSTITUTIONAL LAW.**

CONSTITUTIONS - HISTORY. *See* **CONSTITUTIONAL HISTORY.**

CONSTITUTIONS - INTERPRETATION AND CONSTRUCTION. *See* **CONSTITUTIONAL LAW.**

Construcción de conocimiento y educación virtual / Miguel Angel Campos Hernández, coordinador. 1. ed. Ciudad Universitaria, México, D.F. : Universidad Nacional Autónoma de México, 2000. vii, 189 p. : ill. ; 23 cm. On cover: Facultad de Filosofía y Letras, Universidad Nacional Autónoma de México. Proceedings from a conference held October 24-25, 2000. Includes bibliographical references. ISBN 968-36-8809-8
1. *Learning - Congresses.* 2. *Knowledge, Theory of - Congresses.* 3. *Educational technology - Congresses.* 4. *Distance education - Congresses.* I. Campos Hernández, Miguel Angel. II. Universidad Nacional Autónoma de México. Facultad de Filosofía y Letras.
LB1060 .C658 2000

Constructing a language.
Tomasello, Michael. Cambridge, Mass. : Harvard University Press, 2003.
P118 .T558 2003

Constructing clienthood in social work and human services : interaction, identities, and practices / edited by Christopher Hall ... [et al.]. London ; New York : Jessica Kingsley Publishers, c2003. 272 p. ; 24 cm. Includes bibliographical references (p. 234-255) and indexes. ISBN 1-84310-073-8 (pbk. : alk. paper) DDC 361.3/2
1. *Social case work.* 2. *Social work administration.* 3. *Social interaction.* I. Hall, Christopher, 1948-
HV40 .C6615 2003

Constructing "race" and "ethnicity" in America.
Yanow, Dvora. Armonk, N.Y. : M.E. Sharpe, c2003.
HM753 .Y36 2003

CONSTRUCTION. *See* **ARCHITECTURE; ENGINEERING.**

La construction de l'inconscient colonial en Alsace.
Amougou, Emmanuel. Paris : L'Harmattan, 2002.

CONSTRUCTION INDUSTRY - MANAGEMENT.
Moore, David (David R.) Project management. Oxford, [Eng.] ; Malden, MA : Blackwell Science, c2002.

The construction of communities in the early Middle Ages : texts, resources and artefacts / edited by Richard Corradini, Max Diesenberger, Helmut Reimitz. Leiden ; Boston : Brill, 2003. x, 417 p., [24] p. of plates : ill., facsims. ; 25 cm. (The transformation of the Roman world, 1386-4165 ; v. 12) "This volume is a result of the European Science Foundation programme 'The Transformation of the Roman World'"--P. [vii]. Includes bibliographical references (p. [351]-396) and index. CONTENTS: The construction of communities and the persistence of paradox : an introduction / Walter Pohl -- Structures and resources of power i early medieval Europe / Dick Harrison -- Gens. Terminology and perception of the 'Germanic' peoples from late Antiquity to the early Middles Ages / Hans Liebeschuetz -- The 'gold hoards' of the early migration period in south-eastern Europe and the late Roman Empire / Michael Schmauder -- The nomad's greed for gold : from the fall of the Burgundians to the Avar treasure / Matthias Hardt -- Alaricus rex : legitimizing a Gothic king / Hagith Sivan -- Changes in the topography of power : from civitates to urbes regiae in Hispania / Gisela Ripoll -- Deconstructing the Merovingian family / Ian Wood -- Hair, sacrality and symbolic capital in the Frankish kingdoms / Maximilian Diesenberger -- The ritual significance of vessels in the formation of Merovingian christian communities / Bonnie Effros -- Social networks and identities in Frankish historiography. New aspects of the textual history of Gregory of Tours' Historiae / Helmut Reimitz -- The rhetoric of crisis. Computus and Liber annalis in early nineth-century Fulda / Richard Corradini -- The history of Ibn Habib and ethnogenesis in Al-Andalus / Ann Christys. ISBN 90-04-11862-4
1. *Social history - Medieval, 500-1500.* 2. *Civilization, Medieval.* 3. *Europe - History - 476-1492.* 4. *Europe - History - To 476.* 5. *Community - History - To 1500.* I. Corradini, Richard. II. Diesenberger, Max. III. Reimitz, Helmut. IV. Series.
HN11 .C66 2003

Constructive change. Boise, Idaho : Center for Constructive Change, c1996- v. : ill. ; 22 cm. Frequency: Quarterly. Vol. 1, no. 1 (spring 1996)- . Title from cover. "A publication of the Society for Constructive Change." Continued by: Constructivism in the human sciences ISSN: 1520-2984 (DLC) 98641995 (OCoLC)39388959.
1. *Constructivism (Psychology) - Periodicals.* 2. *Personal construct theory - Periodicals.* I. Society for Constructive Change. II. Center for Constructive Change (Boise, Idaho) III. Title: Constructivism in the human sciences
BF698.9.P47 C66

Constructivism in the human sciences.
Constructive change. Boise, Idaho : Center for Constructive Change, c1996-
BF698.9.P47 C66

CONSTRUCTIVISM (PHILOSOPHY).
Stecker, Robert, 1928- Interpretation and construction. Malden, MA : Blackwell, 2003.
BD241 .S78 2003

CONSTRUCTIVISM (PSYCHOLOGY) - PERIODICALS.
Constructive change. Boise, Idaho : Center for Constructive Change, c1996-
BF698.9.P47 C66

CONSUMER ADVERTISING. *See* **ADVERTISING.**

CONSUMER AFFAIRS DEPARTMENTS. *See* **CONSUMER PROTECTION; CUSTOMER RELATIONS.**

CONSUMER BEHAVIOR.
Wertime, Kent. Building brands & believers. Chichester : Wiley, 2002.

CONSUMER BEHAVIOR - PSYCHOLOGICAL ASPECTS.
Zaltman, Gerald. How customers think. Boston, Mass. : Harvard Business School Press, c2003.
HF5415.32 .Z35 2003

CONSUMER DEMAND. *See* **CONSUMPTION (ECONOMICS).**

CONSUMER EDUCATION. *See also* **HOME ECONOMICS.**
Privacy [electronic resource]. [Washington, D.C.] : Federal Trade Commission, Bureau of Consumer Protection, Office of Consumer and Business Education, [2002]

Privacy [electronic resource]. [Washington, D.C.] : Federal Trade Commission, Bureau of Consumer Protection, Office of Consumer and Business Education, [2002]

Privacy [electronic resource]. [Washington, D.C.] : Federal Trade Commission, Bureau of Consumer Protection, Office of Consumer and Business Education, [2002]

CONSUMER GOODS - MARKETING. *See* **MARKETING.**

CONSUMER PROTECTION - UNITED STATES.
Privacy [electronic resource]. [Washington, D.C.] : Federal Trade Commission, Bureau of Consumer Protection, Office of Consumer and Business Education, [2002]

United States. Congress. Senate. Committee on Commerce, Science, and Transportation. Subcommittee on Consumer Affairs, Foreign Commerce, and Tourism. Customer choice in automotive repair shops. Washington : U.S. G.P.O. : For sale by the Supt. of Docs., U.S. G.P.O., [Congressional Sales Office], 2003.

CONSUMER SPENDING. *See* **CONSUMPTION (ECONOMICS).**

CONSUMERS - INFORMATION SERVICES - ACCESS CONTROL - UNITED STATES.
Privacy [electronic resource]. [Washington, D.C.] : Federal Trade Commission, Bureau of Consumer Protection, Office of Consumer and Business Education, [2002]

CONSUMERS - PSYCHOLOGY.
Psychology and consumer culture. 1st ed. Washington, DC : American Psychological Association, c2004.
HC110.C6 P76 2004

Zaltman, Gerald. How customers think. Boston, Mass. : Harvard Business School Press, c2003.
HF5415.32 .Z35 2003

CONSUMERS - UNITED STATES.
McLuhan, Marshall, 1911- The mechanical bride. Corte Madera, CA : Gingko Press, 2002.

CONSUMPTION (ECONOMICS) - UNITED STATES - PSYCHOLOGICAL ASPECTS.
Psychology and consumer culture. 1st ed. Washington, DC : American Psychological Association, c2004.
HC110.C6 P76 2004

Contact the other side.
Konstantinos, 1972- 1st ed. St. Paul, Minn. : Llewellyn Publications, 2001.
BF1275.D2 K66 2001

Contacts of humans with aliens

CONTACTS OF HUMANS WITH ALIENS. *See* **HUMAN-ALIEN ENCOUNTERS.**

CONTEMPLATION. *See* **MEDITATION.**

The contemporary American family.
Sabourin, Teresa Chandler. Thousand Oaks, Calif. : Sage Publications, c2003.
HQ536 .S213 2003

Contemporary American Indian studies
Mould, Tom, 1969- Choctaw prophecy. Tuscaloosa : University of Alabama Press, c2003.
E99.C8 M68 2003

CONTEMPORARY ART. *See* **ART, MODERN - 20TH CENTURY.**

Contemporary artists and their critics
Newton, Stephen J. Painting, psychoanalysis, and spirituality. New York : Cambridge University Press, 2001.
ND1158.P74 N48 2001

Contemporary cultural theory.
Milner, Andrew, 1950- 3rd ed. Crows Nest, N.S.W. : Allen & Unwin, 2002.

CONTEMPORARY PAINTING. *See* **PAINTING, MODERN - 20TH CENTURY.**

Contemporary peacemaking : conflict, violence and peace processes / edited by John Darby and Roger Mac Ginty. Houndmills, Basingstoke ; New York : Palgrave Macmillan, 2003. xiii, 296 p. ; 24 cm. Includes bibliographical references (p. 275-285) and index. ISBN 1403901384 (hardback : alk. paper) ISBN 1403901392 (pbk. : alk. paper) DDC 327.1/72
1. Pacific settlement of international disputes. 2. Peace. I. Darby, John (John P.) II. Mac Ginty, Roger, 1970-
JZ6010 .C665 2003

Contemporary political theory
Smith, Rogers M., 1953- Stories of peoplehood. Cambridge ; New York : Cambridge University Press, 2003.
JA75.7 .S65 2003

Contemporary problems of proof from a document.
Wrocławskie Sympozjum Badań Pisma (9th : 2000 : Wrocław, Poland) Wroclaw : University of Wroclaw, Faculty of Law, Administration, and Economy, Department of Criminalistics, 2002.
BF891 .W76 2000

Contemporary psychology (Praeger Publishers)
Lewis, Paddy Greenwall, 1945- Helping children cope with the death of a parent. Westport, Conn. : Praeger, 2004.
BF723.G75 L49 2004

Resilience for today. Westport, CT : Praeger, 2003.
BF698.35.R47 R47 2003

Contemporary studies in philosophy and the human sciences
Merleau-Ponty, Maurice, 1908-1961. [Union de l'âme et du corps chez Malebranche, Biran et Bergson. English] The incarnate subject. Amherst, N.Y. : Humanity Books, 2001.
B2430.M379 U513 2001

Contemporary systems thinking
Van Gigch, John P. Metadecisions. New York : Kluwer Academic/Plenum Publishers, c2003.
HM701 .V36 2003

Contemporary youth issues
Buckley, Maureen A., 1964- Mentoring children and adolescents. Westport, Conn. : Praeger, 2003.
BF637.C6 B8 2003

CONTEMPT OF THE WORLD. *See* **ASCETICISM.**

CONTENDING, VERBAL. *See* **VERBAL SELF-DEFENSE.**

El contenido de la felicidad.
Savater, Fernando. 1. ed. Madrid : Aguilar : Santillana, 2002.

CONTENTIOUSNESS. *See* **QUARRELING.**

CONTENTMENT. *See also* **HAPPINESS; PEACE OF MIND.**
Mazumdar, Krishna, 1949- Determinants of human well-being. New York : Nova Science Publishers, c2003.
HB171 .M462 2003

Contes de l'Egypte ancienne : anthologie / présentation, notes, chronologie et dossier par Emmanuelle Rémond-Dalyac. Paris : Flammarion, c2002. 128 p. ; 18 cm. (Etonnants classiques, 1269-8822 ; 2119) ISBN 2-08-072119-4 DDC 890

1. Tales - Egypt. 2. Mythology, Egyptian. I. Rémond-Dalyac, Emmanuelle. II. Series.

Contested pasts : the politics of memory / edited by Katharine Hodgkin and Susannah Radstone. London ; New York : Routledge, 2003. xv, 264 p. : ill. ; 25 cm. (Routledge studies in memory and narrative) Includes bibliographical references and index. ISBN 0-415-28647-6 (alk. paper) DDC 153.1/2
1. Memory - Social aspects. 2. Memory - Political aspects. I. Hodgkin, Katharine, 1961- II. Radstone, Susannah. III. Series.
BF378.S65 C65 2003

Context and cognition.
Foxall, G. R. 1st ed. Reno, NV : Context Press, 2004.
BF199 .F69 2004

CONTEXT (LINGUISTICS).
Giora, Rachel, 1945- On our mind. New York : Oxford University Press, c2003.
BF455 .G525 2003

Kecskés, István. Situation-bound utterances in L1 and L2. Berlin ; New York : Mouton de Gruyter, 2002.
P95.45 .K4 2002

Wort und (Kon)text. Frankfurt : Lang, 2001.
P325.5.C65 W678 2001

CONTEXTUALIZATION (CHRISTIAN THEOLOGY). *See* **CHRISTIANITY AND CULTURE.**

Continental feminism reader / edited by Ann J. Cahill and Jennifer Hansen. Lanham, Md. : Rowman & Littlefield Publishers, c2003. ix, 327 p. ; 24 cm. Includes bibliographical references and index. ISBN 0-7425-2308-X (alk. paper) ISBN 0-7425-2309-8 (pbk : alk. paper) DDC 305.3
1. Gender identity. 2. Sex differences (Psychology) 3. Feminism. I. Cahill, Ann J. II. Hansen, Jennifer, 1970-
HQ1075 .C668 2003

CONTINENTAL PHILOSOPHY. *See also* **PHILOSOPHY, EUROPEAN.**

(8) Lyotard. New York ; London : Routledge, 2002.

CONTINGENCY (PHILOSOPHY).
Vallicella, William F. A paradigm theory of existence. Dordrecht ; Boston : Kluwer Academic, c2002.
BD331 .V36 2002

CONTINUING EDUCATION. *See* **ADULT EDUCATION.**

CONTINUUM MECHANICS. *See* **SOUND.**

CONTRACT BRIDGE - PROBLEMS, EXERCISES, ETC.
Brecher, Erwin. Hocus-pocus. London : Panacea Press, 2001.
GV1282.3 .B725 2001

CONTRACTING OUT. *See* **PUBLIC CONTRACTS.**

CONTRACTS. *See* **PUBLIC CONTRACTS.**

CONTRACTS, EXPORT SALES. *See* **EXPORT SALES CONTRACTS.**

Contrada, Richard J.
Self, social identity, and physical health. New York : Oxford University Press, 1999.
R726.5 .S46 1999

Contrera, Malena Segura. Mídia e pânico : saturação da informação, violência e crise cultural na mídia / Malena Segura Contrera. 1. ed. São Paulo : Annablume : FAPESP, 2002. 126 p. : ill. ; 21 cm. Includes bibliographical references. ISBN 85-7419-240-6
1. Violence in mass media. 2. Mass media - Psychological aspects. 3. Mass media and culture. I. Title.

Contretemps
Dagognet, François. Changement de perspective. Paris : Table ronde, c2002.

Contributions in philosophy
(no. 88) Parmenides. [Nature. English & Greek] Parmenides of Elea. Westport, Conn. : Praeger, 2003.
B235.P23 N3713 2003

Contributions in psychology
(no. 41) Castro, Vanessa Smith, 1969- Acculturation and psychological adaptation. Westport, Conn. : Greenwood Press, 2003.
HM841 .C37 2003

Contributions to management science
Psychoanalysis and management. Heidelberg : Physica-Verlag, c1994.
BF175.4.S65 P777 1994

Contributions to phenomenology
(v. 48) Husserl's Logical investigations reconsidered. Dordrecht ; Boston : Kluwer Academic Publishers, c2003.
B3279.H93 L64346 2003

Contributions to psychological acoustics.
Oldenburger Symposion zur Psychologischen Akustik (8th : 2000) 1. ed. Oldenburg : BIS, Bibliotheks- und Informationssystem der Universität Oldenburg, 2000.
BF251 .O44 2000

Contributions to the study of popular culture
(no. 78) Reading Harry Potter. Westport, Conn. ; London : Praeger Publishers, 2003.
PR6068.O93 Z84 2003

CONTRITION. *See* **REPENTANCE.**

CONTROL (PSYCHOLOGY). *See also* **BRAINWASHING; DOMINANCE (PSYCHOLOGY).**
Alper, Gerald. Like a movie. 1st ed. St. Paul, Minn. : Paragon House, 2004.
BF632.5 .A44 2004

Braiker, Harriet B., 1948- Who's pulling your strings? New York : McGraw-Hill, c2004.
BF632.5 .B69 2004

Carter, Jay. Nasty women. Chicago : Contemporary Books, c2003.
BF632.5 .C365 2003

Cook, Margaret, 1944- Lords of creation. London : Robson, 2002.

Grachev, Georgiĭ. Manipulirovanie lichnost'iu. Moskva : Algoritm, 2002.
BF632.5 .G73 2002

Grolnick, Wendy S. The psychology of parental control. Mahwah, N.J. : L. Erlbaum Associates, 2003.
HQ755.85 .G74 2003

CONTROL (PSYCHOLOGY) IN MOTION PICTURES.
Alper, Gerald. Like a movie. 1st ed. St. Paul, Minn. : Paragon House, 2004.
BF632.5 .A44 2004

CONTROL THEORY.
Chaos control. Berlin ; New York : Springer, c2003.
QA402.3 .C48 2003

Sousa, Joao M. C. Fuzzy decision making in modeling and control. Singapore ; River Edge, N.J. : World Scientific, 2002.

Convergences (Cambridge, Mass.)
Kaplan, Amy. The anarchy of empire in the making of U.S. culture. Cambridge, Mass. : Harvard University Press, 2002.
E661.7 .K37 2002

Convergences (Université de Metz. Centre d'étude des périodiques de langue allemande)
(v. 17.) Grunewald, Michel, 1942- Moeller van den Brucks Geschichtsphilosophie. Bern ; New York : P. Lang, c2001.
DD247.M59 G78 2001

CONVERSATION. *See also* **INTERVIEWS.**
Broth, Matthias, 1965- Agents secrets. Uppsala, Sweden : Uppsala Universitet, c2002.

Hopper, Robert. Gendering talk. East Lansing : Michigan State University Press, c2003.
HQ1075 .H67 2003

Raam, Gabriel. Omanut ha-śiḥah. Tel-Aviv : Yedi'ot aharonot : Sifre hemed, c2003.
P95.45 .R33 2003

Studies in language and social interaction. Mahwah, N.J. ; London : Lawrence Erlbaum, 2003.

CONVERSATION ANALYSIS.
Kecskés, István. Situation-bound utterances in L1 and L2. Berlin ; New York : Mouton de Gruyter, 2002.
P95.45 .K4 2002

Sawyer, R. Keith (Robert Keith) Improvised dialogues. Westport, Conn. : Ablex Pub., 2003.
P95.45 .S3 2003

CONVERSATION - PSYCHOLOGICAL ASPECTS.
Iliev, Vladimir. Psikhologiia na razgovora. 1. izd. Pleven : Lege Artis, 2002.
BF637.C45 I45 2002

Conversations pour demain
(no 17) Babin, Pierre. La fabrique du sexe. Paris : Textuel, [1999]
BF175.5.S48 B23 1999

Conversations with Huston Smith on the spiritual life.
Smith, Huston. The way things are. Berkeley : University of California Press, c2003.
BL43.S64 A5 2003

Conversations with public intellectuals series
Macdonald, Dwight. Interviews with Dwight Macdonald. Jackson : University Press of Mississippi, c2003.
E169.1 .M1363 2003

Conversing with the planets.
Aveni, Anthony F. Rev. ed. Boulder, Colo. : University Press of Colorado, c2002.
QB981 .A99 2002

CONVERSION. See **REPENTANCE.**

CONVERSION - COMPARATIVE STUDIES.
McLaughlin, Michael T. Knowledge, consciousness and religious conversion in Lonergan and Aurobindo. Roma : Editrice Pontificia Universita Gregoriana, 2003.

Convertible dreams.
Corrigan, Patricia, 1948- 1st ed. St. Louis, MO : Virginia Pub., c2001.
BF637.C5 C675 2001

CONVERTS. See **CONVERSION.**

CONVICTION. See **TRUTH.**

Convivencia y globalización.
Ojeda Awad, Alonso. [1a ed.]. [Bogotá] : Universidad Pedagógica Nacional, [2002]

Conway, D. J. (Deanna J.) Magickal, mystical creatures : invite their powers into your life / D.J. Conway. 2nd ed. St. Paul, Minn. : Llewellyn Publications, 2003. 259 p. : ill. ; 23 cm. Rev. ed. of: Magickal, mythical, mystical beasts. 1996. Includes bibliographical references (p. 247-252) and index. ISBN 1-56718-149-X
1. Magic. 2. Animals, Mythical - Miscellanea. 3. Ritual. I. Conway, D. J. (Deanna J.). Magickal, mythical, mystical beasts. II. Title.
BF1623.A55 C67 2003

Magickal, mythical, mystical beasts.
Conway, D. J. (Deanna J.) Magickal, mystical creatures. 2nd ed. St. Paul, Minn. : Llewellyn Publications, 2003.
BF1623.A55 C67 2003

Conyne, Robert K.
Ecological counseling. Alexandria, VA : American Counseling Association, 2003.
BF637.C6 E26 2003

Cook, Ellen Piel, 1952-.
Ecological counseling. Alexandria, VA : American Counseling Association, 2003.
BF637.C6 E26 2003

Cook, Margaret, 1944- Lords of creation : the demented world of men in power / Margaret Cook. London : Robson, 2002. vii, 336 p., [8] p. of plates : ill. ; 24 cm. Includes bibliographical references and index. ISBN 1-86105-552-8 DDC 155.632
1. Men - Psychology. 2. Control (Psychology) I. Title.

Cook, Sybol.
Race and racism in continental philosophy. Bloomington : Indiana University Press, c2003.
HT1523 .R2514 2003

Cook, Thomas H. The interrogation / Thomas Cook. Rockland, MA : Wheeler Pub., 2002. 317 p. ; 24 cm. (Wheeler large print book series) ISBN 1-58724-199-4 DDC 813/.54
1. Police questioning - Fiction. 2. Children - Crimes against - Fiction. 3. Large type books. I. Title. II. Series.
PS3553.O55465 I58 2002

COOKE, GEORGE ALFRED, 1825-1905.
Davenport, Anne Ashley. St. George's Hall. Pasadena : Mike Caveney's Magic Words, c2001.
BF1623 .D38 2001

COOKERY. See also **DINNERS AND DINING; FOOD.**
Wolke, Robert L. What Einstein told his cook. 1st ed. New York : W.W. Norton & Co., c2002.
TX652 .W643 2002

COOKERY, CHINESE.
Lam, Kam Chuen. The Feng Shui kitchen. 1st ed. Boston : Journey Editions, c2000.
TX724.5.C4 L36 2000

COOKERY (HERBS). See **HERBS.**

COOKERY (MARIJUANA). See **MARIJUANA.**

COOKERY, YORUBA.
Ká má baa gbàgbé. [Nigeria] : Jadeas Productions, [2003]

Cool men and the second sex.
Fraiman, Susan. New York : Columbia University Press, c2003.
HQ1090 .F73 2003

Coolican, Hugh. Introduction to research methods and statistics in psychology / Hugh Coolican. 2nd ed. London : Hodder & Stoughton, c1996. 290 p. : ill. ; 25 cm. Includes bibliographical references (p. [282]-284) and index. ISBN 0-340-67937-9 DDC 150/.7/2
1. Psychology - Research - Methodology. 2. Psychometrics. I. Title.
BF76.5 .C663 1996

Research methods and statistics in psychology / Hugh Coolican. 3rd ed. London : Hodder & Stoughton, 1999. xii, 591 p. : ill. ; 25 cm. Includes bibliographical references (p. [567]-580) and index. ISBN 0-340-74760-9 DDC 150.72
1. Psychology - Research - Methodology. 2. Psychometrics. I. Title.
BF76.5 .C664 1999

Coon, Dennis. Essentials of psychology / Dennis Coon. 9th ed. Australia ; Belmont, CA : Thoomson Learning/Wadsworth, c2003. xxxvi, 621, [117] p. : col. ill. ; 28 cm. Includes bibliographical references (p. R-1-R-51) and index. ISBN 0-534-59787-4 DDC 150
1. Psychology. I. Title.
BF121 .C624 2003

Cooper, Cary L. A brief history of stress / Cary L. Cooper and Philip Dewe. 1st ed. Oxford, U.K. ; Malden, MA : Blackwell Pub., 2004. p. cm. (Blackwell brief histories of psychology ; 1) Includes bibliographical references and index. CONTENTS: From early beginnings to the 20th century -- The 20th century -- From the 1950s to Richard Lazarus -- The work of Richard Lazarus -- Work stress and occupational health psychology. ISBN 1-4051-0744-8 (alk. paper) ISBN 1405107456 (pbk : alk. paper) DDC 155.9/042/09
1. Stress (Psychology) - Research - Methodology - History. I. Dewe, Philip. II. Title. III. Series.
BF575.S75 C646 2004

Cooper, Colin, 1954- Individual differences / Colin Cooper. 2nd ed. London : Arnold ; New York : Co-published in the U.S. of America by Oxford University Press, 2002. x, 357 p. : ill. ; 24 cm. Includes bibliographical references (p. [326]-346) and indexes. ISBN 0-340-80816-0 (pbk.) DDC 155.2/2
1. Individual differences. I. Title.
BF697 .C59 2002

Cooper, Judy.
Dilemmas in the consulting room. London ; New York : Karnac, 2002.

Cooper, Myra, 1957- The psychology of bulimia nervosa : a cognitive perspective / Myra Cooper. Oxford ; New York : Oxford University Press, 2003. 337 p. : ill. ; 24 cm. Includes bibliographical references (p. [279]-332) and index. ISBN 0-19-263265-5 DDC 616.852630651
1. Bulimia. 2. Bulimia - Treatment. 3. Cognitive therapy. I. Title.
RC552.B84 C66 2003

Cooper, Patrinella. Gypsy magic : a Romany book of spells, charms, and fortune-telling / Patrinella Cooper. Boston : Weiser Books, 2002. xiii, 162 p. : ill. ; 23 cm. Includes bibliographical references (p. 161). ISBN 1-57863-261-7 (pbk. : alk. paper) DDC 133.4/3/08991497
1. Magic, Romani. I. Title.
BF1622.R65 C66 2002

COOPERATION (PSYCHOLOGY). See **COOPERATIVENESS.**

COOPERATIVENESS.
Barash, David P. The survival game. 1st ed. New York : Times Books, 2003.
HM1111 .B37 2003

Goals and life lessons support materials [electronic resource]. Greenwood Village, CO : FasTracKids International, [1998]
BF637.S4

Morton, Adam. The importance of being understood. London ; New York : Routledge, 2003.
BF637.C45 M65 2003

COOPERATIVENESS - CONGRESSES.
Dahlem Workshop on Genetic and Cultural Evolution of Cooperation (90th : 2002 : Berlin, Germany) Genetic and cultural evolution of cooperation. Cambridge, Mass. : MIT Press in cooperation with Dahlem University Press, c2003.
BF637.H4 D25 2002

Cope, Mick. Lead yourself : be where others will follow : who's steering your boat? / Mick Cope. Cambridge , MA : Perseus Pub., c2001 (2002 printing) xvi, 221 p. : ill. ; 21 cm. "A Momentum book." Includes bibliographical references (p. 215) and index. ISBN 0-7382-0653-9 (pbk.) DDC 158/.4
1. Leadership. I. Title.
BF637.L4 C58 2001

COPING BEHAVIOR. See **ADJUSTMENT (PSYCHOLOGY).**

Coping with anger.
Scheunemann, Pam, 1955- Edina, MN : Abdo Pub., 2004.
BF575.A5 S34 2004

Coping with anxiety.
Bourne, Edmund J. Oakland, CA : New Harbinger, c2003.
BF575.A6 B68 2003

Coping with chaos : analysis of chaotic data and the exploitation of chaotic systems / [edited by] Edward Ott, Tim Sauer, James A. Yorke. New York : J. Wiley, c1994. xii, 418 p. : ill. ; 26 cm. (Wiley series in nonlinear science) "Bibliography" p. 396-414. Includes bibliographical references and index. ISBN 0-471-02556-9 (alk. paper) DDC 003/.7
1. Chaotic behavior in systems. 2. Numerical calculations. I. Ott, Edward. II. Sauer, Tim. III. Yorke, James A. IV. Series.
Q172.5.C45 C67 1994

Coping with public tragedy / edited by Marcia Lattanzi-Licht and Kenneth J. Doka ; foreword by Jack D. Gordon. Washington, DC : Hospice Foundation of America ; New York : Brunner-Routledge, c2003. vi, 314 p. : ill. ; 23 cm. (Living with grief) Includes bibliographical references. ISBN 0-415-94601-8 ISBN 1-89334-904-7 (pbk.) DDC 155.9/35
1. Disasters - Psychological aspects. 2. Disasters - Social aspects. 3. Crisis intervention (Mental health services) I. Lattanzi-Licht, Marcia E. II. Doka, Kenneth J. III. Series.
BF789.D5 C67 2003

Copjec, Joan. Imagine there's no woman : ethics and sublimation / Joan Copjec. Cambridge, Mass. : MIT Press, 2002. viii, 261 p. : ill. ; 24 cm. Includes bibliographical references (p. 232-251) and index. ISBN 0-262-03299-6 (hc. : alk. paper) DDC 170
1. Ethics. 2. Feminist ethics. I. Title.
BJ1012 .C68 2002

COPTIC CHURCH BUILDINGS - EGYPT.
Be thou there. Cairo ; New York : American University in Cairo Press, c2003.

COPTIC CHURCH - DOCTRINES.
Be thou there. Cairo ; New York : American University in Cairo Press, c2001.

COPYRIGHT AND ELECTRONIC DATA PROCESSING.
Matsuura, Jeffrey H., 1957- Managing intellectual assets in the digital age. Boston, MA : Artech House, c2003.
K1401 .M378 2003

COPYRIGHT - COMPUTER PROGRAMS.
Matsuura, Jeffrey H., 1957- Managing intellectual assets in the digital age. Boston, MA : Artech House, c2003.
K1401 .M378 2003

COPYRIGHT - LAW AND LEGISLATION. See **COPYRIGHT.**

Coquio, Eloise.
Constantine, Storm. Bast and Sekhmet. London : R. Hale, c1999.

CORBETT, JIM, 1875-1955.
MAN-EATING LEOPARD OF RUDRAPRAYAG.
Olivetti, Alberto. Gara e bellezza. Fiesole, Firenze : Cadmo, c2002.

Corcoran, Jacqueline. Clinical applications of evidence-based family interventions / Jacqueline Corcoran. Cambridge, U.K. ; New York : Oxford University Press, 2003. xiv, 352 p. : ill. ; 25 cm. Includes bibliographical references (p. 321-344) and index. ISBN 0-19-514952-1 (hardcover : alk. paper) DDC 362.82/86
1. Family social work. 2. Family psychotherapy. I. Title.
HV697 .C67 2003

Cordovero, Moses ben Jacob, 1522-1570. Sefer Mesilot teshuvah : bo yevo'ar ... 'inyan ha-yets.ha-r., [z.o. yetser ha-ra'] mahuto, takhlit beri'ato, ofane kibusho ... 'inyan ha-teshuvah ... sigufe teshuvah, ba'ale teshuvah... / 'arukh mi-kitve ... Mosheh Kordo'ero ... ; ne'erakh ye-hukhan li-defus 'a. y. Shemu'el Yitshak Gad ha-Kohen Yudaikin. Bene

Berak : Da'at kedoshim, 762 [2002] 224 p. ; 25 cm.
Running title: Mesilot teshuvah.
1. Yetzer hara (Judaism) 2. Repentance - Judaism. 3. Cabala.
I. Yudaikin, Shemu'el Yitshak Gad, ha-Kohen. II. Title. III.
Title: Mesilot teshuvah
BM645.R45 C67 2002

CORDOVERO, MOSES BEN JACOB, 1522-1570 - INFLUENCE.
Sack, Bracha, 1933- Shomer ha-pardes. Be'er Sheva' : Universitat Ben-Guryon ba-Negev, c2002.

Coren, Stanley. The pawprints of history : dogs and the course of human events / Stanley Coren ; illustrations by Andy Bartlett. New York ; London : Free Press, c2002. xiii, 322 p. : ill. ; 24 cm. Includes bibliographical references (p. [311]-316) and index. Table of contents URL: http://www.loc.gov/catdir/toc/fy031/2002283337.html ISBN 0-7432-2228-8 DDC 636.7
1. Dogs - Behavior. 2. Dogs. 3. Dogs - History. 4. Human-animal relationships. I. Bartlett, Andy. II. Title.

Sensation and perception / Stanley Coren, Lawrence M. Ward, James T. Enns. 6th ed. Hoboken, NJ : J. Wiley & Sons, c2004. x, 598 p. : ill. (some col.) ; 27 cm. One transparent sheet inserted. Includes bibliographical references (p. 509-576) and index. Publisher description URL: http://www.loc.gov/catdir/desc ription/wiley038/2003049725.html Table of contents URL: http://www.loc.gov/catdir/toc/wiley032/2003049725.html ISBN 0-471-27255-8 (cloth) DDC 153.7
1. Senses and sensation. 2. Perception. I. Ward, Lawrence M. II. Enns, James T. III. Title.
BF233 .C59 2004

Corey, Gerald. Theory and practice of group counseling / Gerald Corey. 6th ed. Australia ; Belmont, CA : Thomson/Brooks/Cole, c2004. xix, 522 p. ; 25 cm. Includes bibliographical references and indexes. ISBN 0-534-59697-5 (student ed.) DDC 158/.35
1. Group counseling. 2. Small groups. I. Title.
BF637.C6 C576 2004

Coriando, Paola-Ludovica, 1969-.
Heidegger, Martin, 1889-1976. Was heisst Denken? Frankfurt am Main : Vittorio Klostermann, c2002.
B3279 .H45 1976 Bd.8

Corlett, J. Angelo, 1958- Race, racism, & reparations / J. Angelo Corlett. Ithaca : Cornell University Press, c2003. xi, 252 p. ; 24 cm. Includes bibliographical references (p. 227-247) and index. ISBN 0-8014-4160-9 (cloth) ISBN 0-8014-8889-3 (pbk.) DDC 305.8
1. Race. 2. Ethnic groups. 3. Racism. 4. Indians of North America - Social conditions. 5. African Americans - Social conditions. 6. Minorities - Government policy - United States. 7. Reparation - United States. I. Title. II. Title: Race, racism, and reparations
HT1523 .C67 2003

Responsibility and punishment / by J. Angelo Corlett. Dordrecht ; Boston : Kluwer Academic Publishers, c2001. ix, 168 p. ; 25 cm. (Library of ethics and applied philosophy ; v. 9) Includes bibliographical references (p. [152]-165) and index. ISBN 0-7923-7167-4 (alk. paper) DDC 170
1. Responsibility. 2. Retribution. 3. Punishment. I. Title. II. Series.
BJ1451 .C67 2001

Corley, M. Deborah. Embracing recovery from chemical dependency : a personal recovery plan / M. Deborah Corley, Jennifer P. Schneider, Richard M. Irons. Sottsdale, AZ : Gentle Path Press, c2003. p. cm. CONTENTS: Denial and other forms of brain trickery -- Double your pleasure, double your trouble : combining drugs and behabiurs -- Embrace the process -- Damage to the body from drug abuse --Recognizing and limiting damage to relationships, career, and the soul -- Healing relationships through accountability -- A new plan -- Creating your recovery support community -- Relapse prevention planning -- Maintaining long-term recovery. ISBN 1-929866-05-4 DDC 616.86/0651
1. Twelve-step programs. 2. Compulsive behavior. 3. Alcoholics - Rehabilitation. 4. Narcotic addicts - Rehabilitation. I. Schneider, Jennifer P. II. Irons, Richard, M.D. III. Title.
BF632 .C63 2003

Corm, Georges. Orient-Occident, la fracture imaginaire / Georges Corm. Paris : Découverte, 2002. 186 p. ; 22 cm. (Cahiers libres) ISBN 2-7071-3838-X DDC 320
1. East and West. 2. Islam and world politics. 3. World politics. 4. International relations. 5. Civilization, Western. I. Title.

Cormier, L. Sherilyn (Louise Sherilyn), 1946-
Counseling strategies and interventions / Sherry Cormier, Harold Hackney. 6th ed. Boston : Pearson, 2004. p. cm. Includes bibliographical references and index.

ISBN 0-205-37052-7 DDC 158/.3
1. Counseling. I. Hackney, Harold, 1935- II. Title.
BF637.C6 H25 2004

Cormorant security studies
The challenges of high command. Houndmills, Basingstoke ; New York : Palgrave Macmillan, 2003.
UB210 .C477 2003

Cornbleth, Catherine. Hearing America's youth : social identities in uncertain times / Catherine Cornbleth. New York : P. Lang, c2003. xiii, 177 p. ; 23 cm. (Adolescent cultures, school & society, 1091-1464 ; v. 23) Includes bibliographical references and index. ISBN 0-8204-5711-6 (pbk. : alk. paper) DDC 305.235/0973
1. Identity (Psychology) in adolescence - United States. 2. Adolescent psychology - United States. 3. National characteristics, American. 4. Group identity - Research - United States. 5. Race awareness in adolescence - United States. I. Title. II. Series.
BF724.3.I3 .C67 2003

Cornblit, Oscar. Violencia social, genocidio y terrorismo / Óscar Cornblit. 1. ed. México, D.F. : Fondo de Cultura Económica, 2002. 158 p. ; 18 cm. (Colección Popular ; 618) (Serie breves) Includes bibliographical references (p. 153-156). ISBN 950-557-518-1
1. Violence. 2. Genocide. 3. Terrorism. I. Title. II. Series: Colección popular (Fondo de Cultura Económica (Mexico)) ; 618. III. Series: Serie Breves (Fondo de Cultura Económica (Mexico))
HM886 .C67 2002

Cornelius, Peter, 1824-1874.
Barbier von Bagdad Er lebt, er lebt.
Hann, Georg. Georg Hann [sound recording]. [Germany] : Preiser Records, p2001.

Barbier von Bagdad. Mein Sohn, sei Allahs Friede hier.
Hann, Georg. Georg Hann [sound recording]. [Germany] : Preiser Records, p2001.

Cornell studies in the history of psychiatry
Rudnytsky, Peter L. Reading psychoanalysis. Ithaca : Cornell University Press, 2002.
BF173 .R794 2002

CORNERS, COMMERCIAL. See **STOCK EXCHANGES.**

Cornette, Joël.
Palais et pouvoir. Vincennes : Presses universitaires de Vincennes, c2003.

Cornils, Stanley P. Your healing journey through grief : a practical guide to grief management / by Stanley Cornils. San Francisco, CA : Robert D. Reed Publishers, c2003. 170 p. : ill. ; 24 cm. Includes bibliographical references (p. [150]-169). ISBN 1-931741-16-6 DDC 155.9/37
1. Grief. 2. Bereavement - Psychological aspects. 3. Death - Psychological aspects. 4. Loss (Psychology) I. Title.
BF575.G7 C677 2003

Corona M., Eduardo.
Relaciones hombre-fauna. México, D.F. : CONACULTA, INAH ; Plaza y Valdes, 2002.
QL85 .R453 2002

CORONERS. See **MEDICAL EXAMINERS (LAW).**

Corpo, ciência e mercado.
Silva, Ana Márcia. Campinas : Editora da UFSC : Editora Autores Associados, 2001.
GT495 .S55 2001

Il corpo pensa.
Giuffrida, Angela, 1943- Roma : Prospettiva, c2002.

CORPORATE ACQUISITIONS. See **CONSOLIDATION AND MERGER OF CORPORATIONS.**

CORPORATE ALLIANCES. See **STRATEGIC ALLIANCES (BUSINESS).**

CORPORATE BUYOUTS. See **CONSOLIDATION AND MERGER OF CORPORATIONS.**

CORPORATE CULTURE.
Brunsson, Nils, 1946- The organization of hypocrisy. 2nd ed. Oslo : Abstrakt ; Malmö, Sweden : Liber ; Herndon, VA : [Distributor] Copenhagen Business School Press, c2002.

Fekete, Sandra. Companies are people, too. Hoboken, N.J. : John Wiley & Sons, c2003.
HD58.7 .F43 2003

Gender, identity and the culture of organizations. London ; New York : Routledge, 2002.
HD58.7 .G46 2002

Harris, O. Jeff. Organizational behavior. New York : Best Business Books, c2002.

HD58.7 .H36943 2002

Holmes, Andrew, 1965- The chameleon consultant. Aldershot ; Burlington, VT : Gower, 2002.

Human resources in the 21st century. Hoboken, N.J. : J. Wiley & Sons, c2003.
HD31 .H81247 2003

Khademian, Anne M., 1961- Working with culture. Washington, D.C. : CQ Press, c2002.
JF1351 .K487 2002

Mauzy, Jeff. Creativity, Inc.. Boston, Mass. : Harvard Business School Press, c2003.
HD53 .M375 2003

Personality and work. 1st ed. San Francisco, CA : Jossey-Bass, c2003.
BF698.9.O3 P47 2003

Sethi, S. Prakash. Setting global standards. Hoboken, N.J. : J. Wiley, c2003.
HD62.4 .S48 2003

The trust process in organizations. Cheltenham, UK ; Northampton, MA : Edward Elgar, c2003.
HD58.7 .T744 2003

Vardi, Yoav, 1944- Misbehavior in organizations. Mahwah, NJ ; London : Lawrence Erlbaum, 2004.
HD58.7 .V367 2004

CORPORATE CULTURE - UNITED STATES.
Job stress in a changing workforce. 1st ed. Washington, DC ; London : American Psychological Association, c1994.
HF5548.85 .J654 1994

Corporate entrepreneurship.
Sathe, Vijay. Cambridge : Cambridge University Press, 2003.

CORPORATE GOVERNANCE.
Carey, Dennis. How to run a company. 1st ed. New York : Crown Business, c2003.
HD38.2 .C374 2003

Management. Cambridge, Mass. : MIT Press, 2003.
HD31 .M2928 2003

Manville, Brook, 1950- A company of citizens. Boston : Harvard Business School Press, c2003.
HD58.7 .M3714 2003

CORPORATE MANAGEMENT. See **INDUSTRIAL MANAGEMENT.**

CORPORATE MERGERS. See **CONSOLIDATION AND MERGER OF CORPORATIONS.**

CORPORATE OFFICERS. See **EXECUTIVES.**

CORPORATE POWER.
Kleiner, Art. Who really matters. 1st ed. New York ; London : Currency/Doubleday, 2003.
HD2741 .K478 2003

CORPORATE REORGANIZATIONS. See **CONSOLIDATION AND MERGER OF CORPORATIONS.**

CORPORATE REORGANIZATIONS - MANAGEMENT.
Lees, Stan. Global acquisitions. Houndmills [England] ; New York : Palgrave Macmillan, 2003.
HD58.8 .L424 2003

CORPORATE STATE. See **FASCISM.**

CORPORATE TAKEOVERS. See **CONSOLIDATION AND MERGER OF CORPORATIONS.**

CORPORATION EXECUTIVES. See **EXECUTIVES.**

CORPORATION LAW. See **CORPORATE REORGANIZATIONS.**

CORPORATIONS. See also **CONSOLIDATION AND MERGER OF CORPORATIONS; CORPORATE REORGANIZATIONS; INTERNATIONAL BUSINESS ENTERPRISES; STOCKS.**
Beyond Keynes. Cheltenham ; Northampton, Mass. : Edward Elgar, c2002.

CORPORATIONS, BUSINESS. See **CORPORATIONS.**

CORPORATIONS - CONSOLIDATION. See **CONSOLIDATION AND MERGER OF CORPORATIONS.**

CORPORATIONS - FINANCE. See **CORPORATE REORGANIZATIONS.**

CORPORATIONS, INTERNATIONAL. *See* **INTERNATIONAL BUSINESS ENTERPRISES.**

CORPORATIONS - MANAGEMENT. *See* **INDUSTRIAL MANAGEMENT.**

CORPORATIONS - MERGERS. *See* **CONSOLIDATION AND MERGER OF CORPORATIONS.**

CORPORATIONS - MORAL AND ETHICAL ASPECTS.
Garten, Jeffrey E., 1946- The politics of fortune. Boston : Harvard Business School Press, c2002.
HD57.7 .G377 2002

CORPORATIONS - PERSONNEL MANAGEMENT. *See* **PERSONNEL MANAGEMENT.**

CORPORATIONS, PUBLIC. *See* **CORPORATIONS.**

CORPORATIONS - REORGANIZATION. *See* **CORPORATE REORGANIZATIONS.**

CORPORATIONS - SOCIOLOGICAL ASPECTS. *See* **CORPORATE CULTURE.**

Corps de lumière.
Musiol, Marie-J. (Marie-Jeanne), 1950- Hull, Québec : Axe Néo-7, art contemporain, [2001?]

Le corps peut-il nous rendre heureux?.
Frey, Jean-Marie. Nantes : Pleins feux, [2002]

CORPULENCE. *See* **OBESITY.**

Corpus des œuvres de philosophie en langue française
Silhon, sieur de (Jean), 1596?-1667. De la certitude des connaissances humaines. [Paris] : Fayard, c2002.

CORPUS HERMETICUM.
Proto, Antonino, 1925- Ermete Trismegisto. Milano : Mimesis, 2000.
BF1598.H6 P76 2000

CORPUS HERMETICUM - EXHIBITIONS.
Magia, alchimia, scienza dal '400 al '700. Firenze : Centro Di, 2002.
BF1598.H6 M34 2002

Corpus philosophorum Medii Aevi. Philosophi Byzantini
(7.) Gemistus Plethon, George, 15th cent. [Magika logia tōn apo Zōroastrou magōn. French & Greek] Magika logia tōn apo Zōroastrou magōn. Athēnai : Akadēmia Athēnōn, 1995.
BF1762 .G45 1995

Corradini, Richard.
The construction of communities in the early Middle Ages. Leiden ; Boston : Brill, 2003.
HN11 .C66 2003

CORRECTIONAL INDUSTRIES. *See* **PRISON INDUSTRIES.**

CORRECTIONS. *See* **PUNISHMENT.**

CORRECTNESS, POLITICAL. *See* **POLITICAL CORRECTNESS.**

Un corredo per la vita.
Tromellini, Pina. Milano : Salani editore, c2002.

CORRELATION OF FORCES. *See* **FORCE AND ENERGY.**

CORRELATION (STATISTICS). *See* **FACTOR ANALYSIS.**

Corrigan, Patricia, 1948- Convertible dreams / by Patricia Corrigan. 1st ed. St. Louis, MO : Virginia Pub., c2001. 200 p. ; 22 cm. ISBN 1-89144-214-7 DDC 814/.6
1. Conduct of life. I. Title.
BF637.C5 C675 2001

Corrington, Robert S., 1950- Wilhelm Reich : psychoanalyst and radical naturalist / Robert S. Corrington. 1st ed. New York : Farrar, Straus and Giroux, 2003. xvii, 297 p. : ill. ; 23 cm. Includes bibliographical references (p. [253]-285) and index. Publisher description URL: http://www.loc.gov/catdir/description/hol031/2002044767.html ISBN 0-374-25002-2 DDC 150.19/5/092
1. Reich, Wilhelm, - 1897-1957. 2. Psychoanalysts - United States - Biography. I. Title.
BF109.R38 C67 2003

CORRUPTION.
Celli, Pier Luigi. Breviario di cinismo ben temperato. 1. ed. Roma : Fazi, 2002.

Cortez, Ana. The playing card oracles : a source book for divination / Ana Cortez ; illustrations and essays by C.J. Freeman. Denver, CO : Two Sisters Press, c2002. xix, 257 p. : ill. (some col.) ; 23 cm. ISBN 0-9719861-0-X DDC 133.0/242
1. Divination cards. I. Freeman, C. J. II. Title.
BF1778.5 .C67 2002

Coscienza e realtà.
Manzotti, Riccardo. Bologna : Società editrice il mulino, c2001.
BF311 .M35 2001

COSMETIC SURGERY. *See* **SURGERY, PLASTIC.**

COSMETICS. *See also* **BEAUTY, PERSONAL.**
Aucoin, Kevyn. Making faces. 1st ed. Boston : Little, Brown, c1997.
RA778 .A873 1997

Cosmic grooves.
Hodges, Jane. San Francisco, Calif. : Chronicle Books, c2001.
BF1726 .H59 2001

COSMOGONY. *See* **CREATION.**

Cosmological crossroads.
Aegean Summer School on Cosmology (1st : 2001 : Samos Island, Greece) Berlin ; New York : Springer, c2002.
QB985 .A44 2001

COSMOLOGY.
Aegean Summer School on Cosmology (1st : 2001 : Samos Island, Greece) Cosmological crossroads. Berlin ; New York : Springer, c2002.
QB985 .A44 2001

Aveni, Anthony F. Conversing with the planets. Rev. ed. Boulder, Colo. : University Press of Colorado, c2002.
QB981 .A99 2002

Baryshev, Yurij. Discovery of cosmic fractals. River Edge, N.J. : World Scientific, c2002.
QB981 .B285 2002

Börner, G. The early universe. 4th ed. Berlin : London : Springer, c2003.

Castagnino, M. (Mario) Tempo e universo. Roma : Armando, c2000.
BD632 .C37 2000

Chmykhov, M. O. (Mykola Oleksandrovych) Vid IAītsia-raïtsia do ideï Spasytelia. Kyïv : "Lybid'", 2001.
BD518.U38 C48 2001

Clow, Barbara Hand, 1943- Catastrophobia. Rochester, Vt. : Bear & Company, c2001.
BF1999 .C587 2001

Harrison, Edward Robert. Masks of the universe. 2nd ed. Cambridge, U.K. ; New York : Cambridge University Press, 2003.
QB981 .H324 2003

Hawking, S. W. (Stephen W.). [Cambridge lectures] The theory of everything. Beverly Hills, CA : New Millennium Press, c2002, 1996.
QB985 .H39 2002

Holmes, Barbara Ann, 1943- Race and the cosmos. Harrisburg, Pa. : Trinity Press International, c2002.
BR563.N4 H654 2002
1. Black author.

Laszlo, Ervin, 1932- The connectivity hypothesis. Albany : State University of New York Press, c2003.
Q175 .L2854 2003

Lurquin, Paul F. The origins of life and the universe. New York : Columbia University Press, c2003.
QH325 .L87 2003

Mircea, Corneliu. Originarul. Bucureşti : Paideia, 2000.
BD638 .M573 2000

Panti, Cecilia, 1964- Moti, virtù e motori celesti nella cosmologia di Roberto Grossatesta. Firenze : SISMEL : Edizioni del Galluzzo, 2001.
B765.G74 P36 2001

Redfield, James. God and the evolving universe. New York : Jeremy P. Tarcher/Putnam, c2002.
BD541 .R43 2002

Tokar, David A. Hans Kayser's Lehrbuch der Harmonik. 2002.

Tsiolkovskiĭ, K. (Konstantin), 1857-1935. Geniĭ sredi lĭudeĭ. Moskva : Mysl', 2002.

TL781.85.T84 A25 2002

Ul'rikh, I. V. Zhizn' cheloveka. Moskva : Izd-vo "Litan", 1999.

Wind, Edgar, 1900- Das Experiment und die Metaphysik. 1. Aufl. Frankfurt am Main : Suhrkamp, 2001.

COSMOLOGY, ANCIENT.
Aveni, Anthony F. Conversing with the planets. Rev. ed. Boulder, Colo. : University Press of Colorado, c2002.
QB981 .A99 2002

COSMOLOGY, BABYLONIAN.
Aveni, Anthony F. Conversing with the planets. Rev. ed. Boulder, Colo. : University Press of Colorado, c2002.
QB981 .A99 2002

COSMOLOGY, CHINESE.
Nielsen, Bent. A companion to Yi jing numerology and cosmology. London ; New York : RoutledgeCurzon, 2003.

COSMOLOGY, EGYPTIAN.
Jenkins, John Major. Galactic alignment. Rochester, Vt. : Bear & Co., 2002.
F1435.3.R3 J45 2002

Vlora, Nedim R., 1943- Le porte del cielo. Bari : M. Adda, c2001.
BF1674 .V56 2001

COSMOLOGY - PHILOSOPHY.
Damiani, Anthony, 1922-1984. Astronoesis. Burdett, N.Y. : Published for Wisdom's Goldenrod, Ltd. by Larson Publications, c2000.
BD418.3 .D347 2000

Domnikov, S. D. (Sergeĭ Dmitrievich) Mat'-zemlia i TSar'-gorod. Moskva : Aleteĭia, 2002.
B4235.H57 D65 2002

Cospito, Giuseppe, 1966- Il "gran Vico" : presenza, immagini e suggestioni vichiane nei testi della cultura italiana pre-risorgimentale (1799-1839) / Giuseppe Cospito. Genova : Name, c2002. 259 p. ; 21 cm. (Storia delle idee e delle istituzioni politiche, Età contemporanea. Studi e testi. Sezione studi ; 5) Includes bibliographical references (p. [227]-250) and index. ISBN 88-87298-34-3 DDC 195
1. Vico, Giambattista, - 1668-1744 - Influence. 2. Cattaneo, Carlo, - 1801-1869. 3. Philosophy, Italian - 19th century. 4. History - Philosophy. I. Title. II. Series: Storia delle idee e delle istituzioni politiche, Età contemporanea. Sezione Studi ; 5.

COST CONTROL. *See* **VALUE ANALYSIS (COST CONTROL).**

COST EFFECTIVENESS. *See* **VALUE ANALYSIS (COST CONTROL).**

Costa, Icléia Thiesen Magalhães.
Memória, cultura e sociedade. Rio de Janeiro : 7Letras, 2002.
BF378.S65 M457 2002

Costa, Marcella.
Bosco Coletsos, Sandra. La struttura parentale nelle fiabe dei fratelli Grimm. Alessandria : Edizioni dell'Orso, 2001.

Costa, Paul T.
Recent advances in psychology and aging. Amsterdam ; Boston : Elsevier, 2003.
BF724.8 .R43 2003

COSTA RICA - ETHNIC RELATIONS.
Castro, Vanessa Smith, 1969- Acculturation and psychological adaptation. Westport, Conn. : Greenwood Press, 2003.
HM841 .C37 2003

Costello, E. Thomas.
A guide to getting it. 1st ed. Portland, Or. : Clarity of Vision Pub., 2002.
BF637.S8 G84 2002

Costes, Alain. Lacan, le fourvoiement linguistique : la métaphore introuvable / Alain Costes. Paris : Presses universitaires de France, 2003. 235 p. ; 22 cm. (Voix nouvelles en psychanalyse) Includes bibliographical references (p. 225-[230]) and indexes. ISBN 2-13-052914-3 DDC 150
1. Lacan, Jacques, - 1901- - Contributions in psycholinguistics. 2. Psycholinguistics. I. Title. II. Series.

COSTUME. *See* **CLOTHING AND DRESS; FASHION; MASKS.**

COSTUME DESIGN.
Fiore, Ann Marie. Understanding aesthetics for the merchandising and design professional. New York : Fairchild, c1997.

Costume design.
Simard-Laflamme, Carole. Habit Habitat Habitus. Trois-Rivières, Québec, Canada : Editions d'art Le Sabord, [2002]
TT507 .S653 2002

COSTUME - PSYCHOLOGICAL ASPECTS.
Fiore, Ann Marie. Understanding aesthetics for the merchandising and design professional. New York : Fairchild, c1997.

Lee, Michelle. Fashion victim. 1st ed. New York : Broadway Books, 2003.
GT524 .L44 2003

Simard-Laflamme, Carole. Habit Habitat Habitus. Trois-Rivières, Québec, Canada : Editions d'art Le Sabord, [2002]
TT507 .S653 2002

Cotroneo, Girolamo. Le idee del tempo : l'etica, la bioetica, i diritti, la pace / Girolamo Cotroneo. Soveria Mannelli (Catanzaro) : Rubbettino, c2002. 125 p. ; 21 cm. (Saggi ; 99) Includes bibliographical references. ISBN 88-498-0303-6 DDC 174
1. Bioethics. 2. Euthanasia. 3. Peace. I. Title. II. Series: Saggi (Soveria Mannelli, Italy) ; 99.

Cotsakis, Spiros, 1963-.
Aegean Summer School on Cosmology (1st : 2001 : Samos Island, Greece) Cosmological crossroads. Berlin ; New York : Springer, c2002.
QB985 .A44 2001

Cottle, Thomas J. Beyond self-esteem : narratives of self knowledge and devotion to others / Thomas J. Cottle. New York : P. Lang, c2003. p. cm. (Adolescent cultures, school and society ; vol. 25) Includes bibliographical references and index. ISBN 0-8204-6718-9 (alk. paper : pbk.) DDC 155.2
1. Self. 2. Identity (Psychology) 3. Self - Social aspects. 4. Self-esteem. I. Title. II. Series: Adolescent cultures, school & society ; v. 25.
BF697 .C675 2003

A sense of self : the work of affirmation / Thomas J. Cottle. Amherst : University of Massachusetts Press, c2003. x, 209 p. ; 25 cm. Includes bibliographical references (p. 193-209). CONTENTS: 1. The act of affirmation -- 2. The relational aspect of affirmation -- 3. The gaze of affirmation -- 4. The miraculous stranger -- 5 The construction of affirmation -- 6. Average, expectable environments -- 7. The affirmation curriculum. ISBN 1-55849-367-0 (alk. paper) DDC 155.2/5
1. Identity (Psychology) I. Title.
BF697 .C68 2003

Couchot, Edmond, 1932-.
Les dons de l'image. Paris : Harmattan, 2003.

La couleur des idées
Petitdemange, Guy. Philosophes et philosophies du XXe siècle. Paris : Seuil, c2003.
B804 .P45 2003

COUNCIL OF EUROPE COUNTRIES. See **EUROPE.**

COUNSELING. See also **COUNSELORS; INTERVIEWING; PSYCHOANALYTIC COUNSELING.**
Adlerian, cognitive, and constructivist therapies. New York : Springer Pub., c2003.
BF637.C6 A335 2003

Anti-discriminatory counselling practice. London ; Thousand Oaks, Calif. : SAGE Publications, 2003.
BF637.C6 A49 2003

Bulkeley, Kelly, 1962- Dreams of healing. New York : Paulist Press, c2003.
BF1099.N53 B85 2003

Cormier, L. Sherilyn (Louise Sherilyn), 1946- Counseling strategies and interventions. 6th ed. Boston : Pearson, 2004.
BF637.C6 H25 2004

Counseling diverse populations. 3rd ed. Boston, Mass. : McGraw-Hill, c2004.
BF637.C6 C6372 2004

Dowling, Linda Culp. Mentor manager, mentor parent. Burneyville, OK : ComCon Books., c2002.
BF637.C6 D6185 2002

Drummond, Robert J. Appraisal procedures for counselors and helping professionals. 5th ed. Upper Saddle River, N.J. : Merrill/Prentice Hall, 2003.
BF176 .D78 2003

Ecological counseling. Alexandria, VA : American Counseling Association, 2003.
BF637.C6 E26 2003

Fall, Kevin A. Theoretical models of counseling and psychotherapy. New York : Brunner-Routledge, 2003.
BF637.C6 F324 2003

Frame, Marsha Wiggins. Integrating religion and spirituality into counseling. Australia ; Pacific Grove, CA : Thomson/Brooks/Cole, c2003.
BF637.C6 F64 2003

Gladding, Samuel T. Community and agency counseling. 2nd ed. Upper Saddle River, N.J. : Pearson : Merrill Prentice Hall, c2004.
BF637.C6 G528 2004

Handbook of counselling psychology. 2nd ed. London ; Thousand Oaks, Calif. : SAGE Publications, 2003.
BF637.C6 H316 2003

Handbook of motivational counseling. Chichester, West Sussex, England ; Hoboken, NJ : J. Wiley, c2004.
BF637.C6 H3172 2004

Hays, Kate F. You're on!. 1st ed. Washington, DC : American Psychological Association, c2003.
BF637.C6 H366 2003

Kottler, Jeffrey A. Introduction to therapeutic counseling. 5th ed. Australia ; Pacific Grove, CA : Thomson-Brooks/Cole, c2004.
BF637.C6 K678 2004

Milner, Judith, senior lecturer. Assessment in counselling. Houndmills, Basingstoke, Hampshire ; New York : Palgrave Macmillan, 2003.
BF637.C6 M5249 2003

Murdock, Nancy L. Theories of counseling and psychotherapy. Upper Saddle River, N.J. : Merrill/Prentice Hall, 2004.
BF637.C6 M846 2004

Nelson-Jones, Richard. Basic counselling skills. London ; Thousand Oaks, Calif. : SAGE Publications, 2003.
BF637.C6 N433 2003

Sommers-Flanagan, John, 1957- Counseling and psychotherapy. Hoboken, NJ : John Wiley & Sons, 2004.
BF637.C6 S69 2004

Tuckwell, Gill, 1948- Racial identity, White counsellors and therapists. Buckingham ; Philadelphia : Open University Press, 2002.
BF637.C6 T84 2002

What's the good of counselling & psychotherapy? London ; Thousand Oaks, Calif. : SAGE Publications, 2002.
BF637.C6 W465 2002

Counseling and psychotherapy.
Sommers-Flanagan, John, 1957- Hoboken, NJ : John Wiley & Sons, 2004.
BF637.C6 S69 2004

COUNSELING - CASE STUDIES.
Frame, Marsha Wiggins. Integrating religion and spirituality into counseling. Australia ; Pacific Grove, CA : Thomson/Brooks/Cole, c2003.
BF637.C6 F64 2003

Murdock, Nancy L. Theories of counseling and psychotherapy. Upper Saddle River, N.J. : Merrill/Prentice Hall, 2004.
BF637.C6 M846 2004

COUNSELING - COMPUTER NETWORK RESOURCES.
Technology in counselling and psychotherapy. New York : Palgrave Macmillan, 2003.
BF637.C6 T467 2003

Tyler, J. Michael. Using technology to improve counseling practice. Alexandria, VA : American Counseling Association, 2003.
BF637.C6 T89 2003

COUNSELING - COMPUTER PROGRAMS.
Technology in counselling and psychotherapy. New York : Palgrave Macmillan, 2003.
BF637.C6 T467 2003

Tyler, J. Michael. Using technology to improve counseling practice. Alexandria, VA : American Counseling Association, 2003.
BF637.C6 T89 2003

Counseling diverse populations / [edited by] Donald R. Atkinson, Gail Hackett. 3rd ed. Boston, Mass. : McGraw-Hill, c2004. p. cm. Includes bibliographical references and indexes. Publisher description URL: http://www.loc.gov/catdir/description/mh031/2003048730.html Table of contents URL: http://www.loc.gov/catdir/toc/mh031/2003048730.html ISBN 0-697-36184-5 (alk. paper) DDC 158/.3/08
1. Counseling. 2. Aged - Counseling of. 3. Women - Counseling of. 4. Handicapped - Counseling of. 5. Gays - Counseling of. I. Atkinson, Donald R. II. Hackett, Gail.
BF637.C6 C6372 2004

COUNSELING - EVALUATION.
Engels, Dennis W. The professional counselor. 3d ed. / Dennis W. Engels and associates. Alexandria, VA : American Counseling Association, c2004.
BF637.C6 P78 2004

COUNSELING - GREAT BRITAIN.
Clinical counselling in voluntary and community settings. New York, NY : Brunner-Routledge, 2003.
BF637.C6 C456 2003

COUNSELING - HISTORY.
Gladding, Samuel T. Community and agency counseling. 2nd ed. Upper Saddle River, N.J. : Pearson : Merrill Prentice Hall, c2004.
BF637.C6 G528 2004

Jacobs, Michael, 1941-. Sigmund Freud. 2nd ed. London ; Thousand Oaks, Calif. : SAGE Publications, 2003.
BF109.F74 J33 2003

COUNSELING - NIGERIA.
Professional concerns arising from twenty years of counselling practice in Nigeria. Garki, Abuja, Nigeria : Official Printers, Jayawahs Communications, 1996.
BF637.C6 P775 1996

COUNSELING - RELIGIOUS ASPECTS.
Frame, Marsha Wiggins. Integrating religion and spirituality into counseling. Australia ; Pacific Grove, CA : Thomson/Brooks/Cole, c2003.
BF637.C6 F64 2003

COUNSELING - RESEARCH - METHODOLOGY.
McLeod, John, 1951- Doing counselling research. 2nd ed. London ; Thousand Oaks, CA : Sage Publications, 2003.
BF637.C6 M37894 2003

Counseling strategies and interventions.
Cormier, L. Sherilyn (Louise Sherilyn), 1946- 6th ed. Boston : Pearson, 2004.
BF637.C6 H25 2004

COUNSELING - TEXTBOOKS.
Hill, Clara E., 1948- Helping skills. 2nd ed. Washington, DC : American Psychological Association, 2004.
BF637.C6 H46 2004

Counselling & psychotherapy in focus
Smith, David Livingston, 1953- Psychoanalysis in focus. London ; Thousand Oaks, Calif. : SAGE Publications, 2003.
BF173 .S569 2003

Counselling Association of Nigeria.
Professional concerns arising from twenty years of counselling practice in Nigeria. Garki, Abuja, Nigeria : Official Printers, Jayawahs Communications, 1996.
BF637.C6 P775 1996

COUNSELORS - RATING OF.
Engels, Dennis W. The professional counselor. 3d ed. / Dennis W. Engels and associates. Alexandria, VA : American Counseling Association, c2004.
BF637.C6 P78 2004

COUNTER CULTURE. See **CONFLICT OF GENERATIONS; CONFORMITY; SOCIAL HISTORY - 1970-; SUBCULTURE.**

Counterpoints (New York, N.Y.)
(v. 116.) From girls in their elements to women in science. New York : P. Lang, 2003.
BF378.S65 F76 2003

(v. 278.) Multiple intelligences reconsidered. New York, NY : P. Lang, c2004.
BF432.3 .M86 2004

Counterpoints (Oxford University Press)
Creativity and development. New York : Oxford University Press, 2003.
BF408 .C7545 2003

COUNTRY AND WESTERN MUSIC. See **COUNTRY MUSIC.**

COUNTRY MUSIC - 1991-2000 - JUVENILE LITERATURE.
Sanders, Mark D. I hope you dance!. Nashville, Tenn. : Rutledge Hill Press, 2003.
BF410 .S26 2003

COUNTRY MUSIC - UNITED STATES. See **COUNTRY MUSIC.**

Coupland, Justine.
Discourse, the body, and identity. Basingstoke, Hampshire ; New York : Palgrave Macmillan, 2003.
HM636 .D57 2003

COUPLES. *See* **GAY COUPLES; MARRIED PEOPLE.**

COUPLES - ANECDOTES.
Bianchi, Carlos J. (Carlos Juan) Relatos de la pareja. Buenos Aires : Corregidor, c2001.

COUPLES - BIOGRAPHY.
Buschey, Monika. "An jenem Tag im blauen Mond September". Düsseldorf : Artemis & Winkler, c2000.

COUPLES, DUAL-INCOME. *See* **DUAL-CAREER FAMILIES.**

COUPLES - PSYCHOLOGY.
Vezin, Annette. [Egéries dans l'ombre des créateurs. English] The 20th-century muse. New York : Harry N. Abrams, 2003.
N71 .V4913 2003

COUPLES, TWO-CAREER. *See* **DUAL-CAREER FAMILIES.**

Couprie, Dirk, 1940- Anaximander in context : new studies in the origins of Greek philosophy / Dirk L. Couprie, Robert Hahn, and Gerard Naddaf. Albany : State University of New York Press, c2003. xiii, 290 p. : ill., maps ; 24 cm. (SUNY series in ancient Greek philosophy) Includes bibliographical references (p. 255-272) and indexes. ISBN 0-7914-5537-8 (alk. paper) ISBN 0-7914-5538-6 (pbk. : alk. paper) DDC 182
1. Anaximander. 2. Philosophy, Ancient. I. Hahn, Robert, 1952- II. Naddaf, Gerard, 1950- III. Title. IV. Series.
B208.Z7 C68 2003

COURAGE. *See also* **HEROES; MORALE.**
Allyn, David (David Smith) I can't believe I just did that. New York : Jeremy P. Tarcher/Penguin, 2004.
BF575.E53 A45 2004

Lacroix, Michel. Le courage réinventé. Paris : Flammarion, c2003.

Mantle, Mickey, 1931- The quality of courage. Lincoln : University of Nebraska Press, [1999]
GV865.A1 M317 1999

Le courage réinventé.
Lacroix, Michel. Paris : Flammarion, c2003.

COURT EPIC, GERMAN - HISTORY AND CRITICISM.
Hübner, Gert. Erzählform im höfischen Roman. Tübingen : Francke, 2003.

Court festivals of the European Renaissance : art, politics, and performance / edited by J.R. Mulryne and Elizabeth Goldring. Aldershot ; Burlington, VT : Ashgate, c2002. xxii, 401 p. : ill., maps, ports. : 24 cm. Includes bibliographical references and index. ISBN 0-7546-0628-7 DDC 791.609409031
1. Festivals - Europe - History - 16th century. 2. Festivals - Europe - History - 17th century. 3. Renaissance. 4. Pageants - Europe - History - 16th century. 5. Pageants - Europe - History - 17th century. I. Mulryne, J. R. (James Ronald) II. Goldring, Elizabeth, 1970-

COURTING. *See* **COURTSHIP.**

COURTS. *See* **JUSTICE, ADMINISTRATION OF.**

COURTS AND COURTIERS. *See* **LADIES-IN-WAITING; PRINCESSES; QUEENS.**

COURTSHIP. *See* **MARRIAGE; MATE SELECTION.**

COURTSHIP - MISCELLANEA.
The love almanac. New York : Welcome Books : Distributed to the trade in the U.S. and Canada by Andrews McMeel Distribution Service, 2003.
BF575.L8 L6675 2003

COURTSHIP - RELIGIOUS ASPECTS - JUDAISM.
Gorfine, Yehudit. Be-karov etslekh. Petaḥ Tiḳvah : Mar'ot, 2002.

Cousens, Elizabeth M.
Ending civil wars. Boulder, Colo. : Lynne Rienner, 2002.
JZ6368 .E53 2002

Couser, G. Thomas. Vulnerable subjects : ethics and life writing / G. Thomas Couser. Ithaca : Cornell University Press, 2004. xv, 234 p. ; 23 cm. Includes bibliographical references (p. [219]-230) and index. ISBN 0-8014-4185-4 (cloth : alk. paper) ISBN 0-8014-8863-X (pbk. : alk. paper) DDC 920/.001
1. Autobiography - Moral and ethical aspects. 2. Ethics. I. Title.
CT25 .C698 2004

Cousineau, Phil.
Smith, Huston. The way things are. Berkeley : University of California Press, c2003.
BL43.S64 A5 2003

The soul aflame. Berkeley, Calif. : Conari Press, 2000.
BL624.2 .S675 2000

Čovek izmedu istorijskog i ličnog vremena.
Litvinović, Gorjana. Beograd : Institut za psihologiju, 2001.
BF697 .L543 2001

COVENANTS NOT TO COMPETE. *See* **COMPETITION.**

Coward, Harold G. Yoga and psychology : language, memory, and mysticism / Harold Coward. Albany : State University of New York Press, 2002. x, 115 p. : ill. ; 23 cm. (SUNY series in religious studies) Includes bibliographical references (p. 93-95) and index. ISBN 0-7914-5499-1 (alk. paper) ISBN 0-7914-5500-9 (pbk. : alk. paper) DDC 181/.45
1. Patañjali. - Yogasūtra. 2. Freud, Sigmund, - 1856-1939. 3. Jung, C. G. - (Carl Gustav), - 1875-1961. 4. Psychology and religion. 5. Yoga. 6. East and West. I. Title. II. Series.
BF51 .C69 2002

Cowen, Lauren. Daughters & mothers / by Lauren Cowen and Jayne Wexler. Philadelphia [Penn.] : Courage Books, c1997. 127 p. : ill. ; 25 x 29 cm. ISBN 0-7624-0110-9 DDC 306.874/3
1. Mothers and daughters. 2. Parent and child. I. Wexler, Jayne. II. Title. III. Title: Daughters and mothers
HQ755.85 .C695 1997

Cowley, Robert.
What ifs? of American history. New York : G.P. Putnam's, c2003.
E179 .W535 2003

Cowper, Donald.
Trainor, Norm, 1946- The eight best practices of high-performing salespeople. Toronto ; New York : Wiley, c2000.
HF5438.25 .T72 2000

Cox, Bonnie. The lightbearer : a true story of love, death, and lessons learned on the other side / Bonnie Cox. Seattle, Wash. : Black Heron Press, c2003. 221 p. ; 23 cm. ISBN 0-930773-65-9 DDC 133.9/1
1. Psychic ability. 2. Parapsychology. I. Title.
BF1031 .C637 2003

Cox, Christoph, 1965- Nietzsche : naturalism and interpretation / Christoph Cox. Berkeley : University of California Press, c1999. xvi, 270 p. ; 23 cm. Includes bibliographical references (p. [247]-260) and index. ISBN 0-520-21553-2 (alk. paper) DDC 193
1. Nietzsche, Friedrich Wilhelm, - 1844-1900 - Contributions in theory of knowledge. 2. Nietzsche, Friedrich Wilhelm, - 1844-1900 - Contributions in ontology. 3. Nietzsche, Friedrich, - 1844-1900. 4. Knowledge, Theory of. 5. Ontology. I. Title.
B3318.K7 C68 1999

Cox, Richard J.
Archives and the public good. Westport, Conn. ; London : Quorum Books, 2002.

Cox, Robert S., 1958- Body and soul : a sympathetic history of American spiritualism / Robert S. Cox. Charlottesville : University of Virginia Press, 2003. viii, 286 p. : ill. ; 24 cm. Includes bibliographical references (p. [237]-282) and index. CONTENTS: Sleepwalking and sympathy -- Celestial symptoms -- Transparent spirits -- Angels' language -- Vox populi -- Invisible world -- Shades. ISBN 0-8139-2230-5 (alk. paper) DDC 133.9/0973
1. Spiritualism - United States - History - 19th century. 2. United States - Race relations - United States - History - 19th century. I. Title.
BF1242.U6 C69 2003

Cox, W. Miles.
Handbook of motivational counseling. Chichester, West Sussex, England ; Hoboken, NJ : J. Wiley, c2004.
BF637.C6 H3172 2004

Coyne, Tami. The spiritual chicks question everything : learn to risk, release, and soar / Tami Coyne and Karen Weissman. York Beach, ME : Red Wheel/Weiser, 2002. xx, 204 p. ; 19 cm. ISBN 1-59003-023-0 (pbk.) DDC 248.8/43
1. Spiritual life. 2. Women - Religious life. I. Weissman, Karen. II. Title.
BL625.7 .C69 2002

Cozby, Paul C. Methods in behavioral research / Paul C. Cozby. 8th ed. Boston : McGraw-Hill, c2004. 396 p. : ill. ; 24 cm. Includes bibliographical references (p. 376-386) and index. Publisher description URL: http://www.loc.gov/catdir/description/mh031/2003051308.html ISBN 0-07-252342-5 DDC 150/.7/2
1. Psychology - Research - Methodology. 2. Social sciences - Research - Methodology. I. Title.
BF76.5 .C67 2004

CPS (CHILD PROTECTIVE SERVICES). *See* **CHILD WELFARE.**

Crabtree, Andy. Designing collaborative systems : a practical guide to ethnography / Andy Crabtree. London ; [New York] : Springer, c2003. xi, 178 p. : ill. ; 24 cm. (Computer supported cooperative work) Includes bibliographical references (p. 169-176) and index. ISBN 1-85233-718-4 (alk. paper) DDC 004.2/1
1. System design. 2. Human-computer interaction. I. Title. II. Series.
QA76.9.S88 C725 2003

The crack in the cosmic egg.
Pearce, Joseph Chilton. Rochester, Vt. : Park Street Press, c2002.
BD331 .P3915 2002

The cradle of thought.
Hobson, R. Peter. New York : Oxford University Press, 2004.
BF720.C63 H63 2004

Hobson, R. Peter. London : Macmillan, 2002.
BF720.C63 H63 2002

The craft of information visualization.
Bederson, Benjamin. San Francisco, Calif. : Morgan Kaufmann ; Oxford : Elsevier Science, 2003.

Craig, Kenneth D., 1937-.
Pain. Mahwah, N.J. : Lawrence Erlbaum, 2003.
BF515 .P29 2003

Craighead, W. Edward.
The concise Corsini encyclopedia of psychology and behavioral science. 3rd ed. Hoboken, NJ : John Wiley & Sons, 2004.
BF31 .E52 2004

CRANIOLOGY. *See* **PHRENOLOGY.**

Crash cultures.
Arthurs, Jane. Bristol, UK ; Portland, OR : Intellect, 2002.

CRASHES, AIRPLANE. *See* **AIRCRAFT ACCIDENTS.**

CRASHES, FINANCIAL. *See* **FINANCIAL CRISES.**

Crass, Chris.
Monkeywrenching the new world order [sound recording]. Oakland, Calif : AK Press ; San Francisco, CA : Alternative Tentacles Records, 2001.

Craven, Rhonda.
International advances in self research. Greenwich, CT : Information Age Pub., 2003.
BF697 .I675 2003

Crawford, Charles (Charles B.).
Evolutionary psychology, public policy, and personal decisions. Mahwah, N.J. : Lawrence Erlbaum Associates, 2004.
BF698.95 .E96 2004

Crawford, Robert G. (Robert George), 1927- What is religion? / Robert Crawford. London ; New York : Routledge, 2002. x, 234 p. ; 22 cm. Includes bibliographical references (p. [216]-225) and index. ISBN 0-415-22670-8 ISBN 0-415-22671-6 (pbk.) DDC 200
1. Religion. I. Title.
BL48 .C722 2002

Craze, Richard, 1950- Mix & match animal & star signs / Richard Craze. 1st ed. Hauppauge, NY : Barron's, 2000. 128 p. : ill. (chiefly col.) ; 28 cm. "This unique flip guide shows you how to read Eastern and Western horoscopes together in order to deepen your understanding of yourself, your friends, and your loved ones". "A Quarto book". ISBN 0-7641-5302-1 DDC 133.5
1. Astrology, Chinese. 2. Astrology. I. Title. II. Title: Mix and match animal and star signs
BF1714.C5 C76 2000

Creamer, Robert W.
Mantle, Mickey, 1931- The quality of courage. Lincoln : University of Nebraska Press, [1999]
GV865.A1 M317 1999

Creasman, Elaine.
Girlfriends. Lincolnwood, Ill. : New Seasons, c2003.
BF575.F66 G57 2003

Create a life that tickles your soul.
Zoglio, Suzanne Willis. Doylestown, Pa. : Tower Hill Press, c1999.
BF724.65.S44 Z65 1999

Created or constructed?.
Storkey, Elaine, 1943- Carlisle [Eng.] : Paternoster Press, 2000.

Creating community with food and drink in Merovingian Gaul.
Effros, Bonnie, 1965- 1st ed. New York ; Houndmills, England : Palgrave Macmillan, 2002.
GT2853.F7 E34 2002

Creating effective & successful teams.
Keen, Thomas R. West Lafayette, Ind. : Ichor Business Books, c2003.
HD66 .K396 2003

Creating effective and successful teams.
Keen, Thomas R. Creating effective & successful teams. West Lafayette, Ind. : Ichor Business Books, c2003.
HD66 .K396 2003

Creating leaderful organizations.
Raelin, Joseph A., 1948- 1st ed. San Francisco : Berrett-Koehler, c2003.
HD57.7 .R34 2003

Creating magical tools.
Cicero, Chic, 1936- 2nd ed. St. Paul, Minn. : Llewellyn Publications, 1999.
BF1623.R7 C48 1999b

Creating racism : psychiatry's betrayal / by Citizens Commission on Human Rights. Los Angeles, CA : Citizens Commission on Human Rights, 1995. 25 p. : ill. ; 28 cm. Caption title: Psychiatry's betrayal in the guise of help. Paper wrappers, stapled.
1. Racism. 2. Cultural psychiatry. 3. Psychiatrists - Attitudes. I. Citizens Commission on Human Rights International. II. Title: Psychiatry's betrayal in the guise of help
RC455.4.E8 C74x 1995

Creating with others.
McNiff, Shaun. 1st ed. Boston, Mass. : Shambhala Publications, 2003.
BF408 .M336 2003

CREATION.
Freund, Philip, 1909- Myths of creation. London : Peter Owen ; Chester Springs, PA : Distributed in the USA by Dufour Editions, 2003.
BL226 .F74 2003

CREATION - BIBLICAL TEACHING.
Giberson, Karl. Species of origins. Lanham, Md. : Rowman & Littlefield, c2002.
BL240.3 .G53 2002

CREATION (LITERARY, ARTISTIC, ETC.). *See also* **CREATIVE ABILITY; PLANNING.**
Allis, Michael, 1964- Parry's creative process. Aldershot : Ashgate, 2003.

Austin, Robert D. (Robert Daniel), 1962- Artful making. Upper Saddle River, NJ : Financial Times/Prentice Hall, 2003.
HD53 .A96 2003

Baron Supervielle, Silvia. Le pays de l'écriture. Paris : Seuil, c2002.

Bimont, Bernard. Je veux que l'on soit homme. Brive : Ecritures, [2002]

Cameron, Julia. The sound of paper. New York : Jeremy P. Tarcher, 2004.
BF408 .C1758 2004

The creation of art. New York, NY : Cambridge University Press, 2003.
N71 .C754 2003

Cullen, Cheryl Dangel. The art of design. 1st ed. Cincinnati, OH : How Design Books, c2003.
NC998.4 .C846 2003

Dobkin de Rios, Marlene. LSD, spirituality, and the creative process. Rochester, Vt. : Park Street Press, c2003.
BF209.L9 D57 2003

Dobyns, Stephen, 1941- Best words, best order. 2nd ed. New York : Palgrave Macmillan, 2003.

Drankov, V. L. (Vladimir L'vovich) Priroda khudozhestvennogo talanta. Sankt-Peterburg : Sankt-Peterburgskiĭ gos. universitet kul'tury i iskusstv, 2001.
BF408 .D66 2001

Drankov, V. L. (Vladimir L'vovich) Priroda khudozhestvennogo talanta. Sankt-Peterburg : Sankt-Peterburgskiĭ gosudarstvennyĭ universitet kul'tury i iskusstv, 2001.

Esin, Sergeĭ. Poputnye mysli. Moskva : Literaturnyĭ in-t im. A. M. Gor'kogo, 2002.

PN145 .E755 2002
La figure des héros dans la création contemporaine. Paris : Harmattan, c2002.

Fritz, Robert, 1943- Your life as art. 1st ed. Newfane, VT : Newfane Press, c2003.
BF637.S4 F753 2003

Galin, A. L. (Aleksandr Latypovich) Psikhologicheskie osobennosti tvorcheskogo povedeniia. Novosibirsk : Novosibirskiĭ gos. universitet, 2001.
BF408 .G315 2001

Gaudin, Thierry. Discours de la méthode créatrice. Gordes : Relié, c2003.

Gerber, Nancy, 1956- Portrait of the mother-artist. Lanham, Md. : Lexington Books, 2003.
PS374.M547 G47 2003

Goux, Jean-Paul. La voix sans repos. Monaco : Rocher, c2003.

Hague, Angela. Fiction, intuition, & creativity. Washington, D.C. : Catholic University of America Press, c2003.
PR826 .H28 2003

Hannas, Wm. C., 1946- The writing on the wall. Philadelphia : University of Pennsylvania Press, c2003.
P381.E18 H36 2003

Haugen Sørensen, Arne, 1932- Samtaler på en bjergtop. 1. oplag. Højbjerg : Hovedland, c2002.

Iannitelli, Leda Muhana. Guiding choreography [microform]. 1994.

Jacob, Suzanne. Ecrire comment pourquoi. Paroisse Notre-Dame-des-Neiges, Québec : Éditions Trois-Pistoles, c2002.
PN56.C69 J23 2002

Jouffroy, Alain, 1928- [Mots et moi] Les mots et moi ; Nantes : Pleins feux, c2002.

Khrestomatiia po psikhologii khudozhestvennogo tvorchestva. Izd., 2. Moskva : Izd-vo Magistr, 1998.
BF408 .K476 1998

Kupka, František, 1871-1957. [Création dans les arts plastiques. Czech. German] Die Schöpfung in der bildenden Kunst. Ostfildern-Ruit : Hatje Cantz, c2001.

Les lieux de l'imaginaire. Montréal : Liber, 2002.

Lindauer, Martin S. Aging, creativity, and art. New York : Kluwer Academic/Plenum Publishers, c2003.
BF724.85.C73 L56 2003

Makeieff, Macha. Poétique du désastre. Arles : Actes sud, c2001.

McNiff, Shaun. Creating with others. 1st ed. Boston, Mass. : Shambhala Publications, 2003.
BF408 .M336 2003

Me-ayin nahalti et shiri. Tel Aviv : Yedi'ot aḥaronot : Sifre ḥemed, c2002.

Medina, Narciso. El suspendido vuelo del ángel creador. La Habana : Ediciones Alarcos, 2003.
1. Black author.

Newton, Stephen J. Painting, psychoanalysis, and spirituality. New York : Cambridge University Press, 2001.
ND1158.P74 N48 2001

Pessoa, Fernando, 1888-1935. [Erostratus. Portuguese & English] Heróstrato e a busca da imortalidade. Lisboa : Assírio e Alvim, c2000.

Pressfield, Steven. The war of art. Warner Books ed. New York : Warner Books, c2002, (2003 printing).
BF408 .P69 2003

Przybylak, Feliks. Inskrypcje ulotności. Wrocław : Oficyna Wydawnicza ATUT-Wrocławskie Wydawn. Oświatowe, 2002.
PN56.C69 P79 2002

Roland, Alan, 1930- Dreams and drama. 1st US ed. Middletown, CT : Wesleyan University Press, 2003.
BF408 .R65 2003

Roland, Alan, 1930- Dreams and drama. 1st US ed. Middletown, CT : Wesleyan University Press, 2003.
BF408 .R65 2003

Sarnoff, Irving, 1922- Intimate creativity. Madison, Wis. : University of Wisconsin Press, c2002.
BF411 .S27 2002

Sawyer, R. Keith (Robert Keith) Improvised dialogues. Westport, Conn. : Ablex Pub., 2003.

P95.45 .S3 2003
Tharp, Twyla. The creative habit. New York : Simon & Schuster, c2003.
BF408 .T415 2003

Thélot, Claude. L'origine des génies. Paris : Seuil, c2003.

Tusa, John. On creativity. London : Methuen, 2003.

Vezin, Annette. [Egéries dans l'ombre des créateurs. English] The 20th-century muse. New York : Harry N. Abrams, 2003.
N71 .V4913 2003

CREATION (LITERARY, ARTISTIC, ETC.) - PSYCHOLOGICAL ASPECTS.
Bodalev, A. A. Kak stanovi͡atsi͡a velikimi ili vydai͡ushchimisi͡a? Moskva : In-t psikhoterapii, 2003.
BF724.5 .B64 2003

Ivanov, S. P. (Sergeĭ Petrovich) Psikhologii͡a khudozhestvennogo deĭstvii͡a sub"ekta. Moskva : Moskovskiĭ psikhologo-sotsial'nyĭ institut ; Voronezh : Izd-vo NPO "MODĖK", 2002.
BF408 .I93 2002

Rasti͡annikov, A. V. Refleksivnoe razvitie kompetentnosti v sovmestnom tvorchestve. Moskva : PER SĖ, 2002.
BF408 .R235 2002

Stepanov, S. I͡U. (Sergeĭ I͡Ur'evich) Refleksivnai͡a praktika tvorcheskogo razvitii͡a cheloveka i organizatsiĭ. Moskva : Nauka, 2000.
BF408 .S75 2000

CREATION (LITERARY, ARTISTIC, ETC.) - SOCIAL ASPECTS.
Group creativity. Oxford ; New York : Oxford University Press, 2003.
BF408 .G696 2003

Menger, Pierre-Michel. Portrait de l'artiste en travailleur. Paris : Seuil, c2002.

Sawyer, R. Keith (Robert Keith) Group creativity. Mahwah, N.J. : L. Erlbaum Associates, 2003.
BF408 .S285 2003

CREATION - MYTHOLOGY.
Freund, Philip, 1909- Myths of creation. London : Peter Owen ; Chester Springs, PA : Distributed in the USA by Dufour Editions, 2003.
BL226 .F74 2003

Giberson, Karl. Species of origins. Lanham, Md. : Rowman & Littlefield, c2002.
BL240.3 .G53 2002

The creation of art : new essays in philosophical aesthetics / edited by Berys Gaut, Paisley Livingston. New York, NY : Cambridge University Press, 2003. 295 p. : ill. ; 24 cm. Includes bibliographical references and index. Publisher description URL: http://www.loc.gov/catdir/description/cam031/2002067420.html Table of contents URL: http://www.loc.gov/catdir/toc/cam031/2002067420.html ISBN 0-521-81234-8 DDC 700/.1
1. Art - Philosophy. 2. Creation (Literary, artistic, etc.) 3. Aesthetics. I. Gaut, Berys Nigel. II. Livingston, Paisley, 1951-
N71 .C754 2003

Création/réel. Convergences
(cahier no 1) La figure des héros dans la création contemporaine. Paris : Harmattan, c2002.

CREATIONISM. *See* **CREATION.**

CREATIVE ABILITY. *See also* **CREATION (LITERARY, ARTISTIC, ETC.); CREATIVE THINKING; GENIUS; INSPIRATION.**
Amašukeli, Elguja. Dro da šemokmedi. T'bilisi : "Merani", 2000.
BF408 .A475 2000

Bardy, Jean. Regard sur "l'évolution créatrice". Paris : Harmattan, c2003.

Beyond knowledge. Mahwah, N.J. : L. Erlbaum Associates, 2003.
BF412 .B44 2003

Boden, Margaret A. The creative mind. 2nd ed. London ; New York : Routledge, 2003.
BF408 .B55 2003

Creativity and development. New York : Oxford University Press, 2003.
BF408 .C7545 2003

Creativity and music education. Edmonton, Canada : Canadian Music Educators' Association, c2002.

Creativity. 1st ed. Washington, DC : American Psychological Association, c2004.

BF408 .C7548 2004

Dobkin de Rios, Marlene. LSD, spirituality, and the creative process. Rochester, Vt. : Park Street Press, c2003.
BF209.L9 D57 2003

Drankov, V. L. (Vladimir L'vovich) Priroda khudozhestvennogo talanta. Sankt-Peterburg : Sankt-Peterburgskiĭ gos. universitet kul'tury i iskusstv, 2001.
BF408 .D66 2001

Drankov, V. L. (Vladimir L'vovich) Priroda khudozhestvennogo talanta. Sankt-Peterburg : Sankt-Peterburgskiĭ gosudarstvennyĭ universitet kul'tury i iskusstv, 2001.

Ecriture et maladie. Paris : Editions Imago, c2003.

Fritz, Robert, 1943- Your life as art. 1st ed. Newfane, VT : Newfane Press, c2003.
BF637.S4 F753 2003

Gaudin, Thierry. Discours de la méthode créatrice. Gordes : Relié, c2003.

Graham, Douglas, 1950- Ideation. Hoboken, N.J. : John Wiley & Sons, Inc., c2004.
BF408 .G664 2004

Granovskaia, R. M. (Rada Mikhaĭlovna) Konflikt i tvorchestvo v zerkale psikhologii. Moskva : Genezis, 2002.
BF637.I48 G72 2002

Hannas, Wm. C., 1946- The writing on the wall. Philadelphia : University of Pennsylvania Press, c2003.
P381.E18 H36 2003

Harris, Chris. Building innovative teams. Houndmills [England] ; New York : Palgrave Macmillan, 2003.
HD66 .H3744 2003

Harvard business essentials. Boston, Mass. : Harvard Business School Press, c2003.
HD45 .H3427 2003

High culture. Albany : State University of New York Press, c2003.
HV4998 .H544 2003

I͡Akovleva, E. L. (Evgeniia Leonovna) Psikhologiia razvitiia tvorcheskogo potentsiala lichnosti. Moskva : Moskovskiĭ psikhologo-sotsial'nyĭ institut : Izd-vo "Flinta" / 1997.
BF408 .I15 1997

Ikram Azam, 1940- Towards the third millennium. Islamabad : Pakistan Futuristics Foundation & Institute, c1999.
BF408 .I445 1999

Khrestomatiia po psikhologii khudozhestvennogo tvorchestva. Izd., 2. Moskva : Izd-vo Magistr, 1998.
BF408 .K476 1998

Koberg, Don, 1930- The universal traveler. 4th ed. Menlo Park, Calif. : Crisp Learning, c2003.
BF441 .K55 2003

McNiff, Shaun. Creating with others. 1st ed. Boston, Mass. : Shambhala Publications, 2003.
BF408 .M336 2003

Piirto, Jane, 1941- Understanding creativity. Scottsdale, Ar. : Great Potential Press : 2004.
BF408 .P87 2004

Ponomarenko, V. A. (Vladimir Aleksandrovich) Sozidatel'naia psikhologiia. Moskva : Moskovskiĭ psikhologo-sotsial'nyĭ institut ; Voronezh : Izd-vo NPO "MODĖK", 2000.
BF408 .P572 2000

Shoham, S. Giora, 1929- Art, crime, and madness. Brighton [England] ; Portland, Or. : Sussex Academic Press, 2002, c2003.
N71.5 .S53 2003

Shoham, S. Giora, 1929- Ṭeruf, setiyah vi-yetsirah. [Israel] : Miśrad ha-biṭaḥon, [2002]

Skloot, Floyd. In the shadow of memory. Lincoln : University of Nebraska Press, c2003.
PS3569.K577 Z47 2003

Sternberg, Robert J. Wisdom, intelligence, and creativity synthesized. Cambridge, UK ; New York : Cambridge University Press, 2003.
BF431 .S7385 2003

Tharp, Twyla. The creative habit. New York : Simon & Schuster, c2003.
BF408 .T415 2003

CREATIVE ABILITY IN ART. *See* **CREATION (LITERARY, ARTISTIC, ETC.).**

CREATIVE ABILITY IN BUSINESS. *See also* **SUCCESS IN BUSINESS.**
Amidon, Debra M., 1946- The innovation superhighway. Amsterdam ; Boston ; London : Butterworth-Heinemann, c2003.
HD53 .A462 2003

Austin, Robert D. (Robert Daniel), 1962- Artful making. Upper Saddle River, NJ : Financial Times/Prentice Hall, 2003.
HD53 .A96 2003

Barker, Alan, 1956- The alchemy of innovation. London : Spiro Press, 2002.

Ceserani, Jonne, 1954- Big ideas. London ; Sterling, VA : Kogan Page Limited, 2002.
HD53 .C46 2002

Christensen, Clayton M. The innovator's solution. Boston, Mass. : Harvard Business School Press, c2003.

Davenport, Thomas H. What's the big idea? Boston, Mass. : Harvard Business School Press, c2003.
HD53 .D38 2003

Graham, Douglas, 1950- Ideation. Hoboken, N.J. : John Wiley & Sons, Inc., c2004.
BF408 .G664 2004

Grulke, Wolfgang. Lessons in radical innovation. International ed. London : Financial Times Prentice Hall, 2002.

Hamel, Gary. Leading the revolution. Rev. and updated hardcover ed. [Boston, Mass.] : Harvard Business School Press, c2002.

Howkins, John, 1945- The creative economy. London : Allen Lane, 2001.

Mauzy, Jeff. Creativity, Inc.. Boston, Mass. : Harvard Business School Press, c2003.
HD53 .M375 2003

Mezias, Stephen J. Organizational dynamics of creative destruction. Houndmills [England] ; New York : Palgrave Macmillan, 2002.
HB615 .M49 2002

Sathe, Vijay. Corporate entrepreneurship. Cambridge : Cambridge University Press, 2003.

Von Stamm, Bettina. The innovation wave. Chichester : John Wiley & Sons, c2003.

Von Stamm, Bettina. Managing innovation, design and creativity. Chichester, England ; Hoboken, NJ : J. Wiley, c2003.
HD45 .V65 2003

CREATIVE ABILITY IN BUSINESS - CASE STUDIES.
Von Stamm, Bettina. Managing innovation, design and creativity. Chichester, England ; Hoboken, NJ : J. Wiley, c2003.
HD45 .V65 2003

CREATIVE ABILITY IN LITERATURE.
Gerber, Nancy, 1956- Portrait of the mother-artist. Lanham, Md. : Lexington Books, c2003.
PS374.M547 G47 2003

CREATIVE ABILITY IN OLD AGE.
Lindauer, Martin S. Aging, creativity, and art. New York : Kluwer Academic/Plenum Publishers, c2003.
BF724.85.C73 L56 2003

CREATIVE ABILITY IN SCIENCE.
Lambert, Ladina Bezzola. Imagining the unimaginable. Amsterdam ; New York, NY : Rodopi, 2002.
QB29 .L35 2002

CREATIVE ABILITY IN TECHNOLOGY. *See* **TECHNOLOGICAL INNOVATIONS.**

CREATIVE ABILITY - PROBLEMS, EXERCISES, ETC.
Epstein, Robert, 1953- The big book of creativity games. New York : McGraw-Hill, c2000.
BF408 .E67 2000

CREATIVE ABILITY - SOCIAL ASPECTS.
Dubina, I. N. (Igor' Nikolaevich) Tvorchestvo kak fenomen sotsial'nykh kommunikatsiĭ. Novosibirsk : Sibirskoe otd-nie RAN, 2000.
BF411 .D82 2000

Creative dissent : psychoanalysis in evolution / edited by Alan Roland, Barry Ulanov, and Claude Barbre. Westport, Conn. : Praeger Publishers, 2003. p. cm. Includes bibliographical references and index. ISBN 0-275-98061-8 (alk. paper) DDC 150.19/5
1. Psychoanalysis. 2. Psychoanalysis - History. I. Roland, Alan, 1930- II. Ulanov, Barry. III. Barbre, Claude.

BF173 .C794 2003

The creative economy.
Howkins, John, 1945- London : Allen Lane, 2001.

Creative envy.
Byington, Carlos Amadeu Botelho, 1933- [Inveja criativa. English] 1st American ed. Wilmette, Ill. : Chiron Publications, 2004.
BF575.E65 B95 2004

The creative habit.
Tharp, Twyla. New York : Simon & Schuster, c2003.
BF408 .T415 2003

The creative mind.
Boden, Margaret A. 2nd ed. London ; New York : Routledge, 2003.
BF408 .B55 2003

CREATIVE THINKING.
Beyond knowledge. Mahwah, N.J. : L. Erlbaum Associates, 2003.
BF412 .B44 2003

Creativity and development. New York : Oxford University Press, 2003.
BF408 .C7545 2003

Gordon, Barry, M.D. Intelligent memory. New York : Viking, 2003.
BF371 .G66 2003

Hugl, Ulrike. Qualitative Inhaltsanalyse und Mind-Mapping. Wiesbaden : Gabler, 1995.

Monahan, Tom. The do-it-yourself lobotomy. New York : J. Wiley, c2002.
BF408 .M59 2002

Pressfield, Steven. The war of art. Warner Books ed. New York : Warner Books, c2002, (2003 printing).
BF408 .P69 2003

Rantanen, Kalevi. Simplified TRIZ. Boca Raton : St. Lucie Press, c2002.
TA153 .R26 2002

Ruggiero, Vincent Ryan. The art of thinking. 7th ed. New York : Pearson/Longman, c2004.
BF441 .R84 2004

Sternberg, Robert J. Wisdom, intelligence, and creativity synthesized. Cambridge, UK ; New York : Cambridge University Press, 2003.
BF431 .S7385 2003

Tharp, Twyla. The creative habit. New York : Simon & Schuster, c2003.
BF408 .T415 2003

Zaltman, Gerald. How customers think. Boston, Mass. : Harvard Business School Press, c2003.
HF5415.32 .Z35 2003

CREATIVE THINKING (EDUCATION). *See* **CREATIVE THINKING.**

CREATIVE THINKING - PROBLEMS, EXERCISES, ETC.
Bagley, Michael T. Red square & green squigglies. Woodcliff Lake, NJ : Green Squiggliess Press, c1996.
BF408 .B327 1996

Epstein, Robert, 1953- The big book of creativity games. New York : McGraw-Hill, c2000.
BF408 .E67 2000

Mallon, Brenda. A year of creativity. Kansas City, Mo. : Andrews McMeel Pub., c2003.
BF408 .M234 2003

CREATIVE THINKING - SOCIAL ASPECTS.
Group creativity. Oxford ; New York : Oxford University Press, 2003.
BF408 .G696 2003

Sawyer, R. Keith (Robert Keith) Group creativity. Mahwah, N.J. : L. Erlbaum Associates, 2003.
BF408 .S285 2003

Creative visualization.
Gawain, Shakti, 1948- [Rev. ed.]. Navato, Calif. : Nataraj Pub./New World Library, c2002.
BF367 .G34 2002

CREATIVE WRITING.
Jacob, Suzanne. Ecrire comment pourquoi. Paroisse Notre-Dame-des-Neiges, Québec : Éditions Trois-Pistoles, c2002.
PN56.C69 J23 2002

Stafford, Kim Robert. The muses among us. Athens : University of Georgia Press, c2003.
PE1408 .S6667 2003

CREATIVENESS. *See also* **CREATIVE ABILITY.**
Dobkin de Rios, Marlene. LSD, spirituality, and the

creative process. Rochester, Vt. : Park Street Press, c2003.
BF209.L9 D57 2003

CREATIVITY. *See* **CREATIVE ABILITY.**

Creativity and development / R. Keith Sawyer ... [et al.]. New York : Oxford University Press, 2003. x, 244 p. ill. ; 25 cm. (Counterpoints) Includes bibliographical references and index. ISBN 0-19-514899-1 ISBN 0-19-514900-9 DDC 153.3/5
1. Creative thinking. 2. Creative ability. 3. Developmental psychology. I. Sawyer, R. Keith (Robert Keith) II. Series: Counterpoints (Oxford University Press)
BF408 .C7545 2003

Creativity and music education / Timothy Sullivan, Lee Willingham, editors. Edmonton, Canada : Canadian Music Educators' Association, c2002. xxi, 249 p. : ill., music ; 25 cm. (Research to practice ; v. 1) Includes bibliographical references. ISBN 0-920630-11-1
1. Music - Instruction and study. 2. Creative ability. I. Sullivan, Timothy, 1954- II. Willingham, Lee. III. Canadian Music Educators' Association. IV. Series.

Creativity : from potential to realization / edited by Robert J. Sternberg, Elena L. Grigorenko, and Jerome L. Singer. 1st ed. Washington, DC : American Psychological Association, c2004. p. cm. Includes bibliographical references and index. CONTENTS: Heisenberg's haiku, Madonna's math : why it is hard to be creative in -- Everyone of the house / James C. Kaufman and John Baer -- The artistic personality : a systems perspective / Sami Abuhamdeh and Mihaly Csikszentmihalyi -- The general-specificity of creativity : a multivariate approach / Todd Lubart and Jacques-Henri Guignard -- Everyone has creative potential / Mark A. Runco -- The evolved fluid specificity of human creative talent / Gregory J. Feist -- Creativity as a constrained stochastic process / Dean Keith Simonton -- Inventors : the ordinary genius next door / Sheila J. Henderson -- Artistic scientists and scientific artists : the link between polymathy and creativity / Robert Root-Bernstein and Michele Root Berstein -- Why creativity is domain general, why it looks domain specific, and why the distinction doesn't matter / Jonathan A. Plucker and Ronald A. Beghetto -- Vertical and horizontal mentoring for creativity / Mia Keinanen and Howard Gardner -- Concluding comments : cross-over creativity or domain specificity? / Jerome L. Singer. ISBN 1-59147-120-6 DDC 153.3/5
1. Creative ability. I. Sternberg, Robert J. II. Grigorenko, Elena. III. Singer, Jerome L.
BF408 .C7548 2004

Creativity games.
Epstein, Robert, 1953- The big book of creativity games. New York : McGraw-Hill, c2000.
BF408 .E67 2000

CREATIVITY IN LITERATURE.
Gerber, Nancy, 1956- Portrait of the mother-artist. Lanham, Md. : Lexington Books, c2003.
PS374.M547 G47 2003

Lives in translation. 1st ed. New York ; Houndmills, England : Palgrave Macmillan, 2003.
P115.25 .L58 2003

Creativity, Inc.
Mauzy, Jeff. Boston, Mass. : Harvard Business School Press, c2003.
HD53 .M375 2003

Creatures of the supernatural in Scotland.
Fleming, Maurice. Not of this world. Edinburgh : Mercat, 2002.

Credere in dialogo.
Sartorio, Ugo. Padova : Edizioni Messaggero, 2002.

Credito italiano.
Metamorfosi della città. Milano : Garzanti / Scheiwiller, 1995 (1996 printing)
HT111 .M472 1995

CREMATION. *See* **FUNERAL RITES AND CEREMONIES.**

Creppell, Ingrid. Toleration and identity : foundations in early modern thought / Ingrid Creppell. New York ; London : Routledge, 2003. xi, 212 p. ; 24 cm. Includes bibliographical references (p. 163-206) and index. CONTENTS: Introduction : basic reconceptions -- Language and identity : making toleration a norm -- Bodin and the state : structuring a political self -- Montaigne and the body : self-reflection in time -- Locke and society : boundaries of recognition -- Defoe and the individual : forms of public judgment -- Rebuilding toleration. ISBN 0-415-93301-3 (hb.) ISBN 0-415-93302-1 (pb.) DDC 179/.9
1. Toleration. 2. Group identity. 3. Social conflict. I. Title.
HM1271 .C73 2003

CREPUSCOLARISMO. *See* **MODERNISM (LITERATURE).**

Cresswell, Jamie.
New religious movements. London ; New York : Routledge in association with the Institute of Oriental Philosophy European Centre, 1999.
BL80.2 .N397 1999

CRIME. *See* **CRIMINOLOGY; SEX CRIMES.**

CRIME AND CRIMINALS. *See* **CRIME.**

CRIME DETECTION. *See* **CRIMINAL INVESTIGATION.**

CRIME INVESTIGATION. *See* **CRIMINAL INVESTIGATION.**

CRIME - ITALY - CASE STUDIES.
Lucarelli, Carlo, 1960- Misteri d'Italia. Torino : Einaudi, c2002.

CRIME SCENES. *See* **CRIMINAL INVESTIGATION.**

CRIME - STUDY AND TEACHING. *See* **CRIMINOLOGY.**

CRIME VICTIMS. *See* **VICTIMS OF CRIMES.**

CRIMES. *See* **CRIME.**

CRIMES AGAINST HUMANITY. *See* **MURDER; SLAVERY.**

CRIMINAL ANTHROPOLOGY. *See* **CRIMINAL PSYCHOLOGY.**

CRIMINAL ANTHROPOLOGY - HISTORY.
Simon, Jürgen, 1966- Kriminalbiologie und Zwangssterilisation. Münster ; New York : Waxmann, c2001.

CRIMINAL ANTHROPOMETRY. *See* **CRIMINAL ANTHROPOLOGY.**

CRIMINAL INVESTIGATION. *See* **LEGAL DOCUMENTS - IDENTIFICATION; POLICE QUESTIONING.**

CRIMINAL INVESTIGATION - PERIODICALS.
Document, various specification. Wrocław : University of Wrocław, Faculty of Law and Administration, Department of Criminalistics, 2000-
BF905.C7 D63

CRIMINAL INVESTIGATIONS. *See* **CRIMINAL INVESTIGATION.**

CRIMINAL JUSTICE, ADMINISTRATION OF. *See* **AMNESTY; CRIME; LAW ENFORCEMENT.**

Criminal justice (LFB Scholarly Publishing LLC)
Champion, David R. Narcissism and entitlement. New York : LFB Scholarly Pub. LLC, c2003.
BF692.15 .C47 2003

Wilkinson, Deanna Lyn, 1968- Guns, violence, and identity among African American and Latino youth. New York : LFB Scholarly Pub., 2003.
HQ799.2.V56 W55 2003

CRIMINAL LAW. *See* **CRIME; LIBEL AND SLANDER.**

CRIMINAL PROCEDURE. *See* **ORDEAL; TRIAL PRACTICE.**

CRIMINAL PSYCHIATRY. *See* **CRIMINAL PSYCHOLOGY.**

CRIMINAL PSYCHOLOGY. *See also* **OPPRESSION (PSYCHOLOGY).**
Rhodes, Henry T. F. (Henry Taylor Fowkes), b. 1892. Le génie et le crime. Paris, France : Harmattan, c2002.

CRIMINAL PSYCHOLOGY - PERIODICALS.
Document, various specification. Wrocław : University of Wrocław, Faculty of Law and Administration, Department of Criminalistics, 2000-
BF905.C7 D63

CRIMINAL RESTITUTION. *See* **REPARATION.**

CRIMINALS. *See also* **CRIME; CRIMINOLOGY; TERRORISTS.**
Rhodes, Henry T. F. (Henry Taylor Fowkes), b. 1892. Le génie et le crime. Paris, France : Harmattan, c2002.

CRIMINALS - PSYCHOLOGY. *See* **CRIMINAL PSYCHOLOGY.**

CRIMINOLOGY. *See* **CRIME.**

CRIMINOLOGY - GERMANY - HISTORY - 20TH CENTURY.
Simon, Jürgen, 1966- Kriminalbiologie und Zwangssterilisation. Münster ; New York : Waxmann, c2001.

Crisand, Ekkehard. Psychologie der Persönlichkeit : eine Einführung / von Ekkehart Crisand. 8., durchgesehene Aufl. Heidelberg : I.H. Sauer-Verlag, 2000. 101 p. : ill. ; 21 cm. (Arbeitshefte Führungspsychologie ; Bd. 1) Includes bibliographical references (p. 101). ISBN 3-7938-7228-9
1. Personality. 2. Typology (Psychology) I. Title. II. Series.
BF698 .C715 2000

La crise de l'esprit.
Jannoud, Claude. Lausanne, Suisse : Age d'homme, c2001.

CRISES. *See* **FINANCIAL CRISES.**

CRISES, FINANCIAL. *See* **FINANCIAL CRISES.**

CRISES INTERVENTION (MENTAL HEALTH SERVICES).
Beristain, Carlos M. Apoyo psicosocial en catátrofes colectivas. 1a. ed. Caracas, Venezuela : Asociación Venezolana de Psicología Social-AVESPO : Comisión de Estudios de Posgrado, Facultad de Hunanidades y Educación, Universidad Central de Venezuela, 2000.

CRISIS INTERVENTION (MENTAL HEALTH SERVICES).
Bulkeley, Kelly, 1962- Dreams of healing. New York : Paulist Press, c2003.
BF1099.N53 B85 2003

Coping with public tragedy. Washington, DC : Hospice Foundation of America ; New York : Brunner-Routledge, c2003.
BF789.D5 C67 2003

Mental health and mass violence [electronic resource]. [Bethesda, MD : National Institute of Mental Health, 2002]

CRISIS MANAGEMENT. *See* **CONFLICT MANAGEMENT.**

Crisp, Roger, 1961-.
Aristotle. [Nicomachean ethics. English] Nicomachean ethics. Cambridge, U.K. ; New York : Cambridge University Press, c2002 (2002 printing)
B430.A5 C7513 2000

Crítica cult.
Souza, Eneida Maria de. Belo Horizonte : Editora UFMG, 2002.
PN94 .S68 2002

Crítica de la razón científica.
Mires, Fernando. 1a ed. Caracas : Editorial Nueva Sociedad, 2002.

CRITICAL CARE MEDICINE. *See* **TERMINAL CARE.**

Critical communication theory.
Jansen, Sue Curry. Lanham, Md. ; Oxford : Rowman & Littlefield, c2002.
HM651 .J36 2002

Critical consciousness.
Mustakova-Possardt, Elena, 1960- Westport, Conn. ; London : Praeger, 2003.
BL53 .M98 2003

Critical faith.
Kuipers, Ronald Alexander. Amsterdam ; New York, NY : Rodopi, 2002.

Critical fictions.
Fichtelberg, Joseph. Athens : University of Georgia Press, c2003.
PS366.S35 F53 2003

CRITICAL INCIDENT TECHNIQUE.
Critical incidents in group counseling. Alexandria, VA : American Counseling Association, 2004.
BF637.C6 C72 2004

Critical incidents in group counseling / [edited by Lawrence E. Tyson, Rachelle Prusse, Jim Whitledge. Alexandria, VA : American Counseling Association, 2004. p. cm. ISBN 1-55620-190-7 (alk. paper) DDC 158/.35
1. Group counseling. 2. Critical incident technique. I. Tyson, Lawrence E. II. Prusse, Rachelle. III. Whitledge, Jim.
BF637.C6 C72 2004

Critical media studies.
Jansen, Sue Curry. Critical communication theory. Lanham, Md. ; Oxford : Rowman & Littlefield, c2002.
HM651 .J36 2002

CRITICAL PEDAGOGY.
Chomsky, Noam. Chomsky on democracy & education. New York ; London : RoutledgeFalmer, 2003.
LB885.C5215 C46 2003

CRITICAL PHENOMENA (PHYSICS).
Sornette, D. Why stock markets crash. Princeton, N.J. : Princeton University Press, c2003.
HB3722 .S66 2003

[Critical psychology (Lawrence & Wishart)] Critical psychology. London : Lawrence & Wishart, c2001-
v. ; 22 cm. Frequency: Three times per year. [Issue 1]- . Other title: International journal of critical psychology. Spine title: IJCP. Issues 2-5> have also distinctive titles. Editor: Valerie Walkerdine. Latest issue consulted: Issue 5, published 2002. First issue unnumbered and called: Launch issue. ISSN 1471-4167
1. Critical psychology - Periodicals. 2. Communism and psychology - Periodicals. I. Walkerdine, Valerie. II. Title: International journal of critical psychology III. Title: IJCP
BF39.9 .C75

CRITICAL PSYCHOLOGY - PERIODICALS.
[Critical psychology (Lawrence & Wishart)] Critical psychology. London : Lawrence & Wishart, c2001-
BF39.9 .C75

Critical reviews and annotated bibliographies series
Gender perspectives on property and inheritance. Oxford : Oxfam, c2001.
HB715 .G45 2001

Critical studies
(no. 18) Feminism/femininity in Chinese literature. Amsterdam ; New York : Rodopi, 2002.

CRITICAL THEORY.
Jansen, Sue Curry. Critical communication theory. Lanham, Md. ; Oxford : Rowman & Littlefield, c2002.
HM651 .J36 2002

CRITICAL THINKING.
Flage, Daniel E., 1951- The art of questioning. Upper Saddle River, N.J. : Pearson/Prentice Hall, c2004.
BF441 .F55 2004

Goodman, Steven. Teaching youth media. New York : Teachers College Press, c2003.
LB1043 .G59 2003

Ruggiero, Vincent Ryan. The art of thinking. 7th ed. New York : Pearson/Longman, c2004.
BF441 .R84 2004

White, Curtis, 1951- The middle mind. 1st ed. [San Francisco] : HarperSanFrancisco, c2003.

CRITICALLY ILL. See TERMINALLY ILL.

CRITICALLY ILL CHILDREN. See TERMINALLY ILL CHILDREN.

CRITICISM. See also AESTHETICS; CANON (LITERATURE); HERMENEUTICS; LITERATURE - HISTORY AND CRITICISM.
Burke, Kenneth, 1897- On human nature. Berkeley : University of California Press, c2003.
B945.B771 R84 2003

Dobyns, Stephen, 1941- Best words, best order. 2nd ed. New York : Palgrave Macmillan, 2003.

Morales Villaroel, Oscar. Huellas y relatos. Caracas : [s.n.], 2001.

Radhakrishnan, R. (Rajagopalan) Theory in an uneven world. Oxford ; Malden, MA : Blackwell, 2003.

Starobinski, Jean. La relation critique. Ed. rev. et augm. [Paris] : Gallimard, c2001.
PN81 .S69 2001

Wortham, Simon. Samuel Weber. Aldershot, England ; Burlington, VT : Ashgate, c2003.
PN81 .W64 2003

Xu, Fen. Zou xiang hou xian dai yu hou zhi min. Di 1 ban. Beijing : Zhongguo she hui ke xue chu ban she : Xin hua shu dian jing xiao, 1996.
PN81 .H76 1996 <Asian China>

CRITICISM - HISTORY - 20TH CENTURY.
Souza, Eneida Maria de. Crítica cult. Belo Horizonte : Editora UFMG, 2002.
PN94 .S68 2002

CRITICISM (PHILOSOPHY).
Levent, Jean-Marc. Les ânes rouges. Paris : Harmattan, 2003.

CRITICISM - TECHNIQUE. See CRITICISM.

A critique of moral knowledge.
Simon, Yves René Marie, 1903-1961. [Critique de la connaissance morale. English] New York : Fordham University Press, 2002.
BJ1249 .S4513 2002

Crnkovic, Gordana.
Kazaaam! splat! ploof!. Lanham, Md. ; Oxford : Rowman & Littlefield, c2003.

D1055 .K39 2003

CROATIA - ETHNIC RELATIONS.
Mir u Hrvatskoj--rezultati istraživanja. Zagreb : Hrvatski Caritas ; Split : Franjevački in-t za kulturu mira, 2001.
HN638.A8 M57 2001

CROATIA - SOCIAL CONDITIONS.
Mir u Hrvatskoj--rezultati istraživanja. Zagreb : Hrvatski Caritas ; Split : Franjevački in-t za kulturu mira, 2001.
HN638.A8 M57 2001

Crockatt, Richard. America embattled : September 11, anti-Americanism, and the global order / Richard Crockatt. London ; New York : Routledge, 2003. xvi, 205 p. ; 23 cm. Includes bibliographical references (p. [186]-194) and index. ISBN 0-415-28341-8 (HB) ISBN 0-415-28342-6 (PB : alk. paper) DDC 327.73
1. United States - Foreign relations - 2001- 2. United States - Foreign relations - 1989- 3. National characteristics, American. 4. Anti-Americanism. 5. United States - Foreign public opinion. 6. September 11 Terrorist Attacks, 2001 - Causes. 7. September 11 Terrorist Attacks, 2001 - Influence. 8. War on Terrorism, 2001- 9. Islamic fundamentalism - Political aspects. 10. Globalization - Political aspects. I. Title.
E902 .C76 2003

CROCKERY. See POTTERY.

Croix, Laurence. La douleur en soi : de l'organique à l'inconscient / Laurence Croix. Ramonville Saint-Agne (France) : Erès, c2002. 302 p. ; 22 cm. (Point hors ligne) Includes bibliographical references (p. [289]-299). ISBN 2-86586-993-8 DDC 150
1. Suffering. 2. Pain. 3. Pain - Physiological aspects. 4. Neurophysiology. I. Title. II. Series.

Cronin, W. Jean. Going for the gold : a parent's playbook for behavior change / W. Jean Cronin, Linda M. Bessire. Longmont, CO : Sopris West, c2003. viii, 47 p. : ill. ; 28 cm. Includes bibliographical references (p. 47). ISBN 1-57035-520-7 DDC 649/.64
1. Behavior modification. 2. Motivation (Psychology) in children. 3. Parenting. I. Bessire, Linda M. II. Title.
BF637.B4 C76 2003

Cross, Amanda. Children's dream dictionary / Amanda Cross. London : Hamlyn ; New York : Distributed in the U.S. by Sterling Pub., 2002. 143 p. : col. ill. ; 19 cm. ISBN 0-600-60409-8 DDC 154.6/3/083
1. Children's dreams - Dictionaries. 2. Dream interpretation - Dictionaries. I. Title.
BF1099.C55 C76 2002

CROSS-CULTURAL COMMUNICATION. See INTERCULTURAL COMMUNICATION.

CROSS-CULTURAL COUNSELING.
Brammer, Robert. Diversity in counseling. Australia ; Belmont, CA : Thomson : Brooks/Cole, c2004.
BF637.C6 B677 2004

Culturally responsive interventions. New York : Brunner-Routledge, 2003.
BF637.C6 C777 2003

Handbook of multicultural competencies in counseling & psychology. Thousand Oaks, Calif. : Sage Publications, c2003.
BF637.C6 H3173 2003

Multicultural counseling competencies 2003. Alexandria, VA : Association for Multicultural Counseling and Development, 2003.
BF637.C6 M8367 2003

Practicing multiculturalism. Boston, MA : Allyn and Bacon, c2004.
BF637.C6 P7 2004

CROSS-CULTURAL ORIENTATION. See also INTERCULTURAL COMMUNICATION.
Lewis, Richard D. The cultural imperative. Yarmouth, Me. : Intercultural Press, c2003.
GN357 .L49 2003

Studien zu antiken Identitäten. Würzburg : Ergon Verlag, c2001.
DG78 .S78 2001

Cross-cultural perspectives in human development : theory, research, and applications / edited by T.S. Saraswathi. New Delhi ; Thousand Oaks, Calif. : Sage Publications, 2003. p. cm. Includes index. Table of contents URL: http://www.loc.gov/catdir/toc/ecip045/2003013078.html CONTENTS: Introduction / T.S. Saraswathi -- Ecocultural perspective on human psychological development / John W. Berry -- Wanted, a contextualized psychology : plea for a cultural psychology based on action theory / Lutz H. Eckensberger -- Ontogeny as the interface between biology and culture : evolutionary considerations / Heidi Keller -- Theoretical frameworks in cross-cultural developmental psychology : an attempt at integration / Pierre R. Dasen -- Human development across cultures : a contextual-functional analysis and implications for interventions / Cigdem Kagitcibasi -- Conceptualizing human development and education in sub-Saharan Africa at the interface of indigenous and exogenous influences / A. Bame Nsamenang -- Modernization and changes in adolescent social life / Alice Schlegel -- Adolescence without family disengagement : the daily family lives of Indian middle class teenagers / Reed Larson, Suman Verma, Jodi Dworkin -- From research project to nationwide program : the mother-child education program of Turkey / Sevda Bekman -- Counting on everyday mathematics / Anita Rampal -- Current issues and trends in early childhood education / Lilian G. Katz. ISBN 0-7619-9768-7 ISBN 0-7619-9769-5 (pbk.) DDC 155
1. Developmental psychology. 2. Ethnopsychology. I. Saraswati, T. S.
BF713.5 .C76 2003

CROSS-CULTURAL PSYCHOLOGY. See ETHNOPSYCHOLOGY.

CROSS-CULTURAL STUDIES.
Culture and international history. New York : Berghahn Books, 2003.
JZ1251 .C84 2003

Crouch, Chris. Simple works : simple ideas to make life better / Chris Crouch, Susan Drake. Memphis, TN : Black Pants Pub., c2001. 138 p. ; 23 cm. ISBN 0-9703736-2-7 (alk. paper) DDC 158.1
1. Quality of life. I. Drake, Susan M. II. Title.
BF637.C5 C78 2001

Crouch, Roxie J. Anger management : a 10-week small-group counseling program for students in grades 3-6 / Roxie J. Crouch ; illustrated by Kurt Deppenschmidt. Warminster, PA : Mar*co Products, c2000. 48 p. : ill. ; 28 cm. "Includes the no-temper Treasure Island game". ISBN 1-57543-095-9
1. Anger in children - Study and teaching (Elementary) I. Deppenschmidt, Kurt. II. Title.
BF723.A4 C76 2000

Crouter, Ann C.
Children's influence on family dynamics. Mahwah, N.J. : Lawrence Erlbaum Associates, 2003.
HQ518 .C535 2003

Crow, Graham.
Social conceptions of time. Houndmills, Basingstoke, Hampshire ; New York : Palgrave MacMillan, 2002.
HM656 .S63 2002

CROWDS. See also DEMONSTRATIONS.
Cantril, Hadley, 1906-1969. The psychology of social movements. New Brunswick, [N.J.] : Transaction Publishers, c2002.
HM881 .C36 2002

Crowley, Aleister, 1875-1947.
[Clavicula Salomonis. English.] The Goetia. York Beach, Me. : Samuel Weiser, 1995.
BF1611 .C5413 1995

DuQuette, Lon Milo, 1948- [Magick of Thelma] The magick of Aleister Crowley. Boston, MA : Weiser Books, 2003.
BF1611 .D87 2003

DuQuette, Lon Milo, 1948- Understanding Aleister Crowley's thoth tarot. Boston, MA : Weiser Books, 2003.
BF1879.T2 D873 2003

Crowley, Tony. Standard English and the politics of language / Tony Crowley. 2nd ed. New York : Palgrave Macmillan, c2003. xi, 292 p. : ill. ; 23 cm. Includes bibliographical references (p. 270-286) and index. ISBN 0-333-99035-8 ISBN 0-333-99036-6 (pbk.) DDC 428
1. Standard language. 2. English language - Standardization. 3. Language and languages. I. Title.
P368 .C76 2003

Crowley, Vivianne. The magickal life : a wiccan priestess shares her secrets / Vivianne Crowley. New York : Penguin Compass, 2003. viii, 306 p. : ill. ; 22 cm. Includes bibliographical references (p. [305]-306). ISBN 0-14-219624-X DDC 133.4/3
1. Magic. 2. Witchcraft. I. Title.
BF1611 .C77 2003

CROWN LANDS. See PUBLIC LANDS.

Crowston, Kevin.
Organizing business knowledge. Cambridge, Mass. : MIT Press, c2003.
HD30.2 .T67 2003

Crowther, Paul. Philosophy after postmodernism : civilized values and the scope of knowledge / Paul Crowther. London ; New York : Routledge, 2003. viii, 235 p. ; 24 cm. (Routledge studies in twentieth-century philosophy ; 16) Includes bibliographical references (p. [222]-

Cruddas, Leora.
230) and index. ISBN 0-415-31036-9 (alk. paper) DDC 190/.9/051
1. Postmodernism. 2. Civilization - Philosophy. 3. Knowledge, Theory of. 4. Values. I. Title. II. Series: Routledge studies in twentieth century philosophy ; 16.
B831.2 .C76 2003

Cruddas, Leora. Girls' voices : supporting girls' learning and emotional development / Leora Cruddas and Lynda Haddock. Stoke on Trent ; Sterling VA : Trentham Books, 2003. x, 135 p. ; 23 cm. Includes bibliographical references (p. 125-127) and index. ISBN 1-85856-277-5 DDC 371.823520941
1. Girls - Education - England. 2. Girls - Psychology. I. Haddock, Lynda. II. Title.
LA631.82 .C783 2003

Cruickshank, Justin, 1969- Realism and sociology : anti-foundationalism, ontology and social research / Justin Cruickshank. London ; New York : Routledge, 2003. viii, 173 p. ; 24 cm. (Routledge studies in critical realism ; 5) Includes bibliographical references (p. [161]-168) and index. ISBN 0-415-26190-2 DDC 301/.01
1. Sociology - Methodology. 2. Sociology - Philosophy. 3. Realism. 4. Ontology. I. Title. II. Series.
HM511 .C78 2003

CRUSADES.
Sinclair, Andrew, 1935- The secret scroll. Edinburgh : Birlinn, 2002.

CRUSADES - FIRST, 1096-1099.
The 1000s. San Diego, Calif. : Greenhaven Press, c2001.
CB354.3 .A16 2001

CRUSADES IN LITERATURE.
Heng, Geraldine. Empire of magic. New York : Columbia University Press, c2003.
PR321 .H46 2003

Crutchfield, James P. (James Patrick).
Evolutionary dynamics. Oxford ; New York : Oxford University Press, 2003.
QH366.2 .E867 2003

Cruz Andreotti, Gonzalo.
Ángeles, demonios y genios en el mundo Mediterráneo. Madrid : Ediciones Clásicas, 2000.

Cruz, Mariano de la, 1921-1999. Mens sana in corpore insepulto : últimes converses amb Mariano de la Cruz / Jaume Boix, Arcadi Espada ; pròleg de Carlos Castilla del Pino. 1. ed. Barcelona : Edicions 62, 2002. 216 p. ; 23 cm. (Biografies i memòries ; 52) Includes index. ISBN 84-297-5123-8
1. Cruz, Mariano de la, - 1921-1999 - Interviews. 2. Psychiatrists - Spain - Interviews. 3. Psychiatry. I. Boix Angelats, Jaume, 1952- II. Espada, Arcadio, 1957- III. Castilla del Pino, Carlos, 1922- IV. Title. V. Series.

CRUZ, MARIANO DE LA, 1921-1999 - INTERVIEWS.
Cruz, Mariano de la, 1921-1999. Mens sana in corpore insepulto. 1. ed. Barcelona : Edicions 62, 2002.

Cryer, Frederick H. Biblical and pagan societies / Frederick H. Cryer, Marie-Louise Thomsen ; edited by Bengt Ankarloo and Stuart Clark. Philadelphia : University of Pennsylvania Press, 2001. xvii, 168 p., [2] p. of plates : ill. ; 25 cm. (Witchcraft and magic in Europe) Includes bibliographical references (p. [153]-164) and index. ISBN 0-8122-3615-7 (alk. paper) ISBN 0-8122-1785-3 (pbk. : alk. paper) DDC 133.4/3/0933
1. Witchcraft - Middle East - History. 2. Magic, Assyro-Babylonian. 3. Magic, Jewish. I. Thomsen, Marie-Louise. II. Ankarloo, Bengt, 1935- III. Clark, Stuart. IV. Title. V. Series.
BF1567 .C79 2001

Cryer, Gretchen.
Vint/age 2001 conference : [videorecording]. New York, c2001.

CRYER, GRETCHEN.
Vint/age 2001 conference : [videorecording]. New York, c2001.

Crying.
Kennedy, Michelle. Hauppauge, N.Y. : Barron's, c2003.
BF720.C78 .K46 2003

CRYING IN CHILDREN.
Kennedy, Michelle. Crying. Hauppauge, N.Y. : Barron's, c2003.
BF720.C78 .K46 2003

CRYING IN INFANTS.
Kennedy, Michelle. Crying. Hauppauge, N.Y. : Barron's, c2003.
BF720.C78 .K46 2003

The crystal children.
Virtue, Doreen, 1958- Carlsbad, Calif. : Hay House, c2003.
BF1045.C45 V57 2003

CRYSTAL GAZING.
Hawk, Ambrose. Exploring scrying. Franklin Lakes, NJ : New Page Books, c2001.
BF1335 .H39 2001

CRYSTALLOGRAPHY. *See* **CRYSTALS.**

CRYSTALS - MISCELLANEA.
Gillotte, Galen, 1952- Sacred stones of the goddess. 1st ed. St. Paul, Minn. : Llewellyn Publications, 2003.
BF1611 .G55 2003

CRYSTALS - PSYCHIC ASPECTS.
Knight, Brenda, 1958- Gem magic. Gloucester, MA : Fair Winds Press, 2003.
BF1442.P74 K65 2004

Csáky, Moritz.
Die Verortung von Gedächtnis. Wien : Passagen, c2001.

CSBMS (INTERNATIONAL RELATIONS). *See* **CONFIDENCE AND SECURITY BUILDING MEASURES (INTERNATIONAL RELATIONS).**

Cuadernos de estrategia
(117) Panorama estratégico, 2001-2002. [Madrid] : Ministerio de Defensa, 2002.

CUBAN LITERATURE - 20TH CENTURY - HISTORY AND CRITICISM.
Vadillo, Alicia E. Santería y Vodú. Madrid : Biblioteca Nueva, c2002.
PQ7372 .V33 2002

Cuerpos frágiles, mujeres prodigiosas.
Martoccia, María, 1957- Buenos Aires : Editorial Sudamericana, c2002.

Cuevas Sosa, Andrés Alejandro, 1939- How do religious figures induce the establishment of sects? : a testimonial essay on the surprising and explicit way in which religious figures communicate with human beings and induce them to feel, think, speak and do whatever they want them to do / Alejandro Cuevas-Sosa ; [translated from Spanish into English by Kathryn Kovacik]. 2nd ed. Leicestershire : Upfront Pub., 2002. 490 p ; 21 cm. Includes bibliographical references (p. 489-490). ISBN 1-84426-057-7 DDC 200/.1/9
1. Spiritualism. 2. Psychology, Religious. 3. Spirits - Miscellanea. 4. Sects. 5. Psychotherapy. 6. Consciousness - Religious aspects. I. Title.
BF1272 .C84 2002

Cuin, Joao. A luz de um novo dia / by Joao Cuin. Sao Paulo : DPL, c 2001. 100 p. ; 21 cm. Subtitle from cover: ao resgatar debitos mais ou menos pesados, de existencias anteriores, capacitamo-nos para um futuro vitorioso. ISBN 85-7501-040-9
1. Self-realization - Religious aspects. 2. Spiritual life. I. Title. II. Title: ao resgatar debitos mais ou menos pesados, de existencias anteriores, capacitamo-nos para um futuro vitorioso

Cujātā, 1935- Karratum perratum : Cujātāviṉ cintaṉaikaḷ / Cujātā. 1. patippu. Ceṉṉai : Vicā Paplikēṣaṉs, 2000. 296 p. ; 19 cm. SUMMARY: Articles on 20th century Tamil literature, politics, and motion pictures. In Tamil.
1. Tamil literature - 20th century - History and criticism. 2. Tamil Nadu (India) - Politics and government - 20th century. 3. Motion pictures - India - Tamil Nadu. I. Title. II. Title: Cujātāviṉ cintaṉaikaḷ
PL4758.9.S8758+

Cujātāviṉ cintaṉaikaḷ.
Cujātā, 1935- Karratum perratum. 1. patippu. Ceṉṉai : Vicā Paplikēṣaṉs, 2000.
PL4758.9.S8758+

Cullen, Cheryl Dangel. The art of design : inspired by fine art, illustration, and film / Cheryl Dangel Cullen. 1st ed. Cincinnati, OH : How Design Books, c2003. 144 p. : col. ill. ; 24 x 31 cm. ISBN 1-58180-337-0 (pob) DDC 741.6/09/04
1. Commercial art - History - 20th century - Themes, motives. 2. Graphic arts - History - 20th century - Themes, motives. 3. Creation (Literary, artistic, etc.) I. Title.
NC998.4 .C846 2003

CULT. *See* **CULTS.**

Les cultes médiatiques : culture fan et oeuvres cultes / sous la direction de Philippe Le Guern. Rennes : Presses universitaires de Rennes, [2002] 378 p. ; 24 cm. (Collection Le sens social, 1269-8644) Includes bibliographical references. Chiefly French; some English. ISBN 2-86847-648-1 DDC 790
1. Mass media - Audiences. 2. Fans (Persons) 3. Popular culture. I. Le Guern, Philippe. II. Series: Sens social (Rennes, France)

The cultic milieu : oppositional subcultures in an age of globalization / edited by Jeffrey Kaplan and Heléne Lööw. Walnut Creek : AltaMira Press, c2002. 353 p. ; 24 cm. Includes bibliographical references and index. Table of contents URL: http://www.loc.gov/catdir/toc/fy032/2002001962.html CONTENTS: The cult, the cultic milieu and secularization / Colin Campbell -- Diggers, wolves, ents, elves and expanding universes / Bron Taylor -- The historical communal roots of ultraconservative groups / Timothy Miller -- Neo-shamanism, psychic phenomena and media trickery / László Kürti -- The gothic milieu / Massimo Introvigne -- Black and white unite in fight? / Mattias Gardell -- The idea of purity / Heléne Lööw -- Thriving in a cultic milieu / Frederick J. Simonelli -- The postwar paths of occult national socialism / Jeffrey Kaplan -- The modern anti-cult movement in historical perspective / J. Gordon Melton -- "Who watches the watchman?" / Laird Wilcox. ISBN 0-7591-0203-1 (alk. paper) ISBN 0-7591-0204-X (pbk. : alk. paper) DDC 306/.1
1. Parapsychology. 2. Cults. I. Kaplan, Jeffrey, 1954- II. Lööw, Heléne.
BP603 .C835 2002

Cultivating citizens : soulcraft and citizenship in contemporary America / edited by Dwight D. Allman and Michael D. Beaty. Lanham : Lexington Books, c2002. xxv, 167 p. ; 23 cm. (Applications of political theory) Includes bibliographical references (p. 151-156) and index. ISBN 0-7391-0452-7 (hc : alk. paper) ISBN 0-7391-0453-5 (paper : alk. paper) DDC 323.6
1. Citizenship. 2. Ethics. 3. Civics. 4. Democracy - United States. 5. Theological virtues. 6. Epicureans (Greek philosophy) 7. Political science - Philosophy. I. Allman, Dwight D., 1957- II. Beaty, Michael D. III. Series.
JK1759 .C85 2002

Cultivating minds.
Fuhrer, Urs, 1950- 1st ed. New York, NY : Taylor & Francis, 2003.
BF697.5.S65 F84 2003

CULTS. *See also* **CHRISTIAN SAINTS - CULT; NEW AGE MOVEMENT; RELIGIOUS CALENDARS; SATANISM; SECTS.**
Challenging religion. London ; New York : Routledge, 2003.
BL60 .C437 2003

The cultic milieu. Walnut Creek : AltaMira Press, c2002.
BP603 .C835 2002

Galovic, Jelena. Los grupos místico-espirituales de la actualidad. México : Plaza y Valdés, 2002.
BL625 .G346 2002

Hunt, Stephen, 1954- Alternative religions. Aldershot, Hampshire, England ; Burlington, VT : Ashgate, c2003.
BP603 .H87 2003

New religious movements. London ; New York : Routledge in association with the Institute of Oriental Philosophy European Centre, 1999.
BL80.2 .N397 1999

Pinto Cañon, Ramiro. Grupos gnósticos. Madrid : Entinema, 2002.

Saliba, John A. Understanding new religious movements. 2nd ed. Walnut Creek, CA ; Oxford : Altamira Press, c2003.
BP603 .S25 2003

Spencer, John, 1954- Mysteries and magic. London : Orion, 2000.

Xie jiao zhen xiang. Di 1 ban. Beijing : Dang dai shi jie chu ban she, 2001.
BT1315.2 .X54 2001

CULTS - HAITI. *See* **VOODOOISM.**

Cults in our midst.
Singer, Margaret Thaler. Rev. ed. San Francisco : Jossey-Bass, c2003.
BP603 .S56 2003

Cults in our midst : the continuing fight against their hidden menace.
Singer, Margaret Thaler. Cults in our midst. Rev. ed. San Francisco : Jossey-Bass, c2003.
BP603 .S56 2003

CULTS - MOROCCO.
Hell, Bertrand. Le tourbillon des génies. Paris : Flammarion, 2002.

CULTS - PSYCHOLOGY.
Lewis, James R. Legitimating new religions. New Brunswick, N.J. : Rutgers University Press, c2003.

BP603 .L49 2003

Singer, Margaret Thaler. Cults in our midst. Rev. ed. San Francisco : Jossey-Bass, c2003.
BP603 .S56 2003

CULTS - RUSSIA (FEDERATION).
Balagushkin, E. G. (Evgeniĭ Gennadʹevich) Netraditsionnye religii v sovremennoĭ Rossii. Moskva : Rossiĭskaia akademiia nauk, Institut filosofii, 1999-2002.
BL980.R8 B35 1999

Novye religioznye obʺedineniia Rossii destruktivnogo i okkulʹtnogo kharaktera. Izd. 3-e, dop. Belgorod : Missionerskiĭ otdel Moskovskogo Patriarkhata Russkoĭ Pravoslavnoĭ TSerkvi, 2002.
BF1434.R8 N67 2002

CULTS - SOUTHERN STATES. *See* **VOODOOISM.**

CULTS - UNITED STATES - HISTORY - 20TH CENTURY.
Constantine, Alex. Virtual government. 1st ed. Venice, CA : Feral House, 1997.
BF633 .C67 1997

CULTS - UNITED STATES - PSYCHOLOGY.
Singer, Margaret Thaler. Cults in our midst. Rev. ed. San Francisco : Jossey-Bass, c2003.
BP603 .S56 2003

Cultura e identidade : perspectivas interdisciplinares / Joanildo A. Burity (org.). Rio de Janeiro, RJ, Brasil : DP & A Editores, 2002. 187 p. ; 21 cm. Includes bibliographical references. CONTENTS: Os desafios da história cultural / Sylvia Couceiro -- Mudança cultural, mudança religiosa e mudança política: para onde caminhamos? / Joanildo A. Burity -- Cultura autoritária e aventura da brasilidade / Paulo Henrique Martins -- O sertão e a identidade nacional em Capistrano de Abreu / Isabel Cristina Martins Guillen -- Caras no espelho: identidade nordestina através da literatura / Nara Maria de Maria Antunes -- O desencontro do ser e do lugar: a migração para São Paulo / Helenilda Cavalcanti -- O narcisismo e a violência na atualidade / Ruth Vasconcelos. ISBN 85-7490-117-2
1. Culture - Philosophy. 2. Group identity. 3. Brazil - Civilization. 4. National characteristics, Brazilian. I. Burity, Joanildo A.

Cultura tedesca
(3) Bosco Coletsos, Sandra. La struttura parentale nelle fiabe dei fratelli Grimm. Alessandria : Edizioni dell'Orso, 2001.

CULTURAL ANTHROPOLOGY. *See* **ETHNOLOGY.**

CULTURAL ASSIMILATION. *See* **ASSIMILATION (SOCIOLOGY).**

CULTURAL CHANGE. *See* **SOCIAL CHANGE.**

CULTURAL DIVERSITY POLICY. *See* **MULTICULTURALISM.**

Cultural encounters in late antiquity and the Middle Ages
(v. 1) De Sion exibit lex et verbum domini de Hierusalem. Turnhout, Belgium : Brepols, c2001.

CULTURAL EVOLUTION. *See* **SOCIAL EVOLUTION.**

Cultural foundations of political psychology.
Roazen, Paul, 1936- New Brunswick, N.J. : Transaction Publishers, c2003.
JA74.5 .R63 2003

CULTURAL HERITAGE. *See* **CULTURAL PROPERTY.**

Cultural-historical psychology.
Toomela, Aaro. Tartu : Tartu University Press, c2000.
BF109.V95 T66 2000

The cultural imperative.
Lewis, Richard D. Yarmouth, Me. : Intercultural Press, c2003.
GN357 .L49 2003

Cultural intelligence.
Earley, P. Christopher. Stanford, Calif. : Stanford University Press, 2003.
HD57.7 .E237 2003

CULTURAL LAG. *See* **COMPENSATORY EDUCATION.**

CULTURAL LIFE. *See* **INTELLECTUAL LIFE.**

Cultural lives of law
Valverde, Mariana, 1955- Law's dream of a common knowledge. Princeton, N.J. ; Woodstock, Oxfordshire : Princeton University Press, c2003.

K380 .V35 2003

Cultural memory in the present
Adorno, Theodor W., 1903-1969. [Ob nach Auschwitz noch sich leben lasse. English] Can one live after Auschwitz? Stanford, Calif. : Stanford University Press, 2003.
B3199.A33 O213 2003

Henry, Michel, 1922- [C'est moi la vérité. English] I am the truth. Stanford, Calif : Stanford University Press, 2003.
BR100 .H39813 2003

Huyssen, Andreas. Present pasts. Stanford, Calif. : Stanford University Press, 2003.
BD181.7 .H89 2003

Lévinas, Emmanuel. [De l'evasion. English] On escape = Stanford, Calif. : Stanford University Press, 2003.
BD331 .L459613 2003

Ricciardi, Alessia. The ends of mourning. Stanford, Calif. : Stanford University Press, 2003.
PN56.D4 R53 2003

The cultural nature of human development.
Rogoff, Barbara. Oxford ; New York : Oxford University Press, 2003.
HM686 .R64 2003

CULTURAL PATRIMONY. *See* **CULTURAL PROPERTY.**

CULTURAL PLURALISM POLICY. *See* **MULTICULTURALISM.**

CULTURAL POLICY. *See* **MUSIC AND STATE.**

CULTURAL PROPERTY.
Claiming the stones/naming the bones. Los Angeles : Getty Research Institute, c2002.
CC135 .C48 2002

CULTURAL PROPERTY - PROTECTION.
Brown, Michael F. (Michael Fobes), 1950- Who owns native culture? Cambridge, Mass. : Harvard University Press, 2003.
K1401 .B79 2003

CULTURAL PROPERTY - REPATRIATION.
Claiming the stones/naming the bones. Los Angeles : Getty Research Institute, c2002.
CC135 .C48 2002

CULTURAL PSYCHIATRY.
Clément, Catherine, 1939- Le divan et le grigri. Paris : Jacob, c2002.

Creating racism. Los Angeles, CA : Citizens Commission on Human Rights, 1995.
RC455.4.E8 C74x 1995

CULTURAL RELATIONS.
Culture and international history. New York : Berghahn Books, 2003.
JZ1251 .C84 2003

Habitar la tierra. Buenos Aires : Grupo Editor Altamira, 2002.
CB358 .H32 2002

CULTURAL RELATIVISM. *See* **ETHNOCENTRISM.**

CULTURAL SOCIOLOGY. *See* **CULTURE.**

CULTURAL TRANSFORMATION. *See* **SOCIAL CHANGE; SOCIAL EVOLUTION.**

Culturally responsive interventions : innovative approaches to working with diverse populations / Julie R. Ancis, editor. New York : Brunner-Routledge, 2003. p. cm. Includes bibliographical references and index. Table of contents URL: http://www.loc.gov/catdir/toc/ecip043/2003010665.html ISBN 0-415-93332-3 ISBN 0-415-93333-1 (pbk). DDC 158/.3
1. Cross-cultural counseling. I. Ancis, Julie R.
BF637.C6 C777 2003

Culturas híbridas.
García Canclini, Néstor. Nueva edición actualizada. Buenos Aires : Paidós, 2001.

CULTURE. *See also* **CHRISTIANITY AND CULTURE; CIVILIZATION; EDUCATION; INTELLECTUAL LIFE; INTERCULTURAL COMMUNICATION; LANGUAGE AND CULTURE; LEARNING AND SCHOLARSHIP; PERSONALITY AND CULTURE; POLITICAL CULTURE; POLITICS AND CULTURE; PSYCHOANALYSIS AND CULTURE; RELIGION AND CULTURE; SOCIAL EVOLUTION; SUBCULTURE.**

Abbinnett, Ross. Culture and identity. London ; Thousand Oaks, Ca. : SAGE, 2003.
HM621 .A23 2003

Alexander, Jeffrey C. The meanings of social life. New York : Oxford University Press, 2003.
HM585 .A5 2003

Barrett, Stanley R. Culture meets power. Westport, Conn. ; London : Praeger, 2002.
HM1256 .B27 2002

Culture of prejudice. Peterborough, Ont. : Broadview Press, 2003.

Elkins, James, 1955- Visual studies. New York : Routledge, 2003.
N72.S6 E45 2003

Kūle, M. (Maija) Phenomenology and culture. Riga : Institute of Philosophy and Sociology, 2002.

Kulʹtura i vlastʹ v usloviiakh kommunikatsionnoĭ revoliutsii XX veka. Moskva : "AIRO-XX", 2002.
HM621 .K858 2002

Lewis, Richard D. The cultural imperative. Yarmouth, Me. : Intercultural Press, c2003.
GN357 .L49 2003

Michalon, Clair. Histoire de différences, différence d'histoires. Saint-Maur : Sépia, c2002.

Milner, Andrew, 1950- Contemporary cultural theory. 3rd ed. Crows Nest, N.S.W. : Allen & Unwin, 2002.

Moreno-Riaño, Gerson, 1971- Political tolerance, culture, and the individual. Lewiston, N.Y. : E. Mellen Press, c2002.
JA74.5 .M653 2002

Roazen, Paul, 1936- Cultural foundations of political psychology. New Brunswick, N.J. : Transaction Publishers, c2003.
JA74.5 .R63 2003

Stróżewski, Władysław. Wokół piękna. Kraków : Universitas, c2002.

Wagner de Reyna, Alberto. El privilegio de ser latinoamericano. 1. ed. Córdoba, Argentina : Editorial Alejandro Korn, c2002.
F1408.3 .W35 2002

Culture, 1922.
Manganaro, Marc, 1955- Princeton, N.J. : Princeton University Press, c2002.
PR888.C84 M36 2002

Culture and children's intelligence : cross-cultural analysis of the WISC-III / edited by James Georgas ... [et al.]. Amsterdam ; Boston : Academic Press, c2003. xxxii, 336 p. : ill. ; 24 cm. Includes bibliographical references and indexes. Publisher description URL: http://www.loc.gov/catdir/description/els031/2003104541.html Table of contents URL: http://www.loc.gov/catdir/toc/els031/2003104541.html ISBN 0-12-280055-9 (alk. paper) DDC 155.4/1393
1. Wechsler Intelligence Scale for Children - Cross-cultural studies. I. Georgas, James, 1934-
BF432.5.W42 C85 2003

CULTURE AND CHRISTIANITY. *See* **CHRISTIANITY AND CULTURE.**

Culture and civilisation in the Middle East.
Kemal, Salim. The philosophical poetics of Alfarabi, Avicenna and Averroes. London ; New York : RoutledgeCurzon, 2003.

Culture and cognition.
Ross, Norbert. Thousand Oaks, CA : Sage Publications, c2004.
BF311 .R6542 2004

Culture and competence : contexts of life success / edited by Robert J. Sternberg and Elena L. Grigorenko. Washington, DC : American Psychological Association, 2004. p. cm. Includes bibliographical references and index. Table of contents URL: http://www.loc.gov/catdir/toc/ecip047/2003016804.html ISBN 1-59147-097-8 DDC 153.9
1. Cognition and culture. I. Sternberg, Robert J. II. Grigorenko, Elena.
BF311 .C845 2004

Culture and identity.
Abbinnett, Ross. London ; Thousand Oaks, Ca. : SAGE, 2003.
HM621 .A23 2003

Culture and international history / edited by Jessica C.E. Gienow-Hecht and Frank Schumacher. New York : Berghahn Books, 2003. xiii, 304 p. : ill. ; 24 cm. (Explorations in culture and international history series) Includes bibliographical references and index. CONTENTS: On the diversity of knowledge and the community of thought: culture and international history / Jessica C. E. Gienow-

Hecht -- The power of culture in international relations / Beate Jahn -- The great derby race: strategies of cultural representation at nineteenth-century world exhibitions / Wolfram Kaiser -- Manliness and "realism": the use of gendered tropes in the debates on the Philippine-American and Vietnam wars / Fabian Hilfrich -- A family affair?: gender, the U. S. information agency, and cold war ideology, 1945-1960 / Laura A. Belmonte -- France and Germany after the great war: businessmen, intellectuals and artists in non-governmental European networks / Guido Müller -- Small Atlantic world: U. S. philanthropy and the expanding international exchange of scholars after 1945 / Oliver Schmidt -- Atlantic alliances: cross-cultural communication and the 1960s student revolution / Philipp Gassert -- Forecasting the future: future studies as international networks of social analysis in the 1960s and 1970s in Western Europe and the United States / Alexander Schmidt-Gernig -- Cultural approaches to international relations: a challenge? / Volker Depkat -- States, international systems, and intercultural transfer: a commentary / Eckart Conze -- "Total culture" and the state-private network: a commentary / Scott Lucas -- Gender, tropes, and images: a commentary / Marc Frey -- Internationalizing ideologies: a commentary / Seth Fein -- The invention of state and diplomacy: the first political testament of Frederick III, elector of Brandenburg (1698) / Volker Depkat -- The rat race for progress: a Punch cartoon of the opening of the 1851 Crystal Palace exhibition / Wolfram Kaiser -- Race and imperialism: an essay from the Chicago Broad ax / Fabian Hilfrich -- A document from the Harvard international summer school / Scott Lucas -- Max Lerner's "Germany has a foreign policy" / Thomas Reuther -- Excerpt from Johan Galtung's "On the future of the international system" / Alexander Schmidt-Gernig -- The "children and war" virtual forum: voices of youth and international relations / Marie Thorsten. ISBN 1-57181-382-9 (cloth : alk. paper) DDC 303.48/2
1. International relations and culture. 2. History - Philosophy. 3. Cross-cultural studies. 4. Cultural relations. 5. Social evolution. I. Gienow-Hecht, Jessica C. E., 1964- II. Schumacher, Frank, 1965- III. Series.
JZ1251 .C84 2003

CULTURE AND LAW.
On interpretation. Madison, Wis. : University of Wisconsin Press for the University of Wisconsin Law School, c2002.

CULTURE AND PERSONALITY. *See* **PERSONALITY AND CULTURE.**

CULTURE AND PSYCHOANALYSIS. *See* **PSYCHOANALYSIS AND CULTURE.**

CULTURE AND RELIGION. *See* **RELIGION AND CULTURE.**

Culture clubs.
Minsos, Susan Felicity, 1944- Edmonton : Spotted Cow Press, c2002.

CULTURE CONFLICT. *See also* **MARGINALITY, SOCIAL.**
Edwards, Charlene. Voices from Vietnam. Bayside, NY : Bayside, c2002.

LeBaron, Michelle, 1956- Bridging cultural conflicts. 1st ed. San Francisco, CA : Jossey-Bass, c2003.
BF698.9.C8 L43 2003

The meanings of violence. London ; New York : Routledge, 2003.
HM1116 .M436 2003

Menéndez, Eduardo L. La parte negada de la cultura. Barcelona : Edicions Bellaterra, c2002.
HM1121 .M46 2002

Ruthven, Malise, 1942- A fury for God. London ; New York : Granta, 2002.
HV6432 .R87 2002

CULTURE - CONGRESSES.
[Nuevos paradigmas. English.] New paradigms, culture, and subjectivity. Cresskill, N.J. : Hampton Press, c2002.
BD161 .N8413 2002

CULTURE, CORPORATE. *See* **CORPORATE CULTURE.**

La culture : de l'universel au particulier : la recherche des origines, la nature de la culture, la construction des identités / coordonné par Nicolas Journet. Auxerre : Sciences humaines éditions, c2002. viii, 370 p. : ill. ; 22 cm. Includes bibliographical references (p. 349-355) and indexes. ISBN 2-912601-17-7 DDC 300
1. Group identity. 2. Identity (Psychology) 3. Multiculturalism. I. Journet, Nicolas, 1950-

CULTURE, EVOLUTION OF. *See* **SOCIAL EVOLUTION.**

CULTURE - HISTORY.
Dostovernost' i dokazatel'nost' v issledovaniĭakh po teorii i istorii kul'tury. Moskva : RGGU, 2002.

HM621 .D68 2002

Steedman, Carolyn. Dust. New Brunswick, N.J. : Rutgers University Press, 2002, c2001.
CD947 .S73 2002

CULTURE IN LITERATURE.
Excursions in Chinese culture. Hong Kong : Chinese University Press, c2002.

Heng, Geraldine. Empire of magic. New York : Columbia University Press, c2003.
PR321 .H46 2003

Manganaro, Marc, 1955- Culture, 1922. Princeton, N.J. : Princeton University Press, c2002.
PR888.C84 M36 2002

Culture meets power.
Barrett, Stanley R. Westport, Conn. ; London : Praeger, 2002.
HM1256 .B27 2002

Culture of fear.
Füredi, Frank, 1947- Rev. ed. London ; New York : Continuum, 2002.
BF575.F2 F86 2002

The culture of Islam.
Rosen, Lawrence, 1941- Chicago : University of Chicago Press, 2002.
DT312 R64 2002

Culture of prejudice : arguments in critical social science / edited by Judith C. Blackwell, Murray Smith, and John Sorenson. Peterborough, Ont. : Broadview Press, 2003. 359 p. ; 23 cm. Includes bibliographical references and index. ISBN 1-55111-490-9 DDC 303.3/85
1. Prejudices. 2. Culture. I. Blackwell, Judith C., 1944- II. Smith, Murray E. G. (Murray Edward George), 1950- III. Sorenson, John, 1952-

CULTURE - PHILOSOPHY.
Chacon, Vamireh. O humanismo ibérico. [Lisboa?] : Imprensa Nacional-Casa da Moeda, [1998]
B821 .C43 1998

Connolly, William E. Neuropolitics. Minneapolis, MN : University of Minnesota Press, c2002.

Cultura e identidade. Rio de Janeiro, RJ, Brasil : DP & A Editores, 2002.

Dostovernost' i dokazatel'nost' v issledovaniĭakh po teorii i istorii kul'tury. Moskva : RGGU, 2002.
HM621 .D68 2002

Esin, A. B. (Andreĭ Borisovich) Literaturovedenie. Kulturologiĭa. Moskva : Flinta ; Nauka, 2002.

Göller, Thomas. Kulturverstehen. Würzburg : Königshausen & Neumann, c2000.
BF311 .G586 2000

Kultur, Handlung, Wissenschaft. 1. Aufl. Weilerswist : Velbrück Wissenschaft, 2002.
B67 .K853 2002

Lévinas, Emmanuel. [Humanisme de l'autre homme. English] Humanism of the other. Urbana : University of Illinois Press, c2003.
B2430.L48 H8413 2003

Manganaro, Marc, 1955- Culture, 1922. Princeton, N.J. : Princeton University Press, c2002.
PR888.C84 M36 2002

Pedroza, Ludim. The ritual of music contemplation. 2002.

Qizilsaflī, Muḥammad Taqī. Qarn-i rawshanfikrān. Chāp-i 1. Tihrān : Markaz-i Bayn al-Milalī-i Guftugū-yi Tamaddun'hā : Hirmis, 1380 [2001]

Rojek, Chris. Stuart Hall. Cambridge, UK : Polity in association with Blackwell, 2003.
HM621 .R64 2003

Sampaio, Luiz Sergio Coelho de, 1933- Filosofia da cultura. Rio de Janeiro : Editora Agora da Ilha, 2002.

Schweppenhäuser, Gerhard. Die Fluchtbahn des Subjekts. Münster : Lit, 2001.

Souza, Eneida Maria de. Crítica cult. Belo Horizonte : Editora UFMG, 2002.
PN94 .S68 2002

Storey, John, 1950- Inventing popular culture. Malden, MA : Blackwell Pub., 2003.
CB19 .S7455 2003

White, Morton Gabriel, 1917- A philosophy of culture. Princeton, N.J. : Princeton University Press, c2002.

B945.W453 P48 2002

CULTURE - POLITICAL ASPECTS.
Kul'tura i vlast' v usloviĭakh kommunikatsionnoĭ revoliŭtsii XX veka. Moskva : "AIRO-XX", 2002.
HM621 .K858 2002

CULTURE, POPULAR. *See* **POPULAR CULTURE.**

CULTURE - PSYCHOLOGICAL ASPECTS.
De Munck, Victor C. Culture, self, and meaning. Prospect Heights, Ill. : Waveland Press, c2000.
BF697.5.S65 M86 2000

Fuhrer, Urs, 1950- Cultivating minds. 1st ed. New York, NY : Taylor & Francis, 2003.
BF697.5.S65 F84 2003

Culture, self, and meaning.
De Munck, Victor C. Prospect Heights, Ill. : Waveland Press, c2000.
BF697.5.S65 M86 2000

CULTURE - SEMIOTIC MODELS.
Une introduction aux sciences de la culture. 1. ed. Paris : Presses universitaires de France ; [Paris] : Institut Ferdinand-de-Saussure, 2002.

CULTURE - STUDY AND TEACHING.
Foucault, cultural studies, and governmentality. Albany : State University of New York Press, c2003.
JC330 .F63 2003

Psicologia social nos estudos culturais. Petrópolis : Editora Voces, c2003.
HM1033 .P75 2003

The culture tools series
Smith, Shawn T., 1967- Surviving aggressive people. 1st Sentient Publications ed. Boulder, CO : Sentient Publications, 2003.
BF575.A3 S55 2003

Cultures et civilisations médiévales
(25) Dans l'eau, sous l'eau. [Paris] : Presses de l'Université de Paris-Sorbonne, 2002.
CB353 .D27 2002

Cultures of the death drive.
Sánchez-Pardo, Esther. Durham [N.C.] : Duke University Press, c2003.
BF175.5.D4 S26 2003

CULTUS. *See* **CULTS.**

Cummings, Sarah.
Gender perspectives on property and inheritance. Oxford : Oxfam, c2001.
HB715 .G45 2001

Cummings, Stephen. Recreating strategy / Steven Cummings. London ; Thousand Oaks : Sage Publications, 2002. xiii, 354 p. : ill. ; 25 cm. Includes bibliographical references (p. [323]-346) and index. ISBN 0-7619-7010-X (pbk.) ISBN 0-7619-7009-6 DDC 658.4/012
1. Strategic planning. 2. Management. I. Title.
HD30.28 .C855 2002

Cumpeta, Silvio. I dialoghi dell'ego / Silvio Cumpeta. Gorizia : Biblioteca statale isontina, c2001. 143 p. ; 24 cm. (Biblioteca di studi goriziani ; 7) DDC 858
1. Philosophy, Modern. 2. Imaginary conversations. I. Title. II. Series.

Cuneiform monographs
(18) Brown, David, 1968- Mesopotamian planetary astronomy-astrology. Groningen : Styx, 2000.
BF1714.A86 B76 2000

Cunha, Maria Teresa Santos.
Destinos das letras. Passo Fundo : Universidade de Passo Fundo, 2002.
P211 .D47 2002

Cunliffe, Barry W.
Archaeology. Oxford : Published for The British Academy by Oxford University Press, c2002.

Cunning-folk.
Davies, Owen, 1969- London ; New York : Hambledon and London, 2003.
BF1622.G7 D385 2002

Cunningham, Ian, 1943- The wisdom of strategic learning : the self managed learning solution / Ian Cunningham. London ; New York : McGraw-Hill, c1994. xiv, 296 p. : ill. ; 25 cm. (McGraw-Hill developing organizations series) Includes bibliographical references and index. ISBN 0-07-707894-2 DDC 658.4/06
1. Organizational change - Management. 2. Learning. I. Title. II. Series.
HD58.8 .C857 1994

Cunningham, Scott, 1956-.
Art of divination.
Cunningham, Scott, 1956- Divination for beginners.

2nd ed. St. Paul, MN : Llewellyn Publications, 2003.
BF1751 .C86 2003

Divination for beginners : reading the past, present & future / Scott Cunningham. 2nd ed. St. Paul, MN : Llewellyn Publications, 2003. xiii, 240 p. : ill. ; 21 cm. Rev. ed. of: The art of divination. c1993. Includes bibliographical references (p. 225-234) and index. ISBN 0-7387-0384-2 DDC 133.3
1. Divination. I. Cunningham, Scott, 1956- Art of divination. II. Title.
BF1751 .C86 2003

[Wicca. Spanish]
Wicca : una guía para la práctica individual / Scott Cunningham ; traducción al español por Héctor Ramírez y Edgar Rojas. 1. ed. St. Paul, Minn. : Llewellyn Español, 2003. p. cm. Includes bibliographical references and index. ISBN 0-7387-0306-0 DDC 299
1. Witchcraft. 2. Magic. 3. Ritual. I. Title.
BF1566 .C8618 2003

Cuomo, Chris J. The philosopher queen : feminist essays on war, love, and knowledge / Chris Cuomo. Lanham, Md. ; Oxford : Rowman & Littlefield, c2003. xiii, 161 p. : ill. ; 24 cm. Includes bibliographical references (p. 153-158) and index. ISBN 0-7425-1380-7 (hbk. : alk. paper) ISBN 0-7425-1381-5 (pbk. : alk. paper) DDC 305.42/01
1. Feminist theory. 2. Feminism. I. Title.
HQ1190 .C866 2003

Ćurčić, Vojislav.
Seminar "Adolescencija: kontinuitet i/ili discontinuitet u razvoju" (1997 : Belgrade, Serbia) Adolescencija. Beograd : KBC "Dr Dragiša Mišović", 1997.
BF724 .S399 1997

Curcio, Kimberly Panisset. Man of light : the extraordinary healing life of Mauricio Panisset / Kimberly Panisset Curcio. 1st ed. New York : SelectBooks, c2002. xii, 186 p. : ill. ; 23 cm. Includes bibliographical references (p. 175). ISBN 1-59079-013-8 DDC 130/.92
1. Panisset, Mauricio. 2. Parapsychology and medicine. 3. Healers - Biography. 4. Spiritual healing. 5. Mental healing. 6. Spiritual life. I. Title.
BF1045.M44 C87 2002

CURING (MEDICINE). *See* **HEALING.**

Curiositas : Welterfahrung und ästhetische Neugierde in Mittelalter und früher Neuzeit / mit Beiträgen von Lorraine Daston ... [et al.] ; herausgegeben von Klaus Krüger. Göttingen : Wallstein, c2002. 180 p. : ill. ; 21 cm. (Göttinger Gespräche zur Geschichtswissenschaft ; Bd. 15) Includes bibliographical references. 1 English, 3 German contributions. ISBN 3-89244-522-2 (pbk.)
1. Curiosity - History. 2. Philosophy, Medieval. 3. Philosophy, Modern - 17th century. I. Daston, Lorraine, 1951- II. Krüger, Klaus, 1957- III. Title: Welterfahrung und ästhetische Neugierde in Mittelalter und früher Neuzeit IV. Series: Göttinger Gespräche zur Geschichtswissenschaft (Series) ; Bd. 15.
BF323.C8 C872 2002

CURIOSITIES AND WONDERS. *See also* **DISASTERS; MONSTERS.**
Cohl, H. Aaron. The book of mosts. 1st ed. New York : St. Martin's Press, 1997.
AG243 .C586 1997

Fanthorpe, R. Lionel. The world's most mysterious objects. Toronto ; Tonawanda NY : Dundurn Press, 2002.

Lucarelli, Carlo, 1960- Misteri d'Italia. Torino : Einaudi, c2002.

Mooney, Julie. The world of Ripley's believe it or not!. New York : Black Dog & Leventhal, c1999.
AG243 .M653 1999

Mysterious places. San Diego, CA : Greenhaven Press, 2004.
BF1031 .M96 2004

Nickell, Joe. The mystery chronicles. Lexington, Ky. : University Press of Kentucky, c2004.
BF1031 .N517 2004

Townsend, John. Mysterious disappearances. Chicago, IL : Raintree, 2004.
BF1389.D57 T69 2004

Townsend, John. Mysterious encounters. Chicago, IL : Raintree, 2004.
BF2050 .T69 2004

Townsend, John, 1955- Mysteries of body and mind. Chicago, IL : Raintree, 2004.

BF1031 .T65 2004

CURIOSITIES AND WONDERS IN LITERATURE.
Royle, Nicholas, 1963- The uncanny. Manchester (UK) ; New York : Manchester University Press, 2003.
PN49 .R75 2002

CURIOSITIES AND WONDERS - IRELAND.
DeFaoíte, Dara. Paranormal Ireland. Ashbourne, Co. Meath : Maverick House, c2002.
BF1031 .D344 2002

deFaoíte, Dara. Paranormal Ireland. Northampton : Maverick House, 2002.

CURIOSITIES AND WONDERS - JUVENILE LITERATURE.
Townsend, John. Mysterious encounters. Chicago, IL : Raintree, 2004.
BF2050 .T69 2004

Townsend, John, 1955- Mysteries of body and mind. Chicago, IL : Raintree, 2004.
BF1031 .T65 2004

CURIOSITY - HISTORY.
Curiositas. Göttingen : Wallstein, c2002.
BF323.C8 C872 2002

Curran, Thomas J., 1929-.
Harmond, Richard P. A history of Memorial Day. New York : P. Lang, c2002.
E642 .H37 2002

CURRENCY. *See* **MONEY.**

CURRENCY QUESTION. *See* **MONEY.**

Current perspectives in psychology
Rumbaugh, Duane M., 1929- Intelligence of apes and other rational beings. New Haven : Yale University Press, c2003.
QL737.P96 R855 2003

Zigler, Edward, 1930- The first three years & beyond. New Haven : Yale University Press, c2002.
HQ767.9 .Z543 2002

Current theory and research in motivation
(v. 47) Nebraska Symposium on Motivation (2001) Evolutionary psychology and motivation. Lincoln, Neb. ; London : University of Nebraska Press, c2001.
BF701 .N43 2001

Currents of encounter
(v. 19) Kuipers, Ronald Alexander. Critical faith. Amsterdam ; New, York, NY : Rodopi, 2002.

Currie, Gregory. Recreative minds : imagination in philosophy and psychology / Gregory Currie, Ian Ravenscroft. Oxford : Clarendon Press ; New York : Oxford University Press, 2002. x, 233 p. ; 24 cm. Includes bibliographical references (p. [205]-227) and index. ISBN 0-19-823809-6 (pbk. : alk. paper) ISBN 0-19-823808-8 (alk. paper) DDC 128/.3
1. Imagination (Philosophy) 2. Imagination. I. Ravenscroft, Ian. II. Title.
BH301.I53 C87 2002

Currie, Stephen, 1960-.
The 1500s. San Diego, Calif : Greenhaven Press, c2001.
CB367 .A165 2001

The curse of the self.
Leary, Mark R. New York : Oxford University Press, 2004.
BF697 .L33 2004

CURSING AND BLESSING. *See* **BLESSING AND CURSING.**

Curtis, Donald. Your thoughts can change your life / Donald Curtis. New York : Warner Books, 1996. 221 p. : ill. ; 20 cm. Originally published: Englewood Cliffs, N.J. : Prentice Hall, 1961. Includes index. ISBN 0-446-67196-7 (pbk.) DDC 299/.93
1. New Thought. I. Title.
BF639 .C885 1996

Customer choice in automotive repair shops.
United States. Congress. Senate. Committee on Commerce, Science, and Transportation. Subcommittee on Consumer Affairs, Foreign Commerce, and Tourism. Washington : U.S. G.P.O. : For sale by the Supt. of Docs., U.S. G.P.O., [Congressional Sales Office], 2003.

CUSTOMER RELATIONS - TECHNOLOGICAL INNOVATIONS.
Burke, Dan, 1965- Business @ the speed of stupid. Cambridge, MA : Perseus Pub., c2001.

HD45 .B7995 2001

CUSTOMER SERVICES.
Christensen, Clayton M. The innovator's solution. Boston, Mass. : Harvard Business School Press, c2003.

CUSTOMERS (CONSUMERS). *See* **CONSUMERS.**

Cutler, Howard C.
Bstan-'dzin-rgya-mtsho, Dalai Lama XIV, 1935- The art of happiness at work. New York : Riverhead Books, 2003.
BF481 .B76 2003

Cutting-Gray, Joanne.
Extreme beauty. London ; New York : Continuum, 2002.
BH39 .E98 2002

Cvetkovich, Ann, 1957- An archive of feelings : trauma, sexuality, and lesbian public cultures / Ann Cvetkovich. Durham : Duke University Press, 2003. xi, 355 p. : ill. ; 24 cm. (Series Q) Filmography (p. [327]-328). Includes bibliographical references (p. [329]-344) and index. CONTENTS: Introduction -- The everyday life of queer trauma -- Trauma and touch : butch-femme sexualities -- Sexual trauma/queer memory : incest, lesbianism, and therapeutic culture -- Transnational trauma and queer diasporic publics -- AIDS activism and public feelings : documenting Act Up's lesbians -- Legacies of activism, legacies of trauma : mourning and militancy revisited -- In the archive of lesbian feelings -- Epilogue : whose feelings count? ISBN 0-8223-3076-8 (cloth : alk. paper) ISBN 0-8223-3088-1 (pbk. : alk. paper) DDC 306.76/63
1. Lesbianism. 2. Sex. 3. Psychic trauma - Cross-cultural studies. I. Title. II. Series.
HQ75.5 .C89 2003

The cyber spellbook.
Knight, Sirona, 1955- Franklin Lakes, NJ : New Page Books, c2002.
BF1571 .T425 2002

CYBERCOMMERCE. *See* **ELECTRONIC COMMERCE.**

CYBERNETICS. *See also* **COMPUTERS.**
Reig, Ramón. El éxtasis cibernético. 1. ed. Madrid : Ediciones Libertarias, 2001.

Von Foerster, Heinz, 1911- Understanding systems. New York : Kluwer Academic/Plenum Publishers ; Heidelberg : Carl-Auer-Systeme Verlag, c2002.

CYBERSPACE. *See also* **COMPUTERS.**
Communication and cyberspace. 2nd ed. Creskill, N.J. : Hampton Press, c2003.
P96.D36 C66 2003

Deciphering cyberspace. Thousand Oaks, Calif. : Sage Publications, c2003.
TK5102.2 .D43 2003

Knight, Sirona, 1955- The cyber spellbook. Franklin Lakes, NJ : New Page Books, c2002.
BF1571 .T425 2002

Lovink, Geert. Uncanny networks. Cambridge, Mass. : MIT Press, c2002.
HM851 .L688 2002

Malvido Arriaga, Adriana. Por la vereda digital. 1. ed. México : CONACULTA (Consejo Nacional para la Cultura y las Artes), 1999.
QA76.9.C66 M35 1999

Il cyborg.
Caronia, Antonio. Milano : Shake edizioni underground, c2001.
Q335 .C34 2001

CYBORGS.
Caronia, Antonio. Il cyborg. Milano : Shake edizioni underground, c2001.
Q335 .C34 2001

Clark, Andy, 1957- Natural-born cyborgs. Oxford ; New York : Oxford University Press, c2003.
T14.5 .C58 2003

CYCLOPEAN REMAINS. *See* **MEGALITHIC MONUMENTS.**

CYCLOPEDIAS. *See* **ENCYCLOPEDIAS AND DICTIONARIES.**

CYNICISM.
Lichev, Valeri. TSinichnoto, ili, Igrata na vlast i udovolstvie. Sofiia : EON-2000, 2000.
B809.5 .L53 2000

CYNICISM - BULGARIA.
Lichev, Valeri. TSinichnoto, ili, Igrata na vlast i udovolstvie. Sofiia : EON-2000, 2000.
B809.5 .L53 2000

CYRENE (ANCIENT CITY). *See* **CYRENE (EXTINCT CITY).**

CYRENE (EXTINCT CITY).
Calame, Claude. [Mythe et histoire dans l'antiquité grecque. English] Myth and history in ancient Greece. Princeton, N.J. : Princeton University Press, c2003.
BL783 .C3513 2003

Cyrulnik, Boris. Dialogue sur la nature humaine / Boris Cyrulnik, Edgar Morin. La Tour d'Aigues : Editions de l'Aube, c2000. 69 p. ; 19 cm. (Série V.O.) (La collection Monde en cours/intervention) ISBN 2-87678-557-9
1. *Human behavior. I. Morin, Edgar. II. Title. III. Series. IV. Series: Monde en cours. Série Intervention.*
BF57 .C97 2000

Czas kryzysu, czas prezełomu.
Lobkowicz, Nikolaus. Kraków : Wydawnictwo WAM : Znak, 1996.

CZECHY (CZECH REPUBLIC). *See* **BOHEMIA (CZECH REPUBLIC).**

Czigler, István.
Az Általánostól a különösig. [Budapest] : Gondolat : MTA Pszichológiai Kutatóintézet, c2002.
BF128.H8 A44 2002

Człowiek - symbol - historia
Radzimiński, Andrzej. Życie i obyczajowość średniowiecznego duchowieństwa. Warszawa : Wydawn. DiG, 2002.
BX1565 .R32 2002

D., ISADORA.
Delaisi de Parseval, Geneviève. Le Roman familial d'Isadora D.. Paris : Odile Jacob, c2002.

Da, Lu.
Bu ping ze ming. Di 2 ban. Beijing : Zhongguo cheng shi chu ban she, 2001.

Da oriente e da occidente.
Peri, Vittorio. Roma : Editrice Antenore, 2002.
BR162.3 .P475 2002

Da shi jie du Zhonghua wen hua jing dian cong shu
Liang Qichao, Zhang Taiyan jie du Zhonghua wen hua jing dian. Di 1 ban. Shenyang Shi : Liao Hai chu ban she, 2003.
PL2262.2 .L54 2003

Da'at u-tevunah.
Śiḥot musar Da'at u-tevunah. Ashdod : Sh. ben E. Bamnolker, 761 [2001]
BJ1280 .B34 2001

Dackweiler, Regina-Maria.
Gewalt-Verhältnisse. Frankfurt ; New York : Campus, c2002.

Dacquino, Giacomo, 1930- Bisogno d'amore : superare l'immaturità psicoaffettiva / Giacomo Dacquino. 1. ed. Milano : Mondadori, 2002. 190 p. (Saggi) ISBN 88-04-50345-9 DDC 155.2/5
1. *Self-perception. 2. Psychosexual development. 3. Sex. I. Title. II. Series: Saggi (Arnoldo Mondadori editore)*
BF697.5.S43 D33 2002

Daddy, up and down.
Stenson, Lila. 1st ed. Snowmass Village, CO : Peaceful Village Pub., 2002.
BF723.G75 S74 2002

DADS. *See* **FATHERS.**

The daffodil principle.
Edwards, Jaroldeen. Salt Lake City, Utah : Shadow Mountain, 2004.
BF637.S4 E4 2004

Dagognet, François. Changement de perspective : le dedans et le dehors / François Dagognet. Paris : Table ronde, c2002. 190 p. ; 21 cm. (Contretemps) Includes bibliographical references. ISBN 2-7103-2521-7 DDC 194
1. *Knowledge, Theory of. 2. Philosophy. I. Title. II. Series.*

Daher, Douglas, 1949- And the passenger was death : the drama and trauma of losing a child / Douglas Daher. Amityville, N.Y. : Baywood Pub., c2003. vii, 118 p. : ports ; 23 cm. Includes bibliographical references (p. 111) and index. ISBN 0-89503-244-9 (pbk. : alk. paper) DDC 155.9/37
1. *Grief. 2. Bereavement - Psychological aspects. 3. Children - Death - Psychological aspects. 4. Loss (Psychology) I. Title.*
BF575.G7 D34 2003

Dahl, Bernhoff A., 1938- Optimize your life with the one-page strategic planner / by Bernhoff A. Dahl. Bangor, Me. : Wind-Breaker Press, c2003. p. cm. Includes bibliographical references and index. ISBN 0-936232-02-1 (Trade paperback : alk. paper) DDC 158.1
1. *Success - Psychological aspects. 2. Planning - Psychological aspects. 3. Goal (Psychology) I. Title.*

BF637.S8 D26 2003

Dahlem Workshop on Genetic and Cultural Evolution of Cooperation (90th : 2002 : Berlin, Germany) Genetic and cultural evolution of cooperation / edited by Peter Hammerstein Cambridge, Mass. : MIT Press in cooperation with Dahlem University Press, c2003. xiv, 485 p. : ill. ; 24 cm. "Report of the 90th Dahlem Workshop on Genetic and Cultural Evolution of Cooperation, Berlin, June 23-28, 2002." Includes bibliographical references and indexes. ISBN 0-262-08326-4 (alk. paper) DDC 302/.14
1. *Cooperativeness - Congresses. I. Hammerstein, Peter, 1949- II. Title.*
BF637.H4 D25 2002

Dahlin, Olov, 1962- Zvinorwadza : being a patient in the religious and medical plurality of the Mberengwa district, Zimbabwe / Olov Dahlin. Frankfurt am Main ; New York : P. Lang, c2002. 295 p. : ill., maps ; 21 cm. (European university studies. Series XXIII, Theology ; vol. 748 = Europäische Hochschulschriften. Reihe XXIII, Theologie, 0721-3409 ; Bd. 748) Thesis (doctoral)--Universität, Stockholm. Includes bibliographical references (p. [265]-271) and index. ISBN 3-631-39576-0 (Frankfurt : pbk.) ISBN 0-8204-5989-5 (New York : pbk.)
1. *Sick - Psychology. 2. Diseases - Zimbabwe - Mberengwa District - Religious aspects. 3. Care of the sick. 4. Healers - Zimbabwe - Mberengwa District. 5. Medical care - Zimbabwe - Mberengwa District. I. Title. II. Series: Europäische Hochschulschriften. Reihe XXIII, Theologie ; Bd. 748.*
R726.5 .D34 2002

Dai, David Yun.
Motivation, emotion, and cognition. Mahwah, N.J. : L. Erlbaum Associates, 2004.
BF431 .M72 2004

The Dalai Lama's book of transformation.
Bstan-'dzin-rgya-mtsho, Dalai Lama XIV, 1935- London : Thorsons, c2000.

Dalal, Farhad. Race, colour and the process of racialization : new perspectives from group analysis, psychoanalysis, and sociology / Farhad Dalal. Hove, [England] ; New York : Brunner-Routledge, 2002. ix, 251 p. : ill. ; 24 cm. Includes bibliographical references (p. [230]-237) and index. ISBN 1-58391-291-6 ISBN 1-58391-292-4 (pbk.) DDC 155.8/2
1. *Psychoanalysis and racism. 2. Race - Psychological aspects. 3. Race awareness. 4. Racism. I. Title.*
BF175.4.R34 D35 2002

Dalby, Andrew, 1947- Language in danger : the loss of linguistic diversity and the threat to our future / Andrew Dalby. New York : Columbia University Press, c2003. xii, 328 p. : maps ; 24 cm. Includes bibliographical references (p. 303-311) and index. ISBN 0-231-12900-9 (cloth : alk. paper) DDC 417/.7
1. *Language obsolescence. 2. Language spread. 3. Language and languages. I. Title.*
P40.5.L33 D35 2003

Dalle tenebre alla luce.
Ferrara, Franco, 1938- Cosenza, Italia : Brenner, c2002.

Dalton, Thomas Carlyle.
The life cycle of psychological ideas. New York : Kluwer Academic/Plenum, 2004.
BF38 .L54 2004

D'Alvia, Rodolfo. Psicoanálisis psicosomática ida y atleuv [sic.] / Rodolfo D'Alvia. Buenos Aires : Editorial Dunken, 2002. 210 p. ; 23 cm. On title page word "vuelta" is written backwards. Includes bibliographical references. Library's copy gift from author. ISBN 9875189782
1. *Medicine, Psychosomatic. 2. Mind and body. 3. Psychoanalysis. I. Title. II. Title: Psicoanálisis psicosomática ida y vuelta III. Title: Ida y vuelta*

Daly, Martin, 1944-.
Nebraska Symposium on Motivation (2001) Evolutionary psychology and motivation. Lincoln, Neb. ; London : University of Nebraska Press, c2001.
BF701 .N43 2001

Damiani, Anthony, 1922-1984. Astronoesis : philosophy's empirical context : astrology's transcendental ground / Anthony J. Damiani. Burdett, N.Y. : Published for Wisdom's Goldenrod, Ltd. by Larson Publications, c2000. xviii, 393 p. : ill. (some col.) ; 21 cm. Includes bibliographical references (p. 367-370) and indexes. Table of contents URL: http://www.loc.gov/catdir/toc/fy033/00133946.html ISBN 0-943914-00-0 DDC 191
1. *Philosophy of mind. 2. Astrology - Philosophy. 3. Cosmology - Philosophy. I. Wisdom's Goldenrod, Ltd. II. Title.*
BD418.3 .D347 2000

Dampierre, Gérald de (Spirit).
Winter, Jean, 1909-1939 (Spirit) Dites-leur que la mort n'existe pas. Chambéry : Exergue, c1997, [1998]

BF1290 .W56 1997

Damrau, Karin.
Unschaerferelationen. Wiesbaden : Nelte, c2002.
BF469 .U5 2002

Damson, Werner.
Loch, Wolfgang. "Mit Freud über Freud hinaus". Tübingen : Edition Diskord, c2001.
BF173 .L554 2001

Dan shen gao bai / Fang Fang, Wang Xiaoming zhu bian. Di 1 ban. Beijing : Beijing chu ban she, 2001. 2, 4, 341 p. ; 21 cm. ISBN 7-200-04291-9
1. *Single women - China. 2. Man-woman relationships. I. Fang, Fang. II. Wang, Xiaoming.*
HQ800.2 .D36 2001

Dan shen gui zu.
Hu, Liuming, 1950- Di 1 ban. [Wuhan Shi] : Chang jiang wen yi chu ban she, [2000]
PL2863.L58 D365 2000

DANCE. *See also* **BALLET; BELLY DANCE; CHOREOGRAPHY; JAZZ DANCE.**
Big Dance [videorecording]. Buffalo, N.Y. : Kineticvideo.com, c1998.
Medina, Narciso. El suspendido vuelo del ángel creador. La Habana : Ediciones Alarcos, 2003.
1. *Black author.*

The peak performance series. Vol. [4] [videorecording]. Longwood, Fla. : Pamela Bolling Enterprises, c1999.

DANCE COMPANIES - CANADA.
Big Dance [videorecording]. Buffalo, N.Y. : Kineticvideo.com, c1998.

DANCE IN TELEVISION. *See* **DANCE IN MOTION PICTURES, TELEVISION, ETC.**

DANCE ON TELEVISION. *See* **DANCE IN MOTION PICTURES, TELEVISION, ETC.**

DANCE - PSYCHOLOGICAL ASPECTS.
Iannitelli, Leda Muhana. Guiding choreography [microform]. 1994.

DANCES. *See* **DANCE.**

DANCING. *See* **DANCE.**

DANCING IN MOTION PICTURES, TELEVISION, ETC. *See* **DANCE IN MOTION PICTURES, TELEVISION, ETC.**

DANCING IN MOVING-PICTURES, TELEVISION, ETC. *See* **DANCE IN MOTION PICTURES, TELEVISION, ETC.**

Dancing naked - in fuzzy red slippers.
Rutlen, Carmen Richardson, 1948- 1st ed. Fort Bragg, CA : Cypress House, c2003.
BF637.S4 R877 2003

DANDARA (EGYPT) - ANTIQUITIES.
Cauville, Sylvie. Le zodiaque d'Osiris. Leuven : Peeters, 1997.
BL2450.O7 C399 1997

Dandola, John, 1951-.
Pettibone, John W. The ghosts of Hammond castle. Glen Ridge, N.J. : Tory Corner Editions, c2001.
BF1474 .P48 2001

Dandyk, Alfred. Unaufrichtigkeit : die existentielle Psychoanalyse Sartres im Kontext der Philosophiegeschichte / Alfred Dandyk. Würzburg : Königshausen & Neumann, c2002. 185 p. ; 24 cm. Includes bibliographical references (p. 183-185). ISBN 3-8260-2349-8 (pbk.)
1. *Sartre, Jean Paul, - 1905- 2. Existentialism. 3. Psychoanalytic interpretation. I. Title.*

Dane, J.
Driekwart eeuw psychotechniek in Nederland. Assen : Van Gorcum, 2001.
HF5548.8 .D73 2001

Dane, Lance.
Pinkney, Andrea Marion. [Kāmasūtra. English.] The Kama Sutra illuminated. New York, N.Y. : Abrams, c2002.

Danesi, Marcel, 1946- Forever young : the teen-aging of modern culture / Marcel Danesi. Toronto : University of Toronto Press, c2003. x, 139 p. ; 24 cm. Includes bibliographical references (p. [127]-135) and index. ISBN 0-8020-8851-1 (bound) ISBN 0-8020-8620-9 (pbk.) DDC 306
1. *Adolescence - Social aspects. 2. Popular culture. I. Title.*

Dang dai shen mei wen hua shu xi
Xiao, Ying. Xing xiang yu sheng cun. Beijing di 1 ban. Beijing : Zuo jia chu ban she : Jing xiao Xin hua shu dian Beijing fa xing suo, 1996.

NX583.A1 H756 1996 <Asian China>

Dang dai Zhongguo qing nian de guo jia min zu yi shi yan jiu.
Cheng zhang de Zhongguo. Di 1 ban. Beijing : Ren min chu ban she, 2002.
HQ799.2.P6 C449 2002

Daniel, Jack L. (Jack Lee), 1942- We fish : the journey to fatherhood / Jack L. Daniel and Omari C. Daniel. Pittsburgh, Pa. : University of Pittsburgh Press, c2003. viii, 206 p. ; 24 cm. Includes index. ISBN 0-8229-4198-8
1. African Americans - Kinship - Pennsylvania. 2. African Americans - Socialization - Pennsylvania. 3. Fathers and sons. 4. Fishing - Pennsylvania. 5. Black author. I. Daniel, Omari C. II. Title. III. Title: Journey to fatherhood

Daniel, Jessica Henderson.
The complete guide to mental health for women. 1st ed. Boston : Beacon Press, c2003.
RC451.4.W6 C65 2003

Daniel, Omari C.
Daniel, Jack L. (Jack Lee), 1942- We fish. Pittsburgh, Pa. : University of Pittsburgh Press, c2003.
1. Black author.

DANIELE, GRACIELA, 1939-.
Vint/age 2001 conference : [videorecording]. New York, c2001.

Daniele, Graciela, 1939- panelist.
Vint/age 2001 conference : [videorecording]. New York, c2001.

Daniell, Beth, 1947- A communion of friendship : literacy, spiritual practice, and women in recovery / Beth Daniell. Carbondale : Southern Illinois University Press, c2003. xiii, 201 p. ; 22 cm. (Studies in writing & rhetoric) Includes bibliographical references (p. 185-191) and index. ISBN 0-8093-2487-3 (alk. paper) DDC 808/.042/082
1. English language - Rhetoric - Study and teaching - United States. 2. Twelve-step programs - United States. 3. Women - Education - United States. 4. Female friendship - United States. 5. Adult education - United States. 6. Narrative therapy. 7. Literacy - United States. 8. Spiritual life. I. Title. II. Series.
PE1405.U6 D36 2003

Daniels, Joni T. Power tools for women : plugging into the essential skills for work and life / Joni Daniels. 1st ed. New York : Three Rivers Press, c2002. x, 322 p. ; 21 cm. Includes index. ISBN 0-609-80955-5 (pbk.) ISBN 0-609-60837-1 DDC 646.7/0082
1. Women - Life skills guides. 2. Women - Psychology. 3. Success. I. Title.
HQ1221 .D26 2002

Daniels, Kooch. Tarot d'amour : find love, sex, and romance in the cards / Kooch Daniels & Victor Daniels. Boston, MA : Weiser Books, 2003. vii, 247 p. : ill. ; 23 cm. Includes bibliographical references (p. 247-248). ISBN 1-57863-292-7 DDC 133.3/2424
1. Tarot. I. Daniels, Victor. II. Title.
BF1879.T2 D35 2003

Daniels, Victor.
Daniels, Kooch. Tarot d'amour. Boston, MA : Weiser Books, 2003.
BF1879.T2 D35 2003

Dans l'eau, sous l'eau : le monde aquatique au moyen âge / Danièle James-Raoul et Claude Thomasset [eds.]. [Paris] : Presses de l'Université de Paris-Sorbonne, 2002. 432 p. : ill. ; 24 cm. (Cultures et civilisations médiévales, 0760-7113 ; 25) Includes bibliographical references and indexes. ISBN 2-8405-0216-X DDC 900
1. Civilization, Medieval. 2. Water and civilization. 3. Aquatic organisms - Symbolic aspects. I. James-Raoul, Danièle. II. Thomasset, Claude Alexandre. III. Title: Monde aquatique au moyen âge IV. Series.
CB353 .D27 2002

Danse avec le diable.
Lacotte, Daniel. [Paris] : Hachette, c2002.
BF1584.E85 L33 2002

Dansereau, Fred, 1946-.
Multi-level issues in organizational behavior and strategy. Amsterdam : London : JAI, 2003.

DANTE ALIGHIERI, 1265-1321. DIVINA COMMEDIA.
Studi sulle società e le culture del Medioevo per Girolamo Arnaldi. [Firenze] : All'insegna del giglio, 2002.
DG443 .S78 2002

Dante's path.
Schaub, Bonney Gulino. New York, N.Y. : Gotham Books, 2003.
BF204.7 .S33 2003

Dantlgraber, Josef.
Loch, Wolfgang. "Mit Freud über Freud hinaus". Tübingen : Edition Diskord, c2001.
BF173 .L554 2001

Danto, Arthur Coleman, 1924- The abuse of beauty : aesthetics and the concept of art / Arthur C. Danto. Chicago : Open Court, c2003. xxiii, 167 p. : ill. ; 24 cm. (Paul Carus lectures series ; 21) Includes index. ISBN 0-8126-9539-9 (hbk. : alk. paper) ISBN 0-8126-9540-2 (pbk. : alk. paper) DDC 111/.85
1. Aesthetics. 2. Art - Philosophy. I. Title. II. Series: Paul Carus lectures ; 21st ser.
BH39 .D3489 2003

Danzig, Robert J., 1932- Every child deserves a champion : including the child within you! / Bob Danzig, with Callie Rucker Oettinger. Washington, DC : Child & Family Press, c2003. p. cm. Originally published: South Orange, NJ : Professional Bi-Cultural Develpment, 2002. Table of contents URL: http://www.loc.gov/catdir/toc/ecip048/2003018507.html ISBN 0-87868-885-4 (alk. paper) DDC 177/.7
1. Encouragement. 2. Self-confidence. 3. Achievement motivation in children. 4. Mentoring. 5. Heroes. 6. Kindness. I. Oettinger, Callie Rucker. II. Title.
BF637.E53 D36 2003

There is only one you : you are unique in the universe / Bob Danzig. Washington, D.C. : Child and Family Press, c2003. p. cm. SUMMARY: A celebration of the many things that each person can do, as well as what each one deserves, accompanied by quotations from famous people such as Mother Teresa, Ovid, Wayne Gretsky, and Walt Whitman. ISBN 0-87868-884-6 (alk. paper) DDC 158.1
1. Individuality in children - Juvenile literature. 2. Individuality. I. Title.
BF723.I56 D36 2003

Dao jie cai gen tan.
Hong, Zicheng, fl. 1596. [Cai gen tan] Di 1 ban. Beijing Shi : Zong jiao wen hua chu ban she, 1996 (1997 printing)
BJ1558.C5 H85 1996 <Asian China>

DAO ZANG - CONCORDANCES.
Schipper, Kristofer Marinus. Dao zang suo yin. Di 1 ban. Shanghai : Shanghai shu dian chu ban she : Xin hua shu dian Shanghai fa xing suo fa xin, 1996.
BL1900.T387 S35 1996 <Orien China>

Dao zang suo yin.
Schipper, Kristofer Marinus. Di 1 ban. Shanghai : Shanghai shu dian chu ban she : Xin hua shu dian Shanghai fa xing suo fa xin, 1996.
BL1900.T387 S35 1996 <Orien China>

Daoism.
Miller, James, 1968- Oxford : Oneworld, c2003.
BL1920 .M55 2003

Darbo, Patrika. 365 glorious nights of love and romance / Patrika Darbo with Lorraine Zenka. 1st ed. New York : ReganBooks, c2002. xiv, 208 p., [8] p. of plates : ill. ; 24 cm. Includes bibliographical references. ISBN 0-06-001382-6 (alk. paper) DDC 306.4
1. Darbo, Patrika. 2. Sex instruction for women. 3. Sexual attraction. 4. Self-confidence. 5. Body image in women. 6. Overweight women - United States - Biography. 7. Actresses - United States - Biography. I. Zenka, Lorraine. II. Title. III. Title: Three hundred sixty-five glorious nights of love and romance
HQ46 .D35 2002

DARBO, PATRIKA.
Darbo, Patrika. 365 glorious nights of love and romance. 1st ed. New York : ReganBooks, c2002.
HQ46 .D35 2002

Darby, John (John P.).
Contemporary peacemaking. Houndmills, Basingstoke ; New York : Palgrave Macmillan, 2003.
JZ6010 .C665 2003

Dare to forgive.
Hallowell, Edward M. Deerfield Beach, Fla. : Health Communications, 2004.
BF637.F67 H35 2004

DARK AGES. See MIDDLE AGES.

The dark archetype.
Dumars, Denise. Franklin Lakes, N.J. : New Page Books, c2003.
BF1623.G63 D86 2003

Dark continents.
Khanna, Ranjana, 1966- Durham, NC : Duke University Press, 2003.
BF175.4.S65 K43 2003

DARK MATTER (ASTRONOMY).
Börner, G. The early universe. 4th ed. Berlin : London : Springer, c2003.

Dark moon mysteries.
Roderick, Timothy, 1963- Aptos, Calif. : New Brighton Books, 2003.
BF1623.M66 R63 2003

DARK NIGHT OF THE SOUL. See MYSTICISM.

Dark Star (Firm).
Quiet rumours. Edinburgh : San Francisco : AK Press/Dark Star, 2002.

The dark worship.
Newton, Toyne. London : Vega, 2002.
BF1531 .N49 2002

The darkened room.
Owen, Alex, 1948- Chicago : University of Chicago, 2004.
BF1275.W65 O94 2004

Darkhe tsedek.
Gantserski, Betsal'el Shelomoh, ha-Levi. Sefer Darkhe tsedek. Tifrah : Mishp. Gantserski, 762 [2001 or 2002]

Darlington, Cynthia L. The female brain / Cynthia Darlington. London ; New York : Taylor & Francis, c2002. xii, 211 p. : ill. ; 25 cm. (Conceptual advances in brain research ; v. 6) Includes bibliographical references and index. ISBN 0-415-27721-3 (hbk) ISBN 0-415-27722-1 (pbk) DDC 612.82
1. Brain - Psychology. 2. Psychophysiology. 3. Brain - Sex differences. 4. Sex differences (Psychology) I. Title. II. Series.
QP402 .D366 2002

Darmaillacq, Dominique.
Merleau-Ponty, Maurice, 1908-1961. L'institution dans l'histoire personnelle et publique ; [Paris] : Belin, c2003.
B2430.M3763 I88 2003

Därmann, Iris.
Fremderfahrung und Repräsentation. 1. Aufl. Weilerswist : Velbrück, 2002.

Darwin, Charles, 1809-1882. Autobiographies / Charles Darwin ; edited by Michael Neve and Sharon Messenger ; with an introduction by Michael Neve. London : Penguin, 2002. xxvi, 97 p. ; 20 cm. (Penguin classics) ISBN 0-14-043390-2 DDC 576.8092
1. Darwin, Charles, - 1809-1882. 2. Naturalists - England - Biography. 3. Evolution (Biology) I. Neve, Michael. II. Messenger, Sharon. III. Title.

ON THE ORIGIN OF SPECIES.
Vallejo, Fernando. La tautología darwinista. 1a. ed. México : Universidad Nacional Autónoma de México, 1998.

DARWIN, CHARLES, 1809-1882.
Darwin, Charles, 1809-1882. Autobiographies. London : Penguin, 2002.

DARWINISM. See EVOLUTION (BIOLOGY).

Dasanirnayee.
Veṅkaṭanāthārya. [Daśanirṇayī] Vaidikasārvabhaumanāmnā suprasiddhaiḥ Veṅkaṭanāthāryaiḥ Vaidikakarmānuṣṭhānasaukaryāya viracitā Daśanirṇayī. 1st ed. Mumbai : Śrīmadahobilamathena, 1998.
BL1226.72 .V36 1998

Daśanirṇayī.
Veṅkaṭanāthārya. [Daśanirṇayī] Vaidikasārvabhaumanāmnā suprasiddhaiḥ Veṅkaṭanāthāryaiḥ Vaidikakarmānuṣṭhānasaukaryāya viracitā Daśanirṇayī. 1st ed. Mumbai : Śrīmadahobilamathena, 1998.
BL1226.72 .V36 1998

Daston, Lorraine, 1951-.
Curiositas. Göttingen : Wallstein, c2002.
BF323.C8 C872 2002

DATA MINING.
Data mining. Hershey : Idea Group, c2002.
QA76.9.D343 D36 2002

Data mining : a heuristic approach / [edited by] Hussein A. Abbass, Ruhul A. Sarker, Charles S. Newton. Hershey : Idea Group, c2002. iv, 300 p. : ill. ; 26 cm. Includes bibliographical references and index. Table of contents URL: http://www.loc.gov/catdir/toc/fy031/2001039775.html ISBN 1-930708-25-4 DDC 006.3
1. Data mining. 2. Database searching. 3. Heuristic programming. I. Abbass, Hussein A. II. Sarker, Ruhul A. III. Newton, Charles S. (Charles Sinclair), 1942-
QA76.9.D343 D36 2002

DATA MINING - CONGRESSES.
International Workshop MLDM 2003 (2003 : Leipzig, Germany) Machine learning and data mining in pattern recognition. Berlin ; New York : Springer, c2003.

Q327 .I67 2003

DATA NETWORKS, COMPUTER. *See* **COMPUTER NETWORKS.**

DATA PROTECTION - LAW AND LEGISLATION. *See* **PRIVACY, RIGHT OF.**

DATA PROTECTION - UNITED STATES.
Privacy [electronic resource]. [Washington, D.C.] : Federal Trade Commission, Bureau of Consumer Protection, Office of Consumer and Business Education, [2002]

DATA REGULATION. *See* **DATA PROTECTION.**

DATA TRANSMISSION SYSTEMS. *See* **COMPUTER NETWORKS.**

DATABASE MANAGEMENT.
Intelligent support systems. Hershey, PA : IRM Press, c2002.
QA76.9.D3 I5495 2002

DATABASE SEARCHING. *See also* **DATA MINING.**
Data mining. Hershey : Idea Group, c2002.
QA76.9.D343 D36 2002

Kelly, Brian, 1956- iSearch. Boston, MA : Allyn and Bacon, c2003.
BF76.78 .K45 2003

Schlein, Alan M. Find it online. 3rd ed. Tempe, AZ : Facts on Demand Press, c2003.

DATING (SOCIAL CUSTOMS). *See* **MAN-WOMAN RELATIONSHIPS.**

Daughters & mothers.
Cowen, Lauren. Philadelphia [Penn.] : Courage Books, c1997.
HQ755.85 .C695 1997

Daughters and mothers.
Cowen, Lauren. Daughters & mothers. Philadelphia [Penn.] : Courage Books, c1997.
HQ755.85 .C695 1997

Dautenhahn, Kerstin.
Imitation in animals and artifacts. Cambridge, Mass. : MIT Press, c2002.
BF357 .I47 2002

Davenport, Anne Ashley. St. George's Hall : behind the scenes at England's home of mystery / Anne Davenport, John Salisse. Pasadena : Mike Caveney's Magic Words, c2001. 474 p. : ill. (some col.) ; 27 cm. (Magical pro-files ; 10th) "The tenth in a series of magical pro-files." Includes bibliographical references ((p. 455-457)) and index. Table of contents URL: http://www.loc.gov/catdir/toc/fy032/2001135447.html DDC 793.8/09421
1. Maskelyne, John Nevil, - 1839-1917. 2. Cooke, George Alfred, - 1825-1905. 3. St. George's Hall (London, England) - History. 4. Magic - England - History. 5. Magicians - England - Biography. I. Salisse, John. II. Title. III. Series.
BF1623 .D38 2001

Davenport, Donna S. Singing mother home : a psychologist's journey through anticipatory grief / Donna S. Davenport. Denton, Tex. : University of North Texas Press, c2002. xv, 157 p., [4] p. of plates : ill., music, geneal. table ; 24 cm. Includes bibliographical references (p. 155-157). ISBN 1-57441-162-4 DDC 155.9/37
1. Grief. 2. Bereavement - Psychological aspects. 3. Loss (Psychology) 4. Mothers - Death - Psychological aspects. 5. Mothers and daughters. I. Title.
BF575.G7 D365 2002

Davenport, Thomas H. What's the big idea? : creating and capitalizing on the best management thinking / Thomas H. Davenport, Laurence Prusak, with H. James Wilson. Boston, Mass. : Harvard Business School Press, c2003. xi, 242 p. : ill. ; 25 cm. Includes bibliographical references (p. 223-230) and index. CONTENTS: Winning with ideas : how business ideas are linked to business success -- The idea practitioners : who introduces ideas to organizations? -- Ideas at work : it's the content that counts -- The guide to gurus : where good management ideas come from -- Market savvy : how ideas interact with markets -- Will it fit? : find ideas that fit your organization, then sell them -- The reengineering tsunami : a case story of an idea that became a tidal wave -- Knowledge management : a case story of a "P-Cycle" movement -- Idea-based leadership : how can your organization lead with ideas? -- Appendix A : A select survey of business and management ideas -- Appendix B : The idea practitioners -- Appendix C : The top two hundred business gurus. ISBN 1-57851-931-4 (alk. paper) DDC 658
1. Creative ability in business. 2. Knowledge management. 3. Success in business. I. Prusak, Laurence. II. Wilson, H. James. III. Title.
HD53 .D38 2003

David, A. Rosalie (Ann Rosalie) Religion and magic in ancient Egypt / Rosalie David. London : Penguin, 2002. xvii, 487 p., [32] p. of plates : ill., maps ; 20 cm. Includes bibliographical references (p. 434-453) and index. ISBN 0-14-026252-0 DDC 299.31
1. Magic, Egyptian. 2. Egypt - Religion. I. Title.

Davidson, Jeffrey P. The 60 second procrastinator / Jeff Davidson. Avon, MA : Adams Media Corp., c2003. p. cm. Includes bibliographical references. ISBN 1-58062-923-7 DDC 155.2/32
1. Procrastination. I. Title. II. Title: Sixty second procrastinator
BF637.P76 D38 2003

Davidson, Matthew, 1972-.
Plantinga, Alvin. Essays in the metaphysics of modality. Oxford ; New York : Oxford University Press, 2003.
B945.P553 M48 2003

Davidson, Richard J.
Handbook of affective sciences. Oxford ; New York : Oxford University Press, 2003.
BF511 .H35 2003

Davidson, Tish. Prejudice / Tish Davidson. New York : Franklin Watts, c2003. 80 p. : col. ill. ; 21 cm. (Life balance) Includes bibliographical references (p. 72-75) and index. CONTENTS: What is prejudice? -- The root of prejudice -- The anatomy of discrimination -- Prejudice in action -- Fighting discrimination. ISBN 0-531-12252-2 DDC 303.3/85
1. Prejudices - Juvenile literature. 2. Hate - Juvenile literature. 3. Discrimination - Juvenile literature. I. Title. II. Series.
BF575.P9 D38 2003

Davies, Brenda, M.D. Chakra power beads : tapping the power of energy stones to unlock your inner potential / Brenda Davies. Berkeley, Calif. : Ulysses Press, c2001. xv, 99 p. ; 22 cm. Includes bibliographical references (p. [98]-99). ISBN 1-56975-261-3
1. Chakras - Miscellanea. 2. Gems - Miscellanea. I. Title.
BF1442.C53 D36 2001

Davies, John.
Towards the semantic web. Chichester, England ; Hoboken, N.J. : J. Wiley, c2003.
TK5105.88815 .T68 2003

Davies, Martin L.
Breaking the disciplines. London ; New York : I.B. Tauris, 2003.
BD175 .B74 2003

Davies, Owen, 1969- Cunning-folk : popular magic in English history / Owen Davies. London ; New York : Hambledon and London, 2003. xiv, 246 p. : ill. ; 24 cm. Includes bibliographical references (p. [219]-237) and index. ISBN 1-85285-297-6 DDC 133.430942
1. Magic - England - History. 2. Magicians - England - History. 3. Witchcraft - England - History. 4. Witches - England - History. I. Title. II. Title: Popular magic in English history
BF1622.G7 D385 2002

Davies, Stephen, 1950-.
Art and essence. Westport, Conn. ; London : Praeger, 2003.
BH39 .A685 2003

Davies, Wendy, 1942-.
Archaeology. Oxford : Published for The British Academy by Oxford University Press, c2002.

Davis, Audrey Craft. Metaphysical techniques that really work / Audrey Craft Davis. Nevada City, CA : Blue Dolphin Pub., 2004. p. cm. Originally published: Mailbu, CA : Valley of the Sun, c1996. CONTENTS: Thoughts and treasure-mapping -- Different kinds of spirits -- Subconscious mind : your obedient servant -- Astral projection -- Ultimate power-pak -- I've got your number -- Is it my right to prosper? -- Mastery of psychic or soul energy -- Metaphysical healing -- Reincarnation : have we lived before? -- Communicating with the dead. ISBN 1-57733-128-1 (pbk. : alk. paper) DDC 133.9
1. Occultism. 2. Spiritualism. 3. Psychic ability. I. Title.
BF1411 .D38 2004

Davis, Charles, 1923- Religion and the making of society : essays in social theology / Charles Davis. New York, NY, USA : Cambridge University Press, 1994. xiv, 208 p. : 23 cm. (Cambridge studies in ideology and religion) Includes bibliographical references and index. Publisher description URL: http://www.loc.gov/catdir/description/cam025/93010224.html Table of contents URL: http://www.loc.gov/catdir/toc/cam024/93010224.html ISBN 0-521-44310-5 ISBN 0-521-44789-5 (pbk.) DDC 261
1. Christian sociology. 2. Religion and sociology. 3. Religion and politics. 4. Ideology - Religious aspects. I. Title. II. Series.
BT738 .D36 1994

Davis, Daniel Leifeld. Your angry child : a guide for parents / Daniel L. Davis. New York : Haworth Press, c2004. p. cm. Includes bibliographical references and index. Table of contents URL: http://www.loc.gov/catdir/toc/ecip043/2003009815.html CONTENTS: Introduction -- The impact of anger problems. The problem of aggression and hostility. In todays society. The effect of aggression and hostility. On the family. Resistance and oppositional behavior -- The working of anger. Temperament and anger. Thinking and anger. The development of thought processes. Moral reasoning. Appraisal and expectations : developing styles of angry thinking. Anger and attachment. Anger and the antisocial child. Animal cruelty and fire setting -- Influences on anger. The development of anger and other characteristics. Media and the development of violence -- Responses to anger. The response of anger. Resilience -- Anger and emotional problems. Attention-deficit hyperactivity disorder. Oppositional defiant disorder. Conduct disorders. Mood disorders. Suicide. Anger and substance abuse -- Anger in children and preteens. Hot thoughts and cool thoughts. Feelings. Cooling down. Anger plans. What if all this stuff fails? -- Anger in teenagers. Adolescents and behavior management. Contracts. Grounding. Independence. Three containers. Talking it through the family. Its not what is that matters : its what we believe. Problem solving -- Building on the positives. Strength building and positive role models. Diversity and the power of others. Values. ISBN 0-7890-1223-5 (hard : alk. paper) ISBN 0-7890-1224-3 (soft : alk. paper) DDC 649/.153
1. Anger in children. 2. Anger in adolescence. 3. Parent and child. 4. Child psychology. 5. Adolescent psychology. I. Title.
BF723.A4 D38 2004

Davis, Frederick, 1931- The Jew and deicide : the origin of an archetype / Frederick B. Davis. Lanham, Md. : University Press of America, c2003. x, 119 p. ; 22 cm. Includes bibliographical references and index. ISBN 0-7618-2542-8 (pbk. : alk. paper) DDC 261.2/6
1. Jesus Christ - Passion - Role of Jews. 2. Bible. - N.T. - Gospels - Criticism, interpretation, etc. 3. Judaism (Christian theology) - History of doctrines - Early church, ca. 30-600. 4. Antisemitism - Psychological aspects. 5. Archetype (Psychology) 6. Christianity and antisemitism. 7. Jews in the New Testament. I. Title.
BS2555.6.J44 D38 2003

Davis, Kenneth C.
Don't know much.
Davis, Kenneth C. History. 1st ed. New York : HarperCollins, c2003.
E178.25 .D37 2003

Don't know much about history.
Davis, Kenneth C. History. 1st ed. New York : HarperCollins, c2003.
E178.25 .D37 2003

History : everthing you need to know about American history but never learned / by Kenneth C. Davis. 1st ed. New York : HarperCollins, c2003. xxi, 678 p. ; 24 cm. (Don't know much about) Rev. ed. of: Don't know much about history. Includes bibliographical references (p. [631]-655) and index. ISBN 0-06-008381-6 (acid-free paper) DDC 973
1. United States - History - Miscellanea. I. Davis, Kenneth C. Don't know much about history. II. Title. III. Title: Don't know much about history IV. Series: Davis, Kenneth C. Don't know much.
E178.25 .D37 2003

Davis, Sampson. The pact : three young men make a promise and fulfill a dream / Sampson Davis, George Jenkins, and Rameck Hunt ; with Lisa Frazier Page. Waterville, ME : Thorndike Press, 2002. 357 p. (large print) ; 23 cm. ISBN 0-7862-4889-0
1. Davis, Sampson. 2. Jenkins, George. 3. Hunt, Rameck. 4. African American physicians - Biography. 5. Dentists - United States - Personal Narratives. 6. Physicians - United States - Personal Narratives. 7. Blacks - United States - Personal Narratives. 8. Large type books. 9. Black author. I. Jenkins, George. II. Hunt, Rameck. III. Title.

DAVIS, SAMPSON.
Davis, Sampson. The pact. Waterville, ME : Thorndike Press, 2002.
1. Black author.

Davis, Stephen F.
Handbook of research methods in experimental psychology. Malden, MA ; Oxford : Blackwell Pub., 2003.
BF76.5 .H35 2003

Davis, Stephen J.
Be thou there. Cairo ; New York : American University in Cairo Press, c2001.

Davis, Susan V. (Susan Voeller), 1966-.
LePla, F. Joseph, 1955- Brand driven. London : Kogan Page, 2003.

Davydov, ÎU. P. (ÎUriĭ Pavlovich) Norma protiv sily : problema miroregulirovaniîa / ÎU.P. Davydov. Moskva : Nauka, 2002. 285 p. : 22 cm. At head of title: Rossiĭskaîa akademiîa nauk, Institut Soedinennykh Shtatov Ameriki i Kanady. Includes bibliographical references. ISBN 5020131342
1. International relations. 2. Rule of law. 3. Law and politics. 4. International law. 5. International organization. 6. Power (Social sciences) I. Institut Soedinennykh Shtatov Ameriki i Kanady (Rossiĭskaîa akademiîa nauk) II. Title.

Dawes, Edwin A. Stanley Collins : conjurer, collector, and iconoclast / by Edwin A. Dawes. Washington, DC : Kaufman and Co., c2002. 1 v. (various pagings) : ill. ; 29 cm. + 1 computer optical disc (4 3/4 in.). CD-ROM includes a short film, "Stanley Collins: The Shuffler." Includes bibliographical references and index.
1. Collins, Stanley, - 1881-1966. 2. Magicians - England - Biography. 3. Magic tricks. I. Title.

Dawkins, Richard, 1941- The extended phenotype : the long reach of the gene / Richard Dawkins ; [with a new afterword by Daniel Dennett]. Rev. ed. Oxford ; New York : Oxford University Press, 1999. viii, 313 p. ; 20 cm. Includes bibliographical references (p. 269-289) and indexes. CONTENTS: Necker cubes and buffaloes -- Genetic determinism and gene selectionism -- Constraints on perfection -- Arms races and manipulation -- The active germ-line replicator -- Organisms, groups and memes: replicators or vehicles? -- Selfish wasp or selfish strategy? -- Outlaws and modifiers -- Selfish DNA, jumping genes, and a Lamarckian scare -- An agony in five fits -- The genetical evolution of animal artefacts -- Host phenotypes of parasite genes -- Action at a distance -- Rediscovering the organism. ISBN 0-19-288051-9 DDC 576.8/2
1. Natural selection. 2. Gene expression. 3. Genetics. 4. Evolution (Biology) I. Dennett, Daniel Clement. II. Title.
QH375 .D38 1999

Dawson, Christopher, 1889-1970. The making of Europe : an introduction to the history of European unity / Christopher Dawson ; [with an introduction by Alexander Murray]. Washington, D.C. : Catholic University of America Press, 2002, 1932. xxxix, 282 p. ; 22 cm. (The works of Christopher Dawson) Originally published: London : Sheed and Ward, 1932. With new introd. Includes bibliographical references (p. 257-269) and index. SUMMARY: Christopher Dawson concludes that the period of the fourth to the eleventh centuries, commonly known as the Dark Ages, is not a barren prelude to the creative energy of the medieval world. Instead, he argues that it is better described as "ages of dawn" for it is in this rich and confused period that the complex and creative interaction of the Roman empire, the Christian Church, the classical tradition, and barbarous societies provided the foundation for a vital, unified European culture. In an age of fragmentation and the emergence of new nationalist forces, Dawson argued that if "our civilization is to survive, it is essential that it should develop a common European consciousness and sense of historic and organic unity." But he was clear that this unity required sources deeper and more complex than the political and economic movements on which so many had come to depend, and he insisted, prophetically, that Europe would need to recover its Christian roots if it was to survive. In a time of cultural and political ambiguity, The making of Europe is an indispensable work for understanding not only the rich sources but also the contemporary implications of the very idea of Europe. CONTENTS: pt. 1. The foundations -- 1. The Roman empire -- 2. The Catholic church -- 3. The classical tradition and Christianity -- 4. The barbarians -- 5. The barbarian invasions and the fall of the empire in the West -- pt. 2. The ascendancy of the East -- 6. The Christian empire and the rise of the Byzantine culture -- 7. The awakening of the East and the revolt of the subject nationalities -- 8. The rise of Islam -- 9. The expansion of Moslem culture -- 10. The Byzantine Renaissance and the revival of the Eastern empire -- pt. 3. The formation of Western christendom -- 11. The Western church and the conversion of the barbarians -- 12. The restoration of the Western empire and Carolingian renaissance -- 13. The age of the Vikings and the conversion of the North -- 14. The rise of the mediaeval unity. ISBN 0-8132-1083-6 (pbk. : alk. paper) DDC 940.1
1. Civilization, Medieval. 2. Church history - Middle Ages, 600-1500. I. Title. II. Title: Introduction to the history of European unity III. Series: Dawson, Christopher, 1889-1970. Works. 2001.
CB353 .D3 2002

Works. 2001.
Dawson, Christopher, 1889-1970. The making of Europe. Washington, D.C. : Catholic University of America Press, 2002, 1932.
CB353 .D3 2002

Dawson, Douglas E. The only bad mistake you make is the one you never learn from : lessons from the battle front / Douglas E. Dawson. Mt. Holly, N.C. : Elias Alexander Press, c2002. ix, 124 p. ; 21 cm. Includes index. ISBN 0-9712680-5-3 DDC 155.2/4
1. Errors - Psychological aspects. I. Title.
BF323.E7 D38 2002

Dawson, Michael Robert William, 1959- Minds and machines : connectionism and psychological modeling / Michael R.W. Dawson. Malden, MA : Blackwell Pub., c2003. p. cm. Includes bibliographical references and index. Table of contents URL: http://www.loc.gov/catdir/toc/ecip041/2003005918.html ISBN 1405113480 (hardcover : alk. paper) ISBN 1405113499 (pbk. : alk. paper) DDC 153
1. Connectionism. 2. Cognitive science. I. Title.
BF311 .D345 2003

Dawson, Peg. Executive skills in children and adolescents : a practical guide to assessment and intervention / Peg Dawson, Richard Guare. New York : Guilford Press, 2004. p. cm. (The Guilford practical intervention in the schools series) Includes bibliographical references and index. Table of contents URL: http://www.loc.gov/catdir/toc/ecip046/2003015732.html CONTENTS: Overview of executive skills -- Assessing executive skills -- Linking assessment to intervention -- Interventions to promote executive skills -- Coaching students with executive skill deficits -- Classroom-wide interventions -- Applications to specific populations. ISBN 1-57230-928-8 (pbk. : alk. paper) DDC 155.4/13
1. Executive ability in children. 2. Executive ability in adolescence. 3. Self-management (Psychology) for teenagers. 4. Self-management (Psychology) for children. I. Guare, Richard. II. Title. III. Series.
BF723.E93 D39 2004

Dāwūd, Muḥammad ʻĪsá. al-Jafr li-Sayyidinā ʻAlī : asrār al-hā' fī al-Jafr / Muḥammad ʻĪsá Dāwūd. al-Muhandisīn [Giza] : Madbūlī al-Ṣaghīr, [2003] 335 p. ; 24 cm. In Arabic. ISBN 977-286-162-3
1. ʻAlī ibn Abī Ṭālib, - Caliph, - 600 (ca.)-661. - Jafr al-jāmiʻ wa-al-nūr al-lāmiʻ. 2. Divination. 3. Occultism, Islamic. 4. Hā' (The Arabic letter) 5. Arab coutries - 21st century. I. Title.
BF1771+

DAY. *See* **NIGHT.**

DAY DREAMS. *See* **FANTASY.**

Day, Eileen.
[I'm good at helping. Spanish]
Soy bueno para ayudar / Eileen Day ; traducción de Sol Robledo. Chicago : Heinemann Library, 2003. p. cm. (Soy bueno para--) Includes index. SUMMARY: Explains what it means and how it feels to be helpful, and shows how to help at home and in other locations. ISBN 1403409323 ISBN 1403435758 (pbk.) DDC 177/.7
1. Helping behavior in children - Juvenile literature. 2. Helpfulness. 3. Spanish language materials. I. Title. II. Series: Day, Eileen. Soy bueno para.
BF723.H45 D3918 2003

Soy bueno para.
Day, Eileen. [I'm good at helping. Spanish] Soy bueno para ayudar. Chicago : Heinemann Library, 2003.
BF723.H45 D3918 2003

The day our world changed : children's art of 9/11 / introduction by Rudolph W. Giuliani ; [edited by] Robin F. Goodman & Andrea Henderson Fahnestock ; forewords by Harold S. Koplewicz & Robert R. Macdonald ; esssys by Debbie Almontaser ... [et al.]. New York : Harry N. Abrams Inc., 2002. 128 p. : col. ill. ; 28 cm. CONTENTS: Foreword / Robert R. Macdonald -- Foreword / Harold S. Koplewicz, M.D. -- Introduction / Rudolph W. Giuliani -- Day our world changed: children's art of 9/11 / Robin F. Goodman, Ph. D., A.T.R.-BC -- Children as witnesses to history / Sarah M. Henry, Ph. D. -- Horror through innocent eyes / Pete Hamill -- School in the towers' shadow / Senator Charles E. Schumer -- Our art is the enemy of death / Tim Rollins -- Sunday after 9/11 / Reverend Alan Gibson -- Growing up Arab-American / Debbie Almontaser -- New friend at the firehouse / Jane Rosenthal, Craig Hatkoff -- Firefighter's new friend / Lieutenant Victor J. Navarra -- Spiritual resistance through art / Rabbi Peter J. Rubinstein -- Memories will shape the future / Arthur L. Carter -- Resilience of our children / Senator Jon S. Corzine -- Foundation for a new America / Imam Abdul Malik -- Stronger & more united than ever / Governor George E. Pataki ISBN 0-8109-3544-9 DDC 155.935083
1. September 11 Terrorist Attacks, 2001 - Psychological aspects. 2. Child psychology. 3. Children's art. 4. Terrorism in art. I. Goodman, Robin F. II. Henderson, Andrea. III. Almontaser, Debbie. IV. New York University. Child Study Center. V. Museum of the City of New York. VI. Title.

Day, Stacey B. Man and Mu : the cradle of becoming and unbecoming : desiderata for human science / by Stacey B. Day. N[ew] Y[ork] : International Foundation for Biosocial Development and Human Health ; Oviedo, Fla. : Disctributed by C.E.P., c1997. xii, 181 p. : ill. ; 29 cm. ISBN 0-934314-00-4 DDC 128
1. Life. 2. Human beings. I. Title.
BD431 .D37 1997

Dāyah, Muḥammad Riḍwān.
Ibn Khātimah, Aḥmad ibn ʻAlī, d. ca. 1369. [Poems] Dīwān Ibn Khātimah al-Anṣārī. al-Ṭabʻah 1. Bayrūt : Dār al-Fikr al-Muʻāṣir ; Dimashq : Dār al-Fikr, 1994.
PJ7760.I2454 *<Orien Arab>*

DAYS. *See* **FASTS AND FEASTS; FESTIVALS; HOLIDAYS.**

D'Cruz, Doreen, 1950- Loving subjects : narratives of female desire / Doreen D'Cruz. New York : P. Lang, c2002. x, 295 p. ; 24 cm. (American university studies. IV, English language and literature ; vol. 195) Includes bibliographical references (p. [275]-288) and index. ISBN 0-8204-5802-3 (alk. paper) DDC 823/.9109353
1. English fiction - Women authors - History and criticism. 2. Women and literature - Great Britain - History - 20th century. 3. Women and literature - United States - History - 20th century. 4. American fiction - Women authors - History and criticism. 5. American fiction - 20th century - History and criticism. 6. English fiction - 20th century - History and criticism. 7. Psychological fiction - History and criticism. 8. Psychoanalysis and literature. 9. Desire in literature. 10. Narration (Rhetoric) 11. Love in literature. I. Title. II. Series: American university studies. Series IV, English language and literature ; v. 195.
PR888.W6 D39 2002

De Anda, Diane. Stress management for adolescents : a cognitive-behavioral program : program guide / Diane de Anda. Champaign, Ill. : Research Press, 2002. iii, 141 p. : ill. ; 28 cm. ISBN 0-87822-444-0 (pbk.) ISBN 0-87822-483-1 (program guide) DDC 155.5/18
1. Stress in adolescence - Study and teaching (Secondary) - Activity programs. 2. Stress management for teenagers - Study and teaching (Secondary) - Activity programs. I. Title.
BF724.3.S86 D4 2002

De Angeles, Ly, 1951- Witchcraft : theory and practice / Ly de Angeles. 1st ed. St. Paul, Minn. : Llewellyn Publications, 2000 (2003 printing) xxvi, 256 p. ; 23 cm. Includes bibliographical references (p. 237-243) and index. ISBN 1-56718-782-X (alk. paper) DDC 133.4/3
1. Witchcraft. I. Title.
BF1566 .D38 2000

De Bergerac, Olivia. The dolphin within : awakening human potential / Olivia De Bergerac. East Roseville, NSW, Australia : Simon & Schuster, 1998. 192 p. : ill. ; 23 cm. Includes bibliographical references (p. 180-185) and index. ISBN 0-7318-0688-3
1. Dolphins - Miscellanea. 2. Mind and body - Miscellanea. 3. Spiritual life - Miscellanea. 4. Human-animal relationships - Miscellanea. I. Title.
BF1999 .D335 1998

DE BONO, EDWARD, 1933-.
Dudgeon, Piers. Breaking out of the box. London : Headline, 2001.
BF109.D39 D83 2001

De Courtivron, Isabelle.
Lives in translation. 1st ed. New York ; Houndmills, England : Palgrave Macmillan, 2003.
P115.25 .L58 2003

De Darwin à Piaget.
Ottavi, Dominique. Paris : CNRS, c2001.

De Falk, Samuel Hayyim, ca. 1710-1782.
Yoman.
Oron, Michal. Mi-'Ba'al shed' le-'Ba'al Shem'. Yerushalayim : Mosad Byaliḳ : Bet ha-sefer le-mada'e ha-Yahadut 'a. sh. Ḥayim Rozenberg, Universiṭat Tel-Aviv, c763 [2002]

DE FALK, SAMUEL HAYYIM, CA. 1710-1782 - CRITICISM AND INTERPRETATION.
Oron, Michal. Mi-'Ba'al shed' le-'Ba'al Shem'. Yerushalayim : Mosad Byaliḳ : Bet ha-sefer le-mada'e ha-Yahadut 'a. sh. Ḥayim Rozenberg, Universiṭat Tel-Aviv, c763 [2002]

De Frankenstein ao transgênero.
Campos, Maria Consuelo Cunha. Rio de Janeiro : Editora Agora da Ilha, 2001.

De Grandis, Francesca. What kind of goddess are you? / by Francesca De Grandis. Naperville, Ill. : Sourcebooks, Inc., 2004. p. cm. Includes bibliographical references. Table of contents URL: http://www.loc.gov/catdir/toc/ecip048/2003020087.html CONTENTS: All fun and light and power -- What the heck is in this book? -- What's a nice woman like you doing in a book like this? -- What kind of goddess are you? -- The cosmic spa for goddesses -- The quizzes -- The mother goddess quiz -- The girlfriend goddess quiz -- Goddess of love quiz -- The activist goddess quiz -- Goddess-just-wants-to-have-fun quiz -- Corporate goddess quiz -- Sex goddess quiz -- The out-to-change-the-world

goddess quiz -- The trickster goddess quiz -- Bad girl goddess quiz -- Princess goddess quiz -- The thirteen modern goddesses -- The mother goddess -- The girlfriend goddess -- Goddess of love -- The activist goddess -- Goddess-just-wants-to-have-fun -- Corporate goddess -- Sex goddess -- The out-to-change-the-world goddess -- The trickster goddess -- Bad girl goddess -- Princess goddess -- Goddess of wrath and unintentional destruction -- The ultimate goddess -- Certificates of divine stature and how to make them easily -- Goddess compatibility (and how we can all be in divine harmony) -- How to throw a goddess party -- Games for goddesses -- Presto! instant sex magic! -- The "I can't hear you" game -- The big secret -- How to be (at least a bit of) a bad girl goddess, version #1: the train wreck boogie -- How to be (at least a bit of) a bad girl goddess, version #2 -- Bless your secret magic weapon -- Princess pink day -- Cosmic coincidence used for fortune telling -- Cosmic coincidental fortune telling stories -- Love, love, and more love -- Modern resources for modern goddesses. ISBN 1402201656 (alk. paper) DDC 201/.43
1. Goddesses - Miscellanea. 2. Women - Miscellanea. 3. Magic, Celtic. 4. Goddess religion. I. Title.
BF1623.G63 D4 2004

De Jong, Mayke.
Topographies of power in the early Middle Ages. Leiden ; Boston : Brill, 2001.
D117 .T67 2001

De Kluyver, Cornelis A. Strategy : a view from the top / Cornelis A. de Kluyver, John A. Pearce II ; foreword by Peter F. Drucker. Upper Saddle River, N.J. : Prentice Hall, c2003. xvii, 142 p. : ill. ; 24 cm. Includes bibliographical references and index. ISBN 0-13-008360-7 (pbk.) DDC 658.4/012
1. Executives. 2. Leadership. 3. Management. I. Pearce, John A. II. Title.
HD38.2 .D425 2003

De la aurora.
Zambrano, María. Córdoba, Argentina : Alción Editora, c1999.

De la certitude des connaissances humaines.
Silhon, sieur de (Jean), 1596?-1667. [Paris] : Fayard, c2002.

De la manière de négocier avec les souverains.
Callières, Monsieur de (François), 1645-1717. Genève : Droz, c2002.

De la paternité et des psychoses.
Lefèvre, Alain, 1947- Paris : Harmattan, c2002-

De l'évasion.
Lévinas, Emmanuel. [De l'evasion. English] On escape = Stanford, Calif. : Stanford University Press, 2003.
BD331 .L459613 2003

De magistro.
Augustine, Saint, Bishop of Hippo. Paderborn : F. Schöningh, 2002.
BR65.A5 G4 2002

De Manhattan à Bagdad.
Arkoun, Mohammed. Paris : Desclée de Brouwer, 2003.
JC319 .A72 2003

De Martino, Ernesto, 1908-1965. Il mondo magico : prolegomeni a una storia del magismo / Ernesto De Martino. 1. ed. Torino : Bollati Boringhieri, 1997. liv, 279 p. ; 22 cm. (Saggi. Storia e scienze sociali) Includes bibliographical references (p. [liii]-liv) and index. ISBN 88-339-1048-2
1. Magic - History. I. Title. II. Series: Saggi (Bollati Boringhieri (Firm)). Storia, filosofia e scienze sociali.
BF1589 .D46 1997

De Mente, Boye. Asian face reading : unlocking the secrets hidden in the human face / Boye de Mente. Boston, MA : Tuttle Pub., 2003. p. cm. ISBN 1-58290-067-1 (pbk.) DDC 138
1. Physiognomy - China. 2. Physiognomy - Japan. 3. Facial expression - China. 4. Facial expression - Japan. I. Title.
BF851 .D37 2003

De Muijnck, Wim. Dependencies, connections, and other relations : a theory of mental causation / by Wim de Muijnck. Dordrecht ; Boston : Kluwer Academic Publishers, c2003. xxxiii, 284 p. ; 25 cm. (Philosophical studies series ; v. 93) Includes bibliographical references (p. [261]-271) and indexes. ISBN 1402013914 (alk. paper) DDC 128/.2
1. Philosophy of mind. 2. Mind and body. 3. Causation. I. Title. II. Series.
BD418.3 .D4 2003

De Munck, Victor C. Culture, self, and meaning / Victor de Munck. Prospect Heights, Ill. : Waveland Press, c2000. v, 113 p. : ill. ; 23 cm. Includes bibliographical references (p. 99-106) and index. ISBN 1-57766-137-0 DDC 302.5
1. Self - Social aspects. 2. Culture - Psychological aspects. 3. Meaning (Psychology) I. Title.
BF697.5.S65 M86 2000

De Pace, Anna. La scepsi, il sapere e l'anima : dissonanze nella cerchia laurenziana / Anna De Pace. Milano : LED, c2002. 314 p. ; 24 cm. (Il filarete / Università degli studi di Milano, Pubblicazioni della Facoltà di lettere e filosofia ; 208) Includes bibliography (p. 281-306), bibliographical references and name index. Number of series appears on spine. A. De Pace teaches at the University of Milan. ISBN 88-7916-187-3 DDC 195
1. Ficino, Marsilio, - 1433-1499 - Criticism and interpretation. 2. Poliziano, Angelo, - 1454-1494 - Criticism and interpretation. 3. Pico della Mirandola, Giovanni, - 1463-1494 - Criticism and interpretation. 4. Philosophy, Renaissance. 5. Philosophy, Italian. 6. Neoplatonism. I. Title. II. Series: Filarete ; 208.

De quebradores y cumplidores.
Viveros, M. (Mara) 1a ed. [Colombia] : CES Universidad Nacional de Colombia : Fundación Ford : Profamilia Colombia, 2002.

De Rosa, Giuseppe. Fatica e gioia di credere : i misteri della fede cristiana / Giuseppe De Rosa. Leumann (Torino) : ElleDiCi ; Roma : La civiltà cattolica, c2002. 348 p. ; 21 cm. (Credere oggi ; [11]) Includes indexes (p. 329-341). ISBN 88-01-02447-9 DDC 230
1. Faith. I. Title. II. Series: Collana credere oggi ; [11].

DE SARLO, FRANCESCO, 1864-1937.
Sava, Gabriella. La psicologia filosofica in Italia. Galatina (Lecce) : Congedo, 2000.
BF38 .S235 2000

De Sion exibit lex et verbum domini de Hierusalem : essays on medieval law, liturgy, and literature in honour of Amnon Linder / edited by Yitzhak Hen. Turnhout, Belgium : Brepols, c2001. viii, 214 p. ; 25 cm. (Cultural encounters in late antiquity and the Middle Ages ; v. 1) "List of the published writings of Amnon Linder": p. [211]-214. Includes bibliographical references. In English; one essay in French. ISBN 2-503-51091-4
1. Linder, Amnon. 2. Catholic Church - Liturgy - History - Middle Ages, 600-1500. 3. Civilization, Medieval. 4. Law, Medieval. 5. Literature, Medieval. I. Hen, Yitzhak. II. Title: Essays on medieval law, liturgy, and literature III. Series.

De St. Aubin, Ed.
The generative society. 1st ed. Washington, DC : American Psychological Association, c2003.
BF724.5 .G45 2003

DEAD. See **FUNERAL RITES AND CEREMONIES; SUICIDE VICTIMS.**

DEAD, COMMUNICATION WITH THE. See **SPIRITUALISM.**

DEADLY SINS. See **ENVY; SADNESS.**

DEADLY SINS - PSYCHOLOGY.
Naranjo, Claudio. [Eneagrama de la sociedad. English] The enneagram of society. Nevada City, Calif. : Gateways Books and Tapes, 2004.
BF698.35.E54 N3813 2004

DEAF CHILDREN - MEANS OF COMMUNICATION.
Goldin-Meadow, Susan. The resilience of language. New York ; Hove [England] : Psychology Press, 2003.
P118 .G57 2003

DEAF - EDUCATION.
Oxford handbook of deaf studies, language, and education. Oxford ; New York : Oxford University Press, c2003.
HV2380 .O88 2003

DEAF - MEANS OF COMMUNICATION.
Oxford handbook of deaf studies, language, and education. Oxford ; New York : Oxford University Press, c2003.
HV2380 .O88 2003

DEAF-MUTES. See **DEAF.**

DEAF - SOCIAL CONDITIONS.
Oxford handbook of deaf studies, language, and education. Oxford ; New York : Oxford University Press, c2003.
HV2380 .O88 2003

Deaf studies, language, and education.
Oxford handbook of deaf studies, language, and education. Oxford ; New York : Oxford University Press, c2003.
HV2380 .O88 2003

DEAFNESS - PATIENTS. See **DEAF.**

DEALERS (RETAIL TRADE). See **AUTOMOBILE DEALERS.**

DEALERSHIPS, AUTOMOBILE. See **AUTOMOBILE DEALERS.**

Dealing with bullies.
Scheunemann, Pam, 1955- Edina, MN : Abdo Pub., 2004.
BF637.B85 S37 2004

Dealing with conflict.
Hart, Lois Borland. The manager's pocket guide to dealing with conflict. Amherst, Mass. : HRD Press, c1999.
BF637.I48 H38 1999

Dealing with losses.
Weiss, Stefanie Iris. Everything you need to know about dealing with losses. Rev. ed. New York : Rosen Pub. Group, 2000.
BF724.3.L66 W45 2000

DeAmicis, Lahni.
DeAmicis, Ralph. Feng shui American style. New York : Paraview Special Editions, c2003.
BF1779.F4 .D42 2003

DeAmicis, Ralph. Feng shui American style : the magic of successful design / Ralph & Lahni DeAmicis. New York : Paraview Special Editions, c2003. 255 p. : ill. ; 23 cm. ISBN 1-931044-44-9 (pbk.)
1. Feng shui. I. DeAmicis, Lahni. II. Title.
BF1779.F4 .D42 2003

Dear friend.
BenShea, Noah. Naperville, Ill. : Sourcebooks, c2003.
BF575.F66 B446 2003

Dearborn, Dorothy, 1927- New Brunswick haunted houses-- and other tales of strange and eerie events / by Dorothy Dearborn ; illustrated by Carol Taylor. Saint John, NB : Neptune Pub., c2000. 128 p. : ill. ; 22 cm. Spine title: New Brunswick haunted houses. ISBN 1-89627-021-2 DDC 133.1/09715/1
1. Ghosts - New Brunswick. 2. Haunted places - New Brunswick. I. Title. II. Title: New Brunswick haunted houses
BF1472.N48 D44 2000

Deary, Ian J.
Matthews, Gerald. Personality traits. 2nd ed. New York : Cambridge University Press, 2003.
BF698 .M3434 2003

DEATH. See also **BEREAVEMENT; CHILDREN AND DEATH; CHILDREN - DEATH; INFANTS (NEWBORN) - DEATH; INFANTS - DEATH; PARENTS - DEATH; TERMINAL CARE; TERMINALLY ILL.**

Bahr, Hans-Dieter. Den Tod denken. München : Fink, 2002.

Bame Bame, Michael. Death and everlasting life. Nairobi, Kenya : All Africa Conference of Churches, 1994.

Burt, Robert, 1939- Death is that man taking names. Berkeley : University of California Press ; New York : Milbank Memorial Fund, c2002.
R726.8 .B875 2002

Celebrity death certificates. Jefferson, N.C. : McFarland, c2003.

Death and denial. Westport, Conn. ; London : Praeger, 2002.
BD444 .D377 2002

Dennison, Amy. Our dad died. Minneapolis, MN : Free Spirit Pub., c2003.
BF723.G75 D46 2003

Extreme beauty. London ; New York : Continuum, 2002.
BH39 .E98 2002

Ferrater Mora, José, 1912- [Selections. English. 2003] Three Spanish philosophers. Albany : State University of New York Press, c2003.
B4568.U54 F3913 2003

Han, Byung-Chul. Tod und Alterität. München : Fink, c2002.
BD444 .H36 2002

Hanus, Michel. La Mort aujourd'hui. Paris : Frison-Roche, c2000.

Johnson, Marvin. Where's Jess? Rev. Omaha, NE : Centering Corp. Resource, 2003.
BF723.G75 J645 2003

Le Fèvre, Jean-Yves. Eloge de la mort. Monaco : Rocher, c2002.

Leland, Kurt. The unanswered question. Charlottesville, VA : Hampton Roads Pub., c2002.

BF1045.N4 L45 2002

Merdalor, Jean. Pensées mortelles. Port-au-Prince, Haiti : Editions Choucoune, 1999.
1. Black author.

Mortalism. Amherst, N.Y. : Prometheus Books, 2003.
BD431 .M886 2003

Nosmas, Alma. La mort élégante. Paris : Horay, c2003.

Reid, Howard. In search of the immortals. London : Headline, 1999.

Smith, William A. (William Aloysius), 1929- Reflections on death, dying, and bereavement. Amityville, N.Y. : Baywood Pub., c2003.
BD444 .S57 2003

Valabrega, Jean-Paul. Les mythes, conteurs de l'inconscient. Paris : Payot, 2001.
BD542 .V353 2001

Yan, Xianglin, 1960- Si wang mei xue. Di 1 ban. Shanghai : Xue lin chu ban she, 1998.

Zeichen des Todes in der psychoanalytischen Erfahrung. Tübingen : Edition Diskord, c2000.

DEATH AND CHILDREN. *See* **CHILDREN AND DEATH.**

Death and denial : interdisciplinary perspectives on the legacy of Ernest Becker / edited by Daniel Liechty. Westport, Conn. ; London : Praeger, 2002. xvi, 301 p. ; 24 cm. Includes bibliographical references (p. [281]-293) and index. ISBN 0-275-97420-0 (alk. paper) DDC 128/.5/092 1. Becker, Ernest. 2. Death. 3. Death - Psychological aspects. I. Liechty, Daniel, 1954-
BD444 .D377 2002

Death and dying.
Peacock, Carol Antoinette. New York : Franklin Watts, c2004.
BF575.G7 P3783 2004

Death and everlasting life.
Bame Bame, Michael. Nairobi, Kenya : All Africa Conference of Churches, 1994.

DEATH, APPARENT. *See* **NEAR-DEATH EXPERIENCES.**

DEATH (BIOLOGY).
Klarsfeld, André. [Biologie de la mort. English] The biology of death. Ithaca, NY : Comstock Pub. Associates/Cornell University Press, 2004.
QH530 .K5613 2004

The death book.
Stalfelt, Pernilla. [Döden boken. English] Toronto, Ont. : Groundwood Books / Douglas & McIntyrenfrom ; Berkeley, CA : Distrituted by Publishers Group West, c2002.
BF723.D3 S7313 2002

DEATH CERTIFICATES.
Celebrity death certificates. Jefferson, N.C. : McFarland, c2003.

DEATH - HISTORY - ART.
Mörgeli, Christoph. "Über dem Grabe geboren". Bern : Benteli, 2002.

Death, immortality, and ideology.
Oron, Israel. Mayet, almayet ye-ide'ologyah. [Israel] : Miśrad ha-biṭaḥon, [2002]

DEATH IN ART.
Yan, Xianglin, 1960- Si wang mei xue. Di 1 ban. Shanghai : Xue lin chu ban she, 1998.

DEATH IN DREAMS.
Grubbs, Geri A., 1943- Bereavement dreaming and the individuating soul. Berwick, Me. : Nicolas-Hays, 2004.
BF1099.D4 G78 2004

DEATH IN LITERATURE.
Greene, Virginie Elisabeth, 1959- Le sujet et la mort dans La mort Artu. Saint-Genouph : Nizet, 2002.

Lis, Izabela. Śmierć w literaturze staroserbskiej. Poznań : Wydawn. Nauk. Uniwersytetu im. Adama Mickiewicza w Poznaniu, 2003.
PG1406 .L59 2003

Ricciardi, Alessia. The ends of mourning. Stanford, Calif. : Stanford University Press, 2003.
PN56.D4 R53 2003

Yan, Xianglin, 1960- Si wang mei xue. Di 1 ban. Shanghai : Xue lin chu ban she, 1998.

DEATH IN MOTION PICTURES.
Ricciardi, Alessia. The ends of mourning. Stanford, Calif. : Stanford University Press, 2003.

PN56.D4 R53 2003

DEATH INSTINCT.
Sánchez-Pardo, Esther. Cultures of the death drive. Durham [N.C.] : Duke University Press, c2003.
BF175.5.D4 S26 2003

Death is that man taking names.
Burt, Robert, 1939- Berkeley : University of California Press ; New York : Milbank Memorial Fund, c2002.
R726.8 .B875 2002

DEATH - MISCELLANEA.
Grant, Robert J. Universe of worlds. Virginia Beach, Va. : A.R.E. Press, 2005.
BF1261.2 .G73 2005

Konstantinos, 1972- Contact the other side. 1st ed. St. Paul, Minn. : Llewellyn Publications, 2001.
BF1275.D2 K66 2001

Death of a parent.
Umberson, Debra. Cambridge ; New York : Cambridge University Press, 2003.
BF789.D4 U48 2003

DEATH OF PARENTS. *See* **PARENTS - DEATH.**

DEATH - PHILOSOPHY. *See* **DEATH.**

DEATH - PSYCHOLOGICAL ASPECTS. *See also* **BEREAVEMENT - PSYCHOLOGICAL ASPECTS.**
Cornils, Stanley P. Your healing journey through grief. San Francisco, CA : Robert D. Reed Publishers, c2003.
BF575.G7 C677 2003

Death and denial. Westport, Conn. ; London : Praeger, 2002.
BD444 .D377 2002

Harrison, Robert Pogue. The dominion of the dead. Chicago : University of Chicago Press, 2003.
BF789.D4 H375 2003

Hedtke, Lorraine, 1957- Re-membering lives. Amityville, N.Y. : Baywood Pub. Co., 2004.
BF789.D4 H4 2004

Hendlin, Steven J. Overcoming the inheritance taboo. New York : Plume, 2004.
BF789.D4 H4235 2004

Herzog, Edgar. [Psyche und Tod. English] Psyche and death. New ed. / edited and designed by C.L. Sebrell. Woodstock, Conn. : Spring Publications, c2000.

Kastenbaum, Robert. Death, society, and human experience. 8th ed. Boston, MA : Allyn and Bacon, 2004.
BF789.D4 K36 2004

Kastenbaum, Robert. On our way. Berkeley : University of California Press, c2004.
BF789.D4 .K365 2004

Living beyond loss. 2nd ed. New York : W.W. Norton, 2004.
BF575.D35 L54 2004

Living with suicide [electronic resource]. [Alexandria, Va.] : PBS Online ; [New York, N.Y.] : Web Lab
BF789.D4

Meier, Levi. Seven heavens. [S.l.] : Devora Publishing, c2002.
BF789.D4 M39 2002

Neeld, Elizabeth Harper, 1940- Seven choices. New York : Warner Books, c2003.
BF575.G7 N44 2003

Oron, Israel. Mayet, almayet ye-ide'ologyah. [Israel] : Miśrad ha-biṭaḥon, [2002]

Ricciardi, Alessia. The ends of mourning. Stanford, Calif. : Stanford University Press, 2003.
PN56.D4 R53 2003

A teen's guide to coping. Minneapolis : Fairview Press, 2003.
BF789.D4 T44 2003

Walter, Carolyn Ambler. The loss of a life partner. New York : Columbia University Press, c2003.
BF575.G7 W3435 2003

With eyes open [electronic resource]. San Francisco : KQED ; [Alexandria, Va.] : PBS
BF789.D4

Wood, Robert S. (Robert Snyder), 1930- Peaceful passing. Sedona, AZ : In Print Pub., c2000.
BF789.D4 W66 2000

DEATH - PSYCHOLOGICAL ASPECTS - CASE STUDIES.
Polcz, Alaine. Gyermek a halál kapujában. Budapest : PONT, c2001.
BF723.D3 P65 2001

DEATH - PSYCHOLOGICAL ASPECTS - DICTIONARIES.
Adams, Christine A. ABC's of grief. Amityville, N.Y. : Baywood, c2003.
BF575.G7 A32 2003

DEATH - PSYCHOLOGICAL ASPECTS - HISTORY.
The psychology of death in fantasy and history. Westport, CT : Praeger, 2004.
BF789.D4 P79 2004

DEATH - PSYCHOLOGICAL ASPECTS - JUVENILE LITERATURE.
Stalfelt, Pernilla. [Döden boken. English] The death book. Toronto, Ont. : Groundwood Books / Douglas & McIntyrenfrom ; Berkeley, CA : Distrituted by Publishers Group West, c2002.
BF723.D3 S7313 2002

DEATH - PSYCHOLOGICAL ASPECTS - TEXTBOOKS.
DeSpelder, Lynne Ann, 1944- The last dance. 7th ed. Boston : McGraw-Hill, 2005.
BF789.D4 D53 2005

DEATH - PSYCHOLOGY. *See* **DEATH - PSYCHOLOGICAL ASPECTS.**

DEATH - RELIGIOUS ASPECTS - CHRISTIANITY.
Babarinde, A. O. The end of man. Lagos, Nigeria : Christ Foundation Baptist Church, 2001.
1. Black author.

Locke, Hubert G. Searching for God in godforsaken times and places. Grand Rapids, Mich. : W.B. Eerdmans Pub., c2003.
BT774 .L63 2003
1. Black author.

DEATH ROW INMATES - PALESTINE - PSYCHOLOGY.
Oron, Israel. Mayet, almayet ye-ide'ologyah. [Israel] : Miśrad ha-biṭaḥon, [2002]

DEATH ROW PRISONERS. *See* **DEATH ROW INMATES.**

DEATH - SOCIAL ASPECTS.
Harrison, Robert Pogue. The dominion of the dead. Chicago : University of Chicago Press, 2003.
BF789.D4 H375 2003

Kastenbaum, Robert. Death, society, and human experience. 8th ed. Boston, MA : Allyn and Bacon, 2004.
BF789.D4 K36 2004

Kastenbaum, Robert. On our way. Berkeley : University of California Press, c2004.
BF789.D4 .K365 2004

Wood, Robert S. (Robert Snyder), 1930- Peaceful passing. Sedona, AZ : In Print Pub., c2000.
BF789.D4 W66 2000

DEATH - SOCIAL ASPECTS - FRANCE.
Hanus, Michel. La Mort aujourd'hui. Paris : Frison-Roche, c2000.

DEATH - SOCIAL ASPECTS - TEXTBOOKS.
DeSpelder, Lynne Ann, 1944- The last dance. 7th ed. Boston : McGraw-Hill, 2005.
BF789.D4 D53 2005

DEATH - SOCIAL ASPECTS - UNITED STATES.
Burt, Robert, 1939- Death is that man taking names. Berkeley : University of California Press ; New York : Milbank Memorial Fund, c2002.
R726.8 .B875 2002

Death, society, and human experience.
Kastenbaum, Robert. 8th ed. Boston, MA : Allyn and Bacon, 2004.
BF789.D4 K36 2004

Death, value, and meaning series
Adams, J. Robert. Prospects for immortality. Amityville, N.Y. : Baywood Pub., c2003.
BD421 .A33 2003

Hedtke, Lorraine, 1957- Re-membering lives. Amityville, N.Y. : Baywood Pub. Co., 2004.
BF789.D4 H4 2004

Smith, William A. (William Aloysius), 1929- Reflections on death, dying, and bereavement. Amityville, N.Y. : Baywood Pub., c2003.

Death, value, and meaning series
BD444 .S57 2003
Stetson, Brad. Living victims, stolen lives. Amityville, N.Y. : Baywood Pub., c2003.
HV6533.C2 S73 2003

Debiec, Jacek.
The self. New York : New York Academy of Sciences, 2003.
BF697

Debolsillo
Margarit i Tayà, Remei. Acerca de la mujer. 1. ed. Barcelona : Plaza & Janés, 2002.

Debras, Sylvie. Lectrices au quotidien : femmes et presse quotidienne, la dissension / Sylvie Debras ; préface de Josiane Jouët ; Postface de Jean-François Barbier-Bouvet. Paris : L'Harmattan, c2003. 222 p. ; 22 cm. (Collection Communication et civilisation) Includes bibliographical references. ISBN 2-7475-3919-9 DDC 300
1. Women and journalism. 2. Women - Press coverage. 3. Newspaper reading. 4. Newspapers. 5. Knowledge, Sociology of. I. Title. II. Series: Communication et civilisation.

Debunked!.
Charpak, Georges. [Devenez sorciers, devenez savants English] Baltimore : Johns Hopkins University Press, 2004.
BF1409.5 .C4313 2004

Decade of behavior
Behavior genetics principles. Washington, DC : American Psychological Association, 2004.
BF698.9.B5 B44 2004

DECEIT. See **DECEPTION.**

DECENTRALIZATION IN GOVERNMENT. See **PUBLIC ADMINISTRATION.**

DECEPTION - PSYCHOLOGICAL ASPECTS.
Garifullin, Ramil', 1962- Illiuzionizm lichnosti. Kazan' : [s.n.], 1997.
BF491 .G37 1997

Svechnikov, Vladimir. Sotsiokul'turnyĭ analiz mistifikatsii. Saratov : Saratovskiĭ gos. tekhn. universitet, 2000.
BF637.D42 S94 2000

DECEPTION - SOCIAL ASPECTS.
Svechnikov, Vladimir. Sotsiokul'turnyĭ analiz mistifikatsii. Saratov : Saratovskiĭ gos. tekhn. universitet, 2000.
BF637.D42 S94 2000

Decher, Friedhelm. Besuch vom Mittagsdämon : Philosophie der Langeweile / Friedhelm Decher. 1. Aufl. Lüneburg : zu Klampen, 2000. 157 p. ; 19 cm. Includes bibliographical references (p. 145-157). ISBN 3-924245-93-2
1. Boredom - History. I. Title.
BF575.B67 .D43 2000

Deci, Edward L.
Handbook of self-determination research. Soft cover ed. Rochester, NY : University of Rochester Press, 2004.
BF575.A88 H36 2004

Decide & conquer.
Robbins, Stephen P., 1943- Upper Saddle River : Prentice Hall Financial Times, 2003.
BF448 .R63 2003

Decide and conquer.
Robbins, Stephen P., 1943- Decide & conquer. Upper Saddle River : Prentice Hall Financial Times, 2003.
BF448 .R63 2003

Deciphering cyberspace : making the most of digital communication technology / Leonard Shyles [editor]. Thousand Oaks, Calif. : Sage Publications, c2003. xix, 415 p. : ill. ; 24 cm. Includes bibliographical references (p. 367-400) and index. Table of contents URL: http://www.loc.gov/catdir/toc/fy035/2002006992.html CONTENTS: Radio and television broadcasting ; Computers in communication : concepts and applications ; Sending messages across the network / Leonard Shyles -- Children in cyberspace / Mark R. Banschick, Josepha Silman Banschick -- Social and psychological uses of the Internet / JoAnn Magdoff, Jeffrey B. Rubin -- Connected learning in the information age / Thomas A. McCain, Leigh Maxwell -- Adopting instructional technologies / Judy C. Pearson -- Law and regulation, part I : individual interests / Keith Lee, Janessa Light -- Law and regulation, part II : business interests / Janessa Light, Katherine Neikirk. ISBN 0-7619-2219-9 (cloth) ISBN 0-7619-2220-2 (pbk) DDC 303.48/33
1. Telecommunication - History. 2. Cyberspace. 3. Information society. I. Shyles, Leonard, 1948-
TK5102.2 .D43 2003

DECISION-MAKING. See **CHOICE (PSYCHOLOGY); PROBLEM SOLVING.**

DECISION MAKING.
Berg, Barbara A. How to escape the no-win trap. New York : McGraw-Hill, c2004.
BF448 .B46 2004

Berry, Joy Wilt. Saying no. New York : Scholastic, c2001.
BF723.R4 B37 2001

Burke, Dan, 1965- Business @ the speed of stupid. Cambridge, MA : Perseus Pub., c2001.
HD45 .B7995 2001

Dennett, Daniel Clement. Freedom evolves. New York ; London : Viking, 2003.
BJ1461 .D427 2003

Enç, Berent. How we act. Oxford : Clarendon Press ; New York : Oxford University Press, 2003.
B105.A35 E63 2003

Etc. frequency processing and cognition. Oxford ; New York : Oxford University Press, c2002.
BF448 .E83 2002

Greenway, A. Roger. Risk management planning handbook. 2nd ed. Rockville, MD : ABS Consulting, Government Institutes, c2002.
HD61 .G733 2002

Greve, Henrich R. Organizational learning from performance feedback. Cambridge : Cambridge University Press, 2003.

Koutsoukis, Nikitas-Spiros. Decision modelling and information systems. Boston : Kluwer Academic Publishers, c2003.
T57.95 .K68 2003

Lempert, Robert J. Shaping the next one hundred years, Santa Monica, CA : RAND, 2003.
T57.6 .L46 2003

Lindgren, Mats, 1959- Scenario planning. Houndmills [England] ; New York : Palgrave Macmillan, 2002.
HD30.28 .L543 2002

Marcum, Dave. BusinessThink. New York : Wiley, c2002.
HF5386 .M3087 2002

McAfee, R. Preston. Competitive solutions. Princeton, N.J. : Princeton University Press, c2002.
HD30.28 .M3815 2002

Miller, John G., 1958- QBQ!. Denver, CO : Denver Press, c2001.
BF611 .M55 2001

The new economic diplomacy. Aldershot, Hampshire, England ; Burlington, VT : Ashgate, c2003.
HF1359 .N4685 2003

Psikhologicheskie problemy priniatiia reshenii̇a. IAroslavl' : IAroslavskiĭ gos. universitet, 2001.
BF448 .P78 2001

Raiffa, Howard, 1924- Negotiation analysis. Cambridge, MA : Belknap Press of Harvard University Press, 2002.
HD58.6 .R342 2002

Rescher, Nicholas. Sensible decisions. Lanham, Md. ; Oxford : Rowman & Littlefield Publishers, c2003.
B945.R453 S46 2003

Robbins, Stephen P., 1943- Decide & conquer. Upper Saddle River : Prentice Hall Financial Times, 2003.
BF448 .R63 2003

Schauer, Frederick F. Profiles, probabilities, and stereotypes. Cambridge, Mass. : Belknap Press of Harvard University Press, 2003.
HM1096 .S34 2003

Schwartz, Barry, 1946- The tyranny of choice. 1st ed. New York : ECCO, 2004.
BF611 .S38 2004

Sen, Amartya Kumar. Rationality and freedom. Cambridge, Mass. : Belknap Press of Harvard University Press, 2002.
HB846.8 .S466 2002

Sousa, Joao M. C. Fuzzy decision making in modeling and control. Singapore ; River Edge, N.J. : World Scientific, c2002.

Thinking. Hoboken, NJ : Wiley, c2003.
BF441 .T466 2003

Van Gigch, John P. Metadecisions. New York : Kluwer Academic/Plenum Publishers, c2003.

HM701 .V36 2003

Yates, J. Frank (Jacques Frank), 1945- Decision management. 1st ed. San Francisco : Jossey-Bass, c2003.
HD30.23 .Y386 2003

Zahariadis, Nikolaos, 1961- Ambiguity and choice in public policy. Washington, D.C. : Georgetown University Press, c2003.
H97 .Z34 2003

DECISION-MAKING, CONSUMER. See **CONSUMER BEHAVIOR.**

DECISION MAKING - GRAPHIC METHODS.
Hugl, Ulrike. Qualitative Inhaltsanalyse und Mind-Mapping. Wiesbaden : Gabler, 1995.

Decision-making group interaction.
Patton, Bobby R., 1935- 4th ed. Boston : Allyn and Bacon, c2003.
HM736 .P37 2003

DECISION MAKING - PHILOSOPHY.
Pettit, Philip, 1945- Rules, reasons, and norms. Oxford : Oxford University Press ; New York : Clarendon Press, 2002.
B105.T54 P48 2002

DECISION MAKING - PSYCHOLOGICAL ASPECTS.
Phillips, Nicola. The big difference. Cambridge, MA : Perseus Pub., c2001.
BF619 .P48 2001

The psychology of economic decisions. Oxford [England] ; New York : Oxford University Press, 2003-
HB74.P8 P725 2003

Decision management.
Yates, J. Frank (Jacques Frank), 1945- 1st ed. San Francisco : Jossey-Bass, c2003.
HD30.23 .Y386 2003

Decision modelling and information systems.
Koutsoukis, Nikitas-Spiros. Boston : Kluwer Academic Publishers, c2003.
T57.95 .K68 2003

DECISION SUPPORT SYSTEMS.
Burke, Dan, 1965- Business @ the speed of stupid. Cambridge, MA : Perseus Pub., c2001.
HD45 .B7995 2001

Decker, Dru Scott, 1942- Stress that motivates : self-talk secrets for success / Dru Scott. Rev. ed. Menlo Park, CA : Crisp Publications, c2002. viii, 112 p. : ill. ; 26 cm. (A Fifty-Minute series book) Includes bibliographical references (p. 110). ISBN 1-56052-537-1
1. Stress (Psychology) 2. Stress management. 3. Self-talk. 4. Motivation (Psychology) I. Title. II. Series: Fifty-Minute series.
BF575.S75 D38 2002

Decoding the ethics code.
Fisher, Celia B. Thousand Oaks, Calif. : Sage Publications, c2003.
BF76.4 .F57 2003

DECOLONIZATION.
Bessis, Sophie, 1947- [Occident et les autres. English] Western supremacy. London ; New York : Zed Books, 2003.
CB245 .B4613 2003

DECOLONIZATION IN LITERATURE.
Xu, Zou xiang hou xian dai yu hou zhi min. Di 1 ban. Beijing : Zhongguo she hui ke xue chu ban she : Xin hua shu dian jing xiao, 1996.
PN81 .H76 1996 <Asian China>

DECOLONIZATION - PSYCHOLOGICAL ASPECTS - CONGRESSES.
Psychanalyse et décolonisation. Paris : L'Harmattan, c1999.
BF175.4.C84 P76 1999

DECONSTRUCTION.
Bertram, Georg W., 1967- Hermeneutik und Dekonstruktion. München : Fink, c2002.
BD241 .B47 2002

Hägglund, Martin. Kronofobi. Stockholm : B. Östlings Bokförlag Symposion, 2002.

The deconstruction of dualism in theology.
McCulloch, Gillian. Carlisle : Paternoster Press, 2002.

Decorating with funky shui.
O'Neil, Jennifer. Kansas City, MO : Andrews McMeel, 2004.
BF1779.F4 O54 2004

DECORATION AND ORNAMENT. See **DESIGN; GEMS; ILLUMINATION OF BOOKS AND MANUSCRIPTS; ILLUSTRATION OF**

BOOKS; MURAL PAINTING AND DECORATION.

DECORATION AND ORNAMENT - PHILOSOPHY.
Vom Parergon zum Labyrinth. Wien : Böhlau, c2001.
NK1505 .V65 2001

DECORATION DAY. See **MEMORIAL DAY.**

DECORATIVE ART. See **DECORATION AND ORNAMENT.**

DECORATIVE ARTS. See **COSTUME; DECORATION AND ORNAMENT; FOLK ART; GLASS ART; POTTERY.**

DECORATIVE DESIGN. See **DECORATION AND ORNAMENT.**

DEDUCTION (LOGIC). See **LOGIC.**

DEDUCTIVE LOGIC. See **LOGIC.**

Dee, John, 1527-1608.
[Selections. 2003]
John Dee / edited by Gerald Suster. Berkeley, Calif. : North Atlantic Books, c2003. p. cm. (Western esoteric masters series) Originally published: Wellingborough, U.K. : Crucible, 1986. Includes bibliographical references (p.   ). ISBN 1-55643-472-3 (pbk.) DDC 001
1. Dee, John, - 1527-1608 - Diaries. 2. Science - Early works to 1800. I. Suster, Gerald. II. Title. III. Series.
BF1598.D5 A25 2003

DEE, JOHN, 1527-1608.
Szőnyi, György Endre. John Dee's occultism. Albany : State University of New York Press, 2004.
BF1598.D5 S98 2004

DEE, JOHN, 1527-1608 - DIARIES.
Dee, John, 1527-1608. [Selections. 2003] John Dee . Berkeley, Calif. : North Atlantic Books, c2003.
BF1598.D5 A25 2003

Dee, Jonathan. Isis : queen of Egyptian magic : her book of divination and spells / Jonathan Dee. New York : Sterling Pub., [2003?] 160 p. : col. ill. ; 25 cm. Includes index. ISBN 1402703961 DDC 133.4/3/0932
1. Magic, Egyptian. 2. Incantations, Egyptian. 3. Divination - Egypt. 4. Isis (Egyptian deity) I. Title.
BF1591 .D44 2003

Deely, John N. The impact on philosophy of semiotics : the quasi-error of the external world : with a dialogue between a 'semiotist' and a 'realist' / John Deely. South Bend, Ind. : St. Augustine's Press, 2003. viii, 267 p. ; 23 cm. Includes bibliographical references (p. 209-249) and index. ISBN 1-58731-375-8 (hardcover : alk. paper) DDC 121/.68
1. Postmodernism. 2. Semiotics. 3. Realism. I. Title.
B831.2 .D437 2003

The deeper dimension of Yoga.
Feuerstein, Georg. Boston : Shambhala, 2003.
B132.Y6 F4875 2003

DEFAMATION. See **LIBEL AND SLANDER.**

DeFaoíte, Dara. Paranormal Ireland : an investigation into the other side of Irish life / by Dara deFaoíte. Ashbourne, Co. Meath : Maverick House, c2002. 300 p. : ill ; 20 cm. Includes bibliography (p. [302-303]). ISBN 0-9542945-0-5 DDC 130/.9415
1. Parapsychology - Ireland. 2. Curiosities and wonders - Ireland. I. Title.
BF1031 .D344 2002

deFaoíte, Dara. Paranormal Ireland : an investigation into the other side of Irish life / by Dara deFaoíte. Northampton : Maverick House, 2002. 260 p. : ill ; 21 cm. Includes bibliography (p. [302-303]). ISBN 0-9542945-0-5 DDC 001.9409415
1. Parapsychology - Ireland. 2. Curiosities and wonders - Ireland. I. Title.

DEFENSE MECHANISMS (PSYCHOLOGY). See **FANTASY; REPRESSION (PSYCHOLOGY); RESISTANCE (PSYCHOANALYSIS).**

Défi à la pudeur.
Bonnet, Gérard. Paris : Albin Michel, c2003.
HQ784.S45 .B66 2003

Defiance and compliance.
El-Kholy, Heba Aziz. New York : Berghahn Books, 2002.
HQ1793.Z9 C353 2002

Defining difference : race and racism in the history of psychology / edited by Andrew S. Winston. 1st ed. Washington, DC : American Psychological Association, c2004. xi, 303 p. ; 26 cm. Includes bibliographical references and indexes. CONTENTS: Type and essence : prologue to the history of psychology and race / Fredric Weizmann -- The concept of race in the life and thought of Francis Galton / Raymond E. Fancher -- The historical problematization of "mixed race" in psychological and human-scientific discourses / Thomas Teo -- "Inharmoniously adapted to each other" : science and racial crosses / William H. Tucker -- "It's an American thing" : the "race" and intelligence controversy from a British perspective / Graham Richards -- Race and psychology in South Africa / Johann Louw and Don Foster -- Constructing difference : heredity, intelligence, and race in textbooks, 1930-1970 / Andrew S. Winston, Bethany Butzer, and Mark D. Ferris -- Antiracist work in the desegregation era : the scientific activism of Kenneth Bancroft Clark / Layli Phillips -- "Racially stuffed shirts and other enemies of mankind" : Horace Mann Bond's parody of segregationist psychology in the 1950s / John P. Jackson, Jr. ISBN 1-59147-027-7 (alk. paper) DDC 155.8/2/09
1. Racism in psychology - United States - History. 2. Racism in psychology - History. 3. Psychology - United States - History. 4. Psychology - History. I. Winston, Andrew S.
BF76.45 .D44 2004

DEFINITION (LOGIC). See **SEMANTICS (PHILOSOPHY).**

Definitional dictionary of Indian philosophy.
Bhāratīya darśana paribhāṣā kośa = Naī Dillī : Vaijñānika tathā Takanīkī Śabdāvalī Āyoga, Mānava Saṃsādhana Vikāsa Mantrālaya, Śikshā Vibhāga, Bhārata Sarakāra, 1999-
B131 .B498 1999

Definitive visual guide to the world's wildlife.
Animal. 1st American ed. New York : DK ; [Washington, D.C.] : Smithsonian Institution, 2001.

DeFoore, Bill, 1950- Anger : deal with it, heal with it, stop it from killing you / William Gray DeFoore. [Rev.]. Deerfield Beach, Fla. : Health Communications, 2004. p. cm. ISBN 0-7573-0111-8 DDC 152.4/7
1. Anger. I. Title.
BF575.A5 D45 2004

Defying the odds.
Israel-Curley, Marcia. 1st ed. Woodstock, N.Y. : Overlook Press, 2002.
HB615 .I75 2002

DEGENERATION.
Eidelberg, Paul. Clash of two decadent civilizations. Shaarei Tikva, Israel : ACPR Publications, 2002.
BM537 .E53 2002

Degrees of knowledge.
Maritain, Jacques, 1882-1973. [Degrés du savoir. English] Distinguish to unite, or, The degrees of knowledge. Notre Dame, Ind. : University of Notre Dame Press, 1998, c1995.
BD162 .M273 1998

Dehm-Gauwerky, Barbara.
Zeichen des Todes in der psychoanalytischen Erfahrung. Tübingen : Edition Diskord, c2000.

Dei, Héctor Daniel. The human being in history : freedom, power, and shared ontological meaning / H. Daniel Dei ; translated by James G. Colbert. Lanham, Md. : Lexington Books, c2003. xi, 134 p. : ill. ; 24 cm. Includes bibliographical references and index. ISBN 0-7391-0685-6 (alk. paper) DDC 128
1. Philosophical anthropology. 2. Liberty. 3. Power (Philosophy) 4. Postmodernism. I. Colbert, James G., 1938- II. Title.
BD450 .D395 2003

DEISM. See **COSMOLOGY.**

DEITIES. See **GODS.**

DÉJÀ VU.
Brown, Alan S. The déjà vu experience. New York : Psychology Press, 2004.
BF378.D45 B76 2004

The déjà vu experience.
Brown, Alan S. New York : Psychology Press, 2004.
BF378.D45 B76 2004

DeJean, Joan E.
Montpensier, Anne-Marie-Louise d'Orléans, duchesse de, 1627-1693. [Correspondence. English & French] Against marriage. Chicago : University of Chicago Press, 2002.
DC130.M8 A4 2002

DEJECTION. See **MELANCHOLY; SADNESS.**

Del alma y el arte.
Krebs, Víctor J., 1957- Caracas, Venezuela : Museo de Bellas Artes, 1997.
N70 .K74 1997

Del Bufalo, Erik. Deleuze et Laruelle : de la schizo-analyse à la non-philosophie / Erik del Bufalo. Paris : Kimé, 2003. 261 p. ; 21 cm. (Bibliothèque de non-philosophie) Includes bibliographical references. ISBN 2-8417-4291-1 DDC 194
1. Laruelle, François. 2. Deleuze, - M. - (J.) 3. Theory (Philosophy) 4. Philosophy, Modern - 20th century. I. Title. II. Series.

Del Moro, Franco. Il dubbio necessario : liberare la coscienza dai limiti della razionalità e del materialismo / Franco Del Moro ; introduzione di Renato Curcio. 1. ed. Murazzano (CN) : Ellin Selae, 2002. 134 p. ; 21 cm. (I libri di Ellin Selae) Collection of already publ. articles, now revised and enlarged. Includes bibliographical references. DDC 128
1. Spiritual life. 2. Civilization, Modern - 21st century. I. Title.

Del proceso y de la paz.
Giraldo Hurtado, Luis Guillermo, 1944- [Colombia? : s.n., 2001] (Manizales : Edigr@ficas)

Delaisi de Parseval, Geneviève. Le Roman familial d'Isadora D. / Geneviève Delaisi de Parseval. Paris : Odile Jacob, c2002. 215 p. : ill. ; 22 cm. Includes bibliographical references. ISBN 2-7381-1202-1 DDC 150
1. D., Isadora. 2. Psychoanalysis. 3. Analysands - France. I. Title.

Deleuze et Laruelle.
Del Bufalo, Erik. Paris : Kimé, 2003.

Deleuze, Gilles.
Actual and the virtual.
Deleuze, Gilles. [Dialogues. English] Dialogues II. 2nd ed. New York : Columbia University Press, 2002.
B2430.D453 D4313 2002

[Dialogues. English]
Dialogues II / Gilles Deleuze and Claire Parnet ; translated by Hugh Tomlinson and Barbara Habberjam. "The actual and the virtual" / translated by Eliot Ross Albert. 2nd ed. New York : Columbia University Press, 2002. xiii, 162 p. ; 22 cm. Originally published: New York : Columbia University Press, 1987. This new edition contains a previously untranslated essay, "The actual and the virtual"--Publisher's info. Includes bibliographical references (p. [153]-159) and index. ISBN 0-231-12669-7 (alk. paper) DDC 084/.1
1. Deleuze, Gilles - Interviews. 2. Philosophy. 3. Aesthetics. 4. Psychoanalysis and philosophy. I. Parnet, Claire. II. Deleuze, Gilles. Actual and the virtual. III. Title. IV. Title: Actual and the virtual. V. Title: Dialogues two VI. Title: Dialogues 2
B2430.D453 D4313 2002

DELEUZE, GILLES - INTERVIEWS.
Deleuze, Gilles. [Dialogues. English] Dialogues II. 2nd ed. New York : Columbia University Press, 2002.
B2430.D453 D4313 2002

DELEUZE, M. (J.).
Del Bufalo, Erik. Deleuze et Laruelle. Paris : Kimé, 2003.

Deliberate success.
Allenbaugh, Eric. Franklin Lakes, NJ : Career Press, c2002.
HF5386 .A5434 2002

DELINQUENCY. See **CRIME.**

DELIVERY OF GOODS.
Ludwig, Timothy D. Intervening to improve the safety of occupational driving. New York : Haworth Press, 2000.
HE5614 .I586 2000

DELIVERY OF HEALTH CARE. See **MEDICAL CARE.**

DELIVERY OF MEDICAL CARE. See **MEDICAL CARE.**

Della magia d'amore.
Casoni, Guido, 1561-1642. Torino : Res, 2002.
BF575.L8 C3 2002

Della Senta, Tarcisio.
No matter, never mind. Amsterdam : Philadelphia : John Benjamins Pub. Co., c2002.
QP411 .N598 2002

Dellasega, Cheryl. Girl wars : 12 strategies that will end female bullying / Cheryl Dellasega & Charisse Nixon. New York : Simon & Schuster, c2003. 242 p. ; 22 cm. "A Fireside book." ISBN 0-7432-4987-9 (alk. paper) DDC 302.3/4
1. Bullying. 2. Girls - Psychology. 3. Teenage girls - Psychology. I. Nixon, Charisse. II. Title.
BF637.B85 D45 2003

DelMonte, M. M. (Michael M.).
The embodiment of mind. Delft : Eburon, c1998.

Delphinidae

BF161 .E43 1998

DELPHINIDAE. *See* **DOLPHINS.**

DELPHININAE. *See* **DOLPHINS.**

Delrieu, Alain. Sigmund Freud : index thématique / Alain Delrieu. 2e éd. rev., augm. et mise à jour. Paris : Anthropos : Diffusion Economica, c2001. xxii, 1568 p. : 24 cm. (Psychanalyse) "Livres, articles, correspondances, minutes de la Société psychanalytique de Vienne (traductions françaises), 888 concepts et notions"--Cover. Includes bibliographical references and index. ISBN 2-7178-4248-9 DDC 150.19/52/092
  1. Freud, Sigmund, - 1856-1939 - Indexes. I. Title. II. Series.
BF109.F74 D45 2001

DELSARTE SYSTEM. *See* **EXPRESSION.**

Delumeau, Jean.
El miedo. Medellín, Colombia : Corporación Región, 2002.
BF575.F2 M494 2002

DELUSIONS. *See* **HALLUCINATIONS AND ILLUSIONS.**

Demamah ye-ḥerut ba-yogah ha-Ḳelasit.
Grinshpon, Yohanan, 1948- [Tel Aviv] : Miśrad ha-biṭaḥon, [2002]

DEMAND (ECONOMIC THEORY). *See* **CONSUMPTION (ECONOMICS); PRODUCTION (ECONOMIC THEORY).**

Demandt, Alexander, 1937-.
Gelehrte in der Antike. Köln : Böhlau, c2002.

DeMarco, Michael. Dugout days : untold tales and leadership lessons from the extraordinary career of Billy Martin / Michael DeMarco. New York : AMACOM, c2001. xxxiii, 302 p. : ill. ; p. 26 cm. Includes bibliographical references and index. ISBN 0-8144-0561-4 DDC 796.357/092
  1. Martin, Billy, - 1928- 2. Baseball managers - United States - Biography. 3. Leadership. I. Title.
GV865.M35 D46 2001

DEMATERIALIZATION, SPONTANEOUS (PARAPSYCHOLOGY). *See* **DISAPPEARANCES (PARAPSYCHOLOGY).**

DEMBOWSKI, PETER F. (PETER FLORIAN), 1925-.
Philologies old and new. Princeton : The Edward C. Armstrong Monographs, 2001.

Demel, Bernhard.
Sankt Georg und sein Bilderzyklus in Neuhaus/Böhmen (Jindřichuv Hradec). Marburg : N.G. Elwert, c2002.
BR1720.G4 S26 2002

Dement'ev, V. V. Neprîamaîa kommunikatsiîa i ee zhanry / V.V. Dement'ev ; pod redaktsieĭ V.E. Gol'dina. Saratov : Izd-vo Saratovskogo universiteta, 2000. 245 p. ; 20 cm. At head of title: Golovnoĭ sovet po filologii Ministerstva obrazovaniîa Rossiĭskoĭ Federatsii. Institut russkogo îazyka, literatury i zhurnalistiki pri filologicheskom fakul'tete Saratovskogo gosudarstvennogo universiteta im. N.G. Chernyshevskogo. Includes bibliographical references (p. [226]-245). ISBN 5292025348
  1. Language and languages. 2. Communication. I. Gol'din, V. E. II. Title.
P106 .D4554 2000

Deming, Alison Hawthorne, 1946-.
The colors of nature. 1st ed. Minneapolis, Minn. : Milkweed Editions, 2002.
QH81 .C663 2002

Demmin, Herbert S., 1959- The ghosts of consciousness : thought and the spiritual path / by Herbert S. Demmin. St. Paul, Minn. : Paragon House, c2003. p. cm. (Omega books) Includes bibliographical references and index. Table of contents URL: http://www.loc.gov/catdir/toc/ecip046/2003015114.html CONTENTS: Thinking -- It's slinky time! -- The phenomenology of thinking -- The development of reflective thinking -- More me -- Say thank you to your ghosts -- The embodiments of consciousness -- Eleven ghostly illusions -- The king and I. ISBN 1-55778-825-1 (pbk. : alk. paper) DDC 153.4/2
  1. Thought and thinking. 2. Self-perception. 3. Consciousness. I. Title. II. Series: Omega book (New York, N.Y.)
BF441 .D395 2003

Demo, Pedro. Dialética da felicidade / Pedro Demo. Petrópolis : Editora Vozes, 2001. 3 v. ; 21 cm. Includes bibliographical references. CONTENTS: v. 1. Olhar sociológico pós-moderno -- v. 2. Insolúvel busca de solução -- v. 3. Felicidade possível. ISBN 85-326-2553-3 (v. 1) ISBN 85-326-2564-9 (v. 2) ISBN 85-326-2567-3 (v. 3)
  1. Dialectic. 2. Happiness. 3. Self-realization. I. Title.

DEMOCRACY. *See also* **LIBERTY.**
Baritono, Raffaella. La democrazia vissuta. Torino : La Rosa, c2001.

Chomsky, Noam. Chomsky on democracy & education. New York ; London : RoutledgeFalmer, 2003.
LB885.C5215 C46 2003

Cladis, Mark Sydney. Public vision, private lives. Oxford ; New York : Oxford University Press, 2003.
JC179.R9 C53 2003

Connolly, William E. Identity/difference. Expanded ed. Minneapolis : University of Minnesota Press, c2002.
JA74 .C659 2002

Fromm, Erich, 1900- Escape from freedom. 1st Owl books ed. New York : H. Holt, 1994.
HM271 .F74 1994

Gutmann, Amy. Identity in democracy. Princeton, N.J. : Princeton University Press, c2003.
JF529 .G886 2003

Karauri, Mathew Adams, 1947- Rulers, leaders, and people. Nairobi : Karma Pub. Co., 2001.
  1. Black author.

Liberty and democracy. Stanford, CA : Hoover Institution Press, c2002.
JC423 .L5178 2002

Lipson, Charles. Reliable partners. Princeton, N.J. : Princeton University Press, c2003.
JC423 .L583 2003

Manville, Brook, 1950- A company of citizens Boston : Harvard Business School Press, c2003.
HD58.7 .M3714 2003

Markell, Patchen, 1969- Bound by recognition. Princeton, N.J. : Princeton University Press, c2003.
JC575 .M37 2003

Peace, prosperity, and democracy at the cutting edge. New York : Nova Science Publishers, c2003.

Tonn, Joan C. Mary P. Follett. New Haven [Conn.] : Yale University Press, c2003.
HN57 .T695 2003

Turner, Stephen P., 1951- Liberal democracy 3.0. London ; Thousand Oaks, Calif. : SAGE Publications, 2003.
JC423 .T87 2003

Zakaria, Fareed. The future of freedom. 1st ed. New York : W.W. Norton, c2003.
JC423 .Z35 2003

DEMOCRACY - CONGO (DEMOCRATIC REPUBLIC).
Le dialogue intercongolais. Bruxelles ; Nairobi : International Crisis Group, [2001]

Masangana Diamaka, Robin, 1962- Dialogue politique. Paris : Editoo.com, 2002.
  1. Black author.

DEMOCRACY - CONGRESSES.
Die Öffentlichkeit der Vernunft und die Vernunft der Öffentlichkeit. 1. Aufl. Frankfurt am Main : Suhrkamp, 2001.
B3258.H324 O34 2001

DEMOCRACY - GUATEMALA.
Acuerdos de paz y seguridad democrática en Guatemala. 1. ed. [Guatemala] : USAC, DIGI, [2002]

DEMOCRACY - UNITED STATES.
Cultivating citizens. Lanham : Lexington Books, c2002.
JK1759 .C85 2002

Machan, Tibor R. The passion for liberty. Lanham, Md. : Rowman & Littlefield, c2003.
JC599.U5 M263 2003

DEMOCRACY - UNITED STATES - HISTORY.
Hansen, Jonathan M. The lost promise of patriotism. Chicago : University of Chicago Press, c2003.
E661 .H316 2003

Democratic management.
Sen, Asim, 1935- Lanham, Md. ; Oxford : University Press of America, c2003.
HD30.65 .S46 2003

La democrazia vissuta.
Baritono, Raffaella. Torino : La Rosa, c2001.

DEMONIAC POSSESSION.
Aluko, Jonathan O. The spirit of this age. [[Akure, Nigeria : Christ Liberation Publications, c1996]
BL480 .A494 1996
  1. Black author.

Koroma, Abu F. Exposing and destroying the dark satanic kingdom. [Freetown, Sierra Leone? : s.n.], c2000.
  1. Black author.

Ofoegbu, Mike. Exposing satanic manipulations. [Lagos, Nigeria : Holy Ghost Anointed Books Ministries, c1998]
  1. Black author.

Possessions and exorcisms. San Diego, Calif. : Greenhaven Press, 2004.
BF1555 .P68 2004

DEMONIAC POSSESSION - FRANCE - HISTORY.
Ferber, Sarah, 1957- Demonic possession and exorcism in early modern France. London ; New York, NY : Routledge, 2004.
BF1517.F5 F47 2004

DEMONIC POSSESSION. *See* **DEMONIAC POSSESSION.**

Demonic possession and exorcism in early modern France.
Ferber, Sarah, 1957- London ; New York, NY : Routledge, 2004.
BF1517.F5 F47 2004

Demonio, religión y sociedad entre España y América / Fermín del Pino Díaz, coordinador. Madrid : Consejo Superior de Investigaciones Científicas, 2002. 389 p. ; 24 cm. (Biblioteca de dialectología y tradiciones populares ; XXXV) Includes bibliographical references. ISBN 84-00-08049-1
  1. Devil. 2. Supernatural. 3. Good and evil. 4. Demonology - Spain - History. 5. Demonology - America - History. 6. Demonology - Western Hemisphere - History. I. Pino, Fermín del., coord. II. Consejo Superior de Investigaciones Científicas (Spain) III. Series.

DEMONOLOGY. *See also* **AMULETS; CHARMS; DEMONIAC POSSESSION; DEVIL; EXORCISM; POLTERGEISTS.**
Aluko, Jonathan O. The spirit of this age. [[Akure, Nigeria : Christ Liberation Publications, c1996]
BL480 .A494 1996
  1. Black author.

Ángeles, demonios y genios en el mundo Mediterráneo. Madrid : Ediciones Clásicas, 2000.

Egbunu, Fidelis Eleojo. Be not afraid, only believe. Enugu, Nigeria : Snaap Press, 2001.
  1. Black author.

Koroma, Abu F. Exposing and destroying the dark satanic kingdom. [Freetown, Sierra Leone? : s.n.], c2000.
  1. Black author.

Newton, Toyne. The dark worship. London : Vega, 2002.
BF1531 .N49 2002

Ofoegbu, Mike. Exposing satanic manipulations. [Lagos, Nigeria : Holy Ghost Anointed Books Ministries, c1998]
  1. Black author.

DEMONOLOGY - AMERICA - HISTORY.
Demonio, religión y sociedad entre España y América. Madrid : Consejo Superior de Investigaciones Científicas, 2002.

DEMONOLOGY - CATHOLIC CHURCH.
Proja, Giovanni Battista. Uomini, diavoli, esorcismi. Roma : Città nuova, 2002.

DEMONOLOGY, CHRISTIAN. *See* **DEMONOLOGY.**

DEMONOLOGY - COMPARATIVE STUDIES. *See* **DEMONOLOGY.**

DEMONOLOGY - EARLY WORKS TO 1800.
Borromeo, Federico, 1564-1631. Manifestazioni demoniache. Milano : Terziaria : ASEFI, 2001.
BF1520 .B67 2001

DEMONOLOGY - EUROPE.
Werewolves, witches, and wandering spirits. Kirksville, MO : Truman State University Press, c2002.
GR135 .W47 2002

DEMONOLOGY - FRANCE - LORRAINE - HISTORY - 16TH CENTURY.
Diedler, Jean-Claude. Le testament de Maître Persin. [Metz] : Editions serpenoise, [2000]
BF1517.F5 D515 2000

DEMONOLOGY - FRANCE - LORRAINE - HISTORY - 17TH CENTURY.
Diedler, Jean-Claude. Le testament de Maître Persin. [Metz] : Editions serpenoise, [2000]

BF1517.F5 D515 2000

DEMONOLOGY IN THE BIBLE.
Proja, Giovanni Battista. Uomini, diavoli, esorcismi. Roma : Città nuova, 2002.

DEMONOLOGY - INDIA - TULUNADU.
Marike, Navīn Kumār. Tuḷunāḍinalli Koraga taniya. Puttūru, Da. Ka. : Śrī Mahāśakti Sangha, 2000.
BF1517.I5 M37 2000

DEMONOLOGY, ISLAMIC. *See* **ZĀR.**

DEMONOLOGY - SLAVIC COUNTRIES.
Levkievskaiā, E. E. (Elena Evgen'evna) Slaviānskiĭ obereg. Moskva : Indrik, 2002.
BL480 .L38 2002

DEMONOLOGY - SPAIN - HISTORY.
Demonio, religión y sociedad entre España y América. Madrid : Consejo Superior de Investigaciones Científicas, 2002.

DEMONOLOGY - WESTERN HEMISPHERE - HISTORY.
Demonio, religión y sociedad entre España y América. Madrid : Consejo Superior de Investigaciones Científicas, 2002.

DEMONS. *See* **DEMONOLOGY.**

DEMONSTRATIONS - WASHINGTON (D.C.) - HISTORY - 20TH CENTURY.
Barber, Lucy G. (Lucy Grace), 1964- Marching on Washington. Berkeley : University of California Press, c2002.
E743 .B338 2002

Demuth, Volker. Topische Ästhetik : Körperwelten, Kunsträume, Cyberspace / Volker Demuth. Würzburg : Königshausen & Neumann, c2002. 247 p. : ill. ; 24 cm. ISBN 3-8260-2281-5 (pbk.)
1. Space and time. 2. Aesthetics. I. Title.

DEMYTHOLOGIZATION. *See* **MYTH.**

DENBIGH (WALES).
Michael, Pamela. Care and treatment of the mentally ill in North Wales, 1800-2000. Cardiff : University of Wales Press, 2003.

Denborough, David.
Queer counselling and narrative practice. Adelaide : Dulwich Centre Publications, c2002.

Dench, Geoff. Minorities in the open society / Geoff Dench ; with a new introduction by the author. New Brunswick, N.J. : Transaction Publishers, 2003. xxxi, 275 p. ; 23 cm. Originally published: London ; New York : Routledge & Kegan Paul, 1986, in series: Reports of the Institute of Community Studies. Includes bibliographical references (p. 262-268) and index. ISBN 0-7658-0979-6 (pbk. : alk. paper) DDC 323.1
1. Minorities - Civil rights. 2. Ethnic groups - Civil rights. 3. Ethnicity. 4. Ethnic relations. I. Title.
JF1061 .D46 2003

DENDROLOGY. *See* **TREES.**

Deng, Minxuan.
Shi, Sheng. Fan Zhongyan li shen xing shi jiu jiu fang lüe. Di 1 ban. Beijing : Zhongguo xi ju chu ban she, 2001.
DS751.6.F3 S5 2001

Deniau, Jean-François, 1928- La gloire à vingt ans : récits / Jean François Deniau. [Paris] : XO editions, c2003. 265 p. : ill. (some col.) ; 24 cm. Includes bibliographical references. ISBN 2-8456-3146-4 DDC 920
1. Biography. 2. Youth - Biography. 3. Young adults - Biography. 4. Fame. 5. Success. I. Title.

Denise, Jan. Naked relationships / Jan Denise. Charlottesville, VA : Hampton Roads Pub., c2002. xvii, 135 p. : ill. ; 21 cm. ISBN 1-57174-306-5 (alk. paper) DDC 158.2
1. Intimacy (Psychology) 2. Self-actualization (Psychology) 3. Man-woman relationships. I. Title.
BF575.I5 D46 2002

Denisovskiĭ, G. M. Politicheskaiā tolerantnost' v reformiruemom rossiĭskom obshchestve vtoroĭ poloviny 90-kh godov / G.M Denisovskiĭ, P.M. Kozyreva. Moskva : TSentr obshchechelovecheskikh tsennosteĭ, 2002. 112 p. ; 21 cm. Includes bibliographical references (p. 109-111). ISBN 5887900849
1. Political culture - Russia (Federation) 2. Political psychology. 3. Toleration. 4. Russia (Federation) - Politics and government - 1991- I. Kozyreva, P. M. II. Title.
JN6699.A15 D46 2002

Das Denken und sein Gehalt.
Lenk, Hans. München : Oldenbourg, 2001.
BF441 .L455 2001

Lenk, Hans. München : Oldenbourg, 2001.

Denker, Alfred, 1960-.
Hegel's Phenomenology of spirit. Amherst, N.Y. : Humanity Books, 2003.
B2929 .H349 2003

Denkwelten um 1700 : zehn intellektuelle Profile / herausgegeben von Richard van Dülmen und Sina Rauschenbach. Köln : Böhlau, 2002. 219 p. : ill. ; 24 cm. ISBN 3-412-07102-1
1. Thought and thinking - History - 17th century. 2. Thought and thinking - History - 18th century. 3. Intellectual life - 17th century. 4. Intellectual life - 18th century. I. Dülmen, Richard van. II. Rauschenbach, Sina.
BF441 .D46 2002

Dennett, Daniel Clement.
Dawkins, Richard, 1941- The extended phenotype. Rev. ed. Oxford ; New York : Oxford University Press, 1999.
QH375 .D38 1999

Freedom evolves / Daniel C. Dennett. New York ; London : Viking, 2003. xiii, 347 p. : ill. ; 25 cm. Includes bibliographical references (p. [311]-324) and index. ISBN 0-670-03186-0 (alk. paper) DDC 123/.5
1. Free will and determinism. 2. Decision making. I. Title.
BJ1461 .D427 2003

Dennett, Preston E., 1965- California ghosts : true accounts of hauntings in the Golden State / by Preston E. Dennett. Atglen, PA : Schiffer Pub., 2004. p. cm. Table of contents URL: http://www.loc.gov/catdir/toc/ecip048/2003019880.html ISBN 0-7643-1972-8 (pbk.) DDC 133.1/09794
1. Ghosts - California. I. Title.
BF1472.U6 D46 2004

Extraterrestrial visitations : true accounts of contact / Preston Dennett. 1st ed. St. Paul, Minn. : Llewellyn Publications, 2001. xvii, 270 p. ; 20 cm. Includes bibliographical references (p. 259-266) and index. ISBN 1-56718-220-8 DDC 001.942
1. Human-alien encounters. 2. Alien abduction. I. Title.
BF2050 .D46 2001

Denning-Bolle, Sara J.
The Persistence of religions. Malibu : Undena Publications, 1996.

Denning, Melita.
Magical philosophy
(bk. 5.) Denning, Melita. Mysteria magica. 3rd ed. St. Paul, Minn. : Llewellyn Publications, 2004.
BF1611 .D395 2004

Mysteria magica : fundamental techniques of high magick / Melita Denning & Osborne Phillips. 3rd ed. St. Paul, Minn. : Llewellyn Publications, 2004. p. cm. (Llewellyn's aurum solis series) (The magical philosophy ; v. 3, bk. 5) Includes bibliographical references. ISBN 0-7387-0169-6 DDC 133.4/3
1. Magic. I. Phillips, Osborne. II. Title. III. Series. IV. Series: Denning, Melita. Magical philosophy ; bk. 5.
BF1611 .D395 2004

Dennison, Allie.
Dennison, Amy. Our dad died. Minneapolis, MN : Free Spirit Pub., c2003.
BF723.G75 D46 2003

Dennison, Amy. Our dad died : the true story of three kids whose lives changed / as told by Amy, Allie, and David Dennison. Minneapolis, MN : Free Spirit Pub., c2003. p. cm. SUMMARY: Three children, ages eight (twins) and four, describe how their lives changed when their father died suddenly two years earlier and offer practical advice for overcoming loss and moving on with life. CONTENTS: Finding out that dad died -- The night he died -- The day before the funeral -- The funeral -- After the funeral -- The first week -- Two weeks -- Six weeks -- Two months -- Three months -- Four months -- Six months -- Eight months -- The cemetery -- One year -- Fifteen months -- Seventeen months -- A year and a half -- Twenty-two months -- Messages from dad -- Grandparents -- The future -- Suggestions -- Letters to dad. ISBN 1-57542-135-6 DDC 155.9/37/083
1. Grief in children - Juvenile literature. 2. Bereavement in children - Juvenile literature. 3. Fathers - Death - Psychological aspects - Juvenile literature. 4. Loss (Psychology) in children - Juvenile literature. 5. Children and death - Juvenile literature. 6. Grief. 7. Fathers - Death. 8. Loss (Psychology) 9. Death. 10. Children's writings. I. Dennison, Allie. II. Dennison, David. III. Title.
BF723.G75 D46 2003

Dennison, David.
Dennison, Amy. Our dad died. Minneapolis, MN : Free Spirit Pub., c2003.
BF723.G75 D46 2003

DENOMINATIONS, CHRISTIAN. *See* **CHRISTIAN SECTS.**

DENOMINATIONS, RELIGIOUS. *See* **RELIGIONS; SECTS.**

DENTAL PERSONNEL. *See* **DENTISTS.**

DENTISTS - UNITED STATES - PERSONAL NARRATIVES.
Davis, Sampson. The pact. Waterville, ME : Thorndike Press, 2002.
1. Black author.

Denzin, Norman K.
9-11 in American culture. Walnut Creek ; Oxford : AltaMira Press, c2003.
HV6432.7 .A13 2003

Collecting and interpreting qualitative materials. 2nd ed. Thousand Oaks, Calif. : Sage, c2003.
H62 .C566 2003

Strategies of qualitative inquiry. 2nd ed. Thousand Oaks, CA : Sage, c2003.
H61 .S8823 2003

DEONTOLOGY. *See* **ETHICS.**

Dépayser la pensée : dialogues hétérotopiques avec François Jullien sur son usage philosophique de la Chine / textes recueillis et publiés sous la direction de Thierry Marchaisse ; avec la collaboration de Le Huu Khoa. Paris : Empêcheurs de penser en rond, 2003. 246 p. ; 21 cm. ISBN 2-8467-1067-8 DDC 194
1. Jullien, François, - 1951- 2. Philosophy. 3. China. I. Marchaisse, Thierry. II. Le, Huu Khoa.

Dependencies, connections, and other relations.
De Muijnck, Wim. Dordrecht ; Boston : Kluwer Academic Publishers, c2003.
BD418.3 .D4 2003

DEPENDENCY (PSYCHOLOGY). *See* **AUTONOMY (PSYCHOLOGY).**

Depew, David J., 1942-.
Evolution and learning. Cambridge, Mass. : MIT Press, c2003.
BF698.95 .E95 2003

Deppenschmidt, Kurt.
Crouch, Roxie J. Anger management. Warminster, PA : Mar*co Products, c2000.
BF723.A4 C76 2000

DEPRESSION, MENTAL. *See* **MELANCHOLY; SADNESS.**

Depreux, Philippe. Charlemagne et les Carolingiens / Philippe Depreux. Paris : Tallandier : Historia, 2002. 159 p. : col. ill., geneal. tables ; 27 cm. (La France au fil de ses rois) Includes bibliographical references. ISBN 2-235-02320-7 DDC 944
1. Charlemagne, - Emperor, - 742-814. 2. France - Kings and rulers - Biography. 3. Holy Roman Empire - Kings and rulers - Biography. 4. France - History - To 987. 5. Holy Roman Empire - History - To 1517. 6. Civilization, Medieval. I. Title. II. Series.
DC73 .D38 2002

Depuis Lacan / sous la direction de Patrick Guyomard, René Major. Paris : Aubier, c2000. 348 p. ; 23 cm. (La psychanalyse prise au mot) "Colloque de Cerisy"--Cover. Includes bibliographical references. ISBN 2-7007-2410-0
1. Psychoanalysis. 2. Lacan, Jacques, - 1901- I. Guyomard, Patrick. II. Major, René. III. Series.
BF173 .D44 2000

Der Ursprung der Gewalt im Denken des Marquis de Sade.
Stobbe, Heinz-Günther, 1948- Vom Geist der Übertretung und Vernichtung. Regensburg : Friedrich Pustet, c2002.

Derekh la-'aliyah.
Segal, Yehudah Zeraḥyah, ha-Levi. Sefer Doreshe H.. Tel-Aviv : Talmiday ye-shmom'e likho, 763 [2003]
BJ1287.S43 D66 2003

Deretić, Jovan. Kratka istorija srpske književnosti / Jovan Deretić. 3., prerađeno i dop. izd. Novi Sad : Svetovi, 2001. 346 p. ; 21 cm. (Biblioteka AZ) Includes index. In Serbian (Cyrillic).
1. Serbian literature - History and criticism. I. Title. II. Series.

Dermine, François-Marie, 1949- Mistici, veggenti e medium : esperienze dell'aldilà a confronto / François-Marie Dermine. Città del Vaticano : Libreria editrice vaticana, c2002. 492 p. ; 21 cm. (Collana "Esperienza e fenomenologia mistica") Includes bibliographical references (p. [479]-484). ISBN 88-209-7274-3 DDC 248
1. Spiritualism - Comparative studies. 2. Future life. I. Title.

DERRIDA, JACQUES.
Derroudida, Jacques. Le repas du grand homme. Paris : Harmattan, 2002.

Hägglund, Martin. Kronofobi. Stockholm : B. Östlings Bokförlag Symposion, 2002.

Jankovic, Zoran. Au-delà du signe. Paris : Harmattan, c2003.

Kropotov, S. L. (Sergeĭ Leonidovich) Ėkonomika teksta v neklassicheskoĭ filosofii iskusstva. Ekaterinburg : Gumanitarnyĭ universitet, 1999.
B831.2 .K76 1999

DERRIDA, JACQUES - CRITICISM AND INTERPRETATION.
Lévesque, Claude, 1927- Par-delà le masculin et le féminin. Paris : Aubier, 2002.

Derroudida, Jacques. Le repas du grand homme / Jacques Derroudida. Paris : Harmattan, 2002. 79 p. ; 22 cm. ISBN 2-7475-2543-0 DDC 844
1. Derrida, Jacques 2. Roudinesco, Eizabeth, - 1944- 3. Imaginary conversations. I. Title.

Dervin, Brenda.
Communication, a different kind of horserace. Cresskill, N.J. : Hampton Press, c2003.
P87.3.C37 C66 2003

DERY, ARIE, 1959-.
Sefer Shaʻagat Aryeh. Yerushalayim : Yerid ha-sefarim, 761 [2000 or 2001]

Des blessures et des jeux.
Auffret, Séverine. Arles : Actes sud, c2003.

Des odyssées à travers le temps : voyages, migrations, découvertes / sous la direction de Jean-Paul Barbiche ; en collaboration avec Annie Blondel et Rita Ranson. Paris : Harmattan, c2002. 458 p. ; 24 cm. Includes bibliographical references. Issued by: Université du Havre, CERIL. Faculté des Affaires Internationales. ISBN 2-7475-3170-8 DDC 900
1. Civilization - History. 2. Historiography. I. Barbiche, Jean-Paul, 1946- II. Université du Havre. Centre d'études et de recherches inter-langues.

Des sociétés.
Figures de la marge. Rennes : Presses universtaires de Rennes, [2002]

Osty, Florence. Le désir de métier. Rennes [France] : Presses universitaires de Rennes, [2003]

Desāī, Punitā Nāgarajī.
Śaṅkarācārya. [Bhajagovinda. Gujarati & Sanskrit] Mohamudgarastotram. Adyatana āvṛtti. Amadāvāda : Sarasvatī Pustaka Bhaṇḍāra, 1998/99 [i.e. 1999]
B133.S463 B5315 1998

Desarrollo de los valores en las instituciones educativas / directoras Itziar Elexpuru Albizuri, Concepción Medrano Samaniego ; equipo investigador: Elena Quevedo Torrientes ... [et al.]. Bilbao : Mensajero, 2001. 276 p. ; 24 cm. ISBN 84-271-2425-2
1. Values. 2. Social values. 3. Educational sociology. I. Elexpuru Albizuri, Itziar. II. Medrano Samaniego, Concepción. III. Quevedo Torrientes, Elena.

Descartes' baby.
Bloom, Paul, 1963- New York : Basic Books, 2004.
BF311 .B555 2004

DESCARTES, RENE, 1596-1650. PASSIONS DE L'AME.
Passion and virtue in Descartes. Amherst, N.Y. : Humanity Books, 2003.
B1868.P37 P37 2003

Descartes, René, 1596-1650.
[Regulae ad directionem ingenii. French]
Règles pour la direction de l'esprit / Descartes ; traduction et notes par Jacques Brunschwig ; préface, dossier et glossaire par Kim Sang Ong-Van-Cung. Paris : Librairie générale française, c2002. 255 p. : ill. ; 18 cm. (Le livre de poche. Classiques de la philosophie ; 4672) ISBN 2-253-06753-9 DDC 194
1. Reasoning. 2. Science - Methodology. I. Brunschwig, Jacques. II. Ong-Van-Cung, Kim Sang. III. Title. IV. Series: Classiques de la philosophie ; 4672.

DESCARTES, RENÉ, 1596-1650.
Clarke, Desmond M. Descartes's theory of mind. Oxford ; New York : Oxford University Press, 2003.

Landucci, Sergio, 1938- La mente in Cartesio. Milano : FrancoAngeli, c2002.

Wohlers, Christian. Wie unnütz ist Descartes? Würzburg : Königshausen & Neumann, c2002.

DESCARTES, RENÉ, 1596-1650 - CONTRIBUTIONS IN THEORY OF KNOWLEDGE.
Araujo, Marcelo de. Scepticism, freedom and autonomy. Berlin : De Gruyter, 2003.

DESCARTES, RENÉ, 1596-1650 - ETHICS.
Araujo, Marcelo de. Scepticism, freedom and autonomy. Berlin : De Gruyter, 2003.

Descartes's theory of mind.
Clarke, Desmond M. Oxford ; New York : Oxford University Press, 2003.

DESCENT AND DISTRIBUTION. *See* **INHERITANCE AND SUCCESSION.**

Descent of men.
Jones, Steve, 1944- Y. Boston : Houghton Mifflin, 2003.
GN281 .J62 2003

DESCENTS. *See* **INHERITANCE AND SUCCESSION.**

Descobrindo o Brasil
Russo, Jane. O mundo psi no Brasil. Rio de Janeiro : Jorge Zahar Editor, c2002.
BF173 .R877 2002

DESCRIPTIVE SOCIOLOGY. *See* **SOCIAL HISTORY.**

The design and analysis of computer experiments.
Santner, Thomas J., 1947- New York : Springer, 2003.
QA279 .S235 2003

DESIGN, DECORATIVE. *See* **DECORATION AND ORNAMENT.**

Design for Six Sigma.
Yang, Kai. New York ; London : McGraw-Hill, c2003.
TS156 .Y33 2003

DESIGN, INDUSTRIAL. *See* **VALUE ANALYSIS (COST CONTROL).**

DESIGN, INDUSTRIAL - PSYCHOLOGICAL ASPECTS.
Norman, Donald A. Emotional design. New York : Basic Books, 2004.
BF531 .N67 2004

Norman, Donald A. [Psychology of everyday things] The design of everyday things. 1st Basic paperback ed. [New York] : Basic Books, c2002.

The design of everyday things.
Norman, Donald A. [Psychology of everyday things] 1st Basic paperback ed. [New York] : Basic Books, c2002.

DESIGN PERCEPTION. *See* **PATTERN PERCEPTION.**

DESIGN - PSYCHOLOGICAL ASPECTS.
Norman, Donald A. Emotional design. New York : Basic Books, 2004.
BF531 .N67 2004

Designing collaborative systems.
Crabtree, Andy. London ; [New York] : Springer, c2003.
QA76.9.S88 C725 2003

Designing effective organisational structures in construction.
Moore, David (David R.) Project management. Oxford, [Eng.] ; Malden, MA : Blackwell Science, c2002.

Designing information spaces : the social navigation approach / Kristina Hook, David Benyon, and Alan J. Munro (eds.). London ; New York : Springer, 2003. xiv, 454 p. : ill. (some col.) ; 24 cm. (Computer supported cooperative work, 1431-1496) Includes bibliographical references (p. 427-450) and index. ISBN 1-85233-661-7 (alk. paper) DDC 303.48/33
1. Computers and civilization. 2. Human-computer interaction. 3. Information technology - Social aspects. I. Hook, Kristina. II. Benyon, David. III. Munro, Alan J., 1965- IV. Series.
QA76.9.C66 D49 2003

Designing sociable robots.
Breazeal, Cynthia L. Cambridge, Mass. : MIT Press, c2002.
TA167 .B74 2002

Designing stress resistant organizations.
Lin, Zhiang. Boston : Kluwer Academic Publishers, c2003.
HD58.8 .L58 2003

Le désir de métier.
Osty, Florence. Rennes [France] : Presses universitaires de Rennes, [2003]

DESIRE.
Ring, Susan. Needs and wants. Mankato, Minn. : Yellow Umbrella Books, c2003.
BF723.M56 R56 2003

Zupančič, Alenka. Esthétique du désir, éthique de la jouissance. Lecques : Théétète, c2002.

DESIRE IN LITERATURE.
D'Cruz, Doreen, 1950- Loving subjects. New York : P. Lang, c2002.
PR888.W6 D39 2002

DESIRE - JUVENILE LITERATURE.
Ring, Susan. Needs and wants. Mankato, Minn. : Yellow Umbrella Books, c2003.
BF723.M56 R56 2003

DESIRE (PHILOSOPHY).
Zupančič, Alenka. Esthétique du désir, éthique de la jouissance. Lecques : Théétète, c2002.

Desmond, William, 1951- Art, origins, otherness : between philosophy and art / William Desmond. Albany : State University of New York Press, c2003. xi, 306 p. ; 23 cm. Includes bibliographical references and index. ISBN 0-7914-5746-X (pbk. : alk. paper) ISBN 0-7914-5745-1 (alk. paper) DDC 111/.85
1. Aesthetics. 2. Art - Philosophy. 3. Other (Philosophy) I. Title.
BH39 .D4535 2003

Desolation and enlightenment.
Katznelson, Ira. New York : Columbia University Press, c2003.
JA71 .K35 2003

DeSpelder, Lynne Ann, 1944- The last dance : encountering death and dying / Lynne Ann DeSpelder, Albert Lee Strickland. 7th ed. Boston : McGraw-Hill, 2005. p. cm. Includes bibliographical references and index. ISBN 0-07-292096-3 DDC 155.9/37
1. Death - Psychological aspects - Textbooks. 2. Death - Social aspects - Textbooks. I. Strickland, Albert Lee. II. Title.
BF789.D4 D53 2005

DESPOTISM.
Tyrannis und Verführung. Wien : Turia + Kant, 2000.
JC381 .T973 2000

DESPOTISM IN LITERATURE.
Tyrannis und Verführung. Wien : Turia + Kant, 2000.
JC381 .T973 2000

Dess, Nancy Kimberly.
Evolutionary psychology and violence. Westport, Conn. : Praeger, 2003.
HM1116 .E96 2003

Destination success.
Bain, Dwight, 1960- Grand Rapids, Mich. : F.H. Revell, c2003.
BF637.S8 B314 2003

Destini personali.
Bodei, Remo, 1938- Milano : Feltrinelli, 2002.

Destinos das letras : história, educação e escrita epistolar / Maria Helena Camara Bastos, Maria Teresa Santos Cunha, Ana Chrystina Venancio Mignot, org. Passo Fundo : Universidade de Passo Fundo, 2002. 277 p. ; 21 cm. ISBN 85-7515-057-X
1. Written communication. 2. Letter writing. 3. Civilization - History. 4. Education. I. Bastos, Maria Helena Camara. II. Cunha, Maria Teresa Santos. III. Mignot, Ana Chrystina Venancio.
P211 .D47 2002

DESTINY. *See* **FATE AND FATALISM.**

DESTRUCTION OF THE JEWS (1939-1945). *See* **HOLOCAUST, JEWISH (1939-1945).**

Destructive emotions.
Goleman, Daniel. New York : Bantam Books, c2003.
BL65.E46 G65 2003

DETECTIVE AND MYSTERY STORIES. *See* **GHOST STORIES.**

DETECTIVES. *See* **CRIMINAL INVESTIGATION; WOMEN DETECTIVES.**

DETENTION OF PERSONS. *See* **PREVENTIVE DETENTION.**

DETENTION, PREVENTIVE. *See* **PREVENTIVE DETENTION.**

Determinants of human well-being.
Mazumdar, Krishna, 1949- New York : Nova Science Publishers, c2003.
HB171 .M462 2003

DETERMINATION (PERSONALITY TRAIT).
Roads to recovery. St. Leonards, NSW : Allen & Unwin, 1997.

BF698.35.D48 R63 1997

DETERMINISM (PHILOSOPHY).
Hardin, Russell, 1940- Indeterminacy and society. Princeton, N.J. : Princeton University Press, c2003.
HM1111 .H37 2003

Detienne, Marcel.
[Ecriture d'Orphée. English]
The writing of Orpheus : Greek myth in cultural context / Marcel Detienne ; translated by Janet Lloyd. Baltimore : Johns Hopkins University Press, 2002, c2003. xv, 199 p. ; 24 cm. Includes bibliographical references (p. [191]-193) and index. CONTENTS: The genealogy of a body of thought -- What the Greeks called "myth" -- Mythology, writing, and forms of historicity -- The practices of myth-analysis -- The Danaids among themselves : Marriage founded upon violence -- A kitchen garden for women, or how to engender on one's own -- Misogynous Hestia, or the city in its autonomy -- Even talk is in some ways divine -- An ephebe and an olive tree -- The crane and the labyrinth -- The finger of Orestes -- At Lycaon's table -- An inventive writing, the voice of Orpheus, and the games of Palamedes -- The double writing of mythology (between the Timaeus and the Critias) -- Orpheus rewrites the city gods. ISBN 0-8018-6954-4 (hardcover : alk. paper) DDC 292.1/3
1. Mythology, Greek. I. Title.
BL783 .D4813 2003

Deus a força que cura!.
Trasferetti, José Antônio. Campinas, SP : Editora Átomo, 2002.

Deutsch, Werner.
Psycholinguistik. Berlin : W. de Gruyter, c2003.

Deutsche Bibliothek der Wissenschaften.
Philosophische Analyse
(Bd. 8.) Hüntelmann, Rafael. Existenz und Modalität. Frankfurt a. M. ; New York : Hänsel-Hohenhausen, c2002.
BD331 .H86 2002

Deutschland und der Westen Europas im Mittelalter / herausgegeben von Joachim Ehlers. Stuttgart : Thorbecke, c2002. 586 p. : ill. ; 24 cm. (Vorträge und Forschungen ; Bd. 56) Includes bibliographical references and index. Contributions in German, English and French. ISBN 3-7995-6656-2
1. Germany - History - To 1517. 2. Germany - Civilization. 3. Europe - History. 4. Europe - Civilization. 5. Civilization, Medieval. 6. Middle Ages. I. Ehlers, Joachim, 1936- II. Series.

Les deux corps du moi.
Guillerault, Gérard. Paris : Gallimard, c1996.
BF175.5.B64 G86 1996

Le deuxième sexe : une relecture en trois temps, 1949-1971-1999 / sous la direction de Cécile Coderre et Marie-Blanche Tahon. Montréal : Éditions du Remue-ménage, 2001. 175 p. ; 23 cm. Includes bibliographical references (p. 161-171). ISBN 289091187X DDC 305.4
1. Beauvoir, Simone de, - 1908- Deuxième sexe. 2. Beauvoir, Simone de, - 1908- - Criticism and interpretation. 3. Beauvoir, Simone de, - 1908- - Influence. 4. Feminism. I. Coderre, Cécile. II. Tahon, Marie-Blanche.

DEVELOPED COUNTRIES - RELATIONS - DEVELOPING COUNTRIES.
Lal, Vinay. Empire of knowledge. London ; Sterling, Va. : Pluto Press, 2002.
HN16 .L35 2002

DEVELOPING COUNTRIES - ECONOMIC CONDITIONS.
Goudge, Paulette. The power of whiteness. London : Lawrence & Wishart, 2003.

Group behaviour and development. Oxford ; New York : Oxford University Press, 2002.
HD58.7 .G76 2002

DEVELOPING COUNTRIES - FORECASTING.
Riding the next wave. Indianapolis, Ind. : Hudson Institute ; [Washington, DC : Distributed by the Brookings Institution Press], c2001.
HM901 .R43 2001

DEVELOPING COUNTRIES - HISTORY - CONGRESSES.
Psychanalyse et décolonisation. Paris : LHarmattan, c1999.
BF175.4.C84 P76 1999

DEVELOPING COUNTRIES - RELATIONS - DEVELOPED COUNTRIES.
Lal, Vinay. Empire of knowledge. London ; Sterling, Va. : Pluto Press, 2002.
HN16 .L35 2002

Developing effective engineering leadership.
Morrison, Raymond E. London : Institution of Electrical Engineers, c2003.

The developing person through the life span.
Berger, Kathleen Stassen. 6th ed. New York : Worth Publishers, 2004.
BF713 .B463 2004

DEVELOPMENT, CHARACTER. See **PERSONALITY DEVELOPMENT.**

DEVELOPMENT, CHILD. See **CHILD DEVELOPMENT.**

DEVELOPMENT, INFANT. See **INFANTS - DEVELOPMENT.**

The development of animal form.
Minelli, Alessandro. Cambridge ; New York : Cambridge University Press, 2003.
QH491 .M559 2003

Development of children's knowledge about the mind.
Flavell, John H. Worcester, Mass. : Clark University Press, 2003.
BF723.C5 F623 2003

The development of face processing in infancy and early childhood : current perspectives / [edited by] Olivier Pascalis and Alan Slater. New York : Nova Science, 2003. p. cm. Includes bibliographical references and index. Table of contents URL: http://www.loc.gov/catdir/toc/ecip045/2003013226.html ISBN 1-59033-775-1 (hardcover) DDC 155.42/2375
1. Face perception in infants. 2. Face perception in children. I. Pascalis, Olivier. II. Slater, Alan.
BF720.F32 D48 2003

Development of national, ethnolinguistic and religious identities in children and adolescents.
Razvitie natsional'noĭ, ėtnolingvisticheskoĭ i religioznoĭ identichnosti u deteĭ i podrostkov = Moskva : In-t psikhologii RAN, 2001.
BF723.C5 R39 2001

The development of science and technology in nineteenth-century Britain.
Cardwell, D. S. L. (Donald Stephen Lowell) Aldershot, Great Britain ; Burlington, VT : Ashgate/Variorum, c2003.
Q127.G4 C37 2003

The development of the social self / [edited by] Mark Bennett & Fabio Sani. 1st ed. London ; New York : Psychology Press, 2003. p. cm. Includes bibliographical references and index. Table of contents URL: http://www.loc.gov/catdir/toc/ecip045/2003013111.html CONTENTS: Children and social identity / Mark Bennett and Fabio Sani -- The development of a sense of "we" : the emergence and implications of children's collective identity / Diane Ruble ... [et al.] -- Developmental aspects of social identity / Fabio Sani and Mark Bennett -- Gender as a social category : intergroup processes and gender-role development / Kimberly Powlishta -- The gender wars : a self-categorization perspective on the development of gender identity / Barbara David, Diane Grace and Michele Ryan -- The development of national identity and social identity processes : do social identity theory and self-categorization theory provide useful heuristic frameworks for developmental research? / Martyn Barrett, Evanthia Lyons, and Arantza del Valle -- Ethnic minority identity and social context / Maykel Verkuyten -- Social identity processes and children's ethnic prejudice / Drew Nesdale -- The development and self-regulation of intergroup attitudes in children / Adam Rutland -- Reducing stepfamily conflict : the importance of inclusive social identity / Brenda Banker ... [et al.] -- The development of social identity : what develops? / Dominic Abrams -- Towards a developmental social psychology of the social self / Kevin Durkin. ISBN 1-84169-294-8 (hardcover : alk. paper) DDC 155.4/182
1. Self in children. 2. Self - Social aspects. 3. Identity (Psychology) 4. Identification. 5. Social interaction. I. Bennett, Mark, 1956 Dec. 10- II. Sani, Fabio, 1961-
BF723.S24 D48 2003

Development of verb inflection in first language acquisition : a cross-linguistic perspective / edited by Dagmar Bittner, Wolfgang U. Dressler, Marianne Kilani-Schoch. Berlin ; New York : Mouton de Gruyter, 2003. xl, 424 p. : ill. ; 24 cm. (Studies on language acquisition ; 21) Includes bibliographical references and index. ISBN 3-11-017823-0 (cloth : alk. paper) DDC 401/.93
1. Language acquisition. 2. Grammar, Comparative and general - Verb. 3. Grammar, Comparative and general - Inflection. I. Bittner, Dagmar. II. Dressler, Wolfgang U., 1939- III. Kilani-Schoch, Marianne, 1953- IV. Series.
P118 .D465 2003

Development of western resources
Seeing nature through gender. Lawrence : University Press of Kansas, c2003.

GF21 .S44 2003

DEVELOPMENT, PERSONALITY. See **PERSONALITY DEVELOPMENT.**

DEVELOPMENT (PSYCHOLOGY). See **DEVELOPMENTAL PSYCHOLOGY.**

DEVELOPMENT, PSYCHOSEXUAL. See **PSYCHOSEXUAL DEVELOPMENT.**

DEVELOPMENT, SUSTAINABLE. See **SUSTAINABLE DEVELOPMENT.**

DEVELOPMENTAL BIOLOGY. See also **AGING; CHILD DEVELOPMENT; HUMAN GROWTH.**
Barbieri, Marcello. The organic codes. Cambridge, UK. ; New York : Cambridge University Press, 2003.
QH331 .B247 2003

Minelli, Alessandro. The development of animal form. Cambridge ; New York : Cambridge University Press, 2003.
QH491 .M559 2003

West-Eberhard, Mary Jane. Developmental plasticity and evolution. Oxford ; New York : Oxford University Press, 2003.
QH546 .W45 2003

Developmental influences on adult intelligence.
Schaie, K. Warner (Klaus Warner), 1928- [Update]. New York : Oxford University Press, 2004.
BF724.55.C63 S32 2004

DEVELOPMENTAL LINGUISTICS. See **LANGUAGE ACQUISITION.**

Developmental plasticity and evolution.
West-Eberhard, Mary Jane. Oxford ; New York : Oxford University Press, 2003.
QH546 .W45 2003

DEVELOPMENTAL PSYCHOBIOLOGY. See also **CHILD DEVELOPMENT; DEVELOPMENTAL PSYCHOLOGY.**
Canault, Nina. Comment le désir de naître vient au fœtus. Paris : Desclée de Brouwer, c2001.

Papalia, Diane E. Human development. 9th ed. Boston : McGraw-Hill, c2004.
BF713 .P35 2004

DEVELOPMENTAL PSYCHOLINGUISTICS. See **LANGUAGE ACQUISITION.**

DEVELOPMENTAL PSYCHOLOGY. See also **AGING - PSYCHOLOGICAL ASPECTS; ATTACHMENT BEHAVIOR; CHILD PSYCHOLOGY; LIFE CHANGE EVENTS; LIFE CYCLE, HUMAN; MATURATION (PSYCHOLOGY); PSYCHOSEXUAL DEVELOPMENT.**
Ageev, Valentin. Psikhologii͡a transtsendirovanii͡a. Almaty: "Qazaq Universiteti", 2002.
BF713 .A34 1998

Berger, Kathleen Stassen. The developing person through the life span. 6th ed. New York : Worth Publishers, 2004.
BF713 .B463 2004

Between culture and biology. Cambridge, U.K. ; New York : Cambridge University Press, 2002.
BF721 .B4138 2002

Beyond the century of the child. Philadelphia : University of Pennsylvania Press, c2003.
HQ767.87 .B49 2003

Creativity and development. New York : Oxford University Press, 2003.
BF408 .C7545 2003

Cross-cultural perspectives in human development. New Delhi ; Thousand Oaks, Calif. : Sage Publications, 2003.
BF713.5 .C76 2003

Dialogicality in development. Westport, Conn. : Praeger, 2003.
BF713 .D53 2003

The elusive child. London ; New York : Karnac, c2002.

Greene, Sheila, 1946- The psychological development of girls and women. London ; New York : Routledge, 2003.
HQ1206 .G767 2003

Handbook of developmental psychology. London : Thousand Oaks, Calif. : SAGE Publications, 2003.
BF713 .H364 2003

Papalia, Diane E. Human development. 9th ed. Boston : McGraw-Hill, c2004.

Developmental psychology

BF713 .P35 2004
Rogoff, Barbara. The cultural nature of human development. Oxford ; New York : Oxford University Press, 2003.
HM686 .R64 2003

Sanders, Robert, 1946- Sibling relationships. New York : Palgrave Macmillan, 2004.
BF723.S43 S159 2004

Shultz, Thomas R. Computational developmental psychology. Cambridge, Mass. : MIT Press, c2003.
BF713 .S35 2003

Washburn, Michael, 1943- Embodied spirituality in a sacred world. Albany : State University of New York Press, 2003.
BF204.7 .W372 2003

White, Sheldon Harold, 1928- Developmental psychology as a human enterprise. Worcester, Mass. : Clark University Press, c2001.
BF713 .W48 2001

Developmental psychology as a human enterprise.
White, Sheldon Harold, 1928- Worcester, Mass. : Clark University Press, c2001.
BF713 .W48 2001

DEVELOPMENTAL PSYCHOLOGY - CONGRESSES.

Issledovaniia obucheniia i razvitiia v kontekste kul'turno-istoricheskogo podkhoda. Moskva : Smysl, 2002.
BF712.5 .I88 2002

Mezhdunarodnaia psikhologicheskaia konferentsiia "Psikhicheskoe razvitie v ontogeneze--zakonomernosti i vozmozhnye periodizatsii" (1999 : Moscow, Russia) Problemy psikhologii razvitiia. Moskva : RGGU, 2000.
BF712.5 .M49 2000

Psikhologiia razvitiia i vozrastnaia psikhologiia. Moskva : Izd-vo MNEPU, 2001-
BF712.5 .P75 2001

Strukturbildung und Lebensstil. München : Ernst Reinhardt, c2002.

DEVELOPMENTAL PSYCHOLOGY - DICTIONARIES - RUSSIAN.

Slovar'-spravochnik po vozrastnoĭ i pedagogicheskoĭ psikhologii. Moskva : Pedagog. ob-vo Rossii, 2001.
BF712.7 .S56 2001

DEVELOPMENTAL PSYCHOLOGY - EXAMINATIONS, QUESTIONS, ETC.

The best test preparation for the CLEP, College-Level Examination Program, human growth & development. Piscataway, N.J. : Research & Education Association, c2003.
BF713 .B49 2003

DEVELOPMENTAL PSYCHOLOGY - NEW ZEALAND.

Bird, Lise. Human development in Aotearoa. Sidney ; New York : McGraw-Hill, c2000.
BF713 .B57 2000

DEVELOPMENTAL PSYCHOLOGY - PHILOSOPHY.

Salkind, Neil J. An introduction to theories of human development. Thousand Oaks, Calif. : Sage Publications, c2004.
BF713 .S245 2004

DEVELOPMENTAL PSYCHOLOGY - SOCIAL ASPECTS.

Bergman, Lars R. Studying individual development in an interindividual context. Mahwah, N.J. : L. Erlbaum Associates, 2003.
BF713 .B464 2003

Dialogicality in development. Westport, Conn. : Praeger, 2003.
BF713 .D53 2003

DEVELOPMENTAL PSYCHOLOGY - TEXTBOOKS.

Kail, Robert V. Human development. 3rd ed. Belmont, CA : Thomson/Wadsworth, c2004.
BF713 .K336 2004

Oakley, Lisa. Cognitive development. New York : Psychology Press, 2004.
BF311 .O12 2004

Yingling, Julie. A lifetime of communication. Mahwah, N.J. : Lawrence Erlbaum Associates, 2004.
BF637.C45 Y56 2004

DEVELOPMENTAL STUDIES PROGRAMS. *See* **BASIC WRITING (REMEDIAL EDUCATION).**

DEVELOPMENTALLY DISABLED CHILDREN - BRAZIL - FAMILY RELATIONSHIPS.

Caniato, Benilde Justo. Um testemunho de mãe. 2a. ed. São Paulo : Lato Senso, 2001.
HV901.B6 C36 2001

Developments in Indian philosophy from Eighteenth century onwards.
Krishna, Daya. New Delhi : Project of History of Indian Science, Philosophy, and Culture : Centre for Studies in Civilizations : Distributed by Motilal Banarsidass, 2002.
B131+

Le développement des habiletés de l'enfant.
Fagard, Jacqueline. Paris : CNRS, c2001.
RJ133 .F34 2001

Deveson, Anne. Resilience / Anne Deveson. Crows Nest, NSW : Allen & Unwin, 2003. viii, 296 p. ; 21 cm. Includes bibliographical references (p. 287-288) and index. ISBN 1-86448-634-1 DDC 155.24
1. Resilience (Personality trait) I. Title.

DEVIANCY. *See* **DEVIANT BEHAVIOR.**

DEVIANT BEHAVIOR. *See also* **CONFORMITY.**
Shoham, S. Giora, 1929- Ṭeruf, setiyah ṿi-yetsirah. [Israel] : Miśrad ha-biṭaḥon, [2002]

DEVIANT BEHAVIOR - CONGRESSES.

Transgressões. Rio de Janeiro, RJ : Espaço Brasileiro de Estudos Psicanalíticos : Contra Capa, 2002.

DEVIL.

Demonio, religión y sociedad entre España y América. Madrid : Consejo Superior de Investigaciones Científicas, 2002.

The Devil and the land of the holy cross.
Souza, Laura de Mello e. [Diabo e a Terra de Santa Cruz. English] 1st University of Texas Press ed. Austin : University of Texas Press : Teresa Lozano Long Institute of Latin American Studies, 2003.
BF1584.B7 S6813 2003

DEVIL - CHRISTIANITY.

Anselm, Saint, Archbishop of Canterbury, 1033-1109. [Dialogues. English. Selections] Three philosophical dialogues. Indianapolis, IN : Hackett Pub., c2002.
B765.A81 .A2513 2002

The devil hath been raised.
Trask, Richard B. Rev. ed. Danvers, Mass. : Yeoman Press, c1997.
BF1576 .T73 1997

DEVIL-WORSHIP. *See* **SATANISM.**

Devil-worship in France with Diana Vaughan and the question of modern palladism.
Waite, Arthur Edward, 1857-1942. Boston, MA : Weiser Books, 2003.
BF1548 .W2 2003

Devin, Lee, 1938-.
Austin, Robert D. (Robert Daniel), 1962- Artful making. Upper Saddle River, NJ : Financial Times/Prentice Hall, 2003.
HD53 .A96 2003

DeVita, Elizabeth. The empty room : surviving the loss of a brother or sister / Elizabeth DeVita. New York : Scribner 2004. p. cm. Includes bibliographical references. ISBN 0-7432-0151-5 DDC 155.9/37/0855
1. Bereavement - Psychological aspects. 2. Brothers and sisters - Death - Psychological aspects. I. Title.
BF575.G7 D48 2004

DEVOTEES. *See* **FANS (PERSONS).**

DEVOTIONAL CALENDARS.

Vanzant, Iyanla. Until today!. New York : Simon & Schuster, c2000.
BL625.2 .V369 2000

Walters, J. Donald. Secrets of comfort and joy. [Nevada City, CA] : Crystal Clarity, 2000.
BF575.H27 W362 2000

What can happen when we pray. Minneapolis : Augsburg Fortress, c2001.

DEVOTIONAL EXERCISES.

Johnson, Kevin Wayne. Give God the glory!. Hillsborough, NJ : Writing for the Lord Ministries, c2001.
1. Black author.

DEVOTIONS (CABALA). *See* **KAVVANOT (CABALA).**

Devout sceptics : conversations on faith and doubt / compiled by Bel Mooney. London : Hodder & Stoughton, 2003. 192 p. ; 24 cm. ISBN 0-340-86202-5 DDC 212.1
1. God - Proof. 2. Belief and doubt. 3. Religion. 4. Skepticism.

Dewe, Philip.
Cooper, Cary L. A brief history of stress. 1st ed. Oxford, U.K. ; Malden, MA : Blackwell Pub., 2004.
BF575.S75 C646 2004

Dewender, Thomas.
Imagination, Fiktion, Kreation. München : Saur, c2003.
BH301.I53 I534 2003

The Dewey color system.
Sadka, Dewey. 1st ed. New York : Three Rivers Press, 2004.
BF789.C7 S23 2004

DEWEY, JOHN, 1859-1952.
Fesmire, Steven, 1967- John Dewey and moral imagination. Bloomington, IN : Indiana University Press, c2003.
BJ1031 .F47 2003

Lekan, Todd, 1967- Making morality. 1st ed. Nashville, TN : Vanderbilt University Press, 2003.
BJ1031 .L45 2003

Dexter, Rosalyn. Good vibes : feng shui : unveiling the myths / Rosalyn Dexter. London : Robson, 2001. 175 p. : ill. ; 19 cm. ISBN 1-86105-426-2 DDC 133.3337
1. Feng shui. I. Title.

Dhātusāmya meṃ manobhāvoṃ kā sthāna.
Pracetā Jyoti. 1. saṃskaraṇa. Nāgapura : Viśvabhāratī Prakāśana, 2001.
BF204.5 .P73 2001

Di Ciaccia, Antonio. Jacques Lacan : un insegnamento sul sapere dell'inconscio / Antonio Di Ciaccia, Massimo Recalcati. Milano : B. Mondadori, 2000. vii, 247 p. ; 17 cm. (Testi e pretesti) Includes bibliographical references and index. ISBN 88-424-9518-2 DDC 150
1. Lacan, Jacques, - 1901- I. Recalcati, Massimo. II. Title. III. Series: Testi e pretesti (Milan, Italy)
BF109.L28 D53 2000

Di Ciaccia, Francesco.
Borromeo, Federico, 1564-1631. Manifestazioni demoniache. Milano : Terziaria : ASEFI, 2001.
BF1520 .B67 2001

Di fronte e attraverso
(581) Sini, Carlo, 1933- La scrittura e il debito. Milano : Jaca book, 2002.

Di Silvestre, Ettore. I concetti della fisica attraverso il tempo / Ettore Di Silvestre. Pisa : ETS, 2000. 315 p. : ill. ; 24 cm. Includes bibliographical references (p. [301]-302) and indexes. ISBN 88-467-0318-9 DDC 530
1. Physics. I. Title.

Le diable chez l'évêque.
Modestin, Georg. Lausanne : Université de Lausanne, Section d'histoire, Faculté des lettres, 1999.
BF1584.S9 M64 1999

La diachronie en psychanalyse.
Green, André. Paris : Minuit, c2000.
BF468 .G66 2000

DIAGNOSIS. *See* **DIAGNOSIS, LABORATORY.**

DIAGNOSIS, LABORATORY - CHILE.

Rodríguez, Luis. Patologías complejas (versión preliminar). [Santiago, Chile] : Corporación de Promoción Universitaria, [1995]

DIAGNOSTIC LABORATORY TESTS. *See* **DIAGNOSIS, LABORATORY.**

DIALECTIC.

Collette, Bernard. Dialectique et hénologie chez Plotin. Bruxelles : Ousia, c2002.
B693.Z7 C655 2002

Demo, Pedro. Dialética da felicidade. Petrópolis : Editora Vozes, 2001.

Dixsaut, Monique. Métamorphoses de la dialectique dans les dialogues de Platon. Paris : Vrin, c2001.
B398.D5 D598 2001

Tietz, Udo. Ontologie und Dialektik. Wien : Passagen, c2003.
B3279.H49 T54 2003

DIALECTIC (LOGIC). *See* **LOGIC.**

DIALECTICAL THEOLOGY.

Kuropka, Nicole. Philipp Melanchthon. Tübingen : Mohr Siebeck, c2002.
BR339 .K86 2002

Dialectique et hénologie chez Plotin.
Collette, Bernard. Bruxelles : Ousia, c2002.
B693.Z7 C655 2002

Dialektika Vygotskogo.
Morozov, S. M. (Stanislav Mikhaĭlovich) Moskva : Smysl, 2002.

BF109.V95 M67 2002
Dialética da felicidade.
Demo, Pedro. Petrópolis : Editora Vozes, 2001.

I dialoghi dell'ego.
Cumpeta, Silvio. Gorizia : Biblioteca statale isontina, c2001.

Dialogi l͡i͡ubvi.
Maksimov, Andreĭ, 1959- Moskva : Delovoĭ ėkspress, 1999.
BF575.L8 M336 1999

Dialogi un vēstules.
Plato. [Selections. Latvian] Platons dialogi un vēstules = [Rīga] : Zinātne, c1999.

Dialogicality in development / edited by Ingrid E. Josephs. Westport, Conn. : Praeger, 2003. xvii, 223 p. : ill. ; 25 cm. (Advances in child development within culturally structured environments) Includes bibliographical references and index. ISBN 1-56750-576-7 (alk. paper) DDC 155
1. Developmental psychology. 2. Developmental psychology - Social aspects. I. Josephs, Ingrid E., 1961- II. Series.
BF713 .D53 2003

Diálogo de civilizaciones Oriente-Occidente : aporte al entendimiento internacional / María Jesús Merinero, coord. [Madrid] : Biblioteca Nueva ; [Cáceres, España] : Universidad de Extremadura, c2002. 155 p. ; 21 cm. (Ensayos / Biblioteca Nueva) Includes bibliographical references. ISBN 84-974209-1-8
1. East and West. 2. Middle East - Foreign relations - United States. 3. Christianity and other religions - Spain. 4. Christianity and other religions - Judaism. 5. Christianity and other religions - Islam. 6. Civilization, Oriental - History. I. Merinero, María Jesús. II. Series.

DIALOGUE. See also **DRAMA.**
Tonoiu, Vasile. Omul dialogal. București : Editura Fundației Culturale Române, 1995.

Le dialogue intercongolais : poker menteur ou negociation politique? Bruxelles ; Nairobi : International Crisis Group, [2001] iii, 38 p. : maps ; 30 cm. (ICG rapport Afrique ; no. 37) "16 novembre 2001." Includes bibliographical references.
1. Congo (Democratic Republic) - Politics and government - 1997- 2. Sud-Kivo (Congo) - Ethnic relations. 3. Nord-Kivo (Congo) - Ethnic relations. 4. Violence - Congo (Democratic Republic) 5. Peacekeeping forces - Congo (Democratic Republic) 6. Democracy - Congo (Democratic Republic) 7. Peace. I. International Crisis Group. II. Series: ICG Africa report ; no. 37.

Dialogue politique.
Masangana Diamaka, Robin, 1962- Paris : Editoo.com, 2002.

Dialogue sur la nature humaine.
Cyrulnik, Boris. La Tour d'Aigues : Editions de l'Aube, c2000.
BF57 .C97 2000

Dialogues 2.
Deleuze, Gilles. [Dialogues. English] Dialogues II. 2nd ed. New York : Columbia University Press, 2002.
B2430.D453 D4313 2002

Dialogues II.
Deleuze, Gilles. [Dialogues. English] 2nd ed. New York : Columbia University Press, 2002.
B2430.D453 D4313 2002

Dialogues two.
Deleuze, Gilles. [Dialogues. English] Dialogues II. 2nd ed. New York : Columbia University Press, 2002.
B2430.D453 D4313 2002

Diamond in the rough.
Farber, Barry J. New York : Berkley Books, c1995.
BF637.S8 F34 1995

Diamond power.
Farber, Barry J. Franklin Lakes, NJ : Career Press, 2004.
BF637.S8 F342 2004

DIAPHRAGM. See **VOICE.**

Diario íntimo de un fracaso.
Téllez, Edgar. 1. ed. Bogotá, D.C., Colombia : Planeta, 2002.

Diaz, Raul.
Alonso, Graciela. Hacia una pedagogía de las experiencias de las mujeres. 1. ed. Buenos Aires : Miño y Dávila, 2002.

Dibrot Tsevi.
Vaisfish, Tsevi ben Shemu'el A. L. Sefer Dibrot Tsevi. Yerushalayim : Makhon le-hotsaʼat sefarim ʻa. sh. Rabi Naḥum mi-Shadik, 762- [2002-

Diccionario de los sueños.
Jiménez Castillo, Mario. St. Paul, Minn. : Llewellyn Español, 2003.
BF1095 .J56 2003

DICKERING. See **NEGOTIATION.**

Dickerson, Karle. Girl chat : the fine art of talk, talk, talk / by Karle Dickerson. New York : Scholastic, c2001. 105 p. : ill. ; 17 cm. ISBN 0-439-18745-1
1. Interpersonal communication in children - Juvenile literature. 2. Girls - Psychology - Juvenile literature. I. Title.
BF723.C57 D53 2001

Dickinson, Rachel. The witch's handbook / by Rachel Dickinson. New York : Price Stern Sloan, c2002. 87 p. : col. ill. ; 15 cm. Includes bibliographical references (p. 84-85). ISBN 0-8431-4917-5
1. Witchcraft - Juvenile literature. I. Title.
BF1571 .D53 2002

DICTIONARIES. See **ENCYCLOPEDIAS AND DICTIONARIES.**

Dictionary of astrology.
Agarwal, G. S., 1936- New Delhi : Sagar Publications, 2002.
BF1714.H5 A33 2002

Dictionary of cognitive science.
[Vocabulaire de sciences cognitives. English.] New York : Psychology Press, 2003.
BF311 .V56713 2003

Dictionary of stroke structures in graphoanalysis / the IGAS Instruction Department. New, 3rd ed. Chicago : International Graphoanalysis Society, 1998. viii, 86 p. : ill. ; 28 cm. Includes index. DDC 155.2/82/03
1. Graphology - Dictionaries. I. International Graphoanalysis Society. Instruction Dept.
BF889.5 .D53 1998

Dictionary on Indian religions.
Rengarajan, T., 1962- Delhi : Eastern Book Linkers, 2003.
BL2001.2 .R46 2003

Dictionnaire amoureux de la justice.
Vergès, Jacques. Paris : Plon, c2002.

Dictionnaire de la jouissance.
Moulinier, Didier. Paris : L'Harmattan, c1999.
BF575.H27 M68 1999

Dictionnaire de psychologie.
Sillamy, Norbert. [Nouv. éd.]. Paris : Larousse, 2003.
BF31 .S5 2003

DIDACTICS. See **TEACHING.**

Didato, Salvatore V. The big book of personality tests : 100 easy-to-score quizzes that reveal the real you / Salvatore V. Didato. New York : Black Dog & Leventhal Publishers, c2003. p. cm. CONTENTS: The real you -- In the mood for love -- A happy home -- Social senses -- On the job -- The smell of success -- Thought in action -- Your emotional wellness. ISBN 1-57912-281-7 DDC 155.2/83
1. Personality tests. I. Title.
BF698.5 .D53 2003

Didier-Weill, Alain. Lila et la lumière de Vermeer : la psychanalyse à l'école des artistes / Alain Didier-Weill. Paris : Denoël, c2003. 165 p. : ill. ; 23 cm. (L'espace analytique) Includes bibliographical references. ISBN 2-207-25439-9 DDC 150
1. Psychoanalysis and art. 2. Psychoanalysis and music. I. Title. II. Series.

Didion, Joan. Where I was from / Joan Didion. 1st ed. New York : Alfred A. Knopf : Distributed by Random House, 2003. 226 p. ; 21 cm. ISBN 0-679-43332-5 DDC 979.4
1. California - History. 2. California - Social conditions. 3. California - In literature. 4. California - Social conditions. 5. National characteristics, American. I. Title.
F861 .D53 2003

Die when you choose with dignity and and ease.
Wood, Robert S. (Robert Snyder), 1930- Peaceful passing. Sedona, AZ : In Print Pub., c2000.
BF789.D4 W66 2000

Diedler, Jean-Claude. Le testament de Maître Persin : l'imaginaire et les croyances des anciennes populations rurales, XVe-XVIIe siècles / Jean-Claude Diedler. [Metz] : Editions serpenoise, [2000] 325 p. ; 22 cm. Includes bibliographical references (p. [313]-317) and indexes. ISBN 2-87692-446-3
1. Demonology - France - Lorraine - History - 16th century. 2. Demonology - France - Lorraine - History - 17th century. 3. Witchcraft - France - Lorraine - History - 16th century. 4. Witchcraft - France - Lorraine - History - 17th century. 5. Peasantry - France - Lorraine - History - 16th century. 6. Peasantry - France - Lorraine - History - 17th century. I. Title.

BF1517.F5 D515 2000
Diehl, Paul F. (Paul Francis).
Regional conflict management. Lanham, Md. : Rowman & Littlefield, c2003.
JZ5330 .R437 2003

Diesenberger, Max.
The construction of communities in the early Middle Ages. Leiden ; Boston : Brill, 2003.
HN11 .C66 2003

DIET. See **FOOD; FOOD HABITS.**

DIETARIES. See **FOOD.**

DIETHYLAMINE. See **LSD (DRUG).**

Dietz-Uhler, Beth.
Sternberg, Robert J. The psychologist's companion. 4th ed. Cambridge, U.K. ; New York : Cambridge University Press, 2003.
BF76.8 .S73 2003

Dieu dans le vaudou haïtien.
Hurbon, Laënnec. Nouv. éd. Paris : Maisonneuve et Larose, 2002.

Dieu, l'homme et la réincarnation.
Hubaut, Michel. Paris : Desclée de Brouwer, c1998.

Les dieux ne sont jamais loin.
Jerphagnon, Lucien, 1921- Paris : Desclée de Brouwer, c2002.

Díez Calzada, José A.
El lenguaje y la mente humana. 1. ed. Barcelona : Ariel Editorial, 2002.

DIFFERENCE (PHILOSOPHY).
Clam, Jean. Was heisst, sich an Differenz statt an Identität orientieren? Konstanz : UVK Verlagsgesellschaft, c2002.

Connolly, William E. Identity/difference. Expanded ed. Minneapolis : University of Minnesota Press, c2002.
JA74 .C659 2002

Kearney, Richard. Strangers, Gods, and monsters. London ; New York : Routledge, 2003.
BD236 .K43 2003

Lenger, Hans-Joachim. Vom Abschied. Bielefeld : Transcript, c2001.
B105.D5 L46 2001

Lyotard. New York ; London : Routledge, 2002.

Markell, Patchen, 1969- Bound by recognition. Princeton, N.J. : Princeton University Press, c2003.
JC575 .M37 2003

DIFFERENCE (PSYCHOLOGY).
Kearney, Richard. Strangers, Gods, and monsters. London ; New York : Routledge, 2003.
BD236 .K43 2003

Studien zu antiken Identitäten. Würzburg : Ergon Verlag, c2001.
DG78 .S78 2001

DIFFERENCE (PSYCHOLOGY) IN LITERATURE.
Arenas, Fernando, 1963- Utopias of otherness. Minneapolis : University of Minnesota Press, c2003.
DP681 .A74 2003

DIFFERENTIABLE DYNAMICAL SYSTEMS. See also **CHAOTIC BEHAVIOR IN SYSTEMS.**
Zhusubaliyev, Zhanybai T. Bifurcations and chaos in piecewise-smooth dynamical systems. River Edge, New Jersey : World Scientific, c2003.

DIFFERENTIAL PSYCHOLOGY. See **DIFFERENCE (PSYCHOLOGY).**

DIFFERENTIATION (DEVELOPMENTAL PSYCHOLOGY). See **DIFFERENCE (PSYCHOLOGY).**

DiGaetani, John Louis, 1943- Wagner and suicide / by John Louis DiGaetani. Jefferson, N.C. : McFarland, c2003. viii, 195 p. : ill. ; 23 cm. Includes bibliographical references (p. 187-192) and index. CONTENTS: Wagner's bipolar life : mania and depression -- Die Fliegender Hollander : the isolated personality -- Tannhauser : the artistic personality and suicide -- Lohengrin : the dream persona from another world -- Tristan und Isolde : suicide as the best alternative -- Die Meistersinger von Nurnberg : mania and reconciliation -- The Ring cycle : suicide as threat and triumph -- Parsifal : beyond polarity -- Suicide in opera and drama -- Wagner, the decadents, and the modern British novel. ISBN 0-7864-1477-4 (softcover : alk. paper) DDC 782.1/092
1. Wagner, Richard, - 1813-1883 - Mental health. 2. Wagner, Richard, - 1813-1883 - Operas. 3. Composers - Mental health. 4. Suicide. I. Title.

DiGeronimo, Theresa Foy.
ML410.W13 D45 2003

DiGeronimo, Theresa Foy.
Ladner, Joyce A. Launching our Black children for success. 1st ed. San Francisco : Jossey-Bass, c2003.
BF723.S77 L33 2003

Digging holes in popular culture : archaeology and science fiction / edited by Miles Russell ; with a preface by Douglas Adams. Oxford : Oxbow, 2002. xv, 174 p. : ill. ; 24 cm. (Occasional papers Bournemouth University. School of Conservation Sciences ; 7) Includes bibliographical references. ISBN 1-84217-063-5 DDC 930.101
1. Archaeology in literature. 2. Popular culture. I. Russell, Miles. II. Bournemouth University. School of Conservation Sciences. III. Series.
PN3433.6 .D54 2002

DIGITAL ART.
Reck, H. U. Mythos Medienkunst. Köln : König, c2002.

DIGITAL COMMUNICATIONS. See **COMPUTER NETWORKS.**

DIGITAL COMPUTER SIMULATION. See **ARTIFICIAL INTELLIGENCE; VIRTUAL COMPUTER SYSTEMS.**

DIGITAL COMPUTER SIMULATION - CONGRESSES.
International Conference on Simulation in Engineering Education (2001 : Phoenix, Ariz.) Proceedings of the International Conference on Simulation and Multimedia in Engineering Education & Virtual Worlds and Simulation. San Diego, CA : Society for Computer Simulation International, c2001.

DIGITAL SIMULATION. See **DIGITAL COMPUTER SIMULATION.**

DIGNITIES (ASTROLOGY).
Hazel, Elizabeth. Tarot decoded. Boston, MA : Weiser Books, 2004.
BF1879.T2 H339 2004

DIGNITY.
Collste, Göran. Is human life special? Bern ; Oxford : Peter Lang, 2002.

Dignity at work.
Rennie Peyton, Pauline, 1952- 1st ed. Hove, East Sussex ; New York : Brunner-Routledge, 2003.
BF637.B85 R46 2003

DIGNITY - RELIGIOUS ASPECTS.
Collste, Göran. Is human life special? Bern ; Oxford : Peter Lang, 2002.

DIGS (ARCHAEOLOGY). See **EXCAVATIONS (ARCHAEOLOGY).**

Dijalog o ljepoti.
Gučetić, Nikola Vitov, 1549-1610. [Dialogo della bellezza. Serbo-Croatian & Italian] Dvojezično izd. Zagreb : Društvo hrvatskih književnika, 1995.
BH301.L65 G8318 1995

Dikṣita, Mathurā Prasāda, 1878-1978. [Kelikutūhala. Hindi & Sanskrit]
Kelikutūhalam : bhāṣānuvādasahitam / Mathurāprasāda Dīkṣitaḥ. Vārāṇasī : Krshaḍāsa Akādamī, 2002. 7, 183 p. ; 22 cm. (Kṛṣṇadāsa Saṃskrta sīrīja ; 173) SUMMARY: Sanskrit text with Hindi translation on art of love. Includes index. Hindi and Sanskrit. ISBN 81-218-0090-0
1. Love. 2. Sex. 3. Sexual intercourse. I. Title. II. Series: Kṛṣṇadāsa Saṃskrta sīrīja ; 173.
HQ470.S3 D55155 2002

DiLalla, Lisabeth F.
Behavior genetics principles. Washington, DC : American Psychological Association, 2004.
BF698.9.B5 B44 2004

DILEMMA.
Foot, Philippa. Moral dilemmas and other topics in moral philosophy. Oxford ; New York : Clarendon Press, 2002.

Dilemma's in menselijke interactie.
Huls, Erica. Utrecht : Lemma, 2001.

Dilemmas in the consulting room / edited by Helen Alfillé and Judy Cooper. London ; New York : Karnac, 2002. xiii, 212 p. ; 23 cm. Includes bibliographical references (p. 185-199) and index. ISBN 1-85575-268-9
1. Psychoanalysis. I. Alfillé, Helen. II. Cooper, Judy.

Dilemmas of reconciliation : cases and concepts / edited by Carol A.L. Prager and Trudy Govier. Waterloo, Ont. : Wilfrid Laurier University Press, 2003. vi, 360 p. : ill. ; 223 cm. Includes bibliographical references and index. ISBN 0-88920-415-2 (pbk.) DDC 172/.4
1. Reconciliation. 2. International relations - Moral and ethical aspects. 3. Political ethics. I. Govier, Trudy. II. Prager, Carol A. L. (Anne Leuchs), 1939-

Dilley, Whitney Crothers.
Feminism/femininity in Chinese literature. Amsterdam ; New York : Rodopi, 2002.

Dillon, John M. The heirs of Plato : a study of the Old Academy, 347-274 B.C. / John Dillon. Oxford : Clarendon Press ; New York : Oxford University Press, 2003. x, 252 p. ; 22 cm. Includes bibliographical references (p. 239-244) and indexes. ISBN 0-19-823766-9 (alk. paper) DDC 184
1. Platonists - History. 2. Philosophy, Ancient. I. Title.
B517 .D536 2003

DiMatteo, Larry A. The law of international business transactions / Larry A. DiMatteo. Mason, OH : Thomson/South-Western West, c2003. xxiii, 527 p. : ill. ; 26 cm. ISBN 0-324-04097-0 DDC 343.73/087
1. Export sales contracts - United States. 2. Foreign trade regulation - United States. 3. Export sales contracts. 4. Foreign trade regulation. 5. Risk. I. Title.
KF915 .D56 2003

Dimen, Muriel. Sexuality, intimacy, power / Muriel Dimen. Hillsdale, NJ : Analytic Press, 2003. viii, 328 p. ; 24 cm. (Relational perspectives book series ; v. 22) Includes bibliographical references (p. 299-316) and index. ISBN 0-88163-368-2 DDC 155.3
1. Feminist psychology. 2. Dualism. I. Title. II. Series.
BF201.4 .D556 2003

The dimensional thinker.
Bruce, William C. 1st ed. Tyler, TX : Home Tree Media, 2000.
BF441 .B/99 2000

Dimensions of mystical experiences.
Hood, Ralph W. Amsterdam ; New York, NY : Rodopi, 2001.

Dimitrievich, Vladimir. V plenu germeticheskogo kruga : o psikhologii Karla IUnga i proze Germana Gesse / Vladimir Dimitrievich ; Ob analiticheskoĭ psikhologii Karla IUnga : vzgli͡ad s pozitsiĭ svi͡atootecheskogo ucheniia o spasenii dushi / Mikhail Medvedev, Tatʹi͡ana Kalashnikova. Permʹ : Panagii͡a, 2001. 126 p. ; 21 cm. (TSerkovʹ i obrazovanie ; vyp. 7) Errata slip tipped in. Includes bibliographical references (p. 125).
1. Jung, C. G. - (Carl Gustav), - 1875-1961. 2. Hesse, Hermann, - 1877-1962. 3. Jungian psychology - Religious aspects - Orthodox Eastern Church. 4. Orthodox Eastern Church - Doctrines. I. Medvedev, Mikhail. Ob analiticheskoĭ psikhologii Karla IUnga. 2001 II. Kalashnikova, T. P. (Tatʹi͡ana Pavlovna) III. Title. IV. Series.
BF173.J85 D56 2001

DING AN SICH.
Caropreso, Paolo. Von der Dingfrage zur Frage nach Gott. Berlin ; New York : W. de Gruyter, 2003.

Dinge im Fluss, Fluss der Verzeichnungen.
Sturm, Hermann, 1936- Frankfurt a.M. : Anabas-Verlag, 2002.

Dingwall, Robert.
Murphy, Elizabeth. Qualitative methods and health policy research. Hawthorne, N.Y. : Aldine de Gruyter, c2003.
RA394 .M87 2003

DINING. See **DINNERS AND DINING.**

DINNERS AND DINING. See **DRINKING CUSTOMS; FOOD.**

DINNERS AND DINING - FRANCE - HISTORY.
Effros, Bonnie, 1965- Creating community with food and drink in Merovingian Gaul. 1st ed. New York ; Houndmills, England : Palgrave Macmillan, 2002.
GT2853.F7 E34 2002

DiPiero, Thomas, 1956- White men aren't / Thomas DiPiero. Durham : Duke University Press, 2002. viii, 338 p. ; 25 cm. Includes bibliographical references (p. [309]-330) and index. CONTENTS: Introduction. Believing is seeing -- Complex Oedipus : reading Sophocles, testing Freud -- Missing links -- The fair sex : it's not what you think -- In defense of the phallus -- White men aren't. ISBN 0-8223-2933-6 (cloth : alk. paper) ISBN 0-8223-2961-1 (pbk. : alk. paper) DDC 305.31
1. White men - Psychology. 2. Men - Identity. 3. White men in literature. 4. Masculinity. 5. Masculinity in literature. I. Title. II. Title: White men are not
HQ1090 .D567 2002

DIPLOMACY.
Callières, Monsieur de (François), 1645-1717. De la manière de négocier avec les souverains. Genève : Droz, c2002.

DIPLOMATIC PROTECTION. See **INTERVENTION (INTERNATIONAL LAW).**

DIPLOMATICS. See **ARCHIVES.**

DIRECT ACTION. See **TERRORISM.**

Direct broadcast satellite service in the multichannel video distribution market.
United States. Congress. House. Committee on the Judiciary. Washington : U.S. G.P.O. For sale by the Supt. of Docs., U.S. G.P.O. [Congressional Sales Office], 2003.

DIRECT BROADCAST SATELLITE TELEVISION - UNITED STATES.
United States. Congress. House. Committee on the Judiciary. Direct broadcast satellite service in the multichannel video distribution market. Washington : U.S. G.P.O. For sale by the Supt. of Docs., U.S. G.P.O. [Congressional Sales Office], 2003.

United States. Congress. Senate. Committee on the Judiciary. Subcommittee on Antitrust, Business Rights, and Competition. Dominance in the sky. [Washington] : U.S. G.P.O. : For sale by the Supt. of Docs., U.S. G.P.O. [Congressional Sales Office], 2003.

DIRECT-TO-HOME SATELLITE TELEVISION. See **DIRECT BROADCAST SATELLITE TELEVISION.**

Directed self-placement : principles and practices / edited by Daniel Royer, Roger Gilles. Cresskill, N.J. : Hampton Press, c2003. viii, 264 p. ; ill. ; 24 cm. (Research and teaching in rhetoric and composition) Includes bibliographical references and indexes. ISBN 1-57273-532-5 (cloth) ISBN 1-57273-533-3 (pbk.) DDC 808/.042/071173
1. English language - Rhetoric - Study and teaching. 2. English language - Rhetoric - Study and teaching - United States - Case studies. 3. Report writing - Study and teaching (Higher) 4. Advanced placement programs (Education) 5. Basic writing (Remedial education) 6. Educational evaluation. 7. Self-evaluation. I. Royer, Daniel. II. Gilles, Roger. III. Series.
PE1404 .D57 2003

Directory.
Uganda Law Society. Kampala : The Society, [1999-
KTW3.3 .U345

Directory of child-family research centres in developing countries and Eastern Europe.
Psychology, IUPsyS global resource [electronic resource]. Hove, East Sussex, UK : published on behalf of the international Union of Psychological Science by Psychology Press Ltd., 2000-
BF76.5 .P79

The directory of ethnic minority professionals in psychology.
American Psychological Association. 4th ed. Washington, D.C. : American Psychological Association, c2001.
BF30 .A493 2001

Directory of health psychology in Latin America.
Psychology, IUPsyS global resource [electronic resource]. Hove, East Sussex, UK : published on behalf of the international Union of Psychological Science by Psychology Press Ltd., 2000-
BF76.5 .P79

Directory of international psychological organizations.
Psychology, IUPsyS global resource [electronic resource]. Hove, East Sussex, UK : published on behalf of the international Union of Psychological Science by Psychology Press Ltd., 2000-
BF76.5 .P79

DIRECTV (FIRM).
United States. Congress. Senate. Committee on the Judiciary. Subcommittee on Antitrust, Business Rights, and Competition. Dominance in the sky. [Washington] : U.S. G.P.O. : For sale by the Supt. of Docs., U.S. G.P.O. [Congressional Sales Office], 2003.

Disabilities.
Adekanmbi, Joseph. Ibadan [Nigeria] : Goalim Publishers, 2001.

DISABILITY PENSIONS. See **DISABILITY RETIREMENT.**

DISABILITY, READING. See **READING DISABILITY.**

DISABILITY RETIREMENT - LAW AND LEGISLATION - UNITED STATES - MISCELLANEA.
Questions and answers about disability and service retirement plans under the Americans with Disabilities Act (ADA) [electronic resource]. [Washington,

D.C.] : U.S. Equal Employment Opportunity Commission, [1995]

DISABLED. *See* **HANDICAPPED.**

DISABLED PEOPLE. *See* **HANDICAPPED.**

DISAPPEARANCES (PARAPSYCHOLOGY).
Herbst, Judith. Vanished. Minneapolis : Lerner Publications Co., 2005.
BF1389.D57 H47 2005

Townsend, John. Mysterious disappearances. Chicago, IL : Raintree, 2004.
BF1389.D57 T69 2004

DISAPPEARANCES (PARAPSYCHOLOGY) - JUVENILE LITERATURE.
Herbst, Judith. Vanished. Minneapolis : Lerner Publications Co., 2005.
BF1389.D57 H47 2005

Townsend, John. Mysterious disappearances. Chicago, IL : Raintree, 2004.
BF1389.D57 T69 2004

DISARMAMENT. *See also* **PEACE.**
Myrdal, Alva Reimer, 1902- "Något kan man väl göra. Stockholm : Carlssons, c2002.

DISASTER PLANNING. *See* **EMERGENCY MANAGEMENT.**

DISASTER PREPAREDNESS. *See* **EMERGENCY MANAGEMENT.**

DISASTER PREVENTION. *See* **EMERGENCY MANAGEMENT.**

DISASTER RELIEF - NEW YORK (STATE) - NEW YORK.
Kendra, James M. Elements of community resilience in the World Trade Center attack. [Newark, Del.?] : Disaster Research Center, University of Delaware, 2001.

DISASTER RELIEF - PLANNING. *See* **EMERGENCY MANAGEMENT.**

DISASTER VICTIMS - PSYCHOLOGY.
Beristain, Carlos M. Apoyo psicosocial en catátrofes colectivas. 1a. ed. Caracas, Venezuela : Asociación Venezolana de Psicología Social-AVESPO : Comisión de Estudios de Posgrado, Facultad de Hunanidades y Educación, Universidad Central de Venezuela, 2000.

DISASTERS. *See* **ACCIDENTS.**

DISASTERS - PLANNING. *See* **EMERGENCY MANAGEMENT.**

DISASTERS - PREPAREDNESS. *See* **EMERGENCY MANAGEMENT.**

DISASTERS - PRESS COVERAGE.
Ross, Gina, 1947- Beyond the trauma vortex. Berkeley, Calif. : North Atlantic Books, c2003.
PN4784.D57 R67 2003

DISASTERS - PSYCHOLOGICAL ASPECTS.
Beristain, Carlos M. Apoyo psicosocial en catátrofes colectivas. 1a. ed. Caracas, Venezuela : Asociación Venezolana de Psicología Social-AVESPO : Comisión de Estudios de Posgrado, Facultad de Hunanidades y Educación, Universidad Central de Venezuela, 2000.

Bulkeley, Kelly, 1962- Dreams of healing. New York : Paulist Press, c2003.
BF1099.N53 B85 2003

Coping with public tragedy. Washington, DC : Hospice Foundation of America ; New York : Brunner-Routledge, c2003.
BF789.D5 C67 2003

Helping children and adolescents cope with violence and disasters [electronic resource]. Bethesda, MD : Office of Communications and Public Liaison, [2001]

Helping children and adolescents cope with violence and disasters [electronic resource]. Bethesda, MD : Office of Communications and Public Liaison, [2001]

Terrorism and disaster. Cambridge, UK ; New York : Cambridge University Press, 2003.
RC552.P67 T476 2003

DISASTERS - SOCIAL ASPECTS.
Coping with public tragedy. Washington, DC : Hospice Foundation of America ; New York : Brunner-Routledge, c2003.
BF789.D5 C67 2003

DISCERNMENT (CHRISTIAN THEOLOGY).
Farrington, Debra K. Hearing with the heart. 1st ed. San Francisco : Jossey-Bass, c2003.
BV4509.5 .F37 2003

Goldsmith, Joel S., 1892-1964. Spiritual discernment. Atlanta, Ga. : Acropolis Books, c2002.
BF639.G56886 2002

Disciplines and nations.
Cherchi, Marcello. Pittsburgh, Pa. : Center for Russian and East European Studies, University Center for International Studies, University of Pittsburgh, c2002.

DISCLOSURE OF SELF. *See* **SELF-DISCLOSURE.**

DISCONTENT.
Dolnick, Barrie. Instructions for your discontent. New York : Simple Abundance Press/Scribner, c2003.
BF637.C4 D65 2003

Discours de la méthode créatrice.
Gaudin, Thierry. Gordes : Relié, c2003.

Discours psychanalytique.
Cathelineau, Pierre-Christophe, 1961- Lacan, lecteur d'Aristote. 2. éd., rev. et corr. Paris : Éditions de l'Association freudienne internationale, c2001 (2002 printing)

Discourse + organization.
Discourse and organization. London ; Thousand Oaks, Calif. : Sage Publications, 1998.
HD58.7 .D57 1998

DISCOURSE ANALYSIS.
Gender identity and discourse analysis. Amsterdam ; Philadelphia : John Benjamins Pub., c2002.
HQ1075 .G428 2002

Wort und (Kon)text. Frankfurt : Lang, 2001.
P325.5.C65 W678 2001

DISCOURSE ANALYSIS, NARRATIVE. *See also* **NARRATION (RHETORIC).**
Rukmini Bhaya Nair. Narrative gravity. New Delhi ; New York : Oxford University Press, 2002.
P302.7 .R85 2002

Rukmini Bhaya Nair. Narrative gravity. London ; New York : Routledge, 2003.
P302.7 .R85 2003

Discourse analysis of Chinese referring expressions.
Shi, Yili. Lewiston, N.Y. : E. Mellen Press, c2002.
P325.5.R44 S53 2002

DISCOURSE ANALYSIS - PSYCHOLOGICAL ASPECTS.
Cherepanova, I. IU. (Irina IUr'evna) Dom koldun'i. Perer., dop. i ispravlennoe izd. Moskva : KSP+, 2001.
BF1156.S8 C53 2001

Problemy interpretat︠s︡ionnoĭ lingvistiki. Novosibirsk : Novosibirskiĭ gos. pedagog. universitet, 2001.
P128.E95 P762 2001

Rukmini Bhaya Nair. Narrative gravity. New Delhi ; New York : Oxford University Press, 2002.
P302.7 .R85 2002

Rukmini Bhaya Nair. Narrative gravity. London ; New York : Routledge, 2003.
P302.7 .R85 2003

Sakita, Tomoko I. Reporting discourse, tense, and cognition. 1st ed. Amsterdam ; Boston : Elsevier, 2002.
P301.5.I53 S25 2002

Discourse and cognition.
Edwards, Derek. London ; Thousand Oaks, Calif. : SAGE Publications, 1997.
BF201.3 .E39 1997

Discourse and organization / edited by David Grant, Tom Keenoy and Cliff Oswick. London ; Thousand Oaks, Calif. : Sage Publications, 1998. viii, 248 p. : ill. ; 24 cm. Cover title: Discourse + organization. Includes bibliographical references (p. [222]-243) and index. CONTENTS: Introduction : Organizational discourse : of diversity, dichotomy and multi-disciplinarity / David Grant, Tom Keenoy and Cliff Oswick -- Discourse on discourse : redeeming the meaning of talk / Robert J. Marshak -- Workplace conversations : the text of organizing / Jill Woodilla -- Emotional discourse in organizations / Iain L. Mangham -- Talk and action : conversations and narrative in interorganizational collaboration / Cynthia Hardy, Thomas B. Lawrence and Nelson Phillips -- Same old story or changing stories? Folkloric, modern and postmodern mutations / Yiannis Gabriel -- As God created the Earth ... a saga that makes sense? / Miriam Salzer-Mörling -- Struggle with sense / Anne Wallemacq and David Sims -- Linearity, control and death / Gibson Burrell -- Organization is a conversation / Gerrit Broekstra -- Metaphor, meaning and language / Didier Cazal and Dawn Inns -- Organizational analysis as discourse analysis : a critique / Mike Reed -- Discourse, organizations and paradox / Richard Dunford and Ian Palmer. ISBN 0-7619-5670-0 ISBN 0-7619-5671-9 (pbk.) DDC 302.35
1. Organizational behavior. 2. Interpersonal relations. I. Grant, David. II. Keenoy, Tom. III. Oswick, Cliff. IV. Title: Discourse + organization.
HD58.7 .D57 1998

Discourse approaches to politics, society, and culture (v. 2) Gender identity and discourse analysis. Amsterdam ; Philadelphia : John Benjamins Pub., c2002.
HQ1075 .G428 2002

DISCOURSE GRAMMAR. *See* **DISCOURSE ANALYSIS.**

Discourse, the body, and identity / edited by Justine Coupland and Richard Gwyn. Basingstoke, Hampshire ; New York : Palgrave Macmillan, 2003. xii, 260 p. : ill. ; 23 cm. Includes bibliographical references and indexes. cat 20030410 psg ISBN 0-333-96900-6 (cloth) DDC 306.4
1. Body, Human - Social aspects. 2. Sociolinguistics. 3. Body language. 4. Identity (Psychology) I. Coupland, Justine. II. Gwyn, Richard, PhD.
HM636 .D57 2003

Discover true north.
Bruce, Anne, 1952- New York : McGraw-Hill, c2004.
BF637.S4 B82 2004

Discover your gold mind.
Shabazz, David L. Clinton, S.C. : Awesome Records, c2001.
BF637.S8 S428 2001

Discover yourself.
Too, Lillian. Carlsbad, Calif. : Hay House, c2002 (2003 printing)
BF697.5.S43 T66 2002

Discovering psychology.
Hockenbury, Don H. 3rd ed. New York : Worth Publishers, c2004.
BF121 .H587 2003

Discovery of cosmic fractals.
Baryshev, Yurij. River Edge, N.J. : World Scientific, c2002.
QB981 .B285 2002

The discovery of spoken language.
Jusczyk, Peter W. 1st MIT Press pbk. ed. Cambridge, Mass. : MIT Press, 2000.
BF720.S67 J87 2000

DISCRIMINATION. *See also* **MINORITIES; RACE DISCRIMINATION.**
Anti-discriminatory counselling practice. London ; Thousand Oaks, Calif. : SAGE Publications, 2003.
BF637.C6 A49 2003

Ataöv, Türkkaya. Discrimination & conflict. Haarlem : SOTA, 2000.

Fuller, Robert W. Somebodies and nobodies. Gabriola Island, Canada : New Society Publishers, 2003.
HM821 .F84 2003

Discrimination & conflict.
Ataöv, Türkkaya. Haarlem : SOTA, 2000.

DISCRIMINATION AGAINST DISABLED PERSONS. *See* **DISCRIMINATION AGAINST THE HANDICAPPED.**

DISCRIMINATION AGAINST HANDICAPPED PERSONS. *See* **DISCRIMINATION AGAINST THE HANDICAPPED.**

DISCRIMINATION AGAINST OLDER WORKERS. *See* **AGE DISCRIMINATION IN EMPLOYMENT.**

DISCRIMINATION AGAINST OVERWEIGHT WOMEN.
Stenzel, Lucia Marques. Obesidade. 1a ed. Porto Alegre : EDIPUCRS, 2002.

DISCRIMINATION AGAINST THE DISABLED. *See* **DISCRIMINATION AGAINST THE HANDICAPPED.**

DISCRIMINATION AGAINST THE HANDICAPPED - PREVENTION - LAW AND LEGISLATION.
Questions and answers about disability and service retirement plans under the Americans with Disabilities Act (ADA) [electronic resource]. [Washington, D.C.] : U.S. Equal Employment Opportunity Commission, [1995]

Discrimination and conflict.
Ataöv, Türkkaya. Discrimination & conflict. Haarlem : SOTA, 2000.

Discrimination in employment

DISCRIMINATION IN EMPLOYMENT. *See* **AGE DISCRIMINATION IN EMPLOYMENT.**

DISCRIMINATION IN EMPLOYMENT - PREVENTION - LAW AND LEGISLATION.
Questions and answers about disability and service retirement plans under the Americans with Disabilities Act (ADA) [electronic resource]. [Washington, D.C.] : U.S. Equal Employment Opportunity Commission, [1995]

Questions and answers [electronic resource]. [Washington, D.C.] : U.S. Equal Employment Opportunity Commission, [2000?]

DISCRIMINATION - JUVENILE LITERATURE.
Davidson, Tish. Prejudice. New York : Franklin Watts, c2003.
BF575.P9 D38 2003

DISCRIMINATION, RACIAL. *See* **RACE DISCRIMINATION.**

DISCS, SOUND. *See* **SOUND RECORDINGS.**

DISCURSIVE PSYCHOLOGY.
Edwards, Derek. Discourse and cognition. London ; Thousand Oaks, Calif. : SAGE Publications, 1997.
BF201.3 .E39 1997

DISCUSSION. *See* **NEGOTIATION.**

DISEASES. *See* **HEALTH; MENTAL ILLNESS; SICK.**

DISEASES - CAUSES AND THEORIES OF CAUSATION. *See* **ACCIDENTS; HEALTH BEHAVIOR.**

DISEASES, MENTAL. *See* **MENTAL ILLNESS.**

DISEASES - ZIMBABWE - MBERENGWA DISTRICT - RELIGIOUS ASPECTS.
Dahlin, Olov, 1962- Zvinorwadza. Frankfurt am Main ; New York : P. Lang, c2002.
R726.5 .D34 2002

DISGUST. *See* **AVERSION.**

DISK RECORDING. *See* **SOUND - RECORDING AND REPRODUCING.**

DISKS, SOUND. *See* **SOUND RECORDINGS.**

Diskurs, Macht und Geschichte.
Maset, Michael. Frankfurt/Main ; New York : Campus, c2002.
BF24.30.F724 M37 2002

Diskurspiratinnen.
Ernst, Waltraud, 1964- Wien : Milena, c1999.
HQ1154 .E7 1999

Diskussionsbeiträge im Schnittpunkt von Musik, Medizin, Physiologie und Psychologie.
Mensch & Musik. Augsburg : Wissner, c2002.
ML3830 .M46 2002

DISLIKE. *See* **AVERSION.**

Disney's learning series
Disney's Mickey Mouse toddler [electronic resource]. Burbank, CA : Disney Interactive, c2000.
BF719

Disney's Mickey Mouse toddler [electronic resource]. Burbank, CA : Disney Interactive, c2000. 1 CD-ROM : 4 3/4 in. + 1 program manual (insert). (Disney's learning series) Title on container: Toddler with active leveling advantage. System requirements for Windows: 133MHz Pentium class processor or faster; Windows 95/98. System requirements for Macintosh: iMac G3 or better; System 8.1 through 9.0. Title from disc label. Includes free CD-ROM entitled: Disney's a bug's life. Ages 18 months to 3 years. SUMMARY: While interacting with Mickey and his friends, children may learn about numbers, letters, colors and shapes as well as other age appropriate skills. Contains activities that build self-confidence by means of continuous positive reinforcement from Mickey and his friends. Production level cataloging. ISBN 1-57350-326-6
1. Infant psychology - Juvenile software. 2. Infants - Development - Juvenile software. 3. Toddlers - Psychology - Juvenile software. I. Title: Mickey Mouse toddler II. Title: Toddler III. Title: Toddler with active leveling advantage IV. Series.
BF719

DISORDERS OF EATING. *See* **EATING DISORDERS.**

DISORDERS, PANIC. *See* **PANIC DISORDERS.**

DISPOSITION OF RECORDS. *See* **RECORDS - MANAGEMENT.**

DISPOSITION (PHILOSOPHY).
Gundersen, Lars Bo. Dispositional theories of knowledge. Aldershot, England ; Burlington, VT : Ashgate, c2003.
BD161 .G86 2003

Molnar, George, d. 1999. Powers. Oxford ; New York : Oxford University Press, 2003.
BD541 .M54 2003

Dispositional theories of knowledge.
Gundersen, Lars Bo. Aldershot, England ; Burlington, VT : Ashgate, c2003.
BD161 .G86 2003

DISPUTE PROCESSING. *See* **DISPUTE RESOLUTION (LAW).**

DISPUTE RESOLUTION (LAW).
Lipsky, David B., 1939- Emerging systems for managing workplace conflict. 1st ed. San Francisco : Jossey-Bass, c2003.
HD42 .L564 2003

DISPUTE SETTLEMENT. *See* **CONFLICT MANAGEMENT; DISPUTE RESOLUTION (LAW).**

DISPUTING. *See* **QUARRELING; VERBAL SELF-DEFENSE.**

DISRELISH. *See* **AVERSION.**

Disseminations
Alford, C. Fred. Levinas, the Frankfurt school and psychoanalysis. 1st US ed. Middletown, CT : Wesleyan University Press, c2002.

Eigen, Michael. Rage. Middletown, Conn. : Wesleyan University Press, c2002.
RC569.5.A53 E38 2002

Roland, Alan, 1930- Dreams and drama. 1st US ed. Middletown, CT : Wesleyan University Press, 2003.
BF408 .R65 2003

Roland, Alan, 1930- Dreams and drama. 1st US ed. Middletown, CT : Wesleyan University Press, 2003.
BF408 .R65 2003

The vitality of objects. 1st US ed. Middletown, Conn. : Wesleyan University Press, 2002.
BF173 .V55 2002

Dissertationes psychologicae Universitatis Tartuensis
(7) Toomela, Aaro. Cultural-historical psychology. Tartu : Tartu University Press, c2000.
BF109.V95 T66 2000

DISTANCE EDUCATION - CONGRESSES.
Construcción de conocimiento y educación virtual. 1. ed. Ciudad Universitaria, México, D.F. : Universidad Nacional Autónoma de México, 2000.
LB1060 .C658 2000

Distant mental influence.
Braud, William. Charlottesville, VA : Hampton Roads Pub., c2003.
BF1045.S33 B74 2003

DISTASTE. *See* **AVERSION.**

Distinguish to unite.
Maritain, Jacques, 1882-1973. [Degrés du savoir. English] Distinguish to unite, or, The degrees of knowledge. Notre Dame, Ind. : University of Notre Dame Press, 1998, c1995.
BD162 .M273 1998

Distinguish to unite, or, The degrees of knowledge.
Maritain, Jacques, 1882-1973. [Degrés du savoir. English] Notre Dame, Ind. : University of Notre Dame Press, 1998, c1995.
BD162 .M273 1998

Distinguished contributions in psychology
Schneider, David J., 1940- The psychology of stereotyping. New York : Guilford Press, c2004.
BF323.S63 S36 2003

DISTRIBUTIVE JUSTICE.
Hurley, S. L. (Susan L.) Justice, luck, and knowledge. Cambridge, Mass. : Harvard University Press, 2003.
BJ1451 .H87 2003

Distrust : manifestations and management / [edited by] Russell Hardin. New York : Russell Sage Foundation, 2004. p. cm. (Russell Sage Foundation series on trust ; v. 6) Includes bibliographical references and index. ISBN 0-87154-350-8 DDC 302/.1
1. Trust. I. Hardin, Russell, 1940- II. Series.
BF575.T7 D57 2004

Distsiplinarnyĭ sanatoriĭ.
Limonov, Ėduard. Sankt-Peterburg : Amfora, 2002.
CB428 .L556 2002

Dites-leur que la mort n'existe pas.
Winter, Jean, 1909-1939 (Spirit) Chambéry : Exergue, c1997, [1998]

BF1290 .W56 1997

Die Diva.
Bronfen, Elisabeth. München : Schirmer/Mosel, c2002.
BJ1470.5 .B76 2002

Divagazioni filosofiche del reverendo Giuseppe Petich tratte dai frammenti del suo "Zibaldone".
Petich, Giuseppe, 1869-1953. Roma : Bulzoni, 2002.

Le divan et le grigri.
Clément, Catherine, 1939- Paris : Jacob, c2002.

DiVanna, Joseph A. Synconomy : adding value in a world of continuously connected business / Joseph A. DiVanna. Houndmills [England] ; New York : Palgrave Macmillan, 2003. xviii, 231 p. : ill. ; 25 cm. Includes bibliographical references (p. 220-226) and index. ISBN 1403911150 DDC 658/.049
1. International business enterprises. 2. Technological innovations. 3. Value. 4. Organizational behavior. I. Title.
HD64.2 .D575 2003

Divano
(85.) Canfora, Luciano. Manifesto della libertà. Palermo : Sellerio, c1994.
JC585 .C29 1994

DiVersa (Mexico City, Mexico)
(4.) Vallejo, Fernando. La tautología darwinista. 1a. ed. México : Universidad Nacional Autónoma de México, 1998.

Diversity in counseling.
Brammer, Robert. Australia ; Belmont, CA : Thomson : Brooks/Cole, c2004.
BF637.C6 B677 2004

DIVERSITY IN THE WORKPLACE.
Job stress in a changing workforce. 1st ed. Washington, DC ; London : American Psychological Association, c1994.
HF5548.85 .J654 1994

DIVINATION.
Buckland, Raymond. Coin divination. 1st ed. St. Paul, Minn. : Llewellyn Publications, 2000.
BF1779.C56 B83 2000

Cunningham, Scott, 1956- Divination for beginners. 2nd ed. St. Paul, MN : Llewellyn Publications, 2003.
BF1751 .C86 2003

Dāwūd, Muḥammad 'Īsá. al-Jafr li-Sayyidinā 'Alī. al-Muhandisīn [Giza] : Madbūlī al-Ṣaghīr, [2003]
BF1771+

Eason, Cassandra. [Complete book of divination] A complete guide to divination. London : Piatkus, 1998 (2002 [printing])

Eason, Cassandra. The complete guide to divination. Berkeley, Calif. : Crossing Press, 2003.
BF1751 .E27 2003

Guide to the Golden Dawn Enochian skrying tarot. St. Paul, Minn. : Llewellyn, 2004.
BF1623.E55 G65 2004

Hathaway, Robert A. Runes from the New World. 2nd ed. [San Diego, Calif.?] : R.A. Hathaway, c2002.
BF1891.R85 H38 2002

Kosarin, Jenni. The everything divining the future book. Avon, MA : Adams Media, c2003.
BF1773 .K67 2003

Llewellyn, A. Bronwyn (Anita Bronwyn) Shakespeare oracle. Gloucester, Mass. : Fair Winds Press, 2003.
BF1879.T2 L59 2003

Madigan, M. A., 1962- Symbols of the craft. 1st ed. St. Paul, Minn. : Llewellyn Publications, 2003.
BF1773 .M29 2003

Magic and modernity. Stanford, Calif. : Stanford University Press, 2003.
GN475.3 .M34 2003

McNaughton, Mary. Synchro-signs. Charlottesville, VA : Hampton Roads Pub., 2003.
BF1773 .M38 2003

Mountfort, Paul Rhys. Ogam, the Celtic oracle of the trees. Rochester, Vt. : Destiny Books, c2002.
PB1217 .M68 2002

Divination & portents in the Roman world.
Divination and portents in the Roman world. Odense : Odense University Press, c2000.
BF1768 .D57 2000

Divination and portents in the Roman world / edited by Robin Lorsch Wildfang and Jacob Isager. Odense : Odense University Press, c2000. 79 p. (Odense University classical studies, 0107-1378 ; v. 21) Spine title: Divination & portents in the Roman world. Revised papers

from a colloquium held at the Dept. of Greek and Roman Studies, Odense University, May 1998. Includes bibliographical references. ISBN 87-7838-462-1
1. Divination - Rome - Congresses. 2. Omens - Rome - Congresses. 3. Rome - Religion - Congresses. I. Wildfang, Robin Lorsch. II. Isager, Jacob, 1944- III. Syddansk universitet. Dept. of Greek and Roman Studies. IV. Title: Divination & portents in the Roman world V. Series.
BF1768 .D57 2000

DIVINATION CARDS.
Buckland, Raymond. Book of alchemy. 1st ed. St. Paul, Minn. : Llewellyn Publications, 2003.
BF1778.5 .B83 2003

Cortez, Ana. The playing card oracles. Denver, CO : Two Sisters Press, c2002.
BF1778.5 .C67 2002

Rogers, Barb, 1947- Mystic glyphs. York Beach, ME : Red Wheel/Weiser, 2003.
BF1778.5 .R64 2003

DIVINATION CARDS - MISCELLANEA.
Lott, Lynn. Madame Dora's fortune-telling cards. Gloucester, Mass. : Fair Winds Press, 2003.
BF1878 .L78 2003

DIVINATION - CHINA.
Karcher, Stephen L. Ta chuan. 1st ed. New York : St. Martin's Press, 2000.
BF1773.2.C5 K368 2000

Schilling, Dennis R. Spruch und Zahl. Aalen : Scientia, 1998.
BF1770.C5 S42 1998

Tai ji wen hua. Xianggang : Zhongguo zhe xue wen hua xie jin hui, [2001-
BF1770.C5 T35

DIVINATION - CHINA - TIBET.
The Tibetan oracle. 1st ed. New York : Harmony Books, c1998.
BF1773.2.C5 T43 1998

DIVINATION - EGYPT.
Dee, Jonathan. Isis. New York : Sterling Pub., [2003?]
BF1591 .D44 2003

Divination for beginners.
Cunningham, Scott, 1956- 2nd ed. St. Paul, MN : Llewellyn Publications, 2003.
BF1751 .C86 2003

DIVINATION - HISTORY.
Wood, Michael, 1936- The road to Delphi. 1st ed. New York : Farrar, Straus and Giroux, 2003.
PN56.O63 W66 2003

DIVINATION - HISTORY - CONGRESSES.
Prayer, magic, and the stars in the ancient and late antique world. University Park, Pa. : Pennsylvania State University Press, 2003.
BF1591 .P73 2003

DIVINATION IN LITERATURE.
Wood, Michael, 1936- The road to Delphi. 1st ed. New York : Farrar, Straus and Giroux, 2003.
PN56.O63 W66 2003

DIVINATION - NIGERIA.
Adeosun, Kola A. [Oro ti obi n ṣo. English] What the kolanut is saying. Ibadan, Nigeria : Creative Books, 1999.
BF1779.K6 A33 1999

DIVINATION - ROME - CONGRESSES.
Divination and portents in the Roman world. Odense : Odense University Press, c2000.
BF1768 .D57 2000

The divine and the demonic.
Dwyer, Graham, 1959- London ; New York : RoutledgeCurzon, 2003.
BL1226.82.E94 D89 2003

DIVINE HEALING. *See* **SPIRITUAL HEALING.**

DIVINE MESSENGERS. *See* **ANGELS.**

DIVINE OFFICE. *See* **COMPLINE.**

Divine Pymander.
Hermes, Trismegistus. Rev. ed. Quakertown, PA : Philosophical Pub. Co., 2001.
BF1598.H5 E5 2001

Divine Pymander ; Asiatic mystery ; Smaragdine table ; Song of Brahm.
Hermes, Trismegistus. Divine Pymander. Rev. ed. Quakertown, PA : Philosophical Pub. Co., 2001.
BF1598.H5 E5 2001

Divine therapy.
Sayers, Janet. Oxford ; New York : Oxford University Press, 2003.
BF175.4.R44 S28 2003

Divining the future book.
Kosarin, Jenni. The everything divining the future book. Avon, MA : Adams Media, c2003.
BF1773 .K67 2003

DIVORCE.
Maushart, Susan, 1958- Wifework. 1st U.S. ed. New York : Bloomsbury : Distributed to the trade by Holtzbrinck Publishers, 2002.
HQ759 .M3944 2002

Simon, Rita James. Global perspectives on social issues. Lanham : Lexington Books, c2003.
HQ503 .S56 2003

DIVORCE - GOVERNMENT POLICY.
Simon, Rita James. Global perspectives on social issues. Lanham : Lexington Books, c2003.
HQ503 .S56 2003

DIVORCE (JEWISH LAW).
Kohen, Yekutiel. Mishpaṭ ha-shalom. Yerushalayim : Mekhon Sha'ar ha-mishpaṭ : Hanhalat bate ha-din ha-rabaniyim, 762 [2001 or 2002]

DIVORCE - SOCIAL ASPECTS.
Simon, Rita James. Global perspectives on social issues. Lanham : Lexington Books, c2003.
HQ503 .S56 2003

DIVORCED PEOPLE. *See* **DIVORCE.**

Divre ḥayim.
Ḥayim Yeroḥam ben Shimshon Meshulam Feybish, mi-Snatin. Sefer Asefat divre ḥakhamim. Yerushalayim : Mekhon Sod yesharim, 761 [2001]

Dīwān Ibn Khātimah al-Anṣārī.
Ibn Khātimah, Aḥmad ibn ʿAlī, d. ca. 1369. [Poems] al-Ṭabʿah 1. Bayrūt : Dār al-Fikr al-Muʿāṣir ; Dimashq : Dār al-Fikr, 1994.
PJ7760.I2454 <Orien Arab>

Dixon-Cooper, Hazel, 1947- Love on a rotten day : an astrological survival guide to romance / Hazel Dixon-Cooper. New York : Simon and Schuster, 2004. p. cm. "A Fireside book." ISBN 0-7432-2563-5 (pbk.) DDC 133.5/83067
1. Astrology. 2. Love - Miscellanea. I. Title.
BF1729.L6 D59 2004

Dixon, Mark R., 1970- Visual Basic for behavioral psychologists / by Mark R. Dixon and Otto H. MacLin ; foreword by Steven C. Hayes. Reno, NV : Context Press, c2003. 279 p. : ill. ; 23 cm. Includes bibliographical references and index. Table of contents URL: http://www.loc.gov/catdir/toc/ecip042/2003008255.html ISBN 1-87897-844-6 DDC 150.19/43/02855133
1. Psychology - Research - Methodology - Software. I. MacLin, Otto H., 1958- II. Title.
BF76.5 .D59 2003

Dixon, Thomas. From passions to emotions : the creation of a secular psychological category / Thomas Dixon. Cambridge ; New York, NY : Cambridge University Press, 2003. x, 287 p. ; 24 cm. Includes bibliographical references and index. ISBN 0-521-82729-9 DDC 152.401
1. Emotions. 2. Emotions (Philosophy) I. Title.

Dixsaut, Monique. Métamorphoses de la dialectique dans les dialogues de Platon / Monique Dixsaut. Paris : Vrin, c2001. 384 p. ; 18 cm. (Bibliothèque d'histoire de la philosophie) Inlcudes bibliographical references (p. [355]-367) and indexes. ISBN 2-7116-1507-3 DDC 100
1. Plato - Dialogues. 2. Dialectic. 3. Philosophy, Ancient. I. Title. II. Series.
B398.D5 D598 2001

Ḍiyara Kalyāṇa, mero kathā mero gīta / [lekhana/sampādana Kalyāṇa Gautama]. 1. saṃskaraṇa. [Kathmandu] : Sañjanā Gautama, 2059- [2002- v. <1 > ; 23 cm. In Nepali. SUMMARY: Compilation of letters included in a radio program expressing personal suffering and loneliness of individuals.
1. Suffering - Nepal. 2. Loneliness - Nepal. I. Gautama, Kalyāna. II. Title: Mero kathā mero gīta
BF789.S8+

DiZerega, Gus. Pagans & Christians : the personal spiritual experience / Gus diZerega. 1st ed. St. Paul, Minn. : Llewellyn Publications, 2001. xxii, 242 p. ; 23 cm. Includes bibliographical references (p. 233-237) and index. CONTENTS: Introduction : Spiritual truth for Christians and Pagans -- pt. 1. The nature of Pagan spirituality. What is Pagan religion? : the world of spirit -- Spirit and humanity in Pagan religion -- What is Wiccan Paganism? -- pt. 2. Christian criticisms of Wicca. Suffering and evil in the material world -- Malice, suffering, and evil -- Biblical inerrancy and scriptural authority -- Spiritual truth and human experience -- pt. 3. Pagan criticisms of Christianity. Spirit and nature : a Christian blindness -- Toleration and violence : a Christian dilemma -- pt. 4. Conclusion. Spiritual truth for Christians and Pagans : a Pagan perspective. ISBN 1-56718-228-3 DDC 299
1. Witchcraft. 2. Experience (Religion) 3. Neopaganism - Relations - Christianity. 4. Christianity and other religions - Neopaganism. I. Title. II. Title: Pagans and Christians
BF1566 .D59 2001

Djiokou, Sadrack.
Emtcheu, André. Psychologie et révélation. Yaoundé, Cameroun : Editions SHERPA, c2001.
1. Black author.

Dliasin, G. G. (Gennadiĭ Gennad'vich) Azbuka Germesa Trismegista, ili, Molekuli︠a︡rnai︠a︡ taĭnost' myshleniia / G.G. Dliasin. Izd. 2-e. Moskva : Izd-vo "Belye al'vy", 2002. 141 p. : ill. ; 21 cm. (Otkrytii︠a︡ XXI veka) Includes bibliographical references (p. 139-141). ISBN 5761901269
1. Hermetism. 2. Hermes, - Trismegistus. I. Title. II. Title: Azbuka Germesa Trismegista III. Title: Molekuli︠a︡rnai︠a︡ taĭnost' myshleniia IV. Series.
BF1616 .D58 2002

Dnipropetrovs'kyĭ natsional'nyĭ universytet. Istoriohrafichni ta dzhereloznavchi problemy istoriï Ukraïny. Dnipropetrovs'k : Vyd-vo Dnipropetrovs'koho universytetu, 2000.
DK508.46 .I84 2000

The do-it-yourself lobotomy.
Monahan, Tom. New York : J. Wiley, c2002.
BF408 .M59 2002

Dobeneck, Holger von. Das Sloterdijk Alphabet : eine lexikalische Einführung in Sloterdijks Gedankenkosmos / Holger Frhr. von Dobeneck. Würzburg : Königshausen & Neumann, c2002. 133 p. ; 24 cm. ISBN 3-8260-2199-1 (pbk.)
1. Sloterdijk, Peter, - 1947- - Language - Glossaries, etc. 2. Philosophy. I. Title.

Dobkin de Rios, Marlene. LSD, spirituality, and the creative process / Marlene Dobkin de Rios and Oscar Janiger. Rochester, Vt. : Park Street Press, c2003. x, 246 p. : col. ill. ; 23 cm. Includes bibliographical references (p. 235-240) and index. CONTENTS: A brief history of LSD research -- Janiger's remarkable experiment -- (Un)characteristics of the LSD experience -- Analyzing the results of the study -- LSD, art, and the creative process -- LSD and spirituality -- Psychedelics and culture -- The future of LSD : the redemptive path. ISBN 0-89281-973-1 DDC 154.4
1. LSD (Drug) - Longitudinal studies. 2. Creative ability. 3. Creation (Literary, artistic, etc.) 4. Spiritual life. 5. Lysergic Acid Diethylamide - pharmacology. 6. Creativeness. 7. Hallucinogens - pharmacology. 8. Longitudinal Studies. I. Janiger, Oscar. II. Title.
BF209.L9 D57 2003

Dobosz, Artur. Tożsamość metamorficzna a komunikacja językowa / Artur Dobosz. Poznań : Wydawn. Naukowe Instytutu Filozofii Uniwersytetu im. Adama Mickiewicza w Poznaniu, 2002. 277 p. ; 24 cm. (Pisma filozoficzne ; t. 84) Includes bibliographical references. ISBN 83-7092-073-X
1. Identity (Philosophical concept) I. Title. II. Series.

Dobson, James C., 1936-.
Hide or seek.
Dobson, James C., 1936- The new hide or seek. Pbk. ed. Grand Rapids, Mich. : F.H. Revell, 2001.
BF723.S3 D6 2001

Life on the edge / James Dobson. Nashville : Word Pub., c2000. 110 p. : col. ill. ; 20 cm. ISBN 0-8499-1629-1
1. Life change events - Psychological aspects. 2. Life change events - Religious aspects - Christianity. 3. Teenagers - Conduct of life. 4. Young adults - Conduct of life. 5. Teenagers - Religious life. 6. Young adults - Religious life. 7. Conduct of life. 8. Christian life. I. Title.
BF637.L53 D63 2000

The new hide or seek : building confidence in your child / James Dobson. Pbk. ed. Grand Rapids, Mich. : F.H. Revell, 2001. 230 p. ; 22 cm. Rev. ed. of: Hide or seek. Includes bibliographical references (p. 227-230). ISBN 0-8007-5680-0 DDC 649/.1/019
1. Self-esteem in children. I. Dobson, James C., 1936- Hide or seek. II. Title.
BF723.S3 D6 2001

Dobyns, Stephen, 1941- Best words, best order : essays on poetry / Stephen Dobyns. 2nd ed. New York : Palgrave Macmillan, 2003. xiv, 398 p. ; 21 cm. Includes bibliographical references (p.[369]-386) and index. First edition published by St. Martin's Press, 1996. CONTENTS: Deceptions -- Metaphor and the authenticating act of memory -- Writing the reader's life -- Notes on free verse -- Pacing : the ways a poem moves -- Function of tone -- Voices one listens to -- Traffic between two worlds -- Rilke's growth as a poet -- Mandelstam : the poem as event -- Chekhov's sense of writing as seen through his letters -- Ritsos and the metaphysical moment -- Cemetery night -- Maker's

manipulation of time -- Passerby in the birdless street -- Problem of beauty and the requirements of art. ISBN 1403961476
1. Poetry. 2. Creation (Literary, artistic, etc.) 3. Poetics. 4. Criticism. I. Title.

Dockett, Kathleen H., 1942-.
Psychology and Buddhism. New York : Kluwer Academic/Plenum Publishers, c2003.
BQ4570.P76 P78 2003

DOCTORS. *See* **PHYSICIANS.**

DOCTORS OF MEDICINE. *See* **PHYSICIANS.**

DOCTRINAL THEOLOGY. *See* **THEOLOGY, DOCTRINAL.**

DOCTRINES, CHRISTIAN. *See* **THEOLOGY, DOCTRINAL.**

DOCUMENT MARKUP LANGUAGES. *See* **HTML (DOCUMENT MARKUP LANGUAGE); XML (DOCUMENT MARKUP LANGUAGE).**

Document, various specification. Wrocław : University of Wrocław, Faculty of Law and Administration, Department of Criminalistics, 2000- v. : ill. 25 cm. Frequency: Quarterly. Nr 1/2000- . Vols. for 2001-<2002> have title: Document, various specifications. Latest issue consulted: Nr 5/2002. 2000 and 2001 complete in single issue; issues bear whole numbering. ISSN 1642-283X
1. Graphology - Periodicals. 2. Criminal psychology - Periodicals. 3. Criminal investigation - Periodicals. 4. Legal documents - Identification - Periodicals. I. Uniwersytet Wrocławski. Katedra Kryminalistyki. II. Title: Document, various specifications
BF905.C7 D63

Document, various specifications.
Document, various specification. Wrocław : University of Wrocław, Faculty of Law and Administration, Department of Criminalistics, 2000-
BF905.C7 D63

Documenta missionalia
(28) McLaughlin, Michael T. Knowledge, consciousness and religious conversion in Lonergan and Aurobindo. Roma : Editrice Pontificia Universita Gregoriana, 2003.

DOCUMENTARIES AND FACTUAL FILMS AND PROGRAMS.
Big Dance [videorecording]. Buffalo, N.Y. : Kineticvideo.com, c1998.

DOCUMENTARY PHOTOGRAPHY. *See* **WAR PHOTOGRAPHY.**

DOCUMENTATION. *See* **ARCHIVES.**

Documenti di storia
(28) Maghi, streghe e alchimisti a Siena e nel suo territorio (1458-1571). Monteriggioni (Siena) : Il leccio, c1999.
BF1622.I8 M295 1999

Documentos (Universidad Nacional de Quilmes)
Simonetti, José María, 1942- El fin de la inocencia. Bernal, Argentina : Universidad Nacional de Quilmes, 2002.
JF1081.S57 2002

DOCUMENTS. *See* **ARCHIVES; LEGAL DOCUMENTS.**

DOCUMENTS, IDENTIFICATION OF. *See* **LEGAL DOCUMENTS - IDENTIFICATION.**

DOCUMENTS, LEGAL. *See* **LEGAL DOCUMENTS.**

DODGERS, DRAFT. *See* **DRAFT RESISTERS.**

DOG. *See* **DOGS.**

DOG BREEDERS - BIOGRAPHY.
Wells, Celia Townsend, 1932- Brood bitch. West Lafayette, Ind. : Purdue University Press, c2003.
SF422.82.W44 A3 2003

Dog days and dandelions.
Barnette, Martha. 1st ed. New York : St. Martin's Press, 2003.
PE1583.B37 2003

DOG SPECIALISTS. *See* **DOG BREEDERS.**

Dogan, Mattei.
Elite configurations at the apex of power. Leiden ; Boston : Brill, 2003.
JC330.3.E45 2003

DOGMA, DEVELOPMENT OF. *See* **THEOLOGY, DOCTRINAL - HISTORY.**

DOGMATIC THEOLOGY. *See* **THEOLOGY, DOCTRINAL.**

DOGS.
Coren, Stanley. The pawprints of history. New York ; London : Free Press, c2002.

Haraway, Donna Jeanne. The companion species manifesto. Chicago, Ill. : Prickly Paradigm ; Bristol : University Presses Marketing, 2003.

Pregosin, Ann. The dogs who grew me. Sterling, Va. : Capital Books, c2002.
SF426.2.P74 2002

DOGS - ANECDOTES.
Pregosin, Ann. The dogs who grew me. Sterling, Va. : Capital Books, c2002.
SF426.2.P74 2002

DOGS - BEHAVIOR.
Coren, Stanley. The pawprints of history. New York ; London : Free Press, c2002.

Dogs don't bite when a growl will do.
Weinstein, Matt. 1st ed. New York : Perigee, 2003.
BF637.C5 W445 2003

DOGS - HISTORY.
Coren, Stanley. The pawprints of history. New York ; London : Free Press, c2002.

DOGS - MISCELLANEA.
Weinstein, Matt. Dogs don't bite when a growl will do. 1st ed. New York : Perigee, 2003.
BF637.C5 W445 2003

DOGS - RELIGIOUS ASPECTS.
Ezell, Jessica. Reunion. Walpole, NH : Stillpoint Pub., c1996.
BF1283.E94 A3 1996

The dogs who grew me.
Pregosin, Ann. Sterling, Va. : Capital Books, c2002.
SF426.2.P74 2002

Doing counselling research.
McLeod, John, 1951- 2nd ed. London ; Thousand Oaks, CA : Sage Publications, 2003.
BF637.C6 M37894 2003

Doing oral history.
Ritchie, Donald A., 1945- 2nd ed. Oxford ; New York : Oxford University Press, c2003.
D16.14.R57 2003

Doing survey research.
Nardi, Peter M. Boston ; London : Allyn and Bacon, c2003.
HN29.N25 2003

Doise, Willem, 1935- Human rights as social representations / Willem Doise. London ; New York : Routledge, 2002. viii, 166 p. ; 25 cm. (Routledge research international series in social psychology) Includes bibliographical references (p. [155]-161) and index. ISBN 0-415-27928-3 (alk. paper) DDC 323
1. Human rights. 2. Social psychology. I. Title. II. Series.
JC571.D65 2002

Doka, Kenneth J.
Coping with public tragedy. Washington, DC : Hospice Foundation of America ; New York : Brunner-Routledge, c2003.
BF789.D5 C67 2003

Dokumente und Schriften der Europäischen Akademie Otzenhausen
(Bd. 101) Afanasjev, Valeri, 1963- Russische Geschichtsphilosophie auf dem Prüfstand. Münster : Lit, [2002]

Dolan, Mia. I know why we're here : the true story of an ordinary woman's extraordinary gift / Mia Dolan. 1st U.S. ed. New York : Harmony Books, 2004. p. cm. ISBN 1400052165 (hardcover) DDC 133.8/092
1. Dolan, Mia. 2. Psychics - Great Britain - Biography. I. Title.
BF1283.D485 A3 2004

DOLAN, MIA.
Dolan, Mia. I know why we're here. 1st U.S. ed. New York : Harmony Books, 2004.
BF1283.D485 A3 2004

Dołęga, Zofia. Samotność młodzieży : analiza teoretyczna i studia empiryczne / Zofia Dołęga. Wyd. 1. Katowice : Wydawn. Uniwersytetu Śląskiego, 2003. 205 p. : ill. ; 24 cm. (Prace naukowe Uniwersytetu Śląskiego w Katowicach, 0208-6336 ; nr. 2070) Summary in English and Russian. Includes bibliographical references (p. [172]-201) ISBN 83-226-1186-2
1. Loneliness in adolescence. 2. Adolescent psychology. I. Title. II. Series.
BF724.3.L64 D65 2003

Dolgin, Aleksandr. Pragmatika kul'tury / Aleksandr Dolgin. Moskva : Fond nauchnykh issledovaniĭ "Pragmatika kul'tury", 2002. 166 p. ; 22 cm. Includes bibliographical references (p. 165-[167]) ISBN 5733302232
1. Value. 2. Exchange. 3. Money. 4. Economics - Sociological aspects. 5. Social psychology. 6. Symbolism (Psychology) 7. Social exchange. I. Title.

Dolnick, Barrie. Instructions for your discontent : how bad times can make life better / Barrie Dolnick ; with a foreword by Sarah Ban Breathnach. New York : Simple Abundance Press/Scribner, c2003. viii, 223 p. ; 23 cm. Includes index. Publisher description URL: http://www.loc.gov/catdir/desc ription/simon034/2003041567.html ISBN 0-7432-1442-0 DDC 158.1
1. Change (Psychology) 2. Discontent. I. Title.
BF637.C4 D65 2003

The dolphin within.
De Bergerac, Olivia. East Roseville, NSW, Australia : Simon & Schuster, 1998.
BF1999.D335 1998

DOLPHINS - MISCELLANEA.
De Bergerac, Olivia. The dolphin within. East Roseville, NSW, Australia : Simon & Schuster, 1998.
BF1999.D335 1998

Dolto, Françoise.
Essais.
Farago, France. Sören Kierkegaard. 1. éd. Paris : Houdiard, c2002.

Serres, Michel. L'incandescent. [Paris] : Pommier, c2003.

Dolto-Tolitch, Catherine.
Guillerault, Gérard. Les deux corps du moi. Paris : Gallimard, c1996.
BF175.5.B64 G86 1996

Dom koldun'i.
Cherepanova, I. ĨU. (Irina ĨUr'evna) Perer., dop. i ispravlennoe izd. Moskva : KSP+, 2001.
BF1156.S8 C53 2001

Domagala, Edward. L'ermeneutica dell'esperienza dell'amore in Max Scheler : l'itinerario verso la comprensione dell'altro e il pensare dialogico / Edward Domagala. Romae : [s.n.], 2000. 352 p. ; 24 cm. At head of title: Pontificia studiorum universitas A.S. Thoma Aq. in Urbe. "Dissertatio ad lauream in Facultate philosophiae apud pontificiam universitatem s. Thomae in Urbe." Includes bibliographical references (p. [307]-345). In Italian; summaries in German and French. DDC 193
1. Scheler, Max, - 1874-1928. 2. Phenomenology. 3. Love. 4. Hermeneutics. I. Pontificia Studiorum Universitas a Sancto Thoma Aquinate in Urbe. II. Title.

Domb, Ellen.
Rantanen, Kalevi. Simplified TRIZ. Boca Raton : St. Lucie Press, c2002.
TA153.R26 2002

DOMESTIC ANIMALS. *See* **CATS; DOGS; HORSES; LIVESTOCK; PETS.**

DOMESTIC ANIMALS - RELIGIOUS ASPECTS - EGYPTIAN RELIGION.
Eyre, Christopher. The cannibal hymn. Liverpool : Liverpool University Press, 2002.

DOMESTIC ARCHITECTURE. *See* **ARCHITECTURE, DOMESTIC.**

DOMESTIC ARCHITECTURE - INDIA.
Asalī prācīna Vaidika vāstu śāstra. 1. saṃskaraṇa. Dillī : Manoja Pôketa Buksa, [2002?]
BF1729.A7 A83 2002

Śukla, Kamalākānta, 1911- Vāstusārasaṅgrahaḥ. 1. saṃskaraṇam. Vārāṇasī : Sampūrṇānanda Saṃskṛta Viśvavidyālaye, 2002.
BF1729.A7+

DOMESTIC ECONOMY. *See* **HOME ECONOMICS.**

DOMESTIC MARKETING. *See* **MARKETING.**

DOMESTIC PARTNERS. *See* **GAY COUPLES.**

DOMESTIC RELATIONS. *See* **FAMILY.**

DOMESTIC SCIENCE. *See* **HOME ECONOMICS.**

DOMESTICATION. *See* **DOMESTIC ANIMALS.**

Domfrancesco, Francesco.
Memorie di luce.
Donfrancesco, Francesco. Una poetica dell'analisi. Bergamo : Moretti & Vitali, 2000.

DOMICILE. *See* **CITIZENSHIP.**

DOMICILES. *See* **DWELLINGS.**

Dominance in the sky.
United States. Congress. Senate. Committee on the Judiciary. Subcommittee on Antitrust, Business Rights, and Competition. [Washington] : U.S. G.P.O.

For sale by the Supt. of Docs., U.S. G.P.O. [Congressional Sales Office], 2003.

Dominance on the ground.
United States. Congress. Senate. Committee on the Judiciary. Subcommittee on Antitrust, Business Rights, and Competition. Washington : U.S. G.P.O. : For sale by the Supt. of Docs., U.S. G.P.O. [Congressional Sales Office], 2003.

DOMINANCE (PSYCHOLOGY).
Gould, Roger V. Collision of wills. Chicago : University of Chicago Press, 2003.
HM1121 .G68 2003

Lorenzi-Cioldi, Fabio, 1955- Les représentations des groupes dominants et dominés. Grenoble : Presses universitaires de Grenoble, c2002.
HM716 .L674 2002

DOMINICAN LITERATURE. See **DOMINICAN POETRY.**

DOMINICAN POETRY - COLLECTIONS.
La palabra como cuerpo del delito. Santo Domingo, República Dominicana : Biblioteca Nacional "Dr. Pedro Henríquez Ureña", 2001.

DOMINICANS POETS - BIOGRAPHY.
La palabra como cuerpo del delito. Santo Domingo, República Dominicana : Biblioteca Nacional "Dr. Pedro Henríquez Ureña", 2001.

The dominion of the dead.
Harrison, Robert Pogue. Chicago : University of Chicago Press, 2003.
BF789.D4 H375 2003

Domnikov, S. D. (Sergeĭ Dmitrievich) Matʹ-zemlia i TSarʹ-gorod : Rossiia kak traditsionnoe obshchestvo / S.D. Domnikov. Moskva : Aleteĭa, 2002. 671 p. ; 22 cm. (Slavianskie drevnosti) ISBN 5893210964
1. Philosophy - Russia - History. 2. Cosmology - Philosophy. 3. Slavs - Religion. 4. Mythology, Slavic. I. Title. II. Title: Rossiia kak traditsionnoe obshchestvo III. Series.
B4235.H57 D65 2002

Donaldson, Christopher.
McLuhan's wake [videorecording]. [Montreal, Quebec] : Primitive Entertainment/National Film Board of Canada, c2002.

DONATIONS. See **GIFTS.**

Donchenko, E. A. (Elena Andreevna) Arkhetypy sotsialʹnoho zhyttia i polityka : hlybynni rehuliatyvy psykhopolitychnoho povsiakdennia / Olena Donchenko, I︠U︡riĭ Romanenko. Kyïv : Lybidʹ, 2001. 334 p. : ill. ; 20 cm. Includes bibliographical references. ISBN 9660601794
1. Political psychology. 2. Identity (Psychology) - Political aspects. 3. Social psychology. 4. Archetype (Psychology) 5. Ukraine - Social conditions - 1991- I. Romanenko, I︠U︡riĭ. II. Title.
JA74.5 .D65 2001

Donegani, Jean-Marie.
Aux frontières des attitudes. Paris, France : Harmattan, c2002.

Doner, Kalia.
Holinger, Paul C. What babies say before they can talk. New York : Simon & Schuster, c2003.
BF720.C65 H64 2003

Donfrancesco, Francesco. Una poetica dell'analisi / Francesco Donfrancesco ; prefazione di James Hillman. Bergamo : Moretti & Vitali, 2000. 174 p. : ill. ; 21 cm. (Il tridente. Saggi ; 15) Originally published 1993 with the title Memorie di luce, now completely revised and enlarged. Includes bibliographical references (p. 69-174). ISBN 88-7186-168-X DDC 155
1. Psychoanalysis and art. 2. Art and mental illness. I. Domfrancesco, Francesco. Memorie di luce. II. Title. III. Series.

Dong fang mei xue dui xi fang de ying xiang.
Chen, Wei, 1957- Di 1 ban. Shanghai : Xue lin chu ban she, 1999.
BH221.C6 C444 1999

Dongfang meixue duixifang de yingxiang.
Chen, Wei, 1957- Dong fang mei xue dui xi fang de ying xiang = Di 1 ban. Shanghai : Xue lin chu ban she, 1999.
BH221.C6 C444 1999

La donna associata allo zelo sacerdotale.
Alberione, James, 1884-1971. Cinisello Balsamo, Milano : San Paolo, c2001.

Les dons de l'image / sous la direction de Alain Cambier ; Edmond Couchot ... [et al.]. Paris : Harmattan, 2003. 313 p. ; 22 cm. (Les rendez-vous d'Archimède) Includes bibliographical references (p. [307]-313). ISBN 2-7475-3868-0 DDC 194
1. Optical images. 2. Visual perception. I. Couchot, Edmond, 1932- II. Cambier, Alain. III. Series.

Don't give me that attitude!.
Borba, Michele. 1st ed. San Francisco : Jossey-Bass, c2004.
BF723.A76 B67 2004

Don't know much about history.
Davis, Kenneth C. History. 1st ed. New York : HarperCollins, c2003.
E178.25 .D37 2003

Dooley, Brendan Maurice, 1953- Morandi's last prophecy and the end of Renaissance politics / Brendan Dooley. Princeton, N.J. ; Woodstock : Princeton University Press, c2002. xii, 238 p. : ill. ; 24 cm. Includes bibliographical references and index. Table of contents URL: http://www.loc.gov/catdir/toc/prin031/2001045848.html Publisher description URL: http://www.loc.gov/catdir/desc ription/prin021/2001045848.html ISBN 0-691-04864-9 (cloth : alk. paper) DDC 133.5/0945/63209032
1. Morandi, Orazio, - d. 1630. 2. Astrologers - Italy - Biography. 3. Astrology - History - 17th century. 4. Europe - Intellectual life - 17th century. I. Title.
BF1679.8.M59 D66 2002

Dooley, Deborah. Journeying into wholeness with map & skills / Deborah Dooley. [Meno Park, Calif. : Delphi Press, c2003] 317 p. ; 26 cm. ISBN 0-9725268-0-3
1. Maturation (Psychology) 2. Self-actualization (Psychology) 3. Healing. I. Title.
BF710 .D64 2003

Doors to other worlds.
Buckland, Raymond. 1st ed. St. Paul, Minn. : Llewellyn, 2000.

Doreal, M.
The emerald tablets of Thoth-the-Atlantean. Sedalia, Colo. : Brotherhood of the White Temple, c2002.
BF1999 .E44 2002

Doreshe H.
Segal, Yehudah Zeraḥyah, ha-Levi. Sefer Doreshe H.. Tel-Aviv : Talmidav ve-shmom'e liḵho, 763 [2003]
BJ1287.S43 D66 2003

Doreshe Ha-shem.
Segal, Yehudah Zeraḥyah, ha-Levi. Sefer Doreshe H.. Tel-Aviv : Talmidav ve-shmom'e liḵho, 763 [2003]
BJ1287.S43 D66 2003

Dorff, Elliot N. Love your neighbor and yourself : a Jewish approach to modern personal ethics / Elliot N. Dorff. 1st ed. Philadelphia, PA : Jewish Publication Society, 2003. xviii, 366 p. ; 24 cm. Includes bibliographical references (p. 347-359) and index. ISBN 0-8276-0759-8 DDC 296.3/6
1. Ethics, Jewish. 2. Conduct of life. 3. Jewish way of life. 4. Philosophy, Jewish. I. Title.
BJ1285 .D67 2003

Dornseiff, Johannes. Tractatus absolutus : Selbstaufklärung des Denkens / Johannes Dornseiff. 1. Aufl. Berlin : Frieling, 2000. 892 p. ; 25 cm. (Frieling Philosophie) Includes bibliographical references and index. ISBN 3-8280-1099-7 (cl.)
1. Philosophy. I. Title.

D'Oro, Giuseppina, 1964- Collingwood and the metaphysics of experience / Giuseppina D'Oro. London ; New York : Routledge, 2002. 179 p. ; 25 cm. (Routledge studies in twentieth-century philosophy ; 13) Includes bibliographical references (p. [165]-171) and index. ISBN 0-415-23971-0 DDC 110/.92
1. Collingwood, R. G. - (Robin George), - 1889-1943 - Contributions in metaphysics. 2. Metaphysics. I. Title. II. Series.
B1618.C74 D67 2002

Dostovernostʹ i dokazatelʹnostʹ v issledovaniiakh po teorii i istorii kulʹtury / [sostavitelʹ i otvetstvennyĭ redaktor M.K. Knabe]. Moskva : RGGU, 2002. 2 v. ; 21 cm. Includes bibliographical references. ISBN 5728103464
1. Culture - Philosophy. 2. Civilization - Philosophy. 3. Culture - History. I. Knabe, G. S. (Georgiĭ Stepanovich)
HM621 .D68 2002

Dottori, Riccardo.
Gadamer, Hans Georg, 1900- Die Lektion des Jahrhunderts. Münster : Lit, [2002]

DOUBLE BIND (PSYCHOLOGY).
Berg, Barbara A. How to escape the no-win trap. New York : McGraw-Hill, c2004.
BF448 .B46 2004

A double life.
Burton, Sarah, 1963- London : Viking ; New York : Penguin Putnam, 2003.

DOUBLE (PARAPSYCHOLOGY).
Lecouteux, Claude. [Fées, sorcières et loups-garous au Moyen Age. English] Witches, werewolves, and fairies. 1st U.S. ed. Rochester, Vt. : Inner Traditions, 2003.
BF1045.D67 L4313 2003

Douglas, Nik. The Tantric Dakini oracle / Nik Douglas and Penny Slinger. Rochester, Vt. : Destiny Books, 2003. p. cm. Table of contents URL: http://www.loc.gov/catdir/toc/ecip045/2003013166.html CONTENTS: Method of the Celtic cross -- Method of the tree of life -- Method of the great universe map -- Approaching the oracle -- Part II: brief meanings of the individual cards -- Part III: the secret Dakini oracle -- Part IV: readings -- Sample I: Traditional tarot method -- Transfer to tree of life chart -- Sample II: Traditional tarot method -- Transfer to tree of life chart -- Sample III: Direct reading onto tree of life chart -- Sample IV: Direct reading onto map of the great universe -- Sample V: Direct reading onto tree of life chart. ISBN 0-89281-137-4 DDC 133.3/2424
1. Tarot. 2. Tarot cards. 3. Tantrism. I. Slinger, Penny. II. Title.
BF1879.T2 D695 2003

Douglas, Tom, 1953-.
Beavers, Brett. Something worth leaving behind. Nashville, Tenn. : Rutledge Hill Press, c2002.
BF637.S8 B383 2002

DOUGLASS, ANNA MURRAY, D. 1882 - FICTION.
Rhodes, Jewell Parker. Douglass' women. New York, NY : Atria Books, c2002.
1. Black author.

DOUGLASS, FREDERICK, 1818-1895 - FICTION.
Rhodes, Jewell Parker. Douglass' women. New York, NY : Atria Books, c2002.
1. Black author.

Douglass' women.
Rhodes, Jewell Parker. New York, NY : Atria Books, c2002.

La douleur en soi.
Croix, Laurence. Ramonville Saint-Agne (France) : Erès, c2002.

DOULL, JAMES - CONTRIBUTIONS IN THE PHILOSOPHY OF LIBERTY.
Philosophy and freedom. Toronto : University of Toronto Press, c2003.

Douno, Beinsa, 1864-1944. In the kingdom of living nature / Beinsa Douno (The Master Peter Dunov) Sofia : Bialo Bratstvo, c2000. 117 p. : 1 col. ill. ; 18 cm. "This is a translation by Vessela Nestorova of the original Bulgarian lectures of the Master Beinsa Douno." ISBN 954744008X
1. Human evolution - Miscellanea. 2. Panslavism - Miscellanea. I. Title.

Douzet, André. Nouvelles lumières sur Rennes-le-Château / André Douzet. Chêne-Bourg (Suisse) : Acquarius, c1998- v. <1 > : ill. (some col.) ; 21 cm. Includes bibliographical references (v. 1, p. 187-188). ISBN 2-88165-048-1 DDC 133/.0944/154
1. Occultism - France - Rennes-le-Château. 2. Saunière, Bérenger, - 1852-1917. 3. Mary Magdalene, - Saint - Miscellanea. 4. Treasure-trove - France - Rennes-le-Château. 5. Rennes-le-Château (France) - History - Miscellanea. I. Title.
BF1434.F8 D69 1998

Dover mesharim.
Mermelshṭain, Avraham Yitsḥak David. Ḳuntres Dover mesharim. Hotsaʾah 2. [Brooklyn] : A.Y.D. Mermelshṭain, 762 [2001]

Dow, Sheila C.
Beyond Keynes. Cheltenham ; Northampton, Mass. : Edward Elgar, c2002.

Dowler, Lorraine.
Gendered landscapes. University Park, PA : Center for Studies in Landscape History, c2000.

Dowling, Linda Culp. Mentor manager, mentor parent : how to develop responsible people and build successful relationships at work and at home / Linda Culp Dowling, Cecile Culp Mielenz. Burneyville, OK : ComCon Books., c2002. viii, 236 p. : ill. ; 24 cm. ISBN 0-9722782-4-9 DDC 158.2
1. Mentoring. 2. Counseling. 3. Mentoring in business. 4. Mentoring in the professions. 5. Child rearing. I. Mielenz, Cecile Culp. II. Title.
BF637.C6 D6185 2002

Downs, Hugh.
My America. New York : Scribner, c2002.
E169.1 .M968 2002

Downs, Timothy M.
Patton, Bobby R., 1935- Decision-making group interaction. 4th ed. Boston : Allyn and Bacon, c2003.

HM736 .P37 2003

DOWSING.
Applegate, George. The complete book of dowsing. Shaftesbury, Dorset ; Rockport, Mass. : Element, c1997.
BF1628 .A67 1997

Grace, Raymon. The future is yours. Charlottesville, VA : Hampton Roads Pub., c2003.
BF639 .G64 2003

Dr. Freud.
Young Dr. Freud [electronic resource]. [Alexandria, Va.?] : PBS, 2002.
BF109.F74

Dr. Tatiana's sex advice to all creation.
Judson, Olivia. 1st ed. New York : Metropolitan Books, 2002.
HQ25 .J83 2002

DRAFT DODGERS. *See* DRAFT RESISTERS.

DRAFT RESISTERS - FICTION.
Kingston, Maxine Hong. The fifth book of peace. 1st ed. New York : Alfred A. Knopf, 2003.
PS3561.I52 F44 2003

O dragão pousou no espaço.
Wanderley, Lula. Rio de Janerio : Rocco, 2002. A.

DRAGONS. *See* ANIMALS, MYTHICAL.

DRAGONS - CHINA - FOLKLORE.
Suckling, Nigel. Legends & lore. New York : Friedman/Fairfax Publishers ; Distributed by Sterling Pub., c2002.
BF1714.C5 S93 2002

Drake, Susan M.
Crouch, Chris. Simple works. Memphis, TN : Black Pants Pub., c2001.
BF637.C5 C78 2001

DRAMA CRITICISM.
Inédits et commentaires. Paris : L'Arche, 2002.

DRAMA - HISTORY AND CRITICISM.
Inédits et commentaires. Paris : L'Arche, 2002.

Land/scape/theater. Ann Arbor : University of Michigan, c2002.
PN2020 .L32 2002

Mangan, Michael, 1953- Staging masculinities. Houndmills, Basingstoke, Hampshire : New York : Palgrave Macmillan, 2003.
PN1650.M44 M36 2003

Roland, Alan, 1930- Dreams and drama. 1st US ed. Middletown, CT : Wesleyan University Press, 2003.
BF408 .R65 2003

Roland, Alan, 1930- Dreams and drama. 1st US ed. Middletown, CT : Wesleyan University Press, 2003.
BF408 .R65 2003

Rolland, Romain, 1866-1944. Le théâtre du peuple. Nouvelle éd. Bruxelles : Complexe, c2003.
PN1655 .R68 2003

Texte et théâtralité. Nancy : Presses universitaires de Nancy, 2000.

DRAMA IN EDUCATION.
Ressler, Paula. Dramatic changes. Portsmouth, NH : Heinemann, c2002.
PN3171 .R47 2002

DRAMA, MODERN. *See* DRAMA.

DRAMA - PHILOSOPHY. *See* DRAMA.

DRAMA - PSYCHOLOGICAL ASPECTS.
Tucker, Kenneth. Shakespeare and Jungian typology. Jefferson, N.C. ; London : McFarland & Co., c2003.
PR3065 .T83 2003

Dramatic changes.
Ressler, Paula. Portsmouth, NH : Heinemann, c2002.
PN3171 .R47 2002

DRAMATIC MUSIC. *See* OPERAS.

Drankov, V. L. (Vladimir L'vovich) Priroda khudozhestvennogo talanta / V.L. Drankov. Sankt-Peterburg : Sankt-Peterburgskiĭ gos. universitet kul'tury i iskusstv, 2001. 323 p. : ill. ; 20 cm. Includes bibliographical references.
1. Creation (Literary, artistic, etc.) 2. Creative ability. 3. Pushkin, Aleksandr Sergeevich, - 1799-1837. 4. Lermontov, Mikhail I͡Ur'evich, - 1814-1841. 5. Chaliapin, Fyodor Ivanovich, - 1873-1938. I. Title.
BF408 .D66 2001

Priroda khudozhestvennogo talanta / V.L. Drankov. Sankt-Peterburg : Sankt-Peterburgskiĭ gosudarstvennyĭ universitet kul'tury i iskusstv, 2001. 323 p. : ill. ; 20 cm. Includes bibliographical references. At head of title: Ministerstvo Kul'tury Rossiĭskoĭ Federatsii. Sankt-Peterburgskiĭ gos. universitet kul'tury i iskusstv.
1. Pushkin, Aleksandr Sergeevich, - 1799-1837 - Criticism and interpretation. 2. Chaliapin, Fyodor Ivanovich, - 1873-1938 - Criticism and interpretation. 3. Lermontov, Mikhail I͡Ur'evich, - 1814-1841 - Criticism and interpretation. 4. Creation (Literary, artistic, etc.) 5. Creative ability. I. Russia (Federation). Ministerstvo kul'tury. II. Title.

Drapeau, Anne Seibold.
Galford, Robert M., 1952- The trusted leader. New York ; London : Free Press, c2002.
HD57.7 .G33 2002

DRAW-A-FAMILY TEST.
Draw-a-family test in psychological research. Lublin : Towarzystwo Naukowe Katolickiego Uniwersytetu Lubelskiego, 2002.
BF698.8.D68 D73 2002

Draw-a-family test in psychological research / edited by Bogusława Lachowska, Mariola Łaguna. Lublin : Towarzystwo Naukowe Katolickiego Uniwersytetu Lubelskiego, 2002. 160 p. : col. ill. ; 24 cm. (Źródła i monografie / Towarzystwo Naukowe Katolickiego Uniwersytetu Lubelskiego ; 230) Includes bibliographical references. ISBN 83-7306-078-2
1. Draw-A-Family Test. I. Laguna, Mariola. II. Lachowska, Bogusława. III. Series: Źródła i monografie (Katolicki Uniwersytet Lubelski. Towarzystwo Naukowe) ; 230.
BF698.8.D68 D73 2002

DRAWING. *See* CHILDREN'S DRAWINGS.

DRAWING - PSYCHOLOGICAL ASPECTS.
Revoir, Katherine Q. Spiritual doodles & mental leapfrogs. Boston, MA : Red Wheel, 2002.
BF697.5.S427 R48 2002

DRAWING, PSYCHOLOGY OF. *See* GRAPHOLOGY.

DRAWINGS. *See* DRAWING.

DRAWINGS, CHILDREN'S. *See* CHILDREN'S DRAWINGS.

DRAY, KARINE.
Dray, Maryvonne. Karine après la vie. Paris : Albin Michel, c2002.

Dray, Maryvonne. Karine après la vie : le témoignage de Maryvonne et Yvon Dray sur l'incroyable aventure de leur fille dans l'au-delà / [Maryvonne et Yvon Dray] ; présenté par Didier van Cauwelaert. Paris : Albin Michel, c2002. 171 p. : ill. ; 23 cm. Includes bibliographical references. ISBN 2-226-13430-1 DDC 130
1. Dray, Karine. 2. Spirit writings. 3. Future life. 4. Spiritualism. I. Dray, Yvon. II. Cauwelaert, Didier van, 1960- III. Title.

Dray, Yvon.
Dray, Maryvonne. Karine après la vie. Paris : Albin Michel, c2002.

Drayer, Ruth. Numerology : the power in numbers : a right & left brain approach / Ruth Abrams Drayer. 3rd ed. Mesilla, N.M. : Jewels of Light Pub., 2002. 236 p. : ill. ; 22 cm. Includes bibliographical references (p. 215-216). ISBN 0-9640321-3-9 (pbk.) DDC 133.3/35
1. Numerology. 2. Symbolism of numbers. I. Title.
BF1623.P9 D72 2002

DREAM ANALYSIS. *See* DREAM INTERPRETATION.

Dream book.
Bluestone, Sarvananda. The world dream book. Rochester, Vt. : Destiny Books, c2002.
BF1091 .B616 2002

Dream dictionary San Diego, CA : Thunder Bay Press, 2003. p. cm. ISBN 1-57145-994-4 DDC 154.6/3/03
1. Dream interpretation - Dictionaries. 2. Symbolism (Psychology) - Dictionaries.
BF1091 .D69 2003

The dream in native American and other primitive cultures.
Lincoln, Jackson Steward, 1902-1941. [Dream in primitive cultures] Mineola, N.Y. : Dover Publications, 2003.
BF1078 .L5 2003

A dream in the world.
Van Löben Sels, Robin E., 1938- New York, NY : Brunner-Routledge, 2003.
BF175.5.D74 V36 2003

DREAM INTERPRETATION.
Abadie, M. J. (Marie-Jeanne) Teen dream power. Rochester, Vt. : Bindu Books, 2003.
BF1099 .T43 2003

Abadie, M. J. (Marie-Jeanne) Teen dream power. Rochester, Vt. : Bindu Books, 2003.
BF1099 .T43 2003

Abiṭbul, Yosef Ḥayim, d. 1998. Ma'agar ha-halomot u-fitronam. Kiryat Gat : Elisha' Abiṭbul, 762 [2002]
BM496.9.D73 A25 2002

Bluestone, Sarvananda. The world dream book. Rochester, Vt. : Destiny Books, c2002.
BF1091 .B616 2002

Bulkeley, Kelly, 1962- Dreams of healing. New York : Paulist Press, c2003.
BF1099.N53 B85 2003

Clarke, Robert B. The four gold keys. Charlottesville, VA : Hampton Roads Pub., c2002.
BF175.5.D74 C58 2002

Dreaming and the self. Albany : State University of New York Press, c2003.
BF1091 .D735 2003

Edgar, Iain R. Guide to imagework. London ; New York : Routledge, 2004.
BF367 .E34 2004

Gibson, Clare K., 1964- The secret life of dreams. San Diego, Calif. : Thunder Bay Press, 2004.
BF1091 .G49 2004

Gillentine, Julie. Tarot & dream interpretation. 1st ed. St. Paul, Minn. : Llewellyn Publications 2003.
BF1879.T2 G585 2003

Gollub, Dan. Interpreting and understanding dreams. Comack, N.Y. : Nova Science Publishers, c1998.
BF1091 .G653 1998

Goodison, Lucy. The dreams of women. 1st American ed. New York : W.W. Norton, 1996.
BF1078 .G475 1996

Hamilton-Parker, Craig. Fantasy dreaming. New York : Sterling Pub., c2002.
BF1091 .H347 2002

Iskusstvo snovideniĭ = Sankt-Peterburg : Skifii͡a, 2002.
NX180.D74 I74 2002

Kallen, Stuart A., 1955- Dreams. San Diego, Calif. : Lucent Books, 2004.
BF1099.C55 K35 2004

Ochs, Vanessa L. The Jewish dream book. Woodstock, VT : Jewish Lights Publishing, 2003.
BF1078 .O24 2003

Smirnov, Terentiĭ. Psikhologii͡a snovideniĭ. Moskva : "KSP+", 2001.
BF175.5.D74 S5 2001

Steiner, Rudolf, 1861-1925. [Lectures. English. Selections] Sleep and dreams. 1st ed. Great Barrington, MA : SteinerBooks, 2003.
BF1091 .S715213 2003

Sullivan, Kathleen, 1941- Recurring dream symbols. New York : Paulist Press, c2004.
BF1091 .S813 2004

DREAM INTERPRETATION - CASE STUDIES.
Burch, Wanda Easter, 1947- She who dreams. Novato, Calif. : New World Library, c2003.
BF1099.W65 B87 2003

Van Löben Sels, Robin E., 1938- A dream in the world. New York, NY : Brunner-Routledge, 2003.
BF175.5.D74 V36 2003

DREAM INTERPRETATION - DICTIONARIES.
Cross, Amanda. Children's dream dictionary. London : Hamlyn ; New York : Distributed in the U.S. by Sterling Pub., 2002.
BF1099.C55 C76 2002

Dream dictionary San Diego, CA : Thunder Bay Press, 2003.
BF1091 .D69 2003

MacGregor, Rob. Dreams. Philadelphia, Pa. : Running Press, c2002.
BF1091 .M314 2002

Phillips, Sara. Dream symbols. Philadelphia, Pa. : Courage Books, c2002.
BF1091 .P46 2002

DREAM INTERPRETATION - DICTIONARIES - JUVENILE LITERATURE.
Collier-Thompson, Kristi. The girls' guide to dreams. New York : Sterling Pub., c2003.
BF1099.C55 C65 2003

DREAM INTERPRETATION - DICTIONARIES - LATVIAN.
Senie latviešu sapņu skaidrojumi. [Rīga] : Tapals, 2002.
BF1098.L35 S46 2002

DREAM INTERPRETATION - DICTIONARIES - SPANISH.
Jiménez Castillo, Mario. Diccionario de los sueños. St. Paul, Minn. : Llewellyn Español, 2003.
BF1095 .J56 2003

DREAM INTERPRETATION - HISTORY.
Dreams and history. 1st ed. New York, NY : Brunner-Routledge, 2003.
BF1078 .D735 2003

Marinelli, Lydia. Dreaming by the book. New York : Other Press, c2003.
BF175.5.D74 F7436 2003

Marinelli, Lydia. Träume nach Freud. Wien : Turia + Kant, c2002.

DREAM INTERPRETATION - HISTORY - TO 1500.
Walde, Christine, 1960- Antike Traumdeutung und moderne Traumforschung. Düsseldorf : Artemis & Winkler, c2001.

DREAM INTERPRETATION IN RABBINICAL LITERATURE.
Ochs, Vanessa L. The Jewish dream book. Woodstock, VT : Jewish Lights Publishing, 2003.
BF1078 .O24 2003

Shekalim, Rami. Torat ha-ḥalom ba-Yahadut. Tel Aviv : R. Shekalim, 762, 2002.

DREAM INTERPRETATION - JUVENILE LITERATURE.
Kallen, Stuart A., 1955- Dreams. San Diego, Calif. : Lucent Books, 2004.
BF1099.C55 K35 2004

Dream magic.
Knight, Sirona, 1955- 1st ed. San Francisco : HarperSanFrancisco, c2000.
BF1621 .K65 2000

The dream of civilized warfare.
Robertson, Linda R. (Linda Raine), 1946- Minneapolis : University of Minnesota Press, c2003.
D606 .R63 2003

Dream symbols.
Phillips, Sara. Philadelphia, Pa. : Courage Books, c2002.
BF1091 .P46 2002

The dreambody in relationships.
Mindell, Arnold, 1940- Portland, OR : Lao Tse Press ; Oakland, CA : Distributed to the trade by Words Distributing Co., c2002.
BF637.N66 M56 2002

The dreamer's way.
Guiley, Rosemary. New York : Berkley Books, 2004.
BF1099.S36 G85 2004

DREAMING. See **DREAMS.**

Dreaming and the self : new perspectives on subjectivity, identity, and emotion / edited by Jeannette Marie Mageo. Albany : State University of New York Press, c2003. vi, 234 p. ; 23 cm. (SUNY series in dream studies) Includes bibliographical references (p. 199-222) and index. Table of contents URL: http://www.loc.gov/catdir/toc/fy038/2002030973.html ISBN 0-7914-5788-5 (pbk.) ISBN 0-7914-5787-7 DDC 154.6/3
1. Dreams. 2. Dream interpretation. 3. Self. 4. Identity (Psychology) I. Mageo, Jeannette Marie. II. Series.
BF1091 .D735 2003

Dreaming by the book.
Marinelli, Lydia. New York : Other Press, c2003.
BF175.5.D74 F7436 2003

Dreaming of Cockaigne.
Pleij, Herman. [Dromen van Cocagne. English] New York : Columbia University Press, c2001.
CB353 .P5413 2001

Dreamlife.
Goodwin, Rufus. 1st ed. Great Barrington, MA : Lindisfarne Books, 2004.
BF1081 .G66 2004

DREAMS. See also **CHILDREN'S DREAMS; FANTASY; WOMEN'S DREAMS.**
Kallen, Stuart A., 1955- San Diego, Calif. : Lucent Books, 2004.
BF1099.C55 K35 2004

MacGregor, Rob. Philadelphia, Pa. : Running Press, c2002.
BF1091 .M314 2002

DREAMS.
Abadie, M. J. (Marie-Jeanne) Teen dream power. Rochester, Vt. : Bindu Books, 2003.
BF1099 .T43 2003

Bluestone, Sarvananda. The world dream book. Rochester, Vt. : Destiny Books, c2002.
BF1091 .B616 2002

Bulkeley, Kelly, 1962- Dreams of healing. New York : Paulist Press, c2003.
BF1099.N53 B85 2003

Clarke, Robert B. The four gold keys. Charlottesville, VA : Hampton Roads Pub., c2002.
BF175.5.D74 C58 2002

Collier-Thompson, Kristi. The girls' guide to dreams. New York : Sterling Pub., c2003.
BF1099.C55 C65 2003

Dreaming and the self. Albany : State University of New York Press, c2003.
BF1091 .D735 2003

Giachery, Emerico. L'avventura del sogno. Roma : A. Stango, 2002.

Gollub, Dan. Interpreting and understanding dreams. Comack, N.Y. : Nova Science Publishers, c1998.
BF1091 .G653 1998

Goodison, Lucy. The dreams of women. 1st American ed. New York : W.W. Norton, 1996.
BF1078 .G475 1996

Goodwin, Rufus. Dreamlife. 1st ed. Great Barrington, MA : Lindisfarne Books, 2004.
BF1081 .G66 2004

Guiley, Rosemary. The dreamer's way. New York : Berkley Books, 2004.
BF1099.S36 G85 2004

Halpern, Leslie, 1960- Dreams on film. Jefferson, NC : London : McFarland, 2003.

Hamilton-Parker, Craig. Fantasy dreaming. New York : Sterling Pub., c2002.
BF1091 .H347 2002

Herzog, Edgar. [Psyche und Tod. English] Psyche and death. New ed. / edited and designed by C.L. Sebrell. Woodstock, Conn. : Spring Publications, c2000.

Jovanović, Tihomir. Nepoznati svet snova. Beograd : IPA "Miroslav", 2000.
BF1078 .J69 2000

Kallen, Stuart A., 1955- Dreams. San Diego, Calif. : Lucent Books, 2004.
BF1099.C55 K35 2004

Knight, Sirona, 1955- Dream magic. 1st ed. San Francisco : HarperSanFrancisco, c2000.
BF1621 .K65 2000

Lincoln, Jackson Steward, 1902-1941. [Dream in primitive cultures] The dream in native American and other primitive cultures. Mineola, N.Y. : Dover Publications, 2003.
BF1078 .L5 2003

Mindell, Arnold, 1940- The dreambody in relationships. Portland, OR : Lao Tse Press ; Oakland, CA : Distributed to the trade by Words Distributing Co., c2002.
BF637.N66 M56 2002

Smirnov, Terentiĭ. Psikhologiia snovideniĭ. Moskva : "KSP+", 2001.
BF175.5.D74 S5 2001

Steiner, Rudolf, 1861-1925. [Lectures. English. Selections] Sleep and dreams. 1st ed. Great Barrington, MA : SteinerBooks, 2003.
BF1091 .S715213 2003

Le système et le rêve. Paris : Harmattan, c2002.
BF1078 .S97 2002

Dreams and drama.
Roland, Alan, 1930- 1st US ed. Middletown, CT : Wesleyan University Press, 2003.
BF408 .R65 2003

Roland, Alan, 1930- 1st US ed. Middletown, CT : Wesleyan University Press, 2003.
BF408 .R65 2003

Dreams and history / [edited by] Daniel Pick and Lyndal Roper. 1st ed. New York, NY : Brunner-Routledge, 2003. p. cm. Includes bibliographical references and index. Table of contents URL: http://www.loc.gov/catdir/toc/ecip041/2003006202.html CONTENTS: How Freud wrote and revised his Interpretation of dreams / by Ilse Grubrich-Simitis ; translated from the German by Arnold J. Pomerans -- Dreams and desire in ancient and early Christian thought -- Interpreting dreams in medieval literature / by Hans-Jurgen Bachorski ; translated from the German by Pamela E. Selwyn -- Women's dreams in early modern England / by Patricia Crawford -- Samuel Taylor Coleridge and the pains of sleep / by Jennifer Ford -- The meaning of dream books / by Maureen Perkins -- Artists and the dream in nineteenth-century Paris : towards a prehistory of surrealism / by Stefanie Heracus ; translated from the German by Deborah Laurie Cohen -- Policing dreams : history and the moral uses of the unconscious / by Rhodri Hayward -- The dreambook in Russia / by Faith Wigzell -- A nice type of the English scientist : Tansley and Freud / by Laura Cameron and John Forrester -- Psychoanalysis, dreams, history : an interview with Hanna Segal by Daniel Pick and Lyndal Roper -- A dream to dream / by Edna O'Shaughnessy -- The shark behind the sofa : recent developments in the theory of dreams / by Susan Budd. ISBN 1-58391-282-7 (alk. paper) ISBN 1-58391-283-5 (pbk. : alk. paper) DDC 154.6/3/09
1. Dreams - History. 2. Dream interpretation - History. I. Pick, Daniel. II. Roper, Lyndal.
BF1078 .D735 2003

DREAMS AND THE ARTS.
Iskusstvo snovideniĭ = Sankt-Peterburg : Skifiia, 2002.
NX180.D74 I74 2002

DREAMS - CASE STUDIES.
Maisel, Eric, 1947- Sleep thinking. Holbrook, Mass. : Adams Media Corp., c2000.
BF1099.P75 M35 2000

DREAMS - DICTIONARIES.
Zolar. Zolar's encyclopedia and dictionary of dreams. Fully rev. and updated for the 21st century. New York : Simon & Schuster, 2004.
BF1091 .Z65 2004

DREAMS - ENCYCLOPEDIAS.
Zolar. Zolar's encyclopedia and dictionary of dreams. Fully rev. and updated for the 21st century. New York : Simon & Schuster, 2004.
BF1091 .Z65 2004

DREAMS - FOLKLORE.
Sny i videniia v narodnoĭ kul'ture. Moskva : RGGU, 2002.
BF1078 .S563 2002

Dreams from God.
Gemmen, Heather. Colorado Springs, Colo. : Faith Kidz, 2003.
BF1099.B5 G46 2003

DREAMS - HISTORY.
Dreams and history. 1st ed. New York, NY : Brunner-Routledge, 2003.
BF1078 .D735 2003

Rossi, Paolo, 1923- Bambini, sogni, furori. 1. ed. in "Campi del sapere.". Milano : Feltrinelli, 2001.
BF41 .R67 2001

DREAMS - HISTORY - TO 1500.
Walde, Christine, 1960- Antike Traumdeutung und moderne Traumforschung. Düsseldorf : Artemis & Winkler, c2001.

DREAMS IN ART.
Iskusstvo snovideniĭ = Sankt-Peterburg : Skifiia, 2002.
NX180.D74 I74 2002

DREAMS IN LITERATURE.
Giachery, Emerico. L'avventura del sogno. Roma : A. Stango, 2002.

DREAMS IN MOTION PICTURES.
Halpern, Leslie, 1960- Dreams on film. Jefferson, NC : London : McFarland, 2003.

DREAMS IN THE BIBLE.
Gemmen, Heather. Dreams from God. Colorado Springs, Colo. : Faith Kidz, 2003.
BF1099.B5 G46 2003

Na'or, Betsal'el. Bringing down dreams. 1st ed. Spring Valley, NY : Orot, c2002.
BF1099 .N28 2002

Quaglia, Rocco. I sogni della Bibbia. Roma : Borla, c2002.

Shekalim, Rami. Torat ha-ḥalom ba-Yahadut. Tel Aviv : R. Shekalim, 762, 2002.

DREAMS IN THE BIBLE - JUVENILE LITERATURE.
Gemmen, Heather. Dreams from God. Colorado Springs, Colo. : Faith Kidz, 2003.
BF1099.B5 G46 2003

DREAMS - INTERPRETATION.
Cifali, Mario. Trois rêves freudiens. Paris : Eshel, c1999.

Dreams of healing

BF175.5.O33 C54 1999

Dreams of healing.
Bulkeley, Kelly, 1962- New York : Paulist Press, c2003.
BF1099.N53 B85 2003

The dreams of women.
Goodison, Lucy. 1st American ed. New York : W.W. Norton, 1996.
BF1078 .G475 1996

Dreams on film.
Halpern, Leslie, 1960- Jefferson, NC : London : McFarland, 2003.

DREAMS - RELIGIOUS ASPECTS.
Guiley, Rosemary. The dreamer's way. New York : Berkley Books, 2004.
BF1099.S36 G85 2004

Steiner, Rudolf, 1861-1925. [Lectures. English. Selections] Sleep and dreams. 1st ed. Great Barrington, MA : SteinerBooks, 2003.
BF1091 .S715213 2003

DREAMS - RELIGIOUS ASPECTS - CHRISTIANITY - CASE STUDIES.
Van Löben Sels, Robin E., 1938- A dream in the world. New York, NY : Brunner-Routledge, 2003.
BF175.5.D74 V36 2003

DREAMS - RELIGIOUS ASPECTS - HISTORY - CONGRESSES.
Prayer, magic, and the stars in the ancient and late antique world. University Park, Pa. : Pennsylvania State University Press, 2003.
BF1591 .P73 2003

DREAMS - RELIGIOUS ASPECTS - JUDAISM.
Abiṭbul, Yosef Ḥayim, d. 1998. Ma'agar ha-halomot u-fitronam. Kiryat Gat : Elisha' Abiṭbul, 762 [2002]
BM496.9.D73 A25 2002

Na'or, Betsal'el. Bringing down dreams. 1st ed. Spring Valley, NY : Orot, c2002.
BF1078 .N28 2002

Ochs, Vanessa L. The Jewish dream book. Woodstock, VT : Jewish Lights Publishing, 2003.
BF1078 .O24 2003

Shekalim, Rami. Torat ha-halom ba-Yahadut. Tel Aviv : R. Shekalim, 762, 2002.

DREAMS - THERAPEUTIC USE.
Burch, Wanda Easter, 1947- She who dreams. Novato, Calif. : New World Library, c2003.
BF1099.W65 B87 2003

DREAMS - THERAPEUTIC USE - CASE STUDIES.
Van Löben Sels, Robin E., 1938- A dream in the world. New York, NY : Brunner-Routledge, 2003.
BF175.5.D74 V36 2003

Dreller, Larry. Secrets of a medium / Larry Dreller. Boston, MA : Weiser Books, 2003. xi, 129 p. ; 22 cm. Includes bibliographical references (p. [125]-129). Table of contents URL: http://www.loc.gov/catdir/toc/ecip042/2003008669.html CONTENTS: The survival hypothesis -- Mugged by death -- What is a medium? -- Into the invisible realm -- Spirituality, soulwash, and repair -- The grand conclusion -- Meditational exercises. ISBN 1-57863-283-8 DDC 133.9/1
1. Parapsychology. 2. Mediums. 3. Spiritual life. I. Title.
BF1031 .D69 2003

DRESS. See **CLOTHING AND DRESS.**

Dressler, Wolfgang U., 1939-.
Development of verb inflection in first language acquisition. Berlin ; New York : Mouton de Gruyter, 2003.
P118 .D465 2003

Dretske, Fred I. Perception, knowledge, and belief : selected essays / Fred Dretske. Cambridge, U.K. ; New York : Cambridge University Press, 2000. xii, 284 p. ; 23 cm. (Cambridge studies in philosophy) Includes bibliographical references and index. Sample text URL: http://www.loc.gov/catdir/samples/cam032/99015973.html Publisher description URL: http://www.loc.gov/catdir/description/cam029/99015973.html Table of contents URL: http://www.loc.gov/catdir/toc/cam025/99015973.html ISBN 0-521-77181-1 ISBN 0-521-77742-9 (pbk.) DDC 121/.092
1. Knowledge, Theory of. 2. Philosophy of mind. I. Title. II. Series.
BD161 .D73 2000

Drew, A. J. God/goddess : exploring and celebrating the two sides of wiccan deity / by AJ Drew & Patricia Telesco. Franklin Lakes, N.J. : New Page Books, 2003. p. cm. ISBN 1-56414-692-8 (pbk.) DDC 299/.94
1. Witchcraft. 2. Gods - Miscellanea. 3. Goddesses - Miscellanea. I. Telesco, Patricia, 1960- II. Title.
BF1571 .D73 2003

Wicca for couples : making magick together / by A.J. Drew. Franklin Lakes, NJ : New Page Books, c2002. 223 p. ; 21 cm. Includes bibliographical references (p. 215-216) and index. ISBN 1-56414-620-0 (pbk.) DDC 299
1. Witchcraft. 2. Love - Miscellanea. I. Title.
BF1572.L6 D74 2002

Wicca spellcraft for men : a spellbook for male pagans / A.J. Drew. Franklin Lakes, N.J. : New Page Books, c2001. 255 p. ; 21 cm. Includes bibliographical references (p. 247-249) and index. ISBN 1-56414-495-X DDC 133.4/4
1. Witchcraft. 2. Men - Miscellanea. I. Title.
BF1571.5.M45 D75 2001

A Wiccan Bible : exploring the mysteries of the craft from birth to summerland / by A.J. Drew. Franklin Lakes, N.J. : New Page Books, c2003. 430 p. : ill., map ; 26 cm. Includes bibliographical references (p. 419-424) and index. ISBN 1-56414-666-9 (pbk.) DDC 299
1. Witchcraft. I. Title.
BF1571 .D74 2003

Drewery, Wendy.
Bird, Lise. Human development in Aotearoa. Sidney ; New York : McGraw-Hill, c2000.
BF713 .B57 2000

Drews, Annette. Guardians of the society : witches among the Kunda and the Yoruba / Annette Drews. Leipzig, Germany : Institut für Afrikanistik, Universität Leipzig, 2000. 24 p. ; 30 cm. (University of Leipzig papers on Africa. Politics and economics series ; no. 31) Includes bibliographical references (p. 23-24). ISBN 3-932632-57-5 (pbk.) DDC 133.4/096894
1. Witchcraft - Zambia. 2. Witchcraft - Nigeria. 3. Human reproduction - Effect of witchcraft on - Zambia. 4. Human reproduction - Effect of witchcraft on - Nigeria. 5. Matrilineal kinship - Zambia. 6. Patrilineal kinship - Nigeria. 7. Kunda (African people) - Zambia - Religion. 8. Yoruba (African people) - Nigeria - Religion. I. Title. II. Series.
BF1584.Z33 D44 2000

Drews, Sibylle.
Die Gegenwart der Psychoanalyse, die Psychoanalyse der Gegenwart. 2. Aufl. Stuttgart : Klett-Cotta, 2002.

Dri med śel goṅ daṅ śel phreṅ, 1725-.
Cai hui gong xu ming jian.
Xizang fo jiao cai hui cai su yi shu. Di 1 ban. Beijing : Zhongguo Zang xue chu ban she : Xin hua shu dian Beijing fa xing suo fa xing, 1997.
ND1489 .X593 1997

Driekwart eeuw psychotechniek in Nederland : de magie van het testen / Pieter J. van Strien en Jacques Dane (red.) ; met medewerking van Peter van Drunen ... [et al.]. Assen : Van Gorcum, 2001. x, 229 p. : ill. ; 25 cm. Festschrift to celebrate the 75th anniversary of Nederlandse Stichting voor Psychotechniek (NSvP). Errata slip inserted. Includes bibliographical references. ISBN 90-232-3677-7
1. Nederlandse Stichting voor Psychotechniek - History. 2. Psychology, Industrial - Netherlands. 3. Work - Psychological aspects. 4. Personnel management - Netherlands. I. Strien, P. J. van. II. Dane, J. III. Nederlandse Stichting voor Psychotechniek.
HF5548.8 .D73 2001

DRINKERS, PROBLEM. See **ALCOHOLICS.**

DRINKING CUSTOMS - EUROPE - HISTORY - TO 1500.
Verdon, Jean. Boire au moyen âge. [Paris] : Perrin, c2002.

DRINKS. See **BEVERAGES.**

DRIVE (PSYCHOLOGY). See **MOTIVATION (PSYCHOLOGY).**

Driver, Betty, 1920- Betty : the autobiography / Betty Driver with Daran Little. Large print ed. Long Preston : Magna, 2000. 346 p. ; 23 cm. Originally published: London: Granada Media, 2000. ISBN 0-7505-1700-X DDC 791.45028092
1. Driver, Betty, 1920- 2. Television actors and actresses - Great Britain - Biography. 3. Large type books. I. Little, Daran. II. Title.

DRIVER, BETTY, 1920-.
Driver, Betty, 1920- Betty. Large print ed. Long Preston : Magna, 2000.

Dro da šemokmedi.
Amašukeli, Elguja. T'bilisi : "Merani", 2000.
BF408 .A475 2000

Droit, Roger-Pol. Fous comme des sages : scènes grecques et romaines / Roger-Pol Droit, Jean-Philippe de Tonnac. Paris : Seuil, c2002. 227, [1] p. ; 21 cm. Includes bibliographical references (p. 227-[228]). ISBN 2-02-052473-2 DDC 180
1. Philosophy, Ancient. I. Tonnac, Jean-Philippe de. II. Title.

Drop of dreams.
Okanoue, Toshiko. Tucson, AZ : Nazraeli Press, c2002.

DRUG ADDICTS. See **NARCOTIC ADDICTS.**

DRUG INDUSTRY. See **PHARMACEUTICAL INDUSTRY.**

DRUG TRADE. See **PHARMACEUTICAL INDUSTRY.**

Drügh, Heinz J., 1965-.
Hermetik. Tübingen : M. Niemeyer Verlag, c2002.
BF1586 .H47 2002

DRUGS. See **GENERIC DRUGS.**

DRUGS, GENERIC. See **GENERIC DRUGS.**

DRUGS - GENERIC SUBSTITUTION. See **GENERIC DRUGS.**

DRUGS - PATENTS - UNITED STATES.
United States. Congress. House. Committee on Energy and Commerce. Subcommittee on Health. Examining issues related to competition in the pharmaceutical marketplace. Washington : U.S. G.P.O. : For sale by the Supt. of Docs., U.S. G.P.O. [Congressional Sales Office], 2002.

DRUIDS AND DRUIDISM.
Imbrogno, Philip J, Celtic mysteries in New England. 1st ed. St. Paul, Minn. : Llewellyn Publications, 2000.
BF2050 I435 2000

Mountfort, Paul Rhys. Ogam, the Celtic oracle of the trees. Rochester, Vt. : Destiny Books, c2002.
PB1217 .M68 2002

Snyder, Christopher A. (Christopher Allen), 1966- The Britons. Malden, MA ; Oxford : Blackwell Pub., 2003.
DA140 .S73 2003

DRUIDS AND DRUIDISM - MISCELLANEA.
The lost books of Merlyn. 1st ed. St. Paul, Minn : Llewellyn Publications, 1998 (2003 printing)
BF1622.C45 L67 1998

Druḳ, Yaʻaḳov ben Zalman. Ohel Yaʻaḳov : daʻat hokhmah u-musar be-farashiyot ha-Torah u-mo'ade ha-shanah / me-et Yaʻaḳov b. a.a.m. ye-r. Zalman Druḳ. Yerushala[yi]m : Y. ben Z. Druḳ, 762 [2002] 3 v. ; 24 cm. CONTENTS: ḥeleḳ 1. Shabat Sukot-15 bi-Shevaṭ -- ḥeleḳ 2. Shekalim-Shevi'i shel Pesaḥ -- ḥeleḳ 3. 27 Nisan-15 be-Av.
1. Bible. - O.T. - Pentateuch - Sermons. 2. Festival-day sermons, Jewish. 3. Ethics, Jewish. 4. Jewish sermons, Hebrew. I. Title.
BS1225.4 .D77 2002

Drummond, Robert J. Appraisal procedures for counselors and helping professionals / Robert J. Drummond. 5th ed. Upper Saddle River, N.J. : Merrill/Prentice Hall, 2003. p. cm. Includes bibliographical references and indexes. CONTENTS: Historical and philosophical foundations of appraisal -- Legal and ethical issues -- Statistical concepts -- Measurement concepts -- Process and procedures in testing -- Ability and intelligence testing -- Aptitude testing -- Achievement testing and alternate forms of assessment -- Career and employment testing -- Personality assessment -- Clinical assessment -- Assessment of development -- Environmental assessment -- Computer use in assessment -- Assessing diverse populations -- Assessment issues in education -- Communicating test results. ISBN 0-13-049416-X DDC 150/.28/7
1. Psychological tests. 2. Educational tests and measurements. 3. Counseling. I. Title.
BF176 .D78 2003

DRUNKARDS. See **ALCOHOLICS.**

DRUNKS. See **ALCOHOLICS.**

Dryden, Windy.
Handbook of counselling psychology. 2nd ed. London ; Thousand Oaks, Calif. : SAGE Publications, 2003.
BF637.C6 H316 2003

DTV Premium
Burkhart, Dagmar. Ehre. Originalausg. München : Deutscher Taschenbuch Verlag, c2002.
BJ1533.H8 B87 2002

Du bist die Göttin.
Haen, Renate. 1. Aufl. Bergish Gladbach : Bastei Lübbe, 1999.

Du ḳensṭ oykh!.
Fridman, Aharon (Aharon ben Yehoshu'a) [Gam atah yakhol. Yiddish] Nyu Yorḳ : Lev Yiśroel, 762, 2002.

Du libre arbitre.
Fourier, Charles, 1772-1837. Bordeaux : Saints Calus, 2003.

Du père à la lettre.
Yankelevich, Héctor, 1946- Ramonville Saint-Agne : Erès, c2003.

Du plaisir, de la douleur et de quelques autres.
Bard, Xavier, 1935- Paris, France : Harmattan, c2002.

Du shu wen cong
He, Zhaowu. Wei cao ji. Di 1 ban. Beijing : Sheng huo, du shu, xin zhi san lian shu dian, 1999.
D16.8 .H42 1999

Du surréalisme considéré dans ses rapports au totalitarisme et aux tables tournantes.
Clair, Jean, 1940- [Paris] : Mille et une nuits, 2003.

Du Weiming wen ji.
Tu, Wei-ming. [Selections. 2002] Wuhan Shi : Wuhan chu ban she, 2002.
B5233.C6 T813 2002

DUAL-CAREER COUPLES. See **DUAL-CAREER FAMILIES.**

DUAL-CAREER FAMILIES. See **WORK AND FAMILY.**

DUAL-CAREER FAMILIES - PSYCHOLOGIC ASPECT.
Hobfoll, Stevan E. [Work won't love you back. Chinese] Top shuang xin jia ting. Chu ban. Taibei Shi : Ye qiang chu ban she, 1997.

DUAL-CAREER MARRIAGE. See **DUAL-CAREER FAMILIES.**

DUAL-INCOME COUPLES. See **DUAL-CAREER FAMILIES.**

DUALISM. See also **MATERIALISM; MIND AND BODY.**
Clarke, Desmond M. Descartes's theory of mind. Oxford ; New York : Oxford University Press, 2003.

Dimen, Muriel. Sexuality, intimacy, power. Hillsdale, NJ : Analytic Press, 2003.
BF201.4 .D556 2003

DUALISM (RELIGION) - CHRISTIANITY.
McCulloch, Gillian. The deconstruction of dualism in theology. Carlisle : Paternoster Press, 2002.

Il dubbio necessario.
Del Moro, Franco. 1. ed. Murazzano (CN) : Ellin Selae, 2002.

DUBIN, RICHARD.
Vint/age 2001 conference : [videorecording]. New York, c2001.

Dubin, Richard, panelist.
Vint/age 2001 conference : [videorecording]. New York, c2001.

Dubina, I. N. (Igor' Nikolaevich) Tvorchestvo kak fenomen sotsial'nykh kommunikatsiĭ / I.N. Dubina ; otvetstvennyĭ redaktor, L.A. Koshcheĭ. Novosibirsk : Sibirskoe otd-nie RAN, 2000. 191 p. ; 21 cm. Includes bibliographical references. ISBN 5769204087
1. Creative ability - Social aspects. I. Koshcheĭ, L. A. (Lĭubov' Alekseevna) II. Title.
BF411 .D82 2000

Duby, Georges. Qu'est-ce que la société féodale? / Georges Duby. Paris : Flammarion, c2002. lxxviii, 1754 p. ; 20 cm. (Mille & une pages) Includes bibliographical references (p. xxxv-lvii) and index. Collection of works originally published 1971-1983. CONTENTS: Société aux XIe et XII siècles dans la région mâconnaise -- Économie rurale et la vie des campagnes dans l'Occident médiéval -- Hommes et structures du Moyen Age. I. La société chevaleresque -- Hommes et structures du Moyen Age. II. Seigneurs et paysans -- Mâle Moyen Age -- Dialogues. ISBN 2-08-210036-7
1. Social history - Medieval, 500-1500. 2. Feudalism. 3. Civilization, Medieval. 4. Social institutions - France - History. 5. Agriculture - Economic aspects - Europe - History. I. Title. II. Series.

Duchesne, Sophie.
Aux frontières des attitudes. Paris, France : Harmattan, c2002.

Ducret, Alix. La vie au moyen âge / sous la direction d'Alix Ducret. Courtaboeuf : Didro, c2002. 227 p. : ill. ; 21 cm. (Collection Les mystères de l'histoire) ISBN 2-910726-55-X DDC 944
1. Civilization, Medieval. 2. Middle Ages. 3. Europe - Social life and customs - To 1492. I. Title. II. Series.

Ducret, Jean-Jacques, 1946- Jean Piaget, 1868-1979 : une décennie de recherches sur les mécanismes de construction cognitive / Jean-Jacques Ducret. Genève, Switzerland : Service de la recherche en éducation, c2000. 537 p. : ill. ; 24 cm. (SRED/Cahier 7/Mai 2000) Includes bibliographical references (p. 536-537). ISBN 2940238065
1. Cognition. 2. Piaget, Jean, - 1896- I. Service de la recherche en éducation (Geneva, Switzerland) II. Title. III. Series: Cahiers du SRED ; no. 7.
BF311 .D813 2000

Dudgeon, Piers. Breaking out of the box : the biography of Edward de Bono / Piers Dudgeon. London : Headline, 2001. 312 p. : ill. ; 24 cm. Includes bibliographical references (p. 299-301) and index. Table of contents URL: http://www.loc.gov/catdir/toc/fy038/2001430615.html ISBN 0-7472-7142-9 DDC 150/.92
1. De Bono, Edward, - 1933- 2. Lateral thinking. 3. Businessmen - Great Britain - Biography. I. Title.
BF109.D39 D83 2001

Dudley-Grant, G. Rita, 1951-.
Psychology and Buddhism. New York : Kluwer Academic/Plenum Publishers, c2003.
BQ4570.P76 P78 2003

DUELING. See **COMBAT.**

Duesterberg, Thomas James, 1950-.
Riding the next wave. Indianapolis, Ind. : Hudson Institute : [Washington, DC : Distributed by the Brookings Institution Press], c2001.
HM901 .R43 2001

Dufour, Adrian. Ciencia y logica de mundos posibles / Adrian Dufour ; Pref. de Evandro Agazzi. Bern : Lang, 2001. xx, 321 p. ; 21 cm. (Publications universitaires Europeennes / Serie 20, Philosophie ; v. 609 = Europäische Hochschulschriften / Reihe XX. Philosophie, 0721-3417 ; 609 = European university studies / Series XX, Philosophy ; v. 609) Includes bibliographical references (p. 305 - 321). ISBN 3-906758-16-8 (pbk.)
1. Knowledge, Theory of. 2. Science - Philosophy. 3. Metaphysics. I. Title. II. Series: Europäische Hochschulschriften. Reihe XX, Philosophie ; Bd. 609.

Dufourmantelle, Anne. La sauvagerie maternelle / Anne Dufourmantelle. Paris : Calmann-Lévy, c2001. 220 p. ; 22 cm. Includes bibliographical references (p. [217]-218). ISBN 2-7021-3246-4 DDC 150
1. Motherhood - Psychological aspects. 2. Psychoanalysis. I. Title.

Dugan, Ellen, 1963- Elements of witchcraft : natural magick for teens / Ellen Dugan. 1st ed. St. Paul, Minn. : Llewellyn Publications, 2003. xviii, 255 p. : ill. ; 23 cm. Includes bibliographical references (p. 243-245) and index. ISBN 0-7387-0393-1 DDC 133.4/3
1. Witchcraft. 2. Teenagers - Miscellanea. I. Title.
BF1571.5.T44 D86 2003

Duggal, S. K. (Sudarshan Kumar), 1937-.
Agarwal, G. S., 1936- Dictionary of astrology. New Delhi : Sagar Publications, 2002.
BF1714.H5 A33 2002

Dugin, Aleksandr. Ėvoliutsiia paradigmal'nykh osnovaniĭ nauki / Aleksandr Dugin. Moskva : Arktogeia, 2002. 412 p. ; 17 cm. Includes bibliographical references (p. 384-409) ISBN 5818600130
1. Science - Philosophy. 2. Paradigm (Theory of knowledge) 3. Knowledge, Theory of. I. Title.
Q174.8 .D845 2002

DUGIN, ALEKSANDR.
Maler, Arkadiĭ. Strategii sakral'nogo smysla. Moskva : Parad izdatel'skiĭ dom, 2003.

Dugout days.
DeMarco, Michael. New York : AMACOM, c2001.
GV865.M35 D46 2001

Duitch, Suri. The big idea : a step-by-step guide to creating effective policy reports / written by Suri Duitch. New York : City Limits Community Information Service, c2002. iv, 127 p. : ill. ; 22 cm.
1. Report writing. I. City Limits Community Information Service. II. Title. III. Title: Step-by-step guide to creating effective policy reports

Dukhovnost' kak faktor uspeshnoĭ sotsial'noĭ adaptatsii cheloveka.
Borodiuk, N. R. (Nelli Rafkatovna) Moskva : [s.n.], 2000.
BF335 .B67 2000

Dukhovnye korni russkogo naroda.
Beliaev, G. G. Moskva : Bylina, 2002.
DK32 .B358 2002

Dukhovnyĭ potentsial liudyny.
Savchyn, Myroslav, 1950- Ivano-Frankivs'k : Plaĭ, 2001.

BF698 .S288 2001

DULIA. See **CHRISTIAN SAINTS - CULT.**

Dülmen, Richard van.
Denkwelten um 1700. Köln : Böhlau, 2002.
BF441 .D46 2002

Dumars, Denise. The dark archetype : exploring the shadow side of the divine / by Denise Dumars & Lori Nyx. Franklin Lakes, N.J. : New Page Books, c2003. p. cm. Includes bibliographical references and index. ISBN 1-56414-693-6 (pbk.) DDC 202/.112
1. Magic. 2. Gods - Miscellanea. 3. Goddesses - Miscellanea. I. Nyx, Lori. II. Title.
BF1623.G63 D86 2003

DUMÉZIL, GEORGES, 1898-.
Poitevin, Michel. Georges Dumézil, un naturel comparatiste. Paris : Harmattan, c2002.

Dumoulin, Olivier. Le rôle social de l'historien : de la chaire au prétoire / Olivier Dumoulin. Paris : Albin Michel, 2002, c2003. 343 p. ; 23 cm. (Bibliothèque Albin Michel Histoire, 1158-6443) Includes bibliographical references. ISBN 2-226-13484-0 DDC 900
1. Historiography. 2. Historians. I. Title. II. Series: Bibliothèque Albin Michel de l'histoire.
D13.2 .D85 2002

Dunbar, R. I. M. (Robin Ian MacDonald), 1947-.
Barrett, Louise. Human evolutionary psychology. Princeton, N.J. : Princeton University Press, c2002.
BF698.95 .B37 2002

DUNCAN, ISADORA, 1877-1927.
Francis, Elizabeth, 1959- Feminism and modernism [microform]. [1994]

Dunk, Hermann Walther von der. Mensen, machten, mogelijkheden : historische beschouwingen / H.W. von der Dunk. Amsterdam : B. Bakker, 2002. 303 p. ; 20 cm. Includes bibliographical references (p. 293-300) and index. ISBN 90-351-2400-6
1. Historiography. I. Title.

Die dunkle Spur im Denken.
Kneer, Markus, 1972- Paderborn : Schöningh, 2003.
DS145 .K64 2003

Dunlap, Linda L. What all children need : theory and application / Linda L. Dunlap. Lanham, Md. : University Press of America, c2002. xi, 299 p. ; 22 cm. Includes bibliographical references (p. [239]-291) and index. ISBN 0-7618-2273-9 (pbk. : alk. paper) DDC 649/.1
1. Child care. 2. Child development. 3. Early childhood education. 4. Social work with children. I. Title.
HQ778.5 .D85 2002

DUNMORE, JOHN MURRAY, EARL OF, 1732-1809.
Skidmore, Warren. Lord Dunmore's little war of 1774. Bowie, Md. : Heritage Books, 2002.

Dunn, Dana. A short guide to writing about psychology / Dana S. Dunn. Upper Saddle River, NJ : Pearson/Longman, 2003. p. cm. (The short guide series) Includes bibliographical references and index. ISBN 0-321-09424-7 (alk. paper) DDC 808/.06615
1. Psychology - Authorship. 2. Report writing. I. Title.
BF76.8 .D86 2003

Dunn-Rankin, Peter.
Scaling methods. 2nd ed. / Peter Dunn-Rankin ... [et al.]. Mahwah, N.J. : L. Erlbaum Associates, 2004.
BF39.2.S34 S33 2004

Scaling methods.
Scaling methods. 2nd ed. / Peter Dunn-Rankin ... [et al.]. Mahwah, N.J. : L. Erlbaum Associates, 2004.
BF39.2.S34 S33 2004

Dunne, Michael, 1962-.
Internationales Eriugena-Colloquium (10th : Maynooth and Dublin : 2002) History and eschatology in John Scottus Eriugena and his time. Leuven : University Press, 2002.

Dŭnov, Petŭr, 1864-1944. Svetlina na misŭlta / Petŭr Dŭnov. Sofiia : Kulturna asotsiatsiia Beĭnsa Dunò, 1998. 154 p. ; 20 cm. ISBN 9545780509
1. Bialo bratstvo (Bulgaria) I. Title.
BF641 .D79 1998

Dunwich, Gerina. Dunwich's guide to gemstone sorcery : using stones for spells, amulets, rituals, and divination / by Gerina Dunwich. Franklin Lakes, NJ : New Page Books, c2003. 221 p. : ill. ; 24 cm. Includes bibliographical references (p. 209-214) and index. ISBN 1-56414-672-3 (pbk.) DDC 133/.25538
1. Gems - Miscellanea. 2. Precious stones - Psychic aspects. 3. Magic. I. Title. II. Title: Guide to gemstone sorcery
BF1442.P74 D86 2003

Dunwich, Gerina.
Exploring spellcraft : how to create and cast effective spells / Gerina Dunwich. Franklin Lakes, NJ : New Page Books, c2001. 220 p. : ill. ; 21 cm. Includes bibliographical references (p. 214-216) and index. ISBN 1-56414-494-1 (pbk.) ISBN 1-56414-480-1 (paper) DDC 133.4/4
1. Witchcraft. 2. Charms. 3. Magic. I. Title.
BF1566 .D866 2001

Herbal magick : a witch's guide to herbal folklore and enchantments / by Gerina Dunwich. Franklin Lakes, NJ : New Page Books, c2002. 240 p. : ill. ; 21 cm. Includes bibliographical references (p. 229-231) and index. ISBN 1-56414-575-1 (pbk.) DDC 133.4/3
1. Witchcraft. 2. Herbs - Miscellanea. I. Title. II. Title: Herbal magic
BF1572.P43 D85 2002

The pagan book of Halloween : a complete guide to the magick, incantations, recipes, spells, and lore / Gerina Dunwich. New York : Penguin/Compass, 2000. xv, 189 p. : ill. ; 18 cm. Includes bibliographical references (p. 179-183) and index. ISBN 0-14-019616-1 DDC 394.2646
1. Witchcraft. 2. Halloween. 3. Charms. 4. Magic. I. Title.
BF1566 .D867 2000

A witch's guide to ghosts and the supernatural / by Gerina Dunwich. Franklin Lakes, NJ : New Page Books, c2002. 239 p. : ill. ; 21 cm. Includes bibliographical references (p. 230-232) and index. ISBN 1-56414-616-2 (pbk.) DDC 133
1. Ghosts. 2. Witchcraft. 3. Magic. 4. Charms. I. Title.
BF1471 .D86 2002

Dunwich's guide to gemstone sorcery.
Dunwich, Gerina. Franklin Lakes, NJ : New Page Books, c2003.
BF1442.P74 D86 2003

Dupaigne, Bernard. Afghanistan, rêve de paix / Bernard Dupaigne. Paris : Buchet-Chastel, 2002. 150 p. : map ; 19 cm. (Au fait) ISBN 2-283-01911-7 DDC 958
1. Peace. 2. Afghanistan - Politics and government - 2001- 3. Afghanistan - Social conditions - 20th century. I. Title. II. Series.

Duplessis, Yvonne, 1912- Surréalisme et paranormal : l'aspect expérimental du surréalisme / Yvonne Duplessis ; [préface de Hubert Larcher]. Agnières : JMG, 2002. 291 p. : ill. ; 20 cm. (Collection Démons et merveilles) Includes bibliographical references (p. 259-284). ISBN 2-912507-76-6 DDC 809
1. Parapsychology. 2. Surrealism. 3. Supernatural in art. 4. Psychology and art. I. Title. II. Series.
BF1023 .D87 2002

Dupouey, Patrick. Est-ce le cerveau qui pense? / Patrick Dupouey. Nantes : Pleins feux, [2002]. 62 p. ; 21 cm. (Lundis philo, 1285-3542 ; 20) ISBN 2-8472-9041-9 DDC 194
1. Philosophy of mind. 2. Neurosciences - Philosophy. I. Title. II. Series.

DuQuette, Lon Milo, 1948-
[Magick of Thelma]
The magick of Aleister Crowley : a handbook of the rituals of Thelema / Lon Milo Duquette. Boston, MA : Weiser Books, 2003. p. cm. Includes bibliographical references and index. Table of contents URL: http://www.loc.gov/catdir/toc/ecip046/2003015150.html ISBN 1-57863-299-4 DDC 133.4/3
1. Magic. 2. Occultism. 3. Crowley, Aleister, - 1875-1947. I. Title.
BF1611 .D87 2003

Understanding Aleister Crowley's thoth tarot / Lon Milo DuQuette. Boston, MA : Weiser Books, 2003. p. cm. Includes bibliographical references and index. URL: http://www.loc.gov/catdir/toc/ecip045/2003014475.html ISBN 1-57863-276-5 DDC 133.3/2424
1. Tarot. 2. Crowley, Aleister, - 1875-1947. I. Title.
BF1879.T2 D873 2003

Duran, Magdelena, 1960- ill.
The jewel of friendship. Berkeley, CA : Dharma Pub., 2002.
BQ1462.E5 J48 2002

Durand, Gilbert, 1921-.
Sciences et archétypes. Paris : Dervy, 2002.

Durand, Jacques, 1947-.
Phonetics, phonology, and cognition. Oxford : Oxford University Press, 2002.
P221 .P475 2002

DURATION, INTUITION OF. See **TIME PERCEPTION.**

Durell, Sandi.
Vint/age 2001 conference : [videorecording]. New York, c2001.

Durham, Diana. The return of King Arthur : finishing the quest for wholeness, inner strength, and self knowledge / by Diana Durham. New York : Jeremy P. Tarcher/Penguin, 2004. p. cm. Includes bibliographical references. ISBN 1-58542-297-5 (alk. paper) DDC 158.1
1. Self-actualization (Psychology) 2. Jungian psychology. 3. Arthurian romances - History and criticism. 4. Grail - Legends - History and criticism. I. Title.
BF637.S4 D88 2004

Đurić, Mihailo.
Kriza i perspektive filozofije. 1. izd. Beograd : Tersit, 1995.
B99.S462 K75 1995

Durilka.
Meniaĭlov, Alekseĭ. Moskva : "Kraft+", 2003.

Durschmied, Erik. From Armageddon to the fall of Rome : how the myth makers changed the world / Erik Durschmied. London : Hodder & Stoughton, c2002. 434 p. : ill., maps ; 23 cm. Includes bibliographical references (p. [410]-416) and index. ISBN 0-340-82176-0 DDC 355.00901
1. Military history, Ancient. 2. History, Ancient. I. Title.

Unsung heroes : the twentieth century's forgotten history-makers / Erik Durschmied. London : Hodder & Stoughton, 2003. 467 p. : [8] p. of plates : ill. ; 24 cm. Includes bibliographical references (p. [445]-451) and index. ISBN 0-340-82519-7 DDC 904.7
1. History, Modern - 20th century - Sources. 2. Heroes. 3. War. I. Title.

Dusha.
Kovalenko, A. P. Moskva : Veteran otchizny : Megatron, 2000.
BF1999 .K685 2000

Düsing, Klaus.
Aufklärungen. Berlin : Duncker und Humblot, c2002.

Dust.
Steedman, Carolyn. New Brunswick, N.J. : Rutgers University Press, 2002, c2001.
CD947 .S73 2002

Duszak, Anna.
Us and others. Amsterdam ; Philadelphia : John Benjamins Pub., c2002.
HM753 .U72 2002

DUTCH LITERATURE - TO 1500 - HISTORY AND CRITICISM.
Besamusca, Bart. The book of Lancelot. Cambridge : D.S. Brewer, 2003.
PT5568 .B47 2003

Dvadt͡satyĭ vek : metodologicheskie problemy istoricheskogo poznanii͡a.
XX vek. Moskva : INION RAN, 2001-

Dvivedī, Bhojarāja. Ācārya Varāhamihira kā jyotisha mem yogadāna / Bhojarāja Dvivedī. 1. saṃskaraṇa. Naī Dillī : Rañjana Pablikes̄ansa, 2002. 345, [1] p. : ill. ; 22 cm. In Hindi; includes passages in English and Sanskrit. SUMMARY: Study on the life and contribution of Varāhamihira, 505-587, to Hindu astrology. Includes bibliographical references (p. [334]-[346]).
1. Varāhamihira, - 505-587. 2. Hindu astrology. 3. Astrologers - India - Biography. I. Title.
BF1679.8.V37 D85 2002

Dvivedī, Brajavallabha.
Lāla, Mukuta Bihārī. [Sāmyayogamīmāṃsā. Hindi & Sanskrit] Sāmyayogamīmāṃsā. 1. saṃskaraṇa. Vārāṇasī : Śaivabhāratī Śodhapratiṣṭhānam, 2001.
BL1237.32+

Dvivedī, Govindarāma.
Gulābavijaya. Śrī Muhūrtarāja. Dvitīyāvṛtti. Ji. Dhāra, Ma. Pra. : Rājendra Pravacana Kāryālaya, 1996.
BF1714.J28+

Dvoĭnai͡a spiral' istorii.
Kantor, Karl Moiseevich. Moskva : I͡Azyk slavi͡anskoĭ kul'tury, 2002-
D16.8 .K224 2002

DWELLINGS. See **ARCHITECTURE, DOMESTIC; HAUNTED HOUSES; MANSIONS.**

DWELLINGS - INDIA - HISTORY.
Khadiratna, Dayanidhi. Brhat śilpaśāstra, bā, Grhabandha bijñāna ; Grhabandha gaṇanā o śubhastambhāropaṇa bicāra. Kaṭaka : Dharmagrantha Shtora, [1995?]
TH4809.I4 K48 1995

Dwyer, Graham, 1959- The divine and the demonic : supernatural affliction and its treatment in North India / Graham Dwyer. London ; New York : RoutledgeCurzon, 2003. xiii, 190 p. : ill., maps ; 23 cm. Includes bibliographical references (p. 176-187) and index. ISBN 0-415-29749-4 (alk. paper) DDC 133.4/2/09544
1. Exorcism. 2. Spirit possession - India - Sawai Madhopur (District) 3. Hinduism - India - Sawai Madhopur (District) - Customs and practices. I. Title.
BL1226.82.E94 D89 2003

DYBBUK.
Chajes, Jeffrey Howard. Between worlds. Philadelphia : University of Pennsylvania Press, c2003.
BM729.D92 C53 2003

Dyer, Wayne W. The power of intention : learning to co-create your world your way / Wayne W. Dyer. Carlsbad, Calif. : Hay House, c2004. p. cm. Table of contents URL: http://www.loc.gov/catdir/toc/ecip046/2003014622.html CONTENTS: The essentials of intention -- Putting intention to work -- The connection. ISBN 1401902154 ISBN 1401902162 (tradepaper) DDC 158.1
1. Intentionalism. I. Title.
BF619.5 .D94 2004

DYFED (WALES) - GENEALOGY.
Nanteos. Llandysul, Wales : Gomer, [2001]
DA738.N36 N36 2001

DYING. See **DEATH.**

DYING PERSONS. See **TERMINALLY ILL.**

A dynamic model of multilingualism.
Herdina, Philip. Clevedon, England Buffalo, N.Y. : Multilingual Matters, 2002.
P115.4 .H47 2002

Dynamic structure of reality.
Zubiri, Xavier. [Estructura dinámica de la realidad. English] Urbana : University of Illinois Press, c2003.
B4568.Z83 E7713 2003

The dynamic workplace.
Allcorn, Seth. Westport, Conn. ; London : Praeger, 2003.
HF5547.2 .A43 2003

DYNAMICS. See **CHAOTIC BEHAVIOR IN SYSTEMS; FORCE AND ENERGY; PHYSICS.**

Dynamics of dissipation / P. Garbaczewski, R. Olkiewicz (eds.). Berlin ; New York : Springer, c2002. x, 512 p. : ill. ; 25 cm. (Lecture notes in physics, 0075-8450 ; 597) Includes bibliographical references and index. ISBN 3-540-44111-5 (acid-free paper) DDC 003/.857
1. Open systems (Physics) 2. Chaotic behavior in systems. 3. Energy dissipation. I. Garbaczewski, P. II. Olkiewicz, R. (Robert), 1962- III. Series.
QC174.85 .D96 2002

The dynamics of human aggression.
Rizzuto, Ana-María. New York, NY : Brunner-Routledge, 2003.
BF175.5.A36 R59 2003

The dynamics of persuasion.
Perloff, Richard M. 2nd ed. Mahwah, N.J. : Lawrence Erlbaum Associates, 2003.
BF637.P4 .P39 2003

Dynamics of the soul.
Saraydarian, Torkom. Cave Creek, Ariz. : T.S.G. Pub., c2001.
BF1999 .S3352 2001

Dynamique des formes et représentations.
Hayat, Michaël. Paris : Harmattan, c2002.
B105.R4 H392 2002

DYSLEXIA.
Dyslexia, fluency, and the brain. Timonium, Md. : York Press, 2001.
RC394.W6 D958 2001

Raĭnov, Vasil G. Za psikhosemantichnata spet͡sifika na ezikovoto vŭzpriĭatie. Sofii͡a : Akademichno izd-vo "Prof. Marin Drinov", 1998.
P37 .R27 1998

Dyslexia, fluency, and the brain / edited by Maryanne Wolf. Timonium, Md. : York Press, 2001. xxv, 423 p. : ill. ; 23 cm. Includes bibliographical references and index. ISBN 0-912752-60-2 DDC 616.85/53
1. Dyslexia. 2. Reading disability - Physiological aspects. 3. Brain. I. Wolf, Maryanne.
RC394.W6 D958 2001

Dyson, Anne Haas. The brothers and sisters learn to write : popular literacies in childhood and school cultures / Anne Haas Dyson. New York : Teachers College Press, c2003. viii, 256 p. : ill. ; 24 cm. (Language and literacy series) Includes bibliographical references and index. ISBN 0-8077-4281-3 (cloth : alk. paper) ISBN 0-8077-4280-5 (pbk. : alk. paper) DDC 302.2/244
1. Children - Language. 2. Educational sociology - United States. 3. Popular culture - United States. 4. Semiotics. 5.

Literacy. I. Title. II. Series: Language and literacy series (New York, N.Y.)
LB1139.L3 D97 2003

Dyson, Michael Eric. Why I love black women / Michael Eric Dyson. New York : Basic Civitas Books, c2003. xxi, 314 p. ; 22 cm. Includes index. ISBN 0-465-01763-0
1. Women, Black. 2. African American women. 3. Self-esteem in women. I. Title.

DYSTOPIAS. *See* **UTOPIAS.**

Dziecko w rodzinie i społeczeństwie / Katedra Historii Edukacji i Wychowania w Rodzinie AB ... [et al.]. Bydgoszsz : Wydawnictwo Uczelniane Bydgoskiej, 2002. 2 v. : ill. ; 24 cm. Includes bibliographical references. Summaries in English, French and German. CONTENTS: tom. 1. Starożytność, średniowiecze / redakcja, Juliusz Jundziłł, Dorota Żołądź-Strzelczyk -- tom. 2. Dzieje nowożytne / redakcja, Krzysztof Jakubiak, Wiesław Jamrożek. ISBN 83-7096-439-7 (tom. 1) ISBN 83-7096-440-0 (tom. 2)
1. Children - History. 2. Children - Social conditions. 3. Children - Legal status, laws, etc. 4. Education. 5. Child care. 6. Children in art. 7. Education. 8. Family. I. Jundziłł, Juliusz. II. Żołądź, Dorota. III. Jakubiak, Krzysztof. IV. Jamrożek, Wiesław.

Džin, Kristina.
Girardi Jurkić, Vesna. Egipatska religija i antička Istra = Pula : Arheološki Muzej Istre, 2001.

Eagly, Alice Hendrickson.
The psychology of gender. 2nd ed. New York : Guilford Press, 2004.
BF692.2 .P764 2004

Earley, P. Christopher. Cultural intelligence : individual interactions across cultures / P. Christopher Earley, Soon Ang. Stanford, Calif. : Stanford University Press, 2003. xv, 379 p. : ill. ; 23 cm. Includes bibliographical references (p. 313-356) and index. ISBN 0-8047-4300-2 (cloth : alk. paper) ISBN 0-8047-4312-6 (pbk. : alk. paper) DDC 658.3/0089
1. Leadership - Cross-cultural studies. 2. Social intelligence. 3. Social interaction. 4. Management - Cross-cultural studies. I. Ang, Soon. II. Title.
HD57.7 .E237 2003

Early category and concept development : making sense of the blooming, buzzing confusion / edited by David H. Rakison and Lisa M. Oakes. Oxford ; New York : Oxford University Press, 2003. xxi, 442 p. : ill. ; 25 cm. Includes bibliographical references and indexes. ISBN 0-19-514293-4 (cloth : alk. paper) ISBN 0-19-514294-2 (pbk. : alk. paper) DDC 155.42/2323
1. Cognition in infants. 2. Perception in infants. I. Rakison, David H., 1969- II. Oakes, Lisa M., 1963-
BF720.C63 E27 2003

Early child development in the 21st century : profiles of current research initiatives / edited by Jeanne Brooks-Gunn, Allison Sidle Fuligni, Lisa J. Berlin. New York : Teachers College Press, c2003. ix, 437 p. : ill. ; 23 cm. Includes bibliographical references (p. 369-402) and index. CONTENTS: Themes in developmental research: historical roots and promise for the future / Allison Sidle Fuligni, Jeanne Brooks-Gunn, and Lisa J. Berlin -- The profiles project / Allison Sidle Fuligni and Jeanne Brooks-Gunn -- Early childhood intervention research initiatives / Lisa J. Berlin, Colleen R. O'Neal, and Jeanne Brooks-Gunn -- Initiatives on the transition to school / Allison Sidle Fuligni and Christy Brady-Smith -- Family support initiatives / Allison Sidle Fuligni and Jeanne Brooks-Gunn -- Pre- and perinatal home visitation interventions / Lisa McCabe and Jeanne Brooks-Gunn -- Child welfare and mental health initiatives / Janis Kupersmidt, Lisa McCabe, and Donna Bryant -- Early child care initiatives: pt I. NICHD study of early child care / NICHD Early Child Care Research Network ; pt II. three early child care initiatives / Phyllis Gyamfi, Natasha Cabrera, and Jodie Roth -- Welfare-to-work initiatives / Christy Brady Smith ... [et al.] -- Neighborhood-based initiatives / Tama Leventhal and Jeanne Brooks-Gunn -- Initiatives on children with special needs / Kathleen Hebbeler and Donna Spiker -- Four new national longitudinal surveys on children / Allison Sidle Fuligni ... [et al.] -- Synthesis: issues and imperatives in research on early childhood development / Allison Sidle Fuligni and Jeanne Brooks-Gunn. ISBN 0-8077-4337-2 (cloth : alk. paper) ISBN 0-8077-4336-4 (pbk. : alk. paper) DDC 305.231
1. Child development. 2. Early childhood education. I. Brooks-Gunn, Jeanne. II. Fuligni, Allison Sidle. III. Berlin, Lisa.
LB1115 .E27 2003

EARLY CHILDHOOD EDUCATION.
Dunlap, Linda L. What all children need. Lanham, Md. : University Press of America, c2002.
HQ778.5 .D85 2002

Early child development in the 21st century. New York : Teachers College Press, c2003.
LB1115 .E27 2003

EARLY CHRISTIAN LITERATURE. *See* **CHRISTIAN LITERATURE, EARLY.**

Early decisions are vital to progress in ongoing negotiations.
United States. General Accounting Office. World Trade Organization [electronic resource]. [Washington, D.C.] : U.S. General Accounting Office, [2002]

Early English Text Society.
Adam, of Eynsham, fl. 1196-1232. [Visio Monachi de Eynsham. English (Middle English) & Latin] The revelation of the Monk of Eynsham. Oxford : Published for the Early English Text Society by the Oxford University Press, 2002.

Early English Text Society (Series)
(no. 318.) Adam, of Eynsham, fl. 1196-1232. [Visio Monachi de Eynsham. English (Middle English) & Latin] The revelation of the Monk of Eynsham. Oxford : Published for the Early English Text Society by the Oxford University Press, 2002.

EARLY MAN. *See* **PREHISTORIC PEOPLES.**

Early psychological thought.
Green, Christopher D. Westport, Conn. ; London : Praeger, 2003.
BF91 .G74 2003

Early studies of Giordano Bruno / edited by Paul Richard Blum. Bristol : Thoemmes, 2000. 6 v. (2260 p.) ; 22 cm. Includes bibliographical references. Translated from more than one language. ISBN 1-85506-857-5 DDC 195
1. Bruno, Giordano, - 1548-1600. 2. Philosophy, Italian. 3. Philosophy, Renaissance. I. Blum, Paul Richard. II. Series: Medieval and Renaissance philosophy.

The early universe.
Börner, G. 4th ed. Berlin : London : Springer, c2003.

Early warning.
Gilad, Benjamin. New York, NY : American Management Association, c2003.
HD61 .G533 2003

EARTH. *See* **WATER.**

Earth bodies.
Mazis, Glen A., 1951- Earthbodies. Albany, NY : State University of New York Press, 2002.
BJ1695 .M39 2002

EARTH - COLLISIONS WITH COMETS. *See* **COMETS - COLLISIONS WITH EARTH.**

EARTH - EFFECT OF HUMAN BEINGS ON. *See* **NATURE - EFFECT OF HUMAN BEINGS ON.**

Earth magic.
Weinstein, Marion. Rev. ed. Franklin Lakes, NJ : New Page Books, c2003.
BF1566 .W46 2003

EARTH - SATELLITE. *See* **MOON.**

EARTH STATIONS (SATELLITE TELECOMMUNICATION). *See* **DIRECT BROADCAST SATELLITE TELEVISION.**

Earthbodies.
Mazis, Glen A., 1951- Albany, NY : State University of New York Press, 2002.
BJ1695 .M39 2002

EARTHENWARE. *See* **POTTERY.**

Eason, Cassandra.
[Complete book of divination]
A complete guide to divination / Cassandra Eason. London : Piatkus, 1998 (2002 [printing]) xii, 276 p. : ill. ; 20 cm. Originally published as: The complete book of divination. 1998. Includes bibliographical references and index. ISBN 0-7499-2304-0 DDC 133.3
1. Divination. I. Title.

The complete guide to divination : how to foretell the future using the most popular methods of prediction / Cassandra Eason. Berkeley, Calif. : Crossing Press, 2003. 314 p. : ill. ; 23 cm. Originally published: London : Judy Piatkus (Publishers) Ltd., 1998. Includes bibliographical references (p. 303-305) and index. Table of contents URL: http://www.loc.gov/catdir/toc/ecip044/2003011013.html CONTENTS: Tarot cards -- Playing cards -- The I Ching -- The Viking runes -- Crystal divination -- Tree divination -- Tea leaf divination -- Numerology -- Pendulum dowsing -- Palmistry. ISBN 1-58091-138-2 DDC 133.3
1. Divination. I. Title.
BF1751 .E27 2003

The complete guide to psychic development : 100 ways to tap into your psychic potential / Cassandra Eason. Berkeley, Calif. : Crossing Press, c2003. 338 p. : ill. ; 23 cm. Originally published: London : Judy Piatkus Publishers, 1997. Includes bibliographical references (p. 329-332) and index. CONTENTS: Developing your psychic powers -- Developing your existing powers -- Divination -- Harnessing natural energies -- Ritual magic -- Magic alphabets and charms -- Other dimensions-- Healing. ISBN 1-58091-150-1 DDC 133.8
1. Psychic ability - Problems, exercises, etc. I. Title. II. Title: Psychic development
BF1031 .E295 2003

A practical guide to witchcraft and magick spells / Cassandra Eason. London ; New York : Quantum, c2001. 320 p. : ill. ; 24 cm. Includes bibliographical references (p. 297-301) and indexes. Cover subtitle: "take advantage of the natural forces of life." ISBN 0-572-02704-4 (pbk.)
1. Magic. 2. Witchcraft. I. Title.

EAST AND WEST. *See also* **INTERCULTURAL COMMUNICATION.**
Anderson, Walt, 1933- The next enlightenment. 1st ed. New York : St. Martin's Press, 2003.
BL476 .A53 2003

Antinomies of modernity. Durham : Duke University Press, 2003.
CB358 .A59 2003

Arkoun, Mohammed. De Manhattan à Bagdad. Paris : Desclée de Brouwer, 2003.
JC319 .A72 2003

Bessis, Sophie, 1947- [Occident et les autres. English] Western supremacy. London ; New York : Zed Books, 2003.
CB245 .B4613 2003

Chen, Wei, 1957- Dong fang mei xue dui xi fang de ying xiang = Di 1 ban. Shanghai : Xue lin chu ban she, 1999.
BH221.C6 C444 1999

Corm, Georges. Orient-Occident, la fracture imaginaire. Paris : Découverte, 2002.

Coward, Harold G. Yoga and psychology. Albany : State University of New York Press, 2002.
BF51 .C69 2002

Diálogo de civilizaciones Oriente-Occidente. [Madrid] : Biblioteca Nueva ; [Cáceres, España] : Universidad de Extremadura, 2002.

The emerging monoculture. Westport, Conn. : Praeger, 2003.
HM843 .E44 2003

Europe and the Asia-Pacific. London ; New York : RoutledgeCurzon, 2003.
D1065.A78 E97 2003

Fuller, Graham E., 1937- The future of political Islam. New York ; Houndmills, Basingstoke : Palgrave, 2003.
BP173.7 .F85 2003

Globalization and civilizations. London ; New York : Routledge, 2002.
CB430 .G58 2002

Grant, George, 1954- The blood of the moon. Nashville, Tenn. : Thomas Nelson Publishers, 2002.
DS62 .G73 2002

Gunn, Geoffrey C. First globalization. Lanham, Md. : Rowman & Littlefield, c2003.
CB251 .G87 2003

Guo, Yanli. Zhong xi wen hua peng zhuang yu jin dai wen xue = Di 1 ban. Jinan Shi : Shandong jiao yu chu ban she, 1999.
PL2274 .G86 1999

Kamal, Niraj. Arise, Asia!. Delhi : Wordsmiths, 2003.
CB251 .K285 2003

Kanygin, IUriĭ Mikhaĭlovich. Poi︠a︡s mira. Kiev : MAUP, 2001.

Mabrūk, Muḥammad Ibrāhīm, 1943- al-Islām wa-al-gharb al-Amrīkī. al-Ṭabʻah al-ʻArabīyah 1. al-Qāhirah : Markaz al-Ḥaḍārah al-ʻArabīyah, 2002.

Nuwayhiḍ, Walīd. Min Kābūl ilá Niyūyūrk. al-Ṭabʻah 1. Bayrūt : Dār Ibn Ḥazm, 2002.
BP172+

Rosen, Lawrence, 1941- The culture of Islam. Chicago : University of Chicago Press, 2002.
DT312 R64 2002

Scholz, Piotr O. Die Sehnsucht nach Tausendundeiner Nacht. Stuttgart : Thorbecke, c2002.

Shayegan, Darius. La lumière vient de l'Occident. [La Tour-d'Aigues] : Éditions de l'Aube, c2001.

East and West

CB 430

Ṭaḥḥān, Aḥmad. Tajā'īd fī wajh al-zaman al-'Arabī. al-Ṭab'ah 1. Bayrūt : Dār al-Fārābī, 2001.

Valle, Alexandre del. Le totalitarisme islamiste à l'assaut des démocraties. Paris : Syrtes, c2002.

Van de Weyer, Robert. Islam and the West. Alresford, Hampshire : O Books, c2001.
CB251 .V36 2001

Van de Weyer, Robert. The shared well. 1st ed. Washington, D.C. : Brassey's, c2002.
BL65.P7 V36 2002

EAST AND WEST - PSYCHOLOGICAL ASPECTS.
L'incubo globale. Bergamo : Moretti & Vitali, c2002.

EAST ASIA - LANGUAGES - WRITING.
Hannas, Wm. C., 1946- The writing on the wall. Philadelphia : University of Pennsylvania Press, c2003.
P381.E18 H36 2003

EAST - CIVILIZATION. *See* **CIVILIZATION, ORIENTAL.**

EAST EUROPE. *See* **EUROPE, EASTERN.**

EAST (FAR EAST). *See* **EAST ASIA.**

EAST (MIDDLE EAST). *See* **MIDDLE EAST.**

EASTERN CIVILIZATION. *See* **CIVILIZATION, ORIENTAL.**

EASTERN EUROPE. *See* **EUROPE, EASTERN.**

EASTERN HEMISPHERE. *See* **AFRICA; ASIA; EUROPE.**

EASTERN MEDITERRANEAN. *See* **MIDDLE EAST.**

EASTERN QUESTION. *See* **EAST AND WEST; WORLD POLITICS.**

Easting, Robert.
Adam, of Eynsham, fl. 1196-1232. [Visio Monachi de Eynsham. English (Middle English) & Latin] The revelation of the Monk of Eynsham. Oxford : Published for the Early English Text Society by the Oxford University Press, 2002.

The easy guide to repertory grids.
Jankowicz, Devi. Chichester, West Sussex, England ; Hoboken, N.J. : Wiley, 2003.
BF698.8.R38 J36 2003

Easy guide to the Chinese system of astrology.
Burns, Debbie. Chinese horoscopes. Sydney : Lansdowne, 2000, c1998.

Easy way
Melucci, Nancy J. Psychology the easy way. Hauppauge, N.Y. : Barron's Educational Series, c2004.
BF121 .M45 2004

EATING. *See* **DINNERS AND DINING; FOOD HABITS.**

EATING DISORDERS. *See* **BULIMIA.**

EATING DISORDERS - ADJUVANT TREATMENT - CASE STUDIES.
Rabinor, Judith Ruskay, 1942- A starving madness. Carlsbad, CA : Gurze Books, c2002.
RC552.E18 R33 2001

EATING DISORDERS IN WOMEN - PSYCHOLOGICAL ASPECTS.
Género, desarrollo psicosocial y trastornos de la imagen corporal. Madrid : Instituto de la Mujer, 2001.

EATING DISORDERS IN WOMEN - SOCIAL ASPECTS.
Género, desarrollo psicosocial y trastornos de la imagen corporal. Madrid : Instituto de la Mujer, 2001.

EATING DISTURBANCES. *See* **EATING DISORDERS.**

EATING DYSFUNCTIONS. *See* **EATING DISORDERS.**

EATING, PATHOLOGICAL. *See* **EATING DISORDERS.**

Eaton, Robert C. The octavolateralis system and Mauthner cell interactions and questions [microform] / Robert C. Eaton, Arthur N. Popper. [Washington, D.C. : National Aeronautics and Space Administration, 1997] p. 124-130. ([NASA contractor report] ; NASA-CR-204741) Caption title. Shipping list no.: 98-0356-M. Originally published: [New York : Karger Medical and Scientific Publishers], 1995. Includes bibliographical references (p. 129-130). Microfiche. [Washington, D.C. : National Aeronautics and Space Administration, 1997] 1 microfiche : negative.
1. Fishes - Physiology. 2. Hearing. 3. Auditory perception. I. Popper, Arthur N. II. United States. National Aeronautics and Space Administration. III. Title. IV. Title: Brain, behavior and evolution. 1995. V. Series: NASA contractor report ; NASA CR-204741.

Ebeling, Richard M.
Von Mises, Ludwig, 1881-1973. Between the two World Wars. Indianapolis, Ind. : Liberty Fund, c2002.
HB101.V66A25 2002

Eberlein, Undine. Einzigartigkeit : das romantische Individualitätskonzept der Moderne / Undine Eberlein. Frankfurt ; New York : Campus, c2000. 400 p. ; 21 cm. Slightly revised version of the author's thesis (Freie Universität Berlin, 1998). Includes bibliographical references (p. 389-400). ISBN 3-593-36606-1 (chlorfrei)
1. Individuality. 2. Self. 3. Individualism. I. Title.
BF697 .E463 2000

Ebert, Christa, 1947-.
Individualitätskonzepte in der russischen Kultur. Berlin : Berlin Verlag Arno Spitz, c2002.
PG2987.I48 .I53 2002

ECCLESIASTICAL ARCHITECTURE. *See* **CHURCH ARCHITECTURE.**

ECCLESIASTICAL FASTS AND FEASTS. *See* **FASTS AND FEASTS.**

ECCLESIASTICAL HISTORY. *See* **CHURCH HISTORY.**

ECCLESIASTICAL RITES AND CEREMONIES. *See* **RITES AND CEREMONIES; SACRAMENTS.**

ECHEA. *See* **VASES, ACOUSTIC.**

ECHEIA. *See* **VASES, ACOUSTIC.**

Echekwube, A. O. (Anthony Onyebuchi) A metaphysical analysis of the concept of reincarnation : towards global harmony and peace / Anthony O. Echekwube. Ekpoma, Nigeria : Ambrose Alli University Publishing House, 2002. v, 42 p. ; 21 cm. "An inaugural lecture, Series 15, delivered at Ambrose Alli University, Ekpoma, Nigeria on Thursday, 26th September, 2002". Includes bibliographical references (p. 38-42). ISBN 978-2100-41-2
1. Reincarnation. 2. Peace (Philosophy) 3. Black author. I. Title.

ECHOSTAR (FIRM).
United States. Congress. Senate. Committee on the Judiciary. Subcommittee on Antitrust, Business Rights, and Competition. Dominance in the sky. [Washington] : U.S. G.P.O. : For sale by the Supt. of Docs., U.S. G.P.O. [Congressional Sales Office], 2003.

Echterhoff, Gerald.
Kontexte und Kulturen des Erinnerns. Konstanz : UVK Verlagsgesellschaft, 2002.
BF378.S65 K65 2002

ECKART, DIETRICH, 1868-1923.
Bärsch, Claus-Ekkehard. Die politische Religion des Nationalsozialismus. 2., vollst. überarb. Aufl. München : W. Fink, c2002.

Eckblad, John. If your life were a business, would you invest in it? : the 13-step program for managing your life like the best CEOs manage their companies / John Eckblad and David Kiel. New York : McGraw-Hill, c2003. xxvii, 260 p. : ill. ; 25 cm. Includes bibliographical references and index. ISBN 0-07-141039-2 DDC 158.1
1. Self-actualization (Psychology) 2. Life skills. 3. Success. I. Kiel, David. II. Title.
BF637.S4 E38 2003

ECKISTS.
Twitchell, Paul, 1908-1971. [Stranger by the river. Croation] Stranac na rijeci. Minneapolis, MN : ECKANKAR, c1994.

ECOFEMINISM.
McCulloch, Gillian. The deconstruction of dualism in theology. Carlisle : Paternoster Press, 2002.

Ecological counseling : an innovative approach to conceptualizing person-environment interaction / edited by Robert K. Conyne, Ellen P. Cook. Alexandria, VA : American Counseling Association, 2003. p. cm. Includes bibliographical references and index. Table of contents URL: http://www.loc.gov/catdir/toc/ecip046/2003014837.html ISBN 1-55620-199-0 (alk. paper) DDC 158/.3
1. Counseling. 2. Environmental psychology. I. Conyne, Robert K. II. Cook, Ellen Piel, 1952-
BF637.C6 E26 2003

ECOLOGICAL ENGINEERING. *See* **HUMAN ECOLOGY.**

ECOLOGICALLY SUSTAINABLE DEVELOPMENT. *See* **SUSTAINABLE DEVELOPMENT.**

ECOLOGY. *See also* **HUMAN ECOLOGY.**
Boff, Leonardo. Ethos mundial. Brasília : Letraviva, 2000.

ECOLOGY - PHILOSOPHY.
Maiorescu, Toma George, 1928- Îmblâzirea fiarei din om sau ecosofia. 3a ediţia revăzută şi completată. Bucureşti : Lumina Lex, 2002.

Philosophie der natürlichen Mitwelt. Würzburg : Königshausen & Neumann, 2002.

Roach, Catherine M., 1965- Mother/nature. Bloomington, IN : Indiana University Press, c2003.
BD581 .R59 2003

ECOLOGY - SOCIAL ASPECTS. *See* **HUMAN ECOLOGY.**

ECONOMETRICS.
Beyond Keynes. Cheltenham ; Northampton, Mass. : Edward Elgar, c2002.

ECONOMIC ASSISTANCE. *See also* **INTERNATIONAL RELIEF.**
Boyce, James K. Investing in peace. Oxford : Oxford University Press, 2002.

ECONOMIC CONDITIONS. *See* **ECONOMIC HISTORY.**

ECONOMIC DEVELOPMENT. *See also* **DEVELOPING COUNTRIES.**
Anderson, Terry Lee, 1946- Property rights. Stanford, Calif. : Hoover Institution Press, c2003.
HB701 .A44 2003

Group behaviour and development. Oxford ; New York : Oxford University Press, 2002.
HD58.7 .G76 2002

Peace, prosperity, and democracy at the cutting edge. New York : Nova Science Publishers, c2003.

Rihani, Samir, 1938- Complex systems theory and development practice. London ; New York : Zed Books, 2002.
HB71 .R485 2002

ECONOMIC DEVELOPMENT - ENVIRONMENTAL ASPECTS. *See* **SUSTAINABLE DEVELOPMENT.**

ECONOMIC DEVELOPMENT, SUSTAINABLE. *See* **SUSTAINABLE DEVELOPMENT.**

ECONOMIC FORECASTING. *See also* **BUSINESS FORECASTING.**
Beyond Keynes. Cheltenham ; Northampton, Mass. : Edward Elgar, c2002.

Riding the next wave. Indianapolis, Ind. : Hudson Institute ; [Washington, DC : Distributed by the Brookings Institution Press], c2001.
HM901 .R43 2001

Some significant 21st century trends and issues. Islamabad : Pakistan Futuristics Foundation & Institute, 1998.
CB161 .S62 1998

ECONOMIC FORECASTING - RUSSIA (FEDERATION).
Tumusov, F. S. (Fedot Semenovich) Budushchee mira i Rossii. Moskva : "Mysl'", 2000.
HC340.12.Z7 S2357 2000

ECONOMIC HISTORY. *See also* **QUALITY OF LIFE.**
Rihani, Samir, 1938- Complex systems theory and development practice. London ; New York : Zed Books, 2002.
HB71 .R485 2002

ECONOMIC HISTORY - 20TH CENTURY.
Beyond Keynes. Cheltenham ; Northampton, Mass. : Edward Elgar, c2002.

Emmott, Bill. 20:21 vision. London : Allen Lane, 2003.

Lal, Vinay. Empire of knowledge. London ; Sterling, Va. : Pluto Press, 2002.
HN16 .L35 2002

ECONOMIC INDICATORS. *See* **ECONOMIC FORECASTING.**

ECONOMIC MAN. *See also* **ECONOMICS.**
Mazumdar, Krishna, 1949- Determinants of human well-being. New York : Nova Science Publishers, c2003.

HB171 .M462 2003

Oakley, Allen. Reconstructing economic theory. Cheltenham, UK ; Northampton, MA, USA : E. Elgar Pub., c2002.
HB74.P8 O15 2002

ECONOMIC POLICY. *See also* **ECONOMIC SANCTIONS; FREE ENTERPRISE; INTERNATIONAL ECONOMIC RELATIONS; NATIONAL SECURITY.**
Barbieri, Katherine, 1965- The liberal illusion. Ann Arbor : University of Michigan Press, c2002.
HF1379 .B363 2002

Beyond Keynes. Cheltenham ; Northampton, Mass. : Edward Elgar, c2002.

Peace, prosperity, and democracy at the cutting edge. New York : Nova Science Publishers, c2003.

ECONOMIC POLICY, FOREIGN. *See* **INTERNATIONAL ECONOMIC RELATIONS.**

ECONOMIC RELATIONS, FOREIGN. *See* **INTERNATIONAL ECONOMIC RELATIONS.**

ECONOMIC SANCTIONS. *See* **INTERNATIONAL ECONOMIC RELATIONS.**

ECONOMIC SANCTIONS - BURUNDI.
Le Burundi aprés la suspension de l'embargo. [Nairobi?] : International Crisis Group, [1999]

ECONOMIC SUSTAINABILITY. *See* **SUSTAINABLE DEVELOPMENT.**

ECONOMIC THEORY. *See* **ECONOMICS.**

ECONOMICS. *See also* **BUSINESS; CAPITALISM; ECONOMIC HISTORY; INDIVIDUALISM; INDUSTRIES; LAND USE; PROPERTY.**
Rihani, Samir, 1938- Complex systems theory and development practice. London ; New York : Zed Books, 2002.
HB71 .R485 2002

Von Mises, Ludwig, 1881-1973. Between the two World Wars. Indianapolis, Ind. : Liberty Fund, c2002.
HB101.V66A25 2002

Economics as social theory
The philosophy of Keynes' economics. London ; New York : Routledge, 2003.
HB99.7 .P45 2003

Economics, cognition, and society
Nelson, Phillip J., 1929- Signaling goodness. Ann Arbor : University of Michigan Press, c2003.
HV31 .N45 2003

ECONOMICS - FORECASTING. *See* **ECONOMIC FORECASTING.**

ECONOMICS, INTERNATIONAL. *See* **INTERNATIONAL ECONOMIC RELATIONS.**

ECONOMICS, MATHEMATICAL.
Foley, Duncan K. Unholy trinity. London ; New York : Routledge, 2003.
HB135 .F65 2003

Vind, Karl. Independence, additivity, uncertainty. Berlin ; New York : Springer, c2003.
HB135 .V56 2003

ECONOMICS - PHILOSOPHY.
Búfalo, Enzo del. Individuo, mercado y utopía. 1. ed. Caracas : Monte Ávila Editores Lationoamericana : Universidad Central de Venezuela, Centro de Investigaciones Post-Doctorales FACES, 1998.
BD222 .B86 1998

Read, Jason. The micro-politics of capital. Albany : State University of New York Press, c2003.
HB97.5 .R42 2003

Zhang, Xiong, 1953- Jing ji zhe xue. Di 1 ban. [Kunming] : Yunnan ren min chu ban she, 2002.
D16.8 .Z536 2002

ECONOMICS - PSYCHOLOGICAL ASPECTS.
Frey, Bruno S. Happiness and economics. Princeton, N.J. : Princeton University Press, c2002.
BF575.H27 F75 2002

Oakley, Allen. Reconstructing economic theory. Cheltenham, UK ; Northampton, MA, USA : E. Elgar Pub., c2002.
HB74.P8 O15 2002

The psychology of economic decisions. Oxford [England] ; New York : Oxford University Press, 2003-

HB74.P8 P725 2003

ECONOMICS - RELIGIOUS ASPECTS - JUDAISM.
Tamari, Meir. Maśa u-matan be-emunah. Yerushalayim : Śimhonim, [761, 2001]

ECONOMICS - SOCIOLOGICAL ASPECTS.
Dolgin, Aleksandr. Pragmatika kul'tury. Moskva : Fond nauchnykh issledovaniĭ "Pragmatika kul'tury", 2002.

Oakley, Allen. Reconstructing economic theory. Cheltenham, UK ; Northampton, MA, USA : E. Elgar Pub., c2002.
HB74.P8 O15 2002

Economy of text in non-classical philosophy of art.
Kropotov, S. L. (Sergeĭ Leonidovich) Ekonomika teksta v neklassicheskoĭ filosofii iskusstva. Ekaterinburg : Gumanitarnyĭ universitet, 1999.
B831.2 .K76 1999

ECOPHYSIOLOGY. *See* **ADAPTATION (PHYSIOLOGY).**

Ecrire comment pourquoi.
Jacob, Suzanne. Paroisse Notre-Dame-des-Neiges, Québec : Éditions Trois-Pistoles, c2002.
PN56.C69 J23 2002

Ecrire (Notre-Dame-des Neiges, Québec)
Jacob, Suzanne. Ecrire comment pourquoi. Paroisse Notre-Dame-des-Neiges, Québec : Éditions Trois-Pistoles, c2002.
PN56.C69 J23 2002

L'écriture de Freud.
Altounian, Janine. Paris : Presses universitaires de France, 2003.
BF173.F73 A48 2003

Ecriture et maladie : du bon usage des maladies / sous la direction d'Arlette Bouloumié : préface de Michel Tournier. Paris : Editions Imago, 2003. 351 p. ; 23 cm. Includes bibliographical references. ISBN 2-911416-76-7 DDC 809
1. Authors - Diseases. 2. Authors - Mental health. 3. Literature and mental illness. 4. Creative ability. I. Bouloumié, Arlette. II. Tournier, Michel.

Ecritures (Editions Alternatives)
Marchand, Valère-Marie. Les alphabets de l'oubli. Paris : Editions Alternatives, 2002.
P211 .M373 2002

ECSTASY.
Lewis, I. M. Ecstatic religion. 3rd ed. London ; New York : Routledge, 2003.
BL626 .L48 2003

Ecstatic religion.
Lewis, I. M. 3rd ed. London ; New York : Routledge, 2003.
BL626 .L48 2003

EDEN.
Morgan, Shemu'el. 'Ets ha-da'at. Pedu'el : Sh. Morgan, [1998?]

Eder, Klaus, 1946-.
Collective identities in action. Aldershot, England ; Burlington, VT : Ashgate, c2002.
GN495.6 .C635 2002

Edgar, Iain R. Guide to imagework : imagination-based research methods / Iain R. Edgar. London ; New York : Routledge, 2004. p. cm. (ASA research methods in social anthropology) Includes bibliographical references and index. ISBN 0-415-23537-5 ISBN 0-415-23538-3 (pbk.) DDC 153.3
1. Imagery (Psychology) - Methodology. 2. Dream interpretation. 3. Gestalt psychology. 4. Psychodrama. 5. Social psychology - Research. 6. Ethopsychology - Research. I. Title. II. Series: ASA research methods in social anthropology (Routledge (Firm))
BF367 .E34 2004

Edgar, Robin A. In my mother's kitchen : an introduction to the healing power of reminiscence / Robin A. Edgar. 2nd ed. Charlotte, N.C. : Tree House Enterprises, 2003. xi, 113 p. : ill. ; 22 cm. Includes bibliographical references (p. 110-112). Table of contents URL: http://www.loc.gov/catdir/toc/ecip043/2003009191.html ISBN 0-9723770-7-7 (pbk. : alk. paper) DDC 153.1/2
1. Reminiscing. 2. Healing - Psychological aspects. 3. Bereavement. I. Title.
BF378.R44 E34 2003

The edge of surrealism.
Caillois, Roger, 1913- Durham : Duke University Press, 2003.
HM590 .C35 2003

Edgeworth, Brendan. Law, modernity, postmodernity : legal change in the contracting state / Brendan Edgeworth. Aldershot, England ; Burlington, VT : Ashgate/Dartmouth, c2003. viii, 304 p. : ill. ; 25 cm. Includes bibliographical references (p. [279]-296) and index. ISBN 1-84014-009-7 (alk. paper) DDC 340/.115
1. Sociological jurisprudence. 2. Postmodernism. 3. Social change. I. Title.
K370 .E34 2003

Edice Každodenní život
(sv. 14) Člověk českého středověku. Vyd. 1. Praha : Argo, 2002.

Edice Psychologie
Utváření a vývoj osobnosti. Vyd. 1. V Brně : Barrister & Principal, 2002.
BF723.P4 U88 2002

EDIFICES. *See* **BUILDINGS.**

Edinger, Edward F. Science of the soul : a Jungian perspective / Edward F. Edinger ; edited by Daryl Sharp and J. Gary Sparks. Toronto, Ont. : Inner City Books, c2002. 125 p. : ill. ; 22 cm. (Studies in Jungian psychology by Jungian analysts) "Science of the soul, encounter with the greater personality, the therapeutic life, the vocation of depth psychotherapy, the transference phenomenon". Includes bibliographical references (p. 119-120) and index. ISBN 1-89457-403-6 (pbk.)
1. Jungian psychology. I. Sharp, Daryl, 1936- II. Sparks, J. Gary (John Gary), 1948- III. Title. IV. Series.
BF173 .E27 2002

EDISON, THOMAS A. (THOMAS ALVA), 1847-1931.
Jonnes, Jill, 1952- Empires of light. 1st ed. New York : Random House, c2003.
TK18 .J66 2003

Edison's Eve.
Wood, Gaby. 1st American ed. New York : A.A. Knopf, 2002.
TJ211 .W65 2002

Edition Akzente
Sauerländer, Willibald. Die Luft auf der Spitze des Pinsels. München : Hanser, 2002.

Edition Suhrkamp
(2279) Pfaller, Robert. Die Illusionen der anderen. 1. Aufl. Frankfurt : Suhrkamp, 2002.

EDITORIAL PHOTOGRAPHY. *See* **PHOTOJOURNALISM.**

Edkins, Jenny. Trauma and the memory of politics / Jenny Edkins. Cambridge ; New York : Cambridge University Press, 2003. xvii, 265 p. : ill. ; 23 cm. Includes bibliographical references (p. 234-249) and index. ISBN 0-521-82696-9 ISBN 0-521-53420-8 (PBK.) DDC 616.8521
1. Psychic trauma. 2. Memory. 3. Memorials x Psychological aspects. 4. Monuments - Psychological aspects. I. Title.
BF175.5.P75 E35 2003

EDMUND, OF EYNSHAM.
Adam, of Eynsham, fl. 1196-1232. [Visio Monachi de Eynsham. English (Middle English) & Latin] The revelation of the Monk of Eynsham. Oxford : Published for the Early English Text Society by the Oxford University Press, 2002.

Edo-e kara shomotsu made / Asano Kagyū hen. Jidō kōen / Sueda Masu ; kaisetsu Morishita Misako. Tōkyō : Kyūzansha, 1997. 2, 66, 265, 5 p. ill. ; 22 cm. (Nihon "kodomo no rekishi" sōsho ; 19) Reprint (1st work). Originally published: Tōkyō : Hōseidō, Shōwa 9 [1934] Reprint (2nd work). Originally published: Tōkyō : Seisui Shobō, Shōwa 17 [1942] (Shōkokumin bunka shinsho ; 2) ISBN 4-906563-42-2
1. Children - Japan - History. 2. Ukiyoe. 3. Illustration of books - Japan - Edo period, 1600-1868. 4. Parks. 5. Games. I. Asano, Kagyū. II. Sueda, Masu. Jidō kōen. III. Title: Jidō kōen IV. Series. V. Series: Shōkokumin bunka shinsho ; 2.
HQ792.J3 N54 1997 v.19

Educación ambiental.
Murillo de Martínez, Ivelisse. 2. ed. Tegucigalpa, Honduras : Copicentro Douglas, 2000.

Educación, ciudadanía y participación : transformar las prácticas : el enfoque de resiliencia / Graciela Frigerio ... [et al.]. 1. ed. Buenos Aires : Novedades Educativas, 2002. 123 p. : ill. ; 24 cm. (Ensayos y experiencias ; t. 44) Includes bibliographical references. Cover title. ISBN 987538058X
1. Education - Philosophy. 2. Educational psychology. 3. Education - Citizen participation. I. Frigerio, Graciela.

Educating boys, learning gender
Boys, literacies, and schooling. Buckingham [England] ; Philadelphia : Open University Press, 2002.

Educating the educators

LC1390 .B69 2002

Educating the educators.
Read, Malcolm K. (Malcolm Kevin), 1945- 1st American ed. Newark : University of Delaware Press ; Cranbury, NJ : Associated University Presses, 2003.
PC4064.R43 A3 2003

EDUCATION. *See also* **ADULT EDUCATION; COMPENSATORY EDUCATION; CULTURE; DISTANCE EDUCATION; EDUCATORS; ENVIRONMENTAL EDUCATION; HOME AND SCHOOL; LEARNING; LEARNING AND SCHOLARSHIP; LEARNING, PSYCHOLOGY OF; LITERACY; LYCEUMS; MASS MEDIA IN EDUCATION; MORAL EDUCATION; RELIGIOUS EDUCATION; SEX DIFFERENCES IN EDUCATION; TEACHING; UNIVERSITIES AND COLLEGES.**
Destinos das letras. Passo Fundo : Universidade de Passo Fundo, 2002.
P211 .D47 2002

Dziecko w rodzinie i społeczeństwie. Bydgoszsz : Wydawnictwo Uczelniane Akademii Bydgoskiej, 2002.

Myrdal, Alva Reimer, 1902- "Något kan man väl göra. Stockholm : Carlssons, c2002.

EDUCATION - AIMS AND OBJECTIVES. *See also* **EDUCATIONAL SOCIOLOGY.**
Meighan, Roland. John Holt. 2nd ed. Nottingham : Educational Heretics Press, 2002.
LB885.H64 M454 2002

EDUCATION - AIMS AND OBJECTIVES - UNITED STATES.
McKnight, Douglas. Schooling, the Puritan imperative, and the molding of an American national identity. Mahwah, N.J. ; London : L. Erlbaum Associates, 2003.
LC311 .M24 2003

Education and mind in the knowledge age.
Bereiter, Carl. Mahwah, N.J. : L. Erlbaum Associates, 2002.
LB1057 .B47 2002

EDUCATION AND SOCIOLOGY. *See* **EDUCATIONAL SOCIOLOGY.**

EDUCATION, CHARACTER. *See* **MORAL EDUCATION.**

EDUCATION - CHINA.
Cai, Yuanpei, 1868-1940. [Selections. 1996] Cai Yuanpei juan. Di 1 ban. Shijiazhuang Shi : Hebei jiao yu chu ban she, 1996.
BJ117 .T74 1996 <Asian China>

EDUCATION - CITIZEN PARTICIPATION.
Educación, ciudadanía y participación. 1. ed. Buenos Aires : Novedades Educativas, 2002.

EDUCATION, COMPENSATORY. *See* **COMPENSATORY EDUCATION.**

EDUCATION - CURRICULA. *See* **WOMEN'S STUDIES.**

EDUCATION - ECONOMIC ASPECTS - GREAT BRITAIN.
Read, Malcolm K. (Malcolm Kevin), 1945- Educating the educators. 1st American ed. Newark : University of Delaware Press ; Cranbury, NJ : Associated University Presses, 2003.
PC4064.R43 A3 2003

EDUCATION, ELEMENTARY.
Pound, Linda. Supporting musical development in the early years. Buckingham ; Philadelphia : Open University Press, 2003.
MT1 .P66 2003

EDUCATION, ETHICAL. *See* **MORAL EDUCATION.**

EDUCATION, HIGHER. *See* **UNIVERSITIES AND COLLEGES.**

EDUCATION, MORAL. *See* **MORAL EDUCATION.**

EDUCATION, MOVEMENT. *See* **MOVEMENT EDUCATION.**

EDUCATION, MUSICAL. *See* **MUSIC - INSTRUCTION AND STUDY.**

EDUCATION OF ADULTS. *See* **ADULT EDUCATION.**

EDUCATION OF CHILDREN. *See* **EDUCATION.**

EDUCATION OF GIRLS. *See* **WOMEN - EDUCATION.**

EDUCATION OF WOMEN. *See* **WOMEN - EDUCATION.**

EDUCATION - PHILOSOPHY.
Cahn, Steven M. Puzzles & perplexities. Lanham, Md. ; Oxford : Rowman & Littlefield, c2002.
BD41 .C26 2002

Chomsky, Noam. Chomsky on democracy & education. New York ; London : RoutledgeFalmer, 2003.
LB885.C5215 C46 2003

Codas, Enrique, 1932- En los caminos de la historia. [Asunción, Paraguay] : El Lector, c2002.
F2695.G83 C63 2002

Educación, ciudadanía y participación. 1. ed. Buenos Aires : Novedades Educativas, 2002.

Korczak, Janusz, 1878-1942. [Works. Hebrew. 1996] Ketavim. [Tel Aviv] : Yad ṿa-shem : ha-Agudah ʻa. sh. Yanush Ḳortsʼaḳ be-Yiśraʼel : Bet Loḥame ha-geṭaʼot ʻa. sh. Yitshak Ḳatsenelson : ha-Ḳibuts ha-meʼuḥad, [1996-
LB775.K627 K48 1996 <Hebr>

Wingerter, J. Richard. Teaching, learning, and the meditative mind. Lanham, Md. ; Oxford : University Press of America, c2003.
LB1025.3 .W55 2003

EDUCATION, PRIMITIVE. *See* **EDUCATION.**

EDUCATION - PSYCHOLOGY. *See* **EDUCATIONAL PSYCHOLOGY.**

EDUCATION - QUOTATIONS, MAXIMS, ETC.
The educator's book of quotes. Thousand Oaks, Calif. : Corwin Press, c2003.
PN6084.E38 E38 2003

EDUCATION, SECONDARY.
Shilony, Tamar. Model menṭali shel morim menusim ṿe-tironim be-miḳtsoʻot madaʻiyim ṿe-humaniyim le-gabe lemidah be-ḳerev yeladim. [Israel : h. mo. l., 1994?]

EDUCATION - SOCIAL ASPECTS.
Moita Lopes, Luiz Paulo da. Identidades fragmentadas. Campinas, SP, Brasil : Mercado de Letras, [2002]
HM753 .M65 2002

EDUCATION - SOCIAL ASPECTS - GREAT BRITAIN.
Read, Malcolm K. (Malcolm Kevin), 1945- Educating the educators. 1st American ed. Newark : University of Delaware Press ; Cranbury, NJ : Associated University Presses, 2003.
PC4064.R43 A3 2003

EDUCATION, THEOLOGICAL. *See* **THEOLOGY - STUDY AND TEACHING.**

EDUCATIONAL ACCELERATION. *See* **ADVANCED PLACEMENT PROGRAMS (EDUCATION).**

EDUCATIONAL ACHIEVEMENT. *See* **ACADEMIC ACHIEVEMENT.**

EDUCATIONAL AIMS AND OBJECTIVES. *See* **EDUCATION - AIMS AND OBJECTIVES.**

EDUCATIONAL ANTHROPOLOGY.
Moita Lopes, Luiz Paulo da. Identidades fragmentadas. Campinas, SP, Brasil : Mercado de Letras, [2002]
HM753 .M65 2002

EDUCATIONAL CHANGE.
Bereiter, Carl. Education and mind in the knowledge age. Mahwah, N.J. : L. Erlbaum Associates, 2002.
LB1057 .B47 2002

EDUCATIONAL EVALUATION.
Directed self-placement. Cresskill, N.J. : Hampton Press, c2003.
PE1404 .D57 2003

EDUCATIONAL GOALS. *See* **EDUCATION - AIMS AND OBJECTIVES.**

EDUCATIONAL INNOVATIONS. *See* **EDUCATIONAL TECHNOLOGY.**

EDUCATIONAL OBJECTIVES. *See* **EDUCATION - AIMS AND OBJECTIVES.**

EDUCATIONAL PSYCHOLOGY. *See also* **CHILD PSYCHOLOGY; INTELLIGENCE LEVELS; LEARNING, PSYCHOLOGY OF; LISTENING; THOUGHT AND THINKING.**
Bulayhid, Muná bint Ṣāliḥ. Thartharat muʻallimāt. al-Ṭabʻah 1. al-Riyāḍ : Maktabat al-ʻUbaykān, 2001.
BJ1291 .B85 2001

Cerezo Manrique, Miguel Ángel. Los comienzos de la psicopedagogía en España, 1882-1936. Madrid : Biblioteca Nueva, c2001.

Educación, ciudadanía y participación. 1. ed. Buenos Aires : Novedades Educativas, 2002.

Healy, Jane M. Your child's growing mind. 3rd ed. New York : Broadway Books, 2004.
BF318 .H4 2004

Lampert, Khen. Compassionate education. Lanham, Md. : University Press of America, c2003.

Montagner, Hubert. L'enfant, la vraie question de l'école. Paris : Jacob, c2002.

Shilony, Tamar. Model menṭali shel morim menusim ṿe-tironim be-miḳtsoʻot madaʻiyim ṿe-humaniyim le-gabe lemidah be-ḳerev yeladim. [Israel : h. mo. l., 1994?]

EDUCATIONAL PSYCHOLOGY - CONGRESSES.
Issledovaniia obucheniia i razvitiia v kontekste kulʼturno-istoricheskogo podkhoda. Moskva : Smysl, 2002.
BF712.5 .I88 2002

EDUCATIONAL PSYCHOLOGY - DICTIONARIES - RUSSIAN.
Slovarʼ-spravochnik po vozrastnoĭ i pedagogicheskoĭ psikhologii. Moskva : Pedagog. ob-vo Rossii, 2001.
BF712.7 .S56 2001

The educational psychology series
Beyond knowledge. Mahwah, N.J. : L. Erlbaum Associates, 2003.
BF412 .B44 2003

Motivation, emotion, and cognition. Mahwah, N.J. : L. Erlbaum Associates, 2004.
BF431 .M72 2004

EDUCATIONAL PURPOSES. *See* **EDUCATION - AIMS AND OBJECTIVES.**

EDUCATIONAL SOCIOLOGY. *See also* **EDUCATION - AIMS AND OBJECTIVES; SCHOOL ENVIRONMENT.**
Desarrollo de los valores en las instituciones educativas. Bilbao : Mensajero, 2001.

Moita Lopes, Luiz Paulo da. Identidades fragmentadas. Campinas, SP, Brasil : Mercado de Letras, [2002]
HM753 .M65 2002

Social justice, education, and identity. London ; New York : RoutledgeFalmer, 2003.
LC191 .S6564 2003

EDUCATIONAL SOCIOLOGY - UNITED STATES.
Dyson, Anne Haas. The brothers and sisters learn to write. New York : Teachers College Press, c2003.
LB1139.L3 D97 2003

EDUCATIONAL TECHNOLOGY - CONGRESSES.
Construcción de conocimiento y educación virtual. 1. ed. Ciudad Universitaria, México, D.F. : Universidad Nacional Autónoma de México, 2000.
LB1060 .C658 2000

EDUCATIONAL TESTS AND MEASUREMENTS. *See also* **CHARACTER TESTS; PSYCHOLOGICAL TESTS.**
Drummond, Robert J. Appraisal procedures for counselors and helping professionals. 5th ed. Upper Saddle River, N.J. : Merrill/Prentice Hall, 2003.
BF176 .D78 2003

Weigle, Sara Cushing. Assessing writing. Cambridge ; New York, NY : Cambridge University Press, 2002.
PE1065 .W35 2002

The educator's book of quotes / John Blaydes. Thousand Oaks, Calif. : Corwin Press, c2003. x, 226 p. ; 26 cm. CONTENTS: Inspiration -- The art of teaching -- Children -- Character -- Managing change -- Advice for life -- Principles for principals -- For a good laugh -- Inspirational leadership -- Success -- Communication -- Balancing the time crunch -- Pearls of wisdom -- Creating a culture of excellence -- Encouragement for the soul -- Education is the key. ISBN 0-7619-3862-1 (cloth) ISBN 0-7619-3863-X (pbk.) DDC 370
1. Education - Quotations, maxims, etc. 2. Conduct of life - Quotations, maxims, etc. I. Blaydes, John.
PN6084.E38 E38 2003

EDUCATORS - GREAT BRITAIN - BIOGRAPHY.
Farrer, Frances, 1950- Sir George Trevelyan and the new spiritual awakening. Edinburgh : Floris, 2002.

Edut, Ophira.
Edut, Tali. Astrostyle. New York : Simon & Schuster, c2003.
BF1729.T44 E38 2003

Edut, Tali. Astrostyle : star-studded advice for love, life, and looking good / Tali and Ophira Edut. New York : Simon & Schuster, c2003. p. cm. "A Fireside book." Includes bibliographical references (p.   ). ISBN 0-7432-4985-2 (alk. paper) DDC 133.5
1. Astrology. 2. Teenagers - Miscellanea. I. Edut, Ophira. II. Title.
BF1729.T44 E38 2003

Edward C. Armstrong monographs on medieval literature
(12.) Philologies old and new. Princeton : The Edward C. Armstrong Monographs, 2001.

Edward, J. J. Self actualization / J.J. Edward. [S.l. : s.n., 1998?] (Islamabad : Shahkar Publications) 194 p. ; 22 cm. Includes bibliographical references (p. 180-194).
1. Self-actualization (Psychology) I. Title.
BF637.S4 E39 1998

Edward, John (John J.) After life : answers from the other side / John Edward with Natasha Stoynoff. New York : Princess Books, c2003. xx, 211 p. ; 24 cm. Table of contents URL: http://www.loc.gov/catdir/toc/ecip044/2003011255.html ISBN 1-932128-06-9 ISBN 1-932128-07-7 (pbk.) DDC 133.9/1/092
1. Edward, John - (John J.) 2. Mediums - United States - Biography. I. Stoynoff, Natasha. II. Title.
BF1283.E34 A3 2003

EDWARD, JOHN (JOHN J.).
Edward, John (John J.) After life. New York : Princess Books, c2003.
BF1283.E34 A3 2003

Edwards, Charlene. Voices from Vietnam : the tragedies and triumphs of Americans and Vietnamese--two peoples forever entwined by the legacy of war / written and photographed by Charlene Edwards ; with a foreword by Robin Moore. Bayside, NY : Bayside, c2002. 264 p. : ill. (some col.), col. map ; 25 cm. Includes index. ISBN 0-9714020-3-5
1. Vietnamese Conflict, 1961-1975 - Personal narratives. 2. Vietnamese Conflict, 1961-1975 - Sources. 3. Culture conflict. I. Title.

Edwards, Derek. Discourse and cognition / Derek Edwards. London ; Thousand Oaks, Calif. : SAGE Publications, 1997. vii, 356 p. ; 24 cm. Includes bibliographical references (p. [325]-347) and index. Table of contents URL: http://www.loc.gov/catdir/toc/fy038/96071381.html ISBN 0-8039-7696-8 ISBN 0-8039-7697-6 (pbk.) DDC 153
1. Discursive psychology. I. Title.
BF201.3 .E39 1997

Edwards, Jaroldeen. The daffodil principle / text by Jaroldeen Asplund Edwards ; illustrations by Anne Marie Oborn. Salt Lake City, Utah : Shadow Mountain, 2004. p. cm. ISBN 1-59038-224-2 (alk. paper) DDC 158.1
1. Self-actualization (Psychology) 2. Success - Psychological aspects. I. Title.
BF637.S4 E4 2004

EDWARDS, JONATHAN, 1703-1758 - CONTRIBUTIONS IN HISTORY OF PHILOSOPHY.
Zakai, Avihu. Jonathan Edwards's philosophy of history. Princeton, N.J. : Princeton University Press, c2003.
B873 .Z35 2003

Edwards, Kathryn A., 1964-.
Werewolves, witches, and wandering spirits. Kirksville, MO : Truman State University Press, c2002.
GR135 .W47 2002

Edwards, Rem Blanchard.
Hartman, Robert S., 1910-1973. [Conocimiento del bien. English] The knowledge of good. Amsterdam ; New York, NY : Rodopi, c2002.
BD232 .H324 2002

E'eśeh lo 'ezer.
Yahav, Avino'am Shemu'el. Kuntres E'eśeh lo 'ezer. Betar 'Ilit : A. S. Yahav, 761, 2001.

EFFECTIVE TEACHING.
Meighan, Roland. John Holt. 2nd ed. Nottingham : Educational Heretics Press, 2002.
LB885.H64 M454 2002

Schultz, Katherine. Listening. New York : Teachers College Press, c2003.

LB1027 .S36638 2003

The effects of marriage and maternal education in reducing child poverty.
Rector, Robert. Washington, D.C. : Heritage Foundation, 2002.

EFFICIENT MARKET THEORY. *See* **STOCK EXCHANGES.**

Effron, Marc.
Human resources in the 21st century. Hoboken, N.J. : J. Wiley & Sons, c2003.
HD31 .H81247 2003

Effros, Bonnie, 1965- Creating community with food and drink in Merovingian Gaul / Bonnie Effros. 1st ed. New York ; Houndmills, England : Palgrave Macmillan, 2002. xviii, 174 p. : ill. : 22 cm. (New Middle Ages) Includes bibliographical references (p. [97]-167) and index. ISBN 0-312-22736-1 DDC 306.4/0944
1. Merovingians - Food - Social aspects. 2. Dinners and dining - France - History. 3. Fasts and feasts - France - History. 4. Civilization, Medieval. 5. France - Social life and customs. I. Title. II. Series: New Middle Ages (Palgrave (Firm))
GT2853.F7 E34 2002

Éfirov, S. A. (Svetozar Aleksandrovich) Sotsial'noe soglasie : utopii͡a ili shans? / S.A. Éfirov. Moskva : Izd-vo In-ta sotsiologii RAN, 2002. 104 p. ; 21 cm. At head of title: Rossiĭskaia akademiia nauk. Institut sotsiologii. Includes bibliographical references (p. 98-99). ISBN 5896970544
1. Negotiation. 2. Conflict management. I. Title.

Egbunu, Fidelis Eleojo. Be not afraid, only believe : Christian remedy to fear of spirits: the Igala case / by Fidelis Eleojo Egbunu. Enugu, Nigeria : Snaap Press, 2001. xvi, 127 p. : ill. ; 22 cm. Includes bibliographical references (p. 102-109). ISBN 9780491023
1. Demonology. 2. Spirits. 3. Fear - Religious aspects. 4. Fear - Religious aspects - Christianity. 5. Christian life - Catholic authors. 6. Igala (African people) - Religion. 7. Black author. I. Title.

Egéries dans l'ombre des créateurs.
Vezin, Annette. Paris : Martinière, 2002.
NX165 .V49 2002

Egipatska religija i antička Istra.
Girardi Jurkić, Vesna. Pula : Arheološki Muzej Istre, 2001.

Les églises de l'ancien diocèse de Lodève au Moyen-Age.
Alzieu, Gérard. Montpellier : Editions P. Clerc, 1998.
BX1532.L63 A695 1998

The ego and the social order.
Comfort, Kenneth Jerold. Cohoes, N.Y. : Public Administration Institute of New York State, 2000.
BF175.5.E35 C65 2000

EGO EROTISM. *See* **NARCISSISM.**

EGO (PSYCHOLOGY). *See also* **AUTONOMY (PSYCHOLOGY); IDENTITY (PSYCHOLOGY).**
Comfort, Kenneth Jerold. The ego and the social order. Cohoes, N.Y. : Public Administration Institute of New York State, 2000.
BF175.5.E35 C65 2000

Gross, Peter, 1941- Ich-Jagd. 1. Aufl., Originalausg. Frankfurt am Main : Suhrkamp, 1999.
BF175.5.E35 G76 1999

EGOISM. *See also* **NARCISSISM.**
Genuss und Egoismus. Berlin : Akademie Verlag, c2002.

Leary, Mark R. The curse of the self. New York : Oxford University Press, 2004.
BF697 .L33 2004

Wolf, Jean-Claude. Ethik und Politik ohne Gewissheiten. Freiburg, Schweiz : Universitätsverlag, c2002.

EGOISM IN LITERATURE.
Genuss und Egoismus. Berlin : Akademie Verlag, c2002.

Egypt.
Gahlin, Lucia. London : Lorenz, 2001.

EGYPT - ANTIQUITIES.
Pinch, Geraldine. Magic in ancient Egypt. London : British Museum Press, c1994.

EGYPT - CIVILIZATION - TO 332 B.C.
Rozanov, V. V. (Vasiliĭ Vasil'evich), 1856-1919. Vozrozhdaiushchiĭsia Egipet. Moskva : Izd-vo "Respublika", 2002.

EGYPT - RELIGION.
Be thou there. Cairo ; New York : American University in Cairo Press, c2001.

Cauville, Sylvie. Le zodiaque d'Osiris. Leuven : Peeters, 1997.
BL2450.O7 C399 1997

Constantine, Storm. Bast and Sekhmet. London : R. Hale, c1999.

David, A. Rosalie (Ann Rosalie) Religion and magic in ancient Egypt. London : Penguin, 2002.

Gahlin, Lucia. Egypt. London : Lorenz, 2001.

Girardi Jurkić, Vesna. Egipatska religija i antička Istra = Pula : Arheološki Muzej Istre, 2001.

Görg, Manfred. Die Barke der Sonne. Freiburg im Breisgau : Herder, 2001.
BL2450.R2 G647 2001

Rozanov, V. V. (Vasiliĭ Vasil'evich), 1856-1919. Vozrozhdaiushchiĭsia Egipet. Moskva : Izd-vo "Respublika", 2002.

Schweizer, Andreas, 1946- Seelenführer durch den verborgenen Raum. München : Kösel, 1994.

Vlora, Nedim R., 1943- Le porte del cielo. Bari : M. Adda, c2001.
BF1674 .V56 2001

Wilkinson, Richard H. The complete gods and goddesses of ancient Egypt. New York : Thames & Hudson, 2003.

EGYPT - RELIGIOUS LIFE AND CUSTOMS.
St. George, E. A. (Elizabeth Ann), 1937- Hathor, the cow goddess. London : Spook Enterprises, c2001.

Egyptian birth signs.
Constantine, Storm. London : Thorsons, 2002.

The Egyptian book of the dead.
[Book of the dead. English.] London : Cassell, 2001.
PJ1555.E5 B83 2001

EGYPTIAN MAGIC. *See* **MAGIC, EGYPTIAN.**

Egyptian Magic.
Jacq, Christian. [Monde magique de l'Egypte ancienne] Magic and mystery in ancient Egypt. London : Souvenir Press, 1998, 2002.

Egyption religion and ancient Istria.
Girardi Jurkić, Vesna. Egipatska religija i antička Istra = Pula : Arheološki Muzej Istre, 2001.

Ehbrecht, Wilfried.
Der weite Blick des Historikers. Köln : Böhlau, c2002.
D116 .W44 2002

Ehlers, Joachim, 1936-.
Deutschland und der Westen Europas im Mittelalter. Stuttgart : Thorbecke, c2002.

Ehre.
Burkhart, Dagmar. Originalausg. München : Deutscher Taschenbuch Verlag, c2002.
BJ1533.H8 B87 2002

Ehyeh.
Green, Arthur, 1941- Woodstock, Vt. : Jewish Lights Publishing, c2003.
BM525 .G84 2003

Eichler, Margrit.
Feminist utopias. Toronto : Inanna Publications and Education, 2002.

Eidam, Heinz. Moral, Freiheit und Geschichte : Aspekte eines Problemzusammenhanges / Heinz Eidam. Würzburg : Königshausen & Neumann, 2001. 140 p. ; 24 cm. Lectures. Includes bibliographical references. ISBN 3-8260-1979-2 (pbk.)
1. Ethics. 2. Liberty - Moral and ethical aspects. I. Title.

Eidelberg, Paul. Clash of two decadent civilizations : toward an Hebraic alternative / Paul Eidelberg. Shaarei Tikva, Israel : ACPR Publications, 2002. 54 p. ; 25 cm. (ACPR Policy Paper ; 144) SUMMARY: "This essay has three parts. Part I discusses the decadence of Islamic civilization. Part II discusses the decadence of Western civilization. Part III discusses the basis of Hebraic civilization, showing how it transcends East and West. Part I portrays Islam's decline as rooted in hate. Part II reveals the West's decline as rooted in indifference. Part III reveals Hebraic civilization as rooted in Hesed - kindness."--Executive summary, p. 5. ISBN 9657165458
1. Civilization - Jewish influences. 2. Degeneration. 3. Social conflict. 4. Hate - Religious aspects. 5. Indifferentism (Religion) 6. Judaism - Influence. 7. Civilization, Modern - 20th century. 8. Islam - Relations. 9. Jews - Civilization. 10. Civilization, Western. 11. Civilization, Islamic. I. Title. II.

Eidôlon (Talence, France)
Series: Policy papers (Merkaz Ari'el le-meḥḳere mediniyut) ; 144.
BM537 .E53 2002

Eidôlon (Talence, France)
(57-58.) La fin des temps. Talence : Université Michel de Montaigne, Bordeaux III, L.A.P.R.I.L., 2000-[2001]

Eigen, Michael. Rage / Michael Eigen. Middletown, Conn. : Wesleyan University Press, c2002. 192 p. ; 23 cm. (Disseminations) Includes bibliographical references (p. 181-192). ISBN 0-8195-6585-7 (cloth : alk. paper) ISBN 0-8195-6586-5 (pbk. : alk. paper) DDC 616.85/82
1. Anger - Case studies. 2. Hostility (Psychology) - Case studies. 3. Psychotherapy - Case studies. I. Title. II. Series.
RC569.5.A53 E38 2002

The eight best practices of high-performing salespeople.
Trainor, Norm, 1946- Toronto ; New York : Wiley, c2000.
HF5438.25 .T72 2000

EIGHTFOLD PATH.
Smith, Jean, 1938- The beginner's guide to walking the Buddha's eightfold path. New York : Bell Tower, 2002.
BQ4320 .S65 2002

Eiguer, Alberto. L'éveil de la conscience féminine / Alberto Eiguer. Paris : Bayard, c2002. 252 p. ; 21 cm. Includes bibliographical references (p. 241-[246]). ISBN 2-227-13954-4 DDC 150
1. Women - Identity. 2. Women - Psychology. I. Title.

La famille de l'adolescent : le retour des ancêtres / Alberto Eiguer. Paris : In press, c2001. 215 p. ; 23 cm. (Collection Adolescence et psychanalyse) Includes bibliographical references (p. [207]-215). ISBN 2-912404-66-5
1. Adolescent psychology. 2. Adjustment (Psychology) in adolescence. 3. Adolescent psychotherapy. 4. Teenagers - Family relationships. 5. Family psychotherapy. 6. Family - Psychological aspects. 7. Genealogy. I. Title.

Eilan, Naomi.
Agency and self-awareness. Oxford : Clarendon Press ; New York : Oxford University Press, 2003.

Eilers, Dana D. The practical pagan / by Dana D. Eilers. Franklin Lakes, NJ : New Page Books, c2002. 251 p. : ill. ; 21 cm. Includes bibliographical references (p. 241-243) and index. ISBN 1-56414-601-4 DDC 299
1. Occultism. 2. Paganism. I. Title.
BF1411 .E34 2002

Eimermacher, Karl.
Kul'tura i vlast' v usloviīakh kommunikatsionnoĭ revoliūtsii XX veka. Moskva : "AIRO-XX", 2002.
HM621 .K858 2002

Einaudi tascabili. Stile libero
(1047) Lucarelli, Carlo, 1960- Misteri d'Italia. Torino : Einaudi, c2002.

Einfalt, Michael.
Konstrukte nationaler Identität. Würzburg : Ergon, c2002.
DC34 .K67 2002

Einführung in die Hermeneutik.
Hufnagel, Erwin, 1940- [Neuaufl.]. St. Augustin : Gardez! Verlag, c2000.

EINSTEIN, ALBERT, 1879-1955.
Galison, Peter Louis. Einstein's clocks, Poincaré's maps. 1st ed. New York : W.W. Norton, c2003.
QB209 .G35 2003

Einstein Bücher.
Zwischen Rauschen und Offenbarung. Berlin : Akademie Verlag, c2002.
PN56.V55 Z89 2002

Einstein's clocks, Poincaré's maps.
Galison, Peter Louis. 1st ed. New York : W.W. Norton, c2003.
QB209 .G35 2003

Einzigartigkeit.
Eberlein, Undine. Frankfurt ; New York : Campus, c2000.
BF697 .E463 2000

Eiseman, Leatrice. The color answer book : the leading lady of color answers your every question / Leatrice Eiseman. Sterling, Va. : Capital Books, c2003. p. cm. Includes index. Table of contents URL: http://www.loc.gov/catdir/toc/ecip041/2003006694.html ISBN 1-931868-25-5 DDC 155.9/1145
1. Color - Psychological aspects. I. Title.
BF789.C7 E375 2003

Eisen, Jeffrey S., 1940- Oneness perceived : a window into enlightenment / Jeffrey S. Eisen. St. Paul, Minn. : Paragon House, c2003. xxvii, 254 p. ; 23 cm. (The Omega books) Includes bibliographical references. Table of contents URL.: http://www.loc.gov/catdir/toc/ecip041/2003005334.html CONTENTS: Section one. Oneness and perception -- Oneness -- The impossibility of knowing -- The structure of illusion -- Perceiving the mind -- The second realm -- Section two. Underpinnings of the physical world -- Time, space and existence -- Emergent phenomena and the nature of the universe -- Section three. Evolution and origins -- Life -- Evolution -- Section four. Self/psyche -- Thingness and the perceived self -- The evolving self, oneness perceiving -- Self-realization -- Section five. Consciousness -- The way the universe knows itself -- Consciousness and the structure of selves -- Beyond perception -- Section six. The intelligence of the universe -- Proto-evolution and the intelligence of the universe -- Oneness, God, and spirituality -- Oneness, consciousness, and existence. ISBN 1-55778-826-X (pbk. : alk. paper) DDC 150.19/8
1. Consciousness. 2. Experience. I. Title. II. Series: Omega book (New York, N.Y.)
BF311 .E39 2003

Eisenbach-Stangl, Irmgard, 1948-.
Das äussere und innere Ausland. Wien : WUV, Universitätsverlag, c2000.
BF335 .A9 2000

Eitel, Ernest John, 1838-1908.
Feng Shui, or, The rudiments of natural science in China.
Eitel, Ernest John, 1838-1908. What is Feng-Shui? Mineola, N.Y. : Dover Publications, 2003.
BF1779.F4 E4 2003

What is Feng-Shui? : the classic nineteenth-century interpretation / Ernest J. Eitel. Mineola, N.Y. : Dover Publications, 2003. vii, 69 p. ; 22 cm. Originally published: Feng Shui, or, The rudiments of natural science in China. Hong Kong : Trubner & Co., 1873. Publisher description URL: http://www.loc.gov/catdir/enhancements/fy0735/2003043987.html ISBN 0-486-43189-4 (pbk.) DDC 133.3/3337
1. Feng shui. I. Eitel, Ernest John, 1838-1908. Feng Shui, or, The rudiments of natural science in China. II. Title.
BF1779.F4 E4 2003

Eižens finks.
Rīgas gaišreģis Eižens Finks. Rīgā : Jumava, c2002.
BF1997.F56 R54 2002

EJECTION (PSYCHOLOGY). See **PERCEPTION.**

Ekel : Darstellung und Deutung in den Wissenschaften und Künsten / Beiträge von Werner Kübler ... [et al.] ; Herausgeber dieses Bandes ist Hermes A. Kick. 1. Aufl. Hürtgenwald : G. Pressler, c2003. 185 p. : ill. (some col.) ; 25 cm. (Schriften zu Psychopathologie, Kunst und Literatur ; 7) Papers presented at a symposium, held Sept. 8-9, 2000, at the Psychiatrische Klinik, Universität Heidelberg. Includes bibliographical references. ISBN 3-87646-101-4
1. Aversion - Congresses. I. Kübler, Werner. II. Kick, Hermes A. (Hermes Andreas) III. Universität Heidelberg. Psychiatrische Klinik. IV. Series.
BF575.A886 E34 2003

Ėkonomika teksta v neklassicheskoĭ filosofii iskusstva.
Kropotov, S. L. (Sergeĭ Leonidovich) Ekaterinburg : Gumanitarnyĭ universitet, 1999.
B831.2 .K76 1999

El-Haik, Basem.
Yang, Kai. Design for Six Sigma. New York ; London : McGraw-Hill, c2003.
TS156 .Y33 2003

El-Kholy, Heba Aziz. Defiance and compliance : negotiating gender in low-income Cairo / Heba Aziz El-Kholy. New York : Berghahn Books, 2002. xi, 265 p. ; 24 cm. (New directions in anthropology ; 15) Includes bibliographical references (p. 237-258) and index. ISBN 1-57181-390-X (cloth : alk. paper) ISBN 1-57181-391-8 (pbk. : alk. paper) DDC 305.42/0962/16
1. Women - Egypt - Cairo - Social conditions. 2. Women - Egypt - Cairo - Economic conditions. 3. Cairo (Egypt) - Social life and customs. 4. Poor - Egypt - Cairo. 5. Sex role - Egypt - Cairo. 6. Social conflict - Egypt - Cairo. I. Title. II. Series.
HQ1793.Z9 C353 2002

El-Khouri, Bassam.
Bergman, Lars R. Studying individual development in an interindividual context. Mahwah, N.J. : L. Erlbaum Associates, 2003.
BF713 .B464 2003

El-Ojeili, Chamsy. From left communism to postmodernism : reconsidering emancipatory discourse / Chamsy el-Ojeili. Lanham, Md. ; Oxford : University Press of America, c2003. vi, 290 p. ; 24 cm. Includes bibliographical references (p. [251]-238) and index. ISBN 0-7618-2584-3 (cloth : alk. paper) DDC 335
1. Socialism. 2. Postmodernism. I. Title.
HX44.5 .E46 2003

El que busca encuentra.
Morales Tomas, Marco Antonio. Guatemala : ESEDIR : Editorial Saqil Tzij, 1999.

Elbert, Thomas.
Biologische Grundlagen der Psychologie. Göttingen ; Seattle : Hogrefe, 2001.
QP360 .B565 2001

Elbom, David.
Likut le-ʻidud ye-ḥizuḳ. Yerushalayim : [ḥ. mo. l.], 756 [1995 or 1996]

Elbro, Carsten.
Precursors of functional literacy. Amsterdam : Philadelphia : J. Benjamins Pub., c2002.
P118.7 .P74 2002

ELDERLY PERSONS. See **AGED.**

ELDERLY WOMEN. See **AGED WOMEN.**

Eldershaw, Jane. The little book of moods / Jane Eldershaw. Avon, MA : Adams Media, 2004. p. cm. ISBN 1-59337-060-1 DDC 152.4
1. Conduct of life. 2. Mood (Psychology) I. Title.
BF637.C5 E383 2004

Elderwoman.
McCain, Marian Van Eyk. Forres : Findhorn Press, 2002.

Eleazar ben Judah, of Worms, 1176 (ca.)-1238. Sefer Sode razaya ... / le-rabenu ... Elʻazar mi-Germaiza ; uve-rosho Sod ha-yiḥud li-Yehuda he-Ḥasid ; u-sevivam Sodot shamayim : perushim ye-heʼarot ... me-et Shelomoh ... b. r. Yahya ... Koraḥ. Bene-Beraḳ : Ḳoraḥ, 759 [1998 or 1999] 26, 126 p. ; 25 cm. Cover title: Sode razaya. Spine title: Sode razaya: ye-saviv lo Sodot shamayim. Reprint of the Biłgoraj, Veinberg 1935 or 1936 ed. SUMMARY: Reprint of the original t.p.: ... "yotsʼim le-ʼor ... ʻal yede Yiśraʼel Ḳamelhar." Abstract in English at end.
1. Cabala. I. Ḳamelhar, Yiśraʼel. II. Judah ben Samuel, ca. 1150-1217. Sod ha-yiḥud. III. Ḳoraḥ, Shelomoh ben Yahya. Sodot shamayim. IV. Title. V. Title: Sode razaya VI. Title: Sode razaya: ye-saviv lo Sodot shamayim
BM525 .E432 1999

ELECTION (THEOLOGY).
'Gottes auserwählte Völker'. Frankfurt am Main ; New York : Lang, c2001.
BT810.2 .G65 2001

ELECTRA (GREEK MYTHOLOGY) IN LITERATURE.
Liddelow, Eden. After Electra. Melbourne : Australian Scholarly, 2002, c2001.

ELECTRIC COMMUNICATION. See **TELECOMMUNICATION.**

ELECTRIC ENGINEERING. See **ELECTRIFICATION.**

ELECTRIC ENGINEERING - HISTORY.
Jonnes, Jill, 1952- Empires of light. 1st ed. New York : Random House, c2003.
TK18 .J66 2003

ELECTRIC POWER DEVELOPMENT. See **ELECTRIFICATION.**

ELECTRIC POWER - HISTORY.
Jonnes, Jill, 1952- Empires of light. 1st ed. New York : Random House, c2003.
TK18 .J66 2003

ELECTRIC POWER-PLANTS. See **NUCLEAR POWER PLANTS.**

ELECTRIC POWER SUPPLY. See **ELECTRIC POWER.**

ELECTRIC UTILITIES. See **ELECTRIFICATION.**

ELECTRICAL ENGINEERING. See **ELECTRIC ENGINEERING.**

ELECTRIFICATION - HISTORY.
Jonnes, Jill, 1952- Empires of light. 1st ed. New York : Random House, c2003.
TK18 .J66 2003

ELECTRONIC APPARATUS AND APPLIANCES. See **COMPUTERS.**

ELECTRONIC BOOKS.
Why they fight [electronic resource]. Carlisle, PA : Strategic Studies Institute, U.S. Army War College, [2003]
U22

ELECTRONIC BRAINS. *See* **ARTIFICIAL INTELLIGENCE; COMPUTERS.**

ELECTRONIC CALCULATING-MACHINES. *See* **COMPUTERS.**

ELECTRONIC CIRCUITS. *See* **INTEGRATED CIRCUITS.**

ELECTRONIC COMMERCE.
Allen, Robert G. Multiple streams of internet income. New York : Wiley, c2001.
HF5548.32 .A45 2001

Burke, Dan, 1965- Business @ the speed of stupid. Cambridge, MA : Perseus Pub., c2001.
HD45 .B7995 2001

Hayes-Roth, Frederick, 1947- Radical simplicity. Upper Saddle River, N.J. ; London : Prentice Hall PTR, 2003.

Reig, Ramón. El éxtasis cibernético. 1. ed. Madrid : Ediciones Libertarias, 2001.

ELECTRONIC COMMERCE - PSYCHOLOGICAL ASPECTS.
Ratnasingam, Pauline. Inter-organizational trust in business-to-business e-commerce. Hershey, PA : IRM Press, c2003.
HF5548.32 .R378 2003

ELECTRONIC COMMERCE - PSYCHOLOGICAL ASPECTS - CASE STUDIES.
Ratnasingam, Pauline. Inter-organizational trust in business-to-business e-commerce. Hershey, PA : IRM Press, c2003.
HF5548.32 .R378 2003

ELECTRONIC COMPUTERS. *See* **COMPUTERS.**

ELECTRONIC DATA PROCESSING. *See* **ARTIFICIAL INTELLIGENCE; DATA PROTECTION.**

ELECTRONIC DATA PROCESSING - DISTRIBUTED PROCESSING. *See* **COMPUTER NETWORKS.**

ELECTRONIC DIGITAL COMPUTERS. *See* **VIRTUAL COMPUTER SYSTEMS.**

ELECTRONIC INFORMATION RESOURCE LITERACY.
Web of deception. Medford, N.J : CyberAge Books, c2002.
ZA4201 .W43 2002

ELECTRONIC INFORMATION RESOURCE SEARCHING.
Villamora, Grace Avellana. Super searchers on Madison Avenue. Medford, N.J. : CyberAge Books/ Information Today, c2003.
HF5415.2 .V497 2003

ELECTRONIC INFORMATION RESOURCES. *See* **COMPUTER NETWORK RESOURCES.**

ELECTRONIC OFFICE MACHINES. *See* **COMPUTERS.**

ELECTRONIC PUBLICATIONS.
Privacy [electronic resource]. [Washington, D.C.] : Federal Trade Commission, Bureau of Consumer Protection, Office of Consumer and Business Education, [2002]

Privacy [electronic resource]. [Washington, D.C.] : Federal Trade Commission, Bureau of Consumer Protection, Office of Consumer and Business Education, [2002]

Privacy [electronic resource]. [Washington, D.C.] : Federal Trade Commission, Bureau of Consumer Protection, Office of Consumer and Business Education, [2002]

Electronic report from the Economic Research Service.
King, John L. Concentration and technology in agricultural input industries [electronic resource]. [Washington, D.C.] : U.S. Dept of Agriculture, [2001].

ELECTRONIC SYSTEMS. *See* **COMPUTER NETWORKS; COMPUTERS; TELEVISION.**

Elementary experimental design for the life sciences.
Ruxton, Graeme D. Oxford : Oxford University Press, 2003.

ELEMENTARY PARTICLES (PHYSICS). *See* **PARTICLES (NUCLEAR PHYSICS).**

Elemente der Metaphysik.
Plessner, Helmuth, 1892- Berlin : Akademie, 2002.
BD113 .P56 2002

Elements of community resilience in the World Trade Center attack.
Kendra, James M. [Newark, Del.?] : Disaster Research Center, University of Delaware, 2001.

The elements of Islamic metaphysics (Bidāyat al-Ḥikmah).
Ṭabāṭabā'ī, Sayyid Muhammad Ḥusayn. London : ICAS, 2003.

Elements of philosophy
Timmons, Mark, 1951- Moral theory. Lanham, Md. : Rowman & Littlefield Publishers, c2002.
BJ1012 .T56 2002

The elements of ritual.
Lipp, Deborah, 1961- 1st ed. St. Paul, Minn. : Llewellyn Publications, 2003.
BF1571 .L56 2003

Elements of witchcraft.
Dugan, Ellen, 1963- 1st ed. St. Paul, Minn. : Llewellyn Publications, 2003.
BF1571.5.T44 D86 2003

ELEPHANTS.
Scigliano, Eric, 1953- Love, war, and circuses. Boston : Houghton Mifflin, 2002.
QL737.P98 S42 2002

Élettörténet és identitás.
Pataki, Ferenc, 1928- Budapest : Osiris Kiadó, 2001.
BF697.5.S65 P38 2001

ELEVENTH CENTURY. *See also* **ONE THOUSAND, A.D.**
The 1000s. San Diego, Calif. : Greenhaven Press, c2001.
CB354.3 .A16 2001

Elexpuru Albizuri, Itziar.
Desarrollo de los valores en las instituciones educativas. Bilbao : Mensajero, 2001.

Elf-help books
Engelhardt, Lisa, 1953- Elf-help for dealing with difficult people. St. Meinrad, IN : One Caring Place/ Abbey Press, c2002.
BF637.I48 E54 2002

Elf-help books for kids
Mundy, Michaelene. Getting out of a stress mess!. St. Meinrad, IN : One Caring Place, c2000.
BF723.S75 M86 2000

Wigand, Molly. Help is here for facing fear. St. Meinrad, IN : One Caring Place/Abbey Press, c2000.
BF723.F4 W54 2000

Elf-help for coping with pain.
Fone, Anne Calodich. St. Meinrad, Ind. : Abbey Press, c2002.
BF515 .F69 2002

Elf-help for dealing with difficult people.
Engelhardt, Lisa, 1953- St. Meinrad, IN : One Caring Place/Abbey Press, c2002.
BF637.I48 E54 2002

Elfenbein, Stefan W., 1964- Die veränderte Rolle der New York Times : Einfluss in Politik, Wirtschaft und Gesellschaft seit Veröffentlichung der Pentagon Papers / Stefan W. Elfenbein. Frankfurt am Main ; New York : P. Lang, c1996. xiii, 207 p. ; 21 cm. (Europäische Hochschulschriften. Reihe XXXI, Politikwissenschaft, 0721-3654 ; Bd. 292 = Publications universitaires européennes. Série XXXI. Sciences politiques ; vol. 292 = European university studies. Series XXXI, Political science ; vol. 292) Originally presented as the author's thesis (doctoral)--Freie Universität Berlin, 1995. Includes bibliographical references (p. 201-207). ISBN 3-631-49694-X DDC 071/.471
1. New York times. 2. Press and politics - United States - History - 20th century. 3. United States - Politics and government - 20th century. I. Title. II. Series: Europäische Hochschulschriften. Reihe XXXI, Politikwissenschaft ; Bd. 292.
PN4899.N42 N375 1996

An Elgar reference collection
Conflict prevention and resolution in water systems. Cheltenham, UK ; Northampton, MA, USA : E. Elgar Pub., c2002.
HD1691 .C664 2002

Migration, diasporas, and transnationalism. Cheltenham, UK ; Northampton, MA : Edward Elgar, 1999.
JV6032 .M54 1999

Elias, Maurice J. Bullying, peer harassment, and victimization in the schools / Maurice J. Elias, Joseph E. Zins. New York : Haworth Press, 2003. p. cm. Includes bibliographical references and index. Table of contents URL: http://www.loc.gov/catdir/toc/ecip046/2003015572.html ISBN 0-7890-2228-1 (alk. paper) ISBN 0-7890-2229-X (pbk. : alk. paper) DDC 373.15/8
1. Bullying. 2. Aggressiveness in children. 3. Aggressiveness in adolescence. 4. School psychology. I. Zins, Joseph E. II. Title.
BF637.B85 E45 2003

ELIAS, NORBERT.
The civilized organization. Amsterdam ; Philadelphia : John Benjamins, c2002.
HD58.7 .C593 2002

Eliav-Feldon, Miriam, 1946-.
Nashim, zekenim ṿa-taf. Yerushalayim : Merkaz Zalman Shazar le-toldot Yiśra'el, [2001]

Eliminating stress, finding inner peace.
Weiss, Brian L. (Brian Leslie), 1944- Carlsbad, Calif. : Hay House, c2003.
BF575.S75 W44 2003

Elior, Rachel. Ḥerut 'al ha-luḥot : ha-maḥashevah ha-Ḥasidit, mekoroteha ha-nistiyim ṿi-yesodoteha ha-Ḳabaliyim / Rahel Eli'or. [Tel Aviv] : Miśrad ha-biṭaḥon, [1999] 283 p. ; 21 cm. (Sifriyat "Universiṭah meshuderet") Title on t.p. verso: Hasidic thought. Includes bibliographical references (p. [271]-283). ISBN 9650510095
1. Hasidism - History. 2. Cabala. I. Title. II. Title: Hasidic thought III. Series.

ELIOT, T. S. (THOMAS STEARNS), 1888-1965 - CRITICISM AND INTERPRETATION.
Strandberg, Åke. The Orphic voice. Uppsala : Acta Universitatis Upsaliensis, 2002.
PS3509.L43 Z87 2002

Elite configurations at the apex of power / edited by Mattei Dogan. Leiden ; Boston : Brill, 2003. ii, 301 p. ; 24 cm. (International studies in sociology and social anthropology, 0074-8684 ; v. 85) Includes bibliographical references and index. ISBN 90-04-12808-5 DDC 305.5/2
1. Political leadership. 2. Elite (Social sciences) 3. Power (Social sciences) I. Dogan, Mattei. II. Series.
JC330.3 .E45 2003

ELITE (SOCIAL SCIENCES).
Elite configurations at the apex of power. Leiden ; Boston : Brill, 2003.
JC330.3 .E45 2003

García de León, María Antonia. Herederas y heridas. 1a ed. [Madrid] : Ediciones Cátedra, Universitat de València, Instituto de la Mujer, 2002.
HD6054.2.S7 G37 2002

Papcke, Sven, 1939- Gesellschaft der Eliten. 1. Aufl. Münster : Westfälisches Dampfboot, 2001.
HM821 .P37 2001

Rosero Garcés, F. (Fernando) Líderes sociales en el siglo XXI. Quito : Ediciones Abya-Yala, 2002.

ELITE (SOCIAL SCIENCES) - UNITED STATES - PUBLIC OPINION - HISTORY - 20TH CENTURY.
Horowitz, David A. America's political class under fire. New York ; London : Routledge, 2003.
HN90.S6 H67 2003

Elite strata in Israeli government bureaucracy : varieties of directors general and styles of administration.
Frankenburg, Reuven. Revadim 'elyonim ba-minhal ha-tsiburi ha-Yiśre'eli. [Israel : ḥ. mo. l., 1999?]

ELITES (SOCIAL SCIENCES). *See* **ELITE (SOCIAL SCIENCES).**

Eliyahu, Mordekhai. Sefer Śifte tsedeḳ : ma'amre Ḥazal 'al ha shemirat ha-lashon bi-yeme avot ha-'olam veha-ḳadmonim / nilḳat ṿe-ne'erakh 'a. y. Mordekhai b.R. Avraham Eliyahu. Rekhasim : M. Eliyahu, 762 [2002] 449 p. ; 24 cm. Running title: Śifte tsedeḳ.
1. Libel and slander. 2. Gossip. 3. Ethics, Jewish. I. Title. II. Title: Śifte tsedeḳ

Eliyahu, Saliman. Sefer Kerem Shelomoh : ṿe-hu perush ulo ... u-meva'er ... et divre ha-sef. ha-ḳ. 'Ets ḥayim ... Hayim Viṭal she-ḳibel mi-pi ... ha-Ari she-ḳibel mi-pi Eliyahu / ḥibro ... Salaman Eliyahu. Yerushala[y]im : Hevrat Ahavat shalom, 762 [2001 or 2002] 6 v. in 3 : facsims. ; 25 cm. (Sifre Mekhon "Ahavat shalom" Yad Shemu'el Franḳo ; mis. 5) Running title: Kerem Shelomoh. Includes bibliographical references.
1. Viṭal, Ḥayyim ben Joseph, -1542 or 3-1620. - 'Ets ḥayim. 2. Cabala. I. Luria, Isaac ben Solomon, 1534-1572. II. Viṭal, Hayyim ben Joseph, 1542 or 3-1620. 'Ets ḥayim. III. Title. IV. Title: 'Ets ḥayim. V. Title: Kerem Shelomoh VI. Series: Sifre Mekhon "Ahavat shalom" Yerushalayim.

Elkaïm-Sartre, Arlette.
Sartre, Jean Paul, 1905- [Imaginaire. English] The imaginary. London : New York : Routledge, 2003.

Elkins, James, 1955

BF408 .S263 2003

Elkins, James, 1955- Visual studies : a skeptical introduction / James Elkins. New York : Routledge, 2003. ix, 230 p. : ill. ; 24 cm. Includes bibliographical references (p. 203-222) and index. ISBN 0-415-96680-9 (HB : alk. paper) ISBN 0-415-96681-7 (PB : alk. paper) DDC 700/.1
1. Art and society. 2. Culture. 3. Visual communication. 4. Visual perception. 5. Visual literacy. 6. Communication and culture. I. Title.
N72.S6 E45 2003

Ellampsis
Ivinskai͡a, A. (Anna) Svet prelomlennogo vremeni v ikonnom prostranstve. Moskva : Khristianskiĭ Vostok, 2002.
N8189.G72 I95 2002

Eller, Cynthia (Cynthia Lorraine) Am I a woman? : a skeptic's guide to gender / Cynthia Eller. Boston : Beacon Press, c2003. 146 p. : ill. ; 23 cm. Includes bibliographical references (p. 137-138) and index. Publisher description URL: http://www.loc.gov/catdir/description/hm031/2003002564.html CONTENTS: What is a woman? -- Under the axis : the physiology of sex -- Feeling for others : women and emotion -- Walking the walk : acting like a woman -- Who's looking? : the judgment of others -- Why this matters. ISBN 0-8070-7508-6 (alk. paper) DDC 305.42/01
1. Feminist theory. 2. Sex role. 3. Sex differences (Psychology) I. Title.
HQ1190 .E424 2003

Elliott, Anthony. Psychoanalytic theory : an introduction / Anthony Elliott. 2nd ed. Durham, NC : Duke University Press, 2002. xii, 196 p. ; 24 cm. Includes bibliographical references (p. 184-189) and index. ISBN 0-8223 3007-5 (alk. paper) ISBN 0-8223-3018-0 (pbk. : alk. paper) DDC 150.19/5
1. Psychoanalysis. I. Title.
BF173 .E63 2002

Social theory since Freud : traversing social imaginaries / Anthony Elliott. 1st ed. London ; New York : Routledge, 2004. p. cm. Includes bibliographical references and index. ISBN 0-415-27164-9 (hardback) ISBN 0-415-27163-0 (softcover) DDC 150.19/5
1. Social sciences and psychoanalysis - History. 2. Freud, Sigmund, - 1856-1939. I. Title.
BF175.4.S65 E455 2004

Elliott, Carl, 1961- Better than well : American medicine meets the American dream / Carl Elliott ; foreword by Peter D. Kramer. 1st ed. New York : W.W. Norton, c2003. xxi, 357 p. ; 25 cm. Includes bibliographical references (p. 305-332) and index. Table of contents URL: http://www.loc.gov/catdir/toc/fy037/2002015947.html CONTENTS: The perfect voice -- The true self -- The face behind the mask -- The loneliness of the late night television watcher -- The identity bazaar -- Three ways to feel homesick -- Pilgrims and strangers -- Resident aliens -- Amputees by choice -- Bringing up baby -- Second acts -- Conclusion: the tyranny of happiness. ISBN 0-393-05201-X (hbk.) DDC 306.4/61/0973
1. Social medicine - United States. 2. Medical innovations - Social aspects - United States. 3. National characteristics, American. I. Title.
RA418.3.U6 E455 2003

Elliott, Charles H., 1948- Overcoming anxiety for dummies / by Charles H. Elliott and Laura L. Smith. New York : Wiley Pub., c2003. xx, 331 p. : ill. ; 24 cm. (--For dummies) Includes bibliographical references (p. [311]-313) and index. Publisher description URL: http://www.loc.gov/catdir/desc ription/wiley038/2002110284.html Table of contents URL: http://www.loc.gov/catdir/toc/wiley031/2002110284.html ISBN 0-7645-5447-6 DDC 152.4/6
1. Anxiety. 2. Fear. 3. Stress (Psychology) 4. Stress management I. Smith, Laura L. II. Title. III. Series.
BF575.A6 E46 2003

Ellis, Arthur R.
Hartman, Robert S., 1910-1973. [Conocimiento del bien. English] The knowledge of good. Amsterdam ; New York, NY : Rodopi, c2002.
BD232 .H324 2002

Ellis, Bill, 1950- Lucifer ascending : the occult in folklore and popular culture / Bill Ellis. Lexington : University Press of Kentucky, c2003. p. cm. Includes bibliographical references (p.   ) and index. Table of contents URL: http://www.loc.gov/catdir/toc/ecip042/2003008810.html ISBN 0-8131-2289-9 DDC 133.4
1. Satanism. 2. Occultism. 3. Superstition. I. Title.
BF1548 .E44 2003

Ellis, Marc H. Israel and Palestine out of the ashes : the search for Jewish identity in the twenty-first century / Marc H. Ellis. London ; Sterling, Va. : Pluto Press, c2002. xi, 198 p. ; 22 cm. Includes bibliographical references and index. CONTENTS: Jewish memory in the post-Holocaust era -- Innocence, settlers and state policy -- The prophetic in the post-Holocaust era -- A Jewish witness in exile. ISBN 0-7453-1957-2 ISBN 0-7453-1956-4 (pbk.) DDC 956.04
1. Arab-Israeli conflict - Moral and ethical aspects. 2. Israel - Moral conditions. 3. Holocaust, Jewish (1939-1945) - Influence. 4. Judaism and politics. 5. Israel - Politics and government. 6. Ethics, Jewish. 7. Israel - Ethnic relations. I. Title.
DS119.76 .E56 2002

ELOCUTION. *See* **EXPRESSION; GESTURE; VOICE.**

Eloge de la mort.
Le Fèvre, Jean-Yves. Monaco : Rocher, c2002.

ELOHIM. *See* **GOD (JUDAISM) - NAME.**

ELOQUENCE. *See* **EXPRESSION.**

The elusive child / edited by Lesley Caldwell. London ; New York : Karnac, c2002. ix, 220 p. ; 23 cm. (Winnicott studies monograph series) Includes bibliographical references (p. 205-214) and index. ISBN 1-85575-296-4
1. Winnicott, D. W. - (Donald Woods), - 1896-1971. 2. Freud, Sigmund, - 1856-1939. 3. Developmental psychology. 4. Child development - Psychological aspects. 5. Mass media and children. 6. Adolescent psychological. 7. Adoption - Psychological aspects. I. Caldwell, Lesley. II. Title. III. Series.

The elusive quest.
Porter, Norman, 1952- Belfast : Blackstaff, 2003.

Elusive Rothschild.
Rose, Kenneth, 1924- London : Weidenfeld & Nicolson, 2003.

Elzenberg, Henryk, 1887-1967. Kłopot z istnieniem : aforyzmy w porządku czasu / Henryk Elzenberg. Wyd. 1., popr. i uzup. Toruń : Wydawn. Uniwersytetu Mikołaja Kopernika, 2002. 532 p. ; 21 cm. Includes indexes. ISBN 83-231-1411-0
1. Philosophy. I. Title.

EMANCIPATION. *See* **LIBERTY.**

EMANCIPATION OF WOMEN. *See* **WOMEN'S RIGHTS.**

EMBARRASSMENT.
Allyn, David (David Smith) I can't believe I just did that. New York : Jeremy P. Tarcher/Penguin, 2004.
BF575.E53 A45 2004

EMBARRASSMENT IN CHILDREN - JUVENILE LITERATURE.
Berry, Joy Wilt. Let's talk about feeling embarrassed. New York : Scholastic, c2002.
BF723.E44 B47 2002

Tell me this isn't happening. New York : Scholastic, c1999.
BF723.E44 T45 1999

EMBARRASSMENT - PREVENTION.
Allyn, David (David Smith) I can't believe I just did that. New York : Jeremy P. Tarcher/Penguin, 2004.
BF575.E53 A45 2004

Emblematik und Mnemonik der frühen Neuzeit im Zusammenspiel Johannes Buno und Johann Justus Winckelmann.
Strasser, Gerhard F. Wiesbaden : Harrassowitz Wolfenbüttel : Herzog August Bibliothek, c2000.
PN6348.5 .S873 2000

Emblems.
Cherchi, Gavina, 1957- Tra le immagini. Fiesole (Firenze) : Cadmo ; Siena : Centro Mario Rossi per gli studi filosofici, 2002.

EMBLEMS - GERMANY - HISTORY - 17TH CENTURY.
Strasser, Gerhard F. Emblematik und Mnemonik der frühen Neuzeit im Zusammenspiel Johannes Buno und Johann Justus Winckelmann. Wiesbaden : Harrassowitz Wolfenbüttel : Herzog August Bibliothek, c2000.
PN6348.5 .S873 2000

Embodied spirituality in a sacred world.
Washburn, Michael, 1943- Albany : State University of New York Press, 2003.
BF204.7 .W372 2003

The embodiment of mind : Eastern and Western perspectives / M.M. DelMonte & Y. Haruki (editors). Delft : Eburon, c1998. 169 p. : ill. ; 24 cm. Part I contains papers presented at a conference held at the Manoir d'Youville, Chateauquay, Quebec, and entitled Body over Mind or Mind over Body: Does it Matter? Part II contains papers presented at a symposium entitled Does the Concept of Embodiment offer Something New in Psychology?, which took place at the XXVI International Congress of Psychology in Montreal. Includes bibliographical references. ISBN 90-5166-638-1 DDC 158.1
1. Mind and body - Congresses. 2. Psychology - Philosophy - Congresses. I. DelMonte, M. M. (Michael M.) II. Haruki, Yutaka, 1933-
BF161 .E43 1998

Embracing fear.
Rutledge, Thom. 1st ed. [San Francisco] : HarperSanFrancisco, c2002.
BF575.F2 R88 2002

Embracing recovery from chemical dependency.
Corley, M. Deborah. Sottsdale, AZ : Gentle Path Press, c2003.
BF632 .C63 2003

Embracing the ties that bind.
Obley, Carole J. [Philadelphia] : Xlibris, c2003.
BF1275.S44 O25 2003

Embracing the witch and the goddess.
Roundtree, Kathryn. London ; New York : Routledge, 2003.
BF1584.N45 R68 2003

EMBRYOLOGY. *See* **EPIGENESIS; GENETICS.**

Emde, Robert N.
Revealing the inner worlds of young children. New York : Oxford University Press, 2003.
BF723.S74 A37 2003

The emerald tablets of Thoth-the-Atlantean : a literal translation of one of the most ancient and secret of the great works of the ancient wisdom / translated by Doreal. Together with An interpretation of the emerald tablets / by Dr. Doreal. Sedalia, Colo. : Brotherhood of the White Temple, c2002. 192 p. ; ill. ; 27 cm. Attributed to Hermes Trismegistus. "In addition, Two tablets not printed previously, Facsimile of original tablet's cover, Map of Atlantis, Three articles on Atlantis by Doreal: Secrets of Atlantis, Atlantis and Lemuria, Atlantis and its part in the new age." DDC 135/.45
1. Medicine, Magic, mystic, and spagiric. I. Hermes, Trismegistus. II. Doreal, M. III. Brotherhood of the White Temple.
BF1999 .E44 2002

EMERGENCIES. *See* **ACCIDENTS.**

EMERGENCY MANAGEMENT. *See also* **DISASTER RELIEF.**
Bird, David F. Quality Air Force in an emergency [electronic resource]. Maxwell Air Force Base, Ala. : Air War College, Air University, [1996]

Granot, Hayim. Terror bombing. Tel Aviv : Dekel Pub. House, 2002.
HV6431 .G73 2002

Terrorism and disaster. Cambridge, UK ; New York : Cambridge University Press, 2003.
RC552.P67 T476 2003

EMERGENCY MANAGEMENT - NEW YORK (STATE) - NEW YORK.
Kendra, James M. Elements of community resilience in the World Trade Center attack. [Newark, Del.?] : Disaster Research Center, University of Delaware, 2001.

Emergency management series
Granot, Hayim. Terror bombing. Tel Aviv : Dekel Pub. House, 2002.
HV6431 .G73 2002

EMERGENCY PLANNING. *See* **EMERGENCY MANAGEMENT.**

EMERGENCY PREPAREDNESS. *See* **EMERGENCY MANAGEMENT.**

EMERGENCY RELIEF. *See* **DISASTER RELIEF.**

The emerging monoculture : assimilation and the "model minority" / edited by Eric Mark Kramer. Westport, Conn. : Praeger, 2003. xxi, 332 p. ; 25 cm. Includes bibliographical references (p. [293]-308) and indexes. ISBN 0-275-97312-3 (alk. paper) DDC 303.48/2
1. Assimilation (Sociology) 2. Acculturation. 3. Globalization. 4. Urbanization. 5. North and south. 6. East and West. 7. Eurocentrism. 8. Minorities. I. Kramer, Eric Mark.
HM843 .E44 2003

EMERGING NATIONS. *See* **DEVELOPING COUNTRIES.**

Emerging systems for managing workplace conflict.
Lipsky, David B., 1939- 1st ed. San Francisco : Jossey-Bass, c2003.
HD42 .L564 2003

EMIGRANT REMITTANCES.
Migration, diasporas, and transnationalism. Cheltenham, UK ; Northampton, MA : Edward Elgar, 1999.
JV6032 .M54 1999

EMIGRANTS. *See* **IMMIGRANTS.**

EMIGRATION AND IMMIGRATION. *See also* **ASSIMILATION (SOCIOLOGY).**
Migration, diasporas, and transnationalism. Cheltenham, UK ; Northampton, MA : Edward Elgar, 1999.
JV6032 .M54 1999

EMIGRATION AND IMMIGRATION - FORECASTING.
Growing global migration and its implications for the United States [electronic resource]. Electronic document. [Washington, D.C.? : National Intelligence Council, 2001]
CB161 .G768

EMIGRATION AND IMMIGRATION LAW. *See* **NATURALIZATION.**

EMIGRATION AND IMMIGRATION - LAW AND LEGISLATION. *See* **EMIGRATION AND IMMIGRATION LAW.**

EMIGRATION AND IMMIGRATION LAW - UNITED STATES - POPULAR WORKS.
McLaughlin, Bob. [USA immigration & orientation. Spanish] USA inmigración y orientación. 1a. ed. en español. Satellite Beach, Fla. : Wellesworth Pub., c2001.

EMIGRATION AND IMMIGRATION - SOCIAL ASPECTS.
Amodélé, Jons. The new Jews. Banjul, The Gambia : Vinasha Publishing, 2000.
1. Black author.

Beyond integration. Lund, Sweden : Nordic Academic Press, c2001.
JV6225 .B49 2001

EMISSARIES OF LIGHT.
Twyman, James F. Emissary of light. Forres : Findhorn, 2002.

Emissary of light.
Twyman, James F. Forres : Findhorn, 2002.

EMMENAGOGUES. *See* **MENSTRUATION.**

Emmons, Robert A.
The psychology of gratitude. New York : Oxford University Press, 2004.
BF575.G68 P79 2003

Emmott, Bill. 20:21 vision : the lessons of the 20th century for the 21st / Bill Emmott. London : Allen Lane, 2003. viii, 326 p. ; 24 cm. Includes bibliographical references and index. ISBN 0-7139-9519-X DDC 909.83
1. Economic history - 20th century. 2. World politics - 20th century. 3. Twenty-first century - Forecasts. 4. Twentieth century. 5. Globalization - Social aspects. 6. Capitalism - Social aspects. 7. International relations - Forecasting. 8. United States - Foreign relations - Forecasting. I. Title.

EMOTION.
Johansen, Heidi Leigh. What I look like when I am angry. 1st ed. New York : PowerStart Press, 2004.
BF723.A4 J63 2004

Emotion and motivation / edited by Marilynn B. Brewer and Miles Hewstone. Malden, MA : Blackwell Pub., 2004. p. cm. Includes bibliographical references and index. Table of contents URL: http://www.loc.gov/catdir/toc/ecip044/2003011036.html ISBN 1405110686 (pbk. : alk. paper) DDC 152.4
1. Emotions - Social aspects. 2. Motivation (Psychology) - Social aspects. I. Brewer, Marilynn B., 1942- II. Hewstone, Miles.
BF531 .E4826 2004

Emotion as meaning.
Opdahl, Keith M., 1934- Lewisburg [Pa.] : Bucknell University Press ; London ; Cranbury, NJ : Associated University Presses, c2002.
PN56.E6 O54 2002

EMOTIONAL CONDITIONING. *See* **BRAINWASHING.**

Emotional connections.
Butterfield, Perry M., 1932- Washington, DC : Zero To Three, 2004.
BF720.E45 B879 2004

Butterfield, Perry M., 1932- 1st ed. Washington, DC : Zero To Three Press, c2003.
BF720.E45 B88 2003

Emotional design.
Norman, Donald A. New York : Basic Books, 2004.
BF531 .N67 2004

EMOTIONAL HEALTH. *See* **MENTAL HEALTH.**

Emotional intelligence.
Andrews, Linda Wasmer. New York : Franklin Watts, 2004.
BF576 .A53 2004

Matthews, Gerald. Cambridge, Mass. : MIT Press, c2002.
BF576 .M28 2002

EMOTIONAL INTELLIGENCE.
Andrews, Linda Wasmer. Emotional intelligence. New York : Franklin Watts, 2004.
BF576 .A53 2004

Kaluzniacky, Eugene. Managing psychological factors in information systems work. Hershey PA : Information Science Pub., c2004.
BF576 .K358 2004

Matthews, Gerald. Emotional intelligence. Cambridge, Mass. : MIT Press, c2002.
BF576 .M28 2002

Tallon, Robert, 1947- From awareness to action. Scranton, Pa. : University of Scranton Press, 2003.
BF698.35.E54 T35 2003

Williams, Redford B., 1940- The type E personality. Emmaus, Pa. : Rodale, c2004.
BF576.3 .W55 2004

EMOTIONAL INTELLIGENCE - JUVENILE LITERATURE.
Andrews, Linda Wasmer. Emotional intelligence. New York : Franklin Watts, 2004.
BF576 .A53 2004

EMOTIONAL INTELLIGENCE - STUDY AND TEACHING (ELEMENTARY).
Self-science. 2nd ed., rev. and updated. San Mateo, Calif. : Six Seconds, c1998.
BF697 .S84 1998

EMOTIONAL PROBLEMS OF CHILDREN.
Children's fears of war and terrorism. Olney, MD : Association for Childhood Education International, c2003.
BF723.W3 C48 2003

Emotional progression in sacred choral music.
Lathan, Mark J., 1961- 2001.

EMOTIONAL STRESS. *See* **STRESS (PSYCHOLOGY).**

EMOTIONAL TRAUMA. *See* **PSYCHIC TRAUMA.**

The emotionally abusive relationship.
Engel, Beverly. New Jersey : J. Wiley, c2002.

EMOTIONS. *See also* **AFFECT (PSYCHOLOGY); ANGER; ANXIETY; AUTONOMY (PSYCHOLOGY); AVERSION; BASHFULNESS; CHARACTER TESTS; CONTROL (PSYCHOLOGY); DESIRE; EMOTIONS IN INFANTS; ENTHUSIASM; ENVY; FEAR; GRIEF; HAPPINESS; INTIMACY (PSYCHOLOGY); LAUGHTER; LOVE; MELANCHOLY; MOOD (PSYCHOLOGY); PAIN; PLEASURE; PREJUDICES; REJECTION (PSYCHOLOGY); SADNESS; SELF-CONFIDENCE; SURPRISE IN CHILDREN; TRUST.**
Andrews, Linda Wasmer. Emotional intelligence. New York : Franklin Watts, 2004.
BF576 .A53 2004

Ben-Ze'ev, Aharon. Be-sod ha-regashot. Lod : Zemorah-Bitan, 2001.

Bu ping ze ming. Di 2 ban. Beijing : Zhongguo cheng shi chu ban she, 2001.

Clough, Joy. The characters within. Chicago, IL : ACTA Publications, c1997.
BF531 .C52 1997

Communication and emotion. Mahwah, N.J. ; London : Lawrence Erlbaum, c2003.
BF637.C45 C6375 2003

Dixon, Thomas. From passions to emotions. Cambridge ; New York, NY : Cambridge University Press, 2003.

Ėmotsii cheloveka v normal'nykh i stressornykh uslovii͡akh. Grodno : Grodnenskiĭ gos. universitet im. ĪAnki Kupaly, 2001.
BF531 .E54 2001

Fortenbaugh, William W. (William Wale) Aristotle on emotion. 2nd ed. London : Duckworth, 2002.

B491.E7 F67 2002

Gorman, Phil, 1965- Motivation and emotion. 1st ed. New York : Routledge, 2003.
BF503 .G67 2003

Handbook of affective sciences. Oxford ; New York : Oxford University Press, 2003.
BF511 .H35 2003

Johansen, Heidi Leigh. [What I look like when I am angry. Spanish & English] What I look like when I am angry = 1st ed. New York : Rosen PowerKids Press, 2004.
BF723.A4 J6318 2004

Johansen, Heidi Leigh. [What I look like when I am happy. Spanish & English] What I look like when I am happy = 1st ed. New York : Rosen Pub. Group's, 2004.
BF723.H37 J6418 2004

Kaluzniacky, Eugene. Managing psychological factors in information systems work. Hershey PA : Information Science Pub., c2004.
BF576 .K358 2004

Kundtz, David, 1937- Nothing's wrong. Boston, MA : Conari Press, 2004.
BF692.5 .K86 2004

Little, Graham. The public emotions. Sydney : ABC Books for the Australian Broadcasting Corporation, 1999.
BF531 .L58 1999

Logik und Leidenschaft. Berlin : D. Reimer Verlag, c2002.

Madell, Geoffrey. Philosophy, music and emotion. Edinburgh : Edinburgh University Press, c2002.

McGaugh, James L. Memory and emotion. New York : Columbia University Press, 2003.
BF378.A87 M34 2003

Memory and emotion. Oxford University Press : New York, 2003.
BF378.A87 M46 2003

Nakonečný, Milan. Lidské emoce. Vyd. 1. Praha : Academia, 2000.
BF536 .N35 2000

Nelson, Robin, 1971- Afraid. Minneapolis, MN : Lerner Publications Co., c2004.
BF723.F4 N45 2004

Nelson, Robin, 1971- Angry. Minneapolis, MN : Lerner Publications Co., c2004.
BF723.A4 N45 2004

Nelson, Robin, 1971- Happy. Minneapolis, MN : Lerner Publications Co., c2004.
BF723.H37 N45 2004

Nelson, Robin, 1971- Sad. Minneapolis, MN : Lerner Publications Co., c2004.
BF723.S15 N45 2004

Passion and virtue in Descartes. Amherst, N.Y. : Humanity Books, 2003.
B1868.P37 P37 2003

Randolph, Joanne. What I look like when I am confused. 1st ed. New York : PowerStart Press, 2004.
BF723.I63 R36 2004

Randolph, Joanne. [What I look like when I am confused. Spanish & English] What I look like when I am confused = 1st ed. New York : Rosen Pub. Group's PowerKids Press, 2004.
BF723.I63 R3618 2004

Randolph, Joanne. What I look like when I am sad. 1st ed. New York : PowerStart Press, 2004.
BF723.S15 R36 2004

Randolph, Joanne. [What I look like when I am sad. Spanish & English] What I look like when I am sad = 1st ed. New York : Rosen Pub. Group's PowerKids Press, 2004.
BF723.S15 R3618 2004

The regulation of emotion. Mahwah, NJ : Lawrence Erlbaum, 2003.
BF531 .R45 2003

Rotner, Shelley. Lots of feelings. Brookfield, Conn. : Millbrook Press, c2003.
BF723.E6 R68 2003

Santangelo, Paolo. Sentimental education in Chinese history. Leiden ; Boston : Brill, 2003.
BF538.C48 S25 2003

Shepherd, Joanne. What I look like when I am scared. New York : Rosen Pub. Group's PowerStart Press, 2004.

Emotions

BF723.F4 S54 2004
Shepherd, Joanne. [What I look like when I am scared. Spanish & English] What I look like when I am scared = 1st ed. New York : Rosen Pub. Group's PowerKids Press, 2004.
BF723.F4 S5418 2004

Shepherd, Joanne. What I look like when I am surprised. 1st ed. New York : Rosen Pub. Group's PowerStart Press, 2004.
BF723.S87 S44 2004

Shepherd, Joanne. [What I look like when I am surprised. Spanish & English] What I look like when I am surprised = 1st ed. New York : Rosen Pub. Group's PowerKids Press, 2004.
BF723.S87 S4418 2004

Shuman, Carol. Jenny is scared. Washington, DC : Magination Press, c2003.
BF723.F4 S58 2003

Tolchard, Guylaine. The H-factor. Cary, N.C. : Process Viewpoint Pub., c2002.
BF511 .T65 2002

Warhol, Robyn R. Having a good cry. Columbus : Ohio State University Press, c2003.
PN56.5.W64 W375 2003

Zautra, Alex. Emotions, stress, and health. Oxford ; New York : Oxford University Press, 2003.
R726.7 .Z38 2003

EMOTIONS AND COGNITION.
Goleman, Daniel. Destructive emotions. New York : Bantam Books, c2003.
BL65.E46 G65 2003

Modell, Arnold H., 1924- Imagination and the meaningful brain. Cambridge, Mass. : MIT Press, c2003.
BF408 .M58 2003

Motivation, emotion, and cognition. Mahwah, N.J. : L. Erlbaum Associates, 2004.
BF431 .M72 2004

Norman, Donald A. Emotional design. New York : Basic Books, 2004.
BF531 .N67 2004

Emotions and sociology / edited by Jack Barbalet. Oxford ; Malden, MA : Blackwell Pub./Sociological Review, 2002. 175 p. ; 23 cm. (Sociological review monographs) Includes bibliographical references and index. CONTENTS: Introduction : why emotions are crucial / Jack Barbalet -- The two traditions in the sociology of emotions / Chris Shilling -- Secure states : towards a political sociology of emotion / Mabel Berezin -- Predicting emotions in groups : some lessons from September 11 / Theodore D. Kemper -- Emotions and economics / Jocelyn Pixley -- Corporate emotions and emotions in corporations / Helena Flam -- Managing the emotions of competition and recognition in academia / Charlotte Bloch -- Science and emotions / Jack Barbalet -- Complex emotions : relations, feelings and images in emotional experience / Ian Burkitt. ISBN 1405105577 DDC 302
1. Emotions - Sociological aspects. 2. Emotions - Social aspects. 3. Social structure. 4. Social interaction. 5. Social psychology. I. Barbalet, J. M., 1946- II. Series: Sociological review monograph.

EMOTIONS - COMPUTER SIMULATION - CONGRESSES.
Emotions in humans and artifacts. Cambridge, Mass. : MIT Press, c2002.
BF531 .E517 2002

EMOTIONS - CONGRESSES.
Emotions in humans and artifacts. Cambridge, Mass. : MIT Press, c2002.
BF531 .E517 2002

Feelings and emotions. New York : Cambridge University Press, 2003.
BF531 .F445 2003

EMOTIONS - EARLY WORKS TO 1850.
Hutcheson, Francis, 1694-1746. An essay on the nature and conduct of the passions and affections. Indianapolis : Liberty Fund, c2002.
B1501 .E6 2002

EMOTIONS - ECONOMIC ASPECTS.
Hochschild, Arlie Russell, 1940- The managed heart. 20th anniversary ed. Berkeley, Calif. : University of California Press, 2003.
BF531 .H62 2003

EMOTIONS IN CHILDREN. *See also*
BEREAVEMENT IN CHILDREN.
Butterfield, Perry M., 1932- Emotional connections. Washington, DC : Zero To Three, 2004.

BF720.E45 B879 2004
Xypas, Constantin. Les stades du développement affectif selon Piaget. Paris : Harmattan, c2001.

EMOTIONS IN CHILDREN - JUVENILE LITERATURE.
Rotner, Shelley. Lots of feelings. Brookfield, Conn. : Millbrook Press, c2003.
BF723.E6 R68 2003

EMOTIONS IN CHILDREN - STUDY AND TEACHING (HIGHER).
Butterfield, Perry M., 1932- Emotional connections. 1st ed. Washington, DC : Zero To Three Press, c2003.
BF720.E45 B88 2003

Emotions in humans and artifacts / edited by Robert Trappl, Paolo Petta, and Sabine Payr. Cambridge, Mass. : MIT Press, c2002. viii, 390 p. : ill. ; 26 cm. (A Bradford book) Includes bibliographical references (p. [367]-368) and index. Papers from a conference. CONTENTS: Emotions: from brain research to computer game development / Robert Trappl and Sabine Payr -- A theory of emotion, its functions, and its adaptive value / Edmund T. Rolls -- How many separately evolved emotional beasties live within us? / Aaron Sloman -- Designing emotions for activity selection in autonomous agents / Lola D. Cañamero -- Emotions: meaningful mappings between the individual and its world / Kirstie L. Bellman -- On making believable emotional agents believable / Andrew Ortony -- What does it mean for a computer to "have" emotions? / Rosalind W. Picard -- The role of elegance in emotion and personality: reasoning for believable agents / Clark Elliott -- The role of emotions in a tractable architecture for situated cognizers / Paolo Petta -- The Wolfgang system: a role of "emotions" to bias learning and problem solving when learning to compose music / Douglas Riecken -- A Baysian heart: computer recognition and simulation of emotion / Eugene Ball -- Creating emotional relationships with virtual characters / Andrew Stern. ISBN 0-262-20142-9 (alk. paper) DDC 152.4
1. Emotions - Congresses. 2. Emotions - Physiological aspects - Congresses. 3. Emotions - Computer simulation - Congresses. I. Trappl, Robert. II. Petta, Paolo, 1963- III. Payr, Sabine, 1956- IV. Series: Bradford book.
BF531 .E517 2002

EMOTIONS IN INFANTS.
Butterfield, Perry M., 1932- Emotional connections. Washington, DC : Zero To Three, 2004.
BF720.E45 B879 2004

EMOTIONS IN INFANTS - STUDY AND TEACHING (HIGHER).
Butterfield, Perry M., 1932- Emotional connections. 1st ed. Washington, DC : Zero To Three Press, c2003.
BF720.E45 B88 2003

EMOTIONS IN LITERATURE.
Cockcroft, Robert, 1939- Rhetorical affect in early modern writing. New York : Palgrave Macmillan, 2003.
PR428.E56 C63 2003

Fichtelberg, Joseph. Critical fictions. Athens : University of Georgia Press, c2003.
PS366.S35 F53 2003

Opdahl, Keith M., 1934- Emotion as meaning. Lewisburg [Pa.] : Bucknell University Press ; London ; Cranbury, NJ : Associated University Presses, c2002.
PN56.E6 O54 2002

Santangelo, Paolo. Sentimental education in Chinese history. Leiden ; Boston : Brill, 2003.
BF538.C48 S25 2003

Tait, Peta, 1953- Performing emotions. Aldershot ; Burlington Vt. : Ashgate, c2002.
PG3458.Z9 D774 2002

EMOTIONS (PHILOSOPHY).
Bard, Xavier, 1935- Du plaisir, de la douleur et de quelques autres. Paris, France : Harmattan, c2002.

Dixon, Thomas. From passions to emotions. Cambridge ; New York, NY : Cambridge University Press, 2003.

EMOTIONS - PHYSIOLOGICAL ASPECTS.
Ėmotsii cheloveka v normal'nykh i stressornykh uslovii͡akh. Grodno : Grodnenskiĭ gos. universitet im. I͡Anki Kupaly, 2001.
BF531 .E54 2001

Gorman, Phil, 1965- Motivation and emotion. 1st ed. New York : Routledge, 2003.
BF503 .G67 2003

EMOTIONS - PHYSIOLOGICAL ASPECTS - CONGRESSES.
Emotions in humans and artifacts. Cambridge, Mass. : MIT Press, c2002.

BF531 .E517 2002
EMOTIONS - RELIGIOUS ASPECTS.
Goleman, Daniel. Destructive emotions. New York : Bantam Books, c2003.
BL65.E46 G65 2003

EMOTIONS - SEX DIFFERENCES.
Shields, Stephanie A. Speaking from the heart. Cambridge, U.K. ; New York : Cambridge University Press, 2002.
BF531 .S55 2002

EMOTIONS - SOCIAL ASPECTS.
Emotion and motivation. Malden, MA : Blackwell Pub., 2004.
BF531 .E4826 2004

Emotions and sociology. Oxford ; Malden, MA : Blackwell Pub./Socological Review, 2002.

The regulation of emotion. Mahwah, NJ : Lawrence Erlbaum, 2003.
BF531 .R45 2003

Shields, Stephanie A. Speaking from the heart. Cambridge, U.K. ; New York : Cambridge University Press, 2002.
BF531 .S55 2002

La soif d'émotion. Paris : Plon, c1999.
BF531 .S637 1999

EMOTIONS - SOCIAL ASPECTS - CONGRESSES.
Feelings and emotions. New York : Cambridge University Press, 2003.
BF531 .F445 2003

EMOTIONS - SOCIAL ASPECTS - TEXTBOOKS.
The social life of emotions. New York : Cambridge University Press, 2004.
BF531 .S634 2004

EMOTIONS - SOCIOLOGICAL ASPECTS.
Emotions and sociology. Oxford ; Malden, MA : Blackwell Pub./Socological Review, 2002.

Hochschild, Arlie Russell, 1940- The commercialization of intimate life. Berkeley : University of California Press, 2003.
HM1106 .H63 2003

Emotions, stress, and health.
Zautra, Alex. Oxford ; New York : Oxford University Press, 2003.
R726.7 .Z38 2003

Ėmotsii cheloveka v normal'nykh i stressornykh uslovii͡akh / pod obshcheĭ redaktsieĭ A.I I͡Arotskogo, I.A. Krivolapchuka. Grodno : Grodnenskiĭ gos. universitet im. I͡Anki Kupaly, 2001. 493 p. : ill. ; 21 cm. Includes bibliographical references (p. 469-491). ISBN 9854173046
1. Emotions. 2. Emotions - Physiological aspects. 3. Stress (Psychology) I. I͡Arotskiĭ, A. I. II. Krivolapchuk, I. A. (Igor' Ivanovich) III. Hrodzenski dz͡ar͡zhaŭny universitėt im͡ia I͡A. Kupaly.
BF531 .E54 2001

EMPATHY.
Ickes, William John. Everyday mind reading. Amherst, N.Y. : Prometheus Books, 2003.
BF575.E55 I35 2003

EMPATHY IN ART.
Makeieff, Macha. Poétique du désastre. Arles : Actes sud, c2001.

Empire of knowledge.
Lal, Vinay. London ; Sterling, Va. : Pluto Press, 2002.
HN16 .L35 2002

Empire of magic.
Heng, Geraldine. New York : Columbia University Press, c2003.
PR321 .H46 2003

Empires of light.
Jonnes, Jill, 1952- 1st ed. New York : Random House, c2003.
TK18 .J66 2003

Empires of time.
Aveni, Anthony F. Rev. ed. Boulder, Colo. : University Press of Colorado, c2002.
QB209 .A94 2002

EMPLOYEE COMPETITIVE BEHAVIOR. *See* **INCENTIVES IN INDUSTRY.**

EMPLOYEE DEVELOPMENT. *See* **EMPLOYEES - TRAINING OF.**

EMPLOYEE INCENTIVES. *See* **INCENTIVES IN INDUSTRY.**

EMPLOYEE LOYALTY.
Cohen, Aaron, 1952- Multiple commitments in the workplace. Mahwah, New Jersey : Lawrence Erlbaum Associates, 2003.
HD58.7 .C6213 2003

EMPLOYEE MEDICAL TESTING. *See* **EMPLOYEES - MEDICAL EXAMINATIONS.**

EMPLOYEE MORALE. *See* **INCENTIVES IN INDUSTRY.**

EMPLOYEE MOTIVATION. *See also* **INCENTIVES IN INDUSTRY.**
Galford, Robert M., 1952- The trusted leader. New York ; London : Free Press, c2002.
HD57.7 .G33 2002

Harvard business essentials. Hiring and keeping the best people. Boston : Harvard Business School Press, c2002.
HF5549.5.S38 H37 2002

Hiam, Alexander. Making horses drink. [Irvine, Calif.] : Entrepreneur Press, c2002.
HD57.7 .H52 2002

Hochschild, Arlie Russell, 1940- The managed heart. 20th anniversary ed. Berkeley, Calif. : University of California Press, 2003.
BF531 .H62 2003

Rampersad, Hubert K. Total performance scorecard. Amsterdam ; Boston ; London : Butterworth-Heinemann, c2003.
HD62.15 .R3598 2003

EMPLOYEE RETENTION.
Harvard business essentials. Hiring and keeping the best people. Boston : Harvard Business School Press, c2002.
HF5549.5.S38 H37 2002

EMPLOYEE SELECTION.
Harvard business essentials. Hiring and keeping the best people. Boston : Harvard Business School Press, c2002.
HF5549.5.S38 H37 2002

EMPLOYEE TRAINING. *See* **EMPLOYEES - TRAINING OF.**

EMPLOYEES. *See* **PERSONNEL MANAGEMENT; PROFESSIONAL EMPLOYEES.**

EMPLOYEES - ATTITUDES.
Personality and work. 1st ed. San Francisco, CA : Jossey-Bass, c2003.
BF698.9.O3 P47 2003

EMPLOYEES - COUNSELING OF.
Bell, Chip R. Managers as mentors. 2nd ed., completely rev. and expanded. San Francisco, Calif : Berrett-Koehler Publishers, c2002.
HF5385 .B45 1996

Frost, Peter J. Toxic emotions at work. Boston : Harvard Business School Press, c2003.
HD42 .F76 2003

EMPLOYEES - MEDICAL EXAMINATIONS - LAW AND LEGISLATION - UNITED STATES - MISCELLANEA.
Questions and answers [electronic resource]. [Washington, D.C.] : U.S. Equal Employment Opportunity Commission, [2000?]

EMPLOYEES, TRAINING OF. *See* **EMPLOYEES - TRAINING OF.**

EMPLOYEES - TRAINING OF.
Bell, Chip R. Managers as mentors. 2nd ed., completely rev. and expanded. San Francisco, Calif : Berrett-Koehler Publishers, c2002.
HF5385 .B45 1996

EMPLOYEES - TRAINING OF - PROBLEMS, EXERCISES, ETC.
Epstein, Robert, 1953- The big book of creativity games. New York : McGraw-Hill, c2000.
BF408 .E67 2000

EMPLOYER-SUPPORTED EDUCATION. *See* **EMPLOYEES - TRAINING OF.**

EMPLOYMENT DISCRIMINATION. *See* **DISCRIMINATION IN EMPLOYMENT.**

EMPLOYMENT (ECONOMIC THEORY). *See* **DISCRIMINATION IN EMPLOYMENT.**

EMPLOYMENT MANAGEMENT. *See* **PERSONNEL MANAGEMENT.**

Empowering your life with wicca.
Knight, Sirona, 1955- Indianapolis, IN : Alpha Books, c2003.

BF1571 .K56 2003

EMPRESSES. *See* **QUEENS.**

The empty room.
DeVita, Elizabeth. New York : Scribner 2004.
BF575.G7 D48 2004

Emtcheu, André. Psychologie et révélation : du fétichisme à la foi en Afrique noire / André Emtcheu et Sadrack Djioukou. Yaoundé, Cameroun : Editions SHERPA, c2001. 125 p. ; 23 cm. "Novembre 2001." Includes bibliographical references (p. [121]-125). ISBN 9956320056
1. Africa, Sub-Saharan - Religion. 2. Africa, Sub-Saharan - Religious life and customs. 3. Christianity and culture - Africa, Sub-Saharan. 4. Superstition - Religious aspects - Christianity. 5. Fetishism. 6. Psychology, Religious. 7. Black author. I. Djiokou, Sadrack. II. Title.

En el ojo de la batalla.
Romero, Pedro G., 1964- Valencia : Universitat de València, 2002.

En los caminos de la historia.
Codas, Enrique, 1932- [Asunción, Paraguay] : El Lector, c2002.
F2695.G83 C63 2002

En marge
Colloque des Invalides (5th : 2001 : Hôtel des invalides) Ce que je ne sais pas. Tusson, Charente : Du Lérot, [2002?]
PQ145 .C65 2001

Enç, Berent. How we act : causes, reasons, and intentions / Berent Enç. Oxford : Clarendon Press ; New York : Oxford University Press, 2003. xii, 252 p. : ill. ; 22 cm. Includes bibliographical references (p. [235]-243) and index. ISBN 0-19-925602-0 DDC 128.4
1. Act (Philosophy) 2. Causation. 3. Reasoning. 4. Will. 5. Decision making. I. Title.
B105.A35 E63 2003

Enchanted feminism.
Salomonsen, Jone, 1956- London ; New York : Routledge, 2002.
BF1577.C2 S25 2002

An enchanted life.
Telesco, Patricia, 1960- Franklin Lakes, N.J. : New Page Books, c2002.
BF1621 .T42 2002

ENCHANTERS. *See* **MAGICIANS.**

Enciclopedia iberoamericana de filosofía
(24) La filosofía medieval. Madrid : Trotta, 2002.
B721 .F47 2002

Encontro de mulheres.
Marraccini, Eliane Michelini. São Paulo : Casa do Psicólogo, c2001.

Encountering Buddhism : Western psychology and Buddhist teachings / edited by Seth Robert Segall. Albany : State University of New York Press, 2003. ix, 214 p. ; 23 cm. (SUNY series in transpersonal and humanistic psychology) Includes bibliographical references and index. ISBN 0-7914-5735-4 (alk. paper) ISBN 0-7914-5736-2 (pbk. : alk. paper) DDC 294.3/375
1. Buddhism and psychoanalysis. 2. Psychotherapy - Religious aspects - Buddhism. 3. Spiritual life - Buddhism. 4. Buddhism - United States - History - 20th century. I. Segall, Seth Robert. II. Series.
BQ4570.P755 E62 2003

ENCOUNTERS OF HUMANS WITH ALIENS. *See* **HUMAN-ALIEN ENCOUNTERS.**

Encounters (Rutgers University Press)
Steedman, Carolyn. Dust. New Brunswick, N.J. : Rutgers University Press, 2002, c2001.
CD947 .S73 2002

Encounters with Asia
Hannas, Wm. C., 1946- The writing on the wall. Philadelphia : University of Pennsylvania Press, c2003.
P381.E18 H36 2003

ENCOUNTERS WITH UNIDENTIFIED FLYING OBJECTS. *See* **UNIDENTIFIED FLYING OBJECTS - SIGHTINGS AND ENCOUNTERS.**

ENCOURAGEMENT.
Danzig, Robert J., 1932- Every child deserves a champion. Washington, DC : Child & Family Press, c2003.
BF637.E53 D36 2003

The encyclopaedia of Celtic myth and legend.
Matthews, John, 1948- London : Rider, 2002.
BL915 .M377 2002

An encyclopædia of occultism.
Spence, Lewis, 1874-1955. Mineola, N.Y. : Dover Publications, 2003.
BF1025 .S7 2003

Encyclopaedia of psychoanalysis
(4) The Ship of thought. London : Karnac, 2002.

Encyclopedia and dictionary of dreams.
Zolar. Zolar's encyclopedia and dictionary of dreams. Fully rev. and updated for the 21st century. New York : Simon & Schuster, 2004.
BF1091 .Z65 2004

The encyclopedia of alien encounters.
Baker, Alan. London : Virgin, 1999.

The encyclopedia of extraterrestrial encounters.
Story, Ronald. New York : New American Library, c2001.
TL789.16 .S76 2001

Encyclopedia of extraterrestrials and otherworldly beings.
Clark, Jerome. Extraordinary encounters. Santa Barbara, Calif. : ABC-CLIO, c2000.
BF2050 .C57 2000

Encyclopedia of psychological assessment / edited by Rocio Fernandez-Ballesteros. London ; Thousand Oaks, Calif. : SAGE Publications, 2003. 2 v. (1164 p.) : ill. ; 26 cm. Includes bibliographical references and index. CONTENTS: v. 1. A-L -- v. 2. M-Z. ISBN 0-7619-5494-5 (set) DDC 150/.28/7
1. Psychometrics - Encyclopedias. 2. Psychological tests - Encyclopedias. I. Fernández Ballesteros, Rocío.
BF39 .E497 2003

Encyclopedia of the unusual and unexplained.
Steiger, Brad. The Gale encyclopedia of the unusual and unexplained. Detroit : Thomson/Gale, c2003.
BF1025 .S79 2003

The encyclopedia of vampires, werewolves, and other monsters.
Guiley, Rosemary. New York, NY : Facts on File, 2004.
BF1556 .G86 2004

ENCYCLOPEDIAS AND DICTIONARIES, ENGLISH. *See* **ENCYCLOPEDIAS AND DICTIONARIES.**

ENCYCLOPEDIAS AND DICTIONARIES - EUROPE - HISTORY.
West, William. Theatres and encyclopedias in early modern Europe. Cambridge : Cambridge University Press, 2002.

End of a beginning in natural history.
Gould, Stephen Jay. I have landed. 1st ed. New York : Harmony Books, 2002.
QH45.5 .G735 2002

The end of dissatisfaction?.
McGowan, Todd. Albany : State University of New York Press, c2004.
BF175.4.C84 M4 2004

The end of everything : postmodernism and the vanishing of the human : Lyotard, Haraway, Plato, Heidegger, Habermas, McLuhan / foreword by Will Self ; introduction by Stuart Sim ; edited by Richard Appignanesi. Cambridge : Icon, 2003. vi, 250 p. ; 20 cm. Includes bibliographical references and index. CONTENTS: Lyotard and the inhuman / Start Sim -- Donna Haraway and GM foods / George Myerson -- Plato and the Internet / Kieron O'Hara -- Heidegger, Habermas and the mobile phone / George Myerson -- Marshall McLuhan and virtuality / Christopher Horrocks. ISBN 1-84046-421-6 DDC 306.46
1. Postmodernism. 2. Technology - Social aspects. I. Appignanesi, Richard, 1940-

The end of man.
Babarinde, A. O. Lagos, Nigeria : Christ Foundation Baptist Church, 2001.

END OF THE WORLD.
Engleman, Dennis Eugene, 1948- Ultimate things. Ben Lomond, Calif. : Conciliar Press, c1995.
BT876 .E54 1995

Expecting Armageddon. New York : Routledge, 2000.
BL503 .E97 2000

Gäbler, Ulrich. Zeiten des Endes. Basel : Schwabe & Co., c2002.

Konstantinovskaia, L. V. (Liudmila Vasil'evna) Kogda prikhodiat proroki. Moskva : Klassiks Stil', 2002.
BF1796 .K66 2002

Nocam. Nostradamus. Champagne-sur-Oise : Kapsos, 1998.

End of the world.

BF1815.N8 A2668 1998

Van Auken, John. The end times. New York : Signet Book, c2001. [Updated ed.].
BF1791 .V36 2001

END OF THE WORLD IN LITERATURE.
La fin des temps. Talence : Université Michel de Montaigne, Bordeaux III, L.A.P.R.I.L., 2000-[2001]

END OF THE WORLD - MISCELLANEA.
Weidner, Jay. The mysteries of the great cross of Hendaye. Rochester, Vt. : Destiny Books, 2003.
BF1999 .W435 2003

The end times.
Van Auken, John. New York : Signet Book, c2001. [Updated ed.].
BF1791 .V36 2001

ENDANGERED ECOSYSTEMS. *See* **NATURE CONSERVATION.**

ENDANGERED SPECIES. *See* **NATURE CONSERVATION.**

Das Ende des Hermetismus : historische Kritik und neue Naturphilosophie in der Spätrenaissance : Dokumentation und Analyse der Debatten um die Datierung der hermetischen Schriften von Genebrard bis Casaubon, (1567-1614) / Martin Mulsow (Hrsg.). Tübingen : Mohr Siebeck, c2002. ix, 405 p. : ill. ; 24 cm. (Religion und Aufklärung, 1436-2600 ; Bd. 9) Includes bibliographical references and indexes. Contributions in German and English; some original Renaissance texts in Italian and Latin. ISBN 3-16-147778-2 (pbk.).
1. Hermetism - History - 16th century. 2. Philosophy, Renaissance. 3. Science - Philosophy - History - 16th century. I. Mulsow, Martin. II. Series.
BF1587 .E53 2002

Ending civil wars : the implementation of peace agreements / edited by Stephen John Stedman, Donald Rothchild, Elizabeth M. Cousens. Boulder, Colo. : Lynne Rienner, 2002. xiii, 729 p. ; 24 cm. "A project of the International Peace Academy and CISAC". Includes bibliographical references (p. 683-698) and index. CONTENTS: Evaluation issues in peace implementation / George Downs and Stephen John Stedman -- Strategy and transitional authority / Michael W. Doyle -- The challenges of strategic coordination / Bruce D. Jones -- Settlement terms and postagreement stability / Donald Rothchild -- Disarmament and demobilization / Joanna Spear -- Economic priorities for successful peace implementation / Susan L. Woodward -- The role of postsettlement elections / Terrence Lyons -- Human rights and sustainable peace / Tonya L. Putnam -- Refugee repatriation / Howard Adelman -- Civilian security / Charles T. Call and William Stanley -- Building local capacity : from implementation to peacebuilding / John Prendergast and Emily Plumb -- Peace in stages : the role of an implementation regime in Nicaragua / Caroline A. Hartzell -- Assessing El Salvador's transition from civil war to peace / Charles T. Call -- Broad participation, diffuse responsibility : peace implementation in Guatemala / William Stanley and David Holiday -- Implementing the Arusha Peace Agreement on Rwanda / Gilbert M. Khadiagala -- Implementing Cambodia's peace agreement / Sorpong Peou -- From missed opportunities to overcompensation : implementing the Dayton Agreement on Bosnia / Elizabeth M. Cousens -- Peace by unconventional means : Lebanon's Taif Agreement / Marie-Joëlle Zahar -- Liberia : a warlord's peace / Adekeye Adebajo -- Flawed mediation, chaotic implementation : the 1987 Indo-Sri Lanka Peace Agreement / Sumantra Bose -- Policy implications / Stephen John Stedman. ISBN 1-58826-058-5 (alk. paper) ISBN 1-58826-083-6 (pbk. : alk. paper) DDC 303.6/4
1. Civil war - Political aspects. 2. Peace. 3. Intervention (International law) - Political aspects. I. Stedman, Stephen John. II. Rothchild, Donald S. III. Cousens, Elizabeth M.
JZ6368 .E53 2002

The ends of mourning.
Ricciardi, Alessia. Stanford, Calif. : Stanford University Press, 2003.
PN56.D4 R53 2003

ENEMY ALIENS. *See* **ALIENS.**

ENERGY. *See* **FORCE AND ENERGY.**

Energy and the unexpected.
Laidler, Keith James, 1916- Oxford ; New York : Oxford University Press, c2002.
QC72 .L35 2002

ENERGY DISSIPATION.
Dynamics of dissipation. Berlin ; New York : Springer, c2002.
QC174.85 .D96 2002

ENERGY INDUSTRIES. *See* **PETROLEUM INDUSTRY AND TRADE.**

L'enfant, la vraie question de l'école.
Montagner, Hubert. Paris : Jacob, c2002.

Enforcement guidance on disability-related inquiries and medical examinations of employees under the Americans with Disabilities Act (ADA).
Questions and answers [electronic resource]. [Washington, D.C.] : U.S. Equal Employment Opportunity Commission, [2000?]

ENFORCEMENT OF LAW. *See* **LAW ENFORCEMENT.**

Engaging humor.
Oring, Elliott, 1945- Urbana : University of Illinois Press, c2003.
PN6147 .O74 2003

Engel, Antke. Wider die Eindeutigkeit : Sexualität und Geschlecht im Fokus queerer Politik der Repräsentation / Antke Engel. Frankfurt/Main ; New York : Campus, c2002. 255 p. ; 23 cm. (Reihe "Politik der Geschlechterverhältnisse" ; Bd. 20) Originally presented as the author's thesis (doctoral - Potsdam) under the title: Repräsentation als Intervention. Queer/feministische Politik der VerUneindeutigung von Geschlecht und Sexualität. Includes bibliographical references. ISBN 3-593-37117-0 (pbk.)
1. Sexual orientation. 2. Gender identity. I. Title. II. Series.

Engel, Beverly. The emotionally abusive relationship : how to stop being abused and how to stop abusing / Beverly Engel. New Jersey : J. Wiley, c2002. v, 266 p. ; 25 cm. Includes bibliographical references (p. 258-260) and index. ISBN 0-471-21297-0
1. Psychological abuse. 2. Interpersonal relations. I. Title.

Honor your anger : how transforming your anger style can change your life / Beverly Engel. Hoboken, N.J. : J. Wiley & Sons, 2003. p. cm. Includes bibliographical references and index. Publisher description URL: http://www.loc.gov/catdir/desc ription/wiley038/2003005796.html Table of contents URL: http://www.loc.gov/catdir/toc/wiley031/2003005796.html CONTENTS: One of the most important changes you will ever make -- The first steps to discovering your anger style -- Discovering your primary anger style -- Variations on a theme: discovering your secondary anger style -- Changing your anger style -- The first steps to change -- Modifying or transforming an aggressive style -- From passive to assertive -- From passive-aggressive to assertiveness -- Transforming the projective-aggressive style -- Dealing with other people's anger -- Getting beyond our anger. ISBN 0-471-27316-3 DDC 152.4/7
1. Anger. I. Title.
BF575.A5 E54 2003

Engelhard, Kristina.
Aufklärungen. Berlin : Duncker und Humblot, c2002.

Engelhardt, Lisa, 1953- Elf-help for dealing with difficult people / written by Lisa O. Engelhardt ; illustrated by R.W. Alley. St. Meinrad, IN : One Caring Place/Abbey Press, c2002. 1 v. (unpaged) : ill. ; 16 cm. (Elf-help books) ISBN 0-87029-366-4 DDC 158.2
1. Interpersonal conflict. 2. Conflict management. I. Title. II. Series.
BF637.I48 E54 2002

Engels, Dennis W. The professional counselor : portfolio, competencies, performance guidelines, and assessment. 3d ed. / Dennis W. Engels and associates. Alexandria, VA : American Counseling Association, c2004. p. cm. Rev. ed. of: The professional counselor / edited by Dennis W. Engels, Joseph D. Dameron. "Written by faculty of the Counseling Program, Department of Counseling, Development, and Higher Education, College of Education, University of North Texas, Denton, Texas." Includes bibliographical references (p.   ). Table of contents URL: http://www.loc.gov/catdir/toc/ecip046/2003014714.html ISBN 1-55620-229-6 DDC 158/.3
1. Counseling - Evaluation. 2. Counselors - Rating of. I. University of North Texas. Counseling Program. II. Title. III. Title: Professional counselor.
BF637.C6 P78 2004

Engfer, Hans-Jürgen.
Neuzeitliches Denken. Berlin ; New York : De Gruyter, 2002.

ENGINEERING. *See* **ELECTRIC ENGINEERING; SURVEYING.**

ENGINEERING - COMPUTER-ASSISTED INSTRUCTION - CONGRESSES.
International Conference on Simulation in Engineering Education (2001 : Phoenix, Ariz.) Proceedings of the International Conference on Simulation and Multimedia in Engineering Education & Virtual Worlds and Simulation. San Diego, CA : Society for Computer Simulation International, c2001.

ENGINEERING - COMPUTER SIMULATION - CONGRESSES.
International Conference on Simulation in Engineering Education (2001 : Phoenix, Ariz.) Proceedings of the International Conference on Simulation and Multimedia in Engineering Education & Virtual Worlds and Simulation. San Diego, CA : Society for Computer Simulation International, c2001.

ENGINEERING - COMPUTER SIMULATION - STUDY AND TEACHING - CONGRESSES.
International Conference on Simulation in Engineering Education (2001 : Phoenix, Ariz.) Proceedings of the International Conference on Simulation and Multimedia in Engineering Education & Virtual Worlds and Simulation. San Diego, CA : Society for Computer Simulation International, c2001.

ENGINEERING DESIGN.
Inclusive design. London ; New York : Springer, c2003.
TA174 .I464 2003

ENGINEERING, ELECTRICAL. *See* **ELECTRIC ENGINEERING.**

ENGINEERING - MANAGEMENT.
Morrison, Raymond E. Developing effective engineering leadership. London : Institution of Electrical Engineers, c2003.

ENGINEERING - METHODOLOGY.
Rantanen, Kalevi. Simplified TRIZ. Boca Raton : St. Lucie Press, c2002.
TA153 .R26 2002

ENGINEERING, SOCIAL. *See* **SOCIAL ENGINEERING.**

ENGLAND - HISTORY. *See* **GREAT BRITAIN - HISTORY.**

ENGLAND - POLITICS AND GOVERNMENT. *See* **GREAT BRITAIN - POLITICS AND GOVERNMENT.**

ENGLAND - SOCIAL LIFE AND CUSTOMS.
Hoggart, Richard, 1918- Everyday language & everyday life. New Brunswick, N.J. ; London : Transaction Publishers, c2003.
PE1074.8 .H64 2003

ENGLAND - SOCIAL LIFE AND CUSTOMS - 1066-1485.
Radulescu, Raluca, 1974- The gentry context for Malory's Morte Darthur. Cambridge [England] ; Rochester, NY : D.S. Brewer, 2003.
PR2047 .R33 2003

Englebert, Clear. Feng shui demystified / by Clear Englebert. Freedom, Calif. : Crossing Press, c2000. 190 p. : ill. ; 20 cm. Includes bibliographical references (p. [171]-179), ISBN 1-58091-078-5 (pbk.) DDC 133.3/337
1. Feng shui. I. Title.
BF1779.F4 E54 2000

Engleman, Dennis Eugene, 1948- Ultimate things : an Orthodox Christian perspective on the end times / by Dennis Eugene Engleman. Ben Lomond, Calif. : Conciliar Press, c1995. 296 p. ; 22 cm. Includes bibliographical references (p. 281-284) and index. ISBN 0-9622713-9-X DDC 236/.9
1. Orthodox Eastern Church - Doctrines. 2. End of the world. 3. Eschatology. I. Title.
BT876 .E54 1995

ENGLISH AUTHORS. *See* **AUTHORS, ENGLISH.**

ENGLISH CHILDREN'S STORIES. *See* **CHILDREN'S STORIES, ENGLISH.**

ENGLISH CHRISTIAN LITERATURE, MIDDLE. *See* **CHRISTIAN LITERATURE, ENGLISH (MIDDLE).**

ENGLISH DRAMA - EARLY MODERN, 1500-1700.
West, William. Theatres and encyclopedias in early modern Europe. Cambridge : Cambridge University Press, 2002.

ENGLISH DRAMA - FILM AND VIDEO ADAPTATIONS.
Shakespeare, the movie, II: popularizing the plays on film, TV, video, and DVD. London ; New York : Routledge, 2003.
PR3093 .S543 2003

ENGLISH DRAMA - HISTORY AND CRITICISM.
Mangan, Michael, 1953- Staging masculinities. Houndmills, Basingstoke, Hampshire ; New York : Palgrave Macmillan, 2003.
PN1650.M44 M36 2003

ENGLISH FICTION. *See* **CHILDREN'S STORIES, ENGLISH.**

ENGLISH FICTION - 20TH CENTURY - HISTORY AND CRITICISM.
D'Cruz, Doreen, 1950- Loving subjects. New York : P. Lang, c2002.
PR888.W6 D39 2002

Liddelow, Eden. After Electra. Melbourne : Australian Scholarly, 2002, c2001.

Vinet, Dominique. Romanesque britannique et psyché. Paris : L'Harmattan, c2003.

ENGLISH FICTION - HISTORY AND CRITICISM - THEORY, ETC.
Hague, Angela. Fiction, intuition, & creativity. Washington, D.C. : Catholic University of America Press, c2003.
PR826 .H28 2003

ENGLISH FICTION - WOMEN AUTHORS - HISTORY AND CRITICISM.
D'Cruz, Doreen, 1950- Loving subjects. New York : P. Lang, c2002.
PR888.W6 D39 2002

Liddelow, Eden. After Electra. Melbourne : Australian Scholarly, 2002, c2001.

ENGLISH HYMNS. *See* **HYMNS, ENGLISH.**

ENGLISH LANGUAGE - CHRESTOMATHIES. *See* **READERS.**

ENGLISH LANGUAGE - CONSONANTS - JUVENILE LITERATURE.
Gemmen, Heather. Dreams from God. Colorado Springs, Colo. : Faith Kidz, 2003.
BF1099.B5 G46 2003

ENGLISH LANGUAGE - DIALECTS. *See* **ENGLISH LANGUAGE - VARIATION.**

ENGLISH LANGUAGE - DICTIONARIES - GUJARATI.
Mansūrī, Jī. Āra. Manovijñānano śabdakośa. Āvrtti 1. Amadāvāda : Mayūra Prakāśana, 2003.
BF31+

ENGLISH LANGUAGE - EARLY MODERN, 1500-1700 - RHETORIC.
Cockcroft, Robert, 1939- Rhetorical affect in early modern writing. New York : Palgrave Macmillan, 2003.
PR428.E56 C63 2003

ENGLISH LANGUAGE - ENGLAND - IDIOMS.
Hoggart, Richard, 1918- Everyday language & everyday life. New Brunswick, N.J. ; London : Transaction Publishers, c2003.
PE1074.8 .H64 2003

ENGLISH LANGUAGE - ENGLAND - USAGE.
Hoggart, Richard, 1918- Everyday language & everyday life. New Brunswick, N.J. ; London : Transaction Publishers, c2003.
PE1074.8 .H64 2003

ENGLISH LANGUAGE - ETYMOLOGY - DICTIONARIES.
Barnette, Martha. Dog days and dandelions. 1st ed. New York : St. Martin's Press, 2003.
PE1583 .B37 2003

ENGLISH LANGUAGE - ETYMOLOGY - POPULAR WORKS. *See* **ENGLISH LANGUAGE - ETYMOLOGY.**

ENGLISH LANGUAGE - GREAT BRITAIN.
Hargraves, Orin. Mighty fine words and smashing expressions. Oxford ; New York : Oxford University Press, 2003.
PE1711 .H37 2003

ENGLISH LANGUAGE - HISTORY. *See* **ENGLISH LANGUAGE - ETYMOLOGY.**

ENGLISH LANGUAGE IN THE UNITED STATES. *See* **ENGLISH LANGUAGE - UNITED STATES.**

ENGLISH LANGUAGE - MIDDLE ENGLISH, 1100-1500 - RHETORIC.
Thompson, Anne Booth. Everyday saints and the art of narrative in the South English legendary. Aldershot, England ; Burlington, Vt. : Ashgate, c2003.
PR2143.S543 T48 2003

ENGLISH LANGUAGE - READERS. *See* **READERS.**

ENGLISH LANGUAGE - RELATIVE CLAUSES.
Fernández, Eva M. Bilingual sentence processing. Amsterdam ; Philadelphia : J. Benjamins Pub., 2003.
P115.4 .F47 2003

ENGLISH LANGUAGE - REMEDIAL TEACHING. *See* **BASIC WRITING (REMEDIAL EDUCATION).**

ENGLISH LANGUAGE - RHETORIC.
Lanham, Richard A. Analyzing prose. 2nd ed. London ; New York : Continuum, 2003.
PE1421 .L295 2003

Stafford, Kim Robert. The muses among us. Athens : University of Georgia Press, c2003.
PE1408 .S6667 2003

ENGLISH LANGUAGE - RHETORIC - STUDY AND TEACHING.
Directed self-placement. Cresskill, N.J. : Hampton Press, c2003.
PE1404 .D57 2003

ENGLISH LANGUAGE - RHETORIC - STUDY AND TEACHING - UNITED STATES.
Daniell, Beth, 1947- A communion of friendship. Carbondale : Southern Illinois University Press, c2003.
PE1405.U6 D36 2003

ENGLISH LANGUAGE - RHETORIC - STUDY AND TEACHING - UNITED STATES - CASE STUDIES.
Directed self-placement. Cresskill, N.J. : Hampton Press, c2003.
PE1404 .D57 2003

ENGLISH LANGUAGE - SOCIAL ASPECTS - ENGLAND.
Hoggart, Richard, 1918- Everyday language & everyday life. New Brunswick, N.J. ; London : Transaction Publishers, c2003.
PE1074.8 .H64 2003

ENGLISH LANGUAGE - SPOKEN ENGLISH - ENGLAND.
Hoggart, Richard, 1918- Everyday language & everyday life. New Brunswick, N.J. ; London : Transaction Publishers, c2003.
PE1074.8 .H64 2003

ENGLISH LANGUAGE - SPOKEN ENGLISH - UNITED STATES.
Spears, Richard A. NTC's dictionary of everyday American English expressions. Lincolnwood, Ill. : National Textbook Co., c1994.
PE2839 .S65 1994

ENGLISH LANGUAGE - STANDARDIZATION.
Crowley, Tony. Standard English and the politics of language. 2nd ed. New York : Palgrave Macmillan, c2003.
P368 .C76 2003

ENGLISH LANGUAGE - STUDY AND TEACHING (HIGHER). *See* **BASIC WRITING (REMEDIAL EDUCATION).**

ENGLISH LANGUAGE - STYLE.
Lanham, Richard A. Analyzing prose. 2nd ed. London ; New York : Continuum, 2003.
PE1421 .L295 2003

ENGLISH LANGUAGE - UNITED STATES.
Hargraves, Orin. Mighty fine words and smashing expressions. Oxford ; New York : Oxford University Press, 2003.
PE1711 .H37 2003

ENGLISH LANGUAGE - UNITED STATES - IDIOMS.
Spears, Richard A. NTC's dictionary of everyday American English expressions. Lincolnwood, Ill. : National Textbook Co., c1994.
PE2839 .S65 1994

ENGLISH LANGUAGE - UNITED STATES - TERMS AND PHRASES.
Spears, Richard A. NTC's dictionary of everyday American English expressions. Lincolnwood, Ill. : National Textbook Co., c1994.
PE2839 .S65 1994

ENGLISH LANGUAGE - VARIATION - ENGLAND.
Hoggart, Richard, 1918- Everyday language & everyday life. New Brunswick, N.J. ; London : Transaction Publishers, c2003.
PE1074.8 .H64 2003

ENGLISH LANGUAGE - WORD HISTORY. *See* **ENGLISH LANGUAGE - ETYMOLOGY.**

ENGLISH LANGUAGE - WRITTEN ENGLISH - ABILITY TESTING.
Weigle, Sara Cushing. Assessing writing. Cambridge ; New York, NY : Cambridge University Press, 2002.
PE1065 .W35 2002

ENGLISH LITERATURE. *See* **ENGLISH DRAMA; ENGLISH FICTION.**

ENGLISH LITERATURE - 19TH CENTURY - HISTORY AND CRITICISM.
Literature, science, psychoanalysis, 1830-1970. Oxford ; New York : Oxford University Press, 2003.
PN55 .L58 2003

ENGLISH LITERATURE - 20TH CENTURY - HISTORY AND CRITICISM.
Literature, science, psychoanalysis, 1830-1970. Oxford ; New York : Oxford University Press, 2003.
PN55 .L58 2003

Manganaro, Marc, 1955- Culture, 1922. Princeton, N.J. : Princeton University Press, c2002.
PR888.C84 M36 2002

ENGLISH LITERATURE - EARLY MODERN, 1500-1700.
Lee-Browne, Patrick. The Renaissance. New York : Facts on File, c2003.

ENGLISH LITERATURE - EARLY MODERN, 1500-1700 - HISTORY AND CRITICISM.
Cockcroft, Robert, 1939- Rhetorical affect in early modern writing. New York : Palgrave Macmillan, 2003.
PR428.E56 C63 2003

ENGLISH LITERATURE - MIDDLE ENGLISH, 1100-1500. *See* **CHRISTIAN LITERATURE, ENGLISH (MIDDLE); ROMANCES, ENGLISH.**

ENGLISH LITERATURE - MIDDLE ENGLISH, 1100-1500 - HISTORY AND CRITICISM.
Heng, Geraldine. Empire of magic. New York : Columbia University Press, c2003.
PR321 .H46 2003

ENGLISH POETRY. *See* **SONNETS, ENGLISH.**

ENGLISH PROVERBS. *See* **PROVERBS, ENGLISH.**

ENGLISH ROMANCES. *See* **ROMANCES, ENGLISH.**

ENGLISH SONNETS. *See* **SONNETS, ENGLISH.**

Engwall, Lars.
The expansion of management knowledge. Stanford, Calif. : Stanford Business Books, c2002.
HD31 .E873 2002

O enigma da esfinge.
Moser, Antônio. 3a ed. Petrópolis : Editora Vozes, 2002, c2001.

ENIGMAS. *See* **CURIOSITIES AND WONDERS.**

Enihma lidera.
Mykytenko, Svitlana. Enihma lidera, abo, Shcho może obitsi͡aty politychna kar'i͡era poriadniĭ li͡udyni, okrim vtraty pori͡adnosti. Kyïv : Vyd-vo "Molod'", 2001.
JC330.3 .M95 2001

Enihma lidera, abo, Shcho może obitsi͡aty politychna kar'i͡era poriadniĭ li͡udyni, okrim vtraty pori͡adnosti.
Mykytenko, Svitlana. Kyïv : Vyd-vo "Molod'", 2001.
JC330.3 .M95 2001

ENLIGHTENMENT.
Sutcliffe, Adam. Judaism and Enlightenment. Cambridge ; New York : Cambridge University Press, 2003.
BM290 .S88 2003

Zakai, Avihu. Jonathan Edwards's philosophy of history. Princeton, N.J. : Princeton University Press, c2003.
B873 .Z35 2003

Enlivening the chakra of the heart.
Lowndes, Florin. [Belebung des Herzchakra. English] London : Sophia Books : Rudolf Steiner Press, c1998.
BF1442.C53 L6913 1998

ENMITY. *See* **HOSTILITY (PSYCHOLOGY).**

The enneagram.
Offiong, Maria I. [Nigeria] : Modern Business Press, 1998.

ENNEAGRAM.
Bartlett, Carolyn, 1950- The Enneagram field guide. Portland, OR : Enneagram Consortium, c2003.
BF698.35.E54 B38 2003

Naranjo, Claudio. [Eneagrama de la sociedad. English] The enneagram of society. Nevada City, Calif. : Gateways Books and Tapes, 2004.

Enneagram.
BF698.35.E54 N3813 2004
Offiong, Maria I. The enneagram. [Nigeria] : Modern Business Press, 1998.
1. Black author.
Tallon, Robert, 1947- From awareness to action. Scranton, Pa. : University of Scranton Press, 2003.
BF698.35.E54 T35 2003

The Enneagram field guide.
Bartlett, Carolyn, 1950- Portland, OR : Enneagram Consortium, c2003.
BF698.35.E54 B38 2003

The enneagram of society.
Naranjo, Claudio. [Eneagrama de la sociedad. English] Nevada City, Calif. : Gateways Books and Tapes, 2004.
BF698.35.E54 N3813 2004

ENNEAGRAM - SOCIAL ASPECTS.
Naranjo, Claudio. [Eneagrama de la sociedad. English] The enneagram of society. Nevada City, Calif. : Gateways Books and Tapes, 2004.
BF698.35.E54 N3813 2004

Enns, James T.
Coren, Stanley. Sensation and perception. 6th ed. Hoboken, NJ : J. Wiley & Sons, c2004.
BF233 .C59 2004

The thinking eye, the seeing brain : explorations in visual cognition / James Enns. New York : W.W. Norton, 2004. p. cm. Includes bibliographical references and indexes. ISBN 0-393-97721-8 (pbk.) DDC 152.14
1. Visual perception. I. Title.
BF241 .E56 2004

ENNUI. See **BOREDOM.**

ENOCHIAN MAGIC.
Guide to the Golden Dawn Enochian skrying tarot. St. Paul, Minn. : Llewellyn, 2004.
BF1623.E55 G65 2004

Ensaios : construção do conhecimento, subjetividad, interdisciplinaridade / Francisca Bezerra de Oliveira, Maria Lucienete Fortunato, organizadoras. João Pessoa : Editora Universitária, 2001. 224 p. ; 21 cm. Includes bibliographical references. ISBN 85-237-0317-9
1. Knowledge, Theory of. 2. Subjectivity. 3. Interdisciplinary approach to knowledge. I. Oliveira, Francica Bezerra de. II. Fortunato, Maria Lucinete.

Ensaios sobre a intolerância : inquisição, marranismo e anti-semitismo : homenagem a Anita Novinsky / Lina Gorenstein e Maria Luiza Tucci Carneiro, organizadoras. São Paulo, SP, Brasil : Humanitas, FFLCH/USP : FAPESP : LEI-Laboratório de Estudos sobre a Intolerância, 2002. 440 p. : ill., maps ; 22 cm. Includes bibliographical references. Limited ed. of 500 copies. ISBN 85-7506-083-X
1. Novinsky, Anita. 2. Prejudices. 3. Inquisition. 4. Antisemitism. I. Silva, Lina Gorenstein Ferreira da, 1951- II. Carneiro, Maria Luiza Tucci.

Ensayo (Ediciones Libertarias)
(129.) Reig, Ramón. El éxtasis cibernético. 1. ed. Madrid : Ediciones Libertarias, 2001.

Ensayos / Biblioteca Nueva
Diálogo de civilizaciones Oriente-Occidente. [Madrid] : Biblioteca Nueva : [Cáceres, España] : Universidad de Extremadura, c2002.

Ensayos (Biblioteca Nueva (Firm))
Vadillo, Alicia E. Santería y Vodú. Madrid : Biblioteca Nueva, c2002.
PQ7372 .V33 2002

Ensayos braudelianos.
Aguirre Rojas, Carlos Antonio. Rosario, Argentina : Prohistoria : M. Suárez ; México : Asociación Nacional de Profesores de Historia de México, 2000.
D15.B62 A38 2000

Ensayos sobre la corrupción y la ilegalidad del poder.
Simonetti, José María, 1942- El fin de la inocencia. Bernal, Argentina : Universidad Nacional de Quilmes, 2002.
JF1081 S57 2002

L'enseignement de la théologie dans les ordres mendiants à Paris au XIIIe siècle.
Goglin, Jean-Marc. Paris : Editions franciscaines, c2002.

Der enteignete Mythos.
Weiler, Gerda, 1921- Königstein : Helmer, [1996]

ENTERPRISES. See **BUSINESS ENTERPRISES.**

ENTERTAINERS. See **DANCERS; MAGICIANS; MUSICIANS.**

ENTERTAINING. See **DINNERS AND DINING; GAMES.**

ENTHUSIASM. See **FANATICISM.**

Enthusiasm!.
Pliskin, Zelig. 1st ed. Brooklyn, N.Y. : Shaar Press : Distributed by Mesorah Publications, 2002.

ENTHUSIASM.
Pliskin, Zelig. Enthusiasm!. 1st ed. Brooklyn, N.Y. : Shaar Press : Distributed by Mesorah Publications, 2002.

ENTHUSIASM - RELIGIOUS ASPECTS - JUDAISM.
Pliskin, Zelig. Enthusiasm!. 1st ed. Brooklyn, N.Y. : Shaar Press : Distributed by Mesorah Publications, 2002.

ENTHUSIASTS (FANS). See **FANS (PERSONS).**

The enticement of religion.
Bolle, Kees W. Notre Dame, Ind. : University of Notre Dame Press, c2002.
BL48 .B585 2002

ENTITLEMENT ATTITUDES.
Champion, David R. Narcissism and entitlement. New York : LFB Scholarly Pub. LLC, c2003.
BF692.15 .C47 2003

Entre 2 siglos.
Marías, Julián, 1914- Entre dos siglos. Madrid : Alianza Editorial, c2002.
PQ6663.A72183 E68 2002

Entre dos siglos.
Marías, Julián, 1914- Madrid : Alianza Editorial, c2002.
PQ6663.A72183 E68 2002

ENTREPRENEURS. See **BUSINESSPEOPLE.**

ENTREPRENEURSHIP.
Israel-Curley, Marcia. Defying the odds. 1st ed. Woodstock, N.Y. : Overlook Press, 2002.
HB615 .I75 2002

Mezias, Stephen J. Organizational dynamics of creative destruction. Houndmills [England] ; New York : Palgrave Macmillan, 2002.
HB615 .M49 2002

Pearlman, Lou. Bands, brands and billions. New York : London : McGraw-Hill, 2002.

Sathe, Vijay. Corporate entrepreneurship. Cambridge : Cambridge University Press, 2003.

Entretien avec Philippe Forest.
Jouffroy, Alain, 1928- [Mots et moi] Les mots et moi ; Nantes : Pleins feux, c2002.

Die Entstehung des Neuen in der Adoleszenz.
King, Vera. Opladen : Leske + Budrich, c2002.

Envejecimiento y cultura : cursos del instituto / coordinado por Pedro García Barreno, Alberto Portera Sánchez. [Madrid] : Instituto de España, c2001. 289 p. : ill. (some col.) ; 24 cm. Includes bibliographical references (p. 285-289). ISBN 84-85559-70-3
1. Aged - Social aspects. 2. Aged - Medical care. 3. Aged - Psychology. I. García Barreno, Pedro. II. Portera Sánchez, Alberto.

ENVIRONMENT. See **ADAPTATION (BIOLOGY); ECOLOGY; NATURE AND NURTURE.**

ENVIRONMENT (AESTHETICS).
Rothenberg, David, 1962- Always the mountains. Athens : University of Georgia Press, c2002.
GF21 .R68 2002

ENVIRONMENT, EFFECT OF HUMAN BEINGS ON. See **NATURE - EFFECT OF HUMAN BEINGS ON.**

ENVIRONMENT, HUMAN. See **HUMAN ECOLOGY.**

ENVIRONMENT, SCHOOL. See **SCHOOL ENVIRONMENT.**

Environmental arts and humanities series
Brosman, Catharine Savage, 1934- Finding higher ground. Reno : University of Nevada Press, c2003.
F787 .B76 2003

ENVIRONMENTAL BIOLOGY. See **ECOLOGY.**

ENVIRONMENTAL ECONOMICS.
Foley, Duncan K. Unholy trinity. London ; New York : Routledge, 2003.
HB135 .F65 2003

ENVIRONMENTAL EDUCATION.
Flores Bedregal, Teresa. Comunicación para el desarrollo sostenible. La Paz : Plural Editores : LIDEMA : Konrad-Adenauer-Stiftung, c2002.

Learning toward an ecological consciousness. New York : Palgrave Macmillan, 2003.
BF353 .L42 2003

Leff, Enrique. Saber ambiental. 3a ed. correg. y aument. México : PNUMA ; Siglo Veintiuno, 2002.

Murillo de Martínez, Ivelisse. Educación ambiental. 2. ed. Tegucigalpa, Honduras : Copicentro Douglas, 2000.

ENVIRONMENTAL EDUCATION - HONDURAS.
Murillo de Martínez, Ivelisse. Educación ambiental. 2. ed. Tegucigalpa, Honduras : Copicentro Douglas, 2000.

ENVIRONMENTAL ENGINEERING. See **HUMAN ENGINEERING.**

ENVIRONMENTAL ETHICS.
Roach, Catherine M., 1965- Mother/nature. Bloomington, IN : Indiana University Press, c2003.
BD581 .R59 2003

ENVIRONMENTAL HEALTH.
Saúde e ambiente sustentável. Rio de Janeiro, RJ : Editora Fiocruz : Abrasco, 2002.

ENVIRONMENTAL PERCEPTION. See **GEOGRAPHICAL PERCEPTION.**

ENVIRONMENTAL POLICY.
Mason, Colin, 1926- The 2030 spike. London ; Sterling, VA : Earthscan Publications, 2003.
CB161 .M384 2003

Saúde e ambiente sustentável. Rio de Janeiro, RJ : Editora Fiocruz : Abrasco, 2002.

ENVIRONMENTAL PSYCHOLOGY.
Adeleye, Modupe, 1980- From our hearts. Rochester, N.Y. : Mo-Biz Publishing Co., 2003.
BF353 .A33 2003

Ecological counseling. Alexandria, VA : American Counseling Association, 2003.
BF637.C6 E26 2003

Identity and the natural environment. Cambridge, Mass. : MIT Press, 2004.
BF353 .I34 2004

Learning toward an ecological consciousness. New York : Palgrave Macmillan, 2003.
BF353 .L42 2003

Psychological theories for environmental issues. Aldershot, Hants, England ; Burlington, VT : Ashgate, 2003.
BF353 .P774 2003

Zeer, Darrin. Office Feng Shui. San Francisco : Chronicle Books, 2004.
BF1779.F4 Z44 2004

ENVIRONMENTAL RISK ASSESSMENT.
Saúde e ambiente sustentável. Rio de Janeiro, RJ : Editora Fiocruz : Abrasco, 2002.

ENVIRONMENTAL SCIENCES. See **ECOLOGY.**

ENVIRONMENTALISM - HISTORY.
Thinking about the environment. Lanham, Md. : Lexington Books, c2002.
GE50 .T48 2002

ENVIRONMENTALISM - PHILOSOPHY.
Preston, Christopher J. Grounding knowledge. Athens, Ga. : University of Georgia Press, c2003.
BD161 .P746 2003

Environmentally sustainable buildings : challenges and policies / Organisation for Economic Co-operation and Development. Paris : Organisation for Economic Co-operation and Development, 2003. 195 p. : ill. ; 23 cm. "This report has been prepared by ... Takahiko Hasegawa"--P. 3. Includes bibliographical references (p. 179-188). ISBN 92-64-19825-3
1. Buildings - Environmental aspects. 2. Sustainable architecture. 3. Architecture - Environmental aspects. I. Hasegawa, Takahiko. II. Organisation for Economic Co-operation and Development.

Envy.
Epstein, Joseph, 1937- New York : New York Public Library ; Oxford University Press, 2003.
BF575.E65 E67 2003

ENVY.
Byington, Carlos Amadeu Botelho, 1933- [Inveja criativa. English] Creative envy. 1st American ed. Wilmette, Ill. : Chiron Publications, 2004.

BF575.E65 B95 2004

Keppe, Norberto R. [Origem Das Enfermidades. English] The origin of illness. 1st American ed. Englewood Cliffs, N.J. : Campbell Hall Press, 2002.
RC460 .K4713 2002

ENVY.
Epstein, Joseph, 1937- Envy. New York : New York Public Library ; Oxford University Press, 2003.
BF575.E65 E67 2003

Envy, anger & sweet revenge.
Silverman, Stephen M. New York : Red Rock Press, c2002.
BF575.E65 S55 2002

Envy, anger, and sweet revenge.
Silverman, Stephen M. Envy, anger & sweet revenge. New York : Red Rock Press, c2002.
BF575.E65 S55 2002

ENVY - MISCELLANEA.
Silverman, Stephen M. Envy, anger & sweet revenge. New York : Red Rock Press, c2002.
BF575.E65 S55 2002

Enzyklopädie der Psychologie
(Themenbereich C, Serie I, Bd. 6) Biologische Grundlagen der Psychologie. Göttingen ; Seattle : Hogrefe, 2001.
QP360 .B565 2001

Enzyklopädie deutscher Geschichte
(Bd. 68) Angenendt, Arnold. Grundformen der Frömmigkeit im Mittelalter. München : Oldenbourg, 2003.

Ephraim, Charles Wm. The pathology of Eurocentrism : the burden and responsibilites of being Black / Charles Wm. Ephraim. Trenton, NJ : Africa World Press, c2003. xix, 468 p. ; 22 cm. Includes bibliographical references (p. [445]-455) and index. ISBN 0-86543-754-8 ISBN 0-86543-755-6 (pbk.) DDC 305.896/073
1. Blacks. 2. Racism. I. Title.
HT1581 .E64 2003

EPIC POETRY, GERMAN. See **COURT EPIC, GERMAN.**

EPICTETUS.
  MANUAL 1-26.
  Simplicius, of Cilicia. [Commentarius in Enchiridion Epicteti. 1-26. English] On Epictetus' "Handbook 1-26". Ithaca, N.Y. : Cornell University Press, 2002.
  B561.M523 S5613 2002

EPICUREANS (GREEK PHILOSOPHY).
Cultivating citizens. Lanham : Lexington Books, c2002.
JK1759 .C85 2002

EPIDEMIOLOGY. See **DISEASES.**

EPIGENESIS - MATHEMATICAL MODELS.
Barbieri, Marcello. The organic codes. Cambridge, UK. ; New York : Cambridge University Press, 2003.
QH331 .B247 2003

EPIGRAMS. See **APHORISMS AND APOTHEGMS; MAXIMS.**

Epimeleia
(n.F., Bd. 3) Erkennen und Leben. Hildesheim [Germany] ; New York : Olms, 2002.
BD435 .E75 2002

Epistemologica.
Scuto, Giuseppe. Milano : FrancoAngeli, c2002.

Epistemologiczne założenia ontologii Christiana Wolffa.
Paź, Bogusław. Wrocław : Wydawn. Uniwersytetu Wrocławskiego, 2002.

EPISTEMOLOGY. See also **KNOWLEDGE, THEORY OF.**
Rescher, Nicholas. Albany : State University of New York Press, c2003.
BD161 .R477 2003

Epistemology : an anthology / edited by Ernest Sosa and Jaegwon Kim ; with the assistance of Matthew McGrath. Malden, Mass. : Blackwell Publishers, 2000. x, 590 p. : ill. ; 25 cm. (Blackwell philosophy anthologies ; 11) Includes bibliographical references and index. CONTENTS: The problem of the external world / Barry Stroud -- Proof of an external world / G.E. Moore -- Skepticism, naturalism and transcendental arguments / P.F. Strawson -- An argument for skepticism / Peter Unger -- Is justified true belief knowledge? / Edmund Gettier -- A proposed definition of propositional knowledge / Peter Klein -- Selections from Thought / Gilbert Harman -- Knowledge and skepticism / Robert Nozick -- The myth of the given / Roderick M. Chisholm -- Does empirical knowledge have a foundation? ; Epistemic principles / Wilfrid Sellars -- The raft and the pyramid / Ernest Sosa -- A coherence theory of truth and knowledge / Donald Davidson -- Evidentialism / Richard Feldman and Earl Conee -- Skepticism and rationality / Richard Foley -- Epistemic norms / John Pollock -- A foundherentist theory of empirical justification / Susan Haack -- Foundationalism, epistemic principles and the Cartesian Circle / James Van Cleve -- Can empirical knowledge have a foundation? / Laurence BonJour -- Reflective knowledge in the best circles / Ernest Sosa -- Epistemology naturalized / W.V. Quine -- What is "naturalized epistemology"? / Jaegwon Kim -- Why reason can't be naturalized / Hilary Putnam -- The old skepticism, the new foundationalism, and naturalized epistemology / Robert Audi -- What is justified belief? / Alvin I. Goldman -- How to think about reliability / William P. Alston -- The generality problem for reliabilism / Earl Conee and Richard Feldman -- Externalism and epistemology naturalized / Keith Lehrer -- Externalism and skepticism / Richard Fumerton -- Knowledge and the internal / John McDowell -- Knowledge and the social articulation of the space of reasons / Robert Brandom -- Epistemic folkways and scientific epistemology / Alvin I. Goldman -- Warrant : a first approximation / Alvin Plantinga -- Virtues of the mind / Linda Zagzebski --Virtues and vices of virtue epistemology / John Greco -- Solving the skeptical problem / Keith DeRose -- Elusive knowledge / David Lewis -- Contextualist solutions to epistemological problems : scepticims, gettier and the lottery / Stewart Cohen -- Epistemological realism / Michael Williams -- Justification, meta-epistemology and meaning / Paul Moser -- Reflective equilibrium, analytic epistemology, and the problem of cognitive diversity / Stephen Stich. ISBN 0-631-19723-0 (alk. paper) ISBN 0-631-19724-9 (pbk. : alk. paper) DDC 121
1. Knowledge, Theory of. I. Sosa, Ernest. II. Kim, Jaegwon. III. McGrath, Matthew. IV. Series.
BD161 .E615 2000

Epistemology and method in law.
Samuel, Geoffrey, 1947- Aldershot, Hampshire, England : Burlington, VT : Ashgate, c2003.
K213 .S259 2003

Epîtres des Freres de la Pureté. XXXVI.
Ikhwān al-Ṣafā'. [Rasā'il. 36. French & Arabic] Les révolutions et les cycles . Louvain-la-Neuve : Bruylant-Academia ; Beyrouth : Al-Bouraq Editions, 1996.

Epîtres (Paris, France)
Godfrind, Jacqueline. Comment la féminité vient aux femmes. Paris : Presses universitaires de France, c2001.
BF175.5.F45 G63 2001

Eppler, Mark, 1946- The Wright way : 7 problem-solving principles from the Wright brothers that can make your business soar! / Mark Eppler. New York : AMACOM, c2004. xvi, 205 p., [8] p. of plates : ill. ; 24 cm. Includes bibliographical references (p. 196-198) and index. ISBN 0-8144-0797-8 DDC 658.4/03
1. Wright, Orville, 1871-1948 - Philosophy. 2. Wright, Wilbur, 1867-1912 - Philosophy. 3. Aeronautics - Research - United States - History. 4. Problem solving. 5. Success in business. 6. Aeronautical engineers - United States - Biography. I. Title.
TL540.W7 E64 2004

Epstein, Joseph, 1937- Envy : the seven deadly sins / Joseph Epstein. New York : New York Public Library ; Oxford University Press, 2003. cm. Includes bibliographical references and index. ISBN 0-19-515812-1 (hardcover) DDC 179/.8
1. Envy. I. Title.
BF575.E65 E67 2003

Epstein, Richard A. Skepticism and freedom : a modern case for classical liberalism / Richard A. Epstein. Chicago : University of Chicago Press, c2003. viii, 311 p. ; 24 cm. (Studies in law and economics) Includes bibliographical references (p. 265-293) and index. CONTENTS: Two forms of skepticism: The system of liberty -- Moral relativism -- Moral incrementalism -- Conceptual skepticism -- A preference for preferences -- Metapreferences, relative preferences, and the prisoner's dilemma game -- Behavioral anomalies -- Cognitive biases. ISBN 0-226-21304-8 (cloth : alk. paper) DDC 340/.1
1. Liberty. 2. Skepticism. 3. Law - Philosophy. I. Title. II. Series.
K487.L5 E67 2003

Epstein, Robert, 1953- The big book of creativity games : quick, fun activities for jumpstarting innovation / Robert Epstein. New York : McGraw-Hill, c2000. xiii, 223 p. : ill. ; 24 cm. (The big book of business games series) Includes index. Publisher description URL: http://www.loc.gov/catdir/description/mh021/00712122.html Table of contents URL: http://www.loc.gov/catdir/toc/mh021/00712122.html ISBN 0-07-136176-6 (alk. paper) DDC 153.3/5
1. Creative ability - Problems, exercises, etc. 2. Creative thinking - Problems, exercises, etc. 3. Employees - Training of - Problems, exercises, etc. I. Title. II. Title: Creativity games III. Series.
BF408 .E67 2000

EQUAL EMPLOYMENT OPPORTUNITY. See **DISCRIMINATION IN EMPLOYMENT.**

EQUAL OPPORTUNITY IN EMPLOYMENT. See **DISCRIMINATION IN EMPLOYMENT.**

EQUALITY. See also **INDIVIDUALISM; LIBERTY; SOCIAL JUSTICE.**
Freiheit, Gleichheit und Autonomie. Wien : Oldenbourg ; Berlin : Akademie Verlag, 2003.
JC575 .F74 2003

Fuller, Robert W. Somebodies and nobodies. Gabriola Island, Canada : New Society Publishers, 2003.
HM821 .F84 2003

Kimmel, Michael S. The gendered society. 2nd ed. New York : Oxford University Press, 2004.
HQ1075 .K547 2004

Lal, Vinay. Empire of knowledge. London ; Sterling, Va. : Pluto Press, 2002.
HN16 .L35 2002

Markell, Patchen, 1969- Bound by recognition. Princeton, N.J. : Princeton University Press, c2003.
JC575 .M37 2003

Sen, Asim, 1935- Democratic management. Lanham, Md. ; Oxford : University Press of America, c2003.
HD30.65 .S46 2003

EQUITIES. See **STOCKS.**

EQUITY CAPITAL. See **STOCKS.**

EQUITY FINANCING. See **STOCKS.**

EQUITY MARKETS. See **STOCK EXCHANGES.**

EQUUS. See **HORSES.**

EQUUS CABALLUS. See **HORSES.**

Er shi shi ji Zhongguo xue shu wen hua sui bi da xi. Di 3 ji
Jiang, Kongyang. Jiang Kongyang xue shu wen hua sui bi. Beijing di 1 ban. Beijing : Zhongguo qing nian chu ban she, 2000.
BH39 .J435 2000

Wen, Yiduo, 1899-1946. Wen Yiduo xue shu wen hua sui bi. Beijing di 1 ban. Beijing : Zhongguo qing nian chu ban she, 2001.
PL2272.5 .W46 2001

Zhang, Shunhui. Zhang Shunhui xue shu wen hua sui bi. Beijing di 1 ban. Beijing : Zhongguo qing nian chu ban she, 2001.
PL2272.5 .Z427 2001

Zhu, Ziqing, 1898-1948. Zhu Ziqing xue shu wen hua sui bi. Beijing di 1 ban. Beijing : Zhongguo qing nian chu ban she, 2000.

Erben, David L.
Adrift in the technological matrix. Lewisburg, PA : Bucknell University Press ; London : Associated University Presses, c2003.

Erdas, Franco Epifanio. Partecipazione e differenza : l'"identità" come progetto / Franco Epifanio Erdas. Roma : Bulzoni, c2002. 327 p. ; 21 cm. (Biblioteca di cultura ; 621) Includes bibliographical references (p. 305-319) and index. ISBN 88-8319-710-0 DDC 306
1. Ethnicity. 2. Pluralism (Social sciences) I. Title. II. Series: Biblioteca di cultura (Bulzoni editore) ; 621.

Eretica
Feo, Giovanni. Prima degli etruschi. Roma : Stampa alternativa, 2001.
BL813.E8 F46 2001

Erfundenes und Erlebtes.
Honegger, Gottfried, 1917- München : Chorus, c2002.

Erfundenes und Erlebtes : Briefe an - .
Honegger, Gottfried, 1917- Erfundenes und Erlebtes. München : Chorus, c2002.

Ergänzungsbände zum Reallexikon der germanischen Altertumskunde
(Bd. 37) Runica, Germanica, Mediaevalia. Berlin ; W. de Gruyter, 2003.

ERGONOMICS. See **HUMAN ENGINEERING.**

ERGOT ALKALOIDS. See **LSD (DRUG).**

Eric Voegelin Institute series in political philosophy
Rhodes, James M. Eros, wisdom, and silence. Columbia, Mo. : University of Missouri Press, c2003.
B398.L9 .R46 2003

Ericsson, Carl W.
Morrison, Raymond E. Developing effective engineering leadership. London : Institution of Electrical Engineers, c2003.

ERIGENA, JOHANNES SCOTUS, CA. 810-CA. 877 - CONGRESSES.
Internationales Eriugena-Colloquium (10th : Maynooth and Dublin : 2002) History and eschatology in John Scottus Eriugena and his time. Leuven : University Press, 2002.

ERIUGENA, JOHANNES SCOTTUS, CA.810-CA.877 - CONGRESSES.
Internationales Eriugena-Colloquium (10th : Maynooth and Dublin : 2002) History and eschatology in John Scottus Eriugena and his time. Leuven : University Press, 2002.

Erjavec, Aleš.
Postmodernism and the postsocialist condition. Berkeley : University of California Press, c2003.
N6494.P66 P684 2003

Erkennen und Leben : philosophische Beiträge zum Lebensbezug menschlicher Erkenntnis / herausgegeben von Horst Seidl ; unter Mitwirkung von Nikolaos Avgelis ... [et al.]. Hildesheim [Germany] ; New York : Olms, 2002. 267 p. ; 21 cm. (Epimeleia ; n.F., Bd. 3) (Philosophische Texte und Studien, 0175-9574 ; Bd. 66) "... in der Eppimeleia-Reihe..." -- t.p. Includes bibliographical references. CONTENTS: Hat Wissenschaft eine Orientierungsfunktion? / Jürgen Mittelstrass -- Die anfängliche Einheit von Lebensform und Denkform / Rainer Marten -- Richtigkeit und Wahrheit der praktischen Vernunft / George Cottier -- Sapere e vita: sul problema delle fondazione della verità / Antonio Livi -- Universelle Minimalmoral als Grundlage der Technikbewertung / Dr Günter Ropohl -- Werte-Erziehung in Elternhaus und Schule: eine Lebensfrage / Siegfried Uhl -- Aristoteles' Phronesis: universelle Einsicht für das konkrete Leben / Karl-Heinz Nusser -- Weisheit als theoretische Lebensform nach traditioneller Auffassung / Horst Seidl -- Philosophie als Lebensweise: Zum Verhältnis von Erkenntnis und Leben in Lukians platonischem Dialog 'Hermotimos' / Till Kinzel -- Der Begriff des Gewissens bei Johann Gottlieb Fichte und die moderne Diskursethik / Wolfgang Schrader -- Wahrheit, Gewissen, Geschichtlichkeit: John Henry Newman über Erkennen und Realisieren / Hanna-Barbara Gerl-Falkovitz -- Ungewissheit im Wagnis des Denkens: der Zusammenhang von Erkenntnis, Leben und Moral bei Peter Wust / Alexander Lohner -- Sprache und Leben: Bemerkungen zu Wittgenstein / Nikolaos Avgelis. ISBN 3-487-11760-6 (pbk.)
1. Life. 2. Knowledge, Theory of. I. Seidl, Horst, 1938- II. Augeles, Nikos. III. Series. IV. Series: Philosophische Texte und Studien, 0175-9574 ; Bd. 66
BD435 .E75 2002

Erlanger, Gad.
[Mazalot, ha-Yahadut ya-ani. English]
Signs of the times : the zodiac in Jewish tradition / by Gad Erlanger ; translated by Yakov Kooper. Jerusalem ; New York : Feldheim Pub., 2000. xii, 276 p. ; 24 cm. ISBN 1-58330-437-1 DDC 133.5/946
1. Jewish astrology. 2. Zodiac - Religious aspects - Judaism. I. Kooper, Yakov. II. Title.
BF1714.J4 E74 2001

Erler, Mary Carpenter.
Gendering the master narrative. Ithaca : Cornell University Press, c2003.
HQ1143 .G46 2003

L'ermeneutica dell'esperienza dell'amore in Max Scheler.
Domagala, Edward. Romae : [s.n.], 2000.

Ermete Trismegisto.
Proto, Antonino, 1925- Milano : Mimesis, 2000.
BF1598.H6 P76 2000

Erneling, Christina E., 1951-.
The mind as a scientific object. New York : Oxford University Press, c2004.
BF311 .M552 2004

Ernest Gellner.
Gellner, Ernest. [Essays. Selections] London ; New York : Routledge, 2003.
B1626.G441 G76 2003

Ernst, Ulrich, 1944-.
Kunst und Erinnerung. Köln : Böhlau, 2003.
PN674 .K86 2003

Ernst, Waltraud, 1964- Diskurspiratinnen : wie feministische Erkenntnisprozesse die Wirklichkeit verändern / Waltraud Ernst. Wien : Milena, c1999. 284 p. ; 21 cm. (Reihe Frauenforschung ; Bd. 38) Includes bibliographical references (p. 268-283) and index. ISBN 3-85286-071-7
1. Feminism. 2. Knowledge, Theory of. 3. Social change. I. Title. II. Series.
HQ1154 .E7 1999

Eros, wisdom, and silence.
Rhodes, James M. Columbia, Mo. : University of Missouri Press, c2003.
B398.L9 .R46 2003

EROTIC ART - INDIA.
Pinkney, Andrea Marion. [Kāmasūtra. English.] The Kama Sutra illuminated. New York, N.Y. : Abrams, c2002.

EROTIC ART, PRIMITIVE. See **EROTIC ART.**

EROTIC LITERATURE.
Pinkney, Andrea Marion. [Kāmasūtra. English.] The Kama Sutra illuminated. New York, N.Y. : Abrams, c2002.

EROTICA. See **EROTIC ART.**

EROTICA - PHILOSOPHY.
Marion, Jean-Luc, 1946- Le phénomène érotique. Paris : Grasset, c2003.
BH301.L65 M37 2003

EROTICISM. See **EROTICA; SEXUAL EXCITEMENT.**

EROTISM, EGO. See **NARCISSISM.**

ERRORS, LOGICAL. See **FALLACIES (LOGIC).**

ERRORS - PSYCHOLOGICAL ASPECTS.
Dawson, Douglas E. The only bad mistake you make is the one you never learn from. Mt. Holly, N.C. : Elias Alexander Press, c2002.
BF323.E7 D38 2002

Die erscheinende Welt : Festschrift für Klaus Held / herausgegeben von Heinrich Hüni und Peter Trawny. Berlin : Duncker & Humblot, c2002. 774 p. ; 1 ill. ; 24 cm. (Philosophische Schriften, 0935-6053 ; Bd. 49) Includes bibliographical references. 1 English, 41 German contributions. CONTENTS: I. Natur und Leib -- II. Ethik und Politik -- III. Geschichte und Kultur -- IV. Sprache und Dichtung -- V. Phänomenologie des Bewusstseins. ISBN 3-428-10896-5 (pbk.)
1. Philosophy. 2. History - Philosophy. 3. Language and languages - Philosophy. 4. Ethics. 5. Phenomenology. I. Hüni, Heinrich. II. Trawny, Peter, 1964- III. Held, Klaus, 1936- IV. Series.

Ershova, N. N.
Psikhologii︠a︡ sub"ektnosti. Kirov : Vi︠a︡tskiĭ gos. pedagog. universitet, 2001.
BF697 .P75 2001

ERUDITION. See **LEARNING AND SCHOLARSHIP.**

Ervø, Søren.
Moulding masculinities. Aldershot, Hants, England ; Burlington, VT : Ashgate, c2003.
BF692.5 .M68 2003

Erzählform im höfischen Roman.
Hübner, Gert. Tübingen : Francke, 2003.

Escape from freedom.
Fromm, Erich, 1900- 1st Owl books ed. New York : H. Holt, 1994.
HM271 .F74 1994

ESCHATOLOGY. See also **DEATH - RELIGIOUS ASPECTS; END OF THE WORLD; FUTURE LIFE.**
Bame Bame, Michael. Death and everlasting life. Nairobi, Kenya : All Africa Conference of Churches, 1994.

Engleman, Dennis Eugene, 1948- Ultimate things. Ben Lomond, Calif. : Conciliar Press, c1995.
BT876 .E54 1995

Gäbler, Ulrich. Zeiten des Endes. Basel : Schwabe & Co., c2002.

Zolla, Elémire. Catàbasi e anàstasi. Alpignano, [Italy] : Tallone Editore, 2001.

ESCHATOLOGY - BIBLICAL TEACHING - CONGRESSES.
Internationales Eriugena-Colloquium (10th : Maynooth and Dublin : 2002) History and eschatology in John Scottus Eriugena and his time. Leuven : University Press, 2002.

ESCHATOLOGY, JEWISH. See also **MESSIANIC ERA (JUDAISM).**
Korah, Shelomoh ben Yahya. Netsah hayenu. Bene Berak : S. Korah, 762 [2001 or 2002]

Escrita psi. Natal/RN : Universidade Potiguar, 2002- v. : 23 cm. Vol. 1, n. 1 (2002)- .
1. Psychology - Periodicals. I. Universidade Potiguar.

BF5 .E83

Escritos de sociología política.
Allard Olmos, Briseida, 1951- Mujer y poder. [Panamá] : Instituto de la Mujer - Universidad de Panamá, 2002.
HQ1154 .A62 2002

Escuchamos.
Jordan, Denise. [We can listen. Spanish] Chicago : Heinemann Library, c2004.
BF323.L5 J6718 2004

Esedra
(21) Olivetti, Alberto. Gara e bellezza. Fiesole, Firenze : Cadmo, c2002.

Esfeld, Michael. Holism in philosophy of mind and philosophy of physics / by Michael Esfeld. Dordrecht ; Boston : Kluwer Academic Publishers, c2001. xiv, 366 p. ; 25 cm. (Synthese library ; v. 298) Includes bibliographical references (p. [321]-351) and indexes. ISBN 0-7923-7003-1 (alk. paper) DDC 149
1. Holism. 2. Philosophy of mind. 3. Quantum theory. I. Title. II. Series.
B818 .E74 2001

Eshevskiĭ, S. V. (Stepan Vasil'evich).
Selections. 2002.
Russkai︠a︡ rasovai︠a︡ teorii︠a︡ do 1917 goda. Moskva : Feri-V, 2002.

Esin, A. B. (Andreĭ Borisovich) Literaturovedenie. Kulturologii︠a︡ : izbrannye trudy / A.B. Esin. Moskva : Flinta ; Nauka, 2002. 351 p. : port. ; 21 cm. Bibliography: p. (344-349). ISBN 5893494547 (Flinta) ISBN 5020029564 (Nauka)
1. Russian literature - 19th century - History and criticism. 2. Russian literature - 20th century - History and criticism. 3. Culture - Philosophy. I. Title.

Esin, Sergeĭ. Poputnye mysli : opyt issledovanii︠a︡ o pisatel'skom trude / Sergeĭ Esin. Moskva : Literaturnyĭ in-t im. A. M. Gor'kogo, 2002. 174 p. ; 21 cm. Includes bibliographical references (p. 165-174) ISBN 5706000506
1. Authorship. 2. Authors - Psychology. 3. Authorship - Psychological aspects. 4. Authorship in literature. 5. Creation (Literary, artistic, etc.) I. Title.
PN145 .E755 2002

L'esistenza ferita.
Moravia, Sergio, 1940- 1. ed. in "Campi del sapere.". Milano : Feltrinelli, 1999.
BF41 .M67 1999

ESKIMOS. See **INUIT.**

Eslin, Jean-Claude, 1935- Saint Augustin : l'homme occidental / Jean-Claude Eslin. Paris : Michalon, c2002. 121 p. ; 19 cm. (Le bien commun) Includes bibliographical references. ISBN 2-8418-6170-8 DDC 100
1. Augustine, - Saint, Bishop of Hippo. 2. Philosophy, Ancient. 3. Philosophers, Ancient. I. Title. II. Series: Collection Le bien commun.

ESOTERIC BUDDHISM. See **TANTRIC BUDDHISM.**

L'espace analytique
Didier-Weill, Alain. Lila et la lumière de Vermeer. Paris : Denoël, c2003.

L'espace intérieur
Jambet, Christian. L'acte d'être. [Paris] : Fayard, c2002.

Espaço & debate
Borges, Edson. Racismo, preconceito e intolerância. [São Paulo, Brazil] : Atual, c2002.

Espaço Brasileiro de Estudos Psicanalíticos.
Transgressões. Rio de Janeiro, RJ : Espaço Brasileiro de Estudos Psicanalíticos : Contra Capa, 2002.

Espada, Arcadio, 1957-.
Cruz, Mariano de la, 1921-1999. Mens sana in corpore insepulto. 1. ed. Barcelona : Edicions 62, 2002.

Español Llorens, Joaquim. El orden frágil de la arquitectura / Joaquim Español. Barcelona : Fundación Caja de Arquitectos, c2001. 215 p. : ill. ; 22 x 24 cm. (Colección Arquíthesis ; no. 9) Includes bibliographical references (p. 209-213) and index. ISBN 84-931388-5-1
1. Architecture - Philosophy. 2. Architecture and philosophy. I. Title. II. Series.

Espasa hoy
Rojas Marcos, Luis, 1943- Más allá del 11 de septiembre. [Madrid] : Espasa, c2002.
HV6432.7 .R64 2002

Espectros del psicoanalisis. Mexico, D.F. : Editorial la Tinta en el Divan, 1997- v. : ill. ; 21 cm. Frequency: Annual. No. 1 (verano 1997)- . Vols. for 1998-<1999> bear

also thematic titles. Latest issue consulted: No. 3 (verano 1999).
1. Psychoanalysis - Periodicals. 2. Psychoanalysis and culture - Periodicals.
BF173.A2 E75

El espejismo de la reconciliación política.
Loveman, Brian. 1. ed. Santiago : LOM Ediciones : DIBAM, 2002.

L'esperienza del dolore.
Natoli, Salvatore. 1. ed. nell'"Universale economica"--Saggi. Milano : Feltrinelli, 2002.

Espiritualidade.
Boff, Leonardo. 2a ed. Rio de Janeiro : Sextante, c2001.

Espíritus y fantasmas.
Southall, R. H. (Richard H.), 1972- [How to be a ghost hunter. Spanish] 1. ed. St. Paul, Minn. : Llewellyn Español, 2003.
BF1461.S6618 2003

Esprits libres (Monaco, Monaco)
Goux, Jean-Paul. La voix sans repos. Monaco : Rocher, c2003.

Esquire presents / edited by A.J. Jacobs. 1st ed. New York : Three Rivers Press, c2003. p. cm. ISBN 0-609-80976-8 (trade pbk.) DDC 155.9
1. Life change events - Psychological aspects.
BF637.L53 E77 2003

An essay on the nature and conduct of the passions and affections.
Hutcheson, Francis, 1694-1746. Indianapolis : Liberty Fund, c2002.
B1501.E6 2002

Essays for Colin Tapper / edited by Peter Mirfield and Roger Smith. London : LexisNexis, 2003. ix, 223 p. ; 25 cm. Includes bibliographical references (p. 211-218) and index. ISBN 0-406-96439-4 DDC 340
1. Evidence (Law) 2. Intellectual property. 3. Computers - Law and legislation. I. Mirfield, Peter. II. Smith, Roger, 1948- III. Tapper, Colin.

Essays in cognitive psychology
Brown, Alan S. The déjà vu experience. New York : Psychology Press, 2004.
BF378.D45 B76 2004

Essays in developmental psychology
Goldin-Meadow, Susan. The resilience of language. New York ; Hove [England] : Psychology Press, 2003.
P118.G57 2003

Essays in honor of Burleigh Wilkins : from history to justice / edited by Aleksandar Jokić. New York : Peter Lang, c2001. viii, 363 p. ; 24 cm. (American university studies. Series V. Philosophy ; v. 102) Includes bibliographical references. ISBN 0-8204-5161-4 (alk. paper) DDC 191
1. Wilkins, Burleigh Taylor. 2. Political science - Philosophy. 3. History - Philosophy. I. Wilkins, Burleigh Taylor. II. Jokić, Aleksandar. III. Series: American university studies. Series V, Philosophy ; v. 192.
JA71.E694 2001

Essays in honor of Peter Florian Dembowski.
Philologies old and new. Princeton : The Edward C. Armstrong Monographs, 2001.

Essays in linguistics in honor of Tomasz P. Krzeszowski.
Language function, structure, and change. Frankfurt am Main ; New York : Lang, c2002.
P125.L36 2002

Essays in the metaphysics of modality.
Plantinga, Alvin. Oxford ; New York : Oxford University Press, 2003.
B945.P553 M48 2003

Essays on medieval law, liturgy, and literature.
De Sion exibit lex et verbum domini de Hierusalem. Turnhout, Belgium : Brepols, c2001.

Essence of the art of karate.
Webster-Doyle, Terrence, 1940- One encounter, one chance. 1st Weatherhill ed. Trumbull, CT : Weatherhill, 2000.
GV1114.3.W43 2000

ESSENCES AND ESSENTIAL OILS. *See* **INCENSE.**

ESSENCES AND ESSENTIAL OILS - MISCELLANEA.
Heath, Maya, 1948- Magical oils by moonlight. Franklin Lakes, NJ : New Page Books, 2004.
BF1442.E77 H43 2004

Essential behaviour analysis.
Leslie, Julian C. London : Arnold ; New York : Oxford University Press, c2002.
BF199.L42 2002

Essential energy balancing 2.
Stein, Diane, 1948- Essential energy balancing II. Berkeley, Calif. : Crossing Press, c2003.
BF1045.K37 S735 2003

Essential energy balancing II.
Stein, Diane, 1948- Berkeley, Calif. : Crossing Press, c2003.
BF1045.K37 S735 2003

Essential energy balancing two.
Stein, Diane, 1948- Essential energy balancing II. Berkeley, Calif. : Crossing Press, c2003.
BF1045.K37 S735 2003

The essential Max Muller.
Muller, F. Max (Friedrich Max), 1823-1900. 1st ed. New York ; Houndmills, England : Palgrave Macmillan, 2002.
BL50.M785 2002

The essential Nostradamus.
Hogue, John. London : Vega, c2002.
BF1815.N8 H58 2002

ESSENTIAL OILS. *See* **ESSENCES AND ESSENTIAL OILS.**

Essential psychology series
Leslie, Julian C. Essential behaviour analysis. London : Arnold ; New York : Oxford University Press, c2002.
BF199.L42 2002

Essentials of 16PF assessment.
Cattell, Heather Birkett. Hoboken, NJ : John Wiley & Sons, 2003.
BF698.8.S5 C265 2003

Essentials of psychological assessment series
Cattell, Heather Birkett. Essentials of 16PF assessment. Hoboken, NJ : John Wiley & Sons, 2003.
BF698.8.S5 C265 2003
Lichtenberger, Elizabeth O. Essentials of WPPSI-III assessment. Hoboken, N.J. : John Wiley & Sons, 2003.
BF432.5.W424 L53 2003

Essentials of psychology.
Coon, Dennis. 9th ed. Australia ; Belmont, CA : Thoomson Learning/Wadsworth, c2003.
BF121.C624 2003
Kassin, Saul M. 1st ed. Upper Saddle River, NJ : Prentice Hall, 2003.
BF121.K335 2003

Essentials of WPPSI-III assessment.
Lichtenberger, Elizabeth O. Hoboken, N.J. : John Wiley & Sons, 2003.
BF432.5.W424 L53 2003

Ésser i moral.
Peiró, Agustí. 1. ed. [Valencia] : Brosquil Edicions, 2002.

ESSEX (WHALESHIP) - JUVENILE LITERATURE.
Philbrick, Nat. Revenge of the whale. New York : G.P. Putnam, 2002.
G530.E77 P454 2002

Est-ce le cerveau qui pense?.
Dupouey, Patrick. Nantes : Pleins feux, [2002].

Estadística aplicada a la investigación social.
Morales Tomas, Marco Antonio. Una gráfica dice más que mil palabras = Guatemala : ESEDIR : Editorial Saqil Tzij, 1999.

Estante USP--Brasil 500 anos
(no. 6) Psiquiatria, loucura e arte. São Paulo, SP, Brasil : Edusp, c2002.

ESTATES, ADMINISTRATION OF. *See* **ADMINISTRATION OF ESTATES.**

ESTATES (SOCIAL ORDERS). *See* **SOCIAL CLASSES.**

Estep, Myrna. A theory of immediate awareness : self organization and adaptation in natural intelligence / Myrna Estep. Dordrecht ; Boston : Kluwer Academic Publishers, 2003. p. cm. Includes bibliographical references and index. ISBN 1402011865 (alk. paper) DDC 153.7
1. Awareness. 2. Intellect. I. Title.
BF311.E79 2003

Esterbauer, Reinhold.
Orte des Schönen. Würzburg : Königshausen & Neumann, c2003.

BH23.O78 2003

Estetica & ermeneutica
(1) Chiurazzi, Gaetano. Modalità ed esistenza. Torino : Trauben, c2001.
BD314.C458 2001

Ėsteticheskoe vosprii͡atie i detskai͡a fantazii͡a.
Saleev, Vadim Alekseevich. Minsk : Natsional'nyĭ in-t obrazovaniii͡a, 1999.
BF723.P36 S25 1999

Ėstetika.
Bychkov, V. V. (Viktor Vasil'evich) Moskva : Gardariki, 2002.

Esteyka czterech żywiołów : ziemia, woda, ogień, powietrze / redakcja Krystyna Wilkoszewska. Kraków : Universitas, c2002. 302 p. : ill. (some col.) ; 27 cm. Includes bibliographical references (p. 277-286) and index. ISBN 83-7052-604-7
1. Aesthetics. 2. Four elements (Philosophy) in art. I. Wilkoszewska, Krystyna.

ESTHETICS. *See* **AESTHETICS.**

Une esthétique contemporaine de l'album de jeunesse.
Beguery, Jocelyne. Paris : Harmattan, c2002.

Esthétique du désir, éthique de la jouissance.
Zupančič, Alenka. Lecques : Théétète, c2002.

Estivals, Robert. Théorie générale de la schématisation / Robert Estivals. Paris : Harmattan, c2002- v. : ill. ; 22 cm. Includes bibliographical references. PARTIAL CONTENTS: 1. Epistémologie des sciences cognitives -- 3. Théorie de la communication. ISBN 2-7475-2641-0 DDC 800
1. Cognitive science. 2. Knowledge, Theory of. 3. Schemas (Psychology) I. Title.

ESTOPPEL. *See* **EVIDENCE (LAW).**

ESTRANGEMENT (PHILOSOPHY). *See* **ALIENATION (PHILOSOPHY).**

Estudios de adquisición y socialización en la lengua materna
(1) La Adquisición de la lengua materna. México : Universidad Nacional Autónoma de México : Centro de Investigaciones y Estudios Superiores en Antropología Social, 2001.
P118.A227 2001

Estudios sobre la violencia : teoría y práctica / Witold Jacorzynski, coordinador. 1. ed. México, D.F. : CIESAS : M.A. Porrúa, 2002. 243 p. ; 23 cm. Includes bibliographical references (p. 233-243). ISBN 9707013036 DDC 303.6/0972
1. Violence - Mexico. 2. Violence. I. Jacorzynski, Witold.
HN120.Z9 V538 2002

Estudos CDAPH. Série história & ciências sociais
Gênero em matizes. Bragança Paulista, SP : EDUSF, [2002]

Estudos gerais. Série universitária
Chacon, Vamireh. O humanismo ibérico. [Lisboa?] : Imprensa Nacional-Casa da Moeda, [1998]
B821.C43 1998

Eṣù ou Exu?.
Salles, Alexandre de. Rio de Jaeiro : Ilú Aiye, 2001.

Esuleke, Kayode Idowu, Chief, Baale Esu of Osogbo.
Adeosun, Kola A. [Oro ti obi n so. English] What the kolanut is saying. Ibadan, Nigeria : Creative Books, 1999.
BF1779.K6 A33 1999

"Et il me montra un fleuve d'eau de la vie" - Apocalypse de saint Jean 22:1.
Aivanhov, Omraam Mikhaël. Fréjus : Prosveta, [2002]

Et l'homme créa l'animal.
Baratay, Eric. Paris : O. Jacob, c2003.

Etc. frequency processing and cognition / [edited by] Peter Sedlmeier and Tilmann Betsch. Oxford ; New York : Oxford University Press, c2002. viii, 324 p. : ill. ; 25 cm. Includes bibliographical references and index. CONTENTS: Frequency processing and cognition: introduction and overview -- Frequency processing: a twenty-five year perspective -- Encoding, representing, and estimating event frequencies: a multiple strategy perspective -- In the year 2054: innumeracy defeated -- Frequency judgements and retrieval structures: splitting, zooming, and merging the units of the empirical world -- Experiential and contextual heuristics in frequency judgement: ease of recall and response scales -- Tversky and Kahneman's availability approach to frequency judgement: a critical analysis -- Memory models approach to frequency and probability judgement: applications of Minerva 2 and Minerva DM -- Associative learning and frequency judgements: the PASS model -- Frequency, contingency and

the information processing theory of conditioning -- Effects of processing fluency on estimates of probability and frequency -- Frequency judgements of emotions: the cognitive basis of personality assessment -- Online strategies versus memory-based strategies in frequency estimation -- Frequency learning and order effects in belief updating -- Psychophysics metaphor in calibration research -- Frequency effects in consumer decision making -- Free word associations and the frequency of co-occurrence in language use -- Technology needs psychology: how natural frequencies foster insight in medical and legal experts -- Frequency processing and cognition: stock-taking and outlook. ISBN 0-19-850863-8 (hbk : alk. paper) DDC 153.4
1. Decision making. 2. Judgment. I. Sedlmeier, Peter. II. Betsch, Tilmann. III. Title: Frequency processing and cognition
BF448 .E83 2002

ETERNAL LIFE. *See* **FUTURE LIFE.**

ETERNAL RETURN.
Lomax, J. Harvey, 1948- The paradox of philosphical education. Lanham, Md. ; Oxford : Lexington Books, c2003.
B3313.J43 L66 2003

Eternally bad.
Robbins, Trina. Berkeley, Calif. : Conari Press, c2001.
BF1623.G63 .R63 2001

ETERNITY. *See* **FUTURE LIFE.**

Etheric anatomy.
Anderson, Victor H. 1917- 1st American pbk. ed. Albany, Calif. : Acorn Guild Press, 2004.
BF1389.A7 A53 2004

ETHERIC WORLD INTELLIGENCES. *See* **GUIDES (SPIRITUALISM).**

Ethical argumentation.
Walton, Douglas N. Lanham, Md. ; Oxford : Lexington Books, c2003.
BJ1012 .W357 2003

Ethical conflicts in psychology / [edited by] Donald N. Bersoff. 3rd ed. Washington, DC : American Psychological Association, c2003. xxvi, 573 p. ; 28 cm. Includes bibliographical references and index. ISBN 1-59147-050-1 (pbk. : alk. paper) ISBN 1-59147-051-X (alk. paper) DDC 174/.915
1. Psychology - Moral and ethical aspects. 2. Psychologists - Professional ethics. I. Bersoff, Donald N.
BF76.4 .E814 2003

The ethical dimension of psychoanalysis.
Meissner, W. W. (William W.), 1931- Albany : State University of New York Press, c2003.
BF173 .M3592 2003

ETHICAL EDUCATION. *See* **MORAL EDUCATION; RELIGIOUS EDUCATION.**

ETHICAL THEOLOGY. *See* **CHRISTIAN ETHICS.**

ETHICS. *See also* **ASCETICISM; CHARACTER; CONDUCT OF LIFE; CONSCIENCE; FEMINIST ETHICS; GOOD AND EVIL; JUDGMENT (ETHICS); MORAL EDUCATION; PEACE; PLEASURE; POWER (PHILOSOPHY); SELF-REALIZATION; VALUES; WILL.**
Ackeren, Marcel van. Das Wissen vom Guten. Amsterdam ; Philadelphia : B.R. Gruner, c2003.
B398.V57 A33 2003

Apel, Karl-Otto. The response of discourse ethics to the moral challenge of the human situation as such and especially today. Leuven : Peeters, 2001.
BJ1012 .A64 2001

Aristotle. [Nicomachean ethics. English] Nicomachean ethics. Cambridge, U.K. ; New York : Cambridge University Press, c2002 (2002 printing)
B430.A5 C7513 2000

Arpaly, Nomy. Unprincipled virtue. Oxford ; New York : Oxford University Press, 2003.
BJ45 .A76 2003

Art and morality. London ; New York : Routledge, 2003.
BH39 .A695 2003

Badiou, Alain. L'éthique. Caen : Nous, c2003.

Barylko, Jaime. Los valores y las virtudes. Buenos Aires : Emecé Editoral, c2002.

Bilbeny, Norbert. Por una causa común. 1. ed. Barcelona : Gedisa Editorial, c2002.

HM1271 .B553 2002

Boff, Leonardo. Ethos mundial. Brasília : Letraviva, 2000.

Braun, Edmund. Der Mensch vor seinem eigenen Anspruch. Würzburg : Königshausen & Neumann, 2002.

Brunero, María Alicia. Etica desde el otro: Buenos Aires : Grupo Editorial Lumen, c2002.

Cacciatore, Giuseppe, 1945- L'etica dello storicismo. Lecce : Milella, 2000.

Carter, Matt. T.H. Green and the development of ethical socialism. Thorverton : Imprint Academic, 2003.
B1638.E8 C37 2003

Celli, Pier Luigi. Breviario di cinismo ben temperato. 1. ed. Roma : Fazi, 2002.

Changeux, Jean-Pierre. [Ce qui nous fait penser. English] What makes us think? Princeton, N.J. : Princeton University Press, c2000.
BJ45 .C4313 2000

Collen, Lindsey. Natir imin. Port Louis, Mauritius : Ledikasyon pu travayer, [2000]

Copjec, Joan. Imagine there's no woman. Cambridge, Mass. : MIT Press, 2002.
BJ1012 .C68 2002

Couser, G. Thomas. Vulnerable subjects. Ithaca : Cornell University Press, 2004.
CT25 .C698 2004

Cultivating citizens. Lanham : Lexington Books, c2002.
JK1759 .C85 2002

Eidam, Heinz. Moral, Freiheit und Geschichte. Würzburg : Königshausen & Neumann, 2001.

Die erscheinende Welt. Berlin : Duncker & Humblot, c2002.

Ethik ohne Dogmen. Paderborn : Mentis, 2001.

Fabelo Corzo, José Ramón. Los valores y sus desafíos actuales. Puebla : Universidad Autónoma de Puebla, 2001.

Fesmire, Steven, 1967- John Dewey and moral imagination. Bloomington, IN : Indiana University Press, c2003.
BJ1031 .F47 2003

Fonseca, Eduardo Giannetti da, 1957- Nada é tudo. Rio de Janeiro, RJ, Brasil : Editora Campus, c2000.
F2521 .F64 2000

Foot, Philippa. Moral dilemmas and other topics in moral philosophy. Oxford ; New York : Clarendon Press, 2002.

Forrester, Mary Gore, 1940- Moral beliefs and moral theory. Dordrecht ; Boston : Kluwer Academic Publishers, c2002.
BJ1012 .F615 2002

Fortitude et servitude. Paris : Kimé, c2003.

Groarke, Louis. The good rebel. Madison [N.J.] : Fairleigh Dickinson University Press ; London ; Cranbury, NJ : Associated University Presses, c2002.
B808.67 .G76 2002

Grundherr, Michael von. Kants Ethik in modernen Gesellschaften. Hamburg : Lit, 2003.

Hartmann, Nicolai, 1882-1950. [Struktur des ethischen Phänomens. English] Moral phenomena. New Brunswick, N.J. : Transaction Publishers, c2002, 1932.
BJ1012 .H342 2002

Hösle, Vittorio, 1960- Philosophie und Öffentlichkeit. Würzburg : Königshausen & Neumann, 2003.

Hossenfelder, Malte. Der Wille zum Recht und das Streben nach Glück. Originalausg. München : C.H. Beck, c2002.

Hume, David, 1711-1776. [Enquiry concerning the principles of morals. German] Eine Untersuchung der Grundlagen der Moral. Göttingen : Vandenhoeck & Ruprecht, c2002.

Hutcheson, Francis, 1694-1746. An essay on the nature and conduct of the passions and affections. Indianapolis : Liberty Fund, c2002.
BJ1501 .E6 2002

Illies, Christian. The grounds of ethical judgement. Oxford : Clarendon, 2003.

Internationales Eriugena-Colloquium (10th : Maynooth and Dublin : 2002) History and eschatology in John Scottus Eriugena and his time. Leuven : University Press, 2002.

Kaplow, Louis. Fairness versus welfare. Cambridge, MA : Harvard University Press, 2002.
K247 .K37 2002

Karg, Hans Hartmut. Theoretische Ethik. Hamburg : Kovac, c1996-<c1999>
BJ1114 .K32 1997

Kovesi, Julius. Values and evaluations. New York ; Bern : P. Lang, c1998.
BD232 .K68 1998

Krollmann, Fritz-Peter, 1963- Ethik und Ästhetik. Essen : Blaue Eule, 2002.

Kuropka, Nicole. Philipp Melanchthon. Tübingen : Mohr Siebeck, c2002.
BR339 .K86 2002

Lee, Simon (Simon F.) Uneasy ethics. London : Pimlico, 2003.

Lekan, Todd, 1967- Making morality. 1st ed. Nashville, TN : Vanderbilt University Press, 2003.
BJ1031 .L45 2003

Lomax, J. Harvey, 1948- The paradox of philosphical education. Lanham, Md. ; Oxford : Lexington Books, c2003.
B3313.J43 L66 2003

Luo, Guojie. [Selections. 2000] Luo Guojie wen ji. Di 1 ban. Baoding Shi : Hebei da xue chu ban she, 2000.
BJ1390 .L892 2000

Maesschalck, M. (Marc) Normes et contextes. Hildesheim ; New York : G. Olms, 2001.
BJ1063 .M34 2001

Markt - Medien - Moral. Bochum : Projekt-Verlag, 2001.

Mazis, Glen A., 1951- Earthbodies. Albany, NY : State University of New York Press, 2002.
BJ1695 .M39 2002

McClure, Joyce Kloc, 1955- Finite, contingent, and free. Lanham, Md. ; Oxford : Rowman & Littlefield Publishers, c2003.
BJ1012 .M316 2003

McLeod, Carolyn. Self-trust and reproductive autonomy. Cambridge, Mass. : MIT Press, c2002.
RG133.5 .M39 2002

Mensch, James R. Ethics and selfhood. Albany, NY : State University of New York Press, c2003.
B945.M4853 E84 2003

Mustakova-Possardt, Elena, 1960- Critical consciousness. Westport, Conn. ; London : Praeger, 2003.
BL53 .M98 2003

Oracle (Writer) The Oracle teachings. 1st ed. Kaua'i, Hawai'i : Oracle Productions, c1996.
BF637.S4 O72 1996

The Oxford handbook of practical ethics. Oxford ; New York : Oxford University Press, 2003.
BJ1031 .O94 2003

Passion and virtue in Descartes. Amherst, N.Y. : Humanity Books, 2003.
B1868.P37 P37 2003

Peiró, Agustí. Ésser i moral. 1. ed. [Valencia] : Brosquil Edicions, 2002.

Philosophie der natürlichen Mitwelt. Würzburg : Königshausen & Neumann, 2002.

Premoli De Marchi, Paola. Etica dell'assenso. Milano : FrancoAngeli, c2002.

Prichard, H. A. (Harold Arthur), 1871-1947. Moral writings. Oxford : Clarendon Press ; New York : Oxford University Press, 2002.

Prudentia und Contemplatio. Paderborn : Ferdinand Schöningh, 2002.

Przełęcki, Marian, 1923- O rozumności i dobroci. Warszawa : "Semper", 2002.
B833 .P79 2002

Przemycki, Piotr, 1965- W stronę Bogoczłowieczeństwa. Łódź : "Ibidem", 2002.
B4238.B44 P79 2002

Pufendorf, Samuel, Freiherr von, 1632-1694. [De officio hominis et civis. English] The whole duty of man, according to the law of nature. Indianapolis, Ind. : Liberty Fund, c2003.

K457.P8 D4313 2003

Railton, Peter Albert. Facts, values, and norms. Cambridge, U.K. ; New York : Cambridge University Press, 2003.
BJ1012 .R33 2003

Rhonheimer, Martin, 1950- Die Perspektive der Moral. Berlin : Akademie Verlag, c2001.

Savater, Fernando. El contenido de la felicidad. 1. ed. Madrid : Aguilar : Santillana, 2002.

Schleiermacher, Friedrich, 1768-1834. Lectures on philosophical ethics. Cambridge ; New York : Cambridge University Press, 2002.

Schröder, Winfried, Dr. phil. Moralischer Nihilismus. Stuttgart-Bad Canstatt : Frommann-Holzboog, c2002.

The search for a holistic approach to human existence and development. [Nigeria?] : Osigwe Anyiam-Osigwe Foundation, [1999?]
B53 .E46 1999

Sequeri, Pier Angelo. L'umano alla prova. Milano : V & P Università, c2002.
BD222.S47 U6 2002

Shafer-Landau, Russ. Whatever happened to good and evil? New York ; Oxford : Oxford University Press, 2004.
BJ1401 .S46 2004

Simplicius, of Cilicia. [Commentarius in Enchiridion Epicteti. 1-26. English] On Epictetus' "Handbook 1-26". Ithaca, N.Y. : Cornell University Press, 2002.
B561.M523 S5613 2002

Singer, Marcus George, 1926- The ideal of a rational morality. Oxford : Clarendon Press ; Oxford ; New York : Oxford University Press, 2002.
BJ1012 .S48 2002

Singer, Peter, 1946- One world. New Haven, Conn. : London : Yale University Press, 2002.

Smith, R. Scott, 1957- Virtue ethics and moral knowledge. Aldershot, England ; Burlington, VT : Ashgate, c2003.
BJ1012 .S5195 2003

Solovyov, Vladimir Sergeyevich, 1853-1900. [Essays. English. Selections] The heart of reality. Notre Dame, Ind. : University of Notre Dame Press, c2003.
B4262.A5 W69 2003

Stepanenko, Valeriĭ. Etyka v problemnykh i analitychnykh zadachakh. Kyiv : Libra, 1998.

Stobbe, Heinz-Günther, 1948- Vom Geist der Übertretung und Vernichtung. Regensburg : Friedrich Pustet, c2002.

Swanton, Christine, 1947- Virtue ethics. Oxford ; New York : Oxford University Press, 2003.
BJ1531 .S93 2003

Teichman, Jenny. Philosophers' hobbies and other essays. Carlton, Vic. : Black Jack Press, 2003.

Thurnherr, Urs. Vernetzte Ethik. Freiburg : Alber, 2001.

Timmons, Mark, 1951- Moral theory. Lanham, Md. : Rowman & Littlefield Publishers, c2002.
BJ1012 .T56 2002

Varieties of ethical reflection. Lanham, Md. ; Oxford : Lexington Books, c2002.
BJ1031 .V37 2002

Vogler, Candace A. Reasonably vicious. Cambridge, Mass. : Harvard University Press, 2002.
BJ1031 .V64 2002

Von Foerster, Heinz, 1911- Understanding systems. New York : Kluwer Academic/Plenum Publishers ; Heidelberg : Carl-Auer-Systeme Verlag, c2002.

Walton, Douglas N. Ethical argumentation. Lanham, Md. ; Oxford : Lexington Books, c2003.
BJ1012 .W357 2003

Werder, Lutz von. Lehrbuch der philosophischen Lebenskunst für das 21. Jahrhundert. Berlin : Schibri-Verlag, c2000.

Wolf, Jean-Claude. Ethik und Politik ohne Gewissheiten. Freiburg, Schweiz : Universitätsverlag, c2002.

Xie, Sizhong. Su zhi yu ming yun. Di 1 ban. Beijing : Zuo jia chu ban she, 2002.
BD450 .X54 2002

ETHICS, ANCIENT.
Fortenbaugh, William W. (William Wale) Aristotle on emotion. 2nd ed. London : Duckworth, 2002.

B491.E7 F67 2002

Ethics and epics.
Matilal, Bimal Krishna. New Delhi ; New York : Oxford University Press, 2002.
B131 .M398 2002b

ETHICS AND LAW. See LAW AND ETHICS.

Ethics and selfhood.
Mensch, James R. Albany, NY : State University of New York Press, c2003.
B945.M4853 E84 2003

ETHICS - CHINA.
Sheng yu xiang jie. Di 1 ban. [Peking] : Xian zhuang shu ju, 1995.
BJ117 .S486 1995 <Orien China>

Yan, Zhitui, 531-591. Yan shi jia xun zhu ping. Di 1 ban. Beijing Shi : Xue yuan chu ban she, 2000.
BJ117 .Y4 2000

Zhuang, Huiming. Yan shi jia xun yi zhu. Di 1 ban. Shanghai : Shanghai gu ji chu ban she : Xin hua shu dian Shanghai fa xing suo fa xing, 1999.

ETHICS - CHINA - HISTORY.
Cai, Yuanpei, 1868-1940. [Selections. 1996] Cai Yuanpei juan. Di 1 ban. Shijiazhuang Shi : Hebei jiao yu chu ban she, 1996.
BJ117 .T74 1996 <Asian China>

ETHICS, CHINESE. See ETHICS - CHINA.

ETHICS, CHRISTIAN. See CHRISTIAN ETHICS.

ETHICS - CONGRESSES.
Die Öffentlichkeit der Vernunft und die Vernunft der Öffentlichkeit. 1. Aufl. Frankfurt am Main : Suhrkamp, 2001.
B3258.H324 O34 2001

Personal and moral identity. Dordrecht ; Boston : Kluwer Academic Publishers, c2002.
BJ45 .P47 2002

ETHICS, JEWISH.
Aboab, Isaac, 14th cent. [Menorat ha-ma'or. Ladino] Una cala en la literatura religiosa sefardí. Granada : Universidad de Granada, 2001.
BJ1287.A152 L33 2001

Adler, Yitshak Eliyahu, ha-Kohen. Sefer Kibud ve-hidur. Ofakim : Y.E. ha-Kohen Adler, 754 [1994]

Admur ha-G. ha-K., Shelita. ['Avodat 'avodah (Torah)] Sefer 'Avodat 'avodah. Kiryat Tohsh, Kanada : N. M. Hershkovitsh, 763 [2002 or 2003]

Algazi, Solomon ben Abraham, 1610?-ca. 1683. Sefer Ahavat 'olam. Bruklin : Sifre Algazi, 760 [2000]

Alshekh, Moses, 16th cent. [Torat Mosheh. Selections] Sefer 'Orot ha-Alshekh. Yerushalayim : [h. mo. l.], 763 [2002 or 2003]

Alter, Judah Aryeh Leib, 1847-1905. [Selections. 2000] Penine Sefat Emet. Ofrah : Mekhon Shovah, [2000?-2003?]
BM198.2 .A55 2000

Ari'av, David ben Nahman, ha-Kohen. Le-re'akha kamokha. Mahad. 2. Yerushalayim : David ben Nahman ha-Kohen Ari'av, 760- [2000 or

Aviner, Shelomoh Hayim, ha-Kohen. Be-ahavah uve-emunah. Yerushalayim : [h. mo. l.], 760-762 [1999 or 2000-2001 or 2002]
BM565 .A93 1999

Aviner, Shelomoh Hayim, ha-Kohen. Perurim mi-shulhan gavoah. Yerushalayim : Sifriyat Hayah, 762 [2001 or 2002]

Baifus, Ya'akov Yisra'el, ha-Kohen. [Lekah tov (Hayim shel Torah)] Yalkut Lekah tov. Rekhasim : "Tashbar ha-Rav", 760- [1999 or 2000-

Bardah, Asher. Sefer Otsrot av. [Bene Berak?] : A. Bardah, 762- [2001 or 2002-
BS1225.54 .B37 2001

Berlin, Naphtali Zevi Judah, 1817-1893. [Selections. 2001] Otsrot ha-Netsiv. Yerushalayim : Ben Arzah, 762 [2001 or 2002]
BM755.B52 A25 2001

Blokh, Avraham Yitshak ben Y. L. (Avraham Yitshak ben Yosef Leyb), d. 1941. Sefer Shi'ure da'at. Yerushalayim : Feldhaim ; Wickliffe, Ohio : Peninei Daas Publications, 761 [2001]

Blokh, Yosef Zalman. Igeret 'al ha-bitahon. Monsi : [h. mo. l.], 5761 [2000 or 2001]
BM729.T7 .B56 2000

Chouchena, Emmanuel. L'homme, espoir de dieu. Paris : Trajectoire, 2001.

Dorff, Elliot N. Love your neighbor and yourself. 1st ed. Philadelphia, PA : Jewish Publication Society, 2003.
BJ1285 .D67 2003

Druk, Ya'akov ben Zalman. Ohel Ya'akov. Yerushala[yi]m : Y. ben Z. Druk, 762 [2002]
BS1225.4 .D77 2002

Eliyahu, Mordekhai. Sefer Sifte tsedek. Rekhasim : M. Eliyahu, 762 [2002]

Ellis, Marc H. Israel and Palestine out of the ashes. London ; Sterling, Va. : Pluto Press, c2002.
DS119.76 .E56 2002

Fridlander, Hayim ben Mosheh. Sefer Sifte hayim. Bene-Berak : ha-Rabanit Fridlander, 763- [2002 or 2003-

Gantserski, Betsal'el Shelomoh, ha-Levi. Sefer Darkhe tsedek. Tifrah : Mishp. Gantserski, 762 [2001 or 2002]

Globerman, Daniyel Aharon. Yalkut Sefer ha-Hinukh. Modi'in 'Ilit : D. A. Globerman, Kolel "Libo hafets", 761 [2000 or 2001]
BM520.8.A32 G4 2001

Golan, Mor Yosef. Sefer ha-Neshamah ba-guf. Itamar : M.Y. Golan, 762 [2001 or 2002]

Goldberg, Avraham Yehoshu'a, 1856-1921. Sefer Kitve paz. Yerushalayim : ha-Mishpahah, 763, c2003.

Hayim Yerohem ben Shimshon Meshulam Feybish, mi-Snatin. Sefer Asefat divre hakhamim. Yerushalayim : Mekhon Sod yesharim, 761 [2001]

Hayun, Yehudah ben Mordekhai. Masekhet ha-hayim. Bene Berak : Y. Hayun, 762 [2001 or 2002]

He lakhem hamishah sefari... [Brooklyn, NY : Renaissance Hebraica, 2000?]

Hurwitz, Joseph, d. 1919. Sefer Madregat ha-adam. Hotsa'ah hadashah mefo'eret menukedet u-metukenet. Yerushalayim : Yeshivat Ner Shemu'el, 762 [2002]

Karelits, Hayim Sha'ul ben Me'ir. Sefer Ahat sha'alti. Bene Berak : Mish. Karelits, 762 [2002]

Kohen, Yekutiel. Mishpat ha-shalom. Yerushalayim : Mekhon Sha'ar ha-mishpat : Hanhalat bate ha-din ha-rabaniyim, 762 [2001 or 2002]

Koll, Shmuel, 1938- Sefer Ra'yonot u-mesarim. Yerushalayim : S. Kol, 761- [2001-

Kuntres Kevod ha-Torah. Bene Berak : ha-Mehaber, 761 [2000 or 2001]

Lamdan, Elimelekh. Torapiah. Yerushalayim : Feldhaim, 762 [2002]

Levin, Yitshak, 1938- Sefer Netivot Yitshak. [Bene Berak] : Y. Levin, [2000-

Likut le-'idud ve-hizuk. Yerushalayim : [h. mo. l.], 756 [1995 or 1996]

Lugasi, Ya'akov Yisra'el. Mishpete Yisra'el. Mahadurah hadashah be-tosefet le-hag ha-Pesah. Yerushalayim : Y. Y. Lugasi, 761 [2001]

Lugasi, Ya'akov Yisra'el. Yalkut Or ha-hayim ha-kadosh. Yerushalayim : [h. mo. l], 762 [2001 or 2002]

Luz, Ehud. [Ma'avak be-nahal Yabok. English] Wrestling with an angel. New Haven : Yale University Press, c2003.
DS143 .L8913 2003

Maimonides, Moses, 1135-1204. [Selections] Sefer Musarim ve-de'ot leha-Rambam. Bene Berak : [h. mo. l], 761 [2000 or 2001]

Malkah, Asher. 'Arakhim ve-hinukh. Hefah : A. Malkah, [5760 i.e. 2000]

Mar'eh Kohen. Yerushalayim : Makhon le-heker mishnat ha-Re'iyah Kuk be-shituf 'im "Bet ha-Rav", c762 [2001 or 2002]

Medan, Barukh. Sefer Birkat Me'ir. Netivot : Barukh Medan, 763 [2002 or 2003]

Mermelshtain, Avraham Yitshak David. Kuntres Dover mesharim. Hotsa'ah 2. [Brooklyn] : A.Y.D. Mermelshtain, 762 [2001]

Miler, Avigdor Hakohen. Sefer Torat Avigdor. Bene Brak : [h. mo. l], 762- [2001 or 2002-

Ethics, Jewish.

Miller, Avigdor. [Lev Avigdor] Sefer Lev Avigdor. Bruklin, N.Y. : S. Miller, 762, c2002.
BM538.P4 .M45 2001

[Mishnah. Avot. 2001.] Sefer Bet ginze. Yerushalayim : R. M. Lurya, 762 [2001 or 2002]

Mitelman, Yiśra'el Yehudah. Ḳuntres Ḥazaḳ ve-nitḥazeḳ. Ashdod : T. T. di-ḥaside Belza, 762 [2002]

Mosheh ben Ḥayim, Ḳoznitser, d. 1874. Sefer Ahavat Yiśra'el. Yotse le-or me-ḥadash. Yerushalayim : Mekhon Sod yesharim, 760 [2000]

Mosheh ben Ḥayim, Ḳoznitser, d. 1874. Sefer 'Ahavat Yiśra'el. Bruḳlin : [Yehoshu'a Pinḥas Bukhinger], 762 [2001]

Mosheh ben Shelomoh El'azar. Sefer Yede Mosheh ve-Torah or. Bene Beraḳ : Sifre Or ha-ḥayim, [760 i.e. 2000]

Otsrot rabotenu mi-Brisḳ. Bene Beraḳ : Sh. L., molut u-mishar bi-sefarim, 762 [2001 or 2002]
BM602 .O+

Passamaneck, Stephen M. Police ethics and the Jewish tradition. Springfield, Ill. : C.C. Thomas, c2003.
HV7924 .P37 2003

Pinḥasi, Raḥamim. Sefer Ḥesed ve-raḥamim. Yerushalayim : R. Pinḥasi, 762 [2001 or 2002]

Pinter, Leib. Sefer 'Aśarah nisyonot. Brooklyn, N.Y. : E.Y.L. Pinter, c[2002?]

Rosenberg, Shelley Kapnek. Raising a mensch. 1st ed. Philadelphia : Jewish Publication Society, 2003.
BF723.M54 R68 2003

Rozner, Shelomoh. Sh. u-t. La-ḥafets be-ḥayim. Mahad. 3, be-tosefet 13 she'elot be-ḥeleḳ 3. Yerushalayim : Kolel shemirat ha-lashon : le-haśig, Sh. Rozner, 762 [2001 or 2002]

Salanter, Israel, 1810-1883. Sefer Torat rabi Yiśra'el mi-Salant. Yerushalayim : [ḥ. mo. l], 763 [2003]

Sefer Ḳedushat ha-dibur. Bene Beraḳ : Yehudah Yosef Ha-levi Gruber, 761- [2001-]

Sefer Sha'agat Aryeh. Yerushalayim : Yerid ha-sefarim, 761 [2000 or 2001]

Segal, Yehudah Zeraḥyah, ha-Levi. Sefer Doreshe H.. Tel-Aviv : Talmiday ve-shmom'e liḳho, 763 [2003]
BJ1287.S43 D66 2003

Shakh, El'azar Menaḥem Man. Sefer Mi-torato de-rabi El'azar. [Bene Beraḳ] : le-haśig mishpaḥat Kohen, [763 i.e. 2003]

Shemu'elevits, Ḥayim, 1901-1979. Sefer Śiḥot musar. Mahad. ḥadashah u-metuḳenet. Yerushalayim : Bene va-ḥatane ha-meḥaber, 762, c2002.
BJ1287.S56 S5 2002

Shooter, Jonathan. The wisdom within. Southfield, MI : Targum Press ; Nanuet, NY : Distributed by Feldheim Publishers, 2002.

Shtern, Shemu'el Eli'ezer. Sefer Sene bo'er ba-esh. Bene Beraḳ : Mekhon "Mayim ḥayim", 762 [2002]

Śiḥot musar Da'at u-tevunah. Ashdod : Sh. ben E. Bamnolḳer, 761 [2001]
BJ1280 .B34 2001

Sofer, Mikha'el Uri. Sefer 'Olamot shel ṭohar. Mahad. 2. Bene Beraḳ : M.U. Sofer, 761 [2000 or 2001]
BM726 .S633 2000

Tamari, Meir. Maśa u-matan be-emunah. Yerushalayim : Simḥonim, [761, 2001]

Tsuri'el, Mosheh Yeḥi'el. Otsrot ha-musar. Yerushalayim : Yerid ha-sefarim, 763, 2002.

Va'eḳnin, Yosef ben Avraham. Sefer Ka-sheleg yalbinu. Yerushalayim : Y. Va'eḳnin, 763 [2002 or 2003]

Vaisfish, Tsevi ben Shemu'el A. L. Sefer Dibrot Tsevi. Yerushalayim : Makhon le-hotsa'at sefarim 'a. sh. Rabi Naḥum mi-Shadiḳ, 762- [2002-

Vakhtfoigel, Nathan. Sefer No'am ha-musar. Laiḳud : [ḥ. mo. l.], 762 [2001 or 2002]
BJ1285 .V35 2001

Vaserman, Asher ben Avraham Betsal'el. Sefer Mishnat avot. Bene Beraḳ : A. Vaserman, 760- [2000-

Wasserman, Elhanan Bunim, 1875-1941. Ḳovets ma'amre 'Iḳvata de-Meshiḥa .... Yerushalayim : Yeshivat Or Elḥanan, 762 [2001 or 2002]

Yahav, Avino'am Shemu'el. Ḳuntres E'eśeh lo 'ezer. Betar 'Ilit : A. S. Yahav, 761, 2001.

Yalḳut Ṭuv ha-peninim. Yerushala[y]im : P. Y. Liberman, 762 [2001 or 2002]
BS1225.53 .Y35 2001

Yanai, Me'ir. Orot ha-tamtsit. Yerushalayim : Nezer David - Ari'el, 761 [2000 or 2001]

Yosef, Yitsḥaḳ. [Yalḳut Yosef (Kibud av va-em)] Sefer Yalḳut Yosef. Yerushalayim : Mekhon "Ḥazon 'Ovadyah", 761 [2001]
BM523.5.R4 Y72 2001

Ziegler, Reuven. By his light. 2nd ed. Jersey City, NJ : KTAV Pub. House ; Alon Shevut, Israel : Yeshivat Har Etzion, 2003.
BM723 .Z54 2003

ETHICS, MEDICAL. See **MEDICAL ETHICS.**

ETHICS, MODERN.
Schweitzer, Albert, 1875-1965. Vorträge, Vorlesungen, Aufsätze. München : C.H. Beck, c2003.

ETHICS, MODERN - 17TH CENTURY.
Araujo, Marcelo de. Scepticism, freedom and autonomy. Berlin : De Gruyter, 2003.

ETHICS, MODERN - 18TH CENTURY.
Caropreso, Paolo. Von der Dingfrage zur Frage nach Gott. Berlin ; New York : W. de Gruyter, 2003.

ETHICS, MODERN - 20TH CENTURY.
Nazarchuk, A. V. (Aleksandr Viktorovich) Ėtika globaliziruiushchegosi︠a︡ obshchestva. Moskva : DirectMedii︠a︡ Pablishing, 2002.
B3199.A634 N39 2002

ETHICS, PRACTICAL. See **CONDUCT OF LIFE.**

ETHICS, PRIMITIVE. See **ETHICS.**

Ethik ohne Dogmen : Aufsätze für Günther Patzig / Achim Stephan, Klaus Peter Rippe (Hrsg.). Paderborn : Mentis, 2001. 284 p. ; 24 cm. Includes bibliographical references. "Der Anlass dieses Buches ist der 75. Geburtstag Günther Patzigs ..."--Vorwort. ISBN 3-89785-195-4 (hd. bd.) DDC 171.5
1. Ethics. 2. Utilitarianism. I. Patzig, Günther. II. Stephan, Achim. III. Rippe, Klaus Peter, 1959-

Ethik und Ästhetik.
Krollmann, Fritz-Peter, 1963- Essen : Blaue Eule, 2002.

Ethik und Politik ohne Gewissheiten.
Wolf, Jean-Claude. Freiburg, Schweiz : Universitätsverlag, c2002.

Ethik und politische Philosophie
(6) Wolf, Jean-Claude. Ethik und Politik ohne Gewissheiten. Freiburg, Schweiz : Universitätsverlag, c2002.

L'éthique.
Badiou, Alain. Caen : Nous, c2003.

ETHNIC ATTITUDES. See also **RACE AWARENESS.**
Song, Miri, 1964- Choosing ethnic identity. Cambridge, UK : Polity Press ; Oxford ; Malden, MA : Blackwell Publishing, 2003.
GN495.6 .S65 2003

ETHNIC ATTITUDES - EUROPE.
Kazaaam! splat! ploof!. Lanham, Md. ; Oxford : Rowman & Littlefield, c2003.
D1055 .K39 2003

ETHNIC CONFLICT.
Collective identities in action. Aldershot, England ; Burlington, VT : Ashgate, c2002.
GN495.6 .C635 2002

Imagine coexistence. 1st ed. San Francisco : Jossey-Bass, c2003.
HM1121 .I42 2003

The meanings of violence. London ; New York : Routledge, 2003.
HM1116 .M436 2003

The territorial management of ethnic conflict. 2nd rev. and expanded ed. London ; Portland, OR : F. Cass, 2003.
GN496 .T47 2003

ETHNIC DIVERSITY. See **PLURALISM (SOCIAL SCIENCES).**

ETHNIC DIVERSITY POLICY. See **MULTICULTURALISM.**

ETHNIC GROUPS. See also **MINORITIES.**
Corlett, J. Angelo, 1958- Race, racism, & reparations. Ithaca : Cornell University Press, c2003.
HT1523 .C67 2003

ETHNIC GROUPS - CIVIL RIGHTS.
Dench, Geoff. Minorities in the open society. New Brunswick, N.J. : Transaction Publishers, 2003.
JF1061 .D46 2003

ETHNIC GROUPS - PSYCHOLOGY. See **ETHNOPSYCHOLOGY.**

ETHNIC MEDICINE. See **TRADITIONAL MEDICINE.**

ETHNIC MINORITIES. See **MINORITIES.**

Ethnic minority professionals in psychology.
American Psychological Association. The directory of ethnic minority professionals in psychology. 4th ed. Washington, D.C. : American Psychological Association, c2001.
BF30 .A493 2001

ETHNIC PSYCHOLOGY. See **ETHNOPSYCHOLOGY.**

ETHNIC RELATIONS. See also **ETHNIC ATTITUDES; MINORITIES; RACE RELATIONS.**
Dench, Geoff. Minorities in the open society. New Brunswick, N.J. : Transaction Publishers, 2003.
JF1061 .D46 2003

Fenton, Steve, 1942- Ethnicity. Cambridge : Polity ; Oxford ; Malden, MA : Blackwell, c2003.
GN495.6 .F46 2003

Race, nature, and the politics of difference. Durham : Duke University Press, c2003.
HT1521 .R2355 2003

ETHNICITY. See also **BLACKS - RACE IDENTITY; MULTICULTURALISM; PLURALISM (SOCIAL SCIENCES).**
Fenton, Steve, 1942- Cambridge : Polity ; Oxford ; Malden, MA : Blackwell, c2003.
GN495.6 .F46 2003

ETHNICITY.
Castro, Vanessa Smith, 1969- Acculturation and psychological adaptation. Westport, Conn. : Greenwood Press, 2003.
HM841 .C37 2003

Catanio, Percy Antonio Galimbertti. O caminho que o dekassegui sonhou (dekassegui no yumē-ji). São Paulo : EDUC, FAPESP; Londrina : UEL, 2002.

Chelovek kak sub"ekt kul'tury. Moskva : Nauka, 2002.

Claiming the stones/naming the bones. Los Angeles : Getty Research Institute, c2002.
CC135 .C48 2002

Collective identities in action. Aldershot, England ; Burlington, VT : Ashgate, c2002.
GN495.6 .C635 2002

The colors of nature. 1st ed. Minneapolis, Minn. : Milkweed Editions, 2002.
QH81 .C663 2002

Dench, Geoff. Minorities in the open society. New Brunswick, N.J. : Transaction Publishers, 2003.
JF1061 .D46 2003

Erdas, Franco Epifanio. Partecipazione e differenza. Roma : Bulzoni, c2002.

Fenton, Steve, 1942- Ethnicity. Cambridge : Polity ; Oxford ; Malden, MA : Blackwell, c2003.
GN495.6 .F46 2003

Gervasoni, Marco, 1968- Le armi di Orfeo. [Scandicci] (Firenze) : La nuova Italia, 2002.
ML3917.E85 G479 2002

Identities. New York ; Oxford : Berghahn Books, 2002.
HM716 .I34 2002

Making and breaking of borders. Helsinki : Finnish Literature Society, 2003.
JC323 .M35 2003

Making sense of collectivity. London ; Sterling, Va. : Pluto Press, 2002.
HM753 .M35 2002

Nagel, Joane. Race, ethnicity, and sexuality. New York : Oxford University Press, 2003.
HQ21 .N195 2003

Perspectives on Las Américas. Maden, MA : Blackwell Pub., c2003.
F1410 .P48 2003

Pompeo, Francesco. Il mondo è poco. Roma : Meltemi, c2002.

GN495.6 .P66 2002

Razvitie nat͡sional'noĭ, ėtnolingvisticheskoĭ i religioznoĭ identichnosti u deteĭ i podrostkov = Moskva : In-t psikhologii RAN, 2001.
BF723.C5 R39 2001

Song, Miri, 1964- Choosing ethnic identity. Cambridge, UK : Polity Press ; Oxford ; Malden, MA : Blackwell Publishing, 2003.
GN495.6 .S65 2003

Yanow, Dvora. Constructing "race" and "ethnicity" in America. Armonk, N.Y. : M.E. Sharpe, c2003.
HM753 .Y36 2003

ETHNOCENTRISM - POLITICAL ASPECTS.
Toshchenko, Zhan Terent'evich. Tri osobennykh lika vlasti. Moskva : RGGU, 2002.
JC330 .T674 2002

ETHNOGRAPHY. See **ETHNOLOGY.**

ETHNOLOGY. See also **BLACKS; ETHNIC GROUPS; FOLKLORE; HUMAN TERRITORIALITY; INDIGENOUS PEOPLES; LANGUAGE AND LANGUAGES; RACE RELATIONS; WHITES.**
Between tradition and postmodernity. Warsaw : Wydawnictwo DiG, 2003.

Menéndez, Eduardo L. La parte negada de la cultura. Barcelona : Edicions Bellaterra, c2002.
HM1121 .M46 2002

ETHNOLOGY - AFRICA. See **AFRICANS.**

ETHNOLOGY - AMERICA. See **INDIANS.**

ETHNOLOGY - ASIA. See **ASIANS.**

ETHNOLOGY - BENIN. See **YORUBA (AFRICAN PEOPLE).**

ETHNOLOGY - BRAZIL. See **BRAZILIANS.**

ETHNOLOGY - CONGRESSES.
Gender, vlast', kul'tura. Saratov : Saratovskiĭ gos. tekhn. universitet, 2000.
HQ1075 .G4667 2000

ETHNOLOGY - EUROPE, EASTERN. See **SLAVS.**

ETHNOLOGY - GAMBIA. See **WOLOF (AFRICAN PEOPLE).**

ETHNOLOGY - INDONESIA. See **INDONESIANS.**

ETHNOLOGY - ISRAEL. See **JEWS.**

ETHNOLOGY - ITALY. See **ROMANS.**

ETHNOLOGY - JAPAN. See **JAPANESE.**

ETHNOLOGY - KOREA. See **KOREANS.**

ETHNOLOGY - LATIN AMERICA. See **LATIN AMERICANS.**

ETHNOLOGY - METHODOLOGY.
Expressions of ethnography. Albany, NY : State University of New York Press, c2003.
GN33 .E97 2003

Gray, Ann, 1946- Research practice for cultural studies. London ; Thousand Oaks, Calif. : SAGE, 2003.
H62 .G73 2003

ETHNOLOGY - MOROCCO.
Rosen, Lawrence, 1941- The culture of Islam. Chicago : University of Chicago Press, 2002.
DT312 R64 2002

ETHNOLOGY - NIGERIA. See **IGALA (AFRICAN PEOPLE); YORUBA (AFRICAN PEOPLE).**

ETHNOLOGY - PALESTINE. See **PALESTINIAN ARABS.**

ETHNOLOGY - PHILIPPINES. See **FILIPINOS.**

ETHNOLOGY - PHILOSOPHY.
Between tradition and postmodernity. Warsaw : Wydawnictwo DiG, 2003.

Carneiro, Robert L. (Robert Leonard), 1927- Evolutionism in cultural anthropology. Boulder, Colo. : Westview Press, 2003.
GN360 .C37 2003

Fremderfahrung und Repräsentation. 1. Aufl. Weilerswist : Velbrück, 2002.

Gellner, Ernest. [Essays. Selections] Ernest Gellner. London ; New York : Routledge, 2003.
B1626.G441 G76 2003

Kessidi, F. Kh. Filosofskie i ėticheskie problemy genetiki cheloveka. Moskva : Martis, 1994.

BF341 .K45 1994

Napier, A. David. The age of immunology. Chicago : University of Chicago Press, 2003.
GN345 .N36 2003

Tadtaev, Kh. B. (Khristofor Bagratovich) Ėtnos, nat͡siia, rasa. Saratov : Saratovskiĭ gos. universitet, 2001.
GN345 .T33 2001

ETHNOLOGY - RESEARCH.
Expressions of ethnography. Albany, NY : State University of New York Press, c2003.
GN33 .E97 2003

ETHNOLOGY - RUSSIA (FEDERATION). See **RUSSIANS.**

ETHNOLOGY - SENEGAL. See **WOLOF (AFRICAN PEOPLE).**

ETHNOLOGY - SPAIN. See **SPANIARDS.**

ETHNOLOGY - UNITED STATES. See **ASIAN AMERICANS; CHINESE AMERICANS.**

ETHNOLOGY - YUGOSLAVIA. See **SERBS.**

ETHNOMEDICINE. See **TRADITIONAL MEDICINE.**

ETHNOPSYCHOLOGY. See also **ETHNOCENTRISM; PERSONALITY AND CULTURE; RACE AWARENESS; SUBCULTURE.**
Chelovek kak sub"ekt kul'tury. Moskva : Nauka, 2002.

Cross-cultural perspectives in human development. New Delhi ; Thousand Oaks, Calif. : Sage Publications, 2003.
BF713.5 .C76 2003

Kochetkov, V. V. (Vladimir Viktorovich) Psikhologiia mezhkul'turnykh razlichiĭ. Moskva : PER SĖ, 2002.
GN502 .K6 2002

Lincoln, Jackson Steward, 1902-1941. [Dream in primitive cultures] The dream in native American and other primitive cultures. Mineola, N.Y. : Dover Publications, 2003.
BF1078 .L5 2003

Paquette, Didier. La mascarade interculturelle. Paris : Harmattan, c2002.

Razvitie nat͡sional'noĭ, ėtnolingvisticheskoĭ i religioznoĭ identichnosti u deteĭ i podrostkov = Moskva : In-t psikhologii RAN, 2001.
BF723.C5 R39 2001

Shweder, Richard A. Why do men barbecue? Cambridge, Mass. : Harvard University Press, 2003.
GN502 .S59 2003

ETHNOPSYCHOLOGY - HISTORY.
Guthrie, Robert V. Even the rat was white a historical view of psychology. Classic ed., 2nd ed. Boston, MA : Allyn and Bacon, 2004.
BF105 .G87 2004

ETHNOPSYCHOLOGY - NORTH AMERICA.
Many faces of gender. Boulder : University Press of Colorado ; Calgary, Alta., Canada : University of Calgary Press, c2002.
E98.P95 M35 2002

Ethnoscapes
Psychological theories for environmental issues. Aldershot, Hants, England ; Burlington, VT : Ashgate, 2003.
BF353 .P774 2003

ETHOLOGISTS - ENGLAND - BIOGRAPHY.
Morris, Desmond. The naked eye. London : Ebury Press, 2000.
QL31.M79 A3 2000

ETHOLOGY. See **CHARACTER; ETHICS; HUMAN BEHAVIOR.**

ETHOLOGY, COMPARATIVE. See **PSYCHOLOGY, COMPARATIVE.**

ETHOPSYCHOLOGY - RESEARCH.
Edgar, Iain R. Guide to imagework. London ; New York : Routledge, 2004.
BF367 .E34 2004

Ethos mundial.
Boff, Leonardo. Brasília : Letraviva, 2000.

Etica dell'assenso.
Premoli De Marchi, Paola. Milano : FrancoAngeli, c2002.

L'etica dello storicismo.
Cacciatore, Giuseppe, 1945- Lecce : Milella, 2000.

Etica desde el otro.
Brunero, María Alicia. Buenos Aires : Grupo Editorial Lumen, c2002.

Ėtika globaliziruiushchegosia obshchestva.
Nazarchuk, A. V. (Aleksandr Viktorovich) Moskva : DirectMedia Pablishing, 2002.
B3199.A634 N39 2002

ETIQUETTE. See **CONVERSATION; DINNERS AND DINING.**

Ėtnos, nat͡siia, rasa.
Tadtaev, Kh. B. (Khristofor Bagratovich) Saratov : Saratovskiĭ gos. universitet, 2001.
GN345 .T33 2001

Etonnants classiques
(2119) Contes de l'Egypte ancienne. Paris : Flammarion, c2002.

Etrangeté apprivoisée.
Charles, Monique. Borges, ou, L'étrangeté apprivoisée. Paris : Harmattan, c2002.

Etre et liberté selon Platon.
Binayemotlagh, Saïd. Paris : Harmattan, 2002.
B395 .B553 2002

ETRURIA - ANTIQUITIES.
Leland, Charles Godfrey, 1824-1903. [Etruscan roman remains in popular tradition] Etruscan Roman remains and the old religion. London ; New York : Kegan Paul ; New York : Distributed by Columbia University Press, 2002.
DG223 .L54 2002

ETRURIANS. See **ETRUSCANS.**

Etruscan Roman remains.
Leland, Charles Godfrey, 1824-1903. [Etruscan roman remains in popular tradition] Etruscan Roman remains and the old religion. London ; New York : Kegan Paul ; New York : Distributed by Columbia University Press, 2002.
DG223 .L54 2002

Etruscan Roman remains and the old religion.
Leland, Charles Godfrey, 1824-1903. [Etruscan roman remains in popular tradition] London ; New York : Kegan Paul ; New York : Distributed by Columbia University Press, 2002.
DG223 .L54 2002

ETRUSCANS - RELIGION.
Feo, Giovanni. Prima degli etruschi. Roma : Stampa alternativa, 2001.
BL813.E8 F46 2001

'Ets ha-da'at.
Morgan, Shemu'el. Pedu'el : Sh. Morgan, [1998?]

'Ets ha-da'at tov.
Vital, Ḥayyim ben Joseph, 1542 or 3-1620. Yerushalayim : Hotsa'at Ahavat shalom, 761 [2000 or 2001]

'Ets ha-da'at tov : ha-shalem.
Vital, Ḥayyim ben Joseph, 1542 or 3-1620. 'Ets ha-da'at tov. Yerushalayim : Hotsa'at Ahavat shalom, 761 [2000 or 2001]

'Ets ha-tidhar.
['Ets ha-tidhar.] Sidur kavanot 'Ets ha-tidhar. Yerushalayim : Kolel Shemen śaśon, [1998?]
1. Keri'at shema 'al ha-mitah.

[**'Ets ha-tidhar.**] Sidur kavanot 'Ets ha-tidhar : keri'at shema 'al ha-miṭah ... / 'a. p. siduro shel Shalom Mizraḥi Didye Shar'abi ; ne'erakh ve-nisdar 'a. y. Tidhar Elon. Yerushalayim : Kolel Shemen śaśon, [1998?] 124, 26 p. ; 25 cm. Cover title: 'Ets ha-tidhar, 'anaf keri'at shema she-'al ha-miṭah.
1. Cabala. 2. Judaism - Ari rite - Liturgy - Texts. 3. Keri'at shema 'al ha-miṭah. I. Azulai, Tidhar Elon. II. Sharabi, Shalom, 1720-1777. III. Title: 'Ets ha-tidhar IV. Title: 'Ets ha-tidhar, 'anaf keri'at shema' she-'al ha-miṭah

'Ets ha-tidhar, 'anaf keri'at shema' she-'al ha-miṭah.
['Ets ha-tidhar.] Sidur kavanot 'Ets ha-tidhar. Yerushalayim : Kolel Shemen śaśon, [1998?]
1. Keri'at shema 'al ha-mitah.

'Ets ḥayim.
Eliyahu, Saliman. Sefer Kerem Shelomoh. Yerushala[y]im : Ḥevrat Ahavat shalom, 762 [2001 or 2002]

Etudes d'histoire moderne
(2) Taric Zumsteg, Fabienne. Les sorciers à l'assaut du village. Lausanne : Editions du Zèbre, 2000.
BF1584.S9 T37 2000

Etudes musulmanes
(37) Arnaldez, Roger. Fakhr al-Dîn al-Râzî. Paris : J. Vrin, 2002.

Etudes psychanalytiques.
Fierens, Christian. Lecture de l'étourdit. Paris : Harmattan, c2002.
BF109.L28 F53 2002

Etuk, Emma S., 1948- Friends : what would I do without them? : finding real and valuable friendships in an unfriendly world / Emma S. Etuk. Washington, D.C. : Emida International, c1999. xv, 268 p. ; 21 cm. Includes bibliographical references and index. ISBN 1-88129-302-5 (pbk.) DDC 177/.62
1. Friendship. 2. Friendship - Religious aspects - Christianity. 3. Black author. I. Title.
BF575.F66 E77 1999

Etyka v problemnykh i analitychnykh zadachakh.
Stepanenko, Valeriĭ. Kyïv : Libra, 1998.

EUGENIC STERILIZATION. *See* **STERILIZATION, EUGENIC.**

EUGENICS. *See* **STERILIZATION, EUGENIC.**

EUGENICS - GERMANY - HISTORY - 20TH CENTURY.
Simon, Jürgen, 1966- Kriminalbiologie und Zwangssterilisation. Münster ; New York : Waxmann, c2001.

EURASIA. *See also* **ASIA; EUROPE.**
Kanygin, IUriĭ Mikhaĭlovich. Poi͡as mira. Kiev : MAUP, 2001.

EURASIAN SCHOOL.
Maler, Arkadiĭ. Strategii sakral'nogo smysla. Moskva : Parad izdatel'skiĭ dom, 2003.

EUROCENTRISM.
The emerging monoculture. Westport, Conn. : Praeger, 2003.
HM843.E44 2003

EUROPA (GREEK MYTHOLOGY).
Lombard, René-André. Le nom de l'Europe. Grenoble : Thot, c2001.

Europaea memoria. Reihe 1. Studien
(Bd. 17) Maesschalck, M. (Marc) Normes et contextes. Hildesheim ; New York : G. Olms, 2001.
BJ1063.M34 2001

Europäische Hochschulschriften. Reihe III, Geschichte und ihre Hilfswissenschaften
(Bd. 829.) Hähner, Olaf. Historische Biographik. Frankfurt am Main ; New York : Lang, 1999.

(Bd. 859.) Ceballos Gómez, Diana Luz, 1962- Zauberei und Hexerei. Frankfurt am Main ; New York : Peter Lang, c2000.
BF1584.S7 C43 2000

Europäische Hochschulschriften. Reihe XX, Philosophie
(Bd. 609.) Dufour, Adrian. Ciencia y logica de mundos posibles. Bern : Lang, 2001.

Europäische Hochschulschriften. Reihe XXIII, Theologie
(Bd. 748.) Dahlin, Olov, 1962- Zvinorwadza. Frankfurt am Main ; New York : P. Lang, c2002.
R726.5.D34 2002

Europäische Hochschulschriften. Reihe XXXI, Politikwissenschaft
(Bd. 292.) Elfenbein, Stefan W., 1964- Die veränderte Rolle der New York Times. Frankfurt am Main ; New York : P. Lang, c1996.
PN4899.N42 N375 1996

Europas Aufbruch in die Neuzeit 1450-1650.
Bastl, Beatrix, 1954- Darmstadt : Primus, c2002.
D208.B37 2002

Europe and the Asia-Pacific : culture, identity and representations of region / edited by Stephanie Lawson. London ; New York : RoutledgeCurzon, 2003. x, 257 p. : ill. ; 25 cm. Includes bibliographical references and index. ISBN 0-415-29724-9 (alk. paper) DDC 303.48/2405
1. Europe - Relations - Asia. 2. Asia - Relations - Europe. 3. East and West. I. Lawson, Stephanie.
D1065.A78 E97 2003

EUROPE - ANTIQUITIES.
Fire in archaeology. Oxford : Archaeopress, 2002.
DA90.B86 suppl. v.1089

EUROPE - CIVILIZATION.
Deutschland und der Westen Europas im Mittelalter. Stuttgart : Thorbecke, c2002.

Frantzen, Allen J., 1947- Bloody good. Chicago : University of Chicago Press, 2004.

D523.F722 2004

Marías, Julián, 1914- Entre dos siglos. Madrid : Alianza Editorial, c2002.
PQ6663.A72183 E68 2002

Medieval cultures in contact. New York : Fordham University Press, 2003.
CB351.M3922 2003

EUROPE - CIVILIZATION - 16TH CENTURY.
The 1500s. San Diego, Calif : Greenhaven Press, c2001.
CB367.A165 2001

La renaissance. [Paris] : Sedes, 2002.

EUROPE - CIVILIZATION - 18TH CENTURY.
Mauriès, Patrick, 1952- Cabinets of curiosities. New York : Thames & Hudson, c2002.
AM221.M38 2002

EUROPE - CIVILIZATION - 19TH CENTURY.
Mauriès, Patrick, 1952- Cabinets of curiosities. New York : Thames & Hudson, c2002.
AM221.M38 2002

EUROPE - CIVILIZATION - 476-1492. *See* **CIVILIZATION, MEDIEVAL.**

EUROPE - CIVILIZATION - AMERICAN INFLUENCES.
Kazaaam! splat! ploof!. Lanham, Md. ; Oxford : Rowman & Littlefield, c2003.
D1055.K39 2003

EUROPE - CIVILIZATION - ORIENTAL INFLUENCES.
Gunn, Geoffrey C. First globalization. Lanham, Md. ; Rowman & Littlefield, c2003.
CB251.G87 2003

EUROPE - COURT AND COURTIERS.
Scholars and courtiers. Aldershot ; Burlington, Vt. : Ashgate/Variorum, c2002.
AZ183.E8 S36 2002

EUROPE - DESCRIPTION AND TRAVEL.
Brosman, Catharine Savage, 1934- Finding higher ground. Reno : University of Nevada Press, c2003.
F787.B76 2003

EUROPE, EASTERN. *See* **SLAVIC COUNTRIES.**

EUROPE, EASTERN - CIVILIZATION.
Medieval cultures in contact. New York : Fordham University Press, 2003.
CB351.M3922 2003

EUROPE, EASTERN - HISTORY - 1918-1945.
Schaller, Helmut Wilhelm, 1940- Der Nationalsozialismus und die slawische Welt. Regensburg : Pustet, c2002.
DD256.5.S259 2002

EUROPE, EASTERN - SOCIAL CONDITIONS.
Medieval cultures in contact. New York : Fordham University Press, 2003.
CB351.M3922 2003

EUROPE - ECONOMIC CONDITIONS - 16TH CENTURY.
A companion to the worlds of the Renaissance. Malden, MA : Blackwell Publishers, 2002.
CB367.C65 2002

Urban achievement in early modern Europe. Cambridge ; New York : Cambridge University Press, 2001.
HT131.U688 2001

EUROPE - ECONOMIC CONDITIONS - 17TH CENTURY.
Urban achievement in early modern Europe. Cambridge ; New York : Cambridge University Press, 2001.
HT131.U688 2001

EUROPE - ECONOMIC CONDITIONS - 18TH CENTURY.
Lukowski, Jerzy. The European nobility in the eighteenth century. Houndmills [England] ; New York : Palgrave Macmillan, 2003.
HT653.E9 L85 2003

Urban achievement in early modern Europe. Cambridge ; New York : Cambridge University Press, 2001.
HT131.U688 2001

EUROPE - ETHNIC RELATIONS.
Sutcliffe, Adam. Judaism and Enlightenment. Cambridge ; New York : Cambridge University Press, 2003.
BM290.S88 2003

EUROPE - HISTORIOGRAPHY.
Venner, Dominique. Histoire et tradition des Européens. Monaco : Rocher, c2002.
D80.V46 2002

EUROPE - HISTORY.
Carlyle, Thomas, 1795-1881. Historical essays. Berkeley ; London : University of California Press, c2002.
D208.C34 2002

Deutschland und der Westen Europas im Mittelalter. Stuttgart : Thorbecke, c2002.

Venner, Dominique. Histoire et tradition des Européens. Monaco : Rocher, c2002.
D80.V46 2002

EUROPE - HISTORY - 1492-1517 - CONGRESSES.
La Renaissance. Paris : Presses de l'université de Paris-Sorbonne, 2003.

EUROPE - HISTORY - 1492-1648.
Bastl, Beatrix, 1954- Europas Aufbruch in die Neuzeit 1450-1650. Darmstadt : Primus, c2002.
D208.B37 2002

The European Renaissance and Reformation, 1350-1600. Detroit, MI : Gale Group, 2001.
CB359.W67 2001

EUROPE - HISTORY - 1517-1648 - CONGRESSES.
La Renaissance. Paris : Presses de l'université de Paris-Sorbonne, 2003.

EUROPE - HISTORY - 15TH CENTURY.
La renaissance. [Paris] : Sedes, 2002.

EUROPE - HISTORY - 16TH CENTURY.
La renaissance. [Paris] : Sedes, 2002.

EUROPE - HISTORY - 476-1492.
The construction of communities in the early Middle Ages. Leiden ; Boston : Brill, 2003.
HN11.C66 2003

Medieval Europe, 814-1350. Detroit, MI : Gale Group, c2002.
D102.M38 2001

EUROPE - HISTORY - TO 476.
The construction of communities in the early Middle Ages. Leiden ; Boston : Brill, 2003.
HN11.C66 2003

EUROPE - INTELLECTUAL LIFE.
Moss, Ann, 1938- Printed commonplace-books and the structuring of Renaissance thought. Oxford : Clarendon Press ; New York : Oxford University Press, 1996.
PA2047.M67 1996

Scholars and courtiers. Aldershot ; Burlington, Vt. : Ashgate/Variorum, c2002.
AZ183.E8 S36 2002

Urban achievement in early modern Europe. Cambridge ; New York : Cambridge University Press, 2001.
HT131.U688 2001

Der weite Blick des Historikers. Köln : Böhlau, c2002.
D116.W44 2002

EUROPE - INTELLECTUAL LIFE - 16TH CENTURY - CONGRESSES.
La Renaissance. Paris : Presses de l'université de Paris-Sorbonne, 2003.

EUROPE - INTELLECTUAL LIFE - 17TH CENTURY.
Baldriga, Irene. L'occhio della lince. Roma : Accademia nazionale dei Lincei, 2002.

Dooley, Brendan Maurice, 1953- Morandi's last prophecy and the end of Renaissance politics. Princeton, N.J. ; Woodstock : Princeton University Press, c2002.
BF1679.8.M59 D66 2002

Sutcliffe, Adam. Judaism and Enlightenment. Cambridge ; New York : Cambridge University Press, 2003.
BM290.S88 2003

Urban achievement in early modern Europe. Cambridge ; New York : Cambridge University Press, 2001.
HT131.U688 2001

EUROPE - INTELLECTUAL LIFE - 18TH CENTURY.
Sutcliffe, Adam. Judaism and Enlightenment. Cambridge ; New York : Cambridge University Press, 2003.

BM290 .S88 2003

Urban achievement in early modern Europe. Cambridge ; New York : Cambridge University Press, 2001.
HT131 .U688 2001

EUROPE - INTELLECTUAL LIFE - HISTORY.
Gibbons, B. J. Spirituality and the occult. London ; New York : Routledge, 2001.
BF1434.E85 G53 2001

EUROPE - LITERATURES. *See* **EUROPEAN LITERATURE.**

EUROPE - RELATIONS - ASIA.
Europe and the Asia-Pacific. London ; New York : RoutledgeCurzon, 2003.
D1065.A78 E97 2003

Gunn, Geoffrey C. First globalization. Lanham, Md. : Rowman & Littlefield, c2003.
CB251 .G87 2003

EUROPE - RELATIONS - UNITED STATES.
Kazaaam! splat! ploof!. Lanham, Md. ; Oxford : Rowman & Littlefield, c2003.
D1055 .K39 2003

EUROPE - SOCIAL CONDITIONS.
Année mille An Mil. Aix-en-Provence : Publications de l'université de Provence, 2002.

Medieval cultures in contact. New York : Fordham University Press, 2003.
CB351 .M3922 2003

EUROPE - SOCIAL CONDITIONS - 16TH CENTURY.
A companion to the worlds of the Renaissance. Malden, MA : Blackwell Publishers, 2002.
CB367 .C65 2002

EUROPE - SOCIAL CONDITIONS - 18TH CENTURY.
Lukowski, Jerzy. The European nobility in the eighteenth century. Houndmills [England] ; New York : Palgrave Macmillan, 2003.
HT653.E9 L85 2003

EUROPE - SOCIAL LIFE AND CUSTOMS.
Religion et mentalités au Moyen Age. Rennes : Presses universitaires de Rennes, c2003.
BR141 .R45 2003

EUROPE - SOCIAL LIFE AND CUSTOMS - 16TH CENTURY.
Lee-Browne, Patrick. The Renaissance. New York : Facts on File, c2003.

EUROPE - SOCIAL LIFE AND CUSTOMS - TO 1492.
Ducret, Alix. La vie au moyen âge. Courtaboeuf : Didro, c2002.

EUROPE - TERRITORIAL EXPANSION.
Medieval cultures in contact. New York : Fordham University Press, 2003.
CB351 .M3922 2003

EUROPE, WESTERN - SOCIAL POLICY.
Brush, Lisa Diane. Gender and governance. Walnut Creek, CA ; Oxford : AltaMira Press, c2003.
JC330 .B75 2003

EUROPE X HISTORIOGRAPHY.
Der weite Blick des Historikers. Köln : Böhlau, c2002.
D116 .W44 2002

European Association of Archaeologists Annual Meeting (6th : 2000 : Lisbon, Portugal).
Fire in archaeology. Oxford : Archaeopress, 2002.
DA90 .B86 suppl. v.1089

European culture and society
Lukowski, Jerzy. The European nobility in the eighteenth century. Houndmills [England] ; New York : Palgrave Macmillan, 2003.
HT653.E9 L85 2003

EUROPEAN LITERATURE. *See* **GERMANIC LITERATURE.**

EUROPEAN LITERATURE - MEDIEVAL, 500-1500. *See* **LITERATURE, MEDIEVAL.**

EUROPEAN LITERATURE - MODERN PERIOD, 1500-. *See* **EUROPEAN LITERATURE.**

EUROPEAN LITERATURE - RENAISSANCE, 1450-1600 - HISTORY AND CRITICISM.
Cité des hommes, cité de Dieu. Genève : Droz, 2003.
PN723 .C584 2003

European monographs in social psychology
Monteil, Jean-Marc. Social context and cognitive performance. Hove, East Sussex, UK : Psychology Press, c1999.
BF311 .M59 1999

The European nobility in the eighteenth century.
Lukowski, Jerzy. Houndmills [England] ; New York : Palgrave Macmillan, 2003.
HT653.E9 L85 2003

European perspectives
Agacinski, Sylviane. [Passeur de temps. English] Time passing. New York : Columbia University Press, c2003.
BD638 .A27713 2003

Kristeva, Julia, 1941- [Révolte intime. English] Intimate revolt. New York : Columbia University Press, c2002.
PN56.P92 K7513 2002

EUROPEAN PHILOSOPHY. *See* **PHILOSOPHY, EUROPEAN.**

The European Renaissance and Reformation, 1350-1600 / edited by Norman J. Wilson. Detroit, MI : Gale Group, 2001. xxix, 522 p. : ill., maps ; 29 cm. (World eras ; v. 1) Includes bibliographical references (p. 477-484) and indexes. CONTENTS: World events -- Geography -- The arts -- Communication, transportation, and exploration -- Social class system and the economy -- Politics, law, and the military -- Leisure, recreation, and daily life -- Family and social trends -- Religion and philosophy -- Science, technology, and health. ISBN 0-7876-1706-7 (alk. paper) DDC 940.2/1
1. Renaissance. 2. Reformation. 3. Religion and culture - Europe - History. 4. Europe - History - 1492-1648. I. Wilson, Norman J. II. Series.
CB359 .W67 2001

EUROPEAN WAR, 1914-1918. *See* **WORLD WAR, 1914-1918.**

EUROPEAN WAR, 1939-1945. *See* **WORLD WAR, 1939-1945.**

Eusterschulte, Anne.
Philosophie der natürlichen Mitwelt. Würzburg : Königshausen & Neumann, 2002.

EUTHANASIA.
Cotroneo, Girolamo. Le idee del tempo. Soveria Mannelli (Catanzaro) : Rubbettino, c2002.

EUTHENICS. *See* **EUGENICS.**

EVALUATION OF LITERATURE. *See* **CRITICISM; LITERATURE - HISTORY AND CRITICISM.**

EVANGELISTIC WORK. *See also* **WITNESS BEARING (CHRISTIANITY).**
Sartorio, Ugo. Credere in dialogo. Padova : Edizioni Messaggero, 2002.

Evans, Bob.
Stewardson, John (John E.) Success is the best revenge. Toronto : Productive Publications, c1994.

Evans, Hilary, 1929- From other worlds : aliens, abductions, and UFOs / Hilary Evans. Pleasantville, N.Y. : Reader's Digest, c1998. 188. [4] p. : ill. (chiefly col.) ; 28 cm. Includes bibliographical references (p. [191-192]) and index. ISBN 0-7621-0107-5 (hardcover) ISBN 0-7621-0108-3 (pbk.) DDC 001.942
1. Human-alien encounters. 2. Alien abduction. 3. Unidentified flying objects. I. Title.
BF2050 .E93 1998

Evans, Jonathan St. B. T., 1948-.
Perspectives on thinking and reasoning. Hove, UK ; Hillsdale : Lawrence Erlbaum Associates, c1995.
BF441 .P48 1995

Evans, Rand B.
The life cycle of psychological ideas. New York : Kluwer Academic/Plenum, 2004.
BF38 .L54 2004

Eve returns Adam's rib.
Sutcliffe, Eileen, 1934- Calgary : Loraleen Enterprises, c2002.

L'éveil de la conscience féminine.
Eiguer, Alberto. Paris : Bayard, c2002.

Even shetiyah.
Milshtein, Mosheh. Sefer Even shetiyah. Bruḳlin : [Lee Printing corp.], 758- [1998-

Even the rat was white a historical view of psychology.
Guthrie, Robert V. Classic ed., 2nd ed. Boston, MA : Allyn and Bacon, 2004.
BF105 .G87 2004

EVENTS, LIFE CHANGE. *See* **LIFE CHANGE EVENTS.**

L'éventuel et le possible.
Kyelem, Apollinaire. [Ouagadougou : Presses universitaires de Ouagadougou, 2002]

Every child deserves a champion.
Danzig, Robert J., 1932- Washington, DC : Child & Family Press, c2003.
BF637.E53 D36 2003

Every day Tao.
Willoughby, Leonard. Boston, MA : Weiser Books, 2001.
BL1920 .W55 2001

Everyday experience and conditional reasoning.
Artman, Lavee. ha-Nisayon ha-yomyomi u-fitron heseḳe tenai ya-hakhalah lo-teḳefim. [Israel : h. mo. l., 1999?]

Everyday language & everyday life.
Hoggart, Richard, 1918- New Brunswick, N.J. ; London : Transaction Publishers, c2003.
PE1074.8 .H64 2003

Everyday language and everyday life.
Hoggart, Richard, 1918- Everyday language & everyday life. New Brunswick, N.J. ; London : Transaction Publishers, c2003.
PE1074.8 .H64 2003

Everyday mind reading.
Ickes, William John. Amherst, N.Y. : Prometheus Books, 2003.
BF575.E55 I35 2003

Everyday moon magic.
Morrison, Dorothy, 1955- St. Paul, Minn. : Llewellyn Publications, 2003.
BF1623.M66 M67 2003

Everyday saints and the art of narrative in the South English legendary.
Thompson, Anne Booth. Aldershot, England ; Burlington, Vt. : Ashgate, c2003.
PR2143.S543 T48 2003

The everything divining the future book.
Kosarin, Jenni. Avon. MA : Adams Media, c2003.
BF1773 .K67 2003

The everything feng shui decluttering book.
Jones, Katina Z. Avon, MA : Adams Media, c2004.
BF1779.F4 J663 2004

Everything happens for a reason.
Kirshenbaum, Mira. New York : Harmony Books, 2004.
BF637.L53 K57 2004

Everything I need to know I learned from other women.
Hateley, B. J. Gallagher (Barbara J. Gallagher), 1949- York Beach, ME : Conari Press, c2002.
HQ1206 .H345 2002

The everything love signs book.
Kosarin, Jenni. Avon, MA : Adams Media, c2004.
BF1729.L6 K67 2004

The everything psychic book.
Hathaway, Michael R. Avon, Mass. : Adams Media Corp., c2003.
BF1031 .H2955 2003

The everything self-esteem book.
Sherfield, Robert M. Avon, MA : Adams Media Corp., c2004.
BF697.5.S46 S52

The everything series
Hathaway, Michael R. The everything psychic book. Avon, Mass. : Adams Media Corp., c2003.
BF1031 .H2955 2003

Everything .series.
Hathaway, Michael R. The everything psychic book. Avon, Mass. : Adams Media Corp., c2003.
BF1031 .H2955 2003

Jones, Katina Z. The everything feng shui decluttering book. Avon, MA : Adams Media, c2004.
BF1779.F4 J663 2004

The everything series
Kosarin, Jenni. The everything divining the future book. Avon, MA : Adams Media, c2003.
BF1773 .K67 2003

Everything series
Kosarin, Jenni. The everything love signs book. Avon, MA : Adams Media, c2004.
BF1729.L6 K67 2004

Sherfield, Robert M. The everything self-esteem book. Avon, MA : Adams Media Corp., c2004.
BF697.5.S46 S52

Everything you need to know about dealing with losses.
Weiss, Stefanie Iris. Rev. ed. New York : Rosen Pub. Group, 2000.
BF724.3.L66 W45 2000

EVIDENCE, DOCUMENTARY. *See* **LEGAL DOCUMENTS - IDENTIFICATION.**

EVIDENCE (LAW). *See also* **ORDEAL; WITNESSES.**
Essays for Colin Tapper. London : LexisNexis, 2003.

EVIL. *See* **GOOD AND EVIL.**

Evil eye.
Mishra, Archana, 1962- Casting the evil eye. New Delhi : Namita Gokhale Editions, Roli Books, 2003.
BF1584.A-Z1.Z7 2003+

EVIL IN MOTION PICTURES. *See* **GOOD AND EVIL.**

EVIL INCLINATION (JUDAISM). *See* **YETZER HARA (JUDAISM).**

EVIL SPIRITS. *See* **DEMONOLOGY.**

EVIL SPIRITS, EXPULSION OF. *See* **EXORCISM.**

Evlampiev, I. I. (Igor' Ivanovich).
Florovsky, Georges, 1893-1979. [Selections. Russian. 2002] Vera i kul'tura. Sankt-Peterburg : Izd-vo Russkogo Khristianskogo gumanitarnogo instituta, 2002.
BX260 .F552 2002

EVOCATION.
Grimassi, Raven, 1951- The witch's familiar. 1st ed. St. Paul, Minn. : Llewellyn Publications, 2003.
BF1557 .G75 2003

Évoliutsiia i soznanie.
Beskova, I. A. Moskva : "Indrik", 2002.
B808.9 .B476 2002x

Évoliutsiia paradigmal'nykh osnovaniĭ nauki.
Dugin, Aleksandr. Moskva : Arktogeia, 2002.
Q174.8 .D845 2002

EVOLUTION. *See also* **CREATION; EVOLUTION (BIOLOGY); SOCIAL EVOLUTION.**
Bichakjian, Bernard H. Language in a Darwinian perspective. Frankfurt am Main ; New York : Peter Lang, c2002.
P142 .B53 2002

Consciousness evolving. Amsterdam ; Philadelphia, Pa. : John Benjamins Pub., c2002.
B808.9 .C665 2002

Freund, Philip, 1909- Myths of creation. London : Peter Owen ; Chester Springs, PA : Distributed in the USA by Dufour Editions, 2003.
BL226 .F74 2003

Giberson, Karl. Species of origins. Lanham, Md. : Rowman & Littlefield, c2002.
BL240.3 .G53 2002

Humphrey, Nicholas. The mind made flesh. Oxford ; New York : Oxford University Press, 2002.
BF701 .H86 2002

Linguistic evolution through language acquisition. Cambridge ; New York : Cambridge University Press, 2002.
P118 .L565 2002

Naturalism, evolution, and intentionality. Calgary, Alta., Canada : University of Calgary Press, c2001.
BD418.3 .N35 2001

Palmer, Trevor, 1944- Perilous planet earth. Cambridge, U.K. ; New York : Cambridge University Press, 2003.
QE506 .P35 2003

Redfield, James. God and the evolving universe. New York : Jeremy P. Tarcher/Putnam, c2002.
BD541 .R43 2002

Evolution and cognition
Atran, Scott, 1952- In gods we trust. Oxford ; New York : Oxford University Press, 2002.
BL53 .A88 2002

Trivers, Robert. Natural selection and social theory. New York : Oxford University Press, 2002.
GN365.9 .T76 2002

Evolution and learning : the Baldwin effect reconsidered / edited by Bruce H. Weber and David J. Depew. Cambridge, Mass. : MIT Press, c2003. x, 341 p. : ill. ; 24 cm. (Life and mind) Based on a conference held in Nov. 1999 at Bennington College. "A Bradford book." Includes bibliographical references and index. CONTENTS: Baldwin boosters, Baldwin skeptics -- Baldwin and his many effects / David J. Depew -- Baldwin effects and the expansion of the explanatory repertoire in evolutionary biology / Stephen M. Downes -- Between Baldwin skepticism and Baldwin boosterism / Peter Godfrey-Smith -- The Baldwin effect: a crane, not a skyhook / Daniel Dennett -- Multilevel selection in a complex adaptive system: the problem of language origins / Terrence W. Deacon -- Postscript on the Baldwin effect and niche construction / Peter Godfrey-Smith, Daniel Dennett, and Terrence W. Deacon -- Evolution, development, and the individual acquisition of traits: what we've learned since Baldwin / Celia L. Moore -- Baldwin and beyond: organic selection and genetic assimilation / Brian K. Hall -- On having a hammer / Susan Oyama -- Beyond the Baldwin effect: James Mark Baldwin's "Social Heredity," epigenetic inheritance, and niche construction / Paul E. Griffiths -- The Baldwin effect in the age of computation / Ruben R. Puentedura -- Role of predator-induced polyphenism in the evolution of cognition: a baldwinian speculation / Scott F. Gilbert -- Baldwin and biosemiotics: what intelligence is for / Jesper Hoffmeyer and Kalevi Kull -- The hierarchic logic of emergence: untangling the interdependence of evolution and self-organization / Terrence W. Deacon -- Emergence of mind and the Baldwin effect / Bruce H. Weber. ISBN 0-262-23229-4 (hc. : alk. paper) DDC 155.7
1. Baldwin, James Mark, - 1861-1934. 2. Evolutionary psychology. 3. Learning, Psychology of. I. Weber, Bruce H. II. Depew, David J., 1942- III. Series.
BF698.95 .E95 2003

EVOLUTION (BIOLOGY). *See also* **EPIGENESIS; HUMAN EVOLUTION.**
Barbieri, Marcello. The organic codes. Cambridge, UK. ; New York : Cambridge University Press, 2003.
QH331 .B247 2003

Boulter, Michael Charles. Extinction. New York : Columbia University Press, c2002.
QE721.2.E97 B68 2002

Consciousness evolving. Amsterdam ; Philadelphia, Pa. : John Benjamins Pub., c2002.
B808.9 .C665 2002

Darwin, Charles, 1809-1882. Autobiographies. London : Penguin, 2002.

Dawkins, Richard, 1941- The extended phenotype. Rev. ed. Oxford ; New York : Oxford University Press, 1999.
QH375 .D38 1999

Evolutionary dynamics. Oxford ; New York : Oxford University Press, 2003.
QH366.2 .E867 2003

Fenchel, Tom. Origin and early evolution of life. Oxford ; New York : Oxford University Press, 2002.
QH325 .F42 2002

Francis, Richard C., 1953- Why men won't ask for directions. Princeton, N.J. : Princeton University Press, 2004.
BF698.95 .F73 2004

Goodall, Jane. Performance and evolution in the age of Darwin. London ; New York : Routledge, 2002.
NX180.S3 G66 2002

Gould, Stephen Jay. I have landed. 1st ed. New York : Harmony Books, 2002.
QH45.5 .G735 2002

Mayr, Ernst, 1904- What evolution is. New York : Basic Books, c2001.
QH366.2 .M3933 2001

Minelli, Alessandro. The development of animal form. Cambridge ; New York : Cambridge University Press, 2003.
QH491 .M559 2003

Origination of organismal form. Cambridge, Mass. : MIT Press, c2003.
QH491 .O576 2003

Reichholf, Josef. Warum wir siegen wollen. München : Deutscher Taschenbuch, c2001.

Shlain, Leonard. Sex, time, and power. New York ; London : Viking, 2003.
HQ23 .S45 2003

Trivers, Robert. Natural selection and social theory. New York : Oxford University Press, 2002.
GN365.9 .T76 2002

Vallejo, Fernando. La tautología darwinista. 1a. ed. México : Universidad Nacional Autónoma de México, 1998.

Wallace, David Rains, 1945- The Klamath knot. 20th anniversary ed. Berkeley : University of California Press, [2003]
QH105.C2 W344 2003

West-Eberhard, Mary Jane. Developmental plasticity and evolution. Oxford ; New York : Oxford University Press, 2003.
QH546 .W45 2003

Evolution, gender, and rape / edited by Cheryl Brown Travis. Cambridge, Mass. : MIT Press, c2003. vi, 454 p. : ill. ; 24 cm. "A Bradford book." Includes bibliographical references and index. CONTENTS: Talking about and selling difference / Cheryl Brown Travis -- Female sexuality and the myth of male control / Christine M. Drea and Kim Wallen -- Power asymmetries between the sexes, mate preferences, and components of fitness / Patricia Adair Gowaty -- Does self-report make sense as an investigative method in evolutionary psychology? / Stephanie A. Shields and Pamela Steinke -- Understanding rape / Ethel Tobach and Rachel Reed -- Pop sociobiology reborn : the evolutionary psychology of sex and violence / A. Leah Vickers and Philip Kitcher. CONTENTS: Of vice and men : a case study in evolutionary psychology / Jerry A. Coyne -- Evolutionary models of why men rape : acknowledging the complexities / Mary P. Koss -- Theory and data on rape and evolution / Cheryl Brown Travis -- Unnatural history of rape / Michael Kimmel -- Violence against science : rape and evolution / Elisabeth A. Lloyd -- Origins of sex differences in human behavior : evolved dispositions versus social roles / Alice H. Eagly and Wendy Wood -- Evolutionary value of the man (to) child affiliative bond : closer to obligate than to facultative / Wade C. Mackey. CONTENTS: Rape-free versus rape-prone : how culture makes a difference / Peggy Reeves Sanday -- "What is rape?"-toward a historical, ethnographic approach / Emily Martin -- Understanding rape : a metatheoretical framework / Jacquelyn W. White and Lori A. Post -- Coming full circle : refuting biological determinism / Sue V. Rosser. ISBN 0-262-20143-7 (hard. : alk. paper) ISBN 0-262-70090-5 (pbk. : alk. paper) DDC 364.15/32
1. Thornhill, Randy. - Natural history of rape. 2. Rape. 3. Men - Sexual behavior. 4. Human evolution. I. Travis, Cheryl Brown, 1944-
HV6558 .E92 2003

Evolution, history and destiny.
Washington, Johnny. New York : Peter Lang, c2002.
E185.625 .W37 2002

The evolution of desire.
Buss, David M. Rev. ed. New York : BasicBooks, c2003.

Evolutionary aesthetics / Eckart Voland, Karl Grammer, eds. Berlin ; New York : Springer, c2003. x, 377 p. : ill. (some col.) ; 24 cm. Includes bibliographical references and index. ISBN 3-540-43670-7 (alk. paper) DDC 111/.85
1. Aesthetics - Psychological aspects. 2. Evolutionary psychology. I. Voland, Eckart, 1949- II. Grammer, Karl, 1950-
BH301.P78 E96 2003

Evolutionary dynamics : exploring the interplay of selection, accident, neutrality, and function / editors, James P. Crutchfield, Peter Schuster. Oxford ; New York : Oxford University Press, 2003. xxxiv, 452 p. : ill. ; 25 cm. (Santa Fe Institute studies in the sciences of complexity) Includes bibliographical references and index. CONTENTS: Preface: Dynamics of evolutionary processes / James P. Crutchfield and Peter Schuster -- The sloshing bucket: how the physical realm controls evolution / Niles Eldredge -- Developmental morphospaces and evolution / Gunther J. Eble -- The dynamics of large biological systems: a statistical physics view of macroevolution / Stefan Bornholdt -- On the population genetics of punctuation / Aviv Bergman and Marcus W. Feldman -- When evolution is revolution / James P. Crutchfield -- Evolution and speciation in a hyperspace: the roles of neutrality, selection, mutation, and random drift / Sergey Gavrilets -- Molecular insights into evolution of phenotypes / Peter Schuster -- The nearly neutral theory with special reference to interactions at the molecular level / Tomoko Ohta -- Spectral landscape theory / Peter F. Stadler -- Quasispecies evolution on dynamic fitness landscapes / Nigel Snoad and Martin Nilsson -- Recombination and bistability in finite populations / Lionel Barnett -- On the dynamic persistence of cooperation: how lower individual fitness induces higher survivability / Guy Sella and Michael Lachmann -- Coevolution of strategies in n-person prisoner's dilemma / Kristian Lindgren and Johann Johansson -- Evolutionary design of collective computation in cellular automata / James P. Crutchfield, Melanie Mitchell and Rajarshi Das. ISBN 0-19-514264-0 ISBN 0-19-514265-9 (pbk.) DDC 576.8
1. Evolution (Biology) I. Crutchfield, James P. (James Patrick) II. Schuster, Peter, 1939- III. Series: Proceedings volume in the Santa Fe Institute studies in the sciences of complexity.
QH366.2 .E867 2003

EVOLUTIONARY ECONOMICS.
Evolutionary economics and human nature. Cheltenham : Edward Elgar, c2003.

Evolutionary economics and human nature / edited by John Laurent, with a preface by Geoffrey M. Hodgson. Cheltenham : Edward Elgar, c2003. xiii, 220 p. : ill. ; 24 cm. Includes bibliographical references and index. ISBN 1-84064-923-2 Prentice/Hall DDC 330.1
1. Evolutionary economics. 2. Psychology. I. Laurent, John.

EVOLUTIONARY PSYCHOLOGY. *See also* **GENETIC PSYCHOLOGY.**
Buss, David M. 2nd ed. Boston, MA : Allyn and Bacon, 2003.
BF698.95 .B87 2003

Gaulin, Steven J. C. 2nd ed. Upper Saddle River, N.J. : Pearson/Prentice Hall, c2004.
BF698.95 .G38 2004

Workman, Lance. New York : Cambridge University Press, 2004.
BF698.95 .W67 2004

EVOLUTIONARY PSYCHOLOGY.
Barrett, Louise. Human evolutionary psychology. Princeton, N.J. : Princeton University Press, c2002.
BF698.95 .B37 2002

Bertelsen, Preben. Free will, consciousness, and the self. New York : Berghahn Books, 2003.
BF621 .B47 2003

Bridgeman, Bruce. Psychology & evolution. Thousand Oaks, Calif. : SAGE Publications, c2003.
BF698.95 .B75 2003

Buss, David M. Evolutionary psychology. 2nd ed. Boston, MA : Allyn and Bacon, 2003.
BF698.95 .B87 2003

Evolution and learning. Cambridge, Mass. : MIT Press, c2003.
BF698.95 .E95 2003

Evolutionary aesthetics. Berlin ; New York : Springer, c2003.
BH301.P78 E96 2003

Evolutionary psychology, public policy, and personal decisions. Mahwah, N.J. : Lawrence Erlbaum Associates, 2004.
BF698.95 .E96 2004

Francis, Richard C., 1953- Why men won't ask for directions. Princeton, N.J. : Princeton University Press, 2004.
BF698.95 .F73 2004

Gaulin, Steven J. C. Evolutionary psychology. 2nd ed. Upper Saddle River, N.J. : Pearson/Prentice Hall, c2004.
BF698.95 .G38 2004

Humphrey, Nicholas. How to solve the mind-- body problem. Thorverton, UK ; Bowling Green, OH : Imprint Academic, c2000.
BF698.95 .H86 2000

Laland, Kevin N. Sense and nonsense. Oxford ; New York : Oxford University Press, 2002.
BF701 .L34 2002

Readings in evolutionary psychology. Boston : Pearson/Allyn and Bacon, c2004.
BF698.95 .R43 2004

Sterelny, Kim. Thought in a hostile world. Malden, MA : Blackwell, 2003.
BF698.95 .S74 2003

Evolutionary psychology and motivation.
Nebraska Symposium on Motivation (2001) Lincoln, Neb. ; London : University of Nebraska Press, c2001.
BF701 .N43 2001

Evolutionary psychology and violence : a primer for policymakers and public policy advocates / edited by Richard W. Bloom and Nancy Dess ; foreword by Joseph Graves, Jr. Westport, Conn. : Praeger, 2003. xiii, 288 p. : ill. ; 24 cm. (Psychological dimensions to war and peace) Includes bibliographical references and index. ISBN 0-275-97467-7 (alk. paper) DDC 303.6
1. Violence - Psychological aspects. 2. Social conflict - Psychological aspects. 3. Genetic psychology. 4. Violence - Government policy. 5. Social conflict - Government policy. I. Bloom, Richard W., 1944- II. Dess, Nancy Kimberly. III. Series.
HM1116 .E96 2003

EVOLUTIONARY PSYCHOLOGY - CONGRESSES.
From mating to mentality. New York, NY : Psychology Press, 2003.
BF698.95 .F76 2003

Evolutionary psychology, public policy, and personal decisions / edited by Charles Crawford, Catherine Salmon. Mahwah, N.J. : Lawrence Erlbaum Associates, 2004. p. cm. Sequel to: Handbook of evolutionary psychology. Includes bibliographical references and indexes. ISBN 0-8058-4377-9 (cloth : alk. paper) ISBN 0-8058-4946-7 (pbk. : alk. paper) DDC 155.7
1. Evolutionary psychology. I. Crawford, Charles (Charles B.) II. Salmon, Catherine.
BF698.95 .E96 2004

EVOLUTIONARY PSYCHOLOGY - TEXTBOOKS.
Workman, Lance. Evolutionary psychology. New York : Cambridge University Press, 2004.
BF698.95 .W67 2004

Evolutionism in cultural anthropology.
Carneiro, Robert L. (Robert Leonard), 1927- Boulder, Colo. : Westview Press, 2003.
GN360 .C37 2003

Evolving connectionist systems.
Kasabov, Nikola K. London ; New York : Springer, c2003.
QA76.87 .K39 2003

Evropeĭskiĭ universitet v Sankt-Peterburge. Fakul'tet politicheskikh nauk i sotsiologii.
Kharkhordin, Oleg, 1964- Oblichat' i litsemerit'. Sankt-Peterburg : Evropeĭskiĭ universitet v Sankt-Peterburge ; Moskva : Letniĭ Sad, 2002.
B2430.F724 K43 2002

EX-CULTISTS. *See* **CULTS.**

EX-MILITARY PERSONNEL. *See* **VETERANS.**

Ex Oriente Lux
Jagaddeva. [Svapnacintāmaṇi. Russian] Volshebnoe sokrovishche snovideniĭ. Moskva : Ladomir, 1996.
BF1088.S26 J34 1996

EX-PRESIDENTS. *See* **PRESIDENTS.**

EX-SERVICE MEN. *See* **VETERANS.**

Examiner's manual.
Mather, Nancy. Woodcock-Johnson III tests of cognitive abilities examiner's manual. Itasca, IL : Riverside Pub., c2001.
BF432.5 .W66 M33 2001

Examiner's manual for the Stoelting Brief Nonverbal Intelligence Test.
Roid, Gale H. S-BIT, Stoelting Brief Nonverbal Intelligence Test. Wood Dale, IL : Stoelting Co., c1999.
BF432.5 .S85 R65 1999

Examining issues related to competition in the pharmaceutical marketplace.
United States. Congress. House. Committee on Energy and Commerce. Subcommittee on Health. Washington : U.S. G.P.O. : For sale by the Supt. of Docs., U.S. G.P.O. [Congressional Sales Office], 2002.

EXAMPLE. *See* **INFLUENCE (PSYCHOLOGY).**

EXCAVATION SITES (ARCHAEOLOGY). *See* **EXCAVATIONS (ARCHAEOLOGY).**

EXCAVATIONS (ARCHAEOLOGY).
Mauerschau. Remshalden-Grunbach : Greiner, 2002.

Mithen, Steven J. After the ice. London : Weidenfeld & Nicolson, 2003.

Theory and practice in late antique archaeology. Leiden ; Boston : Brill, 2003.
CC72.4 .T46 2003

EXCAVATIONS (ARCHAEOLOGY) - VIRGINIA - JAMES RIVER VALLEY.
Gallivan, Martin D., 1968- James River chiefdoms. Lincoln : University of Nebraska Press, c2003.
E99.P85 G35 2003

EXCHANGE. *See also* **CEREMONIAL EXCHANGE; MONEY.**
Dolgin, Aleksandr. Pragmatika kul'tury. Moskva : Fond nauchnykh issledovaniĭ "Pragmatika kul'tury", 2002.

EXCHANGE THEORY (SOCIOLOGY). *See* **POWER (SOCIAL SCIENCES); SOCIAL INTERACTION.**

EXCHANGES, SECURITIES. *See* **STOCK EXCHANGES.**

EXCHANGES, STOCK. *See* **STOCK EXCHANGES.**

EXCITEMENT, SEXUAL. *See* **SEXUAL EXCITEMENT.**

Exclusions in feminist thought : challenging the boundaries of womanhood / edited by Mary Brewer. Brighton [England] ; Portland, Or. : Sussex Academic Press, 2002. vi, 261 p. ; 24 cm. Includes bibliographical references and index. ISBN 1-902210-63-8 (alk. paper) DDC 305.42
1. Feminism. I. Brewer, Mary F.
HQ1206 .E98 2002

Excursions in Chinese culture : festschrift in honor of William R. Schultz / edited by Marie Chan, Chia-lin Pao Tao, Jing-shen Tao. Hong Kong : Chinese University Press, c2002. ix, 232 p. ; 24 cm. Includes bibliographical references. ISBN 962-201-915-3
1. Schultz, William, - 1925- 2. Cixi, - Empress dowager of China, - 1835-1908. 3. Culture in literature. 4. Politics and culture - China. 5. Chinese literature - History and criticism. I. Schultz, William, 1925- II. Chan, Marie, 1944- III. Bao, Jialin. IV. Tao, Jinsheng, 1933-

EXECRATION. *See* **BLESSING AND CURSING.**

EXECUTIVE ABILITY. *See also* **PLANNING.**
Carey, Dennis. How to run a company. 1st ed. New York : Crown Business, c2003.
HD38.2 .C374 2003

Finkelstein, Sydney. Why smart executives fail and what you can learn from their mistakes. New York ; London : Portfolio, 2003.
HD38.2 .F56 2003

Garten, Jeffrey E., 1946- The politics of fortune. Boston : Harvard Business School Press, c2002.
HD57.7 .G377 2002

Leadership. Greenwich, Conn. : Information Age Pub., c2002.
HD57.7 .L4313 2002

Sathe, Vijay. Corporate entrepreneurship. Cambridge : Cambridge University Press, 2003.

Winter, Graham. High performance leadership. Singapore ; New York : John Wiley & Sons (Asia), c2003.

Woolfe, Lorin. The Bible on leadership. New York : American Management Association, c2002.
HD57.7 .W666 2002

EXECUTIVE ABILITY IN ADOLESCENCE.
Dawson, Peg. Executive skills in children and adolescents. New York : Guilford Press, 2004.
BF723.E93 D39 2004

EXECUTIVE ABILITY IN CHILDREN.
Dawson, Peg. Executive skills in children and adolescents. New York : Guilford Press, 2004.
BF723.E93 D39 2004

EXECUTIVE COACHING - PRACTICE.
Fairley, Stephen. Getting started in personal and executive coaching. Hoboken, N.J. : J. Wiley & Sons, 2003.
BF637.P36 F35 2003

EXECUTIVE OFFICERS, CHIEF. *See* **CHIEF EXECUTIVE OFFICERS.**

EXECUTIVE POWER. *See* **AMNESTY; PRESIDENTS.**

Executive skills in children and adolescents.
Dawson, Peg. New York : Guilford Press, 2004.
BF723.E93 D39 2004

EXECUTIVES. *See also* **CHIEF EXECUTIVE OFFICERS; FINANCIAL EXECUTIVES; GOVERNMENT EXECUTIVES.**
Bell, Chip R. Managers as mentors. 2nd ed., completely rev. and expanded. San Francisco, Calif : Berrett-Koehler Publishers, c2002.
HF5385 .B45 1996

De Kluyver, Cornelis A. Strategy. Upper Saddle River, N.J. : Prentice Hall, c2003.
HD38.2 .D425 2003

Kline, Theresa, 1960- Teams that lead. Mahwah, N.J. : L. E. Associates, 2003
HD57.7 .K549 2003

Ward, Andrew. The leadership lifecycle. Houndmills [England] ; New York : Palgrave Macmillan, 2003.
HD57.7 .W367 2003

EXECUTIVES - JOB STRESS.
Frost, Peter J. Toxic emotions at work. Boston : Harvard Business School Press, c2003.
HD42 .F76 2003

EXECUTIVES - PSYCHOLOGY.
Finkelstein, Sydney. Why smart executives fail and what you can learn from their mistakes. New York ; London : Portfolio, 2003.
HD38.2 .F56 2003

EXECUTORS AND ADMINISTRATORS - RUSSIA.
Meniaĭlov, Alekseĭ. Durilka. Moskva : "Kraft+", 2003.

EXEMPLA. *See* **LEGENDS.**

EXERCISE.
Chuckrow, Robert. The tai chi book. Boston : YMAA Publication Center, c1998.
GV504 .C536 1998

EXERCISE THERAPY.
Breathing spaces. New York : Columbia University Press, c2003.
RA781.8 .B73 2003

Exercises in constructive imagination.
Bencivenga, Ermanno, 1950- Dordrecht ; Boston : Kluwer Academic Publishers, c2001.
B3613.B3853 E93 2001

Exercises in psychological testing.
Condon, Margaret E. Boston : Allyn and Bacon, c2002.
BF176 .T47 2002

The existence of the external world.
Vernes, Jean-René. Ottawa : University of Ottawa Press, c2000.

EXISTENTIAL ETHICS.
Peiró, Agustí. Ésser i moral. 1. ed. [Valencia] : Brosquil Edicions, 2002.

EXISTENTIAL PHENOMENOLOGY.
Fletcher, John Wright. A hermeneutic study of generational music. 2002.

EXISTENTIAL PSYCHOLOGY.
Romanova, A. P. (Anna Petrovna) Stanovlenie religioznogo kompleksa. Astrakhan : Izd-vo Astrakhanskogo pedagog. universiteta, 1999.
BF51 .R66 1999

EXISTENTIALISM.
Dandyk, Alfred. Unaufrichtigkeit. Würzburg : Königshausen & Neumann, c2002.

Fotiade, Ramona. Conceptions of the absurd. Oxford : Legenda, 2001.

Existenz und Modalität.
Hüntelmann, Rafael. Frankfurt a. M. ; New York : Hänsel-Hohenhausen, c2002.
BD331 .H86 2002

Exorcising our demons.
Zika, Charles. Leiden ; Boston : Brill, 2003.
BF1584.E85 Z55 2003

EXORCISM. *See also* **ZĀR.**
Chajes, Jeffrey Howard. Between worlds. Philadelphia : University of Pennsylvania Press, c2003.
BM729.D92 C53 2003

Dwyer, Graham, 1959- The divine and the demonic. London ; New York : RoutledgeCurzon, 2003.
BL1226.82.E94 D89 2003

Koroma, Abu F. Exposing and destroying the dark satanic kingdom. [Freetown, Sierra Leone? : s.n.], c2000.
1. Black author.

Possessions and exorcisms. San Diego, Calif. : Greenhaven Press, 2004.
BF1555 .P68 2004

Proja, Giovanni Battista. Uomini, diavoli, esorcismi. Roma : Città nuova, 2002.

EXORCISM - FRANCE - HISTORY.
Ferber, Sarah, 1957- Demonic possession and exorcism in early modern France. London ; New York, NY : Routledge, 2004.
BF1517.F5 F47 2004

EXOTICISM IN ART.
Tythacott, Louise. Surrealism and the exotic. London ; New York : Routledge, 2003.
NX456.5.S8 T98 2003

Exp Psychol dnlm.
[Experimental psychology (Online)] Experimental psychology [electronic resource]. Göttingen, Germany : Hogrefe & Huber, c2002-
BF3

Expand the pie.
Lum, Grande. Seattle, WA : Castle Pacific Pub. ; Cambridge, MA : ThoughtBridge, c2003.
BF637.N4 L86 2003

The expansion of management knowledge : carriers, flows, and sources / edited by Kerstin Sahlin-Andersson and Lars Engwall. Stanford, Calif. : Stanford Business Books, c2002. xvi, 373 p. ; 24 cm. Includes bibliographical references (p. [307]-347) and index. ISBN 0-8047-4197-2 (cloth : alk. paper) ISBN 0-8047-4199-9 (pbk. : alk. paper) DDC 658.4/038
1. Management. 2. Management - Research. 3. Business education. 4. Business consultants. 5. Knowledge management. I. Sahlin-Andersson, Kerstin. II. Engwall, Lars.
HD31 .E873 2002

EXPANSION (UNITED STATES POLITICS). *See* **IMPERIALISM.**

EXPECTATION (PHILOSOPHY) - CONGRESSES.
Workshop on Adaptive Behavior in Anticipatory Learning Systems (1st : 2002 : Edinburgh, Scotland) Anticipatory behavior in adaptive learning systems. Berlin ; New York : Springer, c2003.
Q325.5 .W65 2003

Expecting Armageddon : essential readings in failed prophecy / edited by Jon R. Stone. New York : Routledge, 2000. x, 284 p. : ill. ; 24 cm. Includes bibliographical references. CONTENTS: Introduction / Jon R. Stone -- Unfulfilled prophecies and disappointed messiahs / Leon Festinger, Henry W. Riecken, and Stanley Schachter -- Prophecy fails again : a report of a failure to replicate / Jane Allyn Hardyck and Marcia Braden -- Prophetic failure and Chiliastic identity : the case of Jehovah's Witnesses / Joseph F. Zygmunt -- When prophecies fail : a theoretical perspective on the comparative evidence / Joseph F. Zygmunt -- The effects of prophetic disconfirmation of the committed / Neil Weiser -- Prophecy continues to fail : a Japanese sect / Takaaki Sanada and Edward Norbeck -- When the bombs drop : reactions to disconfirmed prophecy in a millennial sect / Robert W. Balch, Gwen Farnsworth, and Sue Wilkins -- Spiritualization and reaffirmation : what really happens when prophecy fails / J. Gordon Melton -- Had prophecy failed? Contrasting perspectives of the Millerites and Shakers / Lawrence Foster -- How do movements survive failures of prophecy? / Anthony B. van Fossen -- "It separated the wheat from the chaff." The "1975" prophecy and its impact among Dutch Jehovah's Witnesses / Richard Singelenberg -- Coping with apocalypse in Canada : experiences of endtime in La Mission de l'Esprit Saint and the Institute of Applied Metaphysics / Susan J. Palmer and Natalie Finn -- When Festinger fails : prophecy and the Watchtower / Matthew N. Schmalz -- When prophecy is not validated : explaining the unexpected in a messianic campaign / William Shaffir -- Fifteen years of failed prophecy : coping with cognitive dissonance in a Baha'i sect / Robert W. Balch ... [et al.] ISBN 0-415-92330-1 (alk. paper) ISBN 0-415-92331-X (pbk.) DDC 291.2/117
1. End of the world. 2. Prophecies. I. Stone, Jon R., 1959-
BL503 .E97 2000

EXPERIENCE. *See also* **EXPERIENTIAL LEARNING; FACTS (PHILOSOPHY); LIFE CHANGE EVENTS.**
Eisen, Jeffrey S., 1940- Oneness perceived. St. Paul, Minn. : Paragon House, c2003.
BF311 .E39 2003

Mongeau, Pierre, 1954- Survivre. Sainte-Foy : Presses de l'Université du Québec, 2002.
BF122 .M66 2002

Understanding experience. London ; New York : Routledge, 2003.
B105.E9 U53 2003

The view from within. Thorverton, UK : Bowling Green, OH : Imprint Academic, 2000.
BF311 .V512 2000

EXPERIENCE-BASED LEARNING. *See* **EXPERIENTIAL LEARNING.**

EXPERIENCE (RELIGION). *See also* **SPIRIT POSSESSION.**
DiZerega, Gus. Pagans & Christians. 1st ed. St. Paul, Minn. : Llewellyn Publications, 2001.
BF1566 .D59 2001

Forsthoefel, Thomas A. Knowing beyond knowledge. Alderhot, England ; Burlington, VT. : Ashgate, 2002.
B132.A3 F66 2002

Hood, Adam, 1960- Baillie, Oman and Macmurray. Aldershot, England ; Burlington, VT : Ashgate, c2003.
BR110 .H575 2003

Religious experience and the end of metaphysics. Bloomington, Ind. : Indiana University Press, c2003.
BL53 .R444 2003

EXPERIENCE (RELIGION) - COMPARATIVE STUDIES.
McLaughlin, Michael T. Knowledge, consciousness and religious conversion in Lonergan and Aurobindo. Roma : Editrice Pontificia Universita Gregoriana, 2003.

EXPERIENCE (RELIGION) IN WOMEN.
Callahan, Sidney Cornelia. Women who hear voices. New York : Paulist Press, 2003.
BV5091.R4 C35 2003

EXPERIENCES, NEAR-DEATH. *See* **NEAR-DEATH EXPERIENCES.**

EXPERIENCES, STRESSFUL LIFE. *See* **LIFE CHANGE EVENTS.**

EXPERIENTIAL LEARNING - CONGRESSES.
Adaptivity and learning. New York : Springer, 2003.
BF318 .A33 2003

Das Experiment und die Metaphysik.
Wind, Edgar, 1900- 1. Aufl. Frankfurt am Main : Suhrkamp, 2001.

EXPERIMENTAL DESIGN.
Christensen, Larry B., 1941- Experimental methodology. 9th ed. Boston, MA : Allyn and Bacon, 2004.
BF181 .C48 2004

John, Peter William Meredith. Statistical design and analysis of experiments. Philadelphia : Society for Industrial and Applied Mathematics, c1998.
QA279 .J65 1998

Ruxton, Graeme D. Elementary experimental design for the life sciences. Oxford : Oxford University Press, 2003.

Santner, Thomas J., 1947- The design and analysis of computer experiments. New York : Springer, 2003.
QA279 .S235 2003

Yang, Kai. Design for Six Sigma. New York ; London : McGraw-Hill, c2003.
TS156 .Y33 2003

Experimental methodology.
Christensen, Larry B., 1941- 9th ed. Boston, MA : Allyn and Bacon, 2004.
BF181 .C48 2004

EXPERIMENTAL PSYCHOLOGISTS. *See* **PSYCHOLOGY, EXPERIMENTAL.**

EXPERIMENTAL PSYCHOLOGY. *See also* **PSYCHOLOGY, EXPERIMENTAL.**
[Experimental psychology (Online)] Experimental psychology [electronic resource]. Göttingen, Germany : Hogrefe & Huber, c2002-
BF3

Handbook of research methods in experimental psychology. Malden, MA ; Oxford : Blackwell Pub., 2003.
BF76.5 .H35 2003

[**Experimental psychology (Online)**] Experimental psychology [electronic resource]. Göttingen, Germany : Hogrefe & Huber, c2002- Frequency: Four no. a year. Vol. 49, no. 1 (2002)- . Title from table of contents screen (publisher's Website, viewed Aug. 26, 2003). Latest issue consulted: Vol. 50, no. 3 (2003). Online version of the print publication. Mode of access: World Wide Web. URL: http://www.psycinfo.com/library/browse/index.cfm?fuseaction=toc&jrn=zea URL: http://www.hhpub.com/journals/exppsy/ Available in other form: Experimental psychology ISSN: 1618-3169 (DLC) 2002243131 (OCoLC)49275526. Continues: Zeitschrift für experimentelle Psychologie (Online).
1. Psychology - Periodicals. 2. Psychology, Experimental - Periodicals. I. Title: Exp Psychol dnlm II. Title: Experimental psychology III. Title: Zeitschrift für experimentelle Psychologie (Online)
BF3

Experiments in mental suggestion.
Vasil'ev, Leonid Leonidovich. [Rev. ed.]. Charlottesville, VA : Hampton Roads Pub., c2002.
BF1156.S8 V313 2002

EXPERT SYSTEMS (COMPUTER SCIENCE). *See also* **KNOWLEDGE ACQUISITION (EXPERT SYSTEMS).**
Internet-based intelligent information processing systems. Singapore ; River Edge, NJ : World Scientific, 2003.

Knowledge-based information retrieval and filtering from the Web. Boston : Kluwer Academic Publishers, c2003.

TK5105.888 .K58 2003

EXPERTISE ACQUISITION (EXPERT SYSTEMS). *See* **KNOWLEDGE ACQUISITION (EXPERT SYSTEMS).**

EXPERTISE - POLITICAL ASPECTS.
Turner, Stephen P., 1951- Liberal democracy 3.0. London ; Thousand Oaks, Calif. : SAGE Publications, 2003.
JC423 .T87 2003

Explaining linguistics
(4) Word order and scrambling. Malden, MA : Blackwell Pub., 2003.
P295 .W65 2003

EXPLANATION (LINGUISTICS).
Problemy interpretatsionnoĭ lingvistiki. Novosibirsk : Novosibirskiĭ gos. pedagog. universitet, 2001.
P128.E95 P762 2001

EXPLANATORY ADEQUACY (LINGUISTICS). *See* **EXPLANATION (LINGUISTICS).**

EXPLANATORY (LINGUISTICS). *See* **EXPLANATION (LINGUISTICS).**

Exploration of visual data.
Zhou, Xiang Sean. Boston ; London : Kluwer Academic Publishers, c2003.
T385 .Z55 2003

EXPLORATION (PROSPECTING). *See* **PROSPECTING.**

Explorations in culture and international history series
Culture and international history. New York : Berghahn Books, 2003.
JZ1251 .C84 2003

Explorations in language acquisition and use.
Krashen, Stephen D. Portsmouth, NH : Heinemann, c2003.
P51 .K666 2003

Explorations in philosophy.
Mohanty, Jitendranath, 1928- New Delhi ; New York : Oxford University Press, c2001-
B131.M54 M63 2001

Explorations in sociology
(v. 63.) Social relations and the life course. Houndmills, Basingstoke New York : Palgrave Macmillan, 2003.
HM741 .S64 2003

(v.62) Social conceptions of time. Houndmills, Basingstoke, Hampshire ; New York : Palgrave MacMillan, 2002.
HM656 .S63 2002

Exploratory and confirmatory factor analysis.
Thompson, Bruce, 1951- 1st ed. Washington, DC : American Psychological Association, c2004.
BF39.2.F32 T48 2004

EXPLORATORY BEHAVIOR. *See* **CURIOSITY.**

Exploring candle magick.
Telesco, Patricia, 1960- Franklin Lakes, NJ : New Page Books, c2001.
BF1623.C26 T45 2001

Exploring cognitive development.
Garton, Alison, 1950- 1st ed. Oxford, UK ; Malden, MA : Blackwell Pub., 2004.
BF723.P8 G37 2004

Exploring consciousness.
Carter, Rita, 1949- Berkeley : University of California Press, c2002.
BF311 .C289 2002

Exploring scrying.
Hawk, Ambrose. Franklin Lakes, NJ : New Page Books, c2001.
BF1335 .H39 2001

Exploring spellcraft.
Dunwich, Gerina. Franklin Lakes, NJ : New Page Books, c2001.
BF1566 .D866 2001

Exploring the work of Christopher Bollas.
The vitality of objects. 1st US ed. Middletown, Conn. : Wesleyan University Press, 2002.
BF173 .V55 2002

Exploring the "zone".
Miller, Larry, 1947- Gretna, La. : Pelican, 2001.
BF1045.S83 M55 2001

Exploring tough issues
Hibbert, Adam, 1968- Why do people bully? Chicago, Ill. : Raintree, 2004.
BF637.B85 H53 2004

Exploring Wicca.
Sabrina, Lady. Franklin Lakes, NJ : New Page Books, c2001.

EXPORT AND IMPORT CONTROLS. *See* **FOREIGN TRADE REGULATION.**

EXPORT SALES. *See* **EXPORT SALES CONTRACTS.**

EXPORT SALES CONTRACTS.
DiMatteo, Larry A. The law of international business transactions. Mason, OH : Thomson/South-Western West, c2003.
KF915 .D56 2003

EXPORT SALES CONTRACTS - UNITED STATES.
DiMatteo, Larry A. The law of international business transactions. Mason, OH : Thomson/South-Western West, c2003.
KF915 .D56 2003

Exposing and destroying the dark satanic kingdom.
Koroma, Abu F. [Freetown, Sierra Leone? : s.n.], c2000.

Exposing satanic manipulations.
Ofoegbu, Mike. [Lagos, Nigeria : Holy Ghost Anointed Books Ministries, c1998]

EXPOSITION COLONIALE, AGRICOLE ET INDUSTRIELLE DE STRASBOURG (1924).
Amougou, Emmanuel. La construction de l'inconscient colonial en Alsace. Paris : L'Harmattan, 2002.
  1. Black author.

EXPRESSION. *See* **FACIAL EXPRESSION; RHETORIC.**

EXPRESSION - HISTORY.
Zwischen Rauschen und Offenbarung. Berlin : Akademie Verlag, c2002.
PN56.V55 Z89 2002

EXPRESSION (PHILOSOPHY).
Ménasé, Stéphanie. Passivité et création. Paris : Presses universitaires de France, c2003.

Expressions of ethnography : novel approaches to qualitative methods / [edited by] Robin Patric Clair. Albany, NY : State University of New York Press, c2003. xiii, 303 p. : ill. ; 23 cm. Includes bibliographical references and index. ISBN 0-7914-5823-7 (alk. paper) ISBN 0-7914-5824-5 (pbk. : alk. paper) DDC 305.8/007/2
  1. Ethnology - Methodology. 2. Ethnology - Research. 3. Qualitative research. I. Clair, Robin Patric.
GN33 .E97 2003

EXPRESSIVE BEHAVIOR. *See* **EXPRESSION.**

EXPULSION OF EVIL SPIRITS. *See* **EXORCISM.**

El éxtasis cibernético.
Reig, Ramón. 1. ed. Madrid : Ediciones Libertarias, 2001.

The extended phenotype.
Dawkins, Richard, 1941- Rev. ed. Oxford ; New York : Oxford University Press, 1999.
QH375 .D38 1999

EXTENDIBLE MARKUP LANGUAGE (DOCUMENT MARKUP LANGUAGE). *See* **XML (DOCUMENT MARKUP LANGUAGE).**

EXTENSIBLE MARKUP LANGUAGE (DOCUMENT MARKUP LANGUAGE). *See* **XML (DOCUMENT MARKUP LANGUAGE).**

EXTERMINATION, JEWISH (1939-1945). *See* **HOLOCAUST, JEWISH (1939-1945).**

EXTERNAL TRADE. *See* **INTERNATIONAL TRADE.**

EXTERNALISM (PHILOSOPHY OF MIND).
McCulloch, Gregory. The life of the mind. London ; New York : Routledge, 2003.
BD418.3 .M363 2003

New essays on semantic externalism and self-knowledge. Cambridge, Mass. : MIT Press, c2003.
BD418.3 .N49 2003

Rowlands, Mark. The body in mind. Cambridge, U.K. ; New York : Cambridge University Press, 1999.
BD418.3 .R78 1999

EXTINCT ANIMALS. *See* **EXTINCTION (BIOLOGY).**

EXTINCT CITIES - LIBYA. *See* **CYRENE (EXTINCT CITY).**

EXTINCT LANGUAGES. *See* **ALPHABET; WRITING.**

Extinction.
Boulter, Michael Charles. New York : Columbia University Press, c2002.
QE721.2.E97 B68 2002

EXTINCTION (BIOLOGY).
Boulter, Michael Charles. Extinction. New York : Columbia University Press, c2002.
QE721.2.E97 B68 2002

EXTRAGALACTIC NEBULAE. *See* **GALAXIES.**

Extraordinary encounters.
Clark, Jerome. Santa Barbara, Calif. : ABC-CLIO, c2000.
BF2050 .C57 2000

EXTRASENSORY PERCEPTION. *See also* **TELEPATHY.**
French, Christopher C. Paranormal perception? London : Institute for Cultural Research, 2001.

Soskin, Julie. Are you psychic? London : Carroll & Brown, 2002.
BF1031 .S674 2002

Targ, Russell. Limitless mind. Novato, Calif. : New World Library, c2004.
BF1389.R45 T37 2004

EXTRATERRESTRIAL BEINGS.
Herbst, Judith. Aliens. Minneapolis : Lerner Publications, 2005.
BF2050 .H465 2005

Pinotti, Roberto, 1944- Oltre. Firenze : Olimpia, c2002.

EXTRATERRESTRIAL ENCOUNTERS WITH HUMANS. *See* **HUMAN-ALIEN ENCOUNTERS.**

EXTRATERRESTRIAL INTELLIGENCE. *See* **LIFE ON OTHER PLANETS.**

EXTRATERRESTRIAL LIFE. *See* **LIFE ON OTHER PLANETS.**

Extraterrestrial visitations.
Dennett, Preston E., 1965- 1st ed. St. Paul, Minn. : Llewellyn Publications, 2001.
BF2050 .D46 2001

EXTRATERRESTRIALS. *See* **LIFE ON OTHER PLANETS.**

EXTRAVERSION. *See* **SELF-DISCLOSURE.**

Extreme 1-8.
Glasmeier, Michael, 1951- Köln : Salon, 2001.

Extreme beauty : aesthetics, politics, death / edited by James E. Swearingen and Joanne Cutting-Gray. London ; New York : Continuum, 2002. xii, 259 p. : ill. ; 24 cm. (Textures) Includes bibliographical references (p. [245]-254) and index. ISBN 0-8264-6009-7 ISBN 0-8264-6010-0 (pbk.) DDC 111/.85
  1. Aesthetics. 2. Arts - Philosophy. 3. Political science - Philosophy. 4. Death. I. Swearingen, James E., 1939- II. Cutting-Gray, Joanne. III. Series: Textures (New York, N.Y.)
BH39 .E98 2002

Extreme success.
Fettke, Rich. New York : Fireside Book, c2002.
BF637.S8 F46 2002

EXTRINSIC EVIDENCE. *See* **EVIDENCE (LAW).**

Der exzentrische Blick : Gespräch über Physiognomik / herausgegeben von Claudia Schmölders. Berlin : Akademie Verlag, 1996. 258 p. : ill. ; 25 cm. Proceedings of a colloquium held at the Herzog August Bibliothek, Wolfenbüttel, in April 1994, under the title "Physiognomik interdisziplinär." Includes bibliographical references and index. ISBN 3-05-002685-5 DDC 138
  1. Physiognomy - History - Congresses. I. Schmölders, Claudia.
BF853 .E98 1996

Eyal, Tsevi. Mi she-taʻam yayin Hungari : ḥayim shel taʻam, ḥayim shel mashmaʻut / Tsevi Eyal ve-Eli Ṭayib ; [iyurim, Uriʼel Berkovits']. Tel Aviv : Yediʻot aḥaronot : Sifre ḥemed, c2002. 173 p. : ill. (some col.) ; 20 cm. Includes also vocalized poems. ISBN 9655111709
  1. Jewish way of life. 2. Conduct of life. 3. Spiritual life - Judaism. I. Ṭayeb, Eli. II. Berkovits', Uriʼel. III. Title. IV. Title: Ḥayim shel ṭaʻam, ḥayim shel mashmaʻut

EYE - PSYCHOLOGICAL ASPECTS.
Marshall, Evan, 1956- The eyes have it. New York : Citadel Press, c2003.
BF637.N66 M37 2003

EYE - SURGERY. *See* **EYELIDS - SURGERY.**

Eye witness of demons in the temple.
Aluko, Jonathan O. The spirit of this age. [[Akure, Nigeria : Christ Liberation Publications, c1996]
BL480 .A494 1996
1. Black author.

EYEBALL. *See* **EYE.**

EYELIDS - SURGERY - PSYCHOLOGICAL ASPECTS.
Western eyes [videorecording]. New York, NY : First Run/Icarus Films, 2000.

EYES. *See* **EYE.**

The eyes have it.
Marshall, Evan, 1956- New York : Citadel Press, c2003.
BF637.N66 M37 2003

The eyes of shame.
Ayers, Mary, 1960- 1st ed. Hove, East Sussex ; New York : Brunner-Routledge, 2003.
BF175.5.O24 A94 2003

EYEWITNESS IDENTIFICATION. *See* **WITNESSES.**

Eyre, Christopher. The cannibal hymn : a cultural and literary study / Christopher Eyre. Liverpool : Liverpool University Press, 2002. xiv, 272 p. : ill. ; 24 cm. Includes bibliographical references (p. [229]-253) and index. Includes hieroglyphic texts. ISBN 0-85323-696-8 ISBN 0-85323-706-9 (PBK.) DDC 299.31
1. Pyramid texts. 2. Funeral rites and ceremonies - Egypt. 3. Incantations, Egyptian. 4. Future life. 5. Animal sacrifice - Egypt. 6. Domestic animals - Religious aspects - Egyptian religion. 7. Fasts and feasts - Egyptian religion. I. Title.

EYRE, JANE (FICTITIOUS CHARACTER).
Adeleye, Modupe, 1980- From our hearts. Rochester, N.Y. : Mo-Biz Publishing Co., 2003.
BF353 .A33 2003

Ezell, Jessica. Reunion : the extraordinary story of a messenger of love & healing / by Jessica Ezell. Walpole, NH : Stillpoint Pub., c1996. 221 p. : ill. ; 23 cm. ISBN 1-88347-817-0 (alk. paper) DDC 133.9
1. Ezell, Jessica. 2. Dogs - Religious aspects. 3. Spiritualists - United States - Biography. I. Title.
BF1283.E94 A3 1996

EZELL, JESSICA.
Ezell, Jessica. Reunion. Walpole, NH : Stillpoint Pub., c1996.
BF1283.E94 A3 1996

Ėzotericheskai︠a︡ filosofii︠a︡ : ot germetizma k teosofii / pod redaktsieĭ L.A. Mirskoĭ. Rostov-na-Donu : Foliant, 2002. 2 v. ; 21 cm. Includes bibliographical references. CONTENTS: ch. 1. Germetizm i "germeticheskie nauki" -- ch. 2. Misticheskiĭ opyt i okkul'tnye teorii. ISBN 594593030X (set) ISBN 5945930318 (t. 1) ISBN 5945930326 (t. 2)
1. Occultism. 2. Theosophy. I. Mirskai︠a︡, L. A. (Li︠u︡dmila Anatol'evna) II. I︠U︡zhno-rossiĭskiĭ gumanitarnyĭ institut.
BF1416 .E96 2002

Fabbianelli, Faustino.
Reinhold, Karl Leonhard, 1757-1823. [Ueber den Begriff der Philosophie. Italian] Concetto e fondamento della filosofia. Roma : Edizioni di storia e letteratura, 2002.

Fabelo Corzo, José Ramón. Los valores y sus desafíos actuales / José Ramón Fabelo Corzo. Puebla : Universidad Autónoma de Puebla, 2001. 294 p. ; 12 cm. Includes bibliographical references. ISBN 968-863-516-2
1. Values. 2. Ethics. 3. Conduct of life. I. Title.

Fabiani, Paolo, 1968- La filosofia dell'immaginazione in Vico e Malebranche / Paolo Fabiani. Firenze : Firenze University Press, 2002. 368 p. ; 24 cm. (Tesi ; 1) Electronic ed. available at: http://digital.casalini.it/fulltext/is.asp?isbn=8884530342. Includes bibliographical references (p. [367]-368). URL: http://digital.casalini.it/fulltext/is.asp?isbn=8884530342 ISBN 88-8453-034-2 DDC 128
1. Vico, Giambattista, - 1668-1744. 2. Malebranche, Nicolas, - 1638-1715. 3. Imagination (Philosophy) I. Title. II. Series: Tesi (Firenze University Press) ; 1.
B3583.F25 F55 2002

FABLES, GERMAN.
Bosco Coletsos, Sandra. La struttura parentale nelle fiabe dei fratelli Grimm. Alessandria : Edizioni dell'Orso, 2001.

Fabrega, Horacio. Origins of psychopathology : the phylogenetic and cultural basis of mental illness / Horacio Fábrega, Jr. New Brunswick, N.J. : Rutgers University Press, c2002. xv, 410 p. ; 25 cm. Includes bibliographical references (p. 375-399) and index. ISBN 0-8135-3023-7 DDC 616.89/071
1. Mental illness - Etiology. 2. Genetic psychology. 3. Mental illness - Genetic aspects. 4. Mental illness - Etiology - Social aspects. I. Title.
RC454.4 .F33 2002

La fabrique du sexe.
Babin, Pierre. Paris : Textuel, [1999]
BF175.5.S48 B23 1999

Fábula (Tusquets Editores)
(182.) Tusquets, Oscar, 1941- Más que discutible. 1a. ed. en Fabula. Barcelona : Fabula Tusquets Editores, 2002.

FACE. *See* **BEAUTY, PERSONAL; EYE; PHYSIOGNOMY.**

Face à la mort
Hanus, Michel. La Mort aujourd'hui. Paris : Frison-Roche, c2000.

FACE - CARE AND HYGIENE.
Aucoin, Kevyn. Making faces. 1st ed. Boston : Little, Brown, c1997.
RA778 .A873 1997

Bridges, Lillian. Face reading in Chinese medicine. St. Louis, MO : Churchill Livingstone, 2003.
BF851 .B69 2003

Faire face. Paris : Gallimard, [2002]

FACE - EXPRESSION. *See* **FACIAL EXPRESSION.**

FACE IN ART.
Faire face. Paris : Gallimard, [2002]

FACE IN LITERATURE.
Faire face. Paris : Gallimard, [2002]

FACE PERCEPTION.
Faire face. Paris : Gallimard, [2002]

FACE PERCEPTION IN CHILDREN.
The development of face processing in infancy and early childhood. New York : Nova Science, 2003.
BF720.F32 D48 2003

FACE PERCEPTION IN INFANTS.
The development of face processing in infancy and early childhood. New York : Nova Science, 2003.
BF720.F32 D48 2003

Face reading.
Sertori, J. M. London : Hodder & Stoughton, 2000.

Face reading in Chinese medicine.
Bridges, Lillian. St. Louis, MO : Churchill Livingstone, 2003.
BF851 .B69 2003

Facetas das pós-modernidade : a questão da modernidade ; caderno 2 / org Eloá Heise. São Paulo : Universidade de São Paulo, Faculdade De Filosofia Letras e Ciências Humanas, 1996. 233 p. ; 22 cm. (Questão da modernidade ; caderno 2) Includes bibliographical references. ISBN 85-86087-03-3
1. Postmodernism. I. Heise, Elóa. II. Series

FACETIAE. *See* **ANECDOTES; WIT AND HUMOR.**

FACIAL EXERCISES.
Bridges, Lillian. Face reading in Chinese medicine. St. Louis, MO : Churchill Livingstone, 2003.
BF851 .B69 2003

FACIAL EXPRESSION.
Bridges, Lillian. Face reading in Chinese medicine. St. Louis, MO : Churchill Livingstone, 2003.
BF851 .B69 2003

Johansen, Heidi Leigh. What I look like when I am angry. 1st ed. New York : PowerStart Press, 2004.
BF723.A4 J63 2004

Johansen, Heidi Leigh. [What I look like when I am angry. Spanish & English] What I look like when I am angry = 1st ed. New York : Rosen PowerKids Press, 2004.
BF723.A4 J6318 2004

Johansen, Heidi Leigh. What I look like when I am happy. 1st ed. New York : PowerStart Press, 2004.
BF723.H37 J64 2004

Johansen, Heidi Leigh. [What I look like when I am happy. Spanish & English] What I look like when I am happy = 1st ed. New York : Rosen Pub. Group's, 2004.
BF723.H37 J6418 2004

Randolph, Joanne. What I look like when I am confused. 1st ed. New York : PowerStart Press, 2004.
BF723.I63 R36 2004

Randolph, Joanne. [What I look like when I am confused. Spanish & English] What I look like when I am confused = 1st ed. New York : Rosen Pub. Group's PowerKids Press, 2004.
BF723.I63 R3618 2004

Randolph, Joanne. What I look like when I am sad. 1st ed. New York : PowerStart Press, 2004.
BF723.S15 R36 2004

Randolph, Joanne. [What I look like when I am sad. Spanish & English] What I look like when I am sad = 1st ed. New York : Rosen Pub. Group's PowerKids Press, 2004.
BF723.S15 R3618 2004

Shepherd, Joanne. What I look like when I am scared. New York : Rosen Pub. Group's PowerStart Press, 2004.
BF723.F4 S54 2004

Shepherd, Joanne. [What I look like when I am scared. Spanish & English] What I look like when I am scared = 1st ed. New York : Rosen Pub. Group's PowerKids Press, 2004.
BF723.F4 S5418 2004

Shepherd, Joanne. What I look like when I am surprised. 1st ed. New York : Rosen Pub. Group's PowerStart Press, 2004.
BF723.S87 S44 2004

Shepherd, Joanne. [What I look like when I am surprised. Spanish & English] What I look like when I am surprised = 1st ed. New York : Rosen Pub. Group's PowerKids Press, 2004.
BF723.S87 S4418 2004

FACIAL EXPRESSION - CHINA.
De Mente, Boye. Asian face reading. Boston, MA : Tuttle Pub., 2003.
BF851 .D37 2003

Henning, Hai Lee Yang. Mian xiang. London : Vega, 2001.
BF851 .H46 2001

FACIAL EXPRESSION - JAPAN.
De Mente, Boye. Asian face reading. Boston, MA : Tuttle Pub., 2003.
BF851 .D37 2003

FACILITIES, HEALTH. *See* **HEALTH FACILITIES.**

Facing the world with soul.
Sardello, Robert J., 1942- 2nd ed. Great Barrington, MA : Lindisfarne Books, c2003.
BF637.C5 S27 2003

Fact meets fiction
Gott, Robert. One in a million. Littleton, Mass. : Sundance, c2001.
BF1175 .G68 2001

Fact or fiction (Greenhaven Press)
Haunted houses. San Diego, Calif. : Greenhaven Press, 2004.
BF1475 .H32 2004

Mysterious places. San Diego, CA : Greenhaven Press, 2004.
BF1031 .M96 2004

Possessions and exorcisms. San Diego, Calif. : Greenhaven Press, 2004.
BF1555 .P68 2004

FACTOR ANALYSIS - TEXTBOOKS.
Thompson, Bruce, 1951- Exploratory and confirmatory factor analysis. 1st ed. Washington, DC : American Psychological Association, c2004.
BF39.2.F32 T48 2004

FACTOR, GENERAL (PSYCHOLOGY). *See* **GENERAL FACTOR (PSYCHOLOGY).**

FACTORIAL ANALYSIS. *See* **FACTOR ANALYSIS.**

FACTORY MANAGEMENT. *See* **QUALITY CONTROL.**

FACTS, MISCELLANEOUS. *See* **CURIOSITIES AND WONDERS.**

FACTS (PHILOSOPHY).
Putnam, Hilary. The collapse of the fact/value dichotomy and other essays. Cambridge, MA : Harvard University Press, 2002.
B945.P873 C65 2002

Facts, values, and norms.
Railton, Peter Albert. Cambridge, U.K. ; New York : Cambridge University Press, 2003.
BJ1012 .R33 2003

FACULTY (EDUCATION). *See* **EDUCATORS.**

Faery healing.
McArthur, Margie. Aptos, Calif. : New Brighton Books, 2003.
BF1552 .M36 2003

Faery magick.
Knight, Sirona, 1955- Franklin Lakes, NJ : New Page Books, c2003.
BF1552 .K55 2003

Fagard, Jacqueline. Le développement des habiletés de l'enfant : coordination bimanuelle et latéralité / Jacqueline Fagard. Paris : CNRS, c2001. 387 p. : ill. ; 24 cm. Includes bibliographical references (p. [283]-356) and indexes. ISBN 2-271-05943-7
1. Motor ability in children. 2. Motor learning. 3. Laterality. 4. Cerebral dominance. I. Title.
RJ133 .F34 2001

Fahlenbrach, Kathrin. Protest-Inszenierungen : visuelle Kommunikation und kollektive Identitäten in Protestbewegungen / Kathrin Fahlenbrach. 1. Aufl. Wiesbaden : Westdeutscher Verlag, 2002. 271 p. : ill. ; 21 cm. Includes bibliographical references (p. [245]-265). ISBN 3-531-13754-9 (pbk.)
1. Protest movements. 2. Group identity. 3. Visual communication. 4. Student protesters. I. Title.

FAILURE (PSYCHOLOGY). *See also* **SUCCESS.**
Finkelstein, Sydney. Why smart executives fail and what you can learn from their mistakes. New York ; London : Portfolio, 2003.
HD38.2 .F56 2003

FAILURE (PSYCHOLOGY) - RELIGIOUS ASPECTS - CHRISTIANITY.
Aransiola, Moses Olanrewaju. The roots and solutions to peculiar problems (dealing with bad luck, lost opportunities and failure). 1st ed.
1. Black author.

FAIR EMPLOYMENT PRACTICE. *See* **DISCRIMINATION IN EMPLOYMENT.**

Fairchild, Dennis. The fortune telling handbook : the interactive guide to tarot, palm reading, and more / by Dennis Fairchild ; illustrated by Julie Paschkis. 1st ed. Philadelphia, PA : Running Press, c2003. 127 p., [8] p. of plates : ill. (some col.) ; 23 cm. Includes a set of punch-out tarot cards. ISBN 0-7624-1444-8 (pbk.) DDC 133.3
1. Fortune-telling. 2. Tarot. 3. Graphology. 4. Numerology. 5. Palmistry. I. Paschkis, Julie. II. Title.
BF1861 .F35 2003

Faire face / coordonné par Daniel Bougnoux. Paris : Gallimard, [2002] 264 p. : ill. ; 24 cm. (Les cahiers de médiologie ; 15) ISBN 2-07-076609-8 DDC 300
1. Face - Care and hygiene. 2. Face in literature. 3. Face in art. 4. Face perception. I. Bougnoux, Daniel. II. Series.

FAIRIES. *See also* **GOBLINS.**
Franklin, Anna. The illustrated encyclopedia of fairies. London : Vega, 2002.
GR549 .F73 2002

Hoffman, Nancy, 1955- San Diego, Calif. : Lucent Books, 2004.
BF1552 .H64 2004

FAIRIES.
Froud, Brian. Good faeries/bad faeries. London : Pavilion, 2000.

Hoffman, Nancy, 1955- Fairies. San Diego, Calif. : Lucent Books, 2004.
BF1552 .H64 2004

Knight, Sirona, 1955- Faery magick. Franklin Lakes, NJ : New Page Books, c2003.
BF1552 .K55 2003

Lecouteux, Claude. [Fées, sorcières et loups-garous au Moyen Age. English] Witches, werewolves, and fairies. 1st U.S. ed. Rochester, Vt. : Inner Traditions, 2003.
BF1045.D67 L4313 2003

FAIRIES - ENCYCLOPEDIAS.
Franklin, Anna. The illustrated encyclopedia of fairies. London : Vega, 2002.
GR549 .F73 2002

FAIRIES - GREAT BRITAIN.
McArthur, Margie. Faery healing. Aptos, Calif. : New Brighton Books, 2003.
BF1552 .M36 2003

FAIRIES - JUVENILE LITERATURE.
Hoffman, Nancy, 1955- Fairies. San Diego, Calif. : Lucent Books, 2004.
BF1552 .H64 2004

Philip, Neil. The little people. New York ; London : Harry N. Abrams, 2002.

Fairley, Stephen. Getting started in personal and executive coaching : how to create a thriving coaching practice / Stephen Fairley, Chris E. Stout. Hoboken, N.J. : J. Wiley & Sons, 2003. p. cm. Publisher description URL: http://www.loc.gov/catdir/description/wiley039/2003014094.html Table of contents URL: http://www.loc.gov/catdir/toc/wiley032/2003014094.html CONTENTS: Decisions, decisions-- personal coaching or business coaching? -- The 15 largest markets where coaches are making money right now -- Building a successful business requires a solid plan -- It takes money to make money : financing your business -- What to buy on a budget : creating your financial plan -- Target your market or waste your time -- You only get one chance : 7 tools for making a great first impression -- Relationships and referrals : networking, strategic referral partners, and centers of influence -- Key strategies for finding your first 10 clients -- Why most marketing fails : the top 10 marketing mistakes beginning coaches make -- From counseling to coaching : constructing a connection, bridging the gap, and defining differences -- Harnessing the power of internet marketing, e-zines, and websites -- The 7 secrets of highly successful coaches. ISBN 0-471-42624-5 (pbk.) DDC 650.1
1. Personal coaching - Practice. 2. Executive coaching - Practice. I. Stout, Chris E. II. Title.
BF637.P36 F35 2003

FAIRNESS.
Kaplow, Louis. Fairness versus welfare. Cambridge, MA : Harvard University Press, 2002.
K247 .K37 2002

Fairness versus welfare.
Kaplow, Louis. Cambridge, MA : Harvard University Press, 2002.
K247 .K37 2002

Fairview Health Services.
Helping kids cope. Minneapolis : Fairview Press, 2003.
BF723.G75 H35 2003

A teen's guide to coping. Minneapolis : Fairview Press, 2003.
BF789.D4 T44 2003

Fairview Hospice.
Helping kids cope. Minneapolis : Fairview Press, 2003.
BF723.G75 H35 2003

A teen's guide to coping. Minneapolis : Fairview Press, 2003.
BF789.D4 T44 2003

FAIRY TALES - JUVENILE LITERATURE.
Philip, Neil. The little people. New York ; London : Harry N. Abrams, 2002.

FAITH.
Aïvanhov, Omraam Mikhaël. L'amour plus grand que la foi. Fréjus : Prosveta, c2000.

Aïvanhov, Omraam Mikhaël. La foi qui transporte les montagnes. Fréjus : Prosveta, c1999.

De Rosa, Giuseppe. Fatica e gioia di credere. Leumann (Torino) : ElleDiCi ; Roma : La civiltà cattolica, c2002.

Faith in the age of uncertainty. New Delhi : Published by Indialog Publications in association with the India International Centre, 2002.
BL626.3+

Gotz, Ignacio L. Faith, humor, and paradox. Westport, Conn. : Praeger, 2002.
BL51 .G6854 2002

Holmes, Ernest, 1887-1960. [This thing called life] The art of life. New York : J.P. Tarcher/Penguin, c2004.
BF645 .H572 2004

Hood, Adam, 1960- Baillie, Oman and Macmurray. Aldershot, England ; Burlington, VT : Ashgate, c2003.
BR110 .H575 2003

Locke, Hubert G. Searching for God in godforsaken times and places. Grand Rapids, Mich. : W.B. Eerdmans Pub., c2003.
BT774 .L63 2003
1. Black author.

Sabalat, Tina. Pascals "Wette". Marburg : Tectum, 2000.

Sartorio, Ugo. Credere in dialogo. Padova : Edizioni Messaggero, 2002.

Wagner de Reyna, Alberto. El privilegio de ser latinoamericano. 1. ed. Córdoba, Argentina : Editorial Alejandro Korn, c2002.

F1408.3 .W35 2002

Williams, Jaime Andrés. El argumento de la apuesta de Blaise Pascal. 1. ed. Pamplona : Ediciones Universidad de Navarra, 2002.

FAITH AND REASON.
Kuipers, Ronald Alexander. Critical faith. Amsterdam ; New, York, NY : Rodopi, 2002.

Logik und Leidenschaft. Berlin : D. Reimer Verlag, c2002.

FAITH AND REASON - CHRISTIANITY.
Salamucha, Jan. [Selections. English. 2003] Knowledge and faith. Amsterdam ; New York, NY : Rodopi, 2003.

FAITH-CURE. *See* **SPIRITUAL HEALING.**

FAITH HEALERS. *See* **HEALERS.**

FAITH HEALING. *See* **SPIRITUAL HEALING.**

Faith, humor, and paradox.
Gotz, Ignacio L. Westport, Conn. : Praeger, 2002.
BL51 .G6854 2002

Faith in the age of uncertainty / edited by Sima Sharma ; with a foreword by Dr. Karan Singh. New Delhi : Published by Indialog Publications in association with the India International Centre, 2002. 228 p. : ill. (some col.) ; 23 cm. SUMMARY: Contributed articles. Includes bibliographical references. ISBN 81-87981-10-5
1. Faith. 2. Reasoning. 3. Induction (Logic) I. Sharma, Sima.
BL626.3+

FAITH (JUDAISM).
Golan, Mor Yosef. Sefer ha-Neshamah ba-guf. Itamar : M.Y. Golan, 762 [2001 or 2002]

Mosheh ben Ḥayim, Koznitser, d. 1874. Sefer ʻAhavat Yiśraʼel. Bruḳlin : [Yehoshuʻa Pinḥas Bukhinger], 762 [2001]

Pinter, Leib. Sefer ʻAśarah nisyonot. Brooklyn, N.Y. : E.Y.L. Pinter, c[2002?]

Wasserman, Elhanan Bunim, 1875-1941. Ḳovets maʼamre ʻIḳvata de-Meshiḥa .... Yerushalayim : Yeshivat Or Elḥanan, 762 [2001 or 2002]

Fakhr al-Dîn al-Râzî.
Arnaldez, Roger. Paris : J. Vrin, 2002.

Faking it.
Miller, William Ian, 1946- Cambridge ; New York : Cambridge University Press, 2003.
BF697 .M525 2003

Falkenburg, Brigitte, 1953-.
Wind, Edgar, 1900- Das Experiment und die Metaphysik. 1. Aufl. Frankfurt am Main : Suhrkamp, 2001.

Fall, Kevin A. Theoretical models of counseling and psychotherapy / Kevin A. Fall, Janice Miner Holden, Andre Marquis. New York : Brunner-Routledge, 2003. p. cm. Includes bibliographical references and index. Table of contents URL: http://www.loc.gov/catdir/toc/ecip044/2003011781.html ISBN 1-58391-068-9 DDC 158.3
1. Counseling. 2. Psychotherapy. I. Holden, Janice Miner. II. Marquis, Andre, Ph. D. III. Title.
BF637.C6 F324 2003

FALLACIES (LOGIC).
Schreiber, Scott G. (Scott Gregory), 1952- Aristotle on false reasoning. Albany : State University of New York Press, 2003.
B491.R4 S37 2003

Faller, Stefan.
Studien zu antiken Identitäten. Würzburg : Ergon Verlag, c2001.
DG78 .S78 2001

FALLIBILITY. *See* **ERRORS.**

FALSE MEMORY SYNDROME.
Campbell, Sue, 1956- Relational remembering. Lanham, Md. ; Oxford : Rowman & Littlefield, c2003.
BF378.A87 C36 2003

False necessity.
Unger, Roberto Mangabeira. False necessity--anti-necessitarian social theory in the service of radical democracy. New ed. London ; New York : Verso, 2001.

False necessity - anti-necessitarian social theory in the service of radical democracy.
Unger, Roberto Mangabeira. New ed. London ; New York : Verso, 2001.

FALSE PERSONATION - UNITED STATES - PREVENTION.
Privacy [electronic resource]. [Washington, D.C.] :

Federal Trade Commission, Bureau of Consumer Protection, Office of Consumer and Business Education, [2002]

Privacy [electronic resource]. [Washington, D.C.] : Federal Trade Commission, Bureau of Consumer Protection, Office of Consumer and Business Education, [2002]

Fält, Olavi K.
Looking at the other. Oulu, Finland : University of Oulu, 2002.

FAME.
Deniau, Jean-François, 1928- La gloire à vingt ans. [Paris] : XO editions, c2003.

Pessoa, Fernando, 1888-1935. [Erostratus. Portuguese & English] Heróstrato e a busca da imortalidade. Lisboa : Assírio e Alvim, c2000.

FAME - HISTORY.
Bronfen, Elisabeth. Die Diva. München : Schirmer/Mosel, c2002.
BJ1470.5 .B76 2002

FAME - SOCIAL ASPECTS.
Bronfen, Elisabeth. Die Diva. München : Schirmer/Mosel, c2002.
BJ1470.5 .B76 2002

Familiar dialogues in Englyssh and Frenche.
Becker, Monika. Trier : Wissenschaftlicher Verlag Trier, c2003.

FAMILIAR SPIRITS. See also **FAMILIARS (SPIRITS)**
Tyson, Donald, 1954- 1st ed. St. Paul, Minn. : Llewellyn Publications, 2004.
BF1557 .T97 2004

FAMILIARS (SPIRITS).
Grimassi, Raven, 1951- The witch's familiar. 1st ed. St. Paul, Minn. : Llewellyn Publications, 2003.
BF1557 .G75 2003

Tyson, Donald, 1954- Familiar spirits. 1st ed. St. Paul, Minn. : Llewellyn Publications, 2004.
BF1557 .T97 2004

Familie im Wandel / [mit Beiträgen u.a. von Christine Bergmann ... et al.]. Flensburg : Flensburger Hefte, [2002] 189 p. : ill. ; 21 cm. (Flensburger Hefte ; 78) "Herbst 2002"--P. [2] of cover. ISBN 3-935679-08-4 (pbk.)
1. Family. I. Series.

FAMILIES. See **FAMILY.**
FAMILIES, DUAL-CAREER. See **DUAL-CAREER FAMILIES.**
FAMILIES, JEWISH. See **JEWISH FAMILIES.**

La famille de l'adolescent.
Eiguer, Alberto. Paris : In press, c2001.

FAMILY. See also **AIRCRAFT ACCIDENT VICTIMS' FAMILIES; BROTHERS AND SISTERS; CHILDREN; DIVORCE; DOUBLE BIND (PSYCHOLOGY); DUAL-CAREER FAMILIES; HOME; HOUSEHOLDS; JEWISH FAMILIES; MARRIAGE; PARENT AND CHILD; PARENTS; SONS; WORK AND FAMILY.**
Archard, David. Children, family, and the state. Aldershot, Hants, England ; Burlington, VT : Ashgate, 2003.
HQ789 .A695 2003

Carrington, Victoria. New times. Dordrecht : Boston : London : Kluwer Academic, c2002.
HQ728 .C314 2002

Children's influence on family dynamics. Mahwah, N.J. : Lawrence Erlbaum Associates, 2003.
HQ518 .C535 2003

Chvojka, Erhard. Geschichte der Grosselternrollen. Wien : Böhlau, 2003.
HQ759.9 .C45 2003

Dziecko w rodzinie i społeczeństwie. Bydgoszsz : Wydawnictwo Uczelniane Akademii Bydgoskiej, 2002.

Familie im Wandel. Flensburg : Flensburger Hefte, [2002]

Gallop, Jane, 1952- Living with his camera. Durham : Duke University Press, 2003.
TR140.B517 G35 2003

Hochschild, Arlie Russell, 1940- The commercialization of intimate life. Berkeley : University of California Press, 2003.

HM1106 .H63 2003

Lareau, Annette. Unequal childhoods. Berkeley : University of California Press, c2003.
HQ767.9 .L37 2003

Lewis, Jane (Jane E.) Should we worry about family change? Toronto : University of Toronto Press, c2003.

Life as we know it. 1st Washington Square Press trade pbk. ed. New York : Washington Square Press, 2003.

Rozin, V. M. Lı͡ubov' i seksual'nost' v kul'ture, sem'e i vzgli͡adakh na polovoe vospitanie. Moskva : Logos : Vysshai͡a shkola, 1999.
BF575.L8 R69 1999

Rubin, Gabrielle, 1921- Le roman familial de Freud. Paris : Payot, 2002.

Social relations and the life course. Houndmills, Basingstoke New York : Palgrave Macmillan, 2003.
HM741 .S64 2003

Wallat, Cynthia. Family-institution interaction. New York : P. Lang, c2002.
HQ755.85 .W35 2002

FAMILY AND STATE. See **FAMILY POLICY.**
FAMILY AND WORK. See **WORK AND FAMILY.**
FAMILY CAREGIVERS. See **CAREGIVERS.**

FAMILY - CHINA.
Taofen, 1895-1944. Taofen "Du zhe xin xiang". Di 1 ban. Beijing : Zhongguo cheng shi chu ban she, 1998.

FAMILY IN LITERATURE.
Bosco Coletsos, Sandra. La struttura parentale nelle fiabe dei fratelli Grimm. Alessandria : Edizioni dell'Orso, 2001.

Family-institution interaction.
Wallat, Cynthia. New York : P. Lang, c2002.
HQ755.85 .W35 2002

FAMILY LIFE EDUCATION. See **HOME ECONOMICS; SEX INSTRUCTION.**

Family matters (John Wiley & Sons)
Nicolson, Paula. Having it all? Chichester, West Sussex, England ; Hoboken, NJ : J. Wiley, c2002.
HQ1206 .N645 2002

FAMILY POLICY. See also **CHILD WELFARE.**
Lewis, Jane (Jane E.) Should we worry about family change? Toronto : University of Toronto Press, c2003.

FAMILY POLICY - UNITED STATES.
Zigler, Edward, 1930- The first three years & beyond. New Haven : Yale University Press, c2002.
HQ767.9 .Z543 2002

FAMILY - PSYCHOLOGICAL ASPECTS.
Bedi, Ashok. Retire your family karma. Berwick, Me. : Nicolas-Hays, 2003.
BF637.S4 B423 2003

Eiguer, Alberto. La famille de l'adolescent. Paris : In press, c2001.

Quaglia, Rocco. Immagini dell'uomo. Roma : Armando, c2000.

Utváření a vývoj osobnosti. Vyd. 1. V Brně : Barrister & Principal, 2002.
BF723.P4 U88 2002

FAMILY PSYCHOTHERAPY.
Boyd-Franklin, Nancy. Black families in therapy. 2nd ed. New York : Guilford Press, c2003.
RC451.5.N4 B69 2003

Corcoran, Jacqueline. Clinical applications of evidence-based family interventions. Cambridge, U.K. ; New York : Oxford University Press, 2003.
HV697 .C67 2003

Eiguer, Alberto. La famille de l'adolescent. Paris : In press, c2001.

Feminist family therapy. 1st ed. Washington, DC : American Psychological Association, c2003.
RC488.5 .F453 2003

Mindell, Arnold, 1940- The dreambody in relationships. Portland, OR : Lao Tse Press ; Oakland, CA : Distributed to the trade by Words Distributing Co., c2002.
BF637.N66 M56 2002

FAMILY RELATIONSHIPS. See **FAMILY.**

FAMILY RESEARCH. See **FAMILY - RESEARCH.**

FAMILY - RESEARCH - CZECH REPUBLIC.
Utváření a vývoj osobnosti. Vyd. 1. V Brně : Barrister & Principal, 2002.

BF723.P4 U88 2002

FAMILY REUNIONS. See **FAMILY.**

Family secrets.
Kuhn, Annette. New ed. London ; New York : Verso, 2002.
CT274 .K84 2002

FAMILY - SERVICES FOR. See **FAMILY SERVICES.**

FAMILY SERVICES - UNITED STATES.
The subject of care. Lanham, Md. ; Oxford : Rowman & Littlefield Publishers, c2002.
HQ1206 .S9 2002

FAMILY - SOCIAL ASPECTS. See **FAMILY.**
FAMILY - SOCIAL CONDITIONS. See **FAMILY.**

FAMILY SOCIAL WORK.
Corcoran, Jacqueline. Clinical applications of evidence-based family interventions. Cambridge, U.K. ; New York : Oxford University Press, 2003.
HV697 .C67 2003

FAMILY - UNITED STATES.
Life as we know it. 1st Washington Square Press trade pbk. ed. New York : Washington Square Press, 2003.

Sabourin, Teresa Chandler. The contemporary American family. Thousand Oaks, Calif. : Sage Publications, c2003.
HQ536 .S213 2003

Struening, Karen, 1960- New family values. Lanham : Rowman & Littlefield Publishers, c2002.
HQ536 .S82 2002

FAMILY VIOLENCE.
Mills, Linda G. Insult to injury. Princeton, N.J. : Princeton University Press, c2003.
HV6626 .M55 2003

FAMOUS PEOPLE. See **CELEBRITIES.**

Fan jing.
Zeng, Guofan, 1811-1872. Di 1 ban. Beijing : Zhongguo Hua qiao chu ban she, 2001.
BJ1618.C5 H44 2001

Fan, Xiangyong.
Xu, Wenjing, 1667-1756? Guan cheng shi ji. Di 1 ban. Beijing : Zhonghua shu ju : Xin hua shu dian Beijing fa xing suo fa xing, 1998.
PL2461.Z6 H77 1998

FAN, ZHONGYAN, 989-1052.
Shi, Sheng. Fan Zhongyan li shen xing shi jiu jiu fang lüe. Di 1 ban. Beijing : Zhongguo xi ju chu ban she, 2001.
DS751.6.F3 S5 2001

Fan Zhongyan li shen xing shi jiu jiu fang lüe.
Shi, Sheng. Di 1 ban. Beijing : Zhongguo xi ju chu ban she, 2001.
DS751.6.F3 S5 2001

FANATICISM - HISTORY.
Religion et exclusion, XIIe-XVIIIe siècle. Religion et exclusion, douzième-dix-huitième siècle. Aix-en-Provence : Publications de l'Université de Provence, 2001.
BL238 .R448 2001

Rossi, Paolo, 1923- Bambini, sogni, furori. 1. ed. in "Campi del sapere.". Milano : Feltrinelli, 2001.
BF41 .R67 2001

Fanatismo dentro de nuestra sociedad.
Pinto Cañón, Ramiro. Grupos gnósticos. Madrid : Entinema, 2002.

FANCY DRESS. See **COSTUME.**

Fang, Fang.
Dan shen gao bai. Di 1 ban. Beijing : Beijing chu ban she, 2001.
HQ800.2 .D36 2001

Fang, Ning.
Cheng zhang de Zhongguo. Di 1 ban. Beijing : Ren min chu ban she, 2002.
HQ799.2.P6 C449 2002

Fang, Xinliang.
He, Bingsong, 1890-1946. [Works. 1996] He Bingsong wen ji. Di 1 ban. Beijing : Shang wu yin shu guan, 1996.
DS734.7 .H664

Fang yuan bing fa / Wu Xinming bian zhu. Di 1 ban. Beijing : Jin cheng chu ban she, 1998. 2, 10, 514 p. ; 20 cm. ISBN 7-80084-223-1
1. Interpersonal relations. 2. Success. I. Wu, Xinming.

Fanon.
Gibson, Nigel C. Cambridge, U.K. : Polity Press in association with Blackwell Pub. ; Malden, MA : Distributed in the USA by Blackwell Pub., 2003.
CT2628.F35 G53 2003

FANON, FRANTZ, 1925-1961.
Gibson, Nigel C. Fanon. Cambridge, U.K. : Polity Press in association with Blackwell Pub. ; Malden, MA : Distributed in the USA by Blackwell Pub., 2003.
CT2628.F35 G53 2003

FANON, FRANTZ, 1925-1961 - POLITICAL AND SOCIAL VIEWS.
Gibson, Nigel C. Fanon. Cambridge, U.K. : Polity Press in association with Blackwell Pub. ; Malden, MA : Distributed in the USA by Blackwell Pub., 2003.
CT2628.F35 G53 2003

FANS (PERSONS).
Les cultes médiatiques. Rennes : Presses universitaires de Rennes, [2002]

La "fantasia, che è l'occhio dell'ingegno".
Sanna, Manuela. Napoli : A. Guida editore, c2001.
B3583 .S26 2001

Fantasies of flight.
Ogilvie, Daniel M. New York : Oxford University Press, 2003.
BF1385 .O35 2003

Fantasm. Melbourne : Freudian School of Melbourne, 2000. 245 p. : ill. ; 21 cm. (Papers of the Freudian School of Melbourne ; 21) At head of title: Lacanian psychoanalytic writings. Includes bibliographical references. ISBN 0-9578825-0-5
1. Lacan, Jacques, - 1901- 2. Psychoanalysis. I. Freudian School of Melbourne. II. Title: Lacanian psychoanalytic writings

FANTASTIC FICTION. See **GHOST STORIES.**

FANTASTIC, THE.
Imagination, Fiktion, Kreation. München : Saur, c2003.
BH301.I53 I534 2003

FANTASTIC, THE (AESTHETICS). See **FANTASTIC, THE.**

FANTASTIC, THE - RELIGIOUS ASPECTS.
Imagination, Fiktion, Kreation. München : Saur, c2003.
BH301.I53 I534 2003

FANTASY.
Heuermann, Hartmut. Welt und Bewusstsein. Frankfurt am Main ; New York : Peter Lang, c2002.

Langens, Thomas A. Tagträume, Anliegen und Motivation. Göttingen ; Seattle : Hogrefe, c2002.

Fantasy dreaming.
Hamilton-Parker, Craig. New York : Sterling Pub., c2002.
BF1091 .H347 2002

FANTASY FICTION, ENGLISH - HISTORY AND CRITICISM.
Gupta, Suman, 1966- Re-reading Harry Potter. Houndmills, Basingstoke ; New York : Palgrave Macmillan, 2003.
PR6068.O93 Z68 2003

Harry Potter's world. New York ; London : RoutledgeFalmer, 2003.
PR6068.O93 Z73 2003

The ivory tower and Harry Potter. Columbia : University of Missouri Press, 2002.
PR6068.O93 Z734 2002

Reading Harry Potter. Westport, Conn. ; London : Praeger Publishers, 2003.
PR6068.O93 Z84 2003

FANTASY - HISTORY.
Masson, J. Moussaieff (Jeffrey Moussaieff), 1941- The assault on truth. 1st Ballantine Books ed. New York : Ballantine Books, 2003.
BF109.F74 M38 2003

The psychology of death in fantasy and history. Westport, CT : Praeger, 2004.
BF789.D4 P79 2004

FANTASY LITERATURE - HISTORY AND CRITICISM.
Imagination, Fiktion, Kreation. München : Saur, c2003.
BH301.I53 I534 2003

The fantasy principle.
Adams, Michael Vannoy, 1947- New York : Brunner-Routledge, 2004.
BF173.J85 A33 2004

Fantham, Elaine.
Caesar against liberty? Cambridge : Francis Cairns, c2003.

Fanthorpe, P. A.
Fanthorpe, R. Lionel. The world's most mysterious objects. Toronto ; Tonawanda NY : Dundurn Press, 2002.

Fanthorpe, R. Lionel. The world's most mysterious objects / Lionel and Patricia Fanthorpe. Toronto ; Tonawanda NY : Dundurn Press, 2002. 240 p. : ill. ; 23 cm. "A Hounslow book." Includes bibliographical references (p. [237]-240). ISBN 1-55002-403-5 DDC 001.94
1. Curiosities and wonders. I. Fanthorpe, P. A. II. Title.

FAR EAST. See **EAST ASIA.**

FĀRĀBĪ.
Kemal, Salim. The philosophical poetics of Alfarabi, Avicenna and Averroes. London ; New York : RoutledgeCurzon, 2003.

Farago, France. Sören Kierkegaard : l'épreuve de soi / France Farago. 1. éd. Paris : Houdiard, c2002. 125 p. : 22 cm. (Essais) Includes bibliographical references. ISBN 2-912673-17-8 DDC 198
1. Kierkegaard, Søren, - 1813-1855. 2. Self (Philosophy) I. Title. II. Series: Dolto, Françoise. Essais.

Farber, Barry J. Diamond in the rough / Barry J. Farber. New York : Berkley Books, c1995. xxii, 234 p. ; 21 cm. Includes bibliographical references (p. [233]-234). ISBN 0-425-14733-9
1. Success. 2. Self-esteem. I. Title.
BF637.S8 F34 1995

Diamond power : gems of wisdom from America's greatest marketer / by Barry Farber. Franklin Lakes, NJ : Career Press, 2004. p. cm. Includes bibliographical references. ISBN 1-56414-698-7 (pbk.) DDC 158
1. Success - Psychological aspects. I. Title.
BF637.S8 F342 2004

Farcet, Gilles, 1959- Manuel de l'anti-sagesse : traité de l'échec sur la voie spirituelle / Gilles Farcet. [Gordes] : Relié, c2002. 218 p. ; 23 cm. ISBN 2-914916-00-0 DDC 290
1. Spirituality. 2. Spiritual life. I. Title.

FAREWELLS. See **SEPARATION (PSYCHOLOGY).**

FARM ANIMALS. See **DOMESTIC ANIMALS; LIVESTOCK.**

Farmer, Sharon A.
Gender and difference in the Middle Ages. Minneapolis : University of Minnesota Press, c2003.
HQ1143 .G44 2003

FARMING. See **AGRICULTURE.**

Farrar, Janet. Progressive witchcraft : spirituality, mysteries, and training in modern wicca / by Janet Farrar & Gavin Bone. Franklin Lakes, NJ : New Page Books, 2004. p. cm. Includes bibliographical references and index. ISBN 1-56414-719-3 DDC 299/.94
1. Witchcraft. I. Bone, Gavin. II. Title.
BF1571 .F346 2004

Farrer, Frances, 1950- Sir George Trevelyan and the new spiritual awakening / Frances Farrer. Edinburgh : Floris, 2002. 203 p., [8] p. of plates : ill. ; 23 cm. Includes bibliographical references (p. [181]) and index. ISBN 0-86315-377-1 DDC 291.4092
1. Trevelyan, George. 2. Educators - Great Britain - Biography. 3. Spirituality. I. Title.

FARRIERY. See **HORSES.**

Farrington, Debra K. Hearing with the heart : a gentle guide for discerning God's will for your life / Debra K. Farrington. 1st ed. San Francisco : Jossey-Bass, c2003. xvii, 247 p. ; 19 cm. Includes bibliographical references (p. 221-230) and index. CONTENTS: The hearing heart -- Navigating the obstacle course -- The prayerful heart -- The attentive heart -- Learning with the heart -- Discerning companions -- The thoughtful and imaginative heart -- Hearts together -- The engaged heart. ISBN 0-7879-5959-6 (alk. paper) DDC 248.4
1. Christian life. 2. Discernment (Christian theology) 3. God - Will. I. Title.
BV4509.5 .F37 2003

Farrugia, Francis.
La connaissance sociologique. Paris : Harmattan, c2002.
HM651 .C65 2002

Farson, Richard Evans, 1926- Whoever makes the most mistakes wins : the paradox of innovation / Richard Farson and Ralph Keyes. New York ; London : Free Press, c2002. xiv, 129 p. ; 20 cm. ISBN 0-7432-2592-9 DDC 658.4/09
1. Technological innovations. 2. Success in business. 3. Success. I. Keyes, Ralph. II. Title.
HD45 .F357 2002

Farzānagī dar āyinah-i zamān.
Kāviyānī, Shīvā. Tihrān : Nigāh, 2001.

La fascinación de Oriente.
Merlo Lillo, Vicente. 1. ed. Barcelona : Editorial Kairós, 2002.

FASCISM. See also **NATIONAL SOCIALISM.**
Bošković, Hijacint. Filozofski izvori fašizma i nacionalnog socijalizma. 2. izd. Zagreb : Dom i svijet, 2000.
B804 .B66 2000

FASCISM - ITALY.
Franchi, Franco. La libertà nel fascismo. Roma : Europa : Settimo sigillo, c2002.

FASCISTS - GERMANY. See **NAZIS.**

FASHION. See **CLOTHING AND DRESS; COSTUME.**

FASHION - PSYCHOLOGICAL ASPECTS.
Lee, Michelle. Fashion victim. 1st ed. New York : Broadway Books, 2003.
GT524 .L44 2003

Fashion victim.
Lee, Michelle. 1st ed. New York : Broadway Books, 2003.
GT524 .L44 2003

FAST DAYS. See **FASTS AND FEASTS.**

FASTING. See **FASTS AND FEASTS.**

FasTracKids International Ltd.
Goals and life lessons support materials [electronic resource]. Greenwood Village, CO : FasTracKids International, [1998]
BF637.S4

FASTS AND FEASTS. See **FESTIVALS; HOLIDAYS.**

FASTS AND FEASTS - EGYPTIAN RELIGION.
Eyre, Christopher. The cannibal hymn. Liverpool : Liverpool University Press, 2002.

FASTS AND FEASTS - FRANCE - HISTORY.
Effros, Bonnie, 1965- Creating community with food and drink in Merovingian Gaul. 1st ed. New York ; Houndmills, England : Palgrave Macmillan, 2002.
GT2853.F7 E34 2002

FASTS AND FEASTS IN THE BIBLE. See **FASTS AND FEASTS - JUDAISM.**

FASTS AND FEASTS - JEWS. See **FASTS AND FEASTS - JUDAISM.**

FASTS AND FEASTS - JUDAISM.
Levin, Yitshak, 1938- Sefer Netivot Yitshak. [Bene Berak] : Y. Levin, [2000-

Lugasi, Ya'akov Yiśra'el. Mishpete Yiśra'el. Mahadurah ḥadashah be-tosefet le-hag ha-Pesaḥ. Yerushalayim : Y. Y. Lugasi, 761 [2001]

Malkah, Asher. 'Arakhim ve-ḥinukh. Ḥefah : A. Malkah, [5760 i.e. 2000]

FASTS AND FEASTS - JUDAISM - PRAYER-BOOKS AND DEVOTIONS.
Naphtali ben Isaac, ha-Kohen, 1649-1719. Sefer Bet Rahel. Yerushalayim : Ahavat Shalom, 761 [2001]
BM665 .N257 2001

FATALISM. See **FATE AND FATALISM.**

FATALLY ILL. See **TERMINALLY ILL.**

FATE AND FATALISM.
Tan, Amy The opposite of fate. New York : Putnam c2003.
PS3570.A48 Z47 2003

Washington, Johnny. Evolution, history and destiny. New York : Peter Lang, c2002.
E185.625 .W37 2002

FATE AND FATALISM - RELIGIOUS ASPECTS. See **TRUST IN GOD.**

FATE AND FATALISM - RELIGIOUS ASPECTS - CHRISTIANITY.
Meier, Jürgen. Karma und Christentum. Dornach : Verlag am Goetheanum, c2001.

Father and child

FATHER AND CHILD. *See also* **FATHERS AND SONS.**
Brodeur, Claude, 1924- Le père. Paris : L'Harmattan, 2001.
HQ756 .B76 2001

Nuland, Sherwin B. Lost in America. 1st ed. New York : Knopf : Distributed by Random House, 2003.
F128.9.J5 N85 2003

Il "valore" del padre. Torino : UTET libreria, 2001.
BF723.P25 V35 2001

FATHERHOOD.
Le figure del padre. Roma : Armando editore, c2001.

Fthenakis, Wassilios E. Die Rolle des Vaters in der Familie. Stuttgart : Kohlhammer, 2002.

Liaudet, Jean-Claude. Telle fille, quel père? Paris : Archipel, c2002.

FATHERHOOD - PSYCHOLOGICAL ASPECTS.
Fthenakis, Wassilios E. Die Rolle des Vaters in der Familie. Stuttgart : Kohlhammer, 2002.

Lefèvre, Alain, 1947- De la paternité et des psychoses. Paris : Harmattan, c2002-

FATHERS. *See also* **GAY FATHERS.**
Brodeur, Claude, 1924- Le père. Paris : L'Harmattan, 2001.
HQ756 .B76 2001

Le figure del padre. Roma : Armando editore, c2001.

Fthenakis, Wassilios E. Die Rolle des Vaters in der Familie. Stuttgart : Kohlhammer, 2002.

Il "valore" del padre. Torino : UTET libreria, 2001.
BF723.P25 V35 2001

FATHERS AND DAUGHTERS.
Liaudet, Jean-Claude. Telle fille, quel père? Paris : Archipel, c2002.

FATHERS AND SONS.
Daniel, Jack L. (Jack Lee), 1942- We fish. Pittsburgh, Pa. : University of Pittsburgh Press, c2003.
1. Black author.

Gottlieb, Andrew R. Sons talk about their gay fathers. New York : Harrington Park Press, c2003.
HQ76.13 .G67 2003

Kaufman, Barry Neil. No regrets. Novato, Calif. : HJ Kramer/New World Library, 2003.
BF575.G7 K385 2003

Souceray, Joe. Waterline. Boston : D.R. Godine, 2002.
PN4874.S576 A3 2002

Veerman, David. When your father dies. Nashville, Tenn. : Thomas Nelson, c2003.
BF575.G7 V44 2003

FATHERS AND SONS - UNITED STATES.
McEnroe, Colin. My father's footsteps. New York : Warner Books, c2003.
PS3563.C3615 M9 2003

FATHERS - DEATH.
Dennison, Amy. Our dad died. Minneapolis, MN : Free Spirit Pub., c2003.
BF723.G75 D46 2003

FATHERS - DEATH - PSYCHOLOGICAL ASPECTS.
Andrews, John, 1966- For all those left behind. Edinburgh : Mainstream Pub., c2002.
BF789.D4 A55 2002

Kaufman, Barry Neil. No regrets. Novato, Calif. : HJ Kramer/New World Library, 2003.
BF575.G7 K385 2003

McEnroe, Colin. My father's footsteps. New York : Warner Books, c2003.
PS3563.C3615 M9 2003

Veerman, David. When your father dies. Nashville, Tenn. : Thomas Nelson, c2003.
BF575.G7 V44 2003

FATHERS - DEATH - PSYCHOLOGICAL ASPECTS - JUVENILE LITERATURE.
Dennison, Amy. Our dad died. Minneapolis, MN : Free Spirit Pub., c2003.
BF723.G75 D46 2003

Stenson, Lila. Daddy, up and down. 1st ed. Snowmass Village, CO : Peaceful Village Pub., 2002.
BF723.G75 S74 2002

FATHERS IN LITERATURE.
Brodeur, Claude, 1924- Le père. Paris : L'Harmattan, 2001.

HQ756 .B76 2001

FATHERS - PSYCHOLOGY.
Fthenakis, Wassilios E. Die Rolle des Vaters in der Familie. Stuttgart : Kohlhammer, 2002.

Liaudet, Jean-Claude. Telle fille, quel père? Paris : Archipel, c2002.

Fatica e gioia di credere.
De Rosa, Giuseppe. Leumann (Torino) : ElleDiCi ; Roma : La civiltà cattolica, c2002.

FATNESS. *See* **OBESITY.**

Faulconer, James E.
Transcendence in philosophy and religion. Bloomington, IN : Indiana University Press, c2003.
B56 .T73 2003

Faulstich, Werner.
Liebe als Kulturmedium. München : Fink, c2002.

Zeit in den Medien, Medien in der Zeit. München : Fink, c2002.

FAUNA. *See* **ANIMALS.**

Fausto Neto, Antônio.
Comunicação e corporeidades. Brazil : Editora Universitaria : Compas, 2000.

Faux titre
(no. 220) Consenstein, Peter. Literary memory, consciousness, and the group Oulipo. Amsterdam ; New York, NY : Rodopi, 2002.

Favaloro, René G., 1923-.
El milagro y el valor de la vida. 1. ed. Buenos Aires : Patria Grande, 2000.

FCC should include call quality in its annual report on competition in mobile phone services.
United States. General Accounting Office. Telecommunications [electronic resource]. [Washington, D.C.] : U.S. General Accounting Office, [2003]

FEAR. *See also* **ANXIETY; BASHFULNESS.**
Bourne, Edmund J. Coping with anxiety. Oakland, CA : New Harbinger, c2003.
BF575.A6 B68 2003

Buianov, M. I. (Mikhail Ivanovich), vrach. Strakh. Moskva : Rossiĭskoe ob-vo medikov-literatorov, 2002.
BF575.F2 B85 2002

Elliott, Charles H., 1948- Overcoming anxiety for dummies. New York : Wiley Pub., c2003.
BF575.A6 E46 2003

Ferrières, Madeleine. Histoire des peurs alimentaires. Paris : Editions du Seuil, c2002.

Füredi, Frank, 1947- Culture of fear. Rev. ed. London ; New York : Continuum, 2002.
BF575.F2 F86 2002

Leonard, Marcia. I feel scared. Nashville, Tenn. : CandyCane Press, 2003.
BF575.F2 L455 2003

Meiners, Cheri J., 1957- When I feel afraid. Minneapolis, MN : Free Spirit Pub., 2003.
BF723.F4 M45 2003

Mellinger, David. The monster in the cave. 1st ed. New York : Berkley Books, 2003.
BF575.F2 M45 2003

Nelson, Robin, 1971- Afraid. Minneapolis, MN : Lerner Publications Co., c2004.
BF723.F4 N45 2004

Psychology of fear. New York : Nova Science Publishers, 2003.
BF575.F2 P79 2003

Rutledge, Thom. Embracing fear. 1st ed. [San Francisco] : HarperSanFrancisco, c2002.
BF575.F2 R88 2002

Sapadin, Linda. Master your fears. Hoboken, N.J. : John Wiley & Sons, 2004.
BF575.F2 S26 2004

Shepherd, Joanne. What I look like when I am scared. New York : Rosen Pub. Group's PowerStart Press, 2004.
BF723.F4 S54 2004

Shepherd, Joanne. [What I look like when I am scared. Spanish & English] What I look like when I am scared = 1st ed. New York : Rosen Pub. Group's PowerKids Press, 2004.
BF723.F4 S5418 2004

Shuman, Carol. Jenny is scared. Washington, DC : Magination Press, c2003.

BF723.F4 S58 2003

Webb, Wyatt. Five steps for overcoming fear and self-doubt. Carlsbad, Calif. : Hay House, 2004.
BF575.F2 W42 2004

FEAR (CHILD PSYCHOLOGY). *See* **FEAR IN CHILDREN.**

FEAR - CONGRESSES.
El miedo. Medellín, Colombia : Corporación Región, 2002.
BF575.F2 M494 2002

FEAR IN CHILDREN.
Children's fears of war and terrorism. Olney, MD : Association for Childhood Education International, c2003.
BF723.W3 C48 2003

FEAR IN CHILDREN - JUVENILE LITERATURE.
Meiners, Cheri J., 1957- When I feel afraid. Minneapolis, MN : Free Spirit Pub., 2003.
BF723.F4 M45 2003

Nelson, Robin, 1971- Afraid. Minneapolis, MN : Lerner Publications Co., c2004.
BF723.F4 N45 2004

Shepherd, Joanne. What I look like when I am scared. New York : Rosen Pub. Group's PowerStart Press, 2004.
BF723.F4 S54 2004

Shepherd, Joanne. [What I look like when I am scared. Spanish & English] What I look like when I am scared = 1st ed. New York : Rosen Pub. Group's PowerKids Press, 2004.
BF723.F4 S5418 2004

Shuman, Carol. Jenny is scared. Washington, DC : Magination Press, c2003.
BF723.F4 S58 2003

Wigand, Molly. Help is here for facing fear. St. Meinrad, IN : One Caring Place/Abbey Press, c2000.
BF723.F4 W54 2000

FEAR - JUVENILE LITERATURE.
Leonard, Marcia. I feel scared. Nashville, Tenn. : CandyCane Press, 2003.
BF575.F2 L455 2003

FEAR OF DEATH.
Pyszczynski, Thomas A. In the wake of 9/11. Washington, DC : American Psychological Association, c2003.
HV6432 .P97 2003

FEAR OF FAILURE. *See* **FAILURE (PSYCHOLOGY).**

FEAR OF SUCCESS. *See* **SUCCESS.**

FEAR - POLITICAL ASPECTS - CONGRESSES.
El miedo. Medellín, Colombia : Corporación Región, 2002.
BF575.F2 M494 2002

FEAR - RELIGIOUS ASPECTS.
Egbunu, Fidelis Eleojo. Be not afraid, only believe. Enugu, Nigeria : Snaap Press, 2001.
1. Black author.

FEAR - RELIGIOUS ASPECTS - CHRISTIANITY.
Egbunu, Fidelis Eleojo. Be not afraid, only believe. Enugu, Nigeria : Snaap Press, 2001.
1. Black author.

FEAR - SOCIAL ASPECTS - CONGRESSES.
El miedo. Medellín, Colombia : Corporación Región, 2002.
BF575.F2 M494 2002

FEASTS. *See* **FASTS AND FEASTS.**

FEATURE FILMS - HISTORY AND CRITICISM. *See* **MOTION PICTURES.**

Feder, Ellen K.
The subject of care. Lanham, Md. ; Oxford : Rowman & Littlefield Publishers, c2002.
HQ1206 .S9 2002

Federal Prison Industries Competition in Contracting Act of 2003.
United States. Congress. House. Committee on the Judiciary. [Washington, D.C. : U.S. G.P.O., 2003]

FEDERAL PRISON INDUSTRIES, INC.
United States. Congress. House. Committee on the Judiciary. Federal Prison Industries Competition in Contracting Act of 2003. [Washington, D.C. : U.S. G.P.O., 2003]

Federal Trade Commission [electronic resource].
United States. General Accounting Office.

[Washington, D.C.] : U.S. General Accounting Office, [2002]

FEDERAL WRITERS' PROJECT - HISTORY.
Hirsch, Jerrold, 1948- Portrait of America. Chapel Hill : University of North Carolina Press, c2003.
E175.4.W9 H57 2003

Fedi, Laurent.
Renouvier, Charles, 1815-1903. Sur le peuple, l'église et la république. Paris : Harmattan, c2002.

FEELING. *See* **PERCEPTION; TOUCH.**

Feeling embarrassed.
Berry, Joy Wilt. Let's talk about feeling embarrassed. New York : Scholastic, c2002.
BF723.E44 B47 2002

Feeling worried.
Berry, Joy Wilt. Let's talk about feeling worried. New York : Scholastic Inc., c2002.
BF723.W67 B47 2002

FEELINGS. *See* **EMOTIONS.**

Feelings and emotions : the Amsterdam symposium / edited by Antony S.R. Manstead, Nico Frijda, Agneta Fischer. New York : Cambridge University Press, 2003. pm. cm. (Studies in emotion and social interaction) Symposium held in June 2001 in Amsterdam, Netherlands. Publisher description URL: http://www.loc.gov/catdir/description/cam032/2003043960.html Table of contents URL: http://www.loc.gov/catdir/toc/cam031/2003043960.html ISBN 0-521-81652-1 ISBN 0-521-52101-7 (pb.) DDC 152.4
1. Emotions - Congresses. 2. Emotions - Social aspects - Congresses. I. Manstead, A. S. R. II. Frijda, Nico H. III. Fischer, Agneta, 1958- IV. Series.
BF531 .F445 2003

Feigenbaum, A. V. (Armand Vallin) The power of management capital : utilizing the new drivers of innovation, profitability, and growth in a demanding global economy / Armand V. Feigenbaum and Donald S. Feigenbaum. New York ; Toronto : McGraw-Hill, c2003. xiii, 201 p. : ill. ; 23 cm. Includes index. ISBN 0-07-021733-5
1. Industrial management. 2. Leadership. I. Feigenbaum, Donald S. II. Title.
HD31 .F45 2003

Feigenbaum, Donald S.
Feigenbaum, A. V. (Armand Vallin) The power of management capital. New York ; Toronto : McGraw-Hill, c2003.
HD31 .F45 2003

Feigenbaum, Susanne.
Prepositions in their syntactic, semantic, and pragmatic context. Amsterdam ; Philadelphia, PA : J. Benjamins Pub., c2002.
P285 .P74 2002

Fekete, Mária. Pszichológia és pszichopatológia jogászoknak / Fekete Mária, Grád András. Budapest : HVG-ORAC, c2002. 479 p. ; 20 cm. Includes bibliographical references (p. [474]-479). ISBN 9639404462
1. Psychoanalysis. 2. Psychology, Pathological. I. Grád, András. II. Title.
BF173 .F349 2002

Fekete, Sandra. Companies are people, too : discover, develop, and grow your organization's true personality / Sandra Fekete with LeeAnna Keith. Hoboken, N.J. : John Wiley & Sons, c2003. xi, 254 p. : ill., forms ; 24 cm. Includes bibliographical references (p. 245-247) and index. Table of contents URL: http://www.loc.gov/catdir/toc/wiley031/2002153129.html CONTENTS: Every company has a personality -- Companies are people, too : the concept and promise -- Discover your company's personality -- Profiles of practicality -- Profiles of action -- Profiles of idealism -- Profiles of competence -- Discover your leadership personality -- Personality and cultural diversity -- Personality and culture : a cautionary tale -- Finding a face for your personality -- Up close and personal -- Defining vision, mission, and values -- Living in harmony with your company's values -- The physical dimensions of your company -- When things change -- Sizing up the competition, partners, and clients -- What if you don't like who you are? -- Being yourself on purpose. ISBN 0-471-23610-1 (cloth : alk. paper) DDC 658
1. Organizational behavior. 2. Corporate culture. I. Keith, LeAnna. II. Title.
HD58.7 .F43 2003

Feldbaum, Rebecca Bram. If there's anything I can do-- : a bookful of personal experiences and good ideas on how to help those who have suffered loss / Rebecca Bram Feldbaum. Jerusalem, Israel ; Nanuet, NY : Feldheim Publishers, 2003. xvii, 254 p. ; 24 cm. ISBN 1-58330-577-7 DDC 155.9/37
1. Grief. 2. Bereavement - Psychological aspects. 3.

Husbands - Death - Psychological aspects. 4. Loss (Psychology) 5. Jews - Social life and customs. I. Title.
BF575.G7 F46 2003

Feldhūns, Ā. (Ābrams).
Plato. [Selections. Latvian] Platons dialogi un vēstules = [Rīga] : Zinātne, c1999.

Feldman, Robert S. (Robert Stephen), 1947-.
Nonverbal behavior in clinical settings. Oxford ; New York : Oxford University Press, 2003.
RC489.N65 N66 2003

The regulation of emotion. Mahwah, NJ : Lawrence Erlbaum, 2003.
BF531 .R45 2003

Feldman, Ruth Duskin.
Papalia, Diane E. Human development. 9th ed. Boston : McGraw-Hill, c2004.
BF713 .P35 2004

Feldman, Seymour. Philosophy in a time of crisis : Don Isaac Abravanel, defender of the faith / Seymour Feldman. London ; New York : RoutledgeCurzon, 2003. vi, 213 p. ; 25 cm. Includes bibliographical references (p. [206]-210) and index. ISBN 0-7007-1590-8 DDC 296.3/092
1. Abravanel, Isaac, - 1437-1508. 2. León, - Hebreo, - b. ca. 1460. - Dialoghi d'amore. 3. Judaism - Doctrines. 4. Philosophy, Jewish. 5. Philosophy, Medieval. 6. Love. I. Title.
BM755.A25 F45 2003

FELDSHUH, TOVAH.
Vint/age 2001 conference : [videorecording]. New York, c2001.

Feldshuh, Tovah, panelist.
Vint/age 2001 conference : [videorecording]. New York, c2001.

FELIS. *See* **CATS.**

FELIS CATUS. *See* **CATS.**

FELIS DOMESTICA. *See* **CATS.**

FELIS SILVESTRIS CATUS. *See* **CATS.**

FELONIES. *See* **CRIME.**

Feltham, Colin, 1950-.
Psychoanalytic knowledge. New York : Palgrave Macmillan, 2003.
BF173 .P7763 2003

What's the good of counselling & psychotherapy? London ; Thousand Oaks, Calif. : SAGE Publications, 2002.
BF637.C6 W465 2002

The female brain.
Darlington, Cynthia L. London ; New York : Taylor & Francis, c2002.
QP402 .D366 2002

FEMALE DETECTIVES. *See* **WOMEN DETECTIVES.**

FEMALE FRIENDSHIP.
Appel, Dee. Friend to friend. Sisters, Or. : Multnomah Publishers, c2002.
BF575.F66 A66 2002

Girlfriends. Lincolnwood, Ill. : New Seasons, c2003.
BF575.F66 G57 2003

Heim, Pat. In the company of women. New York : J.P. Tarcher/Putnam, c2001.
HD6053 .H387 2001

Laing, Kathleen. Girlfriends' getaway. 1st ed. Colorado Springs, Colo. : WaterBrook Press, 2002.
BF575.F66 L35 2002

Rind, Patricia. Women's best friendships. New York : Haworth Press, c2002.
BF575.F66 R56 2002

FEMALE FRIENDSHIP - MISCELLANEA.
Bodger, Lorraine. 500 reasons why you're my best friend. Kansas City, Mo. : Andrews McMeel Pub., c2003.
BF575.F66 B63 2003

FEMALE FRIENDSHIP - RELIGIOUS ASPECTS - CHRISTIANITY.
Appel, Dee. Friend to friend. Sisters, Or. : Multnomah Publishers, c2002.
BF575.F66 A66 2002

FEMALE FRIENDSHIP - UNITED STATES.
Daniell, Beth, 1947- A communion of friendship. Carbondale : Southern Illinois University Press, c2003.
PE1405.U6 D36 2003

FEMALE GODS. *See* **GODDESSES.**

FEMALE HOMOSEXUALS. *See* **LESBIANS.**

Female impersonation.
Tyler, Carole-Anne. New York : Routledge, c2003.
HQ1190 .T95 2003

FEMALE-MALE RELATIONSHIPS. *See* **MAN-WOMAN RELATIONSHIPS.**

FEMALE STUDIES. *See* **WOMEN'S STUDIES.**

FEMALES. *See* **WOMEN.**

Femenilidades / Joel Birman (organização). Rio de Janeiro : Espaço Brasileiro de Estudos Psicanalíticos : Contra Capa, c2002. 115 p. ; 24 cm. (Coleção Espaço Brasileiro de Estudos Psicanalíticos) Includes bibliographical references (p. 107-115). ISBN 85-86011-51-7
1. Women - Psychology. 2. Femininity. 3. Psychoanalysis. 4. Women - Sexual behavior. I. Birman, Joel. II. Series.

FEMENINSM.
Serret, Estela. Identidad femenina y proyecto ético. 1. ed. México : UNAM, PUEG : Universidad Autónoma Metropolitana, Azcapotzalco : M.A. Porrúa, 2002.

FEMININE BEAUTY (AESTHETICS). *See also* **BEAUTY, PERSONAL.**
Western eyes [videorecording]. New York, NY : First Run/Icarus Films, 2000.

Feminine voices : toward a new millennium / Ma. Concepcion O. Abaya, editor. [Manila?] : NCCA, c2001- v. : ports. ; 18 x 26 cm. "A bio-bibliographical guide to women writers in fiction, general nonfiction, poetry, journalism, drama, literary criticism, screenplay, and other fields."
1. Feminism. 2. Philippine literature - Women authors - Biography. 3. Philippine literature - Bio-bibliography. 4. Women authors, Filipino - 20th century - Biography. 5. Authors, Filipino - 20th century - Biography. I. Abaya, Ma. Concepcion O. (Maria Concepcion O.) II. National Commission on Culture and the Arts (Philippines)

FEMININITY. *See also* **WOMEN.**
Balancing the scales. Lanham, Md. ; Oxford : University Press of America, c2003.
HQ1075 .B3417 2003

Budgeon, Shelley, 1967- Choosing a self. Westport, Conn. : Praeger, 2003.
HQ1229 .B83 2003

Femenilidades. Rio de Janeiro : Espaço Brasileiro de Estudos Psicanalíticos : Contra Capa, c2002.

Giuffrida, Angela, 1943- Il corpo pensa. Roma : Prospettiva, c2002.

Godfrind, Jacqueline. Comment la féminité vient aux femmes. Paris : Presses universitaires de France, c2001.
BF175.5.F45 G63 2001

Gromkowska, Agnieszka. Kobiecość w kulturze globalnej. POznań : Wolumin, 2002.

Studies on femininity. London ; New York : Karnac, 2003.

Tyler, Carole-Anne. Female impersonation. New York : Routledge, c2003.
HQ1190 .T95 2003

FEMININITY OF GOD.
Christ, Carol P. She who changes. 1st ed. New York ; Houndmills, England : Palgrave Macmillan, 2003.
BD372 .C48 2003

FEMININITY OF GOD IN LITERATURE.
Matthews, Caitlin, 1952- King Arthur and the goddess of the land. 2nd ed. Rochester, Vt. : Inner Traditions, 2002.
PB2273.M33 M36 2002

FEMININITY (PHILOSOPHY).
Le Dœuff, Michèle. The philosophical imaginary. London : Continuum, 2002.

Feminino e masculino.
Muraro, Rose Marie. Rio de Janeiro : Sextante, 2002.
HQ801 .M87 2002

FEMINISM. *See also* **FEMINIST THEORY; FEMINISTS; PSYCHOANALYSIS AND FEMINISM; WOMEN - HISTORY; WOMEN - SOCIAL CONDITIONS.**
Adeleke, Veronica I. Concept of gender equality as a paradox in Nigeria's democratic experience. Ikeja [Nigeria] : Dept. of Political Science and Sociology, Babcock University, 2002.
1. Black author.

Adkins, Lisa, 1966- Revisions. Buckingham [UK] ; Philadelphia : Open University Press, 2002.

HQ1075 .A24 2002

African women and feminism. Trenton, NJ : Africa World Press, c2003.
HQ1787 .A372 2003

Allard Olmos, Briseida, 1951- Mujer y poder. [Panamá] : Instituto de la Mujer - Universidad de Panamá, 2002.
HQ1154 .A62 2002

Alonso, Graciela. Hacia una pedagogía de las experiencias de las mujeres. 1. ed. Buenos Aires : Miño y Dávila, 2002.

Brush, Lisa Diane. Gender and governance. Walnut Creek, CA ; Oxford : AltaMira Press, c2003.
JC330 .B75 2003

Continental feminism reader. Lanham, Md. : Rowman & Littlefield Publishers, c2003.
HQ1075 .C668 2003

Cuomo, Chris J. The philosopher queen. Lanham, Md. ; Oxford : Rowman & Littlefield, c2003.
HQ1190 .C866 2003

Le deuxième sexe. Montréal : Éditions du Remue-ménage, 2001.

Ernst, Waltraud, 1964- Diskurspiratinnen. Wien : Milena, c1999.
HQ1154 .E7 1999

Exclusions in feminist thought. Brighton [England] ; Portland, Or. : Sussex Academic Press, 2002.
HQ1206 .E98 2002

Feminine voices [Manila?] : NCCA, c2001-

The feminism and visual culture reader. London ; New York : Routledge, 2003.
HQ1121 .F46 2003

Feminist futures. London ; New York : Zed Books ; New York : Distributed in the USA exclusively by Palgrave, c2003.
HQ1161 .F455 2003

Feminist utopias. Toronto : Inanna Publications and Education, 2002.

Fernandes, Leela. Transforming feminist practice. 1st ed. San Francisco : Aunt Lute Books, 2003.
HQ1154 .F495 2003

Field, Lynda. Woman power. Shaftesbury, Dorset ; Boston : Element, 1999.
HQ1206 .F4623 1999

Francis, Elizabeth, 1959- Feminism and modernism [microform]. [1994]

Gender. London ; New York : Routledge, 2002.
HQ1075 .G426 2002

Goldrick-Jones, Amanda, 1956- Men who believe in feminism. Westport, Conn. ; London : Praeger, 2002.
HQ1236 .G57 2002

Gromkowska, Agnieszka. Kobiecość w kulturze globalnej. POznań : Wolumin, 2002.

Hirdman, Yvonne, 1943- Genus. 1. uppl. Malmö : Liber, 2001.

Kricheldorf, Beate, 1949- Verantwortung, nein danke!. 2., unveränderte Aufl. Frankfurt/Main : R.G. Fischer, 2001, c1998.

Larrea, Martha Victoria. Movimiento femenino. Ibarra, Ecuador : [s.n.], 1997.

Leonel, Vange, 1963- Grrrls. São Paulo : Edições GLS, c2001.

Lister, Ruth, 1949- Citizenship. 2nd ed. Basingstoke, Hampshire ; New York : Palgrave Macmillan, 2003.
HQ1236 .L57 2003

Longstaff, Bill, 1934- Confessions of a matriarchist. Calgary : Ballot Pub., 2003.

Méndez, José Luis, 1941- El irresistible encanto de Betty la fea. San Juan, P.R. : Ediciones Milenio, 2001.

Milner, Andrew, 1950- Contemporary cultural theory. 3rd ed. Crows Nest, N.S.W. : Allen & Unwin, 2002.

Myrdal, Alva Reimer, 1902- "Något kan man väl göra. Stockholm : Carlssons, c2002.

Orenstein, Peggy. Women on work, love, children & life. London : Piatkus, 2000.

Quiet rumours. Edinburgh : San Francisco : AK Press/Dark Star, 2002.

Rowland, Susan, 1962- Jung. Cambridge, UK : Polity ; Malden, MA : Blackwell, 2002.

BF175.4.F45 R69 2002

Schlafly, Phyllis. Feminist fantasies. Dallas : Spence Publishing Co., 2003.
HQ1150 .S34 2003

Stange, Mary Zeiss. Woman the hunter. Boston : Beacon Press, c1997.
SK14 .S88 1997

The subject of care. Lanham, Md. ; Oxford : Rowman & Littlefield Publishers, c2002.
HQ1206 .S9 2002

Thompson, Patricia J. In bed with Procrustes. New York : P. Lang, c2003.
HQ1190 .T52 2002 bk. 2

Tooley, James. The miseducation of women. London ; New York : Continuum, 2002.
HQ1154 .T64 2002

Women's rights. San Diego, Calif. : Greenhaven Press, c2002.
HQ1236 .W6526 2002

Yuracko, Kimberly A., 1969- Perfectionism and contemporary feminist values. Bloomington : Indiana University Press, c2003.
HQ1206 .Y87 2003

FEMINISM AND ARCHITECTURE.
Building gender = Wien : Edition Selene, 2002.

FEMINISM AND EDUCATION.
Alonso, Graciela. Hacia una pedagogía de las experiencias de las mujeres. 1. ed. Buenos Aires : Miño y Dávila, 2002.

Tooley, James. The miseducation of women. London ; New York : Continuum, 2002.
HQ1154 .T64 2002

FEMINISM AND LITERATURE - CHINA.
Feminism/femininity in Chinese literature. Amsterdam ; New York : Rodopi, 2002.

Feminism and modernism [microform].
Francis, Elizabeth, 1959- [1994]

FEMINISM AND PSYCHOANALYSIS. See PSYCHOANALYSIS AND FEMINISM.

FEMINISM AND THE ARTS.
The feminism and visual culture reader. London ; New York : Routledge, 2003.
HQ1121 .F46 2003

The feminism and visual culture reader / edited by Amelia Jones. London ; New York : Routledge, 2003. xxix, 560 p. : ill., ports. ; 25 cm. (In sight) Includes bibliographical references and index. ISBN 0-415-26705-6 ISBN 0-415-26706-4 (pbk.) DDC 305.42
1. Feminism. 2. Feminism and the arts. 3. Visual communication. 4. Popular culture. I. Jones, Amelia. II. Series
HQ1121 .F46 2003

FEMINISM - BRAZIL.
Gênero em matizes. Bragança Paulista, SP : EDUSF, [2002]

FEMINISM - CONGRESSES.
Wissen Macht Geschlecht. Zürich : Chronos, c2002.

FEMINISM - ECUADOR.
Larrea, Martha Victoria. Movimiento femenino. Ibarra, Ecuador : [s.n.], 1997.

Feminism/femininity in Chinese literature / edited by Peng-hsiang Chen ; Whitney Crothers Dilley. Amsterdam ; New York : Rodopi, 2002. xii, 219 p. ; 24 cm. (Critical studies ; no. 18) Includes bibliographical references (p. [211]-219). ISBN 90-420-0727-3
1. Chinese literature - History and criticism. 2. Feminism in literature. 3. Feminism and literature - China. I. Chen, Huihua. II. Dilley, Whitney Crothers. III. Series.

FEMINISM - HEALTH ASPECTS.
McLeod, Carolyn. Self-trust and reproductive autonomy. Cambridge, Mass. : MIT Press, c2002.
RG133.5 .M39 2002

FEMINISM - HISTORY - 20TH CENTURY.
Tooley, James. The miseducation of women. London ; New York : Continuum, 2002.
HQ1154 .T64 2002

FEMINISM IN LITERATURE.
Feminism/femininity in Chinese literature. Amsterdam ; New York : Rodopi, 2002.

FEMINISM - LATIN AMERICA.
Allard Olmos, Briseida, 1951- Mujer y poder. [Panamá] : Instituto de la Mujer - Universidad de Panamá, 2002.
HQ1154 .A62 2002

Larrea, Martha Victoria. Movimiento femenino. Ibarra, Ecuador : [s.n.], 1997.

FEMINISM - MORAL AND ETHICAL ASPECTS.
See also **FEMINIST ETHICS**.
McLeod, Carolyn. Self-trust and reproductive autonomy. Cambridge, Mass. : MIT Press, c2002.
RG133.5 .M39 2002

FEMINISM - PHILOSOPHY. See FEMINIST THEORY.

FEMINISM - SWEDEN.
Hirdman, Yvonne, 1943- Genus. 1. uppl. Malmö : Liber, 2001.

Feminismos
(71) García de León, María Antonia. Herederas y heridas. 1a ed. [Madrid] : Ediciones Cátedra, Universitat de València, Instituto de la Mujer, 2002.
HD6054.2.S7 G37 2002

Feminismus und Gerechtigkeit.
Schwickert, Eva-Maria. Berlin : Akademie Verlag, c2000.

FEMINIST ARCHAEOLOGY.
Ancient queens. Walnut Creek, Calif. ; Oxford : AltaMira Press, c2003.
HQ1127 .A53 2003

Feminist constructions
Campbell, Sue, 1956- Relational remembering. Lanham, Md. ; Oxford : Rowman & Littlefield, c2003.
BF378.A87 C36 2003

Potter, Nancy Nyquist, 1954- How can I be trusted? Lanham, Md. ; Oxford : Rowman & Littlefield, c2002.
BJ1500.T78 P68 2002

The subject of care. Lanham, Md. ; Oxford : Rowman & Littlefield Publishers, c2002.
HQ1206 .S9 2002

FEMINIST CRITICISM.
Rishoi, Christy, 1958- From girl to woman. Albany : State University of New York Press, c2003.
HQ1186.A9 R57 2003

FEMINIST ETHICS.
Copjec, Joan. Imagine there's no woman. Cambridge, Mass. : MIT Press, 2002.
BJ1012 .C68 2002

Schwickert, Eva-Maria. Feminismus und Gerechtigkeit. Berlin : Akademie Verlag, c2000.

FEMINIST ETHICS - CONGRESSES.
Wissen Macht Geschlecht. Zürich : Chronos, c2002.

Feminist family therapy : empowerment in social context / edited by Louise B. Silverstein and Thelma Jean Goodrich. 1st ed. Washington, DC : American Psychological Association, c2003. xix, 393 p. : ill. ; 26 cm. (Psychology of women book series) Includes bibliographical references and indexes. ISBN 1-59147-021-8 DDC 616.89/156
1. Family psychotherapy. 2. Feminist therapy. I. Silverstein, Louise B. II. Goodrich, Thelma Jean, 1940- III. Series.
RC488.5 .F453 2003

Feminist fantasies.
Schlafly, Phyllis. Dallas : Spence Publishing Co., 2003.
HQ1150 .S34 2003

Feminist futures : re-imagining women, culture and development / efited by Kum-Kum Bhavnani, John Foran and Priya A. Kurian. London ; New York : Zed Books ; New York : Distributed in the USA exclusively by Palgrave, c2003. xvii, 309 p. ; 25 cm. Includes bibliographical references (p. [275]-298) and index. ISBN 1-84277-028-4 (cased) ISBN 1-84277-029-2 (limp) DDC 305.42
1. Feminism. 2. Women - Social conditions - Cross-cultural studies. 3. Sex role - Cross-cultural studies. I. Bhavnani, Kum-Kum. II. Foran, John. III. Kurian, Priya A.
HQ1161 .F455 2003

FEMINIST PSYCHOLOGY.
The complete guide to mental health for women. 1st ed. Boston : Beacon Press, c2003.
RC451.4.W6 C65 2003

Dimen, Muriel. Sexuality, intimacy, power. Hillsdale, NJ : Analytic Press, 2003.
BF201.4 .D556 2003

Gonick, Marnina. Between femininities. Albany : State University of New York Press, c2003.
HQ777 .G65 2003

Greene, Sheila, 1946- The psychological development of girls and women. London ; New York : Routledge, 2003.

HQ1206 .G767 2003

Henehan, Mary Pat. Integrating spirit and psyche. New York ; London : Haworth Pastoral Press, c2003.
RC489.F45 H46 2003

Korsström, Tuva. Kan kvinnor tänka? Stockholm/ Stehag : Symposion, 2002.

Rider, Elizabeth A. Our voices. Belmont, CA : Wadsworth, c2000.
HQ1206 .R54 2000

FEMINIST PSYCHOLOGY - CONGRESSES.
Konferentsiia "Gendernyĭ podkhod v psikhologicheskom konsul'tirovanii" (2002 : Evropeĭskiĭ Gumanitarnyĭ Universitet) Gendernyĭ podkhod v psikhologicheskikh issledovaniiakh i konsul'tirovanii. Minsk : Evropeĭskiĭ Gumanitarnyĭ Universitet, 2002.
BF201.4 .K66 2002

FEMINIST SOCIOLOGY. See **FEMINIST THEORY.**

FEMINIST STUDIES. See **WOMEN'S STUDIES.**

FEMINIST THEOLOGY.
Christ, Carol P. She who changes. 1st ed. New York ; Houndmills, England : Palgrave Macmillan, 2003.
BD372 .C48 2003

FEMINIST THEORY.
African women and feminism. Trenton, NJ : Africa World Press, c2003.
HQ1787 .A372 2003

Braidotti, Rosi. [Nomadic subjects. Italian] Soggetto nomade. Roma : Donzelli, 1995.

Cuomo, Chris J. The philosopher queen. Lanham, Md. ; Oxford : Rowman & Littlefield, c2003.
HQ1190 .C866 2003

Eller, Cynthia (Cynthia Lorraine) Am I a woman? Boston : Beacon Press, c2003.
HQ1190 .E424 2003

Heinamaa, Sara, 1960- Toward a phenomenology of sexual difference. Lanham, Md. ; Oxford : Rowman & Littlefield Publishers, c2003.
HQ1208 .B3523 2003

Kītā, Va. Gender. Calcutta : Stree, 2002.
HQ1075 .K576 2002

Le Dœuff, Michèle. The philosophical imaginary. London : Continuum, 2002.

Mills, Linda G. Insult to injury. Princeton, N.J. : Princeton University Press, c2003.
HV6626 .M55 2003

Songe-Möller, Vigdis. Philosophy without women. London : Continuum, c2002.

Thompson, Patricia J. In bed with Procrustes. New York : P. Lang, c2003.
HQ1190 .T52 2002 bk. 2

Tyler, Carole-Anne. Female impersonation. New York : Routledge, c2003.
HQ1190 .T95 2003

Violence and the body. Bloomington : Indiana University Press, c2003.
HM1116 .V557 2003

FEMINIST THEORY - CONGRESSES.
Wissen Macht Geschlecht. Zürich : Chronos, c2002.

FEMINIST THERAPY.
Feminist family therapy. 1st ed. Washington, DC : American Psychological Association, c2003.
RC488.5 .F453 2003

Henehan, Mary Pat. Integrating spirit and psyche. New York ; London : Haworth Pastoral Press, c2003.
RC489.F45 H46 2003

Working with the stories of women's lives. Adelaide : Dulwich Centre Publications, 2001.
HQ1185 .W68 2001

Feminist utopias : re-visioning our futures / edited by Margrit Eichler, June Larkin, Sheila Neysmith. Toronto : Inanna Publications and Education, 2002. 260 p. ; 23 cm. Includes bibliographical references. ISBN 0-9681290-7-2 (pbk.) DDC 305.42
1. Feminism. I. Eichler, Margrit. II. Neysmith, Sheila M., 943- III. Larkin, June, 1952-

FEMINISTS - FRANCE - BIOGRAPHY.
Aller, Annelies van, 1946- Levenskunst van twee vrouwen. Budel : Damon, c2001.
PS3527.I865 Z536 2001

FEMINISTS - UNITED STATES - BIOGRAPHY.
Gallop, Jane, 1952- Living with his camera. Durham : Duke University Press, 2003.
TR140.B517 G35 2003

FEMINITY.
Haen, Renate. Du bist die Göttin ; 1. Auf. Bergish Gladbach : Bastei Lübbe, 1999.

Femme/butch : new considerations of the way we want to go / Michelle Gibson, Deborah T. Meem, editors. New York : Harrington Park Press, 2002. 184 p. : ill. ; 22 cm. "Femme/Butch: new considerations of the way we want to go has been co-published simultaneously as Journal of lesbian studies, volume 6, Number 2, 2002." Includes bibliographical references and index. ISBN 1-56023-300-1 (cloth : alk. paper) ISBN 1-56023-301-X (pbk. : alk. paper) DDC 305.48/9664
1. Lesbians. 2. Lesbians - Identity. 3. Gender identity. 4. Lesbianism. I. Gibson, Michelle. II. Meem, Deborah T. (Deborah Townsend), 1949-
HQ75.5 .F459 2002

FENCES. See **HEDGES.**

Fenchel, Tom. Origin and early evolution of life / Tom Fenchel. Oxford New York : Oxford University Press, 2002. viii, 171 p., 7 p. of plates : ill. (some col.) ; 24 cm. Spine title: Origin & early evolution of life. Includes bibliographical references (p. [157]-159). ISBN 0-19-852635-0 (alk. paper) ISBN 0-19-852533-8 (alk. paper : pbk.) DDC 576.8/3
1. Life - Origin. 2. Evolution (Biology) I. Title. II. Title: Origin & early evolution of life
QH325 .F42 2002

Feng Shui.
Fretwell, Sally. Novato, Calif. : New World Library, [2002]
BF1779.F4 F74 2002

Feng shui.
Sandifer, Jon. London : Piatkus, 1999.

Summers, Selena, 1945- [Feng shui in 5 minutes. Spanish] 1. ed. St. Paul, Minn. : Llewellyn Español, 2003.
BF1779.F4 S84518 2003

Winnie-the-Pooh's little book of feng shui. London : Methuen Children's, 1999.

FENG SHUI.
Beattie, Antonia. Feng shui dictionary. San Diego, Calif. : Thunder Bay Press, c2003.
BF1779.F4 B43 2003

Bradler, Christine M. [Feng Shui Symbole des Ostens. English] Feng shui symbols. New York : Sterling Pub., c2001.
BF1779.F4 .B7313 2001

Bramble, Cate. Architect's guide to feng shui. Amsterdam ; Boston ; London : Architectural Press, 2003.
BF1779.F4 B73 2003

Clayton, Emily. Space clearing. San Diego, Calif. : Thunder Bay Press, c2003.
BF1779.F4 C58 2003

DeAmicis, Ralph. Feng shui American style. New York : Paraview Special Editions, c2003.
BF1779.F4 .D42 2003

Dexter, Rosalyn. Good vibes. London : Robson, 2001.

Eitel, Ernest John, 1838-1908. What is Feng-Shui? Mineola, N.Y. : Dover Publications, 2003.
BF1779.F4 E4 2003

Englebert, Clear. Feng shui demystified. Freedom, Calif. : Crossing Press, c2000.
BF1779.F4 E54 2000

Fretwell, Sally. Feng Shui. Novato, Calif. : New World Library, [2002]
BF1779.F4 F74 2002

Hsu, Shan-Tung, 1942- The yin & yang of love. 1st ed. St. Paul, Minn. : Llewellyn Publications, 2003.
BF1779.F4 H763 2003

Hsu, Shan-Tung, 1942- [Yin & yang of love. Spanish] Feng shui para el amor. 1. ed. St. Paul, Minn. : Llewellyn Espanol, 2003.
BF1779.F4 H76318 2003

Jones, Katina Z. The everything feng shui decluttering book. Avon, MA : Adams Media, c2004.
BF1779.F4 J663 2004

Lam, Kam Chuen. The Feng Shui kitchen. 1st ed. Boston : Journey Editions, c2000.
TX724.5.C4 L36 2000

Lambert, Mary. Feng shui guide to harmonious living. [New York] : Friedman/Fairfax : Distributed by Sterling, c2002.
BF1779.F4 L357 2002

The Learning Annex presents feng shui. 1st ed. New York, NY : J. Wiley, 2004.
BF1779.F4 L42 2004

Levitt, Susan. Teen feng shui. Rochester, Vt. : Bindu Books, c2003.
BF1779.F4 L465 2003

Lum, Alan S.F. (Alan Sun Fai) The centuries old philosophy and practice of traditional Chinese feng shui and the more advanced Flying Star feng shui. Honolulu : Lum Pub., c2002.
BF1779.F4 L86 2002

Mitchell, Shawne, 1958- [Exploring feng shui] Simple feng shui. New York : Gramercy Books, 2004.
BF1779.F4 M58 2004

O'Neil, Jennifer. Decorating with funky shui. Kansas City, MO : Andrews McMeel, 2004.
BF1779.F4 O54 2004

Sandifer, Jon. Feng shui. London : Piatkus, 1999.

Stasney, Sharon. Feng Shui living. New York : Sterling Pub., c2003.
BF1779.F4 S792 2003

Stasney, Sharon. Feng shui your work spaces. New York, NY : Sterling Pub. Co., c2004.
BF1779.F4 S796 2004

Summers, Selena, 1945- [Feng shui in 5 minutes. Spanish] Feng shui. 1. ed. St. Paul, Minn. : Llewellyn Español, 2003.
BF1779.F4 S84518 2003

Watson, Sylvia. Feng shui with what you have. Avon, MA : Adams Media, c2004.
BF1779.F4 W37 2004

Winnie-the-Pooh's little book of feng shui. London : Methuen Children's, 1999.

Wong, Angi Ma. Feng shui dos & taboos for love. Carlsbad, Calif. : Hay House, c2002.
BF1779.F4 W67 2002

Zeer, Darrin. Office Feng Shui. San Francisco : Chronicle Books, 2004.
BF1779.F4 Z44 2004

Feng shui American style.
DeAmicis, Ralph. New York : Paraview Special Editions, c2003.
BF1779.F4 .D42 2003

FENG SHUI - CHINA - HISTORY.
Bruun, Ole. Fengshui in China. Honolulu : University of Hawai'i Press, c2003.
BF1779.F4 B78 2003

Bruun, Ole, 1953- Fengshui in China. Copenhagen, Denmark : NIAS Press, c2003.

Feng shui demystified.
Englebert, Clear. Freedom, Calif. : Crossing Press, c2000.
BF1779.F4 E54 2000

Feng shui dictionary.
Beattie, Antonia. San Diego, Calif. : Thunder Bay Press, c2003.
BF1779.F4 B43 2003

Feng shui dos & taboos for love.
Wong, Angi Ma. Carlsbad, Calif. : Hay House, c2002.
BF1779.F4 W67 2002

Feng shui dos and taboos for love.
Wong, Angi Ma. Feng shui dos & taboos for love. Carlsbad, Calif. : Hay House, c2002.
BF1779.F4 W67 2002

Feng shui guide to harmonious living.
Lambert, Mary. [New York] : Friedman/Fairfax : Distributed by Sterling, c2002.
BF1779.F4 L357 2002

FENG SHUI - HUMOR.
Winnie-the-Pooh's little book of feng shui. London : Methuen Children's, 1999.

The Feng Shui kitchen.
Lam, Kam Chuen. 1st ed. Boston : Journey Editions, c2000.
TX724.5.C4 L36 2000

Feng Shui living.
Stasney, Sharon. New York : Sterling Pub., c2003.
BF1779.F4 S792 2003

Feng shui para el amor.
Hsu, Shan-Tung, 1942- [Yin & yang of love. Spanish] 1. ed. St. Paul, Minn. : Llewellyn Espanol, 2003.
BF1779.F4 H76318 2003

Feng shui symbols.
Bradler, Christine M. [Feng Shui Symbole des Ostens. English] New York : Sterling Pub., c2001.
BF1779.F4 .B7313 2001

Feng shui with what you have.
Watson, Sylvia. Avon, MA : Adams Media, c2004.
BF1779.F4 W37 2004

Feng shui your work spaces.
Stasney, Sharon. New York, NY : Sterling Pub. Co., c2004.
BF1779.F4 S796 2004

Feng, Youlan, 1895- Xin shi xun : sheng huo fang fa xin lun / Feng Youlan zhu. Di 1 ban. Beijing : Beijing da xue chu ban she : Jing xiao zhe Xin hua shu dian, 1996. 156 p. ; 21 cm. ISBN 7-301-03212-9
1. Conduct of life. I. Title.
BJ1588.C5 F42 1996 <Asian China>

Fengshui in China.
Bruun, Ole. Honolulu : University of Hawai'i Press, c2003.
BF1779.F4 B78 2003

Bruun, Ole, 1953- Copenhagen, Denmark : NIAS Press, c2003.

FENNOSCANDIA. *See* **SCANDINAVIA.**

La fenomelogia tra essenza ed esistenza.
Ledda, Antonio. 1. ed. Roma : Carocci editore, 2002.

Fenomenologīiā smekha : karikatura, parodiīā, grotesk v sovremennoĭ kul'ture / [otv. redaktor i sostavitel' Shestakov V.P.]. Moskva : Rossiĭskiĭ institut kul'turologii, 2002. 269 p. : ill. ; 25 cm. ISBN 593719022X
1. Parody. 2. Russian wit and humor, Pictorial. 3. Laughter. I. Shestakov, Vīācheslav Pavlovich.
PN6149.P3 F45 2002

Fensel, Dieter.
Towards the semantic web. Chichester, England ; Hoboken, N.J. : J. Wiley, c2003.
TK5105.88815 .T68 2003

Fenster, Bob. Well, duh! : our stupid world and welcome to it / Bob Fenster. Kansas City, MO : Andrews McMeel Pub., 2004. p. cm. ISBN 0-7407-4176-4 DDC 904
1. Stupidity - History. 2. Stupidity - Anecdotes. I. Title.
BF431 .F37 2004

Fenton, Sasha. Astrology for wimps / Sasha Fenton. New York : Sterling Pub., c2003. 128 p. : col. ill. ; 28 cm. (For wimps series) Includes index. Publisher description URL: http://www.loc.gov/catdir/description/ste031/2003045750.html ISBN 1402703848 DDC 133.5
1. Astrology. I. Title. II. Series.
BF1708.1 .F453 2003

How to be psychic / Sasha Fenton. New York : Sterling Pub., c2003. 150 p. : 1 ill. ; 21 cm. "A Sterling/Zambezi book." Includes index. ISBN 1402707789 DDC 133.8
1. Psychic ability. I. Title.
BF1031 .F46 2003

Super tarot : how to link tarot cards to reveal the future / Sasha Fenton. New York : Sterling Pub., 2003. 150 p. : ill. ; 23 cm. "A Sterling/Zambezi book". Includes index. ISBN 1402705735 (pbk.) DDC 133.3/2424
1. Tarot. I. Title. II. Title: How to link tarot cards to reveal the future
BF1879.T2 F465 2003

Fenton, Steve, 1942- Ethnicity / Steve Fenton. Cambridge : Polity ; Oxford ; Malden, MA : Blackwell, c2003. x, 220 p. ; 23 cm. (Key concepts) Includes bibliographical references (p. [198]-209) and index. CONTENTS: Ethnos: descent and culture communities -- Discourses of ethnicity in three settings: USA, the UK and Malaysia -- The demise of race: the emergence of 'ethnic' -- The primordialism debate -- Key points in the ethnicity literature -- Migration, ethnicity and mobilization -- Conditions of ethnicity: global economy and precarious states -- States, nations and the ethnic majority: a problem of modernity -- Ethnicity and modernity: general conclusions. ISBN 0-7456-2286-0 (hb) ISBN 0-7456-2287-9 (pb) DDC 305.8
1. Ethnicity. 2. Ethnic relations. 3. Race relations. I. Title. II. Series: Key concepts (Polity Press)
GN495.6 .F46 2003

Feo, Giovanni. Prima degli etruschi : i miti della grande dea e dei giganti alle origini della civiltà in Italia / Giovanni Feo. Roma : Stampa alternativa, 2001. 149 p. : ill. (some col.) ; 21 cm. (Eretica) Includes bibliographical references. ISBN 88-7226-638-6 DDC 291

1. Mythology, Roman. 2. Etruscans - Religion. I. Title. II. Series.
BL813.E8 F46 2001

FERAL ANIMALS. *See* **DOMESTIC ANIMALS.**

Ferber, Sarah, 1957- Demonic possession and exorcism in early modern France / Sarah Ferber. London ; New York, NY : Routledge, 2004. p. cm. Includes bibliographical references. ISBN 0-415-21264-2 (hardcover) ISBN 0-415-21265-0 (pbk.) DDC 235/.4/0944
1. Demoniac possession - France - History. 2. Exorcism - France - History. I. Title.
BF1517.F5 F47 2004

FERENCZI, SÁNDOR, 1873-1933 - CORRESPONDENCE - HISTORY AND CRITICISM.
Junker, Helmut, 1934- Unter Übermenschen. Tübingen : Edition Diskord, c1997.
BF109.F74 J85 1997

Ferens, Dominika, 1964-.
Odmiany odmieńca. Katowice : "Śląsk", 2002.
HQ23 .O36 2002

Ferguson, Everett, 1933- Backgrounds of early Christianity / Everett Ferguson. 3rd ed. Grand Rapids, Mich. : W.B. Eerdmans, c2003. xxii, 648 p. : ill., map ; 25 cm. Includes bibliographical references and indexes. ISBN 0-8028-2221-5
1. Christianity - Origin. 2. Rome - History - Republic, 510-30 B.C. 3. Philosophy, Ancient. 4. Judaism - History - Post-exilic period, 586 B.C.-210 A.D. I. Title.

FERMENTATION. *See* **BREWING.**

Fernandes, Leela. Transforming feminist practice : non-violence, social justice and the possibilities of a spiritualized feminism / by Leela Fernandes. 1st ed. San Francisco : Aunt Lute Books, 2003. 146 p. ; 22 cm. Includes bibliographical references (p. 139-146). ISBN 1-87996-067-2 DDC 305.42
1. Feminism. 2. Social action. 3. Social justice. 4. Nonviolence. 5. Spirituality. I. Title.
HQ1154 .F495 2003

Fernández-Armesto, Felipe. Civilizations : culture, ambition, and the transformation of nature / Felipe Fernández-Armesto. New York : Free Press, c2001. xii, 545 p. ; 25 cm. Includes bibliographical references (p. [469]-505) and index. CONTENTS: Itch to civilize -- Waste land: desert, tundra, ice: Helm of ice, ice worlds and tundra as human habitats -- Death of earth, adaptation and counteradaptation in deserts of sand -- Leaves of grass, barely cultivable grasslands, Sweepings of the wind, prairie and grassy savanna -- Highway of civilizations, Eurasian steppe -- Under the rain, civilization in tropical lowlands and postglacial forests: Wild woods, postglacial and temperate woodland -- Hearts of darkness, tropical lowlands -- Shining fields of mud, alluvial soils in drying climates: Lone and level sands, misleading cases in the Near East -- Of shoes and rice, transcending environments of origin in China and India -- Mirrors of sky, civilizing highlands: Gardens of the clouds, highland civilizations of the new world -- Climb to paradise, highland civilizations of the old world -- Water margins, civilizations shaped by the sea: Allotments of the gods, small-island civilizations -- View from the shore: nature of seaboard civilizations -- Chasing the monsoon, seaboard civilizations of maritime Asia -- Tradition of Ulysses, Greek and Roman seaboards -- Breaking the waves, domestication of the oceans: Almost the last environment, rise of oceanic civilizations -- Refloating Atlantis, making of Atlantic civilization -- Atlantic and after, Atlantic supremacy and the global outlook. ISBN 0-7432-0248-1 ISBN 0-7432-0249-X (pbk.) DDC 909
1. Civilization - History. 2. Human geography. 3. Human ecology. 4. Nature - Effect of human beings on. 5. Ambition - History. I. Title.
CB151 .F47 2001

Fernández Ballesteros, Rocío.
Encyclopedia of psychological assessment. London ; Thousand Oaks, Calif. : SAGE Publications, 2003.
BF39 .E497 2003

Fernández Christlieb, Fátima. La responsabilidad de los medios de comunicación / Fátima Fernández Christlieb. 1a. ed. México : Paidós, 2002. 193 p. ; 23 cm. (Paidós croma ; 4) Includes bibliographical references (p. [189]-193). ISBN 968-853-496-X
1. Mass media - Social aspects - Mexico. 2. Mass media - Political aspects - Mexico. 3. Responsibility. 4. Journalism - Social aspects - Mexico. I. Title. II. Series.

Fernández, Eva M. Bilingual sentence processing : relative clause attachment in English and Spanish / Eva M. Fernández. Amsterdam ; Philadelphia : J. Benjamins Pub., 2003. xiv, 292 p. : ill. ; 23 cm. (Language acquisition & language disorders, 0925-0123 ; v. 29) Includes bibliographical references (p. [273]-284) and indexes. ISBN 1-58811-345-0 DDC 404/.2
1. Bilingualism - Psychological aspects. 2. English language - Relative clauses. 3. Spanish language - Relative clauses. 4. Psycholinguistics. I. Title. II. Series.
P115.4 .F47 2003

Fernández, Horacio.
Romero, Pedro G., 1964- En el ojo de la batalla. Valencia : Universitat de València, 2002.

Ferraiuolo, Augusto. "Pro exoneratione sua propria coscientia" : le accuse per stregoneria nella Capua del XVII-XVIII secolo / Augusto Ferraiuolo. Milano : F. Angeli, c2000. 192 p. ; 23 cm. (Collana di antropologia culturale e sociale ; 48) Includes bibliographical references (p. 190-192). ISBN 88-464-2119-1
1. Witchcraft - Italy - Capua - History. 2. Magic - Italy - Capua - History. I. Title. II. Series: Antropologia culturale e sociale. Serie "Studi e ricerche" ; 48.
BF1584.I8 F44 2000

Ferrara, Franco, 1938- Dalle tenebre alla luce / Franco Ferrara. Cosenza, Italia : Brenner, c2002. 196 p. : ill. ; 21 cm. Includes bibliographical references. DDC 133
1. Hermetism. I. Title.

Ferrari, Michel, Ph. D.
Beyond knowledge. Mahwah, N.J. : L. Erlbaum Associates, 2003.
BF412 .B44 2003

Ferrari, Mirella.
Peri, Vittorio. Da oriente e da occidente. Roma : Editrice Antenore, 2002.
BR162.3 .P475 2002

Ferrarotti, Franco.
Le figure del padre. Roma : Armando editore, c2001.

Ferrater Mora, José, 1912- [Selections. English. 2003]
Three Spanish philosophers : Unamuno, Ortega, Ferrater Mora / José Ferrater Mora ; edited and with an introduction by J.M. Terricabras. Albany : State University of New York Press, c2003. vii, 268 p. ; 23 cm. (SUNY series in Latin American and Iberian thought and culture) Includes bibliographical references and indexes. ISBN 0-7914-5714-1 (pbk.) ISBN 0-7914-5713-3 DDC 196/.1
1. Unamuno, Miguel de, - 1864-1936. 2. Ortega y Gasset, José, - 1883-1955. 3. Death. I. Terricabras, Josep-Maria, 1946- II. Title. III. Series.
B4568.U54 F3913 2003

Ferrero, Ernesto. Lezioni napoleoniche : sulla natura degli uomini, le tecniche del buon governo e l'arte di gestire le sconfitte / Ernesto Ferrero. 1. ed. Milano : Mondadori, 2002. 165 p. ; 19 cm. Includes bibliographical references (p. 163-165). ISBN 88-04-51044-7 DDC 944
1. Napoleon - I, - Emperor of the French, - 1769-1821. 2. Leadership. I. Title.

Ferrières, Madeleine. Histoire des peurs alimentaires : du Moyen Age à l'aube du XXe siècle / Madeleine Ferrières. Paris : Editions du Seuil, c2002. 472 p. ; 21 cm. (Univers historique) Includes bibliographical references (p. 441-[464]) and index. ISBN 2-02-047661-4 DDC 900
1. Food habits - Psychological aspects. 2. Food habits - History. 3. Fear. 4. Food - Safety measures. I. Title. II. Series.

Ferry, Luc. Qu'est-ce qu'une vie réussie? / Luc Ferry. Paris : Grasset, c2002. 486 p. ; 23 cm. Includes bibliographical references. ISBN 2-246-53551-4 DDC 194
1. Success. 2. Philosophy. I. Title.
BJ1612 .F47 2002

FERTILE CRESCENT. *See* **MIDDLE EAST.**

Fesmire, Steven, 1967- John Dewey and moral imagination : pragmatism in ethics / Steven Fesmire. Bloomington, IN : Indiana University Press, c2003. xii, 167 p. ; 25 cm. Includes bibliographical references (p. [153]-160) and index. CONTENTS: Habit and character -- The pragmatic turn -- Pragmatism's reconstruction of reason -- Imagination in pragmatist ethics -- Dramatic rehearsal -- The Deweyan ideal -- The moral artist. ISBN 0-253-34233-3 (alk. paper) ISBN 0-253-21598-6 (pbk. : alk. paper) DDC 171/.2
1. Dewey, John, - 1859-1952. 2. Ethics. 3. Pragmatism. 4. Imagination (Philosophy) I. Title.
BJ1031 .F47 2003

FESTIVAL-DAY SERMONS, JEWISH.
Druḳ, Ya'aḳov ben Zalman. Ohel Ya'aḳov. Yerushala[yi]m : Y. ben Z. Druḳ, 762 [2002]
BS1225.4 .D77 2002

Yalḳuṭ Ṭuv ha-peninim. Yerushala[y]im : P. Y. Liberman, 762 [2001 or 2002]
BS1225.53 .Y35 2001

Festival of Yoruba arts and culture.
Ká má baa gbàgbé. [Nigeria] : Jadeas Productions, [2003]

FESTIVALS. *See* **FASTS AND FEASTS; PAGEANTS.**

FESTIVALS - EUROPE - HISTORY - 16TH CENTURY.
Court festivals of the European Renaissance. Aldershot ; Burlington, VT : Ashgate, c2002.

FESTIVALS - EUROPE - HISTORY - 17TH CENTURY.
Court festivals of the European Renaissance. Aldershot ; Burlington, VT : Ashgate, c2002.

FESTIVALS - JEWS. *See* **FASTS AND FEASTS - JUDAISM.**

Festschrift für Manfred Korfmann.
Mauerschau. Remshalden-Grunbach : Greiner, 2002.

FETAL BEHAVIOR.
Canault, Nina. Comment le désir de naître vient au foetus. Paris : Desclée de Brouwer, c2001.

FETISHISM.
Emtcheu, André. Psychologie et révélation. Yaoundé, Cameroun : Editions SHERPA, c2001.
  1. Black author.

Fettke, Rich. Extreme success : the 7-part program that shows you how to succeed without struggle / Rich Fettke ; foreword by Richard Carlson. New York : Fireside Book, c2002. 284 p. : ill. ; 22 cm. Publisher description URL: http://www.loc.gov/catdir/description/simon031/2003544993.html ISBN 0-7432-2953-3 ISBN 0-7432-2314-4 (pbk.) DDC 158.1
  1. Success - Psychological aspects. 2. Achievement motivation. I. Title.
BF637.S8 F46 2002

FETUS.
Canault, Nina. Comment le désir de naître vient au foetus. Paris : Desclée de Brouwer, c2001.

Fetzer, James H., 1940-.
Consciousness evolving. Amsterdam ; Philadelphia, Pa. : John Benjamins Pub., c2002.
B808.9 .C665 2002

Feuchtwang, Stephan.
Bruun, Ole, 1953- Fengshui in China. Copenhagen, Denmark : NIAS Press, c2003.

FEUDAL TENURE. *See* **LAND TENURE.**

FEUDALISM.
Duby, Georges. Qu'est-ce que la société féodale? Paris : Flammarion, c2002.

Feuerstein, Georg. The deeper dimension of Yoga : theory and practice / Georg Feuerstein. Boston : Shambhala, 2003. xv, 415 p. ; 23 cm. Includes bibliographical references (p. 377-386) and index. ISBN 1-57062-935-8 DDC 181/.45
  1. Yoga. I. Title.
B132.Y6 F4875 2003

Feyereisen, Pierre.
Qu'est-ce-donc qu'apprendre? Lausanne : Delachaux et Niestlé, 1999.
BF318 .Q84 1999

Fichtelberg, Joseph. Critical fictions : sentiment and the American market, 1780-1870 / Joseph Fichtelberg. Athens : University of Georgia Press, c2003. x, 280 p. ; 24 cm. Includes bibliographical references and index. ISBN 0-8203-2434-5 (alk. paper) DDC 810.9/353
  1. American prose literature - 1783-1850 - History and criticism. 2. Sentimentalism in literature. 3. American prose literature - 19th century - History and criticism. 4. Literature and society - United States - History - 19th century. 5. Literature and society - United States - History - 18th century. 6. Social problems in literature. 7. Middle class in literature. 8. Liberalism in literature. 9. Sympathy in literature. 10. Emotions in literature. I. Title.
PS366.S35 F53 2003

FICINO, MARSILIO, 1433-1499 - CRITICISM AND INTERPRETATION.
De Pace, Anna. La scepsi, il sapere e l'anima. Milano : LED, c2002.

FICTION. *See* **GHOST STORIES; LEGENDS; ROMANTICISM.**

FICTION - AUTHORSHIP.
Tan, Amy The opposite of fate. New York : Putnam c2003.
PS3570.A48 Z47 2003

FICTION - HISTORY AND CRITICISM. *See also* **PSYCHOLOGICAL FICTION.**
Opdahl, Keith M., 1934- Emotion as meaning. Lewisburg [Pa.] : Bucknell University Press ; London ; Cranbury, NJ : Associated University Presses, c2002.
PN56.E6 O54 2002

FICTION - HISTORY AND CRITICISM - THEORY, ETC.
Hague, Angela. Fiction, intuition, & creativity. Washington, D.C. : Catholic University of America Press, c2003.
PR826 .H28 2003

Fiction, intuition, & creativity.
Hague, Angela. Washington, D.C. : Catholic University of America Press, c2003.
PR826 .H28 2003

Fiction, intuition, and creativity.
Hague, Angela. Fiction, intuition, & creativity. Washington, D.C. : Catholic University of America Press, c2003.
PR826 .H28 2003

FICTION - PHILOSOPHY. *See* **FICTION.**

FICTION, PSYCHOLOGICAL. *See* **PSYCHOLOGICAL FICTION.**

FICTION - TECHNIQUE. *See* **FIRST PERSON NARRATIVE; PSYCHOLOGICAL FICTION.**

FICTION - TECHNIQUE - CONGRESSES.
Colloque des Invalides (5th : 2001 : Hôtel des invalides) Ce que je ne sais pas. Tusson, Charente : Du Lérot, [2002?]
PQ145 .C65 2001

FICTION WRITING. *See* **FICTION - TECHNIQUE.**

FICTITIOUS ANIMALS. *See* **ANIMALS, MYTHICAL.**

FICTITIOUS CHARACTERS.
Adeleye, Modupe, 1980- From our hearts. Rochester, N.Y. : Mo-Biz Publishing Co., 2003.
BF353 .A33 2003

Fiebach, Joachim.
Herrschaft des Symbolischen. Berlin : Vistas, c2002.

Fiedler, Klaus, 1951-.
Bless, Herbert. Social cognition. Hove, East Sussex, UK ; New York : Psychology Press, 2003.
BF323.S63 B55 2003

Stereotyping as inductive hypothesis testing / Klaus Fiedler & Eva Walther. Hove (UK) ; New York : Psychology Press, c2003. p. cm. Includes bibliographical references. Table of contents URL: http://www.loc.gov/catdir/toc/ecip043/2003010529.html CONTENTS: The topic of social hypothesis testing -- Stereotyping as a cognitive-environmental learning process : delineating the conceptual framework -- Learning of social hypotheses stereotypes as illusory correlations -- The auto-verification of social hypotheses -- Information search in the "inner world" : the origin of stereotypes in memory -- Testing social hypotheses in trivariate problem space : further variants of environmental stereotype learning -- Explicit and implicit hypothesis testing in a complex environment -- The vicissitudes of information sampling in a fallible environment : an integrative framework -- Epilogue: Locating CELA in modern stereotype research. ISBN 0-86377-832-1 DDC 303.3/85/072
  1. Stereotype (Psychology) - Research - Methodology. 2. Social sciences - Research - Methodology. I. Walther, Eva, 1964- II. Title.
BF323.S63 F54 2003

Field, Lynda. Woman power / Lynda Field. Shaftesbury, Dorset ; Boston : Element, 1999. 1 v. (various pagings) ; 10 cm. ISBN 1-86204-632-8 (pb) DDC 305.42
  1. Feminism. I. Title.
HQ1206 .F4623 1999

Field notes.
White, Sharon. Center City, Minn. : Hazelden, 2002.
BF575.G7 W485 2002

FIELD SPORTS. *See* **HUNTING; SPORTS.**

Fierens, Christian. Lecture de l'étourdit : Lacan 1972 / Christian Fierens. Paris : Harmattan, c2002. 304 p. : ill. ; 22 cm. (Collection Etudes psychanalytiques) Includes bibliographical references (p. [299]-301). ISBN 2-7475-2985-1 DDC 150
  1. Lacan, Jacques, - 1901- 2. Psychoanalysis. I. Title. II. Series: Etudes psychanalytiques.
BF109.L28 F53 2002

Fiet's vase and other stories of survival, Europe 1939-1945.
Gold, Alison Leslie. New York : Jeremy P. Tarcher/Penguin, c2003.
D804.3 .G64 2003

Fiévé, Pascal.
Fourier, Charles, 1772-1837. Du libre arbitre. Bordeaux : Saints Calus, 2003.

Fifteen-second principle.
Secunda, Al. The 15-second principle. Franklin Lakes, NJ : Career Press, 2004.
BF637.S4 S43 2004

The fifth book of peace.
Kingston, Maxine Hong. 1st ed. New York : Alfred A. Knopf, 2003.
PS3561.I52 F44 2003

FIFTH GENERATION COMPUTERS. *See* **ARTIFICIAL INTELLIGENCE.**

Fifty key thinkers in psychology.
Sheehy, Noel, 1955- London ; New York : Routledge, 2003.
BF109.A1 S49 2003

Fifty-Minute series.
Braham, Barbara J. Finding your purpose. Rev. ed. Menlo Park, CA : Crisp Publications, c2003.
BF637.S4 B67 2003

Decker, Dru Scott, 1942- Stress that motivates. Rev. ed. Menlo Park, CA : Crisp Publications, c2002.
BF575.S75 D38 2002

FIGHTER PILOTS.
Robertson, Linda R. (Linda Raine), 1946- The dream of civilized warfare. Minneapolis : University of Minnesota Press, c2003.
D606 .R63 2003

FIGHTING. *See* **COMBAT; WAR.**

FIGHTING (PSYCHOLOGY).
Johnston, Marianne. [Dealing with fighting. Spanish] Como tratar las peleas. New York : PowerKids Press, 2005.
BF637.I48 J6418 2005

FIGHTING (PSYCHOLOGY) - JUVENILE LITERATURE.
Johnston, Marianne. [Dealing with fighting. Spanish] Como tratar las peleas. New York : PowerKids Press, 2005.
BF637.I48 J6418 2005

Figueiredo, Luís Cláudio M. (Luís Cláudio Mendonça), 1945- Antonio Gomes Penna : razão e história / Luís Cláudio Figueiredo. Brasília, DF : Conselho Federal de Psicologia ; Rio de Janeiro, RJ : Imago, 2002. 99 p. : 1 ill. ; 21 cm. (Coleção Pioneiros da psicologia brasileira ; 9) Includes bibliographical references (p. 99). ISBN 85-312-0810-6
  1. Penna, Antonio Gomes, - 1917- 2. Psycholosgists - Brazil - Biography. 3. Psychology - Brazil - History. I. Title. II. Series.

Le figure del padre : ricerche interdisciplinari / [testi di] Franco Ferrarotti ... [et al.]. Roma : Armando editore, c2001. 219 p. ; 24 cm. (Antropologia culturale) Includes bibliographical references. ISBN 88-8358-105-9 DDC 306
  1. Fathers. 2. Fatherhood. I. Ferrarotti, Franco. II. Series.

La figure des héros dans la création contemporaine / [rédaction en chef Kazem Shahryari]. Paris : Harmattan, c2002. 160 p. : ill. ; 22 cm. (Collection Création/réel) (Convergences ; cahier no 1) "Ce numéro est co-réalisé avec les XIXème Rencontres Charles-Dullin"--P. [7]. ISBN 2-7475-2246-6 DDC 790
  1. Creation (Literary, artistic, etc.) 2. Heroes in art. I. Shahryari, Kazem. II. Series. III. Series: Création/réel. Convergences ; cahier no 1

FIGURE-GROUND PERCEPTION. *See* **PATTERN PERCEPTION; SPACE PERCEPTION.**

Figures
Marion, Jean-Luc, 1946- Le phénomène érotique. Paris : Grasset, c2003.
BH301.L65 M37 2003

Figures de la marge : marginalité et identité dans le monde contemporain / textes réunis et présentés par Hélène Menegaldo. Rennes : Presses universitaires de Rennes, [2002] 193 p. ; 24 cm. (Collection des "sociétés", 1242-8523) Includes bibliographical references (p. 185-189). ISBN 2-86847-686-4 DDC 300
  1. Marginality, Social. 2. Identity (Philosophical concept) I. Menegaldo, Hélène. II. Series: Des sociétés.

Les figures de l'organisation.
Guillo, Dominique. 1. éd. Paris : Presses universitaires de France, 2003.

FIGURES OF SPEECH.
Barnette, Martha. Dog days and dandelions. 1st ed. New York : St. Martin's Press, 2003.
PE1583 .B37 2003

Giora, Rachel, 1945- On our mind. New York : Oxford University Press, c2003.

Figures of speech.

BF455 .G525 2003
Hargraves, Orin. Mighty fine words and smashing expressions. Oxford ; New York : Oxford University Press, 2003.
PE1711 .H37 2003
Hoggart, Richard, 1918- Everyday language & everyday life. New Brunswick, N.J. ; London : Transaction Publishers, c2003.
PE1074.8 .H64 2003
Spears, Richard A. NTC's dictionary of everyday American English expressions. Lincolnwood, Ill. : National Textbook Co., c1994.
PE2839 .S65 1994

Figuring space.
Châtelet, Gilles. [Enjeux du mobile. English] Dordrecht ; Boston : Kluwer, c2000.
B67 .C4313 2000

Filarete
(208.) De Pace, Anna. La scepsi, il sapere e l'anima. Milano : LED, c2002.

Filber, Ya'aḳov, ha-Leṿi.
Mar'eh Kohen. Yerushalayim : Makhon le-ḥeḳer mishnat ha-Re'iyah Ḳuḳ be-shituf 'im "Bet ha-Rav", c762 [2001 or 2002]

Filho, Amilcar Torrão. Tríbades galantes, fanchonos militantes : homossexuais que fizeram história / Amilcar Torrão Filho ; [apresentação, Ronaldo Vainfas]. São Paulo : Edições GLS, 2000. 294 p. ; 21 cm. Includes bibliographical references (p. 283-293) ISBN 85-86755-24-9
1. Homosexuality - History. 2. Gays - History. 3. Celebrities. I. Title.

FILIPINO AUTHORS. *See* **AUTHORS, FILIPINO.**

FILIPINO WOMEN AUTHORS. *See* **WOMEN AUTHORS, FILIPINO.**

FILIPINOS - CANADA - CULTURAL ASSIMILATION.
Western eyes [videorecording]. New York, NY : First Run/Icarus Films, 2000.

FILIPINOS - CANADA - ETHNIC IDENTITY.
Western eyes [videorecording]. New York, NY : First Run/Icarus Films, 2000.

FILM ACTORS. *See* **MOTION PICTURE ACTORS AND ACTRESSES.**

FILM ADAPTATIONS.
Shakespeare, the movie, II: popularizing the plays on film, TV, video, and DVD. London ; New York : Routledge, 2003.
PR3093 .S543 2003

FILM STARS. *See* **MOTION PICTURE ACTORS AND ACTRESSES.**

FILMS. *See* **MOTION PICTURES.**

Filmstudien (Mainz, Rhineland-Palatinate, Germany)
(Bd. 24.) Bühler, Gerhard, 1959- Postmoderne auf dem Bildschirm, auf der Leinwand. Sankt Augustin : Gardez!, c2002.

La filosofia antica.
Trabattoni, Franco. 1a ed. Roma : Carocci, 2002.

La filosofia come scienza della vita.
Tapergi, Fausto, 1909- 1a ed. Milano : Spirali, 2001.

Filosofia da cultura.
Sampaio, Luiz Sergio Coelho de, 1933- Rio de Janeiro : Editora Agora da Ilha, 2002.

La filosofia dell'immaginazione in Vico e Malebranche.
Fabiani, Paolo, 1968- Firenze : Firenze University Press, 2002.
B3583.F25 F55 2002

Filosofia e scienza cognitiva.
Marconi, Diego, 1947- 1. ed. Roma-Bari : Editori Laterza, 2001.
BF311 .M36 2001

Filosofia e scienza nel Cinquecento e nel Seicento. Ser. 1.: Studi
(58) Landucci, Sergio, 1938- La mente in Cartesio. Milano : FrancoAngeli, 2002.

La filosofía medieval / edición de Francisco Bertelloni, Giannina Burlando. Madrid : Trotta, 2002. 378 p. ; 23 cm. (Enciclopedia iberoamericana de filosofía ; 24) Includes bibliographical references and indexes. ISBN 84-8164-535-4 DDC 189
1. Philosophy, Medieval. 2. Philosophy, Spanish - History. I. Bertelloni, Francisco. II. Burlando Bravo, Giannina. III. Series.

B721 .F47 2002

Filosofia (Pisa, Italy)
(50-51.) Materiali per un lessico della ragione. Pisa : Edizioni ETS, c2001.

Filosofía, retórica e interpretación / Helena Beristáin, Mauricio Beuchot (compiladores). México, D.F. : Universidad Nacional Autónoma de México, 2000. 178 p. : ill. ; 20 cm. Includes bibliographical references. ISBN 968-36-8483-1
1. Philosophy. 2. Rhetoric. 3. Interpretation (Philosophy) I. Beristáin, Helena. II. Beuchot, Mauricio.

Filosofia. Ricerche
La persona e i nomi dell'essere. Milano : V&P Università, c2002.
B29 .P414 2002

Sequeri, Pier Angelo. L'umano alla prova. Milano : V & P Università, c2002.
BD222.S47 U6 2002

Filosofia (Rome, Italy)
Marconi, Diego, 1947- Filosofia e scienza cognitiva. 1. ed. Roma-Bari : Editori Laterza, 2001.
BF311 .M36 2001

Filosofia, storia, istituzioni.
Sichirollo, Livio. Nuova ed. [Urbino] : Università degli studi di Urbino, [2001]

La filosofía y el lenguaje en la historia.
Beuchot, Mauricio. México, D.F. : UNAM, 2000.

Filosofiia.
Bahniuk, Anatoliĭ. Rivne : [s.n.], 1997.

Filosofiia i teoriia istorii.
Rozov, N. S. (Nikolaĭ Sergeevich) Moskva : Logos, 2002-
D16.8 .R873 2002

Filosofskaia psikhologiia.
Sergeev, K. K. (Konstantin Konstantinovich) Tol'iatti : "Sovremennik", 1999.
BF38 .S47 1999

Filosofskie i ėticheskie problemy genetiki cheloveka.
Kessidi, F. Kh. Moskva : Martis, 1994.
BF341 .K45 1994

Filosofsko-metodologicheskie osnovy gumanitarnogo znaniia : sbornik aspirantskikh rabot / [pod redaktsieĭ A.L. Zorina, S.IU. Nekliudova]. Moskva : Rossiĭskiĭ gosudarstvennyĭ gumanitarnyĭ universitet, 2001. 302 p. ; 20 cm. Includes bibliographical references. ISBN 5728102689
1. Knowledge, Theory of - Congresses. 2. Humanities - Methodology - Congresses. I. Zorin, A. L. (Andreĭ L.) II. Nekliudov, S. IU.
BD166 .F489 2001

Filozofija minima.
Mićunović, Dragoljub. Beograd : "Filip Višnjić", 2001.
H61.15 .M5 2001

Filozofski izvori fašizma i nacionalnog socijalizma.
Bošković, Hijacint. 2. izd. Zagreb : Dom i svijet, 2000.
B804 .B66 2000

El fin de la inocencia.
Simonetti, José María, 1942- Bernal, Argentina : Universidad Nacional de Quilmes, 2002.
JF1081 S57 2002

El fin del sexo y otras mentiras.
Moreno, María, 1947- Buenos Aires : Editorial Sudamericana, c2002.

La fin des temps / L.A.P.R.I.L. ; articles recueillis par Gérard Peylet. Talence : Université Michel de Montaigne, Bordeaux III, L.A.P.R.I.L., 2000-[2001] 2 v. : col. ill. ; 24 cm. (Eidôlon, 0242-5300 ; 57-58) Includes bibliographical references. ISBN 2-903440-57-3 ISBN 2-903440-58-1 (v. 2) DDC 809
1. Apocalyptic literature. 2. End of the world in literature. 3. Future life in literature. 4. Mythology, Greek. I. Peylet, Gérard. II. Université Michel de Montaigne. III. Université de Bordeaux III. Laboratoire pluridisciplinaire de recherches sur l'imagination littéraire. IV. Series: Eidôlon (Talence, France) ; 57-58.

FINANCE. *See* **MONEY.**

FINANCE, PERSONAL.
Broussard, Cheryl D. What's money got to do with it? Oakland, CA : MetaMedia Pub., [c2002]
1. Black author.

The financial condition of the airline industry.
United States. Congress. House. Committee on Transportation and Infrastructure. Subcommittee on Aviation. Washington : U.S. G.P.O. : For sale by the Supt. of Docs., U.S. G.P.O. [Congressional Sales Office], 2002.

FINANCIAL CRASHES. *See* **FINANCIAL CRISES.**

FINANCIAL CRISES - HISTORY.
Sornette, D. Why stock markets crash. Princeton, N.J. : Princeton University Press, c2003.
HB3722 .S66 2003

FINANCIAL CRISES - UNITED STATES - HISTORY.
Sornette, D. Why stock markets crash. Princeton, N.J. : Princeton University Press, c2003.
HB3722 .S66 2003

FINANCIAL EXECUTIVES - UNITED STATES - BIOGRAPHY.
O'Loughlin, James. The real Warren Buffett. London ; Yarmouth, ME : Nicholas Brealey, 2003.

FINANCIAL PANICS. *See* **FINANCIAL CRISES.**

Financial Times Prentice Hall books.
Austin, Robert D. (Robert Daniel), 1962- Artful making. Upper Saddle River, NJ : Financial Times/Prentice Hall, 2003.
HD53 .A96 2003

Kennedy, Kevin (Kevin John), 1955- Going the distance. Upper Saddle River, NJ : Prentice Hall/Financial Times, c2003.
HD57.7 .K465 2003

Fincher, Richard D., 1951-.
Lipsky, David B., 1939- Emerging systems for managing workplace conflict. 1st ed. San Francisco : Jossey-Bass, c2003.
HD42 .L564 2003

Find it online.
Schlein, Alan M. 3rd ed. Tempe, AZ : Facts on Demand Press, c2003.

Finding higher ground.
Brosman, Catharine Savage, 1934- Reno : University of Nevada Press, c2003.
F787 .B76 2003

Finding the inner you.
Sullivan, Karen. 1st ed. Hauppauge, N.Y. : Barrons Educational Series, 2003.
BF697.5.S43 S95 2003

Finding the real me : true tales of sex and gender diversity / Tracie O'Keefe and Katrina Fox, editors. 1st ed. San Francisco, CA : Jossey-Bass, c2003. xx, 293 p. ; 23 cm. CONTENTS: Paradox is paradise for me / Cynthya Briankate -- Lessons of life / Nero -- A rose in bloom / April Rose Schneider -- A journey to androgyny / Norrie May-Welby -- Bad hair days : the story / Rebecca J. Dittman -- Robyn's journey / Robyn Walters -- Japan : a sexually unique country / Masae Torai -- So, which one is the opposite sex? : the sometimes spiritual journey of a metagender / Phillip Andrew Bernhardt-House -- A personal transsexual perspective of transition / Sarah J. Rutherford -- Peter's story / Peter Hberle -- The headache is in your head / Tucker Lieberman -- Reflections of a pagan heart / Laura Anne Seabrook -- Time for a good transgender story / Kam Wai Kui -- Melanie : my story / Melanie McMullan -- Confessions of a she-male merchant marine / Vera Sepulveda -- Dream on, and don't wake up to the nightmare of reality / Natalie Murphy -- Jack's story / Jack Powell -- Tracy's story / Tracy Deichmann -- The second transition / Christine Burns -- An other gendered boy / Joe Samson -- Masks and redemptive transformation / Jennifer Fraser -- Rikki's story / Rikki Arundel -- The constructed life / E. Tristan Booth -- A journey to self-acceptance / Andy Colson -- The never ending tango / katrina c. rose -- Butch : a work in progress / Jay Copestake. ISBN 0-7879-6547-2 (alk. paper) DDC 306.77
1. Transsexualism. 2. Transsexuals - Biography. 3. Transsexuals - Identity. 4. Gender identity. I. O'Keefe, Tracie. II. Fox, Katrina.
HQ77.7 .F56 2003

Finding your purpose.
Braham, Barbara J. Rev. ed. Menlo Park, CA : Crisp Publications, c2003.
BF637.S4 B67 2003

Findlay, John M. (John Malcolm), 1942- Active vision : the psychology of looking and seeing / John M. Findlay and Iain D. Gilchrist. Oxford ; New York : Oxford University Press, 2003. xiii, 220 p. : ill. ; 25 cm. (Oxford psychology series ; 37) Includes bibliographical references (p. [181]-213) and index. CONTENTS: Preface Ch. 1 Passive vision and active vision -- Ch. 2 Background to active vision -- Ch. 3 Visual selection, covert attention and eye movements -- Ch. 4 Visual orienting -- Ch. 5 Visual sampling during text reading -- Ch. 6 Visual search -- Ch. 7 Natural scenes and activities -- Ch. 8 Human neuropsychology -- Ch. 9 Space constancy and trans-saccadic integration -- References -- Index. ISBN 0-19-852480-3 ISBN

0-19-852479-X (PBK.) DDC 152.14
1. Visual perception. I. Gilchrist, Iain D. II. Title. III. Series: Oxford psychology series ; no. 37.
BF241 .F56 2003

FINE ARTS. See **ART; ARTS.**

Finite, contingent, and free.
McClure, Joyce Kloc, 1955- Lanham, Md. ; Oxford : Rowman & Littlefield Publishers, c2003.
BJ1012 .M316 2003

FINITE, THE.
Hägglund, Martin. Kronofobi. Stockholm : B. Östlings Bokförlag Symposion, 2002.

Fink, Bruce, 1956- Lacan to the letter : reading Ecrits closely / Bruce Fink. Minneapolis, MN : University of Minnesota Press, c2004. p. ; cm. Includes bibliographical references and index. CONTENTS: Lacanian technique in "the direction of the treatment" -- Lacan's critique of the ego psychology troika : Hartmann, Kris, and Loewenstein -- Reading "The instance of the letter in the unconscious or reason since Freud" -- Reading "Subversion of the subject" -- The Lacanian phallus and the square root of negative one -- Hors texte-knowledge and jouissance: a commentary on seminar XX. ISBN 0-8166-4320-2 (hc : alk. paper) ISBN 0-8166-4321-0 (pb : alk. paper) DDC 150.19/5
1. Lacan, Jacques, - 1901- - Ecrits. 2. Psychoanalysis. 3. Lacan, Jacques, - 1901- - Ecrits. 4. Psychoanalytic Theory. I. Title.
BF173 .L1434 2004

Finkelstein, Sydney. Why smart executives fail and what you can learn from their mistakes / Sydney Finkelstein. New York ; London : Portfolio, 2003. x, 321 p. ; 24 cm. Includes bibliographical references (p. 293-310) and index. ISBN 1-59184-010-4 (alk. paper) DDC 658.4/09
1. Executive ability. 2. Business failures. 3. Executives - Psychology. 4. Failure (Psychology) 5. Success in business. I. Title.
HD38.2 .F56 2003

FINKS, EIŽENS, 1885-1958.
Rīgas gaišregis Eižens Finks. Jauns papildināts izdevums. [Rīga] : Jumava, c2002.
BF1283.F55 R66 2002

Rīgas gaišregis Eižens Finks. Rīgā : Jumava, c2002.
BF1997.F56 R54 2002

Finlay, Frank.
Recasting German identity. Rochester, NY : Camden House, 2002.
DD239 .R43 2002

Finley, Guy. An apprentice of the heart : lessons in life only love can teach / by Guy Finley. Ashland, Ore. : White Cloud Press, 2004. p. cm. ISBN 1-88399-158-7 (pbk.) DDC 152.4/1
1. Love. I. Title. II. Title: Lessons in life only love can teach
BF575.L8 F524 2004

Finn-Stevenson, Matia.
Zigler, Edward, 1930- The first three years & beyond. New Haven : Yale University Press, c2002.
HQ767.9 .Z543 2002

FINNO-UGRIC LANGUAGES. See **HUNGARIAN LANGUAGE.**

O fio da espada.
Gaulle, Charles de, 1890-1970. [Fil de l'épée. Portuguese] Rio de Janeiro : Biblioteca do Exército Editora, 2001.

Fiore, Ann Marie. Understanding aesthetics for the merchandising and design professional / Ann Marie Fiore, Patricia Anne Kimle. New York : Fairchild, c1997. xx, 439 p. : ill. ; 26 cm. Includes bibliographical references (p. 420-429) and index. ISBN 1-56367-082-8
1. Costume design. 2. Aesthetics. 3. Clothing trade. 4. Textile fabrics. 5. Costume - Psychological aspects. 6. Clothing and dress - Psychological aspects. 7. Clothing and dress - Marketing. I. Kimle, Patricia Anne. II. Title.

Fiorentino, Leah.
The child's right to play. Westport, Conn. : Praeger, 2003.
BF717 .C44 2003

FIRE. See also **SMOKE.**
Fire in archaeology. Oxford : Archaeopress, 2002.
DA90 .B86 suppl. v.1089

FIRE DEPARTMENTS - OFFICIALS AND EMPLOYEES. See **FIRE FIGHTERS.**

FIRE FIGHTERS - NEW YORK (STATE) - NEW YORK.
Monahan, Brian. From ground zero to ground hero. [Newark, Del.?] : Disaster Research Center, University of Delaware, 2001.

Fire in archaeology : papers from a session held at the European Association of Archaeologists sixth annual meeting in Lisbon 2000 / edited by Dragos Gheorghiu. Oxford : Archaeopress, 2002. iv, 154 p. ; 30 cm. (BSR International series ; 1089) Includes bibliographical references. Contributions in English and French; French articles have English abstracts. ISBN 1-84171-467-4
1. Fire. 2. Civilization - History. 3. Europe - Antiquities. I. Gheorghiu, Dragos. II. European Association of Archaeologists Annual Meeting (6th : 2000 : Lisbon, Portugal) III. Series.
DA90 .B86 suppl. v.1089

FIRE - RELIGIOUS ASPECTS. See **CANDLES AND LIGHTS.**

FIREARMS - SOCIAL ASPECTS.
Wilkinson, Deanna Lyn, 1968- Guns, violence, and identity among African American and Latino youth. New York : LFB Scholarly Pub., 2003.
HQ799.2.V56 W55 2003

FIREFIGHTERS. See **FIRE FIGHTERS.**

Fireman, Gary D.
Narrative and consciousness. Oxford ; New York : Oxford University Press, c2003.
BF311 .N26 2003

FIREMEN. See **FIRE FIGHTERS.**

Firkowska-Mankiewicz, Anna. Intelligence and success in life / Anna Firkowska-Mankiewicz ; translated by Helena Grzegołowska-Klarkowska. Warsaw : IFiS Publishers, 2002. 232 p. : ill. ; 24 cm. Includes bibliographical references (p. [193]-205). ISBN 83-87632-03-1 DDC 153.9/09438/41
1. Gifted persons - Poland - Warsaw - Longitudinal studies. 2. Success in business - Poland - Warsaw. 3. Successful people - Poland - Warsaw. I. Title.
BF412 F57 2002

FIRMS. See **BUSINESS ENTERPRISES.**

FIRST AID IN ILLNESS AND INJURY. See **ACCIDENTS.**

FIRST CONTACT OF ABORIGINAL PEOPLES WITH WESTERNERS. See **INDIANS OF NORTH AMERICA - FIRST CONTACT WITH EUROPEANS.**

First globalization.
Gunn, Geoffrey C. Lanham, Md. : Rowman & Littlefield, c2003.
CB251 .G87 2003

FIRST HOUSE (ASTROLOGY). See **ASCENDANT (ASTROLOGY).**

First language acquisition.
Clark, Eve V. Cambridge, U.K. ; New York : Cambridge University Press, 2003.
P118 .C547 2003

FIRST LOVES. See **LOVE.**

FIRST PERSON NARRATIVE - CONGRESSES.
Colloque des Invalides (5th : 2001 : Hôtel des invalides) Ce que je ne sais pas. Tusson, Charente : Du Lérot, [2002?]
PQ145 .C65 2001

Narrative and consciousness. Oxford ; New York : Oxford University Press, c2003.
BF311 .N26 2003

The first relationship.
Stern, Daniel N. Cambridge, Mass. : Harvard University Press, 2002, 1977.
BF720.M68 S74 2002

First Run/Icarus Films.
Western eyes [videorecording]. New York, NY : First Run/Icarus Films, 2000.

First step nonfiction
Nelson, Robin, 1971- Afraid. Minneapolis, MN : Lerner Publications Co., c2004.
BF723.F4 N45 2004

Nelson, Robin, 1971- Angry. Minneapolis, MN : Lerner Publications Co., c2004.
BF723.A4 N45 2004

Nelson, Robin, 1971- Happy. Minneapolis, MN : Lerner Publications Co., c2004.
BF723.H37 N45 2004

Nelson, Robin, 1971- Sad. Minneapolis, MN : Lerner Publications Co., c2004.
BF723.S15 N45 2004

The first three years & beyond.
Zigler, Edward, 1930- New Haven : Yale University Press, c2002.

HQ767.9 .Z543 2002

First three years and beyond.
Zigler, Edward, 1930- The first three years & beyond. New Haven : Yale University Press, c2002.
HQ767.9 .Z543 2002

FIRST WORLD WAR. See **WORLD WAR, 1914-1918.**

Fisch und Frosch.
Bruyn, Gerd de. Fisch und Frosch, oder, Die Selbstkritik der Moderne. Gütersloh ; Berlin : Bertelsmann Fachzeitschriften ; Basel ; Boston ; Berlin : Birkhäuser, c2001.

Fisch und Frosch, oder, Die Selbstkritik der Moderne.
Bruyn, Gerd de. Gütersloh ; Berlin : Bertelsmann Fachzeitschriften ; Basel ; Boston ; Berlin : Birkhäuser, c2001.

Fischer, Agneta, 1958-.
Feelings and emotions. New York : Cambridge University Press, 2003.
BF531 .F445 2003

Fischer, Bernd Jürgen, 1952-.
Albanian identities. Bloomington : Indiana University Press, 2002.
DR950 .A385 2002

Fischer-Lichte, Erika.
Wahrnehmung und Medialität. Tübingen : Francke, c2001.
PN2039 .W347 2001

Fischer, Norman, 1946- Taking our places : the Buddhist path to truly growing up / Norman Fischer. 1st ed. San Francisco : HarperSanFrancisco, c2003. 198 p. ; 22 cm. Publisher description URL: http://www.loc.gov/catdir/description/hc042/2003545385.html Table of contents URL: http://www.loc.gov/catdir/toc/fy041/2003545385.html ISBN 0-06-050551-6 DDC 294.3/444
1. Maturation (Psychology) 2. Growth. 3. Self actualization (Psychology). I. Title.
BF710 .F57 2003

Fisette, Denis, 1954-.
Husserl's Logical investigations reconsidered. Dordrecht ; Boston : Kluwer Academic Publishers, c2003.
B3279.H93 L64346 2003

FISH. See **FISHES.**

Fishbein, Harold D. Peer prejudice and discrimination : the origins of prejudice / Harold D. Fishbein. 2nd ed. Mahwah, N.J. : L. Erlbaum, 2002. xv, 335 p. ; 24 cm. Includes bibliographical references (p. 301-319) and indexes. ISBN 0-8058-3771-X (alk. paper) ISBN 0-8058-3772-8 (pbk. : alk. paper) DDC 303.3/85
1. Prejudices in children. 2. Prejudices. 3. Prejudices in children - Prevention. I. Title.
BF723.P75 F57 2002

Fisher, Celia B. Decoding the ethics code : a practical guide for psychologists / Celia B. Fisher. Thousand Oaks, Calif. : Sage Publications, c2003. xxxiii, 283 p. ; 26 cm. Includes bibliographical references (p. 265-271) and index. Table of contents URL: http://www.loc.gov/catdir/toc/ecip041/2003006141.html CONTENTS: A code of ethics for psychology : how did we get here? -- The introduction and applicability section, preamble, and general principles : what do they mean? -- Changes from the 1992 ethics code : what you may need to know right now -- Standards for resolving ethical issues -- Standards on competence -- Standards on human relations -- Standards on privacy and confidentiality -- Standards on advertising and other public statements -- Standards on record keeping and fees -- Standards on education and training -- Standards on research and publication -- Standards on assessment -- Standards on therapy -- The APA Ethics Code and ethical decision making. ISBN 0-7619-2619-4 (pbk. : alk. paper) DDC 174/.915
1. Psychologists - Professional ethics. 2. Psychology - Moral and ethical aspects. I. Title.
BF76.4 .F57 2003

Fisher, Helen E. Why we love : the nature and chemistry of romantic love / Helen Fisher. 1st ed. New York : Henry Holt and Company, 2004. p. cm. Includes bibliographical references and index. ISBN 0-8050-6913-5 DDC 152.4/1
1. Love. 2. Love - Physiological aspects. 3. Human evolution. 4. Sex. 5. Sex differences. I. Title.
BF575.L8 F53 2004

Fisher, Peter S. Industrial incentives : competition among American states and cities / Peter S. Fisher, Alan H. Peters. Kalamazoo, Mich. : W.E. Upjohn Institute for Employment Research, 1998. xiii, 307 p. : ill. ; 23 cm. Includes bibliographical references (p. 277-287) and indexes. ISBN 0-88099-183-6 (pbk. : alk. paper) ISBN

Fisheries

0-88099-184-4 (hardcover : alk. paper) DDC 338.973
1. *Incentives in industry - United States.* 2. *Industrial promotion - United States.* 3. *Competition - United States.* I. *Peters, Alan H.* II. *Title.*
HF5549.5.I5 F57 1998

FISHERIES. See **FISHES.**

FISHERS. See **FISHING.**

FISHES. See **FISHING.**

FISHES - PHYSIOLOGY.
Eaton, Robert C. The octavolateralis system and Mauthner cell interactions and questions [microform]. [Washington, D.C. : National Aeronautics and Space Administration, 1997]

FISHING. See **FISHES.**

FISHING - MISCELLANEA.
Andrews, John, 1966- For all those left behind. Edinburgh : Mainstream Pub., c2002.
BF789.D4 A55 2002

FISHING - PENNSYLVANIA.
Daniel, Jack L. (Jack Lee), 1942- We fish. Pittsburgh, Pa. : University of Pittsburgh Press, c2003.
1. *Black author.*

Fiske, Susan T. The handbook of social psychology. 4th ed. Boston : McGraw-Hill ; New York : Distributed exclusively by Oxford University Press, c1998.
HM251 .H224 1998

Fitness, Julie.
From mating to mentality. New York, NY : Psychology Press, 2003.
BF698.95 .F76 2003

Fitzgerald, Helen. The grieving child : a parent's guide / Helen Fitzgerald. 2nd ed. New York : Simon & Schuster, 2003. p. cm. "A Fireside book." Includes bibliographical references and index. ISBN 0-671-76762-3 (alk. paper) DDC 155.9/37/083
1. *Children and death.* 2. *Bereavement in children.* 3. *Grief in children.* 4. *Child rearing.* I. *Title.*
BF723.D3 F58 2003

Fitzhugh, Ben.
Beyond foraging and collecting. New York : Kluwer Academic/Plenum Publishers, c2002.
GN388 .B49 2002

FIVE CIVILIZED TRIBES. See **CHOCTAW INDIANS.**

Five hundred reasons why you're my best friend.
Bodger, Lorraine. 500 reasons why you're my best friend. Kansas City, Mo. : Andrews McMeel Pub., c2003.
BF575.F66 B63 2003

Five steps for overcoming fear and self-doubt.
Webb, Wyatt. Carlsbad, Calif. : Hay House, 2004.
BF575.F2 W42 2004

Flage, Daniel E., 1951- The art of questioning : an introduction to critical thinking / Daniel E. Flage. Upper Saddle River, N.J. : Pearson/Prentice Hall, c2004. xvii, 503 p. : ill. ; 24 cm. Includes bibliographical references and index. ISBN 0-13-093699-5 DDC 160
1. *Critical thinking.* 2. *Questioning.* I. *Title.*
BF441 .F55 2004

FLAGEOLET TONES. See **HARMONICS (MUSIC).**

Flahault, François, 1943- Le sentiment d'exister / François Flahault. Paris : Descartes & Cie, c2002. 824 p. ; 21 cm. (Collection "Essai") Includes bibliographical references. ISBN 2-8444-6034-8 DDC 100
1. *Self-knowledge, Theory of.* I. *Title.* II. *Series: Collection "Essai" (Descartes & Cie)*
BD438.5 .F54 2002

Flaherty, Jane S. Lifetime leadership : leaving your legacy : a day-by-day inspirational guide for leaders / Jane S. Flaherty & Peter B. Stark. San Diego : Bentley Press, c2001. 320 p. ; 23 cm. Spine title: Lifetime leadership, leaving your legacy. ISBN 1-931324-00-X DDC 158/.4
1. *Leadership - Problems, exercises, etc.* I. *Stark, Peter B.* II. *Title.* III. *Title: Lifetime leadership, leaving your legacy*
BF637.L4 F57 2001

Stark, Peter B. The only negotiating guide you'll ever need. 1st ed. New York : Broadway Books, 2003.
BF637.N4 S725 2003

Flahive, Gerry.
Western eyes [videorecording]. New York, NY : First Run/Icarus Films, 2000.

Flamant, Nicolas. Une anthropologie des managers / Nicolas Flamant. Paris : Presses universitaires de France, c2002. 217 p. ; 22 cm. (Sciences sociales et sociétés)

Includes bibliographical references (p. [215]-217). ISBN 2-13-052865-1
1. *Management.* I. *Title.* II. *Series.*
HD33 .F525 2002

Flanagan, Owen J.
Narrative and consciousness. Oxford ; New York : Oxford University Press, c2003.
BF311 .N26 2003

Flathman, Richard E. Freedom and its conditions : discipline, autonomy, and resistance / Richard E. Flathman. New York : Routledge, c2003. x, 193 p. ; 24 cm. Includes bibliographical references (p. 187-188) and index. CONTENTS: Discipline, freedom and resistance: preliminary reflections by way of an engagement with Foucault -- The self against and for itself I: Montaigne on freedom, discipline, and resistance -- The self against and for itself II: Nietzsche as theorist of disciplined freedom of action and free-spiritedness -- Stuart Hampshire on freedoms and unfreedoms of mind and of action -- Stuart Hampshire on freedoms and unfreedoms of action : freedom, discipline, and resistance. ISBN 0-415-94561-5 (cloth : alk. paper) ISBN 0-415-94562-3 (pbk. : alk. paper) DDC 320/.01/1
1. *Liberty.* 2. *Liberty - Philosophy.* I. *Title.*
JC585 .F553 2003

Flavell, John H. Development of children's knowledge about the mind / John H. Flavell ; drawing by Leonard Baskin. Worcester, Mass. : Clark University Press, 2003. p. cm. (Heinz werner lecture series ; 2003, 25) Includes bibliographical references. Table of contents URL: http://www.loc.gov/catdir/toc/ecip046/2003015252.html ISBN 0-914206-39-7 (pbk. : alk. paper) DDC 155.4/13
1. *Cognition in children.* 2. *Knowledge, Theory of, in children.* I. *Title.* II. *Series: Heinz Werner lectures ; 2003.*
BF723.C5 F623 2003

Flem, Lydia.
[Homme Freud. English]
Freud the man : an intellectual biography / Lydia Felm ; translated by Susan Fairfield. New York : Other Press, c2003. xi, 223 p. ; 24 cm. Includes bibliographical references (p. [203]-213) and index. CONTENTS: Creation day by day -- Through the train window -- The archeologist -- The conquistador : Athens, Rome, Jerusalem -- The man without a country -- The man of the book -- In the witch's kitchen -- The shade of the poet -- The metaphor man -- The friend. ISBN 1-59051-037-2 (alk. paper) DDC 150.19/52/092
1. *Freud, Sigmund, 1856-1939.* 2. *Psychoanalysts - Austria - Biography.* 3. *Psychoanalysis - History.* I. *Title.*
BF109.F74 F4813 2003

La voix des amants / Lydia Flem. [Paris] : Seuil, c2002. 145 p. ; 18 cm. (La librairie du XXIe siècle) ISBN 2-02-041424-4 DDC 844
1. *Voice.* 2. *Operas - Characters.* 3. *Psychoanalysis.* I. *Title.* II. *Series.*

Fleming, Jenny.
Government reformed. Aldershot, England ; Burlington, VT : Ashgate, c2003.
JF1525.O73 G686 2003

Fleming, Maurice. Not of this world : creatures of the supernatural in Scotland / Maurice Fleming ; illustrated by Alan McGowan. Edinburgh : Mercat, 2002. xv, 172 p. : ill. ; 22 cm. Includes bibliographical references (p. 170-172). ISBN 1-84183-040-2 DDC 398.46909411
1. *Animals, Mythical - Scotland.* 2. *Supernatural.* I. *Title.* II. *Title: Creatures of the supernatural in Scotland*

FLEMISH LITERATURE - TO 1830. See **DUTCH LITERATURE.**

Flensburger Hefte
(78) Familie im Wandel. Flensburg : Flensburger Hefte, [2002]

Fletcher, John Wright. A hermeneutic study of generational music : the band Nirvana and cultural change in America : a dissertation ... / by John Wright Fletcher. 2002. Thesis (doctoral)--Duquesne University, 2002. Includes bibliographical references. Photocopy. Ann Arbor, Mich. : UMI Dissertation Services, 2003. 22 cm.
1. *Nirvana (Musical group)* 2. *Rock music fans - United States.* 3. *Generation X.* 4. *Grunge music - Social aspects - United States.* 5. *Rock music - Social aspects - United States.* 6. *Subculture - United States.* 7. *Conflict of generations - United States.* 8. *Hermeneutics.* 9. *Existential phenomenology.* I. *Title.*

FLEXIBILITY (PSYCHOLOGY). See **ADAPTABILITY (PSYCHOLOGY).**

Flickstein, Matthew. Journey to the center : a meditation workbook / Matthew Flickstein ; foreword by Bhante Gunaratana. Somerville, MA : Wisdom Publications, c1998. xi, 211 p. : ill. ; 26 cm. Includes bibliographical references (p. 209) and index. ISBN

0-86171-141-6 (pbk.) DDC 158.1/2
1. *Self-actualization (Psychology)* 2. *Meditation.* I. *Title.*
BF637.S4 F58 1998

FLIGHT. See **AERONAUTICS.**

FLIGHT CREWS - CASE STUDIES.
Zentner, John J., 1965- The art of wing leadership and aircrew morale in combat [electronic resource]. Maxwell Air Force Base, Ala. : Air University Press, [2001]

Florenskaia, O. Psikhologiia bytovogo shrifta / O. Florenskaia. Sankt-Peterburg : Krasnyĭ matros, 2001. 56 p. : ill. ; 17 cm. (Krasnyĭ matros : vyp. 35) ISBN 5718703108
1. *Graphology - Russia (Federation)* 2. *Signs and signboards - Russia (Federation) - Lettering.* 3. *Graffiti - Russia (Federation)* 4. *Writing - Psychological aspects.* I. *Title.* II. *Series.*
BF896 .F66 2001

Flores Bedregal, Teresa. Comunicación para el desarrollo sostenible / Teresa Flores Bedregal. La Paz : Plural Editores : LIDEMA : Konrad-Adenauer-Stiftung, c2002. 84 p. : ill. ; 21 cm. Abstract in English. ISBN 9990564353
1. *Communication in the environmental sciences.* 2. *Communication in economic development.* 3. *Sustainable development - Study and teaching.* 4. *Sustainable development - Study and teaching (Higher) - Bolivia.* 5. *Environmental education.* I. *Title.*

Flores, Valeria.
Alonso, Graciela. Hacia una pedagogía de las experiencias de las mujeres. 1. ed. Buenos Aires : Miño y Dávila, 2002.

Florovsky, Georges, 1893-1979.
[Selections. Russian. 2002]
Vera i kul'tura : izbrannye trudy po bogosloviiu i filosofii / prot. Georgiĭ Florovskiĭ ; [otv. redaktory D.K. Burlaka, I.I. Evlampiev]. Sankt-Peterburg : Izd-vo Russkogo Khristianskogo gumanitarnogo instituta, 2002. 862 p. ; 21 cm. Includes bibliographical references. CONTENTS: Georgiĭ Florovskiĭ: put' bogoslova / I.I. Evlampiev -- Khitrost' razuma -- Smysl' istorii i smysl zhizni -- Vechnoe i prekhodiashchee v uchenii russkikh slavianofilov -- Chelovecheskaia mudrost' i Premudrost' Bozhiia -- V mire iskanii i bluzhdaniĭ -- Dva Zaveta -- Pamiati prof. P.I. Novgorodtseva -- Metafizicheskie predposylki utopizma -- Dom Otchiĭ -- Filaret, mitropolit Moskovskiĭ -- Tvar' i tvarnost' -- Ideia tvoreniia v khristianskoĭ filosofii -- Opravdanie znaniia -- Evkharistiia i sobornost' -- Zhil li Khristos? -- Spor o nemetskom idealizme -- Evoliutsiia i épigenez -- Bogoslovskie otryvki -- O pochitanii Sofii, Premudrosti Bozhieĭ, v Vizantii i na Rusi Promysel Sviatogo Dukha v Bogootkrovenii -- Problematika khristianskogo vossoedineniia -- O granitsakh tserkvi -- Sobornost' Tserkvi -- O voskresenii mertvykh -- Tserkov': ee priroda i zadacha -- Patriarkh Ieremiia II i luteranskie bogoslovy -- Sotsial'naia problema v Vostochnoĭ Pravoslavnoĭ Tserkvi -- Utrata bibleĭskogo myshleniia -- Otkrovenie i istolkovanie -- Evangelie Voskreseniia -- Khristianstvo i tsivilizatsiia -- Vera i kul'tura -- Zatrudneniia istorika-khristianina -- Poslushanie i svidetel'stvo -- "Neprestanno molites'" -- Emil Brunner: Der Mittler: zur Bexinnung über den Christusglauben -- Protivorechiia origenizma -- Charles Gore: Jesus of Nazareth -- Slovo v den' Svetlago Khristova Voskreseniia -- O pochesti gornego prizvaniia -- Khristianin v Tserkvi -- Ot Rozhdestva Khristova -- Taĭna Favorskogo sveta -- Syny i naemniki -- Svetozarnaia noch' -- Smert' i zhizn' -- Soblazn uchenikov -- Pr. protoiereĭ Georgiĭ Vasil'evich Florovskiĭ / A. Vedemikov. ISBN 5888121355
1. *Orthodox Eastern Church - Doctrines.* 2. *Philosophy, Russian.* 3. *Christianity and culture.* I. *Burlaka, D. K.* II. *Evlampiev, I. I. (Igor' Ivanovich)* III. *Title.*
BX260 .F552 2002

Die Fluchtbahn des Subjekts.
Schweppenhäuser, Gerhard. Münster : Lit, 2001.

Flying Dutchmen.
Jormakka, Kari. [Olandesi volanti. English] Basel ; Boston : Birkhäuser, 2002.
NA1148 .J6713 2002

FLYING-MACHINES. See **AERONAUTICS.**

FLYING PERSONNEL. See **FLIGHT CREWS.**

FLYING SAUCERS. See **UNIDENTIFIED FLYING OBJECTS.**

Flying Star feng shui.
Lum, Alan S.F. (Alan Sun Fai) The centuries old philosophy and practice of traditional Chinese feng shui and the more advanced Flying Star feng shui. Honolulu : Lum Pub., c2002.
BF1779.F4 L86 2002

Fo jiao mei xue.
Qi, Zhixiang. Di 1 ban. Shanghai : Shanghai ren min chu ban she : Xin hua shu dian Shanghai fa xing suo jing xiao, 1997.
BQ4570.A72 C45 1997 <Asian China>

Focus on contemporary issues
Fudge, Erica. Animal. London : Reaktion, 2002.
QL85 .F83 2002

Marar, Ziyad. The happiness paradox. London : Reaktion, 2003.

Fodor, Jerry A. Hume variations / Jerry A. Fodor. Oxford : Clarendon Press ; New York : Oxford University Press, 2003. 165 p. ; 21 cm. (Lines of thought) Includes bibliographical references (p. [159]-162) and index. ISBN 0-19-926405-8 DDC 128.2
1. Hume, David, - 1711-1776. - Treatise of human nature. 2. Philosophy of mind. I. Title. II. Series.
B1489 .F63 2003

Fogelin, Robert J. Walking the tightrope of reason : the precarious life of a rational animal / Robert Fogelin. Oxford ; New York : Oxford University Press, 2003. xii, 203 p. ; 19 cm. Includes bibliographical references (p. [171]-194) and index. ISBN 0-19-516026-6 (cloth) DDC 128/.33
1. Reason. 2. Skepticism. 3. Metaphysics. I. Title.
BC177 .F64 2003

Fogg, B. J. Persuasive technology : using computers to change what we think and do / B.J. Fogg. Amsterdam ; Boston : Morgan Kaufmann Publishers, / c2003. xxviii, 283 p. : ill. ; 23 cm. (The Morgan Kaufmann series in interactive technologies) Includes bibliographical references and index. Publisher description URL: http://www.loc.gov/catdir/description/els031/2002110617.html Table of contents URL: http://www.loc.gov/catdir/toc/els031/2002110617.html ISBN 1-55860-643-2 (pbk. : alk. paper) DDC 153.8/52/0285
1. Persuasion (Psychology) - Computer programs. 2. Human-computer interaction. I. Title. II. Series.
BF637.P4 F55 2003

Fogiel, M. (Max).
The best test preparation for the Advanced Placement Examination. Piscataway, N.J. : Research & Education Association, c2003.
BF78 .B48 2003

The best test preparation for the CLEP, College-Level Examination Program, human growth & development. Piscataway, N.J. : Research & Education Association, c2003.
BF713 .B49 2003

Fohr, S. D., 1943-.
Guénon, René. [Etats multiples de l'être. English] The multiple states of the being. 2nd English ed. Ghent, NY : Sophia Perennis, c2001.
BD312 .G813 2001

La foi qui transporte les montagnes.
Aïvanhov, Omraam Mikhaël. Fréjus : Prosveta, c1999.

Fokus
(Bd. 26) Becker, Monika. Familiar dialogues in Englyssh and Frenche. Trier : Wissenschaftlicher Verlag Trier, c2003.

Folb, Sherry.
Powers, Marilyn. The bridge between two lifetimes. Phoenix, AZ : Sophia Publications, c1999.
BF724.6 .P68 1999

Foley, Duncan K. Unholy trinity : labor, capital, and land in the new economy / Duncan K. Foley. London ; New York : Routledge, 2003. viii, 98 p. ; 23 cm. (The Graz Schumpeter lectures ; 6) Includes bibliographical references (p. [92]-94) and index. ISBN 0-415-31079-2 DDC 330.1
1. Economics, Mathematical. 2. System theory. 3. Complexity (Philosophy) 4. Labor economics. 5. Environmental economics. 6. Land use - Economic aspects. 7. Capitalism. I. Title. II. Series.
HB135 .F65 2003

La folie du chaman.
Lioger, Richard. Paris : Presses universitaires de France, c2002.

Folio, M. Rhonda. PDMS-2 : Peabody Developmental Motor Scales / M. Rhonda Folio, Rebecca R. Fewell. 2nd ed. Austin : Pro-Ed, c2000. 1 case : 25 x 32 x 21 cm. Title from case. Includes bibliographical references. CONTENTS: Examiner's manual (xv, 119 p.) -- Guide to item administration (52 p.) -- Motor activities program (vi, 167 p.) -- 25 examiner record booklets -- 25 profile/summary forms -- 1 Peabody motor development chart (65 x 94 cm. folded to 22 x 24 cm.) -- 30 manipulatives in a fishnet bag -- 1 roll of maskin tape. DDC 155.42/223
1. Peabody Developmental Motor Scales-2. I. Title.
BF723.M6 .F65 2000

Foliothèque
(108) Meyer, Michel. Michel Meyer présente Manifestes du surréalisme d'André Breton. Paris : Gallimard, 2002.
NX600.S9 B735 2002

FOLK ART - EUROPE - HISTORY.
Jones, Malcolm, 1953- The secret middle ages. Stroud : Sutton, 2002.

FOLK BELIEFS. *See* **FOLKLORE; SUPERSTITION.**

FOLK DANCING, MEXICAN.
Galovic, Jelena. Los grupos místico-espirituales de la actualidad. México : Plaza y Valdés, 2002.
BL625 .G346 2002

FOLK LITERATURE. *See* **LEGENDS; TALES.**

FOLK LITERATURE, CHINESE - HISTORY AND CRITICISM.
Zheng, Chengduo, 1898-1958. Zhongguo su wen xue shi. Di 1 ban. Beijing : Dong fang chu ban she, 1996.
PL2445 .C44 1996

FOLK LITERATURE - EUROPE - HISTORY AND CRITICISM.
Werewolves, witches, and wandering spirits. Kirksville, MO : Truman State University Press, c2002.
GR135 .W47 2002

FOLK-LORE. *See* **FOLKLORE.**

FOLK MEDICINE. *See* **TRADITIONAL MEDICINE.**

FOLK MUSIC - UNITED STATES. *See* **COUNTRY MUSIC.**

FOLK-PSYCHOLOGY. *See* **ETHNOPSYCHOLOGY.**

FOLK SONGS, UKRAINIAN.
Malaniuk, Ira. Arien und Lieder [sound recording]. [Germany] : Preiser Records, p2000.

FOLK TALES. *See* **LEGENDS; TALES.**

FOLKLORE. *See also* **FAIRIES; FOLK LITERATURE; GRAFFITI; GRAIL; MONSTERS; MYTHOLOGY; ORAL TRADITION; SUPERSTITION; TRADITIONAL MEDICINE.**
Morales Villaroel, Oscar. Huellas y relatos. Caracas : [s.n.], 2001.

FOLKLORE - BELARUS.
Kazakova, I. V. (Iryna Valer'eŭna) Mifalahemy i mahiĭa ŭ belaruskim abradavym fal'klory. Minsk : "BOFF", 1997.
GR203.4 .K39 1997

FOLKLORE - EUROPE. *See also* **TRISTAN (LEGENDARY CHARACTER).**
Werewolves, witches, and wandering spirits. Kirksville, MO : Truman State University Press, c2002.
GR135 .W47 2002

FOLKLORE - ITALY.
Leland, Charles Godfrey, 1824-1903. [Etruscan roman remains in popular tradition] Etruscan Roman remains and the old religion. London ; New York : Kegan Paul ; New York : Distributed by Columbia University Press, 2002.
DG223 .L54 2002

FOLKLORE - JUVENILE LITERATURE.
Philip, Neil. The little people. New York ; London : Harry N. Abrams, 2002.

FOLKLORE - LATVIA - DICTIONARIES - LATVIAN.
Senie latviešu sapņu skaidrojumi. [Rīga] : Tapals, 2002.
BF1098.L35 S46 2002

FOLKLORE - MOROCCO.
Hell, Bertrand. Le tourbillon des génies. Paris : Flammarion, c2002.

FOLKLORE - POLITICAL ASPECTS - UNITED STATES.
Azoulay, Paul. Uncle Sam. Anglet : Atlantica, c2002.

FOLKLORE - PSYCHOLOGICAL ASPECTS.
Heuscher, Julius E. (Julius Ernest), 1918- Psychology, folklore, creativity, and the human dilemma. Springfield, Ill. : Charles C Thomas Publisher, c2003.
BF637.C5 H475 2003

FOLKLORE - SLAVIC COUNTRIES - SOURCES.
Levkievskaia, E. E. (Elena Evgen'evna) Slavi͡anskiĭ obereg. Moskva : Indrik, 2002.
BL480 .L38 2002

FOLKTALES. *See* **TALES.**

FOLKWAYS. *See* **SOCIAL NORMS.**

FOLLETT, MARY PARKER, 1868-1933.
Baritono, Raffaella. La democrazia vissuta. Torino : La Rosa, c2001.

Tonn, Joan C. Mary P. Follett. New Haven [Conn.] : Yale University Press, c2003.
HN57 .T695 2003

La follia dei cristiani.
Ruggiero, Fabio. Roma : Città nuova, c2002.
BR166 .R84 2002

Following directions [electronic resource].
Semel, Eleanor Messing. Macintosh/Windows version. Winooski, VT : Laureate Learning Systems, c2000.
BF637.L36

Following our bliss.
Lattin, Don. 1st ed. New York : HarperCollins, c2003.

Fomenko, A. T.
Nosovskiĭ, G. V. (Gleb Vladimirovich), 1958- Rekonstruktsii͡a vseobshcheĭ istorii. Moskva : FID "Delovoĭ ėkspress", 2002.
DK38 .N68 2002

FONDANE, BENJAMIN, 1898-1944.
Fotiade, Ramona. Conceptions of the absurd. Oxford : Legenda, 2001.

Fone, Anne Calodich. Elf-help for coping with pain / written by Anne Calodich Fone ; illustrated by R.W. Alley. St. Meinrad, Ind. : Abbey Press, c2002. 1 v. (unpaged) : ill. ; 16 cm. ISBN 0-87029-368-0 DDC 248.8/6
1. Pain - Psychological aspects. I. Title.
BF515 .F69 2002

Fonseca, Eduardo Giannetti da, 1957- Nada é tudo : ética, economia e brasilidade / Eduardo Giannetti. Rio de Janeiro, RJ, Brasil : Editora Campus, c2000. 252 p. : 21 cm. Most of the articles were previously published in the Brazilian newspaper Folha de S. Paulo between 1995 and 2000. Includes index. ISBN 85-352-0582-9
1. Brazil - Politics and government. 2. Brazil - Economic conditions. 3. Ethics. 4. Science. I. Title.
F2521 .F64 2000

Fontana, David. Psychology, religion, and spirituality / David Fontana. Malden, MA : BPS Blackwell, 2003. ix, 260 p. ; 24 cm. Includes bibliographical references (p. [230]-250) and index. CONTENTS: Why the psychology of religion? -- Definitions and meanings -- Introspection and inner experience -- Approaches to the psychology of religion and spirituality -- Religious beliefs and practices -- Approaches to spiritual development -- Spirituality and the brain -- The origins of religious belief -- Religious expression in myth and the creative arts -- Varieties of religious and spiritual experience -- Concepts of self, soul, and brain -- Religion, health, and well-being. ISBN 1405108053 ISBN 1405108061 (pbk.) DDC 200/.1/9
1. Psychology, Religious. 2. Spirituality - Psychology. I. Title.
BL53 .F57 2003

FOOD. *See* **BEVERAGES.**

FOOD ANIMALS. *See* **LIVESTOCK.**

FOOD BINGE-PURGE BEHAVIOR. *See* **BULIMIA.**

FOOD CUSTOMS. *See* **FOOD HABITS.**

FOOD HABITS - HISTORY.
Ferrières, Madeleine. Histoire des peurs alimentaires. Paris : Editions du Seuil, c2002.

FOOD HABITS - PSYCHOLOGICAL ASPECTS.
Ferrières, Madeleine. Histoire des peurs alimentaires. Paris : Editions du Seuil, c2002.

FOOD - SAFETY MEASURES.
Ferrières, Madeleine. Histoire des peurs alimentaires. Paris : Editions du Seuil, c2002.

FOOD SUPPLY. *See* **AGRICULTURE.**

FOODS. *See* **FOOD.**

FOODWAYS. *See* **FOOD HABITS.**

The fool's pilgrimage.
Hoeller, Stephan A. [Royal road] 2nd Quest ed. Wheaton, Ill. : Quest Books/Theosophical Pub. House, 2004.
BF1879.T2 H6 2004

Foot, Philippa. Moral dilemmas and other topics in moral philosophy / Philippa Foot. Oxford ; New York : Clarendon Press, 2002. 218 p. ; 23 cm. Includes bibliographical references and index. ISBN 0-19-925283-1 ISBN 0-19-925284-X (pbk)
1. Ethics. 2. Dilemma. I. Title.

Foot, Rosemary, 1948-.
Order and justice in international relations. Oxford ; New York : Oxford University Press, 2003.
JZ1308 .O73 2003

FOOTBALL. *See* **SOCCER.**

FOOTBALL (SOCCER). *See* **SOCCER.**

For all those left behind.
Andrews, John, 1966- Edinburgh : Mainstream Pub., c2002.
BF789.D4 A55 2002

--For dummies
Elliott, Charles H., 1948- Overcoming anxiety for dummies. New York : Wiley Pub., c2003.
BF575.A6 E46 2003

For the glory of God.
Stark, Rodney. Princeton, N.J. : Princeton University Press, c2003.
BL221 .S747 2003

For wimps series
Fenton, Sasha. Astrology for wimps. New York : Sterling Pub., c2003.
BF1708.1 .F453 2003

Fora de col·lecció
(5) Peiró, Agustí. Ésser i moral. 1. ed. [Valencia] : Brosquil Edicions, 2002.

Foran, John.
Feminist futures. London ; New York : Zed Books ; New York : Distributed in the USA exclusively by Palgrave, c2003.
HQ1161 .F455 2003

Forbes Inc.
Zhongguo, shui zui fu. Di 1 ban. Beijing : Qi ye guan li chu ban she, 2001.
HC426.5.A2 Z457 2001

FORCE AND ENERGY.
Haché, Alain, 1970- The physics of hockey. Baltimore : Johns Hopkins University Press, 2002.
QC28 .H23 2002

Laidler, Keith James, 1916- Energy and the unexpected. Oxford ; New York : Oxford University Press, c2002.
QC72 .L35 2002

FORCE AND ENERGY - MISCELLANEA.
Stein, Diane, 1948- Essential energy balancing II. Berkeley, Calif. : Crossing Press, c2003.
BF1045.K37 S735 2003

FORCED INDOCTRINATION. *See* **BRAINWASHING.**

Ford, Loren. Human relations : a game plan for improving personal adjustment / Loren Ford. 3rd ed. Upper Saddle River, N.J. : Pearson/Prentice Hall, c2004. xi, 309 p. : ill. ; 28 cm. Includes bibliographical references (p. 299-303) and index. ISBN 0-13-183205-0 DDC 158
1. Adjustment (Psychology) 2. Interpersonal communication. 3. Interpersonal relations. 4. Self-perception. 5. Life change events. I. Title.
BF335 .F67 2004

Fordham series in medieval studies
(no. 1) Medieval cultures in contact. New York : Fordham University Press, 2003.
CB351 .M3922 2003

Fordulópont könyvek
Polcz, Alaine. Gyermek a halál kapujában. Budapest : PONT, c2001.
BF723.D3 P65 2001

FORECASTING. *See also* **ECONOMIC FORECASTING; PROPHECY.**
Konstantinovskaia, L. V. (Liudmila Vasil'evna) Kogda prikhodiat proroki. Moskva : Klassiks Stil', 2002.
BF1796 .K66 2002

Kuz'menko, Volodymyr. Na porozi nadtsyvilizatsii. L'viv : "Universum", 1998.
HM901 .K89 1998

Schauer, Frederick F. Profiles, probabilities, and stereotypes. Cambridge, Mass. : Belknap Press of Harvard University Press, 2003.
HM1096 .S34 2003

FORECASTING, BUSINESS. *See* **BUSINESS FORECASTING.**

Forecasting your life events.
Rushman, Carol. The art of predictive astrology. 1st ed. St. Paul, Minn. : Llewellyn Publications, 2003, c2002.
BF1720.5 .R87 2002

FOREIGN AFFAIRS. *See* **INTERNATIONAL RELATIONS.**

FOREIGN AID PROGRAM. *See* **MILITARY ASSISTANCE.**

FOREIGN ASSISTANCE. *See* **MILITARY ASSISTANCE.**

FOREIGN-BORN POPULATION. *See* **IMMIGRANTS.**

FOREIGN COMMERCE. *See* **INTERNATIONAL TRADE.**

FOREIGN ECONOMIC POLICY. *See* **INTERNATIONAL ECONOMIC RELATIONS.**

FOREIGN ECONOMIC RELATIONS. *See* **INTERNATIONAL ECONOMIC RELATIONS.**

FOREIGN LANGUAGES. *See* **LANGUAGE AND LANGUAGES; LANGUAGES, MODERN.**

FOREIGN POLICY. *See* **INTERNATIONAL RELATIONS.**

FOREIGN POPULATION. *See* **ALIENS; IMMIGRANTS; MINORITIES.**

FOREIGN RELATIONS. *See* **INTERNATIONAL RELATIONS.**

FOREIGN RESIDENTS. *See* **ALIENS.**

FOREIGN SALES CORPORATIONS. *See* **EXPORT SALES CONTRACTS.**

FOREIGN TRADE. *See* **INTERNATIONAL TRADE.**

FOREIGN TRADE CONTROL. *See* **FOREIGN TRADE REGULATION.**

FOREIGN TRADE REGULATION.
DiMatteo, Larry A. The law of international business transactions. Mason, OH : Thomson/South-Western West, c2003.
KF915 .D56 2003

FOREIGN TRADE REGULATION - UNITED STATES.
DiMatteo, Larry A. The law of international business transactions. Mason, OH : Thomson/South-Western West, c2003.
KF915 .D56 2003

FOREIGNERS. *See* **ALIENS; IMMIGRANTS.**

Foreman-Wernet, Lois.
Communication, a different kind of horserace. Cresskill, N.J. : Hampton Press, c2003.
P87.5.C37 C66 2003

Forensic files
Mason, Paul, 1967- Investigating the supernatural. Chicago, Ill. : Heinemann Library, 2004.
BF1029 .M37 2004

Forensic focus
(23.) Castillo, Heather. Personality disorder. London ; Philadelphia : J. Kingsley Pub., 2003.
RC554 .C37 2003

FORENSIC PATHOLOGISTS - FICTION.
Cameron, Stella. Cold day in July. Waterville, Me. : Wheeler Pub. ; Bath, England : Chivers Press, 2002.
PS3553.A4345 C65 2002

FORENSIC PATHOLOGY. *See* **FORENSIC PATHOLOGISTS; MEDICAL EXAMINERS (LAW).**

FORENSIC SCIENCES. *See* **CRIMINAL INVESTIGATION.**

FORENSIC SCIENTISTS. *See* **FORENSIC PATHOLOGISTS; MEDICAL EXAMINERS (LAW).**

FORENSICS (PUBLIC SPEAKING). *See* **PERSUASION (RHETORIC).**

Foreseeing the future.
Christino, Karen. Amherst, MA : One Reed Publications, c2002.
BF1679.8.A31 C56 2002

Foreseen (Observatory).
La soif d'émotion. Paris : Plon, c1999.
BF531 .S637 1999

FOREST, PHILIPPE - INTERVIEWS.
Jouffroy, Alain, 1928- [Mots et moi] Les mots et moi ; Nantes : Pleins feux, c2002.

FORESTS AND FORESTRY. *See* **TREES.**

Forever young.
Danesi, Marcel, 1946- Toronto : University of Toronto Press, c2003.

FORGIVENESS. *See also* **AMNESTY.**
Forgiveness and the healing process. Hove, East Sussex ; New York : Brunner-Routledge, c2003.
BF637.F67 F66 2003

Hallowell, Edward M. Dare to forgive. Deerfield Beach, Fla. : Health Communications, 2004.
BF637.F67 H35 2004

Murphy, Jeffrie G. Getting even. Oxford ; New York : Oxford University Press, 2003.
BF637.F67 M87 2003

Schimmel, Solomon. Wounds not healed by time. Oxford ; New York : Oxford University Press, 2002.
BJ1476 .S34 2002

Spring, Janis Abrahms. How can I forgive you? 1st ed. New York : HarperCollins, 2004.
BF637.F67 S67 2004

Tipping, Colin C. Radical forgiveness. Atlanta, GA : GOLDENeight Publishers, c1997.
BF637.F67 T57 1997

Worthington, Everett L., 1946- Forgiving and reconciling. Rev. ed. Downers Grove, Ill. : InterVarsity Press, c2003.
BF637.F67 W67 2003

Forgiveness and the healing process : a central therapeutic concern / [edited by] Cynthia Ransley and Terri Spy. Hove, East Sussex ; New York : Brunner-Routledge, c2003. p. cm. Includes bibliographical references and index. Table of contents URL: http://www.loc.gov/catdir/toc/ecip044/2003011790.html CONTENTS: Forgiveness : themes and issues / Cynthia Ransley -- Christianity, therapy, and forgiveness / Terri Spy -- Be cautious about forgiveness / Cynthia ransley -- Four:the role of forgiveness in working with couples / Jane Cooper -- And Maria Gilbert -- Organisations and forgiveness : the challenge / Michael Carroll -- Transformation, healing or forgiveness? : assisting victims of crime through restorative practice / Guy Masters -- In the aftermath of political trauma : what price forgiveness? / Fathima Moosa, Gill Eagle, and Gill Straker -- My journey towards healing and forgiveness with the aid of therapy / Joy Green -- Letting go : a question of forgiveness? / Cynthia Ransley and Terri Spy. ISBN 1-58391-182-0 (alk. paper) ISBN 1-58391-183-9 (pbk. : alk. paper) DDC 155.9/2
1. Forgiveness. 2. Forgiveness - Therapeutic use. 3. Forgiveness - Religious aspects. I. Ransley, Cynthia. II. Spy, Terri.
BF637.F67 F66 2003

FORGIVENESS - CROATIA.
Mir u Hrvatskoj--rezultati istraživanja. Zagreb : Hrvatski Caritas ; Split : Franjevački in-t za kulturu mira, 2001.
HN638.A8 M57 2001

FORGIVENESS - RELIGIOUS ASPECTS.
Forgiveness and the healing process. Hove, East Sussex ; New York : Brunner-Routledge, c2003.
BF637.F67 F66 2003

FORGIVENESS - RELIGIOUS ASPECTS - JUDAISM.
Va'eknin, Yosef ben Avraham. Sefer Ka-sheleg yalbinu. Yerushalayim : Y. Va'eknin, 763 [2002 or 2003]

FORGIVENESS - THERAPEUTIC USE.
Forgiveness and the healing process. Hove, East Sussex ; New York : Brunner-Routledge, c2003.
BF637.F67 F66 2003

Forgiving and reconciling.
Worthington, Everett L., 1946- Rev. ed. Downers Grove, Ill. : InterVarsity Press, c2003.
BF637.F67 W67 2003

FORM PERCEPTION. *See* **PATTERN PERCEPTION; PICTURE PERCEPTION.**

FORMAL DISCIPLINE. *See* **MEMORY.**

Formas artísticas y sociedad de masas.
Tomás Ferré, Facundo. Madrid : Antonio Machado Libros, c2001.

FORMATION, CHARACTER. *See* **PERSONALITY DEVELOPMENT.**

The formation of the scientific mind.
Bachelard, Gaston. [Formation de l'esprit scientifique. English] Manchester : Clinamen, c2002.

Formes sémiotiques
Une introduction aux sciences de la culture. 1. ed. Paris : Presses universitaires de France ; [Paris] : Institut Ferdinand-de-Saussure, 2002.

The formula.
Sylvest, Vernon M. Fairfield, Iowa : Sunstar Pub., c1996.
BF161 .S95 1996

Formule magiche.
Astori, Roberta. Milano : Mimesis, c2000.
BF1591 .A88 2000

Forrester, Mary Gore, 1940- Moral beliefs and moral theory / Mary Gore Forrester. Dordrecht ; Boston : Kluwer Academic Publishers, c2002. xiii, 292 p. ; 25 cm. (Library of ethics and applied philosophy ; v. 10) Includes bibliographical references (p. 275-281) and index. ISBN 140200687X (alk. paper) DDC 171/.2
1. Ethics. I. Title. II. Series.
BJ1012 .F615 2002

Forsthoefel, Thomas A. Knowing beyond knowledge : epistemologies of religious experience in classical and modern Advaita / Thomas A. Forsthoefel. Alderhot, England ; Burlington, VT. : Ashgate, 2002. xi199 p. ; 25 cm. (Ashgate world philosophies series) Includes bibliographical references (183-195) and index. ISBN 0-7546-0625-2 (alk. paper) DDC 181/.482
1. Advaita. 2. Knowledge, Theory of. 3. Experience (Religion) I. Title. II. Series.
B132.A3 F66 2002

Fortenbaugh, William W. Theophrastean studies / William W. Fortenbaugh. Stuttgart : Steiner, 2003. 345 p. ; 25 cm. (Philosophie der Antike, 0943-5921 ; Bd. 17) ISBN 3-515-07808-8 (hd.bd.)
1. Theophrastus - Criticism and interpretation. 2. Peripatetics. 3. Philosophy, Ancient. I. Title. II. Series.
B626.T34 F678 2003

Fortenbaugh, William W. (William Wale) Aristotle on emotion : a contribution to philosophical psychology, rhetoric, poetics, politics and ethics / W.W. Fortenbaugh. 2nd ed. London : Duckworth, 2002. 142 p. ; 22 cm. Includes bibliographical references and indexes. ISBN 0-7156-3167-5 DDC 128.3
1. Aristotle, - 384-322 B.C. 2. Emotions. 3. Ethics, Ancient. I. Title.
B491.E7 F67 2002

Fortis, Jean-Michel.
Une introduction aux sciences de la culture. 1. ed. Paris : Presses universitaires de France ; [Paris] : Institut Ferdinand-de-Saussure, 2002.

Fortitude et servitude : lectures de l'éthique IV de Spinoza / sous la direction de Chantal Jaquet, Pascal Sévérac, Ariel Suhamy. Paris : Kimé, c2003. 187 p. ; 22 cm. (Collection Philosophie, épistémologie) Includes bibliographical references. ISBN 2-8417-4298-9 DDC 193
1. Spinoza, Benedictus de, - 1632-1677. - Ethica - Part 4. 2. Ethics. I. Jaquet, Chantal. II. Sévérac, Pascal. III. Suhamy, Ariel. IV. Series.

Fortunato, Maria Lucinete.
Ensaios. Jōao Pessoa : Editora Universitária, 2001.

FORTUNE. *See also* **FATE AND FATALISM; SUCCESS.**
Bharadwaj, Monisha. The Indian luck book. London : Kyle Cathie, 2001.
BF1778 .B43 2001

Lears, T. J. Jackson, 1947- Something for nothing. New York : Viking, 2003.
HV6715 .L415 2003

Nwokogba, Isaac E. Seeds of luck. Cranston, R.I. : Writers' Collective, 2003.
BF1778 .N96 2003

Piven, Joshua. As luck would have it. 1st ed. New York : Villard, c2003.
BF1778 .P58 2003

FORTUNE - MORAL AND ETHICAL ASPECTS.
Hurley, S. L. (Susan L.) Justice, luck, and knowledge. Cambridge, Mass. : Harvard University Press, 2003.
BJ1451 .H87 2003

Fortune teller's dictionary.
Beattie, Antonia. San Diego : Thunder Bay, 2003.
BF1861 .B43 2003

FORTUNE-TELLERS - LATVIA - BIOGRAPHY.
Rīgas gaišregis Eižens Finks. Rīgā : Jumava, c2002.
BF1997.F56 R54 2002

FORTUNE-TELLING. *See also* **FORTUNE-TELLERS.**
Kallen, Stuart A., 1955- San Diego, Calif. : Lucent Books, 2004.
BF1861 .K35 2004

FORTUNE-TELLING.
Fairchild, Dennis. The fortune telling handbook. 1st ed. Philadelphia, PA : Running Press, c2003.
BF1861 .F35 2003

Messenger, Charles M. Nine Wind Tonalamatl Tolteca-fate papers. [United States] : C.M. Messenger, c2002-
BF1861 .M47 2002

FORTUNE TELLING.
Shaw, Maria, 1963- Maria Shaw's star gazer. 1st ed. St. Paul, Minn. : Llewellyn Publications, 2003.
BF1411 .S52 2003

FORTUNE-TELLING BY BIRTHDAY.
Camp, Robert (Robert L.) [Destiny cards] Cards of your destiny. Naperville, Ill. : Sourcebooks, 2004.
BF1878 .C265 2004

FORTUNE-TELLING BY BOOKS.
Bolt, Carol, 1963- Mom's book of answers. New York : Stewart, Tabori & Chang, 2004.
BF1891.B66 B649 2004

FORTUNE-TELLING BY CARDS. *See also* **TAROT.**
Bonewitz, Ra. Wisdom of the Maya. 1st St. Martin's ed. New York : St. Martin's Press, 2000.
BF1878 .B66 2000

Camp, Robert (Robert L.) [Destiny cards] Cards of your destiny. Naperville, Ill. : Sourcebooks, 2004.
BF1878 .C265 2004

Hepburn, Rae. Tea leaf fortune cards. 1st ed. Boston : Journey Editions, c2000.
BF1881 .H47 2000

Kelly, Dorothy, 1952 Aug. 6- Tarot card combinations. Boston, MA : York Beach, ME : Weiser Books, 2003, c1995.
BF1879.T2 K45 2003

Lott, Lynn. Madame Dora's fortune-telling cards. Gloucester, Mass. : Fair Winds Press, 2003.
BF1878 .L78 2003

FORTUNE-TELLING BY DREAMS.
Jagaddeva. [Svapnacintāmaṇi. Russian] Volshebnoe sokrovishche snovideniĭ. Moskva : Ladomir, 1996.
BF1088.S26 J34 1996

FORTUNE-TELLING BY PENDULUM.
Cohen, Maxi. The art of the pendulum. [Kansas City, Mo.] : Andrews McMeel, [c2002]
BF1779.P45 C64 2002

Sonnenberg, Petra. [Pendelen van A tot Z. English] The great pendulum book. New York, NY : Sterling Pub. Co., 2003.
BF1779.P45 S6613 2003

FORTUNE-TELLING BY RUNES.
Aswynn, Freya, 1949- Northern mysteries & magick. 2nd ed. St. Paul, Minn. : Llewellyn Publications, 1998 (2002 printing)
BF1623.R89 A78 1998

Hathaway, Robert A. Runes from the New World. 2nd ed. [San Diego, Calif.?] : R.A. Hathaway, c2002.
BF1891.R85 H38 2002

Mountfort, Paul Rhys. Nordic runes. Rochester, Vt. : Destiny Books, 2003.
BF1779.R86 M68 2003

Seachrist, Brian. The runic oracle. Riverview, FL : Green Warden Foundation, c1999.
BF1891.R85 S43 1999

FORTUNE-TELLING BY TEA LEAVES.
Hepburn, Rae. Tea leaf fortune cards. 1st ed. Boston : Journey Editions, c2000.
BF1881 .H47 2000

FORTUNE-TELLING - DICTIONARIES.
Beattie, Antonia. Fortune teller's dictionary. San Diego : Thunder Bay, 2003.
BF1861 .B43 2003

The fortune telling handbook.
Fairchild, Dennis. 1st ed. Philadelphia, PA : Running Press, c2003.
BF1861 .F35 2003

FORTUNE TELLING - HISTORY.
Kallen, Stuart A., 1955- Fortune-telling. San Diego, Calif. : Lucent Books, 2004.
BF1861 .K35 2004

FORTUNE-TELLING - INDIA.
Bharadwaj, Monisha. The Indian luck book. London : Kyle Cathie, 2001.
BF1778 .B43 2001

FORTUNE-TELLING - JUVENILE LITERATURE.
Kallen, Stuart A., 1955- Fortune-telling. San Diego, Calif. : Lucent Books, 2004.
BF1861 .K35 2004

FORTUNE-TELLING - ROMANIA - TRANSYLVANIA.
Keszeg, Vilmos. Jóslások a mezőségen. Sepsiszentgyörgy : BON AMI, 1997.
BF1868.H8 K47 1997

FORTUNE TELLING - RUSSIA (FEDERATION) - SIBERIA.
Stepanova, Natal'i͡a (Natal'i͡a Ivanovna) Gadanii͡a sibirskoĭ tselitel'nitsy. Moskva : RIPOL klassik, 1999.
BF1866 .S73 1999

Fortunes of history.
Kelley, Donald R., 1931- New Haven : Yale University Press, c2003.
D16 .K26 2003

FORTUNETELLING. *See* **FORTUNE-TELLING.**

Forty years of Philippine psychology / edited by Allan B.I. Bernardo, Madelene A. Sta. Maria, Allen L. Tan. Diliman, Quezon City, Philippines : Psychological Association of the Philippines, c2002. 407 p. : ill. ; 23 cm. "This book is being published by the Psychological Association of the Philippines in commemoration of its 40th anniversary"--P. [4] of cover. Includes bibliographical references. ISBN 971-92567-1-0
1. Psychology - Philippines. I. Bernardo, Allan B. I. II. Sta. Maria, Madelene A. III. Tan, Allen L. IV. Psychological Association of the Philippines. V. Title: 40 years of Philippine psychology
BF108 .F67 2002

Forum europäische Ethnologie
(Bd. 1) Inspecting Germany. Münster : Lit, c2002.
DD76 .I57 2002

Forum Musikpädagogik
(Bd. 51) Mensch & Musik. Augsburg : Wissner, c2002.
ML3830 .M46 2002

Forzano, Lori-Ann B.
Gravetter, Frederick J. Research methods for the behavioral sciences. Belmont, CA : Wadsworth, c2003.
BF76.5 .G73 2003

Fosl, Peter S.
Baggini, Julian. The philosopher's toolkit. Malden, MA : Blackwell Publishers, 2003.
BC177 .B19 2003

Fosshage, James L.
Lichtenberg, Joseph D. A spirit of inquiry. Hillsdale, NJ : Analytic Press, 2002.
RC506 .L5238 2002

FOSSIL HOMINIDS.
Kingdon, Jonathan. Lowly origin. Princeton : Princeton University Press, c2003.
GN282 .K54 2003

Pievani, Telmo. Homo sapiens e altre catastrofi. Roma : Meltemi, c2002.

FOSTER HOME CARE. *See* **ADOPTION.**

Fotiade, Ramona. Conceptions of the absurd : from surrealism to the existential thought of Chestov and Fondane / Ramona Fotiade. Oxford : Legenda, 2001. 259 p. ; 22 cm. Includes bibliographical references (p. [239]-254) and index. Includes passages in French. ISBN 1-900755-47-5 DDC 149
1. Shestov, Lev, - 1866-1938. 2. Fondane, Benjamin, - 1898-1944. 3. Absurd (Philosophy) 4. Absurd (Philosophy) in literature. 5. Surrealism. 6. Existentialism. I. Title.

Foucault au Collège de France : un itinéraire / sous la direction de Guillaume Le Blanc et Jean Terrel. Pessac : Presses universitaires de Bordeaux, c2003. 227 p. ; 24 cm. (Histoire des pensées, 1245-2955) Includes bibliographical references (p. 217-221) and indexes. ISBN 2-86781-295-X DDC 194
1. Foucault, Michel. 2. Collège de France - Curricula. 3. Philosophy, Modern - 20th century. I. Le Blanc, Guillaume. II. Terrel, Jean. III. Series.
B2430.F724 F6855 2003

Foucault, cultural studies, and governmentality / edited by Jack Z. Bratich, Jeremy Packer, Cameron McCarthy. Albany : State University of New York Press, c2003. viii, 369 p. : ill. ; 24 cm. Includes bibliographical references and indexes. ISBN 0-7914-5663-3 (alk. paper) ISBN 0-7914-5664-1 (pbk. : alk. paper) DDC 306.2
1. Foucault, Michel. 2. Power (Social sciences) 3. State, The. 4. Culture - Study and teaching. I. Bratich, Jack Z., 1969- II. Packer, Jeremy, 1970- III. McCarthy, Cameron.
JC330 .F63 2003

FOUCAULT, MICHEL.
Foucault au Collège de France. Pessac : Presses universitaires de Bordeaux, c2003.
B2430.F724 F6855 2003

Foucault, cultural studies, and governmentality. Albany : State University of New York Press, c2003.
JC330 .F63 2003

Kropotov, S. L. (Sergeĭ Leonidovich) Ėkonomika teksta v neklassicheskoĭ filosofii iskusstva. Ekaterinburg : Gumanitarnyĭ universitet, 1999.
B831.2 .K76 1999

Maset, Michael. Diskurs, Macht und Geschichte. Frankfurt/Main ; New York : Campus, c2002.
BF24.30.F724 M37 2002

FOUCAULT, MICHEL - CONTRIBUTIONS IN SOCIAL SCIENCES.
Kharkhordin, Oleg, 1964- Oblichat' i litsemerit'. Sankt-Peterburg : Evropeĭskiĭ universitet v Sankt-Peterburge ; Moskva : Letniĭ Sad, 2002.
B2430.F724 K43 2002

FOUCAULT, MICHEL - INFLUENCE.
The sciences in enlightened Europe. Chicago : University of Chicago Press, 1999.
Q127.E8 S356 1999

Foundations of archaeological inquiry
Style, function, transmission. Salt Lake City : University of Utah Press, c2003.
CC173 .S79 2003

The foundations of mind.
Mandler, Jean Matter. Oxford ; New York : Oxford University Press, 2004.
BF720.C63 M36 2004

Foundations of philosophy in India
Gupta, Bina, 1947- CIT consciousness. New Delhi ; New York : Oxford University Press, 2003.
BF311+

Foundations of social cognition : a festschrift in honor of Robert S. Wyer, Jr. / edited by Galen V. Bodenhausen, Alan J. Lambert. Mahwah, N.J. : L. Erlbaum, 2003. viii, 302 p. : ill. ; 24 cm. Includes bibliographical references and indexes. ISBN 0-8058-4132-6 (alk. paper) DDC 302/.12
1. Social perception. I. Wyer, Robert S. II. Bodenhausen, Galen V. (Galen Von), 1961- III. Lambert, Alan J.
BF323.S63 F68 2003

The founding fathers and the politics of character.
Trees, Andrew S., 1968- Princeton, N.J. : Princeton University Press, c2004.
E302.1 .T74 2004

FOUNDLINGS - FICTION.
Quindlen, Anna. Blessings. 1st large print ed. New York : Random House Large Print, c2002.
PS3567.U336 B59 2002b

FOUR ELEMENTS (PHILOSOPHY) IN ART.
Estetyka czterech żywiołów. Kraków : Universitas, c2002.

The four gold keys.
Clarke, Robert B. Charlottesville, VA : Hampton Roads Pub., c2002.
BF175.5.D74 C58 2002

Four lessons of psychoanalysis.
Safouan, Moustafa. New York : Other Press, c2004.
BF175 .S19 2004

The four temperaments.
Baron, Renee. 1st St. Martin's Griffin ed. New York : St. Martin's Griffin, 2004.
BF698.3 .B365 2004

FOUR TEMPERAMENTS.
Baron, Renee. The four temperaments. 1st St. Martin's Griffin ed. New York : St. Martin's Griffin, 2004.
BF698.3 .B365 2004

The four things that matter most.
Byock, Ira. New York : Free Press, 2004.
BF637.C45 B93 2004

Fourier, Charles, 1772-1837. Du libre arbitre / Charles Fourier. Suivi de, Charles Fourier et l'utopie / par Franck Malécot ; édition établie par Pascal Fiévé. Bordeaux : Saints Calus, 2003. 142 p. : port. ; 18 cm. (Bibliotheca Fritillaria ; [1]) Includes bibliographical references. ISBN 2-914314-01-9 DDC 194
1. Fourier, Charles, - 1772-1837. 2. Free will and determinism. 3. Utopian socialism - France. I. Fiévé, Pascal. II. Malécot, Franck. Charles Fourier et l'utopie. III. Title.

FOURIER, CHARLES, 1772-1837.
Fourier, Charles, 1772-1837. Du libre arbitre. Bordeaux : Saints Calus, 2003.

FOURTH WORLD. See DEVELOPING COUNTRIES.

Fous comme des sages.
Droit, Roger-Pol. Paris : Seuil, c2002.

Fox, Katrina.
Finding the real me. 1st ed. San Francisco, CA : Jossey-Bass, c2003.
HQ77.7 .F56 2003

Fox, Nik Farrell. The new Sartre : explorations in postmodernism / Nik Farrell Fox. New York ; London : Continuum, 2003. ix, 195 p. ; 24 cm. Includes bibliographical references, chronology, and index. ISBN 0-8264-6183-2 ISBN 0-8264-6184-0 (pbk.) DDC 194
1. Sartre, Jean Paul, - 1905- 2. Postmodernism. 3. Philosophers - France. I. Title.

Foxall, G. R. Context and cognition : interpreting complex behavior / Gordon R. Foxall. 1st ed. Reno, NV : Context Press, 2004. p. cm. Includes bibliographical references. ISBN 1-87897-846-2 (pbk.) DDC 150.19/43
1. Behaviorism (Psychology) I. Title.
BF199 .F69 2004

Foxcroft, Cheryl.
An introduction to psychological assessment in the South African context. Cape Town, South Africa : Oxford University Press Southern Africa, 2001.
BF39 .I58 2001

Foxman, Paul. The worried child : recognizing anxiety in children and helping them heal / Paul Foxman. 1st ed. Alameda, CA : Hunter House, c2004. p. cm. Includes bibliographical references and index. Table of contents URL: http://www.loc.gov/catdir/toc/ecip047/2003016843.html ISBN 0-89793-420-2 (pbk.) DDC 155.4/1246
1. Anxiety in children. I. Title.
BF723.A5 F69 2004

FRACTALS.
Baryshev, Yurij. Discovery of cosmic fractals. River Edge, N.J. : World Scientific, c2002.
QB981 .B285 2002

Pickover, Clifford A. Chaos in Wonderland. 1st ed. New York : St. Martin's Press, 1994.
Q172.5.C45 P53 1994

The fractious nation? : unity and division in contemporary American life / Jonathan Rieder, editor ; Steven Steinlight, associate editor. Berkeley : University of California Press, c2003. vii, 295 p. ; 24 cm. Includes bibliographical references and index. ISBN 0-520-23662-9 (cloth : alk. paper) ISBN 0-520-23663-7 (pbk. : alk. paper) ISBN 0-520-22043-9 DDC 973.931
1. National characteristics, American. 2. United States - Politics and government - 1989- 3. Political culture - United States. 4. Citizenship - Social aspects - United States. 5. United States - Moral conditions. 6. United States - Social conditions - 1980- 7. Social conflict - United States. 8. Pluralism (Social sciences) - United States. I. Rieder, Jonathan. II. Steinlight, Steven.
E169.12 .F69 2003

El frágil absoluto, o, Por qué merece la pena luchar por el legado cristiano?.
Žižek, Slavoj, 1949- [Fragile absolute. Spanish] 1. ed. Valencia : Pre-Textos, 2002.
BT1102 .Z58

Fraiman, Susan. Cool men and the second sex / Susan Fraiman. New York : Columbia University Press, c2003. xxiii, 212 p. : ill. ; 23 cm. (Gender and culture) Includes bibliographical references (p. [161]-204) and index. ISBN 0-231-12962-9 (cloth) ISBN 0-231-12963-7 (paper) DDC 305.31
1. Men - Identity. 2. Men - Attitudes. 3. Gender identity. 4. Masculinity. I. Title. II. Series.
HQ1090 .F73 2003

Fraley, R. Chris. How to conduct behavioral research over the internet : a beginner's guide to HTML and CGI/PERL / R. Chris Fraley. New York : Guilford Press, 2005. p. cm. (Methodology in the social sciences) Includes bibliographical references and index. ISBN 1-57230-997-0 (pbk.) DDC 150/.285/4678

1. Internet research. 2. Psychology - Research - Methodology. 3. Social sciences - Research - Methodology. 4. Psychology - Research - Data processing. 5. Social sciences - Research - Data processing. 6. HTML (Document markup language) 7. CGI (Computer network protocol) 8. Perl (Computer program language) I. Title. II. Series.
BF76.6.I57 F73 2005

Fralix, Patti. How to thrive in spite of mess, stress and less! / by Patti Fralix. 1st ed. Raleigh, NC : Triunity Publishers, c2002. xiv, 143 p. ; 20 cm. ISBN 0-9719737-0-9 DDC 158
1. Self-actualization (Psychology) 2. Success - Psychological aspects. I. Title.
BF637.S4 F72 2002

Frame, Marsha Wiggins. Integrating religion and spirituality into counseling : a comprehensive approach / Marsha Wiggins Frame. Australia ; Pacific Grove, CA : Thomson/Brooks/Cole, c2003. xiv, 340 p. ; 24 cm. Includes bibliographical references (p. 299-327) and index. ISBN 0-534-53093-1 DDC 158/.3
1. Counseling. 2. Counseling - Religious aspects. 3. Counseling - Case studies. 4. Psychology and religion. 5. Spirituality. I. Title.
BF637.C6 F64 2003

Framework for teaching across differences.
Schultz, Katherine. Listening. New York : Teachers College Press, c2003.
LB1027 .S36638 2003

La France au fil de ses rois
Depreux, Philippe. Charlemagne et les Carolingiens. Paris : Tallandier : Historia, 2002.
DC73 .D38 2002

FRANCE - COURT AND COURTIERS - HISTORY - 17TH CENTURY.
Montpensier, Anne-Marie-Louise d'Orléans, duchesse de, 1627-1693. [Correspondence. English & French] Against marriage. Chicago : University of Chicago Press, 2002.
DC130.M8 A4 2002

FRANCE - ETHNIC IDENTITY.
Konstrukte nationaler Identität. Würzburg : Ergon, c2002.
DC34 .K67 2002

FRANCE - ETHNIC RELATIONS.
Amougou, Emmanuel. La construction de l'inconscient colonial en Alsace. Paris : L'Harmattan, 2002.
1. Black author.

FRANCE - HISTORY - 18TH CENTURY.
Carlyle, Thomas, 1795-1881. Historical essays. Berkeley ; London : University of California Press, c2002.
D208 .C34 2002

FRANCE - HISTORY - LOUIS XIV, 1643-1715.
Montpensier, Anne-Marie-Louise d'Orléans, duchesse de, 1627-1693. [Correspondence. English & French] Against marriage. Chicago : University of Chicago Press, 2002.
DC130.M8 A4 2002

FRANCE - HISTORY, MILITARY.
Gaulle, Charles de, 1890-1970. [Fil de l'épée. Portuguese] O fio da espada. Rio de Janeiro : Biblioteca do Exército Editora, 2001.

FRANCE - HISTORY - THIRD REPUBLIC, 1870-1940.
Huteau, Michel. Psychologie, psychiatrie et société sous la troisième république. Paris : Harmattan, c2002.

FRANCE - HISTORY - TO 987. See also CAROLINGIANS; MEROVINGIANS.
Depreux, Philippe. Charlemagne et les Carolingiens. Paris : Tallandier : Historia, 2002.
DC73 .D38 2002

FRANCE - KINGS AND RULERS - BIOGRAPHY.
Depreux, Philippe. Charlemagne et les Carolingiens. Paris : Tallandier : Historia, 2002.
DC73 .D38 2002

FRANCE - LITERATURES. See FRENCH LITERATURE.

FRANCE - OCCUPATIONS. See OCCUPATIONS - FRANCE.

FRANCE - SOCIAL CONDITIONS - 1945-1995.
Limonov, Ėduard. Distsiplinarnyĭ sanatoriĭ. Sankt-Peterburg : Amfora, 2002.
CB428 .L556 2002

FRANCE - SOCIAL LIFE AND CUSTOMS.
Effros, Bonnie, 1965- Creating community with food

and drink in Merovingian Gaul. 1st ed. New York ; Houndmills, England : Palgrave Macmillan, 2002.
GT2853.F7 E34 2002

Franchi, Franco. La libertà nel fascismo / Franco Franchi. Roma : Europa : Settimo sigillo, c2002. 101 p. ; 20 cm. (I quaderni di Storia verità ; 9) Includes bibliographical references and index. DDC 945
1. Fascism - Italy. 2. Liberty. 3. Italy - Politics and government - 1922-1945. I. Title. II. Series.

Francia, Luis, 1945-.
Vestiges of war. New York : New York University Press, 2000.
DS679 .V47 2000

Francis-Cheung, Theresa. Teen tarot / Theresa Francis-Cheung and Terry Silvers. Avon, MA : Adams Media Corp., 2003. p. cm. SUMMARY: Explains the meaning of different tarot cards and how teenagers can use tarot cards to help solve problems related to family life, school, work, dating, physical health and appearance, and dreams. ISBN 1-58062-916-4 DDC 133.3/2424
1. Tarot - Juvenile literature. 2. Tarot. I. Silvers, Terry. II. Title.
BF1879.T2 F7 2003

Francis, Elizabeth, 1959- Feminism and modernism [microform] : gender and cultural politics in America, 1910-1940 / by Elizabeth Francis. [1994] vii, 310 leaves : ill. Thesis (Ph.D.)--Brown University, 1994. Vita. Bibliography: leaves 282-304. Microfiche. Ann Arbor, Mich. : University Microfilms International, 1994. 4 microfiches ; 11 x 15 cm. "94-33356." CONTENTS: Introduction: Representing the modern woman -- From event to monument: Isadora Duncan, the body and modernity -- "The Secret treachery of words": Margaret Anderson and the politics of self-expression -- Floyd Dell's fantasy of modernist heterosexuality -- Josephine Herbst and the uses of the usable past -- Conclusion: Language and experience.
1. Duncan, Isadora - 1877-1927. 2. Feminism. 3. Modernism (Aesthetics) 4. Gender identity. I. Title.

Francis, Linda.
Zukav, Gary. The mind of the soul. New York : Free Press, 2003.
BF611 .Z85 2003

Francis, Richard C., 1953- Why men won't ask for directions : the seductions of sociobiology / Richard C. Francis. Princeton, N.J. : Princeton University Press, 2004. p. cm. Includes bibliographical references and index. ISBN 0-691-05757-5 (alk. paper) DDC 155.7
1. Evolutionary psychology. 2. Evolution (Biology) 3. Sex. 4. Sex differences. I. Title.
BF698.95 .F73 2004

FRANCS-TIREURS. *See* **GUERRILLAS.**

Frank, Claudine, 1957-.
Caillois, Roger, 1913- The edge of surrealism. Durham : Duke University Press, 2003.
HM590 .C35 2003

Frank, Daniel H., 1950-.
The Cambridge companion to medieval Jewish philosophy. Cambridge, UK ; New York : Cambridge University Press, 2003.
B755 .C36 2003

Frank, David A.
Rowland, Robert C., 1954- Shared land/conflicting identity. East lansing : Michigan State University Press, 2002.
DS119.7 .R685 2003

Frank, Erica.
Bowman, Marjorie A. Women in medicine. 3rd ed. New York ; Berlin : Springer, c2002.
R692 .B69 2002

Frank, Lawrence K. (Lawrence Kelso), 1890-1968.
Hartley, Ruth E. (Ruth Edith), b.1909 Understanding children's play, London : Routledge, 2000.
BF717 .H3 2000

Frank M. Covey, Jr. Loyola lectures in political analysis
Klosko, George. Jacobins and utopians. Notre Dame, Ind. : University of Notre Dame Press, c2003.
JC491 .K54 2003

Frankenburg, Reuven. Revadim 'elyonim ba-minhal ha-tsiburi ha-Yiśre'eli : sugim shel menahalim kelaliyim ve-signonot nihul / me-et Re'uven Frankenburg. [Israel : h. mo. l., 1999?] 237, xiii p. ; 30 cm. Added title page title: Elite strata in Israeli government bureaucracy : varieties of directors general and styles of administration. Thesis (Ph. D)--ha-Universiṭah ha-'Ivrit bi-Yerushalayim, 1999. Includes bibliographical references (199-211). Abstract also in English.
1. Government executives - Israel. 2. Management. 3. Public administration - Israel. I. Title. II. Title: Elite strata in Israeli government bureaucracy : varieties of directors general and styles of administration

Frankfort-Nachmias, Chava. Social statistics for a diverse society / Chava Frankfort-Nachmias, Anna Leon-Guerrero. 3rd ed. Thousand Oaks, Calif. : Pine Forge Press, c2002. xxxi, 569 p. : ill. ; 24 cm. + 1 computer disc (3 1/2 in.). (The Pine Forge Press series in research methods and statistics) Computer disc in pocket. Includes bibliographical references and index. CONTENTS: The what and why of statistics -- Organization of information: frequency distributions -- Graphic presentation -- Measures of central tendency -- Measures of variability -- Relationships between two variables: cross-tabulation -- Measures of association for nominal and ordinal variables -- Bivariate regression and correlation -- Organization or information and measurement of relationships; a review of descriptive data analysis -- The normal distribution -- Sampling and sampling distributions -- Estimation -- Testing hypotheses -- The chi-square test -- Reviewing inferential statistics. ISBN 0-7619-8743-6 (cloth : alk. paper) ISBN 0-7619-8777-0 (text + CD-ROM) DDC 519.5
1. Social sciences - Statistical methods. 2. Statistics. I. Leon-Guerrero, Anna. II. Title. III. Series.
HA29 .N25 2002

FRANKFURT, HARRY G., 1929-.
Moral responsibility and alternative possibilities. Aldershot, England ; Burlington, VT : Ashgate, c2003.
BJ1451 .M6472 2003

FRANKFURT SCHOOL OF SOCIOLOGY.
Alford, C. Fred. Levinas, the Frankfurt school and psychoanalysis. 1st US ed. Middletown, CT : Wesleyan University Press, c2002.

Frankl, Viktor Emil. Man's search for ultimate meaning / Viktor E. Frankl ; foreword by Swanee Hunt. Cambridge, Mass. : Perseus Pub., c2000. 191 p. : ill. ; 22 cm. "The present text is a revised, updated version of the original Austrian edition, Der Unbewusste Gott, c1948 Viktor E. Frankl; and the English translation, The Unconscious God, c1975 Viktor E. Frankl"--T.p. verso. Includes bibliographical references (p. 155-186) and index. ISBN 0-7382-0354-8 DDC 150.19/5
1. Psychiatry and religion. 2. Psychotherapy. 3. Logotherapy. I. Frankl, Viktor Emil. Unbewusste Gott. II. Frankl, Viktor Emil. Unconscious god. III. Title.
RC455.4.R4 F7 2000

Unbewusste Gott.
Frankl, Viktor Emil. Man's search for ultimate meaning. Cambridge, Mass. : Perseus Pub., c2000.
RC455.4.R4 F7 2000

Unconscious god.
Frankl, Viktor Emil. Man's search for ultimate meaning. Cambridge, Mass. : Perseus Pub., c2000.
RC455.4.R4 F7 2000

Franklin, Anna. The illustrated encyclopedia of fairies / Anna Franklin ; illustrated by Paul Mason and Helen Field. London : Vega, 2002. 288 p. : ill. (some col.) ; 28 cm. Includes bibliographical references. ISBN 1-84333-624-3 DDC 398.21
1. Fairies - Encyclopedias. 2. Monsters - Encyclopedias. 3. Sacred space - Encyclopedias. I. Title. II. Title: Fairies
GR549 .F73 2002

Fransella, Fay. A manual for repertory grid technique / Fay Fransella, Richard Bell, and Don Bannister. 2nd ed. Hoboken, NJ : Wiley, c2004. p. cm. Includes bibliographical references (p.   ) and indexes. Publisher description URL: http://www.loc.gov/catdir/desc ription/wiley0310/2003014732.html Table of contents URL: http://www.loc.gov/catdir/toc/wiley03/2003014732.html ISBN 0-470-85489-8 ISBN 0-470-85490-1 (pbk.) DDC 155.2/8
1. Repertory grid technique. I. Bell, Richard. II. Bannister, D. (Donald) III. Title.
BF698.8.R38 F72 2004

Frantzen, Allen J., 1947- Bloody good : chivalry, sacrifice, and the Great War / Allen J. Frantzen. Chicago : University of Chicago Press, 2004. xv, 335 p. : ill. (some col.) ; 24 cm. Includes bibliographical references (p. 267-323) and index. CONTENTS: Chivalry and sacrifice -- Violence and abjection -- The making of a knight: St. Edmund, virgin and martyr -- Chivalry and sacrifice : a chronicle of scales -- Antisacrifice: the hidden cost of chivalry -- "Modest stillness and humility": the nineteenth century and the chivalry of duty -- "Teach them how to war": postcards, chivalry, and sacrifice -- "Greater love than this": memorials of the Great War --Circles of grief: chivalry and the heart of sacrifice. ISBN 0-226-26085-2 (hardcover : alk. paper) DDC 940.3/1
1. World War, 1914-1918. 2. Chivalry. 3. Sacrifice. 4. Masculinity. 5. Europe - Civilization. I. Title.
D523 .F722 2004

Franzoi, Stephen L. Psychology : a journey of discovery / Stephen Franzoi. Cincinnati, Ohio : Atomic Dog Pub., c2002. xx, 667 p. : ill. ; 28 cm. Includes bibliographical references (p. 578-640) and indexes. ISBN 1-931442-09-6 DDC 150
1. Psychology. I. Title.
BF121 .F67 2002

Psychology : the discovery experience / Stephen Franzoi. Cincinnati, Ohio : Atomic Dog Pub., c2003. xxii, 634 p. : ill. (some col.) ; 28 cm. Includes bibliographical references (p. 537-605) and index. ISBN 1-59260-037-9 (pbk.) DDC 150
1. Psychology. I. Title.
BF121 .F675 2003

Fraser, Robin, 1941-.
Hope, Jeremy. Beyond budgeting. Boston : Harvard Business School Press, c2003.
HD31 .H635 2003

FRAUD. *See* **FALSE PERSONATION.**

Frayne, Jill. Starting out in the afternoon : a mid-life journey into wild land / Jill Frayne. Toronto : Random House Canada, c2002. 247 p. : 1 map ; 20 cm. ISBN 0-679-31119-X DDC 917.104/648
1. Frayne, Jill - Travel - Canada. 2. Middle age - Psychological aspects. 3. Canada - Description and travel. I. Title.

FRAYNE, JILL - TRAVEL - CANADA.
Frayne, Jill. Starting out in the afternoon. Toronto : Random House Canada, c2002.

FREAKS. *See* **MONSTERS.**

Frederiksen, Bodil Folke, 1943- Popular culture, family relations, and issues of everyday democracy : a study of youth in Pumwani / Bodil Folke Frederiksen. [Nairobi] : Institute for Development Studies, University of Nairobi, [2000] ii, 30 p. ; 21 cm. (IDS WP ; no. 530) "November 2000." Includes bibliographical references. DDC 305.235/096762/5
1. Youth - Kenya - Nairobi. 2. Popular culture. I. Title. II. Series: Working paper (University of Nairobi. Institute for Development Studies) ; no. 530.
HQ799.K42 N354 2000

Fredrick, David, 1959-.
The Roman gaze. Baltimore : Johns Hopkins University Press, 2002.
BF637.C45 R64 2002

FREE ENTERPRISE.
Von Mises, Ludwig, 1881-1973. Between the two World Wars. Indianapolis, Ind. : Liberty Fund, c2002.
HB101.V66A25 2002

FREE ENTERPRISE - UNITED STATES.
Monkeywrenching the new world order [sound recording]. Oakland, Calif : AK Press ; San Francisco, CA : Alternative Tentacles Records, 2001.

FREE MARKETS. *See* **FREE ENTERPRISE.**

FREE MATERIAL. *See* **GIFTS.**

A free spirit.
Shine, Betty, 1929- London : HarperCollinsPublishers, 2001.

FREE WILL AND DETERMINISM.
Anselm, Saint, Archbishop of Canterbury, 1033-1109. [Dialogues. English. Selections] Three philosophical dialogues. Indianapolis, IN : Hackett Pub., c2002.
B765.A81 .A2513 2002

Bertelsen, Preben. Free will, consciousness, and the self. New York : Berghahn Books, 2003.
BF621 .B47 2003

Between chance and choice. Thorverton, UK ; Charlottesville, VA : Imprint Academic, c2002.
BJ1461 .B48 2002

Clarke, Randolph K. Libertarian accounts of free will. Oxford ; New York : Oxford University Press, c2003.
BJ1461 .C53 2003

Dennett, Daniel Clement. Freedom evolves. New York ; London : Viking, 2003.
BJ1461 .D427 2003

Fourier, Charles, 1772-1837. Du libre arbitre. Bordeaux : Saints Calus, 2003.

Moral responsibility and alternative possibilities. Aldershot, England ; Burlington, VT : Ashgate, c2003.
BJ1451 .M6472 2003

Schlosser, Herta. Der Mensch als Wesen der Freiheit. Vallendar-Schönstatt : Patris Verlag, 2002.

Shubniakov, B. P. Svoboda kak sotsial'nyĭ i dukhovno-psikhicheskiĭ fenomen. IAroslavl' : DIA-press, 2000.

Tan, Amy The opposite of fate. New York : Putnam c2003.

PS3570.A48 Z47 2003

Voluntary action. Oxford ; New York : Oxford University Press, 2003.
BF621 .V658 2003

Zöller, Rainer. Die Vorstellung vom Willen in der Morallehre Senecas. Leipzig : K.G. Saur, 2003.
PA6686 .Z65 2003

FREE WILL AND DETERMINISM IN LITERATURE.
Muñoz Llamosas, Virginia. La intervención divina en el hombre a través de la literatura griega de época arcaica y clásica. Amsterdam : Hakkert, 2002.
PA3015.R5 M87 2002

Free will, consciousness, and the self.
Bertelsen, Preben. New York : Berghahn Books, 2003.
BF621 .B47 2003

Free, Wynn, 1946- The reincarnation of Edgar Cayce? : interdimensional communication and global transformation / by Wynn Free and David Wilcock. Berkeley, Calif. : Frog, 2004. p. cm. Includes bibliographical references. CONTENTS: David Wilcock : from academia to interdimensional student -- Bainbridge, Cayce, Wilcock : common soul, separate bodies -- The Cayce legacy and the Wilcock promise -- Ra Ra the gang's all here -- The story of Ra-ta -- The great pyramid of Giza -- Enter history, prophecy fulfilled -- Common threads -- Predictions and prophecies -- The Ra readings, introduction -- The advent of the Wilcock readings : level two -- Ra counsels Wilcock -- Ra client readings -- Ra's view of television and the media -- Ra on "your attitude is everything" -- Ra on healing the original wound and reconnecting with God -- Ra on ascension and the birth of the Christ within us all -- A scientific blueprint of ascension -- La pièce de résistance, Ra's pledge. ISBN 1-58394-083-9 (pbk.) DDC 133.8/092
1. Wilcock, David, - 1973- 2. Ra - (Spirit) 3. Wilcock, David, - 1973- Pre-existence. 4. Cayce, Edgar, - 1877-1945. 5. Prophecies (Occultism) I. Wilcock, David, 1973- II. Title.
BF1815.W49 F74 2004

Freedheim, Donald K.
Handbook of psychology. Hoboken, N.J. : John Wiley, c2003.
BF121 .H1955 2003

Freedman, Carl Howard. The incomplete projects : Marxism, modernity, and the politics of culture / Carl Freedman. Middletown, Conn. : Wesleyan University Press, c2002. xvi, 203 p. ; 24 cm. Includes bibliographical references and index. ISBN 0-8195-6554-7 (cloth : alk. paper) ISBN 0-8195-6555-5 (alk. paper) DDC 306.3/45
1. Socialism and culture. 2. Popular culture. 3. Marxist criticism. I. Title.
HX523 .F74 2002

Freedman, Rita Jackaway. Bodylove : learning to like our looks and ourselves : a practical guide for women / Rita Freedman. Updated ed. Carlsbad, CA : Gürze Books, c2002. 327 p. : ill. ; 21 cm. Includes bibliographical references (p. 305-309) and index. ISBN 0-936077-43-3 (pbk.) DDC 155.6/33
1. Body image in women. 2. Beauty, Personal. 3. Self-esteem in women. 4. Women - Psychology. I. Title.
BF697.5.B63 F74 2002

FREEDOM. See LIBERTY.

Freedom and its conditions.
Flathman, Richard E. New York : Routledge, c2003.
JC585 .F553 2003

Freedom evolves.
Dennett, Daniel Clement. New York ; London : Viking, 2003.
BJ1461 .D427 2003

FREEDOM (PSYCHOLOGY). See AUTONOMY (PSYCHOLOGY).

FREEHOLD. See LAND TENURE.

Freeman, C. J.
Cortez, Ana. The playing card oracles. Denver, CO : Two Sisters Press, c2002.
BF1778.5 .C67 2002

Freeman, Sue Joan Mendelson, 1944-.
Women on power. Boston : Northeastern University Press, c2001.
HQ1233 .W597 2001

FREEMASONRY - HISTORY.
Masonería. Quito : [O. Valenzuela Muñoz], 2001.

FREEMASONRY - SYMBOLISM.
Hall, Manly Palmer, 1901- The secret teachings of all ages. Reader's ed. New York : Jeremy P. Tarcher/Putnam, 2003.
BF1411 .H3 2003

Masonería. Quito : [O. Valenzuela Muñoz], 2001.

Ovason, David. [Secret zodiacs of Washington DC] The secret architecture of our nation's capital. 1st Perennial ed. New York, NY : Perennial, 2002.

FREEMASONRY - UNITED STATES - HISTORY.
Ovason, David. [Secret zodiacs of Washington DC] The secret architecture of our nation's capital. 1st Perennial ed. New York, NY : Perennial, 2002.

FREEMASONS - COSTUMES, SUPPLIES, ETC.
Masonería. Quito : [O. Valenzuela Muñoz], 2001.

FREGE, GOTTLOB, 1848-1925.
Greimann, Dirk. Freges Konzeption der Wahrheit. Hildesheim ; New York : Georg Olms, c2003.
B3318.T78 G74 2003

Freges Konzeption der Wahrheit.
Greimann, Dirk. Hildesheim ; New York : Georg Olms, c2003.
B3318.T78 G74 2003

Freiheit, Gleichheit und Autonomie / herausgegeben von Herlinde Pauer-Studer und Herta Nagl-Docekal. Wien : Oldenbourg ; Berlin : Akademie Verlag, 2003. 395 p. ; 22 cm. (Wiener Reihe ; Bd. 11) Includes bibliographical references and index. German and English. ISBN 3-7029-0462-X (Oldenbourg : pbk.) ISBN 3-05-003601-X (Akademie Verlag : pbk.)
1. Equality. 2. Justice. 3. Liberty. I. Pauer-Studer, Herlinde. II. Nagl-Docekal, Herta. III. Series: Wiener Reihe (R. Oldenbourg Verlag) ; Bd. 11.
JC575 .F74 2003

Freiheit wovon, Freiheit wozu?.
Meyer, Gerd. Opladen : Leske + Budrich, 2002.

Freiling, Tom.
Abraham Lincoln's daily treasure. Grand Rapids, Mich. : F.H. Revell, c2002.
E457.2 .F787 2002

Freksa, C.
Spatial cognition III. Berlin ; New York : Springer, c2003.
Q387 .S73 2003

Fremderfahrung und Repräsentation / herausgegeben von Iris Därmann und Christoph Jamme. 1. Aufl. Weilerswist : Velbrück, 2002. 325 p. ; 22 cm. Includes bibliographical references. ISBN 3-934730-40-X (pbk.)
1. Ethnology - Philosophy. 2. Anthropology - Philosophy. 3. Alienation (Philosophy) 4. Xenophobia. I. Därmann, Iris. II. Jamme, Christoph.

FRENCH AUTHORS. See AUTHORS, FRENCH.

FRENCH-CANADIAN LITERATURE - HISTORY AND CRITICISM.
Jacob, Suzanne. Ecrire comment pourquoi. Paroisse Notre-Dame-des-Neiges, Québec : Éditions Trois-Pistoles, c2002.
PN56.C69 J23 2002

FRENCH CHILDREN'S LITERATURE. See CHILDREN'S LITERATURE, FRENCH.

French, Christopher C. Paranormal perception? : a critical evaluation / Christopher C. French. London : Institute for Cultural Research, 2001. 28 p. ; 21 cm. (Monograph series / Institute for Cultural Research ; no. 42) Includes bibliographical references. ISBN 0-904674-34-7
1. Extrasensory perception. 2. Parapsychology. I. Title. II. Series: ICR monograph series ; no. 42.

FRENCH DRAMA - HISTORY AND CRITICISM.
Rolland, Romain, 1866-1944. Le théâtre du peuple. Nouvelle éd. Bruxelles : Complexe, c2003.
PN1655 .R68 2003

French, Jeffrey A.
Nebraska Symposium on Motivation (2001) Evolutionary psychology and motivation. Lincoln, Neb. ; London : University of Nebraska Press, c2001.
BF701 .N43 2001

FRENCH LITERATURE. See CHILDREN'S LITERATURE, FRENCH; FRENCH DRAMA.

FRENCH LITERATURE - CANADA. See FRENCH-CANADIAN LITERATURE.

FRENCH LITERATURE - HISTORY AND CRITICISM - CONGRESSES.
Colloque des Invalides (5th : 2001 : Hôtel des invalides) Ce que je ne sais pas. Tusson, Charente : Du Lérot, [2002?]
PQ145 .C65 2001

French, Marilyn, 1929- From Eve to dawn : a history of women / Marilyn French. Toronto : McArthur, 2002-3 v. : col. maps ; 24 cm. Maps on lining papers. Includes bibliographical references. PARTIAL CONTENTS: v. 1. Origins. ISBN 1-55278-268-9 (v. 1) DDC 305.4/09
1. Women - History. 2. Sex role - History. I. Title.

French, Peter A.
Renaissance and early modern philosophy. Malden, MA ; Oxford : Blackwell Pub., c2002.
B775 .R46 2002

FRENCH PHILOSOPHY. See PHILOSOPHY, FRENCH.

Frenken, Ralph, 1965-.
Die Psychohistorie des Erlebens. Kiel : Oetker-Voges, c2000.

Frequency processing and cognition.
Etc. frequency processing and cognition. Oxford ; New York : Oxford University Press, c2002.
BF448 .E83 2002

Frères et soeurs une maladie d'amour.
Rufo, Marcel. Paris : Fayard, 2002.

Frerichs, Hajo H.
Grundlagen und Modelle für den Hörgerichteten Spracherwerb. Villingen-Schwenningen : Neckar, c1995.

FRESCO PAINTING. See MURAL PAINTING AND DECORATION.

Fretwell, Sally. Feng Shui : back to balance : an easy, commonsense approach to revitalizing your home, business, and relationships / Sally Fretwell. Novato, Calif. : New World Library, [2002] x, 197 p. : ill ; 23 cm. Includes bibliographical references (p. 197). ISBN 1-57731-221-X DDC 133.3/337
1. Feng shui. I. Title.
BF1779.F4 F74 2002

Freud and faith.
Bingaman, Kirk A. Albany, NY : State University of New York Press, c2003.
BF175.4.R44 B56 2003

Freud-Bibliographien.
Stock, Karl F. Graz : Stock & Stock, 1998.
BF109.F73 S76 1998

Freud [electronic resource] : conflict & culture. Washington, DC : Library of Congress Title in HTML header: Sigmund Freud. Mode of access: World Wide Web. Title from home page (viewed on Apr. 10, 2003; last updated Feb. 6, 2002). SUMMARY: Online version of an exhibition that was held at the Library of Congress from October 15, 1998 to January 16, 1999 and curated by Michael S. Roth. Examines Sigmund Freud's life, and his key ideas and their influence on modern culture. Features photographs, prints, manuscripts, and home movies. URL: http://www.loc.gov/exhibits/freud/
1. Psychoanalysis. 2. Psychoanalysis - History. 3. Freud, Sigmund, - 1856-1939. I. Roth, Michael S., 1957- II. Library of Congress. III. Title: Sigmund Freud
BF173

Freud, Heidegger.
Berto, G. (Graziella) Milano : Bompiani, c1998.
BF175.4.P45 B46 1998

Freud, le sujet social / sous la direction de Annick Le Guen, Georges Pragier et Ilana Reiss-Schimmel ; avec la participation de C. Le Guen. 1re éd. Paris : Presses universitaires de France, 2002. 162 p. ; 25 cm. (Monographies de la "Revue française de psychanalyse.." Section Jeudi) Includes bibliographical references (p. [159]-162). ISBN 2-13-052386-2 DDC 150
1. Freud, Sigmund, - 1856-1939. 2. Psychoanalysis. I. Le Guen, Annick. II. Pragier, Georges. III. Reiss-Schimmel, Ilana. IV. Series.

FREUD, MARTHA, 1861-1951.
Behling, Katja, 1963- Martha Freud. Berlin : Aufbau Taschenbuch Verlag, 2002.
BF109.F73 B455 2002

Freud, Sigmund, 1856-1939.
Analyzing Freud. New York : New Directions, c2002.
BF109.F74 A845 2002

[Essays. English. Selections]
The uncanny / Sigmund Freud ; translated by David McLintock ; with an introduction by Hugh Haughton. New York : Penguin Books, 2003. p. cm. (Penguin classics) Includes bibliographical references. CONTENTS: Screen memories -- The creative writer and daydreaming -- Family romances -- Leonardo da Vinci and a memory of his childhood -- The uncanny. ISBN 0-14-243747-6 DDC 150.19/52
1. Psychoanalysis. I. McLintock, David. II. Haughton, Hugh, 1948- III. Title. IV. Series.
BF109.F75 A25 2003

KINDHEITSERINNERUNG DES LEONARDO DA VINCI.
Halpern, Richard, 1954- Shakespeare's perfume.

Philadelphia : University of Pennsylvania Press, c2002.
PR2848 .H25 2002

TRAUMDEUTUNG.
Marinelli, Lydia. Dreaming by the book. New York : Other Press, c2003.
BF175.5.D74 F7436 2003

[Zur Psychopathologie des Alltagslebens. English]
The psychopathology of everyday life / Sigmund Freud ; translated by Anthea Bell with an introduction by Paul Keegan. New York : Penguin Books, 2003. xlviii, 264 p. ; 20 cm. (Penguin classics) Includes bibliographical references. ISBN 0-14-243743-3 DDC 150.19/52
1. Psychoanalysis. 2. Memory. 3. Repression (Psychology) 4. Paragrammatism. 5. Freud, Sigmund, - 1856-1939. I. Title. II. Series.
BF173 .F82513 2003

FREUD, SIGMUND, 1856-1939.
Behling, Katja, 1963- Martha Freud. Berlin : Aufbau Taschenbuch Verlag, 2002.
BF109.F73 B455 2002

Berto, G. (Graziella) Freud, Heidegger. Milano : Bompiani, c1998.
BF175.4.P45 B46 1998

Bocock, Robert. Sigmund Freud. Rev. ed. London ; New York : Routledge, 2002.
BF173.F85 B63 2002

Brickman, Celia. Aboriginal populations in the mind. New York : Columbia University Press, c2003.
BF173 .B79 2003

Britton, Celia. Race and the unconscious. Oxford : Legenda, 2002.

Chebili, Saïd. La tâche civilisatrice de la psychanalyse selon Freud. Paris : L'Harmattan, c2002.

Coward, Harold G. Yoga and psychology. Albany : State University of New York Press, 2002.
BF51 .C69 2002

Elliott, Anthony. Social theory since Freud. 1st ed. London ; New York : Routledge, 2004.
BF175.4.S65 E455 2004

The elusive child. London ; New York : Karnac, c2002.

Flem, Lydia. [Homme Freud. English] Freud the man. New York : Other Press, c2003.
BF109.F74 F4813 2003

Freud [electronic resource]. Washington, DC : Library of Congress
BF173

Freud, le sujet social. 1re éd. Paris : Presses universitaires de France, 2002.

Freud, Sigmund, 1856-1939. [Zur Psychopathologie des Alltagslebens. English] The psychopathology of everyday life. New York : Penguin Books, 2003.
BF173 .F82513 2003

Goldberg, Arnold, 1929- Misunderstanding Freud. New York : Other Press, 2004.
BF173 .G59 2004

Jacobs, Michael, 1941-. Sigmund Freud. 2nd ed. London ; Thousand Oaks, Calif. : SAGE Publications, 2003.
BF109.F74 J33 2003

Kaus, Rainer J. Psychoanalyse und Sozialpsychologie. Heidelberg : C. Winter, c1999.
BF109.F74 K38 1999

Kaus, Rainer J. Psychoanalyse und Sozialpsychologie. Heidelberg : C. Winter, c1999.
BF109.F74 K38 1999

MacIntyre, Alasdair C. The unconscious. Rev. ed. New York : Routledge, 2004.
BF315 .M23 2004

Małyszek, Tomasz, 1971- Romans Freuda i Gradivy. Wrocław : Wydawn. Uniwersytetu Wrocławskiego, 2002.
BF173.F85 M255 2002

Masson, J. Moussaieff (Jeffrey Moussaieff), 1941- The assault on truth. 1st Ballantine Books ed. New York : Ballantine Books, 2003.
BF109.F74 M38 2003

Psychoanalytic knowledge. New York : Palgrave Macmillan, 2003.
BF173 .P7763 2003

Pulman, Bertrand. Anthropologie et psychanalyse. Paris : Presses universitaires de France, 2002.
GN502 .P85 2002

Rereading Freud. Albany : State University of New York Press, 2004.
BF109.F74 R47 2004

Rubin, Gabrielle, 1921- Le roman familial de Freud. Paris : Payot, 2002.

Safouan, Moustafa. Four lessons of psychoanalysis. New York : Other Press, c2004.
BF175 .S19 2004

Schafer, Roy. Insight and interpretation. New York : Other Press, c2003.
BF173 .S3277 2003

Traverso, Paola. "Psiche è una parola greca--". Genova, Italy : Compagnia dei librai, 2000.
BF109.F74 T73 2000

Young-Bruehl, Elisabeth. Where do we fall when we fall in love? New York : Other Press, c2003.
BF173 .Y68 2003

Young Dr. Freud [electronic resource]. [Alexandria, Va.?] : PBS, 2002.
BF109.F74

FREUD, SIGMUND, 1856-1939 - BIBLIOGRAPHY.
Stock, Karl F. Freud-Bibliographien. Graz : Stock & Stock, 1998.
BF109.F73 S76 1998

FREUD, SIGMUND, 1856-1939 - CORRESPONDENCE.
Analyzing Freud. New York : New Directions, c2002.
BF109.F74 A845 2002

FREUD, SIGMUND, 1856-1939 - CORRESPONDENCE - HISTORY AND CRITICISM.
Junker, Helmut, 1934- Unter Übermenschen. Tübingen : Edition Diskord, c1997.
BF109.F74 J85 1997

FREUD, SIGMUND, 1856-1939 - INDEXES.
Delrieu, Alain. Sigmund Freud. 2e éd. rev., augm. et mise à jour. Paris : Anthropos : Diffusion Economica, c2001.
BF109.F74 D45 2001

FREUD, SIGMUND, 1856-1939 - LANGUAGE.
Altounian, Janine. L'écriture de Freud. Paris : Presses universitaires de France, 2003.
BF173.F73 A48 2003

FREUD, SIGMUND, 1856-1939 - POLITICAL AND SOCIAL VIEWS.
Bocock, Robert. Sigmund Freud. Rev. ed. London ; New York : Routledge, 2002.
BF173.F85 B63 2002

FREUD, SIGMUND, 1856-1939 - PUBLIC OPINION - FRANCE.
Bolzinger, André. La réception de Freud en France. Paris : L'Harmattan, c1999.
BF175 .B575 1999

FREUD, SIGMUND, 1856-1939 - RELIGION.
Bingaman, Kirk A. Freud and faith. Albany, NY : State University of New York Press, c2003.
BF175.4.R44 B56 2003

Maciejewski, Franz. Psychoanalytisches Archiv und jüdisches Gedächtnis. 1. Aufl. Wien : Passagen Verlag, 2002.

FREUD, SIGMUND, 1856-1939 - VIEWS ON DREAMS.
Iskusstvo snovideniĭ = Sankt-Peterburg : Skifiâ, 2002.
NX180.D74 I74 2002

Freud the man.
Flem, Lydia. [Homme Freud. English] New York : Other Press, c2003.
BF109.F74 F4813 2003

Freudian School of Melbourne.
Fantasm. Melbourne : Freudian School of Melbourne, 2000.

Freud's theory and its use in literary and cultural studies.
Berg, Henk de, 1963- Rochester, NY : Camden House, 2003.
PN56.P92 B36 2003

Freund, Philip, 1909- Myths of creation / Philip Freund ; illustrated by Milton Charles. London : Peter Owen ; Chester Springs, PA : Distributed in the USA by Dufour Editions, 2003. vi, 304 p. : ill. ; 22 cm. Includes index. ISBN 0-7206-1202-0 DDC 291.24
1. Creation. 2. Creation - Mythology. 3. Evolution. I. Title.
BL226 .F74 2003

Freundlich, Lawrence S.
Mellody, Pia. The intimacy factor. 1st ed. [San Francisco, CA] : HarperSanFrancisco, c2003.
BF575.I5 M45 2003

Frey, Bruno S. Happiness and economics : how the economy and institutions affect well-being / Bruno S. Frey and Alois Stutzer. Princeton, N.J. : Princeton University Press, c2002. viii, 220 p. : ill. ; 24 cm. Includes bibliographical references (p. [195]-214) and index. Table of contents URL: http://www.loc.gov/catdir/toc/prin031/2001095821.html Publisher description URL: http://www.loc.gov/catdir/desc ription/prin022/2001095821.html ISBN 0-691-06997-2 (cloth : alk. paper) ISBN 0-691-06998-0 (pbk. : alk. paper) DDC 174
1. Happiness - Economic aspects. 2. Economics - Psychological aspects. 3. Well-being. I. Stutzer, Alois. II. Title.
BF575.H27 F75 2002

Frey, Jean-Marie. Le corps peut-il nous rendre heureux? / Jean-Marie Frey. Nantes : Pleins feux, [2002] 84 p. ; 21 cm. (Lundis philo, 1285-3542 ; 19) Includes bibliographical references. ISBN 2-8472-9040-0 DDC 194
1. Body, Human (Philosophy) 2. Pleasure. I. Title. II. Series.

FRIARS - FRANCE - PARIS - HISTORY.
Goglin, Jean-Marc. L'enseignement de la théologie dans les ordres mendiants à Paris au XIIIe siècle. Paris : Editions franciscaines, c2002.

Friday, Jonathan. Aesthetics and photography / Jonathan Friday. Aldershot, England ; Burlington, VT : Ashgate, c2002. x, 175 p. : ill. ; 24 cm. (Aesthetics and the philosophy of art) Includes bibliographical references (p. 165-170) and index. ISBN 0-7546-0427-6 (hbk.) ISBN 0-7546-0428-4 (pbk.) DDC 770/.1
1. Photography - Philosophy. 2. Aesthetics. I. Title. II. Series.
TR183 .F75 2002

Fridlander, Ḥayim ben Mosheh. Sefer Śifte ḥayim : midot ve-avodat H. : pirḳe hadrakhah be-midot uve-ʻavodat elokim ḥayim .... / ME-et Ḥayim b. mo. ha-r. R. Mosheh Fridlander. Bene-Beraḳ : ha-Rabanit Fridlander, 763- [2002 or 2003- v. ; 24 cm. Running title: Śifte ḥayim. Includes bibliographical references. PARTIAL CONTENTS: [1] Midot ye-ʻavodat H. pt.1.
1. Worship (Judaism) 2. Ethics, Jewish. I. Title. II. Title: Śifte ḥayim

Fridlund, Alan J.
Gleitman, Henry. Psychology. 6th ed. New York : W.W. Norton, c2004.
BF121 .G58 2004

Fridman, Aharon (Aharon ben Yehoshuʻa)
[Gam atah yakhol. Yiddish]
Du kenst oykh! : matslieḥ zayn in vos du vilst / farfast durkh, Arn Friedman ; ibergearbet oyf Idish durkh, Moysheh Yitshok Shtayn. Nyu York : Lev Yiśroel, 762, 2002. 383 p. ; 24 cm. Spine title: Gam atah yakhol!
1. Success - Religious aspects - Judaism. 2. Conduct of life. I. Shtayn, Moysheh Yitshok. II. Title. III. Title: Gam atah yakhol!

Frie, Roger, 1965-.
Understanding experience. London ; New York : Routledge, 2003.
B105.E9 U53 2003

Fried, Katrina.
The love almanac. New York : Welcome Books : Distributed to the trade in the U.S. and Canada by Andrews McMeel Distribution Service, 2003.
BF575.L8 L6675 2003

Fried Schnitman, Dora.
[Nuevos paradigmas. English.] New paradigms, culture, and subjectivity. Cresskill, N.J. : Hampton Press, c2002.
BD161 .N8413 2002

Frieden, der noch nicht erfüllte Auftrag.
Naumann, Klaus, 1939- Hamburg : Mittler & Sohn, c2002.
UA710 .N38 2002

Friederici, Angela D.
Working on working memory. Leipzig : Leipziger Universitätsverlag, 2000.
BF378.S54 W675 2000

Friedman, Bonnie, 1958- The thief of happiness : the story of an extraordinary psychotherapy / Bonnie Friedman. Boston, Mass. : Beacon Press, 2002. 276 p. ; 24 cm. Publisher description URL: http://www.loc.gov/catdir/description/hm031/2001002562.html ISBN 0-8070-7242-7 (alk. paper) DDC 616.89/14/092
1. Friedman, Bonnie, - 1958- 2. Analysands - United States - Biography. 3. Psychotherapy - Case studies. I. Title.
RC464.F75 A3 2002

FRIEDMAN, BONNIE, 1958-.
Friedman, Bonnie, 1958- The thief of happiness.
Boston, Mass. : Beacon Press, 2002.
RC464.F75 A3 2002

Friedman, Milton, 1912- Capitalism and freedom / Milton Friedman ; with the assistance of Rose D. Friedman ; with a new preface by the author. 40th anniversary ed. Chicago : University of Chicago Press, 2002. xvi, 208 p. ; 21 cm. Originally published: Chicago : University of Chicago Press, [1962] Includes bibliographical references and index. ISBN 0-226-26420-3 (cloth : alk. paper) ISBN 0-226-26421-1 (paper : alk. paper) DDC 330.12/2
  1. Capitalism. 2. State, The. 3. Liberty. 4. United States - Economic policy. I. Friedman, Rose D. II. Title.
HB501 .F7 2002

Friedman, Rose D.
Friedman, Milton, 1912- Capitalism and freedom. 40th anniversary ed. Chicago : University of Chicago Press, 2002.
HB501 .F7 2002

Friedman, Russell L.
The medieval heritage in early modern metaphysics and modal theory, 1400-1700. Dordrecht ; Boston : Kluwer Academic Publishers, c2003.
BD111 .M47 2003

Friedman, Susan Stanford.
Analyzing Freud. New York : New Directions, c2002.
BF109.F74 A845 2002

Friedrich-Ebert-Stiftung.
Conflict management. Nairobi : Friedrich Ebert Stiftung : Centre for Conflict Research : Association of Local Government Authorities of Kenya, 2000.

Friedrich-Ebert-Stiftung (India).
South Asia, 2010. Delhi : Konark Publishers, 2002.

Friend to friend.
Appel, Dee. Sisters, Or. : Multnomah Publishers, c2002.
BF575.F66 A66 2002

FRIENDLINESS. See **FRIENDSHIP.**

Friends.
Etuk, Emma S., 1948- Washington, D.C. : Emida International, c1999.
BF575.F66 E77 1999

Friends and friendship / Rita Schulman, Rhoda Cohen, George H. Pollock, editors. Madison, Conn. : Psychosocial Press, 2003. p. cm. Includes bibliographical references and index. ISBN 1-88784-141-5 DDC 302.3/4
  1. Friendship. I. Schulman, Rita. II. Cohen, Rhoda, 1933- III. Pollock, George H.
BF575.F66 F695 2003

Friends for life.
Jonas, Susan. 1st ed. New York : William Morrow & Co., c1997.
HQ755.85 .J65 1997

FRIENDSHIP. See also **FEMALE FRIENDSHIP; LOVE.**
Haynes, Cyndi. [Book of friendship] New York : Gramercy Books, 2003.
BF575.F66 H39 2003

FRIENDSHIP.
Bolton, Martha, 1951- The "official" friends book. West Monroe, LA : Howard Pub., 2003.
BF575.F66 B65 2003

Etuk, Emma S., 1948- Friends. Washington, D.C. : Emida International, c1999.
BF575.F66 E77 1999
  1. Black author.

Friends and friendship. Madison, Conn. : Psychosocial Press, 2003.
BF575.F66 F695 2003

Gingras, Sandy, 1958- How to be a friend. Harvey Cedars, NJ : Down the Shore Pub., 2003.
BF575.F66 G56 2003

Haynes, Cyndi. [Book of friendship] Friendship. New York : Gramercy Books, 2003.
BF575.F66 H39 2003

Honey from my heart for you. Nashville, Tenn. : J. Countryman, c2002.
BF575.F66 H66 2002

Jordan, Denise. We can be friends. Chicago, Ill. : Heinemann Library, c2003.
BF723.F68 J67 2003

Manning, Martha. A place to land. 1st ed. New York : Ballantine Books, 2003.

BF575.F66 M26 2003
Tiberghien, Gilles A., 1953- Amitier. Paris : Desclée de Brouwer, c2002.

Walters, J. Donald. Secrets of friendship. Nevada City, CA : Crystal Clarity Publishers, c2001.
BF575.F66 WW355 2001

FRIENDSHIP BETWEEN WOMEN. See **FEMALE FRIENDSHIP.**

FRIENDSHIP IN CHILDREN - JUVENILE LITERATURE.
Thomas, Pat, 1959- My friends and me. 1st ed. Hauppauge, N.Y. : Barron's Educational Series, c2001.
BF723.F68 T48 2001

FRIENDSHIP IN WOMEN. See **FEMALE FRIENDSHIP.**

FRIENDSHIP - JUVENILE LITERATURE.
The jewel of friendship. Berkeley, CA : Dharma Pub., 2002.
BQ1462.E5 J48 2002

Jordan, Denise. We can be friends. Chicago, Ill. : Heinemann Library, c2003.
BF723.F68 J67 2003

FRIENDSHIP - MISCELLANEA.
BenShea, Noah. Dear friend. Naperville, Ill. : Sourcebooks, c2003.
BF575.F66 B446 2003

Brown, H. Jackson, 1940- On friendship. Nashville, Tenn. : Rutledge Hill Press, c1996.
BF575.F66 B76 1996

FRIENDSHIP - RELIGIOUS ASPECTS - CHRISTIANITY.
Etuk, Emma S., 1948- Friends. Washington, D.C. : Emida International, c1999.
BF575.F66 E77 1999
  1. Black author.

Friese, Heidrun, 1958-.
Identities. New York ; Oxford : Berghahn Books, 2002.
HM716 .I34 2002

Frigerio, Graciela.
Educación, ciudadanía y participación. 1. ed. Buenos Aires : Novedades Educativas, 2002.

FRIGHT. See **FEAR.**

Frijda, Nico H.
Feelings and emotions. New York : Cambridge University Press, 2003.
BF531 .F445 2003

Frink, Lisa.
Many faces of gender. Boulder : University Press of Colorado ; Calgary, Alta., Canada : University of Calgary Press, c2002.
E98.P95 M35 2002

Frish, Daniyel.
Matok mi devash.
[Zohar ḥadash. Lamentations. 2000.] Zohar ḥadash Megilat Ekhah. "Hotsa'ah meyuḥedet li-yeme ben ha-metsarim". Yerushalayim : Mekhon Da'at Yosef, 761 [2000 or 2001]
BM525.A6 Z6 2001

[Zohar ḥadash.] Sefer Zohar ḥadash. Yerushalayim : Mekhon Da'at Yosef ; Brooklyn, N.Y. (225 Division Ave., Brooklyn 11211) : Le-haśig, B. Daskal, 760- [1999 or 2000-
BM525.A6 Z6+

Fritz, Robert, 1943- Your life as art / Robert Fritz. 1st ed. Newfane, VT : Newfane Press, c2003. x, 240 p. : ill. ; 23 cm. ISBN 0-9725536-0-6 (pbk.) DDC 158.1
  1. Self-actualization (Psychology) 2. Creative ability. 3. Creation (Literary, artistic, etc.) I. Title.
BF637.S4 F753 2003

Frolova, ĪU. G.
Konferentsiīa "Gendernyĭ podkhod v psikhologicheskom konsul'tirovanii" (2002 : Evropeĭskiĭ Gumanitarnyĭ Universitet) Gendernyĭ podkhod v psikhologicheskikh issledovaniīakh i konsul'tirovanii. Minsk : Evropeĭskiĭ Gumanitarnyĭ Universitet, 2002.
BF201.4 .K66 2002

From an ontological point of view.
Heil, John. Oxford : Clarendon Press ; New York : Oxford University Press, 2003.
BD306 .F76 2003

From Armageddon to the fall of Rome.
Durschmied, Erik. London : Hodder & Stoughton, c2002.

From awareness to action.
Tallon, Robert, 1947- Scranton, Pa. : University of Scranton Press, 2003.
BF698.35.E54 T35 2003

From boys to men.
Karras, Ruth Mazo, 1957- Philadelphia : University of Pennsylvania Press, c2003.
HQ775 .K373 2003

From child sexual abuse to adult sexual risk : trauma, revictimization, and intervention / edited by Linda J. Koenig ... [et al.]. 1st ed. Washington, DC : American Psychological Association, c2004. xv, 346 p. : ill. ; 27 cm. Includes bibliographical references and indexes.
CONTENTS: Pt. 1. Introduction. Child sexual abuse and adult sexual risk : where are we now? / Lynda S. Doll, Linda J. Koenig, and David W. Purcell -- pt. 2. Child sexual abuse and sexual risk in adulthood. Child sexual abuse and adult sexual relationships : review and perspective / Julia R. Heiman and Amy R. Heard-Davison -- Child sexual abuse and adult sexual revictimization / Cindy L. Rich, Amy M. Combs-Lane, Heidi S. Resnick, and Dean G. Kilpatrick -- Sexual abuse of girls and HIV infection among women : are they related? / Linda J. Koenig and Hollie Clark -- Sexual abuse of boys : short- and long-term associations and implications for HIV prevention / David W. Purcell, Robert M. Malow, Curtis Dolezal, and Alex Carballo-Diéguez -- pt. 3. Theoretical bases for adult risk and revictimization : cognitive, social, and behavioral mediators. Cognitive and attitudinal paths from childhood trauma to adult HIV risk / Kathryn Quina, Patricia J. Morokoff, Lisa L. Harlow, and Eileen L. Zurbriggen -- The link between child sexual abuse and risky sexual behavior : the role of disassociative tendencies, information-processing effects, and consensual sex decision mechanisms / Eileen L. Zurbriggen and Jennifer J. Freyd -- Toward a social-narrative model of revictimization / Steven Jay Lynn, Judith Pintar, Rachael Fite, Karen Eckjanson, and Jane Stafford -- Child sexual abuse and alcohol use among women : setting the stage for risky sexual behavior / Sharon C. Wilsnack, Richard W. Wilsnack, Arlinda F. Kristjanson, Nancy D. Vogeltanz-Holm, and T. Robert Harris -- Translating traumatic experiences into language : implications for child abuse and long-term health / James W. Pennebaker and Lori D. Stone -- pt. 4. Interventions to promote healthier sexual outcomes among child sexual abuse survivors. Integrating HIV/AIDS prevention activities into psychotherapy for child sexual abuse survivors / John Briere -- Child sexual abuse and HIV : an integrative risk-reduction approach / Dorothy Chin, Gail E. Wyatt, Jennifer Vargas Carmona, Tamra Burns Loeb, and Hector F. Myers -- Trauma-focused versus present-focused models of group therapy for women sexually abused in childhood / David Spiegel, Catherine Classen, Elisabeth Thurston, and Lisa Butler -- Sexual assault revictimization : toward effective risk-reduction programs / Lisa Marmelstein Blackwell, Steven Jay Lynn, Holly Vanderhoff, and Christine Gidycz -- pt. 5. Conclusion. Child sexual abuse and adult sexual risk : where do we go from here? / Ann O'Leary, Linda J. Koenig, and Lynda S. Doll. ISBN 1-59147-030-7 (hardcover : alk. paper) DDC 616.85/ 8369
  1. Adult child sexual abuse victims - Sexual behavior. 2. Adult child sexual abuse victims - Rehabilitation. 3. Hygiene, Sexual. 4. Sexually transmitted diseases - Psychological aspects. 5. AIDS (Disease) - Transmission. 6. Risk-taking (Psychology) I. Koenig, Linda J.
RC569.5.A28 F76 2004

From chivalry to terrorism.
Braudy, Leo. New York : Alfred A. Knopf : Distributed by Random House, 2003.
HQ1090 .B7 2003

From dawn to dusk.
Hubback, Judith. Wilmette, Ill. : Chiron Publications, 2003.
BF109.H77 A3 2003

From Eve to dawn.
French, Marilyn, 1929- Toronto : McArthur, 2002-

From girl to woman.
Rishoi, Christy, 1958- Albany : State University of New York Press, c2003.
HQ1186.A9 R57 2003

From girls in their elements to women in science : rethinking socialization through memory-work / Judith S. Kaufman ... [et al.]. New York : P. Lang, 2003. 166 p. : ill. ; 23 cm. (Counterpoints ; v. 116) Includes bibliographical references (p. [153]-160) and index. ISBN 0-8204-4512-6 (alk. paper) DDC 153.1/2/082
  1. Memory - Social aspects. 2. Human information processing - Social aspects. 3. Cognition and culture. 4. Social perception. 5. Women scientists - Psychology. 6. Socialization. I. Kaufman, Judith S., 1955- II. Series: Counterpoints (New York, N.Y.) ; v. 116.
BF378.S65 F76 2003

From ground zero to ground hero.
Monahan, Brian. [Newark, Del.?] : Disaster Research Center, University of Delaware, 2001.

From Kabila to Kabila : prospects for peace in the Congo. Nairobi ; Brussels : International Crisis Group, 2001. iv, 25 p. : col. map ; 29 cm. (ICG Africa report ; no. 27) "16 March 2001" Includes bibliographical references.
1. Kabila, Laurent-Désiré - Assassination. 2. Congo (Democratic Republic) - Politics and government - 1997- 3. Congo (Democratic Republic) - History - 1997- 4. Peace. I. International Crisis Group. II. Series.

From left communism to post-modernism.
El-Ojeili, Chamsy. Lanham, Md. ; Oxford : University Press of America, c2003.
HX44.5 .E46 2003

From mating to mentality : evaluating evolutionary psychology / edited by Kim Sterelny and Julie Fitness. New York, NY : Psychology Press, 2003. p. cm. Includes bibliographical references and index. ISBN 1-84169-096-1 DDC 155.7
1. Evolutionary psychology - Congresses. I. Sterelny, Kim. II. Fitness, Julie.
BF698.95 .F76 2003

From one brother to another. Volume 2 : voices of African American men / edited by Jeremiah A. Wright, Jr. Valley Forge, PA : Judson Press, c2003. xv, 223 p. ; 16 cm. ISBN 0-8170-1362-8
1. African American men - Prayer-books and devotions - English. 2. African American men - Conduct of life. 3. African American men - Religious life. 4. Meditations. I. Wright, Jeremiah A., Jr.

From other worlds.
Evans, Hilary, 1929- Pleasantville, N.Y. : Reader's Digest, c1998.
BF2050 .E93 1998

From our hearts.
Adeleye, Modupe, 1980- Rochester, N.Y. : Mo-Biz Publishing Co., 2003.
BF353 .A33 2003

From passions to emotions.
Dixon, Thomas. Cambridge ; New York, NY : Cambridge University Press, 2003.

From promise to practice : strengthening UN capacities for the prevention of violent conflict / edited by Chandra Lekha Sriram, Karin Wermester. Boulder ; London : L. Rienner Publishers, 2003. xii, 429 p. ; 24 cm. "A project of the International Peace Academy"--Cover. Includes bibliographical references (p. 393-403) and index. CONTENTS: From risk to response : phases of conflict, phases of conflict prevention / Chandra Lekha Sriram and Karin Wermester -- Third-party incentives and the phases of conflict prevention / Donald Rothchild -- Quiet diplomacy and recurring "ethnic clashes" in Kenya / Stephen Brown -- Zanzibar : a multilevel analysis of conflict prevention / Paul J. Kaiser -- Fiji : peacemaking in a multiethnic state / Ralph R. Premdas -- Javakheti, Georgia : why conflict prevention? / Anna Matveeva -- East Timor : the path to self-determination / Tamrat Samuel -- Colombia : international involvement in protracted peacemaking / Marc W. Chernick -- Tajikistan : bad peace agreements and prolonged civil conflict / Kathleen Collins -- Liberia : legacies and leaders / George Klay Kieh, Jr. -- Preventing conflict escalation in Burundi / Mohammed Omar Maundi -- Insights from the cases : opportunities and challenges for preventive actors / Chandra Lekha Sriram -- From promise to practice? Conflict prevention at the UN / Karin Wermester. ISBN 1-58826-135-2 (alk. paper) ISBN 1-58826-112-3 (pbk. : alk. paper) DDC 341.5
1. United Nations. 2. Conflict management. 3. Peacekeeping forces. I. Sriram, Chandra Lekha, 1971- II. Wermester, Karin. III. International Peace Academy.
JZ6368 .S68 2003

From syntax to discourse.
Hamann, Cornelia, 1953- Dordrecht, The Netherlands ; Boston : Kluwer Academic Publishers, c2002.
P118 .H327 2002

From the coven of witchcraft to Christ.
Soku, Leonard. Rev. ed. [Accra, Ghana? : s.n., c2000]
BV4935 .S6 F76 2000

From the viewpoint of the Lvov-Warsaw school.
Jadacki, Jacek Juliusz. Amsterdam ; New York, NY : Rodopi, 2003.

Froment Meurice, Marc. Incitations / Marc Froment-Meurice. Paris : Galilée, c2002. 187 p. ; 25 cm. (Collection La philosophie en effet, 0768-2395) Includes bibliographical references. ISBN 2-7186-0596-0 DDC 194
1. Philosophy. 2. Philosophy, French. I. Title. II. Series: Collection La philosophie en effet (Editions Galilée)

Fromm, Erich, 1900- Escape from freedom / Erich H. Fromm. 1st Owl books ed. New York : H. Holt, 1994. xviii, 301 p. ; 21 cm. "An Owl book." Originally published: New York : Farrar & Reinhart, 1941. Includes bibliographical references and index. ISBN 0-8050-3149-9 (alk. paper) DDC 323.44
1. Liberty. 2. Democracy. 3. Totalitarianism. 4. Social psychology. I. Title.
HM271 .F74 1994

FROMM, ERICH, 1900-.
Kaus, Rainer J. Psychoanalyse und Sozialpsychologie. Heidelberg : C. Winter, c1999.
BF109.F74 K38 1999

Kaus, Rainer J. Psychoanalyse und Sozialpsychologie. Heidelberg : C. Winter, c1999.
BF109.F74 K38 1999

Meyer, Gerd. Freiheit wovon, Freiheit wozu? Opladen : Leske + Budrich, 2002.

Frömmigkeit im Mittelalter : politisch-soziale Kontexte, visuelle Praxis, körperliche Ausdrucksformen / herausgegeben von Klaus Schreiner in Zusammenarbeit mit Marc Müntz. München : Fink, c2002. 566 p. : ill. ; 24 cm. Internat. conference proceedings. Includes bibliographical references and indexes. 16 German, 2 English contributions. ISBN 3-7705-3625-8 (pbk.)
1. Church history - Middle Ages, 600-1500. 2. Christian life - History - Middle Ages, 600-1500. I. Schreiner, Klaus.

FRONTIER AND PIONEER LIFE - HISTORY. See **FRONTIER AND PIONEER LIFE.**

FRONTIER AND PIONEER LIFE - UNITED STATES.
Linklater, Andro. Measuring America. New York : Walker & Co., 2002.
E161.3 .L46 2002

Nye, David E., 1946- America as second creation. Cambridge : MIT Press, c2003.
E179.5 .N94 2003

FRONTIER AND PIONEER LIFE - UNITED STATES - HISTORIOGRAPHY.
Nye, David E., 1946- America as second creation. Cambridge : MIT Press, c2003.
E179.5 .N94 2003

FRONTIER THESIS.
Gutfeld, Arnon. American exceptionalism. Brighton [England] ; Portland, Or. : Sussex Academic Press, 2002.
E169.1 .G956 2002

Frosh, Stephen. Key concepts in psychoanalysis / Stephen Frosh. London : British Library, 2002. 112 p. ; 24 cm. Includes bibliographical references. ISBN 0-7123-0890-3 DDC 150.19/5
1. Psychoanalysis. I. British Library. II. Title.
BF173 .F898 2002

Key concepts in psychoanalysis / Stephen Frosh. New York : New York University Press, 2003. 112 p. ; 25 cm. Includes bibliographical references. CONTENTS: Unconscious -- Repression -- Defence -- Projection -- Splitting -- Phantasy -- Identification -- Oedipus complex -- Interpretation -- Resistance -- Transference -- Countertransference. ISBN 0-8147-2728-X (alk. paper) ISBN 0-8147-2729-8 (pbk. : alk. paper) DDC 150.19/5
1. Psychoanalysis. I. Title.
BF173 .F898 2003

Frost, Gavin. The magic power of white witchcraft : revised for the millennium / Gavin Frost, and Yvonne Frost. Paramus, NJ : Prentice Hall, c1999. xiv, 256 p. : ill. ; 23 cm. Includes bibliographical references and index. ISBN 0-7352-0093-9 DDC 133.4/3
1. Witchcraft. I. Frost, Yvonne. II. Title.
BF1561 .F76 1999

A witch's grimoire of ancient omens, portents, talismans, amulets, and charms / Gavin Frost and Yvonne Frost. Rev. and updated ed. New York : Reward Books, c2002. xxvi, 230 p. : ill. ; 23 cm. Includes bibliographical references and index. ISBN 0-7352-0326-1 (pbk.) DDC 133.4/3
1. Witchcraft - Handbooks, manuals, etc. 2. Magic - Handbooks, manuals, etc. I. Frost, Yvonne. II. Title.
BF1566 .F83 2002

A witch's guide to psychic healing : applying traditional therapies, rituals, and systems / Gavin and Yvonne Frost. Boston, MA : Weiser Books, 2003. p. cm. Includes index. Table of contents URL: http://www.loc.gov/catdir/toc/ecip046/2003016097.html CONTENTS: The healers -- Modified wiccan healing therapies -- Additional wiccan healing techniques -- Miracle, magic, or witchcraft? -- Depression, psychiatry, and soul retrieval -- Fifteen assumptions about your healing reality -- Meditation -- Wiccan illness diagnosis -- A witch's guide to nutrition and exercise -- True stories of wiccan self-healing -- True stories of wiccan healing from a distance -- Live for life. ISBN 1-57863-295-1 DDC 615.8/528
1. Witchcraft. 2. Spiritual healing. 3. Medicine, Magic, mystic, and spagiric. I. Frost, Yvonne. II. Title.
BF1572.S65 F76 2003

Frost, Peter J. Toxic emotions at work : how compassionate managers handle pain and conflict / Peter J. Frost. Boston : Harvard Business School Press, c2003. xii, 251 p. ; 25 cm. Includes bibliographical references (p. 227-239) and index. CONTENTS: Emotional pain in organizations -- Sources of toxicity in organizations -- The work of the toxin handler -- The toll on toxin handlers -- Healing the handlers -- At the interface : what handlers and their organizations can do -- Leaders handling pain -- The compassionate company : architecting responses to pain -- Looking through the lens of pain. ISBN 1-57851-257-3 (alk. paper) DDC 658.3/14
1. Conflict management. 2. Job stress. 3. Employees - Counseling of. 4. Executives - Job stress. 5. Stress management. 6. Work - Psychological aspects. 7. Psychology, Industrial. I. Title.
HD42 .F76 2003

Frost, Yvonne.
Frost, Gavin. The magic power of white witchcraft. Paramus, NJ : Prentice Hall, c1999.
BF1561 .F76 1999

Frost, Gavin. A witch's grimoire of ancient omens, portents, talismans, amulets, and charms. Rev. and updated ed. New York : Reward Books, c2002.
BF1566 .F83 2002

Frost, Gavin. A witch's guide to psychic healing. Boston, MA : Weiser Books, 2003.
BF1572.S65 F76 2003

FROTTAGE (SEXUALITY). See **SEXUAL EXCITEMENT.**

Froud, Brian. Good faeries/bad faeries / Brian Froud ; edited by Terri Windling. London : Pavilion, 2000. 1 v. : ill. (some col.) ; 30 cm. ISBN 1-86205-302-2 DDC 398.45
1. Fairies. I. Windling, Terri. II. Title.

Frühe Hexenverfolgung in Ravensburg und am Bodensee / herausgegeben von Andreas Schmauder ; mit Beiträgen von Wolfgang Behringer ... [et al.]. Konstanz : UVK Verlagsgesellschaft, c2001. 149 p. : ill. (some col.), maps ; 25 cm. (Historische Stadt Ravensburg, 1615-5750 ; Bd. 2) ISBN 3-89669-812-5
1. Institoris, Heinrich, - 1430-1505. - Malleus maleficarum. 2. Witchcraft - Germany - Ravensburg. 3. Trials (Witchcraft) - Germany - Ravensburg. 4. Witches - Germany - Ravensburg. I. Schmauder, Andreas. II. Series: Historische Stadt Ravensburg (Series) ; Bd. 2.
BF1583 .F784 2001

Frühneuzeit-Studien
(n.F. 2) Seelenmaschinen. Wien : Böhlau Verlag, c2000.
BF381 .S44 2000

Frydenberg, Erica, 1943-.
Beyond coping. Oxford ; New York : Oxford University Press, 2002.
BF335 .B49 2002

Frykman, Maja Povrzanović.
Beyond integration. Lund, Sweden : Nordic Academic Press, c2001.
JV6225 .B49 2001

FTC consumer alert
Privacy [electronic resource]. [Washington, D.C.] : Federal Trade Commission, Bureau of Consumer Protection, Office of Consumer and Business Education, [2002]

Privacy [electronic resource]. [Washington, D.C.] : Federal Trade Commission, Bureau of Consumer Protection, Office of Consumer and Business Education, [2002]

Privacy [electronic resource]. [Washington, D.C.] : Federal Trade Commission, Bureau of Consumer Protection, Office of Consumer and Business Education, [2002]

Fthenakis, Wassilios E. Die Rolle des Vaters in der Familie / Wassilios E. Fthenakis, Beate Minsel. Stuttgart : Kohlhammer, 2002. 349 p. : ill. ; 21 cm. (Schriftenreihe des Bundesministeriums für Familie, Senioren, Frauen und Jugend ; Bd. 213) Includes bibliographical references. ISBN 3-17-017470-3 (pbk.)
1. Fatherhood. 2. Fathers. 3. Fatherhood - Psychological aspects. 4. Fathers - Psychology. 5. Sex role. I. Minsel, Beate. II. Title. III. Series.

Fu gui yu ying er.
Ke, Yunlu. Di 1 ban. Shanghai : Shanghai ren min chu ban she : Xin hua shu dian Shanghai fa xing suo jing xiao, 1996.
BD431 .K6134 1996 <Asian China>

"Fubusi" Zhongguo da lu 50 fu hao pai hang bang.
Zhongguo, shui zui fu. Di 1 ban. Beijing : Qi ye guan li chu ban she, 2001.
HC426.5.A2 Z457 2001

Fuchs, Elinor.
Land/scape/theater. Ann Arbor : University of Michigan, c2002.
PN2020 .L32 2002

Fuchs-Jolie, Stephan.
Wolfram, von Eschenbach, 12th cent. Titurel. Berlin ; New York : Walter de Gruyter, 2002.

Fuchs, Ralf-Peter.
Wahrheit, Wissen, Erinnerung. Münster : Lit, [2002]

Fudge, Erica. Animal / Erica Fudge. London : Reaktion, 2002. 182 p. : ill. ; 21 cm. (Focus on contemporary issues) Includes bibliographical references (p. 167-[180]). ISBN 1-86189-134-2 DDC 306.4
1. Human-animal relationships. 2. Animals in art. 3. Animals in literature. I. Title. II. Series.
QL85 .F83 2002

FUERZAS ARMADAS REVOLUCIONARIAS DE COLOMBIA.
Giraldo Hurtado, Luis Guillermo, 1944- Del proceso y de la paz. [Colombia? : s.n., 2001] (Manizales : Edigr@ficas)

Téllez, Edgar. Diario íntimo de un fracaso. 1. ed. Bogotá, D.C., Colombia : Planeta, 2002.

Valencia, León. Adiós a la política, bienvenido la guerra. [Bogotá, Colombia?] : Intermedio, c2002.

Yusty, Miguel. Negociar en medio de la guerra. [Cali, Colombia] : Editorial Universidad Santiago de Cali, 2002.

FUGING TUNES. See **HYMNS, ENGLISH.**

FUGUING TUNES. See **HYMNS, ENGLISH.**

Fuguiyuyinger.
Ke, Yunlu. Fu gui yu ying er. Di 1 ban. Shanghai : Shanghai ren min chu ban she : Xin hua shu dian Shanghai fa xing suo jing xiao, 1996.
BD431 .K6134 1996 <Asian China>

Fuhrer, Therese.
Augustine, Saint, Bishop of Hippo. De magistro = Paderborn : F. Schöningh, 2002.
BR65.A5 G4 2002

Fuhrer, Urs, 1950- Cultivating minds : identity as meaning-making practice / Urs Fuhrer. 1st ed. New York, NY : Taylor & Francis, 2003. p. cm. Includes bibliographical references and index. CONTENTS: The semiotic mediation of the self -- The self as act -- The rediscovery of Georg Simmel's work on culture -- Simmelian cultivation : the mutuality of the person-culture process -- Identity, culture, and development under transactional issues -- Cultivating meanings as mediating possibilities for the self -- Behavior settings as media for children's cultivation -- The writing on the wall : cultural piracy to struggle with the self. ISBN 0-415-30713-9 DDC 155.2/5
1. Identity (Psychology) - Social aspects. 2. Culture - Psychological aspects. 3. Meaning (Psychology) I. Title.
BF697.5.S65 F84 2003

FULCANELLI, PSEUD. MYSTÈRE DES CATHÉDRALES.
Weidner, Jay. The mysteries of the great cross of Hendaye. Rochester, Vt. : Destiny Books, 2003.
BF1999 .W435 2003

FULFILLMENT (ETHICS). See **SELF-REALIZATION.**

Fuligni, Allison Sidle.
Early child development in the 21st century. New York : Teachers College Press, c2003.
LB1115 .E27 2003

Fuller, Graham E., 1937- The future of political Islam / by Graham E. Fuller. New York ; Houndmills, Basingstoke : Palgrave, 2003. xix, 227 p. ; 24 cm. Includes bibliographical references (p. [215]-220) and index. Publisher description URL: http://www.loc.gov/catdir/description/hol031/2003041024.html ISBN 1403961360 (cl.) DDC 320.5/5
1. Islam and politics - History - 20th century. 2. Islamic fundamentalism. 3. East and West. I. Title.
BP173.7 .F85 2003

Fuller, Matthew. Behind the blip : essays on the culture of software / Matthew Fuller. Brooklyn, NY, USA : Autonomedia, c2003. 165 p. ; 23 cm. Includes bibliographical references. ISBN 1-57027-139-9 (pbk.) DDC 004/.01/9
1. Computer software - Human factors. 2. Human-computer interaction. 3. User interfaces (Computer systems) I. Title.
QA76.76.H85 F85 2003

Fuller, Robert W. Somebodies and nobodies : overcoming the abuse of rank / Robert W. Fuller. Gabriola Island, Canada : New Society Publishers, 2003. xx, 187 p. ; 24 cm. Includes bibliographical references (p. 159-173) and index. ISBN 0-86571-486-X DDC 305.5/6
1. Discrimination. 2. Equality. 3. Social stratification. 4. Marginality, Social. I. Title.
HM821 .F84 2003

Fullerton, Carol S.
Terrorism and disaster. Cambridge, UK ; New York : Cambridge University Press, 2003.
RC552.P67 T476 2003

Fultner, Barbara.
Habermas, Jürgen. [Wahrheit und Rechtfertigung. English] Truth and justification. Cambridge, Mass. : MIT Press, c2003.
B3258.H323 W3413 2003

FULTON, EILEEN.
Vint/age 2001 conference : [videorecording]. New York, c2001.

Fulton, Eileen, panelist.
Vint/age 2001 conference : [videorecording]. New York, c2001.

Fumagalli Beonio Brocchieri, Mariateresa, 1933-
Profilo del pensiero medievale / Mariateresa Fumagalli Beonio Brocchieri ; in collaborazione con Gianluca Briguglia. 1. ed. Roma : Laterza, 2002. xix, 139 p. ; 24 cm. (Manuali di base ; 4) Includes bibliography (p. [123]-136) and name index. ISBN 88-420-6706-7 DDC 189
1. Philosophy, Medieval. 2. Philosophy, Medieval, in literature. I. Title. II. Series.

FUNCTIONAL ANALYSIS (LINGUISTICS). See **FUNCTIONALISM (LINGUISTICS).**

FUNCTIONAL LINGUISTICS. See **FUNCTIONALISM (LINGUISTICS).**

FUNCTIONAL-STRUCTURAL ANALYSIS (LINGUISTICS). See **FUNCTIONALISM (LINGUISTICS).**

FUNCTIONALISM (LINGUISTICS).
Poggio, Rosauta Maria Galvão Fagundes. Processos de gramaticalização de preposições do Latim ao Português. Salvador : EDUFBA, 2002.

FUNCTIONS, KERNEL. See **KERNEL FUNCTIONS.**

FUNCTIONS OF COMPLEX VARIABLES. See **KERNEL FUNCTIONS.**

Fundación Casa de la Reconciliación.
2001, año de las Naciones Unidas del diálogo entre civilizaciones. Guatemala : Fundación Casa de la Reconciliación : MINUGUA, 2001.
JX1952 .A233 2001

Fundacja na Rzecz Nauki Polskiej.
Małyszek, Tomasz, 1971- Romans Freuda i Gradivy. Wrocław : Wydawn. Uniwersytetu Wrocławskiego, 2002.
BF173.F85 M255 2002

Fundamental issues in archaeology
Beyond foraging and collecting. New York : Kluwer Academic/Plenum Publishers, c2002.
GN388 .B49 2002

FUNDAMENTAL RIGHTS. See **CIVIL RIGHTS.**

FUNDAMENTAL THEOLOGY. See **THEOLOGY, DOCTRINAL.**

FUNDAMENTALISM, ISLAMIC. See **ISLAMIC FUNDAMENTALISM.**

FUNDAMENTALISMS, RELIGIOUS. See **RELIGIOUS FUNDAMENTALISM.**

FUNDAMENTALIST MOVEMENTS, RELIGIOUS. See **RELIGIOUS FUNDAMENTALISM.**

Fundamental'nye problemy psikhologii : lichnost' v istoricheskoĭ psikhologii : materialy nauchnoĭ konferentsii, 23-25 aprelia 2002 goda / pod obshcheĭ redaktsieĭ V.M. Allakhverdova, O.V. Zashchirinskoĭ. Sankt-Peterburg : Izd-vo S.-Peterburgskogo universiteta, 2002. 136 p. ; 20 cm. "Nauchnoe izdanie"--Colophon. ISBN 5288030847
1. Psychology - Congresses. I. Allakhverdov, V. M. (Viktor Mikhaĭlovich) II. Zashchirinskaiā, Oksana Vladimirovna.
BF20 .F86 2002

Fundamentals of psychology.
Kosslyn, Stephen Michael, 1948- 2nd ed. Boston : Allyn and Bacon, c2005.
BF121 .K585 2005

Funder, David Charles. The personality puzzle / David C. Funder. 3rd ed. New York : Norton, c2004. p. cm. Includes bibliographical references (   ) and indexes. ISBN 0-393-97996-2 DDC 155.2
1. Personality. I. Title.
BF698 .F84 2004

Pieces of the personality puzzle. 3rd ed. New York : Norton, c2004.
BF698 .P525 2004

FUNERAL DIRECTORS. See **UNDERTAKERS AND UNDERTAKING.**

FUNERAL HOMES. See **UNDERTAKERS AND UNDERTAKING.**

FUNERAL INDUSTRY. See **UNDERTAKERS AND UNDERTAKING.**

FUNERAL RITES AND CEREMONIES - EGYPT.
[Book of the dead. English.] The Egyptian book of the dead. London : Cassell, 2001.
PJ1555.E5 B83 2001

Eyre, Christopher. The cannibal hymn. Liverpool : Liverpool University Press, 2002.

FUNERAL RITES AND CEREMONIES - FRANCE.
Hanus, Michel. La Mort aujourd'hui. Paris : Frison-Roche, c2000.

FUNERALS. See **FUNERAL RITES AND CEREMONIES.**

Funes, Mariana. Laughing matters : live creatively with laughter / Mariana Funes. Dublin : Newleaf, 2000. xvi, 243 p. : ill., tables ; 22 cm. Includes bibliographical references and index. ISBN 0-7171-2893-8 DDC 152.42
1. Laughter. 2. Self-actualization (Psychology) I. Title.

Füredi, Frank, 1947- Culture of fear : risk-taking and the morality of low expectation / Frank Furedi. Rev. ed. London ; New York : Continuum, 2002. xviii, 205 p. ; 23 cm. Includes bibliographical references (p. 195-198) and index. ISBN 0-8264-5929-3 ISBN 0-8264-5930-7 (pbk.) DDC 302/.12
1. Fear. 2. Uncertainty. 3. Risk. I. Title.
BF575.F2 F86 2002

A fury for God.
Ruthven, Malise, 1942- London ; New York : Granta, 2002.
HV6432 .R87 2002

FUSION OF CORPORATIONS. See **CONSOLIDATION AND MERGER OF CORPORATIONS.**

Füssel, Ronald. Hexen und Hexenverfolgung in Thüringen / Roland Füssel. Erfurt : Landeszentrale für Politische Bildung Thüringen, 2001. 115 p. : ill., 1 col. map ; 21 cm. (Thüringen gestern & heute ; 11) Includes bibliographical references (p. 113-114). ISBN 3-931426-53-X
1. Witchcraft - Germany - Thuringia - History. 2. Trials (Witchcraft) - Germany - Thuringia. 3. Thuringia (Germany) - History. I. Title. II. Series.
BF1583 .F87 2001

Futbolsofía.
Goñi Zubieta, Carlos. Madrid : Ediciones del Laberinto, [2002]

FUTHARK. See **RUNES.**

FUTHORC. See **RUNES.**

FUTHORK. See **RUNES.**

Futura
Cimatti, Felice. La mente silenziosa. 1. ed. Roma : Editori riuniti, 2002.

The future is yours.
Grace, Raymon. Charlottesville, VA : Hampton Roads Pub., c2003.
BF639 .G64 2003

FUTURE LIFE. See also **SOUL.**
Babarinde, A. O. The end of man. Lagos, Nigeria : Christ Foundation Baptist Church, 2001.
1. Black author.

[Book of the dead. English.] The Egyptian book of the dead. London : Cassell, 2001.
PJ1555.E5 B83 2001

Botschaften aus dem Jenseits. [Düsseldorf] : Droste, c2002.

Braude, Stephen E., 1945- Immortal remains. Lanham, Md. ; Oxford : Rowman & Littlefield, c2003.

BF1311.F8 B73 2003

Browne, Sylvia. Life on the other side. New York : Dutton, c2000.
BF1311.F8 B77 2000b

Dermine, François-Marie, 1949- Mistici, veggenti e medium. Città del Vaticano : Libreria editrice vaticana, c2002.

Dray, Maryvonne. Karine après la vie. Paris : Albin Michel, c2002.

Eyre, Christopher. The cannibal hymn. Liverpool : Liverpool University Press, 2002.

Han, Byung-Chul. Tod und Alterität. München : Fink, c2002.
BD444 .H36 2002

Hill, Craig C., 1957- In God's time. Grand Rapids, Mich. : W.B. Eerdmans, c2002.
BT903 .H55 2002

Jordan, Kathie. The birth called death. 1st ed. Ashland, Or. : RiverWood Books, 2003.
BF1311.F8 B57 2003

Kastenbaum, Robert. On our way. Berkeley : University of California Press, c2004.
BF789.D4 .K365 2004

Leland, Kurt. The unanswered question. Charlottesville, VA : Hampton Roads Pub., c2002.
BF1045.N4 L45 2002

My proof of survival. 1st ed. St. Paul, Minn. : Llewellyn Publications, 2003.
BF1311.F8 M9 2003

Novak, Peter, 1958- The lost secret of death. Charlottesville, VA : Hampton Roads Pub., 2003.
BF1999 .N73 2003

Nwokogba, Isaac, 1957- Voices from beyond. Cranston, R.I. : Writers' Collective, 2003.
BF1261.2 .N96 2003

Reid, Howard. In search of the immortals. London : Headline, 1999.

Smullyan, Raymond M. Who knows? Bloomington : Indiana University Press, c2003.
BL50 .S59 2003

Staume, David, 1961- The beginner's guide for the recently deceased. 1st ed. St. Paul, Minn. : Llewellyn Publications, 2004.
BF1311.F8 S78 2004

Zolla, Elémire. Catàbasi e anàstasi. Alpignano, [Italy] : Tallone Editore, 2001.

FUTURE LIFE - CHRISTIANITY.
Bame Bame, Michael. Death and everlasting life. Nairobi, Kenya : All Africa Conference of Churches, 1994.

FUTURE LIFE IN LITERATURE.
La fin des temps. Talence : Université Michel de Montaigne, Bordeaux III, L.A.P.R.I.L., 2000-[2001]

FUTURE LIFE - JUDAISM.
Chajes, Jeffrey Howard. Between worlds. Philadelphia : University of Pennsylvania Press, c2003.
BM729.D92 C53 2003

FUTURE LIFE - MISCELLANEA.
Grant, Robert J. Universe of worlds. Virginia Beach, Va. : A.R.E. Press, 2005.
BF1261.2 .G73 2005

Future of childhood series
Children in the city. London : Routledge/Falmer, 2003.

The future of freedom.
Zakaria, Fareed. 1st ed. New York : W.W. Norton, c2003.
JC423 .Z35 2003

The future of marketing : critical 21st-century perspectives / edited by Philip J. Kitchen. Houndmills [England] ; New York : Palgrave Macmillan, 2003. xxi, 196 p. : ill. ; 23 cm. Includes bibliographical references (p. 180-189) and index. ISBN 0-333-99286-5 DDC 658.8/001/12
1. Marketing - Forecasting. 2. Twenty-first century - Forecasts. I. Kitchen, Philip J.
HF5415 .F945 2003

The future of political Islam.
Fuller, Graham E., 1937- New York ; Houndmills, Basingstoke : Palgrave, 2003.
BP173.7 .F85 2003

Future of revolt.
Kristeva, Julia, 1941- [Révolte intime. English]

Intimate revolt. New York : Columbia University Press, c2002.
PN56.P92 K7513 2002

FUZZY DECISION MAKING.
Sousa, Joao M. C. Fuzzy decision making in modeling and control. Singapore ; River Edge, N.J. : World Scientific, 2002.

Fuzzy decision making in modeling and control.
Sousa, Joao M. C. Singapore ; River Edge, N.J. : World Scientific, 2002.

G FACTOR (PSYCHOLOGY). See **GENERAL FACTOR (PSYCHOLOGY).**

The G8 and global governance series
The new economic diplomacy. Aldershot, Hampshire, England ; Burlington, VT : Ashgate, c2003.
HF1359 .N4685 2003

Gäbler, Ulrich. Zeiten des Endes : Ende der Zeiten? / Ulrich Gäbler. Basel : Schwabe & Co., c2002. 16 p. ; 21 cm. (Basler Universitätsreden ; 100. Heft) Includes bibliographical references. "Rektoratsrede gehalten an der Jahresfeier der Universität Basel am 29. November 2002."
1. Eschatology. 2. End of the world. I. Title. II. Series.

Gackenbach, Jayne, 1946-.
Psychology and the Internet. San Diego, Calif. : Academic Press, c1998.
BF637.C45 P79 1998

Gadamer et Derrida.
Jankovic, Zoran. Au-delà du signe. Paris : Harmattan, c2003.

Gadamer, Hans Georg, 1900- Die Lektion des Jahrhunderts : ein Interview von Riccardo Dottori / Hans-Georg Gadamer. Münster : Lit, [2002] i, 161 p. : col. ill. ; 24 cm. (Wissenschaftliche Paperbacks. Philosophie; Bd. 2) Includes bibliographical references. ISBN 3-8258-5049-8 (br.) ISBN 3-8258-5768-9 (gb.)
1. Gadamer, Hans Georg, - 1900- - Interviews. 2. Philosophy, Modern - 20th century. I. Dottori, Riccardo. II. Title. III. Series: Wissenschaftliche Paperbacks ; Bd. 2. IV. Series: Wissenschaftliche Paperbacks. Philosophie.

[Problème de la conscience historique. German]
Das Problem des historischen Bewusstseins / Hans-Georg Gadamer ; aus dem Französischen rückübersetzt von Tobias Nikolaus Klass. Tübingen : Mohr Siebeck, 2001. 55 p. ; 24 cm. University lectures published in French in 1963 under the title "Le probleme de la conscience historique" by Publications universitaires de Louvain and Editions Beatrice Nauwelaerts, Paris. The original manuscript got lost, this book is a re-translation into German from the French new edition of 1996 du Seuil, Paris. ISBN 3-16-147590-9 (pbk.)
1. Humanities - Methodology. 2. Hermeneutics. 3. History - Philosophy. I. Title.

GADAMER, HANS GEORG, 1900-.
Jankovic, Zoran. Au-delà du signe. Paris : Harmattan, c2003.

GADAMER, HANS GEORG, 1900- - INTERVIEWS.
Gadamer, Hans Georg, 1900- Die Lektion des Jahrhunderts. Münster : Lit, [2002]

Gadaniĩa sibirskoĩ tselitel'nitsy.
Stepanova, Natal'ia (Natal'ia Ivanovna) Moskva : RIPOL klassik, 1999.
BF1866 .S73 1999

Gaddis, John Lewis.
Order and justice in international relations. Oxford ; New York : Oxford University Press, 2003.
JZ1308 .O73 2003

GAELS. See **CELTS.**

GAGÁ (CULT). See **VOODOOISM.**

Gagné, Patricia.
Gendered sexualities. New York : JAI, 2002.
HQ1075.A27 vol. 6

Gagosian Gallery.
Kiefer, Anselm, 1945- Merkaba. New York : Gagosian Gallery, c2002.
N6888.K43 A4 2002

Gahlin, Lucia. Egypt : gods, myths and religion : a fascinating guide to the alluring world of ancient Egyptian myths and religion / Lucia Gahlin. London : Lorenz, 2001. 256 p. : ill. (chiefly col.), col. ports. ; 31 cm. Includes bibliographical references and index. SUMMARY: Ancient Egypt was a mystical society with a broad and deep belief in the afterlife and the existence of many gods to appease and worship. Everyday objects and animals were deified and worshipped. Even the kings were considered a divine embodiment of the gods. The tombs, burial sites and artifacts

are an enduring testimony to this fascinating religion. Less documented, but no less fascinating, was the beliefs of the ordinary people of Egypt: magic, rituals, festivals, taboos, superstitions, dreams and oracles reveal how far religion influenced and enriched their lives. Finally the book looks at a voice of dissent in the 3000 period: Pharoah, Alchenaten, who defied thousands of years of culture and history to revolutionize Egyptian religion to outlaw Polytheism and allow worship of only one god. CONTENTS: State religion: Gods and goddesses -- Myths and their settings -- Kingship and the gods -- Temples and priests -- Akhenaten's religious revolution -- Religion in life and death: Funerary religion -- Tombs -- Popular religion -- Mythologizing ancient Egypt. ISBN 0-7548-0565-4 DDC 299.31
1. Mythology, Egyptian. 2. Gods, Egyptian. 3. Egypt - Religion. I. Title.

Gajda, Stanisław.
Język w przestrzeni społecznej. Opole : Uniwersytet Opolski, 2002.
P40 .J492 2002

Galactic alignment.
Jenkins, John Major. Rochester, Vt. : Bear & Co., 2002.
F1435.3.R3 J45 2002

GALATIANS. See **CELTS.**

GALAXIES. See **STARS.**

GALAXIES - EVOLUTION.
Börner, G. The early universe. 4th ed. Berlin : London : Springer, c2003.

The Gale encyclopedia of the unusual and unexplained.
Steiger, Brad. Detroit : Thomson/Gale, c2003.
BF1025 .S79 2003

Galende, Emiliano. Sexo y amor : anhelos e incertidumbres de la intimidad actual / Emiliano Galende. 1a ed. Buenos Aires : Paidós, 2001. 213 p. ; 23 cm. (Paidós contextos ; 69) Includes bibliographical references. ISBN 950-12-6969-8
1. Intimacy (Psychology) 2. Love. 3. Sex (Psychology) 4. Interpersonal relations. I. Title. II. Series.

Galenorn, Yasmine, 1961- Magical meditations : guided imagery for the pagan path / Yasmine Galenorn. [New ed.]. Berkeley, Calif. : Crossing Press, c2003. xvi, 207 p. : ill. ; 21 cm. Rev ed. of: Tracing the witch's wheel. 1997. Includes bibliographical references (p.201-202) and index. ISBN 1-58091-155-2 DDC 299/.94
1. Meditations. 2. Witchcraft. 3. Magic. I. Galenorn, Yasmine, 1961-. Tracing the witch's wheel. II. Title.
BF1561 .G35 2003

Sexual ecstasy & the divine : the passion & pain of our bodies / Yasmine Galenorn. Berkeley, Calif. : Crossing Press, c2003. xiii, 274 p. ; 21 cm. Includes bibliographical references (p. 263-266) and index. ISBN 1-58091-113-7 DDC 299
1. Witchcraft and sex. I. Title. II. Title: Sexual ecstasy and the divine
BF1572.S4 G35 2003

Trancing the witch's wheel.
Galenorn, Yasmine, 1961- Magical meditations. [New ed.]. Berkeley, Calif. : Crossing Press, c2003.
BF1561 .G35 2003

Galford, Robert M., 1952- The trusted leader : bringing out the best in your people and your company / Robert Galford, Anne Siebold Drapeau. New York ; London : Free Press, c2002. xiv, 271 p. : ill. ; 24 cm. Includes bibliographical references (p. 253-257) and index. ISBN 0-7432-3539-8 DDC 174/.4
1. Leadership - Moral and ethical aspects. 2. Business ethics. 3. Organizational behavior - Moral and ethical aspects. 4. Industrial management - Moral and ethical aspects. 5. Employee motivation. 6. Trust. I. Drapeau, Anne Seibold. II. Title.
HD57.7 .G33 2002

Galĩmaa, Ñamaagĩn.
Khurmetbek, Khalikiĩn. Ül bichigdmélüüd. Ulaanbaatar : "Monsudar" Khévlëliĩn Gazar, 2001.
QA465 .K48 2001

Galin, A. L. (Aleksandr Latypovich)
Psikhologicheskie osobennosti tvorcheskogo povedeniĩa / A.L. Galin. Novosibirsk : Novosibirskiĩ gos. universitet, 2001. 233 p. : ill. ; 21 cm. At head of title: Ministerstvo obrazovaniĩa Rossiĩskoĩ Federatsii. Novosibirskiĩ gosudarstvennyĩ universitet. Institut po perepodgotovke i povysheniĩu kvalifikatsii prepodavateleĩ gumanitarnykh i sotsial'nykh nauk. Includes bibliographical references (p. 228-232).
1. Creation (Literary, artistic, etc.) I. Novosibirskiĩ gosudarstvennyĩ universitet. Institut po perepodgotovke i povysheniĩu kvalifikatsii prepodavateleĩ gumanitarnykh i sotsial'nykh nauk. II. Title.

BF408 .G315 2001

Galison, Peter Louis. Einstein's clocks, Poincaré's maps : empires of time / Peter Galison. 1st ed. New York : W.W. Norton, c2003. 389 p. : ill. ; 22 cm. Includes bibliographical references (p. [355]-370) and index. CONTENTS: Synchrony -- Coal, chaos, and convention -- The electric worldmap -- Poincaré's maps -- Einstein's clocks -- The place of time. ISBN 0-393-02001-0 DDC 529
1. Einstein, Albert, - 1879-1955. 2. Poincaré, Henri, - 1854-1912. 3. Time. 4. Relativity (Physics) I. Title.
QB209 .G35 2003

Gallagher, Shaun, 1948-.
Models of the self. Thorverton, UK : Imprint Academic, c1999.
BF697 .M568 1999

Gallant, Mary J. Coming of age in the Holocaust : the last survivors remember / Mary J. Gallant. Lanham, Md. : University Press of America, c2002. 323 p. ; 22 cm. Includes bibliographical references (p. [309]-317) and index. ISBN 0-7618-2403-0 (pbk. : alk. paper) DDC 940.53/18/0922
1. Holocaust, Jewish (1939-1945) - Personal narratives. 2. Holocaust, Jewish (1939-1945) - Psychological aspects. 3. Holocaust survivors - Psychology. 4. Holocaust survivors - Interviews. 5. Stress management. 6. Adjustment (Psychology) I. Title.
D804.3 .G353 2002

GALLERIES, ART. See **ART MUSEUMS.**

Gallivan, Martin D., 1968- James River chiefdoms : the rise of social inequality in the Chesapeake / Martin D. Gallivan. Lincoln : University of Nebraska Press, c2003. xvii, 295 p. : ill., maps ; 24 cm. Includes bibliographical references (p. [255]-287) and index. ISBN 0-8032-2186-X (cloth : alk. paper) DDC 975.5004/973
1. Powhatan Indians - Kings and rulers. 2. Powhatan Indians - First contact with Europeans. 3. Powhatan Indians - Antiquities. 4. Excavations (Archaeology) - Virginia - James River Valley. 5. Chiefdoms - Virginia - James River Valley. 6. Indians of North America - History - Colonial period, ca. 1600-1775. 7. Virginia - History - Colonial period, ca. 1600-1775. 8. James River Valley (Va.) - Antiquities. 9. Great Britain - Colonies - America. I. Title.
E99.P85 G35 2003

Gallop, Jane, 1952- Living with his camera / Jane Gallop ; photography by Dick Blau. Durham : Duke University Press, 2003. 197 p. : ill. ; 24 cm. Includes bibliographical references (p. [183]-194) and index. CONTENTS: Observations of a photographed mother -- The unhappy woman and the empty chair -- The photographer's desire -- Art in the family. ISBN 0-8223-3102-0 (cloth : alk. paper) DDC 306.8
1. Blau, Dick, - 1943- 2. Gallop, Jane, - 1952- 3. Family. 4. Photographers - United States - Biography. 5. Feminists - United States - Biography. I. Blau, Dick, 1943- II. Title.
TR140.B517 G35 2003

GALLOP, JANE, 1952-.
Gallop, Jane, 1952- Living with his camera. Durham : Duke University Press, 2003.
TR140.B517 G35 2003

Galovic, Jelena. Los grupos místico-espirituales de la actualidad / Jelena Galovic. México : Plaza y Valdés, 2002. 616 p. ; 23 cm. ISBN 9707221046 DDC 149.3
1. Mysticism - History - 20th century. 2. Spirituality - History - 20th century. 3. Nahua dance. 4. Folk dancing, Mexican. 5. Cults. 6. Sects. I. Title.
BL625 .G346 2002

Galuske, Ralf A. W.
Virtual lesions. Oxford ; New York : Oxford University Press, c2002.
RC350.B72 V57 2002

Gam atah yakhol!.
Fridman, Aharon (Aharon ben Yehoshu'a) [Gam atah yakhol. Yiddish] Du ḳenst oykh!. Nyu York : Lev Yiśroel, 762, 2002.

Gambhīra vedanta 'a cī 'a maṁ myā".
Khan'' Kyo', Cha rā Ū", Ran' kun' : Yuṁ krañ'' khyak' Cā pe : Chak' svay' ran', Ū" Khan'' Kyo' Cā pe, 2002.
BF1434.B93 K43 2002

Gambin, Felice.
Velásquez, Andrés, fl. 1553-1615. Libro de la melancholía. Viareggio (Lucca) : M. Baroni, [2002]
BF575.M44 V453 2002

Gambini, Roberto, 1944- Soul & culture / Roberto Gambini, foreword by David H. Rosen. 1st ed. College Station : Texas A&M University Press, 2003. xiv, 140 p., [16] p. of plates : ill. (some col.) ; 23 cm. (Carolyn and Ernest Fay series in analytical psychology ; no. 9) Includes bibliographical references (p. [131]-133) and index. CONTENTS: The collective unconscious comes to the newspaper -- Soul making in the new world -- Urban trees as mirrors of the soul -- The alchemy of cement in a modern city -- Bringing soul back to education : dreams in the classroom. ISBN 1-58544-214-3 (alk. paper) DDC 150.19/54
1. Personality and culture. 2. Psychoanalysis and culture. 3. Personality. 4. Psychoanalytic interpretation. 5. Jungian psychology. 6. Subconsciousness. I. Title. II. Title: Soul and culture III. Series.
BF698.9.C8 G35 2003

GAMBLING - SOCIAL ASPECTS - UNITED STATES.
Lears, T. J. Jackson, 1947- Something for nothing. New York : Viking, 2003.
HV6715 .L415 2003

GAMBLING - UNITED STATES - PUBLIC OPINION - HISTORY.
Lears, T. J. Jackson, 1947- Something for nothing. New York : Viking, 2003.
HV6715 .L415 2003

Gambra, José Miguel. La analogía en general : síntesis tomista de Santiago M. Ramírez / José Miguel Gambra. 1. ed. Pamplona : EUNSA, 2002. 305 p. ; 24 cm. (Colección de pensamiento medieval y renacentista ; 28) Includes bibliographical references (p. [297]-305). ISBN 84-313-1986-0
1. Ramírez, Santiago María, - 1891-1967. 2. Analogy. 3. Knowledge, Theory of. I. Title. II. Series.

The game of life.
Harry, Lou, 1963- Philadelphia : Running Press, c2003.
BF637.S4 H357 2003

GAME THEORY.
Barash, David P. The survival game. 1st ed. New York : Times Books, 2003.
HM1111 .B37 2003

McAfee, R. Preston. Competitive solutions. Princeton, N.J. : Princeton University Press, c2002.
HD30.28 .M3815 2002

Raiffa, Howard, 1924- Negotiation analysis. Cambridge, MA : Belknap Press of Harvard University Press, 2002.
HD58.6 .R342 2002

GAMES. See also **GAMBLING; PLAY; SPORTS.**
Broich, Josef, 1948- Körper- und Bewegungsspiele. 1. Aufl. 1999. Köln : Maternus, 1999.

Edo-e kara shomotsu made. Tōkyō : Kyūzansha, 1997.
HQ792.J3 N54 1997 v.19

GAMES FOR CHILDREN. See **GAMES.**

GAMES OF CHANCE. See **GAMBLING.**

GAMES, PRIMITIVE. See **GAMES.**

GAMES - ROME.
Wisdom, Stephen. Gladiators 100 BC-AD 200. Oxford : Osprey, 2001 (2002 printing)

Gamezo, M. V. (Mikhail Viktorovich).
Slovar'-spravochnik po vozrastnoĭ i pedagogicheskoĭ psikhologii. Moskva : Pedagog. ob-vo Rossii, 2001.
BF712.7 .S56 2001

GAMING. See **GAMBLING.**

Gamon, David.
Bragdon, Allen D. Use it or lose it!. 2nd ed., updated and expanded. New York : Walker & Co., 2004.
BF724.85.C64 B73 2004

Building mental muscle : conditioning exercises for the six intelligence zones / David Gamon and Allen D. Bragdon. Rev. and updated ed. New York : Walker & Co., 2003. p. cm. (Brain waves books) Includes bibliographical references and index. ISBN 0-8027-7669-8 (pbk. : alk. paper) DDC 153
1. Thought and thinking - Problems, exercises, etc. 2. Brain - Popular works. I. Bragdon, Allen D. II. Title. III. Series.
BF441 .G35 2003

Gandossy, Robert P.
Human resources in the 21st century. Hoboken, N.J. : J. Wiley & Sons, c2003.
HD31 .H81247 2003

Ganeri, Jonardon.
Matilal, Bimal Krishna. Ethics and epics. New Delhi ; New York : Oxford University Press, 2002.
B131 .M398 2002b

Gaṅgānāthajhā-granthamālā
(20.) Varāhamihira, 505-587. Bṛhatsaṃhitā. 1. saṃskaraṇam. Vārāṇasī : Sampūrṇānanda Saṃskṛta Viśvavidyālaye, 2002-
BF1714.H5+

GANJA. See **MARIJUANA.**

Gans, Deborah. The organic approach to architecture / Deborah Gans and Zehra Kuz. New York ; Chichester : Wiley, 2002. 208 p. : ill., plans ; 29 cm. Includes bibliographical references. ISBN 0-470-84791-3 DDC 720.108
1. Organic architecture. 2. Architecture - Environmental aspects. I. Kuz, Zehra. II. Title.

Gantsersḳi, Betsal'el Shelomoh, ha-Leyi. Sefer Darkhe tsedeḳ : 'al ha-mitsvah la-dun be-tsedeḳ ... "be-tsedeḳ tishpot 'amitekha"... / [Betsal'el Shelomoh ha-Leyi Gantsersḳi] Tifraḥ : Mishp. Gantsersḳi, 762 [2001 or 2002] 64 p. ; 24 cm. Running title: Darkhe tsedek.
1. Golden rule. 2. Ethics, Jewish. I. Title. II. Title: Darkhe tsedek

GANZHEIT (PSYCHOLOGY). See **WHOLE AND PARTS (PSYCHOLOGY).**

Gao, Guofan. Zhongguo wu shu shi / Gao Guofan zhu. Di 1 ban. Shanghai Shi : Shanghai san lian shu dian, 1999. 2, 5, 9, 6, 764 p. : ill. ; 21 cm. (Zhonghua ben tu wen hua cong shu) Includes bibliographical references. ISBN 7-5426-1043-0
1. Witchcraft - China - History. I. Title. II. Series: Zhonghua ben tu wen hua cong shu (Shanghai, China)
BF1584.C5 G36 1999

GAP, GENERATION. See **CONFLICT OF GENERATIONS.**

Gara e bellezza.
Olivetti, Alberto. Fiesole, Firenze : Cadmo, c2002.

GARAGES (AUTO REPAIR). See **AUTOMOBILE REPAIR SHOPS.**

Garano, Lorna.
Bourne, Edmund J. Coping with anxiety. Oakland, CA : New Harbinger, c2003.
BF575.A6 B68 2003

Garay, Judith.
Big Dance [videorecording]. Buffalo, N.Y. : Kineticvideo.com, c1998.

Garbaczewski, P.
Dynamics of dissipation. Berlin ; New York : Springer, c2002.
QC174.85 .D96 2002

García Barreno, Pedro.
Envejecimiento y cultura. [Madrid] : Instituto de España, c2001.

García Canclini, Néstor. Culturas híbridas : estrategias para entrar y salir de la modernidad / Néstor García Canclini. Nueva edición actualizada. Buenos Aires : Paidós, 2001. 349 p. : il. ; 24 cm. (Paidós estado y sociedad ; 87) Incluye referencias bibliográficas (p. [337]-346) e índice. ISBN 950-12-5487-9
1. Latin America - Civilization - 20th century. 2. Civilization, Modern - 20th century. 3. Postmodernism. 4. Arts and society - Latin America. 5. Popular culture - Latin America. 6. Latin America - Cultural policy. I. Title. II. Series.

García de León, María Antonia. Herederas y heridas : sobre las elites profesionales femeninas / María Antonia García de León ; prólogo de Carmen Alborch. 1a ed. [Madrid] : Ediciones Cátedra, Universitat de València, Instituto de la Mujer, 2002. 300 p. ; 21 cm. (Feminismos ; 71) Includes bibliographical references (p. 287-293) and index. ISBN 84-376-2017-1
1. Women in the professions - Spain. 2. Women journalists - Spain. 3. Women in the professions. 4. Upper class women. 5. Elite (Social sciences) 6. Power (Social sciences) I. Title. II. Title: Sobre las elites profesionales femeninas III. Series.
HD6054.2.S7 G37 2002

Gardell, Mattias. Gods of the blood : the pagan revival and white separatism / Mattias Gardell. Durham : Duke University Press, 2003. x, 445 p. : ill. ; 25 cm. Includes bibliographical references (p. [399]-429) and index. CONTENTS: The transforming landscapes of American racism -- The smorgasbord of the revolutionary white-racist counterculture -- The pagan revival -- Wolf-Age pagans : the Odinist call of Aryan revolutionary paganism -- By the spear of Odin : the rise of Wotansvolk -- Ethnic Asatrú -- Hail Loki! Hail Satan! Hail Hitler! : darkside Asatrú, Satanism, and occult National Socialism -- Globalization, Aryan paganism, and romantic men with guns. ISBN 0-8223-3059-8 (alk. paper) ISBN 0-8223-3071-7 (pbk. : alk. paper) DDC 322.4/2/0973
1. White supremacy movements - Religious aspects. 2. Paganism. 3. White supremacy movements - United States. 4. Paganism - United States. I. Title.
BL65.W48 G37 2003

Gardere, Jeffrey Roger. Love prescription : ending the war between Black men and women / Jeffrey Gardere. New York : Kensington Pub., c2002. vii, 293 p. ; 24 cm. "Dafina Books." Includes index. ISBN 0-7582-0251-2
1. Man-woman relationships. 2. African American women -

Attitudes. 3. African American men - Attitudes. 4. Black author.
I. Title.

Gardner, Gerald Brosseau, 1884-1964. The meaning
of witchcraft / G.B. Gardner. Boston : Weiser Books,
2004. p. cm. Originally published: 1st ed. London : Aquarian
Press, 1959. Includes bibliographical references. ISBN 1-
57863-309-5 DDC 133.4/3
1. Witchcraft. I. Title.
BF1566 .G3 2004

Gardner, Howard. Changing minds : the art and
science of changing our own and other peoples
minds / Howard Gardner. Boston, Mass. : Harvard
Business School Press, 2004. p. cm. Includes
bibliographical references and index. Table of contents URL:
http://www.loc.gov/catdir/toc/ecip048/2003019437.html
CONTENTS: The contents of the mind -- The forms of the
mind -- The power of early theories -- Leading a diverse
population -- Leading an institution : how to deal with a
uniform population -- The creative geniuses change minds
indirectly through science, scholarly breakthroughs, and works
of art -- Mind changing in a formal setting -- Mind changing up
close -- Changing ones own mind -- Epilogue : the future of
mind changing. ISBN 1-57851-709-5 DDC 153.8/5
*1. Change (Psychology) 2. Persuasion (Psychology) 3.
Influence (Psychology) I. Title.*
BF637.C4 G37 2004

MULTIPLE INTELLIGENCES.
Multiple intelligences reconsidered. New York,
NY : P. Lang, c2004.
BF432.3 .M86 2004

GARDNER, MARTIN, 1914-.
WHYS OF A PHILOSOPHICAL SCRIVENER.
Smullyan, Raymond M. Who knows?
Bloomington : Indiana University Press, c2003.
BL50 .S59 2003

Gardner, Sebastian.
Art and morality. London ; New York : Routledge,
2003.
BH39 .A695 2003

Garga, Hariśa Kumāra, 1959- Jyotisha tattva vivecanī
saṃhitā / Hariśa Kumāra Garga. 1. saṃskaraṇa. Dillī :
Hariśa Kumāra Garga, 2002. xxxi, 567 p. : ill. ; 25 cm. In
Hindi; includes passages in Sanskrit. SUMMARY: On Hindu
astrology.
1. Hindu astrology. I. Title.
BF1714.H5 G365 2002

Garga, Pushpalatā.
Smārikā. Jayapura : Yoga Sādhanā Āśrama, 2001.
BL1175.A4955 S62 2001

Garifullin, Ramil', 1962- Illiuzionizm lichnosti : kak
novaia filosofsko-psikhologicheskaia
kontseptsiia : psikhologiia obmana, manipuliatsii,
kodirovaniia : nauchnaia monografiia / Ramil'
Garifullin. Kazan' : [s.n.], 1997. 403 p. : ill. ; cm. Added
title page title: Personal illusionism. Summary and table of
contents in English. Includes bibliographical references (p.
393-396). ISBN 5879981246
*1. Hallucinations and illusions. 2. Manipulative behavior. 3.
Deception - Psychological aspects. I. Title. II. Title: Personal
illusionism*
BF491 .G37 1997

**Garland reference library of social science. Pedagogy
and popular culture.**
Harry Potter's world. New York ; London :
RoutledgeFalmer, 2003.
PR6068.O93 Z73 2003

GARMENT INDUSTRY. See **CLOTHING TRADE.**

GARMENTS. See **CLOTHING AND DRESS.**

Garotas iradas.
Leonel, Vange, 1963- Grrrls. São Paulo : Edições
GLS, c2001.

Garrison, Cal. The old girls' book of dreams : how to
make your wishes come true day by day and night by
night / Cal Garrison. Boston, MA : Red Wheel, 2003.
xvi, 176 p. ; 20 cm. Table of contents URL: http://
www.loc.gov/catdir/toc/ecip042/2003007753.html ISBN 1-
59003-062-1 DDC 133.4/3
1. Astrology. 2. Witchcraft. 3. Women - Miscellanea. I. Title.
BF1729.W64 G37 2003

Garten, Jeffrey E., 1946- The politics of fortune : a new
agenda for business leaders / Jeffrey E. Garten.
Boston : Harvard Business School Press, c2002. 211
p. ; 22 cm. Includes bibliographical references (p. [187]-198)
and index. CONTENTS: A new world -- Precedents for
leadership -- Rebuilding the reputation of CEOs -- Protecting
the homeland -- Restoring integrity to markets -- Preserving
economic security -- Sustaining free trade -- Reducing global
poverty -- Expanding corporate citizenship -- Influencing
foreign policy -- Improving business education -- The

challenge ahead. ISBN 1-57851-878-4 (alk. paper) DDC
658.4/08
*1. Leadership. 2. Chief executive officers - Attitudes. 3.
Executive ability. 4. Business ethics. 5. Social responsibility of
business. 6. Corporations - Moral and ethical aspects. 7.
International trade - Moral and ethical aspects. 8. Industrial
management - Moral and ethical aspects. 9. Business and
politics - Moral and ethical aspects. 10. Industries - Security
measures. 11. National security - United States. I. Title.*
HD57.7 .G377 2002

Garton, Alison, 1950- Exploring cognitive
development : the child as problem solver / Alison F.
Garton. 1st ed. Oxford, UK ; Malden, MA : Blackwell
Pub., 2004. p. cm. Includes bibliographical references and
indexes. Table of contents URL: http://www.loc.gov/catdir/
toc/ecip047/2003017215.html CONTENTS: Theoretical
overview -- Strategy use and learning in problem solving --
Social problem solving -- What the child brings to the task --
Summary, review, and implications. ISBN 0-631-23457-8 (alk.
paper) ISBN 0-631-23458-6 (pbk. : alk. paper) DDC 155.4/
1343
1. Problem solving in children. I. Title.
BF723.P8 G37 2004

Gass, Robert H.
Perspectives on persuasion, social influence, and
compliance gaining. Boston, MA : Allyn and Bacon,
2003.
BF637.P4 P415 2003

GASTRONOMY. See **DINNERS AND DINING;
FOOD.**

Gatto, Ludovico.
Studi sulle società e le culture del Medioevo per
Girolamo Arnaldi. [Firenze] : All'insegna del giglio,
2002.
DG443 .S78 2002

**Gaudeamus (Moscow, Russia). Khrestomatiia dlia
vuzov.**
Ol'shanskiĭ, D. V. (Dmitriĭ Vadimovich) Psikhologiia
sovremennoĭ rossiĭskoĭ politiki. Moskva :
Akademicheskiĭ proekt, 2001.
JN6699.A15 O46 2001

Gaudemar, Martine de.
Leibniz, Gottfried Wilhelm, Freiherr von, 1646-1716.
Réfutation inédite de Spinoza. Arles [France] : Actes
Sud ; [Montréal] : Leméac, 1999.

Gaudin, Thierry. Discours de la méthode créatrice :
entretiens / Thierry Gaudin, François L'Yvonnet.
Gordes : Relié, c2003. 172, [1] p. ; 19 cm. (Ose savoir,
1631-5588) Includes bibliographical references (p. 163-[173]).
ISBN 2-909698-88-2 DDC 194
*1. Gaudin, Thierry - Interviews. 2. L'Yvonnet, François -
Interviews. 3. Creative ability. 4. Creation (Literary, artistic,
etc.) I. L'Yvonnet, François. II. Title. III. Series.*

GAUDIN, THIERRY - INTERVIEWS.
Gaudin, Thierry. Discours de la méthode créatrice.
Gordes : Relié, c2003.

Gaulin, Steven J. C. Evolutionary psychology / Steven
J.C. Gaulin and Donald H. McBurney. 2nd ed. Upper
Saddle River, N.J. : Pearson/Prentice Hall, c2004. xiv,
402 p. : ill. ; 25 cm. Rev. ed. of: Psychology. c2001. Includes
bibliographical references (p. 382-396) and index. Table of
contents URL: http://www.loc.gov/catdir/toc/ecip045/
2003013178.html ISBN 0-13-111529-4 DDC 155.7
*1. Evolutionary psychology. 2. Human evolution. I. McBurney,
Donald, 1938- II. Gaulin, Steven J. C. Psychology. III. Title.*
BF698.95 .G38 2004

Psychology.
Gaulin, Steven J. C. Evolutionary psychology. 2nd
ed. Upper Saddle River, N.J. : Pearson/Prentice
Hall, c2004.
BF698.95 .G38 2004

Gaulle, Charles de, 1890-1970.
[Fil de l'épée. Portuguese]
O fio da espada / Charles de Gaulle ; tradução de
Petrônio R. G. Muniz. Rio de Janeiro : Biblioteca
do Exército Editora, 2001. 145 p. ; 22 cm. (Colecção
General Benício ; 378) (Biblioteca do Exército Editora
Publiccação ; v 714) Includes bibliographical references.
Translation of: Le fil de l'epée. ISBN 85-7011-288-2
*1. War. 2. Leadership. 3. France - History, Military. I. <uniz,
Petrônio R. G. II. Title. III. Series: Publicação (Biblioteca do
Exército (Brazil)) ; 714.*

GAULS. See **CELTS.**

Gaura, Guruprasada.
Prthuyaśas. Ṣaṭpañcāśikā. 1. saṃskarana. Vārāṇasī :
Caukhambā Surabhāratī Prakāśana ; Dillī :
Caukhambā Saṃskṛta Pratiṣṭhāna, 2002.
BF1714.H5 P7 2002

Gaurico, Pomponio, 1481 or 82-1528.
Ammonius, Hermiae. Commentaria in quinque voces
Porphyrii. Stuttgart : Frommann-Holzboog, 2002.

Gaut, Berys Nigel.
The creation of art. New York, NY : Cambridge
University Press, 2003.
N71 .C754 2003

**GAUTAMA BUDDHA - PRE-EXISTENCE -
JUVENILE LITERATURE.**
The jewel of friendship. Berkeley, CA : Dharma Pub.,
2002.
BQ1462.E5 J48 2002

Gautama, Kalyāṇa.
Diyara Kalyāṇa, mero kathā mero gīta. 1. saṃskarana.
[Kathmandu] : Sañjanā Gautama, 2059-   [2002-
BF789.S8+

Gavalchin, John. Temporality in music : a conceptual
model based on the phenomenology of Paul Ricoeur /
John Gavalchin. 2000. vii, 169 leaves : music. Thesis (Ph.
D.)--New York University, 2000. Includes bibliographical
references (leaves 166-169). Photocopy. Ann Arbor, Mich. :
UMI Dissertation Services, 2001. vii, 169 p. : music ; 22 cm.
*1. Ricœur, Paul - Influence. 2. Hermeneutics. 3. Time in music.
4. Time perception. 5. Music - Philosophy and aesthetics. I.
Title.*

Gavrilov, D. A. Bogi slavian, iazychestvo, traditsiia /
D.A. Gavrilov, A. E. Nagovitsyn. [Moskva] : Refl-
buk, 2002. 463 p. : ill. ; 21 cm. (Sozvezdiia mudrosti) ISBN
5879830543 (seriia) ISBN 5879831116 (Refl-buk)
*1. Slavs - Religion. 2. Gods, Slavic. 3. Mythology, Slavic. I.
Nagovitsyn, A. E. (Alekseĭ Evgen'evich) II. Title. III. Series:
Astrum sapientiae.*
BL930 .G38 2002

Gawain, Shakti, 1948- Creative visualization : use the
power of your imagination to create what you want in
your life / Shakti Gawain. [Rev. ed.]. Novato, Calif. :
Nataraj Pub./New World Library, c2002. xvi, 175 p. :
ill. ; 22 cm. "25th anniversary edition"--Cover. Includes
bibliographical references (p. 172-174). ISBN 1-57731-229-5
(alk. paper) DDC 153.3/2
*1. Visualization. 2. Affirmations. 3. Self-actualization
(Psychology) I. Title.*
BF367 .G34 2002

The path of transformation : how healing ourselves
can change the world / Shakti Gawain. Rev. ed.
Novato, Calif. : Nataraj Pub., 2000. xviii, 245 p. ; 22 cm.
Originally published: 1993. Includes bibliographical references
(p. 241-244). ISBN 1-57731-154-X DDC 158.1
1. Conduct of life. I. Title.
BJ1581 .G35 2000

Reflections in the light : daily thoughts and
affirmations / Shakti Gawain ; compiled by Denise
Grimshaw. Rev. ed. Novato, Calif. : Nataraj Pub.,
c2003. p. cm. "Based in part on Creative visualization ... and
Living in the light"--T.p. verso. Includes index. ISBN 1-
57731-410-7 DDC 158.1/28
*1. Self-actualization (Psychology) 2. Conduct of life. 3.
Affirmations. I. Grimshaw, Denise. II. Title.*
BF637.S4 G393 2003

Gawor, Leszek. Katastrofizm konsekwentny : o
poglądach Mariana Zdziechowskiego i Stanisława
Ignacego Witkiewicza / Leszek Gawor. Lublin :
Wydawn. Uniwersytetu Marii Curie Skłodowskiej,
1998. 117 p. ; 24 cm. Includes bibliographical references.
ISBN 83-227-1152-2
*1. Zdziechowski, Marjan, - 1861-1938 - Philosophy. 2.
Witkiewicz, Stanisław Ignacy, - 1885-1939 - Philosophy. 3.
Philosophy. I. Title.*
B4691.Z384 G38 1998

GAY ACTIVISTS. See **LESBIAN ACTIVISTS.**

GAY COUPLES.
Pimental-Habib, Richard L. The power of a partner.
1st ed. Los Angeles, CA : Alyson Books, 2002.
HQ76.25 .P56 2002

GAY COUPLES - COUNSELING OF.
Pimental-Habib, Richard L. The power of a partner.
1st ed. Los Angeles, CA : Alyson Books, 2002.
HQ76.25 .P56 2002

GAY FATHERS - FAMILY RELATIONSHIPS.
Gottlieb, Andrew R. Sons talk about their gay fathers.
New York : Harrington Park Press, c2003.
HQ76.13 .G67 2003

GAY MEN.
Califia-Rice, Patrick, 1954- Speaking sex to power.
1st ed. San Francisco : Cleis Press, c2002.
HQ76.25 .C32 2002

**GAY MEN - UNITED STATES - PSYCHOLOGY -
CASE STUDIES.**

Bailey, J. Michael. The man who would be queen. Washington, D.C. : Joseph Henry Press, c2003.
HQ76.2.U5 B35 2003

GAY PARENTS. See **CHILDREN OF GAY PARENTS; GAY FATHERS.**

GAY PARENTS' CHILDREN. See **CHILDREN OF GAY PARENTS.**

GAY PEOPLE. See **GAYS.**

GAY PERSONS. See **GAYS.**

Gay witchcraft.
Penczak, Christopher. Boston, MA : Weiser Books, 2003.
BF1571.5.G39 P46 2003

GAY WOMEN. See **LESBIANS.**

Gayle, Noga Agnus.
Bailey, Gordon, 1946- Ideology. Peterborough, Ont. : Broadview Press, 2003.

Gaylin, Willard. Hatred : the psychological descent into terror / Willard Gaylin. 1st ed. New York : Public Affairs, c2003. viii, 261 p. ; 22 cm. Includes bibliographical references and index. ISBN 1-58648-166-5 DDC 152.4
1. Hate. I. Title.
BF575.H3 G39 2003

Gayon, Jean.
Barsotti, Bernard. Bachelard critique de Husserl. Paris : Harmattan, c2002.
B2430.B254 B37 2002

GAYS. See **GAY MEN; LESBIANS.**

GAYS - COUNSELING OF.
Counseling diverse populations. 3rd ed. Boston, Mass. : McGraw-Hill, c2004.
BF637.C6 C6372 2004

Queer counselling and narrative practice. Adelaide : Dulwich Centre Publications, c2002.

GAYS, FEMALE. See **LESBIANS.**

GAYS - HISTORY.
Filho, Amilcar Torrão. Tríbades galantes, fanchonos militantes. São Paulo : Edições GLS, 2000.

GAYS, MALE. See **GAY MEN.**

GAYS - MENTAL HEALTH.
Ritter, Kathleen. Handbook of affirmative psychotherapy with lesbians and gay men. New York : Guilford Press, c2002.
RC451.4.G39 R55 2002

GAYS - MENTAL HEALTH SERVICES.
Ritter, Kathleen. Handbook of affirmative psychotherapy with lesbians and gay men. New York : Guilford Press, c2002.
RC451.4.G39 R55 2002

GAYS - MISCELLANEA.
Penczak, Christopher. Gay witchcraft. Boston, MA : Weiser Books, 2003.
BF1571.5.G39 P46 2003

GAZE - PSYCHOLOGICAL ASPECTS.
Ayers, Mary, 1960- The eyes of shame. 1st ed. Hove, East Sussex ; New York : Brunner-Routledge, 2003.
BF175.5.O24 A94 2003

Marshall, Evan, 1956- The eyes have it. New York : Citadel Press, c2003.
BF637.N66 M37 2003

The Roman gaze. Baltimore : Johns Hopkins University Press, 2002.
BF637.C45 R64 2002

Gefangen, auch im Erinnern.
Kraut, Bernhard, 1960- Wien : Edition Selene, c2002.

Die Gegenwart der Psychoanalyse, die Psychoanalyse der Gegenwart / herausgegeben von Werner Bohleber und Sibylle Drews. 2. Aufl. Stuttgart : Klett-Cotta, 2002. 611 p. : ill. ; 24 cm. Includes bibliographical references. ISBN 3-608-94349-8
1. Psychoanalysis. I. Bohleber, Werner. II. Drews, Sibylle.

Geier, Alfred, 1930- Plato's erotic thought : the tree of the unknown / Alfred Geier. Rochester, NY : University of Rochester Press, 2002. 237 p. : ill. ; 24 cm. (Rochester studies in philosophy ; 3) Includes bibliographical references (p. [233]-237) and index. ISBN 1-58046-068-2 (alk. paper) DDC 184
1. Plato - Contributions in concept of love. 2. Plato. - Symposium. 3. Plato. - Lysis. 4. Plato. - Phaedrus. 5. Love. I. Title. II. Series.
B398.L9 G45 2002

Geiger, John, 1960- Chapel of extreme experience / by John Geiger. 1st ed. Toronto, Ont. : Gutter Press, c2002. 120 p. : ill. ; 21 cm. "A short history of flicker"--Cover p. 1. Includes bibliographical references (p. 108-117) and index. ISBN 1-89635-636-2 DDC 152.14
1. Stroboscopes - Physiological effect. 2. Stroboscopes - Psychological aspects. 3. Hallucinations and illusions. 4. Optical illusions. I. Title.
QP495 .G45 2002

Geiger, Wolfgang. Geschichte und Weltbild : Plädoyer für eine interkulturelle Hermeneutik / Wolfgang Geiger. 1. Aufl. Frankfurt am Main : Humanities Online, c2002. 390 p. ; 21 cm. Includes bibliographical references. ISBN 3-934157-00-9 (pbk.)
1. Historiography. 2. Hermeneutics. I. Title.

Geist, Gehirn, Maschine.
Tetens, Holm, 1948- Stuttgart : Reclam, c1994.
BF163 .T48 1994x

Geist und Gehirn.
Zoglauer, Thomas. Göttingen : Vandenhoeck & Ruprecht, 1998.
BF163 .Z64 1998

Gelb, Michael. More balls than hands : juggling your way to success by learning to love your mistakes / Michael J. Gleb. New York, NY : Prentice Hall, 2003. p. cm. Includes index. ISBN 0-7352-0337-7 (alk. paper) DDC 158.1
1. Success - Psychological aspects. 2. Success in business. I. Title.
BF637.S8 G39 2003

Gelehrte in der Antike : Alexander Demandt zum 65. Geburtstag / herausgegeben von Andreas Goltz, Andreas Luther und Heinrich Schlange-Schöningen. Köln : Böhlau, c2002. 330 p. ; 24 cm. Includes bibliographical references. ISBN 3-412-02802-9
1. Learning and scholarship - Greece. 2. Learning and scholarship - Rome. 3. Philosophy, Ancient. 4. Classical literature - History and criticism. I. Demandt, Alexander, 1937- II. Goltz, Andreas. III. Luther, Andreas. IV. Schlange-Schöningen, Heinrich, 1960-

Gelfand, Michele J.
The handbook of negotiation. Stanford, Calif. : Stanford Business Books, c2004.
BF637.N4 H365 2004

Gelfert, Hans-Dieter, 1937- Typisch amerikanisch : wie die Amerikaner wurden, was sie sind / Hans-Dieter Gelfert. Originalausg. München : Beck, c2002. 193 p. : ill. ; 19 cm. (Beck'sche Reihe ; 1502) Includes bibliographical references (p. 177-[194]). ISBN 3-406-49406-4
1. National characteristics, American. 2. United States - Social life and customs. I. Title. II. Series: Beck'sche Reihe ; 1502.
E169.1 .G44 2002

Geller, E. Scott, 1942-.
Ludwig, Timothy D. Intervening to improve the safety of occupational driving. New York : Haworth Press, 2000.
HE5614 .I586 2000

Gellner, Ernest.
[Essays. Selections]
Ernest Gellner : selected philosophical themes / Ernest Gellner. London ; New York : Routledge, 2003. 3 v. ; 23 cm. Includes bibliographical references and indexes. CONTENTS: v. 1. Cause and meaning in the social sciences -- v. 2. Contemporary thought and politics -- v. 3. The Devil in modern philosophy. ISBN 0-415-30295-1 (set : alk. paper) ISBN 0-415-30296-X (v. 1 : alk. paper) ISBN 0-415-30297-8 (v. 2 : alk. paper) ISBN 0-415-30298-6 (v. 3 : alk. paper) DDC 192
1. Philosophy. 2. Political science - Philosophy. 3. Social sciences - Philosophy. 4. Ethnology - Philosophy. I. Title. II. Title: Selected philosophical themes
B1626.G441 G76 2003

Gelpi, Christopher, 1966- The power of legitimacy : assessing the role of norms in crisis bargaining / Christopher Gelpi. Princeton, N.J. : Princeton University Press, c2003. xii, 209 p. : ill. ; 25 cm. Includes bibliographical references (p. [191]-200) and index. ISBN 0-691-09248-6 (cloth : alk. paper) DDC 327.1/7
1. Conflict management. 2. Security, International. 3. International relations - Moral and ethical aspects. 4. International relations - Psychological aspects. 5. International relations - Decision making. I. Title.
JZ5595.5 .G45 2003

Gelunbu xue shu wen ku
(3) Li, Xiaobing. Wo zai, wo si. Di 1 ban. Beijing : Dong fang chu ban she : Xin hua shu dian jing xiao, 1996.
CB425 .L39 1996 <Orien China>

Gelven, Michael. What happens to us when we think : transformation and reality / Michael Gelven. Albany : State University of New York Press, c2003. 149 p. ; 23 cm. Includes index. ISBN 0-7914-5747-8 (alk. paper) ISBN 0-7914-5748-6 (pbk. : alk. paper) DDC 110
1. Metaphysics - Psychological aspects. 2. Thought and thinking. 3. Change. I. Title.
BD111 .G45 2003

Gem magic.
Knight, Brenda, 1958- Gloucester, MA : Fair Winds Press, 2003.
BF1442.P74 K65 2004

GEM MINERALS. See **PRECIOUS STONES.**

GEMATRIA.
Bardah, Asher. Sefer Otsrot av. [Bene Berak?] : A. Bardah, 762- [2001 or 2002-
BS1225.54 .B37 2001

Glazerson, Matityahu. Migdele ha-te'omim be-diluge otiyot ba-Torah. Yerushalayim : Yerid ha-sefarim, 2002.

Gemistus Plethon, George, 15th cent.
[Magika logia tōn apo Zōroastrou magōn. French & Greek]
Magika logia tōn apo Zōroastrou magōn : exēgēsis eis ta auta logia / Geōrgiou Gemistou Plēthōnos = Oracles Chaldaïques / recension de Georges Gémist Pléthon ; édition critique avec introduction, traduction, et commentaire par Brigitte Tambrun-Krasker ; la recension arabe des Magika logia par Michel Tardieu. Athēnai : Akadēmia Athēnōn, 1995. lxxx, 187 p. ; 24 cm. (Corpus philosophorum Medii Aevi. Vyzantinoi philosophoi. Philosophi Byzantini ; 7) Text in Greek, Arabic, and French. Includes bibliographical references (p. [xv]-xxx) and indexes. ISBN 9607099400
1. Julianus, - the Theurgist. - Chaldean oracles. 2. Oracles - Early works to 1800. I. Tambrun-Krasker, Brigitte. II. Tardieu, Michel. III. Title. IV. Title: Oracles Chaldaïques V. Series: Oracles magiques des mages disciples de Zoroastre VI. Series: Corpus philosophorum Medii Aevi. Philosophi Byzantini ; 7.
BF1762 .G45 1995

Gemmen, Heather. Dreams from God : d / written by Heather Gemmen and Mary McNeil ; illustrated by Margeaux Lucas. Colorado Springs, Colo. : Faith Kidz, 2003. p. cm. (Rocket readers. Rise and shine) SUMMARY: Illustrates the letter d with a story depicting different dreams in the Bible. ISBN 0-7814-3982-5 DDC 248.2/9
1. Dreams in the Bible - Juvenile literature. 2. English language - Consonants - Juvenile literature. 3. Dreams in the Bible. 4. Reading readiness. I. McNeil, Mary (Mary S.) II. Lucas, Margeaux, ill. III. Title. IV. Series: Gemmen, Heather. Rocket readers. Rise and shine.
BF1099.B5 G46 2003

Rocket readers. Rise and shine.
Gemmen, Heather. Dreams from God. Colorado Springs, Colo. : Faith Kidz, 2003.
BF1099.B5 G46 2003

GEMS. See **PRECIOUS STONES.**

GEMS - MISCELLANEA.
Davies, Brenda, M.D. Chakra power beads. Berkeley, Calif. : Ulysses Press, c2001.
BF1442.C53 D36 2001

Dunwich, Gerina. Dunwich's guide to gemstone sorcery. Franklin Lakes, NJ : New Page Books, c2003.
BF1442.P74 D86 2003

GEMSTONES. See **PRECIOUS STONES.**

Gendai tetsugaku ga wakaru. Tōkyō : Asahi Shinbunsha, 2002. 176 p. : ill. ; 26 cm. (AERA Mook ; no. 76) Cover title. "Asahi Shimbun extra report & analysis special number 76, 2002"--Cover. Includes bibliographical references. ISBN 4-02-274126-0
1. Philosophy, Modern - 20th century. I. Title: Aera (Tokyo, Japan) II. Series.
B804 .G43 2002

Gender.
Kītā, Va. Calcutta : Stree, 2002.
HQ1075 .K576 2002

Gender : a sociological reader / edited by Stevi Jackson and Sue Scott. London ; New York : Routledge, 2002. xiv, 465 p. ; 25 cm. (Routledge student readers) Includes bibliographical references and index. ISBN 0-415-20180-2 (pbk.) DDC 305.3
1. Sex role. 2. Sex - Social aspects. 3. Feminism. I. Jackson, Stevi. II. Scott, Sue. III. Series.
HQ1075 .G426 2002

Gender and aging [electronic resource].
Velkoff, Victoria Averil. [Washington, D.C.] : U.S. Dept. of Commerce, Economics and Statistics Administration, Bureau of the Census, [1998]

Gender and archaeology series
(v. 5) Ancient queens. Walnut Creek, Calif. ; Oxford : AltaMira Press, c2003.

HQ1127 .A53 2003

Gender and culture
Fraiman, Susan. Cool men and the second sex. New York : Columbia University Press, c2003.
HQ1090 .F73 2003

Gender and difference in the Middle Ages / Sharon Farmer and Carol Braun Pasternack, editors. Minneapolis : University of Minnesota Press, c2003. xxvii, 354 p. ; 24 cm. (Medieval cultures ; v. 32) Includes bibliographical references. CONTENTS: On the history of the early phallus / Daniel Boyarin -- Gender irregularity as entertainment: institutionalized transvestism at the Caliphal Court in medieval Baghdad / Everett K. Rowson -- Reconfiguring the prophet Daniel: gender, sanctity, and castration in Byzantium / Kathryn M. Ringrose -- Negotiating gender in Anglo-Saxon England / Carol Braun Pasternack -- Male friendship and the suspicion of sodomy in twelfth-century France / Mathew S. Kuefler -- Crucified by the virtues: monks, lay brothers, and women in the thirteenth-century Cistercian saints' lives / Martha G. Newman -- "Because the other is a poor woman she shall be called his wench": gender, sexuality, and social status in late medieval England / Ruth Mazo Karras -- Re-orienting desire: writing on gender trouble in fourteenth-century Egypt / Michael Uebel -- Manual labor, begging, and conflicting gender expectations in thirteenth-century Paris / Sharon Farmer -- Female homoerotic discourse and religion in medieval Germanic culture / Ulrike Wiethaus -- Nonviolent Christianity and the strangeness of female power in Geoffrey Chaucer's Man of law's tale / Elizabeth Robertson. ISBN 0-8166-3893-4 (HC : alk. paper) ISBN 0-8166-3894-2 (PB : alk. paper) DDC 305.3/09/02
1. Women - History - Middle Ages, 500-1500. 2. Sex role - History - To 1500. 3. Sex differences - Philosophy - History. 4. Social history - Medieval, 500-1500. 5. Civilization, Medieval. I. Farmer, Sharon A. II. Pasternack, Carol Braun. III. Series.
HQ1143 .G44 2003

Gender and governance.
Brush, Lisa Diane. Walnut Creek, CA ; Oxford : AltaMira Press, c2003.
JC330 .B75 2003

Gender, development and money / edited by Caroline Sweetman. Oxford : Oxfam, 2001. 96 p. ; 25 cm. (Oxfam focus on gender) Cover title. Includes bibliographical references. CONTENTS: Editorial / Caroline Sweetman -- Gender biases in finance / Irene van Staveren -- Rural women earning income in Indonesian factories : the impact on gender relations / Peter Hancock -- Just another job? : paying for domestic work / Bridget Anderson -- Conceptualising women's empowerment in societies in Cameroon : how does money fit in? / Joyce B. Endeley -- Pathways to empowerment? : reflections on microfinance and transformation in gender relations in South Asia / Juliet Hunt and Nalini Kasynathan -- Mama Cash : investing in the future of women / Lilianne Ploumen -- Money that makes a change : community currencies, North and South / Gill Seyfang -- "More and more technology, women have to go home" : changing skill demands in manufacturing and Caribbean women's access to training / Daphne Jayasinghe -- An income of one's own : a radical vision of welfare policies in Europe and beyond / Ingrid Robeyns -- Resources / compiled by Erin Murphy Graham. ISBN 0-85598-453-8 DDC 305.3
1. Gender identity. 2. Women in development. 3. Money - Social aspects. 4. Women - Economic conditions. 5. Sex role - Economic aspects. 6. Income distribution. I. Sweetman, Caroline.

GENDER DIFFERENCES. See **SEX DIFFERENCES.**

GENDER IDENTITY.
Augustin, Nicole. "Bewegung in Widersprüchen, Widersprüche in Bewegung bringen". Pfaffenweiler : Centaurus-Verlagsgesellschaft, 1998.
LC2873.G3 A94 1998

Boys, literacies, and schooling. Buckingham [England] ; Philadelphia : Open University Press, 2002.
LC1390 .B69 2002

Burggraf, Jutta. Qué quiere decir género? 1. ed. San Jose, Costa Rica : Promesa, 2001.

Campos, Maria Consuelo Cunha. De Frankenstein ao transgênero. Rio de Janeiro : Editora Agora da Ilha, 2001.

Castel, Pierre-Henri. La métamorphose impensable. Paris : Gallimard, c2003.
HQ77.9 .C38 2003

Cealey Harrison, Wendy. Beyond sex and gender. London ; Thousand Oaks, Calif. : SAGE, 2002.
HQ1075 .C43 2002

Continental feminism reader. Lanham, Md. : Rowman & Littlefield Publishers, c2003.

HQ1075 .C668 2003

Engel, Antke. Wider die Eindeutigkeit. Frankfurt/Main ; New York : Campus, c2002.

Femme/butch. New York : Harrington Park Press, 2002.
HQ75.5 .F459 2002

Finding the real me. 1st ed. San Francisco, CA : Jossey-Bass, c2003.
HQ77.7 .F56 2003

Fraiman, Susan. Cool men and the second sex. New York : Columbia University Press, c2003.
HQ1090 .F73 2003

Francis, Elizabeth, 1959- Feminism and modernism [microform]. [1994]

Gender, development and money. Oxford : Oxfam, 2001.

Gender identity and discourse analysis. Amsterdam ; Philadelphia : John Benjamins Pub., c2002.
HQ1075 .G428 2002

Gender, identity and the culture of organizations. London ; New York : Routledge, 2002.
HD58.7 .G46 2002

Gender nonconformity, race, and sexuality. Madison : University of Wisconsin Press, [2002]
HQ1075 .G4645 2002

Gender perspectives on property and inheritance. Oxford : Oxfam, c2001.
HB715 .G45 2001

Gender, place, and memory in the modern Jewish experience. London ; Portland, Or. : Vallentine Mitchell, 2003.
DS143 .G36 2003

Gendered sexualities. New York : JAI, 2002.
HQ1075.A27 vol. 6

Geschlecht und Globalisierung. Königstein : Ulrike Helmer Verlag, c2001.

Karras, Ruth Mazo, 1957- From boys to men. Philadelphia : University of Pennsylvania Press, c2003.
HQ775 .K373 2003

Kimmel, Michael S. The gendered society. 2nd ed. New York : Oxford University Press, 2004.
HQ1075 .K547 2004

Odmiany odmieńca. Katowice : "Śląsk", 2002.
HQ23 .O36 2002

Ressler, Paula. Dramatic changes. Portsmouth, NH : Heinemann, c2002.
PN3171 .R47 2002

Sexual faces. Madison, Conn. : International Universities Press, c2002.
BF175.5.S48 S47 2002

Gender identity and discourse analysis / edited by Lia Litosseliti, Jane Sunderland. Amsterdam ; Philadelphia : John Benjamins Pub., c2002. vii, 335 p. ; 23 cm. (Discourse approaches to politics, society, and culture ; v. 2) Includes bibliographical references and indexes. ISBN 90-272-2692-X (Europe) ISBN 1-58811-213-6 (US)
1. Sex role. 2. Gender identity. 3. Discourse analysis. I. Litosseliti, Lia. II. Sunderland, Jane. III. Series.
HQ1075 .G428 2002

Gender, identity and the culture of organizations / edited by Iiris Aaltio and Albert J. Mills. London ; New York : Routledge, 2002. xii, 226 p. : ill. ; 25 cm. (Management, organizations and society) Includes bibliographical references and index. ISBN 0-415-27000-6 ISBN 0-415-27001-4 (pbk.) DDC 302.3/5
1. Corporate culture. 2. Gender identity. 3. Organizational change. I. Aaltio-Marjosola, Iiris. II. Mills, Albert J., 1945- III. Series: Management, organizations and society (London, England)
HD58.7 .G46 2002

GENDER IDENTITY DISORDERS. See **TRANSSEXUALISM.**

GENDER IDENTITY - HISTORY.
Hirdman, Yvonne, 1943- Genus. 1. uppl. Malmö : Liber, 2001.

GENDER IDENTITY IN LITERATURE.
Campos, Maria Consuelo Cunha. De Frankenstein ao transgênero. Rio de Janeiro : Editora Agora da Ilha, 2001.

Tait, Peta, 1953- Performing emotions. Aldershot ; Burlington Vt. : Ashgate, c2002.

PG3458.Z9 D774 2002

GENDER IDENTITY - NORTH AMERICA.
Many faces of gender. Boulder : University Press of Colorado ; Calgary, Alta., Canada : University of Calgary Press, c2002.
E98.P95 M35 2002

GENDER IDENTITY - PERIODICALS.
Sexualities, evolution & gender. Sheffield, England : BrunnerRoutledge, 2003-
BF309 .P78

GENDER IDENTITY - PSYCHOLOGICAL ASPECTS.
Bailey, J. Michael. The man who would be queen. Washington, D.C. : Joseph Henry Press, c2003.
HQ76.2.U5 B35 2003

GENDER IDENTITY - SWEDEN - HISTORY.
Hirdman, Yvonne, 1943- Genus. 1. uppl. Malmö : Liber, 2001.

The gender lens series
Brush, Lisa Diane. Gender and governance. Walnut Creek, CA ; Oxford : AltaMira Press, c2003.
JC330 .B75 2003

Gender nonconformity, race, and sexuality : charting the connections / Toni Lester, editor. Madison : University of Wisconsin Press, [2002] ix, 232 p. : ill. ; 24 cm. Includes bibliographical references and index. CONTENTS: "This immoral practice" : the prehistory of homophobia in Black nationalist thought / Martin Summers -- The gendered and racialized space within Australian prisons / Francine Pinnuck and Shannon Dowling -- "More feminine than 999 men out of 1,000" : measuring sex roles and gender nonconformity in psychology / Peter Hegarty -- Race, sexuality, and the question of multiple, marginalized identities in U.S. and European discrimination law / Toni Lester -- Definitional dilemmas : male or female? Black or white? The law's failure to recognize intersexuals and multiracials / Julie Greenberg -- Classical in difference : Isadora Duncan and Bill T. Jones / Carol Martin -- Claude Cahun and Lee Miller : problematizing the surrealist territories of gender and ethnicity / Whitney Chadwick -- "The culture of lesbianism" : intersections of gender, ethnicity, and sexuality in the life of a Chicana lesbian / Katie Gilmartin -- How we learn who we are / Mary C. Gentile -- Diasporic epic fragments : or, how I grew into skin / Geeta Patel -- Education of another kind" : Lorraine Hansberry in the fifties / Michael Anderson. ISBN 0-299-18140-5 (cloth) ISBN 0-299-18144-8 (paper) DDC 305.3
1. Sex role. 2. Minorities - Sexual behavior. 3. Stereotype (Psychology) 4. Gender identity. I. Lester, Toni P., 1955-
HQ1075 .G4645 2002

Gender on planet Earth.
Oakley, Ann. Oxford : Polity, 2002.

Gender perspectives on minority sexual identities.
Odmiany odmieńca. Katowice : "Śląsk", 2002.
HQ23 .O36 2002

Gender perspectives on property and inheritance : a global source book / [edited by Sarah Cummings ... et al.] Oxford : Oxfam, c2001. 142 p. ; 24 cm. (Gender, society & development) (Critical reviews and annotated bibliographies series) Includes bibliographical references and index. CONTENTS: Introduction: women and property, women as property / Maitrayee Mukhopadhyay -- Disjuncture in law and practice: women's inheritance of land in Latin America / Carmen Diana Deere and Magdalena Léon -- Changing the meaning of marriage: women and family law in Côte d'Ivoire / Jeanne Maddox Toungara -- Family laws and gender discrimination: advocacy for legal reforms in the Arab region / Lina Abou-Habib -- Women, tenure and land reform: the case of Namaqualand's reserves / Fiona Archer and Shamim Meer -- Does land ownership make a difference? Women's roles in agriculture in Kerala, India / Shoba Arun. ISBN 0-85598-461-9 ISBN 90-6832-714-3 (KIT) DDC 333.3082
1. Inheritance and succession. 2. Gender identity. 3. Property - Sex differences. I. Cummings, Sarah. II. Series. III. Series: Critical reviews and annotated bibliographies series
HB715 .G45 2001

Gender, place, and memory in the modern Jewish experience : re-placing ourselves / editors, Judith Tydor Baumel, Tova Cohen. London ; Portland, Or. : Vallentine Mitchell, 2003. xxii, 297 p. : ill. ; 24 cm. (Parkes-Wiener series on Jewish studies, 1368-5449) Includes bibliographical references and index. ISBN 0-85303-488-5 (cloth) ISBN 0-85303-489-3 (pbk). DDC 909/.04924/0082
1. Jews - Identity. 2. Jews - Europe - Identity. 3. Jews - United States - Identity. 4. Jews - Israel - Identity. 5. Gender identity. 6. Jewish women authors - United States. 7. Jewish women - Social conditions - 20th century. 8. Women - Israel. I. Baumel, Judith Tydor, 1959- II. Cohen, Tova. III. Series.
DS143 .G36 2003

GENDER ROLE. *See* **SEX ROLE.**

GENDER (SEX). *See* **SEX.**

Gender, sexuality and violence in organizations.
Hearn, Jeff. London ; Thousand Oaks : SAGE, 2001.

Gender, society & development
Gender perspectives on property and inheritance. Oxford : Oxfam, c2001.
HB715 .G45 2001

Gender, vlast', kul'tura : sot︠s︡ial'no-antropologicheskiĭ podkhod : mezhvuzovskiĭ nauchnyĭ sbornik po materialam konferent︠s︡ii (maĭ 2000 g.) / [redakt︠s︡ionnai︠a︡ kollegii︠a︡ E.R. I︠A︡rskai︠a︡-Smirnova (otv. redaktor) ... et al.]. Saratov : Saratovskiĭ gos. tekhn. universitet, 2000. 174 p. ; 21 cm. Includes bibliographical references. ISBN 5743307938
1. Sex role - Congresses. 2. Sex differences (Psychology) - Congresses. 3. Social perception - Sex differences - Congresses. 4. Ethnology - Congresses. I. I︠A︡rskai︠a︡-Smirnova, Elena. II. Saratovskiĭ gosudarstvennyĭ tekhnicheskiĭ universitet. III. Mezhvuzovskai︠a︡ nauchnai︠a︡ konferent︠s︡ii︠a︡ "Gender, vlast', kul'tura: sot︠s︡ial'no-antropologicheskiĭ podkhod" (2000 : Saratov, Russia)
HQ1075 .G4667 2000

Gendered landscapes : an interdisciplinary exploration of past place and space / editors: Bonj Szczygiel, Josephine Carubia, Lorraine Dowler. University Park, PA : Center for Studies in Landscape History, c2000. 167 p. : ill. ; 28 cm. Includes bibliographical references. ISBN 1-88890-102-0
1. Human geography. 2. Sex role. 3. Spatial behavior. 4. Space and time. 5. Geographical perception. 6. Personal space. 7. Social interaction. I. Szczygiel, Bonj. II. Carubia, Josephine. III. Dowler, Lorraine. IV. Center for Studies in Landscape History.

Gendered sexualities / edited by Patricia Gagné, Richard Tewksbury. New York : JAI, 2002. vi, 273 p. ; 23 cm. (Advances in gender research ; v. 6) Includes bibliographical references and index. CONTENTS: Introduction : Advancing gender research at the intersection of gender and sexuality / Patricia Gagné and Richard Tewksbury -- Add penis and stir : a cookbook approach to gender identity / Carol S. Lindquist -- The gender of desire : the sexual fantasies of women and men / Michael S. Kimmel and Rebecca F. Plante -- Voicing gender : the performance of gender in the context of phone sex lines / Christine Mattley -- The Playboy playmate paradox : the case against the objectification of women / James K. Beggan and Scott T. Allison -- Four renditions of doing female drag : feminine appearing conceptual variations of a masculine theme / Steven P. Schacht -- Queering sexuality and doing gender : transgender men's identification with gender and sexuality / Salvador Vidal-Ortiz -- Fracturing transgender : intersectional constructions and identization / K.L. Broad. ISBN 0-7623-0820-6 (alk. paper) DDC 305.3
1. Gender identity. 2. Sex. 3. Sex role. 4. Transsexuals - Identity. I. Gagné, Patricia. II. Tewksbury, Richard A. III. Series.
HQ1075.A27 vol. 6

The gendered society.
Kimmel, Michael S. 2nd ed. New York : Oxford University Press, 2004.
HQ1075 .K547 2004

Gendering talk.
Hopper, Robert. East Lansing : Michigan State University Press, c2003.
HQ1075 .H67 2003

Gendering the master narrative : women and power in the Middle Ages / edited by Mary C. Erler and Maryanne Kowaleski. Ithaca : Cornell University Press, c2003. viii, 269 p. : ill. 24 cm. Includes bibliographical references (p. 229-256) and index. CONTENTS: A new economy of power relations: female agency in the middle ages / Mary C. Erler and Maryanne Kowaleski -- Women and power through the family revisited / Jo Ann McNamara -- Women and confession: from empowerment to pathology / Dyan Elliott -- "With the heat of the hungry heart": empowerment and Ancrene wisse / Nicholas Watson -- Powers of record, powers of example: hagiography and women's history / Jocelyn Wogan-Browne -- Who is the master of this narrative? Maternal patronage of the cult of St. Margaret / Wendy R. Larson -- "The wise mother": the image of St. Anne teaching the Virgin Mary / Pamela Sheingorn -- Did goddesses empower women? the case of dame nature / Barbara Newman -- Women in the late medieval English parish / Katherine L. French -- Public exposure? consorts and ritual in late medieval Europe: the example of the entrance of the dogaresse of Venice / Holly S. Hurlburt -- Women's influence on the design of urban homes / Sarah Rees Jones -- Looking closely: authority and intimacy in the late medieval urban home / Felicity Riddy. ISBN 0-8014-4112-9 (alk. paper) ISBN 0-8014-8830-3 (pbk. : alk. paper) DDC 305.4/09/02
1. Women - History - Middle Ages, 500-1500. 2. Literature, Medieval - Women authors - History and criticism. 3. Women and literature - History - To 1500. 4. Social history - Medieval, 500-1500. 5. Power (Social sciences) 6. Narration (Rhetoric) 7. Women in literature. 8. Rhetoric, Medieval. I. Erler, Mary Carpenter. II. Kowaleski, Maryanne.
HQ1143 .G46 2003

Gendernyĭ kaleĭdoskop / [pod obshcheĭ redakt︠s︡ieĭ M.M. Malyshevoĭ]. Moskva : "Academia", 2001. 519 p. : ill. ; 21 cm. At head of title: Rossiĭskai︠a︡ akademii︠a︡ nauk. Moskovskiĭ t︠s︡entr gendernykh issledovaniĭ. Institut sot︠s︡ial'no-ėkonomicheskikh problem narodonaselenii︠a︡. Includes bibliographical references. ISBN 5874441018
1. Man-woman relationships. 2. Man-woman relationships - Russia (Federation) I. Malysheva, M. M. II. Moskovskiĭ t︠s︡entr gendernykh issledovaniĭ. III. Institut sot︠s︡ial'no-ėkonomicheskikh problem narodonaselenii︠a︡ (Rossiĭskai︠a︡ akademii︠a︡ nauk)

Gendernyĭ podkhod v psikhologicheskikh issledovanii︠a︡kh i konsul'tirovanii.
Konferent︠s︡ii︠a︡ "Gendernyĭ podkhod v psikhologicheskom konsul'tirovanii" (2002 : Evropeĭskiĭ Gumanitarnyĭ Universitet) Minsk : Evropeĭskiĭ Gumanitarnyĭ Universitet, 2002.
BF201.4 .K66 2002

Gendt, Anne-Marie Emma Alberta de, 1952- L'art d'éduquer les nobles damoiselles : le Livre du chevalier de la Tour Landry / Anne Marie De Gendt. Paris : Champion, 2003. 290 p. ; 23 cm. (Essais sur le Moyen Age, 0181-317X ; 28) Includes bibliographical references (p. [253]-271) and indexes. ISBN 2-7453-0668-5 DDC 809
1. La Tour Landry, Geoffroy de, - 14th cent. - Livre du chevalier de La Tour Landry pour l'enseignement de ses filles. 2. Conduct of life. 3. Women - Education, Medieval. I. Title. II. Series: Collection Essais sur le Moyen Age. ; 28.

GENE EXPRESSION.
Dawkins, Richard, 1941- The extended phenotype. Rev. ed. Oxford ; New York : Oxford University Press, 1999.
QH375 .D38 1999

GENEALOGY. *See also* **BIOGRAPHY.**
Eiguer, Alberto. La famille de l'adolescent. Paris : In press, c2001.

GENERAL ABILITY (PSYCHOLOGY). *See* **GENERAL FACTOR (PSYCHOLOGY).**

GENERAL EDUCATION. *See* **LITERACY.**

GENERAL FACTOR (PSYCHOLOGY).
The scientific study of general intelligence. 1st ed. Amsterdam ; Boston : Pergamon, 2003.
BF433.G45 S35 2003

GENERAL INTELLIGENCE (PSYCHOLOGY). *See* **GENERAL FACTOR (PSYCHOLOGY).**

GENERALS - CONFEDERATE STATES OF AMERICA - QUOTATIONS.
Jackson, Stonewall, 1824-1863. Stonewall Jackson's book of maxims. Nashville, Tenn. : Cumberland House, 2002.
E467.1.J15 J17 2002

Generating buy-in.
Walton, Mark S., 1950- New York : American Management Association, c2004.
HD30.3 .W35 2004

GENERATION, BABY BOOM. *See* **BABY BOOM GENERATION.**

GENERATION GAP. *See* **CONFLICT OF GENERATIONS.**

GENERATION X.
Fletcher, John Wright. A hermeneutic study of generational music. 2002.

GENERATIONS. *See also* **CONFLICT OF GENERATIONS.**
Generationswechsel und historischer Wandel. München : Oldenbourg, 2003.

Generationswechsel und historischer Wandel / Andreas Schulz/Gundula Grebner (Hrsg.) München : Oldenbourg, 2003. 147 p. ; 23 cm. (Historische Zeitschrift. Beihefte ; Bd. 36) Includes bibliographical references. ISBN 3-486-64436-X
1. Generations. 2. Intergenerational relations - Cross-cultural studies. 3. Conflict of generations. 4. Social change. 5. Civilization - History. I. Schulz, Andreas. II. Grebner, Gundula. III. Series.

GENERATIVE GRAMMAR. *See* **GOVERNMENT-BINDING THEORY (LINGUISTICS).**

GENERATIVE ORGANS, MALE. *See* **PENIS.**

The generative society : caring for future generations / edited by Ed de St. Aubin, Dan P. McAdams, and Tae-Chang Kim. 1st ed. Washington, DC : American Psychological Association, c2003. xiii, 292 p. : ill. ; 26 cm. Includes bibliographical references and indexes. Table of contents URL: http://www.loc.gov/catdir/toc/ecip044/2003011064.html CONTENTS: The generative society : an introduction / Ed de St. Aubin, Dan P. McAdams, and Tae-Chang Kim -- What is generativity? / Dan P. McAdams and Regina L. Logan -- Generativity and culture : what meaning can do / John Kotre -- Reflections on generativity and society : a sociologist's perspective / Kai Erikson -- The propagation of genes and memes : generativity through culture in Japan and the USA / Ed de St. Aubin -- Generativity as social responsibility : the role of generations in societal continuity and change / Takatoshi Imada -- The generative life cycle model : integration of Japanese folk images and generativity / Yoko Yamada -- Rope of ashes : global aging, generativity, and education / Ronald Manheimer -- Generativity behind bars : some "redemptive truth" about prison society / -- Shadd Maruna, Thomas P. Lebel, and Charles S. Lanier -- American religion, generativity, and the theraputic culture / Michele Dillon and Paul Wink -- Generativity and gender : the politics of care / Bonnie J. Miller-McLemore -- Guarding the next generation : the politics of generativity / Bill E. Peterson -- Generativity and the politics of intergenerational fairness / Takeshi Sasaki -- Volunteerism and the generative society / Mark Snyder and E. Gil Clary -- An ethical analysis of Erikson's concept of generativity / Don Browning -- Erik Erikson on generativity : a biographer's perspective / Lawrence J. Friedman -- The generative society : an epilogue / Ed de St. Aubin, Dan P. McAdams, and Tae-Chang Kim. ISBN 1-59147-034-X (alk. paper) DDC 155.6
1. Adulthood - Psychological aspects. 2. Children and adults. 3. Social psychology. I. De St. Aubin, Ed. II. McAdams, Dan P. III. Kim, T'ae-ch'ang.
BF724.5 .G45 2003

Generic drug entry prior to patent expiration.
United States. Congress. House. Committee on Energy and Commerce. Subcommittee on Health. Examining issues related to competition in the pharmaceutical marketplace. Washington : U.S. G.P.O. : For sale by the Supt. of Docs., U.S. G.P.O. [Congressional Sales Office], 2002.

GENERIC DRUGS - GOVERNMENT POLICY - UNITED STATES.
United States. Congress. House. Committee on Energy and Commerce. Subcommittee on Health. Examining issues related to competition in the pharmaceutical marketplace. Washington : U.S. G.P.O. : For sale by the Supt. of Docs., U.S. G.P.O. [Congressional Sales Office], 2002.

GENERIC EQUIVALENT (DRUGS). *See* **GENERIC DRUGS.**

GENERIC PRODUCTS. *See* **GENERIC DRUGS.**

GENERICS (DRUGS). *See* **GENERIC DRUGS.**

Género, desarrollo psicosocial y trastornos de la imagen corporal / Isabel Martínez Benlloch, coordinadora. Madrid : Instituto de la Mujer, 2001. 429 p. ; 24 cm. (Estudios ; 71) "NIPO: 207-01-080-0"--T.p. verso. Includes bibliographical references (p. 342-360). ISBN 84-7799-970-8 (pbk.)
1. Women - Psychology. 2. Body image in women. 3. Self-perception in women. 4. Body image in adolescence. 5. Eating disorders in women - Psychological aspects. 6. Eating disorders in women - Social aspects. 7. Anorexia nervosa. 8. Bulimia. I. Martínez Benlloch, Isabel. II. Series: Serie "Estudios" (Instituto de la Mujer (Spain)) ; 71.

Gênero em matizes / Heloisa Buarque de Almeida, ... [et al.], organizadoras. Bragança Paulista, SP : EDUSF, [2002] 412 p. ; 21 cm. (Estudos CDAPH. Série história & ciências sociais) Includes bibliographical references. ISBN 85-86965-35-9
1. Sex role - Brazil. 2. Feminism - Brazil. 3. Sex differences. I. Almeida, Heloísa Buarque de. II. Series.

GENEROSITY. *See* **GIFTS.**

GENET, JEAN, 1910-.
Shoham, S. Giora, 1929- Ṭeruf, seṭiyah vi-yetsirah. [Israel] : Miśrad ha-biṭaḥon, [2002]

Genetic and cultural evolution of cooperation.
Dahlem Workshop on Genetic and Cultural Evolution of Cooperation (90th : 2002 : Berlin, Germany) Cambridge, Mass. : MIT Press in cooperation with Dahlem University Press, c2003.
BF637.H4 D25 2002

GENETIC PSYCHOLOGY. *See also* **INTELLIGENCE LEVELS; MATURATION (PSYCHOLOGY).**

Akif'ev, A. P. Genetika i sud'by. Moskva : TSentrpoligraf, 2001.
GN281 .A45 2001

Armstrong, Gordon Scott, 1937- Theatre and consciousness. New York ; Oxford : Peter Lang, c2003.
BH301.P78 A75 2003

Atran, Scott, 1952- In gods we trust. Oxford ; New York : Oxford University Press, 2002.
BL53 .A88 2002

Barber, Nigel, 1955- The science of romance. Amherst, N.Y. : Prometheus Books, 2002.
HQ21 .B184 2002

Evolutionary psychology and violence. Westport, Conn. : Praeger, 2003.
HM1116 .E96 2003

Fabrega, Horacio. Origins of psychopathology. New Brunswick, N.J. : Rutgers University Press, c2002.
RC454.4 .F33 2002

Humphrey, Nicholas. The mind made flesh. Oxford ; New York : Oxford University Press, 2002.
BF701 .H86 2002

Humphrey, Nicholas. The mind made flesh. Oxford ; New York : Oxford University Press, 2002.

Maksymenko, S. D. (Serhiĭ Dmytrovych) Rozvytok psykhiky v ontohenezi. Kyïv : "Forum", 2002.
BF706 .M34 2002

Marcus, Gary F. (Gary Fred) The birth of the mind. New York : Basic Books, 2004.
BF701 .M32 2004

GENETIC PSYCHOLOGY - CONGRESSES.
Nebraska Symposium on Motivation (2001) Evolutionary psychology and motivation. Lincoln, Neb. ; London : University of Nebraska Press, c2001.
BF701 .N43 2001

GENETIC PSYCHOLOGY - PERIODICALS.
Sexualities, evolution & gender. Sheffield, England : BrunnerRoutledge, 2003-
BF309 .P78

GENETICS. See also **ADAPTATION (BIOLOGY); EPIGENESIS; NATURE AND NURTURE; VARIATION (BIOLOGY).**
Andrieu, Bernard. L'interprétation des gènes. Paris : Harmattan, 2002.

Dawkins, Richard, 1941- The extended phenotype. Rev. ed. Oxford ; New York : Oxford University Press, 1999.
QH375 .D38 1999

GENETICS AND ENVIRONMENT. See **NATURE AND NURTURE.**

GENETICS, BEHAVIORAL.
Humphrey, Nicholas. The mind made flesh. Oxford ; New York : Oxford University Press, 2002.
BF701 .H86 2002

GENETICS - HISTORY.
Akif'ev, A. P. Genetika i sud'by. Moskva : TSentrpoligraf, 2001.
GN281 .A45 2001

Genetika i sud'by.
Akif'ev, A. P. Moskva : TSentrpoligraf, 2001.
GN281 .A45 2001

Le génie et le crime.
Rhodes, Henry T. F. (Henry Taylor Fowkes), b. 1892. Paris, France : Harmattan, c2002.

Geniĭ sredi lĭudeĭ.
TSiolkovskiĭ, K. (Konstantin), 1857-1935. Moskva : Mysl', 2002.
TL781.85.T84 A25 2002

Genis, Aleksandr, 1953- Ivan Petrovich umer : stat'i i rassledovaniia / Aleksandr Genis. Moskva : Novoe literaturnoe obozrenie, 1999. 334. [2] p. : ill. ; 23 cm. Includes bibliographical references (p. 330-[335]). ISBN 5867930777
1. Russian literature - 20th century - History and criticism. 2. Popular culture - Soviet Union. 3. Popular culture - Russia (Federation) 4. Popular culture. I. Title.
PG3021 .G46 1999

GENIUS. See also **CREATION (LITERARY, ARTISTIC, ETC.).**
Bloom, Harold. New York : Warner Books, c2002.
BF412 .B58 2002

GENIUS.
Beyond knowledge. Mahwah, N.J. : L. Erlbaum Associates, 2003.

BF412 .B44 2003

Bloom, Harold. Genius. New York : Warner Books, c2002.
BF412 .B58 2002

Mensch & Musik. Augsburg : Wissner, c2002.
ML3830 .M46 2002

Rhodes, Henry T. F. (Henry Taylor Fowkes), b. 1892. Le génie et le crime. Paris, France : Harmattan, c2002.

Thélot, Claude. L'origine des génies. Paris : Seuil, c2003.

GENIUS AND MENTAL ILLNESS.
Rhodes, Henry T. F. (Henry Taylor Fowkes), b. 1892. Le génie et le crime. Paris, France : Harmattan, c2002.

Shoham, S. Giora, 1929- Ṭeruf, setiyah vi-yetsirah. [Israel] : Miśrad ha-biṭaḥon, [2002]

GENIUS - CASE STUDIES.
Murray, Charles A. Human accomplishment. New York : HarperCollins, 2003.
BF416.A1 M87 2003

GENIUS (COMPANION SPIRIT). See **GUARDIAN ANGELS.**

GENIUS - SOVIET UNION - CASE STUDIES.
Spivak, M. L. Posmertnaia diagnostika genial'nosti. Moskva : Agraf, 2001.
BF416.A1 S68 2001

GENIUSES. See **GIFTED PERSONS.**

GENOCIDE. See also **HOLOCAUST, JEWISH (1939-1945).**
Cornblit, Oscar. Violencia social, genocidio y terrorismo. 1. ed. México, D.F. : Fondo de Cultura Económica, 2002.
HM886 .C67 2002

Gentaz, Edouard.
Touching for knowing. Amsterdam ; Philadelphia : John Benjamins Pub., c2003.
BF275 .T69 2003

Gentieu, Penny.
Acredolo, Linda P. My first baby signs. [New York] : HarperFestival, c2002.
BF720.C65 A27 2002

GENTILE, GIOVANNI, 1875-1944.
Scazzola, Andrea. Giovanni Gentile e il Rinascimento. Napoli : Vivarium, 2002.

Gentner, Dedre.
Language in mind. Cambridge, Mass. : MIT Press, c2003.
P37 .L357 2003

The gentry context for Malory's Morte Darthur.
Radulescu, Raluca, 1974- Cambridge [England] : Rochester, NY : D.S. Brewer, 2003.
PR2047 .R33 2003

GENTRY - ENGLAND - HISTORY - TO 1500.
Radulescu, Raluca, 1974- The gentry context for Malory's Morte Darthur. Cambridge [England] : Rochester, NY : D.S. Brewer, 2003.
PR2047 .R33 2003

GENTRY IN LITERATURE.
Radulescu, Raluca, 1974- The gentry context for Malory's Morte Darthur. Cambridge [England] : Rochester, NY : D.S. Brewer, 2003.
PR2047 .R33 2003

GENTRY, LANDED. See **GENTRY.**

Gentzler, Edwin, 1951-.
Translation and power. Amherst : University of Massachusetts Press, 2002.
P306.97.S63 T7 2002

Genus.
Hirdman, Yvonne, 1943- 1. uppl. Malmö : Liber, 2001.

Genuss und Egoismus : zur Kritik ihrer geschichtlichen Verknüpfung / herausgegeben von Wolfgang Klein und Ernst Müller. Berlin : Akademie Verlag, c2002. xx, 364 p. ; 25 cm. (LiteraturForschung) Festschrift in honor of Manfred Naumann's 75th birthday. Includes bibliographical references and index. ISBN 3-05-003569-2 (hd.bd.)
1. Naumann, Manfred. 2. Egoism. 3. Philosophy, Modern. 4. Egoism in literature. I. Klein, Wolfgang. II. Müller, Ernst. III. Naumann, Manfred. IV. Title: Zur Kritik ihrer geschichtlichen Verknüpfung V. Series.

GEODESY. See **SURVEYING.**

GEODETIC ASTRONOMY. See **TIME.**

GEOGRAPHICAL PERCEPTION. See also **SPACE PERCEPTION.**

Gendered landscapes. University Park, PA : Center for Studies in Landscape History, c2000.

GEOGRAPHICAL PERCEPTION - PERIODICALS.
Spatial cognition and computation. [Dordrecht], The Netherlands : Kluwer Academic, c1999-
BF469 .S674

Géographie contemporaine
Le territoire pensé. Sainte-Foy : Presses de l'Université du Québec, 2003.

GEOLOGY AND RELIGION. See **RELIGION AND SCIENCE.**

GEOMANCY. See **ASTROLOGICAL GEOMANCY.**

GEOMETRIC FUNCTION THEORY. See **KERNEL FUNCTIONS.**

GEOMETRICAL DRAWING. See **DESIGN; PERSPECTIVE.**

Geopoliticheskiĭ rakurs.
Medvedko, Leonid Ivanovich. Rossiia, Zapad, Islam. Zhukovskiĭ ; Moskva : Kuchkovo pole, 2003.
BP173.5 .M44 2003

GEOPOLITICS. See also **WORLD POLITICS.**
Arkoun, Mohammed. De Manhattan à Bagdad. Paris : Desclée de Brouwer, 2003.
JC319 .A72 2003

Le territoire pensé. Sainte-Foy : Presses de l'Université du Québec, 2003.

GEOPOLITICS - RUSSIA (FEDERATION).
Maler, Arkadiĭ. Strategii sakral'nogo smysla. Moskva : Parad izdatel'skiĭ dom, 2003.

Georg Hann [sound recording].
Hann, Georg. [Germany] : Preiser Records, p2001.

Georgas, James, 1934-.
Culture and children's intelligence. Amsterdam ; Boston : Academic Press, c2003.
BF432.5.W42 C85 2003

George, Demetra, 1946- Asteroid goddesses : the mythology, psychology, and astrology of the re-emerging feminine / Demetra George and Douglas Bloch. Berwick, Me. : Ibis Press, 2003. p. cm. Originally published: San Diego, Calif. : ACS Publications, c1986. With new pref. Includes bibliographical references. ISBN 0-89254-082-6 (trade paper : alk. paper) DDC 33.5/398
1. Asteroids - Miscellanea. 2. Goddesses - Miscellanea. 3. Astrology and mythology. 4. Astrology and psychology. I. Bloch, Douglas, 1949- II. Title.
BF1724.5 .G46 2003

GEORGE, SAINT, D. 303 - ART.
Sankt Georg und sein Bilderzyklus in Neuhaus/ Böhmen (Jindřichův Hradec). Marburg : N.G. Elwert, c2002.
BR1720.G4 S26 2002

GEORGE, SAINT, D. 303 - CULT - CZECH REPUBLIC - JINDŘICHŮV HRADEC.
Sankt Georg und sein Bilderzyklus in Neuhaus/ Böhmen (Jindřichův Hradec). Marburg : N.G. Elwert, c2002.
BR1720.G4 S26 2002

Georges Dumézil, un naturel comparatiste.
Poitevin, Michel. Paris : Harmattan, c2002.

Georgia ghosts.
Roberts, Nancy, 1924- Winston-Salem N.C. : John F. Blair, Publisher, c1997, 2002.
BF1472.U6 R6318 1997

Georgiev, Lĭuben, 1933- Sreshti s Vangĭa / Lĭuben Georgiev. Sofia : Knigo-TSvĭat, 1996. 96 p. ; 20 cm. ISBN 9548409062
1. Vanga, - 1911- 2. Clairvoyants - Bulgaria. I. Title.
BF1283.V33 G46 1996

Geōrgios, Synkellos, fl. 800.
[Ecloga chronographica English]
The chronography of George Synkellos : a Byzantine chronicle of universal history from the creation / translated with introduction and notes by William Adler, Paul Tuffin. Oxford ; New York : Oxford University Press, 2002. lxxxviii, 638 p. ; 24 cm. Includes bibliographical references and index. ISBN 0-19-924190-2 DDC 930
1. Synkellos, George. - Ecloga chronographica. 2. Bible - Chronology. 3. History, Ancient. I. Adler, William. II. Tuffin, Paul. III. Title.

Gerard, Pierre.
Workshop on Adaptive Behavior in Anticipatory Learning Systems (1st : 2002 : Edinburgh, Scotland)

Anticipatory behavior in adaptive learning systems. Berlin ; New York : Springer, c2003.
Q325.5 .W65 2003

Gerber, Nancy, 1956- Portrait of the mother-artist : class and creativity in contemporary American fiction / Nancy Gerber. Lanham, Md. : Lexington Books, c2003. xv, 99 p. ; 24 cm. Includes bibliographical references (p. 24) and index. ISBN 0-7391-0544-2 (alk. paper) DDC 813/.5093520431
  1. American fiction - 20th century - History and criticism. 2. Mothers in literature. 3. Creation (Literary, artistic, etc.) 4. Creative ability in literature. 5. Mother and child in literature. 6. Social classes in literature. 7. Women artists in literature. 8. Creativity in literature. 9. Motherhood in literature. 10. Artists in literature. I. Title.
PS374.M547 G47 2003

GERBERG, JUDITH.
Vint/age 2001 conference : [videorecording]. New York, c2001.

Gerberg, Judith, panelist.
Vint/age 2001 conference : [videorecording]. New York, c2001.

GERIATRICS. *See* **AGED - HEALTH AND HYGIENE; AGED - MEDICAL CARE.**

Germain-Thiant, Myriam. La relation à l'autre : l'implication distanciée (ID) / Myriam Germain-Thiant, Martine Gremillet-Parent. Lyon : Chronique sociale, [2002] 122 p. : 22 cm. (Savoir communiquer) Includes bibliographical references. ISBN 2-85008-449-2 DDC 300
  1. Interpersonal communication. I. Gremillet-Parent, Martine. II. Title. III. Title: Implication distanciée (ID) IV. Series.

German 20th century philosophical writings / edited by Wolfgang Schirmacher. New York : Continuum, 2003. xx, 268 p. ; 22 cm. (The German library ; v. 77) Includes bibliographical references (p. [265]) and index. ISBN 0-8264-1358-7 (alk. paper) ISBN 0-8264-1359-5 (pbk. : alk. paper) DDC 193
  1. Philosophy. I. Schirmacher, Wolfgang. II. Title: German twentieth century philosophical writings III. Series.
B29 .G397 2003

GERMAN COURT EPIC. *See* **COURT EPIC, GERMAN.**

GERMAN LANGUAGE - IDIOMS.
Stein, Stephan, 1963- Textgliederung. Berlin ; New York : Walter de Gryuter, 2003.

GERMAN LANGUAGE - RHETORIC.
Stein, Stephan, 1963- Textgliederung. Berlin ; New York : Walter de Gryuter, 2003.

GERMAN LANGUAGE - SEMANTICS.
Rauschen. Würzburg : Königshausen & Neumann, c2001.

GERMAN LANGUAGE - STYLE.
Stein, Stephan, 1963- Textgliederung. Berlin ; New York : Walter de Gryuter, 2003.

The German library
  (v. 77) German 20th century philosophical writings. New York : Continuum, 2003.
B29 .G397 2003

GERMAN LITERATURE. *See* **GERMAN POETRY.**

GERMAN LITERATURE - 20TH CENTURY - HISTORY AND CRITICISM.
Recasting German identity. Rochester, NY : Camden House, 2002.
DD239 .R43 2002

GERMAN LITERATURE - HISTORY AND CRITICISM.
Rauschen. Würzburg : Königshausen & Neumann, c2001.

GERMAN PHILOLOGY.
Botschaften verstehen. Frankfurt am Main ; New York : P. Lang, c2000.
P91.25 .B688 2000

GERMAN PHILOSOPHY. *See* **PHILOSOPHY, GERMAN.**

GERMAN POETRY - MIDDLE HIGH GERMAN, 1050-1500. *See* **COURT EPIC, GERMAN.**

GERMAN POETRY - MIDDLE HIGH GERMAN, 1050-1500 - HISTORY AND CRITICISM.
Hübner, Gert. Erzählform im höfischen Roman. Tübingen : Francke, 2003.

German twentieth century philosophical writings.
German 20th century philosophical writings. New York : Continuum, 2003.
B29 .G397 2003

GERMANIC LANGUAGES. *See also* **ENGLISH LANGUAGE; GERMAN LANGUAGE.**
Runica, Germanica, Mediaevalia. Berlin : W. de Gruyter, 2003.

GERMANIC LITERATURE - HISTORY AND CRITICISM.
Runica, Germanica, Mediaevalia. Berlin : W. de Gruyter, 2003.

Germanistische Medienwissenschaft
  (T. 6.) Kommunikation, Kunst und Kultur. Bern ; New York : Peter Lang, c2002.

GERMANY - ARMED FORCES.
Naumann, Klaus, 1939- Frieden, der noch nicht erfüllte Auftrag. Hamburg : Mittler & Sohn, c2002.
UA710 .N38 2002

GERMANY - BIOGRAPHY.
Alt möcht ich werden--. 1. Aufl. Berlin : Aufbau-Verlag, c1994.
HQ1064.G3 A72 1994x

GERMANY - CIVILIZATION.
Deutschland und der Westen Europas im Mittelalter. Stuttgart : Thorbecke, c2002.

GERMANY - CIVILIZATION - 19TH CENTURY.
Renaissance der Kulturgeschichte? Dresden : Verlag der Kunst, 2001.
AM101.B4856 R36 2001

GERMANY - ETHNIC IDENTITY.
Konstrukte nationaler Identität. Würzburg : Ergon, c2002.
DC34 .K67 2002

GERMANY - ETHNIC RELATIONS.
Inspecting Germany. Münster : Lit, c2002.
DD76 .I57 2002

Recasting German identity. Rochester, NY : Camden House, 2002.
DD239 .R43 2002

GERMANY - HISTORIOGRAPHY.
Der weite Blick des Historikers. Köln : Böhlau, c2002.
D116 .W44 2002

GERMANY - HISTORY.
Runica, Germanica, Mediaevalia. Berlin : W. de Gruyter, 2003.

GERMANY - HISTORY - HISTORIOGRAPHY.
Reemtsma, Jan Philipp. Wie hätte ich mich verhalten? München : Beck, c2001.
HM216 .R38 2001

GERMANY - HISTORY - TO 1517.
Deutschland und der Westen Europas im Mittelalter. Stuttgart : Thorbecke, c2002.

GERMANY - INTELLECTUAL LIFE.
Der weite Blick des Historikers. Köln : Böhlau, c2002.
D116 .W44 2002

GERMANY - INTELLECTUAL LIFE - 19TH CENTURY.
Le leggi del pensiero tra logica, ontologia e psicologia. Milano : UNICOPLI, 2002.

GERMANY - INTELLECTUAL LIFE - 20TH CENTURY.
Le leggi del pensiero tra logica, ontologia e psicologia. Milano : UNICOPLI, 2002.

Recasting German identity. Rochester, NY : Camden House, 2002.
DD239 .R43 2002

GERMANY - LITERATURES. *See* **GERMAN LITERATURE.**

GERMANY - MILITARY POLICY - 20TH CENTURY.
Naumann, Klaus, 1939- Frieden, der noch nicht erfüllte Auftrag. Hamburg : Mittler & Sohn, c2002.
UA710 .N38 2002

GERMANY - MILITARY POLICY - 21ST CENTURY.
Naumann, Klaus, 1939- Frieden, der noch nicht erfüllte Auftrag. Hamburg : Mittler & Sohn, c2002.
UA710 .N38 2002

GERMANY - POLITICS AND GOVERNMENT - 1933-1945.
Bärsch, Claus-Ekkehard. Die politische Religion des Nationalsozialismus. 2., vollst. überarb. Aufl. München : W. Fink, c2002.

Schaller, Helmut Wilhelm, 1940- Der Nationalsozialismus und die slawische Welt. Regensburg : Pustet, c2002.
DD256.5 .S259 2002

GERMANY - RELATIONS - POLAND.
Polacy i niemcy. òznań : Wydawn. Poznańskie, 2003.
DK4121 .P65 2003

GERMANY - SOCIAL CONDITIONS - 20TH CENTURY.
Jarausch, Konrad Hugo. Shattered past. Princeton, N.J. : Princeton University Press, c2003.
DD86 .J253 2003

GERMANY - SOCIAL LIFE AND CUSTOMS.
Inspecting Germany. Münster : Lit, c2002.
DD76 .I57 2002

GERMPLASM RESOURCES, ANIMAL. *See* **LIVESTOCK - GERMPLASM RESOURCES.**

Geroimenko, Vladimir, 1955-.
Visualizing the semantic Web. London ; [New York] : Springer, c2003.
TK5105.888 .V55 2003

GERONTOLOGY. *See also* **AGING.**
Invitation to the life course. Amityville, N.Y. : Baywood Pub. Co., c2003.
HQ1061 .I584 2003

Gerow, Edwin.
The Persistence of religions. Malibu : Undena Publications, 1996.

Gerő, Zsuzsa. A gyermekrajzok esztétikuma : és más írások / Gerő Zsuzsa ; [szerkesztette, Vass Zoltán]. Budapest : Flaccus Kiadó, 2003. 232 p. : ill. (some col.) ; 21 cm. ISBN 9639412139
  1. Children's drawings - Psychological aspects. 2. Child psychology. I. Vass, Zoltán. II. Title.
BF723.D7 G47 2003

Gersh, Stephen.
The Platonic tradition in the Middle Ages. Berlin ; New York : W. de Gruyter, 2002.

Gertler, Brie.
Privileged access. Aldershot ; Burlington, VT : Ashgate, c2003.

Gervais, Bertrand, 1957-.
Les lieux de l'imaginaire. Montréal : Liber, 2002.

Gervasoni, Marco, 1968- Le armi di Orfeo : musica, mitologie nazionali e religioni politiche nell'Europa del Novecento / Marco Gervasoni. [Scandicci] (Firenze) : La nuova Italia, 2002. xii, 275 p. ; 22 cm. (Nuovi orchi) Includes bibliographical references and index. ISBN 88-221-4054-0 DDC 780
  1. Music and state - Europe. 2. Music - Europe - Religious aspects. 3. Ethnicity. 4. Nationalism in music. I. Title. II. Series.
ML3917.E85 G479 2002

Geschichte der Grosselternrollen.
Chvojka, Erhard. Wien : Böhlau, 2003.
HQ759.9 .C45 2003

Geschichte der Schrift.
Haarmann, Harald. Originalausg. München : C.H. Beck, c2002.

Geschichte im Kulturprozess.
Rüsen, Jörn. Köln : Böhlau, c2002.
D16.8 .R913 2002

Geschichte im Zeichen der Erinnerung.
Patzel-Mattern, Katja. Stuttgart : Franz Steiner, 2002.

Geschichte und Weltbild.
Geiger, Wolfgang. 1. Aufl. Frankfurt am Main : Humanities Online, c2002.

Geschlecht, Magie und Hexenverfolgung / herausgegeben von Ingrid Ahrendt-Schulte ... [et al.] ; in Zusammenarbeit mit dem Institut für Geschichtliche Landeskunde und Historische Hilfswissenschaften der Universität Tübingen. Bielefeld : Verlag für Regionalgeschichte, 2002. 278 p. : ill. ; 25 cm. (Hexenforschung, 0948-7131 ; Bd. 7) Includes bibliographical references and index. ISBN 3-89534-407-9 DDC 133.4/3/094
  1. Witchcraft - Europe - History. 2. Persecution - Europe - History. 3. Trials (Witchcraft) - Europe - History. 4. Women - Europe - History. I. Ahrendt-Schulte, Ingrid, 1942- II. Universität Thubingen. Institut für Geschichtliche Landeskunde und Historische Hilfswissenschaften. III. Series: Hexenforschung ; Bd. 7.

Geschlecht und Globalisierung : ein kulturwissenschaftlicher Streifzug durch transnationale Räume / herausgegeben von Sabine Hess und Ramona Lenz. Königstein : Ulrike Helmer Verlag, c2001. 244 p. : ill ; 21 cm. (Aktuelle

Frauenforschung) Includes bibliographical references. In German and English. ISBN 3-89741-089-3 (pbk.)
1. Gender identity. 2. Globalization - Social aspects. I. Hess, Sabine, 1969- II. Lenz, Ramona, 1975- III. Series.

Gesellschaft der Eliten.
Papcke, Sven, 1939- 1. Aufl. Münster : Westfälisches Dampfboot, 2001.
HM821 .P37 2001

GESTALT PSYCHOLOGY. See also WHOLE AND PARTS (PSYCHOLOGY).
Edgar, Iain R. Guide to imagework. London ; New York : Routledge, 2004.
BF367 .E34 2004

Salber, Wilhelm. Psychästhetik. Köln : König, c2002.

GESTURE.
Beauperin, Yves. Anthropologie du geste symbolique. Paris : Harmattan, c2002.
BL60 .B339 2002

Goldin-Meadow, Susan. Hearing gesture. Cambridge, Mass. : Belknap Press of Harvard University Press, 2003.
P117 .G65 2003

Goldin-Meadow, Susan. The resilience of language. New York ; Hove [England] : Psychology Press, 2003.
P118 .G57 2003

[Gesture (Amsterdam, Netherlands)] Gesture.
Amsterdam ; Philadelphia : John Benjamins Pub., 2001- v. : ill. ; 22 cm. Frequency: Semiannual. Vol. 1, no. 1 (2001)- . Latest issue consulted: Vol. 2, no. 2 (2002). Accompanied by CD-ROM containing full-text and supplementary audio-visual data, <v. 2 (2002)-> Also available on CD-ROM and online via the World Wide Web. Subscription required for online access and full text. URL: http://www.benjamins.nl/cgi-bin/t%5Fseriesview.cgi?series=GEST Available in other form: Gesture (Amsterdam, Netherlands : CD-ROM) ISSN: 1569-9773 (OCoLC)50850967. ISSN 1568-1475
1. Body language - Periodicals. 2. Gesture - Periodicals. 3. Gestures - Periodicals. I. Title: Gesture (Amsterdam, Netherlands : CD-ROM)
BF637.N66 G47

Gesture (Amsterdam, Netherlands : CD-ROM).
[Gesture (Amsterdam, Netherlands)] Gesture. Amsterdam ; Philadelphia : John Benjamins Pub., 2001-
BF637.N66 G47

GESTURE IN ART.
Rehm, Ulrich. Stumme Sprache der Bilder. München : Deutscher Kunstverlag, 2002.

GESTURE - PERIODICALS.
[Gesture (Amsterdam, Netherlands)] Gesture. Amsterdam ; Philadelphia : John Benjamins Pub., 2001-
BF637.N66 G47

GESTURE - PSYCHOLOGICAL ASPECTS.
Beattie, Geoffrey. Visible thoughts. Hove, East Sussex ; New York, NY : Routledge, 2003.
BF637.N66 B43 2003

GESTURE - RELIGIOUS ASPECTS.
Beauperin, Yves. Anthropologie du geste symbolique. Paris : Harmattan, c2002.
BL60 .B339 2002

GESTURES - PERIODICALS.
[Gesture (Amsterdam, Netherlands)] Gesture. Amsterdam ; Philadelphia : John Benjamins Pub., 2001-
BF637.N66 G47

GESUALDO, CARLO, PRINCIPE DI VENOSA, 1560 (CA.)-1613.
Shoham, S. Giora, 1929- Ṭeruf, setiyah ṿi-yetsirah. [Israel] : Miśrad ha-biṭaḥon, [2002]

Get a grip on your dream.
Jeff, Peter. [Grand Rapids, MI] : Possibility Press, c2000.
BF637.S8 J45 2000

Get over it and on with it!.
McKinney Hammond, Michelle, 1957- 1st ed. Colorado Springs, Colo. : WaterBrook Press, 2002.
BV4908.5 .M357 2002

Getting & staying married the Torah way.
Greiper, BenTzion. Getting and staying married / BenTzion Greiper. Brooklyn, NY : B.T. Greiper, [2001?]
HQ734 .G745 2001

Getting and staying married / BenTzion Greiper.
Greiper, BenTzion. Brooklyn, NY : B.T. Greiper, [2001?]
HQ734 .G745 2001

Getting even.
Murphy, Jeffrie G. Oxford ; New York : Oxford University Press, 2003.
BF637.F67 M87 2003

Getting hurt.
Berry, Joy Wilt. Let's talk about getting hurt. New York : Scholastic, c2002.
BF723.W67 B475 2002

Getting it done : postagreement negotiation and international regimes / edited by Bertram I. Spector and I. William Zartman. Washington, D.C. : United States Institute of Peace Press, 2003. xviii, 312 p. : 24 cm. Includes bibliographical references and index. ISBN 1-929223-43-9 (cloth : alk. paper) ISBN 1-929223-42-0 (paper : alk. paper) DDC 341
1. International law. 2. Treaties. 3. International cooperation. 4. Negotiation. I. Spector, Bertram I. (Bertram Irwin), 1949- II. Zartman, I. William.
KZ1321 .G48 2003

Getting out of a stress mess!.
Mundy, Michaelene. St. Meinrad, IN : One Caring Place, c2000.
BF723.S75 M86 2000

Getting started in personal and executive coaching.
Fairley, Stephen. Hoboken, N.J. : J. Wiley & Sons, 2003.
BF637.P36 F35 2003

Gewalt-Verhältnisse : feministische Perspektiven auf Geschlecht und Gewalt / Regina-Maria Dackweiler, Reinhild Schäfer (Hg.). Frankfurt ; New York : Campus, c2002. 250 p. ; 23 cm. (Reihe "Politik der Geschlechterverhältnisse" ; Bd. 19) Includes bibliographical references. ISBN 3-593-37116-2 (pbk.)
1. Violence. 2. Women - Violence against. I. Dackweiler, Regina-Maria. II. Schäfer, Reinhild. III. Series.

Geyer, Michael, 1947-.
Jarausch, Konrad Hugo. Shattered past. Princeton, N.J. : Princeton University Press, c2003.
DD86 .J253 2003

Ghana journal of psychology. Legon : The Ghana Psychological Association, 2001- v. ; 25 cm. Vol. 1, no. 1 (Aug. 2001)- . Title from cover.
1. Psychology - Ghana - Periodicals. 2. Psychology - Periodicals. I. Ghana Psychological Association.

Ghana Psychological Association.
Ghana journal of psychology. Legon : The Ghana Psychological Association, 2001-

Ghayr ṣāliḥ lil-zawāj.
Jiddāwī, ʻAbd al-Munʻim. al-Qāhirah : Dār Akhbār al-Yawm, 1994-

Gheorghiu, Dragos.
Fire in archaeology. Oxford : Archaeopress, 2002.
DA90 .B86 suppl. v.1089

Gheraṇḍasaṃhitā. English & Sanskrit.
The original Yoga. 2nd rev. ed. New Delhi : Munshiram Manoharlal Publishers, 1999.
B132.Y6 O74 1999

Ghose, Aurobindo, 1872-1950. Records of Yoga / Aurobindo. 1st ed. Pondicherry : Sri Aurobindo Ashram, 2001. 2 v. (1515 p.) ; 25 cm. SUMMARY: Diary on Yoga from 1909-1927. Includes passages in Sanskrit. ISBN 81-7058-650-X (v. 1) ISBN 81-7058-652-6 (v. 2)
1. Ghose, Aurobindo, - 1872-1950 - Diaries. 2. Yoga. I. Title.
B132.Y6+

GHOSE, AUROBINDO, 1872-1950.
McLaughlin, Michael T. Knowledge, consciousness and religious conversion in Lonergan and Aurobindo. Roma : Editrice Pontificia Universita Gregoriana, 2003.

Ranchan, Som P., 1932- Aurotherapy. Delhi : Indian Publishers Distributors, 2001.
BF173.A25 R36 2001

Vrinte, Joseph, 1949- The perennial quest for a psychology with a soul. 1st ed. Delhi : Motilal Banarsidass Publishers, 2002.
BF311+

GHOSE, AUROBINDO, 1872-1950 - DIARIES.
Ghose, Aurobindo, 1872-1950. Records of Yoga. 1st ed. Pondicherry : Sri Aurobindo Ashram, 2001.
B132.Y6+

Ghosh, Shyam.
The original Yoga. 2nd rev. ed. New Delhi : Munshiram Manoharlal Publishers, 1999.
B132.Y6 O74 1999

The ghost hunter's Bible.
Brandon, Trent. Definitive ed. [Ohio?] : Zerotime Paranormal and Supernatural Research, 2002.
BF1461 .B695 2002

The ghost hunter's handbook.
Summer, Lori. New York : Price Stern Sloan, c2002.
BF1461 .S88 2002

GHOST STORIES - CALIFORNIA - SAN FRANCISCO.
Haunted San Francisco. 1st ed. San Francisco : Heritage House Publishers, 2004.
BF1472.U6 H385 2004

GHOSTS. See also HAUNTED PLACES; POLTERGEISTS.
Kallen, Stuart A., 1955- San Diego, Calif. : Lucent Books, c2004.
BF1461 .K33 2004

Martin, Michael, 1948- Mankato, Minn. : Edge Books, 2004.
BF1461 .M365 2004

GHOSTS.
Brandon, Trent. The book of ghosts. Mineva, Ohio : Zerotime Pub., c2003.
BF1461 .B6949 2003

Brandon, Trent. The ghost hunter's Bible. Definitive ed. [Ohio?] : Zerotime Paranormal and Supernatural Research, 2002.
BF1461 .B695 2002

Browne, Sylvia. Visits from the afterlife. New York : Dutton, c2003.
BF1461 .B77 2003

Dunwich, Gerina. A witch's guide to ghosts and the supernatural. Franklin Lakes, NJ : New Page Books, c2002.
BF1471 .D86 2002

Kallen, Stuart A., 1955- Ghosts. San Diego, Calif. : Lucent Books, c2004.
BF1461 .K33 2004

Martin, Michael, 1948- Ghosts. Mankato, Minn. : Edge Books, 2004.
BF1461 .M365 2004

Townsend, John, 1955- Mysterious signs. Chicago, IL : Raintree, c2004.
BF1461 .T69 2004

Warren, Joshua P. How to hunt ghosts. New York : Simon & Schuster, c2003.
BF1471 .W37 2003

Zhao, Xi. Xu wu piao miao de gui shen shi jie. Di 1 ban. Beijing : Zong jiao wen hua chu ban she, 2001.
BL1812.G63 Z436 2001

GHOSTS - ALABAMA - MOBILE.
Parker, Elizabeth. Mobile ghosts. 1st ed. Spanish Fort, Ala. : Apparition Pub., c2001.
BF1472.U6 P36 2001

GHOSTS - CALIFORNIA.
Dennett, Preston E., 1965- California ghosts. Atglen, PA : Schiffer Pub., 2004.
BF1472.U6 D46 2004

GHOSTS - CALIFORNIA - CALABASAS.
Wlodarski, Robert James. Spirits of the Leonis adobe. West Hills, CA : G-Host Pub., c2002.
BF1472.U6 W59 2002

GHOSTS - CALIFORNIA - SAN FRANCISCO.
Haunted San Francisco. 1st ed. San Francisco : Heritage House Publishers, 2004.
BF1472.U6 H385 2004

GHOSTS - CANADA.
Smith, Barbara, 1947- Canadian ghost stories. Edmonton, Alta. : Lone Pine Pub., 2001.
BF1472.C3 S533 2001

GHOSTS - COLORADO.
Martin, MaryJoy, 1955- Twilight dwellers. 2nd ed. Boulder, Colo. : Pruett, 2003.
BF1472.U6 M37 2003

GHOSTS - FICTION. See GHOST STORIES.

GHOSTS - GEORGIA.
Bender, William N. Haunted Atlanta and beyond. Athens, Ga. : Hill Street Press, 2004.
BF1472.U6 B46 2004

Roberts, Nancy, 1924- Georgia ghosts. Winston-Salem N.C. : John F. Blair, Publisher, c1997, 2002.

BF1472.U6 R6318 1997

GHOSTS - GEORGIA - ATLANTA.
Bender, William N. Haunted Atlanta and beyond. Athens, Ga. : Hill Street Press, 2004.
BF1472.U6 B46 2004

GHOSTS - HAWAII.
Grant, Glen. Glen Grant's chicken skin tales. Honolulu, Hawaii : Mutual Pub., c1998.
BF1472.U6 G72 1998

GHOSTS - HUDSON RIVER VALLEY (N.Y. AND N.J.).
Richardson, Judith. Possessions. Cambridge, Mass. : Harvard University Press, 2003.
BF1472.U6 R54 2003

GHOSTS IN LITERATURE.
Richardson, Judith. Possessions. Cambridge, Mass. : Harvard University Press, 2003.
BF1472.U6 R54 2003

GHOSTS - JUVENILE LITERATURE.
Andrews, Ted, 1952- Spirits, ghosts & guardians. 1st ed. Jackson, Tenn. : Dragonhawk Pub., c2002.
BF1461 .A53 2002

Kallen, Stuart A., 1955- Ghosts. San Diego, Calif. : Lucent Books, c2004.
BF1461 .K33 2004

Martin, Michael, 1948- Ghosts. Mankato, Minn. : Edge Books, 2004.
BF1461 .M365 2004

Netzley, Patricia D. Haunted houses. San Diego, Calif. : Lucent Books, c2000.
BF1461 .N48 2000

Summer, Lori. The ghost hunter's handbook. New York : Price Stern Sloan, c2002.
BF1461 .S88 2002

Townsend, John, 1955- Mysterious signs. Chicago, IL : Raintree, c2004.
BF1461 .T69 2004

GHOSTS - MASSACHUSETTS - BOSTON.
Nadler, Holly Mascott. Ghosts of Boston town. Camden, Me. : Down East Books, c2002.
BF1472.U6 N32 2002

GHOSTS - MASSACHUSETTS - GLOUCESTER.
Pettibone, John W. The ghosts of Hammond castle. Glen Ridge, N.J. : Tory Corner Editions, c2001.
BF1474 .P48 2001

GHOSTS - MICHIGAN.
Hunter, Gerald S. Haunted Michigan. 1st. ed. Chicago, IL : Lake Claremont Press, 2000.
BF1472.U6 H86 2000

GHOSTS - NEW BRUNSWICK.
Dearborn, Dorothy, 1927- New Brunswick haunted houses-- and other tales of strange and eerie events. Saint John, NB : Neptune Pub., c2000.
BF1472.N48 D44 2000

GHOSTS - NEW ENGLAND.
Pitkin, David J. Ghosts of the Northeast. Salem, NY : Aurora Publications, c2002.
BF1472.U6 P57 2002

GHOSTS - NEW JERSEY.
Martinelli, Patricia A. Haunted New Jersey. Mechanicsburg, PA : Stackpole Books, 2005.
BF1472.U6 M38 2004

GHOSTS - NEW YORK (STATE) - WARWICK.
Reis, Donna. Seeking ghosts in the Warwick Valley. Atglen, PA : Schiffer Pub., c2002.
BF1472.U6 R45 2002

GHOSTS - NOVA SCOTIA.
Walsh, Darryll. Ghosts of Nova Scotia. East Lawrencetown, N.S. : Pottersfield Press, c2000.
BF1472.C3 W35 2000

Ghosts of Boston town.
Nadler, Holly Mascott. Camden, Me. : Down East Books, c2002.
BF1472.U6 N32 2002

The ghosts of consciousness.
Demmin, Herbert S., 1959- St. Paul, Minn. : Paragon House, c2003.
BF441 .D395 2003

The ghosts of Hammond castle.
Pettibone, John W. Glen Ridge, N.J. : Tory Corner Editions, c2001.
BF1474 .P48 2001

Ghosts of Nova Scotia.
Walsh, Darryll. East Lawrencetown, N.S. : Pottersfield Press, c2000.
BF1472.C3 W35 2000

Ghosts of the Northeast.
Pitkin, David J. Salem, NY : Aurora Publications, c2002.
BF1472.U6 P57 2002

GHOSTS - RESEARCH - METHODOLOGY.
Southall, R. H. (Richard H.), 1972- [How to be a ghost hunter. Spanish] Espíritus y fantasmas. 1. ed. St. Paul, Minn. : Llewellyn Español, 2003.
BF1461 .S6618 2003

GHOSTS - SOUTHERN STATES.
Boogers and boo-daddies. Winston-Salem, N.C. : John F. Blair, Publisher, c2004.
BF1472.U6 B66 2004

GHOSTS - SUPERIOR, LAKE, REGION.
Bishop, Hugh E., 1940- Haunted Lake Superior. 1st ed. Duluth, Minn. : Lake Superior Port Cities, c2003.
BF1472.U6 B565 2003

Ghosts talk.
Byrd, Da Juana. 1st ed. Cedar Hills, Tex. : Byrd Pub., c2002.
BF1031 .B97 2002

GHOSTS - UNITED STATES.
Smith, Terry (Terry L.), 1961- Haunted inns of America. Birmingham, Ala. : Crane Hill Publishers, c2003.
BF1474.5 .S65 2003

Giachery, Emerico. L'avventura del sogno / Emerico Giachery. Roma : A. Stango, 2002. 93 p. ; 21 cm. (Saggistica) ISBN 88-87274-84-3 DDC 854
1. Dreams. 2. Dreams in literature. I. Title. II. Series: Saggistica (Antonio Stango editore)

Gianfaldoni, Paolo. Benvenuto a Pisa / Paolo Gianfaldoni. [Fornacette, Pisa] : CLD iniziative speciali, c2000. 94 p. : ill. (some col.) ; 24 cm. Includes bibliographical references (p. 64-65). ISBN 88-87748-22-5 DDC 945
1. Pisa (Italy) - Civilization. 2. Civilization, Medieval. 3. Architecture, Medieval - Italy - Pisa. 4. Pisa (Italy) - Buildings, structures, etc. I. Title.

Giannini, John L., 1921- Compass of the soul : typology's four archetypal directions as guides to a fuller life / John L. Giannini. Gainesville, Fla. : Center for Applications of Psychological Type, 2003. p. cm. Includes bibliographical references. ISBN 0-935652-70-1 DDC 155.2/64
1. Typology (Psychology) 2. Temperament. 3. Myers-Briggs Type Indicator. I. Title.
BF698.3 .G53 2003

Giardina, Ric. Become a life balance master / Ric Giardina. Hillsboro, Or. : Beyond Words Pub., 2003. p. cm. Includes bibliographical references. CONTENTS: Your life balance equation -- Why bother with balance? -- The four myths of life balance -- A few fundamentals -- The importance of support -- The habit cycles -- Your life balance categories -- The life balance equation process -- Mastering life balance -- The balance masters factorial -- Meditate x 7 -- Act x 6 -- Socialize x 5 -- Train x 4 -- Ethos x 3 -- Reflect x 2 -- Sabbath x 1 -- The balance master tools. ISBN 1-58270-098-2 DDC 158
1. Self-actualization (Psychology) 2. Quality of life. I. Title.
BF637.S4 G486 2003

Gibbons, B. J. Spirituality and the occult : from the Renaissance to the twentieth century / B.J. Gibbons. London ; New York : Routledge, 2001. 196 p. ; 24 cm. Includes bibliographical references (p. [145]-189) and index. ISBN 0-415-24448-X (hbk) ISBN 0-415-24449-8 (pbk.) DDC 133/.094
1. Occultism - Europe - History. 2. Europe - Intellectual life - History. I. Title.
BF1434.E85 G53 2001

Gibbs, Terri.
Honey from my heart for you. Nashville, Tenn. : J. Countryman, c2002.
BF575.F66 H66 2002

Giberson, Karl. Species of origins : America's search for a creation story / Karl W. Giberson and Donald A. Yerxa. Lanham, Md. : Rowman & Littlefield, c2002. ix, 277 p. ; 24 cm. (American intellectual culture) Includes bibliographical references (p. 253-270) and index. ISBN 0-7425-0764-5 (alk. paper) ISBN 0-7425-0765-3 (pbk. : alk. paper) DDC 231.7/652/0973
1. Religion and science. 2. Creation - Biblical teaching. 3. Creation - Mythology. 4. Evolution. I. Yerxa, Donald A., 1950- II. Title. III. Series.
BL240.3 .G53 2002

Gibson, Arthur, 1943- Metaphysics and transcendence / Arthur Gibson. London ; New York : Routledge, 2003. x, 276 p. ; 24 cm. (Routledge studies in religion ; 5) Includes bibliographical references (p. [255]-269) and indexes. ISBN 0-415-32128-X (alk. paper) DDC 110
1. Philosophical theology. 2. Metaphysics. I. Title. II. Series.
BT40 .G53 2003

Gibson, Clare K., 1964- The secret life of dreams : decoding the messages from your subconscious / Clare Gibson. San Diego, Calif. : Thunder Bay Press, 2004. p. cm. Includes bibliographical references and index. ISBN 1-59223-101-2 DDC 154.6/3
1. Dream interpretation. I. Title.
BF1091 .G49 2004

Gibson, Marion, 1970-.
Witchcraft and society in England and America, 1550-1750. Ithaca, NY : Cornell University Press, 2003.
BF1581 .W56 2003

Gibson, Michelle.
Femme/butch. New York : Harrington Park Press, 2002.
HQ75.5 .F459 2002

Gibson, Nigel C. Fanon : the postcolonial imagination / Nigel C. Gibson. Cambridge, U.K. : Polity Press in association with Blackwell Pub. ; Malden, MA : Distributed in the USA by Blackwell Pub., 2003. xi, 252 p. ; 24 cm. (Key contemporary thinkers) Includes bibliographical references (p. [239]-241) and index. ISBN 0-7456-2260-7 ISBN 0-7456-2261-5 (pbk.) DDC 320.5/092
1. Fanon, Frantz, - 1925-1961. 2. Fanon, Frantz, - 1925-1961 - Political and social views. 3. Blacks - Race identity. 4. Racism. I. Title. II. Series: Key contemporary thinkers (Cambridge, England)
CT2628.F35 G53 2003

Gibson, Stephanie B.
Communication and cyberspace. 2nd ed. Creskill, N.J. : Hampton Press, c2003.
P96.D36 C66 2003

Gidirinskiĭ, V. I. (Viktor Il'ich) Vvedenie v russkuiu filosofiiu : tipologicheskiĭ aspekt / V.I. Gidirinskiĭ. Moskva : Russkoe slovo, 2003. 316 p. ; 22 cm. At head of title: Moskovskiĭ gumanitarnyĭ in-t im. E.R. Dashkovoĭ. "Rekomendovano Otdeleniem po filosofii, politologii i religiovedeniiu Uchebno-metodicheskogo ob"edineniia universitetov Rossii v kachestve uchebnogo posobiia dlia studentov i aspirantov vysshikh uchebnykh zavedeniĭ gumanitarnogo profilia." "Uchebnoe posobie k spetskursu"-- Colophon. Includes bibliographical references. ISBN 5948531104 (Russkoe slovo) ISBN 5899030267 (MGI im. E.R. Dashkovoĭ)
1. Philosophy, Russian. 2. Philosophy, Russian - Study and teaching (Higher) - Russia (Federation) I. Moskovskiĭ gumanitarnyĭ institut im. E.R. Dashkovoĭ. II. Title.
B4201 .G536 2003

Gienow-Hecht, Jessica C. E., 1964-.
Culture and international history. New York : Berghahn Books, 2003.
JZ1251 .C84 2003

Gifford, Paul, 1944-.
2000 years and beyond. London ; New York : Routledge, 2003.
BR53 .T86 2003

GIFT EXCHANGE. *See* **CEREMONIAL EXCHANGE.**

Gift for women of all ages.
Walker, Jamie. 101 ways black women can learn to love themselves. Washington, D.C. : J.D. Publishing, c2002.
1. Black author.

The gift of renewal.
Whalen, Charles E., Jr. 1st ed. Gainesville, GA : Warren Featherbone Foundation, c2003 (Gainesville, GA : Matthews Print.)
BF637.S4 W47 2003

GIFTED ADULTS. *See* **GIFTED PERSONS.**

GIFTED PERSONS.
Beyond knowledge. Mahwah, N.J. : L. Erlbaum Associates, 2003.
BF412 .B44 2003

Bloom, Harold. Genius. New York : Warner Books, c2002.
BF412 .B58 2002

GIFTED PERSONS - CASE STUDIES.
Murray, Charles A. Human accomplishment. New York : HarperCollins, 2003.
BF416.A1 M87 2003

GIFTED PERSONS - POLAND - WARSAW - LONGITUDINAL STUDIES.
Firkowska-Mankiewicz, Anna. Intelligence and success in life. Warsaw : IFiS Publishers, 2002.

BF412 F57 2002

GIFTED PERSONS - PSYCHOLOGY.
Lechevalier, Bernard. Le cerveau de Mozart. Paris : O. Jacob, c2003.
ML3838 .L39 2003

GIFTED PERSONS - SOVIET UNION - BIOGRAPHY.
Spivak, M. L. Posmertnaia diagnostika genial'nosti. Moskva : Agraf, 2001.
BF416.A1 S68 2001

GIFTS - MISCELLANEA.
Stellas, Constance. The astrology gift guide. New York : Signet, c2002.
BF1729.G53 S74 2002

Giger, H. R. (Hansruedi), 1940-.
Akron, 1948- H.R. Giger tarot. Köln : Evergreen, c2000.

Gilad, Benjamin. Early warning : using competitive intelligence to anticipate market shifts, control risk, and create powerful strategies / Ben Gilad. New York, NY : American Management Association, c2003. xv, 268 p. : ill. ; 24 cm. Includes bibliographical references and index. Table of contents URL: http://www.loc.gov/catdir/toc/fy038/2003006506.html ISBN 0-8144-0786-2 (hardcover) DDC 658.15/5
1. Risk management. 2. Risk. 3. Strategic planning. I. Title.
HD61 .G533 2003

Gilbert, Daniel Todd.
The handbook of social psychology. 4th ed. Boston : McGraw-Hill ; New York : Distributed exclusively by Oxford University Press, c1998.
HM251 .H224 1998

Gilbert, Muriel. L'identité narrative : une reprise à partir de Freud de la pensée de Paul Ricœur / Muriel Gilbert. Genève : Labor et Fides, c2001. 277 p. ; 23 cm. (Le champ éthique ; no 36) Includes bibliographical references (p. [271]-277) and index. ISBN 2-8309-1019-2
1. Ricœur, Paul. 2. Psychoanalysis. 3. Identity (Psychology) I. Title. II. Series.

Gilbert, Toni. Messages from the archetypes : using tarot for healing and spiritual growth : a guidebook for personal and professional use / by Toni Gilbert ; with Mark Robert Waldman. Ashland, Or. : White Cloud Press, c2003. p. cm. Includes bibliographical references. CONTENTS: Exploring tarot -- Dream work, guided imagery and tarot -- Tarot as an inheritance -- Conscious archetypal energy and healing -- Getting started -- The tarot counselor -- Tarot case stories -- Archetypal levels in tarot counseling -- Levels of the major arcana -- Levels of the court cards -- Levels of the minor arcana. ISBN 1-88399-157-9 DDC 133.3/2424
1. Tarot. 2. Archetype (Psychology) 3. Self-realization. I. Waldman, Mark Robert. II. Title.
BF1879.T2 G53 2003

Gilchrist, Iain D.
Findlay, John M. (John Malcolm), 1942- Active vision. Oxford ; New York : Oxford University Press, 2003.
BF241 .F56 2003

Giles, David, 1964- Media psychology / David Giles. Mahwah, N.J. : Lawrence Erlbaum Associates Publishers, 2003. x, 324 p. : ill. ; 24 cm. Includes bibliographical references (283-308) and index. Table of contents URL: http://www.loc.gov/catdir/toc/fy037/2003042390.html ISBN 0-8058-4048-6 (cloth : acid-free paper) ISBN 0-8058-4049-4 (pbk. : acid-free paper) DDC 302.23/01/9
1. Mass media - Psychological aspects. I. Title.
P96.P75 G55 2003

Gilhooley, James J. Making hope visible / James Gilhooley. Allahabad : Holy Family International, [2003] 375 p. ; 22 cm. Library copy signed by the author. ISBN 81-87269-09-X
1. Christian life. I. Title.

Gill, Harjeet Singh, 1935- Signification in Buddhist and French traditions / Harjeet Singh Gill. New Delhi : Harman Pub. House, 2001. 204 p. ; 25 cm. Includes bibliographical references (p. [201]-204). ISBN 81-86622-44-6
1. Abelard, Peter, - 1079-1142 - Contributions in theology. 2. Abelard, Peter, - 1079-1142 - Contributions in ethics. 3. Signification (Logic) 4. Buddhist logic. 5. Philosophy, Medieval. I. Title.
BC25 .G55 2001

Gill, Michèle.
Rham, Cat de. The spirit of yoga. London : Thorsons, 2001.

Gillentine, Julie. Tarot & dream interpretation / Julie Gillentine ; foreword by Rachel Pollack. 1st ed. St. Paul, Minn. : Llewellyn Publications 2003. xii, 226 p. : ill. ; 23 cm. (Special topics in tarot) Includes bibliographical references (p. 221-222) and index. ISBN 0-7387-0220-X DDC 133.3/2424
1. Tarot. 2. Dream interpretation. I. Title. II. Title: Tarot and dream interpretation III. Series.
BF1879.T2 G585 2003

Gilles, Roger.
Directed self-placement. Cresskill, N.J. : Hampton Press, c2003.
PE1404 .D57 2003

Gilligan, Carol, 1936- The birth of pleasure / Carol Gilligan. 1st ed. New York : A.A. Knopf, 2002. xiii, 253 p. ; 25 cm. Includes bibliographical references (p. 239-245) and index. ISBN 0-679-44037-2 DDC 152.4/1
1. Love. 2. Man-woman relationships. 3. Intimacy (Psychology) I. Title.
BF575.L8 G56 2002

GILLIGAN, CAROL, 1936- - CONTRIBUTIONS IN PSYCHOLOGY OF FEMININITY.
Schwickert, Eva-Maria. Feminismus und Gerechtigkeit. Berlin : Akademie Verlag, c2000.

Gillman, Karen. Mr. and Dr. talking it over : communication for professional couples / by Karen Gillman. Lima, Ohio : Wyndham Hall Press, c2002. 154 p. ; 22 cm. Includes bibliographical references (p. 147-151). ISBN 1-55605-346-0
1. Interpersonal communication. 2. Interpersonal conflict. 3. Man-woman relationships. I. Title. II. Title: Mister and Doctor talking it over
BF637.C45 G55 2002

Gillotte, Galen, 1952- Sacred stones of the goddess : using earth energies for magical living / [Galen Gillotte]. 1st ed. St. Paul, Minn. : Llewellyn Publications, 2003. xii, 276 p. ; 23 cm. Includes bibliographical references (p. 273-276). ISBN 0-7387-0400-8 (pbk. : alk. paper) DDC 133.4/3
1. Magic. 2. Charms. 3. Precious stones - Miscellanea. 4. Crystals - Miscellanea. 5. Witchcraft. 6. Goddess religion. I. Title.
BF1611 .G55 2003

Gilly, Carlos.
Magia, alchimia, scienza dal '400 al '700. Firenze : Centro Di, 2002.
BF1598.H6 M34 2002

Gilman, Charlotte Perkins, 1860-1935. Concerning children / Charlotte Perkins Gilman. A reprint of the 1900 ed. / with an introduction by Michael S. Kimmel. Walnut Creek, CA : Rowman & Littlefield, c2003. xxx, 298 p. : ill. ; 22 cm. (Classics in gender studies) Originally published: Boston : Small, Maynard, 1900. Includes bibliographical references. ISBN 0-7591-0388-7 (cloth : alk. paper) ISBN 0-7591-0389-5 (pbk. : alk. paper) DDC 649/.1
1. Child rearing. I. Title. II. Series.
HQ769 .G5 2003

Gimeno, Antonio.
Žižek, Slavoj, 1949- [Fragile absolute. Spanish] El frágil absoluto, o, Por qué merece la pena luchar por el legado cristiano? 1. ed. Valencia : Pre-Textos, 2002.
BT1102 .Z58

La ginestra
(10) A che servono i simboli? Milano : FrancoAngeli, c2002.

Gingras, Sandy, 1958- How to be a friend / by Sandy Gingras. Harvey Cedars, NJ : Down the Shore Pub., 2003. p. cm. ISBN 0-945582-99-4 DDC 177/.62
1. Friendship. I. Title.
BF575.F66 G56 2003

Ginzburg, Yitshak. Rectifying the state of Israel : a political platform based on the Kabbalah / Yitzchak Ginsburgh. 1st ed. Jerusalem : Gal Einai ; Cedarhurst, NY : For information address, Gal Einai Institute, c2002. xii, 230 p. : ill. ; 24 cm. (Teachings of Kabbalah series) Includes bibliographical references and index. ISBN 9657146054
1. Cabala. 2. Israel - Politics and government. I. Title.

Ginze Armoni.
Armoni, Mosheh Ḥayim. Sefer Ginze Armoni. Yerushalayim : ʻAmutat "Naḥalat-Raḥel", 762 [2002]
BM670.S5 A756 2002

Giora, Rachel, 1945- On our mind : salience, context, and figurative language / Rachel Giora. New York : Oxford University Press, c2003. ix, 259 p. ; 24 cm. Includes bibliographical references (p. 213-242) and indexes. CONTENTS: Prologue -- Salience and context -- Lexical access -- Irony -- Metaphors and idioms -- Jokes -- Innovation -- Evidence from other research -- Coda: unaddressed questions, food for future thought. ISBN 0-19-513616-0 (cloth : alk. paper) DDC 401/.9
1. Psycholinguistics. 2. Figures of speech. 3. Context (Linguistics) I. Title.
BF455 .G525 2003

Giovanni Gentile e il Rinascimento.
Scazzola, Andrea. Napoli : Vivarium, 2002.

Gipertekst istorii.
Sokolov, B. G. (Boris Georgievich) Sankt-Peterburg : Sankt-Peterburgskoe filosofskoe obshchestvo, 2001.
D16.9 .S65 2001

Giraldo Hurtado, Luis Guillermo, 1944- Del proceso y de la paz / Luis Guillermo Giraldo Hurtado. [Colombia? : s.n., 2001] (Manizales : Edigr@ficas) 46 p. ; 22 cm. ISBN 958-33-2668-2
1. Fuerzas Armadas Revolucionarias de Colombia. 2. Colombia - Politics and government - 1974- 3. Negotiation. I. Title.

Girardi Jurkić, Vesna. Egipatska religija i antička Istra = Egyptian religion and ancient Istria : izložba = exhibition / Vesna Girardi-Jurkić, Kristina Džin, Igor Uranić. Pula : Arheološki Muzej Istre, 2001. 28 p. : ill. ; 17 x 24 cm. Exhibition catalogue. Parallel text in Croatian and English.
1. Egypt - Religion. I. Džin, Kristina. II. Uranić, Igor. III. Title. IV. Title: Egyption religion and ancient Istria

Girl chat.
Dickerson, Karle. New York : Scholastic, c2001.
BF723.C57 D53 2001

Girl wars.
Dellasega, Cheryl. New York : Simon & Schuster, c2003.
BF637.B85 D45 2003

The girl who was reborn.
Nissanka, H. S. S. [Năvata upan dăriya. English] Colombo : S. Godage Brothers, 2001.
BL515+

Girlfriends : [a bond between girlfriends is unbreakable] / [contributing writers, Elaine Creasman ... et al.]. Lincolnwood, Ill. : New Seasons, c2003. 1 v. (unpaged) : col. ill. ; 19 cm. ISBN 0-7853-8059-0
1. Female friendship. I. Creasman, Elaine.
BF575.F66 G57 2003

Girlfriends' getaway.
Laing, Kathleen. 1st ed. Colorado Springs, Colo. : WaterBrook Press, 2002.
BF575.F66 L35 2002

GIRLS. See **TEENAGE GIRLS; YOUNG WOMEN.**

GIRLS - EDUCATION. See **WOMEN - EDUCATION.**

GIRLS - EDUCATION - ENGLAND.
Cruddas, Leora. Girls' voices. Stoke on Trent ; Sterling VA : Trentham Books, 2003.
LA631.82 .C783 2003

GIRLS - EDUCATION - GERMANY.
Augustin, Nicole. "Bewegung in Widersprüchen, Widersprüche in Bewegung bringen". Pfaffenweiler : Centaurus-Verlagsgesellschaft, 1998.
LC2873.G3 A94 1998

The girls' guide to dreams.
Collier-Thompson, Kristi. New York : Sterling Pub., c2003.
BF1099.C55 C65 2003

The girls' guide to tarot.
Olmstead, Kathleen. New York : Sterling Pub., c2002.
BF1879.T2 O38 2002

GIRLS - PSYCHOLOGY.
Cruddas, Leora. Girls' voices. Stoke on Trent ; Sterling VA : Trentham Books, 2003.
LA631.82 .C783 2003

Dellasega, Cheryl. Girl wars. New York : Simon & Schuster, c2003.
BF637.B85 D45 2003

Gonick, Marnina. Between femininities. Albany : State University of New York Press, c2003.
HQ777 .G65 2003

Greene, Sheila, 1946- The psychological development of girls and women. London ; New York : Routledge, 2003.
HQ1206 .G767 2003

Underwood, Marion K. Social aggression among girls. New York ; London : Guilford Press, c2003.
BF723.A35 U53 2003

GIRLS - PSYCHOLOGY - JUVENILE LITERATURE.
Dickerson, Karle. Girl chat. New York : Scholastic, c2001.

Girls' voices.
Cruddas, Leora. Stoke on Trent ; Sterling VA : Trentham Books, 2003.
LA631.82 .C783 2003

Giuffrida, Angela, 1943- Il corpo pensa : umanità o femminità? / Angela Giuffrida. Roma : Prospettiva, c2002. 254 p. ; 20 cm. (Mosaico ; 10) Includes bibliographical references. ISBN 88-8022-084-5 DDC 128
1. Femininity. 2. Sex differences (Psychology) 3. Women - Psychology. I. Title. II. Series: Mosaico (Rome, Italy) ; 10.

Giuliani, Rudolph W. Leadership / Rudolph W. Giuliani. London : Little, Brown, 2002. 407 p. ; 24 cm. Includes index. ISBN 0-316-86101-4 DDC 658.4092
1. Giuliani, Rudolph W. 2. Leadership. 3. September 11 Terrorist Attacks, 2001. I. Title.

GIULIANI, RUDOLPH W.
Giuliani, Rudolph W. Leadership. London : Little, Brown, 2002.

Giussani, Luigi. PerCorso / Luigi Giussani. Milano : Rizzoli, c1997- 3 v. ; 23 cm. "Nona edizione: marzo 2001"--Vol. 1. Includes bibliographical references and indexes. PARTIAL CONTENTS: 1. Il senso religioso -- 2. All'origine della pretesa cristiana -- 3. Perché la Chiesa. ISBN 88-17-84518-3 ISBN 88-17-86841-8 DDC 232
1. Jesus Christ - Divinity. 2. Religion. 3. Christianity - Origin. 4. Church. I. Title. II. Title: Senso religioso. III. Title: All'origine della pretesa cristiana. IV. Title: Perché la Chiesa.

Give God the glory!.
Johnson, Kevin Wayne. Hillsborough, NJ : Writing for the Lord Ministries, c2001.

Givens, Gretchen Zita. Black women in the field : experiences understanding ourselves and others through qualitative research / Gretchen Givens Generett, Rhonda Baynes Jeffries. Cresskill, N.J. : Hampton Press, c2003. xii, 154 p. ; 24 cm. (Understanding education and policy) Includes bibliographical references and indexes. CONTENTS: Look back and wonder : African-American women during North Carolina's struggles in education / Sheryl Conrad Cozart -- I can't hear myself think : one student's journey into mainstream English / Joanne Kilgour Dowdy -- Giving voice to those who look like us but are not us / Jennifer Obidah -- African-American women, child sexual abuse, and career development : are you listening / Linda Quinn -- What's in a myth? Qualitative research as a means of (re)creating the myth / Gretchen Givens Generett -- Insider, outsider, or exotic other? Identity, performance, reflexivity, and postcritical ethnography / Paula Groves -- Getting in and gaining trust : one African-American researcher's journey through the ethnographic rites of passage / Trevy A. McDonald -- "I yam what I yam" : examing qualitative research through the ethnographic self, the literary "other," and the academy / Rhonda Baynes Jeffries. ISBN 1-57273-483-3 (c : alk. paper) ISBN 1-57273-484-1 (p : alk. paper) DDC 378.1/2/08996073
1. African American women college teachers. 2. African American women - Race identity. 3. Qualitative research. I. Jeffries, Rhonda B. (Rhonda Baynes), 1965- II. Title. III. Series.
LC2781.5 .G58 2003

Givhan, Walter D. The time value of military force in modern warfare [electronic resource] : the airpower advantage / Walter D. Givhan. Maxwell Air Force Base, Ala. : Air University Press, [1996] System requirements: Adobe Acrobat Reader. Mode of access: Internet from the Air University Press web site. Address as of 10/22/03: http://aupress.au.af.mil/SAAS%5FTheses/Givhan/givhan.pdf; current access is available via PURL. Title from title screen (viewed on Oct. 22, 2003). "March 1996." Thesis--School of Advanced Airpower Studies, Maxwell Air Force Base, Ala., 1994-95. Includes bibliographical references. URL: http://purl.access.gpo.gov/GPO/LPS38818 Available in other form: Givhan, Walter D. The time value of military force in modern warfare : the airpower advantage ix, 53 p. (OCoLC)34533130.
1. Air warfare. 2. Time - Psychological aspects. I. Air University (U.S.). Press. II. Air University (U.S.). Air Command and Staff College. School of Advanced Airpower Studies. III. Title. IV. Title: Givhan, Walter D. The time value of military force in modern warfare : the airpower advantage ix, 53 p.

Givhan, Walter D. The time value of military force in modern warfare : the airpower advantage ix, 53 p.
Givhan, Walter D. The time value of military force in modern warfare [electronic resource]. Maxwell Air Force Base, Ala. : Air University Press, [1996]

Gladding, Samuel T. Community and agency counseling / Samuel T. Gladding, Deborah W. Newsome. 2nd ed. Upper Saddle River, N.J. : Pearson : Merrill Prentice Hall, c2004. xx, 460 p. : ill. ; 24 cm. Includes bibliographical references and indexes. ISBN 0-13-093312-0 DDC 361/.06
1. Counseling. 2. Counseling - History. I. Newsome, Deborah W. II. Title.
BF637.C6 G528 2004

Gladiators 100 BC-AD 200.
Wisdom, Stephen. Oxford : Osprey, 2001 (2002 printing)

GLADIATORS - ROME.
Wisdom, Stephen. Gladiators 100 BC-AD 200. Oxford : Osprey, 2001 (2002 printing)

GLADNESS. *See* **HAPPINESS.**

Glas i konsten.
Rosén, Ingrid. Stockholm : Carlssons, c2000.

Glasenapp, Jörn.
Liebe als Kulturmedium. München : Fink, c2002.

Glasmeier, Michael, 1951- Extreme 1-8 : Vorträge zur Kunst / Michael Glasmeier ; herausgegeben vom Institut für Kunstwissenschaft an der Hochschule für Bildende Künste Braunschweig. Köln : Salon, 2001. 240 p. : ill. ; 19 cm. Includes bibliographical references (p. 228 - 230) and index. ISBN 3-89770-123-5 (pbk.)
1. Art. 2. Aesthetics. I. Hochschule für Bildende Künste Braunschweig. Institut für Kunstwissenschaft. II. Title.

GLASS ART - HISTORY.
Wentscher, Herbert, 1951- Vor dem Schirm. 1. Aufl. [Freiburg im Breisgau] : Modo, 2002.

GLASSWARE IN ART.
Rosén, Ingrid. Glas i konsten. Stockholm : Carlssons, c2000.

Glazerson, Matityahu. Migdele ha-te'omim be-diluge otiyot ba-Torah : aḳtu'alyah be-diluge otiyot ba-torah / me-et Matityahu Glazerson. Yerushalayim : Yerid ha-sefarim, 2002. 314 p. ; 23 cm.
1. World Trade Center (New York, N.Y.) 2. Bible. - O.T. - Prophecies. 3. Bible. - O.T. - Miscellanea. 4. Ciphers in the Bible. 5. Gematria. 6. Cabala. 7. September 11 Terrorist Attacks, 2001 - Religious aspects - Judaism. 8. September 11 Terrorist Attacks, 2001 - Biblical teaching. 9. Arab-Israeli conflict - 1993- - Peace - Biblical teaching. 10. World politics - 21st century - Biblical teaching. 11. Israel - Politics and government - Biblical teaching. 12. Israel - History - Prophecies. I. Title.

Gleason, Katherine.
Zimmermann, Denise. The complete idiot's guide to wicca and witchcraft. 2nd ed. Indianapolis, IN : Alpha, c2003.
BF1566 .Z55 2003

Gleditsch, Nils Petter, 1942-.
Globalization and armed conflict. Lanham, Md. : Rowman & Littlefield, c2003.
JZ5538 .G58 2003

Gleitman, Henry. Psychology / Henry Gleitman, Alan J. Fridlund, Daniel Reisberg. 6th ed. New York : W.W. Norton, c2004. 1 v. (various pagings) : ill. (mostly col.) ; 29 cm. Includes bibliographical references (p. B27-B82) and index. ISBN 0-393-97767-6 DDC 150
1. Psychology. I. Fridlund, Alan J. II. Reisberg, Daniel. III. Title.
BF121 .G58 2004

Glen Grant's chicken skin tales.
Grant, Glen. Honolulu, Hawaii : Mutual Pub., c1998.
BF1472.U6 G72 1998

Glendinning, Chellis. Off the map : an expedition deep into empire and the global economy / Chellis Glendinning. Gabriola Island, BC : New Society Publishers, c2002. xvii, 187 p. ; 23 cm. Includes bibliographical references (p. 181-187). ISBN 0-86571-463-0 DDC 338.6/048
1. Competition, International - Psychological aspects. 2. Imperialism - Psychological aspects. 3. Radical economics. I. Title.
HF1414 .G553 2002

Glener, Doug. Wisdom's blossoms : tales of the saints of India / Doug Glener & Sarat Komaragiri. Boston, Mass. : Shambhala, 2002. xiii, 194 p. : ill., map ; 22 cm. Includes bibliographical references (p. [189]-191). ISBN 1-57062-884-X DDC 294/.092/2
1. Saints - India. 2. India - Religion. 3. Spiritual life. I. Komaragiri, Sarat. II. Title.
BL2003 .G64 2002

Glenn, Phillip J.
Studies in language and social interaction. Mahwah, N.J. ; London : Lawrence Erlbaum, 2003.

Glickman, Marshall. Beyond the breath : extraordinary mindfulness through whole-body Vipassana meditation / by Marshall Glickman. 1st ed. Boston : Journey Editions ; North Clarendon, VT : Distributed by Tuttle Pub., 2002. xiv, 224 p. ; 22 cm. Includes bibliographical references (p. 214-216) and index. ISBN 1-58290-043-4 (pbk.) DDC 294.3/4435
1. Vipaśyanā (Buddhism) 2. Meditation - Buddhism. 3. Religious life - Buddhism. 4. Buddhism - Doctrines. I. Title.
BQ5630.V5 G54 2002

A glimpse of heaven.
Wills-Brandon, Carla, 1956- Avon, MA : Adams Media Corp., c2003.
BF1031 .W68 2003

A glimpse of Jesus.
Manning, Brennan. 1st ed. [San Francisco] : HarperSanFrancisco, c2003.
BV4647.S43 M36 2003

Glinz, Hans, 1913- Languages and their use in our life as human beings : a theory of speech and language on a Saussurean basis / Hans Glinz ; translation of the first three chapters and organisation of the publication, Kurt R. Jankowsky. Münster : Nodus, c2002. 284 p. : ill. ; 21 cm. Includes bibliographical references (p. 282-284) and index. ISBN 3-89323-289-3 (pbk.)
1. Language and languages. 2. Sociolinguistics. I. Title.
P107 .G58 2002

Global acquisitions.
Lees, Stan. Houndmills [England] ; New York : Palgrave Macmillan, 2003.
HD58.8 .L424 2003

Global capitalism and its discontents.
Monkeywrenching the new world order [sound recording]. Oakland, Calif ; AK Press ; San Francisco, CA : Alternative Tentacles Records, 2001.

GLOBAL CLIMATE CHANGES. *See* **CLIMATIC CHANGES.**

GLOBAL CLIMATIC CHANGES. *See* **CLIMATIC CHANGES.**

GLOBAL COMMERCE. *See* **INTERNATIONAL TRADE.**

GLOBAL CORPORATIONS. *See* **INTERNATIONAL BUSINESS ENTERPRISES.**

Global issues series (Palgrave Macmillan (Firm))
Approaches to peacebuilding. Houndmills, Basingstoke, Hampshire ; New York : Palgrave Macmillan, 2002.
JZ5538 .A675 2002

Global perspectives
Perspectives on Las Américas. Maden, MA : Blackwell Pub., c2003.
F1410 .P48 2003

Global perspectives on mentoring : transforming contexts, communities, and cultures / edited by Frances K. Kochan and Joseph T. Pascarelli. Greenwich : Information Age Pub., 2004. p. cm. (Perspectives in mentoring) Includes bibliographical references. ISBN 1-930608-39-X (hardcover) ISBN 1-930608-38-1 (pbk.) DDC 371.102
1. Mentoring. I. Kochan, Frances K. II. Pascarelli, Joseph T. III. Series.
BF637.M48 G57 2004

Global perspectives on social issues.
Simon, Rita James. Lanham : Lexington Books, c2003.
HQ503 .S56 2003

Global security concerns : anticipating the twenty-first century xii, 327 p.
Global security concerns [electronic resource]. Maxwell Air Force Base, Ala. : Air University Press, [1996]

Global security concerns [electronic resource] : anticipating the twenty-first century / Karl P. Magyar, editor. Maxwell Air Force Base, Ala. : Air University Press, [1996] System requirements: Adobe Acrobat Reader. Mode of access: Internet from the Air University Press web site. Address as of 4/29/03: http://aupress.au.af.mil/Books/Magyar%5FGlobalScty/Magyar.pdf; current access is available via PURL. Title from title screen (viewed on Apr. 29, 2003). "March 1996." Includes bibliographical references. URL: http://purl.access.gpo.gov/GPO/LPS30370 Available in other form: Global security concerns : anticipating the twenty-first century xii, 327 p. (OCoLC)34411592.
1. War - Forecasting. 2. Twenty-first century - Forecasts. 3. Security, International. I. Magyar, K. P. (Karl P.) II. Air University (U.S.). Press. III. Title: Global security concerns : anticipating the twenty-first century xii, 327 p.

GLOBAL TRADE. *See* **INTERNATIONAL TRADE.**

GLOBALIZATION.
Abrahamsson, Hans, 1949- Understanding world

order and structural change. Basingstoke, Hampshire : New York : Palgrave Macmillan, 2003.
HF1359 .A24 2003

Bessis, Sophie, 1947- [Occident et les autres. English] Western supremacy. London ; New York : Zed Books, 2003.
CB245 .B4613 2003

The emerging monoculture. Westport, Conn. : Praeger, 2003.
HM843 .E44 2003

Globalization and armed conflict. Lanham, Md. : Rowman & Littlefield, c2003.
JZ5538 .G58 2003

Globalization and civilizations. London ; New York : Routledge, 2002.
CB430 .G58 2002

Howard, Bradley Reed. Indigenous peoples and the state. DeKalb : Northern Illinois University Press, c2003.
GN380 .H68 2003

La Branche, Stéphane. Mondialisation et terrorisme identitaire, ou, Comment l'Occident tente de transformer le monde. Paris : Harmattan, c2003.
JC330 .L2 2003

Lees, Stan. Global acquisitions. Houndmills [England] ; New York : Palgrave Macmillan, 2003.
HD58.8 .L424 2003

Lewis, Richard D. The cultural imperative. Yarmouth, Me. : Intercultural Press, c2003.
GN357 .L49 2003

Lie, Rico. Spaces of intercultural communication. Creskill, N.J. : Hampton Press, c2003.
GN345.6 .L54 2003

Making and breaking of borders. Helsinki : Finnish Literature Society, 2003.
JC323 .M35 2003

Monkeywrenching the new world order [sound recording]. Oakland, Calif : AK Press ; San Francisco, CA : Alternative Tentacles Records, 2001.

Ojeda Awad, Alonso. Convivencia y globalización. [1a ed.]. [Bogotá] : Universidad Pedagógica Nacional, [2002]

Pabón, Carlos. Nación postmortem. 1. ed. San Juan, P.R. : Ediciones Callejón, 2002.

Pessanha, Rodolfo Gomes. O irracionalismo--, dos Estados Unidos da América à globalizaçãp. Niterói : Muiraquitã, c1998.

Pompeo, Francesco. Il mondo è poco. Roma : Meltemi, c2002.
GN495.6 .P66 2002

Tumusov, F. S. (Fedot Semenovich) Budushchee mira i Rossii. Moskva : "Mysl'", 2000.
HC340.12.Z7 S2357 2000

Vidal, Jordi. Résistance au chaos. Paris : Allia, 2002.

Globalization and armed conflict / edited by Gerald Schneider, Katherine Barbieri, and Nils Petter Gleditsch. Lanham, Md. : Rowman & Littlefield, c2003. xiii, 365 p. : ill. ; 23 cm. Includes bibliographical references (p. 325-352) and index. ISBN 0-7425-1831-0 (cl. : alk. paper) ISBN 0-7425-1832-9 (pbk. : alk. paper) DDC 303.6
1. Peace. 2. Security, International. 3. International trade. 4. Globalization. I. Schneider, Gerald, 1962- II. Barbieri, Katherine, 1965- III. Gleditsch, Nils Petter, 1942-
JZ5538 .G58 2003

Globalization and civilizations / edited by Mehdi Mozaffari. London ; New York : Routledge, 2002. xiv, 274 p. ; 24 cm. Includes bibliographical references and index. CONTENTS: Civilizations and the twenty-first century : some theoretical considerations / Robert W. Cox -- Globalization, civilizations and world order : a world-constructivist approach / Mehdi Mozaffari -- The first normative global revolution? The uncertain political future of globalization / Richard Falk -- Standards of civilization today / Gerrit W. Gong -- Globalization, markets and democracy : an anthropological linkage / Michael Mousseau -- European civilization : properties and challenges / Edgar Morin -- The crisis of European civilization : an inter-war diagnosis / Jan Ifversen --The Eastern perception of the west / Djamshid Behnam -- Islamic civilization between Medina and Athena / Mehdi Mozaffari -- What is "Chinese" about Chinese civilization? Culture, institutions and globalization / Xiaoming Huang -- Globalization and Indian civilization : questionable continuities / Niels Brimnes. ISBN 0-415-28614-X (hbk.) ISBN 0-415-28615-8 (pbk.) DDC 909.82
1. Civilization, Modern - 1950- 2. Globalization. 3. Civilization - Philosophy. 4. East and West. I. Mozaffari, Mehdi.

CB430 .G58 2002

Globalization and welfare
The young, the old, and the state. Cheltenham, UK ; Northampton, MA : E. Elgar Pub., c2003.
HQ778.5 .Y69 2003

Globalization and well-being.
Helliwell, John F. Vancouver : UBC Press, 2002.
HF1359 .H43 2002

GLOBALIZATION - ECONOMIC ASPECTS.
Beyond Keynes. Cheltenham ; Northampton, Mass. : Edward Elgar, c2002.

McMurtry, John, 1939- Value wars. London ; Sterling, Va. : Pluto Press, c2002.
HF1359 .M39 2002

GLOBALIZATION - MORAL AND ETHICAL ASPECTS.
McMurtry, John, 1939- Value wars. London ; Sterling, Va. : Pluto Press, c2002.
HF1359 .M39 2002

Singer, Peter, 1946- One world. New Haven, Conn. : London : Yale University Press, 2002.

Varieties of ethical reflection. Lanham, Md. ; Oxford : Lexington Books, c2002.
BJ1031 .V37 2002

GLOBALIZATION - POLITICAL ASPECTS.
Crockatt, Richard. America embattled. London ; New York : Routledge, 2003.
E902 .C76 2003

Hirsh, Michael, 1957- At war with ourselves. New York : Oxford University Press, 2003.
E895 .H57 2003

GLOBALIZATION - RELIGIOUS ASPECTS.
Religion and global culture. Lanham, MD ; Oxford : Lexington Books, c2003.
BL65.C8 R444 2003

GLOBALIZATION - SOCIAL ASPECTS.
Clark, Harold A. The age of intimacy. Laredo, TX : EBookcase.com, c2000.

Emmott, Bill. 20:21 vision. London : Allen Lane, 2003.

Geschlecht und Globalisierung. Königstein : Ulrike Helmer Verlag, c2001.

Habitar la tierra. Buenos Aires : Grupo Editor Altamira, 2002.
CB358 .H32 2002

Helliwell, John F. Globalization and well-being. Vancouver : UBC Press, 2002.
HF1359 .H43 2002

McMurtry, John, 1939- Value wars. London ; Sterling, Va. : Pluto Press, c2002.
HF1359 .M39 2002

Udovik, S. L. (Sergeĭ Leonidovich) Globalizatsiĭa. [Moscow] : Refl-buk ; [Kiev] : Vakler, 2002.
CB430 .U36 2002

Globalizatsiĭa.
Udovik, S. L. (Sergeĭ Leonidovich) [Moscow] : Refl-buk ; [Kiev] : Vakler, 2002.
CB430 .U36 2002

Globalvision, Inc.
Children and human rights. Part 1 [videorecording]. Derry, N.H. : Chip Taylor Communications, 1995.

Peace and conflict resolution. Part 1 [videorecording]. Derry, N.H. : Chip Taylor Communications, 1996.

Peace and conflict resolution. Part 2 [videorecording]. Derry, N.H. : Chip Taylor Communications, 1997.

Globerman, Daniyel Aharon. Yalḳut Sefer ha-Ḥinukh : mafteaḥ 'inyanim mi-Sefer ha-Ḥinukh be-'inyene midot ye-de'ot / ne'erakh 'al yede Daniyel Aharon Globerman. Modi'in 'Ilit : D. A. Globerman, Kolel "Libo ḥafets", 761 [2000 or 2001] 12, 167 p. ; 25 cm.
1. Ethics, Jewish. 2. Commandments, Six hundred and thirteen - Indexes. I. Title. II. Title: Sefer ha-ḥinukh.
BM520.8.A32 G4 2001

Globus symbolicus.
Janz, Nathalie. [Lausanne : Université de Lausanne, 1999]

La gloire à vingt ans.
Deniau, Jean-François, 1928- [Paris] : XO editions, c2003.

GLOOMINESS. See SADNESS.

Gloria.
Trevi, Gloria. México, D.F. : Planeta, c2002.

ML420.T725 A3 2002

Gloria romanorum.
Alföldi, Maria R.- Stuttgart : Franz Steiner Verlag, 2001.
DG78 .A546 2001

GLORY. See FAME.

GLOTTOPOLITICS. See LANGUAGE POLICY.

Gloyna, Tanja. Kosmos und System : Schellings Weg in die Philosophie / Tanja Gloyna. Stuttgart-Bad Cannstatt : Frommann-Holzboog, c2002. vii, 301 p. ; 20 cm. (Schellingiana ; Bd. 15) Previously issued as author's dissertation, 1999, Freie Universität Berlin. Includes bibliographical references (p. 279-295) and indexes. ISBN 3-7728-2199-5 (pbk.)
1. Schelling, Friedrich Wilhelm Joseph von, - 1775-1854. 2. Philosophy. I. Title. II. Series.
B2898 .G56 2002

Gluck, Christoph Willibald, Ritter von, 1714-1787. Operas. Selections.
Malaniuk, Ira. Arien und Lieder [sound recording]. [Germany] : Preiser Records, p2000.

GLYPTICS. See GEMS.

GNAWA (BROTHERHOOD).
Hell, Bertrand. Le tourbillon des génies. Paris : Flammarion, c2002.

GNOMES (MAXIMS). See APHORISMS AND APOTHEGMS; MAXIMS.

GNOSTICISM.
Pinto Cañon, Ramiro. Grupos gnósticos. Madrid : Entinema, 2002.

GOAL (PSYCHOLOGY).
Dahl, Bernhoff A., 1938- Optimize your life with the one-page strategic planner. Bangor, Me. : Wind-Breaker Press, c2003.
BF637.S8 D26 2003

Koberg, Don, 1930- The universal traveler. 4th ed. Menlo Park, Calif. : Crisp Learning, c2003.
BF441 .K55 2003

Secunda, Al. The 15-second principle. Franklin Lakes, NJ : Career Press, 2004.
BF637.S4 S43 2004

Silverman, Robin Landew. Reaching your goals. New York : F. Watts, 2003.
BF505.G6 S57 2003

Tips, Jack. Passion play. 1st ed. Austin, Tex. : Apple-A-Day Press, c2002.
BF503 .T56 2002

GOAL (PSYCHOLOGY) - JUVENILE LITERATURE.
Silverman, Robin Landew. Reaching your goals. New York : F. Watts, 2003.
BF505.G6 S57 2003

GOAL (PSYCHOLOGY) - PROBLEMS, EXERCISES, ETC.
Silber, Lee T. Aim first!. Mission, Kan. : SkillPath Publications, c1999.
BF505.G6 S55 1999

GOAL SETTING IN PERSONNEL MANAGEMENT. See INCENTIVES IN INDUSTRY.

Goals and life lessons support materials [electronic resource]. Greenwood Village, CO : FasTracKids International, [1998] 1 CD-ROM ; 4 3/4 in. System requirements: Any computer with Microsoft Word or compatable document reading software; CD-ROM drive. Title from disc label. SUMMARY: Contains documents to be used with the Goals and Life Lessons CD-ROMs covering general "lifetime" instructions such as personal interaction, goal setting, and handling personal feelings. DDC 158.1
1. Self-actualization (Psychology) 2. Individuality. 3. Peer pressure. 4. Cooperativeness. 5. Interpersonal relations. I. FasTracKids International Ltd.
BF637.S4

GOALS, EDUCATIONAL. See EDUCATION - AIMS AND OBJECTIVES.

GOBLINS - COLORADO.
Martin, MaryJoy, 1955- Twilight dwellers. 2nd ed. Boulder, Colo. : Pruett, 2003.
BF1472.U6 M37 2003

GOD. See also **HOLY SPIRIT; HOLY, THE; METAPHYSICS; MIRACLES; MONOTHEISM; MYTH; RELIGION; THEOLOGY; TRINITY; TRUST IN GOD.**
Buxani, Shyam D. Salam. 1st ed. New York : SAU Salam Foundation, c2003.

God

González, Angel Luis. Ser y participación. 3. ed. revisada y ampliada. Pamplona : Ediciones Universidad de Navarra, c2001.
BX4700.T6 G66 2001

Hurbon, Laënnec. Dieu dans le vaudou haïtien. Nouv. éd. Paris : Maisonneuve et Larose, 2002.
1. Black author.

Lowman, Pete. A long way east of Eden. Carlisle : Paternoster, 2002.

Smullyan, Raymond M. Who knows? Bloomington : Indiana University Press, c2003.
BL50 .S59 2003

God and the evolving universe.
Redfield, James. New York : Jeremy P. Tarcher/Putnam, c2002.
BD541 .R43 2002

GOD - ATTRIBUTES.
Mozia, Michael Ifeanyinachukwu. Holiness & divine mercy (the key to heaven). Ibadan, Oyo State, Nigeria : St. Pauls, 2002.
1. Black author.

God/goddess.
Drew, A. J. Franklin Lakes, N.J. : New Page Books, 2003.
BF1571 .D73 2003

GOD (JUDAISM).
Pinter, Leib. Sefer 'Aśarah nisyonot. Brooklyn, N.Y. : E.Y.L. Pinter, c[2002?]

Sack, Bracha, 1933- Shomer ha-pardes. Be'er Sheva' : Universitat Ben-Guryon ba-Negev, c2002.

GOD (JUDAISM) - NAME - EARLY WORKS TO 1800.
Sefer 'Amude ha-Kabalah. Yerushalayim : Nezer Sheraga, 761 [2001]

GOD - KNOWABLENESS.
Maritain, Jacques, 1882-1973. [Degrés du savoir. English] Distinguish to unite, or, The degrees of knowledge. Notre Dame, Ind. : University of Notre Dame Press, 1998, c1995.
BD162 .M273 1998

Sabalat, Tina. Pascals "Wette". Marburg : Tectum, 2000.

GOD - MISCELLANEA.
Walsch, Neale Donald. The new revelations. New York : Atria Books, c2002.
BF1999 .W2287 2002

Walsch, Neale Donald. Tomorrow's God. 1st ed. New York : Atria Books, 2004.
BF1999 .W2288 2004

GOD - NAME. *See* GOD (JUDAISM) - NAME.

GOD - PROOF.
Devout sceptics. London : Hodder & Stoughton, 2003.

Sabalat, Tina. Pascals "Wette". Marburg : Tectum, 2000.

Salamucha, Jan. [Selections. English. 2003] Knowledge and faith. Amsterdam ; New York, NY : Rodopi, 2003.

GOD - PROOF - HISTORY OF DOCTRINES - 17TH CENTURY.
Williams, Jaime Andrés. El argumento de la apuesta de Blaise Pascal. 1. ed. Pamplona : Ediciones Universidad de Navarra, 2002.

GOD - WILL.
Farrington, Debra K. Hearing with the heart. 1st ed. San Francisco : Jossey-Bass, c2003.
BV4509.5 .F37 2003

Trasferetti, José Antônio. Deus a força que cura!. Campinas, SP : Editora Átomo, 2002.

GODDESS MOVEMENT. *See* GODDESS RELIGION.

The goddess path.
Monaghan, Patricia. 1st ed. St. Paul, Minn. : Llewellyn, 1999.
BL473.5 .M665 1999

GODDESS RELIGION.
Brondwin, C. C., 1945- Clan of the Goddess. Franklin Lakes, NJ : New Page Books, c2002.
BF1623.G63 B76 2002

Christ, Carol P. She who changes. 1st ed. New York ; Houndmills, England : Palgrave Macmillan, 2003.
BD372 .C48 2003

De Grandis, Francesca. What kind of goddess are you? Naperville, Ill. : Sourcebooks, Inc., 2004.

BF1623.G63 D4 2004

Gillotte, Galen, 1952- Sacred stones of the goddess. 1st ed. St. Paul, Minn. : Llewellyn Publications, 2003.
BF1611 .G55 2003

Knight, Sirona, 1955- Empowering your life with wicca. Indianapolis, IN : Alpha Books, c2003.
BF1571 .K56 2003

Lipp, Deborah, 1961- The elements of ritual. 1st ed. St. Paul, Minn. : Llewellyn Publications, 2003.
BF1571 .L56 2003

Monaghan, Patricia. The goddess path. 1st ed. St. Paul, Minn. : Llewellyn, 1999.
BL473.5 .M665 1999

Paige, Anthony. Rocking the goddess. New York : Citadel Press, c2002.
BF1571.5.C64 P35 2002

Roderick, Timothy, 1963- Dark moon mysteries. Aptos, Calif. : New Brighton Books, 2003.
BF1623.M66 R63 2003

Rose, Sharron. Path of the priestess. Rochester, VT. : Inner Traditions, c2002.
BL625.7 .R67 2002

Sermonti, Giuseppe. Il mito della grande madre. Milano : Mimesis, c2002.

Sophia, 1955- The ultimate guide to goddess empowerment. Kansas City : Andrews McMeel Pub., c2003.
BF1621 .S67 2003

Spiraldancer. Moon rites. South Melbourne : [Great Britain] : Lothian, 2002.

Wishart, Catherine, 1965- Teen goddess. 1st ed. St. Paul, Minn. : Llewellyn Publications, c2003.
BF1623.G63 W57 2003

GODDESS RELIGION - NEW ZEALAND.
Roundtree, Kathryn. Embracing the witch and the goddess. London ; New York : Routledge, 2003.
BF1584.N45 R68 2003

GODDESS RELIGION - TURKEY.
Sermonti, Giuseppe. Il mito della grande madre. Milano : Mimesis, c2002.

GODDESSES.
Monaghan, Patricia. The goddess path. 1st ed. St. Paul, Minn. : Llewellyn, 1999.
BL473.5 .M665 1999

GODDESSES, EGYPTIAN. *See also* HATHOR (EGYPTIAN DEITY); ISIS (EGYPTIAN DEITY); SEKHMET (EGYPTIAN DEITY).
Wilkinson, Richard H. The complete gods and goddesses of ancient Egypt. New York : Thames & Hudson, 2003.

GODDESSES IN LITERATURE.
Matthews, Caitlin, 1952- King Arthur and the goddess of the land. 2nd ed. Rochester, Vt. : Inner Traditions, 2002.
PB2273.M33 M36 2002

GODDESSES - MISCELLANEA.
Brondwin, C. C., 1945- Clan of the Goddess. Franklin Lakes, NJ : New Page Books, c2002.
BF1623.G63 B76 2002

De Grandis, Francesca. What kind of goddess are you? Naperville, Ill. : Sourcebooks, Inc., 2004.
BF1623.G63 D4 2004

Drew, A. J. God/goddess. Franklin Lakes, N.J. : New Page Books, 2003.
BF1571 .D73 2003

Dumars, Denise. The dark archetype. Franklin Lakes, N.J. : New Page Books, c2003.
BF1623.G63 D86 2003

George, Demetra, 1946- Asteroid goddesses. Berwick, Me. : Ibis Press, 2003.
BF1724.5 .G46 2003

Robbins, Trina. Eternally bad. Berkeley, Calif. : Conari Press, c2001.
BF1623.G63 .R63 2001

Wishart, Catherine, 1965- Teen goddess. 1st ed. St. Paul, Minn. : Llewellyn Publications, c2003.
BF1623.G63 W57 2003

Godek, Gregory J. P., 1955- 10,000 ways to say I love you : the biggest collection of romantic ideas ever gathered in one place / Gregory J.P. Godek. Naperville, Ill. : Casablanca Press, c1999. 761 p. ; 16 cm. ISBN 1-57071-434-7 (pbk.)
1. Love - Miscellanea. 2. Intimacy (Psychology) - Miscellanea. I. Title. II. Title: Ten thousand ways to say I love you

BF575.L8 G63 1999

Godfrind, Jacqueline. Comment la féminité vient aux femmes / Jacqueline Godfrind. Paris : Presses universitaires de France, c2001. 148 p. ; 22 cm. (Epîtres) Includes bibliographical references (p. [145]-148). ISBN 2-13-051423-5
1. Femininity. I. Title. II. Series: Epîtres (Paris, France)
BF175.5.F45 G63 2001

Godoy, Cristina.
Historiografía y memoria colectiva. 1. ed. Madrid ; Buenos Aires : Miño y Dávila, 2002.

GODS. *See* GODDESSES; MYTH; MYTHOLOGY; RELIGIONS.

GODS, AFRO-BRAZILIAN.
Beniste, José. As águas de Oxalá = Rio de Janeiro, RJ, [Brazil] : Editora Bertrand Brasil, c2001 (2002 printing)
BL2592.C35 B46 2001

GODS, BUDDHIST. *See also* AVALOKITEŚVARA (BUDDHIST DEITY).
Xing, Li. Guanyin. Beijing di 2 ban. Beijing : Xue yuan chu ban she, 2001.
BQ4710.A8 X564 2001

GODS, EGYPTIAN. *See also* OSIRIS (EGYPTIAN DEITY); RA (EGYPTIAN DEITY).
Gahlin, Lucia. Egypt. London : Lorenz, 2001.

Wilkinson, Richard H. The complete gods and goddesses of ancient Egypt. New York : Thames & Hudson, 2003.

GODS, GREEK, IN LITERATURE.
Muñoz Llamosas, Virginia. La intervención divina en el hombre a través de la literatura griega de época arcaica y clásica. Amsterdam : Hakkert, 2002.
PA3015.R5 M87 2002

GODS - MISCELLANEA.
Drew, A. J. God/goddess. Franklin Lakes, N.J. : New Page Books, 2003.
BF1571 .D73 2003

Dumars, Denise. The dark archetype. Franklin Lakes, N.J. : New Page Books, c2003.
BF1623.G63 D86 2003

GODS, NORSE.
Aswynn, Freya, 1949- Northern mysteries & magick. 2nd ed. St. Paul, Minn. : Llewellyn Publications, 1998 (2002 printing)
BF1623.R89 A78 1998

Gods of the blood.
Gardell, Mattias. Durham : Duke University Press, 2003.
BL65.W48 G37 2003

GODS, SLAVIC.
Asov, A. I. (Aleksandr Igorevich) Sviashchennye prarodiny slavian. Moskva : Veche, 2002.
BL930 .A863 2002

Gavrilov, D. A. Bogi slavian, iazychestvo, traditsiia. [Moskva] : Refl-buk, 2002.
BL930 .G38 2002

GOEBBELS, JOSEPH, 1897-1945.
Bärsch, Claus-Ekkehard. Die politische Religion des Nationalsozialismus. 2., vollst. überarb. Aufl. München : W. Fink, c2002.

The Goetia.
[Clavicula Salomonis. English.] York Beach, Me. : Samuel Weiser, 1995.
BF1611 .C5413 1995

Goffen, Rona, 1944- Renaissance rivals : Michelangelo, Leonardo, Raphael, Titian / Rona Goffen. New Haven : University Press, c2002. viii, 521 p. : ill. (some col.) ; 26 cm. Includes bibliographical references (p. [478]-496) and index. ISBN 0-300-09434-5 DDC 709/.45/09024
1. Michelangelo Buonarroti, - 1475-1564. 2. Art, Renaissance - Italy. 3. Competition (Psychology) I. Title.
N6915 .G54 2002

GOGH, VINCENT VAN, 1853-1890.
Shoham, S. Giora, 1929- Ṭeruf, seṭiyah vi-yetsirah. [Israel] : Miśrad ha-biṭaḥon, [2002]

Goglin, Jean-Marc. L'enseignement de la théologie dans les ordres mendiants à Paris au XIIIe siècle / Jean-Marc Goglin. Paris : Editions franciscaines, c2002. 107, [1] p. ; 22 cm. Includes bibliographical references (p. 97-[108]). ISBN 2-85020-110-3 DDC 230
1. Catholic Church - France - Paris - History. 2. Theology - Study and teaching - France - Paris - History. 3. Church history - Middle Ages, 600-1500. 4. Friars - France - Paris - History. I. Title.

Going for the gold.
Cronin, W. Jean. Longmont, CO : Sopris West, c2003.
BF637.B4 C76 2003

Going native or going naive?.
Wernitznig, Dagmar. Lanham, MD : University Press of America, c2003.
E98.P99 W47 2003

GOING PUBLIC (SECURITIES). *See* **STOCKS.**

Going the distance.
Kennedy, Kevin (Kevin John), 1955- Upper Saddle River, NJ : Prentice Hall/Financial Times, c2003.
HD57.7 .K465 2003

Golan, Mor Yosef. Sefer ha-Neshamah ba-guf : ḥokhmah u-musar : ... ma'amre Ḥazal ... tsadiḳim ṿa-Ḥasidim ... / ḳibatsṭiv ṿa-'arakhtiṿ Mor Yosef Golan. Itamar : M.Y. Golan, 762 [2001 or 2002] 311 p. ; 24 cm.
1. Hasidism. 2. Aggada. 3. Ethics, Jewish. 4. Faith (Judaism) I. Title. II. Title: Neshamah ba-guf

Golant, Susan K.
Heim, Pat. In the company of women. New York : J.P. Tarcher/Putnam, c2001.
HD6053 .H387 2001

GOLD. *See* **MONEY.**

Gold, Alison Leslie. Fiet's vase and other stories of survival, Europe 1939-1945 / Alison Leslie Gold. New York : Jeremy P. Tarcher/Penguin, c2003. 244 p. : ill., music ; 22 cm. Includes bibliographical references (p. 239-241). ISBN 1-58542-259-2 DDC 940.53/18/0922
1. Holocaust, Jewish (1939-1945) 2. Holocaust, Jewish (1939-1945) - Biography. 3. Jews - Europe - Biography. 4. Holocaust, Jewish (1939-1945) - Influence. 5. Memory. I. Title.
D804.3 .G64 2003

Gold, Stuart Avery.
Wowisms. 1st ed. New York : Newmarket Press, c2003.
BF637.S8 W7 2003

Goldberg, Arnold, 1929- Misunderstanding Freud / by Arnold Goldberg. New York : Other Press, 2004. p. cm. Includes bibliographical references and index.
CONTENTS: Misunderstanding Freud -- Gaps, barriers and splits : the psychoanalytic search for connection -- Psychoanalysis as an understanding psychology -- Understanding others -- Enactment as understanding and as misunderstanding -- Form versus content -- Interpretation is it : there is no beyond -- The mutuality of meaning -- Representation and the place of the mind -- Postmodern psychoanalysis -- Me and Max -- A world of possibilities : two philosophic approaches to psychoanalysis -- An odd couple : Martin Heidegger and Heinz Kohut. ISBN 1-59051-112-3 (alk. paper) DDC 150.19/52
1. Psychoanalysis. 2. Freud, Sigmund, - 1856-1939. 3. Self psychology. 4. Kohut, Heinz. I. Title.
BF173 .G59 2004

Goldberg, Avraham Yehoshuʻa, 1856-1921. Sefer Kitve paz : ḥidushim, derashot u-mikhtaṿe Torah be-'inyene halakhah agadah u-musar : Yerushalayim : ha-Mishpaḥah, 763, c2003. 510 p. : facsim. ; 25 cm. Running title: Kitve paz.
1. Goldberg, Avraham Yehoshuʻa, - 1856-1921. 2. Bible - O.T. - Pentateuch - Sermons. 3. Jewish sermons, Hebrew. 4. Ethics, Jewish. 5. Jewish law. I. Title. II. Title: Kitve paz

GOLDBERG, AVRAHAM YEHOSHUʻA, 1856-1921.
Goldberg, Avraham Yehoshuʻa, 1856-1921. Sefer Kitve paz. Yerushalayim : ha-Mishpaḥah, 763, c2003.

Goldberg, Bruce, 1948- Self-hypnosis : easy ways to hypnotize your problems away / by Bruce Goldberg. Franklin Lakes, NJ : New Page Books, c2001. vii, 182 p. ; 21 cm. Includes bibliographical references (p. 177-180) and index. ISBN 1-56414-541-7 DDC 154.7
1. Mental suggestion. I. Title.
BF1156.S8 G65 2001

The golden laws.
Ōkawa, Ryūhō, 1956- [Ōgon no hō. English] New York : Lantern Books, c2002.
BP605.K55 O33 2001

GOLDEN PARACHUTES (EXECUTIVE COMPENSATION). *See* **CONSOLIDATION AND MERGER OF CORPORATIONS.**

GOLDEN RULE.
Gantsersḳi, Betsal'el Shelomoh, ha-Leṿi. Sefer Darkhe tsedeḳ. Tifraḥ : Mishp. Gantsersḳi, 762 [2001 or 2002]

Goldenson, Robert M.
Hartley, Ruth E. (Ruth Edith), b.1909 Understanding children's play, London : Routledge, 2000.
BF717 .H3 2000

Goldin-Meadow, Susan. Hearing gesture : how our hands help us think / Susan Goldin-Meadow. Cambridge, Mass. : Belknap Press of Harvard University Press, 2003. xiv, 280 p. : ill. ; 24 cm. Includes bibliographical references (p. [251]-269) and index. ISBN 0-674-01072-8 (alk. paper) DDC 302.2/22
1. Gesture. 2. Thought and thinking. 3. Cognition in children. 4. Communication. I. Title.
P117 .G65 2003

Language in mind. Cambridge, Mass. : MIT Press, c2003.
P37 .L357 2003

The resilience of language : what gesture creation in deaf children can tell us about how all children learn language / Susan Goldin-Meadow. New York ; Hove [England] : Psychology Press, 2003. xxi, 262 p. : ill. ; 24 cm. (Essays in developmental psychology) Includes bibliographical references (p. 233-250) and indexes. ISBN 1-84169-026-0 DDC 401/.93
1. Language acquisition. 2. Gesture. 3. Deaf children - Means of communication. I. Title. II. Series.
P118 .G57 2003

Gol'din, V. E.
Dement'ev, V. V. Nepri͡amai͡a kommunikat͡sii͡a i ee zhanry. Saratov : Izd-vo Saratovskogo universiteta, 2000.
P106 .D4554 2000

Goldman, Ellen. As others see us : body movement and the art of successful communication / Ellen Goldman. New York : Brunner-Routledge, 2003. p. cm. Includes bibliographical references (p.   ) and index. ISBN 0-415-94918-1 (pbk.) DDC 153.6/9
1. Body language. 2. Nonverbal communication. I. Title.
BF637.N66 G65 2003

Goldrick-Jones, Amanda, 1956- Men who believe in feminism / Amanda Goldrick-Jones. Westport, Conn. ; London : Praeger, 2002. x, 209 p. ; 25 cm. Includes bibliographical references (p. [189]-202) and index. Includes web resources. ISBN 0-275-96822-7 (alk. paper) DDC 305.42
1. Women's rights. 2. Men - Attitudes. 3. Feminism. I. Title.
HQ1236 .G57 2002

Goldring, Elizabeth, 1970-.
Court festivals of the European Renaissance. Aldershot ; Burlington, VT : Ashgate, c2002.

Goldsmith, H. Hill.
Handbook of affective sciences. Oxford ; New York : Oxford University Press, 2003.
BF511 .H35 2003

Goldsmith, Joan.
Cloke, Ken, 1941- The art of waking people up. 1st ed. San Francisco : Jossey-Bass, c2003.
HF5385 .C54 2003

Goldsmith, Joel S., 1892-1964. Spiritual discernment : the healing consciousness / Joel S. Goldsmith ; edited by Lorraine Sinkler. Atlanta, Ga. : Acropolis Books, c2002. xi, 220 p. ; 22 cm. Includes bibliographical references.
CONTENTS: Peeling off the onion skins -- God must be an experience, not a concept -- The nature of Spiritual discernment -- Immortality unveiled -- Judge not according to the appearance -- The middle path -- Is -- Mind imbued with truth -- The Christ kingdom -- Rejecting appearances and concepts -- The infinite way of life -- The transition to Christhood. ISBN 1-88905-163-2 (pbk.) DDC 299/.93
1. Spiritual life. 2. Discernment (Christian theology) 3. Spiritual healing. 4. New Thought. I. Sinkler, Lorraine. II. Title.
BF639.G56886 2002

Goldsmith, Marshall.
Human resources in the 21st century. Hoboken, N.J. : J. Wiley & Sons, c2003.
HD31 .H81247 2003

Goldsmith, Martin. The zodiac by degrees : 360 new symbols / Martin Goldsmith. Boston, MA : Weiser Books, 2004. p. cm. Includes bibliographical references.
CONTENTS: Aries -- Taurus -- Gemini -- Cancer -- Leo -- Virgo -- Libra -- Scorpio -- Sagittarius -- Capricorn -- Aquarius -- Pisces. ISBN 1-57863-304-4 DDC 133.5/2
1. Astrology. 2. Zodiac. I. Title.
BF1708.1 .G62 2004

Goldstein, Sam, 1952-.
Brooks, Robert B. The power of resilience. Chicago : Contemporary Books, c2004.
BF698.35.R47 B76 2004

Goleman, Daniel. Destructive emotions : how can we overcome them? : a scientific dialogue with the Dalai Lama / narrated by Daniel Goleman ; with contributions by Richard J. Davidson ... [et al.]. New York : Bantam Books, c2003. xxiii, 404 p. : ill. ; 25 cm. Includes bibliographical references and index. ISBN 0-553-80171-6 DDC 294.3/375
1. Emotions - Religious aspects. 2. Mental health - Religious aspects. 3. Emotions and cognition. 4. Spiritual life. 5. Psychology and religion. I. Title.
BL65.E46 G65 2003

Golin, Al, 1929- Trust or consequences : build trust today or lose your market tomorrow / Al Golin. New York : American Management Association, c2004. viii, 248 p. ; 24 cm. Includes index. CONTENTS: Trust trends -- More than a nice-sounding word -- Damage done -- Fix it before it breaks -- If you can't do it, please say so -- Human touch -- Humility -- Speed, truth, and other good ways to respond to bad times -- Tough trust decisions -- Media -- Great acts of trust -- Acts of distrust -- Ten commandments of organizational trust ISBN 0-8144-7208-7 (hardcover) DDC 174/.4
1. Business ethics. 2. Trust. 3. Reliability. I. Title.
HF5387 .G65 2004

Golinski, Jan.
The sciences in enlightened Europe. Chicago : University of Chicago Press, 1999.
Q127.E8 S356 1999

Gollac, M. (Michel).
Baudelot, Christian. Travailler pour être heureux? [Paris] : Fayard, c2003.

Göller, Thomas. Kulturverstehen : Grundprobleme einer epistemologischen Theorie der Kulturalität und kulturellen Erkenntnis / Thomas Göller. Würzburg : Königshausen & Neumann, c2000. 535 p. ; 24 cm. Includes bibliographical references (p. [458]-521) and indexes. ISBN 3-8260-1675-0 (säurefrei)
1. Cognition and culture. 2. Culture - Philosophy. I. Title.
BF311 .G586 2000

Gollub, Dan. Interpreting and understanding dreams / Dan Gollub. Commack, N.Y. : Nova Science Publishers, c1998. 155 p. ; 23 cm. Table of contents URL: http://www.loc.gov/catdir/toc/fy041/2003544927.html ISBN 1-56072-397-1 DDC 154.6/3
1. Dream interpretation. 2. Dreams. I. Title.
BF1091 .G653 1998

Golomb, Claire. The child's creation of a pictorial world / Claire Golomb. 2nd ed. Mahwah, N.J. : L. Erlbaum Associates, 2004. xii, 388 p. : ill. ; 29 cm. Includes bibliographical references (p. [363]-373) and indexes. ISBN 0-8058-4371-X (alk. paper) ISBN 0-8058-4372-8 (pbk. : alk. paper) DDC 155.4
1. Children's drawings - Psychological aspects. I. Title.
BF723.D7 G64 2004

Goltz, Andreas.
Gelehrte in der Antike. Köln : Böhlau, c2002.

Gombay, Andre, 1933-.
Passion and virtue in Descartes. Amherst, N.Y. : Humanity Books, 2003.
B1868.P37 P37 2003

Gomes, Peter J. The good life : truths that last in times of need / Peter J. Gomes. 1st ed. San Francisco : HarperSanFrancisco, c2002. x, 373 p. ; 24 cm. Includes bibliographical references (p. [357]-364) and index.
CONTENTS: A more excellent way -- The smart and the good -- Living for goodness' sake -- Failure : what's good about it? -- Success : how do I know when I've made it? -- Discipline : the practice of perfection -- Freedom : from what and for what? -- Virtues : ways, means, and ends -- Faith : substance and evidence -- Hope : unreasonable and indispensable -- Love : being and doing. ISBN 0-06-000075-9 DDC 170/.44
1. Conduct of life. 2. Christian ethics. 3. Virtues. I. Title.
BJ1581.2 .G575 2002

Gómez Alzate, Camilo.
Al oído de Uribe. 1a. ed. Bogotá, Colombia : Editorial Oveja Negra, 2002.

Gonce, John Wisdom.
Harms, Daniel. The Necronomicon files. Boston, MA : Weiser Books, c2003.
BF1999 .H37515 2003

Goñi Zubieta, Carlos. Futbolsofía : filosofar a través del fútbol / Carlos Goñi Zubieta. Madrid : Ediciones del Laberinto, [2002] 156 p. ; 21 cm. (Colección Hermes ; no. 19) ISBN 84-8483-069-1
1. Soccer - Philosophy. 2. Philosophy. I. Title. II. Series: Colección Hermes (Ediciones del Laberinto) ; no. 19.

Gonick, Marnina. Between femininities : ambivalence, identity, and the education of girls / Marnina Gonick. Albany : State University of New York Press, c2003. x, 225 p. ; 24 cm. (SUNY series, second thoughts) Includes bibliographical references (p. 189-214) and index. ISBN 0-7914-5829-6 (alk. paper) ISBN 0-7914-5830-X (pbk. : alk. paper) DDC 305.23
1. Girls - Psychology. 2. Maturation (Psychology) 3. Feminist psychology. I. Title. II. Series.

González, Angel Luis.
HQ777 .G65 2003

González, Angel Luis. Ser y participación : estudio sobre la cuarta vía de Tomás de Aquino / Ángel Luis González. 3. ed. revisada y ampliada. Pamplona : Ediciones Universidad de Navarra, c2001. 305 p. ; 22 cm. (Filosófica ; núm. 31) Includes bibliographical references (p. 281-294) and index. ISBN 84-313-1902-X
1. Thomas, - Aquinas, Saint, - 1225?-1274. 2. Philosophy, Medieval. 3. God. I. Title. II. Series: Colección filosófica (Universidad de Navarra. Facultad de Filosofía y Letras) ; 31.
BX4700.T6 G66 2001

González Ayesta, Cruz. Hombre y verdad : gnoseología y antropología del conocimiento en las Q.D. De Veritate / Cruz González Ayesta. 1. ed. Pamplona : Universidad de Navarra, Ediciones, 2002. 176 p. ; 24 cm. (Filosófica ; 172) Includes bibliographical references (p. 171-176). ISBN 84-313-1995-X
1. Thomas, - Aquinas, Saint, - 1225?-1274. - Quaestiones disputatae de veritate. 2. Thomas, - Aquinas, Saint, - 1225?-1274 - Criticism and interpretation. 3. Knowledge, Theory of. 4. Truth - Religious aspects - Christianity. I. Title. II. Series: Colección filosófica (Universidad de Navarra. Facultad de Filosofía y Letras) ; 172.

González Wagner, Carlos.
Jornadas de Roles Sexuales y de Género (2nd : 1995 : Madrid, Spain) Mujer, ideología y población. 1. ed. Madrid : Ediciones Clásicas, 1998.
HQ1075 .J67 1995

GOOD AND EVIL.
Badiou, Alain. L'éthique. Caen : Nous, c2003.

I concetti del male. Torino : Einaudi, c2002.

Connolly, William E. Identity/difference. Expanded ed. Minneapolis : University of Minnesota Press, c2002.
JA74 .C659 2002

Demonio, religión y sociedad entre España y América. Madrid : Consejo Superior de Investigaciones Científicas, 2002.

Hartman, Robert S., 1910-1973. [Conocimiento del bien. English] The knowledge of good. Amsterdam ; New York, NY : Rodopi, c2002.
BD232 .H324 2002

Piazza, Giovanni. Sofferenza e senso. Torino : Camilliane, c2002.

Shafer-Landau, Russ. Whatever happened to good and evil? New York ; Oxford : Oxford University Press, 2004.
BJ1401 .S46 2004

GOOD AND EVIL (JUDAISM). See YETZER HARA (JUDAISM).

GOOD AND EVIL - SOCIAL ASPECTS - NIGERA.
Ofoegbu, Mike. Exposing satanic manipulations. [Lagos, Nigeria : Holy Ghost Anointed Books Ministries, c1998]
1. Black author.

Good and mad.
Middelton-Moz, Jane, 1947- Deerfield Beach, Fla. : Health Communications Inc., c2003.
BF575.A5 M519 2003

Good faeries/bad faeries.
Froud, Brian. London : Pavilion, 2000.

Good fortune.
Knight, Michele. Kansas City, Mo. : Andrews McMeel Pub., c2002.
BF1726 .K55 2002

The good life.
Gomes, Peter J. 1st ed. San Francisco : HarperSanFrancisco, c2002.
BJ1581.2 .G575 2002

Good morning world.
Tubali, Shy. [Selections] Boker tov 'olam. Tel Aviv : Yedi'ot aharonot : Sifre hemed, c2003.

The good rebel.
Groarke, Louis. Madison [N.J.] : Fairleigh Dickinson University Press ; London ; Cranbury, NJ : Associated University Presses, c2002.
B808.67 .G76 2002

Good sex.
Knight, Michele. Kansas City, Mo. : Andrews McMeel Pub., c2002.
BF1729.S4 .K58 2002

Good teachers carry on.
Anderson, Mary Beth, 1952- St. Joseph, Mich. : Cosmic Concepts Press, c2003.
BF1261.2 .A45 2003

Good vibes.
Dexter, Rosalyn. London : Robson, 2001.

Goodall, Jane. Performance and evolution in the age of Darwin : out of the natural order / Jane R. Goodall. London ; New York : Routledge, 2002. xi, 266 p. : ill. ; 23 cm. Includes bibliographical references and index. ISBN 0-415-24377-7 ISBN 0-415-24378-5 (PBK.) DDC 792.7
1. Evolution (Biology) 2. Theater and society - History - 19th century. 3. Science and the arts - History - 19th century. I. Title.
NX180.S3 G66 2002

Goodhue, John D., 1957-.
Brenden, Ann E. Persuasive computer presentations. Chicago, Ill. : Law Practice Management Section, American Bar Association, c2001.
KF320.A9 B74 2001

Goodier, Steve. Lessons of the turtle : living right side up / Steve Goodier. Divide, CO : Life Support System Pub., c2002. 122 p. ; 17 cm. ISBN 1-929664-15-X (softcover) DDC 158.1
1. Conduct of life. 2. Change (Psychology) I. Title.
BF637.C5 G67 2002

A life that makes a difference : 60-second readings that truly matter / Steve Goodier. 1st ed. Divide, CO : Life Support System Pub., c2002. 165 p. ; 22 cm. Includes index. ISBN 1-929664-17-6 DDC 158.1
1. Conduct of life. 2. Self-actualization (Psychology) I. Title.
BF637.C5 G68 2002

Goodison, Lucy. The dreams of women : exploring and interpreting women's dreams / Lucy Goodison. 1st American ed. New York : W.W. Norton, 1996. xiv, 353 p. ; 21 cm. Includes bibliographical references and index. ISBN 0-393-03917-X DDC 154.6/3/082
1. Dreams. 2. Women - Psychology. 3. Dream interpretation. I. Title.
BF1078 .G475 1996

Goodman, Robin F.
The day our world changed. New York : Harry N. Abrams Inc., 2002.

Goodman, Steven. Teaching youth media : a critical guide to literacy, video production & social change / Steven Goodman ; foreword by Maxine Greene. New York : Teachers College Press, c2003. xiii, 129 p. : ill. ; 24 cm. (The series on school reform) Includes bibliographical references (p. 113-118) and index. CONTENTS: Framing the inner-city teenager: criminals, consumers, and the literacy gap -- Cameras and guns in the streets: teaching critical literacy in the documentary workshop -- Dreams and nightmares: a case study of video in a classroom -- Conclusion: Reimagining the school day. ISBN 0-8077-4289-9 (cloth : alk. paper) ISBN 0-8077-4288-0 (pbk. : alk. paper) DDC 371.33
1. Mass media in education - United States. 2. Media literacy - United States. 3. Critical thinking. I. Title. II. Series.
LB1043 .G59 2003

Goodrich, Thelma Jean, 1940-.
Feminist family therapy. 1st ed. Washington, DC : American Psychological Association, c2003.
RC488.5 .F453 2003

Goodwin, Rufus. Dreamlife : how dreams happen / Rufus Goodwin. 1st ed. Great Barrington, MA : Lindisfarne Books, 2004. p. cm. Includes bibliographical references. CONTENTS: Dreamland -- Hard science of dreams -- Dreams of the blind -- Dream idiom -- The pact against vitalism -- Medieval dream theory -- The skunk dream -- Freud's fraud -- Is life a dream? -- Dreamlight bridge between body and mind -- Transpersonal powers of dreams -- Dreams as windows of light : a workbook. ISBN 1-58420-019-7 DDC 154.6/3
1. Dreams. 2. Mind and body. I. Title.
BF1081 .G66 2004

Goodwyn, Susan.
Acredolo, Linda P. My first baby signs. [New York] : HarperFestival, c2002.
BF720.C65 A27 2002

Gopālācārya, Pa. Ca.
Veṅkaṭanāthārya. [Daśanirṇayī] Vaidikasārvabhaumanāmnā suprasiddhaiḥ Veṅkaṭanāthāryaiḥ Vaidikakarmānuṣṭhānasaukaryāya viracitā Daśanirṇayī. 1st ed. Mumbai : Śrīmadahobilamathena, 1998.
BL1226.72 .V36 1998

Gopālakṛṣṇa, Pi. Es. Mīguriñci mīkutelusā? / Pi. Es. Gopālakṛṣṇa. Hyderabad : Media House Publications, 2002. 163 p. ; 23 cm. In Telugu. SUMMARY: On self-actualization (psychology); compilation of radio talks.
1. Self-actualization (psychology) I. Title.
BF637.S4 G655 2002

Gorbatova, M. M.
Sibirskaia psikhologiia segodnia. Kemerovo : Kemerovskiĭ gos. universitet, 2002.

BF20 .S53 2002

Gordon, Andrew S. Strategy representation : an analysis of planning knowledge / Andrew S. Gordon. Mahwah, NJ. : L. Erlbaum, 2003. p. cm. Includes bibliographical references and index. ISBN 0-8058-4527-5 (alk. paper) DDC 153.2
1. Mental representation. 2. Planning. 3. Reasoning (Psychology). I. Title.
BF316.6 .G67 2003

Gordon, Barry, M.D. Intelligent memory : understanding and improving the memory that makes us smarter / Barry Gordon and Lisa Berger. New York : Viking, 2003. p. cm. Includes index. ISBN 0-670-03240-9 (alk. paper) DDC 153.1/2
1. Memory. 2. Thought and thinking. 3. Creative thinking. 4. Problem solving. I. Berger, Lisa. II. Title.
BF371 .G66 2003

Gordon, Claire, 1968- Are you smarter than you think? : 160 ways to test and enhance your natural intelligence / Claire Gordon. New York : Penguin Compass, c2003. 192 p. : col. ill. ; 22 cm. Includes bibliographical references and index. ISBN 0-14-200321-2 DDC 153.9
1. Multiple intelligences. I. Title.
BF432.3 .G67 2003

Gordon, Rochelle.
Your birthday sign through time. New York : Atria Books, c2002.
BF1728.A2 Y57 2002

Gordon, Sharon. Big - small / by Sharon Gordon. New York : Benchmark Books, 2003. p. cm. (Bookworms: Just the opposite) SUMMARY: Two siblings compare the sizes of things they are familiar with, from the buses they ride to the beds they sleep in. ISBN 0-7614-1568-8 DDC 153.7/52
1. Size perception - Juvenile literature. 2. Size judgment - Juvenile literature. 3. Size. I. Title. II. Series: Gordon, Sharon. Bookworms. Just the opposite.
BF299.S5 G67 2003

Bookworms. Just the opposite.
Gordon, Sharon. Big - small. New York : Benchmark Books, 2003.
BF299.S5 G67 2003

Gore, Lesley, 1946-.
Vint/age 2001 conference : [videorecording]. New York, c2001.

GORE, LESLEY, 1946-.
Vint/age 2001 conference : [videorecording]. New York, c2001.

Gorfine, Yehudit. Be-karov etslekh : behirat ben/t zug u-madrikh la-yots'im / 'orekhet, Yehudit Gorfain. Petaḥ Tiḳvah : Mar'ot, 2002. 230 p. : ill. ; 25 cm. Title on verso of t.p.: Please God by you = BekarovEtzlech : choosing a spouse & a guide to dating. Includes bibliographical references (p. 230). ISBN 9659045107
1. Mate selection - Religious aspects - Judaism. 2. Courtship - Religious aspects - Judaism. 3. Marriage brokerage. 4. Man-woman relationships. 5. Judaism - Customs and practices. 6. Israel - Religious life and customs. I. Title. II. Title: Be-karov etslekha III. Title: Please God by you = BekarovEtzlech : choosing a spouse & a guide to dating IV. Title: BekarovEtzlech

Görg, Manfred. Die Barke der Sonne : Religion im alten Ägypten / Manfred Görg. Freiburg im Breisgau : Herder, 2001. 212 p. : ill. ; 20 cm. (Kleine Bibliothek der Religionen ; Bd. 7) ISBN 3-451-23847-0
1. Ra (Egyptian deity) 2. Egypt - Religion. I. Title. II. Series.
BL2450.R2 G647 2001

GORGE-PURGE SYNDROME. See BULIMIA.

Gor'kov, L. P. (Lev Petrovich).
Schrieffer, J. R. (John Robert), 1931- [Papers. Selections] Selected papers of J. Robert Schrieffer. River Edge, NJ : World Scientific, c2002.
QC21.3 .S37 2002

Gorman, Phil, 1965- Motivation and emotion / Phil Gorman. 1st ed. New York : Routledge, 2003. p. cm. (Routledge modular psychology series) Includes bibliographical references and index. Table of contents URL: http://www.loc.gov/catdir/toc/ecip045/2003014341.html ISBN 0-415-22770-4 ISBN 0-415-22769-0 (pbk.) DDC 153.8
1. Motivation (Psychology) 2. Motivation (Psychology) - Physiological aspects. 3. Emotions. 4. Emotions - Physiological aspects. I. Title. II. Series: Routledge modular psychology.
BF503 .G67 2003

Gosden, Chris, 1955- Prehistory : a very short introduction / Chris Gosden. Oxford ; New York : Oxford University Press, 2003. 131 p. : ill., maps ; 18 cm. (Very short introductions) CONTENTS: Includes bibliographical references (p. 121-123) and index. ISBN 0-19-

280343-3
1. History, Ancient. 2. Civilization, Ancient. I. Title. II. Series.

Goss, Stephen, 1966-.
Technology in counselling and psychotherapy. New York : Palgrave Macmillan, 2003.
BF637.C6 T467 2003

GOSSIP.
Eliyahu, Mordekhai. Sefer Śifte tsedek. Rekhasim : M. Eliyahu, 762 [2002]

Rozner, Shelomoh. Sh. u-t. La-ḥafets be-ḥayim. Mahad. 3, be-tosefet 13 she'elot be-ḥelek 3. Yerushalayim : Kolel shemirat ha-lashon : le-hasig, Sh. Rozner, 762 [2001 or 2002]

Gostev, A. A. (Andreĭ Andreevich) Obraznai͡a sfera cheloveka v poznanii i perezhivanii dukhovnykh smyslov / A.A. Gostev. Moskva : In-t psikhologii RAN, 2001. 85 p. ; 21 cm. Includes bibliographical references. ISBN 5927000193
1. Imagery (Psychology) 2. Image (Theology) 3. Asceticism - Orthodox Eastern Church. I. Title.
BF367 .G565 2001

GOSUDARSTVENNYĬ REFLEKSOLOGICHESKIĬ INSTITUT PO IZUCHENIIU MOZGA (RUSSIA).
Spivak, M. L. Posmertnai͡a diagnostika genial'nosti. Moskva : Agraf, 2001.
BF416.A1 S68 2001

Gott, Robert.
Not a chance.
Gott, Robert. One in a million. Littleton, Mass. : Sundance, c2001.
BF1175 .G68 2001

One in a million / Robert Gott. Littleton, Mass. : Sundance, c2001. 96 p. : ill. ; 20 cm. (Fact meets fiction) "A Black Dog book"--T.p. verso. Originally published: St. Leonards, N.S.W. : Horwitz Martin, 1999. Companion volume: Not a chance / Robert Gott. Includes index. SUMMARY: True stories of incredible coincidences and survival against the odds. ISBN 0-7608-8034-4 (pbk.) DDC 001.94
1. Coincidence - Psychic aspects - Juvenile literature. 2. Coincidence. 3. Chance. 4. Survival. I. Gott, Robert. Not a chance. II. Title. III. Series.
BF1175 .G68 2001

'Gottes auserwählte Völker' :
Erwählungsvorstellungen und kollektive Selbstfindung in der Geschichte / herausgegeben von Alois Mosser. Frankfurt am Main ; New York : Lang, c2001. 296 p. ; 23 cm. (Pro Oriente, 1437-367X ; Bd. 1) Papers from a meeting held in Sept. 1998. Includes bibliographical references. ISBN 3-631-34647-6 (säurefrei)
1. Election (Theology) 2. Group identity. I. Mosser, Alois. II. Series: Pro Oriente (Frankfurt am Main, Germany) ; Bd. 1.
BT810.2 .G65 2001

Gotteshauch oder künstliche Seele.
Kather, Regine, 1955- Stuttgart : Akademie der Diözese Rottenburg-Stuttgart, c2000.

Gottesman, Irving I.
Behavior genetics principles. Washington, DC : American Psychological Association, 2004.
BF698.9.B5 B44 2004

GOTTFRIED, VON STRASSBURG, 13TH CENT. TRISTAN.
A companion to Gottfried von Strassburg's "Tristan". Rochester, NY : Camden House, 2003.
PT1526 .C66 2003

Hübner, Gert. Erzählform im höfischen Roman. Tübingen : Francke, 2003.

Göttinger Gespräche zur Geschichtswissenschaft (Series)
(Bd. 14.) Begriffsgeschichte, Diskursgeschichte, Metapherngeschichte. Göttingen : Wallstein, 2002.
D13 .B45 2002

(Bd. 15.) Curiositas. Göttingen : Wallstein, c2002.
BF323.C8 C872 2002

Gottlieb, Alexander.
Gottlieb, Jeff, 1954- Spriggles. Petoskey, Mich. : Mountain Watch Press, c2002.
BF723.M56 G68 2002

Gottlieb, Andrew R. Sons talk about their gay fathers : life curves / Andrew R. Gottlieb. New York : Harrington Park Press, c2003. xviii, 183 p. ; 22 cm. (Haworth gay & lesbian studies) Includes bibliographical references (p. 165-174) and index. ISBN 1-56023-178-5 (alk. paper) ISBN 1-56023-179-3 (softcover : alk. paper) DDC 306.874/2
1. Gay fathers - Family relationships. 2. Fathers and sons. 3. Children of gay parents - Psychology. 4. Sons - Psychology. I. Title. II. Series.

HQ76.13 .G67 2003

Gottlieb, Jeff, 1954- Spriggles : inspiration / by Jeff and Martha Gottlieb ; illustrations by Alexander Gottlieb. Petoskey, Mich. : Mountain Watch Press, c2002. 1 v. (unpaged) : col. ill. ; 17 x 23 cm. "Motivational books for children." Cover title. SUMMARY: Spriggles combines "spirit" and "giggles" to help inspire children to set goals, be persistent, pursue challenges, and learn to share. 3-8. ISBN 1-930439-05-9
1. Motivation (Psychology) in children - Juvenile literature. I. Gottlieb, Martha. II. Gottlieb, Alexander. III. Title. IV. Title: Inspiration
BF723.M56 G68 2002

Gottlieb, Martha.
Gottlieb, Jeff, 1954- Spriggles. Petoskey, Mich. : Mountain Watch Press, c2002.
BF723.M56 G68 2002

Gottlieb, Marvin R. Managing group process / Marvin R. Gottlieb. Westport, Conn. ; London : Praeger, 2003. xiii, 233 p. : ill., forms ; 24 cm. Includes bibliographical references (p. [223]-227) and index. ISBN 1-56720-511-9 (alk. paper) DDC 658.4/036
1. Teams in the workplace. 2. Group facilitation. 3. Management. I. Title.
HD66 .G6778 2003

Göttner-Abendroth, Heide. Die tanzende Göttin : Prinzipien einer matriarchalen Ästhetik / Heide Göttner-Abendroth. 6. vollst. überarb. Neuaufl. München : Frauenoffensive, 2001, c1982. 175 p. : ill. ; 22 cm. Includes bibliographical references. ISBN 3-88104-344-6 (pbk.)
1. Aesthetics. 2. Matriarchy in art. 3. Patriarchy in literature. I. Title.

Gottschild, Brenda Dixon. The Black dancing body : a geography from coon to cool / Brenda Dixon Gottschild. New York : Palgrave Macmillan, 2003. xvii, 332 p. : ill. ; 26 cm. Includes bibliographical references and index. ISBN 0-312-24047-3 DDC 793.3/089/96073
1. African American dance - History. 2. African American dancers. 3. Body image. 4. Black author. I. Title.
GV1624.7.A34 G68 2003

Gotz, Ignacio L. Faith, humor, and paradox / Ignacio L. Gotz. Westport, Conn. : Praeger, 2002. 136 p. ; 25 cm. Includes bibliographical references (p. [123]-131) and index. ISBN 0-275-97895-8 (alk. paper) DDC 210
1. Religion - Philosophy. 2. Religion - Humor. 3. Faith. 4. Paradox. I. Title.
BL51 .G6854 2002

Goudge, Paulette. The power of whiteness : racism in third world development and aid / Paulette Goudge. London : Lawrence & Wishart, 2003. 224 p. ; 22 cm. Includes bibliographical references (p. 215-224). Cover title: The whiteness of power. ISBN 0-85315-957-2 DDC 338.90091724
1. International relief - Developing countries. 2. Racism. 3. Developing countries - Economic conditions. I. Title.

Gould, Lewis L. The modern American presidency / Lewis L. Gould ; foreword by Richard Norton Smith. Lawrence : University Press of Kansas, c2003. xv, 301 p. : ill. ; 24 cm. Includes bibliographical references and indexes. Table of contents URL: http://www.loc.gov/catdir/toc/fy036/2002154108.html CONTENTS: The age of Cortelyou : William McKinley and Theodore Roosevelt -- The lawyer and the professor : William Howard Taft and Woodrow Wilson -- The modern presidency recedes : Warren G. Harding, Calvin Coolidge, and Herbert Hoover -- The modern presidency revives and grows : Franklin D. Roosevelt -- The presidency in the Cold War era : Harry S. Truman and Dwight D. Eisenhower -- The souring of the modern presidency : John F. Kennedy and Lyndon B. Johnson -- The rise of the continuous campaign : Richard Nixon -- The modern presidency under siege : Gerald Ford and Jimmy Carter -- The modern presidency in a Republican age : Ronald Reagan and George H.W. Bush -- Perils of the modern presidency : Bill Clinton. ISBN 0-7006-1252-1 (alk. paper) DDC 973.9/092/2
1. Presidents - United States - History - 20th century. 2. Presidents - United States - Biography. 3. United States - Politics and government - 20th century. 4. United States - Politics and government - 1897-1901. I. Title.
E176.1 .G68 2003

Gould, Roger V. Collision of wills : how ambiguity about social rank breeds conflict / Roger V. Gould ; foreword by Peter Bearman. Chicago : University of Chicago Press, 2003. xvi, 203 p. ; 23 cm. Includes bibliographical references (p. 183-193) and index. CONTENTS: Conflict, honor, and hierarchy -- Dominance relations -- Strife out of symmetry -- Solidarity and group conflict -- Conflict and social structure -- Honor and the individual. ISBN 0-226-30548-1 (alk. paper) ISBN 0-226-30550-3 (paper : alk. paper) DDC 303.6
1. Social conflict. 2. Interpersonal conflict. 3. Violence. 4. Social groups. 5. Group identity. 6. Social control. 7. Dominance (Psychology) I. Title.
HM1121 .G68 2003

Gould, Stephen Jay. I have landed : the end of a beginning in natural history / Stephen Jay Gould. 1st ed. New York : Harmony Books, 2002. xi, 418 p. : ill. ; 25 cm. Includes bibliographical references and index. Table of contents URL: http://www.loc.gov/catdir/toc/fy031/2002024145.html CONTENTS: I have landed -- No science without fancy, no art without facts : the lepidoptery of Vladimir Nabokov -- Jim Bowie's letter and Bill Buckner's legs -- True embodiment of everything that's excellent -- Art meets science in The heart of the Andes : Church paints, Humboldt dies, Darwin writes, and nature blinks in the fateful year of 1859 -- Darwinian gentleman at Marx's funeral : resolving evolution's oddest coupling -- Pre-Adamite in a nutshell -- Freud's evolutionary fantasy -- Jew and the jewstone -- When fossils were young -- Syphilis and the shepherd of Atlantis -- Darwin and the munchkins of Kansas -- Darwin's more stately mansion -- Darwin for all reasons -- When less is truly more -- Darwin's cultural degree -- Without and within of smart mice -- What does the dreaded "E" word mean anyway? -- First day of the rest of our life -- Nartex of San Marco and the pangenetic paradigm -- Linnaeus's luck? -- Abscheulich! (atrocious) -- Tales of a feathered tail -- Evolutionary perspective on the concept of native plants -- Age-old fallacies of thinking and stinking -- Geometer of race -- Great physiologist of Heidelberg -- Good people of Halifax -- Apple brown betty -- Woolworth Building -- September 11, '01. ISBN 0-609-60143-1 (hc) DDC 578
1. Natural history. 2. Evolution (Biology) I. Title. II. Title: End of a beginning in natural history
QH45.5 .G735 2002

Goux, Jean-Paul. La voix sans repos : essai / Jean-Paul Goux. Monaco : Rocher, c2003. 142 p. ; 21 cm. (Esprits libres) Includes bibliographical references (p. [141]). ISBN 2-268-04437-8 DDC 809
1. Creation (Literary, artistic, etc.) 2. Literature - History and criticism - Theory, etc. I. Title. II. Series: Esprits libres (Monaco, Monaco)

GOVERNMENT. See **POLITICAL SCIENCE.**

GOVERNMENT AND BINDING (LINGUISTICS). See **GOVERNMENT-BINDING THEORY (LINGUISTICS).**

GOVERNMENT AND THE PRESS. See **PRESS AND POLITICS.**

GOVERNMENT-BINDING THEORY (LINGUISTICS).
Hamann, Cornelia, 1953- From syntax to discourse. Dordrecht, The Netherlands ; Boston : Kluwer Academic Publishers, c2002.
P118 .H327 2002

GOVERNMENT CONTRACTS. See **PUBLIC CONTRACTS.**

GOVERNMENT EXECUTIVES - ISRAEL.
Frankenburg, Reuven. Revadim 'elyonim ba-minhal ha-tsiburi ha-Yiśre'eli. [Israel : ḥ. mo. l., 1999?]

GOVERNMENT INFORMATION.
Helping children and adolescents cope with violence and disasters [electronic resource]. Bethesda, MD : Office of Communications and Public Liaison, [2001]

GOVERNMENT INVESTIGATORS - FICTION.
Kava, Alex. The soul catcher. Waterville, Me. : Thorndike Press, 2003, 2002.
PS3561.A8682 S6 2003

GOVERNMENT PROCUREMENT. See **GOVERNMENT PURCHASING.**

GOVERNMENT PUBLICATIONS.
Privacy [electronic resource]. [Washington, D.C.] : Federal Trade Commission, Bureau of Consumer Protection, Office of Consumer and Business Education, [2002]

Privacy [electronic resource]. [Washington, D.C.] : Federal Trade Commission, Bureau of Consumer Protection, Office of Consumer and Business Education, [2002]

Privacy [electronic resource]. [Washington, D.C.] : Federal Trade Commission, Bureau of Consumer Protection, Office of Consumer and Business Education, [2002]

Questions and answers about disability and service retirement plans under the Americans with Disabilities Act (ADA) [electronic resource]. [Washington, D.C.] : U.S. Equal Employment Opportunity Commission, [1995]

GOVERNMENT PURCHASING - UNITED STATES.
United States. Congress. House. Committee on the

Judiciary. Federal Prison Industries Competition in Contracting Act of 2003. [Washington, D.C. : U.S. G.P.O., 2003]

Government reformed : values and new political institutions / edited by Ian Holland and Jenny Fleming. Aldershot, England ; Burlington, VT : Ashgate, c2003. x, 292 p. ; 23 cm. (Law, ethics and governance series) Includes bibliographical references (p. [261]-285) and index. ISBN 0-7546-2242-8 (alk. paper) DDC 320/.6
1. Organizational change. 2. Public administration. 3. Values. I. Holland, Ian. II. Fleming, Jenny. III. Series: Law, ethics and governance.
JF1525.O73 G686 2003

GOVERNMENT, RESISTANCE TO. See **CIVIL WAR; INSURGENCY.**

GOVERNMENT, RESISTANCE TO - UNITED STATES.
Suprynowicz, Vin. The ballad of Carl Drega. Reno, NV : Mountain Media, 2002.

Govier, Trudy.
Dilemmas of reconciliation. Waterloo, Ont. : Wilfrid Laurier University Press, 2003.

Govinden, Devarakshanam Betty.
Her-stories. Pietermaritzburg, South Africa : Cluster, 2002.

Gow, Andrew.
Apps, Lara. Male witches in early modern Europe. Manchester ; New York : Manchester University Press ; New York : Distributed exclusively in the USA by Palgrave, 2003.
BF1584.E85 A66 2003

Gower, Paul L.
Psychology of fear. New York : Nova Science Publishers, 2003.
BF575.F2 P79 2003

GRAAL. See **GRAIL.**

Grabhorn, Lynn, 1931- Planet two : Earth in a higher frequency : are you ready? / Lynn Grabhorn. Charlottesville, VA : Hampton Roads Pub. Co., 2004. p. cm. ISBN 1-57174-407-X (5-1/2x8-1/2 : alk. paper) DDC 133.9
1. Spiritual life - Miscellanea. I. Title.
BF1999.G678 2004

GRABOVOĬ, GRIGORIĬ.
Sudakov, Vladimir Ivanovich. Spasitel'. Moskva : TERRA-Sport, 2001.
BF1027.G73 S83 2001

Grabowsky, Ingo.
Kul'tura i vlast' v uslovii︠a︡kh kommunikat︠s︡ionnoĭ revoli︠u︡t︠s︡ii XX veka. Moskva : "AIRO-XX", 2002.
HM621.K858 2002

Grace, Raymon. The future is yours : do something about it / Raymon Grace. Charlottesville, VA : Hampton Roads Pub., c2003. xiv, 216 p. : ill. ; 22 cm. Table of contents URL: http://www.loc.gov/catdir/toc/ecip044/2003012423.html ISBN 1-57174-390-1 (pbk. : acid-free paper) DDC 131
1. New Thought. 2. Mental healing. 3. Dowsing. I. Title.
BF639.G64 2003

GRACE (THEOLOGY). See **SACRAMENTS.**

Grachev, Georgiĭ. Manipulirovanie lichnost'i︠u︡ : organizat︠s︡ii︠a︡, sposoby i tekhnologii informat︠s︡ionno-psikhologicheskogo vozdeĭstvii︠a︡ / Georgiĭ Grachev, Igor' Mel'nik. Moskva : Algoritm, 2002. 284 p. ; 21 cm. Includes bibliographical references (p. 265-283). ISBN 5926500680
1. Manipulative behavior. 2. Persuasion (Psychology) 3. Control (Psychology) I. Mel'nik, Igor', kandidat psikhologicheskikh nauk. II. Title.
BF632.5.G73 2002

Gracia, Jason. Motivated in minutes : 1,001 tips & ideas to help you get motivated / Jason Gracia. Madison, Wis. : Gracia Enterprises, c2002. iv, 284 p. : ill. ; 22 cm. ISBN 0-9714733-1-5
1. Motivation (Psychology) I. Title.
BF503.G73 2002

Grád, András.
Fekete, Mária. Pszichológia és pszichopatológia jogászoknak. Budapest : HVG-ORAC, c2002.
BF173.F349 2002

GRADUATE RECORD EXAMINATION - STUDY GUIDES.
Kellogg, Ronald Thomas. The best test preparation for the Graduate Record Examination, GRE psychology. Piscataway, N.J. : Research and Education Association, [2000]
BF78.K45 2000

Graduate study in psychology.
Kuther, Tara L. Springfield, Ill. : Charles C. Thomas, 2004.
BF77.K85 2004

GRADUATE WORK IN PSYCHOLOGY. See **PSYCHOLOGY - STUDY AND TEACHING (GRADUATE).**

Graevenitz, Gerhart von.
Die Unvermeidlichkeit der Bilder. Tübingen : G. Narr, c2001.
N72.A56 U58 2001x

Graf, Wilfried.
Kritik der Gewalt. Wien : Promedia, c2002.
D860.K75 2002

GRAFFITI - RUSSIA (FEDERATION).
Florenskai︠a︡, O. Psikhologii︠a︡ bytovogo shrifta. Sankt-Peterburg : Krasnyĭ matros, 2001.
BF896.F66 2001

Una gráfica dice más que mil palabras.
Morales Tomas, Marco Antonio. Guatemala : ESEDIR : Editorial Saqil Tzij, 1999.

Grafologie, cesta do hlubin duše.
Veličková, Helena. Vyd. 1. Praha : Academia, 2002.
BF896.V45 2002

Graham, Daniel W.
Presocratic philosophy. Aldershot, Hants, England ; Burlington, VT : Ashgate, 2002.
B187.5.P743 2002

Graham, Douglas, 1950- Ideation : the birth and death of ideas / Douglas Graham, Thomas T. Bachman. Hoboken, N.J. : John Wiley & Sons, Inc., c2004. p. cm. CONTENTS: Section A: Introduction: why ideas matter -- The mothers and fathers of invention -- Taxonomy of innovation -- Section A: The life cycle of ideas. Innovate: the birth of an idea -- Register: the first step for every new idea -- Protect: ensure recognition and reward -- Develop: improve your idea -- Value: what is your idea worth -- Market: finding investors and customers -- The death of an idea -- Section C: The innovation industry. A call to action -- The individual innovation imperative -- The corporate innovation imperative -- Academic innovation imperative -- Creative innovation imperative -- The global innovation imperative -- Section D: A vision for the future. The providers of innovation -- The merchants of innovation -- The consumers of innovation. ISBN 0-471-47944-6 (cloth) DDC 153.2
1. Creative ability. 2. Creative ability in business. 3. Intellectual property. I. Bachman, Thomas T. II. Title.
BF408.G664 2004

GRAIL.
Mörschel, Thomas. Die Historia vom heiligen Gral. Saarbrücken : Logos, 1994-

Nanteos. Llandysul, Wales : Gomer, [2001]
DA738.N36 N36 2001

Phillips, Graham. [Search for the Grail] The chalice of Magdalene. Rochester, Vt. : Bear & Company, 2004.
BF1442.G73 P48 2004

Sinclair, Andrew, 1935- The secret scroll. Edinburgh : Birlinn, 2002.

Tribbe, Frank C. The Holy Grail mystery solved. 1st ed. Lakeville, Minn. : Galde Press, 2003.
BF1442.G73 T75 2003

GRAIL - LEGENDS - HISTORY AND CRITICISM.
Durham, Diana. The return of King Arthur. New York : Jeremy P. Tarcher/Penguin, 2004.
BF637.S4 D88 2004

GRAIL - ROMANCES - HISTORY AND CRITICISM.
Besamusca, Bart. The book of Lancelot. Cambridge : D.S. Brewer, 2003.
PT5568.B47 2003

Grainger, Roger. Group spirituality : a workshop approach / Roger Grainger. Hove, East Sussex ; New York : Brunner-Routledge, 2003. viii, 175 p. : ill. ; 22 cm. Includes bibliographical references (p. [163]-167) and index. CONTENTS: The spirituality of groups -- The space between -- Story into archetype -- Dreaming -- Down to earth. ISBN 1-58391-917-1 (pbk. : alk. paper) ISBN 1-58391-916-3 (hbk : alk. paper) DDC 291.4/46
1. Small groups - Religious aspects. 2. Spiritual life. I. Title.
BL628.4.G73 2003

GRAL. See **GRAIL.**

GRAMMAR. See **GRAMMAR, COMPARATIVE AND GENERAL.**

GRAMMAR, COMPARATIVE AND GENERAL. See also **CONDITIONALS (LOGIC); LANGUAGE AND LANGUAGES.**
Grammatical theory and philosophy of language in antiquity. Leuven ; Sterling, Va. : Peeters, 2002.
P63.G73 2002

GRAMMAR, COMPARATIVE AND GENERAL - CONDITIONALS.
Artman, Lavee. ha-Nisayon ha-yomyomi u-fitron heseke tenai ya-hakhalah lo-teḳefim. [Israel : ḥ. mo. l., 1999?]

GRAMMAR, COMPARATIVE AND GENERAL - CONTEXT. See **CONTEXT (LINGUISTICS).**

GRAMMAR, COMPARATIVE AND GENERAL - DEIXIS. See also **INDEXICALS (SEMANTICS).**
Grounding. Berlin ; Hawthorne, N.Y. : M. de Gruyter, 2002.
P165.G76 2002

GRAMMAR, COMPARATIVE AND GENERAL - INDIRECT DISCOURSE.
Sakita, Tomoko I. Reporting discourse, tense, and cognition. 1st ed. Amsterdam ; Boston : Elsevier, 2002.
P301.5.I53 S25 2002

GRAMMAR, COMPARATIVE AND GENERAL - INFLECTION.
Development of verb inflection in first language acquisition. Berlin ; New York : Mouton de Gruyter, 2003.
P118.D465 2003

GRAMMAR, COMPARATIVE AND GENERAL - MORPHOLOGY.
Reading complex words. New York : Kluwer Academic/Plenum Publishers, c2003.
P37.5.R42 R43 2003

GRAMMAR, COMPARATIVE AND GENERAL - PHONOLOGY.
Phonetics, phonology, and cognition. Oxford : Oxford University Press, 2002.
P221.P475 2002

GRAMMAR, COMPARATIVE AND GENERAL - PREPOSITIONS.
Kessler, Klaus. Raumkognition und Lokalisationsäusserungen. Wiesbaden : Deutscher Universitäts-Verlag, 2000.
BF469.K47 2000

Poggio, Rosauta Maria Galvão Fagundes. Processos de gramaticalização de preposições do Latim ao Português. Salvador : EDUFBA, 2002.

Prepositions in their syntactic, semantic, and pragmatic context. Amsterdam ; Philadelphia, PA : J. Benjamins Pub., c2002.
P285.P74 2002

GRAMMAR, COMPARATIVE AND GENERAL - SENTENCES - PSYCHOLOGICAL ASPECTS.
Vasishth, Shravan, 1964- Working memory in sentence comprehension. New York ; London : Routledge, 2003.
PK1933.V28 2003

GRAMMAR, COMPARATIVE AND GENERAL - SYNTAX.
Chipere, Ngoni, 1965- Understanding complex sentences. New York : Palgrave Macmillan, 2003.
P295.C485 2003

Hamann, Cornelia, 1953- From syntax to discourse. Dordrecht, The Netherlands ; Boston : Kluwer Academic Publishers, c2002.
P118.H327 2002

Prepositions in their syntactic, semantic, and pragmatic context. Amsterdam ; Philadelphia, PA : J. Benjamins Pub., c2002.
P285.P74 2002

GRAMMAR, COMPARATIVE AND GENERAL - TENSE.
Sakita, Tomoko I. Reporting discourse, tense, and cognition. 1st ed. Amsterdam ; Boston : Elsevier, 2002.
P301.5.I53 S25 2002

GRAMMAR, COMPARATIVE AND GENERAL - VERB.
Development of verb inflection in first language acquisition. Berlin ; New York : Mouton de Gruyter, 2003.
P118.D465 2003

GRAMMAR, COMPARATIVE AND GENERAL - WORD ORDER.

Word order and scrambling. Malden, MA : Blackwell Pub., 2003.
P295 .W65 2003

GRAMMAR, PHILOSOPHICAL. *See* **GRAMMAR, COMPARATIVE AND GENERAL.**

GRAMMAR, UNIVERSAL. *See* **GRAMMAR, COMPARATIVE AND GENERAL.**

Grammatical theory and philosophy of language in antiquity / edited by Pierre Swiggers and Alfons Wouters. Leuven ; Sterling, Va. : Peeters, 2002. vi, 347 p. ; 25 cm. (Orbis/Supplementa ; t. 19) Includes bibliographical references and indexes. ISBN 90-429-1143-3 (pbk.) ISBN 2-87723-643-9 (Peeters France) DDC 415
1. Grammar, Comparative and general. 2. Philosophy, Ancient. I. Swiggers, Pierre. II. Wouters, Alfons. III. Series: Orbis (Louvain, Belgium). Supplementa ; t. 19.
P63 .G73 2002

Grammer, Karl, 1950-.
Evolutionary aesthetics. Berlin ; New York : Springer, c2003.
BH301.P78 E96 2003

Il "gran Vico".
Cospito, Giuseppe, 1966- Genova : Name, c2002.

Grandas, Teresa.
Romero, Pedro G., 1964- En el ojo de la batalla. Valencia : Universitat de València, 2002.

GRANDPARENT AND CHILD.
Chvojka, Erhard. Geschichte der Grosselternrollen. Wien : Böhlau, 2003.
HQ759.9 .C45 2003

GRANDPARENTING.
Chvojka, Erhard. Geschichte der Grosselternrollen. Wien : Böhlau, 2003.
HQ759.9 .C45 2003

GRANDPARENTS.
Chvojka, Erhard. Geschichte der Grosselternrollen. Wien : Böhlau, 2003.
HQ759.9 .C45 2003

Grandy, David.
Burton, Dan. Magic, mystery, and science. Bloomington : Indiana University Press, 2003.
BF1411 .B885 2003

Grani mira
Moiseev, N. N. (Nikita Nikolaevich) Kak daleko do zavtrashnego dni︠a︡--. Moskva : Taĭdeks Ko, 2002.
DK49 .M64 2002

Grani nashego vremeni
Vinokurov, Igorʹ. Ne smotrite im v glaza!. Moskva : AiF-Print, 2001.
BF1466 .V56 2001

Granot, Hayim. Terror bombing : the new urban threat : practical approaches for response agencies & security / Hayim Granot, Jay Levinson. Tel Aviv : Dekel Pub. House, 2002. 143 p. ; 27 cm. (Emergency management series) Includes bibliographical references and index. ISBN 9657178010 DDC 363.34/97
1. Terrorism. 2. Terrorism - Psychological aspects. 3. Bombings. 4. Emergency management. I. Levinson, Jay. II. Title. III. Series.
HV6431 .G73 2002

Granovskai︠a︡, R. M. (Rada Mikhaĭlovna) Konflikt i tvorchestvo v zerkale psikhologii / R.M. Granovskai︠a︡. Moskva : Genezis, 2002. 573 p. : ill. ; 21 cm. Includes bibliographical references (p. 566-573). ISBN 5852970565
1. Interpersonal conflict. 2. Social conflict. 3. Conflict (Psychology) 4. Creative ability. I. Title.
BF637.I48 G72 2002

Grant, David.
Discourse and organization. London ; Thousand Oaks, Calif. : Sage Publications, 1998.
HD58.7 .D57 1998

Grant, George, 1954- The blood of the moon : understanding the historic struggle between Islam and Western civilization / George Grant. Nashville, Tenn. : Thomas Nelson Publishers, 2002. xii, 207 p. : maps ; 22 cm. Includes bibliographical references (p. 197-203) and index. ISBN 0-7852-6543-0 (pbk.) DDC 956
1. Middle East - Politics and government. 2. East and West. 3. Islam and politics. I. Title.
DS62 .G73 2002

Grant, Glen. Glen Grant's chicken skin tales : 49 favorite ghost stories from Hawaii. Honolulu, Hawaii : Mutual Pub., c1998. viii, 184 p. : ill. ; 23 cm. ISBN 1-56647-228-8 (pbk.) DDC 133.1/09969
1. Ghosts - Hawaii. 2. Haunted places - Hawaii. I. Title. II. Title: Chicken skin tales
BF1472.U6 G72 1998

GRANT, MICKI.
Vint/age 2001 conference : [videorecording]. New York, c2001.

Grant, Micki, panelist.
Vint/age 2001 conference : [videorecording]. New York, c2001.

Grant, Robert J. Universe of worlds : further explorations of the soul's existence after death / by Robert J. Grant. Virginia Beach, Va. : A.R.E. Press, 2005. p. cm. Includes bibliographical references (p.   ). ISBN 0-87604-446-1 (trade pbk.) DDC 133.9
1. Spiritualism. 2. Future life - Miscellanea. 3. Death - Miscellanea. I. Title.
BF1261.2 .G73 2005

GRANTS-IN-AID, INTERNATIONAL. *See* **INTERNATIONAL RELIEF.**

GRAPHIC ARTS. *See* **COMMERCIAL ART; DRAWING; PAINTING; PRINTING.**

GRAPHIC ARTS - HISTORY - 20TH CENTURY - THEMES, MOTIVES.
Cullen, Cheryl Dangel. The art of design. 1st ed. Cincinnati, OH : How Design Books, c2003.
NC998.4 .C846 2003

GRAPHIC COMMUNICATION. *See* **VISUAL COMMUNICATION.**

GRAPHIC DESIGN (GRAPHIC ARTS). *See* **GRAPHIC ARTS.**

GRAPHICS. *See* **GRAPHIC ARTS.**

Graphics programming with Perl.
Verbruggen, Martien. Greenwich : Manning, c2002.
T385 .V465 2002

GRAPHOLOGY.
Fairchild, Dennis. The fortune telling handbook. 1st ed. Philadelphia, PA : Running Press, c2003.
BF1861 .F35 2003

Gullan-Whur, Margaret. The secrets of your handwriting. [New ed.]. London : Thorsons, 1998.
BF891 .G846 1998

Imberman, Arlyn. Signature for success. Kansas City, Mo. : Andrews McMeel Pub., 2003.
BF891 .I46 2003

Müller, Arno, 1930- Berühmte Frauen. Wien : Braumüller, 2002.

Veličková, Helena. Grafologie, cesta do hlubin duše. Vyd. 1. Praha : Academia, 2002.
BF896 .V45 2002

GRAPHOLOGY - CONGRESSES.
Wrocławskie Sympozjum Badań Pisma (9th : 2000 : Wrocław, Poland) Contemporary problems of proof from a document. Wroclaw : University of Wroclaw, Faculty of Law, Administration, and Economy, Department of Criminalistics, 2002.
BF891 .W76 2000

GRAPHOLOGY - DICTIONARIES.
Dictionary of stroke structures in graphoanalysis. New, 3rd ed. Chicago : International Graphoanalysis Society, 1998.
BF889.5 .D53 1998

GRAPHOLOGY - PERIODICALS.
Document, various specification. Wrocław : University of Wrocław, Faculty of Law and Administration, Department of Criminalistics, 2000-
BF905.C7 D63

GRAPHOLOGY - RUSSIA (FEDERATION).
Florenskai︠a︡, O. Psikhologii︠a︡ bytovogo shrifta. Sankt-Peterburg : Krasnyĭ matros, 2001.
BF896 .F66 2001

Grasskamp, Walter. Ist die Moderne eine Epoche? : Kunst als Modell / Walter Grasskamp. München : C.H. Beck, c2002. 182 p. : ill. ; 19 cm. (Beck'sche Reihe ; 1500) Collection of author's texts, some published previously. Includes bibliographical references (p. 173-182). ISBN 3-406-49404-8 (pbk.)
1. Modernism (Art) 2. Postmodernism. 3. Art, Modern - 20th century. I. Title.

Grathoff, Richard, 1934-.
Schutz, Alfred, 1899-1959. Werkausgabe. Konstanz : UVK, Verlagsgesellschaft, 2003-
BD431 .S284916 2003

GRATITUDE.
Nelson, Noelle C. The power of appreciation. Hillsboro, Or. : Beyond Words Pub., c2003.
BF575.G68 N45 2003

The psychology of gratitude. New York : Oxford University Press, 2004.
BF575.G68 P79 2003

Graven images
(v. 5) On interpretation. Madison, Wis. : University of Wisconsin Press for the University of Wisconsin Law School, c2002.

Gravetter, Frederick J. Research methods for the behavioral sciences / Frederick J Gravetter, Lori-Ann B. Forzano. Belmont, CA : Wadsworth, c2003. xxiii, 478 p. : ill. ; 24 cm. Includes bibliographical references and index. ISBN 0-534-54911-X DDC 150/.7/2
1. Psychology - Research - Methodology. 2. Social sciences - Research - Methodology. I. Forzano, Lori-Ann B. II. Title.
BF76.5 .G73 2003

GRAVITATION. *See* **RELATIVITY (PHYSICS).**

Gravity and grace.
Weil, Simone, 1909-1943. [Pesanteur et la grâce. English] 1st complete English language ed. / with an introduction and postscript by Gustave Thibon. London ; New York : Routledge, 2002.
B2430.W473 P413 2002

Gray, Ann, 1946- Research practice for cultural studies : ethnographic methods and lived cultures / Ann Gray. London ; Thousand Oaks, Calif. : SAGE, 2003. 207 p. ; 24 cm. Includes bibliographical references (p. [191]-198) and index. ISBN 0-7619-5174-1 ISBN 0-7619-5175-X (pbk.) DDC 300.72
1. Social sciences - Research - Methodology. 2. Ethnology - Methodology. I. Title.
H62 .G73 2003

Gray, John, 1948-
[Men are from Mars, women are from Venus. Spanish]
Els homes són de Mart, les dones són de Venus / John Gray ; traducció de Rudolf Ortega. 1. ed. Barcelona : Edicions 62, c2001. 329 p. ; 24 cm. (Llibres a l'abast ; 368) Translation of: Men are from Mars, women from Venus. ISBN 84-297-4997-7
1. Man-woman relationships. 2. Communication in marriage. 3. Interpersonal relations. I. Ortega, Rudolf. II. Title. III. Series.

Straw dogs : thoughts on humans and other animals / John Gray. London : Granta, 2002. x, 246 p. ; 23 cm. Includes bibliographical references (p. 201-230) and index. ISBN 1-86207-512-3 DDC 128
1. Human beings. 2. Self (Philosophy) I. Title.

Gray, Richard T. About face : German physiognomic thought from Lavater to Auschwitz / Richard T. Gray. Detroit : Wayne State University Press, c2004. p. cm. (Kritik) Includes bibliographical references (p.   ) and index. Table of contents URL: http://www.loc.gov/catdir/toc/ecip047/2003017664.html ISBN 0-8143-3179-3 DDC 138/.0943
1. Physiognomy - Germany - History. I. Title. II. Series: Kritik (Detroit, Mich.)
BF851 .G73 2004

Grayson, Andrew, 1963-.
Oates, John, 1946- Cognitive and language development in children. Milton Keynes, U.K. : Open University ; Malden, MA : Blackwell Pub., 2004.
BF723.C5 O38 2004

The Graz Schumpeter lectures
(6) Foley, Duncan K. Unholy trinity. London ; New York : Routledge, 2003.
HB135 .F65 2003

GRE (EDUCATIONAL TEST). *See* **GRADUATE RECORD EXAMINATION.**

GRE psychology.
Kellogg, Ronald Thomas. The best test preparation for the Graduate Record Examination, GRE psychology. Piscataway, N.J. : Research and Education Association, [2000]
BF78 .K45 2000

GRÉAL. *See* **GRAIL.**

GREAT APES. *See* **APES.**

GREAT BRITAIN - ANTIQUITIES, CELTIC.
Snyder, Christopher A. (Christopher Allen), 1966- The Britons. Malden, MA ; Oxford : Blackwell Pub., 2003.
DA140 .S73 2003

GREAT BRITAIN - ARMED FORCES - HISTORY - 20TH CENTURY.
The challenges of high command. Houndmills, Basingstoke ; New York : Palgrave Macmillan, 2003.
UB210 .C477 2003

GREAT BRITAIN - BIOGRAPHY.
Rose, Kenneth, 1924- Elusive Rothschild. London : Weidenfeld & Nicolson, 2003.

GREAT BRITAIN - CHURCH HISTORY - 449-1066.
Bradley, Ian C. The Celtic way. [2nd ed.]. London : Darton Longman & Todd, 2003.
BR748 .B73 2003

GREAT BRITAIN - CIVILIZATION - TO 1066.
Snyder, Christopher A. (Christopher Allen), 1966- The Britons. Malden, MA ; Oxford : Blackwell Pub., 2003.
DA140 .S73 2003

GREAT BRITAIN - COLONIES - AMERICA.
Gallivan, Martin D., 1968- James River chiefdoms. Lincoln : University of Nebraska Press, c2003.
E99.P85 G35 2003

GREAT BRITAIN - ETHNIC IDENTITY.
Konstrukte nationaler Identität. Würzburg : Ergon, c2002.
DC34 .K67 2002

GREAT BRITAIN - HISTORY, MILITARY - 20TH CENTURY - CASE STUDIES.
The challenges of high command. Houndmills, Basingstoke ; New York : Palgrave Macmillan, 2003.
UB210 .C477 2003

GREAT BRITAIN - HISTORY - TO 449.
Snyder, Christopher A. (Christopher Allen), 1966- The Britons. Malden, MA ; Oxford : Blackwell Pub., 2003.
DA140 .S73 2003

GREAT BRITAIN - IN LITERATURE.
Matthews, Caitlín, 1952- King Arthur and the goddess of the land. 2nd ed. Rochester, Vt. : Inner Traditions, 2002.
PB2273.M33 M36 2002

Matthews, Caitlín, 1952- Mabon and the guardians of Celtic Britain. Rochester, Vt. : Inner Traditions, c2002.
PB2273.M33 M37 2002

GREAT BRITAIN - INTELLECTUAL LIFE - 16TH CENTURY.
Lee-Browne, Patrick. The Renaissance. New York : Facts on File, c2003.

GREAT BRITAIN - POLITICS AND GOVERNMENT - 20TH CENTURY.
Sandys, Celia. We shall not fail. New York : Portfolio ; London : Penguin Books, 2003.
DA566.9.C5 S266 2003

GREAT GODDESS RELIGION. See **GODDESS RELIGION.**

The great hedge of India.
Moxham, Roy. Large print ed. Oxford : ISIS, 2001.

Great minds series
Bronowski, Jacob, 1908-1974. The identity of man. Amherst, N.Y. : Prometheus Books, 2002.
BD450 .B653 2002

GREAT MOTHER GODDESS RELIGION. See **GODDESS RELIGION.**

The great pendulum book.
Sonnenberg, Petra. [Pendelen van A tot Z. English] New York, NY : Sterling Pub. Co., 2003.
BF1779.P45 S6613 2003

Great speeches in history series
Women's rights. San Diego, Calif. : Greenhaven Press, c2002.
HQ1236 .W6526 2002

Grebner, Gundula.
Generationswechsel und historischer Wandel. München : Oldenbourg, 2003.

Grechishnikov, S. E. (Sergeĭ Egorovich) Magiia kak sotsiokul'turnyĭ fenomen / S.E. Grechishnikov. Kaluga : GUP "Oblizdat", 1999. 149 p. ; 20 cm. Includes bibliographical references (p. 138-149). ISBN 5896530617
1. Magic. 2. Magic - Social aspects. I. Title.
BF1616 .G74 1999

Les grecs et la vieillesse.
Catrysse, Andrée. Paris : L'Harmattan, c2003.

GREEK LITERATURE. See **BYZANTINE LITERATURE; CLASSICAL LITERATURE.**

GREEK LITERATURE, BYZANTINE. See **BYZANTINE LITERATURE.**

GREEK LITERATURE - HISTORY AND CRITICISM.
Muñoz Llamosas, Virginia. La intervención divina en el hombre a través de la literatura griega de época arcaica y clásica. Amsterdam : Hakkert, 2002.
PA3015.R5 M87 2002

GREEK LITERATURE, MEDIEVAL AND LATE. See **BYZANTINE LITERATURE.**

GREEK PHILOLOGY. See **GREEK LITERATURE.**

Greek theories of elementary cognition.
Beare, John I. (John Isaac), d. 1918 Mansfield Centre, Conn. : Martino Pub., 2004.
BF91 .B3 2004

Green, André. La diachronie en psychanalyse / André Green. Paris : Minuit, c2000. 267 p. ; 22 cm. (Collection "Critique") Includes bibliographical references. ISBN 2-7073-1706-3
1. Time - Psychological aspects. I. Title. II. Series.
BF468 .G66 2000

Time in psychoanalysis : some contradictory aspects / André Green ; translated by Andrew Weller. London ; New York : Free Association Books, 2002. vi, 178 p. ; 23 cm. Includes bibliographical references (p. 170-172) and index. Translated from the French. Table of contents URL: http://www.loc.gov/catdir/toc/fy037/2003538284.html ISBN 1-85343-551-1 ISBN 1-85343-550-3 (PBK.) DDC 150.195
1. Time - Psychological aspects. 2. Time perception. 3. Psychoanalysis and philosophy. I. Title.
BF468 .G6713 2002

Green, Arthur, 1941- Ehyeh : a kabbalah for tomorrow / Arthur Green. Woodstock, Vt. : Jewish Lights Publishing, c2003. xvi, 192 p. : ill. ; 24 cm. Includes bibliographical references (p. 187-192). ISBN 1-58023-125-X DDC 296.1/6
1. Cabala. 2. Mysticism - Judaism. 3. Spiritual life - Judaism. I. Title.
BM525 .G84 2003

Green, Christopher D. Early psychological thought : ancient accounts of mind and soul / Christopher D. Green and Philip R. Groff. Westport, Conn. ; London : Praeger, 2003. xi, 194 p. : ill. ; 25 cm. Includes bibliographical references (p. [181]-188) and index. ISBN 0-313-31845-X (alk. paper) DDC 150/.9
1. Psychology - History. 2. Philosophy of mind - History. 3. Philosophy, Ancient. I. Groff, Philip R., 1966- II. Title.
BF91 .G74 2003

GREEN, THOMAS HILL, 1836-1882 - CONTRIBUTIONS IN ETHICS.
Carter, Matt. T.H. Green and the development of ethical socialism. Thorverton : Imprint Academic, 2003.
B1638.E8 C37 2003

Greenberg, Arthur. The art of chemistry : myths, medicines, and materials / Arthur Greenberg. Hoboken, N.J. : Wiley-Interscience, c2003. xix, 357 p., [16] p. of plates : ill. (some col.) ; 29 cm. Includes bibliographical references and index. SUMMARY: The Art of chemistry employs 187 figures to illuminate 72 essays on the mythical origins, experiments, and adventurous explorers in the annals of chemistry. Each of the eight sections tracks chemistry's incremental progress from myth to modern science, featuring the figures and diagrams that early chemists used to explain their craft. Readers will meet the deadly basilisk and the fabulous phoenix that populated the lore of pre-modern chemistry, learn the contributions to chemistry of Benjamin Franklin, and encounter Antoine Lavoisier, the father of modern chemistry. Greenberg also examines our fundamental connections with science through two personal essays, one on an adolescent friend who became a world-renowned entomology professor and the other on his quest to discover his own chemical heritage. CONTENTS: Spiritual and myphological roots -- Stills, cupels and weapons -- Medicines, purges and ointments -- Emerging science -- Two revolutions in France -- Young country and a young theory -- Specialization and systemization -- Some fun -- Epilogue. ISBN 0-471-07180-3 (cloth : alk. paper) DDC 540/.9
1. Chemistry - History. 2. Alchemy. 3. Medicine - History. I. Title.
QD11 .G735 2003

Greenberg, Jeff, 1954-.
Pyszczynski, Thomas A. In the wake of 9/11. Washington, DC : American Psychological Association, c2003.
HV6432 .P97 2003

Greenberg, Jerrold S. Comprehensive stress management / Jerrold S. Greenberg. 8th ed. Boston : McGraw-Hill, [2003?] xx, 412 p. : ill. ; 28 cm. + 1 computer optical disc (4 3/4 in.). Includes bibliographical references (p. 379-397) and index. System requirements for accompanying computer optical disc: Windows: Pentium, 2X CD ROM, 24 MB RAM, 800x600 resolution; Macintosh: Power PC or higher, Mac OS 7.5, 2X CD-ROM, 24 MB RAM, 800x600 resolution. ISBN 0-07-255707-9 (alk. paper) DDC 155.9/042
1. Stress (Psychology) 2. Stress (Physiology) 3. Stress (Psychology) - Prevention. 4. Stress management. I. Title.
BF575.S75 G66 2003

Greene, Herb. Painting the mental continuum : perception and meaning in the making / Herb Greene. Berkeley, Calif. : Berkeley Hills Books ; [Berkeley, Calif.] : Distributed by Publishers Group West, c2003. 284 p. : ill. (some col.) ; 22 x 29 cm. Includes bibliographical references (p. 277-281) and index. ISBN 1-89316-355-5 (alk. paper) DDC 750/.1/9
1. Whitehead, Alfred North, - 1861-1947 - Influence. 2. Art - Psychology. 3. Art - Philosophy. I. Title.
N71 .G683 2003

Greene, Kathryn.
Privacy and disclosure of HIV in interpersonal relationships. Mahwah, N.J. : Lawrence Erlbaum Associates, 2003.
RA643.8 .P755 2003

Greene, Kenneth V.
Nelson, Phillip J., 1929- Signaling goodness. Ann Arbor : University of Michigan Press, c2003.
HV31 .N45 2003

Greene, Sheila, 1946- The psychological development of girls and women : rethinking change in time / Sheila Greene. London ; New York : Routledge, 2003. viii, 167 p. ; 25 cm. (Women and psychology) Includes bibliographical references (p. [147]-160) and index. ISBN 0-415-17861-4 (hb) ISBN 0-415-17862-2 (pb) DDC 155.6/33
1. Women - Psychology. 2. Girls - Psychology. 3. Developmental psychology. 4. Feminist psychology. I. Title. II. Series.
HQ1206 .G767 2003

Greene, Virginie Elisabeth, 1959- Le sujet et la mort dans La mort Artu / Virginie Greene. Saint-Genouph : Nizet, 2002. 418 p. ; 22 cm. Includes bibliographical references (p. [391]-416). ISBN 2-7078-1274-9 DDC 809
1. Mort Artu. 2. Arthurian romances - History and criticism. 3. Death in literature. I. Title.

Greenway, A. Roger. Risk management planning handbook : a comprehensive guide to hazard assessment, accidental release prevention, consequence analysis, and general duty clause compliance / A. Roger Greenway. 2nd ed. Rockville, MD : ABS Consulting, Government Institutes, c2002. xxiv, 314 p. : ill. ; 28 cm. Includes bibliographical references and index. ISBN 0-86587-841-2 DDC 658.15/5
1. Risk management. 2. Risk assessment. 3. Decision making. I. Title.
HD61 .G733 2002

Greer, Jane, 1951- The afterlife connection : a therapist reveals how to communicate with departed loved ones / Jane Greer. 1st ed. New York : St. Martin's Press, 2003. 260 p. : ill. ; 22 cm. Includes bibliographical references (p. [255]-257). ISBN 0-312-30652-0 DDC 133.9
1. Spiritualism. I. Title.
BF1261.2 .G74 2003

Greer, John Michael. The new encyclopedia of the occult / John Michael Greer. St. Paul, MN : Llewellyn Publications, 2003. p. cm. Includes bibliographical references. ISBN 1-56718-336-0 DDC 133/.03
1. Occultism - North America - Encyclopedias. 2. Occultism - Western Europe - Encyclopedias. 3. Occultism - History - North America - Encyclopedias. 4. Occultism - History - Western Europe - Encyclopedias. I. Title.
BF1407 .G74 2003

Greer, Mary K. (Mary Katherine) Understanding the tarot court / Mary K. Greer & Tom Little. 1st ed. St. Paul, Minn. : Llewellyn Publications, 2004. p. cm. Includes bibliographical references and index. ISBN 0-7387-0286-2 DDC 133.3/2424
1. Tarot. I. Little, Tom, 1961- II. Title.
BF1879.T2 G75 2004

Gregg, Samuel, 1969- On ordered liberty : a treatise on the free society / Samuel Gregg. Lanham, MD : Lexington Books, c2003. xvi, 127 p. ; 23 cm. (Religion, politics, and society in the new millennium) Includes bibliographical references and index. ISBN 0-7391-0622-8 (cloth : alk. paper) ISBN 0-7391-0668-6 (pbk. : alk. paper) DDC 320/.01/1
1. Liberty. 2. Liberalism. 3. Liberty - Religious aspects. I. Title. II. Series.
JC585 .G744 2003

Gregor, Frances Mary.
Campbell, Marie L. (Marie Louise), 1936- Mapping social relations. Aurora, Ont. : Garamond Press, c2002.

Gregory, Carol.
Monahan, Brian. From ground zero to ground hero. [Newark, Del.?] : Disaster Research Center, University of Delaware, 2001.

Gregory, Leland. Hey idiot! : chronicles of human stupidity / Leland Gregory. Kansas City, MO : Andrews McMeel Pub., 2003. p. cm. Publisher description URL: http://www.loc.gov/catdir/desc ription/ simon033/2003052448.html ISBN 0-7407-3902-6 DDC 081
1. Stupidity - Anecdotes. I. Title.
BF431 .G7825 2003

Gregory Palamas, Saint, 1296-1359.
Vizantijska filozofija u srednjevekovnoj Srbiji. Beograd : Stubovi kulture, 2002.

Gregory, Robert J., 1943- Psychological testing : history, principles, and applications / Robert J. Gregory. 4th ed. Boston, MA : Allyn and Bacon, 2004. p. cm. Includes bibliographical references and index. ISBN 0-205-35472-6 DDC 150/.28/7
1. Psychological tests. 2. Psychological tests - History. I. Title.
BF176 .G74 2004

Greimann, Dirk. Freges Konzeption der Wahrheit / Dirk Greimann. Hildesheim ; New York : Georg Olms, c2003. 305 p. ; 24 cm. (Studien und Materialien zur Geschichte der Philosophie, 0585-5802 ; Bd. 63) Revised version of the author's thesis (Habilitationsschrift)--Ludwig-Maximilans-Universität, München, 2000. Includes bibliographical references (p. [293]-300) and index. ISBN 3-487-11851-3 (pbk.)
1. Frege, Gottlob, - 1848-1925. 2. Truth. 3. Knowledge, Theory of. I. Title. II. Series.
B3318.T78 G74 2003

Greiper, BenTzion. Getting and staying married / BenTzion Greiper. Brooklyn, NY : B.T. Greiper, [2001?] 106 p. ; 22 cm. Cover title: Getting & staying married the Torah way.
1. Marriage. 2. Marriage - Religious aspects - Judaism. 3. Jewish families - Religious life. 4. Interpersonal relations. 5. Interpersonal communication. I. Title. II. Title: Getting & staying married the Torah way
HQ734 .G745 2001

Gremillet-Parent, Martine.
Germain-Thiant, Myriam. La relation à l'autre. Lyon : Chronique sociale, [2002]

Grene, Marjorie Glicksman, 1910-.
The philosophy of Marjorie Grene. Chicago : Open Court, c2002.
B945.G734 P47 2002

GRENE, MARJORIE GLICKSMAN, 1910-.
The philosophy of Marjorie Grene. Chicago : Open Court, c2002.
B945.G734 P47 2002

Grenville, Bruce.
Randolph, Jeanne, 1943- Why stoics box. Toronto : YYZ Books, 2003.

Grenzen des Verstehens : philosophische und humanwissenschaftliche Perspektiven / herausgegeben von Gudrun Kühne-Bertram und Gunter Scholtz. Göttingen : Vandenhoeck & Ruprecht, c2002. 272 p. ; 24 cm. Includes bibliographical references and index. German and English. ISBN 3-525-30138-3
1. Comprehension (Theory of knowledge) 2. Comprehension. 3. Hermeneutics. 4. Phenomenology. I. Kühne-Bertram, Gudrun, 1952- II. Scholtz, Gunter.
BD181.5 .G74 2002

Grenzen sprengen, Mittle finden.
21. Goldegger Dialoge. 1. Aufl. Goldegg : Kulturverein Schloss Goldegg, 2002.

Greve, Henrich R. Organizational learning from performance feedback : a behavioral perspective on innovation and change / Henrich R. Greve. Cambridge : Cambridge University Press, 2003. x, 215 p. : ill. ; 24 cm. Includes bibliographical references (p. 187-212) and index. ISBN 0-521-81831-1 ISBN 0-521-53491-7 (PBK.) DDC 658.403
1. Decision making. 2. Organizational learning. 3. Strategic planning. I. Title.

Grhabandha bijñāna.
Khadiratna, Dayanidhi. Brhat śilpaśāstra, bā, Grhabandha bijñāna ; Grhabandha gaṇanā o śubhastambhāropaṇa bicāra. Kaṭaka : Dharmagrantha Shtora, [1995?]
TH4809.I4 K48 1995

Grhabandha gaṇanā o śubhastambhāropaṇa bicāra.
Khadiratna, Dayanidhi. Brhat śilpaśāstra, bā, Grhabandha bijñāna ; Grhabandha gaṇanā o śubhastambhāropaṇa bicāra. Kaṭaka : Dharmagrantha Shtora, [1995?]
TH4809.I4 K48 1995

GRIEF.
Beem, Ellen Evaline, 1957- Bereavement. [Leiden : Universiteit Leiden, 2000]
BF575.G7 B422 2000

Cornils, Stanley P. Your healing journey through grief. San Francisco, CA : Robert D. Reed Publishers, c2003.
BF575.G7 C677 2003

Daher, Douglas, 1949- And the passenger was death. Amityville, N.Y. : Baywood Pub., c2003.
BF575.G7 D34 2003

Davenport, Donna S. Singing mother home. Denton, Tex. : University of North Texas Press, c2002.
BF575.G7 D365 2002

Dennison, Amy. Our dad died. Minneapolis, MN : Free Spirit Pub., c2003.
BF723.G75 D46 2003

Feldbaum, Rebecca Bram. If there's anything I can do--. Jerusalem, Israel ; Nanuet, NY : Feldheim Publishers, 2003.
BF575.G7 F46 2003

Grubbs, Geri A., 1943- Bereavement dreaming and the individuating soul. Berwick, Me. : Nicolas-Hays, 2004.
BF1099.D4 G78 2004

Hedtke, Lorraine, 1957- Re-membering lives. Amityville, N.Y. : Baywood Pub. Co., 2004.
BF789.D4 H4 2004

Hjelmstad, Lois Tschetter. The last violet. Englewood, Colo. : Mulberry Hill Press, c2002.
BF575.G7 H575 2002

Isaacs, Diane R. Molly & Monet. Seattle, WA : Peanut Butter Pub., c1999.
BF575.G7 I86 1999

Johnson, Marvin. Where's Jess? Rev. Omaha, NE : Centering Corp. Resource, 2003.
BF723.G75 J645 2003

Kaufman, Barry Neil. No regrets. Novato, Calif. : HJ Kramer/New World Library, 2003.
BF575.G7 K385 2003

Kuebelbeck, Amy, 1964- Waiting with Gabriel. Chicago, Ill. : Loyola Press, c2003.
BF575.G7 K83 2003

Lathan, Mark J., 1961- Emotional progression in sacred choral music. 2001.

Meier, Levi. Seven heavens. [S.l.] : Devora Publishing, c2002.
BF789.D4 M39 2002

Murray, Donald Morison, 1924- The lively shadow. 1st ed. New York : Ballantine Books, 2003.
BF575.G7 M868 2003

Natoli, Salvatore. L'esperienza del dolore. 1. ed. nell'"Universale economica"--Saggi. Milano : Feltrinelli, 2002.

Neeld, Elizabeth Harper, 1940- Seven choices. New York : Warner Books, c2003.
BF575.G7 N44 2003

Peacock, Carol Antoinette. Death and dying. New York : Franklin Watts, c2004.
BF575.G7 P3783 2004

Schnall, Maxine. What doesn't kill you makes you stronger. Cambridge, MA : Perseus Pub., c2002.
BF575.D35 S36 2002

A teen's guide to coping. Minneapolis : Fairview Press, 2003.
BF789.D4 T44 2003

Veerman, David. When your father dies. Nashville, Tenn. : Thomas Nelson, c2003.
BF575.G7 V44 2003

Walter, Carolyn Ambler. The loss of a life partner. New York : Columbia University Press, c2003.
BF575.G7 W3435 2003

Weiss, Stefanie Iris. Everything you need to know about dealing with losses. Rev. ed. New York : Rosen Pub. Group, 2000.
BF724.3.L66 W45 2000

Wilkins, David, 1944- United by tragedy. Nampa, Idaho : Pacific Press Pub. Association, c2003.
BF575.G7 W555 2003

GRIEF - DICTIONARIES.
Adams, Christine A. ABC's of grief. Amityville, N.Y. : Baywood, c2003.
BF575.G7 A32 2003

GRIEF - EUROPE - CASE STUDIES.
Groben, Joseph. Requiem für ein Kind. 2. Aufl. Köln : Dittrich, 2002.

BF575.G7 G76 2002

GRIEF IN ADOLESCENCE.
Liotta, Alfred J. When students grieve. Horsham, PA : LRP Publications, 2003.
BF724.3.D43 L56 2003

Myers, Edward, 1950- When will I stop hurting? Lanham, Md. : Scarecrow Press, 2004.
BF724.3.G73 M94 2004

Perschy, Mary Kelly, 1942- Helping teens work through grief. 2nd ed. New York : Brunner-Routledge, 2004.
BF724.3.G73 P47 2004

GRIEF IN ADOLESCENCE - JUVENILE LITERATURE.
Weiss, Stefanie Iris. Everything you need to know about dealing with losses. Rev. ed. New York : Rosen Pub. Group, 2000.
BF724.3.L66 W45 2000

GRIEF IN CHILDREN.
Fitzgerald, Helen. The grieving child. 2nd ed. New York : Simon & Schuster, 2003.
BF723.D3 F58 2003

Helping kids cope. Minneapolis : Fairview Press, 2003.
BF723.G75 H35 2003

Kanyer, Laurie A., 1959- 25 things to do when grandpa passes away, mom and dad get divorced, or the dog dies. Seatte Wash., : Parenting Press, 2004.
BF723.G75 K36 2003

Liotta, Alfred J. When students grieve. Horsham, PA : LRP Publications, 2003.
BF724.3.D43 L56 2003

Rathkey, Julia Wilcox. What children need when they grieve. 1st ed. New York : Three Rivers Press, 2004.
BF723.G75 R38 2004

Wakenshaw, Martha. Caring for your grieving child. Oakland, Calif. : New Harbinger ; London : Hi Marketing, 2002.
BF723.G75 W35 2002

GRIEF IN CHILDREN - JUVENILE LITERATURE.
Dennison, Amy. Our dad died. Minneapolis, MN : Free Spirit Pub., c2003.
BF723.G75 D46 2003

Johnson, Marvin. Where's Jess? Rev. Omaha, NE : Centering Corp. Resource, 2003.
BF723.G75 J645 2003

Stenson, Lila. Daddy, up and down. 1st ed. Snowmass Village, CO : Peaceful Village Pub., 2002.
BF723.G75 S74 2002

GRIEF - JUVENILE LITERATURE.
Peacock, Carol Antoinette. Death and dying. New York : Franklin Watts, c2004.
BF575.G7 P3783 2004

GRIEF - MISCELLANEA.
Kolb, Janice E. M. In corridors of eternal time. Nevada City, Calif. : Blue Dolphin Pub., 2003.
BF1997.K65 A3 2003b

GRIEF - PHYSIOLOGICAL ASPECTS.
Beem, Ellen Evaline, 1957- Bereavement. [Leiden : Universiteit Leiden, 2000]
BF575.G7 B422 2000

GRIEF THERAPY.
Perschy, Mary Kelly, 1942- Helping teens work through grief. 2nd ed. New York : Brunner-Routledge, 2004.
BF724.3.G73 P47 2004

GRIEF THERAPY - POPULAR WORKS.
Wakenshaw, Martha. Caring for your grieving child. Oakland, Calif. : New Harbinger ; London : Hi Marketing, 2002.
BF723.G75 W35 2002

GRIEF - UNITED STATES.
Barzach, Amy Jaffe. Accidental courage, boundless dreams. 1st ed. West Hartford, CT : Aurora Pub., c2001.
BF575.G7 B375 2001

The grieving child.
Fitzgerald, Helen. 2nd ed. New York : Simon & Schuster, 2003.
BF723.D3 F58 2003

Grigorenko, Elena.
Creativity. 1st ed. Washington, DC : American Psychological Association, c2004.
BF408 .C7548 2004

Culture and competence. Washington, DC : American Psychological Association, 2004.
BF311 .C845 2004

Grigorovich, A. A. (Aleksandr Anatol'evich) Misteriía zvezd : putevoditel' po sud'be / A. Grigorovich. Moskva : MK-Periodika, 2002. 222 p. : ill., maps (some col.) ; 25 cm. ISBN 5946690124
1. Astrology. I. Title.
BF1708.6 .G75 2002

Grimassi, Raven, 1951- Spirit of the witch : religion & spirituality in contemporary witchcraft / Raven Grimassi. 1st ed. St. Paul, Minn. : Llewellyn Publications, 2003. xiv, 243 p. : ill. ; 23 cm. Includes bibliographical references (p. 235-239) and index. ISBN 0-7387-0338-9 DDC 133.4/3
1. Witchcraft. 2. Spiritual life. I. Title.
BF1566 .G737 2003

The witch's familiar : spiritual partnerships for successful magic / Raven Grimassi. 1st ed. St. Paul, Minn. : Llewellyn Publications, 2003. xxi, 156 p. : ill. ; 23 cm. Includes bibliographical references (p. 153-154) and index. ISBN 0-7387-0339-7 (pbk.) DDC 133.4/3
1. Familiars (Spirits) 2. Magic. 3. Evocation. I. Title.
BF1557 .G75 2003

Grimbert, Joan T.
Philologies old and new. Princeton : The Edward C. Armstrong Monographs, 2001.

GRIMM, JACOB, 1785-1863.
Bosco Coletsos, Sandra. La struttura parentale nelle fiabe dei fratelli Grimm. Alessandria : Edizioni dell'Orso, 2001.

GRIMM, WILHELM, 1786-1859.
Bosco Coletsos, Sandra. La struttura parentale nelle fiabe dei fratelli Grimm. Alessandria : Edizioni dell'Orso, 2001.

Grimoire for the apprentice wizard.
Zell-Ravenheart, Oberon, 1942- Franklin Lakes, NJ : New Page Books, 2004.
BF1611 .Z45 2004

Grimoire for the green witch.
Aoumiel. 1st ed. St. Paul, Minn. : Llewellyn Publications, c2003.
BF1572.P43 A583 2003

The grimoire of Lady Sheba.
Lady Sheba. Llewellyn's centennial ed. St. Paul, Minn. : Llewellyn Publications, 2001.
BF1566 .L335 2001

Grimshaw, Denise.
Gawain, Shakti, 1948- Reflections in the light. Rev. ed. Novato, Calif. : Nataraj Pub., c2003.
BF637.S4 G393 2003

Grimwood, Irene. Land girls at the old rectory / Irene Grimwood. Large print ed. Oxford : ISIS, 2001. 78 p. (large print) : map ; 25 cm. (Isis reminiscence series) Originally published: Ipswich: Old Pond, 2000. ISBN 0-7531-9698-0 DDC 941.084092
1. Grimwood, Irene. 2. Women's Land Army - Biography. 3. World War, 1939-1945 - Women - Great Britain. 4. World War, 1939-1945 - Social aspects - Great Britain. 5. Large type books. I. Title. II. Series: Isis reminiscence series.

GRIMWOOD, IRENE.
Grimwood, Irene. Land girls at the old rectory. Large print ed. Oxford : ISIS, 2001.

Grinshpon, Yohanan, 1948- Demamah ve-ḥerut ba-yogah ha-Ḳelasit / Yoḥanan Grinshpon. [Tel Aviv] : Miśrad ha-biṭaḥon, [2002] 144 p. ; 21 cm. (Sifriyat universiṭah meshuderet) Title on verso of t.p.: Silence and liberation in Classical Yoga. ISBN 965051175X
1. Patañjali. - Yogasūtra. 2. Yoga. I. Title. II. Title: Silence and liberation in Classical Yoga III. Series: Sidrat "universiṭah meshuderet"

Groarke, Louis. The good rebel : understanding freedom and morality / Louis Groarke. Madison [N.J.] : Fairleigh Dickinson University Press ; London ; Cranbury, NJ : Associated University Presses, c2002. 326 p. ; 24 cm. Includes bibliographical references (p. 303-318) and index. ISBN 0-8386-3899-6 (alk. paper) DDC 170
1. Autonomy (Philosophy) 2. Ethics. I. Title.
B808.67 .G76 2002

Groben, Joseph. Requiem für ein Kind : Trauer und Trost berühmter Eltern / Joseph Groben. 2. Aufl. Köln : Dittrich, 2002. 429 p. : ill. ; 25 cm. Includes bibliographical references and index. ISBN 3-920862-32-5
1. Grief - Europe - Case studies. 2. Bereavement - Europe - Psychological aspects - Case studies. 3. Children of celebrities - Death - Psychological aspects - Case studies. 4. Celebrities - Europe - Psychology - Case studies. 5. Parents - Europe - Psychology - Case studies. I. Title.
BF575.G7 G76 2002

Grobon, Guillemette.
Paroles brutes à la recherche d'un trésor. Genouilleux : Passe du vent, c2003.

Grodal, Birgit.
Vind, Karl. Independence, additivity, uncertainty. Berlin ; New York : Springer, c2003.
HB135 .V56 2003

Groebner, Valentin.
Negotiating the gift. Göttingen : Vandenhoeck & Ruprecht, c2003.

Groff, Philip R., 1966-.
Green, Christopher D. Early psychological thought. Westport, Conn. ; London : Praeger, 2003.
BF91 .G74 2003

Groĭs, Boris.
Postmodernism and the postsocialist condition. Berkeley : University of California Press, c2003.
N6494.P66 P684 2003

Groĭsman, A. L. (Alekseĭ L'vovich).
Khrestomatiía po psikhologii khudozhestvennogo tvorchestva. Izd., 2. Moskva : Izd-vo Magistr, 1998.
BF408 .K476 1998

Grolnick, Wendy S. The psychology of parental control : how well-meant parenting backfires / Wendy S. Grolnick. Mahwah, N.J. : L. Erlbaum Associates, 2003. xiii, 182 p. ; 24 cm. Includes bibliographical references (p. 153-167) and indexes. Table of contents URL: http://www.loc.gov/catdir/toc/fy032/2001051087.html ISBN 0-8058-3540-7 (cloth : alk. paper) ISBN 0-8058-3541-5 (pbk. : alk. paper) DDC 306.874
1. Parent and child - Psychological aspects. 2. Parenting - Psychological aspects. 3. Control (Psychology) 4. Parents - Psychology. I. Title.
HQ755.85 .G74 2003

Gromkowska, Agnieszka. Kobiecość w kulturze globalnej : rekonstrukcje i reprezentacje / Agnieszka Gromkowska. POznań : Wolumin, 2002. 251 p. ; 24 cm. Includes bibliographical references (p. 243-251). In Polish with table of contents in English. ISBN 83-88536-40-0
1. Feminism. 2. Women - Identity. 3. Femininity. I. Title.

Groningen studies in cultural change
(v. 1) The metamorphosis of magic from late antiquity to the early modern period. Leuven ; Dudley, MA : Peeters, 2002.
BF1589 .M55 2002

(v. 4) Antiquity renewed. Leuven, Netherlands ; Dudley, MA : Peeters, 2003.
CB365 .A58 2003

Gronke, Horst.
Philosophieren aus dem Diskurs. Würzburg : Königshausen & Neumann, c2002.

GROOMING FOR WOMEN. *See* **BEAUTY, PERSONAL.**

GROOMING, PERSONAL. *See* **BEAUTY, PERSONAL.**

Groos, Arthur.
Perceval = New York : Routledge, 2002.
PN686.P4 P46 2002

Grosbard, Ofer, 1954-
[Yiśra'el 'al ha-sapah. English]
Israel on the couch : the psychology of the peace process / Ofer Grosbard ; with a foreword by Vamik D. Volkan. Albany : State University of New York Press, c2003. xvii, 195 p. ; 23 cm. (SUNY series in Israeli studies) Includes index. ISBN 0-7914-5605-6 (alk. paper) ISBN 0-7914-5606-4 (pbk. : alk. paper) DDC 956.05/3
1. Arab-Israeli conflict - Peace - Psychological aspects. 2. National characteristics, Israeli - Psychological aspects. 3. Conflict management - Israel. 4. Israel - Politics and government - Psychological aspects. 5. Peace - Psychological aspects. 6. Attitude (Psychology) 7. Political psychology. I. Title. II. Series.
DS126.5 .G694 2003

Yiśra'el 'al ha-sapah : ha-psikhologyah shel tahalikh ha-shalom / 'Ofer Grozbard. Tel-Aviv : Yedi'ot aḥaronot : Sifre ḥemed, c2000. 382 p. ; 23 cm. Title on verso of t.p.: Israel on the couch : the psychology of the peace process. ISBN 9654488663
1. Conflict management - Israel. 2. Arab-Israeli conflict - 1993- - Peace - Psychological aspects. 3. National characteristics, Israeli - Psychological aspects. 4. Israel - Politics and government - Psychological aspects. 5. Peace - Psychological aspects. 6. Attitude (Psychology) I. Title. II. Title: Psikhologyah shel tahalikh ha-shalom III. Title: Israel on the couch : the psychology of the peace process IV. Title: Psychology of the peace process

Gross, Esther. You are not alone : a three-dimensional Torah approach to overcoming anxiety / Esther Gross. Jerusalem, Israel ; Nanuet, NY : Feldheim, 2002. 199 p. : ill. ; 24 cm. "Of trials and triumphs: a worksheet," (1 folded leaf), inserted. Includes bibliographical references. ISBN 1-58330-533-5
1. Panic disorders - Popular works. 2. Anxiety - Religious aspects - Judaism. 3. Self-help techniques. I. Title.

Gross, Peter, 1941- Ich-Jagd : im Unabhängigkeitsjahrhundert / Peter Gross. 1. Aufl., Originalausg. Frankfurt am Main : Suhrkamp, 1999. 341, [1] p. ; 18 cm. (Edition Suhrkamp ; 2065) Subtitle on cover: Ein Essay. Includes bibliographical references (p. 327-[342]). ISBN 3-518-12065-4
1. Ego (Psychology) I. Title. II. Title: Ich Jagd
BF175.5.E35 G76 1999

Grosseteste, Robert, 1175?-1253.
Panti, Cecilia, 1964- Moti, virtù e motori celesti nella cosmologia di Roberto Grossatesta. Firenze : SISMEL : Edizioni del Galluzzo, 2001.
B765.G74 P36 2001

GROSSETESTE, ROBERT, 1175?-1253.
Panti, Cecilia, 1964- Moti, virtù e motori celesti nella cosmologia di Roberto Grossatesta. Firenze : SISMEL : Edizioni del Galluzzo, 2001.
B765.G74 P36 2001

Grotberg, Edith Henderson, 1928-.
Resilience for today. Westport, CT : Praeger, 2003.
BF698.35.R47 R47 2003

Groth-Marnat, Gary.
Beutler, Larry E. Integrative assessment of adult personality. 2nd ed. New York : Guilford Press, 2003.
BF698.4 .B42 2003

Grounding knowledge.
Preston, Christopher J. Athens, Ga. : University of Georgia Press, c2003.
BD161 .P746 2003

Grounding : the epistemic footing of deixis and reference / edited by Frank Brisard. Berlin ; Hawthorne, N.Y. : M. de Gruyter, 2002. xxxiv, 475 p. : ill. ; 24 cm. (Cognitive linguistics research ; 21) Some of the papers presented during the 7th International Pragmatics Conference, held in Budapest, Hungary in July 2000. Includes bibliographical references and index. ISBN 3-11-017369-7 (alk. paper) DDC 415
1. Cognitive grammar. 2. Grammar, Comparative and general - Deixis. 3. Reference (Linguistics) I. Brisard, Frank. II. International Pragmatics Conference (7th : 2000 : Budapest, Hungary) III. Series.
P165 .G76 2002

The grounds of ethical judgement.
Illies, Christian. Oxford : Clarendon, 2003.

Group behaviour and development : is the market destroying cooperation? / edited by Judith Heyer, Frances Stewart, and Rosemary Thorp. Oxford ; New York : Oxford University Press, 2002. xvii, 364 p. ; 24 cm. (Queen Elizabeth House series in development studies) "A study prepared for Queen Elizabeth House, International Development Centre, University of Oxford (QEH) and the World Institute for Development Economics Research of the United Nations University (UNU/WIDER)." Includes bibliographical references and index. CONTENTS: Group behaviour and development / Judith Heyer ... [et al.] -- Dynamic interactions between the macro-environment, development thinking, and group behaviour / Frances Stewart -- Individual motivation, its nature, determinants, and consequences for within-group behaviour / Sabina Alkire and Séverine Deneulin -- Collective action for local-level effort regulation : an assessment of recent experiences in Senegalese small-scale fisheries / Frederic Gaspart and Jean-Philippe Platteau -- Leaders and intermediaries as economic development agents in producers' associations / Tito Bianchi -- Group behaviour and development : a comparison of farmers' organizations in South Korea and Taiwan / Larry Burmeister, Gustav Ranis, and Michael Wang -- Has the Coffee Federation become redundant? Collective action and the market in Colombian development / Rosemary Thorp -- Producer groups and the decollectivization of the Mongolian pastoral economy / David Sneath -- The hidden side of group behaviour : a gender analysis of community forestry in South Asia / Bina Agarwal -- Informal women's groups in rural Bangladesh : operation and outcomes / Simeen Mahmud -- Sex workers in Calcutta and the dynamics of collective action : political activism, community identity, and group behaviour / Nandini Gooptu -- Non-market relationships in health care / Maureen Mackintosh and Lucy Gilson -- Institutional cultures and regulatory relationships in a liberalizing health care system : a Tanzanian case study / Paula Tibandebage and Maureen Mackintosh -- The case of indigenous NGOs in Uganda's health sector / Christy Cannon Lorgen -- Conclusions / Judith Heyer, Frances Stewart, and Rosemary Thorp. ISBN 0-19-925691-8 ISBN 0-19-925692-6 (pbk.) DDC 302.3/5

1. Organizational behavior. 2. Organizational behavior - Developing countries. 3. Associations, institutions, etc. 4. Associations, institutions, etc. - Developing countries. 5. Economic development. 6. Developing countries - Economic conditions. I. Heyer, Judith. II. Stewart, Frances, 1940- III. Thorp, Rosemary. IV. Series.
HD58.7 .G76 2002

Group cohesion, trust and solidarity / edited by Shane R. Thye, Edward J. Lawler ; managing editor, Theresa H. Woodhouse. 1st ed. Amsterdam ; New York : JAI, 2002. xii, 253 p. : ill. ; 23 cm. (Advances in group processes ; v. 19) Includes bibliographical references. ISBN 0-7623-0898-2 DDC 302.3
1. Social groups. 2. Trust. 3. Solidarity. I. Thye, Shane R. II. Lawler, Edward J.

GROUP COUNSELING.
Corey, Gerald. Theory and practice of group counseling. 6th ed. Australia ; Belmont, CA : Thomson/Brooks/Cole, c2004.
BF637.C6 C576 2004

Critical incidents in group counseling. Alexandria, VA : American Counseling Association, 2004.
BF637.C6 C72 2004

Group creativity.
Sawyer, R. Keith (Robert Keith) Mahwah, N.J. : L. Erlbaum Associates, 2003.
BF408 .S285 2003

Group creativity : innovation through collaboration / edited by Paul B. Paulus and Bernard A. Nijstad. Oxford ; New York : Oxford University Press, 2003. xiii, 346 p. : ill. ; 25 cm. Includes bibliographical references and index. CONTENTS: 1. Group creativity : an introduction / Paul B. Paulus and Bernard A. Nijstad -- 2. The constraining effects of initial ideas / Steven M. Smith -- 3. Diversity and creativity in work groups : a dynamic perspective on the affective and cognitive processes that link diversity and performance / Frances J. Milliken, Caroline A. Bartel, and Terri R. Kurtzberg -- 4. Better than individuals? : the potential benefits of dissent and diversity for group creativity / Charlan J. Nemeth and Brendan Nemeth-Brown -- 5. Group creativity and collective choice / Garold Stasser and Zachary Birchmeier -- 6. Ideational creativity in groups : lessons from research on brainstorming / Paul B. Paulus and Vincent R. Brown -- 7. Cognitive stimulation and interference in idea generating groups / Bernard A. Nijstad, Michael Diehl, and Wolfgang Stroebe -- 8. Electronic brainstorming : theory, research, and future directions / Alan R. Dennis and Mike L. Williams -- 9. Is the social psychology of creativity really social? : moving beyond a focus on the individual / Beth A. Hennessey -- 10. Newcomer innovation in work teams / John M. Levine, Hoon-Seok Choi, and Richard L. Moreland -- 11. The group as mentor : social capital and the systems model of creativity / Charles Hooker, Jeanne Nakamura, and Mihaly Csikszentmihalyi -- 12. Creativity and innovation implementation in teams Michael A. West -- 13. Learning from direct and indirect experience in organizations : the effects of experience, content, timing, and distribution / Linda Argote, and Aimé Kane -- 14. Creative cultures, nations, and civilizations : strategies and results / Dean Keith Simonton -- 15. Group creativity : common themes and future directions / Bernard A. Nijstad and Paul B. Paulus. ISBN 0-19-514730-8 (alk. paper) DDC 302.3/4
1. Creative thinking - Social aspects. 2. Creation (Literary, artistic, etc.) - Social aspects. 3. Group problem solving. I. Paulus, Paul B. II. Nijstad, Bernard Arjan, 1971-
BF408 .G696 2003

GROUP DECISION MAKING.
Patton, Bobby R., 1935- Decision-making group interaction. 4th ed. Boston : Allyn and Bacon, c2003.
HM736 .P37 2003

GROUP FACILITATION.
Gottlieb, Marvin R. Managing group process. Westport, Conn. ; London : Praeger, 2003.
HD66 .G6778 2003

GROUP IDENTITY.
Abbinnett, Ross. Culture and identity. London ; Thousand Oaks, Ca. : SAGE, 2003.
HM621 .A23 2003

Burack, Cynthia, 1958- Healing identities. Ithaca : Cornell University Press, 2004.
BF175.4.F45 B87 2004

El buscador de oro. [Madrid] : Lengua de Trapo Ediciones, c2002.

Catanio, Percy Antonio Galimberti. O caminho que o dekassegui sonhou (dekassegui no yumê-ji). São Paulo : EDUC, FAPESP; Londrina : UEL, 2002.

Claiming the stones/naming the bones. Los Angeles : Getty Research Institute, c2002.
CC135 .C48 2002

Collective identities in action. Aldershot, England ; Burlington, VT : Ashgate, c2002.
GN495.6 .C635 2002

Creppell, Ingrid. Toleration and identity. New York ; London : Routledge, 2003.
HM1271 .C73 2003

Cultura e identidade. Rio de Janeiro, RJ, Brasil : DP & A Editores, 2002.

La culture. Auxerre : Sciences humaines éditions, c2002.

Fahlenbrach, Kathrin. Protest-Inszenierungen. 1. Aufl. Wiesbaden : Westdeutscher Verlag, 2002.

'Gottes auserwählte Völker'. Frankfurt am Main ; New York : Lang, c2001.
BT810.2 .G65 2001

Gould, Roger V. Collision of wills. Chicago : University of Chicago Press, 2003.
HM1121 .G68 2003

Gutmann, Amy. Identity in democracy. Princeton, N.J. : Princeton University Press, c2003.
JF529 .G886 2003

Identidades, sujetos y subjetividades. Buenos Aires : Prometeo Libros, c2002.

Identities. New York ; Oxford : Berghahn Books, 2002.
HM716 .I34 2002

Lie, Rico. Spaces of intercultural communication. Creskill, N.J. : Hampton Press, c2003.
GN345.6 .L54 2003

Litvinović, Gorjana. Čovek između istorijskog i ličnog vremena. Beograd : Institut za psihologiju, 2001.
BF697 .L543 2001

Lorenzi-Cioldi, Fabio, 1955- Les représentations des groupes dominants et dominés. Grenoble : Presses universitaires de Grenoble, c2002.
HM716 .L674 2002

Making sense of collectivity. London ; Sterling, Va. : Pluto Press, 2002.
HM753 .M35 2002

Markell, Patchen, 1969- Bound by recognition. Princeton, N.J. : Princeton University Press, c2003.
JC575 .M37 2003

Matheus, Tiago Corbisier. Ideais na adolescência. 1a ed. São Paulo, SP : Annablume, 2002.

Migration, diasporas, and transnationalism. Cheltenham, UK ; Northampton, MA : Edward Elgar, 1999.
JV6032 .M54 1999

Moita Lopes, Luiz Paulo da. Identidades fragmentadas. Campinas, SP, Brasil : Mercado de Letras, [2002]
HM753 .M65 2002

Pataki, Ferenc, 1928- Élettörténet és identitás. Budapest : Osiris Kiadó, 2001.
BF697.5.S65 P38 2001

Political communications in greater China. London ; New York : RoutledgeCurzon, 2003.
JF1525.C59 P65 2003

Race, nature, and the politics of difference. Durham : Duke University Press, 2003.
HT1521 .R2355 2003

Self and social identity. Malden, MA : Blackwell Pub., 2003.
BF697.5.S43 S429 2003

Sobre las identidades. Pamplona : Universidad Pública de Navarra, [2001]

Sociología de la identidad. México : Miguel Angel Porrúa : Universidad Autónoma Metropolitana, Unidad Iztapalapa, 2002.

Song, Miri, 1964- Choosing ethnic identity. Cambridge, UK : Polity Press ; Oxford ; Malden, MA : Blackwell Publishing, 2003.
GN495.6 .S65 2003

Le territoire pensé. Sainte-Foy : Presses de l'Université du Québec, 2003.

Us and others. Amsterdam ; Philadelphia : John Benjamins Pub., c2002.
HM753 .U72 2002

GROUP IDENTITY - CROSS-CULTURAL STUDIES.
Us and others. Amsterdam ; Philadelphia : John Benjamins Pub., c2002.
HM753 .U72 2002

GROUP IDENTITY - FRANCE.
Osty, Florence. Le désir de métier. Rennes [France] : Presses universitaires de Rennes, [2003]

GROUP IDENTITY - LATIN AMERICA.
Latin America writes back. New York : Routledge, 2002.
PQ7081.A1 L336 2002

GROUP IDENTITY - POLITICAL ASPECTS.
Lamizet, Bernard. Politique et identité. Lyon : Presses universitaires de Lyon, 2002.

GROUP IDENTITY - POLITICAL ASPECTS - ISRAEL.
Rowland, Robert C., 1954- Shared land/conflicting identity. East lansing : Michigan State University Press, 2002.
DS119.7 .R685 2003

GROUP IDENTITY - RESEARCH - UNITED STATES.
Cornbleth, Catherine. Hearing America's youth. New York : P. Lang, c2003.
BF724.3.I3 .C67 2003

GROUP IDENTITY - ROME.
Studien zu antiken Identitäten. Würzburg : Ergon Verlag, c2001.
DG78 .S78 2001

GROUP IDENTITY - UNITED STATES.
Yanow, Dvora. Constructing "race" and "ethnicity" in America. Armonk, N.Y. : M.E. Sharpe, c2003.
HM753 .Y36 2003

GROUP PROBLEM SOLVING.
Group creativity. Oxford ; New York : Oxford University Press, 2003.
BF408 .G696 2003

Sawyer, R. Keith (Robert Keith) Group creativity. Mahwah, N.J. : L. Erlbaum Associates, 2003.
BF408 .S285 2003

GROUP RELATIONS TRAINING.
Katz, Judy H., 1950- White awareness. 2nd ed., rev. Norman : University of Oklahoma Press, c2003.
HT1523 .K37 2003

Group spirituality.
Grainger, Roger. Hove, East Sussex ; New York : Brunner-Routledge, 2003.
BL628.4 .G73 2003

GROUPS, ETHNIC. *See* **ETHNIC GROUPS.**

Groups in music.
Pavlicevic, Mercedes. London ; New York : Jessica Kingsley Publishers, 2003.
ML3920 .P2279 2003

GROUPS, SMALL. *See* **SMALL GROUPS.**

Growing global migration and its implications for the United States 42 p.
Growing global migration and its implications for the United States [electronic resource]. Electronic document. [Washington, D.C.? : National Intelligence Council, 2001]
CB161 .G768

Growing global migration and its implications for the United States / approved for publication by the National Foreign Intelligence Board under the authority of the Director of Central Intelligence. [Washington, D.C.?] : The Board, 2001. 42 p. : col. ill., col. maps ; 28 cm. "March 2001." "NIE 2001-02D." Includes bibliographical references. Also available via the World Wide Web (paper copy downloaded). SUMMARY: Examines the growing global movement of people and its implications for the United States. Study examines the political, economic, social, and security issues raised by increased migration, including the extent to which some countries may try to use migration as leverage in bilateral relations.
1. National security - United States - Forecasting. 2. Twenty-first century - Forecasts. I. United States. Central Intelligence Agency. II. United States. National Foreign Intelligence Board.

Growing global migration and its implications for the United States [electronic resource]. Electronic document. [Washington, D.C.? : National Intelligence Council, 2001] (NIE ; 2001-02D) System requirements: Adobe Acrobat Reader. Mode of access: Internet from the NIC web site. Address as of 3/26/03: http://www.odci.gov/nic/graphics/migration.pdf; current access is available via PURL. Title from title screen (viewed on Mar. 26, 2003). Text file (.pdf). "This estimate was approved for publication by the National Foreign Intelligence Board under the authority of the Director of Central Intelligence." "March 2001." Includes bibliographical references. URL: http://purl.access.gpo.gov/

GPO/LPS29038 Available in other form: Growing global migration and its implications for the United States 42 p. (OCoLC)48128862.
1. Emigration and immigration - Forecasting. 2. Twenty-first century - Forecasts. 3. National security - United States - Forecasting. I. United States. National Intelligence Council. II. United States. National Foreign Intelligence Board. III. Title: Growing global migration and its implications for the United States 42 p. IV. Series: NIE (Series) ; 2001-02 D.
CB161 .G768

Growing hope.
Thoele, Sue Patton. York Beach, ME : Conari Press, 2004.
BF575.H56 T48 2004

GROWTH. *See also* **HUMAN GROWTH.**
Fischer, Norman, 1946- Taking our places. 1st ed. San Francisco : HarperSanFrancisco, c2003.
BF710 .F57 2003

GROWTH, PERSONAL. *See* **SELF-ACTUALIZATION (PSYCHOLOGY).**

GROWTH (PSYCHOLOGY). *See* **MATURATION (PSYCHOLOGY); SUCCESS.**

Grrrls.
Leonel, Vange, 1963- São Paulo : Edições GLS, c2001.

Grrrls, garotas iradas.
Leonel, Vange, 1963- Grrrls. São Paulo : Edições GLS, c2001.

Grubbs, Geri A., 1943- Bereavement dreaming and the individuating soul / Geri A. Grubbs. Berwick, Me. : Nicolas-Hays, 2004. p. cm. CONTENTS: Understanding death -- By way of Gilgamesh -- Liminality and transcendence -- Bereavement dreaming -- From dismemberment to union : my story -- Saying our goodbyes : a young wife's story -- The heroic dimension : a mother's story -- A calling from the inner room : a brother's story -- Holiday for the dead -- Your bereavement dream sanctuary -- The herb of renewed life. ISBN 0-89254-079-6 (pbk. : alk. paper) DDC 155.9/37
1. Death in dreams. 2. Grief. 3. Bereavement - Psychological aspects. 4. Individuation (Psychology) I. Title.
BF1099.D4 G78 2004

Gruber, Eberhard.
Simone Weil, la passion de la raison. Paris : Harmattan, c2003.
B2430.W474 S55 2003

Gruber, Yehudah Yosef, ha-Leyi.
Sefer Kedushat ha-dibur. Bene Beraḳ : Yehudah Yosef Ha-leyi Gruber, 761- [2001-]

Grubin, David.
Young Dr. Freud [electronic resource]. [Alexandria, Va.?] : PBS, 2002.
BF109.F74

Gruenwald, Ithamar. Rituals and ritual theory in ancient Israel / by Ithamar Gruenwald. Leiden ; Boston : Brill, 2003. xiii, 278 p. ; 24 cm. (Brill reference library of ancient Judaism ; v. 10) Includes bibliographical references (p. [267]-274) and index. ISBN 90-04-12627-9 DDC 296.4/9
1. Bible - Criticism, interpretation, etc. 2. Judaism - Liturgy - Philosophy. 3. Ritual. 4. Judaism - History - To 70 A.D. I. Title. II. Series.
BM660 .G78 2003

Grulke, Wolfgang. Lessons in radical innovation : out of the box - straight to the bottom line / Wolfgang Grulke with Gus Silber. International ed. London : Financial Times Prentice Hall, 2002. xvi, 297 p. : ill., ports. ; 25 cm. Previous ed.: Benmore, South Africa : @One Communications, 2001. ISBN 0-273-65948-0 DDC 658.4063
1. Creative ability in business. I. Silber, Gus. II. Title.

Der Grund, die Not und die Freude des Bewusstseins : Beiträge zum Internationalen Symposion in Venedig zu Ehren von Wolfgang Marx / herausgegeben von Martin Asiáin ... [et al.]. Würzburg : Königshausen & Neumann, c2002. 211 p. ; 24 cm. Includes bibliographical references (p. [201]-205). ISBN 3-8260-2224-6 (pbk.)
1. Consciousness - Congresses. 2. Transcendentalism - Congresses. 3. Subjectivity - Congresses. 4. Philosophy, Modern - Congresses. I. Marx, Wolfgang. II. Asiáin, Martin, 1962-
B808.9 .G78 2002

Grundformen der Frömmigkeit im Mittelalter.
Angenendt, Arnold. München : Oldenbourg, 2003.

Grundherr, Michael von. Kants Ethik in modernen Gesellschaften / Michael von Grundherr. Hamburg : Lit, 2003. 109 p. ; 21 cm. (Philosophie und Ökonomik ; Bd. 4) Includes bibliographical references (p. [105]-109). ISBN 3-8258-6500-2 (pbk.) DDC 193
1. Kant, Immanuel, - 1724-1804. 2. Ethics. I. Title. II. Series.

Grundlagen und Modelle für den Hörgerichteten Spracherwerb / Hajo H. Frerichs, Joachim M.H. Neppert (Herausgeber). Villingen-Schwenningen : Neckar, c1995. 123 p. : ill. ; 21 cm. (Wissenschaftliche Beiträge aus Forschung, Lehre und Praxis zur Rehabilitation behinderter Kinder und Jugendlicher ; 42) Includes bibliographical references (p. 107-122). ISBN 3-7883-0281-X
1. Audio-lingual method (Language teaching) 2. Language acquisition. 3. Hearing impaired children - Education. I. Neppert, Joachim. II. Frerichs, Hajo H. III. Series.

Die Grundsteinmeditation als Schulungsweg : das Wirken der Weihnachtstagung in achtzig Jahren / Sergej O. Prokofieff (Hrsg.) ; mit einem Geleitwort von Marjorie Spock ; und Beiträgen von Werner Barfod ... [et al.]. Dornach : Verlag am Goetheanum, c2002. 414 p. : ill. ; 23 cm. Includes bibliographical references. ISBN 3-7235-1164-3 (pbk.)
1. Meditation. 2. Anthroposophy. 3. Christmas. I. Prokofieff, Sergej O., 1954- II. Barfod, Werner.

Grünewald, Lars. Zwölf Weltanschauungen : und ihre Anordnung in zwei Kreissystemen / Lars Grünewald. 1. Aufl. Borchen : Ch. Möllmann, 2001. 93 p. : ill. ; 21 cm. Includes bibliographical references. ISBN 3-931156-68-0
1. Philosophy. I. Title. II. Title: 12 Weltanschauungen

Grunewald, Michel, 1942- Moeller van den Brucks Geschichtsphilosophie / Michel Grunewald. Bern ; New York : P. Lang, c2001. 2 v. ; 21 cm. (Convergences, 1421-2854 ; vol. 17) Includes bibliographical references and indexes. Abstract in English and French. CONTENTS: Bd. 1. Ewige Urzeugung, ewige Anderswerdung, ewige Weitergabe / Michel Grunewald -- Bd. 2. Rasse und Nation : Meinungen über deutsche Dinge ; Der Untergang des Abendlandes / Arthur Moeller van den Bruck. ISBN 3-906765-43-1 DDC 901
1. Moeller van den Bruck, Arthur, - 1876-1925. 2. National socialism - History. 3. History - Philosophy. 4. Nationalism - Germany. 5. Historians - Germany. I. Moeller van den Bruck, Arthur, 1876-1925. II. Title. III. Series: Convergences (Université de Metz. Centre d'étude des périodiques de langue allemande) ; v. 17.
DD247.M59 G78 2001

GRUNGE MUSIC - SOCIAL ASPECTS - UNITED STATES.
Fletcher, John Wright. A hermeneutic study of generational music. 2002.

GRUNGE ROCK MUSIC. *See* **GRUNGE MUSIC.**

Grupos gnósticos.
Pinto Cañon, Ramiro. Madrid : Entinema, 2002.

Los grupos místico-espirituales de la actualidad.
Galovic, Jelena. México : Plaza y Valdés, 2002.
BL625 .G346 2002

Gscheidel, Karoline.
Augustin, Nicole. "Bewegung in Widersprüchen, Widersprüche in Bewegung bringen". Pfaffenweiler : Centaurus-Verlagsgesellschaft, 1998.
LC2873.G3 A94 1998

Gu dai de mei, jin dai de mei, xian dai de mei.
Chou, Laixiang. Di 1 ban. Changchun Shi : Dongbei shi fan da xue chu ban she : Jilin sheng Xin hua shu dian fa xing, 1996.
BH39 .C5455 1996 <Orien China>

Gu dai zuo jia lun.
Zhao, Yaotang. Di 1 ban. Jinan : Shandong you yi chu ban she, 1994.
PL2277 .C355 1994 <Asian China>

Gu dian wen xue yan jiu de hui gu yu zhan wang.
Shi ji zhi jiao de dui hua. Di 1 ban. Shanghai : Shanghai gu ji chu ban she : Xin hua shu dian Shanghai fa xing suo fa xing, 2000.

GUAIRÁ (PARAGUAY) - HISTORY.
Codas, Enrique, 1932- En los caminos de la historia. [Asunción, Paraguay] : El Lector, c2002.
F2695.G83 C63 2002

Gualandri, Isabella.
Tra IV e V secolo. Milano : Cisalpino, 2002.

Guan cheng shi ji.
Xu, Wenjing, 1667-1756? Di 1 ban. Beijing : Zhonghua shu ju : Xin hua shu dian Beijing fa xing suo fa xing, 1998.
PL2461.Z6 H77 1998

Guan, Dongsheng.
Taofen, 1895-1944. Taofen "Du zhe xin xiang". Di 1 ban. Beijing : Zhongguo cheng shi chu ban she, 1998.

Guan yin's chakra meditations.
LeBeau, Kara R. Boulder, Colo. : Mahasimhananda Press, c2001.

BF1442.C53 L43 2001

Guan yu li shi xing gai nian de zhe xue chan shi.
Han, Zhen. Li shi zhe xue. Di 1 ban. Kunming : Yunnan ren min chu ban she, 2002.
D16.8 .H3597 2002

"Guan zhui bian" yu Du Fu xin jie.
Motsch, Monika, 1942- [Mit Bambusrohr und Ahle von Qian Zhongshus Guanzhuibian zu einer Neubetrachtung Du Fus. Chinese] Di 1 ban. Shijiazhuang Shi : Hebei jiao yu chu ban she, 1997 (2002 printing)
PL2749.C8 Z85 1997

Guanyin.
Xing, Li. Beijing di 2 ban. Beijing : Xue yuan chu ban she, 2001.
BQ4710.A8 X564 2001

GUARDIAN ANGELS.
Sargent, Denny, 1956- Your guardian angel and you. York Beach, ME : Red Wheel/Weiser, 2004.
BF1275.G85 S27 2004

GUARDIAN ANGELS - JUVENILE LITERATURE.
Andrews, Ted, 1952- Spirits, ghosts & guardians. 1st ed. Jackson, Tenn. : Dragonhawk Pub., c2002.
BF1461 .A53 2002

Il guardiano della storiografia.
Sasso, Gennaro. 2. ed. [Bologna] : Società editrice il Mulino, c2002.

Guardians of the Celtic way.
Kelly, Jill. Rochester, Vt. : Bear & Co., c2003.
BF1411 .K45 2003

Guardians of the society.
Drews, Annette. Leipzig, Germany : Institut für Afrikanistik, Universität Leipzig, 2000.
BF1584.Z33 D44 2000

Guare, Richard.
Dawson, Peg. Executive skills in children and adolescents. New York : Guilford Press, 2004.
BF723.E93 D39 2004

Guareschi, Nueza Maria de Fátima.
Psicologia social nos estudos culturais. Petrópolis : Editora Voces, c2003.
HM1033 .P75 2003

GUARINI, GUARINO, 1624-1683 - CRITICISM AND INTERPRETATION.
Scott, John Beldon, 1946- Architecture for the shroud. Chicago : University of Chicago Press, c2003.
NA5621.T823 S36 2003

As águas de Oxalá.
Beniste, José. Rio de Janeiro, RJ, [Brazil] : Editora Bertrand Brasil, c2001 (2002 printing)
BL2592.C35 B46 2001

GUATEMALA - POLITICS AND GOVERNMENT - 1945-1985.
Acuerdos de paz y seguridad democrática en Guatemala. 1. ed. [Guatemala] : USAC, DIGI, [2002]

GUATEMALA - POLITICS AND GOVERNMENT - 1985-.
Acuerdos de paz y seguridad democrática en Guatemala. 1. ed. [Guatemala] : USAC, DIGI, [2002]

GUATEMALA - SOCIAL CONDITIONS.
Acuerdos de paz y seguridad democrática en Guatemala. 1. ed. [Guatemala] : USAC, DIGI, [2002]

Gučetić, Nikola Vitov, 1549-1610.
Dialogo d'amore. Serbo Croatian & Italian.
Gučetić, Nikola Vitov, 1549-1610. [Dialogo della bellezza. Serbo-Croatian & Italian] Dijalog o ljepoti = Dvojezično izd. Zagreb : Društvo hrvatskih književnika, 1995.
BH301.L65 G8318 1995

[Dialogo della bellezza. Serbo-Croatian & Italian]
Dijalog o ljepoti = Dialogo della bellezza ; Dijalog o ljubavi = Dialogo d'amore / Nikola Vitov Gučetić ; prijevod s talijanskoga Natka Badurina ; stručna redakcija Sanja Roić ; pogovor Ljerka Schiffler. Dvojezično izd. Zagreb : Društvo hrvatskih književnika, 1995. 360 p. : ill. ; 19 cm. (Bridge collection. Classical and contemporary Croatian writers ; 8/1995) Includes bibliographical references (p. 354-359). Serbo-Croatian (roman) translation and Italian original in parallel columns.
1. Plato - Views on love. 2. Aesthetics. 3. Love. I. Badurina, Natka. II. Roić, Sanja, 1953- III. Šifler-Premec, Ljerka, 1941- IV. Gučetić, Nikola Vitov, 1549-1610. Dialogo d'amore. Serbo-Croatian & Italian. V. Title. VI. Series: Bridge (Belgrade, Serbia) ; 1955/8.

BH301.L65 G8318 1995

Gudai de mei, jindai de mei, xiandai de mei.
Chou, Laixiang. Gu dai de mei, jin dai de mei, xian dai de mei. Di 1 ban. Changchun Shi : Dongbei shi fan da xue chu ban she : Jilin sheng Xin hua shu dian fa xing, 1996.
BH39 .C5455 1996 <Orien China>

Guénon, René.
[Etats multiples de l'être. English]
The multiple states of the being / Rene Guenon ; translated by Henry D. Fohr ; edited by Samuel D. Fohr. 2nd English ed. Ghent, NY : Sophia Perennis, c2001. xiv, 98 p. ; 23 cm. (Collected works of Rene Guenon) Includes bibliographical references and index. Originally published in French as Les Etats multiples de l'être in 1932. Translated from French. CONTENTS: Infinity & possibility -- Possibles & compossibles -- Being & non-being -- Foundation of the theory of the multiple states -- Relationships of unity & multiplicity -- Analogous considerations drawn from the study of the dream state -- The possibilities of individual consciousness -- Mentality as the characteristic element of human individuality -- The hierarchy of individual faculties -- The limits of the indefinite -- Principles of distinction between the states of being -- The two chaoses -- The spiritual hierarchies -- Reply to objections drawn from the plurality of beings -- The realization of the being through knowledge -- Knowledge & consciousness -- Necessity & contingency -- The metaphysical notion of freedom. ISBN 0-900588-59-4 (pbk. : alk. paper) ISBN 0-900588-60-8 (cloth : alk. paper) DDC 111
1. Guénon, René. 2. Ontology. I. Fohr, S. D., 1943- II. Title. III. Series: Guénon, René. Works. English. 2001.
BD312 .G813 2001

Works. English. 2001.
Guénon, René. [Etats multiples de l'être. English] The multiple states of the being. 2nd English ed. Ghent, NY : Sophia Perennis, c2001.
BD312 .G813 2001

GUÉNON, RENÉ.
Guénon, René. [Etats multiples de l'être. English] The multiple states of the being. 2nd English ed. Ghent, NY : Sophia Perennis, c2001.
BD312 .G813 2001

GUERILLAS. *See* **GUERRILLAS.**

Guerra Manzo, Enrique. Caciquismo y orden público en Michoacán, 1920-1940 / Enrique Guerra Manzo. 1. ed. México : El Colegio de México, Centro de Estudios Sociológicos, c2002. 311 p. : ill., maps ; 21 cm. Includes bibliographical references (p. 297-311). CONTENTS: Capitulo I. La disputa por el poder local en Michoacán -- Los grupos de poder en la década de 1920 -- El mugiquismo : la experiencia radical 1920-1922 -- Los grupos conservadores -- La gubernatura de Lázaro Cárdenas, 1928-1932 : una vía moderada -- Cárdenas y el Poder Judicial -- El control del Poder Legislativo -- El control de las masas : la Confederación Revolucionaria, Michoacana del trabajo, 1929-1932 -- Relaciones con el centro -- La CRMDT y los gobernadores poscadenistas, 1932-1938 -- Capitulo II. El arte de la mediación y la evasión del empaquetamiento en Taretan -- La lucha por la tierra -- El faccionalismo taretano y el problema del orden público -- Los intermediarios políticos y las organizaciones campesinas -- Capítulo III. El liderazgo agrario en el bajío Zamorano -- Antecedentes : porfiriato y revolución -- Ascenso del agrarismo 1920-1932 -- Descenso de los terratenientes: el caso de la familia García Martínez -- El poder del intermediario -- El poder en los ejidos -- Las fuentes institucionales del poder -- La disputa por el poder político -- Capítulo IV. Maestros rurales e intermediarios políticos en la batalla por las almas y las clientelas -- La política educativa del Estado posrevolucionario -- Política educativa y maestros rurales en Michoacán -- Caciques, pedagogos y maestros en la Cañada de los Once pueblos -- La escuela rural en la ciénaga de Zacapu y los pueblos del lago de CONTENTS: Pátzcuaro -- Maestros e intermediarios en la lucha por las clientelas en el municipio de Zamora -- Capítulo V. El caciquismo y las formas de la mediacińń política -- Kulakis, caciques y rancheros en los ejidos -- Las limitaciones del concepto de cacique -- Caciques e intermediarios formales. ISBN 968-12-1065-4 DDC 320.97235
1. Caciques (Indian leaders) - Mexico - Michoacán de Ocampo - History. 2. Land tenure - Mexico - Michoacán de Ocampo - History. 3. Power (Social sciences) 4. Michoacán de Ocampo (Mexico) - Politics and government. 5. Mexico - Politics and government - 1910-1946. I. Title.
F1219.3.P7 G84 2002

Guerrilla Girls (Group of artists).
Bitches, bimbos, and ballbreakers. New York, N.Y. : Penguin Books, 2003.
HQ1206 .B444 2003

GUERRILLAS - COLOMBIA.
Al oído de Uribe. 1a. ed. Bogotá, Colombia : Editorial Oveja Negra, 2002.

Téllez, Edgar. Diario íntimo de un fracaso. 1. ed. Bogotá, D.C., Colombia : Planeta, 2002.

Valencia, León. Adiós a la política, bienvenido la guerra. [Bogotá, Colombia?] : Intermedio, c2002.

Yusty, Miguel. Negociar en medio de la guerra. [Cali, Colombia] : Editorial Universidad Santiago de Cali, 2002.

"Guiados por el espíritu".
Noriega, José. Roma : Pontificia università lateranense ; [Milano] : Mursia, 2000.

Guide for humanists.
Hogan, Patrick Colm. Cognitive science, literature, and the arts. New York ; London : Routledge, 2003.
PN56.P93 H64 2003

GUIDE-POSTS. *See* **SIGNS AND SIGNBOARDS.**

Guide pour un apprenti philosophe.
Schlanger, Jacques. Paris : Presses universitaires de France, 2002.

Guide to gemstone sorcery.
Dunwich, Gerina. Dunwich's guide to gemstone sorcery. Franklin Lakes, NJ : New Page Books, c2003.
BF1442.P74 D86 2003

A guide to getting it : achieving abundance / E. Thomas Costello ... [et al.] ; foreword by Bijan Anjomi ; Marilyn Schwader, editor. 1st ed. Portland, Or. : Clarity of Vision Pub., 2002. x, 150 p. : ill. ; 23 cm. ISBN 0-9716712-1-4 DDC 158.1
1. Success - Psychological aspects. I. Costello, E. Thomas. II. Schwader, Marilyn. III. Title: Achieving abundance
BF637.S8 G84 2002

Guide to imagework.
Edgar, Iain R. London ; New York : Routledge, 2004.
BF367 .E34 2004

Guide to the Golden Dawn Enochian skrying tarot : your complete system for divination, skrying, and ritual magick / Chic Cicero ... [et al.]. St. Paul, Minn. : Llewellyn, 2004. p. cm. Includes bibliographical references. ISBN 0-7387-0201-3 DDC 133.3/2424
1. Enochian magic. 2. Tarot. 3. Divination. 4. Hermetic Order of the Golden Dawn. I. Cicero, Chic, 1936-
BF1623.E55 G65 2004

A guide to the hidden wisdom of kabbalah.
Laĭtman, Mikhaėl'. Thornhill, Ont. : Laitman Kabbalah Publishers, 2002.

GUIDEPOSTS. *See* **SIGNS AND SIGNBOARDS.**

GUIDES, SPIRIT. *See* **GUIDES (SPIRITUALISM).**

GUIDES (SPIRITUALISM).
Sargent, Denny, 1956- Your guardian angel and you. York Beach, ME : Red Wheel/Weiser, 2004.
BF1275.G85 S27 2004

Guiding choreography [microform].
Iannitelli, Leda Muhana. 1994.

Guiley, Rosemary. The dreamer's way : using proactive dreaming to heal and transform your life / Rosemary Ellen Guiley. New York : Berkley Books, 2004. p. cm. ISBN 0-425-19423-X DDC 154.6/3
1. Dreams. 2. Self-realization. 3. Dreams - Religious aspects. 4. Self-realization - Religious aspects. I. Title.
BF1099.S36 G85 2004

The encyclopedia of vampires, werewolves, and other monsters / Rosemary Ellen Guiley. New York, NY : Facts on File, 2004. p. cm. Includes bibliographical references and index. ISBN 0-8160-4685-9 (pbk. : alk. paper) DDC 133.4/23
1. Vampires - Encyclopedias. 2. Werewolves - Encyclopedias. 3. Monsters - Encyclopedias. I. Title.
BF1556 .G86 2004

The Guilford practical intervention in the schools series
Dawson, Peg. Executive skills in children and adolescents. New York : Guilford Press, 2004.
BF723.E93 D39 2004

The Guilford series on social and emotional development
Bierman, Karen L. Peer rejection. New York : Guilford Press, 2004.
BF723.R44 B54 2003

Underwood, Marion K. Social aggression among girls. New York ; London : Guilford Press, c2003.
BF723.A35 U53 2003

Guillaumin, Jean-Yves.
Boethius, d. 524. [De consolatione philosophiae. French] La consolation de philosophie. Paris : Belles lettres, 2002.

Guillerault, Gérard. Les deux corps du moi : schéma corporel et image du corps en psychanalyse / Gérard Guillerault ; [ouvrage publié sous la direction de Catherine Dolto-Tolitch]. Paris : Gallimard, c1996. 294 p. : ill. ; 23 cm. Includes bibliographical references. ISBN 2-07-074611-9
1. Body image. 2. Psychoanalysis. I. Dolto-Tolitch, Catherine. II. Title.
BF175.5.B64 G86 1996

Guillo, Dominique. Les figures de l'organisation : sciences de la vie et sciences sociales au XIXe siècle / Dominique Guillo. 1. éd. Paris : Presses universitaires de France, c2003. xiv, 428 p. ; 22 cm. (Sociologies) Includes bibliographical references (p. [413]-423) and index. ISBN 2-13-050140-0 DDC 300
1. Sociobiology. 2. Life sciences - History. 3. Social sciences - History. I. Title. II. Series.

Guillou, Jan, 1944- Häxornas försvarare : ett historiskt reportage / Jan Guillou. [Stockholm?] : Piratförlaget, c2002. 351 p. : ill. ; 22 cm. Includes bibliographical references (p. 351). ISBN 91-642-0037-X
1. Witches - Sweden - History - 17th century. 2. Trials (Witchcraft) - Sweden - History - 17th century. 3. Witches - Europe - History - 17th century. 4. Trials (Witchcraft) - Europe - History - 17th century. I. Title.
BF1584.S8 G85 2002

Gulābavijaya. Śrī Muhūrtarāja : Śrī Rājendra Hindī ṭīkā / saṅkalanakarttā Gulābavijayajī Mahārāja ; Hindī-ṭīkā lekhaka Jayaprabhavijayajī "Śramaṇa" Mahārāja ; [sampādaka evaṃ Saṃskṛta vyākhyākāra Govindarāmajī Dvivedī]. Dvitīyāvṛtti. Ji. Dhāra, Ma. Pra. : Rājendra Pravacana Kāryālaya, 1996. 32, 444 p. : ill. ; 25 cm. Paramapūjya vyākhyāna vācaspati Ācāryadeva Śrīmadvijaya Yatīndrasūrīśvarajī dīkṣā śatābdī ke upalakṣya meṃ saṃ. 1954-2054. SUMMARY: Treatise, on the proper time for religious observances according to Jaina astrology; includes Rajendra Hindi commentary. In Sanskrit; commentary in Hindi.
1. Jaina astrology. 2. Jainism - Rituals. I. Dvivedī, Govindarāma. II. Jayaprabhavijaya, Śramaṇa. Rājendra. III. Title. IV. Title: Muhūrtarāja
BF1714.J28+

Gullan-Whur, Margaret.
Discover graphology.
Gullan-Whur, Margaret. The secrets of your handwriting. [New ed.]. London : Thorsons, 1998.
BF891 .G846 1998

The secrets of your handwriting : a straightforward and practical guide to handwriting analysis / Margaret Gullan-Whur. [New ed.]. London : Thorsons, 1998. 176 p : ill. ; 22 cm. Rev. ed. of: Discover graphology. 1991. Includes bibliographical references (p. [174]) and index. ISBN 0-7225-3733-6 DDC 155.282
1. Graphology. I. Gullan-Whur, Margaret. Discover graphology. II. Title.
BF891 .G846 1998

Gumbiner, Jann. Adolescent assessment / Jann Gumbiner. Hoboken, N.J. : J. Wiley & Sons, c2003. xvi, 271 p. : ill. ; 26 cm. Includes bibliographical references (p. 255-262) and index. Publisher description URL: http://www.loc.gov/catdir/desc ription/wiley0310/2003000581.html Table of contents URL: http://www.loc.gov/catdir/toc/wiley031/2003000581.html ISBN 0-471-41981-8 (alk. paper) DDC 155.5/18/0287
1. Behavioral assessment of teenagers. 2. Teenagers - Psychological testing. I. Title.
BF724.25 .G86 2003

Gundersen, Lars Bo. Dispositional theories of knowledge : a defence of aetiological foundationalism / Lars Bo Gundersen. Aldershot, England ; Burlington, VT : Ashgate, c2003. 150 p. ; 24 cm. (Ashgate new critical thinking in philosophy) Includes bibliographical references (p. [143]-147) and index. ISBN 0-7546-3051-X (hardback) DDC 121
1. Knowledge, Theory of. 2. Disposition (Philosophy) 3. Modality (Theory of knowledge) I. Title. II. Series.
BD161 .G86 2003

Gunn, Geoffrey C. First globalization : the Eurasian exchange, 1500 to 1800 / Geoffrey C. Gunn. Lanham, Md. : Rowman & Littlefield, c2003. xviii, 342 p. ; 23 cm. (World social change) Includes bibliographical references (p. 285-323) and index. CONTENTS: The discovery canon -- Historical confabulators and literary geographers -- Observations on nature -- Catholic cosmologies -- Mapping Eurasia -- Enlightenment views of Asian Governance -- Civilizational encounters -- Livelihoods. ISBN 0-7425-2661-5

(cloth : alk. paper) ISBN 0-7425-2662-3 (pbk. : alk. paper) DDC 303.48/2504
1. East and West. 2. Europe - Relations - Asia. 3. Asia - Relations - Europe. 4. Europe - Civilization - Oriental influences. 5. Asia - Foreign public opinion, Western. I. Title. II. Series.
CB251 .G87 2003

GUNNING. See **HUNTING.**

Gunning, Stephanie, 1962-.
Mitchell, Shawne, 1958- [Exploring feng shui] Simple feng shui. New York : Gramercy Books, 2004.
BF1779.F4 M58 2004

GUNS. See **FIREARMS.**

Guns, violence, and identity among African American and Latino youth.
Wilkinson, Deanna Lyn, 1968- New York : LFB Scholarly Pub., 2003.
HQ799.2.V56 W55 2003

Günther, Klaus, 1957-.
Die Öffentlichkeit der Vernunft und die Vernunft der Öffentlichkeit. 1. Aufl. Frankfurt am Main : Suhrkamp, 2001.
B3258.H324 O34 2001

Günzel, Stephan, 1971- Anteile : Analytik, Hermeneutik, Politik / Stephan Günzel. Weimar : Verlag und Datenbank für Geisteswissenschaften, 2002. 135 p. ; 21 cm. Includes bibliographical references and index. ISBN 3-89739-297-6 (pbk.)
1. Philosophy, Modern - 20th century. I. Title.

Günzler, Claus, 1937-.
Schweitzer, Albert, 1875-1965. Vorträge, Vorlesungen, Aufsätze. München : C.H. Beck, c2003.

Guo, Qiyong, 1947-.
Tu, Wei-ming. [Selections. 2002] Du Weiming wen ji. Wuhan Shi : Wuhan chu ban she, 2002.
B5233.C6 T813 2002

Guo, Yanli. Zhong xi wen hua peng zhuang yu jin dai wen xue = Chinese and western cultural interaction and modern literature / Guo Yanli zhu. Di 1 ban. Jinan Shi : Shandong jiao yu chu ban she, 1999. 5, 3, 615 p. : ill. ; 21 cm. Includes bibliographical references. ISBN 7-5328-2797-6
1. Chinese literature - Western influences. 2. Literature, Comparative - Chinese and European. 3. Literature, Comparative - European and Chinese. 4. Literature, Modern - 20th century - History and criticism. 5. East and West. I. Title. II. Title: Chinese and western cultural interaction and modern literature
PL2274 .G86 1999

Guoron Ajquijay, Pedro. Retomemos la palabra-- : comunicación tradicional, comunicación alternativa, comunicación intercultural, comunicación interpersonal, comunicación grupal / Pedro Guoron Ajquijay, Federico Roncal Martínez. Guatemala, Guatemala : Editorial Saqil Tzij, 1995. 102 p. : ill. ; 21 cm. Includes bibliographical references (p. 101-102).
1. Communication. 2. Communication - Social aspects - Guatemala. I. Roncal Martínez, Federico. II. Title.

Gupta, Bina, 1947- CIT consciousness / Bina Gupta. New Delhi ; New York : Oxford University Press, 2003. xi, 203 p. ; 22 cm. (Foundations of philosophy in India) Includes bibliographical references (p. [187]-194) and index. ISBN 0-19-566113-3
1. Consciousness - Religious aspects - Hinduism. 2. Philosophy, Indic. I. Title. II. Series.
BF311+

Mohanty, Jitendranath, 1928- Explorations in philosophy. New Delhi ; New York : Oxford University Press, c2001-
B131.M54 M63 2001

Gupta, Śāligrāma.
Saṅkhyāparaka śabda kośa. 1. saṃskaraṇa. Ilāhābāda : Sāhitya Bhavana, 2002.
BF1623.P9+

Gupta, Suman, 1966- Re-reading Harry Potter / Suman Gupta. Houndmills, Basingstoke ; New York : Palgrave Macmillan, 2003. vii, 185 p. ; 22 cm. Includes bibliographical references (p. 177-182) and index. ISBN 1403912645 ISBN 1403912653 (pbk.) DDC 823/.914
1. Rowling, J. K. - Criticism and interpretation. 2. Rowling, J. K. - Characters - Harry Potter. 3. Children - Books and reading - English-speaking countries. 4. Children's stories, English - History and criticism. 5. Fantasy fiction, English - History and criticism. 6. Potter, Harry (Fictitious character) 7. Wizards in literature. 8. Magic in literature. I. Title.
PR6068.O93 Z68 2003

GURUS.
Sant Baba Ishar Singh Ji. Hardwar : Nanak-Dar Sant Baba Nand Singh Sant Baba Ishar Singh Spiritual Mission, 2002.
BL2017.9.I84 S27 2002

Gutfeld, Arnon. American exceptionalism : the effects of plenty on the American experience / Arnon Gutfeld. Brighton [England] ; Portland, Or. : Sussex Academic Press, 2002. xx. 252 p. ; 24 cm. Includes bibliographical references (p. 234-244) and index. ISBN 1-903900-08-5 (alk. paper) DDC 973
1. National characteristics, American. 2. Indians, Treatment of. 3. Indians of North America - Government relations. 4. Nature - Effect of human beings on - United States - History. 5. Frontier thesis. 6. United States - Civilization. 7. United States - Civilization - European influences. 8. United States - Territorial expansion. 9. Political culture - United States. I. Title.
E169.1 .G956 2002

Guthrie, Robert V. Even the rat was white a historical view of psychology / Robert V. Guthrie ; with new foreword by William H. Grier. Classic ed., 2nd ed. Boston, MA : Allyn and Bacon, 2004. xxi, 282 p. : ill. ; 23 cm. Includes bibliographical references (p. 254-270) and index. Table of contents URL: http://www.loc.gov/catdir/toc/fy037/2003041826.html ISBN 0-205-39264-4 DDC 150/.89/96073
1. Psychology - History. 2. African American psychologists. 3. Ethnopsychology - History. 4. Anthropometry - History. 5. Blacks - Psychology. I. Title.
BF105 .G87 2004

Gutiérrez, Javiera, 1964-.
Martoccia, María, 1957- Cuerpos frágiles, mujeres prodigiosas. Buenos Aires : Editorial Sudamericana, c2002.

Gutmann, Amy. Identity in democracy / Amy Gutmann. Princeton, N.J. : Princeton University Press, c2003. 246 p. ; 24 cm. Includes bibliographical references and index. ISBN 0-691-09652-X (alk. paper) DDC 322.4
1. Pressure groups. 2. Group identity. 3. Democracy. I. Title.
JF529 .G886 2003

Gutmann, Mathias.
Kultur, Handlung, Wissenschaft. 1. Aufl. Weilerswist : Velbrück Wissenschaft, 2002.
B67 .K853 2002

Gutmann, Matthew C., 1953-.
Perspectives on Las Américas. Maden, MA : Blackwell Pub., c2003.
F1410 .P48 2003

Guttman, Howard M. When goliaths clash : managing executive conflict to build a more dynamic organization / Howard M. Guttman. New York ; London : AMACOM, c2003. xvii, 250 p. ; 24 cm. Includes bibliographical references and index. ISBN 0-8144-0749-8 DDC 658.4/053
1. Conflict management. 2. Organizational change. I. Title.
HD42 .G88 2003

Guyomard, Patrick.
Depuis Lacan. Paris : Aubier, c2000.
BF173 .D44 2000

Gwyn, Richard, PhD.
Discourse, the body, and identity. Basingstoke, Hampshire ; New York : Palgrave Macmillan, 2003.
HM636 .D57 2003

Gyermek a halál kapujában.
Polcz, Alaine. Budapest : PONT, c2001.
BF723.D3 P65 2001

A gyermekrajzok esztétikuma.
Gerő, Zsuzsa. Budapest : Flaccus Kiadó, 2003.
BF723.D7 G47 2003

Gypsy magic.
Cooper, Patrinella. Boston : Weiser Books, 2002.
BF1622.R65 C66 2002

Gypsy witchcraft & magic.
Buckland, Raymond. 1st ed. St. Paul, Minn. : Llewellyn Publications, 2001, c1998.

Gypsy witchcraft and magic.
Buckland, Raymond. Gypsy witchcraft & magic. 1st ed. St. Paul, Minn. : Llewellyn Publications, 2001, c1998.

Gyug, Richard, 1954-.
Medieval cultures in contact. New York : Fordham University Press, 2003.
CB351 .M3922 2003

H. D. (Hilda Doolittle), 1886-1961.
Analyzing Freud. New York : New Directions, c2002.
BF109.F74 A845 2002

H. D. (HILDA DOOLITTLE), 1886-1961 - CORRESPONDENCE.
Analyzing Freud. New York : New Directions, c2002.
BF109.F74 A845 2002

The H-factor.
Tolchard, Guylaine. Cary, N.C. : Process Viewpoint Pub., c2002.
BF511 .T65 2002

HĀ' (THE ARABIC LETTER).
Dāwūd, Muḥammad 'Īsá. al-Jafr li-Sayyidinā 'Alī. al-Muhandisīn [Giza] : Madbūlī al-Ṣaghīr, [2003]
BF1771+

Haanel, Charles F. (Charles Francis), b. 1866. The master key system / by Charles F. Haanel ; edited by Anthony R. Michalski. 1st ed. Wilkes-Barre, Pa. : Kallisti Pub., c2000. vii, 226 p. : ill. ; 21 cm.
1. New Thought. I. Michalski, Anthony R. II. Title.
BF639 .H132 2000

Haarmann, Harald. Geschichte der Schrift / Harald Haarmann. Originalausg. München : C.H. Beck, c2002. 128 p. : ill. ; 18 cm. (C.H. Beck Wissen in der Beck'schen Reihe) Includes bibliographical references and index. ISBN 3-406-47998-7 (pbk.)
1. Writing - History. I. Title. II. Series: Beck'sche Reihe. Wissen.

Habermas, Jürgen. Kommunikatives Handeln und detranszendentalisierte Vernunft / Jürgen Habermas. Stuttgart : Reclam, c2001. 87 p. ; 15 cm. (Universal-Bibliothek ; 18164) Includes bibliographical references. ISBN 3-15-018164-X (pbk.)
1. Communication - Philosophy. 2. Philosophy, Modern - 20th century. I. Title. II. Series: Universal-Bibliothek (Stuttgart, Germany) ; Nr. 18164.
P91 .H33 2001

Die Öffentlichkeit der Vernunft und die Vernunft der Öffentlichkeit. 1. Aufl. Frankfurt am Main : Suhrkamp, 2001.
B3258.H324 O34 2001

[Wahrheit und Rechtfertigung. English]
Truth and justification / Jürgen Habermas ; edited and with translations by Barbara Fultner. Cambridge, Mass. : MIT Press, c2003. xxii, 327 p. ; 24 cm. (Studies in contemporary German social thought) Includes bibliographical references (p. [293]-319) and index. ISBN 0-262-08318-3 (hc : alk. paper) DDC 100
1. Philosophy. I. Fulmer, Barbara. II. Title. III. Series.
B3258.H323 W3413 2003

HABERMAS, JÜRGEN - CONGRESSES.
Die Öffentlichkeit der Vernunft und die Vernunft der Öffentlichkeit. 1. Aufl. Frankfurt am Main : Suhrkamp, 2001.
B3258.H324 O34 2001

HABIT. See also **FOOD HABITS; HEALTH BEHAVIOR.**
Claiborn, James. The habit change workbook. Oakland, CA : New Harbinger Publications : Distributed in the U.S.A. by Publishers Group West, c2001.
BF337.B74 C57 2001

Robey, Dan. The power of positive habits. Miami, Fla. : Abritt Pub. Group, c2003.
BF335 .R56 2003

HABIT BREAKING - PROBLEMS, EXERCISES, ETC.
Claiborn, James. The habit change workbook. Oakland, CA : New Harbinger Publications : Distributed in the U.S.A. by Publishers Group West, c2001.
BF337.B74 C57 2001

The habit change workbook.
Claiborn, James. Oakland, CA : New Harbinger Publications : Distributed in the U.S.A. by Publishers Group West, c2001.
BF337.B74 C57 2001

Habit Habitat Habitus.
Simard-Laflamme, Carole. Trois-Rivières, Québec, Canada : Editions d'art Le Sabord, [2002]
TT507 .S653 2002

Habitar la tierra / Casalla ... [et al.]. Buenos Aires : Grupo Editor Altamira, 2002. 248 p. ; 22 cm. (Biblioteca de Filosofía) Includes bibliographical references. ISBN 9879423364
1. Civilization, Modern - Philosophy. 2. Civilization, Modern - Psychological aspects. 3. Civilization, Modern - Religious aspects. 4. Postmodernism - Religious aspects. 5. Postmodernism - Psychological aspects. 6. Globalization - Social aspects. 7. Power (Social sciences) 8. Social change - Latin America. 9. Urbanization - Philosophy. 10. Cultural relations. 11. Technology and civilization. I. Casalla, Mario C. II. Series: Biblioteca de filosofía (Buenos Aires, Argentina)
CB358 .H32 2002

Habu, Junko, 1959-.
Beyond foraging and collecting. New York : Kluwer Academic/Plenum Publishers, c2002.
GN388 .B49 2002

Haché, Alain, 1970- The physics of hockey / Alain Haché. Baltimore : Johns Hopkins University Press, 2002. xiii, 184 p. : ill. ; 23 cm. Includes bibliographical references (p. 177) and index. CONTENTS: Introduction -- On ice -- Skating -- Shooting -- Collisions and protective gear -- Keeping the net -- The game -- Appendix. ISBN 0-8018-7071-2 DDC 530
1. Physics. 2. Hockey. 3. Force and energy. I. Title.
QC28 .H23 2002

Hachet, Pascal. Psychanalyse d'un choc esthétique : la villa Palagonia et ses visiteurs / Pascal Hachet. Paris, France : Harmattan, c2002. 144 p. ; 22 cm. (Collection "Psychanalyse et civilisations". Série "Trouvailles et retrouvailles") Includes bibliographical references. ISBN 2-7475-2853-7 DDC 150
1. Villa Palagonia (Bagheria, Italy) 2. Monsters in art. 3. Psychoanalysis and art. 4. Aesthetics, Modern - 18th century. I. Title. II. Series: Psychanalyse et civilisations. Série Trouvailles et retrouvailles.

Hacia una pedagogía de las experiencias de las mujeres.
Alonso, Graciela. 1. ed. Buenos Aires : Miño y Dávila, 2002.

Hackett, Gail.
Counseling diverse populations. 3rd ed. Boston, Mass. : McGraw-Hill, c2004.
BF637.C6 C6372 2004

Hackett, Jeremiah.
Medieval Europe, 814-1350. Detroit, MI : Gale Group, c2002.
D102 .M38 2001

Hackney, Harold, 1935-.
Cormier, L. Sherilyn (Louise Sherilyn), 1946- Counseling strategies and interventions. 6th ed. Boston : Pearson, 2004.
BF637.C6 H25 2004

HaCohen, Ruth.
Katz, Ruth, 1927- Tuning the mind. New Brunswick, N.J. : Transaction Publishers, c2003.
ML3838 .K28 2003

Haddad, Gérard. Le jour où Lacan m'a adopté : mon analyse avec Lacan / Gérard Haddad. Paris : Bernard Grasset, c2002. 374 p. ; 23 cm. ISBN 2-246-42911-0
1. Haddad, Gérard. 2. Lacan, Jacques, - 1901- 3. Psychoanalysis. I. Title.

HADDAD, GÉRARD.
Haddad, Gérard. Le jour où Lacan m'a adopté. Paris : Bernard Grasset, c2002.

Haddock, Lynda.
Cruddas, Leora. Girls' voices. Stoke on Trent ; Sterling VA : Trentham Books, 2003.
LA631.82 .C783 2003

HADEWIJCH, 13TH CENT.
Van Löben Sels, Robin E., 1938- A dream in the world. New York, NY : Brunner-Routledge, 2003.
BF175.5.D74 V36 2003

Hadikin, Ruth. The bullying culture : cause, effect, harm reduction / Ruth Hadikin, Muriel O'Driscoll. Oxford ; Boston : Books for Midwives, 2000. 179 p. : ill. Includes bibliographical references (p. 172-173) and index. ISBN 0-7506-5201-2 DDC 658.3/145
1. National Health Service (Great Britain) 2. Midwifery - organization & administration - Great Britain. 3. Prejudice - Great Britain. 4. Social Behavior - Great Britain. 5. State Medicine - Great Britain. 6. Workplace - psychology - Great Britain. 7. Bullying in the workplace. 8. Midwifery. 9. Midwives - Supervision of. I. O'Driscoll, Muriel. II. Title.
BF637.B85 H33 2000

Hadjistavropoulos, Thomas.
Pain. Mahwah, N.J. : Lawrence Erlbaum, 2003.
BF515 .P29 2003

HAECCEITY (PHILOSOPHY). See **INDIVIDUATION (PHILOSOPHY).**

Haegel, Florence.
Aux frontières des attitudes. Paris, France : Harmattan, c2002.

Haen, Renate. Du bist die Göttin ; weiblichkeit im Neuen Zeitalter / Renate Haen. 1. Auf. Bergish Gladbach : Bastei Lübbe, 1999. 316 p. ; 18 cm. (Bastei-Lübbe-Taschenbuch; 70136) Includes bibliographical references (p. 308-[310])
1. Feminity. 2. Women - Psychology. I. Title. II. Title: Weiblichkeit im Neuen Zeitalter III. Series. IV. Series: Atlantis

HAFTAROT - COMMENTARIES.
Koll, Shmuel, 1938- Sefer Ra'yonot u-mesarim. Yerushalayim : S. Kol, 761- [2001-

HAGADAH (TALMUD). See **AGGADA.**

Hagberg, Karen A., 1943- Stage presence from head to toe : a manual for musicians / Karen A. Hagberg. Lanham, Md. : Scarecrow Press, 2003. xiv, 109 p. : ill. ; 23 cm. Includes bibliographical references (p. 103-105) and index. CONTENTS: Stage presence -- The soloist -- The page turner -- The small ensemble (no conductor) -- The large vocal ensemble -- The orchestra -- The conductor as leader -- On the day of the concert -- The stage and its furnishings -- Nonperforming personnel -- Auditions and competitions -- How to teach stage presence. ISBN 0-8108-4777-9 (pbk. : alk. paper) DDC 781.4/3
1. Music - Performance. 2. Concerts - Handbooks, manuals, etc. 3. Concert etiquette. 4. Self-confidence. I. Title.
ML3795 .H13 2003

Hagen, Elizabeth P., 1915-.
Lohman, David F. Cognitive Abilities Test, form 6, all levels. Chicago (8420 Bryn Mawr, Chicago 60631) : Riverside Pub., c2001.
BF432.5.C64 L64 2001

Lohman, David F. Interpretive guide for teachers and counselors. Itasca, IL : Riverside Pub., c2001.
BF432.5.C64 L65 2001

Hagen, Steve, 1945- Buddhism is not what you think : finding freedom beyond beliefs / Steve Hagen. 1st ed. [San Francisco] : HarperSanFrancisco, c2003. xv, 255 p. : ill. ; 22 cm. ISBN 0-06-050723-3 (cloth) DDC 294.3
1. Buddhism - Doctrines. 2. Truth - Religious aspects - Buddhism. I. Title.
BQ4570.F7 H34 2003

HAGGADA (TALMUD). See **AGGADA.**

HAGGADAH (TALMUD). See **AGGADA.**

HAGGLING. See **NEGOTIATION.**

Hägglund, Martin. Kronofobi : essäer om tid och ändlighet / Martin Hägglund. Stockholm : B. Östlings Bokförlag Symposion, 2002. 241 p. ; 22 cm. Includes bibliographical references (p. 236-240) and index. ISBN 91-7139-573-3
1. Derrida, Jacques. 2. Time. 3. Finite, The. 4. Deconstruction. I. Title.

HAGIOGRAPHY.
Lozito, Vito. Agiografia, magia, superstizione. Bari : Levante, [1999]
BF1775 .L69 1999

Pérez-Embid Wamba, Javier. Hagiología y sociedad en la España medieval. Huelva : Universidad de Huelva, 2002.
BX4659.S8 P47 2002

Thompson, Anne Booth. Everyday saints and the art of narrative in the South English legendary. Aldershot, England ; Burlington, Vt. : Ashgate, c2003.
PR2143.S543 T48 2003

Hagiología y sociedad en la España medieval.
Pérez-Embid Wamba, Javier. Huelva : Universidad de Huelva, 2002.
BX4659.S8 P47 2002

Hague, Angela. Fiction, intuition, & creativity : studies in Brontë, James, Woolf, and Lessing / Angela Hague. Washington, D.C. : Catholic University of America Press, c2003. ix, 329 p. ; 24 cm. Includes bibliographical references (p. 311-320) and index. ISBN 0-8132-1314-2 DDC 823.009
1. English fiction - History and criticism - Theory, etc. 2. Fiction - History and criticism - Theory, etc. 3. Creation (Literary, artistic, etc.) 4. Intuition. I. Title. II. Title: Fiction, intuition, and creativity
PR826 .H28 2003

Hahn, Lewis Edwin, 1908-.
The philosophy of Marjorie Grene. Chicago : Open Court, c2002.
B945.G734 P47 2002

Hahn, Robert, 1952-.
Couprie, Dirk, 1940- Anaximander in context. Albany : State University of New York Press, c2003.
B208.Z7 C68 2003

Hahnel, Robin.
Monkeywrenching the new world order [sound recording]. Oakland, Calif : AK Press ; San Francisco, CA : Alternative Tentacles Records, 2001.

Hähner, Olaf. Historische Biographik : die Entwicklung einer geschichtswissenschaftlichen Darstellungsform von der Antike bis ins 20. Jahrhundert / Olaf Hähner. Frankfurt am Main ; New York : Lang, 1999. xii, 289 p. ; 21 cm. (Europäische Hochschulschriften. Reihe III, Geschichte und ihre Hilfswissenschaften = Publications universitaires européennes. Série III, Histoire, sciences auxiliares de l'histoire = European university studies. Series III, History and allied sciences ; Bd. 829) ISBN 3-631-34650-6
1. Biography - History. 2. Historiography. I. Title. II. Series: Europäische Hochschulschriften. Reihe III, Geschichte und ihre Hilfswissenschaften ; Bd. 829.

HAITI - CIVILIZATION - PHILOSOPHY.
Merdalor, Jean. Pensées mortelles. Port-au-Prince, Haiti : Editions Choucoune, 1999.
1. Black author.

HAITI - RELIGION.
Hurbon, Laënnec. Dieu dans le vaudou haïtien. Nouv. éd. Paris : Maisonneuve et Larose, 2002.
1. Black author.

Hakarat ha-tov.
Kuntres Kevod ha-Torah. Bene Berak : ha-Mehaber, 761 [2000 or 2001]

HAKOHEN, NOAH RAPHAEL.
Jarashow, Jonathan. The silent psalms of our son. Jerusalem, Israel : Feldheim Publishers, c2001.

HALACHA. See **JEWISH LAW.**

Halachic residue in the Zohar.
Ta-Shma, Israel M. ha-Nigleh sheba-nistar. Nusah murhav. [Tel Aviv] : ha-Kibuts ha-me'uhad, c2001.

HALAKHA. See **JEWISH LAW.**

Halász, László, 1933-.
Az Általánostól a különösig. [Budapest] : Gondolat : MTA Pszichológiai Kutatóintézet, c2002.
BF128.H8 A44 2002

Halbertal, Moshe. Ben Torah le-hokhmah : Rabi Menahem ha-Me'iri u-va'ale ha-halakhah ha-Maimonim be-Provans / Mosheh Halbertal. Yerushalayim : Hotsa'at sefarim 'a. sh. Y. L. Magnes, ha-Universitah ha-'Ivrit, 760, 2000. 239 p. ; 23 cm. Added title page title: Between Torah and wisdom : Rabbi Menachem ha-Meiri and the Maimonidean halakhists in Provence. Includes bibliographical references (p. 232-232) and indexes. ISBN 9654930552
1. Meiri, Menahem ben Solomon, - 1249-1306. 2. Maimonides, Moses, - 1135-1204. 3. Philosophy, Jewish. 4. Judaism - France - History - To 1500. 5. Jewish law - Philosophy. 6. Philosophy, Medieval. I. Title. II. Title: Between Torah and wisdom : Rabbi Menachem ha-Meiri and the Maimonidean halakhists in Provence
BM755.M54 H35 2000

Halbwachs et la mémoire sociale.
Namer, Gérard. Paris : L'Harmattan, c2000.
BF378.S65 N36 2000

HALBWACHS, MAURICE, 1877-1945.
Kontexte und Kulturen des Erinnerns. Konstanz : UVK Verlagsgesellschaft, 2002.
BF378.S65 K65 2002

Namer, Gérard. Halbwachs et la mémoire sociale. Paris : L'Harmattan, c2000.
BF378.S65 N36 2000

Haldane, John. An intelligent person's guide to religion / John Haldane. London : Duckworth, 2003. 224 p. ; 18 cm. Includes bibliographical references (p. 218-220) and index. ISBN 0-7156-2867-4
1. Religion. I. Title.

Spirituality, philosophy and education. London ; New York : RoutledgeFalmer, 2003.
BV4501.3 .S65 2003

Halfon, Eliyahu ben Hayim.
Ateret Shelomoh.
Halfon, Eliyahu ben Hayim. Shir ha-shirim. [Israel] : Or tsah hadpasah ve-hafatsah shel sipre Yahadut, [2001]

Shir ha-shirim : 'im perush "'Ateret Shelomoh" / liket ve-'arakh be-tseruf be'urim ve-hashlamot ... Eliyahu b. r. Hayim Halfon. [Israel] : Or tsah hadpasah ve-hafatsah shel sipre Yahadut, [2001] "Ve-hu likutim 'al ha-sefer be-hamishah derakhim : 1. Derekh Peshat, 2. derekh Remaz, 3. derekh Derash, 4. derekh Hasidut 5. derekh Sod, 6. perush "ma'gale tsedek" ce-derekh Sod ..."--On t.p.
1. Bible. - O.T. - Song Of Solomon - Commentaries - History and criticism. 2. Cabala. I. Halfon, Eliyahu ben Hayim. 'Ateret Shelomoh. II. Abi-Hasira, Jacob ben Masoud, 1808-1880. Ma'gele tsedek. III. Title. IV. Title: Bible. O.T. Song of Solomon. 2003.

Halikhot Teman.
Kafah, Yosef, 1917- Mahad. 5, metukenet. Yerushalayim : Mekhon Ben-Tsevi le-heker kehilot Yiśra'el ba-Mizrah : Yad Yitshak ben-Tsevi : ha-Universitah ha-'Ivrit bi-Yerushalayim, 2002.

Hall, Adelaide S. (Adelaide Susan), b. 1857.
[Glossary of important symbols in their Hebrew, pagan, and Christian forms]
Important symbols in their Hebrew, pagan, and Christian forms / compiled by Adelaide S. Hall. Berwick, Me. : Ibis Press, 2003. p. cm. Originally published: A glossary of important symbols in their Hebrew, pagan, and Christian forms. Boston : Bates & Guild Co., 1912. Includes bibliographical references and index. ISBN 0-89254-074-5 (pbk. : alk. paper) DDC 302.2/223
1. Symbolism. I. Title.
BF1623.S9 H35 2003

HALL, CAROL, 1936-.
Vint/age 2001 conference : [videorecording]. New York, c2001.

Hall, Carol, 1936- panelist.
Vint/age 2001 conference : [videorecording]. New York, c2001.

Hall, Christopher, 1948-.
Constructing clienthood in social work and human services. London ; New York : Jessica Kingsley Publishers, c2003.
HV40 .C6615 2003

Hall, Judy, 1943- The intuition handbook : access your hidden powers and transform your life / Judy Hall. London : Vega, 2003. 320 p. : ill. ; 16 cm. Includes bibliographical references (p. 318) and index. Publisher description URL: http://www.loc.gov/catdir/description/ste031/2003464617.html ISBN 1-84333-696-0 DDC 153.44
1. Intuition. 2. Self-actualization (Psychology) 3. Success. I. Title.
BF315.5 .H35 2003

Hall, L. Michael. The sourcebook of magic : a comprehensive guide to the technology of NLP / L. Michael Hall & Barbara P. Belnap. Wales, UK ; Williston, VT : Crown House Pub. Ltd., 2002. xix, 312 p. ; 24 cm. Includes bibliographical references (p. 293-299) and index. ISBN 1-89983-622-5
1. Neurolinguistic programming. I. Belnap, Barbara P. II. Title.
BF637.N46 H36 2002

Hall, Manly Palmer, 1901- The secret teachings of all ages : an encyclopedic outline of Masonic, Hermetic, Qabbalistic, and Rosicrucian symbolical philosophy : being an interpretation of the secret teachings concealed within the rituals, allegories, and mysteries of the ages / by Manly P. Hall ; color illustrations by J. Augustus Knapp. Reader's ed. New York : Jeremy P. Tarcher/Putnam, 2003. p. cm. Originally published: Los Angeles, Calif : Philosophical Research Society, 1928. Includes bibliographical references and index. ISBN 1-58542-250-9 (alk. paper) DDC 135/.4
1. Occultism - History. 2. Symbolism. 3. Mysteries, Religious. 4. Secret societies. 5. Freemasonry - Symbolism. 6. Hermetism. 7. Cabala. I. Title.
BF1411 .H3 2003

Hall, Nancy Wilson.
Zigler, Edward, 1930- The first three years & beyond. New Haven : Yale University Press, c2002.
HQ767.9 .Z543 2002

Hall, Rowan.
Telesco, Patricia, 1960- Animal spirit. Franklin Lakes, NJ : New Page Books, c2002.
BF1623.A55 T445 2002

HALL, STUART.
Rojek, Chris. Stuart Hall. Cambridge, UK : Polity in association with Blackwell, 2003.
HM621 .R64 2003

Halle Saint-Pierre (Museum).
Art spirite, mediumnique, visionnaire. [Paris] : Hoëbeke, c1999.
BF1313 .A78 1999

HALLOWEEN.
Dunwich, Gerina. The pagan book of Halloween. New York : Penguin/Compass, 2000.
BF1566 .D867 2000

Hallowell, Edward M. Dare to forgive / Edward M. Hallowell. Deerfield Beach, Fla. : Health Communications, 2004. p. cm. Includes bibliographical references. ISBN 0-7573-0010-3 (tp) DDC 155.9/2
1. Forgiveness. I. Title.
BF637.F67 H35 2004

HALLUCINATIONS AND ILLUSIONS.
Garifullin, Ramil', 1962- Illi͡uzionizm lichnosti. Kazanʹ : [s.n.], 1997.
BF491 .G37 1997

Geiger, John, 1960- Chapel of extreme experience. 1st ed. Toronto, Ont. : Gutter Press, c2002.
QP495 .G45 2002

HALLUCINATIONS AND ILLUSIONS - PSYCHOLOGY.
Carter, Rita, 1949- Exploring consciousness. Berkeley : University of California Press, c2002.
BF311 .C289 2002

HALLUCINOGENIC DRUGS. See **LSD (DRUG).**

HALLUCINOGENS - PHARMACOLOGY.
Dobkin de Rios, Marlene. LSD, spirituality, and the creative process. Rochester, Vt. : Park Street Press, c2003.
BF209.L9 D57 2003

HaloEyes. Tarot : the Halo method / by HaloEyes. Bloomington : 1stBooks Library, c2002. xii, 154 p. : ill. ; 23 cm. Includes index. ISBN 1403320845 (pbk. : acid-free paper) ISBN 1403320853 (hardcover) ISBN 1403320837 (e-book) DDC 133..3/2424
1. Tarot. 2. Tarot cards. I. Title.
BF1879.T2 H3355 2002

Halpern, Diane F.
Weiten, Wayne, 1950- Psychology. 6th ed. Australia ; Belmont, CA : Thomson/Wadsworth, c2004.
BF121 .W38 2004

Halpern, Leslie, 1960- Dreams on film : the cinematic struggle between art and science / Leslie Halpern ; foreword by Robert Smither. Jefferson, NC ; London : McFarland, 2003. viii, 201 p. ill. ; 23 cm. Filmography : p. 181-190. Includes bibliographical references and index. ISBN 0-7864-1596-7 (pbk.)
1. Dreams in motion pictures. 2. Dreams. I. Title.

Halpern, Richard, 1954- Shakespeare's perfume : sodomy and sublimity in the Sonnets, Wilde, Freud, and Lacan / Richard Halpern. Philadelphia : University of Pennsylvania Press, c2002. 125 p. ; 23 cm. ([New cultural studies]) Series statement on jacket. Includes bibliographical references (p. [117]-121) and index. CONTENTS: Shakespeare's perfume -- Theory to die for : Oscar Wilde's The portrait of Mr. W.H. -- Freud's Egyptian Renaissance : Leonardo da Vinci and a memory of his childhood -- Lacan's anal thing : the ethics of psychoanalysis. ISBN 0-8122-3661-0 (acid-free paper) DDC 820.9/353
1. Shakespeare, William, - 1564-1616. - Sonnets. 2. Shakespeare, William, - 1564-1616 - In literature. 3. Wilde, Oscar, - 1854-1900. - Portrait of Mr W.H. 4. Freud, Sigmund, - 1856-1939. - Kindheitserinnerung des Leonardo da Vinci. 5. Lacan, Jacques, - 1901- - Ethique de la psychanalyse, 1959-1960. 6. Sonnets, English - History and criticism - Theory, etc. 7. Psychoanalysis and literature. 8. Sublime, The, in literature. 9. Sodomy in literature. I. Title. II. Series.
PR2848 .H25 2002

Hamann, Cornelia, 1953- From syntax to discourse : pronominal clitics, null subjects and infinitives in child language / by Cornelia Hamann. Dordrecht, The Netherlands ; Boston : Kluwer Academic Publishers, c2002. xix, 369 p. : ill. ; 23 cm. (Studies in theoretical psycholinguistics ; v. 29) Includes bibliographical references (p. 345-360) and index. ISBN 1402004397 (acid-free paper) ISBN 1402004400 (pbk.) DDC 401/.93
1. Language acquisition. 2. Grammar, Comparative and general - Syntax. 3. Government-binding theory (Linguistics) I. Title. II. Series.
P118 .H327 2002

Hamel, Gary. Leading the revolution : how to thrive in turbulent times by making innovation a way of life / Gary Hamel. Rev. and updated hardcover ed. [Boston, Mass.] : Harvard Business School Press, c2002. 337 p. : ill. ; 24 cm. "Fully revised, with a new introduction"-- Cover. "This revised and updated hardcover edition is here reprinted by arrangement with Plume ..." -- T.p. verso. Includes bibliographical references and index.
1. Creative ability in business. 2. Strategic planning. I. Title.

Hamel, Jean-Marie. Living from the inside out : how to get to the heart of everything that matters / Jean-Marie Hamel. 1st ed. New York : Harmony Books, 2004. p. cm. Includes bibliographical references and index. CONTENTS: Surrendering who you are not -- Opening to who you are -- Choosing your attitude -- Loving fearlessly -- Redefining success -- Co-creating a masterpiece -- Using everything as a learning experience -- Enjoying a soulful life. ISBN 1400052742 (hardcover) DDC 158.1
1. Self-actualization (Psychology) I. Title.
BF637.S4 H34 2004

Hamilton, Bernard, 1932- The Christian world of the Middle Ages / Bernard Hamilton. Stroud, Glos : Sutton, 2003. xxvii, 256 p. [16] p. of plates : ill. (some col.), maps, ports. ; 26 cm. Includes bibliographical references (p. 242-245) and index. Errata slip is inserted. ISBN 0-7509-2405-5 DDC 270.3
1. Civilization, Christian - History. 2. Church history - Primitive and early church, ca. 30-600. 3. Church history - Middle Ages, 600-1500. I. Title.

Hamilton-Parker, Craig. Fantasy dreaming / Craig Hamilton-Parker ; with illustrations by Steinar Lund and Lynne Milton. New York : Sterling Pub., c2002. 144 p. : col. ill. ; 24 cm. Includes index. Publisher description URL: http://www.loc.gov/catdir/description/ste031/2003268513.html ISBN 0-8069-5478-7 DDC 154.6/3
1. Dream interpretation. 2. Symbolism (Psychology) 3. Dreams. I. Title.
BF1091 .H347 2002

Hammerstein, Peter, 1949-.
Dahlem Workshop on Genetic and Cultural Evolution of Cooperation (90th : 2002 : Berlin, Germany) Genetic and cultural evolution of cooperation. Cambridge, Mass. : MIT Press in cooperation with Dahlem University Press, c2003.
BF637.H4 D25 2002

The Hampton Press communication series. Communication alternatives
Communication, a different kind of horserace. Cresskill, N.J. : Hampton Press, c2003.
P87.3.C37 C66 2003

The Hampton Press communication series. Communication and public space
Communication and cyberspace. 2nd ed. Creskill, N.J. : Hampton Press, c2003.
P96.D36 C66 2003

Han, Byung-Chul. Tod und Alterität / Byung-Chul Han. München : Fink, c2002. 240 p. ; 22 cm. Includes bibliographical references (p. 235-240). ISBN 3-7705-3660-6
1. Death. 2. Future life. I. Title.
BD444 .H36 2002

Han, Zhen. Li shi zhe xue : guan yu li shi xing gai nian de zhe xue chan shi / Han Zhen, Meng Wuqi zhu. Di 1 ban. Kunming : Yunnan ren min chu ban she, 2002. 2, 10, 255 p. : 22 cm. (Zhe xue li lun chuang xin cong shu = Philosophy series : new ideas and innovations) Cover title also in English: Philosophy of history : the philosophical interpretation of historicity. Includes bibliographical references. ISBN 7-222-03111-1
1. History - Philosophy. I. Meng, Wuqi, 1966- II. Title. III. Title: Guan yu li shi xing gai nian de zhe xue chan shi IV. Title: Philosophy of history : the philosophical interpretation of historicity V. Series: Zhe xue li lun chuang xin cong shu.
D16.8 .H3597 2002

Hanan, Patrick.
Writing and materiality in China. Cambridge, Mass. : Published by Harvard University Asia Center for Harvard-Yenching Institute : distributed by Harvard University Press, 2003.
PL2262 .W74 2003

The hand.
Tallis, Raymond. Edinburgh : Edinburgh University Press, c2003.
BF908 .T35 2003

HAND.
Tallis, Raymond. The hand. Edinburgh : Edinburgh University Press, c2003.
BF908 .T35 2003

HAND-TO-HAND FIGHTING. See **SELF-DEFENSE.**

HAND-TO-HAND FIGHTING, ORIENTAL. See **KARATE.**

A handbook for constructive living.
Reynolds, David K. Honolulu : University of Hawaii Press, 2002.
RC489.M65 R438 2002

Handbook of adolescent psychology.
Lerner, Richard M. 2nd ed. Hoboken, N.J. : John Wiley & Sons, 2004.
BF724 .L367 2004

Handbook of affective sciences / edited by Richard J. Davidson, Klaus R. Scherer, H. Hill Goldsmith. Oxford ; New York : Oxford University Press, 2003. xvii, 1199 p. : ill. (some col.) ; 29 cm. (Series in affective science) Includes bibliographical references and index. ISBN 0-19-512601-7 (alk. paper) DDC 152.4
1. Affect (Psychology) 2. Emotions. I. Davidson, Richard J. II. Scherer, Klaus R. III. Goldsmith, H. Hill. IV. Title: Affective sciences V. Series.
BF511 .H35 2003

Handbook of affirmative psychotherapy with lesbians and gay men.
Ritter, Kathleen. New York : Guilford Press, c2002.
RC451.4.G39 R55 2002

Handbook of closeness and intimacy / [edited by] Debra J. Mashek, Arthur P. Aron. Mahwah, N.J. : Lawrence Erlbaum Associates, 2004. p. cm. Includes bibliographical references and index. ISBN 0-8058-4284-5 (case : alk. paper) ISBN 0-8058-4285-3 (paperbound : alk.

paper) DDC 158.2
1. Intimacy (Psychology) I. Mashek, Debra J. II. Aron, Arthur.
BF575.I5 H36 2004

Handbook of counseling women / Mary Kopala, Merle A. Keitel, editors. Thousand Oaks, Calif. ; London : Sage Publications, c2003. xiii, 645 p. : ill. ; 26 cm. Includes bibliographical references and indexes. ISBN 0-7619-2640-2 DDC 616.89/14/082
1. Women - Mental health. 2. Psychotherapy. 3. Women - Counseling of. I. Kopala, Mary. II. Keitel, Merle A.
RC451.4.W6 H36 2003

Handbook of counselling psychology / edited by Ray Woolfe, Windy Dryden, Sheelagh Strawbridge. 2nd ed. London ; Thousand Oaks, Calif. : SAGE Publications, 2003. xviii, 709 p. ; 25 cm. Includes bibliographical references and index. ISBN 0-7619-7207-2 (pbk.) ISBN 0-7619-7206-4 DDC 158/.3
1. Counseling. I. Woolfe, Ray. II. Dryden, Windy. III. Strawbridge, Sheelagh.
BF637.C6 H316 2003

Handbook of developmental psychology / edited by Jaan Valsiner and Kevin J. Connolly. London : Thousand Oaks, Calif. : SAGE Publications, 2003. xxvii, 682 p. : ill. ; 26 cm. Includes bibliographical references and index. ISBN 0-7619-6231-X
1. Developmental psychology. I. Valsiner, Jaan. II. Connolly, Kevin J.
BF713 .H364 2003

Handbook of hope. Snyder, C. R. San Diego, Calif. : Academic Press, c2000.
BF575.H56 S69 2000

Handbook of motivational counseling : concepts, approaches, and assessment / edited by W. Miles Cox and Eric Klinger. Chichester, West Sussex, England ; Hoboken, NJ : J. Wiley, c2004. xxii, 515 p. : ill. ; 26 cm. Includes bibliographical references and indexes. Publisher description URL: http://www.loc.gov/catdir/desc ription/wiley037/2003005298.html Table of contents URL: http://www.loc.gov/catdir/toc/wiley031/2003005298.html CONTENTS: Motivation and the theory of current concerns / Eric Klinger and W. Miles Cox -- Motivation and addiction : the role of incentive processes in understanding and treating addictive disorders / Suzette V. Glasner -- Behavioral economics : basic concepts and clinical applications / Christopher J. Correia -- Personal project pursuit : on human doings and well beings / Brian R. Little and Neil C. Chambers -- Goal conflicts : concepts, findings, and consequences for psychotherapy / Johannes Michalak, Thomas Heidenreich, and Jurgen Hoyer -- Motivational counseling in an extended functional context : personality systems interaction theory and assessment / Reiner Kaschel and Julius Kuhl -- A motivational model of alcohol use : determinants of use and change / W. Miles Cox and Eric Klinger -- Measuring motivation : the motivational structure questionnaire and personal concerns inventory / W. Miles Cox and Eric Klinger -- The motivational structure questionnaire and personal concerns inventory: psychometric properties / Eric Klinger and W. Miles Cox -- Volitional and emotional correlates of the motivational structure questionnaire : further evidence for construct validity / Nicola Baumann -- Systematic motivational counseling : the motivational structure questionnaire in action / W. Miles Cox and Eric Klinger -- Systematic motivational counseling in groups : clarifying motivational structure during psychotherapy / Bernhard M. Schroer, Arno Fuhrmann and Renate de Jong-Meyer -- Systematic motivational analysis as part of a self-help technique aimed at personal goal attainment / Renate de Jong-Meyer -- Systematic motivational counseling at work : improving employee performance, satisfaction, and socialization / Loriann Roberson and David M. Sluss -- Systematic motivational counseling in rehabilitation settings / S. Vincent Miranti and Allen W. Heinemann -- Assessing and changing motivation to offend / Mary McMurran -- Enhancing motivation for psychotherapy : the elaboration of positive perspectives (EPOS) to develop clients' goal structure / Ulrike Willutzki and Christoph Koban -- Viktor E. Frankl's existential analysis and logotherapy / Manfred Hillmann -- Changing alcohol expectancies : techniques for altering motivations for drinking / Barry T. Jones -- The motivational drinker's check-up : a brief intervention for early stage problem drinkers / Maria J. Emmen ... [et al.] -- Motivational enhancement as a brief intervention for college student drinkers / Arthur W. Blume and G. Alan Marlatt -- Community reinforcement approach and contingency management interventions for substance abuse / Conrad J. Wong, Hendrée E. Jones, and Maxine L. Stitzer -- Goal setting as a motivational technique for neurorehabilitation / Siegfried Gauggel and Martina Hoop -- Motivational interviewing in health promotion and behavioral medicine / Ken Resnicow ... [et al.] -- Motivational counseling: taking stock and looking ahead / W. Miles Cox and Eric Klinger. ISBN 0-470-84517-1 (alk. paper) DDC 158/.3
1. Counseling. 2. Psychotherapy. 3. Motivation (Psychology) I. Cox, W. Miles. II. Klinger, Eric, 1933-
BF637.C6 H3172 2004

Handbook of multicultural competencies in counseling & psychology / editors, Donald B. Pope-Davis ... [et al.]. Thousand Oaks, Calif. : Sage Publications, c2003. xvi, 650 p. : ill. ; 26 cm. Includes bibliographical references and indexes. ISBN 0-7619-2306-3 DDC 158/.3
1. Cross-cultural counseling. I. Pope-Davis, Donald B.
BF637.C6 H3173 2003

The handbook of negotiation : theoretical advances and cross-cultural perspectives / edited by Michele J. Gelfand and Jeanne M. Brett. Stanford, Calif. : Stanford Business Books, c2004. p. cm. Includes bibliographical references and index. CONTENTS: Basic psychological processes -- Social processes in negotiation -- Negotiation in context -- Epilogue. ISBN 0-8047-4586-2 (cloth : alk. paper) DDC 302.3
1. Negotiation. 2. Conflict management. 3. Negotiation - Cross-cultural studies. 4. Conflict management - Cross-cultural studies. I. Gelfand, Michele J. II. Brett, Jeanne M.
BF637.N4 H365 2004

Handbook of nonverbal assessment / edited by R. Steve McCallum. New York : Kluwer Academic/Plenum Publishers, c2003. xvi, 390 p. : ill. ; 26 cm. Includes bibliographical references and index. ISBN 0-306-47715-7 DDC 153.9/324
1. Intelligence tests for preliterates. I. McCallum, R. Steve.
BF432.5.I55 H36 2003

Handbook of organizational performance : behavior analysis and management / C. Merle Johnson, William K. Redmon, Thomas C. Mawhinney, editors. New York : Haworth Press, c2001. xix, 475 p. : ill. ; 22 cm. Includes bibliographical references and index. CONTENTS: Introduction to organizational performance : behavior analysis and management / C. Merle Johnson, Thomas C. Mawhinney, William K. Redmon -- Principles of learning : respondent and operant conditioning and human behavior / Alan Poling, Diane Braatz -- Developing performance appraisals : criteria for what and how performance is measured / Judith L. Komaki, Michelle Reynard Minnich -- Within-group research designs : going beyond program evaluation questions / Judith L. Komaki, Sonia M. Goltz -- Schedules of reinforcement in organizational performance, 1971-1994 : application, analysis, and synthesis / Donald A. Hantula -- Training and development in organizations : a review of the organizational behavior management literature / Richard Perlow -- Leadership : behavior, context, and consequences / Thomas C. Mawhinney -- The management of occupational stress / Terry A. Beehr, Steve M. Jex, Papia Ghosh -- Pay for performance / Phillip K. Duncan, Dee Tinley Smoot -- The safe performance approach to preventing job-related illness and injury / Beth Sulzer-Azaroff, Kathleen Blake McCann, Todd C. Harris -- Actively caring for occupational safety : extending the performance management paradigm / E. Scott Geller -- A behavioral approach to sales management / Mark J. Martinko, William W. Casey, Paul Fadil -- Marketing behaviorally based solutions / Leslie Wilk Braksick, Julie M. Smith -- Organizational behavior management and organization development : potential paths to reciprocation / James L. Eubanks -- Social learning analysis of behavioral management / Robert Waldersee, Fred Luthans -- Ethics and behavior analysis in management / Howard C. Berthold Jr. -- Organizational culture and behavioral systems analysis / William K. Redmon, Matthew A. Mason. ISBN 0-7890-1086-0 (hard : alk. paper) ISBN 0-7890-1087-9 (soft : alk. paper) DDC 658.3
1. Organizational behavior. 2. Personnel management. I. Johnson, C. Merle. II. Redmon, William K. III. Mawhinney, Thomas C.
HD58.7 .H364 2001

Handbook of peace, prosperity and democracy
(v. 1) Peace, prosperity, and democracy at the cutting edge. New York : Nova Science Publishers, c2003.

Handbook of psychological and educational assessment of children : intelligence, aptitude, and achievement / edited by Cecil R. Reynolds and Randy W. Kamphaus. 2nd ed. New York, N.Y. : Guilford Press, 2003. p. cm. Includes bibliographical references and index. Table of contents URL: http://www.loc.gov/catdir/toc/ecip041/2003006119.html CONTENTS: General issues -- Assessment of intelligence and learning styles/strategies -- Assessment of academic skills -- Special topics in mental testing. ISBN 1-57230-883-4 (alk. paper) DDC 155.4/028/7
1. Psychological tests for children. 2. Achievement tests. I. Reynolds, Cecil R., 1952- II. Kamphaus, Randy W.
BF722 .H33 2003

Handbook of psychological and educational assessment of children : personality, behavior, and context / edited by Cecil R. Reynolds and Randy W. Kamphaus. 2nd ed. New York : Guilford Press, 2003. p. cm. Includes bibliographical references and index. Table of contents URL: http://www.loc.gov/catdir/toc/ecip041/2003005957.html ISBN 1-57230-884-2 (alk. paper) DDC 155.4/028/7
1. Psychological tests for children. 2. Achievement tests. I. Reynolds, Cecil R., 1952- II. Kamphaus, Randy W.
BF722 .H33 2003b

Handbook of psychology / Irving B. Weiner, editor-in-chief. Hoboken, N.J. : John Wiley, c2003. 12 v. : ill. ; 29 cm. Includes bibliographical references and indexes. CONTENTS: v. 1. History of psychology / Donald K. Freedheim, volume editor -- v. 2. Research methods in psychology / John A. Schinka, Wayne F. Velicer, volume editors -- v. 3. Biological psychology / Michela Gallagher, Randy J. Nelson, volume editors -- v. 4. Experimental psychology / Alice F. Healy, Robert W. Proctor, volume editors -- v. 5. Personality and social psychology / Theodore Millon, Melvin J. Lerner, volume editors -- v. 6. Developmental psychology / Richard M. Lerner, M. Ann Easterbrooks, Jayanthi Mistry, volume editors -- v. 7. Educational psychology / William M. Reynolds, Gloria E. Miller, volume editors -- v. 8. Clinical psychology / George Stricker, Thomas A. Widiger, volume editors -- v. 9. Health psychology / Arthur M. Nezu, Christine Maguth Nezu, Pamela A. Geller, volume editors -- v. 10. Assessment psychology / John R. Graham, Jack A. Naglieri, volume editors -- v. 11. Forensic psychology / Alan M. Goldstein, volume editor -- v. 12. Industrial and organizational psychology / Walter C. Borman, Daniel R. Ilgen, Richard J. Klimoski, volume editors. ISBN 0-471-17669-9 (set) DDC 150
1. Psychology. I. Weiner, Irving B. II. Freedheim, Donald K.
BF121 .H1955 2003

Handbook of qualitative research. Strategies of qualitative inquiry. 2nd ed. Thousand Oaks, CA : Sage, c2003.
H61 .S8823 2003

Handbook of research methods in experimental psychology / edited by Stephen F. Davis. Malden, MA ; Oxford : Blackwell Pub., 2003. viii, 507 p. : ill. ; 26 cm. (Blackwell handbooks of research methods in psychology) Includes bibliographical references and indexes. CONTENTS: Psychology's experimental foundations / C. James Goodwin -- Current and future trends in experimental psychology / E.J. Capaldi and Robert W. Proctor -- Traditional nomothetic approaches / Richard J. Harris -- Traditional idiographic approaches / Bryan K. Saville and William Buskist -- The importance of effect magnitude / Roger E. Kirk -- The changing face of research methods / Randolph A. Smith and Stephen F. Davis -- Ethical issues in psychological research with human participants / Richard L. Miller -- Research with animals / Jesse E. Purdy, Scott A. Bailey, and Steven J. Schapiro -- Cross-cultural research / David Matsumoto -- Comparative psychology / Mauricio R. Papini -- Animal learning and animal cognition / Lewis Barker and Jeffrey S. Katz -- Sensation and perception research methods / Lauren Fruh VanSickle Scharff -- Taste / Scott A. Bailey -- Olfaction / W. Robert Batsell, Jr. -- Physiological psychology / Brenda J. Anderson ... [et al.] -- Research methods in human memory / Deanne L. Westerman and David G. Payne -- Research methods in cognition / David G. Payne and Deanne L. Westerman -- Motivation / Melissa Burns -- Audition / Henry E. Heffner and Rickye S. Heffner -- Psychophysics / H.R. Schiffman. ISBN 0-631-22649-4 (hardcover : alk. paper) DDC 150/.7/24
1. Psychology - Research - Methodology. 2. Psychology, Experimental - Research - Methodology. I. Davis, Stephen F. II. Title: Experimental psychology III. Series.
BF76.5 .H35 2003

The handbook of risk / edited by Ben Warwick. Hoboken, N.J. : Wiley, c2003. vii, 274 p. : ill. ; 24 cm. Includes bibliographical references and index. Table of contents URL: http://www.loc.gov/catdir/toc/wiley031/2002012151.html ISBN 0-471-06412-2 DDC 658.15/5
1. Risk. 2. Risk management. I. Warwick, Ben.
HB615 .H266 2003

Handbook of self-determination research / Edward L. Deci & Richard M. Ryan, editors. Soft cover ed. Rochester, NY : University of Rochester Press, 2004. p. cm. Includes bibliographical references and indexes. ISBN 1-58046-156-5 (pbk. : alk. paper) DDC 155.2/5
1. Autonomy (Psychology) I. Deci, Edward L. II. Ryan, Richard M.
BF575.A88 H36 2004

Handbook of self-regulation : research, theory, and applications / edited by Roy F. Baumeister, Kathleen D. Vohs. New York : Guilford Press, 2004. p. cm. Includes bibliographical references and index. Table of contents URL: http://www.loc.gov/catdir/toc/ecip048/2003020013.html ISBN 1-57230-991-1 (alk.paper) DDC 153.8
1. Self-control. I. Baumeister, Roy F. II. Vohs, Kathleen D.
BF632 .H262 2004

The handbook of social psychology / [edited by] Daniel T. Gilbert, Susan T. Fiske, Gardner Lindzey. 4th ed. Boston : McGraw-Hill ; New York :

Distributed exclusively by Oxford University Press, c1998. 2 v. : ill. ; 26 cm. Includes bibliographical references and indexes. CONTENTS: v. 1. Major developments in five decades of social psychology / Edward E. Jones -- The social being in social psychology / Shelley E. Taylor -- Experimentation in social psychology / Elliot Aronson, Timothy D. Wilson, Marilynn B. Brewer -- Survey methods / Norbert Schwarz, Robert M. Groves, Howard Schuman -- Measurement / Charles M. Judd, Gary H. McClelland -- Data analysis in social psychology / David A. Kenny, Deborah A. Kashy, Niall Bolger -- Attitude structure and function / Alice H. Eagly, Shelly Chaiken -- Attitude change : multiple roles for persuasion variables / Richard E. Petty, Duane T. Wegener -- Mental representation and memory / Eliot R. Smith -- Control and automaticity in social life / Daniel M. Wegner, John A. Bargh -- Behavioral decision making and judgment / Robyn M. Dawes -- Motivation / Thane S. Pittman -- Emotions / Robert B. Zajonc -- Understanding personality and social behavior : a functionalist strategy / Mark Snyder, Nancy Cantor -- The self / Roy F. Baumeister -- Social development in childhood and adulthood / Diane N. Ruble, Jacqueline J. Goodnow -- Gender / Kay Deaux, Marianne LaFrance -- CONTENTS: v. 2. Nonverbal communication / Bella M. DePaulo, Howard S. Friedman -- Language and social behavior / Robert M. Krauss, Chi-Yue Chiu -- Ordinary personology / Daniel T. Gilbert -- Social influence : social norms, conformity, and compliance / Robert B. Cialdini, Melanie R. Trost -- Attraction and close relationships / Ellen Berscheid, Harry T. Reis -- Altruism and prosocial behavior / C. Daniel Batson -- Aggression and antisocial behavior / Russell G. Geen -- Stereotyping, prejudice, and discrimination / Susan T. Fiske -- Small groups / John M. Levine, Richard L. Moreland -- Social conflict / Dean G. Pruitt -- Social stigma / Jennifer Crocker, Brenda Major, Claude Steele -- Intergroup relations / Marilynn B. Brewer, Rupert J. Brown -- Social justice and social movements / Tom R. Tyler, Heather J. Smith -- Health behavior / Peter Salovey, Alexander J. Rothman, Judith Rodin -- Psychology and law / Phoebe C. Ellsworth, Robert Mauro -- Understanding organizations : concepts and controversies / Jeffrey Pfeffer -- Opinion and action in the realm of politics / Donald R. Kinder -- Social psychology and world politics / Philip E. Tetlock -- The cultural matrix of social psychology / Alan Page Fiske ... [et al.] -- Evolutionary social psychology / David M. Buss, Douglas T. Kenrick. ISBN 0-19-521376-9 (set : acid-free paper) ISBN 0-07-023709-3 (v. 1) ISBN 0-07-023710-7 (v. 2) DDC 302
1. Social psychology. I. Gilbert, Daniel Todd. II. Fiske, Susan T. III. Lindzey, Gardner.
HM251 .H224 1998

Handbook of violence / [edited by] Lisa A. Rapp-Paglicci, Albert R. Roberts, John S. Wodarski. New York : Wiley, c2002. xx, 460 p. ; 26 cm. Includes bibliographical references and indexes. CONTENTS: Violence within families through the life span -- Adolescent dating violence -- Children and adolescents from violent homes -- Domestic violence in African American homes -- Domestic violence in Latino cultures -- Children and adolescents exposed to community violence -- Assessing violent behavior -- Conduct disorder and substance abuse -- Girls' delinquency and violence: making the case for gender-responsive programming -- Youth gang violence -- Youth violence: chronic violent juvenile offenders -- School bullying: an overview -- Public concern and focus on school violence -- Reducing school violence: a social capacity framework -- School violence among culturally diverse populations -- Preventing workplace violence -- Workplace violence: prevention and intervention, theory and practice -- Domestic violence in the workplace. ISBN 0-471-41467-0 (cloth : alk. paper) DDC 303.6
1. Violence. 2. Violence - Prevention. I. Rapp-Paglicci, Lisa A. II. Roberts, Albert R. III. Wodarski, John S.
HM1116 .H36 2002

Handbücher zur Sprach- und Kommunikationswissenschaft
(Bd. 24.) Psycholinguistik. Berlin : W. de Gruyter, c2003.

Handel, George Frideric, 1685-1759. Operas. Selections.
Malaniuk, Ira. Arien und Lieder [sound recording]. [Germany] : Preiser Records, p2000.

HANDICAPPED. See **DISCRIMINATION AGAINST THE HANDICAPPED; SICK.**

HANDICAPPED CHILDREN. See **DEVELOPMENTALLY DISABLED CHILDREN.**

HANDICAPPED - COUNSELING OF.
Counseling diverse populations. 3rd ed. Boston, Mass. : McGraw-Hill, c2004.
BF637.C6 C6372 2004

HANDICAPPED PEOPLE. See **HANDICAPPED.**

HANDICRAFT. See **OCCUPATIONS.**

HANDWRITING. See **WRITING.**

HANDWRITING ANALYSIS. See **GRAPHOLOGY.**

Handy, Charles B. 21 ideas for managers : practical wisdom for managing your company and yourself / Charles Handy. 1st ed. San Francisco : Jossey-Bass, c2000. xxi, 200 p. : ill. ; 24 cm. Includes index. Table of Contents URL: http://www.loc.gov/catdir/toc/onix07/00008841.html CONTENTS: A world of differences -- The "e" factors -- The secret contract -- The territorial itch -- The inside-out donut -- The Johari window -- The actor's roles -- Marathons or horse races -- The self-fulfilling prophecy -- The stroking formula -- Parents, adults, and children -- Power politics -- Teams and captains -- Outward and visible signs -- Tribes and their ways -- Find your God -- Counting and costing -- The customer is always there -- Curiosity made the cat -- Shamrocks galore. ISBN 0-7879-5219-2 DDC 658
1. Management. 2. Self-management (Psychology) I. Title. II. Title: Twenty-one ideas for managers
HD31 .H31259 2000

Hanegbi, Me'ir.
Steinsaltz, Adin. [Be'ur Tanya. English] Opening the Tanya. 1st ed. San Francisco : Jossey-Bass, c2003.
BM198.2.S563 S7413 2003

Hankins, James. Humanism and platonism in the Italian Renaissance / James Hankins. Roma : Edizioni di storia e letteratura, 2003- v. ; 25 cm. (Storia e letteratura ; 215) Includes bibliographical references and index. CONTENTS: 1. Humanism. ISBN 88-8498-076-3 DDC 850
1. Bruni, Leonardo, - 1369-1444. 2. Humanism - Italy - History. 3. Renaissance - Italy. 4. Platonists - Italy - History. 5. Philosophy, Renaissance. I. Title. II. Series: Storia e letteratura (Edizioni di storia e letteratura) ; 215.

Hann, Georg. Georg Hann [sound recording] : die letzten Aufnahmen. [Germany] : Preiser Records, p2001. 1 sound disc : digital, mono. ; 4 3/4 in. Subtitle from insert: Seine letzten Aufnahmen. For bass-baritone with orchestra, bass-baritone with chorus and orchestra, bass-baritone with piano, vocal duet with orchestra, vocal trio with orchestra, vocal quintet with orchestra. Georg Hann, bass-baritone ; various soloists, choirs, orchestras, and conductors. Recorded from 1949 to 1959. Compact disc. Program notes by Clemens Höslinger in German with English translation ([3] p.) in container. Sung in German. Both Verdi arias sung in German. CONTENTS: Zar und Zimmermann: O santa justitia ; Den hohen Herrscher / Lortzing -- Der Wildschütz: Lass er doch hören ; Ich habe Numero Eins : Fünftausend Taler / Lortzing -- Der Barbier von Bagdad: Mein Sohn, sei Allahs Frieden ; Er lebt, er lebt / Cornelius -- Nabucco: Warum klagt ihr? / Verdi -- Falstaff: Die Ehre! Gauner / Verdi -- Der Zigeunerbaron: Ja, das Schreiben und das Lesen / Joh. Strauss -- Der Bettelstudent: Ach, wie hab' sie ja nur / Millöcker -- Meeresleuchten / Loewe, Siebel -- Odins Meeresritt / Loewe, Schreiber.
1. Operas - Excerpts. 2. Solo cantatas. 3. Songs. 4. Vocal duets with orchestra. 5. Vocal trios with orchestra. 6. Vocal quintets with orchestra. 7. Songs (Low voice) with piano. I. Lortzing, Albert, 1801-1851. Zar und Zimmermann. O sancta justitia, ich möchte rasen. II. Lortzing, Albert, 1801-1851. Zar und Zimmermann. Hohen Herrscher würdig zu empfangen. III. Lortzing, Albert, 1801-1851. Wildschütz. Lass Er doch hören. IV. Lortzing, Albert, 1801-1851. Wildschütz Ich habe Numero Eins. V. Lortzing, Albert, 1801-1851. Wildschütz. Fünftausend Taler. VI. Cornelius, Peter, 1824-1874. Barbier von Bagdad. Mein Sohn, sei Allahs Friede hier. VII. Cornelius, Peter, 1824-1874. Barbier von Bagdad Er lebt, er lebt. VIII. Verdi, Giuseppe, 1813-1901. Nabucco. Del futuro nel bujo discerno. German. IX. Verdi, Giuseppe, 1813-1901. Falstaff. Onore! Ladri! German. X. Strauss, Johann, 1825-1899. Zigeunerbaron Ja, das Schreiben und das Lesen. XI. Millöcker, Carl, 1842-1899. Bettelstudent Ach, ich hab' sie ja nur. XII. Loewe, Carl, 1796-1869. Lieder, op. 145. Meeresleuchten. XIII. Loewe, Carl, 1796-1869. Odins Meeresritt. XIV. Title. XV. Title: Letzten Aufnahmen XVI. Title: Seine letzten Aufnahmen

Hannas, Wm. C., 1946- The writing on the wall : how Asian orthography curbs creativity / William C. Hannas. Philadelphia : University of Pennsylvania Press, c2003. 348 p. ; 24 cm. (Encounters with Asia) Includes bibliographical references (p. [323]-336) and index. ISBN 0-8122-3711-0 (cloth : alk. paper) DDC 495
1. Creation (Literary, artistic, etc.) 2. Creative ability. 3. East Asia - Languages - Writing. I. Title. II. Series.
P381.E18 H36 2003

Hans Holzer's the supernatural.
Holzer, Hans, 1920- Franklin Lakes, NJ : New Page Books, c2003.
BF1031 .H672 2003

Hans Jonas-Zentrum e.V.
Philosophieren aus dem Diskurs. Würzburg : Königshausen & Neumann, c2002.

Hans Kayser's Lehrbuch der Harmonik.
Tokar, David A. 2002.

Hansard-Weiner, Sonja.
On interpretation. Madison, Wis. : University of Wisconsin Press for the University of Wisconsin Law School, c2002.

Hansen, Chad, 1942-.
Toropov, Brandon. The complete idiot's guide to Taoism. Indianapolis, IN : Alpha, c2002.
BL1920 .T67 2002

Hansen, Jennifer, 1970-.
Continental feminism reader. Lanham, Md. : Rowman & Littlefield Publishers, c2003.
HQ1075 .C668 2003

Hansen, Jonathan M. The lost promise of patriotism : debating American identity, 1890-1920 / Jonathan M. Hansen. Chicago : University of Chicago Press, c2003. xxii, 255 p. ; 24 cm. Includes bibliographical references (p. 191-246) and index. CONTENTS: Patriotism properly understood -- Room of one's own -- Democracy as associated learning -- Ex uno plura -- To make democracy safe for the world -- Fighting words -- The twilight of ideals. ISBN 0-226-31583-5 (alk. paper) ISBN 0-226-31584-3 DDC 973.91
1. United States - Politics and government - 1865-1933. 2. United States - Foreign relations - 1865-1921. 3. National characteristics, American. 4. Patriotism - United States - History. 5. Democracy - United States - History. 6. Political culture - United States - History. 7. United States - Intellectual life. 8. Intellectuals - United States - History. 9. Political activists - United States - History. I. Title.
E661 .H316 2003

Hansen, Mark Victor.
Chicken soup for the soul celebrates sisters. Deerfield Beach, Fla. : Health Communications, 2004.
BF723.S43 C43 2004

HANUKKAH.
Levin, Yitshak, 1938- Sefer Netivot Yitshak. [Bene Berak] : Y. Levin, [2000-

Hanus, Michel. La Mort aujourd'hui / Michel Hanus. Paris : Frison-Roche, c2000. 242 p. ; 21 cm. (Face à la mort) ISBN 2-87671-355-1 DDC 300
1. Death. 2. Death - Social aspects - France. 3. Funeral rites and ceremonies - France. 4. Undertakers and undertaking - France. I. Title. II. Series.

Hanvik, Jan Michael.
Big Dance [videorecording]. Buffalo, N.Y. : Kineticvideo.com, c1998.

HAPPINESS. See also **MENTAL HEALTH; PLEASURE.**
Tabensky, Pedro Alexis, 1964- Aldershot, Hampshire, England ; Burlington, VT : Ashgate, c2003.
BJ1481 .T25 2003

HAPPINESS.
Baudelot, Christian. Travailler pour être heureux? [Paris] : Fayard, c2003.

Boethius, d. 524. [De consolatione philosophiae. English] Consolation of philosophy. Indianapolis, IN : Hackett Pub. Co., c2001.
B659.C2 E52 2001

Bstan-'dzin-rgya-mtsho, Dalai Lama XIV, 1935- The art of happiness at work. New York : Riverhead Books, 2003.
BF481 .B76 2003

Carr, Alan, Dr. Positive psychology. London ; New York : Brunner-Routledge, 2004.
BF121 .C355 2004

Carson, Richard David. Taming your gremlin. Rev. ed. New York : Quill, 2003.
BF575.H27 C38 2003

Chetkin, Len. 100 thoughts that lead to happiness. Charlottesville, VA : Hampton Roads Pub., c2002.
BF637.C5 C477 2002

Colantuono, Susan L. Make room for joy. Charlestown, RI : Interlude Productions, c2000.
BF575.H27 C64 2000

Demo, Pedro. Dialética da felicidade. Petrópolis : Editora Vozes, 2001.

Holmes, Ernest, 1887-1960. [This thing called life] The art of life. New York : J.P. Tarcher/Penguin, c2004.
BF645 .H572 2004

Honey from my heart for you. Nashville, Tenn. : J. Countryman, c2002.
BF575.F66 H66 2002

Johansen, Heidi Leigh. What I look like when I am happy. 1st ed. New York : PowerStart Press, 2004.

BF723.H37 J64 2004

Johansen, Heidi Leigh. [What I look like when I am happy. Spanish & English] What I look like when I am happy = 1st ed. New York : Rosen Pub. Group's, 2004.
BF723.H37 J6418 2004

Kelen, Jacqueline. Le bonheur. Paris : Oxus, c2003.

Leonard, Marcia. I feel happy. Nashville, Tenn. : CandyCane Press, 2003.
BF575.H27 L465 2003

MacDonald, Lucy, 1953- Learn to be an optimist. San Francisco : Chronicle Books, 2004.
BF698.35.O57 M23 2004

Marar, Ziyad. The happiness paradox. London : Reaktion, 2003.

Nelson, Robin, 1971- Happy. Minneapolis, MN : Lerner Publications Co., c2004.
BF723.H37 N45 2004

Niẓām al-Dīn, 'Irfān. Lā lil-ikti'āb na'am lil-farḥ!!? al-Ṭab'ah 1. [Beirut?] : al-Mu'assasah al-'Arabīyah-al-Urūbbīyah lil-Ṣiḥāfah wa-al-Nashr, 2001.

Reyes, Arnoldo Juan. Una alternativa para ser feliz. Ciudad de La Habana, Cuba : Editorial Científico-Técnica, 2001, c2000.

Savater, Fernando. El contenido de la felicidad. 1. ed. Madrid : Aguilar : Santillana, 2002.

Tabensky, Pedro Alexis, 1964- Happiness. Aldershot, Hampshire, England ; Burlington, VT : Ashgate, c2003.
BJ1481 .T25 2003

Happiness and economics.
Frey, Bruno S. Princeton, N.J. : Princeton University Press, c2002.
BF575.H27 F75 2002

HAPPINESS - ECONOMIC ASPECTS.
Frey, Bruno S. Happiness and economics. Princeton, N.J. : Princeton University Press, c2002.
BF575.H27 F75 2002

HAPPINESS IN CHILDREN - JUVENILE LITERATURE.
Johansen, Heidi Leigh. What I look like when I am happy. 1st ed. New York : PowerStart Press, 2004.
BF723.H37 J64 2004

Johansen, Heidi Leigh. [What I look like when I am happy. Spanish & English] What I look like when I am happy = 1st ed. New York : Rosen Pub. Group's, 2004.
BF723.H37 J6418 2004

Nelson, Robin, 1971- Happy. Minneapolis, MN : Lerner Publications Co., c2004.
BF723.H37 N45 2004

Happiness is the best revenge.
Spezzano, Charles. Townsend, Wiltshire, England : Vision Products Limited, c1997.
BF575.D35 S68 1997

HAPPINESS - JUVENILE LITERATURE.
Leonard, Marcia. I feel happy. Nashville, Tenn. : CandyCane Press, 2003.
BF575.H27 L465 2003

Thomson, Emma. Little book of happiness. 1st ed. London : Hodder Children's, 2001.
BF575.H27 .T56 2001

The happiness paradox.
Marar, Ziyad. London : Reaktion, 2003.

HAPPINESS - PROBLEMS, EXERCISES, ETC.
Reeve, Susyn. Choose peace & happiness. Boston, MA : Red Wheel, 2003.
BF637.P3 R44 2003

HAPPINESS - RELIGIOUS ASPECTS - BUDDHISM.
Bstan-'dzin-rgya-mtsho, Dalai Lama XIV, 1935- The art of happiness at work. New York : Riverhead Books, 2003.
BF481 .B76 2003

HAPPINESS - SONGS AND MUSIC.
Sanders, Mark D. I hope you dance!. Nashville, Tenn. : Rutledge Hill Press, 2003.
BF410 .S26 2003

Happy.
Nelson, Robin, 1971- Minneapolis, MN : Lerner Publications Co., c2004.
BF723.H37 N45 2004

HAPTIC SENSE. *See* **TOUCH.**
HAPTICS. *See* **TOUCH.**

Haraway, Donna Jeanne. The companion species manifesto : dogs, people, and significant otherness / Donna Haraway. Chicago, Ill. : Prickly Paradigm ; Bristol : University Presses Marketing, 2003. 100 p. : ill. ; 18 cm. ISBN 0-9717575-8-5 DDC 636.70887
1. Dogs. 2. Pet owners - Psychology. 3. Human-animal relationships. I. Title.

Hardie, Titania. Titania's book of hours : a celebration of the witch's year / Titania Hardie ; photographs by Sara Morris. London : Quadrille, 2002. 120 p. : col. ill. ; 23 cm. Includes index. ISBN 1-903845-84-X DDC 133.43
1. Witchcraft. 2. Calendar. 3. Seasons - Mythology. I. Title.

Titania's magical compendium : spells and rituals to bring a little magic into your life / Titania Hardie ; photographs by Sara Morris. San Diego, Calif. : Thunder Bay Press, 2003. p. cm. Includes index. ISBN 1-59223-144-6 DDC 133.4/3
1. Magic. 2. Witchcraft. I. Title.
BF1611 .H235 2003

Hardin, Russell, 1940-.
Distrust. New York : Russell Sage Foundation, 2004.
BF575.T7 D57 2004

Indeterminacy and society / Russell Hardin. Princeton, N.J. : Princeton University Press, c2003. xii, 166 p. ; 25 cm. Includes bibliographical references (p. 151-158) and index. ISBN 0-691-09176-5 (alk. paper) DDC 302
1. Social interaction. 2. Choice (Psychology) 3. Determinism (Philosophy) I. Title.
HM1111 .H37 2003

Harding, M. Esther (Mary Esther), 1888-1971. The parental image : its injury and reconstruction : a study in analytical psychology / M. Esther Harding ; edited by Daryl Sharp. 3rd ed. Toronto : Inner City Books, c2003. 159 p. : ill. ; 22 cm. (Studies in Jungian psychology by Jungian analysts ; 106) Includes bibliographical references: (p. 152-154) and index. ISBN 1-89457-407-9 DDC 155.9/24
1. Parental influences. 2. Parent and child. I. Sharp, Daryl, 1936- II. Title. III. Series.

Hardman, David.
Thinking. Hoboken, NJ : Wiley, c2003.
BF441 .T466 2003

HARDWARE, COMPUTER. *See* **COMPUTERS.**

Hare, Jenny. Think love / Jenny Hare. London : Vega, 2002. 176 p. : ill. ; 20 cm. Includes bibliographical references (p. 165-166) and index. Publisher description URL: http://www.loc.gov/catdir/description/ste031/2003447870.html ISBN 1-84333-009-1 DDC 152.4/1
1. Love. I. Title.
BF575.L8 H338 2002

Harf-Lancner, Laurence.
Progrès, réaction, décadence dans l'Occident médiéval. Genève : Droz, 2003.
PN681 .P764 2003

Hargraves, Orin. Mighty fine words and smashing expressions : making sense of transatlantic English / Orin Hargraves. Oxford ; New York : Oxford University Press, 2003. xiii, 305 p. ; 24 cm. Includes bibliographical references (p. 289-292) and indexes. ISBN 0-19-515704-4 DDC 428/.00941
1. English language - Great Britain. 2. English language - United States. 3. Figures of speech. 4. Americanisms. I. Title.
PE1711 .H37 2003

Harkai Schiller, Pál, 1908-1949. A lélektan feladata / Harkai Schiller Pál. Budapest : Osiris Kiadó, 2002. 313 p. : 1 port. ; 19 cm. (Osiris könyvtár. Pszichológia) Includes bibliographical references and index. ISBN 963-389-309-7 ISSN 1219-7718
1. Psychology. I. Title. II. Series.
BF128.H8 H37 2002

Harker, Lesley.
Thomas, Pat, 1959- My friends and me. 1st ed. Hauppauge, N.Y. : Barron's Educational Series, c2001.
BF723.F68 T48 2001

Harley, Trevor A. The psychology of language : from data to theory / Trevor A. Harley. Hove, East Sussex, UK : Erlbaum (UK) Taylor & Francis, c1995. xiv, 482 p. : ill. Includes bibliographical references (p. 403-467) and indexes. CONTENTS: What is language? What is psycholinguistics? -- The speech system and spoken word recognition -- Visual word recognition -- Word pronunciation and dyslexia -- Syntax and parsing -- Semantics -- Comprehension: understanding and remembering the message -- Speech production and aphasia -- The structure of the language system -- Language, thought, and the precursors of language -- Language development -- New directions. ISBN 0-86377-381-8 (hbk) ISBN 0-86377-382-6 (pbk)
1. Psycholinguistics. I. Title.

HARLOW, HARRY FREDERICK, 1905-.
Blum, Deborah Love at Goon Park. New York : Berkley Books, 2004.
BF109.H346 B58 2004

Blum, Deborah. Love at Goon Park. Cambridge, MA : Perseus Pub., c2002.
BF109.H346 B58 2002

Harmon, Paul, 1942- Business process change : a manager's guide to improving, redesigning, and automating processes / Paul Harmon. Amsterdam ; Boston : Morgan Kaufmann, c2003. xxi, 529 p. : ill. ; 24 cm. Includes bibliographical references (p. 503-506) and index. ISBN 1-55860-758-7
1. Organizational change - Management. 2. Information technology - Management. 3. Strategic planning. 4. Reengineering (Management) I. Title.
HD58.8 .H37 2003

Harmond, Richard P. A history of Memorial Day : unity, discord and the pursuit of happiness / Richard P. Harmond and Thomas J. Curran. New York : P. Lang, c2002. xii, 154 p. : ill. ; 24 cm. (American university studies. Series IX. History, 0740-0462 ; v. 191) Includes bibliographical references and index. ISBN 0-8204-3959-2 (alk. paper) DDC 394.262
1. Memorial Day - History. 2. Memorial Day - Social aspects. 3. National characteristics, American. I. Curran, Thomas J., 1929- II. Title. III. Series.
E642 .H37 2002

HARMONICS (MUSIC).
Tokar, David A. Hans Kayser's Lehrbuch der Harmonik. 2002.

HARMONY OF THE SPHERES.
Tokar, David A. Hans Kayser's Lehrbuch der Harmonik. 2002.

HARMONY (PHILOSOPHY).
Pliskin, Zelig. Harmony with others. 1st ed. Brooklyn, N.Y. : Shaar Press : Distributed by Mesorah Publications, 2002.

HARMONY (PHILOSOPHY) - RELIGIOUS ASPECTS.
Pliskin, Zelig. Harmony with others. 1st ed. Brooklyn, N.Y. : Shaar Press : Distributed by Mesorah Publications, 2002.

Harmony with others.
Pliskin, Zelig. 1st ed. Brooklyn, N.Y. : Shaar Press : Distributed by Mesorah Publications, 2002.

Harms, Daniel. The Necronomicon files : the truth behind Lovecraft's legend / Daniel Harms and John Wisdom Gonce III. Boston, MA : Weiser Books, c2003. xxvi, 342 p. : ill. ; 23 cm. Includes bibliographical references and index. Table of contents URL: http://www.loc.gov/catdir/toc/ecip042/2003008089.html CONTENTS: H.P. Lovecraft and the Necronomicon / Daniel Harms -- "Many a quaint and curious volume ..." -- : the Necronomicon made flesh / Daniel Harms -- Evaluating Necronomicon rumors / Daniel Harms -- The evolution of sorcery : a brief history of modern magick / John Wisdom Gonce III -- Lovecraftian magic--sources and heirs / John Wisdom Gonce III -- A plague of Necronomicons / John Wisdom Gonce III -- Simon, Slater, and the gang : true origins of the Necronomicon / John Wisdom Gonce III -- The chaos of confusion / John Wisdom Gonce III -- The Necronomicon and psychic attack / John Wisdom Gonce III -- Unspeakable cuts : the Necronomicon on film / John Wisdom Gonce III -- Call of the cathode ray tube : the Necronomicon on television / John Wisdom Gonce III. ISBN 1-57863-269-2 (pbk.) DDC 133
1. Occultism. 2. Lovecraft, H. P. - (Howard Phillips), - 1890-1937. I. Gonce, John Wisdom. II. Title.
BF1999 .H37515 2003

Harper, Valerie, 1940-.
Vint/age 2001 conference : [videorecording]. New York, c2001.

HARPER, VALERIE, 1940-.
Vint/age 2001 conference : [videorecording]. New York, c2001.

Harré, Rom. Cognitive science : a philosophical introduction / Rom Harré. London ; Thousand Oaks, Calif. : SAGE Publications, 2002. xxii, 314 p. : ill. ; 25 cm. Includes bibliographical references (p. 305-310) and index. ISBN 0-7619-4746-9 ISBN 0-7619-4747-7 (pbk.) DDC 153
1. Cognition. 2. Cognitive psychology. 3. Cognitive science. 4. Cognitive science - Philosophy. I. Title.
BF311 .H347 2002

Harrell, Keith D. Attitude is everything for success : say it, believe it, receive it / Keith D. Harrell. Carlsbad, CA : Hay House, 2004. p. cm. Table of contents URL: http://www.loc.gov/catdir/toc/ecip045/

Harriger, Katy J. (Katy Jean)
2003012609.html ISBN 1401902014 DDC 153.8/5
1. Attitude (Psychology) I. Title.
BF327 .H373 2004

Harriger, Katy J. (Katy Jean).
Separation of powers. Washington, D.C. : CQ Press, a division of Congressional Quarterly Inc., c2003.
JK305 .S465 2003

Harriman, Richard A.
Mauzy, Jeff. Creativity, Inc.. Boston, Mass. : Harvard Business School Press, c2003.
HD53 .M375 2003

Harris, Bill, 1950- Thresholds of the mind : how holosync audio technology can transform your life / Bill Harris ; [foreword by Harville Hendrix].
Beaverton : Centerpointe Press, c2002. xxi, 193 p. : ill. ; 23 cm. ISBN 0-9721780-0-7
1. Behavior modification. 2. Brain stimulation. 3. Meditation. I. Title.
BF637.B4 H36 2002

Harris, Chris. Building innovative teams : strategies and tools for developing and integrating high performance innovative groups / Chris Harris. Houndmills [England] ; New York : Palgrave Macmillan, 2003. xi, 244 p. : ill. ; 24 cm. Includes bibliographical references (p. 239-240) and index. ISBN 1403903867 (alk. paper) DDC 658.4/02
1. Teams in the workplace. 2. Creative ability. I. Title.
HD66 .H3744 2003

HARRIS-MANNES, CAROL.
Vint/age 2001 conference : [videorecording]. New York, c2001.

Harris-Mannes, Carol, panelist.
Vint/age 2001 conference : [videorecording]. New York, c2001.

Harris, Maxine. The twenty-four carat Buddha and other fables : stories of self-discovery / by Maxine Harris ; with illustrations by Tracey Hedrick Graham and Molly Ennis. Baltimore, Md. : Sidran Institute Press, 2003. p. cm. Table of contents URL: http://www.loc.gov/catdir/toc/ecip046/2003014739.html CONTENTS: The diver -- Just one string -- Gold and silver -- Inktomi -- The travelers -- The alchemist -- The pot of misery -- The silver flute -- Better safe than sorry -- The burden -- The puzzler -- The twenty-four carat Buddha -- The cave of truth -- The contest -- The gift of choices -- A language of your own -- The most evil man in town -- The gambler's lesson -- The options trader -- Two gifts -- Roots for Tanya -- Perfect vision -- The wizard's message -- Speak to me. ISBN 1-88696-814-4 (pbk. : alk. paper) DDC 158.1
1. Self-realization - Miscellanea. I. Title.
BF637.S4 H355 2003

Harris, Mike, 1947-.
Berg, Wendy, 1951- Polarity magic. St. Paul, Minn. : Llewellyn Publications, 2003.
BF1589 .B47 2003

Harris, Nicholas, 1956- How big? / by Nicholas Harris. San Diego, CA : Blackbirch Press, 2004. p. cm. (How?) SUMMARY: Compares the sizes of animals, insects. vehicle, mountains, and planets, using pictures and text. Includes bibliographical references and index. ISBN 1410300684 (lib. bdg. : alk. paper) ISBN 1410301974 (pbk. : alk. paper) DDC 153.7/52
1. Size perception - Juvenile literature. 2. Size judgment - Juvenile literature. 3. Size. I. Title. II. Series.
BF299.S5 H37 2004

Harris, O. Jeff. Organizational behavior / O. Jeff Harris, Sandra J. Hartman. New York : Best Business Books, c2002. xvii, 478 p. : ill. ; 24 cm. Includes bibliographical references and indexes. ISBN 0-7890-1500-5 (soft : alk. paper) ISBN 0-7890-1204-9 (alk. paper) DDC 658
1. Organizational behavior. 2. Corporate culture. 3. Management. I. Hartman, Sandra J. II. Title.
HD58.7 .H36943 2002

Harris, Webb.
Lamb, William, 1944 Apr. 22- The secrets of your rising sign. Gloucester, MA : Fair Winds Press, 2004.
BF1717 .L36 2004

Harrison, Chris.
Pound, Linda. Supporting musical development in the early years. Buckingham ; Philadelphia : Open University Press, 2003.
MT1 .P66 2003

Harrison, Edward Robert. Masks of the universe : changing ideas on the nature of the cosmos / Edward Harrison. 2nd ed. Cambridge, U.K. ; New York : Cambridge University Press, 2003. ix, 331 p. : ill. ; 24 cm. Includes bibliographical references (p. [311]-323) and index. ISBN 0-521-77351-2 DDC 523.1
1. Cosmology. I. Title.
QB981 .H324 2003

Harrison, Lindsay.
Browne, Sylvia. Life on the other side. New York : Dutton, c2000.
BF1311.F8 B77 2000b

Browne, Sylvia. Visits from the afterlife. New York : Dutton, c2003.
BF1461 .B77 2003

Harrison, Robert Pogue. The dominion of the dead / Robert Pogue Harrison. Chicago : University of Chicago Press, 2003. xiii, 208 p. ; 23 cm. Includes bibliographical references (p. 183-198) and index. CONTENTS: The earth and its dead -- Hic jacet -- What is a house? -- The voice of grief -- The origin of our basic words -- Choosing your ancestor -- Hic non est -- The names of the dead -- The afterlife of the image. ISBN 0-226-31791-9 (hardcover : alk. paper) DDC 306.9
1. Death - Psychological aspects. 2. Death - Social aspects. I. Title.
BF789.D4 H375 2003

Harry, Lou, 1963- The game of life : how to succeed in real life no matter where you land / by Lou Harry. Philadelphia : Running Press, c2003. 160 p. : ill. ; 22 cm. ISBN 0-7624-1445-6 DDC 158.1
1. Self-actualization (Psychology) 2. Success. I. Title.
BF637.S4 H357 2003

Harry Potter's world : multidisciplinary critical perspectives / edited by Elizabeth E. Heilman. New York ; London : RoutledgeFalmer, 2003. ix, 308 p. ; 24 cm. (Pedagogy and popular culture) Includes bibliographical references and index. ISBN 0-415-93373-0 (hbk.) ISBN 0-415-93374-9 (pbk.) DDC 823/.914
1. Rowling, J. K. - Criticism and interpretation. 2. Rowling, J. K. - Characters - Harry Potter. 3. Children's stories, English - History and criticism. 4. Fantasy fiction, English - History and criticism. 5. Potter, Harry (Fictitious character) 6. Wizards in literature. 7. Magic in literature. I. Heilman, Elizabeth E. II. Series: Garland reference library of social science. Pedagogy and popular culture.
PR6068.O93 Z73 2003

Harskamp, Anton van, 1946-.
The many faces of individualism. Leuven, Belgium ; Sterling, Va. : Peeters, 2001.
B824 .M354 2001

Hart, Lois Borland. The manager's pocket guide to dealing with conflict / by Lois B. Hart. Amherst, Mass. : HRD Press, c1999. iv, 114 p. : ill. ; 18 cm. Includes bibliographical references (p. 105-107) and index. ISBN 0-87425-480-9
1. Interpersonal conflict. 2. Conflict management. 3. Conflict (Psychology) I. Title. II. Title: Dealing with conflict
BF637.I48 H38 1999

Hartley, Ruth E. (Ruth Edith), b.1909 Understanding children's play, by Ruth E. Hartley, Lawrence K. Frank, Robert M. Goldenson ; prefatory note by Newton Bigelow. London : Routledge, 2000. xvi, 372 p. ; ill.. 23 cm. (The international library of psychology. Developmental psychology ; 32) Originally published: New York : Columbia University Press, 1952. Includes bibliographical references (p. [356]-362) and index. ISBN 0-415-20990-0 DDC 136.7470
1. Play - Psychological aspects. 2. Child psychology. I. Frank, Lawrence K. (Lawrence Kelso), 1890-1968. II. Goldenson, Robert M. III. Title. IV. Series: International library of psychology. V. Series: International library of psychology. Developmental psychology ; v. 32.
BF717 .H3 2000

Hartman, Geoffrey H. Scars of the spirit : the struggle against inauthenticity / Geoffrey Hartman. New York ; Houndmills, England : Palgrave, 2002. xii, 260 p. : 25 cm. Includes bibliographical references (p. [237]-254) and index. ISBN 0-312-29569-3 (hbk.) DDC 128
1. Authenticity (Philosophy) I. Title.
B105.A8 H37 2002

Hartman, Robert S., 1910-1973.
[Conocimiento del bien. English]
The knowledge of good : critique of axiological reason / Robert S. Hartman ; edited by Arthur R. Ellis, Rem B. Edwards. Amsterdam ; New York, NY : Rodopi, c2002. xiv, 470 p. ; 24 cm. (Value inquiry book series ; v. 126) (Value inquiry book series. Hartman Institute axiology studies) "An expanded translation by the author based on his Conocimiento del bien: Critica de la razón axiológica." ISBN 90-420-1220-X
1. Values. 2. Good and evil. I. Ellis, Arthur R. II. Edwards, Rem Blanchard. III. Title. IV. Series. V. Series: Value inquiry book series. Hartman Institute axiology studies
BD232 .H324 2002

Hartman, Sandra J.
Harris, O. Jeff. Organizational behavior. New York : Best Business Books, c2002.
HD58.7 .H36943 2002

Hartmann, Nicolai, 1882-1950.
[Struktur des ethischen Phänomens. English]
Moral phenomena : volume one of Ethics / Nicolai Hartmann ; with a new introduction by Andreas A.M. Kinneging. New Brunswick, N.J. : Transaction Publishers, c2002, 1932. xxxvi, 358 p. ; 23 cm. Originally published: Vol. 1 of Ethics. New York : MacMillan, 1932, in series: Library of philosophy. With new introd. Includes bibliographical references and index. ISBN 0-7658-0909-5 (pbk. : alk. paper) DDC 170
1. Ethics. I. Title.
BJ1012 .H342 2002

HARTMANN, VON AUE, 12TH CENT. IWEIN.
Hübner, Gert. Erzählform im höfischen Roman. Tübingen : Francke, 2003.

Hartwig, Myriam, 1971-.
Liebe und Abhängigkeit. Weinheim : Juventa, 2001.

Haruki, Yutaka, 1933-.
The embodiment of mind. Delft : Eburon, c1998.
BF161 .E43 1998

Harvard business essentials. Hiring and keeping the best people. Boston : Harvard Business School Press, c2002. xiv, 170 p. ; 24 cm. (The Harvard business essentials series) Includes bibliographical references (p. 161-164) and index. ISBN 1-57851-875-X (alk. paper) DDC 658.3/1
1. Employee selection. 2. Employee retention. 3. Employee motivation. I. Harvard Business School. II. Title: Hiring and keeping the best people III. Series.
HF5549.5.S38 H37 2002

Harvard business essentials. Managing change and transition. Boston, Mass. : Harvard Business School Press, c2003. vi, 138 p. : ill. ; 24 cm. (The Harvard business essentials series) Includes bibliographical references (p. 125-131) and index. CONTENTS: Introduction : the dimensions of change -- Are you change-ready? -- Seven steps to change -- Implementation -- Social and human factors -- Helping people adapt -- Toward continous change. ISBN 1-57851-874-1 (alk. paper) DDC 658.1/6
1. Organizational change. 2. Organizational change - Management. I. Series.
HD58.8 .M2544 2003

Harvard business essentials : managing creativity and innovation. Boston, Mass. : Harvard Business School Press, c2003. xv, 174 p. : ill. ; 24 cm. (The Harvard business essentials series) Includes bibliographical references (p. 163-165) and index. CONTENTS: Types of innovation : several types on many fronts -- The S-curve : a concept and its lessons -- Idea generation : opening the genie's bottle -- Recognizing opportunities : don't let the good ones slip by -- Moving innovation to market : will it fly? -- Creativity and creative groups : two keys to innovation -- Enhancing creativity : enriching the organization and workplace -- What leaders must do : making a difference. ISBN 1-59139-112-1 (alk. paper) DDC 658.5/14
1. Technological innovations - Management. 2. New products - Management. 3. Creative ability. I. Title: Managing creativity and innovation II. Series.
HD45 .H3427 2003

The Harvard business essentials series
Harvard business essentials. Hiring and keeping the best people. Boston : Harvard Business School Press, c2002.
HF5549.5.S38 H37 2002

Harvard business essentials. Managing change and transition. Boston, Mass. : Harvard Business School Press, c2003.
HD58.8 .M2544 2003

Harvard business essentials. Boston, Mass. : Harvard Business School Press, c2003.
HD45 .H3427 2003

Harvard business review.
Harvard business review on breakthrough leadership. Boston, Mass. : [Great Britain] : Harvard Business School Press, c2001.

Harvard business review on breakthrough leadership. Boston, Mass. : [Great Britain] : Harvard Business School Press, c2001. vii, 190 p. ; 21 cm. (The Harvard business review paperback series) Articles reprinted from Harvard business review. Includes index. ISBN 1-57851-805-9 DDC 658.4092
1. Leadership. I. Title: Harvard business review. II. Series.

The Harvard business review paperback series
Harvard business review on breakthrough leadership. Boston, Mass. : [Great Britain] : Harvard Business School Press, c2001.

Harvard Business School.
Harvard business essentials. Hiring and keeping the best people. Boston : Harvard Business School Press, c2002.
HF5549.5.S38 H37 2002

Harvard-Yenching Institute monograph series
(58) Writing and materiality in China. Cambridge, Mass. : Published by Harvard University Asia Center for Harvard-Yenching Institute ; distributed by Harvard University Press, 2003.
PL2262 .W74 2003

Harvey, Andrew, 1952- A walk with four spiritual guides : Krishna, Buddha, Jesus, and Ramakrishna / Andrew Harvey. Woodstock, VT : SkyLight Paths Pub., c2003. xiii, 168 p. : ill. ; 23 cm. Includes bibliographical references (p. 166-168). CONTENTS: Krishna -- Buddha -- Jesus -- Ramakrishna. ISBN 1-89336-173-X (hardcover) DDC 291.4
1. Spiritual life. 2. Religions. I. Title.
BL624 .H3445 2003

Harvey, Elizabeth D.
Sensible flesh. Philadelphia, PA : University of Pennsylvania Press, 2003.
BF275 .S46 2003

Hasegawa, Takahiko.
Environmentally sustainable buildings. Paris : Organisation for Economic Co-operation and Development, 2003.

Hasidic thought.
Elior, Rachel. Ḥerut ʻal ha-luḥot. [Tel Aviv] : Miśrad ha-biṭaḥon, [1999]

HASIDISM.
Alter, Judah Aryeh Leib, 1847-1905. [Selections. 2000] Penine Śefat Emet. Ofrah : Mekhon Shovah, [2000?-2003?]
BM198.2 .A55 2000

Golan, Mor Yosef. Sefer ha-Neshamah ba-guf. Itamar : M.Y. Golan, 762 [2001 or 2002]

Ḥayim Yeroḥam ben Shimshon Meshulam Feybish, mi-Snatin. Sefer Asefat divre ḥakhamim. Yerushalayim : Mekhon Sod yesharim, 761 [2001]

Miṭelman, Yiśraʼel Yehudah. Ḳuntres Ḥazak ve-nitḥazek. Ashdod : T. T. di-ḥaside Belza, 762 [2002]

Mosheh ben Ḥayim, Koznitser, d. 1874. Sefer Ahavat Yiśraʼel. Yotse le-or me-hadash. Yerushalayim : Mekhon Sod yesharim, 760 [2000]

Mosheh ben Ḥayim, Koznitser, d. 1874. Sefer ʻAhavat Yiśraʼel. Bruḳlin : [Yehoshuʻa Pinḥas Bukhinger], 762 [2001]

Segal, Yehudah Zeraḥyah, ha-Levi. Sefer Doreshe H.. Tel-Aviv : Talmiday ve-shmomʻe liḳho, 763 [2003]
BJ1287.S43 D66 2003

Steinsaltz, Adin. [Beʼur Tanya. English] Opening the Tanya. 1st ed. San Francisco : Jossey-Bass, c2003.
BM198.2.S563 S7413 2003

HASIDISM - CANADA - QUEBEC - BOISBRAIND (KIRYAS TOSH).
Admur ha-G. ha-K., Sheliṭa. [ʻAvodat ʻavodah (Torah)] Sefer ʻAvodat ʻavodah. Ḳiryat Ṭohsh, Ḳanada : N. M. Hershḳoviṭsh, 763 [2002 or 2003]

HASIDISM - HISTORY.
Elior, Rachel. Ḥerut ʻal ha-luḥot. [Tel Aviv] : Miśrad ha-biṭaḥon, [1999]

HASSIDISM. *See* **HASIDISM.**

Hassin, Ran R.
The new unconscious. New York : Oxford University Press, 2004.
BF315 .N47 2004

Hasty, Will.
A companion to Gottfried von Strassburg's "Tristan". Rochester, NY : Camden House, 2003.
PT1526 .C66 2003

Hasumi, Shiguehiko.
La modernité après le post-moderne. Paris : Maisonneuve & Larose, [2002]

HATE.
Ben-Zeʼev, Aharon. Be-sod ha-regashot. Lod : Zemorah-Bitan, 2001.

Gaylin, Willard. Hatred. 1st ed. New York : Public Affairs, c2003.
BF575.H3 G39 2003

Hating in the first person plural. New York : Other Press, c2003.
RC506 .H285 2003

HATE - JUVENILE LITERATURE.
Davidson, Tish. Prejudice. New York : Franklin Watts, c2003.
BF575.P9 D38 2003

HATE - RELIGIOUS ASPECTS.
Eidelberg, Paul. Clash of two decadent civilizations. Shaarei Tikva, Israel : ACPR Publications, 2002.
BM537 .E53 2002

Hateley, B. J. Gallagher (Barbara J. Gallagher), 1949- Everything I need to know I learned from other women / BJ Gallagher. York Beach, ME : Conari Press, c2002. xii, 270 p. ; 20 cm. ISBN 1-57324-859-2 DDC 305.4
1. Women - Psychology. 2. Women - Conduct of life. I. Title.
HQ1206 .H345 2002

Hathaway, Michael R. The everything psychic book : tap into your inner power and discover your inherent abilities / Michael R. Hathaway. Avon, Mass. : Adams Media Corp., c2003. xii, 289 p. ; 24 cm. (The everything series) Includes bibliographical references (p. 274-277). CONTENTS: What is psychic ability? -- Early psychic experiences -- In tune with your guides -- Keep yourself grounded -- Psychic development training -- Working with your chakras -- Relying on your guides -- Clairvoyance or psychic sight -- Clairaudience or psychic hearing -- Clairsentience or psychic feeling -- Astral projection and telekinetic powers -- Psychic work in your sleep -- It's in the cards and the stars -- A plethora of psychic tools -- The art of dowsing -- Creative psychic talents -- Psychic healing and medical intuition -- The psychic gifts of children -- Getting help from the pros -- Let your psychic ability grow and flourish. ISBN 1-58062-969-5 DDC 133.8
1. Psychic ability. I. Title. II. Series. III. Series: Everything series.
BF1031 .H2955 2003

Hathaway, Robert A. Runes from the New World / by Robert A. Hathaway. 2nd ed. [San Diego, Calif.?] : R.A. Hathaway, c2002. i, 116 p. : ill. ; 23 cm. DDC 133.3/3
1. Fortune-telling by runes. 2. Divination. 3. Runes. I. Title.
BF1891.R85 H38 2002

HATHOR (EGYPTIAN DEITY).
St. George, E. A. (Elizabeth Ann), 1937- Hathor, the cow goddess. London : Spook Enterprises, c2001.

Hathor, the cow goddess.
St. George, E. A. (Elizabeth Ann), 1937- London : Spook Enterprises, c2001.

HATHOR THE GREAT (EGYPTIAN DEITY). *See* **HATHOR (EGYPTIAN DEITY).**

Hating in the first person plural : psychoanalytic essays on racism, homophobia, misogyny, and terror / edited by Donald Moss. New York : Other Press, c2003. xxxiv, 336 p. ; 24 cm. Includes bibliographical references. ISBN 1-59051-014-3 DDC 152.4
1. Hate. 2. Psychoanalysis. 3. Racism. I. Moss, Donald, 1949-
RC506 .H285 2003

HATRED. *See also* **HATE.**
Gaylin, Willard. 1st ed. New York : Public Affairs, c2003.
BF575.H3 G39 2003

Hatwell, Yvette.
Touching for knowing. Amsterdam ; Philadelphia : John Benjamins Pub., c2003.
BF275 .T69 2003

Hatyár, Helga.
Magyarok és nyelvtörvények. Budapest : Teleki László Alapítvány, 2002.
PH2073 .K66 2002

Hauck, Dennis William. The international directory of haunted places : ghostly abodes, sacred sites, and other supernatural locations / Dennis William Hauck. New York : Penguin Books, 2000. ix, 275 p. : ill. ; 24 cm. Includes bibliographical references (p. [253]-254) and index. ISBN 0-14-029635-2 DDC 133.1/09
1. Haunted places - Guidebooks. I. Title. II. Title: Haunted places
BF1471 .H38 2000

HAUERWAS, STANLEY, 1940-.
Smith, R. Scott, 1957- Virtue ethics and moral knowledge. Aldershot, England ; Burlington, VT : Ashgate, c2003.
BJ1012 .S5195 2003

Haugaard, Mark, 1961-.
Making sense of collectivity. London ; Sterling, Va. : Pluto Press, 2002.
HM753 .M35 2002

Haugen Sørensen, Arne, 1932- Samtaler på en bjergtop : om skabelsesproces og verdensanskuelse i kunsten / Arne Haugen Sørensen og Leo Tandrup ; forlagsredaktion, Steen Piper. 1. oplag. Højbjerg : Hovedland, c2002. 227 p. : col. ill. ; 25 cm. Includes bibliographical references. ISBN 87-7739-591-3
1. Art - Philosophy. 2. Creation (Literary, artistic, etc.) I. Tandrup, Leo. II. Piper, Steen. III. Title.

Haughton, Hugh, 1948-.
Freud, Sigmund, 1856-1939. [Essays. English. Selections] The uncanny. New York : Penguin Books, 2003.
BF109.F75 A25 2003

Haunted Atlanta and beyond.
Bender, William N. Athens, Ga. : Hill Street Press, 2004.
BF1472.U6 B46 2004

HAUNTED CASTLES - MASSACHUSETTS - GLOUCESTER.
Pettibone, John W. The ghosts of Hammond castle. Glen Ridge, N.J. : Tory Corner Editions, c2001.
BF1474 .P48 2001

HAUNTED HOTELS - GEORGIA.
Roberts, Nancy, 1924- Georgia ghosts. Winston-Salem N.C. : John F. Blair, Publisher, c1997, 2002.
BF1472.U6 R6318 1997

HAUNTED HOTELS - UNITED STATES - GUIDEBOOKS.
Smith, Terry (Terry L.), 1961- Haunted inns of America. Birmingham, Ala. : Crane Hill Publishers, c2003.
BF1474.5 .S65 2003

Haunted houses.
Netzley, Patricia D. San Diego, Calif. : Lucent Books, c2000.
BF1461 .N48 2000

Haunted houses. San Diego, Calif. : Greenhaven Press, 2004.
BF1475 .H32 2004

Vinokurov, Igorʼ. Ne smotrite im v glaza!. Moskva : AiF-Print, 2001.
BF1466 .V56 2001

Wlodarski, Robert James. The haunted Whaley house, Old Town, San Diego, California. 2nd ed. West Hills, Calif. : G-HOST Pub., 2004.
BF1472.U6 W584

HAUNTED HOUSES - CALIFORNIA - CALABASAS.
Wlodarski, Robert James. Spirits of the Leonis adobe. West Hills, Calif. : G-Host Pub., c2002.
BF1472.U6 W59 2002

HAUNTED HOUSES - GEORGIA.
Roberts, Nancy, 1924- Georgia ghosts. Winston-Salem N.C. : John F. Blair, Publisher, c1997, 2002.
BF1472.U6 R6318 1997

HAUNTED HOUSES - JUVENILE LITERATURE.
Netzley, Patricia D. Haunted houses. San Diego, Calif. : Lucent Books, c2000.
BF1461 .N48 2000

Haunted houses / Terry O'Neill, book editor. San Diego, Calif. : Greenhaven Press, 2004. p. cm. (Fact or fiction) Includes bibliographical references and index. ISBN 0-7377-1068-3 (alk. paper) ISBN 0-7377-1067-5 (pbk. : alk. paper) DDC 133.1/22
1. Haunted houses. I. O'Neill, Terry, 1944- II. Series: Fact or fiction (Greenhaven Press)
BF1475 .H32 2004

HAUNTED HOUSES - UNITED STATES - JUVENILE LITERATURE.
Wlodarski, Robert James. The haunted Whaley house, Old Town, San Diego, California. 2nd ed. West Hills, Calif. : G-HOST Pub., 2004.
BF1472.U6 W584

Haunted inns of America.
Smith, Terry (Terry L.), 1961- Birmingham, Ala. : Crane Hill Publishers, c2003.
BF1474.5 .S65 2003

Haunted Lake Superior.
Bishop, Hugh E., 1940- 1st ed. Duluth, Minn. : Lake Superior Port Cities, c2003.
BF1472.U6 B565 2003

HAUNTED LOCALITIES. *See* **HAUNTED PLACES.**

Haunted Michigan.
Hunter, Gerald S. 1st ed. Chicago, IL : Lake Claremont Press, 2000.

BF1472.U6 H86 2000

Haunted New Jersey.
Martinelli, Patricia A. Mechanicsburg, PA : Stackpole Books, 2005.
BF1472.U6 M38 2004

HAUNTED PLACES. *See also* **GHOSTS; HAUNTED CASTLES; HAUNTED HOTELS; HAUNTED HOUSES.**
Hauck, Dennis William. The international directory of haunted places. New York : Penguin Books, 2000.
BF1471 .H38 2000

HAUNTED PLACES - ALABAMA - MOBILE.
Parker, Elizabeth. Mobile ghosts. 1st ed. Spanish Fort, Ala. : Apparition Pub., c2001.
BF1472.U6 P36 2001

HAUNTED PLACES - GUIDEBOOKS.
Hauck, Dennis William. The international directory of haunted places. New York : Penguin Books, 2000.
BF1471 .H38 2000

HAUNTED PLACES - HAWAII.
Grant, Glen. Glen Grant's chicken skin tales. Honolulu, Hawaii : Mutual Pub., c1998.
BF1472.U6 G72 1998

HAUNTED PLACES - HUDSON RIVER VALLEY (N.Y. AND N.J.).
Richardson, Judith. Possessions. Cambridge, Mass. : Harvard University Press, 2003.
BF1472.U6 R54 2003

HAUNTED PLACES - MASSACHUSETTS - BOSTON.
Nadler, Holly Mascott. Ghosts of Boston town. Camden, Me. : Down East Books, c2002.
BF1472.U6 N32 2002

HAUNTED PLACES - MICHIGAN.
Hunter, Gerald S. Haunted Michigan. 1st ed. Chicago, IL : Lake Claremont Press, 2000.
BF1472.U6 H86 2000

HAUNTED PLACES - NEW BRUNSWICK.
Dearborn, Dorothy, 1927- New Brunswick haunted houses-- and other tales of strange and eerie events. Saint John, NB : Neptune Pub., c2000.
BF1472.N48 D44 2000

HAUNTED PLACES - NEW ENGLAND.
Pitkin, David J. Ghosts of the Northeast. Salem, NY : Aurora Publications, c2002.
BF1472.U6 P57 2002

HAUNTED PLACES - NEW YORK (STATE) - WARWICK.
Reis, Donna. Seeking ghosts in the Warwick Valley. Atglen, PA : Schiffer Pub., c2002.
BF1472.U6 R45 2002

HAUNTED PLACES - NOVA SCOTIA.
Walsh, Darryll. Ghosts of Nova Scotia. East Lawrencetown, N.S. : Pottersfield Press, c2000.
BF1472.C3 W35 2000

Haunted San Francisco : the city's best ghost stories / compiled and edited by Rand Richards. 1st ed. San Francisco : Heritage House Publishers, 2004. p. cm. Includes index. Table of contents URL: http://www.loc.gov/catdir/toc/ecip046/2003015644.html ISBN 1-87936-704-1 DDC 133.1/09794/61
1. Ghosts - California - San Francisco. 2. Ghost stories - California - San Francisco. I. Richards, Rand, 1949-
BF1472.U6 H385 2004

The haunted Whaley house, Old Town, San Diego, California.
Wlodarski, Robert James. 2nd ed. West Hills, Calif. : G-HOST Pub., 2004.
BF1472.U6 W584

Hauschild, Thomas.
Inspecting Germany. Münster : Lit, c2002.
DD76 .I57 2002

Staschen, Heidi. Hexen. Originalausg. Krummwisch [Germany] : Königsfurt, 2001.

Havemann, Ernest.
Kagan, Jerome. Kagan & Segal's psychology. 9th ed. Belmont, CA : Thomson/Wadsworth, c2004.
BF121 .K22 2004

Haverkamp, Anselm.
Blumenberg, Hans. Ästhetische und metaphorologische Schriften. 1. Aufl. Frankfurt : Suhrkamp, 2001.

Haviland, James J. This book is no joke! : the critical role of humor in communication / James J. Haviland. [Philadelphia?] : Xlibris, c2001. 122 p. ; 22 cm. Includes bibliographical references (p. [120]-122). ISBN 0-7388-1849-6 (softcover) DDC 153.6

1. Interpersonal communication. 2. Wit and humor - Psychological aspects. I. Title.
BF637.C45 H38 2001

Having a good cry.
Warhol, Robyn R. Columbus : Ohio State University Press, c2003.
PN56.5.W64 W375 2003

Having it all?.
Nicolson, Paula. Chichester, West Sussex, England ; Hoboken, NJ : J. Wiley, c2002.
HQ1206 .N645 2002

HAWAII - FICTION.
Kingston, Maxine Hong. The fifth book of peace. 1st ed. New York : Alfred A. Knopf, 2003.
PS3561.I52 F44 2003

Hawk, Ambrose. Exploring scrying : how to divine the future and make the most of it / Ambrose Hawk. Franklin Lakes, NJ : New Page Books, c2001. xiii, 162 p. : ill. ; 21 cm. Includes bibliographical references (p. 155-158) and index. ISBN 1-56414-503-4 DDC 133.3/22
1. Crystal gazing. I. Title.
BF1335 .H39 2001

Hawke, Elen, 1947- An alphabet of spells / Elen Hawke. St. Paul, MN : Llewellyn Publications, 2003. xiii, 130 p. ; 15 cm. Includes index. ISBN 0-7387-0466-0 DDC 133.4/4
1. Witchcraft. 2. Charms. 3. Magic. I. Title.
BF1566 .H376 2003

Hawker, Gloria Ann. Morning glory : diary of an alien abductee / by Gloria Ann Hawker. Merrimack, NH : Write to Print, c2001. iv, 375 p. : ill. ; 23 cm. ISBN 0-9714272-3-2 DDC 001.942
1. Alien abduction. 2. Hawker, Gloria Ann. I. Title.
BF2050 .H373 2001

HAWKER, GLORIA ANN.
Hawker, Gloria Ann. Morning glory. Merrimack, NH : Write to Print, c2001.
BF2050 .H373 2001

Hawking, S. W. (Stephen W.).
[Cambridge lectures]
The theory of everything : the origin and fate of the universe / Stephen W. Hawking. Beverly Hills, CA : New Millennium Press, c2002, 1996. xii, 176 p. ; 22 cm. Originally published: The Cambridge lectures: life works. West Hollywood, CA : Dove Books, c1996. Includes index. CONTENTS: First lecture-ideas about the universe -- Second lecture-the expanding universe -- Third lecture-black holes -- Fourth lecture-black holes ain't so black -- Fifth lecture-the origin and fate of the universe -- Sixth lecture-the direction of time -- Seventh lecture-the theory of everything. ISBN 1-89322-454-6 (Hardcover) DDC 523.1
1. Cosmology. 2. Science - Philosophy. I. Title. II. Title: Origin and fate of the universe
QB985 .H39 2002

On the shoulders of giants. Philadelphia : Running Press, c2002.
QC6.2 .O5 2002

Haworth gay & lesbian studies
Gottlieb, Andrew R. Sons talk about their gay fathers. New York : Harrington Park Press, c2003.
HQ76.13 .G67 2003

Häxornas försvarare.
Guillou, Jan, 1944- [Stockholm?] : Piratförlaget, c2002.
BF1584.S8 G85 2002

Hay, Louise L. I can do it! : how to use affirmations to change your life / Louise L. Hay. Carlsbad, CA : Hay House, c2004. p. cm. CONTENTS: Health -- Forgiveness -- Prosperity/wealth -- Creativity -- Relationships/romance -- Job success -- Stress-free living -- Self-esteem. ISBN 1401902197 DDC 158
1. Affirmations. 2. Self-talk. 3. Change (Psychology) I. Title.
BF697.5.S47 H388 2004

Hayat, Michaël. Dynamique des formes et représentations : vers une biosymbolique de l'humain / Michaël Hayat. Paris : Harmattan, c2002. 6 v. ; 22 cm. (Collection L'ouverture philosophique) "Volume 1 de l'ouvrage général ..." Includes bibliographical references. CONTENTS: v. 1. Vers une philosophie matérialiste de la représentation -- v. 2. Représentation et anti-représentation : des beaux-arts à l'art contemporain -- v. 3. Arts assistés par machine et art contemporain : vers une nouvelle philosophie de l'art? -- v. 4. Psychanalyse et biologie -- v. 5. Dynamique des formes et représentation : pour une biopsychologie de la pensée -- v. 6. Philosophie, biosymbolique de l'humain et représentation du réel. ISBN 2-7475-3079-5 (v. 1) ISBN 2-7475-3075-2 (v. 2) ISBN 2-7475-3078-7 (v. 3) ISBN 2-7475-3077-9 (v. 4) ISBN 2-7475-3076-0 (v. 5) ISBN 2-7475-3081-7 (v. 6)

1. Representation (Philosophy) 2. Mental representation. 3. Art and science. I. Title. II. Series.
B105.R4 H392 2002

Hayes-Roth, Frederick, 1947- Radical simplicity : transforming computers into me-centric appliances / Frederick Hayes-Roth, Daniel Amor. Upper Saddle River, N.J. ; London : Prentice Hall PTR, 2003. xxvii, 328 p. : ill. ; 23 cm. (Hewlett-Packard Press strategic books) Includes bibliographical references and index. ISBN 0-13-100291-0 DDC 004.678
1. Human-computer interaction. 2. User interfaces (Computer systems) 3. Internet. 4. World Wide Web. 5. Electronic commerce. I. Amor, Daniel. II. Title.

Ḥayim shel ṭaʻam, ḥayim shel mashmaʻut.
Eyal, Tsevi. Mi she-taʻam yayin Hungari. Tel Aviv : Yediʻot aharonot : Sifre ḥemed, c2002.

Ḥayim Yeroḥam ben Shimshon Meshulam Feybish, mi-Snaṭin. Sefer Asefat divre ḥakhamim : she-nidpas be-sof sefer Divre ḥayim / ḥubar ʻal yede ... Ḥayim Yeroḥam ... mi-Snaṭin. Yerushalayim : Mekhon Sod yesharim, 761 [2001] 92, 42, 3 p. ; 24 cm. Cover title: Asefat divre ḥakhamim. Running title: Or zoreaḥ. Includes also: Ḳunṭres Or zoreaḥ, 42 p. at end.
1. Hasidism. 2. Jewish sermons, Hebrew. 3. Ethics, Jewish. I. Title. II. Title: Divre ḥayim. III. Title: Ḳunṭres Or zoreaḥ. IV. Title: Asefat divre ḥakhamim V. Title: Or zoreaḥ

Haynes, Andrew.
Trainor, Norm, 1946- The eight best practices of high-performing salespeople. Toronto ; New York : Wiley, c2000.
HF5438.25 .T72 2000

Haynes, Cyndi.
[Book of friendship]
Friendship : making life better / Cyndi Haynes. New York : Gramercy Books, 2003. 324 p. ; 19 cm. ISBN 0-517-22266-3 DDC 158.2/5
1. Friendship. I. Title.
BF575.F66 H39 2003

Hays, Kate F. You're on! : consulting for peak performance / Kate F. Hays and Charles H. Brown, Jr. 1st ed. Washington, DC : American Psychological Association, c2003. p. cm. Includes bibliographical references and index. CONTENTS: Part I: Setting the stage -- The roots of performance consultation -- The back story : research in performance consultation -- Part II: Domain-specific information -- Unique aspects of the business domain -- Unique aspects of the high risk domain -- Unique aspects of the performing arts domain -- Part III: Key factors in performance -- The foundations of excellent performance -- Getting it right : preparation -- Keeping your head : mental skills -- The microscopic nightmare of infinity : the experience of stress -- Reframe and relax : coping with stress -- You're on! -- Part IV: What do performers want? -- The help they need : assistance performers desire -- The ideal consultant -- Consultant efforts that hinder performance -- Part V: Consultants need : training, ethics, and practice -- A good fit : training, competence, and ethics -- The consultant as performer. ISBN 1-59147-078-1 (hardcover : alk. paper) DDC 158/.3
1. Counseling. 2. Performance - Psychological aspects. 3. Success - Psychological aspects. I. Brown, Charles H. II. Title.
BF637.C6 H366 2003

Ḥayun, Yehudah ben Mordekhai. Masekhet ha-ḥayim : divre gedole ha-dorot ʻal kol teḳufah u-teḳufah be-ḥaye ha-adam / Yehuda Ḥayun. Bene Beraḳ : Y. Ḥayun, 762 [2001 or 2002] 2 v. ; 24 cm. Cover title: Sefer Masekhet ha-ḥayim.
1. Ethics, Jewish. 2. Jews - Conduct of life. I. Title. II. Title: Sefer Masekhet ha-ḥayim

HAZARDOUS GEOGRAPHIC ENVIRONMENTS. *See* **DISASTERS.**

Hazel, Elizabeth. Tarot decoded : understanding and using dignities and correspondences / Elizabeth Hazel. Boston, MA : Weiser Books, 2004. p. cm. Includes bibliographical references and index. CONTENTS: Forms of dignity -- Elementary elements -- Elemental court cards -- Modal dignities -- Numeric dignities -- Planetary trumps as free agents -- Elemental trumps and the outer planets -- Planetary and zodiacal dignities -- The cosmic axis and other spreads -- Locational dignities -- Directional scanning -- Demonstrations. ISBN 1-57863-302-8 DDC 133.3/2424
1. Tarot. 2. Dignities (Astrology) 3. Hermetic Order of the Golden Dawn. I. Title.
BF1879.T2 H339 2004

HCI models, theories, and frameworks.
Carroll, John M. San Francisco, Calif. : Morgan Kaufmann, 2003.

He, Bingsong, 1890-1946.
[Works. 1996]
He Bingsong wen ji / Liu Yinsheng, Fang Xinliang bian. Di 1 ban. Beijing : Shang wu yin shu guan,

1996. 5 v. : ill. ; 21 cm. CONTENTS: Di 1 juan. Zhong gu Ou zhou shi, Jin shi Ou zhou shi -- ti 2 juan. Lun wen bian, jiao yu bian, sui bi za wen bian, xu ba bian, han dian bian, bao gao bian, bu yi -- di 3 juan. Xin shi xue, Xi yang shi xue shi, Li shi jiao xue fa -- ti 4 juan. Li shi yan jiu fa, tong shi xin yi, Zhe dong xue pai ni yuan, Qin shi huang di, cong li shi dao zhe xue, Meiguo zheng fu jian she zhi jing guo, Lashite Yan shi kao, Meiguo jiao yu zhi du, Ho Bingsong nian pu -- ti 5 juan. Chu zhong wai guo shi, gao zhong wai guo shi. ISBN 7-100-01914-1 (v. 1) ISBN 7-100-01958-3 (v. 2) ISBN 7-100-01959-1 (v. 3) ISBN 7-100-02038-7 (v. 4) ISBN 7-100-02039-5 (v. 5)
1. China - Historiography. 2. Historiography. I. Liu, Yinsheng. II. Fang, Xinliang. III. Title.
DS734.7 .H664

He Bingsong wen ji.
He, Bingsong, 1890-1946. [Works. 1996] Di 1 ban. Beijing : Shang wu yin shu guan, 1996.
DS734.7 .H664

He, Jun.
Zeng, Guofan, 1811-1872. Fan jing. Di 1 ban. Beijing : Zhongguo Hua qiao chu ban she, 2001.
BJ1618.C5 H44 2001

He lakhem ḥamishah sefari. / [Avraham Prizak, mo. l.]. [Brooklyn, NY : Renaissance Hebraica, 2000?] 1 v. (various pagings) ; 15 cm. Reprints. Originally published: Lunéville, 1807. CONTENTS: Masekhet Derekh erets -- Sefer ha-gan / Yitshaḳ ben Eli'ezer -- Orḥot ḥayim / Asher ben Yeḥi'el -- Zikhron teru'ah / Mordekhai Brandes -- Binah la-'itim.
1. Ethics, Jewish. 2. Shofar calls. I. Yitshaḳ ben Eli'ezer, 15th cent. Sefer ha-gan. II. Asher ben Jehiel, ca. 1250-1327. Orḥot ḥayim. III. Brandes, Mordekhai. Zikhron teru'ah. IV. Title: Masekhet Derekh erets. V. Title: Binah la-'itim.

He, Zhaowu. Wei cao ji / He Zhaowu. Di 1 ban. Beijing : Sheng huo, du shu, xin zhi san lian shu dian, 1999. 1, 2, 537 p. ; 19 cm. (Du shu wen cong) Includes bibliographical references. ISBN 7-108-01268-5
1. History - Philosophy. I. Title. II. Series.
D16.8 .H42 1999

HEAD. See **BRAIN; FACE; PHRENOLOGY.**

Head, Tom.
Mysterious places. San Diego, CA : Greenhaven Press, 2004.
BF1031 .M96 2004

Possessions and exorcisms. San Diego, Calif. : Greenhaven Press, 2004.
BF1555 .P68 2004

Headlines in history
The 1000s. San Diego, Calif. : Greenhaven Press, c2001.
CB354.3 .A16 2001

Headlines in history (San Diego, Calif.)
The 1500s. San Diego, Calif : Greenhaven Press, c2001.
CB367 .A165 2001

HEADS OF STATE. See **PRESIDENTS; PRIME MINISTERS.**

HEALERS - BIOGRAPHY.
Curcio, Kimberly Panisset. Man of light. 1st ed. New York : SelectBooks, c2002.
BF1045.M44 C87 2002

HEALERS - ZIMBABWE - MBERENGWA DISTRICT.
Dahlin, Olov, 1962- Zvinorwadza. Frankfurt am Main ; New York : P. Lang, c2002.
R726.5 .D34 2002

HEALING. See also **HEALERS.**
Dooley, Deborah. Journeying into wholeness with map & skills. [Meno Park, Calif. : Delphi Press, c2003]
BF710 .D64 2003

Sylvest, Vernon M. The formula. Fairfield, Iowa : Sunstar Pub., c1996.
BF161 .S95 1996

Healing chakra.
Lee, Ilchi. Las Vegas, NV : Healing Society, c2002.
BF1442.C53 L44 2002

HEALING - GREAT BRITAIN - MISCELLANEA.
McArthur, Margie. Faery healing. Aptos, Calif. : New Brighton Books, 2003.
BF1552 .M36 2003

Healing identities.
Burack, Cynthia, 1958- Ithaca : Cornell University Press, 2004.
BF175.4.F45 B87 2004

HEALING (IN RELIGION, FOLK-LORE, ETC.). See **HEALING - RELIGIOUS ASPECTS.**

Healing magic.
Bennett, Robin Rose. New York : Sterling Pub., 2004.
BF1572.S65 B46 2004

HEALING - MISCELLANEA.
Scully, Nicki, 1943- Alchemical healing. Rochester, Vt. : Bear & Co., 2003.
BF1999 .S369 2003

The healing power of humor.
Klein, Allen. Waterville, Me. : Thorndike Press, 2003.
BF575.L3 K56 2003

HEALING - PSYCHOLOGICAL ASPECTS.
Edgar, Robin A. In my mother's kitchen. 2nd ed. Charlotte, N.C. : Tree House Enterprises, 2003.
BF378.R44 E34 2003

Moerman, Daniel E. Meaning, medicine, and the "placebo effect". Cambridge ; New York : Cambridge University Press, 2002.
R726.5 .M645 2002

HEALING - RELIGIOUS ASPECTS. See **SPIRITUAL HEALING.**

HEALING - RELIGIOUS ASPECTS - BUDDHISM.
Psychology and Buddhism. New York : Kluwer Academic/Plenum Publishers, c2003.
BQ4570.P76 P78 2003

HEALING - RELIGIOUS ASPECTS - CHRISTIANITY.
Trasferetti, José Antônio. Deus a força que cura!. Campinas, SP : Editora Átomo, 2002.

HEALING - RELIGIOUS ASPECTS - ISLAM.
Sengers, Gerda. Vrouwen en demonen. Amsterdam : Het Spinhuis, 2000.
BF1275.F3 S46 2000

Sengers, Gerda. Women and demons. Leiden ; Boston : Brill, 2003.
BF1275.F3 S463 2003

HEALING - RELIGIOUS ASPECTS - JUDAISM.
Va'eḵnin, Yosef ben Avraham. Sefer Ka-sheleg yalbinu. Yerushalayim : Y. Va'eḵnin, 763 [2002 or 2003]

HEALING, SPIRITUAL. See **SPIRITUAL HEALING.**

HEALTH. See also **DISEASES; MENTAL HEALTH; SELF-CARE, HEALTH; STRESS MANAGEMENT.**
Carr, Alan, Dr. Positive psychology. London ; New York : Brunner-Routledge, 2004.
BF121 .C355 2004

Ke, Yunlu. Fu gui yu ying er. Di 1 ban. Shanghai : Shanghai ren min chu ban she : Xin hua shu dian Shanghai fa xing suo jing xiao, 1996.
BD431 .K6134 1996 <Asian China>

HEALTH ATTITUDES. See **HEALTH BEHAVIOR.**

HEALTH BEHAVIOR. See **SELF-CARE, HEALTH.**

HEALTH BEHAVIOR - CONGRESSES.
Self, social identity, and physical health. New York : Oxford University Press, 1999.
R726.5 .S46 1999

HEALTH CARE. See **MEDICAL CARE.**

HEALTH CARE DELIVERY. See **MEDICAL CARE.**

HEALTH CARE ETHICS. See **MEDICAL ETHICS.**

HEALTH CARE FACILITIES. See **HEALTH FACILITIES.**

HEALTH CARE INSTITUTIONS. See **HEALTH FACILITIES.**

HEALTH CARE POLICY. See **MEDICAL POLICY.**

HEALTH CARE, SELF. See **SELF-CARE, HEALTH.**

HEALTH EDUCATION OF WOMEN. See **WOMEN - HEALTH AND HYGIENE.**

HEALTH FACILITIES. See **HOSPITALS.**

HEALTH FACILITIES - PERSONNEL MANAGEMENT.
Sperry, Len. Becoming an effective health care manager. Baltimore, Md. : Health Professions Press, c2003.
RA971 .S72 2003

HEALTH HABITS. See **HEALTH BEHAVIOR.**

Health, healing and the amuse system.
McGhee, Paul E. 3rd ed. Dubuque, Iowa : Kendall/Hunt Pub., c1999.
BF575.L3 M38 1999

HEALTH INSTITUTIONS. See **HEALTH FACILITIES.**

Health of the telecommunication sector.
United States. Congress. House. Committee on Energy and Commerce. Subcommittee on Telecommunications and the Internet. Washington : U.S. G.P.O. : For sale by the Supt. of Docs., U.S. G.P.O. [Congressional Sales Office], 2003.

United States. Congress. House. Committee on Energy and Commerce. Subcommittee on Telecommunications and the Internet. Washington : U.S. G.P.O. : For sale by the Supt. of Docs., U.S. G.P.O., [Congressional Sales Office], 2003.

HEALTH OF WOMEN. See **WOMEN - HEALTH AND HYGIENE.**

HEALTH POLICY. See **MEDICAL POLICY.**

HEALTH RECORDS. See **MEDICAL RECORDS.**

Health reference series
Attention deficit disorder sourcebook. 1st ed. Detroit, MI : Omnigraphics, c2002.
RJ506.H9 A885 2002

HEALTH - RELIGIOUS ASPECTS - CHRISTIANITY.
Webster, Alison R. Wellbeing. London : SCM, c2002.

HEALTH SELF-CARE. See **SELF-CARE, HEALTH.**

HEALTH SERVICES. See **MEDICAL CARE.**

HEALTH SERVICES ADMINISTRATION.
Martin, Vivien, 1947- Leading change in health and social care. London ; New York : Routledge, 2003.
RA971 .M365 2003

Sperry, Len. Becoming an effective health care manager. Baltimore, Md. : Health Professions Press, c2003.
RA971 .S72 2003

HEALTH SERVICES ADMINISTRATORS.
Sperry, Len. Becoming an effective health care manager. Baltimore, Md. : Health Professions Press, c2003.
RA971 .S72 2003

HEALTHS, DRINKING OF. See **DRINKING CUSTOMS.**

Healy, Jane M. Your child's growing mind : a practical guide to brain development and learning from birth to adolescence / Jane Healy. 3rd ed. New York : Broadway Books, 2004. p. cm. Includes bibliographical references and index. ISBN 0-7679-1615-8 DDC 155.4/13
1. Learning, Psychology of. 2. Child rearing. 3. Educational psychology. 4. Pediatric neuropsychology. I. Title.
BF318 .H4 2004

HEARING. See also **AUDITORY PERCEPTION; LISTENING.**
Eaton, Robert C. The octavolateralis system and Mauthner cell interactions and questions [microform]. [Washington, D.C. : National Aeronautics and Space Administration, 1997]

Moore, Brian C. J. An introduction to the psychology of hearing. 5th ed. Amsterdam ; Boston : Academic Press, c2003.
BF251 .M66 2003

Hearing America's youth.
Cornbleth, Catherine. New York : P. Lang, c2003.
BF724.3.I3 .C67 2003

HEARING DISORDERS IN CHILDREN. See **HEARING IMPAIRED CHILDREN.**

Hearing gesture.
Goldin-Meadow, Susan. Cambridge, Mass. : Belknap Press of Harvard University Press, 2003.
P117 .G65 2003

HEARING IMPAIRED. See **DEAF.**

HEARING IMPAIRED CHILDREN - EDUCATION.
Grundlagen und Modelle für den Hörgerichteten Spracherwerb. Villingen-Schwenningen : Neckar, c1995.

Hearing with the heart.
Farrington, Debra K. 1st ed. San Francisco : Jossey-Bass, c2003.

BV4509.5 .F37 2003

Hearn, Jeff. Gender, sexuality and violence in organizations : the unspoken forces of organization violations / Jeff Hearn and Wendy Parkin. London ; Thousand Oaks : SAGE, 2001. xiv, 202 p. : ill. ; 24 cm. Includes bibliographical references (p. [174]-197) and index. ISBN 0-7619-5911-4 ISBN 0-7619-5912-2 (PBK.) DDC 302.35
1. Sexual harassment of women. 2. Sex discrimination in employment. 3. Sexual division of labor. 4. Sex role in the work environment. 5. Bullying in the workplace. 6. Violence in the workplace. 7. Organizational behavior. I. Title.

A heart, a cross & a flag.
Noonan, Peggy, 1950- New York : Free Press, c2003.
E903 .N66 2003

Heart, a cross, and a flag.
Noonan, Peggy, 1950- A heart, a cross & a flag. New York : Free Press, c2003.
E903 .N66 2003

The heart of mentoring.
Stoddard, David A., 1953- Colorado Springs, Colo. : NavPress, 2003.
BF637.C6 S773 2003

The heart of reality.
Solovyov, Vladimir Sergeyevich, 1853-1900. [Essays. English. Selections] Notre Dame, Ind. : University of Notre Dame Press, c2003.
B4262.A5 W69 2003

Heart of the matter.
Austin, Linda S., 1951- New York : Atria Books, c2003.
BF575.L8 A97 2003

Heath, Maya, 1948- Magical oils by moonlight : understanding essential oils, their blends and uses, discover the power of the moon phases, learn the meanings of oils, choose the appropriate day and time / by Maya Heath. Franklin Lakes, NJ : New Page Books, 2004. p. cm. Includes index. ISBN 1-56414-733-9 (pbk.) DDC 133.4/3
1. Essences and essential oils - Miscellanea. 2. Moon - Phases - Miscellanea. 3. Magic. I. Title.
BF1442.E77 H43 2004

Heath, Sue.
Social conceptions of time. Houndmills, Basingstoke, Hampshire ; New York : Palgrave MacMillan, 2002.
HM656 .S63 2002

HEATHENISM. See **PAGANISM.**

HEAVEN.
Zolla, Elémire. Catàbasi e anàstasi. Alpignano, [Italy] : Tallone Editore, 2001.

Hebert, Karen.
The peak performance series. Vol. [4] [videorecording]. Longwood, Fla. : Pamela Bolling Enterprises, c1999.

HEBREW JEWISH SERMONS. See **JEWISH SERMONS, HEBREW.**

HEBREW LANGUAGE - ALPHABET - MISCELLANEA.
Ashcroft-Nowicki, Dolores. Illuminations. 1st ed. St. Paul, Minn. : Llewellyn Publications, 2003.
BF1623.C2 A84 2003

HEBREW LANGUAGE - ALPHABET - RELIGIOUS ASPECTS - JUDAISM.
Seidman, Richard. The oracle of Kabbalah. 1st ed. New York : St. Martin's Press, 2001.
PJ4589 .S42 2001

HEBREW LAW. See **JEWISH LAW.**

HEBREW LITERATURE. See **RABBINICAL LITERATURE.**

HEBREWS. See **JEWS.**

Hecht, Heiko.
Looking into pictures. Cambridge, Mass. : MIT Press, c2003.
BF243 .L66 2003

Heck, Alexander. Auf der Suche nach Anerkennung : Deutung, Bedeutung, Ziele und Kontexte von Anerkennung im gesellschaftstheoretischen Diskurs / Alexander Heck. Münster : Lit, c2003. vii, 428 p. ; 21 cm. (Politische Soziologie ; Bd. 17) Thesis (doctoral)-- Universität, Münster (Westfalen), 2002. Includes bibliographical references. ISBN 3-8258-6515-0 (pbk.)
1. Recognition (Philosophy) 2. Identity (Philosophical concept) I. Title. II. Series.

Hecker, JayEtta Z. Commercial aviation [electronic resource] : financial condition and industry responses affect competition / statement of JayEtta Hecker, Director, Physical Infrastructure Issues. [Washington, D.C.] : U.S. General Accounting Office, [2002] (Testimony : GAO-03-171 T) Running title: Airline financial condition. System requirements: Adobe Acrobat Reader. Mode of access: Internet from GPO Access web site. Address as of 06/10/03: http://frwebgate.access.gpo.gov/cgi- bin/getdoc.cgi?dbname=gao&docid=f:d03171t.pdf; current access available via PURL. Title from title screen (viewed on June 10, 2003). "For release ... October 2, 2002." Paper version available from: General Accounting Office, 441 G St., NW, Rm. LM, Washington, D.C. 20548. Includes bibliographical references. URL: http://purl.access.gpo.gov/GPO/LPS31847 Available in other form: Commercial aviation : financial condition and industry responses affect competition 16 p. (OCoLC)50814215.
1. Aeronautics, Commercial - United States. 2. Competition - United States. I. United States. General Accounting Office. II. Title. III. Title: Airline financial condition IV. Title: Commercial aviation : financial condition and industry responses affect competition 16 p. V. Series.

Heckmann, Heinz-Dieter.
Physicalism and mental causation. Exeter, UK ; Charlottesville, VA : Imprint Academic, c2003.
B825 .P494 2003

Hederman, Mark Patrick. Tarot : talisman or taboo? : reading the world as symbol / Mark Patrick Hederman. Dublin : Currach Press, 2003. 240 p., [24] p. of plates : ill. ; 22 cm. Includes bibliographical references. ISBN 1-85607-902-3
1. Tarot. 2. Major arcana (Tarot) I. Title.

HEDGES - INDIA - HISTORY.
Moxham, Roy. The great hedge of India. Large print ed. Oxford : ISIS, 2001.

HEDONISM. See **PLEASURE.**

Hedtke, Lorraine, 1957- Re-membering lives : conversations with the dying and the bereaved / Lorraine Hedtke, John Winslade. Amityville, N.Y. : Baywood Pub. Co., 2004. p. cm. (Death, value, and meaning series) Includes bibliographical references (p.   ) and index. ISBN 0-89503-285-6 (cloth) DDC 155.9/37
1. Death - Psychological aspects. 2. Terminally ill - Psychology. 3. Bereavement - Psychological aspects. 4. Grief. I. Winslade, John. II. Title. III. Title: Remembering lives IV. Series.
BF789.D4 H4 2004

Heertum, Cis van.
Magia, alchimia, scienza dal '400 al '700. Firenze : Centro Di, 2002.
BF1598.H6 M34 2002

HEGEL, GEORG WILHELM FRIEDRICH, 1770-1831. PHANOMENOLOGIE DES GEISTES.
Hegel's Phenomenology of spirit. Amherst, N.Y. : Humanity Books, 2003.
B2929 .H349 2003

HEGEL, GEORG WILHELM FRIEDRICH, 1770-1831.
Köhler, Manfred. Apokalypse oder Umkehr? Marburg : Tectum, 2000.

Hegel's Phenomenology of spirit : new critical essays / edited by Alfred Denker and Michael Vater. Amherst, N.Y. : Humanity Books, 2003. 359 p. ; 23 cm. Includes bibliographical references and index. ISBN 1-59102-056-5 (paper : alk. paper) DDC 193
1. Hegel, Georg Wilhelm Friedrich, - 1770-1831. - Phanomenologie des Geistes. 2. Spirit. 3. Consciousness. 4. Truth. I. Denker, Alfred, 1960- II. Vater, Michael G., 1944- III. Title: Phenomenology of spirit
B2929 .H349 2003

Hehle, Christine. Boethius in St. Gallen : die Bearbeitung der "Consolatio philosophiae" durch Notker Teutonicus zwischen Tradition und Innovation / von Christine Hehle. Tübingen : Niemeyer, 2002. x, 400 p. : ill. (some col.), facsims. ; 24 cm. (Münchener Texte und Untersuchungen zur deutschen Literatur des Mittelalters, 0580-1362 ; Bd. 122) Includes bibliographical references (p. [353]-383) and indexes. 1 p. of plate tipped in. Text in German, with excerpts in Old High German and Latin. ISBN 3-484-89122-X (cl.)
1. Boethius, - d. 524. - De consolatione philosophiae. 2. Notker - Labeo, - ca. 950-1022. 3. Kloster St. Gallen. 4. Philosophy, Medieval. I. Title. II. Series.

HEIDEGGER, MARTIN, 1889-1976. BEITRÄGE ZUR PHILOSOPHIE.
Vallega-Neu, Daniela, 1966- Heidegger's contributions to philosophy. Bloomington, IN : Indiana University Press, c2003.
B3279.H48 B454 2003

[Essays. English. Selections]
Supplements : from the earliest essays to Being and time and beyond / Martin Heidegger ; edited by John van Buren. Albany : State University of New York Press, c2002. ix, 206 p. ; 23 cm. (SUNY series in contemporary continental philosophy) Includes bibliographical references (p. 201-203). ISBN 0-7914-5505-X (alk. paper) ISBN 0-7914-5506-8 (pbk. : alk. paper) DDC 193
1. Philosophy. I. Van Buren, John, 1956- II. Title. III. Series.
B3279.H47 E5 2002d

SEIN AND ZEIT.
Alackapally, Sebastian, 1961- Being and meaning. 1st ed. Delhi : Motilal Banarsidass Publishers, 2002.
PK541.B48 A43 2002

SEIN UND ZEIT.
Carman, Taylor, 1965- Heidegger's analytic. Cambridge, UK ; New York : Cambridge University Press, 2003.
B3279.H48 S459 2003

Was heisst Denken? / Martin Heidegger ; [herausgegeben von Paola-Ludovika Coriando]. Frankfurt am Main : Vittorio Klostermann, c2002. 271 p. ; 21 cm. (Gesamtausgabe. I. Abteilung, Veröffentlichte Schriften 1910-1976 / Martin Heidegger ; Bd. 8) Anhang contains two texts (part of the 11th lecture and an undelivered 12th lecture) that were not included in the 1954 ed.--Cf. p. [267]. ISBN 3-465-03199-7 (alk. paper) ISBN 3-465-03198-9 (pbk. : alk. paper)
1. Thought and thinking. I. Coriando, Paola-Ludovica, 1969- II. Title. III. Series: Heidegger, Martin, 1889-1976. Works. 1975 ; Bd. 8.
B3279 .H45 1976 Bd.8

Works. 1975
(Bd. 8.) Heidegger, Martin, 1889-1976. Was heisst Denken? Frankfurt am Main : Vittorio Klostermann, c2002.
B3279 .H45 1976 Bd.8

HEIDEGGER, MARTIN, 1889-1976.
Berto, G. (Graziella) Freud, Heidegger. Milano : Bompiani, c1998.
BF175.4.P45 B46 1998

Clam, Jean. Was heisst, sich an Differenz statt an Identität orientieren? Konstanz : UVK Verlagsgesellschaft, c2002.

Jankovic, Zoran. Au-delà du signe. Paris : Harmattan, c2003.

Tietz, Udo. Ontologie und Dialektik. Wien : Passagen, c2003.
B3279.H49 T54 2003

Heidegger's analytic.
Carman, Taylor, 1965- Cambridge, UK ; New York : Cambridge University Press, 2003.
B3279.H48 S459 2003

Heidegger's contributions to philosophy.
Vallega-Neu, Daniela, 1966- Bloomington, IN : Indiana University Press, c2003.
B3279.H48 B454 2003

Heijden, A. H. C. van der. Attention in vision : perception, communication, and action / A.H.C. van der Heijden. 1st ed. New York : Psychology Press, 2003. p. cm. Includes bibliographical references and index. Table of contents URL: http://www.loc.gov/catdir/toc/ecip043/2003010585.html ISBN 1-84169-348-0 DDC 152.14
1. Visual perception. 2. Selectivity (Psychology) 3. Attention. I. Title.
BF241 .H42 2003

Heil, John. From an ontological point of view / John Heil. Oxford : Clarendon Press ; New York : Oxford University Press, 2003. xv, 267 p. : ill. ; 25 cm. Includes bibliographical references (p. [250]-259) and index. ISBN 0-19-925974-7 DDC 111
1. Ontology. I. Title.
BD306 .F76 2003

Heiliger Geist als Lebenskraft in Kirche und Menschheit.
Cho, Hyeon-Kweon Stephan, 1962- Frankfurt am Main ; New York : Peter Lang, c2002.
BT121.3 .C56 2002

Heilinger, Rudolf.
Stock, Karl F. Freud-Bibliographien. Graz : Stock & Stock, 1998.
BF109.F73 S76 1998

Heilman, Elizabeth E.
Harry Potter's world. New York ; London : RoutledgeFalmer, 2003.
PR6068.O93 Z73 2003

Heim, Pat. In the company of women : turning workplace conflict into powerful alliances / Pat Heim and Susan Murphy, with Susan K. Golant. New York :

J.P. Tarcher/Putnam, c2001. 335 p. ; 24 cm. Includes bibliographical references (p. 326-332). CONTENTS: Pt. 1. Conflict : why women behave the way they do. The golden triangle : relationships, power, and self-esteem -- The power dead-even rule -- From the xx files : the origins of woman-to-woman conflict -- Lessons from childhood -- The bitch factor : indirect aggression -- Pt. 2. Colleagues : finding powerful allies and friends among women in the workplace -- The goal is the relationship -- Loosening power dead-even double binds -- How to have healthy conflict with another woman -- Handling conflict with style -- How to be an effective female leader -- Building a dream team -- A final word -- Appendix A. Books on self-esteem -- Appendix B. Conflict Styles Questionnaire answer key. ISBN 1-58542-115-4 (alk. paper) DDC 650.1/3
1. Women employees. 2. Women - Communication. 3. Women - Psychology. 4. Female friendship. 5. Teams in the workplace. I. Murphy, Susan, 1947- II. Golant, Susan K. III. Title.
HD6053 .H387 2001

Heimann, Mikael.
Regression periods in human infancy. Mahwah, N.J. : Lawrence Erlbaum Associates, 2003.
BF720.R43 R44 2003

Heinamaa, Sara, 1960- Toward a phenomenology of sexual difference : Husserl, Merleau-Ponty, Beauvoir / Sara Heinamaa. Lanham, Md. ; Oxford : Rowman & Littlefield Publishers, c2003. xxi, 159 p. ; 23 cm. Includes bibliographical references (p. 137-151) and index. ISBN 0-8476-9784-3 (hbk. : alk. paper) ISBN 0-8476-9785-1 (pbk. : alk. paper) DDC 305.3/01
1. Beauvoir, Simone de, - 1908- - Deuxieme sexe. 2. Beauvoir, Simone de, - 1908- - Criticism and interpretation. 3. Husserl, Edmund, - 1859-1938. 4. Merleau-Ponty, Maurice, - 1908-1961. 5. Sex differences - Philosophy. 6. Body, Human (Philosophy) 7. Phenomenology. 8. Feminist theory. I. Title.
HQ1208 .B3523 2003

Heinegg, Peter.
Mortalism. Amherst, N.Y. : Prometheus Books, 2003.
BD431 .M886 2003

HEINRICH, VON VELDEKE, 12TH CENT. ENEIDE.
Hübner, Gert. Erzählform im höfischen Roman. Tübingen : Francke, 2003.

Heintz, Jean Georges.
Colloque de Strasbourg (14th : 1995) Oracles et prophéties dans l'Antiquité. Strasbourg : Publications de l'Université de Strasbourg II, 1997.
BF1761 .C65 1995

Heinz Kohut.
Strozier, Charles B. 1st pbk. ed. New York : Other Press, 2004.
BF109.K6 S77 2004

Heinz Werner lectures
(2003.) Flavell, John H. Development of children's knowledge about the mind. Worcester, Mass. : Clark University Press, 2003.
BF723.C5 F623 2003

(v. 24.) White, Sheldon Harold, 1928- Developmental psychology as a human enterprise. Worcester, Mass. : Clark University Press, c2001.
BF713 .W48 2001

Heinzmann, Wilhelm.
Runica, Germanica, Mediaevalia. Berlin : W. de Gruyter, 2003.

HEIRS. See **INHERITANCE AND SUCCESSION.**

The heirs of Plato.
Dillon, John M. Oxford : Clarendon Press ; New York : Oxford University Press, 2003.
B517 .D536 2003

Heise, Elóa.
Facetas das pós-modernidade. São Paulo : Universidade de São Paulo, Faculdade De Filosofia Letras e Ciências Humanas, 1996.

Heiwagaku ga wakaru. Tōkyō : Asahi Shinbunsha, 2002. 176 p. : ill. ; 26 cm. (AERA Mook ; no. 83) Cover title. "Asahi Shimbun extra report & analysis special number 83, 2002"--Cover. Includes a directory of universities and graduate schools in Japan which offer peace studies (p. [150-151]). Includes bibliographical references. "Heiwagaku ga wakaru bukku gaido gojū": p. 154-[160]. ISBN 4-02-274133-3
1. Peace. 2. Peace - Research. 3. World politics. I. Title: Aera (Tokyo, Japan) II. Series.
JZ5534 .H44 2002

Held, Jutta.
Intellektuelle in der Frühen Neuzeit. München : Fink, c2002.

Held, Klaus, 1936-.
Die erscheinende Welt. Berlin : Duncker & Humblot, c2002.

Die Heldenschilde.
Portaleone, Abraham ben David, 1542-1612. [Shilṭe Ha Gibborim. German] Frankfurt am Main : Lang, 2002.

HELL.
Smullyan, Raymond M. Who knows? Bloomington : Indiana University Press, c2003.
BL50 .S59 2003

Zolla, Elémire. Catàbasi e anàstasi. Alpignano, [Italy] : Tallone Editore, 2001.

Hell, Bertrand. Le tourbillon des génies : au Maroc avec les Gnawa / Bertrand Hell. Paris : Flammarion, c2002. 371 p. : ill. ; 22 cm. Includes bibliographical references (p. [365]-367). ISBN 2-08-211581-X DDC 297.40964
1. Gnawa (Brotherhood) 2. Folklore - Morocco. 3. Cults - Morocco. 4. Spirit possession. 5. Sufism - Rituals. 6. Morocco - Religious life and customs. I. Title. II. Title: Au Maroc avec les Gnawa

Hell hath no fury : women's letters from the end of the affair / edited by Anna Holmes ; foreword by Francine Prose. 1st Carroll & Graf ed. New York : Carroll & Graf Publishers, 2002. xxviii, 403 p. ; 22 cm. Includes bibliographical references (p. 369-387) and index. ISBN 0-7867-1037-3 DDC 306.7
1. Man-woman relationships - Case studies. 2. Separation (Psychology) - Case studies. 3. Women - Correspondence. I. Holmes, Anna (Anna Elizabeth)
HQ801 .H45 2002

HELLENISTIC JUDAISM. See **JUDAISM - HISTORY - POST-EXILIC PERIOD, 586 B.C.-210 A.D.**

Helliwell, John F. Globalization and well-being / John F. Helliwell. Vancouver : UBC Press, 2002. 104 p. ; 20 cm. Includes bibliographical references (p. 94-101) and index. ISBN 0-7748-0992-2 DDC 337
1. Globalization - Social aspects. 2. Quality of life. 3. Canada - Social conditions - 1991- 4. Political planning - Canada. I. Title.
HF1359 .H43 2002

Hellyer, Marcus.
Spee, Friedrich von, 1591-1635. [Cautio criminalis. English] Cautio criminalis, or, A book on witch trials. Charlottesville : University of Virginia Press, 2003.
BF1583.A2 S6813 2003

Helmont, Franciscus Mercurius van, 1614-1699.
Orio de Miguel, Bernardino, 1936- Leibniz y el pensamiento hermético. Valencia : Universidad Politécnica de Valéncia, Editorial U.P.V., [2002]

HELMONT, FRANCISCUS MERCURIUS VAN, 1614-1699.
Orio de Miguel, Bernardino, 1936- Leibniz y el pensamiento hermético. Valencia : Universidad Politécnica de Valéncia, Editorial U.P.V., [2002]

Helmuth Plessner.
Kämpf, Heike. 1. Aufl. Düsseldorf : Parerga, 2001.
B3323.P564 K36 2001

Help is here for facing fear.
Wigand, Molly. St. Meinrad, IN : One Caring Place/ Abbey Press, c2000.
BF723.F4 W54 2000

HELPFULNESS.
Day, Eileen. [I'm good at helping. Spanish] Soy bueno para ayudar. Chicago : Heinemann Library, 2003.
BF723.H45 D3918 2003

HELPING BEHAVIOR. See also **COUNSELING.**
Krieglstein, Werner J., 1941- Compassion. Amsterdam ; New York : Rodopi, c2002.

Śliwak, Jacek. Osobowość altruistyczna. Wyd. 1. Lublin : Red. Wydawnictw Katolickiego Uniwersytetu Lubelskiego, 2001.
BF637.H4 S58 2001

HELPING BEHAVIOR IN CHILDREN - JUVENILE LITERATURE.
Day, Eileen. [I'm good at helping. Spanish] Soy bueno para ayudar. Chicago : Heinemann Library, 2003.
BF723.H45 D3918 2003

HELPING BEHAVIOR - TEXTBOOKS.
Hill, Clara E., 1948- Helping skills. 2nd ed. Washington, DC : American Psychological Association, 2004.
BF637.C6 H46 2004

Helping children and adolescents cope with violence and disaster 1 v.
Helping children and adolescents cope with violence and disasters [electronic resource]. Bethesda, MD : Office of Communications and Public Liaison, [2001]

Helping children and adolescents cope with violence and disasters [electronic resource] / from the National Institute of Mental Health. Bethesda, MD : Office of Communications and Public Liaison, [2001] (NIH publication ; no. 01-3519) (Fact sheet) World Wide Web Resource System requirements: Adobe Acrobat Reader. Mode of access: Internet from the NIMH web site. Address as of 8/14/03: http://www.nimh.nih.gov/publicat/violence.pdf; current access available via PURL. Title from title screen (viewed on Aug. 14, 2003). SUMMARY: The National Institute of Mental Health (NIMH), a component of the U.S. Department of Health and Human Services National Institutes of Health, provides information on how to help school children of all ages cope with violence and disasters. NIMH discusses such topics as posttraumatic stress disorder and children's reactions to trauma, and suggests ways to help trauma survivors. URL: http://purl.access.gpo.gov/GPO/LPS35195 Available in other form: Helping children and adolescents cope with violence and disaster 1 v. (OCoLC)48960735. DDC 342.0418 DDC 362.88 DDC 363.34019 DDC 303.6019 DDC 305.235
1. United States. Dept. of Health and Human Services. National Institutes of Health. National Institute of Mental Health. 2. Children and violence - Psychological aspects. 3. Youth and violence - Psychological aspects. 4. Disasters - Psychological aspects. 5. Government information 6. Children and violence 7. Disasters - Psychological aspects 8. Violence - Psychological aspects 9. Youth I. National Institute of Mental Health (U.S.) II. National Institute of Mental Health (U.S.). Office of Communications and Public Liaison. III. Title: Helping children and adolescents cope with violence and disaster 1 v. IV. Series.

Helping children cope with the death of a parent.
Lewis, Paddy Greenwall, 1945- Westport, Conn. : Praeger, 2004.
BF723.G75 L49 2004

Helping kids cope : when a loved one is sick and preparing to die / Fairview Hospice, Fairview Health Services. Minneapolis : Fairview Press, 2003. p. cm. Includes bibliographical references. Table of contents URL: http://www.loc.gov/catdir/toc/ecip048/2003019923.html ISBN 1-57749-141-6 (pbk. : alk. paper) DDC 155.9/37/083
1. Bereavement in children. 2. Grief in children. 3. Children and death. 4. Child rearing. I. Fairview Hospice. II. Fairview Health Services.
BF723.G75 H35 2003

Helping skills.
Hill, Clara E., 1948- 2nd ed. Washington, DC : American Psychological Association, 2004.
BF637.C6 H46 2004

Helping teens work through grief.
Perschy, Mary Kelly, 1942- 2nd ed. New York : Brunner-Routledge, 2004.
BF724.3.G73 P47 2004

Helping your angry child.
Nemeth, Darlyne Gaynor. Oakland, Calif. : New Harbinger, c2003.
BF723.A4 N46 2003

HEMI-INATTENTION (NEUROLOGY). See **NEGLECT (NEUROLOGY).**

HEMIINATTENTION (NEUROLOGY). See **NEGLECT (NEUROLOGY).**

HEMISPATIAL NEGLECT (NEUROLOGY). See **NEGLECT (NEUROLOGY).**

Hemming, Jan. Begabung und Selbstkonzept : eine qualitative Studie unter semiprofessionellen Musikern in Rock und Pop / Jan Hemming. Münster : Lit, [2002?] 233 p. : ill. ; 21 cm. (Beiträge zur Musikpsychologie ; Bd. 3) Revision of the author's thesis (doctoral)--Bremen, 2000. Includes bibliographical references (p. 221-233). ISBN 3-8258-5586-4
1. Popular music - Psychological aspects. 2. Musical ability. 3. Self-perception. 4. Musicians - Psychology. 5. Rock musicians - Psychology. I. Title. II. Series.
ML3838 .H46 2002

Hen, Yitzhak.
De Sion exibit lex et verbum domini de Hierusalem. Turnhout, Belgium : Brepols, c2001.

Nashim, zekenim va-taf. Yerushalayim : Merkaz Zalman Shazar le-toldot Yiśra'el, [2001]

Henderson, Andrea.
The day our world changed. New York : Harry N. Abrams Inc., 2002.

Henderson, Joseph L. (Joseph Lewis), 1903-
Transformation of the psyche : the symbolic alchemy of the splendor solis / Joseph L. Henderson and Dyane N. Sherwood. New York : Brunner-Routledge, 2003.
p. cm. Includes bibliographical references (p.   ) and index.

Hendlin, Steven J.
Table of contents URL: http://www.loc.gov/catdir/toc/ecip044/2003011351.html ISBN 1-58391-950-3 DDC 150.19/54
1. Jungian psychology. 2. Alchemy - Psychological aspects. 3. Jung, C. G. - (Carl Gustav), - 1875-1961. I. Sherwood, Dyane N. II. Title.
BF173 .H4346 2003

Hendlin, Steven J. Overcoming the inheritance taboo : how to preserve relationships and transfer possessions / Steven J. Hendlin. New York : Plume, 2004. p. cm. Includes bibliographical references and index. ISBN 0-452-28476-7 (trade pbk.) DDC 306.87
1. Death - Psychological aspects. 2. Inheritance and succession - Psychological aspects. I. Title.
BF789.D4 H4235 2004

Henehan, Mary Pat. Integrating spirit and psyche : using women's narratives in psychotherapy / Mary Pat Henehan. New York ; London : Haworth Pastoral Press, c2003. xvii, 256 p. : ill. ; 23 cm. Includes bibliographical references (p. 221-246) and index. ISBN 0-7890-1209-X (hbk.) ISBN 0-7890-1210-3 (pbk.) DDC 616.89/14/082
1. Feminist therapy. 2. Feminist psychology. 3. Women - Psychology. 4. Autobiography - Therapeutic use. 5. Narrative therapy. 6. Personal construct therapy. I. Title.
RC489.F45 H46 2003

Heng, Geraldine. Empire of magic : medieval romance and the politics of cultural fantasy / Geraldine Heng. New York : Columbia University Press, c2003. xii, 521 p. ; 24 cm. Includes bibliographical references (p. [467]-498) and index. CONTENTS: Introduction: In the beginning was romance... -- Cannibalism, the First Crusade, and the genesis of medieval romance: Geoffrey of Monmouth's History of the kings of Britain -- The romance of England: Richard Coer de Lyon and the politics of race, religion, sexuality, and nation -- Warring against modernity: masculinity and chivalry in crisis; or, the alliterative Morte Arthure's romance examining of the Crusades -- Beauty and the East, a modern love story: women, children, and imagined communities in The man of law's tale and its others -- Eye on the world: Mandeville's pleasure zones; or, cartography, anthropology, and medieval travel romance. ISBN 0-231-12526-7 (cloth : alk. paper) ISBN 0-231-12527-5 (paper : alk. paper) DDC 820.9/001
1. Romances, English - History and criticism. 2. English literature - Middle English, 1100-1500 - History and criticism. 3. Politics and literature - England - History - To 1500. 4. Literature and society - England - History - To 1500. 5. Civilization, Medieval, in literature. 6. Imperialism in literature. 7. Crusades in literature. 8. Culture in literature. 9. Magic in literature. I. Title.
PR321 .H46 2003

Henn, Martin J., 1968-. Parmenides. [Nature. English & Greek] Parmenides of Elea. Westport, Conn. : Praeger, 2003.
B235.P23 N3713 2003

Henna.
Weinberg, Norma Pasekoff, 1941- Henna from head to toe!. Pownal, Vt. : Storey Books, c1999.
GT2343 .W45 1999

HENNA.
Weinberg, Norma Pasekoff, 1941- Henna from head to toe!. Pownal, Vt. : Storey Books, c1999.
GT2343 .W45 1999

Henna from head to toe!.
Weinberg, Norma Pasekoff, 1941- Pownal, Vt. : Storey Books, c1999.
GT2343 .W45 1999

Henning, Hai Lee Yang. Mian xiang : the Chinese art of face reading / Henning Hai Lee Yang. London : Vega, 2001. 228 p. : ill. ; 16 cm. Spine title: Chinese art of face reading. Includes index. ISBN 1-84333-020-2 DDC 138
1. Physiognomy - China. 2. Facial expression - China. I. Title. II. Title: Chinese art of face reading. III. Title: Chinese art of face reading
BF851 .H46 2001

Henry, Dale. The proverbial Cracker Jack : how to get out of the box and become the prize / Dale Henry. Hagerstown, Md. : Autumn House Pub., c2002. 224 p. ; ill. ; 24 cm. ISBN 1-87895-140-8 DDC 158
1. Self-actualization (Psychology) 2. Success - Psychological aspects. I. Title.
BF637.S4 H857 2002

Henry, Michel, 1922-
[C'est moi la vérité. English]
I am the truth : toward a philosophy of Christianity / Michel Henry ; translated by Susan Emanuel. Stanford, Calif : Stanford University Press, 2003. 282 p. ; 24 cm. (Cultural memory in the present) Includes bibliographical references. CONTENTS: Introduction: What do we mean by Christianity? -- Truth of the world -- The truth according to Christianity -- This truth called life -- The self-generation of life as generation of the first living -- The phenomenology of Christ -- Man as "son of God" -- Man as "son within the son" -- Forgetting the condition of son: "me, i"/"me, ego" -- The second birth -- The Christian ethic -- The paradoxes of Christianity -- The word of God, scripture -- Christianity and the world -- Conclusion: Christianity and the modern world. ISBN 0-8047-3775-4 (cloth : alk. paper) ISBN 0-8047-3780-0 (pbk. : alk. paper) DDC 230/.01
1. Christianity - Philosophy. 2. Man (Christian theology) 3. Truth - Religious aspects - Christianity. 4. Christian life. I. Title. II. Series.
BR100 .H39813 2003

Henson, Mitch.
[Clavicula Salomonis. English.] Lemegeton. Jacksonville, FL : Metatron Books, 1999.

HEORTOLOGY. See FASTS AND FEASTS.

Hepburn, Rae. Tea leaf fortune cards / Rae Hepburn ; illustrations by Shawna Alexander. 1st ed. Boston : Journey Editions, c2000. 89 p. : ill. ; 17 cm. + 4 packs of cards. ISBN 1-88520-376-4
1. Fortune-telling by tea leaves. 2. Fortune-telling by cards. I. Title.
BF1881 .H47 2000

Hepfer, Karl.
Hume, David, 1711-1776. [Enquiry concerning the principles of morals. German] Eine Untersuchung der Grundlagen der Moral. Göttingen : Vandenhoeck & Ruprecht, c2002.

Her-stories : hidden histories of women of faith in Africa / edited by Isabel Aphawo Phiri, Devarakshanam Betty Govinden & Sarojini Nadar. Pietermaritzburg, South Africa : Cluster, 2002. 428 p. : 21 cm. Includes bibliographical references. ISBN 1-87505-333-6 (pbk.) DDC 248.843
1. Women in Christianity. 2. Women and religion - Africa. 3. Women - Religious life. I. Phiri, Isabel Aphawo. II. Govinden, Devarakshanam Betty. III. Nadar, Sarojini.

HERACLES (GREEK MYTHOLOGY). See also HERCULES (ROMAN MYTHOLOGY).
Hercules. New York : Dell, c1997.
BL820.H5 H47 1997

HERALDRY. See EMBLEMS; KNIGHTS AND KNIGHTHOOD.

Herbal magic.
Dunwich, Gerina. Herbal magick. Franklin Lakes, NJ : New Page Books, c2002.
BF1572.P43 D85 2002

Herbal magick.
Dunwich, Gerina. Franklin Lakes, NJ : New Page Books, c2002.
BF1572.P43 D85 2002

Herbert, David, 1939- Religion and civil society : rethinking public religion in the contemporary world / David Herbert. Aldershot, Hampshire, England ; Burlington, VT : Ashgate, c2003. x, 322 p. ; 24 cm. (Ashgate religion, culture & society series) Includes bibliographical references and index. ISBN 0-7546-1332-1 ISBN 0-7546-1339-9 (pbk.) DDC 306.6
1. Religion and sociology. 2. Civil society. 3. Religion and culture. I. Title. II. Series.
BL60 .H457 2003

Herbert Quandt Stiftung.
The silent revolution. Bad Homburg v.d. Höhe : Herbert Quandt Foundation, 2000.
HQ1075 .S55 2000

HERBS - MISCELLANEA.
Aoumiel. Grimoire for the green witch. 1st ed. St. Paul, Minn. : Llewellyn Publications, c2003.
BF1572.P43 A583 2003

Dunwich, Gerina. Herbal magick. Franklin Lakes, NJ : New Page Books, c2002.
BF1572.P43 D85 2002

Wood, Jamie. The Wicca herbal. Berkeley, Calif. : Celestial Arts, c2003.
BF1572.P43 W66 2003

HERBS - THERAPEUTIC USE.
Blumenthal, Mark. Popular herbs in the U.S. market. Austin : American Botanical Council, 1997.

Carvalho, Angela Maria B., 1954- A magia das ervas e seu axé. São Paulo, SP : Madras, 2003.
1. Black author.

Herbst, Judith. Aliens / by Judith Herbst. Minneapolis : Lerner Publications, 2005. p. cm. (The unexplained) Includes index. SUMMARY: Investigates several well-known accounts of alien abduction as well as theories aimed at explaining why such reports could be true. Table of contents URL: http://www.loc.gov/catdir/toc/ecip046/2003015808.html CONTENTS: Snatch and grab -- You are getting ver-r-ry sleepy (and confused) -- Wake up and see the aliens -- Why us? ISBN 0-8225-0960-1 (lib. bdg. : alk. paper) DDC 001.942
1. Human-alien encounters - Juvenile literature. 2. Life on other planets - Juvenile literature. 3. Alien abduction. 4. Human-alien encounters. 5. Extraterrestrial beings. 6. Unidentified flying objects. I. Title. II. Series: Unexplained (Lerner Publications)
BF2050 .H465 2005

Vanished / by Judith Herbst. Minneapolis : Lerner Publications Co., 2005. v. cm. (The unexplained) Includes bibliographical references and index. CONTENTS: Amelia and gas gauge -- Chris and the triangle -- Dan's daring disappearance -- Prison break. ISBN 0-8225-1631-4 (lib. bdg. : alk. paper) ISBN 0-8225-2404-X (pbk. : alk. paper) DDC 001.94
1. Disappearances (Parapsychology) - Juvenile literature. 2. Disappearances (Parapsychology) 3. Missing persons. I. Title. II. Series: Unexplained (Lerner Publications)
BF1389.D57 H47 2005

HERCULES (ROMAN MYTHOLOGY). See also HERACLES (GREEK MYTHOLOGY).
Hercules. New York : Dell, c1997.
BL820.H5 H47 1997

Hercules : the complete myths of a legendary hero / with an afterword by Georges Moroz ; [map by Heather Saunders ; interior art by Chris Spollen]. New York : Dell, c1997. 132 p. ; 18 cm. (Laurel-leaf books) Includes bibliography: p. 132. SUMMARY: A retelling of the life and many exploits of the Greek hero Heracles, called Hercules by the Romans, from his birth to his eventual deification. ISBN 0-440-22732-1 DDC 292.2/113
1. Heracles (Greek mythology) 2. Hercules (Roman mythology) 3. Mythology, Greek. 4. Mythology, Roman. I. Moroz, Georges.
BL820.H5 H47 1997

HERDER, JOHANN GOTTFRIED, 1744-1803 - CONTRIBUTIONS IN PHILOSOPHY OF HISTORY.
Barnard, Frederick M., 1921- Herder on nationality, humanity, and history. Montreal : McGill-Queen's University Press, c2003.

HERDER, JOHANN GOTTFRIED, 1744-1803 - CONTRIBUTIONS IN POLITICAL SCIENCE.
Barnard, Frederick M., 1921- Herder on nationality, humanity, and history. Montreal : McGill-Queen's University Press, c2003.

Herder on nationality, humanity, and history.
Barnard, Frederick M., 1921- Montreal : McGill-Queen's University Press, c2003.

Herder Spektrum
(Bd. 5169) Maier, Johann. Judentum von A bis Z. Freiburg im Breisgau : Herder, 2001.

HERDERS. See LIVESTOCK.

Herdina, Philip. A dynamic model of multilingualism : perspectives of change in psycholinguistics / Philip Herdina and Ulrike Jessner. Clevedon, England Buffalo, N.Y. : Multilingual Matters, 2002. x, 182 p. : ill. ; 22 cm. (Multilingual matters ; 121) Includes bibliographical references (p. 162-179) and index. ISBN 1-85359-468-7 (alk. paper) ISBN 1-85359-467-9 (pbk. : alk. paper) DDC 306.44/6
1. Multilingualism - Psychological aspects. 2. Psycholinguistics. 3. Second language acquisition. 4. System theory. I. Jessner, Ulrike. II. Title. III. Title: Perspectives of change in psycholinguistics IV. Series: Multilingual matters series (2002) ; 121.
P115.4 .H47 2002

Herding, Klaus.
Psychische Energien bildender Kunst. 1. Aufl. Köln : DuMont, 2002.

Herederas y heridas.
García de León, María Antonia. 1a ed. [Madrid] : Ediciones Cátedra, Universitat de València, Instituto de la Mujer, 2002.
HD6054.2.S7 G37 2002

HEREDITARY SUCCESSION. See INHERITANCE AND SUCCESSION.

HEREDITY. See EUGENICS; GENETICS; NATURE AND NURTURE; VARIATION (BIOLOGY).

HEREDITY AND ENVIRONMENT. See NATURE AND NURTURE.

HERESIES, CHRISTIAN. See CHRISTIAN SECTS.

HERESY.
Xie jiao zhen xiang. Di 1 ban. Beijing : Dang dai shi jie chu ban she, 2001.

BT1315.2 .X54 2001

HERITAGE PROPERTY. *See* **CULTURAL PROPERTY.**

Herman, George A. (George Arthur), 1953-.
Organizing business knowledge. Cambridge, Mass. : MIT Press, c2003.
HD30.2 .T67 2003

A hermeneutic study of generational music.
Fletcher, John Wright. 2002.

HERMENEUTICS.
Antropología e interpretación. Tucumán, Argentina : Instituto de Estudios Antropológicos y Filosofía de la Religión, Facultad de Filosofía y Letras, Universidad Nacional de Tucumán, c2001.
BD450 .A564 2001

Bertram, Georg W., 1967- Hermeneutik und Dekonstruktion. München : Fink, c2002.
BD241 .B47 2002

Cherchi, Gavina, 1957- Tra le immagini. Fiesole (Firenze) : Cadmo ; Siena : Centro Mario Rossi per gli studi filosofici, 2002.

Domagala, Edward. L'ermeneutica dell'esperienza dell'amore in Max Scheler. Romae : [s.n.], 2000.

Fletcher, John Wright. A hermeneutic study of generational music. 2002.

Gadamer, Hans Georg, 1900- [Problème de la conscience historique. German] Das Problem des historischen Bewusstseins. Tübingen : Mohr Siebeck, 2001.

Gavalchin, John. Temporality in music. 2000.

Geiger, Wolfgang. Geschichte und Weltbild. 1. Aufl. Frankfurt am Main : Humanities Online, c2002.

Grenzen des Verstehens. Göttingen : Vandenhoeck & Ruprecht, c2002.
BD181.5 .G74 2002

Hufnagel, Erwin, 1940- Einführung in die Hermeneutik. [Neuaufl.]. St. Augustin : Gardez! Verlag, c2000.

Jankovic, Zoran. Au-delà du signe. Paris : Harmattan, c2003.

Krollmann, Fritz-Peter, 1963- Ethik und Ästhetik. Essen : Blaue Eule, 2002.

Küle, M. (Maija) Phenomenology and culture. Riga : Institute of Philosophy and Sociology, 2002.

Luft, Sandra Rudnick, 1934- Vico's uncanny humanism. Ithaca, N.Y. : Cornell University Press, 2003.
B3581.P73 L84 2003

On interpretation. Madison, Wis. : University of Wisconsin Press for the University of Wisconsin Law School, c2002.

Pagnini, Marcello. Letteratura ed ermeneutica. Firenze : L.S. Olschki, 2002.

Piazza, Giovanni. Sofferenza e senso. Torino : Camilliane, c2002.

Rosen, Stanley, 1929- Hermeneutics as politics. 2nd ed. New Haven, Conn. : Yale University Press, 2003.
BD241 .R81 2003

Roush, Sherry. Hermes' lyre. Toronto : University of Toronto Press, c2002.

The sacred and the profane. Aldershot, Hants, England ; Burlington, VT : Ashgate, c2003.
BD241 .S312 2003

Slavskaia, A. N. Lichnost' kak sub"ekt interpretatsii. Dubna : "Feniks+", 2002.
BF698 .S54 2002

Stecker, Robert, 1928- Interpretation and construction. Malden, MA : Blackwell, 2003.
BD241 .S78 2003

Transcendence in philosophy and religion. Bloomington, IN : Indiana University Press, c2003.
B56 .T73 2003

Hermeneutics as politics.
Rosen, Stanley, 1929- 2nd ed. New Haven, Conn. : Yale University Press, 2003.
BD241 .R81 2003

HERMENEUTICS - RELIGIOUS ASPECTS.
The sacred and the profane. Aldershot, Hants, England ; Burlington, VT : Ashgate, c2003.
BD241 .S312 2003

Hermeneutik und Dekonstruktion.
Bertram, Georg W., 1967- München : Fink, c2002.
BD241 .B47 2002

Hermes' lyre.
Roush, Sherry. Toronto : University of Toronto Press, c2002.

Hermes, Trismegistus. Divine Pymander : including The Asiatic mystery ; The Smaragdine table ; and The Song of Brahm / [edited by] Paschal Beverly Randolph. Rev. ed. Quakertown, PA : Philosophical Pub. Co., 2001. 176 p. : ill. ; 22 cm. DDC 135/.45
I. Randolph, Paschal Beverly, 1825-1874. II. Title. III. Title: Asiatic mystery. IV. Title: Smaragdine table. V. Title: Song of Brahm. VI. Title: Divine Pymander ; Asiatic mystery ; Smaragdine table ; Song of Brahm
BF1598.H5 E5 2001

Hermes, Trismegistus.
The emerald tablets of Thoth-the-Atlantean. Sedalia, Colo. : Brotherhood of the White Temple, c2002.
BF1999 .E44 2002

Hermes Trismegistus.
Magia, alchimia, scienza dal '400 al '700. Firenze : Centro Di, 2002.
BF1598.H6 M34 2002

HERMES, TRISMEGISTUS.
Dliasin, G. G. (Gennadiĭ Gennad'vich) Azbuka Germesa Trismegista, ili, Molekuliarnaia taĭnost' myshleniia. Izd. 2-e. Moskva : Izd-vo "Belye al'vy", 2002.
BF1616 .D58 2002

Proto, Antonino, 1925- Ermete Trismegisto. Milano : Mimesis, 2000.
BF1598.H6 P76 2000

HERMES, TRISMEGISTUS - EXHIBITIONS.
Magia, alchimia, scienza dal '400 al '700. Firenze : Centro Di, 2002.
BF1598.H6 M34 2002

HERMETIC ORDER OF THE GOLDEN DAWN.
Guide to the Golden Dawn Enochian skrying tarot. St. Paul, Minn. : Llewellyn, 2004.
BF1623.E55 G65 2004

Hazel, Elizabeth. Tarot decoded. Boston, MA : Weiser Books, 2004.
BF1879.T2 H339 2004

HERMETIC ORDER OF THE GOLDEN DAWN - RITUALS.
Cicero, Chic, 1936- Creating magical tools. 2nd ed. St. Paul, Minn. : Llewellyn Publications, 1999.
BF1623.R7 C48 1999b

Hermetic philosophy
(bk. 2) Baines, John. [Hombre estelar. English] The stellar man. 2nd ed. New York : John Baines Institute, Inc., 2002.
BF1621 .B3513 2002

HERMETICISM. *See* **HERMETISM.**

Hermetik : literarische Figurationen zwischen Babylon und Cyberspace / herausgegeben von Nicola Kaminski, Heinz J. Drügh und Michael Herrmann ; unter Mitarbeit von Andreas Beck. Tübingen : M. Niemeyer Verlag, c2002. x, 244 p. : ill. ; 22 cm. (Untersuchungen zur deutschen Literaturgeschichte, 0083-4564 ; Bd. 113) Papers presented at a colloquium held in honor of the 60th birthday of Hans-Georg Kemper, May 26, 2001, in Tübingen, Germany. Includes bibliographical references and index. cat 20030128 rsb ISBN 3-484-32113-X (pbk.)
1. Hermetism - Congresses. 2. Hermetism in literature - Congresses. 3. Alchemy in literature - Congresses I. Kemper, Hans-Georg. II. Kaminski, Nicola. III. Drügh, Heinz J., 1965- IV. Herrmann, Michael. V. Series.
BF1586 .H47 2002

HERMETISM.
The alchemy reader. Cambridge, U.K. New York : Cambridge University Press, 2003.
QD26 .A585 2003

Baines, John. [Hombre estelar. English] The stellar man. 2nd ed. New York : John Baines Institute, Inc., 2002.
BF1621 .B3513 2002

Dliasin, G. G. (Gennadiĭ Gennad'vich) Azbuka Germesa Trismegista, ili, Molekuliarnaia taĭnost' myshleniia. Izd. 2-e. Moskva : Izd-vo "Belye al'vy", 2002.
BF1616 .D58 2002

Ferrara, Franco, 1938- Dalle tenebre alla luce. Cosenza, Italia : Brenner, c2002.

Hall, Manly Palmer, 1901- The secret teachings of all ages. Reader's ed. New York : Jeremy P. Tarcher/Putnam, 2003.
BF1411 .H3 2003

HERMETISM - CONGRESSES.
Hermetik. Tübingen : M. Niemeyer Verlag, c2002.
BF1586 .H47 2002

HERMETISM - EUROPE - MANUSCRIPTS - EXHIBITIONS.
Magia, alchimia, scienza dal '400 al '700. Firenze : Centro Di, 2002.
BF1598.H6 M34 2002

HERMETISM - HISTORY - 16TH CENTURY.
Das Ende des Hermetismus. Tübingen : Mohr Siebeck, c2002.
BF1587 .E53 2002

HERMETISM - HISTORY - CONGRESSES.
Antike Weisheit und kulturelle Praxis. Göttingen : Vandenhoeck & Ruprecht, 2001.
BF1586 .A58 2001

HERMETISM IN LITERATURE.
Proto, Antonino, 1925- Ermete Trismegisto. Milano : Mimesis, 2000.
BF1598.H6 P76 2000

HERMETISM IN LITERATURE - CONGRESSES.
Hermetik. Tübingen : M. Niemeyer Verlag, c2002.
BF1586 .H47 2002

Herrmann, Theo.
Psycholinguistik. Berlin : W. de Gruyter, c2003.

Hernes, Tor.
Autopoietic organization theory. Oslo, Norway : Abstrakt forlag ; Malmö, Sweden : Liber Ekonomi ; Herndon, VA, USA : Copenhagen Business School Press, c2003.
HD31 .A825 2003

HEROES.
Danzig, Robert J., 1932- Every child deserves a champion. Washington, DC : Child & Family Press, c2003.
BF637.E53 D36 2003

Durschmied, Erik. Unsung heroes. London : Hodder & Stoughton, 2003.

Robertson, Linda R. (Linda Raine), 1946- The dream of civilized warfare. Minneapolis : University of Minnesota Press, c2003.
D606 .R63 2003

HEROES - CASE STUDIES - JUVENILE LITERATURE.
Survivors. New York : Scholastic, c2002.
BF637.S8 S8317 2002

HEROES IN ART.
La figure des héros dans la création contemporaine. Paris : Harmattan, c2002.

HEROES IN LITERATURE.
Matthews, Caitlin, 1952- Mabon and the guardians of Celtic Britain. Rochester, Vt. : Inner Traditions, c2002.
PB2273.M33 M37 2002

HEROES - NEW YORK (STATE) - NEW YORK.
Monahan, Brian. From ground zero to ground hero. [Newark, Del.?] : Disaster Research Center, University of Delaware, 2001.

Heroic leadership.
Lowney, Chris. Chicago : Loyola Press, c2003.
HD57.7 .L69 2003

HEROINES IN LITERATURE.
Bhāvamiśra, 19th cent. [Śṛṅgārasarasī. Hindi & Sanskrit] Śṛṅgārasarasī. Saṃskaraṇa 1. Vrndāvana : Vrndāvana Śodha Saṃsthāna, 2001.
PK2916+

HEROISM. *See* **HEROES.**

Heróstrato e a busca da imortalidade.
Pessoa, Fernando, 1888-1935. [Erostratus. Portuguese & English] Lisboa : Assírio e Alvim, c2000.

Herrera, Gioconda.
Masculinidades en Ecuador. Quito, Ecuador : FLACSO ; [S.l.] : UNFPA, 2001.
BF692.5 .M388 2001

Masculinidades en Ecuador. Quito, Ecuador : FLACSO ; [s.l.] : UNFPA, 2001.
BF692.5 .M37 2001

Herrmann, Michael.
Hermetik. Tübingen : M. Niemeyer Verlag, c2002.

Herrmann, Theo.
BF1586 .H47 2002

Herrmann, Theo.
Psycholinguistik. Berlin : W. de Gruyter, c2003.

Herrschaft des Symbolischen : Bewegungsformen gesellschaftlicher Theatralität : Europa, Asien, Afrika / herausgegeben von Joachim Fiebach und Wolfgang Mühl-Benninghaus. Berlin : Vistas, c2002. 366 p. : ill. ; 21 cm. (Berliner Theaterwissenschaft, 0948-7646 ; Bd. 8) Includes bibliographical references. ISBN 3-89158-336-2 (pbk.)
1. Theater and society. 2. Symbolism. I. Fiebach, Joachim. II. Mühl-Benninghaus, Wolfgang. III. Series.

Hertel, Paula.
Memory and emotion. Oxford University Press : New York, 2003.
BF378.A87 M46 2003

Ḥerut ʻal ha-luḥot.
Elior, Rachel. [Tel Aviv] : Miśrad ha-biṭaḥon, [1999]

Herzog August Bibliothek.
Strasser, Gerhard F. Emblematik und Mnemonik der frühen Neuzeit im Zusammenspiel Johannes Buno und Johann Justus Winckelmann. Wiesbaden : Harrassowitz Wolfenbüttel : Herzog August Bibliothek, c2000.
PN6348.5 .S873 2000

Herzog, Edgar.
[Psyche und Tod. English]
Psyche and death : death-demons in folklore, myths, and modern dreams / by Edgar Herzog ; translated from the German by David Cox and Eugene Rolfe ; with a new preface by C.L. Sebrell. New ed. / edited and designed by C.L. Sebrell. Woodstock, Conn. : Spring Publications, c2000. iv, 225 p. ; 22 cm. Translation of: Psyche und Tod. Includes bibliographical references (p. [226]-[228]). ISBN 0-88214-515-0
1. Death - Psychological aspects. 2. Mythology. 3. Dreams. I. Sebrell, C. L. II. Title.

Ḥesed ye-raḥamim.
Pinḥasi, Raḥamim. Sefer Ḥesed ye-raḥamim. Yerushalayim : R. Pinḥasi, 762 [2001 or 2002]

Hess-Lüttich, Ernest W. B.
Botschaften verstehen. Frankfurt am Main ; New York : P. Lang, c2000.
P91.25 .B688 2000

Medien, Texte und Maschinen. 1. Aufl. Wiesbaden : Westdeutscher Verlag, c2001.

Hess, Sabine, 1969-.
Geschlecht und Globalisierung. Königstein : Ulrike Helmer Verlag, c2001.

HESSE, HERMANN, 1877-1962.
Dimitrievich, Vladimir. V plenu germeticheskogo kruga. Perm' : Panagiia, 2001.
BF173.J85 D56 2001

HETEROSEXISM.
Segrest, Mab, 1949- Born to belonging. New Brunswick, NJ : Rutgers University Press, c2002.
HQ75.25 .S44 2002

Heuermann, Hartmut. Welt und Bewusstsein : eine Topographie der inneren Erfahrung / Hartmut Heuermann. Frankfurt am Main ; New York : Peter Lang, c2002. 490 p. ; 21 cm. Includes bibliographical references. ISBN 3-631-39388-1 (pbk.)
1. Thought and thinking. 2. Fantasy. I. Title.

HEURISTIC PROGRAMMING.
Data mining. Hershey : Idea Group, c2002.
QA76.9.D343 D36 2002

Heuscher, Julius E. (Julius Ernest), 1918- Psychology, folklore, creativity, and the human dilemma / by Julius E. Heuscher. Springfield, Ill. : Charles C Thomas Publisher, c2003. xxiv, 364 p. : ill. ; 26 cm. Includes bibliographical references (p. 359-364). ISBN 0-398-07410-0 (hbk.) ISBN 0-398-07411-9 (pbk.) DDC 158
1. Conduct of life. 2. Psychology and literature. 3. Folklore - Psychological aspects. I. Title.
BF637.C5 H475 2003

Hewstone, Miles.
Emotion and motivation. Malden, MA : Blackwell Pub., 2004.
BF531 .E4826 2004

Self and social identity. Malden, MA : Blackwell Pub., 2003.
BF697.5.S43 S429 2003

Social cognition. Malden, MA : Blackwell Pub., 2003.
BF316.6 .S65 2003

Hexen.
Staschen, Heidi. Originalausg. Krummwisch [Germany] : Königsfurt, 2001.

Hexen und Hexenverfolgung in Thüringen.
Füssel, Ronald. Erfurt : Landeszentrale für Politische Bildung Thüringen, 2001.
BF1583 .F87 2001

Hexenforschung
(Bd. 7.) Geschlecht, Magie und Hexenverfolgung. Bielefeld : Verlag für Regionalgeschichte, 2002.

Hey idiot!.
Gregory, Leland. Kansas City, MO : Andrews McMeel Pub., 2003.
BF431 .G7825 2003

Heyer, Judith.
Group behaviour and development. Oxford ; New York : Oxford University Press, 2002.
HD58.7 .G76 2002

Hiam, Alexander. Making horses drink : how to lead and succeed in business / by Alex Hiam. [Irvine, Calif.] : Entrepreneur Press, c2002. xi, 244 p. ; 21 cm. Includes index. Table of contents URL: http://www.loc.gov/catdir/toc/fy032/2002019155.html ISBN 1-89198-450-0 DDC 658.4/09
1. Leadership. 2. Employee motivation. 3. Success in business. I. Title.
HD57.7 .H52 2002

Hibbert, Adam, 1968- Why do people bully? / Adam Hibbert. Chicago, Ill. : Raintree, 2004. v. cm. (Exploring tough issues) Includes bibliographical references and index. Table of contents URL: http://www.loc.gov/catdir/toc/ecip048/2003018548.html CONTENTS: What is bullying? -- When does bullying happen? -- What are the causes of bullying? -- What does bullying do? -- How are bullies stopped? ISBN 0-7398-6681-8 DDC 302.3
1. Bullying - Juvenile literature. 2. Bullying. I. Title. II. Series.
BF637.B85 H53 2004

Hickman, Martha Whitmore, 1925- Wade in the water : 52 reflections on the faith we sing / Martha Whitmore Hickman. Nashville, TN : Abingdon Press, 2003. 72 p. ; 22 cm. Includes index. ISBN 0-687-02797-7 (pbk. : alk. paper) DDC 264/.076023
1. United Methodist Church (U.S.) - Hymns - History and criticism. 2. Hymns, English - History and criticism. 3. Meditations. I. Title. II. Title: 52 reflections on the faith we sing
BV310 .H53 2003

Hiepko, Andreas.
Rauschen. Würzburg : Königshausen & Neumann, c2001.

HIEROGLYPHICS. See also ALPHABET.
Marchand, Valère-Marie. Les alphabets de l'oubli. Paris : Editions Alternatives, 2002.
P211 .M373 2002

Higate, Paul.
Military masculinities. Westport, Conn. : Praeger, 2003.
U21.5 .M4975 2003

HIGGLING. See NEGOTIATION.

HIGH ACHIEVERS. See SUCCESSFUL PEOPLE.

High culture : reflections on addiction and modernity / edited by Anna Alexander and Mark S. Roberts. Albany : State University of New York Press, c2003. xiii, 402 p. ; 23 cm. (SUNY series, hot topics) Includes bibliographical references and index. ISBN 0-7914-5553-X (alk. paper) ISBN 0-7914-5554-8 (pbk. : alk. paper) DDC 394.1/4
1. Substance abuse. 2. Creative ability. 3. Inspiration. 4. Civilization, Modern. I. Alexander, Anna, 1956- II. Roberts, Mark S. III. Series.
HV4998 .H544 2003

HIGH ENERGY PHYSICS. See PARTICLES (NUCLEAR PHYSICS).

HIGH HOLIDAYS.
Levin, Yitsḥak, 1938- Sefer Netivot Yitsḥak. [Bene Beraḳ] : Y. Levin, [2000-

HIGH PERFORMANCE COMPUTING.
Roland, Alex, 1944- Strategic computing. Cambridge, Mass. : MIT Press, c2002.
QA76.88 .R65 2002

High performance leadership.
Winter, Graham. Singapore ; New York : John Wiley & Sons (Asia), c2003.

HIGH SCHOOL TEACHERS.
Shilony, Tamar. Model mentali shel morim menusim ye-tironim be-miktso'ot mada'iyim ye-humaniyim le-gabe lemidah be-ḳerev yeladim. [Israel : h. mo. l., 1994?]

Un hijo no puede morir.
Roccatagliata Orsini, Susana. 3. ed. Santiago de Chile : Grijalbo, 2000.
BF723.D3 R6 2000

HIKING. See MOUNTAINEERING.

Hildegard of Bingen's spiritual remedies.
Strehlow, Wighard, 1937- Rochester, Vt. : Healing Arts Press, c2002.
BT732.5 .S87 2002

HILDEGARD, SAINT, 1098-1179.
Strehlow, Wighard, 1937- Hildegard of Bingen's spiritual remedies. Rochester, Vt. : Healing Arts Press, c2002.
BT732.5 .S87 2002

Hilel, Yaʻaḳov Mosheh. Sefer Ahavat shalom : arbaʻah maʻamarim ha-medabrim nikhbadot odot gedulat ... maran ha-Rashash ... / she-ḥibarti Yaʻaḳov Mosheh Hilel. [Hotsaʼah 2], ʻim hosafot rabot. Yerushala[y]im : ha-Makhon le-hotsaʼat sefarim ye-khitve yad "Ahavat Shalom", 762 [2002] 30, 370 p. : facsims. ; 25 cm. (Sifre Mekhon "Ahavat shalom" Yerushalayim ; 300) Running title: Ahavat shalom. Includes bibliographical references.
1. Sharabi, Shalom, - 1720-1777. 2. Cabala. 3. Judaism - Ari rite. I. Title. II. Title: Ahavat shalom III. Series.

Sefer Shorshe ha-Yam : beʻurim ve-ḥidushim le-sefer ha-ḳadosh "ʻEts Ḥayim" she-neʼemru be-shiʻurim ... di-Yeshivat "Ḥevrat Ahavat shalom" ... : Shaʻar ha-tiḳun / Yaʻaḳov Mosheh Hilel. Yerushalayim : ha-Makhon le-hotsaʼat sefarim "Ahavat shalom", 759-[1999- v. ; 25 cm. Cover title: Shorshe ha-Yam.
1. Vital, Ḥayyim ben Joseph, - 1542 or 3-1620. - Shaʻar ha-tiḳun. 2. Cabala. I. Title. II. Title: Shorshe ha-Yam III. Title: Shorshe ha-Yam
BM525.V532 H5 1999

Shenot Ḥayim.
Vital, Ḥayyim ben Joseph, 1542 or 3-1620. ʻEts ha-daʻat tov. Yerushalayim : Hotsaʼat Ahavat shalom, 761 [2000 or 2001]

Hilgard, Ernest Ropiequet, 1904-.
Atkinson & Hilgard's introduction to psychology. 14th ed. Australia ; Belmont, CA : Wadworth/Thomson Learning, c2003.
BF121 .I57 2003

Hilgard's introduction to psychology.
Atkinson & Hilgard's introduction to psychology. 14th ed. Australia ; Belmont, CA : Wadworth/Thomson Learning, c2003.
BF121 .I57 2003

Hill, Clara E., 1948- Helping skills : facilitating exploration, insight, and action / Clara E. Hill. 2nd ed. Washington, DC : American Psychological Association, 2004. p. cm. Includes bibliographical references and index. ISBN 1-59147-104-4 (hardcover : alk. paper) DDC 158/.3
1. Counseling - Textbooks. 2. Helping behavior - Textbooks. I. Title.
BF637.C6 H46 2004

Hill, Craig C., 1957- In God's time : the Bible and the future / Craig C. Hill. Grand Rapids, Mich. : W.B. Eerdmans, c2002. viii, 229 p. : ill. ; 23 cm. Includes bibliographical references (p. 210-213) and indexes. ISBN 0-8028-6090-7 (pbk.) DDC 236
1. Future life. I. Title.
BT903 .H55 2002

Hill, Darryl B., 1963-.
About psychology. Albany : State University of New York Press, c2003.
BF38 .A28 2003

Hill, Linda A. (Linda Annette), 1956- Becoming a manager : how new managers master the challenges of leadership / Linda A. Hill. 2nd ed. Boston, Mass. : Harvard Business School Press, c2003. xix, 420 p. : ill. ; 24 cm. Includes bibliographical references (p. 387-410) and index. ISBN 1-59139-182-2 (alk. paper) DDC 658.4/09
1. Career changes. 2. Management. I. Title.
HF5384 .H55 2003

Hillard, John, 1946-.
Beyond Keynes. Cheltenham ; Northampton, Mass. : Edward Elgar, c2002.

HILLBILLY MUSIC. See COUNTRY MUSIC.

Hillix, William A. (William Allen), 1927-.
Rumbaugh, Duane M., 1929- Respondents, operants, and emergents [microform]. [Washington, D.C. : National Aeronautics and Space Administration, 1997]

Hillman, James.
L'incubo globale. Bergamo : Moretti & Vitali, c2002.

Hills, Richard Leslie, 1936-.
Cardwell, D. S. L. (Donald Stephen Lowell) The development of science and technology in nineteenth-century Britain. Aldershot, Great Britain ; Burlington, VT : Ashgate/Variorum, c2003.
Q127.G4 C37 2003

HINDI LANGUAGE - PSYCHOLOGICAL ASPECTS.
Vasishth, Shravan, 1964- Working memory in sentence comprehension. New York ; London : Routledge, 2003.
PK1933 .V28 2003

HINDI LANGUAGE - SENTENCES.
Vasishth, Shravan, 1964- Working memory in sentence comprehension. New York ; London : Routledge, 2003.
PK1933 .V28 2003

HINDU ART. See **ART, HINDU.**

HINDU ASTROLOGY.
Asalī prācīna Vaidika vāstu śāstra. 1. saṃskaraṇa. Dillī : Manoja Pôkeṭa Buksa, [2002?]
BF1729.A7 A83 2002

Bansal, Ashwinie Kumar. Vastu. Hauppauge, NY : Barron's, 2002.
BF1779.V38 B36 2002

Bloomfield, Andrew, 1960- How to practice Vedic astrology. Rochester, Vt. : Destiny Books, 2003.
BF1714.H5 B585 2003

Dvivedī, Bhojarāja. Ācārya Varāhamihira kā jyotisha meṃ yogadāna. 1. saṃskaraṇa. Naī Dillī : Rañjana Pablikeśansa, 2002.
BF1679.8.V37 D85 2002

Garga, Harīśa Kumāra, 1959- Jyotisha tattva vivecanī saṃhitā. 1. saṃskaraṇa. Dillī : Harīśa Kumāra Garga, 2002.
BF1714.H5 G365 2002

Johnsen, Linda, 1954- A thousand suns. St. Paul, MN : Yes International Publishers, 2003.
BF1714.H5 J665 2003

[Keralapraśnasaṅgraha. Hindi & Sanskrit.] Keralapraśnasaṅgrahaḥ. 1. saṃskaraṇa. Purī : Paramānandaprakāśanam, 1999.
BF1714.H5+

Lomaśa, Maharṣi. [Lomaśa saṃhitā. Hindi & Sanskrit] Lomaśa saṃhitā. Saṃskaraṇa 1. Ilāhābāda : Hindī Sāhitya Sammelana, Prayāga, 2002.
BF1714.H5+

[Mānasāgarī. Hindi & Sanskrit.] Mānasāgarī. Saṃskaraṇa 1. Haridvāra : Raṇadhīra Prakāśana, 2000.
BF1714.H5+

Parsai, K. B. [Predictive astrology] Star guide to predictive astrology. New Delhi : Rupa & Co., c2001.
BF1720.5 .P37 2001

Śarmā, Kisanalāla. Lāla kitāba. 1. saṃskaraṇa. Dillī : Manoja Pôkeṭa Buksa, [2000?]
BF1714.H5+

Śāstrī, Girijā Śaṅkara. Ācārya Varāhamihira. 1. saṃskaraṇa, Ilāhābāda : Jyotiṣa Karmakāṇḍa evaṃ Adhyātma Śodha Saṃsthāna, 2001.
BF1679.8.V37 S27 2001

Śāstrī, Girijā Śaṅkara. Bhāratīya Kuṇḍalī-vimarśa. 1. saṃskaraṇa. Ilāhābāda : Jyotiṣa Karmakāṇḍa evaṃ Adhyātma Śodha Saṃsthāna, 2002.
BF1714.H5+

Śāstrī, Umeśa. Vyāsasūtram. Jayapura : Yūnika Tredarsa, 2002.
BF1714.H5 S287 2002

Śāstrī, Vinoda, 1959- Jyotisha-vijñāna-nirjharī. Jayapura : Rājasthāna Saṃskṛta Akādamī, [2002?]
BF1714.H5 S288 2002

Veṅkaṭanāthārya. [Daśanirṇayī] Vaidikasārvabhaumanāmnā suprasiddhaiḥ Veṅkaṭanāthāryaiḥ Vaidikakarmānuṣṭhānasaukaryāya viracitā Daśanirṇayī. 1st ed. Mumbai : Śrīmadahobilamathena, 1998.
BL1226.72 .V36 1998

Whelan, Bilkis. Vastu in 10 simple lessons. 1st ed. New York : Watson-Guptill Publications, 2002.
BF1779.V38 W48 2002

Wilhelm, E. (Ernst) Vault of the heavens. 1st ed. [S.l.] : Kāla Occult Publishers, 2001.
BF1714.H5 W55 2001

HINDU ASTROLOGY - DICTIONARIES.
Agarwal, G. S., 1936- Dictionary of astrology. New Delhi : Sagar Publications, 2002.
BF1714.H5 A33 2002

HINDU ASTROLOGY - EARLY WORKS TO 1800.
Mantreśvara. Phaladīpikā. 1. saṃskaraṇa. Vārāṇasī : Caukhambā Surabhāratī Prakāśana, 2002.
BF1714.H5+

Nīlakaṇṭha, 16th cent. [Tājikanīlakaṇṭhī. English & Sanskrit] Tajik Nilkanthi = 1st ed. New Delhi : Ranjan Publications, 2001.
BF1714.H5 N4813 2001

Prthuyaśas. Ṣaṭpañcāśikā. 1. saṃskaraṇa. Vārāṇasī : Caukhambā Surabhāratī Prakāśana ; Dillī : Caukhambā Saṃskṛta Pratiṣṭhāna, 2002.
BF1714.H5 P7 2002

Vaidyanāthadīkṣita, 15th cent. [Jātakapārijāta] Jātakapārijātaḥ. 1. saṃskaraṇa. Vārāṇasī : Caukhambā Surabhāratī Prakāśana ; Dillī : Caukhambā Saṃskṛti Pratiṣṭhāna, 2001.
BF1714.H5 V253 2001

Varāhamihira, 505-587. Bṛhatsaṃhitā. 1. saṃskaraṇam. Vārāṇasī : Sampūrṇānanda Saṃskṛta Viśvavidyālaye, 2002-
BF1714.H5+

HINDU ASTROLOGY - HISTORY.
Śāstrī, Girijā Śaṅkara. Jyotisha tattva-viveka. 1. saṃskaraṇa, Ilāhābāda : Jyotisha Karmakāṇḍa evaṃ Adhyātma Śodha Saṃsthāna, 2001.
BF1714.H5 S277 2001

HINDU COSMOLOGY.
Jenkins, John Major. Galactic alignment. Rochester, Vt. : Bear & Co., 2002.
F1435.3.R3 J45 2002

HINDU EPISTEMOLOGY. See **KNOWLEDGE, THEORY OF (HINDUISM).**

HINDU LITERATURE - TRANSLATIONS INTO ENGLISH.
Robinson, Edward Jewitt. Tamil wisdom. New Delhi : Asian Educational Services, 2001.
BJ1571 .R63 2001

HINDU SYMBOLISM.
Bharadwaj, Monisha. The Indian luck book. London : Kyle Cathie, 2001.
BF1778 .B43 2001

Bühnemann, Gudrun. Maṇḍalas and Yantras in the Hindu traditions. Leiden ; Boston : Brill, 2003.
BL2015.M3 B85 2003

Kollar, L. Peter (Laszlo Peter), 1926- Symbolism in Hindu architecture as revealed in the Shri Minakshi Sundareswar. New Delhi : Aryan Books International, 2001.
NA6002 .K65 2001

Varshney, D. C., 1933- Hindū vijñāna evaṃ vidhi. 1. saṃskaraṇa. Lakhanaū : Nyū Rôyala Buka Kampanī, 2001.
BL1215.S36 V27 2001

HINDU TEMPLES. See **TEMPLES, HINDU.**

Hindū vijñāna evaṃ vidhi.
Varshney, D. C., 1933- 1. saṃskaraṇa. Lakhanaū : Nyū Rôyala Buka Kampanī, 2001.
BL1215.S36 V27 2001

HINDUISM. See also **KNOWLEDGE, THEORY OF (HINDUISM); TEMPLES, HINDU; YOGA.**
Terrin, Aldo N. (Aldo Natale) Mistiche dell'Occidente. 1. ed. Brescia : Morcelliana, 2001.
BP605.N48 T477 2001

HINDUISM AND SCIENCE.
Varshney, D. C., 1933- Hindū vijñāna evaṃ vidhi. 1. saṃskaraṇa. Lakhanaū : Nyū Rôyala Buka Kampanī, 2001.
BL1215.S36 V27 2001

HINDUISM - INDIA - SAWAI MADHOPUR (DISTRICT) - CUSTOMS AND PRACTICES.
Dwyer, Graham, 1959- The divine and the demonic. London ; New York : RoutledgeCurzon, 2003.
BL1226.82.E94 D89 2003

HINDUISM - PSYCHOLOGY.
Bedi, Ashok. Retire your family karma. Berwick, Me. : Nicolas-Hays, 2003.
BF637.S4 B423 2003

Vishnu on Freud's desk. Delhi ; Oxford : Oxford University Press, 1999 (2002 [printing])

HINDUISM - RELATIONS - CHRISTIANITY.
McLaughlin, Michael T. Knowledge, consciousness and religious conversion in Lonergan and Aurobindo. Roma : Editrice Pontificia Universita Gregoriana, 2003.

HINDUISM - RITUALS.
Veṅkaṭanāthārya. [Daśanirṇayī] Vaidikasārvabhaumanāmnā suprasiddhaiḥ Veṅkaṭanāthāryaiḥ Vaidikakarmānuṣṭhānasaukaryāya viracitā Daśanirṇayī. 1st ed. Mumbai : Śrīmadahobilamathena, 1998.
BL1226.72 .V36 1998

HINDUSTANI LANGUAGE. See **HINDI LANGUAGE.**

Hin'" Lat'. Ca dha ba va manomaya / Hin'" Lat'. Kyok' taṃ tā", [Rangoon] : Yuṃ kraññ' khyak' Cā pe : Pran'' khyi re", Rve Nan'" Mhan' kū Cā 'up' Tuik', 2002. 130 p. ; 19 cm. In Burmese. SUMMARY: Occultism in Burma; articles.
1. Occultism - Burmese. I. Title.
BF1434.B93 H56 2002

Hinterhuber, H. (Hartmann) Die Seele : Natur- und Kulturgeschichte von Psyche, Geist und Bewusstsein / Hartmann Hinterhuber. Wien ; New York : Springer, c2001. xii, 242 p. : ill. ; 25 cm. Includes bibliographical references (p. [229]-237) and index. ISBN 3-211-83667-5
1. Soul. 2. Soul - History of doctrines. 3. Philosophy of mind. 4. Neurosciences. 5. Psychology and religion. I. Title. II. Title: Natur- und Kulturgeschichte von Psyche, Geist und Bewusstsein

Hinton, Perry R. (Perry Roy), 1954-.
SPSS explained. London ; New York : Routledge, 2004.
BF39 .S68 2004

Statistics explained / by Perry R. Hinton. 2nd ed. New York : Routledge, 2004. p. cm. Includes bibliographical references and index. ISBN 0-415-33284-2 ISBN 0-415-33285-0 (pbk.) DDC 519.5
1. Psychometrics - Textbooks. I. Title.
BF39 .H54 2004

Hinz, Jessica.
Hinz, Michael. Learn to balance your life. San Francisco : Chronicle Books, 2004.
BF637.S4 H55 2004

Hinz, Michael. Learn to balance your life : a practical guide to having it all / by Michael Hinz and Jessica Hinz. San Francisco : Chronicle Books, 2004. p. cm. Includes index. ISBN 0-8118-4301-7 DDC 158.1
1. Self-actualization (Psychology) I. Hinz, Jessica. II. Title.
BF637.S4 H55 2004

HIP-HOP CULTURE. See **HIP-HOP.**

HIP-HOP - MISCELLANEA.
Marriott, Rob. Astrology uncut. 1st trade pbk. ed. New York : One World, 2004.
BF1711 .M45 2004

HIPPOLOGY. See **HORSES.**

Hirata, Helena Sumiko.
[División sexual del trabajo. Portuguese]
Nova divisão sexual do trabalho? : um olhar voltado para a empresa e a sociedade / Helena Hirata ; tradução, Wanda Caldeira Brant. 1a ed. São Paulo : Boitempo, 2002. 335 p. ; 21 cm. (Coleção Mundo do trabalho) Includes bibliographical references. ISBN 85-85934-90-5
1. Sexual division of labor. 2. Man-woman relationships. 3. Interpersonal relations and culture. 4. Technological innovations - Social aspects. I. Title. II. Series: Coleção Mundo do trabalho (Boitempo Editorial)
HD6060.6 .H5717 2002

Hirdman, Yvonne, 1943- Genus : om det stabilas föränderliga former / Yvonne Hirdman. 1. uppl. Malmö : Liber, 2001. 216 p. : ill. ; 24 cm. Includes bibliographical references (p. 205-215). ISBN 91-47-06223-1
1. Feminism. 2. Feminism - Sweden. 3. Gender identity - History. 4. Gender identity - Sweden - History. 5. Sex role - History. 6. Sex role - Sweden - History. I. Title.
Myrdal, Alva Reimer, 1902- "Något kan man väl göra. Stockholm : Carlssons, c2002.

Hiring and keeping the best people.
Harvard business essentials. Hiring and keeping the best people. Boston : Harvard Business School Press, c2002.
HF5549.5.S38 H37 2002

HIROSE, KYOKUSŌ, 1807-1863.
Bolitho, Harold. Bereavement and consolation. New Haven : Yale University Press, c2003.
DS822.2 .B65 2003

Hirsch, Jerrold, 1948- Portrait of America : a cultural history of the Federal Writers' Project / Jerrold Hirsch. Chapel Hill : University of North Carolina Press, c2003. xii, 293 p. ; 25 cm. Includes bibliographical references (p. [239]-281) and index. ISBN 0-8078-2817-3 (cloth : alk. paper) ISBN 0-8078-5489-1 (pbk. : alk. paper) DDC 973.917
1. Federal Writers' Project - History. 2. National characteristics, American. 3. United States - Historiography. 4. United States - Intellectual life - 20th century. 5. United States - Civilization - 1918-1945. I. Title.
E175.4.W9 H57 2003

Hirschmann, Kris, 1967- Leadership / Kris Hirschmann. Chicago, IL : Raintree, 2003. v. cm. (Character education) Includes bibliographical references and index. Table of contents URL: http://www.loc.gov/catdir/toc/ecip041/2003005899.html CONTENTS: What is leadership? -- Having a vision -- It's about the team -- Lead by example -- Take charge -- Be decisive -- Commitment -- Attitude -- Communication -- Consistency -- Flexibility -- Respect others -- Know Your limits. ISBN 0-7398-7006-8 ISBN 1410903257 (pbk.) DDC 303.3/4
1. Leadership - Juvenile literature. 2. Leadership. I. Title. II. Series: Character education (Raintree (Firm))
BF723.L4 H57 2003

Hirsh, Michael, 1957- At war with ourselves : why America is squandering its chance to build a better world / Michael Hirsh. New York : Oxford University Press, 2003. xiv, 288 p. ; 24 cm. Includes bibliographical references (p. [259]-274) and index. ISBN 0-19-515269-7 DDC 327.73
1. National characteristics, American. 2. Globalization - Political aspects. 3. United States - Foreign relations - 2001- 4. United States - Foreign relations - Philosophy. I. Title. II. Title: Why America is squandering its chance to build a better world
E895 .H57 2003

HISPANIC AMERICAN WOMEN - PSYCHOLOGY.
Nogales, Ana, 1951- Latina power!. New York : Simon & Schuster, c2003.
BF637.S8 N64 2003

HISPANIC AMERICAN YOUNG MEN - NEW YORK - NEW YORK - SOCIAL CONDITIONS.
Wilkinson, Deanna Lyn, 1968- Guns, violence, and identity among African American and Latino youth. New York : LFB Scholarly Pub., 2003.
HQ799.2.V56 W55 2003

HISPANIC AMERICANS.
Perspectives on Las Américas. Maden, MA : Blackwell Pub., c2003.
F1410 .P48 2003

Hispanic issues (Routledge (Firm))
(28.) Latin America writes back. New York : Routledge, 2002.
PQ7081.A1 L336 2002

HISPANIC STUDIES SPECIALISTS. See **HISPANISTS.**

Hispanisms
Zubiri, Xavier. [Estructura dinámica de la realidad. English] Dynamic structure of reality. Urbana : University of Illinois Press, c2003.
B4568.Z83 E7713 2003

HISPANISTS - GREAT BRITAIN - BIOGRAPHY.
Read, Malcolm K. (Malcolm Kevin), 1945- Educating the educators. 1st American ed. Newark : University of Delaware Press ; Cranbury, NJ : Associated University Presses, 2003.
PC4064.R43 A3 2003

Histoire de différences, différence d'histoires.
Michalon, Clair. Saint-Maur : Sépia, c2002.

Histoire de la pensée politique médiévale (300-1450).
Canning, Joseph. [History of medieval political thought, 300-1450. French] Fribourg, Suisse : Editions universitaires ; Paris : Cerf, [2003]

Histoire de la psychologie française.
Nicolas, Serge. Paris : In press, c2002.
BF108.F8 N536 2002

Histoire des pensées
Foucault au Collège de France. Pessac : Presses universitaires de Bordeaux, c2003.
B2430.F724 F6855 2003

Histoire des peurs alimentaires.
Ferrières, Madeleine. Paris : Editions du Seuil, c2002.

Histoire et tradition des Européens.
Venner, Dominique. Monaco : Rocher, c2002.
D80 .V46 2002

Historia en tiempo de mujeres.
López, Carmen Adela, 1935- Madres e hijas. Caracas, Venezuela : Vadell Hermanos, 2002.

Historia (LOM Ediciones)
Loveman, Brian. El espejismo de la reconciliación política. 1. ed. Santiago : LOM Ediciones : DIBAM, 2002.

Die Historia vom heiligen Gral.
Mörschel, Thomas. Saarbrücken : Logos, 1994-

Historia (Wiesbaden, Germany). Einzelschriften
(Heft 153.) Alföldi, Maria R.- Gloria romanorum. Stuttgart : Franz Steiner Verlag, 2001.
DG78 .A546 2001

Historía y sentido : exploraciones en teoría historiográfica / Ezequiel Adamovsky (ed.) ; María Ines Mudrovcic ... [et al.]. Buenos Aires : Ediciones El Cielo por Asalto, c2001. 157 p. ; 23 cm. ISBN 9879035224
1. Historiography. I. Adamovsky, Ezequiel, 1971- II. Mudrovcic, María Inés.

HISTORIANS. See also **ARCHAEOLOGISTS; RELIGION HISTORIANS.**
Dumoulin, Olivier. Le rôle social de l'historien. Paris : Albin Michel, 2002, c2003.
D13.2 .D85 2002

Les historiens. Paris : A. Colin, 2003.
D14 .H523 2003

History and historians in the twentieth century. Oxford : Published for the British Academy by Oxford University Press, 2002.

HISTORIANS - EUROPE.
Kelley, Donald R., 1931- Fortunes of history. New Haven : Yale University Press, c2003.
D16 .K26 2003

Sasso, Gennaro. Il guardiano della storiografia. 2. ed. [Bologna] : Società editrice il Mulino, c2002.

HISTORIANS - EUROPE - BIOGRAPHY.
Pallares-Burke, Maria Lucia G. The new history. Cambridge, UK ; Malden, MA : Polity in association with Blackwell Publishers Ltd., 2002.
D14 .P35 2002

HISTORIANS - FRANCE - BIOGRAPHY.
Aguirre Rojas, Carlos Antonio. Ensayos braudelianos. Rosario, Argentina : Prohistoria ; M. Suárez ; México : Asociación Nacional de Profesores de Historia de México, 2000.
D15.B62 A38 2000

HISTORIANS - GERMANY.
Grunewald, Michel, 1942- Moeller van den Brucks Geschichtsphilosophie. Bern ; New York : P. Lang, c2001.
DD247.M59 G78 2001

HISTORIANS - GREAT BRITAIN - BIOGRAPHY.
Pallares-Burke, Maria Lucia G. The new history. Cambridge, UK ; Malden, MA : Polity in association with Blackwell Publishers Ltd., 2002.
D14 .P35 2002

HISTORIANS - INTERVIEWS.
Pallares-Burke, Maria Lucia G. The new history. Cambridge, UK ; Malden, MA : Polity in association with Blackwell Publishers Ltd., 2002.
D14 .P35 2002

HISTORIANS OF RELIGION. See **RELIGION HISTORIANS.**

The historian's toolbox.
Williams, Robert Chadwell, 1938- Armonk, N.Y. : M.E. Sharpe, c2003.
D16 .W62 2003

HISTORIC BUILDINGS.
Baumann, Günter, 1962- Meisterwerke der Architektur. Stuttgart : Reclam, c2001.
NA200 .B33 2001

HISTORIC SITES. See **MONUMENTS.**

HISTORICAL CRITICISM. See **HISTORIOGRAPHY.**

Historical dictionaries of religions, philosophies, and movements
(no. 47) Bailey, Michael David, 1971- Historical dictionary of witchcraft. 1st ed. Lanham, Md. : Scarecrow Press, 2003.
BF1566 .B25 2003

Historical dictionary of witchcraft.
Bailey, Michael David, 1971- 1st ed. Lanham, Md. : Scarecrow Press, 2003.
BF1566 .B25 2003

Historical essays.
Carlyle, Thomas, 1795-1881. Berkeley ; London : University of California Press, c2002.
D208 .C34 2002

HISTORICAL LINGUISTICS.
Language evolution. Oxford ; New York : Oxford University Press, 2003.
P140 .L256 2003

Poggio, Rosauta Maria Galvão Fagundes. Processos de gramaticalização de preposições do Latim ao Português. Salvador : EDUFBA, 2002.

Historical marble : studies in art history.
Marmur dziejowy. Poznań : Wydawnictwo Poznańskiego Towarzystwa Przyjaciół Nauk, 2002.

HISTORICAL MATERIALISM.
Historical materialism and social evolution. New York : Palgrave Macmillan, 2002.
HX523 .H565 2002

Huang, Minlan. Xue shu jiu guo. Di 1 ban. Zhengzhou Shi : Henan ren min chu ban she, 1995.
D16.9 .H795 1995 <Asian China>

Historical materialism and social evolution / edited by Paul Blackledge and Graeme Kirkpatrick. New York : Palgrave Macmillan, 2002. viii, 244 p. ; 23 cm. Includes bibliographical references and index. CONTENTS: Historical materialism and social evolution / Paul Blackledge and Graeme Kirkpatrick -- Historical materialism : from social evolution to revolutionary politics / Paul Blackledge -- Social Darwinism and socialist Darwinism in Germany ; 1860 to 1900 / Ted Benton -- A Darwinian historical materialism / Paul Nolan -- Analytical Marxism and the debate on social evolution / Alan Carling -- History, exploitation and oppression / Alex Callinicos -- Progress and technology in Habermas's theory of social evolution / Graeme Kirkpatrick -- The possible wonders of technology : beyond Habermas towards Marcuse : a critical framework for technological progress / Giuseppe Tassone -- Lean production and economic evolution in capitalism / Tony Smith. ISBN 0-333-99562-7 (cloth) DDC 335.4/119
1. Communism and culture. 2. Communism and society. 3. Historical materialism. 4. Social Darwinism. 5. Human evolution. I. Blackledge, Paul, 1967- II. Kirkpatrick, Graeme, 1963-
HX523 .H565 2002

HISTORICAL MONUMENTS. See **MONUMENTS.**

HISTORICAL RECORD PRESERVATION. See **ARCHIVES.**

HISTORICAL SOCIOLOGY. See **CULTURE.**

HISTORICISM.
Jenkins, Keith, 1943- Refiguring history. London : New York : Routledge, 2003 .
D16.8 .J385 2003

Les historiens / Stéphane Audoin-Rouzeau, ... [et al.] ; ouvrage coordonné par Véronique Sales. Paris : A. Colin, 2003. 349 p. ; 24 cm. Includes bibliographical references. ISBN 2-200-26286-8 DDC 900
1. Historians. 2. Historiography. I. Audoin-Rouzeau, Stéphane. II. Sales, Véronique.
D14 .H523 2003

Historiografía y memoria colectiva : tiempos y territorios / Cristina Godoy, compiladora ; Hayden White, prefacio ; Godoy ... [et al.]. 1. ed. Madrid ; Buenos Aires : Miño y Dávila, 2002. 264 p. : ill. ; 23 cm. Ensayos de Cristina Godoy, Ludmila da Silva Catela, Matilde Bruera, Isabel Fernández Acevedo, Beatriz Andrés, Diana Wang, Daniel Feierstein, Elizabeth Martínez de Aguirre, Silvia Pampinella, Pablo Montini, Claudio Conenna, Sylvia Saítta, Roxana C. Mauri Nicastro, Carolina Kaufmann, Gabriela Aguila, Cristina Viano, Pablo Francescutti. Includes bibliographical references. ISBN 950-9467-89-8
1. Historiography - Social aspects. 2. Historiography - Social aspects - Argentina. 3. Argentina - Historiografía. 4. Memory - Social aspects. 5. Memory - Social aspects - Argentina. I. Godoy, Cristina. II. White, Hayden V., 1928-

HISTORIOGRAPHERS. See **HISTORIANS.**

HISTORIOGRAPHY.
Adediran, A. A. The problem with the past. Ile-Ife, Nigeria : Obafemi Awolowo University Press, c2002.
1. Black author.

Aguirre Rojas, Carlos Antonio. Ensayos braudelianos. Rosario, Argentina : Prohistoria ; M. Suárez ; México : Asociación Nacional de Profesores de Historia de México, 2000.
D15.B62 A38 2000

Begriffsgeschichte, Diskursgeschichte, Metapherngeschichte. Göttingen : Wallstein, 2002.
D13 .B45 2002

Beuchot, Mauricio. La filosofía y el lenguaje en la historia. México, D.F. : UNAM, 2000.

Breisach, Ernst. On the future of history. Chicago : University of Chicago Press, c2003.
HM449 .B74 2003

Carlyle, Thomas, 1795-1881. Historical essays. Berkeley ; London : University of California Press, c2002.
D208 .C34 2002

Clark, J. C. D. Our shadowed present. London : Atlantic, 2003.

Des odyssées à travers le temps. Paris : Harmattan, c2002.

Dumoulin, Olivier. Le rôle social de l'historien. Paris : Albin Michel, 2002, c2003.
D13.2 .D85 2002

Dunk, Hermann Walther von der. Mensen, machten, mogelijkheden. Amsterdam : B. Bakker, 2002.

Geiger, Wolfgang. Geschichte und Weltbild. 1. Aufl. Frankfurt am Main : Humanities Online, c2002.

Hähner, Olaf. Historische Biographik. Frankfurt am Main ; New York : Lang, 1999.

He, Bingsong, 1890-1946. [Works. 1996] He Bingsong wen ji. Di 1 ban. Beijing : Shang wu yin shu guan, 1996.
DS734.7 .H664

História y sentido. Buenos Aires : Ediciones El Cielo por Asalto, c2001.

Les historiens. Paris : A. Colin, 2003.
D14 .H523 2003

History and historians in the twentieth century. Oxford : Published for the British Academy by Oxford University Press, 2002.

Istoriohrafichni ta dzhereloznavchi problemy istoriï Ukraïny. Dnipropetrovs'k : Vyd-vo Dnipropetrovs'koho universytetu, 2000.
DK508.46 .I84 2000

Jenkins, Keith, 1943- Refiguring history. London : New York : Routledge, 2003 .
D16.8 .J385 2003

Kelley, Donald R., 1931- Fortunes of history. New Haven : Yale University Press, c2003.
D16 .K26 2003

Kiesewetter, Hubert, 1939- Irreale oder reale Geschichte? Herbolzheim : Centaurus, 2002.

Krockow, Christian, Graf von. Die Zukunft der Geschichte. München : List, c2002.
D16.8 .K722 2002

Mali, Joseph. Mythistory. Chicago : The University of Chicago Press, c2003.
D13 .M268 2003

Maset, Michael. Diskurs, Macht und Geschichte. Frankfurt/Main ; New York : Campus, c2002.
BF24.30.F724 M37 2002

Michelet, Jules, 1798-1874. La cité des vivants et des morts. [Paris] : Belin, c2002.

Nikolaev, Alekseĭ. Istoricheskie t͡sikly. Vologda : [s.n.], c2002.
D16.15 .N55 2002

Nosovskiĭ, G. V. (Gleb Vladimirovich), 1958- Rekonstrukt͡sii͡a vseobshcheĭ istorii. Moskva : FID "Delovoĭ ėkspress", 2002.
DK38 .N68 2002

Pallares-Burke, Maria Lucia G. The new history. Cambridge, UK ; Malden, MA : Polity in association with Blackwell Publishers Ltd., 2002.
D14 .P35 2002

Ritchie, Donald A., 1945- Doing oral history. 2nd ed. Oxford ; New York : Oxford University Press, c2003.
D16.14 .R57 2003

Rüsen, Jörn. Geschichte im Kulturprozess. Köln : Böhlau, c2002.
D16.8 .R913 2002

Sasso, Gennaro. Il guardiano della storiografia. 2. ed. [Bologna] : Società editrice il Mulino, c2002.

Sommer, Barbara W. The oral history manual. Walnut Creek, CA ; Oxford : Altamira Press, c2002.
D16.14 .S69 2002

Vainfas, Ronaldo. Os protagonistas anônimos da história. Rio de Janeiro : Editora Campus, 2002.
D16 .V35 2002

Wahrheit, Wissen, Erinnerung. Münster : Lit, [2002]

Western historical thinking. New York : Berghahn Books, 2002.

D16.9 .W454 2002

What is history now? Houndmills [England] ; New York : Palgrave Macmillan, 2002.
D16.8 .W5 2002

Williams, Robert Chadwell, 1938- The historian's toolbox. Armonk, N.Y. : M.E. Sharpe, c2003.
D16 .W62 2003

XX vek. Moskva : INION RAN, 2001-

HISTORIOGRAPHY - ASIA - HISTORY.
Turning points in historiography. Rochester, NY : University of Rochester Press, 2002.
D13 .T87 2002

HISTORIOGRAPHY - EUROPE - HISTORY.
Ionov, I. N. (Igor' Nikolaevich) Teorii͡a t͡sivilizat͡siĭ. Sankt-Peterburg : Aleteĭi͡a, 2002.
CB19 .I656 2002

Turning points in historiography. Rochester, NY : University of Rochester Press, 2002.
D13 .T87 2002

HISTORIOGRAPHY - FRANCE.
Religion et mentalités au Moyen Age. Rennes : Presses universitaires de Rennes, c2003.
BR141 .R45 2003

HISTORIOGRAPHY - GERMANY - HISTORY - 20TH CENTURY.
Jarausch, Konrad Hugo. Shattered past. Princeton, N.J. : Princeton University Press, c2003.
DD86 .J253 2003

HISTORIOGRAPHY - GREECE - HISTORY.
Alonso-Nuñez, José Miguel. The idea of universal history in Greece. Amsterdam : J.C. Gieben, 2002.
D13.5.G8 A46 2002

HISTORIOGRAPHY - HISTORY.
Turning points in historiography. Rochester, NY : University of Rochester Press, 2002.
D13 .T87 2002

HISTORIOGRAPHY - RUSSIA.
Nosovskiĭ, G. V. (Gleb Vladimirovich), 1958- Rekonstrukt͡sii͡a vseobshcheĭ istorii. Moskva : FID "Delovoĭ ėkspress", 2002.
DK38 .N68 2002

HISTORIOGRAPHY - RUSSIA - HISTORY.
Ionov, I. N. (Igor' Nikolaevich) Teorii͡a t͡sivilizat͡siĭ. Sankt-Peterburg : Aleteĭi͡a, 2002.
CB19 .I656 2002

HISTORIOGRAPHY - SOCIAL ASPECTS.
Historiografía y memoria colectiva. 1. ed. Madrid ; Buenos Aires : Miño y Dávila, 2002.

HISTORIOGRAPHY - SOCIAL ASPECTS - ARGENTINA.
Historiografía y memoria colectiva. 1. ed. Madrid ; Buenos Aires : Miño y Dávila, 2002.

HISTORIOGRAPHY - SOCIAL ASPECTS - UNITED STATES - HISTORY - 19TH CENTURY.
Pfitzer, Gregory M. Picturing the past. Washington [D.C.] : Smithsonian Institution Press, c2002.
E175 .P477 2002

Historisch-anthropologische Studien
(Bd. 12) Linck, Gudula. Leib und Körper. Frankfurt am Main ; New York : P. Lang, c2001.
B105.B64 L58 2001

Historische Biographik.
Hähner, Olaf. Frankfurt am Main ; New York : Lang, 1999.

Historische Chronologie des Abendlandes.
Brincken, Anna-Dorothee von den. Stuttgart : Kohlhammer, 2000.

Historische Stadt Ravensburg (Series)
(Bd. 2.) Frühe Hexenverfolgung in Ravensburg und am Bodensee. Konstanz : UVK Verlagsgesellschaft, c2001.
BF1583 .F784 2001

Historische Zeitschrift. Beihefte
(Bd. 36) Generationswechsel und historischer Wandel. München : Oldenbourg, 2003.

HISTORY. *See also* **ARCHAEOLOGY; BIOGRAPHY; CHURCH HISTORY; CONSTITUTIONAL HISTORY; LITERATURE AND HISTORY; SOCIAL HISTORY; WORLD HISTORY.**
Davis, Kenneth C. 1st ed. New York : HarperCollins, c2003.

E178.25 .D37 2003

HISTORY.
History and historians in the twentieth century. Oxford : Published for the British Academy by Oxford University Press, 2002.

HISTORY, ANCIENT.
Clow, Barbara Hand, 1943- Catastrophobia. Rochester, Vt. : Bear & Company, c2001.
BF1999 .C587 2001

Durschmied, Erik. From Armageddon to the fall of Rome. London : Hodder & Stoughton, c2002.

Geōrgios, Synkellos, fl. 800. [Ecloga chronographica English] The chronography of George Synkellos. Oxford ; New York : Oxford University Press, 2002.

Gosden, Chris, 1955- Prehistory. Oxford ; New York : Oxford University Press, 2003.

Hyland, Ann. The horse in the ancient world. Stroud : Sutton, 2003.

Ikas, Wolfgang-Valentin. Martin von Troppau (Martinus Polonus), O.P. (1278) in England. Wiesbaden : Reichert, 2002.

Mithen, Steven J. After the ice. London : Weidenfeld & Nicolson, 2003.

HISTORY, ANCIENT - HISTORIOGRAPHY.
Alonso-Nuñez, José Miguel. The idea of universal history in Greece. Amsterdam : J.C. Gieben, 2002.
D13.5.G8 A46 2002

Mali, Joseph. Mythistory. Chicago : The University of Chicago Press, c2003.
D13 .M268 2003

History and eschatology in John Scottus Eriugena and his time.
Internationales Eriugena-Colloquium (10th : Maynooth and Dublin : 2002) Leuven : University Press, 2002.

History and historians in the twentieth century / edited by Peter Burke. Oxford : Published for the British Academy by Oxford University Press, 2002. x, 253 p. ; 25 cm. (British Academy centenary monograph)
Includes index. ISBN 0-19-726268-6 DDC 907.2
1. History. 2. Historiography. 3. Historians. I. Burke, Peter, 1937- II. British Academy. III. Series.

HISTORY AND LITERATURE. *See* **LITERATURE AND HISTORY.**

HISTORY AND POETRY. *See* **LITERATURE AND HISTORY.**

HISTORY - AUTHORSHIP. *See* **HISTORIOGRAPHY.**

HISTORY - BIOGRAPHY. *See* **BIOGRAPHY.**

HISTORY, CHURCH. *See* **CHURCH HISTORY.**

HISTORY - CRITICISM. *See* **HISTORIOGRAPHY.**

HISTORY, ECCLESIASTICAL. *See* **CHURCH HISTORY.**

HISTORY, ECONOMIC. *See* **ECONOMIC HISTORY.**

HISTORY - HISTORIOGRAPHY. *See* **HISTORIOGRAPHY.**

HISTORY - METHODOLOGY. *See also* **ORAL HISTORY.**
Istoriohrafichni ta dzhereloznavchi problemy istoriï Ukraïny. Dnipropetrovs'k : Vyd-vo Dnipropetrovs'koho universytetu, 2000.
DK508.46 .I84 2000

Kelley, Donald R., 1931- Fortunes of history. New Haven : Yale University Press, c2003.
D16 .K26 2003

Kiesewetter, Hubert, 1939- Irreale oder reale Geschichte? Herbolzheim : Centaurus, 2002.

Nikolaev, Alekseĭ. Istoricheskie t͡sikly. Vologda : [s.n.], c2002.
D16.15 .N55 2002

Rozov, N. S. (Nikolaĭ Sergeevich) Filosofii͡a i teorii͡a istorii. Moskva : Logos, 2002-
D16.8 .R873 2002

Turning points in historiography. Rochester, NY : University of Rochester Press, 2002.
D13 .T87 2002

Vainfas, Ronaldo. Os protagonistas anônimos da história. Rio de Janeiro : Editora Campus, 2002.

History - Methodology

D16 .V35 2002

Western historical thinking. New York : Berghahn Books, 2002.
D16.9 .W454 2002

Williams, Robert Chadwell, 1938- The historian's toolbox. Armonk, N.Y. : M.E. Sharpe, c2003.
D16 .W62 2003

HISTORY, MODERN. *See* **RENAISSANCE.**

HISTORY, MODERN - 20TH CENTURY. *See* **WORLD WAR, 1914-1918; WORLD WAR, 1939-1945.**

HISTORY, MODERN - 20TH CENTURY - SOURCES.
Durschmied, Erik. Unsung heroes. London : Hodder & Stoughton, 2003.

HISTORY, MODERN - HISTORIOGRAPHY.
Mali, Joseph. Mythistory. Chicago : The University of Chicago Press, c2003.
D13 .M268 2003

HISTORY, NATURAL. *See* **NATURAL HISTORY.**

History of computing
Roland, Alex, 1944- Strategic computing. Cambridge, Mass. : MIT Press, c2002.
QA76.88 .R65 2002

A history of Memorial Day.
Harmond, Richard P. New York : P. Lang, c2002.
E642 .H37 2002

A history of modern psychology.
Schultz, Duane P. 8th ed. Belmont, CA : Thomson/Wadsworth, c2004.
BF95 .S35 2004

History of psychology.
Hothersall, David. 4th ed. Boston : McGraw-Hill, c2004.
BF95 .H67 2004

A history of psychology.
Leahey, Thomas Hardy. 6th ed. Upper Saddle River, N.J. : Prentice Hall, 2004.
BF81 .L4 2004

History of science, philosophy, and culture in Indian civilization. Volume X. Towards independence (pt. 1) Krishna, Daya. Developments in Indian philosophy from Eighteenth century onwards. New Delhi : Project of History of Indian Science, Philosophy, and Culture : Centre for Studies in Civilizations : Distributed by Motilal Banarsidass, 2002.
B131+

History of the concept of mind.
MacDonald, Paul S., 1951- Aldershot ; Burlington, VT : Ashgate, c2003.

History of the International Union of Psychological Science (IUPsyS).
International Union of Psychological Science. Hove, East Sussex ; Philadelphia, PA : Psychology Press, c2000.
BF11 .I62 2000

History of the Psychology Department at the University of Texas at Austin.
Texas psychology. Austin : The University of Texas at Austin, c2002.
BF80.7.U62 T48 2002

HISTORY - PERIODIZATION.
Nikolaev, Alekseĭ. Istoricheskie t͡sikly. Vologda : [s.n.], c2002.
D16.15 .N55 2002

Nosovskiĭ, G. V. (Gleb Vladimirovich), 1958- Rekonstrukt͡sii͡a vseobshcheĭ istorii. Moskva : FID "Delovoĭ ėkspress", 2002.
DK38 .N68 2002

HISTORY - PHILOSOPHY.
Adediran, A. A. The problem with the past. Ile-Ife, Nigeria : Obafemi Awolowo University Press, c2002.
1. Black author.

Alonso-Nuñez, José Miguel. The idea of universal history in Greece. Amsterdam : J.C. Gieben, 2002.
D13.5.G8 A46 2002

Altomare, Vincenzo. Alla ricerca dell'uomo tra Bibbia e modernità. 1. ed. Cosenza : Progetto 2000, c2000.

Barnard, Frederick M., 1921- Herder on nationality, humanity, and history. Montreal : McGill-Queen's University Press, c2003.

Begriffsgeschichte, Diskursgeschichte, Metapherngeschichte. Göttingen : Wallstein, 2002.

D13 .B45 2002

Cacciatore, Giuseppe, 1945- L'etica dello storicismo. Lecce : Milella, 2000.

Cioran, E. M. (Emile M.), 1911- [Histoire et utopie. Romanian] Istorie și utopie. București : Humanitas, 2002.

Clark, J. C. D. Our shadowed present. London : Atlantic, 2003.

Codas, Enrique, 1932- En los caminos de la historia. [Asunción, Paraguay] : El Lector, c2002.
F2695.G83 C63 2002

Cospito, Giuseppe, 1966- Il "gran Vico". Genova : Name, c2002.

Culture and international history. New York : Berghahn Books, 2003.
JZ1251 .C84 2003

Die erscheinende Welt. Berlin : Duncker & Humblot, c2002.

Essays in honor of Burleigh Wilkins. New York : Peter Lang, c2001.
JA71 .E694 2001

Gadamer, Hans Georg, 1900- [Problème de la conscience historique. German] Das Problem des historischen Bewusstseins. Tübingen : Mohr Siebeck, 2001.

Grunewald, Michel, 1942- Moeller van den Brucks Geschichtsphilosophie. Bern ; New York : P. Lang, c2001.
DD247.M59 G78 2001

Han, Zhen. Li shi zhe xue. Di 1 ban. Kunming : Yunnan ren min chu ban she, 2002.
D16.8 .H3597 2002

He, Zhaowu. Wei cao ji. Di 1 ban. Beijing : Sheng huo, du shu, xin zhi san lian shu dian, 1999.
D16.8 .H42 1999

Huang, Minlan. Xue shu jiu guo. Di 1 ban. Zhengzhou Shi : Henan ren min chu ban she, 1995.
D16.9 .H795 1995 <Asian China>

Huyssen, Andreas. Present pasts. Stanford, Calif. : Stanford University Press, 2003.
BD181.7 .H89 2003

Identities. New York ; Oxford : Berghahn Books, 2002.
HM716 .I34 2002

Ionov, I. N. (Igor' Nikolaevich) Teorii͡a t͡sivilizat͡siĭ. Sankt-Peterburg : Aletei͡a, 2002.
CB19 .I656 2002

Jarausch, Konrad Hugo. Shattered past. Princeton, N.J. : Princeton University Press, c2003.
DD86 .J253 2003

Jenkins, Keith, 1943- Refiguring history. London : New York : Routledge, 2003 .
D16.8 .J385 2003

Kantor, Karl Moiseevich. Dvoĭnai͡a spiral' istorii. Moskva : I͡Azyk slavi͡anskoĭ kul'tury, 2002-
D16.8 .K224 2002

Karl Jaspers on philosophy of history and history of philosophy. Amherst, N.Y. : Humanity Books, 2003.
B3279.J34 K292 2003

Kelley, Donald R., 1931- Fortunes of history. New Haven : Yale University Press, c2003.
D16 .K26 2003

Kovesi, Julius. Values and evaluations. New York ; Bern : P. Lang, c1998.
BD232 .K68 1998

Krockow, Christian, Graf von. Die Zukunft der Geschichte. München : List, c2002.
D16.8 .K722 2002

Lal, Vinay. Empire of knowledge. London ; Sterling, Va. : Pluto Press, 2002.
HN16 .L35 2002

Maset, Michael. Diskurs, Macht und Geschichte. Frankfurt/Main ; New York : Campus, 2002.
BF24.30.F724 M37 2002

Michelet, Jules, 1798-1874. La cité des vivants et des morts. [Paris] : Belin, c2002.

Nikolaev, Alekseĭ. Istoricheskie t͡sikly. Vologda : [s.n.], c2002.
D16.15 .N55 2002

Pallares-Burke, Maria Lucia G. The new history. Cambridge, UK ; Malden, MA : Polity in association with Blackwell Publishers Ltd., 2002.

D14 .P35 2002

Patzel-Mattern, Katja. Geschichte im Zeichen der Erinnerung. Stuttgart : Franz Steiner, 2002.

Pistes didactiques et chemins historiques. Paris : Harmattan, 2003.

Progrès, réaction, décadence dans l'Occident médiéval. Genève : Droz, 2003.
PN681 .P764 2003

Robin, Régine, 1936- La mémoire saturée. Paris : Stock, 2003.
D16.8 .R59 2003

Rozov, N. S. (Nikolaĭ Sergeevich) Filosofii͡a i teorii͡a istorii. Moskva : Logos, 2002-
D16.8 .R873 2002

Rüsen, Jörn. Geschichte im Kulturprozess. Köln : Böhlau, c2002.
D16.8 .R913 2002

Sokolov, B. G. (Boris Georgievich) Gipertekst istorii. Sankt-Peterburg : Sankt-Peterburgskoe filosofskoe obshchestvo, 2001.
D16.9 .S65 2001

Steedman, Carolyn. Dust. New Brunswick, N.J. : Rutgers University Press, 2002, c2001.
CD947 .S73 2002

Stiehler, Gottfried. Mensch und Geschichte. Köln : PapyRossa, c2002.
D16.8 .S75 2002

Turning points in historiography. Rochester, NY : University of Rochester Press, 2002.
D13 .T87 2002

Ul'rikh, I. V. Zhizn' cheloveka. Moskva : Izd-vo "Litan", 1999.

Venner, Dominique. Histoire et tradition des Européens. Monaco : Rocher, c2002.
D80 .V46 2002

Der weite Blick des Historikers. Köln : Böhlau, c2002.
D116 .W44 2002

Western historical thinking. New York : Berghahn Books, 2002.
D16.9 .W454 2002

What is history now? Houndmills [England] ; New York : Palgrave Macmillan, 2002.
D16.8 .W5 2002

Wilson, Edmund, 1895-1972. To the Finland station. New York : New York Review of Books, 2003.
HX36 .W5 2003

Zakai, Avihu. Jonathan Edwards's philosophy of history. Princeton, N.J. : Princeton University Press, c2003.
B873 .Z35 2003

Zerubavel, Eviatar. Time maps. Chicago : University of Chicago Press, 2003.
BD638 .Z48 2003

Zhang, Xiong, 1953- Jing ji zhe xue. Di 1 ban. [Kunming] : Yunnan ren min chu ban she, 2002.
D16.8 .Z536 2002

HISTORY - PSYCHOLOGICAL ASPECTS.
Murray, Charles A. Human accomplishment. New York : HarperCollins, 2003.
BF416.A1 M87 2003

Die Psychohistorie des Erlebens. Kiel : Oetker-Voges, c2000.

HISTORY - RELIGIOUS ASPECTS - CHRISTIANITY.
Kantor, Karl Moiseevich. Dvoĭnai͡a spiral' istorii. Moskva : I͡Azyk slavi͡anskoĭ kul'tury, 2002-
D16.8 .K224 2002

HISTORY - RESEARCH.
Kelley, Donald R., 1931- Fortunes of history. New Haven : Yale University Press, c2003.
D16 .K26 2003

Williams, Robert Chadwell, 1938- The historian's toolbox. Armonk, N.Y. : M.E. Sharpe, c2003.
D16 .W62 2003

HISTORY - RUSSIA - PHILOSOPHY.
Afanasjev, Valeri, 1963- Russische Geschichtsphilosophie auf dem Prüfstand. Münster : Lit, [2002]

HISTORY - SOURCES. *See* **ARCHIVES; TIME CAPSULES.**

HISTORY - STUDY AND TEACHING.
Williams, Robert Chadwell, 1938- The historian's toolbox. Armonk, N.Y. : M.E. Sharpe, c2003.
D16 .W62 2003

HISTRIONICS. *See* **THEATER.**

Hite, Sheilaa, 1958- Secrets of a psychic counselor : insightful guidance & inspiring true stories of love, prosperity, and success / Sheilaa Hite. Needham, Mass. : Moment Point Press ; [Oakland, Calif.] : Distributed to the trade by Words Distributing Co., c2003. 155 p. ; 21 cm. Table of contents URL: http://www.loc.gov/catdir/toc/ecip042/2003008318.html CONTENTS: Score! : turning failure into success -- The wonder of you : learning to love yourself -- Sold! : how to sell anything quickly -- Ready for love : attracting someone special -- Thanks, but no thanks : getting rid of negative people -- The it factor : increasing your personal magnetism -- Let's clear the air : getting rid of negative energy -- Money matters : drawing prosperity to your life -- Enough is enough : claiming and using your personal power -- The glass slipper : getting your prince (or princess) to commit -- Affirmations: Me-on being great : Risk ; Psalm 23. ISBN 1-930491-03-4 (alk. paper) DDC 133.8
1. Psychic readings - Case studies. 2. Self-realization - Miscellanea. 3. Success - Miscellanea. I. Title.
BF1045.R43 H58 2003

HITLER, ADOLF, 1889-1945.
Bärsch, Claus-Ekkehard. Die politische Religion des Nationalsozialismus. 2., vollst. überarb. Aufl. München : W. Fink, c2002.

Roberts, Andrew, 1963- Hitler and Churchill. London : Weidenfeld & Nicolson, 2003.

Hitler and Churchill.
Roberts, Andrew, 1963- London : Weidenfeld & Nicolson, 2003.

HIV INFECTIONS. *See* **AIDS (DISEASE).**

HIV INFECTIONS - PATIENTS. *See* **HIV-POSITIVE PERSONS.**

HIV PATIENTS. *See* **HIV-POSITIVE PERSONS.**

HIV-POSITIVE PERSONS.
Privacy and disclosure of HIV in interpersonal relationships. Mahwah, N.J. : Lawrence Erlbaum Associates, 2003.
RA643.8 .P755 2003

HIV-POSITIVE PERSONS - SEXUAL BEHAVIOR.
Klitzman, Robert. Mortal secrets. Baltimore : Johns Hopkins University Press, 2003.
RA643.8 .K56 2003

Hjelmstad, Lois Tschetter. The last violet : mourning my mother / Lois Tschetter Hjelmstad. Englewood, Colo. : Mulberry Hill Press, c2002. xi, 146 p. : ill. ; 22 cm. Includes index. ISBN 0-9637139-7-3 DDC 155.9/37
1. Grief. 2. Bereavement - Psychological aspects. 3. Mothers - Death - Psychological aspects. 4. Mothers and daughters. 5. Loss (Psychology) 6. Hjelmstad, Lois Tschetter. I. Title.
BF575.G7 H575 2002

Hjelmstad, Lois Tschetter. The last violet. Englewood, Colo. : Mulberry Hill Press, c2002.
BF575.G7 H575 2002

Hnatyszyn, Andriy.
Malaniuk, Ira. Arien und Lieder [sound recording]. [Germany] : Preiser Records, p2000.

HOBBYISTS. *See* **COLLECTORS AND COLLECTING; FANS (PERSONS).**

Hobfoll, Ivonne H.
Hobfoll, Stevan E. [Work won't love you back. Chinese] Top shuang xin jia ting. Chu ban. Taibei Shi : Ye qiang chu ban she, 1997.

Hobfoll, Stevan E.
[Work won't love you back. Chinese]
Top shuang xin jia ting / Stevan E. Hobfoll, Ivonne H. Hobfoll Chu ; Nan Zhiguo, Liu si yi. Chu ban. Taibei Shi : Ye qiang chu ban she, 1997. 330 p. ; 21 cm. (Shi yong xin li xue) ISBN 9576834902
1. Psychology. 2. Dual-career families - Psychologic aspect. I. Hobfoll, Ivonne H. II. Nan, Zhiguo. III. Liu, Si. IV. Title. V. Title: Shuang xin jia ting

HOBGOBLINS. *See* **GOBLINS.**

Hobson, R. Peter. The cradle of thought : exploring the origins of thinking / Peter Hobson. New York : Oxford University Press, 2004. p. cm. Includes bibliographical references (p.) and index. ISBN 0-19-521954-6 DDC 155.42/234
1. Cognition in infants. 2. Social interaction in infants. 3. Thought and thinking. 4. Autism. I. Title.
BF720.C63 H63 2004

The cradle of thought / Peter Hobson. London : Macmillan, 2002. xviii, 296 p. ; ill. ; 24 cm. Includes bibliographical references (p. [275]-291) and index. ISBN 0-333-76633-4
1. Cognition in infants. 2. Social interaction in infants. 3. Thought and thinking. 4. Autism. I. Title.
BF720.C63 H63 2002

Hoc hic et nunc.
Reina, Maria Elena. [Firenze] : Leo S. Olschki, 2002.

Hoch, John, 1971-.
Pellegrini, Anthony D. Observing children in their natural worlds. 2nd ed. Mahwah, N.J. : L. Erlbaum Associates, 2004.
BF722 .P45 2004

Hochman, Judith. Image and word in Ahsen's image psychology / Judith Hochman. New York : Brandon House, c2000. xvi, 206 p. ; 23 cm. Cover title: Image & word. Includes bibliographical references (p. 195-200) and index. ISBN 0-913412-81-3 DDC 153.3/2
1. Imagery (Psychology) 2. Psycholinguistics. 3. Ahsen, Akhter. I. Title. II. Title: Image & word
BF367 .H63 2000

Hochschild, Arlie Russell, 1940- The commercialization of intimate life : notes from home and work / Arlie Russell Hochschild. Berkeley : University of California Press, 2003. ix, 313 p. ; 24 cm. Includes bibliographical references (p. 281-302) and index. Table of contents URL: http://www.loc.gov/catdir/toc/fy036/2002152224.html ISBN 0-520-21487-0 (alk. paper) ISBN 0-520-21488-9 (pbk. : alk. paper) DDC 302
1. Interpersonal relations and culture. 2. Emotions - Sociological aspects. 3. Social pressure. 4. Man-woman relationships. 5. Self. 6. Family. I. Title.
HM1106 .H63 2003

The managed heart : commercialization of human feeling / Arlie Russell Hochschild. 20th anniversary ed. Berkeley, Calif. : University of California Press, 2003. xii, 327 p. ; 21 cm. Originally published: Berkeley : University of California Press, c1983. Includes bibliographical references (p. 287-315) and index. ISBN 0-520-23933-4 (alk. paper) DDC 152.4
1. Emotions - Economic aspects. 2. Work - Psychological aspects. 3. Employee motivation. I. Title.
BF531 .H62 2003

Hochschule für Bildende Künste Braunschweig. Institut für Kunstwissenschaft.
Glasmeier, Michael, 1951- Extreme 1-8. Köln : Salon, 2001.

Hockenbury, Don H. Discovering psychology / Don H. Hockenbury, Sandra E. Hockenbury. 3rd ed. New York : Worth Publishers, c2004. xxxvii, 576, [119] p. : ill. (some col.) ; 29 cm. Includes bibliographical references (R-1-R-49) and indexes. ISBN 0-7167-5895-4 ISBN 0-7167-5704-4 (pbk.) DDC 150
1. Psychology - Textbooks. I. Hockenbury, Sandra E. II. Title.
BF121 .H587 2004

Psychology / Don H. Hockenbury, Sandra E. Hockenbury. 3rd ed. New York : Worth Publishers , c2003. xl, 662, [132] p. : ill. (some col.) ; 29 cm. Includes bibliographical references (R-1-R-57)and indexes. ISBN 0-7167-5129-1 DDC 150
1. Psychology - Textbooks. I. Hockenbury, Sandra E. II. Title.
BF121 .H59 2003

Hockenbury, Sandra E.
Hockenbury, Don H. Discovering psychology. 3rd ed. New York : Worth Publishers, c2004.
BF121 .H587 2004

Hockenbury, Don H. Psychology. 3rd ed. New York : Worth Publishers , c2003.
BF121 .H59 2003

HOCKEY.
Haché, Alain, 1970- The physics of hockey. Baltimore : Johns Hopkins University Press, 2002.
QC28 .H23 2002

Hocus-pocus.
Brecher, Erwin. London : Panacea Press, 2001.
GV1282.3 .B725 2001

Hodge, Stephen, 1947-.
The Tibetan oracle. 1st ed. New York : Harmony Books, c1998.
BF1773.2.C5 T43 1998

Hodges, Carolyn R., 1947- Making schools work : negotiating educational meaning and transforming the margins / Carolyn R. Hodges and Olga M. Welch. New York : P. Lang, c2003. viii, 101 p. ; 23 cm. (Adolescent cultures, school & society ; v. 8) Includes bibliographical references (p. [95]-101). ISBN 0-8204-3981-9 (pbk. : alk. paper) DDC 370.11/1
1. Compensatory education - United States - Longitudinal studies. 2. Academic achievement - United States - Longitudinal studies. 3. Children with social disabilities - Education (Secondary) - United States - Longitudinal studies. 4. African American high school students - Longitudinal studies. 5. Identity (Psychology) 6. Black author. I. Welch, Olga M. II. Title. III. Series.
LC213.2 .H63 2003

Hodges, Jane. Cosmic grooves / by Jane Hodges. San Francisco, Calif. : Chronicle Books, c2001. 12 v. ; 13 cm. + 12 sound discs (digital ; 4 3/4 in.) CONTENTS: [1] Aquarius, Jan. 21-Feb. 20 -- [2] Pisces, Feb. 21-Mar. 20 -- [3] Aries, Mar. 21-Apr. 20 -- [4] Taurus, Apr. 21-May 21 -- [5] Gemini, May 22-June 21 -- [6] Cancer, June 22-July 22 -- [7] Leo, July 23-Aug. 23 -- [8] Virgo, Aug. 24-Sept. 22 -- [9] Libra, Sept. 23-Oct. 23 -- [10] Scorpio, Oct. 24-Nov. 22 -- [11] Sagittarius, Nov. 23-Dec. 21 -- [12] Capricorn, Dec. 22-Jan. 20. ISBN 0-8118-3077-2
1. Zodiac. 2. Astrology. I. Title.
BF1726 .H59 2001

Hodgkin, Katharine, 1961-.
Contested pasts. London ; New York : Routledge, 2003.
BF378.S65 C665 2003

Hoeller, Stephan A.
[Royal road]
The fool's pilgrimage : Kabbalistic meditations on the tarot / Stephan A. Hoeller. 2nd Quest ed. Wheaton, Ill. : Quest Books/Theosophical Pub. House, 2004. p. cm. Originally published: The royal road. Wheaton, Ill. : Theosophical Pub. House, c1975. ISBN 0-8356-0839-5 DDC 133.3/2424
1. Tarot. 2. Cabala. I. Title.
BF1879.T2 H6 2004

Hoenen, M. J. F. M., 1957-.
The Platonic tradition in the Middle Ages. Berlin ; New York : W. de Gruyter, 2002.

Hoffman, David A., 1947-.
Bringing peace into the room. 1st ed. San Francisco : Jossey-Bass, 2003.
HM1126 .B75 2003

Hoffman, Nancy, 1955- Fairies / by Nancy Hoffman. San Diego, Calif. : Lucent Books, 2004. v. cm. (The mystery library) Includes bibliographical references and index. Table of contents URL: http://www.loc.gov/catdir/toc/ecip041/2003006836.html CONTENTS: What are fairies? -- The origin of fairy folk -- The evolution of the fairy faith -- Human encounters with fairies -- The search for fairies. ISBN 1-56006-973-2 (alk. paper) DDC 133.1/4
1. Fairies - Juvenile literature. 2. Fairies. I. Title. II. Series: Mystery library (Lucent Books)
BF1552 .H64 2004

Hoffmann, Arne. Sind Frauen bessere Menschen? : Plädoyer für einen selbstbewussten Mann / Arne Hoffmann. Berlin : Schwarzkopf & Schwarzkopf, 2001. 603 p. ; 21 cm. (Schwarzkopf & Schwarzkopf Debatte) Includes bibliographical references (p. 565-587). ISBN 3-89602-382-9 (pbk.)
1. Sex role. 2. Social role. 3. Socialization. 4. Sex differences (Psychology) 5. Sexism. I. Title. II. Series.
HQ1075 .H64 2001

Hoffmann, Monika, 1972- Selbstliebe : ein grundlegendes Prinzip von Ethos / Monika Hoffmann. Paderborn : Schöningh, c2002. 381 p. : ill. ; 24 cm. (Abhandlungen zur Philosophie, Psychologie, Soziologie der Religion und Ökumenik, 0343-7310 ; Neuen Folge, Heft 50) Originally presented as the author's thesis (Doctoral-Regensburg). Includes bibliographical references (p. [348]-381) and index. ISBN 3-506-70200-9 (pbk.)
1. Self-acceptance - Religious aspects - Christianity. 2. Narcissism. I. Title. II. Series: Abhandlungen zur Philosophie, Psychologie, Soziologie der Religion und Ökumenik ; n.F., Heft 50.
BF575.S37 H66 2002

Hofmann, Dorothea. Der Komponist als Heros : Mechanismen zur Bildung von kulturellem Gedächtnis / Dorothea Hofmann. Essen : Die Blaue Eule, c2003. 255 p. : music ; 21 cm. (Musikwissenschaft/Musikpädagogik in der Blauen Eule ; Bd. 62) Includes bibliographical references. ISBN 3-89924-030-8 (pbk.)
1. Music - History and criticism. 2. Music - Social aspects. 3. Memory - Social aspects. I. Title. II. Series.

Hofmann, Gabriele.
Mensch & Musik. Augsburg : Wissner, c2002.
ML3830 .M46 2002

Hofmann, Michael, 1932-.
Psychoanalysis and management. Heidelberg : Physica-Verlag, c1994.
BF175.4.S65 P777 1994

Hofstadler, Beate, 1961- KörperNormen, KörperFormen : Männer über Körper, Geschlecht und Sexualität / Beate Hofstadler, Birgit Buchinger. Wien : Turia + Kant, c2001. 270 p., 16 p. of plates : ill. (some col.) ; 24 cm. (Kultur.wissenschaft ; Bd. 4) Includes bibliographical references (p. 266-269). ISBN 3-85132-294-0
1. Body image in men - Austria. 2. Masculinity - Austria. I. Buchinger, Birgit. II. Title. III. Series: Kultur.wissenschaft (Vienna, Austria) ; Bd. 4.
BF692.5 .H64 2001

Hogan, Kevin. Can't get through : eight barriers to communication / Kevin Hogan, Ron Stubbs. Gretna, La. : Pelican Pub. Co., c2003. 174 p. ; 22 cm. Includes bibliographical references. ISBN 1-58980-075-3 DDC 153.6
1. Interpersonal communication. I. Stubbs, Ron. II. Title.
BF637.C45 H635 2003

Hogan, Patrick Colm. Cognitive science, literature, and the arts : a guide for humanists / Patrick Colm Hogan. New York ; London : Routledge, 2003. 244 p. ; 24 cm. Includes bibliographical references (p. [227]-233) and index. ISBN 0-415-94244-6 ISBN 0-415-94245-4 (PBK.) DDC 809
1. Psychology in literature. 2. Psychology in art. 3. Cognitive science. 4. Literature - History and criticism. I. Title. II. Title: Guide for humanists
PN56.P93 H64 2003

Hoggart, Richard, 1918- Everyday language & everyday life / Richard Hoggart. New Brunswick, N.J. ; London : Transaction Publishers, c2003. xvi, 181 p. ; 24 cm. Includes index. ISBN 0-7658-0176-0 (acid-free paper) DDC 306.44/0942
1. English language - Spoken English - England. 2. Aphorisms and apothegms - History and criticism. 3. English language - Social aspects - England. 4. Proverbs, English - History and criticism. 5. English language - Variation - England. 6. English language - England - Idioms. 7. English language - England - Usage. 8. Working class - England - Language. 9. Speech and social status - England. 10. England - Social life and customs. 11. Maxims - History and criticism. 12. Figures of speech. I. Title. II. Title: Everyday language and everyday life
PE1074.8 .H64 2003

Hogue, John. The essential Nostradamus : prophecies for the 21st century and beyond / John Hogue. London : Vega, c2002. 272 p. : ill. ; 16 cm. Includes bibliographical references (p. 262-263) and index. Publisher description URL: http://www.loc.gov/catdir/description/ste031/2003428835.html ISBN 1-84333-597-2 DDC 133.3092
1. Nostradamus, - 1503-1566 - Prophecies. 2. Twenty-first century - Forecasts. I. Nostradamus, 1503-1566. II. Hogue, John. III. Title.
BF1815.N8 H58 2002

Hogue, John. The essential Nostradamus. London : Vega, c2002.
BF1815.N8 H58 2002

Hohlfeldt, Antônio.
Comunicação e corporeidades. Brazil : Editora Universitaria : Compas, 2000.

Hojas de ruta.
Bucay, Jorge, 1949- 1a ed. Buenos Aires : Editorial Sudamericana : Editorial Del nuevo extremo, 2001.

Holá, Lenka. Mediace : způsob řešení mezilidských konfliktu / Lenka Holá. Vyd. 1. Praha : Grada Pub., 2003. 190 p. : ill. ; 23 cm. (Psyché) Includes bibliographical references (p. 182-190). ISBN 80-247-0467-6
1. Interpersonal conflict. 2. Mediation. I. Title. II. Series: Psyché (Prague, Czech Republic)
BF637.I48 H63 2003

Holden, George W.
Texas psychology. Austin : The University of Texas at Austin, c2002.
BF80.7.U62 T48 2002

Holden, Janice Miner.
Fall, Kevin A. Theoretical models of counseling and psychotherapy. New York : Brunner-Routledge, 2003.
BF637.C6 F324 2003

HOLIDAYS. *See* **FASTS AND FEASTS; MEMORIAL DAY.**

HOLIDAYS - HISTORY.
Aveni, Anthony F. The book of the year. Oxford ; New York : Oxford University Press, 2003.
GT3930 .A94 2003

HOLIDAYS, JEWISH. *See* **FASTS AND FEASTS - JUDAISM.**

HOLIDAYS - JEWS. *See* **FASTS AND FEASTS - JUDAISM.**

HOLINESS.
Mozia, Michael Ifeanyinachukwu. Holiness & divine mercy (the key to heaven). Ibadan, Oyo State, Nigeria : St. Pauls, 2002.
1. Black author.

Holiness & divine mercy (the key to heaven).
Mozia, Michael Ifeanyinachukwu. Ibadan, Oyo State, Nigeria : St. Pauls, 2002.

Holiness and divine mercy (the key to heaven).
Mozia, Michael Ifeanyinachukwu. Holiness & divine mercy (the key to heaven). Ibadan, Oyo State, Nigeria : St. Pauls, 2002.
1. Black author.

Holinger, Paul C. What babies say before they can talk : the nine signals infants use to express their feelings / Paul C. Holinger, with Kalia Doner. New York : Simon & Schuster, c2003. xix, 266 p. : ill. ; 22 cm. "A Fireside book." Includes bibliographical references (p. 253-258) and index. ISBN 0-7434-0667-2 DDC 155.42/2369
1. Nonverbal communication in infants. 2. Interpersonal communication in infants. I. Doner, Kalia. II. Title.
BF720.C65 H64 2003

HOLISM.
Esfeld, Michael. Holism in philosophy of mind and philosophy of physics. Dordrecht ; Boston : Kluwer Academic Publishers, c2001.
B818 .E74 2001

Holismus in der Philosophie. 1. Aufl. Weilerswist : Velbrück Wissenschaft, c2002.

Pint, A. A. (Aleksandr Aleksandrovich) Nas mnogo, no my odno. Moskva : Shkola kholicheskoĭ psikhologii, 2003.
BF202 .P56 2003

White, Morton Gabriel, 1917- A philosophy of culture. Princeton, N.J. : Princeton University Press, c2002.
B945.W453 P48 2002

Holism in philosophy of mind and philosophy of physics.
Esfeld, Michael. Dordrecht ; Boston : Kluwer Academic Publishers, c2001.
B818 .E74 2001

Holismus in der Philosophie : ein zentrales Motiv der Gegenwartsphilosophie / herausgegeben von Georg W. Bertram und Jasper Liptow. 1. Aufl. Weilerswist : Velbrück Wissenschaft, c2002. 224 p. ; 23 cm. Includes bibliographical references (p. 218-223). ISBN 3-934730-52-3 (pbk.)
1. Holism. 2. Philosophy, Modern. I. Bertram, Georg W., 1967- II. Liptow, Jasper.

HOLISTIC MEDICINE. *See also* **HEALTH; MIND AND BODY; SELF-CARE, HEALTH.**
Blumenthal, Mark. Popular herbs in the U.S. market. Austin : American Botanical Council, 1997.

Bryden, Barbara E., 1954- Sundial. Gainesville, FL : Center for Applications of Psychological Type, 2003.
BF698.3 .B79 2003

Holl, Adolf, 1930- Brief an die gottlosen Frauen / Adolf Holl. Wien : Zsolnay, 2002. 206 p. ; 21 cm. Includes bibliographical references. ISBN 3-552-05203-8 (hd.bd.)
1. Women - Religious life. 2. Skepticism. I. Title.

Holland, Eileen. Spells for the solitary witch / Eileen Holland. Boston, MA : Weiser Books, 2004. p. cm. Includes index. CONTENTS: Inner work -- Goals, hopes, wishes -- Love -- Life-enhancement -- Problem solving -- Magickal candle gardens -- Tea potions. ISBN 1-57863-294-3 DDC 133.4/4
1. Witchcraft. 2. Magic. I. Title.
BF1566 .H643 2004

A witch's book of answers / Eileen Holland & Cerelia. York Beach, ME : Weiser Books, 2003. x, 370 p. ; 23 cm. Includes bibliographical references (p. 363-366) and index. ISBN 1-57863-280-3 (pbk.) DDC 133.4/3
1. Witchcraft. I. Cerelia. II. Title.
BF1566 .H647 2003

Holland, Ian.
Government reformed. Aldershot, England ; Burlington, VT : Ashgate, c2003.
JF1525.O73 G686 2003

Höller, Christian, 1966-.
Pop unlimited? Wien : Turia + Kant, 2001.
NX456.5.P6 P67 2001

Hollis, James, 1940- On this journey we call our life : living the questions / James Hollis. Toronto, Ont. : Inner City Books, c2003. 157 p. ; 22 cm. (Studies in Jungian psychology by Jungian analysts) Includes bibliographical references (p. 149-151) and index. ISBN 1-89457-404-4 DDC 158.1
1. Self-perception. 2. Individuation (Psychology) 3. Jungian psychology. I. Title. II. Series.
BF697.5.S43 H65 2003

On this journey we call our life : living the questions / James Hollis. Toronto : Inner City Books, c2003. 157 p. ; 22 cm. (Studies in Jungian psychology by Jungian analysts) Includes bibliographical references and index. ISBN 1-89457-404-4 (pbk.) DDC 155.2
1. Self-perception. 2. Individuation (Psychology) 3. Jungian psychology. I. Title. II. Series.

Hollis-Sawyer, Lisa A., 1963-.
Condon, Margaret E. Exercises in psychological testing. Boston : Allyn and Bacon, c2002.
BF176 .T47 2002

Hollywood's most wanted.
Conner, Floyd, 1951- 1st ed. Washington, D.C. : Brassey's, c2002.
PN1998 .C54 2002

Holman, David.
The new workplace. Chichester, UK ; Hoboken, NJ : Wiley, c2003.
HD6955 .N495 2003

Holman, David (David J.).
Management and language. London ; Thousand Oaks : SAGE, 2003.
HD30.3 .H65 2003

Holmes, Andrew, 1965- The chameleon consultant : culturally intelligent consultancy / Andrew Holmes. Aldershot ; Burlington, VT : Gower, 2002. xii, 158 p. : ill. ; 25 cm. Includes bibliographical references and index. ISBN 0-566-08407-4 DDC 658.46
1. Business consultants. 2. Corporate culture. I. Title.

Holmes, Anna (Anna Elizabeth).
Hell hath no fury. 1st Carroll & Graf ed. New York : Carroll & Graf Publishers, 2002.
HQ801 .H45 2002

Holmes, Barbara Ann, 1943- Race and the cosmos : an invitation to view the world differently / Barbara A. Holmes. Harrisburg, Pa. : Trinity Press International, c2002. xvii, 188 p. ; 23 cm. Includes bibliographical references (p. 175-182) and index. CONTENTS: Introduction: Treading new ground -- Coming to awareness -- Liberation theology and beyond -- Science, theology, and culture : the perils and possibilities of shared discourses -- "Dem as could fly home" : indigenous wisdom and science -- Race, cosmology, and inclusion -- Quantum contexts and dominance -- A community called beloved -- The search for meaning -- Conclusion: When we consider how our lives are spent. ISBN 1-56338-377-2 (pbk. : alk. paper) DDC 261.8/348
1. African Americans - Religion. 2. Race - Religious aspects - Christianity. 3. Religion and science. 4. Cosmology. 5. Black author. I. Title.
BR563.N4 H654 2002

Holmes, Ernest, 1887-1960.
[This thing called life]
The art of life : (formerly published as This thing called life) / Ernest Holmes. New York : J.P. Tarcher/Penguin, c2004. p. cm. Originally published: This thing called life. New York : Dodd, Mead, 1943. ISBN 1-58542-267-3 (pbk. : alk. paper) DDC 299/.93
1. New Thought. 2. Success. 3. Happiness. 4. Faith. I. Title.
BF645 .H572 2004

HOLOCAUST (CHRISTIAN THEOLOGY).
Locke, Hubert G. Searching for God in godforsaken times and places. Grand Rapids, Mich. : W.B. Eerdmans Pub., c2003.
BT774 .L63 2003
1. Black author.

Holocaust girls.
Wisenberg, S. L. (Sandi L.) Lincoln : University of Nebraska Press, c2002.
DS143 .W645 2002

HOLOCAUST, JEWISH (1939-1945). *See also* **HOLOCAUST (CHRISTIAN THEOLOGY).**
Adorno, Theodor W., 1903-1969. [Ob nach Auschwitz noch sich leben lasse. English] Can one live after Auschwitz? Stanford, Calif. : Stanford University Press, 2003.
B3199.A33 O213 2003

Gold, Alison Leslie. Fiet's vase and other stories of survival, Europe 1939-1945. New York : Jeremy P. Tarcher/Penguin, c2003.
D804.3 .G64 2003

Katznelson, Ira. Desolation and enlightenment. New York : Columbia University Press, c2003.
JA71 .K35 2003

HOLOCAUST, JEWISH (1939-1945) - BIOGRAPHY.
Gold, Alison Leslie. Fiet's vase and other stories of survival, Europe 1939-1945. New York : Jeremy P. Tarcher/Penguin, c2003.
D804.3 .G64 2003

HOLOCAUST, JEWISH (1939-1945) - HISTORIOGRAPHY.
Jarausch, Konrad Hugo. Shattered past. Princeton, N.J. : Princeton University Press, c2003.
DD86 .J253 2003

Kraft, Robert Nathaniel. Memory perceived. Westport, Conn. : Praeger, 2002.
D804.195 .K73 2002

Stier, Oren Baruch, 1966- Committed to memory. 1st ed. Amherst : University of Massachusetts Press, 2003.
D804.3 .S79 2003

HOLOCAUST, JEWISH (1939-1945), IN LITERATURE.
Stier, Oren Baruch, 1966- Committed to memory. 1st ed. Amherst : University of Massachusetts Press, 2003.
D804.3 .S79 2003

HOLOCAUST, JEWISH (1939-1945), IN MOTION PICTURES.
Stier, Oren Baruch, 1966- Committed to memory. 1st ed. Amherst : University of Massachusetts Press, 2003.
D804.3 .S79 2003

HOLOCAUST, JEWISH (1939-1945) - INFLUENCE.
Ellis, Marc H. Israel and Palestine out of the ashes. London ; Sterling, Va. : Pluto Press, c2002.
DS119.76 .E56 2002

Gold, Alison Leslie. Fiet's vase and other stories of survival, Europe 1939-1945. New York : Jeremy P. Tarcher/Penguin, c2003.
D804.3 .G64 2003

Kraft, Robert Nathaniel. Memory perceived. Westport, Conn. : Praeger, 2002.
D804.195 .K73 2002

Reading, Anna. The social inheritance of the Holocaust. Houndmills [England] ; New York : Palgrave Macmillan, 2002.
D804.3 .R42 2002

Stier, Oren Baruch, 1966- Committed to memory. 1st ed. Amherst : University of Massachusetts Press, 2003.
D804.3 .S79 2003

Wisenberg, S. L. (Sandi L.) Holocaust girls. Lincoln : University of Nebraska Press, c2002.
DS143 .W645 2002

HOLOCAUST, JEWISH (1939-1945) - PERSONAL NARRATIVES.
Gallant, Mary J. Coming of age in the Holocaust. Lanham, Md. : University Press of America, c2002.
D804.3 .G353 2002

Kraft, Robert Nathaniel. Memory perceived. Westport, Conn. : Praeger, 2002.
D804.195 .K73 2002

HOLOCAUST, JEWISH (1939-1945) - PSYCHOLOGICAL ASPECTS.
Gallant, Mary J. Coming of age in the Holocaust. Lanham, Md. : University Press of America, c2002.
D804.3 .G353 2002

Kraft, Robert Nathaniel. Memory perceived. Westport, Conn. : Praeger, 2002.
D804.195 .K73 2002

Recasting German identity. Rochester, NY : Camden House, 2002.
DD239 .R43 2002

HOLOCAUST MEMORIALS.
Stier, Oren Baruch, 1966- Committed to memory. 1st ed. Amherst : University of Massachusetts Press, 2003.
D804.3 .S79 2003

HOLOCAUST SURVIVORS - INTERVIEWS.
Gallant, Mary J. Coming of age in the Holocaust. Lanham, Md. : University Press of America, c2002.
D804.3 .G353 2002

HOLOCAUST SURVIVORS - PSYCHOLOGY.
Gallant, Mary J. Coming of age in the Holocaust. Lanham, Md. : University Press of America, c2002.
D804.3 .G353 2002

Holt, Jason, 1971- Blindsight and the nature of consciousness / Jason Holt. Peterborough, Ont. : Broadview Press, c2003. 153 p. ; 23 cm. Includes bibliographical references (p. 147-153). ISBN 1-55111-351-1 DDC 126
1. Visual perception - Philosophy. 2. Consciousness. I. Title.

HOLT, JOHN CALDWELL, 1923-.
Meighan, Roland. John Holt. 2nd ed. Nottingham : Educational Heretics Press, 2002.
LB885.H64 M454 2002

Holt, Lynn, 1959- Apprehension : reason in the absence of rules / Lynn Holt. Aldershot, Hants, England ; Burlington, VT : Ashgate, c2002. vi, 120 p. ; 24 cm. Includes bibliographical references and index. ISBN 0-7546-0663-5 (alk. paper) ISBN 0-7546-0664-3 (pbk. : alk. paper) DDC 128/.33
1. Reason. 2. Intuition. I. Title.
BC177 .H655 2002

Holt, W. V. America by trial / by William Holt. München : Tuduv, c2001. xiv, 227 p. ; 21 cm. ISBN 3-88073-588-3 (pbk.)
1. United States - Moral conditions. 2. United States - Social conditions - 1980- 3. United States - Social policy - 1993- 4. Liberty. 5. Capitalism. 6. Toleration. I. Title.

HOLY DAYS. *See* **FASTS AND FEASTS.**

HOLY GHOST. *See* **HOLY SPIRIT.**

HOLY GRAIL. *See* **GRAIL.**

The Holy Grail mystery solved.
Tribbe, Frank C. 1st ed. Lakeville, Minn. : Galde Press, 2003.
BF1442.G73 T75 2003

The holy longing.
Zweig, Connie. New York : Jeremy P. Tarcher/Putnam, c2003.
BL53 .Z84 2003

HOLY OFFICE. *See* **INQUISITION.**

HOLY PLACES. *See* **SACRED SPACE.**

HOLY PLACES, CHRISTIAN. *See* **CHRISTIAN SHRINES.**

HOLY ROMAN EMPIRE. CONSTITUTIO CRIMINALIS CAROLINA.
Ströhmer, Michael, 1968- Von Hexen, Ratsherren und Juristen. Paderborn : Bonifatius, c2002.
BF1583 .S77 2002

HOLY ROMAN EMPIRE - HISTORY - TO 1517.
Depreux, Philippe. Charlemagne et les Carolingiens. Paris : Tallandier : Historia, 2002.
DC73 .D38 2002

HOLY ROMAN EMPIRE - KINGS AND RULERS - BIOGRAPHY.
Depreux, Philippe. Charlemagne et les Carolingiens. Paris : Tallandier : Historia, 2002.
DC73 .D38 2002

Morrissey, Robert John, 1947- [Empereur à la barbe fleurie. English] Charlemagne & France. English language ed. Notre Dame, Ind. : University of Notre Dame Press, c2003.
DC73 .M7513 2003

HOLY SHROUD.
Scott, John Beldon, 1946- Architecture for the shroud. Chicago : University of Chicago Press, c2003.
NA5621.T823 S36 2003

Tribbe, Frank C. The Holy Grail mystery solved. 1st ed. Lakeville, Minn. : Galde Press, 2003.
BF1442.G73 T75 2003

HOLY SPIRIT.
Cho, Hyeon-Kweon Stephan, 1962- Heiliger Geist als Lebenskraft in Kirche und Menschheit. Frankfurt am Main ; New York : Peter Lang, c2002.
BT121.3 .C56 2002

HOLY SPIRIT - HISTORY OF DOCTRINES - MIDDLE AGES, 600-1500.
Noriega, José. "Guiados por el espíritu". Roma : Pontificia università lateranense ; [Milano] : Mursia, 2000.

Holy terrors.
Lincoln, Bruce. Chicago : University of Chicago Press, 2003.
BL65.T47 L56 2003

HOLY, THE. *See* **SACRED SPACE.**

HOLY, THE - CONGRESSES.
Il sacro nel Rinascimento. Firenze : F. Cesati, c2002.
PN49 .S337 2002

HOLY, THE, IN LITERATURE - CONGRESSES.
Il sacro nel Rinascimento. Firenze : F. Cesati, c2002.
PN49 .S337 2002

Holzer, Hans, 1920- Hans Holzer's the supernatural : explaining the unexplained. Franklin Lakes, NJ : New Page Books, c2003. 219 p. : ill., maps ; 23 cm. Includes bibliographical references (p. 207-209) and index. ISBN 1-56414-661-8 (pbk.) DDC 133
1. Parapsychology. 2. Supernatural. I. Title. II. Title: Supernatural
BF1031 .H672 2003

Hombre y verdad.
González Ayesta, Cruz. 1. ed. Pamplona : Universidad de Navarra, Ediciones, 2002.

HOME. *See* **FAMILY; HOME ECONOMICS; MARRIAGE.**

HOME AND SCHOOL - UNITED STATES.
Kunjufu, Jawanza. Black students-Middle class teachers. Chicago, Ill. : African American Images, c2002.
1. Black author.

HOME BUILDING INDUSTRY. *See* **CONSTRUCTION INDUSTRY.**

HOME DESIGN. *See* **ARCHITECTURE, DOMESTIC.**

HOME ECONOMICS. *See* **FOOD; HOUSEHOLDS.**

HOME ECONOMICS - PHILOSOPHY.
Thompson, Patricia J. In bed with Procrustes. New York : P. Lang, c2003.
HQ1190 .T52 2002 bk. 2

HOME HEALTH CAREGIVERS. *See* **CAREGIVERS.**

HOME - MISCELLANEA.
Moorey, Teresa. Magic house. 1st US ed. New York, NY : Ryland Peters & Small, 2003.
BF1623.H67 M66 2003

HOME SATELLITE TELEVISION. *See* **DIRECT BROADCAST SATELLITE TELEVISION.**

HOME VIDEO SYSTEMS. *See* **DIRECT BROADCAST SATELLITE TELEVISION.**

HOMELESS ADULTS. *See* **HOMELESS PERSONS.**

HOMELESS CHILDREN - UNITED STATES - BIOGRAPHY.
Summer, Lauralee, 1976- Learning joy from dogs without collars. New York ; London : Simon & Schuster, c2003.
HV4505 .S86 2003

HOMELESS PEOPLE. *See* **HOMELESS PERSONS.**

HOMELESS PERSONS. *See* **HOMELESS CHILDREN.**

HOMELESS PERSONS - UNITED STATES - PSYCHOLOGY.
Summer, Lauralee, 1976- Learning joy from dogs without collars. New York ; London : Simon & Schuster, c2003.
HV4505 .S86 2003

HOMELESSNESS. *See* **HOMELESS PERSONS.**

HOMER.
ODYSSEY.
Shay, Jonathan. Odysseus in America. New York : Scribner, c2002.
RC550 .S533 2002

HOMES. *See* **DWELLINGS.**

Els homes són de Mart, les dones són de Venus.
Gray, John, 1948- [Men are from Mars, women are from Venus. Spanish] 1. ed. Barcelona : Edicions 62, c2001.

HOMESTEADING. *See* **FRONTIER AND PIONEER LIFE.**

HOMICIDE. *See* **MURDER.**

HOMICULTURE. *See* **EUGENICS.**

HOMILETICAL ILLUSTRATIONS. *See* **LEGENDS.**

HOMINIDS. *See* **HUMAN BEINGS.**

L'homme, espoir de dieu.
Chouchena, Emmanuel. Paris : Trajectoire, 2001.

L'homme sans gravité.
Melman, Charles, 1931- Paris : Denoël, c2002.

HOMO SAPIENS. *See* **HUMAN BEINGS.**

Homo sapiens e altre catastrofi.
Pievani, Telmo. Roma : Meltemi, c2002.

HOMOPHOBIA.
Califia-Rice, Patrick, 1954- Speaking sex to power. 1st ed. San Francisco : Cleis Press, c2002.
HQ76.25 .C32 2002

HOMOPLASY. *See* **EVOLUTION (BIOLOGY).**

HOMOSEXUAL COUPLES. *See* **GAY COUPLES.**

HOMOSEXUALITY. *See also* **HOMOSEXUALITY, MALE.**
Califia-Rice, Patrick, 1954- Speaking sex to power. 1st ed. San Francisco : Cleis Press, c2002.
HQ76.25 .C32 2002

Leonel, Vange, 1963- Grrrls. São Paulo : Edições GLS, c2001.

Moser, Antônio. O enigma da esfinge. 3a ed. Petrópolis : Editora Vozes, 2002, c2001.

Odmiany odmieńca. Katowice : "Śląsk", 2002.
HQ23 .O36 2002

Queer counselling and narrative practice. Adelaide : Dulwich Centre Publications, c2002.

Sexual faces. Madison, Conn. : International Universities Press, c2002.
BF175.5.S48 S47 2002

HOMOSEXUALITY AND EDUCATION.
Ressler, Paula. Dramatic changes. Portsmouth, NH : Heinemann, c2002.
PN3171 .R47 2002

HOMOSEXUALITY - HISTORY.
Filho, Amilcar Torrão. Tríbades galantes, fanchonos militantes. São Paulo : Edições GLS, 2000.

HOMOSEXUALITY IN LITERATURE.
Vadillo, Alicia E. Santería y Vodú. Madrid : Biblioteca Nueva, c2002.
PQ7372 .V33 2002

HOMOSEXUALITY, MALE - PSYCHOLOGICAL ASPECTS.
Bailey, J. Michael. The man who would be queen. Washington, D.C. : Joseph Henry Press, c2003.
HQ76.2.U5 B35 2003

HOMOSEXUALS. *See* **GAYS.**

HOMOSEXUALS, FEMALE. *See* **LESBIANS.**

HOMOSEXUALS, MALE. *See* **GAY MEN.**

Honegger, Gottfried, 1917- Erfundenes und Erlebtes : Briefe an Leonardo da Vinci, Sonia Delaunay, Vincent van Gogh, Marcel Duchamp, Giovanni Pisanello, Henri Matisse, René Magritte, Mark Rothko, Fernand Léger, Yves Klein, Domenico Ghirlandaio, Kasimir Malewitch, Edvard Munch, Sophie Taeuber, Alberto Giacometti, Giorigio de Chirico, Sam Francis, Barnett Newman, Rembrandt van Rijn, Piet Mondrian, Josef Beuys, Roy Lichtenstein, Ljubow Popowa, Hans Arp, Eugène Delacroix / Gottfried Honegger. München : Chorus, c2002. 119 p. : ill. ; 25 cm. (Kunst Theorie) Cover title: Erfundenes und Erlebtes : Briefe an-- . Fictitious letters by the commercial artist. Includes bibliographical references. ISBN 3-931876-43-8 (hd.bd.)
1. Art - Philosophy. 2. Aesthetics. I. Title. II. Title: Erfundenes und Erlebtes : Briefe an-- III. Series.

Honey from my heart for you / [project editor, Terri Gibbs] ; illustrated by Debra Jordan Bryan. Nashville, Tenn. : J. Countryman, c2002. 1 v. (unpaged) : col. ill. ; 17 cm. ISBN 0-8499-9530-2
1. Friendship. 2. Sharing. 3. Happiness. I. Gibbs, Terri. II. Bryan, Debra Jordan.
BF575.F66 H66 2002

HONEYMOONS. *See* **MARRIAGE.**

Hong, Joon-kee, 1962- Der Subjektbegriff bei Lacan und Althusser : ein philosophisch-systematischer Versuch zur Rekonstruktion ihrer Theorien / Joon-kee Hong. Frankfurt am Main ; New York : Peter Lang , c2000. 267 p. ; 21 cm. (Philosophie und Geschichte der Wissenschaften, 0724-4479 ; Bd. 43) Originally presented as the author's thesis (doctoral)--Bremen, Univ., 1999. Includes bibliographical references (p. 257-267). ISBN 3-631-34675-1 (pbk. : säurefrei)
1. Lacan, Jacques, - 1901- 2. Althusser, Louis. I. Title. II. Series.
BF109.L28 H66 2000

Hong, Zicheng, fl. 1596.
[Cai gen tan]
Dao jie cai gen tan : zhe zhe di zhi gui / Hong Yingming zhu ; Ying Han bian yi. Di 1 ban. Beijing Shi : Zong jiao wen hua chu ban she, 1996 (1997 printing) 11, 395 p. ; 21 cm. ISBN 7-80123-039-6
1. Conduct of life. I. Ying, Han. II. Title.
BJ1558.C5 H85 1996 <Asian China>

Ru jie cai gen tan : Ren zhe di shu yu / Hong Yingming zhu ; Ying Han bian yi. Di 1 ban. Beijing Shi : Zong jiao wen hua chu ban she, 1996 (1997 printing) 11, 400 p. ; 21 cm. ISBN 7-80123-037-X
1. Conduct of life. I. Ying, Han. II. Title.
BJ1558.C5 H85 1996b <Asian China>

Honig, S.
Naphtali ben Isaac, ha-Kohen, 1649-1719. Sefer Bet Rahel. Yerushalayim : Ahavat Shalom, 761 [2001]
BM665 .N257 2001

Honigman, Andrew, 1970-.
My proof of survival. 1st ed. St. Paul, Minn. : Llewellyn Publications, 2003.
BF1311.F8 M9 2003

HONOR.
Burkhart, Dagmar. Ehre. Originalausg. München : Deutscher Taschenbuch Verlag, c2002.
BJ1533.H8 B87 2002

Honor your anger.
Engel, Beverly. Hoboken, N.J. : J. Wiley & Sons, 2003.
BF575.A5 E54 2003

La honte est-elle immorale?.
Ogien, Ruwen. Paris : Bayard, c2002.

Hood, Adam, 1960- Baillie, Oman and Macmurray : experience and religious belief / Adam Hood. Aldershot, England ; Burlington, VT : Ashgate, c2003. x, 216 p. ; 24 cm. (Ashgate new critical thinking in religion, theology & biblical studies) Includes bibliographical references (p. [205]-212) and index. ISBN 0-7546-3135-4 (alk. paper) DDC 248.2/092/2
1. Baillie, John, - 1886-1960. 2. Oman, John, - 1860-1939. 3. Macmurray, John, - 1891- 4. Experience (Religion) 5. Faith. I. Title. II. Series: Ashgate new critical thinking in religion, theology, and biblical studies.
BR110 .H575 2003

Hood, Ralph W. Dimensions of mystical experiences : empirical studies and psychological links / Ralph W. Hood, Jr. Amsterdam ; New York, NY : Rodopi, 2001. ii, 184 p. : 22 cm. (International series in the psychology of religion ; 11) Includes bibliographical references (p. [164]-178) and indexes. ISBN 90-420-1339-7 (pbk.)
1. Mysticism. 2. Psychology, Religious. I. Title. II. Series.

Hood-Williams, John.
Cealey Harrison, Wendy. Beyond sex and gender. London ; Thousand Oaks, Calif. : SAGE, 2002.
HQ1075 .C43 2002

HOODOO (CULT). *See* **VOODOOISM.**

Hook, Kristina.
Designing information spaces. London ; New York : Springer, 2003.
QA76.9.C66 D49 2003

Hooks, Bell. Rock my soul : Black people and self-esteem / Bell Hooks. New York, NY : Atria Books, c2003. xiii, 226 p. ; 23 cm. ISBN 0-7434-5605-X
1. Self-esteem. 2. African Americans - Social conditions - 1975- 3. Black author. I. Title.

Hoole book of Kyng Arthur and of his noble knyghtes of the Rounde Table.
Malory, Thomas, Sir, 15th cent. [Morte d'Arthur] Le morte Darthur, or, The hoole book of Kyng Arthur and of his noble knyghtes of the Rounde Table. 1st ed. New York ; London : Norton, c2004.
PR2041 .M37 2004

HOORNEMAN, MARGARET.
Vint/age 2001 conference : [videorecording]. New York, c2001.

Hoorneman, Margaret, panelist.
Vint/age 2001 conference : [videorecording]. New York, c2001.

Hoover Institution Press publication
(515.) Anderson, Terry Lee, 1946- Property rights. Stanford, Calif. : Hoover Institution Press, c2003.
HB701 .A44 2003

Hope.
Zournazi, Mary. Annandale, N.S.W. : Pluto Press, 2002.

HOPE.
Snyder, C. R. Handbook of hope. San Diego, Calif. : Academic Press, c2000.
BF575.H56 S69 2000

Takahashi, Keiko, 1956- Kibō no genri = Tōkyō : Sanpō Shuppan, 1997.
BD216 .T35 1997

Thoele, Sue Patton. Growing hope. York Beach, ME : Conari Press, 2004.
BF575.H56 T48 2004

Zournazi, Mary. Hope. Annandale, N.S.W. : Pluto Press, 2002.

Hope, Jeremy. Beyond budgeting : how managers can break free from the annual performance trap / Jeremy Hope, Robin Fraser. Boston : Harvard Business School Press, c2003. xxii, 232 p. : ill. : 24 cm. Includes bibliographical references (p. 217-220) and index. CONTENTS: The annual performance trap -- Breaking free -- How three organizations introduced adaptive processes -- Principles of adaptive processes -- Insights into implementation -- How three organizations removed the barriers to change -- Principles of radical decentralization -- Insights into changing centralized mind-sets -- The roles of systems and tools -- The vision of a management model fit for the twenty-first century. ISBN 1-57851-866-0 (alk. paper) DDC 658
1. Management. I. Fraser, Robin, 1941- II. Title.
HD31 .H635 2003

Hopf, Christel.
Liebe und Abhängigkeit. Weinheim : Juventa, 2001.

Höpfl, Heather.
Interpreting the maternal organisation. London ; New York : Routledge, 2003.
HM786 .I58 2003

Hopper, Robert. Gendering talk / Robert Hopper. East Lansing : Michigan State University Press, c2003. xi, 251 p. ; 23 cm. Includes bibliographical references. CONTENTS: The conversation -- The arrangement between the sexes -- Flirting -- Hey baby, you bitch -- Coupling as progressive commitment -- Coupling as a difference engine -- Talk about women, talk about men -- Making women look bad -- How women and men talk -- How gender creeps into talk -- Leveling the playing field -- Return to laughter. ISBN 0-87013-636-4 (pbk. : alk. paper) DDC 302.2
1. Sex role. 2. Communication - Sex differences. 3. Communication and sex. 4. Man-woman relationships. 5. Interpersonal communication. 6. Conversation. I. Title.
HQ1075 .H67 2003

Hopper, Robert, 1945-.
Studies in language and social interaction. Mahwah, N.J. : London : Lawrence Erlbaum, 2003.

Horgan, John, 1953- Rational mysticism : dispatches from the border between science and spirituality / John Horgan. Boston : Houghton Mifflin, 2003. 292 p. : 24 cm. Includes bibliographical references (p. 241-272) and index. ISBN 0-618-06027-8 DDC 291.1/75
1. Mysticism. 2. Religion and science. I. Title.
BL625 .H67 2003

Hornig, Christian. Wollheims Traum : Beiträge zur Kunstwissenschaft / Christian Hornig. Gauting : Lynx, c2001. 162 p. : ill. (some col.) ; 26 cm. Includes bibliographical references (p. 155-161) and index. ISBN 3-936169-00-4 (hd.bd.)
1. Wollheim, Gert H., - 1894-1974. 2. Art - History. I. Title.

Hornung, Erik.
Schweizer, Andreas, 1946- Seelenführer durch den verborgenen Raum. München : Kösel, 1994.

HOROLOGY. *See* **TIME.**

HOROSCOPES.
Constantine, Storm. Egyptian birth signs. London : Thorsons, 2002.

Omarr, Sydney. [Astrology, love, sex, and you] Sydney Omarr's astrology, love, sex, and you. New York : Signet, c2002.
BF1729.S4 O58 2002

Orosz, László Wladimir. A jelen és az idő. Debrecen : Stalker Stúdió, 2001.
BF1999 .O69 2000

Suckling, Nigel. Legends & lore. New York : Friedman/Fairfax Publishers : Distributed by Sterling Pub., c2002.
BF1714.C5 S93 2002

Your birthday sign through time. New York : Atria Books, c2002.
BF1728.A2 Y57 2002

HOROSCOPY. *See* **ASTROLOGY.**

Horowitz, David A. America's political class under fire : the twentieth century's great culture war / by David A. Horowitz. New York ; London : Routledge, 2003. xii, 290 p. ; 24 cm. Includes bibliographical references (p. [229]-275) and index. ISBN 0-415-94690-5 (hbk. : alk. paper) ISBN 0-415-94691-3 (pbk. : alk. paper) DDC 305.5/0973/0904
1. Social classes - United States - History - 20th century. 2. Elite (Social sciences) - United States - Public opinion - History - 20th century. 3. Classism - United States. 4. Intellectuals - United States - Public opinion. 5. Public opinion - United States - History - 20th century. 6. United States - Politics and government - 20th century. I. Title.
HN90.S6 H67 2003

Horowitz, Leonard M.
IIP, inventory of interpersonal problems manual. [San Antonio, TX?] : Psychological Corp., c2000.
BF698.5 .I36 2000

HOROWITZ, SHABBETAI SHEFTEL BEN AKIVA, D. 1619.
Sack, Bracha, 1933- Shomer ha-pardes. Be'er Sheva' : Universiṭat Ben-Guryon ba-Negev, c2002.

Horrigan, Marianne.
Imbrogno, Philip J. Celtic mysteries in New England. 1st ed. St. Paul, Minn. : Llewellyn Publications, 2000.
BF2050 I435 2000

HORROR. *See also* **FEAR.**
Lhomme-Rigaud, Colette. L'adolescent et ses monstres. Ramonville Saint-Agne : Erès, c2002.

HORROR TALES. *See* **GHOST STORIES.**

HORSE. *See* **HORSES.**

The horse in the ancient world.
Hyland, Ann. Stroud : Sutton, 2003.

Horse wise.
Kimball, Cheryl. Boston, MA : Conari Press, 2004.
BF637.C5 K55 2004

HORSES - HISTORY - TO 1500.
Hyland, Ann. The horse in the ancient world. Stroud : Sutton, 2003.

HORSES - MIDDLE EAST - HISTORY - TO 1500.
Hyland, Ann. The horse in the ancient world. Stroud : Sutton, 2003.

HORSES - PSYCHOLOGY - MISCELLANEA.
Kimball, Cheryl. Horse wise. Boston, MA : Conari Press, 2004.
BF637.C5 K55 2004

Horton, Ian, 1940-.
Applied psychology. London ; Thousand Oaks, Calif. : SAGE Publications, 2003.
BF636 .A62 2003

Hösle, Vittorio, 1960- Philosophie und Öffentlichkeit / Vittorio Hösle. Würzburg : Königshausen & Neumann, c2003. 141 p. ; 24 cm. Includes bibliographical references (p. 141). ISBN 3-8260-2445-1 (pbk.)
1. *Philosophy, Modern - 20th century.* 2. *Ethics.* 3. *Political science - Philosophy.* I. *Title.*

HOSPITAL MEDICAL RECORDS. *See* **MEDICAL RECORDS.**

HOSPITAL RECORDS. *See* **MEDICAL RECORDS.**

HOSPITALS. *See* **PSYCHIATRIC HOSPITALS.**

HOSPITALS - HISTORY.
Michael, Pamela. Care and treatment of the mentally ill in North Wales, 1800-2000. Cardiff : University of Wales Press, 2003.

HOSPITALS - PSYCHIATRIC SERVICES. *See* **PSYCHIATRIC HOSPITALS.**

Hossenfelder, Malte. Der Wille zum Recht und das Streben nach Glück : Grundlegung einer Ethik des Wollens / Malte Hossenfelder. Originalausg. München : C.H. Beck, c2000. 215 p. ; 19 cm. (Beck'sche Reihe ; 1383) Includes bibliographical references and index. ISBN 3-406-45923-4 (pbk.)
1. *Ethics.* 2. *Humanistic ethics.* I. *Title.*

HOSTILE BEHAVIOR. *See* **HOSTILITY (PSYCHOLOGY).**

HOSTILE TAKEOVERS OF CORPORATIONS. *See* **CONSOLIDATION AND MERGER OF CORPORATIONS.**

HOSTILITIES. *See* **WAR; WAR (INTERNATIONAL LAW).**

HOSTILITY (PSYCHOLOGY). *See* **FIGHTING (PSYCHOLOGY).**

HOSTILITY (PSYCHOLOGY) - CASE STUDIES.
Eigen, Michael. Rage. Middletown, Conn. : Wesleyan University Press, c2002.
RC569.5.A53 E38 2002

Hot love spells.
Sophia, 1955- The little book of hot love spells. Kansas City, Mo. : Andrews McMeel Pub., c2002.
BF1623.L6 S66 2002

Hot topics (Berlin, Germany)
Adaptive agents and multi-agent systems. Berlin ; New York : Springer, c2003.
QA76.76.I58 A312 2003

Hôtel des invalides (France).
Colloque des Invalides (5th : 2001 : Hôtel des invalides) Ce que je ne sais pas. Tusson, Charente : Du Lérot, [2002?]
PQ145 .C65 2001

HOTELS. *See* **HAUNTED HOTELS.**

Hothersall, David. History of psychology / David Hothersall. 4th ed. Boston : McGraw-Hill, c2004. xiii, 610 p. : ill. ; 24 cm. Includes bibliographical references (p. 541-590) and indexes. Publisher description URL: http://www.loc.gov/catdir/description/mh031/2003046392.html Table of contents URL: http://www.loc.gov/catdir/toc/mh031/2003046392.html ISBN 0-07-284965-7 (alk. paper) DDC 150/.9
1. *Psychology - History.* I. *Title.*
BF95 .H67 2004

Hotho, Heinrich Gustav, 1802-1873. Vorstudien für Leben und Kunst / Heinrich Gustav Hotho ; herausgegeben und eingeleitet von Bernadette Collenberg-Plotnikov. Stuttgart : Frommann-Holzboog, 2002. lxxxv, 329 p. ; 22 cm. (Spekulation und Erfahrung. Abteilung I. Texte ; Bd. 5) Includes bibliography (p. 309-314) and indexes. Original publication, Stuttgart: Cotta, 1835. ISBN 3-7728-1488-3 (cl.)
1. *Aesthetics.* I. *Collenberg-Plotnikov, Bernadette, 1963-* II. *Title.* III. *Series.*

Hottois, Gilbert, 1946- Species technica ; suivi d'un Dialogue philosophique autour de Species Technica vingt ans plus tard / par Gilbert Hottois. Paris : Vrin, 2002. 347 p. ; 22 cm. (Pour demain, 0180-4847)
CONTENTS: Species technica -- Dialogue autour de Species Technica vingt ans plus tard. ISBN 2-7116-1565-0 DDC 194
1. *Philosophy, Modern - 20th century.* 2. *Hottois, Gilbert, - 1946- - Interviews.* 3. *Philosophers, Modern - Belgium - Interviews.* I. *Title.* II. *Series.*

HOTTOIS, GILBERT, 1946- - INTERVIEWS.
Hottois, Gilbert, 1946- Species technica ; Paris : Vrin, 2002.

Hou xian dai zhu yi wen hua cong shu
(2) Ma, Wenqi. Shui yue jing hua. Di 1 ban. Beijing : Zhongguo she hui chu ban she, 1994.
PN2039 .M28 1994 <Orien China>

Hou xian dai zhu yi yu dang dai hui hua.
Li, Yi. Zou xiang he chu. Di 1 ban. Beijing : Zhongguo she hui chu ban she : Xin hua shu dian Beijing fa xing suo jing xiao, 1994.
ND196.P66 L5 1994 <Orien China>

Hou xian dai zhu yi yu dang dai xi ju.
Ma, Wenqi. Shui yue jing hua. Di 1 ban. Beijing : Zhongguo she hui chu ban she, 1994.
PN2039 .M28 1994 <Orien China>

Houdé, Olivier.
[Vocabulaire de sciences cognitives. English.] Dictionary of cognitive science. New York : Psychology Press, 2003.
BF311 .V56713 2003

Houdeshell, Seth, 1974-.
Miller, Scott D. Staying on top and keeping the sand out of your pants. Deerfield Beach, Fla. : Health Communications, c2003.
BF637.S8 M565 2003

HOURS OF LABOR. *See* **HOLIDAYS.**

HOURS (TIME). *See* **TIME.**

Housden, Roger.
The Tibetan oracle. 1st ed. New York : Harmony Books, c1998.
BF1773.2.C5 T43 1998

HOUSE FURNISHINGS. *See* **POTTERY.**

HOUSE MARKS. *See* **STREET ADDRESSES.**

HOUSE NUMBERS. *See* **STREET ADDRESSES.**

HOUSE-RAISING PARTIES. *See* **DWELLINGS.**

HOUSEHOLD ANIMALS. *See* **PETS.**

HOUSEHOLD ECOLOGY. *See* **DWELLINGS.**

HOUSEHOLD MANAGEMENT. *See* **HOME ECONOMICS.**

HOUSEHOLD MOVING. *See* **MOVING, HOUSEHOLD.**

HOUSEHOLD SCIENCE. *See* **HOME ECONOMICS.**

HOUSEHOLD SURVEYS. *See* **HOUSEHOLDS.**

HOUSEHOLDS. *See* **FAMILY; HOME ECONOMICS.**

HOUSEHOLDS - MISCELLANEA.
Moorey, Teresa. Magic house. 1st US ed. New York, NY : Ryland Peters & Small, 2003.
BF1623.H67 M66 2003

HOUSEHUSBANDS. *See* **FATHERS; HUSBANDS.**

Houser, Marcel.
Bergeret, Jean. La sexualité infantile et ses mythes. Paris : Dunod, c2001.

HOUSES. *See* **ARCHITECTURE, DOMESTIC; DWELLINGS.**

HOUSES (ASTROLOGY).
Your birthday sign through time. New York : Atria Books, c2002.
BF1728.A2 Y57 2002

HOUSEWIVES. *See* **MOTHERS.**

HOUSING. *See* **DWELLINGS; HOUSEHOLDS.**

Housley, William, 1970- Interaction in multidisciplinary teams / William Housley. Aldershot, England ; Burlington, VT : Ashgate, c2003. vi, 141 p. : ill. ; 23 cm. (Cardiff papers in qualitative research) Includes bibliographical references (p. 135-139) and index. ISBN 0-7546-1796-3 (alk. paper) DDC 361.3
1. *Social service - Teamwork.* 2. *Teams in the workplace.* I. *Title.* II. *Series.*
HV41 .H667 2003

Ḥovat ha-levavot ha-mefo'ar.
Baḥya ben Joseph ibn Paḳuda, 11th cent. [Hidāyah ilá farā'iḍ al-ḳulūb] Torat ḥovat ha-levavot ha-mefo'ar. Nyu Yorḳ : Y. Vais : Star Ḳompozishan : [Hotsa'at Ateret], 760 [2000]

How?
Harris, Nicholas, 1956- How big? San Diego, CA : Blackbirch Press, 2004.
BF299.S5 H37 2004

How big?.
Harris, Nicholas, 1956- San Diego, CA : Blackbirch Press, 2004.
BF299.S5 H37 2004

How can I be trusted?.
Potter, Nancy Nyquist, 1954- Lanham, Md. ; Oxford : Rowman & Littlefield, c2002.
BJ1500.T78 P68 2002

How can I forgive you?.
Spring, Janis Abrahms. 1st ed. New York : HarperCollins, 2004.
BF637.F67 S67 2004

How customers think.
Zaltman, Gerald. Boston, Mass. : Harvard Business School Press, c2003.
HF5415.32 .Z35 2003

How do religious figures induce the establishment of sects?.
Cuevas Sosa, Andrés Alejandro, 1939- 2nd ed. Leicestershire : Upfront Pub., 2002.
BF1272 .C84 2002

How do you compare?.
Williams, Andrew N. 1st Perigee ed. New York : Perigee Book, 2004.
BF698.5 .W55 2004

How Germans negotiate.
Smyser, W. R., 1931- Washington, D.C. : U.S. Institute of Peace Press, 2003.
BF637.N4 S59 2003

How healthy are we? : a national study of well-being at midlife / edited by Orville Gilbert Brim, Carol D. Ryff, and Ronald C. Kessler. Chicago, Ill. : University of Chicago Press, c2003. p. cm. (The John D. and Catherine T. MacArthur Foundation series on mental health and development. Studies on successful midlife development) Includes bibliographical references and indexes. Table of contents URL: http://www.loc.gov/catdir/toc/ecip045/2003012636.html ISBN 0-226-07475-7 (cloth : alk. paper) DDC 305.244/0973
1. *Middle age - Psychological aspects.* 2. *Middle age - Social aspects.* 3. *Middle age - Health and hygiene.* I. *Brim, Orville Gilbert, 1923-* II. *Ryff, Carol D.* III. *Kessler, Ronald C.* IV. *Series.*
BF724.6 .H69 2003

How images think.
Burnett, Ron, 1947- Cambridge, Mass. : MIT Press, 2004.
BF241 .B79 2004

How religion works.
Pyysiäinen, Ilkka. Leiden ; Boston : Brill, 2001.
BL53 .P98 2001

How three twentieth century masterworks depict grief in time of war.
Lathan, Mark J., 1961- Emotional progression in sacred choral music. 2001.

How to be a friend.
Gingras, Sandy, 1958- Harvey Cedars, NJ : Down the Shore Pub., 2003.
BF575.F66 G56 2003

How to be psychic.
Fenton, Sasha. New York : Sterling Pub., c2003.
BF1031 .F46 2003

How to build a mind.
Aleksander, Igor. New York : Columbia University Press, 2001.
Q335 .A44225 2001

How to conduct behavioral research over the internet.
Fraley, R. Chris. New York : Guilford Press, 2005.
BF76.6.I57 F73 2005

How to connect in business in 90 seconds or less.
Boothman, Nicholas. New York : Workman Pub., 2002.
HD69.S8 B66 2002

How to escape the no-win trap.
Berg, Barbara A. New York : McGraw-Hill, c2004.
BF448 .B46 2004

How to get a really great job!.
Varner, Don. Toronto : Productive Publications, 1998.

How to hunt ghosts.
Warren, Joshua P. New York : Simon & Schuster, c2003.
BF1471 .W37 2003

How to link tarot cards to reveal the future.
Fenton, Sasha. Super tarot. New York : Sterling Pub., 2003.
BF1879.T2 F465 2003

How to make peace.
Laurel, Alicia Bay, 1949- 1st ed. Layton, Utah : G. Smith, Publisher, c2004.
BF637.P3 L38 2004

How to persuade people who don't want to be persuaded.
Bauer, Joel. 1960- Hoboken, N.J. : John Wiley & Sons, 2004.
BF637.P4 B32 2004

How to practice Vedic astrology.
Bloomfield, Andrew, 1960- Rochester, Vt. : Destiny Books, 2003.
BF1714.H5 B585 2003

How to prepare for mechanical aptitude & spatial relations tests.
Wiesen, Joel P. (Joel Peter) Hauppauge, NY : Barron's, 2003.
BF433.M4 W535 2003

How to prepare for the AP psychology advanced placement examination.
McEntarffer, Robert. Barron's how to prepare for the AP pscyhology advanced placement examination. Hauppauge, N.Y. : Barron's, c2004.
BF78 .M34 2004

How to run a company.
Carey, Dennis. 1st ed. New York : Crown Business, c2003.
HD38.2 .C374 2003

How to say it when you don't know what to say.
Kaplan, Robbie Miller. Prentice Hall Press ed. Upper Saddle River, NJ : Prentice Hall Press, 2004.
BF637.C54 K36 2004

How to solve the mind - body problem.
Humphrey, Nicholas. Thorverton, UK ; Bowling Green, OH : Imprint Academic, c2000.
BF698.95 .H86 2000

How to think straight about psychology.
Stanovich, Keith E., 1950- 7th ed. Boston, MA : Allyn and Bacon, 2004.
BF76.5 .S68 2004

How to thrive in spite of mess, stress and less!.
Fralix, Patti. 1st ed. Raleigh, NC : Triunity Publishers, c2002.
BF637.S4 F72 2002

How we act.
Enç, Berent. Oxford : Clarendon Press ; New York : Oxford University Press, 2003.
B105.A35 E63 2003

How we have changed : America since 1950 / [edited] by Rick Phalen. Gretna, La. : Pelican Pub. Co., 2003. 232 p. ; 24 cm. Includes index. Table of contents URL: http://www.loc.gov/catdir/toc/fy038/2002015406.html ISBN 1-58980-110-5 (alk. paper) DDC 973.92
1. United States - Civilization - 1945- 2. United States - Social conditions - 1945- 3. National characteristics, American. 4. Celebrities - United States - Interviews. I. Phalen, Richard C., 1937-
E169.12 .H677 2003

Howard, Bradley Reed. Indigenous peoples and the state : the struggle for native rights / Bradley Reed Howard. DeKalb : Northern Illinois University Press, c2003. 252 p. ; 24 cm. Includes bibliographical references (p. [215]-245) and index. ISBN 0-87580-290-7 (alk. paper) DDC 323.1/1
1. Indigenous peoples. 2. Human rights. 3. Self-determination, National. 4. Racism. 5. Globalization. I. Title.
GN380 .H68 2003

Howard, Kerry. The book of love and happiness : how to find and keep love in your life / Kerry Howard, Mavis Klein, Julia Lampshire ; illustrations by Natacha Ledwidge. New York : Ryland Peters & Small, Inc., 2004. p. cm. Includes bibliographical references and index. CONTENTS: The love coach / by Kerry Howard -- Know yourself -- What's your love-ability? -- Believe in love -- Love goals -- The right chemistry -- Love now -- Communicating love / by Julia Lampshire -- First impressions -- Being a good listener -- Where are you coming from? -- Building rapport -- Communicating sex -- Getting what you want -- Communicate now -- The astrology of love / by Mavis Klein -- The signs of love -- The transits of life -- Do it now. ISBN 1-84172-590-0 DDC 158.2
1. Love. I. Klein, Mavis. II. Lampshire, Julia. III. Title.
BF575.L8 H69 2004

Howard, Michael, 1922 Nov. 29- The invention of peace and the reinvention of war / Michael Howard. Rev. and extended ed. London : Profile, 2002, c2001. 126 p. ; 20 cm. Previous ed.: published as The invention of peace, 2000. ISBN 1-86197-409-4 DDC 327.172
1. Peace. 2. Security, International. 3. War - History. I. Howard, Michael, 1922 Nov. 29- Invevntion of peace. II. Title.

Invervntion of peace.
Howard, Michael, 1922 Nov. 29- The invention of peace and the reinvention of war. Rev. and extended ed. London : Profile, 2002, c2001.

HOWE, TINA.
Vint/age 2001 conference : [videorecording]. New York, c2001.

Howe, Tina, panelist.
Vint/age 2001 conference : [videorecording]. New York, c2001.

Howkins, John, 1945- The creative economy : how people make money from ideas / John Howkins. London : Allen Lane, 2001. xviii, 263 p. ; 25 cm. Includes bibliographical references and index. ISBN 0-7139-9403-7 DDC 658.575
1. Creative ability in business. 2. New products - Management. 3. Intellectual property. 4. Technological innovations - Management. I. Title.

Howlett, Robert J., 1954-.
Internet-based intelligent information processing systems. Singapore ; River Edge, NJ : World Scientific, 2003.

H.R. Giger tarot.
Akron, 1948- Köln : Evergreen, c2000.

Hrodzenski dziarzhaŭny universitėt imia IA. Kupaly.
Ėmotsii cheloveka v normal'nykh i stressornykh usloviiakh. Grodno : Grodnenskiĭ gos. universitet im. IAnki Kupaly, 2001.
BF531 .E54 2001

Hsu, Shan-Tung, 1942- The yin & yang of love : feng shui for relationships / Shan-Tung Hsu. 1st ed. St. Paul, Minn. : Llewellyn Publications, 2003. xiii, 198 p. : ill. ; 21 cm. Includes index. ISBN 0-7387-0347-8 DDC 133.3/337
1. Feng shui. 2. Love. I. Title. II. Title: Yin and yang of love
BF1779.F4 H763 2003

[**Yin & yang of love. Spanish**]
Feng shui para el amor / Shan-Tung Hsu ; traducido por Héctor Ramírez Silva y Edgar Rojas. 1. ed. St. Paul, Minn. : Llewellyn Espanol, 2003. xiii, 201 p. : ill. ; 21 cm. Includes index. ISBN 0-7387-0381-8 DDC 133.3/337
1. Feng shui. 2. Love. I. Title.
BF1779.F4 H76318 2003

HTML and XHTML, the definitive guide.
Musciano, Chuck. 5th ed. Beijing ; Sebastopol [Calif.] : O'Reilly, 2002.

HTML (DOCUMENT MARKUP LANGUAGE).
Fraley, R. Chris. How to conduct behavioral research over the internet. New York : Guilford Press, 2005.
BF76.6.I57 F73 2005

Musciano, Chuck. HTML and XHTML, the definitive guide. 5th ed. Beijing ; Sebastopol [Calif.] : O'Reilly, 2002.

Hu, Guocheng.
Tou shi Meiguo. Di 1 ban. Beijing : Zhongguo she hui ke xue chu ban she : Jing xiao Xin hua shu dian, 2002.
E175.8 .T78 2002

Hu, Liuming, 1950- Dan shen gui zu : dang dai du shi dan shen nü ren de qing gan qing su / Hu Liuming zhu. Di 1 ban. [Wuhan Shi] : Chang jiang wen yi chu ban she, [2000] 2, 4, 319 p. ; 21 cm. Cover title. ISBN 7-5354-1958-5
1. Single women - China. 2. Man-woman relationships. I. Title.
PL2863.L58 D365 2000

Hu, Shihou. Hua jia ji : wen xue san lun / Hu Shihou zhu. Di 1 ban. Kaifeng Shi : Henan da xue chu ban she, 1998. 2, 5, 259 p. ; 21 cm. Cover title: Huajia ji. Includes bibliographical references. ISBN 7-81041-411-9
1. Chinese literature - History and criticism. I. Title. II. Title: Huajia ji

Hu, Zhi, 1891-1962. Bai hua wen xue shi / Hu Shi zhu. Di 1 ban. Beijing : Dong fang chu ban she, 1996. 345 p. ; 21 cm. (Min guo xue shu jing dian wen ku ; 30) In Chinese. ISBN 7-5060-0708-8
1. Chinese literature - History and criticism. I. Title.

Hua jia ji.
Hu, Shihou. Di 1 ban. Kaifeng Shi : Henan da xue chu ban she, 1998.

Huajia ji.
Hu, Shihou. Hua jia ji. Di 1 ban. Kaifeng Shi : Henan da xue chu ban she, 1998.

Huang, Hao.
Cai, Zhichun. Huo fo zhuan shi. Di 1 ban. Beijing : Hua wen chu ban she : Xin hua shu dian jing xiao, 2000.
BL515 .C345 2000

Huang, Kejian.
[Selections. 1998]
Huang Kejian zi xuan ji / Wang Kejian zhu. Di 1 ban. Guilin Shi : Guangxi shi fan da xue chu ban she, 1998. 2, 2, 2, 2, 421 p. : ill. ; 23 cm. (Kua shi ji xue ren wen cun) "'Jiu wu' guo jia zhong dian tu shu chu ban gui hua." Includes bibliographical references. List of the author's works: p. 416-421. Table of contents also in English. ISBN 7-5633-2812-2
1. Philosophy. 2. Philosophy, Chinese. I. Title. II. Series.
B99.C52 H765 1998

Huang Kejian zi xuan ji.
Huang, Kejian. [Selections. 1998] Di 1 ban. Guilin Shi : Guangxi shi fan da xue chu ban she, 1998.
B99.C52 H765 1998

Huang, Minlan. Xue shu jiu guo : zhi shi fen zi li shi guan yu Zhongguo zheng zhi / [Huang Minlan zhu]. Di 1 ban. Zhengzhou Shi : Henan ren min chu ban she, 1995. 3, 5, 290 p. ; 21 cm. (Zhongguo zhi shi fen zi cong shu) Includes bibliographical references. ISBN 7-215-03510-7
1. Historical materialism. 2. History - Philosophy. 3. Intellectuals - China. I. Title. II. Title: Zhi shi fen zi li shi guan yu Zhonggu zheng zhi III. Series.
D16.9 .H795 1995 <Asian China>

Huang, Shizhong. Hun bian, dao de yu wen xue : fu xin hun bian mu ti yan jiu / Huang Shizhong zhu. Di 1 ban. Beijing : Ren min wen xue chu ban she, 2000. 2, 319 p. ; 21 cm. (Yang gu wen cong) ISBN 7-02-003100-5
1. Chinese literature - History and criticism. 2. Love in literature. 3. Marriage in literature. I. Title. II. Series.

Huang, Thomas S., 1936-.
Zhou, Xiang Sean. Exploration of visual data. Boston ; London : Kluwer Academic Publishers, c2003.
T385 .Z55 2003

Huang, Yongnian.
[Selections. 2000]
Wen shi tan wei : Huang Yongnian zi xuan ji. Di 1 ban. Beijing : Zhonghua shu ju, 2000. 2, 612 p. : facsims. ; 21 cm. Includes bibliographical references. ISBN 7-101-02326-6
1. China - History. 2. China - Civilization. 3. Chinese literature - History and criticism. I. Title. II. Title: Huang Yongnian zi xuan ji
DS736 .H795 2000

Huang Yongnian zi xuan ji.
Huang, Yongnian. [Selections. 2000] Wen shi tan wei. Di 1 ban. Beijing : Zhonghua shu ju, 2000.

DS736 .H795 2000

Huard, Raymond.
Renouvier, Charles, 1815-1903. Sur le peuple, l'église et la république. Paris : Harmattan, c2002.

Hubaut, Michel. Dieu, l'homme et la réincarnation / Michel Hubaut. Paris : Desclée de Brouwer, c1998. 207 p. ; 22 cm. Includes bibliographical references. ISBN 2-220-04176-X DDC 200
1. Reincarnation. I. Title.

Hubback, Judith. From dawn to dusk : autobiography of Judith Hubback. Wilmette, Ill. : Chiron Publications, 2003. p. cm. Includes bibliographical references and index. Table of contents URL: http://www.loc.gov/catdir/toc/ecip044/2003012118.html CONTENTS: Family background : roots and origins -- The nineteen twenties : mostly Paris -- The nineteen thirties -- Vienna -- Cambridge -- Transition to war -- The Second World War -- Transition to peace -- New opportunities -- Moving on -- Wives who went to college -- The fifties : a kind of wilderness -- A possible way forward -- Being and becoming -- Analytical psychologist in London -- Late years and a few reflections. ISBN 1-88860-225-2 (pbk.) DDC 150.19/54/092
1. Hubback, Judith. 2. Jungian psychology - England. 3. Psychoanalysts - England - Biography. I. Title.
BF109.H77 A3 2003

HUBBACK, JUDITH.
Hubback, Judith. From dawn to dusk. Wilmette, Ill. : Chiron Publications, 2003.
BF109.H77 A3 2003

Hubble, Mark A., 1951-.
Miller, Scott D. Staying on top and keeping the sand out of your pants. Deerfield Beach, Fla. : Health Communications, c2003.
BF637.S8 M565 2003

Hubig, Christoph, 1952-.
Neuzeitliches Denken. Berlin ; New York : De Gruyter, 2002.

Hübner, Benno. Sinn in Sinn-loser Zeit : metaphysische Verrechnung : eine Abrechnung / Benno Hübner. Wien : Passagen, c2002. 368 p. ; 24 cm. (Passagen Philosophie) Includes bibliographical references. ISBN 3-85165-525-7 (pbk.)
1. Consciousness - Philosophy. 2. Metaphysics. I. Title. II. Series.

Hübner, Gert. Erzählform im höfischen Roman : Studien zur Fokalisierung im "Eneas", im "Iwein" und im "Tristan" / Gert Hübner. Tübingen : Francke, 2003. ix, 458 p. ; 24 cm. (Bibliotheca Germanica, 0067-7477 ; 44) Includes bibliographical references (p. [408]-453) and index. Revision of the author's Habilitationsschrift--Otto-Friedrich-Universität, Bamberg, 2002. ISBN 3-7720-2035-6 (cl.)
1. Heinrich, - von Veldeke, - 12th cent - Eneide. 2. Gottfried, - von Strassburg, - 13th cent - Tristan. 3. Hartmann, - von Aue, - 12th cent - Iwein. 4. Court epic, German - History and criticism. 5. German poetry - Middle High German, 1050-1500 - History and criticism. 6. Romances, German - History and criticism. 7. Arthurian romances - History and criticism. I. Title. II. Series.

Huddy, Leonie.
Oxford handbook of political psychology. Oxford ; New York : Oxford University Press, 2003.
JA74.5 .H355 2003

Hudson, Carson O. These detestable slaves of the devill : a concise guide to witchcraft in colonial Virginia / by Carson O. Hudson, Jr. Haverford, PA : Infinity Pub., c2001. vi, 74 p. ; 22 cm. Includes bibliographical references (p. 71-74). ISBN 0-7414-0859-7 DDC 133.4/3/09755
1. Witchcraft - Virginia - History - Colonial period, ca. 1600-1775. 2. Virginia - History - Colonial period, ca. 1600-1775. I. Title.
BF1577.V8 H83 2001

Hudson Institute.
Riding the next wave. Indianapolis, Ind. : Hudson Institute ; [Washington, DC : Distributed by the Brookings Institution Press], c2001.
HM901 .R43 2001

HUDSON RIVER VALLEY (N.Y. AND N.J.) - BIOGRAPHY.
Philip, Cynthia Owen. Wilderstein and the Suckleys. Rhinebeck, N.Y. : Wilderstein Preservation, 2001.
F129.W747 P48 2001

HUDSON RIVER VALLEY (N.Y. AND N.J.) - SOCIAL LIFE AND CUSTOMS.
Philip, Cynthia Owen. Wilderstein and the Suckleys. Rhinebeck, N.Y. : Wilderstein Preservation, 2001.
F129.W747 P48 2001

Richardson, Judith. Possessions. Cambridge, Mass. : Harvard University Press, 2003.

BF1472.U6 R54 2003

HUDSON VALLEY (N.Y. AND N.J.). See HUDSON RIVER VALLEY (N.Y. AND N.J.).

Huellas y relatos.
Morales Villaroel, Oscar. Caracas : [s.n.], 2001.

Huellas y sombras.
Pérez-Jofre, Ignacio. Sada, A Coruña : Ediciós do Castro, [2001]
ND195 .P368 2001

Huffman, Karen. Psychology in action / Karen Huffman. 7th ed. Hoboken, NJ : John Wiley & Sons, c2004. xxvii, 595, [111] p. : ill. (chiefly col.) ; 29 cm. Includes bibliographical references (p. R1-R58) and indexes. Publisher description URL: http://www.loc.gov/catdir/description/wiley037/2003269787.html Table of contents URL: http://www.loc.gov/catdir/toc/wiley032/2003269787.html ISBN 0-471-26326-5 (alk. paper) DDC 150
1. Psychology. I. Title.
BF121 .H78 2004

Hufnagel, Erwin, 1940- Einführung in die Hermeneutik / Erwin Hufnagel. [Neuaufl.]. St. Augustin : Gardez! Verlag, c2000. 392 p. ; 21 cm. (Hermeneutik im Gardez! ; Bd. 1) Includes bibliographical references. ISBN 3-89796-023-0 (pbk)
1. Hermeneutics. I. Title.

Huggins, Laura E., 1976-.
Anderson, Terry Lee, 1946- Property rights. Stanford, Calif. : Hoover Institution Press, c2003.
HB701 .A44 2003

Hughes, Richard T. (Richard Thomas), 1943- Myths America lives by / Richard T. Hughes ; foreword by Robert N. Bellah. Urbana : University of Illinois Press, c2003. xv, 203 p. ; 24 cm. Includes bibliographical references and index. ISBN 0-252-02860-0 (acid-free paper) DDC 973
1. United States - History - Philosophy. 2. United States - Foreign relations - Philosophy. 3. United States - History - Religious aspects - Christianity. 4. National characteristics, American. 5. Nationalism - United States. 6. Myth - Political aspects - United States. I. Title.
E175.9 .H84 2003

Hughes, Robert.
Apollon, Willy. After Lacan. Albany : State University of New York Press, 2002.
RC506 .A65 2002

Hugl, Ulrike. Qualitative Inhaltsanalyse und Mind-Mapping : ein neuer Ansatz für Datenauswertung und Organisationsdiagnose / Ulrike Hugl. Wiesbaden : Gabler, 1995. xviii, 299 p. : ill. ; 21 cm. (Neue betriebswirtschaftliche Forschung ; 151) Includes bibliographical references (p. 285-299). ISBN 3-409-13194-9
1. Problem solving - Graphic methods. 2. Decision making - Graphic methods. 3. Creative thinking. 4. Thought and thinking. I. Title. II. Series.

Huglo, Marie-Pascale, 1961-.
Passions du passé. Paris : L'Harmattan, c2000.
BF378.S65 P37 2000

Huguet, Pascal.
Monteil, Jean-Marc. Social context and cognitive performance. Hove, East Sussex, UK : Psychology Press, c1999.
BF311 .M59 1999

Huls, Erica. Dilemma's in menselijke interactie : een inleiding in de strategische mogelijkheden van taalgebruik / Erica Huls. Utrecht : Lemma, 2001. 204 p. : ill. ; 24 cm. Includes bibliographical references (p. [195]-198). ISBN 90-5189-895-9
1. Social interaction. 2. Pragmatics. 3. Communication - Social aspects. 4. Intercultural communication. I. Title.

Hulsman, Cornelis.
Be thou there. Cairo ; New York : American University in Cairo Press, c2001.

Human accomplishment.
Murray, Charles A. New York : HarperCollins, 2003.
BF416.A1 M87 2003

HUMAN ACTION. See HUMAN BEHAVIOR.

HUMAN-ALIEN CONTACTS. See HUMAN-ALIEN ENCOUNTERS.

HUMAN-ALIEN ENCOUNTERS. See also LIFE ON OTHER PLANETS.
Bergmark, Janet, 1955- In the presence of aliens. 1st ed. St. Paul, Minn. : Llewellyn Publications, 1997.
BF2050 .B47 1997

Dennett, Preston E., 1965- Extraterrestrial visitations. 1st ed. St. Paul, Minn. : Llewellyn Publications, 2001.

BF2050 .D46 2001

Evans, Hilary, 1929- From other worlds. Pleasantville, N.Y. : Reader's Digest, c1998.
BF2050 .E93 1998

Herbst, Judith. Aliens. Minneapolis : Lerner Publications, 2005.
BF2050 .H465 2005

Larkins, Lisette. Calling on extraterrestrials. Charlottesville, VA : Hampton Roads Pub., c2003.
BF2050 .L365 2003

Larkins, Lisette. Talking to extraterrestrials. Charlottesville, VA : Hampton Roads Pub., c2002.
BF2050 .L37 2002

Legends of the star ancestors. Rochester, Vt. : Bear & Co., c2002.
BF2050 .L44 2002

Mishlove, Jeffrey, 1946- The PK man. Charlottesville, VA : Hampton Roads, [c2000]
BF1027.O94 M57 2000

Moffitt, John F. (John Francis), 1940- Picturing extraterrestrials. Amherst, N.Y. : Prometheus Press, c2003.
BF2050 .M64 2003

Townsend, John. Mysterious encounters. Chicago, IL : Raintree, 2004.
BF2050 .T69 2004

HUMAN-ALIEN ENCOUNTERS - ENCYCLOPEDIAS.
Baker, Alan. The encyclopedia of alien encounters. London : Virgin, 1999.

Clark, Jerome. Extraordinary encounters. Santa Barbara, Calif. : ABC-CLIO, c2000.
BF2050 .C57 2000

Story, Ronald. The encyclopedia of extraterrestrial encounters. New York : New American Library, c2001.
TL789.16 .S76 2001

HUMAN-ALIEN ENCOUNTERS - JUVENILE LITERATURE.
Herbst, Judith. Aliens. Minneapolis : Lerner Publications, 2005.
BF2050 .H465 2005

Townsend, John. Mysterious encounters. Chicago, IL : Raintree, 2004.
BF2050 .T69 2004

HUMAN-ALIEN ENCOUNTERS - NEW ENGLAND.
Imbrogno, Philip J. Celtic mysteries in New England. 1st ed. St. Paul, Minn. : Llewellyn Publications, 2000.
BF2050 I435 2000

HUMAN ANATOMY. See BODY, HUMAN.

HUMAN-ANIMAL COMMUNICATION.
Brunke, Dawn Baumann. Animal voices. Rochester, Vt. : Bear & Co., c2002.
QL776 .B78 2002

Shine, Betty, 1929- A free spirit. London : HarperCollinsPublishers, 2001.

HUMAN-ANIMAL RELATIONSHIPS. See also ANIMALS; ANIMALS AND CIVILIZATION.
Alger, Janet M., 1937- Cat culture. Philadelphia : Temple University Press, 2003.
SF446.5 .A36 2003

Baratay, Eric. Et l'homme créa l'animal. Paris : O. Jacob, c2003.

Brüder, Bestien, Automaten. 1. Aufl. Erlangen : H. Fischer, c2002.

Coren, Stanley. The pawprints of history. New York ; London : Free Press, c2002.

Fudge, Erica. Animal. London : Reaktion, 2002.
QL85 .F83 2002

Haraway, Donna Jeanne. The companion species manifesto. Chicago, Ill. : Prickly Paradigm ; Bristol : University Presses Marketing, 2003.

Pregosin, Ann. The dogs who grew me. Sterling, Va. : Capital Books, c2002.
SF426.2 .P74 2002

Relaciones hombre-fauna. México, D.F. : CONACULTA, INAH ; Plaza y Valdes, 2002.
QL85 .R453 2002

Representing animals. Bloomington : Indiana University Press, c2002.

Human-animal relationships

QL85 .R46 2002

Scigliano, Eric, 1953- Love, war, and circuses. Boston : Houghton Mifflin, 2002.
QL737.P98 S42 2002

Shepard, Paul, 1925- Where we belong. Athens : University of Georgia Press, c2003.
GF21 .S524 2003

Tallis, Raymond. The hand. Edinburgh : Edinburgh University Press, c2003.
BF908 .T35 2003

Wells, Celia Townsend, 1932- Brood bitch. West Lafayette, Ind. : Purdue University Press, c2003.
SF422.82.W44 A3 2003

Ziolkowska, Aleksandra. Podróże z moją kotką. Wyd. 1. Warszawa : Wydawn. Nowy Świat, 2002.

HUMAN-ANIMAL RELATIONSHIPS - MISCELLANEA.
De Bergerac, Olivia. The dolphin within. East Roseville, NSW, Australia : Simon & Schuster, 1998.
BF1999 .D335 1998

HUMAN ASSISTED REPRODUCTION. See **HUMAN REPRODUCTIVE TECHNOLOGY.**

HUMAN BEHAVIOR. See also **CONSUMER BEHAVIOR; DEVIANT BEHAVIOR; HEALTH BEHAVIOR; HELPING BEHAVIOR; PSYCHOLOGY, COMPARATIVE; RISK-TAKING (PSYCHOLOGY); WORK.**
Cyrulnik, Boris. Dialogue sur la nature humaine. La Tour d'Aigues : Editions de l'Aube, c2000.
BF57 .C97 2000

Khzardzhi͡an, S. M. (Sanatruk M.) Bioprogrammy v prirode i politike. Pushchino : ONTI PNTS RAN, 1996.
BF199 .K43 1996

Mongeau, Pierre, 1954- Survivre. Sainte-Foy : Presses de l'Université du Québec, 2002.
BF122 .M66 2002

Morris, Desmond. The naked eye. London : Ebury Press, 2000.
QL31.M79 A3 2000

HUMAN BEHAVIOR - PHILOSOPHY.
Katznelson, Ira. Desolation and enlightenment. New York : Columbia University Press, c2003.
JA71 .K35 2003

The human being in history.
Dei, Héctor Daniel. Lanham, Md. : Lexington Books, c2003.
BD450 .D395 2003

HUMAN BEINGS. See also **ANTHROPOLOGY; ETHNOLOGY; NATURE - EFFECT OF HUMAN BEINGS ON; PREHISTORIC PEOPLES; WOMEN.**
Boncinelli, Edoardo. Io sono, tu sei. 1. ed. Milano : Mondadori, 2002.

Cioran, E. M. (Emile M.), 1911- [Précis de décomposition. Romanian] Tratat de descompunere. București : Humanitas, 2002, c1996.

Day, Stacey B. Man and Mu. N[ew] Y[ork] : International Foundation for Biosocial Development and Human Health ; Oviedo, Fla. : Disctributed by C.E.P., c1997.
BD431 .D37 1997

Gray, John, 1948- Straw dogs. London : Granta, 2002.

Redfield, James. God and the evolving universe. New York : Jeremy P. Tarcher/Putnam, c2002.
BD541 .R43 2002

Xie, Sizhong. Su zhi yu ming yun. Di 1 ban. Beijing : Zuo jia chu ban she, 2002.
BD450 .X54 2002

Zons, Raimar. Die Zeit des Menschen. 1. Aufl., Originalausg. Frankfurt : Suhrkamp, c2001.

HUMAN BEINGS AND ANIMALS. See **HUMAN-ANIMAL RELATIONSHIPS.**

HUMAN BEINGS - ANIMAL NATURE.
Chebili, Saïd. La tâche civilisatrice de la psychanalyse selon Freud. Paris : L'Harmattan, c2002.

HUMAN BEINGS - ATTITUDE AND MOVEMENT. See **BIPEDALISM; MOVEMENT EDUCATION.**

HUMAN BEINGS - CONSTITUTION. See **BODY, HUMAN.**

HUMAN BEINGS - DISEASES. See **DISEASES.**

HUMAN BEINGS - ECOLOGY. See **HUMAN ECOLOGY.**

HUMAN BEINGS - EFFECT OF ENVIRONMENT ON. See **HUMAN ECOLOGY; NATURE AND NURTURE.**

HUMAN BEINGS - EFFECT OF SATURN ON.
Schostak, Sherene. Surviving saturn's return. 1st ed. New York : McGraw-Hill, 2004.
BF1724.2.S3 S36 2004

HUMAN BEINGS - EFFECT OF TECHNOLOGICAL INNOVATIONS ON.
Tenner, Edward. Our own devices. 1st ed. New York : Alfred A. Knopf, 2003.
T14.5 .T4588 2003

HUMAN BEINGS - EFFECT OF THE MOON ON.
Pagés Larraya, Fernando. Liturgia lunar de la locura. Córdoba, Argentina : Comunicarte Editorial, c2002.

Pharr, Daniel. The moon & everyday living. 2nd ed. St. Paul, Minn. : LLewellyn, 2002.
BF1723 .P48 2002

Townley, John, 1945- Lunar returns. 1st ed. St. Paul, Minn. : Llewellyn Publications, 2003.
BF1723 .T69 2003

HUMAN BEINGS - FOOD HABITS. See **FOOD HABITS.**

HUMAN BEINGS - FORECASTING.
Tolsdorf, Samuel, 1926- The theory of reality. Vancouver, B.C. : Leumas Publications, [1998]
BF1999 .T62 1998

HUMAN BEINGS - INFLUENCE ON NATURE. See **NATURE - EFFECT OF HUMAN BEINGS ON.**

HUMAN BEINGS - MISCELLANEA.
Baines, John. [Hombre estelar. English] The stellar man. 2nd ed. New York : John Baines Institute, Inc., 2002.
BF1621 .B3513 2002

Nicheva, Nina. Prez vremeto i prostranstvoto. [Bulgaria] : Gutoranov i sin, [1998?]
BF1999 .N46 1998

HUMAN BEINGS ON OTHER PLANETS. See **LIFE ON OTHER PLANETS.**

HUMAN BEINGS - ORIGIN. See also **HUMAN EVOLUTION.**
Baur, Manfred, 1959- Die Odyssee des Menschen. München : Ullstein, c2001.

Jones, Steve, 1944- Y. Boston : Houghton Mifflin, 2003.
GN281 .J62 2003

Kingdon, Jonathan. Lowly origin. Princeton : Princeton University Press, c2003.
GN282 .K54 2003

HUMAN BEINGS - SPIRITUAL ASPECTS.
The search for a holistic approach to human existence and development. [Nigeria?] : Osigwe Anyiam-Osigwe Foundation, [1999?]
B53 .E46 1999

HUMAN BIOLOGY. See **HUMAN BEHAVIOR; MEDICINE; PHYSICAL ANTHROPOLOGY; PSYCHOLOGY.**

HUMAN BODY. See **BODY, HUMAN.**

HUMAN CAPITAL.
Management. Cambridge, Mass. : MIT Press, 2003.
HD31 .M2928 2003

HUMAN COMFORT. See also **HUMAN ENGINEERING; QUALITY OF LIFE.**
Walters, J. Donald. Secrets of comfort and joy. [Nevada City, CA] : Crystal Clarity, 2000.
BF575.H27 W362 2000

HUMAN-COMPUTER INTERACTION. See also **USER INTERFACES (COMPUTER SYSTEMS).**
Adrift in the technological matrix. Lewisburg, PA : Bucknell University Press ; London : Associated University Presses, c2003.

Bederson, Benjamin. The craft of information visualization. San Francisco, Calif. : Morgan Kaufmann ; Oxford : Elsevier Science, 2003.

Carroll, John M. HCI models, theories, and frameworks. San Francisco, Calif. : Morgan Kaufmann, 2003.

Clark, Andy, 1957- Natural-born cyborgs. Oxford ; New York : Oxford University Press, c2003.

T14.5 .C58 2003

Crabtree, Andy. Designing collaborative systems. London ; [New York] : Springer, c2003.
QA76.9.S88 C725 2003

Designing information spaces. London ; New York : Springer, 2003.
QA76.9.C66 D49 2003

Fogg, B. J. Persuasive technology. Amsterdam ; Boston : Morgan Kaufmann Publishers, / c2003.
BF637.P4 F55 2003

Fuller, Matthew. Behind the blip. Brooklyn, NY, USA : Autonomedia, c2003.
QA76.76.H85 F85 2003

Hayes-Roth, Frederick, 1947- Radical simplicity. Upper Saddle River, N.J. ; London : Prentice Hall PTR, 2003.

Human factors engineering program review model [microform]. Rev. 1. Washington, DC : Division of System Analysis and Regulatory Effectiveness, Office of Nuclear Regulatory Research, U.S. Nuclear Regulatory Commission : Supt. of Docs., U.S. G.P.O. [distributor], 2002.

Lengen, Haiko van. Bücher im virtuellen Warenkorb. Berlin : Verlag für Wirtschaftskommunikation, c2001.

Schreck, Jorg. Security and privacy in user modeling. Dordrecht ; Boston ; London : Kluwer Academic Publishers, c2003.
QA76.9.A25 S353 2003

Sharing expertise. Cambridge, Mass. : MIT Press, c2003.
HD30.2 .S53 2003

Virtual reality. Frankfurt am Main ; New York : P. Lang, c2001.
QA76.9.H85 V5815 2001

Visualizing argumentation. London ; New York : Springer, 2003.
QA76.9.H85 V67 2003

HUMAN CONTACTS WITH ALIENS. See **HUMAN-ALIEN ENCOUNTERS.**

Human development.
Kail, Robert V. 3rd ed. Belmont, CA : Thomson/Wadsworth, c2004.
BF713 .K336 2004

Papalia, Diane E. 9th ed. Boston : McGraw-Hill, c2004.
BF713 .P35 2004

Human development in Aotearoa.
Bird, Lise. Sidney ; New York : McGraw-Hill, c2000.
BF713 .B57 2000

HUMAN DIGNITY. See **DIGNITY.**

HUMAN ECOLOGY. See also **NATURE - EFFECT OF HUMAN BEINGS ON; QUALITY OF LIFE; SOCIAL PSYCHOLOGY.**
Arsuaga, Juan Luis de. [Collar del neandertal. English] The Neanderthal's necklace. New York : Four Walls Eight Windows, c2002.
GN285 .A7713 2002

Fernández-Armesto, Felipe. Civilizations. New York : Free Press, c2001.
CB151 .F47 2001

Kittredge, William. The nature of generosity. 1st Vintage Departures ed. New York : Vintage, 2001, c2000.
PS3561.I87 Z472 2001

Leff, Enrique. Saber ambiental. 3a ed. correg. y aument. México : PNUMA ; Siglo Veintiuno, 2002.

Maiorescu, Toma George, 1928- Îmblâzirea fiarei din om sau ecosofia. 3a ediția revăzută și completată. București : Lumina Lex, 2002.

Pievani, Telmo. Homo sapiens e altre catastrofi. Roma : Meltemi, c2002.

HUMAN ECOLOGY - PHILOSOPHY.
Rothenberg, David, 1962- Always the mountains. Athens : University of Georgia Press, c2002.
GF21 .R68 2002

Seeing nature through gender. Lawrence : University Press of Kansas, c2003.
GF21 .S44 2003

Shepard, Paul, 1925- Where we belong. Athens : University of Georgia Press, c2003.
GF21 .S524 2003

HUMAN ENCOUNTERS WITH ALIENS. *See* **HUMAN-ALIEN ENCOUNTERS.**

HUMAN ENGINEERING.
Norman, Donald A. [Psychology of everyday things] The design of everyday things. 1st Basic paperback ed. [New York] : Basic Books, c2002.

HUMAN ENGINEERING - STUDY AND TEACHING - RUSSIA (FEDERATION) - TVERSKAIA OBLAST' - HISTORY.
Shikun, A. A. (Alekseĭ Alekseevich) Istoriia i razvitie psikhologicheskogo obrazovaniia v gorode Tveri i oblasti. Tver' : Tverskoĭ gos. universitet : Mezhdunarodnaia akademiia psikhologicheskikh nauk, 1999.
BF80.7.R8 S55 1999

HUMAN ENVIRONMENT. *See* **HUMAN ECOLOGY.**

HUMAN EVOLUTION. *See also* **GENETIC PSYCHOLOGY.**
Akif'ev, A. P. Genetika i sud'by. Moskva : TSentrpoligraf, 2001.
GN281 .A45 2001

Arsuaga, Juan Luis de. [Collar del neandertal. English] The Neanderthal's necklace. New York : Four Walls Eight Windows, c2002.
GN285 .A7713 2002

Baur, Manfred, 1959- Die Odyssee des Menschen. München : Ullstein, c2001.

Beskova, I. A. Ėvoliutsiia i soznanie. Moskva : "Indrik", 2002.
B808.9 .B476 2002x

Beyond foraging and collecting. New York : Kluwer Academic/Plenum Publishers, c2002.
GN388 .B49 2002

Buss, David M. Evolutionary psychology. 2nd ed. Boston, MA : Allyn and Bacon, 2003.
BF698.95 .B87 2003

Evolution, gender, and rape. Cambridge, Mass. : MIT Press, c2003.
HV6558 .E92 2003

Fisher, Helen E. Why we love. 1st ed. New York : Henry Holt and Company, 2004.
BF575.L8 F53 2004

Gaulin, Steven J. C. Evolutionary psychology. 2nd ed. Upper Saddle River, N.J. : Pearson/Prentice Hall, c2004.
BF698.95 .G38 2004

Historical materialism and social evolution. New York : Palgrave Macmillan, 2002.
HX523 .H565 2002

Une introduction aux sciences de la culture. 1. ed. Paris : Presses universitaires de France ; [Paris] : Institut Ferdinand-de-Saussure, 2002.

Jones, Steve, 1944- Y. Boston : Houghton Mifflin, 2003.
GN281 .J62 2003

Kingdon, Jonathan. Lowly origin. Princeton : Princeton University Press, c2003.
GN282 .K54 2003

Leary, Timothy Francis, 1920- Musings on human metaporphoses. Berkeley, CA : Ronin, c2003.

Picq, Pascal G. A la recherche de l'homme. Paris : Nil, c2002.
GN281 .P48 2002

Pievani, Telmo. Homo sapiens e altre catastrofi. Roma : Meltemi, c2002.

Sandvoss, Ernst. Vom homo sapiens zum homo spaciens. Berlin : Logos, c2002.

Shlain, Leonard. Sex, time, and power. New York ; London : Viking, 2003.
HQ23 .S45 2003

Style, function, transmission. Salt Lake City : University of Utah Press, c2003.
CC173 .S79 2003

Washington, Johnny. Evolution, history and destiny. New York : Peter Lang, c2002.
E185.625 .W37 2002

HUMAN EVOLUTION - MISCELLANEA.
Atwater, P. M. H. [Children of the new millennium] The new children and near-death experiences. Rochester, Vt. : Bear & Co., 2003.
BF1045.N42 A88 2003

Douno, Beinsa, 1864-1944. In the kingdom of living nature. Sofia : Bialo Bratstvo, c2000.

Miller, Larry, 1947- Exploring the "zone". Gretna, La. : Pelican, 2001.
BF1045.S83 M55 2001

HUMAN EVOLUTION - RELIGIOUS ASPECTS.
Anderson, Walt, 1933- The next enlightenment. 1st ed. New York : St. Martin's Press, 2003.
BL476 .A53 2003

Human evolutionary psychology.
Barrett, Louise. Princeton, N.J. : Princeton University Press, c2002.
BF698.95 .B37 2002

Human experience.
Russon, John Edward, 1960- Albany : State University of New York Press, c2003.
BF204.5 .R87 2003

Human factors engineering program review model [microform] / prepared by J. O'Hara ... [et al.]. Rev. 1. Washington, DC : Division of System Analysis and Regulatory Effectiveness, Office of Nuclear Regulatory Research, U.S. Nuclear Regulatory Commission : Supt. of Docs., U.S. G.P.O. [distributor], 2002. xviii, 106 p. : ill. ; 28 cm. Technical. Shipping list no.: 2002-0493-M. "Date published: May 2002." Includes bibliographical references (p. 89-94). "NUREG-0711." W6546. Microfiche. [Washington, D.C.?] : Supt. of Docs., U.S. G.P.O., [2002] 2 microfiches : negative. Also available via Internet from the NRC web site. Address as of 9/22/03: http://www.nrc.gov/reading-rm/doc-co llections/nuregs/staff/sr0711/ml021560629.pdf; current access available via PURL. URL: http://purl.access.gpo.gov/GPO/LPS36221
1. Nuclear power plants - Human factors. 2. Human-computer interaction. I. O'Hara, J. II. Brookhaven National Laboratory. Energy Sciences and Technology Dept. III. U.S. Nuclear Regulatory Commission. Division of Systems Analysis and Regulatory Effectiveness.

HUMAN FACTORS IN ENGINEERING DESIGN. *See* **HUMAN ENGINEERING.**

HUMAN FEMALES. *See* **WOMEN.**

HUMAN GENETICS. *See also* **GENETIC PSYCHOLOGY.**
Jones, Steve, 1944- Y. Boston : Houghton Mifflin, 2003.
GN281 .J62 2003

Ridley, Matt. Nature via nurture. 1st ed. New York : HarperCollins, c2003.
QH438.5 .R535 2003

Sykes, Bryan. Adam's curse. London ; New York : Bantam, 2003.

HUMAN GEOGRAPHY. *See also* **HUMAN ECOLOGY; HUMAN TERRITORIALITY.**
Allen, John, 1951- Lost geographies of power. Malden, MA ; Oxford : Blackwell Pub., 2003.
GF50 .A453 2003

Fernández-Armesto, Felipe. Civilizations. New York : Free Press, c2001.
CB151 .F47 2001

Gendered landscapes. University Park, PA : Center for Studies in Landscape History, c2000.

Le territoire pensé. Sainte-Foy : Presses de l'Université du Québec, 2003.

HUMAN GROWTH. *See* **LIFE CYCLE, HUMAN.**

HUMAN GROWTH - EXAMINATIONS, QUESTIONS, ETC.
The best test preparation for the CLEP, College-Level Examination Program, human growth & development. Piscataway, N.J. : Research & Education Association, c2003.
BF713 .B49 2003

HUMAN INFORMATION PROCESSING. *See* **SELECTIVITY (PSYCHOLOGY).**

HUMAN INFORMATION PROCESSING (CHILD PSYCHOLOGY). *See* **HUMAN INFORMATION PROCESSING IN CHILDREN.**

HUMAN INFORMATION PROCESSING IN CHILDREN - JUVENILE LITERATURE.
Randolph, Joanne. What I look like when I am confused. 1st ed. New York : PowerStart Press, 2004.
BF723.I63 R36 2004

Randolph, Joanne. [What I look like when I am confused. Spanish & English] What I look like when I am confused = 1st ed. New York : Rosen Pub. Group's PowerKids Press, 2004.
BF723.I63 R3618 2004

HUMAN INFORMATION PROCESSING - SOCIAL ASPECTS.
From girls in their elements to women in science. New York : P. Lang, 2003.
BF378.S65 F76 2003

Wyer, Robert S. Social comprehension and judgment. Mahwah, N.J. : L. Erlbaum Associates, Publishers, 2004.
BF323.S63 W94 2004

HUMAN INTELLIGENCE. *See* **INTELLECT.**

HUMAN INTERACTION. *See* **SOCIAL INTERACTION.**

Human learning.
Ormrod, Jeanne Ellis. 4th ed. Upper Saddle River, N.J. : Merrill, c2004.
BF318 .O76 2004

HUMAN LIFE CYCLE. *See* **LIFE CYCLE, HUMAN.**

HUMAN-MACHINE SYSTEMS. *See also* **USER INTERFACES (COMPUTER SYSTEMS).**
Breazeal, Cynthia L. Designing sociable robots. Cambridge, Mass. : MIT Press, c2002.
TA167 .B74 2002

The new workplace. Chichester, UK ; Hoboken, NJ : Wiley, c2003.
HD6955 .N495 2003

HUMAN MECHANICS.
The Alexander technique [videorecording]. New York, N.Y. : Wellspring Media, c1999.

Human memory.
Neath, Ian, 1965- 2nd ed. Australia ; Belmont, CA : Thomson/Wadsworth, c2003.
BF371 .N43 2003

HUMAN PHYSIOLOGY. *See* **BODY, HUMAN; HUMAN REPRODUCTION.**

HUMAN RACE. *See* **HUMAN BEINGS.**

HUMAN RELATIONS. *See also* **INTERPERSONAL RELATIONS.**
Ford, Loren. 3rd ed. Upper Saddle River, N.J. : Pearson/Prentice Hall, c2004.
BF335 .F67 2004

HUMAN REPRODUCTION - EFFECT OF WITCHCRAFT ON - NIGERIA.
Drews, Annette. Guardians of the society. Leipzig, Germany : Institut für Afrikanistik, Universität Leipzig, 2000.
BF1584.Z33 D44 2000

HUMAN REPRODUCTION - EFFECT OF WITCHCRAFT ON - ZAMBIA.
Drews, Annette. Guardians of the society. Leipzig, Germany : Institut für Afrikanistik, Universität Leipzig, 2000.
BF1584.Z33 D44 2000

HUMAN REPRODUCTION - MORAL AND ETHICAL ASPECTS.
McLeod, Carolyn. Self-trust and reproductive autonomy. Cambridge, Mass. : MIT Press, c2002.
RG133.5 .M39 2002

HUMAN REPRODUCTION - TECHNOLOGICAL INNOVATIONS. *See* **HUMAN REPRODUCTIVE TECHNOLOGY.**

HUMAN REPRODUCTIVE TECHNOLOGY - MORAL AND ETHICAL ASPECTS.
McLeod, Carolyn. Self-trust and reproductive autonomy. Cambridge, Mass. : MIT Press, c2002.
RG133.5 .M39 2002

HUMAN RESILIENCE. *See* **RESILIENCE (PERSONALITY TRAIT).**

HUMAN RESOURCE DEVELOPMENT. *See* **EDUCATION.**

HUMAN RESOURCE MANAGEMENT. *See* **PERSONNEL MANAGEMENT.**

Human resources in the 21st century / editors, Marc Effron, Robert Gandossy, Marshall Goldsmith ; foreword by Rosabeth Moss Kanter. Hoboken, N.J. : J. Wiley & Sons, c2003. xvii, 332 p. : ill. ; 24 cm. Includes bibliographical references (p. 295-306) and index. Table of contents URL: http://www.loc.gov/catdir/toc/wiley/031/2002153112.html ISBN 0-471-43421-3 (cloth : alk. paper) DDC 658.3
1. Management. 2. Personnel management. 3. Corporate culture. 4. Organizational change. 5. Leadership. I. Effron, Marc. II. Gandossy, Robert P. III. Goldsmith, Marshall.
HD31 .H81247 2003

HUMAN RIGHTS. *See also* **CHILDREN'S RIGHTS; CIVIL RIGHTS; WOMEN'S RIGHTS.**
Ataöv, Türkkaya. Discrimination & conflict. Haarlem : SOTA, 2000.

Children and human rights. Part 1 [videorecording]. Derry, N.H. : Chip Taylor Communications, 1995.

Doise, Willem, 1935- Human rights as social representations. London ; New York : Routledge, 2002.
JC571 .D65 2002

Howard, Bradley Reed. Indigenous peoples and the state. DeKalb : Northern Illinois University Press, c2003.
GN380 .H68 2003

Peace and conflict resolution. Part 1 [videorecording]. Derry, N.H. : Chip Taylor Communications, 1996.

Peace and conflict resolution. Part 2 [videorecording]. Derry, N.H. : Chip Taylor Communications, 1997.

The politics of memory. London ; New York : Zed Books, c2000.
JC571 .P642 2000

Truth v. justice. Princeton, N.J. : Princeton University Press, c2000.
DT1945 .T78 2000

Human rights as social representations.
Doise, Willem, 1935- London ; New York : Routledge, 2002.
JC571 .D65 2002

HUMAN RIGHTS - SOUTH AFRICA.
Truth v. justice. Princeton, N.J. : Princeton University Press, c2000.
DT1945 .T78 2000

HUMAN SCIENCES. *See* **SOCIAL SCIENCES.**

HUMAN SERVICES. *See also* **DISASTER RELIEF; FAMILY SERVICES; SOCIAL SERVICE.**
The young, the old, and the state. Cheltenham, UK ; Northhampton, MA : E. Elgar Pub., c2003.
HQ778.5 .Y69 2003

HUMAN SERVICES PERSONNEL. *See* **SOCIAL WORKERS.**

HUMAN SERVICES - RESEARCH - METHODOLOGY.
Campbell, Marie L. (Marie Louise), 1936- Mapping social relations. Aurora, Ont. : Garamond Press, c2002.

HUMAN SETTLEMENTS. *See* **CITIES AND TOWNS; COMMUNITY; LAND SETTLEMENT.**

Human spatial memory : remembering where / edited by Gary L. Allen. Mahwah, NJ : Lawrence Erlbaum Associates, 2003. p. cm. Includes bibliographical references and index. ISBN 0-8058-4218-7 (cloth : alk. paper) DDC 153.1/3
1. Space perception - Congresses. 2. Spatial behavior - Congresses. 3. Spatial ability - Congresses. I. Allen, Gary L.
BF469 .H86 2003

HUMAN TERRITORIALITY.
Le territoire pensé. Sainte-Foy : Presses de l'Université du Québec, 2003.

The territorial management of ethnic conflict. 2nd rev. and expanded ed. London ; Portland, OR : F. Cass, 2003.
GN496 .T47 2003

HUMAN TERRITORIALITY - QUÉBEC (PROVINCE).
Le territoire pensé. Sainte-Foy : Presses de l'Université du Québec, 2003.

HUMANE SOCIETIES. *See* **CHILD WELFARE.**

HUMANISM. *See also* **HUMANITIES; LEARNING AND SCHOLARSHIP; PHILOSOPHICAL ANTHROPOLOGY; RENAISSANCE.**
2000 years and beyond. London ; New York : Routledge, 2003.
BR53 .T86 2003

Antropología e interpretación. Tucumán, Argentina : Instituto de Estudios Antropológicos y Filosofía de la Religión, Facultad de Filosofía y Letras, Universidad Nacional de Tucumán, c2001.
BD450 .A564 2001

Lévinas, Emmanuel. [Humanisme de l'autre homme. English] Humanism of the other. Urbana : University of Illinois Press, c2003.
B2430.L48 H8413 2003

Luft, Sandra Rudnick, 1934- Vico's uncanny humanism. Ithaca, N.Y. : Cornell University Press, 2003.
B3581.P73 L84 2003

HUMANISM - 20TH CENTURY.
The search for a holistic approach to human existence and development. [Nigeria?] : Osigwe Anyiam-Osigwe Foundation, [1999?]
B53 .E46 1999

Sepúlveda, Jesús. El jardín de las peculiaridades. Buenos Aires : Ediciones del Leopardo, [2002]

Humanism and platonism in the Italian Renaissance.
Hankins, James. Roma : Edizioni di storia e letteratura, 2003-

HUMANISM - ITALY - HISTORY.
Hankins, James. Humanism and platonism in the Italian Renaissance. Roma : Edizioni di storia e letteratura, 2003-

Humanism of the other.
Lévinas, Emmanuel. [Humanisme de l'autre homme. English] Urbana : University of Illinois Press, c2003.
B2430.L48 H8413 2003

HUMANISM - PORTUGAL.
Chacon, Vamireh. O humanismo ibérico. [Lisboa?] : Imprensa Nacional-Casa da Moeda, [1998]
B821 .C43 1998

O humanismo ibérico.
Chacon, Vamireh. [Lisboa?] : Imprensa Nacional-Casa da Moeda, [1998]
B821 .C43 1998

HUMANISTIC ETHICS.
Hossenfelder, Malte. Der Wille zum Recht und das Streben nach Glück. Originalausg. München : C.H. Beck, c2000.

HUMANISTIC PSYCHOLOGY. *See also* **SELF-ACTUALIZATION (PSYCHOLOGY).**
Cohen, David, 1946- Carl Rogers. London : Constable, 1997.
BF109.R63 C64 1997

HUMANISTIC PSYCHOLOGY - HISTORY - 20TH CENTURY.
Milton, Joyce. The road to Malpsychia. 1st ed. San Francisco : Encounter Books, 2002.
BF204 .M54 2002

HUMANISTS - EUROPE.
Moss, Ann, 1938- Printed commonplace-books and the structuring of Renaissance thought. Oxford : Clarendon Press ; New York : Oxford University Press, 1996.
PA2047 .M67 1996

Humanitas (Minas Gerais, Brazil)
(79.) Souza, Eneida Maria de. Crítica cult. Belo Horizonte : Editora UFMG, 2002.
PN94 .S68 2002

HUMANITIES. *See also* **ARTS; PHILOSOPHY.**
Marías, Julián, 1914- Entre dos siglos. Madrid : Alianza Editorial, c2002.
PQ6663.A72183 E68 2002

HUMANITIES - METHODOLOGY.
Gadamer, Hans Georg, 1900- Problème de la conscience historique. German] Das Problem des historischen Bewusstseins. Tübingen : Mohr Siebeck, 2001.

HUMANITIES - METHODOLOGY - CONGRESSES.
Filosofsko-metodologicheskie osnovy gumanitarnogo znaniia. Moskva : Rossiĭskiĭ gosudarstvennyĭ gumanitarnyĭ universitet, 2001.
BD166 .F489 2001

HUMANITY (HUMAN BEINGS). *See* **HUMAN BEINGS.**

HUMANKIND. *See* **HUMAN BEINGS.**

HUMANS. *See* **HUMAN BEINGS.**

Hume, David, 1711-1776.
[Enquiry concerning the principles of morals. German]
Eine Untersuchung der Grundlagen der Moral / David Hume ; eingeleitet, übersetzt und erläutert von Karl Hepfer. Göttingen : Vandenhoeck & Ruprecht, c2002. lxxvi, 164 p. ; 21 cm. (Sammlung Philosophie ; Bd. 2) Includes bibliographical references and index. ISBN 3-525-30601-6 (kart.)
1. Ethics. I. Hepfer, Karl. II. Title.

TREATISE OF HUMAN NATURE.
Fodor, Jerry A. Hume variations. Oxford : Clarendon Press ; New York : Oxford University Press, 2003.
B1489 .F63 2003

Hume variations.
Fodor, Jerry A. Oxford : Clarendon Press ; New York : Oxford University Press, 2003.
B1489 .F63 2003

Humeniuk, O. IE. (Oksana IEvstakhïvna)
Psykholohiia IA-kontseptsii : monohrafiia / Oksana Humeniuk. Ternopil' : Ekonomichna dumka, 2002. 185 p. : ill. ; 21 cm. Includes bibliographical references and index. ISBN 9666541017
1. Self-perception. I. Title.
BF697.5.S43 H84 2002

HUMOR. *See* **ANECDOTES; WIT AND HUMOR.**

HUMORISTS, AMERICAN - 20TH CENTURY - BIOGRAPHY.
McEnroe, Colin. My father's footsteps. New York : Warner Books, c2003.
PS3563.C3615 M9 2003

Humphrey, James Harry, 1911- Child development through sports / James H. Humphrey. Binghamton, N.Y. ; London : Haworth Press, c2003. x, 141 p. ; 23 cm. Includes bibliographical references (p. 133-135) and index. ISBN 0-7890-1827-6 (hardcover : alk. paper) ISBN 0-7890-1828-4 (softcover : alk. paper) DDC 796/.083
1. Sports for children. 2. Child development. I. Title.
GV709.2 .H845 2003

Childhood stress in contemporary society / James H. Humphrey. New York : Haworth Press, 2004. p. cm. Includes bibliographical references and index. ISBN 0-7890-2265-6 (hard : alk. paper) ISBN 0-7890-2266-4 (pbk. : alk. paper) DDC 155.4/18
1. Stress in children. 2. Child rearing. I. Title.
BF723.S75 H842 2004

Humphrey, Melanie Friedersdorf.
Stenson, Lila. Daddy, up and down. 1st ed. Snowmass Village, CO : Peaceful Village Pub., 2002.
BF723.G75 S74 2002

Humphrey, Nicholas. How to solve the mind-- body problem / Nicholas Humphrey. Thorverton, UK ; Bowling Green, OH : Imprint Academic, c2000. 112 p. : ill. ; 26 cm. (Journal of consciousness studies 1355-8250 ; 7, no. 4) Includes bibliographical references. ISBN 0-907845-08-8 (pbk.) DDC 128/.2
1. Evolutionary psychology. 2. Consciousness. I. Title. II. Series.
BF698.95 .H86 2000

The inner eye / Nicholas Humphrey ; with illustrations by Mel Calman. Oxford ; New York : Oxford University Press, c2002. 188 p. : ill. ; 20 cm. Originally published: London : Faber and Faber, 1986. Includes bibliographical references (p. 179-183) and index. ISBN 0-19-280245-4 DDC 126
1. Consciousness. 2. Thought and thinking. 3. Intellect. I. Title.
BF311 .H778 2002

The mind made flesh : essays from the frontiers of psychology and evolution / Nicholas Humphrey. Oxford ; New York : Oxford University Press, 2002. x, 366 p. : ill. ; 22 cm. Includes bibliographical references (p. [340]-361) and index. ISBN 0-19-280227-5 (pbk. : alk. paper)
1. Genetic psychology. 2. Self. 3. Consciousness. 4. Evolution. 5. Psychology. 6. Genetics, Behavioral. I. Title.
BF701 .H86 2002

The mind made flesh : essays from the frontiers of psychology and evolution / Nicholas Humphrey. Oxford ; New York : Oxford University Press, 2002. x, 366 p. : ill., port. ; 22 cm. Includes bibliographical references (p. [340]-361) and index. ISBN 0-19-280227-5 (pbk. : alk. paper)
1. Genetic psychology. 2. Self. I. Title.

Hun bian, dao de yu wen xue.
Huang, Shizhong. Di 1 ban. Beijing : Ren min wen xue chu ban she, 2000.

HUNA - MISCELLANEA.
Anderson, Victor H. 1917- Etheric anatomy. 1st American pbk. ed. Albany, Calif. : Acorn Guild Press, 2004.
BF1389.A7 A53 2004

HUNGARIAN LANGUAGE - REFORM.
Magyarok és nyelvtörvények. Budapest : Teleki László Alapítvány, 2002.
PH2073 .K66 2002

HUNGARIAN LANGUAGE - STANDARDIZATION.
Magyarok és nyelvtörvények. Budapest : Teleki László Alapítvány, 2002.
PH2073 .K66 2002

Hüni, Heinrich.
Die erscheinende Welt. Berlin : Duncker & Humblot, c2002.

Hüning, Dieter.
Societas rationis. Berlin : Duncker & Humblot, c2002.
B29 .S633 2002

Hunt, Rameck.
Davis, Sampson. The pact. Waterville, ME : Thorndike Press, 2002.
1. Black author.

HUNT, RAMECK.
Davis, Sampson. The pact. Waterville, ME : Thorndike Press, 2002.
1. Black author.

Hunt, Stephen, 1954- Alternative religions : a sociological introduction / Stephen J. Hunt. Aldershot, Hampshire, England ; Burlington, VT : Ashgate, c2003. xix, 268 p. : ill. ; 25 cm. Includes bibliographical references (p. [239]-255) and index. ISBN 0-7546-3409-4 (alk. paper) ISBN 0-7546-3410-8 (pbk. : alk. paper) DDC 306.6
1. Cults. 2. Sects. 3. Religions. 4. Religion and sociology. 5. Christianity and other religions. I. Title.
BP603 .H87 2003

Hüntelmann, Rafael. Existenz und Modalität : eine Studie zur analytischen Modalontologie / Rafael Hüntelmann. Frankfurt a. M. ; New York : Hänsel-Hohenhausen, c2002. 189 p. ; 22 cm. (Deutsche Bibliothek der Wissenschaften. Philosphische Analyse ; Bd. 8 = German library of sciences. Philosophical analysis ; Bd. 8) Includes bibliographical references (p. [185]-189). ISBN 3-8267-0027-9
1. Ontology. 2. Possibility. 3. Analysis (Philosophy) I. Title. II. Series: Deutsche Bibliothek der Wissenschaften. Philosophische Analyse ; Bd. 8.
BD331 .H86 2002

Hunter-Gault, Charlayne.
Children and human rights. Part 1 [videorecording]. Derry, N.H. : Chip Taylor Communications, 1995.

Peace and conflict resolution. Part 1 [videorecording]. Derry, N.H. : Chip Taylor Communications, 1996.

Peace and conflict resolution. Part 2 [videorecording]. Derry, N.H. : Chip Taylor Communications, 1997.

Hunter, Gerald S. Haunted Michigan : recent encounters with active spirits / Gerald S. Hunter. 1st. ed. Chicago, IL : Lake Claremont Press, 2000. ix, 207 p. : ill. ; 22 cm. Includes index. ISBN 1-89312-110-0 DDC 133.1/09774
1. Ghosts - Michigan. 2. Haunted places - Michigan. I. Title.
BF1472.U6 H86 2000

Hunter, Ian, 1949-.
Pufendorf, Samuel, Freiherr von, 1632-1694. [De officio hominis et civis. English] The whole duty of man, according to the law of nature. Indianapolis, Ind. : Liberty Fund, c2003.
K457.P8 D4313 2003

HUNTING AND GATHERING SOCIETIES.
Beyond foraging and collecting. New York : Kluwer Academic/Plenum Publishers, c2002.
GN388 .B49 2002

HUNTING - MORAL AND ETHICAL ASPECTS.
Stange, Mary Zeiss. Woman the hunter. Boston : Beacon Press, c1997.
SK14 .S88 1997

HUNTING - PHILOSOPHY.
Stange, Mary Zeiss. Woman the hunter. Boston : Beacon Press, c1997.
SK14 .S88 1997

HUNTING, PRIMITIVE. See **HUNTING.**

Huo fo zhuan shi.
Cai, Zhichun. Di 1 ban. Beijing : Hua wen chu ban she : Xin hua shu dian jing xiao, 2000.
BL515 .C345 2000

Huo, Songlin. Tang yin ge lun wen ji / Huo Songlin zhu. [Shijiazhuang Shi] : Hebei jiao yu chu ban she, [2000?] 433 p. ; 23 cm. Fu can kao wen xian. ISBN 7-5434-4018-0 (set)
1. Chinese poetry - History and criticism. 2. Chinese literature - History and criticism. I. Title.
PL2866.O236 A6 2000 v.1

Tang yin ge sui bi ji / Huo Songlin zhu. [Shijiazhuang Shi] : Hebei jiao yu chu ban she, [2000?] 8, 633 p. : ill. ; 23 cm. ISBN 7-5434-4018-0 (set)
1. Chinese poetry - History and criticism. 2. Chinese literature - History and criticism. I. Title.
PL2866.O236 A6 2000 v.4

Huotari, Maija-Leena. Trust in knowledge management and systems in organizations / Maija-Leena Huotari, Mirja Iivonen. Hershey, PA ; London : Idea Group Publishing, c2004. xviii, 352 p. : ill. ; 26 cm. Includes bibliographical references and index. ISBN 1-59140-126-7 (hardcover) ISBN 1-59140-220-4 (paperback) ISBN 1-59140-127-5 (ebook) DDC 658.4/038
1. Knowledge management. 2. Trust. 3. Strategic alliances (Business) 4. Business communication. 5. Information resources management. I. Iivonen, Mirja. II. Title.
HD30.2 .H865 2004

ḤURBAN (1939-1945). See **HOLOCAUST, JEWISH (1939-1945).**

ḤURBN (1939-1945). See **HOLOCAUST, JEWISH (1939-1945).**

Hurbon, Laënnec. Dieu dans le vaudou haïtien / Laënnec Hurbon ; préface de Geneviève Calame-Griaule. Nouv. éd. Paris : Maisonneuve et Larose, 2002. 268 p. : ill. ; 21 cm. (Références Maisonneuve et Larose) Includes bibliographical references (p. [259]-268). ISBN 2-7068-1619-8
1. Catholic Church - Relations - Voodooism. 2. Haiti - Religion. 3. Voodooism. 4. God. 5. Voodooism - Haiti - Relations - Catholic Church. 6. Black author. I. Calame-Griaule, Geneviève. II. Title. III. Series.

Hurley, Jennifer A., 1973-.
Women's rights. San Diego, Calif. : Greenhaven Press, c2002.
HQ1236 .W6526 2002

Hurley, Jessica, 1970- Burn this book-- : and move on with your life / Jessica Hurley. Kansas City, Mo. : Andrews McMeel, c2002. xi p., 99 leaves ; 19 cm. ISBN 0-7407-2699-4 DDC 158.1
1. Self-actualization (Psychology) I. Title.
BF637.S4 H87 2002

Hurley, S. L. (Susan L.) Justice, luck, and knowledge / S.L. Hurley. Cambridge, Mass. : Harvard University Press, 2003. viii, 341 p. : ill. ; 25 cm. Includes bibliographical references (p. 321-329) and index. ISBN 0-674-01029-9 (alk. paper) DDC 172
1. Responsibility. 2. Distributive justice. 3. Fortune - Moral and ethical aspects. I. Title.
BJ1451 .H87 2003

Hurrell, Andrew.
Order and justice in international relations. Oxford ; New York : Oxford University Press, 2003.
JZ1308 .O73 2003

Hurrell, Joseph J.
Job stress in a changing workforce. 1st ed. Washington, DC ; London : American Psychological Association, c1994.
HF5548.85 .J654 1994

Hurson, Didier. Alexander Mitscherlich, 1908-1982 : psychanalyse, société et histoire / Didier Hurson. Paris : Presses de l'Université de Paris-Sorbonne, 2002. 263 p. ; 24 cm. (Monde germanique, histoires et cultures) Includes bibliographical references (p. 241-256) and index. Includes a cited passage in German with French translation. ISBN 2-8405-0242-9 DDC 300
1. Mitscherlich, Alexander, - 1908- 2. Psychoanalysts - Germany - Biography. 3. Psychoanalysis. I. Title. II. Series: Monde germanique.

Hurt, William.
The Alexander technique [videorecording]. New York, N.Y. : Wellspring Media, c1999.

Hurwitz, Joseph, d. 1919. Sefer Madregat ha-adam / mi-maʼamare ... Yosef Yozl Hurvits. Hotsaʼah hadashah mefoʼeret menukedet u-metukenet. Yerushalayim : Yeshivat Ner Shemuʼel, 762 [2002] 21, 279, 275 p. ; 24 cm. Running title: Madregat ha-adam. Vocalized.
1. Ethics, Jewish. I. Title. II. Title: Madregat ha-adam

HUSBAND AND WIFE (JEWISH LAW).
Kohen, Yekutiel. Mishpaṭ ha-shalom. Yerushalayim : Mekhon Shaʼar ha-mishpaṭ : Hanhalat bate ha-din ha-rabaniyim, 762 [2001 or 2002]

HUSBANDRY. See **AGRICULTURE.**

HUSBANDS. See **MATE SELECTION.**

HUSBANDS - DEATH - PSYCHOLOGICAL ASPECTS.
Feldbaum, Rebecca Bram. If there's anything I can do--. Jerusalem, Israel ; Nanuet, NY : Feldheim Publishers, 2003.
BF575.G7 F46 2003

HUSSERL, EDMUND, 1859-1938.
LOGISCHE UNTERSUCHUNGEN.
Husserl's Logical investigations reconsidered. Dordrecht ; Boston : Kluwer Academic Publishers, c2003.
B3279.H93 L64346 2003

HUSSERL, EDMUND, 1859-1938.
Barsotti, Bernard. Bachelard critique de Husserl. Paris : Harmattan, c2002.
B2430.B254 B37 2002

Heinamaa, Sara, 1960- Toward a phenomenology of sexual difference. Lanham, Md. ; Oxford : Rowman & Littlefield Publishers, c2003.
HQ1208 .B3523 2003

Ledda, Antonio. La fenomelogia tra essenza ed esistenza. 1. ed. Roma : Carocci editore, 2002.

Husserl's Logical investigations reconsidered / [edited by] Denis Fisette. Dordrecht ; Boston : Kluwer Academic Publishers, c2003. vi, 235 p. : ill. ; 25 cm. (Contributions to phenomenology ; v. 48) Includes bibliographical references (p. [223]-232) and index. ISBN 1402013892 (alk. paper) DDC 160
1. Husserl, Edmund, - 1859-1938. - Logische Untersuchungen. 2. Logic. 3. Knowledge, Theory of. 4. Phenomenology. I. Fisette, Denis, 1954- II. Series.
B3279.H93 L64346 2003

Hutcheson, Francis, 1694-1746. An essay on the nature and conduct of the passions and affections : with illustrations on the moral sense / Francis Hutcheson ; edited with an introduction by Aaron Garrett. Indianapolis : Liberty Fund, c2002. xxv, 226 p. : ill., port. ; 24 cm. (Natural law and enlightenment classics) (The collected works of Francis Hutcheson) Includes bibliographical references and index. ISBN 0-86597-386-5 (hbk.) ISBN 0-86597-387-3 (pbk. : alk. paper) DDC 171/.2
1. Emotions - Early works to 1850. 2. Ethics. I. Title. II. Series. III. Series: Hutcheson, Francis, 1694-1746. Works. 2002.
B1501 .E6 2002

Works. 2002.
Hutcheson, Francis, 1694-1746. An essay on the nature and conduct of the passions and affections. Indianapolis : Liberty Fund, c2002.
B1501 .E6 2002

Huteau, Michel. Psychologie, psychiatrie et société sous la troisième république : la biocratie d'Edouard Toulouse, 1865-1947 / Michel Huteau. Paris : Harmattan, c2002. 304 p. : ill. ; 24 cm. (Collection "Histoire des sciences humaines") Includes bibliographical references (p. [279]-293) and index. ISBN 2-7475-3082-5 DDC 300
1. Toulouse, Edouard, - b. 1865. 2. Psychology - France - History. 3. Psychiatry - France - History. 4. France - History - Third Republic, 1870-1940. I. Title. II. Series.

Hüttel, Barbara.
Re-Visionen. Berlin : Akademie Verlag, c2002.

Huttel, Richard.
Re-Visionen. Berlin : Akademie Verlag, c2002.

Huyssen, Andreas. Present pasts : urban palimpsests and the politics of memory / Andreas Huyssen. Stanford, Calif. : Stanford University Press, 2003. xii, 177 p. : ill. ; 24 cm. (Cultural memory in the present) Includes bibliographical references (p. [165]-177). CONTENTS: Present pasts : media, politics, amnesia -- Monumental seduction : Christo in Berlin -- The voids of Berlin -- After the war : Berlin as palimpsest -- Fear of mice : the Times Square redevelopment -- Memory sites in an expanded field : the memory park in Buenos Aires -- Doris Salcedo's memory sculpture Unland : the orphan's tunic -- Of mice and mimesis : reading Spiegelman with Adorno -- Rewritings and new beginnings : W.G. Sebald and the literature on the air war -- Twin memories : after-images of nine/eleven. ISBN 0-8047-4560-9 (alk. paper) ISBN 0-8047-4561-7 (pbk. : alk. paper) DDC 901
1. Memory (Philosophy) 2. History - Philosophy. 3. Memory - Social aspects. 4. Cities and towns - Psychological aspects. 5. Memory in literature. I. Title. II. Series.
BD181.7 .H89 2003

HYDROLOGY. See **WATER.**

HYGIENE. See **BEAUTY, PERSONAL; HEALTH.**

HYGIENE, SEXUAL. See also **SEX INSTRUCTION; SEXUALLY TRANSMITTED DISEASES.**
From child sexual abuse to adult sexual risk. 1st ed. Washington, DC : American Psychological Association, c2004.
RC569.5.A28 F76 2004

Hyland, Ann. The horse in the ancient world / Ann Hyland. Stroud : Sutton, 2003. xxi, 210 p., [20] p. of plates : ill., maps ; 24 cm. Includes bibliographical references (p. 193-201) and indexes. ISBN 0-7509-2160-9 (ALK. PAPER) DDC 636.100935
1. Horses - Middle East - History - To 1500. 2. Horses - History - To 1500. 3. Animals and civilization - Middle East - History - To 1500. 4. History, Ancient. I. Title.

HYMNS, ENGLISH - HISTORY AND CRITICISM.
Hickman, Martha Whitmore, 1925- Wade in the water. Nashville, TN : Abingdon Press, 2003.
BV310 .H53 2003

HYPERACTIVE CHILD SYNDROME. *See* **ATTENTION-DEFICIT HYPERACTIVITY DISORDER.**

HYPERKINESIA IN CHILDREN. *See* **ATTENTION-DEFICIT HYPERACTIVITY DISORDER.**

HYPERKINETIC SYNDROME. *See* **ATTENTION-DEFICIT HYPERACTIVITY DISORDER.**

HYPERTEXT MARKUP LANGUAGE (DOCUMENT MARKUP LANGUAGE). *See* **HTML (DOCUMENT MARKUP LANGUAGE).**

Hypnosis.
Bobgan, Martin, 1930- Santa Barbara, Calif. : EastGate Publishers, c2001.
BF1152 .B63 2001

HYPNOTIC AGE REGRESSION.
Bongard, Jerry. The near birth experience. New York : Marlowe & Co. ; [Emeryville, CA?] : Distributed by Publishers Group West, c2000.
BF1156.R45 B66 2000

HYPNOTIC AGE REGRESSION - CASE STUDIES.
Kent, James H., 1939- Past life memories as a Confederate soldier. Huntsville, AR : Ozark Mountain Publishers, c2003.
BF1156.R45 K45 2003

HYPNOTICALLY INDUCED AGE REGRESSION. *See* **HYPNOTIC AGE REGRESSION.**

HYPNOTISM. *See also* **HYPNOTIC AGE REGRESSION; REINCARNATION THERAPY.**
Bobgan, Martin, 1930- Hypnosis. Santa Barbara, Calif. : EastGate Publishers, c2001.
BF1152 .B63 2001

Markham, Ursula. The beginner's guide to self-hypnosis. London : Vega, 2002.
BF1141 .M36 2002

I am dynamite.
Rapport, Nigel, 1956- London ; New York : Routledge, 2003.

I am the truth.
Henry, Michel, 1922- [C'est moi la vérité. English] Stanford, Calif : Stanford University Press, 2003.
BR100 .H39813 2003

I can do it!.
Hay, Louise L. Carlsbad, CA : Hay House, c2004.
BF697.5.S47 H388 2004

I can't believe I just did that.
Allyn, David (David Smith) New York : Jeremy P. Tarcher/Penguin, 2004.
BF575.E53 A45 2004

I feel angry.
Leonard, Marcia. Nashville, Tenn. : CandyCane Press, 2003.
BF575.A5 L465 2003

I feel happy.
Leonard, Marcia. Nashville, Tenn. : CandyCane Press, 2003.
BF575.H27 L465 2003

I feel sad.
Leonard, Marcia. Nashville, Tenn. : CandyCane Press, 2003.
BF575.S23 L46 2003

I feel scared.
Leonard, Marcia. Nashville, Tenn. : CandyCane Press, 2003.
BF575.F2 L455 2003

I have landed.
Gould, Stephen Jay. 1st ed. New York : Harmony Books, 2002.
QH45.5 .G735 2002

I hope you dance!.
Sanders, Mark D. Nashville, Tenn. : Rutledge Hill Press, 2003.
BF410 .S26 2003

I know why we're here.
Dolan, Mia. 1st U.S. ed. New York : Harmony Books, 2004.
BF1283.D485 A3 2004

IA vam pomogu
Stepanova, Natal'i͡a (Natal'i͡a Ivanovna) Gadanii͡a sibirskoĭ tselitel'nitsy. Moskva : RIPOL klassik, 1999.
BF1866 .S73 1999

IA vsegda byl idealistom - .
Shchedrovitskiĭ, G. P. (Georgiĭ Petrovich), 1929-1994. Moskva : Put', 2001.
BF109.S44 A3 2001

Iadicola, Peter. Violence, inequality, and human freedom / Peter Iadicola and Anson Shupe. 2nd ed. Lanham, Md. ; Oxford : Rowman & Littlefield Publishers, Inc., c2003. ix, 405 p. : ill. ; 24 cm. Includes bibliographical references and index. ISBN 0-7425-1923-6 (hbk. : alk. paper) ISBN 0-7425-1924-4 (pbk. : alk. paper) DDC 303.6
1. Violence. 2. Civil rights. I. Shupe, Anson D. II. Title.
HM886 .I18 2003

I͡Akovleva, E. L. (Evgenii͡a Leonovna) Psikhologii͡a razvitii͡a tvorcheskogo potentsiala lichnosti / E.L. I͡Akovleva. Moskva : Moskovskiĭ psikhologo-sotsial'nyĭ institut : Izd-vo "Flinta" / 1997. 222, [1] p. ; 21 cm. Authorized for instructional purposes. Includes bibliographical references (p. 214-[223]). ISBN 5895020046 ISBN 5893490320
1. Creative ability. I. Title.
BF408 .I15 1997

I͡Anitskiĭ, M. S. (Mikhail Sergeevich).
Sibirskai͡a psikhologii͡a segodni͡a. Kemerovo : Kemerovskiĭ gos. universitet, 2002.
BF20 .S53 2002

T͡Sennostnye orientat͡sii lichnosti kak dinamicheskai͡a sistema / M.S. I͡Anitskiĭ. Kemerovo : Kuzbassvuzizdat, 2000. 202 p. : ill. ; 21 cm. Includes bibliographical references (p. 189-202). ISBN 5202017170
1. Personality. 2. Values. I. Title.
BF698 .I18 2000

Iannitelli, Leda Muhana. Guiding choreography [microform] : a process-oriented, person-centered approach with contributions from psychoanalytic, cognitive, and humanistic psychology / by Leda Muhana Iannitelli. 1994. x, 292 leaves : ill. Thesis (Ed. D.)--Temple University, 1994. Bibliography: leaves 279-290. Microfiche. Ann Arbor, Mich. : University Microfilms International, 1994. 4 microfiches ; 11 x 15 cm. "94-22651"
1. Dance - Psychological aspects. 2. Choreography - Study and teaching. 3. Creation (Literary, artistic, etc.) I. Title.

I͡Aroslavskiĭ gosudarstvennyĭ universitet im. P.G. Demidova.
Psikhologicheskie problemy prini͡atii͡a reshenii͡a. I͡Aroslavl' : I͡Aroslavskiĭ gos. universitet, 2001.
BF448 .P78 2001

I͡Arotskiĭ, A. I.
Ėmot͡sii cheloveka v normal'nykh i stressornykh uslovii͡akh. Grodno : Grodnenskiĭ gos. universitet im. I͡Anki Kupaly, 2001.
BF531 .E54 2001

I͡Arskai͡a-Smirnova, Elena.
Gender, vlast', kul'tura. Saratov : Saratovskiĭ gos. tekhn. universitet, 2000.
HQ1075 .G4667 2000

I͡Astrebit͡skai͡a, Alla L'vovna.
XX vek. Moskva : INION RAN, 2001-

I͡Azycheskai͡a zari͡a.
Shcheglov, A. (Alekseĭ) Moskva : [Izdatel'stvo "PROBEL-2000"], 2002.
BL980.R5 S53 2002

I͡Azyk, semiotika, kul'tura. Malai͡a serii͡a
Bernshteĭn, Boris Moiseevich. Pigmalion naiznanku. Moskva : I͡Azyki slavi͡anskoĭ kul'tury, 2002.
N5300 .B614 2002

Ibay, Manny. Thank you, Tony Robbins : how Tony's success programs helped me design my life so I can do what I want, when I want / Manny Ibay. 1st Destini Books ed. Santa Monica, Calif. : Destini Books, 2002. 238 p. ; 22 cm. ISBN 0-9717700-7-7 DDC 158.1
1. Success - Psychological aspects. I. Title.
BF637.S8 I23 2002

IBN EZRA, ABRAHAM BEN MEÏR, 1092-1167 - CONTRIBUTIONS IN SCIENCE.
Sela, Shlomo. Abraham Ibn Ezra and the rise of medieval Hebrew science. Leiden ; Boston, MA : Brill, 2003.
BM538.S3 S45 2003

Ibn Gaon, Shem Tov ben Abraham, 13th/14th cent. Bade ha aron.
Sefer 'Amude ha-Kabalah. Yerushalayim : Nezer Sheraga, 761 [2001]

Keter Shem Tov.
Sefer 'Amude ha-Kabalah. Yerushalayim : Nezer Sheraga, 761 [2001]

Ibn Khāṭimah, Aḥmad ibn 'Alī, d. ca. 1369. Faṣl al adīl baynaal raqīb wa al washi wa al adhil.
Ibn Khāṭimah, Aḥmad ibn 'Alī, d. ca. 1369. [Poems] Dīwān Ibn Khāṭimah al-Anṣārī. al-Ṭab'ah 1. Bayrūt : Dār al-Fikr al-Mu'āṣir ; Dimashq : Dār al-Fikr, 1994.
PJ7760.I2454   <Orien Arab>

[Poems]
Dīwān Ibn Khāṭimah al-Anṣārī : Aḥmad ibn 'Alī ibn Khāṭimah al-Anṣārī al-Andalusī ; wa-Risālat al-Faṣl al-'Ādil bayna al-raqīb wa-al-wāshī wa-al-'ādhil / ḥaqqaqahu wa-sharaḥahu wa-qaddama la-hu Muḥammad Riḍwān al-Dāyah. al-Ṭab'ah 1. Bayrūt : Dār al-Fikr al-Mu'āṣir ; Dimashq : Dār al-Fikr, 1994. 240 p. ; 24 cm. Includes bibliographical references and index. In Arabic.
1. Love - Early works to 1800. I. Dāyah, Muḥammad Riḍwān. II. Ibn Khāṭimah, Aḥmad ibn 'Alī, d. ca. 1369. Faṣl al-'ādil baynaal-raqīb wa-al-washī wa-al-'ādhil. III. Title.
PJ7760.I2454   <Orien Arab>

**Ibn Shem Tov, Shem Tov ben Joseph ben Shem Tov, 15th cent.
Emunot.**
Sefer 'Amude ha-Kabalah. Yerushalayim : Nezer Sheraga, 761 [2001]

Torat ha sefirot.
Sefer 'Amude ha-Kabalah. Yerushalayim : Nezer Sheraga, 761 [2001]

ICG Africa report
(no. 27) From Kabila to Kabila. Nairobi ; Brussels : International Crisis Group, 2001.

(no. 37.) Le dialogue intercongolais. Bruxelles ; Nairobi : International Crisis Group, [2001]

(no. 44) Storm clouds over Sun City. Brussels ; Nairobi : International Crisis Group, 2002.

ICG Burundi report
(no. 3.) Le Burundi aprés la suspension de l'embargo. [Nairobi?] : International Crisis Group, [1999]

Ich-Jagd.
Gross, Peter, 1941- 1. Aufl., Originalausg. Frankfurt am Main : Suhrkamp, 1999.
BF175.5.E35 G76 1999

Ich Jagd.
Gross, Peter, 1941- Ich-Jagd. 1. Aufl., Originalausg. Frankfurt am Main : Suhrkamp, 1999.
BF175.5.E35 G76 1999

ICHTHYOLOGY. *See* **FISHES.**

Icing Ivy.
Marshall, Evan, 1956- Waterville, Me. : Thorndike Press, 2003, c2002.
PS3563.A72236 I27 2003

Ickes, William John. Everyday mind reading : understanding what other people think and feel / William Ickes. Amherst, N.Y. : Prometheus Books, 2003. p. cm. Includes bibliographical references. ISBN 1-59102-119-7 DDC 155.6
1. Empathy. I. Title.
BF575.E55 I35 2003

ICONOGRAPHY. *See* **ART.**

ICONS, BYZANTINE - GREECE - ATHOS.
Ivinskai͡a, A. (Anna) Svet prelomlennogo vremeni v ikonnom prostranstve. Moskva : Khristianskiĭ Vostok, 2002.
N8189.G72 I95 2002

ICONS, BYZANTINE - GREECE - CRETE.
Ivinskai͡a, A. (Anna) Svet prelomlennogo vremeni v ikonnom prostranstve. Moskva : Khristianskiĭ Vostok, 2002.
N8189.G72 I95 2002

ICR monograph series
(no. 42.) French, Christopher C. Paranormal perception? London : Institute for Cultural Research, 2001.

Ida y vuelta.
D'Alvia, Rodolfo. Psicoanálisis psicosomática ida y atleuv [sic.]. Buenos Aires : Editorial Dunken, 2002.

The idea of identification.
Woodward, Gary C. Albany : State University of New York Press, c2003.
BF697.5.S65 W66 2003

The idea of universal history in Greece.
Alonso-Nuñez, José Miguel. Amsterdam : J.C. Gieben, 2002.
D13.5.G8 A46 2002

Ideais na adolescência.
Matheus, Tiago Corbisier. 1a ed. São Paulo, SP : Annablume, 2002.

IDEAL BEAUTIFUL WOMEN. *See* **FEMININE BEAUTY (AESTHETICS).**

The ideal of a rational morality.
Singer, Marcus George, 1926- Oxford : Clarendon Press ; Oxford ; New York : Oxford University Press, 2002.
BJ1012 .S48 2002

IDEAL STATES. *See* **UTOPIAS.**

IDEALISM. *See also* **MATERIALISM; TRANSCENDENTALISM.**
Krollmann, Fritz-Peter, 1963- Ethik und Ästhetik. Essen : Blaue Eule, 2002.

Ideas and insights from the world's foremost business thinkers.
Best practice. Cambridge, MA : Perseus Publishing, c2003.

Ideas and Moral Messages from the Weekly Haftarot.
Koll, Shmuel, 1938- Sefer Ra'yonot u-mesarim. Yerushalayim : S. Kol, 761- [2001-

Ideas in context
(66) Sutcliffe, Adam. Judaism and Enlightenment. Cambridge ; New York : Cambridge University Press, 2003.
BM290 .S88 2003

Ideation.
Graham, Douglas, 1950- Hoboken, N.J. : John Wiley & Sons, Inc., c2004.
BF408 .G664 2004

Le idee del tempo.
Cotroneo, Girolamo. Soveria Mannelli (Catanzaro) : Rubbettino, c2002.

Idee w Rosji
Przesmycki, Piotr, 1965- W stronę Bogoczłowieczeństwa. Łódź : "Ibidem", 2002.
B4238.B44 P79 2002

Idei i napravleniia otechestvennogo liubomudriia.
Zamaleev, A. F. (Aleksandr Fazlaevich) Sankt-Peterburg : Izdatel'sko-torgovyĭ dom "Letniĭ sad", 2003.
B4201 .Z33 2003

Identidad femenina y proyecto ético.
Serret, Estela. 1. ed. México : UNAM, PUEG : Universidad Autónoma Metropolitana, Azcapotzalco : M.A. Porrúa, 2002.

Identidades fragmentadas.
Moita Lopes, Luiz Paulo da. Campinas, SP, Brasil : Mercado de Letras, [2002]
HM753 .M65 2002

Identidades, sujetos y subjetividades / Leonor Arfuch, compiladora. Buenos Aires : Prometeo Libros, c2002. 190 p. ; 20 cm. Includes bibliographical references (p. 185-190) ISBN 950-9217-26-3
1. Sociology, Urban. 2. Group identity. I. Arfuch, Leonor.

IDENTIFICATION.
The development of the social self. 1st ed. London ; New York : Psychology Press, 2003.
BF723.S24 D48 2003

Woodward, Gary C. The idea of identification. Albany : State University of New York Press, c2003.
BF697.5.S65 W66 2003

IDENTIFICATION NUMBERS, PERSONAL.
Privacy [electronic resource]. [Washington, D.C.] : Federal Trade Commission, Bureau of Consumer Protection, Office of Consumer and Business Education, [2002]

Privacy [electronic resource]. [Washington, D.C.] : Federal Trade Commission, Bureau of Consumer Protection, Office of Consumer and Business Education, [2002]

Privacy [electronic resource]. [Washington, D.C.] : Federal Trade Commission, Bureau of Consumer Protection, Office of Consumer and Business Education, [2002]

IDENTIFICATION NUMBERS, PERSONAL - UNITED STATES.
Privacy [electronic resource]. [Washington, D.C.] : Federal Trade Commission, Bureau of Consumer Protection, Office of Consumer and Business Education, [2002]

Privacy [electronic resource]. [Washington, D.C.] : Federal Trade Commission, Bureau of Consumer Protection, Office of Consumer and Business Education, [2002]

IDENTIFICATION OF DOCUMENTS. *See* **LEGAL DOCUMENTS - IDENTIFICATION.**

Identification of nonlinear physiological systems.
Westwick, D. T. (David T.) Piscataway, NJ : IEEE Press ; Hoboken, NJ : Wiley-Interscience, c2003.
QP33.6.M36 W475 2003

Identità e la differenza negli uomini e in natura.
Boncinelli, Edoardo. Io sono, tu sei. 1. ed. Milano : Mondadori, 2002.

Identitaten.
Identities. New York ; Oxford : Berghahn Books, 2002.
HM716 .I34 2002

Identitäten und Alteritäten
(Bd. 11) Konstrukte nationaler Identität. Würzburg : Ergon, c2002.
DC34 .K67 2002

(Bd. 9.) Studien zu antiken Identitäten. Würzburg : Ergon Verlag, c2001.
DG78 .S78 2001

Identitäten und Alteritäten. Altertumswissenschaftliche Reihe
(Bd. 2.) Studien zu antiken Identitäten. Würzburg : Ergon Verlag, c2001.
DG78 .S78 2001

L'identité narrative.
Gilbert, Muriel. Genève : Labor et Fides, c2001.

Identities : time, difference, and boundaries / edited by Heidrun Friese. New York ; Oxford : Berghahn Books, 2002. xiv, 273 p. ; 24 cm. (Making sense of history ; vol. 2) Chiefly written by members of the Forschungsgruppe Historische Sinnbildung, Universität Bielefeld. Based in part on Identitaten, ed. by Aleida Assmann and Heidrun Friese. 1998. Includes bibliographical references and index. CONTENTS: Identity : desire, name, and difference / Heidrun Friese -- Identity and selfhood as a problematique / Peter Wagner -- Personal and collective identity / Jurgen Straub -- Identities of the West : reason, myths, limits of tolerance / Barbara Henry -- The praxis of cognition and the representation of difference / Martin Fuchs -- Constructions of cultural identity and problems of translation / Shingo Shimada -- The performance of hysteria / Elisabeth Bronfen -- The "Jewess Pallas Athena" : horizons of selfconception in the 19th and 20th centuries / Barbara Hahn -- Collective identity as a dual discursive construction / Gerd Baumann -- Historical culture in (post-)colonial context : the genesis of national identification figures in francophone Western Africa / Hans-Jurgen Lusebrink -- Identity as progress : the longevity of nationalism / Christian Geulen -- Culture and history in comparative fundamentalism / Emanuel Sivan. ISBN 1-57181-474-4 (hbk. : alk. paper) ISBN 1-57181-507-4 (pbk. : alk. paper) DDC 305.8
1. Group identity. 2. Identity (Psychology) 3. Ethnicity. 4. Nationalism. 5. History - Philosophy. I. Friese, Heidrun, 1958- II. Assmann, Aleida. III. Universität Bielefeld. Forschungsgruppe Historische Sinnbildung. IV. Title: Identitaten. V. Series.
HM716 .I34 2002

Identity.
White, Vernon. London : SCM, c2002.

Identity and the natural environment : the psychological significance of nature / edited by Susan Clayton and Susan Opotow. Cambridge, Mass. : MIT Press, 2004. p. cm. Includes bibliographical references and index. ISBN 0-262-03311-9 (hc : alk. paper) ISBN 0-262-53206-9 (pbk. : alk. paper) DDC 155.9/1
1. Environmental psychology. 2. Identity (Psychology) I. Clayton, Susan. II. Opotow, Susan.
BF353 .I34 2004

Identity, cause, and mind.
Shoemaker, Sydney. Expanded ed. Oxford : Clarendon Press ; New York : Oxford University Press, c2003.
B29 .S5135 2003

IDENTITY, COLLECTIVE. *See* **GROUP IDENTITY.**

IDENTITY, COMMUNITY. *See* **GROUP IDENTITY.**

Identity/difference.
Connolly, William E. Expanded ed. Minneapolis : University of Minnesota Press, c2002.
JA74 .C659 2002

IDENTITY, GROUP. *See* **GROUP IDENTITY.**

Identity in democracy.
Gutmann, Amy. Princeton, N.J. : Princeton University Press, c2003.
JF529 .G886 2003

Identity in modern society.
Simon, Bernd. Oxford, UK ; Malden, MA : Blackwell Pub., 2004.
BF697 .S546 2004

IDENTITY, NATIONAL. *See* **NATIONALISM.**

The identity of man.
Bronowski, Jacob, 1908-1974. Amherst, N.Y. : Prometheus Books, 2002.
BD450 .B653 2002

IDENTITY (PHILOSOPHICAL CONCEPT).
Beyond integration. Lund, Sweden : Nordic Academic Press, c2001.
JV6225 .B49 2001

Cohen, Jeffrey Jerome. Medieval identity machines. Minneapolis : University of Minnesota Press, c2003.
CB353 .C64 2003

Connolly, William E. Identity/difference. Expanded ed. Minneapolis : University of Minnesota Press, c2002.
JA74 .C659 2002

Dobosz, Artur. Tożsamość metamorficzna a komunikacja językowa. Poznań : Wydawn. Naukowe Instytutu Filozofii Uniwersytetu im. Adama Mickiewicza w Poznaniu, 2002.

Figures de la marge. Rennes : Presses universitaires de Rennes, [2002]

Heck, Alexander. Auf der Suche nach Anerkennung. Münster : Lit, c2003.

Kearney, Richard. Strangers, Gods, and monsters. London ; New York : Routledge, 2003.
BD236 .K43 2003

Sequeri, Pier Angelo. L'umano alla prova. Milano : V & P Università, c2002.
BD222.S47 U6 2002

Sobre las identidades. Pamplona : Universidad Pública de Navarra, [2001]

Social justice, education, and identity. London ; New York : RoutledgeFalmer, 2003.
LC191 .S6564 2003

White, Vernon. Identity. London : SCM, c2002.

Woodward, Gary C. The idea of identification. Albany : State University of New York Press, c2003.
BF697.5.S65 W66 2003

IDENTITY (PHILOSOPHICAL CONCEPT) - RELIGIOUS ASPECTS - CHRISTIANITY.
White, Vernon. Identity. London : SCM, c2002.

IDENTITY (PSYCHOLOGIA).
Sociología de la identidad. México : Miguel Angel Porrúa : Universidad Autónoma Metropolitana, Unidad Iztapalapa, 2002.

IDENTITY (PSYCHOLOGY). *See also* **EGO (PSYCHOLOGY); GENDER IDENTITY; GROUP IDENTITY.**
Arenas, Fernando, 1963- Utopias of otherness. Minneapolis : University of Minnesota Press, c2003.
DP681 .A74 2003

Brosman, Catharine Savage, 1934- Finding higher ground. Reno : University of Nevada Press, c2003.
F787 .B76 2003

Chelovek kak sub"ekt kul'tury. Moskva : Nauka, 2002.

Children in the city. London : Routledge/Falmer, 2003.

Cohen, Jeffrey Jerome. Medieval identity machines. Minneapolis : University of Minnesota Press, c2003.
CB353 .C64 2003

Cottle, Thomas J. Beyond self-esteem. New York : P. Lang, c2003.
BF697 .C675 2003

Cottle, Thomas J. A sense of self. Amherst : University of Massachusetts Press, c2003.
BF697 .C68 2003

La culture. Auxerre : Sciences humaines éditions, c2002.

The development of the social self. 1st ed. London ; New York : Psychology Press, 2003.

Identity (Psychology)

BF723.S24 D48 2003

Discourse, the body, and identity. Basingstoke, Hampshire ; New York : Palgrave Macmillan, 2003.
HM636 .D57 2003

Dreaming and the self. Albany : State University of New York Press, c2003.
BF1091 .D735 2003

Gilbert, Muriel. L'identité narrative. Genève : Labor et Fides, c2001.

Hodges, Carolyn R., 1947- Making schools work. New York : P. Lang, c2003.
LC213.2 .H63 2003
1. Black author.

Identities. New York ; Oxford : Berghahn Books, 2002.
HM716 .I34 2002

Identity and the natural environment. Cambridge, Mass. : MIT Press, 2004.
BF353 .I34 2004

Kearney, Richard. Strangers, Gods, and monsters. London ; New York : Routledge, 2003.
BD236 .K43 2003

Litvinović, Gorjana. Čovek između istorijskog i ličnog vremena. Beograd : Institut za psihologiju, 2001.
BF697 .L543 2001

Lives in translation. 1st ed. New York ; Houndmills, England : Palgrave Macmillan, 2003.
P115.25 .L58 2003

Lord, Robert G. (Robert George), 1946- Leadership processes and follower self-identity. Mahwah, N.J. ; London : Lawrence Erlbaum, 2004.
HM1261 .L67 2004

McNally, David, 1946- Be your own brand. 1st ed. San Francisco, CA : Berrett-Koehler, c2002.
BF697 .M385 2002

Miller, William Ian, 1946- Faking it. Cambridge ; New York : Cambridge University Press, 2003.
BF697 .M525 2003

Moessinger, Pierre Le jeu de l'identité. 1re éd. Paris : Presses universitaires de France, 2000.
BF697.5.S43 M634 2000

Perspectives on Las Américas. Maden, MA : Blackwell Pub., c2003.
F1410 .P48 2003

Psychology and consumer culture. 1st ed. Washington, DC : American Psychological Association, c2004.
HC110.C6 P76 2004

Read, Malcolm K. (Malcolm Kevin), 1945- Educating the educators. 1st American ed. Newark : University of Delaware Press ; Cranbury, NJ : Associated University Presses, 2003.
PC4064.R43 A3 2003

Self and social identity. Malden, MA : Blackwell Pub., 2003.
BF697.5.S43 S429 2003

Simon, Bernd. Identity in modern society. Oxford, UK ; Malden, MA : Blackwell Pub., 2004.
BF697 .S546 2004

Studien zu antiken Identitäten. Würzburg : Ergon Verlag, c2001.
DG78 .S78 2001

IDENTITY (PSYCHOLOGY) - CONGRESSES.
Advances in identity and research. New York : Kluwer Academic/Plenum Publishers, c2003.
BF697 .A347 2003

Personal and moral identity. Dordrecht ; Boston : Kluwer Academic Publishers, c2002.
BJ45 .P47 2002

Self, social identity, and physical health. New York : Oxford University Press, 1999.
R726.5 .S46 1999

IDENTITY (PSYCHOLOGY) IN ADOLESCENCE - UNITED STATES.
Cornbleth, Catherine. Hearing America's youth. New York : P. Lang, c2003.
BF724.3.I3 .C67 2003

IDENTITY (PSYCHOLOGY) IN YOUTH.
Tonolo, Giorgio. Adolescenza e identità. Bologna : Il mulino, c1999.
BF724.3.I3 T65 1999

Wilkinson, Deanna Lyn, 1968- Guns, violence, and identity among African American and Latino youth. New York : LFB Scholarly Pub., 2003.

HQ799.2.V56 W55 2003

IDENTITY (PSYCHOLOGY) - POLITICAL ASPECTS.
Donchenko, E. A. (Elena Andreevna) Arkhetypy sotsial'noho zhyttia i polityka. Kyïv : Lybid', 2001.
JA74.5 .D65 2001

Lamizet, Bernard. Politique et identité. Lyon : Presses universitaires de Lyon, 2002.

IDENTITY (PSYCHOLOGY) - SOCIAL ASPECTS.
Fuhrer, Urs, 1950- Cultivating minds. 1st ed. New York, NY : Taylor & Francis, 2003.
BF697.5.S65 F84 2003

Pataki, Ferenc, 1928- Élettörténet és identitás. Budapest : Osiris Kiadó, 2001.
BF697.5.S65 P38 2001

Simon, Bernd. Identity in modern society. Oxford, UK ; Malden, MA : Blackwell Pub., 2004.
BF697 .S546 2004

Viatkina, G. V. Razvitie individual'nosti lichnosti v sovremennykh usloviiakh. Moskva : In-t molodezhi, 1997.
BF697 .V52 1997

IDENTITY, SOCIAL. See **GROUP IDENTITY.**

IDEOLOGY. See also **POLITICAL CORRECTNESS.**
Bailey, Gordon, 1946- Peterborough, Ont. : Broadview Press, 2003.

IDEOLOGY.
Bailey, Gordon, 1946- Ideology. Peterborough, Ont. : Broadview Press, 2003.

Clark, J. C. D. Our shadowed present. London : Atlantic, 2003.

Jansen, Sue Curry. Critical communication theory. Lanham, Md. ; Oxford : Rowman & Littlefield, c2002.
HM651 .J36 2002

Oron, Israel. Mayet, almayet ye-ide'ologyah. [Israel] : Miśrad ha-biṭaḥon, [2002]

IDEOLOGY - EUROPE.
Lurati, Ottavio. Per modo di dire--. Bologna : CLUEB, c2002.

IDEOLOGY - RELIGIOUS ASPECTS.
Davis, Charles, 1923- Religion and the making of society. New York, NY, USA : Cambridge University Press, 1994.
BT738 .D36 1994

IDIOCY. See **STUPIDITY.**

IDOLS AND IMAGES.
Die Unvermeidlichkeit der Bilder. Tübingen : G. Narr, c2001.
N72.A56 U58 2001x

Idowu, Adeyemi I.
Professional concerns arising from twenty years of counselling practice in Nigeria. Garki, Abuja, Nigeria : Official Printers, Jayawahs Communications, 1996.
BF637.C6 P775 1996

Idrobo Díaz, Hugo, 1954- La joda de la paz en Colombia : radiografía social de América Hispana / Hugo Idrobo Díaz. 1. ed. Cali, Colombia : [s.n.], 2002?] 251 p. ill. ; 21 cm. ISBN 958-33-4089-8 (pbk.)
1. Colombia - Politics and government - 1974- 2. Colombia - Economic conditions - 1970- 3. Colombia - Social conditions - 1970- 4. Social conflict - Colombia - History - 20th century. 5. Peace. I. Title. II. Title: Radiografía social de América Hispana

IEE management of technology series
(21) Morrison, Raymond E. Developing effective engineering leadership. London : Institution of Electrical Engineers, c2003.

IEEE Engineering in Medicine and Biology Society.
Westwick, D. T. (David T.) Identification of nonlinear physiological systems. Piscataway, NJ : IEEE Press ; Hoboken, NJ : Wiley-Interscience, c2003.
QP33.6.M36 W475 2003

IEEE Press series in biomedical engineering
Westwick, D. T. (David T.) Identification of nonlinear physiological systems. Piscataway, NJ : IEEE Press ; Hoboken, NJ : Wiley-Interscience, c2003.
QP33.6.M36 W475 2003

If heaven is so wonderful - why come here?.
Brooker, John L., 1923- Nevada City, CA : Blue Dolphin, 2004.
BF1261.2 .B76 2004

If the horse is dead, get off!.
Sills, Judith. New York : Viking, 2004.
BF637.S38 S55 2004

If there's anything I can do - .
Feldbaum, Rebecca Bram. Jerusalem, Israel ; Nanuet, NY : Feldheim Publishers, 2003.
BF575.G7 F46 2003

If you want to be a witch.
McCoy, Edain, 1957- 1st ed. St. Paul, Minn. : Llewellyn Publications, 2004.
BF1571 .M455 2004

If your life were a business, would you invest in it?.
Eckblad, John. New York : McGraw-Hill, c2003.
BF637.S4 E38 2003

IFA (RELIGION).
Karade, Akinkugbe. Path to priesthood. Brooklyn, N.Y. : Kânda Mukûtu Books, c2001.
BL2523.I33 K37 2001
1. Black author.

IFSR international series on systems science and engineering
(v. 17.) Von Foerster, Heinz, 1911- Understanding systems. New York : Kluwer Academic/Plenum Publishers ; Heidelberg : Carl-Auer-Systeme Verlag, c2002.

IGALA (AFRICAN PEOPLE) - RELIGION.
Egbunu, Fidelis Eleojo. Be not afraid, only believe. Enugu, Nigeria : Snaap Press, 2001.
1. Black author.

IGARA (AFRICAN PEOPLE). See **IGALA (AFRICAN PEOPLE).**

IGARA (AFRICAN TRIBE). See **IGALA (AFRICAN PEOPLE).**

IGARRA (AFRICAN PEOPLE). See **IGALA (AFRICAN PEOPLE).**

Igeret 'al ha-biṭaḥon.
Blokh, Yosef Zalman. Monsi : [ḥ. mo. l.], 5761 [2000 or 2001]
BM729.T7 .B56 2000

Iggers, Georg G.
Turning points in historiography. Rochester, NY : University of Rochester Press, 2002.
D13 .T87 2002

Ignorance and liberty.
Infantino, Lorenzo, 1948- [Ignoranza e libertà. English] London ; New York : Routledge, 2003.
HB95 .I4913 2003

IGNORANCE (THEORY OF KNOWLEDGE) IN LITERATURE - CONGRESSES.
Colloque des Invalides (5th : 2001 : Hôtel des invalides) Ce que je ne sais pas. Tusson, Charente : Du Lérot, [2002?]
PQ145 .C65 2001

Igrata na vlast i udovolstvie.
Lichev, Valeri. TSinichnoto, ili, Igrata na vlast i udovolstvie. Sofiia : EON-2000, 2000.
B809.5 .L53 2000

IIP, inventory of interpersonal problems manual /
Leonard M. Horowitz ... [et al.]. [San Antonio, TX?] : Psychological Corp., c2000. vii, 100 p. : ill. ; 28 cm. Includes bibliographical references (p. 93-98). ISBN 0-15-813251-3 DDC 158.2/028/7
1. Interpersonal conflict - Testing. 2. Interpersonal relations - Testing. I. Horowitz, Leonard M. II. Title: Inventory of interpersonal problems
BF698.5 .I36 2000

Iivonen, Mirja.
Huotari, Maija-Leena. Trust in knowledge management and systems in organizations. Hershey, PA ; London : Idea Group Publishing, c2004.
HD30.2 .H865 2004

IJCP.
[Critical psychology (Lawrence & Wishart)] Critical psychology. London : Lawrence & Wishart, c2001-
BF39.9 .C75

IJCT.
International journal of cognition and technology. Amsterdam ; Philadelphia : John Benjamins, c2002-
BF309 .I58

Ikas, Wolfgang-Valentin. Martin von Troppau (Martinus Polonus), O.P. (1278) in England : Überlieferungs- und wirkungsgeschichtliche Studien zu dessen Papst- und Kaiserchronik / von Wolfgang-Valentin Ikas. Wiesbaden : Reichert, 2002. xiv. 417 p. : ill. (some col.) ; 24 cm. (Wissensliteratur im Mittelalter ; Bd. 40) Previously issued as author's dissertation, 2001, Bayerische Julius-Maximilians-Universität Würzburg. On t.p.:

"1278" is preceded by a dagger. Includes bibliographical references (p. [365]-402) and indexes. ISBN 3-89500-313-1 (cl.)
1. Martinus, - Polonus, - d. 1279. - Chronicon pontificum et imperatorum. 2. History, Ancient. I. Title. II. Series.

Ikhwān al-Ṣafāʾ.
[Rasāʾil. 36. French & Arabic]
Les révolutions et les cycles : (Epîtres des freres de la Pureté, XXXVI) / Ikhwân al-Ṣafâʾ ; traduction de l'arabe, introduction, notes et lexique par Gedefroid de Callataÿ. Louvain-la-Neuve : Bruylant-Academia ; Beyrouth : Al-Bouraq Editions, 1996. 207 p : ill. ; 20 cm. (Sagesses musulmanes ; 3) Includes bibliographical references (p. [151]-169) and index. ISBN 2-8416-1040-3
1. Astronomy, Arab - Early works to 1800. 2. Astrology, Arab - Early works to 1800. 3. Science - Early works to 1800. 4. Islam - Early works to 1800. I. Callataÿ, Godefroid de. II. Title. III. Title: Epîtres des Freres de la Pureté. XXXVI IV. Series.

Ikram Azam, 1940-.
Some significant 21st century trends and issues. Islamabad : Pakistan Futuristics Foundation & Institute, 1998.
CB161 .S62 1998

Towards the third millennium : seven types of creativity / Ikram Azam. Islamabad : Pakistan Futuristics Foundation & Institute, c1999. iv, 336 p. ; 22 cm. Includes bibliographical references. DDC 153.3/5
1. Creative ability. I. Title.
BF408 .I445 1999

ʿIḳvata de-Meshiḥa.
Wasserman, Elhanan Bunim, 1875-1941. Ḳovets maʾamre ʿIḳvata de-Meshiḥa .... Yerushalayim : Yeshivat Or Elḥanan, 762 [2001 or 2002]

Ilardi, Massimo. In nome della strada : libertà e violenza / Massimo Ilardi. Roma : Meltemi, c2002. 143 p. : ill. ; 19 cm. (Melusine ; 1) Includes bibliographical references. ISBN 88-8353-150-7 DDC 307
1. Liberty. 2. Urban violence. 3. Public spaces. I. Title. II. Series: Melusine (Rome, Italy) ; 1.

Iliev, Vladimir. Psikhologiia na razgovora / Vladimir Iliev ; retsenzenti, Iliia Stoĭkov, Zarko Angelov. 1. izd. Pleven : Lege Artis, 2002. 171 p. ; 20 cm. Summary in English. Includes bibliographical references (p. 165-168) and index. ISBN 9549933229
1. Conversation - Psychological aspects. 2. Interpersonal communication. I. Title.
BF637.C45 I45 2002

Illies, Christian. The grounds of ethical judgement : new transcendental arguments in moral philosophy / Christian Illies. Oxford : Clarendon, 2003. viii, 214 p. ; 22 cm. (Oxford philosophical monographs) Includes bibliographical references (p.[199]-209) index. ISBN 0-19-823832-0 DDC 170
1. Judgment (Ethics) 2. Ethics. 3. Transcendentalism. I. Title. II. Series.

ILLITERACY. See **LITERACY.**

Illiuzionizm lichnosti.
Garifullin, Ramil', 1962- Kazan' : [s.n.], 1997.
BF491 .G37 1997

ILLNESS. See **DISEASES.**

ILLNESSES. See **DISEASES.**

ILLOCUTIONARY ACTS (LINGUISTICS). See **SPEECH ACTS (LINGUISTICS).**

ILLUMINATION OF BOOKS AND MANUSCRIPTS - EUROPE.
Clegg, Justin. The medieval Church. London : British Library, 2003.

Illuminations.
Ashcroft-Nowicki, Dolores. 1st ed. St. Paul, Minn. : Llewellyn Publications, 2003.
BF1623.C2 A84 2003

Die Illusionen der anderen.
Pfaller, Robert. 1. Aufl. Frankfurt : Suhrkamp, 2002.

ILLUSIONISTS (MAGICIANS). See **MAGICIANS.**

ILLUSIONS. See **HALLUCINATIONS AND ILLUSIONS.**

ILLUSTRATED BOOKS - UNITED STATES - HISTORY - 19TH CENTURY.
Pfitzer, Gregory M. Picturing the past. Washington [D.C.] : Smithsonian Institution Press, c2002.
E175 .P477 2002

ILLUSTRATED CHILDREN'S BOOKS. See **PICTURE BOOKS FOR CHILDREN.**

The illustrated encyclopedia of fairies.
Franklin, Anna. London : Vega, 2002.
GR549 .F73 2002

ILLUSTRATION OF BOOKS. See **DRAWING; ILLUMINATION OF BOOKS AND MANUSCRIPTS; ILLUSTRATED BOOKS.**

ILLUSTRATION OF BOOKS - JAPAN - EDO PERIOD, 1600-1868.
Edo-e kara shomotsu made. Tōkyō : Kyūzansha, 1997.
HQ792.J3 N54 1997 v.19

ILLUSTRIOUS PEOPLE. See **CELEBRITIES.**

'Imʿ chokʿ mangalā kyamʿ'".
'Oṅʿ Mranʿ, ʾAṅʿgyanʿnīyā Ūʿ. Mantale" : Krīʿ pvāʿʿ re" Cā ʿupʿ Tuikʿ, 2002.
BF1779.A88 O56 2002

I'm rich beyond my wildest dreams - "I am. I am. I am".
Pauley, Thomas L. New York : Berkley Books, 2003.
BF639 .P28 2003

Image & word.
Hochman, Judith. Image and word in Ahsen's image psychology. New York : Brandon House, c2000.
BF367 .H63 2000

Image and word in Ahsen's image psychology.
Hochman, Judith. New York : Brandon House, c2000.
BF367 .H63 2000

IMAGE, BODY. See **BODY IMAGE.**

The image of spiritual liberty in the western Sufi movement following Hazrat Inayat Khan.
Jironet, Karin. Leuven : Peeters, 2002.
BP189.2 .J57 2002

IMAGE (PHILOSOPHY).
Die Unvermeidlichkeit der Bilder. Tübingen : G. Narr, c2001.
N72.A56 U58 2001x

IMAGE PROCESSING - CONGRESSES.
International Workshop MLDM 2003 (2003 : Leipzig, Germany) Machine learning and data mining in pattern recognition. Berlin ; New York : Springer, c2003.
Q327 .I67 2003

IMAGE (THEOLOGY).
Gostev, A. A. (Andreĭ Andreevich) Obraznaia sfera cheloveka v poznanii i perezhivanii dukhovnykh smyslov. Moskva : In-t psikhologii RAN, 2001.
BF367 .G565 2001

IMAGERY, MENTAL. See **IMAGERY (PSYCHOLOGY).**

IMAGERY (PSYCHOLOGY). See also **ARCHETYPE (PSYCHOLOGY); BODY IMAGE; VISUALIZATION.**
Burnett, Ron, 1947- How images think. Cambridge, Mass. : MIT Press, 2004.
BF241 .B79 2004

Gostev, A. A. (Andreĭ Andreevich) Obraznaia sfera cheloveka v poznanii i perezhivanii dukhovnykh smyslov. Moskva : In-t psikhologii RAN, 2001.
BF367 .G565 2001

Hochman, Judith. Image and word in Ahsen's image psychology. New York : Brandon House, c2000.
BF367 .H63 2000

Wunenburger, Jean-Jacques. La vie des images. [Nouvelle édition augmentée]. Grenoble : Presses universitaires de Grenoble, 2002.
BF367 .W85 2002

IMAGERY (PSYCHOLOGY) - METHODOLOGY.
Edgar, Iain R. Guide to imagework. London ; New York : Routledge, 2004.
BF367 .E34 2004

IMAGERY (PSYCHOTHERAPY).
Braud, William. Distant mental influence. Charlottesville, VA : Hampton Roads Pub., c2003.
BF1045.S33 B74 2003

IMAGES, MENTAL. See **IMAGERY (PSYCHOLOGY).**

IMAGINAL COMMUNICATION. See **VISUAL COMMUNICATION.**

The imaginary.
Sartre, Jean Paul, 1905- [Imaginaire. English] London ; New York : Routledge, 2003.
BF408 .S263 2003

IMAGINARY ANIMALS. See **ANIMALS, MYTHICAL.**

IMAGINARY CONVERSATIONS.
Aller, Annelies van, 1946- Levenskunst van twee vrouwen. Budel : Damon, c2001.
PS3527.I865 Z536 2001

Becker, Monika. Familiar dialogues in Englyssh and Frenche. Trier : Wissenschaftlicher Verlag Trier, c2003.

Cumpeta, Silvio. I dialoghi dell'ego. Gorizia : Biblioteca statale isontina, c2001.

Derroudida, Jacques. Le repas du grand homme. Paris : Harmattan, 2002.

Walsch, Neale Donald. The new revelations. New York : Atria Books, c2002.
BF1999 .W2287 2002

Walsch, Neale Donald. Tomorrow's God. 1st ed. New York : Atria Books, 2004.
BF1999 .W2288 2004

IMAGINARY HISTORIES.
What ifs? of American history. New York : G.P. Putnam's, c2003.
E179 .W535 2003

IMAGINARY PLACES IN LITERATURE.
Les lieux de l'imaginaire. Montréal : Liber, 2002.

IMAGINARY WARS AND BATTLES. See **PROPHECIES.**

IMAGINATION. See also **CREATION (LITERARY, ARTISTIC, ETC.); FANTASY; IMAGERY (PSYCHOLOGY); VISUALIZATION.**
Adams, Michael Vannoy, 1947- The fantasy principle. New York : Brunner-Routledge, 2004.
BF173.J85 A33 2004

Aleksander, Igor. How to build a mind. New York : Columbia University Press, 2001.
Q335 .A44225 2001

Currie, Gregory. Recreative minds. Oxford : Clarendon Press ; New York : Oxford University Press, 2002.
BH301.I53 C87 2002

Imagination and its pathologies. Cambridge, Mass. : MIT Press, c2003.
BF408 .I455 2003

Itinéraires de l'imaginaire. Paris : L'Harmattan, c1999.
BF408 .I86 1999

Jensen, Anders Fogh. Metaforens magt. 1. opl. Århus : Modtryk, 2001.

Lambert, Ladina Bezzola. Imagining the unimaginable. Amsterdam ; New York, NY : Rodopi, 2002.
QB29 .L35 2002

Les lieux de l'imaginaire. Montréal : Liber, 2002.

Makeieff, Macha. Poétique du désastre. Arles : Actes sud, c2001.

McNiff, Shaun. Creating with others. 1st ed. Boston, Mass. : Shambhala Publications, 2003.
BF408 .M336 2003

Modell, Arnold H., 1924- Imagination and the meaningful brain. Cambridge, Mass. : MIT Press, c2003.
BF408 .M58 2003

Sartre, Jean Paul, 1905- [Imaginaire. English] The imaginary. London ; New York : Routledge, 2003.
BF408 .S263 2003

Starobinski, Jean. La relation critique. Ed. rev. et augm. [Paris] : Gallimard, c2001.
PN81 .S69 2001

Imagination and its pathologies / edited by James Phillips and James Morley. Cambridge, Mass. : MIT Press, c2003. viii, 276 p. : ill. ; 24 cm. Includes bibliographical references and index. CONTENTS: Imagination: looking in the right place (and in the right way) / Paul B. Lieberman -- Imagination and its pathologies: domain of the unreal or a fundamental dimension of human reality? / Edwin L. Hersch -- Narrative and the ethics of remembrance / Richard Kearney -- Imagination, fantasy, hallucination, and memory / Edward S. Casey -- The texture of the real: Merleau-Ponty on imagination and psychopathology / James Morley -- The creative role of fantasy in adaptation / Ethel Spector Person -- The Madonna imago: a new interpretation of its pathology / M.C. Dillon -- The impossibility of female mourning / Jennifer Hansen -- Depression, depth, and the imagination / Jennifer Church -- The unconscious as a hermeneutic myth: a defense of the imagination / J. Melvin Woody -- A phenomenological psychological approach to

research on hallucination / Amadeo Giorgi -- Narrative in play: the structure of the imagination in psychotherapy with young children / Robert S. Kruger -- On the dialectics of imagination: Nijinsky's sublime defeat / Pascal Sauvayre and Barbara Forbes -- Was St. Anthony crazy?: visionary experiences and the desert fathers / Greg Mahr. ISBN 0-262-16214-8 DDC 153.3
1. Imagination. 2. Mental illness. 3. Imagination (Philosophy) 4. Psychiatry - Philosophy. I. Phillips, James, 1938- II. Morley, James, 1957-
BF408 .I455 2003

Imagination and the meaningful brain.
Modell, Arnold H., 1924- Cambridge, Mass. : MIT Press, c2003.
BF408 .M58 2003

Imagination, Fiktion, Kreation : das kulturschaffende Vermögen der Phantasie / herausgegeben von Thomas Dewender und Thomas Welt. München : Saur, c2003. 407 p. : ill. ; 25 cm. ISBN 3-598-73010-1
1. Imagination (Philosophy) 2. Fantastic, The. 3. Fantasy literature - History and criticism. 4. Fantastic, The - Religious aspects. I. Dewender, Thomas. II. Welt, Thomas.
BH301.I53 I534 2003

IMAGINATION IN LITERATURE.
Les lieux de l'imaginaire. Montréal : Liber, 2002.

IMAGINATION (PHILOSOPHY).
Auffret, Séverine. Des blessures et des jeux. Arles : Actes sud, c2003.

Currie, Gregory. Recreative minds. Oxford : Clarendon Press ; New York : Oxford University Press, 2002.
BH301.I53 C87 2002

Fabiani, Paolo, 1968- La filosofia dell'immaginazione in Vico e Malebranche. Firenze : Firenze University Press, 2002.
B3583.F25 F55 2002

Fesmire, Steven, 1967- John Dewey and moral imagination. Bloomington, IN : Indiana University Press, c2003.
BJ1031 .F47 2003

Imagination and its pathologies. Cambridge, Mass. : MIT Press, c2003.
BF408 .I455 2003

Imagination, Fiktion, Kreation. München : Saur, c2003.
BH301.I53 I534 2003

Imagination, philosophy, and the arts. London ; New York : Routledge, 2003.
BH301.I53 I53 2003

Les lieux de l'imaginaire. Montréal : Liber, 2002.

Was kostet den Kopf? Marburg : Tectum Verlag, 2001.

Imagination, philosophy, and the arts / edited by Matthew Kieran and Dominic McIver Lopes. London ; New York : Routledge, 2003. x, 320 p. : 24 cm. Includes bibliographical references (p. 305-316) and index. ISBN 0-415-30516-0 DDC 111/.85
1. Imagination (Philosophy) 2. Arts - Philosophy. 3. Aesthetics. I. Kieran, Matthew, 1968- II. Lopes, Dominic.
BH301.I53 I53 2003

Imagine coexistence : restoring humanity after violent ethnic conflict / Antonia Chayes and Martha Minow, Editors. 1st ed. San Francisco : Jossey-Bass, c2003. xxiii, 350 p. ; 24 cm. Includes bibliographical references and index. CONTENTS: Constructing coexistence : a survey of coexistence projects in areas of ethnic conflict / Aneelah Afzali and Laura Colleton -- The process toward reconciliation / Carlos E. Sluzki -- On hidden ground : one coexistence strategy in Central Africa / Marc Sommers and Elizabeth McClintock -- Grand visions and small projects : coexistence efforts in southeastern Europe / Diana Chigas and Brian Ganson -- Imagine coexistence pilot projects in Rwanda and Bosnia / Cynthia Burns, Laura McGrew, and Ilija Todorovic -- Evaluating coexistence : insights and challenges / Eileen F. Babbitt -- Freedom's hidden price : framing the obstacles to economic coexistence / Sven M. Spengemann -- Bureaucratic obstacles to imagining coexistence / Antonia Chayes -- The culture of corruption in the postconflict and developing world / Glenn T. Ware and Gregory P. Noone -- Education for coexistence / Martha Minow -- Coexistence and repair / Elizabeth V. Spelman -- Religion as an aid and a hindrance to postconflict coexistence work / Marc Gopin -- Engaging with the arts to promote coexistence / Cynthia Cohen -- Fostering coexistence in identity-based conflicts : toward a narrative approach / Sara Cobb -- The art of the possible : parallelism as an approach to promoting coexistence / Lauren Elizabeth Guth. ISBN 0-7879-6577-4 (alk. paper) DDC 305.8
1. Ethnic conflict. 2. Political violence. 3. Conflict management. 4. International relations. 5. Peace. I. Chayes, Antonia Handler, 1929- II. Minow, Martha, 1954-
HM1121 .I42 2003

Imagine there's no woman.
Copjec, Joan. Cambridge, Mass. : MIT Press, 2002.
BJ1012 .C68 2002

Imagining the unimaginable.
Lambert, Ladina Bezzola. Amsterdam ; New York, NY : Rodopi, 2002.
QB29 .L35 2002

Imberman, Arlyn. Signature for success : how to analyze handwriting and improve your career, your relationships, and your life / Arlyn Imberman and June Rifkin. Kansas City, Mo. : Andrews McMeel Pub., 2003. p. cm. Includes bibliographical references. Publisher description URL: http://www.loc.gov/catdir/description/simon033/2003052152.html ISBN 0-7407-3842-9 DDC 155.2/82
1. Graphology. I. Rifkin, June. II. Title.
BF891 .I46 2003

Îmblâzirea fiarei din om sau ecosofia.
Maiorescu, Toma George, 1928- 3a ediţia revăzută şi completată. Bucureşti : Lumina Lex, 2002.

Imbrogno, Philip J. Celtic mysteries in New England / Philip J. Imbrogno & Marianne Horrigan. 1st ed. St. Paul, Minn. : Llewellyn Publications, 2000. 164 p., [6] p. of plates : ill. (some col.) ; 23 cm. Includes index. ISBN 1-56718-357-3 DDC 001.94
1. Druids and Druidism. 2. Human-alien encounters - New England. 3. Unidentified flying objects - Sightings and encounters - New England. 4. Megalithic monuments - New England. 5. Civilization, Celtic - Miscellanea. I. Horrigan, Marianne. II. Title.
BF2050 I435 2000

IMITATION - CONGRESSES.
Imitation in animals and artifacts. Cambridge, Mass. : MIT Press, c2002.
BF357 .I47 2002

Imitation in animals and artifacts / edited by Kerstin Dautenhahn and Chrystopher L. Nehaniv. Cambridge, Mass. : MIT Press, c2002. xv, 607 p. : ill. ; 26 cm. (Complex adaptive systems) "A Bradford book." Papers presented at a meeting held in Edinburgh, Scotland, Apr. 7-9, 1999. Includes bibliographical references and index. ISBN 0-262-04203-7 (alk. paper) DDC 591.5/14
1. Imitation - Congresses. 2. Learning in animals - Congresses. 3. Machine learning - Congresses. I. Nehaniv, Chrystopher L., 1963- II. Dautenhahn, Kerstin. III. Series.
BF357 .I47 2002

Immagini dell'uomo.
Quaglia, Rocco. Roma : Armando, c2000.

IMMEDIATE MEMORY. See **SHORT-TERM MEMORY.**

IMMERSION, BAPTISMAL. See **BAPTISM.**

IMMIGRANTS. See **ALIENS.**

IMMIGRANTS - FRANCE - ALSACE.
Amougou, Emmanuel. La construction de l'inconscient colonial en Alsace. Paris : L'Harmattan, 2002.
1. Black author.

IMMIGRANTS - LEGAL STATUS, LAWS, ETC.
See **EMIGRATION AND IMMIGRATION LAW.**

IMMIGRANTS - UNITED STATES.
McLaughlin, Bob. [USA immigration & orientation. Spanish] USA inmigración y orientación. 1a. ed. en español. Satellite Beach, Fla. : Wellesworth Pub., c2001.

IMMIGRATION. See **EMIGRATION AND IMMIGRATION.**

IMMIGRATION LAW. See **EMIGRATION AND IMMIGRATION LAW.**

Immoral balance.
Voldeck, Joseph F., 1967- Santa Fe, NM : Sunstone Press, 2003.
BF1999 .V63 2003

IMMORALITY.
I concetti del male. Torino : Einaudi, c2002.

Immortal remains.
Braude, Stephen E., 1945- Lanham, Md. ; Oxford : Rowman & Littlefield, c2003.
BF1311.F8 B73 2003

IMMORTALITY. See **FUTURE LIFE.**

IMMORTALITY (PHILOSOPHY).
Adams, J. Robert. Prospects for immortality. Amityville, N.Y. : Baywood Pub., c2003.
BD421 .A33 2003

IMMUNOLOGICAL DEFICIENCY SYNDROMES. See **AIDS (DISEASE).**

IMMUNOLOGY.
Napier, A. David. The age of immunology. Chicago : University of Chicago Press, 2003.
GN345 .N36 2003

Imobighe, Thomas A. The OAU (AU) and OAS in regional conflict management : a comparative assessment / T.A. Imobighe. Ibadan : Spectrum Books ; Oxford, UK : USA distributor, African Books Collective, 2003. xix, 192 p. ; 22 cm. Includes bibliographical references (p. 175-179) and index. ISBN 9780293744
1. African Union - Evaluation. 2. Organization of American States - Evaluation. 3. Conflict management - International cooperation - Case studies. 4. Intervention (International law) - Case studies. 5. Armed Forces - Operations other than war - Case studies. 6. Conflict management. I. Title.
JZ6374 .I46 2003

IMPACT OF COMETS ON EARTH. See **COMETS - COLLISIONS WITH EARTH.**

The impact on philosophy of semiotics.
Deely, John N. South Bend, Ind. : St. Augustine's Press, 2003.
B831.2 .D437 2003

Impact, studies in language and society
(15.) Boxer, Diana, 1948- Applying sociolinguistics. Amsterdam ; Philadelphia : J. Benjamins Pub., c2002.
P40 .B678 2002

Imperial ascent.
Bayers, Peter L., 1966- Boulder, Colo. : University Press of Colorado, c2003.
GV200.19.P78 B39 2003

IMPERIALISM. See **DECOLONIZATION.**

IMPERIALISM - HISTORY.
Antinomies of modernity. Durham : Duke University Press, 2003.
CB358 .A59 2003

Bessis, Sophie, 1947- [Occident et les autres. English] Western supremacy. London ; New York : Zed Books, 2003.
CB245 .B4613 2003

IMPERIALISM - HISTORY - 18TH CENTURY.
York, Neil Longley. Turning the world upside down. Westport, Conn. ; London : Praeger, 2003.
E210 .Y67 2003

IMPERIALISM IN LITERATURE.
Heng, Geraldine. Empire of magic. New York : Columbia University Press, c2003.
PR321 .H46 2003

Kaplan, Amy. The anarchy of empire in the making of U.S. culture. Cambridge, Mass. : Harvard University Press, 2002.
E661.7 .K37 2002

Remembering Africa. Portsmouth, NH : Heinemann, c2002.
DT14 .R46 2002

IMPERIALISM IN MOTION PICTURES.
Kaplan, Amy. The anarchy of empire in the making of U.S. culture. Cambridge, Mass. : Harvard University Press, 2002.
E661.7 .K37 2002

IMPERIALISM - PSYCHOLOGICAL ASPECTS.
Glendinning, Chellis. Off the map. Gabriola Island, BC : New Society Publishers, c2002.
HF1414 .G553 2002

Khanna, Ranjana, 1966- Dark continents. Durham, NC : Duke University Press, 2003.
BF175.4.S65 K43 2003

IMPERIALISM - SOCIAL ASPECTS - UNITED STATES - HISTORY.
Kaplan, Amy. The anarchy of empire in the making of U.S. culture. Cambridge, Mass. : Harvard University Press, 2002.
E661.7 .K37 2002

IMPERSONAL JUDGMENT. See **JUDGMENT (LOGIC).**

IMPERSONATION. See **FALSE PERSONATION.**

IMPERSONATION (LAW). See **FALSE PERSONATION.**

Implementing collaboration technologies in industry : case examples and lessons learned / Bjo rn Erik Munkvold (ed.). London ; New York : Springer,

c2003. xii, 308 p. : ill. ; 23 cm. (Computer supported cooperative work, 1431-1496) Includes bibliographical references and index. ISBN 1-85233-418-5 (alk. paper) DDC 658.4/038
1. Information technology - Management. 2. Communication in organizations. 3. Teams in the workplace. 4. Business networks. 5. Computer networks. I. Munkvold, Bjo rn Erik, 1962- II. Series.
HD30.2 .I38 2003

Implication distanciée (ID).
Germain-Thiant, Myriam. La relation à l'autre. Lyon : Chronique sociale, [2002]

IMPORT AND EXPORT CONTROLS. See **FOREIGN TRADE REGULATION.**

The importance of being understood.
Morton, Adam. London ; New York : Routledge, 2003.
BF637.C45 M65 2003

Important symbols in their Hebrew, pagan, and Christian forms.
Hall, Adelaide S. (Adelaide Susan), b. 1857. [Glossary of important symbols in their Hebrew, pagan, and Christian forms] Berwick, Me. : Ibis Press, 2003.
BF1623.S9 H35 2003

IMPOSTORS AND IMPOSTURE.
Nickell, Joe. The mystery chronicles. Lexington, Ky. : University Press of Kentucky, c2004.
BF1031 .N517 2004

IMPOVERISHED PEOPLE. See **POOR.**

IMPRECATION. See **BLESSING AND CURSING.**

IMPROMPTU THEATER. See **IMPROVISATION (ACTING).**

Improving your memory for dummies.
Arden, John Boghosian. New York : Wiley Pub., c2002.
BF385 .A47 2002

IMPROVISATION (ACTING).
Sawyer, R. Keith (Robert Keith) Improvised dialogues. Westport, Conn. : Ablex Pub., 2003.
P95.45 .S3 2003

Improvised dialogues.
Sawyer, R. Keith (Robert Keith) Westport, Conn. : Ablex Pub., 2003.
P95.45 .S3 2003

In bed with Procrustes.
Thompson, Patricia J. New York : P. Lang, c2003.
HQ1190 .T52 2002 bk. 2

In corridors of eternal time.
Kolb, Janice E. M. Nevada City, Calif. : Blue Dolphin Pub., 2003.
BF1997.K65 A3 2003b

In darkness and secrecy : the anthropology of assault sorcery and witchcraft in Amazonia / edited by Neil L. Whitehead and Robin Wright. Durham, NC : Duke University Press, 2004. p. cm. Includes bibliographical references and index. CONTENTS: The anthropology of assault sorcery and witchcraft / Neil L. Whitehead and Robin Wright -- The order of dark shamans among the Warao / Johannes Wilbert -- Dark shamans and the shamanic state : sorcery as political process in Guyana and the Venezuelan Amazon / Silvia Vidal and Neil L. Whitehead -- The wicked and the wise men : witches and prophets in the history of the Northwest Amazon / Robin Wright -- Sorcery beliefs, transmission of shamanic knowledge, and therapeutic practice among the Desana of the Upper Rio Negro Region, Brazil / Dominique Buchillet -- The glorious tyranny of silence and the resonance of shamanic breath / George Mentore -- A blend of blood and tobacco : shamans and jaguars among the Parakan of Eastern Amazonia / Carlos Fausto -- The wars within Xinguano witchcraft and the balance of power / Michael Heckenberger -- Siblings and sorcerers : the paradox of kinship among the Kulina / Don Pollock -- Being alone amid others : sorcery and morality amongst the Arara, Carib, Brazil / Nio Teixeira Pinto -- Sorcery and shamanism in Cashinahua discourse and praxis, Purus River, Brazil / Elsje Lagrou -- The enemy within : child sorcery, revolution, and the evils of modernization in Eastern Peru / Fernando Santos-Granero. ISBN 0-8223-3333-3 (cloth : alk. paper) ISBN 0-8223-3345-7 (pbk. : alk. paper) DDC 133.4/3/09811
1. Witchcraft - Amazon River Region. 2. Magic - Amazon River Region. I. Whitehead, Neil L. II. Wright, Robin, 1950-
BF1566 .I5 2004

In extenso (Larousse (Firm))
Sillamy, Norbert. Dictionnaire de psychologie. [Nouv. éd.]. Paris : Larousse, 2003.
BF31 .S5 2003

In God's time.
Hill, Craig C., 1957- Grand Rapids, Mich. : W.B. Eerdmans, c2002.
BT903 .H55 2002

In gods we trust.
Atran, Scott, 1952- Oxford ; New York : Oxford University Press, 2002.
BL53 .A88 2002

In my mother's kitchen.
Edgar, Robin A. 2nd ed. Charlotte, N.C. : Tree House Enterprises, 2003.
BF378.R44 E34 2003

In nome della strada.
Ilardi, Massimo. Roma : Meltemi, c2002.

In Porphyrium.
Ammonius, Hermiae. Commentaria in quinque voces Porphyrii. Stuttgart : Frommann-Holzboog, 2002.

In search of the immortals.
Reid, Howard. London : Headline, 1999.

IN-SERVICE TRAINING. See **EMPLOYEES - TRAINING OF.**

In sight
The feminism and visual culture reader. London ; New York : Routledge, 2003.
HQ1121 .F46 2003

In the company of women.
Heim, Pat. New York : J.P. Tarcher/Putnam, c2001.
HD6053 .H387 2001

In the grip of disease.
Lloyd, G. E. R. (Geoffrey Ernest Richard), 1933- Oxford ; New York : Oxford University Press, 2003.
B187.M4 L56 2003

In the kingdom of living nature.
Douno, Beinsa, 1864-1944. Sofia : Bialo Bratstvo, c2000.

In the presence of aliens.
Bergmark, Janet, 1955- 1st ed. St. Paul, Minn. : Llewellyn Publications, 1997.
BF2050 .B47 1997

In the shadow of memory.
Skloot, Floyd. Lincoln : University of Nebraska Press, c2003.
PS3569.K577 Z47 2003

In the wake of 9/11.
Pyszczynski, Thomas A. Washington, DC : American Psychological Association, c2003.
HV6432 .P97 2003

Inaugural lecture series (Obafemi Awolowo University)
(159). Adediran, A. A. The problem with the past. Ile-Ife, Nigeria : Obafemi Awolowo University Press, c2002.

Inayat Khan, 1882-1927. Rassa shastra : Inayat Khan on the mysteries of love, sex, and marriage / Hazrat Inaya Khan. Berwick, ME : Ibis Press : York Beach, ME : distributed to the trade by Red Wheel/Weiser, 2003. p. cm. Previous edition published in 1938 under title: Rassa shastra : the science of life's creative forces. ISBN 0-89254-071-0 (paper : alk. paper) DDC 297.4/4
1. Sex (Psychology) 2. Love. 3. Marriage. I. Title. II. Title: Inayat Khan on the mysteries of love, sex, and marriage
BF692 .I5 2003

INAYAT KHAN, 1882-1927.
Jironet, Karin. The image of spiritual liberty in the western Sufi movement following Hazrat Inayat Khan. Leuven : Peeters, 2002.
BP189.2 .J57 2002

Inayat Khan on the mysteries of love, sex, and marriage.
Inayat Khan, 1882-1927. Rassa shastra. Berwick, ME : Ibis Press : York Beach, ME : distributed to the trade by Red Wheel/Weiser, 2003.
BF692 .I5 2003

INCA INDIANS. See **INCAS.**

L'incandescent.
Serres, Michel. [Paris] : Pommier, c2003.

INCANTATIONS. See also **BLESSING AND CURSING.**
Knight, Sirona, 1955- Dream magic. 1st ed. San Francisco : HarperSanFrancisco, c2000.
BF1621 .K65 2000

Sophia, 1955- The little book of hot love spells. Kansas City, Mo. : Andrews McMeel Pub., c2002.

BF1623.L6 S66 2002

INCANTATIONS, EGYPTIAN.
[Book of the dead. English.] The Egyptian book of the dead. London : Cassell, 2001.
PJ1555.E5 B83 2001

Dee, Jonathan. Isis. New York : Sterling Pub., [2003?]
BF1591 .D44 2003

Eyre, Christopher. The cannibal hymn. Liverpool : Liverpool University Press, 2002.

The incarnate subject.
Merleau-Ponty, Maurice, 1908-1961. [Union de l'âme et du corps chez Malebranche, Biran et Bergson. English] Amherst, N.Y. : Humanity Books, 2001.
B2430.M379 U513 2001

INCAS - RELIGION - MISCELLANEA.
Polich, Judith Bluestone, 1948- Return of the children of light. Santa Fe, N.M. : Linkage Publications, c1999.
BF1812.P4 P65 1999

Incense.
Neal, Carl F., 1965- 1st ed. St. Paul, Minn. : Llewellyn Publications, 2003.
BF1623.I52 N43 2003

INCENSE - MISCELLANEA.
Neal, Carl F., 1965- Incense. 1st ed. St. Paul, Minn. : Llewellyn Publications, 2003.
BF1623.I52 N43 2003

INCENTIVE (PSYCHOLOGY). See **REINFORCEMENT (PSYCHOLOGY).**

INCENTIVES IN INDUSTRY.
Cloke, Ken, 1941- The art of waking people up. 1st ed. San Francisco : Jossey-Bass, c2003.
HF5385 .C54 2003

INCENTIVES IN INDUSTRY - UNITED STATES.
Fisher, Peter S. Industrial incentives. Kalamazoo, Mich. : W.E. Upjohn Institute for Employment Research, 1998.
HF5549.5.I5 F57 1998

Incitations.
Froment Meurice, Marc. Paris : Galilée, c2002.

Inclusive design : design for the whole population / edited by John Clarkson ... [et al.]. London ; New York : Springer, c2003. 608 p. : ill. ; 25 cm. Includes bibliographical references and index. ISBN 1-85233-700-1 (pbk. : alk. paper) DDC 620/.0042
1. Engineering design. 2. People with disabilities. 3. Barrier-free design. 4. Universal design. 5. Architecture - Philosophy. I. Clarkson, John, 1961-
TA174 .I464 2003

INCOME.
Allen, Robert G. Multiple streams of internet income. New York : Wiley, c2001.
HF5548.32 .A45 2001

INCOME DISTRIBUTION.
Gender, development and money. Oxford : Oxfam, 2001.

Monkeywrenching the new world order [sound recording]. Oakland, Calif : AK Press ; San Francisco, CA : Alternative Tentacles Records, 2001.

The incomplete projects.
Freedman, Carl Howard. Middletown, Conn. : Wesleyan University Press, c2002.
HX523 .F74 2002

L'inconscient à ciel ouvert de la psychose.
Soler, Colette. Toulouse : Presses universitaires du Mirail, c2002.

L'inconscio antinomico : sviluppi e prospettive dell'opera di Matte Blanco / a cura di Pietro Bria e Fiorangela Oneroso. Milano : F. Angeli, c1999. 319 p. : ill. ; 22 cm. (Psicoanalisi contemporanea. 4, Studi interdisciplinari ; 1) Includes bibliographical references. ISBN 88-464-1495-0 DDC 150
1. Subconsciousness - Congresses. 2. Matte Blanco, Ignacio. I. Bria, Pietro. II. Oneroso Di Lisa, Fiorangela. III. Series: Psicoanalisi contemporanea. Sez. 4, Studi interdisciplinari ; 1.
BF315 .I56 1999

L'incubo globale : prospettive junghiane a proposito dell'11 settembre / a cura di Luigi Zoja ; [scritti di] James Hillman ... [et al.] ; traduzioni di Luciano Perez. Bergamo : Moretti & Vitali, c2002. 221 p. ; 21 cm. (Il tridente. Saggi ; 23) Includes bibliographical references. ISBN 88-7186-213-9 DDC 150
1. East and West - Psychological aspects. 2. Terrorism - Psychological aspects. 3. War on Terrorism, 2001- 4. Jungian psychology. 5. September 11 Terrorist Attacks, 2001. I. Hillman, James. II. Zoja, Luigi. III. Series.

Inculturation (Christian theology)

INCULTURATION (CHRISTIAN THEOLOGY). *See* **CHRISTIANITY AND CULTURE.**

Independence, additivity, uncertainty.
Vind, Karl. Berlin ; New York : Springer, c2003.
HB135 .V56 2003

INDEPENDENCE (PSYCHOLOGY). *See* **AUTONOMY (PSYCHOLOGY).**

Indeterminacy and society.
Hardin, Russell, 1940- Princeton, N.J. : Princeton University Press, c2003.
HM1111 .H37 2003

INDEXICALITY (SEMANTICS). *See* **INDEXICALS (SEMANTICS).**

INDEXICALS (SEMANTICS).
Indexikalität und sprachlicher Weltbezug. Paderborn : Mentis, c2002.

Indexikalität und sprachlicher Weltbezug / Matthias Kettner, Helmut Pape (Hrsg.). Paderborn : Mentis, c2002. 284 p. ill. ; 24 cm. Includes bibliographical references (p. [271]-280). ISBN 3-89785-149-0 (pbk.)
1. Reference (Linguistics) 2. Indexicals (Semantics) 3. Reference (Philosophy) I. Kettner, Matthias, 1955- II. Pape, Helmut.

La (indi)gestión cultural : una cartografía de los procesos culturales contemporáneos / Mónica Lacarrieu, Marcelo Alvarez, compiladores ; George Yúdice ... [et al.]. 1. ed. Bs. As., Argentina : Ediciones Ciccus-La Crujía, 2002. 247 p. ; 23 cm. (Colección Signo) Includes bibliographical references. ISBN 9871004087
1. Popular culture. I. Lacarrieu, Mónica B. II. Alvarez, Marcelo. III. Yúdice, George. IV. Title: Indigestión cultural V. Series: Colección Signo (Buenos Aires, Argentina)
HM621 .I535 2002

India. Commission for Scientific and Technical Terminology.
Bhāratīya darśana paribhāshā kośa = Naī Dillī : Vaijñānika tathā Takanīkī Śabdāvalī Āyoga, Mānava Saṃsādhana Vikāsa Mantrālaya, Śikshā Vibhāga, Bhārata Sarakāra, 1999-
B131 .B498 1999

INDIA - HISTORY - BRITISH OCCUPATION, 1765-1947.
Moxham, Roy. The great hedge of India. Large print ed. Oxford : ISIS, 2001.

INDIA - RELIGION.
Glener, Doug. Wisdom's blossoms. Boston, Mass. : Shambhala, 2002.
BL2003 .G64 2002

INDIA - RELIGION - DICTIONARIES.
Rengarajan, T., 1962- Dictionary on Indian religions. Delhi : Eastern Book Linkers, 2003.
BL2001.2 .R46 2003

Saṅkhyāparaka śabda kośa. 1. saṃskaraṇa. Ilāhābāda : Sāhitya Bhavana, 2002.
BF1623.P9+

India. Small Scale Industries.
Millennium projects. 1st ed. New Delhi : Small Scale Industries, Ministry of Small Scale Industries, Agro & Rural Industries, Govt. of India, 2000-
HD2346.I5 M45 2000

Indian Institute of Language Studies.
Perspectives in linguistics. New Delhi : Indian Institute of Language Studies : Distributed by Creative Books, 2003.

The Indian luck book.
Bharadwaj, Monisha. London : Kyle Cathie, 2001.
BF1778 .B43 2001

Indian philosophers and postmodern thinkers.
Olson, Carl. New Delhi : New York : Oxford University Press, 2002.
B131 .O57 2002

Indian philosophy of knowledge.
Shastri, L. C., 1933- 1st ed. Delhi, India : Global Vision Pub. House, 2002.
B132.K6 S48 2002

INDIAN PHILOSOPHY - UNITED STATES.
Wernitznig, Dagmar. Going native or going naive? Lanham, MD : University Press of America, c2003.
E98.P99 W47 2003

INDIAN POTTERY - PERU.
Statnekov, Daniel K., 1943- Animated earth. 2nd ed. Berkeley Calif. : North Atlantic Books, 2003.
BF1999 .S719 2003

INDIAN SUB-CONTINENT. *See* **SOUTH ASIA.**

BIBLIOGRAPHIC GUIDE

INDIAN WOMEN - NORTH AMERICA - SOCIAL CONDITIONS.
Many faces of gender. Boulder : University Press of Colorado ; Calgary, Alta., Canada : University of Calgary Press, c2002.
E98.P95 M35 2002

Indiana series in the philosophy of religion
Religious experience and the end of metaphysics. Bloomington, Ind. : Indiana University Press, c2003.
BL53 .R444 2003

Transcendence in philosophy and religion. Bloomington, IN : Indiana University Press, c2003.
B56 .T73 2003

INDIANS - CIVILIZATION. *See* **INDIANS.**

INDIANS - HISTORY.
The 1000s. San Diego, Calif. : Greenhaven Press, c2001.
CB354.3 .A16 2001

INDIANS IN POPULAR CULTURE.
Wernitznig, Dagmar. Going native or going naive? Lanham, MD : University Press of America, c2003.
E98.P99 W47 2003

INDIANS - KINGS AND RULERS. *See* **CACIQUES (INDIAN LEADERS).**

INDIANS OF CENTRAL AMERICA. *See* **MAYAS.**

INDIANS OF MEXICO. *See* **AZTECS; MAYAS.**

INDIANS OF NORTH AMERICA - CULTURE. *See* **INDIANS OF NORTH AMERICA.**

INDIANS OF NORTH AMERICA - ETHNOLOGY. *See* **INDIANS OF NORTH AMERICA.**

INDIANS OF NORTH AMERICA - FIRST CONTACT WITH EUROPEANS - VIRGINIA - JAMESTOWN.
Price, David, 1961- Love and hate in Jamestown. 1st ed. New York : Alfred A. Knopf : Distributed by Random House, 2003.
F234.J3 P68 2003

INDIANS OF NORTH AMERICA - FIRST CONTACT WITH OCCIDENTAL CIVILIZATION. *See* **INDIANS OF NORTH AMERICA - FIRST CONTACT WITH EUROPEANS.**

INDIANS OF NORTH AMERICA - GOVERNMENT RELATIONS.
Gutfeld, Arnon. American exceptionalism. Brighton [England] ; Portland, Or. : Sussex Academic Press, 2002.
E169.1 .G956 2002

INDIANS OF NORTH AMERICA - HISTORY - COLONIAL PERIOD, CA. 1600-1775.
Gallivan, Martin D., 1968- James River chiefdoms. Lincoln : University of Nebraska Press, c2003.
E99.P85 G35 2003

INDIANS OF NORTH AMERICA - PSYCHOLOGY.
Many faces of gender. Boulder : University Press of Colorado ; Calgary, Alta., Canada : University of Calgary Press, c2002.
E98.P95 M35 2002

INDIANS OF NORTH AMERICA - PUBLIC OPINION.
Wernitznig, Dagmar. Going native or going naive? Lanham, MD : University Press of America, c2003.
E98.P99 W47 2003

INDIANS OF NORTH AMERICA - SEXUAL BEHAVIOR.
Many faces of gender. Boulder : University Press of Colorado ; Calgary, Alta., Canada : University of Calgary Press, c2002.
E98.P95 M35 2002

INDIANS OF NORTH AMERICA - SOCIAL CONDITIONS.
Corlett, J. Angelo, 1958- Race, racism, & reparations. Ithaca : Cornell University Press, c2003.
HT1523 .C67 2003

INDIANS OF NORTH AMERICA - SOUTHERN STATES. *See* **CHOCTAW INDIANS.**

INDIANS OF NORTH AMERICA - UNITED STATES. *See* **INDIANS OF NORTH AMERICA.**

INDIANS OF NORTH AMERICA - VIRGINIA. *See* **POWHATAN INDIANS.**

INDIANS OF NORTH AMERICA - WOMEN. *See* **INDIAN WOMEN - NORTH AMERICA.**

INDIANS OF SOUTH AMERICA - ANDES REGION. *See* **INCAS.**

INDIANS OF THE UNITED STATES. *See* **INDIANS OF NORTH AMERICA.**

INDIANS - PHILOSOPHY. *See* **INDIAN PHILOSOPHY.**

INDIANS - POTTERY. *See* **INDIAN POTTERY.**

INDIANS, TREATMENT OF.
Gutfeld, Arnon. American exceptionalism. Brighton [England] ; Portland, Or. : Sussex Academic Press, 2002.
E169.1 .G956 2002

INDIC LITERATURE. *See* **TAMIL LITERATURE; TIBETAN LITERATURE.**

INDICES (SEMANTICS). *See* **INDEXICALS (SEMANTICS).**

INDIFFERENCE, RELIGIOUS. *See* **INDIFFERENTISM (RELIGION).**

INDIFFERENTISM (RELIGION).
Eidelberg, Paul. Clash of two decadent civilizations. Shaarei Tikva, Israel : ACPR Publications, 2002.
BM537 .E53 2002

INDIGENIZATION (CHRISTIAN THEOLOGY). *See* **CHRISTIANITY AND CULTURE.**

INDIGENOUS CLERGY. *See* **CLERGY.**

INDIGENOUS MEDICINE. *See* **TRADITIONAL MEDICINE.**

INDIGENOUS PEOPLES.
Howard, Bradley Reed. Indigenous peoples and the state. DeKalb : Northern Illinois University Press, c2003.
GN380 .H68 2003

Indigenous peoples and the state.
Howard, Bradley Reed. DeKalb : Northern Illinois University Press, c2003.
GN380 .H68 2003

INDIGENOUS PEOPLES - GOVERNMENT RELATIONS. *See* **INDIGENOUS PEOPLES.**

INDIGENOUS PEOPLES - LEGAL STATUS, LAWS, ETC.
Brown, Michael F. (Michael Fobes), 1950- Who owns native culture? Cambridge, Mass. : Harvard University Press, 2003.
K1401 .B79 2003

INDIGENOUS PEOPLES - PSYCHOLOGY. *See* **ETHNOPSYCHOLOGY.**

INDIGENOUS POPULATIONS. *See* **INDIGENOUS PEOPLES.**

INDIGENOUS WOMEN.
Working with the stories of women's lives. Adelaide : Dulwich Centre Publications, 2001.
HQ1185 .W68 2001

Indigestión cultural.
La (indi)gestión cultural. 1. ed. Bs. As., Argentina : Ediciones Ciccus-La Crujía, 2002.
HM621 .I535 2002

INDIGNATION. *See* **ANGER.**

Individual differences.
Cooper, Colin, 1954- 2nd ed. London : Arnold ; New York : Co-published in the U.S. of America by Oxford University Press, 2002.
BF697 .C59 2002

INDIVIDUAL DIFFERENCES.
Cooper, Colin, 1954- Individual differences. 2nd ed. London : Arnold ; New York : Co-published in the U.S. of America by Oxford University Press, 2002.
BF697 .C59 2002

INDIVIDUAL DIFFERENCES IN ADOLESCENCE - LONGITUDINAL STUDIES.
Nature, nurture, and the transition to early adolescence. Oxford ; New York : Oxford University Press, 2003.
BF341 .N387 2003

INDIVIDUAL DIFFERENCES IN CHILDREN.
Individual differences in theory of mind. New York : Psychology Press, 2003.
BF723.P48 I53 2003

Individual differences in theory of mind : implications for typical and atypical development / edited by Betty Repacholi and Virginia Slaughter. New York : Psychology Press, 2003. p. cm. (Macquarie monographs in cognitive science) Includes bibliographical references and index. ISBN 1-84169-093-7 DDC 155.4/13

1. Philosophy of mind in children. 2. Individual differences in children. I. Repacholi, Betty. II. Slaughter, Virginia. III. Series.
BF723.P48 I53 2003

INDIVIDUALISM.
Baritono, Raffaella. La democrazia vissuta. Torino : La Rosa, c2001.

Búfalo, Enzo del. Individuo, mercado y utopía. 1. ed. Caracas : Monte Ávila Editores Lationoamericana : Universidad Central de Venezuela, Centro de Investigaciones Post-Doctorales FACES, 1998.
BD222 .B86 1998

Eberlein, Undine. Einzigartigkeit. Frankfurt ; New York : Campus, c2000.
BF697 .E463 2000

The many faces of individualism. Leuven, Belgium ; Sterling, Va. : Peeters, 2001.
B824 .M354 2001

Rapport, Nigel, 1956- I am dynamite. London ; New York : Routledge, 2003.

Souchon, Gisèle. Nietzsche. Paris : Harmattan, c2003.

Tucci, Antonio. Individualità e politica. Napoli : Edizioni scientifiche italiane, 2002.

Venne, Jean-François, 1972- Le lien social dans le modèle de l'individualisme privé. Paris : L'Harmattan, c2002.

INDIVIDUALISM - CASE STUDIES.
Rapport, Nigel, 1956- I am dynamite. London ; New York : Routledge, 2003.

Individualità e politica.
Tucci, Antonio. Napoli : Edizioni scientifiche italiane, 2002.

Individualitätskonzepte in der russischen Kultur /
Christa Ebert (Hrsg.). Berlin : Berlin Verlag Arno Spitz, c2002. 243 p. ; 23 cm. Includes bibliographical references. ISBN 3-8305-0111-0 (pbk.)
1. Russian literature - History and criticism. 2. Individuality in literature. 3. Self in literature. 4. National characteristics, Russian. I. Ebert, Christa, 1947-
PG2987.I48 .I53 2002

INDIVIDUALITY. See also **CONFORMITY; PERSONALITY; SELF.**
Ageev, Valentin. Vvedenie v psikhologiiu chelovecheskoĭ unikal'nosti. Tomsk : Izd-vo "Peleng", 2002.
BF697 .A353 2002

Boncinelli, Edoardo. Io sono, tu sei. 1. ed. Milano : Mondadori, 2002.

Budgeon, Shelley, 1967- Choosing a self. Westport, Conn. : Praeger, 2003.
HQ1229 .B83 2003

Chelovek kak sub"ekt kul'tury. Moskva : Nauka, 2002.

Danzig, Robert J., 1932- There is only one you. Washington, D.C. : Child and Family Press, c2003.
BF723.I56 D36 2003

Eberlein, Undine. Einzigartigkeit. Frankfurt ; New York : Campus, c2000.
BF697 .E463 2000

Goals and life lessons support materials [electronic resource]. Greenwood Village, CO : FasTracKids International, [1998]
BF637.S4

Markell, Patchen, 1969- Bound by recognition. Princeton, N.J. : Princeton University Press, c2003.
JC575 .M37 2003

Vi͡atkina, G. V. Razvitie individual'nosti lichnosti v sovremennykh uslovii͡akh. Moskva : In-t molodezhi, 1997.
BF697 .V52 1997

Whyte, William Hollingsworth. The organization man. Philadelphia : University of Pennsylvania Press, c2002, 1956.
BF697 .W47 2002

INDIVIDUALITY IN CHILDREN - JUVENILE LITERATURE.
Danzig, Robert J., 1932- There is only one you. Washington, D.C. : Child and Family Press, c2003.
BF723.I56 D36 2003

INDIVIDUALITY IN LITERATURE.
Individualitätskonzepte in der russischen Kultur. Berlin : Berlin Verlag Arno Spitz, c2002.
PG2987.I48 .I53 2002

INDIVIDUALS (PHILOSOPHY). See **INDIVIDUATION (PHILOSOPHY).**

INDIVIDUATION. See **INDIVIDUATION (PHILOSOPHY).**

INDIVIDUATION (PHILOSOPHY).
The many faces of individualism. Leuven, Belgium ; Sterling, Va. : Peeters, 2001.
B824 .M354 2001

INDIVIDUATION (PSYCHOLOGY).
Grubbs, Geri A., 1943- Bereavement dreaming and the individuating soul. Berwick, Me. : Nicolas-Hays, 2004.
BF1099.D4 G78 2004

Hollis, James, 1940- On this journey we call our life. Toronto, Ont. : Inner City Books, c2003.
BF697.5.S43 H65 2003

Hollis, James, 1940- On this journey we call our life. Toronto : Inner City Books, c2003.

Miller, Jeffrey C., 1951- The transcendent function. Albany : State University of New York Press, c2003.
BF175.5.I53 M55 2003

Zlatanović, Ljubiša, 1958- Jung, jastvo i individuacija. 1. izd. Niš : Studenski informativno-izdavački centar Niš, 2001.
BF109.J8 Z53 2001

Individuo, mercado y utopía.
Búfalo, Enzo del. 1. ed. Caracas : Monte Ávila Editores Lationoamericana : Universidad Central de Venezuela, Centro de Investigaciones Post-Doctorales FACES, 1998.
BD222 .B86 1998

INDO-ARYAN LANGUAGES. See **SANSKRIT LANGUAGE.**

INDO-EUROPEANS. See **CELTS; SLAVS.**

INDOCTRINATION, FORCED. See **BRAINWASHING.**

INDOLOGY - DICTIONARIES.
Saṅkhyāparaka śabda kośa. 1. saṃskaraṇa. Ilāhābāda : Sāhitya Bhavana, 2002.
BF1623.P9+

INDONESIA - FOREIGN RELATIONS - UNITED STATES.
Kivimäki, Timo. US-Indonesian hegemonic bargaining. Aldershot ; Burlington, VT : Ashgate, 2003.

INDUCTION (LOGIC).
Artman, Lavee. ha-Nisayon ha-yomyomi u-fitron heseḵe tenai ya-hakhalah lo-teḵefim. [Israel : ḥ. mo. l., 1999?]

Faith in the age of uncertainty. New Delhi : Published by Indialog Publications in association with the India International Centre, 2002.
BL626.3+

INDUCTIVE LOGIC. See **INDUCTION (LOGIC).**

Inductive synthesis of functional programs.
Schmid, U. (Ute) Berlin ; New York : Springer, c2003.
QA76.6 .S3855 2003

INDUSTRIAL ADMINISTRATION. See **INDUSTRIAL MANAGEMENT.**

INDUSTRIAL ARTS. See **AGRICULTURE; ENGINEERING; TECHNOLOGY.**

INDUSTRIAL CONCENTRATION. See also **COMPETITION; CONSOLIDATION AND MERGER OF CORPORATIONS.**
King, John L. Concentration and technology in agricultural input industries [electronic resource]. [Washington, D.C.] : U.S. Dept of Agriculture, [2001].

INDUSTRIAL DESIGN. See **DESIGN, INDUSTRIAL.**

INDUSTRIAL DEVELOPMENT PROJECTS. See **INDUSTRIAL PROMOTION.**

INDUSTRIAL ENGINEERING. See also **HUMAN ENGINEERING; PSYCHOLOGY, INDUSTRIAL; QUALITY CONTROL.**
Process management. Springer-verlag, Berlin, Heidelberg ; New York : Springer, c2003.
HD31 .P756 2003

Industrial incentives.
Fisher, Peter S. Kalamazoo, Mich. : W.E. Upjohn Institute for Employment Research, 1998.
HF5549.5.I5 F57 1998

INDUSTRIAL MANAGEMENT. See also **BUSINESS; MARKETING.**
Best practice. Cambridge, MA : Perseus Publishing, c2003.

Brunsson, Nils, 1946- The organization of hypocrisy. 2nd ed. Oslo : Abstrakt ; Malmö, Sweden : Liber ; Herndon, VA : [Distributor] Copenhagen Business School Press, c2002.

Carey, Dennis. How to run a company. 1st ed. New York : Crown Business, c2003.
HD38.2 .C374 2003

Christensen, Clayton M. The innovator's solution. Boston, Mass. : Harvard Business School Press, c2003.

Cohen, Allan R. The portable MBA in management. 2nd ed. New York : J. Wiley, c2002.
HD31 .C586 2002

Feigenbaum, A. V. (Armand Vallin) The power of management capital. New York ; Toronto : McGraw-Hill, c2003.
HD31 .F45 2003

Kennedy, Kevin (Kevin John), 1955- Going the distance. Upper Saddle River, NJ : Prentice Hall/Financial Times, c2003.
HD57.7 .K465 2003

Krames, Jeffrey A. The Jack Welch lexicon of leadership. 1st ed. New York : McGraw-Hill, 2001, c2002.
HD57.7 .K726 2001

Making time. Oxford ; New York : Oxford University Press, 2002.
HD69.T54 M34 2002

McAfee, R. Preston. Competitive solutions. Princeton, N.J. : Princeton University Press, c2002.
HD30.28 .M3815 2002

Process management. Springer-verlag, Berlin, Heidelberg ; New York : Springer, c2003.
HD31 .P756 2003

INDUSTRIAL MANAGEMENT - CASE STUDIES.
Barker, Alan, 1956- The alchemy of innovation. London : Spiro Press, 2002.

INDUSTRIAL MANAGEMENT - COMMUNICATION SYSTEMS.
Burke, Dan, 1965- Business @ the speed of stupid. Cambridge, MA : Perseus Pub., c2001.
HD45 .B7995 2001

INDUSTRIAL MANAGEMENT - MORAL AND ETHICAL ASPECTS.
Galford, Robert M., 1952- The trusted leader. New York ; London : Free Press, c2002.
HD57.7 .G33 2002

Garten, Jeffrey E., 1946- The politics of fortune. Boston : Harvard Business School Press, c2002.
HD57.7 .G377 2002

INDUSTRIAL ORGANIZATION. See **INDUSTRIAL MANAGEMENT.**

INDUSTRIAL PRODUCTION. See **INDUSTRIES.**

INDUSTRIAL PROMOTION - UNITED STATES.
Fisher, Peter S. Industrial incentives. Kalamazoo, Mich. : W.E. Upjohn Institute for Employment Research, 1998.
HF5549.5.I5 F57 1998

INDUSTRIAL PSYCHOLOGISTS. See **PSYCHOLOGY, INDUSTRIAL.**

INDUSTRIAL PSYCHOLOGY. See **PSYCHOLOGY, INDUSTRIAL.**

INDUSTRIAL PUBLICITY. See **ADVERTISING.**

INDUSTRIAL RELATIONS. See also **EMPLOYEES; MANAGEMENT.**
The new workplace. Chichester, UK ; Hoboken, NJ : Wiley, c2003.
HD6955 .N495 2003

Nooteboom, B. Trust. Cheltenham, UK ; Northampton, MA : E. Elgar Pub., c2002.
HD2758.5 .N66 2002

INDUSTRIALIZATION. See **DEVELOPING COUNTRIES.**

INDUSTRIES. See **PRISON INDUSTRIES.**

INDUSTRIES - SECURITY MEASURES.
Garten, Jeffrey E., 1946- The politics of fortune. Boston : Harvard Business School Press, c2002.
HD57.7 .G377 2002

INDUSTRIES - SIZE. *See* **SMALL BUSINESS.**

INDUSTRY. *See* **INDUSTRIES.**

INDUSTRY (PSYCHOLOGY). *See* **WORK.**

INEBRIATES. *See* **ALCOHOLICS.**

Inédits et commentaires / Serge Valletti ... [et al.].
Paris : L'Arche, 2002. 413 p. : ill. ; 21 cm. (LEXI/textes ; 6) ISBN 2-85181-521-0 DDC 809
1. Drama criticism. 2. Drama - History and criticism. I. Valletti, Serge. II. Théâtre National de la Colline.

INEFFICIENCY, INTELLECTUAL. *See* **STUPIDITY.**

INFANCY. *See* **INFANTS.**

INFANT AND MOTHER. *See* **MOTHER AND INFANT.**

INFANT DEVELOPMENT. *See* **INFANTS - DEVELOPMENT.**

INFANT PSYCHOLOGY. *See also* **EMOTIONS IN INFANTS.**
Mijolla-Mellor, Sophie de. Le besoin de savoir. Paris : Dunod, c2002.
BF723.S4 M556 2002

INFANT PSYCHOLOGY - JUVENILE SOFTWARE.
Disney's Mickey Mouse toddler [electronic resource]. Burbank, CA : Disney Interactive, c2000.
BF719

Infantino, Lorenzo, 1948-
[Ignoranza e libertà. English]
Ignorance and liberty / Lorenzo Infantino. London ; New York : Routledge, 2003. viii, 210 p. ; 25 cm. (Routledge studies in social and political thought ; 37) Includes bibliographical references (p. [193]-205) and index. ISBN 0-415-28573-9 (alk. paper) DDC 323.44
1. Liberalism. 2. Liberty. 3. Civil society. I. Title. II. Series.
HB95 .I4913 2003

INFANTS - DEATH - PSYCHOLOGICAL ASPECTS.
Kuebelbeck, Amy, 1964- Waiting with Gabriel. Chicago, Ill. : Loyola Press, c2003.
BF575.G7 K83 2003

INFANTS - DEVELOPMENT. *See also* **INFANT PSYCHOLOGY.**
Zigler, Edward, 1930- The first three years & beyond. New Haven : Yale University Press, c2002.
HQ767.9 .Z543 2002

INFANTS - DEVELOPMENT - JUVENILE SOFTWARE.
Disney's Mickey Mouse toddler [electronic resource]. Burbank, CA : Disney Interactive, c2000.
BF719

INFANTS (NEWBORN) - DEATH - PSYCHOLOGICAL ASPECTS.
Kuebelbeck, Amy, 1964- Waiting with Gabriel. Chicago, Ill. : Loyola Press, c2003.
BF575.G7 K83 2003

INFANTS (NEWBORN) - HISTORY.
Mörgeli, Christoph. "Über dem Grabe geboren". Bern : Benteli, 2002.

INFANTS - PSYCHOLOGY. *See* **INFANT PSYCHOLOGY.**

The infinite organization.
Broom, Michael F. 1st ed. Palo Alto, Calif. : Davies-Black, c2002.
HD58.7 .B755 2002

INFIRMARIES. *See* **HOSPITALS.**

Influence of Hermes Trismegistus.
Magia, alchimia, scienza dal '400 al '700. Firenze : Centro Di, 2002.
BF1598.H6 M34 2002

INFLUENCE (PSYCHOLOGY). *See also* **CONFORMITY; IMITATION; PERSUASION (PSYCHOLOGY); SOCIAL INFLUENCE.**
Gardner, Howard. Changing minds. Boston, Mass. : Harvard Business School Press, 2004.
BF637.C4 G37 2004

Perspectives on persuasion, social influence, and compliance gaining. Boston, MA : Allyn and Bacon, 2003.
BF637.P4 P415 2003

Influsso di Eremete Trismegisto.
Magia, alchimia, scienza dal '400 al '700. Firenze : Centro Di, 2002.
BF1598.H6 M34 2002

INFOMEDIARIES - UNITED STATES.
Privacy [electronic resource]. [Washington, D.C.] : Federal Trade Commission, Bureau of Consumer Protection, Office of Consumer and Business Education, [2002]

INFORMAL CAREGIVERS. *See* **CAREGIVERS.**

Information and organization design series
Lin, Zhiang. Designing stress resistant organizations. Boston : Kluwer Academic Publishers, c2003.
HD58.8 .L58 2003

INFORMATION NETWORKS. *See* **COMPUTER NETWORKS.**

INFORMATION POLICY - ECONOMIC ASPECTS.
Public policy in knowledge-based economies. Cheltenham, UK ; Northampton, MA : Edward Elgar, c2003.
HC79.I55 P83 2003

INFORMATION PROCESSING.
Johnson, Addie. Attention. Thousand Oaks, Calif. : Sage Publications, c2004.
BF321 .J56 2004

INFORMATION PROCESSING, HUMAN. *See* **HUMAN INFORMATION PROCESSING.**

INFORMATION PROCESSING IN CHILDREN. *See* **HUMAN INFORMATION PROCESSING IN CHILDREN.**

INFORMATION RESOURCES MANAGEMENT.
Huotari, Maija-Leena. Trust in knowledge management and systems in organizations. Hershey, PA ; London : Idea Group Publishing, c2004.
HD30.2 .H865 2004

Process management. Springer-verlag, Berlin, Heidelberg ; New York : Springer, c2003.
HD31 .P756 2003

INFORMATION SCIENCE - GOVERNMENT POLICY. *See* **INFORMATION POLICY.**

INFORMATION SERVICES. *See* **ARCHIVES; RESEARCH.**

INFORMATION SERVICES AND STATE. *See* **INFORMATION POLICY.**

INFORMATION SERVICES - ORGANIZATION & ADMINISTRATION.
Kaluzniacky, Eugene. Managing psychological factors in information systems work. Hershey PA : Information Science Pub., c2004.
BF576 .K358 2004

INFORMATION SOCIETY.
Deciphering cyberspace. Thousand Oaks, Calif. : Sage Publications, c2003.
TK5102.2 .D43 2003

Lovink, Geert. Uncanny networks. Cambridge, Mass. : MIT Press, c2002.
HM851 .L688 2002

Public policy in knowledge-based economies. Cheltenham, UK ; Northampton, MA : Edward Elgar, c2003.
HC79.I55 P83 2003

INFORMATION STORAGE AND RETRIEVAL SYSTEMS. *See also* **COMPUTERS; EXPERT SYSTEMS (COMPUTER SCIENCE); MULTIMEDIA SYSTEMS.**
Knowledge-based information retrieval and filtering from the Web. Boston : Kluwer Academic Publishers, c2003.
TK5105.888 .K58 2003

INFORMATION SUPERHIGHWAY. *See* **ELECTRONIC COMMERCE; INFORMATION TECHNOLOGY.**

INFORMATION TECHNOLOGY. *See also* **KNOWLEDGE MANAGEMENT.**
Lempert, Robert J. Shaping the next one hundred years. Santa Monica, CA : RAND, 2003.
T57.6 .L46 2003

Information technology and business process reengineering.
Tsai, Hui-Liang. Information technology. Westport, Conn. : Praeger, 2003.
HD58.87 .T73 2003

INFORMATION TECHNOLOGY - MANAGEMENT.
Harmon, Paul, 1942- Business process change. Amsterdam ; Boston : Morgan Kaufmann, c2003.
HD58.8 .H37 2003

Implementing collaboration technologies in industry. London ; New York : Springer, c2003.
HD30.2 .I38 2003

Sharing expertise. Cambridge, Mass. : MIT Press, c2003.
HD30.2 .S53 2003

Tsai, Hui-Liang. Information technology and business process reengineering. Westport, Conn. : Praeger, 2003.
HD58.87 .T73 2003

INFORMATION TECHNOLOGY - SOCIAL ASPECTS.
Designing information spaces. London ; New York : Springer, 2003.
QA76.9.C66 D49 2003

Lovink, Geert. Uncanny networks. Cambridge, Mass. : MIT Press, c2002.
HM851 .L688 2002

INFORMATION THEORY. *See* **KNOWLEDGE REPRESENTATION (INFORMATION THEORY); LANGUAGE AND LANGUAGES; TELECOMMUNICATION.**

INFORMATION THEORY IN PSYCHOLOGY. *See* **HUMAN INFORMATION PROCESSING.**

INFORMATION VISUALIZATION.
Bederson, Benjamin. The craft of information visualization. San Francisco, Calif. : Morgan Kaufmann ; Oxford : Elsevier Science, 2003.

INGARDEN, ROMAN, 1893- - PHILOSOPHY.
Vergara, Gloria, 1964- Tiempo y verdad en la literatura. 1a. ed. México, D.F. : Universidad Iberoamericana, 2001.

Ingensiep, Hans Werner, 1953-.
Philosophie der natürlichen Mitwelt. Würzburg : Königshausen & Neumann, 2002.

Inglis, John, 1954-.
Medieval philosophy and the classical tradition. London ; New York : Curzon, c2002.
B721 .M4535 2002

Ingram, Susan. Zarathustra's sisters : women's autobiography and the shaping of cultural history / Susan Ingram. Toronto ; Buffalo : University of Toronto Press, c2003. viii, 197 p. : ports. ; 24 cm. Includes bibliographical references and index. CONTENTS: Lou Andreas-Salomé -- Simone de Beauvoir -- Maitreyi Devi -- Asja Lacis -- Nadezhda Mandel'shtam -- Romola Nijinsky. ISBN 0-8020-3690-2 DDC 809/.93592072/0904
1. Nietzsche, Friedrich Wilhelm, - 1844-1900. 2. Autobiography - Women authors. 3. Women authors - Biography - History and criticism. 4. Prose literature - Women authors - History and criticism. 5. Man-woman relationships. I. Title.
PN471 .I537 2003

Inhelder, Bärbel.
Piaget, Jean, 1896- [Développement des quantités chez l'enfant. English] The child's construction of quantities. London ; New York : Routledge, 1997.
BF723.P5 P5 1997

INHERITANCE AND SUCCESSION.
Gender perspectives on property and inheritance. Oxford : Oxfam, c2001.
HB715 .G45 2001

INHERITANCE AND SUCCESSION - PSYCHOLOGICAL ASPECTS.
Hendlin, Steven J. Overcoming the inheritance taboo. New York : Plume, 2004.
BF789.D4 H4235 2004

INHIBITION.
Pressfield, Steven. The war of art. Warner Books ed. New York : Warner Books, c2002, (2003 printing).
BF408 .P69 2003

INITIALS. *See* **ILLUMINATION OF BOOKS AND MANUSCRIPTS.**

INITIATION RITES - RELIGIOUS ASPECTS. *See* **BAPTISM.**

INJURIES. *See* **ACCIDENTS.**

Inmigración y orientación.
McLaughlin, Bob. [USA immigration & orientation. Spanish] USA inmigración y orientación. 1a. ed. en español. Satellite Beach, Fla. : Wellesworth Pub., c2001.

Inner coach, outer power.
Varnum, Keith. Phoenix, Ariz. : New Dimensions Pub., c2002.
BF1999 .V36 2002

The inner eye.
Humphrey, Nicholas. Oxford ; New York : Oxford University Press, c2002.

BF311 .H778 2002

Inner pathways to the divine.
Toland, Diane. Hygiene, CO : SunShine Press Publications, c2001.
BF1879.T2 .T65 2001

INNER PEACE. *See* **PEACE OF MIND.**

Inner peace for busy women.
Borysenko, Joan. Carlsbad, Calif. : Hay House, 2003.
BF637.P3 B673 2003

INNOVATION RELAY CENTERS. *See* **TECHNOLOGICAL INNOVATIONS.**

The innovation superhighway.
Amidon, Debra M., 1946- Amsterdam ; Boston ; London : Butterworth-Heinemann, c2003.
HD53 .A462 2003

The innovation wave.
Von Stamm, Bettina. Chichester : John Wiley & Sons, c2003.

INNOVATIONS, INDUSTRIAL. *See* **TECHNOLOGICAL INNOVATIONS.**

INNOVATIONS, MEDICAL. *See* **MEDICAL INNOVATIONS.**

INNOVATIONS, TECHNOLOGICAL. *See* **TECHNOLOGICAL INNOVATIONS.**

The innovator's solution.
Christensen, Clayton M. Boston, Mass. : Harvard Business School Press, c2003.

Innovatsii v psikhologii : materialy pervykh mezhdunarodnykh psikhologicheskikh chteniĭ (4-5 oktiabria 2001 g.) / [otvetstvennyĭ redaktor S.I. Kudinov]. Biĭsk : Nauchno-izdatel'skiĭ tsentr Biĭskogo pedagog. gos. universiteta, 2001- v. <1 > ; 21 cm. At head of title: Ministerstvo obrazovaniia Rossiĭskoĭ Federatsii, Biĭskiĭ pedagogicheskiĭ gosudarstvennyĭ universitet im. V.M. Shukshina. Altaĭskoe otdelenie Rossiĭskogo psikhologicheskogo obshchestva. Soiuz studentov, Altaĭske otdelenie RPO. Includes bibliographical references. ISBN 5851272627
1. Psychology - Congresses. I. Kudinov, S. I. II. Biĭskiĭ pedagogicheskiĭ gosudarstvennyĭ universitet im. V.M. Shukshina. III. Rossiĭskoe psikhologicheskoe obshchestvo. Altaĭskoe otdelenie. IV. Soiuz studentov Rossiĭskogo psikhologicheskogo obshchestva. Altaĭske otdelenie.
BF20 .I45 2001

INNUIT. *See* **INUIT.**

INQUISITION.
Ensaios sobre a intolerância. São Paulo, SP, Brasil : Humanitas, FFLCH/USP : FAPESP : LEI-Laboratório de Estudos sobre a Intolerância, 2002.

INQUISITION - ITALY - PISA - HISTORY.
Caterina e il diavolo. Pisa : ETS, c1999.
BF1584.I8 C38 1999

INQUISITION - MALTA - HISTORY - 16TH CENTURY.
Cassar, Carmel. Witchcraft, sorcery, and the Inquisition. Msida, Malta : Mireva Publications, 1996.
BF1584.M35 C37 1996

INQUISITIVENESS. *See* **CURIOSITY.**

INSANITY. *See also* **PSYCHIATRY.**
Symington, Neville. A pattern of madness. London ; New York : Karnac, 2002.

INSANITY AND ART. *See* **ART AND MENTAL ILLNESS.**

INSCRIPTIONS. *See* **GRAFFITI; PETROGLYPHS.**

INSCRIPTIONS, RUNIC. *See also* **RUNES.**
Runica, Germanica, Mediaevalia. Berlin : W. de Gruyter, 2003.

INSECURITY (PSYCHOLOGY). *See* **SECURITY (PSYCHOLOGY).**

INSERVICE TRAINING. *See* **EMPLOYEES - TRAINING OF.**

Insight and interpretation.
Schafer, Roy. New York : Other Press, c2003.
BF173 .S3277 2003

INSIGHT - ANECDOTES.
Scalzi, John, 1969- Uncle John's presents Book of the dumb. San Diego, CA : Portable Press, 2003.
BF431 .S273 2003

INSIGHT (BUDDHISM). *See* **VIPAŚYANĀ (BUDDHISM).**

INSIGHT - HUMOR.
Scalzi, John, 1969- Uncle John's presents Book of the dumb. San Diego, CA : Portable Press, 2003.
BF431 .S273 2003

INSIGHT - TESTING.
Mangieri, John N. Yale Assessment of Thinking. San Francisco : Jossey-Bass, c2003.
BF442 .M34 2003

Insights and intuitions.
Saberi, Reza, 1941- Lanham, Md. : University Press of America, 2003.
BF1999 .S225 2003

Inskrypcje ulotności.
Przybylak, Feliks. Wrocław : Oficyna Wydawnicza ATUT-Wrocławskie Wydawn. Oświatowe, 2002.
PN56.C69 P79 2002

Inspecting Germany : internationale Deutschland-Ethnographie der Gegenwart / Thomas Hauschild, Bernd Jürgen Warneken (Hg.). Münster : Lit, c2002. 568 p. : ill. ; 23 cm. (Forum europäische Ethnologie ; Bd. 1) Includes bibliographical references (p. 553-566). ISBN 3-8258-6123-6
1. National characteristics, German. 2. Germany - Social life and customs. 3. Germany - Ethnic relations. 4. Multiculturalism - Germany. I. Hauschild, Thomas. II. Warneken, Bernd Jürgen, 1945- III. Series.
DD76 .I57 2002

INSPIRATION. *See also* **CREATION (LITERARY, ARTISTIC, ETC.).**
Gottlieb, Jeff, 1954- Spriggles. Petoskey, Mich. : Mountain Watch Press, c2002.
BF723.M56 G68 2002

INSPIRATION.
High culture. Albany : State University of New York Press, c2003.
HV4998 .H544 2003

Makeieff, Macha. Poétique du désastre. Arles : Actes sud, c2001.

Walker, Jamie. 101 ways black women can learn to love themselves. Washington, D.C. : J.D. Publishing, c2002.
1. Black author.

INSPIRATION IN LITERATURE.
Me-ayin nahalti et shiri. Tel Aviv : Yedi'ot aharonot : Sifre ḥemed, c2002.

L'inspiration philosophique
Clair, André. Sens de l'existence. Paris : Armand Colin, c2002.

INSPIRATION - SONGS AND MUSIC - JUVENILE LITERATURE.
Sanders, Mark D. I hope you dance!. Nashville, Tenn. : Rutledge Hill Press, 2003.
BF410 .S26 2003

Instant karma.
Kipfer, Barbara Ann. New York : Workman Pub., c2003.
BF637.C5 K56 2003

Instant notes in cognitive psychology.
Andrade, Jackie, 1964- New York, NY : Garland Science/BIOS Scientific Publishers, 2004.
BF201 .A53 2004

INSTINCT. *See* **ORIENTATION (PHYSIOLOGY); PSYCHOLOGY, COMPARATIVE.**

INSTITORIS, HEINRICH, 1430-1505. MALLEUS MALEFICARUM.
Frühe Hexenverfolgung in Ravensburg und am Bodensee. Konstanz : UVK Verlagsgesellschaft, c2001.
BF1583 .F784 2001

Institut de France.
Leonardo, da Vinci, 1452-1519. [Selections. English. 1999] The manuscripts of Leonardo da Vinci in the Institut de France. Milano : Ente raccolta vinciana, 1999-
Q113 .L3513 1999

Institut für Vergleichende Städtegeschichte.
Der weite Blick des Historikers. Köln : Böhlau, c2002.
D116 .W44 2002

Institut nauchnoĭ informatsii po obshchestvennym naukam (Rossiĭskaia akademiia nauk).
XX vek. Moskva : INION RAN, 2001-

Institut obshchegumanitarnykh issledovaniĭ.
Burlakova, N. S. Proektivnye metody. Moskva : In-t obshchegumanitarnykh issledovaniĭ, 2001.
BF698.7 .B87 2001

Institut psikhologii (Rossiĭskaia akademiia nauk).
Razvitie natsional'noĭ, etnolingvisticheskoĭ i religioznoĭ identichnosti u deteĭ i podrostkov = Moskva : In-t psikhologii RAN, 2001.
BF723.C5 R39 2001

Tvorcheskoe nasledie A.V. Brushlinskogo i O.K. Tikhomirova i sovremennaia psikhologiia myshleniia (k 70-letiiu so dnia rozhdeniia). Moskva : In-t psikhologii RAN, 2003.
BF109.B86 T86 2003

Institut Soedinennykh Shtatov Ameriki i Kanady (Rossiĭskaia akademiia nauk).
Davydov, IU. P. (IUriĭ Pavlovich) Norma protiv sily. Moskva : Nauka, 2002.

Institut sotsial'no-ekonomicheskikh problem narodonaseleniia (Rossiĭskaia akademiia nauk).
Gendernyĭ kaleĭdoskop. Moskva : "Academia", 2001.

Institute for Personality and Ability Testing.
Russell, Mary T. The 16PF fifth edition administrator's manual. 3rd ed. Champaign, Ill. : Institute for Personality and Ability Testing, 2002.
BF698.8.S5 A37 2002

INSTITUTION BUILDING.
Chanaa, Jane. Security sector reform. Oxford ; New York : Oxford University Press for the International Institute for Strategic Studies, 2002.
HV6419 .C52 2002

L'institution dans l'histoire personnelle et publique.
Merleau-Ponty, Maurice, 1908-1961. [Paris] : Belin, c2003.
B2430.M3763 I88 2003

Institution, la passivité.
Merleau-Ponty, Maurice, 1908-1961. L'institution dans l'histoire personnelle et publique ; [Paris] : Belin, c2003.
B2430.M3763 I88 2003

Institution of Electrical Engineers.
Morrison, Raymond E. Developing effective engineering leadership. London : Institution of Electrical Engineers, c2003.

INSTITUTIONAL LINGUISTICS. *See* **LANGUAGE POLICY.**

INSTITUTIONS, ASSOCIATIONS, ETC. *See* **ASSOCIATIONS, INSTITUTIONS, ETC.**

INSTITUTIONS, HEALTH. *See* **HEALTH FACILITIES.**

INSTITUTIONS, SOCIAL. *See* **SOCIAL INSTITUTIONS.**

Instituto Español de Estudios Estratégicos.
Panorama estratégico, 2001-2002. [Madrid] : Ministerio de Defensa, 2002.

INSTRUCTION. *See also* **EDUCATION; TEACHING.**
The peak performance series. Vol. [4] [videorecording]. Longwood, Fla. : Pamela Bolling Enterprises, c1999.

INSTRUCTIONAL OBJECTIVES. *See* **EDUCATION - AIMS AND OBJECTIVES.**

INSTRUCTIONAL SYSTEMS. *See* **EDUCATIONAL TECHNOLOGY; TEACHING.**

INSTRUCTIONAL TECHNOLOGY. *See* **EDUCATIONAL TECHNOLOGY.**

Instructions for your discontent.
Dolnick, Barrie. New York : Simple Abundance Press/Scribner, c2003.
BF637.C4 D65 2003

Instytut filosofiï NAN Ukraïny im. H. Skovorody.
Suspil'stvo na porozi XXI stolittia. Kyïv : Ukraïns'kyĭ TSentr dukhovnoĭ kul'tury, 1999.

Instytut psykholohiï im. H.S. Kostiuka.
Aktual'ni problemy psykholohiï. Kyïv : In-tyt psykholohiï im. H.S. Kostiuka, 2001-
BF8.U38 A38

Smul'son, M. L. (Maryna Lazarivna) Psykholohiia rozvytku intelektu. Kyïv : Instytut psykholohiï im. H.S. Kostiuka APN Ukraïny, 2001.
BF431 .S68 2001

Insult to injury.
Mills, Linda G. Princeton, N.J. : Princeton University Press, c2003.
HV6626 .M55 2003

INSULTS. *See* **INVECTIVE.**

INSULTS, VERBAL. *See* **INVECTIVE.**

INSURANCE CLAIMS. *See* **WORKERS' COMPENSATION CLAIMS.**

INSURANCE, DISABILITY. *See* **DISABILITY RETIREMENT.**

INSURANCE, HEALTH. *See* **MEDICAL CARE.**

INSURGENCY. *See* **GOVERNMENT, RESISTANCE TO; TERRORISM.**

INSURGENCY - COLOMBIA.
Al oído de Uribe. 1a. ed. Bogotá, Colombia : Editorial Oveja Negra, 2002.

Téllez, Edgar. Diario íntimo de un fracaso. 1. ed. Bogotá, D.C., Colombia : Planeta, 2002.

INSURGENCY - CONGO (DEMOCRATIC REPUBLIC) - HISTORY - 20TH CENTURY.
Masangana Diamaka, Robin, 1962- Dialogue politique. Paris : Editoo.com, 2002.
1. Black author.

INTAGLIOS. *See* **GEMS.**

INTANGIBLE PROPERTY. *See* **COPYRIGHT; INTELLECTUAL PROPERTY.**

INTEGRATED CIRCUITS - VERY LARGE SCALE INTEGRATION.
Qu, Gang, 1969- Intellectual property protection in VLSI designs. Boston, Mass. : London : Kluwer Academic, c2003.

Integrating gender and culture in parenting / Toni Schindler Zimmerman, editor. New York : Haworth Press, 2003. p. cm. "Integrating gender and culture in parenting has been co-published simultaneously as Journal of feminist family therapy, volume 14, numbers 3/4 2003." Includes bibliographical references (p.   ) and index. Table of contents URL: http://www.loc.gov/catdir/toc/ecip043/2003009781.html ISBN 0-7890-2241-9 (hard cover : alk. paper) ISBN 0-7890-2242-7 (soft cover : alk. paper) DDC 649/.1
1. Prejudices in children - Prevention. 2. Parenting - Study and teaching. I. Zimmerman, Toni Schindler. II. Title: Journal of feminist family therapy.
BF723.P75 I57 2003

Integrating religion and spirituality into counseling.
Frame, Marsha Wiggins. Australia ; Pacific Grove, CA : Thomson/Brooks/Cole, c2003.
BF637.C6 F64 2003

Integrating spirit and psyche.
Henehan, Mary Pat. New York ; London : Haworth Pastoral Press, c2003.
RC489.F45 H46 2003

INTEGRATION, RACIAL. *See* **RACE RELATIONS.**

Integrative assessment of adult personality.
Beutler, Larry E. 2nd ed. New York : Guilford Press, 2003.
BF698.4 .B42 2003

Integrator 2.0.
Kohn, Arthur J. The integrator for Introductory psychology 2.0 [electronic resource]. Pacific Grove, Calif. : Brooks/Cole, c1998.
BF121

The integrator for Introductory psychology 2.0 [electronic resource].
Kohn, Arthur J. Pacific Grove, Calif. : Brooks/Cole, c1998.
BF121

INTELLECT. *See also* **CREATION (LITERARY, ARTISTIC, ETC.); GENERAL FACTOR (PSYCHOLOGY); KNOWLEDGE, THEORY OF; LOGIC; MEMORY; PERCEPTION; REASON; STUPIDITY; THOUGHT AND THINKING.**
Andrews, Linda Wasmer. Intelligence. New York : Franklin Watts, c2003.
BF431 .A576 2003

Estep, Myrna. A theory of immediate awareness. Dordrecht ; Boston : Kluwer Academic Publishers, 2003.
BF311 .E79 2003

Humphrey, Nicholas. The inner eye. Oxford ; New York : Oxford University Press, c2002.
BF311 .H778 2002

International handbook of intelligence. Cambridge ; New York : Cambridge University Press, 2003.
BF431 .I59 2003

Motivation, emotion, and cognition. Mahwah, N.J. : L. Erlbaum Associates, 2004.

BF431 .M72 2004

Ornstein, Robert E. (Robert Evan), 1942- Multimind. Cambridge, MA : ISHK, 2003.
BF431 .O68 2003

Ruggiero, Vincent Ryan. Making your mind matter. Lanham, Md. : Rowman & Littlefield, c2003.
BF431 .R78 2003

The scientific study of general intelligence. 1st ed. Amsterdam ; Boston : Pergamon, 2003.
BF433.G45 S35 2003

Smul′son, M. L. (Maryna Lazarivna) Psykholohiía rozvytku intelektu. Kyïv : Instytut psykholohiï im. H.S. Kostíuka APN Ukraïny, 2001.
BF431 .S68 2001

Sternberg, Robert J. Wisdom, intelligence, and creativity synthesized. Cambridge, UK ; New York : Cambridge University Press, 2003.
BF431 .S7385 2003

INTELLECT - GENETIC ASPECTS.
Jensen, Arthur Robert. Intelligence, race, and genetics. Boulder, Colo. : Westview Press, c2002.
BF431 .J396 2002

INTELLECT - JUVENILE LITERATURE.
Andrews, Linda Wasmer. Intelligence. New York : Franklin Watts, c2003.
BF431 .A576 2003

INTELLECT - SOCIAL ASPECTS.
The mind as a scientific object. New York : Oxford University Press, c2004.
BF311 .M552 2004

Trufanov, A. A. (Andreĭ Andreevich) Osnovy teorii intelligentnosti. Kazan′ : ZAO "Novoe znanie", 2002.
BF431 .T78 2002

Intellection in the mirror of time.
Kāviyānī, Shīvā. Farzānagī dar āyinah-i zamān. Tihrān : Nigāh, 2001.

INTELLECTRONICS. *See* **ARTIFICIAL INTELLIGENCE.**

INTELLECTUAL CAPITAL. *See also* **KNOWLEDGE MANAGEMENT.**
Amidon, Debra M., 1946- The innovation superhighway. Amsterdam ; Boston ; London : Butterworth-Heinemann, c2003.
HD53 .A462 2003

Read, Jason. The micro-politics of capital. Albany : State University of New York Press, c2003.
HB97.5 .R42 2003

INTELLECTUAL LIFE. *See* **LEARNING AND SCHOLARSHIP; POPULAR CULTURE.**

INTELLECTUAL LIFE - 17TH CENTURY.
Denkwelten um 1700. Köln : Böhlau, 2002.
BF441 .D46 2002

INTELLECTUAL LIFE - 18TH CENTURY.
Denkwelten um 1700. Köln : Böhlau, 2002.
BF441 .D46 2002

INTELLECTUAL LIFE - HISTORY.
Neuzeitliches Denken. Berlin ; New York : De Gruyter, 2002.

INTELLECTUAL PROPERTY. *See also* **COPYRIGHT.**
Beverley-Smith, Huw. Commercial appropriation of personality. Cambridge, UK ; New York : Cambridge University Press, 2002.
K627 .B48 2002

Brown, Michael F. (Michael Fobes), 1950- Who owns native culture? Cambridge, Mass. : Harvard University Press, 2003.
K1401 .B79 2003

Claiming the stones/naming the bones. Los Angeles : Getty Research Institute, c2002.
CC135 .C48 2002

Essays for Colin Tapper. London : LexisNexis, 2003.

Graham, Douglas, 1950- Ideation. Hoboken, N.J. : John Wiley & Sons, Inc., c2004.
BF408 .G664 2004

Howkins, John, 1945- The creative economy. London : Allen Lane, 2001.

Intellectual property rights in animal breeding and genetics. Wallingford ; New York : CABI, c2002.

King, John L. Concentration and technology in agricultural input industries [electronic resource]. [Washington, D.C.] : U.S. Dept of Agriculture, [2001].

Matsuura, Jeffrey H., 1957- Managing intellectual assets in the digital age. Boston, MA : Artech House, c2003.
K1401 .M378 2003

Monotti, Ann Louise. Universities and intellectual property. Oxford ; New York : Oxford University Press, 2003.
KF4225.U55 M66 2003

Qu, Gang, 1969- Intellectual property protection in VLSI designs. Boston, Mass. : London : Kluwer Academic, c2003.

Rahnasto, Ilkka. Intellectual property rights, external effects, and antitrust law. Oxford ; New York : Oxford University Press, 2003.

INTELLECTUAL PROPERTY - MORAL AND ETHICAL ASPECTS.
Claiming the stones/naming the bones. Los Angeles : Getty Research Institute, c2002.
CC135 .C48 2002

Intellectual property protection in VLSI designs.
Qu, Gang, 1969- Boston, Mass. : London : Kluwer Academic, c2003.

Intellectual property rights, external effects, and antitrust law.
Rahnasto, Ilkka. Oxford ; New York : Oxford University Press, 2003.

Intellectual property rights in animal breeding and genetics / edited by Max Rothschild and Scott Newman. Wallingford ; New York : CABI, c2002. xx, 272 p. : ill. ; 24 cm. Includes bibliographical references and index. ISBN 0-85199-641-8 DDC 636.0821
1. Livestock - Germplasm resources - Patents. 2. Intellectual property. I. Rothschild, Max Frederick, 1952- II. Newman, Scott.

INTELLECTUALS.
Jansen, Sue Curry. Critical communication theory. Lanham, Md. ; Oxford : Rowman & Littlefield, c2002.
HM651 .J36 2002

INTELLECTUALS - CHINA.
Huang, Minlan. Xue shu jiu guo. Di 1 ban. Zhengzhou Shi : Henan ren min chu ban she, 1995.
D16.9 .H795 1995 <Asian China>

INTELLECTUALS - HISTORY.
Intellektuelle in der Frühen Neuzeit. München : Fink, c2002.

INTELLECTUALS - IRAN - INTERVIEWS.
Qizilsaflī, Muḥammad Taqī. Qarn-i rawshanfikrān. Chāp-i 1. Tihrān : Markaz-i Bayn al-Milalī-i Guftugū-yi Tamaddun′hā : Hirmis, 1380 [2001]

INTELLECTUALS - UNITED STATES - HISTORY.
Hansen, Jonathan M. The lost promise of patriotism. Chicago : University of Chicago Press, c2003.
E661 .H316 2003

INTELLECTUALS - UNITED STATES - INTERVIEWS.
Macdonald, Dwight. Interviews with Dwight Macdonald. Jackson : University Press of Mississippi, c2003.
E169.1 .M1363 2003

INTELLECTUALS - UNITED STATES - PUBLIC OPINION.
Horowitz, David A. America's political class under fire. New York ; London : Routledge, 2003.
HN90.S6 H67 2003

Intellektuelle in der Frühen Neuzeit / Jutta Held (Hrsg.). München : Fink, c2002. 207 p. : ill. ; 23 cm. Includes bibliographical references. ISBN 3-7705-3731-9 (pbk.)
1. Intellectuals - History. 2. Renaissance. I. Held, Jutta.

INTELLIGENCE. *See also* **INTELLECT.**
Andrews, Linda Wasmer. New York : Franklin Watts, c2003.
BF431 .A576 2003

Intelligence and success in life.
Firkowska-Mankiewicz, Anna. Warsaw : IFiS Publishers, 2002.
BF412 F57 2002

INTELLIGENCE, ARTIFICIAL. *See* **ARTIFICIAL INTELLIGENCE.**

INTELLIGENCE LEVELS. *See* **GENIUS.**

INTELLIGENCE LEVELS - SOCIAL ASPECTS.
Jensen, Arthur Robert. Intelligence, race, and genetics. Boulder, Colo. : Westview, 2002.

INTELLIGENCE LEVELS - TESTING. *See* **INTELLIGENCE TESTS.**

INTELLIGENCE OF ANIMALS. *See* **PSYCHOLOGY, COMPARATIVE.**

Intelligence of apes and other rational beings.
Rumbaugh, Duane M., 1929- New Haven : Yale University Press, c2003.
QL737.P96 R855 2003

INTELLIGENCE QUOTIENT. *See* **INTELLIGENCE LEVELS.**

Intelligence, race, and genetics.
Jensen, Arthur Robert. Boulder, Colo. : Westview Press, c2002.
BF431 .J396 2002

Jensen, Arthur Robert. Boulder, Colo. : Westview, 2002.

INTELLIGENCE TESTING. *See* **INTELLIGENCE TESTS.**

INTELLIGENCE TESTS. *See also* **COGNITIVE ABILITIES TEST.**
Carter, Philip J. IQ and psychometric tests. London ; Sterling, VA : Kogan Page Ltd., 2004.
BF431.3 .C362 2004

Carter, Philip J. Maximize your brainpower. West Sussex, England ; New York : John Wiley & Sons, Ltd, 2002.
BF431.3 .C3647 2002

Carter, Philip J. More IQ testing. Chichester, West Sussex, England ; New York : John Wiley & Sons, Ltd, 2002.
BF431.3 .C367 2002

Race and IQ. Expanded ed. New York : Oxford University Press, 1999.
BF432.A1 R3 1999

Russell, Kenneth, 1928- The Times book of IQ tests. Book 1. London : Kogan Page, 2001.

Russell, Kenneth, 1928- The Times book of IQ tests. Book 2. London ; Milford, CT : Kogan Page, 2002.

Russell, Kenneth A. The Times book of IQ tests. Book 3. London ; Sterling, VA : Kogan Page Ltd., 2003.
BF431.3 .R87 2003

INTELLIGENCE TESTS FOR PRELITERATES.
Handbook of nonverbal assessment. New York : Kluwer Academic/Plenum Publishers, c2003.
BF432.5.I55 H36 2003

INTELLIGENCE TESTS - SOCIAL ASPECTS.
Jensen, Arthur Robert. Intelligence, race, and genetics. Boulder, Colo. : Westview, 2002.

INTELLIGENCES, ETHERIC WORLD. *See* **GUIDES (SPIRITUALISM).**

INTELLIGENT AGENT SOFTWARE. *See* **INTELLIGENT AGENTS (COMPUTER SOFTWARE).**

INTELLIGENT AGENTS (COMPUTER SOFTWARE).
Adaptive agents and multi-agent systems. Berlin ; New York : Springer, c2003.
QA76.76.I58 A312 2003

INTELLIGENT MACHINES. *See* **ARTIFICIAL INTELLIGENCE.**

Intelligent memory.
Gordon, Barry, M.D. New York : Viking, 2003.
BF371 .G66 2003

Intelligent robots and autonomous agents
Breazeal, Cynthia L. Designing sociable robots. Cambridge, Mass. : MIT Press, c2002.
TA167 .B74 2002

INTELLIGENT SOFTWARE AGENTS. *See* **INTELLIGENT AGENTS (COMPUTER SOFTWARE).**

Intelligent support systems : knowledge management / [edited by] Vijayan Sugumaran. Hershey, PA : IRM Press, c2002. vii, 301 p. : ill. ; 26 cm. Includes bibliographical references and index. ISBN 1-931777-00-4 (paper) DDC 006.3
1. Database management. 2. Artificial intelligence. 3. Knowledge management. I. Sugumaran, Vijayan, 1960-
QA76.9.D3 I5495 2002

INTELLIGENTSIA. *See* **INTELLECTUALS.**

Les intemporels
Kelen, Jacqueline. Le bonheur. Paris : Oxus, c2003.

Marguier, Florence. Le plaisir. Paris : Oxus, c2003.

INTENSION (PHILOSOPHY). *See* **SEMANTICS (PHILOSOPHY).**

INTENTIONALISM.
Dyer, Wayne W. The power of intention. Carlsbad, Calif. : Hay House, c2004.
BF619.5 .D94 2004

Voluntary action. Oxford ; New York : Oxford University Press, 2003.
BF621 .V658 2003

INTENTIONALITY (PHILOSOPHY).
Naturalism, evolution, and intentionality. Calgary, Alta., Canada : University of Calgary Press, c2001.
BD418.3 .N35 2001

Schueler, G. F. Reasons and purposes. Oxford : Oxford University Press, 2003.

Voluntary action. Oxford ; New York : Oxford University Press, 2003.
BF621 .V658 2003

Inter-act.
Verderber, Kathleen S., 1949- 10th ed. New York : Oxford University Press, 2004.
BF637.C45 V47 2004

Inter-organizational trust for business-to-business e-commerce.
Ratnasingam, Pauline. Inter-organizational trust in business-to-business e-commerce. Hershey, PA : IRM Press, c2003.
HF5548.32 .R378 2003

Inter-organizational trust in business-to-business e-commerce.
Ratnasingam, Pauline. Hershey, PA : IRM Press, c2003.
HF5548.32 .R378 2003

Interact.
Verderber, Kathleen S., 1949- Inter-act. 10th ed. New York : Oxford University Press, 2004.
BF637.C45 V47 2004

Interaction effects in multiple regression.
Jaccard, James. 2nd ed. Thousand Oaks, Calif. : Sage Publications, c2003.
HA31.3 .J33 2003

Interaction in multidisciplinary teams.
Housley, William, 1970- Aldershot, England ; Burlington, VT : Ashgate, c2003.
HV41 .H667 2003

INTERACTION, SOCIAL. *See* **SOCIAL INTERACTION.**

INTERACTIVE ART.
Braun-Thürmann, Holger. Künstliche Interaktion. 1. Aufl. Wiesbaden : Westdeutscher Verlag, 2002.

INTERACTIVE COMPUTER SYSTEMS.
Lengen, Haiko van. Bücher im virtuellen Warenkorb. Berlin : Verlag für Wirtschaftskommunikation, c2001.

INTERACTIVE MULTIMEDIA.
Malvido Arriaga, Adriana. Por la vereda digital. 1. ed. México : CONACULTA (Consejo Nacional para la Cultura y las Artes), 1999.
QA76.9.C66 M35 1999

Production methods. London ; New York : Springer, c2003.
QA76.76.I59 P76 2003

Sutcliffe, Alistair, 1951- Multimedia and virtual reality. Mahwah, N.J. ; London : Lawrence Erlbaum, c2003.
QA76.76.I59 S88 2003

INTERCULTURAL COMMUNICATION.
Huls, Erica. Dilemma's in menselijke interactie. Utrecht : Lemma, 2001.

Lie, Rico. Spaces of intercultural communication. Creskill, N.J. : Hampton Press, c2003.
GN345.6 .L54 2003

Napier, A. David. The age of immunology. Chicago : University of Chicago Press, 2003.
GN345 .N36 2003

Pompeo, Francesco. Il mondo è poco. Roma : Meltemi, c2002.
GN495.6 .P66 2002

Rüsen, Jörn. Geschichte im Kulturprozess. Köln : Böhlau, c2002.
D16.8 .R913 2002

INTERCULTURAL COMMUNICATION - CASE STUDIES.

Kochetkov, V. V. (Vladimir Viktorovich) Psikhologiia mezhkul'turnykh razlichiĭ. Moskva : PER SE, 2002.
GN502 .K6 2002

Paquette, Didier. La mascarade interculturelle. Paris : Harmattan, c2002.

INTERCULTURAL COMMUNICATION IN LITERATURE.
Paquette, Didier. La mascarade interculturelle. Paris : Harmattan, c2002.

INTERCULTURAL COMMUNICATION IN MOTION PICTURES.
Paquette, Didier. La mascarade interculturelle. Paris : Harmattan, c2002.

INTERDEPENDENCE OF NATIONS. *See* **INTERNATIONAL ECONOMIC RELATIONS; INTERNATIONAL RELATIONS.**

INTERDISCIPLINARY APPROACH TO KNOWLEDGE.
Ensaios. João Pessoa : Editora Universitária, 2001.

INTEREST (PSYCHOLOGY). *See* **CURIOSITY.**

Interfaces.
Chazal, Gérard. Seyssel [France] : Champ Vallon, c2002.
HM1111 .C49 2002

INTERFACES, USER (COMPUTER SYSTEMS). *See* **USER INTERFACES (COMPUTER SYSTEMS).**

INTERGENERATIONAL RELATIONS. *See* **CHILDREN AND ADULTS; CONFLICT OF GENERATIONS.**

INTERGENERATIONAL RELATIONS - CROSS-CULTURAL STUDIES.
Generationswechsel und historischer Wandel. München : Oldenbourg, 2003.

INTERGROUP CONFLICT. *See* **INTERGROUP RELATIONS.**

INTERGROUP RELATIONS - COSTA RICA.
Castro, Vanessa Smith, 1969- Acculturation and psychological adaptation. Westport, Conn. : Greenwood Press, 2003.
HM841 .C37 2003

INTERIOR DECORATION. *See* **MURAL PAINTING AND DECORATION.**

INTERMEDIATE STATE. *See* **DEATH - RELIGIOUS ASPECTS.**

INTERNAL SECURITY. *See also* **INSURGENCY.**
Chanaa, Jane. Security sector reform. Oxford ; New York : Oxford University Press for the International Institute for Strategic Studies, 2002.
HV6419 .C52 2002

International advances in self research : speaking to the future / edited by Herbert W. Marsh, Rhonda G. Craven, and Dennis M. McInerney. Greenwich, CT : Information Age Pub., 2003. p. cm. Includes bibliographical references. ISBN 1-59311-005-7 ISBN 1-59311-004-9 (pbk.) DDC 155.2
1. Self. I. Marsh, Herbert W. II. Craven, Rhonda. III. McInerney, D. M. (Dennis M.), 1948-
BF697 .I675 2003

International and cultural psychology series
Psychology and Buddhism. New York : Kluwer Academic/Plenum Publishers, c2003.
BQ4570.P76 P78 2003

International Association for Media and Communication Research (Series)
Lie, Rico. Spaces of intercultural communication. Creskill, N.J. : Hampton Press, c2003.
GN345.6 .L54 2003

International brief (United States. Bureau of the Census)
(IB/98-3.) Velkoff, Victoria Averil. Gender and aging [electronic resource]. [Washington, D.C.] : U.S. Dept. of Commerce, Economics and Statistics Administration, Bureau of the Census, [1998]

INTERNATIONAL BUSINESS ENTERPRISES.
DiVanna, Joseph A. Syncronomy. Houndmills [England] ; New York : Palgrave Macmillan, 2003.
HD64.2 .D575 2003

INTERNATIONAL BUSINESS ENTERPRISES - MANAGEMENT.
New challenges for international leadership. Santa Monica, Calif. : RAND, 2003.
HD57.7 .N488 2003

International business enterprises - Management.

Sethi, S. Prakash. Setting global standards. Hoboken, N.J. : J. Wiley, c2003.
HD62.4 .S48 2003

INTERNATIONAL COMPETITION. *See* **COMPETITION, INTERNATIONAL.**

International Conference on Motivation (8th : 2002 Moscow, Russia) 8th International Conference on Motivation : Workshop on achievement and task motivation, Moscow, June 12-15, 2002 : abstracts / [redaktor D.A. Leont'ev]. Moscow : Russian State University for Humanities, 2002. 143 p. ; 21 cm. "Nauchnoe izdanie"--Colophon. ISBN 5893571266
1. Motivation (Psychology) - Congresses. I. Leont'ev, D. A. II. Rossiĭskiĭ gosudarstvennyĭ gumanitarnyĭ universitet. III. Title. IV. Title: Workshop on achievement and task motivation
BF501.5 .I58 2002

International Conference on Simulation and Multimedia in Engineering Education & Virtual Worlds and Simulation. International Conference on Simulation in Engineering Education (2001 : Phoenix, Ariz.) Proceedings of the International Conference on Simulation and Multimedia in Engineering Education & Virtual Worlds and Simulation. San Diego, CA : Society for Computer Simulation International, c2001.

International Conference on Simulation in Engineering Education (2001 : Phoenix, Ariz.) Proceedings of the International Conference on Simulation and Multimedia in Engineering Education & Virtual Worlds and Simulation : Phoenix, Arizona, Crowne Plaza Hotel, January 7-11, 2001 / edited by Hamid Vakilzadian, Christopher Landauer, Kirstie L. Bellman ; sponsored by the Society for Modeling and Simulation International. San Diego, CA : Society for Computer Simulation International, c2001. x, 308 p. : ill. ; 28 cm. (Simulation series ; v. 33, no. 2) Spine title: International Conference on Simulation and Multimedia in Engineering Education & Virtual Worlds and Simulation. "2001 International Conference on Simulation in Engineering Education (ICSEE'2001." "2001 International Conference on Virtual Worlds and Simulation ... fourth Virtual Worlds and Simulation Conference (VWSim'01)"--P. iii & iv. Includes bibliographical references and index. ISBN 1-56555-224-5
1. Engineering - Computer simulation - Study and teaching - Congresses. 2. Multimedia systems - Congresses. 3. Engineering - Computer simulation - Congresses. 4. Digital computer simulation - Congresses. 5. Engineering - Computer-assisted instruction - Congresses. 6. Virtual computer systems - Congresses. 7. Virtual reality in medicine - Congresses. 8. Virtual reality - Congresses. I. Vakilzadian, Hamid. II. Landauer, Christopher. III. Bellman, Kirstie L. IV. Society for Computer Simulation. V. Virtual Worlds and Simulation Conference (4th : 2001 : Phoenix, Ariz.) VI. Title. VII. Title: International Conference on Simulation and Multimedia in Engineering Education & Virtual Worlds and Simulation VIII. Title: Proceedings of the International Conference on Virtual Worlds and Simulation IX. Title: Virtual Worlds and Simulation X. Series.

International Conference on Simulation of Adaptive Behavior (7th : 2002 : University of Edinburgh). Workshop on Adaptive Behavior in Anticipatory Learning Systems (1st : 2002 : Edinburgh, Scotland) Anticipatory behavior in adaptive learning systems. Berlin ; New York : Springer, c2003.
Q325.5 .W65 2003

International Congress of Psychology. Psychology, IUPsyS global resource [electronic resource]. Hove, East Sussex, UK : published on behalf of the international Union of Psychological Science by Psychology Press Ltd., 2000-
BF76.5 .P79

INTERNATIONAL COOPERATION. Getting it done. Washington, D.C. : United States Institute of Peace Press, 2003.
KZ1321 .G48 2003

The new economic diplomacy. Aldershot, Hampshire, England ; Burlington, VT : Ashgate, c2003.
HF1359 .N4685 2003

INTERNATIONAL CORPORATIONS. *See* **INTERNATIONAL BUSINESS ENTERPRISES.**

International Crisis Group. Le Burundi aprés la suspension de l'embargo. [Nairobi?] : International Crisis Group, [1999]

Le dialogue intercongolais. Bruxelles ; Nairobi : International Crisis Group, [2001]

From Kabila to Kabila. Nairobi ; Brussels : International Crisis Group, 2001.

Storm clouds over Sun City. Brussels ; Nairobi : International Crisis Group, 2002.

The international directory of haunted places. Hauck, Dennis William. New York : Penguin Books, 2000.
BF1471 .H38 2000

INTERNATIONAL ECONOMIC POLICY. *See* **INTERNATIONAL ECONOMIC RELATIONS.**

INTERNATIONAL ECONOMIC RELATIONS. *See also* **ECONOMIC SANCTIONS; INTERNATIONAL TRADE.**
Abrahamsson, Hans, 1949- Understanding world order and structural change. Basingstoke, Hampshire : New York : Palgrave Macmillan, 2003.
HF1359 .A24 2003

Barbieri, Katherine, 1965- The liberal illusion. Ann Arbor : University of Michigan Press, c2002.
HF1379 .B363 2002

McMurtry, John, 1939- Value wars. London ; Sterling, Va. : Pluto Press, c2002.
HF1359 .M39 2002

The new economic diplomacy. Aldershot, Hampshire, England ; Burlington, VT : Ashgate, c2003.
HF1359 .N4685 2003

INTERNATIONAL ECONOMIC RELATIONS - CASE STUDIES.
The new economic diplomacy. Aldershot, Hampshire, England ; Burlington, VT : Ashgate, c2003.
HF1359 .N4685 2003

INTERNATIONAL ECONOMICS. *See* **INTERNATIONAL ECONOMIC RELATIONS.**

INTERNATIONAL FINANCE.
Beyond Keynes. Cheltenham ; Northampton, Mass. : Edward Elgar, c2002.

INTERNATIONAL GRANTS-IN-AID. *See* **INTERNATIONAL RELIEF.**

International Graphoanalysis Society. Instruction Dept. Dictionary of stroke structures in graphoanalysis. New, 3rd ed. Chicago : International Graphoanalysis Society, 1998.
BF889.5 .D53 1998

International handbook of intelligence / Robert J. Sternberg, editor. Cambridge ; New York : Cambridge University Press, 2003. p. cm. Includes bibliographical references and index. Publisher description URL: http://www.loc.gov/catdir/description/cam032/2003048462.html Table of contents URL: http://www.loc.gov/catdir/toc/cam031/2003048462.html ISBN 0-521-80815-4 ISBN 0-521-00402-0 (pbk.) DDC 153.9
1. Intellect. I. Sternberg, Robert J.
BF431 .I59 2003

International Institute for Strategic Studies. Chanaa, Jane. Security sector reform. Oxford ; New York : Oxford University Press for the International Institute for Strategic Studies, 2002.
HV6419 .C52 2002

International journal of cognition and technology. Amsterdam ; Philadelphia : John Benjamins, c2002- v. ; 22 cm. Frequency: 2 issues per year. Vol. 1, no. 1 (2002)- . Other title: IJCT. "Official publication of the Cognitive Technology Society." Latest issue consulted: vol. 1, no. 2 (2002). Publication suspended 2003- ISSN 1569-2167
1. Cognitive science - Periodicals. I. Cognitive Technology Society. II. Title: Cognition and technology III. Title: IJCT
BF309 .I58

International journal of critical psychology. [Critical psychology (Lawrence & Wishart)] Critical psychology. London : Lawrence & Wishart, c2001-
BF39.9 .C75

International Journal of Psychology. Psychology, IUPsyS global resource [electronic resource]. Hove, East Sussex, UK : published on behalf of the international Union of Psychological Science by Psychology Press Ltd., 2000-
BF76.5 .P79

International journal of psychology. Psychology, IUPsyS global resource [electronic resource]. Hove, East Sussex, UK : published on behalf of the international Union of Psychological Science by Psychology Press Ltd., 2000-
BF76.5 .P79

INTERNATIONAL LAW. *See also* **CIVIL WAR; INTERVENTION (INTERNATIONAL LAW); NATURALIZATION; SOVEREIGNTY; WAR (INTERNATIONAL LAW); WATER RIGHTS (INTERNATIONAL LAW).**
Davydov, IU. P. (I︠U︡riĭ Pavlovich) Norma protiv sily. Moskva : Nauka, 2002.

Getting it done. Washington, D.C. : United States Institute of Peace Press, 2003.
KZ1321 .G48 2003

International library of philosophy
Art and morality. London ; New York : Routledge, 2003.
BH39 .A695 2003

Morton, Adam. The importance of being understood. London ; New York : Routledge, 2003.
BF637.C45 M65 2003

International library of psychology.
Hartley, Ruth E. (Ruth Edith), b.1909 Understanding children's play, London : Routledge, 2000.
BF717 .H3 2000

International library of psychology. Developmental psychology
(v. 32.) Hartley, Ruth E. (Ruth Edith), b.1909 Understanding children's play, London : Routledge, 2000.
BF717 .H3 2000

International library of sociology
Witkin, Robert W. (Robert Winston) Adorno on popular culture. London ; New York : Routledge, 2003.
B3199.A34 W58 2003

The international library of studies on migration
(9) Migration, diasporas, and transnationalism. Cheltenham, UK ; Northampton, MA : Edward Elgar, 1999.
JV6032 .M54 1999

INTERNATIONAL MIGRATION. *See* **EMIGRATION AND IMMIGRATION.**

International Nietzsche studies
Rée, Paul, 1849-1901. [Ursprung der moralischen Empfindungen. English] Basic writings. Urbana : University of Illinois Press, c2003.
B3323.R343 U67 2003

INTERNATIONAL OFFENSES. *See* **TERRORISM.**

INTERNATIONAL ORGANIZATION. *See also* **WORLD POLITICS.**
Davydov, IU. P. (I︠U︡riĭ Pavlovich) Norma protiv sily. Moskva : Nauka, 2002.

Ojeda Awad, Alonso. Convivencia y globalización. [1a ed.]. [Bogotá] : Universidad Pedagógica Nacional, [2002]

International Peace Academy.
From promise to practice. Boulder ; London : L. Rienner Publishers, 2003.
JZ6368 .S68 2003

International peace operations.
Christoff, Joseph A. Issues in implementing international peace operations [electronic resource]. [Washington, D.C.] : U.S. General Accounting Office, [2002]

International political economy series (Palgrave Macmillan (Firm))
Abrahamsson, Hans, 1949- Understanding world order and structural change. Basingstoke, Hampshire : New York : Palgrave Macmillan, 2003.
HF1359 .A24 2003

INTERNATIONAL POLITICS. *See* **WORLD POLITICS.**

International Pragmatics Conference (7th : 2000 : Budapest, Hungary).
Grounding. Berlin ; Hawthorne, N.Y. : M. de Gruyter, 2002.
P165 .G76 2002

International Psychoanalysis Association. Committee on Women and Psychoanalysis.
Studies on femininity. London ; New York : Karnac, 2003.

INTERNATIONAL RELATIONS. *See also* **BALANCE OF POWER; COMPETITION, INTERNATIONAL; CONFIDENCE AND SECURITY BUILDING MEASURES (INTERNATIONAL RELATIONS); INTERNATIONAL ECONOMIC RELATIONS; NATIONAL SECURITY; NATIONALISM; PEACE; PEACEFUL CHANGE (INTERNATIONAL RELATIONS); WAR; WORLD POLITICS.**
Christoff, Joseph A. Issues in implementing international peace operations [electronic resource].

[Washington, D.C.] : U.S. General Accounting Office, [2002]

Corm, Georges. Orient-Occident, la fracture imaginaire. Paris : Découverte, 2002.

Davydov, I︠U︡. P. (I︠U︡riĭ Pavlovich) Norma protiv sily. Moskva : Nauka, 2002.

Imagine coexistence. 1st ed. San Francisco : Jossey-Bass, c2003.
HM1121 .I42 2003

Kritik der Gewalt. Wien : Promedia, c2002.
D860 .K75 2002

Order and justice in international relations. Oxford ; New York : Oxford University Press, 2003.
JZ1308 .O73 2003

Panorama estratégico, 2001-2002. [Madrid] : Ministerio de Defensa, 2002.

Policymaking and peace. Lanham, Md. : Lexington Books, c2003.
JZ5538 .P65 2003

Power, postcolonialism, and international relations. London ; New York : Routledge, 2002.
JV51 .P69 2002

United States. General Accounting Office. World Trade Organization [electronic resource]. [Washington, D.C.] : U.S. General Accounting Office, [2002]

INTERNATIONAL RELATIONS AND CULTURE.
Culture and international history. New York : Berghahn Books, 2003.
JZ1251 .C84 2003

International relations and the "third debate" : postmodernism and its critics / edited by Darryl S.L. Jarvis. Westport, Conn. : Praeger, 2002. xii, 209 p. ; 24 cm. Includes bibliographical references (p. [199]-202) and index. ISBN 0-275-96000-5 (alk. paper) DDC 327.1/01
1. International relations - Philosophy. 2. Postmodernism. I. Jarvis, D. S. L. (Darryl S. L.), 1963-
JZ1306 .I577 2002

INTERNATIONAL RELATIONS - DECISION MAKING.
Gelpi, Christopher, 1966- The power of legitimacy. Princeton, N.J. : Princeton University Press, c2003.
JZ5595.5 .G45 2003

INTERNATIONAL RELATIONS - FORECASTING.
Emmott, Bill. 20:21 vision. London : Allen Lane, 2003.

INTERNATIONAL RELATIONS - HISTORY.
Maoz, Zeev. Bound by struggle. Ann Arbor : University of Michigan Press, c2002.
JZ5595 .M366 2002

INTERNATIONAL RELATIONS - MORAL AND ETHICAL ASPECTS.
Dilemmas of reconciliation. Waterloo, Ont. : Wilfrid Laurier University Press, 2003.
Gelpi, Christopher, 1966- The power of legitimacy. Princeton, N.J. : Princeton University Press, c2003.
JZ5595.5 .G45 2003

INTERNATIONAL RELATIONS - PHILOSOPHY.
International relations and the "third debate". Westport, Conn. : Praeger, 2002.
JZ1306 .I577 2002

Katznelson, Ira. Desolation and enlightenment. New York : Columbia University Press, c2003.
JA71 .K35 2003

INTERNATIONAL RELATIONS - PSYCHOLOGICAL ASPECTS.
Gelpi, Christopher, 1966- The power of legitimacy. Princeton, N.J. : Princeton University Press, c2003.
JZ5595.5 .G45 2003

INTERNATIONAL RELIEF - DEVELOPING COUNTRIES.
Goudge, Paulette. The power of whiteness. London : Lawrence & Wishart, 2003.

International Renaissance Foundation (Ukraine). Transformation of the Humanities Program.
Stepanenko, Valeriĭ. Etyka v problemnykh i analitychnykh zadachakh. Kyïv : Libra, 1998.

INTERNATIONAL RIVERS.
Conflict prevention and resolution in water systems. Cheltenham, UK ; Northampton, MA, USA : E. Elgar Pub., c2002.
HD1691 .C664 2002

INTERNATIONAL SALES. *See* **EXPORT SALES CONTRACTS.**

International series in the psychology of religion
(11) Hood, Ralph W. Dimensions of mystical experiences. Amsterdam ; New York, NY : Rodopi, 2001.

International Society for Theoretical Psychology. Conference (9th : 2001 : Calgary, Alta.) Theoretical psychology : critical contributions / edited by Niamh Stephenson ... [et al.]. Concord, Ont. : Captus Press, c2003. xviii, 452 p. ; 26 cm. "Selected proceedings of the 9th Biennial Conference of the International Society for Theoretical Psychology, Calgary, Alberta, Canada Jun. 3-8, 2001". Includes bibliographical references and index. ISBN 1-55322-055-2 DDC 150/.1
1. Psychology - Philosophy - Congresses. 2. Psychology - Methodology - Congresses. I. Stephenson, Niamh. II. Title.

INTERNATIONAL STANDARD BOOK NUMBERS. *See* **BOOKS.**

International studies in sociology and social anthropology
(v. 85) Elite configurations at the apex of power. Leiden ; Boston : Brill, 2003.
JC330.3 .E45 2003

(v. 86) Sengers, Gerda. Women and demons. Leiden ; Boston : Brill, 2003.
BF1275.F3 S463 2003

International survey on cognitive science.
Psychology, IUPsyS global resource [electronic resource]. Hove, East Sussex, UK : published on behalf of the international Union of Psychological Science by Psychology Press Ltd., 2000-
BF76.5 .P79

International survey on ethics codes in psychology.
Psychology, IUPsyS global resource [electronic resource]. Hove, East Sussex, UK : published on behalf of the international Union of Psychological Science by Psychology Press Ltd., 2000-
BF76.5 .P79

INTERNATIONAL TRADE. *See also* **COMPETITION, INTERNATIONAL.**
Barbieri, Katherine, 1965- The liberal illusion. Ann Arbor : University of Michigan Press, c2002.
HF1379 .B363 2002

Globalization and armed conflict. Lanham, Md. : Rowman & Littlefield, c2003.
JZ5538 .G58 2003

United States. General Accounting Office. World Trade Organization [electronic resource]. [Washington, D.C.] : U.S. General Accounting Office, [2002]

INTERNATIONAL TRADE CONTROL. *See* **FOREIGN TRADE REGULATION.**

INTERNATIONAL TRADE - LAW AND LEGISLATION. *See* **FOREIGN TRADE REGULATION.**

INTERNATIONAL TRADE - MORAL AND ETHICAL ASPECTS.
Garten, Jeffrey E., 1946- The politics of fortune. Boston : Harvard Business School Press, c2002.
HD57.7 .G377 2002

McMurtry, John, 1939- Value wars. London ; Sterling, Va. : Pluto Press, c2002.
HF1359 .M39 2002

INTERNATIONAL TRADE REGULATION. *See* **FOREIGN TRADE REGULATION.**

INTERNATIONAL TRAVEL REGULATIONS. *See* **EMIGRATION AND IMMIGRATION LAW.**

International Union of Psychological Science. History of the International Union of Psychological Science (IUPsyS) / Mark R. Rosenzweig ... [et al.]. Hove, East Sussex ; Philadelphia, PA : Psychology Press, c2000. xiii, 290 p. : ill. ; 23 cm. Includes bibliographical references and index. ISBN 1-84169-197-6 DDC 150/.6/01
1. International Union of Psychological Science - History. I. Rozenzweig, Mark R II. Title.
BF11 .I62 2000

Psychology, IUPsyS global resource [electronic resource]. Hove, East Sussex, UK : published on behalf of the international Union of Psychological Science by Psychology Press Ltd., 2000-
BF76.5 .P79

INTERNATIONAL UNION OF PSYCHOLOGICAL SCIENCE.
Psychology, IUPsyS global resource [electronic resource]. Hove, East Sussex, UK : published on behalf of the international Union of Psychological Science by Psychology Press Ltd., 2000-
BF76.5 .P79

INTERNATIONAL UNION OF PSYCHOLOGICAL SCIENCE - HISTORY.
International Union of Psychological Science. History of the International Union of Psychological Science (IUPsyS). Hove, East Sussex ; Philadelphia, PA : Psychology Press, c2000.
BF11 .I62 2000

International Workshop MLDM 2003 (2003 : Leipzig, Germany) Machine learning and data mining in pattern recognition : third international conference, MLDM 2003, Leipzig, Germany, July 5-7, 2003, proceedings / Petra Perner, Azriel Rosenfeld (eds.). Berlin ; New York : Springer, c2003. xii, 440 p. : ill. ; 24 cm. (Lecture notes in computer science, 0302-9743 ; 2734. Lecture notes in artificial intelligence) Includes bibliographical references and index. ISBN 3-540-40504-6 (alk. paper) DDC 006.3/1
1. Pattern perception - Congresses. 2. Machine learning - Congresses. 3. Data mining - Congresses. 4. Image processing - Congresses. I. Title. II. Series: Lecture notes in computer science ; 2734. III. Series: Lecture notes in computer science. Lecture notes in artificial intelligence.
Q327 .I67 2003

International Workshop on Multiple Classifier Systems (4th : 2003 : Guildford, England) Multiple classifier systems : 4th international workshop, MCS 2003, Guildford, UK, June 11-13, 2003 : proceedings / Terry Windeatt, Fabio Roli (eds.). Berlin ; New York : Springer, c2003. x, 406 p. : ill. ; 24 cm. (Lecture notes in computer science, 0302-9743 ; 2709) Includes bibliographical references and index. ISBN 3-540-40369-8 (softcover : alk. paper) DDC 006.3/1
1. Machine learning - Congresses. 2. Neural networks (Computer science) - Congresses. 3. Pattern perception - Congresses. I. Windeatt, Terry. II. Roli, Fabio, 1962- III. Title. IV. Series.
Q325.5 .I574 2003

Internationale Assoziation von Philosophinnen. Symposion (9th : 2000 : Zurich, Switzerland).
Wissen Macht Geschlecht. Zürich : Chronos, c2002.

Internationale Forschungen zur allgemeinen und vergleichenden Literaturwissenschaft
(58) Lambert, Ladina Bezzola. Imagining the unimaginable. Amsterdam ; New York, NY : Rodopi, 2002.
QB29 .L35 2002

Internationale Hochschulschriften
(Bd. 372) Simon, Jürgen, 1966- Kriminalbiologie und Zwangssterilisation. Münster ; New York : Waxmann, 2001.

Internationales Eriugena-Colloquium (10th : Maynooth and Dublin : 2002) History and eschatology in John Scottus Eriugena and his time : proceedings of the Tenth International Conference of the Society for the Promotion of Eriugenian Studies, [held at] Maynooth and Dublin, August 16-20, 2002 / edited by James McEvoy and Michael Dunne. Leuven : University Press, 2002. xviii, 645 p. ; 25 cm. (Ancient and medieval philosophy. Series 1 ; 30) Includes bibliographical references and indexes. Text in English and Italian ISBN 90-5867-241-7 DDC 189
1. Erigena, Johannes Scotus, - ca. 810-ca. 877 - Congresses. 2. Eriugena, Johannes Scottus, - ca.810-ca.877 - Congresses. 3. Bible - Hermeneutics - Congresses. 4. Eschatology - Biblical teaching - Congresses. 5. Theology, Doctrinal - History - Middle Ages, 600-1500 - Congresses. 6. Philosophy, Medieval - Congresses. 7. Ethics. I. Dunne, Michael, 1962- II. McEvoy, J. J. III. Society for the Promotion of Eriugenian Studies. IV. Title. V. Title: John Scotus Eriugena and his time VI. Series.

INTERNATIONALISM. *See also* **NATIONALISM.**
Clark, Harold A. The age of intimacy. Laredo, TX : EBookcase.com, c2000.

Migration, diasporas, and transnationalism. Cheltenham, UK ; Northampton, MA : Edward Elgar, 1999.
JV6032 .M54 1999

INTERNET.
Allen, Robert G. Multiple streams of internet income. New York : Wiley, c2001.
HF5548.32 .A45 2001

Burke, Dan, 1965- Business @ the speed of stupid. Cambridge, MA : Perseus Pub., c2001.
HD45 .B7995 2001

Hayes-Roth, Frederick, 1947- Radical simplicity. Upper Saddle River, N.J. ; London : Prentice Hall PTR, 2003.

Piscitelli, Alejandro. Meta-cultura. Buenos Aires : La Crujía, 2002.
P96.T42 P575

INTERNET ADDRESSES - DIRECTORIES.
Schlein, Alan M. Find it online. 3rd ed. Tempe, AZ : Facts on Demand Press, c2003.

INTERNET AND CHILDREN.
Children in the digital age. Westport, Conn. : Praeger, 2002.
HQ784.M3 C455 2002

Internet-based intelligent information processing systems / editors, R. J. Howlett ... [et al.]. Singapore ; River Edge, NJ : World Scientific, 2003. xxxviii, 402 p. : ill. ; 24 cm. (Series on innovative intelligence ; v.3) Includes bibliographical references and index. ISBN 981-238-281-X
1. Expert systems (Computer science) 2. Internet searching. I. Howlett, Robert J., 1954- II. Series.

INTERNET BOOKSTORES - GERMANY.
Lengen, Haiko van. Bücher im virtuellen Warenkorb. Berlin : Verlag für Wirtschaftskommunikation, c2001.

INTERNET BOOKSTORES - GREAT BRITAIN.
Lengen, Haiko van. Bücher im virtuellen Warenkorb. Berlin : Verlag für Wirtschaftskommunikation, c2001.

INTERNET - CENSORSHIP - DATA PROCESSING.
Knowledge-based information retrieval and filtering from the Web. Boston : Kluwer Academic Publishers, c2003.
TK5105.888 .K58 2003

INTERNET COMMERCE. *See* **ELECTRONIC COMMERCE.**

INTERNET FRAUD.
Web of deception. Medford, N.J : CyberAge Books, c2002.
ZA4201 .W43 2002

Internet power searching.
Bradley, Phil, 1959- 2nd ed. New York : Neal-Schuman Publishers, c2002.
ZA4201 .B69 2002

INTERNET - PSYCHOLOGICAL ASPECTS.
Psychologie des Internet. Wien : WUV, Universitätsverlag, 2001.
BF637.C45 P759 2001

Psychology and the Internet. San Diego, Calif. : Academic Press, c1998.
BF637.C45 P79 1998

INTERNET RESEARCH.
Fraley, R. Chris. How to conduct behavioral research over the internet. New York : Guilford Press, 2005.
BF76.6.I57 F73 2005

INTERNET RESOURCES. *See* **COMPUTER NETWORK RESOURCES.**

INTERNET SEARCHING.
Bradley, Phil, 1959- Internet power searching. 2nd ed. New York : Neal-Schuman Publishers, c2002.
ZA4201 .B69 2002

Clegg, Brian. The professional's guide to mining the Internet. 2nd ed. London : Kogan Page ; Sterling, VA : Stylus Pub., 2001.
ZA4230 .C56 2001

Internet-based intelligent information processing systems. Singapore ; River Edge, NJ : World Scientific, 2003.

Kelly, Brian, 1956- iSearch. Boston, MA : Allyn and Bacon, c2003.
BF76.78 .K45 2003

Knowledge-based information retrieval and filtering from the Web. Boston : Kluwer Academic Publishers, c2003.
TK5105.888 .K58 2003

Villamora, Grace Avellana. Super searchers on Madison Avenue. Medford, N.J. : CyberAge Books/Information Today, c2003.
HF5415.2 .V497 2003

Web of deception. Medford, N.J : CyberAge Books, c2002.
ZA4201 .W43 2002

INTERNET - SOCIAL ASPECTS.
Lovink, Geert. Uncanny networks. Cambridge, Mass. : MIT Press, c2002.
HM851 .L688 2002

Internships in psychology : the APAGS workbook for writing successful applications and finding the right match / edited by Carol Williams-Nickelson and Mitchell J. Prinstein ; with contributions by Shane J. Lopez and W. Gregory Keilin. Washington, D.C. : American Psychological Association, c2004. xii, 142 p. ; 28 cm. Includes bibliographical references (p. 111-113). ISBN 1-59147-036-6
1. Psychology - Study and teaching (Internship) I. Williams-Nickelson, Carol. II. Prinstein, Mitchell J., 1970- III. Lopez, Shane J. IV. Keilin, W. Gregory. V. American Psychological Association of Graduate Students. VI. Title: APAGS workbook for writing successful applications and finding the right match
BF77 .I67 2004

INTERORGANIZATIONAL RELATIONS.
Ratnasingam, Pauline. Inter-organizational trust in business-to-business e-commerce. Hershey, PA : IRM Press, c2003.
HF5548.32 .R378 2003

INTERPERSONAL COMMUNICATION. *See also* **BODY LANGUAGE; DOUBLE BIND (PSYCHOLOGY); SELF-DISCLOSURE.**
Beebe, Steven A., 1950- 4th ed. Boston, MA : Allyn and Bacon, 2004.
BF637.C45 B43 2004

Canary, Daniel J. 3rd ed. Boston : Bedford/St. Martin's, c2003.
BF637.C45 C34 2003

Trenholm, Sarah, 1944- 5th ed. New York : Oxford University Press, 2003.
BF637.C45 T72 2003

INTERPERSONAL COMMUNICATION.
Adler, Ronald B. (Ronald Brian), 1946- Interplay. New York : Oxford University Press, 2004. 9th ed.
BF637.C45 A33 2004

Bjornson, Lawrence E. Secrets of power conversation. [S.l.] : L.E. Bjornson, c2002.
BF637.C45 B575 2002

Boothman, Nicholas. How to connect in business in 90 seconds or less. New York : Workman Pub., 2002.
HD69.S8 B66 2002

Broussard, Cheryl D. What's money got to do with it? Oakland, CA : MetaMedia Pub., [c2002]
1. Black author.

Byock, Ira. The four things that matter most. New York : Free Press, 2004.
BF637.C45 B93 2004

Canary, Daniel J. Interpersonal communication. 3rd ed. Boston : Bedford/St. Martin's, c2003.
BF637.C45 C34 2003

Chelovek kak sub"ekt kul'tury. Moskva : Nauka, 2002.

Clayton, Charles Walker, 1951- Connections!. Radcliffe, IA : Ide House Publishers, 2004.
BF637.C45 C54 2004

Cohen, Norman H. (Norman Harris), 1941- The mentee's guide to mentoring. Amherst, Mass. : HRD Press, c1999.

Communication and emotion. Mahwah, N.J. ; London : Lawrence Erlbaum, c2003.
BF637.C45 C6375 2003

Ford, Loren. Human relations. 3rd ed. Upper Saddle River, N.J. : Pearson/Prentice Hall, c2004.
BF335 .F67 2004

Germain-Thiant, Myriam. La relation à l'autre. Lyon : Chronique sociale, [2002]

Gillman, Karen. Mr. and Dr. talking it over. Lima, Ohio : Wyndham Hall Press, c2002.
BF637.C45 G55 2002

Greiper, BenTzion. Getting and staying married / BenTzion Greiper. Brooklyn, NY : B.T. Greiper, [2001?]
HQ734 .G745 2001

Haviland, James J. This book is no joke!. [Philadelphia?] : Xlibris, c2001.
BF637.C45 H38 2001

Hogan, Kevin. Can't get through. Gretna, La. : Pelican Pub. Co., c2003.
BF637.C45 H635 2003

Hopper, Robert. Gendering talk. East Lansing : Michigan State University Press, c2003.
HQ1075 .H67 2003

Iliev, Vladimir. Psikhologiia na razgovora. 1. izd. Pleven : Lege Artis, 2002.
BF637.C45 I45 2002

Kaplan, Robbie Miller. How to say it when you don't know what to say. Prentice Hall Press ed. Upper Saddle River, NJ : Prentice Hall Press, 2004.
BF637.C54 K36 2004

Lichtenberg, Joseph D. A spirit of inquiry. Hillsdale, NJ : Analytic Press, 2002.
RC506 .L5238 2002

Lumsden, Gay. Communicating with credibility and confidence. 2nd ed. Australia ; Belmont, CA : Thomson/Wadsworth, c2003.
BF637.C45 L85 2003

Petronio, Sandra Sporbert. Boundaries of privacy. Albany : State University of New York Press, c2002.
BF697.5.S427 P48 2002

Plung, Daniel L. Professional communication. Mason, Ohio : Thomson/South-Western, c2004.
HF5718 .P58 2004

Raam, Gabriel. Omanut ha-śiḥah. Tel-Aviv : Yedi'ot aharonot : Sifre ḥemed, c2003.
P95.45 .R33 2003

Rosenberg, Marshall B. Nonviolent communication. 2nd ed. Encinitas, CA : PuddleDancer Press, 2003.
BF637.C45 R645 2003

Studies in language and social interaction. Mahwah, N.J. ; London : Lawrence Erlbaum, 2003.

Tonoiu, Vasile. Omul dialogal. București : Editura Fundației Culturale Române, 1995.

Trenholm, Sarah, 1944- Interpersonal communication. 5th ed. New York : Oxford University Press, 2003.
BF637.C45 T72 2003

Tvorogova, N. D. (Nadezhda Tvorogova) Obshchenie. Moskva : Smysl, 2002.
BF637.C45 T88 2002

Verderber, Kathleen S., 1949- Inter-act. 10th ed. New York : Oxford University Press, 2004.
BF637.C45 V47 2004

INTERPERSONAL COMMUNICATION - CONGRESSES.
Psikhologiia otnosheniĭ. Vladimir : Vladimirskiĭ gos. pedagogicheskiĭ universitet, 2001.
BF637.C45 P74 2001

INTERPERSONAL COMMUNICATION IN CHILDREN. *See also* **LANGUAGE ACQUISITION.**
Meyer, John, 1964- Kids talking. Lanham, MD : Rowman & Littlefield, c2003.
BF723.C57 M49 2003

INTERPERSONAL COMMUNICATION IN CHILDREN - JUVENILE LITERATURE.
Dickerson, Karle. Girl chat. New York : Scholastic, c2001.
BF723.C57 D53 2001

INTERPERSONAL COMMUNICATION IN INFANTS.
Acredolo, Linda P. My first baby signs. [New York] : HarperFestival, c2002.
BF720.C65 A27 2002

Holinger, Paul C. What babies say before they can talk. New York : Simon & Schuster, c2003.
BF720.C65 H64 2003

INTERPERSONAL COMMUNICATION - TEXTBOOKS.
Beebe, Steven A., 1950- Interpersonal communication. 4th ed. Boston, MA : Allyn and Bacon, 2004.
BF637.C45 B43 2004

Yingling, Julie. A lifetime of communication. Mahwah, N.J. : Lawrence Erlbaum Associates, 2004.
BF637.C45 Y56 2004

INTERPERSONAL CONFLICT. *See also* **SOCIAL CONFLICT.**
Canary, Daniel J. Interpersonal communication. 3rd ed. Boston : Bedford/St. Martin's, c2003.
BF637.C45 C34 2003

Engelhardt, Lisa, 1953- Elf-help for dealing with difficult people. St. Meinrad, IN : One Caring Place/Abbey Press, c2002.
BF637.I48 E54 2002

Gillman, Karen. Mr. and Dr. talking it over. Lima, Ohio : Wyndham Hall Press, c2002.
BF637.C45 G55 2002

Gould, Roger V. Collision of wills. Chicago : University of Chicago Press, 2003.
HM1121 .G68 2003

Granovskaia, R. M. (Rada Mikhaĭlovna) Konflikt i tvorchestvo v zerkale psikhologii. Moskva : Genezis, 2002.

BF637.I48 G72 2002

Hart, Lois Borland. The manager's pocket guide to dealing with conflict. Amherst, Mass. : HRD Press, c1999.
BF637.I48 H38 1999

Holá, Lenka. Mediace. Vyd. 1. Praha : Grada Pub., 2003.
BF637.I48 H63 2003

Kowalski, Robin M. Complaining, teasing, and other annoying behaviors. New Haven : Yale University Press, c2003.
HM1106 .K69 2003

Křivohlavý, Jaro. Konflikty mezi lidmi. Vyd. 2., přepracované, v Portalu 1. Praha : Portal, 2002.
BF637.I48 K75 2002

Nay, W. Robert. Taking charge of anger. New York : Guilford Press, c2003.
BF575.A5 N39 2003

Paleg, Kim. When anger hurts your relationship. Oakland, CA : New Harbinger Publications, c2001.
BF575.A5 P35 2001

VanSant, Sondra. Wired for conflict. Gainesville, Fla. : Center for Applications of Psychological Type, c2003.
BF698.3 .V36 2003

INTERPERSONAL CONFLICT - JUVENILE LITERATURE.
Johnston, Marianne. [Dealing with fighting. Spanish] Como tratar las peleas. New York : PowerKids Press, 2005.
BF637.I48 J6418 2005

INTERPERSONAL CONFLICT - TESTING.
IIP, inventory of interpersonal problems manual. [San Antonio, TX?] : Psychological Corp., c2000.
BF698.5 .I36 2000

INTERPERSONAL CONFRONTATION - JUVENILE LITERATURE.
Johnston, Marianne. [Dealing with fighting. Spanish] Como tratar las peleas. New York : PowerKids Press, 2005.
BF637.I48 J6418 2005

INTERPERSONAL PERCEPTION. *See* **SOCIAL PERCEPTION.**

INTERPERSONAL RELATIONS. *See also* **COMPETITION (PSYCHOLOGY); COUPLES; DISCRIMINATION; FRIENDSHIP; HELPING BEHAVIOR; INTERGENERATIONAL RELATIONS; INTERPERSONAL COMMUNICATION; INTERPERSONAL CONFLICT; INTERPERSONAL CONFRONTATION; INTIMACY (PSYCHOLOGY); MAN-WOMAN RELATIONSHIPS; OBJECT RELATIONS (PSYCHOANALYSIS); PARENT AND CHILD; SEPARATION (PSYCHOLOGY); SOCIAL PERCEPTION; VERBAL SELF-DEFENSE.**
Alborch Bataller, Carmen. Malas. 3. ed. [Madrid] : Aguilar, 2002.

Austin, Linda S., 1951- Heart of the matter. New York : Atria Books, c2003.
BF575.L8 A97 2003

Bianchi, Carlos J. (Carlos Juan) Relatos de la pareja. Buenos Aires : Corregidor, c2001.

Birtchnell, John. The two of me. Hove, East Sussex [England] ; New York : Routledge, 2003.
BF311 .B533 2003

Boothman, Nicholas. How to connect in business in 90 seconds or less. New York : Workman Pub., 2002.
HD69.S8 B66 2002

Byock, Ira. The four things that matter most. New York : Free Press, 2004.
BF637.C45 B93 2004

Canary, Daniel J. Interpersonal communication. 3rd ed. Boston : Bedford/St. Martin's, c2003.
BF637.C45 C34 2003

Carter, Jay. Nasty women. Chicago : Contemporary Books, c2003.
BF632.5 .C365 2003

Cohen, Norman H. (Norman Harris), 1941- The mentee's guide to mentoring. Amherst, Mass. : HRD Press, c1999.

Discourse and organization. London ; Thousand Oaks, Calif. : Sage Publications, 1998.
HD58.7 .D57 1998

Engel, Beverly. The emotionally abusive relationship. New Jersey : J. Wiley, c2002.

Fang yuan bing fa. Di 1 ban. Beijing : Jin cheng chu ban she, 1998.

Ford, Loren. Human relations. 3rd ed. Upper Saddle River, N.J. : Pearson/Prentice Hall, c2004.
BF335 .F67 2004

Galende, Emiliano. Sexo y amor. 1a ed. Buenos Aires : Paidós, 2001.

Goals and life lessons support materials [electronic resource]. Greenwood Village, CO : FasTracKids International, [1998]
BF637.S4

Gray, John, 1948- [Men are from Mars, women are from Venus. Spanish] Els homes són de Mart, les dones són de Venus. 1. ed. Barcelona : Edicions 62, c2001.

Greiper, BenTzion. Getting and staying married / BenTzion Greiper. Brooklyn, NY : B.T. Greiper, [2001?]
HQ734 .G745 2001

Johnston, Marianne. [Dealing with fighting. Spanish] Como tratar las peleas. New York : PowerKids Press, 2005.
BF637.I48 J6418 2005

Kowalski, Robin M. Complaining, teasing, and other annoying behaviors. New Haven : Yale University Press, c2003.
HM1106 .K69 2003

Krieglstein, Werner J., 1941- Compassion. Amsterdam ; New York : Rodopi, c2002.

Lowry, Don. Keys to personal success. Riverside, Calif. : True Colors, Inc. ; c2001.
BF637.S8 .L77 2001

Lumsden, Gay. Communicating with credibility and confidence. 2nd ed. Australia ; Belmont, CA : Thomson/Wadsworth, c2003.
BF637.C45 L85 2003

Mellody, Pia. The intimacy factor. 1st ed. [San Francisco, CA] : HarperSanFrancisco, c2003.
BF575.I5 M45 2003

Mindell, Arnold, 1940- The dreambody in relationships. Portland, OR : Lao Tse Press ; Oakland, CA : Distributed to the trade by Words Distributing Co., c2002.
BF637.N66 M56 2002

Pimental-Habib, Richard L. The power of a partner. 1st ed. Los Angeles, CA : Alyson Books, 2002.
HQ76.25 .P56 2002

Reyes, Arnoldo Juan. Una alternativa para ser feliz. Ciudad de La Habana, Cuba : Editorial Científico-Técnica, 2001, c2000.

Richmond, Virginia P., 1949- Nonverbal behavior in interpersonal relations. 5th ed. Boston, Mass. : Pearson, 2004.
BF637.N66 R53 2004

Rosenberg, Marshall B. Nonviolent communication. 2nd ed. Encinitas, CA : PuddleDancer Press, 2003.
BF637.C45 R645 2003

Rozin, V. M. Li︠u︡bov' i seksual'nost' v kul'ture, sem'e i vzgli︠a︡dakh na polovoe vospitanie. Moskva : Logos : Vysshai︠a︡ shkola, 1999.
BF575.L8 R69 1999

Social relations and the life course. Houndmills, Basingstoke New York : Palgrave Macmillan, 2003.
HM741 .S64 2003

Somogyi, Gábor. Libikóka. [Budapest?] : Honestus-Press, 2002.
BF575.L8 S623 2002

Tipping, Colin C. Radical forgiveness. Atlanta, GA : GOLDENeight Publishers, c1997.
BF637.F67 T57 1997

Tonoiu, Vasile. Omul dialogal. București : Editura Fundației Culturale Române, 1995.

Verderber, Kathleen S., 1949- Inter-act. 10th ed. New York : Oxford University Press, 2004.
BF637.C45 V47 2004

Whalen, Charles E., Jr. The gift of renewal. 1st ed. Gainesville, GA : Warren Featherbone Foundation, c2003 (Gainesville, GA : Matthews Print.)

BF637.S4 W47 2003

INTERPERSONAL RELATIONS AND CULTURE.
Hirata, Helena Sumiko. [División sexual del trabajo. Portuguese] Nova divisão sexual do trabalho? 1a ed. São Paulo : Boitempo, 2002.
HD6060.6 .H5717 2002

Hochschild, Arlie Russell, 1940- The commercialization of intimate life. Berkeley : University of California Press, 2003.
HM1106 .H63 2003

INTERPERSONAL RELATIONS - CASE STUDIES.
Maksimov, Andreĭ, 1959- Dialogi li︠u︡bvi. Moskva : Delovoĭ ėkspress, 1999.
BF575.L8 M336 1999

INTERPERSONAL RELATIONS - CONGRESSES.
Psikhologii︠a︡ otnosheniĭ. Vladimir : Vladimirskiĭ gos. pedagogicheskiĭ universitet, 2001.
BF637.C45 P74 2001

INTERPERSONAL RELATIONS IN CHILDREN.
Meyer, John, 1964- Kids talking. Lanham, MD : Rowman & Littlefield, c2003.
BF723.C57 M49 2003

INTERPERSONAL RELATIONS - JUVENILE LITERATURE.
Morrison, Toni. The book of mean people. 1st ed. New York : Hyperion Books for Children, c2002.
1. Black authors.

INTERPERSONAL RELATIONS - PSYCHIC ASPECTS.
Braud, William. Distant mental influence. Charlottesville, VA : Hampton Roads Pub., c2003.
BF1045.S33 B74 2003

INTERPERSONAL RELATIONS - RELIGIOUS ASPECTS - JUDAISM.
Mermelshṭain, Avraham Yitshak David. Kuntres Dover mesharim. Hotsa'ah 2. [Brooklyn] : A.Y.D. Mermelshṭain, 762 [2001]

Mosheh ben Ḥayim, Koznitser, d. 1874. Sefer Ahavat Yiśra'el. Yotse le-or me-ḥadash. Yerushalayim : Mekhon Sod yesharim, 760 [2000]

Mosheh ben Ḥayim, Koznitser, d. 1874. Sefer 'Ahavat Yiśra'el. Bruḳlin : [Yehoshu'a Pinḥas Bukhinger], 762 [2001]

INTERPERSONAL RELATIONS - TESTING.
IIP, inventory of interpersonal problems manual. [San Antonio, TX?] : Psychological Corp., c2000.
BF698.5 .I36 2000

INTERPERSONAL RELATIONS - UNITED STATES.
Longing to tell. 1st ed. New York : Farrar, Straus and Giroux, 2003.
E185.625 .L66 2003

INTERPERSONAL RELATIONSHIPS - GERMANY.
Liebe und Abhängigkeit. Weinheim : Juventa, 2001.

Interplay.
Adler, Ronald B. (Ronald Brian), 1946- New York : Oxford University Press, 2004. 9th ed.
BF637.C45 A33 2004

INTERPRETATION. *See* **HERMENEUTICS.**

Interpretation and construction.
Stecker, Robert, 1928- Malden, MA : Blackwell, 2003.
BD241 .S78 2003

L'interprétation des gènes.
Andrieu, Bernard. Paris : Harmattan, 2002.

INTERPRETATION, DREAM. *See* **DREAM INTERPRETATION.**

INTERPRETATION OF PICTURES. *See* **PICTURE INTERPRETATION.**

INTERPRETATION (PHILOSOPHY).
Filosofía, retórica e interpretación. México, D.F. : Universidad Nacional Autónoma de México, 2000.

Interpretation und Argument / herausgegeben von Helmut Linneweber-Lammerskitten und Georg Mohr. Würzburg : Königshausen & Neumann, c2002. ix, 403 p. ; 24 cm. "Gerhard Seel zum 60. Geburtstag"--P. [v]. Includes bibliographical references. 14 German, 6 English, 5 French contributions. ISBN 3-8260-2274-2 (hd.bd.)
1. Philosophy. I. Linneweber-Lammerskitten, Helmut. II. Mohr, Georg. III. Seel, Gerhard, 1940-

INTERPRETING AND TRANSLATING. *See* **TRANSLATING AND INTERPRETING.**

Interpreting and understanding dreams.
Gollub, Dan. Comack, N.Y. : Nova Science Publishers, c1998.
BF1091 .G653 1998

Interpreting Kant's critiques.
Ameriks, Karl, 1947- Oxford : Clarendon Press ; New York : Oxford University Press, 2003.
B2779 .A64 2003

Interpreting the maternal organisation / edited by Heather Höpfl and Monika Kostera. London ; New York : Routledge, 2003. xxiii, 239 p. : ill. ; 25 cm. (Routledge studies in human resource development ; 4) Includes bibliographical references and index. ISBN 0-415-28574-7 (alk. paper) DDC 302.3/5
1. Organization - Philosophy. 2. Organizational sociology. 3. Organizational behavior. 4. Sex role in the work environment. I. Höpfl, Heather. II. Kostera, Monika, 1963- III. Series.
HM786 .I58 2003

Interpreting the modern world
Making sense of collectivity. London ; Sterling, Va. : Pluto Press, 2002.
HM753 .M35 2002

Interpretive guide for teachers and counselors.
Lohman, David F. Itasca, IL : Riverside Pub., c2001.
BF432.5.C64 L65 2001

INTERPROFESSIONAL RELATIONS. See PROFESSIONS.

The interrogation.
Cook, Thomas H. Rockland, MA : Wheeler Pub., 2002.
PS3553.O55465 I58 2002

INTERSTELLAR MATTER. See DARK MATTER (ASTRONOMY).

INTERSUBJECTIVITY.
Lévinas, Emmanuel. [Humanisme de l'autre homme. English] Humanism of the other. Urbana : University of Illinois Press, c2003.
B2430.L48 H8413 2003

La intervención divina en el hombre a través de la literatura griega de época arcaica y clásica.
Muñoz Llamosas, Virginia. Amsterdam : Hakkert, 2002.
PA3015.R5 M87 2002

Intervening to improve the safety of occupational driving.
Ludwig, Timothy D. New York : Haworth Press, 2000.
HE5614 .I586 2000

INTERVENTION (CRIMINAL PROCEDURE). See REPARATION.

INTERVENTION (INTERNATIONAL LAW).
Chanaa, Jane. Security sector reform. Oxford ; New York : Oxford University Press for the International Institute for Strategic Studies, 2002.
HV6419 .C52 2002

INTERVENTION (INTERNATIONAL LAW) - CASE STUDIES.
Imobighe, Thomas A. The OAU (AU) and OAS in regional conflict management. Ibadan : Spectrum Books ; Oxford, UK : USA distributor, African Books Collective, 2003.
JZ6374 .I46 2003

INTERVENTION (INTERNATIONAL LAW) - POLITICAL ASPECTS.
Ending civil wars. Boulder, Colo. : Lynne Rienner, 2002.
JZ6368 .E53 2002

Intervention philosophique
Civilisation et barbarie. 1re éd. Paris : Presses universitaires de France, c2002.

INTERVIEWING. See COUNSELING; INTERVIEWS.

INTERVIEWING - HANDBOOKS, MANUALS, ETC.
Sommer, Barbara W. The oral history manual. Walnut Creek, CA ; Oxford : Altamira Press, c2002.
D16.14 .S69 2002

INTERVIEWING IN LAW ENFORCEMENT. See POLICE QUESTIONING.

INTERVIEWS. See also INTERVIEWING.
Nosmas, Alma. La mort élégante. Paris : Horay, c2003.

INTERVIEWS - GREAT BRITAIN.
Archer, Margaret Scotford. Structure, agency and the internal conversation. Cambridge, U.K. ; New York : Cambridge University Press, 2003.
HM708 .A73 2003

Interviews with Dwight Macdonald.
Macdonald, Dwight. Jackson : University Press of Mississippi, c2003.
E169.1 .M1363 2003

INTESTACY. See INHERITANCE AND SUCCESSION.

INTESTATE SUCCESSION. See INHERITANCE AND SUCCESSION.

Intimacy.
Rosenthal, Don. Doughcloyne, Wilton, Cork : Collins Press, 1999.
BF575.I5 R67 1999

The intimacy factor.
Mellody, Pia. 1st ed. [San Francisco, CA] : HarperSanFrancisco, c2003.
BF575.I5 M45 2003

INTIMACY (PSYCHOLOGY). See also LOVE; SEPARATION (PSYCHOLOGY).
Clark, Harold A. The age of intimacy. Laredo, TX : EBookcase.com, c2000.

Denise, Jan. Naked relationships. Charlottesville, VA : Hampton Roads Pub., c2002.
BF575.I5 D46 2002

Galende, Emiliano. Sexo y amor. 1a ed. Buenos Aires : Paidós, 2001.

Gilligan, Carol, 1936- The birth of pleasure. 1st ed. New York : A.A. Knopf, 2002.
BF575.L8 G56 2002

Handbook of closeness and intimacy. Mahwah, N.J. : Lawrence Erlbaum Associates, 2004.
BF575.I5 H36 2004

Liebe und Abhängigkeit. Weinheim : Juventa, 2001.

Longing to tell. 1st ed. New York : Farrar, Straus and Giroux, 2003.
E185.625 .L66 2003

Mellody, Pia. The intimacy factor. 1st ed. [San Francisco, CA] : HarperSanFrancisco, c2003.
BF575.I5 M45 2003

Rosenthal, Don. Intimacy. Doughcloyne, Wilton, Cork : Collins Press, 1999.
BF575.I5 R67 1999

Sarnoff, Irving, 1922- Intimate creativity. Madison, Wis. : University of Wisconsin Press, c2002.
BF411 .S27 2002

INTIMACY (PSYCHOLOGY) IN LITERATURE.
Kristeva, Julia, 1941- [Révolte intime. English] Intimate revolt. New York : Columbia University Press, c2002.
PN56.P92 K7513 2002

INTIMACY (PSYCHOLOGY) - MISCELLANEA.
Godek, Gregory J. P., 1955- 10,000 ways to say I love you. Naperville, Ill. : Casablanca Press, c1999.
BF575.L8 G63 1999

Intimate creativity.
Sarnoff, Irving, 1922- Madison, Wis. : University of Wisconsin Press, c2002.
BF411 .S27 2002

Intimate revolt.
Kristeva, Julia, 1941- [Révolte intime. English] New York : Columbia University Press, c2002.
PN56.P92 K7513 2002

INTOLERANCE. See FANATICISM.

INTRAPSYCHIC CONFLICT. See CONFLICT (PSYCHOLOGY).

Introducing child psychology.
Schaffer, H. Rudolph. Malden, MA : Blackwell Pub. Ltd., 2004.
BF721 .S349 2004

Une introduction aux sciences de la culture / sous la direction de François Rastier et Simon Bouquet ; avec le concours de Jean-Michel Fortis. 1. ed. Paris : Presses universitaires de France ; [Paris] : Institut Ferdinand-de-Saussure, 2002. vi, 290 p. : ill. ; 22 cm. (Formes sémiotiques, 0767-1970) Includes bibliographical references. ISBN 2-13-052897-X DDC 300
1. Culture - Semiotic models. 2. Anthropological linguistics. 3. Cognitive science. 4. Human evolution. 5. Semiotics. I. Rastier, François. II. Bouquet, Simon. III. Fortis, Jean-Michel. IV. Series.

Introduction to astrology.
Kūshyār, d. ca. 961. [Introduction to astrology] Kūšyār ibn Labbān's introduction to astrology. Tokyo : Institue for the Study of Languages and Cultures of Asia and Africa, 1997.
BF1714.I84 K87 1997

Introduction to behavioral research methods.
Leary, Mark R. 4th ed. Boston, MA : Allyn and Bacon, 2004.
BF76.5 .L39 2004

An introduction to parapsychology.
Irwin, H. J. (Harvey J.) 4th ed. Jefferson, N.C. : McFarland & Co., 2003.
BF1031 .I79 2003

Introduction to personality.
Mischel, Walter. 7th ed. Hoboken, NJ : J. Wiley & Sons, c2004.
BF698 .M555 2004

Introduction to philosophy in an African perspective.
Chukwu, Cletus N. Eldoret, Kenya : Zapf Chancery, 2002.

An introduction to psychological assessment in the South African context / edited by Cheryl Foxcroft & Gert Roodt. Cape Town, South Africa : Oxford University Press Southern Africa, 2001. xxviii, 398 p. : ill. ; 22 cm. Includes bibliographical references (p. 369-389) and index. ISBN 0-19-571856-9
1. Psychometrics - South Africa. 2. Psychological tests - South Africa. I. Foxcroft, Cheryl. II. Roodt, G.
BF39 .I58 2001

Introduction to psychology.
Atkinson & Hilgard's introduction to psychology. 14th ed. Australia ; Belmont, CA : Wadworth/Thomson Learning, c2003.
BF121 .I57 2003

Introduction to research methods and statistics in psychology.
Coolican, Hugh. 2nd ed. London : Hodder & Stoughton, c1996.
BF76.5 .C663 1996

Introduction to the history of European unity.
Dawson, Christopher, 1889-1970. The making of Europe. Washington, D.C. : Catholic University of America Press, 2002, 1932.
CB353 .D3 2002

An introduction to the psychology of hearing.
Moore, Brian C. J. 5th ed. Amsterdam ; Boston : Academic Press, c2003.
BF251 .M66 2003

An introduction to theories of human development.
Salkind, Neil J. Thousand Oaks, Calif. : Sage Publications, c2004.
BF713 .S245 2004

Introduction to therapeutic counseling.
Kottler, Jeffrey A. 5th ed. Australia ; Pacific Grove, CA : Thomson-Brooks/Cole, c2004.
BF637.C6 K678 2004

Introduzione alla filosofia di Giordano Bruno.
Vecchiotti, Icilio. Urbino : QuattroVenti, c2000.
B783.Z7 V43 2000

INTUITION. See also INSIGHT.
Hague, Angela. Fiction, intuition, & creativity. Washington, D.C. : Catholic University of America Press, c2003.
PR826 .H28 2003

Hall, Judy, 1943- The intuition handbook. London : Vega, 2003.
BF315.5 .H35 2003

Holt, Lynn, 1959- Apprehension. Aldershot, Hants, England ; Burlington, VT : Ashgate, c2002.
BC177 .H655 2002

North, Dia. The smart spot. Boston, MA : Red Wheel, 2003.
BF637.S8 N655 2003

The intuition handbook.
Hall, Judy, 1943- London : Vega, 2003.
BF315.5 .H35 2003

INTUITION OF DURATION. See TIME PERCEPTION.

INTUITION (PSYCHOLOGY). See PERCEPTION.

INUIT - PSYCHOLOGY.
Many faces of gender. Boulder : University Press of Colorado ; Calgary, Alta., Canada : University of Calgary Press, c2002.
E98.P95 M35 2002

INUIT - SEXUAL BEHAVIOR.
Many faces of gender. Boulder : University Press of Colorado ; Calgary, Alta., Canada : University of Calgary Press, c2002.

E98.P95 M35 2002

INUIT WOMEN - SOCIAL CONDITIONS.
Many faces of gender. Boulder : University Press of Colorado : Calgary, Alta., Canada : University of Calgary Press, c2002.
E98.P95 M35 2002

INUPIK. *See* **INUIT.**

INVALIDS. *See* **HANDICAPPED.**

INVASION OF PRIVACY. *See* **PRIVACY, RIGHT OF.**

INVECTIVE.
Johnston, Marianne. [Dealing with insults. Spanish] Como tratar los insultos. New York : PowerKids Press, 2005.
BF637.V47 J6418 2005

INVECTIVE - JUVENILE LITERATURE.
Johnston, Marianne. [Dealing with insults. Spanish] Como tratar los insultos. New York : PowerKids Press, 2005.
BF637.V47 J6418 2005

INVECTIVE - PSYCHOLOGICAL ASPECTS.
Jay, Timothy. Why we curse. Philadelphia : John Benjamins Publishing Company, c2000.
BF463.I58 J38 2000

Inventing popular culture.
Storey, John, 1950- Malden, MA : Blackwell Pub., 2003.
CB19 .S7455 2003

The invention of peace and the reinvention of war.
Howard, Michael, 1922 Nov. 29- Rev. and extended ed. London : Profile, 2002, c2001.

The invention of telepathy, 1870-1901.
Luckhurst, Roger. Oxford ; New York : Oxford University Press, 2002.
BF1171 .L77 2002

INVENTIONS. *See* **TECHNOLOGICAL INNOVATIONS.**

Inventory of interpersonal problems.
IIP, inventory of interpersonal problems manual. [San Antonio, TX?] : Psychological Corp., c2000.
BF698.5 .I36 2000

Investigación social y estadística aplicada
(módulo 1) Morales Tomas, Marco Antonio. El que busca encuentra = Guatemala : ESEDIR : Editorial Saqil Tzij, 1999.
(módulo 2) Valle Bonilla, Otto René. Que no le cuenten cuentos = Guatemala : ESEDIR : Editorial Saqil Tzij, 1999.
(módulo 3) Morales Tomas, Marco Antonio. Una gráfica dice más que mil palabras = Guatemala : ESEDIR : Editorial Saqil Tzij, 1999.

Investigando a relação oral/escrito e as teorias do letramento.
Marcuschi, Luiz Antônio. Campinas, SP : Mercado de Letras, 2001.

Investigating the supernatural.
Mason, Paul, 1967- Chicago, Ill. : Heinemann Library, 2004.
BF1029 .M37 2004

INVESTIGATIONS. *See* **CRIMINAL INVESTIGATION.**

INVESTIGATORS, GOVERNMENT. *See* **GOVERNMENT INVESTIGATORS.**

Investing in peace.
Boyce, James K. Oxford : Oxford University Press, 2002.

INVESTMENTS - UNITED STATES.
United States. Congress. House. Committee on Energy and Commerce. Subcommittee on Telecommunications and the Internet. Health of the telecommunication sector. Washington : U.S. G.P.O. : For sale by the Supt. of Docs., U.S. G.P.O. [Congressional Sales Office], 2003.

The invisible bag.
Solar, Melanie B. Greenwell Springs, LA : Solar Pub., 2000.
BF723.C47 S65 2000

INVISIBLE WORLD. *See* **SPIRITS.**

Invitation to psychology.
Wade, Carole. 3rd ed. Upper Saddle River, NJ : Pearson/Prentice Hall, 2004.
BF121 .W265 2004

Invitation to the life course : toward new understandings of later life / edited by Richard A. Settersten, Jr. Amityville, N.Y. : Baywood Pub. Co., c2003. viii, 355 p. ; 24 cm. (Society and aging series) Includes bibliographical references and indexes. ISBN 0-89503-269-4 DDC 305.26
1. Gerontology. 2. Aging. 3. Life cycle, Human. I. Settersten, Richard A. II. Series.
HQ1061 .I584 2003

INVOCATION OF CHRISTIAN SAINTS. *See* **CHRISTIAN SAINTS - CULT.**

INVOLUNTARY STERILIZATION. *See* **STERILIZATION, EUGENIC.**

INVOLUNTARY TREATMENT. *See* **STERILIZATION, EUGENIC.**

Io sono, tu sei.
Boncinelli, Edoardo. 1. ed. Milano : Mondadori, 2002.

Ionov, I. N. (Igor' Nikolaevich) Teoriia tsivilizatsiĭ : ot antichnosti do kontsa XIX veka / I.N. Ionov, V.M. Khachaturi͡an. Sankt-Peterburg : Aleteĭi͡a, 2002. 382 p. ; 22 cm. Includes bibliographical references. ISBN 5893294173
1. Civilization - Philosophy - History. 2. Historiography - Europe - History. 3. Historiography - Russia - History. 4. Philosophy, Russian - History. 5. History - Philosophy. I. Khachaturi͡an, V. M. (Valeri͡ia Marlenovna) II. Title.
CB19 .I656 2002

IQ. *See* **INTELLIGENCE LEVELS.**

IQ and psychometric tests.
Carter, Philip J. London ; Sterling, VA : Kogan Page Ltd., 2004.
BF431.3 .C362 2004

IQ TESTS. *See* **INTELLIGENCE TESTS.**

IRAN - INTELLECTUAL LIFE - 20TH CENTURY.
Qizilsaflī, Muḥammad Taqī. Qarn-i rawshanfikrān. Chāp-i 1. Tihrān : Markaz-i Bayn al-Milalī-i Guftugū-yi Tamaddunʹhā : Hirmis, 1380 [2001]

Iranzo, Juan Manuel.
Sobre las identidades. Pamplona : Universidad Pública de Navarra, [2001]

IRAQ - ARMED FORCES - UNIT COHESION.
Why they fight [electronic resource]. Carlisle, PA : Strategic Studies Institute, U.S. Army War College, [2003]
U22

IRAQ WAR, 2003.
Cannon, Carl M. The pursuit of happiness in times of war. Lanham, MD ; Oxford : Rowman & Littlefield ; [Lanham, Md.] : Distributed by National Book Network, c2004.
E183 .C25 2004

IRAQ WAR, 2003 - PSYCHOLOGICAL ASPECTS.
Why they fight [electronic resource]. Carlisle, PA : Strategic Studies Institute, U.S. Army War College, [2003]
U22

IRGUN TSEVAʹI LEʹUMI.
Oron, Israel. Mayet, almayet ye-ideʹologyah. [Israel] : Miśrad ha-biṭaḥon, [2002]

Irigaray, Luce.
[Voie de l'amour. English]
The way of love / Luce Irigaray ; translated by Heidi Bostic and Stephen Pluháček. London ; New York : Continuum, 2002. xxii, 174 p. ; 20 cm. ISBN 0-8264-5982-X
1. Love. 2. Sex differences. I. Bostic, Heidi. II. Pluháček, Stephen. III. Title.
BF575.L8 I7513 2002

The way of love / Luce Irigaray ; translated by Heidi Bostic and Stephen Pluháček. London ; New York : Continuum, 2002. xxii, 174 p. ; 20 cm. ISBN 0-8264-5982-X DDC 128.46
1. Love. 2. Sex differences. I. Bostic, Heidi. II. Pluháček, Stephen. III. Title.

Irish Jesus, Roman Jesus.
Snyder, Graydon F. Harrisburg, Pa. : Trinity Press International, c2002.
BR737.C4 S69 2002

Irons, Richard, M.D.
Corley, M. Deborah. Embracing recovery from chemical dependency. Sottsdale, AZ : Gentle Path Press, c2003.
BF632 .C63 2003

O irracionalismo - , dos Estados Unidos da América à globalização.
Pessanha, Rodolfo Gomes. Niterói : Muiraquitã, c1998.

IRRATIONALISM (PHILOSOPHY). *See* **ABSURD (PHILOSOPHY).**

Irreale oder reale Geschichte?.
Kiesewetter, Hubert, 1939- Herbolzheim : Centaurus, 2002.

Irrelevance reasoning in knowledge based systems [miroform].
Levy, Alon Y. (Alon Yitzchak) [Washington, DC : National Aeronautics and Space Administration] ; Springfield, VA : Available from the National Technical Information Service, [1998]

El irresistible encanto de Betty la fea.
Méndez, José Luis, 1941- San Juan, P.R. : Ediciones Milenio, 2001.

IRREVERSIBLE PROCESSES. *See* **OPEN SYSTEMS (PHYSICS).**

Irwin, H. J. (Harvey J.) An introduction to parapsychology / Harvey J. Irwin. 4th ed. Jefferson, N.C. : McFarland & Co., 2003. p. cm. Includes bibliographical references and indexes. ISBN 0-7864-1833-8 (pbk. : alk. paper) DDC 133.8
1. Parapsychology - Textbooks. I. Title.
BF1031 .I79 2003

Is human life special?.
Collste, Göran. Bern ; Oxford : Peter Lang, 2002.

Isaacs, Diane R. Molly & Monet : a story about surviving the loss of a loved one / Diane R. Isaacs. Seattle, WA : Peanut Butter Pub., c1999. 94 p. : ill. ; 22 cm. ISBN 0-89716-857-7 (pbk.) DDC 155.9/37
1. Grief. 2. Bereavement - Psychological aspects. 3. Spouses - Death - Psychological aspects. 4. Loss (Psychology) I. Title. II. Title: Molly and Monet
BF575.G7 I86 1999

Isager, Jacob, 1944-.
Divination and portents in the Roman world. Odense : Odense University Press, c2000.
BF1768 .D57 2000

Isaković, Alija.
Biserje. 3., dop. izd. Sarajevo : Ljiljan, 1998.

Iscoe, Louise.
Texas psychology. Austin : The University of Texas at Austin, c2002.
BF80.7.U62 T48 2002

iSearch.
Kelly, Brian, 1956- Boston, MA : Allyn and Bacon, c2003.
BF76.78 .K45 2003

iSearch psychology 2003.
Kelly, Brian, 1956- iSearch. Boston, MA : Allyn and Bacon, c2003.
BF76.78 .K45 2003

ĪSHARA SIṄGHA, 1905-1975.
Sant Baba Ishar Singh Ji. Hardwar : Nanak-Dar Sant Baba Nand Singh Sant Baba Ishar Singh Spiritual Mission, 2002.
BL2017.9.I84 S27 2002

ISI guides to the major disciplines
Robinson, Daniel N., 1937- A student's guide to psychology. 1st ed. Wilmington, Del. : ISI Books, c2002.
BF121 .R598 2002

ISIS. *See also* **ISIS (EGYPTIAN DEITY).**
Dee, Jonathan. New York : Sterling Pub., [2003?]
BF1591 .D44 2003

ISIS (EGYPTIAN DEITY).
Dee, Jonathan. Isis. New York : Sterling Pub., [2003?]
BF1591 .D44 2003

Isis reminiscence series.
Grimwood, Irene. Land girls at the old rectory. Large print ed. Oxford : ISIS, 2001.

Iskusstvo snovideniĭ = Arts & dreams / pod redakt͡sieĭ Anastasii Budanok i Viktora Mazina. Sankt-Peterburg : Skifii͡a, 2002. 328 p. : ill. ; 20 cm. Includes bibliographical references. Russian and English. ISBN 5926801400
1. Freud, Sigmund, - 1856-1939 - Views on dreams. 2. Dreams and the arts. 3. Dreams in art. 4. Dream interpretation. I. Budanok, Anastasii͡a. II. Mazin, Viktor. III. Title: Arts & dreams IV. Title: Kabinet Zh
NX180.D74 I74 2002

ISLAM. *See* **ISLAMIC FUNDAMENTALISM.**

ISLAM - 20TH CENTURY. *See also* **ISLAMIC RENEWAL.**
Van de Weyer, Robert. Islam and the West. Alresford, Hampshire : O Books, c2001.

ISLAM - 21ST CENTURY.
Mabrūk, Muḥammad Ibrāhīm, 1943- al-Islām wa-al-gharb al-Amrīkī. al-Ṭabʻah al-ʻArabīyah 1. al-Qāhirah : Markaz al-Ḥaḍārah al-ʻArabīyah, 2002.

ISLAM - AFRICA.
Tijan Bangura, Abubakar. The truth can be discovered in the Qurʼan. [Freetown, Sierra Leone : s.n., 2002]
1. Black author.

ISLAM AND POLITICS.
Grant, George, 1954- The blood of the moon. Nashville, Tenn. : Thomas Nelson Publishers, 2002.
DS62 .G73 2002

Nuwayhiḍ, Walīd. Min Kābūl ilá Niyūyūrk. al-Ṭabʻah 1. Bayrūt : Dār Ibn Ḥazm, 2002.
BP172+

Valle, Alexandre del. Le totalitarisme islamiste à l'assaut des démocraties. Paris : Syrtes, c2002.

ISLAM AND POLITICS - HISTORY.
Van de Weyer, Robert. Islam and the West. Alresford, Hampshire : O Books, c2001.
CB251 .V36 2001

ISLAM AND POLITICS - HISTORY - 20TH CENTURY.
Fuller, Graham E., 1937- The future of political Islam. New York ; Houndmills, Basingstoke : Palgrave, 2003.
BP173.7 .F85 2003

Nuwayhiḍ, Walīd. Min Kābūl ilá Niyūyūrk. al-Ṭabʻah 1. Bayrūt : Dār Ibn Ḥazm, 2002.
BP172+

ISLAM AND TERRORISM.
Valle, Alexandre del. Le totalitarisme islamiste à l'assaut des démocraties. Paris : Syrtes, c2002.

Islam and the West.
Van de Weyer, Robert. Alresford, Hampshire : O Books, c2001.
CB251 .V36 2001

ISLAM AND WORLD POLITICS.
Corm, Georges. Orient-Occident, la fracture imaginaire. Paris : Découverte, 2002.

Medvedko, Leonid Ivanovich. Rossiia, Zapad, Islam. Zhukovskiĭ ; Moskva : Kuchkovo pole, 2003.
BP173.5 .M44 2003

ISLAM - EARLY WORKS TO 1800.
Ikhwān al-Ṣafāʼ. [Rasāʼil. 36. French & Arabic] Les révolutions et les cycles . Louvain-la-Neuve : Bruylant-Academia ; Beyrouth : Al-Bouraq Editions, 1996.

ISLAM - NIGERIA.
Babalola, E. O. African cultural revolution of Islam and Christianity in Yoruba land. Ipaja-Lagos : Eternal Communications, 2002.
1. Black author.

ISLAM - POLITICAL ASPECTS. See ISLAM AND POLITICS.

ISLAM - REFORM. See ISLAMIC RENEWAL.

ISLAM - RELATIONS.
Eidelberg, Paul. Clash of two decadent civilizations. Shaarei Tikva, Israel : ACPR Publications, 2002.
BM537 .E53 2002

ISLAM - RELATIONS - CHRISTIANITY.
Adeniyi, M. O. Yoruba Muslim-Christian understanding. Majiyagbe, Ipaja, Nigeria : Eternal Communications, 2001.
1. Black author.

Mabrūk, Muḥammad Ibrāhīm, 1943- al-Islām wa-al-gharb al-Amrīkī. al-Ṭabʻah al-ʻArabīyah 1. al-Qāhirah : Markaz al-Ḥaḍārah al-ʻArabīyah, 2002.

Nuwayhiḍ, Walīd. Min Kābūl ilá Niyūyūrk. al-Ṭabʻah 1. Bayrūt : Dār Ibn Ḥazm, 2002.
BP172+

Tijan Bangura, Abubakar. The truth can be discovered in the Qurʼan. [Freetown, Sierra Leone : s.n., 2002]
1. Black author.

Van de Weyer, Robert. The shared well. 1st ed. Washington, D.C. : Brassey's, c2002.
BL65.P7 V36 2002

ISLAM - RELATIONS - JUDAISM.
Mabrūk, Muḥammad Ibrāhīm, 1943- al-Islām wa-al-gharb al-Amrīkī. al-Ṭabʻah al-ʻArabīyah 1. al-Qāhirah : Markaz al-Ḥaḍārah al-ʻArabīyah, 2002.

ISLAM - RENEWAL. See ISLAMIC RENEWAL.

al-Islām wa-al-gharb al-Amrīkī.
Mabrūk, Muḥammad Ibrāhīm, 1943- al-Ṭabʻah al-ʻArabīyah 1. al-Qāhirah : Markaz al-Ḥaḍārah al-ʻArabīyah, 2002.

ISLAMIC ASTROLOGY - EARLY WORKS TO 1800.
Kūshyār, d. ca. 961. [Introduction to astrology] Kūshyār ibn Labbān's introduction to astrology. Tokyo : Institue for the Study of Languages and Cultures of Asia and Africa, 1997.
BF1714.184 K87 1997

ISLAMIC CIVILIZATION. See CIVILIZATION, ISLAMIC.

ISLAMIC COUNTRIES - RELATIONS - OCCIDENT.
Mabrūk, Muḥammad Ibrāhīm, 1943- al-Islām wa-al-gharb al-Amrīkī. al-Ṭabʻah al-ʻArabīyah 1. al-Qāhirah : Markaz al-Ḥaḍārah al-ʻArabīyah, 2002.

ISLAMIC EMPIRE - HISTORY - 750-1258. See CRUSADES.

ISLAMIC ETHICS.
Bulayhid, Munā bint Ṣāliḥ. Tharthārāt muʻallimāt. al-Ṭabʻah 1. al-Riyāḍ : Maktabat al-ʻUbaykān, 2001.
BJ1291 .B85 2001

ISLAMIC FUNDAMENTALISM.
Fuller, Graham E., 1937- The future of political Islam. New York ; Houndmills, Basingstoke : Palgrave, 2003.
BP173.7 .F85 2003

Ruthven, Malise, 1942- A fury for God. London ; New York : Granta, 2002.
HV6432 .R87 2002

Valle, Alexandre del. Le totalitarisme islamiste à l'assaut des démocraties. Paris : Syrtes, c2002.

ISLAMIC FUNDAMENTALISM - POLITICAL ASPECTS.
Crockatt, Richard. America embattled. London ; New York : Routledge, 2003.
E902 .C76 2003

ISLAMIC PHILOSOPHY. See PHILOSOPHY, ISLAMIC.

ISLAMIC REFORM. See ISLAMIC RENEWAL.

ISLAMIC RENEWAL - HISTORY - 20TH CENTURY.
Nuwayhiḍ, Walīd. Min Kābūl ilá Niyūyūrk. al-Ṭabʻah 1. Bayrūt : Dār Ibn Ḥazm, 2002.
BP172+

ISLAMISM. See ISLAM.

ISLANDS - NORTH PACIFIC OCEAN. See ISLANDS OF THE PACIFIC.

ISLANDS OF THE PACIFIC - LANGUAGES.
Collected papers on Southeast Asian and Pacific languages. Canberra, ACT : Pacific Linguistics, Research School of Pacific and Asian Studies, Australian National University, 2002.

ISLANDS - PACIFIC OCEAN. See ISLANDS OF THE PACIFIC.

Israel and Palestine out of the ashes.
Ellis, Marc H. London ; Sterling, Va. : Pluto Press, c2002.
DS119.76 .E56 2002

ISRAEL-ARAB BORDER CONFLICTS, 1949- - EGYPT.
Maoz, Zeev. Bound by struggle. Ann Arbor : University of Michigan Press, c2002.
JZ5595 .M366 2002

ISRAEL-ARAB CONFLICTS. See ARAB-ISRAELI CONFLICT.

Israel-Curley, Marcia. Defying the odds : sharing the lessons I learned as a pioneer entrepreneur / Marcia Israel-Curley. 1st ed. Woodstock, N.Y. : Overlook Press, 2002. 270 p., [48] p. of plates : ill. ; 24 cm. Includes index. ISBN 1-58567-307-2 (alk. paper) DDC 658.4/21
1. Entrepreneurship. 2. Businesswomen. 3. Success in business. 4. Women - Psychology. I. Title.
HB615 .I75 2002

ISRAEL - ETHNIC RELATIONS.
Ellis, Marc H. Israel and Palestine out of the ashes. London ; Sterling, Va. : Pluto Press, c2002.
DS119.76 .E56 2002

ISRAEL - ETHNIC RELATIONS - POLITICAL ASPECTS.
Kook, Rebecca B., 1959- The logic of democratic exclusion. Lanham, Md. : Lexington Books, c2002.
E185.615 .K59 2002

ISRAEL - HISTORY. See ARAB-ISRAELI CONFLICT.

ISRAEL - HISTORY - PROPHECIES.
Glazerson, Matityahu. Migdele ha-teʼomim be-diluge otiyot ba-Torah. Yerushalayim : Yerid ha-sefarim, 2002.

ISRAEL - MORAL CONDITIONS.
Ellis, Marc H. Israel and Palestine out of the ashes. London ; Sterling, Va. : Pluto Press, c2002.
DS119.76 .E56 2002

Israel on the couch.
Grosbard, Ofer, 1954- [Yiśraʼel ʻal ha-sapah. English] Albany : State University of New York Press, c2003.
DS126.5 .G694 2003

Israel on the couch : the psychology of the peace process.
Grosbard, Ofer, 1954- Yiśraʼel ʻal ha-sapah. Tel-Aviv : Yediʻot aḥaronot : Sifre ḥemed, c2000.

ISRAEL-PALESTINE CONFLICT. See ARAB-ISRAELI CONFLICT.

ISRAEL - POLITICS AND GOVERNMENT.
Ellis, Marc H. Israel and Palestine out of the ashes. London ; Sterling, Va. : Pluto Press, c2002.
DS119.76 .E56 2002

Ginzburg, Yitshak. Rectifying the state of Israel. 1st ed. Jerusalem : Gal Einai ; Cedarhurst, NY : For information address, Gal Einai Institute, c2002.

ISRAEL - POLITICS AND GOVERNMENT - 1993-.
Kook, Rebecca B., 1959- The logic of democratic exclusion. Lanham, Md. : Lexington Books, c2002.
E185.615 .K59 2002

ISRAEL - POLITICS AND GOVERNMENT - BIBLICAL TEACHING.
Glazerson, Matityahu. Migdele ha-teʼomim be-diluge otiyot ba-Torah. Yerushalayim : Yerid ha-sefarim, 2002.

ISRAEL - POLITICS AND GOVERNMENT - PSYCHOLOGICAL ASPECTS.
Grosbard, Ofer, 1954- [Yiśraʼel ʻal ha-sapah. English] Israel on the couch. Albany : State University of New York Press, c2003.
DS126.5 .G694 2003

Grosbard, Ofer, 1954- Yiśraʼel ʻal ha-sapah. Tel-Aviv : Yediʻot aḥaronot : Sifre ḥemed, c2000.

ISRAEL - RELIGIOUS LIFE AND CUSTOMS.
Gorfine, Yehudit. Be-ḳarov etslekh. Petaḥ Tiḳvah : Marʼot, 2002.

ISRAELI-ARAB CONFLICT. See ARAB-ISRAELI CONFLICT.

ISRAELI NATIONAL CHARACTERISTICS. See NATIONAL CHARACTERISTICS, ISRAELI.

ISRAELI-PALESTINIAN CONFLICT. See ARAB-ISRAELI CONFLICT.

ISRAELITES. See JEWS.

Issledovaniia obucheniia i razvitiia v kontekste kulʼturno-istoricheskogo podkhoda : materialy vtorykh chteniĭ, posviashchennykh pamiati L.S. Vygotskogo, Moskva, 15-17 noiabria 2001 goda / [nauchnaia redaktsiia, E.E. Kravtsova, V.F. Spiridonov, IU.E. Kravchenko]. Moskva : Smysl, 2002. 303 p. : ill. ; 22 cm. Includes bibliographical references. ISBN 5893571274
1. Developmental psychology - Congresses. 2. Educational psychology - Congresses. I. Kravtsova, E. E. II. Spiridonov, V. F. III. Kravchenko, IU. E. IV. Vygotskiĭ, L. S. (Lev Semenovich), 1896-1934. V. Rossiĭskiĭ gosudarstvennyĭ gumanitarnyĭ universitet. Institut psikhologii im. L.S. Vygotskogo.
BF712.5 .I88 2002

Issues & debates
Claiming the stones/naming the bones. Los Angeles : Getty Research Institute, c2002.
CC135 .C48 2002

Issues in implementing international peace operations 21 p.
Christoff, Joseph A. Issues in implementing international peace operations [electronic resource]. [Washington, D.C.] : U.S. General Accounting Office, [2002]

Issues in implementing international peace operations [electronic resource].
Christoff, Joseph A. [Washington, D.C.] : U.S. General Accounting Office, [2002]

Ist die Moderne eine Epoche?.
Grasskamp, Walter. München : C.H. Beck, c2002.

Istituto francescano di spiritualità (Rome, Italy).
Martinelli, Paolo, 1958- Vocazione e stati di vita del cristiano. Roma : Collegio San Lorenzo da Brindisi, 2001.

Istituto italiano per gli studi storici (Series)
Sasso, Gennaro. Il guardiano della storiografia. 2. ed. [Bologna] : Società editrice il Mulino, c2002.

Istoricheskie tsikly.
Nikolaev, Alekseĭ. Vologda : [s.n.], c2002.
D16.15 .N55 2002

Istoricheskoe razvitie kul'tury.
Romanov, V. N. (Vladimir Nikolaevich) Moskva : Savin, 2003.
CB19 .R65 2003

Istorie şi utopie.
Cioran, E. M. (Emile M.), 1911- [Histoire et utopie. Romanian] Bucureşti : Humanitas, 2002.

Istoriĭa drevnegrecheskoĭ filosofii ot Falesa do Aristotelia.
Basov, R. A. Moskva : Letopis' XXI, 2002.
B175.R9 B37 2002

Istoriĭa i razvitie psikhologicheskogo obrazovaniĭa v gorode Tveri i oblasti.
Shikun, A. A. (Alekseĭ Alekseevich) Tver' : Tverskoĭ gos. universitet : Mezhdunarodnaia akademiia psikhologicheskikh nauk, 1999.
BF80.7.R8 S55 1999

Istoriĭa psykholohiï dvadtsiatoho stolittia.
Romenets, V. A. (Vladimir Andreevich) Istoriia psykholohiï XX stolittia. Kyïv : "Lebid'", 1998.
BF105 .R66 1998

Istoriĭa psykholohiï XX stolittia.
Romenets, V. A. (Vladimir Andreevich) Kyïv : "Lebid'", 1998.
BF105 .R66 1998

Istoriohrafichni ta dzhereloznavchi problemy istoriï Ukraïny : obrazy nauky : mizhvuzivs'kyĭ zbirnyk naukovykh prats' / [redaktsiĭna kolehiia, A.H. Bolebrukh (vidp. red.) ... et al.]. Dnipropetrovs'k : Vyd-vo Dnipropetrovs'koho universytetu, 2000. 248 p. : ill. ; 20 cm. At head of title: Ministerstvo osvity i nauky Ukraïny. Dnipropetrovs'kyĭ natsional'nyĭ universytet. Includes bibliographical references. ISBN 9665510606
1. Ukraine - Historiography. 2. Ukraine - History - Sources. 3. Historiography. 4. History - Methodology. I. Bolebrukh, A. G. (Anatoliĭ Grigor'evich) II. Dnipropetrovs'kyĭ natsional'nyĭ universytet.
DK508.46 .I84 2000

It happened to me
(no. 8) Myers, Edward, 1950- When will I stop hurting? Lanham, Md. : Scarecrow Press, 2004.
BF724.3.G73 M94 2004

The IT revolution in architecture
Jormakka, Kari. [Olandesi volanti. English] Flying Dutchmen. Basel ; Boston : Birkhäuser, 2002.
NA1148 .J6713 2002

Palumbo, Maria Luisa. [Nuovi ventri. English] New wombs : electronic bodies and architectural disorders. Basel : Birkhäuser, 2000.
NA2765 .P35 2000

ITALIAN LANGUAGE - TERMS AND PHRASES.
Lurati, Ottavio. Per modo di dire--. Bologna : CLUEB, c2002.

ITALIAN LITERATURE. See **ITALIAN POETRY.**

ITALIAN LITERATURE - TO 1400 - HISTORY AND CRITICISM.
Studi sulle società e le culture del Medioevo per Girolamo Arnaldi. [Firenze] : All'insegna del giglio, 2002.
DG443 .S78 2002

ITALIAN PHILOSOPHY. See **PHILOSOPHY, ITALIAN.**

ITALIAN POETRY - HISTORY AND CRITICISM.
Roush, Sherry. Hermes' lyre. Toronto : University of Toronto Press, c2002.

ITALIC LANGUAGES AND DIALECTS. See **LATIN LANGUAGE.**

ITALIC PEOPLES. See **ETRUSCANS; ROMANS.**

ITALY - ANTIQUITIES, ROMAN.
Antico Gallina, Mariavittoria. I romani. Cinisello Balsamo (Milano) : Silvana, 1998.

ITALY - CIVILIZATION - 1268-1559.
A companion to the worlds of the Renaissance. Malden, MA : Blackwell Publishers, 2002.
CB367 .C65 2002

The Renaissance. London ; New York : Routledge, 2003.
DG445 .R565 2003

ITALY - CIVILIZATION - 476-1268.
Studi sulle società e le culture del Medioevo per Girolamo Arnaldi. [Firenze] : All'insegna del giglio, 2002.
DG443 .S78 2002

ITALY - HISTORY - CAROLINGIAN RULE, 774-887. See **CAROLINGIANS.**

ITALY - INTELLECTUAL LIFE - 1268-1559.
A companion to the worlds of the Renaissance. Malden, MA : Blackwell Publishers, 2002.
CB367 .C65 2002

ITALY - LITERATURES. See **ITALIAN LITERATURE.**

ITALY - POLITICS AND GOVERNMENT - 1922-1945.
Franchi, Franco. La libertà nel fascismo. Roma : Europa : Settimo sigillo, c2002.

ITALY - SOCIAL CONDITIONS - 1268-1559.
A companion to the worlds of the Renaissance. Malden, MA : Blackwell Publishers, 2002.
CB367 .C65 2002

Iterson, Ad van, 1952-.
The civilized organization. Amsterdam ; Philadelphia : John Benjamins, c2002.
HD58.7 .C593 2002

Itinéraires de l'imaginaire / ouvrage coordonné par Marie-Caroline Vanbremeersch ; préface de Sylvia Ostrowetsky. Paris : L'Harmattan, c1999. 264 p. ; 24 cm. (Les cahiers du CEFRESS) Includes bibliographical references. ISBN 2-7384-8527-8
1. Imagination. I. Vanbremeersch, Marie-Caroline, 1944- II. Series.
BF408 .I86 1999

Itinéraires du savoir
Conche, Marcel. Confession d'un philosophe. Paris : Albin Michel, c2003.
B804 .C66 2003

It's all in the cards.
Mangiapane, John. New York : Sterling Pub., c2004.
BF1879.T2 M332 2004

IUPsyS global resource.
Psychology, IUPsyS global resource [electronic resource]. Hove, East Sussex, UK : published on behalf of the international Union of Psychological Science by Psychology Press Ltd., 2000-
BF76.5 .P79

I͡Uzhno-rossiĭskiĭ gumanitarnyĭ institut.
Ezotericheskaia filosofiia. Rostov-na-Donu : Foliant, 2002.
BF1416 .E96 2002

Ivan Petrovich umer.
Genis, Aleksandr, 1953- Moskva : Novoe literaturnoe obozrenie, 1999.
PG3021 .G46 1999

Ivanich, Clarke M.
Stress. New York : Nova Science Publishers, c2002.
BF575.S75

Ivannikov, V. A. (Vi͡acheslav Andreevich)
Psikhologicheskie mekhanizmy volevoĭ reguliatsii : uchebnoe posobie / V.A. Ivannikov. [2. izd.]. Moskva : Izd-vo URAO, 1998. 140, [1] p. ; 21 cm. Includes bibliographical references (p. 136-[141]). ISBN 5204001484
1. Will - History - 20th century. I. Title.
BF616 .I93 1998

Ivanov, S. P. (Sergeĭ Petrovich) Psikhologiia khudozhestvennogo deĭstviia sub"ekta / S.P. Ivanov. Moskva : Moskovskiĭ psikhologo-sotsial'nyĭ institut ; Voronezh : Izd-vo NPO "MODĖK", 2002. 638 p. : ill. ; 21 cm. (Biblioteka psikhologa) At head of title: Rossiĭskaia akademiia obrazovaniia. Moskovskiĭ psikhologo-sotsial'nyĭ institut. Includes bibliographical references (p. 611-[637]). ISBN 5895023428 (MPSI) ISBN 5893954165 (NPO "MODĖK")
1. Creation (Literary, artistic, etc.) - Psychological aspects. 2. Self psychology. I. Rossiĭskaia akademiia obrazovaniia. II. Moskovskiĭ psikhologo-sotsial'nyĭ institut. III. Title. IV. Series.
BF408 .I93 2002

Ivanova, Anna (Anna N.) Kakŭv trud e nuzhen na choveka? : psikhologichni problemi na sŭdŭrzhanieto na truda / Anna Ivanova. Sofiia : Akademichno izd-vo "Prof. Marin Drinov", 2000. 171 p. ; 21 cm. Added title page title: Was für Arbeit braucht der Mensch? Summary and table of contents in German. Includes bibliographical references (p. 157-167). ISBN 9544306846
1. Work - Psychological aspects. I. Title. II. Title: Was für Arbeit braucht der Mensch?
BF481 .I82 2000

Ivanova, E. V. (Elena Vladimirovna) Ved'my : nauchnyĭ skaz ob arkhetipakh zhenskogo povedeniia / E.V. Ivanova. Ekaterinburg : Ural'skiĭ gos. universitet, 2002. 128, [1] p. ; 21 cm. Includes bibliographical references (p. 127-[129]). ISBN 5752507987
1. Witches - Russia (Federation) - History. 2. Women - Russia (Federation) - History. 3. Mythology, Slavic. 4. Women - Russia (Federation) - Psychology. 5. Archetype (Psychology) I. Title.
BF1584.R9 I85 2002

Ivashkevich, O. V. (Ol'ga Vladimirovna).
Saleev, Vadim Alekseevich. Ėsteticheskoe vospriiatie i detskaia fantaziia. Minsk : Natsional'nyĭ in-t obrazovaniia, 1999.
BF723.P36 S25 1999

Ivinskaia, A. (Anna) Svet prelomlennogo vremeni v ikonnom prostranstve / A. Ivinskaia. Moskva : Khristianskiĭ Vostok, 2002. 172 p. : col. ill. ; 30 cm. (Ėllampsis) Includes bibliographical references. ISBN 5869881161
1. Icons, Byzantine - Greece - Athos. 2. Icons, Byzantine - Greece - Crete. 3. Mural painting and decoration, Byzantine - Greece - Crete. 4. Space (Art) 5. Composition (Art) I. Title. II. Series.
N8189.G72 I95 2002

The ivory tower and Harry Potter : perspectives on a literary phenomenon / Lana A. Whited, editor. Columbia : University of Missouri Press, 2002. x, 408 p. ; 24 cm. Includes bibliographical references (p. 369-389) and index. CONTENTS: Pt. 1. Harry's cousins in the magical realm. Harry Potter and the secret password: finding our way in the magical genre / Amanda Cockrell ; The education of a wizard: Harry Potter and his predecessors / Pat Pinsent -- Pt. 2. Harry's roots in epic, myth, and folklore. In medias res: Harry Potter as hero-in-progress / Mary Pharr ; Of magicals and muggles: reversals and revulsions at Hogwarts / Jann Lacoss ; Harry Potter: fairy tale prince, real boy, and archetypal hero / M. Katherine Grimes -- Pt. 3. Harry's other literary relatives. Harry Potter and the extraordinariness of the ordinary / Roni Natov ; Harry Potter, Tom Brown, and the British school story: lost in transit? / David K. Steege -- Pt. 4. Greater than gold in Gringotts: questions of authority and values. Crowning the king: Harry Potter and the construction of authority / Farah Mendlesohn ; What would Harry do? J.K. Rowling and Lawrence Kohlberg's theories of moral development / Lana A. Whited, with M. Katherine Grimes -- Pt. 5. Gender issues and Harry Potter. Hermione Granger and the heritage of gender / Eliza T. Dresang ; Locating Harry Potter in the "boys' book" market / Terri Doughty -- Pt. 6. Harry's language: taking issue with words. You say "jelly," I say "jell-o"? Harry Potter and the transfiguration of language / Philip Nel ; Harry Potter and the tower of Babel: translating the magic / Nancy K. Jentsch -- Pt. 7. Commodity and culture in the world of Harry Potter. Specters of Thatcherism: contemporary British culture in J.K. Rowling's Harry Potter series / Karin E. Westman ; Harry Potter and the technology of magic / Elizabeth Teare ; Apprentice wizards welcome: fan communities and the culture of Harry Potter / Rebecca Sutherland Borah. ISBN 0-8262-1443-6 DDC 823/.914
1. Rowling, J. K. - Characters - Harry Potter. 2. Children's stories, English - History and criticism. 3. Fantasy fiction, English - History and criticism. 4. Potter, Harry (Fictitious character) 5. Wizards in literature. 6. Magic in literature. I. Whited, Lana A., 1958-
PR6068.O93 Z734 2002

Izabrani ogledi.
Jerotić, Vladeta. [Selections 2000] Beograd: Srpska književna zadruga, 2000.
BF109.J47 A25 2000

Jaccard, James. Interaction effects in multiple regression / James Jaccard, Robert Turrisi. 2nd ed. Thousand Oaks, Calif. : Sage Publications, c2003. vii, 92 p. : ill. ; 22 cm. (Quantitative applications in the social sciences ; 72) Includes bibliographical references (p. 89-91) and index. ISBN 0-7619-2742-5 (pbk.) DDC 519.5/36/0243
1. Regression analysis. 2. Social sciences - Statistical methods. I. Turrisi, Robert. II. Title. III. Series: Sage university papers series. Quantitative applications in the social sciences ; no. 07-072.
HA31.3 .J33 2003

The Jack Welch lexicon of leadership.
Krames, Jeffrey A. 1st ed. New York : McGraw-Hill, 2001, c2002.

Jackson, Buddy, ill.
  HD57.7 .K726 2001
Jackson, Buddy, ill.
  Sanders, Mark D. I hope you dance!. Nashville,
  Tenn. : Rutledge Hill Press, 2003.
  BF410 .S26 2003
Jackson, Gordon, 1949-.
  Never scratch a tiger with a short stick. Colorado
  Springs, Colo. : NavPress, c2003.
  BF637.L4 N48 2003
Jackson, Holbrook, 1874-1948.
  [Anatomy of bibliomania. Portuguese. Selections]
  O tato : uma das cinco portas do amor ao livro /
  Holbrook Jackson. São Paulo : Imprensa Oficial do
  Estado, 2002. 22 p. ; 19 cm. (Plaquetas da Oficina ; 55)
  1. Bibliomania. 2. Senses and sensation. 3. Book collecting. 4.
  Books and reading. I. Title. II. Series.
  Z992 .J33 2002
Jackson, J. S. Bye-bye, bully! : a kid's guide for dealing
  with bullies / written by J.S. Jackkson ; illustrated by
  R.W. Alley. St. Meinrad, IN. : Abbey Press, c2003. 1
  v. (unpaged) : col. ill. ; 21 cm. ISBN 0-87029-369-9
  1. Bullying - Juvenile literature. I. Alley, R. W. (Robert W.) II.
  Title.
  BF637.B85 J33 2003
Jackson, Sherri L., 1962- Research methods and
  statistics : a critical thinking approach / Sherri L.
  Jackson. Australia ; Belmont, CA : Thomson/
  Wadsworth, c2003. xix, 357 p. : ill. ; 25 cm. Includes
  bibliographical references (p. 341-342) and index. ISBN 0-
  534-55423-7 DDC 150/.7/2
  1. Psychology - Research - Methodology. 2. Psychometrics. I.
  Title.
  BF76.5 .J29 2003
Jackson, Stevi.
  Gender. London ; New York : Routledge, 2002.
  HQ1075 .G426 2002
Jackson, Stonewall, 1824-1863. Stonewall Jackson's
  book of maxims / edited by James I. Robertson Jr.
  Nashville, Tenn. : Cumberland House, 2002. 144 p.,
  [16] p. of plates : ill. ; 22 cm. Includes bibliographical
  references (p. 125-140) and index. ISBN 1-58182-296-0 DDC
  973.7/3/092
  1. Jackson, Stonewall, - 1824-1863 - Quotations. 2. Generals -
  Confederate States of America - Quotations. 3. Conduct of
  life - Quotations, maxims, etc. I. Robertson, James I. II. Title.
  E467.1.J15 J17 2002

**JACKSON, STONEWALL, 1824-1863 -
QUOTATIONS.**
  Jackson, Stonewall, 1824-1863. Stonewall Jackson's
  book of maxims. Nashville, Tenn. : Cumberland
  House, 2002.
  E467.1.J15 J17 2002

Jacob, Suzanne. Ecrire comment pourquoi / Suzanne
  Jacob. Paroisse Notre-Dame-des-Neiges, Québec :
  Éditions Trois-Pistoles, c2002. 84 p. : ill. ; 20 cm. (Ecrire)
  ISBN 2895830096
  1. Creation (Literary, artistic, etc.) 2. Creative writing. 3.
  French-Canadian literature - History and criticism. I. Title. II.
  Title: Comment pourquoi III. Series: Ecrire (Notre-Dame-des
  Neiges, Québec)
  PN56.C69 J23 2002

Jacobi, Eleonore.
  [Tarot für Liebe und Partnerschaft. English]
  Tarot for love & relationships / Eleonore Jacobi.
  New York : Sterling Pub. Co., c2003. 144 p. : col.
  ill. ; 22 cm. Includes index. ISBN 1402702531 DDC 133.3/
  2424
  1. Tarot. I. Title. II. Title: Tarot for love and relationships
  BF1879.T2 J3413 2003

Jacobins and utopians.
  Klosko, George. Notre Dame, Ind. : University of
  Notre Dame Press, c2003.
  JC491 .K54 2003

Jacobs, Michael, 1941-. Sigmund Freud / Michael
  Jacobs. 2nd ed. London ; Thousand Oaks, Calif. :
  SAGE Publications, 2003. vii, 168 p. ; 22 cm. (Key figures
  in counselling and psychotherapy) Includes bibliographical
  references (p. [156]-163) and index. ISBN 0-7619-4110-X
  (pbk.) DDC 150.19/52/092
  1. Freud, Sigmund, - 1856-1939. 2. Counseling - History. 3.
  Psychotherapy - History. I. Title. II. Series.
  BF109.F74 J33 2003

Jacobson, Ronald L., 1956-.
  Communication and cyberspace. 2nd ed. Creskill,
  N.J. : Hampton Press, c2003.
  P96.D36 C66 2003

Jacorzynski, Witold.
  Estudios sobre la violencia. 1. ed. México, D.F. :
  CIESAS : M.A. Porrúa, 2002.
  HN120.Z9 V538 2002

Jacq, Christian.
  [Monde magique de l'Egypte ancienne]
  Magic and mystery in ancient Egypt / Christian
  Jacq ; translated by Janet M. Davis. London :
  Souvenir Press, 1998, 2002. 187 p. : ill. ; 20 cm.
  English translation first published in 1985 under the title:
  Egyptian Magic. Retitled with revised translation. "First
  published in France under the title Le Monde magique de
  l'Egypte ancienne." Includes bibliographical references (p.
  [173]-175). ISBN 0-285-63462-3 (pbk.) DDC 133.430932
  1. Magic, Egyptian. I. Title. II. Title: Egyptian Magic

JACQUERIE, 1358. See **PEASANTRY - FRANCE.**

Jacques Lacan.
  Di Ciaccia, Antonio. Milano : B. Mondadori, 2000.
  BF109.L28 D53 2000

Jacques Lacan and feminist epistemology.
  Campbell, Kirsten, 1969- New York, NY : Routledge,
  2004.
  BF175.4.F45 .C37 2004

Jacques Maritain and the many ways of knowing /
  Douglas A. Ollivant, editor ; with an introduction by
  George Anastaplo. Washington, D.C. : American
  Maritain Association : Distributed by the Catholic
  University of America Press, c2002. xii, 330 p. ; 23 cm.
  Includes bibliographical references and index. ISBN
  0-9669226-4-6 (pbk. : alk. paper) DDC 121/.092
  1. Maritain, Jacques, - 1882-1973. 2. Knowledge, Theory of. I.
  Ollivant, Douglas A.
  B2430.M34 J317 2002

Jacquette, Dale.
  Philosophy, psychology, and psychologism.
  Dordrecht ; Boston : Kluwer Academic Publishers,
  c2003.
  BF41 .P553 2003

Jadacki, Jacek Juliusz. From the viewpoint of the
  Lvov-Warsaw school / Jacek Juliusz Jadacki.
  Amsterdam ; New York, NY : Rodopi, 2003. 278 p. ;
  22 cm. (Poznań studies in the philosophy of the sciences and
  the humanities, 0303-8157 ; v. 78) Includes bibliographical
  references (p. [239]-246) and indexes. ISBN 90-420-0904-7
  1. Lvov-Warsaw school of philosophy. 2. Logic, Symbolic and
  mathematical - History - 20th century. 3. Philosophy, Polish -
  20th century. 4. Ontology. 5. Substance (Philosophy) 6. Truth.
  7. Silence (Philosophy) 8. Miscommunication. I. Title. II.
  Series.

  Salamucha, Jan. [Selections. English. 2003]
  Knowledge and faith. Amsterdam ; New York, NY :
  Rodopi, 2003.

Jaeger, C. Stephen.
  Scholars and courtiers. Aldershot ; Burlington, Vt. :
  Ashgate/Variorum, c2002.
  AZ183.E8 S36 2002

al-Jafr li-Sayyidinā 'Alī.
  Dāwūd, Muḥammad 'Īsá. al-Muhandisīn [Giza] :
  Madbūlī al-Ṣaghīr, [2003]
  BF1771+

Jagaddeva.
  [Svapnacintāmaṇi. Russian]
  Volshebnoe sokrovishche snovideniĭ /
  Dzhagaddeva ; perevod s sanskrita stat'ia i
  kommentariĭ A.IA. Syrkin. Moskva : Ladomir,
  1996. 110 p. ; 23 cm. (Ex Oriente Lux) Includes
  bibliographical references (p. [93]-95). ISBN 5862182241
  1. Fortune-telling by dreams. I. Syrkin, A. IA. (Aleksandr
  IAkovlevich), 1930- II. Title. III. Series.
  BF1088.S26 J34 1996

JAGANNĀTHA TEMPLE (DHARĀKOṬA, INDIA).
  Pathy, Dinanath. Art, regional traditions, the Temple
  of Jagannātha. New Delhi : Sundeep Prakashan, 2001.
  NA6002 .P37 2001

**Jahrbuch für internationale Germanistik. Reihe C,
Forschungsberichte**
  (Bd. 7.) Kommunikation, Kunst und Kultur. Bern ;
  New York : Peter Lang, c2002.

Jáidar, Isabel. La psicología : un largo sendero, una
  breve historia / Isabel Jáidar, Lilia Esther Vargas,
  Margarita Baz. 1. ed. México, D.F. : Universidad
  Autónoma Metropolitana, Unidad Xochimilco,
  División de Ciencias Sociales y Humanidades, 2002.
  195 p. ; 22 cm. (Colección La llave ; 24) Includes
  bibliographical references. ISBN 9706544526 (colección)
  ISBN 9703100813
  1. Psychology - History. 2. Psychology - Mexico - Hisotry. I.
  Vargas, Lilia Esther. II. Baz, Margarita. III. Title. IV. Series:
  Colección La llave (Universidad Autónoma Metropolitana.
  Unidad Xochimilco. División de Ciencias Sociales y
  Humanidades) ; 24.

JAINA ASTROLOGY.
  Gulābavijaya. Śrī Muhūrtarāja. Dvitīyāvṛtti. Ji. Dhāra,
  Ma. Pra. : Rājendra Pravacana Kāryālaya, 1996.
  BF1714.J28+

JAINA ASTROLOGY - EARLY WORKS TO 1800.
  Naracandrasūri, 13th cent. [Naracandrajyotiṣa.
  Gujarati & English] Naracandra Jaina jyotiṣa.
  Saṃśodhita adyatana āvṛtti. Amadāvāda : Sarasvatī
  Pustaka Bhaṇḍāra, 2003.
  BF1714.J28+

JAINISM. See **YOGA (JAINISM).**

JAINISM - RITUALS.
  Gulābavijaya. Śrī Muhūrtarāja. Dvitīyāvṛtti. Ji. Dhāra,
  Ma. Pra. : Rājendra Pravacana Kāryālaya, 1996.
  BF1714.J28+

Jakubiak, Krzysztof.
  Dziecko w rodzinie i społeczeństwie. Bydgoszsz :
  Wydawnictwo Uczelniane Akademii Bydgoskiej,
  2002.

Jalagin, Seija.
  Looking at the other. Oulu, Finland : University of
  Oulu, 2002.

Jalongo, Mary Renck.
  The world's children and their companion animals.
  Olney, MD : Association for Childhood Education
  International, 2004.
  BF723.A45 W67 2004

Jambet, Christian. L'acte d'être : la philosophie de la
  révélation chez Mollâ Sadrâ / Christian Jambet.
  [Paris] : Fayard, c2002. 447 p. ; 22 cm. (L'espace intérieur)
  Includes bibliographical references and index. ISBN 2-213-
  61376-1 DDC 297
  1. Ṣadr al-Dīn Shīrāzī, Muḥammad ibn Ibrāhīm, - d. 1641. 2.
  Ontology. 3. Philosophy, Islamic - Greek influences. 4. Sufism.
  5. Shī'ah. I. Title. II. Series.

JAMES BOND (FICTITIOUS CHARACTER). See
  BOND, JAMES (FICTITIOUS CHARACTER).

James, Jacqueline. Take control of your life : and see
  the future change in your hands / Jacqueline James.
  London : Hodder & Stoughton, 1995, c1994. 215 p. :
  ill. ; 20 cm. Includes bibliographical references (p. 213). ISBN
  0-340-63844-3 (pbk) DDC 133.6
  1. Palmistry. I. Title.

James-Raoul, Danièle.
  Dans l'eau, sous l'eau. [Paris] : Presses de
  l'Université de Paris-Sorbonne, 2002.
  CB353 .D27 2002

James River chiefdoms.
  Gallivan, Martin D., 1968- Lincoln : University of
  Nebraska Press, c2003.
  E99.P85 G35 2003

JAMES RIVER VALLEY (VA.) - ANTIQUITIES.
  Gallivan, Martin D., 1968- James River chiefdoms.
  Lincoln : University of Nebraska Press, c2003.
  E99.P85 G35 2003

James, William, 1842-1910.
  [Pragmatism. German]
  Pragmatismus : ein neuer Name für einige alte
  Wege des Denkens / William James ;
  herausgegeben von Klaus Oehler. Berlin :
  Akademie Verlag, c2000. x, 289 p. ; 21 cm. (Klassiker
  Auslegen ; Bd. 21) Contributions in English and German.
  Includes bibliographical references (p. 263-276) and
  indexes. CONTENTS: Die pragmatistische Konzeption der
  Philosophie / Klaus Oehler -- James' Transformation der
  pragmatischen Maxime von Peirce / Kai-Michael Hingst --
  Pragmatismus: zwischen Kritik und Postulat / Ludwig
  Nagl -- William James on the one and the many / Sandra B.
  Rosenthal / The Philosopher's "License" : William James
  and common sense / Charlene Haddock Seigfrid -- James'
  pragmatistische Deutung der Korrespondenztheorie der
  Wahrheit / Kai-Michael Hingst -- James's pragmatism and
  the problem of reference / Ignas K. Skrupskelis --
  Pragmatismus und Religion / Hermann Deuser -- Religious
  faith, intellectual responsibility, and romance / Richard
  Rorty -- Zur Begründungslogik des Pragmatismus : die
  Wahrheit des Gedankens u. die Erfahrung der Bedutung :
  über die Grundlegung der Jamesschen Wahrheitstheorie
  durch seine Psychologie der Symbolerfahrung / Helmut
  Pape. ISBN 3-05-003092-5 (pbk.)
  1. James, William, - 1842-1910. 2. Pragmatism. 3. Psychology.
  4. Philosophy. I. Oehler, Klaus, ed. II. Title. III. Series.

JAMES, WILLIAM, 1842-1910.
  James, William, 1842-1910. [Pragmatism. German]
  Pragmatismus. Berlin : Akademie Verlag, c2000.

Jameson, Fredric. A singular modernity : essay on the
  ontology of the present / Fredric Jameson. London ;
  New York : Verso, 2002. 250 p. ; 20 cm. Includes
  bibliographical references and index. ISBN 1-85984-674-2

(hbk.) ISBN 1-85984-450-2 (pbk.) DDC 149/.97
1. Civilization, Modern - Philosophy. 2. Civilization, Modern - 1950- 3. Modernism (Aesthetics) 4. Modernism (Art) 5. Postmodernism. I. Title.
CB358 .J348 2002

JAMESTOWN (VA.) - BIOGRAPHY.
Price, David, 1961- Love and hate in Jamestown. 1st ed. New York : Alfred A. Knopf : Distributed by Random House, 2003.
F234.J3 P68 2003

JAMESTOWN (VA.) - HISTORY.
Price, David, 1961- Love and hate in Jamestown. 1st ed. New York : Alfred A. Knopf : Distributed by Random House, 2003.
F234.J3 P68 2003

Jamme, Christoph.
Fremderfahrung und Repräsentation. 1. Aufl. Weilerswist : Velbrück, 2002.

Jamrożek, Wiesław.
Dziecko w rodzinie i społeczeństwie. Bydgoszsz : Wydawnictwo Uczelniane Akademii Bydgoskiej, 2002.

Jan Salamucha, knowledge and faith.
Salamucha, Jan. [Selections. English. 2003] Knowledge and faith. Amsterdam ; New York, NY : Rodopi, 2003.

Janaszek-Ivaničková, Halina. Nowa twarz postmodernizmu / Halina Janaszek-Ivaničková. Wyd. 1. Katowice : Wydawn. Uniwersytetu Śląskiego, 2002. 331 p. ; 24 cm. (Prace naukowe Uniwersytetu Śląskiego w Katowicach ; nr. 2025) Errata slip inserted. Includes bibliographical references and index. Summary in English and French. ISBN 83-226-1113-7
1. Postmodernism (Literature) 2. Postmodernism. I. Title. II. Series.

Janesick, Valerie J. "Stretching" exercises for qualitative researchers / Valerie J. Janesick. 2nd ed. Thousand Oaks, Calif. : Sage Publications, c2004. xiii, 271 p. ; 23 cm. Includes bibliographical references (p. 257-261) and index. ISBN 0-7619-2815-4 (cloth : alk. paper) DDC 300/.72
1. Social sciences - Research - Methodology. 2. Observation (Scientific method) 3. Qualitative reasoning. I. Title.
H62 .J346 2004

Janich, Peter.
Kultur, Handlung, Wissenschaft. 1. Aufl. Weilerswist : Velbrück Wissenschaft, 2002.
B67 .K853 2002

Janiger, Oscar.
Dobkin de Rios, Marlene. LSD, spirituality, and the creative process. Rochester, Vt. : Park Street Press, c2003.
BF209.L9 D57 2003

Jankovic, Zoran. Au-delà du signe : Gadamer et Derrida : le dépassement herméneutique et déconstructiviste du Dasein / Zoran Jankovic. Paris : Harmattan, c2003. 246, [1] p. ; 22 cm. (Collection Ouverture philosophique) Includes bibliographical references (p. [237]-[247]). ISBN 2-7475-3908-3 DDC 194
1. Gadamer, Hans Georg, - 1900- 2. Derrida, Jacques. 3. Heidegger, Martin, - 1889-1976. 4. Hermeneutics. I. Title. II. Title: Gadamer et Derrida III. Series: Collection L'ouverture philosophique.

Jankowicz, Devi. The easy guide to repertory grids / Devi Jankowicz. Chichester, West Sussex, England ; Hoboken, N.J. : Wiley, 2003. p. cm. Includes bibliographical references and index. Publisher description URL: http://www.loc.gov/catdir/desc ription/wiley039/2003006941.html Table of contents URL: http://www.loc.gov/catdir/toc/wiley031/2003006941.html ISBN 0-470-85404-9 (pbk. : alk. paper) DDC 155.2/8
1. Repertory grid technique. I. Title.
BF698.8.R38 J36 2003

Jannoud, Claude. La crise de l'esprit / Claude Jannoud. Lausanne, Suisse : Age d'homme, c2001. 116 p. ; 23 cm. (Mobiles philosophiques) ISBN 2-8251-1606-8 DDC 100
1. Philosophy. 2. Civilization, Modern - 21st century. 3. Moral conditions. 4. Postmodernism - Religious aspects. 5. Twenty-first century. 6. Spirituality. I. Title. II. Series.

Janowski, Rahula.
Monkeywrenching the new world order [sound recording]. Oakland, Calif : AK Press ; San Francisco, CA : Alternative Tentacles Records, 2001.

Janse, A. Ridderschap in Holland : portret van een adellijke elite in de late middeleeuwen / Antheun Janse. Hilversum : Verloren, 2001. 514 p. : ill. (some col.), maps ; 25 cm. (Adelsgeschiedenis ; 1) Includes bibliographical references (p. [459]-494) and index. ISBN 90-6550-667-5

1. Knights and knighthood - Netherlands. 2. Civilization, Medieval. 3. Nobility - Netherlands. I. Title. II. Series.
DJ152 .J26 2001

Jansen, Sue Curry. Critical communication theory : power, media, gender, and technology / Sue Curry Jansen. Lanham, Md. : Oxford : Rowman & Littlefield, c2002. x, 275 p. ; 24 cm. (Critical media studies) Includes bibliographical references (p. 257-266) and index. ISBN 0-7425-2372-1 (hbk. : alk. paper) ISBN 0-7425-2373-X (pbk. : alk. paper) DDC 302.2
1. Communication - Social aspects. 2. Critical theory. 3. Knowledge, Sociology of. 4. Ideology. 5. Intellectuals. I. Title. II. Series.
HM651 .J36 2002

Jantzen, Grace. Power, gender, and Christian mysticism / Grace M. Jantzen. Cambridge ; New York : Cambridge University Press, 1995. xvii, 384 p. : ill. ; 23 cm. (Cambridge studies in ideology and religion ; 8) Includes bibliographical references (p. 354-379) and index. Publisher description URL: http://www.loc.gov/catdir/description/cam026/94044562.html Table of contents URL: http://www.loc.gov/catdir/toc/cam024/94044562.html ISBN 0-521-47376-4 (hardback) ISBN 0-521-47926-6 (pbk.) DDC 248.2/2/082
1. Mysticism. 2. Women mystics. 3. Sex - Religious aspects - Christianity. 4. Authority - Religious aspects - Christianity. I. Title. II. Series.
BV5083 .J36 1995

Janz, Nathalie. Globus symbolicus : la philosophie d'Ernst Cassirer : une épistémologie de la troisième voie? / par Nathalie Janz. [Lausanne : Université de Lausanne, 1999] 277 p. ; 30 cm. "Décembre 1999." Thesis (doctoral)--Université de Lausanne, 1999. Includes bibliographical references (p. [242]-271).
1. Cassirer, Ernst, - 1874-1945. 2. Signs and symbols - Philosophy. 3. Knowledge, Theory of. I. Title. II. Title: Philosophie d'Ernst Cassirer : une épistémologie de la troisième voie?

JAPAN - CIVILIZATION - 1600-1868.
Bolitho, Harold. Bereavement and consolation. New Haven : Yale University Press, c2003.
DS822.2 .B65 2003

JAPANESE - BRAZIL.
Catanio, Percy Antonio Galimberttl. O caminho que o dekassegui sonhou (dekassegui no yumê-ji). São Paulo : EDUC, FAPESP; Londrina : UEL, 2002.

JAPANESE LANGUAGE - PHONOLOGY.
Toda, Takako. Second language speech perception and production. Lanham, Md. ; Oxford : University Press of America, c2003.
PL541 .T63 2003

Jaquet, Chantal.
Fortitude et servitude. Paris : Kimé, c2003.

Jarashow, Jonathan. The silent psalms of our son : Noah's holy life above the five senses : in honor of our son, Noah Raphael Hakohen / by Jonathan Jarashow. Jerusalem, Israel : Feldheim Publishers, c2001. 95 p. : ill. ; 23 cm. ISBN 0-9701045-1-0
1. Hakohen, Noah Raphael. 2. Children - Israel - Biography. 3. Tay-Sachs disease. 4. Children - Death. 5. Jewish families - Religious life. 6. Spiritual life - Judaism. I. Title.

Jarausch, Konrad Hugo. Shattered past : reconstructing German histories / Konrad H. Jarausch and Michael Geyer. Princeton, N.J. : Princeton University Press, c2003. xi, 380 p. ; 24 cm. Includes bibliographical references and index. ISBN 0-691-05935-7 (alk. paper) ISBN 0-691-05936-5 (pbk. : alk. paper) DDC 943.08/07/2043
1. Historiography - Germany - History - 20th century. 2. History - Philosophy. 3. Nationalism - Germany - History - 20th century. 4. Holocaust, Jewish (1939-1945) - Historiography. 5. Germany - Social conditions - 20th century. I. Geyer, Michael, 1947- II. Title.
DD86 .J253 2003

El jardín de las peculiaridades.
Sepúlveda, Jesús. Buenos Aires : Ediciones del Leopardo, [2002]

Jarvis, D. S. L. (Darryl S. L.), 1963-.
International relations and the "third debate". Westport, Conn. : Praeger, 2002.
JZ1306 .J577 2002

Jarvis, William E., 1945- Time capsules : a cultural history / by William E. Jarvis. Jefferson, N.C. : McFarland & Co., c2003. vii, 321 p. : ill. ; 23 cm. Includes bibliographical references (p. 265-312) and index. CONTENTS: Introduction : the time capsule experience -- Time capsule milestones in world chronology -- How time capsules work -- Notional and archaeological time capsules -- The time capsule's ancient origins and modern transformations -- The golden age of the grand time capsules,

1935-1982 -- Writing down the ages : ancient writings from yesterday, today, and tomorrow as time capsule experiences -- Keeping time in a perpetual futurescape -- Epilogue : our ideal time capsule. ISBN 0-7864-1261-5 (softcover : alk. paper) DDC 909
1. Time capsules - History. 2. Civilization - History. I. Title.
CB151 .J37 2003

JASPERS, KARL, 1883-1969.
Karl Jaspers on philosophy of history and history of philosophy. Amherst, N.Y. : Humanity Books, 2003.
B3279.J34 K292 2003

JATAKA STORIES, ENGLISH.
The jewel of friendship. Berkeley, CA : Dharma Pub., 2002.
BQ1462.E5 J48 2002

Jataka tales series
The jewel of friendship. Berkeley, CA : Dharma Pub., 2002.
BQ1462.E5 J48 2002

Jātakapārijātaḥ.
Vaidyanāthadīkṣita, 15th cent. [Jātakapārijāta] 1. saṃskaraṇa. Vārāṇasī : Caukhambā Surabhāratī Prakāśana ; Dillī : Caukhambā Saṃskrti Pratiṣṭhāna, 2001.
BF1714.H5 V253 2001

Jaunā viedība.
Mūks, Roberts. Rīga : Daugava, 2002.

Jay, Martin, 1944- Refractions of violence / Martin Jay. New York ; London : Routledge, 2003. ix, 228 p. ; ill. ; 23 cm. Includes bibliographical references (p. 189-217) and index. CONTENTS: Walter Benjamin and the refusal to mourn -- Peace in our time -- Fathers and sons : Jan Phillip Reemtsma -- The ungrateful dead -- When did the Holocaust end? Reflections on historical objectivity -- The conversion of the Rose -- Pen pals with the unicorn killer -- Kwangju : from massacre to Biennale -- Must justice be blind? : images and the law -- Diving into the wreck : aesthetic spectatorship at the turn of the millennium -- Astronomical hindsight : the speed of light and the virtualization of reality -- Returning the gaze : the American response to the French critique of ocularcentrism -- Lafayette's children : the American reception of French liberalism -- Somaesthetics and democracy : John Dewey and body art -- The paradoxes of religious violence -- Fearful symmetries : September 11th and the agonies of the left. ISBN 0-415-96665-5 (HB : alk. paper) ISBN 0-415-96666-3 (PB : alk. paper) DDC 303.6
1. Violence. 2. Civilization, Modern - 20th century. I. Title.
HM1116 .J39 2003

Jay, Timothy. Why we curse : a neuro-psycho-social theory of speech / Timothy Jay. Philadelphia : John Benjamins Publishing Company, c2000. xv, 328 p. : ill. ; 23 cm. Includes bibliographical references (p. [277]-317) and index. ISBN 1-55619-758-6 (alk. paper) DDC 401/.9
1. Invective - Psychological aspects. 2. Blessing and cursing - Psychological aspects. 3. Threat (Psychology) 4. Verbal behavior. I. Title.
BF463.I58 J38 2000

Jayaprabhavijaya, Śramaṇa.
Rajendra.
Gulābavijaya. Śrī Muhūrtarāja. Dvitīyāvrtti. Ji. Dhāra, Ma. Pra. : Rājendra Pravacana Kāryālaya, 1996.
BF1714.J28+

JAZZ DANCE - STUDY AND TEACHING.
The peak performance series. Vol. [4] [videorecording]. Longwood, Fla. : Pamela Bolling Enterprises, c1999.

Je veux que l'on soit homme.
Bimont, Bernard. Brive : Ecritures, [2002]

JEALOUSY. *See also* **ENVY.**
Ruge, Kenneth. The Othello response. New York : Marlowe & Co., 2003.
BF575.J4 R84 2003

Jean, de la Rochelle, d. 1245. Summa de anima / Jean de La Rochelle ; texte critique avec introduction, notes et tables publié par Jacques Guy Bougerol. Paris : J. Vrin, 1995. 298 p. ; 26 cm. (Textes philosophiques du Moyen Age ; 19) Includes bibliographical references and index. ISBN 2-7116-1234-1 DDC 128/.1
1. Soul - Early works to 1800. 2. Philosophical anthropology - Early works to 1800. 3. Philosophy, Medieval. I. Bougerol, Jacques Guy. II. Title. III. Series.
BD420 .J43 1995

Jean, Mark, 1957-.
Smith, Terry (Terry L.), 1961- Haunted inns of America. Birmingham, Ala. : Crane Hill Publishers, c2003.
BF1474.5 .S65 2003

Jean-Paul Sartre.
Mavouangui, David, 1953- Paris : Paari, [2002], c2001.

Jean Piaget, 1868-1979.
Ducret, Jean-Jacques, 1946- Genève, Switzerland : Service de la recherche en éducation, c2000.
BF311 .D813 2000

Jean Piaget Society. Meeting (30th : 2000 : Montréal, Québec) Changing conceptions of psychological life / edited by Cynthia Lightfoot, Chris LaLonde, Michael Chandler. Mahwah, N.J. : L. Erlbaum Associates, 2004. p. cm. Includes bibliographical references and index. ISBN 0-8058-4336-1 (c. : alk. paper) DDC 155.2
1. Self - Congresses. I. Lightfoot, Cynthia. II. LaLonde, Christopher A. III. Chandler, Michael J. IV. Title.
BF697 .J36 2004

Jeannerod, Marc. La nature de l'esprit : sciences cognitives et cerveau / Marc Jeannerod. Paris : Odile Jacob, c2002. 256 p. ; 22 cm. (Sciences) Includes bibliographical references (p. 223-[235]) and index. ISBN 2-7381-1071-1 DDC 150
1. Cognition. I. Title. II. Title: Sciences cognitives et cerveau III. Series: Sciences (Editions Odile Jacob)
BF311 .J435 2002

Jeff, Peter. Get a grip on your dream : 12 ways to squeeze more success out of your goals / Peter Jeff. [Grand Rapids, MI] : Possibility Press, c2000. 144 p. : ill. ; 21 cm. ISBN 0-938716-63-8 DDC 158.1
1. Success - Psychological aspects. I. Title.
BF637.S8 J45 2000

Jeffries, Rhonda B. (Rhonda Baynes), 1965-.
Givens, Gretchen Zita. Black women in the field. Cresskill, N.J. : Hampton Press, c2003.
LC2781.5 .G58 2003

Jeffries, William C. Profiles of the 16 personality types / by William C. Jeffries. Noblesville, IN : Buttermilk Ridge Pub. ; Zionsville, Ind. : Distributed by Executive Strategies International, c2002. 135 p. ; 22 cm. ISBN 0-9723961-0-1 DDC 155.2/64
1. Myers-Briggs Type Indicator. 2. Typology (Psychology) I. Title. II. Title: Profiles of the sixteen personality types
BF698.8.M94 J43 2002

Still true to type : an introduction to type and answers to most frequently asked questions about completing and interpreting the Myers-Briggs Type Indicator / by William C. Jeffries. Noblesville, IN : Buttermilk Ridge Pub. ; Zionsville, Ind. : Distributed by Executive Strategies International, c2002. 205 p. : ill. ; 22 cm. Includes bibliographical references (p. 199-205). ISBN 0-9723961-1-X DDC 155.2/64
1. Myers-Briggs Type Indicator. 2. Typology (Psychology) I. Title.
BF698.8.M94 J435 2002

JEHOVAH. See **GOD (JUDAISM) - NAME.**

A jelen és az idő.
Orosz, László Wladimir. Debrecen : Stalker Stúdió, 2001.
BF1999 .O69 2000

Jenkins, George.
Davis, Sampson. The pact. Waterville, ME : Thorndike Press, 2002.
1. Black author.

JENKINS, GEORGE.
Davis, Sampson. The pact. Waterville, ME : Thorndike Press, 2002.
1. Black author.

Jenkins, John Major. Galactic alignment : the transformation of consciousness according to Mayan, Egyptian, and Vedic Traditions / John Major Jenkins. Rochester, Vt. : Bear & Co., 2002. 300 p. : ill. , maps ; 23 cm. Includes bibliographical references ([P. 271]-293) and index. Table of contents URL: http://www.loc.gov/catdir/toc/fy034/2002006139.html ISBN 1-87918-184-3 DDC 529/.329784152
1. Maya cosmology. 2. Maya astronomy. 3. Maya calendar. 4. Cosmology, Egyptian. 5. Hindu cosmology. I. Title.
F1435.3.R3 J45 2002

Jenkins, Keith, 1943- Refiguring history : new thoughts on an old discipline / Keith Jenkins. London : New York : Routledge, 2003 . 74 p. ; 23 cm. Includes bibliographical references and index. ISBN 0-415-24410-2 (HB : alk. paper) ISBN 0-415-24411-0 (PB : alk. paper) DDC 901
1. History - Philosophy. 2. Historiography. 3. Historicism. I. Title.
D16.8 .J385 2003

Jenny is scared.
Shuman, Carol. Washington, DC : Magination Press, c2003.

BF723.F4 S58 2003

Jensen, Anders Fogh. Metaforens magt : fantasiens fostre og fornunftens fødsler / Anders Fogh Jensen. 1. opl. Århus : Modtryk, 2001. 252 p. : ill. ; 25 cm. Includes bibliographical references (p. 247-250) and index. ISBN 87-7394-654-0
1. Metaphor. 2. Language and culture. 3. Imagination. I. Title.

Jensen, Arthur, 1954-.
Trenholm, Sarah, 1944- Interpersonal communication. 5th ed. New York : Oxford University Press, 2003.
BF637.C45 T72 2003

Jensen, Arthur Robert. Intelligence, race, and genetics : conversations with Arthur R. Jensen / Frank Miele. Boulder, Colo. : Westview Press, c2002. xi, 243 p. : ill. ; 24 cm. "Bibliography of Arthur R. Jensen": p. 191-222. Includes bibloographical references and index. ISBN 0-8133-4008-X (alk. paper) DDC 155.7
1. Intellect - Genetic aspects. 2. Nature and nurture. 3. African-Americans - Intelligence levels. 4. Jensen, Arthur Robert. I. Miele, Frank. II. Title.
BF431 .J396 2002

Intelligence, race, and genetics : conversations with Arthur R. Jensen / Frank Miele. Boulder, Colo. : Westview, 2002. xi, 243 p. : ill. ; 24 cm. Includes bibliography of Jensen's works. Includes bibloographical references and index. ISBN 0-8133-4008-X
1. Jensen, Arthur Robert. 2. Jensen, Arthur Robert - Bibliography. 3. Intelligence tests - Social aspects. 4. Intelligence levels - Social aspects. 5. Psychometrics. 6. Racism in psychology. I. Miele, Frank. II. Title.

The scientific study of general intelligence. 1st ed. Amsterdam ; Boston : Pergamon, 2003.
BF433.G45 S35 2003

JENSEN, ARTHUR ROBERT.
Jensen, Arthur Robert. Intelligence, race, and genetics. Boulder, Colo. : Westview Press, c2002.
BF431 .J396 2002

Jensen, Arthur Robert. Intelligence, race, and genetics. Boulder, Colo. : Westview, 2002.

JENSEN, ARTHUR ROBERT - BIBLIOGRAPHY.
Jensen, Arthur Robert. Intelligence, race, and genetics. Boulder, Colo. : Westview, 2002.

Jeong, Ho-Won.
Approaches to peacebuilding. Houndmills, Basingstoke, Hampshire ; New York : Palgrave Macmillan, 2002.
JZ5538 .A675 2002

Jerotić, Vladeta. Neuroticne pojave naseg vremena / Vladeta Jerotić. 2, dop. izd. Beograd : Zlatousti, 2001. 181 p. ; 22 cm. In Serbian (Cyrillic).
1. Neuroses. I. Title.

[Selections 2000]
Izabrani ogledi / Vladeta Jerotić ; predgovor Pavle Zorić. Beograd: Srpska književna zadruga, 2000. 366 p. ; 19 cm. (Srpska književna zadruga ; kolo 93, knj. 617) In Serbian (Cyrillic). Includes bibliographical references. ISBN 86-379-0734-2
1. Psychiatry. 2. Psychotherapy. 3. Serbian literature - History and criticism. 4. Serbian literature - Psychological aspects. 5. Jungian psychology - Religious aspects - Christianity. 6. Jungian psychology - Religious aspects - Orthodox Eastern Church. I. Zorić, Pavle, 1934- II. Title. III. Series: Srpska književna zadruga (Series) ; kolo 93, knj. 617.
BF109.J47 A25 2000

Jerphagnon, Lucien, 1921- Les dieux ne sont jamais loin / Lucien Jerphagnon. Paris : Desclée de Brouwer, c2002. 223 p. ; 21 cm. ISBN 2-220-05177-3 DDC 100
1. Myth. I. Title.

Jervis, Robert, 1940-.
Oxford handbook of political psychology. Oxford ; New York : Oxford University Press, 2003.
JA74.5 .H355 2003

Jessner, Ulrike.
Herdina, Philip. A dynamic model of multilingualism. Clevedon, England Buffalo, N.Y. : Multilingual Matters, 2002.
P115.4 .H47 2002

JESTS. See **WIT AND HUMOR.**

JESUITS - HISTORY.
Lowney, Chris. Heroic leadership. Chicago : Loyola Press, c2003.
HD57.7 .L69 2003

JESUS CHRIST - BLOOD.
Olorunfemi, Samuel Jimson. Breaking the evil blood covenant. Ibadan, Oyo State, Nigeria : Triumphant Faith Publications, 2001.
1. Black author.

JESUS CHRIST - DIVINITY.
Giussani, Luigi. PerCorso. Milano : Rizzoli, c1997-

JESUS CHRIST - FAMILY.
Be thou there. Cairo ; New York : American University in Cairo Press, c2001.

JESUS CHRIST - FLIGHT INTO EGYPT.
Be thou there. Cairo ; New York : American University in Cairo Press, c2001.

JESUS CHRIST - MISCELLANEA.
Novak, Peter, 1958- The lost secret of death. Charlottesville, VA : Hampton Roads Pub., 2003.
BF1999 .N73 2003

JESUS CHRIST - PASSION - ROLE OF JEWS.
Davis, Frederick, 1931- The Jew and deicide. Lanham, Md. : University Press of America, c2003.
BS2555.6.J44 D38 2003

Jette, Christine, 1953- Professional tarot : the business of reading, consulting & teaching / Christine Jette. 1st ed. St. Paul, Minn. : Llewellyn Publications, 2003. xvii, 215 p. ; 23 cm. Includes bibliographical references (p. 203-208) and index. ISBN 0-7387-0217-X (pbk.) DDC 133.3/2424
1. Tarot. I. Title.
BF1879.T2 J475 2003

Le jeu de l'identité.
Moessinger, Pierre 1re éd. Paris : Presses universitaires de France, 2000.
BF697.5.S43 M634 2000

The Jew and deicide.
Davis, Frederick, 1931- Lanham, Md. : University Press of America, c2003.
BS2555.6.J44 D38 2003

JEW - CONDUCT OF LIFE.
Yanai, Me'ir. Orot ha-tamtsit. Yerushalayim : Nezer Dayid - Ari'el, 761 [2000 or 2001]

The jewel of friendship : a Jataka tale / illustrated by Magdelena Duran. Berkeley, CA : Dharma Pub., 2002. 1 v. (unpaged) : col. ill. ; 28 cm. (Jataka tales series) An adaptation of Manikantha Jataka. SUMMARY: When he is befriended by a serpent king in human form, who later reveals his true nature, a young boy learns that friendship is more precious than the rarest of jewels. ISBN 0-89800-319-9 (pbk.) DDC 294.3/82325
1. Jataka stories, English. 2. Friendship - Juvenile literature. 3. Gautama Buddha - Pre-existence - Juvenile literature. I. Duran, Magdelena, 1960- ill. II. Title: Tipiṭaka. Suttapiṭaka. Khuddakanikāya. Jātaka. Manikanthajataka. III. Series.
BQ1462.E5 J48 2002

JEWELS. See **GEMS; PRECIOUS STONES.**

JEWISH AGED.
Adler, Yitshak Eliyahu, ha-Kohen. Sefer Kibud ye-hidur. Ofakim : Y.E. ha-Kohen Adler, 754 [1994]

JEWISH-ARAB RELATIONS. See **PROPAGANDA, ZIONIST.**

JEWISH-ARAB RELATIONS - 1917-. See **ARAB-ISRAELI CONFLICT.**

JEWISH-ARAB RELATIONS - 1949-. See **ARAB-ISRAELI CONFLICT.**

JEWISH ASTROLOGY.
Erlanger, Gad. [Mazalot, ha-Yahadut ya-ani. English] Signs of the times. Jerusalem ; New York : Feldheim Pub., 2000.
BF1714.J4 E74 2001

Sela, Shlomo. Abraham Ibn Ezra and the rise of medieval Hebrew science. Leiden ; Boston, MA : Brill, 2003.
BM538.S3 S45 2003

JEWISH CATASTROPHE (1939-1945). See **HOLOCAUST, JEWISH (1939-1945).**

Jewish culture and contexts
Chajes, Jeffrey Howard. Between worlds. Philadelphia : University of Pennsylvania Press, c2003.
BM729.D92 C53 2003

JEWISH DEVOTIONAL LITERATURE. See **JUDAISM - PRAYER-BOOKS AND DEVOTIONS.**

The Jewish dream book.
Ochs, Vanessa L. Woodstock, VT : Jewish Lights Publishing, 2003.
BF1078 .O24 2003

JEWISH FAMILIES - RELIGIOUS LIFE.
Greiper, BenTzion. Getting and staying married / BenTzion Greiper. Brooklyn, NY : B.T. Greiper, [2001?]

HQ734 .G745 2001

Jarashow, Jonathan. The silent psalms of our son. Jerusalem, Israel : Feldheim Publishers, c2001.

Yahav, Avino'am Shemu'el. Ḳuntres E'eśeh lo 'ezer. Betar 'Ilit : A. S. Yahav, 761, 2001.

JEWISH HOLIDAYS. See **FASTS AND FEASTS - JUDAISM.**

JEWISH HOLOCAUST (1939-1945). See **HOLOCAUST, JEWISH (1939-1945).**

JEWISH LANGUAGE. See **HEBREW LANGUAGE.**

JEWISH LAW. See also **COMMANDMENTS, SIX HUNDRED AND THIRTEEN; COMMERCIAL LAW (JEWISH LAW); DIVORCE (JEWISH LAW); HUSBAND AND WIFE (JEWISH LAW); PARENT AND CHILD (JEWISH LAW); RESPECT FOR PERSONS (JEWISH LAW); RESPONSA.**
Aviner, Shelomoh Ḥayim, ha-Kohen. Be-ahavah uve-emunah. Yerushalayim : [ḥ. mo. l.], 760-762 [1999 or 2000-2001 or 2002]
BM565 .A93 1999

Goldberg, Avraham Yehoshu'a, 1856-1921. Sefer Kitve paz. Yerushalayim : ha-Mishpaḥah, 763, c2003.

Ḳarelits, Ḥayim Sha'ul ben Me'ir. Sefer Aḥat sha'alti. Bene Beraḳ : Mish. Ḳarelits, 762 [2002]

Marḳ, Shelomoh Zalman ben Neḥemyah. Sefer Ma'aśeh uman. Yerushalayim : Naḥalat kolel "Bet ulpana de-rabenu Yoḥanan, 763 [2002 or 2003]

JEWISH LAW - INFLUENCE.
Ta-Shma, Israel M. ha-Nigleh sheba-nistar. Nusaḥ murḥav. [Tel Aviv] : ha-Ḳibuts ha-me'uḥad, c2001.

JEWISH LAW - INTERPRETATION AND CONSTRUCTION.
Neusner, Jacob, 1932- Analysis and argumentation in Rabbinic Judaism. Lanham, Md. : University Press of America, c2003.
BM496.5 .N4775 2003

JEWISH LAW - PHILOSOPHY.
Halbertal, Moshe. Ben Torah le-ḥokhmah. Yerushalayim : Hotsa'at sefarim 'a. sh. Y. L. Magnes, ha-Universiṭah ha-'Ivrit, 760, 2000.
BM755.M54 H35 2000

JEWISH LEARNING AND SCHOLARSHIP. See also **TALMUD TORAH (JUDAISM).**
Mosheh ben Shelomoh El'azar. Sefer Yede Mosheh ve-Torah or. Bene Beraḳ : Sifre Or ha-ḥayim, [760 i.e. 2000]

Jewish life in Sana.
Ḳafaḥ, Yosef, 1917- Halikhot Teman. Mahad. 5, metuḳenet. Yerushalayim : Mekhon Ben-Tsevi le-ḥeker kehilot Yiśra'el ba-Mizraḥ : Yad Yitsḥaḳ ben-Tsevi : ha-Universiṭah ha-Ivrit bi-Yerushalayim, 2002.

JEWISH LITERATURE. See **MIDRASH; RABBINICAL LITERATURE.**

JEWISH MAGIC. See **MAGIC, JEWISH.**

JEWISH MARTYRS.
[Zohar ḥadash. Lamentations. 2000.] Zohar ḥadash Megilat Ekhah. "Hotsa'ah meyuḥedet li-yeme ben ha-metsarim". Yerushalayim : Mekhon Da'at Yosef, 761 [2000 or 2001]
BM525.A6 Z6 2001

JEWISH MARTYRS - PALESTINE - PSYCHOLOGY.
Oron, Israel. Mavet, almavet ve-ide'ologyah. [Israel] : Miśrad ha-biṭaḥon, [2002]

JEWISH MEDITATIONS.
Mantovani, Massimo. Meditazioni sull'albero della cabala. Milano : Xenia, 2002.

JEWISH PRAYERS. See **JUDAISM - PRAYER-BOOKS AND DEVOTIONS.**

JEWISH RABBIS. See **RABBIS.**

JEWISH RELIGIOUS EDUCATION. See **TALMUD TORAH (JUDAISM).**

JEWISH RELIGIOUS EDUCATION OF CHILDREN.
Brezak, Dov. Chinuch in turbulent times. 1st ed. Brooklyn, N.Y. : Mesorah Publications, c2002.

JEWISH RELIGIOUS POETRY, HEBREW.
Naphtali ben Isaac, ha-Kohen, 1649-1719. Sefer Bet Raḥel. Yerushalayim : Ahavat Shalom, 761 [2001]
BM665 .N257 2001

JEWISH SCHOLARS. See also **RABBIS.**
Adler, Yitsḥaḳ Eliyahu, ha-Kohen. Sefer Kibud ve-hidur. Ofaḳim : Y.E. ha-Kohen Adler, 754 [1994]

JEWISH SECTS. See **HASIDISM.**

JEWISH SERMONS. See **MIDRASH.**

JEWISH SERMONS, HEBREW.
Admur ha-G. ha-Ḳ., Sheliṭa. ['Avodat 'avodah (Torah)] Sefer 'Avodat 'avodah. Ḳiryat Ṭohsh, Ḳanada : N. M. Hershḳovitsh, 763 [2002 or 2003]

Algazi, Solomon ben Abraham, 1610?-ca. 1683. Sefer Ahavat 'olam. Bruḳlin : Sifre Algazi, 760 [2000]

Alter, Judah Aryeh Leib, 1847-1905. [Śefat emet (Torah). Selections] Sefer Śefat emet. Yerushalayim : Mir, 762 [2001 or 2002]

Armoni, Mosheh Ḥayim. Sefer Ginze Armoni. Yerushalayim : 'Amutat "Naḥalat-Raḥel", 762 [2002]
BM670.S5 A756 2002

Bardaḥ, Asher. Sefer Otsrot av. [Bene Beraḳ?] : A. Bardaḥ, 762-   [2001 or 2002-
BS1225.54 .B37 2001

Druḳ, Ya'aḳov ben Zalman. Ohel Ya'aḳov. Yerushala[yi]m : Y. ben Z. Druḳ, 762 [2002]
BS1225.4 .D77 2002

Goldberg, Avraham Yehoshu'a, 1856-1921. Sefer Kitve paz. Yerushalayim : ha-Mishpaḥah, 763, c2003.

Ḥayim Yeroḥam ben Shimshon Meshulam Feybish, mi-Snatin. Sefer Asefat divre ḥakhamim. Yerushalayim : Mekhon Sod yesharim, 761 [2001]

Ḳarelits, Ḥayim Sha'ul ben Me'ir. Sefer Aḥat sha'alti. Bene Beraḳ : Mish. Ḳarelits, 762 [2002]

Ḳoll, Shmuel, 1938- Sefer Ra'yonot u-mesarim. Yerushalayim : S. Ḳol, 761- [2001-

Miler, Avigdor Hakohen. Sefer Torat Avigdor. Bene Braḳ : [ḥ. mo. l], 762- [2001 or 2002-

Vainshṭoḳ, Bentsiyon Mosheh Ya'ir ben Mordekhai David. Sefer Or ha-da'at. Yerushalayim : ha-Makhon le-hotsa'at sifre ha-g. R. M.Y. Vainshṭoḳ, 762 [2001 or 2002]

Vaisfish, Tsevi ben Shemu'el A. L. Sefer Dibrot Tsevi. Yerushalayim : Makhon le-hotsa'at sefarim 'a. sh. Rabi Naḥum mi-Shadiḳ, 762- [2002-

Vital, Ḥayyim ben Joseph, 1542 or 3-1620. 'Ets ha-da'at tov. Yerushalayim : Hotsa'at Ahavat shalom, 761 [2000 or 2001]

Yalḳuṭ Ṭuv ha-peninim. Yerushala[y]im : P. Y. Liberman, 762 [2001 or 2002]
BS1225.53 .Y35 2001

JEWISH SERMONS, HEBREW - ISRAEL.
Shemu'elevits, Ḥayim, 1901-1979. Sefer Śiḥot musar. Mahad. ḥadashah u-metuḳenet. Yerushalayim : Bene va-hatane ha-meḥaber, 762, c2002.
BJ1287.S56 S5 2002

JEWISH SERMONS, HEBREW - NEW YORK (STATE) - LAKEWOOD.
Vakhtfoigel, Nathan. Sefer No'am ha-musar. Laikvud : [ḥ. mo. l.], 762 [2001 or 2002]
BJ1285 .V35 2001

JEWISH WAY OF LIFE.
Alshekh, Moses, 16th cent. [Torat Mosheh. Selections] Sefer 'Orot ha-Alshekh. Yerushalayim : [ḥ. mo. l.], 763 [2002 or 2003]

Dorff, Elliot N. Love your neighbor and yourself. 1st ed. Philadelphia, PA : Jewish Publication Society, 2003.
BJ1285 .D67 2003

Eyal, Tsevi. Mi she-ta'am yayin Hungari. Tel Aviv : Yedi'ot aḥaronot : Sifre ḥemed, c2002.

Maier, Johann. Judentum von A bis Z. Freiburg im Breisgau : Herder, 2001.

Otsrot rabotenu mi-Brisk. Bene Beraḳ : Sh. L., molut u-mishar bi-sefarim, 762 [2001 or 2002]
BM602 .O+

Segal, Yehudah Zeraḥyah, ha-Levi. Sefer Doreshe H.. Tel-Aviv : Talmidav ve-shmom'e likho, 763 [2003]
BJ1287.S43 D66 2003

Shooter, Jonathan. The wisdom within. Southfield, MI : Targum Press ; Nanuet, NY : Distributed by Feldheim Publishers, 2002.

Ziegler, Reuven. By his light. 2nd ed. Jersey City, NJ : KTAV Pub. House ; Alon Shevut, Israel : Yeshivat Har Etzion, 2003.

BM723 .Z54 2003

JEWISH WOMEN AUTHORS - UNITED STATES.
Gender, place, and memory in the modern Jewish experience. London ; Portland, Or. : Vallentine Mitchell, 2003.
DS143 .G36 2003

JEWISH WOMEN - CONDUCT OF LIFE.
Sofer, Mikha'el Uri. Sefer 'Olamot shel ṭohar. Mahad. 2. Bene Beraḳ : M.U. Sofer, 761 [2000 or 2001]
BM726 .S633 2000

JEWISH WOMEN - SOCIAL CONDITIONS - 20TH CENTURY.
Gender, place, and memory in the modern Jewish experience. London ; Portland, Or. : Vallentine Mitchell, 2003.
DS143 .G36 2003

JEWS. See **JUDAISM.**

JEWS - CIVILIZATION.
Eidelberg, Paul. Clash of two decadent civilizations. Shaarei Tikva, Israel : ACPR Publications, 2002.
BM537 .E53 2002

Rozanov, V. V. (Vasiliĭ Vasil'evich), 1856-1919. Vozrozhdaiushchiĭsia Egipet. Moskva : Izd-vo "Respublika", 2002.

JEWS - CONDUCT OF LIFE.
Ashkenazi, Nisim. Ben he-'anan. Tel-Aviv : Gal, 2002.

Ḥayun, Yehudah ben Mordekhai. Masekhet ha-ḥayim. Bene Beraḳ : Y. Ḥayun, 762 [2001 or 2002]

Lugasi, Ya'aḳov Yiśra'el. Yalḳut Or ha-ḥayim ha-ḳadosh. Yerushalayim : [ḥ. mo. l], 762 [2001 or 2002]

JEWS - DIVORCE. See **DIVORCE (JEWISH LAW).**

JEWS - EUROPE - BIOGRAPHY.
Gold, Alison Leslie. Fiet's vase and other stories of survival, Europe 1939-1945. New York : Jeremy P. Tarcher/Penguin, c2003.
D804.3 .G64 2003

JEWS - EUROPE - IDENTITY.
Gender, place, and memory in the modern Jewish experience. London ; Portland, Or. : Vallentine Mitchell, 2003.
DS143 .G36 2003

JEWS - FAMILIES. See **JEWISH FAMILIES.**

JEWS - FASTS AND FEASTS. See **FASTS AND FEASTS - JUDAISM.**

JEWS - FESTIVALS. See **FASTS AND FEASTS - JUDAISM.**

JEWS - IDENTITY.
Gender, place, and memory in the modern Jewish experience. London ; Portland, Or. : Vallentine Mitchell, 2003.
DS143 .G36 2003

Luz, Ehud. [Ma'avaḳ be-naḥal Yaboḳ. English] Wrestling with an angel. New Haven : Yale University Press, c2003.
DS143 .L8913 2003

Wisenberg, S. L. (Sandi L.) Holocaust girls. Lincoln : University of Nebraska Press, c2002.
DS143 .W645 2002

JEWS IN THE NEW TESTAMENT.
Davis, Frederick, 1931- The Jew and deicide. Lanham, Md. : University Press of America, c2003.
BS2555.6.J44 D38 2003

JEWS - ISRAEL - IDENTITY.
Gender, place, and memory in the modern Jewish experience. London ; Portland, Or. : Vallentine Mitchell, 2003.
DS143 .G36 2003

JEWS - LANGUAGES. See **HEBREW LANGUAGE.**

JEWS - LAW. See **JEWISH LAW.**

JEWS - NAZI PERSECUTION. See **HOLOCAUST, JEWISH (1939-1945).**

JEWS - NEW YORK (STATE) - NEW YORK. - BIOGRAPHY.
Nuland, Sherwin B. Lost in America. 1st ed. New York : Knopf ; Distributed by Random House, 2003.
F128.9.J5 N85 2003

JEWS - PALESTINE - HISTORY - 20TH CENTURY.
Oron, Israel. Mavet, almavet ve-ide'ologyah. [Israel] : Miśrad ha-biṭaḥon, [2002]

JEWS - PERSECUTIONS. *See* **HOLOCAUST, JEWISH (1939-1945).**

JEWS - PRAYER-BOOKS AND DEVOTIONS. *See* **JUDAISM - PRAYER-BOOKS AND DEVOTIONS.**

JEWS - PSYCHOLOGY.
Wisenberg, S. L. (Sandi L.) Holocaust girls. Lincoln : University of Nebraska Press, c2002.
DS143 .W645 2002

JEWS - PUBLIC OPINION - HISTORY.
Katznelson, Ira. Desolation and enlightenment. New York : Columbia University Press, c2003.
JA71 .K35 2003

JEWS - RELIGION. *See* **JUDAISM.**

JEWS - RESTORATION. *See* **MESSIANIC ERA (JUDAISM).**

JEWS - RITUAL. *See* **JUDAISM - LITURGY.**

JEWS - SOCIAL LIFE AND CUSTOMS.
Feldbaum, Rebecca Bram. If there's anything I can do--. Jerusalem, Israel ; Nanuet, NY : Feldheim Publishers, 2003.
BF575.G7 F46 2003

Kafaḥ, Yosef, 1917- Halikhot Teman. Mahad. 5, metukenet. Yerushalayim : Mekhon Ben-Tsevi le-ḥeker ḳehilot Yiśra'el ba-Mizraḥ : Yad Yitsḥaḳ ben-Tsevi : ha-Universiṭah ha-Ivrit bi-Yerushalayim, 2002.

Maier, Johann. Judentum von A bis Z. Freiburg im Breisgau : Herder, 2001.

JEWS - UNITED STATES - IDENTITY.
Gender, place, and memory in the modern Jewish experience. London ; Portland, Or. : Vallentine Mitchell, 2003.
DS143 .G36 2003

JEWS - YEMEN - ṢAN'Ā'.
Kafaḥ, Yosef, 1917- Halikhot Teman. Mahad. 5, metukenet. Yerushalayim : Mekhon Ben-Tsevi le-ḥeker ḳehilot Yiśra'el ba-Mizraḥ : Yad Yitsḥaḳ ben-Tsevi : ha-Universiṭah ha-Ivrit bi-Yerushalayim, 2002.

Język w przestrzeni społecznej / redakcja naukowa Stanisław Gajda, Kazimierz Rymut, Urszula Żydek-Bednarczuk. Opole : Uniwersytet Opolski, 2002. 515 p. : ill. (some col.) ; 24 cm. "Bibliografia prac naukowych profesora Władysława Lubasia za lata 1957-2001"--P. [21]-41. ISBN 83-86881-33-X
1. Lubaś, Władysław. 2. Sociolinguistics. 3. Language and languages. I. Gajda, Stanisław. II. Rymut, Kazimierz. III. Żydek-Bednarczuk, Urszula. IV. Lubaś, Władysław. V. Uniwersytet Opolski. Instytut Filologii Polskiej. VI. Opolskie Towarzystwo Przyjaciół Nauk.
P40 .J492 2002

JFE 03-4795.
Lee, Michelle. Fashion victim. 1st ed. New York : Broadway Books, 2003.
GT524 .L44 2003

Jha, Ganganatha, Sir, 1871-1941.
Patañjali. The Yoga-darshana. 2nd ed.--throughly rev. [Fremont, Calif.] : Asian Humanities Press, [2002], 1934.
B132.Y6 P265 2002

Jian lun han yu min zu xing ge.
Zhang, Fan. Mei xue yu yan xue. Di 1 ban. Beijing : Shou du shi fan da xue chu ban she, 1998.
P121 .Z465 1998

Jiang, Kongyang. Jiang Kongyang xue shu wen hua sui bi / Zheng Yuanzhe bian. Beijing di 1 ban. Beijing : Zhongguo qing nian chu ban she, 2000. vii, 4, 368 p. ; 21 cm. (Er shi shi ji Zhongguo xue shu wen hua sui bi da xi. Di 3 ji) Includes bibliographical references. CONTENTS: Di 1 bian. Ren sheng pian -- Di 2 bian. Mei xue pian -- Di 3 bian. Wen hua yi shu pian -- Jiang Kongyang nian pu jian bian -- Ba: Jiang Kongyang de mei xue dao lu. ISBN 7-5006-3732-2
1. Aesthetics. 2. Aesthetics, Chinese. I. Zheng, Yuanzhe, 1964- II. Title. III. Series.
BH39 .J435 2000

Jiang Kongyang xue shu wen hua sui bi.
Jiang, Kongyang. Beijing di 1 ban. Beijing : Zhongguo qing nian chu ban she, 2000.
BH39 .J435 2000

Jiang, Yin. Xue shu de nian lun / Jiang Yin zhu. Di 1 ban. [Beijing] : Zhongguo wen lian chu ban she, 2000. 3, 3, 2, 264 p. ; 20 cm. (Si xiang xue shu sheng huo) Includes bibliographical references.
1. Chinese literature - History and criticism. I. Title. II. Series.
PL2262 .J536 2000

Jibu, Mari.
No matter, never mind. Amsterdam ; Philadelphia : John Benjamins Pub. Co., c2002.

QP411 .N598 2002

Jiddāwī, 'Abd al-Mun'im. Ghayr ṣāliḥ lil-zawāj / bi-qalam 'Abd al-Mun'im al-Jiddāwī. al-Qāhirah : Dār Akhbār al-Yawm, 1994- v. ; 20 cm. (Kitāb al-Yawm.) In Arabic. ISBN 9770804940 (v. 1)
1. Marriage. I. Title.

Jidō kōen.
Edo-e kara shomotsu made. Tōkyō : Kyūzansha, 1997.
HQ792.J3 N54 1997 v.19

Jiménez Castillo, Mario. Diccionario de los sueños / Mario Jiménez Castillo. St. Paul, Minn. : Llewellyn Español, 2003. xxii, 333 p. ; 23 cm. ISBN 0-7387-0313-3 DDC 154.6/3/03
1. Dream interpretation - Dictionaries - Spanish. I. Title.
BF1095 .J56 2003

Jin nian lai Zhongguo de Meiguo yan jiu.
Tou shi Meiguo. Di 1 ban. Beijing : Zhongguo she hui ke xue chu ban she : Jing xiao Xin hua shu dian, 2002.
E175.8 .T78 2002

JINDŘICHUV HRADEC (CZECH REPUBLIC) - CHURCH HISTORY.
Sankt Georg und sein Bilderzyklus in Neuhaus/Böhmen (Jindřichuv Hradec). Marburg : N.G. Elwert, c2002.
BR1720.G4 S26 2002

Jing Chu qing nian ren wen xue zhe wen cong
Li, Jianzhong, 1955- [Selections. 1999] Li Jianzhong zi xuan ji. Di 1 ban. Wuchang : Hua zhong li gong da xue chu ban she, 1999.
PL2284 .L395 1999

Jing ji zhe xue.
Zhang, Xiong, 1953- Di 1 ban. [Kunming] : Yunnan ren min chu ban she, 2002.
D16.8 .Z536 2002

Jironet, Karin. The image of spiritual liberty in the western Sufi movement following Hazrat Inayat Khan / Karin Jironet. Leuven : Peeters, 2002. xiv, 293 p. ; ill. ; 25 cm. (New religious identities in the western world ; 4) Includes bibliographical references and index. ISBN 90-429-1205-7 (pbk.)
1. Inayat Khan, - 1882-1927. 2. Sufism. 3. Sufism - Netherlands. 4. Spirituality. I. Title. II. Series.
BP189.2 .J57 2002

Jñāneśvara, Umeśa Purī.
[Mānasāgarī. Hindi & Sanskrit.] Mānasāgarī. Saṃskaraṇa 1. Haridvāra : Raṇadhīra Prakāśana, 2000.
BF1714.H5+

Joanne Goodman lectures
(2001.) Lewis, Jane (Jane E.) Should we worry about family change? Toronto : University of Toronto Press, c2003.

JOB BIAS. *See* **DISCRIMINATION IN EMPLOYMENT.**

JOB DISCRIMINATION. *See* **DISCRIMINATION IN EMPLOYMENT.**

JOB SATISFACTION. *See also* **BURN OUT (PSYCHOLOGY).**
The new workplace. Chichester, UK ; Hoboken, NJ : Wiley, c2003.
HD6955 .N495 2003

Personality and work. 1st ed. San Francisco, CA : Jossey-Bass, c2003.
BF698.9.O3 P47 2003

Salmon, William A. The mid-career tune-up. New York : Amacom, c2000.
HF5381 .S256 2000

JOB SECURITY.
Salmon, William A. The mid-career tune-up. New York : Amacom, c2000.
HF5381 .S256 2000

JOB STRESS. *See also* **BURN OUT (PSYCHOLOGY).**
Clark, John, 1946- Stress. London ; Rollinsford, NH : Spiro Press, 2002.

Frost, Peter J. Toxic emotions at work. Boston : Harvard Business School Press, c2003.
HD42 .F76 2003

Job stress in a changing workforce : investigating gender, diversity, and family issues / edited by Gwendolyn Puryear Keita and Joseph J. Hurrell, Jr. 1st ed. Washington, DC ; London : American Psychological Association, c1994. xix, 345 p. : ill. ; 25 cm. Includes bibliographical references and indexes. ISBN 1-55798-271-6 (acid-free paper) DDC 158.7
1. Job stress - United States. 2. Work - Psychological aspects.

3. Corporate culture - United States. 4. Work and family - United States. 5. Diversity in the workplace. I. Keita, Gwendolyn Puryear. II. Hurrell, Joseph J.
HF5548.85 .J654 1994

JOB STRESS - NEW YORK (STATE).
Work-related mental stress injuries in the NYS workers' compensation system. [Albany, N.Y. : The Board, 1997]
HF5548.85 .W668 1997

JOB STRESS - UNITED STATES.
Job stress in a changing workforce. 1st ed. Washington, DC ; London : American Psychological Association, c1994.
HF5548.85 .J654 1994

JOBS. *See* **OCCUPATIONS; PROFESSIONS.**

La joda de la paz en Colombia.
Idrobo Díaz, Hugo, 1954- 1. ed. Cali, Colombia : [s.n., 2002?]

Joenniemi, Pertti.
The Nordic peace. Aldershot, England ; Burlington, VT : Ashgate, c2003.
UA646.7 .N672 2003

Johanek, Peter.
Der weite Blick des Historikers. Köln : Böhlau, c2002.
D116 .W44 2002

Johansen, Heidi Leigh. What I look like when I am angry / Heidi Johansen. 1st ed. New York : PowerStart Press, 2004. 24 p. : col. ill. ; 21 cm. (Let's look at feelings) Includes index. SUMMARY: Describes what different parts of the face look like when a person is angry. Table of contents URL: http://www.loc.gov/catdir/toc/ecip043/2003009455.html ISBN 1404275080 DDC 152.4/7
1. Anger in children - Juvenile literature. 2. Anger. 3. Facial expression. 4. Emotion. I. Title. II. Title: Angry III. Series.
BF723.A4 J63 2004

[What I look like when I am angry. Spanish & English]
What I look like when I am angry = Cómo me veo cuando estoy enojado / Heidi Johansen ; translated by Maria Cristina Brusca. 1st ed. New York : Rosen PowerKids Press, 2004. 24 p. : col. ill. ; 22 cm. (Let's look at feelings) SUMMARY: Describes what different parts of the face look like when a person is angry. Spanish and English. Includes index. ISBN 1404275088 (library binding) DDC 152.4/7
1. Anger in children - Juvenile literature. 2. Anger. 3. Facial expression. 4. Emotions. 5. Spanish language materials - Bilingual. I. Title. II. Title: Cómo me veo cuando estoy enojado III. Series.
BF723.A4 J6318 2004

What I look like when I am happy / Heidi Johansen. 1st ed. New York : PowerStart Press, 2004. 24 p. : col. ill. ; 21 cm. (Let's look at feelings) Includes index. SUMMARY: Describes how different parts of the face look when a person is happy. Table of contents URL: http://www.loc.gov/catdir/toc/ecip041/2003005985.html CONTENTS: My mouth -- My eyes -- My cheeks -- My whole face -- Words to know. ISBN 1404225064 DDC 152.4/2
1. Happiness in children - Juvenile literature. 2. Happiness. 3. Facial expression. I. Title. II. Series.
BF723.H37 J64 2004

[What I look like when I am happy. Spanish & English]
What I look like when I am happy = Cómo me veo cuando estoy contento / Heidi Johansen ; traducción al español: Marisa Cristina Brusca. 1st ed. New York : Rosen Pub. Group's, 2004. 24 p. : col. ill. ; 22 cm. (Let's look at feelings) SUMMARY: Describes what different parts of the face look like when a person is happy. Spanish and English. Includes index. CONTENTS: I am happy -- My face -- Words to know. ISBN 1404275061 (lib. bdg.) DDC 152.4/2
1. Happiness in children - Juvenile literature. 2. Happiness. 3. Facial expression. 4. Emotions. 5. Spanish language materials - Bilingual. I. Title. II. Title: Cómo me veo cuando estoy contento III. Series.
BF723.H37 J6418 2004

Johansson, Thomas.
Moulding masculinities. Aldershot, Hants, England ; Burlington, VT : Ashgate, c2003.
BF692.5 .M68 2003

John, Climacus, Saint, 6th cent.
Scala Paradisi. Serbian.
Vizantijska filozofija u srednjevekovnoj Srbiji. Beograd : Stubovi kulture, 2002.

The John D. and Catherine T. MacArthur Foundation series on mental health and development. Studies on successful midlife development

How healthy are we? Chicago, Ill. : University of Chicago Press, c2003.
BF724.6 .H69 2003

John Dee.
Dee, John, 1527-1608. [Selections. 2003] Berkeley, Calif. : North Atlantic Books, c2003.
BF1598.D5 A25 2003

John Dee's occultism.
Szőnyi, György Endre. Albany : State University of New York Press, 2004.
BF1598.D5 S98 2004

John Dewey and moral imagination.
Fesmire, Steven, 1967- Bloomington, IN : Indiana University Press, c2003.
BJ1031 .F47 2003

John F. Blair, Publisher.
Boogers and boo-daddies. Winston-Salem, N.C. : John F. Blair, Publisher, c2004.
BF1472.U6 B66 2004

John Holt.
Meighan, Roland. 2nd ed. Nottingham : Educational Heretics Press, 2002.
LB885.H64 M454 2002

John, Mary. Children's rights and power : charging up for a new century / Mary John. London ; New York : Jessica Kingsley Publishers, 2003. 304 p. ; 24 cm. (Children in charge series ; 9) Includes bibliographical references (p. 271-291) and indexes. ISBN 1-85302-659-X (pbk. : alk. paper) ISBN 1-85302-658-1 (hardback : alk. paper) DDC 305.23
1. Children's rights. 2. Children. 3. Power (Social sciences) I. Title. II. Series.
HQ789 .J64 2003

John, of Damascus, Saint.
Dialectica. Serbian.
Vizantijska filozofija u srednjevekovnoj Srbiji. Beograd : Stubovi kulture, 2002.

John Paul II, Pope, 1920-.
2001, año de las Naciones Unidas del diálogo entre civilizaciones. Guatemala : Fundación Casa de la Reconciliación : MINUGUA, 2001.
JX1952 .A233 2001

John, Peter William Meredith. Statistical design and analysis of experiments / Peter W.M. John. Philadelphia : Society for Industrial and Applied Mathematics, c1998. xxiv, 356 p. ; 23 cm. (Classics in applied mathematics ; 22) "An unabridged republication of the work first published by the Macmillan Company, New York, 1971"--T.p. verso. Includes bibliographical references (p. 339-350) and index. ISBN 0-89871-427-3 (pbk.) DDC 001.4/34
1. Experimental design. I. Title. II. Series.
QA279 .J65 1998

John Scotus Eriugena and his time.
Internationales Eriugena-Colloquium (10th : Maynooth and Dublin : 2002) History and eschatology in John Scottus Eriugena and his time. Leuven : University Press, 2002.

The John W. Houck Notre Dame series in business ethics
Business, religion, & spirituality. Notre Dame, Ind. : University of Notre Dame Press, c2003.
HF5388 .B87 2003

Johns, Richard, 1968- A theory of physical probability / Richard Johns. Toronto : University of Toronto Press, c2002. vi, 259 p. : ill. ; 24 cm. (Toronto studies in philosophy) Includes bibliographical references and index. ISBN 0-8020-3603-1 (bound) DDC 122
1. Chance. 2. Causation. I. Title. II. Series.

Johnsen, Linda, 1954- A thousand suns : designing your future with Vedic astrology / Linda Johnsen. St. Paul, MN : Yes International Publishers, 2003. p. cm. Includes bibliographical references. CONTENTS: Entering the universe of Vedic astrology -- Return to the source : ancient Indian astrology -- Your past lives : how you created your horoscope -- Your karmic report card : what your Vedic chart reveals -- Whats your karma? : setting up your Vedic chart -- Whats your Vedic sign? : finding your nakshatra -- What the planets say : reading the sky -- Shadow planets : the karmic axis -- Planetary patterns : the knots of destiny -- Unfolding time : your planetary cycles -- Vedic subcharts : hidden dimensions of your horoscope -- Karmic counselors : Vedic astrologers at work -- Star temples : making peace with the planets -- Dealing with disaster : when karmic debt comes due -- Reshaping the future : tools for altering destiny -- Vedic astrological prescriptions I : mantric upayas -- Vedic astrological prescriptions II : mental upayas -- Vedic astrological prescriptions III : physical upayas -- Vedic astrological prescriptions IV : tantric upayas -- Astrology in the city of light : the eternal tradition -- The gnostic sky : Jesus and Jyotish -- Fear of foreknowledge : are we ready for the future?

ISBN 0-936663-35-9 DDC 133.5/9445
1. Hindu astrology. I. Title.
BF1714.H5 J665 2003

Johnson, Addie. Attention : theory and practice / Addie Johnson, Robert W. Proctor. Thousand Oaks, Calif. : Sage Publications, c2004. p. cm. Includes bibliographical references and index. Table of contents URL: http://www.loc.gov/catdir/toc/ecip046/2003016015.html CONTENTS: Historical overview of research on attention -- Information processing and the study of attention -- Selective visual attention -- Auditory and crossmodal attention -- Attention and inhibition -- Multiple-task performance -- Memory and attention -- Attention and displays -- Mental workload and situation awareness -- Individual differences in attention -- The cognitive neuroscience of attention -- Disorders of attention. ISBN 0-7619-2760-3 ISBN 0-7619-2761-1 (pbk.) DDC 153.7/33
1. Attention. 2. Information processing. 3. Memory. I. Proctor, Robert W. II. Title.
BF321 .J56 2004

Johnson, C. Merle.
Handbook of organizational performance. New York : Haworth Press, c2001.
HD58.7 .H364 2001

Johnson Cook, Suzan D. (Suzan Denise), 1957- Too blessed to be stressed / Suzan D. Johnson Cook. Nashville, Tenn. : T. Nelson, c1998. x, 177 p. ; 21 cm. Includes bibliographical references (p. 177). ISBN 0-7852-7070-1 (pbk.) DDC 248.8/43
1. Johnson Cook, Suzan D. - (Suzan Denise), - 1957- 2. Women - Religious life. 3. Stress (Psychology) - Religious aspects - Christianity. 4. African American women clergy - Biography. 5. Black author. I. Title.
BV4527 .J65 1998

JOHNSON COOK, SUZAN D. (SUZAN DENISE), 1957-.
Johnson Cook, Suzan D. (Suzan Denise), 1957- Too blessed to be stressed. Nashville, Tenn. : T. Nelson, c1998.
BV4527 .J65 1998
1. Black author.

Johnson, David Martel.
The mind as a scientific object. New York : Oxford University Press, c2004.
BF311 .M552 2004

Johnson, Deborah L., 1956- Letters from the Infinite / as revealed to Deborah L. Johnson, Aptos, CA : New Brighton Books, c2002- v. <1 > : ill. ; 23 cm. PARTIAL CONTENTS: v. 1. The sacred yes. ISBN 0-9718377-0-8 (v. 1 : alk. paper) DDC 299/.93
1. Spiritual life. 2. Spirit writings. 3. Private revelations. 4. Black author. I. Title.
BF1301 .J575 2002

Johnson, Joy.
Johnson, Marvin. Where's Jess? Rev. Omaha, NE : Centering Corp. Resource, 2003.
BF723.G75 J645 2003

Johnson, Kevin Wayne. Give God the glory! : know God and do the will of God concerning your life / Kevin Wayne Johnson. Hillsborough, NJ : Writing for the Lord Ministries, c2001. 167 p. ; 22 cm. Distributed by FaithWorks, a division of National Book Network, Inc. ISBN 0-9705902-0-2 (pbk.)
1. Christian life. 2. Devotional exercises. 3. Black author. I. Title.

Johnson, Kirk A.
Rector, Robert. The effects of marriage and maternal education in reducing child poverty. Washington, D.C. : Heritage Foundation, 2002.

Johnson, Marvin. Where's Jess? : for children who have a brother or sister die / [Marv S. Johnson, Joy K. Johnson ; illustrated by Paris Sieff]. Rev. Omaha, NE : Centering Corp. Resource, 2003. 1 v. (unpaged) : col. ill. ; 18 cm. Cover title. SUMMARY: A young child experiences a variety of feelings after the death of a sibling. ISBN 1-56123-009-X
1. Grief in children - Juvenile literature. 2. Bereavement in children - Juvenile literature. 3. Brothers and sisters - Death - Psychological aspects - Juvenile literature. 4. Children and death - Juvenile literature. 5. Loss (Psychology) in children - Juvenile literature. 6. Grief. 7. Brothers and sisters - Death. 8. Death. 9. Loss (Psychology) I. Johnson, Joy. II. Sieff, Paris, ill. III. Title.
BF723.G75 J645 2003

Johnson, Meredith, ill.
Meiners, Cheri J., 1957- When I feel afraid. Minneapolis, MN : Free Spirit Pub., 2003.
BF723.F4 M45 2003

Johnson, Paul, 1928- Art : a new history / Paul Johnson. 1st ed. New York : HarperCollins, c2003. x, 777 p. : ill. (chiefly col.), ports. ; 26 cm. Includes index. ISBN 0-06-053075-8
1. Art - History. I. Title.

Johnston, Daniel H. Lessons for living : simple solutions for life's problems / Daniel H. Johnston. 1st ed. Macon, Ga. : Dagali Press, c2001. xii, 194 p. : ill. ; 22 cm. Includes bibliographical references (p. 187). ISBN 0-9712165-0-9
1. Self-actualization (Psychology) 2. Success - Psychological aspects. 3. Self-help techniques. I. Title.
BF637.S4 J65 2001

Johnston, Joni E., 1960- The complete idiot's guide to psychology / by Joni E. Johnston. 2nd ed. Indianapolis, IN : Alpha Books, c2003. xxvii, 436 p. ; 24 cm. Includes index. ISBN 1-59257-069-0 DDC 150
1. Psychology. I. Title. II. Title: Psychology
BF121 .J64 2003

Johnston, Marianne.
[Dealing with anger. Spanish]
Como tratar la ira / Marianne Johnston ; traduccion al Español, Mauricio Velazquez de Leon. New York : PowerKids Press, 2005. p. cm. (Biblioteca Solucion de conflictos) Includes index. SUMMARY: A discussion of anger, including suggestions for ways to deal with it directly, channel it to something productive, and avoid its destructiveness. ISBN 1404275509 (lib. bdg.) DDC 152.4/7
1. Anger - Juvenile literature. 2. Anger. 3. Spanish language materials. I. Title. II. Series.
BF575.A5 J6418 2005

[Dealing with bullying. Spanish]
Como tratar a los bravucones / Marianne Johnston ; traduccion al Español, Mauricio Velazquez de Leon. New York : PowerKids Press, 2005. p. cm. (Biblioteca Solucion de conflictos) Includes index. SUMMARY: Describes what is meant by bullying, then goes on to explain why bullies act as they do, how to deal with them, and how to stop being one. ISBN 1404275479 (lib. bdg.) DDC 303.6/9
1. Bullying - Juvenile literature. 2. Bullying. 3. Spanish language materials. I. Title. II. Series.
BF637.B85 J6418 2005

[Dealing with fighting. Spanish]
Como tratar las peleas / Marianne Johnston ; traduccion al Español, Mauricio Velazquez de Leon. New York : PowerKids Press, 2005. p. cm. (Biblioteca Solucion de conflictos) Includes index. SUMMARY: Explains how arguments and quarrels can lead to fights and how to avoid or deflect conflict in interpersonal relations. ISBN 1404275517 (lib. bdg.) DDC 303.6/9
1. Interpersonal conflict - Juvenile literature. 2. Fighting (Psychology) - Juvenile literature. 3. Quarreling - Juvenile literature. 4. Interpersonal confrontation - Juvenile literature. 5. Conflict (Psychology) 6. Fighting (Psychology) 7. Quarreling. 8. Interpersonal relations. 9. Spanish language materials. I. Title. II. Series.
BF637.I48 J6418 2005

[Dealing with insults. Spanish]
Como tratar los insultos / Marianne Johnston ; traduccion al Español, Mauricio Velazquez de Leon. New York : PowerKids Press, 2005. p. cm. (Biblioteca Solucion de conflictos) Includes index. SUMMARY: Explains why some people use words that hurt others, how one can avoid insulting others, and how to productively respond to insult. ISBN 1404275495 (lib. bdg.) DDC 158.2
1. Verbal self-defense - Juvenile literature. 2. Invective - Juvenile literature. 3. Self-defense. 4. Invective. 5. Spanish language materials. I. Title. II. Series.
BF637.V47 J6418 2005

Joines, Vann. Personality adaptations : a new guide to human understanding in psychotherapy and counselling / Vann Joines, Ian Stewart. Nottingham ; Chapel Hill, N.C. : Lifespace, 2002. xvi, 419 p. : ill. ; 21 cm. Includes bibliographical references (p. 392-402) and index. ISBN 1-87024-401-X DDC 155.23
1. Personality. 2. Personality development. I. Stewart, Ian, 1940- II. Title.
BF698.3 .J65 2002

JOINT VENTURES. See **INTERNATIONAL BUSINESS ENTERPRISES.**

JOKES. See **WIT AND HUMOR.**

Jokic, Aleksandar.
Consciousness. Oxford : Clarendon Press ; New York : Oxford University Press, 2003.
B808.9 .C667 2003

Jokić, Aleksandar.
Essays in honor of Burleigh Wilkins. New York : Peter Lang, c2001.

JA71 .E694 2001

JOKING. *See* **WIT AND HUMOR.**

Jolivet, Joëlle.
Roche, Christian. Le bestiaire des philosophes. [Paris] : Seuil, c2001.

Jolley, Janina M.
Mitchell, Mark L. Writing for psychology. 1st ed. Australia ; Belmont, CA : Wadsworth/Thomson, 2004.
BF76.7 .M58 2004

Jolly, Karen Louise. The Middle Ages / Karen Jolly, Catharina Raudvere, Edward Peters ; edited by Bengt Ankarloo and Stuart Clark. Philadelphia : University of Pennsylvania Press, 2002, 2001. 12 300 xiv, 280 p. ; 24 cm. xiv, 280 p. ; 24 cm. (Witchcraft and magic in Europe) Originally published: London : Athlone Press, 2001, in series: Athlone history of witchcraft and magic in Europe. Includes bibliographical references (p. [246]-272) and index. CONTENTS: Medieval magic : definitions, beliefs, practices / Karen Jolly -- Trolldómr in early medieval Scandinavia / Catharina Raudvere -- The medieval church and state on superstition, magic and witchcraft : from Augustine to the sixteenth century / Edward Peters. ISBN 0-8122-3616-5 (alk. paper) ISBN 0-8122-1786-1 (pbk.)
1. Magic - Europe - History - To 1500. 2. Witchcraft - Europe - History - To 1500. 3. Magic - Religious aspects - Christianity. I. Peters, Edward, 1936- II. Raudvere, Catharina. III. Ankarloo, Bengt, 1935- IV. Clark, Stuart. V. Title. VI. Series.
BF1593 .J65 2002

JOLOF (AFRICAN PEOPLE). *See* **WOLOF (AFRICAN PEOPLE).**

Jón Magnússon, 1610-1696. Píslarsaga séra Jóns Magnússonar / Matthías Vi!ar Sæmundsson sá um útgáfuna ; Þór!ur Ingi Gu!jónsson og Jón Torfason bjuggu vi!auka til prentunar. Reykjavík : Mál og menning, 2001. 439 p. : ill., map ; 24 cm. Spine title: Píslarsaga. Includes bibliographical references and index. ISBN 9979321660
1. Witchcraft - Iceland. I. Matthías Vi$ar Sæmundsson. II. Þór$ur Ingi Gu$jónsson. III. Jón Torfason. IV. Title. V. Title: Píslarsaga
BF1584.I2 J66 2001

Jón Torfason.
Jón Magnússon, 1610-1696. Píslarsaga séra Jóns Magnússonar. Reykjavík : Mál og menning, 2001.
BF1584.I2 J66 2001

Jonas, Susan. Friends for life : enriching the bond between mothers and their adult daughters / Susan Jonas and Marilyn Nissenson. 1st ed. New York : William Morrow & Co., c1997. xxvii, 355 p. ; 25 cm. Includes bibliographical references (p. 353-355). ISBN 0-688-14673-2 DDC 306.874/3
1. Mothers and daughters. 2. Parent and adult child. I. Nissenson, Marilyn, 1939- II. Title.
HQ755.85 .J65 1997

Jonathan Edwards' philosophy of history.
Zakai, Avihu. Jonathan Edwards's philosophy of history. Princeton, N.J. : Princeton University Press, c2003.
B873 .Z35 2003

Jonathan Edwards's philosophy of history.
Zakai, Avihu. Princeton, N.J. : Princeton University Press, c2003.
B873 .Z35 2003

Jones, Amelia.
The feminism and visual culture reader. London ; New York : Routledge, 2003.
HQ1121 .F46 2003

Jones, Carol D., 1948- Overcoming anger / Carol D. Jones. Avon, MA : Adams Media, 2004. p. cm. Includes bibliographical references and index. Table of contents URL: http://www.loc.gov/catdir/toc/ecip042/2003008261.html ISBN 1-58062-929-6 DDC 152.4/7
1. Anger. I. Title.
BF575.A5 J66 2004

Jones, Charisse. Shifting : the double lives of Black women in America / Charisse Jones and Kumea Shorter-Gooden. 1st ed. New York : HarperCollins, c2003. x, 340 p. ; 24 cm. Includes bibliographical references (p. [293]-326) and index. ISBN 0-06-009054-5 DDC 306.7/089/96073
1. African American women - Psychology. 2. Adjustment (Psychology) - United States. 3. Racism - United States - Psychological aspects. 4. African American women - Social conditions. 5. African American women - Interviews. I. Shorter-Gooden, Kumea. II. Title.
E185.625 .J657 2003

Jones-Farrow, Hilary.
Big Dance [videorecording]. Buffalo, N.Y. : Kineticvideo.com, c1998.

Jones, Gill, 1942-.
Social relations and the life course. Houndmills, Basingstoke New York : Palgrave Macmillan, 2003.
HM741 .S64 2003

Jones, Katina Z. The everything feng shui decluttering book / Katina Z. Jones. Avon, MA : Adams Media, c2004. p. cm. (An everything series book) Includes bibliographical references. Table of contents URL: http://www.loc.gov/catdir/toc/ecip048/2003019096.html ISBN 1-59337-028-8 DDC 133.3/337
1. Feng shui. I. Title. II. Series: Everything series.
BF1779.F4 J663 2004

Jones, Malcolm, 1953- The secret middle ages / Malcolm Jones. Stroud : Sutton, 2002. xxvi, 374 p. : ill. (some col.) ; 27 cm. Includes bibliographical references and index. ISBN 0-7509-2685-6 DDC 940.1
1. Civilization, Medieval. 2. Civilization, Medieval, in art. 3. Folk art - Europe - History. 4. Art, Medieval - Europe. 5. Punishment - Europe - History - To 1500. I. Title.

Jones, Steve, 1944- Y : the descent of men / Steve Jones. Boston : Houghton Mifflin, 2003. xvii, 252 p. ; 23 cm. Includes bibliographical references (p. [225]-235) and index. Publisher description URL: http://www.loc.gov/catdir/description/hm031/2002027631.html ISBN 0-618-13930-3 DDC 599.93/8
1. Human beings - Origin. 2. Human evolution. 3. Human genetics. 4. Y chromosome. 5. Masculinity. 6. Men - Physiology. I. Title. II. Title: Descent of men
GN281 .J62 2003

Jones, Timothy S.
Marvels, monsters, and miracles. Kalamazoo, Mich. : Medieval Institute Publications, 2002.
GR825 .M218 2002

Jonnes, Jill, 1952- Empires of light : Edison, Tesla, Westinghouse, and the race to electrify the world / Jill Jonnes. 1st ed. New York : Random House, c2003. xiv, 416 p., [16] p. of plates : ill. ; 25 cm. Includes bibliographical references (p. [375]-377) and index. ISBN 0-375-50739-6 (alk. paper) DDC 621.3/09
1. Edison, Thomas A. - (Thomas Alva) - 1847-1931. 2. Tesla, Nikola, - 1856-1943. 3. Westinghouse, George, - 1846-1914. 4. Electric engineering - History. 5. Electrification - History. 6. Electric power - History. 7. Competition - United States. I. Title.
TK18 .J66 2003

Jonscher, Reinhard. Kleine thüringische Geschichte : vom Thüringer Reich bis 1990 / Reinhard Jonscher, Willy Schilling. 3., überarb. und erw. Aufl. Jena : Jenzig-Verlag Köhler, 2001. 353 p. : ill., geneal. tables ; 19 cm. Includes bibliographical references (p. 305-319) and index. ISBN 3-910141-44-7 (pbk.)
1. Thuringia (Germany) - History. I. Schilling, Willy. II. Title.
DD801.T44 J658 2001

Jordan, Amy B. (Amy Beth).
Children in the digital age. Westport, Conn. : Praeger, 2002.
HQ784.M3 C455 2002

Jordan, Denise.
Tu y yo.
Jordan, Denise. [We can listen. Spanish] Escuchamos. Chicago : Heinemann Library, c2004.
BF323.L5 J6718 2004

Jordan, Denise. [Your fair share. Spanish] A partes iguales. Chicago : Heinemann Library, c2004.
BF723.S428 J6718 2003

We can be friends / Denise M. Jordan. Chicago, Ill. : Heinemann Library, c2003. p. cm. (You and me) SUMMARY: Simple text and pictures explain the how, why, where, and when of sharing friendship. ISBN 1403444072 (hardcover) ISBN 1403444137 (pbk.) DDC 177/.62
1. Friendship - Juvenile literature. 2. Friendship. I. Title. II. Series: Jordan, Denise. You and me.
BF723.F68 J67 2003

We can listen / Denise M. Jordan. Chicago, Ill. : Heinemann Library, 2003. p. cm. (You and me) SUMMARY: Simple text and pictures explain when, where, and why we listen. Table of contents URL: http://www.loc.gov/catdir/toc/ecip045/2003012818.html ISBN 1403444080 ISBN 1403444145 (pbk.) DDC 153.6/8
1. Listening - Juvenile literature. 2. Listening. I. Title. II. Series: Jordan, Denise. You and me.
BF323.L5 J67 2003

[We can listen. Spanish]
Escuchamos / Denise M. Jordan ; traducción de Patricia Abello. Chicago : Heinemann Library, c2004. p. cm. (Tú y yo) Includes index. SUMMARY: Simple text and pictures explain when, where, and why we listen. ISBN 1403444315 ISBN 1403444374 DDC 153.6/8
1. Listening - Juvenile literature. 2. Listening. 3. Spanish language materials. I. Title. II. Series: Jordan, Denise. Tú y yo.
BF323.L5 J6718 2004

You and me.
Jordan, Denise. We can be friends. Chicago, Ill. : Heinemann Library, c2003.
BF723.F68 J67 2003

Jordan, Denise. We can listen. Chicago, Ill. : Heinemann Library, 2003.
BF323.L5 J67 2003

Jordan, Denise. Your fair share. Chicago, Ill. : Heinemann Library, 2003.
BF723.S428 J67 2003

Your fair share / Denise M. Jordan. Chicago, Ill. : Heinemann Library, 2003. p. cm. (You and me) SUMMARY: Explains how to share pencils, toys, and chores. Table of contents URL: http://www.loc.gov/catdir/toc/ecip045/2003012816.html ISBN 1403444099 ISBN 1403444153 (pbk.) DDC 177/.7
1. Sharing in children - Juvenile literature. 2. Sharing. I. Title. II. Series: Jordan, Denise. You and me.
BF723.S428 J67 2003

[Your fair share. Spanish]
A partes iguales / Denise M. Jordan ; traducción de Patricia Abello. Chicago : Heinemann Library, c2004. p. cm. (Tú y yo) Includes index. SUMMARY: Explains how to share pencils, toys, and chores. ISBN 1403444323 ISBN 1403444382 DDC 177/.7
1. Sharing in children - Juvenile literature. 2. Sharing. 3. Spanish language materials. I. Title. II. Series: Jordan, Denise. Tú y yo.
BF723.S428 J6718 2003

Jordan, Kathie. The birth called death / Kathie Jordan. 1st ed. Ashland, Or. : RiverWood Books, 2003. p. cm. ISBN 1-88399-177-3 DDC 133.9/01/3
1. Future life. 2. Spiritualism. I. Title.
BF1311.F8 B57 2003

Jormakka, Kari.
Building gender = Wien : Edition Selene, 2002.

[Olandesi volanti. English]
Flying Dutchmen : motion in architecture / Kari Jormakka. Basel ; Boston : Birkhäuser, 2002. 93 p. : ill. (some col.), music ; 19 cm. (The IT revolution in architecture) ISBN 3-7643-6639-7 (pbk.)
1. Architecture - Netherlands - 20th century. 2. Architecture - Technological innovations. 3. Architecture - Philosophy. I. Title. II. Series.
NA1148 .J6713 2002

Jornadas de Roles Sexuales y de Género (2nd : 1995 : Madrid, Spain) Mujer, ideología y población : II Jornadas de Roles Sexuales y de Género : Madrid, 13 al 16 de noviembre de 1995 / Pilar Ortega, Ma. José Rodríguez Mampaso, Carlos G. Wagner (eds.). 1. ed. Madrid : Ediciones Clásicas, 1998. 370 p. ; 22 cm. (Serie ARYS ; 11) Includes bibliographical references. ISBN 84-7882-422-7
1. Sex role - Congresses. 2. Women - Congresses. I. Ortega, Pilar. II. Rodríguez Mampaso, Ma. José (María José) III. González Wagner, Carlos. IV. Title. V. Series: ARYS ; 11.
HQ1075 .J67 1995

Josconiando.
Barrios, Luis. 1st ed. New York : Editorial Aguiar, 2000.

Joseph, Ammu, 1953-.
Terror, counter-terror. London ; New York : Zed Books ; New Delhi : Kali for Women ; New York : Distributed in the U.S. exclusively by Palgrave, 2003.
HQ1236 .T47 2003

Josephs, Ingrid E., 1961-.
Dialogicality in development. Westport, Conn. : Praeger, 2003.
BF713 .D53 2003

Jośī, Gajānana Nārāyaṇa. Bhāratīya tattvajñānācā br̥had itihāsa / Gajānana Nārāyaṇa Jośī. 1. āvr̥ttī. Pune : Marāṭhī Tattvajñāna-Mahākośa Maṇḍala yāñce karitā Śubhadā-Sārasvata Prakāśana, 1994. 12 v. ; 23 cm. SUMMARY: Comprehensive work on ancient and modern Indic philosophy; with some reference to religious movements and reforms of Marathi and other Indian saints. Includes bibliographical references (v. 12, p. 321-341) and index. In Marathi: includes passages in Sanskrit. CONTENTS: 1. Veda, Upanishade, va bhautikavāda --2. Bauddhadarśana -- 3. Cāra darśane (Sāṅkhya, Nyāya, Vaiśeshesika, Jaina) -- 4. Pūrvamīmāṃsāva Śāṅkaravedānta -- 5. Śāṅkarottara Vedānta va Śaivadarśana -- 6. Yoga darśana va Śākta mata -- 7. Mahārāṣṭra santa -- 8. Bhakti-Sampradāya āṇi pramukha Bhāratīya santa -- 9. Ādhunika Bhāratāce tattvajñāna -- 10. Mahārāṣṭrātīla prabodhanakāra -- 11. Ādhunika Bhāratīya tattvacintaka -- 12. Śrīmadbhagavadgītā, Bhāratīya nītiśāstra,

CONTENTS: upasaṃhāra ; Ullekha sūcī / Ananta Jośī. ISBN 81-85239-95-9 (set)
1. Philosophy, Indic. 2. Religion - India - History. 3. Religion - India - Maharashtra - History. 4. Saints - India - Maharashtra. I. Title.
B131 .J674 1994

Jóslások a mezőségen.
Keszeg, Vilmos. Sepsiszentgyörgy : BON AMI, 1997.
BF1868.H8 K47 1997

The Jossey-Bass business & management series
Brown, Duane. Career choice and development. 4th ed. San Francisco, CA : Jossey-Bass, c2002.
HF5381 .C265143 2002

Jouanna, Arlette.
La Renaissance. Paris : Presses de l'université de Paris-Sorbonne, 2003.

Jouffroy, Alain, 1928-.
Entretien avec Philippe Forest.
Jouffroy, Alain, 1928- [Mots et moi] Les mots et moi ; Nantes : Pleins feux, c2002.

[Mots et moi]
Les mots et moi ; suivi de Poèmes ; et d'un entretien avec Philippe Forest / Alain Jouffroy. Nantes : Pleins feux, c2002. 62 p. ; 19 cm. (Auteurs en questions) ISBN 2-912567-86-6 DDC 841
1. Jouffroy, Alain, - 1928 - Interviews. 2. Forest, Philippe - Interviews. 3. Creation (Literary, artistic, etc.) 4. Self (Philosophy) in literature. I. Jouffroy, Alain, 1928- Poèmes. II. Jouffroy, Alain, 1928- Entretien avec Philippe Forest. III. Title. IV. Title: Poèmes. V. Title: Entretien avec Philippe Forest. VI. Series.

Poemes.
Jouffroy, Alain, 1928- [Mots et moi] Les mots et moi ; Nantes : Pleins feux, c2002.

JOUFFROY, ALAIN, 1928- - INTERVIEWS.
Jouffroy, Alain, 1928- [Mots et moi] Les mots et moi ; Nantes : Pleins feux, c2002.

Jouffroy, Théodore, 1796-1842.
[Selections]
La psychologie de Th. Jouffroy / [édité par] Serge Nicolas. Paris : L'Harmattan, c2003. 288 p. ; 22 cm. (Collection "La Philosophie en commun") Includes bibliographical references. ISBN 2-7475-4112-6 DDC 150
1. Jouffroy, Théodore, - 1796-1842 - Contributions in psychology. 2. Psychology - Philosophy. I. Nicolas, Serge. II. Title. III. Series: Philosophie en commun.

JOUFFROY, THÉODORE, 1796-1842 - CONTRIBUTIONS IN PSYCHOLOGY.
Jouffroy, Théodore, 1796-1842. [Selections] La psychologie de Th. Jouffroy. Paris : L'Harmattan, c2003.

Jouissance as ānanda.
Khasnabish, Ashmita, 1959- Lanham, Md. : Lexington Books, c2003.
BF173 .K427 2003

Le jour où Lacan m'a adopté.
Haddad, Gérard. Paris : Bernard Grasset, c2002.

Journal for the psychoanalysis of culture & society.
[Journal for the psychoanalysis of culture & society (Online)] Journal for the psychoanalysis of culture and society [electronic resource]. Columbus, Ohio : Ohio State University Press
BF175.4.C84

[Journal for the psychoanalysis of culture & society (Online)] Journal for the psychoanalysis of culture and society [electronic resource]. Columbus, Ohio : Ohio State University Press Frequency: Semiannual. Print began with vol. 1, no. 1 (spring 1996). Other title: JPCS. Description based on: Vol. 8, no. 1 (spring 2003); title from table of contents (viewed Apr. 9, 2003). Online version of the print publication. Mode of access: World Wide Web. Electronic access restricted to subscribers; requires NYPL IP address. Official publication of the Association for the Psychoanalysis of Culture & Society. URL: http://muse.jhu.edu/journals/journal_for_the_psychoanalysis_of_culture_&_society Available in other form: Journal for the psychoanalysis of culture & society ISSN: 1088-0763 (DLC) 96659228 (OCoLC)34506953. ISSN 1543-3390
1. Psychoanalysis and culture - Periodicals. 2. Psychoanalysis - Periodicals. I. Association for the Psychoanalysis of Culture & Society. II. Project Muse III. Title: JPCS IV. Title: Journal for the psychoanalysis of culture & society
BF175.4.C84

Journal of consciousness studies
(6, no. 2-3) The view from within. Thorverton, UK : Bowling Green, OH : Imprint Academic, 2000.

BF311 .V512 2000
(7, no. 4) Humphrey, Nicholas. How to solve the mind-- body problem. Thorverton, UK ; Bowling Green, OH : Imprint Academic, c2000.
BF698.95 .H86 2000

Journal of feminist family therapy.
Integrating gender and culture in parenting. New York : Haworth Press, 2003.
BF723.P75 I57 2003

JOURNALISM. See also **PHOTOJOURNALISM.**
Meyer, Philip. Precision journalism. 4th ed. Lanham, Md. : Rowman & Littlefield Publishers, c2002.
PN4775 .M48 2002

JOURNALISM, CAMERA. See **PHOTOJOURNALISM.**

JOURNALISM - POLITICAL ASPECTS. See **PRESS AND POLITICS.**

JOURNALISM - SOCIAL ASPECTS - MEXICO.
Fernández Christlieb, Fátima. La responsabilidad de los medios de comunicación. 1a. ed. México : Paidós, 2002.

JOURNALISTIC PHOTOGRAPHY. See **PHOTOJOURNALISM.**

JOURNALISTS. See **TELEVISION JOURNALISTS; WOMEN JOURNALISTS.**

JOURNALISTS - UNITED STATES - BIOGRAPHY.
Soucheray, Joe. Waterline. Boston : D.R. Godine, 2002.
PN4874.S576 A3 2002

Journet, Nicolas, 1950-.
La culture. Auxerre : Sciences humaines éditions, c2002.

The journey from heartbreak to connection.
Anderson, Susan, C.S.W. Berkley trade pbk. ed. New York : Berkley Books, 2003.
BF575.R35 A533 2003

Journey into love.
Comstock, Kari. Ashland, OR : Willow Press, c2000.
BF575.L8 C647 2002

The journey of adulthood.
Bee, Helen L., 1939- 5th ed. Upper Saddle River, NJ : Pearson Prentice Hall, c2004.
BF724.5 .B44 2004

Journey to fatherhood.
Daniel, Jack L. (Jack Lee), 1942- We fish. Pittsburgh, Pa. : University of Pittsburgh Press, c2003.
1. Black author.

Journey to the center.
Flickstein, Matthew. Somerville, MA : Wisdom Publications, c1998.
BF637.S4 F58 1998

Journeying into wholeness with map & skills.
Dooley, Deborah. [Meno Park, Calif. : Delphi Press, c2003]
BF710 .D64 2003

Jovanović, Tihomir. Nepoznati svet snova : mistika, filozofija, nauka, praksa / Tihomir Jovanović. Beograd : IPA "Miroslav", 2000. 191 p. ; 24 cm. (Biblioteka Medicina i budućnost) In Serbian (roman) with summary in English. Include bibliographical references (p. 185-190) ISBN 86-82487-50-0
1. Dreams. I. Title. II. Series.
BF1078 .J69 2000

JOY.
Colantuono, Susan L. Make room for joy. Charlestown, RI : Interlude Productions, c2000.
BF575.H27 C64 2000

Moulinier, Didier. Dictionnaire de la jouissance. Paris : L'Harmattan, c1999.
BF575.H27 M68 1999

Walters, J. Donald. Secrets of comfort and joy. [Nevada City, CA] : Crystal Clarity, 2000.
BF575.H27 W362 2000

Joyce, Patrick, 1945- The rule of freedom : liberalism and the modern city / Patrick Joyce. London : Verso, 2003. xii, 276 p. : ill., maps ; 22 cm. Includes bibliographical references and index. ISBN 1-85984-520-7 DDC 323.44
1. Liberty. 2. Liberalism. I. Title.
JC585 .J69 2003

JPCS.
[Journal for the psychoanalysis of culture & society (Online)] Journal for the psychoanalysis of culture and society [electronic resource]. Columbus, Ohio : Ohio State University Press

BF175.4.C84
Ju, Yueshi.
Zhongguo xiang zheng wen hua. Di 1 ban. Shanghai : Shanghai ren min chu ban she : Xin hua shu dian Shanghai fa xing suo jing xiao, 2001.
DS721 .Z4985 2001

Judah ben Samuel, ca. 1150-1217.
Sod ha yihud.
Eleazar ben Judah, of Worms, 1176 (ca.)-1238. Sefer Sode razaya .... Bene-Beraḳ : Ḳoraḥ, 759 [1998 or 1999]
BM525 .E432 1999

JUDAICA. See **JEWS.**

JUDAISM. See also **COMMANDMENTS, SIX HUNDRED AND THIRTEEN; FASTS AND FEASTS - JUDAISM; JEWS; WORSHIP (JUDAISM).**
Maier, Johann. Judentum von A bis Z. Freiburg im Breisgau : Herder, 2001.

Judaism and Enlightenment.
Sutcliffe, Adam. Cambridge ; New York : Cambridge University Press, 2003.
BM290 .S88 2003

JUDAISM AND POLITICS.
Ellis, Marc H. Israel and Palestine out of the ashes. London ; Sterling, Va. : Pluto Press, c2002.
DS119.76 .E56 2002

JUDAISM AND PSYCHOANALYSIS.
Maciejewski, Franz. Psychoanalytisches Archiv und jüdisches Gedächtnis. 1. Aufl. Wien : Passagen Verlag, 2002.

JUDAISM AND PSYCHOLOGY.
Lamdan, Elimelekh. Torapiah. Yerushalayim : Feldhaim, 762 [2002]

JUDAISM AND SCIENCE - HISTORY.
Sela, Shlomo. Abraham Ibn Ezra and the rise of medieval Hebrew science. Leiden ; Boston, MA : Brill, 2003.
BM538.S3 S45 2003

JUDAISM - ARI RITE.
Hilel, Ya'aḳov Mosheh. Sefer Ahavat shalom. [Hotsa'ah 2], 'im hosafot rabot. Yerushala[y]im : ha-Makhon le-hotsa'at sefarim ye-khitve yad "Ahavat Shalom", 762 [2002]

JUDAISM - ARI RITE - LITURGY. See also **KAVVANOT (CABALA).**
Armoni, Mosheh Ḥayim. Sefer Ginze Armoni. Yerushalayim : 'Amutat "Naḥalat-Raḥel", 762 [2002]
BM670.S5 A756 2002

JUDAISM - ARI RITE - LITURGY - TEXTS.
['Ets ha-tidhar.] Sidur ḳayanot 'Ets ha-tidhar. Yerushalayim : Kolel Shemen śaśon, [1998?]
1. Ḳeri'at shema 'al ha-mitah.

JUDAISM (CHRISTIAN THEOLOGY) - HISTORY OF DOCTRINES - EARLY CHURCH, CA. 30-600.
Davis, Frederick, 1931- The Jew and deicide. Lanham, Md. : University Press of America, c2003.
BS2555.6.J44 D38 2003

JUDAISM - CUSTOMS AND PRACTICES. See also **JUDAISM - ARI RITE.**
Aviner, Shelomoh Ḥayim, ha-Kohen. Be-ahavah uve-emunah. Yerushalayim : [ḥ. mo. l.], 760-762 [1999 or 2000-2001 or 2002]
BM565 .A93 1999

Gorfine, Yehudit. Be-ḳarov etslekh. Petaḥ Tiḳvah : Mar'ot, 2002.

Maier, Johann. Judentum von A bis Z. Freiburg im Breisgau : Herder, 2001.

JUDAISM - DOCTRINES. See also **FAITH (JUDAISM); GOD (JUDAISM).**
Berlin, Naphtali Zevi Judah, 1817-1893. [Selections. 2001] Otsrot ha-Netsiv. Yerushalayim : Ben Arzah, 762 [2001 or 2002]
BM755.B52 A25 2001

Blokh, Avraham Yitshaḳ ben Y. L. (Avraham Yitshaḳ ben Yosef Leyb), d. 1941. Sefer Shi'ure da'at. Yerushalayim : Feldhaim ; Wickliffe, Ohio : Peninei Daas Publications, 761 [2001]

Feldman, Seymour. Philosophy in a time of crisis. London ; New York : RoutledgeCurzon, 2003.
BM755.A25 F45 2003

Maimonides, Moses, 1135-1204. [Selections] Sefer Musarim ve-de'ot leha-Rambam. Bene Beraḳ : [ḥ. mo. l], 761 [2000 or 2001]

Otsrot rabotenu mi-Brisk. Bene Berak : Sh. L., molut u-mishar bi-sefarim, 762 [2001 or 2002]
BM602 .O+

JUDAISM - ESSENCE, GENIUS, NATURE.
Aviner, Shelomoh Hayim, ha-Kohen. Be-ahavah uve-emunah. Yerushalayim : [h. mo. l.], 760-762 [1999 or 2000-2001 or 2002]
BM565 .A93 1999

Chouchena, Emmanuel. L'homme, espoir de dieu. Paris : Trajectoire, 2001.

JUDAISM - EUROPE - HISTORY.
Sutcliffe, Adam. Judaism and Enlightenment. Cambridge ; New York : Cambridge University Press, 2003.
BM290 .S88 2003

JUDAISM - FRANCE - HISTORY - TO 1500.
Halbertal, Moshe. Ben Torah le-hokhmah. Yerushalayim : Hotsa'at sefarim 'a. sh. Y. L. Magnes, ha-Universitah ha-'Ivrit, 760, 2000.
BM755.M54 H35 2000

JUDAISM - FUNCTIONARIES. *See* **RABBIS.**

JUDAISM, HELLENISTIC. *See* **JUDAISM - HISTORY - POST-EXILIC PERIOD, 586 B.C.-210 A.D.**

JUDAISM - HISTORY.
Maier, Johann. Judentum von A bis Z. Freiburg im Breisgau : Herder, 2001.

JUDAISM - HISTORY - 17TH CENTURY.
Sutcliffe, Adam. Judaism and Enlightenment. Cambridge ; New York : Cambridge University Press, 2003.
BM290 .S88 2003

JUDAISM - HISTORY - 18TH CENTURY.
Sutcliffe, Adam. Judaism and Enlightenment. Cambridge ; New York : Cambridge University Press, 2003.
BM290 .S88 2003

JUDAISM - HISTORY - GRECO-ROMAN PERIOD, 332 B.C.-210 A.D. *See* **JUDAISM - HISTORY - POST-EXILIC PERIOD, 586 B.C.-210 A.D.**

JUDAISM - HISTORY - INTER-TESTAMENTAL PERIOD, 140 B.C.-30 A.D. *See* **JUDAISM - HISTORY - POST-EXILIC PERIOD, 586 B.C.-210 A.D.**

JUDAISM - HISTORY - MEDIEVAL AND EARLY MODERN PERIOD, 425-1789.
The Cambridge companion to medieval Jewish philosophy. Cambridge, UK ; New York : Cambridge University Press, 2003.
B755 .C36 2003

Meyuhas Ginio, Alisa, 1937- Kerovim u-rehokim. Tel Aviv : Mif'alim Universitayim, 760 [1999]

JUDAISM - HISTORY - POST-EXILIC PERIOD, 586 B.C.-210 A.D.
Ferguson, Everett, 1933- Backgrounds of early Christianity. 3rd ed. Grand Rapids, Mich. : W.B. Eerdmans, c2003.

JUDAISM - HISTORY - PRE-TALMUDIC PERIOD, 586 B.C.-10 A.D. *See* **JUDAISM - HISTORY - POST-EXILIC PERIOD, 586 B.C.-210 A.D.**

JUDAISM - HISTORY - TO 140 B.C. *See* **JUDAISM - HISTORY - TO 70 A.D.**

JUDAISM - HISTORY - TO 70 A.D.
Gruenwald, Ithamar. Rituals and ritual theory in ancient Israel. Leiden ; Boston : Brill, 2003.
BM660 .G78 2003

JUDAISM - INFLUENCE.
Eidelberg, Paul. Clash of two decadent civilizations. Shaarei Tikva, Israel : ACPR Publications, 2002.
BM537 .E53 2002

Maciejewski, Franz. Psychoanalytisches Archiv und jüdisches Gedächtnis. 1. Aufl. Wien : Passagen Verlag, 2002.

JUDAISM - LITURGY - PHILOSOPHY.
Gruenwald, Ithamar. Rituals and ritual theory in ancient Israel. Leiden ; Boston : Brill, 2003.
BM660 .G78 2003

JUDAISM - LITURGY - SABBATH PRAYERS.
Sharir, Avraham Yiśra'el. Pene Shabat nekablah. Yerushalayim : Avraham Kohen-Erez, 763 [2003]
BM670.L44 S527 2003

JUDAISM - MINHAG ARI. *See* **JUDAISM - ARI RITE.**

JUDAISM - NUSAH ARI. *See* **JUDAISM - ARI RITE.**

JUDAISM - PRAYER-BOOKS AND DEVOTIONS - HEBREW.
Naphtali ben Isaac, ha-Kohen, 1649-1719. Sefer Bet Rahel. Yerushalayim : Ahavat Shalom, 761 [2001]
BM665 .N257 2001

JUDAISM - PUBLIC OPINION. *See* **JEWS - PUBLIC OPINION.**

JUDAISM - RELATIONS - CHRISTIANITY.
Meyuhas Ginio, Alisa, 1937- Kerovim u-rehokim. Tel Aviv : Mif'alim Universitayim, 760 [1999]

JUDAISM - RITUALS. *See* **JUDAISM - LITURGY.**

JUDAISM - STUDY AND TEACHING. *See* **TALMUD TORAH (JUDAISM).**

JUDAISM - WORKS TO 1900.
Portaleone, Abraham ben David, 1542-1612. [Shilte Ha Gibborim. German] Die Heldenschilde. Frankfurt am Main : Lang, 2002.

Judd, Naomi. Naomi's breakthrough guide : 20 choices to transform your life / Naomi Judd. New York : Simon & Schuster, 2004. p. cm. ISBN 0-7432-3662-9 DDC 158.1
1. Self-actualization (Psychology) 2. Judd, Naomi. I. Title.
BF637.S4 J84 2004

Judd, Naomi. Naomi's breakthrough guide. New York : Simon & Schuster, 2004.
BF637.S4 J84 2004

Jude, Brian, 1947- Body language : the South African way / Brian Jude. Johannesburg : Zebra Press, 1998. 132 p. : ill. ; 22 cm. Includes index. ISBN 1-86872-243-0 DDC 153.6/9/0968
1. Body language - South Africa. I. Title.
BF637.N66 J83 1998

JUDGEMENT.
Wyer, Robert S. Social comprehension and judgment. Mahwah, N.J. : L. Erlbaum Associates, Publishers, 2004.
BF323.S63 W94 2004

The judgement of the eye.
Weber, Jürgen, 1928- Wien ; New York : Springer, c2002.
BF241 .W38 2002

JUDGES. *See* **JUSTICE, ADMINISTRATION OF.**

JUDGMENT. *See also* **SIZE JUDGMENT.**
Etc. frequency processing and cognition. Oxford ; New York : Oxford University Press, c2002.
BF448 .E83 2002

Schauer, Frederick F. Profiles, probabilities, and stereotypes. Cambridge, Mass. : Belknap Press of Harvard University Press, 2003.
HM1096 .S34 2003

Thinking. Hoboken, NJ : Wiley, c2003.
BF441 .T466 2003

JUDGMENT (ETHICS).
Illies, Christian. The grounds of ethical judgement. Oxford : Clarendon, 2003.

Löffelmann, Markus. Das Urteil. Würzburg : Königshausen & Neumann, c2002.
BC181 .L64 2002

JUDGMENT (LOGIC). *See also* **FALLACIES (LOGIC); REASONING.**
Löffelmann, Markus. Das Urteil. Würzburg : Königshausen & Neumann, c2002.
BC181 .L64 2002

JUDICIAL PROCESS. *See* **EVIDENCE (LAW).**

JUDO. *See* **KARATE.**

Judson, Olivia. Dr. Tatiana's sex advice to all creation / Olivia Judson. 1st ed. New York : Metropolitan Books, 2002. x, 308 p. ; 22 cm. Includes bibliographical references (p. [260]-297) and index. Publisher description URL: http://www.loc.gov/catdir/description/hol021/2002019591.html CONTENTS: pt. 1. Let slip the whores of war -- 1. A sketch of the battlefield -- 2. The expense is damnable -- 3. Fruits of knowledge -- 4. Swords or pistols -- 5. How to win even if you're a loser -- pt. 2. The evolution of depravity -- 6. How to make love to a cannibal -- 7. Crimes of passion -- 8. Hell hath no fury -- 9. Aphrodisiacs, love potions, and other recipes from Cupid's kitchen -- 10. Till death do us part -- pt. 3. Are men necessary : usually, but not always -- 11. The fornications of kings -- 12. Eve's testicle -- 13. Wholly virgin. ISBN 0-8050-6331-5 DDC 306.7

1. Sex. 2. Sex differences. 3. Sexual behavior in animals. I. Title. II. Title: Sex advice to all creation
HQ25 .J83 2002

JULIANUS, THE THEURGIST. CHALDEAN ORACLES.
Gemistus Plethon, George, 15th cent. [Magika logia tōn apo Zōroastrou magōn. French & Greek] Magika logia tōn apo Zōroastrou magōn. Athēnai : Akadēmia Athēnōn, 1995.
BF1762 .G45 1995

JULLIEN, FRANÇOIS, 1951-.
Dépayser la pensée. Paris : Empêcheurs de penser en rond, 2003.

Jumping Mouse.
Marlow, Mary Elizabeth, 1940- Norfolk, VA : Hampton Roads Pub. Co., c1995.
BF575.T7 M37 1995

Jundziłł, Juliusz.
Dziecko w rodzinie i społeczeństwie. Bydgoszsz : Wydawnictwo Uczelniane Akademii Bydgoskiej, 2002.

Jung.
Bair, Deirdre. Boston : Little, Brown, 2003.
BF109.J8 B35 2003

Rowland, Susan, 1962- Cambridge, UK : Polity ; Malden, MA : Blackwell, 2002.
BF175.4.F45 R69 2002

Jung, C. G. (Carl Gustav), 1875-1961. Transzendente Funktion.
Miller, Jeffrey C., 1951- The transcendent function. Albany : State University of New York Press, c2003.
BF175.5.I53 M55 2003

JUNG, C. G. (CARL GUSTAV), 1875-1961.
Bair, Deirdre. Jung. Boston : Little, Brown, 2003.
BF109.J8 B35 2003

Cabot, Catharine Rush. Jung, my mother and I. Einsiedeln : Daimon, 2001.

Clarke, Robert B. The four gold keys. Charlottesville, VA : Hampton Roads Pub., c2002.
BF175.5.D74 C58 2002

Coward, Harold G. Yoga and psychology. Albany : State University of New York Press, 2002.
BF51 .C69 2002

Dimitrievich, Vladimir. V plenu germeticheskogo kruga. Perm' : Panagiia, 2001.
BF173.J85 D56 2001

Henderson, Joseph L. (Joseph Lewis), 1903- Transformation of the psyche. New York : Brunner-Routledge, 2003.
BF173 .H4346 2003

Menzhulin, V. (Vadim), 1968- Raskoldovyvaia IUnga. Kiev : Izd-vo "Sfera", 2002.
BF173.J85 M46 2002

Rowland, Susan, 1962- Jung. Cambridge, UK : Polity ; Malden, MA : Blackwell, 2002.
BF175.4.F45 R69 2002

Rowland, Susan, 1962- Jung. Cambridge, UK : Polity ; Malden, MA : Blackwell, 2002.
BF175.4.F45 R69 2002

Ryan, Robert E. Shamanism and the psychology of C.G. Jung. London : Vega, 2002.
BF175.4.R44 R93 2002

Shamdasani, Sonu, 1962- C.G. Jung and the making of modern psychology. Cambridge, UK ; New York : Cambridge University Press, 2003.
BF173 .S485 2003

Tucker, Kenneth. Shakespeare and Jungian typology. Jefferson, N.C. ; London : McFarland & Co., c2003.
PR3065 .T83 2003

Weiler, Gerda, 1921- Der enteignete Mythos. Königstein : Helmer, [1996]

Witzig, James Starr. Jungian psychology. [Philadelphia, Pa.?] : Xlibris, c2002.
BF173.J85 W58 2002

Zlatanović, Ljubiša, 1958- Jung, jastvo i individuacija. 1. izd. Niš : Studenski informativno-izdavački centar Niš, 2001.
BF109.J8 Z53 2001

Jung, jastvo i individuacija.
Zlatanović, Ljubiša, 1958- 1. izd. Niš : Studenski informativno-izdavački centar Niš, 2001.
BF109.J8 Z53 2001

Jung, my mother and I.
Cabot, Catharine Rush. Einsiedeln : Daimon, 2001.

JUNGIAN PSYCHOANALYSIS. *See* **JUNGIAN PSYCHOLOGY.**

Jungian psychology.
Witzig, James Starr. [Philadelphia, Pa.?] : Xlibris, c2002.
BF173.J85 W58 2002

JUNGIAN PSYCHOLOGY.
Adams, Michael Vannoy, 1947- The fantasy principle. New York : Brunner-Routledge, 2004.
BF173.J85 A33 2004

Bond, D. Stephenson. The archetype of renewal. Toronto : Inner City Books, c2003.

Clarke, Robert B. The four gold keys. Charlottesville, VA : Hampton Roads Pub., c2002.
BF175.5.D74 C58 2002

Durham, Diana. The return of King Arthur. New York : Jeremy P. Tarcher/Penguin, 2004.
BF637.S4 D88 2004

Edinger, Edward F. Science of the soul. Toronto, Ont. : Inner City Books, c2002.
BF173 .E27 2002

Gambini, Roberto, 1944- Soul & culture. 1st ed. College Station : Texas A&M University Press, 2003.
BF698.9.C8 G35 2003

Henderson, Joseph L. (Joseph Lewis), 1903- Transformation of the psyche. New York : Brunner-Routledge, 2003.
BF173 .H4346 2003

Hollis, James, 1940- On this journey we call our life. Toronto, Ont. : Inner City Books, c2003.
BF697.5.S43 H65 2003

Hollis, James, 1940- On this journey we call our life. Toronto : Inner City Books, c2003.

L'incubo globale. Bergamo : Moretti & Vitali, c2002.

Knox, Jean, 1948- Archetype, attachment, analysis. Hove, East Sussex ; New York : Brunner-Routledge, 2003.
BF175.5.A72 K68 2003

Rowland, Susan, 1962- Jung. Cambridge, UK : Polity ; Malden, MA : Blackwell, 2002.
BF175.4.F45 R69 2002

Ryan, Robert E. Shamanism and the psychology of C.G. Jung. London : Vega, 2002.
BF175.4.R44 R93 2002

Shamdasani, Sonu, 1962- C.G. Jung and the making of modern psychology. Cambridge, UK ; New York : Cambridge University Press, 2003.
BF173 .S485 2003

Tilton, Hereward. The quest for the phoenix. Berlin ; New York : Walter de Gruyter, 2003.
QD24.M3 T558 2003

Witzig, James Starr. Jungian psychology. [Philadelphia, Pa.?] : Xlibris, c2002.
BF173.J85 W58 2002

JUNGIAN PSYCHOLOGY - CASE STUDIES.
Van Löben Sels, Robin E., 1938- A dream in the world. New York, NY : Brunner-Routledge, 2003.
BF175.5.D74 V36 2003

JUNGIAN PSYCHOLOGY - ENGLAND.
Hubback, Judith. From dawn to dusk. Wilmette, Ill. : Chiron Publications, 2003.
BF109.H77 A3 2003

JUNGIAN PSYCHOLOGY - RELIGIOUS ASPECTS - CHRISTIANITY.
Jerotić, Vladeta. [Selections 2000] Izabrani ogledi. Beograd: Srpska književna zadruga, 2000.
BF109.J47 A25 2000

JUNGIAN PSYCHOLOGY - RELIGIOUS ASPECTS - CHRISTIANITY - CASE STUDIES.
Van Löben Sels, Robin E., 1938- A dream in the world. New York, NY : Brunner-Routledge, 2003.
BF175.5.D74 V36 2003

JUNGIAN PSYCHOLOGY - RELIGIOUS ASPECTS - ORTHODOX EASTERN CHURCH.
Dimitrievich, Vladimir. V plenu germeticheskogo kruga. Perm' : Panagiia, 2001.
BF173.J85 D56 2001

Jerotić, Vladeta. [Selections 2000] Izabrani ogledi. Beograd: Srpska književna zadruga, 2000.
BF109.J47 A25 2000

JUNGIAN THEORY. *See* **JUNGIAN PSYCHOLOGY.**

JUNGIAN THEORY.
Rowland, Susan, 1962- Jung. Cambridge, UK : Polity ; Malden, MA : Blackwell, 2002.
BF175.4.F45 R69 2002

Junker, Helmut, 1934- Unter Übermenschen : Freud & Ferenczi : die Geschichte einer Beziehung in Briefen / Helmut Junker. Tübingen : Edition Diskord, c1997. 237 p. ; 22 cm. Includes bibliographical references (p. 235-237). ISBN 3-89295-623-5 DDC 150.19/52/0922
1. Freud, Sigmund, - 1856-1939 - Correspondence - History and criticism. 2. Ferenczi, Sándor, - 1873-1933 - Correspondence - History and criticism. I. Title.
BF109.F74 J85 1997

JUPITER (PLANET) - MISCELLANEA.
Aslan, Madalyn. Madalyn Aslan's Jupiter signs. New York : Viking Studio, 2003.
BF1724.2.J87 A85 2003

JURISDICTION, TERRITORIAL.
The territorial management of ethnic conflict. 2nd rev. and expanded ed. London ; Portland, OR : F. Cass, 2003.
GN496 .T47 2003

JURISPRUDENCE. *See also* **LAW.**
Mill, John Stuart, 1806-1873. Utilitarianism ; 2nd ed. Malden, MA : Blackwell Pub., 2003.
B1602 .A5 2003

JURISTS. *See* **LAWYERS.**

Jusczyk, Peter W. The discovery of spoken language / Peter W. Jusczyk. 1st MIT Press pbk. ed. Cambridge, Mass. : MIT Press, 2000. xii, 314 p. : ill. ; 23 cm. (Language, speech, and communication) "A Bradford book." Includes bibliographical references (p. [255]-300) and indexes. ISBN 0-262-60036-6 (pbk.) ISBN 0-262-10058-4 (hardcover) DDC 401/.93
1. Speech perception in infants. 2. Speech perception in newborn infants. 3. Language acquisition. 4. Psycholinguistics. I. Title. II. Series.
BF720.S67 J87 2000

Jussen, Bernhard.
Negotiating the gift. Göttingen : Vandenhoeck & Ruprecht, c2003.

JUSTICE. *See also* **SOCIAL JUSTICE.**
Freiheit, Gleichheit und Autonomie. Wien : Oldenbourg ; Berlin : Akademie Verlag, 2003.
JC575 .F74 2003

Kaplow, Louis. Fairness versus welfare. Cambridge, MA : Harvard University Press, 2002.
K247 .K37 2002

Markell, Patchen, 1969- Bound by recognition. Princeton, N.J. : Princeton University Press, c2003.
JC575 .M37 2003

Order and justice in international relations. Oxford ; New York : Oxford University Press, 2003.
JZ1308 .O73 2003

Schauer, Frederick F. Profiles, probabilities, and stereotypes. Cambridge, Mass. : Belknap Press of Harvard University Press, 2003.
HM1096 .S34 2003

JUSTICE, ADMINISTRATION OF. *See* **DISPUTE RESOLUTION (LAW).**

JUSTICE, ADMINISTRATION OF - CASE STUDIES.
Vergès, Jacques. Dictionnaire amoureux de la justice. Paris : Plon, c2002.

Justice, luck, and knowledge.
Hurley, S. L. (Susan L.) Cambridge, Mass. : Harvard University Press, 2003.
BJ1451 .H87 2003

JUVENILE DELINQUENCY. *See* **SCHOOL VIOLENCE.**

JUVENILE LITERATURE. *See* **CHILDREN'S LITERATURE.**

Jyotisha tattva vivecanī saṃhitā.
Garga, Harīśa Kumāra, 1959- 1. saṃskaraṇa. Dillī : Harīśa Kumāra Garga, 2002.
BF1714.H5 G365 2002

Jyotisha tattva-viveka.
Śāstrī, Girijā Śaṅkara. 1. saṃskaraṇa. Ilāhābāda : Jyotisha Karmakāṇḍa evaṃ Adhyātma Śodha Saṃsthāna, 2001.
BF1714.H5 S277 2001

Jyotisha-vijñāna-nirjharī.
Śāstrī, Vinoda, 1959- Jayapura : Rājasthāna Saṃskrta Akādamī, [2002?]
BF1714.H5 S288 2002

Ká má baa gbàgbé : a festival of Yoruba arts & culture. [Nigeria] : Jadeas Productions, [2003] 121 p. : ill., map ; 30 cm. Cover title.
1. Yoruba (African people) - History. 2. Yoruba language. 3. Yoruba literature. 4. Yoruba (African people) - Social life and customs. 5. Cookery, Yoruba. 6. Yoruba (African people) - Religion. I. Title: Festival of Yoruba arts and culture

Ka-sheleg yalbinu.
Va'eknin, Yosef ben Avraham. Sefer Ka-sheleg yalbinu. Yerushalayim : Y. Va'eknin, 763 [2002 or 2003]

Kabbalist Rabbi Shabbetai Sheftel Horowitz of Prague.
Sack, Bracha, 1933- Shomer ha-pardes. Be'er Sheva' : Universiṭat Ben-Guryon ba-Negev, c2002.

KABILA, LAURENT-DÉSIRÉ - ASSASSINATION.
From Kabila to Kabila. Nairobi : Brussels : International Crisis Group, 2001.

Kabinet Zh.
Iskusstvo snovideniĭ = Sankt-Peterburg : Skifiia, 2002.
NX180.D74 I74 2002

Kabrin, V. I.
Vserossiĭskaia konferentsiia "Mezhdistsiplinarnyĭ sintez v metodologii gumanitarnykh issledovaniĭ" (2002 : Tomsk, Russia) Lichnost' v paradigmakh i metaforakh. Tomsk : Tomskiĭ gos. universitet, 2002.
BF698 .V74 2002

Kachere text
(no. 10) Soko, Boston. Nchimi chikanga. Blantyre [Malawi] : Christian Literature Association in Malawi, 2002.

Kadishman, Menashe, 1932-.
Me-ayin nahalti et shiri. Tel Aviv : Yedi'ot aharonot ; Sifre hemed, c2002.

Kaenel, Hans-Markus von.
Alföldi, Maria R.- Gloria romanorum. Stuttgart : Franz Steiner Verlag, 2001.
DG78 .A546 2001

Kafaḥ, Yosef, 1917- Halikhot Teman : haye ha-Yehudim be-Tsan'a u-venoteha / me-et Yosef Kafah ; ba-'arikhat Yiśra'el Yesha'yahu. Mahad. 5, metukenet. Yerushalayim : Mekhon Ben-Tsevi le-heker kehilot Yiśra'el ba-Mizrah : Yad Yitshak ben-Tsevi : ha-Universiṭah ha-Ivrit bi-Yerushalayim, 2002. 447 p., [24] p. of plates : ill., port., map ; 25 cm. (Meḥkarim u-meḳorot shel Mekhon Ben-Tsevi) Added title page title: Jewish life in Sana. Includes bibliographical references and indexes. ISBN 9652350885
1. Jews - Yemen - Ṣan'ā'. 2. Jews - Social life and customs. I. Yesh'ayahu, Yiśra'el. II. Title. III. Title: Jewish life in Sana

KAFKA, FRANZ, 1883-1924 - CRITICISM AND INTERPRETATION.
Milmaniene, José E. Clínica del texto. [1. ed.]. Buenos Aires : Editorial Biblos, c2002.

Kagan & Segal's psychology.
Kagan, Jerome. 9th ed. Belmont, CA : Thomson/Wadsworth, c2004.
BF121 .K22 2004

Kagan, Jerome. Kagan & Segal's psychology : an introduction / Jerome Kagan, Julius Segal, Ernest Havemann ; as revised by Don Baucum, Carolyn D. Smith. 9th ed. Belmont, CA : Thomson/Wadsworth, c2004. 702 p. ; 28 cm. Distinctive title: Psychology. Rev. ed.: Psychology. 8th ed. Fort Worth : Harcourt Press, Harcourt Brace College Publishers, c1995. ISBN 0-15-508114-4 (student ed. : pbk.)
1. Psychology. I. Segal, Julius, 1924- II. Havemann, Ernest. III. Baucum, Don. IV. Smith, Carolyn D. V. Kagan, Jerome. Psychology. VI. Title. VII. Title: Psychology.
BF121 .K22 2004

Psychology.
Kagan, Jerome. Kagan & Segal's psychology. 9th ed. Belmont, CA : Thomson/Wadsworth, c2004.
BF121 .K22 2004

Kail, Robert V. Human development : a life-span view / Robert Kail, John Cavanaugh. 3rd ed. Belmont, CA : Thomson/Wadsworth, c2004. xxv, 751 p. : col. ill. ; 29 cm. Includes bibliographical references (p. [669]-730) and indexes. ISBN 0-534-59751-3 DDC 155.2
1. Developmental psychology - Textbooks. I. Cavanaugh, John C. II. Title.
BF713 .K336 2004

Kaiser, Lisa.
Carducci, Bernardo J. The shyness breakthrough. [Emmaus, Pa.] : Rodale, c2003.
BF723.B3 C37 2003

Kaiserliche Rechtsprechung und herrschaftliche Stabilisierung.
Westphal, Siegrid, 1963- Köln : Böhlau, 2002.

Kaiwar, Vasant, 1950-.
Antinomies of modernity. Durham : Duke University Press, 2003.
CB358 .A59 2003

Kak daleko do zavtrashnego dnīa - .
Moiseev, N. N. (Nikita Nikolaevich) Moskva : Taĭdeks Ko, 2002.
DK49 .M64 2002

Kak daleko do zavtrashnego dnīa - : svobodnye razmyshlenīīa, 1917-1993 ; Vospominanīīa o N.N. Moiseeve.
Moiseev, N. N. (Nikita Nikolaevich) Kak daleko do zavtrashnego dnīa--. Moskva : Taĭdeks Ko, 2002.
DK49 .M64 2002

Kak nauchit'sīa ponimat' sebīa i drugikh.
Prakticheskaīa psikhologīīa v testakh, ili, Kak nauchit'sīa ponimat' sebīa i drugikh. Moskva : AST-Press kniga, 2003.
BF176 .P73 2003

Kak stanovīātsīa velikimi ili vydaīushchimisīa?.
Bodalev, A. A. Moskva : In-t psikhoterapii, 2003.
BF724.5 .B64 2003

Kakŭv trud e nuzhen na choveka?.
Ivanova, Anna (Anna N.) Sofīīa : Akademichno izd-vo "Prof. Marin Drinov", 2000.
BF481 .I82 2000

Kalashnikova, T. P. (Tat'īāna Pavlovna).
Dimitrievich, Vladimir. V plenu germeticheskogo kruga. Perm' : Panagīīa, 2001.
BF173.J85 D56 2001

Kaleidoskopische Schriften.
Mersmann, Paul. Hamburg : Maximilian-Gesellschaft, 2002.

Kalisch, Eleonore. Konfigurationen der Renaissance : zur Emanzipationsgeschichte der ars theatrica / von Eleonore Kalisch. Berlin : Vistas, c2002. 267 p. ; 21 cm. (Berliner Theaterwissenschaft, 0948-7646 ; Bd. 9) Includes bibliographical references. ISBN 3-89158-337-0 (pbk.)
1. Theater - History. 2. Renaissance. I. Title. II. Series.

Kallen, Stuart A., 1955- Dreams / by Stuart A. Kallen. San Diego, Calif. : Lucent Books, 2004. v. cm. (The mystery library) Includes bibliographical references and index. CONTENTS: Dream science -- Interpreting dreams -- Dreams and cultures -- Telepathic dreaming -- Dream power. ISBN 1-59018-288-X (alk. paper) DDC 154.6/3
1. Children's dreams - Juvenile literature. 2. Dream interpretation - Juvenile literature. 3. Dreams. 4. Dream interpretation. I. Title. II. Series: Mystery library (Lucent Books)
BF1099.C55 K35 2004

Fortune-telling / by Stuart A. Kallen. San Diego, Calif. : Lucent Books, 2004. p. cm. (The mystery library) SUMMARY: Presents a description and history of some of the most popular methods of predicting the future, including astrology, palm reading, tarot cards, I Ching, and oracles. Includes bibliographical references and index. Table of contents URL: http://www.loc.gov/catdir/toc/ecip043/2003010726.html ISBN 1-59018-289-8 (alk. paper) DDC 133.3
1. Fortune-telling - Juvenile literature. 2. Fortune telling - History. I. Title. II. Series: Mystery library (Lucent Books)
BF1861 .K35 2004

Ghosts / by Stuart A. Kallen. San Diego, Calif. : Lucent Books, c2004. p. cm. (The mystery library) SUMMARY: Provides a history of ghosts, descriptions of different types of hauntings, and information on the people who seek scientific evidence that apparitions are real. Includes bibliographical references and index. Table of contents URL: http://www.loc.gov/catdir/toc/ecip042/2003007624.html CONTENTS: Ghosts throughout the ages -- Haunted hangouts -- Hunting ghosts -- Ghostly communications -- When ghosts attack. ISBN 1-59018-290-1 (hardback : alk. paper) DDC 133.1
1. Ghosts - Juvenile literature. 2. Ghosts. I. Title. II. Series: Mystery library (Lucent Books)
BF1461 .K33 2004

Kallinikos, Jannis. Technology and society : interdisciplinary studies in formal organization / Jannis Kallinikos ; with a foreword by Robert Cooper. Munich : Accedo ; Distributed in the U.S.A. by The Institute of Mind and Behavior, c1996. x, 178 p. ; 21 cm. (Studies of action and organisation (SAO) ; v. 6) Includes bibliographical references ([165]-174) and index. ISBN 3-89265-023-3
1. Organizational behavior. 2. Organizational sociology. I. Title. II. Series: Studies of action and organisation ; v. 6.

Kałuża, Zenon.
La servante et la consolatrice. Paris : Vrin, 2002.
B721 .S479 2002

Kaluzniacky, Eugene. Managing psychological factors in information systems work : an orientation to emotional intelligence / Eugene Kaluzniacky. Hershey PA : Information Science Pub., c2004. p. ; cm. Includes bibliographical references and index. CONTENTS: The Myers-Briggs personality types -- Enneagram personalities -- Thinking style: cognition, creativity and learning -- The deepest inner self --- a foundation for "emotional intelligence" -- Influencing IT -- Emotionally intelligent IT -- A call to action. ISBN 1-59140-198-4 (cloth) ISBN 1-59140-290-5 (pbk.) ISBN 1-59140-199-2 (ebook) DDC 004/.01/9
1. Emotional intelligence. 2. Computer programming - Psychological aspects. 3. Mental Health. 4. Occupational Health. 5. Emotions. 6. Information Services - organization & administration. 7. Personality. 8. Social Behavior. I. Title.
BF576 .K358 2004

The Kama Sutra illuminated.
Pinkney, Andrea Marion. [Kāmasūtra. English.] New York, N.Y. : Abrams, c2002.

Kamal, Niraj. Arise, Asia! : respond to white peril / Niraj Kamal. Delhi : Wordsmiths, 2003. x, 414 p. : ill., maps ; 23 cm. Includes bibliographical references and index. ISBN 81-87412-08-9
1. East and West. I. Title.
CB251 .K285 2003

Ḳamelhar, Yiśra'el.
Eleazar ben Judah, of Worms, 1176 (ca.)-1238. Sefer Sode razaya .... Bene-Beraḳ : Ḳoraḥ, 759 [1998 or 1999]
BM525 .E432 1999

Kamil, Alan C.
Nebraska Symposium on Motivation (2001) Evolutionary psychology and motivation. Lincoln, Neb. ; London : University of Nebraska Press, c2001.
BF701 .N43 2001

Kaminski, Nicola.
Hermetik. Tübingen : M. Niemeyer Verlag, c2002.
BF1586 .H47 2002

Kaminsky, Donna.
Skidmore, Warren. Lord Dunmore's little war of 1774. Bowie, Md. : Heritage Books, 2002.

Kamper, Dietmar, 1936-.
Logik und Leidenschaft. Berlin : D. Reimer Verlag, c2002.

Was kostet den Kopf? Marburg : Tectum Verlag, 2001.

KAMPER, DIETMAR, 1936-.
Logik und Leidenschaft. Berlin : D. Reimer Verlag, c2002.

Was kostet den Kopf? Marburg : Tectum Verlag, 2001.

Kämpf, Heike. Helmuth Plessner : eine Einführung / Heike Kämpf. 1. Aufl. Düsseldorf : Parerga, 2001. 137 p. ; 21 cm. (Philosophie und andere Künste) Includes bibliographical references (p. 134-137). ISBN 3-930450-65-8 (pbk.)
1. Plessner, Helmuth, - 1892- 2. Philosophy, Modern - 20th century. 3. Philosophical anthropology. I. Title. II. Series.
B3323.P564 K36 2001

Kamphaus, Randy W.
Handbook of psychological and educational assessment of children. 2nd ed. New York, N.Y. : Guilford Press, 2003.
BF722 .H33 2003

Handbook of psychological and educational assessment of children. 2nd ed. New York : Guilford Press, 2003.
BF722 .H33 2003b

Kampis, George.
Appraising Lakatos. Dordrecht ; Boston : Kluwer Academic, c2002.
Q175 .A685 2002

Kan kvinnor tänka?.
Korsström, Tuva. Stockholm/Stehag : Symposion, 2002.

Kanalenstein, Ruben. La palabra. Los rostros / Ruben Kanalenstein. Córdoba, Argentina : Alción, 2000. 88 p. ; 22 cm. "Por los territorios del asombro, acceso a los misterios de la Kabalá"--Cover.
1. Cabala. I. Title.

Kaneta, Susumu, 1938-.
Kuno Akira Kyōju kanreki kinen tetsugaku ronbunshū. Tōkyō : Ibunsha, 1995.
B29 .K826 1995 <Orien Japan>

Ḳanevsḳi, Sh. Y. Ḥ. ben Y. Y. (Shemaryahu Yosef Ḥayim ben Y. Y.).
Ari'av, Dayid ben Naḥman, ha-Kohen. Le-re'akha kamokha. Mahad. 2. Yerushalayim : Dayid ben Naḥman ha-Kohen Ari'av, 760- [2000-

Kangxi, Emperor of China, 1654-1722.
Sheng yu xiang jie. Di 1 ban. [Peking] : Xian zhuang shu ju, 1995.
BJ117 .S486 1995 <Orien China>

Kanner, Allen.
Psychology and consumer culture. 1st ed. Washington, DC : American Psychological Association, c2004.
HC110.C6 P76 2004

KANNON (BUDDHIST DEITY). *See* **AVALOKITEŚVARA (BUDDHIST DEITY).**

KANT, IMMANUEL, 1724-1804. KRITIK DER PRAKTISCHEN VERNUNFT.
Ameriks, Karl, 1947- Interpreting Kant's critiques. Oxford : Clarendon Press ; New York : Oxford University Press, 2003.
B2779 .A64 2003

KRITIK DER REINEN VERNUNFT.
Ameriks, Karl, 1947- Interpreting Kant's critiques. Oxford : Clarendon Press ; New York : Oxford University Press, 2003.
B2779 .A64 2003

KRITIK DER URTEILSKRAFT.
Ameriks, Karl, 1947- Interpreting Kant's critiques. Oxford : Clarendon Press ; New York : Oxford University Press, 2003.
B2779 .A64 2003

KANT, IMMANUEL, 1724-1804.
Grundherr, Michael von. Kants Ethik in modernen Gesellschaften. Hamburg : Lit, 2003.

KANT, IMMANUEL, 1724-1804 - CONTRIBUTIONS IN CONCEPT OF DING AN SICH.
Caropreso, Paolo. Von der Dingfrage zur Frage nach Gott. Berlin ; New York : W. de Gruyter, 2003.

KANT, IMMANUEL, 1724-1804 - CONTRIBUTIONS IN CONCEPT OF FAITH.
Caropreso, Paolo. Von der Dingfrage zur Frage nach Gott. Berlin ; New York : W. de Gruyter, 2003.

KANT, IMMANUEL, 1724-1804 - CONTRIBUTIONS IN CONCEPT OF GOD.
Caropreso, Paolo. Von der Dingfrage zur Frage nach Gott. Berlin ; New York : W. de Gruyter, 2003.

KANT, IMMANUEL, 1724-1804 - CONTRIBUTIONS IN ONTOLOGY.
Caropreso, Paolo. Von der Dingfrage zur Frage nach Gott. Berlin ; New York : W. de Gruyter, 2003.

Kantor, Karl Moiseevich. Dvoĭnaīa spiral' istorii : istoriosofīīa proektizma / Karl Kantor. Moskva : IAzyk slavīānskoĭ kul'tury, 2002- v. : ill. ; 25 cm. Includes bibliographical references. Summary in English. PARTIAL CONTENTS: tom 1. Obshchie problemy. ISBN 5944570350
1. History - Philosophy. 2. Social evolution. 3. History - Religious aspects - Christianity. I. Title.
D16.8 .K224 2002

Kants Ethik in modernen Gesellschaften.
Grundherr, Michael von. Hamburg : Lit, 2003.

Kantstudien. Ergänzungshefte
(143) Caropreso, Paolo. Von der Dingfrage zur Frage nach Gott. Berlin ; New York : W. de Gruyter, 2003.

Kanyer, Laurie A., 1959- 25 things to do when grandpa passes away, mom and dad get divorced, or the dog dies : activities to help children suffering loss or change / Laurie A. Kanyer ; illustrated by Jenny Williams. Seatte Wash., : Parenting Press, 2004. p. cm. Includes index. ISBN 1-88473-454-5 ISBN 1-88473-453-7 (pbk.) DDC 155.9/37/083
1. Grief in children. 2. Loss (Psychology) in children. 3. Children - Counseling of. I. Title. II. Title: Twenty five things to do when grandpa passes away, mom and dad get divorced, or the dog dies
BF723.G75 K36 2003

Kanygin, I͡Uriĭ Mikhaĭlovich. Poi͡as mira : Ukraina - Kazakhstan, fundament Evraziĭskogo edinstva / I͡U. M. Kanygin. Kiev : MAUP, 2001. 239 p. : ill. ; 21 cm. With the assistance of Andreĭ Grigor'evich Mali͡arenko--Cf. colophon. Includes bibliographical references. ISBN 9666081040
1. Eurasia. 2. East and West. I. Mali͡arenko, Andreĭ Grigor'evich. II. Title.

Kaplan, Amy. The anarchy of empire in the making of U.S. culture / Amy Kaplan. Cambridge, Mass. : Harvard University Press, 2002. 260 p. ; 25 cm. (Convergences) Includes bibliographical references (p. 215-245) and index. Table of contents URL: http://www.loc.gov/catdir/toc/fy034/2002027254.html ISBN 0-674-00913-4 (alk. paper) DDC 327.73/009/034
1. United States - Foreign relations - 1865-1921. 2. United States - Foreign relations - 1783-1865. 3. United States - Territorial expansion. 4. National characteristics, American. 5. Popular culture - United States - History - 19th century. 6. Popular culture - United States - History - 20th century. 7. Imperialism - Social aspects - United States - History. 8. Imperialism in literature. 9. Imperialism in motion pictures. I. Title. II. Series: Convergences (Cambridge, Mass.)
E661.7 .K37 2002

Kaplan, Jeffrey, 1954-.
The cultic milieu. Walnut Creek : AltaMira Press, c2002.
BP603 .C835 2002

Kaplan, Leonard V.
On interpretation. Madison, Wis. : University of Wisconsin Press for the University of Wisconsin Law School, c2002.

Kaplan, Robbie Miller. How to say it when you don't know what to say : the right words for difficult times / Robbie Miller Kaplan. Prentice Hall Press ed. Upper Saddle River, NJ : Prentice Hall Press, 2004. p. cm. ISBN 0-7352-0375-X DDC 155.9/3
1. Consolation. 2. Interpersonal communication. I. Title.
BF637.C54 K36 2004

Kaplow, Louis. Fairness versus welfare / Louis Kaplow, Steven Shavell. Cambridge, MA : Harvard University Press, 2002. xxii, 544 p. ; 26 cm. Includes bibliographical references (p. [475]-509) and index. ISBN 0-674-00622-4 (alk. paper) DDC 340/.11
1. Fairness. 2. Ethics. 3. Justice. 4. Social policy. 5. Law and economics. I. Shavell, Steven, 1946- II. Title.
K247 .K37 2002

Karade, Akinkugbe. Path to priesthood : the making of an African priest in an American world / Baba Akinkugbe Karade. Brooklyn, N.Y. : Kânda Mukûtu Books, c2001. 111 p. : ill. ; 23 cm. (Classical writings on the Ifa/Yoruba traditional religion) Includes bibliographical references (p. 105-106). ISBN 1-89015-726-0 DDC 299/.6/092
1. Karade, Akinkugbe. 2. Priests - Biography. 3. Ifa (Religion) 4. Yoruba (African people) - Religion. 5. Black author. I. Title. II. Series.
BL2523.I33 K37 2001

KARADE, AKINKUGBE.
Karade, Akinkugbe. Path to priesthood. Brooklyn, N.Y. : Kânda Mukûtu Books, c2001.
BL2523.I33 K37 2001
1. Black author.

Karambolagen.
Karasek, Hellmuth, 1934- 2. Aufl. München : Ullstein Verlag, c2002.

Karasek, Hellmuth, 1934- Karambolagen : Begegnungen mit Zeitgenossen / Hellmuth Karasek. 2. Aufl. München : Ullstein Verlag, c2002. 287 p. ; 21 cm. Includes index. ISBN 3-550-08391-2
1. Karasek, Hellmuth, - 1934- 2. Celebrities. 3. Biography - 20th century. I. Title.

KARASEK, HELLMUTH, 1934-.
Karasek, Hellmuth, 1934- Karambolagen. 2. Aufl. München : Ullstein Verlag, c2002.

Karasev, Nikolaĭ, iereĭ. Put' okkul'tizma : istoriko-bogoslovskie issledovanii͡a / Nikolaĭ Karasev. Moskva : Izd-vo "Prensa", 2003. 335 p. ; 21 cm. (Apologetika) Includes bibliographical references (p. 329-335). ISBN 5948840026
1. Occultism. I. Title. II. Series.
BF1416 .K37 2003

KARATE - PHILOSOPHY.
Webster-Doyle, Terrence, 1940- One encounter, one chance. 1st Weatherhill ed. Trumbull, CT : Weatherhill, 2000.
GV1114.3 .W43 2000

Karauri, Mathew Adams, 1947- Rulers, leaders, and people : a philosophy / Mathew Adams Karauri. Nairobi : Karma Pub. Co., 2001. 85 p. ; 18 cm. ISBN 9966969241 DDC 823/.914
1. Karauri, Mathew Adams, - 1947- - Philosophy. 2. Leadership. 3. Democracy. 4. Black author. I. Title.

KARAURI, MATHEW ADAMS, 1947- - PHILOSOPHY.
Karauri, Mathew Adams, 1947- Rulers, leaders, and people. Nairobi : Karma Pub. Co., 2001.
1. Black author.

Karcher, Stephen L. Ta chuan : the great treatise / Stephen Karcher. 1st ed. New York : St. Martin's Press, 2000. 159 p. : col. ill. ; 25 cm. Subtitle on cover : The key to understanding the I Ching and its place in your life. Includes index. ISBN 0-312-26428-3 DDC 133.3/3
1. Yi jing. 2. Divination - China. I. Title. II. Title: The key to understanding the I Ching and its place in your life
BF1773.2.C5 K368 2000

Ḳarelits, Ḥayim Sha'ul ben Me'ir. Sefer Aḥat sha'alti : ḥidu. T. u-ma'amre hashḳafah / ... Ḥayim Sha'ul b.R. Me'ir Ḳarelits. Bene Beraḳ : Mish. Ḳarelits, 762 [2002] 143 p. ; 24 cm. Running title: Aḥat sha'alti.
1. Jewish law. 2. Jewish sermons, Hebrew. 3. Ethics, Jewish. I. Title. II. Title: Aḥat sha'alti

Karg, Hans Hartmut. Theoretische Ethik / Hans Hartmut Karg. Hamburg : Kovac, c1996-<c1999> 3 v. ; 21 cm. PARTIAL CONTENTS: Bd. 1. Basisformen des Sittlichen -- Bd. 2. Theorie der Versittlichung -- Bd. 3. Methodenlehren und Begründungsformen. ISBN 3-86064-447-5 (v. 1) ISBN 3-86064-521-8 (v. 2) DDC 170
1. Ethics. 2. Social ethics. I. Title.
BJ1114 .K32 1997

Karimi, Simin.
Word order and scrambling. Malden, MA : Blackwell Pub., 2003.
P295 .W65 2003

Karine après la vie.
Dray, Maryvonne. Paris : Albin Michel, c2002.

Karl Jaspers on philosophy of history and history of philosophy / edited by Joseph W. Koterski and Raymond J. Langley. Amherst, N.Y. : Humanity Books, 2003. 316 p. ; 24 cm. Includes bibliographical references and indexes. ISBN 1-59102-002-6 (cloth : alk. paper) DDC 109
1. Jaspers, Karl, - 1883-1969. 2. Philosophy - History. 3. History - Philosophy. I. Koterski, Joseph W. II. Langley, Raymond J., 1935-
B3279.J34 K292 2003

KARMA.
Meier, Jürgen. Karma und Christentum. Dornach : Verlag am Goetheanum, c2001.

Nwokogba, Isaac, 1957- America, here I come. 2nd ed. Cranston, R.I. : Writers' Collective, c2003.
BF1045.K37 N86 2003

Saint-Germain, Jon, 1960- Karmic palmistry. 1st ed. St. Paul, Minn. : Llewellyn Publications, 2003.
BF921 .S215 2003

KARMA - MISCELLANEA.
Stein, Diane, 1948- Essential energy balancing II. Berkeley, Calif. : Crossing Press, 2003.
BF1045.K37 S735 2003

KARMA - PSYCHOLOGY.
Bedi, Ashok. Retire your family karma. Berwick, Me. : Nicolas-Hays, 2003.
BF637.S4 B423 2003

Karma und Christentum.
Meier, Jürgen. Dornach : Verlag am Goetheanum, c2001.

Karmic palmistry.
Saint-Germain, Jon, 1960- 1st ed. St. Paul, Minn. : Llewellyn Publications, 2003.
BF921 .S215 2003

Karṇāṭaka, Vimalā. Śrīmadbhāgavata meṁ Sāṅkhyayoga ke tattva : eka pariśīlana / lekhakā, Vimalā Karṇāṭaka ; Rāmamurti Śarmā kī prastāvanā se vibhūṣitā. 1. saṁskaraṇa. Vārāṇasī : Sampūrṇānanda Saṁskr̥ta Viśvavidyālaya, 2001. 11, 399 p. ; 25 cm. (Viśvavidyālaya-rajatajayantī-granthamālā ; 37) Added title page title: Śrīmadbhāgavata meṅ Sāṅkhya-Yoga ke tattva. Includes bibliographical references. In Hindi; includes passages in Sanskrit. ISBN 81-7270-068-7
1. Puranas. - Bhāgavatapurāṇa - Criticism, interpretation, etc. 2. Sankhya. 3. Yoga. I. Sampūrṇānanda Saṁskr̥ta Viśvavidyālaya. II. Title. III. Title: Śrīmadbhāgavata meṅ Sāṅkhya-Yoga ke tattva IV. Series.
BL1140.4.B437 K27 2001

Karnath, H.-O. (Hans-Otto), 1961-.
The cognitive and neural bases of spatial neglect. Oxford ; New York : Oxford University Press, 2002.

RC394.N44 C64 2002

Karol, Darcie L.
Russell, Mary T. The 16PF fifth edition administrator's manual. 3rd ed. Champaign, Ill. : Institute for Personality and Ability Testing, 2002.
BF698.8.S5 A37 2002

Karpenko, M. (Maksim).
Universum sapiens.
Karpenko, M. (Maksim) Vselennai͡a razumnai͡a = 2. perer. izd. Moskva : MAIK Nauka/Interperiodika, 2001.
BF1036 .K37 2001

Vselennai͡a razumnai͡a = Universum sapiens / Maksim Karpenko. 2. perer. izd. Moskva : MAIK Nauka/Interperiodika, 2001. 382 p. ; 22 cm. (Zemnye fenomeny) Rev. ed. of: Universum sapiens. ISBN 5784600656
1. Parapsychology. 2. Psychokinesis. I. Karpenko, M. (Maksim) Universum sapiens. II. Title. III. Title: Universum sapiens IV. Series: Serii͡a "Zemnye fenomeny"
BF1036 .K37 2001

Karras, Ruth Mazo, 1957- From boys to men : formations of masculinity in late medieval Europe / Ruth Mazo Karras. Philadelphia : University of Pennsylvania Press, c2003. 246 p. ; 24 cm. (The Middle Ages series) Includes bibliographical references (p. [209]-231) and index. ISBN 0-8122-3699-8 (hbk. : alk. paper) ISBN 0-8122-1834-5 (pbk. : alk. paper) DDC 305.31/09/02
1. Boys - Europe - History - To 1500. 2. Young men - Europe - History - To 1500. 3. Masculinity. 4. Men - Socialization. 5. Gender identity. 6. Maturation (Psychology) I. Title. II. Series.
HQ775 .K373 2003

Karratum perratum.
Cujātā, 1935- 1. patippu. Ceṉṉai : Vicā Papḷikēṣaṉs, 2000.
PL4758.9.S8758+

Kartun-Blum, Ruth.
Me-ayin nahalti et shiri. Tel Aviv : Yedi'ot aharonot : Sifre hemed, c2002.

Kasabov, Nikola K. Evolving connectionist systems : methods and applications in bioinformatics, brain study and intelligent machines / Nikola Kasabov. London ; New York : Springer, c2003. xii, 307 p. : ill. ; 24 cm. (Perspectives in neural computing, 1431-6854) Includes bibliographical references (p. 275-289) and index. ISBN 1-85233-400-2 (pbk.) DDC 006.3/2
1. Neural computers. 2. Brain - Computer simulation. 3. Bioinformatics. 4. Artificial intelligence. I. Title. II. Series.
QA76.87 .K39 2003

Kasser, Tim.
Psychology and consumer culture. 1st ed. Washington, DC : American Psychological Association, c2004.
HC110.C6 P76 2004

Kassin, Saul M. Essentials of psychology / Saul Kassin. 1st ed. Upper Saddle River, NJ : Prentice Hall, 2003. p. cm. Includes bibliographical references and index. ISBN 0-13-048946-8 (alk. paper) DDC 150
1. Psychology - Textbooks. I. Title.
BF121 .K335 2003

Psychology / Saul Kassin. 4th ed. Upper Saddle River, NJ : Pearson/Prentice Hall, 2003. p. cm. Includes bibliographical references and index. ISBN 0-13-049641-3 DDC 150
1. Psychology. I. Title.
BF121 .K34 2003

Kastenbaum, Robert. Death, society, and human experience / Robert J. Kastenbaum. 8th ed. Boston, MA : Allyn and Bacon, 2004. p. cm. Includes bibliographical references and index. ISBN 0-205-38193-6 (pbk.) DDC 306.9
1. Death - Psychological aspects. 2. Death - Social aspects. I. Title.
BF789.D4 K36 2004

On our way : the final passage through life and death / Robert Kastenbaum. Berkeley : University of California Press, c2004. p. cm. (Life passages) Includes bibliographical references (p.   ) and index. Table of contents URL: http://www.loc.gov/catdir/toc/ecip041/2003005044.html ISBN 0-520-21880-9 DDC 306.9
1. Death - Psychological aspects. 2. Death - Social aspects. 3. Future life. I. Title. II. Series.
BF789.D4 .K365 2004

Katastrofizm konsekwentny.
Gawor, Leszek. Lublin : Wydawn. Uniwersytetu Marii Curie Skłodowskiej, 1998.
B4691.Z384 G38 1998

Kateb, George.
Mill, John Stuart, 1806-1873. On liberty. New Haven : Yale University Press, c2003.

Kater, Kathy. Real kids come in all sizes : ten essential lessons to build body esteem / Kathy Kater. New York : Broadway Books, 2004. p. cm. ISBN 0-7679-1608-5 DDC 649/.1
1. Body image in children. 2. Self-esteem in children. 3. Child rearing. I. Title.
BF723.B6 K38 2004

Kather, Regine, 1955- Gotteshauch oder künstliche Seele : der Geist im Blick verschiedener Disziplinen / Regine Kather. Stuttgart : Akademie der Diözese Rottenburg-Stuttgart, c2000. 103 p. ; 22 cm. (Kleine Hohenheimer Reihe ; Bd. 40) Includes bibliographical references. ISBN 3-926297-78-6 (pbk.)
1. Soul. I. Title. II. Series.

Was ist Leben? : philosophische Positionen und Perspektiven / Regine Kather. Darmstadt : Wissenschaftliche Buchgesellschaft, c2003. 246 p. ; 23 cm. Includes bibliographical references (p. [233]-246). ISBN 3-534-15619-6
1. Life. I. Title.

Kats, Ḥayim Avraham ben Aryeh Leyb, 18th/19th cent. Pat lehem.
Baḥya ben Joseph ibn Paḳuda, 11th cent. [Hidāyah ilá farā'iḍ al-qulūb] Torat ḥovat ha-levavot ha-mefo'ar. Nyu Yorḳ : Y. Vais : Star Ḳompozishan : [Hotsa'at Ateret], 760 [2000]

Katz, Judy H., 1950- White awareness : handbook for anti-racism training / by Judith H. Katz. 2nd ed., rev. Norman : University of Oklahoma Press, c2003. xi, 212 p. ; 23 cm. Includes bibliographical references (p. 199-208) and index. ISBN 0-8061-3560-3 (pbk. : alk. paper) DDC 305.8
1. Racism. 2. Race discrimination - Psychological aspects. 3. Caucasian race. 4. Group relations training. 5. Race awareness. 6. Racism - United States. I. Title.
HT1523 .K37 2003

Katz, Ruth, 1927- Tuning the mind : connecting aesthetics to cognitive science / Ruth Katz and Ruth HaCohen. New Brunswick, N.J. : Transaction Publishers, c2003. xiv, 317 p. : ill. ; 24 cm. Includes bibliographical references and indexes. ISBN 0-7658-0081-0 (alk. paper) DDC 781/.11
1. Music - Psychological aspects. 2. Cognition. 3. Music - Philosophy and aesthetics. I. HaCohen, Ruth. II. Title.
ML3838 .K28 2003

Katznelson, Ira. Desolation and enlightenment : political knowledge after total war, totalitarianism, and the Holocaust / Ira Katznelson. New York : Columbia University Press, c2003. xvi, 185 p. ; 24 cm. (Leonard Hastings Schoff memorial lectures) Includes bibliographical references and index. ISBN 0-231-11194-0 DDC 301/.01
1. Political science - Philosophy. 2. Human behavior - Philosophy. 3. Political psychology. 4. Political sociology. 5. World politics - 1945-1989. 6. War (Philosophy) 7. International relations - Philosophy. 8. Holocaust, Jewish (1939-1945) 9. Jews - Public opinion - History. I. Title. II. Series: University seminars/Leonard Hastings Schoff memorial lectures.
JA71 .K35 2003

Kaufman, Alan S., 1944-.
Lichtenberger, Elizabeth O. Essentials of WPPSI-III assessment. Hoboken, N.J. : John Wiley & Sons, 2003.
BF432.5.W424 L53 2003

Kaufman, Barry Neil. No regrets : last chance for a father and son / by Barry Neil Kaufman. Novato, Calif. : HJ Kramer/New World Library, 2003. xiv, 336 p. ; 24 cm. Includes bibliographical references (p. 329-334). ISBN 1-932073-02-7 (alk. paper) DDC 155.9/37/092
1. Grief. 2. Bereavement - Psychological aspects. 3. Fathers - Death - Psychological aspects. 4. Loss (Psychology) 5. Fathers and sons. 6. Kaufman, Barry Neil. I. Title.
BF575.G7 K385 2003

KAUFMAN, BARRY NEIL.
Kaufman, Barry Neil. No regrets. Novato, Calif. : HJ Kramer/New World Library, 2003.
BF575.G7 K385 2003

Kaufman, Judith S., 1955-.
From girls in the elements to women in science. New York : P. Lang, 2003.
BF378.S65 F76 2003

Kaufman, Ronald A. Anatomy of success : the ultimate system for achieving your personal and professional goals / Ronald A. Kaufman. Dubuque, Iowa : Kendall/Hunt Pub., c1999. xvi, 284 p. ; 23 cm. Includes index. ISBN 0-7872-5590-4 DDC 158.1
1. Success. 2. Self-actualization (Psychology) I. Title.

BF637.S8 .K379 1999
Kaufman, Scott M.
Kushell, Jennifer. Secrets of the young & successful. New York : Simon & Schuster, c2003.
BF637.S8 K875 2003

Kaufman, Stephen, 1946-.
Racism. Armonk, N.Y. : M.E. Sharpe, c2003.
HT1521 .R323 2003

Kaufmann, Jean-Claude. Premier matin : comment naît une histoire d'amour / Jean-Claude Kaufmann. Paris : Colin, 2002. 254 p. ; 22 cm. (Collection Individu et société) Includes bibliographical references. ISBN 2-200-26422-4 DDC 300
1. Love. I. Title. II. Series.

Kaus, Rainer J. Psychoanalyse und Sozialpsychologie : Sigmund Freud und Erich Fromm / Rainer J. Kaus ; mit einem Vorwort von Léon Wurmser. Heidelberg : C. Winter, c1999. 255 p. ; 22 cm. (Beiträge zur neueren Literaturgeschichte ; Bd. 166) Includes bibliographical references (p. 245-255) and indexes. ISBN 3-8253-0392-6
1. Freud, Sigmund, - 1856-1939. 2. Fromm, Erich, - 1900- 3. Psychoanalysis. 4. Psychology, Social. 5. Freud, Sigmund, - 1856-1939. 6. Fromm, Erich, - 1900- 7. Psychoanalysis. 8. Social psychology. I. Title. II. Series: Beiträge zur neueren Literaturgeschichte ; 3. Folge, Bd. 166.
BF109.F74 K38 1999

Kava, Alex. The soul catcher / Alex Kava. Waterville, Me. : Thorndike Press, 2003, 2002. 592 p. (large print) ; 22 cm. "Thorndike Press large print basic series"--T.p. verso. ISBN 0-7862-4925-0 DDC 813/.6
1. O'Dell, Maggie (Fictitious character) - Fiction. 2. Government investigators - Fiction. 3. Washington (D.C.) - Fiction. 4. Women detectives - Fiction. 5. Serial murders - Fiction. 6. Massachusetts - Fiction. 7. Sects - Fiction. 8. Large type books. I. Title.
PS3561.A8682 S6 2003

KAVANOT (CABALA). See **KAVVANOT (CABALA).**

KAVANOT (ḲABALAH). See **KAVVANOT (CABALA).**

Kāviyānī, Shīvā. Farzānagī dar āyinah-i zamān : dirang bar falsafah, hunar va dānish / Shīvā Kāviyānī. Tihrān : Nigāh, 2001. 174, 11 p. ; 22 cm. Added title page title: Intellection in the mirror of time. Includes bibliographical references and index. In Persian; introduction also in English. ISBN 9643510697
1. Philosophy. 2. Aesthetics. I. Title. II. Title: Intellection in the mirror of time

KAVVANAHS (CABALA). See **KAVVANOT (CABALA).**

KAVVANOT (CABALA).
Armoni, Mosheh Ḥayim. Sefer Ginze Armoni. Yerushalayim : 'Amutat "Naḥalat-Raḥel", 762 [2002]
BM670.S5 A756 2002

Kaye, Bob, pianist.
Vint/age 2001 conference : [videorecording]. New York, c2001.

Kaymak, Uzay.
Sousa, Joao M. C. Fuzzy decision making in modeling and control. Singapore ; River Edge, N.J. : World Scientific, 2002.

KAYSER, HANS, 1891-1964. LEHRBUCH DER HARMONIK.
Tokar, David A. Hans Kayser's Lehrbuch der Harmonik. 2002.

Lehrbuch der Harmonik. English. Selections. 2002.
Tokar, David A. Hans Kayser's Lehrbuch der Harmonik. 2002.

Kazaaam! splat! ploof! : the American impact on European popular culture since 1945 / edited by Sabrina P. Ramet and Gordana P. Crnkovic. Lanham, Md. ; Oxford : Rowman & Littlefield, c2003. viii, 264 p. : ill. ; 24 cm. Includes bibliographical references and indexes. ISBN 0-7425-0000-4 (hbk. : alk. paper) ISBN 0-7425-0001-2 (pbk. : alk. paper) DDC 303.48/24073
1. Europe - Civilization - American influences. 2. Ethnic attitudes - Europe. 3. Popular culture - Europe - History - 20th century. 4. National characteristics, European. 5. National characteristics, American. 6. Europe - Relations - United States - Europe. 7. Europe - Relations - United States. I. Ramet, Sabrina P., 1949- II. Crnkovic, Gordana.
D1055 .K39 2003

Kazakov, Dimitar, 1967-.
Adaptive agents and multi-agent systems. Berlin ; New York : Springer, c2003.
QA76.76.I58 A312 2003

Kazakova, I. V. (Iryna Valer'eŭna) Mifalahemy i mahiia ŭ belaruskim abradavym fal'klory / I.V. Kazakova. Minsk : "BOFF", 1997. 119 p. ; 21 cm. "Navukovae vydanne"--Colophon. Includes bibliographical references. ISBN 985430003X
1. Folklore - Belarus. 2. Rites and ceremonies - Belarus. 3. Mythology. 4. Magic - Belarus. I. Title.
GR203.4 .K39 1997

Kazakova, N. E. (Natal'ia Evgen'evna) Poliprofessionalizm deiatel'nosti vydaiushchegosia psikhologa - akmeologa K.K. Platonova / N.E. Kazakova. Shuia : Vest', 2002. 102 p. : ill. ; 21 cm. Includes bibliographical references (p. 91-101).
1. Platonov, Konstantin Konstantinovich. I. Title.
BF109.P56 K39 2002

Kazan, Lainie.
Vint/age 2001 conference : [videorecording]. New York, c2001.

KAZAN, LAINIE.
Vint/age 2001 conference : [videorecording]. New York, c2001.

Kazerounian, Nadine. Stepping up : women's guide to career development / Nadine Kazerounian. London : McGraw-Hill, c2002. xvii, 325 p. : ill. ; 23 cm. Includes bibliographical references and index. ISBN 0-07-709802-1 DDC 650.14082
1. Career development. 2. Businesswomen. 3. Women executives. 4. Success in business. I. Title.

KDD (INFORMATION RETRIEVAL). See **DATA MINING.**

Ke, Yunlu. Fu gui yu ying er : Ke Yunlu tan xian dai ren zi zai di sheng ming = Fuguiyuyinger / Ke Yunlu zhu. Di 1 ban. Shanghai : Shanghai ren min chu ban she : Xin hua shu dian Shanghai fa xing suo jing xiao, 1996. 7, 2, 2, 254 p. ; 21 cm. (Ming jia xin ji cong shu) ISBN 7-208-02225-9
1. Life. 2. Health. I. Title. II. Title: Ke Yunlu tan xian zi zai di sheng ming III. Title: Fuguiyuyinger IV. Series.
BD431 .K6134 1996 <Asian China>

Ke Yunlu tan xian dai ren zi zai di sheng ming.
Ke, Yunlu. Fu gui yu ying er. Di 1 ban. Shanghai : Shanghai ren min chu ban she : Xin hua shu dian Shanghai fa xing suo jing xiao, 1996.
BD431 .K6134 1996 <Asian China>

Kearney, Richard. Strangers, Gods, and monsters : interpreting otherness / Richard Kearney. London ; New York : Routledge, 2003. x, 294 p. : ill. ; 25 cm. Includes bibliographical references (p. 233-291) and index. ISBN 0-415-27257-2 ISBN 0-415-27258-0 (pbk.) DDC 128
1. Identity (Philosophical concept) 2. Identity (Psychology) 3. Difference (Philosophy) 4. Difference (Psychology) I. Title.
BD236 .K43 2003

Kearney, Robert E., 1947-.
Westwick, D. T. (David T.) Identification of nonlinear physiological systems. Piscataway, NJ : IEEE Press ; Hoboken, NJ : Wiley-Interscience, c2003.
QP33.6.M36 W475 2003

Keats, J. A. (John Augustus).
Cliff, Norman, 1930- Ordinal measurement in the behavioral sciences. Mahwah, N.J. : Lawrence Erlbaum Associates, 2003.
BF39 .C525 2003

Keazor, Henry.
Psychische Energien bildender Kunst. 1. Aufl. Köln : DuMont, 2002.

Kecskés, István. Situation-bound utterances in L1 and L2 / by István Kecskés. Berlin ; New York : Mouton de Gruyter, 2002. viii, 228 p. ; 24 cm. (Studies on language acquisition ; 19) Includes bibliographical references and index. CONTENTS: Introduction -- Lexical and conceptual level -- A dynamic model of meaning -- Context and salience -- The origin of situation-bound utterances -- Distinguishing features of SBUs -- Classification and interpretation of SBUs -- Creativity and formulaicity -- Conceptual socialization -- Easy to learn hard to understand -- Conclusion. ISBN 3-11-017358-1 (cloth : alk. paper) DDC 401/.41
1. Conversation analysis. 2. Context (Linguistics) 3. Second language acquisition. 4. Bilingualism. I. Title. II. Series.
P95.45 .K4 2002

Ḳedushat ha-dibur.
Sefer Ḳedushat ha-dibur. Bene Beraḳ : Yehudah Yosef Ha-levi Gruber, 761- [2001-]

Keefe, Susan A. Water and the Word : baptism and the education of the clergy in the Carolingian empire / Susan A. Keefe. Notre Dame, Ind. : University of Notre Dame Press, c2002. 2 v. ; 27 cm. (Publications in medieval studies) Includes bibliographical references and index. English and Latin. CONTENTS: v. 1. A study of texts and manuscripts -- v. 2. Editions of the texts. ISBN

0-268-01965-7 (v. 1 : alk. paper) ISBN 0-268-01969-X (v. 2 : alk. paper) DDC 274/.03
1. Church history - Middle Ages, 600-1500. 2. Baptism - History. 3. Carolingians - History. 4. Clergy - Education - History. 5. Manuscripts, Latin (Medieval and modern) I. Title. II. Series: Publications in medieval studies (Unnumbered)
BR200 .K44 2002

Keen, Thomas R. Creating effective & successful teams / Thomas R. Keen. West Lafayette, Ind. : Ichor Business Books, c2003. ix, 85 p. : ill. ; 28 cm. Includes bibliographical references (p. 75-79) and index. ISBN 1-55753-289-3 (alk. paper) DDC 658.4/02
1. Teams in the workplace. I. Title. II. Title: Creating effective and successful teams
HD66 .K396 2003

Keenan, Roger.
At-Hlan, Spirit. The voice of At-Hlan. Torquay : Pyramid Pub., c1996.

Keeney, Bradford P.
Kottler, Jeffrey A. American shaman. New York : Brunner-Routledge, 2004.
BF1598.K43 K68 2004

Kottler, Jeffrey A. American shaman. New York : Brunner-Routledge, 2004.
BF1598.K43 K68 2004

Keenoy, Tom.
Discourse and organization. London ; Thousand Oaks, Calif. : Sage Publications, 1998.
HD58.7 .D57 1998

Keeping the warfighting edge.
Leed, Maren. Santa Monica, CA : RAND, 2002.
UB413 .L386 2002

The Kegan Paul library of arcana
Leland, Charles Godfrey, 1824-1903. [Etruscan roman remains in popular tradition] Etruscan Roman remains and the old religion. London ; New York : Kegan Paul ; New York : Distributed by Columbia University Press, 2002.
DG223 .L54 2002

Kegel, Zdzisław.
Wrocławskie Sympozjum Badań Pisma (9th : 2000 : Wrocław, Poland) Contemporary problems of proof from a document. Wroclaw : University of Wroclaw, Faculty of Law, Administration, and Economy, Department of Criminalistics, 2002.
BF891 .W76 2000

Keilin, W. Gregory.
Internships in psychology. Washington, D.C. : American Psychological Association, c2004.
BF77 .I67 2004

Keita, Gwendolyn Puryear.
Job stress in a changing workforce. 1st ed. Washington, DC ; London : American Psychological Association, c1994.
HF5548.85 .J654 1994

Keitel, Merle A.
Handbook of counseling women. Thousand Oaks, Calif. ; London : Sage Publications, c2003.
RC451.4.W6 H36 2003

Keith, LeAnna.
Fekete, Sandra. Companies are people, too. Hoboken, N.J. : John Wiley & Sons, c2003.
HD58.7 .F43 2003

Kelen, Jacqueline. Le bonheur / Jacqueline Kelen. Paris : Oxus, c2003. 160 p. ; 20 cm. (Les intemporels) ISBN 2-8489-8000-1 DDC 844
1. Happiness. I. Title. II. Series.

Kelikutūhalam.
Dīkṣita, Mathurā Prasāda, 1878-1978. [Kelikutūhala. Hindi & Sanskrit] Vārāṇasī : Kṛshṇadāsa Akādamī, 2002.
HQ470.S3 D55155 2002

Keller, Heidi, 1945-.
Between culture and biology. Cambridge, U.K. ; New York : Cambridge University Press, 2002.
BF721 .B4138 2002

Keller, John Robert. Samuel Beckett and the primacy of love / John Robert Keller. Manchester : Manchester University Press, 2002. 226 p. ; 23 cm. Includes bibliographical references and index. ISBN 0-7190-6312-4 ISBN 0-7190-6313-2 (PBK.) DDC 822.912
1. Beckett, Samuel, - 1906- - Criticism and interpretation. 2. Psychoanalysis and literature. I. Title.

Keller, Joyce (Joyce E.) Seven steps to heaven : how to communicate with your departed loved ones in seven easy steps / Joyce Keller. New York : Simon & Schuster, 2003. p. cm. "A Fireside book." Includes bibliographical references. ISBN 0-7432-2560-0 (pbk.) DDC 133.9
1. Spiritualism. I. Title.
BF1261.2 .K45 2003

Keller, Otto, 1838-1920.
[Thiere des klassischen Alterthums in kulturgeschichtlicher Beziehung]
Tiere des klassischen Altertums in kulturgeschichtlicher Beziehung / Otto Keller. Hildesheim : Olms, c2001, 1887. ix, 488 p. : ill. ; 22 cm. Originally published: Thiere des klassischen Alterthums in kulturgeschichtlicher Beziehung. Innsbruck : Wagner'schen Universitäts-Buchhandlung, 1887. Includes bibliographical references and index. ISBN 3-487-09424-X (cl.) DDC 938
1. Civilization, Classical. 2. Animals. I. Title.

Kelley, Donald R., 1931- Fortunes of history : historical inquiry from Herder to Huizinga / Donald R. Kelley. New Haven : Yale University Press, c2003. xiii, 426 p. ; 25 cm. Includes bibliographical references (p. 347-410) and index. CONTENTS: Enlightened history -- History between research and reason -- Expanding horizons -- British initiatives -- German impulses -- French novelties -- German ascendancy -- French visions -- English observances -- Beyond the Canon -- American parallels -- New histories. ISBN 0-300-09578-3 (hard cover : alk. paper) DDC 901
1. History - Research. 2. History - Philosophy. 3. Historians - Europe. 4. History - Methodology. 5. Historiography. 6. Literature and history. I. Title.
D16 .K26 2003

Kellner, Herbert Anton. Musicalische Temperatur der Bachsöhne / Herbert Anton Kellner. Darmstadt : Herbert Anton Kellner, c2001. 93 p. : ill., music ; 21 cm. Includes bibliographical references. CONTENTS: Musicalische Temperatur bei Carl Philipp Emanuel Bach -- Musicalische Temperatur bei Wilhelm Friedemann und Carl Philipp Emanuel Bach. ISBN 3-00-008614-5 (pbk.)
1. Bach, Carl Philipp Emanuel, - 1714-1788 - Criticism and interpretation. 2. Bach, Wilhelm Friedemann, - 1710-1784 - Criticism and interpretation. 3. Symbolism of numbers. I. Title.

Kellogg, Ronald Thomas. The best test preparation for the Graduate Record Examination, GRE psychology / Ronald T. Kellogg, Richard Pisacreta. Piscataway, N.J. : Research and Education Association, [2000] x, 579 p. : ill. ; 26 cm. ISBN 0-87891-599-0
1. Psychology - Examinations - Study guides. 2. Graduate Record Examination - Study guides. 3. Psychology - Examinations, questions, etc. I. Pisacreta, Richard. II. Title. III. Title: GRE psychology
BF78 .K45 2000

Kelly, Brian, 1956- iSearch : psychology / Brian M. Kelly, Linda R. Barr. Boston, MA : Allyn and Bacon, c2003. v, 122 p. : ill. ; 24 cm. Spine title: iSearch psychology 2003. ISBN 0-205-37640-1 (pbk.) DDC 025.06/15
1. Psychology - Computer network resources - Directories. 2. Internet searching. 3. Computer network resources - Evaluation. 4. Citation of electronic information resources. 5. Database searching. I. Barr, Linda R. (Linda Robinson) II. Title. III. Title: Psychology IV. Title: iSearch psychology 2003
BF76.78 .K45 2003

Kelly, Dorothy, 1952 Aug. 6- Tarot card combinations / by Dorothy Kelly ; foreword by Joan Bunning. Boston, MA : York Beach, ME : Weiser Books, 2003, c1995. x, 354 p. : ill. ; 23 cm. Includes index. ISBN 1-57863-293-5 (pbk.) DDC 133.3/2424
1. Tarot. 2. Fortune-telling by cards. I. Title.
BF1879.T2 K45 2003

Kelly, Jill. Guardians of the Celtic way : the path to Arthurian fulfillment / Jill Kelly. Rochester, Vt. : Bear & Co., c2003. xv, 172 p. : ill. ; 21 cm. Includes bibliographical references. Table of contents URL: http://www.loc.gov/catdir/toc/ecip041/2003006502.html CONTENTS: My own love -- The Celtic vows -- The invisible structures of the universe: the great heart light flowing to all worlds -- The tree kingdom: wisdom keepers -- The stone people: astrologers -- The path of experience: the labyrinth, dragon slayer's path -- Animal: the warrior's way, path of justice -- Plant: the learned ones, keepers of the sacred druid groves -- Father sun, mother moon: transformation -- The mother's kingdom: peace on earth, creativity, and love -- Community and family: freedom of the spirit child -- The earth: the fairy kingdom, dragon power, creator flow -- The Arthurian promise: the fulfillment, bird -- Our wish for you. ISBN 1-59143-007-0 (pbk.) DDC 133
1. Occultism. 2. Spiritual life. 3. Celts - Religion. I. Title.
BF1411 .K45 2003

Kelly, Kevin, 1966- Life : a trip towards trust / Kevin Kelly. Ballintubber, Co. Roscommon : Inspiring Irish Publications, 2002. 184 p., [8] p. of plates : ill. ; 22 cm. ISBN 0-9541868-1-8
1. Kelly, Kevin, - 1966- 2. Spiritual life. I. Title.

KELLY, KEVIN, 1966-.
Kelly, Kevin, 1966- Life. Ballintubber, Co. Roscommon : Inspiring Irish Publications, 2002.

Kemal, Salim. The philosophical poetics of Alfarabi, Avicenna and Averroes : the Aristotelian reception / Salim Kemal. London ; New York : RoutledgeCurzon, 2003. vi, 362 p. ; 24 cm. Includes bibliographical references and index. ISBN 0-7007-1348-4 DDC 180
1. Avicenna, - 980-1037. 2. Averroës, - 1126-1198. 3. Aristotle. - Poetics. 4. Fārābī. 5. Aesthetics. I. Title. II. Series: Culture and civilisation in the Middle East.

Kemerovskiĭ gosudarstvennyĭ universitet.
Sibirskai͡a psikhologii͡a segodni͡a. Kemerovo : Kemerovskiĭ gos. universitet, 2002.
BF20 .S53 2002

Kemp, Richard.
Brace, Nicola. SPSS for psychologists. 2nd ed. Mahwah, NJ : Lawrence Erlbaum Associates, 2003.
BF39 .K447 2003

Kemper, Hans-Georg.
Hermetik. Tübingen : M. Niemeyer Verlag, c2002.
BF1586 .H47 2002

Ken Wilber.
Visser, Frank, 1958- [Ken Wilber. English] Albany, NY : State University of New York Press, c2003.
BF109.W54 V5713 2003

Kendra, James M. Elements of community resilience in the World Trade Center attack / James M. Kendra, Tricia Wachtendorf. [Newark, Del.?] : Disaster Research Center, University of Delaware, 2001. 22 leaves ; 29 cm. (Preliminary paper / University of Delaware Disaster Research Center ; #318) "November, 2001." "Presented at the 48th North American Meeting of the Regional Science Association International, November 15-17, 2001, Charleston, S.C."--P. 1. Includes bibliographical references (p. 21-22).
1. New York (N.Y.). - Emergency Operation Center. 2. September 11 Terrorist Attacks, 2001. 3. Emergency management - New York (State) - New York. 4. Disaster relief - New York (State) - New York. 5. Organizational behavior. I. Wachtendorf, Tricia. II. Title. III. Series: Preliminary paper (University of Delaware. Disaster Research Center) ; no. 318.

Kenneally, James J. (James Joseph), 1929- A compassionate conservative : a political biography of Joseph W. Martin, Jr., speaker of the U.S. House of Representatives / James J. Kenneally. Lanham, Md. : Lexington Books, c2003. xiii, 335 p. ; 24 cm. Includes bibliographical references (p. 311-324) and index. ISBN 0-7391-0676-7 (alk. paper) DDC 328.73/092
1. Martin, Joseph W. - (Joseph William), - 1884-1968. 2. United States. - Congress. - House - Speakers - Biography. 3. Legislators - United States - Biography. 4. Conservatism - United States - History - 20th century. 5. United States - Politics and government - 20th century. I. Title.
E748.M375 K46 2003

Kennedy, Bill, 1951-.
Musciano, Chuck. HTML and XHTML, the definitive guide. 5th ed. Beijing ; Sebastopol [Calif.] : O'Reilly, 2002.

Kennedy, Kevin (Kevin John), 1955- Going the distance : why some companies dominate and others fail / Kevin Kennedy, Mary Moore. Upper Saddle River, NJ : Prentice Hall/Financial Times, c2003. xxxii, 253 p. : ill. ; 24 cm. (Financial Times Prentice Hall books) Includes index. ISBN 0-13-046120-2 DDC 658.4
1. Leadership. 2. Technological innovations - Management. 3. Organizational change. 4. Organizational learning. 5. Organizational effectiveness. 6. Strategic planning. 7. Industrial management. I. Moore, Mary, 1947- II. Title. III. Series.
HD57.7 .K465 2003

Kennedy, Michelle. Crying / Michelle Kennedy. Hauppauge, N.Y. : Barron's, c2003. 128 p. : ill. ; 18 cm. (Last straw strategies) "99 tips to bring you back from the end of your rope." Includes bibliographical references (p. 126) and index. ISBN 0-7641-2438-2 (pbk.) DDC 649/.122
1. Crying in infants. 2. Crying in children. 3. Child rearing. I. Title. II. Series: Kennedy, Michelle. Last straw strategies.
BF720.C78 .K46 2003

Last straw strategies.
Kennedy, Michelle. Crying. Hauppauge, N.Y. : Barron's, c2003.
BF720.C78 .K46 2003

Kennedy, Michelle. Sleeping. Hauppauge, N.Y. : Barron's, c2003.
BF723.S45 .K46 2003

Kennedy, Michelle. Tantrums. Hauppauge, N.Y. : Barron's, c2003.

Kennedy, Michelle.
BF723.A4 .K46 2003
Sleeping / Michelle Kennedy. Hauppauge, N.Y. : Barron's, c2003. 128 p. : ill. ; 18 cm. (Last straw strategies) "99 tips to bring you back from the end of your rope." Includes bibliographical references (p. 126) and index. ISBN 0-7641-2440-4 (pbk.) DDC 649/.122
1. Children - Sleep. 2. Child rearing. I. Title. II. Series: Kennedy, Michelle. Last straw strategies.
BF723.S45 .K46 2003

Tantrums / Michelle Kennedy. Hauppauge, N.Y. : Barron's, c2003. 128 p. : ill. ; 18 cm. (Last straw strategies) "99 tips to bring you back from the end of your rope." Includes bibliographical references (p. 126) and index. ISBN 0-7641-2441-2 (pbk.)
1. Temper tantrums in children. 2. Anger in children. 3. Child rearing. I. Title. II. Series: Kennedy, Michelle. Last straw strategies.
BF723.A4 .K46 2003

Kennerley, Mike.
Neely, A. D. (Andy D.) The performance prism. London ; New York : Financial Times/Prentice Hall, 2002.
HF5549.5.P35 N44 2002

Kenrick, Douglas T.
Readings in evolutionary psychology. Boston : Pearson/Allyn and Bacon, c2004.
BF698.95 .R43 2004

Kent, James H., 1939- Past life memories as a Confederate soldier / by James H. Kent. Huntsville, AR : Ozark Mountain Publishers, c2003. 181, [1] p. : ill., maps ; 22 cm. Includes bibliographical references (p. [182]). ISBN 1-88694-084-3
1. Hypnotic age regression - Case studies. 2. Reincarnation - Case studies. 3. United States - History - Civil War, 1861-1865 - Miscellanea. I. Title.
BF1156.R45 K45 2003

KENTENICH, JOSEPH.
Schlosser, Herta. Der Mensch als Wesen der Freiheit. Vallendar-Schönstatt : Patris Verlag, 2002.

KENTUCKY - GENEALOGY.
Skidmore, Warren. Lord Dunmore's little war of 1774. Bowie, Md. : Heritage Books, 2002.

KENTUCKY - HISTORY - TO 1792.
Skidmore, Warren. Lord Dunmore's little war of 1774. Bowie, Md. : Heritage Books, 2002.

Keppe, Norberto R.
[Origem Das Enfermidades. English]
The origin of illness : psychological, physical and social / Norberto R. Keppe ; translated by Susan Berkley and Margaret Pinckard Kowarick. 1st American ed. Englewood Cliffs, N.J. : Campbell Hall Press, 2002. xii, 162 p. : ill. ; 23 cm. Originally published in Brazil in 2000 by Proton Editora Ltda. under the title 'A Origem Das Enfermidades'. ISBN 0-9664302-2-0 DDC 616.89
1. Mental illness - Popular works. 2. Mental illness - Etiology. 3. Mentally ill - Attitudes. 4. Sick - Psychology. 5. Envy. I. Title.
RC460 .K4713 2002

[Keralapraśnasaṅgraha. Hindi & Sanskrit.]
Keralapraśnasaṅgrahaḥ / Keralaṛṣipravartitaḥ ; saṅgrāhakaḥ vyākhyākāraśca Saccidānandamiśraḥ ; Hindīrūpāntaraṇakāraḥ Śivākāntamiśraḥ. 1. saṃskaraṇa. Purī : Paramānandaprakāśanam, 1999. [16], 140 p. ; 21 cm. SUMMARY: Ancient treatise on Hindu astrology. Sanskrit and Hindi.
1. Hindu astrology. I. Mishra, Satchidananda, 1947- II. Title.
BF1714.H5+

Keralapraśnasaṅgrahaḥ.
[Keralapraśnasaṅgraha. Hindi & Sanskrit.] 1. saṃskaraṇa. Purī : Paramānandaprakāśanam, 1999.
BF1714.H5+

Kerem Shelomoh.
Eliyahu, Saliman. Sefer Kerem Shelomoh. Yerushala[y]im : Ḥevrat Ahavat shalom, 762 [2001 or 2002]

KERNEL FUNCTIONS - CONGRESSES.
Conference on Computational Learning Theory (16th : 2003 : Washington, D.C.) Learning theory and Kernel machines. Berlin ; New York : Springer, c2003.
Q325.5 .C654 2003

Ḳerovim u-reḥoḳim.
Meyuhas Ginio, Alisa, 1937- Tel Aviv : Mif'alim Universiṭayim, 760 [1999]

Kessidi, F. Kh. Filosofskie i ėticheskie problemy genetiki cheloveka : analiz diskussiĭ / F.Kh. Kessidi. Moskva : Martis, 1994. 107 p. 22 cm. Includes bibliographical references.
1. Nature and nurture. 2. Sociobiology. 3. Physical anthropology - Philosophy. 4. Ethnology - Philosophy. I. Title.
BF341 .K45 1994

Kessler, Klaus. Raumkognition und Lokalisationsäusserungen : ein konnektionistisches Modell des Verstehens von Richtungspräpositionen / Klaus Kessler ; mit einem Geleitwort von Theo Herrmann und Gert Rickheit. Wiesbaden : Deutscher Universitäts-Verlag, 2000. xvi, 233 p. : ill. ; 21 cm. (Studien zur Kognitionswissenschaft) Originally presented as the author's thesis (doctoral)--Universität, Mannheim, 1998. Includes bibliographical references (p. [213]-226). ISBN 3-8244-4388-0 (pbk.) DDC 153.7/52
1. Space perception. 2. Psycholinguistics. 3. Grammar, Comparative and general - Prepositions. I. Title. II. Series.
BF469 .K47 2000

Kessler, Ronald C.
How healthy are we? Chicago, Ill. : University of Chicago Press, c2003.
BF724.6 .H69 2003

Keszeg, Vilmos. Jóslások a mezőségen : etnomantikai elemzés / Keszeg Vilmos. Sepsiszentgyörgy : BON AMI, 1997. 151 p. : ill. ; 20 cm. Summary in English and Romanian. Includes bibliographical references (p. 135-139). ISBN 9739807216
1. Fortune-telling - Romania - Transylvania. 2. Prophecy. I. Title. II. Title: Prezicerile în Câmpia Transylvaniei
BF1868.H8 K47 1997

Ketavim.
Korczak, Janusz, 1878-1942. [Works. Hebrew. 1996] [Tel Aviv] : Yad va-shem : ha-Agudah 'a. sh. Yanush Ḳorts'aḳ be-Yiśra'el : Bet Loḥame ha-geṭa'ot 'a. sh. Yitsḥaḳ Ḳatsenelson : ha-Ḳibuts ha-me'uḥad, [1996-
LB775.K627 K48 1996 <Hebr>

Kettner, Matthias, 1955-.
Indexikalität und sprachlicher Weltbezug. Paderborn : Mentis, c2002.

Keuss, Jeffrey F., 1965-.
The sacred and the profane. Aldershot, Hants, England ; Burlington, VT : Ashgate, c2003.
BD241 .S312 2003

Kevod ha-Torah.
Ḳunṭres Kevod ha-Torah. Bene Beraḳ : ha-Meḥaber, 761 [2000 or 2001]

Key concepts in psychoanalysis.
Frosh, Stephen. London : British Library, 2002.
BF173 .F898 2002

Frosh, Stephen. New York : New York University Press, 2003.
BF173 .F898 2003

Key concepts (Polity Press)
Fenton, Steve, 1942- Ethnicity. Cambridge : Polity ; Oxford ; Malden, MA : Blackwell, c2003.
GN495.6 .F46 2003

Key contemporary thinkers
Rojek, Chris. Stuart Hall. Cambridge, UK : Polity in association with Blackwell, 2003.
HM621 .R64 2003

Key contemporary thinkers (Cambridge, England)
Gibson, Nigel C. Fanon. Cambridge, U.K. : Polity Press in association with Blackwell Pub. ; Malden, MA : Distributed in the USA by Blackwell Pub., 2003.
CT2628.F35 G53 2003

Key figures in counselling and psychotherapy
Jacobs, Michael, 1941-. Sigmund Freud. 2nd ed. London ; Thousand Oaks, Calif. : SAGE Publications, 2003.
BF109.F74 J33 2003

Key readings in cognition
Cognitive psychology. New York : Psychology Press, 2003.
BF201 .C642 2003

Key sociologists (Routledge (Firm))
Bocock, Robert. Sigmund Freud. Rev. ed. London ; New York : Routledge, 2002.
BF173.F85 B63 2002

Keyes, Ralph.
Farson, Richard Evans, 1926- Whoever makes the most mistakes wins. New York ; London : Free Press, c2002.
HD45 .F357 2002

KEYNES, JOHN MAYNARD, 1883-1946.
Beyond Keynes. Cheltenham ; Northampton, Mass. : Edward Elgar, c2002.

Keynes, uncertainty and the global economy.
Beyond Keynes. Cheltenham ; Northampton, Mass. : Edward Elgar, c2002.

KEYNESIAN ECONOMICS.
Beyond Keynes. Cheltenham ; Northampton, Mass. : Edward Elgar, c2002.

The philosophy of Keynes' economics. London ; New York : Routledge, 2003.
HB99.7 .P45 2003

Keys to personal success.
Lowry, Don. Riverside, Calif. : True Colors, Inc. ; c2001.
BF637.S8 .L77 2001

Khachaturi̇͡an, V. M. (Valeri̇͡a Marlenovna).
Ionov, I. N. (Igor' Nikolaevich) Teorii̇͡a tsivilizatsiĭ. Sankt-Peterburg : Alete͡ĭ͡a, 2002.
CB19 .I656 2002

Khademian, Anne M., 1961- Working with culture : how the job gets done in public programs / Anne M. Khademian. Washington, D.C. : CQ Press, c2002. xii, 148 p. ; 23 cm. (Public affairs and policy administration series) Includes bibliographical references (p. [329]-342) and index. CONTENTS: Working with culture -- Culture as a management tool -- A cultural roots framework -- Extending the cultural roots model -- Detecting cultural commitments : an exercise -- Getting the job done with culture : lessons. ISBN 1-56802-687-0 (pbk. : alk. paper) DDC 351
1. Public administration. 2. Corporate culture. 3. Performance. I. Title. II. Series.
JF1351 .K487 2002

Khadiratna, Dayanidhi. Br̥hat śilpaśāstra, bā, Gr̥habandha bijñāna ; Gr̥habandha gaṇanā o śubhastambhāropaṇa bicāra / Dayānidhi Khadiratna. Kaṭaka : Dharmagrantha Shṭora, [1995?] 5, 179 p. : ill. ; 19 cm. SUMMARY: Comprehensive work on domestic architecture; considerations from Hindu astrology and mensuration. Oriya and Sanskrit (Sanskrit in Oriya script).
1. Dwellings - India - History. 2. Architecture, Hindu. 3. Architecture and cosmology. 4. Mensuration. 5. Architecture, Domestic - India - Designs and plans. I. Title. II. Title: Gr̥habandha gaṇanā o śubhastambhāropaṇa bicāra. III. Title: Br̥hat śilpaśāstra IV. Title: Gr̥habandha bijñāna V. Title: Śilpaśāstra
TH4809.I4 K48 1995

Khalsa, Mahan.
Marcum, Dave. BusinessThink. New York : Wiley, c2002.
HF5386 .M3087 2002

Khan'' Kyo', Cha rā Ū". Gambhīra vedanta 'a cī 'a maṃ myā" / Cha rā Ū" Khan'' Kyo'. Ran' kun' : Yuṃ kraññ' khyak' Cā pe : Chak' svay' ran', Ū" Khan'' Kyo' Cā pe, 2002. 235 p. : ill. ; 21 cm. In Burmese. Cover title. SUMMARY: On occultism as practiced in Burmese; articles.
1. Occultism - Burma. I. Title.
BF1434.B93 K43 2002

Khandekar, Renuka N.
The Book of prayer. New Delhi ; New York, USA : Viking, 2001.
BL560 .B625 2001

Khanna, Ranjana, 1966- Dark continents : psychoanalysis and colonialism / Ranjana Khanna. Durham, NC : Duke University Press, 2003. xiv, 310 p. ; 25 cm. (Post-contemporary interventions) Includes bibliographical references (p. [275]-301) and index. CONTENTS: Genealogies -- Psychoanalysis and archaeology -- Freud in the sacred grove -- Colonial rescriptings -- War, decolonization, psychoanalysis -- Colonial melancholy -- Haunting and the future -- The ethical ambiguities of transnational feminism -- Hamlet in the colonial archive. ISBN 0-8223-3055-5 (cloth : alk. paper) ISBN 0-8223-3067-9 (pbk. : alk. paper) DDC 150.19/5
1. Social sciences and psychoanalysis. 2. Imperialism - Psychological aspects. I. Title. II. Series.
BF175.4.S65 K43 2003

Kharkhordin, Oleg, 1964- Oblichat' i litsemerit' : genealogii̇͡a rossiĭskoĭ lichnosti / Oleg Kharkhordin. Sankt-Peterburg : Evropeĭskiĭ universitet v Sankt-Peterburge ; Moskva : Letniĭ Sad, 2002. 507 p. : ill. ; 21 cm. (Trudy fakul'teta politicheskikh nauk i sotsiologii ; vyp. 5) "Nauchnoe izdanie"--Colophon. At head of title: Evropeĭskiĭ universitet v Sankt-Peterburge, Fakul'tet politicheskikh nauk i sotsiologii. ISBN 5943810773 (Letniĭ sad) ISBN 5943800174 (Evropeĭskiĭ universitet v Sabkt-Peterburge)
1. Foucault, Michel - Contributions in social sciences. 2. National characteristics, Russian. I. Evropeĭskiĭ universitet v Sankt-Peterburge. Fakul'tet politicheskikh nauk i sotsiologii. II. Title. III. Series: Trudy fakul'teta politicheskikh nauk i sotsiologii (Evropeĭskiĭ universitet v Sankt-Peterburge) ; vyp. 5.

B2430.F724 K43 2002

Khasnabish, Ashmita, 1959- Jouissance as ānanda : Indian philosophy, feminist theory, and literature / Ashmita Khasnabish. Lanham, Md. : Lexington Books, c2003. 239 p. ; 24 cm. Includes bibliographical references (p. [229]-234) and index. ISBN 0-7391-0467-5 (cloth : alk. paper) DDC 150.19/5
1. Psychoanalysis. I. Title.
BF173 .K427 2003

Khatri, Srishar K.
South Asia, 2010. Delhi : Konark Publishers, 2002.

KHLYSTY.
Rozanov, V. V. (Vasiliĭ Vasil'evich), 1856-1919. Vozrozhdaiushchiĭsia Egipet. Moskva : Izd-vo "Respublika", 2002.

Khrestomatiia po psikhologii khudozhestvennogo tvorchestva / [redaktor-sostavitel' A.L. Groĭsman]. Izd., 2. Moskva : Izd-vo Magistr, 1998. 199, [1] p. ; 20 cm. Includes bibliographical references (p. 198-[200]).
1. Creative ability. 2. Creation (Literary, artistic, etc.) I. Groĭsman, A. L. (Alekseĭ L'vovich)
BF408 .K476 1998

Khri-bsam-gtan.
Bod Rgya rtsom rig gśib bsdur gyi dpyad brjod. Par theṅs 1. Pe-cin : Mi rigs dpe skrun khaṅ, 2001.
PL3705 (P-PZ22)+

Khristoforova, O. B. (Ol'ga Borisovna).
Sny i videniia v narodnoĭ kul'ture. Moskva : RGGU, 2002.
BF1078 .S563 2002

Khrolenko, A. T. Lingvokul'turovedenie / A.T. Khrolenko. Kursk : Izd-vo GUIPP "Kursk", 2000. 167 p. ; 20 cm. Includes bibliographical references (p. 161-167). ISBN 5885620970
1. Anthropological linguistics. 2. Language and culture. I. Title.
P35 .K524 2000

Khurmetbek, Khalikiĭn. Ül bichigdmelüüd / Khalikiĭn Khurmetbek ; redaktor, Niamaagiĭn Galiimaa. Ulaanbaatar : "Monsudar" Khėvlėliĭn Gazar, 2001. 147 p. : ill. ; 24 cm. (2001 ony shildėg nom) Cover title: Bichigdmėlüüd. "Tanin mėdėkhüĭn nomyg tusgaĭlan khėn nėgėnd bus erdiĭn khün bükhėnd zoriulav." Essays. In Mongolian (Cyrillic script). CONTENTS: 1. bülėg. Khėmzhilzüĭ -- 2. bülėg. Angilalzüĭ -- 3. bülėg. Sėtgėlzüĭ -- 4. bülėg. Protsess sistem. ISBN 9992900482
1. Metrology. 2. Classification. 3. Psychology. 4. Computers. I. Galiimaa, Niamaagiĭn. II. Title. III. Title: Bichigdmėlüüd IV. Series.
QA465 .K48 2001

Khushwant Singh, 1915- Khushwant Singh on women, love & lust / compiled by N. Krishnamurthy. New Delhi : Books Today, c2002. 206 p. ; 21 cm. ISBN 81-87478-40-3 (cover)
1. Women - India - Sexual behavior. 2. Love. 3. Lust. I. Krishnamurthy, N. (Natarajan), 1948- II. Title. III. Title: Women, love & lust
HQ29 .K48 2002

Khushwant Singh on women, love & lust.
Khushwant Singh, 1915- New Delhi : Books Today, c2002.
HQ29 .K48 2002

Khzardzhian, S. M. (Sanatruk M.) Bioprogrammy v prirode i politike : osnovnye printsipy upravleniia iavleniiami prirody i obshchestva / S.M. Khzardzhian. Pushchino : ONTI PNTS RAN, 1996. 84 p. ; 21 cm. ISBN 5201142893
1. Human behavior. 2. Motivation (Psychology) I. Title.
BF199 .K43 1996

Kibō no genri.
Takahashi, Keiko, 1956- Tōkyō : Sanpō Shuppan, 1997.
BD216 .T35 1997

Kibud ye-hidur.
Adler, Yitshak Eliyahu, ha-Kohen. Sefer Kibud ye-hidur. Ofaḳim : Y.E. ha-Kohen Adler, 754 [1994]

Kick, Hermes A. (Hermes Andreas).
Ekel. 1. Aufl. Hürtgenwald : G. Pressler, c2003.
BF575.A886 E34 2003

Kids talking.
Meyer, John, 1964- Lanham, MD : Rowman & Littlefield, c2003.
BF723.C57 M49 2003

Kiefer, Anselm, 1945- Merkaba / Anselm Kiefer ; [catalogue editor, Ealan Wingate]. New York : Gagosian Gallery, c2002. 120 p. : chiefly col. ill. ; 32 cm. Published on the occasion of the exhibition: Anselm Kiefer, Merkaba held November 8-December 14, 2002 at Gagosian Gallery, New York. ISBN 1-88015-483-8 DDC 709/.2
1. Kiefer, Anselm, - 1945- - Exhibitions. 2. Photography, Artistic. 3. Cabala. I. Wingate, Ealan. II. Gagosian Gallery. III. Title. IV. Title: Anselm Kiefer, Merkaba
N6888.K43 A4 2002

KIEFER, ANSELM, 1945- - EXHIBITIONS.
Kiefer, Anselm, 1945- Merkaba. New York : Gagosian Gallery, c2002.
N6888.K43 A4 2002

Kiel, Achim.
Bonewitz, Ra. Wisdom of the Maya. 1st St. Martin's ed. New York : St. Martin's Press, 2000.
BF1878 .B66 2000

Kiel, David.
Eckblad, John. If your life were a business, would you invest in it? New York : McGraw-Hill, c2003.
BF637.S4 E38 2003

Kieran, Matthew, 1968-.
Imagination, philosophy, and the arts. London ; New York : Routledge, 2003.
BH301.I53 I53 2003

KIERKEGAARD, SøREN, 1813-1855.
Farago, France. Sören Kierkegaard. 1. éd. Paris : Houdiard, c2002.

Kiesewetter, Hubert, 1939- Irreale oder reale Geschichte? : ein Traktat über Methodenfragen der Geschichtswissenschaft / Hubert Kiesewetter. Herbolzheim : Centaurus, 2002. 202 p. ; 21 cm. (Reihe Geschichtswissenschaft, 0177-2767 ; Bd. 50) Includes bibliographical references and index. ISBN 3-8255-0378-X (pbk.)
1. Historiography. 2. History - Methodology. I. Title. II. Series.

Kilani-Schoch, Marianne, 1953-.
Development of verb inflection in first language acquisition. Berlin ; New York : Mouton de Gruyter, 2003.
P118 .D465 2003

Kilduff, Martin. Social networks and organizations / Martin Kilduff and Wenpin Tsai. London : SAGE, 2003. 172 p. : ill. ; 25 cm. ISBN 0-7619-6956-X ISBN 0-7619-6957-8 (pbk)
1. Organizational behavior. 2. Social networks. I. Tsai, Wenpin. II. Title.

Kim, Jaegwon.
Epistemology. Malden, Mass. : Blackwell Publishers, 2000.
BD161 .E615 2000

Kim, T'ae-ch'ang.
The generative society. 1st ed. Washington, DC : American Psychological Association, c2003.
BF724.5 .G45 2003

Kimball, Cheryl. Horse wise : thinking outside the stall and other lessons I learned from my horse / Cheryl Kimball. Boston, MA : Conari Press, 2004. p. cm. CONTENTS: Open-minded doesn't mean "sucker for anything" -- Anger and a half-ton horse -- Create the life you want -- Sometimes the walk is faster than the trot -- The honor of being the herd leader -- The importance of having a source of peace -- Equine tutorials -- Learn about how you learn -- A routine isn't a rut -- Teach respect for all living things -- Maintain a sense of humor -- You can lead a horse to water but you don't need a lot of gimmicks to make him drink -- Making life sweeter -- Learning to think "outside the stall" -- Tuning in to your inner horse -- Accept your limitations, but expand your limits -- Give yourself your best time of day -- Transform resistance with persistence -- Be willing to do the adjusting -- Shake yourself up once in a while -- Avoid gossip -- Some people just won't think like you do -- Be sure you want what you ask for -- Be humble. ISBN 1-57324-866-5 (alk. paper) DDC 158.1
1. Conduct of life. 2. Horses - Psychology - Miscellanea. I. Title.
BF637.C5 K55 2004

Kimle, Patricia Anne.
Fiore, Ann Marie. Understanding aesthetics for the merchandising and design professional. New York : Fairchild, c1997.

Kimmel, Michael S. The gendered society / Michael S. Kimmel. 2nd ed. New York : Oxford University Press, 2004. viii, 344 p. : ill. ; 24 cm. Includes bibliographical references (p. 295-333) and index. ISBN 0-19-514975-0 (alk. paper) DDC 305.3
1. Sex role. 2. Sex differences (Psychology) 3. Gender identity. 4. Sex discrimination. 5. Equality. I. Title.
HQ1075 .K547 2004

Kimmerle, Gerd, 1947-.
Zeichen des Todes in der psychoanalytischen Erfahrung. Tübingen : Edition Diskord, c2000.

Kincheloe, Joe L.
Multiple intelligences reconsidered. New York, NY : P. Lang, c2004.
BF432.3 .M86 2004

KINDER- UND HAUSMÄRCHEN.
Bosco Coletsos, Sandra. La struttura parentale nelle fiabe dei fratelli Grimm. Alessandria : Edizioni dell'Orso, 2001.

KINDNESS.
Danzig, Robert J., 1932- Every child deserves a champion. Washington, DC : Child & Family Press, c2003.
BF637.E53 D36 2003

KINESICS. See **BODY LANGUAGE.**

KINESIOLOGY. See **MOVEMENT EDUCATION.**

Kineticvideo.com (Firm).
Big Dance [videorecording]. Buffalo, N.Y. : Kineticvideo.com, c1998.

King Arthur and the goddess of the land.
Matthews, Caitlin, 1952- 2nd ed. Rochester, Vt. : Inner Traditions, 2002.
PB2273.M33 M36 2002

King, Joan C. Cellular wisdom : decoding the body's secret language / Joan C. King. Berkeley : Celestial Arts, 2003. p. cm. Includes bibliographical references and index. Table of contents URL: http://www.loc.gov/catdir/toc/ecip047/2003016394.html CONTENTS: Live from the inside out -- Turn on and turn off -- Shape life moment-by-moment -- Actualize life's potentials -- Tap into renewal -- Claim abundance -- Reach out to others -- Discovering core values -- Witness amplification -- Giving and responding to feedback -- Providing and accepting support -- Protecting the vulnerable -- The richness of diversity -- Accessing genius. ISBN 1-58761-188-0 DDC 158
1. Self-actualization (Psychology) 2. Physiology - Miscellanea. I. Title.
BF637.S4 K548 2003

King, John L. Concentration and technology in agricultural input industries [electronic resource] / John L. King. [Washington, D.C.] : U.S. Dept of Agriculture, [2001]. (Agriculture information bulletin ; no. 763) at head of title: Electronic report from the Economic Research Service. Title from title screen (viewed on Aug. 11, 2003). "March 2001." System requirements: Adobe Acrobat Reader. Mode of access: Internet via the USDA web site. Address as of 08/11/03: http://www.ers.usda.gov/publications/aib763/aib763.pdf; current access is available via PURL. Also available in paper. URL: http://purl.access.gpo.gov/GPO/LPS34611 Available in other form: King, John L. Concentration and technology in agricultural input industries 13 p. (OCoLC)47646892.
1. Agricultural biotechnology - Research. 2. Biotechnology industries. 3. Industrial concentration. 4. Intellectual property. I. United States. Dept. of Agriculture. Economic Research Service. II. Title. III. Title: Electronic report from the Economic Research Service IV. Title: King, John L. Concentration and technology in agricultural input industries 13 p. V. Series.

King, John L. Concentration and technology in agricultural input industries 13 p.
King, John L. Concentration and technology in agricultural input industries [electronic resource]. [Washington, D.C.] : U.S. Dept of Agriculture, [2001].

King, Richard Andrew. The king's book of numerology / Richard Andrew King. Aptos, Calif. : New Brighton Books, 2003- p. cm. PARTIAL CONTENTS: v. 1. Foundations & fundamentals. ISBN 0-9718377-3-2 DDC 133.3/35
1. Numerology. 2. Symbolism of numbers. I. Title. II. Title: Book of numerology
BF1729.N85 K56 2003

King, Ursula. Mysticism and contemporary society : some Teilhardian reflections / Ursula King. [Lewisburg, Pa.] : American Teilhard Association, c2002. 20 p. ; 22 cm. (Teilhard studies ; no. 44) Reprinted from Contemporary Spiritualities, C. & J. Erricker, eds. (New York : Continuum, 2001). Includes bibliographical references. ISBN 0-89012-086-2
1. Teilhard de Chardin, Pierre - Contributions in spirituality. 2. Mysticism - History - 20th century. 3. Spirituality. 4. Religion and sociology. I. Title. II. Series.
B2430.T374 A18 no.44

King, Vera. Die Entstehung des Neuen in der Adoleszenz : Individuation, Generativität und Geschlecht in modernisierten Gesellschaften / Vera King. Opladen : Leske + Budrich, c2002. 285 p. ; 21 cm. Includes bibliographical references (p. 261-285). ISBN 3-8100-3562-9 (pbk.)
1. Adolescence. 2. Adolescent psychology. I. Title.

Kingdon, Jonathan. Lowly origin : where, when, and why our ancestors first stood up / Jonathan Kingdon. Princeton : Princeton University Press, c2003. xx, 396 p. : ill., maps ; 25 cm. Includes bibliographical references and index. Publisher description URL: http://www.loc.gov/catdir/desc ription/prin031/2002072852.html ISBN 0-691-05086-4 (cl : alk. paper) DDC 599.93/8
1. Fossil hominids. 2. Bipedalism - Origin. 3. Human beings - Origin. 4. Human evolution. I. Title.
GN282 .K54 2003

KINGS AND RULERS. *See* **QUEENS.**

KINGS AND RULERS IN LITERATURE.
Malory, Thomas, Sir, 15th cent. [Morte d'Arthur] Le morte Darthur, or, The hoole book of Kyng Arthur and of his noble knyghtes of the Rounde Table. 1st ed. New York ; London : Norton, c2004.
PR2041 .M37 2004

Matthews, Caitlin, 1952- King Arthur and the goddess of the land. 2nd ed. Rochester, Vt. : Inner Traditions, 2002.
PB2273.M33 M36 2002

Wickham-Crowley, Kelley M. Writing the future. Cardiff : University of Wales Press, 2002.

The king's book of numerology.
King, Richard Andrew. Aptos, Calif. : New Brighton Books, 2003-
BF1729.N85 K56 2003

Kingston, Maxine Hong. The fifth book of peace / Maxine Hong Kingston. 1st ed. New York : Alfred A. Knopf, 2003. 401 p. ; 24 cm. ISBN 0-679-44075-5
1. Kingston, Maxine Hong. 2. Vietnamese Conflict, 1961-1975 - Veterans - Interviews. 3. Authors, American - 20th century - Biography. 4. Draft resisters - Fiction. 5. Hawaii - Fiction. 6. Peace. I. Title.
PS3561.I52 F44 2003

KINGSTON, MAXINE HONG.
Kingston, Maxine Hong. The fifth book of peace. 1st ed. New York : Alfred A. Knopf, 2003.
PS3561.I52 F44 2003

Kingwell, Mark, 1963- Practical judgments : essays in culture, politics, and interpretation / Mark Kingwell. Toronto : University of Toronto Press, c2002. xii, 344 p. ; 23 cm. Includes bibliographical references and index. ISBN 0-8020-3675-9 (bound) DDC 081
1. Philosophy. I. Title.

Kinley, Gary J.
Brashears, Deya. Challenging biases-- facing our fears. Dubuque, Iowa : Kendall/Hunt Pub., c1999.
BF575.P9 B735 1999

Kinoetics.
Linson, William. [United States] : Kinoetics Publishing, c2002.
BF637.N66 L56 2002

The Kinsey Institute series
(v. 7) Sexual development in childhood. Bloomington : Indiana University Press, 2003.
BF723.S4 S47 2003

KINSHIP. *See* **FAMILY; MATRILINEAL KINSHIP; PATRILINEAL KINSHIP.**

Kintzler, Catherine.
Peinture et musique. Villeneuve-d'Ascq : Presses universitaires du Septentrion, c2002.

Kipfer, Barbara Ann. Instant karma : 8,879 ways to give yourself and others good fortune right now / Barbara Ann Kipfer. New York : Workman Pub., c2003. 594 p. ; 11 cm. ISBN 0-7611-2804-2 (alk. paper) DDC 291.4/4
1. Conduct of life. I. Title.
BF637.C5 K56 2003

Kiraly, Donald C., 1953- Pathways to translation : pedagogy and process / Donald C.Kiraly. Kent, Ohio : Kent State University Press, c1995. xv, 175 p. : ill. ; 24 cm. (Translation studies ; 3) Includes bibliographical references (p. 164-170) and index. ISBN 0-87338-516-0 (alk. paper) DDC 418/.02/07
1. Translating and interpreting - Study and teaching. 2. Language and languages - Study and teaching. 3. Psycholinguistics. I. Title. II. Series.
P306.5 .K57 1995

Kirasic, K. C. Midlife in context / K.C. Kirasic. Boston : McGraw-Hill, c2004. xix, 219 p. ; 24 cm. (McGraw-Hill series in developmental psychology) Includes bibliographical references (p. 193-209) and indexes. Table of contents URL: http://www.loc.gov/catdir/toc/mh031/2003048842.html ISBN 0-07-245839-9 (alk. paper) DDC 305.244
1. Middle age - Psychological aspects. 2. Middle aged persons - Psychology. 3. Aging - Psychological aspects. 4. Middle age. I. Title. II. Series.
BF724.6 .K55 2004

Kirby, Simon.
Language evolution. Oxford ; New York : Oxford University Press, 2003.
P140 .L256 2003

Kirchenchor St. Barbara, Wien.
Malaniuk, Ira. Arien und Lieder [sound recording]. [Germany] : Preiser Records, p2000.

Kirkpatrick, Graeme, 1963-.
Historical materialism and social evolution. New York : Palgrave Macmillan, 2002.
HX523 .H565 2002

KIRLIAN PHOTOGRAPHY.
Larson, Cynthia Sue. Aura advantage. Avon, MA : Adams Media Corp., c2003.
BF1389.A8 L37 2003

Musiol, Marie-J. (Marie-Jeanne), 1950- Corps de lumière. Hull, Québec : Axe Néo-7, art contemporain, [2001?]

Die Kirschen in Nachbars Garten.
Onken, Julia, 1942- Vollständige Taschenbuchausg. München : Goldmann, 1999.

Kirschner, Paul Arthur, 1951-.
Visualizing argumentation. London ; New York : Springer, 2003.
QA76.9.H85 V67 2003

Kirshenbaum, Mira. Everything happens for a reason : finding the true meaning of the events of our lives / Mira Kirshenbaum. New York : Harmony Books, 2004. p. cm. ISBN 1400051088 (Hardcover) DDC 158
1. Life change events - Psychological aspects. 2. Meaning (Psychology) 3. Conduct of life. I. Title.
BF637.L53 K57 2004

Kitā, Va. Gender / V. Geetha. Calcutta : Stree, 2002. xvi, 149 p. ; 22 cm. (Theorizing feminism) Includes bibliographical references (p. [139]-143) and index. ISBN 81-85604-45-2
1. Sex role. 2. Sex differences. 3. Feminist theory. I. Title. II. Series.
HQ1075 .K576 2002

Kitaev-Smyk, L. A. (Leonid Aleksandrovich) Stress voĭny : frontovye zapiski vracha-psikhologa / Leonid Kitaev-Smyk. Moskva : Ministerstvo kul'tury RF : Rossiĭskiĭ in-t kul'turologii, 2001. 79 p. : ill. ; 22 cm. Col. ill. on end papers. "Nekotorye fragmenty knigi L.A. Kitaeva-Smyka .. pis' im ran'she v zhurnalakh "Arkhetip" (1992, no. 2), "Millennium" (2001, Nos. 2-3, 11), v gazetakh "Moskovskiĭ komsomolets" (1996, 10 okt.), "Ul'ianovskaia pravda (2001, 15-16 avg., 10-11 okt.), a takzhe prochitany po radio "Maiak", "Svoboda", "Ėko Moskvy"--P. 77. Includes bibliographical references. ISBN 5937190181
1. Kitaev-Smyk, L. A. - (Leonid Aleksandrovich) 2. Stress (Psychology) 3. War - Psychological aspects. 4. War neuroses. 5. Post-traumatic stress disorder. 6. Psychologists - Russia (Federation) - Biography. I. Title.

KITAEV-SMYK, L. A. (LEONID ALEKSANDROVICH).
Kitaev-Smyk, L. A. (Leonid Aleksandrovich) Stress voĭny. Moskva : Ministerstvo kul'tury RF : Rossiĭskiĭ in-t kul'turologii, 2001.

Kitchen, Philip J.
The future of marketing. Houndmills [England] ; New York : Palgrave Macmillan, 2003.
HF5415 .F945 2003

Ḳitsur 138 pitḥe ḥokhmah.
Luzzatto, Moshe Ḥayyim, 1707-1747. Yerushalayim : Mekhon Hadrat Yerushalayim, 761 [2000 or 2001]

Ḳitsur Me'ah sheloshim u-shemonah pitḥe ḥokhmah.
Luzzatto, Moshe Ḥayyim, 1707-1747. Ḳitsur 138 pitḥe ḥokhmah. Yerushalayim : Mekhon Hadrat Yerushalayim, 761 [2000 or 2001]

Kittay, Eva Feder.
The subject of care. Lanham, Md. : Oxford : Rowman & Littlefield Publishers, c2002.
HQ1206 .S9 2002

Kittredge, William. The nature of generosity / William Kittredge. 1st Vintage Departures ed. New York : Vintage, 2001, c2000. 276 p. ; 20 cm. Includes bibliographic references. ISBN 0-679-75687-6 (pbk.) DDC 813/.54
1. Kittredge, William - Travel. 2. Authors, American - 20th century - Biography. 3. Social ecology. 4. Human ecology. 5. Altruism. I. Title.
PS3561.I87 Z472 2001

KITTREDGE, WILLIAM - TRAVEL.
Kittredge, William. The nature of generosity. 1st Vintage Departures ed. New York : Vintage, 2001, c2000.
PS3561.I87 Z472 2001

Kitve paz.
Goldberg, Avraham Yehoshuʻa, 1856-1921. Sefer Kitve paz. Yerushalayim : ha-Mishpaḥah, 763, c2003.

Kivimäki, Timo. US-Indonesian hegemonic bargaining : strength of weakness / Timo Kivimäki. Aldershot ; Burlington, VT : Ashgate, 2003. vii, 300 p. : ill. ; 22 cm. Includes bibliographical references and index. ISBN 0-7546-3686-0 DDC 327.598073
1. Negotiation. 2. Indonesia - Foreign relations - United States. 3. United States - Foreign relations - Indonesia. 4. United States - Foreign relations - 20th century. I. Title. II. Title: US Indonesian hegemonic bargaining

Kivisto, Peter, 1948-.
Christiano, Kevin J. Sociology of religion. Walnut Creek, CA : AltaMira Press, c2002.
BL60 .C465 2002

The Klamath knot.
Wallace, David Rains, 1945- 20th anniversary ed. Berkeley : University of California Press, [2003]
QH105.C2 W344 2003

KLAMATH MOUNTAINS (CALIF. AND OR.).
Wallace, David Rains, 1945- The Klamath knot. 20th anniversary ed. Berkeley : University of California Press, [2003]
QH105.C2 W344 2003

Klangmaschine.
Chlada, Marvin, 1970- 2., überarbeitete und erw. Aufl. Aschaffenburg : Alibri ; [Stuttgart] : Lautsprecher, 2001.
ML3470 .C55 2001

Klarsfeld, André.
[Biologie de la mort. English]
The biology of death : origins of mortality / André Klarsfeld & Frédéric Revah ; translated from the French by Lydia Brady. Ithaca, NY : Comstock Pub. Associates/Cornell University Press, 2004. 211 p. : ill. ; 24 cm. Includes bibliographical references (p. [201]-204) and index. ISBN 0-8014-4118-8 (cloth) DDC 571.9/39
1. Death (Biology) 2. Aging. 3. Cell death. I. Revah, Frédéric. II. Title.
QH530 .K5613 2004

Klass, Morton, 1927- Mind over mind : the anthropology and psychology of spirit possession / Morton Klass. Lanham, Md. ; Oxford : Rowman & Littlefield, c2003. xii, 139 p. ; 23 cm. Includes bibliographical references (p. 127-132) and index. CONTENTS: Unanswered questions and unbridgeable chasms -- Culture as against "culture" -- The spirits are willing -- "Not for us to judge" -- Consciousness and dissociation : paradigms lost -- Dissociative disorders and the human mind -- Dissociation and spirit possession. ISBN 0-7425-2676-3 (hbk. : alk. paper) ISBN 0-7425-2677-1 (pbk. : alk. paper) DDC 133.4/26
1. Spirit possession. I. Title.
BF1555 .K58 2003

Klassiker Auslegen
(Bd. 10) Ludwig Wittgenstein, Tractatus logico-philosophicus. Berlin : Akademie Verlag, 2001.

(Bd. 21) James, William, 1842-1910. [Pragmatism. German] Pragmatismus. Berlin : Akademie Verlag, c2000.

Klatt, Andy.
Arsuaga, Juan Luis de. [Collar del neandertal. English] The Neanderthal's necklace. New York : Four Walls Eight Windows, c2002.
GN285 .A7713 2002

Klatt, Norbert. Die Rivalin Gottes : zur Geschichte der Seele als Herrschafts- und Ordnungsidee / Norbert Klatt. Göttingen : N. Klatt, 2000. 274 p. ; 21 cm. Includes bibliographical references (p. 236-257) and index. ISBN 3-928312-11-1 (pbk.)
1. Soul. 2. Transmigration. 3. Philosophy, Ancient. I. Title.

Klein, Allen. The healing power of humor : techniques for getting through loss, setbacks, upsets, disappointments, difficulties, trials, tribulations, and all that not-so-funny stuff / Allen Klein. Waterville, Me. : Thorndike Press, 2003. p. cm. Originally published: c1989. Includes bibliographical references. ISBN 0-7862-5990-6 (lg. print : hc : alk. paper) DDC 152.4/3
1. Laughter. 2. Wit and humor - Psychological aspects. 3. Adjustment (Psychology) I. Title.
BF575.L3 K56 2003

Klein, Barbara Schave. Not all twins are alike : psychological profiles of twinship / Barbara Schave Klein ; forward by Marjorie Ford. Westport, Conn. :

Praeger, 2003. xix, 133 p. : ill. ; 25 cm. Includes bibliographical references (p. 125-129)and index. ISBN 0-275-97584-3 (alk. paper) DDC 155.44/4
1. Twins - Psychology. I. Title.
BF723.T9 K57 2003

Klein, Mavis.
Howard, Kerry. The book of love and happiness. New York : Ryland Peters & Small, Inc., 2004.
BF575.L8 H69 2004

KLEIN, MELANIE.
Sánchez-Pardo, Esther. Cultures of the death drive. Durham [N.C.] : Duke University Press, c2003.
BF175.5.D4 S26 2003

Klein, Wolfgang.
Genuss und Egoismus. Berlin : Akademie Verlag, c2002.

Kleine Bibliothek der Religionen
(Bd. 7) Görg, Manfred. Die Barke der Sonne. Freiburg im Breisgau : Herder, 2001.
BL2450.R2 G647 2001

Kleine Hohenheimer Reihe
(Bd. 40) Kather, Regine, 1955- Gotteshauch oder künstliche Seele. Stuttgart : Akademie der Diözese Rottenburg-Stuttgart, c2000.

Kleine Philosophie des Lachens.
Michel-Andino, Andreas, 1961- Koblenz : Fölbach, c2000.
BF575.L3 M53 2000

Kleine Schriften.
Rix, Helmut, 1926- Bremen : Hempen, 2001.

Kleine thüringische Geschichte.
Jonscher, Reinhard. 3., überarb. und erw. Aufl. Jena : Jenzig-Verlag Köhler, 2001.
DD801.T44 J658 2001

Kleinedler, Steven Racek.
Spears, Richard A. NTC's dictionary of everyday American English expressions. Lincolnwood, Ill. : National Textbook Co., c1994.
PE2839.S65 1994

Kleiner, Art. Who really matters : the Core Group theory of power, privilege, and success / Art Kleiner. 1st ed. New York ; London : Currency/Doubleday, 2003. ix, 277 p. : ill. ; 25 cm. Includes bibliographical references (p. 257-264) and index. ISBN 0-385-48448-8 DDC 650/.01
1. Corporate power. 2. Organizational behavior. 3. Success in business. I. Title.
HD2741.K478 2003

Kleiner, Marcus S., 1973-.
Chlada, Marvin, 1970- Klangmaschine. 2., überarbeitete und erw. Aufl. Aschaffenburg : Alibri ; [Stuttgart] : Lautsprecher, 2001.
ML3470.C55 2001

Kleinöder-Strobel, Susanne, 1969- Die Verfolgung von Zauberei und Hexerei in den fränkischen Markgraftümern im 16. Jahrhundert / Susanne Kleinöder-Strobel. Tübingen : Mohr Siebeck, c2002. xiv, 332 p. : folded map ; 24 cm. (Spätmittelalter und Reformation, 0937-5740 ; neue Reihe, 20) Includes bibliographical references (p. [283]-303) and indexes. ISBN 3-16-147863-0
1. Witchcraft - Germany - Franconia - History - 16th century. 2. Persecution - Germany - Franconia - History - 16th century. 3. Trials (Witchcraft) - Germany - Franconia - History - 16th century. I. Title. II. Series: Spätmittelalter und Reformation ; neue Reihe, 20.
BF1583.K54 2002

Kliem, Ralph L. The organizational engineering approach to project management : the revolution in building and managing effective teams / Ralph L. Kliem, Harris B. Anderson. Boca Raton : St. Lucie Press, c2003. 239 p. : ill. ; 25 cm. Includes bibliographical references (p. 235-236) and index. ISBN 1-57444-322-4 (alk. paper) DDC 658.4/04
1. Teams in the workplace. 2. Project management. I. Anderson, Harris B. II. Title.
HD66.K585 2003

Klimov, R. B. Teoriia stadial'nogo razvitiia iskusstva i stat'i / Rostislav Borisovich Klimov ; sostaviteli Elizaveta Plavinskaia, Mariia Plavinskaia. Moskva : O.G.I., 2002. 498 p. : ill. ; 22 cm. ISBN 5942820600
1. Art - History. I. Plavinskaia, Elizaveta. II. Plavinskaia, Mariia. III. Title.
N5300.K55 2002

Kline, John A. Listening effectively [electronic resource] / John A. Kline. Maxwell Air Force Base, Ala. : Air University Press, [1996] System requirements: Adobe Acrobat Reader. Mode of access: Internet from the Air University Press web site. Address as of 4/28/03: http:// aupress.au.af.mil/Books/b-10/b10.pdf; current access is available via PURL. Title from title screen (viewed on Apr. 28, 2003). "April 1996." URL: http://purl.access.gpo.gov/GPO/LPS30260 Available in other form: Kline, John A. Listening effectively xi, 59 p. (OCoLC)34118153.
1. Listening. I. Air University (U.S.). Press. II. Title. III. Title: Kline, John A. Listening effectively xi, 59 p.

Kline, John A. Listening effectively xi, 59 p.
Kline, John A. Listening effectively [electronic resource]. Maxwell Air Force Base, Ala. : Air University Press, [1996]

Kline, Rex B. Beyond significance testing: reforming data analysis methods in behavioral research / by Rex B. Kline. 1st ed. Washington, DC : American Psychological Association, c2004. p. cm. Includes bibliographical references and index. CONTENTS: Introductory concepts -- Changing times -- Fundamental concepts -- What's wrong with statistical tests and where we go from here -- Effect size estimation in comparative studies -- Parametric effect size indexes -- Nonparametric effect size indexes -- Effect size estimation in one-way designs -- Effect size estimation in multifactor designs -- Other alternatives to statistical tests -- Replication and meta-analysis -- Resampling and Bayesian estimation. ISBN 1-59147-118-4 (alk. paper) DDC 150/.72/4
1. Psychometrics - Textbooks. I. Title.
BF39.K59 2004

Kline, Theresa, 1960- Teams that lead : a matter of market strategy, leadership skills, and executive strength / Theresa J.B. Kline. Mahwah, N.J. : L. E. Associates, 2003 xii, 223 p. : ill. ; 24 cm. Includes bibliographical references (p. 207-213) and indexes. ISBN 0-8058-4237-3 (cloth : alk. paper) ISBN 0-8058-4542-9 (pbk. : alk. paper) DDC 658.4/092
1. Leadership. 2. Executives. 3. Organizational effectiveness. I. Title.
HD57.7.K549 2003

Klinger, Eric, 1933-.
Handbook of motivational counseling. Chichester, West Sussex, England ; Hoboken, NJ : J. Wiley, c2004.
BF637.C6 H3172 2004

Klitzman, Robert. Mortal secrets : truth and lies in the age of AIDS / Robert Klitzman and Ronald Bayer. Baltimore : Johns Hopkins University Press, 2003. 218 p. ; 24 cm. Includes bibliographical references (p. [207]-212) and index. CONTENTS: Getting tested : uncovering the truth -- Sexual partners : sex, love, and disclosure -- Secrets and "secret secrets" : disclosure in families -- Disclosure in other worlds : friends, co-workers, and going public -- Dangerous acts -- Making moral judgments. ISBN 0-8018-7427-0 (acid-free) DDC 362.1/969792
1. AIDS (Disease) - Prevention - Social aspects. 2. Self-disclosure. 3. HIV-positive persons - Sexual behavior. I. Bayer, Ronald. II. Title.
RA643.8.K56 2003

Klíuch k probuzhdeníiu
Klíuchnikov, Sergeĭ. Master zhizni. Moskva : Belovod'e, 2001.
BF637.S4 K556 2001

Klíuchnikov, Sergeĭ. Master zhizni : psikhologicheskaia zashchita v sotsiume / Sergeĭ Klíuchnikov. Moskva : Belovod'e, 2001. 583 p. ; 21 cm. (Klíuch k probuzhdeníiu) Summary in English. Includes bibliographical references (p. 576-[582]). ISBN 5934540173
1. Self-actualization (Psychology) - Social aspects. 2. Self-defense. I. Title. II. Series.
BF637.S4 K556 2001

Kłopot z istnieniem.
Elzenberg, Henryk, 1887-1967. Wyd. 1., popr. i uzup. Toruń : Wydawn. Uniwersytetu Mikołaja Kopernika, 2002.

Klosko, George. Jacobins and utopians : the political theory of fundamental moral reform / George Klosko. Notre Dame, Ind. : University of Notre Dame Press, c2003. xii, 200 p. ; 24 cm. (Frank M. Covey, Jr. Loyola lectures in political analysis) Includes bibliographical references (p. 177-193) and index. ISBN 0-268-03257-2 (hbk. : alk. paper) ISBN 0-268-03258-0 (pbk. : alk. paper) DDC 321/.07
1. Revolutions. 2. Political science - History. 3. Social ethics. 4. Social reformers. 5. Power (Social sciences) I. Title. II. Series.
JC491.K54 2003

KLOSTER ST. GALLEN.
Hehle, Christine. Boethius in St. Gallen. Tübingen : Niemeyer, 2002.

The Kluwer international series in engineering and computer science
(SECS 746) Knowledge-based information retrieval and filtering from the Web. Boston : Kluwer Academic Publishers, c2003.
TK5105.888.K58 2003

The Kluwer international series in video computing
Zhou, Xiang Sean. Exploration of visual data. Boston ; London : Kluwer Academic Publishers, c2003.
T385.Z55 2003

Kluwer international series on HCI
(v. 2.) Schreck, Jorg. Security and privacy in user modeling. Dordrecht ; Boston ; London : Kluwer Academic Publishers, c2003.
QA76.9.A25 S353 2003

Knabe, G. S. (Georgiĭ Stepanovich).
Dostovernost' i dokazatel'nost' v issledovaniiakh po teorii i istorii kul'tury. Moskva : RGGU, 2002.
HM621.D68 2002

Knaus, William J. The procrastination workbook / William Knaus ; foreword by Albert Ellis. Oakland, Calif. : New Harbinger, 2002. vi, 170 p. : ill. ; 28 cm. Includes bibliographical references (p. [171]-172). ISBN 1-57224-295-7 (pbk.) DDC 155.232
1. Procrastination. 2. Procrastination - Problems, exercises, etc. I. Title.
BF637.P76 K55 2002

Kneer, Markus, 1972- Die dunkle Spur im Denken : Rationalität und Antijudaismus / Markus Kneer. Paderborn : Schöningh, 2003. 204 p. ; 24 cm. (Paderborner theologische Studien ; Bd. 34) Slightly rev. version of author's dissertation, 2002, Theologische Fakultät, Paderborn. Includes bibliographical references (p. [194]-200) and indexes. ISBN 3-506-76285-0 (pbk.)
1. Antisemitism. 2. Rationalism. 3. Philosophy, Modern - 20th century. I. Title. II. Series.
DS145.K64 2003

Kniga dlia tekh, komu nravitsia zhit', ili, Psikhologiia lichnostnogo rosta.
Kozlov, Nikolaĭ (Nikolaĭ Ivanovich) Moskva : "AST-Press kniga", 2002.
BF723.P4 K69 2002

The knight.
Baker, Alan. Hoboken, N.J. : Wiley, c2003.
CR4513.B32 2003

Knight, Brenda, 1958- Gem magic : crystals and gemstones for love, luck, and power / Brenda Knight. Gloucester, MA : Fair Winds Press, 2003. p. cm. Table of contents URL: http://www.loc.gov/catdir/toc/ecip048/2003018411.html CONTENTS: The glories and wonder of gems, crystal, and stones -- Gem magic -- Birthstones and astro-gemology -- Crystal power -- Crystal conjuring and stone spells -- Crystal healing and crystal consciousness -- Gem mythology and crystal descriptionary. ISBN 1-59233-024-X DDC 133/.2548
1. Precious stones - Psychic aspects. 2. Crystals - Psychic aspects. I. Title.
BF1442.P74 K65 2004

Knight, Michele. Good fortune : star signs / Michele Knight. Kansas City, Mo. : Andrews McMeel Pub., c2002. 208 p. : ill. (chiefly col.) ; 15 cm. ISBN 0-7407-2900-4 DDC 133.5
1. Zodiac. 2. Astrology. I. Title.
BF1726.K55 2002

Good sex : star signs / Michele Knight. Kansas City, Mo. : Andrews McMeel Pub., c2002. 208 p. : ill. (some col.) ; 15 cm. ISBN 0-7407-2901-2
1. Astrology and sex. 2. Love - Miscellanea. I. Title.
BF1729.S4 K58 2002

Knight, Sirona, 1955- The cyber spellbook : magick in the virtual world / by Sirona Knight and Patricia Telesco. Franklin Lakes, NJ : New Page Books, c2002. 190 p. ; 21 cm. Includes bibliographical references (p. 179-181) and index. ISBN 1-56414-582-4 (pbk.) DDC 133.4/3
1. Witchcraft. 2. Virtual reality. 3. Cyberspace. I. Telesco, Patricia, 1960- II. Title.
BF1571.T425 2002

Dream magic : night spells and rituals for love, prosperity, and personal power / Sirona Knight. 1st ed. San Francisco : HarperSanFrancisco, c2000. xiii, 272 p. ; 21 cm. Includes bibliographical references (p. 265-270). ISBN 0-06-251675-2 DDC 135/.3
1. Magic. 2. Incantations. 3. Dreams. I. Title.
BF1621.K65 2000

Empowering your life with wicca / Sirona Knight. Indianapolis, IN : Alpha Books, c2003. x, 293 p. : ill. ; 23 cm. Includes bibliographical references (p. [285]-288) and index. ISBN 0-02-864437-9 DDC 299/.94
1. Witchcraft. 2. Goddess religion. I. Title.

Knight, Sirona, 1955

BF1571 .K56 2003
Faery magick : spells, potions, and lore from the earth spirits / by Sirona Knight. Franklin Lakes, NJ : New Page Books, c2003. 222 p. : ill. ; 21 cm. Includes bibliographical references (p. 211-215) and index. ISBN 1-56414-595-6 (pbk.) DDC 133.4/3
1. Fairies. I. Title.
BF1552 .K55 2003

A witch like me : the spiritual journeys of today's pagan practitioners / by Sirona Knight. Franklin Lakes, NJ : New Page Books, c2002. 208 p. ; 21 cm. Includes bibliographical references (p. 191-199) and index. SUMMARY: Thirteen men and women explain how they came to walk down the Wiccan path, sharing their insights, feelings, thoughts as well as describing their life-changing experiences. ISBN 1-56414-539-5 (pbk.) DDC 299
1. Witches - United States - Biography. 2. Witchcraft. I. Title.
BF1408 .K55 2002

KNIGHTHOOD. See **KNIGHTS AND KNIGHTHOOD.**

KNIGHTS AND KNIGHTHOOD - EUROPE - HISTORY.
Baker, Alan. The knight. Hoboken, N.J. : Wiley, c2003.
CR4513 .B32 2003

KNIGHTS AND KNIGHTHOOD IN LITERATURE.
Besamusca, Bart. The book of Lancelot. Cambridge : D.S. Brewer, 2003.
PT5568 .B47 2003

Malory, Thomas, Sir, 15th cent. [Morte d'Arthur] Le morte Darthur, or, The hoole book of Kyng Arthur and of his noble knyghtes of the Rounde Table. 1st ed. New York ; London : Norton, c2004.
PR2041 .M37 2004

Philologies old and new. Princeton : The Edward C. Armstrong Monographs, 2001.

KNIGHTS AND KNIGHTHOOD - NETHERLANDS.
Janse, A. Ridderschap in Holland. Hilversum : Verloren, 2001.
DJ152 .J26 2001

KNIGHTS TEMPLAR (MASONIC ORDER) - HISTORY.
Sinclair, Andrew, 1935- The secret scroll. Edinburgh : Birlinn, 2002.

Knižnice dějin a současnosti
(sv. 19.) Smetanka, Z. Archeologické etudy. Praha : [Lidové noviny], 2003.

Knowing beyond knowledge.
Forsthoefel, Thomas A. Alderhot, England ; Burlington, VT. : Ashgate, 2002.
B132.A3 F66 2002

KNOWLEDGE ACQUISITION (EXPERT SYSTEMS).
Towards the semantic web. Chichester, England ; Hoboken, N.J. : J. Wiley, c2003.
TK5105.88815 .T68 2003

Knowledge and faith.
Salamucha, Jan. [Selections. English. 2003] Amsterdam ; New York, NY : Rodopi, 2003.

Knowledge and freedom in Indian philosophy.
Chatterjea, Tara, 1937- Lanham, Md. ; Oxford : Lexington Books, 2002.
B131 .C518 2002

Knowledge-based information retrieval and filtering from the Web / edited by Witold Abramowicz.
Boston : Kluwer Academic Publishers, c2003. xvi, 303 p. : ill. ; 25 cm. (The Kluwer international series in engineering and computer science ; SECS 746) Includes bibliographical references and index. ISBN 1402075235 (alk. paper) DDC 004.6/78
1. World Wide Web. 2. Expert systems (Computer science) 3. Artificial intelligence. 4. Information storage and retrieval systems. 5. Internet searching. 6. Internet - Censorship - Data processing. I. Abramowicz, Witold. II. Series.
TK5105.888 .K58 2003

KNOWLEDGE-BASED SYSTEMS (COMPUTER SCIENCE). See **EXPERT SYSTEMS (COMPUTER SCIENCE).**

KNOWLEDGE, BOOKS OF. See **ENCYCLOPEDIAS AND DICTIONARIES.**

Knowledge, consciousness and religious conversion in Lonergan and Aurobindo.
McLaughlin, Michael T. Roma : Editrice Pontificia Universita Gregoriana, 2003.

KNOWLEDGE DISCOVERY IN DATABASES. See **DATA MINING.**

KNOWLEDGE MANAGEMENT. See also **INFORMATION TECHNOLOGY; ORGANIZATIONAL LEARNING.**
Burke, Dan, 1965- Business @ the speed of stupid. Cambridge, MA : Perseus Pub., c2001.
HD45 .B7995 2001

Davenport, Thomas H. What's the big idea? Boston, Mass. : Harvard Business School Press, c2003.
HD53 .D38 2003

The expansion of management knowledge. Stanford, Calif. : Stanford Business Books, c2002.
HD31 .E873 2002

Huotari, Maija-Leena. Trust in knowledge management and systems in organizations. Hershey, PA ; London : Idea Group Publishing, c2004.
HD30.2 .H865 2004

Intelligent support systems. Hershey, PA : IRM Press, c2002.
QA76.9.D3 I5495 2002

Organizing business knowledge. Cambridge, Mass. : MIT Press, c2003.
HD30.2 .T67 2003

Public policy in knowledge-based economies. Cheltenham, UK ; Northampton, MA : Edward Elgar, c2003.
HC79.I55 P83 2003

Sharing expertise. Cambridge, Mass. : MIT Press, c2003.
HD30.2 .S53 2003

Styhre, Alexander. Understanding knowledge management. Malmö, Sweden : Liber ; Oslo, Norge : Abstrakt ; Herndon, VA : Copenhagen Business School Press, c2003.
HD30.2 .S84 2003

KNOWLEDGE MANAGEMENT - PHILOSOPHY.
Styhre, Alexander. Understanding knowledge management. Malmö, Sweden : Liber ; Oslo, Norge : Abstrakt ; Herndon, VA : Copenhagen Business School Press, c2003.
HD30.2 .S84 2003

The knowledge of good.
Hartman, Robert S., 1910-1973. [Conocimiento del bien. English] Amsterdam ; New York, NY : Rodopi, c2002.
BD232 .H324 2002

Knowledge of things human and divine.
Verene, Donald Phillip, 1937- New Haven, Conn. : Yale University Press, c2003.
B3581.P73 V47 2003

Knowledge power gender : philosophy and the future of the "condition féminine".
Wissen Macht Geschlecht. Zürich : Chronos, c2002.

KNOWLEDGE REPRESENTATION (INFORMATION THEORY).
Spatial cognition III. Berlin ; New York : Springer, c2003.
Q387 .S73 2003

KNOWLEDGE, SOCIOLOGY OF.
Berthier, Denis. Le savoir et l'ordinateur. Paris : Harmattan, c2002.

Breaking the disciplines. London ; New York : I.B. Tauris, 2003.
BD175 .B74 2003

Comunicação e corporeidades. Brazil : Editora Universitaria : Compas, 2000.

La connaissance sociologique. Paris : Harmattan, c2002.
HM651 .C65 2002

Debras, Sylvie. Lectrices au quotidien. Paris : L'Harmattan, c2003.

Jansen, Sue Curry. Critical communication theory. Lanham, Md. ; Oxford : Rowman & Littlefield, c2002.
HM651 .J36 2002

Lal, Vinay. Empire of knowledge. London ; Sterling, Va. : Pluto Press, 2002.
HN16 .L35 2002

Ouyang, Kang, 1953- She hui ren shi lun. Di 1 ban. [Kunming] : Yunnan ren min chu ban she, 2002.
BF323.S63 O93 2002

Public policy in knowledge-based economies. Cheltenham, UK ; Northampton, MA : Edward Elgar, c2003.
HC79.I55 P83 2003

Schutz, Alfred, 1899-1959. Werkausgabe. Konstanz : UVK, Verlagsgesellschaft, 2003-
BD431 .S284916 2003

Turner, Stephen P., 1951- Liberal democracy 3.0. London ; Thousand Oaks, Calif. : SAGE Publications, 2003.
JC423 .T87 2003

Valverde, Mariana, 1955- Law's dream of a common knowledge. Princeton, N.J. ; Woodstock, Oxfordshire : Princeton University Press, c2003.
K380 .V35 2003

Zetterberg, Hans Lennart, 1927- Social theory and social practice. New Brunswick, NJ : Transaction Publishers, c2002.
HM511 .Z48 2002

KNOWLEDGE, THEORY OF. See also **CATEGORIES (PHILOSOPHY); COMPREHENSION (THEORY OF KNOWLEDGE); EXPERTISE; IDEOLOGY; INTELLECT; MODALITY (THEORY OF KNOWLEDGE); OBSERVATION (PSYCHOLOGY); OTHER MINDS (THEORY OF KNOWLEDGE); PARADIGM (THEORY OF KNOWLEDGE); PERCEPTION; SUBJECTIVITY; TRUTH; VALUES.**
Ameriks, Karl, 1947- Interpreting Kant's critiques. Oxford : Clarendon Press ; New York : Oxford University Press, 2003.
B2779 .A64 2003

Andrieu, Bernard. L'interprétation des gènes. Paris : Harmattan, 2002.

Appraising Lakatos. Dordrecht ; Boston : Kluwer Academic, c2002.
Q175 .A685 2002

Araujo, Marcelo de. Scepticism, freedom and autonomy. Berlin : De Gruyter, 2003.

Bachelard, Gaston. [Formation de l'esprit scientifique. English] The formation of the scientific mind. Manchester : Clinamen, c2002.

Barsotti, Bernard. Bachelard critique de Husserl. Paris : Harmattan, c2002.
B2430.B254 B37 2002

Bereiter, Carl. Education and mind in the knowledge age. Mahwah, N.J. : L. Erlbaum Associates, 2002.
LB1057 .B47 2002

Caropreso, Paolo. Von der Dingfrage zur Frage nach Gott. Berlin ; New York : W. de Gruyter, 2003.

Casti, J. L. The one true platonic heaven. Washington, D.C. : Joseph Henry Press, c2003.
Q175 .C4339 2003

Chatterjea, Tara, 1937- Knowledge and freedom in Indian philosophy. Lanham, Md. ; Oxford : Lexington Books, 2002.
B131 .C518 2002

Chattopadhyaya, Gauri, 1950- Advaitic ontology and epistemology. 1st ed. Allahabad : Raka Prakashan, 2001.
B132.A3+

Conoscenza e cognizione. 1. ed. Milano : Guerini e associati, 2002.
BJ45.5 .C66 2002

Cox, Christoph, 1965- Nietzsche. Berkeley : University of California Press, c1999.
B3318.K7 C68 1999

Crowther, Paul. Philosophy after postmodernism. London ; New York : Routledge, 2003.
B831.2 .C76 2003

Dagognet, François. Changement de perspective. Paris : Table ronde, c2002.

Dretske, Fred I. Perception, knowledge, and belief. Cambridge, U.K. ; New York : Cambridge University Press, 2000.
BD161 .D73 2000

Dufour, Adrian. Ciencia y logica de mundos posibles. Bern : Lang, 2001.

Dugin, Aleksandr. Évoliutsiia paradigmal'nykh osnovaniĭ nauki. Moskva : Arktogeia, 2002.
Q174.8 .D845 2002

Ensaios. João Pessoa : Editora Universitária, 2001.

Epistemology. Malden, Mass. : Blackwell Publishers, 2000.

BD161 .E615 2000
Erkennen und Leben. Hildesheim [Germany] ; New York : Olms, 2002.
BD435 .E75 2002

Ernst, Waltraud, 1964- Diskurspiratinnen. Wien : Milena, c1999.
HQ1154 .E7 1999

Estivals, Robert. Théorie générale de la schématisation. Paris : Harmattan, c2002-

Forsthoefel, Thomas A. Knowing beyond knowledge. Alderhot, England ; Burlington, VT. : Ashgate, 2002.
B132.A3 F66 2002

Gambra, José Miguel. La analogía en general. 1. ed. Pamplona : EUNSA, 2002.

González Ayesta, Cruz. Hombre y verdad. 1. ed. Pamplona : Universidad de Navarra, Ediciones, 2002.

Greimann, Dirk. Freges Konzeption der Wahrheit. Hildesheim ; New York : Georg Olms, c2003.
B3318.T78 G74 2003

Gundersen, Lars Bo. Dispositional theories of knowledge. Aldershot, England ; Burlington, VT : Ashgate, c2003.
BD161 .G86 2003

Husserl's Logical investigations reconsidered. Dordrecht ; Boston : Kluwer Academic Publishers, c2003.
B3279.H93 L64346 2003

Jacques Maritain and the many ways of knowing. Washington, D.C. : American Maritain Association : Distributed by the Catholic University of America Press, c2002.
B2430.M34 J317 2002

Janz, Nathalie. Globus symbolicus. [Lausanne : Université de Lausanne, 1999]

Kvanvig, Jonathan L. The value of knowledge and the pursuit of understanding. Cambridge, U.K. ; New York : Cambridge University Press, 2003.
BD232 .K92 2003

Majorek, Marek B. Objektivität, ein Erkenntnisideal auf dem Prüfstand. Tübingen : Francke, c2002.

Maritain, Jacques, 1882-1973. [Degrés du savoir. English] Distinguish to unite, or, The degrees of knowledge. Notre Dame, Ind. : University of Notre Dame Press, 1998, c1995.
BD162 .M273 1998

Nietzsche and the sciences. Dordrecht ; Boston : Kluwer Academic Publishers, c1999-
B3318.K7 N54 1999

O'Callaghan, John (John P.) Thomist realism and the linguistic turn. Notre Dame, Ind. : University of Notre Dame Press, c2003.
BD161 .O3 2003

Paál, Gábor. Was ist schön? Würzburg : Königshausen & Neumann, c2003.
BH39 .P33 2003

Papalotzin, Itzcoatl. Los recuerdos robados a las estrellas muertas. Barcelona : Mtm editor.es, c2002.

Porus, V. N. Ratsional'nost', nauka, kul'tura. Moskva : Universitet Rossiĭskoĭ akademii obrazovaniĭa, Kafedra filosofii, 2002.
Q175.32.K45 P678 2002

Preston, Christopher J. Grounding knowledge. Athens, Ga. : University of Georgia Press, c2003.
BD161 .P746 2003

Ramos, João Baptista. Quinze cartas sobre moralidade & ciência. Brasilia : Thesaurus, 2000.

Rescher, Nicholas. Epistemology. Albany : State University of New York Press, c2003.
BD161 .R477 2003

Roehle, Friedrich, 1916-1995. Die Struktur des Bewusstseins. Frankfurt am Main ; New York : Peter Lang, c2001.

Rosenberg, Jay F. Thinking about knowing. Oxford : Clarendon Press ; New York : Oxford University Press, 2002.
BD161 .R65 2002

Ruben, David-Hillel. Action and its explanation. 1st ed. Oxford : Clarendon Press, 2003.
BF38 .R83 2003

Samuel, Geoffrey, 1947- Epistemology and method in law. Aldershot, Hampshire, England : Burlington, VT : Ashgate, c2003.

K213 .S259 2003
Schürmann, Reiner, 1941- [Des hégémonies brisées. English] Broken hegemonies. Bloomington : Indiana University Press, c2003.
BD162 .S48 2003

Scuto, Giuseppe. Epistemologica. Milano : FrancoAngeli, c2002.

Sepúlveda, Jesús. El jardín de las peculiaridades. Buenos Aires : Ediciones del Leopardo, [2002]

Simon, Yves René Marie, 1903-1961. [Critique de la connaissance morale. English] A critique of moral knowledge. New York : Fordham University Press, 2002.
BJ1249 .S4513 2002

Soukup, Johannes. Metaphysik der Zeit oder Wirklichkeit und Wissen. Deutsche 1. Ausg. Wien : Passagen Verlag. c1998.

Spoerri, Hubert M. Mensch und Kunst. München : Scaneg, c2002.

Styhre, Alexander. Understanding knowledge management. Malmö, Sweden : Liber ; Oslo, Norge : Abstrakt ; Herndon, VA : Copenhagen Business School Press, c2003.
HD30.2 .S84 2003

Sub"ekt, poznanie, deĭatel'nost'. Moskva : Kanon+, 2002.
BD166 .S84 2002

Vernes, Jean-René. The existence of the external world. Ottawa : University of Ottawa Press, c2000.

Von Foerster, Heinz, 1911- Understanding systems. New York : Kluwer Academic/Plenum Publishers ; Heidelberg : Carl-Auer-Systeme Verlag, c2002.

Wilkens, Sander. Die Konvertibilität des Bewusstseins. 1. Aufl. Würzburg ; Boston : Deutscher Wissenschafts-Verlag (DWV), c2002.
BD163 .E45 2002

KNOWLEDGE, THEORY OF - CONGRESSES.
Collège de France. Symposium annuel. La vérité dans les sciences. Paris : Jacob, c2003.

Construcción de conocimiento y educación virtual. 1. ed. Ciudad Universitaria, México, D.F. : Universidad Nacional Autónoma de México, 2000.
LB1060 .C658 2000

Filosofsko-metodologicheskie osnovy gumanitarnogo znaniĭa. Moskva : Rossiĭskiĭ gosudarstvennyĭ gumanitarnyĭ universitet, 2001.
BD166 .F489 2001

Nosov, N. A. Ne-virtualistika. Moskva : Gumanitariĭ, 2001.
BF38 .N67 2001

[Nuevos paradigmas. English.] New paradigms, culture, and subjectivity. Cresskill, N.J. : Hampton Press, c2002.
BD161 .N8413 2002

Die Öffentlichkeit der Vernunft und die Vernunft der Öffentlichkeit. 1. Aufl. Frankfurt am Main : Suhrkamp, 2001.
B3258.H324 O34 2001

KNOWLEDGE, THEORY OF (HINDUISM).
McLaughlin, Michael T. Knowledge, consciousness and religious conversion in Lonergan and Aurobindo. Roma : Editrice Pontificia Universita Gregoriana, 2003.

Miśra, Ānanda, lecturer. Saṃvitprakāśavāda. 1. saṃskaraṇa. Dillī : Bhāratīya Vidyā Prakāśana, 2002.
B132.K6 M58 2002

Shastri, L. C., 1933- Indian philosophy of knowledge. 1st ed. Delhi, India : Global Vision Pub. House, 2002.
B132.K6 S48 2002

KNOWLEDGE, THEORY OF, IN CHILDREN.
Flavell, John H. Development of children's knowledge about the mind. Worcester, Mass. : Clark University Press, 2003.
BF723.C5 F623 2003

KNOWLEDGE, THEORY OF (RELIGION). *See also* **ANALOGY (RELIGION).**
McLaughlin, Michael T. Knowledge, consciousness and religious conversion in Lonergan and Aurobindo. Roma : Editrice Pontificia Universita Gregoriana, 2003.

Knox, Jean, 1948- Archetype, attachment, analysis : Jungian psychology and the emergent mind / Jean Knox. Hove, East Sussex ; New York : Brunner-Routledge, 2003. p. cm. Includes bibliographical references. Table of contents URL: http://www.loc.gov/catdir/toc/

ecip041/2003005123.html CONTENTS: Introduction -- Jung's various models of archetypes -- Archetypes and image schemas, a developmental perspective -- The making of meaning, the formation of internal working models -- Trauma and defences, their roots in relationship -- Reflective function, the mind as an internal object -- The process of change in analysis and the role of the analyst -- Conclusions, science and symbols. ISBN 1-58391-128-6 (alk. paper) ISBN 1-58391-129-4 (pbk. : alk. paper) DDC 150.19/54
1. Archetype (Psychology) 2. Attachment behavior. 3. Jungian psychology. I. Title.
BF175.5.A72 K68 2003

KOBAYASHI, ISSA, 1763-1827.
Bolitho, Harold. Bereavement and consolation. New Haven : Yale University Press, c2003.
DS822.2 .B65 2003

Koberg, Don, 1930- The universal traveler : a soft-systems guide to creativity, problem-solving, and the process of reaching goals / by Don Koberg and Jim Bagnall. 4th ed. Menlo Park, Calif. : Crisp Learning, c2003. p. cm. Includes bibliographical references and index. CONTENTS: Anatomy of the universal traveler -- How the universal traveler can help you -- Introduction to creativity -- Keys to creative behavior -- Blocks to creativity -- Logic makes sense -- Design process -- Travel map -- A word about methods -- General travel tips -- General language guide -- General travel guide -- The universal travel agency -- How to use travel agency -- Tourist traps -- Some generic methods -- Acceptance -- Analysis -- Definition -- Ideation -- Idea-selecting -- Implementation -- Evaluation -- Back home with memorabilia -- Side trips -- Creativity games -- Guide to measurable objectives -- Lessons from problem-solving -- Synectics -- Self-hypnotism -- Criticism -- Communications checklist -- Wiring diagrams -- Wiring ahead. ISBN 1-56052-679-3 (pbk.) DDC 158.1
1. Problem solving. 2. Creative ability. 3. Goal (Psychology) I. Bagnall, Jim. II. Title.
BF441 .K55 2003

Kobiecość w kulturze globalnej.
Gromkowska, Agnieszka. POznań : Wolumin, 2002.

Kobieta - .
Zawadzki, Roman. Warszawa : Wydawn. von borowiecky, 2002.
PN56.5.W64 Z28 2002

Kochan, Frances K.
Global perspectives on mentoring. Greenwich : Information Age Pub., 2004.
BF637.M48 G57 2004

Kochan, Thomas A.
Management. Cambridge, Mass. : MIT Press, 2003.
HD31 .M2928 2003

Kochetkov, V. V. (Vladimir Viktorovich) Psikhologii︠a︡ mezhkul'turnykh razlichiĭ : uchebnoe posobie dli︠a︡ vuzov / V.V. Kochetkov. Moskva : PER SE, 2002. 413 p. : ill. ; 21 cm. (Sovremennoe obrazovanie) Includes bibliographical references. Summary and table of contents in English. ISBN 5929200327
1. Ethnopsychology. 2. National characteristics. 3. Intercultural communication - Case studies. 4. National characteristics, Russian. I. Title. II. Title: Psychology of intercultural differences III. Series.
GN502 .K6 2002

Kocsány, Piroska.
Wort und (Kon)text. Frankfurt : Lang, 2001.
P325.5.C65 W678 2001

Koenig, Linda J.
From child sexual abuse to adult sexual risk. 1st ed. Washington, DC : American Psychological Association, c2004.
RC569.5.A28 F76 2004

Koenig, Yvan.
La magie en Egypte. Paris : Documentation française : Musée du Louvre, c2002.
BF1591 .M3447 2002

Kōfuku no Kagaku (Organization).
Ōkawa, Ryūhō, 1956- [Ōgon no hō. English] The golden laws. New York : Lantern Books, c2002.
BP605.K55 O33 2001

KŌFUKU NO KAGAKU (ORGANIZATION).
Ōkawa, Ryūhō, 1956- [Ai no genten. English] The origin of love. New York : Lantern Books, c2003.
BP605.K55 O29513 2003

Ōkawa, Ryūhō, 1956- [Hito o aishi, hito o ikashi, hito o yuruse. English] Love, nurture, and forgive. New York : Lantern Books, c2002.
BP605.K55 O32413 2002

Ōkawa, Ryūhō, 1956- [Ōgon no hō. English] The golden laws. New York : Lantern Books, c2002.

Kōfuku no Kagaku (Organization)
BP605.K55 O33 2001

Kogda prikhodiat proroki.
Konstantinovskaia, L. V. (Liudmila Vasil'evna) Moskva : Klassiks Stil', 2002.
BF1796.K66 2002

Kohen, Ya'aḳov Yiśra'el.
Shakh, El'azar Menaḥem Man. Sefer Mi-torato de-rabi El'azar. [Bene Beraḳ] : le-haśig mishpahat Kohen, [763 i.e. 2003]

Kohen, Yekutiel. Mishpaṭ ha-shalom : ben shalom ve-gerushin ... / Yekuti'el Kohen. Yerushalayim : Mekhon Sha'ar ha-mishpaṭ : Hanhalat bate ha-din ha-rabaniyim, 762 [2001 or 2002] 300 p. ; 24 cm.
1. Husband and wife (Jewish law) 2. Marriage - Religious aspects - Judaism. 3. Divorce (Jewish law) 4. Ethics, Jewish. I. Title.

Kohl, Jeanette.
Re-Visionen. Berlin : Akademie Verlag, c2002.

KOHLBERG, LAWRENCE, 1927- - CONTRIBUTIONS IN MORAL PHILOSOPHY.
Schwickert, Eva-Maria. Feminismus und Gerechtigkeit. Berlin : Akademie Verlag, c2000.

Köhler, Henning, 1951- War Michel aus Lönneberga aufmerksamkeitsgestört? : der ADS-Mythos und die neue Kindergeneration / Henning Köhler ; mit einem Nachwort von Georg Kühlewind. 2. Aufl. Stuttgart : Freies Geistesleben, 2002. 296 p. ; 23 cm. Includes bibliographical references (p. 289-296). ISBN 3-7725-1937-7 (pbk.)
1. Attention-deficit hyperactivity disorder. 2. Attention-deficit hyperactivity disorder - Diagnosis. I. Title.

Köhler, Manfred. Apokalypse oder Umkehr? : Vorspiel einer Philosophie der Zukunft : von der Überlebenskrise der Menschheit / von Manfred Köhler. Marburg : Tectum, 2000. 214 p. ; 21 cm. Includes bibliographical references (p. 210-214). ISBN 3-8288-8145-9 (pbk.)
1. Hegel, Georg Wilhelm Friedrich, - 1770-1831. 2. Philosophy, Modern - 20th century. 3. Violence. 4. Nihilism (Philosophy) I. Title.

Kohn, Arthur J. The integrator for Introductory psychology 2.0 [electronic resource] / Arthur J. Kohn, Wendy Kohn. Pacific Grove, Calif. : Brooks/Cole, c1998. 1 CD-ROM ; 4 3/4 in. Title on jewel case insert: Integrator 2.0. System requirements for PC: 486DX/66MHz PC; Windows 3.1 or 95. System requirements for Macintosh: 68LC040 processor or better; System 7.1 or later. Title from disc label. SUMMARY: Multimedia introduction to psychology. May be used with the text entitled Introductory Psychology or used independently. Production level cataloging. ISBN 0-534-34924-2
1. Psychology. I. Kohn, Wendy. II. Title. III. Title: Integrator 2.0
BF121

Kohn, Michael L.
Mason, Douglas J. The memory workbook. Oakland, CA : New Harbinger Publications, : c2001. : Distributed in the U.S.A. by Publishers Group West, c2001.
BF724.85.M45 M37 2001

Kohn, Wendy.
Kohn, Arthur J. The integrator for Introductory psychology 2.0 [electronic resource]. Pacific Grove, Calif. : Brooks/Cole, c1998.
BF121

KOHUT, HEINZ.
Goldberg, Arnold, 1929- Misunderstanding Freud. New York : Other Press, 2004.
BF173.G59 2004

Strozier, Charles B. Heinz Kohut. 1st pbk. ed. New York : Other Press, 2004.
BF109.K6 S77 2004

KOLA NUTS - NIGERIA.
Adeosun, Kola A. [Oro ti obi n so. English] What the kolanut is saying. Ibadan, Nigeria : Creative Books, 1999.
BF1779.K6 A33 1999

KOLA TREE. See **KOLA NUTS.**
KOLANUTS. See **KOLA NUTS.**

Kolb, Janice E. M. In corridors of eternal time : a passage through grief : a journal / Janice Gray Kolb. Nevada City, Calif. : Blue Dolphin Pub., 2003. p. cm. Table of contents URL: http://www.loc.gov/catdir/toc/ecip046/2003015769.html ISBN 1-57733-135-4 (pbk. : alk. paper) DDC 155.9/37
1. Kolb, Janice E. M. 2. Pets - Death. 3. Grief - Miscellanea. 4. Cats. 5. Bereavement - Miscellanea. I. Title.
BF1997.K65 A3 2003b

KOLB, JANICE E. M.
Kolb, Janice E. M. In corridors of eternal time. Nevada City, Calif. : Blue Dolphin Pub., 2003.
BF1997.K65 A3 2003b

Koleda, Sergeĭ. Modelirovanie bessoznatel'nogo : praktika NLP v rossiĭskom kontekste / Sergeĭ Koleda. Moskva : In-t obshchegumanitarnykh issledovaniĭ, 2000. 219 p. ; 20 cm. (Seriia Neĭro-lingvisticheskoe programmirovanie ; vyp. 2) "Nauchnoe izdanie"--Colophon. On p. preceding t.p.: Sovremennaia psikhologiia: teoriia i praktika. ISBN 588230086X
1. Neurolinguistic programming. I. Title. II. Series.
BF637.N46 K65 2000

Koll, Shmuel, 1938- Sefer Ra'yonot u-mesarim : le-haftarot ha-shavu'a ... / ḥubar 'al yede Shemu'el ben ... Yehoshu'a Kol ... kolel Ḳuntres Zanvot ha-udim ha-'ashenim ... ḥubar ... 'al yede Shemu'el ... Kol ... nispaḥ Beri'ut ha-'enayim veha-limud ha-intensivi ... me-et Dr. Binyamin Zilberman. Yerushalayim : S. Kol, 761- [2001- v. ; 23 cm. Added title page title: Raayonot umssarim lhaftarot hashavua. CONTENTS: v.1. Be-reshit-Shemot -- v.2. Va-yiḳra-Bamidbar.
1. Haftarot - Commentaries. 2. Jewish sermons, Hebrew. 3. Ethics, Jewish. 4. Smoking - Religious aspects - Judaism. I. Silverman, Bynjamin, Dr. II. Title. III. Title: Zanvot ha-udim ha-'ashenim. IV. Title: Ḳuntres Zanvot ha-udim ha-'ashenim. V. Title: Beri'ut ha-'enayim veha-limud ha-intensivi. VI. Title: Ra'yonot u-mesarim VII. Title: Raayonot umssarim lhaftarot hashavua VIII. Title: Ideas and Moral Messages from the Weekly Haftarot

Kollar, L. Peter (Laszlo Peter), 1926- Symbolism in Hindu architecture as revealed in the Shri Minakshi Sundareswar / L. Peter Kollar ; photographs by Alan Croker. New Delhi : Aryan Books International, 2001. xiv, 97 p., [24] p. of plates : ill. ; 24 cm. Includes bibliographical references (p. [91]-93) and index. ISBN 81-7305-204-2
1. Maturai Arulmiku Mīṇāṭci Cuntarēśvarar Ālayam. 2. Temples, Hindu. 3. Symbolism in architecture - India. 4. Art, Hindu - India. 5. Hindu symbolism. I. Title.
NA6002.K65 2001

Kolo, Festus D.
Professional concerns arising from twenty years of counselling practice in Nigeria. Garki, Abuja, Nigeria : Official Printers, Jayawahs Communications, 1996.
BF637.C6 P775 1996

Kolo, Ibrahim A.
Professional concerns arising from twenty years of counselling practice in Nigeria. Garki, Abuja, Nigeria : Official Printers, Jayawahs Communications, 1996.
BF637.C6 P775 1996

Kolokwia psychologiczne
(t. 10) Psychologia w obliczu zachodzących przemian społeczno-kulturowych. Warszawa : Instytut Psychologii PAN, 2002.
BF20.P79 2002

Komaragiri, Sarat.
Glener, Doug. Wisdom's blossoms. Boston, Mass. : Shambhala, 2002.
BL2003.G64 2002

Komik der Renaissance, Renaissance der Komik / herausgegeben von Barbara Marx, unter Mitarbeit von Sabine Strickrodt und Alexandra Stanislaw-Kemenah. Frankfurt am Main ; New York : P. Lang, c2000. xxiv, 240 p. ; 21 cm. Papers presented at a conference held in Jena, Sept. 29-Oct. 2, 1997. Includes bibliographical references (p.230-232) and index. ISBN 3-631-36567-5 (acid-free paper)
1. Comic, The - Congresses. 2. Renaissance - Congresses. I. Marx, Barbara. II. Strickrodt, Sabine. III. Stanislaw-Kemenah, Alexandra. IV. Title: Renaissance der Komik
BH301.C7.K63 2000

Kommunikation, Kunst und Kultur / herausgegeben von Reiner Matzker und Michael Müller. Bern ; New York : Peter Lang, c2002. 247 p. : ill. ; 23 cm. (Jahrbuch für Internationale Germanistik. Reihe C. Forschungsberichte ; Band 7) (Forschungsberichte zur Internationalen Germanistik. Medienwissenschaft ; Teil 6) Cover title: Medienwissenschaft Kommunikation, Kunst und Kultur. Includes bibliographical references (p. 231-246). ISBN 3-906770-23-0 ISSN 0721-3905
1. Communication and culture. 2. Communication and the arts. 3. Cognitive psychology. I. Matzker, Reiner, 1953- II. Müller, Michael, 1946- III. Title: Medienwissenschaft Kommunikation, Kunst und Kultur IV. Series: Jahrbuch für internationale Germanistik. Reihe C, Forschungsberichte ; Bd. 7. V. Series: Germanistische Medienwissenschaft ; T. 6.

Kommunikative Effizienz.
Roelcke, Thorsten. Heidelberg : Winter, c2002.

Kommunikatives Handeln und detranszendentalisierte Vernunft.
Habermas, Jürgen. Stuttgart : Reclam, c2001.
P91.H33 2001

Kọ́mọ́láfẹ́, Kọ́láwọlé. African traditional religion : understanding Ogboni Fraternity / by Kọ́láwọlé Kọ́mọ́láfẹ́. Lagos : Ifa-Ọ̀rúnmìlà Organisation, 1995. 20 p. : ill. ; 21 cm. Includes bibliographical references (p. 20). Includes texts in Yoruba with English translations. ISBN 978-33199-0-6 DDC 366/.09669
1. Reformed Ogboni Fraternity (Nigeria) 2. Yoruba (African people) - Religion. 3. Nigeria - Religion. I. Title. II. Title: Understanding Ogboni fraternity
BL2480.Y6 K65 1995

Der Komponist als Heros.
Hofmann, Dorothea. Essen : Die Blaue Eule, c2003.

Kompositionsfragen.
Kuhn-Wengenmayr, Annemarie. Frankfurt ; New York : P. Lang, c2001.
N7430.K826 2001

Komsomol'skiĭ-na-Amure gosudarstvennyĭ pedagogicheskiĭ universitet.
Psikhologicheskaia sluzhba v obshchestve. Komsomol'sk-na-Amure : Komsomol'skiĭ-na-Amure gos. pedagogicheskiĭ universitet, 2002.
BF20.P743 2002

Konferentsiia "Gendernyĭ podkhod v psikhologicheskom konsul'tirovanii" (2002 : Evropeĭskiĭ Gumanitarnyĭ Universitet) Gendernyĭ podkhod v psikhologicheskikh issledovaniiakh i konsul'tirovanii : materialy konferentsii / pod redaktsieĭ E.I Krukovich. Minsk : Evropeĭskiĭ Gumanitarnyĭ Universitet, 2002. 98 p. ; 21 cm. Summary in English. Includes bibliographical references. ISBN 985661483X
1. Feminist psychology - Congresses. 2. Psychoanalysis and feminism - Congresses. 3. Sex role - Congresses. 4. Sex differences (Psychology) - Congresses. I. Krukovich, E. I. II. Frolova, I͡U. G. III. Title.
BF201.4.K66 2002

Konferentsiia "Virtualistika-2001" (2001 : Moscow, Russia).
Nosov, N. A. Ne-virtualistika. Moskva : Gumanitariĭ, 2001.
BF38.N67 2001

Konfigurationen der Renaissance.
Kalisch, Eleonore. Berlin : Vistas, c2002.

Konflikt i tvorchestvo v zerkale psikhologii.
Granovskaia, R. M. (Rada Mikhaĭlovna) Moskva : Genezis, 2002.
BF637.I48 G72 2002

Konflikty mezi lidmi.
Křivohlavý, Jaro. Vyd. 2., přepracované, v Portalu 1. Praha : Portal, 2002.
BF637.I48 K75 2002

Kong Meng ren sheng ge yan ji cui.
Confucius. [Selections. Chinese & English. 1998] Wuhan : Wuhan gong ye da xue chu ban she, 1998.

Konserwatyzm.
Protsenko, Oleh. Kyïv : "Smoloskyp", 1998.

Konstantinos, 1972- Contact the other side : 7 methods for afterlife communication / Konstantinos. 1st ed. St. Paul, Minn. : Llewellyn Publications, 2001. vi, 203 p. ; 23 cm. Includes bibliographical references (p. 199) and index. ISBN 1-56718-377-8 DDC 133.9/1
1. Death - Miscellanea. 2. Spiritualism. I. Title.
BF1275.D2 K66 2001

Konstantinovskaia, L. V. (Liudmila Vasil'evna)
Kogda prikhodiat proroki / L.V. Konstantinovskaia. Moskva : Klassiks Stil', 2002. 233, [1] p. : ill., maps ; 27 cm. Includes bibliographical references (p. 233-[234]). ISBN 5946030280
1. Prophets - History. 2. Prophecies (Occultism) - History. 3. End of the world. 4. Forecasting. I. Title.
BF1796.K66 2002

Konstrukte nationaler Identität : Deutschland, Frankreich und Grossbritannien (19. und 20. Jahrhundert) / herausgegeben von Michael Einfalt ... [et al.]. Würzburg : Ergon, c2002. 298 p. : ill. ; 23 cm. (Identitäten und Alteritäten ; Bd. 11) Includes bibliographical references. ISBN 3-89913-232-7
1. National characteristics, French. 2. National characteristics, German. 3. National characteristics, British. 4. France - Ethnic identity. 5. Germany - Ethnic identity. 6. Great Britain - Ethnic identity. I. Einfalt, Michael. II. Series.
DC34.K67 2002

Kontexte und Kulturen des Erinnerns : Maurice Halbwachs und das Paradigma des kollektiven Gedächtnisses / Gerald Echterhoff, Martin Saar (Hg.) ; mit einem Geleitwort von Jan Assmann. Konstanz : UVK Verlagsgesellschaft, 2002. 289 p. : ill. ; 23 cm. (Theorie und Methode. Sozialwissenschaften) Includes bibliographical references and index. Eleven German, 2 English contributions. ISBN 3-89669-814-1 (pbk.).
1. Halbwachs, Maurice, - 1877-1945. 2. Memory - Social aspects. 3. Social psychology. I. Echterhoff, Gerald. II. Saar, Martin. III. Assmann, Jan. IV. Series.
BF378.S65 K65 2002

Kontra, Miklós.
Magyarok és nyelvtörvények. Budapest : Teleki László Alapítvány, 2002.
PH2073 .K66 2002

Die Konvertibilität des Bewusstseins.
Wilkens, Sander. 1. Aufl. Würzburg ; Boston : Deutscher Wissenschafts-Verlag (DWV), c2002.
BD163 .E45 2002

Kook, Abraham Isaac, 1865-1935. Selections. 2001.
Mar'eh Kohen. Yerushalayim : Makhon le-ḥeḳer mishnat ha-Re'iyah Ḳuḳ be-shituf 'im "Bet ha-Rav", c762 [2001 or 2002]

KOOK, ABRAHAM ISAAC, 1865-1935.
Mar'eh Kohen. Yerushalayim : Makhon le-ḥeḳer mishnat ha-Re'iyah Ḳuḳ be-shituf 'im "Bet ha-Rav", c762 [2001 or 2002]

KOOK, ABRAHAM ISAAC, 1865-1935 - PORTRAITS.
Mar'eh Kohen. Yerushalayim : Makhon le-ḥeḳer mishnat ha-Re'iyah Ḳuḳ be-shituf 'im "Bet ha-Rav", c762 [2001 or 2002]

Kook, Rebecca B., 1959- The logic of democratic exclusion : African Americans in the United States and Palestinian citizens in Isreal / Rebecca B. Kook. Lanham, Md. : Lexington Books, c2002. x, 221 p. ; 23 cm. Includes bibliographical references (p. 189-208) and index. CONTENTS: National identity and collective action -- Representing American national identity : the shifting status of African Americans -- National identity in Israel : being a Palestinian in a Jewish state -- The legal construction of membership in Israel -- Reinventing the invisible man : African Americans and the American symbolic indexes of identity -- Nationalizing religion : the Israeli national symbolic matrix -- Re-writing national identity--from Blacks to African Americans -- The crisis of Israeli collective national identity. ISBN 0-7391-0441-1 (alk. paper) ISBN 0-7391-0442-X (pbk. : alk. paper) DDC 323.1/1927405694
1. African Americans - Civil rights. 2. Marginality, Social - United States. 3. National characteristics, American. 4. United States - Race relations - Political aspects. 5. United States - Politics and government - 1989- 6. Palestinian Arabs - Civil rights - Israel. 7. Marginality, Social - Israel. 8. National characteristics, Israeli. 9. Israel - Ethnic relations - Political aspects. 10. Israel - Politics and government - 1993- I. Title.
E185.615 .K59 2002

Kooper, Yakov.
Erlanger, Gad. [Mazalot, ha-Yahadut ya-ani. English] Signs of the times. Jerusalem ; New York : Feldheim Pub., 2000.
BF1714.J4 E74 2001

Koops, W. (Willem).
Beyond the century of the child. Philadelphia : University of Pennsylvania Press, c2003.
HQ767.87 .B49 2003

Kopala, Mary.
Handbook of counseling women. Thousand Oaks, Calif. ; London : Sage Publications, c2003.
RC451.4.W6 H36 2003

Ḳoraḥ, Shelomoh ben Yaḥya. Netsaḥ ḥayenu : toldot ḥaye ha-adam ... 'ad 'aliyato la- meromim ... 'ad tehiyat ha-metim / me-et Shelomoh ... b. r. Yaḥya Ḳoraḥ ... Bene Beraḳ : S. Ḳoraḥ, 762 [2001 or 2002] 163 p. ; 24 cm.
1. Man (Jewish theology) 2. Soul (Judaism) 3. Cabala. 4. Eschatology, Jewish. I. Title.

Sodot shamayim.
Eleazar ben Judah, of Worms, 1176 (ca.)-1238. Sefer Sode razaya .... Bene-Beraḳ : Ḳoraḥ, 759 [1998 or 1999]
BM525 .E432 1999

KORAN AND PHILOSOPHY.
Tijan Bangura, Abubakar. The truth can be discovered in the Qur'an. [Freetown, Sierra Leone? : s.n., 2002]
1. Black author.

Korb-Khalsa, Kathy L., 1958-.
Liptak, John J. The self-esteem program. Plainview, NY : Wellness Reproductions & Pub., c2002.
BF697.5.S46 L57 2002

Korczak, Janusz, 1878-1942. [Works. Hebrew. 1996]
Ketavim / Yanush Ḳorts'aḳ ; mi-Polanit, Yonat ye-Aleksander Sened. [Tel Aviv] : Yad ya-shem : ha-Agudah 'a. sh. Yanush Ḳorts'aḳ be-Yiśra'el : Bet Loḥame ha-geta'ot 'a. sh. Yitsḥaḳ Ḳatsenelson : ha-Ḳibuts ha-me'uḥad, [1996- v. : ill. ; 22 cm. PARTIAL CONTENTS: kerekh 1. Ekh le-ehov yeled. Rega'im ḥinukhiyim. Zekhut ha-yeled li-khevod -- kerekh 2. Prozah piyutit -- kerekh 3. Sipure ha-ḳayetanot -- kerekh 4. Yalde rehov ve-yeled ha-teraklin -- kerekh 5. ha-Tehilah ye-sipurim aḥadim. ISBN 9653940376 (v.2)
1. Child psychology. 2. Child rearing. 3. Education - Philosophy. I. Sened, Yonat. II. Sened, Alexander. III. Title.
LB775.K627 K48 1996 <Hebr>

KOREANS - CANADA - CULTURAL ASSIMILATION.
Western eyes [videorecording]. New York, NY : First Run/Icarus Films, 2000.

KOREANS - CANADA - ETHNIC IDENTITY.
Western eyes [videorecording]. New York, NY : First Run/Icarus Films, 2000.

Korepanova, M. V. (Marina Vasil'evna) Teoriia i praktika stanovleniia i razvitiia obraza IA doshkol'nika : monografiia / M.V. Korepanova. Volgograd : Peremena, 2001. 239 p. ; 21 cm. Includes bibliographical references (p. 227-239). ISBN 5882345073
1. Self-perception in children. 2. Self-perception - Study and teaching (Preschool) I. Title.
BF723.S28 K66 2001

Korfmann, Manfred.
Mauerschau. Remshalden-Grunbach : Greiner, 2002.

KORFMANN, MANFRED.
Mauerschau. Remshalden-Grunbach : Greiner, 2002.

Korhonen, Teppo.
Making and breaking of borders. Helsinki : Finnish Literature Society, 2003.
JC323 .M35 2003

Körner, Hans, 1951-.
Botschaften aus dem Jenseits. [Düsseldorf] : Droste, c2002.

Kornilova, T. V.
Tvorcheskoe nasledie A.V. Brushlinskogo i O.K. Tikhomirova i sovremennaia psikhologiia myshleniia (k 70-letiiu so dnia rozhdeniia). Moskva : In-t psikhologii RAN, 2003.
BF109.B86 T86 2003

Koroma, Abu F. Exposing and destroying the dark satanic kingdom / by Abu F. Koroma. [Freetown, Sierra Leone? : s.n.], c2000. 45 p. : ill. ; 21 cm. Cover title.
1. Demonology. 2. Spiritual warfare. 3. Demoniac possession. 4. Exorcism. 5. Black author. I. Title.

Korotkov, K. (Konstantin), 1952-.
Musiol, Marie-J. (Marie-Jeanne), 1950- Corps de lumière. Hull, Québec : Axe Néo-7, art contemporain, [2001?]

Körper- und Bewegungsspiele.
Broich, Josef, 1948- 1. Aufl. 1999. Köln : Maternus, 1999.

KörperNormen, KörperFormen.
Hofstadler, Beate, 1961- Wien : Turia + Kant, c2001.
BF692.5 .H64 2001

Korsgaard, Christine M. (Christine Marion).
Raz, Joseph. The practice of value. Oxford ; New York : Oxford University Press, 2003.
BD232 .R255 2003

Korsström, Tuva. Kan kvinnor tänka? : en undersökning av det kvinnliga tänkandets villkor / Tuva Korsström. Stockholm/Stehag : Symposion, 2002. 312, [1] p. ; 21 cm. Includes bibliographical references (P. 308-[313]). ISBN 91-7139-531-8
1. Feminist psychology. 2. Sex differences (Psychology) 3. Women authors. 4. Thought and thinking. I. Title.

Kosarin, Jenni. The everything divining the future book : from runes to tarot cards to tealeaves to cyrstals, predict what fate has in store for you / Jenni Kosarin. Avon, MA : Adams Media, c2003. xii, 289 p. : ill. ; 24 cm. (The everything series) Includes bibliographical references (p. 268-270) and index. ISBN 1-58062-866-4 (pbk.) DDC 133.3
1. Divination. I. Title. II. Title: Divining the future book III. Series.
BF1773 .K67 2003

The everything love signs book / Jenni Kosarin. Avon, MA : Adams Media, c2004. p. cm. (An everything series book) ISBN 1-59337-040-7 DDC 133.5/864677
1. Astrology. 2. Love - Miscellanea. 3. Mate selection - Miscellanea. 4. Sex - Miscellanea. I. Title. II. Series: Everything series.
BF1729.L6 K67 2004

Kosek, Jake.
Race, nature, and the politics of difference. Durham : Duke University Press, c2003.
HT1521 .R2355 2003

Koshcheĭ, L. A. (Lĭubov' Alekseevna).
Dubina, I. N. (Igor' Nikolaevich) Tvorchestvo kak fenomen sotsial'nykh kommunikatsiĭ. Novosibirsk : Sibirskoe otd-nie RAN, 2000.
BF411 .D82 2000

Kosminsky, Jane.
The Alexander technique [videorecording]. New York, N.Y. : Wellspring Media, c1999.

Kosmos und System.
Gloyna, Tanja. Stuttgart-Bad Cannstatt : Frommann-Holzboog, c2002.
B2898 .G56 2002

Kosslyn, Stephen Michael, 1948- Fundamentals of psychology : the brain, the person, the world / Stephen M. Kosslyn, Robin S. Rosenberg. 2nd ed. Boston : Allyn and Bacon, c2005. p. cm. Includes bibliographical references and indexes. DDC 150
1. Psychology - Textbooks. I. Rosenberg, Robin S. II. Title.
BF121 .K585 2005

Psychology : the brain, the person, the world / Stephen M. Kosslyn. 2nd ed. Boston, MA : Allyn and Bacon, 2004. p. cm. Includes bibliographical references and index. ISBN 0-205-37609-6 (alk. paper) DDC 150
1. Psychology. I. Title.
BF121 .K59 2004

Kostera, Monika, 1963-.
Interpreting the maternal organisation. London ; New York : Routledge, 2003.
HM786 .I58 2003

Kostina, L. M. (Lĭubov' Mikhaĭlovna) Metody diagnostiki trevozhnosti / L.M. Kostina. Sankt-Peterburg : Rech', 2002. 197 p. : ill. ; 21 cm. (Praktikum po psikhodiagnostike) Includes bibliographical references (p. 193-[196]). ISBN 5926801249
1. Anxiety. 2. Psychodiagnostics. 3. Psychology - Methodology. I. Title. II. Series.
BF575.A6 K65 2002

Kotel'nikova, T.
Psikhologicheskie i pedagogicheskie problemy samorazvitiia lichnosti. Kirov : Viatskiĭ gos. pedagogicheskiĭ universitet, 2002.
BF723.P4 P78 2002

Koterski, Joseph W.
Karl Jaspers on philosophy of history and history of philosophy. Amherst, N.Y. : Humanity Books, 2003.
B3279.J34 K292 2003

Kotler, Philip. Social marketing : improving the quality of life / Philip Kotler, Ned Roberto, Nancy Lee. 2nd ed. Thousand Oaks, Calif. ; London : Sage Publications, c2002. xvi, 438 p. : ill. ; 24 cm. Includes bibliographical references and indexes. CONTENTS: Understanding social marketing. Defining social marketing. Outlining the strategic marketing planning process. Discovering keys to success -- Analyzing the social marketing environment. Determining research needs and resources. Mapping the internal and external environments -- Establishing target audiences, objectives, and goals. Selecting target markets. Setting objectives and goals. Deepening our understanding of the target audience and the competition -- Developing social marketing strategies. Product: designing the market offering. Price: managing costs of behavior change. Place: making access convenient. Promotion: creating messages. Promotion: selecting media channels -- Managing social marketing programs. Developing a plan for evaluation and monitoring. Establishing budgets and finding funding sources. Completing an implementation plan and sustaining behavior. Making ethical decisions. ISBN 0-7619-2434-5 (pbk. : alk. paper) DDC 658.8
1. Social marketing. 2. Behavior modification. I. Roberto, Ned. II. Lee, Nancy, 1932- III. Title.
HF5414 .K67 2002

Kottler, Jeffrey A. American shaman : an odyssey of global healing traditions / Jeffrey Kottler and Jon Carlson with Bradford Keeney. New York : Brunner-Routledge, 2004. p. cm. Includes bibliographical references (p.   ) and index. ISBN 0-415-94821-5 ISBN 0-415-94822-3 (pbk.) DDC 200/.92
1. Shamanism. 2. Spiritual healing. I. Keeney, Bradford P. II. Carlson, Jon. III. Keeney, Bradford P. IV. Title.
BF1598.K43 K68 2004

Introduction to therapeutic counseling : voices from the field / Jeffrey A. Kottler. 5th ed. Australia ; Pacific

Kottler, Jeffrey A.
Grove, CA : Thomson-Brooks/Cole, c2004. xvii, 462 p. : ill. ; 24 cm. Includes bibliographical references (p. 429-446) and index. ISBN 0-534-52339-0 (Student ed. with InfoTrac college ed.) ISBN 0-534-52343-9 (Student ed. without InfoTrac college ed.) DDC 616.89/14
1. Counseling. I. Title.
BF637.C6 K678 2004

Koutsoukis, Nikitas-Spiros. Decision modelling and information systems : the information value chain / by Nikitas-Spiros Koutsoukis, Gautam Mitra. Boston : Kluwer Academic Publishers, c2003. xvi, 366 p. : ill. ; 25 cm. (Operations research/computer science interfaces series ; ORCS 26) Includes bibliographical references and index. ISBN 140207560X DDC 658.4/03
1. Decision making. I. Mitra, Gautam. II. Title. III. Series.
T57.95 .K68 2003

Koval', N. A.
Razvitie lichnosti v kul'turno-obrazovatel'nom prostranstve. Tambov : Tambovskiĭ gos. universitet im. G.R. Derzhavina, 2000.
BF698 .R342 2000

Kovalenko, A. P. Dusha : vse o dushe, o serdt͡se i vole cheloveka / A.P. Kovalenko. Moskva : Veteran otchizny ; Megatron, 2000. 339 p. : ill. ; 22 cm. Includes bibliographical references (p. 336-337). ISBN 5868040716
1. Soul - Miscellanea. I. Title.
BF1999 .K685 2000

Kovesi, Julius. Values and evaluations : essays on ethics and ideology / Julius Kovesi ; edited by Alan Tapper. New York ; Bern : P. Lang, c1998. 223 p. ; 24 cm. (American university studies. Series V. Philosophy, 0739-6392 ; v. 183) Includes bibliographical references (p. [209]-217) and index. ISBN 0-8204-3808-1 (alk. paper) DDC 190
1. Values. 2. Ethics. 3. Theology. 4. History - Philosophy. I. Tapper, Alan. II. Title. III. Series.
BD232 .K68 1998

Ḳovets ma'amre 'Iḳvata de-Meshiḥa ...
Wasserman, Elhanan Bunim, 1875-1941.
Yerushalayim : Yeshivat Or Elḥanan, 762 [2001 or 2002]

Kōvintaṉ, Ka. Tamiḻt tiraippaṭaṅkaḷil āṇ-peṇ pāl pētam / Ka. Kōvintaṉ. 1. patippu. Ceṉṉai : Kumaraṉ Papḷiṣars, 2001. x, 298 p. : ill. ; 22 cm. Cover title: Tamiḻt tiraippaṭaṅkaḷil āṇ-peṉ pālpētam. In Tamil. SUMMARY: Gender differences in Tamil cinema. Includes bibliographical references.
1. Sex differences. 2. Motion pictures - India - Tamil Nadu. I. Title. II. Title: Tamiḻt tiraippaṭaṅkaḷil āṇ-peṇ pālpētam III. Title: Āṇ-peṇ pālpētam
BF692.2 .K68 2001

Kowaleski, Maryanne.
Gendering the master narrative. Ithaca : Cornell University Press, c2003.
HQ1143 .G46 2003

Kowalski, Robin M. Complaining, teasing, and other annoying behaviors / Robin M. Kowalski. New Haven : Yale University Press, c2003. x, 197 p. ; 22 cm. Includes bibliographical references (p. [181]-191) and index. CONTENTS: The offensive side of social interaction -- Complaining -- Teasing and bullying -- Egocentrism, arrogance, and conceit -- Incivility and breaches of propriety -- Excessive worry and reassurance-seeking -- Deceit and betrayal. ISBN 0-300-09971-1 (alk. paper) DDC 302
1. Interpersonal relations. 2. Interpersonal conflict. I. Title.
HM1106 .K69 2003

Kozlov, Nikolaĭ (Nikolaĭ Ivanovich) Kniga dl͡ia tekh, komu nravit͡sia zhit', ili, Psikhologi͡ia lichnostnogo rosta / Nikolaĭ Kozlov. Moskva : "AST-Press kniga", 2002. 348 p. : ill. ; 22 cm. Includes bibliographical references. ISBN 5780510091
1. Personality development. 2. Psychology, Applied. I. Title. II. Title: Psikhologi͡ia lichnostnogo rosta
BF723.P4 K69 2002

Kozomara, Mladen.
Kriza i perspektive filozofije. 1. izd. Beograd : Tersit, 1995.
B99.S462 K75 1995

Kozyreva, P. M.
Denisovskiĭ, G. M. Politicheskai͡a tolerantnost' v reformiruemom rossiĭskom obshchestve vtoroĭ poloviny 90-kh godov. Moskva : T͡Sentr obshchechelovecheskikh t͡sennosteĭ, 2002.
JN6699.A15 D46 2002

KQED-TV (Television station : San Francisco, Calif.)
With eyes open [electronic resource]. San Francisco : KQED ; [Alexandria, Va.] : PBS
BF789.D4

Kraft, Robert Nathaniel. Memory perceived : recalling the Holocaust / Robert N. Kraft. Westport, Conn. : Praeger, 2002. xxii, 211 p. ; 25 cm. (Psychological dimensions to war and peace, 1540-5265) Includes bibliographical references (p. 197-204) and index. ISBN 0-275-97774-9 (alk. paper) DDC 940.53/18/092
1. Holocaust, Jewish (1939-1945) - Personal narratives. 2. Holocaust, Jewish (1939-1945) - Psychological aspects. 3. Holocaust, Jewish (1939-1945) - Influence. 4. Holocaust, Jewish (1939-1945) - Historiography. 5. Memory. I. Title. II. Series.
D804.195 .K73 2002

Kral, Michael J., 1956-.
About psychology. Albany : State University of New York Press, c2003.
BF38 .A28 2003

Kramer, Eric Mark.
The emerging monoculture. Westport, Conn. : Praeger, 2003.
HM843 .E44 2003

Kramer, Matthew H., 1959- The quality of freedom / Matthew H. Kramer. Oxford ; New York : Oxford University Press, 2003. ix, 482 p. ; 24 cm. Includes bibliographical references and index. ISBN 0-19-924756-0 DDC 320/.01/1
1. Liberty. I. Title.
JC585 .K74 2003

Krames, Jeffrey A. The Jack Welch lexicon of leadership / Jeffrey A. Krames. 1st ed. New York : McGraw-Hill, 2001, c2002. xii, 210 p. ; 22 cm. "Over 250 terms, concepts, strategies and initiatives of the legendary leader"--jacket. Includes bibliographical references (p. 205-210) ISBN 0-07-138140-6
1. Welch, Jack, - 1935- 2. Leadership. 3. Industrial management. 4. Competition. I. Title.
HD57.7 .K726 2001

The Rumsfeld way : leadership wisdom of a battle-hardened maverick / Jefferey A. Krames. 1st ed. New York : McGraw-Hill, c2002. ix, 244 p. ; 22 cm. Includes bibliographical references (p. 209-229) and index. CONTENTS: The road to Kandahar -- Rumsfeld: who and why? -- Mission first -- Straight talk -- All the right moves -- Crafting coalitions -- The consequence of values -- The war CEO -- Acquiring and using intelligence -- Mastering the agenda -- The pragmatic leader -- The determined warrior. ISBN 0-07-140641-7 : $18.95 DDC 658.4/092
1. Rumsfeld, Donald, - 1932- 2. Leadership. I. Title.
UB210 .K73 2002

Kramsch, Claire J.
Language acquisition and language socialization. London ; New York : Continuum, 2002.
P118 .L243 2002

Krashen, Stephen D. Explorations in language acquisition and use : the Taipei lectures / Stephen D. Krashen. Portsmouth, NH : Heinemann, c2003. viii, 103 p. : ill. ; 23 cm. Includes bibliographical references (p. 87-96) and index. ISBN 0-325-00554-0 DDC 418/.0071
1. Language and languages - Study and teaching. 2. Language acquisition. I. Title.
P51 .K666 2003

Krasikov, V. I. (Vladimir Ivanovich) Sindrom sushchestvovanii͡a / V.I. Krasikov. Tomsk : [s.n.], 2002. 255 p. ; 21 cm. Includes list of the author's publications (p. 254-[256]) ISBN 5713701948
1. Philosophical anthropology. 2. Life. 3. Vice. I. Title.

Krasnyĭ matros
(vyp. 35) Florenskai͡a, O. Psikhologi͡ia bytovogo shrifta. Sankt-Peterburg : Krasnyĭ matros, 2001.
BF896 .F66 2001

Kratka istorija srpske književnosti.
Deretić, Jovan. 3., prerađeno i dop. izd. Novi Sad : Svetovi, 2001.

Krauss, Sandy. Set yourself free : how to unlock the greatness within you! / Sandy Krauss. North Royalton, Ohio : Success Talks Pub., c1999. x, 163 p. ; 22 cm. Includes bibliographical references (p. 161-162). ISBN 0-9673198-0-3 DDC 158.1
1. Self-actualization (Psychology) 2. Self-esteem. I. Title.
BF637.S4 K73 1999

Kraut, Bernhard, 1960- Gefangen, auch im Erinnern / Bernhard Kraut. Wien : Edition Selene, c2002. 124 p. ; 21 cm. ISBN 3-85266-191-9 (pbk.)
1. Austria - History - 20th century. 2. Austria - Politics and government - 20th century. 3. Memory - Political aspects. 4. Memory - Social aspects. I. Title.

Kravchenko, I͡U. E.
Issledovanii͡a obuchenii͡a i razvitii͡a v kontekste kul'turno-istoricheskogo podkhoda. Moskva : Smysl, 2002.
BF712.5 .I88 2002

Kravt͡sova, E. E.
Issledovanii͡a obuchenii͡a i razvitii͡a v kontekste kul'turno-istoricheskogo podkhoda. Moskva : Smysl, 2002.
BF712.5 .I88 2002

Mezhdunarodnai͡a psikhologicheskai͡a konferent͡sii͡a "Psikhicheskoe razvitie v ontogeneze--zakonomernosti i vozmozhnye periodizat͡sii" (1999 : Moscow, Russia) Problemy psikhologii razvitii͡a. Moskva : RGGU, 2000.
BF712.5 .M49 2000

Kray, Jutta. Adult age differences in task switching : components, generalizability, and modifiability / Jutta Kray. Lengerich : Pabst Science Publishers, 2000. 210 p. : ill. ; 21 cm. (Psychologia universalis ; neue Reihe, Bd. 19) Originally presented as the author's thesis (doctoral)--Freie Universität, Berlin, 1998. Includes bibliographical references (p. 179-193). ISBN 3-934252-51-6 (pbk.) DDC 155.67/13
1. Cognition - Age factors. 2. Aging - Psychological aspects. I. Title. II. Series.
BF724.55.C63 K73 2000

Krayer, Karl J., 1954-.
Lee, William W. Organizing change. San Francisco : Pfeiffer, c2003.
HD58.8 .L423 2003

Krebs, Víctor J., 1957- Del alma y el arte / Víctor J. Krebs. Caracas, Venezuela : Museo de Bellas Artes, 1997. 188 p. : ill. (some col.) ; 23 cm. (Serie Reflexiones en el Museo ; no. 2) Includes bibliographical references (p. [165]-188). ISBN 980-238-176-4
1. Aesthetics. 2. Art - Philosophy. I. Museo de Bellas Artes (Venezuela) II. Title. III. Series.
N70 .K74 1997

Kricheldorf, Beate, 1949- Verantwortung, nein danke! : weibliche Opferhaltung als Strategie und Taktik / Beate Kricheldorf. 2., unveränderte Aufl. Frankfurt/Main : R.G. Fischer, 2001, c1998. 104 p. ; 21 cm. ISBN 3-89501-617-9
1. Women - Social conditions. 2. Feminism. I. Title.

Krieglstein, Werner J., 1941- Compassion : a new philosophy of the other / Werner J. Krieglstein. Amsterdam ; New York : Rodopi, c2002. viii, 248 p. ; 22 cm. (Value inquiry book series ; v. 134) Includes bibliographical references (p. [233]-238) and index. ISBN 90-420-0903-9 (pbk.)
1. Altruism. 2. Caring. 3. Helping behavior. 4. Interpersonal relations. I. Title. II. Series.

Kriminalbiologie und Zwangssterilisation.
Simon, Jürgen, 1966- Münster ; New York : Waxmann, c2001.

Kripal, Jeffrey John, 1962-.
Vishnu on Freud's desk. Delhi ; Oxford : Oxford University Press, 1999 (2002 [printing])

Krishna, Daya. Developments in Indian philosophy from Eighteenth century onwards : classical and western / Daya Krishna. New Delhi : Project of History of Indian Science, Philosophy, and Culture : Centre for Studies in Civilizations : Distributed by Motilal Banarsidass, 2002. xxiii, 416 p. ; 28 cm. (History of science, philosophy, and culture in Indian civilization. Volume X. Towards independence ; pt. 1) Includes bibliographical references and indexes. ISBN 81-87586-08-7
1. Philosophy, Indic. 2. Philosophy, Modern. I. Project of History of Indian Science, Philosophy, and Culture. II. Centre for Studies in Civilization (Delhi, India) III. Title. IV. Series.
B131+

Krishnamurthy, N. (Natarajan), 1948-.
Khushwant Singh, 1915- Khushwant Singh on women, love & lust. New Delhi : Books Today, c2002.
HQ29 .K48 2002

Kristeva, Julia, 1941- .
Avenir d'une revolte. English.
Kristeva, Julia, 1941- [Révolte intime. English] Intimate revolt. New York : Columbia University Press, c2002.
PN56.P92 K7513 2002

Pouvoirs et limites de la psychanalyse. English
(v. 2.) Kristeva, Julia, 1941- [Révolte intime. English] Intimate revolt. New York : Columbia University Press, c2002.
PN56.P92 K7513 2002

[Révolte intime. English]
Intimate revolt / Julia Kristeva ; translated by Jeanine Herman. New York : Columbia University Press, c2002. 291 p. ; 24 cm. (European perspectives) (The powers and limits of psychoanalysis ; v. 2) Includes bibliographical references and index. CONTENTS: pt. 1.

Intimate revolt -- pt. 2. The future of revolt. ISBN 0-231-11414-1 DDC 809/.93353
1. Psychoanalysis and literature. 2. Psychoanalysis in literature. 3. Intimacy (Psychology) in literature. 4. Psychoanalysis and philosophy. I. Kristeva, Julia, 1941- . Avenir d'une révolte. English. II. Title. III. Title: Future of revolt. IV. Series. V. Series: Kristeva, Julia, 1941- Pouvoirs et limites de la psychanalyse. English ; v. 2.
PN56.P92 K7513 2002

Kritik der Gewalt : Friedenspolitik im Zeichen von Krieg und Terror / Anita Bilek, Wilfried J. Graf, Alexander Neumann (Hg.). Wien : Promedia, c2002. 191 p. ; 21 cm. 7 of 13 contributions were published previously. Includes bibliographical references. ISBN 3-85371-192-8 (pbk.)
1. World politics - 1989- 2. International relations. 3. United States - Foreign relations - 1989- 4. War on Terrorism, 2001- 5. Peace. I. Bilek, Anita, 1972- II. Graf, Wilfried III. Neumann, Alexander, 1971-
D860 .K75 2002

Kritik (Detroit, Mich.)
Gray, Richard T. About face. Detroit : Wayne State University Press, c2004.
BF851 .G73 2004

KRITIS.
Padma, N. K., 1956- Navam and the Karṇātak group kṛtis. New Delhi : Kanishka Publishers, Distributors, 2002.
ML338 .P197 2002

Křivohlavý, Jaro. Konflikty mezi lidmi / Jaro Křivohlavý. Vyd. 2., přepracované, v Portalu 1. Praha : Portal, 2002. 189 p. ; 20 cm. Includes bibliographical references (p. 187-189) ISBN 80-7178-642-X
1. Interpersonal conflict. 2. Conflict (Psychology) 3. Conflict management. I. Title.
BF637.I48 K75 2002

Krivolapchuk, I. A. (Igor' Ivanovich).
Ėmotsii cheloveka v normal'nykh i stressornykh uslovii͡akh. Grodno : Grodnenskiĭ gos. universitet im. I͡Anki Kupaly, 2001.
BF531 .E54 2001

Kriza i perspektive filozofije / priredili Danilo N. Basta, Slobodan Žunjić, Mladen Kozomara. 1. izd. Beograd : Tersit, 1995. 554 p. ; 23 cm. (Biblioteka Misao) Includes bibliographical references. In Serbian (Roman), English and German. ISBN 86-7162-006-9
1. Philosophy. I. Basta, Danilo N., 1945- II. Žunjić, Slobodan, 1949- III. Kozomara, Mladen. IV. Đurić, Mihailo. V. Series: Biblioteka misao (Tersit (Firm))
B99.S462 K75 1995

Krockow, Christian, Graf von. Die Zukunft der Geschichte : ein Vermächtnis / Christian Graf von Krockow. München : List, c2002. 207 p. ; 22 cm. Includes bibliographical references. ISBN 3-471-79467-0
1. History - Philosophy. 2. Historiography. I. Title.
D16.8 .K722 2002

Krollmann, Fritz-Peter, 1963- Ethik und Ästhetik : zwei thematische Erörterungen im Horizont der Theorie des Holistischen Idealismus / Fritz-Peter Krollmann. Essen : Blaue Eule, 2002. 146 p. ; 21 cm. (Philosophie in der Blauen Eule ; Bd. 51) Includes bibliographical references. ISBN 3-89924-011-1 (pbk.)
1. Ethics. 2. Aesthetics. 3. Hermeneutics. 4. Idealism. I. Title. II. Series.

Kronofobi.
Hägglund, Martin. Stockholm : B. Östlings Bokförlag Symposion, 2002.

Kropotov, S. L. (Sergeĭ Leonidovich) Ėkonomika teksta v neklassicheskoĭ filosofii iskusstva : Nitsshe, Bataĭ͡a, Fuko, Derrida / S.L. Kropotov. Ekaterinburg : Gumanitarnyĭ universitet, 1999. 404 p. ; 21 cm. Includes bibliographical references. Title, table of contents, and summary also in English. ISBN 5774100405
1. Nietzsche, Friedrich Wilhelm, - 1844-1900. 2. Bataille, Georges, - 1897-1962. 3. Foucault, Michel. 4. Derrida, Jacques. 5. Postmodernism. 6. Art - Philosophy. I. Title. II. Title: Economy of text in non-classical philosophy of art
B831.2 .K76 1999

Krshṇadāsa Saṃskṛta sīrīja
(173.) Dīkṣita, Mathurā Prasāda, 1878-1978. [Kelikutūhala. Hindi & Sanskrit] Kelikutūhalam. Vārāṇasī : Kṛshadāsa Akādamī, 2002.
HQ470.S3 D55155 2002

Krüger, Klaus, 1957-.
Curiositas. Göttingen : Wallstein, c2002.
BF323.C8 C872 2002

Krukovich, E. I.
Konferent͡sii͡a "Gendernyĭ podkhod v psikhologicheskom konsul'tirovanii" (2002 : Evropeĭskiĭ Gumanitarnyĭ Universitet) Gendernyĭ podkhod v psikhologicheskikh issledovanii͡akh i konsul'tirovanii. Minsk : Evropeĭskiĭ Gumanitarnyĭ Universitet, 2002.
BF201.4 .K66 2002

Krzeszowksi, Tomasz P.
Language function, structure, and change. Frankfurt am Main ; New York : Lang, c2002.
P125 .L36 2002

KRZESZOWSKI, TOMASZ P. - BIBLIOGRAPHY.
Language function, structure, and change. Frankfurt am Main ; New York : Lang, c2002.
P125 .L36 2002

Kua shi ji xue ren wen cun
Huang, Kejian. [Selections. 1998] Huang Kejian zi xuan ji. Di 1 ban. Guilin Shi : Guangxi shi fan da xue chu ban she, 1998.
B99.C52 H765 1998

KUAN-YIN (BUDDHIST DEITY). See AVALOKITEŚVARA (BUDDHIST DEITY).

Kubik, Gerhard, 1933-.
Soko, Boston. Nchimi chikanga. Blantyre [Malawi] : Christian Literature Association in Malawi, 2002.
1. Black author.

Kübler, Werner.
Ekel. 1. Aufl. Hürtgenwald : G. Pressler, c2003.
BF575.A886 E34 2003

Kudenko, Daniel, 1968-.
Adaptive agents and multi-agent systems. Berlin ; New York : Springer, c2003.
QA76.76.I58 A312 2003

Kudinov, S. I.
Innovatsii v psikhologii. Biĭsk : Nauchno-izdatel'skiĭ t͡sentr Biĭskogo pedagog. gos. universiteta, 2001-
BF20 .I45 2001

Kuebelbeck, Amy, 1964- Waiting with Gabriel : a story of cherishing a baby's brief life / Amy Kuebelbeck. Chicago, Ill. : Loyola Press, c2003. 174 p. : ill. ; 22 cm. Includes bibliographical references (p. [167]-174). ISBN 0-8294-1603-X DDC 155.9/37
1. Grief. 2. Bereavement - Psychological aspects. 3. Infants (Newborn) - Death - Psychological aspects. 4. Infants - Death - Psychological aspects. 5. Loss (Psychology) I. Title.
BF575.G7 K83 2003

Kugeler, Martin, 1971-.
Process management. Springer-verlag, Berlin, Heidelberg ; New York : Springer, c2003.
HD31 .P756 2003

Kuhlmann, Dörte.
Building gender = Wien : Edition Selene, 2002.

Kuhn, Annette. Family secrets : acts of memory and imagination / Annette Kuhn. New ed. London ; New York : Verso, 2002. ix, 181 p. : ill. ; 19 cm. Includes bibliographical references (p. 180-181). ISBN 1-85984-406-5 DDC 929/.2/0973
1. Kuhn family. 2. Kuhn, Annette. 3. Autobiographical memory. 4. Photography of families. 5. Women - United States - Biography. I. Title.
CT274 .K84 2002

KUHN, ANNETTE.
Kuhn, Annette. Family secrets. New ed. London ; New York : Verso, 2002.
CT274 .K84 2002

KUHN FAMILY.
Kuhn, Annette. Family secrets. New ed. London ; New York : Verso, 2002.
CT274 .K84 2002

Kühn, R. (Reimer), 1955-.
Adaptivity and learning. New York : Springer, 2003.
BF318 .A33 2003

Kuhn, Rudolf, 1939-.
Kuhn-Wengenmayr, Annemarie. Kompositionsfragen. Frankfurt ; New York : P. Lang, c2001.
N7430 .K826 2001

Kuhn-Wengenmayr, Annemarie.
Kompositionsfragen : Beispiele aus fünf Jahrhunderten : Cranach, Dürer, Rubens, Ignaz Günther und Bernini, Schnorr von Carolsfeld, Manet, Marées, Liebermann, Picasso und Raffael / Annemarie Kuhn-Wengenmayr, Rudolf Kuhn. Frankfurt ; New York : P. Lang, c2001. 383 p. : ill. ; 23 cm. (Ars faciendi ; 0940-5097 ; Bd. 10) Includes bibliographical references. ISBN 3-631-37508-5 (pbk.)
1. Composition (Art) 2. Art - Philosophy. I. Kuhn, Rudolf, 1939- II. Title. III. Series.
N7430 .K826 2001

Kühne-Bertram, Gudrun, 1952-.
Grenzen des Verstehens. Göttingen : Vandenhoeck & Ruprecht, c2002.
BD181.5 .G74 2002

Kuipers, Ronald Alexander. Critical faith : toward a renewed understanding of religious life and its public accountability / Ronald A. Kuipers. Amsterdam ; New York, NY : Rodopi, 2002. vi, 331 p. ; 22 cm. (Currents of encounter ; v. 19) Includes bibliographical references (p. [313]-323) and index. CONTENTS: Reconsidering the relationship between faith and reason -- Legitimacy without legitimation? -- Speaking of Spirit -- Religious faith as personal knowledge -- Religion and critical rationality. ISBN 90-420-0853-9 (pbk.)
1. Faith and reason. 2. Christianity - Philosophy. 3. Christian life. I. Title. II. Series.

Kūle, M. (Maija) Phenomenology and culture / Maija Kūle. Riga : Institute of Philosophy and Sociology, 2002. 292 p. : ill. ; 24 cm. Includes bibliographical references (p. [274]-287) and index. ISBN 998462420X
1. Phenomenology. 2. Hermeneutics. 3. Culture. I. Title.

Kultur, Handlung, Wissenschaft : für Peter Janich / herausgegeben von Mathias Gutmann ... [et al.]. 1. Aufl. Weilerswist : Velbrück Wissenschaft, 2002. 362 p. ; 23 cm. Includes bibliographical references. German; one contribution in English. ISBN 3-934730-53-1 (pbk.)
1. Philosophy and science. 2. Culture - Philosophy. I. Janich, Peter. II. Gutmann, Mathias.
B67 .K853 2002

Kultur und Mentalität
Bastl, Beatrix, 1954- Europas Aufbruch in die Neuzeit 1450-1650. Darmstadt : Primus, c2002.
D208 .B37 2002

Kultur und Psychologie in Brasilien.
Stubbe, Hannes, 1941- Bonn : Holos, 2001.
BF108.B6 S783 2001

Kul'tura i vlast'
Kul'tura i vlast' v uslovii͡akh kommunikatsionnoĭ revolŭt͡sii XX veka. Moskva : "AIRO-XX", 2002.
HM621 .K858 2002

Kul'tura i vlast' v uslovii͡akh kommunikatsionnoĭ revolŭt͡sii XX veka : forum nemetskikh i rossiĭskikh issledovateleĭ / pod redakt͡sieĭ Karla Aĭermakhera, Gennadii͡a Bordi͡ugova i Ingo Grabovskogo. Moskva : "AIRO-XX", 2002. 478 p. : ill. ; 25 cm. Includes bibliographical references. Romanized record. CONTENTS: 1. Politika i ideologii͡a -- 2. Literatura -- 3. Iskusstvo -- 4. Subkul'tura i kontrkul'tura -- 5. Intelligent͡sii͡a : refleksii i samorefleksii. ISBN 588735092X
1. Culture. 2. Power (Social sciences) 3. Politics and culture. 4. Communication an culture. 5. Culture - Political aspects. 6. Soviet literature - Political aspects. 7. Soviet Union - Intellectual life. 8. Soviet Union - Politics and government. I. Eimermacher, Karl. II. Bordi͡ugov, G. A. (Gennadiĭ Arkad'evich) III. Grabowsky, Ingo. IV. Title: Kul'tura i vlast' v uslovii͡akh kommunikatsionnoĭ revolŭt͡sii XX veka
HM621 .K858 2002

Kulturstudien
(Bd. 33) Chvojka, Erhard. Geschichte der Grosselternrollen. Wien : Böhlau, 2003.
HQ759.9 .C45 2003

Kulturverstehen.
Göller, Thomas. Würzburg : Königshausen & Neumann, c2000.
BF311 .G586 2000

Kultur.wissenschaft (Vienna, Austria)
(Bd. 4.) Hofstadler, Beate, 1961- KörperNormen, KörperFormen. Wien : Turia + Kant, c2001.
BF692.5 .H64 2001

KUNDA (AFRICAN PEOPLE) - ZAMBIA - RELIGION.
Drews, Annette. Guardians of the society. Leipzig, Germany : Institut für Afrikanistik, Universität Leipzig, 2000.
BF1584.Z33 D44 2000

Kundtz, David, 1937- Nothing's wrong : a man's guide to managing his feelings / David Kundtz. Boston, MA : Conari Press, 2004. p. cm. Includes bibliographical references and index. Table of contents URL:: http://www.loc.gov/catdir/toc/ecip047/2003017458.html ISBN 1-57324-915-7 DDC 155.6/32
1. Men - Psychology. 2. Emotions. I. Title.
BF692.5 .K86 2004

KUNG FU. See KARATE.

Kunin, Seth Daniel. Religion : the modern theories / Seth D. Kunin. Baltimore : Johns Hopkins University Press, 2003. viii, 232 p. ; 24 cm. Includes bibliographical references (p. 223-228) and index. CONTENTS: Karl Marx and cultural materialism -- Emile Durkheim and functionalism -- Max Weber -- Sigmund Freud and the

Kunjufu, Jawanza.

psychological tradition -- Rudolf Otto : the idea of the holy -- Sociology, methodological atheism and secularisation -- Psychological approaches -- Phenomenology and the history of religion -- Feminism, gender and religion -- Anthropological approaches to religion -- Some final words -- Ritual -- Symbolism -- Myth -- Last words. ISBN 0-8018-7727-X ISBN 0-8018-7728-8 (pbk.)
1. Religion. 2. Religion - Philosophy. 3. Religion - Sociological aspects. 4. Philosophy and religion. I. Title.

Kunjufu, Jawanza. Black students-Middle class teachers / by Jawanza Kunjufu. Chicago, Ill. : African American Images, c2002. xii, 164 p. : ill. ; 22 cm. Includes bibliographical references (p. 157-160) and index. CONTENTS: Middle-class schools -- White female teachers -- African American teachers -- Master teachers -- A relevant black curriculum -- African American students -- African American parents -- Models of success. ISBN 0-913543-81-0
1. African American children - Education. 2. Self-esteem in children. 3. Home and school - United States. 4. African Americans - Education. 5. Black author. I. Title.

Kuno, Akira, 1930-.
Kuno Akira Kyōju kanreki kinen tetsugaku ronbunshū. Tōkyō : Ibunsha, 1995.
B29 .K826 1995 <Orien Japan>

Kuno Akira Kyōju kanreki kinen tetsugaku ronbunshū / Takeichi Akihiro, Kaneta Susumu hen. Tōkyō : Ibunsha, 1995. 562 p. ; 22 cm. Includes bibliographical references. ISBN 4-7531-0167-3
1. Philosophy. I. Kuno, Akira, 1930- II. Takeichi, Akihiro, 1933- III. Kaneta, Susumu, 1938- IV. Title: Tetsugaku ronbunshū
B29 .K826 1995 <Orien Japan>

Kunst.
Svendsen, Lars Fr. H., 1970- Oslo : Universitetsforlaget, c2000.
N6490 .S88499 2000

Kunst Theorie
Honegger, Gottfried, 1917- Erfundenes und Erlebtes. München : Chorus, c2002.

Kunst und Erinnerung : memoriale Konzepte in der Erzählliteratur des Mittelalters / Ulrich Ernst und Klaus Ridder (Hg.). Köln : Böhlau, 2003. xvii, 325 p. : ill. ; 24 cm. (Ordo : Studien zur Literatur und Gesellschaft des Mittelalters und der frühen Neuzeit ; Bd. 8) Includes bibliographical references and indexes. ISBN 3-412-09902-3 (pbk.)
1. Literature, Medieval - History and criticism. 2. Memory - Social aspects. 3. Memory in literature. 4. Literature and society. I. Ernst, Ulrich, 1944- II. Ridder, Klaus. III. Series: Ordo (Hildesheim, Germany) ; Bd. 8.
PN674 .K86 2003

Künstliche Interaktion.
Braun-Thürmann, Holger. 1. Aufl. Wiesbaden : Westdeutscher Verlag, 2002.

Kunstwissenschaftliche Bibliothek
(Bd. 17.) Salber, Wilhelm. Psychästhetik. Köln : König, c2002.

(Bd. 20) Reck, H. U. Mythos Medienkunst. Köln : König, c2002.

Kunstwissenschaftliche Bibliothek. Pamphlet.
Salber, Wilhelm. Psychästhetik. Köln : König, c2002.

Kunstwissenschaftliche Studien (Deutscher Kunstverlag)
(Bd. 106.) Rehm, Ulrich. Stumme Sprache der Bilder. München : Deutscher Kunstverlag, 2002.

Ḳunṭres Be-shem omro.
Ḳunṭres Ḳevod ha-Torah. Bene Beraḳ : ha-Meḥaber, 761 [2000 or 2001]

Ḳunṭres Bi-shevile ha-'avodah.
Segal, Yehudah Zeraḥyah, ha-Levi. Sefer Doreshe H.. Tel-Aviv : Talmiday ye-shmom'e liḳho, 763 [2003]
BJ1287.S43 D66 2003

Ḳunṭres Dover mesharim.
Mermelshṭain, Avraham Yitsḥaḳ David. Hotsa'ah 2. [Brooklyn] : A.Y.D. Mermelshṭain, 762 [2001]

Ḳunṭres E'eśeh lo 'ezer.
Yahav, Avino'am Shemu'el. Betar 'Ilit : A. S. Yahav, 761, 2001.

Ḳunṭres ha-Derekh la-'aliyah : tsiyune derekh ba-'avodat D. : ḳovets śiḥot ya-hagigim ....
Segal, Yehudah Zeraḥyah, ha-Levi. Sefer Doreshe H.. Tel-Aviv : Talmiday ye-shmom'e liḳho, 763 [2003]
BJ1287.S43 D66 2003

Ḳunṭres Hakarat ha-ṭov.
Ḳunṭres Ḳevod ha-Torah. Bene Beraḳ : ha-Meḥaber, 761 [2000 or 2001]

Ḳunṭres Ḥazaḳ ye-nitḥazeḳ.
Mitelman, Yiśra'el Yehudah. Ashdod : T. T. di-ḥaside Belza, 762 [2002]

Ḳunṭres Ḳevod ha-Torah : ... din ha-poseḳ mi-mishnato ... : Ḳunṭres Torah mi-tokh ha-deḥaḳ ... : Ḳunṭres Hakarat ha-tov ... : Ḳunṭres Be-shem omro .. Bene Beraḳ : ha-Meḥaber, 761 [2000 or 2001] 128, [101] p. ; 24 cm. Running title: Ḳevod ha-Torah. Running title: Torah mi-tokh ha-deḥaḳ. Running title: Hakarat ha-ṭov.
1. Talmud Torah (Judaism) 2. Ethics, Jewish. I. Title: Ḳunṭres Torah mi-tokh ha-deḥaḳ. II. Title: Ḳunṭres Hakarat ha-ṭov III. Title: Ḳunṭres Be-shem omro. IV. Title: Be-shem omro. V. Title: Ḳevod ha-Torah. VI. Title: Torah mi-tokh ha-deḥaḳ. VII. Title: Hakarat ha-ṭov.

Ḳunṭres Or zoreaḥ.
Ḥayim Yeroḥam ben Shimshon Meshulam Feybish, mi-Snaṭin. Sefer Asefat divre ḥakhamim. Yerushalayim : Mekhon Sod yesharim, 761 [2001]

Ḳunṭres Segulot.
Tsuri'el, Mosheh Yeḥi'el. Otsrot ha-musar. Yerushalayim : Yerid ha-sefarim, 763, 2002.

Ḳunṭres Shenot Ḥayim.
Vital, Ḥayyim ben Joseph, 1542 or 3-1620. 'Ets ha-da'at ṭov. Yerushalayim : Hotsa'at Ahavat shalom, 761 [2000 or 2001]

Ḳunṭres Torah mi-tokh ha-deḥaḳ.
Ḳunṭres Ḳevod ha-Torah. Bene Beraḳ : ha-Meḥaber, 761 [2000 or 2001]

Ḳunṭres Zanvot ha-udim-'ashenim.
Koll, Shmuel, 1938- Sefer Ra'yonot u-mesarim. Yerushalayim : S. Kol, 761- [2001-

Kupdehraben, N.
Malaniuk, Ira. Arien und Lieder [sound recording]. [Germany] : Preiser Records, p2000.

Kupka, František, 1871-1957.
[Création dans les arts plastiques. Czech. German]
Die Schöpfung in der bildenden Kunst / František Kupka ; herausgegeben und übersetzt von Noemi Smolik. Ostfildern-Ruit : Hatje Cantz, c2001. 169 p. : ill. ; 24 cm. (Materialien zur Moderne) CONTENTS: Die Schöpfung in der bildenden Kunst / František Kupka -- Einige Anmerkungen zum Entstehen des Buches ... / Meda Mladek -- Kupka: ein Künstler, der seiner Zeit voraus war / Noemi Smolik. ISBN 3-7757-0824-3
1. Kupka, František, - 1871-1957 - Criticism and interpretation. 2. Creation (Literary, artistic, etc.) I. Smolik, Noemi. II. Mladek, Meda. III. Title. IV. Series.

KUPKA, FRANTIŠEK, 1871-1957 - CRITICISM AND INTERPRETATION.
Kupka, František, 1871-1957. [Création dans les arts plastiques. Czech. German] Die Schöpfung in der bildenden Kunst. Ostfildern-Ruit : Hatje Cantz, c2001.

Küppers, Topsy, 1931- Wolf Messing : Hellseher und Magier / Topsy Küppers. München : Langen Müller, c2002. 374 p. : ill. ; 22 cm. Includes index. ISBN 3-7844-2880-0
1. Messing, Vol'f, - 1899-1974. 2. Psychics - Soviet Union - Biography. I. Title.
BF1027.M47 K87 2002

KURBSKIĬ, ANDREĬ MIKHAĬLOVICH, KNÎAZ', D. 1583.
Zaĭtseva, L. I. Russkie providt͡sy o rossiĭskoĭ gosudarstvennosti. Moskva : In-t ėkonomiki RAN, 1998-
DK49 .Z35 1998

Kurganov, E. Anekdot, simvol, mif : ėtiudy po teorii literatury / Efim Kurganov. Sankt-Peterburg : Izd-vo zhurnala "Zvezda", 2002. 127 p. ; 18 cm. Includes bibliographical references. ISBN 594214026X
1. Russian literature - History and criticism. 2. Symbolism. 3. Anecdotes - History and criticism. 4. Myth in literature. 5. Mythology in literature. 6. Literature - Philosophy. I. Title.

Kurian, Priya A.
Feminist futures. London ; New York : Zed Books ; New York : Distributed in the USA exclusively by Palgrave, c2003.
HQ1161 .F455 2003

Kuropka, Nicole. Philipp Melanchthon : Wissenschaft und Gesellschaft : ein Gelehrter im Dienst der Kirche (1526-1532) / Nicole Kuropka. Tübingen : Mohr Siebeck, c2002. xii, 324 p. : ill. ; 24 cm. (Spätmittelalter und Reformation, 0937-5740 ; neue Reihe, 21) Previously issued as author's dissertation, 2001, Kirchliche Hochschule in Wuppertal. Includes bibliographical references (p. 288-316) and indexes. ISBN 3-16-147898-3 (hd.bd.)
1. Melanchthon, Philipp, - 1497-1560. 2. Dialectical theology. 3. Ethics. I. Title. II. Series: Spätmittelalter und Reformation ; 21.

BIBLIOGRAPHIC GUIDE

300

BR339 .K86 2002

Kurzon, Dennis.
Prepositions in their syntactic, semantic, and pragmatic context. Amsterdam ; Philadelphia, PA : J. Benjamins Pub., c2002.
P285 .P74 2002

Kushell, Jennifer. Secrets of the young & successful : how to get everything you want without waiting a lifetime / Jennifer Kushell with Scott M. Kaufman. New York : Simon & Schuster, c2003. xix, 347 p. ; 22 cm. "A Fireside book." Includes index. ISBN 0-7432-2758-1 DDC 158
1. Success - Psychological aspects. 2. Success in business. I. Kaufman, Scott M. II. Title. III. Title: Secrets of the young and successful
BF637.S8 K875 2003

Kūshyār, d. ca. 961.
[Introduction to astrology]
Kūshyār ibn Labbān's introduction to astrology / edited and translated by Michio Yano. Tokyo : Institue for the Study of Languages and Cultures of Asia and Africa, 1997. xxviii, 319 p. ; 30 cm. (Studia culturae Islamicae, 1340-5306 ; no. 62) Includes bibliographical references (p. xxvi-xxviii).
1. Islamic astrology - Early works to 1800. I. Yano, Michio, 1944- II. Title. III. Title: Introduction to astrology IV. Series.
BF1714.I84 K87 1997

Kūshyār ibn Labbān's introduction to astrology.
Kūshyār, d. ca. 961. [Introduction to astrology] Tokyo : Institue for the Study of Languages and Cultures of Asia and Africa, 1997.
BF1714.I84 K87 1997

Kuther, Tara L. Graduate study in psychology : your guide to success / by Tara L. Luther. Springfield, Ill. : Charles C. Thomas, 2004. p. cm. Includes bibliographical references and index. ISBN 0-398-07478-X ISBN 0-398-07479-8 (pbk.) DDC 150/.71/1
1. Psychology - Study and teaching (Graduate) I. Title.
BF77 .K85 2004

Kuz, Zehra.
Gans, Deborah. The organic approach to architecture. New York ; Chichester : Wiley, 2002.

Kuz'menko, Volodymyr. Na porozi nadtsyvilizatsiï : systemnyĭ analiz aktual'nykh problem suchasnosti : sotsial'nye prognozovaniia ta futurolohiia / Volodymyr Kuz'menko, Oleh Romanchuk. L'viv : "Universum", 1998. 159 p. : ill. ; 21 cm. Added title page title: On the threshold of overcivilization. "Naukove vydannia"--Colophon. At head of title: Tovarystvo universumu. ISBN 9665590901
1. Social prediction. 2. Forecasting. 3. Postmodernism. I. Romanchuk, Oleh. II. Title. III. Title: On the threshold of overcivilization
HM901 .K89 1998

Kvanvig, Jonathan L. The value of knowledge and the pursuit of understanding / Jonathan L. Kvanvig. Cambridge, U.K. ; New York : Cambridge University Press, 2003. xvi, 216 p. ; 24 cm. (Cambridge studies in philosophy) Includes bibliographical references (p. 207-211) and index. ISBN 0-521-82713-2 DDC 121
1. Knowledge, Theory of. 2. Values. I. Title. II. Series.
BD232 .K92 2003

Kvasz, Ladislav.
Appraising Lakatos. Dordrecht ; Boston : Kluwer Academic, c2002.
Q175 .A685 2002

Kyelem, Apollinaire. L'éventuel et le possible / Apollinaire Kyelem ; préface de Joseph Ki-Zerbo. [Ouagadougou : Presses universitaires de Ouagadougou, 2002] Includes bibliographical references (p. 110-114).
1. United Nations - Africa. 2. Africa - Politics and government - 1960- 3. Africa - Social conditions - 1960- 4. Burkina Faso - Politics and government. 5. Conflict management - Africa. 6. Peace. 7. Black author. I. Title.

Kyïvs'kyĭ instytut turyzmu, ekonomiky i prava.
Suspil'stvo na porozi XXI stolittia. Kyïv : Ukraïns'kyĭ TSentr dukhovnoï kul'tury, 1999.

KYRENE (EXTINCT CITY). See CYRENE (EXTINCT CITY).

Kyriazi, Paul. The complete live the James Bond lifestyle seminar / Paul Kyriazi. Los Angeles, CA : Ronin Books, c2002. v, 259 p. ; 22 cm. ISBN 0-9716183-0-5 DDC 158.1
1. Success - Psychological aspects. 2. Men - Psychology. 3. Bond, James (Fictitious character) - Miscellanea. I. Title. II. Title: Live the James Bone lifestyle
BF637.S8 K97 2002

La Branche, Stéphane. Mondialisation et terrorisme identitaire, ou, Comment l'Occident tente de transformer le monde / Stéphane La Branche. Paris : Harmattan, c2003. 285 p. ; 22 cm. (Collection Logiques sociales) Includes bibliographical references (p. 279-284). ISBN 2-7475-3649-1
1. Power (Social sciences) 2. Globalization. 3. Civilization, Western. 4. Violence. I. Title. II. Title: Comment l'occident tente de transformer le monde III. Series: Logiques sociales.
JC330 .L2 2003

La-ḥafets be-ḥayim.
Rozner, Shelomoh. Sh. u-t. La-ḥafets be-ḥayim. Mahad. 3, be-tosefet 13 she'elot be-ḥelek 3. Yerushalayim : Kolel shemirat ha-lashon : le-haśig, Sh. Rozner, 762 [2001 or 2002]

Lā lil-ikti'āb na'am lil-farḥ!!?.
Niẓām al-Dīn, 'Irfān. al-Ṭab'ah 1. [Beirut?] : al-Mu'assasah al-'Arabīyah-al-Ūrūbbīyah lil-Ṣiḥāfah wa-al-Nashr, 2001.

LA TOUR LANDRY, GEOFFROY DE, 14TH CENT. LIVRE DU CHEVALIER DE LA TOUR LANDRY POUR L'ENSEIGNEMENT DE SES FILLES.
Gendt, Anne-Marie Emma Alberta de, 1952- L'art d'éduquer les nobles damoiselles. Paris : Champion, 2003.

LABOR. *See* **WORK; WORKING CLASS.**

LABOR AND LABORING CLASSES. *See* **WORKING CLASS.**

LABOR ECONOMICS.
Beyond Keynes. Cheltenham ; Northampton, Mass. : Edward Elgar, c2002.

Foley, Duncan K. Unholy trinity. London ; New York : Routledge, 2003.
HB135 .F65 2003

LABOR INCENTIVES. *See* **INCENTIVES IN INDUSTRY.**

LABORATORY DIAGNOSIS. *See* **DIAGNOSIS, LABORATORY.**

LABORATORY MEDICINE. *See* **DIAGNOSIS, LABORATORY.**

LABORERS. *See* **EMPLOYEES.**

Laborie, Philippe. Le patient absent de Jacques Lacan : (l'innommable menace) : essai / Philippe Laborie. Paris : Harmattan, c2002. 131 p. ; 22 cm. (Collection Psychanalyse et civilisations. Série Trouvailles et retrouvailles) Includes bibliographical references. ISBN 2-7475-2797-2 DDC 150
1. Lacan, Jacques, - 1901- 2. Psychoanalysis. I. Title. II. Series: Psychanalyse et civilisations. Trouvailles et retrouvailles.

LABORING CLASS. *See* **WORKING CLASS.**

The labyrinth of the continuum.
Leibniz, Gottfried Wilhelm, Freiherr von, 1646-1716. [Selections. English & Latin. 2001] New Haven : Yale University Press, c2001.
B2558 .A78 2001

Lacan en la razón posmoderna.
Alemán, Jorge. Málaga : Miguel Gómez Ediciones, c2000.
BF109.L28 A44 2000

LACAN, JACQUES, 1901-.
ECRITS.
Fink, Bruce, 1956- Lacan to the letter. Minneapolis, MN : University of Minnesota Press, c2004.
BF173 .L1434 2004

Fink, Bruce, 1956- Lacan to the letter. Minneapolis, MN : University of Minnesota Press, c2004.
BF173 .L1434 2004

ETHIQUE DE LA PSYCHANALYSE, 1959-1960.
Halpern, Richard, 1954- Shakespeare's perfume. Philadelphia : University of Pennsylvania Press, c2002.
PR2848 .H25 2002

LACAN, JACQUES, 1901-.
Alemán, Jorge. Lacan en la razón posmoderna. Málaga : Miguel Gómez Ediciones, c2000.
BF109.L28 A44 2000

Apollon, Willy. After Lacan. Albany : State University of New York Press, 2002.
RC506 .A65 2002

Campbell, Kirsten, 1969- Jacques Lacan and feminist epistemology. New York, NY : Routledge, 2004.
BF175.4.F45 .C37 2004

Cathelineau, Pierre-Christophe, 1961- Lacan, lecteur d'Aristote. 2. éd., rev. et corr. Paris : Éditions de l'Association freudienne internationale, c2001 (2002 printing)

Depuis Lacan. Paris : Aubier, c2000.
BF173 .D44 2000

Di Ciaccia, Antonio. Jacques Lacan. Milano : B. Mondadori, 2000.
BF109.L28 D53 2000

Fantasm. Melbourne : Freudian School of Melbourne, 2000.

Fierens, Christian. Lecture de l'étourdit. Paris : Harmattan, c2002.
BF109.L28 F53 2002

Haddad, Gérard. Le jour où Lacan m'a adopté. Paris : Bernard Grasset, c2002.

Hong, Joon-kee, 1962- Der Subjektbegriff bei Lacan und Althusser. Frankfurt am Main ; New York : Peter Lang , c2000.
BF109.L28 H66 2000

Laborie, Philippe. Le patient absent de Jacques Lacan. Paris : Harmattan, c2002.

Leupin, Alexandre, 1948- Lacan today. New York : Other Press, 2004.
BF109.L28 L48 2004

McGowan, Todd. The end of dissatisfaction? Albany : State University of New York Press, c2004.
BF175.4.C84 M4 2004

Moulinier, Didier. Dictionnaire de la jouissance. Paris : L'Harmattan, c1999.
BF575.H27 M68 1999

(Re)-turn. Columbia, Mo. : University of Missouri Press, 2003-
BF173.L15 R48

Safouan, Moustafa. Four lessons of psychoanalysis. New York : Other Press, c2004.
BF175 .S19 2004

LACAN, JACQUES, 1901- - CONTRIBUTIONS IN PSYCHOLINGUISTICS.
Costes, Alain. Lacan, le fourvoiement linguistique. Paris : Presses universitaires de France, 2003.

LACAN, JACQUES, 1901 - -PERIODICALS.
(Re)-turn. Columbia, Mo. : University of Missouri Press, 2003-
BF173.L15 R48

Lacan, le fourvoiement linguistique.
Costes, Alain. Paris : Presses universitaires de France, 2003.

Lacan, lecteur d'Aristote.
Cathelineau, Pierre-Christophe, 1961- 2. éd., rev. et corr. Paris : Éditions de l'Association freudienne internationale, c2001 (2002 printing)

Lacan to the letter.
Fink, Bruce, 1956- Minneapolis, MN : University of Minnesota Press, c2004.
BF173 .L1434 2004

Lacan today.
Leupin, Alexandre, 1948- New York : Other Press, 2004.
BF109.L28 L48 2004

Lacanian psychoanalytic writings.
Fantasm. Melbourne : Freudian School of Melbourne, 2000.

Lacarrieu, Mónica B.
La (indi)gestión cultural. 1. ed. Bs. As., Argentina : Ediciones Ciccus-La Crujía, 2002.
HM621 .I535 2002

Lachman, Gary, 1955- A secret history of consciousness / Gary Lachman. Great Barrington, MA : Lindisfarne Books, 2003. xxxv, 314 p. ; 23 cm. Includes bibliographical references (p. 309-314). CONTENTS: Part one: the search for cosmic consciousness -- R.M. Bucke and the future of humanity -- William James and the anesthetic revelation -- Henri Bergson and the Elan Vital -- The superman -- A.R. Orage and the new age -- Ouspensky's fourth dimension -- Part two: esoteric evolution -- The bishop and the bulldog -- Enter the madame -- Dr. Steiner, I presume? -- From Goethean science to the wisdom of the human being -- Cosmic evolution -- Hypnagogia -- Part three: the archaeology of consciousness -- The invisible mind -- Cracking the egg -- Lost worlds -- Noncerebral consciousness -- The split -- Part four: participatory epistemology -- The shock of metaphor -- The participating mind -- The tapestry of nature -- Thinking about thinking -- The black hole of consciousness -- Other times and places -- Faculty X -- Part five: the presence of origin -- The ascent of Mount Ventoux -- Structures of consciousness -- The mental-rational structure -- The integral structure -- Last words: playing for time. ISBN 1-58420-011-1 DDC 126/.09
1. Consciousness - History. I. Title.
BF311 .L19 2003

Lachmann, Frank M.
Lichtenberg, Joseph D. A spirit of inquiry. Hillsdale, NJ : Analytic Press, 2002.
RC506 .L5238 2002

Lachowska, Bogusława.
Draw-a-family test in psychological research. Lublin : Towarzystwo Naukowe Katolickiego Uniwersytetu Lubelskiego, 2002.
BF698.8.D68 D73 2002

Lacotte, Daniel. Danse avec le diable : une histoire des sorcières / Daniel Lacotte. [Paris] : Hachette, c2002. 237 p. ; 23 cm. Includes bibliographical references (p. 229-235). ISBN 2-01-235574-9 DDC 900
1. Witchcraft - Europe - History. 2. Witches - Europe - History. 3. Warlocks - Europe - History. 4. Witches - Europe - Biography. 5. Warlocks - Europe - Biography. I. Title.
BF1584.E85 L33 2002

Lacroix, Michel. Le courage réinventé / Michel Lacroix. Paris : Flammarion, c2003. 148 p. ; 21 cm. (Essais) Includes bibliographical references. ISBN 2-08-210286-6 DDC 194
1. Courage. I. Title.

Lacy, Norris J.
Perceval = New York : Routledge, 2002.
PN686.P4 P46 2002

LADIES-IN-WAITING - FRANCE - CORRESPONDENCE.
Montpensier, Anne-Marie-Louise d'Orléans, duchesse de, 1627-1693. [Correspondence. English & French] Against marriage. Chicago : University of Chicago Press, 2002.
DC130.M8 A4 2002

The ladies' room reader.
Alvrez, Alicia. Berkeley, Calif. : Conari Press, c2000.
HQ1233 .A68 2000

The ladies' room reader revisited.
Alvrez, Alicia. Berkeley, Calif. : Conari Press ; [Emeryville, Calif.] : Distributed by Publishers Group West, c2002.
HQ1233 .A68 2002

Ladner, Joyce A. Launching our Black children for success : a guide for parents of kids from three to eighteen / Joyce A. Ladner with Theresa Foy DiGeronimo ; foreword by Alvin F. Poussaint. 1st ed. San Francisco : Jossey-Bass, c2003. xvii, 280 p. ; 23 cm. Includes bibliographical references (p. 257-269) and index. Publisher description URL: http://www.loc.gov/catdir/description/wiley038/2003000400.html Table of contents URL: http://www.loc.gov/catdir/toc/wiley031/2003000400.html CONTENTS: Know thyself -- How well do you know your child? -- Building strong identity and positive self-esteem -- Family values -- The power of discipline : its use and abuse -- Countering negative media and peer groups -- Education : they can't take it away from you -- Drugs and violence : no place to hide -- Raising sons and daughters : gender differences -- Role models : how to find and use them -- College preparation, application, and selection -- Coping skills : the key to survival. ISBN 0-7879-6488-3 (alk. paper) DDC 649/.15796073
1. Success in children. 2. Success in adolescence. 3. African American children - Psychology. 4. African American teenagers - Psychology. 5. Child rearing. I. DiGeronimo, Theresa Foy. II. Title.
BF723.S77 L33 2003

LADY OF THE WEST (EGYPTIAN DEITY). *See* **HATHOR (EGYPTIAN DEITY).**

Lady Sheba.
Book of shadows.
Lady Sheba. The grimoire of Lady Sheba. Llewellyn's centennial ed. St. Paul, Minn. : Llewellyn Publications, 2001.
BF1566 .L335 2001

The book of shadows / by Lady Sheba. 1st ed. St. Paul, Minn. : Llewellyn Publications, 2002. 186 p. ; 21 cm. ISBN 0-87542-075-3
1. Witchcraft. I. Title.

The grimoire of Lady Sheba : includes The book of shadows / foreword by Carl Llewellyn Weschcke. Llewellyn's centennial ed. St. Paul, Minn. : Llewellyn Publications, 2001. xvii, 243 p. : ill. ; 24 cm. ISBN 0-87542-076-1 DDC 133.4/3
1. Witchcraft. I. Lady Sheba. Book of shadows. II. Title.

Lady Sheba.
BF1566 .L335 2001

LaFollette, Hugh, 1948-.
The Oxford handbook of practical ethics. Oxford ; New York : Oxford University Press, 2003.
BJ1031 .O94 2003

Lago, Colin, 1944-.
Anti-discriminatory counselling practice. London ; Thousand Oaks, Calif. : SAGE Publications, 2003.
BF637.C6 A49 2003

Laguna, Mariola.
Draw-a-family test in psychological research. Lublin : Towarzystwo Naukowe Katolickiego Uniwersytetu Lubelskiego, 2002.
BF698.8.D68 D73 2002

Laidler, Keith James, 1916- Energy and the unexpected / Keith J. Laidler. Oxford ; New York : Oxford University Press, c2002. xiii, 146 p. : ill. ; 24 cm. Includes bibliographical references (p. [141]-142) and index. ISBN 0-19-852516-8 DDC 531/.6
1. Force and energy. 2. Chance. 3. Chaotic behavior in systems. I. Title.
QC72 .L35 2002

Laing, Kathleen. Girlfriends' getaway : a complete guide to the weekend adventure that turns friends into sisters and sisters into friends / Kathleen Laing & Elizabeth Butterfield. 1st ed. Colorado Springs, Colo. : WaterBrook Press, 2002. x, 178 p. ; 21 cm. Includes bibliographical references (p. 177-178). CONTENTS: The adventure begins -- Discover your girlfriends -- Set up camp -- Follow the map -- Stop for lemonade -- Dig for treasure -- Diamond or lump of coal? -- Enjoy the riches -- Share the wealth -- Epilogue: The adventure continues. ISBN 1-57856-516-2 DDC 158.2/5/082
1. Female friendship. 2. Short vacations. I. Butterfield, Elizabeth. II. Title.
BF575.F66 L35 2002

LAISSEZ-FAIRE. *See* **FREE ENTERPRISE.**

Laïtman, Mikhaël'. A guide to the hidden wisdom of kabbalah : with ten complete kabbalah lessons / by Michael Laitman ; compiled by Benzion Giertz. Thornhill, Ont. : Laitman Kabbalah Publishers, 2002. 193 p. ; 22 cm. Includes index. ISBN 0-9731909-0-6
1. Cabala. I. Title.

LAKATOS, IMRE.
Appraising Lakatos. Dordrecht ; Boston : Kluwer Academic, c2002.
Q175 .A685 2002

LAKATOS, IMRE, D. 1974.
Appraising Lakatos. Dordrecht ; Boston : Kluwer Academic, c2002.
Q175 .A685 2002

Laks, Bernard.
Phonetics, phonology, and cognition. Oxford : Oxford University Press, 2002.
P221 .P475 2002

Lal, Vinay. Empire of knowledge : culture and plurality in the global economy / Vinay Lal. London ; Sterling, Va. : Pluto Press, 2002. xi, 254 p. ; 22 cm. Includes bibliographical references (p. 202-246) and index. ISBN 0-7453-1737-5 (hardback) ISBN 0-7453-1736-7 (paperback) DDC 306/.09/04
1. Social history - 20th century. 2. Economic history - 20th century. 3. World politics - 20th century. 4. Equality. 5. Knowledge, Sociology of. 6. History - Philosophy. 7. Developed countries - Relations - Developing countries. 8. Developing countries - Relations - Developed countries. I. Title.
HN16 .L35 2002

Lāla kitāba.
Śarmā, Kisanalāla. 1. saṃskaraṇa. Dillī : Manoja Pôketa Buksa, [2000?]
BF1714.H5+

Lāla, Mukuṭa Bihārī.
[Sāṃyayogamīmāṃsā. Hindi & Sanskrit]
Sāṃyayogamīmāṃsā : bhāṣānuvāda-samanvitā / lekhako'nuvādakaśca, Mukutavihārīlālaḥ ; sampādakaḥ, Vrajavallabhadvivedah. 1. saṃskaraṇa. Vārāṇasī : Śaivabhāratī Śodhapratiṣṭhānam, 2001. xxii, 230 p. ; 22 cm. (Śodhaprakāśana-granthamālā ; 27) Added title page title: Sāṃyayogamīmāṃsā : with Hindi translation. Includes bibliographical references and indexes. Sanskrit and Hindi. ISBN 81-86768-50-5 (bound) ISBN 81-86768-51-3 (pbk.)
1. Spiritual life - Hinduism. 2. Religion and sociology. 3. Religion and ethics. I. Dvivedī, Brajavallabha. II. Śaivabhāratī-Śodhapratiṣṭhāna. III. Title. IV. Title: Sāṃyayogamīmāṃsā : with Hindi translation V. Series.
BL1237.32+

Laland, Kevin N. Sense and nonsense : evolutionary perspectives on human behaviour / Kevin N. Laland and Gillian R. Brown. Oxford ; New York : Oxford University Press, 2002. ix, 369 p. : ill. ; 23 cm. Spine title: Sense & nonsense. Includes bibliographical references and index. ISBN 0-19-850884-0 DDC 155.7
1. Evolutionary psychology. I. Brown, Gillian R. II. Title. III. Title: Sense & nonsense
BF701 .L34 2002

LaLonde, Christopher A.
Jean Piaget Society. Meeting (30th : 2000 : Montréal, Québec) Changing conceptions of psychological life. Mahwah, N.J. : L. Erlbaum Associates, 2004.
BF697 .J36 2004

Lam, Kai Sin.
Lam, Kam Chuen. The Feng Shui kitchen. 1st ed. Boston : Journey Editions, c2000.
TX724.5.C4 L36 2000

Lam, Kam Chuen. The Feng Shui kitchen : the philosopher's guide to cooking and eating / Lam Kam Chuen with Lam Kai Sin. 1st ed. Boston : Journey Editions, c2000. 159 p. : ill. ; 23 cm. ISBN 1-88520-393-4 (pbk.) DDC 641.5952
1. Cookery, Chinese. 2. Feng shui. I. Lam, Kai Sin. II. Title.
TX724.5.C4 L36 2000

LAMAISM. *See* **BUDDHISM.**

LAMAS - BIOGRAPHY.
Cai, Zhichun. Huo fo zhuan shi. Di 1 ban. Beijing : Hua wen chu ban she : Xin hua shu dian jing xiao, 2000.
BL515 .C345 2000

LAMB, CHARLES, 1775-1834.
Burton, Sarah, 1963- A double life. London : Viking ; New York : Penguin Putnam, 2003.

Lamb, Debora.
LeBeau, Kara R. Guan yin's chakra meditations. Boulder, Colo. : Mahasimhananda Press, c2001.
BF1442.C53 L43 2001

LAMB, MARY, 1764-1847.
Burton, Sarah, 1963- A double life. London : Viking ; New York : Penguin Putnam, 2003.

Lamb, William, 1944 Apr. 22- The secrets of your rising sign : the astrological key to getting what you want / William Lamb with Webb Harris, Jr. Gloucester, MA : Fair Winds Press, 2004. p. cm. ISBN 1-59233-038-X DDC 133.5
1. Ascendant (Astrology) I. Harris, Webb. II. Title.
BF1717 .L36 2004

Lambert, Alan J.
Foundations of social cognition. Mahwah, N.J. : L. Erlbaum, 2003.
BF323.S63 F68 2003

Lambert, Ladina Bezzola. Imagining the unimaginable : the poetics of early modern astronomy / Ladina Bezzola Lambert. Amsterdam ; New York, NY : Rodopi, 2002. ix, 182 p. : ill. ; 25 cm. (Internationale Forschungen zur allgemeinen und vergleichenden Literaturwissenschaft ; 58) Thesis (doctoral)--University of Zurich, 1999. Includes bibliographical references (p. [173]-182). ISBN 90-420-1578-0 (pbk.)
1. Astronomy - History - 17th century. 2. Creative ability in science. 3. Imagination. 4. Metaphor. I. Title. II. Series.
QB29 .L35 2002

Lambert, Mary. Feng shui guide to harmonious living : 101 ways to clear life's clutter / Mary Lambert. [New York] : Friedman/Fairfax ; Distributed by Sterling, c2002. 96 p. : ill. (chiefly col.) ; 24 cm. Originally published: Great Britain : Cico Books Ltd, 2002. Includes bibliographical references (p. 96) and index. ISBN 1-58663-704-5 (pbk.) DDC 133.3/337
1. Feng shui. I. Title.
BF1779.F4 L357 2002

Lamdan, Elimelekh. Torapiah : hadrakhah le-yi'uts be-ruaḥ ha-Torah / Elimelekh Lamdan. Yerushalayim : Feldhaim, 762 [2002] 173 p. ; 24 cm.
1. Ethics, Jewish. 2. Judaism and psychology. I. Title.

Lamiell, James T. Beyond individual and group differences : human individuality, scientific psychology, and William Stern's critical personalism / James T. Lamiell. Thousand Oaks, Calif. : Sage Publications, c2003. xxii, 331 p. : ill. ; 24 cm. Includes bibliographical references (p. 303-318) and indexes. Table of contents URL: http://www.loc.gov/catdir/toc/ecip042/2003008606.html CONTENTS: Introduction: a lost star -- Part I: Historical beginnings -- The problem of individuality and the birth of a "differential" psychology -- The narrowing of perspective in the proliferation of standardized testing and correlational research -- The entrenchment of a "common trait" perspective on human individuality -- Part II : Statistical thinking in the post-wundtian restructuring of scientific psychology -- The emergence of a "neo-galtonian" framework for psychological research : a historical sketch -- Contemporary "nomotheticism" within the neo-galtonian framework : a methodological primer -- Contemporary "nomotheticism" in critical perspective -- Part III: Rethinking the problem -- An introduction to critical personalism -- Some models of personalistic inquiry in contemporary psychology -- Our differences aside : persons, things, individuality, and community. ISBN 0-7619-2172-9 (cloth) DDC 155.2
1. Psychology - History - 20th century. 2. Psychology - History - 19th century. 3. Stern, William, - 1871-1938. I. Title.
BF105 .L36 2003

Lamizet, Bernard. Politique et identité / Bernard Lamizet. Lyon : Presses universitaires de Lyon, 2002. 350 p. ; 24 cm. Includes bibliographical references. ISBN 2-7297-0707-7 DDC 300
1. Identity (Psychology) - Political aspects. 2. Group identity - Political aspects. 3. Political psychology. 4. Political sociology. 5. Minorities - Political activity. I. Title.

Lamoine, Georges.
Ramsay, Chevalier (Andrew Michael), 1686-1743. Les voyages de Cyrus. Paris : Champion, 2002.

Lampenfieber und Angst bei ausübenden Musikern.
Mornell, Adina. Frankfurt am Main : P. Lang, 2002.
ML3830 .M67 2002

Lampert, Khen. Compassionate education : a prolegomena for radical schooling / Khen Lampert. Lanham, Md. : University Press of America, c2003. xxxiii, 258 p. ; 22 cm. Includes bibliographical references (p. [245]-249) and index. ISBN 0-7618-2641-6 (pbk.)
1. Teachers of problem children - United States. 2. Problem children - Education - United States. 3. Children with social disabilities - Education - United States. 4. School environment - United States. 5. Educational psychology. 6. Compassion. 7. Caring. I. Title.

Lampshire, Julia.
Howard, Kerry. The book of love and happiness. New York : Ryland Peters & Small, Inc., 2004.
BF575.L8 H69 2004

LANCELOT DU LAC (LEGENDARY CHARACTER). *See* **LANCELOT (LEGENDARY CHARACTER).**

LANCELOT (LEGENDARY CHARACTER) - ROMANCES - HISTORY AND CRITICISM.
Besamusca, Bart. The book of Lancelot. Cambridge : D.S. Brewer, 2003.
PT5568 .B47 2003

LANCELOT (PROSE ROMANCE).
Besamusca, Bart. The book of Lancelot. Cambridge : D.S. Brewer, 2003.
PT5568 .B47 2003

LAND. *See* **LAND USE.**

Land girls at the old rectory.
Grimwood, Irene. Large print ed. Oxford : ISIS, 2001.

LAND, NATIONALIZATION OF. *See* **LAND TENURE.**

LAND OWNERSHIP. *See* **LAND TENURE.**

LAND QUESTION. *See* **LAND TENURE.**

Land/scape/theater / Elinor Fuchs and Una Chaudhuri, editors. Ann Arbor : University of Michigan, c2002. x, 390 p. : ill. ; 24 cm. (Theater--theory/text/performance) Includes bibliographical references and index. ISBN 0-472-09720-2 (alk. paper) ISBN 0-472-06720-6 (pbk. : alk. paper) DDC 792
1. Theater. 2. Drama - History and criticism. 3. Landscape in literature. I. Fuchs, Elinor. II. Chaudhuri, Una, 1951- III. Series.
PN2020 .L32 2002

LAND SETTLEMENT PATTERNS, PREHISTORIC.
Beyond foraging and collecting. New York : Kluwer Academic/Plenum Publishers, c2002.
GN388 .B49 2002

LAND SETTLEMENT - UNITED STATES - HISTORIOGRAPHY.
Nye, David E., 1946- America as second creation. Cambridge : MIT Press, c2003.
E179.5 .N94 2003

LAND SETTLEMENT - UNITED STATES - HISTORY.
Nye, David E., 1946- America as second creation. Cambridge : MIT Press, c2003.
E179.5 .N94 2003

LAND SURVEYING. *See* **SURVEYING.**

LAND TENURE. See **PEASANTRY.**

LAND TENURE - MEXICO - MICHOACÁN DE OCAMPO - HISTORY.
Guerra Manzo, Enrique. Caciquismo y orden público en Michoacán, 1920-1940. 1. ed. México : El Colegio de México, Centro de Estudios Sociológicos, c2002.
F1219.3.P7 G84 2002

LAND USE. See **PUBLIC LANDS.**

LAND USE - ECONOMIC ASPECTS.
Foley, Duncan K. Unholy trinity. London ; New York : Routledge, 2003.
HB135.F65 2003

LAND USE - PLANNING. See **CITY PLANNING.**

LAND USE, RURAL. See **AGRICULTURE; AGRICULTURE - ECONOMIC ASPECTS; LAND SETTLEMENT; LAND TENURE.**

LAND USE, URBAN - MANAGEMENT. See **CITY PLANNING.**

LAND USE, URBAN - PLANNING. See **CITY PLANNING.**

Landauer, Christopher.
International Conference on Simulation in Engineering Education (2001 : Phoenix, Ariz.) Proceedings of the International Conference on Simulation and Multimedia in Engineering Education & Virtual Worlds and Simulation. San Diego, CA : Society for Computer Simulation International, c2001.

LANDED GENTRY. See **GENTRY.**

LANDOWNERS. See **LAND TENURE; WOMEN LANDOWNERS.**

Landriscina, Luis, 1935-.
El milagro y el valor de la vida. 1. ed. Buenos Aires : Patria Grande, 2000.

LANDSCAPE ARCHITECTURE. See **HEDGES.**

LANDSCAPE ASSESSMENT. See also **LAND USE.**
Shepard, Paul, 1925- Where we belong. Athens : University of Georgia Press, c2003.
GF21.S524 2003

LANDSCAPE IN LITERATURE.
Land/scape/theater. Ann Arbor : University of Michigan, c2002.
PN2020.L32 2002

Landscrapers.
Betsky, Aaron. New York, New York : Thames & Hudson, 2002.

Landucci, Sergio, 1938- La mente in Cartesio / di Sergio Landucci. Milano : FrancoAngeli, c2002. 228 p. ; 23 cm. (Filosofia e scienza nel Cinquecento e nel Seicento. Ser. 1.: Studi ; 58) Includes bibliographical references and index. ISBN 88-464-3894-9 DDC 194
1. Descartes, René, - 1596-1650. 2. Mind and body. 3. Philosophy of mind. I. Title. II. Series.

Lane, Gill.
The situational mentor. Burlington, VT : Gower, 2004.
BF637.M48 S56 2004

Lang, Christoph Maria.
Alt möcht ich werden--. 1. Aufl. Berlin : Aufbau-Verlag, c1994.
HQ1064.G3 A72 1994x

Langens, Thomas A. Tagträume, Anliegen und Motivation / von Thomas A. Langens. Göttingen ; Seattle : Hogrefe, c2002. xi, 217 p. : ill. ; 24 cm. (Motivationsforschung ; 18) ISBN 3-8017-1670-8 (kart.)
1. Motivation (Psychology) 2. Fantasy. I. Title. II. Series.

Langevin, Michael Peter, 1952- Secrets of the Amazon shamans : healing traditions from South America / by Michael Peter Langevin. Franklin Lakes, NJ : New Page Books, c2003. p. cm. Includes bibliographical references (p.   ) and index. ISBN 1-56414-653-7 (pbk.) DDC 299/.8
1. Shamanism - South America. I. Title.
BF1622.S63 L36 2003

Langford, Elizabeth. Mind and muscle : an owner's handbook / Elizabeth Langford ; drawings by Enci Noro. Leuven : Gafant, 1999. xv, 253 p. : ill. ; 24 cm. Includes bibliographical references (p. 251-252). ISBN 90-5350-883-X
1. Mind and body. 2. Body, Human. I. Title.

Langley, Raymond J., 1935-.
Karl Jaspers on philosophy of history and history of philosophy. Amherst, N.Y. : Humanity Books, 2003.
B3279.J34 K292 2003

Language & culture. Lusaka, Zambia : Quest, 1999. 164 p. ; 24 cm. Cover title: Language and culture. Issued as: Quest (Special issue), Vol. XIII, no. 1-2, 1999. Cover title. Includes bibliographical references. In English and French. CONTENTS: Colonialism and linguistic dilemmas in Africa : Cameroon as a paradigm / Godfrey Tangwa -- Colonialism and linguistic dilemmas in Africa : Cameroon as a paradigm (Revisited) / George Echu -- Africa and its linguistic problematic / Lansana Keita -- Cultures do not exist, exploding self-evidence in the investigation of interculturality / Wim van Binsbergen -- Les particularismes culturels négro-africaine face a la dynamique universalisatrice de la technique et de la démocratie / Lazare Marcelin Poame -- L'antériorité des civisilations négres : motif de fierté ou d'orgueil? / Pierre Nzinzi -- Philosophie et tradition / Mahamadé Savadogo -- Kwasi Wiredu and the problems of conceptual decolonization / Sanya Osha.
1. Language and culture - Africa. 2. Language and languages. 3. Multilingualism - Africa. 4. Africa - Languages - Colonial influence. I. Title: Quest (Lusaka, Zambia). Special issue. II. Title: Language and culture

LANGUAGE ACQUISITION. See also **SECOND LANGUAGE ACQUISITION.**
La Adquisición de la lengua materna. México : Universidad Nacional Autónoma de México : Centro de Investigaciones y Estudios Superiores en Antropología Social, 2001.
P118.A227 2001

Clark, Eve V. First language acquisition. Cambridge, U.K. ; New York : Cambridge University Press, 2003.
P118.C547 2003

Development of verb inflection in first language acquisition. Berlin ; New York : Mouton de Gruyter, 2003.
P118.D465 2003

Goldin-Meadow, Susan. The resilience of language. New York ; Hove [England] : Psychology Press, 2003.
P118.G57 2003

Grundlagen und Modelle für den Hörgerichteten Spracherwerb. Villingen-Schwenningen : Neckar, c1995.

Hamann, Cornelia, 1953- From syntax to discourse. Dordrecht, The Netherlands ; Boston : Kluwer Academic Publishers, c2002.
P118.H327 2002

Jusczyk, Peter W. The discovery of spoken language. 1st MIT Press pbk. ed. Cambridge, Mass. : MIT Press, 2000.
BF720.S67 J87 2000

Krashen, Stephen D. Explorations in language acquisition and use. Portsmouth, NH : Heinemann, c2003.
P51.K666 2003

Linguistic evolution through language acquisition. Cambridge ; New York : Cambridge University Press, 2002.
P118.L565 2002

Oates, John, 1946- Cognitive and language development in children. Milton Keynes, U.K. : Open University ; Malden, MA : Blackwell Pub., 2004.
BF723.C5 O38 2004

Precursors of functional literacy. Amsterdam ; Philadelphia : J. Benjamins Pub., c2002.
P118.7.P74 2002

Tomasello, Michael. Constructing a language. Cambridge, Mass. : Harvard University Press, 2003.
P118.T558 2003

Word order and scrambling. Malden, MA : Blackwell Pub., 2003.
P295.W65 2003

Language acquisition & language disorders
(v. 29) Fernández, Eva M. Bilingual sentence processing. Amsterdam ; Philadelphia : J. Benjamins Pub., 2003.
P115.4.F47 2003

Language acquisition and language socialization : ecological perspectives / edited by Claire Kramsch. London ; New York : Continuum, 2002. xvi, 308 p. ; 24 cm. (Advances in applied linguistics) Includes bibliographical references and index. ISBN 0-8264-5371-6 ISBN 0-8264-5372-4 (pbk.) DDC 418
1. Language acquisition - Social aspects. 2. Language and languages - Study and teaching. 3. Socialization. 4. Social ecology. I. Kramsch, Claire J. II. Series.
P118.L243 2002

LANGUAGE ACQUISITION - PARENT PARTICIPATION.
Acredolo, Linda P. My first baby signs. [New York] : HarperFestival, c2002.
BF720.C65 A27 2002

LANGUAGE ACQUISITION - SOCIAL ASPECTS.
Language acquisition and language socialization. London ; New York : Continuum, 2002.
P118.L243 2002

Language and culture.
Language & culture. Lusaka, Zambia : Quest, 1999.
Alefirenko, M. F. Poėticheskaia ėnergiia slova. Moskva : Academia, 2002.
P35.A544 2002

Jensen, Anders Fogh. Metaforens magt. 1. opl. Århus : Modtryk, 2001.

Khrolenko, A. T. Lingvokul'turovedenie. Kursk : Izd-vo GUIPP "Kursk", 2000.
P35.K524 2000

Minsos, Susan Felicity, 1944- Culture clubs. Edmonton : Spotted Cow Press, c2002.

Translation and power. Amherst : University of Massachusetts Press, 2002.
P306.97.S63 T7 2002

Us and others. Amsterdam ; Philadelphia : John Benjamins Pub., c2002.
HM753.U72 2002

LANGUAGE AND CULTURE - AFRICA.
Language & culture. Lusaka, Zambia : Quest, 1999.

LANGUAGE AND CULTURE - EUROPE.
Lurati, Ottavio. Per modo di dire--. Bologna : CLUEB, c2002.

LANGUAGE AND EDUCATION. See also **LANGUAGES, MODERN - STUDY AND TEACHING.**
Linguistic anthropology of education. Westport, Conn. ; London : Praeger, 2003.
P40.8.L55 2003

LANGUAGE AND LANGUAGES. See also **BILINGUALISM; LINGUISTICS; MULTILINGUALISM; SEMANTICS (PHILOSOPHY); SPEECH; TRANSLATING AND INTERPRETING; VOICE; WRITING.**
Augustine, Saint, Bishop of Hippo. De magistro = Paderborn : F. Schöningh, 2002.
BR65.A5 G4 2002

Bahnasāwī, Ḥusām. Ahammīyat al-rabṭ bayna al-tafkīr al-lughawī ʻinda al-ʻArab wa- naẓarīyāt al-baḥth al-lughawī al-ḥadīth. al-Qāhirah : Maktabat al-Thaqāfah al-Dīnīyah, 1994.
PJ6106.B35 1994 <Orien Arab>

Chazal, Gérard. Interfaces. Seyssel [France] : Champ Vallon, c2002.
HM1111.C49 2002

Cherchi, Marcello. Disciplines and nations. Pittsburgh, Pa. : Center for Russian and East European Studies, University Center for International Studies, University of Pittsburgh, 2002.

Chomsky, Noam. Chomsky on democracy & education. New York ; London : RoutledgeFalmer, 2003.
LB885.C5215 C46 2003

Collected papers on Southeast Asian and Pacific languages. Canberra, ACT : Pacific Linguistics, Research School of Pacific and Asian Studies, Australian National University, 2002.

Crowley, Tony. Standard English and the politics of language. 2nd ed. New York : Palgrave Macmillan, c2003.
P368.C76 2003

Dalby, Andrew, 1947- Language in danger. New York : Columbia University Press, c2003.
P40.5.L33 D35 2003

Dement'ev, V. V. Nepriamaia kommunikatsiia i ee zhanry. Saratov : Izd-vo Saratovskogo universiteta, 2000.
P106.D4554 2000

Glinz, Hans, 1913- Languages and their use in our life as human beings. Münster : Nodus, c2002.
P107.G58 2002

Język w przestrzeni społecznej. Opole : Uniwersytet Opolski, 2002.
P40.J492 2002

Language & culture. Lusaka, Zambia : Quest, 1999.

Language and languages

Language function, structure, and change. Frankfurt am Main ; New York : Lang, c2002.
P125 .L36 2002

Ling, Yuanzheng. Xin yu wen jian she shi hua. Di 1 ban. Kaifeng Shi : Henan da xue chu ban she : Henan sheng Xin hua shu dian fa xing, 1995.
PL1175 .L55 1995 <Orien China>

Ludwig Wittgenstein, Tractatus logico-philosophicus. Berlin : Akademie Verlag, 2001.

Magyarok és nyelvtörvények. Budapest : Teleki László Alapítvány, 2002.
PH2073 .K66 2002

Marcuschi, Luiz Antônio. Investigando a relação oral/escrito e as teorias do letramento. Campinas, SP : Mercado de Letras, 2001.

Mélanges David Cohen. Paris : Maisonneuve et Larose, 2003.

Perspectives in linguistics. New Delhi : Indian Institute of Language Studies : Distributed by Creative Books, 2003.

Rix, Helmut, 1926- Kleine Schriften. Bremen : Hempen, 2001.

Russkoe slovo. Penza : Izd-vo PGPU, 1998.
PG2026.B66 R88 1998

Virtual'naia real'nost' v psikhologii i iskusstvennom intellekte. Moskva : Rossiĭskaia Assotsiatsiia iskusstvennogo intellekta, 1998.
BF204.5 .V57 1998

LANGUAGE AND LANGUAGES - ACQUISITION. See **LANGUAGE ACQUISITION.**

LANGUAGE AND LANGUAGES - GOVERNMENT POLICY. See **LANGUAGE POLICY.**

LANGUAGE AND LANGUAGES - GRAMMAR, COMPARATIVE. See **GRAMMAR, COMPARATIVE AND GENERAL.**

LANGUAGE AND LANGUAGES - ORIGIN.
Bichakjian, Bernard H. Language in a Darwinian perspective. Frankfurt am Main ; New York : Peter Lang, c2002.
P142 .B53 2002

Language evolution. Oxford ; New York : Oxford University Press, 2003.
P140 .L256 2003

LANGUAGE AND LANGUAGES - PHILOSOPHY. See also **ANALYSIS (PHILOSOPHY); SPEECH ACTS (LINGUISTICS).**
Beuchot, Mauricio. La filosofía y el lenguaje en la historia. México, D.F. : UNAM, 2000.

Die erscheinende Welt. Berlin : Duncker & Humblot, c2002.

El lenguaje y la mente humana. 1. ed. Barcelona : Ariel Editorial, 2002.

O'Callaghan, John (John P.) Thomist realism and the linguistic turn. Notre Dame, Ind. : University of Notre Dame Press, c2003.
BD161 .O3 2003

Schröder, Jürgen. Die Sprache des Denkens. Würzburg : Königshausen & Neumann, c2001.

Smith, R. Scott, 1957- Virtue ethics and moral knowledge. Aldershot, England ; Burlington, VT : Ashgate, c2003.
BJ1012 .S5195 2003

LANGUAGE AND LANGUAGES - RELIGIOUS ASPECTS.
Muller, F. Max (Friedrich Max), 1823-1900. The essential Max Muller. 1st ed. New York ; Houndmills, England : Palgrave Macmillan, 2002.
BL50 .M785 2002

Müller, Max E., 1935- Wortzauber. Frankfurt : Lembeck, c2001.
P35 .M945 2001

LANGUAGE AND LANGUAGES - RHETORIC. See **RHETORIC.**

LANGUAGE AND LANGUAGES - SENTENCES. See **GRAMMAR, COMPARATIVE AND GENERAL - SENTENCES.**

LANGUAGE AND LANGUAGES - STUDY AND TEACHING. See also **AUDIO-LINGUAL METHOD (LANGUAGE TEACHING).**
Kiraly, Donald C., 1953- Pathways to translation. Kent, Ohio : Kent State University Press, c1995.

P306.5 .K57 1995

Krashen, Stephen D. Explorations in language acquisition and use. Portsmouth, NH : Heinemann, c2003.
P51 .K666 2003

Language acquisition and language socialization. London ; New York : Continuum, 2002.
P118 .L243 2002

LANGUAGE AND LANGUAGES - STYLE.
Sakita, Tomoko I. Reporting discourse, tense, and cognition. 1st ed. Amsterdam ; Boston : Elsevier, 2002.
P301.5.I53 S25 2002

LANGUAGE AND LANGUAGES - TRANSLATING. See **TRANSLATING AND INTERPRETING.**

LANGUAGE AND LANGUAGES - VARIATION.
Chipere, Ngoni, 1965- Understanding complex sentences. New York : Palgrave Macmillan, 2003.
P295 .C485 2003

Language and literacy series (New York, N.Y.)
Dyson, Anne Haas. The brothers and sisters learn to write. New York : Teachers College Press, c2003.
LB1139.L3 D97 2003

LANGUAGE AND STATE. See **LANGUAGE POLICY.**

LANGUAGE ARTS.
Boys, literacies, and schooling. Buckingham [England] ; Philadelphia : Open University Press, 2002.
LC1390 .B69 2002

LANGUAGE AWARENESS IN CHILDREN.
Precursors of functional literacy. Amsterdam : Philadelphia : J. Benjamins Pub., c2002.
P118.7 .P74 2002

LANGUAGE DEVELOPMENT IN CHILDREN. See **LANGUAGE ACQUISITION.**

LANGUAGE DISORDERS.
Raĭnov, Vasil G. Za psikhosemantichnata spetsifika na ezikovoto vŭzpriĭatie. Sofiia : Akademichno izd-vo "Prof. Marin Drinov", 1998.
P37 .R27 1998

Language evolution / edited by Morten H. Christiansen, Simon Kirby. Oxford ; New York : Oxford University Press, 2003. xvii, 395 p. : ill. ; 24 cm. (Studies in the evolution of language ; 3) Includes bibliographical references (p. [338]-383) and index. ISBN 0-19-924484-7 ISBN 0-19-924483-9 (CASED)
1. Historical linguistics. 2. Language and languages - Origin. 3. Anthropological linguistics. I. Christiansen, Morten H., 1963- II. Kirby, Simon. III. Series.
P140 .L256 2003

Language function, structure, and change : essays in linguistics in honor of Tomasz P. Krzeszowski / Wiesław Oleksy (ed.). Frankfurt am Main ; New York : Lang, c2002. 166 p. : ill. ; 21 cm. (Polish studies in English language and literature, 1436-7513 ; v. 5) Includes bibliographical references and index. ISBN 3-631-39587-6 (Frankfurt : pbk.) ISBN 0-8204-5993-3 (New York : pbk.)
1. Krzeszowski, Tomasz P. - Bibliography. 2. Linguistics. 3. Language and languages. I. Krzeszowski, Tomasz P. II. Oleksy, Wiesław. III. Title: Essays in linguistics in honor of Tomasz P. Krzeszowski IV. Series: Polish studies in English language and literature ; v. 5.
P125 .L36 2002

Language in a Darwinian perspective.
Bichakjian, Bernard H. Frankfurt am Main ; New York : Peter Lang, c2002.
P142 .B53 2002

Language in danger.
Dalby, Andrew, 1947- New York : Columbia University Press, c2003.
P40.5.L33 D35 2003

Language in mind : advances in the study of language and thought / edited by Dedre Gentner and Susan Goldin-Meadow. Cambridge, Mass. : MIT Press, c2003. viii, 528 p. : ill. ; 23 cm. "A Bradford book." Includes bibliographical references and index. ISBN 0-262-07243-2 (alk. paper) ISBN 0-262-57163-3 (pbk. : alk. paper) DDC 401/.9
1. Psycholinguistics. 2. Cognition. I. Gentner, Dedre. II. Goldin-Meadow, Susan.
P37 .L357 2003

LANGUAGE OBSOLESCENCE.
Dalby, Andrew, 1947- Language in danger. New York : Columbia University Press, c2003.
P40.5.L33 D35 2003

Language, ontology, and political philosophy in China.
Wagner, Rudolf G. Albany : State University of New York Press, c2003.
B126 .W284 2003

LANGUAGE PLANNING. See **LANGUAGE POLICY.**

LANGUAGE POLICY - SWITZERLAND.
Büchi, Christophe. "Röstigraben". 2. aufl. Zürich : NZZ, c2001.

LANGUAGE SCHOOLS. See **LANGUAGES, MODERN - STUDY AND TEACHING.**

Language, speech, and communication
Jusczyk, Peter W. The discovery of spoken language. 1st MIT Press pbk. ed. Cambridge, Mass. : MIT Press, 2000.
BF720.S67 J87 2000

LANGUAGE SPREAD.
Dalby, Andrew, 1947- Language in danger. New York : Columbia University Press, c2003.
P40.5.L33 D35 2003

LANGUAGES. See **LANGUAGE AND LANGUAGES.**

Languages and their use in our life as human beings.
Glinz, Hans, 1913- Münster : Nodus, c2002.
P107 .G58 2002

LANGUAGES, FOREIGN. See **LANGUAGES, MODERN.**

LANGUAGES IN CONTACT. See **BILINGUALISM.**

LANGUAGES, LIVING. See **LANGUAGES, MODERN.**

LANGUAGES, MODERN - CONVERSATION AND PHRASE BOOKS.
Becker, Monika. Familiar dialogues in Englyssh and Frenche. Trier : Wissenschaftlicher Verlag Trier, c2003.

LANGUAGES, MODERN - STUDY AND TEACHING. See **AUDIO-LINGUAL METHOD (LANGUAGE TEACHING).**

LANGUAGES, MODERN - STUDY AND TEACHING - HISTORY - 16TH CENTURY.
Becker, Monika. Familiar dialogues in Englyssh and Frenche. Trier : Wissenschaftlicher Verlag Trier, c2003.

LANGUAGES, MODERN - STUDY AND TEACHING - HISTORY - 17TH CENTURY.
Becker, Monika. Familiar dialogues in Englyssh and Frenche. Trier : Wissenschaftlicher Verlag Trier, c2003.

LANGUAGES, NATIONAL. See **LANGUAGE POLICY.**

LANGUAGES, OFFICIAL. See **LANGUAGE POLICY.**

Lanham, Richard A. Analyzing prose / Richard A. Lanham. 2nd ed. London ; New York : Continuum, 2003. xviii, 244 p. : ill. ; 25 cm. Includes index. ISBN 0-8264-6189-1 ISBN 0-8264-6190-5 (pbk.) DDC 828/.08
1. English language - Style. 2. English language - Rhetoric. 3. Report writing. I. Title.
PE1421 .L295 2003

Lannoy, Jacques-Dominique de.
Qu'est-ce-donc qu'apprendre? Lausanne : Delachaux et Niestlé, 1999.
BF318 .Q84 1999

Lännström, Anna.
Promise and peril. Notre Dame, Ind. : University of Notre Dame Press, c2003.
BL50 .P65 2003

Lapsley, Daniel K.
Moral development, self, and identity. Mahwah, N.J. : Lawrence Erlbaum Associates, 2004.
BF723.M54 M686 2004

Lareau, Annette. Unequal childhoods : class, race, and family life / Annette Lareau. Berkeley : University of California Press, c2003. xii, 331 p. ; 24 cm. Includes bibliographical references (p. 313-323) and index. CONTENTS: Concerted cultivation and the accomplishment of natural growth -- Social structure and daily life -- The hectic pace of concerted cultivation -- A child's pace -- Children's play is for children -- Developing a child -- Language as a conduit for social life -- Concerted cultivation in organizational spheres -- Concerted cultivation gone awry -- Letting educators lead the way -- Beating with a belt, fearing "the school" -- The power and limits of social class. ISBN 0-520-23763-3 (cloth : alk. paper) ISBN 0-520-23950-4 (pbk. : alk. paper) DDC

305.23
1. Children - Social conditions. 2. Family. I. Title.
HQ767.9 .L37 2003

LARGE TYPE BOOKS.
Cameron, Stella. Cold day in July. Waterville, Me. : Wheeler Pub. ; Bath, England : Chivers Press, 2002.
PS3553.A4345 C65 2002

Chopra, Deepak. The spontaneous fulfillment of desire. New York : Random House Large Print, 2003.
BF1175 .C48 2003b

Cook, Thomas H. The interrogation. Rockland, MA : Wheeler Pub., 2002.
PS3553.O55465 I58 2002

Davis, Sampson. The pact. Waterville, ME : Thorndike Press, 2002.
1. Black author.

Driver, Betty, 1920- Betty. Large print ed. Long Preston : Magna, 2000.

Grimwood, Irene. Land girls at the old rectory. Large print ed. Oxford : ISIS, 2001.

Kava, Alex. The soul catcher. Waterville, Me. : Thorndike Press, 2003, 2002.
PS3561.A8682 S6 2003

Marshall, Evan, 1956- Icing Ivy. Waterville, Me. : Thorndike Press, 2003, c2002.
PS3563.A72236 I27 2003

Meier, Leslie. Birthday party murder. Waterville, Me. : Thorndike Press, 2003.
PS3563.E3455 B57 2003

Moxham, Roy. The great hedge of India. Large print ed. Oxford : ISIS, 2001.

Quindlen, Anna. Blessings. 1st large print ed. New York : Random House Large Print, c2002.
PS3567.U336 B59 2002b

Rogers, Rita. Mysteries. Large print ed. Bath, England : Chivers Press ; Waterville, Me. : Thorndike Press, 2002.
BF1031 .R635 2002

Larkin, June, 1952-.
Feminist utopias. Toronto : Inanna Publications and Education, 2002.

Larkins, Lisette. Calling on extraterrestrials : 11 steps to inviting your own UFO encounters / Lisette Larkins. Charlottesville, VA : Hampton Roads Pub., c2003. x, 245 p. ; 22 cm. Includes bibliographical references (p. 241). ISBN 1-57174-372-3 (pbk. : alk. paper) DDC 001.942
1. Human-alien encounters. I. Title.
BF2050 .L365 2003

Talking to extraterrestrials : communicating with enlightened beings / Lisette Larkins. Charlottesville, VA : Hampton Roads Pub., c2002. xviii, 237 p. ; 22 cm. Includes index. ISBN 1-57174-334-0 (alk. paper) DDC 001.942
1. Human-alien encounters. I. Title.
BF2050 .L37 2002

Larrea, Martha Victoria. Movimiento femenino / Martha Victoria Larrea. Ibarra, Ecuador : [s.n.], 1997. 168 p. : ill. ; 22 cm. Includes bibliographical references (p. 160-161). ISBN 9978401245
1. Feminism. 2. Feminism - Latin America. 3. Feminism - Ecuador. I. Title.

Larson, Cynthia Sue. Aura advantage / Cynthia Sue Larson. Avon, MA : Adams Media Corp., c2003. p. cm. Includes bibliographical references. CONTENTS: What's an aura? -- What your aura does for you -- What's my aura? -- See and feel your aura -- Strengthen and transform your aura -- Attract what you most desire -- Protect yourself -- Aura photography and imaging -- Aura meditations for everyday life -- Color assessment and therapy. ISBN 1-58062-945-8 DDC 133.8/92
1. Aura. 2. Kirlian photography. 3. Color - Psychic aspects. I. Title.
BF1389.A8 L37 2003

LARUELLE, FRANÇOIS.
Del Bufalo, Erik. Deleuze et Laruelle. Paris : Kimé, 2003.

LARYNX. See **VOICE.**

Lasserre, Frédéric, 1967-.
Le territoire pensé. Sainte-Foy : Presses de l'Université du Québec, 2003.

The last dance.
DeSpelder, Lynne Ann, 1944- 7th ed. Boston : McGraw-Hill, 2005.
BF789.D4 D53 2005

LAST THINGS (THEOLOGY). See **ESCHATOLOGY.**

The last violet.
Hjelmstad, Lois Tschetter. Englewood, Colo. : Mulberry Hill Press, c2002.
BF575.G7 H575 2002

Laszlo, Ervin, 1932- The connectivity hypothesis : foundations of an integral science of quantum, cosmos, life, and consciousness / Ervin Laszlo ; foreword by Ralph H. Abraham. Albany : State University of New York Press, c2003. viii, 147 p. ; 23 cm. Includes bibliographical references (p. 133-142) and index. ISBN 0-7914-5785-0 (alk. paper) ISBN 0-7914-5786-9 (pbk. : alk. paper) DDC 501
1. Science - Philosophy. 2. Cosmology. I. Title.
Q175 .L2854 2003

Late antique archaeology
(v. 1) Theory and practice in late antique archaeology. Leiden ; Boston : Brill, 2003.
CC72.4 .T46 2003

LATERAL THINKING.
Dudgeon, Piers. Breaking out of the box. London : Headline, 2001.
BF109.D39 D83 2001

LATERALITY. See also **LEFT AND RIGHT (PSYCHOLOGY).**
Fagard, Jacqueline. Le développement des habiletés de l'enfant. Paris : CNRS, c2001.
RJ133 .F34 2001

Lathan, Mark J., 1961- Emotional progression in sacred choral music : how three twentieth century masterworks depict grief in time of war ; and, Song of hope : a cantata for chorus and orchestra / by Mark J. Lathan. 2001. vii, 115 leaves : music ; 28 cm. Thesis (Ph.D.)--University of California--Los Angeles, 2001. Typescript. Vita. Part Two consists of Song of hope score for SATB chorus with orchestra (leaves 38-115). Includes bibliographical references (leaf 37). Photocopy. Ann Arbor, Mich. : UMI Dissertation Services, 2002. 22 cm. (UMI no. 3032853).
1. Vaughan Williams, Ralph, - 1872-1958. - Dona nobis pacem. 2. Tippett, Michael, - 1905- - Child of our time. 3. Britten, Benjamin, - 1913-1976. - War requiem. 4. Grief. 5. Music - Psychological aspects. 6. Cantatas, Sacred - Scores. I. Lathan, Mark J., 1961- Song of hope. II. Title. III. Title: How three twentieth century masterworks depict grief in time of war IV. Title: Song of hope

Song of hope.
Lathan, Mark J., 1961- Emotional progression in sacred choral music. 2001.

LATIN AMERICA - CIVILIZATION.
Wagner de Reyna, Alberto. El privilegio de ser latinoamericano. 1. ed. Córdoba, Argentina : Editorial Alejandro Korn, c2002.
F1408.3 .W35 2002

LATIN AMERICA - CIVILIZATION - 20TH CENTURY.
García Canclini, Néstor. Culturas híbridas. Nueva edición actualizada. Buenos Aires : Paidós, 2001.

LATIN AMERICA - CIVILIZATION - PHILOSOPHY.
Latin America writes back. New York : Routledge, 2002.
PQ7081.A1 L336 2002

LATIN AMERICA - CULTURAL POLICY.
García Canclini, Néstor. Culturas híbridas. Nueva edición actualizada. Buenos Aires : Paidós, 2001.

LATIN AMERICA - HISTORY.
Perspectives on Las Américas. Maden, MA : Blackwell Pub., c2003.
F1410 .P48 2003

LATIN AMERICA - HISTORY - ERRORS, INVENTIONS, ETC.
Restall, Matthew, 1964- Seven myths of the Spanish conquest. Oxford ; New York : Oxford University Press, 2003.
F1230 .R47 2003

LATIN AMERICA - INTELLECTUAL LIFE.
Britto García, Luis. Conciencia de América Latina. 1. ed. Caracas, Venezuela : Editorial Nueva Sociedad, [2002]

LATIN AMERICA - SOCIAL CONDITIONS.
Britto García, Luis. Conciencia de América Latina. 1. ed. Caracas, Venezuela : Editorial Nueva Sociedad, [2002]

LATIN AMERICA - SOCIAL POLICY.
Amar Amar, José Juan. Políticas sociales y modelos de atención integral a la infancia. Barranquilla, Colombia : Ediciones Uninorte, 2001.

Latin America writes back : postmodernity in the periphery (an interdisciplinary perspective) / edited by Emil Volek. New York : Routledge, 2002. xxviii, 282 p. ; 24 cm. (Hispanic issues ; v. 28) Includes bibliographical references and index. Table of contents URL: http://www.loc.gov/catdir/toc/fy035/2002021347.html CONTENTS: PART I. Macondo or death, but not exactly: the case of unrequited modernity that does not go away -- Traditionalism and modernity in Latin American culture / José Joaquín Brunner -- Modernity and postmodernity in the periphery ; Communications: decentering modernity / Jesús Martín Barbero -- PART II. Changing identities, or "Where do we come from" and "Where are we going?" -- Challenges of postmodernity and globalization: multiple or fragmented identities? / Fernando Ainsa -- Postmodernism and Latin American identity / Jorge Larrain -- Latin American identity, dramatized / José Joaquín Brunner -- PART III. Changing realities, politics, arts: strategies of/for resistance -- Autochthonous cultures and the global market / Mario Roberto Morales -- Post-cities and politics: new urban movements in the two Americas / Armando Silva -- Modern and postmodern aesthetics in contemporary Argentine theatre (1985-1997) / Osvaldo Pelletieri -- Polarized modernity: Latin America at the postmodern juncture / Raúl Bueno -- Latin American writer in these postmodern times / Abelardo Castillo -- PART IV. Changing cultural dossier: some classic texts from the 1990s -- Variations on postmodernity, or, what does the Latin American postboom mean? / Mempo Giardinelli -- Latin America and postmodernity / Nelly Richards -- Critique of global philosophy, five hundred years later / Rafael Ángel Herra -- Cultural topologies / Daniel Altamiranda, Hernán Thomas. ISBN 0-8153-3256-4 (alk. paper) DDC 860.9/113
1. Spanish American literature - 20th century - History and criticism. 2. Latin America - Civilization - Philosophy. 3. Postmodernism. 4. Group identity - Latin America. I. Volek, Emil. II. Series: Hispanic issues (Routledge (Firm)) ; 28.
PQ7081.A1 L336 2002

LATIN AMERICAN LITERATURE. See **SPANISH AMERICAN LITERATURE.**

LATIN AMERICANS - UNITED STATES.
Perspectives on Las Américas. Maden, MA : Blackwell Pub., c2003.
F1410 .P48 2003

LATIN AUTHORS. See **AUTHORS, LATIN.**

LATIN DRAMA. See **LATIN DRAMA (TRAGEDY).**

LATIN DRAMA (TRAGEDY) - HISTORY AND CRITICISM.
Studien zu antiken Identitäten. Würzburg : Ergon Verlag, c2001.
DG78 .S78 2001

LATIN LANGUAGE - PREPOSITIONS.
Poggio, Rosauta Maria Galvão Fagundes. Processos de gramaticalização de preposições do Latim ao Português. Salvador : EDUFBA, 2002.

LATIN LANGUAGE - STUDY AND TEACHING - EUROPE - HISTORY - 16TH CENTURY.
Moss, Ann, 1938- Printed commonplace-books and the structuring of Renaissance thought. Oxford : Clarendon Press ; New York : Oxford University Press, 1996.
PA2047 .M67 1996

LATIN LANGUAGE - STUDY AND TEACHING - EUROPE - HISTORY - 17TH CENTURY.
Moss, Ann, 1938- Printed commonplace-books and the structuring of Renaissance thought. Oxford : Clarendon Press ; New York : Oxford University Press, 1996.
PA2047 .M67 1996

LATIN LANGUAGE - TEXTBOOKS - HISTORY.
Moss, Ann, 1938- Printed commonplace-books and the structuring of Renaissance thought. Oxford : Clarendon Press ; New York : Oxford University Press, 1996.
PA2047 .M67 1996

LATIN LITERATURE. See **CLASSICAL LITERATURE.**

LATIN LITERATURE - HISTORY AND CRITICISM.
Tra IV e V secolo. Milano : Cisalpino, 2002.

LATIN ORIENT. See **CRUSADES.**

LATIN PHILOLOGY. See **LATIN LANGUAGE; LATIN LITERATURE.**

Latina power!.
Nogales, Ana, 1951- New York : Simon & Schuster, c2003.

LATINI (ITALIC PEOPLE). *See* **ROMANS.**

Latour, Bruno. War of the worlds : what about peace? / Bruno Latour ; translated from the French by Charlotte Bigg ; edited by John Tresch. Chicago : Prickly Paradigm Press, c2002. 53 p. ; 18 cm. Includes bibliographical references (p. 53). ISBN 0-9717575-1-8
1. Peace. 2. Social sciences - Philosophy. I. Tresch, John. II. Title.
H61.15 .L38 2002

Lattanzi-Licht, Marcia E.
Coping with public tragedy. Washington, DC : Hospice Foundation of America ; New York : Brunner-Routledge, c2003.
BF789.D5 C67 2003

Lattin, Don. Following our bliss : how the spiritual ideals of the sixties shape our lives today / Don Lattin. 1st ed. New York : HarperCollins, c2003. x, 276 p. : ill. ; 26 cm. Includes bibliographical references (p. 247-257) and index. ISBN 0-06-009394-3 (hc)
1. Religions. 2. Spiritual life. I. Title.

Lau, Clarence K.
Lum, Alan S.F. (Alan Sun Fai) The centuries old philosophy and practice of traditional Chinese feng shui and the more advanced Flying Star feng shui. Honolulu : Lum Pub., c2002.
BF1779.F4 L86 2002

Laughing at nothing.
Marmysz, John, 1964- Albany : State University of New York Press, c2003.
B828.3 .M265 2003

Laughing matters.
Funes, Mariana. Dublin : Newleaf, 2000.

LAUGHTER.
Fenomenologii︠a︡ smekha. Moskva : Rossiĭskiĭ institut kul'turologii, 2002.
PN6149.P3 F45 2002

Funes, Mariana. Laughing matters. Dublin : Newleaf, 2000.

Klein, Allen. The healing power of humor. Waterville, Me. : Thorndike Press, 2003.
BF575.L3 K56 2003

Michel-Andino, Andreas, 1961- Kleine Philosophie des Lachens. Koblenz : Fölbach, c2000.
BF575.L3 M53 2000

LAUGHTER - PSYCHOLOGICAL ASPECTS.
McGhee, Paul E. Health, healing and the amuse system. 3rd ed. Dubuque, Iowa : Kendall/Hunt Pub., c1999.
BF575.L3 M38 1999

LAUNCELOT (LEGENDARY CHARACTER). *See* **LANCELOT (LEGENDARY CHARACTER).**

Launching our Black children for success.
Ladner, Joyce A. 1st ed. San Francisco : Jossey-Bass, c2003.
BF723.S77 L33 2003

Laura Shannon series in French medieval studies.
Morrissey, Robert John, 1947- [Empereur à la barbe fleurie. English] Charlemagne & France. English language ed. Notre Dame, Ind. : University of Notre Dame Press, c2003.
DC73 .M7513 2003

Laureate Learning Systems.
Semel, Eleanor Messing. Following directions [electronic resource]. Macintosh/Windows version. Winooski, VT : Laureate Learning Systems, c2000.
BF637.L36

Laurel, Alicia Bay, 1949- How to make peace : 50 recipes / written, illustrated, and designed by Alicia Bay Laurel. 1st ed. Layton, Utah : G. Smith, Publisher, c2004. p. cm. ISBN 1-58685-416-X DDC 170/.44
1. Peace of mind. I. Title.
BF637.P3 L38 2004

Laurent, John.
Evolutionary economics and human nature. Cheltenham : Edward Elgar, c2003.

Laury, Ritva.
Perspectives in linguistics. New Delhi : Indian Institute of Language Studies : Distributed by Creative Books, 2003.

Lavan, Luke.
Theory and practice in late antique archaeology. Leiden ; Boston : Brill, 2003.
CC72.4 .T46 2003

LAW. *See* **JUSTICE, ADMINISTRATION OF; PUBLICITY (LAW); SEMANTICS (LAW).**

LAW AND ECONOMICS.
Kaplow, Louis. Fairness versus welfare. Cambridge, MA : Harvard University Press, 2002.
K247 .K37 2002

LAW AND ETHICS - CASE STUDIES.
Vergès, Jacques. Dictionnaire amoureux de la justice. Paris : Plon, c2002.

LAW AND LITERATURE.
On interpretation. Madison, Wis. : University of Wisconsin Press for the University of Wisconsin Law School, c2002.

LAW AND MORALS. *See* **LAW AND ETHICS.**

LAW AND POLITICS.
Davydov, I︠U︡. P. (I︠U︡riĭ Pavlovich) Norma protiv sily. Moskva : Nauka, 2002.

Law Development Centre.
The scope magazine. Kampala, Uganda : LDC Publishers, [2001-
K23 .C665

LAW, EMIGRATION. *See* **EMIGRATION AND IMMIGRATION LAW.**

LAW ENFORCEMENT. *See* **CRIMINAL INVESTIGATION.**

LAW ENFORCEMENT - MORAL AND ETHICAL ASPECTS.
Passamaneck, Stephen M. Police ethics and the Jewish tradition. Springfield, Ill. : C.C. Thomas, c2003.
HV7924 .P37 2003

Law, ethics and governance.
Government reformed. Aldershot, England ; Burlington, VT : Ashgate, c2003.
JF1525.O73 G686 2003

LAW, HEBREW. *See* **JEWISH LAW.**

LAW, IMMIGRATION. *See* **EMIGRATION AND IMMIGRATION LAW.**

LAW IN THE BIBLE. *See* **JEWISH LAW.**

LAW - INTERPRETATION AND CONSTRUCTION.
On interpretation. Madison, Wis. : University of Wisconsin Press for the University of Wisconsin Law School, c2002.

Stecker, Robert, 1928- Interpretation and construction. Malden, MA : Blackwell, 2003.
BD241 .S78 2003

LAW, JEWISH. *See* **JEWISH LAW.**

LAW, MEDIEVAL.
De Sion exibit lex et verbum domini de Hierusalem. Turnhout, Belgium : Brepols, c2001.

LAW - METHODOLOGY.
Samuel, Geoffrey, 1947- Epistemology and method in law. Aldershot, Hampshire, England : Burlington, VT : Ashgate, c2003.
K213 .S259 2003

Law, modernity, postmodernity.
Edgeworth, Brendan. Aldershot, England ; Burlington, VT : Ashgate/Dartmouth, c2003.
K370 .E34 2003

LAW, MOSAIC. *See* **JEWISH LAW.**

The law of international business transactions.
DiMatteo, Larry A. Mason, OH : Thomson/South-Western West, c2003.
KF915 .D56 2003

LAW OF SUCCESSION. *See* **INHERITANCE AND SUCCESSION.**

LAW - PHILOSOPHY. *See also* **LAW AND ETHICS.**
Epstein, Richard A. Skepticism and freedom. Chicago : University of Chicago Press, c2003.
K487.L5 E67 2003

LAW PRACTICE. *See* **PRACTICE OF LAW.**

LAW, PRACTICE OF. *See* **PRACTICE OF LAW.**

LAW - PSYCHOLOGICAL ASPECTS.
Valverde, Mariana, 1955- Law's dream of a common knowledge. Princeton, N.J. ; Woodstock, Oxfordshire : Princeton University Press, c2003.
K380 .V35 2003

LAW, SEMITIC. *See* **JEWISH LAW.**

LAW - SOCIAL ASPECTS.
Valverde, Mariana, 1955- Law's dream of a common knowledge. Princeton, N.J. ; Woodstock, Oxfordshire : Princeton University Press, c2003.
K380 .V35 2003

LAW - UGANDA - PERIODICALS.
The scope magazine. Kampala, Uganda : LDC Publishers, [2001-
K23 .C665

Lawaty, Andreas, 1953-.
Polacy i niemcy. òznań : Wydawn. Poznańskie, 2003.
DK4121 .P65 2003

Lawler, Edward J.
Group cohesion, trust and solidarity. 1st ed. Amsterdam ; New York : JAI, 2002.

Lawless, Sue.
Vint/age 2001 conference : [videorecording]. New York, c2001.

LAWMAKERS. *See* **LEGISLATORS.**

Lawrence, D. H. (David Herbert), 1885-1930. Fantasia of the unconscious.
Lawrence, D. H. (David Herbert), 1885-1930. [Psychoanalysis and the unconscious] Psychoanalysis and the unconscious; New York : Cambridge, 2003.
BF173 .L28 2003

[Psychoanalysis and the unconscious]
Psychoanalysis and the unconscious; and, Fantasia of the unconscious New York : Cambridge, 2003. p. cm. (The Cambridge edition of the works of D.H. Lawrence) Includes bibliographical references and index. ISBN 0-521-32791-1 DDC 150
1. Psychoanalysis. 2. Subconsciousness. I. Steele, Bruce. II. Lawrence, D. H. (David Herbert), 1885-1930. Fantasia of the unconscious. III. Title. IV. Series: Lawrence, D. H. (David Herbert), 1885-1930. Works. 1979.
BF173 .L28 2003

Works. 1979.
Lawrence, D. H. (David Herbert), 1885-1930. [Psychoanalysis and the unconscious] Psychoanalysis and the unconscious; New York : Cambridge, 2003.
BF173 .L28 2003

Lawrence, Ruth.
Suicide & risk-taking deaths of children & young people. Surry Hills, NSW : The Commission, c2003.

Lawrence, Shirley Blackwell. The secret science of numerology : the hidden meaning of numbers and letters / by Shirley Blackwell Lawrence. Franklin Lakes, NJ : New Page Books, c2001. 287 p. : ill. ; 26 cm. Includes bibliographical references (p. 275-278) and indexes. ISBN 1-56414-529-8 (pbk.) DDC 133.3/35
1. Numerology. I. Title.
BF1623.P9 L38 2001

Law's dream of a common knowledge.
Valverde, Mariana, 1955- Princeton, N.J. ; Woodstock, Oxfordshire : Princeton University Press, c2003.
K380 .V35 2003

Lawson, Anton E. The neurological basis of learning, development, and discovery : implications for science and mathematics instruction / Anton E. Lawson. Dordrecht ; Boston : Kluwer Academic Publishers, c2003. xvi, 283 p. : ill. ; 25 cm. (Science & technology education library ; v. 18) Includes bibliographical references (p. 261-276) and index. ISBN 1402011806 (alk. paper) DDC 153.1/5
1. Learning, Psychology of. 2. Learning - Physiological aspects. I. Title. II. Series.
BF318 .L365 2003

Lawson, Melinda, 1954- Patriot fires : forging a new American nationalism in the Civil War North / Melinda Lawson. Lawrence : University Press of Kansas, c2002. xv, 265 p. : ill. ; 24 cm. (American political thought) Includes bibliographical references (p. [235]-250) and index. CONTENTS: A union love feast : the sanitary fairs, Civil War patriotism, and national identity -- Let the nation be your bank : Jay Cooke and the war bond drives -- From democracy to loyalty : the partisan construction of national identity -- A profound national devotion : the metropolitan union leagues -- Until the ideas of Massachusetts kiss the gulf of Mexico : the abolitionist vision of nation and patriotism -- Abraham Lincoln and the construction of national patriotism -- Conclusion. ISBN 0-7006-1207-6 (cloth : alk. paper) DDC 973.7/1
1. United States - History - Civil War, 1861-1865 - Social aspects. 2. Nationalism - United States - History - 19th century. 3. Patriotism - United States - History - 19th century. 4. National characteristics, American. 5. United States - Politics and government - 1861-1865. 6. Northeastern States - Social

conditions - 19th century. 7. Northeastern States - Politics and government - 19th century. 8. Political culture - United States - History - 19th century. 9. Political culture - Northeastern States - History - 19th century. I. Title. II. Series.
E468.9 .L39 2002

Lawson, Stephanie.
Europe and the Asia-Pacific. London ; New York : RoutledgeCurzon, 2003.
D1065.A78 E97 2003

Lawson, Valerie A.
Velkoff, Victoria Averil. Gender and aging [electronic resource]. [Washington, D.C.] : U.S. Dept. of Commerce, Economics and Statistics Administration, Bureau of the Census, [1998]

Lawton, Eric.
The soul aflame. Berkeley, Calif. : Conari Press, 2000.
BL624.2 .S675 2000

LAWYERS. See **PRACTICE OF LAW.**

LAWYERS - LEGAL STATUS, LAWS, ETC. See **LAWYERS.**

LAWYERS - UGANDA - DIRECTORIES.
Uganda Law Society. Directory. Kampala : The Society, [1999-
KTW3.3 .U345

LAX, RUTH F.
Vint/age 2001 conference : [videorecording]. New York, c2001.

Lax, Ruth F., panelist.
Vint/age 2001 conference : [videorecording]. New York, c2001.

LAZINESS. See **PROCRASTINATION.**

LDC'S. See **DEVELOPING COUNTRIES.**

Le Blanc, Guillaume.
Foucault au Collège de France. Pessac : Presses universitaires de Bordeaux, c2003.
B2430.F724 F6855 2003

Le Dœuff, Michèle. The philosophical imaginary / Michele Le Doeuff ; translated by Colin Gordon. London : Continuum, 2002. x, 199 p. : ill. ; 22 cm. (Athlone contemporary European thinkers) Originally published: London: Athlone, 2000. Includes bibliographical references and index. Translated from the French. ISBN 0-8264-5991-9 DDC 305.401
1. Woman (Philosophy) 2. Femininity (Philosophy) 3. Philosophy. 4. Philosophers - Attitudes. 5. Philosophers - Relations with women - Psychological aspects. 6. Women philosophers. 7. Feminist theory. I. Title. II. Series.

Le Fanu, Joseph Sheridan, 1814-1873.
Carmilla.
Ashley, Leonard R. N. The complete book of sex magic. Fort Lee, NJ : Barricade Books, 2003.
BF1623.S4 A85 2002

Le Fèvre, Jean-Yves. Eloge de la mort : comme enseignement et outil initiatique / Jean-Yves Le Fèvre, Roger Begey, Jean-Paul Bertrand. Monaco : Rocher, c2002. 201 p. ; 23 cm. Includes bibliographical references. ISBN 2-268-04415-7 DDC 194
1. Death. I. Begey, Roger. II. Bertrand, Jean-Paul. III. Title.

Le Guen, Annick.
Freud, le sujet social. 1re éd. Paris : Presses universitaires de France, 2002.

Le Guern, Philippe.
Les cultes médiatiques. Rennes : Presses universitaires de Rennes, [2002]

Le, Huu Khoa.
Dépayser la pensée. Paris : Empêcheurs de penser en rond, 2003.

Le-reʻakha kamokha.
Ariʻav, Dayid ben Naḥman, ha-Kohen. Mahad. 2. Yerushalayim : Dayid ben Naḥman ha-Kohen Ariʻav, 760- [2000-

LEA series in organization and management.
Lord, Robert G. (Robert George), 1946- Leadership processes and follower self-identity. Mahwah, N.J. ; London : Lawrence Erlbaum, 2004.
HM1261 .L67 2004

Leach, Chris.
Sternberg, Robert J. The psychologist's companion. 4th ed. Cambridge, U.K. ; New York : Cambridge University Press, 2003.
BF76.8 .S73 2003

Leach, Colin Wayne, 1967-.
The social life of emotions. New York : Cambridge University Press, 2004.
BF531 .S634 2004

Leach, Evan A.
Berger, Helen A., 1949- Voices from the pagan census. Columbia, S.C. : University of South Carolina Press, c2003.
BF1573 .B48 2003

Lead yourself.
Cope, Mick. Cambridge , MA : Perseus Pub., c2001 (2002 printing)
BF637.L4 C58 2001

Leader who enables thousand flowers to blossom : successful spiritual leadership of the 21st century.
Tayir, Bracha Klein. ha-Manhig she-meʼafsher le-elef peraḥim li-feroaḥ. Tel Aviv : Yediʻot aḥaronot : Sifre ḥemed, c2002.

LEADERSHIP. See also **COMMAND OF TROOPS; ELITE (SOCIAL SCIENCES).**
Giuliani, Rudolph W. London : Little, Brown, 2002.

Hirschmann, Kris, 1967- Chicago, IL : Raintree, 2003.
BF723.L4 H57 2003

Sadler, Philip, 1930- 2nd ed. London ; Sterling, VA : Kogan Page Ltd., 2003.
HD57.7 .S227 2003

LEADERSHIP.
Adair, John Eric, 1934- Not bosses but leaders. 3rd ed. / John Adair with Peter Reed. London ; Sterling, VA : Kogan Page, 2003.

An, Lizhi. "Zhen guan zheng yao" yu ling dao yi shu. Di 1 ban. Shanghai : Shanghai gu ji chu ban she, 1999.
DS749.3.W813 A63 1999

Bennis, Warren G. On becoming a leader. [Rev. ed.]. Cambridge, MA : Perseus Pub., c2003.
BF637.L4 B37 2003

Best practice. Cambridge, MA : Perseus Publishing, c2003.

Bird, David F. Quality Air Force in an emergency [electronic resource]. Maxwell Air Force Base, Ala. : Air War College, Air University, [1996]

Carey, Dennis. How to run a company. 1st ed. New York : Crown Business, c2003.
HD38.2 .C374 2003

The collaborative work systems fieldbook. San Francisco : Jossey-Bass/Pfeiffer, c2003.
HD66 .C547 2003

Cope, Mick. Lead yourself. Cambridge , MA : Perseus Pub., c2001 (2002 printing)
BF637.L4 C58 2001

De Kluyver, Cornelis A. Strategy. Upper Saddle River, N.J. : Prentice Hall, c2003.
HD38.2 .D425 2003

DeMarco, Michael. Dugout days. New York : AMACOM, c2001.
GV865.M35 D46 2001

Feigenbaum, A. V. (Armand Vallin) The power of management capital. New York ; Toronto : McGraw-Hill, c2003.
HD31 .F45 2003

Ferrero, Ernesto. Lezioni napoleoniche. 1. ed. Milano : Mondadori, 2002.

Garten, Jeffrey E., 1946- The politics of fortune. Boston : Harvard Business School Press, c2002.
HD57.7 .G377 2002

Gaulle, Charles de, 1890-1970. [Fil de l'épée. Portuguese] O fio da espada. Rio de Janeiro : Biblioteca do Exército Editora, 2001.

Giuliani, Rudolph W. Leadership. London : Little, Brown, 2002.

Harvard business review on breakthrough leadership. Boston, Mass. : [Great Britain] : Harvard Business School Press, c2001.

Hiam, Alexander. Making horses drink. [Irvine, Calif.] : Entrepreneur Press, c2002.
HD57.7 .H52 2002

Hirschmann, Kris, 1967- Leadership. Chicago, IL : Raintree, 2003.
BF723.L4 H57 2003

Human resources in the 21st century. Hoboken, N.J. : J. Wiley & Sons, c2003.
HD31 .H81247 2003

Karauri, Mathew Adams, 1947- Rulers, leaders, and people. Nairobi : Karma Pub. Co., 2001.
1. Black author.

Kennedy, Kevin (Kevin John), 1955- Going the distance. Upper Saddle River, NJ : Prentice Hall/ Financial Times, c2003.
HD57.7 .K465 2003

Kline, Theresa, 1960- Teams that lead. Mahwah, N.J. : L. E. Associates, 2003
HD57.7 .K549 2003

Krames, Jeffrey A. The Jack Welch lexicon of leadership. 1st ed. New York : McGraw-Hill, 2001, c2002.
HD57.7 .K726 2001

Krames, Jeffrey A. The Rumsfeld way. 1st ed. New York : McGraw-Hill, c2002.
UB210 .K73 2002

Leadership. Greenwich, Conn. : Information Age Pub., c2002.
HD57.7 .L4313 2002

Leadership in a new era. New York : Paraview Special Editions, c2002.
BF637.L4 .L395 2002

Leading change. Bristol, UK : Policy Press, c2003.

Leading in an upside-down world. Toronto : Dundurn Group, c2003.
BF637.L4 L425 2003

Leading in an upside-down world. Toronto : Dundurn Group, c2003.

Leed, Maren. Keeping the warfighting edge. Santa Monica, CA : RAND, 2002.
UB413 .L386 2002

LePla, F. Joseph, 1955- Brand driven. London : Kogan Page, 2003.

Lowney, Chris. Heroic leadership. Chicago : Loyola Press, c2003.
HD57.7 .L69 2003

Martin, Vivien, 1947- Leading change in health and social care. London ; New York : Routledge, 2003.
RA971 .M365 2003

Morrison, Raymond E. Developing effective engineering leadership. London : Institution of Electrical Engineers, c2003.

Murphy, Emmett C. Leading on the edge of chaos. Paramus, N.J. : Prentice Hall Press, c2002.
HD57.7 .M868 2002

Mykytenko, Svitlana. Enihma lidera, abo, Shcho mozhe obitsi͡ati polity͡chna karʼi͡era pori͡adniĭ li͡udyni, okrim vtraty pori͡adnosti. Kyïv : Vyd-vo "Molod'", 2001.
JC330.3 .M95 2001

New challenges for international leadership. Santa Monica, Calif. : RAND, 2003.
HD57.7 .N488 2003

O'Loughlin, James. The real Warren Buffett. London ; Yarmouth, ME : Nicholas Brealey, 2003.

Phillips, Donald T. (Donald Thomas), 1952- Character in action. Annapolis, Md. : Naval Institute Press, c2003.
VG53 .P49 2003

Raelin, Joseph A., 1948- Creating leaderful organizations. 1st ed. San Francisco : Berrett-Koehler, c2003.
HD57.7 .R34 2003

Roberts, Andrew, 1963- Hitler and Churchill. London : Weidenfeld & Nicolson, 2003.

Rosero Garcés, F. (Fernando) Líderes sociales en el siglo XXI. Quito : Ediciones Abya-Yala, 2002.

Sadler, Philip, 1930- Leadership. 2nd ed. London ; Sterling, VA : Kogan Page Ltd., 2003.
HD57.7 .S227 2003

Safari, J. F. The new art of leadership for Africa 2000. Peramiho, Tanzania : Benedictine Publications Ndanda, 1996.
HM1261 S35 1996
1. Black author.

Sandys, Celia. We shall not fail. New York : Portfolio ; London : Penguin Books, 2003.
DA566.9.C5 S266 2003

Sashkin, Marshall, 1944- Leadership that matters. 1st ed. San Francisco : Berrett-Koehler, c2003.
HD57.7 .S27 2003

Sperry, Len. Becoming an effective health care manager. Baltimore, Md. : Health Professions Press, c2003.

Leadership.

RA971 .S72 2003

Tayir, Bracha Klein. ha-Manhig she-me'afsher le-elef perahim li-feroah. Tel Aviv : Yedi'ot aharonot : Sifre hemed, c2002.

Terry, Larry D. Leadership of public bureaucracies. 2nd ed. Armonk, N.Y. : M.E. Sharpe, c2003.
JF1525.L4 .T47 2003

The trust process in organizations. Cheltenham, UK ; Northampton, MA : Edward Elgar, c2003.
HD58.7 .T744 2003

Vosburgh, Bob. LIFT. [United Ustates?] : 9g Enterprises, c2002.
BF637.L4 V67 2002

Walton, Mark S., 1950- Generating buy-in. New York : American Management Association, c2004.
HD30.3 .W35 2004

Ward, Andrew. The leadership lifecycle. Houndmills [England] ; New York : Palgrave Macmillan, 2003.
HD57.7 .W367 2003

Winter, Graham. High performance leadership. Singapore ; New York : John Wiley & Sons (Asia), c2003.

Women on power. Boston : Northeastern University Press, c2001.
HQ1233 .W597 2001

Woodhead, Roy (Roy M.) Achieving results. London : Thomas Telford, 2002.

Woolfe, Lorin. The Bible on leadership. New York : American Management Association, c2002.
HD57.7 .W666 2002

Zeng, Changyong. Zeng Guofan ling dao fang lüe. Di 1 ban. Beijing Shi : Zhongguo hua qiao chu ban she, 2001.
DS758.23.T74 Z48 2001 East Asian

LEADERSHIP - AFRICA.
Safari, J. F. The new art of leadership for Africa 2000. Peramiho, Tanzania : Benedictine Publications Ndanda, 1996.
HM1261 S35 1996
1. Black author.

LEADERSHIP - CASE STUDIES.
Bennis, Warren G. On becoming a leader. [Rev. ed.]. Cambridge, MA : Perseus Pub., c2003.
BF637.L4 B37 2003

The challenges of high command. Houndmills, Basingstoke ; New York : Palgrave Macmillan, 2003.
UB210 .C477 2003

Zentner, John J., 1965- The art of wing leadership and aircrew morale in combat [electronic resource]. Maxwell Air Force Base, Ala. : Air University Press, [2001]

LEADERSHIP - CROSS-CULTURAL STUDIES.
Earley, P. Christopher. Cultural intelligence. Stanford, Calif. : Stanford University Press, 2003.
HD57.7 .E237 2003

Leadership / edited by Linda L. Neider, Chester A. Schriesheim. Greenwich, Conn. : Information Age Pub., c2002. xii, 228 p. : 24 cm. (The Research in management series) Includes bibliographical references. CONTENTS: Forward and commentary / Linda L. Neider and Chester A. Schriesheim. -- The leader as integrator : the case of Jack Welch at General Electric / Edwin A. Locke. -- Transformational and charismatic leadership : a levels-of-analysis review of theory, measurement, data analysis, and inferences / Francis J. Yammarino, Shelley Dionne, and Jae Uk Chun -- Social exchanges in the workplace : a review of recent developments and future research directions in leader-member exchange theory / Berrin Erdogan and Robert C. Liden. -- Path goal theory of leadership / Martin G. Evans -- Influence tactics and leader effectiveness / Gary Yukl and Carolyn Chavez -- Mentoring in the context of psychological contract breach / Terri A. Scandura and Ethlyn A. Williams -- Contingency model of leadership effectiveness : challenges and achievements / Roya Ayman. ISBN 1-931576-51-3 ISBN 1-931576-50-5 (pbk.) DDC 658.4/092
1. Leadership. 2. Executive ability. I. Neider, Linda L., 1953- II. Schriesheim, Chester. III. Series: Research in management.
HD57.7 .L4313 2002

Leadership in a new era : visionary approaches to the biggest crises of our time / edited by John Renesch. New York : Paraview Special Editions, c2002. xiii, 311 p. ; 23 cm. Includes bibliographical references (p. 291-296) and index. ISBN 1-931044-40-6 (pbk.)
1. Leadership. I. Renesch, John, 1937-
BF637.L4 .L395 2002

LEADERSHIP IN THE BIBLE.
Woolfe, Lorin. The Bible on leadership. New York : American Management Association, c2002.
HD57.7 .W666 2002

LEADERSHIP IN WOMEN.
Women on power. Boston : Northeastern University Press, c2001.
HQ1233 .W597 2001

LEADERSHIP - JUVENILE LITERATURE.
Hirschmann, Kris, 1967- Leadership. Chicago, IL : Raintree, 2003.
BF723.L4 H57 2003

The leadership lifecycle.
Ward, Andrew. Houndmills [England] ; New York : Palgrave Macmillan, 2003.
HD57.7 .W367 2003

LEADERSHIP, MILITARY. See COMMAND OF TROOPS.

LEADERSHIP - MORAL AND ETHICAL ASPECTS.
Galford, Robert M., 1952- The trusted leader. New York ; London : Free Press, c2002.
HD57.7 .G33 2002

Leadership of public bureaucracies.
Terry, Larry D. 2nd ed. Armonk, N.Y. : M.E. Sharpe, c2003.
JF1525.L4 .T47 2003

LEADERSHIP - PROBLEMS, EXERCISES, ETC.
Flaherty, Jane S. Lifetime leadership. San Diego : Bentley Press, c2001.
BF637.L4 F57 2001

Leadership processes and follower self-identity.
Lord, Robert G. (Robert George), 1946- Mahwah, N.J. ; London : Lawrence Erlbaum, 2004.
HM1261 .L67 2004

LEADERSHIP - PSYCHOLOGICAL ASPECTS.
Lord, Robert G. (Robert George), 1946- Leadership processes and follower self-identity. Mahwah, N.J. ; London : Lawrence Erlbaum, 2004.
HM1261 .L67 2004

LEADERSHIP - QUOTATIONS, MAXIMS, ETC.
Never scratch a tiger with a short stick. Colorado Springs, Colo. : NavPress, c2003.
BF637.L4 N48 2003

Leadership that matters.
Sashkin, Marshall, 1944- 1st ed. San Francisco : Berrett-Koehler, c2003.
HD57.7 .S27 2003

Leading change : a guide to whole systems working / Margaret Attwood ... [et al.]. Bristol, UK : Policy Press, c2003. xvi, 207 p. : ill. ; 24 cm. Includes bibliographical references (p. 193-199) and index. ISBN 1-86134-449-X
1. Social service. 2. Leadership. I. Attwood, Margaret.

Leading change in health and social care.
Martin, Vivien, 1947- London ; New York : Routledge, 2003.
RA971 .M365 2003

Leading in an upside-down world : new Canadian perspectives on leadership / edited by J. Patrick Boyer. Toronto : Dundurn Group, c2003. 224 p. : ill. ; 23 cm. Includes bibliographical references (p. [222]-224). ISBN 1-55002-455-8 DDC 158/.4
1. Leadership. 2. Management. 3. Organizational change - Management. I. Boyer, J. Patrick.
BF637.L4 L425 2003

Leading in an upside-down world : new Canadian perspectives on leadership / J. Patrick Boyer, editor. Toronto : Dundurn Group, c2003. 224 p. : ill., ports. ; 23 cm. ISBN 1-55002-455-8 DDC 658.4/092
1. Leadership. 2. Management. 3. Organizational change - Management - Canada. I. Boyer, J. Patrick.

Leading on the edge of chaos.
Murphy, Emmett C. Paramus, N.J. : Prentice Hall Press, c2002.
HD57.7 .M868 2002

Leading the revolution.
Hamel, Gary. Rev. and updated hardcover ed. [Boston, Mass.] : Harvard Business School Press, c2002.

Leahey, Thomas Hardy. A history of psychology : main currents in psychological thought / Thomas Hardy Leahey. 6th ed. Upper Saddle River, N.J. : Prentice Hall, 2004. p. cm. Includes bibliographical references and index. ISBN 0-13-111447-6 DDC 150/.9
1. Psychology - History. I. Title.

BF81 .L4 2004

Leaman, Oliver, 1950-.
The Cambridge companion to medieval Jewish philosophy. Cambridge, UK ; New York : Cambridge University Press, 2003.
B755 .C36 2003

Leaney, Cindy.
Hero club safety.
Leaney, Cindy. Long walk to school. Vero Beach, Fla. : Rourke Pub., 2003.
BF637.B85 L43 2003

Long walk to school : safety outdoors / by Cindy Leaney ; illustrated by Peter Wilks. Vero Beach, Fla. : Rourke Pub., 2003. p. cm. (Hero club safety) SUMMARY: The Hero kids help a boy who is being bullied, as well as the one doing the bullying. ISBN 1-58952-745-3 DDC 371.5/8
1. Bullying - Juvenile literature. 2. Bullying. 3. Bullies. 4. Safety. I. Wilks, Peter, ill. II. Title. III. Series: Leaney, Cindy. Hero club safety.
BF637.B85 L43 2003

Leap of faith (Motion picture).
Peace and conflict resolution. Part 2 [videorecording]. Derry, N.H. : Chip Taylor Communications, 1997.

Lear, Jonathan. Therapeutic action : an earnest plea for irony / Jonathan Lear. New York : Other Press, c2003. 246 p. ; 24 cm. Includes bibliographical references (p. 231-237) and index. CONTENTS: Introduction -- Subjectivity, objectivity and irony -- Internalization -- Love as a drive -- Transference as worldiness -- Revocation. ISBN 1-59051-077-1 (hardcover : alk. paper) DDC 150.19/5
1. Psychoanalytic counseling. 2. Psychoanalysis. I. Title.
BF175.4.C68 L43 2003

Learn to balance your life.
Hinz, Michael. San Francisco : Chronicle Books, 2004.
BF637.S4 H55 2004

Learn to be an optimist.
MacDonald, Lucy, 1953- San Francisco : Chronicle Books, 2004.
BF698.35.O57 M23 2004

LEARNED INSTITUTIONS AND SOCIETIES. See LEARNING AND SCHOLARSHIP.

LEARNED INSTITUTIONS AND SOCIETIES - HISTORY - 17TH CENTURY.
Baldriga, Irene. L'occhio della lince. Roma : Accademia nazionale dei Lincei, 2002.

LEARNED INSTITUTIONS AND SOCIETIES - ITALY - HISTORY - 17TH CENTURY.
Baldriga, Irene. L'occhio della lince. Roma : Accademia nazionale dei Lincei, 2002.

LEARNING. See also EXPERIENTIAL LEARNING; ORGANIZATIONAL LEARNING.
Cunningham, Ian, 1943- The wisdom of strategic learning. London ; New York : McGraw-Hill, c1994.
HD58.8 .C857 1994

LEARNING ABILITY. See LEARNING, PSYCHOLOGY OF.

LEARNING AND SCHOLARSHIP. See CULTURE; EDUCATION; HUMANISM; HUMANITIES; LEARNED INSTITUTIONS AND SOCIETIES; RESEARCH; SCHOLARS.

LEARNING AND SCHOLARSHIP - CHINA.
Liang Qichao, Zhang Taiyan jie du Zhonghua wen hua jing dian. Di 1 ban. Shenyang Shi : Liao Hai chu ban she, 2003.
PL2262.2 .L54 2003

LEARNING AND SCHOLARSHIP - EUROPE - HISTORY.
Moss, Ann, 1938- Printed commonplace-books and the structuring of Renaissance thought. Oxford : Clarendon Press ; New York : Oxford University Press, 1996.
PA2047 .M67 1996

LEARNING AND SCHOLARSHIP - GREECE.
Gelehrte in der Antike. Köln : Böhlau, c2002.

LEARNING AND SCHOLARSHIP - ROME.
Gelehrte in der Antike. Köln : Böhlau, c2002.

Learning Annex (Firm).
The Learning Annex presents feng shui. 1st ed. New York, NY : J. Wiley, 2004.
BF1779.F4 L42 2004

The Learning Annex presents feng shui / the Learning Annex with Meihwa Lin. 1st ed. New York, NY : J. Wiley, 2004. p. cm. ISBN 0-7645-4144-7 (pbk.) DDC 133.3/337

1. Feng shui. I. Lin, Meihwa. II. Learning Annex (Firm) III. Title.
BF1779.F4 L42 2004

Learning as a Self-Organization. 1996.
Rumbaugh, Duane M., 1929- Respondents, operants, and emergents [microform]. [Washington, D.C. : National Aeronautics and Space Administration, 1997]

LEARNING - CONGRESSES.
Construcción de conocimiento y educación virtual. 1. ed. Ciudad Universitaria, México, D.F. : Universidad Nacional Autónoma de México, 2000.
LB1060 .C658 2000

LEARNING DISABILITIES. See **READING DISABILITY.**

LEARNING, EXPERIENTIAL. See **EXPERIENTIAL LEARNING.**

LEARNING IN ANIMALS - CONGRESSES.
Imitation in animals and artifacts. Cambridge, Mass. : MIT Press, c2002.
BF357 .I47 2002

Learning in the field.
Rossman, Gretchen B. 2nd ed. Thousand Oaks, Calif. ; London : Sage Publications, c2003.
H62 .R667 2003

Learning joy from dogs without collars.
Summer, Lauralee, 1976- New York ; London : Simon & Schuster, c2003.
HV4505 .S86 2003

LEARNING, MACHINE. See **MACHINE LEARNING.**

LEARNING - MATHEMATICAL MODELS - CONGRESSES.
Adaptivity and learning. New York : Springer, 2003.
BF318 .A33 2003

LEARNING ORGANIZATIONS. See **ORGANIZATIONAL LEARNING.**

LEARNING - PHYSIOLOGICAL ASPECTS.
Arnold, Margret. Aspekte einer modernen Neurodidaktik. München : Ernst Vögel, 2002.

Lawson, Anton E. The neurological basis of learning, development, and discovery. Dordrecht ; Boston : Kluwer Academic Publishers, c2003.
BF318 .L365 2003

Understanding the brain. Paris : Organisation for Economic Co-operation and Development, 2002.
QP360.5 .U54 2002

LEARNING - PHYSIOLOGICAL ASPECTS - CONGRESSES.
Adaptivity and learning. New York : Springer, 2003.
BF318 .A33 2003

LEARNING PROCESS. See **LEARNING.**

LEARNING - PSYCHOLOGICAL ASPECTS. See **LEARNING, PSYCHOLOGY OF.**

LEARNING, PSYCHOLOGY OF. See also **MOTOR LEARNING.**
Beaver, Diana. NLP for lazy learning. London : Vega, 2002.
BF637.N46 B44 2002

Bereiter, Carl. Education and mind in the knowledge age. Mahwah, N.J. : L. Erlbaum Associates, 2002.
LB1057 .B47 2002

Cabrera, Derek. Remedial genius. 1st ed. Loveland, Colo. : Project N Press, 2001.
BF441 .C23 2001

Cerezo Manrique, Miguel Ángel. Los comienzos de la psicopedagogía en España, 1882-1936. Madrid : Biblioteca Nueva, c2001.

Evolution and learning. Cambridge, Mass. : MIT Press, c2003.
BF698.95 .E95 2003

Healy, Jane M. Your child's growing mind. 3rd ed. New York : Broadway Books, 2004.
BF318 .H4 2004

Lawson, Anton E. The neurological basis of learning, development, and discovery. Dordrecht ; Boston : Kluwer Academic Publishers, c2003.
BF318 .L365 2003

Machado, Armando. The psychology of learning. Upper Saddle River, NJ : Prentice Hall, 2003.
BF318 .M29 2003

Meighan, Roland. John Holt. 2nd ed. Nottingham : Educational Heretics Press, 2002.

LB885.H64 M454 2002

Ormrod, Jeanne Ellis. Human learning. 4th ed. Upper Saddle River, N.J. : Merrill, c2004.
BF318 .O76 2004

Pierce, W. David. Behavior analysis and learning. 3rd ed. Mahwah, N.J. : L. Erlbaum Associates, 2004.
BF199 .P54 2004

Qu'est-ce-donc qu'apprendre? Lausanne : Delachaux et Niestlé, 1999.
BF318 .Q84 1999

Rumbaugh, Duane M., 1929- Respondents, operants, and emergents [microform]. [Washington, D.C. : National Aeronautics and Space Administration, 1997]

The Ship of thought. London : Karnac, 2002.

Sunbeck, Deborah. The complete Infinity walk . Rochester, N.Y. : Leonardo Foundation Press, c2001-
BF318 .S86 2001

Understanding the brain. Paris : Organisation for Economic Co-operation and Development, 2002.
QP360.5 .U54 2002

LEARNING, PSYCHOLOGY OF - CONGRESSES.
Adaptivity and learning. New York : Springer, 2003.
BF318 .A33 2003

LEARNING, PSYCHOLOGY OF - PROBLEMS, EXERCISES, ETC.
Machado, Armando. The psychology of learning. Upper Saddle River, NJ : Prentice Hall, 2003.
BF318 .M29 2003

Learning tarot reversals.
Bunning, Joan. Boston, MA : Weiser Books, 2003.
BF1879.T2 .B834 2003

Learning theory and Kernel machines.
Conference on Computational Learning Theory (16th : 2003 : Washington, D.C.) Berlin ; New York : Springer, c2003.
Q325.5 .C654 2003

Learning toward an ecological consciousness : selected transformative practices / edited by Edmund V. O'Sullivan and Marilyn M. Taylor. New York : Palgrave Macmillan, 2003. p. cm. Includes bibliographical references and index. ISBN 1403963045 (pbk.) ISBN 1403963053 (cloth) DDC 304.2
1. Environmental psychology. 2. Environmental education. I. O'Sullivan, Edmund, 1938- II. Taylor, Marilyn M.
BF353 .L42 2003

Lears, T. J. Jackson, 1947- Something for nothing : luck in America / Jackson Lears. New York : Viking, 2003. xi, 392 p. : ill. ; 24 cm. Includes bibliographical references (p. 335-365) and index. ISBN 0-670-03173-9 (alk. paper) DDC 363.4/2
1. Gambling - Social aspects - United States. 2. Gambling - United States - Public opinion - History. 3. United States - Moral conditions - History. 4. Fortune. I. Title.
HV6715 .L415 2003

Leary, Mark R. The curse of the self : self-awareness, egotism, and the quality of human life / Mark R. Leary. New York : Oxford University Press, 2004. p. cm. Includes bibliographical references (p.   ). ISBN 0-19-517242-6 (alk. paper) DDC 155.2
1. Self. 2. Egoism. 3. Conduct of life. I. Title.
BF697 .L33 2004

Introduction to behavioral research methods / Mark R. Leary. 4th ed. Boston, MA : Allyn and Bacon, 2004. p. cm. Includes bibliographical references and index. ISBN 0-205-39676-3 DDC 150/.7/2
1. Psychology - Research - Methodology. I. Title.
BF76.5 .L39 2004

Leary, Timothy Francis, 1920- Musings on human metaporphoses / Timothy Leary. Berkeley, CA : Ronin, c2003. 128 p. ; 22 cm. ISBN 1-57951-058-2 DDC 599.93/8
1. Human evolution. 2. Life on other planets. I. Title.

LEA's communication series.
Communication and emotion. Mahwah, N.J. ; London : Lawrence Erlbaum, c2003.
BF637.C45 C6375 2003

Privacy and disclosure of HIV in interpersonal relationships. Mahwah, N.J. : Lawrence Erlbaum Associates, 2003.
RA643.8 .P755 2003

LEA's organization and management series
Personality and organizations. Mahwah, N.J. : Lawrence Erlbaum Associates, 2004.
BF698.9.O3 P46 2004

LEA's series on personal relationships
Yingling, Julie. A lifetime of communication. Mahwah, N.J. : Lawrence Erlbaum Associates, 2004.
BF637.C45 Y56 2004

LEAST DEVELOPED COUNTRIES. See **DEVELOPING COUNTRIES.**

LeBaron, Curtis D.
Studies in language and social interaction. Mahwah, N.J. : London : Lawrence Erlbaum, 2003.

LeBaron, Michelle, 1956- Bridging cultural conflicts : a new approach for a changing world / Michelle LeBaron ; foreword by Mohammed Abu-Nimer. 1st ed. San Francisco, CA : Jossey-Bass, c2003. xvi, 332 p. : ill. ; 24 cm. Includes bibliographical references (p. 303-312) and index. CONTENTS: Bridging cultures : uncovering paths that connect us -- Cultural fluency in conflict : an overview -- Cultural fluency in conflict : currencies and starting points -- Mindful awareness as a path to cultural fluency -- Conflict fluency -- Engaging difference -- Deepening the colors : personal practices to help bridge differences -- Out of the fire : interpersonal practices to help bridge differences -- On the larger stage : intergroup practices to help bridge differences -- Third party roles in cultural conflict -- Stepping into shared pictures. ISBN 0-7879-6431-X (alk. paper) DDC 303.6/9
1. Culture conflict. 2. Conflict management. I. Title.
BF698.9.C8 L43 2003

LeBeau, Kara R. Guan yin's chakra meditations / Kara R. LeBeau, with Debora Lamb, and Michelle Stein. Boulder, Colo. : Mahasimhananda Press, c2001. 46 p. : bill. (some col.), 44 cm.
1. Chakras. 2. Buddhist meditations. 3. Mantras. 4. Avalokitesvara (Buddhist deity) I. Lamb, Debora. II. Stein, Michelle. III. Title.
BF1442.C53 L43 2001

Lebrun, Jean Pierre.
Melman, Charles, 1931- L'homme sans gravité. Paris : Denoël, c2002.

Lechaume, Aline.
Le territoire pensé. Sainte-Foy : Presses de l'Université du Québec, 2003.

Lechevalier, Bernard. Le cerveau de Mozart / Bernard Lechevalier ; préface de Jean Cambier. Paris : O. Jacob, c2003. 338 p. : ill. ; 22 cm. Includes bibliographical references (p. [317]-327) and index. ISBN 2-7381-1298-6 DDC 781/.11
1. Mozart, Wolfgang Amadeus, - 1756-1791. 2. Music - Psychological aspects. 3. Neuropsychology. 4. Musical ability. 5. Gifted persons - Psychology. I. Title.
ML3838 .L39 2003

Lechner, Jörg-Johannes, 1966-.
Reiner, Hans, 1896- Philosophieren. Oberried bei Freiburg i. Br. : PAIS-Verlag, c2002.

Leçon sur L'éthique à Nicomaque, d'Aristote.
Ricot, Jacques. 1re ed. Paris : Presses universitaires de France, c2001.
B430 .R536 2001

Lecouteux, Claude.
[Fées, sorcières et loups-garous au Moyen Age. English]
Witches, werewolves, and fairies : shapeshifters and astral doublers in the Middle Ages / Claude Lecouteux ; translated by Clare Frock. 1st U.S. ed. Rochester, Vt. : Inner Traditions, 2003. xxiv, 200 p. : ill. ; 23 cm. Includes bibliographical references (p. 192-195) and index. Table of contents URL : http://www.loc.gov/catdir/toc/ecip043/2003009563.html CONTENTS: The ecstatic journey -- Pagan ecstatics -- An unusual concept of the soul -- -- The double and fairies -- The double and witchcraft -- Metamorphosis : the double and werewolves -- Autoscopy -- Shadow, reflection, and image. ISBN 0-89281-096-3 (pbk.) DDC 133.1/4
1. Double (Parapsychology) 2. Werewolves. 3. Wizards. 4. Fairies. I. Title.
BF1045.D67 L4313 2003

Collection Le temps de l'histoire
Année mille An Mil. Aix-en-Provence : Publications de l'université de Provence, 2002.

Lectrices au quotidien.
Debras, Sylvie. Paris : L'Harmattan, c2003.

Lecture de l'étourdit.
Fierens, Christian. Paris : Harmattan, c2002.
BF109.L28 F53 2002

Lecture notes in computer science
(2533.) ALT 2002 (2002 : Lübeck, Germany) Algorithmic learning theory. Berlin ; New York : Springer, c2002.
QA76.9.A43 A48 2002

Lecture notes in computer science

(2600.) Machine Learning Summer School 2002 (2002 : Canberra, N.C.T.) Advanced lectures on machine learning. Berlin ; New York : Springer, 2003.
Q325.5 .M344 2002

(2636.) Adaptive agents and multi-agent systems. Berlin ; New York : Springer, c2003.
QA76.76.I58 A312 2003

(2654.) Schmid, U. (Ute) Inductive synthesis of functional programs. Berlin ; New York : Springer, c2003.
QA76.6 .S3855 2003

(2684.) Workshop on Adaptive Behavior in Anticipatory Learning Systems (1st : 2002 : Edinburgh, Scotland) Anticipatory behavior in adaptive learning systems. Berlin ; New York : Springer, c2003.
Q325.5 .W65 2003

(2685.) Spatial cognition III. Berlin ; New York : Springer, c2003.
Q387 .S73 2003

(2709) International Workshop on Multiple Classifier Systems (4th : 2003 : Guildford, England) Multiple classifier systems. Berlin ; New York : Springer, c2003.
Q325.5 .I574 2003

(2734.) International Workshop MLDM 2003 (2003 : Leipzig, Germany) Machine learning and data mining in pattern recognition. Berlin ; New York : Springer, c2003.
Q327 .I67 2003

(2777.) Conference on Computational Learning Theory (16th : 2003 : Washington, D.C.) Learning theory and Kernel machines. Berlin ; New York : Springer, c2003.
Q325.5 .C654 2003

Lecture notes in computer science. Lecture notes in artificial intelligence.
Adaptive agents and multi-agent systems. Berlin ; New York : Springer, c2003.
QA76.76.I58 A312 2003

ALT 2002 (2002 : Lübeck, Germany) Algorithmic learning theory. Berlin ; New York : Springer, c2002.
QA76.9.A43 A48 2002

Conference on Computational Learning Theory (16th : 2003 : Washington, D.C.) Learning theory and Kernel machines. Berlin ; New York : Springer, c2003.
Q325.5 .C654 2003

International Workshop MLDM 2003 (2003 : Leipzig, Germany) Machine learning and data mining in pattern recognition. Berlin ; New York : Springer, c2003.
Q327 .I67 2003

Machine Learning Summer School 2002 (2002 : Canberra, N.C.T.) Advanced lectures on machine learning. Berlin ; New York : Springer, 2003.
Q325.5 .M344 2002

Schmid, U. (Ute) Inductive synthesis of functional programs. Berlin ; New York : Springer, c2003.
QA76.6 .S3855 2003

Spatial cognition III. Berlin ; New York : Springer, c2003.
Q387 .S73 2003

Workshop on Adaptive Behavior in Anticipatory Learning Systems (1st : 2002 : Edinburgh, Scotland) Anticipatory behavior in adaptive learning systems. Berlin ; New York : Springer, c2003.
Q325.5 .W65 2003

Lecture notes in control and information sciences
(292) Chaos control. Berlin ; New York : Springer, c2003.
QA402.3 .C48 2003

Lecture notes in physics
(592) Aegean Summer School on Cosmology (1st : 2001 : Samos Island, Greece) Cosmological crossroads. Berlin ; New York : Springer, c2002.
QB985 .A44 2001

(597) Dynamics of dissipation. Berlin ; New York : Springer, c2002.
QC174.85 .D96 2002

LECTURES.
Loch, Wolfgang. "Mit Freud über Freud hinaus". Tübingen : Edition Diskord, c2001.
BF173 .L554 2001

Lectures on philosophical ethics.
Schleiermacher, Friedrich, 1768-1834. Cambridge ; New York : Cambridge University Press, 2002.

Ledda, Antonio. La fenomelogia tra essenza ed esistenza : Husserl e Tommaso d'Aquino a confronto / Antonio Ledda. 1. ed. Roma : Carocci editore, 2002. 220 p. ; 22 cm. (Ricerche ; 114. Filosofia) Includes bibliographical references (p. 217-220). ISBN 88-430-2374-8 DDC 142
1. Husserl, Edmund, - 1859-1938. 2. Thomas, - Aquinas, Saint, - 1225?-1274. 3. Phenomenology. 4. Ontology. I. Title. II. Series: Ricerche (Carocci editore) ; 114. III. Series: Ricerche (Carocci editore). Filosofia.

LeDoux, Joseph E.
The self. New York : New York Academy of Sciences, 2003.
BF697

Lee-Browne, Patrick. The Renaissance : English literature in its historical, cultural and social contexts / Patrick Lee-Browne. New York : Facts on File, c2003. 96 p. : col. ill. ; 26 cm. (Backgrounds to English literature ; v.1) ISBN 0-8160-5125-9 (set) ISBN 0-8160-5126-7 (v.1)
1. Renaissance. 2. English literature - Early modern, 1500-1700. 3. Great Britain - Intellectual life - 16th century. 4. Europe - Social life and customs - 16th century. I. Title.

Lee, Ilchi. Healing chakra : light to awaken my soul / Ilchi Lee. Las Vegas, NV : Healing Society, c2002. xxv, 142 p. : ill. (some col.) ; 24 cm. + self-training booklet. ISBN 0-9720282-4-2 (pbk.) DDC 31
1. Chakras - Miscellanea. I. Title.
BF1442.C53 L44 2002

Lee, Michelle. Fashion victim : our love-hate relationship with dressing, shopping, and the cost of style / Michelle Lee. 1st ed. New York : Broadway Books, 2003. xxv, 294 p. ; 25 cm. Includes index. JFE 03-4795. ISBN 0-7679-1048-6 DDC 391
1. Costume - Psychological aspects. 2. Fashion - Psychological aspects. 3. Clothing trade - Psychological aspects. 4. Advertising - Fashion. 5. Compulsive shopping. 6. Body image in women. 7. Self-esteem in women. I. Title. II. Title: JFE 03-4795
GT524 .L44 2003

Lee, Nancy, 1932-.
Kotler, Philip. Social marketing. 2nd ed. Thousand Oaks, Calif. ; London : Sage Publications, c2002.
HF5414 .K67 2002

Lee, Simon (Simon F.) Uneasy ethics / Simon Lee. London : Pimlico, 2003. 230 p. ; 22 cm. (A Pimlico original ; 585) ISBN 0-7126-0655-6 DDC 170
1. Ethics. I. Title.

Lee, Terence, 1924-.
Psychological theories for environmental issues. Aldershot, Hants, England ; Burlington, VT : Ashgate, 2003.
BF353 .P774 2003

Lee, William W. Organizing change : an inclusive, systemic approach to maintain productivity and achieve results / William W. Lee, Karl J. Krayer. San Francisco : Pfeiffer, c2003. xv, 256 p. : ill. ; 25 cm. + 1 computer optical disc (4 3/4 in.). Includes bibliographical references (p. 241-247) and index. ISBN 0-7879-6443-3 (alk. paper) DDC 658.4/06
1. Organizational change - Management. I. Krayer, Karl J., 1954- II. Title.
HD58.8 .L423 2003

Leed, Maren. Keeping the warfighting edge : an empirical analysis of Army officers' tactical expertise / Maren Leed. Santa Monica, CA : RAND, 2002. xiv, 116 p. : ill. ; 23 cm. "Arroyo Center." "Prepared for the United States Army." "MR-1378-A"--P. [4] of cover. Includes bibliographical references (p. 111-116). Sponsored by the United States Army. DASW01-01-C-0003 ISBN 0-8330-3130-9
1. United States. - Army - Officers. 2. United States. - Army - Officers - Education. 3. United States. - Army - Drill and tactics. 4. Leadership. I. Arroyo Center. II. Rand Corporation. III. Title.
UB413 .L386 2002

Leertouwer, Lammert.
Modern societies & the science of religions. Leiden ; Boston : Brill, 2002.
BL48 .M542 2002

Lees, Stan. Global acquisitions : strategic integration and the human factor / Stan Lees. Houndmills [England] ; New York : Palgrave Macmillan, 2003. xx, 288 p. : ill. ; 24 cm. Includes bibliographical references (p. 277-282) and indexes. ISBN 0-333-77629-1 DDC 658.1/6
1. Organizational change - Management. 2. Consolidation and merger of corporations - Management. 3. Corporate reorganizations - Management. 4. Globalization. I. Title.
HD58.8 .L424 2003

Lefèvre, Alain, 1947- De la paternité et des psychoses : une étude philosophique et psychanalytique / Alain Lefevre. Paris : Harmattan, c2002- v. ; ill. ; 22 cm. (Psychanalyse et civilisations) Includes bibliographical references. PARTIAL CONTENTS: t. 1. Du père. ISBN 2-7475-3981-4 DDC 150
1. Fatherhood - Psychological aspects. 2. Psychoses. 3. Psychoanalysis. I. Title. II. Series.

Leff, Enrique. Saber ambiental : sustentabilidad, racionalidad, conplejidad, poder / por Enrique Leff. 3a ed. correg. y aument. México : PNUMA ; Siglo Veintiuno, 2002. 414 p. ; 21 cm. (Ambiente y democracia) Includes bibliographical references (p. 401-414). ISBN 968-23-2402-5
1. Sustainable development - Environmental aspects. 2. Human ecology. 3. Environmental education. I. United Nations Environment Programme. II. Title. III. Title: Sustentabilidad, racionalidad, conplejidad, poder. IV. Series.

Lefort, Claude.
Merleau-Ponty, Maurice, 1908-1961. L'institution dans l'histoire personnelle et publique ; [Paris] : Belin, c2003.
B2430.M3763 I88 2003

Lefrère, Jean-Jacques.
Colloque des Invalides (5th : 2001 : Hôtel des invalides) Ce que je ne sais pas. Tusson, Charente : Du Lérot, [2002?]
PQ145 .C65 2001

LEFT AND RIGHT (PSYCHOLOGY).
Sunbeck, Deborah. The complete Infinity walk . Rochester, N.Y. : Leonardo Foundation Press, c2001-
BF318 .S86 2001

LEFT AND RIGHT (PSYCHOLOGY) - STUDY AND TEACHING (PRESCHOOL) - ACTIVITY PROGRAMS.
Semel, Eleanor Messing. Following directions [electronic resource]. Macintosh/Windows version. Winooski, VT : Laureate Learning Systems, c2000.
BF637.L36

Lefter, Ion Bogdan. Postmodernism : din dosarul unei "bătălii" culturale / Ion Bogdan Lefter. Pitești : Editura Paralela 45, 2000. 282 p. ; 20 cm. Includes bibliographical references. ISBN 9735932792
1. Postmodernism - Romania. 2. Philosophy, Modern - 20th century. I. Title.

Legacies of social thought
Meadow, Phyllis W., 1924- The new psychoanalysis. Lanham, Md. : Rowman & Littlefield, c2003.
BF173 .M3585 2003

LEGAL DOCUMENTS - IDENTIFICATION - PERIODICALS.
Document, various specification. Wrocław : University of Wrocław, Faculty of Law and Administration, Department of Criminalistics, 2000-
BF905.C7 D63

LEGAL HOLIDAYS. *See* **HOLIDAYS.**

LEGAL INSTRUMENTS. *See* **LEGAL DOCUMENTS.**

LEGAL PROFESSION. *See* **LAWYERS.**

LEGAL TENDER. *See* **MONEY.**

LEGALIZATION. *See* **LEGAL DOCUMENTS.**

LEGENDS. *See* **MYTHOLOGY.**

Legends & lore.
Suckling, Nigel. New York : Friedman/Fairfax Publishers ; Distributed by Sterling Pub., c2002.
BF1714.C5 S93 2002

Legends and lore.
Suckling, Nigel. Legends & lore. New York : Friedman/Fairfax Publishers ; Distributed by Sterling Pub., c2002.
BF1714.C5 S93 2002

LEGENDS - CHINA.
Zhao, Xi. Xu wu piao miao de gui shen shi jie. Di 1 ban. Beijing : Zong jiao wen hua chu ban she, 2001.
BL1812.G63 Z436 2001

LEGENDS - GREAT BRITAIN.
Squire, Charles. Celtic myth and legend. Rev. ed. Franklin Lakes, NJ : New Page Books, c2001.
BL900 .S6 2001

LEGENDS - IRELAND.
Squire, Charles. Celtic myth and legend. Rev. ed. Franklin Lakes, NJ : New Page Books, c2001.

BL900 .S6 2001

LEGENDS, JEWISH. *See* **AGGADA.**

Legends of Indian cinema.
Surendra Kumar. New Delhi : Har-Anand Publications, c2003.
PN1993.5.I4 S87 2003

Legends of the star ancestors : stories of extraterrestrial contact from wisdomkeepers around the world / as spoken to Nancy Red Star. Rochester, Vt. : Bear & Co., c2002. xi, 178 p. : ill. (some col.) ; 23 cm. CONTENTS: The world peace : compassionate enlightenment / Khenpo Rinpoche Kharthur -- A spiritual renewal : the big mother / Rabbi Ohad Ezrah -- Breaking the stone : healing the waters / Desiree Fitzgibbon -- Tribal ink and link : awakening humanity / Luis E. Meija -- Truth : the brotherhood of the snake / Daniel M. Salter -- The geneticists : in solitude / Ana Brito -- High strangeness : spiritual choice / James Lujan -- Guardians of the gate: women's earth wisdom / Colleen Kelly -- Twin hearts : star soul attunement / Dr. Ra-Ja Dove and Dr. Moi-Ra Dove -- Painting in the dreamtime : holding the universe / Jingalu -- A gathering of nations : serving mankind / Sultan Abdul Latif -- Sunbow : world cycles / Naoko Hitomi. ISBN 1-87918-179-7 (pbk.) DDC 001.942
1. Human-alien encounters. I. Red Star, Nancy, 1950-
BF2050 .L44 2002

Leger, Daniel W.
Nebraska Symposium on Motivation (2001)
Evolutionary psychology and motivation. Lincoln, Neb, ; London : University of Nebraska Press, c2001.
BF701 .N43 2001

LEGERDEMAINISTS. *See* **MAGICIANS.**

Le leggi del pensiero tra logica, ontologia e psicologia : il dibattito austrotedesco : 1830-1930 / a cura di Stefano Poggi. Milano : UNICOPLI, 2002. 291 p. ; 22 cm. (Biblioteca di cultura filosofica ; 23) Collected essays. Includes bibliographical references. ISBN 88-400-0803-9 DDC 190
1. Ontology. 2. Thought and thinking. 3. Psychology. 4. Philosophy. 5. Logic. 6. Germany - Intellectual life - 19th century. 7. Germany - Intellectual life - 20th century. 8. Austria - Intellectual life - 19th century. 9. Austria - Intellectual life - 20th century. I. Poggi, Stefano. II. Series: Biblioteca di cultura filosofica (Milan, Italy) ; 23.

LEGISLATION. *See* **LAW.**

LEGISLATORS - UNITED STATES - BIOGRAPHY.
Kenneally, James J. (James Joseph), 1929- A compassionate conservative. Lanham, Md. : Lexington Books, c2003.
E748.M375 K46 2003

Legitimating new religions.
Lewis, James R. New Brunswick, N.J. : Rutgers University Press, c2003.
BP603 .L49 2003

Lehmann, Hartmut, 1936-.
Antike Weisheit und kulturelle Praxis. Göttingen : Vandenhoeck & Ruprecht, 2001.
BF1586 .A58 2001

Lehmkuhl, Ulrike.
Strukturbildung und Lebensstil. München : Ernst Reinhardt, c2002.

Lehrbuch der philosophischen Lebenskunst für das 21. Jahrhundert.
Werder, Lutz von. Berlin : Schibri-Verlag, c2000.

Lehrer.
Augustine, Saint, Bishop of Hippo. De magistro = Paderborn ; F. Schöningh, 2002.
BR65.A5 G4 2002

Leib und Körper.
Linck, Gudula. Frankfurt am Main ; New York : P. Lang, c2001.
B105.B64 L58 2001

Leibniz, Gottfried Wilhelm, Freiherr von, 1646-1716.
Orio de Miguel, Bernardino, 1936- Leibniz y el pensamiento hermético. Valencia : Universidad Politécnica de Valéncia, Editorial U.P.V., [2002]

Leibniz, Gottfried Wilhelm, Freiherr von, 1646-1716.
Réfutation inédite de Spinoza : remarques critiques de Leibniz sur un livre de J.G. Wachter à propos de la philosophie cachée des Hébreux : d'après le manuscrit original de la Bibliothèque royale de Hanovre / Gottfried Wilhelm Leibniz ; lecture et appareil critique de Martine de Gaudemar. Arles [France] : Actes Sud ; [Montréal] : Leméac, 1999. 101 p. ; 18 cm. (Babel ; 368) (Les philosophiques) Translation of: Leibnitii animadversiones ex autographo Bibliothecae regiae Hanoveranae. "Texte tel que l'a traduit Foucher de Careil ...".--P. 11. Includes bibliographical references. ISBN 2-7427-2074-X ISBN 2760920364 (Leméac) DDC 193
1. Spinoza, Benedictus de, - 1632-1677. 2. Cabala. I. Gaudemar, Martine de. II. Wachter, Johann Georg, 1673-1757. Spinozismus im Jüdenthumb. III. Title. IV. Series: Babel (Arles, France) ; 368. V. Series: Babel (Arles, France). Philosophiques.

[Selections. English & Latin. 2001]
The labyrinth of the continuum : writings on the continuum problem, 1672-1686 / G.W. Leibniz ; translated, edited, and with an introduction by Richard T.W. Arthur New Haven : Yale University Press, c2001. lxxxviii, 484 p. ; 25 cm. (The Yale Leibniz) Includes bibliographical references and indexes. Original Latin text with English translation on facing pages. Table of contents URL: http://www.loc.gov/catdir/toc/fy022/2001017973.html ISBN 0-300-07911-7 (alk. paper) DDC 193
1. Philosophy. I. Arthur, Richard, 1950- II. Title. III. Series: Leibniz, Gottfried Wilhelm, Freiherr von, 1646-1716. Selections. Polyglot. 1992.
B2558 .A78 2001

Leibniz, Gottfried Wilhelm, Freiherr von, 1646-1716. Selections. Polyglot. 1992.
Leibniz, Gottfried Wilhelm, Freiherr von, 1646-1716. [Selections. English & Latin. 2001] The labyrinth of the continuum. New Haven : Yale University Press, c2001.
B2558 .A78 2001

LEIBNIZ, GOTTFRIED WILHELM, FREIHERR VON, 1646-1716.
Orio de Miguel, Bernardino, 1936- Leibniz y el pensamiento hermético. Valencia : Universidad Politécnica de Valéncia, Editorial U.P.V., [2002]

Leibniz y el pensamiento hermético.
Orio de Miguel, Bernardino, 1936- Valencia : Universidad Politécnica de Valéncia, Editorial U.P.V., [2002]

Leibowitz, Yeshayahu, 1903- Ben mada' le-filosofyah : ma'amarim, hartsa'ot ye-śiḥot / Yesha'yahu Libovits. Yerushalayim : Aḳademon, 762 [2002] 367 p. : ill. ; 21 cm. Includes bibliographical references.
1. Science - Philosophy. 2. Science - Moral and ethical aspects. 3. Values. I. Title.

Leighton, Jacqueline P.
The nature of reasoning. Cambridge, U.K. ; New York : Cambridge University Press, 2003.
BF442 .N38 2003

Leipzig series in cognitive sciences
(1) Working on working memory. Leipzig : Leipziger Universitätsverlag, 2000.
BF378.S54 W675 2000

Lekan, Todd, 1967- Making morality : pragmatist reconstruction in ethical theory / Todd Lekan. 1st ed. Nashville, TN : Vanderbilt University Press, 2003. x, 205 p. ; 22 cm. (The Vanderbilt library of American philosophy) Includes bibliographical references (p. 195-199) and index. CONTENTS: Introduction: Pragmatic metaethics as revisionism -- A pragmatic account of practical knowledge -- The goods in activities -- Between universalism and particularism -- The boundaries and authority of morality : a pragmatist view -- Pragmatist social criticism. ISBN 0-8265-1420-0 (alk. paper) ISBN 0-8265-1421-9 (pbk. : alk. paper) DDC 171/.2
1. Dewey, John, - 1859-1952. 2. Ethics. 3. Pragmatism. I. Title. II. Series.
BJ1031 .L45 2003

Die Lektion des Jahrhunderts.
Gadamer, Hans Georg, 1900- Münster : Lit, [2002]

Lektorskiĭ, V. A.
Sub"ekt, poznanie, deĭatel'nost'. Moskva : Kanon+, 2002.
BD166 .S84 2002

LEKTORSKIĬ, V. A.
Sub"ekt, poznanie, deĭatel'nost'. Moskva : Kanon+, 2002.
BD166 .S84 2002

Leland, Charles Godfrey, 1824-1903.
[Etruscan roman remains in popular tradition]
Etruscan Roman remains and the old religion : gods, goblins, divination and amulets / Charles Godfrey Leland. London ; New York : Kegan Paul ; New York : Distributed by Columbia University Press, 2002. viii, 385 p. : ill. ; 24 cm. (The Kegan Paul library of arcana) Spine title: Etruscan Roman remains. Originally published: Etruscan roman remains in popular tradition: London : Fisher Unwin, 1892. Includes index. ISBN 0-7103-0762-4 DDC 299.9294
1. Etruria - Antiquities. 2. Folklore - Italy. 3. Superstition. I. Title. II. Title: Etruscan Roman remains III. Series.

DG223 .L54 2002

Leland, Kurt. The unanswered question : death, near-death, and the afterlife / Kurt Leland. Charlottesville, VA : Hampton Roads Pub., c2002. xix, 499 p. ; 23 cm. Includes bibliographical references (p. 485-487) and index. ISBN 1-57174-299-9 (pbk. : alk. paper) DDC 133.9/01/3
1. Near-death experiences. 2. Death. 3. Future life. I. Title.
BF1045.N4 L45 2002

A lélektan feladata.
Harkai Schiller, Pál, 1908-1949. Budapest : Osiris Kiadó, 2002.
BF128.H8 H37 2002

Lemaître, Pascal.
Morrison, Toni. The book of mean people. 1st ed. New York : Hyperion Books for Children, c2002.
1. Black authors.

Lemegeton.
[Clavicula Salomonis. English.] Jacksonville, FL : Metatron Books, 1999.

Lemesurier, Peter, 1936-.
Nostradamus : the next 50 years.
Lemesurier, Peter, 1936- Nostradamus in the 21st century. Rev. ed. London : Piatkus, 2000 (2001 printing).

Nostradamus in the 21st century : and the coming invasion of Europe / Peter Lemesurier. Rev. ed. London : Piatkus, 2000 (2001 printing). 325 p. ; 22 cm. Previous ed. published as: Nostradamus : the next 50 years. 1993. Includes bibliographical references and index. ISBN 0-7499-2163-3 DDC 133.3
1. Nostradamus, - 1503-1566 - Prophecies. 2. Twenty-first century - Forecasts. I. Lemesurier, Peter, 1936- Nostradamus : the next 50 years. II. Title.

LEMGO (GERMANY) - HISTORY.
Ströhmer, Michael, 1968- Von Hexen, Ratsherren und Juristen. Paderborn : Bonifatius, c2002.
BF1583 .S77 2002

Lemire, Laurent.
Picq, Pascal G. A la recherche de l'homme. Paris : Nil, c2002.
GN281 .P48 2002

Lempereur, Alain Pekar.
Callières, Monsieur de (François), 1645-1717. De la manière de négocier avec les souverains. Genève : Droz, c2002.

Lempert, Robert J. Shaping the next one hundred years : new methods for quantitative, long-term policy analysis and bibliography / Robert J. Lempert, Steven W. Popper, Steven C. Bankes. Santa Monica, CA : RAND, 2003. xxi, 187 p. ; 25 cm. "MR-1626." ISBN 0-8330-3275-5 (pbk.) DDC 320/.6/0113
1. System analysis. 2. Decision making. 3. Information technology. I. Popper, Steven W., 1953- II. Bankes, Steven C. III. Title.
T57.6 .L46 2003

Lenard-Cook, Lisa.
Tognetti, Arlene. The complete idiot's guide to tarot. 2nd ed. Indianapolis, IN : Alpha, c2003.
BF1879.T2 T64 2003

Lengen, Haiko van. Bücher im virtuellen Warenkorb : wie deutsche und britische Internet-Buchhandlungen das Internet als interaktives Medium nutzen / Haiko van Lengen. Berlin : Verlag für Wirtschaftskommunikation, c2001. 209 p ; ill. ; 21 cm. Includes bibliographical references (p. 155-160). ISBN 3-934973-11-6
1. Interactive computer systems. 2. Human-computer interaction. 3. Internet bookstores - Great Britain. 4. Internet bookstores - Germany. I. Title.

Lenger, Hans-Joachim. Vom Abschied : ein Essay zur Differenz / Hans-Joachim Lenger. Bielefeld : Transcript, c2001. 240 p. ; 21 cm. Includes bibliographical references (p. 229-240). ISBN 3-933127-75-0 (pbk.)
1. Difference (Philosophy) 2. Philosophy, Modern - 20th century. I. Title.
B105.D5 L46 2001

El lenguaje y la mente humana / Noam Chomsky ... [et al.] ; coordinadores Natalia Català, José A. Díez Calzada y José A. García-Albea. 1. ed. Barcelona : Ariel Editorial, 2002. 253 p. ; 21 cm. (Ariel filosofía) Includes bibliographical references. ISBN 84-344-8762-4
1. Thought and thinking. 2. Psycholinguistics. 3. Language and languages - Philosophy. I. Chomsky, Noam. II. Català, Natàlia. III. Díez Calzada, José A. IV. Series.

LENINISM. *See* **COMMUNISM.**

Lenk, Hans. Das Denken und sein Gehalt / Hans Lenk. München : Oldenbourg, 2001. 395 p. : ill. ; 23 cm. (Scientia nova) Includes bibliographical references (p. [377]-

Lenson, Barry.
392) and index. ISBN 3-486-56472-2 (pbk.)
1. Thought and thinking. I. Title. II. Series.
BF441 .L455 2001

Das Denken und sein Gehalt / Hans Lenk. München : Oldenbourg, 2001. 395 p. : ill. ; 23 cm. (Scientia nova) Includes bibliographical references (p. [377]-392) and index. ISBN 3-486-56472-2 (pbk.)
1. Thought and thinking. I. Title. II. Series.

Lenson, Barry.
Caliandro, Arthur. Lost and found. 1st ed. New York : McGraw-Hill, 2003.
BF637.S4 .C32 2003

Ruge, Kenneth. The Othello response. New York : Marlowe & Co., 2003.
BF575.J4 R84 2003

Lentin, Jérôme.
Mélanges David Cohen. Paris : Maisonneuve et Larose, 2003.

Lenz, Ramona, 1975-.
Geschlecht und Globalisierung. Königstein : Ulrike Helmer Verlag, c2001.

Leon-Guerrero, Anna.
Frankfort-Nachmias, Chava. Social statistics for a diverse society. 3rd ed. Thousand Oaks, Calif. : Pine Forge Press, c2002.
HA29 .N25 2002

LEÓN, HEBREO, B. CA. 1460. DIALOGHI D'AMORE.
Feldman, Seymour. Philosophy in a time of crisis. London ; New York : RoutledgeCurzon, 2003.
BM755.A25 F45 2003

León, Monica Ileana de.
Acuerdos de paz y seguridad democrática en Guatemala. 1. ed. [Guatemala] : USAC, DIGI, [2002]

León Pasquel, Lourdes de.
La Adquisición de la lengua materna. México : Universidad Nacional Autónoma de México : Centro de Investigaciones y Estudios Superiores en Antropología Social, 2001.
P118 .A227 2001

Leonard, Marcia.
I feel.
Leonard, Marcia. I feel angry. Nashville, Tenn. : CandyCane Press, 2003.
BF575.A5 L465 2003

Leonard, Marcia. I feel happy. Nashville, Tenn. : CandyCane Press, 2003.
BF575.H27 L465 2003

Leonard, Marcia. I feel sad. Nashville, Tenn. : CandyCane Press, 2003.
BF575.S23 L46 2003

Leonard, Marcia. I feel scared. Nashville, Tenn. : CandyCane Press, 2003.
BF575.F2 L455 2003

I feel angry / written by Marcia Leonard ; illustrated by Bartholomew. Nashville, Tenn. : CandyCane Press, 2003. p. cm. (I feel) ISBN 0-8249-6526-4 (alk. paper) DDC 152.4/7
1. Anger - Juvenile literature. 2. Anger. I. Bartholomew, ill. II. Title. III. Series: Leonard, Marcia. I feel.
BF575.A5 L465 2003

I feel happy / written by Marcia Leonard ; illustrated by Bartholomew. Nashville, Tenn. : CandyCane Press, 2003. p. cm. ISBN 0-8249-6523-X (alk. paper) DDC 152.4/2
1. Happiness - Juvenile literature. 2. Happiness. I. Bartholomew, ill. II. Title. III. Series: Leonard, Marcia. I feel.
BF575.H27 L465 2003

I feel sad / written by Marcia Leonard ; illustrated by Bartholomew. Nashville, Tenn. : CandyCane Press, 2003. p. cm. (I feel) ISBN 0-8249-6524-8 (alk. paper) DDC 152.4
1. Sadness - Juvenile literature. 2. Sadness. I. Bartholomew, ill. II. Title. III. Series: Leonard, Marcia. I feel.
BF575.S23 L46 2003

I feel scared / written by Marcia Leonard ; illustrated by Bartholomew. Nashville, Tenn. : CandyCane Press, 2003. p. cm. (I feel) ISBN 0-8249-6525-6 (alk. paper) DDC 152.4/6
1. Fear - Juvenile literature. 2. Fear. I. Bartholomew, ill. II. Title. III. Series: Leonard, Marcia. I feel.
BF575.F2 L455 2003

Leonardo
Lovink, Geert. Uncanny networks. Cambridge, Mass. : MIT Press, c2002.
HM851 .L688 2002

Leonardo da Vinci.
Leonardo, da Vinci, 1452-1519. [Selections. English. 1999] The manuscripts of Leonardo da Vinci in the Institut de France. Milano : Ente raccolta vinciana, 1999-
Q113 .L3513 1999

Leonardo, da Vinci, 1452-1519. [Selections. English. 1999]
The manuscripts of Leonardo da Vinci in the Institut de France / translated and annotated by John Venerella. Milano : Ente raccolta vinciana, 1999- v. : ill. ; 24 cm. Eavh vol. designated by a letter, e.g., Manuscript A. Includes bibliographical references and indexes. DDC 509.024
1. Leonardo, - da Vinci, - 1452-1519 - Manuscripts. 2. Science - Early works to 1800. I. Venerella, John. II. Institut de France. III. Title. IV. Title: Leonardo da Vinci
Q113 .L3513 1999

LEONARDO, DA VINCI, 1452-1519 - MANUSCRIPTS.
Leonardo, da Vinci, 1452-1519. [Selections. English. 1999] The manuscripts of Leonardo da Vinci in the Institut de France. Milano : Ente raccolta vinciana, 1999-
Q113 .L3513 1999

Leonel, Vange, 1963- Grrrls : garotas iradas / Vange Leonel ; [prefácio de Fernando Bonassi]. São Paulo : Edições GLS, c2001. 149 p. : port. ; 21 cm. Includes bibliographical references (p. 145-147). ISBN 85-86755-27-3
1. Lesbianism. 2. Lesbians - Identity. 3. Lesbian feminism. 4. Homosexuality. 5. Feminism. I. Bonassi, Fernando, 1962- II. Title. III. Title: Grrrls, garotas iradas IV. Title: Garotas iradas

Leont'ev, D. A.
International Conference on Motivation (8th : 2002 Moscow, Russia) 8th International Conference on Motivation. Moscow : Russian State University for Humanities, 2002.
BF501.5 .I58 2002

Sovremennaĭa psikhologiĭa motivatsii. Moskva : Smysl, 2002.
BF503 .S68 2002

Lepgold, Joseph.
Regional conflict management. Lanham, Md. : Rowman & Littlefield, c2003.
JZ5330 .R437 2003

LePla, F. Joseph, 1955- Brand driven : the route to integrated branding through great leadership / F. Joseph LePla, Susan V. Davis & Lynn M. Parker. London : Kogan Page, 2003. xvi, 334 p. : ill. ; 25 cm. Includes bibliographical references and index. ISBN 0-7494-3797-9 DDC 658.827
1. Brand name products - Management. 2. Leadership. I. Davis, Susan V. (Susan Voeller), 1966- II. Parker, Lynn M., 1956- III. Title.

LERMONTOV, MIKHAIL ĬUR'EVICH, 1814-1841.
Drankov, V. L. (Vladimir L'vovich) Priroda khudozhestvennogo talanta. Sankt-Peterburg : Sankt-Peterburgskiĭ gos. universitet kul'tury i iskusstv, 2001.
BF408 .D66 2001

LERMONTOV, MIKHAIL ĬUR'EVICH, 1814-1841 - CRITICISM AND INTERPRETATION.
Drankov, V. L. (Vladimir L'vovich) Priroda khudozhestvennogo talanta. Sankt-Peterburg : Sankt-Peterburgskiĭ gosudarstvennyĭ universitet kul'tury i iskusstv, 2001.

Lerner, Isha, 1954- The triple goddess tarot : the power of the major arcana, chakra healing, and the divine feminine / Isha Lerner, with Tara McKinney ; illustrated by Mara Friedman. Rochester Vt. : Bear & Co., c2002. xiv, 231 p. : ill. ; 24 cm. + 1 set col. tarot cards. Includes bibliographical references (p. 230-231). CONTENTS: Mythology of the triple goddess through the ages -- Mystery schools, sacred pilgrimage, alchemy, and initiation -- Embodiment of the divine feminine in a new millennium -- How to use the triple goddess tarot in everyday life : layouts and divine play -- The alchemy cards : the royal road to wisdom -- The chakra cards : body and earth attunement through the seven sacred chakras -- What would the goddess do right now? / by Tara McKinney. ISBN 1-87918-194-0 DDC 133.3/2424
1. Tarot. I. McKinney, Tara. II. Title.
BF1879.T2 L4365 2002

Lerner, Richard M. Handbook of adolescent psychology / Richard M. Lerner and Laurence Steinberg. 2nd ed. Hoboken, N.J. : John Wiley & Sons, 2004. p. cm. Includes bibliographical references and index. Publisher description URL: http://www.loc.gov/catdir/desc ription/wiley036/2003049664.html Table of contents URL: http://www.loc.gov/catdir/toc/wiley032/2003049664.html ISBN 0-471-20948-1 (cloth) DDC 155.5

1. Adolescent psychology. I. Steinberg, Laurence D., 1952- II. Title.
BF724 .L367 2004

LESBIAN ACTIVISTS - TRAVEL.
Segrest, Mab, 1949- Born to belonging. New Brunswick, NJ : Rutgers University Press, c2002.
HQ75.25 .S44 2002

LESBIAN FEMINISM.
Leonel, Vange, 1963- Grrrls. São Paulo : Edições GLS, c2001.

LESBIANISM.
Cvetkovich, Ann, 1957- An archive of feelings. Durham : Duke University Press, 2003.
HQ75.5 .C89 2003

Femme/butch. New York : Harrington Park Press, 2002.
HQ75.5 .F459 2002

Leonel, Vange, 1963- Grrrls. São Paulo : Edições GLS, c2001.

LESBIANS.
Califia-Rice, Patrick, 1954- Speaking sex to power. 1st ed. San Francisco : Cleis Press, c2002.
HQ76.25 .C32 2002

Femme/butch. New York : Harrington Park Press, 2002.
HQ75.5 .F459 2002

LESBIANS - IDENTITY.
Femme/butch. New York : Harrington Park Press, 2002.
HQ75.5 .F459 2002

Leonel, Vange, 1963- Grrrls. São Paulo : Edições GLS, c2001.

LESBIANS - MENTAL HEALTH.
Ritter, Kathleen. Handbook of affirmative psychotherapy with lesbians and gay men. New York : Guilford Press, c2002.
RC451.4.G39 R55 2002

Lesebuch.
Albert, Hans, 1921- Tübingen : Mohr Siebeck, 2001.

LeShan, Lawrence L., 1920- The medium, the mystic, and the physicist : toward a general theory of the paranormal / Lawrence LeShan. New York : Helios Press, 2003, c1974. xix, 299 p. ; 21 cm. Originally published: New York : Viking Press, 1974. Includes bibliographical references. ISBN 1-58115-273-6 (pbk.) DDC 133.8
1. Parapsychology. I. Title.
BF1031 .L43 2003

Leslie, Julian C. Essential behaviour analysis / Julian C. Leslie. London : Arnold ; New York : Oxford University Press, c2002. ix, 228 p. : ill. ; 24 cm. (Essential psychology series) Includes bibliographical references (p. [214]-218) and indexes. ISBN 0-340-76273-X (pbk.) DDC 150.19/43
1. Behaviorism (Psychology) I. Title. II. Series.
BF199 .L42 2002

Leslie, Mike, 1956- The magical personality : identify strengths & weaknesses to improve your magic / Mike Leslie. 1st ed. St. Paul, Minn. : Llewellyn, 2002. x, 274 p. : ill. ; 24 cm. Includes bibliographical references (p. 265-267) and index. ISBN 0-7387-0187-4 DDC 133.4/3
1. Magic. 2. Typology (Psychology) - Miscellanea. I. Title.
BF1621 .L47 2002

Lesmes, Jorge.
Téllez, Edgar. Diario íntimo de un fracaso. 1. ed. Bogotá, D.C., Colombia : Planeta, 2002.

LESS DEVELOPED COUNTRIES. See **DEVELOPING COUNTRIES.**

Lesser key of Solomon.
[Clavicula Salomonis. English.] Lemegeton. Jacksonville, FL : Metatron Books, 1999.

Lesser key of Solomon the King.
[Clavicula Salomonis. English.] The Goetia. York Beach, Me. : Samuel Weiser, 1995.
BF1611 .C5413 1995

Lessing, Hans-Ulrich, 1953-.
Plessner, Helmuth, 1892- Elemente der Metaphysik. Berlin : Akademie, 2002.
BD113 .P56 2002

Lessons for living.
Johnston, Daniel H. 1st ed. Macon, Ga. : Dagali Press, c2001.
BF637.S4 J65 2001

Lessons in life only love can teach.
Finley, Guy. An apprentice of the heart. Ashland, Ore. : White Cloud Press, 2004.

BF575.L8 F524 2004

Lessons in radical innovation.
Grulke, Wolfgang. International ed. London : Financial Times Prentice Hall, 2002.

Lessons of the turtle.
Goodier, Steve. Divide, CO : Life Support System Pub., c2002.
BF637.C5 G67 2002

Lester, Toni P., 1955-.
Gender nonconformity, race, and sexuality. Madison : University of Wisconsin Press, [2002]
HQ1075 .G4645 2002

Let's look at feelings
Johansen, Heidi Leigh. What I look like when I am angry. 1st ed. New York : PowerStart Press, 2004.
BF723.A4 J63 2004

Johansen, Heidi Leigh. [What I look like when I am angry. Spanish & English] What I look like when I am angry = 1st ed. New York : Rosen PowerKids Press, 2004.
BF723.A4 J6318 2004

Johansen, Heidi Leigh. What I look like when I am happy. 1st ed. New York : PowerStart Press, 2004.
BF723.H37 J64 2004

Johansen, Heidi Leigh. [What I look like when I am happy. Spanish & English] What I look like when I am happy = 1st ed. New York : Rosen Pub. Group's, 2004.
BF723.H37 J6418 2004

Randolph, Joanne. What I look like when I am confused. 1st ed. New York : PowerStart Press, 2004.
BF723.I63 R36 2004

Randolph, Joanne. [What I look like when I am confused. Spanish & English] What I look like when I am confused = 1st ed. New York : Rosen Pub. Group's PowerKids Press, 2004.
BF723.I63 R3618 2004

Randolph, Joanne. What I look like when I am sad. 1st ed. New York : PowerStart Press, 2004.
BF723.S15 R36 2004

Randolph, Joanne. [What I look like when I am sad. Spanish & English] What I look like when I am sad = 1st ed. New York : Rosen Pub. Group's PowerKids Press, 2004.
BF723.S15 R3618 2004

Shepherd, Joanne. What I look like when I am scared. New York : Rosen Pub. Group's PowerStart Press, 2004.
BF723.F4 S54 2004

Shepherd, Joanne. [What I look like when I am scared. Spanish & English] What I look like when I am scared = 1st ed. New York : Rosen Pub. Group's PowerKids Press, 2004.
BF723.F4 S5418 2004

Shepherd, Joanne. What I look like when I am surprised. New York : Rosen Pub. Group's PowerStart Press, 2004.
BF723.S87 S44 2004

Shepherd, Joanne. [What I look like when I am surprised. Spanish & English] What I look like when I am surprised = 1st ed. New York : Rosen Pub. Group's PowerKids Press, 2004.
BF723.S87 S4418 2004

Let's talk about feeling embarrassed.
Berry, Joy Wilt. New York : Scholastic, c2002.
BF723.E44 B47 2002

Let's talk about feeling worried.
Berry, Joy Wilt. New York : Scholastic Inc., c2002.
BF723.W67 B47 2002

Let's talk about getting hurt.
Berry, Joy Wilt. New York : Scholastic Inc., c2002.
BF723.W67 B475 2002

Let's talk about saying no.
Berry, Joy Wilt. Saying no. New York : Scholastic, c2001.
BF723.R4 B37 2001

LETTER WRITING.
Destinos das letras. Passo Fundo : Universidade de Passo Fundo, 2002.
P211 .D47 2002

Letteratura ed ermeneutica.
Pagnini, Marcello. Firenze : L.S. Olschki, 2002.

Letters from the Infinite.
Johnson, Deborah L., 1956- Aptos, CA : New Brighton Books, c2002-

BF1301 .J575 2002

LETTERS OF THE ALPHABET. *See* **ALPHABET.**

Letture filosofiche.
Verna, Arturo. Padova : Unipress, 2002.

Letzten Aufnahmen.
Hann, Georg. Georg Hann [sound recording]. [Germany] : Preiser Records, p2001.

Leupin, Alexandre, 1948- Lacan today : psychoanalysis, science, religion / by Alexandre Leupin. New York : Other Press, 2004. p. cm. Includes bibliographical references and index. CONTENTS: The structure of the subject -- The schema L -- The schema R -- The graphs of desire -- Topology -- The Borromean knot -- Epistemology -- Epistemology of science, epistemology of humanities -- Lacan's theory of language -- A unified epistemology -- An impossible ethics -- The master, the academic, the psychoanalyst and the hysteric (four discourses) -- The master's discourse -- The university's discourse -- The psychoanalyst's discourse -- The hysteric's discourse -- There is no sexual rapport -- God is real. ISBN 1-89274-690-5 (pbk. : alk. paper) DDC 150.19/5/092
1. Lacan, Jacques, - 1901- I. Title.
BF109.L28 L48 2004

Leutenberg, Estelle A.
Liptak, John J. The self-esteem program. Plainview, NY : Wellness Reproductions & Pub., c2002.
BF697.5.S46 L57 2002

Lev Avigdor.
Miller, Avigdor. [Lev Avigdor] Sefer Lev Avigdor. Bruklin, N.Y. : S. Miller, 762, c2002.
BM538.P4 .M45 2001

Levack, Brian P. The witchcraft sourcebook / Brian Levack. London ; New York : Routledge, 2003. p. cm. Includes bibliographical references and index. Table of contents URL: http://www.loc.gov/catdir/toc/ecip042/2003008535.html ISBN 0-415-19506-3 (pbk. : alk. paper) ISBN 0-415-19505-5 (hardback : alk. paper) DDC 133.4/3/09
1. Witchcraft - History - Sources. 2. Magic - History - Sources. I. Title.
BF1566 .L475 2003

LEVANT. *See* **MIDDLE EAST.**

Levenskunst van twee vrouwen.
Aller, Annelies van, 1946- Budel : Damon, c2001.
PS3527.I865 Z536 2001

Levent, Jean-Marc. Les ânes rouges : généalogie des figures critiques de l'institution philosophique en France / Jean-Marc Levent. Paris : Harmattan, 2003. 286 p. ; 22 cm. (La philosophie en commun) Includes bibliographical references (p. [277]-284). ISBN 2-7475-3727-7 DDC 194
1. Criticism (Philosophy) 2. Philosophy, Modern - 20th century. 3. Philosophy, French - 20th century. I. Title. II. Series.

Lévesque, Claude, 1927- Par-delà le masculin et le féminin / Claude Lévesque. Paris : Aubier, 2002. 317 p. ; 22 cm. (La psychanalyse prise au mot) Includes bibliographical references. CONTENTS: Savoir et non-savoir de la différence sexuelle selon Freud et Lacan -- L'innommable singularité de l'autre : une lecture d'Éperons et d'autres textes de Jacques Derrida -- L'écriture plurielle et la différence sexuelle : autour du Dernier mot de Maurice Blanchot -- Nom propre et identité sexuelle dans les récits de Georges Bataille. ISBN 2-7007-2422-4 DDC 155.3
1. Derrida, Jacques - Criticism and interpretation. 2. Blanchot, Maurice - Criticism and interpretation. 3. Bataille, Georges, - 1897-1962 - Criticism and interpretation. 4. Sex differences (Psychology) 5. Sex (Psychology) I. Title. II. Series: Psychanalyse prise au mot.

Levin, Daniel T.
Thinking and seeing. Cambridge, MA : Mit Press, 2004.
BF241 .T48 2004

Leyin, Yitshak, 1938- Sefer Netivot Yitshak : śihot musar derashot u-ma'amarim ... / hubar me-iti Yitshak ha-Levi Levin ... [Bene Berak] : Y. Levin, [2000- v. ; 25 cm. Running title: Netivot Yitshak.
1. Repentance - Judaism. 2. Ethics, Jewish. 3. High Holidays. 4. Tishri. 5. Fasts and feasts - Judaism. 6. Hanukkah. 7. Purim. I. Title. II. Title: Netivot Yitshak

Lévinas, Emmanuel.
[De l'évasion. English]
On escape = De l'évasion / Emmanuel Lévinas ; translated by Bettina Bergo. Stanford, Calif. : Stanford University Press, 2003. 120 p. ; 21 cm. (Cultural memory in the present) Includes bibliographical references and index. CONTENTS: Note to "getting out of being by a new path" -- Letter from Emmanuel Levinas -- Getting out of being by a new path -- Jacques Rolland -- On escape -- Annotations -- Jacques Rolland. ISBN

0-8047-4139-5 (alk. paper) ISBN 0-8047-4140-9 (pbk. : alk. paper) DDC 111
1. Ontology. I. Title. II. Title: De l'évasion. III. Series.
BD331 .L459613 2003

[Humanisme de l'autre homme. English]
Humanism of the other / Emmanuel Levinas ; Translated from the French by Nidra Poller ; introduction by Richard A. Cohen. Urbana : University of Illinois Press, c2003. xlvi, 83 p. ; 22 cm. Includes bibliographical references and index. ISBN 0-252-02840-6 DDC 144
1. Humanism. 2. Intersubjectivity. 3. Meaning (Philosophy) 4. Culture - Philosophy. I. Poller, Nidra. II. Title.
B2430.L48 H8413 2003

LÉVINAS, EMMANUEL.
Alford, C. Fred. Levinas, the Frankfurt school and psychoanalysis. 1st US ed. Middletown, CT : Wesleyan University Press, c2002.

LÉVINAS, EMMANUEL - CRITICISM AND INTERPRETATION.
Milmaniene, José E. Clínica del texto. [1. ed.]. Buenos Aires : Editorial Biblos, c2002.

Levinas, the Frankfurt school and psychoanalysis.
Alford, C. Fred. 1st US ed. Middletown, CT : Wesleyan University Press, c2002.

Levine, Leslie. Wish it, dream it, do it : turn the life you're living into the life you want / Leslie Levine. New York : Simon & Schuster, c2004. p. cm. "A Fireside book". Includes bibliographical references. ISBN 0-7432-2981-9 (pbk.) DDC 158.1
1. Success - Psychological aspects. 2. Self-actualization (Psychology) I. Title.
BF637.S8 L449 2004

Levinson, Jay.
Granot, Hayim. Terror bombing. Tel Aviv : Dekel Pub. House, 2002.
HV6431 .G73 2002

LEVITATION.
Ogilvie, Daniel M. Fantasies of flight. New York : Oxford University Press, 2003.
BF1385 .O35 2003

LEVITATION - CASE STUDIES.
Ogilvie, Daniel M. Fantasies of flight. New York : Oxford University Press, 2003.
BF1385 .O35 2003

Levitt, Susan. Taoist astrology : a handbook of the authentic Chinese tradition / Susan Levitt with Jean Tang. Rochester, Vt. : Destiny Books, c1997. 216 p. : ill. ; 23 cm. ISBN 0-89281-606-6 (alk. paper) DDC 133.5/949514
1. Taoist astrology. I. Tang, Jean. II. Title.
BF1714.T34 L48 1997

Teen feng shui : design your space, design your life / Susan Levitt. Rochester, Vt. : Bindu Books, c2003. 223 p. : ill. ; 23 cm. ISBN 0-89281-916-2 (pbk.) DDC 133.3/337
1. Feng shui. 2. Taoism. 3. Teenagers. I. Title.
BF1779.F4 L465 2003

Levkievskaia, E. E. (Elena Evgen'evna) Slavianskii obereg : semantika i struktura / E.E. Levkievskaia. Moskva : Indrik, 2002. 334 p. ; 22 cm. (TDKS. Sovremennye issledovaniia) Includes bibliographical references and index. "Nauchnoe izdanie"--Colophon. ISBN 5857591856
1. Demonology - Slavic countries. 2. Folklore - Slavic countries - Sources. 3. Slavic countries - Social life and customs. 4. Semantics. 5. Slavs - Religion. 6. Slavs - Folklore. I. Title. II. Series.
BL480 .L38 2002

Levy, Alon Y. (Alon Yitzchak) Irrelevance reasoning in knowledge based systems [miroform] / by Alon Y. Levy. [Washington, DC : National Aeronautics and Space Administration] ; Springfield, VA : Available from the National Technical Information Service, [1998] 1 v. ([NASA technical memorandum ; 205731]) (Report ; no. STAN-CS-93-1482) Shipping list no: 99-0685-M. "July 1993." Originally published: Stanford, Calif. : Dept. of Computer Science, Stanford University, 1993. Thesis (Ph.D.)--Stanford University, 1993. Microfiche. [Washington, D.C. : National Aeronautics and Space Administration, 1998] 3 microfiches. Available in other form: Levy, Alon Y. Irrelevance reasoning in knowledge based systems xiv, 201 p. (OCoLC)30464410.
1. Artificial intelligence. I. United States. National Aeronautics and Space ASdministration. II. Title. III. Title: Levy, Alon Y. Irrelevance reasoning in knowledge based systems xiv, 201 p. IV. Series. V. Series: Report (Stanford University. Computer Science Dept.) ; no. STAN-CS-93-1482.

Levy, Alon Y. Irrelevance reasoning in knowledge based systems xiv, 201 p.
Levy, Alon Y. (Alon Yitzchak) Irrelevance reasoning in knowledge based systems [miroform]. [Washington, DC : National Aeronautics and Space Administration] ; Springfield, VA : Available from the National Technical Information Service, [1998]

Lévy, Ghyslain. Au-delà du malaise : psychanalyse et barbaries / Ghyslain Lévy. Ramonville Saint-Agne : Erès, c2000. 203 p. ; 21 cm. (Collection "des travaux et des jours") Includes bibliographical references (p. [199]-203). ISBN 2-86586-780-3
1. Psychoanalysis. I. Title. II. Series.
BF175 .L487 2000

Levy, Mark, 1962-.
Bauer, Joel, 1960- How to persuade people who don't want to be persuaded. Hoboken, N.J. : John Wiley & Sons, 2004.
BF637.P4 B32 2004

Lewis-Hall, Jennifer, 1964- Life's a journey--not a sprint : navigating life's challenges and finding your pathway to success / Jennifer Lewis-Hall. Carlsbad, Calif. : Hay House, c2003. 207 p. : ill. ; 24 cm. Includes bibliographical references (p. 205). ISBN 1401901891 ISBN 1401901905 (tradepaper) DDC 158.1
1. Success - Psychological aspects. 2. Success in business. 3. Women - Psychology. I. Title.
BF637.S8 L455 2003

Lewis, I. M. Ecstatic religion : a study of shamanism and spirit possession / I.M. Lewis. 3rd ed. London ; New York : Routledge, 2003. xxiv, 15-200 p. : ill. ; 22 cm. Includes bibliographical references (p. 185-194) and index. ISBN 0-415-30508-X (hb) ISBN 0-415-30124-6 (pbk.) DDC 306.6/9142
1. Ecstasy. 2. Shamanism. 3. Spirit possession. 4. Religion and sociology. I. Title.
BL626 .L48 2003

Lewis, James R. Legitimating new religions / James R. Lewis. New Brunswick, N.J. : Rutgers University Press, c2003. viii, 272 p. : ill. ; 24 cm. Includes bibliographical references (p. 247-259) and index. CONTENTS: Part I : legitimating new religions -- Religious experience and the origins of religion -- Native American prophet religions -- Jesus in India and the forging of tradition -- Science, technology, and the Space Brothers -- Anton Lavey, the Satanic Bible, and the Satanist tradition -- Heaven's Gate and the legitimation of suicide -- The authority of the long ago and the far away -- Part II : legitimating repression -- Atrocity tales as a delegitimation strategy -- Religious insanity -- The cult stereotype as an ideological resource -- Scholarship and the delegitimation of religion. ISBN 0-8135-3323-6 (hardcover : alk. paper) ISBN 0-8135-3324-4 (pbk. : alk. paper) DDC 200/.9/04
1. Cults - Psychology. 2. Psychology, Religious. 3. Authority - Religious aspects. I. Title.
BP603 .L49 2003

Satanism today : an encyclopedia of religion, folklore, and popular culture / James R. Lewis. Santa Barbara, Calif. : ABC-CLIO, c2001. xv, 371 p. : ill. ; 26 cm. Includes bibliographical references and index. ISBN 1-57607-292-4 (hardcover : alk. paper) DDC 133.4/22/03
1. Satanism - Encyclopedias. I. Title.
BF1548 .L49 2001

Lewis, Jane (Jane E.) Should we worry about family change? / Jane Lewis. Toronto : University of Toronto Press, c2003. x, 132 p. : ill. ; 23 cm. (The Joanne Goodman lectures : 2001) Includes bibliographical references (p. [109]-126) and index. ISBN 0-8020-8746-9 (bound) DDC 306.85
1. Family. 2. Social change. 3. Family policy. I. Title. II. Series: Joanne Goodman lectures ; 2001.

Lewis, Paddy Greenwall, 1945- Helping children cope with the death of a parent : a guide for the first year / Paddy Greenwall Lewis and Jessica G. Lippman. Westport, Conn. : Praeger, 2004. p. cm. (Contemporary psychology) Includes bibliographical references and index. ISBN 0-275-98097-9 (alk. paper) DDC 155.9/37/083
1. Bereavement in children. 2. Parents - Death - Psychological aspects. I. Lippman, Jessica G., 1941- II. Title. III. Series: Contemporary psychology (Praeger Publishers)
BF723.G75 L49 2004

Lewis, Richard D. The cultural imperative : global trends in the 21st century / Richard D. Lewis. Yarmouth, Me. : Intercultural Press, c2003. xxiv, 338 p. : ill. ; 24 cm. Includes bibliographical references (p. 319-322) and index. CONTENTS: From 2,000,000B.C. to A.D.2000 : the roots and routes of culture -- Culture and climate -- Culture and religion -- Cross-century worldviews -- Cultural spectacles -- Cultural black holes -- Cognitive processes -- The Pacific Rim : the fourth cultural ecology -- The China phenomenon -- Americanization versus Asianization -- Culture and globalization -- Empires-past, present, and future -- After September 11. ISBN 1-87786-498-6 DDC 306
1. Culture. 2. Cross-cultural orientation. 3. Globalization. 4. Religion and culture. 5. Cognition and culture. I. Title.
GN357 .L49 2003

LEWIS, WENDY, 1959-.
Vint/age 2001 conference : [videorecording]. New York, c2001.

Lewis, Wendy, 1959- panelist.
Vint/age 2001 conference : [videorecording]. New York, c2001.

LEXICOLOGY.
Lexique et motivation. Paris ; Sterling, Va. : Peeters, c2002.
P326 .L45 2002

Lexikon der Lebenskunst.
Brenner, Andreas. Leipzig : Reclam-Verlag, 2002.

Lexique et motivation : perspectives ethnolinguistiques / sous la direction de Véronique de Colombel et Nicole Tersis. Paris ; Sterling, Va. : Peeters, c2002. 263 p. : ill. ; 24 cm. (SELAF ; no 400) (Numéros spéciaux ; 28) Includes bibliographical references. ISBN 90-429-1115-8 (alk. paper) ISBN 2-87723-627-7 (alk. paper) DDC 413/.028
1. Lexicology. 2. Anthropological linguistics. I. Colombel, Véronique de. II. Tersis, Nicole. III. Series: Société d'études linguistiques et anthropologiques de France (Series) ; 400. IV. Series: Numéro spécial (Société d'études linguistiques et anthropologiques de France) ; 28.
P326 .L45 2002

Lezioni napoleoniche.
Ferrero, Ernesto. 1. ed. Milano : Mondadori, 2002.

Lhomme-Rigaud, Colette. L'adolescent et ses monstres / Colette Lhomme-Rigaud. Ramonville Saint-Agne : Erès, c2002. 237 p. : ill. ; 22 cm. (Collection Actualité de la psychanalyse) Includes bibliographical references (p. [225]-227) and index. ISBN 2-7492-0002-4 DDC 150
1. Horror. 2. Parent and teenager. 3. Adolescent analysis. 4. Psychosexual development. 5. Psychology, Pathological. I. Title. II. Series.

Li, Chunlin.
Zhongguo, shui zui fu. Di 1 ban. Beijing : Qi ye guan li chu ban she, 2001.
HC426.5.A2 Z457 2001

Li, Jianzhong, 1955- [Selections. 1999]
Li Jianzhong zi xuan ji. Di 1 ban. Wuchang : Hua zhong li gong da xue chu ban she, 1999. 2, ii, 4, 410 p., [1] leaf of plates : col. ill. ; 21 cm. (Jing Chu qing nian ren wen xue zhe wen cong) Includes bibliographical references. ISBN 7-5609-2043-8
1. Chinese literature - Qin and Han dynasties, 221 B.C.-220 A.D. - History and criticism. 2. Chinese literature - 220-589 - History and criticism. 3. Chinese literature - History and criticism. I. Title. II. Series.
PL2284 .L395 1999

Li Jianzhong zi xuan ji.
Li, Jianzhong, 1955- [Selections. 1999] Di 1 ban. Wuchang : Hua zhong li gong da xue chu ban she, 1999.
PL2284 .L395 1999

Li shi de qi shi
An, Lizhi. "Zhen guan zheng yao" yu ling dao yi shu. Di 1 ban. Shanghai : Shanghai gu ji chu ban she, 1999.
DS794.3.W813 A63 1999

Li shi zhe xue.
Han, Zhen. Di 1 ban. Kunming : Yunnan ren min chu ban she, 2002.
D16.8 .H3597 2002

Li ti wen xue lun.
Li, Tingba. Di 1 ban. Beijing : Guang ming ri bao chu ban she : Xin hua shu dian Beijing fa xing suo jing xiao, 1997.
PL2262 .L47 1997 <Asian China>

Li, Tianming, 1945- Li Tianming di si kao yi shu / Li Tianming zhu ; Rong Ziyou, Liang Peilin bian. Beijing di 1 ban. Beijing : Sheng huo, du shu, xin zhi san lian shu dian, 1996. 8, 361 p. ; 21 cm. Includes bibliographical references. ISBN 7-108-00960-9
1. Thought and thinking. 2. Logic. I. Rong, Ziyou. II. Liang, Peilin. III. Title.

Li Tianming di si kao yi shu.
Li, Tianming, 1945- Beijing di 1 ban. Beijing : Sheng huo, du shu, xin zhi san lian shu dian, 1996.

Li, Tingba. Li ti wen xue lun / Li Tingba zhu. Di 1 ban. Beijing : Guang ming ri bao chu ban she : Xin hua shu dian Beijing fa xing suo jing xiao, 1997. 2, 4, 186 p. : ill. ; 21 cm. Cover title: Liti wenxue lun. Includes bibliographical references. Table of contents also in English. ISBN 7-80091-960-9
1. Chinese literature - History and criticism. I. Title. II. Title: Liti wenxue lun
PL2262 .L47 1997 <Asian China>

Li, Xiaobing. Wo zai, wo si : shi ji zhi jiao di wen hua yu zhe xue / Li Xiaobing. Di 1 ban. Beijing : Dong fang chu ban she : Xin hua shu dian jing xiao, 1996. 2, 2, 320 p. ; 21 cm. (Gelunbu xue shu wen ku ; 3) Colophon title also in pinyin: Wo zai, wosi. Includes bibliographical references. ISBN 7-5060-0755-X
1. Civilization - 20th century. 2. Philosophy, Modern - 20th century. I. Title. II. Title: Shi ji zhi jiao di wen hua yu zhe xue III. Title: Wo zai, wosi IV. Series.
CB425 .L39 1996 <Orien China>

Li, Yi. Zou xiang he chu : hou xian dai zhu yi yu dang dai hui hua / Li Yi zhu. Di 1 ban. Beijing : Zhongguo she hui chu ban she : Xin hua shu dian Beijing fa xing suo jing xiao, 1994. 2, 264 p., [2] p. of plates : ill. ; 19 cm. (Hou xian dai zhu yi wen hua cong shu ; 3) ISBN 7-80088-547-X
1. Painting, Modern - 20th century. 2. Postmodernism. 3. Painting, Chinese. 4. Painting, Modern - 20th century - China. 5. Postmodernism - China. I. Title. II. Title: Hou xian dai zhu yi yu dang dai hui hua
ND196.P66 L5 1994 <Orien China>

Li yi fen shu.
Liu, Shuxian, 1934- Di 1 ban. Shanghai : Shanghai wen yi chu ban she, 2000.
B29 .L68 2000

Li, Zehou. Tan xun yu sui / Li Zehou ; Yang Chunshi bian. Di 1 ban. Shanghai : Shanghai wen yi chu ban she, 2000. 9, 425 p., [2] leaves of plates : col. port. ; 21 cm. (Xue yuan ying hua) Cover title also in pinyin: Tanxin yusui. ISBN 7-5321-1968-8
1. Philosophy, Chinese. 2. Philosophy. 3. Aesthetics. I. Yang, Chunshi, 1948- II. Title. III. Title: Tanxin yusui IV. Series.
B126 .L532 2000

Liang, Peilin.
Li, Tianming, 1945- Li Tianming di si kao yi shu. Beijing di 1 ban. Beijing : Sheng huo, du shu, xin zhi san lian shu dian, 1996.

Liang, Qichao, 1873-1929.
Liang Qichao, Zhang Taiyan jie du Zhonghua wen hua jing dian. Di 1 ban. Shenyang Shi : Liao Hai chu ban she, 2003.
PL2262.2 .L54 2003

Liang Qichao Zhang Taiyan jie du Zhonghua wen hua jing dian.
Liang Qichao, Zhang Taiyan jie du Zhonghua wen hua jing dian. Di 1 ban. Shenyang Shi : Liao Hai chu ban she, 2003.
PL2262.2 .L54 2003

Liang Qichao, Zhang Taiyan jie du Zhonghua wen hua jing dian / Qing Shan, Yu Tang bian. Di 1 ban. Shenyang Shi : Liao Hai chu ban she, 2003. 414 p. ; 21 cm. (Da shi jie du Zhonghua wen hua jing dian cong shu) ISBN 7-80669-361-0
1. Learning and scholarship - China. 2. Chinese literature - History and criticism. 3. Chinese classics - History and criticism. I. Qing, Shan. II. Yu, Tang. III. Liang, Qichao, 1873-1929. IV. Zhang, Taiyan, 1868-1936. V. Title: Liang Qichao Zhang Taiyan jie du Zhonghua wen hua jing dian VI. Series.
PL2262.2 .L54 2003

Liang, Yannian, fl. 1673-1681.
Sheng yu xiang jie. Di 1 ban. [Peking] : Xian zhuang shu ju, 1995.
BJ117 .S486 1995 <Orien China>

Liaudet, Jean-Claude. Telle fille, quel père? / Jean-Claude Liaudet. Paris : Archipel, c2002. 258 p. ; 23 cm. Includes bibliographical references (p. 257-[259]). ISBN 2-8418-7354-4 DDC 150
1. Fathers - Psychology. 2. Fatherhood. 3. Fathers and daughters. 4. Psychoanalysis. I. Title.

LIBEL AND SLANDER. See also PRIVACY, RIGHT OF.
Eliyahu, Mordekhai. Sefer Šifte tsedeḳ. Rekhasim : M. Eliyahu, 762 [2002]

LIBEL AND SLANDER - LAW AND LEGISLATION. See LIBEL AND SLANDER.

LIBEL AND SLANDER - RELIGIOUS ASPECTS - JUDAISM.
Rozner, Shelomoh. Sh. u-t. La-ḥafets be-ḥayim. Maḥad. 3, be-tosefet 13 she'elot be-ḥeleḳ 3. Yerushalayim : Kolel shemirat ha-lashon : le-haśig, Sh. Rozner, 762 [2001 or 2002]

Liberal democracy 3.0.
Turner, Stephen P., 1951- London ; Thousand Oaks, Calif. : SAGE Publications, 2003.
JC423 .T87 2003

Liberal democracy three point zero.
Turner, Stephen P., 1951- Liberal democracy 3.0. London ; Thousand Oaks, Calif. : SAGE Publications, 2003.
JC423 .T87 2003

The liberal illusion.
Barbieri, Katherine, 1965- Ann Arbor : University of Michigan Press, c2002.
HF1379 .B363 2002

LIBERALISM.
Gregg, Samuel, 1969- On ordered liberty. Lanham, MD : Lexington Books, c2003.
JC585 .G744 2003

Infantino, Lorenzo, 1948- [Ignoranza e libertà. English] Ignorance and liberty. London ; New York : Routledge, 2003.
HB95 .I4913 2003

Joyce, Patrick, 1945- The rule of freedom. London : Verso, 2003.
JC585 .J69 2003

LIBERALISM IN LITERATURE.
Fichtelberg, Joseph. Critical fictions. Athens : University of Georgia Press, c2003.
PS366.S35 F53 2003

LIBERALISM - UNITED STATES - HISTORY - 20TH CENTURY.
The achievement of American liberalism. New York : Columbia University Press, c2003.
E806 .M63 2003

LIBERATION. See **LIBERTY.**

LIBERATION MOVEMENTS (CIVIL RIGHTS). See **CIVIL RIGHTS MOVEMENTS.**

Liberman, Pinḥas Yehudah.
Yalḳuṭ Ṭuv ha-peninim. Yerushala[y]im : P. Y. Liberman, 762 [2001 or 2002]
BS1225.53 .Y35 2001

La libertà nel fascismo.
Franchi, Franco. Roma : Europa : Settimo sigillo, c2002.

Libertarian accounts of free will.
Clarke, Randolph K. Oxford ; New York : Oxford University Press, c2003.
BJ1461 .C53 2003

LIBERTARIANISM. See **INDIVIDUALISM; LIBERTY.**

Libertas (Belgrade, Serbia)
Mićunović, Dragoljub. Filozofija minima. Beograd : "Filip Višnjić", 2001.
H61.15 .M5 2001

LIBERTY. See also **CONFORMITY; LIBERALISM; SOCIAL CONTROL.**
Anderson, Terry Lee, 1946- Property rights. Stanford, Calif. : Hoover Institution Press, c2003.
HB701 .A44 2003

Binayemotlagh, Saïd. Etre et liberté selon Platon. Paris : Harmattan, 2002.
B395 .B553 2002

Caesar against liberty? Cambridge : Francis Cairns, c2003.

Canfora, Luciano. Manifesto della libertà. Palermo : Sellerio, c1994.
JC585 .C29 1994

Canto-Sperber, Monique. Les règles de la liberté. [Paris] : Plon, c2003.

Dei, Héctor Daniel. The human being in history. Lanham, Md. : Lexington Books, c2003.
BD450 .D395 2003

Epstein, Richard A. Skepticism and freedom. Chicago : University of Chicago Press, c2003.
K487.L5 E67 2003

Flathman, Richard E. Freedom and its conditions. New York : Routledge, c2003.
JC585 .F553 2003

Franchi, Franco. La libertà nel fascismo. Roma : Europa : Settimo sigillo, c2002.

Freiheit, Gleichheit und Autonomie. Wien : Oldenbourg ; Berlin : Akademie Verlag, 2003.
JC575 .F74 2003

Friedman, Milton, 1912- Capitalism and freedom. 40th anniversary ed. Chicago : University of Chicago Press, 2002.
HB501 .F7 2002

Fromm, Erich, 1900- Escape from freedom. 1st Owl books ed. New York : H. Holt, 1994.
HM271 .F74 1994

Gregg, Samuel, 1969- On ordered liberty. Lanham, MD : Lexington Books, c2003.
JC585 .G744 2003

Holt, W. V. America by trial. München : Tuduv, c2001.

Ilardi, Massimo. In nome della strada. Roma : Meltemi, c2002.

Infantino, Lorenzo, 1948- [Ignoranza e libertà. English] Ignorance and liberty. London ; New York : Routledge, 2003.
HB95 .I4913 2003

Joyce, Patrick, 1945- The rule of freedom. London : Verso, 2003.
JC585 .J69 2003

Kramer, Matthew H., 1959- The quality of freedom. Oxford ; New York : Oxford University Press, 2003.
JC585 .K74 2003

Liberty and democracy. Stanford, CA : Hoover Institution Press, c2002.
JC423 .L5178 2002

Limonov, Ėduard. Distsiplinarnyĭ sanatoriĭ. Sankt-Peterburg : Amfora, 2002.
CB428 .L556 2002

Machan, Tibor R. The passion for liberty. Lanham, Md. : Rowman & Littlefield, c2003.
JC599.U5 M263 2003

Mackenzie, Patrick T. Mind, body, and freedom. Amherst, N.Y. : Humanity Books, 2003.
BF161 .M23 2003

Mill, John Stuart, 1806-1873. On liberty. New Haven : Yale University Press, c2003.
JC585 .M76 2003

Mill, John Stuart, 1806-1873. Utilitarianism ; 2nd ed. Malden, MA : Blackwell Pub., 2003.
B1602 .A5 2003

Nemoianu, Virgil. Tradiție și libertate. București : Curtea Veche, 2001.
JC585 .N42 2001

Osofisan, Femi. Literature and the pressures of freedom. Nigeria : Opon Ifa Readers, 2001.
1. Black author.

Philosophy and freedom. Toronto : University of Toronto Press, c2003.

Preventive detention and individual liberty. New Delhi : South Asia Human Rights Documentation Centre, 2000.
KNS4654 .P74 2000

Schlosser, Herta. Der Mensch als Wesen der Freiheit. Vallendar-Schönstatt : Patris Verlag, 2002.

Sen, Amartya Kumar. Rationality and freedom. Cambridge, Mass. : Belknap Press of Harvard University Press, 2002.
HB846.8 .S466 2002

Sen, Asim, 1935- Democratic management. Lanham, Md. ; Oxford : University Press of America, c2003.
HD30.65 .S46 2003

Shubni͡akov, B. P. Svoboda kak sot͡sialʹnyĭ i dukhovno-psikhicheskiĭ fenomen. I͡Aroslavlʹ : DIA-press, 2000.

Sleinis, E. E. (Edgar Evalt), 1943- Art and freedom. Urbana : University of Illinois Press, c2003.
BH39 .S5518 2003

Struening, Karen, 1960- New family values. Lanham : Rowman & Littlefield Publishers, c2002.
HQ536 .S82 2002

Suprynowicz, Vin. The ballad of Carl Drega. Reno, NV : Mountain Media, 2002.

Tulʹchinskiĭ, G. L. (Grigoriĭ Lʹvovich) Postchelovecheskai͡a personologii͡a. Sankt-Peterburg : Aletei͡a, 2002.
BD331 .T84 2002

Vidal, Jordi. Résistance au chaos. Paris : Allia, 2002.

Von Mises, Ludwig, 1881-1973. Between the two World Wars. Indianapolis, Ind. : Liberty Fund, c2002.

HB101.V66A25 2002

Zakaria, Fareed. The future of freedom. 1st ed. New York : W.W. Norton, c2003.
JC423 .Z35 2003

Liberty and democracy / edited by Tibor R. Machan. Stanford, CA : Hoover Institution Press, c2002. xxvi, 125 p. ; 23 cm. Includes bibliographical references and index. CONTENTS: The democratic ideal / Tibor R. Machan -- Default and dynamic democracy / Loren E. Lomasky -- The first founding father: Aristotle on freedom and popular government / Gregory R. Johnson -- Thoughts on democracy / John Hospers -- Moral worth and the worth of rights / Neera K. Badhwar. ISBN 0-8179-2922-3 (pbk.) DDC 321.8
1. Democracy. 2. Liberty. I. Machan, Tibor R.
JC423 .L5178 2002

LIBERTY - MORAL AND ETHICAL ASPECTS.
Eidam, Heinz. Moral, Freiheit und Geschichte. Würzburg : Königshausen & Neumann, 2001.

LIBERTY OF CONSCIENCE. See **PUBLIC OPINION.**

LIBERTY - PHILOSOPHY.
Flathman, Richard E. Freedom and its conditions. New York : Routledge, c2003.
JC585 .F553 2003

Philosophy and freedom. Toronto : University of Toronto Press, c2003.

LIBERTY - RELIGIOUS ASPECTS.
Gregg, Samuel, 1969- On ordered liberty. Lanham, MD : Lexington Books, c2003.
JC585 .G744 2003

Libikóka.
Somogyi, Gábor. [Budapest?] : Honestus-Press, 2002.
BF575.L8 S623 2002

La librairie du XXIe siècle
Flem, Lydia. La voix des amants. [Paris] : Seuil, c2002.

LIBRARY MATERIALS. See **BOOKS.**

Library of Congress.
Freud [electronic resource]. Washington, DC : Library of Congress
BF173

Library of ethics and applied philosophy
(v. 10) Forrester, Mary Gore, 1940- Moral beliefs and moral theory. Dordrecht ; Boston : Kluwer Academic Publishers, c2002.
BJ1012 .F615 2002

(v. 11) Personal and moral identity. Dordrecht ; Boston : Kluwer Academic Publishers, c2002.
BJ45 .P47 2002

(v. 9) Corlett, J. Angelo, 1958- Responsibility and punishment. Dordrecht ; Boston : Kluwer Academic Publishers, c2001.
BJ1451 .C67 2001

The library of living philosophers
(v. 29) The philosophy of Marjorie Grene. Chicago : Open Court, c2002.
B945.G734 P47 2002

I libri dell'altra scienza
(171) Mantovani, Massimo. Meditazioni sull'albero della cabala. Milano : Xenia, 2002.

Libro de la melancholía.
Velásquez, Andrés, fl. 1553-1615. Viareggio (Lucca) : M. Baroni, [2002]
BF575.M44 V453 2002

LIBYA - ANTIQUITIES. See **CYRENE (EXTINCT CITY).**

Lichev, Aleksandŭr. Russland verstehen : Schlüssel zum russischen Wesen / Alexander Litschev. 1. Aufl. Düsseldorf : Grupello, 2001. 132 p. ; 21 cm. Includes bibliographical references and index. ISBN 3-933749-40-9 (pbk.)
1. National characteristics, Russian. 2. Russia - Civilization. I. Title.

Lichev, Valeri. T͡Sinichnoto, ili, Igrata na vlast i udovolstvie / Valeri Lichev. Sofii͡a : EON-2000, 2000. 254 p. ; 20 cm. (Serii͡a "Filosofska antropologii͡a") Includes bibliographical references (p. 245-[252]). ISBN 9549699056
1. Cynicism. 2. Cynicism - Bulgaria. 3. Slang. 4. Sex. 5. Power (Social sciences) I. Title. II. Title: T͡Sinichnoto III. Title: Igrata na vlast i udovolstvie IV. Series.
B809.5 .L53 2000

Lichnost' kak sub"ekt interpretatsii.
Slavskai͡a, A. N. Dubna : "Feniks+", 2002.
BF698 .S54 2002

Lichnost' v paradigmakh i metaforakh.
Vserossiĭskaia konferentsiia "Mezhdistsiplinarnyĭ sintez v metodologii gumanitarnykh issledovaniĭ" (2002 : Tomsk, Russia) Tomsk : Tomskiĭ gos. universitet, 2002.
BF698 .V74 2002

Lichtenberg, Joseph D. A spirit of inquiry : communication in psychoanalysis / Joseph D. Lichtenberg, Frank M. Lachmann, James L. Fosshage. Hillsdale, NJ : Analytic Press, 2002. 210 p. ; 24 cm. (Psychoanalytic inquiry book series ; v. 19) Includes bibliographical references (p. 191-201) and index. ISBN 0-88163-364-X DDC 616.89/17
1. Psychoanalysis. 2. Psychotherapist and patient. 3. Interpersonal communication. I. Lachmann, Frank M. II. Fosshage, James L. III. Title. IV. Series.
RC506 .L5238 2002

Lichtenberger, Elizabeth O. Essentials of WPPSI-III assessment / Elizabeth O. Lichtenberger and Alan S. Kaufman. Hoboken, N.J. : John Wiley & Sons, 2003. p. cm. (Essentials of psychological assessment series) Includes bibliographical references and index. Publisher description URL: http://www.loc.gov/catdir/desc ription/wiley038/2003053482.html Table of contents URL : http://www.loc.gov/catdir/toc/wiley032/2003053482.html ISBN 0-471-28895-0 (pbk.) DDC 155.42/3393
1. Wechsler Preschool and Primary Scale of Intelligence. I. Kaufman, Alan S., 1944- II. Title. III. Series.
BF432.5.W424 L53 2003

Lichtenstein, Aharon.
Ziegler, Reuven. By his light. 2nd ed. Jersey City, NJ : KTAV Pub. House ; Alon Shevut, Israel : Yeshivat Har Etzion, 2003.
BM723 .Z54 2003

Liddelow, Eden. After Electra : rage, grief and hope in twentieth-century fiction / Eden Liddelow. Melbourne : Australian Scholarly, 2002, c2001. 211 p. ; 25 cm. Includes bibliographical references and index. ISBN 1-74097-005-5
1. English fiction - Women authors - History and criticism. 2. English fiction - 20th century - History and criticism. 3. Self in literature. 4. Electra (Greek mythology) in literature. 5. Psychoanalysis and literature. I. Title.

Líderes sociales en el siglo XXI.
Rosero Garcés, F. (Fernando) Quito : Ediciones Abya-Yala, 2002.

Lidské emoce.
Nakonečný, Milan. Vyd. 1. Praha : Academia, 2000.
BF536 .N35 2000

Lie, Rico. Spaces of intercultural communication : an interdisciplinary introduction to communication, culture, and globalizing/localizing identities / Rico Lie. Creskill, N.J. : Hampton Press, c2003. xiv, 241 p. : ill. ; 24 cm. (International Association for Media and Communication Research) Includes bibliographical references (p. 203-227) and indexes. ISBN 1-57273-498-1 (hbk.) ISBN 1-57273-499-X (pbk.) DDC 303.48/2
1. Intercultural communication. 2. Group identity. 3. Globalization. 4. Television - Social aspects. I. Title. II. Series: International Association for Media and Communication Research (Series)
GN345.6 .L54 2003

Liebe als Kulturmedium / herausgegeben von Werner Faulstich und Jörn Glasenapp. München : Fink, c2002. 184 p. : ill. ; 24 cm. Includes bibliographical references. ISBN 3-7705-3657-6 (pbk.)
1. Love. I. Faulstich, Werner. II. Glasenapp, Jörn.

Liebe und Abhängigkeit : Partnerschaftsbeziehungen junger Frauen / Christel Hopf, Myriam Hartwig (Hrsg.). Weinheim : Juventa, 2001. 211 p. ; 21 cm. Includes bibliographical references. ISBN 3-7799-1078-0 (pbk.)
1. Young women - Germany - Psychology. 2. Intimacy (Psychology) 3. Interpersonal relationships - Germany. I. Hopf, Christel. II. Hartwig, Myriam, 1971-

Liechty, Daniel, 1954-.
Death and denial. Westport, Conn. ; London : Praeger, 2002.
BD444 .D377 2002

Le lien social dans le modèle de l'individualisme privé.
Venne, Jean-François, 1972- Paris : L'Harmattan, c2002.

Les lieux de l'imaginaire / sous la direction de Jean-François Chassay et Bertrand Gervais. Montréal : Liber, 2002. 306 p. ; 23 cm. Includes bibliographical references. ISBN 289578017X DDC 801/.9
1. Imagination in literature. 2. Imagination. 3. Creation (Literary, artistic, etc.) 4. Imaginary places in literature. 5. Imagination (Philosophy) I. Chassay, Jean-François, 1959- II. Gervais, Bertrand, 1957-

LIFE. *See also* **DEATH; PHILOSOPHICAL ANTHROPOLOGY; QUALITY OF LIFE.**
Kelly, Kevin, 1966- Ballintubber, Co. Roscommon : Inspiring Irish Publications, 2002.

LIFE.
Boncinelli, Edoardo. Io sono, tu sei. 1. ed. Milano : Mondadori, 2002.

Burneko, Guy Christian. By the torch of chaos and doubt. Cresskill, N.J. : Hampton Press, c2003.
BD431 .B84 2003

Colantuono, Susan L. Make room for joy. Charlestown, RI : Interlude Productions, c2000.
BF575.H27 C64 2000

Collste, Göran. Is human life special? Bern ; Oxford : Peter Lang, 2002.

Day, Stacey B. Man and Mu. N[ew] Y[ork] : International Foundation for Biosocial Development and Human Health ; Oviedo, Fla. : Disctributed by C.E.P., c1997.
BD431 .D37 1997

Erkennen und Leben. Hildesheim [Germany] ; New York : Olms, 2002.
BD435 .E75 2002

Kather, Regine, 1955- Was ist Leben? Darmstadt : Wissenschaftliche Buchgesellschaft, c2003.

Ke, Yunlu. Fu gui yu ying er. Di 1 ban. Shanghai : Shanghai ren min chu ban she : Xin hua shu dian Shanghai fa xing suo jing xiao, 1996.
BD431 .K6134 1996 <Asian China>

Krasikov, V. I. (Vladimir Ivanovich) Sindrom sushchestvovaniia. Tomsk : [s.n.], 2002.

Merdalor, Jean. Pensées mortelles. Port-au-Prince, Haiti : Editions Choucoune, 1999.
1. Black author.

Mortalism. Amherst, N.Y. : Prometheus Books, 2003.
BD431 .M886 2003

Pollard, Irina. Life, love and children. Boston : Kluwer Academic Publishers, c2002.
R725.5 .P655 2002

Rogers, W. Kim. Reason and life. Lanham, Md. : University Press of America, c2003.
BD431 .R5515 2003

Schutz, Alfred, 1899-1959. Werkausgabe. Konstanz : UVK, Verlagsgesellschaft, 2003-
BD431 .S284916 2003

Slutskiĭ, O. I. (Oleg Isaakovich) Chto posle illiuzii? Moskva : Veche, 2002.
BV4509.R8 S58 2002

Tapergi, Fausto, 1909- La filosofia come scienza della vita. 1a ed. Milano : Spirali, 2001.

Thomson, Garrett. On the meaning of life. Australia ; United States : Thomson/Wadsworth, c2003.
BD431 .T296 2003

LIFE AFTER DEATH. *See* **FUTURE LIFE.**

Life after life.
Moody, Raymond A. Rev. 25th anniversary ed / with a new preface by Melvin Morse and a foreword by Elisabeth Kübler-Ross. London : Rider, 2001.

Life and mind
Evolution and learning. Cambridge, Mass. : MIT Press, c2003.
BF698.95 .E95 2003

Pylyshyn, Zenon W., 1937- Seeing and visualizing. Cambridge, Mass. : MIT Press, 2003.
BF241 .P95 2003

Shapiro, Lawrence A. The mind incarnate. Cambridge, Mass. : MIT Press, 2004.
BF161 .S435 2004

Life as we know it : a collection of personal essays from Salon.com / edited by Jennifer Foote Sweeney. 1st Washington Square Press trade pbk. ed. New York : Washington Square Press, 2003. xvi, 319 p. ; 19 cm. ISBN 0-7434-7686-7 (pbk.)
1. Family. 2. Family - United States. 3. United States - Social life and customs. 4. Alternative lifestyles - United States. I. Sweeney, Jennifer Foote. II. Salon.com (Firm)

Life balance
Andrews, Linda Wasmer. Emotional intelligence. New York : Franklin Watts, 2004.
BF576 .A53 2004

Andrews, Linda Wasmer. Intelligence. New York : Franklin Watts, c2003.
BF431 .A576 2003

Andrews, Linda Wasmer. Meditation. New York : F. Watts, c2003.
BF637.M4 A53 2003

Davidson, Tish. Prejudice. New York : Franklin Watts, c2003.
BF575.P9 D38 2003

Peacock, Carol Antoinette. Death and dying. New York : Franklin Watts, c2004.
BF575.G7 P3783 2004

Silverman, Robin Landew. Reaching your goals. New York : F. Watts, 2003.
BF505.G6 S57 2003

LIFE (BIOLOGY). *See* **BIOLOGY; DEATH (BIOLOGY).**

LIFE CHANGE EVENTS. *See also* **STRESS (PSYCHOLOGY).**
Ford, Loren. Human relations. 3rd ed. Upper Saddle River, N.J. : Pearson/Prentice Hall, c2004.
BF335 .F67 2004

LIFE CHANGE EVENTS - PSYCHOLOGICAL ASPECTS.
Childs-Oroz, Annette. Will you dance? Incline Village, NV : Wandering Feather Press, c2002.
BF637.L53 C45 2002

Dobson, James C., 1936- Life on the edge. Nashville : Word Pub., c2000.
BF637.L53 D63 2000

Esquire presents. 1st ed. New York : Three Rivers Press, c2003.
BF637.L53 E77 2003

Kirshenbaum, Mira. Everything happens for a reason. New York : Harmony Books, 2004.
BF637.L53 K57 2004

O'Hanlon, William Hudson. Thriving through crisis. 1st Perigee ed. New York : Perigee, 2004.
BF789.S8 O35 2004

Spencer, Sabina A., 1951- Life changes. New York : Paraview Special Editions, c2002.
BF637.L53 S64 2002

LIFE CHANGE EVENTS - PSYCHOLOGICAL ASPECTS - PROBLEMS, EXERCISES, ETC.
Spencer, Sabina A., 1951- Life changes. New York : Paraview Special Editions, c2002.
BF637.L53 S64 2002

LIFE CHANGE EVENTS - RELIGIOUS ASPECTS - CHRISTIANITY.
Dobson, James C., 1936- Life on the edge. Nashville : Word Pub., c2000.
BF637.L53 D63 2000

McKinney Hammond, Michelle, 1957- Get over it and on with it!. 1st ed. Colorado Springs, Colo. : WaterBrook Press, 2002.
BV4908.5 .M357 2002
1. Black author.

Life changes.
Spencer, Sabina A., 1951- New York : Paraview Special Editions, c2002.
BF637.L53 S64 2002

Life changing relationships.
Meeks, James T., 1956- Chicago, Ill. : Moody Press, c2002.
HQ801 .M515 2002

LIFE CYCLE, HUMAN. *See also* **ADULTHOOD; CHILDREN; DEVELOPMENTAL PSYCHOLOGY; YOUTH.**
The complete guide to mental health for women. 1st ed. Boston : Beacon Press, c2003.
RC451.4.W6 C65 2003

Invitation to the life course. Amityville, N.Y. : Baywood Pub. Co., c2003.
HQ1061 .I584 2003

Social relations and the life course. Houndmills, Basingstoke New York : Palgrave Macmillan, 2003.
HM741 .S64 2003

LIFE CYCLE, HUMAN - RELIGIOUS ASPECTS - JUDAISM.
Malkah, Asher. ʻArakhim ye-ḥinukh. Ḥefah : A. Malkah, [5760 i.e. 2000]

The life cycle of psychological ideas : understanding prominence and the dynamics of intellectual change / edited by Thomas C. Dalton, Rand B. Evans. New York : Kluwer Academic/Plenum, 2004. p. cm. (PATH

in psychology) Includes bibliographical references and index. ISBN 0-306-47998-2 DDC 150/.1
1. Psychology - Philosophy - History. 2. Psychology - History.
I. Dalton, Thomas Carlyle. II. Evans, Rand B. III. Series.
BF38 .L54 2004

LIFE CYCLES (BIOLOGY). *See* **LIFE CYCLE, HUMAN.**

LIFE EVENTS, STRESSFUL. *See* **LIFE CHANGE EVENTS.**

LIFE EXPERIENCES, STRESSFUL. *See* **LIFE CHANGE EVENTS.**

LIFE, FUTURE. *See* **FUTURE LIFE.**

LIFE HISTORIES. *See* **BIOGRAPHY.**

Life lifters.
Ziglar, Zig. Zig Ziglar's life lifters. Nashville, Tenn. : Broadman & Holman, c2003.
BF637.C5 Z54 2003

Life, love and children.
Pollard, Irina. Boston : Kluwer Academic Publishers, c2002.
R725.5 .P655 2002

LIFE - MISCELLANEA.
Nicheva, Nina. Prez vremeto i prostranstvoto. [Bulgaria] : Gutoranov i sin, [1998?]
BF1999 .N46 1998

Saberi, Reza, 1941- Insights and intuitions. Lanham, Md. : University Press of America, c2003.
BF1999 .S225 2003

LIFE - MORAL AND ETHICAL ASPECTS.
El milagro y el valor de la vida. 1. ed. Buenos Aires : Patria Grande, 2000.

The life of the mind.
McCulloch, Gregory. London ; New York : Routledge, 2003.
BD418.3 .M363 2003

LIFE ON OTHER PLANETS. *See also* **HUMAN-ALIEN ENCOUNTERS.**
Leary, Timothy Francis, 1920- Musings on human metaporphoses. Berkeley, CA : Ronin, c2003.

Pinotti, Roberto, 1944- Oltre. Firenze : Olimpia, c2002.

LIFE ON OTHER PLANETS IN ART.
Moffitt, John F. (John Francis), 1940- Picturing extraterrestrials. Amherst, N.Y. : Prometheus Press, c2003.
BF2050 .M64 2003

LIFE ON OTHER PLANETS - JUVENILE LITERATURE.
Herbst, Judith. Aliens. Minneapolis : Lerner Publications, 2005.
BF2050 .H465 2005

Life on the edge.
Dobson, James C., 1936- Nashville : Word Pub., c2000.
BF637.L53 D63 2000

Life on the other side.
Browne, Sylvia. New York : Dutton, c2000.
BF1311.F8 B77 2000b

LIFE - ORIGIN.
Fenchel, Tom. Origin and early evolution of life. Oxford New York : Oxford University Press, 2002.
QH325 .F42 2002

Lurquin, Paul F. The origins of life and the universe. New York : Columbia University Press, c2003.
QH325 .L87 2003

Life passages
Kastenbaum, Robert. On our way. Berkeley : University of California Press, c2004.
BF789.D4 .K365 2004

LIFE - PHILOSOPHY. *See* **LIFE.**

LIFE, QUALITY OF. *See* **QUALITY OF LIFE.**

LIFE - RELIGIOUS ASPECTS.
Collste, Göran. Is human life special? Bern ; Oxford : Peter Lang, 2002.

LIFE SCIENCES. *See* **AGRICULTURE; BIOLOGY; MEDICINE.**

LIFE SCIENCES - EXPERIMENTS.
Ruxton, Graeme D. Elementary experimental design for the life sciences. Oxford : Oxford University Press, 2003.

LIFE SCIENCES - HISTORY.
Guillo, Dominique. Les figures de l'organisation. 1. éd. Paris : Presses universitaires de France, c2003.

LIFE SCIENTISTS. *See* **NEUROSCIENTISTS.**

LIFE SKILLS. *See also* **CONDUCT OF LIFE; SELF-HELP TECHNIQUES.**
Bucay, Jorge, 1949- Hojas de ruta. 1a ed. Buenos Aires : Editorial Sudamericana : Editorial Del nuevo extremo, 2001.

Chiodi, Michael. The art of building people. 1st ed. St. Paul, Minn. : Chiberry Press, c2003.
BF637.S4 C497 2003

Eckblad, John. If your life were a business, would you invest in it? New York : McGraw-Hill, c2003.
BF637.S4 E38 2003

LIFE, SPIRITUAL. *See* **SPIRITUAL LIFE.**

LIFE STAGES, HUMAN. *See* **LIFE CYCLE, HUMAN.**

A life that makes a difference.
Goodier, Steve. 1st ed. Divide, CO : Life Support System Pub., c2002.
BF637.C5 G68 2002

LIFECYCLE, HUMAN. *See* **LIFE CYCLE, HUMAN.**

Life's a journey - not a sprint.
Lewis-Hall, Jennifer, 1964- Carlsbad, Calif. : Hay House, c2003.
BF637.S8 L455 2003

Life's treasure book on friendship.
Brown, H. Jackson, 1940- On friendship. Nashville, Tenn. : Rutledge Hill Press, c1996.
BF575.F66 B76 1996

Life's treasure book on things that really matter.
Brown, H. Jackson, 1940- On things that really matter. Nashville, Tenn. : Rutledge Hill Press, c1999.
BF637.C5 B777 1999

Lifetime leadership.
Flaherty, Jane S. San Diego : Bentley Press, c2001.
BF637.L4 F57 2001

Lifetime leadership, leaving your legacy.
Flaherty, Jane S. Lifetime leadership. San Diego : Bentley Press, c2001.
BF637.L4 F57 2001

A lifetime of communication.
Yingling, Julie. Mahwah, N.J. : Lawrence Erlbaum Associates, 2004.
BF637.C45 Y56 2004

LIFT.
Vosburgh, Bob. [United Ustates?] : 9g Enterprises, c2002.
BF637.L4 V67 2002

Lifting the mind fog.
Sims, Robert Vincent. [S.l.] : Garden Rebel Books, c1996.
BF637.C5 S5444 1996

LIGHT. *See* **COLOR.**

LIGHT - RELIGIOUS ASPECTS. *See* **CANDLES AND LIGHTS.**

The lightbearer.
Cox, Bonnie. Seattle, Wash. : Black Heron Press, c2003.
BF1031 .C637 2003

Lightfoot, Cynthia.
Jean Piaget Society. Meeting (30th : 2000 : Montréal, Québec) Changing conceptions of psychological life. Mahwah, N.J. : L. Erlbaum Associates, 2004.
BF697 .J36 2004

LIGHTS AND CANDLES. *See* **CANDLES AND LIGHTS.**

LIGHTS, LITURGICAL. *See* **CANDLES AND LIGHTS.**

Like a movie.
Alper, Gerald. 1st ed. St. Paul, Minn. : Paragon House, 2004.
BF632.5 .A44 2004

Likut le-'idud ye-ḥizuḳ : 'etsah ma'aśit ha-mehazeket me'od u-mekhayenet be-derekh ha-limud.
Yerushalayim : [h. mo. l.], 756 [1995 or 1996] 162 p. ; 25 cm. Edited by Dayid Elbom et al.
1. Talmud Torah (Judaism) 2. Ethics, Jewish. I. Elbom, Dayid.

Liḳuṭe Leshem shevo ye-aḥlamah.
Shelomoh ben Ḥayim Ḥaikel. Sefer Liḳute u-ferushe niglot Leshem shevo ye-aḥlamah. Kiryat Sefer : Mosheh Vais, 762 [2002]
BM525 .H4332 2002

Liḳuṭe niglot Leshem shevo ye-aḥlamah.
Shelomoh ben Ḥayim Ḥaikel. Sefer Liḳute u-ferushe niglot Leshem shevo ye-aḥlamah. Kiryat Sefer : Mosheh Vais, 762 [2002]
BM525 .H4332 2002

Lila et la lumière de Vermeer.
Didier-Weill, Alain. Paris : Denoël, c2003.

Lillehammer, Hallvard, 1970-.
Real metaphysics. London : New York : Routledge, 2003.
BD111 .R227 2003

Lilly, Reginald.
Schürmann, Reiner, 1941- [Des hégémonies brisées. English] Broken hegemonies. Bloomington : Indiana University Press, c2003.
BD162 .S48 2003

Lim, C. J. Realms of impossibility. Ground / series creator C.J. Lim. Water. Chichester : Wiley-Academy, 2002. 192 p. : ill. (some col.) ; 15 x 21 cm. ISBN 0-470-84442-6 DDC 721
1. Architecture - Philosophy. 2. Architectural design. I. Title.

LIMITATIONS, CONSTITUTIONAL. *See* **CONSTITUTIONAL LAW.**

LIMITED COMPANIES. *See* **CORPORATIONS.**

Limitless mind.
Targ, Russell. Novato, Calif. : New World Library, c2004.
BF1389.R45 T37 2004

Il limnisco
(9) Bonvecchio, Claudio. La maschera e l'uomo. Milano : F. Angeli, 2002.

Limonov, Ėduard. Distsiplinarnyĭ sanatoriĭ / Ėduard Limonov. Sankt-Peterburg : Amfora, 2002. 245 p. ; 21 cm. ISBN 5942783209
1. Civilization, Western - 20th century. 2. Social control. 3. Social history - 1970- 4. Totalitarianism. 5. Liberty. 6. United States - Social conditions - 1945- 7. France - Social conditions - 1945-1995. I. Title.
CB428 .L556 2002

Lin, Jian. Ren di zi you di zhe xue si suo / Lin Jian zhu. Di 1 ban. Beijing : Zhongguo ren min da xue chu ban she : Jing xiao xin hua shu dian, 1996. 2, 3, 261 p. : ill. ; 21 cm. (Zhongguo ren min da xue bo shi wen ku) Originally presented as the author's thesis (doctoral--Zhongguo ren min da xue). Includes bibliographical references. Table of contents also in English. ISBN 7-300-02261-8
1. Philosophy. I. Title. II. Series.
B99.C52 L55 1996 <Orien China>

Lin, Meihwa.
The Learning Annex presents feng shui. 1st ed. New York, NY : J. Wiley, 2004.
BF1779.F4 L42 2004

Lin, Shu, 1852-1924. Tie bi jin zhen : Lin Shu wen xuan / Xu Guiting xuan zhu. Di 1 ban. Tianjin Shi : Bai hua wen yi chu ban she, 2002. 2, 4, 25, 213 p. ; 21 cm. (Zhongguo jin dai si xiang zhe cong shu) Includes bibliographical references. ISBN 7-5306-3296-5
1. Literature - History and criticism. 2. Chinese literature - History and criticism. I. Xu, Guiting. II. Title. III. Title: Lin Shu wen xuan IV. Series.
PL2718.I5 T54 2002

Lin Shu wen xuan.
Lin, Shu, 1852-1924. Tie bi jin zhen. Di 1 ban. Tianjin Shi : Bai hua wen yi chu ban she, 2002.
PL2718.I5 T54 2002

Lin, Zhiang. Designing stress resistant organizations : computational theorizing and crisis applications / Zhiang Lin, Kathleen M. Carley. Boston : Kluwer Academic Publishers, c2003. xxiii, 211 p. : ill. ; 25 cm. (Information and organization design series) Includes bibliographical references (p. [191]-208) and index. ISBN 1402074360 (acid-free paper) DDC 302.3/5
1. Organizational change. 2. Organizational behavior. I. Carley, Kathleen M. II. Title. III. Series.
HD58.8 .L58 2003

Linck, Gudula. Leib und Körper : zum Selbstverständnis im vormodernen China / Gudula Linck. Frankfurt am Main ; New York : P. Lang, c2001. 277 p. : ill., map ; 22 cm. (Historisch-anthropologische Studien, 1430-0621 ; Bd. 12) Includes bibliographical references (p. 231-247). ISBN 3-631-34035-4 (acid-free paper) DDC 128/.6/0951
1. Body, Human (Philosophy) I. Title. II. Series.
B105.B64 L58 2001

LINCOLN, ABRAHAM, 1809-1865 - ORATORY.
Winger, Stewart Lance. Lincoln, religion, and romantic cultural politics. DeKalb : Northern Illinois University Press, c2003.

E457.2 .W77 2003

LINCOLN, ABRAHAM, 1809-1865 - PHILOSOPHY.
Abraham Lincoln's daily treasure. Grand Rapids, Mich. : F.H. Revell, c2002.
E457.2 .F787 2002

LINCOLN, ABRAHAM, 1809-1865 - POLITICAL AND SOCIAL VIEWS.
Winger, Stewart Lance. Lincoln, religion, and romantic cultural politics. DeKalb : Northern Illinois University Press, c2003.
E457.2 .W77 2003

LINCOLN, ABRAHAM, 1809-1865 - QUOTATIONS.
Abraham Lincoln's daily treasure. Grand Rapids, Mich. : F.H. Revell, c2002.
E457.2 .F787 2002

LINCOLN, ABRAHAM, 1809-1865 - RELIGION.
Abraham Lincoln's daily treasure. Grand Rapids, Mich. : F.H. Revell, c2002.
E457.2 .F787 2002

LINCOLN, ABRAHAM, 1809-1865 - VIEWS ON RELIGION.
Winger, Stewart Lance. Lincoln, religion, and romantic cultural politics. DeKalb : Northern Illinois University Press, c2003.
E457.2 .W77 2003

Lincoln, Bruce. Holy terrors : thinking about religion after September 11 / Bruce Lincoln. Chicago : University of Chicago Press, 2003. xi, 142 p. : ill. : 24 cm. Includes bibliographical references (p. 109-137) and index. ISBN 0-226-48192-1 (cloth : alk. paper) DDC 291.1/787
1. September 11 Terrorist Attacks, 2001. 2. Terrorism - Religious aspects. 3. Religion - Philosophy. 4. Religion and culture. I. Title.
BL65.T47 L56 2003

Lincoln, Jackson Steward, 1902-1941.
[Dream in primitive cultures]
The dream in native American and other primitive cultures / Jackson Steward Lincoln. Mineola, N.Y. : Dover Publications, 2003. xv, 359 p. : ill. : 22 cm. Originally published: The dream in primitive cultures. London : Cresset Press, 1935. Includes bibliographical references (p. 335-342) and index. Publisher description URL: http://www.loc.gov/catdir/desc ription/dover032/2002041668.html ISBN 0-486-42706-4 (pbk.) DDC 154.6/3/09
1. Dreams. 2. Ethnopsychology. I. Title.
BF1078 .L5 2003

Lincoln, religion, and romantic cultural politics.
Winger, Stewart Lance. DeKalb : Northern Illinois University Press, c2003.
E457.2 .W77 2003

Lincoln, Yvonna S.
9-11 in American culture. Walnut Creek ; Oxford : AltaMira Press, c2003.
HV6432.7 .A13 2003

Collecting and interpreting qualitative materials. 2nd ed. Thousand Oaks, Calif. : Sage, c2003.
H62 .C566 2003

Strategies of qualitative inquiry. 2nd ed. Thousand Oaks, CA : Sage, c2003.
H61 .S8823 2003

Lindauer, Martin S. Aging, creativity, and art : a positive perspective on late-life development / Martin S. Lindauer. New York : Kluwer Academic/Plenum Publishers, c2003. xvii, 312 p. : ill. ; 24 cm. (The Plenum series in adult development and aging) Includes bibliographical references (p. 289-308) and index. ISBN 0-306-47756-4 DDC 155.67/1335
1. Creative ability in old age. 2. Creation (Literary, artistic, etc.) 3. Aged artists. 4. Aged - Psychology. I. Title. II. Series.
BF724.85.C73 L56 2003

Linden, Stanton J., 1935-.
The alchemy reader. Cambridge, U.K. New York : Cambridge University Press, 2003.
QD26 .A585 2003

LINDER, AMNON.
De Sion exibit lex et verbum domini de Hierusalem. Turnhout, Belgium : Brepols, c2001.

Lindgren, Mats, 1959- Scenario planning : the link between future and strategy / Mats Lindgren, Hans Bandhold. Houndmills [England] ; New York : Palgrave Macmillan, 2002. xii, 180 p. : ill. ; 24 cm. Includes bibliographical references (p. [173]-[177]) and index. ISBN 0-333-99317-9 (alk. paper) DDC 658.4/012
1. Strategic planning. 2. Decision making. 3. Communication in management. 4. Business planning. I. Bandhold, Hans. II. Title.

HD30.28 .L543 2002

Lindstrom, Pia.
Vint/age 2001 conference : [videorecording]. New York, c2001.

LINDSTROM, PIA.
Vint/age 2001 conference : [videorecording]. New York, c2001.

Lindzey, Gardner.
The handbook of social psychology. 4th ed. Boston : McGraw-Hill : New York : Distributed exclusively by Oxford University Press, c1998.
HM251 .H224 1998

LINEAR PERSPECTIVE. *See* **PERSPECTIVE.**

Lines of thought
Fodor, Jerry A. Hume variations. Oxford : Clarendon Press ; New York : Oxford University Press, 2003.
B1489 .F63 2003

Ling dao zhe bi bei. Zeng Guofan cheng jiu da shi de xue wen
(4) Zeng, Guofan, 1811-1872. Fan jing. Di 1 ban. Beijing : Zhongguo Hua qiao chu ban she, 2001.
BJ1618.C5 H44 2001

Ling, Yuanzheng. Xin yu wen jian she shi hua / Ling Yuanzheng zhu. Di 1 ban. Kaifeng Shi : Henan da xue chu ban she : Henan sheng Xin hua shu dian fa xing, 1995. 6, 2, 343 p. ; 20 cm. In Chinese. Includes bibliographical references (p. 341-342). ISBN 7-81041-120-9
1. Chinese language - Reform. 2. Language and languages. I. Title.
PL1175 .L55 1995 <Orien China>

A linguagem no teatro infantil.
Camarotti, Marco. 2a edição. [Recife : Editora Universitária UFPE, 2002]

LINGUISTIC ANALYSIS (LINGUISTICS). *See* **EXPLANATION (LINGUISTICS).**

LINGUISTIC ANALYSIS (PHILOSOPHY). *See* **ANALYSIS (PHILOSOPHY).**

Linguistic anthropology of education / edited by Stanton Wortham and Betsy Rymes. Westport, Conn. ; London : Praeger, 2003. vi, 279 p. : ill., facsims. ; 25 cm. Includes bibliographical references and index. ISBN 0-89789-823-0 (alk. paper) DDC 306.44/089
1. Language and education. 2. Anthropological linguistics. I. Wortham, Stanton Emerson Fisher, 1963- II. Rymes, Betsy.
P40.8 .L55 2003

LINGUISTIC CHANGE.
Bichakjian, Bernard H. Language in a Darwinian perspective. Frankfurt am Main ; New York : Peter Lang, c2002.
P142 .B53 2002

Linguistic evolution through language acquisition / edited by Ted Briscoe. Cambridge ; New York : Cambridge University Press, 2002. vii, 349 p. : ill. ; 24 cm. Includes bibliographical references and index. CONTENTS: Introduction / Ted Briscoe -- Learned systems of arbitrary reference: the foundation of human linguistic uniqueness / Michael Oliphant -- Bootstrapping grounded word semantics / Luc Steels, Frederic Kaplan -- Linguistic structure and the evolution of words / Robert Worden -- Negotiation and acquisition of recursive grammars as a result of competition among exemplars / John Batali -- Learning, bottlenecks and the evolution of recursive syntax / Simon Kirby -- Theories of cultural evolution and their application to language change / Partha Niyogi -- Learning guided evolution of natural language / William J. Turkel -- Grammatical acquisition and linguistic selection / Ted Briscoe -- Expression/induction models of language evolution: dimensions and issues / James R. Hurford. ISBN 0-521-66299-0 DDC 401
1. Language acquisition. 2. Anthropological linguistics. 3. Evolution. I. Briscoe, E. J., 1959-
P118 .L565 2002

LINGUISTIC SCIENCE. *See* **LINGUISTICS.**

LINGUISTICS. *See also* **CONTEXT (LINGUISTICS); FUNCTIONALISM (LINGUISTICS); GOVERNMENT-BINDING THEORY (LINGUISTICS); GRAMMAR, COMPARATIVE AND GENERAL; MODALITY (LINGUISTICS); REFERENCE (LINGUISTICS); SPEECH ACTS (LINGUISTICS).**
Collected papers on Southeast Asian and Pacific languages. Canberra, ACT : Pacific Linguistics, Research School of Pacific and Asian Studies, Australian National University, 2002.

Language function, structure, and change. Frankfurt am Main ; New York : Lang, c2002.

P125 .L36 2002

Marcuschi, Luiz Antônio. Investigando a relação oral/escrito e as teorias do letramento. Campinas, SP : Mercado de Letras, 2001.

Perspectives in linguistics. New Delhi : Indian Institute of Language Studies : Distributed by Creative Books, 2003.

Rix, Helmut, 1926- Kleine Schriften. Bremen : Hempen, 2001.

Zhang, Fan. Mei xue yu yan xue. Di 1 ban. Beijing : Shou du shi fan da xue chu ban she, 1998.
P121 .Z465 1998

LINGUISTICS - HISTORY.
Bichakjian, Bernard H. Language in a Darwinian perspective. Frankfurt am Main ; New York : Peter Lang, c2002.
P142 .B53 2002

LINGUISTS. *See* **PHILOLOGISTS.**

Lingvokul'turovedenie.
Khrolenko, A. T. Kursk : Izd-vo GUIPP "Kursk", 2000.
P35 .K524 2000

Linklater, Andro. Measuring America : how an untamed wilderness shaped the United States and fulfilled the promise of democracy / Andro Linklater. New York : Walker & Co., 2002. 310 p. : ill. ; 22 cm. Includes bibliographical references (p. 289-292) and index. CONTENTS: 1. The invention of landed property -- 2. Precise confusion -- 3. Who owned America -- 4. Life, liberty, or what -- 5. Simple arithmetic -- 6. A line drawn in the wilderness -- 7. The French dimension -- 8. Democratic decimals -- 9. The birth of the metric system -- 10. Dombey's luck -- 11. The end of Putnam -- 12. The immaculate grid -- 13. The shape of cities -- 14. Hassler's passion -- 15. The dispossessed -- 16. The limit of enclosure -- 17. Four against ten -- 18. Metric triumphant -- Epilogue : the witness tree. ISBN 0-8027-1396-3 DDC 973
1. United States - Geography. 2. United States - Surveys - History. 3. United States - Territorial expansion. 4. National characteristics, American. 5. Public lands - United States - History. 6. Frontier and pioneer life - United States. 7. Ohio River Valley - Geography. 8. Ohio River Valley - Surveys - History. 9. Surveying - United States - History. 10. Surveyors - United States - History. I. Title.
E161.3 .L46 2002

Linn, Denise. Secrets & mysteries : the glory and pleasure of being a woman / Denise Linn. Carlsbad, Calif. : Hay House, c2002. 223 p. : ill. ; 23 cm. Includes bibliographical references (p. 212-214) and index. ISBN 1401901034 (pbk.) DDC 305.4
1. Women - Psychology. 2. Women - Conduct of life. 3. Women - Health and hygiene. 4. Self-realization. I. Title. II. Title: Secrets and mysteries
HQ1206 .L513 2002

Soul coaching : 28 days to discover your authentic self / Denise Linn. Carlsbad, CA : Hay House, 2003. xiii, 206 p. ; 21 cm. Includes bibliographical references. Table of contents URL: http://www.loc.gov/catdir/toc/ecip045/2003012608.html CONTENTS: What is soul coaching? -- Air week : clearing your mental self -- Water week : clearing your emotional self -- Fire week : clearing your spiritual self -- Earth week : clearing your physical self -- Quest : beyond the 28 days. ISBN 1401902316 DDC 158.1
1. Self-actualization (Psychology) - Problems, exercises, etc. 2. Spiritual life - Problems, exercises, etc. I. Title.
BF637.S4 L565 2003

Linnemann, Manuela.
Brüder, Bestien, Automaten. 1. Aufl. Erlangen : H. Fischer, c2000.

Linneweber-Lammerskitten, Helmut.
Interpretation und Argument. Würzburg : Königshausen & Neumann, c2002.

Linson, William. Kinoetics : signs of conflict : our personal body language / by William Linson. [United States] : Kinoetics Publishing, c2002. x, 219 p. : ill. ; 22 x 24 cm. Includes bibliographical references (p. 217-218). ISBN 0-9700739-0-9
1. Body language. 2. Conflict (Psychology) 3. Touch. 4. Nonverbal communication. I. Title.
BF637.N66 L56 2002

Linstead, Stephen.
Text/work. London ; New York : Routledge, 2003.

Lioger, Richard. La folie du chaman : histoire et perspectives de l'ethnopsychanalyse théorique / Richard Lioger. Paris : Presses universitaires de France, c2002. 174 p. ; 24 cm. (Collection "Ethnologies") ISBN 2-13-052870-8 DDC 301
1. Psychoanalysis and religion. 2. Shamanism - Psychology. I. Title. II. Series.

Liotta, Alfred J. When students grieve : a guide to bereavement in the schools / by Alfred J. Liotta. Horsham, PA : LRP Publications, 2003. p. cm. Includes bibliographical references and index. ISBN 1-57834-036-5 DDC 155.9/37/083
1. Teenagers and death. 2. Children and death. 3. Grief in adolescence. 4. Grief in children. 5. Bereavement in adolescence. 6. Bereavement in children. 7. Teenagers - Counseling of. 8. Children - Counseling of. I. Title.
BF724.3.D43 L56 2003

Lipinski, Barbara. The tao of integrity : legal, ethical, and professional issues in psychology / Barbara Lipinski. San Buenaventura, CA : Pacific Meridian Publications, c2001. 267 p. : ill. ; 23 cm. Includes bibliographical references (p. [247]-257) and index. ISBN 1-928702-03-1 DDC 150/.23
1. Psychology - Practice - United States. 2. Psychology - Standards - United States. 3. Psychologists - Professional ethics - United States. 4. Psychologists - Legal status, laws, etc. - United States. I. Title.
BF75 .L655 2001

Lipp, Deborah, 1961- The elements of ritual : air, fire, water & earth in the wiccan circle / Deborah Lipp. 1st ed. St. Paul, Minn. : Llewellyn Publications, 2003. xi, 273 p. : ill. ; 24 cm. Includes bibliographical references and index. ISBN 0-7387-0301-X DDC 299
1. Witchcraft. 2. Neopaganism - Rituals. 3. Goddess religion. I. Title.
BF1571 .L56 2003

Lippe, Toinette, 1939- Nothing left over : a plain and simple life / Toinette Lippe. New York : J.P. Tarcher/Putnam, c2002. 257 p. ; 20 cm. ISBN 1-58542-160-X (alk. paper) DDC 179/.9
1. Lippe, Toinette, - 1939- 2. Simplicity. 3. Conduct of life. I. Title.
BJ1496 .L57 2002

LIPPE, TOINETTE, 1939-.
Lippe, Toinette, 1939- Nothing left over. New York : J.P. Tarcher/Putnam, c2002.
BJ1496 .L57 2002

Lippman, Jessica G., 1941-.
Lewis, Paddy Greenwall, 1945- Helping children cope with the death of a parent. Westport, Conn. : Praeger, 2004.
BF723.G75 L49 2004

Lipsky, David B., 1939- Emerging systems for managing workplace conflict : lessons from American corporations for managers and dispute resolution professionals / David B. Lipsky, Ronald L. Seeber, Richard D. Fincher. 1st ed. San Francisco : Jossey-Bass, c2003. xxiii, 406 p. : ill. ; 24 cm. Includes bibliographical references (p. 371-379) and index. ISBN 0-7879-6434-4 (alk. paper) DDC 658.4/053
1. Conflict management. 2. Dispute resolution (Law) I. Seeber, Ronald Leroy. II. Fincher, Richard D., 1951- III. Title.
HD42 .L564 2003

Lipson, Charles. Reliable partners : how democracies have made a separate peace / Charles Lipson. Princeton, N.J. : Princeton University Press, c2003. 259 p. ; 25 cm. Includes bibliographical references (p. [191]-248) and index. ISBN 0-691-11390-4 (alk. paper) DDC 327.1/7
1. Democracy. 2. Peace. I. Title.
JC423 .L583 2003

Liptak, John J. The self-esteem program : inventories, activities & educational handouts / by John J. Liptak, Kathy L. Khalsa, Estelle A. Leutenberg ; illustrated by Amy L. Brodsky. Plainview, NY : Wellness Reproductions & Pub., c2002. ix, 95 leaves : ill. ; 28 cm. ISBN 1-89327-710-0 DDC 155.2/83
1. Self-esteem - Study and teaching. I. Korb-Khalsa, Kathy L., 1958- II. Leutenberg, Estelle A. III. Title.
BF697.5.S46 L57 2002

Liptow, Jasper.
Holismus in der Philosophie. 1. Aufl. Weilerswist : Velbrück Wissenschaft, c2002.

LIQUIDS. See **BEVERAGES.**

LIQUORS. See **BREWING.**

Lira, Elizabeth.
Loveman, Brian. El espejismo de la reconciliación política. 1. ed. Santiago : LOM Ediciones : DIBAM, 2002.

Lis, Izabela. Śmierć w literaturze staroserbskiej : XII-XIV wiek / Izabela Lis. Poznań : Wydawn. Nauk. Uniwersytetu im. Adama Mickiewicza w Poznaniu, 2003. 127 p. ; 21 cm. (Seria Filologia słowiańska ; nr 9) Includes bibliographical references (p. 118-[121]). Summary in Serbo-Croatian (Cyrillic). ISBN 83-232-1225-2
1. Serbian literature - History and criticism. 2. Death in literature. I. Title. II. Series.

PG1406 .L59 2003

Lisovyĭ, Vasyl'.
Protsenko, Oleh. Konservatyzm. Kyïv : "Smoloskyp", 1998.

List, Monika.
Psychoanalysis and management. Heidelberg : Physica-Verlag, c1994.
BF175.4.S65 P777 1994

Listening.
Schultz, Katherine. New York : Teachers College Press, c2003.
LB1027 .S36638 2003

LISTENING.
Jordan, Denise. We can listen. Chicago, Ill. : Heinemann Library, 2003.
BF323.L5 J67 2003

Jordan, Denise. [We can listen. Spanish] Escuchamos. Chicago : Heinemann Library, c2004.
BF323.L5 J6718 2004

Kline, John A. Listening effectively [electronic resource]. Maxwell Air Force Base, Ala. : Air University Press, [1996]

Schultz, Katherine. Listening. New York : Teachers College Press, c2003.
LB1027 .S36638 2003

The wisdom of listening. Somerville, MA : Wisdom Publications, c2003.
BF323.L5 W57 2003

Listening effectively [electronic resource].
Kline, John A. Maxwell Air Force Base, Ala. : Air University Press, [1996]

LISTENING - JUVENILE LITERATURE.
Jordan, Denise. We can listen. Chicago, Ill. : Heinemann Library, 2003.
BF323.L5 J67 2003

Jordan, Denise. [We can listen. Spanish] Escuchamos. Chicago : Heinemann Library, c2004.
BF323.L5 J6718 2004

Lister, Ruth, 1949- Citizenship : feminist perspectives / Ruth Lister ; consultant editor, Jo Campling. 2nd ed. Basingstoke, Hampshire ; New York : Palgrave Macmillan, 2003. 323 p. ; 24 cm. Includes bibliographical references (p. 249-313) and indexes. ISBN 0-333-94819-X ISBN 0-333-94820-3 (pbk.) DDC 305.4201
1. Women in politics. 2. Citizenship. 3. Political obligation. 4. Feminism. I. Campling, Jo. II. Title.
HQ1236 .L57 2003

LISZT, FRANZ, 1811-1886.
Pedroza, Ludim. The ritual of music contemplation. 2002.

LITERACY.
Dyson, Anne Haas. The brothers and sisters learn to write. New York : Teachers College Press, c2003.
LB1139.L3 D97 2003

Precursors of functional literacy. Amsterdam : Philadelphia : J. Benjamins Pub., c2002.
P118.7 .P74 2002

LITERACY - UNITED STATES.
Daniell, Beth, 1947- A communion of friendship. Carbondale : Southern Illinois University Press, c2003.
PE1405.U6 D36 2003

LITERARY AGENTS - FICTION.
Marshall, Evan, 1956- Icing Ivy. Waterville, Me. : Thorndike Press, 2003, c2002.
PS3563.A72236 I27 2003

LITERARY CANON. See **CANON (LITERATURE).**

LITERARY CLASSICS. See **CANON (LITERATURE).**

LITERARY CRITICISM. See **CRITICISM.**

Literary memory, consciousness, and the group Oulipo.
Consenstein, Peter. Amsterdam ; New York, NY : Rodopi, 2002.

LITERARY MOVEMENTS. See **MODERNISM (LITERATURE); POSTMODERNISM (LITERATURE); ROMANTICISM.**

LITERARY PROPERTY. See **COPYRIGHT.**

Literatur und Anthropologie
(Bd. 7) Die Unvermeidlichkeit der Bilder. Tübingen : G. Narr, c2001.
N72.A56 U58 2001x

Literatura e psicanálise.
Villari, Rafael Andrés. Florianópolis : Editora da UFSC, 2002.

LITERATURE. See also **AUTHORS; AUTHORSHIP; CHILDREN'S LITERATURE; CLASSICAL LITERATURE; CREATION (LITERARY, ARTISTIC, ETC.); CRITICISM; DRAMA; FEMINISM AND LITERATURE; FICTION; FIRST PERSON NARRATIVE; FOLK LITERATURE; JOURNALISM; LEGENDS; POETRY; PROSE LITERATURE; PSYCHOANALYSIS AND LITERATURE; SURREALISM (LITERATURE); WIT AND HUMOR; WOMEN AND LITERATURE.**
Osofisan, Femi. Literature and the pressures of freedom. Nigeria : Opon Ifa Readers, 2001.
1. Black author.

Tomás Ferré, Facundo. Formas artísticas y sociedad de masas. Madrid : Antonio Machado Libros, c2001.

Zhou, Xiuping. Wen xue xin shang yu pi ping. Di 1 ban. Changsha : Zhong nan gong ye da xue chu ban she, 1998.
PL2262 .Z468 1998

LITERATURE - AESTHETICS.
Zong, Baihua. Yi jing. Di 2 ban. Beijing : Beijing da xue chu ban she, 1998.
MLCSC 92/01825 (B)

LITERATURE, ANCIENT. See **CLASSICAL LITERATURE.**

LITERATURE AND HISTORY.
Kelley, Donald R., 1931- Fortunes of history. New Haven : Yale University Press, c2003.
D16 .K26 2003

LITERATURE AND HISTORY - GREAT BRITAIN - HISTORY - TO 1500.
Wickham-Crowley, Kelley M. Writing the future. Cardiff : University of Wales Press, 2002.

LITERATURE AND MENTAL ILLNESS.
Ecriture et maladie. Paris : Editions Imago, c2003.

LITERATURE AND MYTH.
Arenas, Fernando, 1963- Utopias of otherness. Minneapolis : University of Minnesota Press, c2003.
DP681 .A74 2003

Literature and philosophy
Singer, Alan, 1948- Aesthetic reason. University Park, Pa. : Pennsylvania State University Press, c2003.
BH91 .S56 2003

LITERATURE AND POLITICS. See **POLITICS AND LITERATURE.**

LITERATURE AND PSYCHOANALYSIS. See **PSYCHOANALYSIS AND LITERATURE.**

LITERATURE AND RELIGION. See **RELIGION AND LITERATURE.**

LITERATURE AND SCIENCE.
Literature, science, psychoanalysis, 1830-1970. Oxford ; New York : Oxford University Press, 2003.
PN55 .L58 2003

LITERATURE AND SOCIETY.
Kunst und Erinnerung. Köln : Böhlau, 2003.
PN674 .K86 2003

LITERATURE AND SOCIETY - ENGLAND - HISTORY - TO 1500.
Heng, Geraldine. Empire of magic. New York : Columbia University Press, c2003.
PR321 .H46 2003

Radulescu, Raluca, 1974- The gentry context for Malory's Morte Darthur. Cambridge [England] ; Rochester, NY : D.S. Brewer, 2003.
PR2047 .R33 2003

LITERATURE AND SOCIETY - UNITED STATES - HISTORY - 18TH CENTURY.
Fichtelberg, Joseph. Critical fictions. Athens : University of Georgia Press, c2003.
PS366.S35 F53 2003

LITERATURE AND SOCIETY - UNITED STATES - HISTORY - 19TH CENTURY.
Fichtelberg, Joseph. Critical fictions. Athens : University of Georgia Press, c2003.
PS366.S35 F53 2003

LITERATURE AND SOCIOLOGY. See **LITERATURE AND SOCIETY.**

LITERATURE AND STATE. See **POLITICS AND LITERATURE.**

Literature and the pressures of freedom

Literature and the pressures of freedom.
Osofisan, Femi. Nigeria : Opon Ifa Readers, 2001.

LITERATURE, CLASSICAL. *See* **CLASSICAL LITERATURE.**

LITERATURE, COMPARATIVE - 19TH CENTURY.
Svobodnyĭ vzgli͡ad na literaturu. Moskva : Nauka, 2002.

LITERATURE, COMPARATIVE - 20TH CENTURY.
Svobodnyĭ vzgli͡ad na literaturu. Moskva : Nauka, 2002.

LITERATURE, COMPARATIVE - CHINESE AND EUROPEAN.
Guo, Yanli. Zhong xi wen hua peng zhuang yu jin dai wen xue = Di 1 ban. Jinan Shi : Shandong jiao yu chu ban she, 1999.
PL2274 .G86 1999

LITERATURE, COMPARATIVE - CHINESE AND TIBETAN.
Bod Rgya rtsom rig gśib bsdur gyi dpyad brjod. Par theṅs 1. Pe-cin : Mi rigs dpe skrun khaṅ, 2001.
PL3705 (P-PZ22)+

LITERATURE, COMPARATIVE - EUROPEAN AND CHINESE.
Guo, Yanli. Zhong xi wen hua peng zhuang yu jin dai wen xue = Di 1 ban. Jinan Shi : Shandong jiao yu chu ban she, 1999.
PL2274 .G86 1999

LITERATURE, COMPARATIVE - HISTORY AND CRITICISM. *See* **LITERATURE, COMPARATIVE.**

LITERATURE, COMPARATIVE - TIBETAN AND CHINESE.
Bod Rgya rtsom rig gśib bsdur gyi dpyad brjod. Par theṅs 1. Pe-cin : Mi rigs dpe skrun khaṅ, 2001.
PL3705 (P-PZ22)+

LITERATURE - EVALUATION. *See* **CRITICISM; LITERATURE - HISTORY AND CRITICISM.**

LITERATURE - HISTORY AND CRITICISM. *See also* **CANON (LITERATURE).**
Hogan, Patrick Colm. Cognitive science, literature, and the arts. New York ; London : Routledge, 2003.
PN56.P93 H64 2003

Lin, Shu, 1852-1924. Tie bi jin zhen. Di 1 ban. Tianjin Shi : Bai hua wen yi chu ban she, 2002.
PL2718.I5 T54 2002

Pagnini, Marcello. Letteratura ed ermeneutica. Firenze : L.S. Olschki, 2002.

Wen xue yin lun. Di 1 ban. Ha'erbin Shi : Heilongjiang jiao yu chu ban she, 1999.

Zhou, Xiuping. Wen xue xin shang yu pi ping. Di 1 ban. Changsha : Zhong nan gong ye da xue chu ban she, 1998.
PL2262 .Z468 1998

LITERATURE - HISTORY AND CRITICISM - THEORY, ETC.
Goux, Jean-Paul. La voix sans repos. Monaco : Rocher, c2003.

Matt, Peter von. Literaturwissenschaft und Psychoanalyse. Stuttgart : Reclam, c2001.

Souza, Eneida Maria de. Crítica cult. Belo Horizonte : Editora UFMG, 2002.
PN94 .S68 2002

LITERATURE, MEDIEVAL.
De Sion exibit lex et verbum domini de Hierusalem. Turnhout, Belgium : Brepols, c2001.

Pleij, Herman. [Dromen van Cocagne. English] Dreaming of Cockaigne. New York : Columbia University Press, c2001.
CB353 .P5413 2001

LITERATURE, MEDIEVAL - HISTORY AND CRITICISM.
Carmona Fernández, Fernando. La mentalidad literaria medieval. 1. ed. Murcia : Universidad de Murcia, Servicio de Publicaciones, 2001.

Kunst und Erinnerung. Köln : Böhlau, 2003.
PN674 .K86 2003

Progrès, réaction, décadence dans l'Occident médiéval. Genève : Droz, 2003.
PN681 .P764 2003

LITERATURE, MEDIEVAL - WOMEN AUTHORS - HISTORY AND CRITICISM.
Gendering the master narrative. Ithaca : Cornell University Press, c2003.

HQ1143 .G46 2003

LITERATURE, MODERN - 15TH AND 16TH CENTURIES. *See* **EUROPEAN LITERATURE - RENAISSANCE, 1450-1600.**

LITERATURE, MODERN - 20TH CENTURY. *See* **POSTMODERNISM (LITERATURE).**

LITERATURE, MODERN - 20TH CENTURY - HISTORY AND CRITICISM.
Guo, Yanli. Zhong xi wen hua peng zhuang yu jin dai wen xue = Di 1 ban. Jinan Shi : Shandong jiao yu chu ban she, 1999.
PL2274 .G86 1999

LITERATURE, MODERN - HISTORY AND CRITICISM.
Berg, Henk de, 1963- Freud's theory and its use in literary and cultural studies. Rochester, NY : Camden House, 2003.
PN56.P92 B36 2003

Ricciardi, Alessia. The ends of mourning. Stanford, Calif. : Stanford University Press, 2003.
PN56.D4 R53 2003

LITERATURE - MORAL AND RELIGIOUS ASPECTS. *See* **RELIGION AND LITERATURE.**

LITERATURE - PHILOSOPHY.
Kurganov, E. Anekdot, simvol, mif. Sankt-Peterburg : Izd-vo zhurnala "Zvezda", 2002.

Przybylak, Feliks. Inskrypcje ulotności. Wrocław : Oficyna Wydawnicza ATUT-Wrocławskie Wydawn. Oświatowe, 2002.
PN56.C69 P79 2002

Royle, Nicholas, 1963- The uncanny. Manchester (UK) ; New York : Manchester University Press, 2003.
PN49 .R75 2002

Solovyov, Vladimir Sergeyevich, 1853-1900. [Essays. English. Selections] The heart of reality. Notre Dame, Ind. : University of Notre Dame Press, c2003.
B4262.A5 W69 2003

LITERATURE - POLITICAL ASPECTS. *See* **POLITICS AND LITERATURE.**

LITERATURE - PSYCHOLOGY. *See* **AESTHETICS.**

LITERATURE, RENAISSANCE. *See* **EUROPEAN LITERATURE - RENAISSANCE, 1450-1600.**

Literature, science, psychoanalysis, 1830-1970 : essays in honour of Gillian Beer / edited by Helen Small and Trudi Tate. Oxford ; New York : Oxford University Press, 2003. vi, 255 p. : ill. ; 24 cm. Includes bibliographical references and index. "Select bibliography of works by Gillian Beer": p. [245]-248. CONTENTS: Darwin's 'Second sun' : Alexander von Humboldt and the genesis of The voyage of the Beagle / Nigel Leask -- 'And if it be a pretty woman all the better' : Darwin and sexual selection / George Levine -- Ordering creation, or maybe not / Harriet Ritvo -- Chances are : Henry Buckle, Thomas Hardy, and the individual at risk / Helen Small -- The psychology of childhood in Victorian literature and medicine / Sally Shuttleworth -- A Freudian curiosity / Rachel Bowlby -- Freud's theory of metaphor : Beyond the pleasure principle : nineteenth-century science and figurative language / Suzanne Raitt -- On not being able to sleep / Jacqueline Rose -- 'Brownie' Sharpe and the stuff of dreams / Mary Jacobus -- On not knowing why : memorializing the Light Brigade / Trudi Tate -- Sounds of the city : Virginia Woolf and modern noise / Kate Flint -- 'Chloe liked Olivia' : the woman scientist, sex, and suffrage / Maroula Joannou -- The chemistry of truth and the literature of dystopia / Alison Winter -- Coming of age / E. F. Keller. ISBN 0-19-926667-0 DDC 820.935609034
1. Beer, Gillian - Bibliography. 2. English literature - 19th century - History and criticism. 3. English literature - 20th century - History and criticism. 4. Literature and science. 5. Psychoanalysis and literature. 6. Science in literature. 7. Psychoanalysis in literature. 8. Science - History - 19th century. 9. Science - History - 20th century. I. Small, Helen. II. Tate, Trudi.
PN55 .L58 2003

LITERATURE - SOCIAL ASPECTS. *See* **LITERATURE AND SOCIETY.**

LITERATURE - TRANSLATING. *See* **TRANSLATING AND INTERPRETING.**

LITERATURE, VICTORIAN. *See* **ENGLISH LITERATURE - 19TH CENTURY.**

LITERATURE - WOMEN AUTHORS. *See* **FEMINISM AND LITERATURE.**

LITERATURES OF THE SOVIET UNION. *See* **SOVIET LITERATURE.**

LiteraturForschung
Genuss und Egoismus. Berlin : Akademie Verlag, c2002.

Literaturovedenie. Kulturologii͡a.
Esin, A. B. (Andreĭ Borisovich) Moskva : Flinta ; Nauka, 2003.

Literaturwissenschaft und Psychoanalyse.
Matt, Peter von. Stuttgart : Reclam, c2001.

Liti wenxue lun.
Li, Tingba. Li ti wen xue lun. Di 1 ban. Beijing : Guang ming ri bao chu ban she : Xin hua shu dian Beijing fa xing suo jing xiao, 1997.
PL2262 .L47 1997 <Asian China>

Litosseliti, Lia.
Gender identity and discourse analysis. Amsterdam : Philadelphia : John Benjamins Pub., c2002.
HQ1075 .G428 2002

LITTERATEURS. *See* **AUTHORS; LITERARY AGENTS.**

Littérature & politique.
Merleau-Ponty, Maurice, 1908-1961. L'institution dans l'histoire personnelle et publique ; [Paris] : Belin, c2003.
B2430.M3763 I88 2003

Michelet, Jules, 1798-1874. La cité des vivants et des morts. [Paris] : Belin, c2002.

Little book of feng shui.
Winnie-the-Pooh's little book of feng shui. London : Methuen Children's, 1999.

Little book of happiness.
Thomson, Emma. 1st ed. London : Hodder Children's, 2001.
BF575.H27 .T56 2001

The little book of hot love spells.
Sophia, 1955- Kansas City, Mo. : Andrews McMeel Pub., c2002.
BF1623.L6 S66 2002

A little book of mirror magick.
Telesco, Patricia, 1960- Berkeley, Calif. : Crossing Press, c2003.
BF1891.M28 T45 2003

The little book of moods.
Eldershaw, Jane. Avon, MA : Adams Media, 2004.
BF637.C5 E383 2004

Little, Daran.
Driver, Betty, 1920- Betty. Large print ed. Long Preston : Magna, 2000.

Little, Graham. The public emotions : from mourning to hope / Graham Little. Sydney : ABC Books for the Australian Broadcasting Corporation, 1999. 289 p. ; 24 cm. Includes index. ISBN 0-7333-0683-7 DDC 152.4
1. Emotions. 2. Loss (Psychology) 3. Conflict (Psychology) I. Australian Broadcasting Corporation. II. Title.
BF531 .L58 1999

Little, Gregory L.
Little, Lora. Secrets of the ancient world. Virginia Beach, Va. : A.R.E. Press, c2003.
BF1045.A74 L58 2003

Little indulgences.
MacGregor, Cynthia. York Beach, ME : Conari Press, 2003.
BF637.C5 M32 2003

Little, Lora. Secrets of the ancient world : exploring the insights of America's most well-documented psychic, Edgar Cayce / by Lora Little, Gregory L. Little, and John Van Auken. Virginia Beach, Va. : A.R.E. Press, c2003. p. cm. ISBN 0-87604-481-X (pbk.) DDC 133.8/092
1. Parapsychology and archaeology. 2. Antiquities - Miscellanea. 3. Bible - Miscellanea. 4. Cayce, Edgar, - 1877-1945. - Edgar Cayce readings. I. Little, Gregory L. II. Van Auken, John. III. Title.
BF1045.A74 L58 2003

The little people.
Philip, Neil. New York ; London : Harry N. Abrams, 2002.

Little, Tom, 1961-.
Greer, Mary K. (Mary Katherine) Understanding the tarot court. 1st ed. St. Paul, Minn. : Llewellyn Publications, 2004.
BF1879.T2 G75 2004

Littman, Jonathan, 1958-.
Sandys, Celia. We shall not fail. New York : Portfolio ; London : Penguin Books, 2003.

DA566.9.C5 S266 2003
Liturgia lunar de la locura.
Pagés Larraya, Fernando. Córdoba, Argentina : Comunicarte Editorial, c2002.

LITURGICAL CANDLES. See **CANDLES AND LIGHTS.**

LITURGICS. See **FASTS AND FEASTS.**

Litvinović, Gorjana. Čovek između istorijskog i ličnog vremena / Gorjana D. Litvinović. Beograd : Institut za psihologiju, 2001. 217 p. : ill. ; 24 cm. (Psihološke monografije ; 7) In Serbian (Roman). Includes bibliographical references (p. 189-197).
1. Identity (Psychology) 2. Group identity. 3. Perception - Cross-cultural studies. 4. Time perception - Cross-cultural studies. I. Title. II. Series.
BF697 .L543 2001

Liu, Ling.
Shi, Zhecun. Beishan si chuang. Di 1 ban. Shanghai : Shanghai wen yi chu ban she : Xin hua shu dian jing xiao, 2000.
PL2272.5 .S543 2000

Liu, Lydia He.
Writing and materiality in China. Cambridge, Mass. : Published by Harvard University Asia Center for Harvard-Yenching Institute : distributed by Harvard University Press, 2003.
PL2262 .W74 2003

Liu, Peiping. She hui mao dun yu jin dai Zhongguo / Liu Peiping zhu. Di 1 ban. Jinan Shi : Shandong jiao yu chu ban she, 2000. 3, 22, 441 p. ; 22 cm. Cover title: Shehui maodun yu jindai Zhongguo. Includes bibliographical references. ISBN 7-5328-3246-5
1. Social conflict - China - History - 20th century. 2. Social conflict. I. Title. II. Title: Shehui maodun yu jindai Zhongguo
HN733 .L569 2000

Liu, Shi, 1963-.
Yan, Zhitui, 531-591. Yan shi jia xun zhu ping. Di 1 ban. Beijing Shi : Xue yuan chu ban she, 2000.
BJ117 .Y4 2000

Liu, Shuxian, 1934- Li yi fen shu / Liu Shuxian. Di 1 ban. Shanghai : Shanghai wen yi chu ban she, 2000. 6, 2, 382 p., [2] leaves of plates : col. ports. ; 21 cm. (Xue yuan ying hua) Cover title also in pinyin: Liyi fenshu. ISBN 7-5321-2002-3
1. Philosophy. 2. Philosophy, Chinese. I. Title. II. Title: Liyi fenshu III. Series.
B29 .L68 2000

Liu, Si.
Hobfoll, Stevan E. [Work won't love you back. Chinese] Top shuang xin jia ting. Chu ban. Taibei Shi : Ye qiang chu ban she, 1997.

Liu, Yanjie.
Yan, Zhitui, 531-591. Yan shi jia xun zhu ping. Di 1 ban. Beijing Shi : Xue yuan chu ban she, 2000.
BJ117 .Y4 2000

Liu, Yinsheng.
He, Bingsong, 1890-1946. [Works. 1996] He Bingsong wen ji. Di 1 ban. Beijing : Shang wu yin shu guan, 1996.
DS734.7 .H664

Liu, Zaifu, 1941- Shu yuan si xu : Liu Zaifu xue shu si xiang jing cui / Liu Zaifu zhu ; Yang Chunshi bian. Xianggang : Tian di tu shu you xian gong si, 2002. 452 p. ; 21 cm. ISBN 9629937190
1. Chinese literature - History and criticism. I. Yang, Chunshi, 1948- II. Title. III. Title: Liu Zaifu xue shu si xiang jing cui.
PL2879.T653 S58 2002

Liu Zaifu xue shu si xiang jing cui.
Liu, Zaifu, 1941- Shu yuan si xu. Xianggang : Tian di tu shu you xian gong si, 2002.
PL2879.T653 S58 2002

Lĭubov' i seksual'nost' v kul'ture, sem'e i vzgli͡adakh na polovoe vospitanie.
Rozin, V. M. Moskva : Logos : Vysshai͡a shkola, 1999.
BF575.L8 R69 1999

Live questions in ethics and moral philosophy
Archard, David. Children, family, and the state. Aldershot, Hants, England ; Burlington, VT : Ashgate, 2003.
HQ789 .A695 2003

LIVE STOCK. See **LIVESTOCK.**

Live the James Bone lifestyle.
Kyriazi, Paul. The complete live the James Bond lifestyle seminar. Los Angeles, CA : Ronin Books, c2002.

BF637.S8 K97 2002
The lively shadow.
Murray, Donald Morison, 1924- 1st ed. New York : Ballantine Books, 2003.
BF575.G7 M868 2003

Lives in translation : bilingual writers on identity and creativity / edited by Isabelle de Courtivron. 1st ed. New York ; Houndmills, England : Palgrave Macmillan, 2003. 171 p. ; 22 cm. Includes bibliographical references. ISBN 1403960666 (alk. paper) DDC 306.44/6/019
1. Bilingual authors. 2. Bilingualism - Psychological aspects. 3. Identity (Psychology) 4. Creativity in literature. I. De Courtivron, Isabelle.
P115.25 .L58 2003

LIVESTOCK. See **HORSES.**

LIVESTOCK - GERMPLASM RESOURCES - PATENTS.
Intellectual property rights in animal breeding and genetics. Wallingford ; New York : CABI, c2002.

Living beyond loss : death in the family / edited by Froma Walsh, Monica McGoldrick. 2nd ed. New York : W.W. Norton, 2004. p. cm. "A Norton professional book." Includes bibliographical references and index. ISBN 0-393-70438-6 (pbk.) DDC 306.9
1. Loss (Psychology) 2. Death - Psychological aspects. 3. Bereavement - Psychological aspects. I. Walsh, Froma. II. McGoldrick, Monica.
BF575.D35 L54 2004

Living from the inside out.
Hamel, Jean-Marie. 1st ed. New York : Harmony Books, 2004.
BF637.S4 H34 2004

LIVING LANGUAGES. See **LANGUAGES, MODERN.**

Living victims, stolen lives.
Stetson, Brad. Amityville, N.Y. : Baywood Pub., c2003.
HV6533.C2 S73 2003

Living with grief
Coping with public tragedy. Washington, DC : Hospice Foundation of America ; New York : Brunner-Routledge, c2003.
BF789.D5 C67 2003

Living with his camera.
Gallop, Jane, 1952- Durham : Duke University Press, 2003.
TR140.B517 G35 2003

Living with suicide [electronic resource] : shared experiences and voices of loss. [Alexandria, Va.] : PBS Online ; [New York, N.Y.] : Web Lab Began in 1998? Mode of access: World Wide Web. Title from home page (viewed on Nov. 5, 2003). SUMMARY: Presents an open discussion of surviving a loved one's suicide. Created to help persons be free of the stigma and silence surrounding those who must cope. URL: http://www.pbs.org/cgi-bin/weblab/living/discuss.cgi
1. Death - Psychological aspects. 2. Suicide. I. PBS Online. II. Web Lab (Firm) III. Title: Shared experiences and voices of loss
BF789.D4

Livingston, Paisley, 1951-.
The creation of art. New York, NY : Cambridge University Press, 2003.
N71 .C754 2003

Livingstone, Margaret. Vision and art : the biology of seeing / by Margaret Livingstone ; foreword by David Hubel. New York, N.Y. : Harry N. Abrams, c2002. 208 p. : col. ill. ; 29 cm. Includes bibliographical references (p. 204) and index. CONTENTS: 1 Fiat lux: let there be light -- 2 The eye and color vision -- 3 Luminance and night vision -- 4 The first stages of processing color and luminance: where and what -- 5 Acuity and spatial resolution: central and peripheral vision -- 6 The next level of color processing: surround effects -- 7 From 3-D to 2-D: perspective -- 8 From 3-D to 2-D: shading and chiaroscuro -- 9 From 3-D to 2-D: stereopsis -- 10 Illusions of motion -- 11 Color mixing and color resolution -- 12 Television, movies, and computer graphics -- Epilogue -- Talent, music and learning disabilities -- Further reading -- Index -- Credits. ISBN 0-8109-0406-3 DDC 750.1/8
1. Visual perception. 2. Color vision. 3. Painting - Psychology. I. Title.
N7430.5 .L54 2002

Liyi fenshu.
Liu, Shuxian, 1934- Li yi fen shu. Di 1 ban. Shanghai : Shanghai wen yi chu ban she, 2000.
B29 .L68 2000

Llewellyn, A. Bronwyn (Anita Bronwyn) Shakespeare oracle : let the bard predict your future / A. Bronwyn Llewellyn. Gloucester, Mass. : Fair Winds Press,

2003. p. cm. Table of contents URL: http://www.loc.gov/catdir/toc/ecip048/2003018407.html ISBN 1-59233-016-9 DDC 133.3/2424
1. Tarot. 2. Divination. 3. Shakespeare, William, - 1564-1616. I. Title.
BF1879.T2 L59 2003

Llewellyn, Jack H. Coming in first : twelve keys to being a winner every day / Jack H. Llewellyn with J. Donald McKee. Atlanta : Longstreet Press, c2000. 227 p. ; 22 cm. Table of contents URL: http://www.loc.gov/catdir/toc/fy041/00105068.html ISBN 1-56352-630-1 (hardcover : alk. paper) DDC 158.1
1. Success - Psychological aspects. I. McKee, J. Donald. II. Title.
BF637.S8 L56 2000

Llewellyn, Ralph A.
Tipler, Paul Allen, 1933- Modern physics. 4th ed. New York : W.H. Freeman, 2002 printing, c2003.
QC21.3 .T56 2003

Llewellyn's aurum solis series
Denning, Melita. Mysteria magica. 3rd ed. St. Paul, Minn. : Llewellyn Publications, 2004.
BF1611 .D395 2004

Llewellyn's vanguard series
Thorsson, Edred. The truth about Teutonic magick. 2nd ed. Saint Paul, MN : Llewellyn Publications, 1994.
BF1622.G3 T488 1994

Llewellyn's world religion & magic series.
Buckland, Raymond. Witchcraft from the inside. Rev. and enl. 3rd ed. St. Paul, Minn., U.S.A. : Llewellyn Publications, 1995 (2001 printing)
BF1566 .B77 1995

Llibres a l'abast
(368) Gray, John, 1948- [Men are from Mars, women are from Venus. Spanish] Els homes són de Mart, les dones són de Venus. 1. ed. Barcelona : Edicions 62, c2001.

LLILAS Translations from Latin America series
Souza, Laura de Mello e. [Diabo e a Terra de Santa Cruz. English] The Devil and the land of the holy cross. 1st University of Texas Press ed. Austin : University of Texas Press : Teresa Lozano Long Institute of Latin American Studies, 2003.
BF1584.B7 S6813 2003

Lloyd, G. E. R. (Geoffrey Ernest Richard), 1933- In the grip of disease : studies in the Greek imagination / G.E.R. Lloyd. Oxford ; New York : Oxford University Press, 2003. xxi, 258 p. ; 23 cm. Includes bibliographical references (p. [247]-252) and index. Text in English with some Greek. ISBN 0-19-925323-4 DDC 610.938
1. Philosophy, Ancient. 2. Medicine, Greek and Roman. 3. Medicine, Ancient. 4. Medicine - Greece - History. 5. Medicine in literature. I. Title.
B187.M4 L56 2003

Lloyd, Scott.
Blake, Steve. Pendragon. London : Rider, 2002.

LLULL, RAMON, 1232?-1316.
Vega, Amador. Ramon Llull y el secreto de la vida. Madrid : Siruela, 2002.

LOATHING. See **AVERSION.**

Lobkowicz, Nikolaus. Czas kryzysu, czas przełomu / Nikolaus Lobkowicz ; przełożył, Grezegorz Sowinski. Kraków : Wydawnictwo WAM : Znak, 1996. 185 p. ; 20 cm. (Beiträge zur politischen Wissenschaft, 0582-0421 ; Bd. 89) Includes bibliographical references and index. ISBN 83-7097-261-6 ISBN 83-7006-412-4
1. Philosophy, Modern - 20th century. I. Title. II. Series.

Eine Lobrede für Politiker.
Palonen, Kari, 1947- Opladen : Leske + Budrich, 2002.
JF2051.W43 J35 2002

LOCAL GOVERNMENT. See **PUBLIC ADMINISTRATION.**

LOCAL TELEPHONE SERVICE - RATES - UNITED STATES.
United States. General Accounting Office. Telecommunications [electronic resource]. Washington, D.C. : U.S. General Accounting Office, [2002]

LOCALITIES, HAUNTED. See **HAUNTED PLACES.**

Loch, Wolfgang. "Mit Freud über Freud hinaus" : ausgewählte Vorlesungen zur Psychoanalyse / Wolfgang Loch ; bearbeitet und herausgegeben von Josef Dantlgraber und Werner Damson. Tübingen : Edition Diskord, c2001. 143 p. : ill., port. ; 22 cm. University lectures delivered over two semesters, summer 1974

Locke, Hubert G.
and winter 1974/75. Includes bibliographical references. ISBN 3-89295-707-X
1. Psychoanalysis. 2. Lectures. 3. Psychoanalysis. I. Dantlgraber, Josef. II. Damson, Werner. III. Title.
BF173 .L554 2001

Locke, Hubert G. Searching for God in godforsaken times and places : reflections on the Holocaust, racism, and death / Hubert G. Locke. Grand Rapids, Mich. : W.B. Eerdmans Pub., c2003. x, 109 p. ; 24 cm. Includes bibliographical references. ISBN 0-8028-6084-2 (pbk. : alk. paper) DDC 231.7/6
1. Locke, Hubert G. 2. Faith. 3. Holocaust (Christian theology) 4. Death - Religious aspects - Christianity. 5. Racism - Religious aspects - Christianity. 6. Black author. I. Title.
BT774 .L63 2003

LOCKE, HUBERT G.
Locke, Hubert G. Searching for God in godforsaken times and places. Grand Rapids, Mich. : W.B. Eerdmans Pub., c2003.
BT774 .L63 2003
1. Black author.

LOCOMOTION. See **BIPEDALISM.**

LODÈVE (FRANCE) - CHURCH HISTORY.
Alzieu, Gérard. Les églises de l'ancien diocèse de Lodève au Moyen-Age. Montpellier : Editions P. Clerc, 1998.
BX1532.L63 A695 1998

Loewe, Carl, 1796-1869.
 Lieder, op. 145. Meeresleuchten.
Hann, Georg. Georg Hann [sound recording]. [Germany] : Preiser Records, p2001.

 Odins Meeresritt.
Hann, Georg. Georg Hann [sound recording]. [Germany] : Preiser Records, p2001.

Loewenthal, Del, 1947- Post-modernism for psychotherapists : a critical reader / Del Loewenthal and Robert Snell. Hove, East Sussex ; New York : Brunner-Routledge, 2003. p. cm. Includes bibliographical references. ISBN 1-58391-100-6 ISBN 1-58391-101-4 (pbk.) DDC 149l.97/02415
1. Psychology and philosophy. 2. Psychology - Philosophy. 3. Postmodernism. I. Snell, Robert, 1951- II. Title.
BF41 .L64 2003

Löffelmann, Markus. Das Urteil : Grundlegung einer Philosophie des entgrenzten Denkens im Endlichen / Markus Löffelmann. Würzburg : Königshausen & Neumann, c2002. 195 p. ; 24 cm. Includes bibliographical references and index. ISBN 3-8260-2139-8 (pbk.)
1. Judgment (Logic) 2. Judgment (Ethics) 3. Reasoning. I. Title.
BC181 .L64 2002

LOGIC. See also **CATEGORIES (PHILOSOPHY); COMPREHENSION (THEORY OF KNOWLEDGE); CONDITIONALS (LOGIC); FALLACIES (LOGIC); INDUCTION (LOGIC); JUDGMENT (LOGIC); MODALITY (LOGIC); REASONING; SIGNIFICATION (LOGIC); THOUGHT AND THINKING.**
Husserl's Logical investigations reconsidered. Dordrecht ; Boston : Kluwer Academic Publishers, c2003.
B3279.H93 L64346 2003

Le leggi del pensiero tra logica, ontologia e psicologia. Milano : UNICOPLI, 2002.

Li, Tianming, 1945- Li Tianming di si kao yi shu. Beijing di 1 ban. Beijing : Sheng huo, du shu, xin zhi san lian shu dian, 1996.

Rosental, Claude. La trame de l'évidence. 1 éd. Paris : Presses universitaires de France, c2003.

LOGIC AND FAITH. See **FAITH AND REASON.**

LOGIC, DEDUCTIVE. See **LOGIC.**

LOGIC - HISTORY.
Salamucha, Jan. [Selections. English. 2003] Knowledge and faith. Amsterdam ; New York, NY : Rodopi, 2003.

LOGIC, INDUCTIVE. See **INDUCTION (LOGIC).**

LOGIC MACHINES. See **ARTIFICIAL INTELLIGENCE.**

The logic of democratic exclusion.
Kook, Rebecca B., 1959- Lanham, Md. : Lexington Books, c2002.
E185.615 .K59 2002

LOGIC, SYMBOLIC AND MATHEMATICAL. See also **SEMANTICS (PHILOSOPHY).**
Ludwig Wittgenstein, Tractatus logico-philosophicus. Berlin : Akademie Verlag, 2001.

LOGIC, SYMBOLIC AND MATHEMATICAL - HISTORY - 20TH CENTURY.
Jadacki, Jacek Juliusz. From the viewpoint of the Lvov-Warsaw school. Amsterdam ; New York, NY : Rodopi, 2003.

LOGIC, UNIVERSAL. See **LOGIC, SYMBOLIC AND MATHEMATICAL.**

LOGICAL ANALYSIS. See **ANALYSIS (PHILOSOPHY).**

LOGICAL POSITIVISM. See **ANALYSIS (PHILOSOPHY); SEMANTICS (PHILOSOPHY).**

Logical processes in humans and computers.
Wagman, Morton. Westport, Conn. : Praeger, 2003.
BF311 .W26566 2003

LOGICAL SEMANTICS. See **SEMANTICS (PHILOSOPHY).**

Logik und Leidenschaft : Erträge historischer Anthropologie / Christoph Wulf, Dietmar Kamper (Hg.). Berlin : D. Reimer Verlag, c2002. 1129 p. : ill. ; 24 cm. (Reihe Historische Anthropologie ; Sonderband) Includes bibliographical references. ISBN 3-496-02739-8 (pbk.)
1. Kamper, Dietmar, - 1936- 2. Faith and reason. 3. Anthropology - Moral and ethical aspects. 4. Emotions. I. Wulf, Christoph, 1944- II. Kamper, Dietmar, 1936- III. Series.

La logique de l'éternité.
Vallier, Gilles-Félix. 1998.

Logiques sociales.
Amougou, Emmanuel. La construction de l'inconscient colonial en Alsace. Paris : L'Harmattan, 2002.

La Branche, Stéphane. Mondialisation et terrorisme identitaire, ou, Comment l'Occident tente de transformer le monde. Paris : Harmattan, c2003.
JC330 .L2 2003

Namer, Gérard. Halbwachs et la mémoire sociale. Paris : L'Harmattan, c2000.
BF378.S65 N36 2000

Logiques sociales. Sociologie de la connaissance.
La connaissance sociologique. Paris : Harmattan, c2002.
HM651 .C65 2002

LOGOTHERAPY.
Frankl, Viktor Emil. Man's search for ultimate meaning. Cambridge, Mass. : Perseus Pub., c2000.
RC455.4.R4 F7 2000

LOḤAME ḤERUT YIŚRA'EL.
Oron, Israel. Mavet, almavet ye-ide'ologyah. [Israel] : Miśrad ha-biṭaḥon, [2002]

Lohman, David F. Cognitive Abilities Test, form 6, all levels / David F. Lohman, Elizabeth Hagen. Chicago (8420 Bryn Mawr, Chicago 60631) : Riverside Pub., c2001. 128 p. : ill. ; 28 cm. Cover title. Chiefly tables. "Norms booklet"--Cover. DDC 153.9/3
1. Cognitive Abilities Test - Scoring - Statistics. I. Hagen, Elizabeth P., 1915- II. Title.
BF432.5.C64 L64 2001

Interpretive guide for teachers and counselors : form 6 / David F. Lohman, Elizabeth P. Hagen. Itasca, IL : Riverside Pub., c2001. 166 p. : ill. ; 28 cm. Spine title: Cognitive Abilities Test interpretive guide. At head of title: CogAT. Includes bibliographical references (p. 161-166). DDC 153.9/3
1. Cognitive Abilities Test. I. Hagen, Elizabeth P., 1915- II. Title. III. Title: Cognitive Abilities Test interpretive guide
BF432.5.C64 L65 2001

Lohr, Charles H.
Ammonius, Hermiae. Commentaria in quinque voces Porphyrii. Stuttgart : Frommann-Holzboog, 2002.

Lomaśa, Maharṣi.
 [Lomaśa saṃhitā. Hindi & Sanskrit]
Lomaśa saṃhitā / sampādaka evaṃ ṭīkākāra Girijāśaṅkara Śāstrī. Saṃskaraṇa 1. Ilāhābāda : Hindī Sāhitya Sammelana, Prayāga, 2002. 188 p. ; 22 cm. Hindi and Sanskrit. SUMMARY: On Hindu astrology; text with Hindi interpretation.
1. Hindu astrology. I. Śāstrī, Girijā Śaṅkara. II. Title.
BF1714.H5+

Lomaśa saṃhitā.
Lomaśa, Maharṣi. [Lomaśa saṃhitā. Hindi & Sanskrit] Saṃskaraṇa 1. Ilāhābāda : Hindī Sāhitya Sammelana, Prayāga, 2002.
BF1714.H5+

Lomax, J. Harvey, 1948- The paradox of philosphical education : Nietzsche's new nobility and the eternal recurrence in Beyond good and evil / J. Harvey Lomax. Lanham, Md. ; Oxford : Lexington Books, c2003. xiii, 133 p. ; 24 cm. (Applications of political theory) Includes bibliographical references and index. ISBN 0-7391-0476-4 (hbk. : alk. paper) ISBN 0-7391-0477-2 (pbk. : alk. paper) DDC 193
1. Nietzsche, Friedrich Wilhelm, - 1844-1900. - Jenseits von Gut und Bose. 2. Ethics. 3. Nobility. 4. Eternal return. I. Title. II. Series.
B3313.J43 L66 2003

Lombard, René-André. Le nom de l'Europe : souvenir d'un cérémonial millénaire : essai d'archéologie mythique / René-André Lombard. Grenoble : Thot, c2001. 300 p. : ill. ; 21 cm. (Collection Expert) Includes bibliographical references. ISBN 2-911786-42-4 DDC 290
1. Europa (Greek mythology) 2. Bulls - Mythology. 3. Mythology. I. Title.

Lomber, Stephen G.
Virtual lesions. Oxford ; New York : Oxford University Press, c2002.
RC350.B72 V57 2002

London, Herbert Ira.
Riding the next wave. Indianapolis, Ind. : Hudson Institute ; [Washington, DC : Distributed by the Brookings Institution Press], c2001.
HM901 .R43 2001

LONELINESS IN ADOLESCENCE.
Dołęga, Zofia. Samotność młodzieży. Wyd. 1. Katowice : Wydawn. Uniwersytetu Śląskiego, 2003.
BF724.3.L64 D65 2003

LONELINESS - NEPAL.
Diyara Kalyāṇa, mero kathā mero gīta. 1. saṃskaraṇa. [Kathmandu] : Sañjanā Gautama, 2059- [2002-
BF789.S8+

LONERGAN, BERNARD J. F.
McLaughlin, Michael T. Knowledge, consciousness and religious conversion in Lonergan and Aurobindo. Roma : Editrice Pontificia Universita Gregoriana, 2003.

LONG, CHARLES H.
Religion and global culture. Lanham, MD ; Oxford : Lexington Books, c2003.
BL65.C8 R444 2003

The long road of woman's memory.
Addams, Jane, 1860-1935. Urbana : University of Illinois Press, 2002.
HQ1206 .A25 2002

Long walk to school.
Leaney, Cindy. Vero Beach, Fla. : Rourke Pub., 2003.
BF637.B85 L43 2003

A long way east of Eden.
Lowman, Pete. Carlisle : Paternoster, 2002.

A long way from home.
Brokaw, Tom. 1st trade ed. New York : Random House, c2002.
PN4874.B717 A3 2002b

Long, William J., 1956- War and reconciliation : reason and emotion in conflict resolution / William J. Long and Peter Brecke. Cambridge, Mass. : MIT Press, c2003. x, 235 p. : ill. ; 24 cm. Includes bibliographical references (p. [199]-217) and index. ISBN 0-262-12254-5 ISBN 0-262-62168-1 (pbk.) DDC 303.6/9
1. Reconciliation. 2. Peace. 3. Civil war. 4. War (International law) I. Brecke, Peter. II. Title.
JZ5597 .L66 2003

Longacre, Celeste B. Love signs / Celeste B. Longacre. 1st ed. Walpole, NH : Sweet Fern Publications, 2000. 360 p. : ill. ; 23 cm. ISBN 0-930043-13-8
1. Astrology. 2. Love - Miscellanea. I. Title.
BF1729.L6 L66 2000

LONGEVITY. See also **AGING; OLD AGE.**
Overall, Christine, 1949- Aging, death, and human longevity. Berkeley : University of California Press, c2003.
RA564.8 .O95 2003

Longhin, Luigi.
Sentieri della mente. 1. ed. Torino : Bollati Boringhieri, 2001.

LONGING. See **DESIRE.**

Longing to tell : Black women talk about sexuality and intimacy / [compiled by] Tricia Rose. 1st ed. New York : Farrar, Straus and Giroux, 2003. xii, 415 p. ; 24 cm. Includes bibliographical references (p. [401]-404) and index. Publisher description URL: http://www.loc.gov/catdir/description/hol031/2002032541.html ISBN 0-374-19061-5 (alk. paper) DDC 306.7/089/96073
1. African American women - Psychology. 2. African American women - Sexual behavior. 3. African American women - Interviews. 4. Intimacy (Psychology) 5. Love - United States. 6.

Interpersonal relations - United States. 7. Sex role - United States. 8. Racism - United States - Psychological aspects. 9. United States - Race relations - Psychological aspects. I. Rose, Tricia.
E185.625 .L66 2003

LONGITUDINAL STUDIES.
Dobkin de Rios, Marlene. LSD, spirituality, and the creative process. Rochester, Vt. : Park Street Press, c2003.
BF209.L9 D57 2003

Longobardi, Claudio.
Il "valore" del padre. Torino : UTET libreria, 2001.
BF723.P25 V35 2001

Longstaff, Bill, 1934- Confessions of a matriarchist : rebuilding society on feminine principles / Bill Longstaff. Calgary : Ballot Pub., 2003. 225 p. ; 23 cm. Includes bibliographical references and index. ISBN 0-9689029-1-X DDC 305.42
1. Matriarchy. 2. Social evolution. 3. Sex role. 4. Feminism. I. Title. II. Title: Rebuilding society on feminine principles

Lonnet, Antoine.
Mélanges David Cohen. Paris : Maisonneuve et Larose, 2003.

Look me in the eye.
Macdonald, Barbara, 1913- New, expanded ed. Denver, CO : Spinsters Ink Books, 2001.

Looking at the other : historical study of images in theory and practise / Kari Alenius, Olavi K. Fält & Seija Jalagin (eds.). Oulu, Finland : University of Oulu, 2002. 130 p. ; 25 cm. Mode of access: World Wide Web. Includes bibliographical references. ISBN 951-42-6632-3
1. Public opinion. 2. Attitude (Psychology) I. Alenius, Kari. II. Fält, Olavi K. III. Jalagin, Seija. IV. Series: Acta Universitatis Ouluensis. Series B, Humaniora ; no. 42.

Looking beyond.
Van Praagh, James. New York : Simon & Schuster, c2003.
BF1272 .V36 2003

Looking into pictures : an interdisciplinary approach to pictorial space / edited by Heiko Hecht, Robert Schwartz, Margaret Atherton. Cambridge, Mass. : MIT Press, c2003. xviii, 417 p., [4] p. of plates : ill. (some col.) ; 24 cm. "A Bradford book." Includes bibliographical references (p. [379]-403) and index. CONTENTS: Pt. 1. The dual nature of picture perception. In defense of seeing-in / Richard Wollheim ; Conjoint representations and the mental capacity for multiple simultaneous perspectives / Rainer Mausfeld ; Relating direct and indirect perception of spatial layout / H.A. Sedgwick ; The dual nature of picture perception: a challenge to current general accounts of visual perception / Reinhard Niederée and Dieter Heyer ; Perceptual strategies and pictorial content / Mark Rollins -- Pt. 2. The status of perspective. Optical laws or symbolic rules? the dual nature of pictorial systems / John Willats ; Perspective, convention, and compromise / Robert Hopkins ; Resemblance reconceived / Klaus Sachs-Hombach ; What you see is what you get: the problems of linear perspective / Klaus Rehkämper ; Pictures of perspective: theory or therapy? / Patrick Maynard -- Pt. 3. The nature and structure of reconceived pictorial space. Reconceiving perceptual space / James E. Cutting ; Pictorial space / Jan J. Koenderink and Andrea J. van Doorn ; Truth and meaning in pictorial space / Sheena Rogers ; Line and borders of surfaces: grouping and foreshortening / John M. Kennedy, Igor Juricevic, and Juan Bai ; Irreconcilable views / Hermann Kalkofen. ISBN 0-262-08310-8 (alk. paper) DDC 152.14
1. Picture perception - Congresses. 2. Perspective - Congresses. 3. Picture interpretation - Congresses. I. Hecht, Heiko. II. Schwartz, Robert, 1940- III. Atherton, Margaret.
BF243 .L66 2003

Lööw, Heléne.
The cultic milieu. Walnut Creek : AltaMira Press, c2002.
BP603 .C835 2002

Lopes, Dominic.
Imagination, philosophy, and the arts. London ; New York : Routledge, 2003.
BH301.I53 I53 2003

López, Carmen Adela, 1935- Madres e hijas : historia en tiempo de mujeres / Carmen Adela López. Caracas, Venezuela : Vadell Hermanos, 2002. 301 p. ; 22 cm. ISBN 980-212-320-X
1. Mothers and daughters. 2. Women - Psychology. 3. Motherhood - Psychological aspects. I. Title. II. Title: Historia en tiempo de mujeres

López Chávez, Carlos.
Acuerdos de paz y seguridad democrática en Guatemala. 1. ed. [Guatemala] : USAC, DIGI, [2002]

López-Coño, Dagoberto.
La palabra como cuerpo del delito. Santo Domingo, República Dominicana : Biblioteca Nacional "Dr. Pedro Henríquez Ureña", 2001.

López Díaz, Yolanda. Por qué se maltrata al más íntimo? : una perspectiva psicoanalítica del maltrato infantil / Yolanda Lopez Diaz. 1. ed. [Bogota] : Universidad Nacional de Colombia, Sede Bogota, 2002. 142 p. ; 24 cm. (Colección Sede) Includes bibliographical references. ISBN 958-701-137-6
1. Child abuse. 2. Psychoanalysis. I. Title. II. Series.

Lopez, Shane J.
Internships in psychology. Washington, D.C. : American Psychological Association, c2004.
BF77 .I67 2004

Loranger, Armand W. (Armand Walter), 1930- OMNI personality inventories : professional manual : OMNI personality inventory OMNI-IV personality disorder inventory / Armand W. Loranger. Lutz, FL : Psychological Assessment Resources, c2001. vi, 75 p. ; 28 cm. Includes bibliographical references (p. 59-61). DDC 155.2/83
1. OMNI Personality Inventory. 2. OMNI-IV Personality Disorder Inventory. I. Title.
BF698.8.O46 L67 2001

Lord Dunmore's little war of 1774.
Skidmore, Warren. Bowie, Md. : Heritage Books, 2002.

LORD DUNMORE'S WAR, 1774.
Skidmore, Warren. Lord Dunmore's little war of 1774. Bowie, Md. : Heritage Books, 2002.

LORD DUNMORE'S WAR, 1774 - REGISTERS.
Skidmore, Warren. Lord Dunmore's little war of 1774. Bowie, Md. : Heritage Books, 2002.

Lord, Robert G. (Robert George), 1946- Leadership processes and follower self-identity / Robert G. Lord, Douglas J. Brown. Mahwah, N.J. ; London : Lawrence Erlbaum, 2004. xiii, 248 p. : ill. ; 24 cm. (LEA's organization and management series) Includes bibliographical references (p. 218-236) and indexes. ISBN 0-8058-3892-9 (alk. paper) DDC 158/.4
1. Leadership - Psychological aspects. 2. Self-perception. 3. Identity (Psychology) I. Brown, Douglas J. II. Title. III. Series: LEA series in organization and management.
HM1261 .L67 2004

Lords of creation.
Cook, Margaret, 1944- London : Robson, 2002.

Lorenzi-Cioldi, Fabio, 1955- Les représentations des groupes dominants et dominés : collections et agrégats / Fabio Lorenzi-Cioldi. Grenoble : Presses universitaires de Grenoble, c2002. 360 p. ; 21 cm. (Vies sociales, 0986-4547) Includes bibliographical references (p. 311-357). ISBN 2-7061-1047-3
1. Social groups. 2. Dominance (Psychology) 3. Group identity. I. Title. II. Series.
HM716 .L674 2002

Loriga, Vincenzo.
A che servono i simboli? Milano : FrancoAngeli, c2002.

Lortzing, Albert, 1801-1851.
Wildschutz. Funftausend Taler.
Hann, Georg. Georg Hann [sound recording]. [Germany] : Preiser Records, p2001.

Wildschutz Ich habe Numero Eins.
Hann, Georg. Georg Hann [sound recording]. [Germany] : Preiser Records, p2001.

Wildschutz. Lass Er doch horen.
Hann, Georg. Georg Hann [sound recording]. [Germany] : Preiser Records, p2001.

Zar und Zimmermann. Hohen Herrscher wurdig zu empfangen.
Hann, Georg. Georg Hann [sound recording]. [Germany] : Preiser Records, p2001.

Zar und Zimmermann. O sancta justitia, ich mochte rasen.
Hann, Georg. Georg Hann [sound recording]. [Germany] : Preiser Records, p2001.

LOSING (PSYCHOLOGY). See **FAILURE (PSYCHOLOGY).**

Losquadro-Liddle, Tara. Why motor skills matter : improve your child's physical development to enhance learning and self-esteem / Tara Losquadro-Liddle with Laura Yorke. Chicago : Contemporary Books, c2004. xxvii, 206 p. : ill. ; 23 cm. Includes bibliographical references (p. 191-193) and index. Publisher description URL: http://www.loc.gov/catdir/description/mh031/2003046108.html ISBN 0-07-140818-5 (acid-free paper) DDC 155.4/123
1. Motor ability in children. 2. Cognition in children. 3. Self-esteem in children. I. Yorke, Laura. II. Title.

BF723.M6 L67 2004
The loss of a life partner.
Walter, Carolyn Ambler. New York : Columbia University Press, c2003.
BF575.G7 W3435 2003

LOSS OF LOVED ONE BY SEPARATION. See **SEPARATION (PSYCHOLOGY).**

LOSS OF LOVED ONES BY DEATH. See **BEREAVEMENT.**

LOSS (PSYCHOLOGY). See also **BEREAVEMENT; GRIEF; SEPARATION (PSYCHOLOGY).**
Anderson, Susan, C.S.W. The journey from heartbreak to connection. Berkley trade pbk. ed. New York : Berkley Books, 2003.
BF575.R35 A533 2003

Andrews, John, 1966- For all those left behind. Edinburgh : Mainstream Pub., c2002.
BF789.D4 A55 2002

Beem, Ellen Evaline, 1957- Bereavement. [Leiden : Universiteit Leiden, 2000]
BF575.G7 B422 2000

Cornils, Stanley P. Your healing journey through grief. San Francisco, CA : Robert D. Reed Publishers, c2003.
BF575.G7 C677 2003

Daher, Douglas, 1949- And the passenger was death. Amityville, N.Y. : Baywood Pub., c2003.
BF575.G7 D34 2003

Davenport, Donna S. Singing mother home. Denton, Tex. : University of North Texas Press, c2002.
BF575.G7 D365 2002

Dennison, Amy. Our dad died. Minneapolis, MN : Free Spirit Pub., c2003.
BF723.G75 D46 2003

Feldbaum, Rebecca Bram. If there's anything I can do--. Jerusalem, Israel ; Nanuet, NY : Feldheim Publishers, 2003.
BF575.G7 F46 2003

Hjelmstad, Lois Tschetter. The last violet. Englewood, Colo. : Mulberry Hill Press, c2002.
BF575.G7 H575 2002

Isaacs, Diane R. Molly & Monet. Seattle, WA : Peanut Butter Pub., c1999.
BF575.G7 I86 1999

Johnson, Marvin. Where's Jess? Rev. Omaha, NE : Centering Corp. Resource, 2003.
BF723.G75 J645 2003

Kaufman, Barry Neil. No regrets. Novato, Calif. : HJ Kramer/New World Library, 2003.
BF575.G7 K385 2003

Kuebelbeck, Amy, 1964- Waiting with Gabriel. Chicago, Ill. : Loyola Press, c2003.
BF575.G7 K83 2003

Little, Graham. The public emotions. Sydney : ABC Books for the Australian Broadcasting Corporation, 1999.
BF531 .L58 1999

Living beyond loss. 2nd ed. New York : W.W. Norton, 2004.
BF575.D35 L54 2004

Meier, Levi. Seven heavens. [S.l.] : Devora Publishing, c2002.
BF789.D4 M39 2002

Murray, Donald Morison, 1924- The lively shadow. 1st ed. New York : Ballantine Books, 2003.
BF575.G7 M868 2003

Roads to recovery. St. Leonards, NSW : Allen & Unwin, 1997.
BF698.35.D48 R63 1997

Schnall, Maxine. What doesn't kill you makes you stronger. Cambridge, MA : Perseus Pub., c2002.
BF575.D35 S36 2002

Spezzano, Charles. Happiness is the best revenge. Townsend, Wiltshire, England : Vision Products Limited, c1997.
BF575.D35 S68 1997

Stearns, Rob, 1952- Winning smart after losing big. 1st ed. San Francisco, CA : Encounter Books, 2003.
BF575.D35 S74 2003

Umberson, Debra. Death of a parent. Cambridge ; New York : Cambridge University Press, 2003.

Loss (Psychology)

BF789.D4 U48 2003

Walter, Carolyn Ambler. The loss of a life partner. New York : Columbia University Press, c2003.
BF575.G7 W3435 2003

Weiss, Stefanie Iris. Everything you need to know about dealing with losses. Rev. ed. New York : Rosen Pub. Group, 2000.
BF724.3.L66 W45 2000

LOSS (PSYCHOLOGY) IN ADOLESCENCE.
Myers, Edward, 1950- When will I stop hurting? Lanham, Md. : Scarecrow Press, 2004.
BF724.3.G73 M94 2004

LOSS (PSYCHOLOGY) IN ADOLESCENCE - JUVENILE LITERATURE.
Weiss, Stefanie Iris. Everything you need to know about dealing with losses. Rev. ed. New York : Rosen Pub. Group, 2000.
BF724.3.L66 W45 2000

LOSS (PSYCHOLOGY) IN CHILDREN.
Kanyer, Laurie A., 1959- 25 things to do when grandpa passes away, mom and dad get divorced, or the dog dies. Seatte Wash., : Parenting Press, 2004.
BF723.G75 K36 2003

Rathkey, Julia Wilcox. What children need when they grieve. 1st ed. New York : Three Rivers Press, 2004.
BF723.G75 R38 2004

Wakenshaw, Martha. Caring for your grieving child. Oakland, Calif. : New Harbinger ; London : Hi Marketing, 2002.
BF723.G75 W35 2002

LOSS (PSYCHOLOGY) IN CHILDREN - JUVENILE LITERATURE.
Dennison, Amy. Our dad died. Minneapolis, MN : Free Spirit Pub., c2003.
BF723.G75 D46 2003

Johnson, Marvin. Where's Jess? Rev. Omaha, NE : Centering Corp. Resource, 2003.
BF723.G75 J645 2003

Stenson, Lila. Daddy, up and down. 1st ed. Snowmass Village, CO : Peaceful Village Pub., 2002.
BF723.G75 S74 2002

LOSS (PSYCHOLOGY) - RELIGIOUS ASPECTS - CHRISTIANITY.
McKinney Hammond, Michelle, 1957- Get over it and on with it!. 1st ed. Colorado Springs, Colo. : WaterBrook Press, 2002.
BV4908.5 .M357 2002
1. Black author.

LOSS (PSYCHOLOGY) - UNITED STATES.
Barzach, Amy Jaffe. Accidental courage, boundless dreams. 1st ed. West Hartford, CT : Aurora Pub., c2001.
BF575.G7 B375 2001

Lost and found.
Caliandro, Arthur. 1st ed. New York : McGraw-Hill, 2003.
BF637.S4 .C32 2003

LOST ARTICLES - LAW AND LEGISLATION.
See **TREASURE-TROVE.**

The lost books of Merlyn : Druid magic from the age of Arthur / [compiled by] Douglas Monroe. 1st ed. St. Paul, Minn : Llewellyn Publications, 1998 (2003 printing) xxii, 409 p. : ill. ; 23 cm. Based on the Druid text The book of Pheryllt. CONTENTS: The battle of the trees -- The book of Pheryllt -- The Gorchan of Maeldrew. ISBN 1-56718-471-5 (pbk.) DDC 133.4/3/089916
1. Magic, Celtic. 2. Druids and Druidism - Miscellanea. I. Monroe, Douglas, 1957- II. Title: Book of Pheryllt.
BF1622.C45 L67 1998

Lost geographies of power.
Allen, John, 1951- Malden, MA ; Oxford : Blackwell Pub., 2003.
GF50 .A453 2003

Lost in America.
Nuland, Sherwin B. 1st ed. New York : Knopf : Distributed by Random House, 2003.
F128.9.J5 N85 2003

The lost promise of patriotism.
Hansen, Jonathan M. Chicago : University of Chicago Press, c2003.
E661 .H316 2003

The lost secret of death.
Novak, Peter, 1958- Charlottesville, VA : Hampton Roads Pub., 2003.
BF1999 .N73 2003

Lost souls.
Weissman, David, 1936- Albany : State University of New York Press, c2003.
B105.M53 W45 2003

Lots of feelings.
Rotner, Shelley. Brookfield, Conn. : Millbrook Press, c2003.
BF723.E6 R68 2003

Lott, Lynn. Madame Dora's fortune-telling cards : everything you need to know about love, money, sex, relationships, work, & happiness / by Lynn Lott, Rick Naymark, Jane Nelsen. Gloucester, Mass. : Fair Winds Press, 2003. 155 p. ; 15 cm. + 50 cards (col. ; 12 x 8 cm.). Issued in case. Table of contents URL: http://www.loc.gov/catdir/toc/ecip048/2003018405.html ISBN 1-59233-013-4 DDC 133.3/242
1. Fortune-telling by cards. 2. Divination cards - Miscellanea. I. Naymark, Rick. II. Nelsen, Jane. III. Title.
BF1878 .L78 2003

Louden, Jennifer. Comfort secrets for busy women / by Jennifer Louden. Naperville, Ill. : Sourcebooks, c2003. p. cm. Table of contents URL: http://www.loc.gov/catdir/toc/ecip042/2003007707.html ISBN 1402201265 (alk. paper) DDC 158.1/082
1. Conduct of life. 2. Women - Psychology. I. Title.
BF637.C5 L676 2003

Louden, Robert B., 1953-.
Schleiermacher, Friedrich, 1768-1834. Lectures on philosophical ethics. Cambridge ; New York : Cambridge University Press, 2002.

Louise, Kim. True devotion / by Kim Louise. Washington D.C. : BET Publications, 2002. 316 p. ; 18 cm. (Arabesque (Series)) "BET books" Contemporary romance -- Spine ISBN 1-58314-284-3
1. African Americans - Fiction. 2. Man-woman relationships. I. Title. II. Series.

LOUISIANA - FICTION.
Cameron, Stella. Cold day in July. Waterville, Me. : Wheeler Pub. ; Bath, England : Chivers Press, 2002.
PS3553.A4345 C65 2002

Louvre conférences et colloques
La magie en Egypte. Paris : Documentation française : Musée du Louvre, c2002.
BF1591 .M3447 2002

LOVE. *See also* **ATTACHMENT BEHAVIOR; COURTSHIP; FRIENDSHIP; INTIMACY (PSYCHOLOGY); MARRIAGE.**
Ai ni, dan bu xiang xin ni. Di 1 ban. Beijing : Zhongguo hua qiao chu ban she, 2000.
PL2608.L6 A5 2000

Anderson, Rafe. Total palmistry. Boston : Red Wheel, 2003.
BF935.L67 A53 2003

Austin, Linda S., 1951- Heart of the matter. New York : Atria Books, c2003.
BF575.L8 A97 2003

Ben-Ze'ev, Aharon. Be-sod ha-regashot. Lod : Zemorah-Bitan, 2001.

Brenot, Philippe. Le sexe et l'amour. Paris : Jacob, c2003.

Buschey, Monika. "An jenem Tag im blauen Mond September". Düsseldorf : Artemis & Winkler, c2000.

Comstock, Kani. Journey into love. Ashland, OR : Willow Press, c2000.
BF575.L8 C647 2003

Dīkṣita, Mathurā Prasāda, 1878-1978. [Kelikutūhala. Hindi & Sanskrit] Kelikutūhalam. Vārāṇasī : Krshadāsa Akādamī, 2002.
HQ470.S3 D55155 2002

Domagala, Edward. L'ermeneutica dell'esperienza dell'amore in Max Scheler. Romae : [s.n.], 2000.

Feldman, Seymour. Philosophy in a time of crisis. London ; New York : RoutledgeCurzon, 2003.
BM755.A25 F45 2003

Finley, Guy. An apprentice of the heart. Ashland, Ore. : White Cloud Press, 2004.
BF575.L8 F524 2004

Fisher, Helen E. Why we love. 1st ed. New York : Henry Holt and Company, 2004.
BF575.L8 F53 2004

Galende, Emiliano. Sexo y amor. 1a ed. Buenos Aires : Paidós, 2001.

Geier, Alfred, 1930- Plato's erotic thought. Rochester, NY : University of Rochester Press, 2002.

B398.L9 G45 2002

Gilligan, Carol, 1936- The birth of pleasure. 1st ed. New York : A.A. Knopf, 2002.
BF575.L8 G56 2002

Gučetić, Nikola Vitov, 1549-1610. [Dialogo della bellezza. Serbo-Croatian & Italian] Dijalog o ljepoti = Dvojezično izd. Zagreb : Društvo hrvatskih književnika, 1995.
BH301.L65 G8318 1995

Hare, Jenny. Think love. London : Vega, 2002.
BF575.L8 H338 2002

Howard, Kerry. The book of love and happiness. New York : Ryland Peters & Small, Inc., 2004.
BF575.L8 H69 2004

Hsu, Shan-Tung, 1942- The yin & yang of love. 1st ed. St. Paul, Minn. : Llewellyn Publications, 2003.
BF1779.F4 H763 2003

Hsu, Shan-Tung, 1942- [Yin & yang of love. Spanish] Feng shui para el amor. 1. ed. St. Paul, Minn. : Llewellyn Espanol, 2003.
BF1779.F4 H76318 2003

Inayat Khan, 1882-1927. Rassa shastra. Berwick, ME : Ibis Press : York Beach, ME : distributed to the trade by Red Wheel/Weiser, 2003.
BF692 .I5 2003

Irigaray, Luce. [Voie de l'amour. English] The way of love. London ; New York : Continuum, 2002.
BF575.L8 I7513 2002

Irigaray, Luce. The way of love. London ; New York : Continuum, 2002.

Kaufmann, Jean-Claude. Premier matin. Paris : Colin, 2002.

Khushwant Singh, 1915- Khushwant Singh on women, love & lust. New Delhi : Books Today, c2002.
HQ29 .K48 2002

Liebe als Kulturmedium. München : Fink, c2002.

Marion, Jean-Luc, 1946- [Prolégomènes à la charité. English] Prolegomena to charity. 1st ed. New York : Fordham University Press, 2002.
BD436 .M3313 2002

Markus, Georg. Meine Reisen in die Vergangenheit. 2. Aufl. Wien : Amalthea, 2002.
AC35 .M385 2002

Nāgārjuna, Siddha. [Ratiśāstra. English & Sanskrit] Conjugal love in India. Leiden Boston, MA : Brill, 2002.
HQ470.S3 N3413 2002

Ōkawa, Ryūhō, 1956- [Ai no genten. English] The origin of love. New York : Lantern Books, c2003.
BP605.K55 O29513 2003

Pollard, Irina. Life, love and children. Boston : Kluwer Academic Publishers, c2002.
R725.5 .P655 2002

Rhodes, James M. Eros, wisdom, and silence. Columbia, Mo. : University of Missouri Press, c2003.
B398.L9 .R46 2003

Rozin, V. M. Lîubov' i seksual'nost' v kul'ture, sem'e i vzgliadakh na polovoe vospitanie. Moskva : Logos : Vysshaîa shkola, 1999.
BF575.L8 R69 1999

Sarnoff, Irving, 1922- Intimate creativity. Madison, Wis. : University of Wisconsin Press, c2002.
BF411 .S27 2002

Sayers, Janet. Divine therapy. Oxford ; New York : Oxford University Press, 2003.
BF175.4.R44 S28 2003

Scola, Angelo. Uomo-donna. 1. ed. italiana. Genova : Marietti, c2002.

Somogyi, Gábor. Libikóka. [Budapest?] : Honestus-Press, 2002.
BF575.L8 S623 2002

Towler, Solala. Tao paths to love. Kansas City, Mo. : Andrews McMeel Pub., 2002.
BD436 .T65 2002

Vergès, Jacques. Dictionnaire amoureux de la justice. Paris : Plon, c2002.

Xu, Kun. Xing qing nan nü. Beijing di 1 ban. Beijing : Zhong'guo qing nian chu ban she, 2001.

Zhang, Hong. Ai qing de di er zhang mian kong = Di 1 ban. Jinan : Shandong ren min chu ban she, 2001.

The love almanac / edited by Katrina Fried & Lena Tabori. New York : Welcome Books : Distributed to the trade in the U.S. and Canada by Andrews McMeel Distribution Service, 2003. 240 p. : col. ill ; 24 cm. Includes index. ISBN 0-941807-91-6 DDC 306.7
1. Love - Miscellanea. 2. Courtship - Miscellanea. I. Fried, Katrina. II. Tabori, Lena.
BF575.L8 L6675 2003

Love and hate in Jamestown.
Price, David, 1961- 1st ed. New York : Alfred A. Knopf : Distributed by Random House, 2003.
F234.J3 P68 2003

Love at Goon Park.
Blum, Deborah New York : Berkley Books, 2004.
BF109.H346 B58 2004

Blum, Deborah. Cambridge, MA : Perseus Pub., c2002.
BF109.H346 B58 2002

LOVE - CASE STUDIES.
Maksimov, Andreĭ, 1959- Dialogi li︠u︡bvi. Moskva : Delovoĭ ėkspress, 1999.
BF575.L8 M336 1999

LOVE - EARLY WORKS TO 1800.
Casoni, Guido, 1561-1642. Della magia d'amore. Torino : Res, 2002.
BF575.L8 C3 2002

Ibn Khātimah, Aḥmad ibn ʻAlī, d. ca. 1369. [Poems] Dīwān Ibn Khātimah al-Anṣārī. al-Ṭabʻah 1. Bayrūt : Dār al-Fikr al-Muʻāṣir ; Dimashq : Dār al-Fikr, 1994.
PJ7760.I2454   <Orien Arab>

Pinkney, Andrea Marion. [Kāmasūtra. English.] The Kama Sutra illuminated. New York, N.Y. : Abrams, c2002.

Shayzarī, ʻAbd al-Raḥmān ibn Naṣr, 12th cent. Rawḍat al-qulūb wa-nuzhat al-muḥibb wa-al-maḥbūb. Wiesbaden : Harrassowitz, 2003.

LOVE - HEALTH ASPECTS.
Sayers, Janet. Divine therapy. Oxford ; New York : Oxford University Press, 2003.
BF175.4.R44 S28 2003

LOVE - HISTORY - TO 1500.
Rousselot, Pierre, 1878-1915. [Pour l'histoire du problème de l'amour au moyen âge. English] The problem of love in the Middle Ages. Milwaukee : Marquette University Press, [2001?]
B738.L68 R68 2001

LOVE IN LITERATURE.
D'Cruz, Doreen, 1950- Loving subjects. New York : P. Lang, c2002.
PR888.W6 D39 2002

Huang, Shizhong. Hun bian, dao de yu wen xue. Di 1 ban. Beijing : Ren min wen xue chu ban she, 2000.

LOVE-LETTERS. *See* **COURTSHIP.**

LOVE LOSS (PSYCHOLOGY). *See* **SEPARATION (PSYCHOLOGY).**

LOVE - MISCELLANEA.
Dixon-Cooper, Hazel, 1947- Love on a rotten day. New York : Simon and Schuster, 2004.
BF1729.L6 D59 2004

Drew, A. J. Wicca for couples. Franklin Lakes, NJ : New Page Books, c2002.
BF1572.L6 D74 2002

Godek, Gregory J. P., 1955- 10,000 ways to say I love you. Naperville, Ill. : Casablanca Press, c1999.
BF575.L8 G63 1999

Knight, Michele. Good sex. Kansas City, Mo. : Andrews McMeel Pub., c2002.
BF1729.S4 .K58 2002

Kosarin, Jenni. The everything love signs book. Avon, MA : Adams Media, c2004.
BF1729.L6 K67 2004

Longacre, Celeste B. Love signs. 1st ed. Walpole, NH : Sweet Fern Publications, 2000.
BF1729.L6 L66 2000

The love almanac. New York : Welcome Books : Distributed to the trade in the U.S. and Canada by Andrews McMeel Distribution Service, 2003.
BF575.L8 L6675 2003

McCormack, Kathleen. Magic for lovers : find your ideal partner through the power of magic. 1st ed. Hauppauge, NY : Barron's, c2003.
BF1623.L6 M38 2003

Omarr, Sydney. [Astrology, love, sex, and you] Sydney Omarr's astrology, love, sex, and you. New York : Signet, c2002.

BF1729.S4 O58 2002

Sophia, 1955- The little book of hot love spells. Kansas City, Mo. : Andrews McMeel Pub., c2002.
BF1623.L6 S66 2002

Tempest, Raven. Bewitching love potions & charms. London : Cassell Illustrated ; New York, NY : Distributed in the USA by Sterling Pub. Co., c2003.
BF575.L8 .T45 2003

White, Lauren. Spells for a perfect love life. Kansas City, Mo. : Andrews McMeel Pub., 2000.
BF1572.L6 .W45 2000

Wong, Angi Ma. Feng shui dos & taboos for love. Carlsbad, Calif. : Hay House, c2002.
BF1779.F4 W67 2002

Love, nurture, and forgive.
Ōkawa, Ryūhō, 1956- [Hito o aishi, hito o ikashi, hito o yurusu. English] New York : Lantern Books, c2002.
BP605.K55 O32413 2002

Love on a rotten day.
Dixon-Cooper, Hazel, 1947- New York : Simon and Schuster, 2004.
BF1729.L6 D59 2004

LOVE - PHYSIOLOGICAL ASPECTS.
Fisher, Helen E. Why we love. 1st ed. New York : Henry Holt and Company, 2004.
BF575.L8 F53 2004

Love potions and charms.
Tempest, Raven. Bewitching love potions & charms. London : Cassell Illustrated ; New York, NY : Distributed in the USA by Sterling Pub. Co., c2003.
BF575.L8 .T45 2003

Love prescription.
Gardere, Jeffrey Roger. New York : Kensington Pub., c2002.

LOVE - PSYCHOLOGICAL ASPECTS.
Marar, Ziyad. The happiness paradox. London : Reaktion, 2003.

LOVE - RELIGIOUS ASPECTS.
Aïvanhov, Omraam Mikhaël. L'amour plus grand que la foi. Fréjus : Prosveta, c2000.

LOVE - RELIGIOUS ASPECTS - CHRISTIANITY - HISTORY OF DOCTRINES - MIDDLE AGES, 600-1500.
Rousselot, Pierre, 1878-1915. [Pour l'histoire du problème de l'amour au moyen âge. English] The problem of love in the Middle Ages. Milwaukee : Marquette University Press, [2001?]
B738.L68 R68 2001

Love signs.
Longacre, Celeste B. 1st ed. Walpole, NH : Sweet Fern Publications, 2000.
BF1729.L6 L66 2000

LOVE (THEOLOGY). *See* **LOVE - RELIGIOUS ASPECTS - CHRISTIANITY.**

LOVE - UNITED STATES.
Longing to tell. 1st ed. New York : Farrar, Straus and Giroux, 2003.
E185.625 .L66 2003

Love, war, and circuses.
Scigliano, Eric, 1953- Boston : Houghton Mifflin, 2002.
QL737.P98 S42 2002

Love your neighbor and yourself.
Dorff, Elliot N. 1st ed. Philadelphia, PA : Jewish Publication Society, 2003.
BJ1285 .D67 2003

LOVECRAFT, H. P. (HOWARD PHILLIPS), 1890-1937.
Harms, Daniel. The Necronomicon files. Boston, MA : Weiser Books, c2003.
BF1999 .H37515 2003

Loveman, Brian. El espejismo de la reconciliación política : Chile 1990-2002 / Brian Loveman, Elizabeth Lira. 1. ed. Santiago : LOM Ediciones : DIBAM, 2002. 449 p. : ill. ; 21 cm. (Historia) Includes bibliographical references (p. 439-449) and index. ISBN 9568026053
1. Chile - Politics and government - 1988- 2. Reconciliation. I. Lira, Elizabeth. II. Title. III. Series: Historia (LOM Ediciones)

Loving subjects.
D'Cruz, Doreen, 1950- New York : P. Lang, c2002.
PR888.W6 D39 2002

Loving the self-absorbed.
Brown, Nina W. Oakland, Calif. : New Harbinger, c2003.
BF575.N35 B76 2003

Lovink, Geert. Uncanny networks : dialogues with the virtual intelligentsia / Geert Lovink. Cambridge, Mass. : MIT Press, c2002. xv, 374 p. ; 24 cm. (Leonardo) Includes bibliographical references (p. 370-374). ISBN 0-262-12251-0 (hc.) DDC 303.48/34
1. Information society. 2. Computer networks - Social aspects. 3. Internet - Social aspects. 4. Cyberspace. 5. Computers and civilization. 6. Information technology - Social aspects. I. Title. II. Series.
HM851 .L688 2002

LOW BACK PAIN. *See* **BACKACHE.**

LOW-INCOME PEOPLE. *See* **POOR.**

Lowenkopf, Eugene L. The almighty dollar : a psychiatrist looks at money / Eugene L. Lowenkopf. New York : iUniverse, Inc., c2003. xvi, 252 p. ; 24 cm. ISBN 0-595-65702-8 (cloth) ISBN 0-595-27663-6 (pbk.)
1. Money - Psychological aspects. 2. Psychoanalysis. I. Title.

LOWER BACK PAIN. *See* **BACKACHE.**

Lowly origin.
Kingdon, Jonathan. Princeton : Princeton University Press, c2003.
GN282 .K54 2003

Lowman, Pete. A long way east of Eden : could God explain the mess we're in? / Pete Lowman. Carlisle : Paternoster, 2002. x, 390 p. ; 20 cm. Includes bibliographical references and index. ISBN 1-84227-108-3 DDC 306.6
1. God. 2. Religion and sociology. I. Title.

Lowndes, Florin.
[Belebung des Herzchakra. English]
Enlivening the chakra of the heart : the fundamental spiritual exercises of Rudolf Steiner / Florin Lowndes ; [translated by Matthew Barton]. London : Sophia Books : Rudolf Steiner Press, c1998. viii, 199 p. : ill. ; 22 cm. Includes bibliographical references (p. [189]-199). ISBN 1-85584-091-X
1. Chakras - Miscellanea. 2. Spiritual life. I. Title.
BF1442.C53 L6913 1998

Lowney, Chris. Heroic leadership : best practices from a 450-year-old company that changed the world / Chris Lowney. Chicago : Loyola Press, c2003. 330 p. : ill. ; 24 cm. Includes bibliographical references and index. CONTENTS: Of Jesuits and J.P. Morgan -- What leaders do -- The Jesuits : an accidental company with a purposeful vision -- Leadership role models : three unlikely case studies -- To order one's life : self-awareness as the foundation of leadership -- The spiritual exercises : a lifelong development tool -- The whole world becomes our house : how ingenuity sparks innovation, creativity, and a global mindset -- Refuse no talent, nor any man of quality : how love uncovers talent and unites teams -- An uninterrupted life of heroic deeds : how heroism envisions the impossible and does it -- Exceptional daring was essential : when risk-taking vanished, so did the company almost -- The way we do things : four core values, but one integrated life. ISBN 0-8294-1816-4 DDC 658.4/092
1. Jesuits - History. 2. Leadership. I. Title.
HD57.7 .L69 2003

Lowry, Don. Keys to personal success / Don Lowry. Riverside, Calif. : True Colors, Inc. ; c2001. 25 p. : col. ill. ; 22 cm.
1. Success. 2. Interpersonal relations. I. Title.
BF637.S8 .L77 2001

Loy, James M., 1942-.
Phillips, Donald T. (Donald Thomas), 1952- Character in action. Annapolis, Md. : Naval Institute Press, c2003.
VG53 .P49 2003

LOYALTY. *See also* **PATRIOTISM.**
Whyte, William Hollingsworth. The organization man. Philadelphia : University of Pennsylvania Press, c2002, 1956.
BF697 .W47 2002

Lozito, Vito. Agiografia, magia, superstizione / Vito Lozito. Bari : Levante, [1999] 327, 43 p. of plates : ill. (some col.) ; 24 cm. Includes bibliographical references (p. 307-320) and index. ISBN 88-7949-198-9
1. Superstition - Social aspects. 2. Religion and culture. 3. Hagiography. I. Title.
BF1775 .L69 1999

LSD (DRUG) - LONGITUDINAL STUDIES.
Dobkin de Rios, Marlene. LSD, spirituality, and the creative process. Rochester, Vt. : Park Street Press, c2003.
BF209.L9 D57 2003

LSD, spirituality, and the creative process.
Dobkin de Rios, Marlene. Rochester, Vt. : Park Street Press, c2003.
BF209.L9 D57 2003

Lu, Jinhua.
Confucius. [Selections. Chinese & English. 1998] Kong Meng ren sheng ge yan ji cui. Wuhan : Wuhan gong ye da xue chu ban she, 1998.

LU, XUN, 1881-1936.
Wang, Furen. Tu po mang dian. Di 1 ban. Beijing Shi : Zhongguo wen lian chu ban she, 2001.
PL2754.S5 Z89 2001

Lubaś, Władysław.
Język w przestrzeni społecznej. Opole : Uniwersytet Opolski, 2002.
P40 .J492 2002

LUBAŚ, WŁADYSŁAW.
Język w przestrzeni społecznej. Opole : Uniwersytet Opolski, 2002.
P40 .J492 2002

Lucarelli, Carlo, 1960- Misteri d'Italia : i casi di Blu notte / Carlo Lucarelli ; postfazione di Giorgio Boatti. Torino : Einaudi, c2002. 262 p. ; 21 cm. (Einaudi tascabili. Stile libero ; 1047) On cover: Big. Includes the texts of ten mysteries transmitted in 2001 on Rai3 TV in the programme Blu notte-Misteri italiani, concerning Michele Sindona, Roberto Calvi, Enrico Mattei, the massacre of Gioia Tauro, etc. ISBN 88-06-15445-1 DDC 364
1. Crime - Italy - Case studies. 2. Curiosities and wonders. I. Title. II. Title: Blu notte III. Series.

Lucas, John Scott, 1970- Astrology and numerology in medieval and early modern Catalonia : the Tractat de prenostication de la vida natural dels hòmens / by John Scott Lucas Leiden ; Boston : Brill, 2003. p. cm. (The medieval and early modern Iberian world ; v. 18) Includes bibliographical references (p.   ) and index. ISBN 90-04-13242-2 DDC 133.5
1. Astrology - Early works to 1800. 2. Numerology - Spain - Catalonia. 3. Numerology - Early works to 1800. 4. Catalonia (Spain) - Intellectual life. 5. Civilization, Medieval. I. Title. II. Title: Tractat de prenostication de la vida natural dels hòmens. English & Catalan. III. Series.
BF1685 .L83 2003

Lucas, Margeaux, ill.
Gemmen, Heather. Dreams from God. Colorado Springs, Colo. : Faith Kidz, 2003.
BF1099.B5 G46 2003

Luce, Carol L.
Readings in evolutionary psychology. Boston : Pearson/Allyn and Bacon, c2004.
BF698.95 .R43 2004

Luciani Rivero, Rafael Francisco. El misterio de la diferencia : un estudio tipológico de la analogía como estructura originaria de la realidad en Tomás de Aquino, Erich Przywara y Hans Urs von Balthasar y su uso en teología trinitaria / Rafael Francisco Luciani Rivero. Roma : Pontificia università gregoriana, 2001. 628 p. ; 23 cm. (Analecta Gregoriana ; vol. 285. Series Facultatis Theologiae. Sectio B ; n. 101) Includes bibliographical references (p. [577]-612). ISBN 88-7652-931-4 DDC 230
1. Thomas, - Aquinas, Saint, - 1225?-1274. 2. Przywara, Erich, - 1889-1972. 3. Balthasar, Hans Urs von, - 1905- 4. Trinity. 5. Ontology. 6. Analogy (Religion) I. Title. II. Series: Analecta Gregoriana ; v. 285. III. Series: Analecta Gregoriana. Series Facultatis Theologiae. Sectio B ; n. 101.

LUCIFER. See DEVIL.

Lucifer ascending.
Ellis, Bill, 1950- Lexington : University Press of Kentucky, c2003.
BF1548 .E44 2003

LUCK. See FORTUNE.

Luckhurst, Roger. The invention of telepathy, 1870-1901 / Roger Luckhurst. Oxford ; New York : Oxford University Press, 2002. viii, 324 p. : ill. ; 24 cm. Includes bibliographical references (p. [279]-318) and index. ISBN 0-19-924962-8 (alk. paper) DDC 820.935609034
1. Telepathy - History. I. Title.
BF1171 .L77 2002

Lucrèce.
Moreau, Pierre-François, 1948- 1. ed. Paris : Presses universitaires de France, 2002.

LUCRETIUS CARUS, TITUS. DE RERUM NATURA LIBER 3.
Moreau, Pierre-François, 1948- Lucrèce. 1. ed. Paris : Presses universitaires de France, 2002.

LUCY STONE (FICTITIOUS CHARACTER). See STONE, LUCY (FICTITIOUS CHARACTER).

LUDICROUS, THE. See COMIC, THE; WIT AND HUMOR.

Ludwig, Timothy D. Intervening to improve the safety of occupational driving : a behavior-change model and review of empirical evidence / Timothy D. Ludwig, E. Scott Geller ; Thomas C. Mawhinney, editor. New York : Haworth Press, 2000. xii, 127 p. : ill. ; 23 cm. "Co-published simultaneously as Journal [of] organizational behavior management, volume 19, number 4 2000." Includes bibliographical references (p. 114-124) and index. ISBN 0-7890-1004-6 (alk. paper) ISBN 0-7890-1012-7 (alk. paper) DDC 363.12/57
1. Traffic accidents. 2. Delivery of goods. 3. Behavior modification. I. Geller, E. Scott, 1942- II. Mawhinney, Thomas C. III. Title.
HE5614 .I586 2000

Ludwig Wittgenstein, Tractatus logico-philosophicus / herausgegeben von Wilhelm Vossenkuhl. Berlin : Akademie Verlag, 2001. viii, 335 p. : ill. ; 21 cm. (Klassiker Auslegen ; Bd. 10) Includes bibliographical references and indexes. ISBN 3-05-002694-4 (pbk.)
1. Wittgenstein, Ludwig, - 1889-1951. - Tractatus logico-philosophicus. 2. Logic, Symbolic and mathematical. 3. Philosophy. 4. Language and languages. I. Vossenkuhl, Wilhelm, 1945- II. Title: Tractatus logico-philosophicus III. Series.

Die Luft auf der Spitze des Pinsels.
Sauerländer, Willibald. München : Hanser, 2002.

Luft, Sandra Rudnick, 1934- Vico's uncanny humanism : reading the New science between modern and postmodern / Sandra Rudnick Luft. Ithaca, N.Y. : Cornell University Press, 2003. xviii, 213 p. ; 24 cm. Includes bibliographical references and index. ISBN 0-8014-4108-0 (alk. paper) DDC 195
1. Vico, Giambattista, - 1668-1744. - Principi di una scienza nuova. 2. Humanism. 3. Hermeneutics. 4. Poetry. I. Title.
B3581.P73 L84 2003

Lugasi, Yaʻaḳov Yiśraʼel. Mishpeṭe Yiśraʼel / ... ḥubar ve-neʻerakh me-iti Yaʻaḳov Yiśraʼel Lugasi. Mahadurah ḥadashah be-tosefet le-ḥag ha-Pesaḥ. Yerushalayim : Y. Y. Lugasi, 761 [2001] 294, 150 p. ; 23 cm. (Be-emunato yiḥyeh ; 19) Cover title: Mishpeṭe Yiśraʼel : Elul, Rosh ha-shanah, Yom kipur, Sukot, Ḥanukah, Purim, Shavuʻot. Vocalized.
1. Fasts and feasts - Judaism. 2. Ethics, Jewish. 3. Repentance - Judaism. I. Title. II. Title: Mishpeṭe Yiśraʼel : Elul, Rosh ha-shanah, Yom kipur, Sukot, Ḥanukah, Purim, Shavuʻot

Yalḳuṭ Or ha-ḥayim ha-ḳadosh : liḳuṭe musar mi-sefer "Or haḥayim" ... / Yaʻaḳov Iśraʼel Lugasi. Yerushalayim : [ḥ. mo. l], 762 [2001 or 2002] 420 p. ; 24 cm. Running title: Or ha-ḥayim. Vocalized.
1. Aṭṭar, Ḥayyim ben Moses, - 1696-1743. - Or ha-ḥayim. 2. Ethics, Jewish. 3. Jews - Conduct of life. I. Title. II. Title: Or ha-ḥayim

Luhmann, Niklas.
[Beobachtungen der Moderne. English]
Observations on modernity / Niklas Luhmann ; translated by William Whobrey. Stanford, CA : Stanford University Press, 1998. x, 147 p. ; 23 cm. (Writing science) "The publication of this work was assisted by a subsidy from Inter Nationes, Bonn." Includes bibliographical references (p. [136]-147). ISBN 0-8047-3234-5 (cloth : alk. paper) ISBN 0-8047-3235-3 (pbk. : alk. paper) DDC 301/.01
1. Sociology - Philosophy. 2. Postmodernism - Social aspects. I. Title. II. Series.
HM24 .L88813 1998

LUHMANN, NIKLAS.
Autopoietic organization theory. Oslo, Norway : Abstrakt forlag ; Malmö, Sweden : Liber Ekonomi ; Herndon, VA, USA : Copenhagen Business School Press, c2003.
HD31 .A825 2003

Clam, Jean. Was heisst, sich an Differenz statt an Identität orientieren? Konstanz : UVK Verlagsgesellschaft, c2002.

Lukowski, Jerzy. The European nobility in the eighteenth century / Jerzy Lukowski. Houndmills [England] ; New York : Palgrave Macmillan, 2003. x, 243 p. : maps ; 23 cm. (European culture and society) Includes bibliographical references (p. 215-233) and index. ISBN 0-333-65209-6 (hbk.) ISBN 0-333-65210-X (pbk.) DDC 305.5/223/09409033
1. Nobility - Europe - History - 18th century. 2. Power (Social sciences) 3. Europe - Economic conditions - 18th century. 4. Europe - Social conditions - 18th century. I. Title. II. Series.
HT653.E9 L85 2003

Lum, Alan S.F. (Alan Sun Fai) The centuries old philosophy and practice of traditional Chinese feng shui and the more advanced Flying Star feng shui / author, Alan S.F. Lum ; with consultation by Clarence K. Lau. Honolulu : Lum Pub., c2002. 186 p. : ill. ; 26 cm. ISBN 0-9720869-1-9
1. Feng shui. I. Lau, Clarence K. II. Title. III. Title: Traditional Chinese feng shui IV. Title: Flying Star feng shui
BF1779.F4 L86 2002

Lum, Grande. Expand the pie : how to add value to any negotiation / by Grande Lum, Irma Tyler-Wood, Anthony Wanis-St. John. Seattle, WA : Castle Pacific Pub. ; Cambridge, MA : ThoughtBridge, c2003. 215 p. : ill. ; 20 cm. Includes bibliographical references (p. 209-211). ISBN 0-9653869-7-X DDC 302.3
1. Negotiation. I. Tyler-Wood, Irma. II. Wanis-St. John, Anthony. III. Title.
BF637.N4 L86 2003

LUMBAGO. See BACKACHE.

La lumière vient de l'Occident.
Shayegan, Darius. [La Tour-d'Aigues] : Éditions de l'Aube, c2001.
CB 430

Lumsden, Donald L.
Lumsden, Gay. Communicating with credibility and confidence. 2nd ed. Australia ; Belmont, CA : Thomson/Wadsworth, c2003.
BF637.C45 L85 2003

Lumsden, Gay. Communicating with credibility and confidence : diverse people, diverse settings / Gay Lumsden, Donald Lumsden. 2nd ed. Australia ; Belmont, CA : Thomson/Wadsworth, c2003. 408 p. : ill. ; 24 cm. Includes bibliographical references (p. 381-396) and indexes. ISBN 0-534-50944-4 DDC 153.6
1. Interpersonal communication. 2. Body language. 3. Interpersonal relations. 4. Communication - Psychological aspects. I. Lumsden, Donald L. II. Title.
BF637.C45 L85 2003

Lunar returns.
Townley, John, 1945- 1st ed. St. Paul, Minn. : Llewellyn Publications, 2003.
BF1723 .T69 2003

Lundberg, K. C., 1948-.
Murray, Karel, 1954- Straight talk. Portland, Or. : Arnica Pub., c2003.
BF637.C5 M87 2003

Lundis philo
(19) Frey, Jean-Marie. Le corps peut-il nous rendre heureux? Nantes : Pleins feux, [2002]

(20) Dupouey, Patrick. Est-ce le cerveau qui pense? Nantes : Pleins feux, [2002].

Luo, Guojie.
[Selections. 2000]
Luo Guojie wen ji. Di 1 ban. Baoding Shi : Hebei da xue chu ban she, 2000. 2 v. : col. ports. ; 21 cm. Includes bibliographical references. ISBN 7-81028-490-8
1. Communist ethics. 2. Ethics. I. Title.
BJ1390 .L892 2000

Luo Guojie wen ji.
Luo, Guojie. [Selections. 2000] Di 1 ban. Baoding Shi : Hebei da xue chu ban she, 2000.
BJ1390 .L892 2000

Luo, Zongqiang. Luo Zongqiang gu dai wen xue si xiang lun ji / Zhang Yi bian. Di 1 ban. Shantou Shi : Shantou da xue chu ban she, 1999. 4, 8, 2, 656 p. ; 21 cm. (20 shi ji Chao ren wen hua cui ying cong shu) Includes bibliographical references. ISBN 7-81036-385-9
1. Chinese literature - History and criticism. I. Zhang, Yi. II. Title. III. Series.
PL2264 .L95 1999

Luo Zongqiang gu dai wen xue si xiang lun ji.
Luo, Zongqiang. Di 1 ban. Shantou Shi : Shantou da xue chu ban she, 1999.
PL2264 .L95 1999

Lurati, Ottavio. Per modo di dire-- : storia della lingua e antropologia nelle locuzioni italiane ed europee / Ottavio Lurati. Bologna : CLUEB, c2002. 394 p. ; 24 cm. Includes bibliographical references (p. [279]-358) and index. ISBN 88-491-1795-7 DDC 398
1. Italian language - Terms and phrases. 2. Terms and phrases - Europe. 3. Anthropological linguistics. 4. Language and culture - Europe. 5. Ideology - Europe. 6. Political correctness - Europe. I. Title. II. Title: Storia della lingua e antropologia nella locuzioni italiane ed europee

The lure of self-harm.
Portmann, John. Boston : Beacon Press, 2004.
BF637.S37 P67 2004

Luria, Isaac ben Solomon, 1534-1572.
Ben Ratson-Laḥaṭ, Tsiyon. Sefer ha-Nistarot ṿeha-niglot. [Israel? : ḥ. mo. l.], 761 i.e. 2001?]

Eliyahu, Saliman. Sefer Kerem Shelomoh. Yerushala[y]im : Ḥevrat Ahavat shalom, 762 [2001 or 2002]

Lurquin, Paul F. The origins of life and the universe / Paul F. Lurquin. New York : Columbia University Press, c2003. xii, 217 p. : ill. ; 24 cm. Includes bibliographical references (p. [201]-203) and index. ISBN 0-231-12654-9 (cl. : alk. paper) ISBN 0-231-12655-7 (pbk. : alk. paper) DDC 576.8/3
1. Life - Origin. 2. Cosmology. I. Title.
QH325 .L87 2003

Lurya, Mosheh.
[Mishnah. Avot. 2001.] Sefer Bet ginze. Yerushalayim : R. M. Lurya, 762 [2001 or 2002]

Lusardy, Martine.
Art spirite, mediumnique, visionnaire. [Paris] : Hoëbeke, c1999.
BF1313 .A78 1999

LUST.
Khushwant Singh, 1915- Khushwant Singh on women, love & lust. New Delhi : Books Today, c2002.
HQ29 .K48 2002

Luther, Andreas.
Gelehrte in der Antike. Köln : Böhlau, c2002.

A luz de um novo dia.
Cuin, Joao. Sao Paulo : DPL, c 2001.

Luz, Ehud.
[Ma'avaḳ be-naḥal Yaboḳ. English]
Wrestling with an angel : power, morality, and Jewish identity / Ehud Luz ; translated from the Hebrew by Michael Swirsky. New Haven : Yale University Press, c2003. xii, 350 p. ; 25 cm. Includes bibliographical references (p. 283-338) and index. ISBN 0-300-09293-8 (alk. paper) DDC 296.3/6
1. Jews - Identity. 2. Zionism and Judaism. 3. Ethics, Jewish. 4. Power (Social sciences) - Moral and ethical aspects. 5. Sovereignty - Moral and ethical aspects. I. Title.
DS143 .L8913 2003

Luz, Ulrich.
Schweitzer, Albert, 1875-1965. Vorträge, Vorlesungen, Aufsätze. München : C.H. Beck, c2003.

Luzzatto, Moshe Ḥayyim, 1707-1747. Ḳitsur 138 pithe hokhmah : hu kitsur tseruf shel ha-sefer ha-gadol "138 ithe hokhmah" / she-yasad he-hasid ... Mosheh Ḥayim Lutsaṭo ; 'arukh bi-yede Shalom Ulman. Yerushalayim : Mekhon Hadrat Yerushalayim, 761 [2000 or 2001] 187 p. ; 23 cm.
1. Cabala. I. Ulman, Shalom. II. Title. III. Title: Kitsur Me'ah sheloshim u-shemonah pithe ḥokhmah

LVOV-WARSAW SCHOOL OF PHILOSOPHY.
Jadacki, Jacek Juliusz. From the viewpoint of the Lvov-Warsaw school. Amsterdam ; New York, NY : Rodopi, 2003.

LYCANTHROPY. See **WEREWOLVES.**

Lycett, John.
Barrett, Louise. Human evolutionary psychology. Princeton, N.J. : Princeton University Press, c2002.
BF698.95 .B37 2002

LYCEUMS - HISTORY - 17TH CENTURY.
Baldriga, Irene. L'occhio della lince. Roma : Accademia nazionale dei Lincei, 2002.

LYCEUMS - ITALY - HISTORY - 17TH CENTURY.
Baldriga, Irene. L'occhio della lince. Roma : Accademia nazionale dei Lincei, 2002.

Lyman, R. Lee.
Style, function, transmission. Salt Lake City : University of Utah Press, c2003.
CC173 .S79 2003

Lynn, Steven J.
Mellinger, David. The monster in the cave. 1st ed. New York : Berkley Books, 2003.
BF575.F2 M45 2003

LYOTARD, JEAN FRANÇOIS.
Lyotard. New York ; London : Routledge, 2002.

Lyotard : philosophy, politics, and the sublime / edited with an introduction by Hugh J. Silverman. New York ; London : Routledge, 2002. xv, 287 p. : ports. ; 23 cm. (Continental philosophy ; 8) Includes bibliographical references (p. 259-280) CONTENTS: Jean-François Lyotard : between politics and aesthetics / Hugh J. Silverman -- Emma : between philosophy and psychoanalysis / Jean-François Lyotard -- Conversations in postmodern hermeneutics / Shaun Gallagher -- Lyotard, Bakhtin, and radical heterogeneity / Fred Evans -- Lyotard, Levinas, and the phrasing of the ethical / James Hatley -- Lyotard, Gadamer, and the relation between ethics and aesthetics / Gary E. Aylesworth -- Lyotard, Nancy, and the myth of interruption / Michael Naas -- Lyotard, Frank, and the limits of understanding / Erik Vogt -- Interrupting Lyotard : whither the we? / Debra B. Bergoffen -- Lyotard, Heidegger, and "the jews" / James R. Watson -- Lyotard and history without witnesses / Thomas R. Flynn -- Lyotard and "the forgotten" / Stephen David Ross -- Postmodern thinking of transcendence / Richard Brons -- Lyotard : before and after the sublime / Serge Trottein -- Lyotard, Kant, and the in-finite / Wilhelm S. Wurzer -- The suspense / Wayne Froman -- Lyotard and the events of the postmodern sublime / Hugh J. Silverman. ISBN 0-415-91958-4 (hardcover) ISBN 0-415-91959-2 (paperback)
1. Lyotard, Jean François. 2. Aesthetics, Modern - 20th century. 3. Sublime, The. 4. Difference (Philosophy) 5. Postmodernism. I. Silverman, Hugh J. II. Series.

LYSERGIC ACID DIETHYLAMIDE. See **LSD (DRUG).**

LYSERGIC ACID DIETHYLAMIDE - PHARMACOLOGY.
Dobkin de Rios, Marlene. LSD, spirituality, and the creative process. Rochester, Vt. : Park Street Press, c2003.
BF209.L9 D57 2003

LYSERGIDE. See **LSD (DRUG).**

Lyster, William.
Be thou there. Cairo ; New York : American University in Cairo Press, c2001.

L'Yvonnet, François.
Gaudin, Thierry. Discours de la méthode créatrice. Gordes : Relié, c2003.

L'YVONNET, FRANÇOIS - INTERVIEWS.
Gaudin, Thierry. Discours de la méthode créatrice. Gordes : Relié, c2003.

Ma, Changyi. Zhongguo ling hun xin yang / Ma Changyi zhu. Di 1 ban. Shanghai : Shanghai wen yi chu ban she, 1998. 3, 8, 426 p. : ill. (some col.) ; 21 cm. (Bian fu cong shu) Includes bibliographical references. ISBN 7-5321-1688-3
1. Soul. 2. Soul worship - China. 3. China - Religious life and customs. I. Title. II. Series.
BL290 .M28 1998

Ma, Lijun.
Cheng zhang de Zhongguo. Di 1 ban. Beijing : Ren min chu ban she, 2002.
HQ799.2.P6 C449 2002

Ma, Shude, 1944-.
Motsch, Monika, 1942- [Mit Bambusrohr und Ahle von Qian Zhongshus Guanzhuibian zu einer Neubetrachtung Du Fus. Chinese] "Guan zhui bian" yu Du Fu xin jie. Di 1 ban. Shijiazhuang Shi : Hebei jiao yu chu ban she, 1997 (2002 printing)
PL2749.C8 Z85 1997

Ma, Wenqi. Shui yue jing hua : hou xian dai zhu yi yu dang dai xi ju / Ma Wenqi zhu. Di 1 ban. Beijing : Zhongguo she hui chu ban she, 1994. 2, 268 p., [2] p. of plates : ill ; 21 cm. (Hou xian dai yi wen hua cong shu ; 2) ISBN 7-80088-546-1
1. Theater. 2. Postmodernism. I. Title. II. Title: Hou xian dai zhu yi yu dang dai xi ju III. Series.
PN2039 .M28 1994 <Orien China>

Ma'agar ha-ḥalomot u-fitronam.
Abiṭbul, Yosef Ḥayim, d. 1998. Ḳiryat Gat : Elisha' Abiṭbul, 762 [2002]
BM496.9.D73 A25 2002

Ma'amar 'Aśarah haruge malkhut.
[Zohar ḥadash. Lamentations. 2000.] Zohar ḥadash Megilat Ekhah. "Hotsa'ah meyuḥedet li-yeme ben ha-metsarim". Yerushalayim : Mekhon Da'at Yosef, 761 [2000 or 2001]
BM525.A6 Z6 2001

Ma'aśeh uman.
Marḳ, Shelomoh Zalman ben Neḥemyah. Sefer Ma'aśeh uman. Yerushalayim : Nahalat kolel "Bet ulpana de-rabenu Yoḥanan, 763 [2002 or 2003]

Maasen, Sabine, 1960-.
Voluntary action. Oxford ; New York : Oxford University Press, 2003.
BF621 .V658 2003

MABINOGION.
Matthews, Caitlin, 1952- King Arthur and the goddess of the land. 2nd ed. Rochester, Vt. : Inner Traditions, 2002.
PB2273.M33 M36 2002

Matthews, Caitlin, 1952- Mabon and the guardians of Celtic Britain. Rochester, Vt. : Inner Traditions, c2002.

Mabon and the guardians of Celtic Britain.
Matthews, Caitlin, 1952- Rochester, Vt. : Inner Traditions, c2002.
PB2273.M33 M37 2002

Mabrūk, Muḥammad Ibrāhīm, 1943- al-Islām wa-al-gharb al-Amrīkī : bayna ḥatmīyat al-ṣidām wa-imkānīyāt al-ḥiwār : naẓarīyah fī dawāfi' al-ṣidām wa-iḥtimālāt al-mustaqbal / Muḥammad Ibrāhīm Mabrūk. al-Ṭab'ah al-'Arabīyah 1. al-Qāhirah : Markaz al-Ḥaḍārah al-'Arabīyah, 2002. 349 p. ; 24 cm. Includes bibliographical references. In Arabic. ISBN 977-291-370-4
1. Islam - 21st century. 2. Islam - Relations - Christianity. 3. Islam - Relations - Judaism. 4. Islamic countries - Relations - Occident. 5. East and West. I. Title.

Mac Ginty, Roger, 1970-.
Contemporary peacemaking. Houndmills, Basingstoke ; New York : Palgrave Macmillan, 2003.
JZ6010 .C665 2003

MacAdam, Jim.
Prichard, H. A. (Harold Arthur), 1871-1947. Moral writings. Oxford : Clarendon Press ; New York : Oxford University Press, 2002.

Macchi, Laura, 1961-.
Thinking. Hoboken, NJ : Wiley, c2003.
BF441 .T466 2003

Macdonald, Barbara, 1913- Look me in the eye : old women, aging and ageism / Barbara Macdonald with Cynthia Rich. New, expanded ed. Denver, CO : Spinsters Ink Books, 2001. xvi, 182 p. ; 22 cm. Expanded ed. of 2nd ed., c1991, with preface by Lise Weil and new afterword by Cynthia Rich. Includes bibliographical references. ISBN 1-88352-340-0 (pbk.) DDC 305.26
1. Aged women. 2. Aged lesbians. 3. Aged women - Social conditions. 4. Aged women - Psychology. 5. Ageism. 6. Aging. 7. Old age. I. Rich, Cynthia. II. Title. III. Title: Old women, aging and ageism

Macdonald, Bradley J.
Strategies for theory. Albany : State University of New York Press, c2003.
B842 .S77 2003

Macdonald, Dwight. Interviews with Dwight Macdonald / edited by Michael Wreszin. Jackson : University Press of Mississippi, c2003. xxiii, 181 p. : ill. ; 24 cm. (Conversations with public intellectuals series) Includes bibliographical references and index. ISBN 1-57806-533-X (alk. paper) ISBN 1-57806-534-8 (pbk. : alk. paper) DDC 973.93
1. Macdonald, Dwight - Interviews. 2. United States - Intellectual life - 20th century. 3. Popular culture - United States - History - 20th century. 4. United States - Politics and government - 20th century. 5. United States - Social conditions - 20th century. 6. Intellectuals - United States - Interviews. I. Wreszin, Michael. II. Title. III. Series.
E169.1 .M1363 2003

MACDONALD, DWIGHT - INTERVIEWS.
Macdonald, Dwight. Interviews with Dwight Macdonald. Jackson : University Press of Mississippi, c2003.
E169.1 .M1363 2003

MacDonald, Lucy, 1953- Learn to be an optimist : a practical guide to achieving happiness / by Lucy MacDonald. San Francisco : Chronicle Books, 2004. p. cm. Includes index. ISBN 0-8118-4169-3 DDC 158
1. Optimism. 2. Happiness. I. Title.
BF698.35.O57 M23 2004

MacDonald, Paul S., 1951- History of the concept of mind : speculations about soul, mind and spirit from Homer to Hume / Paul S. MacDonald. Aldershot ; Burlington, VT : Ashgate, c2003. xi, 398 p. ; 24 cm. Includes bibliographical references and index. ISBN 0-7546-1364-X ISBN 0-7546-1365-8 (pbk.) DDC 128.209
1. Philosophy of mind - History. 2. Mind and body - History. I. Title.

Macek, Petr, 1956-.
Utváření a vývoj osobnosti. Vyd. 1. V Brně : Barrister & Principal, 2002.
BF723.P4 U88 2002

MacGregor, Cynthia. Little indulgences : more than 400 ways to be good to yourself / Cynthia MacGregor. York Beach, ME : Conari Press, 2003. p. cm. ISBN 1-57324-873-8 DDC 646.7
1. Conduct of life - Miscellanea. 2. Quality of life - Miscellanea. I. Title.
BF637.C5 M32 2003

MacGregor, Megan, 1989-.
MacGregor, Rob. Star power. Franklin Lakes, NJ : New Page Books, c2003.

MacGregor, Rob.
BF1571.5.T44 M23 2003

MacGregor, Rob. Dreams : more than 400 symbols explained / by Rob MacGregor. Philadelphia, Pa. : Running Press, c2002. 253 p. ; 12 cm. (The Running Press pocket guide) ISBN 0-7624-1439-1 DDC 154.6/3
1. Dream interpretation - Dictionaries. 2. Symbolism (Psychology) - Dictionaries. I. Title. II. Series.
BF1091 .M314 2002

Star power : astrology for teens / by Rob MacGregor and Megan MacGregor. Franklin Lakes, NJ : New Page Books, c2003. 272 p. : ill. ; 15 cm. ISBN 1-56414-680-4 (pbk.) DDC 133.4./3
1. Witchcraft. 2. Teenagers - Miscellanea. I. MacGregor, Megan, 1989- II. Title.
BF1571.5.T44 M23 2003

MACH, ERNST, 1838-1916.
Anders, Martin. Präsenz zu denken--. St. Augustin : Gardez!, c2002.
B3303 .A53 2002

Machačová, Helena.
[Behaviorální prevence stresu. English]
Behavioural prevention of stress / Helena Machačová. 1st ed. Prague : Karolinum Press, 1999. 190 p. : ill. ; 23 cm. (Acta Universitatis Carolinae. Philosophica et historica. Monographia, 0567-8307 ; 156) Includes bibliographical references (p. 167-180) and index. ISBN 80-7184-821-2
1. Stress (Psychology) - Prevention. I. Title. II. Series.
BF575.S75 M26513 1999

Machado, Armando. The psychology of learning : a student workbook / Armando Machado. Francisco J. Silva ; forward by William Timberlake. Upper Saddle River, NJ : Prentice Hall, 2003. p. cm. Includes bibliographical references and index. ISBN 0-13-091768-0 DDC 153.1/5
1. Learning, Psychology of. 2. Learning, Psychology of - Problems, exercises, etc. I. Silva, Francisco J. II. Title.
BF318 .M29 2003

Machan, Tibor R.
Liberty and democracy. Stanford, CA : Hoover Institution Press, c2002.
JC423 .L5178 2002

The passion for liberty / Tibor R. Machan. Lanham, Md. : Rowman & Littlefield, c2003. xiii, 243 p. ; 24 cm. Includes bibliographical references and index. CONTENTS: Opposing senses of freedom -- Ethical egoism (or individualism) : personal responsibility -- Why capitalism squares with morality -- Immigration into a free society -- Military defense of a free society -- Liberty, economic v. moral benefits -- Against utilitarianism -- Reflections on the right to private property -- The democratic ideal -- Revisiting the class warfare -- Individual rights, democracy, and government debt -- Exploring extreme violence (torture) -- The norms of military intervention -- Democracy and foreign affairs -- Why abortion is not murder -- Objections and alternatives to affirmative action -- The bill of rights and moral philosophy -- Freedom and the media. ISBN 0-7425-3102-3 (alk. paper) ISBN 0-7425-3103-1 (pbk. : alk. paper) DDC 320/.01/1
1. Liberty. 2. Civil rights - United States. 3. Democracy - United States. I. Title.
JC599.U5 M263 2003

MACHINE INTELLIGENCE. See ARTIFICIAL INTELLIGENCE.

Machine learning and data mining in pattern recognition.
International Workshop MLDM 2003 (2003 : Leipzig, Germany) Berlin ; New York : Springer, c2003.
Q327 .I67 2003

MACHINE LEARNING - CONGRESSES.
Adaptivity and learning. New York : Springer, 2003.
BF318 .A33 2003

ALT 2002 (2002 : Lübeck, Germany) Algorithmic learning theory. Berlin ; New York : Springer, c2002.
QA76.9.A43 A48 2002

Conference on Computational Learning Theory (16th : 2003 : Washington, D.C.) Learning theory and Kernel machines. Berlin ; New York : Springer, c2003.
Q325.5 .C654 2003

Imitation in animals and artifacts. Cambridge, Mass. : MIT Press, c2002.
BF357 .I47 2002

International Workshop MLDM 2003 (2003 : Leipzig, Germany) Machine learning and data mining in pattern recognition. Berlin ; New York : Springer, c2003.
Q327 .I67 2003

International Workshop on Multiple Classifier Systems (4th : 2003 : Guildford, England) Multiple classifier systems. Berlin ; New York : Springer, c2003.
Q325.5 .I574 2003

Machine Learning Summer School 2002 (2002 : Canberra, N.C.T.) Advanced lectures on machine learning. Berlin ; New York : Springer, 2003.
Q325.5 .M344 2002

Workshop on Adaptive Behavior in Anticipatory Learning Systems (1st : 2002 : Edinburgh, Scotland) Anticipatory behavior in adaptive learning systems. Berlin ; New York : Springer, c2003.
Q325.5 .W65 2003

Machine Learning Summer School 2002 (2002 : Canberra, N.C.T.) Advanced lectures on machine learning : Machine Learning Summer School 2002, Canberra, Australia, February 11-22, 2002 : revised lectures / Shahar Mendelson, Alexander J. Smola (eds.) Berlin ; New York : Springer, 2003. 257 p. : ill. ; 23 cm. (Lecture notes in computer science ; 2600. Lecture notes in artificial intelligence) Includes bibliographical references and index. Also available via the World Wide Web. URL: http://link.springer-ny.com/link/service/series/0558/tocs/t2600.htm ISBN 3-540-00529-3 (softcover : alk. paper) DDC 006.3/1
1. Machine learning - Congresses. I. Mendelson, Shahar. II. Smola, Alexander J. III. Title. IV. Series: Lecture notes in computer science ; 2600. V. Series: Lecture notes in computer science. Lecture notes in artificial intelligence.
Q325.5 .M344 2002

MACHINE SYSTEMS, VIRTUAL. See VIRTUAL COMPUTER SYSTEMS.

MACHINE THEORY. See ARTIFICIAL INTELLIGENCE; COMPUTERS; MACHINE LEARNING.

MACHINE TRANSLATING.
Wort und (Kon)text. Frankfurt : Lang, 2001.
P325.5.C65 W678 2001

Machinist, Peter.
Nissinen, Martti. Prophets and prophecy in the ancient Near East. Atlanta, GA : Society of Biblical Literature, c2003.
BF1762 .N58 2003b

Nissinen, Martti. Prophets and prophecy in the ancient Near East. Leiden ; Boston : Brill, 2003.
BF1762 .N58 2003

Maciejewski, Franz. Psychoanalytisches Archiv und jüdisches Gedächtnis : Freud, Beschneidung und Monotheismus / Franz Maciejewski. 1. Aufl. Wien : Passagen Verlag, 2002. 395 p. ; 24 cm. (Passagen Philosophie) Thesis (doctoral) - Universität, Frankfurt, 2002. Includes bibliographical references (p. 381-395) ISBN 3-85165-555-9 (pbk.)
1. Freud, Sigmund, - 1856-1939 - Religion. 2. Judaism and psychoanalysis. 3. Judaism - Influence. 4. Monotheism. 5. Circumcision. 6. Oedipus complex. I. Title. II. Series.

MacIntyre, Alasdair C. The unconscious : a conceptual analysis / Alasdair MacIntyre. Rev. ed. New York : Routledge, 2004. p. cm. Includes bibliographical references and index. ISBN 0-415-33303-2 ISBN 0-415-33304-0 (pbk.) DDC 154.2
1. Subconsciousness. 2. Freud, Sigmund, - 1856-1939. I. Title.
BF315 .M23 2004

MACINTYRE, ALASDAIR C.
Smith, R. Scott, 1957- Virtue ethics and moral knowledge. Aldershot, England ; Burlington, VT : Ashgate, c2003.
BJ1012 .S5195 2003

Mackenzie, Patrick T. Mind, body, and freedom / Patrick T. Mackenzie. Amherst, N.Y. : Humanity Books, 2003. 136 p. ; 24 cm. Includes bibliographical references (p. 131-133) and index. ISBN 1-59102-001-8 (alk. paper) DDC 128/.2
1. Mind and body - Philosophy. 2. Liberty. I. Title.
BF161 .M23 2003

MacLin, Otto H., 1958-.
Dixon, Mark R., 1970- Visual Basic for behavioral psychologists. Reno, NV : Context Press, c2003.
BF76.5 .D59 2003

MACMURRAY, JOHN, 1891-.
Hood, Adam, 1960- Baillie, Oman and Macmurray. Aldershot, England ; Burlington, VT : Ashgate, c2003.
BR110 .H575 2003

Macquarie monographs in cognitive science
Individual differences in theory of mind. New York : Psychology Press, 2003.
BF723.P48 I53 2003

MACROECONOMICS.
Beyond Keynes. Cheltenham ; Northampton, Mass. : Edward Elgar, c2002.

Madalyn Aslan's Jupiter signs.
Aslan, Madalyn. New York : Viking Studio, 2003.
BF1724.2.J87 A85 2003

Madame Dora's fortune-telling cards.
Lott, Lynn. Gloucester, Mass. : Fair Winds Press, 2003.
BF1878 .L78 2003

Madeleva lecture in spirituality
(2003.) Callahan, Sidney Cornelia. Women who hear voices. New York : Paulist Press, 2003.
BV5091.R4 C35 2003

Madell, Geoffrey. Philosophy, music and emotion / Geoffrey Madell. Edinburgh : Edinburgh University Press, c2002. vii, 162 p. : music ; 24 cm. Includes bibliographical references (p. 158-160) and index. ISBN 0-7486-1612-8 DDC 780.1
1. Music - Philosophy and aesthetics. 2. Emotions. I. Title.

Madhubuti, Haki R., 1942- Tough notes : a healing call for creating exceptional Black men : affirmations, meditations, readings, and strategies / Haki R. Madhubuti. 1st ed. Chicago : Third World Press, c2002. xiii, 225 p. ; 23 cm. Includes bibliographical references (p. 213-225). ISBN 0-88378-236-7 (alk. paper) DDC 170/.835/1
1. African American men - Life skills guides. 2. African American men - Psychology. 3. African American men - Social conditions. 4. Conduct of life. 5. Social values - United States. 6. African Americans - Social conditions. 7. Black author. I. Title.
E185.86 .T68 2002

Madigan, M. A., 1962- Symbols of the craft / M.A. Madigan & P.M. Richards. 1st ed. St. Paul, Minn. : Llewellyn Publications, 2003. xxiii, 157 p. : ill. ; 21 cm. ISBN 0-7387-0194-7 DDC 133.3/22
1. Divination. 2. Magic. 3. Charms. 4. Witchcraft. I. Richards, P. M., 1962- II. Title.
BF1773 .M29 2003

MADNESS. See ANGER; MENTAL ILLNESS.

Madness, deviance and creativity.
Shoham, S. Giora, 1929- Teruf, setiyah yi-yetsirah. [Israel] : Miśrad ha-biṭaḥon, [2002]

Madregat ha-adam.
Hurwitz, Joseph, d. 1919. Sefer Madregat ha-adam. Hotsa'ah ḥadashah mefo'eret menuḳedet u-metuḳenet. Yerushalayim : Yeshivat Ner Shemu'el, 762 [2002]

Madres e hijas.
López, Carmen Adela, 1935- Caracas, Venezuela : Vadell Hermanos, 2002.

Madsen, Kim Halskov, 1956-.
Production methods. London ; New York : Springer, c2003.
QA76.76.I59 P76 2003

Maesschalck, M. (Marc) Normes et contextes : les fondements d'une pragmatique contextuelle / Marc Maesschalck. Hildesheim ; New York : G. Olms, 2001. 324 p. ; 24 cm. (Europaea memoria. Reihe 1. Studien ; Bd. 17) Includes bibliographical references and index. ISBN 3-487-11327-9 (pbk.)
1. Norm (Philosophy) 2. Ethics. I. Title. II. Series.
BJ1063 .M34 2001

Maestripieri, Dario.
Primate psychology. Cambridge, MA : Harvard University Press, 2003.
BF671 .P75 2003

Mageia-satanismos.
Tsiakkas, Christophoros A. 3 ekd. Leukōsia : Ekdosē Hieras Monēs Trooditissēs, 2001.
BF1550 .T73 2001

The magenta gamma.
Astartes, Alfa. [Philadelphia] : Xlibris, c2002.
BF1714.O7 A88 2002

Mageo, Jeannette Marie.
Dreaming and the self. Albany : State University of New York Press, c2003.
BF1091 .D735 2003

Magett, Sonya.
Marriott, Rob. Astrology uncut. 1st trade pbk. ed. New York : One World, 2004.
BF1711 .M45 2004

Maghi, streghe e alchimisti a Siena e nel suo territorio (1458-1571) / [a cura di] Maria Assunta Ceppari Ridolfi ; presentazione di Mario Ascheri. Monteriggioni (Siena) : Il leccio, c1999. 143 p. : ill. ; 24 cm. (Documenti di storia ; 28) Italian and Latin. Includes

bibliographical references (p. [135]-137) and index. ISBN 88-86507-39-9
1. Magic - Italy - Siena - History - Sources. 2. Witchcraft - Italy - Siena - History - Sources. 3. Alchemy - Italy - Siena - History - Sources. I. Ceppari Ridolfi, Maria A. II. Series.
BF1622.I8 M295 1999

Magia, alchimia, scienza dal '400 al '700 : l'influsso di Ermete Trismegisto = magic, alchemy and science 15th-18th centuries : the influence of Hermes Trismegistus /ca cura di = edited by Carlos Gilly, Cis van Heertum. Firenze : Centro Di, 2002. 2 v. : ill. (some col.) ; 29 cm. Italian and English. "The Marciana Library is thus happy to accept the proposal of Joost R. Ritman, creator of the Bibliotheca Philosophica Hermetica of Amsterdam, to set up a joint exhibition devoted to the history of the Hermetic tradition..."--P. 10, vol. 1. "Whereas the more extensive first volume of the catalogue consists of lengthier essays and monographs on authors, manuscripts, books and images of importance to the theme of the exhibition, this second volume serves above all as an illustrated guide to the books presented there."--P. 8, vol. 2. Includes bibliographical references. ISBN 88-7038-359-8 (v. 1) ISBN 88-7038-385-7 (v. 2) DDC 135/.45
1. Corpus Hermeticum - Exhibitions. 2. Hermes, - Trismegistus - Exhibitions. 3. Biblioteca nazionale marciana - Exhibitions. 4. Bibliotheca Philosophica Hermetica (Amsterdam, Netherlands) - Exhibitions. 5. Alchemy - Europe - Manuscripts - Exhibitions. 6. Hermetism - Europe - Manuscripts - Exhibitions. 7. Occultism - Europe - Manuscripts - Exhibitions. I. Gilly, Carlos. II. Heertum, Cis van. III. Biblioteca nazionale marciana. IV. Bibliotheca Philosophica Hermetica (Amsterdam, Netherlands) V. Title: Influsso di Eremete Trismegisto. VI. Title: Magic, alchemy and science 15th-18th centuries. VII. Title: Influence of Hermes Trismegistus. VIII. Title: Hermes Trismegistus
BF1598.H6 M34 2002

Magia y belleza.
McCoy, Edain, 1957- [Enchantments. Spanish] 1st ed. St. Paul, Minn. : Llewellyn Español, 2002.
BF1623.B43 E6418 2002

MAGIC. See also AMULETS; CHARMS; MEDICINE, MAGIC, MYSTIC, AND SPAGIRIC; TALISMANS.
Alexander, Skye. 10-minute magic spells. Gloucester, Mass. : Fair Winds Press, 2003.
BF1611 .A43 2003

Alexander, Skye. Magickal astrology. Franklin Lakes, NJ : New Page Books, c2000.
BF1611 .A44 2000

Andrews, Ted, 1952- Magic of believing. 1st ed. Jackson, Tenn. : Dragonhawk Pub., c2000.
BF1611 .A53 2000

Aoumiel. Grimoire for the green witch. 1st ed. St. Paul, Minn. : Llewellyn Publications, c2003.
BF1572.P43 A583 2003

Ashley, Leonard R. N. The complete book of sex magic. Fort Lee, NJ : Barricade Books, 2003.
BF1623.S4 A85 2002

Aswynn, Freya, 1949- Northern mysteries & magick. 2nd ed. St. Paul, Minn. : Llewellyn Publications, 1998 (2002 printing)
BF1623.R89 A78 1998

Brondwin, C. C., 1945- Clan of the Goddess. Franklin Lakes, NJ : New Page Books, c2002.
BF1623.G63 B76 2002

Buckland, Raymond. Color magick. 1st ed., rev. St. Paul, Minn. : Llewellyn Publications, 2002.
BF1623.C6 B83 2002

Carney, John, 1958- The book of secrets. 1st ed. [United States?] : Carney Magic, c2002.
BF1611 .C35 2002

Clément, Catherine, 1939- Le divan et le grigri. Paris : Jacob, c2002.

Conway, D. J. (Deanna J.) Magickal, mystical creatures. 2nd ed. St. Paul, Minn. : Llewellyn Publications, 2003.
BF1623.A55 C67 2003

Crowley, Vivianne. The magickal life. New York : Penguin Compass, 2003.
BF1611 .C77 2003

Cunningham, Scott, 1956- [Wicca. Spanish] Wicca. 1. ed. St. Paul, Minn. : Llewellyn Español, 2003.
BF1566 .C8618 2003

Denning, Melita. Mysteria magica. 3rd ed. St. Paul, Minn. : Llewellyn Publications, 2004.
BF1611 .D395 2004

Dumars, Denise. The dark archetype. Franklin Lakes, N.J. : New Page Books, c2003.

Dunwich, Gerina. Dunwich's guide to gemstone sorcery. Franklin Lakes, NJ : New Page Books, c2003.
BF1442.P74 D86 2003

Dunwich, Gerina. Exploring spellcraft. Franklin Lakes, NJ : New Page Books, c2001.
BF1566 .D866 2001

Dunwich, Gerina. The pagan book of Halloween. New York : Penguin/Compass, 2000.
BF1566 .D867 2000

Dunwich, Gerina. A witch's guide to ghosts and the supernatural. Franklin Lakes, NJ : New Page Books, c2002.
BF1471 .D86 2002

DuQuette, Lon Milo, 1948- [Magick of Thelma] The magick of Aleister Crowley. Boston, MA : Weiser Books, 2003.
BF1611 .D87 2003

Eason, Cassandra. A practical guide to witchcraft and magick spells. London ; New York : Quantum, c2001.

Galenorn, Yasmine, 1961- Magical meditations. [New ed.]. Berkeley, Calif. : Crossing Press, c2003.
BF1561 .G35 2003

Gillotte, Galen, 1952- Sacred stones of the goddess. 1st ed. St. Paul, Minn. : Llewellyn Publications, 2003.
BF1611 .G55 2003

Grechishnikov, S. E. (Sergeĭ Egorovich) Magii︠a︡ kak sotsiokul'turnyĭ fenomen. Kaluga : GUP "Oblizdat", 1999.
BF1616 .G74 1999

Grimassi, Raven, 1951- The witch's familiar. 1st ed. St. Paul, Minn. : Llewellyn Publications, 2003.
BF1557 .G75 2003

Hardie, Titania. Titania's magical compendium. San Diego, Calif. : Thunder Bay Press, 2003.
BF1611 .H235 2003

Hawke, Elen, 1947- An alphabet of spells. St. Paul, MN : Llewellyn Publications, 2003.
BF1566 .H376 2003

Heath, Maya, 1948- Magical oils by moonlight. Franklin Lakes, NJ : New Page Books, 2004.
BF1442.E77 H43 2004

Holland, Eileen. Spells for the solitary witch. Boston, MA : Weiser Books, 2004.
BF1566 .H643 2004

Knight, Sirona, 1955- Dream magic. 1st ed. San Francisco : HarperSanFrancisco, c2000.
BF1621 .K65 2000

Leslie, Mike, 1956- The magical personality. 1st ed. St. Paul, Minn. : Llewellyn, 2002.
BF1621 .L47 2002

Madigan, M. A., 1962- Symbols of the craft. 1st ed. St. Paul, Minn. : Llewellyn Publications, 2003.
BF1773 .M29 2003

Magic and modernity. Stanford, Calif. : Stanford University Press, 2003.
GN475.3 .M34 2003

McColman, Carl. Before you cast a spell. Franklin Lakes, NJ : New Page Books, 2004.
BF1611 .M385 2004

McCormack, Kathleen. Magic for lovers : find your ideal partner through the power of magic. 1st ed. Hauppauge, NY : Barron's, c2003.
BF1623.L6 M38 2003

McCoy, Edain, 1957- [Enchantments. Spanish] Magia y belleza. 1st ed. St. Paul, Minn. : Llewellyn Español, 2002.
BF1623.B43 E6418 2002

Meader, William A., 1955- Shine forth. Mariposa, Calif. : Source Publications, c2004.
BF1611 .M412 2004

Moorey, Teresa. Magic house. 1st US ed. New York, NY : Ryland Peters & Small, 2003.
BF1623.H67 M66 2003

Morrison, Dorothy, 1955- Everyday moon magic. St. Paul, Minn. : Llewellyn Publications, 2003.
BF1623.M66 M67 2003

Neal, Carl F., 1965- Incense. 1st ed. St. Paul, Minn. : Llewellyn Publications, 2003.
BF1623.I52 N43 2003

Richardson, S. Cheryl. Magicka formularia. [Miami, Fla.] : S.C. Richardson, c2001.

Riggs-Bergesen, Catherine. Candle therapy. Kansas City, Mo. : Andrews McMeel Pub., c2003.
BF1623.C26 R54 2003

Roderick, Timothy, 1963- Dark moon mysteries. Aptos, Calif. : New Brighton Books, 2003.
BF1623.M66 R63 2003

Rumstuckle, Cornelius, 1940- The book of wizardry. 1st ed. St. Paul, Minn. : Llewellyn Publications, 2003.
BF1611 .R85 2003

Sophia, 1955- The little book of hot love spells. Kansas City, Mo. : Andrews McMeel Pub., c2002.
BF1623.L6 S66 2002

Sophia, 1955- The ultimate guide to goddess empowerment. Kansas City : Andrews McMeel Pub., c2003.
BF1621 .S67 2003

Styers, Randall. Making magic. New York : Oxford University Press, 2003.
BF1611 .S855 2003

Telesco, Patricia, 1960- Animal spirit. Franklin Lakes, NJ : New Page Books, c2002.
BF1623.A55 T445 2002

Telesco, Patricia, 1960- An enchanted life. Franklin Lakes, N.J. : New Page Books, c2002.
BF1621 .T42 2002

Telesco, Patricia, 1960- Exploring candle magick. Franklin Lakes, NJ : New Page Books, c2001.
BF1623.C26 T45 2001

Telúch, Peter. Amulety a talizmany. Bratislava : Print-Servis, 1998.

Trobe, Kala, 1969- The witch's guide to life. 1st ed. St. Paul, Minn. : Llewellyn Publications, 2003.
BF1566 .T76 2003

Weinstein, Marion. Earth magic. Rev. ed. Franklin Lakes, NJ : New Page Books, c2003.
BF1566 .W46 2003

Weinstein, Marion. Positive magic. Rev. ed. Franklin Lakes, NJ : New Page Books, c2002.
BF1411 .W393 2002

Wishart, Catherine, 1965- Teen goddess. 1st ed. St. Paul, Minn. : Llewellyn Publications, c2003.
BF1623.G63 W57 2003

Wood, Jamie. The Wicca herbal. Berkeley, Calif. : Celestial Arts, c2003.
BF1572.P43 W66 2003

Zell-Ravenheart, Oberon, 1942- Grimoire for the apprentice wizard. Franklin Lakes, NJ : New Page Books, 2004.
BF1611 .Z45 2004

Magic, alchemy and science 15th-18th centuries.
Magia, alchimia, scienza dal '400 al '700. Firenze : Centro Di, 2002.
BF1598.H6 M34 2002

MAGIC - AMAZON RIVER REGION.
In darkness and secrecy. Durham, NC : Duke University Press, 2004.
BF1566 .I5 2004

MAGIC, ANCIENT.
Astori, Roberta. Formule magiche. Milano : Mimesis, c2000.
BF1591 .A88 2000

Perry, Laura, 1965- Ancient spellcraft. Franklin Lakes, NJ : New Page Books, c2002.
BF1591 .P47 2002

Pinch, Geraldine. Magic in ancient Egypt. London : British Museum Press, c1994.

MAGIC, ANCIENT - CONGRESSES.
Prayer, magic, and the stars in the ancient and late antique world. University Park, Pa. : Pennsylvania State University Press, 2003.
BF1591 .P73 2003

Magic and modernity : interfaces of revelation and concealment / edited by Birgit Meyer and Peter Pels. Stanford, Calif. : Stanford University Press, 2003. viii, 390 p. ; 23 cm. Includes bibliographical references and index. CONTENTS: Between science and superstition: religion and the modern subject of the nation in colonial India / Gyan Prakash -- Undying past: spirit possession and the memory of war in southern Mozambique / Alcinda Honwana -- Robert Kaplan and "Juju journalism" in Sierra Leone's rebel war: the primitivizing of an African conflict / Rosalind Shaw -- The citizen's trance: the Haitian revolution and the motor of history / Laurent Dubois -- Hidden forces: colonialism and the politics of magic in the Netherlands Indies / Margaret J.

Wiener -- On witch doctors and spin doctors: the role of "experts" in African and American politics / Peter Geschiere -- The magical power of the (printed) word / Martha Kaplan -- Ghanaian popular cinema and the magic in and of film / Birgit Meyer -- Dr. Jekyll and Mr. Hyde: modern medicine between magic and science / Jojada Verrips -- Spirits of modernity: Alfred Wallace, Edward Tylor, and the visual politics of fact / Peter Pels -- Viscerality, faith, and skepticism: another theory of magic / Michael Taussig. ISBN 0-8047-4463-7 ISBN 0-8047-4464-5 DDC 306.4
1. Magic. 2. Divination. 3. Witchcraft. 4. Spiritualism. I. Meyer, Birgit. II. Pels, Peter.
GN475.3 .M34 2003

Magic and mystery in ancient Egypt.
Jacq, Christian. [Monde magique de l'Egypte ancienne] London : Souvenir Press, 1998, 2002.

MAGIC, ASSYRO-BABYLONIAN.
Cryer, Frederick H. Biblical and pagan societies. Philadelphia : University of Pennsylvania Press, 2001.
BF1567 .C79 2001

MAGIC - BELARUS.
Kazakova, I. V. (Iryna Valerʹeŭna) Mifalahemy i mahiia ŭ belaruskim abradavym falʹklory. Minsk : "BOFF", 1997.
GR203.4 .K39 1997

MAGIC - BIBLIOGRAPHY.
McColman, Carl. The well-read witch. Franklin Lakes, NJ : New Page Books, c2002.
BF1611

MAGIC, CELTIC.
Brondwin, C. C., 1945- Clan of the Goddess. Franklin Lakes, NJ : New Page Books, c2002.
BF1623.G63 B76 2002

De Grandis, Francesca. What kind of goddess are you? Naperville, Ill. : Sourcebooks, Inc., 2004.
BF1623.G63 D4 2004

The lost books of Merlyn. 1st ed. St. Paul, Minn : Llewellyn Publications, 1998 (2003 printing)
BF1622.C45 L67 1998

MAGIC, COPTIC. *See* **MAGIC, EGYPTIAN.**

MAGIC - DICTIONARIES.
Beattie, Antonia. Spells dictionary. San Diego, Calif. : Thunder Bay Press, 2003.
BF1611 .B43 2003

MAGIC - EARLY WORKS TO 1800.
Bruno, Giordano, 1548-1600. Opere magiche. Milano : Adelphi, 2000.
BF1600 .B78 2000

[Clavicula Salomonis. English.] The Goetia. York Beach, Me. : Samuel Weiser, 1995.
BF1611 .C5413 1995

MAGIC, EGYPTIAN.
Clark, Rosemary, 1948- The sacred magic of ancient Egypt. 1st ed. St. Paul, Minn. : Llewellyn Publications, 2003.
BF1591 .C52 2003

Constantine, Storm. Bast and Sekhmet. London : R. Hale, c1999.

David, A. Rosalie (Ann Rosalie) Religion and magic in ancient Egypt. London : Penguin, 2002.

Dee, Jonathan. Isis. New York : Sterling Pub., [2003?]
BF1591 .D44 2003

Jacq, Christian. [Monde magique de l'Egypte ancienne] Magic and mystery in ancient Egypt. London : Souvenir Press, 1998, 2002.

Pinch, Geraldine. Magic in ancient Egypt. London : British Museum Press, c1994.

MAGIC, EGYPTIAN - CONGRESSES.
La magie en Egypte. Paris : Documentation française : Musée du Louvre, c2002.
BF1591 .M3447 2002

MAGIC - ENGLAND - HISTORY.
Davenport, Anne Ashley. St. George's Hall. Pasadena : Mike Caveney's Magic Words, c2001.
BF1623 .D38 2001

Davies, Owen, 1969- Cunning-folk. London ; New York : Hambledon and London, 2003.
BF1622.G7 D385 2002

MAGIC - EUROPE - HISTORY.
Zika, Charles. Exorcising our demons. Leiden ; Boston : Brill, 2003.
BF1584.E85 Z55 2003

MAGIC - EUROPE - HISTORY - TO 1500.
Jolly, Karen Louise. The Middle Ages. Philadelphia : University of Pennsylvania Press, 2002, 2001. 12 300 xiv, 280 p. ; 24 cm.
BF1593 .J65 2002

Magic for lovers : find your ideal partner through the power of magic.
McCormack, Kathleen. 1st ed. Hauppauge, NY : Barron's, c2003.
BF1623.L6 M38 2003

The magic formula.
Roads, Michael J. 1st ed. Cleveland : SilverRoads Pub., 2003.
BF637.S4 R575 2003

MAGIC, GERMANIC.
Thorsson, Edred. The truth about Teutonic magick. 2nd ed. Saint Paul, MN : Llewellyn Publications, 1994.
BF1622.G3 T488 1994

MAGIC - HANDBOOKS, MANUALS, ETC.
Connor, Kerri, 1970- The pocket spell creator. Franklin Lakes, N.J. : New Page Books, c2003.
BF1611 .C724 2003

Frost, Gavin. A witch's grimoire of ancient omens, portents, talismans, amulets, and charms. Rev. and updated ed. New York : Reward Books, c2002.
BF1566 .F83 2002

Morgan, Sheena. The Wicca handbook. London : Vega, 2003.
BF1566 .M716 2003

MAGIC - HISTORY.
Aveni, Anthony F. Behind the crystal ball. Rev. ed. Boulder, Colo. : University Press of Colorado, c2002.
BF1589 .A9 2002

Berg, Wendy, 1951- Polarity magic. St. Paul, Minn. : Llewellyn Publications, 2003.
BF1589 .B47 2003

De Martino, Ernesto, 1908-1965. Il mondo magico. 1. ed. Torino : Bollati Boringhieri, 1997.
BF1589 .D46 1997

The metamorphosis of magic from late antiquity to the early modern period. Leuven ; Dudley, MA : Peeters, 2002.
BF1589 .M55 2002

Szőnyi, György Endre. John Dee's occultism. Albany : State University of New York Press, 2004.
BF1598.D5 S98 2004

MAGIC - HISTORY - SOURCES.
Levack, Brian P. The witchcraft sourcebook. London ; New York : Routledge, 2003.
BF1566 .L475 2003

Magic house.
Moorey, Teresa. 1st US ed. New York, NY : Ryland Peters & Small, 2003.
BF1623.H67 M66 2003

Magic in ancient Egypt.
Pinch, Geraldine. London : British Museum Press, c1994.

Magic in history.
Bailey, Michael David, 1971- Battling demons. University Park, Pa. : Pennsylvania State University Press, c2003.
BF1569 .B35 2003

Prayer, magic, and the stars in the ancient and late antique world. University Park, Pa. : Pennsylvania State University Press, 2003.
BF1591 .P73 2003

MAGIC IN LITERATURE.
Astori, Roberta. Formule magiche. Milano : Mimesis, c2000.
BF1591 .A88 2000

Gupta, Suman, 1966- Re-reading Harry Potter. Houndmills, Basingstoke ; New York : Palgrave Macmillan, 2003.
PR6068.O93 Z68 2003

Harry Potter's world. New York ; London : RoutledgeFalmer, 2003.
PR6068.O93 Z73 2003

Heng, Geraldine. Empire of magic. New York : Columbia University Press, c2003.
PR321 .H46 2003

The ivory tower and Harry Potter. Columbia : University of Missouri Press, 2002.
PR6068.O93 Z734 2002

Reading Harry Potter. Westport, Conn. ; London : Praeger Publishers, 2003.

PR6068.O93 Z84 2003

MAGIC, ISLAMIC. *See* **ZĀR.**

MAGIC - ITALY - CAPUA - HISTORY.
Ferraiuolo, Augusto. "Pro exoneratione sua propria coscientia". Milano : F. Angeli, c2000.
BF1584.I8 F44 2000

MAGIC - ITALY - SIENA - HISTORY - SOURCES.
Maghi, streghe e alchimisti a Siena e nel suo territorio (1458-1571). Monteriggioni (Siena) : Il leccio, c1999.
BF1622.I8 M295 1999

MAGIC, JEWISH.
[Clavicula Salomonis. English.] Lemegeton. Jacksonville, FL : Metatron Books, 1999.

Cryer, Frederick H. Biblical and pagan societies. Philadelphia : University of Pennsylvania Press, 2001.
BF1567 .C79 2001

Oron, Michal. Mi-'Ba'al shed' le-'Ba'al Shem'. Yerushalayim : Mosad Byalik : Bet ha-sefer le-mada'e ha-Yahadut 'a. sh. Hayim Rozenberg, Universitat Tel-Aviv, c763 [2002]

MAGIC, JEWISH - EARLY WORKS TO 1800.
[Clavicula Salomonis. English.] The Goetia. York Beach, Me. : Samuel Weiser, 1995.
BF1611 .C5413 1995

MAGIC - JUVENILE LITERATURE.
Andrews, Ted, 1952- Magic of believing. 1st ed. Jackson, Tenn. : Dragonhawk Pub., c2000.
BF1611 .A53 2000

Rumstuckle, Cornelius, 1940- The book of wizardry. 1st ed. St. Paul, Minn. : Llewellyn Publications, 2003.
BF1611 .R85 2003

MAGIC - MALAWI.
Soko, Boston. Nchimi chikanga. Blantyre [Malawi] : Christian Literature Association in Malawi, 2002.
1. Black author.

MAGIC MEDICINE. *See* **MEDICINE, MAGIC, MYSTIC, AND SPAGIRIC.**

MAGIC MIRRORS.
Telesco, Patricia, 1960- A little book of mirror magick. Berkeley, Calif. : Crossing Press, c2003.
BF1891.M28 T45 2003

MAGIC - MISCELLANEA.
Tempest, Raven. Bewitching love potions & charms. London : Cassell Illustrated ; New York, NY : Distributed in the USA by Sterling Pub. Co., c2003.
BF575.L8 .T45 2003

Magic, mystery, and science.
Burton, Dan. Bloomington : Indiana University Press, 2003.
BF1411 .B885 2003

MAGIC - NEW ZEALAND.
Roundtree, Kathryn. Embracing the witch and the goddess. London ; New York : Routledge, 2003.
BF1584.N45 R68 2003

Magic of believing.
Andrews, Ted, 1952- 1st ed. Jackson, Tenn. : Dragonhawk Pub., c2000.
BF1611 .A53 2000

The magic power of white witchcraft.
Frost, Gavin. Paramus, NJ : Prentice Hall, c1999.
BF1561 .F76 1999

MAGIC - PUERTO RICO.
Romberg, Raquel. Witchcraft and welfare. 1st ed. Austin : University of Texas Press, c2003.
BF1584.P9 R66 2003

MAGIC - RELIGIOUS ASPECTS.
Styers, Randall. Making magic. New York : Oxford University Press, 2003.
BF1611 .S855 2003

MAGIC - RELIGIOUS ASPECTS - CHRISTIANITY.
Jolly, Karen Louise. The Middle Ages. Philadelphia : University of Pennsylvania Press, 2002, 2001. 12 300 xiv, 280 p. ; 24 cm.
BF1593 .J65 2002

Soko, Boston. Nchimi chikanga. Blantyre [Malawi] : Christian Literature Association in Malawi, 2002.
1. Black author.

MAGIC - RELIGIOUS ASPECTS - HISTORY - CONGRESSES.
Prayer, magic, and the stars in the ancient and late antique world. University Park, Pa. : Pennsylvania State University Press, 2003.
BF1591 .P73 2003

MAGIC, ROMANI.
Cooper, Patrinella. Gypsy magic. Boston : Weiser Books, 2002.
BF1622.R65 C66 2002

MAGIC - SCOTLAND - HISTORY - 16TH CENTURY.
Maxwell-Stuart, P. G. Satan's conspiracy. East Linton, Scotland : Tuckwell Press, 2001.
BF1622.S38 M39 2001

MAGIC, SEMITIC. *See* **MAGIC, JEWISH.**

MAGIC - SOCIAL ASPECTS.
Grechishnikov, S. E. (Sergeĭ Egorovich) Magii͡a kak sotsiokul'turnyĭ fenomen. Kaluga : GUP "Oblizdat", 1999.
BF1616.G74 1999

Styers, Randall. Making magic. New York : Oxford University Press, 2003.
BF1611.S855 2003

MAGIC - SPAIN - GRANADA - HISTORY.
Ceballos Gómez, Diana Luz, 1962- Zauberei und Hexerei. Frankfurt am Main ; New York : Peter Lang, c2000.
BF1584.S7 C43 2000

MAGIC TRICKS.
Dawes, Edwin A. Stanley Collins. Washington, DC : Kaufman and Co., c2002.

Mandelberg, Robert. Mystifying mind reading tricks. New York : Sterling Pub., 2002.
GV1553.M35 2002

Magical meditations.
Galenorn, Yasmine, 1961- [New ed.]. Berkeley, Calif. : Crossing Press, c2003.
BF1561.G35 2003

Magical oils by moonlight.
Heath, Maya, 1948- Franklin Lakes, NJ : New Page Books, 2004.
BF1442.E77 H43 2004

The magical personality.
Leslie, Mike, 1956- 1st ed. St. Paul, Minn. : Llewellyn, 2002.
BF1621.L47 2002

Magical pro-files
(10th) Davenport, Anne Ashley. St. George's Hall. Pasadena : Mike Caveney's Magic Words, c2001.
BF1623.D38 2001

MAGICAL THINKING. *See* **CHARMS.**

MAGICIANS - ENGLAND - BIOGRAPHY.
Davenport, Anne Ashley. St. George's Hall. Pasadena : Mike Caveney's Magic Words, c2001.
BF1623.D38 2001

Dawes, Edwin A. Stanley Collins. Washington, DC : Kaufman and Co., c2002.

MAGICIANS - ENGLAND - HISTORY.
Davies, Owen, 1969- Cunning-folk. London ; New York : Hambledon and London, 2003.
BF1622.G7 D385 2002

The magick of Aleister Crowley.
DuQuette, Lon Milo, 1948- [Magick of Thelma] Boston, MA : Weiser Books, 2003.
BF1611.D87 2003

Magicka formularia.
Richardson, S. Cheryl. [Miami, Fla.] : S.C. Richardson, c2001.
BF1611.R53 2001

Magickal astrology.
Alexander, Skye. Franklin Lakes, NJ : New Page Books, c2000.
BF1611.A44 2000

The magickal life.
Crowley, Vivianne. New York : Penguin Compass, 2003.
BF1611.C77 2003

Magickal, mystical creatures.
Conway, D. J. (Deanna J.) 2nd ed. St. Paul, Minn. : Llewellyn Publications, 2003.
BF1623.A55 C67 2003

Magid, Barry. Ordinary mind : exploring the common ground of Zen and psychotherapy / Barry Magid. Boston : Wisdom, c2002. xiii, 190 p. ; 24 cm. Includes bibliographical references (p. 181-184) and index. ISBN 0-86171-306-0 (alk. paper) DDC 294.3/375
1. Religious life - Zen Buddhism. 2. Psychotherapy - Religious aspects - Zen Buddhism. 3. Buddhism and psychoanalysis. I. Title.
BQ9286.M34 2002

La magie en Egypte : à la recherche d'une définition : actes du colloque organisé par le Musée du Louvre, les 29 et 30 septembre 2000 / sous la direction scientifique d'Yvan Koenig. Paris : Documentation française : Musée du Louvre, c2002. 437 p. : ill. ; 24 cm. (Louvre conférences et colloques, 1158-677X) Includes bibliographical references and indexes. ISBN 2-11-005267-8 DDC 133.4/3/0932
1. Magic, Egyptian - Congresses. I. Koenig, Yvan. II. Musée du Louvre. III. Series.
BF1591.M3447 2002

Magii͡a kak sotsiokul'turnyĭ fenomen.
Grechishnikov, S. E. (Sergeĭ Egorovich) Kaluga : GUP "Oblizdat", 1999.
BF1616.G74 1999

Magika logia tōn apo Zōroastrou magōn.
Gemistus Plethon, George, 15th cent. [Magika logia tōn apo Zōroastrou magōn. French & Greek] Athēnai : Akadēmia Athēnōn, 1995.
BF1762.G45 1995

Magill, Richard A.
Motor learning.
Magill, Richard A. Motor learning and control. 7th ed. Boston : McGraw-Hill, c2004.
BF295.M36 2004

Motor learning and control : concepts and applications / Richard A. Magill. 7th ed. Boston : McGraw-Hill, c2004. xiv, 400 p. : ill. ; 25 cm. Rev. ed. of: Motor learning. c2001. Includes bibliographical references (p. 361-380) and indexes. ISBN 0-07-255722-2 (alk. paper) DDC 152.3/34
1. Motor learning. I. Magill, Richard A. Motor learning. II. Title.
BF295.M36 2004

MAGNETIC PROSPECTING.
Neubauer, Wolfgang, 1963- Magnetische Prospektion in der Archäologie. Wien : Verlag der Österreichischen Akademie der Wissenschaften, 2001.

Magnetische Prospektion in der Archäologie.
Neubauer, Wolfgang, 1963- Wien : Verlag der Österreichischen Akademie der Wissenschaften, 2001.

Magnitogorskiĭ gosudarstvennyĭ pedagogicheskiĭ institut.
Psikhologicheskie problemy bytii͡a cheloveka v sovremennom obshchestve. Magnitogorsk : Magnitogorskiĭ gos. universitet, 2001.
BF20.P744 2001

Magnusson, David.
Bergman, Lars R. Studying individual development in an interindividual context. Mahwah, N.J. : L. Erlbaum Associates, 2003.
BF713.B464 2003

Magyar, K. P. (Karl P.).
Global security concerns [electronic resource]. Maxwell Air Force Base, Ala. : Air University Press, [1996]

MAGYAR LANGUAGE. *See* **HUNGARIAN LANGUAGE.**

Magyarok és nyelvtörvények / szerkesztette, Kontra Miklós és Hatyár Helga. Budapest : Teleki László Alapítvány, 2002. 140 p. : ill. ; 24 cm. (A Magyarságkutatás könyvtára, 0865-3925 ; 26) Includes bibliographical references and index. ISBN 963-86291-3-4
1. Hungarian language - Reform. 2. Hungarian language - Standardization. 3. Language and languages. I. Kontra, Miklós. II. Hatyár, Helga. III. Series.
PH2073.K66 2002

A Magyarságkutatás könyvtára
(26) Magyarok és nyelvtörvények. Budapest : Teleki László Alapítvány, 2002.
PH2073.K66 2002

MAHAYANA BUDDHISM. *See* **TANTRIC BUDDHISM.**

Maḥfūẓ, Najlā'.
Iʿtirāfāt al nisa.
Maḥfūẓ, Najlā'. Zawjī wa-al-ukhrá. al-Ṭabʿah 1. al-Qāhirah : al-Dār al-Miṣrīyah al-Lubnānīyah, 2003.
HQ1793.M34 2003

Zawjī wa-al-ukhrá / Najlā' Maḥfūẓ. al-Ṭabʿah 1. al-Qāhirah : al-Dār al-Miṣrīyah al-Lubnānīyah, 2003. 211 p. ; 20 cm. (Iʿtirāfāt al-nisā') In Arabic. ISBN 977-270-774-8
1. Women - Egypt - Social conditions. 2. Social problems - Egypt. I. Title. II. Series: Maḥfūẓ, Najlā'. Iʿtirāfāt al-nisā'.
HQ1793.M34 2003

Mahoney, James, 1968-.
Comparative historical analysis in the social sciences. Cambridge, U.K. ; New York : Cambridge University Press, 2003.
H61.C524 2003

Mai, Manfred, 1953-.
Popvisionen. Frankfurt : Suhrkamp, 2003.
ML3470.P69 2003

Maier, Johann. Judentum von A bis Z : Glauben, Geschichte, Kultur / Johann Maier. Freiburg im Breisgau : Herder, 2001. 462 p. ; 21 cm. (Herder Spektrum ; Bd. 5169) Includes bibliographical references and index. ISBN 3-451-05169-9
1. Judaism - Customs and practices. 2. Judaism - History. 3. Judaism. 4. Jews - Social life and customs. 5. Jewish way of life. I. Series.

MAIER, MICHAEL, 1568?-1622.
Tilton, Hereward. The quest for the phoenix. Berlin ; New York : Walter de Gruyter, 2003.
QD24.M3 T558 2003

Maila, Joseph.
Arkoun, Mohammed. De Manhattan à Bagdad. Paris : Desclée de Brouwer, 2003.
JC319.A72 2003

Maimonides, Moses, 1135-1204.
[Selections]
Sefer Musarim ye-deʿot leha-Rambam : liḳuṭim meha-Rambam ... mi-kol sefarav ... bi-leshono ha-zahav ; yeha-ḥonim ʿalay ... rabotenu gedole ha-aharonim ... uve-"Otsrot ha-melekh" hemah kelulim / ʿa. y. ha-melaket, Eliyahu Roṭ. Bene Beraḳ : [ḥ. mo. l], 761 [2000 or 2001] 2 v. (927 p.) ; 25 cm. Cover title: Musarim ye-deʿot la-Rambam ; kol ʿinyene musar, ʿavodat H. ye-deʿot. Running title: Otsrot ha-melekh. Includes indexes.
1. Maimonides, Moses, - 1135-1204 - Teachings. 2. Philosophy, Jewish. 3. Judaism - Doctrines. 4. Ethics, Jewish. I. Roṭ, Eliyahu. Otsrot ha-melekh. II. Title. III. Title: Musarim ye-deʿot la-Rambam : kol ʿinyene musar, ʿavodat H. ye-deʿot IV. Title: Otsrot ha-melekh

MAIMONIDES, MOSES, 1135-1204.
Halbertal, Moshe. Ben Torah le-ḥokhmah. Yerushalayim : Hotsa'at sefarim ʿa. sh. Y. L. Magnes, ha-Universitah ha-ʿIvrit, 760, 2000.
BM755.M54 H35 2000

MAIMONIDES, MOSES, 1135-1204 - TEACHINGS.
Maimonides, Moses, 1135-1204. [Selections] Sefer Musarim ye-deʿot leha-Rambam. Bene Beraḳ : [ḥ. mo. l], 761 [2000 or 2001]

MAINE DE BIRAN, PIERRE, 1766-1824.
Merleau-Ponty, Maurice, 1908-1961. [Union de l'âme et du corps chez Malebranche, Biran et Bergson. English] The incarnate subject. Amherst, N.Y. : Humanity Books, 2001.
B2430.M379 U513 2001

MAINE - FICTION.
Meier, Leslie. Birthday party murder. Waterville, Me. : Thorndike Press, 2003.
PS3563.E3455 B57 2003

MAINTENANCE. *See* **REPAIRING.**

Maiorescu, Toma George, 1928- Îmblâzirea fiarei din om sau ecosofia / Toma George Maiorescu. 3a ediția revăzută și completată. București : Lumina Lex, 2002. 534 p. ; 23 cm. Includes index.
1. Ecology - Philosophy. 2. Philosophy. 3. Human ecology. I. Title.

Maisel, Eric, 1947- Sleep thinking : the revolutionary program that helps you solve problems, reduce stress, and increase creativity while you sleep / Eric Maisel with Natalya Maisel. Holbrook, Mass. : Adams Media Corp., c2000. x, 230 p. ; 22 cm. Includes bibliographical references (p. 223-226) and index. ISBN 1-58062-445-6 DDC 154.6
1. Problem solving - Miscellanea. 2. Dreams - Case studies. I. Maisel, Natalya. II. Title.
BF1099.P75 M35 2000

Maisel, Natalya.
Maisel, Eric, 1947- Sleep thinking. Holbrook, Mass. : Adams Media Corp., c2000.
BF1099.P75 M35 2000

MAJOR ARCANA (TAROT).
Hederman, Mark Patrick. Tarot. Dublin : Currach Press, 2003.

Osho, 1931-1990. Tarot in the spirit of Zen. 1st ed. New York : St. Martin's Griffin, 2003.

BF1879.T2 O85 2003

MAJOR ORDERS. *See* **CLERGY.**

Major, René.
Depuis Lacan. Paris : Aubier, c2000.
BF173 .D44 2000

Majorek, Marek B. Objektivität, ein Erkenntnisideal auf dem Prüfstand : Rudolf Steiners Geisteswissenschaft als ein Ausweg aus der Sackgasse / Marek B. Majorek. Tübingen : Francke, c2002. 517 p. ; 23 cm. (Basler Studien zur Philosophie, 0941-9918 ; 13) Thesis (Ph. D.)--Universität, Basel, 2001. Includes bibliographical references. ISBN 3-7720-2082-8 (pbk.)
1. Steiner, Rudolf, - 1861-1925. 2. Objectivity. 3. Knowledge, Theory of. I. Title. II. Series.

MAJORITIES. *See* **MINORITIES.**

Make room for joy.
Colantuono, Susan L. Charlestown, RI : Interlude Productions, c2000.
BF575.H27 C64 2000

Makeieff, Macha. Poétique du désastre / Macha Makeïeff. Arles : Actes sud, c2001. 46 p. : col. ill. ; 19 cm. ISBN 2-7427-3567-4 DDC 809
1. Creation (Literary, artistic, etc.) 2. Inspiration. 3. Imagination. 4. Empathy in art. I. Title.

Making and breaking of borders : ethnological interpretations, presentations, representations / edited by Teppo Korhonen, Helena Ruotsala & Eeva Uusitalo. Helsinki : Finnish Literature Society, 2003. 328 p. : ill., maps ; 25 cm. (Studia Fennica. Ethnologica ; 7) Includes bibliographical references. ISBN 951-746-467-3 (pbk.)
1. Boundaries. 2. Ethnicity. 3. Globalization. I. Korhonen, Teppo. II. Ruotsala, Helena. III. Uusitalo, Eeva. IV. Series.
JC323 .M35 2003

Making faces.
Aucoin, Kevyn. 1st ed. Boston : Little, Brown, c1997.
RA778 .A873 1997

Making hope visible.
Gilhooley, James J. Allahabad : Holy Family International, [2003]

Making horses drink.
Hiam, Alexander. [Irvine, Calif.] : Entrepreneur Press, c2002.
HD57.7 .H52 2002

Making magic.
Styers, Randall. New York : Oxford University Press, 2003.
BF1611 .S855 2003

Making morality.
Lekan, Todd, 1967- 1st ed. Nashville, TN : Vanderbilt University Press, 2003.
BJ1031 .L45 2003

The making of Europe
Brown, Peter Robert Lamont. The rise of Western Christendom. 2nd ed. Malden, MA ; Oxford : Blackwell Publishing, 2003.
BR162.3 .B76 2003

Dawson, Christopher, 1889-1970. Washington, D.C. : Catholic University of America Press, 2002, 1932.
CB353 .D3 2002

Making schools work.
Hodges, Carolyn R., 1947- New York : P. Lang, c2003.
LC213.2 .H63 2003

Making sense of collectivity : ethnicity, nationalism, and globalisation / edited by Siniša Malešević and Mark Haugaard. London ; Sterling, Va. : Pluto Press, 2002. 226 p. ; 23 cm. (Interpreting the modern world) Includes bibliographical references and index. CONTENTS: Introduction: The idea of collectivity / Mark Haugaard and Siniša Malešević -- Different societies? Different cultures? What are human collectivities? / Richard Jenkins -- The construction of collective identities and the continual reconstruction of primordiality / S.N. Eisenstadt -- The fundamentals of the theory of ethnicity / John Rex -- Nationalism and modernity / Mark Haugaard -- The morphogenesis of nation / Gordana Uzelac -- Cultural variety or variety of cultures? / Zygmunt Bauman - A disagreement about difference / John A. Hall -- Identity : conceptual, operational and historical critique / Siniša Malešević. ISBN 0-7453-1937-8 (hardback) ISBN 0-7453-1936-X (pbk.) DDC 305.8
1. Group identity. 2. Ethnicity. 3. Nationalism. 4. Pluralism (Social sciences) I. Malešević, Siniša. II. Haugaard, Mark, 1961- III. Series.
HM753 .M35 2002

Making sense of history
Western historical thinking. New York : Berghahn Books, 2002.
D16.9 .W454 2002

(vol. 2) Identities. New York ; Oxford : Berghahn Books, 2002.
HM716 .I34 2002

Making sense of social research.
Williams, Malcolm, 1953- London : SAGE, c2003.

Making time : time and management in modern organizations / edited by Richard Whipp, Barbara Adam and Ida Sabelis. Oxford ; New York : Oxford University Press, 2002. xvii, 222 p. : ill. ; 24 cm. Includes bibliographical references (p. [196]-217) and index. CONTENTS: Choreographing time and management : traditions, developments, and opportunities / Barbara Adam, Richard Whipp, and Ida Sabelis -- Towards a theory of timing : kairology in business networks / Laurids Hedaa and Jan-Åke Törnroos -- Taking time seriously : organizational change, flexibility, and the present time in a new perspective / Christian Noss -- Now's the time? Consumption and time-space disruptions in postmodern virtual worlds / Pamela Odih and David Knights -- Time and management as a morality tale, or 'what's wrong with linear time, damn it?' / Alf Rehn -- Hidden causes for unknown losses : time compression in management / Ida Sabelis -- Cooperation engineered : efficiency in the 'just-in-time' system / Nishimoto Ikuko -- Hanging on the telephone : temporal flexibility and the accessible worker / Emma Bell and Alan Tuckman -- A new time discipline : managing virtual work environments / Heijin Lee and Jonathan Liebenau -- The use of time by management and consumers : an analysis of the computer industry / Paul Sergius Koku -- Contested presents : critical perspectives on 'real-time' management / Ronald E. Purser -- The rhythm of the organization : simultaneity, identity, and discipline in an Australian coastal hotel / Dirk Bunzel -- Interpretative times : the timescape of managerial decision making / Tom Keenoy ... [et al.]. ISBN 0-19-925369-2 ISBN 0-19-925370-6 (pbk.) DDC 658.4093
1. Time management. 2. Industrial management. I. Whipp, Richard. II. Adam, Barbara. III. Sabelis, Ida, 1954-
HD69.T54 M34 2002

Making your mind matter.
Ruggiero, Vincent Ryan. Lanham, Md. : Rowman & Littlefield, c2003.
BF431 .R78 2003

Maksimov, Andreĭ, 1959- Dialogi li︠u︡bvi / Andreĭ Maksimov. Moskva : Delovoĭ ėkspress, 1999. 304 p. : ill. ; 21 cm. ISBN 5896440170
1. Love - Case studies. 2. Man-woman relationships - Case studies. 3. Interpersonal relations - Case studies. 4. Celebrities - Russia (Federation) - Interviews. 5. Married people - Russia (Federation) - Interviews. I. Title.
BF575.L8 M336 1999

Maksymenko, S. D. (Serhiĭ Dmytrovych) Rozvytok psykhiky v ontohenezi / S.D. Maksymenko. Kyïv : "Forum", 2002. 2 v. : ill. ; 22 cm. Summary in English. Title from cover. Includes bibliographical references. CONTENTS: t. 1. Teoretyko-metodolohichni problemy henetychnoï psykhologiï -- t. 2. Modeli︠u︡vanni︠a︡ psykholohichnykh novoutvoren' : henetychniĭ aspekt. ISBN 9667786447
1. Genetic psychology. I. Title.
BF706 .M34 2002

MALADJUSTED CHILDREN. *See* **PROBLEM CHILDREN.**

MALADJUSTMENT (PSYCHOLOGY). *See* **ADJUSTMENT (PSYCHOLOGY).**

Malaniuk, Ira. Arien und Lieder [sound recording] / Ira Malaniuk. [Germany] : Preiser Records, p2000. 1 sound disc : digital, mono., stereo. ; 4 3/4 in. For contralto and orchestra (tracks 1-11), contralto, mixed chorus and orchestra (tracks 12-14), contralto and piano (tracks 15-18). Ira Malaniuk, contralto ; Orchester der Staatsoper in der Volksoper, Hans Swarowsky, conductor ; Kirchenchor St. Barbara, Wien, Andriy Hnatyszyn, conductor ; N. Kupdehraben, piano. Compact disc. Program notes ([7] p.) in German and English by Clemens Höslinger inserted in container. Sung in German, Italian or Ukrainian. CONTENTS: Ach, ich habe sie verloren / Gluck -- Non sò più cosa son, cosa faccio ; Voi, che sapete che cosa è amor ; Deh per questo istante solo / Mozart -- Lodernde Flammen schlagen zum Himmel auf ; Die Hände in schweren Ketten ; O don fatale / Verdi -- Ja, die Liebe hat bunte Flügel ; Draussen am Wall von Sevilla / Bizet -- Die Sonne, sie lachte, der Frühling erwachte / Saint-Saëns -- Ombra mai fu / Handel -- Lied des Schäfers -- Duda -- Der Flirt -- Die Kornfelder -- Wiegenlied -- Für mich ist's alles einerlei -- Gewähre mir Freiheit, o Herr.
1. Operas - Excerpts. 2. Solo cantatas. 3. Songs. 4. Songs (Low voice) with orchestra. 5. Songs (Low voice) with piano. 6. Songs, Ukrainian. 7. Folk songs, Ukrainian. I. Swarowsky, Hans. II. Hnatyszyn, Andriy. III. Kupdehraben, N. IV. Gluck, Christoph Willibald, Ritter von, 1714-1787. Operas.

Selections. V. Mozart, Wolfgang Amadeus, 1756-1791. Operas. Selections. VI. Verdi, Giuseppe, 1813-1901. Operas. Selections. VII. Bizet, Georges, 1838-1875. Operas. Selections. VIII. Saint-Saëns, Camille, 1835-1921. Operas. Selections. IX. Handel, George Frideric, 1685-1759. Operas. Selections. X. Wiener Staatsoper. Orchester. XI. Kirchenchor St. Barbara, Wien. XII. Title.

Malas.
Alborch Bataller, Carmen. 3. ed. [Madrid] : Aguilar, 2002.

MALE COLLEGE STUDENTS - UNITED STATES - PSYCHOLOGY.
Champion, David R. Narcissism and entitlement. New York : LFB Scholarly Pub. LLC, c2003.
BF692.15 .C47 2003

MALE-FEMALE RELATIONSHIPS. *See* **MAN-WOMAN RELATIONSHIPS.**

MALE GAYS. *See* **GAY MEN.**

MALE HOMOSEXUALITY. *See* **HOMOSEXUALITY, MALE.**

MALE LIVESTOCK. *See* **BULLS.**

MALE SEXUAL ABUSE VICTIMS - MENTAL HEALTH.
Spiegel, Josef. Sexual abuse of males. New York : Brunner-Routledge, 2003.
RC569.5.A28 S65 2003

Male witches in early modern Europe.
Apps, Lara. Manchester ; New York : Manchester University Press ; New York : Distributed exclusively in the USA by Palgrave, 2003.
BF1584.E85 A66 2003

MALEBRANCHE, NICOLAS, 1638-1715.
Fabiani, Paolo, 1968- La filosofia dell'immaginazione in Vico e Malebranche. Firenze : Firenze University Press, 2002.
B3583.F25 F55 2002

Merleau-Ponty, Maurice, 1908-1961. [Union de l'âme et du corps chez Malebranche, Biran et Bergson. English] The incarnate subject. Amherst, N.Y. : Humanity Books, 2001.
B2430.M379 U513 2001

Malécot, Franck.
Charles Fourier et l'utopie.
Fourier, Charles, 1772-1837. Du libre arbitre. Bordeaux : Saints Calus, 2003.

MALEDICTION. *See* **BLESSING AND CURSING.**

Maler, Arkadiĭ. Strategii sakral'nogo smysla / Arkadiĭ Maler. Moskva : Parad izdatel'skiĭ dom, 2003. 266 p. ; 21 cm. Includes bibliographical references (p. 263-265). ISBN 5773900491
1. Dugin, Aleksandr. 2. Russkai︠a︡ pravoslavnai︠a︡ ︠t︡serkov' - Doctrines. 3. Conservatism - Russia (Federation) 4. Conservatism - Religious aspects - Russkai︠a︡ pravoslavnai︠a︡ ︠t︡serkov'. 5. Metaphysics. 6. Philosophy, Russian. 7. Tradition (Philosophy) 8. Geopolitics - Russia (Federation) 9. Eurasian school. I. Title.

Der Maler auf seinem Drehstuhl.
Ziegelmüller, Martin, 1935- [Frauenfeld] : Waldgut, c2001.

Malešević, Siniša.
Making sense of collectivity. London ; Sterling, Va. : Pluto Press, 2002.
HM753 .M35 2002

Mali, Joseph. Mythistory : the making of a modern historiography / Joseph Mali. Chicago : The University of Chicago Press, c2003. xiii, 354 p. ; 24 cm. Includes bibliographical references and index. CONTENTS: Where terms begin : myth, history, and mythistory -- The vico road : from Livy to Michelet -- Jacob Burckhardt : mythistorian -- Aby Warburg : history as ancient mythology -- Ernst Kantorowicz : history as new mythology -- Walter Benjamin : history as modern mythology -- Ideareal history : a lesson from Joyce. ISBN 0-226-50262-7 (cloth : alk. paper) DDC 907/.2
1. Historiography. 2. Mythology - Historiography. 3. History, Ancient - Historiography. 4. History, Modern - Historiography. I. Title.
D13 .M268 2003

Maliarenko, Andreĭ Grigor'evich.
Kanygin, I︠U︡riĭ Mikhaĭlovich. Poi︠a︡s mira. Kiev : MAUP, 2003.

MALINOWSKI, BRONISLAW, 1884-1942.
Pulman, Bertrand. Anthropologie et psychanalyse. Paris : Presses universitaires de France, 2002.
GN502 .P85 2002

Malkah, Asher. ʻArakhim ve-ḥinukh : be-farashiyot ha-shavuʻa, be-maʻgal ha-shanah, be-maʻgal ha-ḥayim / Asher Malkah. Ḥefah : A. Malkah, [5760 i.e. 2000] 2 v. (44, 589 p.) ; 25 cm. CONTENTS: ḥeleḳ 1. Bereshit. Shemot. Va-yiḳra -- ḥeleḳ 2. Ba-midbar. Devarim.
1. Bible. - O.T. - Pentateuch - Commentaries. 2. Fasts and feasts - Judaism. 3. Ethics, Jewish. 4. Life cycle, Human - Religious aspects - Judaism. I. Title.

MALL, THE (WASHINGTON, D.C.) - HISTORY - 20TH CENTURY.
Barber, Lucy G. (Lucy Grace), 1964- Marching on Washington. Berkeley : University of California Press, c2002.
E743 .B338 2002

Mallan, Kerry.
Youth cultures. Westport, Conn. : Praeger, 2003.
HQ796 .Y59273 2003

MALLARMÉ, STÉPHANE, 1842-1898 - INFLUENCE - ELIOT.
Strandberg, Åke. The Orphic voice. Uppsala : Acta Universitatis Upsaliensis, 2002.
PS3509.L43 Z87 2002

MALLEABILITY (PSYCHOLOGY). *See* ADAPTABILITY (PSYCHOLOGY).

Mallon, Brenda. A year of creativity : a seasonal guide to new awareness / Brenda Mallon. Kansas City, Mo. : Andrews McMeel Pub., c2003. 256 p. : col. ill. ; 15 cm. ISBN 0-7407-3017-7 DDC 153.3/5
1. Creative thinking - Problems, exercises, etc. 2. Spiritual life. I. Title.
BF408 .M234 2003

Malone, Kareen Ror, 1955-.
Apollon, Willy. After Lacan. Albany : State University of New York Press, 2002.
RC506 .A65 2002

Malone, Thomas W.
Organizing business knowledge. Cambridge, Mass. : MIT Press, c2003.
HD30.2 .T67 2003

Malory, Thomas, Sir, 15th cent.
[Morte d'Arthur]
Le morte Darthur, or, The hoole book of Kyng Arthur and of his noble knyghtes of the Rounde Table : authoritative text, sources and backgrounds, criticism / Sir Thomas Malory ; edited by Stephen H.A. Shepherd. 1st ed. New York ; London : Norton, c2004. lii, 954 p. ; 24 cm. (A Norton critical edition) Includes bibliographical references (p. 945-954). ISBN 0-393-97464-2 (pbk.) DDC 823/.2
1. Malory, Thomas, - Sir, - 15th cent. - Morte d'Arthur. 2. Arthurian romances. 3. Arthurian romances - History and criticism. 4. Knights and knighthood in literature. 5. Kings and rulers in literature. I. Shepherd, S. H. A. II. Title. III. Title: Hoole book of Kyng Arthur and of his noble knyghtes of the Rounde Table IV. Series.
PR2041 .M37 2004

MALORY, THOMAS, SIR, 15TH CENT. MORTE D'ARTHUR.
Malory, Thomas, Sir, 15th cent. [Morte d'Arthur] Le morte Darthur, or, The hoole book of Kyng Arthur and of his noble knyghtes of the Rounde Table. 1st ed. New York ; London : Norton, c2004.
PR2041 .M37 2004

Radulescu, Raluca, 1974- The gentry context for Malory's Morte Darthur. Cambridge [England] ; Rochester, NY : D.S. Brewer, 2003.
PR2047 .R33 2003

MALORY, THOMAS, SIR, 15TH CENT. - POLITICAL AND SOCIAL VIEWS.
Radulescu, Raluca, 1974- The gentry context for Malory's Morte Darthur. Cambridge [England] ; Rochester, NY : D.S. Brewer, 2003.
PR2047 .R33 2003

Malott, Richard W. Principles of behavior / Richard W. Malott, Elizabeth A. Trojan Suarez. 5th ed. Upper Saddle River, N.J. : Pearson/Prentice Hall, 2003. p. cm. Includes bibliographical references and index. CONTENTS: The reinforcer -- Reinforcement -- Escape -- Punishment -- Penalty -- Extinction and recovery -- Differential reinforcement and punishment -- Shaping -- Unlearned reinforcers and aversive conditions -- Special establishing operations -- Learned reinforcers and aversive conditions -- Discrimination -- Complex stimulus control -- Imitation -- Avoidance -- Punishment by prevention -- Ratio schedules -- Time-dependent schedules -- Concurrent contingencies -- Behavioral chains and rate contingencies -- Respondent conditioning -- Analogs to reinforcement and avoidance, part i -- Analogs to reinforcement and avoidance, part ii -- A theory of rule-governed behavior -- Pay for performance -- Moral and legal control -- Maintenance --

Transfer -- Research methods -- Jobs and grad school. ISBN 0-13-048225-0 DDC 150
1. Operant behavior. 2. Psychology. I. Trojan, Elizabeth A. II. Title.
BF319.5.O6 M34 2003

Malpsychia.
Milton, Joyce. The road to Malpsychia. 1st ed. San Francisco : Encounter Books, 2002.
BF204 .M54 2002

Malvido Arriaga, Adriana. Por la vereda digital / Adriana Malvido. 1. ed. México : CONACULTA (Consejo Nacional para la Cultura y las Artes), 1999. 411 p. : ill. (some col.) ; 23 cm. (Teoría y práctica del arte) Includes bibliographical references (p. 405-407). ISBN 9701831403
1. Computers and civilization. 2. Virtual reality. 3. Cyberspace. 4. Interactive multimedia. I. Title. II. Series: Teoría y práctica del arte.
QA76.9.C66 M35 1999

Malysheva, M. M.
Gendernyĭ kaleĭdoskop. Moskva : "Academia", 2001.

Małyszek, Tomasz, 1971- Ästhetik der Psychoanalyse : die Internalisierung der Psychoanalyse in den literarischen Gestalten von Patrick Süskind und Sten Nadolny / Tomasz Małyszek. Wrocław : Wydawn. Uniwersytetu Wrocławskiego, 2000. 215 p. ; 21 cm. (Acta Universitatis Wratislaviensis ; no 2209) Includes bibliographical references (p. [209]-215). ISBN 83-229-2074-1
1. Süskind, Patrick. 2. Nadolny, Sten. 3. Psychoanalysis and literature. I. Title. II. Series.

Romans Freuda i Gradivy : rozważania o psychoanalizie / Tomasz Małyszek. Wrocław : Wydawn. Uniwersytetu Wrocławskiego, 2002. 199 p. ; 21 cm. (Monografie FNP. Seria humanistyczna) Summary in German. At head of title: Fundacja na Rzecz Nauki Polskiej. Includes bibliographical references (p. 190-[193]) and index. ISBN 83-229-2297-3
1. Freud, Sigmund, - 1856-1939. 2. Psychoanalysis. I. Fundacja na Rzecz Nauki Polskiej. II. Title. III. Series: Monografie Fundacji na Rzecz Nauki Polskiej. Seria humanistyczna.
BF173.F85 M255 2002

Mama Gena's School of Womanly Arts.
Thomashauer, Regena. New York : Simon & Schuster, c2002.
HQ1206 .T4673 2002

Mamleev, I︠U︡riĭ. Rossii︠a︡ vechnai︠a︡ / I︠U︡riĭ Mamleev. Moskva : AiF-Print, 2002. 333 p. : ill. ; 21 cm. (Rus' mnogolikai︠a︡) "Rossii︠a︡ v proshlom, nastoi︠a︡shchem, budushchem"--Cover. CONTENTS: ch. 1. Drevo Rossii -- ch. 2. Russkai︠a︡ doktrina -- ch. 3. Filosofskie stat'i, interv'i︠u︡ -- ch. 4. Literaturno-kriticheskie stat'i, interv'i︠u︡ -- Izbrannye stikhi russkikh poėtov o Rossii: S.A. Esenin, A.S. Pushkin, M.I. T︠S︡vetaeva, F.I. Ti︠u︡tchev, A.A. Blok, M.A. Voloshin, A.S. Khomi︠a︡kov. ISBN 5947360098
1. National characteristics, Russian. 2. Russia (Federation) - Civilization. 3. Russia (Federation) - History - Philosophy. 4. Russian literature - History and criticism. 5. Philosophy, Russian. 6. Russia - Poetry. I. Title. II. Series.
DK32 .M355 2002

MAMMARY GLANDS. *See* BREAST.
MAN. *See* HUMAN BEINGS.

Man and Mu.
Day, Stacey B. N[ew] Y[ork] : International Foundation for Biosocial Development and Human Health ; Oviedo, Fla. : Disctributed by C.E.P., c1997.
BD431 .D37 1997

Man and nature in Asia
(no. 8.) Bruun, Ole, 1953- Fengshui in China. Copenhagen, Denmark : NIAS Press, c2003.

MAN-ANIMAL RELATIONSHIPS. *See* HUMAN-ANIMAL RELATIONSHIPS.

MAN (CHRISTIAN THEOLOGY).
Babarinde, A. O. The end of man. Lagos, Nigeria : Christ Foundation Baptist Church, 2001.
1. Black author.

Henry, Michel, 1922- [C'est moi la vérité. English] I am the truth. Stanford, Calif : Stanford University Press, 2003.
BR100 .H39813 2003

Przesmycki, Piotr, 1965- W stronę Bogoczłowieczeństwa. Łódź : "Ibidem", 2002.
B4238.B44 P79 2002

MAN (JEWISH THEOLOGY). *See also* SOUL (JUDAISM).
Ḳoraḥ, Shelomoh ben Yaḥya. Netsaḥ ḥayenu. Bene Beraḳ : S. Ḳoraḥ, 762 [2001 or 2002]

Man of light.
Curcio, Kimberly Panisset. 1st ed. New York : SelectBooks, c2002.
BF1045.M44 C87 2002

MAN ON OTHER PLANETS. *See* LIFE ON OTHER PLANETS.
MAN (PHILOSOPHY). *See* PHILOSOPHICAL ANTHROPOLOGY.
MAN, PREHISTORIC. *See* PREHISTORIC PEOPLES.
MAN, PRIMITIVE. *See* PRIMITIVE SOCIETIES.
MAN (THEOLOGY). *See* MAN (CHRISTIAN THEOLOGY); MAN (JEWISH THEOLOGY); SOUL.

Man tikitzijoj tzijonem chawe.
Valle Bonilla, Otto René. Que no le cuenten cuentos = Guatemala : ESEDIR : Editorial Saqil Tzij, 1999.

The man who would be queen.
Bailey, J. Michael. Washington, D.C. : Joseph Henry Press, c2003.
HQ76.2.U5 B35 2003

MAN-WOMAN RELATIONSHIPS. *See also* MATE SELECTION.
Amores de película. 1. ed. [Madrid] : Aguilar, 2002.
PN1998.2 .A46 2002

Austin, Linda S., 1951- Heart of the matter. New York : Atria Books, c2003.
BF575.L8 A97 2003

Barber, Nigel, 1955- The science of romance. Amherst, N.Y. : Prometheus Books, 2002.
HQ21 .B184 2002

Brown, Nina W. Loving the self-absorbed. Oakland, Calif. : New Harbinger, c2003.
BF575.N35 B76 2003

Dan shen gao bai. Di 1 ban. Beijing : Beijing chu ban she, 2001.
HQ800.2 .D36 2001

Denise, Jan. Naked relationships. Charlottesville, VA : Hampton Roads Pub., c2002.
BF575.I5 D46 2002

Gardere, Jeffrey Roger. Love prescription. New York : Kensington Pub., c2002.
1. Black author.

Gendernyĭ kaleĭdoskop. Moskva : "Academia", 2001.

Gilligan, Carol, 1936- The birth of pleasure. 1st ed. New York : A.A. Knopf, 2002.
BF575.L8 G56 2002

Gillman, Karen. Mr. and Dr. talking it over. Lima, Ohio : Wyndham Hall Press, c2002.
BF637.C45 G55 2002

Gorfine, Yehudit. Be-ḳarov etslekh. Petaḥ Tiḳvah : Mar'ot, 2002.

Gray, John, 1948- [Men are from Mars, women are from Venus. Spanish] Els homes són de Mart, les dones són de Venus. 1. ed. Barcelona : Edicions 62, c2001.

Hirata, Helena Sumiko. [División sexual del trabajo. Portuguese] Nova divisão sexual do trabalho? 1a ed. São Paulo : Boitempo, 2002.
HD6060.6 .H5717 2002

Hochschild, Arlie Russell, 1940- The commercialization of intimate life. Berkeley : University of California Press, 2003.
HM1106 .H63 2003

Hopper, Robert. Gendering talk. East Lansing : Michigan State University Press, c2003.
HQ1075 .H67 2003

Hu, Liuming, 1950- Dan shen gui zu. Di 1 ban. [Wuhan Shi] : Chang jiang wen yi chu ban she, [2000] *PL2863.L58 D365 2000*

Ingram, Susan. Zarathustra's sisters. Toronto ; Buffalo : University of Toronto Press, c2003.
PN471 .I537 2003

Louise, Kim. True devotion. Washington D.C. : BET Publications, 2002.

Meeks, James T., 1956- Life changing relationships. Chicago, Ill. : Moody Press, c2002.
HQ801 .M515 2002
1. Black author.

Muraro, Rose Marie. Feminino e masculino. Rio de Janeiro : Sextante, 2002.

Man-woman relationships

HQ801 .M87 2002

Onken, Julia, 1942- Die Kirschen in Nachbars Garten. Vollständige Taschenbuchausg. München : Goldmann, 1999.

Paleg, Kim. When anger hurts your relationship. Oakland, CA : New Harbinger Publications, c2001.
BF575.A5 P35 2001

Paroles brutes à la recherche d'un trésor. Genouilleux : Passe du vent, c2003.

Rhodes, Jewell Parker. Douglass' women. New York, NY : Atria Books, c2002.
1. Black author.

Sarnoff, Irving, 1922- Intimate creativity. Madison, Wis. : University of Wisconsin Press, c2002.
BF411 .S27 2002

Scola, Angelo. Uomo-donna. 1. ed. italiana. Genova : Marietti, c2002.

Vezin, Annette. Egéries dans l'ombre des créateurs. Paris : Martinière, 2002.
NX165 .V49 2002

Weinberg, George H. Why men won't commit. New York : Atria Books, c2002.
BF619 .W45 2002

MAN-WOMAN RELATIONSHIPS - CASE STUDIES.
Hell hath no fury. 1st Carroll & Graf ed. New York : Carroll & Graf Publishers, 2002.
HQ801 .H45 2002

Maksimov, Andreĭ, 1959- Dialogi li͡ubvi. Moskva : Delovoĭ ėkspress, 1999.
BF575.L8 M336 1999

MAN-WOMAN RELATIONSHIPS - RELIGIOUS ASPECTS - CHRISTIANITY.
Meeks, James T., 1956- Life changing relationships. Chicago, Ill. : Moody Press, c2002.
HQ801 .M515 2002
1. Black author.

MAN-WOMAN RELATIONSHIPS - RUSSIA (FEDERATION).
Gendernyĭ kaleĭdoskop. Moskva : "Academia", 2001.

The managed heart.
Hochschild, Arlie Russell, 1940- 20th anniversary ed. Berkeley, Calif. : University of California Press, 2003.
BF531 .H62 2003

MANAGEMENT. *See also* **BUSINESS; CONFLICT MANAGEMENT; EMERGENCY MANAGEMENT; EXECUTIVES; INDUSTRIAL MANAGEMENT; KNOWLEDGE MANAGEMENT; ORGANIZATION; ORGANIZATIONAL BEHAVIOR; ORGANIZATIONAL CHANGE; PERSONNEL MANAGEMENT; PLANNING; REENGINEERING (MANAGEMENT).**
Adair, John Eric, 1934- Not bosses but leaders. 3rd ed. / John Adair with Peter Reed. London : Sterling, VA : Kogan Page, 2003.

Amidon, Debra M., 1946- The innovation superhighway. Amsterdam ; Boston ; London : Butterworth-Heinemann, c2003.
HD53 .A462 2003

Autopoietic organization theory. Oslo, Norway : Abstrakt forlag ; Malmö, Sweden : Liber Ekonomi ; Herndon, VA, USA : Copenhagen Business School Press, c2003.
HD31 .A825 2003

The collaborative work systems fieldbook. San Francisco : Jossey-Bass/Pfeiffer, c2003.
HD66 .C547 2003

Cummings, Stephen. Recreating strategy. London ; Thousand Oaks : Sage Publications, 2002.
HD30.28 .C855 2002

De Kluyver, Cornelis A. Strategy. Upper Saddle River, N.J. : Prentice Hall, c2003.
HD38.2 .D425 2003

The expansion of management knowledge. Stanford, Calif. : Stanford Business Books, c2002.
HD31 .E873 2002

Flamant, Nicolas. Une anthropologie des managers. Paris : Presses universitaires de France, c2002.
HD33 .F525 2002

Frankenburg, Reuven. Revadim 'elyonim ba-minhal ha-tsiburi ha-Yiśre'eli. [Israel : ḥ. mo. l., 1999?]

Gottlieb, Marvin R. Managing group process. Westport, Conn. ; London : Praeger, 2003.

HD66 .G6778 2003

Handy, Charles B. 21 ideas for managers. 1st ed. San Francisco : Jossey-Bass, c2000.
HD31 .H31259 2000

Harris, O. Jeff. Organizational behavior. New York : Best Business Books, c2002.
HD58.7 .H36943 2002

Hill, Linda A. (Linda Annette), 1956- Becoming a manager. 2nd ed. Boston, Mass. : Harvard Business School Press, c2003.
HF5384 .H55 2003

Hope, Jeremy. Beyond budgeting. Boston : Harvard Business School Press, c2003.
HD31 .H635 2003

Human resources in the 21st century. Hoboken, N.J. : J. Wiley & Sons, c2003.
HD31 .H81247 2003

Leading in an upside-down world. Toronto : Dundurn Group, c2003.
BF637.L4 L425 2003

Leading in an upside-down world. Toronto : Dundurn Group, c2003.

Management and language. London ; Thousand Oaks : SAGE, 2003.
HD30.3 .H65 2003

Management. Cambridge, Mass. : MIT Press, 2003.
HD31 .M2928 2003

Manville, Brook, 1950- A company of citizens. Boston : Harvard Business School Press, c2003.
HD58.7 .M3714 2003

Process management. Springer-verlag, Berlin, Heidelberg ; New York : Springer, c2003.
HD31 .P756 2003

Tonn, Joan C. Mary P. Follett. New Haven [Conn.] : Yale University Press, c2003.
HN57 .T695 2003

Topchik, Gary S. The accidental manager. [1st ed.]. New York : AMACOM, c2004.
HD31 .T6368 2004

The trust process in organizations. Cheltenham, UK ; Northampton, MA : Edward Elgar, c2003.
HD58.7 .T744 2003

Woodhead, Roy (Roy M.) Achieving results. London : Thomas Telford, 2002.

Woolfe, Lorin. The Bible on leadership. New York : American Management Association, c2002.
HD57.7 .W666 2002

Management & language.
Management and language. London ; Thousand Oaks : SAGE, 2003.
HD30.3 .H65 2003

Management and language : the manager as a practical author / [edited by] David Holman and Richard Thorpe. London ; Thousand Oaks : SAGE, 2003. x, 196 p. : ill. ; 25 cm. Cover title: Management & language. Includes bibliographical references and index. ISBN 0-7619-6907-1 ISBN 0-7619-6908-X (PBK.) DDC 658.4
1. Management. I. Holman, David (David J.) II. Thorpe, Richard, 1951- III. Title: Management & language
HD30.3 .H65 2003

MANAGEMENT BY OBJECTIVES.
Sen, Asim, 1935- Democratic management. Lanham, Md. ; Oxford : University Press of America, c2003.
HD30.65 .S46 2003

MANAGEMENT - CROSS-CULTURAL STUDIES.
Earley, P. Christopher. Cultural intelligence. Stanford, Calif. : Stanford University Press, 2003.
HD57.7 .E237 2003

MANAGEMENT - EMPLOYEE PARTICIPATION.
Cohen, Allan R. The portable MBA in management. 2nd ed. New York : J. Wiley, c2002.
HD31 .C586 2002

MANAGEMENT, INDUSTRIAL. *See* **INDUSTRIAL MANAGEMENT.**

Management : inventing and delivering its future / edited by Thomas A. Kochan and Richard L. Schmalensee. Cambridge, Mass. : MIT Press, 2003. xiv, 309 p. : ill. ; 24 cm. "The MIT Sloan School of Management: 50th anniversary." Includes bibliographical references and index. ISBN 0-262-11282-5 (hc. : alk. paper) DDC 658
1. Management. 2. Organizational change. 3. Corporate governance. 4. Personnel management. 5. Human capital. 6. Technological innovations - Management. I. Kochan, Thomas A. II. Schmalensee, Richard. III. Sloan School of Management.

HD31 .M2928 2003

MANAGEMENT OF CONFLICT. *See* **CONFLICT MANAGEMENT.**

MANAGEMENT OF KNOWLEDGE ASSETS. *See* **KNOWLEDGE MANAGEMENT.**

MANAGEMENT OF SELF. *See* **SELF-MANAGEMENT (PSYCHOLOGY).**

The management of water resources
Conflict prevention and resolution in water systems. Cheltenham, UK ; Northampton, MA, USA : E. Elgar Pub., c2002.
HD1691 .C664 2002

Management, organizations and society
Text/work. London ; New York : Routledge, 2003.

Management, organizations and society (London, England)
Gender, identity and the culture of organizations. London ; New York : Routledge, 2002.
HD58.7 .G46 2002

MANAGEMENT - PSYCHOLOGICAL ASPECTS.
Psychoanalysis and management. Heidelberg : Physica-Verlag, c1994.
BF175.4.S65 P777 1994

MANAGEMENT - RESEARCH.
The expansion of management knowledge. Stanford, Calif. : Stanford Business Books, c2002.
HD31 .E873 2002

MANAGEMENT, SELF (PSYCHOLOGY). *See* **SELF-MANAGEMENT (PSYCHOLOGY).**

MANAGEMENT, STRESS. *See* **STRESS MANAGEMENT.**

MANAGERS. *See* **EXECUTIVES.**

Managers as mentors.
Bell, Chip R. 2nd ed., completely rev. and expanded. San Francisco, Calif : Berrett-Koehler Publishers, c2002.
HF5385 .B45 1996

MANAGERS, BASEBALL. *See* **BASEBALL MANAGERS.**

The manager's pocket guide to dealing with conflict.
Hart, Lois Borland. Amherst, Mass. : HRD Press, c1999.
BF637.I48 H38 1999

MANAGING CONFLICT. *See* **CONFLICT MANAGEMENT.**

Managing creativity and innovation.
Harvard business essentials. Boston, Mass. : Harvard Business School Press, c2003.
HD45 .H3427 2003

Managing group process.
Gottlieb, Marvin R. Westport, Conn. ; London : Praeger, 2003.
HD66 .G6778 2003

Managing innovation, design & creativity.
Von Stamm, Bettina. Managing innovation, design and creativity. Chichester, England ; Hoboken, NJ : J. Wiley, c2003.
HD45 .V65 2003

Managing innovation, design and creativity.
Von Stamm, Bettina. Chichester, England ; Hoboken, NJ : J. Wiley, c2003.
HD45 .V65 2003

Managing intellectual assets in the digital age.
Matsuura, Jeffrey H., 1957- Boston, MA : Artech House, c2003.
K1401 .M378 2003

Managing psychological factors in information systems work.
Kaluzniacky, Eugene. Hershey PA : Information Science Pub., c2004.
BF576 .K358 2004

Mānasāgarī.
[Mānasāgarī. Hindi & Sanskrit.] Saṃskaraṇa 1. Haridvāra : Raṇadhīra Prakāśana, 2000.
BF1714.H5+

[Mānasāgarī. Hindi & Sanskrit.] Mānasāgarī : Bhāratīya jyotiṣa kā phalita mahāgrantha / Harajī Kalyāṇa Ṛṣi kṛta ; vyākhyākāra Umeśa Purī "Jñāneśvara". Saṃskaraṇa 1. Haridvāra : Raṇadhīra Prakāśana, 2000. 746 p. ; ill. ; 22 cm. Spine title: Phalita jyotiṣa mahāgrantha. SUMMARY: On Hindu astrology with Hindi interpretation. Sanskrit and Hindi. ISBN 81-86955-90-9
1. Hindu astrology. I. Jñāneśvara, Umeśa Purī. II. Title. III. Title: Phalita jyotiṣa mahāgrantha

BF1714.H5+

Mānasaroga cikitsā.
Upādhyāya, Govindaprasāda. Āyurvedīya mānasaroga cikitsā. 1. saṃskaraṇa. Vārāṇasī : Caukhabā Surabhāratī Prakāśana ; Dillī : Anya Prāptisthāna Caukhambā Saṃskṛta Pratiṣṭhāna, 2000.
R605 .U67 2000

Mancia, Mauro.
Sentieri della mente. 1. ed. Torino : Bollati Boringhieri, 2001.

MANDALA.
Bühnemann, Gudrun. Maṇḍalas and Yantras in the Hindu traditions. Leiden ; Boston : Brill, 2003.
BL2015.M3 B85 2003

Maṇḍalas and Yantras in the Hindu traditions.
Bühnemann, Gudrun. Leiden ; Boston : Brill, 2003.
BL2015.M3 B85 2003

Mandel, Robert Steven, 1943- 9 journeys home : how to get back to yourself : steps, stops, pitfalls, and maps to guide you on your ultimate adventure / Bob Mandel. Berkeley : Celestial Arts, c2003. xi, 156 p. : ill. ; 23 cm. Includes index. Table of contents URL: http://www.loc.gov/catdir/toc/ecip043/2003009982.html ISBN 1-58761-203-8 DDC 158.1
1. Self-actualization (Psychology) I. Title. II. Title: Nine journeys home
BF575.S4 M36 2003

Mandelbaum, Jenny S.
Studies in language and social interaction. Mahwah, N.J. : London : Lawrence Erlbaum, 2003.

Mandelberg, Robert. Mystifying mind reading tricks / Robert Mandelberg ; illustrated by Ferruccio Sardella. New York : Sterling Pub., 2002. 95 p. : ill. ; 21 cm. Includes index. Publisher description URL: http://www.loc.gov/catdir/description/ste021/2002066866.html ISBN 0-8069-8811-8 DDC 793.8
1. Magic tricks. 2. Telepathy. I. Title.
GV1553 .M35 2002

Mandell, Faye. Self-powerment : towards a new way of living / by Faye Mandell. New York : Dutton, c2003. p. cm. Includes bibliographical references. ISBN 0-525-94774-4 (alk. paper) DDC 158.1
1. Self-actualization (Psychology) 2. Self-perception. I. Title.
BF637.S4 M337 2003

Mandler, Jean Matter. The foundations of mind : origins of conceptual thought / by Jean Matter Mandler. Oxford ; New York : Oxford University Press, 2004. p. cm. (Oxford series in cognitive development) Includes bibliographical references and index. Table of contents URL: http://www.loc.gov/catdir/toc/ecip047/2003017304.html CONTENTS: How to build a baby : prologue -- Piaget's sensorimotor infant -- Kinds of representation : seeing and thinking -- Perceptual meaning analysis and image-schemas : the infant as interpreter -- Some image-schemas and their functions -- Some differences between percepts and concepts : the case of the basic level -- Some preverbal concepts -- Concepts as induction machines -- Continuity in the conceptual system : acquisition, breakdown, and reorganization -- Recall of the past -- Language acquisition -- Consciousness and conclusions. ISBN 0-19-517200-0 (alk. paper) DDC 155.42/2323
1. Cognition in infants. 2. Concepts in infants. I. Title. II. Series.
BF720.C63 M36 2004

Manferto, Valeria.
The Splendors of archaeology. Cairo : American University in Cairo Press, 1998.

Mangan, Michael, 1953- Staging masculinities : history, gender, performance / Michael Mangan. Houndmills, Basingstoke, Hampshire : New York : Palgrave Macmillan, 2003. xi, 276 p. ; 21 cm. Includes bibliographical references (p. 249-265) and index. ISBN 0-333-72018-0 (cloth) ISBN 0-333-72019-9 (pbk.) DDC 809/.93352041
1. Men in literature. 2. Masculinity in literature. 3. Drama - History and criticism. 4. English drama - History and criticism. I. Title.
PN1650.M44 M36 2003

Manganaro, Marc, 1955- Culture, 1922 : the emergence of a concept / Marc Manganaro. Princeton, N.J. : Princeton University Press, c2002. 231 p. ; 24 cm. Includes bibliographical references and index. ISBN 0-691-00136-7 ISBN 0-691-00137-5 (PBK) DDC 306.01
1. Culture in literature. 2. English literature - 20th century - History and criticism. 3. American literature - 20th century - History and criticism. 4. Culture - Philosophy. I. Title.
PR888.C84 M36 2002

Mangiapane, John. It's all in the cards : tarot reading made easy / John Mangiapane. New York : Sterling Pub., c2004. p. cm. Includes index. CONTENTS: The tarot deck -- Using tarot spreads -- The major arcana -- The minor arcana -- The court cards -- Tarot combinations -- Runs of suits, numbers, and cards -- Life cards -- Year cards -- Tarot as oracle. ISBN 1402709862 DDC 133.3/2424
1. Tarot. I. Title.
BF1879.T2 M332 2004

Mangieri, John N. Yale Assessment of Thinking : a self-assessment of your skill in the areas of reasoning, insight, and self-knowledge / John N. Mangieri, Cathy Collins Block. San Francisco : Jossey-Bass, c2003. p. cm. Publisher description URL: http://www.loc.gov/catdir/description/wiley039/2003006687.html ISBN 0-7879-6883-8 (alk. paper) DDC 153.9/3
1. Reasoning - Ability testing. 2. Self-perception - Testing. 3. Insight - Testing. 4. Self-evaluation. I. Block, Cathy Collins. II. Title.
BF442 .M34 2003

ha-Manhig she-me'afsher le-elef peraḥim li-feroaḥ.
Tayir, Bracha Klein. Tel Aviv : Yedi'ot aḥaronot : Sifre ḥemed, c2002.

Manifestazioni demoniache.
Borromeo, Federico, 1564-1631. Milano : Terziaria : ASEFI, 2001.
BF1520 .B67 2001

Manifestes du surréalisme d'André Breton.
Meyer, Michel. Michel Meyer présente Manifestes du surréalisme d'André Breton. Paris : Gallimard, 2002.
NX600.S9 B735 2002

Manifesto della libertà.
Canfora, Luciano. Palermo : Sellerio, c1994.
JC585 .C29 1994

MANIPRAVALAM LANGUAGE (MALAYALAM). See **SANSKRIT LANGUAGE.**

MANIPULATIVE BEHAVIOR.
Braiker, Harriet B., 1948- Who's pulling your strings? New York : McGraw-Hill, c2004.
BF632.5 .B69 2004

Garifullin, Ramil', 1962- Illi͡uzionizm lichnosti. Kazan' : [s.n.], 1997.
BF491 .G37 1997

Grachev, Georgiĭ. Manipulirovanie lichnostʹi͡u. Moskva : Algoritm, 2002.
BF632.5 .G73 2002

Perspectives on persuasion, social influence, and compliance gaining. Boston, MA : Allyn and Bacon, 2003.
BF637.P4 P415 2003

MANIPULATORS (MECHANISM). See **ROBOTS.**

Manipulirovanie lichnostʹi͡u.
Grachev, Georgiĭ. Moskva : Algoritm, 2002.
BF632.5 .G73 2002

MANKIND. See **HUMAN BEINGS.**

Mann, A. T., 1943- A new vision of astrology / A.T. Mann. New York : Pocket Books, c2002. xv, 333 p. : ill. ; 21 cm. Includes bibliographical references (p. 316-317) and index. Publisher description URL: http://www.loc.gov/catdir/description/simon034/2003266938.html ISBN 0-7434-5341-7 (pbk.)
1. Astrology. I. Title.
BF1708.1 .M355 2002

[Round art]
The round art of astrology : an illustrated guide to theory and practice / A.T. Mann. London : Vega, c2003. 299 p. : ill. (some col.), map ; 28 cm. Originally published: The round art. Limpsfield, Eng. : Paper Tiger, 1979. Includes bibliographical references (p. 294) and index. ISBN 1-84333-698-7 DDC 133.5
1. Astrology. I. Title.
BF1708.1 .M36 2003

MANNERS AND CUSTOMS. See **BODY, HUMAN - SOCIAL ASPECTS; CLOTHING AND DRESS; COSTUME; DRINKING CUSTOMS; FESTIVALS; FOLKLORE; FOOD HABITS; FRONTIER AND PIONEER LIFE; FUNERAL RITES AND CEREMONIES; GIFTS; HOLIDAYS; ORDEAL; RITES AND CEREMONIES; SEX CUSTOMS; SLEEPING CUSTOMS; SOCIAL NORMS; WOMEN - HISTORY.**

MANNERS AND CUSTOMS IN LITERATURE.
Thompson, Anne Booth. Everyday saints and the art of narrative in the South English legendary. Aldershot, England ; Burlington, Vt. : Ashgate, c2003.
PR2143.S543 T48 2003

Manning, Brennan. A glimpse of Jesus : the stranger to self-hatred / Brennan Manning. 1st ed. [San Francisco] : HarperSanFrancisco, c2003. x, 145 p. ; 22 cm. "Portions of this book were previously published in Stranger to self-hatred, by Brennan Manning, published by Dimension Books"--T.p. verso. Includes bibliographical references. ISBN 0-06-000069-4 DDC 248.4
1. Self-acceptance - Religious aspects - Christianity. 2. Christian life. I. Manning, Brennan. Stranger to self-hatred. II. Title.
BV4647.S43 M36 2003

Stranger to self hatred.
Manning, Brennan. A glimpse of Jesus. 1st ed. [San Francisco] : HarperSanFrancisco, c2003.
BV4647.S43 M36 2003

The wisdom of tenderness : what happens when God's fierce mercy transforms our lives / Brennan Manning. 1st ed. New York : HarperCollins, c2002. 179 p. ; 22 cm. Includes bibliographical references. ISBN 0-06-000070-8 DDC 248.4
1. Witness bearing (Christianity) 2. Christian life. I. Title.
BV4520 .M36 2002

Manning, H. Paul.
Cherchi, Marcello. Disciplines and nations. Pittsburgh, Pa. : Center for Russian and East European Studies, University Center for International Studies, University of Pittsburgh, c2002.

Manning, Martha. A place to land : lost and found in an unlikely friendship / Martha Manning. 1st ed. New York : Ballantine Books, 2003. xvii, 252 p. ; 22 cm. ISBN 0-345-45055-8
1. Friendship. I. Title.
BF575.F66 M26 2003

Mannoni, Octave.
Psychanalyse et décolonisation. Paris : LHarmattan, c1999.
BF175.4.C84 P76 1999

MANNONI, OCTAVE.
Psychanalyse et décolonisation. Paris : LHarmattan, c1999.
BF175.4.C84 P76 1999

Manokha, I. P. (Iryna Petrivna) Psykholohii͡a potaiemnoho "I͡A" / I.P. Manokha. Kyïv : "Polihrafknyha", 2001. 446 p. : ill. ; 21 cm. Includes bibliographical references (p. 424-446). ISBN 9665300709
1. Self-actualization (Psychology) I. Title.
BF637.S4 M338 2001

Manovijñānano śabdakośa.
Mansūrī, Jī. Āra. Āvṛtti 1. Amadāvāda : Mayūra Prakāśana, 2003.
BF31+

MANPOWER PLANNING. See **ORGANIZATIONAL CHANGE.**

MANPOWER UTILIZATION. See **PERSONNEL MANAGEMENT.**

Man's search for ultimate meaning.
Frankl, Viktor Emil. Cambridge, Mass. : Perseus Pub., c2000.
RC455.4.R4 F7 2000

MANSIONS (ASTROLOGY). See **HOUSES (ASTROLOGY).**

MANSIONS - WALES - DYFED - HISTORY.
Nanteos. Llandysul, Wales : Gomer, [2001]
DA738.N36 N36 2001

MANSLAUGHTER. See **MURDER.**

Manstead, A. S. R.
Feelings and emotions. New York : Cambridge University Press, 2003.
BF531 .F445 2003

Mansūrī, Jī. Āra. Manovijñānano śabdakośa : śāḷākôlejanā śikshako-adhyāpako ane vidyārthīo māṭe atyanta upayogī / Jī. Āra. Mansūrī. Āvṛtti 1. Amadāvāda : Mayūra Prakāśana, 2003. iv, 302 p. ; 22 cm. English and Gujarati. "Manovijñānanī paribhāshāonī vyākhyāo, manovaijñānikonā paricayo ane manovijñānanī agatyanī māhitī aṅgenī 2100thī pana vadhu vigato dharāvato Gujarātī bhāshāno ekamātra śabdakośa." SUMMARY: Dictionary of psychology.
1. Psychology - Dictionaries. 2. English language - Dictionaries - Gujarati. I. Title.
BF31+

Mantle, Mickey, 1931- The quality of courage / Mickey Mantle and Robert W. Creamer. Lincoln : University of Nebraska Press, [1999] 185 p. ; 21 cm. "Bison books"--Spine. Originally published: Garden City, N.Y. : Doubleday, 1964. With new introd. ISBN 0-8032-8259-1 (alk. paper) DDC 796.357/092/2
1. New York Yankees (Baseball team) 2. Baseball players - United States - Anecdotes. 3. Baseball players - United States - Biography. 4. Courage. 5. Role models. I. Creamer, Robert W. II. Title.

Mantovani, Massimo.
GV865.A1 M317 1999

Mantovani, Massimo. Meditazioni sull'albero della cabala / Massimo Mantovani. Milano : Xenia, 2002. 252 p. : ill. ; 21 cm. (I libri dell'altra scienza ; 171) Includes bibliographical references. ISBN 88-7273-462-2 DDC 296
1. Cabala. 2. Jewish meditations. 3. Trees - Religious aspects - Judaism. 4. Sefirot (Cabala) 5. Alphabet - Religious aspects - Judaism. I. Title. II. Series.

MANTRAS.
LeBeau, Kara R. Guan yin's chakra meditations. Boulder, Colo. : Mahasimhananda Press, c2001.
BF1442.C53 L43 2001

MANTRAYĀNA BUDDHISM. See **TANTRIC BUDDHISM.**

Mantreśvara. Phaladīpikā : Hindīvyākhyāsahitā / Mantreśvaraviracitā ; vyākhyākāra Hariśaṅkara Pāṭhaka. 1. saṃskaraṇa. Vārāṇasī : Caukhambā Surabhāratī Prakāśana, 2002. 13, 373 p. : ill. ; 22 cm. (Caukhambā Surabhāratī granthamālā ; 349) SUMMARY: Treatise with Hindi intrepretation, on Hindu astrology. In Sanskrit; commentary in Hindi.
1. Hindu astrology - Early works to 1800. I. Pāṭhaka, Hariśaṅkara. II. Title. III. Series.
BF1714.H5+

A manual for repertory grid technique.
Fransella, Fay. 2nd ed. Hoboken, NJ : Wiley, c2004.
BF698.8.R38 F72 2004

MANUAL TRAINING. See **DESIGN; DRAWING.**

Manuali di base
(4) Fumagalli Beonio Brocchieri, Mariateresa, 1933- Profilo del pensiero medievale. 1. ed. Roma : Laterza, 2002.

Manuali di psicologia, psichiatria, psicoterapia
Sentieri della mente. 1. ed. Torino : Bollati Boringhieri, 2001.

Manuel de l'anti-sagesse.
Farcet, Gilles, 1959- [Gordes] : Relié, c2002.

MANUSCRIPT DEPOSITORIES. See **ARCHIVES.**

MANUSCRIPT REPOSITORIES. See **ARCHIVES.**

MANUSCRIPTS. See **ILLUMINATION OF BOOKS AND MANUSCRIPTS; MANUSCRIPTS, MEDIEVAL.**

MANUSCRIPTS - DEPOSITORIES. See **ARCHIVES.**

MANUSCRIPTS, ILLUMINATED. See **ILLUMINATION OF BOOKS AND MANUSCRIPTS.**

MANUSCRIPTS - ILLUSTRATIONS. See **ILLUMINATION OF BOOKS AND MANUSCRIPTS.**

MANUSCRIPTS, LATIN (MEDIEVAL AND MODERN).
Keefe, Susan A. Water and the Word. Notre Dame, Ind. : University of Notre Dame Press, c2002.
BR200 .K44 2002

MANUSCRIPTS, MEDIEVAL. See **MANUSCRIPTS, LATIN (MEDIEVAL AND MODERN).**

MANUSCRIPTS, MEDIEVAL - EUROPE.
Clegg, Justin. The medieval Church. London : British Library, 2003.

The manuscripts of Leonardo da Vinci in the Institut de France.
Leonardo, da Vinci, 1452-1519. [Selections. English. 1999] Milano : Ente raccolta vinciana, 1999-
Q113 .L3513 1999

MANUSCRIPTS - REPOSITORIES. See **ARCHIVES.**

Manusov, Valerie Lynn.
Canary, Daniel J. Interpersonal communication. 3rd ed. Boston : Bedford/St. Martin's, c2003.
BF637.C45 C34 2003

Manville, Brook, 1950- A company of citizens : what the world's first democracy teaches leaders about creating great organizations / Brook Manville, Josiah Ober. Boston : Harvard Business School Press, c2003. xiv, 202 p. ; 22 cm. Includes bibliographical references (p. 177-189) and index. ISBN 1-57851-440-1 DDC 658
1. Organizational behavior. 2. Management. 3. Citizenship. 4. Democracy. 5. Corporate governance. I. Ober, Josiah. II. Title.
HD58.7 .M3714 2003

Many faces of gender : roles and relationships through time in indigenous northern communities / edited By Lisa Frink, Rita S. Shepard, and Gregory A. Reinhardt. Boulder : University Press of Colorado ; Calgary, Alta., Canada : University of Calgary Press, c2002. viii, 257 p. : ill., maps ; 24 cm. Papers from participants in the "Approaches to Gender in the North" symposium at the 25th annual meeting of the Alaska Anthropological Association held in Anchorage, Alaska, March 1998, and from other contributors. Includes bibliographical references and index. CONTENTS: Many faces: an introduction to gender research in indigenous northern North America / Lisa Frink, Rita S. Shepard, and Gregory A. Reinhardt -- Kipijuituq in Netsilik society: changing patterns of gender and patterns of changing gender / Henry Stewart -- Gender equality in a contemporary Indian community / Lillian A. Ackerman -- Celebration of a life: remembering Linda Womkon Badten, Yupik educator / Carol Zane Jolles -- Changing residence patterns and intradomestic role changes: causes and effects in nineteenth-century western Alaska / Rita S. Shepard -- Re-peopling the house: household organization within Deg Hit'an villages, southwest Alaska / Jennifer Ann Tobey -- Fish tales: women and decision making in western Alaska / Lisa Frink -- Child and infant burials in the Arctic / Barbara A. Crass -- Puzzling out gender-specific "sides" to a prehistoric house in Barrow, Alaska / Gregory A. Reinhardt -- Broken eyes and simple grooves: understanding eastern Aleut needle technology through experimental manufacture and use of bone needles / Brian W. Hoffman -- Gender, households, and the material construction of social difference: metal consumption at a classic Thule whaling village / Peter Whitridge -- Gender dynamics in native northwestern North America: perspectives and prospects / Hetty Jo Brumbach and Robert Jarvenpa. ISBN 0-87081-677-2 (hardcover : alk. paper) ISBN 0-87081-687-X (pbk.) ISBN 1-55238-093-9 (University of Calgary Press) DDC 305.3/089/971
1. Indians of North America - Psychology. 2. Indians of North America - Sexual behavior. 3. Indian women - North America - Social conditions. 4. Inuit - Psychology. 5. Inuit - Sexual behavior. 6. Inuit women - Social conditions. 7. Gender identity - North America. 8. Sex role - North America. 9. Sex differences. 10. Ethnopsychology - North America. I. Frink, Lisa. II. Shepard, Rita S. III. Reinhardt, Gregory A. IV. Alaska Anthropological Association. Meeting (25th : 1998 : Anchorage, Alaska)
E98.P95 M35 2002

The many faces of individualism / Anton van Harskamp & Albert W. Musschenga, [editors]. Leuven, Belgium ; Sterling, Va. : Peeters, 2001. vi, 281 p. ; 24 cm. (Morality and the meaning of life ; 12) Includes bibliographical references and index. SUMMARY: Arguments about the definition, the moral and social significance of the concepts of individualism and individualisation are addressed in this collection of essays. ISBN 90-429-0954-4 (alk. paper) DDC 141/.4
1. Individualism. 2. Individuation (Philosophy) 3. Civil society. I. Harskamp, Anton van, 1946- II. Musschenga, A. W., 1950- III. Series.
B824 .M354 2001

The many faces of philosophy : reflections from Plato to Arendt / edited by Amélie Oksenberg Rorty. Oxford ; New York : Oxford University Press, 2003. xxix, 512 p. ; 26 cm. Includes bibliographical references. ISBN 0-19-513402-8 (alk. paper) DDC 100
1. Philosophy. I. Rorty, Amélie.
B72 .M346 2003

Manzoni, Alessandro, 1785-1873. Postille : filosofia / [Alessandro Manzoni] ; a cura di Donatella Martinelli ; premessa di Vittorio Mathieu. Milano : Centro nazionale studi manzoniani, 2002. cxxiv, 410 p., [8] leaves of pl. : ill. ; 23 cm. (Edizione nazionale ed europea delle opere di Alessandro Manzoni ; 20) Includes bibliography and indexes. Texts in French or Italian. DDC 190
1. Manzoni, Alessandro, - 1785-1873 - Knowledge - Philosophy. 2. Philosophy. I. Martinelli, Donatella. II. Title.

MANZONI, ALESSANDRO, 1785-1873 - KNOWLEDGE - PHILOSOPHY.
Manzoni, Alessandro, 1785-1873. Postille. Milano : Centro nazionale studi manzoniani, 2002.

Manzotti, Riccardo. Coscienza e realtà : una teoria della coscienza per costruttori e studiosi di menti e cervelli / Riccardo Manzotti e Vincenzo Tagliasco. Bologna : Società editrice il mulino, c2001. 595 p. : ill. : 22 cm. (Percorsi) ISBN 88-15-08171-2 DDC 126
1. Consciousness. 2. Perception - Physiology. I. Tagliasco, Vincenzo, 1941- II. Title. III. Series: Percorsi (Bologna, Italy)
BF311 .M35 2001

MAO, DUN, 1896- - CRITICISM AND INTERPRETATION.
Zhuang, Zhongqing. Mao Dun de wen lun li cheng. Di 1 ban. Shanghai : Shanghai wen yi chu ban she : Xin hua shu dian jing xiao, 1996.
PL2801.N2 Z64 1996

MAOISM. See **COMMUNISM.**

Maoz, Zeev. Bound by struggle : the strategic evolution of enduring international rivalries / Zeev Maoz and Ben D. Mor. Ann Arbor : University of Michigan Press, c2002. x, 356 p. : ill. ; 24 cm. Includes bibliographical references (p. 321-338) and indexes. ISBN 0-472-11274-0 (Cloth : alk. paper) DDC 327.1/6
1. International relations - History. 2. Israel-Arab Border Conflicts, 1949- - Egypt. 3. Peace. I. Mor, Ben D. II. Title.
JZ5595 .M366 2002

Mapes, James J., 1945- Quantum leap thinking : an owner's guide to the mind / James J. Mapes. Naperville, Ill. : Sourcebooks, c2003. xxiii, 260 p. : ill. ; 23 cm. Includes bibliographical references (p. [251]-252) and index. CONTENTS: What is quantum leap thinking? -- Continuous learning -- Creative thinking -- Managing change -- The fourteen points of quantum leap thinking -- Paradoxical thinking and the power of paradigms -- Exploring truth -- Goals : the pathway to vision -- Vision : the catapult to your future -- The magic of values -- The mind by Mapes -- Positive visualization : the power within -- Turn fear into power -- Risking it all -- Strategies for balance -- Taking inventory -- Teams ; the quantum leap partnership -- The challenge of leadership -- Parting thoughts. ISBN 1402200439 (pbk. : alk. paper) DDC 153.4
1. Thought and thinking. I. Title.
BF441 .M265 2003

Mapping social relations.
Campbell, Marie L. (Marie Louise), 1936- Aurora, Ont. : Garamond Press, c2002.

Mapping your birthchart.
Clement, Stephanie Jean. 1st ed. St. Paul, Minn. : Llewellyn Publications, 2003.
BF1708.1 .C535 2003

MAPS, MENTAL. See **GEOGRAPHICAL PERCEPTION.**

Maps of the mind
Aleksander, Igor. How to build a mind. New York : Columbia University Press, 2001.
Q335 .A44225 2001

McGaugh, James L. Memory and emotion. New York : Columbia University Press, c2003.
BF378.A87 M34 2003

MAQUIS. See **GUERRILLAS.**

Marar, Ziyad. The happiness paradox / Ziyad Marar. London : Reaktion, 2003. 207 p. : ill. ; 21 cm. (Focus on contemporary issues) ISBN 1-86189-182-2 DDC 152.42
1. Happiness. 2. Work - Psychological aspects. 3. Love - Psychological aspects. I. Title. II. Series.

Marchaisse, Thierry.
Dépayser la pensée. Paris : Empêcheurs de penser en rond, 2003.

Marchand, Valère-Marie. Les alphabets de l'oubli : signes & savoirs perdus / Valère-Marie Marchand. Paris : Editions Alternatives, 2002. 158 p. : ill. ; 24 cm. (Ecritures) Includes bibliographical references. ISBN 2-86227-349-X
1. Writing - History. 2. Hieroglyphics. 3. Alphabet. I. Title. II. Series: Ecritures (Editions Alternatives)
P211 .M373 2002

Marching on Washington.
Barber, Lucy G. (Lucy Grace), 1964- Berkeley : University of California Press, c2002.
E743 .B338 2002

Marcinkowski, Frank.
Die Politik der Massenmedien. Köln : Halem, 2001.

Marconi, Diego, 1947- Filosofia e scienza cognitiva / Diego Marconi. 1. ed. Roma-Bari : Editori Laterza, 2001. 167 p. : ill. ; 18 cm. (Biblioteca essenziale Laterza ; 41) (Filosofia) Includes bibliographical references and index. ISBN 88-420-6344-4
1. Cognitive science. I. Title. II. Series. III. Series: Filosofia (Rome, Italy)
BF311 .M36 2001

Marcu, Emanoil.
Cioran, E. M. (Emile M.), 1911- [Histoire et utopie. Romanian] Istorie şi utopie. Bucureşti : Humanitas, 2002.

Marcum, Dave. BusinessThink : rules for getting it right--now, and no matter what! / Dave Marcum, Steve Smith, Mahan Khalsa ; foreword by Stephen R. Covey. New York : Wiley, c2002. xxi, 257 p. : ill. ; 24 cm. Table of contents URL: http://www.loc.gov/catdir/toc/wiley021/2001008001.html CONTENTS: Think! Rule one-check your ego at the door -- Ego alert -- The language of humility. Rule two-create curiosity -- The deep dive for curiosity. Rule three-move off the solution -- Welcome to the main event -- No more guessing! -- Resist the solution reduction! Rule four-get evidence -- Failure at the speed of light : addicted to speed -- In God we trust-everyone else bring

evidence -- Searching for soft evidence -- Digging for Hard Evidence. Rule five-calculate the impact -- Whiteboard economics. Rule six-explore the ripple effect -- Who or what else is effected? Rule seven-slow down for yellow lights -- Let's get real-or let's not play. Rule eight-find the cause -- Why ask why? The last mile -- Pay attention : time, people, and money -- Make a decision-maybe-proof your company -- The age of NOW! Q&A for the businessThink Curious. ISBN 0-471-21993-2 (cloth : alk. paper) DDC 650.1
1. *Success in business.* 2. *Decision making.* I. *Smith, Steve.* II. *Khalsa, Mahan.* III. *Title.* IV. *Title: Rules for getting it right--now, and no matter what!*
HF5386 .M3087 2002

Marcus, Gary F. (Gary Fred) The birth of the mind : how a tiny number of genes creates the complexities of human thought / Gary F. Marcus. New York : Basic Books, 2004. p. cm. Includes bibliographical references and index. Table of contents URL: http://www.loc.gov/catdir/toc/ecip044/2003012545.html CONTENTS: Etched in stone? -- Born to learn -- Brain storms -- Aristotle's impetus -- Copernicus's revenge -- Wiring the mind -- The evolution of mental genes -- Paradox lost -- Final frontiers -- Appendix: methods for reading the genome. ISBN 0-465-04405-0 DDC 155.7
1. *Genetic psychology.* 2. *Psychobiology.* 3. *Nature and nurture.* 4. *Cognitive science.* I. *Title.*
BF701 .M32 2004

Marcuschi, Luiz Antônio. Investigando a relação oral/escrito e as teorias do letramento / Luiz Antonio Marcuschi... [et.al.] ; Ines Signorini (org.). Campinas, SP : Mercado de Letras, 2001. 192 p. : ill. ; 21 cm. (Idéias sobre linguagem) Includes bibliographical references. ISBN 85-85725-80-X
1. *Language and languages.* 2. *Oral communication.* 3. *Written communication.* 4. *Linguistics.* I. *Title.* II. *Series: Coleção Idéias sobre linguagem.*

Mar'eh Kohen : albom ha-Re'iyah Ḳuḳ, zatsal. Mar'eh Kohen. Yerushalayim : Makhon le-ḥeḳer mishnat ha-Re'iyah Ḳuḳ be-shituf 'im "Bet ha-Rav", c762 [2001 or 2002]

Mar'eh Kohen : demuto ye-haguto shel ha-Rav Avraham Yitshak ha-Kohen Ḳuḳ, zatsal / be-'arikhat Ya'aḳov ha-Levi Filber. Yerushalayim : Makhon le-ḥeḳer mishnat ha-Re'iyah Ḳuḳ be-shituf 'im "Bet ha-Rav", c762 [2001 or 2002] 143 p. : ill., ports. (some col.) ; 29 cm. Cover title: Mar'eh Kohen : albom ha-Re'iyah Ḳuḳ, zatsal. Mostly vocalized text. Includes bibliographical references. ISBN 9659015054
1. *Kook, Abraham Isaac, - 1865-1935.* 2. *Kook, Abraham Isaac, - 1865-1935 - Portraits.* 3. *Orthodox Judaism.* 4. *Ethics, Jewish.* 5. *Rabbis - Jerusalem - Biography.* I. *Kook, Abraham Isaac, 1865-1935. Selections. 2001.* II. *Filber, Ya'aḳov, ha-Levi.* III. *Title: Mar'eh Kohen : albom ha-Re'iyah Ḳuḳ, zatsal* IV. *Title: Albom ha-Re'iyah Ḳuḳ, zatsal*

Margarit i Tayà, Remei. Acerca de la mujer / Remei Margarit. 1. ed. Barcelona : Plaza & Janés, 2002. 190, [1] p. ; 18 cm. (Debolsillo) Includes bibliographical references (p. 191). ISBN 84-8450-918-4
1. *Women - Socialization.* 2. *Women - Social conditions.* 3. *Women - Psychology.* I. *Title.* II. *Series.*

MARGINAL PEOPLES. *See* **MARGINALITY, SOCIAL.**

MARGINALITY, SOCIAL.
Figures de la marge. Rennes : Presses universitaires de Rennes, [2002]

Fuller, Robert W. Somebodies and nobodies. Gabriola Island, Canada : New Society Publishers, 2003.
HM821 .F84 2003

Violence and the body. Bloomington : Indiana University Press, c2003.
HM1116 .V557 2003

MARGINALITY, SOCIAL - ISRAEL.
Kook, Rebecca B., 1959- The logic of democratic exclusion. Lanham, Md. : Lexington Books, c2002.
E185.615 .K59 2002

MARGINALITY, SOCIAL - UNITED STATES.
Kook, Rebecca B., 1959- The logic of democratic exclusion. Lanham, Md. : Lexington Books, c2002.
E185.615 .K59 2002

Marguier, Florence. Le plaisir / Florence Marguier. Paris : Oxus, c2003. 161 p. ; 20 cm. (Les intemporels) Includes bibliographical references. ISBN 2-8489-8001-X DDC 844
1. *Pleasure.* I. *Title.* II. *Series.*

Maria Shaw's star gazer.
Shaw, Maria, 1963- 1st ed. St. Paul, Minn. : Llewellyn Publications, 2003.
BF1411 .S52 2003

Marías, Julián, 1914- Entre dos siglos / Julián Marías. Madrid : Alianza Editorial, c2002. 635 p. ; 23 cm. "Entre dos siglos es un conjunto de artículos que permite una recapitulación de es mundo cambiante de nuestor dias, una toma de posesión de una etapa que se cierra y otra que amanece con la incertidumbre que depara el futuro..."--p. 4 of cover. ISBN 84-206-6789-7 DDC 864/.64
1. *Europe - Civilization.* 2. *Civilization - Philosophy.* 3. *Humanities.* 4. *Philosophy, Modern - 20th century.* 5. *Spanish literature - 20th century - History and criticism.* I. *Title.* II. *Title: Entre 2 siglos*
PQ6663.A72183 E68 2002

MARIHUANA. *See also* **MARIJUANA.**
Thorne, Robert. Portland, Or. : Clarus Books Pub., c1998 (1999 printing)
BF209.C3 T48 1998

MARIJUANA - HISTORY.
Thorne, Robert. Marihuana. Portland, Or. : Clarus Books Pub., c1998 (1999 printing)
BF209.C3 T48 1998

MARIJUANA - PSYCHOLOGICAL ASPECTS.
Thorne, Robert. Marihuana. Portland, Or. : Clarus Books Pub., c1998 (1999 printing)
BF209.C3 T48 1998

Marike, Navīn Kumār. Tuḷunāḍinalli Koraga taniya : ondu adhyayana / Navīn Kumār Marike. Puttūru, Da. Ka. : Śrī Mahāśakti Saṅgha, 2000. 61 p. : ill. ; 23 cm. In Kannada. SUMMARY: Study on Koraga Taniya, demon worshipped by Hindus in Tulunadu. Includes bibliographical references (p. 60-61).
1. *Demonology - India - Tulunadu.* 2. *Tulunadu (India) - Religion.* I. *Title.*
BF1517.I5 M37 2000

Marin, Isabel da Silva Kahn, 1954- Violências / Isabel da Silva Kahn Marin. São Paulo : Editora Escuta : FAPESP, 2002. 202 p. ; 21 cm. (Biblioteca de Psicopatologia fundamental) Includes bibliographical references (p. [191]-202). ISBN 85-7137-204-7
1. *Violence - Psychological aspects.* 2. *Aggressiveness.* I. *Title.*

MARINE ACCIDENTS. *See* **SHIPWRECKS.**

MARINE DISASTERS. *See* **SHIPWRECKS.**

Marinelli, Lydia. Dreaming by the book : Freud's Interpretation of dreams and the history of the psychoanalytic movement / Lydia Marinelli, Andreas Mayer ; translated by Susan Fairfield. New York : Other Press, c2003. p. cm. Includes bibliographical references and index. Table of contents URL: http://www.loc.gov/catdir/toc/ecip046/2003015654.html CONTENTS: Between resistance and disagreement: lay and specialist readers -- Unconscious writing : dream analyses in letters -- Conceited doctors and well trained patients -- A 'central office for dreams' : collective research on symbolism -- Reversals of the theory -- Philology, typography, and oedipus complex -- Theory in the dream : the phenomenon of autosymbolism -- Analysis without synthesis -- The visibility of repression -- The return of the author Freud -- Dreaming translators and legitimate interpreters -- Afterword: The interpretation of dreams today -- Appendices: Sources for the history of the interpretation of dreams. ISBN 1-59051-009-7 (alk. paper) DDC 154.6/3
1. *Freud, Sigmund, - 1856-1939. - Traumdeutung.* 2. *Dream interpretation - History.* 3. *Psychoanalysis - History.* I. *Mayer, Andreas.* II. *Title.*
BF175.5.D74 F7436 2003

Träume nach Freud : die "Traumdeutung" und die Geschichte der psychoanalytischen Bewegung / Lydia Marinelli, Andreas Mayer. Wien : Turia + Kant, c2002. 216 p. : ill. ; 24 cm. Includes bibliographical references. ISBN 3-85132-321-1 (pbk.)
1. *Dream interpretation - History.* 2. *Psychoanalysis - History.* I. *Title.*

Marion, Jean-Luc, 1946- Le phénomène érotique : six méditations / Jean-Luc Marion. Paris : Grasset, c2003. 344 p. ; 23 cm. (Figures) ISBN 2-246-55091-2 DDC 194
1. *Erotica - Philosophy.* 2. *Aesthetics.* I. *Title.* II. *Series.*
BH301.L65 M37 2003

[**Prolégomènes à la charité. English**]
Prolegomena to charity / Jean-Luc Marion ; translated by Stephen E. Lewis. 1st ed. New York : Fordham University Press, 2002. xii, 178 p. ; 23 cm. (Perspectives in continental philosophy ; 24) Includes bibliographical references and indexes. ISBN 0-8232-2171-7 ISBN 0-8232-2172-5 (pbk.) DDC 177/.7
1. *Love.* I. *Title.* II. *Series: Perspectives in continental philosophy ; no. 24.*
BD436 .M3313 2002

Marioni, Tom, 1937- Writings on art : 1969-1999 / Tom Marioni. San Francisco, Calif. : Crown Point Press, 2000. 84 p. ; 21 cm. Spine title. ISBN 1-89130-014-8
1. *Art - History.* I. *Title.* II. *Title: Writings on art, Tom Marioni, 1969-1999.*

Maritain, Jacques, 1882-1973.
[**Degrés du savoir. English**]
Distinguish to unite, or, The degrees of knowledge / Jacques Maritain ; translated from the fourth French edition under the supervision of Gerald B. Phelan ; presented by Ralph McInerny. Notre Dame, Ind. : University of Notre Dame Press, 1998, c1995. xxviii, 500 p. : ill. ; 23 cm. (The collected works of Jacques Maritain ; v. 7) "Paperback 1998"--T.p. verso. "First published in 1959 ... by Charles Scribner's Sons"--T.p. verso. Includes bibliographical references and index. ISBN 0-268-00886-8 (pbk.)
1. *Knowledge, Theory of.* 2. *Philosophy of nature.* 3. *Metaphysics.* 4. *God - Knowableness.* 5. *Mysticism.* 6. *Wisdom.* I. *Phelan, Gerald B. (Gerald Bernard), 1892-1965.* II. *Title.* III. *Title: Distinguish to unite* IV. *Title: Degrees of knowledge* V. *Series: Maritain, Jacques, 1882-1973. Works. English. 1995 ; v. 7.*
BD162 .M273 1998

Works. English. 1995
(v. 7.) Maritain, Jacques, 1882-1973. [Degrés du savoir. English] Distinguish to unite, or, The degrees of knowledge. Notre Dame, Ind. : University of Notre Dame Press, 1998, c1995.
BD162 .M273 1998

MARITAIN, JACQUES, 1882-1973.
Jacques Maritain and the many ways of knowing. Washington, D.C. : American Maritain Association : Distributed by the Catholic University of America Press, c2002.
B2430.M34 J317 2002

MARITAL PSYCHOTHERAPY.
Bianchi, Carlos J. (Carlos Juan) Relatos de la pareja. Buenos Aires : Corregidor, c2001.

MARITAL STATUS. *See* **MARRIED PEOPLE; SINGLE PEOPLE; WIDOWS.**

Marḳ, Shelomoh Zalman ben Neḥemyah. Sefer Ma'aśeh uman : liḳuṭ u-verur divre ha-posḳim be-dine shemirah ve-aharayut 'al ha-umanim u-va'ale melakhah be-śim lev le-she'elot aḳtualiyot ... Yerushalayim : Nahalat kolel "Bet ulpana de-rabenu Yoḥanan, 763 [2002 or 2003] 461 p. ; 25 cm. Running title: Ma'aśeh uman.
1. *Work - Religious aspects - Judaism.* 2. *Responsibility.* 3. *Jewish law.* I. *Title.* II. *Title: Ma'aśeh uman*

Mark, Stacey.
Vint/age 2001 conference : [videorecording]. New York, c2001.

Markell, Patchen, 1969- Bound by recognition / Patchen Markell. Princeton, N.J. : Princeton University Press, c2003. xiii, 284 p. ; 24 cm. Includes bibliographical references (p. [249]-276) and index. ISBN 0-691-11381-5 (alk. paper) ISBN 0-691-11382-3 (pbk. : alk. paper) DDC 320/.01
1. *Equality.* 2. *Justice.* 3. *Multiculturalism.* 4. *Difference (Philosophy)* 5. *Group identity.* 6. *Recognition (Philosophy)* 7. *Agent (Philosophy)* 8. *Individuality.* 9. *Democracy.* I. *Title.*
JC575 .M37 2003

MARKET ECONOMY. *See* **CAPITALISM.**

MARKET RESEARCH. *See* **MARKETING RESEARCH.**

MARKET SURVEYS. *See* **CONSUMER BEHAVIOR.**

MARKETING. *See* **NEW PRODUCTS; RETAIL TRADE.**

MARKETING - DATABASES.
Villamora, Grace Avellana. Super searchers on Madison Avenue. Medford, N.J. : CyberAge Books/ Information Today, c2003.
HF5415.2 .V497 2003

MARKETING - FORECASTING.
The future of marketing. Houndmills [England] ; New York : Palgrave Macmillan, 2003.
HF5415 .F945 2003

MARKETING - POLITICAL ASPECTS.
Martín Salgado, Lourdes. Marketing político. Barcelona : Paidós, c2002.

Marketing político.
Martín Salgado, Lourdes. Barcelona : Paidós, c2002.

MARKETING - PSYCHOLOGICAL ASPECTS.
Wertime, Kent. Building brands & believers. Chichester : Wiley, 2002.

Zaltman, Gerald. How customers think. Boston, Mass. : Harvard Business School Press, c2003.

Marketing - Psychological aspects.

HF5415.32 .Z35 2003

MARKETING - RESEARCH. *See* **MARKETING RESEARCH.**

MARKETING RESEARCH - COMPUTER NETWORK RESOURCES.
Villamora, Grace Avellana. Super searchers on Madison Avenue. Medford, N.J. : CyberAge Books/ Information Today, c2003.
HF5415.2 .V497 2003

MARKETING RESEARCH - METHODOLOGY.
Using qualitative research in advertising: strategies, techniques, and applications. Thousand Oaks, Calif. : Sage, c2002.
HF5814 .U78 2002

MARKETS. *See* **STOCK EXCHANGES.**

MARKETS, FREE. *See* **FREE ENTERPRISE.**

MARKETS - RESEARCH. *See* **MARKETING RESEARCH.**

Markham, Ursula. The beginner's guide to self-hypnosis / Ursula Markham. London : Vega, 2002. 144 p. ; 22 cm. Includes index. Publisher description URL: http://www.loc.gov/catdir/description/ste031/2003464301.html ISBN 1-84333-616-2 DDC 154.7
1. Hypnotism. 2. Self-help techniques. 3. Self-care, Health. I. Title.
BF1141 .M36 2002

MÄRKISCHES MUSEUM - HISTORY.
Renaissance der Kulturgeschichte? Dresden : Verlag der Kunst, 2001.
AM101.B4856 R36 2001

Markman, Arthur B.
Medin, Douglas L. Cognitive psychology. 4th ed. Hoboken, NJ : John Wiley & Sons, 2004.
BF201 .M43 2004

Marks, David. The psychology of the psychic / David F. Marks. 2nd ed. Amherst, N.Y. : Prometheus Books, 2000. 336 p. : ill. ; 23 cm. Includes bibliographical references (p. 323-330) and index. ISBN 1-57392-798-8 (pbk. : alk. paper) DDC 133.8/01/9
1. Parapsychology. I. Title.
BF1042 .M33 2000

Markt - Medien - Moral / Herausgeber, Walter Schweidler. Bochum : Projekt-Verlag, 2001. 139 p. ; 21 cm. (Schriftenreihe der Universität Dortmund / Bd. 46. Studium generale ; Bd. 10) Includes bibliographical references. ISBN 3-89733-062-8 (pbk.)
1. Ethics. 2. Mass media - Moral and ethical aspects. 3. Capitalism - Moral and ethical aspects. I. Schweidler, Walter, 1957- II. Series: Schriftenreihe der Universität Dortmund. Studium generale ; Bd. 10. III. Series: Schriftenreihe der Universität Dortmund ; Bd. 46.

Markus, Georg. Meine Reisen in die Vergangenheit / Georg Markus. 2. Aufl. Wien : Amalthea, 2002. 303 p., [8] leaves of plates : ill. ; 25 cm. Includes bibliographical references (p. 298-299) and index. ISBN 3-85002-483-0
1. Music. 2. Love. I. Title.
AC35 .M385 2002

Marlow, Mary Elizabeth, 1940- Jumping Mouse : a story about inner trust / Mary Elizabeth Marlow. Norfolk, VA : Hampton Roads Pub. Co., c1995. 167 p. ; 20 cm. Includes bibliographical references (p. 165-166). SUMMARY: Jumping Mouse journeys to the Sacred Mountain, the heart of his true self, and discovers that which gives his life meaning and purpose. On his journey he is challenged by the stages and initiations one must face in order to trust within: paradox, ambiguity, betrayal, doubt, the leap of faith, the pull of consensus reality, and the subtleties of discernment. Jumping Mouse learns to trust the promptings of his heart. ISBN 1-57174-014-7 (acid-free paper)
1. Trust I. Title.
BF575.T7 M37 1995

Marmur dziejowy : studie z historii sztuki = Historical marble : studies in art history. Poznań : Wydawnictwo Poznańskiego Towarzystwa Przyjaciół Nauk, 2002. 560 p. : ill. ; 24 cm. (Prace Komisji Historii Sztuki ; t. 32 = Publications of the committee for art history ; v. 32) Includes bibliographical references. Festschrift in honor of Professor Zofia Ostrowska-Kębłowska. Polish, with abstract and table of contents in English. ISBN 83-7063-347-1
1. Art - History. 2. Architecture - History. I. Ostrowska-Kębłowska, Zofia. II. Title: Historical marble : studies in art history III. Series: Prace Komisji Historii Sztuki ; t. 32.

Marmysz, John, 1964- Laughing at nothing : humor as a response to nihilism / John Marmysz. Albany : State University of New York Press, c2003. vii, 209 p. ; 23 cm. Includes bibliographical references (p. 195-202) and index. ISBN 0-7914-5840-7 (pbk. : alk. paper) ISBN 0-7914-5839-3 (alk. paper) DDC 149/.8
1. Nihilism (Philosophy) 2. Comic, The. I. Title.

B828.3 .M265 2003

Marot, Sébastien, 1961-
[Art de la mémoire, la territoire et l'architecture] Sub-urbanism and the art of memory / Sébastien Marot. London : Architectural Association, c2003. 82 p. : ill., ports. ; 22 cm. (Architecture landscape urbanism ; 8) Includes bibliographical references. Title and author's name taken from spine as this information is only partialy reproduced on the t.p. Translated from the French. ISBN 1-902902-23-8 DDC 711.58
1. Architecture - Philosophy. 2. Memory (Philosophy) 3. Suburbs. 4. City planning. I. Architectural Association. II. Title. III. Series.

Marquette studies in philosophy
(#24.) Rousselot, Pierre, 1878-1915. [Pour l'histoire du problème de l'amour au moyen âge. English] The problem of love in the Middle Ages. Milwaukee : Marquette University Press, [2001?]
B738.L68 R68 2001

Marquis, Andre, Ph. D.
Fall, Kevin A. Theoretical models of counseling and psychotherapy. New York : Brunner-Routledge, 2003.
BF637.C6 F324 2003

Marr, Hugh K., 1949-.
Pearson, Carol, 1944- PMAI manual. Gainesville, FL : Center for Applications of Psychological Type, c2003.
BF698.8.P37 P43 2003

MARR, NIKOLAĬ ĪAKOVLEVICH, 1864-1934.
Cherchi, Marcello. Disciplines and nations. Pittsburgh, Pa. : Center for Russian and East European Studies, University Center for International Studies, University of Pittsburgh, c2002.

Marraccini, Eliane Michelini. Encontro de mulheres : uma experiência criativa no meio da vida / Eliane Michelini Marraccini. São Paulo : Casa do Psicólogo, c2001. 131 p. ; 21 cm. Inlcudes bibliographical references (p. 129-131).
1. Climacteric - Psychological aspects. 2. Menopause - Psychological aspects. 3. Women - Psychology. I. Title.

MARRIAGE. *See also* **COURTSHIP; DIVORCE; FAMILY; HOME; MATE SELECTION.**
Greiper, BenTzion. Getting and staying married / BenTzion Greiper. Brooklyn, NY : B.T. Greiper, [2001?]
HQ734 .G745 2001

Inayat Khan, 1882-1927. Rassa shastra. Berwick, ME : Ibis Press ; York Beach, ME : distributed to the trade by Red Wheel/Weiser, 2003.
BF692 .I5 2003

Jiddāwī, 'Abd al-Mun'im. Ghayr ṣāliḥ lil-zawāj. al-Qāhirah : Dār Akhbār al-Yawm, 1994-

Maushart, Susan, 1958- Wifework. 1st U.S. ed. New York : Bloomsbury : Distributed to the trade by Holtzbrinck Publishers, 2002.
HQ759 .M3944 2002

Montpensier, Anne-Marie-Louise d'Orléans, duchesse de, 1627-1693. [Correspondence. English & French] Against marriage. Chicago : University of Chicago Press, 2002.
DC130.M8 A4 2002

Shumway, David R. Modern love. New York : New York University Press, c2003.
HQ503 .S54 2003

Simon, Rita James. Global perspectives on social issues. Lanham : Lexington Books, c2003.
HQ503 .S56 2003

MARRIAGE BROKERAGE. *See also* **MATE SELECTION.**
Gorfine, Yehudit. Be-ḳarov etslekh. Petaḥ Tiḳvah : Mar'ot, 2002.

MARRIAGE COUNSELING.
Bianchi, Carlos J. (Carlos Juan) Relatos de la pareja. Buenos Aires : Corregidor, c2001.

MARRIAGE - GOVERNMENT POLICY.
Simon, Rita James. Global perspectives on social issues. Lanham : Lexington Books, c2003.
HQ503 .S56 2003

MARRIAGE IN LITERATURE.
Huang, Shizhong. Hun bian, dao de yu wen xue. Di 1 ban. Beijing : Ren min wen xue chu ban she, 2000.

Shumway, David R. Modern love. New York : New York University Press, c2003.
HQ503 .S54 2003

MARRIAGE IN MOTION PICTURES.
Shumway, David R. Modern love. New York : New York University Press, c2003.

HQ503 .S54 2003

MARRIAGE IN POPULAR CULTURE.
Shumway, David R. Modern love. New York : New York University Press, c2003.
HQ503 .S54 2003

MARRIAGE - RELIGIOUS ASPECTS - JUDAISM.
Greiper, BenTzion. Getting and staying married / BenTzion Greiper. Brooklyn, NY : B.T. Greiper, [2001?]
HQ734 .G745 2001

Kohen, Yekutiel. Mishpaṭ ha-shalom. Yerushalayim : Mekhon Sha'ar ha-mishpaṭ : Hanhalat bate ha-din ha-rabaniyim, 762 [2001 or 2002]

Yahav, Avino'am Shemu'el. Ḳuntres E'eśeh lo 'ezer. Betar 'Ilit : A. S. Yahav, 761, 2001.

MARRIAGE - SOCIAL ASPECTS.
Simon, Rita James. Global perspectives on social issues. Lanham : Lexington Books, c2003.
HQ503 .S56 2003

MARRIED LIFE. *See* **MARRIAGE.**

MARRIED MEN. *See* **HUSBANDS.**

MARRIED PEOPLE. *See* **SPOUSES.**

MARRIED PEOPLE - FINANCE, PERSONAL.
Broussard, Cheryl D. What's money got to do with it? Oakland, CA : MetaMedia Pub., [c2002]
1. Black author.

MARRIED PEOPLE - RUSSIA (FEDERATION) - INTERVIEWS.
Maksimov, Andreĭ, 1959- Dialogi li︠u︡bvi. Moskva : Delovoĭ ėkspress, 1999.
BF575.L8 M336 1999

MARRIED PERSONS. *See* **MARRIED PEOPLE.**

Marriott, Rob. Astrology uncut : a street-smart guide to the stars / Rob Marriott and Sonya Magett. 1st trade pbk. ed. New York : One World, 2004. p. cm. ISBN 0-8129-6793-3 DDC 133.5
1. Astrology. 2. Hip-hop - Miscellanea. I. Magett, Sonya.
BF1711 .M45 2004

Marschark, Marc.
Oxford handbook of deaf studies, language, and education. Oxford ; New York : Oxford University Press, c2003.
HV2380 .O88 2003

Marsella, Anthony J.
Understanding terrorism. 1st ed. Washington, DC : American Psychological Association, 2004.
HV6431 .U35 2004

Marsh, Elizabeth J.
Cognitive psychology. New York : Psychology Press, 2003.
BF201 .C642 2003

Marsh, Herbert W.
International advances in self research. Greenwich, CT : Information Age Pub., 2003.
BF697 .I675 2003

Marshall, Evan, 1956- The eyes have it : revealing their power, messages, and secrets / Evan Marshall. New York : Citadel Press, c2003. 181 p. : ill. ; 21 cm. Includes index. ISBN 0-8065-2445-6 DDC 138
1. Eye - Psychological aspects. 2. Gaze - Psychological aspects. 3. Body language. I. Title.
BF637.N66 M37 2003

Icing Ivy / Evan Marshall. Waterville, Me. : Thorndike Press, 2003, c2002. 336 p. (large print) : ill. ; 22 cm. ISBN 0-7862-5388-6 (pbk. series lg. print : U.S. : sc : alk. paper) ISBN 0-7540-7234-7 (Chivers lg. print : U.K. : hc) ISBN 0-7540-7235-5 (Camden lg. print : U.K. sc) DDC 813/.54
1. Stuart, Jane (Fictitious character) - Fiction. 2. Winky (Fictitious character) - Fiction. 3. Women cat owners - Fiction. 4. Literary agents - Fiction. 5. Cats - Fiction. 6. Large type books. I. Title.
PS3563.A72236 I27 2003

Marshall, Ian, 1954- Peak experiences : walking meditations on literature, nature, and need / Ian Marshall. Charlottesville : University of Virginia Press, 2003. 267 p. ; 24 cm. (Under the sign of nature) Includes bibliographical references (p. [243]-256) and index. ISBN 0-8139-2167-8 DDC 810.9/36
1. Maslow, Abraham H. - (Abraham Harold) - Influence. 2. American literature - History and criticism. 3. Nature in literature. 4. Psychology in literature. 5. Need (Psychology) 6. Mountaineering. I. Title. II. Series.
PS163 .M37 2003

MARSILIUS, OF INGHEN, D. 1396.
Reina, Maria Elena. Hoc hic et nunc. [Firenze] : Leo S. Olschki, 2002.

Marsolek, Chad J.
Rethinking implicit memory. Oxford ; New York : Oxford University Press, c2003.
RC394.M46 R485 2003

Martels, Z. R. W. M. von.
Antiquity renewed. Leuven, Netherlands ; Dudley, MA : Peeters, 2003.
CB365 .A58 2003

Martha Freud.
Behling, Katja, 1963- Berlin : Aufbau Taschenbuch Verlag, 2002.
BF109.F73 B455 2002

MARTIAL ARTS. *See* **SELF-DEFENSE.**

Martin, Barbara Y. Change your aura, change your life : a step-by-step guide to unfolding your spiritual power / Barbara Y. Martin with Dimitri Moraitis. Sunland, CA : WisdomLight Books, c2003. xv, 233 p. : ill. (some col.) ; 26 cm. Includes index. ISBN 0-9702118-1-3 (pbk.) DDC 133.8/92
1. Aura. 2. Color - Psychic aspects. I. Moraitis, Dimitri. II. Title.
BF1389.A8 M37 2003

MARTIN, BILLY, 1928-.
DeMarco, Michael. Dugout days. New York : AMACOM, c2001.
GV865.M35 D46 2001

Martin, Carole A.
Butterfield, Perry M., 1932- Emotional connections. Washington, DC : Zero To Three, 2004.
BF720.E45 B879 2004

Butterfield, Perry M., 1932- Emotional connections. 1st ed. Washington, DC : Zero To Three Press, c2003.
BF720.E45 B88 2003

Martin, Hervé, 1940-.
Religion et mentalités au Moyen Age. Rennes : Presses universitaires de Rennes, c2003.
BR141 .R45 2003

Martin, Jack, 1950- Psychology and the question of agency / Jack Martin, Jeff Sugarman, Janice Thompson. Albany : State University of New York Press, c2003. x, 186 p. ; 23 cm. (SUNY series, alternatives in psychology) Includes bibliographical references (p. 167-174) and index. ISBN 0-7914-5726-5 (pbk.) ISBN 0-7914-5725-7 DDC 155.2
1. Autonomy (Psychology) I. Sugarman, Jeff, 1955- II. Thompson, Janice, 1964- III. Title. IV. Series.
BF575.A88 M37 2003

Martin, Jean-Clet. Parures d'éros : un traité du superficiel / Jean-Clet Martin. Paris : Kimé, 2003. 115 p. ; 21 cm. (Collection "Philosophie en cours") Includes bibliographical references. ISBN 2-8417-4301-2 DDC 194
1. Clothing and dress - Erotic aspects. 2. Sexual excitement - Philosophy. 3. Aesthetics. I. Title. II. Series.

Martin, John Jeffries, 1951-.
The Renaissance. London ; New York : Routledge, 2003.
DG445 .R565 2003

MARTIN, JOSEPH W. (JOSEPH WILLIAM), 1884-1968.
Kenneally, James J. (James Joseph), 1929- A compassionate conservative. Lanham, Md. : Lexington Books, c2003.
E748.M375 K46 2003

Martin, MaryJoy, 1955- Twilight dwellers : ghosts, gases, and goblins of Colorado / MaryJoy Martin. 2nd ed. Boulder, Colo. : Pruett, 2003. p. cm. Includes bibliographical references. ISBN 0-87108-686-7 (alk. paper) DDC 133.1/09788
1. Ghosts - Colorado. 2. Goblins - Colorado. I. Title.
BF1472.U6 M37 2003

Martin, Michael, 1948- Ghosts / by Michael Martin. Mankato, Minn. : Edge Books, 2004. v. cm. (The unexplained) Includes bibliographical references and index. CONTENTS: The mysterious world of ghosts -- The history of ghosts -- Searching for ghosts -- Looking for answers. ISBN 0-7368-2717-X DDC 133.1
1. Ghosts - Juvenile literature. 2. Ghosts. I. Title. II. Series.
BF1461 .M365 2004

Near-death experiences / by Michael Martin. Mankato, Minn. : Edge Books, 2004. v. cm. (The unexplained) Includes bibliographical references and index. CONTENTS: The mysterious world of near-death experiences -- The history of near-death experiences -- Searching for near-death experiences -- Looking for answers -- Features -- The stages of the near-death experience -- Leaving the body behind -- Teenagers and the near-death experience -- An African near-death experience. ISBN 0-7368-2719-6 DDC 133.9/01/3
1. Near-death experiences - Juvenile literature. 2. Near-death experiences. I. Title. II. Series.
BF1045.N4 M375 2004

Martin, Richard P.
Myths of the ancient Greeks. New York : New American Library, 2003.
BL783 .M98 2003

Martín Salgado, Lourdes. Marketing político : arte y ciencia de la persuasión en democracia / Lourdes Martín Salgado. Barcelona : Paidós, c2002. 283 p. ; 20 cm. (Papeles de comunicación ; 37) Inlcudes bibliographical references (p. [269]-283). ISBN 84-493-1238-8
1. Television in politics. 2. Marketing - Political aspects. 3. Political campaigns. 4. Persuasion (Psychology) 5. Communication. I. Title. II. Series.

Martin, Vivien, 1947- Leading change in health and social care / Vivien Martin. London ; New York : Routledge, 2003. vii, 186 p. : ill. ; 25 cm. Includes bibliographical references (p. [179]-181) and index. ISBN 0-415-30545-4 (hbk.) ISBN 0-415-30546-2 (pbk.) DDC 362.1/068
1. Health services administration. 2. Social work administration. 3. Organizational change. 4. Leadership. I. Title.
RA971 .M365 2003

Martin von Troppau (Martinus Polonus), O.P. (1278) in England.
Ikas, Wolfgang-Valentin. Wiesbaden : Reichert, 2002.

Martin, William.
Vint/age 2001 conference : [videorecording]. New York, c2001.

Martinelli, Donatella.
Manzoni, Alessandro, 1785-1873. Postille. Milano : Centro nazionale studi manzoniani, 2002.

Martinelli, Paolo, 1958- Vocazione e stati di vita del cristiano : riflessioni sistematiche in dialogo con Hans Urs von Balthasar / Paolo Martinelli. Roma : Collegio San Lorenzo da Brindisi, 2001. 456 p. ; 24 cm. (Collana Dimensioni spirituali ; 15) Includes bibliographical references (p. [405]-441) and indexes. At head of title: Istituto francescano di spiritualità. DDC 248
1. Balthasar, Hans Urs von, - 1905- 2. Theology, Doctrinal - History - 20th century. 3. Christian life. 4. Spiritual life. I. Istituto francescano di spiritualità (Rome, Italy) II. Title. III. Series.

Martinelli, Patricia A. Haunted New Jersey : ghosts and strange phenomena of the Garden State / Patricia A. Martinelli and Charles A. Stansfield, Jr. Mechanicsburg, PA : Stackpole Books, 2005. p. cm. Includes bibliographical references. ISBN 0-8117-3156-1 (pbk.) DDC 133.1/09749
1. Ghosts - New Jersey. 2. Monsters - New Jersey. I. Stansfield, Charles A. II. Title.
BF1472.U6 M38 2004

Martínez Benlloch, Isabel.
Género, desarrollo psicosocial y trastornos de la imagen corporal. Madrid : Instituto de la Mujer, 2001.

Martinez-Gros, Gabriel.
Palais et pouvoir. Vincennes : Presses universitaires de Vincennes, c2003.

MARTINUS, POLONUS, D. 1279. CHRONICON PONTIFICUM ET IMPERATORUM.
Ikas, Wolfgang-Valentin. Martin von Troppau (Martinus Polonus), O.P. (1278) in England. Wiesbaden : Reichert, 2002.

Martoccia, María, 1957- Cuerpos frágiles, mujeres prodigiosas / María Martoccia, Javiera Gutiérrez. Buenos Aires : Editorial Sudamericana, c2002. 204 p. ; 22 cm. Includes bibliographical references (p. 199-202). CONTENTS: Frida Kahlo : bellas mentiras -- Jacqueline du Pré : el arco del destino -- Virginia Woolf : las razones -- Billie Holiday : el color de la sombra -- Madame Curie : heroína del dolor -- Katherine Mansfield : la herida nómade -- María Callas : la codicia que nutre -- Judy Garland : la adulteración del ser -- Simone Weil : filósofa del hambre. ISBN 950-07-2197-X
1. Women - Biography. 2. Women - Diseases - Psychological aspects - Biography. 3. Mind and body. I. Gutiérrez, Javiera, 1964- II. Title.

Marton, L. Magda.
Az Általánostól a különösig. [Budapest] : Gondolat : MTA Pszichológiai Kutatóintézet, c2002.
BF128.H8 A44 2002

MARTYRS, JEWISH. *See* **JEWISH MARTYRS.**

MARVELOUS, THE. *See* **MIRACLES.**

Marvels, monsters, and miracles : studies in the medieval and early modern imaginations / edited by Timothy S. Jones and David A. Sprunger. Kalamazoo, Mich. : Medieval Institute Publications, 2002. xxv, 306 p. : ill. ; 24 cm. (Studies in medieval culture ; 42) Includes bibliographical references. CONTENTS: The medieval other: the Middle Ages as other / Paul Freedman -- Marvelous peoples or marvelous races?: Race and the Anglo-Saxon Wonders of the east / Greta Austin -- Wonders of the Beast: India in classical and medieval literature / Andrea Rossi-Reder -- The book of John Mandeville and the geography of identity / Martin Camargo -- Froissart's "Debate of the horse and the greyhound": companion animals and signs of social status in the fourteenth century / Kristen M. Figg -- The miracle of the lengthened beam in Apocryphal and hagiographic tradition / Thomas N. Hall -- Falling giants and floating lead: scholastic history in the Middle English Cleanness / Michael W. Twomey -- From monster to martyr: the Old English legend of Saint Christopher / Joyce Tally Lionarons -- Fighting men, fighting monsters: outlawry, masculinity, and identity in the Gesta herewardi / Timothy S. Jones -- Monsters of misogyny: Bigorne and Chicheface- suite et fin? / Malcolm Jones -- Depicting the insane: a thirteenth-century case study / David A. Sprunger -- Magic and metafiction in The Franklin's tale: Chaucer's Clerk of Orléans as double of the Franklin / Paul Battles -- Portentous births and the monstrous imagination in Renaissance culture / Norman R. Smith -- The nude cyclops in the costume book / Mary Baine Campbell. ISBN 1-58044-065-7 ISBN 1-58044-066-5 (pbk.) DDC 809/.02
1. Popular culture - Europe - Religious aspects - Christianity. 2. Civilization, Medieval. 3. Animals, Mythical. 4. Miracles - History of doctrines - Middle Ages, 600-1500. 5. Monsters. I. Jones, Timothy S. II. Sprunger, David A. III. Series.
GR825 .M218 2003

Marx, Barbara.
Komik der Renaissance, Renaissance der Komik. Frankfurt am Main ; New York : P. Lang, c2000.
BH301.C7 .K63 2000

MARX, KARL, 1818-1883.
Read, Jason. The micro-politics of capital. Albany : State University of New York Press, c2003.
HB97.5 .R42 2003

Marx, Wolfgang.
Der Grund, die Not und die Freude des Bewusstseins. Würzburg : Königshausen & Neumann, c2002.
B808.9 .G78 2002

MARXIAN ECONOMICS.
Read, Jason. The micro-politics of capital. Albany : State University of New York Press, c2003.
HB97.5 .R42 2003

MARXISM. *See* **COMMUNISM; SOCIALISM.**

MARXIST CRITICISM.
Freedman, Carl Howard. The incomplete projects. Middletown, Conn. : Wesleyan University Press, c2002.
HX523 .F74 2002

Strategies for theory. Albany : State University of New York Press, c2003.
B842 .S77 2003

MARY, BLESSED VIRGIN, SAINT - APPARITIONS AND MIRACLES.
Van Auken, John. The end times. New York : Signet Book, c2001. [Updated ed.].
BF1791 .V36 2001

MARY, BLESSED VIRGIN, SAINT - APPARITIONS AND MIRACLES - HISTORY - MISCELLANEA.
Roberts, Courtney, 1957- Visions of the Virgin Mary. St. Paul, Minn. : Llewellyn, 2004.
BF1729.R4 R63 2004

MARY, BLESSED VIRGIN, SAINT - SHRINES - EGYPT.
Be thou there. Cairo ; New York : American University in Cairo Press, c2001.

MARY MAGDALENE, SAINT - MISCELLANEA.
Douzet, André. Nouvelles lumières sur Rennes-le-Château. Chêne-Bourg (Suisse) : Acquarius, c1998-
BF1434.F8 D69 1998

Mary P. Follett.
Tonn, Joan C. New Haven [Conn.] : Yale University Press, c2003.
HN57 .T695 2003

Más allá del 11 de septiembre.
Rojas Marcos, Luis, 1943- [Madrid] : Espasa, c2002.
HV6432.7 .R64 2002

Más que discutible.
Tusquets, Oscar, 1941- 1a. ed. en Fabula. Barcelona : Fabula Tusquets Editores, 2002.

Maśa u-matan be-emunah.
Tamari, Meir. Yerushalayim : Śimḥonim, [761, 2001]

Masangana Diamaka, Robin, 1962- Dialogue politique : sur fond du conflit inter-congolais / Robin Masangana Diamaka. Paris : Editoo.com, 2002. 118 p. ; 22 cm. "Texte de l'accord de Lusaka inclus : Communiqué travaux du prédialogue, Pacte républicain signé à Gaberonne." ISBN 2-7477-0025-9
1. United Nations - Congo (Democratic Republic) 2. Congo (Democratic Republic) - Politics and government - 1997- 3. Insurgency - Congo (Democratic Republic) - History - 20th century. 4. Peacekeeping forces - Congo (Democratic Republic) 5. Violence - Congo (Democratic Republic) 6. Military assistance - Congo (Democratic Republic) 7. Democracy - Congo (Democratic Republic) 8. Peace. 9. Black author. I. Title.

La mascarade interculturelle.
Paquette, Didier. Paris : Harmattan, c2002.

La maschera e l'uomo.
Bonvecchio, Claudio. Milano : F. Angeli, 2002.

Masculinidades en Ecuador / X. Andrade y Gioconda Herrera, editores. Quito, Ecuador : FLACSO ; [S.l.] : UNFPA, 2001. 199 p. ; 24 cm. (Agora) ISBN 9978670645
1. Masculinity - Ecuador - Congresses. 2. Men - Ecuador - Congresses. 3. Sex role - Ecuador - Congresses. I. Andrade, X. (Xavier) II. Herrera, Gioconda. III. Series: Agora (FLACSO (Organization). Sede Ecuador)
BF692.5 .M388 2001

Masculinidades en Ecuador / X. Andrade y Gioconda Herrera, editores. Quito, Ecuador : FLACSO ; [s.l.] : UNFPA, 2001. 199 p. ; 24 cm. (Agora) ISBN 9978670645
1. Masculinity - Ecuador - Congresses. 2. Sex role - Ecuador - Congresses. I. Andrade, X. (Xavier) II. Herrera, Gioconda. III. Series: Agora (FLACSO (Organization). Sede Ecuador)
BF692.5 .M37 2001

MASCULINITY. See also ANDROCENTRISM.
Bayers, Peter L., 1966- Imperial ascent. Boulder, Colo. : University Press of Colorado, c2003.
GV200.19.P78 B39 2003

Boys, literacies, and schooling. Buckingham [England] ; Philadelphia : Open University Press, 2002.
LC1390 .B69 2002

DiPiero, Thomas, 1956- White men aren't. Durham : Duke University Press, 2002.
HQ1090 .D567 2002

Fraiman, Susan. Cool men and the second sex. New York : Columbia University Press, c2003.
HQ1090 .F73 2003

Frantzen, Allen J., 1947- Bloody good. Chicago : University of Chicago Press, 2004.
D523 .F722 2004

Jones, Steve, 1944- Y. Boston : Houghton Mifflin, 2003.
GN281 .J62 2003

Karras, Ruth Mazo, 1957- From boys to men. Philadelphia : University of Pennsylvania Press, c2003.
HQ775 .K373 2003

Military masculinities. Westport, Conn. : Praeger, 2003.
U21.5 .M4975 2003

Moulding masculinities. Aldershot, Hants, England ; Burlington, VT : Ashgate, c2003.
BF692.5 .M68 2003

Newell, Waller Randy. The code of man. 1st ed. New York : ReganBooks, c2003.
HQ1090 .N49 2003

Pieroni, Osvaldo. Pene d'amore. Soveria Mannelli : Rubbettino, c2002.

Working with men in the human services. Crows Nest, N.S.W. : Allen & Unwin, c2001.

MASCULINITY - AUSTRIA.
Hofstadler, Beate, 1961- KörperNormen, KörperFormen. Wien : Turia + Kant, c2001.
BF692.5 .H64 2001

MASCULINITY - COLOMBIA - ARMENIA (QUINDÍO) - CASE STUDIES.
Viveros, M. (Mara) De quebradores y cumplidores. 1a ed. [Colombia] : CES Universidad Nacional de Colombia : Fundación Ford : Profamilia Colombia, 2002.

MASCULINITY - COLOMBIA - QUIBDÓ - CASE STUIDES.
Viveros, M. (Mara) De quebradores y cumplidores. 1a ed. [Colombia] : CES Universidad Nacional de Colombia : Fundación Ford : Profamilia Colombia, 2002.

MASCULINITY - ECUADOR - CONGRESSES.
Masculinidades en Ecuador. Quito, Ecuador : FLACSO ; [S.l.] : UNFPA, 2001.
BF692.5 .M388 2001

Masculinidades en Ecuador. Quito, Ecuador : FLACSO ; [s.l.] : UNFPA, 2001.
BF692.5 .M37 2001

MASCULINITY - HISTORY.
Braudy, Leo. From chivalry to terrorism. New York : Alfred A. Knopf : Distributed by Random House, 2003.
HQ1090 .B7 2003

MASCULINITY IN LITERATURE.
DiPiero, Thomas, 1956- White men aren't. Durham : Duke University Press, 2002.
HQ1090 .D567 2002

Mangan, Michael, 1953- Staging masculinities. Houndmills, Basingstoke, Hampshire : New York : Palgrave Macmillan, 2003.
PN1650.M44 M36 2003

MASCULINITY (PSYCHOLOGY). See MASCULINITY.

MASCULINITY - SCANDINAVIA.
Moulding masculinities. Aldershot, Hants, England ; Burlington, VT : Ashgate, c2003.
BF692.5 .M68 2003

Masekhet Derekh erets.
He lakhem ḥamishah sefari.. [Brooklyn, NY : Renaissance Hebraica, 2000?]

Masekhet ha-ḥayim.
Ḥayun, Yehudah ben Mordekhai. Bene Beraḳ : Y. Ḥayun, 762 [2001 or 2002]

Maset, Michael. Diskurs, Macht und Geschichte : Foucaults Analysetechniken und die historische Forschung / Michael Maset. Frankfurt/Main ; New York : Campus, c2002. 268 p. ; 23 cm. (Campus Historische Studien ; Bd. 32) Originally presented as the author's thesis (doctoral)--Universität Kassel. Includes bibliographical references (p. 237-268). ISBN 3-593-37113-8 (pbk.) DDC 194
1. Foucault, Michel. 2. History - Philosophy. 3. Power (Social sciences) 4. Historiography. I. Title. II. Series.
BF24.30.F724 M37 2002

Mashek, Debra J.
Handbook of closeness and intimacy. Mahwah, N.J. : Lawrence Erlbaum Associates, 2004.
BF575.I5 H36 2004

MASKELYNE, JOHN NEVIL, 1839-1917.
Davenport, Anne Ashley. St. George's Hall. Pasadena : Mike Caveney's Magic Words, c2001.
BF1623 .D38 2001

Masks of the universe.
Harrison, Edward Robert. 2nd ed. Cambridge, U.K. ; New York : Cambridge University Press, 2003.
QB981 .H324 2003

MASKS - SYMBOLIC ASPECTS.
Bonvecchio, Claudio. La maschera e l'uomo. Milano : F. Angeli, 2002.

Maslach, Christina.
[Burnout, the cost of caring]
Burnout : the cost of caring / Christina Maslach ; prologue by Philip G. Zimbardo. Cambridge, MA : ISHK, 2003. p. cm. Originally published: Burnout, the cost of caring. Englewood Cliffs, N.J. : Prentice-Hall, c1982 Includes bibliographical references and index. ISBN 1-88353-635-9 (alk. paper) DDC 158.7/23
1. Burn out (Psychology) I. Title.
BF481 .M384 2003

MASLOW, ABRAHAM H. (ABRAHAM HAROLD) - INFLUENCE.
Marshall, Ian, 1954- Peak experiences. Charlottesville : University of Virginia Press, 2003.
PS163 .M37 2003

MASOCHISM. See SUFFERING.

Mason, Colin, 1926- The 2030 spike : countdown to global catastrophe / Colin Mason. London ; Sterling, VA : Earthscan Publications, 2003. iv, 250 p. ; 23 cm. Includes bibliographical references and index. ISBN 1-84407-018-2 (hbk.) DDC 303.49
1. Twenty-first century - Forecasts. 2. Environmental policy. 3. Natural resources. 4. Social prediction. 5. Catastrophical, The. I. Title. II. Title: Two thousand thirty spike III. Title: Two thousand and thirty spike IV. Title: Twenty-thirty spike
CB161 .M384 2003

Mason, Douglas J. The memory workbook : breakthrough techniques to exercise your brain and improve your memory / Douglas J. Mason & Michael L. Kohn ; foreword by Karen A. Clark. Oakland, CA : New Harbinger Publications, ; c2001. : Distributed in the U.S.A. by Publishers Group West, c2001. xiii, 230 p. : ill. ; 28 cm. Includes bibliographical references (p. [221]-230) ISBN 1-57224-258-2 (pbk.) DDC 155.67/1314
1. Memory in old age. 2. Mnemonics. I. Kohn, Michael L. II. Title. III. Title: Breakthrough techniques to exercise your brain and improve your memory
BF724.85.M45 M37 2001

Mason, Paul, 1967- Investigating the supernatural / Paul Mason. Chicago, Ill. : Heinemann Library, 2004. p. cm. (Forensic files) SUMMARY: Introduces the use of forensic science in cases involving the supernatural, such as those involving hauntings, werewolves or vampires, and offers scientific reasons for the alleged supernatural behavior. Includes bibliographical references (p.   ) and index. Table of contents URL: http://www.loc.gov/catdir/toc/ecip047/2003018158.html ISBN 1403448329 (lib. bdg.) ISBN 1403454728 (pbk.) DDC 130
1. Supernatural - Case studies - Juvenile literature. 2. Supernatural. I. Title. II. Series.
BF1029 .M37 2004

Masonería : vestiduras y paramentos masónicos / [recopilación] Oscar Valenzuela Muñoz. Quito : [O. Valenzuela Muñoz], 2001. 172 p. : ill. ; 23 cm. "Textos publicados en la Revista Masónica de Chile, 1955-1957." Includes bibliographical references. ISBN 9978419446
1. Freemasons - Costumes, supplies, etc. 2. Freemasonry - History. 3. Freemasonry - Symbolism. I. Valenzuela Muñoz, Oscar. II. Title: Vestiduras y paramentos masónicos

MASONIC ORDERS. See FREEMASONRY.

MASONRY (SECRET ORDER). See FREEMASONRY.

Masons and the building of Washington D.C.
Ovason, David. [Secret zodiacs of Washington DC] The secret architecture of our nation's capital. 1st Perennial ed. New York, NY : Perennial, 2002.

MASS COMMUNICATION. See COMMUNICATION; COMMUNICATION AND TRAFFIC; TELECOMMUNICATION.

MASS CULTURE. See POPULAR CULTURE.

MASS MEDIA. See also MOTION PICTURES.
La comunicazione nei processi sociali e organizzativi. Nuova ed. aggiornata. Milano, Italy : FrancoAngeli, [2001?], c1997.

Medien, Texte und Maschinen. 1. Aufl. Wiesbaden : Westdeutscher Verlag, c2001.

Zeit in den Medien, Medien in der Zeit. München : Fink, c2002.

MASS MEDIA AND CHILDREN.
Children in the digital age. Westport, Conn. : Praeger, 2002.
HQ784.M3 C455 2002

The elusive child. London ; New York : Karnac, c2002.

MASS MEDIA AND CULTURE.
Contrera, Malena Segura. Mídia e pânico. 1. ed. São Paulo : Annablume : FAPESP, 2002.

Pinheiro, José Moura. Mitos atuais. Salvador : Secretaria da Cultura e Turismo : Fundação Cultural do Estado da Bahia : Empresa Gráfoca da Bahia, 2001.

Ries, Marc, 1956- Medienkulturen. Wien : Sonderzahl, c2002.
P94.6 .R54 2002

Writing and materiality in China. Cambridge, Mass. : Published by Harvard University Asia Center for Harvard-Yenching Institute : distributed by Harvard University Press, 2003.
PL2262 .W74 2003

MASS MEDIA AND FOLKLORE.
Pinheiro, José Moura. Mitos atuais. Salvador : Secretaria da Cultura e Turismo : Fundação Cultural do Estado da Bahia : Empresa Gráfoca da Bahia, 2001.

MASS MEDIA AND TECHNOLOGY.
Piscitelli, Alejandro. Meta-cultura. Buenos Aires : La Crujía, 2002.
P96.T42 P575

MASS MEDIA AND THE ENVIRONMENT.
McLuhan's wake [videorecording]. [Montreal, Quebec] : Primitive Entertainment/National Film Board of Canada, c2002.

MASS MEDIA AND YOUTH.
Youth cultures. Westport, Conn. : Praeger, 2003.
HQ796 .Y59273 2003

MASS MEDIA - AUDIENCES.
Les cultes médiatiques. Rennes : Presses universitaires de Rennes, [2002]

MASS MEDIA CRITICISM.
Wortham, Simon. Samuel Weber. Aldershot, England ; Burlington, VT : Ashgate, c2003.
PN81 .W64 2003

MASS MEDIA IN EDUCATION - UNITED STATES.
Goodman, Steven. Teaching youth media. New York : Teachers College Press, c2003.
LB1043 .G59 2003

MASS MEDIA LITERACY. See **MEDIA LITERACY.**

MASS MEDIA - MORAL AND ETHICAL ASPECTS.
Markt - Medien - Moral. Bochum : Projekt-Verlag, 2001.

MASS MEDIA - OBJECTIVITY.
Stanovich, Keith E., 1950- How to think straight about psychology. 7th ed. Boston, MA : Allyn and Bacon, 2004.
BF76.5 .S68 2004

MASS MEDIA - PHILOSOPHY.
Wahrnehmung und Medialität. Tübingen : Francke, c2001.
PN2039 .W347 2001

MASS MEDIA - POLITICAL ASPECTS - GERMANY.
Die Politik der Massenmedien. Köln : Halem, 2001.

MASS MEDIA - POLITICAL ASPECTS - MEXICO.
Fernández Christlieb, Fátima. La responsabilidad de los medios de comunicación. 1a. ed. México : Paidós, 2002.

MASS MEDIA - PSYCHOLOGICAL ASPECTS.
Contrera, Malena Segura. Mídia e pânico. 1. ed. São Paulo : Annablume ; FAPESP, 2002.

Giles, David, 1964- Media psychology. Mahwah, N.J. : Lawrence Erlbaum Associates Publishers, 2003.
P96.P75 G55 2003

Perloff, Richard M. The dynamics of persuasion. 2nd ed. Mahwah, N.J. : Lawrence Erlbaum Associates, 2003.
BF637.P4 .P39 2003

Reklama. Moskva : Izd-vo Dom "Bakhrakh-M", 2001.

Stanovich, Keith E., 1950- How to think straight about psychology. 7th ed. Boston, MA : Allyn and Bacon, 2004.
BF76.5 .S68 2004

MASS MEDIA - SEMIOTICS.
Medien, Texte und Maschinen. 1. Aufl. Wiesbaden : Westdeutscher Verlag, c2001.

MASS MEDIA - SOCIAL ASPECTS.
Sodré, Muniz. Sociedade mídia e violência. Porto Alegre : Editora Sulina ; EDIPUCRS, c2002.

MASS MEDIA - SOCIAL ASPECTS - MEXICO.
Fernández Christlieb, Fátima. La responsabilidad de los medios de comunicación. 1a. ed. México : Paidós, 2002.

MASS MURDER - PSYCHOLOGICAL ASPECTS.
Mental health and mass violence [electronic resource]. [Bethesda, MD : National Institute of Mental Health, 2002]

MASS POLITICAL BEHAVIOR. See **POLITICAL PARTICIPATION.**

MASS PSYCHOLOGY. See **SOCIAL PSYCHOLOGY.**

MASS SOCIETY. See also **POPULAR CULTURE.**
Tomás Ferré, Facundo. Formas artísticas y sociedad de masas. Madrid : Antonio Machado Libros, c2001.

Massa, Adriana.
Pagés Larraya, Fernando. Liturgia lunar de la locura. Córdoba, Argentina : Comunicarte Editorial, c2002.

MASSACHUSETTS - FICTION.
Kava, Alex. The soul catcher. Waterville, Me. : Thorndike Press, 2003, 2002.
PS3561.A8682 S6 2003

Masson, J. Moussaieff (Jeffrey Moussaieff), 1941-
The assault on truth : Freud's suppression of the seduction theory / Jeffrey Moussaieff Masson. 1st Ballantine Books ed. New York : Ballantine Books, 2003. xxi, 361 p. : ill. ; 21 cm. Includes bibliographical references (p. 201-240) and index. DDC 150.19/52
1. Freud, Sigmund, - 1856-1939. 2. Psychoanalysis - History. 3. Seduction - Psychological aspects - History. 4. Sexually abused children - Mental health - History. 5. Child sexual abuse - History. 6. Fantasy - History. I. Title.
BF109.F74 M38 2003

The master key system.
Haanel, Charles F. (Charles Francis), b. 1866. 1st ed. Wilkes-Barre, Pa. : Kallisti Pub., c2000.
BF639 .H132 2000

Master your fears.
Sapadin, Linda. Hoboken, N.J. : John Wiley & Sons, 2004.
BF575.F2 S26 2004

Master your whole life.
Reed, Bob, 1942- 1st ed. Toronto, Ont. : New Vision Pub., 2000.
BF637.S4 R44 2000

Master zhizni.
Klíuchnikov, Sergeĭ. Moskva : Belovod'e, 2001.
BF637.S4 K556 2001

Mastering the world of psychology.
Wood, Samuel E. Boston : Pearson/Allyn and Bacon, c2004.
BF121 .W656 2004

Mastromarino, Diane, 1978-.
Simple joys. Boulder, Colo. : Blue Mountain Arts, Inc., c2003.
BF637.C5 S5443 2003

Mat'-zemlía i TSar'-gorod.
Domnikov, S. D. (Sergeĭ Dmitrievich) Moskva : Aleteĭía, 2002.
B4235.H57 D65 2002

MATCOM (Alexandria, Va.).
Conflict resolution for school personnel [electronic resource]. [Washington, D.C.?] : U.S. Dept. of Justice, Office of Justice Programs, National Institute of Justice, c1999.

MATE SELECTION. See also **MAN-WOMAN RELATIONSHIPS.**
Meeks, James T., 1956- Life changing relationships. Chicago, Ill. : Moody Press, c2002.
HQ801 .M515 2002
1. Black author.

Shlain, Leonard. Sex, time, and power. New York ; London : Viking, 2003.
HQ23 .S45 2003

MATE SELECTION - MISCELLANEA.
Kosarin, Jenni. The everything love signs book. Avon, MA : Adams Media, c2004.
BF1729.L6 K67 2004

MATE SELECTION - RELIGIOUS ASPECTS - CHRISTIANITY.
Meeks, James T., 1956- Life changing relationships. Chicago, Ill. : Moody Press, c2002.
HQ801 .M515 2002
1. Black author.

MATE SELECTION - RELIGIOUS ASPECTS - JUDAISM.
Gorfine, Yehudit. Be-karov etslekh. Petah Tikvah : Mar'ot, 2002.

MATERIA MEDICA. See **DRUGS.**

MATERIA MEDICA, VEGETABLE.
Carvalho, Angela Maria B., 1954- A magia das ervas e seu axé. São Paulo, SP : Madras, 2003.
1. Black author.

MATERIAL CULTURE. See **ANTIQUITIES; FOLKLORE; TECHNOLOGY.**

Materiali per un lessico della ragione / a cura di Massimo Barale. Pisa : Edizioni ETS, c2001. 2 v. (582 p.) ; 22 cm. (Filosofia ; 50-51) Includes bibliographical references. Vol 1 by M. Barale ... [et al.]; v. 2 by E. Moriconi ... [et al.]. ISBN 88-467-0555-6 ISBN 88-467-0540-8 (v. 1) ISBN 88-467-0541-6 (v. 2) DDC 128
1. Reason - Philosophy. 2. Reasoning. I. Barale, Massimo, 1941- II. Moriconi, Enrico, 1950- III. Series: Filosofia (Pisa, Italy) ; 50-51.

Materialien zur Moderne
Kupka, František, 1871-1957. [Création dans les arts plastiques. Czech. German] Die Schöpfung in der bildenden Kunst. Ostfildern-Ruit : Hatje Cantz, c2001.

MATERIALISM. See also **NATURALISM.**
Physicalism and mental causation. Exeter, UK : Charlottesville, VA : Imprint Academic, c2003.
B825 .P494 2003

MATERIALISM - PSYCHOLOGICAL ASPECTS.
Psychology and consumer culture. 1st ed. Washington, DC : American Psychological Association, c2004.
HC110.C6 P76 2004

MATERNITY. See **MOTHERHOOD.**

MATH. See **MATHEMATICS.**

Math all around me.
Bruce, Lisa. Chicago, Ill. : Raintree, 2003.
BF294 .B78 2003

MATHEMATICAL LOGIC. See **LOGIC, SYMBOLIC AND MATHEMATICAL.**

MATHEMATICAL PHYSICS. See **SOUND.**

MATHEMATICAL STATISTICS. See also **SAMPLING (STATISTICS).**
Blaikie, Norman W. H., 1933- Analyzing quantitative data. London ; Thousand Oaks, CA : Sage Publications Ltd, 2003.
HA29 .B556 2003

MATHEMATICS. See **LOGIC, SYMBOLIC AND MATHEMATICAL.**

MATHEMATICS, MEDIEVAL.
Abbo of Fleury and Ramsay. Oxford ; New York : Oxford University Press, 2002.

MATHEMATICS - PHILOSOPHY.
Appraising Lakatos. Dordrecht ; Boston : Kluwer Academic, c2002.
Q175 .A685 2002

Châtelet, Gilles. [Enjeux du mobile. English] Figuring space. Dordrecht ; Boston : Kluwer, c2000.
B67 .C4313 2000

Mather, Nancy. Woodcock-Johnson III tests of cognitive abilities examiner's manual / Nancy Mather, Richard W. Woodcock. Itasca, IL : Riverside Pub., c2001. xii, 106 p. : ill. ; 28 cm. Spine title: WJ III tests of cognitive abilities examiner's manual. Includes bibliographical references (p. 95-99). DDC 153.9/3
1. Woodcock-Johnson Tests of Cognitive Ability. I. Title. II. Title: Woodcock-Johnson 3 tests of cognitive abilities examiner's manual III. Title: Woodcock-Johnson three tests of cognitive abilities examiner's manual IV. Title: Examiner's manual V. Title: WJ III tests of cognitive abilities examiner's manual
BF432.5.W66 M33 2001

Woodcock, Richard W. Woodcock-Johnson III tests of cognitive abilities. Itasca, IL : Riverside Pub., c2001.
BF432.5.W66 W66 2001

Mathers, S. L. MacGregor (Samuel Liddell MacGregor), 1854-1918.
[Clavicula Salomonis. English.] The Goetia. York Beach, Me. : Samuel Weiser, 1995.
BF1611 .C5413 1995

Matheson, Richard. Mediums rare / Richard Matheson. 1st ed. Baltimore, Md. : Cemetery Dance Publications, 2000. 124 p. ; 24 cm. Includes bibliographical references. ISBN 1-58767-007-0
1. Spiritualism (Channeling) 2. Mediums. I. Title.

Matheus, Tiago Corbisier. Ideais na adolescência : falta (d)e perspectivas na virada do século / Tiago Corbisier Matheus. 1a ed. São Paulo, SP : Annablume, 2002. 199 p. ; 21 cm. (Selo universidade ; 195. Psicologia) "FAPESP." Originally presented as the author's thesis (master's)--Universidade de São Paulo, 2000. Includes bibliographical references (p. [177]-181). ISBN 85-7419-241-4
1. Psychology. 2. Psychoanalysis. 3. Group identity. 4. Adolescence psychology. I. Title. II. Series: Selo universidade ; 195. III. Series: Selo universidade. Psicologia.

Mathews, Patrick, 1962- Never say goodbye : a medium's stories of connecting with your loved ones / Patrick Mathews. 1st ed. St. Paul, Minn. : Llewellyn Publications, 2003. xii, 198 p. ; 23 cm. ISBN 0-7387-0353-2 DDC 133.9/1/092
1. Mathews, Patrick, - 1962- 2. Mediums - United States - Biography. 3. Spiritualism. I. Title.
BF1283.M27 A3 2003

MATHEWS, PATRICK, 1962-.
Mathews, Patrick, 1962- Never say goodbye. 1st ed. St. Paul, Minn. : Llewellyn Publications, 2003.
BF1283.M27 A3 2003

Matière à symbolisation : art, création et psychanalyse / sous la direction de Bernard Chouvier ; avec le concours de Marie Anaut ... [et al.].

Matilal, Bimal Krishna.
Lausanne : Delachaux et Niestlé, c1998. 287 p. : ill. ; 21 cm. (Champs psychanalytiques) "... les principales contributions présentées au colloque "Matière à symbolisation", organisé par le Centre de recherches en psychopathologie et psychologie clinique ... février 1998 à l'Université Lumière Lyon 2"--P. 8. Includes bibliographical references (p. 281-287). ISBN 2-603-01168-5
1. Symbolism (Psychology) 2. Psychology and art. I. Chouvier, Bernard. II. Anaut, Marie. III. Centre de recherches en psychopathologie et psychologie clinique. IV. Title. V. Series.
BF458 .M38 1998

Matilal, Bimal Krishna. Ethics and epics : the collected essays of Bimal Krishna Matilal / edited by Jonardon Ganeri. New Delhi ; New York : Oxford University Press, 2002. vii, 445 p. ; 23 cm. (Philosophy, culture, and religion) Includes bibliographical references and index. ISBN 0-19-565511-7 DDC 181.4
1. Philosophy, Indic. I. Ganeri, Jonardon. II. Title. III. Series.
B131 .M398 2002b

Matisse.
Percheron, René. Paris : Citadelles & Mazenod, c2002.
N6853.M33 P47 2002

Matisse, Henri, 1869-1954.
Percheron, René. Matisse. Paris : Citadelles & Mazenod, c2002.
N6853.M33 P47 2002

MATISSE, HENRI, 1869-1954 - CRITICISM AND INTERPRETATION.
Percheron, René. Matisse. Paris : Citadelles & Mazenod, c2002.
N6853.M33 P47 2002

MATISSE, HENRI, 1869-1954 - KNOWLEDGE - ARCHITECTURE.
Percheron, René. Matisse. Paris : Citadelles & Mazenod, c2002.
N6853.M33 P47 2002

Matiushkina, A. A. (Anna Alekseevna) Reshenie problemy kak poisk smyslov : monografiia / A.A. Matiushkina. Moskva : Izdatel'skii tsentr GUU, 2003. 91 p. ; 21 cm. Includes bibliographical references (p. 81-90). ISBN 5215014094
1. Meaning (Psychology) 2. Thought and thinking. I. Title.
BF463.M4 M33 2003

Matok mi-devash.
[Zohar ḥadash.] Sefer Zohar ḥadash. Yerushalayim : Mekhon Daʻat Yosef ; Brooklyn, N.Y. (225 Division Ave., Brooklyn 11211) : Le-haśig, B. Daskal, 760- [1999 or 2000-
BM525.A6 Z6+

[Zohar ḥadash. Lamentations. 2000.] Zohar ḥadash Megilat Ekhah. "Hotsa'ah meyuhedet li-yeme ben ha-metsarim". Yerushalayim : Mekhon Daʻat Yosef, 761 [2000 or 2001]
BM525.A6 Z6 2001

MATRIARCHY. See also **FAMILY; MATRILINEAL KINSHIP.**
Longstaff, Bill, 1934- Confessions of a matriarchist. Calgary : Ballot Pub., 2003.

MATRIARCHY IN ART.
Göttner-Abendroth, Heide. Die tanzende Göttin. 6. vollst. überarb. Neuaufl. München : Frauenoffensive, 2001, c1982.

MATRILINEAL DESCENT. See **MATRILINEAL KINSHIP.**

MATRILINEAL KINSHIP - ZAMBIA.
Drews, Annette. Guardians of the society. Leipzig, Germany : Institut für Afrikanistik, Universität Leipzig, 2000.
BF1584.Z33 D44 2000

MATRILINY. See **MATRILINEAL KINSHIP.**

MATRIMONY. See **MARRIAGE.**

Matsuura, Jeffrey H., 1957- Managing intellectual assets in the digital age / Jeffrey H. Matsuura. Boston, MA : Artech House, c2003. xi, 233 p. : forms ; 24 cm. (Artech House communications law and policy series) Includes bibliographical references and index. ISBN 1-58053-359-0 (alk. paper) DDC 346.04/8
1. Intellectual property. 2. Copyright and electronic data processing. 3. Copyright - Computer programs. 4. Software protection - Law and legislation. I. Title. II. Series: Artech House communications law and policy library.
K1401 .M378 2003

Matt, Peter von. Literaturwissenschaft und Psychoanalyse / Peter von Matt. Stuttgart : Reclam, c2001. 155 p. ; 15 cm. (Universal-Bibliothek ; Nr. 17626) Originally published in 1972 by Rombach Verlaghaus, Freiburg. With and expanded epilogue and bibliography.

Includes bibliographical references (p. [141]-150) and indexes. ISBN 3-15-017626-3 (pbk.)
1. Psychoanalysis and literature. 2. Literature - History and criticism - Theory, etc. I. Title. II. Series: Universal-Bibliothek (Stuttgart, Germany) ; Nr. 17626.

MATTE BLANCO, IGNACIO.
L'inconscio antinomico. Milano : F. Angeli, c1999.
BF315 .I56 1999

Mattéi, Jean-François.
Civilisation et barbarie. 1re éd. Paris : Presses universitaires de France, c2002.

MATTER. See also **DARK MATTER (ASTRONOMY); SUBSTANCE (PHILOSOPHY).**
Vernes, Jean-René. The existence of the external world. Ottawa : University of Ottawa Press, c2000.

MATTER, DARK (ASTRONOMY). See **DARK MATTER (ASTRONOMY).**

MATTER, NONLUMINOUS (ASTRONOMY). See **DARK MATTER (ASTRONOMY).**

MATTER, UNOBSERVED (ASTRONOMY). See **DARK MATTER (ASTRONOMY).**

MATTER, UNSEEN (ASTRONOMY). See **DARK MATTER (ASTRONOMY).**

Matthews, Boris.
Bedi, Ashok. Retire your family karma. Berwick, Me. : Nicolas-Hays, 2003.
BF637.S4 B423 2003

Matthews, Caitlín, 1952-.
Arthur and the sovereignty of Britain.
Matthews, Caitlín, 1952- King Arthur and the goddess of the land. 2nd ed. Rochester, Vt. : Inner Traditions, 2002.
PB2273.M33 M36 2002

King Arthur and the goddess of the land : the divine feminine in the Mabinogion / Caitlín Matthews. 2nd ed. Rochester, Vt. : Inner Traditions, 2002. xxiii, 360 p. : ill. ; 23 cm. Rev. ed. of: Arthur and the sovereignty of Britain. 1989. Includes bibliographical references and index. ISBN 0-89281-921-9 DDC 891.6/631
1. Mabinogion. 2. Arthurian romances - History and criticism. 3. Tales, Medieval - History and criticism. 4. Tales - Wales - History and criticism. 5. Mythology, Celtic, in literature. 6. Femininity of God in literature. 7. Kings and rulers in literature. 8. Great Britain - In literature. 9. Mythology, Celtic - Wales. 10. Goddesses in literature. I. Matthews, Caitlín, 1952- Arthur and the sovereignty of Britain. II. Title.
PB2273.M33 M36 2002

Mabon and the guardians of Celtic Britain : hero myths in the Mabinogion / Caitlín Matthews. Rochester, Vt. : Inner Traditions, c2002. xxiii, 230 p. : ill., map ; 23 cm. Rev. ed. of: Mabon and the mysteries of Britain. 1987. Includes bibliographical references (p. 218-225) and index. Table of contents URL: http://www.loc.gov/catdir/toc/fy034/2002007635.html ISBN 0-89281-920-0 (pbk.) DDC 891.6/631
1. Mabinogion. 2. Tales, Medieval - History and criticism. 3. Arthurian romances - History and criticism. 4. Tales - Wales - History and criticism. 5. Mythology, Celtic, in literature. 6. Great Britain - In literature. 7. Mythology, Celtic - Wales. 8. Heroes in literature. I. Matthews, Caitlín, 1952- Mabon and the mysteries of Britain. II. Title.
PB2273.M33 M37 2002

Mabon and the mysteries of Britain.
Matthews, Caitlín, 1952- Mabon and the guardians of Celtic Britain. Rochester, Vt. : Inner Traditions, c2002.
PB2273.M33 M37 2002

Matthews, John, 1948- The encyclopaedia of Celtic myth and legend. London : Rider, 2002.
BL915 .M377 2002

Matthews, Christopher, 1945- American : beyond our grandest notions / Chris Matthews. New York : Free Press, c2002. xi, 240 p. : ill. ; 22 cm. Includes bibliographical references (p. 209-230) and index. Table of contents URL: http://www.loc.gov/catdir/toc/simon031/2002034741.html Publisher description URL: http://www.loc.gov/catdir/description/simon031/2002034741.html ISBN 0-7432-4086-3 DDC 973
1. National characteristics, American. 2. United States - Civilization. I. Title.
E169.1 .M429 2002

Matthews, Dawn D.
Attention deficit disorder sourcebook. 1st ed. Detroit, MI : Omnigraphics, c2002.
RJ506.H9 A885 2002

Matthews, Gerald. Emotional intelligence : science and myth / Gerald Matthews, Moshe Zeidner, and Richard D. Roberts. Cambridge, Mass. : MIT Press, c2002. xxi, 697 p. : ill. ; 24 cm. "A Bradford book." Includes bibliographical references (p. [591]-681) and index. ISBN 0-262-13418-7 (alk. paper) DDC 152.4
1. Emotional intelligence. I. Zeidner, Moshe. II. Roberts, Richard D. III. Title.
BF576 .M28 2002

Personality traits / Gerald Matthews, Ian J. Deary, Martha C. Whiteman. 2nd ed. New York : Cambridge University Press, 2003. p. cm. Includes bibliographical references and index. Publisher description URL: http://www.loc.gov/catdir/description/cam032/2003046259.html Table of contents URL: http://www.loc.gov/catdir/toc/cam032/2003046259.html ISBN 0-521-83107-5 ISBN 0-521-53824-6 (pbk.) DDC 155.2/3
1. Personality. I. Deary, Ian J. II. Whiteman, Martha C. III. Title.
BF698 .M3434 2003

Matthews, John, 1948- The encyclopaedia of Celtic myth and legend : an inspirational source book of magic, vision, and lore / John and Caitlín Matthews. London : Rider, 2002. vi, 504 p. ; 25 cm. Includes bibliographical references (p. [494]-499) and index. ISBN 0-7126-1218-1 DDC 299.1/6
1. Mythology, Celtic. I. Matthews, Caitlín, 1952- II. Title.
BL915 .M377 2002

Matthías Vi#ar Sæmundsson.
Jón Magnússon, 1610-1696. Píslarsaga séra Jóns Magnússonar. Reykjavík : Mál og menning, 2001.
BF1584.I2 J66 2001

MATURAI ARUḶMIKU MĪNĀṬCI CUNTARĒŚVARAR ĀLAYAM.
Kollar, L. Peter (Laszlo Peter), 1926- Symbolism in Hindu architecture as revealed in the Shri Minakshi Sundareswar. New Delhi : Aryan Books International, 2001.
NA6002 .K65 2001

MATURATION (PSYCHOLOGY). See also **LIFE CYCLE, HUMAN.**
Bridges, William, 1933- The way of transition. Cambridge, Mass. : Perseus Pub., c2001.
BF335 .B717 2001

Dooley, Deborah. Journeying into wholeness with map & skills. [Meno Park, Calif. : Delphi Press, c2003]
BF710 .D64 2003

Fischer, Norman, 1946- Taking our places. 1st ed. San Francisco : HarperSanFrancisco, c2003.
BF710 .F57 2003

Gonick, Marnina. Between femininities. Albany : State University of New York Press, c2003.
HQ777 .G65 2003

Karras, Ruth Mazo, 1957- From boys to men. Philadelphia : University of Pennsylvania Press, c2003.
HQ775 .K373 2003

Rishoi, Christy, 1958- From girl to woman. Albany : State University of New York Press, c2003.
HQ1186.A9 R57 2003

Matzker, Reiner, 1953-.
Kommunikation, Kunst und Kultur. Bern ; New York : Peter Lang, c2002.

Mauerschau : Festschrift für Manfred Korfmann / herausgegeben von Rüstem Aslan ... [et al.]. Remshalden-Grunbach : Greiner, 2002. 3 v. (xl, 1248 p.) : ill. (some col.), maps ; 30 cm. Includes bibliographical references and index. Papers in English and German with some text in Turkish. ISBN 3-935383-10-X
1. Korfmann, Manfred. 2. Archaeology. 3. Archaeology - Methodology. 4. Archaeologists - Biography. 5. Excavations (Archaeology) I. Korfmann, Manfred. II. Aslan, Rüstem. III. Title: Festschrift für Manfred Korfmann

Mauriès, Patrick, 1952- Cabinets of curiosities / Patrick Mauries. New York : Thames & Hudson, c2002. 256 p. : col. ill. ; 31 cm. Simultaneously published in French. Includes bibliographical references (p. 253) and index. ISBN 0-500-51091-1 DDC 069
1. Collectors and collecting - History. 2. Collectors and collecting - Europe - History. 3. Cabinets of curiosities - Europe - History. 4. Museums - Europe - History. 5. Renaissance. 6. Europe - Civilization - 18th century. 7. Europe - Civilization - 19th century. I. Title.
AM221 .M38 2002

Maushart, Susan, 1958- Wifework : what marriage really means for women / Susan Maushart. 1st U.S. ed. New York : Bloomsbury : Distributed to the trade by Holtzbrinck Publishers, 2002. 278, [1] p. ; 25 cm.

"First published in Australia by the Text Publishing Company, Melbourne, in 2001"--T.p. verso. Includes bibliographical references ([265]-[279]) and index. ISBN 1-58234-202-4 DDC 306.872
1. Wives. 2. Marriage. 3. Divorce. I. Title.
HQ759 .M3944 2002

Mauthner, Melanie L., 1964- Sistering : power and change in female relationships / Melanie L. Mauthner. New York : Palgrave Macmillan, 2002. x, 228 p. ; 23 cm. Includes bibliographical references (p. 203-222) and index. ISBN 0-333-80080-X DDC 306.875
1. Sisters. 2. Sisters - Family relationships. 3. Women - Psychology. I. Title.
BF723.S43 M385 2002

Mauzy, Jeff. Creativity, Inc. : building an inventive organization / Jeff Mauzy, Richard Harriman. Boston, Mass. : Harvard Business School Press, c2003. xvi, 232 p. ; 25 cm. Includes bibliographical references (p. [201]-219) and index. CONTENTS: pt. 1. Creative thinking. The dynamics that underlie creative thinking. Becoming creatively fit as an individual. Breaking and making connections for an enterprise -- pt. 2. Climate. The Climate for creativity in an enterprise. Personal creative climate: the bubble -- pt. 3. Action. Leadership: fostering systemic creativity. Purposeful creativity. Sustaining the change. ISBN 1-57851-207-7 DDC 658.4/063
1. Creative ability in business. 2. Corporate culture. I. Harriman, Richard A. II. Title.
HD53 .M375 2003

Mayet, almayet ye-ide'ologyah.
Oron, Israel. [Israel] : Miśrad ha-biṭaḥon, [2002]

Mavouangui, David, 1953- Jean-Paul Sartre : introduction à sa philosophie de l'existence / David Mavouangui. Paris : Paari, [2002], c2001. 57 p. ; 21 cm. (Collection Germod) ISBN 2-8422-0002-0
1. Sartre, Jean Paul, - 1905- - Ontology. 2. Ontology. I. Title. II. Series.

Mavrodin, Irina.
Cioran, E. M. (Emile M.), 1911- [Précis de décomposition. Romanian] Tratat de descompunere. București : Humanitas, 2002, c1996.

Mawhinney, Thomas C.
Handbook of organizational performance. New York : Haworth Press, c2001.
HD58.7 .H364 2001

Ludwig, Timothy D. Intervening to improve the safety of occupational driving. New York : Haworth Press, 2000.
HE5614 .I586 2000

Mawi Asgedom. The code : the 5 secrets of teen success / Mawi Asgedom. New York : Little, Brown, 2003. 152 p. ; 22 cm. "Megan Tingley books." ISBN 0-316-82633-2 ISBN 0316636899 (pbk.).
1. Success in adolescence - Juvenile literature. 2. Self-esteem - Juvenile literature. 3. Self-actualization - Juvenile literature. 4. Teenagers - Juvenile literature. I. Title. II. Title: 5 secrets of teen success
BF724.3.S9 M34 2003

Maximize your brainpower.
Carter, Philip J. West Sussex, England ; New York : John Wiley & Sons, Ltd, 2002.
BF431.3 .C3647 2002

MAXIMS. *See* **APHORISMS AND APOTHEGMS.**

MAXIMS - HISTORY AND CRITICISM.
Hoggart, Richard, 1918- Everyday language & everyday life. New Brunswick, N.J. ; London : Transaction Publishers, c2003.
PE1074.8 .H64 2003

Maximus, Confessor, Saint, ca. 580-662.
Centuriae quatuor de charitate. Serbian.
Vizantijska filozofija u srednjevekovnoj Srbiji. Beograd : Stubovi kulture, 2002.

MAXIMUS, THE GREEK, SAINT, 1480-1556.
Zaĭtseva, L. I. Russkie providtsy o rossiĭskoĭ gosudarstvennosti. Moskva : In-t ėkonomiki RAN, 1998-
DK49 .Z35 1998

Maxwell, John C., 1947- Today matters : 12 daily practices to guarantee tomorrow's success / John C. Maxwell. New York : Warner Books, 2004. p. cm. CONTENTS: Today often falls to pieces : what is the missing piece? -- Today can become a masterpiece -- Today's attitude gives me possibilities -- Today's values give me direction -- Today's family gives me stability -- Today's health gives me strength -- Today's priorities give me focus -- Today's thinking gives me an advantage -- Today's commitment gives me tenacity -- Today's relationships give me fulfillment -- Today's finances give me options -- Today's faith gives me peace -- Today's growth gives me potential -- Today's generosity gives me significance -- Making today matter. ISBN 0-446-52958-3 DDC 158
1. Success - Psychological aspects. I. Title.
BF637.S8 M3423 2004

Maxwell paper (Air University (U.S.). Air War College)
(no. 2.) Bird, David F. Quality Air Force in an emergency [electronic resource]. Maxwell Air Force Base, Ala. : Air War College, Air University, [1996]

Maxwell-Stuart, P. G. Satan's conspiracy : magic and witchcraft in sixteenth-century Scotland / P.G. Maxwell-Stuart. East Linton, Scotland : Tuckwell Press, 2001. 225 p. ; 24 cm. Includes bibliographical references (p. [216]-222) and index. ISBN 1-86232-136-1 DDC 133.4/3/0941109031
1. Magic - Scotland - History - 16th century. 2. Witchcraft - Scotland - History - 16th century. I. Title.
BF1622.S38 .M39 2001

May, Jon.
Andrade, Jackie, 1964- Instant notes in cognitive psychology. New York, NY : Garland Science/BIOS Scientific Publishers, 2004.
BF201 .A53 2004

MAYA ASTRONOMY.
Jenkins, John Major. Galactic alignment. Rochester, Vt. : Bear & Co., 2002.
F1435.3.R3 J45 2002

MAYA CALENDAR.
Jenkins, John Major. Galactic alignment. Rochester, Vt. : Bear & Co., 2002.
F1435.3.R3 J45 2002

MAYA CHRONOLOGY - MISCELLANEA.
Argüelles, José, 1939- Time and the technosphere. Rochester, Vt. : Bear & Co., c2002.
BF1999 .A6398 2002

MAYA COSMOLOGY.
Jenkins, John Major. Galactic alignment. Rochester, Vt. : Bear & Co., 2002.
F1435.3.R3 J45 2002

MAYA INDIANS. *See* **MAYAS.**

MAYAKOVSKY, VLADIMIR, 1893-1930.
Spivak, M. L. Posmertnaia diagnostika genial'nosti. Moskva : Agraf, 2001.
BF416.A1 S68 2001

MAYANS. *See* **MAYAS.**

MAYAS - CHRONOLOGY. *See* **MAYA CHRONOLOGY.**

MAYAS - MISCELLANEA.
Bonewitz, Ra. Wisdom of the Maya. 1st St. Martin's ed. New York : St. Martin's Press, 2000.
BF1878 .B66 2000

MAYAS - RELIGION - MISCELLANEA.
Polich, Judith Bluestone, 1948- Return of the children of light. Santa Fe, N.M. : Linkage Publications, c1999.
BF1812.P4 P65 1999

Mayer, Andreas.
Marinelli, Lydia. Dreaming by the book. New York : Other Press, c2003.
BF175.5.D74 F7436 2003

Mayr, Ernst, 1904- What evolution is / Ernst Mayr. New York : Basic Books, c2001. xv, 318 p. : ill., maps ; 24 cm. Includes bibliographical references (p. [293]-303) and index. CONTENTS: In what kind of a world do we live? -- What is the evidence for evolution on earth? -- The rise of the living world -- How and why does evolution take place? -- Variational evolution -- Natural selection -- Adaptedness and natural selection : anagenesis -- The units of diversity : species -- Speciation -- Macroevolution -- How did mankind evolve? -- The frontiers of evolutionary biology. ISBN 0-465-04425-5 (hc : alk. paper) DDC 576.8
1. Evolution (Biology) I. Title.
QH366.2 .M3933 2001

Mazin, Viktor.
Iskusstvo snovideniĭ = Sankt-Peterburg : Skifiia, 2002.
NX180.D74 I74 2002

Mazis, Glen A., 1951- Earthbodies : rediscovering our planetary senses / Glen A. Mazis. Albany, NY : State University of New York Press, 2002. xi, 269 p. ; 23 cm. Includes bibliographical references and index. ISBN 0-7914-5417-7 (alk. paper) ISBN 0-7914-5418-5 (pbk. : alk. paper) DDC 128
1. Body, Human (Philosophy) 2. Ethics. I. Title. II. Title: Earth bodies
BJ1695 .M39 2002

Mazumdar, Krishna, 1949- Determinants of human well-being / Krishna Mazumdar. New York : Nova Science Publishers, c2003. xiv, 237 p. : ill. ; 27 cm. Includes bibliographical references (p. [187]-207) and index. CONTENTS: What is human well-being -- Measuring human well-being -- Casual flow between human well-being and per capita gross domestic product -- Determinants of human well-being -- Determining factors of human well-being : the constituent indicators -- Determinants of human well-being : ultimate analysis -- Divergence and convergence of countries in HWB -- Concluding remarks. ISBN 1-59033-654-2 (cloth) DDC 339.4
1. Economic man. 2. Values. 3. Contentment. 4. Self-realization. I. Title.
HB171 .M462 2003

Mazumdar, Sucheta, 1948-.
Antinomies of modernity. Durham : Duke University Press, 2003.
CB358 .A59 2003

Mazza, Nicholas. Poetry therapy : interface of the arts and psychology / by Nicholas Mazza. Boca Raton, Fla : CRC Press, 1999. 202 p. ; 24 cm. (Innovations in psychology) Includes bibliographical references (p. 129-145) and index. ISBN 0-8493-0350-8 (alk. paper) ISBN 1-57444-183-3 (alk. paper) DDC 616.89/166
1. Poetry - Therapeutic use. 2. Psychotherapy. I. Title.
RC489.P6 M39 1999

MBA in management.
Cohen, Allan R. The portable MBA in management. 2nd ed. New York : J. Wiley, c2002.
HD31 .C586 2002

MBA masterclass series
Sadler, Philip, 1930- Leadership. 2nd ed. London ; Sterling, VA : Kogan Page Ltd., 2003.
HD57.7 .S227 2003

McAdams, Dan P.
The generative society. 1st ed. Washington, DC : American Psychological Association, c2003.
BF724.5 .G45 2003

McAfee, R. Preston. Competitive solutions : the strategist's toolkit / R. Preston McAfee. Princeton, N.J. : Princeton University Press, c2002. xx, 404 p. : ill. ; 25 cm. Includes bibliographical references (p. 381-392) and index. CONTENTS: Introduction -- Industry analysis -- Firm strategies -- Differentiation -- Product life cycle -- Cooperation -- Organizational scope -- Incentives -- Antitrust -- Elementary statistics -- Pricing -- Auctions -- Signaling -- Bargaining -- Last words ISBN 0-691-09646-5 (alk. paper) DDC 658.4/012
1. Strategic planning. 2. Business planning. 3. Decision making. 4. Game theory. 5. Pricing. 6. Antitrust law. 7. Industrial management. 8. Competition. 9. Strategic planning - Case studies. I. Title.
HD30.28 .M3815 2002

McArthur, Margie. Faery healing : the lore and the legacy / Margie McArthur. Aptos, Calif. : New Brighton Books, 2003. m. Includes bibliographical references and index. ISBN 0-9718377-5-9 DDC 398/.45/089916041
1. Fairies - Great Britain. 2. Healing - Great Britain - Miscellanea. I. Title.
BF1552 .M36 2003

McBride, Angus.
Wisdom, Stephen. Gladiators 100 BC-AD 200. Oxford : Osprey, 2001 (2002 printing)

McBride, Molly.
The Alexander technique [videorecording]. New York, N.Y. : Wellspring Media, c1999.

McBurney, Donald, 1938-.
Gaulin, Steven J. C. Evolutionary psychology. 2nd ed. Upper Saddle River, N.J. : Pearson/Prentice Hall, c2004.
BF698.95 .G38 2004

McCain, Marian Van Eyk. Elderwoman : reap the wisdom-- feel the power-- embrace the joy / Marian Van Eyk McCain. Forres : Findhorn Press, 2002. 288 p. ; 24 cm. Includes bibliographical references and index. ISBN 1-89917-129-0 DDC 305.26082
1. Aged women - Psychology. 2. Self-actualization (Psychology) I. Title.

McCallum, R. Steve.
Handbook of nonverbal assessment. New York : Kluwer Academic/Plenum Publishers, c2003.
BF432.5.I55 H36 2003

McCandrew, Debra A.
Williamson, James C. Roadways to success. 3rd ed. Upper Saddle River, NJ : Pearson/ Prentice Hall, 2004.
BF637.S8 W5216 2004

McCarthy, Cameron.
Foucault, cultural studies, and governmentality. Albany : State University of New York Press, c2003.
JC330 .F63 2003

McCarthy, Paul.
Bullying. 2nd ed. Annandale, N.S.W. : The Federation Press 2001.
BF637.B85 B85 2001

McClure, Joyce Kloc, 1955- Finite, contingent, and free : a new ethics of acceptance / Joyce Kloc McClure. Lanham, Md. ; Oxford : Rowman & Littlefield Publishers, c2003. x, 155 p. ; 24 cm. Includes bibliographical references (p. 139-146) and index. CONTENTS: Contingency and finitude as conditions of existence -- Freedom and personhood in a non-Newtonian paradigm -- Moral luck and vulnerability -- Vulnerability and acceptance in Our mutual friend : a case study -- An ethics of active acceptance. ISBN 0-7425-1404-8 (hbk. : alk. paper) ISBN 0-7425-1405-6 (pbk. : alk. paper) DDC 171/.3
1. Ethics. 2. Social acceptance. I. Title.
BJ1012 .M316 2003

McCluskey, John William. Amazing mystic tarot / John William McCluskey. 1st ed. East Hampton, N.Y. : Arden Book Co., c2002. 239 p. : ill. ; 21 cm. ISBN 0-9677332-1-9 DDC 133.3/2424
1. Tarot. I. Title.
BF1879.T2 M42 2002

McColman, Carl. Before you cast a spell : understanding the power of magic / by Carl McColman. Franklin Lakes, NJ : New Page Books, 2004. p. cm. Includes index. ISBN 1-56414-716-9 (pbk.) DDC 133.4/3
1. Magic. I. Title.
BF1611 .M385 2004

The well-read witch : essential books for your magickal library / by Carl McColman. Franklin Lakes, NJ : New Page Books, c2002. 287 p. ; 21 cm. Includes bibliographical references (p. 259-280) and index. SUMMARY: The Well-Read Witch can help anyone with a sincere interest in Wiccan ways to find the best books to read, with reviews of over 400 books. ISBN 1-56414-530-1 DDC 016.1334/3
1. Magic - Bibliography. I. Title.
BF1611

When someone you love is Wiccan : a guide to witchcraft and paganism for concerned friends, nervous parents, and curious co-workers / by Carl McColman. Franklin Lakes, NJ : New Page Books, 2003. 221 p. ; 21 cm. Includes index. ISBN 1-56414-622-7 (pbk.) DDC 299
1. Witchcraft. 2. Paganism. I. Title.
BF1566 .M36 2003

McConeghey, Howard. Art and soul / Howard McConeghey ; foreword by Thomas Moore. 1st ed. Putnam, CT : Spring Publications, Inc. ; [New York] : Distributed by Continuum, c2003. viii, 100 p., [16] p. of plates : ill. (some col.) ; 23 cm. (Classics in archetypal psychology ; 7) Includes bibliographical references. ISBN 0-88214-383-2
1. Art - Psychology. 2. Visual perception. 3. Art therapy. 4. Archetype (Psychology) I. Title. II. Series.

McConnell, Carmel. Change activist : make big things happen fast / Carmel McConnell. Cambridge, MA : Perseus Pub., c2001. xiii, 225 p. : ill. ; 21 cm. "A Momentum book". Includes index. ISBN 0-7382-0652-0 (pbk.) DDC 158.7
1. Work - Psychological aspects. 2. Change (Psychology) 3. Success in business. I. Title.
BF481 .M393 2001

McCormack, Kathleen. Magic for lovers : find your ideal partner through the power of magic / Kathleen McCormack ; with an introduction by Barbara Bianco. 1st ed. Hauppauge, NY : Barron's, c2003. 128 p. : col. ill. ; 23 cm. Includes index. ISBN 0-7641-5591-1
1. Magic. 2. Love - Miscellanea. 3. Astrology and sex. I. Title.
BF1623.L6 M38 2003

The tarot workbook : an IQ book for the tarot practitioner / Kathleen McCormack. 1st ed. Hauppauge, NY : Barron's, c2002. 128 p. : col. ill. ; 25 cm. "A Quarto book". Includes index. ISBN 0-7641-2227-4 (pbk.) DDC 133.3/2424
1. Tarot. I. Title.
BF1879.T2 M33 2002

McCoy, Edain, 1957- Advanced witchcraft : go deeper, reach further, fly higher / Edain McCoy. 1st ed. St. Paul, Minn. : Llewellyn, 2004. p. cm. Includes bibliographical references and index. ISBN 0-7387-0513-6 DDC 133.4/3
1. Witchcraft. I. Title.
BF1571 .M45 2004

[Enchantments. Spanish]
Magia y belleza : encantos y pócimas para crear rituales mágicos / Edain McCoy ; traducido al español por Héctor Ramírez y Edgar Rojas. 1st ed. St. Paul, Minn. : Llewellyn Español, 2002. p. cm. Includes bibliographical references (p. 211-215) and index. ISBN 0-7387-0210-2 DDC 133.4/46
1. Magic. 2. Beauty, Personal - Miscellanea. 3. Women - Health and hygiene - Miscellanea. I. Title.
BF1623.B43 E6418 2002

If you want to be a witch : a practical introduction to the craft / Edain McCoy. 1st ed. St. Paul, Minn. : Llewellyn Publications, 2004. p. cm. Includes bibliographical references and index. ISBN 0-7387-0514-4 DDC 133.4/3
1. Witchcraft. I. Title.
BF1571 .M455 2004

McCroskey, James C.
Richmond, Virginia P., 1949- Nonverbal behavior in interpersonal relations. 5th ed. Boston, Mass. : Pearson, 2004.
BF637.N66 R53 2004

McCuish, James (James D.).
Woodhead, Roy (Roy M.) Achieving results. London : Thomas Telford, 2002.

McCulloch, Douglas, 1950- Valuing health in practice : priorities, QALYs, and choice / Douglas McCulloch. Aldershot, Hampshire, England ; Burlington, VT : Ashgate, c2003. 128 p. : ill. ; 22 cm. Includes bibliographical references (p. [106]-121) and index. ISBN 0-7546-1867-6 (alk. paper) DDC 338.4/33621
1. Medical care - Cost effectiveness. 2. Medical care - Quality control. 3. Quality of life. 4. Outcome assessment (Medical care) I. Title.
RA410.5 .M37 2002

McCulloch, Gillian. The deconstruction of dualism in theology : with special reference to ecofeminist theology and new age spirituality / Gillian McCulloch ; foreword by David A.S. Ferguson. Carlisle : Paternoster Press, 2002. x, 281 p. ; 23 cm. (Paternoster biblical and theological monographs) Includes bibliographical references (p. [267]-278) and index. ISBN 1-84227-044-3
1. Ecofeminism. 2. Dualism (Religion) - Christianity. 3. Spiritual life - New Age movement. I. Title. II. Series.

McCulloch, Gregory. The life of the mind : an essay on phenomenological externalism / Gregory McCulloch. London ; New York : Routledge, 2003. xviii, 152 p. ; 24 cm. Includes bibliographical references (p. 141-143) and index. ISBN 0-415-26622-X (hbk.) ISBN 0-415-26623-8 (pbk.) DDC 128/.2
1. Philosophy of mind. 2. Externalism (Philosophy of mind) 3. Mind and body. I. Title.
BD418.3 .M363 2003

McCullough, Michael E.
The psychology of gratitude. New York : Oxford University Press, 2004.
BF575.G68 P79 2003

McDaniel, Patricia (Patricia A.) Shrinking violets and Caspar Milquetoasts : shyness, power, and intimacy in the United States, 1950-1995 / Patricia McDaniel. New York : New York University Press, 2003. p. cm. (The American social experience series) Includes bibliographical references and index. Table of contents URL: http://www.loc.gov/catdir/toc/ecip044/2003011890.html CONTENTS: The emotional culture of shyness from the Middle Ages to the early twentieth century -- "Build him a dais" : shyness and heterosexuality from the roles of the fifties to the rules of the nineties -- Assertive women and timid men? : race, heterosexuality, and shyness -- Shyness from nine to five -- "Intimacy is a difficult art" : the changing role of shyness -- In friendship. ISBN 0-8147-5677-8 (alk. paper) ISBN 0-8147-5678-6 (pbk. : alk. paper) DDC 155.2/32
1. Bashfulness - History. 2. Bashfulness - Social aspects - United States. I. Title. II. Series.
BF575.B3 M34 2003

McElroy, Mark, 1964- Putting the tarot to work / Mark McElroy. 1st ed. St. Paul, Minn. : Llewellyn Publications, 2004. p. cm. Includes index. ISBN 0-7387-0444-X DDC 133.3/2424
1. Tarot cards. 2. Business forecasting - Miscellanea. I. Title.
BF1879.T2 M43 2004

McEnroe, Colin. My father's footsteps : a memoir / Colin McEnroe. New York : Warner Books, c2003. vii, 198 p. ; 22 cm. ISBN 0-446-52933-8 DDC 818/.5402
1. McEnroe, Colin - Family. 2. Humorists, American - 20th century - Biography. 3. Fathers - Death - Psychological aspects. 4. Parent and adult child - United States. 5. Baby boom generation - United States. 6. Fathers and sons - United States. I. Title.
PS3563.C3615 M9 2003

MCENROE, COLIN - FAMILY.
McEnroe, Colin. My father's footsteps. New York : Warner Books, c2003.
PS3563.C3615 M9 2003

McEntarffer, Robert. Barron's how to prepare for the AP pscyhology advanced placement examination / Robert McEntarffer, Allyson J. Weseley. Hauppauge, N.Y. : Barron's, c2004. p. cm. Includes index. ISBN 0-7641-2349-1 DDC 150/.76
1. Psychology - Examinations, questions, etc. 2. Psychology - Examinations - Study guides. 3. Advanced placement programs (Education) I. Weseley, Allyson. II. Title. III. Title: How to prepare for the AP psychology advanced placement examination IV. Title: AP psychology
BF78 .M34 2004

McEvilley, Thomas, 1939- The shape of ancient thought : comparative studies in Greek and Indian philosophies / Thomas McEvilley. New York : Allworth Press : School of Visual Arts, c2002. xxxvi, 732 p. : ill., maps ; 24 cm. Includes bibliographical references (p. 678-702) and index. CONTENTS: Diffusion channels in the pre-Alexandrian period -- The problem of the One and the Many -- The cosmic cycle -- The doctrine of reincarnation -- Platonic monism and Indian thought -- Platonic ethics and Indian yoga -- Plato, Orphics, and Jains -- Plato and kuṇḍalinī -- Cynics and Pāśupatas -- Five questions concerning the ancient Near East -- The elements -- Early pluralisms in Greece and India -- Skepticism, empiricism, and naturalism -- Diffusion channels in the Hellenistic and Roman periods -- Dialectic before Alexander -- Early Greek philosophy and Mādhyamika --Pyrrhonism and Mādhyamika -- The path of the dialectic -- The syllogism -- Peripatetics and Vaiśeṣikas -- The Stoics and Indian thought -- Neoplatonism and the Upaniṣadic-Vedāntic tradition -- Plotinus and Vijñānavāda Buddhism -- Neoplatonism and Tantra -- The ethics of imperturbability. ISBN 1-58115-203-5 DDC 180
1. Philosophy, Ancient. 2. Philosophy, Indic. 3. Philosophy, Comparative. I. Title.
B165 .M22 2002

McEvoy, J. J.
Internationales Eriugena-Colloquium (10th : Maynooth and Dublin : 2002) History and eschatology in John Scottus Eriugena and his time. Leuven : University Press, 2002.

McFadyen, Ian. Mind wars : the battle for your brain / Ian McFadyen. St Leonards, N.S.W., Australia : Allen & Unwin, c2000. vi, 226 p. ; 22 cm. Includes bibliographical references (p. 218-220) and index. ISBN 1-86508-316-X DDC 155.7
1. Behavior evolution. I. Title.
BF701 .M38 2000

McFarlin, Dean B.
Sweeney, Paul D., 1955- Organizational behavior. Boston : McGraw-Hill Irwin, c2002.
HD58.7 .S953 2002

McGaugh, James L. Memory and emotion : the making of lasting memories / James L. McGaugh. New York : Columbia University Press, c2003. xi, 162 p. : ill. ; 24 cm. (Maps of the mind) Includes bibliographical references (p. [139]-155) and index. ISBN 0-231-12022-2 (alk. paper) ISBN 0-231-12023-0 (pbk. : alk. paper) DDC 153.1/2
1. Autobiographical memory. 2. Emotions. I. Title. II. Series.
BF378.A87 M34 2003

McGhee, Paul E. Health, healing and the amuse system : humor as survival training / Paul E. McGhee. 3rd ed. Dubuque, Iowa : Kendall/Hunt Pub., c1999. xx, 281 p. : ill. ; 23 cm. "Formerly known as How to develop your sense of humor: an 8-step humor development training program." Includes bibliographical references (p. 255-266). ISBN 0-7872-5797-4 DDC 152.4/3
1. Laughter - Psychological aspects. 2. Wit and humor - Psychological aspects. 3. Wit and humor - Social aspects. 4. Stress management. 5. Adaptation, Psychological. 6. Wit and Humor - psychology. I. McGhee, Paul E. How to develop your sense of humor. II. Title.
BF575.L3 M38 1999

How to develop your sense of humor.
McGhee, Paul E. Health, healing and the amuse system. 3rd ed. Dubuque, Iowa : Kendall/Hunt Pub., c1999.
BF575.L3 M38 1999

McGill-Queen's studies in the history of ideas
(35) Barnard, Frederick M., 1921- Herder on nationality, humanity, and history. Montreal : McGill-Queen's University Press, c2003.

McGoldrick, Monica.
Living beyond loss. 2nd ed. New York : W.W. Norton, 2004.
BF575.D35 L54 2004

McGovern, James R. And a time for hope : Americans in the Great Depression / James R. McGovern. Westport, Conn. : Praeger, 2000. xii, 354 p. : ill. ; 24 cm. Includes bibliographical references (p. [339]-343) and index. ISBN 0-275-96786-7 (alk. paper) DDC 973.917
1. United States - History - 1933-1945. 2. United States - Social life and customs - 1918-1945. 3. United States - Social conditions - 1933-1945. 4. National characteristics, American. I. Title.
E806 .M45 2000

McGowan, Todd. The end of dissatisfaction? : Jacques Lacan and the emerging society of enjoyment / by Todd McGowan. Albany : State University of New York Press, c2004. p. cm. (SUNY series in psychoanalysis and culture) Includes bibliographical references (p.) and index. ISBN 0-7914-5967-5 (alk. paper) ISBN 0-7914-5968-3 (pbk. : alk. paper) DDC 306.4/8
1. Psychoanalysis and culture. 2. Lacan, Jacques, - 1901- I. Title. II. Series.
BF175.4.C84 M4 2004

McGrade, Arthur Stephen.
The Cambridge companion to medieval philosophy. Cambridge ; New York : Cambridge University Press, 2003.
B721 .C36 2003

McGrath, Matthew.
Epistemology. Malden, Mass. : Blackwell Publishers, 2000.
BD161 .E615 2000

McGraw-Hill developing organizations series
Cunningham, Ian, 1943- The wisdom of strategic learning. London ; New York : McGraw-Hill, c1994.
HD58.8 .C857 1994

McGraw-Hill series in developmental psychology
Kirasic, K. C. Midlife in context. Boston : McGraw-Hill, c2004.
BF724.6 .K55 2004

McGrew, Kevin S. Woodcock-Johnson III technical manual/ Kevin S. McGrew, Richard W. Woodcock. Itasca, IL : Riverside Pub., c2001. xii, 209 p. : ill. ; 28 cm. Spine title: WJ III technical manual. Includes bibliographical references (p. 103-107). DDC 153.9/3
1. Woodcock-Johnson Tests of Cognitive Ability. I. Woodcock, Richard W. II. Title. III. Title: Woodcock-Johnson 3 technical manual IV. Title: Woodcock-Johnson three technical manual V. Title: Technical manual VI. Title: WJ III technical manual
BF432.5.W66 M345 2001

Woodcock, Richard W. Woodcock-Johnson III tests of cognitive abilities. Itasca, IL : Riverside Pub., c2001.
BF432.5.W66 W66 2001

McGuire, Therese.
Balancing the scales. Lanham, Md. ; Oxford : University Press of America, c2003.
HQ1075 .B3417 2003

McInerney, D. M. (Dennis M.), 1948-.
International advances in self research. Greenwich, CT : Information Age Pub., 2003.
BF697 .I675 2003

McIntosh, Jillian Scott, 1959-.
Naturalism, evolution, and intentionality. Calgary, Alta., Canada : University of Calgary Press, c2001.
BD418.3 .N35 2001

McKay, Matthew.
Paleg, Kim. When anger hurts your relationship. Oakland, CA : New Harbinger Publications, c2001.
BF575.A5 P35 2001

The self-nourishment companion : 57 inspiring ways to take care of yourself / Matthew McKay, Catharine Sutker, Kristin Beck. Oakland, CA : New Harbinger Publications, c2001. v, 131 p. ; 18 cm. ISBN 1-57224-242-6 (pbk.) DDC 158.1
1. Self-actualization (Psychology) 2. Relaxation. I. Sutker, Catharine. II. Beck, Kristin. III. Title.
BF637.S4 M3925 2001

McKee, J. Donald.
Llewellyn, Jack H. Coming in first. Atlanta : Longstreet Press, c2000.
BF637.S8 L56 2000

McKenna, Michael.
Moral responsibility and alternative possibilities. Aldershot, England ; Burlington, VT : Ashgate, c2003.
BJ1451 .M6472 2003

McKinney Hammond, Michelle, 1957- Get over it and on with it! : how to get up when life knocks you down / Michelle McKinney Hammond. 1st ed. Colorado Springs, Colo. : WaterBrook Press, 2002. xi, 221, [2] p. ; 22 cm. Includes bibliographical references (p. [223]). ISBN 1-57856-450-6 DDC 248.8/6
1. Life change events - Religious aspects - Christianity. 2. Adjustment (Psychology) - Religious aspects - Christianity. 3. Loss (Psychology) - Religious aspects - Christianity. 4. Black author. I. Title.
BV4908.5 .M357 2002

McKinney, Tara.
Lerner, Isha, 1954- The triple goddess tarot. Rochester Vt. : Bear & Co., c2002.
BF1879.T2 L4365 2002

McKnight, Douglas. Schooling, the Puritan imperative, and the molding of an American national identity : education's "errand into the wilderness" / Douglas McKnight. Mahwah, N.J. ; London : L. Erlbaum Associates, 2003. xiii, 165 p. ; 24 cm. (Studies in curriculum theory) Includes bibliographical references (p. 151-159) and indexes. ISBN 0-8058-4317-5 DDC 370.11/4
1. Moral education - United States. 2. Education - Aims and objectives - United States. 3. National characteristics, American. I. Title. II. Series.
LC311 .M24 2003

McLaughlin, Bob.
[USA immigration & orientation. Spanish]
USA inmigración y orientación / Bob y Mary McLaughlin. 1a. ed. en español. Satellite Beach, Fla. : Wellesworth Pub., c2001. x, 528 p. ; 22 cm. Includes bibliographical references and index. "Traduc[c]ión de la quinta edición en inglés por 'The Spanish Center, Charlotte, North Carolina.'" Text in Spanish. CONTENTS: Libro 1. Iniciarse : resolviendo el proceso de inmigración -- Libro 2. Establecerse : ajustàndose a la vida en los Estados Unidos de América. ISBN 0-9657571-1-0
1. Emigration and immigration law - United States - Popular works. 2. Naturalization - United States - Handbooks, manuals, etc. 3. Aliens - United States. 4. Immigrants - United States. 5. United States - Emigration and immigration. 6. Spanish language materials. I. McLaughlin, Mary. II. Title. III. Title: Inmigración y orientación

McLaughlin, Kristina.
McLuhan's wake [videorecording]. [Montreal, Quebec] : Primitive Entertainment/National Film Board of Canada, c2002.

McLaughlin, Mary.
McLaughlin, Bob. [USA immigration & orientation. Spanish] USA inmigración y orientación. 1a. ed. en español. Satellite Beach, Fla. : Wellesworth Pub., c2001.

McLaughlin, Michael T. Knowledge, consciousness and religious conversion in Lonergan and Aurobindo / Michael T. McLaughlin. Roma : Editrice Pontificia Universita Gregoriana, 2003. 318 p. ; 24 cm. (Documenta missionalia ; 28) Dissertation. Includes bibliographical references (p. [303]-313). ISBN 88-7652-946-2 (pbk.) DDC 291
1. Lonergan, Bernard J. F. 2. Ghose, Aurobindo, - 1872-1950. 3. Christianity and other religions - Hinduism. 4. Hinduism - Relations - Christianity. 5. Knowledge, Theory of (Religion) 6. Knowledge, Theory of (Hinduism) 7. Consciousness - Religious aspects - Christianity. 8. Consciousness - Religious aspects - Hinduism. 9. Conversion - Comparative studies. 10. Experience (Religion) - Comparative studies. I. Title. II. Series.

McLelland, Lilith. Out of the shadows : myths and truths of modern Wicca / Lilith McLelland. New York : Citadel Press, c2002. ix, 245 p. ; 21 cm. Includes bibliographical references (p. 233-237) and index. ISBN 0-8065-2210-0 DDC 299/.94
1. Witchcraft. I. Title.
BF1571 .M46 2002

McLeod, Carolyn. Self-trust and reproductive autonomy / Carolyn McLeod. Cambridge, Mass. : MIT Press, c2002. xiii, 199 p. ; 24 cm. (Basic bioethics) Includes bibliographical references (p. [167]-190) and index. ISBN 0-262-13408-X (hc. : alk. paper) DDC 176
1. Human reproductive technology - Moral and ethical aspects. 2. Human reproduction - Moral and ethical aspects. 3. Autonomy. 4. Medical ethics. 5. Bioethics. 6. Trust. 7. Feminism - Health aspects. 8. Feminism - Moral and ethical aspects. 9. Ethics. I. Title. II. Series.
RG133.5 .M39 2002

McLeod, John, 1951- Doing counselling research / John McLeod. 2nd ed. London ; Thousand Oaks, CA : Sage Publications, 2003. ix, 227 p. ; 25 cm. Includes bibliographical references (p. [195]-219) and index. ISBN 0-7619-4108-8 (pbk.) ISBN 0-7619-4107-X (hbk)
1. Counseling - Research - Methodology. I. Title.
BF637.C6 M37894 2003

McLintock, David.
Freud, Sigmund, 1856-1939. [Essays. English. Selections] The uncanny. New York : Penguin Books, 2003.
BF109.F75 A25 2003

MCLUHAN, MARSHALL, 1911-.
LAWS OF MEDIA.
McLuhan's wake [videorecording]. [Montreal, Quebec] : Primitive Entertainment/National Film Board of Canada, c2002.

The mechanical bride : folklore of industrial man / by Marshall McLuhan. Corte Madera, CA : Gingko Press, 2002. xii, 157 p. : ill. ; 28 cm. ISBN 1-58423-050-9
1. Social psychology. 2. Advertising - Psychological aspects. 3. Consumers - United States. I. Title.

McLuhan's wake [videorecording] / a production of Primitive Entertainment ; produced by Kristina McLaughlin, Michael McMahon. [Montreal, Quebec] : Primitive Entertainment/National Film Board of Canada, c2002. 1 videocassette (94 min.) : sd., col. ; 1/2 in. Directed by Kevin McMahon ; written, conceived, and co-produced by David Sobelman ; editor, Christopher Donaldson. Narrator, Laurie Anderson. VHS. SUMMARY: Illuminates McLuhan's Laws of Media through archival footage of McLuhan speaking and teaching, family photographs, original animation and digital effects. Closed captioned.
1. McLuhan, Marshall, - 1911- - Laws of Media. 2. Video recordings for the hearing impaired. 3. Mass media and the environment. 4. Communication. 5. Semiotics. I. McLaughlin, Kristina. II. McMahon, Michael. III. McMahon, Kevin. IV. Sobelman, David. V. Donaldson, Christopher. VI. Primitive Features Inc. VII. National Film Board of Canada.

McMahon, Kevin.
McLuhan's wake [videorecording]. [Montreal, Quebec] : Primitive Entertainment/National Film Board of Canada, c2002.

McMahon, Michael.
McLuhan's wake [videorecording]. [Montreal, Quebec] : Primitive Entertainment/National Film Board of Canada, c2002.

McManus, Martha Hansen, 1948- Understanding the angry child : coping strategies for you and your child / by Martha Hansen McManus & Shari Steelsmith. Seattle, Wash. : Parenting Press, 2004. p. cm. Includes bibliographical references and index. ISBN 0-943990-71-8 ISBN 0-943990-70-X (pbk.) DDC 649/.1
1. Anger in children. 2. Child rearing. I. Steelsmith, Shari. II. Title.
BF723.A4 M38 2004

McMurtry, John, 1939- Value wars : the Global market versus the life economy / John McMurtry. London ; Sterling, Va. : Pluto Press, c2002. xxv, 277 p. ; 22 cm. Includes index. ISBN 0-7453-1890-8 (hardback) ISBN 0-7453-1889-4 (pbk.) DDC 330.9/049
1. Globalization - Economic aspects. 2. Globalization - Moral and ethical aspects. 3. Globalization - Social aspects. 4. International trade - Moral and ethical aspects. 5. Capitalism - Moral and ethical aspects. 6. Values. 7. International economic relations. I. Title.
HF1359 .M39 2002

McNally, David, 1946- Be your own brand : a breakthrough formula for standing out from the crowd / David McNally and Karl D. Speak. 1st ed. San Francisco, CA : Berrett-Koehler, c2002. x, 148 p. : ill. ; 24 cm. Includes bibliographical references (p. 139) and index. ISBN 1-57675-141-4 DDC 158/.1
1. Identity (Psychology) 2. Brand name products - Miscellanea. I. Speak, Karl D., 1951- II. Title.
BF697 .M385 2002

McNally, Richard J. Remembering trauma / Richard J. McNally. Cambridge, Mass. : Belknap Press of Harvard University Press, 2003. 420 p. ; 24 cm. Includes bibliographical references (p. [313]-408) and index. Table of contents URL: http://www.loc.gov/catdir/toc/fy036/2002028143.html ISBN 0-674-01082-5 DDC 616.85/21
1. Psychic trauma. 2. Post-traumatic stress disorder. 3. Recovered memory. I. Title.
RC552.P67 M396 2003

McNaughton, Mary. Synchro-signs : a new system of divination based on ancient universal symbols and worldwide / Mary McNaughton. Charlottesville, VA : Hampton Roads Pub., 2003. p. cm. Includes bibliographical references. ISBN 1-57174-388-X DDC 133.3/3
1. Divination. I. Title.
BF1773 .M38 2003

McNeil, Mary (Mary S.).
Gemmen, Heather. Dreams from God. Colorado Springs, Colo. : Faith Kidz, 2003.
BF1099.B5 G46 2003

McNiff, Shaun. Creating with others : the practice of imagination in life, art, and the workplace / Shaun McNiff. 1st ed. Boston, Mass. : Shambhala Publications, 2003. xii, 260 p. ; 24 cm. Includes index.

ISBN 1-57062-966-8 (alk. paper) DDC 153.3/5
1. Creative ability. 2. Creation (Literary, artistic, etc.) 3. Imagination. 4. Social groups. 5. Teams in the workplace. I. Title.
BF408 .M336 2003

McQuillar, Tayannah Lee, 1977- Rootwork : using the folk magick of Black America for love, money, and success / Tayannah Lee McQuillar. New York : Simon & Schuster, c2003. xviii, 141 p. ; 22 cm. "A Fireside book." Includes bibliographical references (p. 137) and index. ISBN 0-7432-3534-7 DDC 133.4/3/08996073
1. African American magic. 2. Medicine, Magic, mystic, and spagiric - United States. 3. Witchcraft. 4. Charms. 5. Success in business. 6. Talismans. 7. Voodooism. 8. Black author. I. Title.
BF1622.A34 M37 2003

McVay, Ted E.
Narrative and consciousness. Oxford ; New York : Oxford University Press, c2003.
BF311 .N26 2003

McWilliam, Erica. What about Uranus? : or, how are you on the whole? / Erica McWilliam. Sydney, NSW, Australia : UNSW Press, 2002. 95 p. : ill. ; 15 cm. ISBN 0-86840-773-9 DDC 158
1. Self-actualization (Psychology) I. Title.
BF637.S4 M397 2002

What about Uranus? : or, how are you on the whole? / Erica McWilliam. Sydney : UNSW Press, 2002. 95 p. : ill. ; 15 cm. ISBN 0-86840-773-9
1. Self-actualization (Psychology) I. Title.

MDS. *See* **PHYSICIANS.**

Me-ayin naḥalti et shiri : sofrim u-meshorerim medabrim ʻal meḳorot hashraʼah / ʻorekhet, Rut Karṭun-Blum ; rishumim, Menasheh Ḳadishman. Tel Aviv : Yediʻot aḥaronot : Sifre ḥemed, c2002. 335 p. : ill., ports. ; 23 x 24 cm. Title on t.p. verso: Writers and poets on sources of inspiration.
1. Authors, Israeli. 2. Poets, Israeli. 3. Inspiration in literature. 4. Creation (Literary, artistic, etc.) I. Karṭun-Blum, Ruth. II. Ḳadishman, Menashe, 1932- III. Title: Writers and poets on sources of inspiration

Meader, William A., 1955- Shine forth : the soul's magical destiny / William A. Meader. Mariposa, Calif. : Source Publications, c2004. p. cm. Includes bibliographical references and index. Table of contents URL: http://www.loc.gov/catdir/toc/ecip044/2003012231.html ISBN 0-9635766-5-8 DDC 131
1. Magic. 2. Occultism. I. Title.
BF1611 .M412 2004

Meadow, Phyllis W., 1924- The new psychoanalysis / Phyllis W. Meadow. Lanham, Md. : Rowman & Littlefield, c2003. p. cm. (Legacies of social thought) Includes bibliographical references and index. Table of contents URL: http://www.loc.gov/catdir/toc/ecip042/2003008297.html ISBN 0-7425-2824-3 (cloth : alk. paper) ISBN 0-7425-2825-1 (pbk. : alk. paper) DDC 150.19/5
1. Psychoanalysis. I. Title. II. Series.
BF173 .M3585 2003

Meaning, medicine, and the "placebo effect".
Moerman, Daniel E. Cambridge ; New York : Cambridge University Press, 2002.
R726.5 .M645 2002

The meaning of witchcraft.
Gardner, Gerald Brosseau, 1884-1964. Boston : Weiser Books, 2004.
BF1566 .G3 2004

MEANING (PHILOSOPHY).
Lévinas, Emmanuel. [Humanisme de l'autre homme. English] Humanism of the other. Urbana : University of Illinois Press, c2003.
B2430.L48 H8413 2003

Merdalor, Jean. Pensées mortelles. Port-au-Prince, Haiti : Editions Choucoune, 1999.
1. Black author.

Schiffer, Stephen R. The things we mean. Oxford ; New York : Clarendon, 2003.

MEANING (PSYCHOLOGY). *See also* **LANGUAGE AND LANGUAGES; SEMANTICS (PHILOSOPHY).**
Cabrera, Derek. Remedial genius. 1st ed. Loveland, Colo. : Project N Press, 2001.
BF441 .C23 2001

De Munck, Victor C. Culture, self, and meaning. Prospect Heights, Ill. : Waveland Press, c2000.
BF697.5.S65 M86 2000

Fuhrer, Urs, 1950- Cultivating minds. 1st ed. New York, NY : Taylor & Francis, 2003.

BF697.5.S65 F84 2003

Kirshenbaum, Mira. Everything happens for a reason. New York : Harmony Books, 2004.
BF637.L53 K57 2004

Matiushkina, A. A. (Anna Alekseevna) Reshenie problemy kak poisk smyslov. Moskva : Izdatelʼskiĭ tsentr GUU, 2003.
BF463.M4 M33 2003

Modell, Arnold H., 1924- Imagination and the meaningful brain. Cambridge, Mass. : MIT Press, c2003.
BF408 .M58 2003

The meanings of social life.
Alexander, Jeffrey C. New York : Oxford University Press, 2003.
HM585 .A5 2003

The meanings of violence / edited by Elizabeth A. Stanko. London ; New York : Routledge, 2003. xvii, 250 p. : ill. ; 24 cm. Includes bibliographical references and index. ISBN 0-415-30129-7 (hardcover) ISBN 0-415-30130-0 (papercover) DDC 303.6
1. Violence. 2. Social conflict. 3. Culture conflict. 4. Ethnic conflict. I. Stanko, Elizabeth Anne, 1950-
HM1116 .M436 2003

MEASUREMENT, MENTAL. *See* **PSYCHOMETRICS.**

MEASUREMENT, PSYCHOLOGICAL. *See* **PSYCHOMETRICS.**

Measuring America.
Linklater, Andro. New York : Walker & Co., 2002.
E161.3 .L46 2002

MECHANICAL ABILITY - EXAMINATIONS, QUESTIONS, ETC.
Wiesen, Joel P. (Joel Peter) How to prepare for mechanical aptitude & spatial relations tests. Hauppauge, NY : Barron's, 2003.
BF433.M4 W535 2003

MECHANICAL APTITUDE. *See* **MECHANICAL ABILITY.**

Mechanical aptitude & spatial relations test.
Wiesen, Joel P. (Joel Peter) How to prepare for mechanical aptitude & spatial relations tests. Hauppauge, NY : Barron's, 2003.
BF433.M4 W535 2003

The mechanical bride.
McLuhan, Marshall, 1911- Corte Madera, CA : Gingko Press, 2002.

MECHANICAL DRAWING. *See* **DESIGN, INDUSTRIAL.**

MECHANICAL INTELLIGENCE. *See* **MECHANICAL ABILITY.**

MECHANICAL PERSPECTIVE. *See* **PERSPECTIVE.**

MECHANISM (PHILOSOPHY). *See* **MATERIALISM; NATURALISM.**

Méchoulan, Eric.
Passions du passé. Paris : L'Harmattan, c2000.
BF378.S65 P37 2000

Mecklinger, Axel.
Working on working memory. Leipzig : Leipziger Universitätsverlag, 2000.
BF378.S54 W675 2000

Medan, Barukh. Sefer Birkat Meʼir ; siḥot musar ... / Barukh Medan ... Netivot : Barukh Medan, 763 [2002 or 2003] 436 p. ; 24 cm. Cover title: Birkat Meʼir.
1. Ethics, Jewish. I. Title. II. Title: Birkat Meʼir

Medeiros, Carlos Alberto.
Borges, Edson. Racismo, preconceito e intolerancia. [São Paulo, Brazil] : Atual, c2002.

Medhananda, 1908-1994.
[Au fil de l'eternitè avec Medhananda. English. Selections]
On the threshold of a new age with Medhananda : fragments of conversations recorded in French by Yvonne Artaud / [English translation by Shraddhavan ; drawings by Medhananda]. 1st ed. Pondicherry : Sri Mira Trust, 2000. 199 p. : ill. ; 23 cm. SUMMARY: On spiritualism and Yoga philosophy. ISBN 81-86413-14-6
1. Spiritualism (Philosophy) 2. Yoga. I. Artaud, Yvonne. II. Title.
B841 .M4313 2000

MEDIA LITERACY - UNITED STATES.
Goodman, Steven. Teaching youth media. New York : Teachers College Press, c2003.

LB1043 .G59 2003

Media psychology.
Giles, David, 1964- Mahwah, N.J. : Lawrence Erlbaum Associates Publishers, 2003.
P96.P75 G55 2003

Mediace.
Holá, Lenka. Vyd. 1. Praha : Grada Pub., 2003.
BF637.I48 H63 2003

MEDIATION. *See* **DISPUTE RESOLUTION (LAW).**

Médiation.
Six, Jean François. Paris : Editions du Seuil, c2002.
HM1126 .S59 2002

MEDIATION.
Bringing peace into the room. 1st ed. San Francisco : Jossey-Bass, 2003.
HM1126 .B75 2003

Conflict resolution for school personnel [electronic resource]. [Washington, D.C.?] : U.S. Dept. of Justice, Office of Justice Programs, National Institute of Justice, c1999.

Holá, Lenka. Mediace. Vyd. 1. Praha : Grada Pub., 2003.
BF637.I48 H63 2003

Peace-building. [Harare] : ACPD, 2002.

Six, Jean François. Médiation. Paris : Editions du Seuil, c2002.
HM1126 .S59 2002

MEDIATION, INTERNATIONAL.
Promoting peace. Berne, Switzerland : Staempfli, 2002.

MEDICAL AND HEALTH CARE INDUSTRY. *See* **MEDICAL CARE.**

MEDICAL ANTHROPOLOGY. *See* **TRADITIONAL MEDICINE.**

MEDICAL CARE. *See also* **HEALTH FACILITIES; MENTAL HEALTH SERVICES; SELF-CARE, HEALTH.**
Pharmacum carthusiense. Salzburg, Austria : Institut für Anglistik und Amerikanistik, Universität Salzburg, 2002.
BX2435 .P43 2002

MEDICAL CARE - COST EFFECTIVENESS.
McCulloch, Douglas, 1950- Valuing health in practice. Aldershot, Hampshire, England ; Burlington, VT : Ashgate, c2003.
RA410.5 .M37 2002

MEDICAL CARE - EVALUATION. *See* **OUTCOME ASSESSMENT (MEDICAL CARE).**

MEDICAL CARE FACILITIES. *See* **HEALTH FACILITIES.**

MEDICAL CARE FOR THE AGED. *See* **AGED - MEDICAL CARE.**

MEDICAL CARE - GOVERNMENT POLICY. *See* **MEDICAL POLICY.**

MEDICAL CARE - HISTORY.
Michael, Pamela. Care and treatment of the mentally ill in North Wales, 1800-2000. Cardiff : University of Wales Press, 2003.

MEDICAL CARE INSTITUTIONS. *See* **HEALTH FACILITIES.**

MEDICAL CARE - MORAL AND ETHICAL ASPECTS. *See* **MEDICAL ETHICS.**

MEDICAL CARE - QUALITY CONTROL.
McCulloch, Douglas, 1950- Valuing health in practice. Aldershot, Hampshire, England ; Burlington, VT : Ashgate, c2003.
RA410.5 .M37 2002

MEDICAL CARE - SOCIAL ASPECTS. *See* **SOCIAL MEDICINE.**

MEDICAL CARE - ZIMBABWE - MBERENGWA DISTRICT.
Dahlin, Olov, 1962- Zvinorwadza. Frankfurt am Main ; New York : P. Lang, c2002.
R726.5 .D34 2002

MEDICAL CENTERS. *See* **HOSPITALS.**

MEDICAL DOCTORS. *See* **PHYSICIANS.**

MEDICAL EMERGENCIES. *See* **ACCIDENTS.**

MEDICAL ETHICS. *See also* **MEDICAL RECORDS - ACCESS CONTROL; SOCIAL MEDICINE.**

McLeod, Carolyn. Self-trust and reproductive autonomy. Cambridge, Mass. : MIT Press, c2002.
RG133.5 .M39 2002

Pollard, Irina. Life, love and children. Boston : Kluwer Academic Publishers, c2002.
R725.5 .P655 2002

MEDICAL ETHICS - INTERVIEW.
Changeux, Jean-Pierre. [Ce qui nous fait penser. English] What makes us think? Princeton, N.J. : Princeton University Press, c2000.
BJ45 .C4313 2000

MEDICAL EXAMINERS (LAW). See **FORENSIC PATHOLOGISTS.**

MEDICAL EXAMINERS (LAW) - FICTION.
Cameron, Stella. Cold day in July. Waterville, Me. : Wheeler Pub. ; Bath, England : Chivers Press, 2002.
PS3553.A4345 C65 2002

MEDICAL FACILITIES. See **HEALTH FACILITIES.**

MEDICAL FOLKLORE. See **TRADITIONAL MEDICINE.**

MEDICAL INNOVATIONS - SOCIAL ASPECTS - UNITED STATES.
Elliott, Carl, 1961- Better than well. 1st ed. New York : W.W. Norton, c2003.
RA418.3.U6 E455 2003

MEDICAL LABORATORY DIAGNOSIS. See **DIAGNOSIS, LABORATORY.**

MEDICAL PERSONNEL. See **MIDWIVES; PHYSICIANS.**

MEDICAL PERSONNEL-CAREGIVER RELATIONSHIPS.
Promising practies in the field of caregiving [electronic resource]. [Washington, D.C.] : U.S. Dept. of Health and Human Services, Administration on Aging, [2003?]

MEDICAL POLICY - RESEARCH - METHODOLOGY.
Murphy, Elizabeth. Qualitative methods and health policy research. Hawthorne, N.Y. : Aldine de Gruyter, c2003.
RA394 .M87 2003

MEDICAL PROFESSION. See **MEDICINE; PHYSICIANS.**

MEDICAL RECORDS - ACCESS CONTROL - UNITED STATES - MISCELLANEA.
Questions and answers [electronic resource]. [Washington, D.C.] : U.S. Equal Employment Opportunity Commission, [2000?]

MEDICAL SCIENCES. See **MEDICINE; NEUROSCIENCES.**

MEDICAL SELF-CARE. See **SELF-CARE, HEALTH.**

MEDICAL SERVICES. See **MEDICAL CARE.**

MEDICAL SOCIOLOGY. See **SOCIAL MEDICINE.**

MEDICAL SUPPLIES. See **DRUGS.**

MEDICAL TECHNOLOGY. See **HUMAN REPRODUCTIVE TECHNOLOGY; MEDICAL INNOVATIONS.**

Medications [electronic resource].
Strock, Margaret. [4th ed., rev. Apr. 2002, repr. Sept. 2002]. [Bethesda, Md.] : Dept. of Health and Human Services, Public Health Service, National Institutes of Health, National Institute of Mental Health, 2002.

MEDICINE. See **DISEASES; HEALTH; PHYSICIANS; VIRTUAL REALITY IN MEDICINE.**

MEDICINE, ANCIENT.
Lloyd, G. E. R. (Geoffrey Ernest Richard), 1933- In the grip of disease. Oxford ; New York : Oxford University Press, 2003.
B187.M4 L56 2003

MEDICINE AND PSYCHOLOGY. See also **HEALTH BEHAVIOR; PLACEBO (MEDICINE); PSYCHIATRY.**
Bryden, Barbara E., 1954- Sundial. Gainesville, FL : Center for Applications of Psychological Type, 2003.
BF698.3 .B79 2003

Strock, Margaret. Medications [electronic resource]. [4th ed., rev. Apr. 2002, repr. Sept. 2002]. [Bethesda, Md.] : Dept. of Health and Human Services, Public Health Service, National Institutes of Health, National Institute of Mental Health, 2002.

Sylvest, Vernon M. The formula. Fairfield, Iowa : Sunstar Pub., c1996.
BF161 .S95 1996

MEDICINE AND PSYCHOLOGY - CONGRESSES.
Self, social identity, and physical health. New York : Oxford University Press, 1999.
R726.5 .S46 1999

MEDICINE AND STATE. See **MEDICAL POLICY.**

MEDICINE, AYURVEDA.
Pracetā Jyoti. Dhātusāmya mem manobhāvom kā sthāna. 1. samskarana. Nāgapura : Viśvabhāratī Prakāśana, 2001.
BF204.5 .P73 2001

MEDICINE, AYURVEDIC.
Upādhyāya, Govindaprasāda. Āyurvedīya mānasaroga cikitsā. 1. samskarana. Vārānasī : Caukhabā Surabhāratī Prakāśana ; Dillī : Anya Prāptisthāna Caukhambā Samskrta Pratishthāna, 2000.
R605 .U67 2000

MEDICINE - GREECE - HISTORY.
Lloyd, G. E. R. (Geoffrey Ernest Richard), 1933- In the grip of disease. Oxford ; New York : Oxford University Press, 2003.
B187.M4 L56 2003

MEDICINE, GREEK AND ROMAN.
Lloyd, G. E. R. (Geoffrey Ernest Richard), 1933- In the grip of disease. Oxford ; New York : Oxford University Press, 2003.
B187.M4 L56 2003

MEDICINE - HISTORY.
Greenberg, Arthur. The art of chemistry. Hoboken, N.J. : Wiley-Interscience, c2003.
QD11 .G735 2003

MEDICINE IN LITERATURE.
Lloyd, G. E. R. (Geoffrey Ernest Richard), 1933- In the grip of disease. Oxford ; New York : Oxford University Press, 2003.
B187.M4 L56 2003

MEDICINE - INNOVATIONS. See **MEDICAL INNOVATIONS.**

MEDICINE, LABORATORY. See **DIAGNOSIS, LABORATORY.**

MEDICINE, MAGIC, MYSTIC, AND SPAGIRIC.
Bennett, Robin Rose. Healing magic. New York : Sterling Pub., 2004.
BF1572.S65 B46 2004

Carvalho, Angela Maria B., 1954- A magia das ervas e seu axé. São Paulo, SP : Madras, 2003.
1. Black author.

The emerald tablets of Thoth-the-Atlantean. Sedalia, Colo. : Brotherhood of the White Temple, c2002.
BF1999 .E44 2002

Frost, Gavin. A witch's guide to psychic healing. Boston, MA : Weiser Books, 2003.
BF1572.S65 F76 2003

MEDICINE, MAGIC, MYSTIC, AND SPAGIRIC - UNITED STATES.
McQuillar, Tayannah Lee, 1977- Rootwork. New York : Simon & Schuster, c2003.
BF1622.A34 M37 2003
1. Black author.

MEDICINE - MORAL AND ETHICAL ASPECTS. See **MEDICAL ETHICS.**

MEDICINE, MYSTIC. See **MEDICINE, MAGIC, MYSTIC, AND SPAGIRIC.**

MEDICINE, OCCULT. See **MEDICINE, MAGIC, MYSTIC, AND SPAGIRIC.**

MEDICINE, POPULAR. See **SELF-CARE, HEALTH.**

MEDICINE, PRIMITIVE. See **TRADITIONAL MEDICINE.**

MEDICINE, PSYCHOSOMATIC.
D'Alvia, Rodolfo. Psicoanálisis psicosomática ida y atleuv [sic.]. Buenos Aires : Editorial Dunken, 2002.

MEDICINE, SOCIAL. See **SOCIAL MEDICINE.**

MEDICINE - SOCIAL ASPECTS. See **SOCIAL MEDICINE.**

MEDICINE, SPAGIRIC. See **MEDICINE, MAGIC, MYSTIC, AND SPAGIRIC.**

MEDICINE - TECHNOLOGICAL INNOVATIONS. See **MEDICAL INNOVATIONS.**

Medien, Texte und Maschinen : angewandte Mediensemiotik / Ernst W.B. Hess-Lüttich, Hrsg. 1. Aufl. Wiesbaden : Westdeutscher Verlag, c2001. 264 p. : ill. ; 21 cm. Includes bibliographical references. ISBN 3-531-13622-4
1. Mass media - Semiotics. 2. Mass media. 3. Semiotics. 4. Communication. I. Hess-Lüttich, Ernest W. B.

Medienkulturen.
Ries, Marc, 1956- Wien : Sonderzahl, c2002.
P94.6 .R54 2002

Medienwissenschaft Kommunikation, Kunst und Kulture.
Kommunikation, Kunst und Kultur. Bern ; New York : Peter Lang, c2002.

The medieval and early modern Iberian world
(v. 18) Lucas, John Scott, 1970- Astrology and numerology in medieval and early modern Catalonia. Leiden ; Boston : Brill, 2003.
BF1685 .L83 2003

MEDIEVAL AND MODERN LATIN MANUSCRIPTS. See **MANUSCRIPTS, LATIN (MEDIEVAL AND MODERN).**

Medieval and Renaissance philosophy.
Early studies of Giordano Bruno. Bristol : Thoemmes, 2000.

MEDIEVAL ART. See **ART, MEDIEVAL.**

The medieval Church.
Clegg, Justin. London : British Library, 2003.

MEDIEVAL CIVILIZATION. See **CIVILIZATION, MEDIEVAL.**

Medieval cultures
(v. 32) Gender and difference in the Middle Ages. Minneapolis : University of Minnesota Press, c2003.
HQ1143 .G44 2003

(v. 35) Cohen, Jeffrey Jerome. Medieval identity machines. Minneapolis : University of Minnesota Press, c2003.
CB353 .C64 2003

Medieval cultures in contact / edited by Richard F. Gyug. New York : Fordham University Press, 2003. xxi, 282 p. : ill. ; 23 cm. (Fordham series in medieval studies, 1542-6378 ; no. 1) Includes bibliographical references and index. CONTENTS: Pt. 1. Cultures in contact. Bilingual philology in Bede's exegesis / Carmela Vircillo Franklin ; Conversion or the crown of martyrdom: conflicting goals for fourteenth-century missionaries in central Asia? / James D. Ryan ; Speaking for others: imposing solidarities on the past, the case of Venetian Crete / Sally McKee ; The Church of Dubrovnik and the Pannicculus of Christ: relics between east and west (and men and women) in medieval Dalmatia / Richard F. Gyug ; Medieval Europe and its encounter with the foreign world: late-medieval German witnesses / Albrecht Classen ; Dreams and visions: a comparative analysis of spiritual gifts in medieval Christian and Muslim conversion narratives / Linda G. Jones ; Venetian commerce in the later middle ages: feast or famine? / Alan M. Stahl ; Quidam de sinagoga: the Jew of the Jeu d'Adam / Jennifer R. Goodman ; Minstrel meets clerk in early French literature: medieval romance as the meeting-place between two traditions of verbal eloquence and performance practice / Evelyn Birge Vitz -- Pt. 2. Teaching cultures in contact. Team teaching the literature of the European and Islamic middle ages: the European perspective / Kathryn L. Lynch ; Team teaching the literature of the European and Islamic middle ages: the Islamic perspective / Louise Marlow ; Appendix. Sample syllabus (English 315/Religion 365): Images of the other in the European and Islamic middle ages / Kathryn L. Lynch and Louise Marlow ; Center and periphery in the teaching of medieval history / Teofilo F. Ruiz ; Appendix. Sample syllabus (UCLA: History 121D): Crisis and renewal: from late medieval to early modern, 1300-1525. ISBN 0-8232-2212-8 (hardcover : alk. paper) ISBN 0-8232-2213-6 (pbk. : alk. paper) DDC 909.07
1. Civilization, Medieval. 2. Europe - Civilization. 3. Europe - Social conditions. 4. Europe, Eastern - Civilization. 5. Middle Ages - Historiography. 6. Christianity and other religions. 7. Europe, Eastern - Social conditions. 8. Europe - Territorial expansion. I. Gyug, Richard, 1954- II. Series.
CB351 .M3922 2003

Medieval Europe, 814-1350 / [edited by] Jeremiah Hackett. Detroit, MI : Gale Group, c2002. xxvii, 519 p. : ill., maps ; 29 cm. (World eras ; v. 4) "A Manly, Inc. book." Includes bibliographical references (p. 485-500) and index. ISBN 0-7876-1709-1 (alk. paper) DDC 940.1/4
1. Europe - History - 476-1492. 2. Middle Ages. 3. Civilization, Medieval. I. Hackett, Jeremiah. II. Series.
D102 .M38 2001

The medieval heritage in early modern metaphysics and modal theory, 1400-1700 / edited by Russell L. Friedman and Lauge O. Nielsen. Dordrecht ; Boston : Kluwer Academic Publishers, c2003. vi, 346 p. ; 25 cm. (The new synthese historical library ; v. 53) Includes bibliographical references and index. ISBN 140201631X (hb) DDC 189
1. Metaphysics - History. 2. Modality (Logic) - History. 3. Philosophical theology - History. 4. Philosophy, Medieval. 5. Philosophy, Modern. I. Friedman, Russell L. II. Nielsen, Lauge Olaf. III. Series.
BD111 .M47 2003

Medieval identity machines.
Cohen, Jeffrey Jerome. Minneapolis : University of Minnesota Press, c2003.
CB353 .C64 2003

MEDIEVAL LITERATURE. See **LITERATURE, MEDIEVAL.**

MEDIEVAL MANUSCRIPTS. See **MANUSCRIPTS, MEDIEVAL.**

MEDIEVAL PERIOD. See **MIDDLE AGES.**

MEDIEVAL PHILOSOPHY. See **PHILOSOPHY, MEDIEVAL.**

Medieval philosophy and the classical tradition : in Islam, Judaism and Christianity / edited by John Inglis. London ; New York : Curzon, c2002. x, 317 p. ; 25 cm. Includes bibliographical references and index. Proceedings of colloquium held in April, 1999, University of Dayton. CONTENTS: Introduction. Towards a balanced historiography of medieval philosophy / John Inglis -- Section 1. Historical context. Medieval Islamic philosophy and the classical tradition / Michael E. Marmura -- Section 2. Philosophy. A philosophical odyssey : Ghazzālī's Intentions of the philosophers / Gabriel Said Reynolds ; The relationship between Averroes and al-Ghazālī : as it presents itself in Averroes' early writings, especially in his commentary on al-Ghazālī's al-Mustasfā / Frank Griffel ; Al Ghazali and Halevi on philosophy and the philosophers / Barry S. Kogan -- Section 3. Neoplatonism. Projection and time in Proclus / D. Gregory MacIssac ; Forms of knowledge in the Arabic Plotinus / Peter Adamson ; Secumdum rei vim vel secundum cognoscentium facultatem : knower and known in the Consolation of philosophy of Boethius and the Proslogion of Anselm / Wayne J. Hankey ; Proclean 'remaining' and Avicenna on existence as accident : Neoplatonic Methodology and a defence of 'pre-existing' essences / Sarah Pessin ; Augustine vs Plotinus : the uniqueness of the vision at Ostia / Thomas Williams -- Section 4. Creation. Infinite power and Plenitude : two traditions on neccessity of the eternal / Taneli Kukkonen ; The challenge to medieval Christian philosophy : relating creator to creatures / David B. Burrell -- Section 5. Virtue. Three kinds of objectivity / Jonathan Jacobs ; On defining Maimonides' Aristotelianism / Daniel H. Frank ; Porphyry, Bonaventure and Thomas Aquinas : a Neoplatonic hierarchy of virtures and two Christian appropriations / Joshua P. Hochschild -- Section 6. The Latin reception. William of Auvergne and the Aristotelians : the nature of a servant / Michael Miller ; Is God a "what"? : Avicenna, William of Auvergne, and Aquinas on the Divine essence / John P. Rosheger ; Maimonides and Roger Bacon : did Roger Bacon read Maimonides? / Jeremiah Hackett. ISBN 0-7007-1469-3 DDC 189
1. Philosophy, Medieval. I. Inglis, John, 1954-
B721 .M4535 2002

Medievalia Hispanica
(vol. 7) Burlaeus, Gualterus, 1275-1345? [De vita et moribus philosophorum. Spanish] Vida y costumbres de los viejos filósofos. Madrid : Iberoamericana ; Frankfurt : Vervuert, 2002.

MEDIEVALISM. See also **MIDDLE AGES.**
Cohen, Jeffrey Jerome. Medieval identity machines. Minneapolis : University of Minnesota Press, c2003.
CB353 .C64 2003

Medin, Douglas L. Cognitive psychology / Douglas L. Medin, Brian H. Ross, Arthur B. Markman. 4th ed. Hoboken, NJ : John Wiley & Sons, 2004. p. cm. Includes bibliographical references and index. ISBN 0-471-45820-1 (cloth : alk. paper) DDC 153
1. Cognitive psychology - Textbooks. 2. Cognitive neuroscience - Textbooks. I. Ross, Brian H. II. Markman, Arthur B. III. Title.
BF201 .M43 2004

Medina, Narciso. El suspendido vuelo del ángel creador / Narciso Medina. La Habana : Ediciones Alarcos, 2003. 57 p. : ill. ; 22 x 28 cm. Author's autograph inscription on half t.p.
1. Dance. 2. Creation (Literary, artistic, etc.) 3. Black author. I. Title.

Medioevo e umanesimo
(107, 108) Peri, Vittorio. Da oriente e da occidente. Roma : Editrice Antenore, 2002.
BR162.3 .P475 2002

Meditation.
Andrews, Linda Wasmer. New York : F. Watts, c2003.
BF637.M4 A53 2003

MEDITATION.
Adiswarananda, Swami, 1925- Meditation & its practices. Woodstock, Vt. : SkyLight Paths Pub., 2003.
BL627 .A33 2003

Andrews, Linda Wasmer. Meditation. New York : F. Watts, c2003.
BF637.M4 A53 2003

Buckland, Raymond. Color magick. 1st ed., rev. St. Paul, Minn. : Llewellyn Publications, 2002.
BF1623.C6 B83 2002

Chuckrow, Robert. The tai chi book. Boston : YMAA Publication Center, c1998.
GV504 .C536 1998

Chuckrow, Robert. Tai chi walking. Boston, Mass. : YMAA Publication Center, c2002.

Flickstein, Matthew. Journey to the center. Somerville, MA : Wisdom Publications, c1998.
BF637.S4 F58 1998

Die Grundsteinmeditation als Schulungsweg. Dornach : Verlag am Goetheanum, c2002.

Harris, Bill, 1950- Thresholds of the mind. Beaverton : Centerpointe Press, c2002.
BF637.B4 H36 2002

Spotts, Dane. Super brain power. Seattle, Wash. : LifeQuest Pub. Group, c1998.
BF441 .S68 1998

Tubali, Shy. [Selections] Boker tov 'olam. Tel Aviv : Yedi'ot aharonot : Sifre hemed, c2003.

Wingerter, J. Richard. Teaching, learning, and the meditative mind. Lanham, Md. ; Oxford : University Press of America, c2003.
LB1025.3 .W55 2003

Meditation & its practices.
Adiswarananda, Swami, 1925- Woodstock, Vt. : SkyLight Paths Pub., 2003.
BL627 .A33 2003

Meditation and its practices.
Adiswarananda, Swami, 1925- Meditation & its practices. Woodstock, Vt. : SkyLight Paths Pub., 2003.
BL627 .A33 2003

MEDITATION - BUDDHISM. See also **VIPAŚYANĀ (BUDDHISM).**
Glickman, Marshall. Beyond the breath. 1st ed. Boston : Journey Editions ; North Clarendon, VT : Distributed by Tuttle Pub., 2002.
BQ5630.V5 G54 2002

MEDITATION - JUVENILE LITERATURE.
Andrews, Linda Wasmer. Meditation. New York : F. Watts, c2003.
BF637.M4 A53 2003

Meditations.
Van Praagh, James. New York : Simon & Schuster, 2003.
BF1261.2 .V355 2003

From one brother to another. Volume 2. Valley Forge, PA : Judson Press, c2003.

Galenorn, Yasmine, 1961- Magical meditations. [New ed.]. Berkeley, Calif. : Crossing Press, c2003.
BF1561 .G35 2003

Hickman, Martha Whitmore, 1925- Wade in the water. Nashville, TN : Abingdon Press, 2003.
BV310 .H53 2003

Re-Cord-El, 1943- The pyramid discourses. Columbus, OH : Howie Pub., 2003.
BF1999 .R3956 2003

The soul aflame. Berkeley, Calif. : Conari Press, 2000.
BL624.2 .S675 2000

Van Praagh, James. Meditations. New York : Simon & Schuster, 2003.
BF1261.2 .V355 2003

Weil, Simone, 1909-1943. [Pesanteur et la grâce. English] Gravity and grace. 1st complete English language ed. / with an introduction and postscript by Gustave Thibon. London ; New York : Routledge, 2002.
B2430.W473 P413 2002

Wildman, Laura A. Wiccan meditations. New York : Citadel Press, c2002.
BF1571 .W55 2002

Meditazioni sull'albero della cabala.
Mantovani, Massimo. Milano : Xenia, 2002.

Mediterránea (Madrid, Spain)
(no. 7.) Ángeles, demonios y genios en el mundo Mediterráneo. Madrid : Ediciones Clásicas, 2000.

MEDITERRANEAN REGION, EASTERN. See **MIDDLE EAST.**

MEDITERRANEAN REGION - MISCELLANEA.
Welch, R. W., 1929- Comet of Nostradamus. 1st ed. St. Paul, Minn. : Llewellyn Publications, 2000 (2001 printing)
BF1815.N8 A269 2000

MEDITERRANEAN REGION - RELIGION.
Ángeles, demonios y genios en el mundo Mediterráneo. Madrid : Ediciones Clásicas, 2000.

MEDITERRANEAN SEA REGION. See **MEDITERRANEAN REGION.**

MEDIUM-SIZED BUSINESS. See **SMALL BUSINESS.**

The medium, the mystic, and the physicist.
LeShan, Lawrence L., 1920- New York : Helios Press, 2003, c1974.
BF1031 .L43 2003

MEDIUMS. See also **WOMEN MEDIUMS.**
Dreller, Larry. Secrets of a medium. Boston, MA : Weiser Books, 2003.
BF1031 .D69 2003

Matheson, Richard. Mediums rare. 1st ed. Baltimore, Md. : Cemetery Dance Publications, 2000.

MEDIUMS - BIOGRAPHY.
Brown, Robert, medium. We are eternal. New York : Warner Books, c2003.
BF1283.B717 A3 2003

MEDIUMS - GREAT BRITAIN - BIOGRAPHY.
Shine, Betty, 1929- A free spirit. London : HarperCollinsPublishers, 2001.

MEDIUMS - ICELAND - BIOGRAPHY.
Steinunn Eyjólfsdóttir, 1936- Undir verndarhendi. Reykjavík : Skjaldborg, 1995.
BF1283.B58 S74 1995

Mediums rare.
Matheson, Richard. 1st ed. Baltimore, Md. : Cemetery Dance Publications, 2000.

MEDIUMS - SCOTLAND - BIOGRAPHY.
Smith, Gordon, 1962- Spirit messenger. Carlsbad, Calif. : Hay House, 2004.
BF1283.S616 A3 2004

MEDIUMS - UNITED STATES - BIOGRAPHY.
Edward, John (John J.) After life. New York : Princess Books, c2003.
BF1283.E34 A3 2003

Mathews, Patrick, 1962- Never say goodbye. 1st ed. St. Paul, Minn. : Llewellyn Publications, 2003.
BF1283.M27 A3 2003

Moskowitz-Mateu, Lysa. Psychic diaries. New York : Harper Entertainment, 2003.
BF1283.M66 A3 2003

Medrano Samaniego, Concepción.
Desarrollo de los valores en las instituciones educativas. Bilbao : Mensajero, 2001.

Medvedev, Mikhail.
Ob analiticheskoi psikhologii Karla IUnga. 2001
Dimitrievich, Vladimir. V plenu germeticheskogo kruga. Perm' : Panagiia, 2001.
BF173.J85 D56 2001

Medvedev, V. A. (Vladimir Aleksandrovich).
Russian Imago 2001. Nauchnoe izd. Sankt-Peterburg : Izd-vo "Aleteiia", 2002.
BF175.4.C84 R87 2002

Medvedko, Leonid Ivanovich. Rossiia, Zapad, Islam : "stolknovenie tsivilizatsii"? / L.I. Medvedko. Zhukovskii ; Moskva : Kuchkovo pole, 2003. 509 p. ; 21 cm. (Geopoliticheskii rakurs) Includes bibliographical references and index. ISBN 5860900503
1. Islam and world politics. 2. War and society. 3. War - Religious aspects - Islam. 4. Terrorism. 5. Peace. I. Title. II. Series: Geopoliticheskii rakurs.
BP173.5 .M44 2003

Meeks, James T., 1956- Life changing relationships : bad boys, bad girls / James T. Meeks. Chicago, Ill. : Moody Press, c2002. 106 p. : ill. ; 24 cm. Includes bibliographical references (p. [105]-106). ISBN 0-8024-2994-7 DDC 646.7/7
1. Mate selection. 2. Mate selection - Religious aspects - Christianity. 3. Man-woman relationships. 4. Man-woman relationships - Religious aspects - Christianity. 5. Single women - Psychology. 6. African American women - Life skills guides. 7. Black author. I. Title.
HQ801 .M515 2002

Meem, Deborah T. (Deborah Townsend), 1949-. Femme/butch. New York : Harrington Park Press, 2002.
HQ75.5 .F459 2002

Megale, Nilza Botelho. Santos do povo brasileiro / Nilza Botelho Megale. Petrópolis : Editora Vozes, 2002. 198 p. : ill. ; 21 cm. Includes bibliographical references (p. 195-198). ISBN 85-326-2685-8
1. Christian saints - Cult - Brazil. 2. Christian saints - Biography. 3. Brazil - Religious life and customs. I. Title.

MEGALITHIC MONUMENTS - NEW ENGLAND.
Imbrogno, Philip J. Celtic mysteries in New England. 1st ed. St. Paul, Minn. : Llewellyn Publications, 2000.
BF2050 I435 2000

Mei xue yu yan xue.
Zhang, Fan. Di 1 ban. Beijing : Shou du shi fan da xue chu ban she, 1998.
P121 .Z465 1998

Meier, Jürgen. Karma und Christentum : Wege zu einem christlichen Schicksalsverständnis / Jürgen Meier. Dornach : Verlag am Goetheanum, c2001. 246 p. ; 21 cm. Includes bibliographical references (p. 243-246). ISBN 3-7235-1104-X (pbk.)
1. Karma. 2. Reincarnation - Christianity. 3. Fate and fatalism - Religious aspects - Christianity. I. Title.

Meier, Leslie. Birthday party murder : a Lucy Stone mystery / Leslie Meier. Waterville, Me. : Thorndike Press, 2003. 383 p. (large print) ; 22 cm. (Thorndike Press large print senior lifestyles series) ISBN 0-7862-4993-5 (lg. print : hc : alk. paper) DDC 813/.54
1. Stone, Lucy (Fictitious character) - Fiction. 2. Women detectives - Maine - Fiction. 3. Women - Maine - Fiction. 4. Maine - Fiction. 5. Large type books. I. Title. II. Series.
PS3563.E3455 B57 2003

Meier, Levi. Seven heavens : inspirational stories to elevate your soul / Levi Meier. [S.l.] : Devora Publishing, c2002. 221 p. ; 24 cm. URL: http://www.pitspopany.com ISBN 1-930143-47-8 ISBN 1-930143-47-8
1. Death - Psychological aspects. 2. Loss (Psychology) 3. Grief. I. Title.
BF789.D4 M39 2002

Meighan, Roland. John Holt : personalised learning instead of "uninvited teaching" / by Roland Meighan. 2nd ed. Nottingham : Educational Heretics Press, 2002. 129 p. ; 21 cm. Includes bibliographical references (p. [130]). ISBN 1-900219-23-9
1. Holt, John Caldwell, - 1923- 2. Education - Aims and objectives. 3. Learning, Psychology of. 4. Underachievement - Social aspects. 5. Effective teaching. 6. Teacher effectiveness. I. Title.
LB885.H64 M454 2002

Meine Reisen in die Vergangenheit.
Markus, Georg. 2. Aufl. Wien : Amalthea, 2002.
AC35 .M385 2002

Meiners, Cheri J., 1957-.
Learning to get along.
Meiners, Cheri J., 1957- When I feel afraid. Minneapolis, MN : Free Spirit Pub., 2003.
BF723.F4 M45 2003

When I feel afraid / Cheri J. Meiners ; illustrations by Meredith Johnson. Minneapolis, MN : Free Spirit Pub., 2003. p. cm. (Learning to get along) SUMMARY: Explains that many things can be frightening and provides examples of what one can do to feel less afraid, such as asking for help from a person one trusts. Includes information and extension activities for parents or teachers. ISBN 1-57542-138-0 DDC 152.4/6
1. Fear in children - Juvenile literature. 2. Fear. 3. Conduct of life. I. Johnson, Meredith, ill. II. Title. III. Series: Meiners, Cheri J., 1957- Learning to get along.
BF723.F4 M45 2003

MEIRI, MENAHEM BEN SOLOMON, 1249-1306.
Halbertal, Moshe. Ben Torah le-ḥokhmah. Yerushalayim : Hotsa'at sefarim ʻa. sh. Y. L. Magnes, ha-Universiṭah ha-ʻIvrit, 760, 2000.
BM755.M54 H35 2000

Meis, Markus.
Oldenburger Symposion zur Psychologischen Akustik (8th : 2000) Contributions to psychological acoustics. 1. ed. Oldenburg : BIS, Bibliotheks- und Informationssystem der Universität Oldenburg, 2000.
BF251 .O44 2000

Meiser, Gerhard.
Rix, Helmut, 1926- Kleine Schriften. Bremen : Hempen, 2001.

Meissner, W. W. (William W.), 1931- The ethical dimension of psychoanalysis : a dialogue / W.W. Meissner. Albany : State University of New York Press, c2003. ix, 371 p. ; 23 cm. (SUNY series in psychoanalysis and culture) Includes bibliographical references (p. 325-353) and indexes. ISBN 0-7914-5690-0 (pbk. : alk. paper) ISBN 0-7914-5689-7 (alk. paper) DDC 150.19/5
1. Psychoanalysis - Moral and ethical aspects. I. Title. II. Series.
BF173 .M3592 2003

Rizzuto, Ana-María. The dynamics of human aggression. New York, NY : Brunner-Routledge, 2003.
BF175.5.A36 R59 2003

Meisterwerke der Architektur.
Baumann, Günter, 1962- Stuttgart : Reclam, c2001.
NA200 .B33 2001

Mekenkamp, Monique.
Searching for peace in Central and South Asia. Boulder, Colo. : Lynne Rienner Publishers, 2002.
JZ5597 .S43 2002

Mekhon Daʻat Yosef (Jerusalem).
[Zohar ḥadash. Lamentations. 2000.] Zohar ḥadash Megilat Ekhah. "Hotsaʼah meyuḥedet li-yeme ben ha-metsarim". Yerushalayim : Mekhon Daʻat Yosef, 761 [2000 or 2001]
BM525.A6 Z6 2001

MELANCHOLY. *See* **SADNESS.**

MELANCHOLY - EARLY WORKS TO 1800.
Velásquez, Andrés, fl. 1553-1615. Libro de la melancholía. Viareggio (Lucca) : M. Baroni, [2002]
BF575.M44 V453 2002

MELANCHOLY IN LITERATURE.
Villari, Rafael Andrés. Literatura e psicanálise. Florianópolis : Editora da UFSC, 2002.

MELANCHTHON, PHILIPP, 1497-1560.
Kuropka, Nicole. Philipp Melanchthon. Tübingen : Mohr Siebeck, c2002.
BR339 .K86 2002

Mélanges David Cohen : etudes sur le langage, les langues, les dialectes, les littératures, offertes par ses élèves, ses collègues, ses amis, présentées à l'occasion de son quatre-vingtième anniversaire / textes réunis et édités par Jérôme Lentin & Antoine Lonnet ; avec l'aide d'Aziza Boucherit ... [et al. ; textes de Abderrahman Ayoub ... et al.]. Paris : Maisonneuve et Larose, 2003. liii, 764 p. : ill. ; 24 cm. Includes bibliographical references and index. Chiefly French; also contributions in English and Arabic. ISBN 2-7068-1674-0 DDC 410
1. Semitic languages. 2. Semitic philology. 3. Language and languages. I. Cohen, David, 1922- II. Lentin, Jérôme. III. Lonnet, Antoine.

Melchiorre, Virgilio.
La persona e i nomi dell'essere. Milano : V&P Università, c2002.
B29 .P414 2002

MELCHIORRE, VIRGILIO.
La persona e i nomi dell'essere. Milano : V&P Università, c2002.
B29 .P414 2002

Mele, Alfred R., 1951- Motivation and agency / Alfred R. Mele. Oxford ; New York : Oxford University Press, 2003. xiii, 264 p. ; 24 cm. Includes bibliographical references (p. 247-255). ISBN 0-19-515617-X (alk. paper) DDC 128/.4
1. Agent (Philosophy) 2. Motivation (Psychology) I. Title.
BD450 .M383 2003

Mellinger, David. The monster in the cave : how to face your fear and anxiety and live your life / David Mellinger and Steven Jay Lynn. 1st ed. New York : Berkley Books, 2003. p. cm. Includes bibliographical references and index. ISBN 0-425-19169-9 DDC 616.85/22
1. Fear. 2. Anxiety. I. Lynn, Steven J. II. Title.
BF575.F2 M45 2003

Mellody, Pia. The intimacy factor : the ground rules for overcoming the obstacles to truth, respect, and lasting love / Pia Mellody and Lawrence S. Freundlich. 1st ed. [San Francisco, CA] : HarperSanFrancisco, c2003. xvi, 215 p. ; 24 cm. Includes index. Publisher description URL: http://www.loc.gov/catdir/description/hc042/2003274949.html ISBN 0-06-009577-6 (hardcover) ISBN 0-06-009580-6 (pbk.) DDC 158.2
1. Intimacy (Psychology) 2. Interpersonal relations. I. Freundlich, Lawrence S. II. Title.
BF575.I5 M45 2003

Mellor, D. H.
Real metaphysics. London ; New York : Routledge, 2003.
BD111 .R227 2003

Melman, Charles, 1931- L'homme sans gravité : jouir à tout prix / Charles Melman ; entretiens avec Jean-Pierre Lebrun. Paris : Denoël, c2002. 264 p. ; 23 cm. (Méditations) Includes bibliographical references. ISBN 2-207-25406-2 DDC 300
1. Psychoanalysis and culture. 2. Civilization, Modern - 21st century. 3. Social psychology. I. Lebrun, Jean Pierre. II. Title.

Mel'nik, Igor', kandidat psikhologicheskikh nauk.
Grachev, Georgiĭ. Manipulirovanie lichnost'i͡u. Moskva : Algoritm, 2002.
BF632.5 .G73 2002

Melucci, Nancy J. Psychology the easy way / Nancy J. Melucci. Hauppauge, N.Y. : Barron's Educational Series, c2004. p. cm. (Easy way) Includes bibliographical references and index. ISBN 0-7641-2393-9 DDC 150
1. Psychology. I. Title. II. Series.
BF121 .M45 2004

Melusine (Rome, Italy)
(1.) Ilardi, Massimo. In nome della strada. Roma : Meltemi, c2002.

Melville, Francis. The book of runes : read the secrets in the language of the stones / Roni Jay. 1st ed. Hauppauge, NY : Barrons, c2003. 128 p. : col. ill., col. map ; 21 cm. "A Quarto book"--T.p. verso. Includes index. ISBN 0-7641-5551-2
1. Runes - Miscellanea. I. Title.
BF1891.R85 M45 2003

MEMBERS OF CONGRESS (UNITED STATES). *See* **LEGISLATORS - UNITED STATES.**

MEMBERS OF CONGRESS (UNITED STATES HOUSE OF REPRESENTATIVES). *See* **LEGISLATORS - UNITED STATES.**

MEMBERS OF CONGRESS (UNITED STATES SENATE). *See* **LEGISLATORS - UNITED STATES.**

MEMBERS OF PARLIAMENT. *See* **LEGISLATORS.**

Mémento retrouvé.
Renouvier, Charles, 1815-1903. Sur le peuple, l'église et la république. Paris : Harmattan, c2002.

La mémoire saturée.
Robin, Régine, 1936- Paris : Stock, 2003.
D16.8 .R59 2003

MEMOIRS. *See* **AUTOBIOGRAPHY; BIOGRAPHY.**

Memória, cultura e sociedade / organização, Icléia Thiesen Magalhães Costa, Evelyn Goyannes Dill Orrico. Rio de Janeiro : 7Letras, 2002. 175 p. ; 21 cm. "Mestrado Memória social e documento"--cover. ISBN 85-7388-299-9
1. Memory - Social aspects. I. Costa, Icléia Thiesen Magalhães. II. Orrico, Evelyn G. D.
BF378.S65 M457 2002

MEMORIA TECHNICA. *See* **MNEMONICS.**

Memoria y crítica de la educación
(5) Cerezo Manrique, Miguel Ángel. Los comienzos de la psicopedagogía en España, 1882-1936. Madrid : Biblioteca Nueva, c2001.

MEMORIAL DAY - HISTORY.
Harmond, Richard P. A history of Memorial Day. New York : P. Lang, c2002.
E642 .H37 2002

MEMORIAL DAY - SOCIAL ASPECTS.
Harmond, Richard P. A history of Memorial Day. New York : P. Lang, c2002.
E642 .H37 2002

MEMORIALS. *See* **HOLIDAYS; MONUMENTS.**

MEMORIALS X PSYCHOLOGICAL ASPECTS.
Edkins, Jenny. Trauma and the memory of politics. Cambridge ; New York : Cambridge University Press, 2003.
BF175.5.P75 E35 2003

MEMORY. *See also* **AUTOBIOGRAPHICAL MEMORY; LEARNING, PSYCHOLOGY OF; MNEMONICS; RECOGNITION**

Memory

(PSYCHOLOGY); RECOLLECTION (PSYCHOLOGY); SHORT-TERM MEMORY.
Turkington, Carol. Hoboken, N.J. : J. Wiley and Sons, c2003.
BF385 .T88 2003

MEMORY.
Arden, John Boghosian. Improving your memory for dummies. New York : Wiley Pub., c2002.
BF385 .A47 2002

Consenstein, Peter. Literary memory, consciousness, and the group Oulipo. Amsterdam ; New York, NY : Rodopi, 2002.

Edkins, Jenny. Trauma and the memory of politics. Cambridge ; New York : Cambridge University Press, 2003.
BF175.5.P75 E35 2003

Freud, Sigmund, 1856-1939. [Zur Psychopathologie des Alltagslebens. English] The psychopathology of everyday life. New York : Penguin Books, 2003.
BF173 .F82513 2003

Gold, Alison Leslie. Fiet's vase and other stories of survival, Europe 1939-1945. New York : Jeremy P. Tarcher/Penguin, c2003.
D804.3 .G64 2003

Gordon, Barry, M.D. Intelligent memory. New York : Viking, 2003.
BF371 .G66 2003

Johnson, Addie. Attention. Thousand Oaks, Calif. : Sage Publications, c2004.
BF321 .J56 2004

Kraft, Robert Nathaniel. Memory perceived. Westport, Conn. : Praeger, 2002.
D804.195 .K73 2002

Neath, Ian, 1965- Human memory. 2nd ed. Australia ; Belmont, CA : Thomson/Wadsworth, c2003.
BF371 .N43 2003

Patzel-Mattern, Katja. Geschichte im Zeichen der Erinnerung. Stuttgart : Franz Steiner, 2002.

Rethinking implicit memory. Oxford ; New York : Oxford University Press, c2003.
RC394.M46 R485 2003

Stier, Oren Baruch, 1966- Committed to memory. 1st ed. Amherst : University of Massachusetts Press, 2003.
D804.3 .S79 2003

Strasser, Gerhard F. Emblematik und Mnemonik der frühen Neuzeit im Zusammenspiel Johannes Buno und Johann Justus Winckelmann. Wiesbaden : Harrassowitz Wolfenbüttel : Herzog August Bibliothek, c2000.
PN6348.5 .S873 2000

Tadié, Jean-Yves, 1936- Le sens de la mémoire. Paris : Gallimard, c1999.
BF371 .T32 1999

Toševski, Jovo. Nerazumna mreža. Novi Sad : Prometej ; [Kragujevac] : Jefimija, c2002.

Wyer, Robert S. Social comprehension and judgment. Mahwah, N.J. : L. Erlbaum Associates, Publishers, 2004.
BF323.S63 W94 2004

Memory and emotion.
McGaugh, James L. New York : Columbia University Press, c2003.
BF378.A87 M34 2003

Memory and emotion / edited by Daniel Reisberg and Paula Hertel. Oxford University Press : New York, 2003. p. cm. (Series in affective science) Includes bibliographical references and index. Table of contents URL: http://www.loc.gov/catdir/toc/ecip041/2003006595.html ISBN 0-19-515856-3 (alk. paper) DDC 152.4
1. Autobiographical memory. 2. Emotions. 3. Psychophysiology. 4. Psychiatry. I. Reisberg, Daniel. II. Hertel, Paula. III. Series.
BF378.A87 M46 2003

MEMORY, AUTOBIOGRAPHICAL. See **AUTOBIOGRAPHICAL MEMORY.**

MEMORY DISORDERS.
Rethinking implicit memory. Oxford ; New York : Oxford University Press, c2003.
RC394.M46 R485 2003

MEMORY IN LITERATURE.
Huyssen, Andreas. Present pasts. Stanford, Calif. : Stanford University Press, 2003.
BD181.7 .H89 2003

Kunst und Erinnerung. Köln : Böhlau, 2003.
PN674 .K86 2003

MEMORY IN OLD AGE.
Mason, Douglas J. The memory workbook. Oakland, CA : New Harbinger Publications, ; c2001. : Distributed in the U.S.A. by Publishers Group West, c2001.
BF724.85.M45 M37 2001

Memory perceived.
Kraft, Robert Nathaniel. Westport, Conn. : Praeger, 2002.
D804.195 .K73 2002

MEMORY (PHILOSOPHY).
Huyssen, Andreas. Present pasts. Stanford, Calif. : Stanford University Press, 2003.
BD181.7 .H89 2003

Marot, Sébastien, 1961- [Art de la mémoire, la territoire et l'architecture] Sub-urbanism and the art of memory. London : Architectural Association, c2003.

MEMORY - PHILOSOPHY.
Passions du passé. Paris : L'Harmattan, c2000.
BF378.S65 P37 2000

MEMORY (PHILOSOPHY).
Steedman, Carolyn. Dust. New Brunswick, N.J. : Rutgers University Press, 2002, c2001.
CD947 .S73 2002

MEMORY - POLITICAL ASPECTS.
Contested pasts. London ; New York : Routledge, 2003.
BF378.S65 C665 2003

Kraut, Bernhard, 1960- Gefangen, auch im Erinnern. Wien : Edition Selene, c2002.

MEMORY - PSYCHOLOGICAL ASPECTS.
Reading, Anna. The social inheritance of the Holocaust. Houndmills [England] ; New York : Palgrave Macmillan, 2002.
D804.3 .R42 2002

MEMORY - SOCIAL ASPECTS.
Archaeologies of memory. Malden, MA ; Oxford : Blackwell, 2003.
CC72.4 .A733 2003

Contested pasts. London ; New York : Routledge, 2003.
BF378.S65 C665 2003

From girls in their elements to women in science. New York : P. Lang, 2003.
BF378.S65 F76 2003

Historiografía y memoria colectiva. 1. ed. Madrid ; Buenos Aires : Miño y Dávila, 2002.

Hofmann, Dorothea. Der Komponist als Heros. Essen : Die Blaue Eule, c2003.

Huyssen, Andreas. Present pasts. Stanford, Calif. : Stanford University Press, 2003.
BD181.7 .H89 2003

Kontexte und Kulturen des Erinnerns. Konstanz : UVK Verlagsgesellschaft, 2002.
BF378.S65 K65 2002

Kraut, Bernhard, 1960- Gefangen, auch im Erinnern. Wien : Edition Selene, c2002.

Kunst und Erinnerung. Köln : Böhlau, 2003.
PN674 .K86 2003

Memória, cultura e sociedade. Rio de Janeiro : 7Letras, 2002.
BF378.S65 M457 2002

Namer, Gérard. Halbwachs et la mémoire sociale. Paris : L'Harmattan, c2000.
BF378.S65 N36 2000

Passions du passé. Paris : L'Harmattan, c2000.
BF378.S65 P37 2000

Reading, Anna. The social inheritance of the Holocaust. Houndmills [England] ; New York : Palgrave Macmillan, 2002.
D804.3 .R42 2002

Remembering Africa. Portsmouth, NH : Heinemann, c2002.
DT14 .R46 2002

Wisenberg, S. L. (Sandi L.) Holocaust girls. Lincoln : University of Nebraska Press, c2002.
DS143 .W645 2002

MEMORY - SOCIAL ASPECTS - ARGENTINA.
Historiografía y memoria colectiva. 1. ed. Madrid ; Buenos Aires : Miño y Dávila, 2002.

MEMORY - SOCIAL ASPECTS - CONGRESSES.
Die Verortung von Gedächtnis. Wien : Passagen, c2001.

MEMORY - SOCIAL ASPECTS - HISTORY.
Wahrheit, Wissen, Erinnerung. Münster : Lit, [2002]

MEMORY TRAINING. See **MNEMONICS.**

The memory workbook.
Mason, Douglas J. Oakland, CA : New Harbinger Publications, ; c2001. : Distributed in the U.S.A. by Publishers Group West, c2001.
BF724.85.M45 M37 2001

MEN. See also **BROTHERS; FATHERS; GAY MEN; HUSBANDS; MASCULINITY; SONS; WHITE MEN; YOUNG MEN.**
Military masculinities. Westport, Conn. : Praeger, 2003.
U21.5 .M4975 2003

Sykes, Bryan. Adam's curse. London ; New York : Bantam, 2003.

MEN - ATTITUDES.
Fraiman, Susan. Cool men and the second sex. New York : Columbia University Press, c2003.
HQ1090 .F73 2003

Goldrick-Jones, Amanda, 1956- Men who believe in feminism. Westport, Conn. ; London : Praeger, 2002.
HQ1236 .G57 2002

MEN - ECUADOR - CONGRESSES.
Masculinidades en Ecuador. Quito, Ecuador : FLACSO ; [S.l.] : UNFPA, 2001.
BF692.5 .M388 2001

MEN - IDENTITY.
Bayers, Peter L., 1966- Imperial ascent. Boulder, Colo. : University Press of Colorado, c2003.
GV200.19.P78 B39 2003

DiPiero, Thomas, 1956- White men aren't. Durham : Duke University Press, 2002.
HQ1090 .D567 2002

Fraiman, Susan. Cool men and the second sex. New York : Columbia University Press, c2003.
HQ1090 .F73 2003

Moulding masculinities. Aldershot, Hants, England ; Burlington, VT : Ashgate, c2003.
BF692.5 .M68 2003

Viveros, M. (Mara) De quebradores y cumplidores. 1a ed. [Colombia] : CES Universidad Nacional de Colombia : Fundación Ford : Profamilia Colombia, 2002.

MEN IN BLACK (UFO PHENOMENON). See **UNIDENTIFIED FLYING OBJECTS - SIGHTINGS AND ENCOUNTERS.**

MEN IN LITERATURE.
Mangan, Michael, 1953- Staging masculinities. Houndmills, Basingstoke, Hampshire : New York : Palgrave Macmillan, 2003.
PN1650.M44 M36 2003

MEN - MISCELLANEA.
Drew, A. J. Wicca spellcraft for men. Franklin Lakes, N.J. : New Page Books, c2001.
BF1571.5.M45 D75 2001

MEN - PHYSIOLOGY.
Jones, Steve, 1944- Y. Boston : Houghton Mifflin, 2003.
GN281 .J62 2003

MEN - POLITICAL ASPECTS.
Working with men in the human services. Crows Nest, N.S.W. : Allen & Unwin, c2001.

MEN - PSYCHOLOGY.
Braudy, Leo. From chivalry to terrorism. New York : Alfred A. Knopf : Distributed by Random House, 2003.
HQ1090 .B7 2003

Cook, Margaret, 1944- Lords of creation. London : Robson, 2002.

Kundtz, David, 1937- Nothing's wrong. Boston, MA : Conari Press, 2004.
BF692.5 .K86 2004

Kyriazi, Paul. The complete live the James Bond lifestyle seminar. Los Angeles, CA : Ronin Books, c2002.
BF637.S8 K97 2002

Pieroni, Osvaldo. Pene d'amore. Soveria Mannelli : Rubbettino, c2002.

Weinberg, George H. Why men won't commit. New York : Atria Books, c2002.

BF619 .W45 2002

MEN - RELATIONS WITH WOMEN. *See* **MAN-WOMAN RELATIONSHIPS.**

MEN SEXUAL ABUSE VICTIMS. *See* **MALE SEXUAL ABUSE VICTIMS.**

MEN - SEXUAL BEHAVIOR. *See also* **HOMOSEXUALITY, MALE.**
Evolution, gender, and rape. Cambridge, Mass. : MIT Press, c2003.
HV6558 .E92 2003

MEN - SOCIALIZATION.
Karras, Ruth Mazo, 1957- From boys to men. Philadelphia : University of Pennsylvania Press, c2003.
HQ775 .K373 2003

MEN, WHITE. *See* **WHITE MEN.**

Men who believe in feminism.
Goldrick-Jones, Amanda, 1956- Westport, Conn. ; London : Praeger, 2002.
HQ1236 .G57 2002

MEN-WOMEN RELATIONSHIPS. *See* **MAN-WOMAN RELATIONSHIPS.**

Ménager, Daniel.
Cité des hommes, cité de Dieu. Genève : Droz, 2003.
PN723 .C584 2003

MÉNAGER, DANIEL - BIBLIOGRAPHY.
Cité des hommes, cité de Dieu. Genève : Droz, 2003.
PN723 .C584 2003

Menapace, Mamerto.
El milagro y el valor de la vida. 1. ed. Buenos Aires : Patria Grande, 2000.

Ménasé, Stéphanie.
Merleau-Ponty, Maurice, 1908-1961. L'institution dans l'histoire personnelle et publique ; [Paris] : Belin, c2003.
B2430.M3763 I88 2003

Passivité et création : Merleau-Ponty et l'art moderne / Stéphanie Ménasé. Paris : Presses universitaires de France, c2003. ix, 264 p. : ill. ; 21 cm. (Pratiques théoriques) Includes bibliographical references (p. 249-[257]) and index. ISBN 2-13-052399-4 DDC 194
1. Merleau-Ponty, Maurice, - 1908-1961. 2. Expression (Philosophy) 3. Aesthetics. 4. Phenomenology. I. Title. II. Series.

Mencius.
Selections. Chinese & English. 1998.
Confucius. [Selections. Chinese & English. 1998] Kong Meng ren sheng ge yan ji cui. Wuhan : Wuhan gong ye da xue chu ban she, 1998.

MENDEL'S LAW. *See* **GENETICS.**

Mendelson, Shahar.
Machine Learning Summer School 2002 (2002 : Canberra, N.C.T.) Advanced lectures on machine learning. Berlin ; New York : Springer, 2003.
Q325.5 .M344 2002

Méndez, José Luis, 1941- El irresistible encanto de Betty la fea / José Luis Méndez. San Juan, P.R. : Ediciones Milenio, 2001. 106 p. ; 21 cm. ISBN 1-88174-804-9
1. Yo soy Betty la fea (Television program) 2. Soap operas - Social aspects - Colombia. 3. Soap operas - Colombia - History and criticism. 4. Television and women - Colombia. 5. Feminism. I. Title. II. Title: Betty la fea

MENDICANT ORDERS. *See* **FRIARS.**

MENDING. *See* **REPAIRING.**

MENDIVE, CARLOS (MENDIVE ARBELOA).
Sobre las identidades. Pamplona : Universidad Pública de Navarra, [2001]

Menegaldo, Hélène.
Figures de la marge. Rennes : Presses universitaires de Rennes, [2002]

Menéndez, Eduardo L. La parte negada de la cultura : relativismo, diferencias y racismo / Eduardo L. Menéndez. Barcelona : Edicions Bellaterra, c2002. 421 p. ; 22 cm. (Serie General universitaria ; 16) Includes bibliographical references (p. [397]-421). ISBN 84-7290-186-6
1. Culture conflict. 2. Racism. 3. Ethnology. I. Title. II. Series.
HM1121 .M46 2002

Meng, Wuqi, 1966-.
Han, Zhen. Li shi zhe xue. Di 1 ban. Kunming : Yunnan ren min chu ban she, 2002.
D16.8 .H3597 2002

Menger, Pierre-Michel. Portrait de l'artiste en travailleur : métamorphoses du capitalisme / Pierre-Michel Menger. Paris : Seuil, c2002. 96 p. : ill. ; 21 cm.

(La république des idées) Includes bibliographical references. ISBN 2-02-057892-1 DDC 300
1. Creation (Literary, artistic, etc.) - Social aspects. 2. Capitalism. I. Title. II. Series.

Meniaĭlov, Alekseĭ. Durilka : Zapiski zi︠a︡ti︠a︡ glavravvina : utonchennye priemy skrytogo upravleniia / Alekseĭ Meniaĭlov. Moskva : "Kraft+", 2003. 275 p. ; 21 cm. "Psikhologiia prakticheskoĭ vlasti"--Cover. ISBN 5936750418
1. Executors and administrators - Russia. 2. Philosophy, Russian. 3. National characteristics, Russian. 4. Russia - Civilization. I. Title. II. Title: Zapiski zi︠a︡ti︠a︡ glavravvina III. Title: Utonchennye priemy skrytogo upravleniia

MENOPAUSE.
Spiraldancer. Moon rites. South Melbourne : [Great Britain] : Lothian, 2002.

MENOPAUSE - PSYCHOLOGICAL ASPECTS.
Marraccini, Eliane Michelini. Encontro de mulheres. São Paulo : Casa do Psicólogo, c2001.

Mens sana in corpore insepulto.
Cruz, Mariano de la, 1921-1999. 1. ed. Barcelona : Edicions 62, 2002.

El mensaje de los santos.
Place, Robert Michael. [Gnostic book of saints. Spanish] St. Paul, Minn. : Llewellyn Español, 2003.
BF1879.T2 P5518 2003

Mensch & Musik : Diskussionsbeiträge im Schnittpunkt von Musik, Medizin, Physiologie und Psychologie / Gabriele Hofmann, Claudia Trübsbach (Hg.). Augsburg : Wissner, c2002. 134 p. : ill. ; 24 cm. (Forum Musikpädagogik, 0946-543X ; Bd. 51) Papers principally from an undated symposium at the Volkshochschule München. Includes bibliographical references. CONTENTS: Wirkungen von Musik : Musikpsychologische Forschungsergebnisse / Heiner Gembris -- Genie auf Zeit / Marianne Hassler -- Lampenfieber und Auffüngsängste sind nicht dasselbe ; Was träumen Musiker? Können wir mit Hilfe der neurobiologischen Traumforschung Musiker besser verstehen? / Helmut Möller -- Überlastungsbeschwerden bei Instrumentalmusikern / Albrecht Lahme -- Musik in Anästhesie und Schmerztherapie / Ralph Spintge -- Zwischen den Stühlen : Versuch der Positionsbestimmung einer jungen Alten : der Musiktherapie. ISBN 3-89639-290-5
1. Music - Psychological aspects - Congresses. 2. Music therapy. 3. Musicians - Health and hygiene. 4. Genius. 5. Stage fright. I. Hofmann, Gabriele. II. Trübsbach, Claudia. III. Title: Mensch und Musik IV. Title: Diskussionsbeiträge im Schnittpunkt von Musik, Medizin, Physiologie und Psychologie V. Series.
ML3830 .M46 2002

Der Mensch als Wesen der Freiheit.
Schlosser, Herta. Vallendar-Schönstatt : Patris Verlag, 2002.

Mensch, James R. Ethics and selfhood : alterity and the phenomenology of obligation / James Richard Mensch. Albany, NY : State University of New York Press, c2003. ix, 215 p. ; 23 cm. Includes bibliographical references (p. 205-210) and indexes. ISBN 0-7914-5751-6 (alk. paper) ISBN 0-7914-5752-4 (pbk. : alk. paper) DDC 170
1. Ethics. 2. Phenomenology. 3. Self (Philosophy) 4. Other (Philosophy) I. Title.
B945.M4853 E84 2003

Mensch und Geschichte.
Stiehler, Gottfried. Köln : PapyRossa, c2002.
D16.8 .S75 2002

Mensch und Kunst.
Spoerri, Hubert M. München : Scaneg, c2002.

Mensch und Musik.
Mensch & Musik. Augsburg : Wissner, c2002.
ML3830 .M46 2002

Der Mensch vor seinem eigenen Anspruch.
Braun, Edmund. Würzburg : Königshausen & Neumann, 2002.

Mensen, machten, mogelijkheden.
Dunk, Hermann Walther von der. Amsterdam : B. Bakker, 2002.

MENSES. *See* **MENSTRUATION.**

MENSTRUAL CYCLE. *See* **MENSTRUATION.**

MENSTRUATION - MYTHOLOGY.
Spiraldancer. Moon rites. South Melbourne : [Great Britain] : Lothian, 2002.

MENSURATION.
Khadiratna, Dayanidhi. Brhat śilpaśāstra, bā, Grhabandha bijñāna ; Grhabandha gaṇanā o śubhastambhāropaṇa bicāra. Kaṭaka : Dharmagrantha Shtora, [1995?]

TH4809.14 K48 1995

Mental aerobics - .
Bruce, Barbara. Nashville : Abingdon Press, c2003.
BF632 .B78 2003

Mental causation and the metaphysics of mind : a reader / edited by Neil Campbell. Peterborough, Ont. : Broadview Press, c2003. 301 p. ; 23 cm. Includes bibliographical references. ISBN 1-55111-509-3 DDC 128/.2
1. Philosophy of mind. 2. Mind and body. 3. Causation. I. Campbell, Neil, 1967-

MENTAL CHRONOMETRY. *See* **TIME PERCEPTION.**

MENTAL DISCIPLINE. *See also* **EDUCATION; MEMORY; MNEMONICS.**
Bruce, Barbara. Mental aerobics--. Nashville : Abingdon Press, c2003.
BF632 .B78 2003

Sivananda, Swami. Thought power. 13th ed. Uttaranchal, Himalayas, India : Divine Life Society, 2002.

MENTAL DISEASES. *See* **MENTAL ILLNESS.**

MENTAL DISORDERS. *See* **MENTAL ILLNESS.**

MENTAL EFFICIENCY.
Bruce, Barbara. Mental aerobics--. Nashville : Abingdon Press, c2003.
BF632 .B78 2003

MENTAL FATIGUE. *See* **BOREDOM.**

MENTAL HEALERS. *See* **HEALERS.**

MENTAL HEALING. *See* **HEALERS; MIND AND BODY.**

MENTAL HEALING.
Braud, William. Distant mental influence. Charlottesville, VA : Hampton Roads Pub., c2003.
BF1045.S33 B74 2003

MENTAL HEALING.
Curcio, Kimberly Panisset. Man of light. 1st ed. New York : SelectBooks, c2002.
BF1045.M44 C87 2002

Grace, Raymon. The future is yours. Charlottesville, VA : Hampton Roads Pub., c2003.
BF639 .G64 2003

Nudel, Michael. 21st century's new chakra healing. Los Angeles, CA : Bio-Energy System Services, c2000.
BF1999 .N83 2000

MENTAL HEALING.
Sayers, Janet. Divine therapy. Oxford ; New York : Oxford University Press, 2003.
BF175.4.R44 S28 2003

MENTAL HEALING.
Sayers, Janet. Divine therapy. Oxford ; New York : Oxford University Press, 2003.
BF175.4.R44 S28 2003

Tubali, Shy. [Selections] Boḳer ṭov 'olam. Tel Aviv : Yedi'ot aḥaronot : Sifre ḥemed, c2003.

MENTAL HEALTH. *See* **MENTAL ILLNESS; PERSONALITY; PSYCHIATRY; PSYCHOLOGY; SELF-ACTUALIZATION (PSYCHOLOGY); STRESS (PSYCHOLOGY).**

MENTAL HEALTH.
Kaluzniacky, Eugene. Managing psychological factors in information systems work. Hershey PA : Information Science Pub., c2004.
BF576 .K358 2004

Mental health and mass violence [electronic resource] : evidence-based early psychological intervention for victims/survivors of mass violence : a workshop to reach consensus on best practices / U.S. Department of Health and Human Services ... [et al.]. [Bethesda, MD : National Institute of Mental Health, 2002] (NIH publication : no. 02-5138) System requirements: Adobe Acrobat Reader. Mode of access: Internet from the NIMH web site. Address as of 8/14/03: http://www.nimh.nih.gov/research/massviolence.pdf; current access available via PURL. Title from title screen (viewed on Aug. 14, 2003). URL: http://purl.access.gpo.gov/GPO/LPS34086 Available in other form: Mental health and mass violence v, 109 p. (DLC) 2003431138 (OCoLC)52639006.
1. Crisis intervention (Mental health services) 2. Mass murder - Psychological aspects. 3. Victims of crimes - Psychology. 4. Victims of terrorism - Psychology. 5. Violence. I. United States. Dept. of Health and Human Services. II. National Institute of Mental Health (U.S.) III. Title: Mental health and mass violence v, 109 p. IV. Series.

Mental health and mass violence v, 109 p.
Mental health and mass violence [electronic resource]. [Bethesda, MD : National Institute of Mental Health, 2002]

MENTAL HEALTH CARE. *See* **MENTAL HEALTH SERVICES.**

MENTAL HEALTH COUNSELING. *See* **PSYCHOTHERAPY.**

MENTAL HEALTH FACILITIES. *See* **PSYCHIATRIC HOSPITALS.**

MENTAL HEALTH PERSONNEL. *See* **PSYCHIATRISTS.**

MENTAL HEALTH - RELIGIOUS ASPECTS.
Goleman, Daniel. Destructive emotions. New York : Bantam Books, c2003.
BL65.E46 G65 2003

MENTAL HEALTH SERVICES - BRAZIL - HISTORY.
Psiquiatria, loucura e arte. São Paulo, SP, Brasil : Edusp, c2002.

MENTAL HOSPITALS. *See* **PSYCHIATRIC HOSPITALS.**

MENTAL HYGIENE. *See* **MENTAL HEALTH.**

MENTAL ILLNESS. *See also* **MENTAL HEALTH.**
Imagination and its pathologies. Cambridge, Mass. : MIT Press, c2003.
BF408 .I455 2003

Michael, Pamela. Care and treatment of the mentally ill in North Wales, 1800-2000. Cardiff : University of Wales Press, 2003.

Pagés Larraya, Fernando. Liturgia lunar de la locura. Córdoba, Argentina : Comunicarte Editorial, c2002.

Soler, Colette. L'inconscient à ciel ouvert de la psychose. Toulouse : Presses universitaires du Mirail, c2002.

MENTAL ILLNESS AND ART. *See* **ART AND MENTAL ILLNESS.**

MENTAL ILLNESS - BRAZIL - HISTORY.
Psiquiatria, loucura e arte. São Paulo, SP, Brasil : Edusp, c2002.

MENTAL ILLNESS - ETIOLOGY.
Fabrega, Horacio. Origins of psychopathology. New Brunswick, N.J. : Rutgers University Press, c2002.
RC454.4 .F33 2002

Keppe, Norberto R. [Origem Das Enfermidades. English] The origin of illness. 1st American ed. Englewood Cliffs, N.J. : Campbell Hall Press, 2002.
RC460 .K4713 2002

MENTAL ILLNESS - ETIOLOGY - SOCIAL ASPECTS.
Fabrega, Horacio. Origins of psychopathology. New Brunswick, N.J. : Rutgers University Press, c2002.
RC454.4 .F33 2002

MENTAL ILLNESS - GENETIC ASPECTS.
Fabrega, Horacio. Origins of psychopathology. New Brunswick, N.J. : Rutgers University Press, c2002.
RC454.4 .F33 2002

MENTAL ILLNESS - PATIENTS. *See* **MENTALLY ILL.**

MENTAL ILLNESS - POPULAR WORKS.
Keppe, Norberto R. [Origem Das Enfermidades. English] The origin of illness. 1st American ed. Englewood Cliffs, N.J. : Campbell Hall Press, 2002.
RC460 .K4713 2002

MENTAL ILLNESS - TREATMENT.
Strock, Margaret. Medications [electronic resource]. [4th ed., rev. Apr. 2002, repr. Sept. 2002]. [Bethesda, Md.] : Dept. of Health and Human Services, Public Health Service, National Institutes of Health, National Institute of Mental Health, 2002.

MENTAL IMAGERY (PSYCHOLOGY). *See* **IMAGERY (PSYCHOLOGY).**

MENTAL IMAGES. *See* **IMAGERY (PSYCHOLOGY).**

MENTAL INSTITUTIONS. *See* **PSYCHIATRIC HOSPITALS.**

MENTAL MAPS. *See* **GEOGRAPHICAL PERCEPTION.**

Mental model of teachers with different teaching experience who teach different subject matter about the structure of children's minds and its functioning in learning.
Shilony, Tamar. Model mental̲i shel morim menusim ye-tironim be-miḳtsoʻot madaʻiyim ye-humaniyim le-gabe lemidah be-ḳerev yeladim. [Israel : h. mo. l., 1994?]

MENTAL PATIENTS. *See* **MENTALLY ILL; PSYCHOTHERAPY PATIENTS.**

MENTAL PHILOSOPHY. *See* **PHILOSOPHY; PSYCHOLOGY.**

MENTAL PRAYER. *See* **MEDITATION.**

MENTAL REPRESENTATION.
Gordon, Andrew S. Strategy representation. Mahwah, NJ. : L. Erlbaum, 2003.
BF316.6 .G67 2003

Hayat, Michaël. Dynamique des formes et représentations. Paris : Harmattan, c2002.
B105.R4 H392 2002

O'Callaghan, John (John P.) Thomist realism and the linguistic turn. Notre Dame, Ind. : University of Notre Dame Press, c2003.
BD161 .O3 2003

Pylyshyn, Zenon W., 1937- Seeing and visualizing. Cambridge, Mass. : MIT Press, 2003.
BF241 .P95 2003

MENTAL REPRESENTATION - SOCIAL ASPECTS.
Social cognition. Malden, MA : Blackwell Pub., 2003.
BF316.6 .S65 2003

MENTAL RETARDATION. *See* **INTELLECT.**

MENTAL STEREOTYPE. *See* **STEREOTYPE (PSYCHOLOGY).**

MENTAL STRESS. *See* **STRESS (PSYCHOLOGY).**

MENTAL SUGGESTION. *See also* **BRAINWASHING; SUBLIMINAL PROJECTION.**
Cherepanova, I. IU. (Irina IUrʹevna) Dom kolduni. Perer., dop. i ispravlennoe izd. Moskva : KSP+, 2001.
BF1156.S8 C53 2001

Goldberg, Bruce, 1948- Self-hypnosis. Franklin Lakes, NJ : New Page Books, c2001.
BF1156.S8 G65 2001

Vasilʹev, Leonid Leonidovich. Experiments in mental suggestion. [Rev. ed.]. Charlottesville, VA : Hampton Roads Pub., c2002.
BF1156.S8 V313 2002

MENTAL TELEPATHY. *See* **TELEPATHY.**

MENTAL TESTS. *See* **INTELLIGENCE TESTS; PSYCHOLOGICAL TESTS.**

MENTAL TYPES. *See* **TYPOLOGY (PSYCHOLOGY).**

Der mentale Zugang zur Welt.
Willaschek, Marcus. Frankfurt am Main : Klostermann, 2003.
B835 .W55 2003

La mentalidad literaria medieval.
Carmona Fernández, Fernando. 1. ed. Murcia : Universidad de Murcia, Servicio de Publicaciones, 2001.

Mentalistika.
Akopov, G. V. Samara : Samarskiĭ gos. pedagog. universitet, 2001.
BF108.R8 A478 2001

MENTALLY HANDICAPPED. *See* **MENTALLY ILL.**

MENTALLY ILL. *See* **PSYCHOTHERAPY PATIENTS.**

MENTALLY ILL - ATTITUDES.
Keppe, Norberto R. [Origem Das Enfermidades. English] The origin of illness. 1st American ed. Englewood Cliffs, N.J. : Campbell Hall Press, 2002.
RC460 .K4713 2002

MENTALLY ILL - HOSPITALS. *See* **PSYCHIATRIC HOSPITALS.**

La mente in Cartesio.
Landucci, Sergio, 1938- Milano : FrancoAngeli, c2002.

La mente silenziosa.
Cimatti, Felice. 1. ed. Roma : Editori riuniti, 2002.

The mentee's guide to mentoring.
Cohen, Norman H. (Norman Harris), 1941- Amherst, Mass. : HRD Press, c1999.

MENTICIDE. *See* **BRAINWASHING.**

Mentor manager, mentor parent.
Dowling, Linda Culp. Burneyville, OK : ComCon Books., c2002.
BF637.C6 D6185 2002

Mentored by a millionaire.
Scott, Steve, 1948- Hoboken, N.J. : J. Wiley & Sons, 2004.
BF637.S8 S388 2004

MENTORING.
Buckley, Maureen A., 1964- Mentoring children and adolescents. Westport, Conn. : Praeger, 2003.
BF637.C6 B8 2003

Danzig, Robert J., 1932- Every child deserves a champion. Washington, DC : Child & Family Press, c2003.
BF637.E53 D36 2003

Dowling, Linda Culp. Mentor manager, mentor parent. Burneyville, OK : ComCon Books., c2002.
BF637.C6 D6185 2002

Global perspectives on mentoring. Greenwich : Information Age Pub., 2004.
BF637.M48 G57 2004

The situational mentor. Burlington, VT : Gower, 2004.
BF637.M48 S56 2004

Stoddard, David A., 1953- The heart of mentoring. Colorado Springs, Colo. : NavPress, 2003.
BF637.C6 S773 2003

Mentoring children and adolescents.
Buckley, Maureen A., 1964- Westport, Conn. : Praeger, 2003.
BF637.C6 B8 2003

MENTORING IN BUSINESS.
Bell, Chip R. Managers as mentors. 2nd ed., completely rev. and expanded. San Francisco, Calif : Berrett-Koehler Publishers, c2002.
HF5385 .B45 1996

Cloke, Ken, 1941- The art of waking people up. 1st ed. San Francisco : Jossey-Bass, c2003.
HF5385 .C54 2003

Cohen, Norman H. A step-by-step guide to starting an effective mentoring program. Amherst, Mass. : HRC Press, c2000.
HF5385 .C64 2000

Cohen, Norman H. (Norman Harris), 1941- The mentee's guide to mentoring. Amherst, Mass. : HRD Press, c1999.

Dowling, Linda Culp. Mentor manager, mentor parent. Burneyville, OK : ComCon Books., c2002.
BF637.C6 D6185 2002

MENTORING IN THE PROFESSIONS.
Dowling, Linda Culp. Mentor manager, mentor parent. Burneyville, OK : ComCon Books., c2002.
BF637.C6 D6185 2002

MENUS. *See* **DINNERS AND DINING.**

Menzhulin, V. (Vadim), 1968- Raskoldovyvaia IUnga : ot apologetiki k kritike / V. Menzhulin. Kiev : Izd-vo "Sfera", 2002. 199 p. ; 20 cm. Title on colophon: Rozvorozhuĭuchy IUnga. Summary in Ukrainian. Includes bibliographical references (p. 191-199). ISBN 9667841448
1. Jung, C. G. - (Carl Gustav), - 1875-1961. 2. Psychoanalysis. I. Title. II. Title: Rozvorozhuĭuchy IUnga
BF173.J85 M46 2002

Meo, Giuseppe.
Petich, Giuseppe, 1869-1953. Divagazioni filosofiche del reverendo Giuseppe Petich tratte dai frammenti del suo "Zibaldone". Roma : Bulzoni, 2002.

Meo, Oscar. Mondi possibili : un'indagine sulla costruzione percettiva dell'oggetto estetico / Oscar Meo. Genova : Il melangolo, c2002. 187 p. : ill. ; 21 cm. (Università ; 58) Includes bibliographical references (p. 169-181) and index. ISBN 88-7018-458-7 DDC 701
1. Art - Philosophy. 2. Visual perception. 3. Semiotics. I. Title.
N68.3 .M46 2002

MERCHANDISE, BRANDED. *See* **BRAND NAME PRODUCTS.**

Merdalor, Jean. Pensées mortelles : [essais] / Jean Merdalor. Port-au-Prince, Haiti : Editions Choucoune, 1999. 74 p. ; 21 cm.
1. Haiti - Civilization - Philosophy. 2. Meaning (Philosophy) 3. Life. 4. Death. 5. Conduct of life. 6. Black author. I. Title.

La mère absente.
Tremblay-Dupré, Thérèse. Monaco : Rocher, 2003.

MERGER OF CORPORATIONS. See **CONSOLIDATION AND MERGER OF CORPORATIONS.**

MERGERS, CORPORATE. See **CONSOLIDATION AND MERGER OF CORPORATIONS.**

Merinero, María Jesús.
Diálogo de civilizaciones Oriente-Occidente. [Madrid] : Biblioteca Nueva ; [Cáceres, España] : Universidad de Extremadura, c2002.

Merkaba.
Kiefer, Anselm, 1945- New York : Gagosian Gallery, c2002.
N6888.K43 A4 2002

Merkaz la-'arakhim ba-'asaḳim ye-aḥrayut ḥevratit.
Tamari, Meir. Maśa u-matan be-emunah. Yerushalayim : Śimḥonim, [761, 2001]

MERKAZ LA-'ARAKHIM BA-'ASAḲIM YE-AḤRAYUT ḤEVRATIT.
Tamari, Meir. Maśa u-matan be-emunah. Yerushalayim : Śimḥonim, [761, 2001]

Merleau-Ponty, Maurice, 1908-1961. L'institution dans l'histoire personnelle et publique ; Le problème de la passivité, le sommeil, l'inconscient, la mémoire : notes de cours au collège de France, 1954-1955 / Maurice Merleau-Ponty ; textes établis par Dominique Darmaillacq, Claude Lefort et Stéphanie Ménasé ; préface de Claude Lefort. [Paris] : Belin, c2003. 296 p. ; 22 cm. (Littérature et politique, 0985-9632) Includes bibliographical references. ISBN 2-7011-3301-7 DDC 194
1. Philosophy, Modern - 20th century. 2. Philosophy, Modern - 19th century. 3. Phenomenology. I. Darmaillacq, Dominique. II. Lefort, Claude. III. Ménasé, Stéphanie. IV. Title. V. Title: Problème de la passivité, le sommeil, l'inconscient, la mémoire VI. Title: Institution, la passivité VII. Series: Littérature & politique.
B2430.M3763 I88 2003

[Union de l'âme et du corps chez Malebranche, Biran et Bergson. English]
The incarnate subject : Malebranche, Biran, and Bergson on the union of body and soul / Maurice Merleau-Ponty ; preface by Jacques Taminiaux ; translation by Paul B. Milan ; edited by Andrew G. Bjelland, Jr. and Patrick Burke. Amherst, N.Y. : Humanity Books, 2001. 152 p. : ill. ; 24 cm. (Contemporary studies in philosophy and the human sciences) Includes bibliographical references (p. 137-138) and indexes. ISBN 1-57392-915-8 (cloth : alk. paper) DDC 128
1. Malebranche, Nicolas, - 1638-1715. 2. Maine de Biran, Pierre, - 1766-1824. 3. Bergson, Henri, - 1859-1941. 4. Mind and body. 5. Monism. I. Bjelland, Andrew G. II. Burke, Patrick. III. Title. IV. Series.
B2430.M379 U513 2001

MERLEAU-PONTY, MAURICE, 1908-1961.
Heinamaa, Sara, 1960- Toward a phenomenology of sexual difference. Lanham, Md. ; Oxford : Rowman & Littlefield Publishers, c2003.
HQ1208.B3523 2003

Ménasé, Stéphanie. Passivité et création. Paris : Presses universitaires de France, c2003.

Merleau-Ponty. Paris : Vrin ; Milano : Mimesis, 2001.

Merleau-Ponty : non-philosophie et philosophie avec deux notes inédites sur la musique / [numéro coordonné par Leonard Lawlor] = Non-philosophy and philosophy with two unpublished notes on music / [volume coordinated by Leonard Lawlor] = Non filosofia e filosofia con due note inedite sulla musica / [numero coordinato da Leonard Lawlor]. Paris : Vrin ; Milano : Mimesis, 2001. 414 p. ; 21 cm. (Chiasmi international ; nouv. sér.) Includes bibliographical references. ISBN 2-7116-4305-0 ISBN 88-8483-059-1 DDC 100
1. Merleau-Ponty, Maurice, - 1908-1961. 2. Philosophy. 3. Philosophy, Modern - 20th century. 4. Philosophy, European - 20th century. I. Title: Non-philosophy and philosophy with two unpublished notes on music II. Title: Non filosofia e filosofia con due note inedite sulla musica III. Series.

Merlo Lillo, Vicente. La fascinación de Oriente : el silencio de la meditación y el espacio del corazón / Vicente Merlo. 1. ed. Barcelona : Editorial Kairós, 2002. 277 p. ; 20 cm. (Sabiduría perenne) Includes bibliographical references (p. 257-263). ISBN 84-7245-490-8
1. Philosophy, Asian. 2. Philosophy, Indic. I. Title. II. Series: Colección Sabiduría perenne.

Mermelshṭain, Avraham Yitsḥaḳ Dayid. Ḳuntres Dover mesharim : be-'inyan ona'at devarim yeha-isur le-vazot ule-tsa'er et havero : be-tseruf 'uvdot ye-sipure tsadiḳim : be-Idish / ne'erakh ye-nilḳat ye-yo. l. 'a. y. Avraham Yitsḥaḳ Dayid Mermelshṭain.

Hotsa'ah 2. [Brooklyn] : A.Y.D. Mermelshṭain, 762 [2001] 148 p. ; 24 cm. Cover title: Sefer Dover mesharim. Spine title: Dover mesharim. In Yiddish.
1. Ethics, Jewish. 2. Brotherliness - Religious aspects - Judaism. 3. Interpersonal relations - Religious aspects - Judaism. I. Title. II. Title: Sefer Dover mesharim III. Title: Dover mesharim

Mero kathā mero gītā.
Diyara Kalyāṇa, mero kathā mero gītā. 1. saṃskaraṇa. [Kathmandu] : Sañjanā Gautama, 2059- [2002-
BF789.S8+

MEROVINGIANS - FOOD - SOCIAL ASPECTS.
Effros, Bonnie, 1965- Creating community with food and drink in Merovingian Gaul. 1st ed. New York ; Houndmills, England : Palgrave Macmillan, 2002.
GT2853.F7 E34 2002

Merrell, Floyd, 1937- Sensing corporeally : toward a posthuman understanding / Floyd Merrell. Toronto ; Buffalo : University of Toronto Press, c2003. xiv, 359 p. : ill. ; 24 cm. (Toronto studies in semiotics and communication) Includes bibliographical references (p. [331]-348) and index. ISBN 0-8020-3704-6 DDC 121/.68
1. Semiotics. 2. Consciousness. 3. Comprehension (Theory of knowledge) I. Title. II. Series.
P99.M477 2003

Merrens, Matthew R.
Shaffer, Lary. Research stories for introductory psychology. 2nd ed. Boston, MA : Allyn and Bacon, c2004.
BF76.5.S43 2004

Merritt, Jon.
Bloch, Douglas, 1949- The power of positive talk. Rev. and updated ed. Minneapolis, Minn. : Free Spirit Pub., 2003.
BF723.S3 B56 2003

Mersmann, Paul. Kaleidoskopische Schriften / Paul Mersmann ; mit drei Originalradierungen des Verfassers. Hamburg : Maximilian-Gesellschaft, 2002. 117 p : ill. ; 25 cm. (Veröffentlichung der Maximilian-Gesellschaft für das Jahr ; 2001) Library copy signed by author. ISBN 3-921743-50-8 (geb.)
1. Philosophy. I. Title.

Mertvi pro vartistʹ ʹzhyttiā ne rozkaz̆hutʹ
Andrushkiv, Bohdan, 1947- Po toï bik bezodni, abo, Mertvi pro vartistʹ ʹzhyttiā ne rozkaz̆hutʹ. Ternopilʹ : "Pidruchnyky & posibnyky", 1997.
HV6545.A616 1997

Meschonnic, Henri, 1932-.
La modernité après le post-moderne. Paris : Maisonneuve & Larose, [2002]

Mesilot teshuvah.
Cordovero, Moses ben Jacob, 1522-1570. Sefer Mesilot teshuvah. Bene Beraḳ : Da'at ḳedoshim, 762 [2002]
BM645.R45 C67 2002

Meskimmon, Marsha.
Breaking the disciplines. London ; New York : I.B. Tauris, 2003.
BD175.B74 2003

Mesoamerican worlds
Aveni, Anthony F. Empires of time. Rev. ed. Boulder, Colo. : University Press of Colorado, c2002.
QB209.A94 2002

Mesopotamian planetary astronomy-astrology.
Brown, David, 1968- Groningen : Styx, 2000.
BF1714.A86 B76 2000

Messages from the archetypes.
Gilbert, Toni. Ashland, Or. : White Cloud Press, c2003.
BF1879.T2 G53 2003

Messenger, Charles M. Nine Wind Tonalamatl Tolteca-fate papers : the fifty-two year cycle. [United States] : C.M. Messenger, c2002- v. <1 > : ill. (some col.) ; 28 cm. Cover title: Tonalamatl Tolteca. On cover: Nine Wind, the prophecy calendar. PARTIAL CONTENTS: 1. Ninewind-Tonalamatl Toltecа.
1. Fortune-telling. 2. Tlaxcalan calendar. I. Title. II. Title: Tonalamatl Tolteca III. Title: Nine Wind, the prophecy calendar
BF1861.M47 2002

Messenger, Sharon.
Darwin, Charles, 1809-1882. Autobiographies. London : Penguin, 2002.

MESSIAH. See **MESSIANIC ERA (JUDAISM).**

MESSIAH - JUDASIM.
Wasserman, Elhanan Bunim, 1875-1941. Ḳovets ma'amre 'Iḳvata de-Meshiḥa .... Yerushalayim : Yeshivat Or Elḥanan, 762 [2001 or 2002]

MESSIANIC ERA (JUDAISM).
Wasserman, Elhanan Bunim, 1875-1941. Ḳovets ma'amre 'Iḳvata de-Meshiḥa .... Yerushalayim : Yeshivat Or Elḥanan, 762 [2001 or 2002]

MESSIANISM, POLITICAL - UNITED STATES.
York, Neil Longley. Turning the world upside down. Westport, Conn. ; London : Praeger, 2003.
E210.Y67 2003

MESSING, VOL'F, 1899-1974.
Küppers, Topsy, 1931- Wolf Messing. München : Langen Müller, c2002.
BF1027.M47 K87 2002

Meta-cultura.
Piscitelli, Alejandro. Buenos Aires : La Crujía, 2002.
P96.T42 P575

META KNOWLEDGE. See **METACOGNITION.**

METABOLISM - DISORDERS. See **OBESITY.**

METACOGNITION - CONGRESSES.
Applied metacognition. Cambridge, U.K. ; New York : Cambridge University Press, 2002.
BF311.A638 2002

Thinking and seeing. Cambridge, MA : Mit Press, 2004.
BF241.T48 2004

Metadecisions.
Van Gigch, John P. New York : Kluwer Academic/Plenum Publishers, c2003.
HM701.V36 2003

METAFICTION. See **FICTION; FICTION - TECHNIQUE.**

Metafizicheskaia antropologiia.
Avdeev, V. B. (Vladimir Borisovich) Moskva : Belye al'vy, 2002.
DK510.763.A93 2002

Metáfora y discurso filosófico / edición de José M. Sevilla Fernández, Manuel Barrios Casares. Madrid : Tecnos, 2000. 236 p. : charts ; 21 cm. (Ventana abierta) Includes bibliographical references (p. 225-227) and index. ISBN 84-309-3523-1 (pbk.)
1. Metaphor. 2. Philosophy. I. Sevilla Fernández, José M. II. Barrios Casares, Manuel. III. Series: Colección Ventana abierta.

Metaforens magt.
Jensen, Anders Fogh. 1. opl. Århus : Modtryk, 2001.

MetaLinguistica
(Bd. 7) Wort und (Kon)text. Frankfurt : Lang, 2001.
P325.5.C65 W678 2001

METALS, TRANSMUTATION OF. See **ALCHEMY.**

METAMATHEMATICS. See **LOGIC, SYMBOLIC AND MATHEMATICAL.**

METAMEMORY. See **METACOGNITION.**

Metamorfosi della città / Benno Albrecht ... [et al.] ; a cura di Leonardo Benevolo. Milano : Garzanti / Scheiwiller, 1995 (1996 printing) xvi, 486 p. : ill. (some col.) ; 29 cm. (Civitas europaea) "Credito italiano"--T.p. verso. Includes bibliographical references. ISBN 88-7644-230-8
1. Cities and towns - History. 2. City planning - History. 3. Civilization - History. I. Albrecht, Benno Andres, 1957- II. Benevolo, Leonardo. III. Credito italiano. IV. Series.
HT111.M472 1995

La métamorphose impensable.
Castel, Pierre-Henri. Paris : Gallimard, c2003.
HQ77.9.C38 2003

Metamorphosen der Schönheit.
Penz, Otto. Wien : Turia + Kant, c2001.
GT495.P459 2001

Métamorphoses de la dialectique dans les dialogues de Platon.
Dixsaut, Monique. Paris : Vrin, c2001.
B398.D5 D598 2001

METAMORPHOSIS - FOLKLORE. See **WEREWOLVES.**

The metamorphosis of magic from late antiquity to the early modern period / edited by Jan N. Bremmer and Jan R. Veenstra. Leuven ; Dudley, MA : Peeters, 2002. xiv, 317 p. ; 25 cm. (Groningen studies in cultural change ; v. 1) Errata slip tipped in. Includes bibliographical references (p. [283]-305) and index. ISBN 90-429-1227-8 (alk. paper) DDC 133.4/309
1. Magic - History. I. Bremmer, Jan N. II. Veenstra, Jan R., 1939- III. Series.
BF1589.M55 2002

METAPHOR.
Alefirenko, M. F. Poėticheskaia ėnergiia slova. Moskva : Academia, 2002.
P35 .A544 2002

Blumenberg, Hans. Ästhetische und metaphorologische Schriften. 1. Aufl. Frankfurt : Suhrkamp, 2001.

Jensen, Anders Fogh. Metaforens magt. 1. opl. Århus : Modtryk, 2001.

Lambert, Ladina Bezzola. Imagining the unimaginable. Amsterdam ; New York, NY : Rodopi, 2002.
QB29 .L35 2002

Metáfora y discurso filosófico. Madrid : Tecnos, 2000.

A metaphysical analysis of the concept of reincarnation.
Echekwube, A. O. (Anthony Onyebuchi) Ekpoma, Nigeria : Ambrose Alli University Publishing House, 2002.

Metaphysical techniques that really work.
Davis, Audrey Craft. Nevada City, CA : Blue Dolphin Pub., 2004.
BF1411 .D38 2004

METAPHYSICS. See also **COSMOLOGY; GOD; KNOWLEDGE, THEORY OF; PHILOSOPHY OF MIND; SUBSTANCE (PHILOSOPHY); VALUES.**
D'Oro, Giuseppina, 1964- Collingwood and the metaphysics of experience. London ; New York : Routledge, 2002.
B1618.C74 D67 2002

Dufour, Adrian. Ciencia y logica de mundos posibles. Bern : Lang, 2001.

Fogelin, Robert J. Walking the tightrope of reason. Oxford ; New York : Oxford University Press, 2003.
BC177 .F64 2003

Gibson, Arthur, 1943- Metaphysics and transcendence. London ; New York : Routledge, 2003.
BT40 .G53 2003

Hübner, Benno. Sinn in Sinn-loser Zeit. Wien : Passagen, c2002.

Maler, Arkadiĭ. Strategii sakral'nogo smysla. Moskva : Parad izdatel'skiĭ dom, 2003.

Maritain, Jacques, 1882-1973. [Degrés du savoir. English] Distinguish to unite, or, The degrees of knowledge. Notre Dame, Ind. : University of Notre Dame Press, 1998, c1995.
BD162 .M273 1998

Molnar, George, d. 1999. Powers. Oxford ; New York : Oxford University Press, 2003.
BD541 .M54 2003

Plantinga, Alvin. Essays in the metaphysics of modality. Oxford ; New York : Oxford University Press, 2003.
B945.P553 M48 2003

Plessner, Helmuth, 1892- Elemente der Metaphysik. Berlin : Akademie, 2002.
BD113 .P56 2002

Prudentia und Contemplatio. Paderborn : Ferdinand Schöningh, 2002.

Real metaphysics. London ; New York : Routledge, 2003.
BD111 .R227 2003

Ruffinengo, Pier Paolo, 1937- Ontonèesis. 1. ed. Genova : Marietti, 2002.

Russell, Bertrand, 1872-1970. Russell on metaphysics. London ; New York : Routledge, 2003.
B1649.R91 M86 2003

Salamucha, Jan. [Selections. English. 2003] Knowledge and faith. Amsterdam ; New York, NY : Rodopi, 2003.

Sanna, Manuela. La "fantasia, che è l'occhio dell'ingegno". Napoli : A. Guida editore, c2001.
B3583 .S26 2001

Solodin, A. I. Strategiia ontologicheskoĭ igry. Sankt-Peterburg : Aleteĭa, 2002.
BF237 .S6 2002

Soukup, Johannes. Metaphysik der Zeit oder Wirklichkeit und Wissen. Deutsche 1. Ausg. Wien : Passagen Verlag, c1998.

Stalnaker, Robert. Ways a world might be. Oxford : Clarendon ; New York : Oxford University Press, 2003.

BD111 .S73 2003

Vallicella, William F. A paradigm theory of existence. Dordrecht ; Boston : Kluwer Academic, c2002.
BD331 .V36 2002

Wagner, Rudolf G. Language, ontology, and political philosophy in China. Albany : State University of New York Press, c2003.
B126 .W284 2003

Westphal, Merold. Overcoming onto-theology. 1st ed. New York : Fordham University Press, 2001.
BR100 .W47 2001

Wind, Edgar, 1900- Das Experiment und die Metaphysik. 1. Aufl. Frankfurt am Main : Suhrkamp, 2001.

Witt, Charlotte, 1951- Ways of being. Ithaca : Cornell University Press, 2003.
B434 .W59 2003

Wohlers, Christian. Wie unnütz ist Descartes? Würzburg : Königshausen & Neumann, c2002.

Zur Verwindung der Methaphysik. Bonn : Bouvier, 2002.

Metaphysics and transcendence.
Gibson, Arthur, 1943- London ; New York : Routledge, 2003.
BT40 .G53 2003

METAPHYSICS - HISTORY.
The medieval heritage in early modern metaphysics and modal theory, 1400-1700. Dordrecht ; Boston : Kluwer Academic Publishers, c2003.
BD111 .M47 2003

METAPHYSICS (PARAPSYCHOLOGY). See **PARAPSYCHOLOGY.**

METAPHYSICS - PSYCHOLOGICAL ASPECTS.
Gelven, Michael. What happens to us when we think. Albany : State University of New York Press, c2003.
BD111 .G45 2003

Metaphysik der Zeit oder Wirklichkeit und Wissen.
Soukup, Johannes. Deutsche 1. Ausg. Wien : Passagen Verlag, c1998.

METAPSYCHOLOGY. See **SPIRITUALISM.**

Metcalfe, David.
Raiffa, Howard, 1924- Negotiation analysis. Cambridge, MA : Belknap Press of Harvard University Press, 2002.
HD58.6 .R342 2002

Metchnikoff, Elie, 1845-1916.
 Selections. 2002.
Russkaia rasovaia teoriia do 1917 goda. Moskva : Feri-V, 2002.

METEOROLOGY. See **SEASONS.**

METHOD OF WORK. See **WORK.**

METHODOLOGY. See also **ANALYSIS (PHILOSOPHY); PROBLEM SOLVING; RESEARCH.**
Baggini, Julian. The philosopher's toolkit. Malden, MA : Blackwell Publishers, 2003.
BC177 .B19 2003

Methodology in the social sciences
Fraley, R. Chris. How to conduct behavioral research over the internet. New York : Guilford Press, 2005.
BF76.6.I57 F73 2005

Methods in behavioral research.
Cozby, Paul C. 8th ed. Boston : McGraw-Hill, c2004.
BF76.5 .C67 2004

Metody diagnostiki trevozhnosti.
Kostina, L. M. (Lиubov' Mikhaĭlovna) Sankt-Peterburg : Rech', 2002.
BF575.A6 K65 2002

METOPOSCOPY. See **PHYSIOGNOMY.**

METROLOGY.
Khurmetbek, Khalikiĭn. Ŭl bichigdmėlüüd. Ulaanbaatar : "Monsudar" Khėvlėliĭn Gazar, 2001.
QA465 .K48 2001

Metzinger, Thomas, 1958-
Conscious experience. Paderborn : Schöningh/Imprint Academic, 1995 (Lawrence, Kan. : Allen Press)
BF311 .C6443 1995

MEXICA INDIANS. See **AZTECS.**

MEXICO - HISTORY - CONQUEST, 1519-1540 - HISTORIOGRAPHY.
Restall, Matthew, 1964- Seven myths of the Spanish conquest. Oxford ; New York : Oxford University Press, 2003.

F1230 .R47 2003

MEXICO - POLITICS AND GOVERNMENT - 1910-1946.
Guerra Manzo, Enrique. Caciquismo y orden público en Michoacán, 1920-1940. 1. ed. México : El Colegio de México, Centro de Estudios Sociológicos, c2002.
F1219.3.P7 G84 2002

Meyer-Abich, Klaus Michael, 1936-.
Philosophie der natürlichen Mitwelt. Würzburg : Königshausen & Neumann, 2002.

Meyer, Birgit.
Magic and modernity. Stanford, Calif. : Stanford University Press, 2003.
GN475.3 .M34 2003

Meyer, Gerd. Freiheit wovon, Freiheit wozu? : politische Psychologie und Alternativen humanistischer Politik bei Erich Fromm : Darstellung - Interpretation - Kritik / Gerd Meyer. Opladen : Leske + Budrich, 2002. 216 p. : ill. ; 21 cm. Includes bibliographical references (p. 209-216). ISBN 3-8100-3396-0 (pbk.)
1. Fromm, Erich, - 1900- 2. Political psychology. I. Title.

Meyer, John, 1964- Kids talking : learning relationships and culture with children / John Meyer. Lanham, MD : Rowman & Littlefield, c2003. p. cm. Includes bibliographical references and index. ISBN 0-7425-2705-0 (cloth : alk. paper) ISBN 0-7425-2706-9 (pbk. : alk. paper) DDC 302.3/46/083
1. Interpersonal communication in children. 2. Interpersonal relations in children. I. Title.
BF723.C57 M49 2003

Meyer, Michel. Michel Meyer présente Manifestes du surréalisme d'André Breton. Paris : Gallimard, 2002. 182 p. ; 18 cm. (Foliothèque ; 108) Cover title: Michel Meyer commente Manifestes du surréalisme d'André Breton. Includes bibliographical references. ISBN 2-07-041999-1 DDC 809
1. Breton, André, - 1896-1966. - Manifestes du surréalisme. 2. Surrealism. 3. Arts, Modern - 20th century. I. Title. II. Title: Manifestes du surréalisme d'André Breton III. Title: Michel Meyer commente Manifestes du surréalisme d'André Breton IV. Series.
NX600.S9 B735 2002

Meyer, Philip. Precision journalism : a reporter's introduction to social science methods / Philip Meyer. 4th ed. Lanham, Md. : Rowman & Littlefield Publishers, c2002. viii, 263 p. : ill. ; 24 cm. Includes bibliographical references and index. Table of contents URL: http://www.loc.gov/catdir/toc/fy02/2001048802.html ISBN 0-7425-1087-5 (alk. paper) ISBN 0-7425-1088-3 (pbk. : alk. paper) DDC 070.4/07/23
1. Journalism. 2. Social sciences - Statistical methods. I. Title.
PN4775 .M48 2002

Meyer-Plantureux, Chantal.
Rolland, Romain, 1866-1944. Le théâtre du peuple. Nouvelle éd. Bruxelles : Complexe, c2003.
PN1655 .R68 2003

Meyuhas Ginio, Alisa, 1937- Kerovim u-reḥokim : 'iyunim be-sugyot she-ben Yehudim le-Notsrim bi-Sefarad shel yeme ha-benayim / 'Alizah Meyuhas G'ini'o. Tel Aviv : Mif'alim Universitayim, 760 [1999] 315 p. ; 23 cm. (Ibero-Amerikah) Title on verso of t.p.: Together yet apart : Jews and Christians in the Medieval Iberian Peninsula. Includes bibliographical references (p. 309-310) and index. ISBN 9653720414
1. Spain - History - 711-1492. 2. Judaism - History - Medieval and early modern period, 425-1789. 3. Church history - Middle Ages, 600-1500. 4. Judaism - Relations - Christianity. 5. Christianity and other religions - Judaism. 6. Spain - Ethnic Relations. I. Title. II. Title: Together yet apart : Jews and Christians in the Medieval Iberian Peninsula

Mezhdunarodnaia psikhologicheskaia konferentsiia "Psikhicheskoe razvitie v ontogeneze--zakonomernosti i vozmozhnye periodizatsii" (1999 : Moscow, Russia) Problemy psikhologii razvitiia : materialy mezhdunarodnoĭ psikhologicheskoĭ konferentsii "Psikhicheskoe razvitie v ontogeneze--zakonomernosti i vozmozhnye periodizatsii", Moskva, 19-22 oktiabria 1999 g. / [pod redaktsieĭ Kravtsovoĭ E.E. (glavnyĭ redaktor), Spiridonova V.F.]. Moskva : RGGU, 2000. 382 p. : ill. ; 20 cm. Includes bibliographical references.
1. Developmental psychology - Congresses. I. Kravtsova, E. E. II. Spiridonov, V. F. III. Title.
BF712.5 .M49 2000

Mezhdunarodnyĭ nezavisimyĭ ėkologo-politologicheskiĭ universitet.
Psikhologiia razvitiia i vozrastnaia psikhologiia. Moskva : Izd-vo MNĖPU, 2001-
BF712.5 .P75 2001

Mezhregional'naia Rossiĭskaia nauchno-prakticheskaia konferentsiia "Psikhologicheskie osobennosti preodoleniia ėkstremal'nykh i ėmotsiogennykh situatsiĭ v podrostkovo-iunosheskom vozraste" (2002 : Syktyvkar, Russia)
Psikhologicheskie osobennosti preodoleniia ėkstremal'nykh i ėmotsiogennykh situatsiĭ v podrostkovo-iunosheskom vozraste : materialy Rossiĭskoĭ mezhregional'noĭ nauchno-prakticheskoĭ konferentsii. 26-28 sentiabria 2002 g. Syktyvkar : Syktyvkarskiĭ gos. universitet, 2002. 293 p. : ill. ; 21 cm. ISBN 5872373074
1. Adolescent psychology - Russia (Federation) - Congresses. 2. Youth - Psychology - Congresses. 3. College students - Psychology - Congresses. I. Syktyvkarskiĭ gosudarstvennyĭ universitet. II. Title.
BF724 .M48 2002

Mezhvuzovskaia nauchnaia konferentsiia "Gender, vlast', kul'tura: sotsial'no-antropologicheskiĭ podkhod" (2000 : Saratov, Russia).
Gender, vlast', kul'tura. Saratov : Saratovskiĭ gos. tekhn. universitet, 2000.
HQ1075 .G4667 2000

Mezias, Stephen J. Organizational dynamics of creative destruction : entrepreneurship and the emergence of industries / Stephen J. Mezias and Elizabeth Boyle. Houndmills [England] ; New York : Palgrave Macmillan, 2002. ix, 213 p. : ill. ; 23 cm. Includes bibliographical references (p. 197-210) and index. ISBN 0-333-99862-6 DDC 338/.04
1. Schumpeter, Joseph Alois, - 1883-1950. 2. Entrepreneurship. 3. Creative ability in business. 4. Technological innovations - Economic aspects. 5. New business enterprises. I. Boyle, Elizabeth, 1961- II. Title.
HB615 .M49 2002

Mi-'Ba'al shed' le-'Ba'al Shem'.
Oron, Michal. Yerushalayim : Mosad Byalik : Bet ha-sefer le-mada'e ha-Yahadut 'a. sh. Hayim Rozenberg, Universitat Tel-Aviv, c763 [2002]

Mi she-ṭa'am yayin Hungari.
Eyal, Tsevi. Tel Aviv : Yedi'ot aharonot : Sifre hemed, c2002.

Mi-torato de-rabi El'azar.
Shakh, El'azar Menahem Man. Sefer Mi-torato de-rabi El'azar. [Bene Berak] : le-haśig mishpahat Kohen, [763 i.e. 2003]

Mian xiang.
Henning, Hai Lee Yang. London : Vega, 2001.
BF851 .H46 2001

Michael, Pamela. Care and treatment of the mentally ill in North Wales, 1800-2000 / Pamela Michael. Cardiff : University of Wales Press, 2003. xiii, 252 p. : ill., ports., map ; 22 cm. Includes bibliographical references and index. ISBN 0-7083-1740-5
1. North Wales Hospital for Nervous and Mental Disorders, Denbigh. 2. War - History. 3. Hospitals - History. 4. Mental illness. 5. Medical care - History. 6. Denbigh (Wales) I. Title.

River of words. Berkeley, Calif. : Heyday Books, c2003.
PS595.W374 R58 2003

Michalon, Clair. Histoire de différences, différence d'histoires / Clair Michalon. Saint-Maur : Sépia, c2002. 117 p. : ill. ; 22 cm. Includes bibliographical references. ISBN 2-8428-0069-9 DDC 300
1. Social evolution. 2. Culture. 3. Civilization - History. 4. Civilization - Philosophy. I. Title.

Michalski, Anthony R.
Haanel, Charles F. (Charles Francis), b. 1866. The master key system. 1st ed. Wilkes-Barre, Pa. : Kallisti Pub., c2000.
BF639 .H132 2000

Michel-Andino, Andreas, 1961- Kleine Philosophie des Lachens : ein Essay über das Phänomen des Komischen / Andreas Michel-Andino. Koblenz : Fölbach, c2000. 96 p. : ill. ; 21 cm. ISBN 3-934795-03-X (pbk.)
1. Laughter. 2. Comic, The. I. Title.
BF575.L3 M53 2000

Michel Meyer commente Manifestes du surréalisme d'André Breton.
Meyer, Michel. Michel Meyer présente Manifestes du surréalisme d'André Breton. Paris : Gallimard, 2002.
NX600.S9 B735 2002

Michel Meyer présente Manifestes du surréalisme d'André Breton.
Meyer, Michel. Paris : Gallimard, 2002.
NX600.S9 B735 2002

MICHELANGELO BUONARROTI, 1475-1564.
Goffen, Rona, 1944- Renaissance rivals. New Haven : University Press, c2002.
N6915 .G54 2002

Michelat, Guy.
Aux frontières des attitudes. Paris, France : Harmattan, c2002.

Michelet, Jules, 1798-1874. La cité des vivants et des morts : préfaces et introductions / Michelet ; présentées par Claude Lefort. [Paris] : Belin, c2002. 475 p. ; 22 cm. (Littérature et politique, 0985-9632) ISBN 2-7011-2811-0 DDC 944
1. Historiography. 2. History - Philosophy. I. Title. II. Series: Littérature & politique.

MICHOACÁN DE OCAMPO (MEXICO) - POLITICS AND GOVERNMENT.
Guerra Manzo, Enrique. Caciquismo y orden público en Michoacán, 1920-1940. 1. ed. México : El Colegio de México, Centro de Estudios Sociológicos, c2002.
F1219.3.P7 G84 2002

Mickaharic, Draja. Spiritual cleansing : a handbook of psychic protection / Draja Mickaharic. York Beach, ME : Red Wheel/Weiser, 2003. p. cm. Originally published: York Beach, Me. : S. Weiser, 1982. Includes bibliographical references and indexes. Table of contents URL: http://www.loc.gov/catdir/toc/ecip042/2003008389.html CONTENTS: The spiritual man -- Malochia, or "the evil eye" -- Protection while asleep -- Cleansing with baths -- Cleansing with water -- Cleansing with eggs -- Cleansing with incense -- Quieting a house -- Quieting the mind -- Selecting a spiritual practitioner. ISBN 1-57863-278-1 DDC 131
1. Parapsychology. I. Title.
BF1040 .M53 2003

Mickey Mouse toddler.
Disney's Mickey Mouse toddler [electronic resource]. Burbank, CA : Disney Interactive, c2000.
BF719

The micro-politics of capital.
Read, Jason. Albany : State University of New York Press, c2003.
HB97.5 .R42 2003

MICROCHIPS. See **INTEGRATED CIRCUITS.**

MICROECONOMICS. See also **PRODUCTION (ECONOMIC THEORY).**
Beyond Keynes. Cheltenham ; Northampton, Mass. : Edward Elgar, c2002.

MICROELECTRONICS. See **INTEGRATED CIRCUITS.**

MICROENTERPRISES. See **SMALL BUSINESS.**

Mićunović, Dragoljub. Filozofija minima / Dragoljub Mićunović. Beograd : "Filip Višnjić", 2001. 354 p. ; 21 cm. (Libertas) Includes bibliographical references. In Serbian (Roman). ISBN 86-7363-298-6
1. Social sciences - Philosophy. 2. Political science - Philosophy. 3. Philosophy. I. Title. II. Series: Libertas (Belgrade, Serbia)
H61.15 .M5 2001

The mid-career tune-up.
Salmon, William A. New York : Amacom, c2000.
HF5381 .S256 2000

MID-EAST PEACE PROCESS. See **ARAB-ISRAELI CONFLICT - 1993- - PEACE.**

Middelton-Moz, Jane, 1947- Good and mad : transform anger using mind, body, soul, and humor / Jane Middelton-Moz, Lisa Tener, Peaco Todd ; cartoons by Peaco Todd. Deerfield Beach, Fla. : Health Communications Inc., c2003. xxvii, 281 p. : ill. ; 16 x 23 cm. Includes bibliographical references (p. 277-280). ISBN 0-7573-0102-9 DDC 152.4/7
1. Anger. I. Tener, Lisa. II. Todd, Peaco. III. Title.
BF575.A5 M519 2003

MIDDLE AGE. See also **AGING; CLIMACTERIC.**
Kirasic, K. C. Midlife in context. Boston : McGraw-Hill, c2004.
BF724.6 .K55 2004

MIDDLE AGE - HEALTH AND HYGIENE.
How healthy are we? Chicago, Ill. : University of Chicago Press, c2003.
BF724.6 .H69 2003

MIDDLE AGE - PSYCHOLOGICAL ASPECTS.
Frayne, Jill. Starting out in the afternoon. Toronto : Random House Canada, c2002.

How healthy are we? Chicago, Ill. : University of Chicago Press, c2003.
BF724.6 .H69 2003

Kirasic, K. C. Midlife in context. Boston : McGraw-Hill, c2004.
BF724.6 .K55 2004

Powers, Marilyn. The bridge between two lifetimes. Phoenix, AZ : Sophia Publications, c1999.
BF724.6 .P68 1999

MIDDLE AGE - SOCIAL ASPECTS.
How healthy are we? Chicago, Ill. : University of Chicago Press, c2003.
BF724.6 .H69 2003

MIDDLE AGED PERSONS - PSYCHOLOGY.
Kirasic, K. C. Midlife in context. Boston : McGraw-Hill, c2004.
BF724.6 .K55 2004

Powers, Marilyn. The bridge between two lifetimes. Phoenix, AZ : Sophia Publications, c1999.
BF724.6 .P68 1999

Zoglio, Suzanne Willis. Create a life that tickles your soul. Doylestown, Pa. : Tower Hill Press, c1999.
BF724.65.S44 Z65 1999

MIDDLE AGES. See **ARCHITECTURE, MEDIEVAL; CIVILIZATION, MEDIEVAL; RENAISSANCE.**

The Middle Ages.
Jolly, Karen Louise. Philadelphia : University of Pennsylvania Press, 2002, 2001. 12 300 xiv, 280 p. ; 24 cm.
BF1593 .J65 2002

MIDDLE AGES.
Deutschland und der Westen Europas im Mittelalter. Stuttgart : Thorbecke, c2002.

Ducret, Alix. La vie au moyen âge. Courtaboeuf : Didro, c2002.

Medieval Europe, 814-1350. Detroit, MI : Gale Group, c2002.
D102 .M38 2001

MIDDLE AGES - CIVILIZATION. See **CIVILIZATION, MEDIEVAL.**

MIDDLE AGES - HISTORIOGRAPHY.
Medieval cultures in contact. New York : Fordham University Press, 2003.
CB351 .M3922 2003

MIDDLE AGES - HISTORY. See also **CRUSADES; KNIGHTS AND KNIGHTHOOD.**
The 1000s. San Diego, Calif. : Greenhaven Press, c2001.
CB354.3 .A16 2001

Topographies of power in the early Middle Ages. Leiden ; Boston : Brill, 2001.
D117 .T67 2001

The Middle Ages series
Karras, Ruth Mazo, 1957- From boys to men. Philadelphia : University of Pennsylvania Press, c2003.
HQ775 .K373 2003

MIDDLE AGES - STUDY AND TEACHING.
Cohen, Jeffrey Jerome. Medieval identity machines. Minneapolis : University of Minnesota Press, c2003.
CB353 .C64 2003

MIDDLE CLASS IN LITERATURE.
Fichtelberg, Joseph. Critical fictions. Athens : University of Georgia Press, c2003.
PS366.S35 F53 2003

MIDDLE EAST - CIVILIZATION.
Antinomies of modernity. Durham : Duke University Press, 2003.
CB358 .A59 2003

MIDDLE EAST - FOREIGN RELATIONS - UNITED STATES.
Diálogo de civilizaciones Oriente-Occidente. [Madrid] : Biblioteca Nueva ; [Cáceres, España] : Universidad de Extremadura, c2002.

MIDDLE EAST - LITERATURES.
Nissinen, Martti. Prophets and prophecy in the ancient Near East. Atlanta, GA : Society of Biblical Literature, c2003.
BF1762 .N58 2003b

MIDDLE EAST PEACE PROCESS. See **ARAB-ISRAELI CONFLICT - 1993- - PEACE.**

MIDDLE EAST - POLITICS AND GOVERNMENT.
Grant, George, 1954- The blood of the moon. Nashville, Tenn. : Thomas Nelson Publishers, 2002.
DS62 .G73 2002

MIDDLE EASTERN LITERATURE.
Nissinen, Martti. Prophets and prophecy in the ancient Near East. Leiden ; Boston : Brill, 2003.

BF1762 .N58 2003

MIDDLE EASTERN PEACE PROCESS. *See* **ARAB-ISRAELI CONFLICT - 1993- - PEACE.**

MIDDLE ENGLISH. *See* **ENGLISH LANGUAGE - MIDDLE ENGLISH, 1100-1500.**

MIDDLE ENGLISH CHRISTIAN LITERATURE. *See* **CHRISTIAN LITERATURE, ENGLISH (MIDDLE).**

MIDDLE ENGLISH LITERATURE. *See* **ENGLISH LITERATURE - MIDDLE ENGLISH, 1100-1500.**

The middle mind.
White, Curtis, 1951- 1st ed. [San Francisco] : HarperSanFrancisco, c2003.

MIDEAST. *See* **MIDDLE EAST.**

Midgley, Mary, 1919- The myths we live by / Mary Midgley. London ; New York : Routledge, 2003. x, 192 p. ; 24 cm. Includes bibliographical references and index. ISBN 0-415-30906-9 DDC 191
1. Myth. 2. Symbolism. 3. Philosophy. I. Title.
BL304 .M53 2003

Mídia e pânico.
Contrera, Malena Segura. 1. ed. São Paulo : Annablume : FAPESP, 2002.

MIDLIFE. *See* **MIDDLE AGE.**

MIDLIFE CRISIS.
Powers, Marilyn. The bridge between two lifetimes. Phoenix, AZ : Sophia Publications, c1999.
BF724.6 .P68 1999

Midlife in context.
Kirasic, K. C. Boston : McGraw-Hill, c2004.
BF724.6 .K55 2004

Midrash Ekhah.
[Zohar ḥadash. Lamentations. 2000.] Zohar ḥadash Megilat Ekhah. "Hotsa'ah meyuḥedet li-yeme ben ha-metsarim". Yerushalayim : Mekhon Da'at Yosef, 761 [2000 or 2001]
BM525.A6 Z6 2001

Midrash ha-neʻlam Lamentations.
[Zohar ḥadash. Lamentations. 2000.] Zohar ḥadash Megilat Ekhah. "Hotsa'ah meyuḥedet li-yeme ben ha-metsarim". Yerushalayim : Mekhon Da'at Yosef, 761 [2000 or 2001]
BM525.A6 Z6 2001

Midrash ha-neʻlam Ruth.
[Zohar ḥadash. Lamentations. 2000.] Zohar ḥadash Megilat Ekhah. "Hotsa'ah meyuḥedet li-yeme ben ha-metsarim". Yerushalayim : Mekhon Da'at Yosef, 761 [2000 or 2001]
BM525.A6 Z6 2001

MIDRASH - HISTORY AND CRITICISM - THEORY, ETC.
Neusner, Jacob, 1932- Analysis and argumentation in Rabbinic Judaism. Lanham, Md. : University Press of America, c2003.
BM496.5 .N4775 2003

Midrash Rut.
[Zohar ḥadash. Lamentations. 2000.] Zohar ḥadash Megilat Ekhah. "Hotsa'ah meyuḥedet li-yeme ben ha-metsarim". Yerushalayim : Mekhon Da'at Yosef, 761 [2000 or 2001]
BM525.A6 Z6 2001

Midwest studies in philosophy
(v. 26) Renaissance and early modern philosophy. Malden, MA ; Oxford : Blackwell Pub., c2002.
B775 .R46 2002

MIDWIFERY. *See also* **MIDWIVES.**
Hadikin, Ruth. The bullying culture. Oxford ; Boston : Books for Midwives, 2000.
BF637.B85 H33 2000

MIDWIFERY - ORGANIZATION & ADMINISTRATION - GREAT BRITAIN.
Hadikin, Ruth. The bullying culture. Oxford ; Boston : Books for Midwives, 2000.
BF637.B85 H33 2000

MIDWIVES. *See* **MIDWIFERY.**

MIDWIVES - SUPERVISION OF.
Hadikin, Ruth. The bullying culture. Oxford ; Boston : Books for Midwives, 2000.
BF637.B85 H33 2000

El miedo : reflexiones sobre su dimensión social y cultural / Jean Delumeau ... [et al.]. Medellín, Colombia : Corporación Región, 2002. 246 p. ; 21 cm. "Agosto de 2001 en Medellín...el seminario 'La construcción social del miedo. Una lectura de la experiencia en las ciudades contemporáneas'"--p. 6. Includes bibliographies. CONTENTS: Presentación / M.I. Villa Martínez -- Miedos de ayer y de hoy / J. Delumeau -- Las incidencias del miedo en la política: una mirada desde Hobbes / M.T. Uribe de H. -- Somos ciudades sin muros: el temor y la política en la síntesis tomana / J.G. Ramírez -- Seguridad: historia de una palabra y de un concepto / J. Delumeau -- Las rutas narrativas de los miedos: sujetos cuerpos y memorias / P. Riaño Alcalá -- Miedos y secretos en la memoria de la represión política: un estudio de caso en la frontera argentino-brasileña / A. Grimson -- Nuestros miedos / N. Lechner -- Que te coge el holandés: miedos y conjuros en la ciudad de San Juan / S. Álvarez Curbelo -- Eco del miedo en Santafé de Bogotá e imaginarios de sus ciudadanos / S. Niño Murcia -- La vivienda: los miedos de la ciudad / J. Echavarría -- Caras y contracaras del miedo en Medellín / L.A. Sánchez Medina, M.I. Villa Martínez y A.M. Jaramillo Arbeláez. ISBN 958-813-410-2 (pbk.)
1. Fear - Congresses. 2. Fear - Social aspects - Congresses. 3. Fear - Political aspects - Congresses. I. Delumeau, Jean.
BF575.F2 M494 2002

Miele, Frank.
Jensen, Arthur Robert. Intelligence, race, and genetics. Boulder, Colo. : Westview Press, c2002.
BF431 .J396 2002

Jensen, Arthur Robert. Intelligence, race, and genetics. Boulder, Colo. : Westview, 2002.

Mielenz, Cecile Culp.
Dowling, Linda Culp. Mentor manager, mentor parent. Burneyville, OK : ComCon Books., c2002.
BF637.C6 D6185 2002

Mifalaḥemy i mahiĭa ŭ belaruskim abradavym fal'klory.
Kazakova, I. V. (Iryna Valer'eŭna) Minsk : "BOFF", 1997.
GR203.4 .K39 1997

Migdal Ḥanan'el.
Sefer ʻAmude ha-Kabalah. Yerushalayim : Nezer Sheraga, 761 [2001]

Migdele ha-teʼomim be-diluge otiyot ba-Torah.
Glazerson, Matityahu. Yerushalayim : Yerid ha-sefarim, 2002.

Mighty fine words and smashing expressions.
Hargraves, Orin. Oxford ; New York : Oxford University Press, 2003.
PE1711 .H37 2003

Mignot, Ana Chrystina Venancio.
Destinos das letras. Passo Fundo : Universidade de Passo Fundo, 2002.
P211 .D47 2002

Migration, diasporas, and transnationalism / edited by Steven Vertovec and Robin Cohen. Cheltenham, UK ; Northampton, MA : Edward Elgar, 1999. xxviii, 663 p. ; 25 cm. (The international library of studies on migration ; 9) (An Elgar reference collection) Includes bibliographical references and index. ISBN 1-85898-869-1 DDC 304.8
1. Emigration and immigration. 2. Emigrant remittances. 3. Group identity. 4. Statelessness. 5. Internationalism. 6. Nationalism. I. Vertovec, Steven. II. Cohen, Robin, 1944- III. Series. IV. Series: An Elgar reference collection
JV6032 .M54 1999

MIGRATION, INTERNATIONAL. *See* **EMIGRATION AND IMMIGRATION.**

Miguriñci mikutelusā?.
Gōpālakr̥ṣṇa, Pi. Es. Hyderabad : Media House Publications, 2002.
BF637.S4 G655 2002

Mijolla-Mellor, Sophie de. Le besoin de savoir : théories et mythes magico-sexuels dans l'enfance / Sophie de Mijolla-Mellor. Paris : Dunod, c2002. 231 p. ; 24 cm. (Psychismes) ISBN 2-10-004491-5 DDC 150
1. Sex (Psychology) 2. Infant psychology. 3. Children and sex. I. Title. II. Series.
BF723.S4 M556 2002

Mikhaĭlov, A. D. (Andreĭ Dmitrievich).
Svobodnyĭ vzgli͡ad na literaturu. Moskva : Nauka, 2002.

MIKKYŌ. *See* **TANTRIC BUDDHISM.**

El milagro y el valor de la vida / [René Favaloro, Luis Landriscina, Mamerto Menapace]. 1. ed. Buenos Aires : Patria Grande, 2000. 85 p. : ill. ; 20 cm.17. "Luna Park, 8 de diciembre de 1997." ISBN 950-546-125-9
1. Quality of life. 2. Life - Moral and ethical aspects. 3. Values. I. Favaloro, René G., 1923- II. Landriscina, Luis, 1935- III. Menapace, Mamerto.

Miler, Avigdor Hakohen. Sefer Torat Avigdor : maʼamarim ve-siḥot be-ʻinyene daʻat u-musar ve-ḥokmat ha-yirʼah asher hishmia' le-ḥaverim makshivim ... / Avigdor Hakohen Miller (Miler) Bene Braḳ : [ḥ. mo. l], 762- [2001 or 2002- v. ; 23 cm. Cover title: Torat Avigdor. CONTENTS: [1] Shenat 729 -- [2] Shenot 721, 722, 728.
1. Ethics, Jewish. 2. Jewish sermons, Hebrew. I. Title. II. Title: Torat Avigdor

Miletto, Gianfranco, 1960-.
Portaleone, Abraham ben David, 1542-1612. [Shilte Ha Gibborim. German] Die Heldenschilde. Frankfurt am Main : Lang, 2002.

MILITARISM. *See* **IMPERIALISM.**

MILITARY AID. *See* **MILITARY ASSISTANCE.**

MILITARY ART AND SCIENCE. *See* **ARMED FORCES; COMMAND OF TROOPS; MORALE; WAR.**

MILITARY ASSISTANCE - CONGO (DEMOCRATIC REPUBLIC).
Masangana Diamaka, Robin, 1962- Dialogue politique. Paris : Editoo.com, 2002.
1. Black author.

MILITARY COMBAT. *See* **COMBAT.**

MILITARY HISTORY, ANCIENT.
Durschmied, Erik. From Armageddon to the fall of Rome. London : Hodder & Stoughton, c2002.

MILITARY INTERVENTION. *See* **INTERVENTION (INTERNATIONAL LAW).**

MILITARY LEADERSHIP. *See* **COMMAND OF TROOPS.**

MILITARY LIFE. *See* **SOLDIERS.**

Military masculinities : identity and the state / [edited by] Paul R. Higate ; foreword by Jeff Hearn. Westport, Conn. : Praeger, 2003. xxii, 233 p. ; 25 cm. Includes bibliographical references (p. [217]-223) and index. ISBN 0-275-97558-4 (alk. paper) DDC 306.2/7
1. Sociology, Military. 2. Men. 3. Masculinity. I. Higate, Paul.
U21.5 .M4975 2003

MILITARY OPERATIONS OTHER THAN WAR. *See* **ARMED FORCES - OPERATIONS OTHER THAN WAR.**

MILITARY PERSONNEL. *See* **SOLDIERS.**

MILITARY POLICY. *See* **MILITARY ASSISTANCE; NATIONAL SECURITY.**

MILITARY PSYCHOLOGY. *See* **PSYCHOLOGY, MILITARY.**

MILITARY, THE. *See* **ARMED FORCES.**

Mill, John Stuart, 1806-1873.
On liberty.
Mill, John Stuart, 1806-1873. Utilitarianism ; 2nd ed. Malden, MA : Blackwell Pub., 2003.
B1602 .A5 2003

On liberty / John Stuart Mill ; edited by David Bromwich and George Kateb ; with essays by Jean Bethke Elshtain ... [et al.]. New Haven : Yale University Press, c2003. x, 249 p. ; 22 cm. (Rethinking the Western tradition) Includes bibliographical references (p. [247]-249). ISBN 0-300-09608-9 (cloth) ISBN 0-300-09610-0 (paper) DDC 323.44
1. Liberty. I. Bromwich, David, 1951- II. Kateb, George. III. Title. IV. Series.
JC585 .M76 2003

Utilitarianism ; and, On liberty : including Mill's 'Essay on Bentham', and selections from the writings of Jeremy Bentham and John Austin / edited with an introduction by Mary Warnock. 2nd ed. Malden, MA : Blackwell Pub., 2003. 264 p. ; 24 cm. Includes bibliographical references (p. [252]-254) and index. ISBN 0-631-23351-2 (alk. paper) ISBN 0-631-23352-0 (pbk. : alk. paper) DDC 171/.5
1. Utilitarianism. 2. Liberty. 3. Jurisprudence. I. Bentham, Jeremy, 1748-1832. II. Austin, John, 1790-1859. III. Warnock, Mary. IV. Mill, John Stuart, 1806-1873. On liberty. V. Title. VI. Title: On liberty. VII. Title: Utilitarianism ; and, On liberty
B1602 .A5 2003

Mille & une pages
Duby, Georges. Qu'est-ce que la société féodale? Paris : Flammarion, c2002.

Millennium projects. 1st ed. New Delhi : Small Scale Industries, Ministry of Small Scale Industries, Agro & Rural Industries, Govt. of India, 2000- v. ; 29 cm. SUMMARY: On project profiles and opportunities in small scale industries in India. PARTIAL CONTENTS: v. 1. Mechanical products -- v. 2. Metallurgical products -- 3. Hosiery products
1. Small business - India - Forecasting.. 2. Twenty-first century - Forecasts. I. India. Small Scale Industries.

Miller, Avigdor.
[Lev Avigdor]
Sefer Lev Avigdor : kelalim vi-yesodot nifla'im ba-avodat ha-adam be-ḳinyene ha-shelemut / me-et Avigdor ha-Kohen Miller. Bruḳlin, N.Y. : S. Miller, 762, c2002. 214 p. ; 25 cm. Running title: Lev Avigdor. Includes indexes.
1. Perfectionism (Personality trait) - Religious aspects - Judaism. 2. Choice (Psychology) - Religious aspects - Judaism. 3. Ethics, Jewish. I. Title. II. Title: Lev Avigdor
BM538.P4 .M45 2001

Miller, D. Patrick, 1953- News of a new human nature : the best features and interviews on the new spirituality / by D. Patrick Miller. 1st ed. Berkeley, Calif. : Fearless Books, 2002. xv, 349 p. : ill. ; 23 cm. Includes bibliographical references. ISBN 0-9656809-4-0 DDC 299/.93
1. Self-actualization (Psychology) - Miscellanea. 2. Spirituality - Miscellanea. 3. Self-help techniques - Miscellanea. 4. New Age movement - United States. I. Title.
BF637.S4 M547 2002

Miller, James, 1968- Daoism : a short introduction / James Miller. Oxford : Oneworld, c2003. xviii, 174 p. ; 23 cm. Includes bibliographical references (p. [157]-163) and index. ISBN 1-85168-315-1 DDC 299.514
1. Taoism. I. Title.
BL1920 .M55 2003

Miller, Jeffrey C., 1951- The transcendent function : Jung's model of psychological growth through dialogue with the unconscious / Jeffrey C. Miller. Albany : State University of New York Press, c2003. p. cm. Includes bibliographical references (p.) and index. ISBN 0-7914-5977-2 (alk. paper) ISBN 0-7914-5978-0 (pbk. : alk. paper) DDC 155.2/5
1. Individuation (Psychology) 2. Subconsciousness. I. Jung, C. G. (Carl Gustav), 1875-1961. Transzendente Funktion. II. Title.
BF175.5.I53 M55 2003

Miller, John G., 1958- QBQ! : the question behind the question / John G. Miller. Denver, CO : Denver Press, c2001. 115 p. ; 19 cm. "What to really ask yourself. Practicing personal accountability in business and in life." ISBN 0-9665832-9-9 (pbk) DDC 153.8/3
1. Choice (Psychology) 2. Decision making. 3. Problem solving. 4. Responsibility. I. Title. II. Title: Question behind the question
BF611 .M55 2001

Miller, Larry, 1947- Exploring the "zone" / by Larry Miller with James Redfield. Gretna, La. : Pelican, 2001. 205 p. : ill. ; 22 cm. Includes bibliographical references (p. 205). ISBN 1-56554-717-9 DDC 131
1. Success - Psychic aspects. 2. Mind and body. 3. Supernatural. 4. Human evolution - Miscellanea. I. Redfield, James. II. Title.
BF1045.S83 M55 2001

Miller, Lucy J.
Roid, Gale H. S-BIT, Stoelting Brief Nonverbal Intelligence Test. Wood Dale, IL : Stoelting Co., c1999.
BF432.5.S85 R65 1999

Miller, Scott D. Staying on top and keeping the sand out of your pants : a surfer's guide to the good life / Scott Miller, Mark A. Hubble, and Seth Houdeshell ; with cartoons by John Byrne. Deerfield Beach, Fla. : Health Communications, c2003. vii, 148 p. : ill. ; 19 cm. Includes bibliographical references. ISBN 0-7573-0033-2 DDC 158.1
1. Success - Psychological aspects. 2. Self-actualization (Psychology) I. Hubble, Mark A., 1951- II. Houdeshell, Seth, 1974- III. Title.
BF637.S8 M565 2003

Miller, William Ian, 1946- Faking it / William Ian Miller. Cambridge ; New York : Cambridge University Press, 2003. xi, 290 p. ; 24 cm. Includes bibliographical references (p. 266-277) and index. Publisher description URL: http://www.loc.gov/catdir/description/ cam032/2003043750.html Table of contents URL: http:// www.loc.gov/catdir/toc/cam031/2003043750.html ISBN 0-521-83018-4 (hbk.) DDC 179/.8
1. Identity (Psychology) 2. Social role. 3. Authenticity (Philosophy) 4. Self-doubt. I. Title.
BF697 .M525 2003

MILLIONAIRES - CHINA - BIOGRAPHY.
Zhongguo, shui zui fu. Di 1 ban. Beijing : Qi ye guan li chu ban she, 2001.
HC426.5.A2 Z457 2001

Millöcker, Carl, 1842-1899.
Bettelstudent Ach, ich hab' sie ja nur.
Hann, Georg. Georg Hann [sound recording]. [Germany] : Preiser Records, p2001.

Mills, Albert J., 1945-.
Gender, identity and the culture of organizations. London ; New York : Routledge, 2002.
HD58.7 .G46 2002

Mills, Andy, 1979- Shapesville / Andy Mills and Becky Osborn ; illustrated by Erica Neitz. 1st ed. Carlsbad, CA : Gurze Books, 2003. p. cm. SUMMARY: A celebration of the many different sizes, shapes, and colors of the people who live in Shapesville, where everyone is different and each is a star. Includes discussion questions and a note to parents and educators. ISBN 0-936077-47-6 (hardcover) ISBN 0-936077-44-1 (trade pbk. : alk. paper) DDC 306.4/61
1. Body image in children - Juvenile literature. 2. Body image. I. Osborn, Becky. II. Neitz, Erica, ill. III. Title.
BF723.B6 M55 2003

Mills, Jon, 1964-.
Psychoanalysis at the limit. Albany : State University of New York Press, 2004.
BF173 .P7753 2004

Rereading Freud. Albany : State University of New York Press, 2004.
BF109.F74 R47 2004

Mills, Linda G. Insult to injury : rethinking our responses to intimate abuse / Linda G. Mills. Princeton, N.J. : Princeton University Press, c2003. xiv, 178 p. ; 24 cm. Includes bibliographical references (p. [149]-169) and index. ISBN 0-691-09639-2 (cloth : alk. paper) DDC 362.82/92
1. Family violence. 2. Conjugal violence. 3. Wife abuse. 4. Abusive men. 5. Abusive women. 6. Feminist theory. I. Title.
HV6626 .M55 2003

Milmaniene, José E. Clínica del texto : Kafka, Benjamin, Lévinas / José E. Milmaniene. [1. ed.]. Buenos Aires : Editorial Biblos, c2002. 128 p. ; 23 cm. (Psicología) Includes bibliographical references (p. 127-128). ISBN 950-786-317-6
1. Kafka, Franz, - 1883-1924 - Criticism and interpretation. 2. Benjamin, Walter, - 1892-1940 - Criticism and interpretation. 3. Lévinas, Emmanuel - Criticism and interpretation. 4. Psychoanalysis and literature. 5. Psychology, Applied. I. Title.

Milne, A. A. (Alan Alexander), 1882-1956.
Winnie-the-Pooh's little book of feng shui. London : Methuen Children's, 1999.

Milner, A. D. (A. David).
The cognitive and neural bases of spatial neglect. Oxford ; New York : Oxford University Press, 2002.
RC394.N44 C64 2002

Milner, Andrew, 1950- Contemporary cultural theory / Andrew Milner and Jeff Browitt. 3rd ed. Crows Nest, N.S.W. : Allen & Unwin, 2002. viii, 280 p. ; 22 cm. Previous ed.: London : UCL Press, 1994. Includes bibliographical references (p. 245-264) and index. ISBN 1-86508-808-0 (pbk.)
1. Culture. 2. Structuralism. 3. Socialism. 4. Feminism. 5. Postmodernism. 6. Utilitarianism. I. Browitt, Jeff, 1950- II. Title.

Milner, Judith, senior lecturer. Assessment in counselling : theory, process, and decision-making / Judith Milner and Patrick O'Byrne ; consultant editor, Jo Campling. Houndmills, Basingstoke, Hampshire ; New York : Palgrave Macmillan, 2003. p. cm. Includes bibliographical references and index. ISBN 1403904294 (pbk.) DDC 158/.3
1. Counseling. I. O'Byrne, Patrick. II. Campling, Jo. III. Title.
BF637.C6 M5249 2003

Milosavljević, Boris.
Vizantijska filozofija u srednjevekovnoj Srbiji. Beograd : Stubovi kulture, 2002.

Milshṭein, Mosheh. Sefer Even shetiyah / me-et Mosheh Milshṭein. Bruḳlin : [Lee Printing corp.], 758- [1998- 123 p. ; 24 cm. Spine title: Even shetiyah.
1. Bible. - O.T. - Pentateuch - Commentaries. 2. Cabala. I. Title. II. Title: Even shetiyah

Milton, Joyce. The road to Malpsychia : humanistic psychology and our discontents / Joyce Milton. 1st ed. San Francisco : Encounter Books, 2002. 326 p. ; 24 cm. Includes bibliographical references (p. [295]-309) and index. ISBN 1-89355-479-1 DDC 150.19/8
1. Humanistic psychology - History - 20th century. I. Title. II. Title: Malpsychia
BF204 .M54 2002

Mimesis
Astori, Roberta. Formule magiche. Milano : Mimesis, c2000.
BF1591 .A88 2000

MIMICRY. See IMITATION.

Min Kābūl ilá Niyūyūrk.
Nuwayhiḍ, Walīd. al-Ṭabʻah 1. Bayrūt : Dār Ibn Ḥazm, 2002.

BP172+

Minayo, Maria Cecília de Souza.
Saúde e ambiente sustentável. Rio de Janeiro, RJ : Editora Fiocruz : Abrasco, 2002.

MIND. See **BRAIN; INTELLECT; KNOWLEDGE, THEORY OF; MIND AND BODY; PSYCHOLOGY; REASON; THOUGHT AND THINKING.**

MIND AND BODY. See also **BODY IMAGE; BODY, HUMAN; BODY, HUMAN (PHILOSOPHY); CONSCIOUSNESS; INTENTIONALITY (PHILOSOPHY); OTHER MINDS (THEORY OF KNOWLEDGE); PHRENOLOGY; SELF.**

The Alexander technique [videorecording]. New York, N.Y. : Wellspring Media, c1999.

Andrieu, Bernard. La nouvelle philosophie du corps. Ramonville Saint-Agne : Erès, 2002.

Brossman, Sandra C. The power of oneness. Boston, MA : Red Wheel, 2003.
BF637.S4 B8 2003

Bryden, Barbara E., 1954- Sundial. Gainesville, FL : Center for Applications of Psychological Type, 2003.
BF698.3 .B79 2003

Clarke, Desmond M. Descartes's theory of mind. Oxford ; New York : Oxford University Press, 2003.

D'Alvia, Rodolfo. Psicoanálisis psicosomática ida y atleuv [sic.]. Buenos Aires : Editorial Dunken, 2002.

De Muijnck, Wim. Dependencies, connections, and other relations. Dordrecht ; Boston : Kluwer Academic Publishers, c2003.
BD418.3 .D4 2003

Goodwin, Rufus. Dreamlife. 1st ed. Great Barrington, MA : Lindisfarne Books, 2004.
BF1081 .G66 2004

Landucci, Sergio, 1938- La mente in Cartesio. Milano : FrancoAngeli, c2002.

Langford, Elizabeth. Mind and muscle. Leuven : Garant, 1999.

Martoccia, María, 1957- Cuerpos frágiles, mujeres prodigiosas. Buenos Aires : Editorial Sudamericana, c2002.

McCulloch, Gregory. The life of the mind. London ; New York : Routledge, 2003.
BD418.3 .M363 2003

Mental causation and the metaphysics of mind. Peterborough, Ont. : Broadview Press, c2003.

Merleau-Ponty, Maurice, 1908-1961. [Union de l'âme et du corps chez Malebranche, Biran et Bergson. English] The incarnate subject. Amherst, N.Y. : Humanity Books, 2001.
B2430.M379 U513 2001

Miller, Larry, 1947- Exploring the "zone". Gretna, La. : Pelican, 2001.
BF1045.S83 M55 2001

Modell, Arnold H., 1924- Imagination and the meaningful brain. Cambridge, Mass. : MIT Press, c2003.
BF408 .M58 2003

Models of the self. Thorverton, UK : Imprint Academic, c1999.
BF697 .M568 1999

Nichols, Shaun. Mindreading. Oxford : Clarendon Press ; New York : Oxford University Press, 2003.

Orsucci, Franco. Changing mind. River Edge, NJ : World Scientific, c2002.
BF161 .O77 2002

Pearce, Joseph Chilton. The crack in the cosmic egg. Rochester, Vt. : Park Street Press, c2002.
BD331 .P3915 2002

Das Rätsel von Leib und Seele. Herne : Heitkamp, c1997.
BF163 .R28 1997

Rowlands, Mark. The body in mind. Cambridge, U.K. ; New York : Cambridge University Press, 1999.
BD418.3 .R78 1999

Shapiro, Lawrence A. The mind incarnate. Cambridge, Mass. : MIT Press, 2004.
BF161 .S435 2004

Sylvest, Vernon M. The formula. Fairfield, Iowa : Sunstar Pub., c1996.

BF161 .S95 1996

Weissman, David, 1936- Lost souls. Albany : State University of New York Press, c2003.
B105.M53 W45 2003

Women's minds, women's bodies. Basingstoke : New York : Palgrave Macmillan, 2003.
RA778 .P724 2003

Zoglauer, Thomas. Geist und Gehirn. Göttingen : Vandenhoeck & Ruprecht, 1998.
BF163 .Z64 1998

MIND AND BODY - CONGRESSES.
The embodiment of mind. Delft : Eburon, c1998.
BF161 .E43 1998

MIND AND BODY - HISTORY.
MacDonald, Paul S., 1951- History of the concept of mind. Aldershot ; Burlington, VT : Ashgate, c2003.

MIND AND BODY IN CHILDREN.
Thomas, Patrice Olympius. The power of relaxation. 1st U.S. ed. St. Paul, MN : Redleaf Press, 2003.
BF723.S75 T48 2003

MIND AND BODY IN CHILDREN - PROBLEMS, EXERCISES, ETC.
Thomas, Patrice Olympius. The power of relaxation. 1st U.S. ed. St. Paul, MN : Redleaf Press, 2003.
BF723.S75 T48 2003

MIND AND BODY - INTERVIEW.
Changeux, Jean-Pierre. [Ce qui nous fait penser. English] What makes us think? Princeton, N.J. : Princeton University Press, c2000.
BJ45 .C4313 2000

MIND AND BODY - MISCELLANEA.
Alexander, Jane. The smudging and blessings book. New York: Sterling Pub., 2001.
BF1999 .A6329 2001

De Bergerac, Olivia. The dolphin within. East Roseville, NSW, Australia : Simon & Schuster, 1998.
BF1999 .D335 1998

MIND AND BODY - PHILOSOPHY.
Mackenzie, Patrick T. Mind, body, and freedom. Amherst, N.Y. : Humanity Books, 2003.
BF161 .M23 2003

Tetens, Holm, 1948- Geist, Gehirn, Maschine. Stuttgart : Reclam, c1994.
BF163 .T48 1994x

Mind and muscle.
Langford, Elizabeth. Leuven : Gafant, 1999.

The mind as a scientific object : between brain and culture / edited by Christina E. Erneling and David Martel Johnson. New York : Oxford University Press, c2004. p. cm. Includes bibliographical references and index. Table of contents URL: http://www.loc.gov/catdir/toc/ecip041/2003006897.html ISBN 0-19-513932-1 (alk. paper) ISBN 0-19-513933-X (pbk. : alk. paper) DDC 153
1. Cognitive science. 2. Intellect - Social aspects. 3. Cognition - Social aspects. I. Erneling, Christina E., 1951- II. Johnson, David Martel.
BF311 .M552 2004

Mind, body, and freedom.
Mackenzie, Patrick T. Amherst, N.Y. : Humanity Books, 2003.
BF161 .M23 2003

MIND-BODY RELATIONS (METAPHYSICS).
Braud, William. Distant mental influence. Charlottesville, VA : Hampton Roads Pub., c2003.
BF1045.S33 B74 2003

Carter, Rita, 1949- Exploring consciousness. Berkeley : University of California Press, c2002.
BF311 .C289 2002

MIND CONTROL. See **BRAINWASHING.**

MIND-CURE. See **MIND AND BODY.**

The mind incarnate.
Shapiro, Lawrence A. Cambridge, Mass. : MIT Press, 2004.
BF161 .S435 2004

The mind made flesh.
Humphrey, Nicholas. Oxford ; New York : Oxford University Press, 2002.
BF701 .H86 2002

Humphrey, Nicholas. Oxford ; New York : Oxford University Press, 2002.

Mind, matter, and mystery : questions in science and philosophy / edited by Ranjit Nair. New Delhi : Scientia, 2001. xi, 148 p. ; 23 cm. SUMMARY: Contributed articles. Includes bibliographical references (p. [135]-143) and index. ISBN 81-88155-00-4

1. Philosophy of mind. 2. Philosophy and science. I. Nair, Ranjit.
BD418.3 .M5556 2001

The mind of the soul.
Zukav, Gary. New York : Free Press, 2003.
BF611 .Z85 2003

Mind over mind.
Klass, Morton, 1927- Lanham, Md. ; Oxford : Rowman & Littlefield, c2003.
BF1555 .K58 2003

MIND, PEACE OF. See **PEACE OF MIND.**

MIND, PHILOSOPHY OF. See **PHILOSOPHY OF MIND.**

The mind readers.
Rauscher, William V. Woodbury, N.J. : Mystic Light Press, c2002.
BF1171 .R28 2002

MIND-READING. See **TELEPATHY.**

MIND, THEORY OF. See **PHILOSOPHY OF MIND.**

Mind wars.
McFadyen, Ian. St Leonards, N.S.W., Australia : Allen & Unwin, c2000.
BF701 .M38 2000

Mindell, Arnold, 1940- The dreambody in relationships / Arnold Mindell. Portland, OR : Lao Tse Press ; Oakland, CA : Distributed to the trade by Words Distributing Co., c2002. xii, 148 p. ; 22 cm. (The foundation series) Includes bibliographical references (p. [135]-136) and index. ISBN 1-88707-867-3 (pbk.) DDC 153.6
1. Body language. 2. Interpersonal relations. 3. Dreams. 4. Family psychotherapy. I. Title. II. Series: Mindell, Arnold, 1940- Foundation series.
BF637.N66 M56 2002

Foundation series.
Mindell, Arnold, 1940- The dreambody in relationships. Portland, OR : Lao Tse Press ; Oakland, CA : Distributed to the trade by Words Distributing Co., c2002.
BF637.N66 M56 2002

Minding God.
Peterson, Gregory R., 1966- Minneapolis, MN : Fortress Press, c2003.
BL53 .P42 2003

Minding spirituality.
Sorenson, Randall Lehmann, 1954- Hillsdale, NJ : Analytic Press, 2003.
BF175.4.R44 S67 2003

Mindreading.
Nichols, Shaun. Oxford : Clarendon Press ; New York : Oxford University Press, 2003.

Minds and machines.
Dawson, Michael Robert William, 1959- Malden, MA : Blackwell Pub., c2003.
BF311 .D345 2003

MINDS OF OTHERS (THEORY OF KNOWLEDGE). See **OTHER MINDS (THEORY OF KNOWLEDGE).**

MINE EXAMINATION. See **PROSPECTING.**

MINE VALUATION. See **PROSPECTING.**

Minelli, Alessandro. The development of animal form : ontogeny, morphology, and evolution / Alessandro Minelli. Cambridge ; New York : Cambridge University Press, 2003. xviii, 323 p. : ill. ; 24 cm. Includes bibliographical references (p. 255-312) and index. Publisher description URL: http://www.loc.gov/catdir/description/cam031/2002073694.html Table of contents URL: http://www.loc.gov/catdir/toc/cam031/2002073694.html CONTENTS: The Nature of Development -- Everything begun to the service of development: cellular Darwinism and the origin of animal form -- Development: generic to genetic -- Periodization -- Body regions, their boundaries and complexity -- Differentiation and patterning -- Size factors -- Axes and symmetries -- Segments -- Evo-devo perspectives on homology. ISBN 0-521-80851-0 DDC 571.3/1
1. Developmental biology. 2. Ontogeny. 3. Morphology. 4. Evolution (Biology) I. Title.
QH491 .M559 2003

MINERALS. See **PRECIOUS STONES.**

MINES AND MINERAL RESOURCES. See **PROSPECTING.**

Ming jia xin ji cong shu
Ke, Yunlu. Fu gui yu ying er. Di 1 ban. Shanghai : Shanghai ren min chu ban she : Xin hua shu dian Shanghai fa xing suo jing xiao, 1996.

BD431 .K6134 1996 <Asian China>

MINHAG ARI. See **JUDAISM - ARI RITE.**

MINIATURES (ILLUMINATION OF BOOKS AND MANUSCRIPTS). See **ILLUMINATION OF BOOKS AND MANUSCRIPTS.**

MINIMAL BRAIN DYSFUNCTION IN CHILDREN. See **ATTENTION-DEFICIT HYPERACTIVITY DISORDER.**

Mining autonomy / editors Michael Osman ... [et al.] Cambridge, Mass. : London : MIT Press, c2002. 135 p. : ill. (some col.) ; 31 cm. (Perspecta : the Yale archtectural journal, 0079-0958 ; 33) ISBN 0-262-65061-4 DDC 720.1
1. Architecture - Philosophy. I. Osman, Michael. II. Series.

MINISTERS (CLERGY). See **CLERGY.**

MINISTERS OF THE GOSPEL. See **CLERGY.**

MINNESOTA MULTIPHASIC PERSONALITY INVENTORY.
Sherwood, Nancy E. The MMPI-A content component scales. Minneapolis : University of Minnesota Press, c1997.
BF698.8.M5 S54 1997

MINOR PLANETS. See **ASTEROIDS.**

MINOR PROPHETS. See **PROPHETS.**

MINORITIES. See also **ASSIMILATION (SOCIOLOGY); DISCRIMINATION; ETHNIC ATTITUDES; RACE RELATIONS; RELIGIOUS MINORITIES.**
The emerging monoculture. Westport, Conn. : Praeger, 2003.
HM843 .E44 2003

MINORITIES - CIVIL RIGHTS.
Dench, Geoff. Minorities in the open society. New Brunswick, N.J. : Transaction Publishers, 2003.
JF1061 .D46 2003

MINORITIES - GOVERNMENT POLICY - UNITED STATES.
Corlett, J. Angelo, 1958- Race, racism, & reparations. Ithaca : Cornell University Press, c2003.
HT1523 .C67 2003

Minorities in the open society.
Dench, Geoff. New Brunswick, N.J. : Transaction Publishers, 2003.
JF1061 .D46 2003

MINORITIES - POLITICAL ACTIVITY.
Lamizet, Bernard. Politique et identité. Lyon : Presses universitaires de Lyon, 2002.

MINORITIES - RACE IDENTITY.
Song, Miri, 1964- Choosing ethnic identity. Cambridge, UK : Polity Press ; Oxford ; Malden, MA : Blackwell Publishing, 2003.
GN495.6 .S65 2003

MINORITIES - SEXUAL BEHAVIOR.
Gender nonconformity, race, and sexuality. Madison : University of Wisconsin Press, [2002]
HQ1075 .G4645 2002

MINORITIES - UNITED STATES.
The colors of nature. 1st ed. Minneapolis, Minn. : Milkweed Editions, 2002.
QH81 .C663 2002

MINORITY GROUPS. See **MINORITIES.**

MINORITY PSYCHOLOGISTS - DIRECTORIES.
American Psychological Association. The directory of ethnic minority professionals in psychology. 4th ed. Washington, D.C. : American Psychological Association, c2001.
BF30 .A493 2001

MINORITY PSYCHOLOGISTS - UNITED STATES - DIRECTORIES.
American Psychological Association. The directory of ethnic minority professionals in psychology. 4th ed. Washington, D.C. : American Psychological Association, c2001.
BF30 .A493 2001

Minow, Martha, 1954-.
Imagine coexistence. 1st ed. San Francisco : Jossey-Bass, c2003.
HM1121 .I42 2003

Minsel, Beate.
Fthenakis, Wassilios E. Die Rolle des Vaters in der Familie. Stuttgart : Kohlhammer, 2002.

Minsos, Susan Felicity, 1944- Culture clubs : the art of living together / [S. Minsos]. Edmonton : Spotted Cow Press, c2002. viii, 256 p. ; 22 cm. Also available in an electronic version. Includes bibliographical references (p. 231-249) and index. ISBN 0-9688977-8-9 DDC 303.3/2

1. *Socialization.* 2. *Social groups.* 3. *Social acceptance.* 4. *Language and culture.* I. Title.

Mintz, Anne P.
Web of deception. Medford, N.J : CyberAge Books, c2002.
ZA4201 .W43 2002

Mir u Hrvatskoj--rezultati istraživanja / [uredili Bože Vuleta i Vice J. Batarelo]. Zagreb : Hrvatski Caritas ; Split : Franjevački in-t za kulturu mira, 2001. 1 v. (various pagings) : ill. ; 24 cm. Added title page title: Peace in Croatia--research survey results. Inverted cover title: Peace in Croatia--results of research. Text in Serbo-Croatian (roman) and English, bound back to back and inverted. ISBN 9536915014
1. *Croatia - Social conditions.* 2. *Social surveys - Croatia.* 3. *Reconciliation.* 4. *Forgiveness - Croatia.* 5. *Croatia - Ethnic relations.* I. Vuleta, Bože. II. Batarelo, Vice J. III. Title: Peace in Croatia--research survey results IV. Title: Peace in Croatia--results of research
HN638.A8 M57 2001

MIRACLE WORKERS. See MIRACLES.

MIRACLES. See SPIRITUAL HEALING; SUPERNATURAL.

MIRACLES - HISTORY OF DOCTRINES - MIDDLE AGES, 600-1500.
Marvels, monsters, and miracles. Kalamazoo, Mich. : Medieval Institute Publications, 2002.
GR825 .M218 2002

Miranda, Ary Carvalho de.
Saúde e ambiente sustentável. Rio de Janeiro, RJ : Editora Fiocruz : Abrasco, 2002.

Mircea, Corneliu. Originarul / Corneliu Mircea. București : Paideia, 2000. 263 p. ; 24 cm. Includes bibliographical references. ISBN 9738064120
1. *Origin (Philosophy)* 2. *Beginning.* 3. *Cosmology.* I. Title.
BD638 .M573 2000

Mires, Fernando. Crítica de la razón científica / Fernando Mires. 1a ed. Caracas : Editorial Nueva Sociedad, 2002. 285 p. ; 23 cm. Includes bibliographical references (p. [281]-285). ISBN 980-317-192-5
1. *Science - Philosophy.* 2. *Reason.* 3. *Philosophy, Modern - 20th century.* I. Title.

Mirfield, Peter.
Essays for Colin Tapper. London : LexisNexis, 2003.

Mironova, T. L. (Tat'i͡ana L'vovna) Samosoznanie professionala / T.L. Mironova. Ulan-Udė: Izd-vo Buri͡atskogo gosuniversiteta, 1999. 199 p. ; 20 cm. "Nauchnoe izdanie"--Colophon. Includes bibliographical references (p. 192-199). ISBN 5852132144
1. *Self-perception.* 2. *Professional employees - Psychology.* 3. *Physicians - Psychology.* I. Title.
BF697.5.S43 M57 1999

Mirskai͡a, L. A. (Li͡udmila Anatol'evna).
Ėzotericheskai͡a filosofii͡a. Rostov-na-Donu : Foliant, 2002.
BF1416 .E96 2002

Misbehavior in organizations.
Vardi, Yoav, 1944- Mahwah, NJ ; London : Lawrence Erlbaum, 2004.
HD58.7 .V367 2004

MISCELLANEOUS FACTS. See CURIOSITIES AND WONDERS.

Mischel, Walter. Introduction to personality : toward an integration / Walter Mischel, Yuichi Shoda, Ronald E. Smith. 7th ed. Hoboken, NJ : J. Wiley & Sons, c2004. xxv, 512 p. : ill. (some col.) ; 27 cm. Includes bibliographical references (p. 455-488) and indexes. Publisher description URL: http://www.loc.gov/catdir/desc ription/wiley038/2003053487.html Table of contents URL: http://www.loc.gov/catdir/toc/wiley032/2003053487.html ISBN 0-471-27249-3 (alk. paper) DDC 155.2
1. *Personality.* I. Title.
BF698 .M555 2004

MISCOMMUNICATION.
Jadacki, Jacek Juliusz. From the viewpoint of the Lvov-Warsaw school. Amsterdam ; New York, NY : Rodopi, 2003.

Randolph, Joanne. What I look like when I am confused. 1st ed. New York : PowerStart Press, 2004.
BF723.I63 R36 2004

Randolph, Joanne. [What I look like when I am confused. Spanish & English] What I look like when I am confused = 1st ed. New York : Rosen Pub. Group's PowerKids Press, 2004.
BF723.I63 R3618 2004

MISDEMEANORS. See CRIME.

The miseducation of women.
Tooley, James. London ; New York : Continuum, 2002.
HQ1154 .T64 2002

Mishlove, Jeffrey, 1946- The PK man : a true story of mind over matter / Jeffrey Mishlove ; with an introduction by John E. Mack. Charlottesville, VA : Hampton Roads, [c2000] xx, 283 p. ; 22 cm. Includes bibliographical references (p. 267-272) and index. ISBN 1-57174-183-6 (pbk. : alk. paper) DDC 133.8/092
1. *Owens, Ted.* 2. *Psychics - Biography.* 3. *Psychokinesis.* 4. *Unidentified flying objects - Sightings and encounters.* 5. *Human-alien encounters.* I. Title.
BF1027.O94 M57 2000

Mishnah. Avot. 2000.
Vaserman, Asher ben Avraham Betsal'el. Sefer Mishnat avot. Bene Berak : A. Vaserman, 760-[2000-

[Mishnah. Avot. 2001.] Sefer Bet ginze : kolel perushim ma'amarim u-ve'urim 'al masekhet Avot / me-et Refa'el Mosheh Lurya. Yerushalayim : R. M. Lurya, 762 [2001 or 2002] 339 p. ; 25 cm. Running title: Bet ginze. Includes indexes.
1. *Mishnah. - Avot - Commentaries.* 2. *Ethics, Jewish.* I. Lurya, Mosheh. II. Title. III. Title: Bet ginze

MISHNAH. AVOT - COMMENTARIES.
[Mishnah. Avot. 2001.] Sefer Bet ginze. Yerushalayim : R. M. Lurya, 762 [2001 or 2002]

Vaserman, Asher ben Avraham Betsal'el. Sefer Mishnat avot. Bene Berak : A. Vaserman, 760-[2000-

Mishnat avot.
Vaserman, Asher ben Avraham Betsal'el. Sefer Mishnat avot. Bene Berak : A. Vaserman, 760-[2000-

Mishpaṭ ha-shalom.
Kohen, Yekutiel. Yerushalayim : Mekhon Sha'ar ha-mishpaṭ : Hanhalat bate ha-din ha-rabaniyim, 762 [2001 or 2002]

Mishpeṭe Yiśra'el.
Lugasi, Ya'aḳov Yiśra'el. Mahadurah ḥadashah be-tosefet le-ḥag ha-Pesaḥ. Yerushalayim : Y. Y. Lugasi, 761 [2001]

Mishpeṭe Yiśra'el : Elul, Rosh ha-shanah, Yom kipur, Sukot, Ḥanukah, Purim, Shavu'ot.
Lugasi, Ya'aḳov Yiśra'el. Mishpeṭe Yiśra'el. Mahadurah ḥadashah be-tosefet le-ḥag ha-Pesaḥ. Yerushalayim : Y. Y. Lugasi, 761 [2001]

Mishra, Archana, 1962- Casting the evil eye : witch trials in tribal India / Archana Mishra. New Delhi : Namita Gokhale Editions, Roli Books, 2003. xi, 204 p. : ill. ; 23 cm. SUMMARY: Case studies with special reference to Singhbhūm District, India. ISBN 81-7436-214-2
1. *Witchcraft - India - Singhbhūm - Case studies.* I. Title. II. Title: Evil eye
BF1584.A-Z1.Z7 2003+

Mishra, Satchidananda, 1947-.
[Keralapraśnasaṅgraha. Hindi & Sanskrit.] Keralapraśnasaṅgrahaḥ. 1. saṃskaraṇa. Purī : Paramānandaprakāśanam, 1999.
BF1714.H5+

Misión de las Naciones Unidas de Verificación de los Derechos Humanos y del Cumplimiento de los Compromisos del Acuerdo Global sobre Derechos Humanos en Guatemala.
2001, año de las Naciones Unidas del diálogo entre civilizaciones. Guatemala : Fundación Casa de la Reconciliación : MINUGUA, 2001.
JX1952 .A233 2001

Miśra, Ānanda, lecturer. Saṃvitprakāśavāda : jñāna kī svaprakāśatā kī samasyā para eka prabandha / Ānanda Miśra. 1. saṃskaraṇa. Dillī : Bhāratīya Vidyā Prakāśana, 2002. 228 p. ; 22 cm. Cover title: Saṃvit prakāśavāda. Includes bibliographical references (p. [215]-224) and index. In Hindi; includes passages in Sanskrit. ISBN 81-217-0168-6
1. *Knowledge, Theory of (Hinduism)* 2. *Philosophy, Indic.* I. Title. II. Title: Saṃvit prakāśavāda
B132.K6 M58 2002

Missing believed killed.
Nesbit, Roy Conyers. Stroud : Sutton, 2002.

MISSING PERSONS.
Herbst, Judith. Vanished. Minneapolis : Lerner Publications Co., 2005.
BF1389.D57 H47 2005

Nesbit, Roy Conyers. Missing believed killed. Stroud : Sutton, 2002.

Townsend, John. Mysterious disappearances. Chicago, IL : Raintree, 2004.
BF1389.D57 T69 2004

The missing piece.
Boughton, Harold "Bud" [Lancaster, Ohio] : Lucky Press, c2003.
BF575.S35 B68 2003

MISTAKES. See ERRORS.

Mister and Doctor talking it over.
Gillman, Karen. Mr. and Dr. talking it over. Lima, Ohio : Wyndham Hall Press, c2002.
BF637.C45 G55 2002

Misteri d'Italia.
Lucarelli, Carlo, 1960- Torino : Einaudi, c2002.

Misterii͡a zvezd.
Grigorovich, A. A. (Aleksandr Anatol'evich) Moskva : MK-Periodika, 2002.
BF1708.6 .G75 2002

El misterio de la diferencia.
Luciani Rivero, Rafael Francisco. Roma : Pontificia università gregoriana, 2001.

Mistérios e práticas da lei de Umbanda.
Silva, W. W. da Matta e (Woodrow Wilson da Matta e), 1917- Sao Paulo : Icone Editora, c1999.

Mistiche dell'Occidente.
Terrin, Aldo N. (Aldo Natale) 1. ed. Brescia : Morcelliana, 2001.
BP605.N48 T477 2001

Mistici, veggenti e medium.
Dermine, François-Marie, 1949- Città del Vaticano : Libreria editrice vaticana, c2002.

Mistry, P. J.
Perspectives in linguistics. New Delhi : Indian Institute of Language Studies : Distributed by Creative Books, 2003.

MISTRY, P. J.
Perspectives in linguistics. New Delhi : Indian Institute of Language Studies : Distributed by Creative Books, 2003.

Misunderstanding Freud.
Goldberg, Arnold, 1929- New York : Other Press, 2004.
BF173 .G59 2004

"Mit Freud über Freud hinaus".
Loch, Wolfgang. Tübingen : Edition Diskord, c2001.
BF173 .L554 2001

MIT Press/Bradford Books series in cognitive psychology
Solso, Robert L., 1933- The psychology of art and the evolution of the conscious brain. Cambridge, Mass. : MIT Press, 2003.
BF311 .S652 2003

MIT process handbook.
Organizing business knowledge. Cambridge, Mass. : MIT Press, c2003.
HD30.2 .T67 2003

Mitchell, Juliet, 1940- Siblings : sex and violence / Juliet Mitchell. Cambridge, UK : Polity Press, c2003. p. cm. Includes bibliographical references and index. Table of contents URL: http://www.loc.gov/catdir/toc/ecip042/2003007589.html CONTENTS: Siblings and psychoanalysis : an overview -- Did Oedipus have a sister? -- Sister-brother/brother-sister incest -- Looking sideways : a child is being beaten -- The difference between gender and sexual difference -- Who's been sitting in my chair? -- Attachment and maternal deprivation : how did John Bowlby miss the siblings? -- In our own time : sexuality, psychoanalysis and social change -- Siblings and the engendering of gender. ISBN 0-7456-3220-3 (hb : alk. paper) ISBN 0-7456-3221-1 (pbk. : alk. paper) DDC 155.44/3
1. *Brothers and sisters.* 2. *Sex (Psychology)* 3. *Violence.* 4. *Psychoanalysis.* I. Title.
BF723.S43 M58 2003

Mitchell, Mark L. Writing for psychology : a guide for students / Mark L. Mitchell and Janina M. Jolley, Robert P. O'Shea. 1st ed. Australia ; Belmont, CA : Wadsworth/Thomson, 2004. xv, 208 p. : ill. ; 24 cm. Includes index. ISBN 0-15-508554-9
1. *Communication in psychology - Handbooks, manuals, etc.* 2. *Psychology - Authorship.* I. Jolley, Janina M. II. O'Shea, Robert P. (Robert Paul) III. Title.
BF76.7 .M58 2004

Mitchell, Shawne, 1958-
[Exploring feng shui]
Simple feng shui : ancient principles to bring love, joy, and prosperity into your life / Shawne Mitchell with Stephanie Gunning. New York : Gramercy

Miṭelman, Yiśra'el Yehudah.
Books, 2004. p. cm. Originally published: Exploring feng shui. Franklin Lakes, NJ : New Page Books, c2002. Includes bibliographical references and index. ISBN 0-517-22296-5 DDC 133.3/337
1. Feng shui. I. Gunning, Stephanie, 1962- II. Title.
BF1779.F4 M58 2004

Miṭelman, Yiśra'el Yehudah. Ḳuntres Ḥazaḳ ve-nithazeḳ : asifat ma'amarim ve-'inyanim divre Torah u-musar ... Ashdod : T. T. di-ḥaside Belza, 762 [2002] 90 p. ; 25 cm.
1. Talmud Torah (Judaism) 2. Ethics, Jewish. 3. Hasidism. I. Title.

Mithen, Steven J. After the ice : a global human history 20,000-5000 BC / Steve Mithen. London : Weidenfeld & Nicolson, 2003. xiii, 622 p., [24] p. of plates : ill. (some col.), maps ; 24 cm. Includes bibliographical references (p. [575]-610) and index. ISBN 0-297-64318-5 DDC 930
1. Prehistoric peoples - Social life and customs. 2. Prehistoric peoples - Social conditions. 3. Primitive societies - History. 4. Social evolution. 5. Antiquities, Prehistoric. 6. Civilization, Ancient. 7. History, Ancient. 8. Excavations (Archaeology) I. Title.

Il mito della grande madre.
Sermonti, Giuseppe. Milano : Mimesis, c2002.

Mitos atuais.
Pinheiro, José Moura. Salvador : Secretaria da Cultura e Turismo : Fundação Cultural do Estado da Bahia : Empresa Gráfoca da Bahia, 2001.

Mitra, Gautam.
Koutsoukis, Nikitas-Spiros. Decision modelling and information systems. Boston : Kluwer Academic Publishers, c2003.
T57.95 .K68 2003

MITSCHERLICH, ALEXANDER, 1908-.
Hurson, Didier. Alexander Mitscherlich, 1908-1982. Paris : Presses de l'Université de Paris-Sorbonne, 2002.

Mitteilungen der Prähistorischen Kommission der Österreichischen Akademie der Wissenschaften
(44. Bd.) Neubauer, Wolfgang, 1963- Magnetische Prospektion in der Archäologie. Wien : Verlag der Österreichischen Akademie der Wissenschaften, 2001.

Mitteilungen. Sonderheft (Altnürnberger Landschaft e.V.)
(2002.) Stark, Heinz. Plecher Kirchengeschichte im Mittelalter. Simmelsdorf : Altnürnberger Landschaft, 2002.

Mix & match animal & star signs.
Craze, Richard, 1950- 1st ed. Hauppauge, NY : Barron's, 2000.
BF1714.C5 C76 2000

Mix and match animal and star signs.
Craze, Richard, 1950- Mix & match animal & star signs. 1st ed. Hauppauge, NY : Barron's, 2000.
BF1714.C5 C76 2000

Mixing methods in psychology : the integration of qualitative and quantitative methods in theory and practice / edited by Zazie Todd ... [et al.]. New York : Psychology Press, 2004. p. cm. Includes bibliographical references and index. Table of contents URL: http://www.loc.gov/catdir/toc/ecip047/2003016650.html ISBN 0-415-18649-8 (hbk.) ISBN 0-415-18650-1 (pbk.) DDC 150/.7/2
1. Psychology - Research - Methodology. I. Todd, Zazie.
BF76.5 .M59 2004

Mizuhara, Sohei, 1969-.
The philosophy of Keynes' economics. London ; New York : Routledge, 2003.
HB99.7 .P45 2003

MIZWAHS, SIX HUNDRED AND THIRTEEN. See **COMMANDMENTS, SIX HUNDRED AND THIRTEEN.**

Mladek, Meda.
Kupka, František, 1871-1957. [Création dans les arts plastiques. Czech. German] Die Schöpfung in der bildenden Kunst. Ostfildern-Ruit : Hatje Cantz, c2001.

MMPI.
Sherwood, Nancy E. The MMPI-A content component scales. Minneapolis : University of Minnesota Press, c1997.
BF698.8.M5 S54 1997

MMPI-2/MMPI-A test reports
(3) Sherwood, Nancy E. The MMPI-A content component scales. Minneapolis : University of Minnesota Press, c1997.
BF698.8.M5 S54 1997

The MMPI-A content component scales.
Sherwood, Nancy E. Minneapolis : University of Minnesota Press, c1997.
BF698.8.M5 S54 1997

MNEMONICS. See also **MEMORY.**
Arden, John Boghosian. Improving memory for dummies. New York : Wiley Pub., c2002.
BF385 .A47 2002

Mason, Douglas J. The memory workbook. Oakland, CA : New Harbinger Publications, : c2001. : Distributed in the U.S.A. by Publishers Group West, c2001.
BF724.85.M45 M37 2001

Turkington, Carol. Memory. Hoboken, N.J. : J. Wiley and Sons, c2003.
BF385 .T88 2003

MNEMONICS - HISTORY - TO 1500 - CONGRESSES.
Seelenmaschinen. Wien : Böhlau Verlag, c2000.
BF381 .S44 2000

MNES (INTERNATIONAL BUSINESS ENTERPRISES). See **INTERNATIONAL BUSINESS ENTERPRISES.**

Mniejszościowe orientacje seksualne w perspektywie gender.
Odmiany odmieńca. Katowice : "Śląsk", 2002.
HQ23 .O36 2002

Mnogomernaia psikhika.
Berezina, T. N. Moskva : PER SĖ, 2001.
BF468 .B47 2001

Mo'alem, ahuvi.
Moalem, Shuli. Tel Aviv : Yedi'ot aḥaronot : Sifre ḥemed, c2002.

MOALEM, MOSHEH.
Moalem, Shuli. Mo'alem, ahuvi. Tel Aviv : Yedi'ot aḥaronot : Sifre ḥemed, c2002.

Moalem, Shuli. Mo'alem, ahuvi / Shuli Mo'alem. Tel Aviv : Yedi'ot aḥaronot : Sifre ḥemed, c2002. 222 p. ; 21 cm. Title on verso of t.p.: My beloved, Moalem. SUMMARY: Letters written by author to her husband, an army officer who was killed in the helicopter accident of February 1997. ISBN 9655111040
1. Moalem, Shuli - Correspondence. 2. Moalem, Mosheh. 3. Bereavement. I. Title. II. Title: My beloved, Moalem

MOALEM, SHULI - CORRESPONDENCE.
Moalem, Shuli. Mo'alem, ahuvi. Tel Aviv : Yedi'ot aḥaronot : Sifre ḥemed, c2002.

Mobile ghosts.
Parker, Elizabeth. 1st ed. Spanish Fort, Ala. : Apparition Pub., c2001.
BF1472.U6 P36 2001

Mobile phone call quality.
United States. General Accounting Office. Telecommunications [electronic resource]. [Washington, D.C.] : U.S. General Accounting Office, [2003]

Mobiles philosophiques
Jannoud, Claude. La crise de l'esprit. Lausanne, Suisse : Age d'homme, c2001.

Möckli, Daniel.
Wenger, Andreas. Conflict prevention. Boulder, Colo. ; London : Lynne Rienner Publishers, 2003.
JZ5538 .W46 2003

MODAL LOGIC. See **MODALITY (LOGIC).**

Modalità ed esistenza.
Chiurazzi, Gaetano. Torino : Trauben, c2001.
BD314 .C458 2001

MODALITY (LINGUISTICS).
Wort und (Kon)text. Frankfurt : Lang, 2001.
P325.5.C65 W678 2001

MODALITY (LOGIC).
Chiurazzi, Gaetano. Modalità ed esistenza. Torino : Trauben, c2001.
BD314 .C458 2001

Plantinga, Alvin. Essays in the metaphysics of modality. Oxford ; New York : Oxford University Press, 2003.
B945.P553 M48 2003

MODALITY (LOGIC) - HISTORY.
The medieval heritage in early modern metaphysics and modal theory, 1400-1700. Dordrecht ; Boston : Kluwer Academic Publishers, c2003.
BD111 .M47 2003

MODALITY (THEORY OF KNOWLEDGE).
Gundersen, Lars Bo. Dispositional theories of knowledge. Aldershot, England ; Burlington, VT : Ashgate, c2003.
BD161 .G86 2003

MODEL CITIES. See **CITY PLANNING.**

Model menṭali shel morim menusim ye-ṭironim be-miḳtso'ot mada'iyim ye-humaniyim le-gabe lemidah be-ḳerev yeladim.
Shilony, Tamar. [Israel : h. mo. l., 1994?]

Modelirovanie bessoznatel'nogo.
Koleda, Sergeĭ. Moskva : In-t obshchegumanitarnykh issledovaniĭ, 2000.
BF637.N46 K65 2000

Modell, Arnold H., 1924- Imagination and the meaningful brain / Arnold H. Modell. Cambridge, Mass. : MIT Press, c2003. xiv, 253 p. ; 21 cm. "A Bradford book." Includes bibliographical references (p. [217]-233) and index. ISBN 0-262-13425-X (alk. paper) DDC 150.19/5
1. Imagination. 2. Meaning (Psychology) 3. Emotions and cognition. 4. Mind and body. I. Title.
BF408 .M58 2003

Models of the self / edited by Shaun Gallagher and Jonathan Shear. Thorverton, UK : Imprint Academic, c1999. xviii, 524 p. : ill. ; 26 cm. Includes bibliographical references and index. CONTENTS: Philosophical controversies. 'The self' / Galen Strawson -- Know thyself / Kathleen V. Wilkes -- Unified consciousness and the self / Andrew Brook -- There is no problem of the self / Eric T. Olson -- The self is a semiotic process / John Pickering -- Cognitive and neuroscientific models. Three laws of qualia: what neurology tells us about the biological functions of consciousness, qualia and the self / V.S. Ramachandran & W. Hirstein -- The periconscious substrates of consciousness: affective states and the evolutionary origins of the self / Jaak Panksepp -- Consciousness as self-function / Donald Perlis -- An interpretation of the 'self' from the dynamical systems perspective: a constructivist approach / Jun Tani -- The dialogue of the soul with itself / James Blachowicz -- Developmental and phenomenological constraints. A developmental-ecological perspective on Strawson's 'The self' / George Butterworth -- Mental and bodily awareness in infancy: consciousness of self-existence / Maria Legerstee -- Phenomenology and agency: methodological and theoretical issues in Strawson's 'The self' / Maxine Sheets-Johnstone -- Phenomenal consciousness and self awareness: a phenomenological critique of representational theory / D. Zahavi & J. Parnas -- Pathologies of the self. The self in contextualized action / Shaun Gallagher and Anthony J. Marcel -- On 'being faceless': selfhood and facial embodiment / Jonathan Cole -- Schizophrenia, self-consciousness and the modern mind / Louis A. Sass -- Pathologically divided minds, synchronic unity and models of self / Jennifer Radden -- Meditation-based approaches. What does mysticism have to teach us about consciousness? / Robert Forman -- A rDzogs-chen Buddhist interpretation of the sense of self / Jeremy Hayward -- Consciousness it/self / Steven W. Laycock -- Experiential clarification of the problem of self / Jonathan Shear -- 'I' = awareness / Arthur J. Deikman -- Further methodological questions. Reduction and the self / José Louis Bermúdez -- Subject and object / Mait Edey -- Exceptional persons: on the limits of imaginary cases / Tamar Szabó Gendler -- Being scientific about our selves / Mary Midgley -- Response from keynote author: The self and SESMET / Galen Strawson. ISBN 0-907845-40-1 DDC 155.2
1. Self. 2. Consciousness. 3. Mind and body. I. Gallagher, Shaun, 1948- II. Shear, J. (Jonathan)
BF697 .M568 1999

MODERN AESTHETICS. See **AESTHETICS, MODERN.**

The modern American presidency.
Gould, Lewis L. Lawrence : University Press of Kansas, c2003.
E176.1 .G68 2003

MODERN ARCHITECTURE. See **ARCHITECTURE, MODERN.**

MODERN ART. See **ART, MODERN; MODERNISM (ART).**

MODERN ARTS. See **ARTS, MODERN.**

MODERN CIVILIZATION. See **CIVILIZATION, MODERN.**

MODERN ETHICS. See **ETHICS, MODERN.**

Modern European philosophy
Carman, Taylor, 1965- Heidegger's analytic. Cambridge, UK ; New York : Cambridge University Press, 2003.
B3279.H48 S459 2003

MODERN HISTORY. *See* **HISTORY, MODERN.**

MODERN LANGUAGES. *See* **LANGUAGES, MODERN.**

MODERN LITERATURE. *See* **LITERATURE, MODERN.**

Modern love.
Shumway, David R. New York : New York University Press, c2003.
HQ503 .S54 2003

Modern mantras. 1st ed. Hauppauge, N.Y. : Barron's Educational Series, 2002. 240 p. ; 16 cm. Includes index. ISBN 0-7641-5523-7 DDC 291.3/7
1. Conduct of life - Quotations, maxims, etc. I. Barron's Educational Series, inc.
BF637.C5 M63 2002

MODERN PAINTING. *See* **PAINTING, MODERN.**

MODERN PHILOSOPHERS. *See* **PHILOSOPHERS, MODERN.**

MODERN PHILOSOPHY. *See* **PHILOSOPHY, MODERN.**

Modern physics.
Tipler, Paul Allen, 1933- 4th ed. New York : W.H. Freeman, 2002 printing, c2003.
QC21.3 .T56 2003

Modern societies & the science of religions : studies in honour of Lammert Leertouwer / edited by Gerard Wiegers in association with Jan Platvoet. Leiden ; Boston : Brill, 2002. viii, 397 p. : col. ill. ; 25 cm. (Studies in the history of religions, 0169-8834 ; v. 95) Includes bibliographical references and index. ISBN 90-04-11665-6 (alk. paper) DDC 200/.71
1. Religion. 2. Religions. 3. Religion and sociology. I. Leertouwer, Lammert. II. Wiegers, Gerard Albert, 1959- III. Platvoet, Jan. IV. Title: Modern societies and the science of religions V. Series: Studies in the history of religions ; 95.
BL48 .M542 2002

Modern societies and the science of religions.
Modern societies & the science of religions. Leiden ; Boston : Brill, 2002.
BL48 .M542 2002

MODERNISM (AESTHETICS)
Francis, Elizabeth, 1959- Feminism and modernism [microform]. [1994]

Jameson, Fredric. A singular modernity. London ; New York : Verso, 2002.
CB358 .J348 2002

MODERNISM (ART). *See also* **ART, MODERN - 20TH CENTURY; POSTMODERNISM.**
Grasskamp, Walter. Ist die Moderne eine Epoche? München : C.H. Beck, c2002.

Jameson, Fredric. A singular modernity. London ; New York : Verso, 2002.
CB358 .J348 2002

La modernité après le post-moderne. Paris : Maisonneuve & Larose, [2002]

MODERNISM IN ART. *See* **MODERNISM (ART).**

MODERNISM (LITERATURE). *See also* **POSTMODERNISM (LITERATURE).**
La modernité après le post-moderne. Paris : Maisonneuve & Larose, [2002]

MODERNIST ART. *See* **MODERNISM (ART).**

La modernité après le post-moderne / sous la direction de Henri Meschonnic et de Shiguehiko Hasumi. Paris : Maisonneuve & Larose, [2002] 199 p. ; 24 cm. Includes bibliographical references. ISBN 2-7068-1642-2 DDC 300
1. Arts, Modern - 20th century - France. 2. Arts, Modern - 20th century - Japan. 3. Modernism (Literature) 4. Modernism (Art) 5. Postmodernism. I. Meschonnic, Henri, 1932- II. Hasumi, Shiguehiko.

Modestin, Georg. Le diable chez l'évêque : chasse aux sorciers dans le diocèse de Lausanne, vers 1460 / Georg Modestin. Lausanne : Université de Lausanne, Section d'histoire, Faculté des lettres, 1999. 403 p. : ill., maps ; 22 cm. (Cahiers lausannois d'histoire médiévale ; 25) French and Latin. Includes bibliographical references (p. [375]-389) and index. ISBN 2940110158
1. Witchcraft - Switzerland - Lausanne - History - To 1500. 2. Catholic Church. - Diocese of Lausanne (Switzerland) - History. 3. Church history - Middle Ages, 600-1500. I. Title. II. Series.
BF1584.S9 M64 1999

MODESTY - RELIGIOUS ASPECTS - JUDAISM.
Sofer, Mikha'el Uri. Sefer ʻOlamot shel ṭohar. Mahad. 2. Bene Beraḳ : M.U. Sofer, 761 [2000 or 2001]
BM726 .S633 2000

Moeller van den Bruck, Arthur, 1876-1925.
Grunewald, Michel, 1942- Moeller van den Brucks Geschichtsphilosophie. Bern ; New York : P. Lang, c2001.
DD247.M59 G78 2001

MOELLER VAN DEN BRUCK, ARTHUR, 1876-1925.
Grunewald, Michel, 1942- Moeller van den Brucks Geschichtsphilosophie. Bern ; New York : P. Lang, c2001.
DD247.M59 G78 2001

Moeller van den Brucks Geschichtsphilosophie.
Grunewald, Michel, 1942- Bern ; New York : P. Lang, c2001.
DD247.M59 G78 2001

Moerman, Daniel E. Meaning, medicine, and the "placebo effect" / Daniel E. Moerman. Cambridge ; New York : Cambridge University Press, 2002. xiii, 172 p. : ill. ; 24 cm. (Cambridge studies in medical anthropology ; [9]) Includes bibliographical references (p. 156-168) and index. Publisher description URL: http://www.loc.gov/catdir/description/cam022/2002020167.html Table of contents URL: http://www.loc.gov/catdir/toc/cam022/2002020167.html ISBN 0-521-80630-5 (hbk.) ISBN 0-521-00087-4 (pbk.) DDC 615.5
1. Healing - Psychological aspects. 2. Placebo (Medicine) I. Title. II. Series.
R726.5 .M645 2002

Moessinger, Pierre Le jeu de l'identité / Pierre Moessinger. 1re éd. Paris : Presses universitaires de France, 2000. vii, 171 p. ; 21 cm. (Le sociologue) Includes bibliographical references (p. [165]-171) ISBN 2-13-050127-3 DDC 155.2
1. Identity (Psychology) 2. Self-perception. 3. Social psychology. I. Title. II. Series.
BF697.5.S43 M634 2000

Moffitt, John F. (John Francis), 1940- Picturing extraterrestrials : alien images in modern culture / John F. Moffitt. Amherst, N.Y. : Prometheus Press, c2003. 595 p., [16] p. of plates : ill. ; 24 cm. Includes bibliographical references (p. 561-578) and index. ISBN 1-57392-990-5 (cloth : alk. paper) DDC 704.9/49001942
1. Human-alien encounters. 2. Life on other planets in art. 3. Popular culture. I. Title.
BF2050 .M64 2003

Moghaddam, Fathali M.
Understanding terrorism. 1st ed. Washington, DC : American Psychological Association, 2004.
HV6431 .U35 2004

MOHAMMEDANISM. *See* **ISLAM.**

Mohamudgarastotram.
Śaṅkarācārya. [Bhajagovinda. Gujarati & Sanskrit] Adyatana āvrtti. Amadāvāda : Sarasvatī Pustaka Bhaṇḍāra, 1998/99 [i.e. 1999]
B133.S463 B5315 1998

Mohanty, Jitendranath, 1928- Explorations in philosophy / essays by J.N. Mohanty ; edited by Bina Gupta. New Delhi ; New York : Oxford University Press, c2001- v. : port. ; 23 cm. Includes bibliographical references and index. PARTIAL CONTENTS: v. 1. Indian philosophy -- v. 2. Western philosophy. ISBN 0-19-565083-2 (v. 1) ISBN 0-19-565086-7 (v. 2) DDC 181/.4
1. Philosophy, Indic. 2. Philosophy. 3. Phenomenology. I. Gupta, Bina, 1947- II. Title.
B131.M54 M63 2001

Mohr, Georg.
Interpretation und Argument. Würzburg : Königshausen & Neumann, c2002.

Moiseev, N. N. (Nikita Nikolaevich) Kak daleko do zavtrashnego dnia-- : svobodnye razmyshleniia, 1917-1993 ; Vospominaniia o N.N. Moiseeve / N.N. Moiseev. Moskva : Taĭdeks Ko, 2002. 487 p., [16] p. of plates : ill. ; 22 cm. (Grani mira) (Biblioteka zhurnala "Ekologiia i zhizn'") ISBN 5947020033
1. Twenty-first century - Forecasts. 2. Russia - History - Philosophy. 3. Russia - Forecasting. I. Title. II. Title: Vospominaniia o N.N. Moiseeve. III. Title: Kak daleko do zavtrashnego dnia-- : svobodnye razmyshleniia, 1917-1993. IV. Vospominaniia o N.N. Moiseeve V. Series. VI. Series: Biblioteka zhurnala "Ekologiia i zhizn'"
DK49 .M64 2002

Moita Lopes, Luiz Paulo da. Identidades fragmentadas : a construção discursiva de raça, gênero e sexualidade em sala de aula / Luiz Paulo da Moita Lopes. Campinas, SP, Brasil : Mercado de Letras, [2002] 232 p. ; 21 cm. (Coleção Letramento, educação e sociedade) Includes bibliographical references (p. 219-232). CONTENTS: A construção da diferença e da raça -- A construção da sexualidade e do gênero : masculinidades escolares -- Uma abordagem do discurso : deconstruindo identidades sociais em sala de aula. ISBN 85-85725-86-9
1. Educational anthropology. 2. Educational sociology. 3. Group identity. 4. Education - Social aspects. I. Title. II. Series.
HM753 .M65 2002

Moix, Terenci, 1943-.
Amores de película. 1. ed. [Madrid] : Aguilar, 2002.
PN1998.2 .A46 2002

MOKṢA.
Siṃha, Kīrti Kumāra. Bhāratīya darśana meṃ duḥkha aura mukti. 1. saṃskaraṇa. Ilāhābāda : Śekhara Prakāśana, 2001.
B132.M64 S56 2001

Molekuliarnaia taĭnost' myshleniia.
Dliasin, G. G. (Gennadiĭ Gennad'vich) Azbuka Germesa Trismegista, ili, Molekuliarnaia taĭnost' myshleniia. Izd. 2-e. Moskva : Izd-vo "Belye al'vy", 2002.
BF1616 .D58 2002

MOLESTING OF CHILDREN. *See* **CHILD SEXUAL ABUSE.**

Molly & Monet.
Isaacs, Diane R. Seattle, WA : Peanut Butter Pub., c1999.
BF575.G7 I86 1999

Molly and Monet.
Isaacs, Diane R. Molly & Monet. Seattle, WA : Peanut Butter Pub., c1999.
BF575.G7 I86 1999

Molnár, Anna.
Wort und (Kon)text. Frankfurt : Lang, 2001.
P325.5.C65 W678 2001

Molnar, George, d. 1999. Powers : a study in metaphysics / George Molnar ; edited with an introduction by Stephen Mumford ; and a foreword by D.M. Armstrong. Oxford ; New York : Oxford University Press, 2003. xiv, 238 p. : ill. ; 23 cm. Includes bibliographical references (p. [224]-232) and index. ISBN 0-19-925978-X DDC 110
1. Causation. 2. Power (Philosophy) 3. Disposition (Philosophy) 4. Metaphysics. I. Mumford, Stephen. II. Title.
BD541 .M54 2003

"Mom, Jason's breathing on me!".
Wolf, Anthony E. 1st ed. New York : Ballantine Books, 2003.
BF723.S43 W65 2003

MOMS. *See* **MOTHERS.**

Mom's book of answers.
Bolt, Carol, 1963- New York : Stewart, Tabori & Chang, 2004.
BF1891.B66 B649 2004

Moṅ· Moṅ· Mraṅ·' 'E".
Roṅ· praṅ· lak· choṅ·. Raṅ· kuṅ· : 'Aruṇ· Ū" Cā pe : Phraṅ·" khyi re", Lābh· Mui" Cve Cā pe, 2001.
BF1434.B+

Monaghan, Patricia. The goddess path : myths, invocations & rituals / Patricia Monaghan. 1st ed. St. Paul, Minn. : Llewellyn, 1999. x, 268 p. : ill. ; 24 cm. Includes bibliographical references (p. 259-262) and index. ISBN 1-56718-467-7 (trade paper) DDC 291.2/114
1. Goddesses. 2. Goddess religion. I. Title.
BL473.5 .M665 1999

Monahan, Brian. From ground zero to ground hero : status appropriation and the FDNY / Brian Monahan, Carol Gregory. [Newark, Del.?] : Disaster Research Center, University of Delaware, 2004. 22 leaves ; 29 cm. (Preliminary paper / University of Delaware Disaster Research Center ; #315) Includes bibliographical references (leaf 22).
1. New York (N.Y.). - Fire Dept. 2. September 11 Terrorist Attacks, 2001 - Social aspects. 3. Fire fighters - New York (State) - New York. 4. Heroes - New York (State) - New York. 5. Prestige. 6. Symbolism. I. Gregory, Carol. II. Title. III. Series: Preliminary paper (University of Delaware. Disaster Research Center) ; no. 313.

Monahan, Tom. The do-it-yourself lobotomy : open your mind to greater creative thinking / Tom Monahan. New York : J. Wiley, c2002. vi, 266 p. : ill. ; 24 cm. "An Adweek book." Includes bibliographical references (p.258-259) and index. Publisher description URL: http://www.loc.gov/catdir/desc ription/wiley036/2002284857.html Table of contents URL: http://www.loc.gov/catdir/toc/wiley023/2002284857.html ISBN 0-471-41742-4 (alk. paper) DDC 153.3/5
1. Creative thinking. 2. Brainstorming. 3. Success. I. Title.
BF408 .M59 2002

MONARCHY. *See* **QUEENS.**

Monash romance studies (Newark, Del.)
Read, Malcolm K. (Malcolm Kevin), 1945- Educating the educators. 1st American ed. Newark : University of Delaware Press ; Cranbury, NJ : Associated University Presses, 2003.
PC4064.R43 A3 2003

MONASTIC AND RELIGIOUS LIFE.
Pharmacum carthusiense. Salzburg, Austria : Institut für Anglistik und Amerikanistik, Universität Salzburg, 2002.
BX2435 .P43 2002

MONASTICISM AND RELIGIOUS ORDERS. *See* **FRIARS.**

Monde aquatique au moyen âge.
Dans l'eau, sous l'eau. [Paris] : Presses de l'Université de Paris-Sorbonne, 2002.
CB353 .D27 2002

Monde en cours
Shayegan, Darius. La lumière vient de l'Occident. [La Tour-d'Aigues] : Éditions de l'Aube, c2001.
CB 430

Monde en cours. Série Intervention.
Cyrulnik, Boris. Dialogue sur la nature humaine. La Tour d'Aigues : Editions de l'Aube, c2000.
BF57 .C97 2000

Monde germanique.
Hurson, Didier. Alexander Mitscherlich, 1908-1982. Paris : Presses de l'Université de Paris-Sorbonne, 2002.

Mondi possibili.
Meo, Oscar. Genova : Il melangolo, c2002.
N68.3 .M46 2002

Mondialisation et terrorisme identitaire, ou, Comment l'Occident tente de transformer le monde.
La Branche, Stéphane. Paris : Harmattan, c2003.
JC330 .L2 2003

Il mondo è poco.
Pompeo, Francesco. Roma : Meltemi, c2002.
GN495.6 .P66 2002

Il mondo magico.
De Martino, Ernesto, 1908-1965. 1. ed. Torino : Bollati Boringhieri, 1997.
BF1589 .D46 1997

MONETARY QUESTION. *See* **MONEY.**

MONEY. *See also* **COINS.**
Allen, Robert G. Multiple streams of internet income. New York : Wiley, c2001.
HF5548.32 .A45 2001

Dolgin, Aleksandr. Pragmatika kul'tury. Moskva : Fond nauchnykh issledovaniĭ "Pragmatika kul'tury", 2002.

[Wohlstand entschleiern. English] Unveiling wealth. Dordrecht ; Boston : Kluwer, c2002.
HD75.6 .U58 2002

MONEY, PRIMITIVE. *See* **MONEY.**

MONEY - PSYCHOLOGICAL ASPECTS.
Lowenkopf, Eugene L. The almighty dollar. New York : iUniverse, Inc., c2003.

MONEY - SOCIAL ASPECTS.
Gender, development and money. Oxford : Oxfam, 2001.

Mongeau, Pierre, 1954- Survivre : la dynamique de l'inconfort / Pierre Mongeau et Jacques Tremblay. Sainte-Foy : Presses de l'Université du Québec, 2002. ix, 142 p. : ill. ; 23 cm. Includes bibliographical references (p. [137]-142). ISBN 2760511529 DDC 155.2
1. Psychology. 2. Human behavior. 3. Change (Psychology) 4. Experience. I. Tremblay, Jacques, 1952- II. Title.
BF122 .M66 2002

Moniot, Henri.
Pistes didactiques et chemins historiques. Paris : Harmattan, 2003.

MONISM. *See also* **MATERIALISM.**
Merleau-Ponty, Maurice, 1908-1961. [Union de l'âme et du corps chez Malebranche, Biran et Bergson. English] The incarnate subject. Amherst, N.Y. : Humanity Books, 2001.
B2430.M379 U513 2001

Monkey wrenching the new world order.
Monkeywrenching the new world order [sound recording]. Oakland, Calif : AK Press ; San Francisco, CA : Alternative Tentacles Records, 2001.

Monkeywrenching the new world order [sound recording] : global capitalism and its discontents. Oakland, Calif : AK Press ; San Francisco, CA : Alternative Tentacles Records, 2001. 2 sound discs (128 min.) : digital, mono. ; 4 3/4 in. "An AK Press spoken word compilation." AK Press: AKA 022CD (additional no. on disc: VIRUS 272CD). Various lecturers. SUMMARY: "This double CD ranges over the changing politics of globalization, neoliberalism and world trade, colonialism and debt, militarism and policing, native and indigenous rights and struggles, frankenfood and genetic engineering, capitalism and the fairy-tale economic boom -- and the leading alternatives to and struggles against a system which puts profits over people, unregulated growth over sustainability and money over morals"--Container. CONTENTS: Disc one. Capitalism, world trade, and economics / Howard Zinn (9:20) -- Some reflections on globalization : then and now / Alexander Cockburn (7:44) -- Advice for history teachers / Howard Zinn (2:10) -- Methods of organizing / Howard Zinn (1:44) -- Extending solidarity / Howard Zinn (0:48) -- Conspiracy theories / Howard Zinn (3:59) -- Women, bioengineering, corporations and the State / Vandana Shiva (13:55) -- The WTO, neoliberalism, and global economic policy / Robin Hahnel (3:27) -- Pies, politics and prison / Rahula Janowski (5:07) -- The biotic baking brigade and the global pastry uprising / Agent Apple (6:15) -- A reading from the Seattle N30 Communique from the Acme collective of the black bloc / Craig O'Hara (6:28) -- CONTENTS: Disc two. What is "globalization"? / Noam Chomsky (5:29) -- Poverty, debt and colonialism / Noam Chomsky (4:27) -- Economics, strategy, and class conflict / Michael Albert & Robin Hahnel (5:49) -- Native America, genocide, and the scalp bounty / Ward Churchill (7:16) -- Collective liberation / Chris Crass (12:49) -- Lockdown America / Christian Parenti (14:58) -- Corporate media and its discontents / Normon Solomon (8:15) -- "You fucked up!" : strategic organizing for the new millennia / Alexander Cockburn (2:11) -- Critical mass / Craig O'Hara (3:02). ISBN 1-902593-35-9
1. Anti-globalization movement. 2. Globalization. 3. Income distribution. 4. Social conflict. 5. Free enterprise - United States. 6. Capitalism - United States. 7. United States - Economic policy - 1993-2001. 8. United States - Economic policy - 2001- 9. United States - Politics and government - 1989- 10. United States - Foreign relations - 1989- I. Chomsky, Noam. II. Cockburn, Alexander. III. Zinn, Howard, 1922- IV. Shiva, Vandana. V. Hahnel, Robin. VI. Janowski, Rahula. VII. Agent Apple. VIII. O'Hara, Craig. IX. Albert, Michael, 1947- X. Churchill, Ward. XI. Crass, Chris. XII. Parenti, Christian. XIII. Solomon, Norman, 1951- XIV. Title: Monkey wrenching the new world order XV. Title: Global capitalism and its discontents

Monográfica
(264.) Aboab, Isaac, 14th cent. [Menorat ha-ma'or. Ladino] Una cala en la literatura religiosa sefardí. Granada : Universidad de Granada, 2001.
BJ1287.A152 L33 2001

Monográfica. Crítica literaria.
Aboab, Isaac, 14th cent. [Menorat ha-ma'or. Ladino] Una cala en la literatura religiosa sefardí. Granada : Universidad de Granada, 2001.
BJ1287.A152 L33 2001

Monografie Fundacji na Rzecz Nauki Polskiej. Seria humanistyczna.
Małyszek, Tomasz, 1971- Romans Freuda i Gradivy. Wrocław : Wydawn. Uniwersytetu Wrocławskiego, 2002.
BF173.F85 M255 2002

Motycka, Alina. Nauka o neiświadomość. Wrocław : Leopoldinum, 1998.

Monografije (Stubovi kulture (Firm))
(knj. 3.) Vizantijska filozofija u srednjevekovnoj Srbiji. Beograd : Stubovi kulture, 2002.

Monograph series (Babcock University. Dept. of Political Science and Sociology)
(no. 3.) Adeleke, Veronica I. Concept of gender equality as a paradox in Nigeria's democratic experience. Ikeja [Nigeria] : Dept. of Political Science and Sociology, Babcock University, 2002.

Monograph series (Toronto, Canada)
The occult Webb. Toronto : Colombo & Co., c1999.
BF1408.2.W42 O33 1999

Monographies de la "Revue française de psychanalyse.." Section Société
Freud, le sujet social. 1re éd. Paris : Presses universitaires de France, 2002.

MONOPOLIES. *See* **COMPETITION.**

MONOTHEISM. *See also* **GOD.**
Maciejewski, Franz. Psychoanalytisches Archiv und jüdisches Gedächtnis. 1. Aufl. Wien : Passagen Verlag, 2002.

MONOTHEISM - HISTORY.
Stark, Rodney. For the glory of God. Princeton, N.J. : Princeton University Press, c2003.
BL221 .S747 2003

Monotti, Ann Louise. Universities and intellectual property : ownership and exploitation / Ann Louise Monotti with Sam Ricketson. Oxford ; New York : Oxford University Press, 2003. lxvii, 626 p. ; 24 cm. Includes bibliographical references (p. [571]-605) and index. ISBN 0-19-826594-8 DDC 346.048
1. Intellectual property. 2. Universities and colleges - Law and legislation. I. Ricketson, Sam. II. Title.
KF4225.U55 M66 2003

Monroe, Douglas, 1957-.
The lost books of Merlyn. 1st ed. St. Paul, Minn : Llewellyn Publications, 1998 (2003 printing)
BF1622.C45 L67 1998

The monster in the cave.
Mellinger, David. 1st ed. New York : Berkley Books, 2003.
BF575.F2 M45 2003

MONSTERS. *See also* **DRAGONS.**
Marvels, monsters, and miracles. Kalamazoo, Mich. : Medieval Institute Publications, 2002.
GR825 .M218 2002

MONSTERS, DOUBLE. *See* **MONSTERS.**

MONSTERS - ENCYCLOPEDIAS.
Franklin, Anna. The illustrated encyclopedia of fairies. London : Vega, 2002.
GR549 .F73 2002

Guiley, Rosemary. The encyclopedia of vampires, werewolves, and other monsters. New York, NY : Facts on File, 2004.
BF1556 .G86 2004

MONSTERS IN ART.
Hachet, Pascal. Psychanalyse d'un choc esthétique. Paris, France : Harmattan, c2002.

MONSTERS - NEW JERSEY.
Martinelli, Patricia A. Haunted New Jersey. Mechanicsburg, PA : Stackpole Books, 2005.
BF1472.U6 M38 2004

MONSTROSITIES. *See* **MONSTERS.**

Montagner, Hubert. L'enfant, la vraie question de l'école / Hubert Montagner ; [présentation de Georges Dupon-Lahitte]. Paris : Jacob, c2002. 325 p. : ill. ; 24 cm. Includes bibliographical references. ISBN 2-7381-1169-6 DDC 150
1. Educational psychology. 2. School psychology. 3. Child psychology. I. Title.

Montagu, Ashley, 1905-.
Race and IQ. Expanded ed. New York : Oxford University Press, 1999.
BF432.A1 R3 1999

MONTAUK POINT (N.Y.) - MISCELLANEA.
Moon, Peter. The black sun. New York : Sky Books, c1997.
BF1434.U6 M66 1997

Montauk series
(bk. 4) Moon, Peter. The black sun. New York : Sky Books, c1997.
BF1434.U6 M66 1997

Monte, Christopher F. Beneath the mask : an introduction to theories of personality / Christopher F. Monte, Robert N. Sollod. 7th ed. Hoboken, NJ : J. Wiley & Sons, c2003. xviii, 711 p. : ill. ; 26 cm. Includes bibliographical references (p. 665-688) and indexes. Publisher description URL: http://www.loc.gov/catdir/desc ription/wiley038/2002191098.html Table of contents URL: http://www.loc.gov/catdir/toc/wiley031/2002191098.html ISBN 0-471-26398-2 (alk. paper) DDC 155.2
1. Personality - Philosophy. I. Sollod, Robert N. II. Title.
BF698 .M64 2003

Monteil, Jean-Marc. Social context and cognitive performance : towards a social psychology of cognition / Jean-Marc Monteil and Pascal Huguet. Hove, East Sussex, UK : Psychology Press, c1999. v, 170 p. : ill. ; 24 cm. (European monographs in social psychology, 0892-7286) Includes bibliographical references (p. 145-164) and indexes. ISBN 0-86377-784-8 DDC 153
1. Cognition - Social aspects. 2. Cognition and culture. 3. Thought and thinking - Social aspects. I. Huguet, Pascal. II. Title. III. Series.
BF311 .M59 1999

Montes, Oscar (Montes Padilla).
Téllez, Edgar. Diario íntimo de un fracaso. 1. ed. Bogotá, D.C., Colombia : Planeta, 2002.

Montgomery, Tracy T.
Plung, Daniel L. Professional communication. Mason, Ohio : Thomson/South-Western, c2004.
HF5718 .P58 2004

Montpensier, Anne-Marie-Louise d'Orléans, duchesse de, 1627-1693.
[Correspondence. English & French]
Against marriage : the correspondence of la Grande Mademoiselle / edited and translated by Joan DeJean. Chicago : University of Chicago Press, 2002. xix, 86 p. : ports. ; 23 cm. (The other voice in early modern Europe) Includes bibliographical references (p. 73-82) and index. Text in English and French. ISBN 0-226-53490-1 (cloth : alk. paper) ISBN 0-226-53492-8 (pbk. : alk. paper) DDC 944/.033/0922
1. Montpensier, Anne-Marie-Louise d'Orléans, - duchesse de, - 1627-1693 - Correspondence. 2. Motteville, Françoise de, - d. 1689 - Correspondence. 3. Princesses - France - Correspondence. 4. Ladies-in-waiting - France - Correspondence. 5. France - History - Louis XIV, 1643-1715. 6. France - Court and courtiers - History - 17th century. 7. Marriage. 8. Sex role. I. Motteville, Françoise de, d. 1689. II. DeJean, Joan E. III. Title. IV. Series.
DC130.M8 A4 2002

MONTPENSIER, ANNE-MARIE-LOUISE D'ORLÉANS, DUCHESSE DE, 1627-1693 - CORRESPONDENCE.
Montpensier, Anne-Marie-Louise d'Orléans, duchesse de, 1627-1693. [Correspondence. English & French] Against marriage. Chicago : University of Chicago Press, 2002.
DC130.M8 A4 2002

MONUMENTS. See **MEGALITHIC MONUMENTS.**

MONUMENTS - PSYCHOLOGICAL ASPECTS.
Edkins, Jenny. Trauma and the memory of politics. Cambridge ; New York : Cambridge University Press, 2003.
BF175.5.P75 E35 2003

MOOD (PSYCHOLOGY).
Eldershaw, Jane. The little book of moods. Avon, MA : Adams Media, 2004.
BF637.C5 E383 2004

Moody, Raymond A. Life after life : the investigation of a phenomenon, survival of bodily death / Raymond A. Moody. Rev. 25th anniversary ed / with a new preface by Melvin Morse and a foreword by Elisabeth Kübler-Ross. London : Rider, 2001. xxviii, 175 p. ; 22 cm. Previous ed.: [Covington : Mockingbird], 1975. ISBN 0-7126-0273-9 DDC 133.9013
1. Parapsychology. 2. Reincarnation - Case studies. 3. Reincarnation therapy - Case studies. I. Title.

MOON.
Ross, Helen Elizabeth, 1935- The mystery of the moon illusion. Oxford ; New York : Oxford University Press, 2002.
QP495 .R67 2002

The moon & everyday living.
Pharr, Daniel. 2nd ed. St. Paul, Minn. : LLewellyn, 2002.
BF1723 .P48 2002

Moon and everyday living.
Pharr, Daniel. The moon & everyday living. 2nd ed. St. Paul, Minn. : LLewellyn, 2002.
BF1723 .P48 2002

MOON - MISCELLANEA.
Burk, Kevin, 1967- The complete node book. 1st ed. St. Paul, Minn. : Llewellyn Publications, 2003.
BF1723 .B87 2003

Morrison, Dorothy, 1955- Everyday moon magic. St. Paul, Minn. : Llewellyn Publications, 2003.
BF1623.M66 M67 2003

Pharr, Daniel. The moon & everyday living. 2nd ed. St. Paul, Minn. : LLewellyn, 2002.
BF1723 .P48 2002

Townley, John, 1945- Lunar returns. 1st ed. St. Paul, Minn. : Llewellyn Publications, 2003.
BF1723 .T69 2003

MOON, NEW. See **NEW MOON.**

Moon, Peter. The black sun : Montauk's Nazi-Tibetan connection / Peter Moon ; illustrated by Nina Helms. New York : Sky Books, c1997. 295 p. : ill. ; 22 cm. (Montauk series ; bk. 4) Includes bibliographical references (p. [283]-[286]) and index. ISBN 0-9631889-4-1 (pbk.) DDC 133
1. Occultism - New York (State) - Montauk Point. 2. Montauk Point (N.Y.) - Miscellanea. 3. Nazis - Miscellanea. 4. Tibet (China) - Miscellanea. I. Title. II. Series.
BF1434.U6 M66 1997

MOON - PHASES. See **NEW MOON.**

MOON - PHASES - MISCELLANEA.
Heath, Maya, 1948- Magical oils by moonlight. Franklin Lakes, NJ : New Page Books, 2004.
BF1442.E77 H43 2004

Moon rites.
Spiraldancer. South Melbourne : [Great Britain] : Lothian, 2002.

Mooney, Julie. The world of Ripley's believe it or not! / by Julie Mooney and the editors of Ripley's entertainment. New York : Black Dog & Leventhal, c1999. 159 p. : ill. (some col.) ; 35 cm. Includes index ISBN 1-57912-088-1 DDC 031.02
1. Ripley's believe it or not (New York : 1965) 2. Curiosities and wonders. I. Title. II. Title: Ripley's believe it or not (New York : 1965)
AG243 .M653 1999

Moore, Barbara, 1963- What tarot can do for you : your future in the cards / Barbara Moore. 1st ed. St. Paul, Minn. : Llewellyn Publications, 2004. p. cm. ISBN 0-7387-0173-4 DDC 133.3/2424
1. Tarot. I. Title.
BF1879.T2 M653 2004

Moore, Brian C. J. An introduction to the psychology of hearing / Brian C.J. Moore. 5th ed. Amsterdam ; Boston : Academic Press, c2003. xvi, 413 p. : ill. ; 23 cm. Includes bibliographical references (p. 355-397) and index. Publisher description URL: http://www.loc.gov/catdir/description/els031/2002116780.html Table of contents URL: http://www.loc.gov/catdir/toc/els031/2002116780.html ISBN 0-12-505628-1 (alk. paper) DDC 152.1/5
1. Auditory perception. 2. Hearing. I. Title.
BF251 .M66 2003

Moore, David (David R.) Project management : designing effective organisational structures in construction / David R. Moore. Oxford, [Eng.] ; Malden, MA : Blackwell Science, c2002. 288 p. : ill. ; 25 cm. Includes bibliographical references (p. 281-284) and index. ISBN 0-632-06393-9 (pbk.)
1. Construction industry - Management. 2. Project management. 3. Organizational behavior. I. Title. II. Title: Designing effective organisational structures in construction

Moore, Donald S., 1963-.
Race, nature, and the politics of difference. Durham : Duke University Press, c2003.
HT1521 .R2355 2003

Moore, Mary, 1947-.
Kennedy, Kevin (Kevin John), 1955- Going the distance. Upper Saddle River, NJ : Prentice Hall/Financial Times, c2003.
HD57.7 .K465 2003

Moore, Thomas, 1940- Original self : living with paradox and authenticity / Thomas Moore ; illustrated by Joan Hanley. 1st ed. New York : HarperCollins, c2000. vii, 150 p. : ill. ; 21 cm. Cover title: Original self : living with paradox and originality. Includes bibliographical references (p. 149-150). ISBN 0-06-019542-8 DDC 291.4/32
1. Spiritual life. 2. Psychology, Religious. I. Title. II. Title: Original self : living with paradox and originality
BL624 .M6643 2000

Moorey, Teresa. Magic house : practical magic for a harmonious home / Teresa Moorey. 1st US ed. New York, NY : Ryland Peters & Small, 2003. p. cm. Includes bibliographical references and index. Table of contents URL: http://www.loc.gov/catdir/toc/ecip042/2003008485.html CONTENTS: Your magical toolkit -- A journey through your home -- First impressions -- The heart of the home -- The energy centre -- Nourished in every way -- Creating concentration -- Peace and pleasure -- The nursery -- Bathtime bliss -- Your store-house -- Your head space -- A home for all seasons -- Moving on -- Table of magical correspondences. ISBN 1-84172-484-X DDC 133.4/3
1. Magic. 2. Home - Miscellanea. 3. Households - Miscellanea. 4. Witchcraft. I. Title.
BF1623.H67 M66 2003

Spellbound : the teenage witch's wiccan handbook / Teresa Moorey. Berkeley, CA : Ulysses Press ; Distributed in the U.S.A. by Publishers Group West, 2002. 250 p. : ill., 22 cm. Includes index. ISBN 1-56975-312-1 (pbk.)
1. Witchcraft - Juvenile literature. 2. Teenagers - Miscellanea - Juvenile literature. I. Title.
BF1571.5.T44 M66 2002

MOOTW (MILITARY SCIENCE). See **ARMED FORCES - OPERATIONS OTHER THAN WAR.**

Mor, Ben D.
Maoz, Zeev. Bound by struggle. Ann Arbor : University of Michigan Press, c2002.
JZ5595 .M366 2002

Moraitis, Dimitri.
Martin, Barbara Y. Change your aura, change your life Sunland, CA : WisdomLight Books, c2003.
BF1389.A8 M37 2003

Moral beliefs and moral theory.
Forrester, Mary Gore, 1940- Dordrecht ; Boston : Kluwer Academic Publishers, c2002.
BJ1012 .F615 2002

MORAL CONDITIONS. See also **SEX CUSTOMS.**
Jannoud, Claude. La crise de l'esprit. Lausanne, Suisse : Age d'homme, c2001.

MORAL DEVELOPMENT.
Ashkenazi, Nisim. Ben he-'anan. Tel-Aviv : Gal, 2002.

Moral development, self, and identity. Mahwah, N.J. : Lawrence Erlbaum Associates, 2004.
BF723.M54 M686 2004

Rosenberg, Shelley Kapnek. Raising a mensch. 1st ed. Philadelphia : Jewish Publication Society, 2003.
BF723.M54 R68 2003

Schwickert, Eva-Maria. Feminismus und Gerechtigkeit. Berlin : Akademie Verlag, c2000.

Xypas, Constantin. Les stades du développement affectif selon Piaget. Paris : Harmattan, c2001.

Moral development, self, and identity / Daniel K. Lapsley and Darcia Narvaez, editors. Mahwah, N.J. : Lawrence Erlbaum Associates, 2004. p. cm. Includes bibliographical references and index. ISBN 0-8058-4286-1 (hc : alk. paper) DDC 155.2/5
1. Moral development. I. Blasi, Augusto. II. Lapsley, Daniel K. III. Narváez, Darcia.
BF723.M54 M686 2004

Moral dilemmas and other topics in moral philosophy.
Foot, Philippa. Oxford ; New York : Clarendon Press, 2002.

MORAL EDUCATION. See also **RELIGIOUS EDUCATION.**
Tromellini, Pina. Un corredo per la vita. Milano : Salani editore, c2002.

MORAL EDUCATION - EUROPE - HISTORY.
Moss, Ann, 1938- Printed commonplace-books and the structuring of Renaissance thought. Oxford : Clarendon Press ; New York : Oxford University Press, 1996.
PA2047 .M67 1996

MORAL EDUCATION - UNITED STATES.
McKnight, Douglas. Schooling, the Puritan imperative, and the molding of an American national identity. Mahwah, N.J. ; London : L. Erlbaum Associates, 2003.
LC311 .M24 2003

Moral, Freiheit und Geschichte.
Eidam, Heinz. Würzburg : Königshausen & Neumann, 2001.

MORAL JUDGMENT. See **JUDGMENT (ETHICS).**

Moral phenomena.
Hartmann, Nicolai, 1882-1950. [Struktur des ethischen Phänomens. English] New Brunswick, N.J. : Transaction Publishers, c2002, 1932.
BJ1012 .H342 2002

MORAL PHILOSOPHY. See **ETHICS.**

Moral responsibility and alternative possibilities : essays on the importance of alternative possibilities / edited by David Widerker and Michael McKenna. Aldershot, England ; Burlington, VT : Ashgate, c2003. vi, 364 p. : ill. ; 24 cm. Includes bibliographical references (p. [347]-354) and index. ISBN 0-7546-0495-0 (alk. paper) DDC 123/.5
1. Frankfurt, Harry G., - 1929- 2. Responsibility. 3. Free will and determinism. I. Widerker, David, 1963- II. McKenna, Michael.
BJ1451 .M6472 2003

MORAL THEOLOGY. See **CHRISTIAN ETHICS.**

Moral theory.
Timmons, Mark, 1951- Lanham, Md. : Rowman & Littlefield Publishers, c2002.
BJ1012 .T56 2002

Moral writings.
Prichard, H. A. (Harold Arthur), 1871-1947. Oxford : Clarendon Press ; New York : Oxford University Press, 2002.

MORALE. *See also* **PSYCHOLOGY, MILITARY.**
Why they fight [electronic resource]. Carlisle, PA : Strategic Studies Institute, U.S. Army War College, [2003]
U22

MORALE - CASE STUDIES.
Zentner, John J., 1965- The art of wing leadership and aircrew morale in combat [electronic resource]. Maxwell Air Force Base, Ala. : Air University Press, [2001]

Morales Tomas, Marco Antonio. El que busca encuentra = Nril, ri nikanon (kaqchikel) : conocimiento, método científico y el proceso de la investigación / [elaborado por Marco Antonio Morales Tomas, Otto René Valle Bonilla]. Guatemala : ESEDIR : Editorial Saqil Tzij, 1999. 59 p. : ill. ; 28 cm. (Investigación social y estadística aplicada ; módulo 1) Includes bibliographical references (p. 59). Text in Spanish only.
1. Research - Methodology. 2. Social sciences - Research - Methodology. 3. Science - Methodology. I. Valle Bonilla, Otto René. II. Title. III. Title: Nril, ri nikanon IV. Title: Conocimiento, método científico y el proceso de la investigación V. Title: Que busca encuentra VI. Series.

Una gráfica dice más que mil palabras = B'a-ok nikib'ij k'iy ch'ab'äl chwa jun achib'äl (kaqchikel) : estadística aplicada a la investigación social / [elaborado por Marco Antonio Morales Tomas, Otto René Valle Bonilla]. Guatemala : ESEDIR : Editorial Saqil Tzij, 1999. 26 p. : ill. ; 28 cm. (Investigación social y estadística aplicada ; módulo 3) Includes bibliographical references (p. 26).
1. Social sciences - Research - Methodology. 2. Social sciences - Statistical methods. I. Valle Bonilla, Otto René. II. Title. III. Title: B'a-ok nikib'ij k'iy ch'ab'äl chwa jun achib'äl IV. Title: Estadística aplicada a la investigación social V. Series.

Valle Bonilla, Otto René. Que no le cuenten cuentos = Guatemala : ESEDIR : Editorial Saqil Tzij, 1999.

Morales Villaroel, Oscar. Huellas y relatos / Oscar Morales Villaroel. Caracas : [s.n.], 2001. 170 p. ; 22 cm. Literary sketches.
1. Venezuelan essays. 2. Criticism. 3. Quotations. 4. Aphorisms and apothegms. 5. Folklore. 6. Mythology. I. Title.

Moralischer Nihilismus.
Schröder, Winfried, Dr. phil. Stuttgart-Bad Canstatt : Frommann-Holzboog, c2002.

MORALITY. *See* **ETHICS.**

Morality and the meaning of life
(11) Tudor, Steven. Compassion and remorse. Leuven ; Sterling, Va. : Peeters, 2001.
BJ1475 .T84 2001

(12) The many faces of individualism. Leuven, Belgium ; Sterling, Va. : Peeters, 2001.
B824 .M354 2001

(13) Apel, Karl-Otto. The response of discourse ethics to the moral challenge of the human situation as such and especially today. Leuven : Peeters, 2001.
BJ1012 .A64 2001

MORALS. *See* **CONDUCT OF LIFE; ETHICS.**

MORALS AND LAW. *See* **LAW AND ETHICS.**

MORANDI, ORAZIO, D. 1630.
Dooley, Brendan Maurice, 1953- Morandi's last prophecy and the end of Renaissance politics. Princeton, N.J. ; Woodstock : Princeton University Press, c2002.
BF1679.8.M59 D66 2002

Morandi's last prophecy and the end of Renaissance politics.
Dooley, Brendan Maurice, 1953- Princeton, N.J. ; Woodstock : Princeton University Press, c2002.
BF1679.8.M59 D66 2002

Moravia, Sergio, 1940- L'esistenza ferita : modi d'essere, sofferenze, terapie dell'uomo nell'inquietudine del mondo / Sergio Moravia. 1. ed. in "Campi del sapere.". Milano : Feltrinelli, 1999. 302 p. ; 23 cm. (Campi del sapere) Includes bibliographical references (p. 263-295) and index. ISBN 88-07-10259-5
1. Psychology and philosophy. 2. Psychotherapy. 3. Typology (Psychology) I. Title.
BF41 .M67 1999

MORBIDITY. *See* **DISEASES.**

More balls than hands.
Gelb, Michael. New York, NY : Prentice Hall, 2003.
BF637.S8 G39 2003

More IQ testing.
Carter, Philip J. Chichester, West Sussex, England ; New York : John Wiley & Sons, Ltd, 2002.
BF431.3 .C367 2002

Moreau de Bellaing, Louis.
La connaissance sociologique. Paris : Harmattan, c2002.
HM651 .C65 2002

Moreau, Pierre-François, 1948- Lucrèce : l'âme / Pierre-François Moreau. 1. ed. Paris : Presses universitaires de France, 2002. 127 p. : 18 cm. (Philosophies, 0766-1398 ; 158) Includes bibliographical references. ISBN 2-13-053211-X DDC 180
1. Lucretius Carus, Titus. - De rerum natura - Liber 3. 2. Soul. 3. Philosophy, Ancient. I. Title. II. Series.

Moreno, María, 1947- El fin del sexo y otras mentiras / María Moreno. Buenos Aires : Editorial Sudamericana, c2002. 283 p. ; 23 cm. ISBN 950-07-2323-9
1. Sex. I. Title.

Moreno-Riaño, Gerson, 1971- Political tolerance, culture, and the individual / Gerson Moreno-Riaño. Lewiston, N.Y. : E. Mellen Press, c2002. 144 p. ; 24 cm. (Studies in political science ; v. 6) Includes bibliographical references (p. [135]-142) and index. ISBN 0-7734-6962-1 (v. 6) ISBN 0-7734-7434-X (SPS series) DDC 306.2
1. Political psychology. 2. Toleration. 3. Culture. I. Title. II. Series: Studies in political science (Lewiston, N.Y.) ; v. 6.
JA74.5 .M653 2002

Morgan, Gerald, 1935-.
Nanteos. Llandysul, Wales : Gomer, [2001]
DA738.N36 N36 2001

The Morgan Kaufmann series in interactive technologies
Carroll, John M. HCI models, theories, and frameworks. San Francisco, Calif. : Morgan Kaufmann, 2003.

Fogg, B. J. Persuasive technology. Amsterdam ; Boston : Morgan Kaufmann Publishers, / c2003.
BF637.P4 F55 2003

Morgan, Sheena. The Wicca handbook : a complete guide to witchcraft & magic / Sheena Morgan. London : Vega, 2003. 192 p. : col. ill. ; 29 cm. ISBN 1-84333-697-9
1. Witchcraft - Handbooks, manuals, etc. 2. Magic - Handbooks, manuals, etc. I. Title.
BF1566 .M716 2003

Morgan, Shemu'el. 'Ets ha-da'at : tov o ra'? / Shemu'el Morgan. Pedu'el : Sh. Morgan, [1998?] 173 p. ; 25 cm. Includes bibliographical references.
1. Bible. - O.T. - Genesis II-IV - Criticism, interpretation, etc. 2. Tree of life. 3. Eden. I. Title.

Mörgeli, Christoph. "Über dem Grabe geboren" : Kindsnöte in Medizin und Kunst / Christoph Mörgeli, Uli Wunderlich. Bern : Benteli, 2002. 259 p. : ill. (chiefly col.), ports. ; 31 cm. Includes bibliographical references. ISBN 3-7165-1277-X
1. Art - History. 2. Infants (Newborn) - History. 3. Death - History - Art. I. Wunderlich, Uli. II. Title.

Moriconi, Enrico, 1950-.
Materiali per un lessico della ragione. Pisa : Edizioni ETS, c2001.

Morin, Edgar.
Cyrulnik, Boris. Dialogue sur la nature humaine. La Tour d'Aigues : Editions de l'Aube, c2000.
BF57 .C97 2000

MORITA PSYCHOTHERAPY.
Reynolds, David K. A handbook for constructive living. Honolulu : University of Hawaii Press, 2002.
RC489.M65 R438 2002

Morley, James, 1957-.
Imagination and its pathologies. Cambridge, Mass. : MIT Press, c2003.
BF408 .I455 2003

Mornell, Adina. Lampenfieber und Angst bei ausübenden Musikern : kritische Übersicht über die Forschung / Adina Mornell. Frankfurt am Main : P. Lang, 2002. 120 p. : ill. ; 21 cm. (Schriften zur Musikpsychologie und Musikästhetik, 0938-3820 ; Bd. 14) Includes bibliographical references (p. 105-118) and index. ISBN 3-631-39744-5 (pbk.)
1. Music - Performance - Psychological aspects. 2. Musicians - Psychology. 3. Performance anxiety. 4. Anxiety - Prevention. 5. Stress management. 6. Stress (Psychology) - Prevention. I. Title. II. Series: Schriften zur Musikpsychologie und Musikästhetik ; Bd. 14.
ML3830 .M67 2002

Morning glory.
Hawker, Gloria Ann. Merrimack, NH : Write to Print, c2001.
BF2050 .H373 2001

MOROCCO - RELIGIOUS LIFE AND CUSTOMS.
Hell, Bertrand. Le tourbillon des génies. Paris : Flammarion, c2002.

MOROCCO - SOCIAL LIFE AND CUSTOMS.
Rosen, Lawrence, 1941- The culture of Islam. Chicago : University of Chicago Press, 2002.
DT312 R64 2002

Moroz, Georges.
Hercules. New York : Dell, c1997.
BL820.H5 H47 1997

Morozov, S. M. (Stanislav Mikhaĭlovich) Dialektika Vygotskogo : vnechuvstvennaia real'nost' deiatel'nosti / S.M. Morozov. Moskva : Smysl, 2002. 119 p. ; 22 cm. (Psikhologicheskie issledovaniia) Includes bibliographical references (p. [112]-119). ISBN 5893571290
1. Vygotskiĭ, L. S. - (Lev Semenovich), - 1896-1934. 2. Psychology - Soviet Union - History. I. Title. II. Series.
BF109.V95 M67 2002

MORPHOGENESIS.
Origination of organismal form. Cambridge, Mass. : MIT Press, c2003.
QH491 .O576 2003

MORPHOLOGY.
Minelli, Alessandro. The development of animal form. Cambridge ; New York : Cambridge University Press, 2003.
QH491 .M559 2003

Morris, Desmond. The naked eye : my travels in search of the human species / Desmond Morris. London : Ebury Press, 2000. ix, 278 p., [32] p. of plates : ill. (some col.), col. ports. ; 24 cm. Includes index. ISBN 0-09-187022-4 DDC 301
1. Human behavior. 2. Animal behavior. 3. Ethologists - England - Biography. I. Title.
QL31.M79 A3 2000

Morris, Noelle.
Survivors. New York : Scholastic, c2002.
BF637.S8 S8317 2002

Morrison, Alan, 1946-.
Burke, Dan, 1965- Business @ the speed of stupid. Cambridge, MA : Perseus Pub., c2001.
HD45 .B7995 2001

Morrison, Dorothy, 1955- Everyday moon magic : spells & rituals for abundant living / Dorothy Morrison. St. Paul, Minn. : Llewellyn Publications, 2003. p. cm. Includes bibliographical references and index. ISBN 0-7387-0249-8 DDC 133.4/3
1. Magic. 2. Moon - Miscellanea. I. Title.
BF1623.M66 M67 2003

Morrison, Margaret A.
Using qualitative research in advertising: strategies, techniques, and applications. Thousand Oaks, Calif. : Sage, c2002.
HF5814 .U78 2002

Morrison, Raymond E. Developing effective engineering leadership / Ray Morrison and Carl Ericsson. London : Institution of Electrical Engineers, c2003. 164 p. : ill. ; 24 cm. (IEE management of technology series ; 21) Includes bibliographical references (p. [155]-158) and index. ISBN 0-85296-214-2 DDC 620.0068
1. Engineering - Management. 2. Leadership. I. Ericsson, Carl W. II. Institution of Electrical Engineers. III. Title. IV. Series.

Morrison, Slade.
Morrison, Toni. The book of mean people. 1st ed. New York : Hyperion Books for Children, c2002.
I. Black authors.

Morrison, Toni. The book of mean people / Toni & Slade Morrison ; pictures by Pascal Lemaître. 1st ed. New York : Hyperion Books for Children, c2002. 1 v. (unpaged) : col. ill. ; 25 cm. SCHOMBURG CHILDREN'S COLLECTION ISBN 0-7868-0540-4 (trade) ISBN 0-7868-2471-9 (library)
1. Conduct of life - Juvenile literature. 2. Interpersonal relations - Juvenile literature. 3. Black authors. I. Morrison, Slade. II. Lemaître, Pascal. III. Schomburg Children's Collection. IV. Title.

Morrissey, Robert John, 1947-
[Empereur à la barbe fleurie. English]
Charlemagne & France : a thousand years of mythology / Robert Morrissey ; translated by Catherine Tihanyi. English language ed. Notre Dame, Ind. : University of Notre Dame Press, c2003. xxi, 391 p., [16] p. of plates : ill. (some col.) ; 25 cm. (The Laura Shannon series in French medieval studies) Spine title: Charlemagne and France. Includes

bibliographical references (p. 303-369) and index. ISBN 0-268-02277-1 DDC 944/.014/092
1. Charlemagne, - Emperor, - 742-814 - Influence. 2. Charlemagne, - Emperor, - 742-814 - Legends - History and criticism. 3. Charlemagne, - Emperor, - 742-814 - Romances - History and criticism. 4. Charlemagne, - Emperor, - 742-814 - In literature. 5. Holy Roman Empire - Kings and rulers - Biography. 6. Civilization, Medieval. I. Title. II. Title: Charlemagne and France III. Series: Laura Shannon series in French medieval studies.
DC73 .M7513 2003

Mörschel, Thomas. Die Historia vom heiligen Gral : worinnen nebst anderem berichtet wird von Begebenheiten zu zeiten seiner heiligsten Majestät Arthurus, des Sohnes der Pferde und Königs von Loegrien, Cornwall, Albany und Cambria / zusammengetragen von Thomas Mörschel und mit Illustrationen von Ulrike Schneidewind. Saarbrücken : Logos, 1994- v. : ill. ; 25 cm. (Zwischen Traum und Wirklichkeit ; Bd. 3) PARTIAL CONTENTS: Bd. 1. Schwert und Harfe. ISBN 3-928598-03-1 (v. 1)
1. Grail. I. Schneidewind, Ulrike. II. Title. III. Series.

MORT ARTU.
Greene, Virginie Elisabeth, 1959- Le sujet et la mort dans La mort Artu. Saint-Genouph : Nizet, 2002.

La Mort aujourd'hui.
Hanus, Michel. Paris : Frison-Roche, c2000.

La mort élégante.
Nosmas, Alma. Paris : Horay, c2003.

Mortal secrets.
Klitzman, Robert. Baltimore : Johns Hopkins University Press, 2003.
RA643.8 .K56 2003

Mortalism : readings on the meaning of life / edited by Peter Heinegg. Amherst, N.Y. : Prometheus Books, 2003. 214 pg. ; 23 cm. Includes bibliographical references. ISBN 1-59102-042-5 (pbk. : alk. paper) DDC 128/.5
1. Life. 2. Death. I. Heinegg, Peter.
BD431 .M886 2003

MORTALITY. See **DEATH (BIOLOGY).**

Le morte Darthur, or, The hoole book of Kyng Arthur and of his noble knyghtes of the Rounde Table.
Malory, Thomas, Sir, 15th cent. [Morte d'Arthur] 1st ed. New York ; London : Norton, c2004.
PR2041 .M37 2004

MORTICIANS. See **UNDERTAKERS AND UNDERTAKING.**

Morton, Adam. The importance of being understood : folk psychology as ethics / Adam Morton. London ; New York : Routledge, 2003. ix, 225 p. ; 24 cm. (International library of philosophy) Includes bibliographical references (p. [206]-221) and index. ISBN 0-415-27242-4 (hbk.) ISBN 0-415-27243-2 (pbk.) DDC 150/.1
1. Communication - Psychological aspects. 2. Cooperativeness. 3. Social psychology. I. Title. II. Series.
BF637.C45 M65 2003

MORTUARY CEREMONIES. See **FUNERAL RITES AND CEREMONIES.**

MORTUARY PRACTICE. See **UNDERTAKERS AND UNDERTAKING.**

MOSAIC LAW. See **JEWISH LAW.**

Mosaico (Rome, Italy)
(10.) Giuffrida, Angela, 1943- Il corpo pensa. Roma : Prospettiva, c2002.

Mosekilde, Erik.
Zhusubaliyev, Zhanybai T. Bifurcations and chaos in piecewise-smooth dynamical systems. River Edge, New Jersey : World Scientific, c2003.

Moser, Antônio. O enigma da esfinge : a sexualidade / Antônio Moser. 3a ed. Petrópolis : Editora Vozes, 2002, c2001. 287 p. ; 21 cm. Includes bibliographical references (p. 261-281). ISBN 85-326-2595-9
1. Sex. 2. Sexual ethics. 3. Sex - Religious aspects - Christianity. 4. Homosexuality. I. Title.

Moser, Walter, 1942-.
Passions du passé. Paris : L'Harmattan, c2000.
BF378.S65 P37 2000

Moses ben Shem Tov, de Leon, d. 1305.
Shekel ha kodesh.
Sefer 'Amude ha-Kabalah. Yerushalayim : Nezer Sheraga, 761 [2001]

Moses, Lisa F.
Children's fears of war and terrorism. Olney, MD : Association for Childhood Education International, c2003.

BF723.W3 C48 2003

Mosheh ben Hayim, Koznitser, d. 1874. Sefer Ahavat Yiśra'el : yalkut nifla be-'inyene ahavat Yiśra'el ... : melukat mi-Shas u-midrashim ... / hubar 'a. y. Mosheh [ben] Hayim Koznitser. Yotse le-or me-hadash. Yerushalayim : Mekhon Sod yesharim, 760 [2000] 158 p. ; 24 cm.
1. Brotherliness - Religious aspects - Judaism. 2. Hasidism. 3. Ethics, Jewish. 4. Interpersonal relations - Religious aspects - Judaism. I. Title. II. Title: Ahavat Yiśra'el

Sefer 'Ahavat Yiśra'el : yevo'ar bo mitsvat Ahavat Yiśra'el ... ; Sefer ha-hayim : yevo'ar bo mitsvat ma'alat ha-emunah ... / ... Mosheh ha-Kohen mi-Koznits ... Bruklin : [Yehoshu'a Pinhas Bukhinger], 762 [2001] 2 v. in 1 ; 24 cm. Running title: 'Ahavat Yisra'el. Includes indexes.
1. Hasidism. 2. Brotherliness - Religious aspects - Judaism. 3. Ethics, Jewish. 4. Interpersonal relations - Religious aspects - Judaism. 5. Faith (Judaism) I. Title. II. Title: Sefer ha-Hayim. III. Title: 'Ahavat Yisra'el

Mosheh ben Shelomoh El'azar. Sefer Yede Mosheh ve-Torah or : ... ma'amre Hazal ... le-limud To. ha-k. vela-'asok be-mitsvot ... / mimeni ... Mosheh [ben] ... Shelomoh El'azar. Bene Berak : Sifre Or ha-hayim, [760 i.e. 2000] 225 p. ; 24 cm. Spine title: Yede Mosheh ye-Torah or.
1. Talmud Torah (Judaism) 2. Ethics, Jewish. 3. Jewish learning and scholarship. I. Title. II. Title: Yede Mosheh ye-Torah or

Moshkov, V. A. (Valentin Alekseevich). Selections. 2002.
Russkaia rasovaia teoriia do 1917 goda. Moskva : Feri-V, 2002.

Moskovskiĭ gumanitarnyĭ institut im. E.R. Dashkovoĭ.
Gidirinskiĭ, V. I. (Viktor Il'ich) Vvedenie v russkuiu filosofiiu. Moskva : Russkoe slovo, 2003.
B4201 .G536 2003

Moskovskiĭ psikhologo-sotsial'nyĭ institut.
Ivanov, S. P. (Sergeĭ Petrovich) Psikhologiia khudozhestvennogo deĭstviia sub"ekta. Moskva : Moskovskiĭ psikhologo-sotsial'nyĭ institut ; Voronezh : Izd-vo NPO "MODEK", 2002.
BF408 .I93 2002

Ponomarenko, V. A. (Vladimir Aleksandrovich) Sozidatel'naia psikhologiia. Moskva : Moskovskiĭ psikhologo-sotsial'nyĭ institut ; Voronezh : Izd-vo NPO "MODEK", 2000.
BF408 .P572 2000

Zeĭgarnik, B. V. (Bliuma Vul'fovna) Psikhologiia lichnosti. Moskva : Moskovskiĭ psikhologo-sotsial'nyĭ in-t, 1998.
BF698 .Z43 1998

Moskovskiĭ tsentr gendernykh issledovaniĭ.
Gendernyĭ kaleĭdoskop. Moskva : "Academia", 2001.

Moskowitz-Mateu, Lysa. Psychic diaries : connecting with who you are, why you're here, and what lies beyond / by Lysa Mateu. New York : Harper Entertainment, 2003. p. cm. Publisher description URL: http://www.loc.gov/catdir/description/hc044/2003062475.html ISBN 0-06-055966-7 (alk. paper) DDC 133.9/1
1. Moskowitz-Mateu, Lysa. 2. Mediums - United States - Biography. 3. Psychics - United States - Biography. I. Title.
BF1283.M66 A3 2003

MOSKOWITZ-MATEU, LYSA.
Moskowitz-Mateu, Lysa. Psychic diaries. New York : Harper Entertainment, 2003.
BF1283.M66 A3 2003

Moss, Ann, 1938- Printed commonplace-books and the structuring of Renaissance thought / Ann Moss. Oxford : Clarendon Press ; New York : Oxford University Press, 1996. ix, 345 p. ; 24 cm. Includes bibliographical references (p. [319]-338) and index. ISBN 0-19-815908-0 (acid-free paper) DDC 870.9/004
1. Latin language - Study and teaching - Europe - History - 16th century. 2. Latin language - Study and teaching - Europe - History - 17th century. 3. Thought and thinking - Study and teaching - Europe - History. 4. Quotations, Latin - Study and teaching - Europe - History. 5. Commonplace-books - Study and teaching - Europe - History. 6. Learning and scholarship - Europe - History. 7. Latin language - Textbooks - History. 8. Moral education - Europe - History. 9. Europe - Intellectual life. 10. Humanists - Europe. 11. Renaissance. I. Title.
PA2047 .M67 1996

Moss, Donald, 1949-
Hating in the first person plural. New York : Other Press, c2003.
RC506 .H285 2003

Moss, Henry, 1948-.
The self. New York : New York Academy of Sciences, 2003.
BF697

Mosser, Alois.
'Gottes auserwählte Völker'. Frankfurt am Main ; New York : Lang, c2001.
BT810.2 .G65 2001

MOTHER AND CHILD. See also **MOTHER AND INFANT.**
Rector, Robert. The effects of marriage and maternal education in reducing child poverty. Washington, D.C. : Heritage Foundation, 2002.

Smith, Janna Malamud. A potent spell. Boston : Houghton Mifflin, 2003.
HQ759 .S618 2003

Stern, Daniel N. The first relationship. Cambridge, Mass. : Harvard University Press, 2002, 1977.
BF720.M68 S74 2002

MOTHER AND CHILD IN LITERATURE.
Gerber, Nancy, 1956- Portrait of the mother-artist. Lanham, Md. : Lexington Books, c2003.
PS374.M547 G47 2003

MOTHER AND CHILD - INDONESIA.
Zevalkink, Dina Johanna, 1962- Attachment in Indonesia. [Netherlands? : s.n.], c1997 (Ridderkerk : Ridderprint)
BF575.A86 Z48 1997

MOTHER AND CHILD - UNITED STATES.
The subject of care. Lanham, Md. ; Oxford : Rowman & Littlefield Publishers, c2002.
HQ1206 .S9 2002

MOTHER AND INFANT.
Stern, Daniel N. The first relationship. Cambridge, Mass. : Harvard University Press, 2002, 1977.
BF720.M68 S74 2002

MOTHER AND INFANT - CROSS-CULTURAL STUDIES.
Regression periods in human infancy. Mahwah, N.J. : Lawrence Erlbaum Associates, 2003.
BF720.R43 R44 2003

MOTHER-CHILD RELATIONSHIP. See **MOTHER AND CHILD.**

MOTHER GODDESS RELIGION. See **GODDESS RELIGION.**

MOTHER-INFANT RELATIONSHIP. See **MOTHER AND INFANT.**

Mother/nature.
Roach, Catherine M., 1965- Bloomington, IN : Indiana University Press, c2003.
BD581 .R59 2003

MOTHERHOOD. See **MOTHERS.**

MOTHERHOOD IN LITERATURE.
Gerber, Nancy, 1956- Portrait of the mother-artist. Lanham, Md. : Lexington Books, c2003.
PS374.M547 G47 2003

MOTHERHOOD - PSYCHOLOGICAL ASPECTS.
Dufourmantelle, Anne. La sauvagerie maternelle. Paris : Calmann-Lévy, c2001.

López, Carmen Adela, 1935- Madres e hijas. Caracas, Venezuela : Vadell Hermanos, 2002.

Smith, Janna Malamud. A potent spell. Boston : Houghton Mifflin, 2003.
HQ759 .S618 2003

MOTHERS. See also **MOTHERHOOD.**
Smith, Janna Malamud. A potent spell. Boston : Houghton Mifflin, 2003.
HQ759 .S618 2003

MOTHERS AND DAUGHTERS.
Cowen, Lauren. Daughters & mothers. Philadelphia [Penn.] : Courage Books, c1997.
HQ755.85 .C695 1997

Davenport, Donna S. Singing mother home. Denton, Tex. : University of North Texas Press, c2002.
BF575.G7 D365 2002

Hjelmstad, Lois Tschetter. The last violet. Englewood, Colo. : Mulberry Hill Press, c2002.
BF575.G7 H575 2002

Jonas, Susan. Friends for life. 1st ed. New York : William Morrow & Co., c1997.
HQ755.85 .J65 1997

López, Carmen Adela, 1935- Madres e hijas. Caracas, Venezuela : Vadell Hermanos, 2002.

Mothers and daughters.
Wells, Celia Townsend, 1932- Brood bitch. West Lafayette, Ind. : Purdue University Press, c2003.
SF422.82.W44 A3 2003

MOTHERS - DEATH - PSYCHOLOGICAL ASPECTS.
Davenport, Donna S. Singing mother home. Denton, Tex. : University of North Texas Press, c2002.
BF575.G7 D365 2002

Hjelmstad, Lois Tschetter. The last violet. Englewood, Colo. : Mulberry Hill Press, c2002.
BF575.G7 H575 2002

MOTHERS IN LITERATURE.
Gerber, Nancy, 1956- Portrait of the mother-artist. Lanham, Md. : Lexington Books, c2003.
PS374.M547 G47 2003

MOTHERS - PSYCHOLOGY.
Smith, Janna Malamud. A potent spell. Boston : Houghton Mifflin, 2003.
HQ759 .S618 2003

Moti, virtù e motori celesti nella cosmologia di Roberto Grossatesta.
Panti, Cecilia, 1964- Firenze : SISMEL : Edizioni del Galluzzo, 2001.
B765.G74 P36 2001

MOTION PICTURE ACTORS AND ACTRESSES - BIOGRAPHY.
Amores de película. 1. ed. [Madrid] : Aguilar, 2002.
PN1998.2 .A46 2002

MOTION PICTURE ACTORS AND ACTRESSES - INDIA.
Surendra Kumar. Legends of Indian cinema. New Delhi : Har-Anand Publications, c2003.
PN1993.5.I4 S87 2003

MOTION PICTURE DIRECTION. *See* **MOTION PICTURES - PRODUCTION AND DIRECTION.**

MOTION PICTURE PLAYS - PRODUCTION AND DIRECTION. *See* **MOTION PICTURES - PRODUCTION AND DIRECTION.**

MOTION PICTURE PRODUCTION. *See* **MOTION PICTURES - PRODUCTION AND DIRECTION.**

MOTION PICTURE STARS. *See* **MOTION PICTURE ACTORS AND ACTRESSES.**

MOTION PICTURES. *See* **DANCE IN MOTION PICTURES, TELEVISION, ETC.**

MOTION PICTURES AND YOUTH.
Youth cultures. Westport, Conn. : Praeger, 2003.
HQ796 .Y59273 2003

MOTION PICTURES - COSTUME. *See* **COSTUME.**

MOTION PICTURES - DIRECTION. *See* **MOTION PICTURES - PRODUCTION AND DIRECTION.**

MOTION PICTURES - HISTORY.
Bühler, Gerhard, 1959- Postmoderne auf dem Bildschirm, auf der Leinwand. Sankt Augustin : Gardez!, c2002.

Caballero, Rufo, 1966- Sedición en la pasarela. La Habana, Cuba : Editorial Arte y Literatura, c2001.

MOTION PICTURES - INDIA.
Surendra Kumar. Legends of Indian cinema. New Delhi : Har-Anand Publications, c2003.
PN1993.5.I4 S87 2003

MOTION PICTURES - INDIA - TAMIL NADU.
Cujātā, 1935- Karratum perratum. 1. patippu. Cennai : Vicā Paplikēsans, 2000.
PL4758.9.S8758+

Kōvintan, Ka. Tamilt tiraippatankalil āṇ-peṇ pāl pētam. 1. patippu. Cennai : Kumaran Paplisars, 2001.
BF692.2 .K68 2001

MOTION PICTURES - MISCELLANEA.
Conner, Floyd, 1951- Hollywood's most wanted. 1st ed. Washington, D.C. : Brassey's, c2002.
PN1998 .C54 2002

Roeper, Richard, 1959- 10 sure signs a movie character is doomed, and other surprising movie lists. 1st ed. New York : Hyperion, c2003.
PN1998 .R568 2003

Silverman, Stephen M. Envy, anger & sweet revenge. New York : Red Rock Press, c2002.
BF575.E65 S55 2002

MOTION PICTURES - PRODUCTION AND DIRECTION - INDIA.
Surendra Kumar. Legends of Indian cinema. New Delhi : Har-Anand Publications, c2003.
PN1993.5.I4 S87 2003

Motivated in minutes.
Gracia, Jason. Madison, Wis. : Gracia Enterprises, c2002.
BF503 .G73 2002

Motivation.
Beck, Robert C. (Robert Clarence), 1931- 5th ed. Upper Saddle River, N.J. : Pearson/Prentice Hall, c2004.
BF503 .B38 2004

Motivation and agency.
Mele, Alfred R., 1951- Oxford ; New York : Oxford University Press, 2003.
BD450 .M383 2003

Motivation and emotion.
Gorman, Phil, 1965- 1st ed. New York : Routledge, 2003.
BF503 .G67 2003

MOTIVATION - CONGRESSES.
Nebraska Symposium on Motivation (2001) Evolutionary psychology and motivation. Lincoln, Neb. ; London : University of Nebraska Press, c2001.
BF701 .N43 2001

Motivation, emotion, and cognition : integrative perspectives on intellectual development and functioning / edited by David Yun Dai and Robert J. Sternberg. Mahwah, N.J. : L. Erlbaum Associates, 2004. p. cm. (The educational psychology series) Includes bibliographical references and index. ISBN 0-8058-4556-9 (c : alk. paper) ISBN 0-8058-4557-7 (pbk. : paper) DDC 153.9 1. Intellect. 2. Motivation (Psychology) 3. Emotions and cognition. I. Dai, David Yun. II. Sternberg, Robert J. III. Series.
BF431 .M72 2004

MOTIVATION (PSYCHOLOGY). *See also* **BURN OUT (PSYCHOLOGY); COMPETITION (PSYCHOLOGY); CONFLICT (PSYCHOLOGY); GOAL (PSYCHOLOGY); NEED (PSYCHOLOGY); SELF-ACTUALIZATION (PSYCHOLOGY); THREAT (PSYCHOLOGY).**
Beck, Robert C. (Robert Clarence), 1931- Motivation. 5th ed. Upper Saddle River, N.J. : Pearson/Prentice Hall, c2004.
BF503 .B38 2004

Decker, Dru Scott, 1942- Stress that motivates. Rev. ed. Menlo Park, CA : Crisp Publications, c2002.
BF575.S75 D38 2002

Gorman, Phil, 1965- Motivation and emotion. 1st ed. New York : Routledge, 2003.
BF503 .G67 2003

Gracia, Jason. Motivated in minutes. Madison, Wis. : Gracia Enterprises, c2002.
BF503 .G73 2002

Handbook of motivational counseling. Chichester, West Sussex, England ; Hoboken, NJ : J. Wiley, c2004.
BF637.C6 H3172 2004

Khzardzhi͡an, S. M. (Sanatruk M.) Bioprogrammy v prirode i politike. Pushchino : ONTI PNTS RAN, 1996.
BF199 .K43 1996

Langens, Thomas A. Tagträume, Anliegen und Motivation. Göttingen ; Seattle : Hogrefe, c2002.

Mele, Alfred R., 1951- Motivation and agency. Oxford ; New York : Oxford University Press, 2003.
BD450 .M383 2003

Motivation, emotion, and cognition. Mahwah, N.J. : L. Erlbaum Associates, 2004.
BF431 .M72 2004

Ring, Susan. Needs and wants. Mankato, Minn. : Yellow Umbrella Books, c2003.
BF723.M56 R56 2003

Sovremennai͡a psikhologii͡a motivat͡sii. Moskva : Smysl, 2002.
BF503 .S68 2002

Why they fight [electronic resource]. Carlisle, PA : Strategic Studies Institute, U.S. Army War College, [2003]
U22

MOTIVATION (PSYCHOLOGY) - CONGRESSES.
International Conference on Motivation (8th : 2002 Moscow, Russia) 8th International Conference on Motivation. Moscow : Russian State University for Humanities, 2002.
BF501.5 .I58 2002

MOTIVATION (PSYCHOLOGY) IN CHILDREN.
Cronin, W. Jean. Going for the gold. Longmont, CO : Sopris West, c2003.
BF637.B4 C76 2003

MOTIVATION (PSYCHOLOGY) IN CHILDREN - JUVENILE LITERATURE.
Gottlieb, Jeff, 1954- Spriggles. Petoskey, Mich. : Mountain Watch Press, c2002.
BF723.M56 G68 2002

Ring, Susan. Needs and wants. Mankato, Minn. : Yellow Umbrella Books, c2003.
BF723.M56 R56 2003

MOTIVATION (PSYCHOLOGY) - PHYSIOLOGICAL ASPECTS.
Gorman, Phil, 1965- Motivation and emotion. 1st ed. New York : Routledge, 2003.
BF503 .G67 2003

MOTIVATION (PSYCHOLOGY) - SOCIAL ASPECTS.
Emotion and motivation. Malden, MA : Blackwell Pub., 2004.
BF531 .E4826 2004

Motivationsforschung
(18) Langens, Thomas A. Tagträume, Anliegen und Motivation. Göttingen ; Seattle : Hogrefe, c2002.

MOTOR ABILITY. *See* **MECHANICAL ABILITY.**

MOTOR ABILITY IN CHILDREN.
Fagard, Jacqueline. Le développement des habiletés de l'enfant. Paris : CNRS, c2001.
RJ133 .F34 2001

Losquadro-Liddle, Tara. Why motor skills matter. Chicago : Contemporary Books, c2004.
BF723.M6 L67 2004

MOTOR LEARNING. *See also* **MOVEMENT EDUCATION.**
Coker, Cheryl A. Motor learning and control for practitioners. Boston : McGraw-Hill, c2004.
BF295 .C645 2004

Fagard, Jacqueline. Le développement des habiletés de l'enfant. Paris : CNRS, c2001.
RJ133 .F34 2001

Magill, Richard A. Motor learning and control. 7th ed. Boston : McGraw-Hill, c2004.
BF295 .M36 2004

Steinhauer, Kimberly Marie. The relationship among voice onset, voice quality and fundamental frequency. 2000.

Motor learning and control.
Magill, Richard A. 7th ed. Boston : McGraw-Hill, c2004.
BF295 .M36 2004

Motor learning and control for practitioners.
Coker, Cheryl A. Boston : McGraw-Hill, c2004.
BF295 .C645 2004

Motor learning and performance.
Schmidt, Richard A., 1941- 3rd ed. Champaign, IL : Human Kinetics, 2004.
BF295 .S249 2004

MOTOR LEARNING - TEXTBOOKS.
Schmidt, Richard A., 1941- Motor learning and performance. 3rd ed. Champaign, IL : Human Kinetics, 2004.
BF295 .S249 2004

MOTOR SKILL LEARNING. *See* **MOTOR LEARNING.**

Les mots et moi.
Jouffroy, Alain, 1928- [Mots et moi] Nantes : Pleins feux, c2002.

Motsch, Monika, 1942-
[Mit Bambusrohr und Ahle von Qian Zhongshus Guanzhuibian zu einer Neubetrachtung Du Fus. Chinese]
"Guan zhui bian" yu Du Fu xin jie / [De] Mozhiyijia zhu ; Ma Shude yi. Di 1 ban. Shijiazhuang Shi : Hebei jiao yu chu ban she, 1997 (2002 printing) [1], 3, 4, 279 p. ; 21 cm. (Qian Zhongshu yan jiu cong shu) Gen ju Deguo Meiyin he pan Falankefu Ou Zhou ke xue chu ban she 1994 nian ban yi chu. Includes bibliographical references. ISBN 7-5434-3091-6
1. Chinese literature - History and criticism. 2. Chinese classics - History and criticism. I. Ma, Shude, 1944- II. Qian, Zhongshu, 1910- Guan zhui bian. 1998. III. Title. IV. Series.

Motteville, Françoise de, d. 1689.
Montpensier, Anne-Marie-Louise d'Orléans, duchesse de, 1627-1693. [Correspondence. English & French] Against marriage. Chicago : University of Chicago Press, 2002.
DC130.M8 A4 2002

MOTTEVILLE, FRANÇOISE DE, D. 1689 - CORRESPONDENCE.
Montpensier, Anne-Marie-Louise d'Orléans, duchesse de, 1627-1693. [Correspondence. English & French] Against marriage. Chicago : University of Chicago Press, 2002.
DC130.M8 A4 2002

Motycka, Alina. Nauka o nieświadomość : filozofia nauki wobec kontekstu tworzenia / Alina Motycka. Wrocław : Leopoldinum, 1998. 176 p. ; 21 cm. (Monografie Fundacji na Rzecz Nauki Polskiej. Seria humanistyczna) Includes bibliographical references and index. Summary in English. ISBN 83-85220-86-0
1. Science - Philosophy. 2. Subconsciousness. I. Title. II. Series.

Mould, Tom, 1969- Choctaw prophecy : a legacy of the future / Tom Mould. Tuscaloosa : University of Alabama Press, c2003. xxxvii, 263 p. : ill., map ; 25 cm. (Contemporary American Indian studies) Includes bibliographical references (p. [243]-255) and index. ISBN 0-8173-1225-0 (cloth : alk. paper) ISBN 0-8173-1226-9 (pbk. : alk. paper) DDC 299/.783
1. Choctaw Indians - Religion. 2. Prophecy. 3. Choctaw Indians - Folklore. 4. Oral tradition - Mississippi. I. Title. II. Series.
E99.C8 M68 2003

Moulding masculinities / edited by Søren Ervø and Thomas Johansson. Aldershot, Hants, England ; Burlington, VT : Ashgate, c2003. 2 v. : ill. ; 23 cm. Published in association with Nordic Summer University. "The two "Moulding Masculinities" volumes represent the first major publication in English of Northern Europe studies on masculinities"--V. 1, p. [4] of cover. Articles from several conferences presented by the Nordic Network for Masculinity Studies within the Nordic Summer University, and other seminars. Includes bibliographical references and indexes. CONTENTS: v. 1. Among men -- v. 2. Bending bodies. ISBN 1-84014-804-7 (v. 1) ISBN 1-84014-803-9 (v. 2) DDC 305.32
1. Masculinity. 2. Men - Identity. 3. Body image in men. 4. Body, Human (Philosophy) 5. Masculinity - Scandinavia. I. Ervø, Søren. II. Johansson, Thomas. III. Scandinavian Summer University.
BF692.5 .M68 2003

Moulinier, Didier. Dictionnaire de la jouissance / Didier Moulinier. Paris : L'Harmattan, c1999. 286 p. ; 22 cm. (Collection "La Philosophie en commun") Includes bibliographical references (p. 283-284). ISBN 2-7384-8413-1
1. Joy. 2. Lacan, Jacques, - 1901- 3. Psychoanalysis. 4. Postmodernism. I. Title. II. Series: Philosophie en commun.
BF575.H27 M68 1999

MOUNTAIN CLIMBING. See **MOUNTAINEERING.**

MOUNTAINEERING.
Marshall, Ian, 1954- Peak experiences. Charlottesville : University of Virginia Press, 2003.
PS163 .M37 2003

MOUNTAINEERING - PSYCHOLOGICAL ASPECTS.
Bayers, Peter L., 1966- Imperial ascent. Boulder, Colo. : University Press of Colorado, c2003.
GV200.19.P78 B39 2003

MOUNTAINS - CALIFORNIA. See **KLAMATH MOUNTAINS (CALIF. AND OR.).**

MOUNTAINS - OREGON. See **KLAMATH MOUNTAINS (CALIF. AND OR.).**

Mountfort, Paul Rhys. Nordic runes : understanding, casting, and interpreting the ancient Viking oracle / Paul Rhys Mountfort. Rochester, Vt. : Destiny Books, 2003. viii, 279 p. : ill. ; 23 cm. Includes bibliographical references (p. 273-277) and index. CONTENTS: Runelore -- Odin's gift -- Divine mysteries -- Runes and rune guilds -- The rune poems -- Runes and sagas -- The northern tradition -- Runestaves -- Guide to the staves -- Frey's aett -- Hagal's aett -- Tyr's aett -- Runecasting -- Re-membering the tradition -- The theory of runic divination -- The art of runecasting -- Spreads and castings -- A final word: the rune revival. ISBN 0-89281-093-9 (pbk.) DDC 133.3/3
1. Runes - Miscellanea. 2. Fortune-telling by runes. I. Title.
BF1779.R86 M68 2003

Ogam, the Celtic oracle of the trees : understanding, casting, and interpreting the ancient Druidic alphabet / Paul Rhys Mountfort. Rochester, Vt. : Destiny Books, c2002. 216 p. : ill. ; 23 cm. Includes bibliographical references (p. [209]-212). Table of contents URL: http://www.loc.gov/catdir/toc/fy034/2002073519.html ISBN 0-89281-919-7 DDC 491.6/211
1. Ogham alphabet. 2. Mythology, Celtic. 3. Druids and Druidism. 4. Trees - Mythology. 5. Divination. I. Title.
PB1217 .M68 2002

Moura, Carlos Eugênio Marcondes de.
Verger, Pierre. Saída de Iaô. Sao Paulo : Fundação Pierre Verger : Axis Mundi Editora, 2002.

Mourelatos, Alexander P. D., 1936-.
Presocratic philosophy. Aldershot, Hants, England ; Burlington, VT : Ashgate, 2002.
B187.5 .P743 2002

MOURNING. See **BEREAVEMENT - PSYCHOLOGICAL ASPECTS; GRIEF.**

MOURNING CUSTOMS. See **FUNERAL RITES AND CEREMONIES.**

MOVEMENT (ACTING). See **GESTURE.**

MOVEMENT EDUCATION. See also **MOTOR LEARNING.**
Broich, Josef, 1948- Körper- und Bewegungsspiele. 1. Aufl. 1999. Köln : Maternus, 1999.

MOVEMENT EDUCATION - GERMANY.
Augustin, Nicole. "Bewegung in Widersprüchen, Widersprüche in Bewegung bringen". Pfaffenweiler : Centaurus-Verlagsgesellschaft, 1998.
LC2873.G3 A94 1998

MOVEMENT PERCEPTION (VISION). See **MOTION PERCEPTION (VISION).**

MOVEMENT, PSYCHOLOGY OF. See **MOTION PERCEPTION (VISION); MOTOR LEARNING; MOVEMENT EDUCATION.**

MOVEMENT THERAPY.
Broich, Josef, 1948- Körper- und Bewegungsspiele. 1. Aufl. 1999. Köln : Maternus, 1999.

MOVIES. See **MOTION PICTURES.**

Movimiento femenino.
Larrea, Martha Victoria. Ibarra, Ecuador : [s.n.], 1997.

MOVING, HOUSEHOLD - MISCELLANEA.
Cochrane, David. AstroLocality magic. 1st ed. Gainesville, FL : Cosmic Patterns Software, c2002.
BF1729.M68 C63 2002

MOVING-PICTURE ACTORS AND ACTRESSES. See **MOTION PICTURE ACTORS AND ACTRESSES.**

MOVING-PICTURES. See **MOTION PICTURES.**

Moxham, Roy. The great hedge of India / Roy Moxham. Large print ed. Oxford : ISIS, 2001. 224 p. (large print) : map ; 25 cm. Originally published: London: Constable. ISBN 0-7531-5615-6 DDC 954.03
1. Moxham, Roy - Travel - India. 2. Hedges - India - History. 3. Large type books. 4. India - History - British occupation, 1765-1947. I. Title.

MOXHAM, ROY - TRAVEL - INDIA.
Moxham, Roy. The great hedge of India. Large print ed. Oxford : ISIS, 2001.

Moyaert, Paul, 1952- Begeren en vereren : sublimering en idealisering / Paul Moyaert. Amsterdam : SUN, c2002. 191 p. ; 22 cm. Includes bibliographical references. ISBN 90-5875-020-5
1. Sublimation (Psychology) I. Title.
BF175.5.S92 M69 2002

Mozaffari, Mehdi.
Globalization and civilizations. London ; New York : Routledge, 2002.
CB430 .G58 2002

Mozart, Wolfgang Amadeus, 1756-1791. Operas. Selections.
Malaniuk, Ira. Arien und Lieder [sound recording]. [Germany] : Preiser Records, p2000.

MOZART, WOLFGANG AMADEUS, 1756-1791.
Lechevalier, Bernard. Le cerveau de Mozart. Paris : O. Jacob, c2003.
ML3838 .L39 2003

Mozia, Michael Ifeanyinachukwu. Holiness & divine mercy (the key to heaven) : a theological reflection / by Michael Ifeanyinachukwu Mozia. Ibadan, Oyo State, Nigeria : St. Pauls, 2002. viii, 146 p. : ill. ; 22 cm. Includes bibliographical references (p. 140-141) and index.
1. Catholic Church - Nigeria - Doctrines. 2. Holiness. 3. Christian life. 4. God - Attributes. 5. Black author. I. Title. II. Title: Holiness and divine mercy (the key to heaven)

Mozzhilin, S. I. (Sergeĭ Ivanovich) Obretenie ĪA i vozniknovenie rannikh form sotsialʹnosti / S.I. Mozzhilin. Saratov : Saratovskiĭ gos. sotsialʹno-èkonomicheskiĭ universitet, 2002. 118, [1] p. ; 20 cm. Includes bibliographical references (p. 112-[119]). ISBN 5873092621
1. Self - Social aspects - History. 2. Sex role - History. I. Title.
BF697.5.S65 M69 2002

Mr. and Dr. talking it over.
Gillman, Karen. Lima, Ohio : Wyndham Hall Press, c2002.
BF637.C45 G55 2002

Mran' mā' ruī' rā gehavidhī.
'Oṅ' Mraṅ', 'Aṅ'gyaṅ'nīyā Ū". 'Im' chok' maṅgalā kyam'". Mantale : Krī' pvā' re" Cā 'up' Tuik", 2002.
BF1779.A88 O56 2002

Mran' mā' ruī' rā 'im' khraṃ mre naññ'" paññā.
San'" Ū", Sutagavesī. Ran' kun' : Rvhe Pu ra puid' Cā pe : Phran'' khyi re", Sa mī" Jotika Cā pe, 2000.
BF1773.2.B93 S26 2000

Mraṅ'' Svaṅ', Ū". Ca le cha rā krī" Ū" Puñña bedaṅ' 'a ho te" thap' 'a phvaṅ" kyam'" / Ū" Mraṅ' Svaṅ'. Ran' kun' : Khyui Te" Saṃ Cā pe : [Phran'' khyi re"], Paññā Rvhe Toṅ' Cā 'up' Tuik", 2002. 249 p. : ill. ; 19 cm. In Burmese. SUMMARY: Prose commentary on verse work on astrology of Ca le Ū", Puñña, 1802 or 3-1866 or 7; includes text.
1. Astrology, Burmese. I. Puñña, Ca le Ū", 1802 or 3-1866 or 7. II. Title.
BF1714.B8 M73 2002

Mróz, Lech.
Between tradition and postmodernity. Warsaw : Wydawnictwo DiG, 2003.

Mudimbe-boyi, M. Elisabeth.
Remembering Africa. Portsmouth, NH : Heinemann, c2002.
DT14 .R46 2002

MUDRA. See **GESTURE.**

Mudrovcic, María Inés.
Historia y sentido. Buenos Aires : Ediciones El Cielo por Asalto, c2001.

MUHAMMADANISM. See **ISLAM.**

Mühl-Benninghaus, Wolfgang.
Herrschaft des Symbolischen. Berlin : Vistas, c2002.

Muhūrtarāja.
Gulābavijaya. Śrī Muhūrtarāja. Dvitīyāvṛtti. Ji. Dhāra, Ma. Pra. : Rājendra Pravacana Kāryālaya, 1996.
BF1714.J28+

MUI TSAI. See **SLAVERY.**

Mujer, ideología y población.
Jornadas de Roles Sexuales y de Género (2nd : 1995 : Madrid, Spain) 1. ed. Madrid : Ediciones Clásicas, 1998.
HQ1075 .J67 1995

Mujer y poder.
Allard Olmos, Briseida, 1951- [Panamá] : Instituto de la Mujer - Universidad de Panamá, 2002.
HQ1154 .A62 2002

Mujeres en movimiento.
Musachi, Graciela. Argentina : Fondo de Cultura Económica / Argentina, 2001.

Mujeres y culturas
Piel que habla. Barcelona : Icaria, [2001]
BF697.5.B63 P54 2001

Mūks, Roberts. Jaunā viedība : Heidegers, Hilmans un eņģeļi / Roberts Mūks. Rīga : Dauguva, 2002. 148 p. ; 21 cm. Includes bibliographical references. ISBN 9984644839
1. Mysticism. I. Title.

Müller, Arno, 1930- Berühmte Frauen : von Maria Stuart bis Mutter Teresa : Persönlichkeit, Lebensweg und Handschriftenanalyse / Arno Müller. Wien : Braumüller, 2002. x, 278 p. : ill. ; 29 cm. Includes bibliographical references. ISBN 3-7003-1398-5 (hd. bd.) DDC 920.72
1. Women - Biography. 2. Graphology. I. Title.

Müller, Ernst.
Genuss und Egoismus. Berlin : Akademie Verlag, c2002.

Muller, F. Max (Friedrich Max), 1823-1900. The essential Max Muller : on language, mythology, and religion / edited by Jon R. Stone. 1st ed. New York ; Houndmills, England : Palgrave Macmillan, 2002. xx, 367 p. ; 24 cm. Includes bibliographical references and index. ISBN 0-312-29308-9 (hbk.) ISBN 0-312-29309-7 (pbk.) DDC 200
1. Religion. 2. Mythology. 3. Language and languages - Religious aspects. I. Stone, Jon R., 1959- II. Title.
BL50 .M785 2002

Müller, Gerd (Gerd B.).
Origination of organismal form. Cambridge, Mass. : MIT Press, c2003.
QH491 .O576 2003

Müller, Klaus E., 1935- Wortzauber : eine Ethnologie der Eloquenz / Klaus E. Müller. Frankfurt ; Lembeck, c2001. 159 p. ; 21 cm. Includes bibliographical references (p. 141-159). ISBN 3-87476-380-3 (pbk.)
1. Anthropological linguistics. 2. Speech acts (Linguistics) - Religious aspects. 3. Language and languages - Religious aspects. I. Title.
P35 .M945 2001

Müller, Michael, 1946-.
Kommunikation, Kunst und Kultur. Bern ; New York : Peter Lang, c2002.

Mulligan, Bob. Between astrolgers and clients : the foundation of a relationship / Bob Mulligan. Naples, Fla. : Astrology Co., c2001. ix, 235 p. ; 22 cm. Cover title: Between astrologers & clients. Includes bibliographical references (p. 221-225). ISBN 140102422X (softcover) ISBN 1401024238 (hardcover) DDC 133.5/023
1. Astrologers - Practice. I. Title. II. Title: Between astrologers & clients
BF1711 .M85 2001

Mulryne, J. R. (James Ronald).
Court festivals of the European Renaissance. Aldershot ; Burlington, VT : Ashgate, c2002.

Mulsow, Martin.
Das Ende des Hermetismus. Tübingen : Mohr Siebeck, c2002.
BF1587 .E53 2002

Multi-level issues in organizational behavior and strategy / edited by Fred Dansereau, Francis J. Yammarino. Amsterdam ; London : JAI, 2003. xii, 390 p. : ill. ; 23 cm. (Research in multi-level issues ; v. 2) Includes bibliographical references. ISBN 0-7623-1039-1 DDC 302.35
1. Organizational behavior. I. Dansereau, Fred, 1946- II. Yammarino, Francis J., 1954- III. Series.

MULTICIDE. *See* **MASS MURDER; SERIAL MURDERS.**

Multicultural counseling competencies 2003 :
Association for Multicultural Counseling and Development / edited by Gargi roysircar ... [et al.]. Alexandria, VA : Association for Multicultural Counseling and Development, 2003. p. cm. Includes bibliographical references and index. ISBN 1-55620-231-8 (alk. paper) DDC 158/.3
1. Cross-cultural counseling. 2. Psychiatry, Transcultural. I. Roysircar, Gargi. II. Association for Multicultural Counseling and Development (U.S.) III. Title: Multicultural counseling competencies two thousand three
BF637.C6 M8367 2003

Multicultural counseling competencies two thousand three.
Multicultural counseling competencies 2003. Alexandria, VA : Association for Multicultural Counseling and Development, 2003.
BF637.C6 M8367 2003

MULTICULTURALISM. *See also* **PLURALISM (SOCIAL SCIENCES).**
La culture. Auxerre : Sciences humaines éditions, c2002.

Markell, Patchen, 1969- Bound by recognition. Princeton, N.J. : Princeton University Press, c2003.
JC575 .M37 2003

Pompeo, Francesco. Il mondo è poco. Roma : Meltemi, c2002.
GN495.6 .P66 2002

Shweder, Richard A. Why do men barbecue? Cambridge, Mass. : Harvard University Press, 2003.
GN502 .S59 2003

Sobre las identidades. Pamplona : Universidad Pública de Navarra, [2001]

MULTICULTURALISM - GERMANY.
Inspecting Germany. Münster : Lit, c2002.
DD76 .I57 2002

MULTICULTURALISM - GOVERNMENT POLICY. *See* **MULTICULTURALISM.**

MULTICULTURALISM - UNITED STATES.
The afro-asian century. Durham, N.C. : Duke University Press, 2003.

Multilingual matters series (2002)
(121.) Herdina, Philip. A dynamic model of multilingualism. Clevedon, England Buffalo, N.Y. : Multilingual Matters, 2002.
P115.4 .H47 2002

MULTILINGUALISM. *See* **BILINGUALISM.**

MULTILINGUALISM - AFRICA.
Language & culture. Lusaka, Zambia : Quest, 1999.

MULTILINGUALISM - PSYCHOLOGICAL ASPECTS.
Herdina, Philip. A dynamic model of multilingualism. Clevedon, England Buffalo, N.Y. : Multilingual Matters, 2002.
P115.4 .H47 2002

Multimedia and virtual reality.
Sutcliffe, Alistair, 1951- Mahwah, N.J. ; London : Lawrence Erlbaum, c2003.
QA76.76.I59 S88 2003

MULTIMEDIA (ART).
Reck, H. U. Mythos Medienkunst. Köln : König, c2002.

MULTIMEDIA COMPUTING. *See* **MULTIMEDIA SYSTEMS.**

MULTIMEDIA INFORMATION SYSTEMS. *See* **MULTIMEDIA SYSTEMS.**

MULTIMEDIA KNOWLEDGE SYSTEMS. *See* **MULTIMEDIA SYSTEMS.**

MULTIMEDIA SYSTEMS - CONGRESSES.
International Conference on Simulation in Engineering Education (2001 : Phoenix, Ariz.) Proceedings of the International Conference on Simulation and Multimedia in Engineering Education & Virtual Worlds and Simulation. San Diego, CA : Society for Computer Simulation International, c2001.

Multimind.
Ornstein, Robert E. (Robert Evan), 1942- Cambridge, MA : ISHK, 2003.
BF431 .O68 2003

MULTINATIONAL CORPORATIONS. *See* **INTERNATIONAL BUSINESS ENTERPRISES.**

MULTINATIONAL ENTERPRISES. *See* **INTERNATIONAL BUSINESS ENTERPRISES.**

MULTIPLE BIRTH. *See* **TWINS.**

Multiple classifier systems.
International Workshop on Multiple Classifier Systems (4th : 2003 : Guildford, England) Berlin ; New York : Springer, c2003.
Q325.5 .I574 2003

Multiple commitments in the workplace.
Cohen, Aaron, 1952- Mahwah, New Jersey : Lawrence Erlhaum Associates, 2003.
HD58.7 .C6213 2003

MULTIPLE INTELLIGENCES.
Gordon, Claire, 1968- Are you smarter than you think? New York : Penguin Compass, c2003.
BF432.3 .G67 2003

Multiple intelligences reconsidered. New York, NY : P. Lang, c2004.
BF432.3 .M86 2004

Multiple intelligences reconsidered / edited by Joe L. Kincheloe. New York, NY : P. Lang, c2004. p. cm. (Counterpoints, 1058-1634 ; v. 278) Includes bibliographical references and index. CONTENTS: Twenty-first-century questions about multiple intelligences / Joe L. Kincheloe -- The power of language : a critique of the assumptions and pedagogical implications of Howard Gardner's concept of linguistic intelligence / Kathleen Nolan -- Musical stupidity and the reigning monoculture / Yusef Progler -- Where is the mathematics? Where are the mathematicians? / Peter Appelbaum -- Howard Gardner's theory of visual-spatial intelligence : a critical rethcorizing / Richard Cary -- Bodily-kinesthetic intelligence and the democratic ideal / Donald S. Blumenthal-Jones -- Getting personal : rethinking Gardner's personal intelligences / Joe L. Kincheloe -- The eighth one : naturalistic intelligence / Marla Morris -- Multiplying intelligences : hypermedia and social semiotics / Jay L. Lemke -- Multiple intelligences in early childhood education : a poststructural/feminist analysis / Gaile S. Cannella -- Howard Gardner's third way : toward a postformal redefinition of educational psychology / Danny Weil -- Multiple intelligences are not what they seem to be / Kathleen S. Berry. ISBN 0-8204-7098-8 (pbk. : alk. paper) DDC 153.9
1. Multiple intelligences. 2. Gardner, Howard. - Multiple intelligences. I. Kincheloe, Joe L. II. Series: Counterpoints (New York, N.Y.) ; v. 278.
BF432.3 .M86 2004

MULTIPLE MURDER. *See* **SERIAL MURDERS.**

The multiple states of the being.
Guénon, René. [Etats multiples de l'être. English] 2nd English ed. Ghent, NY : Sophia Perennis, c2001.
BD312 .G813 2001

Multiple streams of internet income.
Allen, Robert G. New York : Wiley, c2001.
HF5548.32 .A45 2001

MULTIVARIATE ANALYSIS.
The analysis and interpretation of multivariate data for social scientists. Boca Raton, Fla. : Chapman & Hall/CRC, c2002.
HA29 .A5824 2002

Mumford, Stephen.
Molnar, George, d. 1999. Powers. Oxford ; New York : Oxford University Press, 2003.
BD541 .M54 2003

Russell, Bertrand, 1872-1970. Russell on metaphysics. London ; New York : Routledge, 2003.
B1649.R91 M86 2003

MUMMIES.
Reid, Howard. In search of the immortals. London : Headline, 1999.

Münchener Texte und Untersuchungen zur deutschen Literatur des Mittelalters
(Bd. 122) Hehle, Christine. Boethius in St. Gallen. Tübingen : Niemeyer, 2002.

Munck, Jean de.
Retroprospectivas psicológicas. Santiago : Ediciones UCSH, [2002]
BF75 .R48 2002

O mundo psi no Brasil.
Russo, Jane. Rio de Janeiro : Jorge Zahar Editor, c2002.
BF173 .R877 2002

Mundy, Michaelene. Getting out of a stress mess! : a guide for kids / written by Michaelene Mundy ; illustrated by R.W. Alley. St. Meinrad, IN : One Caring Place, c2000. 1 v. (unpaged) : col. ill. ; 20 cm. (Elf-help books for kids) ISBN 0-87029-348-6
1. Stress in children - Juvenile literature. 2. Stress management for children - Juvenile literature. I. Alley, R. W. (Robert W.) II. Title. III. Series.
BF723.S75 M86 2000

MUNICIPAL CONTRACTS. *See* **PUBLIC CONTRACTS.**

MUNICIPALITIES. *See* **CITIES AND TOWNS.**

Munkvold, Bjo rn Erik, 1962-.
Implementing collaboration technologies in industry. London ; New York : Springer, c2003.
HD30.2 .I38 2003

Muñoz Llamosas, Virginia. La intervención divina en el hombre a través de la literatura griega de época arcaica y clásica / Virginia Muñoz Llamosas. Amsterdam : Hakkert, 2002. xi, 726 p. ; 25 cm. (Classical and Byzantine monographs ; v. 51) Based on the author's thesis (Ph. D.)--Universidad de Oviedo, 2000. Includes bibliographical references (p. [665]-695) and index. ISBN 90-256-0638-5 ISBN 90-256-1155-9
1. Greek literature - History and criticism. 2. Religion in literature. 3. Providence and government of God in literature. 4. Free will and determinism in literature. 5. Religion and literature - Greece. 6. Gods, Greek, in literature. 7. Philosophy, Ancient. I. Title. II. Series.
PA3015.R5 M87 2002

Munro, Alan J., 1965-.
Designing information spaces. London ; New York : Springer, 2003.
QA76.9.C66 D49 2003

MURAL PAINTING AND DECORATION, BYZANTINE - GREECE - CRETE.
Ivinskaia, A. (Anna) Svet prelomlennogo vremeni v ikonnom prostranstve. Moskva : Khristianskiĭ Vostok, 2002.
N8189.G72 I95 2002

MURAL PAINTING AND DECORATION - CZECH REPUBLIC - JINDŘICHUV HRADEC.
Sankt Georg und sein Bilderzyklus in Neuhaus/Böhmen (Jindřichuv Hradec). Marburg : N.G. Elwert, c2002.
BR1720.G4 S26 2002

MURALS. *See* **MURAL PAINTING AND DECORATION.**

Muraro, Rose Marie. Feminino e masculino : uma nova consciência para o encontro das diferenças / Rose Marie Muraro, Leonardo Boff. Rio de Janeiro : Sextante, 2002. 287 p. : ill. ; 21 cm. Includes bibliographical

references. ISBN 85-7542-018-6
1. *Man-woman relationships.* 2. *Sex differences (Psychology)* I. Boff, Leonardo. II. Title.
HQ801 .M87 2002

MURDER. *See* **MASS MURDER; SERIAL MURDERS.**

MURDER - CALIFORNIA - CASE STUDIES.
Stetson, Brad. Living victims, stolen lives. Amityville, N.Y. : Baywood Pub., c2003.
HV6533.C2 S73 2003

MURDER, MASS. *See* **MASS MURDER.**

MURDERS, SERIAL. *See* **SERIAL MURDERS.**

Murdock, Nancy L. Theories of counseling and psychotherapy : a case approach / Nancy L. Murdock. Upper Saddle River, N.J. : Merrill/Prentice Hall, 2004. p. cm. Includes bibliographical references and index. ISBN 0-13-027163-2 DDC 158/.3
1. *Counseling.* 2. *Psychotherapy.* 3. *Counseling - Case studies.* 4. *Psychotherapy - Case studies.* I. Title.
BF637.C6 M846 2004

Murillo de Martínez, Ivelisse. Educación ambiental : fundamentos teóricos / Ivelisse Murillo de Martínez. 2. ed. Tegucigalpa, Honduras : Copicentro Douglas, 2000. 271, 20 p. : ill., maps ; 28 cm. "Naturaleza, cultura, sociedad, educación ambiental, desarrollo sostenible" Includes bibliographical references.
1. *Environmental education.* 2. *Environmental education - Honduras.* I. Title.

Muris, Timothy J.
United States. Congress. House. Committee on Energy and Commerce. Subcommittee on Health. Examining issues related to competition in the pharmaceutical marketplace. Washington : U.S. G.P.O. : For sale by the Supt. of Docs., U.S. G.P.O. [Congressional Sales Office], 2002.

Murphey, Cecil B.
Wilkins, David, 1944- United by tragedy. Nampa, Idaho : Pacific Press Pub. Association, c2003.
BF575.G7 W555 2003

Murphy, Elizabeth. Qualitative methods and health policy research / Elizabeth Murphy, Robert Dingwall. Hawthorne, N.Y. : Aldine de Gruyter, c2003. vi, 230 p. ; 24 cm. (Social problems and social issues) Includes bibliographical references (p. 209-226) and index. ISBN 0-202-30710-7 DDC 362.1/07/2
1. *Medical policy - Research - Methodology.* 2. *Qualitative research.* I. Dingwall, Robert. II. Title. III. Series.
RA394 .M87 2003

Murphy, Emmett C. Leading on the edge of chaos : the 10 critical elements for success in volatile times / Emmett C. Murphy, Mark A. Murphy. Paramus, N.J. : Prentice Hall Press, c2002. xiv, 226 p. : ill. ; 24 cm. Includes bibliographical references (p. 215-218) and index. ISBN 0-7352-0312-1 DDC 658.4/092
1. *Leadership.* I. *Murphy, Mark A. (Mark Andrew)* II. Title.
HD57.7 .M868 2002

Murphy, Jeffrie G. Getting even : forgiveness and its limits / Jeffrie G. Murphy. Oxford ; New York : Oxford University Press, 2003. ix, 138 p. ; 22 cm. Includes bibliographical references (p. 119-124) and index. ISBN 0-19-515149-6 (alk. paper) DDC 155.9/2
1. *Forgiveness.* I. Title.
BF637.F67 M87 2003

Murphy, Mark A. (Mark Andrew).
Murphy, Emmett C. Leading on the edge of chaos. Paramus, N.J. : Prentice Hall Press, c2002.
HD57.7 .M868 2002

Murphy, Michael, 1930 Sept. 3-.
Redfield, James. God and the evolving universe. New York : Jeremy P. Tarcher/Putnam, c2002.
BD541 .R43 2002

Murphy, Susan, 1947-.
Heim, Pat. In the company of women. New York : J.P. Tarcher/Putnam, c2001.
HD6053 .H387 2001

Murray, Charles A. Human accomplishment : the pursuit of excellence in the arts and sciences, 800 BC to 1950 / Charles Murray. New York : HarperCollins, 2003. p. cm. Includes bibliographical references and index. Publisher description URL: http://www.loc.gov/catdir/description/hc044/2003047820.html ISBN 0-06-019247-X DDC 908/.7/9
1. *Gifted persons - Case studies.* 2. *Genius - Case studies.* 3. *Civilization - History.* 4. *History - Psychological aspects.* I. Title.
BF416.A1 M87 2003

Murray, Donald Morison, 1924- The lively shadow : living with the death of a child / Donald M. Murray. 1st ed. New York : Ballantine Books, 2003. xi, 193 p. : ill. ; 20 cm. ISBN 0-345-44984-3 DDC 155.9/37
1. *Grief.* 2. *Bereavement - Psychological aspects.* 3. *Children - Death - Psychological aspects.* 4. *Loss (Psychology)* I. Title.
BF575.G7 M868 2003

Murray, Elizabeth.
Survivors. New York : Scholastic, c2002.
BF637.S8 S8317 2002

Murray, Karel, 1954- Straight talk : getting off the curb / Karel Murray and K.C. Lundberg. Portland, Or. : Arnica Pub., c2003. 146 p. ; 23 cm. CONTENTS: Knock, Knock -- Sweat pants of life -- Hall of mirrors -- Dog at a dance -- So what if everyone else is doing it? -- Speak up, I can't hear you! -- Getting off the curb -- If you're not careful, you'll raise the perfect underachiever -- Let's pretend -- The bug -- High hopes -- Never what you expect- -- Checkmate -- Surviving your career -- Paper tiger -- It's your move -- Strip plowing -- Godiva chocolate-riding romantic -- The scoreboard -- Getting off the curb workbook. ISBN 0-9726535-0-3 (pbk. : alk. paper) DDC 158.1
1. *Conduct of life.* I. *Lundberg, K. C., 1948-* II. Title.
BF637.C5 M87 2003

Musachi, Graciela. Mujeres en movimiento : eróticas de un siglo a otro / Graciela Musachi. Argentina : Fondo de Cultura Económica / Argentina, 2001. 123 p. ; 20 cm. (Biblioteca de Psicología, Psiquiatría y Psicoanálisis) Includes bibliographical references (p. 115-121). ISBN 950-557-400-2
1. *Women and psychoanalysis - History.* 2. *Psychoanalysis and feminism.* 3. *Women - Sexual behavior.* I. Title. II. Series.

MUSAR MOVEMENT.
Blokh, Avraham Yitsḥaḳ ben Y. L. (Avraham Yitsḥaḳ ben Yosef Leyb), d. 1941. Sefer Shiʻure daʻat. Yerushalayim : Feldhaim : Wickliffe, Ohio : Peninei Daas Publications, 761 [2001]

Musarim ye-deʻot la-Rambam : kol ʻinyene musar, ʻavodat H. ye-deʻot.
Maimonides, Moses, 1135-1204. [Selections] Sefer Musarim ye-deʻot leha-Rambam. Bene Beraḳ : [ḥ. mo. l], 761 [2000 or 2001]

Musciano, Chuck. HTML and XHTML, the definitive guide / Chuck Musciano and Bill Kennedy. 5th ed. Beijing ; Sebastopol [Calif.] : O'Reilly, 2002. xxi, 645 p. : ill. ; 24 cm. + quick reference card (24 x 41 cm. folded to 24 x 14 cm.). "Creating effective Web pages"--cover. Includes index. CONTENTS: HTML, XHTML, and the World Wide Web -- Quick start -- Anatomy of an HTML document -- Text basics -- Rules, images, and multimedia -- Links and webs -- Formatted lists -- Cascading style sheets -- Forms -- Tables -- Frames -- Executable content -- Dynamic documents -- Netscape layout extensions -- XML -- XHTML -- Tips, tricks, and hacks. ISBN 0-596-00382-X
1. *HTML (Document markup language)* 2. *XHTML (Document markup language)* I. *Kennedy, Bill, 1951-* II. Title.

Muse, Charles T.
Williamson, James C. Roadways to success. 3rd ed. Upper Saddle River, NJ : Pearson/ Prentice Hall, 2004.
BF637.S8 W5216 2004

Muse pisane
(2) Caterina e il diavolo. Pisa : ETS, c1999.
BF1584.I8 C38 1999

Musée du Louvre.
La magie en Egypte. Paris : Documentation française : Musée du Louvre, c2002.
BF1591 .M3447 2002

Musek, Janek. Psihološki modeli in teorije osebnosti / Janek Musek. Ljubljana : Filozofska fakulteta Univerze v Ljubljani, 1999. 324 p. : ill. ; 24 cm. Includes bibliographical references (p. 292-319) and index. ISBN 9616200984
1. *Personality.* I. Title.
BF698 .M887 1999

Museo de Bellas Artes (Venezuela).
Krebs, Víctor J., 1957- Del alma y el arte. Caracas, Venezuela : Museo de Bellas Artes, 1997.
N70 .K74 1997

The muses among us.
Stafford, Kim Robert. Athens : University of Georgia Press, c2003.
PE1408 .S6667 2003

Museum of the City of New York.
The day our world changed. New York : Harry N. Abrams Inc., 2002.

MUSEUMS. *See* **ART MUSEUMS.**

MUSEUMS - EUROPE - HISTORY.
Mauriès, Patrick, 1952- Cabinets of curiosities. New York : Thames & Hudson, c2002.
AM221 .M38 2002

MUSIC. *See also* **CONCERTS; POPULAR MUSIC; VOICE.**
Markus, Georg. Meine Reisen in die Vergangenheit. 2. Aufl. Wien : Amalthea, 2002.
AC35 .M385 2002

MUSIC - ACOUSTICS AND PHYSICS. *See also* **HARMONICS (MUSIC).**
Tokar, David A. Hans Kayser's Lehrbuch der Harmonik. 2002.

MUSIC AND ANTHROPOLOGY.
Pedroza, Ludim. The ritual of music contemplation. 2002.

MUSIC AND SOCIETY. *See* **MUSIC AND STATE.**

MUSIC AND STATE - EUROPE.
Gervasoni, Marco, 1968- Le armi di Orfeo. [Scandicci] (Firenze) : La nuova Italia, 2002.
ML3917.E85 G479 2002

MUSIC AND TECHNOLOGY.
Popvisionen. Frankfurt : Suhrkamp, 2003.
ML3470 .P69 2003

MUSIC AND YOUTH.
Youth cultures. Westport, Conn. : Praeger, 2003.
HQ796 .Y59273 2003

MUSIC, CLASSICAL. *See* **MUSIC.**

MUSIC EDUCATION. *See* **MUSIC - INSTRUCTION AND STUDY.**

MUSIC - EUROPE - RELIGIOUS ASPECTS.
Gervasoni, Marco, 1968- Le armi di Orfeo. [Scandicci] (Firenze) : La nuova Italia, 2002.
ML3917.E85 G479 2002

MUSIC FESTIVALS. *See* **CONCERTS.**

MUSIC - GREAT BRITAIN - 19TH CENTURY - HISTORY AND CRITICISM.
Allis, Michael, 1964- Parry's creative process. Aldershot : Ashgate, 2003.

MUSIC - HISTORY AND CRITICISM.
Hofmann, Dorothea. Der Komponist als Heros. Essen : Die Blaue Eule, c2003.

Music in nineteenth-century Britain
Allis, Michael, 1964- Parry's creative process. Aldershot : Ashgate, 2003.

MUSIC - INDIA - HISTORY AND CRITICISM.
Padma, N. K., 1956- Navam and the Karṇāṭak group kṛtis. New Delhi : Kanishka Publishers, Distributors, 2002.
ML338 .P197 2002

MUSIC - INSTRUCTION AND STUDY.
Creativity and music education. Edmonton, Canada : Canadian Music Educators' Association, c2002.

MUSIC - INSTRUCTION AND STUDY - JUVENILE.
Pound, Linda. Supporting musical development in the early years. Buckingham ; Philadelphia : Open University Press, 2003.
MT1 .P66 2003

MUSIC - PERFORMANCE. *See also* **CONCERTS; PERFORMANCE PRACTICE (MUSIC).**
Hagberg, Karen A., 1943- Stage presence from head to toe. Lanham, Md. : Scarecrow Press, 2003.
ML3795 .H13 2003

Pedroza, Ludim. The ritual of music contemplation. 2002.

MUSIC - PERFORMANCE - PSYCHOLOGICAL ASPECTS.
Mornell, Adina. Lampenfieber und Angst bei ausübenden Musikern. Frankfurt am Main : P. Lang, 2002.
ML3830 .M67 2002

MUSIC - PHILOSOPHY AND AESTHETICS.
Gavalchin, John. Temporality in music. 2000.

Katz, Ruth, 1927- Tuning the mind. New Brunswick, N.J. : Transaction Publishers, c2003.
ML3838 .K28 2003

Madell, Geoffrey. Philosophy, music and emotion. Edinburgh : Edinburgh University Press, c2002.

Pedroza, Ludim. The ritual of music contemplation. 2002.

MUSIC - PHYSIOLOGICAL ASPECTS. *See* **VOICE.**

MUSIC, POPULAR. *See* **POPULAR MUSIC.**

MUSIC, POPULAR (SONGS, ETC.). *See* **POPULAR MUSIC.**

MUSIC - PSYCHOLOGICAL ASPECTS.
Katz, Ruth, 1927- Tuning the mind. New Brunswick, N.J. : Transaction Publishers, c2003.
ML3838 .K28 2003

Lathan, Mark J., 1961- Emotional progression in sacred choral music. 2001.

Lechevalier, Bernard. Le cerveau de Mozart. Paris : O. Jacob, c2003.
ML3838 .L39 2003

MUSIC - PSYCHOLOGICAL ASPECTS - CONGRESSES.
Mensch & Musik. Augsburg : Wissner, c2002.
ML3830 .M46 2002

MUSIC - RELIGIOUS ASPECTS.
Tokar, David A. Hans Kayser's Lehrbuch der Harmonik. 2002.

MUSIC - SOCIAL ASPECTS.
Hofmann, Dorothea. Der Komponist als Heros. Essen : Die Blaue Eule, c2003.

Pedroza, Ludim. The ritual of music contemplation. 2002.

MUSIC - SOCIAL ASPECTS - 19TH CENTURY.
Pedroza, Ludim. The ritual of music contemplation. 2002.

MUSIC - SOCIAL ASPECTS - 20TH CENTURY.
Pedroza, Ludim. The ritual of music contemplation. 2002.

MUSIC - STUDY AND TEACHING. *See* **MUSIC - INSTRUCTION AND STUDY.**

MUSIC THEORY.
Tokar, David A. Hans Kayser's Lehrbuch der Harmonik. 2002.

MUSIC THERAPY.
Mensch & Musik. Augsburg : Wissner, c2002.
ML3830 .M46 2002

Pavlicevic, Mercedes. Groups in music. London ; New York : Jessica Kingsley Publishers, 2003.
ML3920 .P2279 2003

MUSIC VIDEOS - HISTORY AND CRITICISM.
Bühler, Gerhard, 1959- Postmoderne auf dem Bildschirm, auf der Leinwand. Sankt Augustin : Gardez!, c2002.

MUSICAL ABILITY.
Hemming, Jan. Begabung und Selbstkonzept. Münster : Lit, [2002?]
ML3838 .H46 2002

Lechevalier, Bernard. Le cerveau de Mozart. Paris : O. Jacob, c2003.
ML3838 .L39 2003

MUSICAL COMPOSITIONS. *See* **MUSIC.**

MUSICAL EDUCATION. *See* **MUSIC - INSTRUCTION AND STUDY.**

MUSICAL GAMES.
Cohn, Arthur, 1910- Musical puzzlemania. Mew York, NY : Carl Fischer, c1998.

MUSICAL INSTRUCTION. *See* **MUSIC - INSTRUCTION AND STUDY.**

MUSICAL PERCEPTION.
Peinture et musique. Villeneuve-d'Ascq : Presses universitaires du Septentrion, c2002.

MUSICAL PERFORMANCE. *See* **MUSIC - PERFORMANCE.**

Musical puzzlemania.
Cohn, Arthur, 1910- Mew York, NY : Carl Fischer, c1998.

Musical quizzical III.
Cohn, Arthur, 1910- Musical puzzlemania. Mew York, NY : Carl Fischer, c1998.

MUSICAL WORKS. *See* **MUSIC.**

Musicalische Temperatur der Bachsöhne.
Kellner, Herbert Anton. Darmstadt : Herbert Anton Kellner, c2001.

MUSICIANS. *See* **COMPOSERS; ROCK MUSICIANS; SINGERS.**

MUSICIANS - HEALTH AND HYGIENE.
Mensch & Musik. Augsburg : Wissner, c2002.
ML3830 .M46 2002

MUSICIANS - PSYCHOLOGY.
Hemming, Jan. Begabung und Selbstkonzept. Münster : Lit, [2002?]
ML3838 .H46 2002

Mornell, Adina. Lampenfieber und Angst bei ausübenden Musikern. Frankfurt am Main : P. Lang, 2002.
ML3830 .M67 2002

Musikwissenschaft/Musikpädagogik in der Blauen Eule
(Bd. 62) Hofmann, Dorothea. Der Komponist als Heros. Essen : Die Blaue Eule, c2003.

MUSIL, ROBERT, 1880-1942 - CRITICISM AND INTERPRETATION.
Anders, Martin. Präsenz zu denken--. St. Augustin : Gardez!, c2002.
B3303 .A53 2002

Musings on human metaporphoses.
Leary, Timothy Francis, 1920- Berkeley, CA : Ronin, c2003.

Musiol, Marie-J. (Marie-Jeanne), 1950- Corps de lumière / Marie-Jeanne Musiol ; avec un texte du professeur Konstantin Korotkov = Bodies of light / Marie-Jeanne Musiol ; with a text by Professor Konstantin Korotkov. Hull, Québec : Axe Néo-7, art contemporain, [2001?] 89 p. : ill. ; 23 cm. Limited ed. of 400 copies, 50 of which are numbered. Includes bibliographical references. Text in French and English. ISBN 2922794032 DDC 778.3
1. Kirlian photography. 2. Aura. I. Korotkov, K. (Konstantin), 1952- II. Axe Néo-7 art contemporain. III. Title. IV. Title: Bodies of light

MUSKOGEAN INDIANS. *See* **CHOCTAW INDIANS.**

MUSLIM CIVILIZATION. *See* **CIVILIZATION, ISLAMIC.**

MUSLIM COUNTRIES. *See* **ISLAMIC COUNTRIES.**

MUSLIM PHILOSOPHY. *See* **PHILOSOPHY, ISLAMIC.**

MUSLIMISM. *See* **ISLAM.**

Mussaud, Véronique.
Six, Jean François. Médiation. Paris : Editions du Seuil, c2002.
HM1126 .S59 2002

Musschenga, A. W., 1950-.
The many faces of individualism. Leuven, Belgium ; Sterling, Va. : Peeters, 2001.
B824 .M354 2001

Personal and moral identity. Dordrecht ; Boston : Kluwer Academic Publishers, c2002.
BJ45 .P47 2002

MUSSULMANISM. *See* **ISLAM.**

Mustafa, Huda Nura. Practicing beauty : crisis, value and the challenge of self-mastery in Dakar, 1970-1994. 1997. x, 355 leaves : ill. (some col.), map ; 29 cm. Thesis (Ph. D.)--Harvard University, 1997. Includes bibliographical references (leaves 341-355). Photocopy. Ann Arbor, Mich. : UMI Dissertation Services, 2003. x, 354 p. ill., map ; 24 cm.
1. Wolof (African people) - Economic conditions. 2. Clothing trade - Senegal - Dakar. 3. Beauty, Personal. 4. Senegal - Economic conditions. I. Title.

Mustakova-Possardt, Elena, 1960- Critical consciousness : a study of morality in global, historical context / Elena Mustakova-Possardt. Westport, Conn. ; London : Praeger, 2003. xix, 218 p. : ill. ; 25 cm. Includes bibliographical references (p. [197]-207) and index. ISBN 0-275-97911-3 (alk. paper) DDC 126
1. Psychology, Religious. 2. Consciousness. 3. Ethics. I. Title.
BL53 .M98 2003

MUTATION (BIOLOGY). *See* **GENETICS; VARIATION (BIOLOGY).**

Mutazioni
(8) Pievani, Telmo. Homo sapiens e altre catastrofi. Roma : Meltemi, c2002.

MUTUAL DEFENSE ASSISTANCE PROGRAM. *See* **MILITARY ASSISTANCE.**

My America : what my country means to me by 150 Americans from all walks of life / edited and with an introduction by Hugh Downs. New York : Scribner, c2002. xvi, 266 p. : ill. ; 24 cm. "A Lisa Drew book." Table of contents URL: http://www.loc.gov/catdir/toc/fy033/2002072794.html CONTENTS: Alan Alda -- Buzz Aldrin -- Shaun Alexander -- Lincoln Almond -- Bill Anderson -- Walter Anderson -- Maya Angelou -- Piers Anthony -- Desi Arnaz Jr. -- Robert Ballard -- Lisa Beamer -- Yogi Berra -- Bruce C. Birch -- Michael Bloomberg -- Barbara Taylor Bradford -- David Brenner -- Dave Brubeck -- Art Buchwald -- George Bush -- Jeb Bush -- Benjamin Cayetano -- Margaret Cho -- Dick Clark -- Jerry Colangelo -- Stephen Coonts -- Catherine Crier -- Walter Cronkite -- Vincent Curcio -- Charlie Daniels -- Michael E. Debakey -- Mark DeCarlo -- Alan Dershowitz -- Anita Diamont -- Phyllis Diller -- Peter C. Doherty -- Duffy Dyer -- Michael D. Eisner -- John Engler -- Steven Englund -- Barbara Fairchild -- Jamie Farr -- Mike Farrell -- Jose Feliciano -- Steve Forbes -- M. J. "Mike" Foster Jr. -- Dan Gable -- Joe Garagiola -- Art Garfunkel -- Leeza Gibbons -- Nikki Giovanni -- Marvin Girouard -- John Glenn -- Andrew J. Goodpaster -- Otto Graham -- Gordon A. Haaland -- Alexander M. Haig Jr. -- Pete Hamill -- Barry Hantman -- Charles B. Harmon -- Paul Harvey -- Tony Hillerman -- John Hoeven -- Jayne Howard-Feldman -- Mike Huckabee -- Janice Huff -- Jon M. Huntsman -- Janis Ian -- Bil Keane -- Frank Keating -- Kitty Kelly -- Coretta Scott King -- Howard Kissel -- Rebecca Kolls -- Michael Korda -- Gunta Krasts-Voutyras -- Richard D. Lamm -- Frances Langford -- Anthony Lewis. CONTENTS: Joseph Lieberman -- Art Linkletter -- Dick Locher -- Anne Graham Lotz -- Frank Mancuso -- Al Martino -- Peter Max -- Theodore E. McCarrick -- Colman McCarthy -- Mike McCurry -- Jayne Meadows -- Howard Metzenbaum -- Kate Mulgrew -- John J. Nance -- Patricia Neal -- Robert Novak -- Michele O'Brien -- George Olah -- Norman Ornstein -- Steve Osunsami -- Bill Owens -- Jack Paar -- George E. Pataki -- Ross Perot -- Regis Philbin -- George Pickett -- Stanley Prusiner -- Sally Quinn -- Sally Jesse Raphael -- Anne W. Richards -- Oral Roberts -- Cliff Robertson -- Ned Rorem -- John G. Rowland -- Mark Russell -- George H. Ryan -- Diane Sawyer -- Laura Schlessinger -- Harrison H. Schmitt -- Patricia S. Schroeder -- Charles E. Schumer -- Diana L. Schwarzbein -- Willard Scot -- Winston E. Scott -- William Shatner -- Artie Shaw -- Jackie W. Sherill -- Paul Simon -- Nancy Snyderman -- Mary Sojourner -- Billy Squier -- Maureen Stapleton -- John Stossel -- Maireid Sullivan -- Karen Tates-Denton -- Edward Teller -- Helen Thomas -- Dick Thornburgh -- Donald Trump -- Stansfield Turner -- Greta Van Susteren -- Jesse Ventura -- Thomas J. Vilsack -- Mort Walker -- Mike Wallace -- Barbara Walters -- Tina Wesson -- Curtis Wilkie -- Roger Williams -- Dan Wooding -- David Wright -- Lucy Yang -- Endnote. ISBN 0-7432-3369-7 DDC 973
1. National characteristics, American. 2. Patriotism - United States. 3. United States - Biography. I. Downs, Hugh.
E169.1 .M968 2002

My beloved, Moalem.
Moalem, Shuli. Mo'alem, ahuvi. Tel Aviv : Yedi'ot aḥaronot : Sifre ḥemed, c2002.

My father's footsteps.
McEnroe, Colin. New York : Warner Books, c2003.
PS3563.C3615 M9 2003

My first baby signs.
Acredolo, Linda P. [New York] : HarperFestival, c2002.
BF720.C65 A27 2002

My friends and me.
Thomas, Pat, 1959- 1st ed. Hauppauge, N.Y. : Barron's Educational Series, c2001.
BF723.F68 T48 2001

My proof of survival : personal accounts of contact with the hereafter / compiled & edited by Andrew Honigman. 1st ed. St. Paul, Minn. : Llewellyn Publications, 2003. p. cm. ISBN 0-7387-0264-1 DDC 133.9/01/3
1. Future life. 2. Spiritualism. I. Honigman, Andrew, 1970-
BF1311.F8 M9 2003

MYERS-BRIGGS TYPE INDICATOR.
Giannini, John L., 1921- Compass of the soul. Gainesville, Fla. : Center for Applications of Psychological Type, 2003.
BF698.3 .G53 2003

Jeffries, William C. Profiles of the 16 personality types. Noblesville, IN : Buttermilk Ridge Pub. ; Zionsville, Ind. : Distributed by Executive Strategies International, c2002.
BF698.8.M94 J43 2002

Jeffries, William C. Still true to type. Noblesville, IN : Buttermilk Ridge Pub. ; Zionsville, Ind. : Distributed by Executive Strategies International, c2002.
BF698.8.M94 J435 2002

VanSant, Sondra. Wired for conflict. Gainesville, Fla. : Center for Applications of Psychological Type, c2003.
BF698.3 .V36 2003

Myers, Edward, 1950- When will I stop hurting? : teens, loss, and grief / Edward Myers ; illustrations by Kelly Adams. Lanham, Md. : Scarecrow Press, 2004. p. cm. (It happened to me ; no. 8) Includes bibliographical

references and index. ISBN 0-8108-4921-6 (alk. paper) DDC 155.9/37/0835
1. Bereavement in adolescence - Psychological aspects. 2. Grief in adolescence. 3. Loss (Psychology) in adolescence. I. Title. II. Series.
BF724.3.G73 M94 2004

Mykytenko, Svitlana. Enihma lidera, abo, Shcho može obitsiaty polityhna kar'iera poriadniĭ lĭudyni, okrim vtraty poriadnosti / Svitlana Mykytenko. Kyïv : Vyd-vo "Molod'", 2001. 413 p. ; 21 cm. ISBN 9667615251
1. Leadership. 2. Political science. I. Title. II. Title: Enihma lidera III. Title: Shcho može obitsiaty polityhna kar'iera poriadniĭ lĭudyni, okrim vtraty poriadnosti
JC330.3 .M95 2001

Myrdal, Alva Reimer, 1902- "Något kan man väl göra : texter 1932-1982 / Alva Myrdal ; texter i urval av Cecilia Åse och Yvonne Hirdman ; inledning av Yvonne Hirdman. Stockholm : Carlssons, c2002. 258 p. ; 23 cm. Includes bibliographical references. Swedish and English. ISBN 91-7203-469-6
1. Myrdal, Alva Reimer, - 1902- 2. Feminism. 3. Education. 4. Disarmament. I. Åse, Cecilia. II. Hirdman, Yvonne, 1943- III. Title.

MYRDAL, ALVA REIMER, 1902-.
Myrdal, Alva Reimer, 1902- "Något kan man väl göra. Stockholm : Carlssons, c2002.

Mysteria magica.
Denning, Melita. 3rd ed. St. Paul, Minn. : Llewellyn Publications, 2004.
BF1611 .D395 2004

Mysteries.
Rogers, Rita. Large print ed. Bath, England : Chivers Press ; Waterville, Me. : Thorndike Press, 2002.
BF1031 .R635 2002

Mysteries and magic.
Spencer, John, 1954- London : Orion, 2000.

Mysteries of body and mind.
Townsend, John, 1955- Chicago, IL : Raintree, 2004.
BF1031 .T65 2004

The mysteries of the great cross of Hendaye.
Weidner, Jay. Rochester, Vt. : Destiny Books, 2003.
BF1999 .W435 2003

MYSTERIES, RELIGIOUS. See also **ORACLES; RITES AND CEREMONIES.**
Hall, Manly Palmer, 1901- The secret teachings of all ages. Reader's ed. New York : Jeremy P. Tarcher/Putnam, 2003.
BF1411 .H3 2003

MYSTERIES, RELIGIOUS - HISTORY.
Berg, Wendy, 1951- Polarity magic. St. Paul, Minn. : Llewellyn Publications, 2003.
BF1589 .B47 2003

Mysterious disappearances.
Townsend, John. Chicago, IL : Raintree, 2004.
BF1389.D57 T69 2004

Mysterious encounters.
Townsend, John. Chicago, IL : Raintree, 2004.
BF2050 .T69 2004

Mysterious places / Tom Head, book editor. San Diego, CA : Greenhaven Press, 2004. p. cm. (Fact or fiction) Includes bibliographical references and index. ISBN 0-7377-1643-6 (alk. paper) ISBN 0-7377-1644-4 (pbk. : alk. paper) DDC 001.94
1. Parapsychology. 2. Curiosities and wonders. I. Head, Tom. II. Series: Fact or fiction (Greenhaven Press)
BF1031 .M96 2004

Mysterious signs.
Townsend, John, 1955- Chicago, IL : Raintree, c2004.
BF1461 .T69 2004

The mystery chronicles.
Nickell, Joe. Lexington, Ky. : University Press of Kentucky, c2004.
BF1031 .N517 2004

Mystery library (Lucent Books)
Hoffman, Nancy, 1955- Fairies. San Diego, Calif. : Lucent Books, 2004.
BF1552 .H64 2004

Kallen, Stuart A., 1955- Dreams. San Diego, Calif. : Lucent Books, 2004.
BF1099.C55 K35 2004

Kallen, Stuart A., 1955- Fortune-telling. San Diego, Calif. : Lucent Books, 2004.
BF1861 .K35 2004

Kallen, Stuart A., 1955- Ghosts. San Diego, Calif. : Lucent Books, c2004.
BF1461 .K33 2004

Netzley, Patricia D. Haunted houses. San Diego, Calif. : Lucent Books, c2000.
BF1461 .N48 2000

The mystery of the moon illusion.
Ross, Helen Elizabeth, 1935- Oxford ; New York : Oxford University Press, 2002.
QP495 .R67 2002

MYSTERY RELIGIONS. See **MYSTERIES, RELIGIOUS.**

Mystic glyphs.
Rogers, Barb, 1947- York Beach, ME : Red Wheel/Weiser, 2003.
BF1778.5 .R64 2003

MYSTIC MEDICINE. See **MEDICINE, MAGIC, MYSTIC, AND SPAGIRIC.**

The mystic thesaurus.
Whitehead, Willis F. Berwick, Me. : Ibis Press, 2003.
BF1411 .W46 2003

MYSTICAL THEOLOGY. See **MYSTICISM.**

MYSTICISM. See also **MYSTICS.**
Ashkenazi, Nisim. Ben he-'anan. Tel-Aviv : Gal, 2002.

Hood, Ralph W. Dimensions of mystical experiences. Amsterdam ; New York, NY : Rodopi, 2001.

Horgan, John, 1953- Rational mysticism. Boston : Houghton Mifflin, 2003.
BL625 .H67 2003

Jantzen, Grace. Power, gender, and Christian mysticism. Cambridge ; New York : Cambridge University Press, 1995.
BV5083 .J36 1995

Maritain, Jacques, 1882-1973. [Degrés du savoir. English] Distinguish to unite, or, The degrees of knowledge. Notre Dame, Ind. : University of Notre Dame Press, 1998, c1995.
BD162 .M273 1998

Mūks, Roberts. Jaunā viedība. Rīga : Daugava, 2002.

Sayers, Janet. Divine therapy. Oxford ; New York : Oxford University Press, 2003.
BF175.4.R44 S28 2003

Thorne, Robert. Marihuana. Portland, Or. : Clarus Books Pub., c1998 (1999 printing)
BF209.C3 T48 1998

Twyman, James F. Emissary of light. Forres : Findhorn, 2002.

Mysticism and contemporary society.
King, Ursula. [Lewisburg, Pa.] : American Teilhard Association, c2002.
B2430.T374 A18 no.44

MYSTICISM - EARLY WORKS TO 1800.
Vizantijska filozofija u srednjevekovnoj Srbiji. Beograd : Stubovi kulture, 2002.

MYSTICISM - HISTORY - 20TH CENTURY.
Galovic, Jelena. Los grupos místico-espirituales de la actualidad. México : Plaza y Valdés, 2002.
BL625 .G346 2002

King, Ursula. Mysticism and contemporary society. [Lewisburg, Pa.] : American Teilhard Association, c2002.
B2430.T374 A18 no.44

MYSTICISM - HISTORY OF DOCTRINES. See **MYSTICISM - HISTORY.**

MYSTICISM - ISLAM. See **SUFISM.**

MYSTICISM - JUDAISM. See also **HASIDISM.**
Chajes, Jeffrey Howard. Between worlds. Philadelphia : University of Pennsylvania Press, c2003.
BM729.D92 C53 2003

Green, Arthur, 1941- Ehyeh. Woodstock, Vt. : Jewish Lights Publishing, c2003.
BM525 .G84 2003

MYSTICS. See **MYSTICISM.**

MYSTICS - ENGLAND - BIOGRAPHY.
Oron, Michal. Mi-'Ba'al shed' le-'Ba'al Shem'. Yerushalayim : Mosad Byaliḳ : Bet ha-sefer le-mada'e ha-Yahadut 'a. sh. Ḥayim Rozenberg, Universiṭat Tel-Aviv, c763 [2002]

Mystifying mind reading tricks.
Mandelberg, Robert. New York : Sterling Pub., 2002.
GV1553 .M35 2002

MYTH. See also **MYTHOLOGY.**
Albanian identities. Bloomington : Indiana University Press, 2002.
DR950 .A385 2002

Cherepanova, I. IU. (Irina IUr'evna) Dom koldun'i. Perer., dop. i ispravlennoe izd. Moskva : KSP+, 2001.
BF1156.S8 C53 2001

Jerphagnon, Lucien, 1921- Les dieux ne sont jamais loin. Paris : Desclée de Brouwer, c2002.

Midgley, Mary, 1919- The myths we live by. London ; New York : Routledge, 2003.
BL304 .M53 2003

Pinheiro, José Moura. Mitos atuais. Salvador : Secretaria da Cultura e Turismo : Fundação Cultural do Estado da Bahia : Empresa Gráfoca da Bahia, 2001.

Restall, Matthew, 1964- Seven myths of the Spanish conquest. Oxford ; New York : Oxford University Press, 2003.
F1230 .R47 2003

Sciences et archétypes. Paris : Dervy, 2002.

Verene, Donald Phillip, 1937- Knowledge of things human and divine. New Haven, Conn. : Yale University Press, c2003.
B3581.P73 V47 2003

Wunenburger, Jean-Jacques. La vie des images. [Nouvelle édition augmentée]. Grenoble : Presses universitaires de Grenoble, 2002.
BF367 .W85 2002

Myth and history in ancient Greece.
Calame, Claude. [Mythe et histoire dans l'antiquité grecque. English] Princeton, N.J. : Princeton University Press, c2003.
BL783 .C3513 2003

MYTH IN LITERATURE.
Kurganov, E. Anekdot, simvol, mif. Sankt-Peterburg : Izd-vo zhurnala "Zvezda", 2002.

MYTH - POLITICAL ASPECTS - UNITED STATES.
Hughes, Richard T. (Richard Thomas), 1943- Myths America lives by. Urbana : University of Illinois Press, c2003.
E175.9 .H84 2003

Les mythes, conteurs de l'inconscient.
Valabrega, Jean-Paul. Paris : Payot, 2001.
BD542 .V353 2001

MYTHICAL ANIMALS. See **ANIMALS, MYTHICAL.**

Mythistory.
Mali, Joseph. Chicago : The University of Chicago Press, c2003.
D13 .M268 2003

MYTHOLOGY. See also **ANIMALS, MYTHICAL; FOLKLORE; GODS; MYTH.**
Clow, Barbara Hand, 1943- Catastrophobia. Rochester, Vt. : Bear & Company, c2001.
BF1999 .C587 2001

Herzog, Edgar. [Psyche und Tod. English] Psyche and death. New ed. / edited and designed by C.L. Sebrell. Woodstock, Conn. : Spring Publications, c2000.

Kazakova, I. V. (Iryna Valer'eŭna) Mifalahemy i mahii͡a ŭ belaruskim abradavym fal'klory. Minsk : "BOFF", 1997.
GR203.4 .K39 1997

Lombard, René-André. Le nom de l'Europe. Grenoble : Thot, c2001.

Morales Villaroel, Oscar. Huellas y relatos. Caracas : [s.n.], 2001.

Muller, F. Max (Friedrich Max), 1823-1900. The essential Max Muller. 1st ed. New York ; Houndmills, England : Palgrave Macmillan, 2002.
BL50 .M785 2002

Pak, Si-in. Alt'ai munhwa kihaeng. Ch'op'an. Sŏul-si : Ch'ŏngnoru, 1995.

Pandian, Jacob. Supernaturalism in human life. New Delhi : Vedams ebooks, [2002]
BF1031.A4-Z+

The Persistence of religions. Malibu : Undena Publications, 1996.

Pinheiro, José Moura. Mitos atuais. Salvador : Secretaria da Cultura e Turismo : Fundação Cultural do Estado da Bahia : Empresa Gráfoca da Bahia, 2001.

Poitevin, Michel. Georges Dumézil, un naturel comparatiste. Paris : Harmattan, c2002.

Ramsay, Chevalier (Andrew Michael), 1686-1743. Les voyages de Cyrus. Paris : Champion, 2002.

Rozanov, V. V. (Vasiliĭ Vasil'evich), 1856-1919. Vo dvore iazychnikov. Moskva : Izd-vo "Respublika", 1999.
BL96 .R69 1999

Zhao, Xi. Xu wu piao miao de gui shen shi jie. Di 1 ban. Beijing : Zong jiao wen hua chu ban she, 2001.
BL1812.G63 Z436 2001

MYTHOLOGY, CELTIC.
Matthews, John, 1948- The encyclopaedia of Celtic myth and legend. London : Rider, 2002.
BL915 .M377 2002

Mountfort, Paul Rhys. Ogam, the Celtic oracle of the trees. Rochester, Vt. : Destiny Books, c2002.
PB1217 .M68 2002

Squire, Charles. Celtic myth and legend. Rev. ed. Franklin Lakes, NJ : New Page Books, c2001.
BL900 .S6 2001

Vega, Phyllis. Celtic astrology. Franklin Lakes, NJ : New Page Books, c2002.
BF1714.C44 V44 2002

MYTHOLOGY, CELTIC, IN LITERATURE.
Matthews, Caitlín, 1952- King Arthur and the goddess of the land. 2nd ed. Rochester, Vt. : Inner Traditions, 2002.
PB2273.M33 M36 2002

Matthews, Caitlín, 1952- Mabon and the guardians of Celtic Britain. Rochester, Vt. : Inner Traditions, c2002.
PB2273.M33 M37 2002

MYTHOLOGY, CELTIC - WALES.
Matthews, Caitlín, 1952- King Arthur and the goddess of the land. 2nd ed. Rochester, Vt. : Inner Traditions, 2002.
PB2273.M33 M36 2002

Matthews, Caitlín, 1952- Mabon and the guardians of Celtic Britain. Rochester, Vt. : Inner Traditions, c2002.
PB2273.M33 M37 2002

MYTHOLOGY, CHINESE.
Xing, Li. Guanyin. Beijing di 2 ban. Beijing : Xue yuan chu ban she, 2001.
BQ4710.A8 X564 2001

MYTHOLOGY, CLASSICAL. See GODS.

MYTHOLOGY, EGYPTIAN.
Contes de l'Egypte ancienne. Paris : Flammarion, c2002.

Gahlin, Lucia. Egypt. London : Lorenz, 2001.

Vlora, Nedim R., 1943- Le porte del cielo. Bari : M. Adda, c2001.
BF1674 .V56 2001

Wilkinson, Richard H. The complete gods and goddesses of ancient Egypt. New York : Thames & Hudson, 2003.

MYTHOLOGY, GREEK. See also EUROPA (GREEK MYTHOLOGY); HERACLES (GREEK MYTHOLOGY).
Burkert, Walter, 1931- [Wilder Ursprung. English] Savage energies. Chicago : University of Chicago Press, c2001.
BL785 .B8513 2001

Calame, Claude. [Mythe et histoire dans l'antiquité grecque. English] Myth and history in ancient Greece. Princeton, N.J. : Princeton University Press, c2003.
BL783 .C3513 2003

Detienne, Marcel. [Ecriture d'Orphee. English] The writing of Orpheus. Baltimore : Johns Hopkins University Press, 2002, c2003.
BL783 .D4813 2003

La fin des temps. Talence : Université Michel de Montaigne, Bordeaux III, L.A.P.R.I.L., 2000-[2001]

Hercules. New York : Dell, c1997.
BL820.H5 H47 1997

Myths of the ancient Greeks. New York : New American Library, 2003.
BL783 .M98 2003

Tamiozzo Villa, Patrizia. L'astrologia e i miti del mondo antico. 1. ed. Roma : Newton & Compton, 2001.
BF1729.M9 T35 2001

MYTHOLOGY, HINDU.
Varshney, D. C., 1933- Hindū vijñāna evaṃ vidhi. 1. saṃskaraṇa. Lakhanaū : Nyū Rôyala Buka Kampanī, 2001.
BL1215.S36 V27 2001

MYTHOLOGY - HISTORIOGRAPHY.
Mali, Joseph. Mythistory. Chicago : The University of Chicago Press, c2003.
D13 .M268 2003

MYTHOLOGY - HISTORY.
Berg, Wendy, 1951- Polarity magic. St. Paul, Minn. : Llewellyn Publications, 2003.
BF1589 .B47 2003

MYTHOLOGY IN LITERATURE.
Kurganov, E. Anekdot, simvol, mif. Sankt-Peterburg : Izd-vo zhurnala "Zvezda", 2002.

MYTHOLOGY, KOREAN.
Pak, Si-in. Alt'ai munhwa kihaeng. Ch'op'an. Sŏul-si : Ch'ŏngnoru, 1995.

MYTHOLOGY - POLITICAL ASPECTS - UNITED STATES.
Azoulay, Paul. Uncle Sam. Anglet : Atlantica, c2002.

MYTHOLOGY - PSYCHOLOGICAL ASPECTS.
Valabrega, Jean-Paul. Les mythes, conteurs de l'inconscient. Paris : Payot, 2001.
BD542 .V353 2001

MYTHOLOGY, ROMAN. See also HERCULES (ROMAN MYTHOLOGY).
Feo, Giovanni. Prima degli etruschi. Roma : Stampa alternativa, 2001.
BL813.E8 F46 2001

Hercules. New York : Dell, c1997.
BL820.H5 H47 1997

Tamiozzo Villa, Patrizia. L'astrologia e i miti del mondo antico. 1. ed. Roma : Newton & Compton, 2001.
BF1729.M9 T35 2001

MYTHOLOGY, SLAVIC.
Asov, A. I. (Aleksandr Igorevich) Sviashchennye prarodiny slavian. Moskva : Veche, 2002.
BL930 .A863 2002

Domnikov, S. D. (Sergeĭ Dmitrievich) Mat'-zemlia i TSar'-gorod. Moskva : Aleteia, 2002.
B4235.H57 D65 2002

Gavrilov, D. A. Bogi slavian, iazychestvo, traditsiia. [Moskva] : Refl-buk, 2002.
BL930 .G38 2002

Ivanova, E. V. (Elena Vladimirovna) Ved'my. Ekaterinburg : Ural'skiĭ gos. universitet, 2002.
BF1584.R9 I85 2002

Petrović, Aleksandar M. Praistorija Srba. Beograd : Pešić i sinovi, 2001.
DR1953 .P48 2001

Tkach, Mykola. Volodymyrovi bohy. Kyïv : Ukraïns'kyĭ tsentr dukhovnoï kul'tury, 2002.
DK75 .T53 2002

Vinšćak, Tomo. Vjerovanja o drveću u hrvata. [Jastrebarsko] : Naklada Slap, c2002.

Mythos Medienkunst.
Reck, H. U. Köln : König, c2002.

MYTHS. See MYTHOLOGY.

Myths America lives by.
Hughes, Richard T. (Richard Thomas), 1943- Urbana : University of Illinois Press, c2003.
E175.9 .H84 2003

Myths of creation.
Freund, Philip, 1909- London : Peter Owen ; Chester Springs, PA : Distributed in the USA by Dufour Editions, 2003.
BL226 .F74 2003

Myths of the ancient Greeks / Richard P. Martin, [editor] ; illustrations by Patrick Hunt. New York : New American Library, 2003. ix, [11], 346 p. : ill., 2 maps ; 21 cm. Includes bibliographical references (p. [323]-324) and index. ISBN 0-451-20685-1 (alk. paper) DDC 398.2/0938/01
1. Mythology, Greek. I. Martin, Richard P.
BL783 .M98 2003

The myths we live by.
Midgley, Mary, 1919- London ; New York : Routledge, 2003.
BL304 .M53 2003

Na porozi nadt͡syvilizat͡siï.
Kuz'menko, Volodymyr. L'viv : "Universum", 1998.
HM901 .K89 1998

Nación postmortem.
Pabón, Carlos. 1. ed. San Juan, P.R. : Ediciones Callejón, 2002.

Nada é tudo.
Fonseca, Eduardo Giannetti da, 1957- Rio de Janeiro, RJ, Brasil : Editora Campus, c2000.
F2521 .F64 2000

Nadar, Sarojini.
Her-stories. Pietermaritzburg, South Africa : Cluster, 2002.

Naddaf, Gerard, 1950-.
Couprie, Dirk, 1940- Anaximander in context. Albany : State University of New York Press, c2003.
B208.Z7 C68 2003

Nadelman, Lorraine, 1924- Research manual in child development / Lorraine Nadelman. 2nd ed. Mahwah, N.J. : Lawrence Erlbaum Associates, Publishers, 2004. xi, 467 p. ill. ; 28 cm. Includes bibliographical references and index. ISBN 0-8058-4041-9 (alk. paper) DDC 155.4/072
1. Child psychology - Research - Textbooks. I. Title.
BF722 .N32 2004

Nadler, Holly Mascott. Ghosts of Boston town : three centuries of true hauntings / Holly Mascott Nadler. Camden, Me. : Down East Books, c2002. 175 p. : ill. ; 22 cm. ISBN 0-89272-535-4 DDC 133.1/09744/61
1. Ghosts - Massachusetts - Boston. 2. Haunted places - Massachusetts - Boston. I. Title.
BF1472.U6 N32 2002

NADOLNY, STEN.
Małyszek, Tomasz, 1971- Ästhetik der Psychoanalyse. Wrocław : Wydawn. Uniwersytetu Wrocławskiego, 2000.

Nāgārjuna, Siddha.
Ratiramana. English & Sanskrit.
Nāgārjuna, Siddha. [Ratiśāstra. English & Sanskrit] Conjugal love in India. Leiden Boston, MA : Brill, 2002.
HQ470.S3 N3413 2002

Nāgārjuna, Siddha.
[Ratiśāstra. English & Sanskrit]
Conjugal love in India : Ratiśāstra and Ratiramaṇa : text, translation, and notes / by Kenneth G. Zysk. Leiden Boston, MA : Brill, 2002. xiv, 319 p. 25 cm. (Sir Henry Wellcome Asian studies ; v. 1) Includes bibliographical references (p. [291]-302) and index. ISBN 90-04-12598-1 DDC 306.7/0954
1. Love. 2. Sex. 3. Sex in marriage. I. Zysk, Kenneth G. II. Nāgārjuna, Siddha Ratiramana. English & Sanskrit. III. Title. IV. Series.
HQ470.S3 N3413 2002

Nagel, Joane. Race, ethnicity, and sexuality : intimate intersections, forbidden frontiers / Joane Nagel. New York : Oxford University Press, 2003. xii, 308 p. : ill. (some col.) ; 24 cm. Includes bibliographical references (p. 265-299) and index. CONTENTS: Sex matters: racing sex and sexing race -- Ethnosexual frontiers: cruising and crossing intimate intersections -- Constructing ethnicity & sexuality: building boundaries and identities -- Sex and conquest: domination and desire on ethnosexual frontiers -- Sex and race: the color of sex in America -- Sex and nationalism: sexually imagined communities -- Sex and war: fighting men, comfort women and the military-sexual complex -- Sex and tourism: travel and romance in ethnosexual destinations -- Sex and globalization: the global economy of desire -- Sex-baiting and race-baiting: the politics of ethnosexuality. CONTENTS: 505 0 Sex matters: racing sex and sexing race -- Ethnosexual frontiers: cruising and crossing intimate intersections -- Constructing ethnicity & sexuality: building boundaries and identities -- Sex and conquest: domination and desire on ethnosexual frontiers -- Sex and race: the color of sex in America -- Sex and nationalism: sexually imagined communities -- Sex and war: fighting men, comfort women and the military-sexual complex -- Sex and tourism: travel and romance in ethnosexual destinations -- Sex and globalization: the global economy of desire -- Sex-baiting and race-baiting ISBN 0-19-512746-3 (cloth : alk. paper) ISBN 0-19-512747-1 (pbk. : alk. paper) DDC 305.8
1. Sex. 2. Race. 3. Ethnicity. 4. Nationalism. I. Title.
HQ21 .N195 2003

Nagel, Stuart S., 1934-.
Peace, prosperity, and democracy at the cutting edge. New York : Nova Science Publishers, c2003.

Policymaking and peace. Lanham, Md. : Lexington Books, c2003.

JZ5538 .P65 2003

Nagl-Docekal, Herta.
Freiheit, Gleichheit und Autonomie. Wien : Oldenbourg ; Berlin : Akademie Verlag, 2003.
JC575 .F74 2003

"Något kan man väl göra.
Myrdal, Alva Reimer, 1902- Stockholm : Carlssons, c2002.

Nagovitsyn, A. E. (Alekseĭ Evgen'evich).
Gavrilov, D. A. Bogi slavian, iazychestvo, traditsiia. [Moskva] : Refl-buk, 2002.
BL930 .G38 2002

Nahl, Astrid van, 1951-.
Runica, Germanica, Mediaevalia. Berlin : W. de Gruyter, 2003.

NAHUA DANCE.
Galovic, Jelena. Los grupos místico-espirituales de la actualidad. México : Plaza y Valdés, 2002.
BL625 .G346 2002

The Nahualli animal oracle.
Rainieri, Caelum. Rochester, Vt. : Bear & Co., 2003.
BF1773 .R35 2003

NAHUAS. See **AZTECS.**

NAIKAN PSYCHOTHERAPY.
Reynolds, David K. A handbook for constructive living. Honolulu : University of Hawaii Press, 2002.
RC489.M65 R438 2002

Na'īm, 'Abd Allāh Aḥmad, 1946-.
The politics of memory. London ; New York : Zed Books, c2000.
JC571 .P642 2000

Nair, Ranjit.
Mind, matter, and mystery. New Delhi : Scientia, 2001.
BD418.3 .M5556 2001

Nair, Sheila, 1959-.
Power, postcolonialism, and international relations. London ; New York : Routledge, 2002.
JV51 .P69 2002

The naked eye.
Morris, Desmond. London : Ebury Press, 2000.
QL31.M79 A3 2000

Naked relationships.
Denise, Jan. Charlottesville, VA : Hampton Roads Pub., c2002.
BF575.I5 D46 2002

Nakonečný, Milan. Lidské emoce / Milan Nakonečný. Vyd. 1. Praha : Academia, 2000. 335 p. : ill. ; 24 cm. ISBN 80-200-0763-6
1. Emotions. I. Title.
BF536 .N35 2000

Name all the animals.
Smith, Alison, 1968- New York : Scribner, c2004.
BF575.G7 S58 2004

Namer, Gérard. Halbwachs et la mémoire sociale / Gérard Namer. Paris : L'Harmattan, c2000. 244 p. ; 22 cm. (Collection Logiques sociales) Includes bibliographical references (p. [243]-244). ISBN 2-7384-9595-8
1. Halbwachs, Maurice, - 1877-1945. 2. Memory - Social aspects. I. Title. II. Series: Logiques sociales.
BF378.S65 N36 2000

NAMES. See **TERMS AND PHRASES.**

Nan, Zhiguo.
Hobfoll, Stevan E. [Work won't love you back. Chinese] Top shuang xin jia ting. Chu ban. Taibei Shi : Ye qiang chu ban she, 1997.

Nanak-Dar Sant Baba Nand Singh Sant Baba Ishar Singh Spiritual Mission (Haridwār, India).
Sant Baba Ishar Singh Ji. Hardwar : Nanak-Dar Sant Baba Nand Singh Sant Baba Ishar Singh Spiritual Mission, 2002.
BL2017.9.I84 S27 2002

Nannipieri, Silvia.
Caterina e il diavolo. Pisa : ETS, c1999.
BF1584.18 C38 1999

Nanteos : a Welsh house and its families / edited by Gerald Morgan ; with chapters by J. Hext-Lewes ... [et al.]. Llandysul, Wales : Gomer, [2001] xiii, 264 p. : ill., maps ; 25 cm. Includes bibliographical references and index. ISBN 1-85902-802-0 DDC 942.9/61
1. Powell family. 2. Nanteos Mansion (Wales) - History. 3. Nanteos Mansion (Wales) - Genealogy. 4. Mansions - Wales - Dyfed - History. 5. Dyfed (Wales) - Genealogy. 6. Grail. I. Morgan, Gerald, 1935-
DA738.N36 N36 2001

NANTEOS MANSION (WALES) - GENEALOGY.
Nanteos. Llandysul, Wales : Gomer, [2001]
DA738.N36 N36 2001

NANTEOS MANSION (WALES) - HISTORY.
Nanteos. Llandysul, Wales : Gomer, [2001]
DA738.N36 N36 2001

Naomi's breakthrough guide.
Judd, Naomi. New York : Simon & Schuster, 2004.
BF637.S4 J84 2004

Na'or, Betsal'el. Bringing down dreams : exploring the lost art of Jewish dream interpretation / Bezalel Naor. 1st ed. Spring Valley, NY : Orot, c2002. 284 p. ; 24 cm. Includes bibliographical references (p. [211]-284). ISBN 0-9674512-5-6
1. Dreams - Religious aspects - Judaism. 2. Dreams in the Bible. I. Title.
BF1078 .N28 2002

Naphtali ben Isaac, ha-Kohen, 1649-1719. Sefer Bet Raḥel : otsar tefilot, teḥinot, piyutim u-seliḥot le-'inyanim u-zemanim shonim / me-et Naftali Kats ; yotse la-or la-rishonah mikhtav yad Rozentalianah be-Amsterdam 'im he'arot u-mekorot 'a. y. Shelomoh Honig. Yerushalayim : Ahavat Shalom, 761 [2001] 2 v. ; 28 cm. (Sifre Mekhon "Ahavat shalom" Yerushalayim ; 281) (Keren Ohel Avraham ye-Sarah ; 16-17) (Sifre ha-ga'on Rabenu Naftali Kats, z. ts. ye-k.l. ; [3]) Spine title: Bet Raḥel.
1. Naphtali ben Isaac, - ha-Kohen, - 1649-1719 - Will. 2. Judaism - Prayer-books and devotions - Hebrew. 3. Fasts and feasts - Judaism - Prayer-books and devotions. 4. Sick - Prayer-books and devotions, Jewish. 5. Piyutim. 6. Jewish religious poetry, Hebrew. 7. Cabala. 8. Wills, Ethical. I. Honig, S. II. Title. III. Title: Zemirot. IV. Title: Seliḥot. V. Title: Bet Raḥel VI. Series. VII. Series: Naphtali ben Isaac, ha-Kohen, 1649-1719. Works. 2001 ; v.3.
BM665 .N257 2001

Works. 2001
(v.3.) Naphtali ben Isaac, ha-Kohen, 1649-1719. Sefer Bet Raḥel. Yerushalayim : Ahavat Shalom, 761 [2001]
BM665 .N257 2001

NAPHTALI BEN ISAAC, HA-KOHEN, 1649-1719 - WILL.
Naphtali ben Isaac, ha-Kohen, 1649-1719. Sefer Bet Raḥel. Yerushalayim : Ahavat Shalom, 761 [2001]
BM665 .N257 2001

Napier, A. David. The age of immunology : conceiving a future in an alienating world / A. David Napier. Chicago : University of Chicago Press, 2003. xxiii, 319 p. : ill. ; 24 cm. Includes bibliographical references (p. [299]-313) and index. Table of contents URL: http://www.loc.gov/catdir/toc/fy036/2002012926.html ISBN 0-226-56812-1 (cloth : alk. paper) DDC 305.8/001
1. Ethnology - Philosophy. 2. Intercultural communication. 3. Self. 4. Change. 5. Immunology. I. Title.
GN345 .N36 2003

NAPOLEON I, EMPEROR OF THE FRENCH, 1769-1821.
Ferrero, Ernesto. Lezioni napoleoniche. 1. ed. Milano : Mondadori, 2002.

Naracandra Jaina jyotisha.
Naracandrasūri, 13th cent. [Naracandrajyotiṣa. Gujarati & English] Samśodhita adyatana āvrtti. Amadāvāda : Sarasvatī Pustaka Bhaṇḍāra, 2003.
BF1714.J28+

Naracandrasūri, 13th cent. [Naracandrajyotiṣa. Gujarati & English]
Naracandra Jaina jyotisha. Samśodhita adyatana āvrtti. Amadāvāda : Sarasvatī Pustaka Bhaṇḍāra, 2003. 161 p. : ill. ; 22 cm. Gujarati and Sanskrit. SUMMARY: On Jaina astrology.
1. Jaina astrology - Early works to 1800. I. Title.
BF1714.J28+

Naranjo, Claudio. [Eneagrama de la sociedad. English]
The enneagram of society / Claudio Naranjo. Nevada City, Calif. : Gateways Books and Tapes, 2004. p. cm. CONTENTS: Passions, pathologies, and neurotic motivations -- The circle of the nine basic characters -- The disturbances of love -- The ills of the world. ISBN 0-89556-159-X DDC 155.26
1. Enneagram. 2. Deadly sins - Psychology. 3. Enneagram - Social aspects. I. Title.
BF698.35.E54 N3813 2004

NARCISM. See **NARCISSISM.**

NARCISSISM.
Brown, Nina W. Loving the self-absorbed. Oakland, Calif. : New Harbinger, c2003.
BF575.N35 B76 2003

Campos, Edemilson Antunes de. A tirania de Narciso. 1. ed. São Paulo, SP, Brasil : Annablume/FAPESP, 2001.

Champion, David R. Narcissism and entitlement. New York : LFB Scholarly Pub. LLC, c2003.
BF692.15 .C47 2003

Hoffmann, Monika, 1972- Selbstliebe. Paderborn : Schöningh, c2002.
BF575.S37 H66 2002

Symington, Neville. A pattern of madness. London ; New York : Karnac, 2002.

Vaknin, Samuel. Narcissism book of quotes [electronic resource]. [Vancouver, B.C.] : Suite 101, [2003?]
BF575.N35

Narcissism and entitlement.
Champion, David R. New York : LFB Scholarly Pub. LLC, c2003.
BF692.15 .C47 2003

Narcissism book of quotes [electronic resource].
Vaknin, Samuel. [Vancouver, B.C.] : Suite 101, [2003?]
BF575.N35

NARCISSISM IN CHILDREN.
Bergeret, Jean. La sexualité infantile et ses mythes. Paris : Dunod, c2001.

NARCISSISM - RELIGIOUS ASPECTS.
Simonetta, Catherine. Renoncement et narcissisme chez Maurice Zundel. Saint-Maurice : Editions Saint-Augustin, c2002.

NARCISSISTIC INJURIES. See **SELF-ESTEEM.**

NARCOTIC ADDICTS - REHABILITATION.
Corley, M. Deborah. Embracing recovery from chemical dependency. Sottsdale, AZ : Gentle Path Press, c2003.
BF632 .C63 2003

Nardi, Peter M. Doing survey research : a guide to quantitative methods / Peter M. Nardi. Boston ; London : Allyn and Bacon, c2003. viii, 228 p. : ill. ; 23 cm. Includes bibliographical references (p. 222-224) and index. ISBN 0-205-34348-1 DDC 300/.723
1. Social surveys. 2. Social sciences - Research - Methodology. 3. Sampling (Statistics) I. Title.
HN29 .N25 2003

Narodnaia bibliotechka. Seriia "Velikorossy"
Shakhmagonov, N. (Nikolaĭ) Somknem riady, chtoby zhila Rossiia. Moskva : Ispo-Servis, 1999.

NARRATION (RHETORIC). See also **FIRST PERSON NARRATIVE.**
D'Cruz, Doreen, 1950- Loving subjects. New York : P. Lang, c2002.
PR888.W6 D39 2002

Gendering the master narrative. Ithaca : Cornell University Press, c2003.
HQ1143 .G46 2003

Thompson, Anne Booth. Everyday saints and the art of narrative in the South English legendary. Aldershot, England ; Burlington, Vt. : Ashgate, c2003.
PR2143.S543 T48 2003

Narrative and consciousness : literature, psychology, and the brain / edited by Gary D. Fireman, Ted E. McVay, Jr., Owen J. Flanagan. Oxford ; New York : Oxford University Press, c2003. xi, 252 p. ; 25 cm. Includes bibliographical references and index. Papers from a conference. CONTENTS: Role of narrative in the development of conscious awareness -- Narrative and the emergence of a consciousness of self -- The development of the self -- The role of narrative in recollection : a view from cognitive and neuropsychology -- Material selves : bodies, memory, and autobiographical narrating -- Rethinking the fictive, reclaiming the real : autobiography, narrative time, and the burden of truth -- Dual-focalization, retrospective fictional autobiography, and the ethics of Lolita -- The pursuit of death in Holocaust narrative -- Community and coherence : narrative contributions to the psychology of conflict and loss -- Empirical evidence for a narrative concept of self -- Sexual identities and narratives of self. ISBN 0-19-514005-2 (alk. paper) ISBN 0-19-516172-6 (pbk. : alk. paper) DDC 153
1. Consciousness - Congresses. 2. First person narrative - Congresses. 3. Autobiographical memory - Congresses. I. Fireman, Gary D. II. McVay, Ted E. III. Flanagan, Owen J.
BF311 .N26 2003

NARRATIVE ART.
Rehm, Ulrich. Stumme Sprache der Bilder. München : Deutscher Kunstverlag, 2002.

NARRATIVE, FIRST PERSON. See FIRST PERSON NARRATIVE.

Narrative gravity.
Rukmini Bhaya Nair. New Delhi ; New York : Oxford University Press, 2002.
P302.7 .R85 2002

Rukmini Bhaya Nair. London ; New York : Routledge, 2003.
P302.7 .R85 2003

NARRATIVE THERAPY.
Daniell, Beth, 1947- A communion of friendship. Carbondale : Southern Illinois University Press, c2003.
PE1405.U6 D36 2003

Henehan, Mary Pat. Integrating spirit and psyche. New York ; London : Haworth Pastoral Press, c2003.
RC489.F45 H46 2003

NARRATIVE WRITING. See NARRATION (RHETORIC).

Narváez, Darcia.
Moral development, self, and identity. Mahwah, N.J. : Lawrence Erlbaum Associates, 2004.
BF723.M54 M686 2004

Nas mnogo, no my odno.
Pint, A. A. (Aleksandr Aleksandrovich) Moskva : Shkola kholisticheskoĭ psikhologii, 2003.
BF202 .P56 2003

NASA contractor report
(NASA CR-204741.) Eaton, Robert C. The octavolateralis system and Mauthner cell interactions and questions [microform]. [Washington, D.C. : National Aeronautics and Space Administration, 1997]

(NASA CR-204798.) Rumbaugh, Duane M., 1929- Respondents, operants, and emergents [microform]. [Washington, D.C. : National Aeronautics and Space Administration, 1997]

[NASA contractor report]
(NASA CR-204997) Three-dimensional user interfaces for immersive virtual reality [microform]. Providence, RI : Brown University Computer Graphics Group, [1997]

[NASA technical memorandum
(205731]) Levy, Alon Y. (Alon Yitzchak) Irrelevance reasoning in knowledge based systems [microform]. [Washington, DC : National Aeronautics and Space Administration] ; Springfield, VA : Available from the National Technical Information Service, [1998]

NASA technical memorandum
(205922.) Washington, Richard. Abstraction planning in real time [microform]. Stanford, Calif. : Stanford University, Dept. of Computer Science, [1994] (Springfield, Va. : U.S. Dept. of Commerce, National Technical Information Service).

Nashim, zeḳenim ṿa-ṭaf : ḳovets ma'amarim li-khevodah shel Shulamit Shahar / 'orkhim, Miri Eli'av-Feldon, Yitshak Hen. Yerushalayim : Merkaz Zalman Shazar le-toldot Yiśra'el, [2001] 184 p. : ill., port. ; 24 cm. Added title page title: Women, children and the elderly : essays in honour of Shulamit Shahar. "Reshimat ketaveha shel Shulamit Shahar": p. 173-175. Includes bibliographical references and index. Text in Hebrew; table of contents also in English. ISBN 965227156X
1. Shahar, Shulamith - Bibliography. 2. Civilization, Medieval. 3. Social history - Medieval, 500-1500. 4. Aged - Family relationship - Europe. 5. Women - Europe - Middle Ages, 500-1500. 6. Children - Europe. 7. Parent and child. I. Eliav-Feldon, Miriam, 1946- II. Hen, Yitzhak. III. Title: Women, children and the elderly : essays in honour of Shulamit Shahar

Nasio, Juan-David.
[Livre de la douleur et de l'amour. English]
The book of love and pain : thinking at the limit with Freud and Lacan / Juan-David Nasio ; translated by David Pettigrew and François Raffoul. Albany : State University of New York, 2003. p. cm. Includes bibliographical references and index. ISBN 0-7914-5925-X (alk. paper) ISBN 0-7914-5926-8 (pbk. : alk. paper) DDC 150.19/5
1. Pain - Psychological aspects. 2. Psychoanalysis. I. Title.
BF515 .N3713 2003

Nasty women.
Carter, Jay. Chicago : Contemporary Books, c2003.
BF632.5 .C365 2003

Nathan, Tobie.
Clément, Catherine, 1939- Le divan et le grigri. Paris : Jacob, c2002.

Nathan-Wlodarski, Anne.
Wlodarski, Robert James. The haunted Whaley house, Old Town, San Diego, California. 2nd ed. West Hills, Calif. : G-HOST Pub., 2004.
BF1472.U6 W584

NATIONAL CHARACTERISTICS. See also ETHNOPSYCHOLOGY.
Kochetkov, V. V. (Vladimir Viktorovich) Psikhologii︠a︡ mezhkul'turnykh razlichiĭ. Moskva : PER SE, 2002.
GN502 .K6 2002

NATIONAL CHARACTERISTICS, AMERICAN.
Azoulay, Paul. Uncle Sam. Anglet : Atlantica, c2002.

Brokaw, Tom. A long way from home. 1st trade ed. New York : Random House, c2002.
PN4874.B717 A3 2002b

Cannon, Carl M. The pursuit of happiness in times of war. Lanham, MD ; Oxford : Rowman & Littlefield ; [Lanham, Md.] : Distributed by National Book Network, c2004.
E183 .C25 2004

Cornbleth, Catherine. Hearing America's youth. New York : P. Lang, c2003.
BF724.3.13 .C67 2003

Crockatt, Richard. America embattled. London ; New York : Routledge, 2003.
E902 .C76 2003

Didion, Joan. Where I was from. 1st ed. New York : Alfred A. Knopf : Distributed by Random House, 2003.
F861 .D53 2003

Elliott, Carl, 1961- Better than well. 1st ed. New York : W.W. Norton, c2003.
RA418.3.U6 E455 2003

The fractious nation? Berkeley : University of California Press, c2003.
E169.12 .F69 2003

Gelfert, Hans-Dieter, 1937- Typisch amerikanisch. Originalausg. München : Beck, c2002.
E169.1 .G44 2002

Gutfeld, Arnon. American exceptionalism. Brighton [England] ; Portland, Or. : Sussex Academic Press, 2002.
E169.1 .G956 2002

Hansen, Jonathan M. The lost promise of patriotism. Chicago : University of Chicago Press, c2003.
E661 .H316 2003

Harmond, Richard P. A history of Memorial Day. New York : P. Lang, c2002.
E642 .H37 2002

Hirsch, Jerrold, 1948- Portrait of America. Chapel Hill : University of North Carolina Press, c2003.
E175.4.W9 H57 2003

Hirsh, Michael, 1957- At war with ourselves. New York : Oxford University Press, 2003.
E895 .H57 2003

How we have changed. Gretna, La. : Pelican Pub. Co., 2003.
E169.12 .H677 2003

Hughes, Richard T. (Richard Thomas), 1943- Myths America lives by. Urbana : University of Illinois Press, c2003.
E175.9 .H84 2003

Kaplan, Amy. The anarchy of empire in the making of U.S. culture. Cambridge, Mass. : Harvard University Press, 2002.
E661.7 .K37 2002

Kazaaam! splat! ploof!. Lanham, Md. ; Oxford : Rowman & Littlefield, c2003.
D1055 .K39 2003

Kook, Rebecca B., 1959- The logic of democratic exclusion. Lanham, Md. : Lexington Books, c2002.
E185.615 .K59 2002

Lawson, Melinda, 1954- Patriot fires. Lawrence : University Press of Kansas, c2002.
E468.9 .L39 2002

Linklater, Andro. Measuring America. New York : Walker & Co., 2002.
E161.3 .L46 2002

Matthews, Christopher, 1945- American. New York : Free Press, c2002.
E169.1 .M429 2002

McGovern, James R. And a time for hope. Westport, Conn. : Praeger, 2000.
E806 .M45 2000

McKnight, Douglas. Schooling, the Puritan imperative, and the molding of an American national identity. Mahwah, N.J. ; London : L. Erlbaum Associates, 2003.
LC311 .M24 2003

My America. New York : Scribner, c2002.
E169.1 .M968 2002

Noonan, Peggy, 1950- A heart, a cross & a flag. New York : Free Press, c2003.
E903 .N66 2003

Nye, David E., 1946- America as second creation. Cambridge : MIT Press, c2003.
E179.5 .N94 2003

Pessanha, Rodolfo Gomes. O irracionalismo--, dos Estados Unidos da América à globalizaçãp. Niterói : Muiraquitã, c1998.

Pfitzer, Gregory M. Picturing the past. Washington [D.C.] : Smithsonian Institution Press, c2002.
E175 .P477 2002

Skeen, Carl Edward. 1816. Lexington : University Press of Kentucky, c2003.
E341 .S57 2003

Taylor, Lawrence Douglas. El nuevo norteamericano. México : Universidad Nacional Autónoma de México, Coordinación de Humanidades : Centro de Investigaciones sobre América del Norte ; Tijuana, B.C. : El Colegio de la Frontera Norte, 2001.
E40 .T39 2001

Trees, Andrew S., 1968- The founding fathers and the politics of character. Princeton, N.J. : Princeton University Press, c2004.
E302.1 .T74 2004

Winger, Stewart Lance. Lincoln, religion, and romantic cultural politics. DeKalb : Northern Illinois University Press, c2003.
E457.2 .W77 2003

York, Neil Longley. Turning the world upside down. Westport, Conn. ; London : Praeger, 2003.
E210 .Y67 2003

NATIONAL CHARACTERISTICS, ARAB - PSYCHOLOGICAL ASPECTS.
Rowland, Robert C., 1954- Shared land/conflicting identity. East lansing : Michigan State University Press, 2002.
DS119.7 .R685 2003

NATIONAL CHARACTERISTICS, BRAZILIAN.
Cultura e identidade. Rio de Janeiro, RJ, Brasil : DP & A Editores, 2002.

NATIONAL CHARACTERISTICS, BRITISH.
Konstrukte nationaler Identität. Würzburg : Ergon, c2002.
DC34 .K67 2002

NATIONAL CHARACTERISTICS, CANADIAN.
Taylor, Lawrence Douglas. El nuevo norteamericano. México : Universidad Nacional Autónoma de México, Coordinación de Humanidades : Centro de Investigaciones sobre América del Norte ; Tijuana, B.C. : El Colegio de la Frontera Norte, 2001.
E40 .T39 2001

NATIONAL CHARACTERISTICS, EUROPEAN.
Kazaaam! splat! ploof!. Lanham, Md. ; Oxford : Rowman & Littlefield, c2003.
D1055 .K39 2003

NATIONAL CHARACTERISTICS, FRENCH.
Büchi, Christophe. "Röstigraben". 2. aufl. Zürich : NZZ, c2001.

Konstrukte nationaler Identität. Würzburg : Ergon, c2002.
DC34 .K67 2002

NATIONAL CHARACTERISTICS, GERMAN.
Büchi, Christophe. "Röstigraben". 2. aufl. Zürich : NZZ, c2001.

Inspecting Germany. Münster : Lit, c2002.
DD76 .I57 2002

Konstrukte nationaler Identität. Würzburg : Ergon, c2002.
DC34 .K67 2002

Polacy i niemcy. òznań : Wydawn. Poznańskie, 2003.
DK4121 .P65 2003

Recasting German identity. Rochester, NY : Camden House, 2002.

DD239 .R43 2002

Smyser, W. R., 1931- How Germans negotiate. Washington, D.C. : U.S. Institute of Peace Press, 2003.
BF637.N4 S59 2003

NATIONAL CHARACTERISTICS, ISRAELI.
Kook, Rebecca B., 1959- The logic of democratic exclusion. Lanham, Md. : Lexington Books, c2002.
E185.615 .K59 2002

NATIONAL CHARACTERISTICS, ISRAELI - PSYCHOLOGICAL ASPECTS.
Grosbard, Ofer, 1954- [Yiśra'el 'al ha-sapah. English] Israel on the couch. Albany : State University of New York Press, c2003.
DS126.5 .G694 2003

Grosbard, Ofer, 1954- Yiśra'el 'al ha-sapah. Tel-Aviv : Yedi'ot aḥaronot : Sifre ḥemed, c2000.

Rowland, Robert C., 1954- Shared land/conflicting identity. East lansing : Michigan State University Press, 2002.
DS119.7 .R685 2003

NATIONAL CHARACTERISTICS, MEXICAN.
Sociología de la identidad. México : Miguel Angel Porrúa : Universidad Autónoma Metropolitana, Unidad Iztapalapa, 2002.

Taylor, Lawrence Douglas. El nuevo norteamericano. México : Universidad Nacional Autónoma de México, Coordinación de Humanidades : Centro de Investigaciones sobre América del Norte ; Tijuana, B.C. : El Colegio de la Frontera Norte, 2001.
E40 .T39 2001

NATIONAL CHARACTERISTICS, POLISH.
Polacy i niemcy. òznań : Wydawn. Poznańskie, 2003.
DK4121 .P65 2003

NATIONAL CHARACTERISTICS, RUSSIAN.
Akopov, G. V. Mentalistika. Samara : Samarskiĭ gos. pedagog. universitet, 2001.
BF108.R8 A478 2001

Belíaev, G. G. Dukhovnye korni russkogo naroda. Moskva : Bylina, 2002.
DK32 .B358 2002

Individualitätskonzepte in der russischen Kultur. Berlin : Berlin Verlag Arno Spitz, c2002.
PG2987.I48 .I53 2002

Kharkhordin, Oleg, 1964- Oblichat' i litsemerit'. Sankt-Peterburg : Evropeĭskiĭ universitet v Sankt-Peterburge ; Moskva : Letniĭ Sad, 2002.
B2430.F724 K43 2002

Kochetkov, V. V. (Vladimir Viktorovich) Psikhologiia mezhkul'turnykh razlichiĭ. Moskva : PER SĖ, 2002.
GN502 .K6 2002

Lichev, Aleksandŭr. Russland verstehen. 1. Aufl. Düsseldorf : Grupello, 2001.

Mamleev, I͡Uriĭ. Rossiia vechnaia. Moskva : AiF-Print, 2002.
DK32 .M355 2002

Meniaĭlov, Alekseĭ. Durilka. Moskva : "Kraft+", 2003.

Shakhmagonov, N. (Nikolaĭ) Somknem riady, chtoby zhila Rossiia. Moskva : Ispo-Servis, 1999.

Shcheglov, A. (Alekseĭ) I͡Azycheskaia zaria. Moskva : [Izdatel'stvo "PROBEL-2000"], 2002.
BL980.R5 S53 2002

Trufanov, A. A. (Andreĭ Andreevich) Osnovy teorii intelligentnosti. Kazan' : ZAO "Novoe znanie", 2002.
BF431 .T78 2002

V'iunov, I͡U. A. Slovo o russkikh. Moskva : Izd-vo IKAR, c2002.

Zhuravlev, V. K. (Vladimir Konstantinovich) Russkiĭ iazyk i russkiĭ kharakter. Moskva : Moskovskiĭ patriarkhat, 2002.
PG2095 .Z48 2002

National Commission on Culture and the Arts (Philippines).
Feminine voices. [Manila?] : NCCA, c2001-

NATIONAL CONSCIOUSNESS. See **NATIONALISM.**

National Egyptian Heritage Revival Association.
Be thou there. Cairo ; New York : American University in Cairo Press, c2001.

National Film Board of Canada.
McLuhan's wake [videorecording]. [Montreal, Quebec] : Primitive Entertainment/National Film Board of Canada, c2002.

Western eyes [videorecording]. New York, NY : First Run/Icarus Films, 2000.

NATIONAL HEALTH SERVICE (GREAT BRITAIN).
Hadikin, Ruth. The bullying culture. Oxford ; Boston : Books for Midwives, 2000.
BF637.B85 H33 2000

NATIONAL HERITAGE. See **CULTURAL PROPERTY.**

NATIONAL HOLIDAYS. See **HOLIDAYS.**

NATIONAL IDENTITY. See **NATIONALISM.**

National Institute of Justice (U.S.).
Conflict resolution for school personnel [electronic resource]. [Washington, D.C.?] : U.S. Dept. of Justice, Office of Justice Programs, National Institute of Justice, c1999.

National Institute of Mental Health (U.S.).
Helping children and adolescents cope with violence and disasters [electronic resource]. Bethesda, MD : Office of Communications and Public Liaison, [2001]

Mental health and mass violence [electronic resource]. [Bethesda, MD : National Institute of Mental Health, 2002]

Strock, Margaret. Medications [electronic resource]. [4th ed., rev. Apr. 2002, repr. Sept. 2002]. [Bethesda, Md.] : Dept. of Health and Human Services, Public Health Service, National Institutes of Health, National Institute of Mental Health, 2002.

National Institute of Mental Health (U.S.). Office of Communications and Public Liaison.
Helping children and adolescents cope with violence and disasters [electronic resource]. Bethesda, MD : Office of Communications and Public Liaison, [2001]

National Institute on Aging.
Aging under the microscope [electronic resource]. Bethesda, MD : National Institute on Aging, National Institutes of Health, [2002]

NATIONAL LANGUAGES. See **LANGUAGE POLICY.**

NATIONAL LIBERATION MOVEMENTS. See **GUERRILLAS; SELF-DETERMINATION, NATIONAL.**

NATIONAL MALL (WASHINGTON, D.C.). See **MALL, THE (WASHINGTON, D.C.).**

NATIONAL PATRIMONY. See **CULTURAL PROPERTY.**

NATIONAL PSYCHOLOGY. See **ETHNOPSYCHOLOGY.**

NATIONAL SECURITY. See **INTERNATIONAL RELATIONS.**

NATIONAL SECURITY - GUATEMALA.
Acuerdos de paz y seguridad democrática en Guatemala. 1. ed. [Guatemala] : USAC, DIGI, [2002]

NATIONAL SECURITY - SCANDINAVIA.
The Nordic peace. Aldershot, England ; Burlington, VT : Ashgate, c2003.
UA646.7 .N672 2003

NATIONAL SECURITY - UNITED STATES.
Garten, Jeffrey E., 1946- The politics of fortune. Boston : Harvard Business School Press, c2002.
HD57.7 .G377 2002

NATIONAL SECURITY - UNITED STATES - FORECASTING.
Growing global migration and its implications for the United States. [Washington, D.C.?] : The Board, 2001.

Growing global migration and its implications for the United States [electronic resource]. Electronic document. [Washington, D.C.? : National Intelligence Council, 2001]
CB161 .G768

NATIONAL SELF-DETERMINATION. See **SELF-DETERMINATION, NATIONAL.**

NATIONAL SOCIALISM. See also **FASCISM; NAZIS.**
Bošković, Hijacint. Filozofski izvori fašizma i nacionalnog socijalizma. 2. izd. Zagreb : Dom i svijet, 2000.
B804 .B66 2000

Reemtsma, Jan Philipp. Wie hätte ich mich verhalten? München : Beck, c2001.
HM216 .R38 2001

NATIONAL SOCIALISM - HISTORY.
Bärsch, Claus-Ekkehard. Die politische Religion des Nationalsozialismus. 2., vollst. überarb. Aufl. München : W. Fink, c2002.

Grunewald, Michel, 1942- Moeller van den Brucks Geschichtsphilosophie. Bern ; New York : P. Lang, c2001.
DD247.M59 G78 2001

Rickels, Laurence A. Nazi psychoanalysis. Minneapolis : University of Minnesota Press, c2002-
BF173 .R49 2002

Schaller, Helmut Wilhelm, 1940- Der Nationalsozialismus und die slawische Welt. Regensburg : Pustet, c2002.
DD256.5 .S259 2002

Simon, Jürgen, 1966- Kriminalbiologie und Zwangssterilisation. Münster ; New York : Waxmann, c2001.

NATIONAL SOCIALISM - RELIGIOUS ASPECTS.
Bärsch, Claus-Ekkehard. Die politische Religion des Nationalsozialismus. 2., vollst. überarb. Aufl. München : W. Fink, c2002.

NATIONAL SOCIALISTS. See **NAZIS.**

National survey and reports on status of psychology.
Psychology, IUPsyS global resource [electronic resource]. Hove, East Sussex, UK : published on behalf of the international Union of Psychological Science by Psychology Press Ltd., 2000-
BF76.5 .P79

National Textbook language dictionaries.
Spears, Richard A. NTC's dictionary of everyday American English expressions. Lincolnwood, Ill. : National Textbook Co., c1994.
PE2839 .S65 1994

NATIONAL TREASURE. See **CULTURAL PROPERTY.**

NATIONALISM. See also **ETHNOCENTRISM; MESSIANISM, POLITICAL; SELF-DETERMINATION, NATIONAL.**
Identities. New York ; Oxford : Berghahn Books, 2002.
HM716 .I34 2002

Making sense of collectivity. London ; Sterling, Va. : Pluto Press, 2002.
HM753 .M35 2002

Migration, diasporas, and transnationalism. Cheltenham, UK ; Northampton, MA : Edward Elgar, 1999.
JV6032 .M54 1999

Nagel, Joane. Race, ethnicity, and sexuality. New York : Oxford University Press, 2003.
HQ21 .N195 2003

Toshchenko, Zhan Terent'evich. Tri osobennykh lika vlasti. Moskva : RGGU, 2002.
JC330 .T674 2002

NATIONALISM - ALBANIA.
Albanian identities. Bloomington : Indiana University Press, 2002.
DR950 .A385 2002

NATIONALISM - CHINA.
Cheng zhong de Zhongguo. Di 1 ban. Beijing : Ren min chu ban she, 2002.
HQ799.2.P6 C449 2002

NATIONALISM - GERMANY.
Grunewald, Michel, 1942- Moeller van den Brucks Geschichtsphilosophie. Bern ; New York : P. Lang, c2001.
DD247.M59 G78 2001

NATIONALISM - GERMANY - HISTORY - 20TH CENTURY.
Jarausch, Konrad Hugo. Shattered past. Princeton, N.J. : Princeton University Press, c2003.
DD86 .J253 2003

NATIONALISM IN MUSIC.
Gervasoni, Marco, 1968- Le armi di Orfeo. [Scandicci] (Firenze) : La nuova Italia, 2002.
ML3917.E85 G479 2002

NATIONALISM - PHILOSOPHY.
Clark, J. C. D. Our shadowed present. London : Atlantic, 2003.

Tadtaev, Kh. B. (Khristofor Bagratovich) Ėtnos, natsiia, rasa. Saratov : Saratovskiĭ gos. universitet, 2001.

GN345 .T33 2001

NATIONALISM - PUERTO RICO.
Pabón, Carlos. Nación postmortem. 1. ed. San Juan, P.R. : Ediciones Callejón, 2002.

NATIONALISM - RUSSIA (FEDERATION).
Avdeev, V. B. (Vladimir Borisovich) Metafizicheskaia antropologiia. Moskva : Belye al'vy, 2002.
DK510.763 .A93 2002

Shakhmagonov, N. (Nikolaĭ) Somknem rı̃ady, chtoby zhila Rossiia. Moskva : Ispo-Servis, 1999.

NATIONALISM - RUSSIA (FEDERATION) - HISTORY.
V'iunov, IU. A. Slovo o russkikh. Moskva : Izd-vo IKAR, c2002.

NATIONALISM - UNITED STATES.
Hughes, Richard T. (Richard Thomas), 1943- Myths America lives by. Urbana : University of Illinois Press, c2003.
E175.9 .H84 2003

NATIONALISM - UNITED STATES - HISTORY - 19TH CENTURY.
Lawson, Melinda, 1954- Patriot fires. Lawrence : University Press of Kansas, c2002.
E468.9 .L39 2002

NATIONALITIES, PRINCIPLE OF. *See* **SELF-DETERMINATION, NATIONAL.**

NATIONALITY (CITIZENSHIP). *See* **CITIZENSHIP.**

Der Nationalsozialismus und die slawische Welt.
Schaller, Helmut Wilhelm, 1940- Regensburg : Pustet, c2002.
DD256.5 .S259 2002

Natir imin.
Collen, Lindsey. Port Louis, Mauritius : Ledikasyon pu travayer, [2000]

NATIVE AMERICANS. *See* **INDIANS OF NORTH AMERICA.**

NATIVE CLERGY. *See* **CLERGY.**

NATIVE PEOPLES. *See* **INDIGENOUS PEOPLES.**

NATIVE RACES. *See* **INDIGENOUS PEOPLES.**

Natoli, Salvatore. L'esperienza del dolore : le forme del patire nella cultura occidentale / Salvatore Natoli. 1. ed. nell'"Universale economica"--Saggi. Milano : Feltrinelli, 2002. 387 p. ; 20 cm. (Saggi universale economica Feltrinelli ; 1699) Includes bibliographical references. ISBN 88-07-81699-7 DDC 128
1. Grief. 2. Suffering. I. Title.

Natur- und Kulturgeschichte von Psyche, Geist und Bewusstsein.
Hinterhuber, H. (Hartmann) Die Seele. Wien ; New York : Springer, c2001.

Natural-born cyborgs.
Clark, Andy, 1957- Oxford ; New York : Oxford University Press, c2003.
T14.5 .C58 2003

NATURAL DISASTERS. *See* **COMETS - COLLISIONS WITH EARTH.**

NATURAL HISTORY. *See also* **BIOLOGY.**
Gould, Stephen Jay. I have landed. 1st ed. New York : Harmony Books, 2002.
QH45.5 .G735 2002

NATURAL HISTORY - KLAMATH MOUNTAINS (CALIF. AND OR.).
Wallace, David Rains, 1945- The Klamath knot. 20th anniversary ed. Berkeley : University of California Press, [2003]
QH105.C2 W344 2003

NATURAL HISTORY - PHILOSOPHY - POPULAR WORKS.
Vallejo, Fernando. La tautología darwinista. 1a. ed. México : Universidad Nacional Autónoma de México, 1998.

NATURAL LAW. *See also* **LIBERTY.**
Pufendorf, Samuel, Freiherr von, 1632-1694. [De officio hominis et civis. English] The whole duty of man, according to the law of nature. Indianapolis, Ind. : Liberty Fund, c2003.
K457.P8 D4313 2003

Natural law and enlightenment classics
Hutcheson, Francis, 1694-1746. An essay on the nature and conduct of the passions and affections. Indianapolis : Liberty Fund, c2002.
B1501 .E6 2002

Pufendorf, Samuel, Freiherr von, 1632-1694. [De officio hominis et civis. English] The whole duty of man, according to the law of nature. Indianapolis, Ind. : Liberty Fund, c2003.
K457.P8 D4313 2003

NATURAL PHILOSOPHY. *See* **PHYSICS.**

NATURAL RESOURCES.
Mason, Colin, 1926- The 2030 spike. London ; Sterling, VA : Earthscan Publications, 2003.
CB161 .M384 2003

NATURAL RESOURCES, COMMUNAL. *See* **PUBLIC LANDS.**

NATURAL SCIENCE. *See* **NATURAL HISTORY; SCIENCE.**

NATURAL SELECTION. *See also* **EVOLUTION (BIOLOGY).**
Dawkins, Richard, 1941- The extended phenotype. Rev. ed. Oxford ; New York : Oxford University Press, 1999.
QH375 .D38 1999

Vallejo, Fernando. La tautología darwinista. 1a. ed. México : Universidad Nacional Autónoma de México, 1998.

Natural selection and social theory.
Trivers, Robert. New York : Oxford University Press, 2002.
GN365.9 .T76 2002

NATURAL THEOLOGY. *See* **CREATION.**

Naturaliser la phénoménologie : essais sur la phénoménologie contemporaine et les sciences cognitives / sous la direction de Jean Petitot ... [et al.] ; avec les contributions de Renaud Barbaras ... [et al.]. Paris : CNRS, c2002. xii, 796 p. : ill. ; 24 cm. (CNRS communication) Includes bibliographical references (p. [725]-771) and indexes. ISBN 2-271-05821-X DDC 194
1. Phenomenology. 2. Cognitive science. I. Petitot, Jean, 1944- II. Barbaras, Renaud. III. Series.

NATURALISM.
Naturalism, evolution, and intentionality. Calgary, Alta., Canada : University of Calgary Press, c2001.
BD418.3 .N35 2001

Papineau, David, 1947- The roots of reason. Oxford : Clarendon Press ; New York : Oxford University Press, 2003.
BD418.3 .P35 2003

Rea, Michael C. (Michael Cannon), 1968- World without design. Oxford : Clarendon Press ; New York : Oxford University Press, 2002.
B828.2 .R43 2002

Naturalism, evolution & intentionality.
Naturalism, evolution, and intentionality. Calgary, Alta., Canada : University of Calgary Press, c2001.
BD418.3 .N35 2001

Naturalism, evolution, and intentionality / edited by Jillian Scott McIntosh. Calgary, Alta., Canada : University of Calgary Press, c2001. iv, 258 p. : ill. ; 22 cm. (Canadian journal of philosophy. Supplementary volume, 0229-7051 ; 27) Spine title: Naturalism, evolution & intentionality. Includes bibliographical references and index. CONTENTS: Introduction : investigating the mind / Jillian S. McIntosh -- Self-directed agents / Wayne D. Christensen and Cliff A. Hooker -- Darwin's algorithm, natural selective history, and intentionality naturalized / Philip P. Hanson -- Adapted minds / Larry Shapiro -- A tale of two froggies / Colin Allen -- The excesses of teleosemantics / Paul Sheldon Davies -- Teleosemantics and the epiphenomenality of content / Eric Saidel -- Monsters among us / Timothy Schroeder -- Why vision is more than seeing / Melvyn A. Goodale -- Our knowledge of colour / Mohan Matthen. ISBN 0-919491-27-8 (alk. paper) DDC 128/.2
1. Philosophy of mind. 2. Naturalism. 3. Evolution. 4. Intentionality (Philosophy) I. McIntosh, Jillian Scott, 1959- II. Title: Naturalism, evolution & intentionality III. Series.
BD418.3 .N35 2001

NATURALISM - HISTORY - 19TH CENTURY.
Van Wyhe, John, 1971- Phrenology and the origins of Victorian scientific naturalism. Burlington, VT : Ashgate, c2003.
BF879 .V36 2003

NATURALISTS - ENGLAND - BIOGRAPHY.
Darwin, Charles, 1809-1882. Autobiographies. London : Penguin, 2002.

NATURALIZATION - UNITED STATES - HANDBOOKS, MANUALS, ETC.
McLaughlin, Bob. [USA immigration & orientation. Spanish] USA inmigración y orientación. 1a. ed. en español. Satellite Beach, Fla. : Wellesworth Pub., c2001.

NATURE.
The colors of nature. 1st ed. Minneapolis, Minn. : Milkweed Editions, 2002.
QH81 .C663 2002

NATURE (AESTHETICS).
Shepard, Paul, 1925- Where we belong. Athens : University of Georgia Press, c2003.
GF21 .S524 2003

NATURE AND NURTURE.
Bailey, J. Michael. The man who would be queen. Washington, D.C. : Joseph Henry Press, c2003.
HQ76.2.U5 B35 2003

Jensen, Arthur Robert. Intelligence, race, and genetics. Boulder, Colo. : Westview Press, c2002.
BF431 .J396 2002

Kessidi, F. Kh. Filosofskie i ėticheskie problemy genetiki cheloveka. Moskva : Martis, 1994.
BF341 .K45 1994

Marcus, Gary F. (Gary Fred) The birth of the mind. New York : Basic Books, 2004.
BF701 .M32 2004

Pinker, Steven, 1954- The blank slate . New York : Viking, 2002.
BF341 .P47 2002

Race and IQ. Expanded ed. New York : Oxford University Press, 1999.
BF432.A1 R3 1999

Ridley, Matt. Nature via nurture. 1st ed. New York : HarperCollins, c2003.
QH438.5 .R535 2003

NATURE AND NURTURE - LONGITUDINAL STUDIES.
Nature, nurture, and the transition to early adolescence. Oxford ; New York : Oxford University Press, 2003.
BF341 .N387 2003

NATURE CONSERVATION - PHILOSOPHY.
Rothenberg, David, 1962- Always the mountains. Athens : University of Georgia Press, c2002.
GF21 .R68 2002

La nature de l'esprit.
Jeanneret, Marc. Paris : Odile Jacob, c2002.
BF311 .J435 2002

NATURE - EFFECT OF HUMAN BEINGS ON. *See also* **HUMAN ECOLOGY.**
Boulter, Michael Charles. Extinction. New York : Columbia University Press, c2002.
QE721.2.E97 B68 2002

Fernández-Armesto, Felipe. Civilizations. New York : Free Press, c2001.
CB151 .F47 2001

Pievani, Telmo. Homo sapiens e altre catastrofi. Roma : Meltemi, c2002.

NATURE - EFFECT OF HUMAN BEINGS ON - UNITED STATES - HISTORY.
Gutfeld, Arnon. American exceptionalism. Brighton [England] ; Portland, Or. : Sussex Academic Press, 2002.
E169.1 .G956 2002

NATURE - FOLKLORE.
Turovich, V. (Vasiliĭ) 1000 primet pogody. Perm' : Izd-vo "Poligrafist", 1997.
BF1777 .T87 1997

NATURE IN ART. *See* **NATURE (AESTHETICS).**

NATURE IN LITERATURE.
Marshall, Ian, 1954- Peak experiences. Charlottesville : University of Virginia Press, 2003.
PS163 .M37 2003

Thinking about the environment. Lanham, Md. : Lexington Books, c2002.
GE50 .T48 2002

NATURE IN ORNAMENT. *See* **DECORATION AND ORNAMENT.**

NATURE - NURTURE. *See* **NATURE AND NURTURE.**

Nature, nurture, and the transition to early adolescence / edited by Stephen A. Petrill ... [et al.]. Oxford ; New York : Oxford University Press, 2003. xi, 329 p. : ill. ; 25 cm. Includes bibliographical references and indexes. ISBN 0-19-515747-8 (alk. paper) DDC 155.4/5
1. Colorado Adoption Project. 2. Nature and nurture - Longitudinal studies. 3. Individual differences in adolescence - Longitudinal studies. 4. Adopted children - Colorado - Psychology - Longitudinal studies. I. Petrill, Stephen A., 1968-

BF341 .N387 2003

The nature of generosity.
Kittredge, William. 1st Vintage Departures ed. New York : Vintage, 2001, c2000.
PS3561.I87 Z472 2001

The nature of reasoning / edited by Robert J. Sternberg, Jacqueline P. Leighton. Cambridge, U.K. ; New York : Cambridge University Press, 2003. p. cm. Includes bibliographical references and index. Table of contents URL: http://www.loc.gov/catdir/toc/cam031/2003041966.html Publisher description URL: http://www.loc.gov/catdir/description/cam031/2003041966.html ISBN 0-521-81090-6 ISBN 0-521-00928-6 (pbk.) DDC 153.4/3
1. Reasoning (Psychology) I. Sternberg, Robert J. II. Leighton, Jacqueline P.
BF442 .N38 2003

NATURE - POLITICAL ASPECTS.
Race, nature, and the politics of difference. Durham : Duke University Press, c2003.
HT1521 .R2355 2003

NATURE PROTECTION. See **NATURE CONSERVATION.**

NATURE VERSUS NURTURE. See **NATURE AND NURTURE.**

Nature via nurture.
Ridley, Matt. 1st ed. New York : HarperCollins, c2003.
QH438.5 .R535 2003

NATUROPATHY.
Blumenthal, Mark. Popular herbs in the U.S. market. Austin : American Botanical Council, 1997.

Nauka o nieświadomość.
Motycka, Alina. Wrocław : Leopoldinum, 1998.

Naumann, Klaus, 1939- Frieden, der noch nicht erfüllte Auftrag / Klaus Naumann. Hamburg : Mittler & Sohn, c2002. 269 p. : ill. ; 25 cm. ISBN 3-8132-0714-5
1. Germany - Military policy - 20th century. 2. Germany - Military policy - 21st century. 3. Germany - Armed Forces. 4. Peace. 5. World politics - 20th century. 6. World politics - 21st century. I. Title.
UA710 .N38 2002

Naumann, Manfred.
Genuss und Egoismus. Berlin : Akademie Verlag, c2002.

NAUMANN, MANFRED.
Genuss und Egoismus. Berlin : Akademie Verlag, c2002.

NAUTICAL ASTRONOMY. See **TIME.**

Navam and the Karṇāṭak group kṛtis.
Padma, N. K., 1956- New Delhi : Kanishka Publishers, Distributors, 2002.
ML338 .P197 2002

NAVARRE (SPAIN) - CIVILIZATION.
Signos de identidad histórica para Navarra. Pamplona : Caja de Ahorros de Navarra, 1996.
DP302.N267 S54 1996

Navarro Jr., Antonio B., 1963-.
Carvalho, Angela Maria B., 1954- A magia das ervas e seu axé. São Paulo, SP : Madras, 2003.
1. Black author.

Nay, W. Robert. Taking charge of anger : how to resolve conflict, sustain relationships, and express yourself without losing control / W. Robert Nay. New York : Guilford Press, c2003. p. cm. Includes bibliographical references and index. Table of contents URL: http://www.loc.gov/catdir/toc/ecip043/2003010342.html CONTENTS: The faces of anger : who do you see in the mirror? -- Behind the mask : understanding anger and its expression -- Understanding your anger triggers -- Anger awareness -- Dampening anger arousal -- Recognizing thoughts that fuel anger -- Rewriting your script : new thinking for new solutions -- Assertive problem solving : expressing anger constructively in conflict situations -- When anger is aimed at you -- Establishing new anger habits -- So you've had a setback : getting back on track -- Appendix 1: Self-assessment of anger questionnaire -- Appendix 2: Personal anger scale. ISBN 1-57230-927-X (hard) ISBN 1-57230-680-7 (pbk.) DDC 152.4/7
1. Anger. 2. Interpersonal conflict. I. Title.
BF575.A5 N39 2003

Naymark, Rick.
Lott, Lynn. Madame Dora's fortune-telling cards. Gloucester, Mass. : Fair Winds Press, 2003.
BF1878 .L78 2003

Nazarchuk, A. V. (Aleksandr Viktorovich) Ėtika globaliziruiushchegosia obshchestva : tendentsii i problemy globalizatsii v svete sotsial'no-ėticheskoĭ kontseptsii K.-O. Apelia / A.V. Nazarchuk. Moskva : DirectMediia Publishing, 2002. 378 p. ; 23 cm. ISBN 5948650014
1. Apel, Karl-Otto. 2. Ethics, Modern - 20th century. 3. Philosophy, Modern - 20th century. 4. Analysis (Philosophy) I. Title.
B3199.A634 N39 2002

Nazhmudinov, G. M.
Shubniakov, B. P. Svoboda kak sotsial'nyĭ i dukhovno-psikhicheskiĭ fenomen. Iaroslavl' : DIA-press, 2000.

Nazi psychoanalysis.
Rickels, Laurence A. Minneapolis : University of Minnesota Press, c2002-
BF173 .R49 2002

NAZIS. See **NATIONAL SOCIALISM.**

NAZIS - MISCELLANEA.
Moon, Peter. The black sun. New York : Sky Books, c1997.
BF1434.U6 M66 1997

NAZISM. See **NATIONAL SOCIALISM.**

Nchimi chikanga.
Soko, Boston. Blantyre [Malawi] : Christian Literature Association in Malawi, 2002.

Ne smotrite im v glaza!.
Vinokurov, Igor'. Moskva : AiF-Print, 2001.
BF1466 .V56 2001

Ne-virtualistika.
Nosov, N. A. Moskva : Gumanitariĭ, 2001.
BF38 .N67 2001

Neal, Carl F., 1965- Incense : crafting & use of magickal scents / Carl F. Neal. 1st ed. St. Paul, Minn. : Llewellyn Publications, 2003. xxvii, 149 p. : ill. ; 24 cm. Includes bibliographical references (p. 141-142) and index. ISBN 0-7387-0336-2
1. Magic. 2. Incense - Miscellanea. I. Title.
BF1623.I52 N43 2003

Neal-Schuman netguide series
Bradley, Phil, 1959- Internet power searching. 2nd ed. New York : Neal-Schuman Publishers, c2002.
ZA4201 .B69 2002

NEANDERTHALS.
Arsuaga, Juan Luis de. [Collar del neandertal. English] The Neanderthal's necklace. New York : Four Walls Eight Windows, c2002.
GN285 .A7713 2002

The Neanderthal's necklace.
Arsuaga, Juan Luis de. [Collar del neandertal. English] New York : Four Walls Eight Windows, c2002.
GN285 .A7713 2002

The near birth experience.
Bongard, Jerry. New York : Marlowe & Co. ; [Emeryville, CA?] : Distributed by Publishers Group West, c2000.
BF1156.R45 B66 2000

Near-death experiences.
Martin, Michael, 1948- Mankato, Minn. : Edge Books, 2004.
BF1045.N4 M375 2004

NEAR-DEATH EXPERIENCES.
Leland, Kurt. The unanswered question. Charlottesville, VA : Hampton Roads Pub., c2002.
BF1045.N4 L45 2002

Martin, Michael, 1948- Near-death experiences. Mankato, Minn. : Edge Books, 2004.
BF1045.N4 M375 2004

NEAR-DEATH EXPERIENCES IN CHILDREN.
Atwater, P. M. H. [Children of the new millennium] The new children and near-death experiences. Rochester, Vt. : Bear & Co., 2003.
BF1045.N42 A88 2003

NEAR-DEATH EXPERIENCES - JUVENILE LITERATURE.
Martin, Michael, 1948- Near-death experiences. Mankato, Minn. : Edge Books, 2004.
BF1045.N4 M375 2004

NEAR-DEATH EXPERIENCES - RELIGIOUS ASPECTS. See **FUTURE LIFE.**

NEAR EAST. See **MIDDLE EAST.**

Neath, Ian, 1965- Human memory : an introduction to research, data, and theory / Ian Neath, Aimée M. Surprenant. 2nd ed. Australia ; Belmont, CA : Thomson/Wadsworth, c2003. xxii, 474 p. : ill. ; 24 cm. Includes bibliographical references (p. 403-440) and indexes. ISBN 0-534-59562-6 DDC 153.1/2
1. Memory. I. Surprenant, Aimée M. II. Title.
BF371 .N43 2003

Nebraska Symposium on Motivation.
Nebraska Symposium on Motivation
(v. 47.) Nebraska Symposium on Motivation (2001) Evolutionary psychology and motivation. Lincoln, Neb. ; London : University of Nebraska Press, c2001.
BF701 .N43 2001

Nebraska Symposium on Motivation (2001)
Evolutionary psychology and motivation / Jeffrey A. French, Alan C. Kamil, and Daniel W. Leger, volume editors ; presenters, Martin Daly ... [et al.] Lincoln, Neb. ; London : University of Nebraska Press, c2001. xxiii, 221 p. : ill. ; 24 cm. (Current theory and research in motivation ; v. 47) (Nebraska Symposium on Motivation ; v. 47) Includes bibliographical references and indexes. CONTENTS: Introduction : Fear and loathing of evolutionary psychology in the social sciences / Daniel W. Leger, Alan C. Kamil, and Jeffrey A. French -- Risk-taking, intrasexual competition, and homicide / Martin Daly and Margo Wilson -- Adaptive design, selective history, and women's sexual motivations / Steven W. Gangestad -- Pheromones and vasanas : the functions of social chemosignals / Martha K. McClintock ... [et al.] -- The adaptive toolbox : toward a Darwinian rationality / Gerd Gigerenzer -- Cognitive strategies and the representation of social relations by monkeys / Robert M. Seyfarth and Dorothy L. Cheney -- Motivation and melancholy : a Darwinian perspective / Randolph M. Nesse. ISBN 0-8032-2926-7
1. Genetic psychology - Congresses. 2. Psychology, Comparative - Congresses. 3. Motivation - congresses. I. French, Jeffrey A. II. Kamil, Alan C. III. Leger, Daniel W. IV. Daly, Martin, 1944- V. Title. VI. Series. VII. Series: Nebraska Symposium on Motivation. Nebraska Symposium on Motivation ; v. 47.
BF701 .N43 2001

NEBULAE, EXTRAGALACTIC. See **GALAXIES.**

NECESSITY (PHILOSOPHY). See **FATE AND FATALISM; TRUTH.**

NECROMANCY. See **MAGIC.**

The Necronomicon files.
Harms, Daniel. Boston, MA : Weiser Books, c2003.
BF1999 .H37515 2003

Nederlandse Stichting voor Psychotechniek.
Driekwart eeuw psychotechniek in Nederland. Assen : Van Gorcum, 2001.
HF5548.8 .D73 2001

NEDERLANDSE STICHTING VOOR PSYCHOTECHNIEK - HISTORY.
Driekwart eeuw psychotechniek in Nederland. Assen : Van Gorcum, 2001.
HF5548.8 .D73 2001

Nedzirdamais kļūst dzirdams.
Raudive, Konstantins, 1909-1974. [Unhörbares wird hörbar. Latvian] Rīga : Zintnieks, c2003.
BF1029 .R3816 2003

NEED (PSYCHOLOGY).
Marshall, Ian, 1954- Peak experiences. Charlottesville : University of Virginia Press, 2003.
PS163 .M37 2003

Ring, Susan. Needs and wants. Mankato, Minn. : Yellow Umbrella Books, c2003.
BF723.M56 R56 2003

NEED (PSYCHOLOGY) - JUVENILE LITERATURE.
Ring, Susan. Needs and wants. Mankato, Minn. : Yellow Umbrella Books, c2003.
BF723.M56 R56 2003

The need to know library
Weiss, Stefanie Iris. Everything you need to know about dealing with losses. Rev. ed. New York : Rosen Pub. Group, 2000.
BF724.3.L66 W45 2000

Needs and wants.
Ring, Susan. Mankato, Minn. : Yellow Umbrella Books, c2003.
BF723.M56 R56 2003

Neeld, Elizabeth Harper, 1940- Seven choices : finding daylight after loss shatters your world / Elizabeth Harper Neeld. New York : Warner Books, c2003. xvi, 462 p. : ill. ; 23 cm. Includes bibliographical references (p. 447-451) and index. ISBN 0-446-69050-3 DDC 155.9/37
1. Bereavement - Psychological aspects. 2. Death - Psychological aspects. 3. Grief. I. Title.

Neely, A. D. (Andy D.)
BF575.G7 N44 2003

Neely, A. D. (Andy D.) The performance prism : the scorecard for measuring and managing business success / Andy Neely, Chris Adams, and Mike Kennerly. London ; New York : Financial Times/ Prentice Hall, 2002. xv, 393 p. : ill. ; 24 cm. + 1 CD-ROM (4 3/4 in.). Includes bibliographical references (p. 374-377) and index. ISBN 0-273-65334-2 DDC 658.4013
1. Performance standards. 2. Organizational effectiveness. 3. Success in business. I. Adams, Chris, 1956- II. Kennerley, Mike. III. Title.
HF5549.5.P35 N44 2002

NEGATION (LOGIC) IN CHILDREN - JUVENILE LITERATURE.
Berry, Joy Wilt. Saying no. New York : Scholastic, c2001.
BF723.R4 B37 2001

NEGLECT (NEUROLOGY).
The cognitive and neural bases of spatial neglect. Oxford ; New York : Oxford University Press, 2002.
RC394.N44 C64 2002

Negociar en medio de la guerra.
Yusty, Miguel. [Cali, Colombia] : Editorial Universidad Santiago de Cali, 2002.

Negotiate this!.
Cohen, Herb. New York : Warner Business Books, c2003.
BF637.N4 C545 2003

NEGOTIATING. *See* **NEGOTIATION.**

Negotiating the gift : pre-modern figurations of exchange / edited by Gadi Algazi, Valentin Groebner and Bernhard Jussen. Göttingen : Vandenhoeck & Ruprecht, c2003. 419 p. ; 25 cm. (Veröffentlichungen des Max-Planck-Instituts für Geschichte ; Bd. 188) Includes bibliographical references and index. ISBN 3-525-35186-0
1. Ceremonial exchange - Europe - Middle Ages, 500-1500. 2. Social history - Medieval, 500-1500. 3. Civilization, Medieval. I. Algazi, Gadi. II. Groebner, Valentin. III. Jussen, Bernhard. IV. Series.

NEGOTIATION. *See also* **CONFLICT MANAGEMENT.**
Callières, Monsieur de (François), 1645-1717. De la manière de négocier avec les souverains. Genève : Droz, c2002.

Cohen, Herb. Negotiate this!. New York : Warner Business Books, c2003.
BF637.N4 C545 2003

Efirov, S. A. (Svetozar Aleksandrovich) Sotsial'noe soglasie. Moskva : Izd-vo In-ta sotsiologii RAN, 2002.

Getting it done. Washington, D.C. : United States Institute of Peace Press, 2003.
KZ1321 .G48 2003

Giraldo Hurtado, Luis Guillermo, 1944- Del proceso y de la paz. [Colombia? : s.n., 2001] (Manizales : Edigr@ficas)

The handbook of negotiation. Stanford, Calif. : Stanford Business Books, c2004.
BF637.N4 H365 2004

Kivimäki, Timo. US-Indonesian hegemonic bargaining. Aldershot ; Burlington, VT : Ashgate, 2003.

Lum, Grande. Expand the pie. Seattle, WA : Castle Pacific Pub. ; Cambridge, MA : ThoughtBridge, c2003.
BF637.N4 L86 2003

Peace and conflict resolution. Part 1 [videorecording]. Derry, N.H. : Chip Taylor Communications, 1996.

Peace and conflict resolution. Part 2 [videorecording]. Derry, N.H. : Chip Taylor Communications, 1997.

Raiffa, Howard, 1924- Negotiation analysis. Cambridge, MA : Belknap Press of Harvard University Press, 2002.
HD58.6 .R342 2002

Smyser, W. R., 1931- How Germans negotiate. Washington, D.C. : U.S. Institute of Peace Press, 2003.
BF637.N4 S59 2003

Stark, Peter B. The only negotiating guide you'll ever need. 1st ed. New York : Broadway Books, 2003.
BF637.N4 S725 2003

United States. General Accounting Office. World Trade Organization [electronic resource]. [Washington, D.C.] : U.S. General Accounting Office, [2002]

Negotiation analysis.
Raiffa, Howard, 1924- Cambridge, MA : Belknap Press of Harvard University Press, 2002.
HD58.6 .R342 2002

NEGOTIATION - COLOMBIA.
Al oído de Uribe. 1a. ed. Bogotá, Colombia : Editorial Oveja Negra, 2002.

Téllez, Edgar. Diario íntimo de un fracaso. 1. ed. Bogotá, D.C., Colombia : Planeta, 2002.

NEGOTIATION - COLOMBIA - 20TH CENTURY.
Yusty, Miguel. Negociar en medio de la guerra. [Cali, Colombia] : Editorial Universidad Santiago de Cali, 2002.

NEGOTIATION - CONGO (DEMOCRATIC REPUBLIC).
Storm clouds over Sun City. Brussels ; Nairobi : International Crisis Group, 2002.

NEGOTIATION - CROSS-CULTURAL STUDIES.
The handbook of negotiation. Stanford, Calif. : Stanford Business Books, c2004.
BF637.N4 H365 2004

NEGOTIATION IN BUSINESS.
The new economic diplomacy. Aldershot, Hampshire, England ; Burlington, VT : Ashgate, c2003.
HF1359 .N4685 2003

Raiffa, Howard, 1924- Negotiation analysis. Cambridge, MA : Belknap Press of Harvard University Press, 2002.
HD58.6 .R342 2002

NEGOTIATIONS. *See* **NEGOTIATION.**

NEGRITUDE. *See* **BLACKS - RACE IDENTITY.**

NEGROES. *See* **BLACKS.**

Nehaniv, Chrystopher L., 1963-.
Imitation in animals and artifacts. Cambridge, Mass. : MIT Press, c2002.
BF357 .I47 2002

Neider, Linda L., 1953-.
Leadership. Greenwich, Conn. : Information Age Pub., c2002.
HD57.7 .L4313 2002

Neidhöfer, Herbert.
Was kostet den Kopf? Marburg : Tectum Verlag, 2001.

NEIGHBORHOOD JUSTICE CENTERS. *See* **DISPUTE RESOLUTION (LAW).**

NEIGHBORHOOD - PSYCHOLOGICAL ASPECTS.
Children in the city. London : Routledge/Falmer, 2003.

NEIGHBORHOOD - SOCIAL ASPECTS.
Wilkinson, Deanna Lyn, 1968- Guns, violence, and identity among African American and Latino youth. New York : LFB Scholarly Pub., 2003.
HQ799.2.V56 W55 2003

NEIGHBORHOODS. *See* **NEIGHBORHOOD.**

Neitz, Erica, ill.
Mills, Andy, 1979- Shapesville. 1st ed. Carlsbad, CA : Gurze Books, 2003.
BF723.B6 M55 2003

Nekhudov, S. IU.
Filosofsko-metodologicheskie osnovy gumanitarnogo znaniia. Moskva : Rossiĭskiĭ gosudarstvennyĭ gumanitarnyĭ universitet, 2001.
BD166 .F489 2001

Nelsen, Jane.
Lott, Lynn. Madame Dora's fortune-telling cards. Gloucester, Mass. : Fair Winds Press, 2003.
BF1878 .L78 2003

Nelson Brissac, Antonio Augusto Arantes.
Peixoto, Nelson Brissac. [São Paulo, SP : Fundação Memorial da América Latina, 1997]

Nelson-Jones, Richard. Basic counselling skills : a helper's manual / Richard Nelson-Jones. London ; Thousand Oaks, Calif. : SAGE Publications, 2003. viii, 206 p. ; 22 cm. Includes bibliographical references (p. [193]-199) and index. ISBN 0-7619-4961-5 (pbk.) ISBN 0-7619-4960-7 DDC 158/.3
1. Counseling. I. Title.
BF637.C6 N433 2003

Nelson, Noelle C. The power of appreciation / Noelle C. Nelson, Jeannine Lemare Calaba. Hillsboro, Or. : Beyond Words Pub., c2003. p. cm. Includes bibliographical references. Table of contents URL: http://www.loc.gov/catdir/toc/ecip046/2003015294.html CONTENTS: The transformative nature of appreciation-- The energy of appreciation -- Becoming an appreciator -- Using appreciation to transform situations and attract desired outcomes -- Five steps to using appreciation for transformation and attraction -- Appreciate your way to loving relationships -- Appreciate your way to rewarding and fulfilling work -- Your children and appreciation -- Appreciate your way to health and healing -- Appreciate your way to positive aging -- Appreciate your way through crisis -- Towards a future of appreciation. ISBN 1-58270-104-0 DDC 179/.9
1. Gratitude. 2. Values - Psychological aspects. I. Calaba, Jeannine Lemare. II. Title.
BF575.G68 N45 2003

Nelson, Phillip J., 1929- Signaling goodness : social rules and public choice / Phillip J. Nelson and Kenneth V. Greene. Ann Arbor : University of Michigan Press, c2003. 261 p. ; 24 cm. (Economics, cognition, and society) Includes bibliographical references (p. 241-251) and index. ISBN 0-472-11347-X (alk. paper) DDC 361.2/5
1. Charities. 2. Altruism. 3. Social norms. 4. Social perception. 5. Political sociology. 6. Public interest. I. Greene, Kenneth V. II. Title. III. Series.
HV31 .N45 2003

Nelson, Robert S., 1947-.
Visuality before and beyond the Renaissance. Cambridge, U.K. ; New York, NY, USA : Cambridge University Press, 2000.
N7430.5 .V54 2000

Nelson, Robin, 1971- Afraid / by Robin Nelson. Minneapolis, MN : Lerner Publications Co., c2004. p. cm. (First step nonfiction) SUMMARY: An introduction to feeling afraid and the things that might make a person feel that way. ISBN 0-8225-3886-5 (pbk. : alk. paper) DDC 152.4/6
1. Fear in children - Juvenile literature. 2. Fear. 3. Emotions. I. Title. II. Series.
BF723.F4 N45 2004

Angry / by Robin Nelson. Minneapolis, MN : Lerner Publications Co., c2004. p. cm. (First step nonfiction) SUMMARY: An introduction to feeling angry and the things that might make a person feel that way. ISBN 0-8225-3887-3 (pbk. : alk. paper) DDC 152.4/7
1. Anger in children - Juvenile literature. 2. Anger. 3. Emotions. I. Title. II. Series.
BF723.A4 N45 2004

Happy / by Robin Nelson. Minneapolis, MN : Lerner Publications Co., c2004. p. cm. (First step nonfiction) SUMMARY: An introduction to feeling happy and the things that might make a person feel that way. ISBN 0-8225-3888-1 (pbk. : alk. paper) DDC 152.4/2
1. Happiness in children - Juvenile literature. 2. Happiness. 3. Emotions. I. Title. II. Series.
BF723.H37 N45 2004

Sad / by Robin Nelson. Minneapolis, MN : Lerner Publications Co., c2004. p. cm. (First step nonfiction) SUMMARY: An introduction to feeling sad and the things that might make a person feel that way. ISBN 0-8225-3890-3 (pbk. : alk. paper) DDC 152.4
1. Sadness in children - Juvenile literature. 2. Sadness. 3. Emotions. I. Title. II. Series.
BF723.S15 N45 2004

Nelson, Sarah M., 1931-.
Ancient queens. Walnut Creek, Calif. ; Oxford : AltaMira Press, c2003.
HQ1127 .A53 2003

Nemeroff, Charles B.
The concise Corsini encyclopedia of psychology and behavioral science. 3rd ed. Hoboken, NJ : John Wiley & Sons, 2004.
BF31 .E52 2004

Nemeth, Darlyne Gaynor. Helping your angry child : worksheets, fun puzzles, and engaging games to help you communicate better : a workbook for you and your family / Darlyne Gaynor Nemeth, Kelly Paulk Ray, Máydel Morín Schexnayder. Oakland, Calif. : New Harbinger, c2003. 196 p. : ill. ; 28 cm. Includes bibliographical references (p. [195]-196). ISBN 1-57224-312-0 (pbk.) DDC 649.64
1. Anger in children. 2. Parenting. 3. Child rearing. I. Ray, Kelly Paulk. II. Schexnayder, Máydel Morín. III. Title.
BF723.A4 N46 2003

Nemeth, Elisabeth.
Philosophie in Aktion. Wien : Turia + Kant, 2000.

Nemoianu, Virgil. Tradiție și libertate / Virgil Nemoianu. București : Curtea Veche, 2001. 534 p. ; 20 cm. Some articles translated from English. ISBN 9738120551
1. Liberty. 2. Pluralism. I. Title.
JC585 .N42 2001

NEO-CONSERVATISM. *See* **CONSERVATISM.**

NEO-FASCISM. *See* **FASCISM.**

NEO-NAZIS. *See* **NAZIS.**

NEO-NAZISM. *See* **NATIONAL SOCIALISM.**

NEO-PAGANISM. *See* **NEOPAGANISM.**

NEO-SLAVISM. *See* **PANSLAVISM.**

NEOCOLONIALISM. *See* **IMPERIALISM.**

NEONATAL DEATH. *See* **INFANTS (NEWBORN) - DEATH.**

NEONATES. *See* **INFANTS (NEWBORN).**

NEONATOLOGY. *See* **INFANTS (NEWBORN).**

NEOPAGANISM. *See* **GODDESS RELIGION.**

NEOPAGANISM - NEW ZEALAND.
Roundtree, Kathryn. Embracing the witch and the goddess. London ; New York : Routledge, 2003.
BF1584.N45 R68 2003

NEOPAGANISM - RELATIONS - CHRISTIANITY.
DiZerega, Gus. Pagans & Christians. 1st ed. St. Paul, Minn. : Llewellyn Publications, 2001.
BF1566 .D59 2001

NEOPAGANISM - RITUALS.
Lipp, Deborah, 1961- The elements of ritual. 1st ed. St. Paul, Minn. : Llewellyn Publications, 2003.
BF1571 .L56 2003

NEOPAGANISM - RUSSIA (FEDERATION) - POLITICAL ASPECTS.
Shcheglov, A. (Alekseĭ) I͡Azycheskaia͡ zari͡a. Moskva : [Izdatelʹstvo "PROBEL-2000"], 2002.
BL980.R5 S53 2002

NEOPAGANISM - UNITED STATES.
Berger, Helen A., 1949- Voices from the pagan census. Columbia, S.C. : University of South Carolina Press, 2003.
BF1573 .B48 2003

NEOPLATONISM.
De Pace, Anna. La scepsi, il sapere e l'anima. Milano : LED, c2002.

NEOTROPICAL REGION. *See* **LATIN AMERICA.**

NEOTROPICS. *See* **LATIN AMERICA.**

NEPAL - LITERATURES. *See* **TIBETAN LITERATURE.**

Nepoznati svet snova.
Jovanović, Tihomir. Beograd : IPA "Miroslav", 2000.
BF1078 .J69 2000

Neppert, Joachim.
Grundlagen und Modelle für den Hörgerichteten Spracherwerb. Villingen-Schwenningen : Neckar, c1995.

Nepri͡amai͡a kommunikat͡sii͡a i ee zhanry.
Dementʹev, V. V. Saratov : Izd-vo Saratovskogo universiteta, 2000.
P106 .D4554 2000

Nerazumna mreža.
Toševski, Jovo. Novi Sad : Prometej ; [Kragujevac] : Jefimija, c2002.

NERVOUS SYSTEM. *See* **NEUROSCIENCES.**

Nesbit, Roy Conyers. Missing believed killed / Roy Conyers Nesbit. Stroud : Sutton, 2002. 183 p. : ill. ; 25 cm. Includes bibliographical references and index. ISBN 0-7509-3003-9 DDC 363.12465
1. Aircraft accidents - Investigation. 2. Missing persons. 3. Air pilots. I. Title.

Neshamah ba-guf.
Golan, Mor Yosef. Sefer ha-Neshamah ba-guf. Itamar : M.Y. Golan, 762 [2001 or 2002]

NETHERLANDS - LITERATURES. *See* **DUTCH LITERATURE.**

Netivot Yitshaḳ.
Leṿin, Yitshaḳ, 1938- Sefer Netivot Yitshaḳ. [Bene Beraḳ] : Y. Leṿin, [2000-

NetLibrary, Inc.
Arthurs, Jane. Crash cultures. Bristol, UK ; Portland, OR : Intellect, 2002.

Netraditsionnye religii v sovremennoĭ Rossii.
Balagushkin, E. G. (Evgeniĭ Gennadʹevich) Moskva : Rossiĭskai͡a akademii͡a nauk, Institut filosofii, 1999-2002.
BL980.R8 B35 1999

NETS, NEURAL (COMPUTER SCIENCE). *See* **NEURAL NETWORKS (COMPUTER SCIENCE).**

Netsaḥ ḥayenu.
Koraḥ, Shelomoh ben Yaḥya. Bene Beraḳ : S. Koraḥ, 762 [2001 or 2002]

NETWORK COMPUTERS. *See* **COMPUTER NETWORKS.**

NETWORKS (ASSOCIATIONS, INSTITUTIONS, ETC.). *See* **ASSOCIATIONS, INSTITUTIONS, ETC.**

NETWORKS, COMPUTER. *See* **COMPUTER NETWORKS.**

NETWORKS, NEURAL (COMPUTER SCIENCE). *See* **NEURAL NETWORKS (COMPUTER SCIENCE).**

Netzley, Patricia D. Haunted houses / Patricia D. Netzley. San Diego, Calif. : Lucent Books, c2000. 96 p. : ill. ; 24 cm. (The mystery library) Includes bibliographical references and index. SUMMARY: Discusses haunted houses, including ghosts and apparitions, poltergeists, communicating with spirits, and investigating hauntings. CONTENTS: Introduction -- Ghosts and apparitions -- Poltergeists -- Communicating with spirits -- Investigating hauntings. ISBN 1-56006-685-7 (alk. paper) DDC 133.1
1. Ghosts - Juvenile literature. 2. Poltergeists - Juvenile literature. 3. Haunted houses - Juvenile literature. I. Title. II. Series: Mystery library (Lucent Books)
BF1461 .N48 2000

Neubauer, Wolfgang, 1963- Magnetische Prospektion in der Archäologie / Wolfgang Neubauer. Wien : Verlag der Österreichischen Akademie der Wissenschaften, 2001. 236 p. : ill. (some col.), plans ; 30 cm. (Mitteilungen der Prähistorischen Kommission / Österreichische Akademie der Wissenschaften, philosophisch-historische Klasse ; Bd. 44, 0065-5376) Includes bibliographical references (p. 231-236). ISBN 3-7001-3009-0 (pbk.)
1. Archaeology. 2. Magnetic prospecting. 3. Prospecting - Geophysical methods. I. Title. II. Series: Mitteilungen der Prähistorischen Kommission der Österreichischen Akademie der Wissenschaften ; 44. Bd.

Neuber, Wolfgang.
Seelenmaschinen. Wien : Böhlau Verlag, c2000.
BF381 .S44 2000

Neue betriebswirtschaftliche Forschung
(151) Hugl, Ulrike. Qualitative Inhaltsanalyse und Mind-Mapping. Wiesbaden : Gabler, 1995.

Neues Bewusstsein : die Energetik der Wandlung : ein Symposiumsband / Paracelsus Akademie Villach (Hg.) ; [mit Beiträgen von Peter Sloterdijk, ... et al.] Wien : Edition Selene, 1999. 155 p. ; 21 cm. Conference proceedings. Includes bibliographical referencers. ISBN 3-85266-125-0 (pbk.)
1. Consciousness - Congresses. I. Sloterdijk, Peter, 1947- II. Paracelsus Akademie Villach.

Neuharth, Dan. Secrets you keep from yourself : how to stop sabotaging your happiness / Dan Neuharth. 1st U.S. ed. New York : St. Martins Press, 2004. p. cm. ISBN 0-312-31247-4 DDC 158.1
1. Self-defeating behavior. 2. Self-actualization (Psychology) I. Title.
BF637.S37 N48 2004

Neumann, Alexander, 1971-.
Kritik der Gewalt. Wien : Promedia, c2002.
D860 .K75 2002

Neumann-Braun, Klaus.
Popvisionen. Frankfurt : Suhrkamp, 2003.
ML3470 .P69 2003

NEUMANN, ERICH.
Weiler, Gerda, 1921- Der enteignete Mythos. Königstein : Helmer, [1996]

NEURAL COMPUTERS. *See also* **ARTIFICIAL INTELLIGENCE.**
Kasabov, Nikola K. Evolving connectionist systems. London ; New York : Springer, c2003.
QA76.87 .K39 2003

NEURAL NETS (COMPUTER SCIENCE). *See* **NEURAL NETWORKS (COMPUTER SCIENCE).**

NEURAL NETWORKS (COMPUTER SCIENCE) - CONGRESSES.
International Workshop on Multiple Classifier Systems (4th : 2003 : Guildford, England) Multiple classifier systems. Berlin ; New York : Springer, c2003.
Q325.5 .I574 2003

NEURAL SCIENCES. *See* **NEUROSCIENCES.**

NEUROLINGUISTIC PROGRAMMING.
Beaver, Diana. NLP for lazy learning. London : Vega, 2002.
BF637.N46 B44 2002

Hall, L. Michael. The sourcebook of magic. Wales, UK ; Williston, VT : Crown House Pub. Ltd., 2002.
BF637.N46 H36 2002

Koleda, Sergeĭ. Modelirovanie bessoznatelʹnogo. Moskva : In-t obshchegumanitarnykh issledovaniĭ, 2000.
BF637.N46 K65 2000

NEUROLINGUISTICS.
Raĭnov, Vasil G. Za psikhosemantichnata spet͡sifika na ezikovoto vŭzpri͡atie. Sofii͡a : Akademichno izd-vo "Prof. Marin Drinov", 1998.
P37 .R27 1998

The neurological basis of learning, development, and discovery.
Lawson, Anton E. Dordrecht ; Boston : Kluwer Academic Publishers, c2003.
BF318 .L365 2003

NEUROLOGICAL SCIENCES. *See* **NEUROSCIENCES.**

NEUROLOGISTS. *See* **PSYCHIATRISTS.**

NEUROPHYSIOLOGY.
Croix, Laurence. La douleur en soi. Ramonville Saint-Agne (France) : Erès, c2002.

Upādhyāya, Govindaprasāda. Āyurvedīya mānasaroga cikitsā. 1. saṃskaraṇa. Vārāṇasī : Caukhabā Surabhāratī Prakāśana ; Dillī : Anya Prāptisthāna Caukhambā Saṃskr̥ta Pratishṭhāna, 2000.
R605 .U67 2000

Neuropolitics.
Connolly, William E. Minneapolis, MN : University of Minnesota Press, c2002.

NEUROPSYCHOLOGY. *See also* **COGNITIVE NEUROSCIENCE; LEARNING - PHYSIOLOGICAL ASPECTS.**
Carter, Rita, 1949- Exploring consciousness. Berkeley : University of California Press, c2002.
BF311 .C289 2002

Changeux, Jean-Pierre. [Ce qui nous fait penser. English] What makes us think? Princeton, N.J. : Princeton University Press, c2000.
BJ45 .C4313 2000

Lechevalier, Bernard. Le cerveau de Mozart. Paris : O. Jacob, c2003.
ML3838 .L39 2003

Neuropsychology and cognition
(22) Reading complex words. New York : Kluwer Academic/Plenum Publishers, c2003.
P37.5.R42 R43 2003

NEUROSCIENCE. *See* **NEUROSCIENCES.**

Neuroscience for the mental health clinician.
Pliszka, Steven R. New York : Guilford Press, c2003.
RC341 .P58 2003

NEUROSCIENCES.
Hinterhuber, H. (Hartmann) Die Seele. Wien ; New York : Springer, c2001.

Orsucci, Franco. Changing mind. River Edge, NJ : World Scientific, c2002.
BF161 .O77 2002

Pliszka, Steven R. Neuroscience for the mental health clinician. New York : Guilford Press, c2003.
RC341 .P58 2003

NEUROSCIENCES - PHILOSOPHY.
Churchland, Patricia Smith. Brain-wise. Cambridge, Mass. : MIT Press, c2002.
RC343 .C486 2002

Dupouey, Patrick. Est-ce le cerveau qui pense? Nantes : Pleins feux, [2002].

NEUROSCIENCES - SOCIAL ASPECTS.
Clark, Andy, 1957- Natural-born cyborgs. Oxford ; New York : Oxford University Press, c2003.
T14.5 .C58 2003

Neuroscientist and a philosopher argue about ethics, human nature, and the brain.
Changeux, Jean-Pierre. [Ce qui nous fait penser. English] What makes us think? Princeton, N.J. : Princeton University Press, c2000.
BJ45 .C4313 2000

NEUROSCIENTISTS - FRANCE - INTERVIEWS.
Changeux, Jean-Pierre. [Ce qui nous fait penser. English] What makes us think? Princeton, N.J. : Princeton University Press, c2000.

BJ45 .C4313 2000

NEUROSES. *See also* **ANXIETY.**
Jerotić, Vladeta. Neuroticne pojave naseg vremena. 2, dop. izd. Beograd : Zlatousti, 2001.

Russon, John Edward, 1960- Human experience. Albany : State University of New York Press, c2003.
BF204.5 .R87 2003

Neuroticne pojave naseg vremena.
Jerotić, Vladeta. 2, dop. izd. Beograd : Zlatousti, 2001.

Neusner, Jacob, 1932- Analysis and argumentation in Rabbinic Judaism / Jacob Neusner. Lanham, Md. : University Press of America, c2003. xxvi, 263 p. ; 24 cm. (Studies in Judaism) Includes bibliographical references. ISBN 0-7618-2527-4 (alk. paper) DDC 296.1/206
1. Talmud - Hermeneutics. 2. Rabbinical literature - History and criticism. 3. Jewish law - Interpretation and construction. 4. Reasoning. 5. Aggada - History and criticism - Theory, etc. 6. Midrash - History and criticism - Theory, etc. I. Title. II. Series.
BM496.5 .N4775 2003

NEUTRALITY. *See* **INTERVENTION (INTERNATIONAL LAW); WAR (INTERNATIONAL LAW).**

Neuzeitliches Denken : Festschrift für Hans Poser zum 65. Geburtstag / herausgegeben von Günter Abel, Hans-Jürgen Engfer und Christoph Hubig. Berlin ; New York : De Gruyter, 2002. xi, 480 p. : ill. ; 24 cm. Includes bibliographical references. 22 German, 3 French, 2 English contributions. ISBN 3-11-017516-9 (hd.bd.)
1. Intellectual life - History. 2. Civilization - History. I. Poser, Hans. II. Abel, Günter. III. Engfer, Hans-Jürgen. IV. Hubig, Christoph, 1952-

Neve, Michael.
Darwin, Charles, 1809-1882. Autobiographies. London : Penguin, 2002.

Never say goodbye.
Mathews, Patrick, 1962- 1st ed. St. Paul, Minn. : Llewellyn Publications, 2003.
BF1283.M27 A3 2003

Never scratch a tiger with a short stick : and other quotations for leaders / compiled by Gordon S. Jackson. Colorado Springs, Colo. : NavPress, c2003. 223 p. ; 19 cm. Includes index. ISBN 1-57683-342-9 DDC 158/.4
1. Leadership - Quotations, maxims, etc. I. Jackson, Gordon, 1949-
BF637.L4 N48 2003

Nevid, Jeffrey S. Psychology and the challenges of life : adjustment in the new millennium / Jeffrey S. Nevid, Spencer A. Rathus. 9th ed. Hoboken, NJ : Wiley, c2005. p. cm. Rev. ed. of: Psychology and the challenges of life / Spencer A. Rathus, Jeffrey S. Nevid. 8th ed. c2002. Includes bibliographical references (p.   ) and indexes. ISBN 0-471-44693-9 (cloth) DDC 1535.2/4
1. Adjustment (Psychology) 2. Psychology. I. Rathus, Spencer A. II. Rathus, Spencer A. Psychology and the challenges of life. III. Title.
BF335 .N475 2005

Psychology : concepts and applications / Jeffrey S. Nevid. Boston, MA : Houghton Mifflin, c2003. xxviii, 665, [102] p. : ill. (some col.) ; 29 cm. Includes bibliographical references (p. A-30-A-72) and index. ISBN 0-618-06143-6 DDC 150
1. Psychology. I. Title.
BF121 .N42 2003

NEW AGE MOVEMENT.
Roads, Michael J. The magic formula. 1st ed. Cleveland : SilverRoads Pub., 2003.
BF637.S4 R575 2003

Rysev, Sergeĭ. Vyshe kryshi. Sankt-Peterburg : Gelikon Plıūs, 2001.
B105.C473 R97 2001

Terrin, Aldo N. (Aldo Natale) Mistiche dell'Occidente. 1. ed. Brescia : Morcelliana, 2001.
BP605.N48 T477 2001

Zukav, Gary. The mind of the soul. New York : Free Press, 2003.
BF611 .Z85 2003

NEW AGE MOVEMENT - UNITED STATES.
Miller, D. Patrick, 1953- News of a new human nature. 1st ed. Berkeley, Calif. : Fearless Books, 2002.
BF637.S4 M547 2002

Wernitznig, Dagmar. Going native or going naive? Lanham, MD : University Press of America, c2003.
E98.P99 W47 2003

New age, orientalismo, mondo pentecostale.
Terrin, Aldo N. (Aldo Natale) Mistiche dell'Occidente. 1. ed. Brescia : Morcelliana, 2001.
BP605.N48 T477 2001

The new art of leadership for Africa 2000.
Safari, J. F. Peramiho, Tanzania : Benedictine Publications Ndanda, 1996.
HM1261 S35 1996

The new astrology for women.
Adams, Jessica. [New ed.]. Pymble, Sydney, N.S.W. : HarperCollins, 1998 (2002 printing)

New Brunswick haunted houses.
Dearborn, Dorothy, 1927- New Brunswick haunted houses-- and other tales of strange and eerie events. Saint John, NB : Neptune Pub., c2000.
BF1472.N48 D44 2000

New Brunswick haunted houses - and other tales of strange and eerie events.
Dearborn, Dorothy, 1927- Saint John, NB : Neptune Pub., c2000.
BF1472.N48 D44 2000

NEW BUSINESS ENTERPRISES.
Mezias, Stephen J. Organizational dynamics of creative destruction. Houndmills [England] ; New York : Palgrave Macmillan, 2002.
HB615 .M49 2002

New chakra healing.
Nudel, Michael. 21st century's new chakra healing. Los Angeles, CA : Bio-Energy System Services, c2000.
BF1999 .N83 2000

New challenges for international leadership : lessons from organizations with global missions / Tora K. Bikson, Gregory F. Treverton, Joy Moini, Gustav Lindstrom. Santa Monica, Calif. : RAND, 2003. 78 p. ; 28 cm. ISBN 0-8330-3345-X (pbk.) DDC 658.4/092
1. Leadership. 2. International business enterprises - Management. 3. Organizational effectiveness. I. Bikson, Tora K., 1940-
HD57.7 .N488 2003

The new children and near-death experiences.
Atwater, P. M. H. [Children of the new millennium] Rochester, Vt. : Bear & Co., 2003.
BF1045.N42 A88 2003

[New cultural studies]
Halpern, Richard, 1954- Shakespeare's perfume. Philadelphia : University of Pennsylvania Press, c2002.
PR2848 .H25 2002

NEW DEAL, 1933-1939.
The achievement of American liberalism. New York : Columbia University Press, c2003.
E806 .M63 2003

New directions in aesthetics
(1) Stecker, Robert, 1928- Interpretation and construction. Malden, MA : Blackwell, 2003.
BD241 .S78 2003

New directions in anthropology
(15) El-Kholy, Heba Aziz. Defiance and compliance. New York : Berghahn Books, 2002.
HQ1793.Z9 C53 2002

The new economic diplomacy : decision-making and negotiation in international economic relations / [edited by] Nicholas Bayne and Stephen Woolcock ; with case studies by Colin Budd ... [et al.]. Aldershot, Hampshire, England ; Burlington, VT : Ashgate, c2003. xiv, 314 p. ; 23 cm. (The G8 and global governance series) This book is based on the 2000-2001 course given at the LSE's International Relations Dept. Includes bibliographical references (p. 300-307) and index. Table of contents URL: http://www.loc.gov/catdir/toc/fy036/2002027785.html CONTENTS: What is economic diplomacy? / Nicholas Bayne and Stephen Woolcock -- Theoretical analysis of economic diplomacy / Stephen Woolcock -- State and non-state actors / Stephen Woolcock -- The practice of economic diplomacy / Nicholas Bayne -- Current challenges to economic diplomacy / Nicholas Bayne -- The ITO, the GATT and the WTO / Stephen Woolcock -- Creating the economic summits / Nicholas Bayne -- G8 summits and their preparation / Colin Budd -- Is trade policy democratic? And should it be? / Phil Evans -- Bilateral economic diplomacy : the United States / Nicholas Bayne -- When the twain meet : an overview of US-Japanese economic relations / Matthew Goodman -- The regional dimension : European economic diplomacy / Stephen Woolcock -- Making EU international environment policy / Patrick Rabe -- International institutions : plurilateralism and multilateralism / Nicholas Bayne -- Economic diplomacy for developing countries / Ivan Mbirimi -- Governments, the international financial institutions and international cooperation / Nigel Wicks -- The world trading system / Richard Carden -- Economic diplomacy in the 2000s / Nicholas Bayne and Stephen Woolcock. ISBN 0-7546-1832-3 (alk. paper) DDC 337
1. International economic relations. 2. International cooperation. 3. Commercial policy. 4. Negotiation in business. 5. Decision making. 6. International economic relations - Case studies. I. Bayne, Nicholas, 1937- II. Woolcock, Stephen. III. Budd, Colin. IV. Series.
HF1359 .N4685 2003

The new encyclopedia of the occult.
Greer, John Michael. St. Paul, MN : Llewellyn Publications, 2003.
BF1407 .G74 2003

New essays on semantic externalism and self-knowledge / edited by Susana Nuccetelli. Cambridge, Mass. : MIT Press, c2003. vii, 317 p. ; 24 cm. "A Bradford book." Includes bibliographical references (p. [295]-306) and index. ISBN 0-262-14083-7 (alk. paper) DDC 121/.4
1. Externalism (Philosophy of mind) 2. Self-knowledge, Theory of. I. Nuccetelli, Susana.
BD418.3 .N49 2003

New family values.
Struening, Karen, 1960- Lanham : Rowman & Littlefield Publishers, c2002.
HQ536 .S82 2002

The new hide or seek.
Dobson, James C., 1936- Pbk. ed. Grand Rapids, Mich. : F.H. Revell, 2001.
BF723.S3 D6 2001

The new history.
Pallares-Burke, Maria Lucia G. Cambridge, UK ; Malden, MA : Polity in association with Blackwell Publishers Ltd., 2002.
D14 .P35 2002

New horizons in public policy
Public policy in knowledge-based economies. Cheltenham, UK ; Northampton, MA : Edward Elgar, c2003.
HC79.I55 P83 2003

NEW INTERNATIONAL ECONOMIC ORDER. *See* **INTERNATIONAL ECONOMIC RELATIONS.**

The new Jews.
Amodélé, Jons. Banjul, The Gambia : Vinasha Publishing, 2000.

New Middle Ages (Palgrave (Firm))
Effros, Bonnie, 1965- Creating community with food and drink in Merovingian Gaul. 1st ed. New York ; Houndmills, England : Palgrave Macmillan, 2002.
GT2853.F7 E34 2002

NEW MOON - MISCELLANEA.
Roderick, Timothy, 1963- Dark moon mysteries. Aptos, Calif. : New Brighton Books, 2003.
BF1623.M66 R63 2003

NEW MOON - RELIGIOUS ASPECTS.
Roderick, Timothy, 1963- Dark moon mysteries. Aptos, Calif. : New Brighton Books, 2003.
BF1623.M66 R63 2003

NEW ORLEANS (LA.) - DESCRIPTION AND TRAVEL.
Brosman, Catharine Savage, 1934- Finding higher ground. Reno : University of Nevada Press, c2003.
F787 .B76 2003

New paradigms, culture, and subjectivity.
[Nuevos paradigmas. English.] Cresskill, N.J. : Hampton Press, c2002.
BD161 .N8413 2002

New perspectives
Ozaniec, Naomi. Chakras. Rev. ed. Shaftesbury : Element, 2000.

NEW PRODUCT DEVELOPMENT. *See* **NEW PRODUCTS.**

NEW PRODUCTS. *See* **DESIGN, INDUSTRIAL.**

NEW PRODUCTS - MANAGEMENT.
Harvard business essentials. Boston, Mass. : Harvard Business School Press, c2003.
HD45 .H3427 2003

Howkins, John, 1945- The creative economy. London : Allen Lane, 2001.

The new psychoanalysis.
Meadow, Phyllis W., 1924- Lanham, Md. : Rowman & Littlefield, c2003.
BF173 .M3585 2003

New religious identities in the western world
(4) Jironet, Karin. The image of spiritual liberty in the western Sufi movement following Hazrat Inayat Khan. Leuven : Peeters, 2002.
BP189.2 .J57 2002

New religious movements : challenge and response / edited by Bryan Wilson and Jamie Cresswell. London ; New York : Routledge in association with the Institute of Oriental Philosophy European Centre, 1999. xviii, 284 p. ; 24 cm. Includes bibliographical references and index. ISBN 0-415-20049-0 ISBN 0-415-20050-4 (pbk.) DDC 291
1. Religions. 2. Cults. 3. Sects. I. Wilson, Bryan R. II. Cresswell, Jamie.
BL80.2 .N397 1999

The new revelations.
Walsch, Neale Donald. New York : Atria Books, c2002.
BF1999 .W2287 2002

NEW RIGHT. *See* **CONSERVATISM.**

The new Sartre.
Fox, Nik Farrell. New York ; London : Continuum, 2003.

New South Wales. Centre for Mental Health.
Suicide & risk-taking deaths of children & young people. Surry Hills, NSW : The Commission, c2003.

The new synthese historical library
(v. 52) Yu, Jiyuan. The structure of being in Aristotle's Metaphysics. Dordrecht, Boston : Kluwer Academic, c2003.
B434 .Y8 2003

(v. 53) The medieval heritage in early modern metaphysics and modal theory, 1400-1700. Dordrecht ; Boston : Kluwer Academic Publishers, c2003.
BD111 .M47 2003

NEW THOUGHT.
Curtis, Donald. Your thoughts can change your life. New York : Warner Books, 1996.
BF639 .C885 1996

Goldsmith, Joel S., 1892-1964. Spiritual discernment. Atlanta, Ga. : Acropolis Books, c2002.
BF639.G56886 2002

Grace, Raymon. The future is yours. Charlottesville, VA : Hampton Roads Pub., c2003.
BF639 .G64 2003

Haanel, Charles F. (Charles Francis), b. 1866. The master key system. 1st ed. Wilkes-Barre, Pa. : Kallisti Pub., c2000.
BF639 .H132 2000

Holmes, Ernest, 1887-1960. [This thing called life] The art of life. New York : J.P. Tarcher/Penguin, c2004.
BF645 .H572 2004

Pauley, Thomas L. I'm rich beyond my wildest dreams-- "I am. I am. I am". New York : Berkley Books, 2003.
BF639 .P28 2003

New times.
Carrington, Victoria. Dordrecht : Boston : London : Kluwer Academic, c2002.
HQ728 .C314 2002

The new unconscious / edited by Ran R. Hassin, James S. Uleman, and John A. Bargh. New York : Oxford University Press, 2004. p. cm. (Oxford series in social cognition and social neuroscience) Includes bibliographical references and index. ISBN 0-19-514995-5 (alk. paper) DDC 154.2
1. Subconsciousness. I. Hassin, Ran R. II. Uleman, James S. III. Bargh, John A. IV. Series.
BF315 .N47 2004

A new vision of astrology.
Mann, A. T., 1943- New York : Pocket Books, c2002.
BF1708.1 .M355 2002

New wombs : electronic bodies and architectural disorders.
Palumbo, Maria Luisa. [Nuovi ventri. English] Basel : Birkhäuser, 2000.
NA2765 .P35 2000

The new workplace : a guide to the human impact of modern working practices / edited by David Holman ... [et al.]. Chichester, UK ; Hoboken, NJ : Wiley, c2003. xiv, 450 p. : ill. ; 25 cm. Includes bibliographical references and indexes. ISBN 0-471-48543-8 DDC 331.2
1. Quality of work life. 2. Job satisfaction. 3. Psychology,
Industrial. 4. Work environment. 5. Work design. 6. Human-machine systems. 7. Industrial relations. I. Holman, David.
HD6955 .N495 2003

NEW WORLD TROPICS. *See* **LATIN AMERICA.**

New York Coalition of Professional Women in the Arts and Media, Inc.
Vint/age 2001 conference : [videorecording]. New York, c2001.

NEW YORK (N.Y.). EMERGENCY OPERATION CENTER.
Kendra, James M. Elements of community resilience in the World Trade Center attack. [Newark, Del.?] : Disaster Research Center, University of Delaware, 2001.

NEW YORK (N.Y.). FIRE DEPT.
Monahan, Brian. From ground zero to ground hero. [Newark, Del.?] : Disaster Research Center, University of Delaware, 2001.

New York Review Books classics
Wilson, Edmund, 1895-1972. To the Finland station. New York : New York Review of Books, 2003.
HX36 .W5 2003

New York (State). Workers' Compensation Board.
Work-related mental stress injuries in the NYS workers' compensation system. [Albany, N.Y. : The Board, 1997]
HF5548.85 .W668 1997

New York (State). Workers' Compensation Board. Mental Stress Injury Committee.
Work-related mental stress injuries in the NYS workers' compensation system. [Albany, N.Y. : The Board, 1997]
HF5548.85 .W668 1997

NEW YORK TIMES.
Elfenbein, Stefan W., 1964- Die veränderte Rolle der New York Times. Frankfurt am Main ; New York : P. Lang, c1996.
PN4899.N42 N375 1996

New York University. Child Study Center.
The day our world changed. New York : Harry N. Abrams Inc., 2002.

NEW YORK YANKEES (BASEBALL TEAM).
Mantle, Mickey, 1931- The quality of courage. Lincoln : University of Nebraska Press, [1999]
GV865.A1 M317 1999

NEWBORN INFANTS. *See* **INFANTS (NEWBORN).**

Newell, Waller Randy. The code of man : love, courage, pride, family, country / Waller R. Newell. 1st ed. New York : ReganBooks, c2003. xxxiii, 269 p. ; 24 cm. Includes index. ISBN 0-06-008751-X (acid-free paper) DDC 305.31
1. Masculinity. I. Title.
HQ1090 .N49 2003

NEWLY INDUSTRIALIZED COUNTRIES. *See* **DEVELOPING COUNTRIES.**

NEWLY INDUSTRIALIZING COUNTRIES. *See* **DEVELOPING COUNTRIES.**

NEWMAN, PHYLLIS, 1935-.
Vint/age 2001 conference : [videorecording]. New York, c2001.

Newman, Phyllis, 1935- panelist.
Vint/age 2001 conference : [videorecording]. New York, c2001.

Newman, Scott.
Intellectual property rights in animal breeding and genetics. Wallingford ; New York : CABI, c2002.

Newman, Stuart.
Origination of organismal form. Cambridge, Mass. : MIT Press, c2003.
QH491 .O576 2003

News of a new human nature.
Miller, D. Patrick, 1953- 1st ed. Berkeley, Calif. : Fearless Books, 2002.
BF637.S4 M547 2002

NEWS PHOTOGRAPHY. *See* **PHOTOJOURNALISM.**

NEWSCASTERS. *See* **TELEVISION JOURNALISTS.**

Newsome, Deborah W.
Gladding, Samuel T. Community and agency counseling. 2nd ed. Upper Saddle River, N.J. : Pearson : Merrill Prentice Hall, c2004.
BF637.C6 G528 2004

NEWSPAPER READING.
Debras, Sylvie. Lectrices au quotidien. Paris : L'Harmattan, c2003.

NEWSPAPERS.
Debras, Sylvie. Lectrices au quotidien. Paris : L'Harmattan, c2003.

Newstead, Stephen E.
Perspectives on thinking and reasoning. Hove, UK : Hillsdale : Lawrence Erlbaum Associates, c1995.
BF441 .P48 1995

Newton, Charles S. (Charles Sinclair), 1942-.
Data mining. Hershey : Idea Group, c2002.
QA76.9.D343 D36 2002

Newton, Stephen J. Painting, psychoanalysis, and spirituality / Stephen James Newton. New York : Cambridge University Press, 2003. 264 p. : ill. ; 26 cm. (Contemporary artists and their critics) Includes bibliographical references (p. 251-255) and index. ISBN 0-521-66134-X DDC 750/.1/9
1. Psychoanalysis and art. 2. Painting - Psychological aspects. 3. Creation (Literary, artistic, etc.) I. Title. II. Series.
ND1158.P74 N48 2001

Newton, Toyne. The dark worship / Toyne Newton. London : Vega, 2002. 176 p., [8] p. of plates : ill. ; 20 cm. Includes bibliographical references (p. 169-171) and index. Publisher description URL: http://www.loc.gov/catdir/description/ste031/2003464302.html ISBN 1-84333-586-7 DDC 133.4/2
1. Demonology. 2. Satanism - History - 20th century. 3. Occultism - History. I. Title.
BF1531 .N49 2002

The next enlightenment.
Anderson, Walt, 1933- 1st ed. New York : St. Martin's Press, 2003.
BL476 .A53 2003

Neysmith, Sheila M., 943-.
Feminist utopias. Toronto : Inanna Publications and Education, 2002.

Nhât Hanh, Thích. No death, no fear : comforting wisdom for life / Thich Nhat Hanh. New York : Riverhead Books, c2002. xii, 194 p. ; 22 cm. ISBN 1-57322-221-6 DDC 294.3/444
1. Spiritual life - Buddhism. 2. Buddhism - Doctrines. I. Title.
BQ4302 .N43 2002

Niagolova, Mariana, 1963-.
Antologiia. 1. izd. Veliko Tŭrnovo : Izd-vo PAN-VT, 2001.
BF108.B9 A58 2001

Nicheva, Nina. Prez vremeto i prostranstvoto / Nina Nicheva. [Bulgaria] : Gutoranov i sin, [1998?] 148 p. ; 20 cm. ISBN 9545071095
1. Space and time - Miscellanea. 2. Human beings - Miscellanea. 3. Life - Miscellanea. I. Title.
BF1999 .N46 1998

Nichols, Shaun. Mindreading : an integrated account of pretence, self-awareness, and understanding other minds / Shaun Nichols and Stephen P. Stich. Oxford : Clarendon Press ; New York : Oxford University Press, 2003. 237 p. : ill. ; 25 cm. (Oxford cognitive science series) Includes bibliographical references (p. [214]-229) and index. ISBN 0-19-823609-3 ISBN 0-19-823610-7 (PBK) DDC 128.2
1. Philosophy of mind. 2. Other minds (Theory of knowledge) 3. Thought and thinking. 4. Mind and body. 5. Telepathy. I. Stich, Stephen P. II. Title. III. Series.

Nickell, Joe. The mystery chronicles : more real-life X-files / Joe Nickell. Lexington, Ky. : University Press of Kentucky, c2004. p. cm. Includes bibliographical references and index. ISBN 0-8131-2318-6 (alk. paper) DDC 001.94
1. Parapsychology - Case studies. 2. Curiosities and wonders. 3. Impostors and imposture. I. Title.
BF1031 .N517 2004

Nicolas, Serge. Histoire de la psychologie française : naissance d'une nouvelle science / Serge Nicolas ; préface de Maurice Reuchlin. Paris : In press, c2002. 360 p. ; 24 cm. (Collection Psycho) Includes bibliographical references and index. ISBN 2-912404-72-X DDC 150
1. Psychology - France - History. 2. Psychologists - France - History. I. Title. II. Series.
BF108.F8 N536 2002

Jouffroy, Théodore, 1796-1842. [Selections] La psychologie de Th. Jouffroy. Paris : L'Harmattan, c2003.

Nicolson, Paula. Having it all? : choices for today's superwoman / Paula Nicolson. Chichester, West Sussex, England ; Hoboken, NJ : J. Wiley, c2002. ix, 209 p. : ill. ; 22 cm. (Family matters) Includes bibliographical references (p. [199]-206) and index. ISBN 0-470-84687-9

DDC 305.42
1. Women - Psychology. 2. Women - Social conditions. I. Title.
II. Title: Choices for today's superwoman III. Series: Family matters (John Wiley & Sons)
HQ1206 .N645 2002

Nicomachean ethics.
Aristotle. [Nicomachean ethics. English] Cambridge, U.K. ; New York : Cambridge University Press, c2002 (2002 printing)
B430.A5 C7513 2000

NICS (NEWLY INDUSTRIALIZED COUNTRIES). See DEVELOPING COUNTRIES.

NIDER, JOHANNES, CA. 1380-1438.
Bailey, Michael David, 1971- Battling demons. University Park, Pa. : Pennsylvania State University Press, c2003.
BF1569 .B35 2003

NIE (Series)
(2001-02 D.) Growing global migration and its implications for the United States [electronic resource]. Electronic document. [Washington, D.C.? : National Intelligence Council, 2001]
CB161 .G768

Nielsen, Bent. A companion to Yi jing numerology and cosmology : Chinese studies of images and numbers from Han (202 BCE-220 CE) to Song (960-1279 CE) / Bent Nielsen. London ; New York : RoutledgeCurzon, 2003. xix, 391 p. : ill. ; 24 cm. "Technical terms and ... bio-bibliographical information on Chinese Yi jing scholars ... organized as a Chinese-English encyclopaedia, arranged alphabetically according to the pinyin romanisation, with Chinese characters appended"--P. 4 of cover. Dynasty names in subtitle also appear in Chinese characters. Includes bibliographical references (p. 352-366) and indexes. In Chinese and English. ISBN 0-7007-1608-4
1. Yi jing. 2. Yi jing - Terminology. 3. Scholars - China - Bio-bibliography. 4. Numerology. 5. Cosmology, Chinese. I. Title.

Nielsen, Lauge Olaf.
The medieval heritage in early modern metaphysics and modal theory, 1400-1700. Dordrecht ; Boston : Kluwer Academic Publishers, c2003.
BD111 .M47 2003

NIELSON, JOHN.
Vint/age 2001 conference : [videorecording]. New York, c2001.

Nielson, John, panelist.
Vint/age 2001 conference : [videorecording]. New York, c2001.

Nietzsche.
Cox, Christoph, 1965- Berkeley : University of California Press, c1999.
B3318.K7 C68 1999

Souchon, Gisèle. Paris : Harmattan, c2003.

Nietzsche and the sciences / edited by Babette E. Babich ; in cooperation with Robert S. Cohen. Dordrecht ; Boston : Kluwer Academic Publishers, c1999- 2 v. ; 25 cm. (Boston studies in the philosophy of science ; v. 203-204) Includes bibliographical references and index. PARTIAL CONTENTS: [v.] 1. Nietzsche, theories of knowledge, and critical theory -- [v.] 2. Nietzsche, epistemology, and philosophy of science. ISBN 0-7923-5778-7 (set) ISBN 0-7923-5742-6 (v. 1 : alk. paper) ISBN 0-7923-5743-4 (v. 2 : alk. paper) DDC 193
1. Nietzsche, Friedrich Wilhelm, - 1844-1900 - Contributions in theory of knowledge. 2. Nietzsche, Friedrich Wilhelm, - 1844-1900 - Contributions in philosophy of science. 3. Knowledge, Theory of. 4. Science - Philosophy. I. Babich, Babette E., 1956- II. Cohen, R. S. (Robert Sonné) III. Series.
B3318.K7 N54 1999

NIETZSCHE, FRIEDRICH, 1844-1900.
Cox, Christoph, 1965- Nietzsche. Berkeley : University of California Press, c1999.
B3318.K7 C68 1999

NIETZSCHE, FRIEDRICH WILHELM, 1844-1900. JENSEITS VON GUT UND BOSE.
Lomax, J. Harvey, 1948- The paradox of philosophical education. Lanham, Md. : Oxford : Lexington Books, c2003.
B3313.J43 L66 2003

[Selections. English. 2003]
Writings from the late notebooks / Friedrich Nietzsche ; edited by Rüdiger Bittner ; translated by Kate Sturge. Cambridge, UK ; New York : Cambridge University Press, c2003. xliii, 286 p. ; 24 cm. (Cambridge texts in the history of philosophy) Includes bibliographical references (p. xxxviii-xl) and indexes. Translated from the German. Sample text URL: http://www.loc.gov/catdir/samples/cam033/2002031057.html Table of contents URL: http://www.loc.gov/catdir/toc/cam031/2002031057.html Publisher description URL: http://www.loc.gov/catdir/description/cam031/2002031057.html ISBN 0-521-80405-1 ISBN 0-521-00887-5 (pb.) DDC 193
1. Philosophy. I. Bittner, Rüdiger, 1945- II. Sturge, Kate. III. Title. IV. Series.
B3312.E5 B58 2003

NIETZSCHE, FRIEDRICH WILHELM, 1844-1900.
Breitschmid, Markus, 1966- Der bauende Geist. Luzern : Quart, 2001.
B3318.A4 B745 2001

Ingram, Susan. Zarathustra's sisters. Toronto ; Buffalo : University of Toronto Press, c2003.
PN471 .I537 2003

Kropotov, S. L. (Sergeĭ Leonidovich) Ėkonomika teksta v neklassicheskoĭ filosofii iskusstva. Ekaterinburg : Gumanitarnyĭ universitet, 1999.
B831.2 .K76 1999

Souchon, Gisèle. Nietzsche. Paris : Harmattan, c2003.

NIETZSCHE, FRIEDRICH WILHELM, 1844-1900 - CONTRIBUTIONS IN ONTOLOGY.
Cox, Christoph, 1965- Nietzsche. Berkeley : University of California Press, c1999.
B3318.K7 C68 1999

NIETZSCHE, FRIEDRICH WILHELM, 1844-1900 - CONTRIBUTIONS IN PHILOSOPHY OF SCIENCE.
Nietzsche and the sciences. Dordrecht ; Boston : Kluwer Academic Publishers, c1999-
B3318.K7 N54 1999

NIETZSCHE, FRIEDRICH WILHELM, 1844-1900 - CONTRIBUTIONS IN THEORY OF KNOWLEDGE.
Cox, Christoph, 1965- Nietzsche. Berkeley : University of California Press, c1999.
B3318.K7 C68 1999

Nietzsche and the sciences. Dordrecht ; Boston : Kluwer Academic Publishers, c1999-
B3318.K7 N54 1999

NIGERIA - CIVILIZATION.
Osofisan, Femi. Literature and the pressures of freedom. Nigeria : Opon Ifa Readers, 2001.
1. Black author.

NIGERIA - POLITICS AND GOVERNMENT.
Adeleke, Veronica I. Concept of gender equality as a paradox in Nigeria's democratic experience. Ikeja [Nigeria] : Dept. of Political Science and Sociology, Babcock University, 2002.
1. Black author.

NIGERIA - RELIGION.
Adeniyi, M. O. Yoruba Muslim-Christian understanding. Majiyagbe, Ipaja, Nigeria : Eternal Communications, 2001.
1. Black author.

Aluko, Jonathan O. The spirit of this age. [[Akure, Nigeria : Christ Liberation Publications, c1996]
BL480 .A494 1996
1. Black author.

Kómoláfé, Kóláwọlé. African traditional religion. Lagos : Ifa-Ọrúnmìlà Organisation, 1995.
BL2480.Y6 K65 1995

Studies in the theology and sociology of Yoruba indigenous religion. Lagos, Nigeria : Concept Publications (Nig.), 2002.

NIGERIA - SOCIAL LIFE AND CUSTOMS.
Opata, Damian U. (Damian Ugwutikiri) Towards a genealogy of African time. Nsukka, Nigeria : AP Express Publishing Company Lt., 2001.
1. Black author.

NIGHT - HISTORY.
Verdon, Jean. [Nuit au Moyen Age. English] Night in the Middle Ages. Notre Dame, Ind. : University of Notre Dame Press, c2002.
HM1033 .V4713 2002

Night in the Middle Ages.
Verdon, Jean. [Nuit au Moyen Age. English] Notre Dame, Ind. : University of Notre Dame Press, c2002.
HM1033 .V4713 2002

NIGHT PRAYER. See COMPLINE.

NIGHT - SOCIAL ASPECTS.
Verdon, Jean. [Nuit au Moyen Age. English] Night in the Middle Ages. Notre Dame, Ind. : University of Notre Dame Press, c2002.
HM1033 .V4713 2002

NIGHTMARES.
Bulkeley, Kelly, 1962- Dreams of healing. New York : Paulist Press, c2003.
BF1099.N53 B85 2003

Nigle she-banistar : the Halachic residue in the Zohar.
Ta-Shma, Israel M. ha-Nigleh sheba-nistar. Nusaḥ murḥav. [Tel Aviv] : ha-Ḳibuts ha-me'uḥad, c2001.

ha-Nigleh sheba-nistar.
Ta-Shma, Israel M. Nusaḥ murḥav. [Tel Aviv] : ha-Ḳibuts ha-me'uḥad, c2001.

NIH publication
(no. 01-3519) Helping children and adolescents cope with violence and disasters [electronic resource]. Bethesda, MD : Office of Communications and Public Liaison, [2001]

(no. 02-2756) Aging under the microscope [electronic resource]. Bethesda, MD : National Institute on Aging, National Institutes of Health, [2002]

(no. 02-3929) Strock, Margaret. Medications [electronic resource]. [4th ed., rev. Apr. 2002, repr. Sept. 2002]. [Bethesda, Md.] : Dept. of Health and Human Services, Public Health Service, National Institutes of Health, National Institute of Mental Health, 2002.

(no. 02-5138) Mental health and mass violence [electronic resource]. [Bethesda, MD : National Institute of Mental Health, 2002]

NIHILISM (PHILOSOPHY).
Köhler, Manfred. Apokalypse oder Umkehr? Marburg : Tectum, 2000.

Marmysz, John, 1964- Laughing at nothing. Albany : State University of New York Press, c2003.
B828.3 .M265 2003

Nihon "kodomo no rekishi" sōsho
(19) Edo-e kara shomotsu made. Tōkyō : Kyūzansha, 1997.
HQ792.J3 N54 1997 v.19

NII teorii arkhitektury i gradostroitel'stva (Rossiĭskaia akademiia arkhitektury i stroitel'nykh nauk).
Arkhitekturnoe soznanie XX-XXI vekov. Moskva : Ėditorial URSS, 2001.
NA712 .A87 2001

Nijstad, Bernard Arjan, 1971-.
Group creativity. Oxford ; New York : Oxford University Press, 2003.
BF408 .G696 2003

Nikolaev, Alekseĭ. Istoricheskie t︠s︡ikly / Alekseĭ Nikolaev. Vologda : [s.n.], c2002. 103 p. ; 20 cm. Chart inserted.
1. History - Periodization. 2. History - Philosophy. 3. Historiography. 4. History - Methodology. I. Title.
D16.15 .N55 2002

Nikolŭkin, Aleksandr Nikolaevich.
Rozanov, V. V. (Vasiliĭ Vasil'evich), 1856-1919. Vo dvore i︠a︡zychnikov. Moskva : Izd-vo "Respublika", 1999.
BL96 .R69 1999

Rozanov, V. V. (Vasiliĭ Vasil'evich), 1856-1919. Vozrozhdai︠u︡shchii︠a︡si︠a︡ Egipet. Moskva : Izd-vo "Respublika", 2002.

Nīlakaṇṭha, 16th cent.
[Tājikanīlakaṇṭhī. English & Sanskrit]
Tajik Nilkanthi = Tājika Nīlakanṭhī / translation & comments by D.P. Saxena. 1st ed. New Delhi : Ranjan Publications, 2001. 334 p. : ill. ; 22 cm. Spine title: Tajik Neelkanthi. SUMMARY: On Hindu astrology; Sanskrit text with English translation. English and Sanskrit.
1. Hindu astrology - Early works to 1800. I. Saxena, D. P. (Dayal Prasad), 1929- II. Title. III. Title: Tājika Nīlakaṇṭhī IV. Title: Tajik Neelkanthi
BF1714.H5 N4813 2001

NIMBY SYNDROME. See LAND USE.

NIN, ANAÏS, 1903-1977.
Aller, Annelies van, 1946- Levenskunst van twee vrouwen. Budel : Damon, c2001.
PS3527.I865 Z536 2001

Nine-eleven in American culture.
9-11 in American culture. Walnut Creek ; Oxford : AltaMira Press, c2003.
HV6432.7 .A13 2003

Nine journeys home.
Mandel, Robert Steven, 1943- 9 journeys home. Berkeley : Celestial Arts, c2003.

BF575.S4 M36 2003

NINE (THE NUMBER).
Padma, N. K., 1956- Navam and the Karṇāṭak group kṛtis. New Delhi : Kanishka Publishers, Distributors, 2002.
ML338 .P197 2002

Nine Wind, the prophecy calendar.
Messenger, Charles M. Nine Wind Tonalamatl Tolteca-fate papers. [United States] : C.M. Messenger, c2002-
BF1861 .M47 2002

Nine Wind Tonalamatl Tolteca-fate papers.
Messenger, Charles M. [United States] : C.M. Messenger, c2002-
BF1861 .M47 2002

Nir Dayid.
Ari'av, Dayid ben Naḥman, ha-Kohen. Le-re'akha kamokha. Mahad. 2. Yerushalayim : Dayid ben Naḥman ha-Kohen Ari'av, 760- [2000-

NIRVANA (MUSICAL GROUP).
Fletcher, John Wright. A hermeneutic study of generational music. 2002.

ha-Nisayon ha-yomyomi u-fitron heseḳe tenai ya-hakhalah lo-teḳefim.
Artman, Lavee. [Israel : ḥ. mo. l., 1999?]

Nissanka, H. S. S.
[Năvata upan dăriya. English]
The girl who was reborn : a case study suggestive of reincarnation / H.S.S. Nissanka. Colombo : S. Godage Brothers, 2001. 192 p. ; 23 cm. ISBN 955-20-4782-X
1. Reincarnation - Case studies. I. Title.
BL515+

Nissenson, Marilyn, 1939-.
Jonas, Susan. Friends for life. 1st ed. New York : William Morrow & Co., c1997.
HQ755.85 .J65 1997

Nissinen, Martti. Prophets and prophecy in the ancient Near East / by Martti Nissinen with contributions by C.L. Seow and Robert K. Ritner ; edited by Peter Machinist. Atlanta, GA : Society of Biblical Literature, c2003. xxi, 273 p. : maps ; 23 cm. (Writings from the ancient world ; no. 12) Includes bibliographical references and index. Table of contents URL: http://www.loc.gov/catdir/toc/ecip012/2003007002.html ISBN 1-58983-027-X (alk. paper) DDC 133.3/0939/4
1. Prophets - Middle East - History. 2. Prophecy - History. 3. Middle East - Literatures. I. Ritner, Robert Kriech, 1953- II. Seow, C. L. (Choon Leong) III. Machinist, Peter. IV. Title. V. Series.
BF1762 .N58 2003b

Prophets and prophecy in the ancient Near East / by Martti Nissinen ; with contributions by C.L. Seow and Robert K. Ritner ; edited by Peter Machinist. Leiden ; Boston : Brill, 2003. xxi, 273 p. : maps ; 25 cm. (Writings from the ancient world ; no. 12) Includes bibliographical references (p. 223-260) and index. ISBN 90-04-12691-0 (cloth binding : alk. paper) DDC 133.3/0939/4
1. Prophets - Middle East - History. 2. Prophecy - History. 3. Middle Eastern literature. I. Machinist, Peter. II. Title. III. Series.
BF1762 .N58 2003

Nixon, Charisse.
Dellasega, Cheryl. Girl wars. New York : Simon & Schuster, c2003.
BF637.B85 D45 2003

Niẓām al-Dīn, 'Irfān. Lā lil-ikti'āb na'am lil-farḥ!!? / 'Irfān Niẓām al-Dīn. al-Tab'ah 1. [Beirut?] : al-Mu'assasah al-'Arabīyah-al-Ūrūbbīyah lil-Ṣiḥāfah wa-al-Nashr, 2001. 244 p. ; 24 cm. SUMMARY: miscellaneous essays. In Arabic.
1. Happiness. 2. Sadness. I. Title.

Nizovskikh, N. A. (Nina Arkad'evna).
Psikhologiia sub"ektnosti. Kirov : Viatskiĭ gos. pedagog. universitet, 2001.
BF697 .P75 2001

NLP for lazy learning.
Beaver, Diana. London : Vega, 2002.
BF637.N46 B44 2002

No death, no fear.
Nhất Hạnh, Thích. New York : Riverhead Books, c2002.
BQ4302 .N43 2002

No matter, never mind : proceedings of toward a science of consciousness : fundamental approaches (Tokyo '99) / edited by Kunio Yasue, Mari Jibu, Tarcisio Della Senta. Amsterdam ; Philadelphia : John Benjamins Pub. Co., c2002. xvi, 389 p. : ill. ; 22 cm. (Advances in consciousness research, 1381-589X ; v. 33) Includes bibliographical references and indexes. ISBN 1-58811-095-8 (US : alk. paper) ISBN 90-272-5153-3 (Eur : alk. paper) DDC 612.8/2
1. Consciousness - Congresses. I. Yasue, Kunio. II. Jibu, Mari. III. Della Senta, Tarcisio. IV. Series.
QP411 .N598 2002

The no-nonsense guide to world history.
Brazier, Chris. Oxford : New Internationalist Publications ; London : in association with Verso, c2001.
D21 .B78 2001

No-nonsense guides (New Internationalist Publications (Firm))
Brazier, Chris. The no-nonsense guide to world history. Oxford : New Internationalist Publications ; London : in association with Verso, c2001.
D21 .B78 2001

No regrets.
Beazley, Hamilton, 1943- Hoboken, N.J. : John Wiley & Sons, c2004.
BF575.R33 B43 2004

Kaufman, Barry Neil. Novato, Calif. : HJ Kramer/ New World Library, 2003.
BF575.G7 K385 2003

No'am ha-musar : Torah, zemanim.
Vakhtfoigel, Nathan. Sefer No'am ha-musar. Laikvud : [ḥ. mo. l.], 762 [2001 or 2002]
BJ1285 .V35 2001

NOBILITY. *See also* **KNIGHTS AND KNIGHTHOOD.**
Lomax, J. Harvey, 1948- The paradox of philosphical education. Lanham, Md. ; Oxford : Lexington Books, c2003.
B3313.J43 L66 2003

NOBILITY - EUROPE - HISTORY - 18TH CENTURY.
Lukowski, Jerzy. The European nobility in the eighteenth century. Houndmills [England] : New York : Palgrave Macmillan, 2003.
HT653.E9 L85 2003

NOBILITY - NETHERLANDS.
Janse, A. Ridderschap in Holland. Hilversum : Verloren, 2001.
DJ152 .J26 2001

NOBILITY OF CHARACTER.
Candido, Antonio. O nobre. São Paulo : Imprensa Oficial do Estado, 2002.
BJ1533.N6 C36 2002

NOBLE CLASS. *See* **NOBILITY.**
NOBLES (SOCIAL CLASS). *See* **NOBILITY.**

O nobre.
Candido, Antonio. São Paulo : Imprensa Oficial do Estado, 2002.
BJ1533.N6 C36 2002

Nocam. Nostradamus : premier décodage daté : le cataclysme annoncé par ses prophéties : Centuries et Sixains / Nocam. Champagne-sur-Oise : Kapsos, 1998. 269 p. : ill. ; 24 cm. (Collection Philosophie et connaissance) Includes bibliographical references. ISBN 2-910056-04-X
1. Nostradamus, - 1503-1566. - Prophéties. 2. End of the world. I. Title. II. Series.
BF1815.N8 A2668 1998

Node book.
Burk, Kevin, 1967- The complete node book. 1st ed. St. Paul, Minn. : Llewellyn Publications, 2003.
BF1723 .B87 2003

Nodl, Martin.
Člověk českého středověku. Vyd. 1. Praha : Argo, 2002.

Noegel, Scott B.
Prayer, magic, and the stars in the ancient and late antique world. University Park, Pa. : Pennsylvania State University Press, 2003.
BF1591 .P73 2003

Nogales, Ana, 1951- Latina power! : using 7 strengths you already have to create the success you deserve / Ana Nogales with Laura Golden Bellotti. New York : Simon & Schuster, c2003. p. cm. "A Fireside book." Includes bibliographical references (p.   ) and index. ISBN 0-7432-3630-0 (pbk.) DDC 158.1/082
1. Success - Psychological aspects. 2. Hispanic American women - Psychology. I. Bellotti, Laura Golden. II. Title.
BF637.S8 N64 2003

NOISE. *See* **SILENCE.**

NOISE - PSYCHOLOGICAL ASPECTS - CONGRESSES.
Oldenburger Symposon zur Psychologischen Akustik (8th : 2000) Contributions to psychological acoustics. 1. ed. Oldenburg : BIS, Bibliotheks- und Informationssystem der Universität Oldenburg, 2000.
BF251 .O44 2000

NOISE - PSYCHOLOGY. *See* **NOISE - PSYCHOLOGICAL ASPECTS.**

Le nom de l'Europe.
Lombard, René-André. Grenoble : Thot, c2001.

NOMINEES, POLITICAL. *See* **POLITICAL CANDIDATES.**

Non filosofia e filosofia con due note inedite sulla musica.
Merleau-Ponty. Paris : Vrin ; Milano : Mimesis, 2001.

NON-MONOGAMOUS RELATIONSHIPS.
Pasini, Willy. I nuovi comportamenti amorosi. 2. ed. Milano : Mondadori, 2002.

Non-philosophy and philosophy with two unpublished notes on music.
Merleau-Ponty. Paris : Vrin ; Milano : Mimesis, 2001.

NON-RESISTANCE TO GOVERNMENT. *See* **GOVERNMENT, RESISTANCE TO.**

NONCITIZENS. *See* **ALIENS.**

NONCLASSICAL MATHEMATICAL LOGIC. *See* **MODALITY (LOGIC).**

NONCONFORMITY. *See* **CONFORMITY.**

NONLINEAR SYSTEMS.
Orsucci, Franco. Changing mind. River Edge, NJ : World Scientific, c2002.
BF161 .O77 2002

Westwick, D. T. (David T.) Identification of nonlinear physiological systems. Piscataway, NJ : IEEE Press ; Hoboken, NJ : Wiley-Interscience, c2003.
QP33.6.M36 W475 2003

NONLINEAR THEORIES. *See* **CHAOTIC BEHAVIOR IN SYSTEMS.**

NONLUMINOUS MATTER (ASTRONOMY). *See* **DARK MATTER (ASTRONOMY).**

A nonpareil book
Soucheray, Joe. Waterline. Boston : D.R. Godine, 2002.
PN4874.S576 A3 2002

NONRELATIVISTIC QUANTUM MECHANICS. *See* **RELATIVITY (PHYSICS).**

Nonverbal behavior in clinical settings / edited by Pierre Philippot, Robert S. Feldman, Erik J. Coats Oxford ; New York : Oxford University Press, 2003. xii, 324 p. : ill. (some col.) ; 24 cm. (Series in affective science) Includes bibliographical references and index. CONTENTS: The role of nonverbal behavior in clinical settings : introduction and overview / Pierre Philippot, Robert S. Feldman, and Erik J. Coats -- Nonverbal social skills and psychopathology / John E. Perez and Ronald E. Riggio -- Of butterflies and roaring thunder : nonverbal communication in interaction and regulation of emotion / Arvid Kappas and Jean Descoteaux -- Changes in nonverbal behavior during the development of therapeutic relationships / Linda Tickle-Degnen and Elizabeth Gavett -- What makes good therapists fail? / Jürg Merten and Rainer Krause -- Selective processing of non-verbal information in anxiety : attentional biases for threat / Karin Mogg and Brendan P. Bradley -- The social and functional aspects of emotional expression during bereavement / George Bonanno and Anthony Papa -- Impairments of facial nonverbal communication after brain damage / Raymond Bruyer -- Nonverbal deficits and interpersonal regulation in alcoholics / Pierre Philippot, Charles Kornreich, and Sylvie Blairy -- Ethology and depression / Antoinette L. Bouhuys -- Nonverbal behavior in schizophrenia / Ann M. Kring and Kelly S. Earnst -- Clinical implications of research in nonverbal behavior of children with autism / Gail McGee and Michael Morrier. ISBN 0-19-514109-1 (cloth : alk. paper) DDC 616.89/14
1. Body language. 2. Psychotherapy. I. Philippot, Pierre, 1960- II. Feldman, Robert S. (Robert Stephen), 1947- III. Coats, Erik J., 1968- IV. Series.
RC489.N65 N66 2003

Nonverbal behavior in interpersonal relations.
Richmond, Virginia P., 1949- 5th ed. Boston, Mass. : Pearson, 2004.
BF637.N66 R53 2004

NONVERBAL COMMUNICATION. *See also* **BODY LANGUAGE; EXPRESSION.**

Nonverbal communication

Goldman, Ellen. As others see us. New York : Brunner-Routledge, 2003.
BF637.N66 G65 2003

Linson, William. Kinoetics. [United States] : Kinoetics Publishing, c2002.
BF637.N66 L56 2002

Pharmacum carthusiense. Salzburg, Austria : Institut für Anglistik und Amerikanistik, Universität Salzburg, 2002.
BX2435 .P43 2002

NONVERBAL COMMUNICATION IN INFANTS.
Acredolo, Linda P. My first baby signs. [New York] : HarperFestival, c2002.
BF720.C65 A27 2002

Holinger, Paul C. What babies say before they can talk. New York : Simon & Schuster, c2003.
BF720.C65 H64 2003

NONVERBAL COMMUNICATION (PSYCHOLOGY). See BODY LANGUAGE.

NONVIOLENCE.
Fernandes, Leela. Transforming feminist practice. 1st ed. San Francisco : Aunt Lute Books, 2003.
HQ1154 .F495 2003

Potorti, David. September 11th Families for Peaceful Tomorrows. New York, NY : RDV Books, c2003.

The power of nonviolence. Boston, Mass. : Beacon Press, c2002.
JZ5538 .P685 2002

La tierra nueva. Río Cuarto, Argentina : Universidad Nacional de Río Cuarto, Facultad de Ciencias Humanas, Centro de Estudios y Actividades para una Cultura de la Paz, 2000.

Nonviolent communication.
Rosenberg, Marshall B. 2nd ed. Encinitas, CA : PuddleDancer Press, 2003.
BF637.C45 R645 2003

Noonan, Peggy, 1950- A heart, a cross & a flag : America today / Peggy Noonan. New York : Free Press, c2003. xv, 270 p. ; 24 cm. (A Wall Street journal book) Collection of articles published in the Wall Street journal from Sept. 2001 to Sept. 2002. Publisher description URL: http://www.loc.gov/catdir/desc ription/simon033/2003048336.html ISBN 0-7432-5005-2 DDC 973.931
1. United States - Politics and government - 2001- 2. September 11 Terrorist Attacks, 2001. 3. National characteristics, American. 4. United States - Social conditions - 1980- 5. War on Terrorism, 2001- I. Title. II. Title: Heart, a cross, and a flag III. Series.
E903 .N66 2003

Nooteboom, B. Trust : forms, foundations, functions, failures, and figures / Bart Nooteboom. Cheltenham, UK ; Northampton, MA : E. Elgar Pub., c2002. xii, 231 p. : ill. ; 25 cm. Includes bibliographical references (p. 211-222) and index. ISBN 1-84064-545-8 DDC 306.3/4
1. Industrial relations. 2. Trust. I. Title.
HD2758.5 .N66 2002

The trust process in organizations. Cheltenham, UK ; Northampton, MA : Edward Elgar, c2003.
HD58.7 .T744 2003

NORD-KIVO (CONGO) - ETHNIC RELATIONS.
Le dialogue intercongolais. Bruxelles ; Nairobi : International Crisis Group, [2001]

NORDEN. See SCANDINAVIA.

NORDIC COUNTRIES. See SCANDINAVIA.

The Nordic peace / edited by Clive Archer, Pertti Joenniemi. Aldershot, England ; Burlington, VT : Ashgate, c2003. viii, 217 p. : map ; 23 cm. Includes bibliographical references and index. ISBN 0-7546-1417-4 (alk. paper) DDC 327.1/72/0948
1. Scandinavia - Strategic aspects. 2. National security - Scandinavia. 3. Scandinavia - Ethnic relations. 4. Peace. I. Archer, Clive. II. Joenniemi, Pertti.
UA646.7 .N672 2003

Nordic runes.
Mountfort, Paul Rhys. Rochester, Vt. : Destiny Books, 2003.
BF1779.R86 M68 2003

Noriega, José. "Guiados por el espíritu" : el Espíritu Santo y el conocimiento moral en Tomás de Aquino / José Noriega. Roma : Pontificia università lateranense ; [Milano] : Mursia, 2000. 609 p. ; 21 cm. (Studi e ricerche) At head of title: Pontificium institutum Joannes Paulus II Studiorum Matrimonii ac Familiae, Thesis ad Doctoratum in Theologia. Includes bibliographical references (p. [565]-594) and index. DDC 231
1. Thomas, - Aquinas, Saint, - 1225?-1274 - Contributions in doctrine of the Holy Spirit. 2. Thomas, - Aquinas, Saint, -

1225?-1274 - Contributions in doctrine of the Trinity. 3. Holy Spirit - History of doctrines - Middle Ages, 600-1500. 4. Trinity - History of doctrines - Middle Ages, 600-1500. 5. Christian life. 6. Christian ethics. I. Title. II. Series: Studi e ricerche (Istituto Giovanni Paolo II per studi su matrimonio e famiglia)

NORM (PHILOSOPHY).
Maesschalck, M. (Marc) Normes et contextes. Hildesheim ; New York : G. Olms, 2001.
BJ1063 .M34 2001

Schürmann, Reiner, 1941- [Des hégémonies brisées. English] Broken hegemonies. Bloomington : Indiana University Press, c2003.
BD162 .S48 2003

Norma protiv sily.
Davydov, IU. P. (IUriĭ Pavlovich) Moskva : Nauka, 2002.

Norman, Donald A. Emotional design : why we love (or hate) everyday things / Donald A. Norman. New York : Basic Books, 2004. p. cm. Includes bibliographical references and index. Table of contents URL: http://www.loc.gov/catdir/toc/ecip043/2003010123.html CONTENTS: The meaning of things. Attractive things work better -- The multiple faces of emotion and design -- Design in practice. Three levels of design : visceral, behavioral and reflective -- Fun and games -- People, places and things -- Emotional machines -- The future of robots -- Epilogue: we are all designers. ISBN 0-465-05135-9 DDC 155.9/11
1. Emotions and cognition. 2. Design - Psychological aspects. 3. Design, Industrial - Psychological aspects. I. Title.
BF531 .N67 2004

[Psychology of everyday things]
The design of everyday things / Donald A. Norman. 1st Basic paperback ed. [New York] : Basic Books, c2002. xxi, 257 p. : ill. ; 21 cm. Previously published as The psychology of everyday things. "With a new introduction by the author"--Cover. Includes bibliographical references (p. 241-247) and index. ISBN 0-465-06710-7
1. Design, Industrial - Psychological aspects. 2. Human engineering. I. Title.

Normes et contextes.
Maesschalck, M. (Marc) Hildesheim ; New York : G. Olms, 2001.
BJ1063 .M34 2001

NORMS, SOCIAL. See SOCIAL NORMS.

NORTH AMERICA - CIVILIZATION - 20TH CENTURY.
Taylor, Lawrence Douglas. El nuevo norteamericano. México : Universidad Nacional Autónoma de México, Coordinación de Humanidades : Centro de Investigaciones sobre América del Norte ; Tijuana, B.C. : El Colegio de la Frontera Norte, 2001.
E40 .T39 2001

NORTH AMERICA - ECONOMIC INTEGRATION.
Taylor, Lawrence Douglas. El nuevo norteamericano. México : Universidad Nacional Autónoma de México, Coordinación de Humanidades : Centro de Investigaciones sobre América del Norte ; Tijuana, B.C. : El Colegio de la Frontera Norte, 2001.
E40 .T39 2001

NORTH AMERICAN INDIANS. See INDIANS OF NORTH AMERICA.

NORTH AND SOUTH.
Antinomies of modernity. Durham : Duke University Press, 2003.
CB358 .A59 2003

Bessis, Sophie, 1947- [Occident et les autres. English] Western supremacy. London ; New York : Zed Books, 2003.
CB245 .B4613 2003

The emerging monoculture. Westport, Conn. : Praeger, 2003.
HM843 .E44 2003

North, Dia. The smart spot : 4 steps to setting intentions and using intuition to achieve success / Dia North. Boston, MA : Red Wheel, 2003. p. cm. Table of contents URL: http://www.loc.gov/catdir/toc/ecip045/2003013677.html CONTENTS: The smart spot process -- Establish your grounding connection -- Set an effective intention -- Access your creative intuition -- Act with intention -- The next step. ISBN 1-59003-038-9 DDC 153.4/4
1. Success - Psychological aspects. 2. Intuition. I. Title.
BF637.S8 N655 2003

NORTH WALES HOSPITAL FOR NERVOUS AND MENTAL DISORDERS, DENBIGH.
Michael, Pamela. Care and treatment of the mentally ill in North Wales, 1800-2000. Cardiff : University of Wales Press, 2003.

NORTHEASTERN STATES - POLITICS AND GOVERNMENT - 19TH CENTURY.
Lawson, Melinda, 1954- Patriot fires. Lawrence : University Press of Kansas, c2002.
E468.9 .L39 2002

NORTHEASTERN STATES - SOCIAL CONDITIONS - 19TH CENTURY.
Lawson, Melinda, 1954- Patriot fires. Lawrence : University Press of Kansas, c2002.
E468.9 .L39 2002

NORTHERN IRELAND - POLITICS AND GOVERNMENT - 1994-.
Porter, Norman, 1952- The elusive quest. Belfast : Blackstaff, 2003.

Northern mysteries & magic.
Aswynn, Freya, 1949- Northern mysteries & magick. 2nd ed. St. Paul, Minn. : Llewellyn Publications, 1998 (2002 printing)
BF1623.R89 A78 1998

Northern mysteries & magick.
Aswynn, Freya, 1949- 2nd ed. St. Paul, Minn. : Llewellyn Publications, 1998 (2002 printing)
BF1623.R89 A78 1998

Northern mysteries and magic.
Aswynn, Freya, 1949- Northern mysteries & magick. 2nd ed. St. Paul, Minn. : Llewellyn Publications, 1998 (2002 printing)
BF1623.R89 A78 1998

Northern mysteries and magick.
Aswynn, Freya, 1949- Northern mysteries & magick. 2nd ed. St. Paul, Minn. : Llewellyn Publications, 1998 (2002 printing)
BF1623.R89 A78 1998

NORTHERN TIER (MIDDLE EAST). See MIDDLE EAST.

Norton, Anne. Bloodrites of the post-structuralists : word, flesh, and revolution / Anne Norton. New York : Routledge, 2002. x, 206 p. : ill. ; 24 cm. Includes bibliographical references (p. 183-196) and index. ISBN 0-415-93458-3 (alk. paper) ISBN 0-415-93459-1 (pbk. : alk. paper) DDC 303.4
1. Social evolution. 2. Authority. 3. Power (Social sciences) 4. Political development. I. Title.
HM626 .N6785 2002

A Norton critical edition
Malory, Thomas, Sir, 15th cent. [Morte d'Arthur] Le morte Darthur, or, The hoole book of Kyng Arthur and his noble knyghtes of the Rounde Table. 1st ed. New York ; London : Norton, c2004.
PR2041 .M37 2004

Norwood, Ann E., 1953-.
Terrorism and disaster. Cambridge, UK ; New York : Cambridge University Press, 2003.
RC552.P67 T476 2003

Nosmas, Alma. La mort élégante : entretiens / Alma Nosmas ; préface Henri Caillavet ; postface Willy Barral. Paris : Horay, c2003. 119 p. ; 24 cm. (Collection Paroles) ISBN 2-7058-0352-1 DDC 844
1. Interviews. 2. Right to die. 3. Death. I. Title. II. Series.

Nosov, N. A. Ne-virtualistika : sovremennai͡a filosofii͡a psikhologii : materialy konferentsii "Virtualistika - 2001". Moskva, vesenni͡ai͡a sessii͡a-11 aprelii͡a 2001 g / N.A. Nosov. Moskva : Gumanitarii, 2001. 55 p. ; 21 cm. (Trudy Laboratorii virtualistiki ; vyp. 12) Includes bibliographical references (p. 52-55). ISBN 5892210421
1. Psychology - Philosophy - Congresses. 2. Knowledge, Theory of - Congresses. 3. Virtual reality - Congresses. I. Konferentsii͡a "Virtualistika-2001" (2001 : Moscow, Russia) II. Title. III. Series.
BF38 .N67 2001

Nosovskiĭ, G. V. (Gleb Vladimirovich), 1958-
Rekonstruktsii͡a vseobshcheĭ istorii : Zhanna D'Ark, Samson i russkai͡a istorii͡a / G.V. Nosovskiĭ, A.T. Fomenko. Moskva : FID "Delovoĭ ėkspress", 2002. 863 p. : ill. (some col.) ; 24 cm. (Novai͡a khronologii͡a) "S prilozheniem 'Arki Slavy Imperatora Maksimiliana I', sozdannoĭ A. Di͡urerom, i s prilozheniem svodnykh khronologicheskikh talits dat i imen praviteleĭ." "Uchebnoe izdanie"--Colophon. Includes bibliographical references (p. 849-861). ISBN 5896440596 (set) ISBN 5896440219 (v.1) ISBN 5896440278 (v.2)
1. Bible - Chronology. 2. Historiography. 3. Historiography - Russia. 4. History - Periodization. 5. Chronology, Historical. 6. World history. I. Fomenko, A. T. II. Title. III. Title: Zhanna d'Ark, Samson i russkai͡a istorii͡a IV. Series: Novai͡a khronologii͡a (Delovoĭ ėkspress (Firm))
DK38 .N68 2002

Nostradamus.
Nocam. Champagne-sur-Oise : Kapsos, 1998.
BF1815.N8 A2668 1998

Vystrecil, Henri. Portet-sur-Garonne : Loubatières, c2002.

Wilson, Ian, 1941- 1st U.S. ed. New York : St. Martin's Press, 2003.
BF1815.N8 W56 2003

Nostradamus, 1503-1566.
Hogue, John. The essential Nostradamus. London : Vega, c2002.
BF1815.N8 H58 2002

PROPHÉTIES.
Nocam. Nostradamus. Champagne-sur-Oise : Kapsos, 1998.
BF1815.N8 A2668 1998

Welch, R. W., 1929- Comet of Nostradamus. 1st ed. St. Paul, Minn. : Llewellyn Publications, 2000 (2001 printing)
BF1815.N8 A269 2000

Propheties. Selections. 2002.
Vystrecil, Henri. Nostradamus. Portet-sur-Garonne : Loubatières, c2002.

NOSTRADAMUS, 1503-1566.
Van Auken, John. The end times. New York : Signet Book, c2001. [Updated ed.].
BF1791 .V36 2001

Vystrecil, Henri. Nostradamus. Portet-sur-Garonne : Loubatières, c2002.

Wilson, Ian, 1941- Nostradamus. 1st U.S. ed. New York : St. Martin's Press, 2003.
BF1815.N8 W56 2003

NOSTRADAMUS, 1503-1566 - PROPHECIES.
Hogue, John. The essential Nostradamus. London : Vega, c2002.
BF1815.N8 H58 2002

Lemesurier, Peter, 1936- Nostradamus in the 21st century. Rev. ed. London : Piatkus, 2000 (2001 printing)

Nostradamus in the 21st century.
Lemesurier, Peter, 1936- Rev. ed. London : Piatkus, 2000 (2001 printing).

Not all twins are alike.
Klein, Barbara Schave. Westport, Conn. : Praeger, 2003.
BF723.T9 K57 2003

Not bosses but leaders.
Adair, John Eric, 1934- 3rd ed. / John Adair with Peter Reed. London ; Sterling, VA : Kogan Page, 2003.

Not of this world.
Fleming, Maurice. Edinburgh : Mercat, 2002.

Notas sobre historia del libro.
Tagle Frías de Cuenca, Matilde. Córdoba, República Argentina : Ediciones del Copista, c1997.
Z4

Nothing left over.
Lippe, Toinette, 1939- New York : J.P. Tarcher/Putnam, c2002.
BJ1496 .L57 2002

Nothing's wrong.
Kundtz, David, 1937- Boston, MA : Conari Press, 2004.
BF692.5 .K86 2004

NOTKER, LABEO, CA. 950-1022.
Hehle, Christine. Boethius in St. Gallen. Tübingen : Niemeyer, 2002.

Notz, William.
Santner, Thomas J., 1947- The design and analysis of computer experiments. New York : Springer, 2003.
QA279 .S235 2003

Nouvel, Jean, 1945-.
Baudrillard, Jean. [Objets singuliers. English] The singular objects of architecture. Minneapolis : University of Minnesota Press, c2002.
NA2500 .B3413 2002

La nouvelle philosophie du corps.
Andrieu, Bernard. Ramonville Saint-Agne : Erès, 2002.

Nouvelles lumières sur Rennes-le-Château.
Douzet, André. Chêne-Bourg (Suisse) : Acquarius, c1998-
BF1434.F8 D69 1998

Nova divisão sexual do trabalho?.
Hirata, Helena Sumiko. [División sexual del trabajo. Portuguese] 1a ed. São Paulo : Boitempo, 2002.
HD6060.6 .H5717 2002

Novaia khronologiia (Delovoĭ ėkspress (Firm))
Nosovskiĭ, G. V. (Gleb Vladimirovich), 1958- Rekonstruktsiia vseobshcheĭ istorii. Moskva : FID "Delovoĭ ėkspress", 2002.
DK38 .N68 2002

Novak, Peter, 1958- The lost secret of death : our divided souls and the afterlife / Peter Novak. Charlottesville, VA : Hampton Roads Pub., 2003. p. cm. Includes bibliographical references and index. CONTENTS: When we all spoke one language : the single world religion of humanity's past -- Two selves in every brain : modern science's binary soul doctrine -- Witnesses of division : near-death experiences -- Descendants of division : past-life regression -- Victims of division : ghosts and poltergeists -- Healers of division : shamanic soul retrieval and out-of-body rescues -- Conquerors of division : psychics and mystics -- That's why they call it a blind spot : cognitive illusions in afterlife experiences -- Why we have two souls : the divine dichotomy and our binary world -- Why would our souls divide at death? the pathology in the system -- Message in the messenger : the encoded history of the Jews -- Forging a self that won't shatter at death : baptism into the authenticity of the third soul -- The old path to the third soul : the one world religion of the pyramid builders -- The Toltec teachings : living voice of the old path -- Forging a new path to immortality : Christ's mission to save the human race -- The third day : consummation. ISBN 1-57174-324-3 (trade paper w/flaps) DDC 133.9/01/3
1. Soul. 2. Future life. 3. Jesus Christ - Miscellanea. I. Title.
BF1999 .N73 2003

NOVELISTS. See **FICTION.**

NOVELISTS, AMERICAN - 20TH CENTURY - BIOGRAPHY.
Tan, Amy The opposite of fate. New York : Putnam c2003.
PS3570.A48 Z47 2003

NOVELISTS, AMERICAN - 20TH CENTURY - FAMILY RELATIONSHIPS.
Tan, Amy The opposite of fate. New York : Putnam c2003.
PS3570.A48 Z47 2003

NOVELLAS (SHORT NOVELS). See **FICTION.**

NOVELS. See **FICTION.**

NOVINSKY, ANITA.
Ensaios sobre a intolerância. São Paulo, SP, Brasil : Humanitas, FFLCH/USP : FAPESP : LEI-Laboratório de Estudos sobre a Intolerância, 2002.

Novosibirskiĭ gosudarstvennyĭ pedagogicheskiĭ universitet.
Problemy interpretatsionnoĭ lingvistiki. Novosibirsk : Novosibirskiĭ gos. pedagog. universitet, 2001.
P128.E95 P762 2001

Novosibirskiĭ gosudarstvennyĭ universitet. Institut po perepodgotovke i povyshenii͡u kvalifikat͡sii prepodavateleĭ gumanitarnykh i sot͡sial'nykh nauk.
Galin, A. L. (Aleksandr Latypovich) Psikhologicheskie osobennosti tvorcheskogo povedenii͡a. Novosibirsk : Novosibirskiĭ gos. universitet, 2001.
BF408 .G315 2001

Novye religioznye ob"edinenii͡a Rossii destruktivnogo i okkul'tnogo kharaktera : spravochnik. Izd. 3-e, dop. Belgorod : Missionerskiĭ otdel Moskovskogo Patriarkhata Russkoĭ Pravoslavnoĭ T͡Serkvi, 2002. 445 p. ; 30 cm. Enl. ed. of: Novye religioznye organizat͡sii Rossii destruktivnogo i okkul'tnogo kharaktera. Izd. 2., perer i dop. 1997. Includes bibliographical references (p. 397-419) and index.
1. Occultism - Russia (Federation) 2. Cults - Russia (Federation) 3. Sects - Russia (Federation) I. Russkai͡a pravoslavnai͡a ͡tserkov'. Moskovskai͡a patriarkhii͡a. Missionerskiĭ otdel. II. Title: Novye religioznye organizat͡sii Rossii destruktivnogo i okkul'tnogo kharaktera.
BF1434.R8 N67 2002

Novye religioznye organizat͡sii Rossii destruktivnogo i okkul'tnogo kharaktera.
Novye religioznye ob"edinenii͡a Rossii destruktivnogo i okkul'tnogo kharaktera. Izd. 3-e, dop. Belgorod : Missionerskiĭ otdel Moskovskogo Patriarkhata Russkoĭ Pravoslavnoĭ T͡Serkvi, 2002.
BF1434.R8 N67 2002

Nowa twarz postmodernizmu.
Janaszek-Ivaničková, Halina. Wyd. 1. Katowice : Wydawn. Uniwersytetu Śląskiego, 2002.

Nril, ri nikanon.
Morales Tomas, Marco Antonio. El que busca encuentra = Guatemala : ESEDIR : Editorial Saqil Tzij, 1999.

NSW Commission for Children & Young People.
Suicide & risk-taking deaths of children & young people. Surry Hills, NSW : The Commission, c2003.

NTC's dictionary of everyday American English expressions.
Spears, Richard A. Lincolnwood, Ill. : National Textbook Co., c1994.
PE2839 .S65 1994

Nub phyogs śer rtogs rig pa'i tshig bum.
Tshe-riṅ-rdo-rje, 'Broṅ-bu. Par theṅs 1. Pe-cin : Mi rigs dpe skrun khaṅ, 1995.

Nuccetelli, Susana.
New essays on semantic externalism and self-knowledge. Cambridge, Mass. : MIT Press, c2003.
BD418.3 .N49 2003

NUCLEAR ASTROPHYSICS.
Börner, G. The early universe. 4th ed. Berlin : London : Springer, c2003.

NUCLEAR ENERGY. See **NUCLEAR POWER PLANTS.**

NUCLEAR FACILITIES. See **NUCLEAR POWER PLANTS.**

NUCLEAR PARTICLES. See **PARTICLES (NUCLEAR PHYSICS).**

NUCLEAR PHYSICS. See **PARTICLES (NUCLEAR PHYSICS).**

NUCLEAR POWER PLANTS - HUMAN FACTORS.
Human factors engineering program review model [microform]. Rev. 1. Washington, DC : Division of System Analysis and Regulatory Effectiveness, Office of Nuclear Regulatory Research, U.S. Nuclear Regulatory Commission : Supt. of Docs., U.S. G.P.O. [distributor], 2002.

NUCLEAR POWER STATIONS. See **NUCLEAR POWER PLANTS.**

NUCLEONS. See **PARTICLES (NUCLEAR PHYSICS).**

Nudel, Eva.
Nudel, Michael. 21st century's new chakra healing. Los Angeles, CA : Bio-Energy System Services, c2000.
BF1999 .N83 2000

Nudel, Michael. 21st century's new chakra healing / Michael Nudel & Eva Nudel. Los Angeles, CA : Bio-Energy System Services, c2000. xiii, 155 p. : ill. ; 22 cm. Includes bibliographical references (p. 153-155). ISBN 0-9677514-1-1 DDC 131
1. Chakras. 2. Mental healing. I. Nudel, Eva. II. Title. III. Title: Twenty-first century's new chakra healing IV. Title: New chakra healing
BF1999 .N83 2000

NUDELMAN, MEYER.
Nuland, Sherwin B. Lost in America. 1st ed. New York : Knopf : Distributed by Random House, 2003.
F128.9.J5 N85 2003

El nuevo norteamericano.
Taylor, Lawrence Douglas. México : Universidad Nacional Autónoma de México, Coordinación de Humanidades : Centro de Investigaciones sobre América del Norte ; Tijuana, B.C. : El Colegio de la Frontera Norte, 2001.
E40 .T39 2001

[Nuevos paradigmas. English.] New paradigms, culture, and subjectivity / edited by Dora Fried Schnitman, Jorge Schnitman. Cresskill, N.J. : Hampton Press, c2002. xxiii, 378 p. : ill. ; 23 cm. (Advances in systems theory, complexity, and the human sciences) Includes bibliographical references and indexes. ISBN 1-57273-261-X ISBN 1-57273-262-8 DDC 001
1. Knowledge, Theory of - Congresses. 2. Subjectivity - Congresses. 3. Science - Congresses. 4. Culture - Congresses. 5. Psychotherapy - Congresses. I. Fried Schnitman, Dora. II. Schnitman, Jorge. III. Title. IV. Series.
BD161 .N8413 2002

Nuland, Sherwin B. Lost in America : a journey with my father / Sherwin B. Nuland. 1st ed. New York : Knopf : Distributed by Random House, 2003. 209 p. ; 22 cm. ISBN 0-375-41294-8 DDC 974.7/275004924
1. Nuland, Sherwin B. 2. Nuland, Sherwin B. - Family relationships. 3. Nudelman, Meyer. 4. Jews - New York (State) - New York. - Biography. 5. Bronx (New York, N.Y.) - Biography. 6. Father and child. I. Title.

Nuland, Sherwin B.

F128.9.J5 N85 2003

NULAND, SHERWIN B.
Nuland, Sherwin B. Lost in America. 1st ed. New York : Knopf : Distributed by Random House, 2003.
F128.9.J5 N85 2003

NULAND, SHERWIN B. - FAMILY RELATIONSHIPS.
Nuland, Sherwin B. Lost in America. 1st ed. New York : Knopf : Distributed by Random House, 2003.
F128.9.J5 N85 2003

Numao, Masayuki, 1961-.
ALT 2002 (2002 : Lübeck, Germany) Algorithmic learning theory. Berlin ; New York : Springer, c2002.
QA76.9.A43 A48 2002

NUMBER SYMBOLISM. *See* **SYMBOLISM OF NUMBERS.**

NUMBERS, HOUSE. *See* **STREET ADDRESSES.**

NUMERALS. *See* **SYMBOLISM OF NUMBERS.**

NUMERICAL CALCULATIONS.
Coping with chaos. New York : J. Wiley, c1994.
Q172.5.C45 C67 1994

Numéro spécial (Société d'études linguistiques et anthropologiques de France)
(28.) Lexique et motivation. Paris ; Sterling, Va. : Peeters, c2002.
P326 .L45 2002

Numerology.
Drayer, Ruth. 3rd ed. Mesilla, N.M. : Jewels of Light Pub., 2002.
BF1623.P9 D72 2002

NUMEROLOGY.
Drayer, Ruth. Numerology. 3rd ed. Mesilla, N.M. : Jewels of Light Pub., 2002.
BF1623.P9 D72 2002

Fairchild, Dennis. The fortune telling handbook. 1st ed. Philadelphia, PA : Running Press, c2003.
BF1861 .F35 2003

King, Richard Andrew. The king's book of numerology. Aptos, Calif. : New Brighton Books, 2003-
BF1729.N85 K56 2003

Lawrence, Shirley Blackwell. The secret science of numerology. Franklin Lakes, NJ : New Page Books, c2001.
BF1623.P9 L38 2001

Nielsen, Bent. A companion to Yi jing numerology and cosmology. London ; New York : RoutledgeCurzon, 2003.

Shaw, Maria, 1963- Maria Shaw's star gazer. 1st ed. St. Paul, Minn. : Llewellyn Publications, 2003.
BF1411 .S52 2003

NUMEROLOGY - EARLY WORKS TO 1800.
Lucas, John Scott, 1970- Astrology and numerology in medieval and early modern Catalonia. Leiden ; Boston : Brill, 2003.
BF1685 .L83 2003

NUMEROLOGY - SPAIN - CATALONIA.
Lucas, John Scott, 1970- Astrology and numerology in medieval and early modern Catalonia. Leiden ; Boston : Brill, 2003.
BF1685 .L83 2003

NUMINOUS, THE. *See* **HOLY, THE.**

NUMISMATICS. *See* **COINS.**

Nunno, Pasquale di.
Petich, Giuseppe, 1869-1953. Divagazioni filosofiche del reverendo Giuseppe Petich tratte dai frammenti del suo "Zibaldone". Roma : Bulzoni, 2002.

I nuovi comportamenti amorosi.
Pasini, Willy. 2. ed. Milano : Mondadori, 2002.

Nuovi orchi
Gervasoni, Marco, 1968- Le armi di Orfeo. [Scandicci] (Firenze) : La nuova Italia, 2002.
ML3917.E85 G479 2002

Nuovi studi storici
(59) Zerbi, Piero. "Philosophi" e "logici". Roma : Istituto storico italiano per il Medio Evo ; Milano : Vita e pensiero, 2002.
B765.A24 Z473 2002

NUPTIALITY. *See* **MARRIAGE.**

NUREMBERG (GERMANY) - CHURCH HISTORY - TO 1500.
Stark, Heinz. Plecher Kirchengeschichte im Mittelalter. Simmelsdorf : Altnürnberger Landschaft, 2002.

NURSE MIDWIVES. *See* **MIDWIVES.**

NURSERY STOCK. *See* **TREES.**

NURSING ETHICS. *See* **MEDICAL ETHICS.**

NURSING SPECIALTIES. *See* **MIDWIFERY.**

NURTURE AND NATURE. *See* **NATURE AND NURTURE.**

NUSAḤ ARI. *See* **JUDAISM - ARI RITE.**

NUTRITION. *See* **FOOD; FOOD HABITS.**

NUTRITION DISORDERS. *See* **OBESITY.**

Nuwayhiḍ, Walīd. Min Kābūl ilá Niyūyūrk : maqālāt 'an ṣirā' al-Islām wa-al-Gharb / Walīd Nuwayhid. al-Ṭab'ah 1. Bayrūt : Dār Ibn Ḥazm, 2002. 140 p. ; 21 cm. Includes index. In Arabic.
1. East and West. 2. Islam and politics. 3. Islam - Relations - Christianity. 4. Christianity and other religions - Islam. 5. Islamic renewal - History - 20th century. 6. Islam and politics - History - 20th century. I. Title.
BP172+

Nwokogba, Isaac, 1957- America, here I come : a spiritual journey / Isaac E. Nwokogba. 2nd ed. Cranston, R.I. : Writers' Collective, c2003. p. cm. Includes bibliographical references. Table of contents URL: http://www.loc.gov/catdir/toc/ecip044/2003011768.html CONTENTS: Returning to earth -- The divine birth -- The day after -- Military training -- War and death -- Period of awakening -- Beginning life lessons -- Life as a teenager -- Searching for the truth -- America, here I come -- Face-to-face with destiny -- Spiritual progress confirmed -- Mind power -- Master and the neophyte -- Cosmic law fulfilled. ISBN 1-59411-022-0 (alk. paper) DDC 133.9
1. Karma. I. Title.
BF1045.K37 N86 2003

Voices from beyond : the God force, the other side, and you / by Isaac Nwokogba. Cranston, R.I. : Writers' Collective, 2003. p. cm. Includes index. ISBN 1-932133-44-5 (alk. paper) DDC 133.9
1. Spiritualism. 2. Future life. 3. Reincarnation. I. Title.
BF1261.2 .N96 2003

Nwokogba, Isaac E. Seeds of luck : the ABCs of creating your heart's desires / Isaac E. Nwokogba. Cranston, R.I. : Writers' Collective, 2003. p. cm. Table of contents URL: http://www.loc.gov/catdir/toc/ecip045/2003014239.html CONTENTS: Sowing the seeds of luck -- Your petition is granted -- Power petition : the nonverbal approach -- Probing the subconscious -- Intuition : the most trusted guide -- Meditation and self-hypnosis -- Behind affirmations -- Recognizing answers to your petitions -- Limitations to petitions -- Fate, destiny, and petitions. ISBN 1-59411-023-9 (alk. paper) DDC 131
1. Fortune. 2. Prayer. I. Title.
BF1778 .N96 2003

Nyborg, Helmuth.
The scientific study of general intelligence. 1st ed. Amsterdam ; Boston : Pergamon, 2003.
BF433.G45 S35 2003

Nye, David E., 1946- America as second creation : technology and narratives of new beginnings / David E. Nye. Cambridge : MIT Press, c2003. x, 371 p. : ill., maps ; 24 cm. Includes bibliographical references (p. [345]-364) and index. ISBN 0-262-14081-0 (hc. : alk. paper) DDC 978/.02
1. Frontier and pioneer life - United States. 2. Frontier and pioneer life - United States - Historiography. 3. Technology - Social aspects - United States - History. 4. Technology - Social aspects - United States - Historiography. 5. Land settlement - United States - History. 6. Land settlement - United States - Historiography. 7. National characteristics, American. 8. United States - Discovery and exploration. 9. United States - Colonization. 10. United States - Historical geography. I. Title.
E179.5 .N94 2003

Nyx, Lori.
Dumars, Denise. The dark archetype. Franklin Lakes, N.J. : New Page Books, c2003.
BF1623.G63 D86 2003

O duši i bogovima.
Popović, Velimir B. Niš : Prosveta, 2001.
BF175.5.A72 P67 2001

O interpretowaniu psychologicznym w kręgu szkoły lwowsko-warszawskiej.
Rzepa, Teresa. Warszawa : Polskie Tow. Semiotyczne, 2002.
BF108.P7 R94 2002

O rozumności i dobroci.
Przełęcki, Marian, 1923- Warszawa : "Semper", 2002.
B833 .P79 2002

Oakes, Lisa M., 1963-.
Early category and concept development. Oxford ; New York : Oxford University Press, 2003.
BF720.C63 E27 2003

Oakley, Allen. Reconstructing economic theory : the problem of human agency / Allen Oakley. Cheltenham, UK ; Northampton, MA, USA : E. Elgar Pub., c2002. xi, 234 p. ; 24 cm. Includes bibliographical references (p. 218-228) and index. ISBN 1-84064-133-9 DDC 330/.01
1. Economics - Psychological aspects. 2. Economics - Sociological aspects. 3. Economic man. I. Title.
HB74.P8 O15 2002

Oakley, Ann. Gender on planet Earth / Ann Oakley. Oxford : Polity, 2002. ix, 291 p. ; 23 cm. Includes bibliographical references and index. ISBN 0-7456-2963-6 ISBN 0-7456-2964-4 (PBK.) DDC 305.3
1. Sex role. 2. Sex discrimination. 3. Power (Social sciences) I. Title.

Oakley, Lisa. Cognitive development / Lisa Oakley. New York : Psychology Press, 2004. p. cm. (Routledge modular psychology series) Includes bibliographical references and index. ISBN 0-415-24234-7 (hbk.) ISBN 0-415-24235-5 (pbk.) DDC 155.4/13
1. Cognition - Textbooks. 2. Developmental psychology - Textbooks. I. Title. II. Series: Routledge modular psychology.
BF311 .O12 2004

Oates, John, 1946- Cognitive and language development in children / John Oates and Andrew Grayson. Milton Keynes, U.K. : Open University ; Malden, MA : Blackwell Pub., 2004. p. cm. (Child development ; 3) Includes bibliographical references and indexes. Table of contents URL: http://www.loc.gov/catdir/toc/ecip047/2003018263.html ISBN 1405110457 (pbk : alk. paper) DDC 155.4/13
1. Cognition in children. 2. Language acquisition. I. Grayson, Andrew, 1963- II. Title. III. Series: Child development (Cambridge, Mass.) ; 3.
BF723.C5 O38 2004

The OAU (AU) and OAS in regional conflict management.
Imobighe, Thomas A. Ibadan : Spectrum Books ; Oxford, UK : USA distributor, African Books Collective, 2003.
JZ6374 .I46 2003

OBEAH (CULT). *See* **VOODOOISM.**

Ober, Josiah.
Manville, Brook, 1950- A company of citizens. Boston : Harvard Business School Press, c2003.
HD58.7 .M3714 2003

Obesidade.
Stenzel, Lucia Marques. 1a ed. Porto Alegre : EDIPUCRS, 2002.

OBESITY - SOCIAL ASPECTS.
Stenzel, Lucia Marques. Obesidade. 1a ed. Porto Alegre : EDIPUCRS, 2002.

Object relations and self psychology.
St. Clair, Michael, 1940- 4th ed. Australia ; Belmont, CA : Thomson/Brooks/Cole, c2004.
BF175.5.O24 S7 2004

OBJECT RELATIONS (PSYCHOANALYSIS). *See also* **INTERPERSONAL RELATIONS.**
Ayers, Mary, 1960- The eyes of shame. 1st ed. Hove, East Sussex ; New York : Brunner-Routledge, 2003.
BF175.5.O24 A94 2003

St. Clair, Michael, 1940- Object relations and self psychology. 4th ed. Australia ; Belmont, CA : Thomson/Brooks/Cole, c2004.
BF175.5.O24 S7 2004

The vitality of objects. 1st US ed. Middletown, Conn. : Wesleyan University Press, 2002.
BF173 .V55 2002

OBJECT RELATIONS THEORY (PSYCHOANALYSIS). *See* **OBJECT RELATIONS (PSYCHOANALYSIS).**

OBJECTIVES, EDUCATIONAL. *See* **EDUCATION - AIMS AND OBJECTIVES.**

OBJECTIVITY.
Majorek, Marek B. Objektivität, ein Erkenntnisideal auf dem Prüfstand. Tübingen : Francke, c2002.

Objektivität, ein Erkenntnisideal auf dem Prüfstand.
Majorek, Marek B. Tübingen : Francke, c2002.

Obley, Carole J. Embracing the ties that bind : connecting with the spirit / Carole J. Obley. [Philadelphia] : Xlibris, c2003. 276 p. ; 22 cm. Includes bibliographical references (p. 267). ISBN 1401089720 ISBN

1401089712 (pbk.) DDC 131
1. Self-realization. 2. Spiritualism. I. Title.
BF1275.S44 O25 2003

Oblichat' i lit͡semerit'
Kharkhordin, Oleg, 1964- Sankt-Peterburg :
Evropeĭskiĭ universitet v Sankt-Peterburge ; Moskva :
Letniĭ Sad, 2002.
B2430.F724 K43 2002

Obraznai͡a sfera cheloveka v poznanii i perezhivanii dukhovnykh smyslov.
Gostev, A. A. (Andreĭ Andreevich) Moskva : In-t psikhologii RAN, 2001.
BF367 .G565 2001

Obrazovatel'nai͡a biblioteka
Udovik, S. L. (Sergeĭ Leonidovich) Globalizat͡sii͡a. [Moscow] : Refl-buk ; [Kiev] : Vakler, 2002.
CB430 .U36 2002

Obretenie I͡A i vozniknovenie rannikh form sot͡sial'nosti.
Mozzhilin, S. I. (Sergeĭ Ivanovich) Saratov : Saratovskiĭ gos. sot͡sial'no-ėkonomicheskiĭ universitet, 2002.
BF697.5.S65 M69 2002

O'Brien, Margaret, 1954-.
Children in the city. London : Routledge/Falmer, 2003.

O'Brien, Michael J. (Michael John), 1950-.
Style, function, transmission. Salt Lake City : University of Utah Press, c2003.
CC173 .S79 2003

O'Brien, Patrick Karl.
Urban achievement in early modern Europe. Cambridge ; New York : Cambridge University Press, 2001.
HT131 .U688 2001

OBSEQUIES. See **FUNERAL RITES AND CEREMONIES.**

OBSERVATION (PSYCHOLOGY).
Pellegrini, Anthony D. Observing children in their natural worlds. 2nd ed. Mahwah, N.J. : L. Erlbaum Associates, 2004.
BF722 .P45 2004

OBSERVATION (SCIENTIFIC METHOD).
Janesick, Valerie J. "Stretching" exercises for qualitative researchers. 2nd ed. Thousand Oaks, Calif. : Sage Publications, c2004.
H62 .J346 2004

Observations on modernity.
Luhmann, Niklas. [Beobachtungen der Moderne. English] Stanford, CA : Stanford University Press, 1998.
HM24 .L88813 1998

Observing children in their natural worlds.
Pellegrini, Anthony D. 2nd ed. Mahwah, N.J. : L. Erlbaum Associates, 2004.
BF722 .P45 2004

Obshchenie.
Tvorogova, N. D. (Nadezhda Tvorogova) Moskva : Smysl, 2002.
BF637.C45 T88 2002

Obshchestvo li͡ubiteleĭ rossiĭskoĭ slovesnosti.
Alefirenko, M. F. Poėticheskai͡a ėnergii͡a slova. Moskva : Academia, 2002.
P35 .A544 2002

O'Byrne, Patrick.
Milner, Judith, senior lecturer. Assessment in counselling. Houndmills, Basingstoke, Hampshire ; New York : Palgrave Macmillan, 2003.
BF637.C6 M5249 2003

O'Callaghan, John (John P.) Thomist realism and the linguistic turn : toward a more perfect form of existence / John P. O'Callaghan. Notre Dame, Ind. : University of Notre Dame Press, c2003. ix, 357 p. ; 25 cm. Includes bibliographical references (p. 337-346) and index.
ISBN 0-268-04217-9 (alk. paper) ISBN 0-268-04218-7 (pbk. : alk. paper) DDC 149/.91
1. Knowledge, Theory of. 2. Mental representation. 3. Language and languages - Philosophy. 4. Thomists. I. Title.
BD161 .O3 2003

Occasional papers Bournemouth University. School of Conservation Sciences
(7) Digging holes in popular culture. Oxford : Oxbow, 2002.
PN3433.6 .D54 2002

Occhino, MaryRose. Beyond these four walls : diary of a psychic medium / MaryRose Occhino. New York : Berkley Books, 2003. p. cm. ISBN 0-425-19410-8 DDC 133.9/1/092
1. Occhino, MaryRose. 2. Parapsychology. 3. Spiritualism. I. Title.
BF1283.O27 A3 2003

OCCHINO, MARYROSE.
Occhino, MaryRose. Beyond these four walls. New York : Berkley Books, 2003.
BF1283.O27 A3 2003

L'occhio della lince.
Baldriga, Irene. Roma : Accademia nazionale dei Lincei, 2002.

OCCIDENTAL ART. See **ART.**

OCCIDENTAL CIVILIZATION. See **CIVILIZATION, WESTERN.**

OCCULT MEDICINE. See **MEDICINE, MAGIC, MYSTIC, AND SPAGIRIC.**

OCCULT SCIENCES. See **OCCULTISM.**

OCCULT, THE. See **OCCULTISM.**

The occult Webb : an appreciation of the life and work of James Webb / compiled by John Robert Colombo ; with contributions by Colin Wilson and Joyce Collin-Smith. Toronto : Colombo & Co., c1999. 100 leaves : ill. ; 22 cm. (The monograph series) (QuasiBook edition) Includes bibliographical references.
1. Webb, James, - 1946- I. Colombo, John Robert, 1936- II. Wilson, Colin, 1931- III. Collin-Smith, Joyce, 1919- IV. Series. V. Series: Monograph series (Toronto, Canada)
BF1408.2.W42 O33 1999

OCCULTISM. See also **ALCHEMY; ASTROLOGY; DIVINATION; FORTUNE-TELLING; HAUNTED PLACES; HERMETISM; MAGIC; NUMEROLOGY; ORACLES; PARAPSYCHOLOGY; PROPHECIES (OCCULTISM); SATANISM; SPIRITUALISM; WITCHCRAFT.**
Bô Yin Râ, 1876-1943. [Buch vom Menschen. English] The book on human nature. Berkeley, Calif. : Kober Press, c2000.
BF1999 .B6516713 2000

Bobgan, Martin, 1930- Hypnosis. Santa Barbara, Calif. : EastGate Publishers, c2001.
BF1152 .B63 2001

Browne, Sylvia. Secrets & mysteries of the world. Carlsbad, Calif. : Hay House, c2005.
BF1411 .B78 2005

Buckland, Raymond. Color magick. 1st ed., rev. St. Paul, Minn. : Llewellyn Publications, 2002.
BF1623.C6 B83 2002

Charlton-Davis, Mark K. Thoughts from the underworld. Los Angeles, Calif. : Amen-Ra Theological Seminary Press, c2001 (Kearney, NE : Morris Pub.)
BF1999 .C5145 2001

Davis, Audrey Craft. Metaphysical techniques that really work. Nevada City, CA : Blue Dolphin Pub., 2004.
BF1411 .D38 2004

DuQuette, Lon Milo, 1948- [Magick of Thelma] The magick of Aleister Crowley. Boston, MA : Weiser Books, 2003.
BF1611 .D87 2003

Eilers, Dana D. The practical pagan. Franklin Lakes, NJ : New Page Books, c2002.
BF1411 .E34 2002

Ellis, Bill, 1950- Lucifer ascending. Lexington : University Press of Kentucky, c2003.
BF1548 .E44 2003

Ėzotericheskai͡a filosofii͡a. Rostov-na-Donu : Foliant, 2002.
BF1416 .E96 2002

Harms, Daniel. The Necronomicon files. Boston, MA : Weiser Books, c2003.
BF1999 .H37515 2003

Karasev, Nikolaĭ, iereĭ. Put' okkul'tizma. Moskva : Izd-vo "Prensa", 2003.
BF1416 .K37 2003

Kelly, Jill. Guardians of the Celtic way. Rochester, Vt. : Bear & Co., c2003.
BF1411 .K45 2003

Meader, William A., 1955- Shine forth. Mariposa, Calif. : Source Publications, c2004.
BF1611 .M412 2004

Orosz, László Wladimir. A jelen és az idő. Debrecen : Stalker Stúdió, 2001.

BF1999 .O69 2000
Rahbar'zādah, Ḥasan. Shinākht-i rūḥ. Chāp-i 1. Tihrān : Nashr-i Pārsā, 1380 [2001 04 2002]

Rogers, Rita. Mysteries. Large print ed. Bath, England : Chivers Press ; Waterville, Me. : Thorndike Press, 2002.
BF1031 .R635 2002

Saraydarian, Torkom. Dynamics of the soul. Cave Creek, Ariz. : T.S.G. Pub., c2001.
BF1999 .S3352 2001

Scully, Nicki, 1943- Alchemical healing. Rochester, Vt. : Bear & Co., 2003.
BF1999 .S369 2003

Shaw, Maria, 1963- Maria Shaw's star gazer. 1st ed. St. Paul, Minn. : Llewellyn Publications, 2003.
BF1411 .S52 2003

Solodin, A. I. Strategii͡a ontologicheskoĭ igry. Sankt-Peterburg : Aleteĭi͡a, 2002.

Spencer, John, 1954- Mysteries and magic. London : Orion, 2000.

Weinstein, Marion. Positive magic. Rev. ed. Franklin Lakes, NJ : New Page Books, c2002.
BF1411 .W393 2002

Whitehead, Willis F. The mystic thesaurus. Berwick, Me. : Ibis Press, 2003.
BF1411 .W46 2003

OCCULTISM AND SCIENCE.
Aveni, Anthony F. Behind the crystal ball. Rev. ed. Boulder, Colo. : University Press of Colorado, c2002.
BF1589 .A9 2002

Charpak, Georges. [Devenez sorciers, devenez savants English] Debunked!. Baltimore : Johns Hopkins University Press, 2004.
BF1409.5 .C4313 2004

OCCULTISM - BURMA.
Khan'' Kyo', Cha rā Ū''. Gambhīra vedanta 'a cī 'a maṃ myā''. Ran' kun' : Yuṃ krañ''' khyak' Cā pe : Chak' svay' ran'', Ū'' Khan'' Kyo' Cā pe, 2002.
BF1434.B93 K43 2002

'Oṅ' Mran'', 'Aṅ'gyan'nīyā Ū''. 'Im' chok' maṅgalā kyam''''. Mantale'' : Krī'' pvā'' re'' Cā 'up' Tuik'', 2002.
BF1779.A88 O56 2002

Roṅ' pran' lak' choṅ'. Ran' kun' : 'Aruṇ' Ū'' Cā pe : Phran'' khyi re'', Lābh' Mui' Cve Cā pe, 2001.
BF1434.B+

San''' Ū'', Sutagavesī. Mran' mā' rui'' rā 'im' khraṃ mre nañn''' pañnā. Ran' kun' : Rvhe Pu ra puid' Cā pe : Phran'' khyi re'', Sa mī'' Jotika Cā pe, 2000.
BF1773.2.B93 S26 2000

OCCULTISM - BURMESE.
Hin''' Lat'. Ca dha ba va manomaya. Kyok' taṃ tā'', [Rangoon] : Yuṃ krañn'' khyak' Cā pe : Pran'' khyi re'', Rve Nan''' Mhan' kū Cā 'up' Tuik', 2002.
BF1434.B93 H56 2002

OCCULTISM - DICTIONARIES.
Spence, Lewis, 1874-1955. An encyclopædia of occultism. Mineola, N.Y. : Dover Publications, 2003.
BF1025 .S7 2003

OCCULTISM - ENCYCLOPEDIAS.
Steiger, Brad. The Gale encyclopedia of the unusual and unexplained. Detroit : Thomson/Gale, c2003.
BF1025 .S79 2003

OCCULTISM - EUROPE - HISTORY.
Gibbons, B. J. Spirituality and the occult. London ; New York : Routledge, 2001.
BF1434.E85 G53 2001

OCCULTISM - EUROPE - HISTORY - CONGRESSES.
Antike Weisheit und kulturelle Praxis. Göttingen : Vandenhoeck & Ruprecht, 2001.
BF1586 .A58 2001

OCCULTISM - EUROPE - MANUSCRIPTS - EXHIBITIONS.
Magia, alchimia, scienza dal '400 al '700. Firenze : Centro Di, 2002.
BF1598.H6 M34 2002

OCCULTISM - FRANCE - HISTORY.
Waite, Arthur Edward, 1857-1942. Devil-worship in France with Diana Vaughan and the question of modern palladism. Boston, MA : Weiser Books, 2003.
BF1548 .W2 2003

OCCULTISM - FRANCE - RENNES-LE-CHÂTEAU.
Douzet, André. Nouvelles lumières sur Rennes-le-Château. Chêne-Bourg (Suisse) : Acquarius, c1998-

BF1434.F8 D69 1998

OCCULTISM - GERMANY - HISTORY.
Treitel, Corinna. A science for the soul. Baltimore :
Johns Hopkins University Press, 2004.
BF1434.G5 T74 2004

OCCULTISM - GREAT BRITAIN - HISTORY - 19TH CENTURY.
Owen, Alex, 1948- The place of enchantment.
Chicago, Ill. : University of Chicago Press, c2004.
BF1429 .O94 2004

OCCULTISM - HISTORY.
Berg, Wendy, 1951- Polarity magic. St. Paul, Minn. :
Llewellyn Publications, 2003.
BF1589 .B47 2003

Burton, Dan. Magic, mystery, and science.
Bloomington : Indiana University Press, 2003.
BF1411 .B885 2003

Hall, Manly Palmer, 1901- The secret teachings of all ages. Reader's ed. New York : Jeremy P. Tarcher/Putnam, 2003.
BF1411 .H3 2003

Newton, Toyne. The dark worship. London : Vega, 2002.
BF1531 .N49 2002

Szőnyi, György Endre. John Dee's occultism.
Albany : State University of New York Press, 2004.
BF1598.D5 S98 2004

OCCULTISM - HISTORY - NORTH AMERICA - ENCYCLOPEDIAS.
Greer, John Michael. The new encyclopedia of the occult. St. Paul, MN : Llewellyn Publications, 2003.
BF1407 .G74 2003

OCCULTISM - HISTORY - WESTERN EUROPE - ENCYCLOPEDIAS.
Greer, John Michael. The new encyclopedia of the occult. St. Paul, MN : Llewellyn Publications, 2003.
BF1407 .G74 2003

OCCULTISM, ISLAMIC.
Dāwūd, Muḥammad 'Īsá. al-Jafr li-Sayyidinā 'Alī al-Muhandisīn [Giza] : Madbūlī al-Ṣaghīr, [2003]
BF1771+

OCCULTISM - JUVENILE LITERATURE.
Shaw, Maria, 1963- Maria Shaw's star gazer. 1st ed.
St. Paul, Minn. : Llewellyn Publications, 2003.
BF1411 .S52 2003

OCCULTISM - NEW YORK (STATE) - MONTAUK POINT.
Moon, Peter. The black sun. New York : Sky Books, c1997.
BF1434.U6 M66 1997

OCCULTISM - NORTH AMERICA - ENCYCLOPEDIAS.
Greer, John Michael. The new encyclopedia of the occult. St. Paul, MN : Llewellyn Publications, 2003.
BF1407 .G74 2003

OCCULTISM - RELIGIOUS ASPECTS - CHRISTIANITY.
Ofoegbu, Mike. Exposing satanic manipulations.
[Lagos, Nigeria : Holy Ghost Anointed Books Ministries, c1998]
1. Black author.

Olorunfemi, Samuel Jimson. Breaking the evil blood covenant. Ibadan, Oyo State, Nigeria : Triumphant Faith Publications, 2001.
1. Black author.

Proja, Giovanni Battista. Uomini, diavoli, esorcismi.
Roma : Città nuova, 2002.

OCCULTISM - RELIGIOUS ASPECTS - ORTHODOX EASTERN CHURCH.
Tsiakkas, Christophoros A. Mageia-satanismos. 3 ekd.
Leukōsia : Ekdosē Hieras Monēs Trooditissēs, 2001.
BF1550 .T73 2001

OCCULTISM - RUSSIA (FEDERATION).
Novye religioznye ob"edineniia Rossii destruktivnogo i okkul'tnogo kharaktera. Izd. 3-e, dop. Belgorod : Missionerskiĭ otdel Moskovskogo Patriarkhata Russkoĭ Pravoslavnoĭ TSerkvi, 2002.
BF1434.R8 N67 2002

OCCULTISM - UNITED STATES.
Starr, Martin P., 1959- The unknown God.
Bolingbrook, IL : Teitan Press, 2003.
BF1997.S73 2003

OCCULTISM - WESTERN EUROPE - ENCYCLOPEDIAS.
Greer, John Michael. The new encyclopedia of the occult. St. Paul, MN : Llewellyn Publications, 2003.
BF1407 .G74 2003

OCCULTISTS. *See* **ASTROLOGERS; ROSICRUCIANS; SPIRITUALISTS; WARLOCKS; WITCHES.**

OCCUPATIONAL HEALTH.
Kaluzniacky, Eugene. Managing psychological factors in information systems work. Hershey PA : Information Science Pub., c2004.
BF576 .K358 2004

OCCUPATIONAL STRESS. *See* **JOB STRESS.**

OCCUPATIONAL TRAINING. *See* **EMPLOYEES - TRAINING OF.**

OCCUPATIONS. *See* **PROFESSIONS; WORK.**

OCCUPATIONS - FRANCE - SOCIOLOGICAL ASPECTS.
Osty, Florence. Le désir de métier. Rennes [France] : Presses universitaires de Rennes, [2003]

Ocherki po filosofii arkhitekturnoĭ formy.
Revzin, G. I. (Grigoriĭ I.) Moskva : O.G.I., 2002.
NA2500 .R464 2002

Ochs, Elizabeth, 1984-.
Ochs, Vanessa L. The Jewish dream book.
Woodstock, VT : Jewish Lights Publishing, 2003.
BF1078 .O24 2003

Ochs, Vanessa L. The Jewish dream book : the key to opening the inner meaning of your dreams / Vanessa L. Ochs with Elizabeth Ochs ; illustrations by Kristina Swarner. Woodstock, VT : Jewish Lights Publishing, 2003. p. cm. Includes bibliographical references. Table of contents URL: http://www.loc.gov/catdir/toc/ecip041/2003006452.html ISBN 1-58023-132-2 (pbk.) DDC 296.7/1
1. Dreams - Religious aspects - Judaism. 2. Dream interpretation. 3. Dream interpretation in rabbinical literature. I. Ochs, Elizabeth, 1984- II. Title.
BF1078 .O24 2003

The octavolateralis system and Mauthner cell interactions and questions [microform].
Eaton, Robert C. [Washington, D.C. : National Aeronautics and Space Administration, 1997]

ODDITIES. *See* **CURIOSITIES AND WONDERS.**

O'DELL, MAGGIE (FICTITIOUS CHARACTER) - FICTION.
Kava, Alex. The soul catcher. Waterville, Me. : Thorndike Press, 2003, 2002.
PS3561.A8682 S6 2003

Odense University classical studies
(v. 21) Divination and portents in the Roman world.
Odense : Odense University Press, c2000.
BF1768 .D57 2000

Odmiany odmieńca : mniejszościowe orientacje seksualne w perspektywie gender = A queer mixture : gender perspectives on minority sexual identities / redakcja, Tomasz Basiuk, Dominika Ferens, Tomasz Sikora. Katowice : "Śląsk", 2002. 218 p. : ill. ; 20 cm. Includes bibliographical references. Polish and English. ISBN 83-7164-344-6
1. Sexual orientation. 2. Gender identity. 3. Homosexuality. I. Basiuk, Tomasz. II. Ferens, Dominika, 1964- III. Sikora, Tomasz. IV. Title: Mniejszościowe orientacje seksualne w perspektywie gender V. Title: Queer mixture : gender perspectives on minority sexual identities VI. Title: Gender perspectives on minority sexual identities
HQ23 .O36 2002

ODORS. *See* **INCENSE.**

O'Driscoll, Muriel.
Hadikin, Ruth. The bullying culture. Oxford ; Boston : Books for Midwives, 2000.
BF637.B85 H33 2000

Oduyoye, Mercy Amba. Les colliers et les perles : réflexion d'une femme sur le christianisme africain / Mercy Amba Oduyoye ; traduit de l'anglais par Marie-Claire Dati. Yaoundé : Editions CLE, c2002. 188 p. ; 21 cm. (Réflexions théologiques du sud) Includes bibliographical references. ISBN 2-7235-0159-0
1. Women in Christianity - Africa. 2. Women - Religious life. 3. Women - Africa - Social conditions. 4. Black author. I. Title. II. Series: Collection "Réflexions théologiques du sud"

Die Odyssee des Menschen.
Baur, Manfred, 1959- München : Ullstein, c2001.

Odysseus in America.
Shay, Jonathan. New York : Scribner, c2002.
RC550 .S533 2002

OECOLOGY. *See* **ECOLOGY.**

OEDIPUS COMPLEX.
Cifali, Mario. Trois rêves freudiens. Paris : Eshel, c1999.

BF175.5.O33 C54 1999
Maciejewski, Franz. Psychoanalytisches Archiv und jüdisches Gedächtnis. 1. Aufl. Wien : Passagen Verlag, 2002.

Oehler, Klaus, ed.
James, William, 1842-1910. [Pragmatism. German] Pragmatismus. Berlin : Akademie Verlag, c2000.

Oettinger, Callie Rucker.
Danzig, Robert J., 1932- Every child deserves a champion. Washington, DC : Child & Family Press, c2003.
BF637.E53 D36 2003

Off the map.
Glendinning, Chellis. Gabriola Island, BC : New Society Publishers, c2002.
HF1414 .G553 2002

OFFENSES AGAINST THE PERSON. *See* **MURDER; SEX CRIMES.**

Die Öffentlichkeit der Vernunft und die Vernunft der Öffentlichkeit : Festschrift für Jürgen Habermas / herausgegeben von Lutz Wingert und Klaus Günther. 1. Aufl. Frankfurt am Main : Suhrkamp, 2001. 706, [1] p. ; 18 cm. (Suhrkamp Taschenbuch Wissenschaft ; 1533) Papers from a symposium held July 1999 at the Johann Wolfgang Goethe-Universität in Frankfurt am Main, Germany, in honor of Jürgen Habermas's 70th birthday. Includes bibliographical references. ISBN 3-518-29133-5 (pbk.)
1. Habermas, Jürgen - Congresses. 2. Knowledge, Theory of - Congresses. 3. Ethics - Congresses. 4. Democracy - Congresses. I. Habermas, Jürgen. II. Wingert, Lutz, 1958- III. Günther, Klaus, 1957- IV. Universität Frankfurt am Main. V. Series.
B3258.H324 O34 2001

Office Feng Shui.
Zeer, Darrin. San Francisco : Chronicle Books, 2004.
BF1779.F4 Z44 2004

OFFICE LAYOUT.
Allcorn, Seth. The dynamic workplace. Westport, Conn. ; London : Praeger, 2003.
HF5547.2 .A43 2003

OFFICE MANAGEMENT.
Allcorn, Seth. The dynamic workplace. Westport, Conn. ; London : Praeger, 2003.
HF5547.2 .A43 2003

The "official" friends book.
Bolton, Martha, 1951- West Monroe, LA : Howard Pub., c2003.
BF575.F66 B65 2003

OFFICIAL LANGUAGES. *See* **LANGUAGE POLICY.**

Offiong, Maria I. The enneagram : gateway to self-discovery / Maria I. Offiong. [Nigeria] : Modern Business Press, 1998. xii, 136 p. : ill. ; 21 cm. Includes bibliographical references (p. 134-136). ISBN 978-2676-39-X
1. Enneagram. 2. Personality assessment. 3. Black author. I. Title.

Ofoegbu, Mike. Exposing satanic manipulations / by Mike Ofoegbu. [Lagos, Nigeria : Holy Ghost Anointed Books Ministries, c1998] viii, 85 p. ; 20 cm. ISBN 978-33401-6-6
1. Good and evil - Social aspects - Nigera. 2. Occultism - Religious aspects - Christianity. 3. Satanism. 4. Demonology. 5. Christian life. 6. Demoniac possession. 7. Spiritual healing. 8. Black author. I. Title.

Ofori Onwona, Samuel. Shadows come to light : prayer as spiritual warfare / Samuel Ofori Onwona. Achimota, Ghana : Africa Christian Press, 2000. 286 p. ; 20 cm. ISBN 9964-87-530-4
1. Prayer - Psychology. 2. Prayer. 3. Prayer - Christianity. 4. Christian life. 5. Theology, Practical. I. Title.
BV215 .O46 2000

Ogam, the Celtic oracle of the trees.
Mountfort, Paul Rhys. Rochester, Vt. : Destiny Books, c2002.
PB1217 .M68 2002

OGHAM ALPHABET.
Mountfort, Paul Rhys. Ogam, the Celtic oracle of the trees. Rochester, Vt. : Destiny Books, c2002.
PB1217 .M68 2002

Ogien, Ruwen. La honte est-elle immorale? / Ruwen Ogien. Paris : Bayard, c2002. 165 p. ; 19 cm. (Le temps d'une question) Includes bibliographical references. ISBN 2-227-02018-0 DDC 194
1. Shame. I. Title. II. Series.

Ogilvie, Daniel M. Fantasies of flight / Daniel M. Ogilvie. New York : Oxford University Press, 2003. p. cm. Includes bibliographical references and index. ISBN 0-19-

515746-X (alk. paper) DDC 154.3
1. Levitation. 2. Levitation - Case studies. I. Title.
BF1385 .O35 2003

Ognev, A. S. (Aleksandr Sergeevich) Teoreticheskie osnovy psikhologii sub"ektogeneza / A.S. Ognev. Voronezh : Izd-vo VF RAGS, 1997. 121 p. ; 21 cm. Includes bibliographical references (p. 112-121). ISBN 5858130755
1. Personality. I. Title.
BF698 .O36 1997

O'Hanlon, William Hudson. Thriving through crisis : turn tragedy and trauma into growth and change / Bill O'Hanlon. 1st Perigee ed. New York : Perigee, 2004. p. cm. Includes bibliographical references. ISBN 0-399-52946-2 DDC 155.9/3
1. Suffering. 2. Self-actualization (Psychology) 3. Life change events - Psychological aspects. I. Title.
BF789.S8 O35 2004

O'Hara, Craig. Monkeywrenching the new world order [sound recording]. Oakland, Calif : AK Press ; San Francisco, CA : Alternative Tentacles Records, 2001.

O'Hara, J. Human factors engineering program review model [microform]. Rev. 1. Washington, DC : Division of System Analysis and Regulatory Effectiveness, Office of Nuclear Regulatory Research, U.S. Nuclear Regulatory Commission : Supt. of Docs., U.S. G.P.O. [distributor], 2002.

O'Hara, Nancy. Serenity in motion : inner peace-- anytime, anywhere / Nancy O'Hara. New York : Warner Books, 2003. p. cm. ISBN 0-446-69085-6 DDC 158.1
1. Peace of mind. I. Title.
BF637.P3 O42 2003

Ohel Ya'aḳov. Druk, Ya'aḳov ben Zalman. Yerushala[yi]m : Y. ben Z. Druk, 762 [2002]
BS1225.4 .D77 2002

OHIO RIVER VALLEY - GEOGRAPHY.
Linklater, Andro. Measuring America. New York : Walker & Co., 2002.
E161.3 .L46 2002

OHIO RIVER VALLEY - SURVEYS - HISTORY.
Linklater, Andro. Measuring America. New York : Walker & Co., 2002.
E161.3 .L46 2002

OHIO VALLEY. See **OHIO RIVER VALLEY.**

OIL INDUSTRIES. See **PETROLEUM INDUSTRY AND TRADE.**

OIL PAINTING. See **PAINTING.**

Ojeda Awad, Alonso. Convivencia y globalización : aportes para la paz / Alonso Ojeda Awad. [1a ed.]. [Bogotá] : Universidad Pedagógica Nacional, [2002] 351 p. ; 21 cm. Includes bibliographical references. ISBN 958-9097-68-5
1. Peace. 2. International organization. 3. Globalization. I. Title.

Okanoue, Toshiko. Drop of dreams / Toshiko Okanoue. Tucson, AZ : Nazraeli Press, c2002. 69 p. : ill. ; 28 cm. Cover: Toshiko Okanoue : works 1950-1956. ISBN 1-59005-035-5
1. Photomontage. 2. Surrealism. I. Title.

Ōkawa, Ryūhō, 1956-
[Ai no genten. English]
The origin of love : on the beauty of compassion / Ryuho Okawa. New York : Lantern Books, c2003. ix, 95 p. ; 22 cm. Translation of: Ai no genten. ISBN 1-59056-052-3 (alk. paper) DDC 299/.93
1. Kōfuku no Kagaku (Organization) 2. Love. I. Title.
BP605.K55 O29513 2003

[Hito o aishi, hito o ikashi, hito o yuruse. English]
Love, nurture, and forgive : a handbook to add a new richness to your life / Ryuho Okawa. New York : Lantern Books, c2002. 100 p. ; 22 cm. Includes bibliographical references. CONTENTS: Love, nurture, and forgive -- How the "Stages of love" philosophy started -- What it means to love others -- Practicing spiritually nurturing love -- Forgiving love -- The spirit on the journey to independence -- Starting from the ordinary -- Independence -- Diverse values -- An encounter with God -- Increasing the value of time -- Rising to an extraordinary level of love. ISBN 1-930051-78-6 (pbk. : alk. paper) DDC 299/.93
1. Kōfuku no Kagaku (Organization) 2. Spiritual life. I. Title.
BP605.K55 O32413 2002

[Ōgon no hō. English]
The golden laws : history through the Eyes of the Eternal Buddha / Ryuho Okawa ; [translated by The Institute for Research in Human Happiness, Ltd.]. New York : Lantern Books, c2002. xii, 229 p. ; 22 cm. "Rev. ed. of: The laws of gold. c1990"--T.p. verso. ISBN 1-930051-61-1 (pbk. : alk. paper) DDC 299/.93
1. Kōfuku no Kagaku (Organization) 2. Spiritual life. I. Ōkawa, Ryūhō, 1956- Ōgon no hō. English. II. Kōfuku no Kagaku (Organization) III. Title.
BP605.K55 O33 2001

Ogon no ho. English.
Okawa, Ryūhō, 1956- [Ōgon no hō. English] The golden laws. New York : Lantern Books, c2002.
BP605.K55 O33 2001

O'Keefe, Tracie. Finding the real me. 1st ed. San Francisco, CA : Jossey-Bass, c2003.
HQ77.7 .F56 2003

Oklahoma Psychological Association. Oklahoma psychology in the twentieth century. [Oklahoma City, OK : Oklahoma Psychological Association, 2003?]
BF77 .O35 2003

Oklahoma psychology in the twentieth century : a five volume history / commissioned by the Oklahoma Psychological Association to commemorate a half century of service to the citizens of Oklahoma ; general editor, Charles Whipple. [Oklahoma City, OK : Oklahoma Psychological Association, 2003?] 5 v. in 1 : ill. ; 30 cm. CONTENTS: v. 1. A history of psychology departments in the universities developed out of the unassigned lands of Indian Territory 1889-2000, University of Oklahoma, Oklahoma State University, University of Central Oklahoma -- v. 2. A history of the psychology departments in the state universities developed out of the territory of the five civilized tribes, 1897-2000, Cameron University, East Central State University, Northeastern State University, Northwestern State University, Southeastern State University -- v. 3. A history of the psychology departments in Oklahoma private and parochial universities, 1894-2000, Oklahoma Baptist University, Oklahoma Christian University, Oklahoma City University, Southern Nazarene University, University of Tulsa -- v. 4. A history of the Oklahoma Psychological Association, and the Oklahoma State Board of Examiners of Human Services, the child guidance centers, and the Federal Aviation Administration in the state of Oklahoma. DDC 150/.71/1766
1. Psychology - Study and teaching (Higher) - Oklahoma - History. 2. Psychology - Oklahoma - History. 3. Psychologists - Oklahoma - History. I. Whipple, Charles M. II. Oklahoma Psychological Association.
BF77 .O35 2003

'Olamot shel ṭohar.
Sofer, Mikha'el Uri. Sefer 'Olamot shel ṭohar. Mahad. 2. Bene Beraḳ : M.U. Sofer, 761 [2000 or 2001]
BM726 .S633 2000

Olaoye, Elaine H. Passions of the soul : poetry and poetry therapy : selected writings in poetry abd psychology on self-development / Elaine H. Olaoye. 2nd ed. Red Bank, N.J. : Northwind Publishers, 2002. 90 p. ; 22 cm. ISBN 1-88076-414-8
1. Self-culture. 2. Psychology, Applied. 3. Poetry - Women authors. 4. Poetry, American - African American authors. 5. Black author. I. Title.

OLD AGE. See also **AGED; AGING.**
Macdonald, Barbara, 1913- Look me in the eye. New, expanded ed. Denver, CO : Spinsters Ink Books, 2001.

OLD AGE ASSISTANCE. See **AGED - MEDICAL CARE.**

OLD AGE - GREECE - HISTORY.
Catrysse, Andrée. Les grecs et la vieillesse. Paris : L'Harmattan, c2003.

OLD AGE - PHILOSOPHY.
Catrysse, Andrée. Les grecs et la vieillesse. Paris : L'Harmattan, c2003.

The old girls' book of dreams.
Garrison, Cal. Boston, MA : Red Wheel, 2003.
BF1729.W64 G37 2003

OLD WOMEN. See **AGED WOMEN.**

Old women, aging and ageism.
Macdonald, Barbara, 1913- Look me in the eye. New, expanded ed. Denver, CO : Spinsters Ink Books, 2001.

Oldenburger Symposion zur Psychologischen Akustik (8th : 2000) Contributions to psychological acoustics : results of the eighth Oldenburg Symposium on Psychological Acoustics / edited by August Schick, Markus Meis, Carsten Reckhardt. 1. ed. Oldenburg : BIS, Bibliotheks- und Informationssystem der Universität Oldenburg, 2000. 601 p. : ill. (some col.) ; 21 cm. ISBN 3-8142-0697-5 DDC 152.1/5
1. Auditory perception - Congresses. 2. Noise - Psychological aspects - Congresses. 3. Sound - Psychological aspects - Congresses. I. Schick, August. II. Meis, Markus. III. Reckhardt, Carsten. IV. Title.
BF251 .O44 2000

OLDER PERSONS. See **AGED.**

OLDER WOMEN. See **AGED WOMEN.**

Olds, Sally Wendkos.
Papalia, Diane E. Human development. 9th ed. Boston : McGraw-Hill, c2004.
BF713 .P35 2004

Oleksy, Wieslaw.
Language function, structure, and change. Frankfurt am Main ; New York : Lang, c2002.
P125 .L36 2002

Oleshkevich, V. I.
Burlakova, N. S. Proektivnye metody. Moskva : In-t obshchegumanitarnykh issledovaniĭ, 2001.
BF698.7 .B87 2001

Olhar acima do horizonte.
Py, Luiz Alberto. Rio de Janeiro : Rocco, 2002.

Oliveira, Francica Bezerra de.
Ensaios. João Pessoa : Editora Universitária, 2001.

Olivetti, Alberto. Gara e bellezza / di Alberto Olivetti. Fiesole, Firenze : Cadmo, c2002. 97 p. ; 17 cm. (Esedra ; 21) Includes bibliographical references and index. CONTENTS: Gara e bellezza -- Arte venatoria, o del contatto. ISBN 88-7923-278-9 DDC 111
1. Corbett, Jim, - 1875-1955. - Man-eating leopard of Rudraprayag. 2. Struggle. 3. Aesthetics. I. Title. II. Series.

Olkiewicz, R. (Robert), 1962-.
Dynamics of dissipation. Berlin ; New York : Springer, c2002.
QC174.85 .D96 2002

Ollivant, Douglas A. Jacques Maritain and the many ways of knowing. Washington, D.C. : American Maritain Association : Distributed by the Catholic University of America Press, c2002.
B2430.M34 J317 2002

Olmstead, Kathleen. The girls' guide to tarot / Kathleen Olmstead ; illustrated by Sandie Turchyn. New York : Sterling Pub., c2002. 128 p. : col. ill. ; 24 cm. Includes index. SUMMARY: Full instructions on how to use tarot cards. Includes ideas for birthdays, parties, storytelling, keeping a journal and designing your own tarot cards. Publisher description URL: http://www.loc.gov/catdir/description/ste021/2002280996.html ISBN 0-8069-8072-9
1. Tarot - Juvenile literature. I. Turchyn, Sandie. II. Title.
BF1879.T2 O38 2002

Olorunfemi, Samuel Jimson. Breaking the evil blood covenant / Samuel Jimson Olorunfemi. Ibadan, Oyo State, Nigeria : Triumphant Faith Publications, 2001. 29 p. ; 17 cm. ISBN 978-34633-7-3
1. Jesus Christ - Blood. 2. Spiritual warfare. 3. Occultism - Religious aspects - Christianity. 4. Satanism. 5. Black author. I. Title.

O'Loughlin, James. The real Warren Buffett : managing capital, leading people / James O'Loughlin. London ; Yarmouth, ME : Nicholas Brealey, 2003. xiv, 260 p. : ill. ; 24 cm. Includes bibliographical references (p. [239]-256) and index. ISBN 1-85788-308-X DDC 658.15092
1. Buffett, Warren. 2. Financial executives - United States - Biography. 3. Leadership. 4. Success in business. I. Title.

Ol'shanskiĭ, D. V. (Dmitriĭ Vadimovich) Psikhologii︠a︡ sovremennoĭ rossiĭskoĭ politiki / D.V. Ol'shanskiĭ. Moskva : Akademicheskiĭ proekt, 2001. 648 p. ; 21 cm. (Gaudeamus. Khrestomatii︠a︡ dli︠a︡ vuzov) Includes bibliographical references. ISBN 5829101467
1. Political culture - Russia (Federation) 2. Political psychology. 3. Russia (Federation) - Politics and government - 1991- I. Title. II. Series: Gaudeamus (Moscow, Russia). Khrestomatii︠a︡ dli︠a︡ vuzov.
JN6699.A15 O46 2001

Olson, Carl. Indian philosophers and postmodern thinkers : dialogues on the margins of culture / Carl Olson. New Delhi ; New York : Oxford University Press, 2002. xv, 331 p. ; 23 cm. Includes bibliographical references (p. [297]-319) and index. ISBN 0-19-565390-4 DDC 181.4
1. Philosophy, Indic. 2. Postmodernism. I. Title.
B131 .O57 2002

Oltre.
Pinotti, Roberto, 1944- Firenze : Olimpia, c2002.

Oltre il paesaggio.
Bonesio, Luisa, 1950- 1. ed. Casalecchio (Bologna) : Arianna, 2002.

OMAN, JOHN, 1860-1939.
Hood, Adam, 1960- Baillie, Oman and Macmurray. Aldershot, England ; Burlington, VT : Ashgate, c2003.
BR110 .H575 2003

Omanut ha-śiḥah.
Raam, Gabriel. Tel-Aviv : Yediʻot aḥaronot : Sifre hemed, c2003.
P95.45 .R33 2003

Omarr, Sydney.
[Astrology, love, sex, and you]
Sydney Omarr's astrology, love, sex, and you. New York : Signet, c2002. 338 p. : ill. ; 18 cm. "Signet astrology." ISBN 0-451-20693-2 (pbk.) DDC 133.5
1. Astrology and sex. 2. Horoscopes. 3. Love - Miscellanea. I. Title. II. Title: Astrology, love, sex, and you
BF1729.S4 O58 2002

Omega book (New York, N.Y.)
Combs, Allan, 1942- The radiance of being. 2nd ed. St. Paul, Minn. : Paragon House, 2002.
BF311 .C575 2002

Demmin, Herbert S., 1959- The ghosts of consciousness. St. Paul, Minn. : Paragon House, c2003.
BF441 .D395 2003

Eisen, Jeffrey S., 1940- Oneness perceived. St. Paul, Minn. : Paragon House, c2003.
BF311 .E39 2003

OMENS. *See also* **SIGNS AND SYMBOLS.**
Śāstrī, Vinoda, 1959- Jyotisha-vijñāna-nirjharī. Jayapura : Rājasthāna Saṃskṛta Akādamī, [2002?]
BF1714.H5 S288 2002

OMENS - ROME - CONGRESSES.
Divination and portents in the Roman world. Odense : Odense University Press, c2000.
BF1768 .D57 2000

OMENS - RUSSIA (FEDERATION).
Turovich, V. (Vasiliĭ) 1000 primet pogody. Perm' : Izd-vo "Poligrafist", 1997.
BF1777 .T87 1997

OMNI-IV PERSONALITY DISORDER INVENTORY.
Loranger, Armand W. (Armand Walter), 1930- OMNI personality inventories. Lutz, FL : Psychological Assessment Resources, c2001.
BF698.8.O46 L67 2001

OMNI personality inventories.
Loranger, Armand W. (Armand Walter), 1930- Lutz, FL : Psychological Assessment Resources, c2001.
BF698.8.O46 L67 2001

OMNI PERSONALITY INVENTORY.
Loranger, Armand W. (Armand Walter), 1930- OMNI personality inventories. Lutz, FL : Psychological Assessment Resources, c2001.
BF698.8.O46 L67 2001

Omul dialogal.
Tonoiu, Vasile. Bucureşti : Editura Fundaţiei Culturale Române, 1995.

On anxiety.
Salecl, Renata, 1962- 1st ed. London ; New York : Routledge, 2004.
BF575.A6 S25 2004

On becoming a leader.
Bennis, Warren G. [Rev. ed.]. Cambridge, MA : Perseus Pub., c2003.
BF637.L4 B37 2003

On behavior.
Pryor, Karen, 1932- 1st ed. North Bend, Wash. : Sunshine Books, c1995.
BF637.B4 P68 1995

On being ill.
Woolf, Virginia, 1882-1941. Ashfield, Mass. : Paris Press, 2002.
PR6045.O72 O5 2002

On Epictetus' "Handbook 1-26".
Simplicius, of Cilicia. [Commentarius in Enchiridion Epicteti. 1-26. English] Ithaca, N.Y. : Cornell University Press, 2002.
B561.M523 S5613 2002

On escape.
Lévinas, Emmanuel. [De l'evasion. English] Stanford, Calif. : Stanford University Press, 2003.
BD331 .L459613 2003

On friendship.
Brown, H. Jackson, 1940- Nashville, Tenn. : Rutledge Hill Press, c1996.
BF575.F66 B76 1996

On human nature.
Burke, Kenneth, 1897- Berkeley : University of California Press, c2003.
B945.B771 R84 2003

On interpretation : studies in culture, law, and the sacred / edited by Andrew D. Weiner and Leonard V. Kaplan ; associate editor, Sonja Hansard-Weiner. Madison, Wis. : University of Wisconsin Press for the University of Wisconsin Law School, c2002. 291 p. : ill. ; 28 cm. (Graven images ; v. 5) Includes bibliographical references. ISBN 0-299-17894-3
1. Law and literature. 2. Culture and law. 3. Religion and law. 4. Law - Interpretation and construction. 5. Hermeneutics. I. Weiner, Andrew D. II. Kaplan, Leonard V. III. Hansard-Weiner, Sonja. IV. University of Wisconsin--Madison. Law School. V. Series.

On liberty.
Mill, John Stuart, 1806-1873. New Haven : Yale University Press, c2003.
JC585 .M76 2003

Mill, John Stuart, 1806-1873. Utilitarianism ; 2nd ed. Malden, MA : Blackwell Pub., 2003.
B1602 .A5 2003

'Oṅ' Mraṅ'', 'Aṅ'gyaṅ'nīyā Ū''. 'Iṃ' chok' maṅgalā kyaṃ'" / pru cu sū 'Aṅ'gyaṅ'nīyā Ū'' 'Oṅ' Mraṅ''. Mantale" : Krī'' pvā'' re'' Cā 'up' Tuik', 2002. 69 p. : ill. ; 20 cm. At head of title: Mraṅ' mā' rui'' rā gehavidhī. At head of title: Buddha vaṅ', mahā vaṅ', rāja vaṅ' myā' nhaṅ' bisukā kyaṃ'" myā" mha kok' nut' taṅ' pra 'ap' so Mraṅ' mā' rui'' rā gehavidhī. In Burmese. SUMMARY : Astrological geomantic considerations and occultism in Burmese architecture. Includes bibliographical references (p. 68-69).
1. Astrological geomancy - Burma. 2. Architecture - Burma. 3. Occultism - Burma. I. Title. II. Title: Mraṅ' mā' rui'' rā gehavidhī III. Title: Buddha vaṅ', mahā vaṅ', rāja vaṅ' myā" nhaṅ'' bisukā kyaṃ'" myā" mha kok' nut' taṅ' pra 'ap' so Mraṅ' mā' rui'' rā gehavidhī
BF1779.A88 O56 2002

On ne choisit pas ses parents.
Pierron, Jean-Philippe. [Paris] : Seuil, c2003.

On ordered liberty.
Gregg, Samuel, 1969- Lanham, MD : Lexington Books, c2003.
JC585 .G744 2003

On our mind.
Giora, Rachel, 1945- New York : Oxford University Press, c2003.
BF455 .G525 2003

On our way.
Kastenbaum, Robert. Berkeley : University of California Press, c2004.
BF789.D4 .K365 2004

On social evaluation : the thought of evaluative activities on social group as subject.
Chen, Xinhan. She hui ping jia lun. Di 1 ban. Shanghai : Shanghai she hui ke xue yuan chu ban she : Xin hua shu dian Shanghai fa xing suo fa xing, 1997.
HM131 .C7135 1997 <Asian China>

On the future of history.
Breisach, Ernst. Chicago : University of Chicago Press, c2003.
HM449 .B74 2003

ON-THE-JOB STRESS. *See* **JOB STRESS.**

ON-THE-JOB TRAINING. *See* **EMPLOYEES - TRAINING OF.**

On the meaning of life.
Thomson, Garrett. Australia ; United States : Thomson/Wadsworth, c2003.
BD431 .T296 2003

On the shoulders of giants : the great works of physics and astronomy / edited, with commentary, by Stephen Hawking. Philadelphia : Running Press, c2002. xiii, 1264 p. : ill. ; 24 cm. Includes bibliographical references. CONTENTS: Nicolaus Copernicus (1473-1543): His life and work; On the revolution of heavenly spheres -- Galileo Galilei (1564-1642): His life and work; Dialogues concerning two sciences -- Johannes Kepler (1571-1630): His life and work; Harmony of the world, Book 5 -- Sir Isaac Newton (1643-1727): His life and work; Principia --- Albert Einstein (1879-1955): His life and work; Selections from The principle of relativity. ISBN 0-7624-1348-4 DDC 520
1. Physics. 2. Astronomy. I. Hawking, S. W. (Stephen W.)
QC6.2 .O5 2002

On the threshold of a new age with Medhananda.
Medhananda, 1908-1994. [Au fil de l'eternitè avec Medhananda. English. Selections] 1st ed. Pondicherry : Sri Mira Trust, 2000.
B841 .M4313 2000

On the threshold of overcivilization.
Kuz'menko, Volodymyr. Na porozi nadt͡syvilizat͡siï. L'viv : "Universum", 1998.
HM901 .K89 1998

On things that really matter.
Brown, H. Jackson, 1940- Nashville, Tenn. : Rutledge Hill Press, c1999.
BF637.C5 B777 1999

On this journey we call our life.
Hollis, James, 1940- Toronto, Ont. : Inner City Books, c2003.
BF697.5.S43 H65 2003

Hollis, James, 1940- Toronto : Inner City Books, c2003.

Oñcēri, Līlā.
Padma, N. K., 1956- Navam and the Karṇāṭak group kṛtis. New Delhi : Kanishka Publishers, Distributors, 2002.
ML338 .P197 2002

One encounter, one chance.
Webster-Doyle, Terrence, 1940- 1st Weatherhill ed. Trumbull, CT : Weatherhill, 2000.
GV1114.3 .W43 2000

ONE-FAMILY HOUSES. *See* **ARCHITECTURE, DOMESTIC; DWELLINGS.**

One hundred one ways black women can learn to love themselves.
Walker, Jamie. 101 ways black women can learn to love themselves. Washington, D.C. : J.D. Publishing, c2002.
1. Black author.

One hundred thoughts that lead to happiness.
Chetkin, Len. 100 thoughts that lead to happiness. Charlottesville, VA : Hampton Roads Pub., c2002.
BF637.C5 C477 2002

One in a million.
Gott, Robert. Littleton, Mass. : Sundance, c2001.
BF1175 .G68 2001

ONE THOUSAND, A.D.
Année mille An Mil. Aix-en-Provence : Publications de l'université de Provence, 2002.

One thousand symbols.
Shepherd, Rowena. 1000 symbols. New York : Thames & Hudson, 2002.
BF458 .S63 2002

One thousands.
The 1000s. San Diego, Calif. : Greenhaven Press, c2001.
CB354.3 .A16 2001

The one true platonic heaven.
Casti, J. L. Washington, D.C. : Joseph Henry Press, c2003.
Q175 .C4339 2003

One world.
Singer, Peter, 1946- New Haven, Conn. : London : Yale University Press, 2002.

O'Neil, Jennifer. Decorating with funky shui : how to lighten up, loosen up, and have fun decorating your home / Jennifer O'Neil and Kitty O'Neil. Kansas City, MO : Andrews McMeel, 2004. p. cm. ISBN 0-7407-4199-3 DDC 133.3/337
1. Feng shui. I. O'Neil, Kitty, 1965- II. Title.
BF1779.F4 O54 2004

O'Neil, Kitty, 1965-.
O'Neil, Jennifer. Decorating with funky shui. Kansas City, MO : Andrews McMeel, 2004.
BF1779.F4 O54 2004

O'Neill, Terry, 1944-.
Haunted houses. San Diego, Calif. : Greenhaven Press, 2004.
BF1475 .H32 2004

Oneness perceived.
Eisen, Jeffrey S., 1940- St. Paul, Minn. : Paragon House, c2003.
BF311 .E39 2003

Oneroso Di Lisa, Fiorangela.
L'inconscio antinomico. Milano : F. Angeli, c1999.
BF315 .I56 1999

Ong-Van-Cung, Kim Sang.
Descartes, René, 1596-1650. [Regulae ad directionem

ingenii. French] Règles pour la direction de l'esprit. Paris : Librairie générale française, c2002.

Onken, Julia, 1942- Die Kirschen in Nachbars Garten : von den Ursachen fürs Fremdgehen und den Bedingungen fürs Daheimbleiben / Julia Onken. Vollständige Taschenbuchausg. München : Goldmann, 1999. 379 p. ; 19 cm. Includes bibliographical references. ISBN 3-442-15026-4
1. Adultery. 2. Man-woman relationships. I. Title.

ONLINE COMMERCE. See **ELECTRONIC COMMERCE.**

The only bad mistake you make is the one you never learn from.
Dawson, Douglas E. Mt. Holly, N.C. : Elias Alexander Press, c2002.
BF323.E7 D38 2002

The only negotiating guide you'll ever need.
Stark, Peter B. 1st ed. New York : Broadway Books, 2003.
BF637.N4 S725 2003

ONOMASIOLOGY. See **REFERENCE (LINGUISTICS).**

Het onschatbare subject.
Rosseel, Eric. Brussel : VUBPress, c2001.
BF697.5.S65 R67 2001

ONTOGENY.
Minelli, Alessandro. The development of animal form. Cambridge ; New York : Cambridge University Press, 2003.
QH491 .M559 2003

Ontologie und Dialektik.
Tietz, Udo. Wien : Passagen, c2003.
B3279.H49 T54 2003

ONTOLOGY. See also **CATEGORIES (PHILOSOPHY); METAPHYSICS; PERSPECTIVE (PHILOSOPHY); PHILOSOPHICAL ANTHROPOLOGY; SPIRITUALISM (PHILOSOPHY); SUBSTANCE (PHILOSOPHY).**
Alackapally, Sebastian, 1961- Being and meaning. 1st ed. Delhi : Motilal Banarsidass Publishers, 2002.
PK541.B48 A43 2002

Balmès, Marc. Pour un plein accès à l'acte d'être avec Thomas d'Aquin et Aristote. Paris : Harmattan, c2003.

Barsotti, Bernard. Bachelard critique de Husserl. Paris : Harmattan, c2002.
B2430.B254 B37 2002

Binayemotlagh, Saïd. Etre et liberté selon Platon. Paris : Harmattan, 2002.
B395 .B553 2002

Blanchette, Oliva. Philosophy of being. Washington, D.C. : Catholic University of America Press, c2003.
BD331 .B565 2003

Carman, Taylor, 1965- Heidegger's analytic. Cambridge, UK ; New York : Cambridge University Press, 2003.
B3279.H48 S459 2003

Caropreso, Paolo. Von der Dingfrage zur Frage nach Gott. Berlin ; New York : W. de Gruyter, 2003.

Chattopadhyaya, Gauri, 1950- Advaitic ontology and epistemology. 1st ed. Allahabad : Raka Prakashan, 2001.
B132.A3+

Chiurazzi, Gaetano. Modalità ed esistenza. Torino : Trauben, c2001.
BD314 .C458 2001

Clair, André. Sens de l'existence. Paris : Armand Colin, c2002.

Clam, Jean. Was heisst, sich an Differenz statt an Identität orientieren? Konstanz : UVK Verlagsgesellschaft, c2002.

Cox, Christoph, 1965- Nietzsche. Berkeley : University of California Press, c1999.
B3318.K7 C68 1999

Cruickshank, Justin, 1969- Realism and sociology. London ; New York : Routledge, 2003.
HM511 .C78 2003

Guénon, René. [Etats multiples de l'être. English] The multiple states of the being. 2nd English ed. Ghent, NY : Sophia Perennis, c2001.
BD312 .G813 2001

Heil, John. From an ontological point of view. Oxford : Clarendon Press ; New York : Oxford University Press, 2003.
BD306 .F76 2003

Hüntelmann, Rafael. Existenz und Modalität. Frankfurt a. M. ; New York : Hänsel-Hohenhausen, c2002.
BD331 .H86 2002

Jadacki, Jacek Juliusz. From the viewpoint of the Lvov-Warsaw school. Amsterdam ; New York, NY : Rodopi, 2003.

Jambet, Christian. L'acte d'être. [Paris] : Fayard, c2002.

Ledda, Antonio. La fenomelogia tra essenza ed esistenza. 1. ed. Roma : Carocci editore, 2002.

Le leggi del pensiero tra logica, ontologia e psicologia. Milano : UNICOPLI, 2002.

Lévinas, Emmanuel. [De l'evasion. English] On escape = Stanford, Calif. : Stanford University Press, 2003.
BD331 .L459613 2003

Luciani Rivero, Rafael Francisco. El misterio de la diferencia. Roma : Pontificia università gregoriana, 2001.

Mavouangui, David, 1953- Jean-Paul Sartre. Paris : Paari, [2002], c2001.

Paź, Bogusław. Epistemologiczne założenia ontologii Christiana Wolffa. Wrocław : Wydawn. Uniwersytetu Wrocławskiego, 2002.

Rea, Michael C. (Michael Cannon), 1968- World without design. Oxford : Clarendon Press ; New York : Oxford University Press, 2002.
B828.2 .R43 2002

Solodin, A. I. Strategii͡a ontologicheskoĭ igry. Sankt-Peterburg : Aletei͡a, 2002.
BF237 .S6 2002

Tietz, Udo. Ontologie und Dialektik. Wien : Passagen, c2003.
B3279.H49 T54 2003

Towards the semantic web. Chichester, England ; Hoboken, N.J. : J. Wiley, c2003.
TK5105.88815 .T68 2003

Vallicella, William F. A paradigm theory of existence. Dordrecht ; Boston : Kluwer Academic, c2002.
BD331 .V36 2002

Witherall, Arthur, 1966- The problem of existence. Aldershot, England ; Brookfield, VT : Ashgate, c2002.
BD331 .W58 2002

Witt, Charlotte, 1951- Ways of being. Ithaca : Cornell University Press, 2003.
B434 .W59 2003

Yu, Jiyuan. The structure of being in Aristotle's Metaphysics. Dordrecht, Boston : Kluwer Academic, c2003.
B434 .Y8 2003

Zubiri, Xavier. [Estructura dinámica de la realidad. English] Dynamic structure of reality. Urbana : University of Illinois Press, 2003.
B4568.Z83 E7713 2003

Ontonòesis.
Ruffinengo, Pier Paolo, 1937- 1. ed. Genova : Marietti, 2002.

Onyechere Osigwe Anyiam-Osigwe memorial lecture series
(1999) The search for a holistic approach to human existence and development. [Nigeria?] : Osigwe Anyiam-Osigwe Foundation, [1999?]
B53 .E46 1999

OOTW (MILITARY SCIENCE). See **ARMED FORCES - OPERATIONS OTHER THAN WAR.**

Opata, Damian U. (Damian Ugwutikiri) Towards a genealogy of African time / Damian Ugwutikiri Opata. Nsukka, Nigeria : AP Express Publishing Company Lt., 2001. v, 93 p. ; 18 cm. Includes bibliographical references (p. 91-93).
1. Time - Social aspects - Nigeria. 2. Time - Philosophy. 3. Time perception. 4. Time - Sociological aspects. 5. Time management. 6. Social interaction - Nigeria. 7. Nigeria - Social life and customs. 8. Black author. I. Title.

Opdahl, Keith M., 1934- Emotion as meaning : the literary case for how we imagine / Keith M. Opdahl. Lewisburg [Pa.] : Bucknell University Press ; London ; Cranbury, NJ : Associated University Presses, c2002. 301 p. ; 24 cm. Includes bibliogaphical references (p. 271-287) and index. ISBN 0-8387-5521-6 (alk. paper) DDC 809/.93350
1. Emotions in literature. 2. Fiction - History and criticism. I. Title.
PN56.E6 O54 2002

OPEN LEARNING. See **ADULT EDUCATION; DISTANCE EDUCATION.**

OPEN PRICE SYSTEM. See **COMPETITION.**

OPEN SYSTEMS (PHYSICS).
Dynamics of dissipation. Berlin ; New York : Springer, c2002.
QC174.85 .D96 2002

Opening Skinner's box.
Slater, Lauren. 1st ed. New York : W.W. Norton, c2004.
BF198.7 .S57 2004

Opening the Tanya.
Steinsaltz, Adin. [Be'ur Tanya. English] 1st ed. San Francisco : Jossey-Bass, c2003.
BM198.2.S563 S7413 2003

OPERA - COSTUME. See **COSTUME.**

Opera omnia
(6) Alberione, James, 1884-1971. La donna associata allo zelo sacerdotale. Cinisello Balsamo, Milano : San Paolo, c2001.

OPERANT BEHAVIOR.
Malott, Richard W. Principles of behavior. 5th ed. Upper Saddle River, N.J. : Pearson/Prentice Hall, 2003.
BF319.5.O6 M34 2003

Rumbaugh, Duane M., 1929- Respondents, operants, and emergents [microform]. [Washington, D.C. : National Aeronautics and Space Administration, 1997]

OPERAS - CHARACTERS.
Flem, Lydia. La voix des amants. [Paris] : Seuil, c2002.

OPERAS - EXCERPTS.
Hann, Georg. Georg Hann [sound recording]. [Germany] : Preiser Records, p2001.

Malaniuk, Ira. Arien und Lieder [sound recording]. [Germany] : Preiser Records, p2000.

OPERATIONS OTHER THAN WAR (MILITARY SCIENCE). See **ARMED FORCES - OPERATIONS OTHER THAN WAR.**

Operations research/computer science interfaces series
(ORCS 26) Koutsoukis, Nikitas-Spiros. Decision modelling and information systems. Boston : Kluwer Academic Publishers, c2003.
T57.95 .K68 2003

Opere magiche.
Bruno, Giordano, 1548-1600. Milano : Adelphi, 2000.
BF1600 .B78 2000

OPERETTAS. See **OPERAS.**

Opevalova, E. V. (Ekaterina Vasil'evna).
Psikhologicheskai͡a sluzhba v obshchestve. Komsomol'sk-na-Amure : Komsomol'skiĭ-na-Amure gos. pedagogicheskiĭ universitet, 2002.
BF20 .P743 2002

OPINION, PUBLIC. See **PUBLIC OPINION.**

Opolskie Towarzystwo Przyjaciół Nauk.
Język w przestrzeni społecznej. Opole : Uniwersytet Opolski, 2002.
P40 .J492 2002

Opon Ifa series.
Osofisan, Femi. Literature and the pressures of freedom. Nigeria : Opon Ifa Readers, 2001.

Opotow, Susan.
Identity and the natural environment. Cambridge, Mass. : MIT Press, 2004.
BF353 .I34 2004

Oppenheim, David.
Revealing the inner worlds of young children. New York : Oxford University Press, 2003.
BF723.S74 A37 2003

The opportunity in every problem.
Taylor, Scott L., 1964- 1st ed. Salt Lake City : Gibbs Smith, c2003.
BF637.S8 T285 2003

The opposite of fate.
Tan, Amy New York : Putnam c2003.
PS3570.A48 Z47 2003

OPPRESSION (PSYCHOLOGY).
Bishop, Anne, 1950- Becoming an ally. 2nd ed. London ; New York : Zed Books ; Halifax, N.S. :

Optical illusions.

Fernwood Pub. ; New York : Distributed in the USA exclusively by Palgrave, 2002.
HM1256 .B57 2002

OPTICAL ILLUSIONS.
Geiger, John, 1960- Chapel of extreme experience. 1st ed. Toronto, Ont. : Gutter Press, c2002.
QP495 .G45 2002

Ross, Helen Elizabeth, 1935- The mystery of the moon illusion. Oxford ; New York : Oxford University Press, 2002.
QP495 .R67 2002

OPTICAL IMAGES.
Les dons de l'image. Paris : Harmattan, 2003.

OPTICS. *See* **COLOR; PERSPECTIVE.**

OPTICS, PSYCHOLOGICAL. *See* **VISUAL PERCEPTION.**

OPTIMISM.
Carr, Alan, Dr. Positive psychology. London ; New York : Brunner-Routledge, 2004.
BF121 .C355 2004

MacDonald, Lucy, 1953- Learn to be an optimist. San Francisco : Chronicle Books, 2004.
BF698.35.O57 M23 2004

Optimize your life with the one-page strategic planner.
Dahl, Bernhoff A., 1938- Bangor, Me. : Wind-Breaker Press, c2003.
BF637.S8 D26 2003

OPTOELECTRONIC DEVICES. *See* **TELEVISION.**

Or ha-daʻat.
Vainshtok, Bentsiyon Mosheh Yaʻir ben Mordekhai David. Sefer Or ha-daʻat. Yerushalayim : ha-Makhon le-hotsaʼat sifre ha-g. R. M.Y. Vainshtok, 762 [2001 or 2002]

Or ha-ḥayim.
Lugasi, Yaʻakov Yiśraʼel. Yalkut Or ha-ḥayim ha-ḳadosh. Yerushalayim : [h. mo. l], 762 [2001 or 2002]

Or zoreaḥ.
Ḥayim Yeroḥam ben Shimshon Meshulam Feybish, mi-Snatin. Sefer Asefat divre ḥakhamim. Yerushalayim : Mekhon Sod yesharim, 761 [2001]

Oracle of ancient knowledge for today.
Bonewitz, Ra. Wisdom of the Maya. 1st St. Martin's ed. New York : St. Martin's Press, 2000.
BF1878 .B66 2000

The oracle of Kabbalah.
Seidman, Richard. 1st ed. New York : St. Martin's Press, 2001.
PJ4589 .S42 2001

The Oracle series
(bk. 2) Oracle (Writer) The Oracle teachings. 1st ed. Kauaʻi, Hawaiʻi : Oracle Productions, c1996.
BF637.S4 O72 1996

The Oracle teachings.
Oracle (Writer) 1st ed. Kauaʻi, Hawaiʻi : Oracle Productions, c1996.
BF637.S4 O72 1996

Oracle (Writer) The Oracle teachings : soul over mind / the Oracle. 1st ed. Kauaʻi, Hawaiʻi : Oracle Productions, c1996. 222 p. : ill. ; 23 cm. (The Oracle series ; bk. 2) ISBN 0-9648443-3-8 (pbk.)
1. Self-actualization (Psychology) 2. Self-realization. 3. Ethics. I. Title. II. Series.
BF637.S4 O72 1996

ORACLES.
Rainieri, Caelum. The Nahualli animal oracle. Rochester, Vt. : Bear & Co., 2003.
BF1773 .R35 2003

Schilling, Dennis R. Spruch und Zahl. Aalen : Scientia, 1998.
BF1770.C5 S42 1998

Wood, Michael, 1936- The road to Delphi. 1st ed. New York : Farrar, Straus and Giroux, 2003.
PN56.O63 W66 2003

Oracles Chaldaïques.
Gemistus Plethon, George, 15th cent. [Magika logia tōn apo Zōroastrou magōn. French & Greek] Magika logia tōn apo Zōroastrou magōn. Athēnai : Akadēmia Athēnōn, 1995.
BF1762 .G45 1995

ORACLES - CONGRESSES.
Colloque de Strasbourg (14th : 1995) Oracles et prophéties dans l'Antiquité. Strasbourg : Publications de l'Université de Strasbourg II, 1997.
BF1761 .C65 1995

ORACLES - EARLY WORKS TO 1800.
Gemistus Plethon, George, 15th cent. [Magika logia tōn apo Zōroastrou magōn. French & Greek] Magika logia tōn apo Zōroastrou magōn. Athēnai : Akadēmia Athēnōn, 1995.
BF1762 .G45 1995

Oracles et prophéties dans l'Antiquité.
Colloque de Strasbourg (14th : 1995) Strasbourg : Publications de l'Université de Strasbourg II, 1997.
BF1761 .C65 1995

ORACLES, GREEK.
Buitenwerf, Rieuwerd. Book III of the Sibylline oracles and its social setting. Leiden ; Boston, MA : Brill, 2003.
BF1769 .B85 2003

ORACLES IN LITERATURE.
Wood, Michael, 1936- The road to Delphi. 1st ed. New York : Farrar, Straus and Giroux, 2003.
PN56.O63 W66 2003

Oracles magiques des mages disciples de Zoroastre.
Gemistus Plethon, George, 15th cent. [Magika logia tōn apo Zōroastrou magōn. French & Greek] Magika logia tōn apo Zōroastrou magōn. Athēnai : Akadēmia Athēnōn, 1995.
BF1762 .G45 1995

ORACULA SIBYLLINA. BOOK 3.
Buitenwerf, Rieuwerd. Book III of the Sibylline oracles and its social setting. Leiden ; Boston, MA : Brill, 2003.
BF1769 .B85 2003

Oracula sibyllina. Book 3. English.
Buitenwerf, Rieuwerd. Book III of the Sibylline oracles and its social setting. Leiden ; Boston, MA : Brill, 2003.
BF1769 .B85 2003

ORAL BIOGRAPHY. *See* **ORAL HISTORY.**

ORAL COMMUNICATION. *See also* **CONVERSATION; ORAL TRADITION; SPEECH.**
Marcuschi, Luiz Antônio. Investigando a relação oral/escrito e as teorias do letramento. Campinas, SP : Mercado de Letras, 2001.

Raam, Gabriel. Omanut ha-śiḥah. Tel-Aviv : Yediʻot aharonot : Sifre ḥemed, c2003.
P95.45 .R33 2003

Roelcke, Thorsten. Kommunikative Effizienz. Heidelberg : Winter, c2002.

ORAL COMMUNICATION - RELIGIOUS ASPECTS - JUDAISM.
Sefer Ḳedushat ha-dibur. Bene Beraḳ : Yehudah Yosef Ha-leyi Gruber, 761- [2001-]

ORAL HABITS. *See* **FOOD HABITS; SMOKING.**

ORAL HISTORY. *See also* **ORAL TRADITION.**
Ritchie, Donald A., 1945- Doing oral history. 2nd ed. Oxford ; New York : Oxford University Press, c2003.
D16.14 .R57 2003

ORAL HISTORY - HANDBOOKS, MANUALS, ETC.
Sommer, Barbara W. The oral history manual. Walnut Creek, CA ; Oxford : Altamira Press, c2002.
D16.14 .S69 2002

The oral history manual.
Sommer, Barbara W. Walnut Creek, CA ; Oxford : Altamira Press, c2002.
D16.14 .S69 2002

ORAL HISTORY - METHODOLOGY.
Ritchie, Donald A., 1945- Doing oral history. 2nd ed. Oxford ; New York : Oxford University Press, c2003.
D16.14 .R57 2003

ORAL HISTORY - METHODOLOGY.
Sommer, Barbara W. The oral history manual. Walnut Creek, CA ; Oxford : Altamira Press, c2002.
D16.14 .S69 2002

ORAL LITERATURE. *See* **FOLK LITERATURE.**

ORAL SELF-DEFENSE. *See* **VERBAL SELF-DEFENSE.**

ORAL TRADITION. *See* **FOLKLORE; ORAL HISTORY.**

ORAL TRADITION - MISSISSIPPI.
Mould, Tom, 1969- Choctaw prophecy. Tuscaloosa : University of Alabama Press, c2003.
E99.C8 M68 2003

ORAL TRANSMISSION. *See* **ORAL COMMUNICATION.**

ORATORY. *See* **EXPRESSION; GESTURE; PERSUASION (RHETORIC).**

Orbis (Louvain, Belgium). Supplementa
(t. 19.) Grammatical theory and philosophy of language in antiquity. Leuven ; Sterling, Va. : Peeters, 2002.
P63 .G73 2002

ORDEAL - RELIGIOUS ASPECTS - JUDAISM.
Pinter, Leib. Sefer ʻAśarah nisyonot. Brooklyn, N.Y. : E.Y.L. Pinter, c[2002?]

El orden frágil de la arquitectura.
Español Llorens, Joaquim. Barcelona : Fundación Caja de Arquitectos, c2001.

Order and justice in international relations / edited by Rosemary Foot, John Gaddis, and Andrew Hurrell. Oxford ; New York : Oxford University Press, 2003. xiv, 313 p. ; 25 cm. Includes bibliographical references (p. [287]-292) and index. CONTENTS: Order and justice in international relations: what is at stake? / Andrew Hurrell -- Order/justice issues at the United Nations / Adam Roberts -- Order, justice, the IMF, and the World Bank / Ngaire Woods -- Order and justice in the international trade system / John Toye -- Order and justice beyond the nation-state: Europe's competing paradigms / Kalypso Nicolaidis and Justine Lacroix -- Order versus justice: an American foreign policy dilemma / John Lewis Gaddis -- Russian perspectives on order and justice / S. Neil MacFarlane -- An uneasy engagement: Chinese ideas of global order and justice in historical perspective / Rana Mitter -- Indian conceptions of order and justice: Nehruvian, Gandhian, Hindutva, and neo-liberal / Kanti Bajpai -- Order, justice, and global Islam / James Piscatori. ISBN 0-19-925120-7 (hard : acid-free paper) ISBN 0-19-925119-3 (pbk. : acid-free paper) DDC 327.1/01
1. International relations. 2. Peace. 3. Security, International. 4. Justice. I. Foot, Rosemary, 1948- II. Gaddis, John Lewis. III. Hurrell, Andrew.
JZ1308 .O73 2003

ORDERS, MAJOR. *See* **CLERGY.**

ORDERS OF KNIGHTHOOD AND CHIVALRY. *See* **KNIGHTS AND KNIGHTHOOD.**

Ordinal measurement in the behavioral sciences.
Cliff, Norman, 1930- Mahwah, N.J. : Lawrence Erlbaum Associates, 2003.
BF39 .C525 2003

Ordinary mind.
Magid, Barry. Boston : Wisdom, c2002.
BQ9286 .M34 2002

Ordo (Hildesheim, Germany)
(Bd. 8.) Kunst und Erinnerung. Köln : Böhlau, 2003.
PN674 .K86 2003

ORDO TEMPLI ORIENTIS.
Starr, Martin P., 1959- The unknown God. Bolingbrook, IL: Teitan Press, 2003.
BF1997.S73 2003

Ordre d'idées
Robin, Régine, 1936- La mémoire saturée. Paris : Stock, 2003.
D16.8 .R59 2003

Ordre philosophique.
Stengers, Isabelle. Penser avec Whitehead. Paris : Seuil, c2002.

Orenstein, Peggy. Women on work, love, children & life / Peggy Orenstein. London : Piatkus, 2000. 322 p. ; 24 cm. "First published as Flux in the USA in 2000." Includes bibliographical references (p. [313]-322). ISBN 0-7499-2140-4 DDC 305.42
1. Women - Interviews. 2. Women - Social conditions. 3. Feminism. 4. Work and family. I. Title.

The organic approach to architecture.
Gans, Deborah. New York ; Chichester : Wiley, 2002.

ORGANIC ARCHITECTURE.
Gans, Deborah. The organic approach to architecture. New York ; Chichester : Wiley, 2002.

The organic codes.
Barbieri, Marcello. Cambridge, UK. ; New York : Cambridge University Press, 2003.
QH331 .B247 2003

Organisation for Economic Co-operation and Development.
Environmentally sustainable buildings. Paris : Organisation for Economic Co-operation and Development, 2002.

Understanding the brain. Paris : Organisation for Economic Co-operation and Development, 2002.

QP360.5 .U54 2002

ORGANISMS, AQUATIC. See **AQUATIC ORGANISMS.**

Organismus und System
(Bd. 3) Virtual reality. Frankfurt am Main ; New York : P. Lang, c2001.
QA76.9.H85 V5815 2001

ORGANIZATION. See also **MANAGEMENT; ORGANIZATIONAL BEHAVIOR; ORGANIZATIONAL CHANGE; PLANNING.**
Autopoietic organization theory. Oslo, Norway : Abstrakt forlag ; Malmö, Sweden : Liber Ekonomi ; Herndon, VA, USA : Copenhagen Business School Press, c2003.
HD31 .A825 2003

ORGANIZATION DEVELOPMENT. See **ORGANIZATIONAL CHANGE.**

The organization man.
Whyte, William Hollingsworth. Philadelphia : University of Pennsylvania Press, c2002, 1956.
BF697 .W47 2002

ORGANIZATION OF AMERICAN STATES - EVALUATION.
Imobighe, Thomas A. The OAU (AU) and OAS in regional conflict management. Ibadan : Spectrum Books ; Oxford, UK : USA distributor, African Books Collective, 2003.
JZ6374 .I46 2003

The organization of hypocrisy.
Brunsson, Nils, 1946- 2nd ed. Oslo : Abstrakt ; Malmö, Sweden : Liber ; Herndon, VA : [Distributor] Copenhagen Business School Press, c2002.

ORGANIZATION - PHILOSOPHY.
Interpreting the maternal organisation. London ; New York : Routledge, 2003.
HM786 .I58 2003

ORGANIZATIONAL BEHAVIOR. See also **CORPORATE CULTURE.**
Harris, O. Jeff. New York : Best Business Books, c2002.
HD58.7 .H36943 2002

Sweeney, Paul D., 1955- Boston : McGraw-Hill Irwin, c2002.
HD58.7 .S953 2002

ORGANIZATIONAL BEHAVIOR.
Allcorn, Seth. The dynamic workplace. Westport, Conn. ; London : Praeger, 2003.
HF5547.2 .A43 2003

Bacon, Terry R. Winning behavior. New York : AMACOM, c2003.
HD58.7 .B3423 2003

Broom, Michael F. The infinite organization. 1st ed. Palo Alto, Calif. : Davies-Black, c2002.
HD58.7 .B755 2002

Brunsson, Nils, 1946- The organization of hypocrisy. 2nd ed. Oslo : Abstrakt ; Malmö, Sweden : Liber ; Herndon, VA : [Distributor] Copenhagen Business School Press, c2002.

The civilized organization. Amsterdam ; Philadelphia : John Benjamins, c2002.
HD58.7 .C593 2002

Cloke, Ken, 1941- The art of waking people up. 1st ed. San Francisco : Jossey-Bass, c2003.
HF5385 .C54 2003

Cohen, Aaron, 1952- Multiple commitments in the workplace. Mahwah, New Jersey : Lawrence Erlbaum Associates, 2003.
HD58.7 .C6213 2003

Discourse and organization. London ; Thousand Oaks, Calif. : Sage Publications, 1998.
HD58.7 .D57 1998

DiVanna, Joseph A. Synconomy. Houndmills [England] ; New York : Palgrave Macmillan, 2003.
HD64.2 .D575 2003

Fekete, Sandra. Companies are people, too. Hoboken, N.J. : John Wiley & Sons, c2003.
HD58.7 .F43 2003

Group behaviour and development. Oxford ; New York : Oxford University Press, 2002.
HD58.7 .G76 2002

Handbook of organizational performance. New York : Haworth Press, c2001.
HD58.7 .H364 2001

Harris, O. Jeff. Organizational behavior. New York : Best Business Books, c2002.
HD58.7 .H36943 2002

Hearn, Jeff. Gender, sexuality and violence in organizations. London ; Thousand Oaks : SAGE, 2001.

Interpreting the maternal organisation. London ; New York : Routledge, 2003.
HM786 .I58 2003

Kallinikos, Jannis. Technology and society. Munich : Accedo : Distributed in the U.S.A. by The Institute of Mind and Behavior, c1996.

Kendra, James M. Elements of community resilience in the World Trade Center attack. [Newark, Del.?] : Disaster Research Center, University of Delaware, 2001.

Kilduff, Martin. Social networks and organizations. London : SAGE, 2003.

Kleiner, Art. Who really matters. 1st ed. New York ; London : Currency/Doubleday, 2003.
HD2741 .K478 2003

Lin, Zhiang. Designing stress resistant organizations. Boston : Kluwer Academic Publishers, c2003.
HD58.8 .L58 2003

Manville, Brook, 1950- A company of citizens. Boston : Harvard Business School Press, c2003.
HD58.7 .M3714 2003

Moore, David (David R.) Project management. Oxford, [Eng.] ; Malden, MA : Blackwell Science, c2002.

Multi-level issues in organizational behavior and strategy. Amsterdam ; London : JAI, 2003.

Organizing business knowledge. Cambridge, Mass. : MIT Press, c2003.
HD30.2 .T67 2003

Psychoanalysis and management. Heidelberg : Physica-Verlag, c1994.
BF175.4.S65 P777 1994

Sweeney, Paul D., 1955- Organizational behavior. Boston : McGraw-Hill Irwin, c2002.
HD58.7 .S953 2002

Text/work. London ; New York : Routledge, 2003.

Thompson, Grahame. Between hierarchies and markets. Oxford ; New York : Oxford University Press, 2003.
HD58.7 .T4786 2003

The trust process in organizations. Cheltenham, UK ; Northampton, MA : Edward Elgar, c2003.
HD58.7 .T744 2003

Vardi, Yoav, 1944- Misbehavior in organizations. Mahwah, NJ ; London : Lawrence Erlbaum, 2004.
HD58.7 .V367 2004

ORGANIZATIONAL BEHAVIOR - DEVELOPING COUNTRIES.
Group behaviour and development. Oxford ; New York : Oxford University Press, 2002.
HD58.7 .G76 2002

ORGANIZATIONAL BEHAVIOR - MORAL AND ETHICAL ASPECTS.
Galford, Robert M., 1952- The trusted leader. New York ; London : Free Press, c2002.
HD57.7 .G33 2002

ORGANIZATIONAL CHANGE.
Brunsson, Nils, 1946- The organization of hypocrisy. 2nd ed. Oslo : Abstrakt ; Malmö, Sweden : Liber ; Herndon, VA : [Distributor] Copenhagen Business School Press, c2002.

Gender, identity and the culture of organizations. London ; New York : Routledge, 2002.
HD58.7 .G46 2002

Government reformed. Aldershot, England ; Burlington, VT : Ashgate, c2003.
JF1525.O73 G686 2003

Guttman, Howard M. When goliaths clash. New York ; London : AMACOM, c2003.
HD42 .G88 2003

Harvard business essentials. Managing change and transition. Boston, Mass. : Harvard Business School Press, c2003.
HD58.8 .M2544 2003

Human resources in the 21st century. Hoboken, N.J. : J. Wiley & Sons, c2003.
HD31 .H81247 2003

Kennedy, Kevin (Kevin John), 1955- Going the distance. Upper Saddle River, NJ : Prentice Hall/ Financial Times, c2003.
HD57.7 .K465 2003

Lin, Zhiang. Designing stress resistant organizations. Boston : Kluwer Academic Publishers, c2003.
HD58.8 .L58 2003

Management. Cambridge, Mass. : MIT Press, 2003.
HD31 .M2928 2003

Martin, Vivien, 1947- Leading change in health and social care. London ; New York : Routledge, 2003.
RA971 .M365 2003

Von Stamm, Bettina. The innovation wave. Chichester : John Wiley & Sons, c2003.

ORGANIZATIONAL CHANGE - MANAGEMENT.
Cunningham, Ian, 1943- The wisdom of strategic learning. London ; New York : McGraw-Hill, c1994.
HD58.8 .C857 1994

Harmon, Paul, 1942- Business process change. Amsterdam ; Boston : Morgan Kaufmann, c2003.
HD58.8 .H37 2003

Harvard business essentials. Managing change and transition. Boston, Mass. : Harvard Business School Press, c2003.
HD58.8 .M2544 2003

Leading in an upside-down world. Toronto : Dundurn Group, c2003.
BF637.L4 L425 2003

Lee, William W. Organizing change. San Francisco : Pfeiffer, c2003.
HD58.8 .L423 2003

Lees, Stan. Global acquisitions. Houndmills [England] ; New York : Palgrave Macmillan, 2003.
HD58.8 .L424 2003

Tsai, Hui-Liang. Information technology and business process reengineering. Westport, Conn. : Praeger, 2003.
HD58.87 .T73 2003

Ward, Andrew. The leadership lifecycle. Houndmills [England] ; New York : Palgrave Macmillan, 2003.
HD57.7 .W367 2003

ORGANIZATIONAL CHANGE - MANAGEMENT - CANADA.
Leading in an upside-down world. Toronto : Dundurn Group, c2003.

ORGANIZATIONAL COMMITMENT.
Cohen, Aaron, 1952- Multiple commitments in the workplace. Mahwah, New Jersey : Lawrence Erlhaum Associates, 2003.
HD58.7 .C6213 2003

ORGANIZATIONAL CULTURE. See **CORPORATE CULTURE.**

ORGANIZATIONAL DEVELOPMENT. See **ORGANIZATIONAL CHANGE.**

Organizational dynamics of creative destruction.
Mezias, Stephen J. Houndmills [England] ; New York : Palgrave Macmillan, 2002.
HB615 .M49 2002

ORGANIZATIONAL EFFECTIVENESS.
Bacon, Terry R. Winning behavior. New York : AMACOM, c2003.
HD58.7 .B3423 2003

Burke, Dan, 1965- Business @ the speed of stupid. Cambridge, MA : Perseus Pub., c2001.
HD45 .B7995 2001

Kennedy, Kevin (Kevin John), 1955- Going the distance. Upper Saddle River, NJ : Prentice Hall/ Financial Times, c2003.
HD57.7 .K465 2003

Kline, Theresa, 1960- Teams that lead. Mahwah, N.J. : L. E. Associates, 2003
HD57.7 .K549 2003

Neely, A. D. (Andy D.) The performance prism. London ; New York : Financial Times/Prentice Hall, 2002.
HF5549.5.P35 N44 2002

New challenges for international leadership. Santa Monica, Calif. : RAND, 2003.
HD57.7 .N488 2003

Ward, William Aidan. Trust and mistrust. Chichester, England ; Hoboken, NJ : John Wiley & Sons, c2003.
HD69.S8 W37 2003

The organizational engineering approach to project management.
Kliem, Ralph L. Boca Raton : St. Lucie Press, c2003.
HD66 .K585 2003

The organizational frontiers series
Personality and work. 1st ed. San Francisco, CA : Jossey-Bass, c2003.
BF698.9.O3 P47 2003

ORGANIZATIONAL INNOVATION. See **ORGANIZATIONAL CHANGE.**

ORGANIZATIONAL LEARNING. See also **KNOWLEDGE MANAGEMENT.**
Greve, Henrich R. Organizational learning from performance feedback. Cambridge : Cambridge University Press, 2003.

Kennedy, Kevin (Kevin John), 1955- Going the distance. Upper Saddle River, NJ : Prentice Hall/Financial Times, c2003.
HD57.7 .K465 2003

Rampersad, Hubert K. Total performance scorecard. Amsterdam ; Boston ; London : Butterworth-Heinemann, c2003.
HD62.15 .R3598 2003

Organizational learning from performance feedback.
Greve, Henrich R. Cambridge : Cambridge University Press, 2003.

ORGANIZATIONAL LEARNING - MANAGEMENT.
Sharing expertise. Cambridge, Mass. : MIT Press, c2003.
HD30.2 .S53 2003

Tsai, Hui-Liang. Information technology and business process reengineering. Westport, Conn. : Praeger, 2003.
HD58.87 .T73 2003

ORGANIZATIONAL SOCIOLOGY.
The civilized organization. Amsterdam ; Philadelphia : John Benjamins, c2002.
HD58.7 .C593 2002

Interpreting the maternal organisation. London ; New York : Routledge, 2003.
HM786 .I58 2003

Kallinikos, Jannis. Technology and society. Munich : Accedo : Distributed in the U.S.A. by The Institute of Mind and Behavior, c1996.

ORGANIZATIONAL STRESS. See **JOB STRESS.**

ORGANIZATIONS. See **ASSOCIATIONS, INSTITUTIONS, ETC.**

ORGANIZATIONS, BUSINESS. See **BUSINESS ENTERPRISES.**

Organizing business knowledge : the MIT process handbook / Thomas W. Malone, Kevin Crowston, and George A. Herman, editors. Cambridge, Mass. : MIT Press, c2003. ix, 619 p. : ill. ; 24 cm. Includes bibliographical references (p. [577]-601) and index. ISBN 0-262-13429-2 (hc. : alk. paper) DDC 658.4/038
1. Knowledge management. 2. Organizational behavior. I. Malone, Thomas W. II. Crowston, Kevin. III. Herman, George A. (George Arthur), 1953- IV. Title: MIT process handbook
HD30.2 .T67 2003

Organizing change.
Lee, William W. San Francisco : Pfeiffer, c2003.
HD58.8 .L423 2003

Organizing for the spirit.
Schlenger, Sunny. 1st ed. San Francisco : Jossey-Bass, c2004.
BF637.S4 S345 2004

Oricha : ritos y prácticas de la religión Yoruba. 1. ed. Barcelona : Editorial Humanitas, 2003. 494 p. : ill. ; 23 cm. ISBN 84-7910-367-1
1. Yoruba (African people) - Cuba. 2. Yoruba (African people) - Religion. 3. Yoruba (African people) - Rites and ceremonies. 4. Orishas. 5. Rites and ceremonies - Cuba.

ORIENT. See **ASIA, SOUTHEASTERN; EAST ASIA; MIDDLE EAST; SOUTH ASIA.**

ORIENT AND OCCIDENT. See **EAST AND WEST.**

Orient-Occident, la fracture imaginaire.
Corm, Georges. Paris : Découverte, 2002.

ORIENTAL CIVILIZATION. See **CIVILIZATION, ORIENTAL.**

ORIENTALISM - HISTORY.
Antinomies of modernity. Durham : Duke University Press, 2003.
CB358 .A59 2003

ORIENTALS. See **ASIANS.**

ORIENTATION. See **ORIENTATION (PHYSIOLOGY).**

ORIENTATION (PHYSIOLOGY).
Schmauks, Dagmar. Orientierung im Raum. Tübingen : Stauffenburg, c2002.
QP443 .S363 2002

ORIENTATION (PSYCHOLOGY). See **GEOGRAPHICAL PERCEPTION; TIME PERCEPTION.**

ORIENTATION, SEXUAL. See **SEXUAL ORIENTATION.**

Orientierung im Raum.
Schmauks, Dagmar. Tübingen : Stauffenburg, c2002.
QP443 .S363 2002

Origin & early evolution of life.
Fenchel, Tom. Origin and early evolution of life. Oxford New York : Oxford University Press, 2002.
QH325 .F42 2002

Origin and early evolution of life.
Fenchel, Tom. Oxford New York : Oxford University Press, 2002.
QH325 .F42 2002

Origin and fate of the universe.
Hawking, S. W. (Stephen W.). [Cambridge lectures] The theory of everything. Beverly Hills, CA : New Millennium Press, c2002, 1996.
QB985 .H39 2002

The origin of illness.
Keppe, Norberto R. [Origem Das Enfermidades. English] 1st American ed. Englewood Cliffs, N.J. : Campbell Hall Press, 2002.
RC460 .K4713 2002

The origin of love.
Ōkawa, Ryūhō, 1956- [Ai no genten. English] New York : Lantern Books, c2003.
BP605.K55 O29513 2003

ORIGIN OF SPECIES. See **EVOLUTION (BIOLOGY).**

ORIGIN (PHILOSOPHY).
Mircea, Corneliu. Originarul. București : Paideia, 2000.
BD638 .M573 2000

Original self.
Moore, Thomas, 1940- 1st ed. New York : HarperCollins, c2000.
BL624 .M6643 2000

Original self : living with paradox and originality.
Moore, Thomas, 1940- Original self. 1st ed. New York : HarperCollins, c2000.
BL624 .M6643 2000

The original Yoga : as expounded in Śivasaṃhitā, Gheraṇḍasaṃhitā and Pātañjala Yogasūtra : original text in Sanskrit / translated, edited, and annotated with an introduction by Shyam Ghosh. 2nd rev. ed. New Delhi : Munshiram Manoharlal Publishers, 1999. xxiii, 262 p. ; 23 cm. Includes index. English and Sanskrit. ISBN 81-215-0891-6 ISBN 81-215-0892-4 (soft) DDC 181/.45
1. Yoga. I. Ghosh, Shyam. II. Patañjali. Yogasūtra. III. Title: Śivasaṃhitā. English & Sanskrit. IV. Title: Gheraṇḍasaṃhitā. English & Sanskrit.
B132.Y6 O74 1999

ORIGINALITY. See **CREATION (LITERARY, ARTISTIC, ETC.).**

Originarul.
Mircea, Corneliu. București : Paideia, 2000.
BD638 .M573 2000

Origination of organismal form : beyond the gene in developmental and evolutionary biology / edited by Gerd B. Müller and Stuart A. Newman. Cambridge, Mass. : MIT Press, c2003. vi, 332 p. : ill. ; 24 cm. (The Vienna series in theoretical biology) "A Bradford book." Includes bibliographical references and index. ISBN 0-262-13419-5 (hc. : alk. paper) DDC 571.3
1. Morphogenesis. 2. Evolution (Biology) I. Müller, Gerd (Gerd B.) II. Newman, Stuart. III. Series.
QH491 .O576 2003

L'origine des génies.
Thélot, Claude. Paris : Seuil, c2003.

The origins of life and the universe.
Lurquin, Paul F. New York : Columbia University Press, c2003.
QH325 .L87 2003

Origins of modern witchcraft.
Aoumiel. 1st ed. St. Paul, Minn. : Llewellyn Publications, 2000 (2002 printing)
BF1566 .A56 2000

Origins of psychopathology.
Fabrega, Horacio. New Brunswick, N.J. : Rutgers University Press, c2002.
RC454.4 .F33 2002

Oring, Elliott, 1945- Engaging humor / Elliott Oring. Urbana : University of Illinois Press, c2003. xii, 208 p. : ill. ; 24 cm. Includes bibliographical references (p. [163]-202) and index. ISBN 0-252-02786-8 (alk. paper) DDC 809.7
1. Wit and humor - History and criticism. 2. Comic, The. I. Title.
PN6147 .O74 2003

Orio de Miguel, Bernardino, 1936- Leibniz y el pensamiento hermético : a propósito de los "Cogitata in genesim" de F.M. van Helmont / Bernardino Orio de Miguel. Valencia : Universidad Politécnica de Valéncia, Editorial U.P.V., [2002] 2 v. (580 p.) : ill. ; 24 cm. (Colección Leibnizius politechnicus ; no. 3) Includes bibliographical references and index. ISBN 84-970514-4-0 (Obra Completa) ISBN 84-970514-5-9 (Tomo 1) ISBN 84-970514-6-7 (Tomo 2)
1. Helmont, Franciscus Mercurius van, - 1614-1699. 2. Leibniz, Gottfried Wilhelm, - Freiherr von, - 1646-1716. 3. Bible. - O.T. - Genesis - Commentaries - History and criticism. 4. Bible. - O.T. - Genesis - Commentaries. 5. Philosophy, Modern - 17th century. I. Leibniz, Gottfried Wilhelm, Freiherr von, 1646-1716. II. Helmont, Franciscus Mercurius van, 1614-1699. III. Title. IV. Series.

ORISHAS.
Beniste, José. As águas de Oxalá = Rio de Janeiro, RJ, [Brazil] : Editora Bertrand Brasil, c2001 (2002 printing)
BL2592.C35 B46 2001

Oricha. 1. ed. Barcelona : Editorial Humanitas, 2003.

Verger, Pierre. Saída de Iaô. Sao Paulo : Fundação Pierre Verger : Axis Mundi Editora, 2002.

Orłowski, Hubert.
Polacy i niemcy. òznań : Wydawn. Poznańskie, 2003.
DK4121 .P65 2003

Ormrod, Jeanne Ellis. Human learning / Jeanne Ellis Ormrod. 4th ed. Upper Saddle River, N.J. : Merrill, c2004. 1 v. (various pagings) : ill. (some col.) ; 25 cm. Includes bibliographical references and indexes. ISBN 0-13-094199-9 DDC 153.1/5
1. Learning, Psychology of. 2. Behaviorism (Psychology) I. Title.
BF318 .O76 2004

ORNAMENT. See **DECORATION AND ORNAMENT.**

ORNAMENTAL ALPHABETS. See **ILLUMINATION OF BOOKS AND MANUSCRIPTS.**

Ornstein, Robert E. (Robert Evan), 1942- Multimind / Robert Ornstein. Cambridge, MA : ISHK, 2003. p. cm. Originally published: Boston : Houghton Mifflin, 1986. Includes bibliographical references. ISBN 1-88353-629-4 (alk. paper) DDC 150
1. Intellect. 2. Brain. I. Title.
BF431 .O68 2003

Oron, Israel. Mavet, almavet ve-ide'ologyah : 'iyun psikhologi ba-she'elah madu'a hiskimu nidone Etsel ve-Lehi Ia-'alot la-gardom / me-et Yiśra'el Oron (Ostri). [Israel] : Miśrad ha-biṭaḥon, [2002] 230 p. : facsims ; 22 cm. Title on verso of t.p. : Death, immortality, and ideology. Includes bibliographical references and index. ISBN 9650511296
1. Irgun tseva'i le'umi. 2. Loḥame ḥerut Yiśra'el. 3. Jews - Palestine - History - 20th century. 4. Jewish martyrs - Palestine - Psychology. 5. Ideology. 6. Political prisoners - Psychology. 7. Death row inmates - Palestine - Psychology. 8. Death - Psychological aspects. 9. Psychohistory. I. Title. II. Title: Death, immortality, and ideology

Oron, Michal. Mi-'Ba'al shed' le-'Ba'al Shem' : Shemu'el Falḳ, ha-Ba'al Shem mi-London / Mikhal Oron. Yerushalayim : Mosad Byalik : Bet ha-sefer le-mada'e ha-Yahadut 'a. sh. Ḥayim Rozenberg, Universitat Tel-Aviv, c763 [2002] 296 p., [8] p. of plates : ill., ports., facsims. ; 24 cm. Title on verso of t.p.: Samuel Falk, the Baal Shem of London. Includes bibliographical references (p. 281-287) and index. Includes "Yomano shel Tsevi Hirsh mi-Ḳalish" (p. 115-192) and "Yomano shel Shemu'el Falk" (p. 193-279). ISBN 9653428500
1. De Falk, Samuel Hayyim, - ca. 1710-1782 - Criticism and interpretation. 2. Mystics - England - Biography. 3. Magic, Jewish. I. De Falk, Samuel Hayyim, ca. 1710-1782. Yoman. II. Tsevi Hirsh, mi-Ḳalish, 18th cent. Yoman. III. Title. IV. Title: Samuel Falk, the Baal Shem of London

Orosz, László Wladimir. A jelen és az idő / Orosz László Wladimir. Debrecen : Stalker Stúdió, 2001. 207 p. : ill. ; 24 cm. ISBN 963-00-8633-6
1. Occultism. 2. Horoscopes. 3. Time. I. Title.
BF1999 .O69 2000

'Orot ha-Alshekh.
Alshekh, Moses, 16th cent. [Torat Mosheh. Selections] Sefer 'Orot ha-Alshekh. Yerushalayim : [ḥ. mo. l.], 763 [2002 or 2003]

Orot ha-tamtsit.
Yanai, Me'ir. Yerushalayim : Nezer Dayid - Ari'el, 761 [2000 or 2001]

The Orphic voice.
Strandberg, Åke. Uppsala : Acta Universitatis Upsaliensis, 2002.
PS3509.L43 Z87 2002

Orrico, Evelyn G. D.
Memória, cultura e sociedade. Rio de Janeiro : 7Letras, 2002.
BF378.S65 M457 2002

Orringer, Nelson R.
Zubiri, Xavier. [Estructura dinámica de la realidad. English] Dynamic structure of reality. Urbana : University of Illinois Press, c2003.
B4568.Z83 E7713 2003

Orsucci, Franco. Changing mind : transitions in natural and artificial environments / Franco F. Orsucci. River Edge, NJ : World Scientific, c2002. xiv, 209 p. : ill., map ; 23 cm. (Studies of nonlinear phenomena in life sciences ; v. 9) Includes bibliographical references (p. 197-206) and index. ISBN 981-238-027-2 (alk. paper) DDC 153
1. Mind and body. 2. Nonlinear systems. 3. Cognitive science. 4. Neurosciences. 5. Complexity (Philosophy) I. Title. II. Series.
BF161 .O77 2002

Orte des Schönen : phänomenologische Annäherungen : für Günther Pöltner zum 60. Geburtstag / herausgegeben von Reinhold Esterbauer. Würzburg : Königshausen & Neumann, c2003. 576 p. ; 24 cm. Includes bibliographical references (p.565]-571) and indexes. ISBN 3-8260-2493-1 (pbk.)
1. Aesthetics. 2. Art - Philosophy. I. Esterbauer, Reinhold. II. Pöltner, Günther.
BH23 .O78 2003

Ortega, Pilar.
Jornadas de Roles Sexuales y de Género (2nd : 1995 : Madrid, Spain) Mujer, ideología y población. 1. ed. Madrid : Ediciones Clásicas, 1998.
HQ1075 .J67 1995

Ortega, Rudolf.
Gray, John, 1948- [Men are from Mars, women are from Venus. Spanish] Els homes són de Mart, les dones són de Venus. 1. ed. Barcelona : Edicions 62, c2001.

ORTEGA Y GASSET, JOSÉ, 1883-1955.
Ferrater Mora, José, 1912- [Selections. English. 2003] Three Spanish philosophers. Albany : State University of New York Press, c2003.
B4568.U54 F3913 2003

ORTHODOX EASTERN CHURCH - DOCTRINES.
Dimitrievich, Vladimir. V plenu germeticheskogo kruga. Perm' : Panagiia, 2001.
BF173.J85 D56 2001

Engleman, Dennis Eugene, 1948- Ultimate things. Ben Lomond, Calif. : Conciliar Press, c1995.
BT876 .E54 1995

Florovsky, Georges, 1893-1979. [Selections. Russian. 2002] Vera i kul'tura. Sankt-Peterburg : Izd-vo Russkogo Khristianskogo gumanitarnogo instituta, 2002.
BX260 .F552 2002

Tsiakkas, Christophoros A. Mageia-satanismos. 3 ekd. Leukōsia : Ekdosē Hieras Monēs Trooditissēs, 2001.
BF1550 .T73 2001

ORTHODOX JUDAISM.
Mar'eh Kohen. Yerushalayim : Makhon le-ḥeker mishnat ha-Re'iyah Ḳuḳ be-shituf 'im "Bet ha-Rav", c762 [2001 or 2002]

Ortiz, Eulogio L.
Peace and conflict resolution. Part 1 [videorecording]. Derry, N.H. : Chip Taylor Communications, 1996.

Peace and conflict resolution. Part 2 [videorecording]. Derry, N.H. : Chip Taylor Communications, 1997.

Osborn, Becky.
Mills, Andy, 1979- Shapesville. 1st ed. Carlsbad, CA : Gurze Books, 2003.

BF723.B6 M55 2003

Ose savoir
Gaudin, Thierry. Discours de la méthode créatrice. Gordes : Relié, c2003.

O'Shea, Robert P. (Robert Paul).
Mitchell, Mark L. Writing for psychology. 1st ed. Australia ; Belmont, CA : Wadsworth/Thomson, 2004.
BF76.7 .M58 2004

Osho, 1931-1990. Tantra, the supreme understanding : discourses on the tantric way of Tilopa's song of Mahamudra / Osho. Delhi : Full Circle, 1999. vii, 271 p. ; 22 cm. ISBN 81-216-0695-0 DDC 299/.93
1. Tilopāda, - 988-1069. 2. Spiritual life. 3. Religious life - Tantric Buddhism. 4. Tantric Buddhism - Doctrines. I. Title.
BP605.R34 T367 1999

Tarot in the spirit of Zen : the game of life / Osho. 1st ed. New York : St. Martin's Griffin, 2003. xv, 206 p. : ill. (some col.) ; 21 cm. Includes deck of cards on two plates at end of book. Publisher description URL: http://www.loc.gov/catdir/description/hol032/2002045208.html ISBN 0-312-31767-0 (pbk.) DDC 133.3/2424
1. Tarot. 2. Major arcana (Tarot) I. Title.
BF1879.T2 O85 2003

OSIRIS. See OSIRIS (EGYPTIAN DEITY).

OSIRIS (EGYPTIAN DEITY).
Cauville, Sylvie. Le zodiaque d'Osiris. Leuven : Peeters, 1997.
BL2450.O7 C399 1997

Osiris könyvtár. Pszichológia
Harkai Schiller, Pál, 1908-1949. A lélektan feladata. Budapest : Osiris Kiadó, 2002.
BF128.H8 H37 2002

Osman, Michael.
Mining autonomy. Cambridge, Mass. : London : MIT Press, c2002.

Osnovy teorii intelligentnosti.
Trufanov, A. A. (Andreĭ Andreevich) Kazan' : ZAO "Novoe znanie", 2002.
BF431 .T78 2002

Osobowość altruistyczna.
Śliwak, Jacek. Wyd. 1. Lublin : Red. Wydawnictw Katolickiego Uniwersytetu Lubelskiego, 2001.
BF637.H4 S58 2001

Osofisan, Femi. Literature and the pressures of freedom : essays, speeches and songs / by Femi Osofisan. Nigeria : Opon Ifa Readers, 2001. xi, 196 p. ; 22 cm. (Opon Ifa readers) Includes bibliographical references (p. 193-195) and index. ISBN 978-33259-7-3 (pbk.)
1. Literature. 2. Liberty. 3. Nigeria - Civilization. 4. Black author. I. Title. II. Series: Opon Ifa series.

Osoznannye snovideniia
Smirnov, Terentiĭ. Psikhologiia snovideniĭ. Moskva : "KSP+", 2001.
BF175.5.D74 S5 2001

Ostendorf, Fritz, 1955-.
Personality and temperament: genetics, evolution, and structure. Lengerich : Pabst Science Publishers, 2001.
BF698 .P3692 2001

Ostrowska-Kębłowska, Zofia.
Marmur dziejowy. Poznań : Wydawnictwo Poznańskiego Towarzystwa Przyjaciół Nauk, 2002.

Ostwalt, Conrad Eugene, 1959- Secular steeples : popular culture and the religious imagination / Conrad Ostwalt. Harrisburg, PA : Trinity Press International, c2003. xi, 231 p. ; 23 cm. Includes bibliographical references (p. 209-223) and index. CONTENTS: Space/place/pre-text -- Megachurches -- Love valley : the sacralization of secular space -- Narrative/text -- Religion and "secular" texts -- Image/post-text -- Movies and the apocalypse -- Conclusion: Theological appropriation of secularization : a cooperative model. DDC 291.1/7
1. Popular culture - Religious aspects. 2. Religion and culture. 3. Secularism. I. Title.
BL65.C8 O88 2003

Osty, Florence. Le désir de métier : engagement, identité et reconnaissance au travail / Florence Osty. Rennes [France] : Presses universitaires de Rennes, [2003] 244 p. : ill. ; 25 cm. (Collection "Des sociétés", 1242-8523) Includes bibliographical references. ISBN 2-86847-760-7 DDC 300
1. Work - Psychological aspects. 2. Group identity - France. 3. Professions - France - Sociological aspects. 4. Occupations - France - Sociological aspects. I. Title. II. Series: Des sociétés.

O'Sullivan, Edmund, 1938-.
Learning toward an ecological consciousness. New York : Palgrave Macmillan, 2003.

BF353 .L42 2003

Oswick, Cliff.
Discourse and organization. London ; Thousand Oaks, Calif. : Sage Publications, 1998.
HD58.7 .D57 1998

Otero, Carlos Peregrin, 1930-.
Chomsky, Noam. Chomsky on democracy & education. New York ; London : RoutledgeFalmer, 2003.
LB885.C5215 C46 2003

The Othello response.
Ruge, Kenneth. New York : Marlowe & Co., 2003.
BF575.J4 R84 2003

OTHER MINDS (THEORY OF KNOWLEDGE).
Nichols, Shaun. Mindreading. Oxford : Clarendon Press ; New York : Oxford University Press, 2003.

OTHER (PHILOSOPHY).
Campos, Edemilson Antunes de. A tirania de Narciso. 1. ed. São Paulo, SP, Brasil : Annablume/FAPESP, 2001.

Desmond, William, 1951- Art, origins, otherness. Albany : State University of New York Press, c2003.
BH39 .D4535 2003

Mensch, James R. Ethics and selfhood. Albany, NY : State University of New York Press, c2003.
B945.M4853 E84 2003

Studien zu antiken Identitäten. Würzburg : Ergon Verlag, c2001.
DG78 .S78 2001

Other realities
(v. 9) The Persistence of religions. Malibu : Undena Publications, 1996.

The other voice in early modern Europe
Montpensier, Anne-Marie-Louise d'Orléans, duchesse de, 1627-1693. [Correspondence. English & French] Against marriage. Chicago : University of Chicago Press, 2002.
DC130.M8 A4 2002

Otkrytiia XXI veka
Dliasin, G. G. (Gennadiĭ Gennad'vich) Azbuka Germesa Trismegista, ili, Molekuliarnaia tainost' myshleniia. Izd. 2-e. Moskva : Izd-vo "Belye al'vy", 2002.
BF1616 .D58 2002

Otsar 'avodat H.
Tsuri'el, Mosheh Yehi'el. Otsrot ha-musar. Yerushalayim : Yerid ha-sefarim, 763, 2002.

Otsar 'avodat ha-Shem.
Tsuri'el, Mosheh Yehi'el. Otsrot ha-musar. Yerushalayim : Yerid ha-sefarim, 763, 2002.

Otsar tefilat 18.
Armoni, Mosheh Ḥayim. Sefer Ginze Armoni. Yerushalayim : 'Amutat "Naḥalat-Raḥel", 762 [2002] BM670.S5 A756 2002

Otsrot av.
Bardaḥ, Asher. Sefer Otsrot av. [Bene Beraḳ?] : A. Bardaḥ, 762- [2001 or 2002- BS1225.54 .B37 2001

Otsrot ha-melekh.
Maimonides, Moses, 1135-1204. [Selections] Sefer Musarim ve-de'ot leha-Rambam. Bene Beraḳ : [ḥ. mo. l], 761 [2000 or 2001]

Otsrot ha-musar.
Tsuri'el, Mosheh Yeḥi'el. Yerushalayim : Yerid ha-sefarim, 763, 2002.

Otsrot ha-Netsiv.
Berlin, Naphtali Ẓevi Judah, 1817-1893. [Selections. 2001] Yerushalayim : Ben Arzah, 762 [2001 or 2002] BM755.B52 A25 2001

Otsrot ha-Netsiv mi-Voloz'in.
Berlin, Naphtali Ẓevi Judah, 1817-1893. [Selections. 2001] Otsrot ha-Netsiv. Yerushalayim : Ben Arzah, 762 [2001 or 2002] BM755.B52 A25 2001

Otsrot rabotenu mi-Brisḳ : amarot ṭehorot, yesodot ne'emanim u-fenine ḳodesh / me-otsrotehem shel sheloshet ha-ro'im ... Ba'al ha-Bet ha-Levi, Rabenu Ḥayim ha-Levi, Yitsḥaḳ Ze'ev ha-Levi Soloyaitsiḳ ; nilḳat ve-ne'erakh mi-tokh sifrehem umi-sifre ye-khitve talmidim. Bene Beraḳ : Sh. L., molut u-mishar bi-sefarim, 762 [2001 or 2002] 304 p. ; 25 cm. Includes bibliographical references.
1. Soloveitchik family. 2. Judaism - Doctrines. 3. Ethics, Jewish. 4. Talmud Torah (Judaism) 5. Jewish way of life. I. Soloveichik, Joseph Baer, 1820-1892. II. Soloveichik, Ḥayyim, 1853-1918. III. Soloveichik, Isaac Ze'ev, ha-Levi, 1886-1960.

Ott, Edward.
Coping with chaos. New York : J. Wiley, c1994.
Q172.5.C45 C67 1994

Ottavi, Dominique. De Darwin à Piaget : pour une histoire de la psychologie de l'enfant / Dominique Ottavi. Paris : CNRS, c2001. 350 p. ; 24 cm. (CNRS Histoire des sciences) Includes bibliographical references (p. [317]-340) and index. ISBN 2-271-05962-3 DDC 150
1. Child psychology. 2. Child development. I. Title. II. Series.

OULAF (AFRICAN PEOPLE). *See* **WOLOF (AFRICAN PEOPLE).**

OULIPO (ASSOCIATION).
Consenstein, Peter. Literary memory, consciousness, and the group Oulipo. Amsterdam ; New York, NY : Rodopi, 2002.

Our dad died.
Dennison, Amy. Minneapolis, MN : Free Spirit Pub., c2003.
BF723.G75 D46 2003

Our own devices.
Tenner, Edward. 1st ed. New York : Alfred A. Knopf, 2003.
T14.5 .T4588 2003

Our shadowed present.
Clark, J. C. D. London : Atlantic, 2003.

Our voices.
Rider, Elizabeth A. Belmont, CA : Wadsworth, c2000.
HQ1206 .R54 2000

Out of the shadows.
McLelland, Lilith. New York : Citadel Press, c2002.
BF1571 .M46 2002

Out there
Townsend, John. Mysterious disappearances. Chicago, IL : Raintree, 2004.
BF1389.D57 T69 2004

Townsend, John. Mysterious encounters. Chicago, IL : Raintree, 2004.
BF2050 .T69 2004

OUTCOME ASSESSMENT (MEDICAL CARE).
McCulloch, Douglas, 1950- Valuing health in practice. Aldershot, Hampshire, England ; Burlington, VT : Ashgate, c2003.
RA410.5 .M37 2002

OUTCOME EVALUATION (MEDICAL CARE). *See* **OUTCOME ASSESSMENT (MEDICAL CARE).**

OUTCOME MEASURES (MEDICAL CARE). *See* **OUTCOME ASSESSMENT (MEDICAL CARE).**

OUTCOMES ASSESSMENT (MEDICAL CARE). *See* **OUTCOME ASSESSMENT (MEDICAL CARE).**

OUTCOMES MEASUREMENT (MEDICAL CARE). *See* **OUTCOME ASSESSMENT (MEDICAL CARE).**

OUTCOMES RESEARCH (MEDICAL CARE). *See* **OUTCOME ASSESSMENT (MEDICAL CARE).**

OUTDOOR LIFE. *See* **MOUNTAINEERING; SPORTS.**

OUTER PLANETS. *See* **JUPITER (PLANET).**

Outer power.
Varnum, Keith. Inner coach, outer power. Phoenix, Ariz. : New Dimensions Pub., c2002.
BF1999 .V36 2002

Outstanding dissertations in linguistics
Vasishth, Shravan, 1964- Working memory in sentence comprehension. New York ; London : Routledge, 2003.
PK1933 .V28 2003

Ouyang, Kang, 1953- She hui ren shi lun : ren lei she hui zi wo ren shi zhi mi de zhe xue tan suo / Ouyang Kang zhu. Di 1 ban. [Kunming] : Yunnan ren min chu ban she, 2002. 2, 10, 415 p. ; 22 cm. (Zhe xue li lun chuang xin cong shu = Philosophy series : new ideas and innovations c) Cover title: Social epistemology : a philosophical study to the riddle of self-cognition of human society. Includes bibliographical references. ISBN 7-222-03115-4
1. Social perception. 2. Knowledge, Sociology of. I. Title. II. Title: Ren lei she hui zi wo ren shi zhi mi de zhe xue tan suo III. Title: Social epistemology : a philosophical study to the riddle of self-cognition of human society IV. Series: Zhe xue li lun chuang xin cong shu.

BF323.S63 O93 2002

Ouyang, Zhesheng, 1962-.
Cai, Yuanpei, 1868-1940. [Selections. 1996] Cai Yuanpei juan. Di 1 ban. Shijiazhuang Shi : Hebei jiao yu chu ban she, 1996.
BJ117 .T74 1996 <Asian China>

Ovason, David.
[Secret zodiacs of Washington DC]
The secret architecture of our nation's capital : the Masons and the building of Washington, D.C. / David Ovason. 1st Perennial ed. New York, NY : Perennial, 2002. viii, 516 p. : ill. (some col.), maps ; 20 cm. Includes bibliographical references (p. 393-465) and index. Originally published in Great Britain by Century Publishing in 1999 under title: The secret zodiacs of Washington, D.C. "A hardcover edition of this book was published in 2000 by HarperCollins Publishers"--Verso t.p. ISBN 0-06-095368-3 (pbk.)
1. Zodiac in art. 2. Freemasonry - Symbolism. 3. Freemasonry - United States - History. 4. Symbolism in architecture - Washington (D.C.) 5. Washington (D.C.) - Buildings, structures, etc. I. Title. II. Title: Masons and the building of Washington D.C.

Overall, Christine, 1949- Aging, death, and human longevity : a philosophical inquiry / Christine Overall. Berkeley : University of California Press, c2003. xi, 264 p. ; 24 cm. Includes bibliographical references (p. 239-253) and index. ISBN 0-520-23298-4 (alk. paper) DDC 305.26
1. Aging. 2. Longevity. 3. Terminal care. I. Title.
RA564.8 .O95 2003

Overcoming anger.
Jones, Carol D., 1948- Avon, MA : Adams Media, 2004.
BF575.A5 J66 2004

Overcoming anxiety for dummies.
Elliott, Charles H., 1948- New York : Wiley Pub., c2003.
BF575.A6 E46 2003

Overcoming onto-theology.
Westphal, Merold. 1st ed. New York : Fordham University Press, 2001.
BR100 .W47 2001

Overcoming the inheritance taboo.
Hendlin, Steven J. New York : Plume, 2004.
BF789.D4 H4235 2004

Overmier, J. Bruce.
Psychology, IUPsyS global resource [electronic resource]. Hove, East Sussex, UK : published on behalf of the international Union of Psychological Science by Psychology Press Ltd., 2000-
BF76.5 .P79

Overmier, Judith A., 1939-.
Psychology, IUPsyS global resource [electronic resource]. Hove, East Sussex, UK : published on behalf of the international Union of Psychological Science by Psychology Press Ltd., 2000-
BF76.5 .P79

OVERTONES (MUSIC). *See* **HARMONICS (MUSIC).**

OVERWEIGHT. *See* **OBESITY.**

OVERWEIGHT PERSONS. *See* **OVERWEIGHT WOMEN.**

OVERWEIGHT WOMEN.
Big Dance [videorecording]. Buffalo, N.Y. : Kineticvideo.com, c1998.

OVERWEIGHT WOMEN - UNITED STATES - BIOGRAPHY.
Darbo, Patrika. 365 glorious nights of love and romance. 1st ed. New York : ReganBooks, c2002.
HQ46 .D35 2002

Owen, Alex, 1948- The darkened room : women, power, and spiritualism in late Victorian England / Alex Owen. Chicago : University of Chicago, 2004. p. cm. Originally published: Philadelphia : University of Pennsylvania Press, c1990, in series: The new cultural studies series. Includes bibliographical references and index. ISBN 0-226-64205-4 (pbk. : alk. paper) DDC 133.9/082/0941
1. Women and spiritualism - England - History - 19th century. 2. Women mediums - England - History - 19th century. I. Title.
BF1275.W65 O94 2004

The place of enchantment : British occultism and the culture of the modern / Alex Owen. Chicago, Ill. : University of Chicago Press, c2004. p. cm. Includes bibliographical references and index. Table of contents URL: http://www.loc.gov/catdir/toc/ecip041/2003006764.html CONTENTS: Culture and the occult at the fin de siecle -- Magicians of the dawn -- Sexual politics -- Modern enchantment and the consciousness of the self -- Occult reality and the fictionalizing mind -- Aleister Crowley in the desert -- After Armageddon -- Occultism and the ambiguities of the modern. ISBN 0-226-64201-1 (hardcover : alk. paper) DDC 133/.0941/09034
1. Occultism - Great Britain - History - 19th century. I. Title.
BF1429 .O94 2004

OWENS, TED.
Mishlove, Jeffrey, 1946- The PK man. Charlottesville, VA : Hampton Roads, [c2000]
BF1027.O94 M57 2000

OWNERSHIP. *See* **PROPERTY.**

OWNERSHIP OF SLAVES. *See* **SLAVERY.**

Oxford cognitive science series
Campbell, John, 1956- Reference and consciousness. Oxford : Clarendon Press ; New York : Oxford University Press, 2002.
BF321 .C36 2002

Nichols, Shaun. Mindreading. Oxford : Clarendon Press ; New York : Oxford University Press, 2003.

Stenning, Keith. Seeing reason. Oxford ; New York : Oxford University Press, 2002.
BF441 .S775 2002

Oxford handbook of deaf studies, language, and education / edited by Marc Marschark and Patricia Elizabeth Spencer. Oxford ; New York : Oxford University Press, c2003. xvi, 505 p. : ill. ; 26 cm. Includes bibliographical references and index. Includes sign language. ISBN 0-19-514997-1 (cloth : alk. paper) DDC 362.4/2
1. Deaf - Social conditions. 2. Deaf - Education. 3. Deaf - Means of communication. 4. Sign language. I. Marschark, Marc. II. Spencer, Patricia Elizabeth. III. Title: Deaf studies, language, and education
HV2380 .O88 2003

Oxford handbook of political psychology / edited by David O. Sears, Leonie Huddy, Robert Jervis. Oxford ; New York : Oxford University Press, 2003. x, 822 p. ; 25 cm. Includes bibliographical references and index. ISBN 0-19-515220-4 (hbk.) ISBN 0-19-516220-X (pbk.) DDC 320/.01/9
1. Political psychology. I. Sears, David O. II. Huddy, Leonie. III. Jervis, Robert, 1940-
JA74.5 .H355 2003

The Oxford handbook of practical ethics / edited by Hugh LaFollette. Oxford ; New York : Oxford University Press, 2003. xvii, 772 p. ; 26 cm. Includes bibliographical references and index. ISBN 0-19-824105-4 (alk. paper) DDC 170
1. Applied ethics. 2. Ethics. I. LaFollette, Hugh, 1948- II. Title: Practical ethics
BJ1031 .O94 2003

Oxford linguistics
Phonetics, phonology, and cognition. Oxford : Oxford University Press, 2002.
P221 .P475 2002

Oxford medical publications
Sayers, Janet. Divine therapy. Oxford ; New York : Oxford University Press, 2003.
BF175.4.R44 S28 2003

Oxford philosophical monographs
Illies, Christian. The grounds of ethical judgement. Oxford : Clarendon, 2003.

Oxford psychology series
(no. 37.) Findlay, John M. (John Malcolm), 1942- Active vision. Oxford ; New York : Oxford University Press, 2003.
BF241 .F56 2003

Oxford series in cognitive development
Mandler, Jean Matter. The foundations of mind. Oxford ; New York : Oxford University Press, 2004.
BF720.C63 M36 2004

Oxford series in social cognition and social neuroscience
The new unconscious. New York : Oxford University Press, 2004.
BF315 .N47 2004

Oxford studies in theoretical linguistics
(3) Phonetics, phonology, and cognition. Oxford : Oxford University Press, 2002.
P221 .P475 2002

Oyěwùmí, Oyèrónké.
African women and feminism. Trenton, NJ : Africa World Press, c2003.
HQ1787 .A372 2003

Ozaniec, Naomi. Chakras : an introductory guide to your energy centres for total health / Naomi Ozaniec. Rev. ed. Shaftesbury : Element, 2000. 128 p. : ill. ; 20 cm. (New perspectives) Previous ed. published as: The

elements of the chakras. Shaftesbury : Element, 1990. Includes bibliographical references and index. ISBN 1-86204-765-0 DDC 181.45
1. Chakras. I. Ozaniec, Naomi. Elements of the chakras. II. Title. III. Series.

Elements of the chakras.
Ozaniec, Naomi. Chakras. Rev. ed. Shaftesbury : Element, 2000.

Ozer, Daniel J.
Pieces of the personality puzzle. 3rd ed. New York : Norton, c2004.
BF698 .P525 2004

Ozurumba, Davy.
The search for a holistic approach to human existence and development. [Nigeria?] : Osigwe Anyiam-Osigwe Foundation, [1999?]
B53 .E46 1999

Paál, Gábor. Was ist schön? : Ästhetik und Erkenntnis / Gábor Paál. Würzburg : Königshausen & Neumann, c2003. 233 p. : ill. ; 24 cm. Includes bibliographical references (p. 218-222) and index. ISBN 3-8260-2425-7 (pbk.)
1. Aesthetics. 2. Knowledge, Theory of. 3. Science - Philosophy. I. Title.
BH39 .P33 2003

Pabón, Carlos. Nación postmortem : ensayos sobre los tiempos de insoportable ambigüedad / Carlos Pabón. 1. ed. San Juan, P.R. : Ediciones Callejón, 2002. 429 p. : ill. ; 22 cm. (Colección Fuga. Ensayos) Includes bibliographical references. ISBN 1-88174-807-3 (pbk.)
1. Nationalism - Puerto Rico. 2. Postmodernism - Puerto Rico. 3. Globalization. 4. Philosophy, Modern - 20th century. 5. Puerto Rico - Intellectual life - 20th century. I. Title.

PACIFIC ISLANDS. *See* **ISLANDS OF THE PACIFIC.**

Pacific linguistics
(530) Collected papers on Southeast Asian and Pacific languages. Canberra, ACT : Pacific Linguistics, Research School of Pacific and Asian Studies, Australian National University, 2002.

PACIFIC OCEAN ISLANDS. *See* **ISLANDS OF THE PACIFIC.**

PACIFIC SETTLEMENT OF INTERNATIONAL DISPUTES.
Contemporary peacemaking. Houndmills, Basingstoke ; New York : Palgrave Macmillan, 2003.
JZ6010 .C665 2003

Promoting peace. Berne, Switzerland : Staempfli, 2002.

Searching for peace in Central and South Asia. Boulder, Colo. : Lynne Rienner Publishers, 2002.
JZ5597 .S43 2002

Wenger, Andreas. Conflict prevention. Boulder, Colo. ; London : Lynne Rienner Publishers, 2003.
JZ5538 .W46 2003

PACIFISM.
The power of nonviolence. Boston, Mass. : Beacon Press, c2002.
JZ5538 .P685 2002

Packer, Jeremy, 1970-.
Foucault, cultural studies, and governmentality. Albany : State University of New York Press, c2003.
JC330 .F63 2003

The pact.
Davis, Sampson. Waterville, ME : Thorndike Press, 2002.

Paderborner theologische Studien
(Bd. 34) Kneer, Markus, 1972- Die dunkle Spur im Denken. Paderborn : Schöningh, 2003.
DS145 .K64 2003

Padma, N. K., 1956- Navam and the Karṇāṭak group kṛtis / [guide], Leela Omcheri ; [author], N.K. Padma. New Delhi : Kanishka Publishers, Distributors, 2002. viii, 283 p. ; 22 cm. SUMMARY: With reference to significance of number nine in the musical compositions of Carnatic music of India; a study. Includes bibliographical references (p. [277]-280) and index. Includes passages in Sanskrit (Sanskrit in roman). ISBN 81-7391-449-4 DDC 781.6/9/0954
1. Carnatic music - History and criticism. 2. Music - India - History and criticism. 3. Nine (The number) 4. Symbolism of numbers. 5. Kritis. I. Õñćeri, Līlā. II. Title.
ML338 .P197 2002

The pagan book of Halloween.
Dunwich, Gerina. New York : Penguin/Compass, 2000.
BF1566 .D867 2000

Pagan theology.
York, Michael, 1939- New York ; London : New York University Press, c2003.
BL85 .Y67 2003

Pagani, Simona.
Il "valore" del padre. Torino : UTET libreria, 2001.
BF723.P25 V35 2001

PAGANISM.
Eilers, Dana D. The practical pagan. Franklin Lakes, NJ : New Page Books, c2002.
BF1411 .E34 2002

Gardell, Mattias. Gods of the blood. Durham : Duke University Press, 2003.
BL65.W48 G37 2003

McColman, Carl. When someone you love is Wiccan. Franklin Lakes, NJ : New Page Books, 2003.
BF1566 .M36 2003

York, Michael, 1939- Pagan theology. New York ; London : New York University Press, c2003.
BL85 .Y67 2003

PAGANISM - HISTORY.
Aoumiel. Origins of modern witchcraft. 1st ed. St. Paul, Minn. : Llewellyn Publications, 2000 (2002 printing)
BF1566 .A56 2000

Ruggiero, Fabio. La follia dei cristiani. Roma : Città nuova, c2002.
BR166 .R84 2002

PAGANISM - KIEVAN RUS.
Tkach, Mykola. Volodymyrovi bohy. Kyïv : Ukraïns'kyĭ tsentr dukhovnoï kul'tury, 2002.
DK75 .T53 2002

PAGANISM - RUSSIA - POLITICAL ASPECTS.
Shcheglov, A. (Alekseĭ) I͡Azycheskai͡a zari͡a. Moskva : [Izdatel'stvo "PROBEL-2000"], 2002.
BL980.R5 S53 2002

PAGANISM - UNITED STATES.
Gardell, Mattias. Gods of the blood. Durham : Duke University Press, 2003.
BL65.W48 G37 2003

Pagans & Christians.
DiZerega, Gus. 1st ed. St. Paul, Minn. : Llewellyn Publications, 2001.
BF1566 .D59 2001

Pagans and Christians.
DiZerega, Gus. Pagans & Christians. 1st ed. St. Paul, Minn. : Llewellyn Publications, 2001.
BF1566 .D59 2001

PAGEANTS. *See* **FESTIVALS.**

PAGEANTS - EUROPE - HISTORY - 16TH CENTURY.
Court festivals of the European Renaissance. Aldershot ; Burlington, VT : Ashgate, c2002.

PAGEANTS - EUROPE - HISTORY - 17TH CENTURY.
Court festivals of the European Renaissance. Aldershot ; Burlington, VT : Ashgate, c2002.

Pagés Larraya, Fernando. Liturgia lunar de la locura / Fernando Pagés Larraya, Adriana Massa. Córdoba, Argentina : Comunicarte Editorial, c2002. 136 p. ; ill. ; 22 cm. On cover: "Con la edición y traducción castellana del Liber de Lunaticis de Theophrast von Hohenheim gen. Paracelsus realizada por Adriana Massa." "Departamento de Publicaciones del Seminario de Antropología Psiquiátrica, Programa de Investigaciones sobre Epidemiología Psiquiátrica, Consejo Nacional de Investigaciones Científicas y Técnicas, 2001." Includes bibliographical references. Spanish and German parallel text. Some English, French and Italian. ISBN 9879280660
1. Mental illness. 2. Human beings - Effect of the moon on. I. Massa, Adriana. II. Paracelsus, 1493-1541. Liber de Lunaticis. Spanish and German. III. Title.

Pagnini, Marcello. Letteratura ed ermeneutica / Marcello Pagnini. Firenze : L.S. Olschki, 2002. v, 356 p. ; 24 cm. (Studi / Accademia toscana di scienze e lettere "La Colombaria" ; 202) Includes bibliographical references and name index. ISBN 88-222-5120-2 DDC 809
1. Hermeneutics. 2. Literature - History and criticism. I. Title. II. Series: Studi (Accademia toscana di scienze e lettere La Colombaria) ; 202.

Paidós contextos
(69) Galende, Emiliano. Sexo y amor. 1a ed. Buenos Aires : Paidós, 2001.

Paidós croma
(4) Fernández Christlieb, Fátima. La responsabilidad de los medios de comunicación. 1a. ed. México : Paidós, 2002.

Paidós estado y sociedad
(87) García Canclini, Néstor. Culturas híbridas. Nueva edición actualizada. Buenos Aires : Paidós, 2001.

Paige, Anthony. Rocking the goddess : campus wicca for the student practitioner / Anthony Paige. New York : Citadel Press, c2002. xiv, 252 p. ; 21 cm. ISBN 0-8065-2356-5 DDC 299/.94
1. Witchcraft. 2. Goddess religion. 3. College students - Miscellanea. I. Title.
BF1571.5.C64 P35 2002

PAIN. *See also* **BACKACHE; SUFFERING.**
Croix, Laurence. La douleur en soi. Ramonville Saint-Agne (France) : Érès, c2002.

PAIN - PHILOSOPHY.
Bard, Xavier, 1935- Du plaisir, de la douleur et de quelques autres. Paris, France : Harmattan, c2002.

PAIN - PHYSIOLOGICAL ASPECTS.
Croix, Laurence. La douleur en soi. Ramonville Saint-Agne (France) : Érès, c2002.

PAIN - PSYCHOLOGICAL ASPECTS.
Fone, Anne Calodich. Elf-help for coping with pain. St. Meinrad, Ind. : Abbey Press, c2002.
BF515 .F69 2002

Nasio, Juan-David. [Livre de la douleur et de l'amour. English] The book of love and pain. Albany : State University of New York, 2003.
BF515 .N3713 2003

Pain. Mahwah, N.J. : Lawrence Erlbaum, 2003.
BF515 .P29 2003

Pain : psychological perspectives / edited by Thomas Hadjistavropoulos, Kenneth D. Craig. Mahwah, N.J. : Lawrence Erlbaum, 2003. p. cm. Includes bibliographical references and index. ISBN 0-8058-4299-3 (alk. paper) DDC 152.1/824
1. Pain - Psychological aspects. I. Hadjistavropoulos, Thomas. II. Craig, Kenneth D., 1937-
BF515 .P29 2003

PAINTED CEILINGS. *See* **MURAL PAINTING AND DECORATION.**

PAINTING. *See* **MURAL PAINTING AND DECORATION.**

PAINTING, BUDDHIST - CHINA - TIBET.
Xizang fo jiao cai hui cai su yi shu. Di 1 ban. Beijing : Zhongguo Zang xue chu ban she : Xin hua shu dian Beijing fa xing suo fa xing, 1997.
ND1489 .X593 1997

PAINTING, CHINESE.
Li, Yi. Zou xiang he chu. Di 1 ban. Beijing : Zhongguo she hui chu ban she : Xin hua shu dian Beijing fa xing suo jing xiao, 1994.
ND196.P66 L5 1994 <Orien China>

PAINTING, DECORATIVE. *See* **DECORATION AND ORNAMENT; MURAL PAINTING AND DECORATION.**

PAINTING, MODERN - 20TH CENTURY.
Li, Yi. Zou xiang he chu. Di 1 ban. Beijing : Zhongguo she hui chu ban she : Xin hua shu dian Beijing fa xing suo jing xiao, 1994.
ND196.P66 L5 1994 <Orien China>

Pérez-Jofre, Ignacio. Huellas y sombras. Sada, A Coruña : Ediciós do Castro, [2001]
ND195 .P368 2001

PAINTING, MODERN - 20TH CENTURY - CHINA.
Li, Yi. Zou xiang he chu. Di 1 ban. Beijing : Zhongguo she hui chu ban she : Xin hua shu dian Beijing fa xing suo jing xiao, 1994.
ND196.P66 L5 1994 <Orien China>

PAINTING, PRIMITIVE. *See* **PAINTING.**

Painting, psychoanalysis, and spirituality.
Newton, Stephen J. New York : Cambridge University Press, 2001.
ND1158.P74 N48 2001

PAINTING - PSYCHOLOGICAL ASPECTS.
Newton, Stephen J. Painting, psychoanalysis, and spirituality. New York : Cambridge University Press, 2001.
ND1158.P74 N48 2001

PAINTING - PSYCHOLOGY.
Livingstone, Margaret. Vision and art. New York, N.Y. : Harry N. Abrams, c2002.
N7430.5 .L54 2002

Painting the mental continuum.
Greene, Herb. Berkeley, Calif. : Berkeley Hills

Painting, Tibetan.

Books ; [Berkeley, Calif.] : Distributed by Publishers Group West, c2003.
N71 .G683 2003

PAINTING, TIBETAN.
Xizang fo jiao cai hui cai su yi shu. Di 1 ban. Beijing : Zhongguo Zang xue chu ban she : Xin hua shu dian Beijing fa xing suo fa xing, 1997.
ND1489 .X593 1997

PAINTINGS. *See* **PAINTING.**

PAINTINGS, MODERN. *See* **PAINTING, MODERN.**

Pak, Si-in. Alt'ai munhwa kihaeng / Pak Si-in chiŭm. Ch'op'an. Sŏul-si : Ch'ŏngnoru, 1995. 381 p. : ill., maps ; 23 cm. Introduction and abstract in English before index. Brief description of several ancient Japanese emperial families in Japanese at the end of the book. Includes bibliographical references and index. ISBN 8979250207 (pbk.)
1. Mythology. 2. Mythology, Korean. I. Title.

La palabra como cuerpo del delito : antología poética de Palabra: Expresión Cultural (PEC), New York / Dió-genes Abréu y Dagoberto López-Coño, [eds.]. Santo Domingo, República Dominicana : Biblioteca Nacional "Dr. Pedro Henríquez Ureña", 2001. 235 p. ; 23 cm. (Serie poesía) (Colección de la Biblioteca Nacional "Dr. Pedro Henríquez Ureña") ISBN 9993431117 (pbk.)
1. Spanish language materials. 2. Dominican poetry - Collections. 3. American poetry - Authors, Dominican. 4. Anthologies. 5. Dominicans poets - Biography. I. Abréu, Diógenes. II. López-Coño, Dagoberto. III. Series: Colección de la Biblioteca Nacional de la República Dominicana. IV. Series: Serie Poesía (Biblioteca Nacional (Dominican Republic))

La palabra. Los rostros.
Kanalenstein, Ruben. Córdoba, Argentina : Alción, 2000.

PALACES.
Palais et pouvoir. Vincennes : Presses universitaires de Vincennes, c2003.

Palais et pouvoir : de Constantinople à Versailles / sous la direction de Marie-France Auzépy et Joël Cornette ; [contributions de Gabriel Martinez-Gros ... et al.]. Vincennes : Presses universitaires de Vincennes, c2003. 370 p. : ill. ; 22 cm. (Temps & espaces) ISBN 2-8429-2131-3 DDC 900
1. Palaces. 2. Power (Social sciences) 3. Architecture and state - History. 4. Architecture and society - History. 5. Power (Social sciences) in art. I. Auzépy, Marie-France. II. Cornette, Joël. III. Martinez-Gros, Gabriel. IV. Series: Temps et espaces.

Paleg, Kim. When anger hurts your relationship : 10 simple solutions for couples who fight / Kim Paleg, Matthew McKay. Oakland, CA : New Harbinger Publications, c2001. 140 p. ; 23 cm. Includes bibliographical references (p. [139]-140). ISBN 1-57224-260-4 (pbk.) DDC 306.7
1. Anger. 2. Interpersonal conflict. 3. Man-woman relationships. I. McKay, Matthew. II. Title.
BF575 .A5 P35 2001

PALEOECOLOGY.
Relaciones hombre-fauna. México, D.F. : CONACULTA, INAH ; Plaza y Valdes, 2002.
QL85 .R453 2002

PALEOGRAPHY. *See* **ILLUMINATION OF BOOKS AND MANUSCRIPTS; RUNES.**

PALEONTOLOGY.
Relaciones hombre-fauna. México, D.F. : CONACULTA, INAH ; Plaza y Valdes, 2002.
QL85 .R453 2002

PALESTINE - HISTORY - 638-1917. *See* **CRUSADES.**

PALESTINE - HISTORY - TO 70 A.D. *See* **JUDAISM - HISTORY - POST-EXILIC PERIOD, 586 B.C.-210 A.D.; JUDAISM - HISTORY - TO 70 A.D.**

PALESTINE-ISRAEL CONFLICT. *See* **ARAB-ISRAELI CONFLICT.**

PALESTINE PROBLEM (1948-). *See* **ARAB-ISRAELI CONFLICT.**

PALESTINIAN ARABS - CIVIL RIGHTS - ISRAEL.
Kook, Rebecca B., 1959- The logic of democratic exclusion. Lanham, Md. : Lexington Books, c2002.
E185.615 .K59 2002

PALESTINIAN ARABS - HISTORY - 20TH CENTURY. *See* **ARAB-ISRAELI CONFLICT.**

PALESTINIAN-ISRAELI CONFLICT. *See* **ARAB-ISRAELI CONFLICT.**

PALESTINIANS. *See* **PALESTINIAN ARABS.**

Pallares-Burke, Maria Lucia G. The new history : confessions and conversations / Maria Lucia Pallares-Burke. Cambridge, UK ; Malden, MA : Polity in association with Blackwell Publishers Ltd., 2002. 247 p. ; 24 cm. Includes bibliographical references and index. ISBN 0-7456-3020-0 (hbk.) ISBN 0-7456-3021-9 (pbk.) DDC 907/.2022
1. Historians - Interviews. 2. Historians - Great Britain - Biography. 3. Historians - Europe - Biography. 4. History - Philosophy. 5. Historiography. I. Title.
D14 .P52 2002

Palmer, Lynne. Prosperity / by Lynne Palmer. Las Vegas : Star Bright Publishers, [c2001] 248 p. : ill. ; 22 cm. ISBN 0-9709498-0-4 DDC 133.5/8332024
1. Astrology and personal finance. I. Title.
BF1729 .F48 P35 2001

Palmer, Trevor, 1944- Perilous planet earth : catastrophes and catastrophism through the ages / Trevor Palmer. Cambridge, U.K. ; New York : Cambridge University Press, 2003. ix, 522 p. : ill. ; 26 cm. Includes bibliographical references (p. 373-501) and index. ISBN 0-521-81928-8 DDC 551.3/97
1. Asteroids - Collisions with Earth. 2. Catastrophes (Geology) 3. Evolution. I. Title.
QE506 .P35 2003

PALMISTRY.
Anderson, Rafe. Total palmistry. Boston : Red Wheel, 2003.
BF935 .L67 A53 2003

Fairchild, Dennis. The fortune telling handbook. 1st ed. Philadelphia, PA : Running Press, c2003.
BF1861 .F35 2003

James, Jacqueline. Take control of your life. London : Hodder & Stoughton, 1995, c1994.

Saint-Germain, Jon, 1960- Karmic palmistry. 1st ed. St. Paul, Minn. : Llewellyn Publications, 2003.
BF921 .S215 2003

Webster, Richard, 1946- [Palm reading for beginners. Spanish] Quiromancia para principiantes. 1. ed. St. Paul, Minn. : Llewellyn Español, 2003.
BF921 .W43 2003

Palonen, Kari, 1947- Eine Lobrede für Politiker : ein Kommentar zu Max Webers "Politik als Beruf" / Kari Palonen. Opladen : Leske + Budrich, 2002. 154 p. ; 21 cm. (Studien zur politischen Gesellschaft ; Bd. 4) Includes bibliographical references (p. 147-154). ISBN 3-8100-3498-3 (pbk.) DDC 324.7
1. Weber, Max, - 1864-1920. - Politik als Beruf. 2. Politics, Practical. 3. Vocational guidance. I. Title. II. Series: Reihe Studien zur politischen Gesellschaft ; Bd. 4.
JF2051 .W43 J35 2002

Palumbo, Maria Luisa.
[Nuovi ventri. English]
New wombs : electronic bodies and architectural disorders / Maria Luisa Palumbo ; [translation into English: Lucinda Byatt]. Basel : Birkhäuser, 2000. 93 p. : ill. ; 19 cm. (The IT revolution in architecture) CONTENTS: Towards a postorganic paradigm -- The dismeasurable body. The man in the circle ; The eyes of olympia: the body as a machine of the senses ; Spaces with figures : the body in prosthesis ; The cyborg: the body without organs -- The project of chaos. Utopia and chaotic attractors ; Urban dismeasurement ; Architectural dismeasurement ; Uprooting ; Fluidity ; A visceral nature ; Virtuality ; Sensitivity -- The logic of complexity. Electronic space ; The corporeal machine ; The architecture of the machine. ISBN 3-7643-6294-4 DDC 720/.1
1. Space (Architecture) 2. Architecture - Philosophy. I. Title. II. Series.
NA2765 .P35 2000

Pami︠a︡tniki psikhologicheskoĭ mysli
Anan'ev, Boris Gerasimovich. Psikhologii︠a︡ chuvstvennogo poznanii︠a︡. Moskva : "Nauka", 2001.
BF233 .A5 2001

PAN-SLAVISM. *See* **PANSLAVISM.**

Pan, Zhichang, 1956- Shi yu si di dui hua / Pan Zhichang zhu zhe. Di 1 ban. Shanghai Shi : Shanghai san lian shu dian : Fa xing Xin hua shu dian Shanghai fa xing suo, 1997. 3, 401 p. ; 21 cm. (Shanghai san lian wen ku) (Shanghai san lian wen ku. Xue shu xi lie) Subtitle in colophon: Shen mei huo dong de ben ti lun nei han ji qi xian dai chan shi. "Shou wang jing shen jia yuan"--Cover. Includes bibliographical references (p. 390-393). Table of contents also in English. ISBN 7-5426-1064-3
1. Aesthetics. I. Title. II. Title: Shen mei huo dong de ben ti lun nei han ji qi xian dai chan shi III. Series. IV. Series: Shanghai san lian wen ku. Xue shu xi lie
BH39 .P2286 1997<Asian China>

Pāṇḍeya, Nāgendra.
Varāhamihira, 505-587. Bṛhatsaṃhitā. 1. saṃskaraṇam. Vārāṇasī : Sampūrṇānanda Saṃskṛta Viśvavidyālaye, 2002-
BF1714 .H5+

Pandian, Anand.
Race, nature, and the politics of difference. Durham : Duke University Press, c2003.
HT1521 .R2355 2003

Pandian, Jacob. Supernaturalism in human life : a discourse on myth, rituals & religion / by J. Pandian. New Delhi : Vedams ebooks, [2002] xi, 279 p. ; 22 cm. Includes bibliographical references (p. [231]-269) and index. ISBN 81-7936-005-9
1. Supernatural. 2. Parapsychology and anthropology. 3. Mythology. 4. Religion and sociology. I. Title.
BF1031 .A4-Z+

Pandora, Katherine, 1958- Rebels within the ranks : psychologists' critique of scientific authority and democratic realities in New Deal America / Katherine Pandora. Cambridge ; New York : Cambridge University Press, 1997. xi, 260 p. ; 23 cm. (Cambridge studies in the history of psychology) Includes bibliographical references (p. 183-251) and index. ISBN 0-521-58358-6 (hardcover) DDC 150/.973/09043
1. Psychology - United States - History - 20th century. I. Title. II. Series.
BF105 .P36 1997

PANEL DISCUSSIONS.
Vint/age 2001 conference : [videorecording]. New York, c2001.

PANIC DISORDERS - POPULAR WORKS.
Gross, Esther. You are not alone. Jerusalem, Israel ; Nanuet, NY : Feldheim, 2002.

PANICS (FINANCE). *See* **FINANCIAL CRISES.**

PANISSET, MAURICIO.
Curcio, Kimberly Panisset. Man of light. 1st ed. New York : SelectBooks, c2002.
BF1045 .M44 C87 2002

Panorama estratégico, 2001-2002 / Instituto Español de Estudios Estratégicos. [Madrid] : Ministerio de Defensa, 2002. 262 p. ; 24 cm. (Cuadernos de estrategia ; 117) ISBN 84-7823-908-1
1. International relations. 2. Peace. 3. Security, International. I. Instituto Español de Estudios Estratégicos. II. Spain. Ministerio de Defensa. III. Series.

Panorama : philosophies of the visible / edited by Wilhelm S. Wurzer. New York : Continuum, 2002. xi, 254 p. ; 24 cm. (Textures) Includes bibliographical references (p. [248]-251) and index. ISBN 0-8264-6003-8 ISBN 0-8264-6004-6 (pbk.) DDC 111/.85
1. Aesthetics. I. Wurzer, Wilhelm S. II. Series: Textures (New York, N.Y.)
BH39 .P2292 2002

PANSLAVISM - MISCELLANEA.
Douno, Beinsa, 1864-1944. In the kingdom of living nature. Sofia : Bialo Bratstvo, c2000.

PANTHEISM. *See* **MONOTHEISM.**

Panti, Cecilia, 1964- Moti, virtù e motori celesti nella cosmologia di Roberto Grossatesta : studio ed edizione dei trattati De sphera, De cometis, De motu supercelestium / Cecilia Panti. Firenze : SISMEL : Edizioni del Galluzzo, 2001. x, 436 p. ; 26 cm. (Testi e studi per il "Corpus philosophorum Medii Aevi" ; 16) Includes Latin texts by Robert Grosseteste (p. 289-345). Includes bibliographical references (p. 385-408) and indexes. ISBN 88-8450-025-7 DDC 113
1. Grosseteste, Robert, - 1175?-1253. 2. Cosmology. I. Grosseteste, Robert, 1175?-1253. II. Title. III. Series.
B765 .G74 P36 2001

PANTOMIME. *See* **BALLET.**

PANTOMIMES WITH MUSIC. *See* **KECAK (DANCE DRAMA); PAGEANTS.**

Papalia, Diane E. Human development / Diane E. Papalia, Sally Wendkos Olds, Ruth Duskin Feldman ; in consultation with Dana Gross. 9th ed. Boston : McGraw-Hill, c2004. 1 v. (various pagings) : ill. (some col.) 29 cm. + 1 CD-ROM (4 3/4 in.). Accompanied by student CD-ROM. Includes bibliographical references (p. B1-B82) and indexes. System requirements for accompanying CD-ROM: Windows 98 or higher, or Mac OS 8.6 or higher, with 48MB RAM, 4X CD-ROM drive, Netscape Navigator 5.x or higer, Microsoft Internet Explorer 5.1 or higher, IE Browser included. ISBN 0-07-282030-6 (hbk. : alk. paper) ISBN 0-07-121501-8 (ISE) DDC 155
1. Developmental psychology. 2. Developmental psychobiology. I. Olds, Sally Wendkos. II. Feldman, Ruth Duskin. III. Title.

BF713 .P35 2004

Papalotzin, Itzcoatl. Los recuerdos robados a las estrellas muertas / Itzcoatl Papalotzin (Agustín). Barcelona : Mtm editor.es, c2002. 180 p. ; 21 cm. ISBN 84-955901-4-X
1. Shamanism. 2. Knowledge, Theory of. I. Title.

Papantonopoulos, E. (Eleftherios).
Aegean Summer School on Cosmology (1st : 2001 : Samos Island, Greece) Cosmological crossroads. Berlin ; New York : Springer, c2002.
QB985 .A44 2001

Papcke, Sven, 1939- Gesellschaft der Eliten : zur Reproduktion und Problematik sozialer Distanz / Sven Papcke. 1. Aufl. Münster : Westfälisches Dampfboot, 2001. 409 p. ; 24 cm. Includes bibliographical references (p. 373-409). ISBN 3-89691-496-0 (pbk.).
1. Elite (Social sciences) 2. Power (Social sciences) 3. Social distance. I. Title.
HM821 .P37 2001

Pape, Helmut.
Indexikalität und sprachlicher Weltbezug. Paderborn : Mentis, c2002.

Papeles de comunicación
(37) Martín Salgado, Lourdes. Marketing político. Barcelona : Paidós, c2002.

Papers of the Langford Latin Seminar
(11) Caesar against liberty? Cambridge : Francis Cairns, c2003.

Papeu, Dēmētrēs, 1947- Astrologiko hēmerologio 2002 / Dēmētrē Papeu. 3. etos ekd. Leukōsia : Ekdoseis Papeu, [2001] 258 p. : ill. ; 24 cm. ISBN 9963-600-73-5
1. Astrology. I. Title.
BF1708.8.G74 P37 2001

Papineau, David, 1947- The roots of reason : philosophical essays on rationality, evolution, and probability / David Papineau. Oxford : Clarendon Press ; New York : Oxford University Press, 2003. viii, 242 p. ; 21 cm. Includes bibliographical references and index. CONTENTS: Normativity and judgement -- The evolution of knowledge -- The evolution of means--end reasoning -- Probability as a guide to life / co-authored with Helen Beebee -- Causation as a guide to life -- Uncertain decisions and the many-minds interpretation of quantum mechanics. ISBN 0-19-924384-0 (alk. paper) DDC 128/.33
1. Philosophy of mind. 2. Naturalism. 3. Reason. I. Title.
BD418.3 .P35 2003

PapyRossa Hochschulschriften
(39) Stiehler, Gottfried. Mensch und Geschichte. Köln : PapyRossa, c2002.
D16.8 .S75 2002

Paquette, Didier. La mascarade interculturelle : interculturalité et sexuation psychique / Didier Paquette. Paris : Harmattan, c2002. 154 p. ; 22 cm. (Collection L'œuvre et la psyché) Includes bibliographical references (p. [149]-151). ISBN 2-7475-3009-4 DDC 300
1. Intercultural communication - Case studies. 2. Intercultural communication in motion pictures. 3. Intercultural communication in literature. 4. Ethnopsychology. 5. Psychoanalysis and culture. 6. Sex differences (Psychology) I. Title. II. Series.

Par-delà le masculin et le féminin.
Lévesque, Claude, 1927- Paris : Aubier, 2002.

Paracelsus, 1493-1541.
Liber de Lunaticis. Spanish and German.
Pagés Larraya, Fernando. Liturgia lunar de la locura. Córdoba, Argentina : Comunicarte Editorial, c2002.

Paracelsus Akademie Villach.
Neues Bewusstsein. Wien : Edition Selene, 1999.

PARACLETE. *See* **HOLY SPIRIT.**

A paradigm theory of existence.
Vallicella, William F. Dordrecht ; Boston : Kluwer Academic, c2002.
BD331 .V36 2002

PARADIGM (THEORY OF KNOWLEDGE).
Dugin, Aleksandr. Evoliutsiia paradigmal'nykh osnovaniĭ nauki. Moskva : Arktogeia, 2002.
Q174.8 .D845 2002

Paradigms of personality assessment.
Wiggins, Jerry S. New York : Guilford Press, 2003.
BF698.4 .W525 2003

PARADISE.
Adam, of Eynsham, fl. 1196-1232. [Visio Monachi de Eynsham. English (Middle English) & Latin] The revelation of the Monk of Eynsham. Oxford : Published for the Early English Text Society by the Oxford University Press, 2002.

PARADOX.
Gotz, Ignacio L. Faith, humor, and paradox. Westport, Conn. : Praeger, 2002.
BL51 .G6854 2002

Paradox and the possibility of knowledge.
Barris, Jeremy. Selinsgrove : Susquehanna University Press, c2003.
BF175.4.P45 B37 2003

The paradox of philosphical education.
Lomax, J. Harvey, 1948- Lanham, Md. ; Oxford : Lexington Books, c2003.
B3313.J43 L66 2003

PARAGRAMMATISM.
Freud, Sigmund, 1856-1939. [Zur Psychopathologie des Alltagslebens. English] The psychopathology of everyday life. New York : Penguin Books, 2003.
BF173 .F82513 2003

Paranormal Ireland.
DeFaoîte, Dara. Ashbourne, Co. Meath : Maverick House, c2002.
BF1031 .D344 2002

deFaoîte, Dara. Northampton : Maverick House, 2002.

Paranormal perception?.
French, Christopher C. London : Institute for Cultural Research, 2001.

PARANORMAL PHENOMENA. *See* **PARAPSYCHOLOGY.**

PARAPSYCHOLOGISTS - RUSSIA (FEDERATION) - BIOGRAPHY.
Sudakov, Vladimir Ivanovich. Spasitel'. Moskva : TERRA-Sport, 2001.
BF1027.G73 S83 2001

PARAPSYCHOLOGY. *See also* **COINCIDENCE - PSYCHIC ASPECTS; DISAPPEARANCES (PARAPSYCHOLOGY); DOUBLE (PARAPSYCHOLOGY); KARMA; OCCULTISM; PSYCHIC ABILITY; PSYCHIC READINGS; REMOTE VIEWING (PARAPSYCHOLOGY).**
Brandon, Trent. The book of ghosts. Mineva, Ohio : Zerotime Pub., c2003.
BF1461 .B6949 2003

Brandon, Trent. The ghost hunter's Bible. Definitive ed. [Ohio?] : Zerotime Paranormal and Supernatural Research, 2002.
BF1461 .B695 2002

Browne, Sylvia. Secrets & mysteries of the world. Carlsbad, Calif. : Hay House, c2005.
BF1411 .B78 2005

Buckland, Raymond. Color magick. 1st ed., rev. St. Paul, Minn. : Llewellyn Publications, 2002.
BF1623.C6 B83 2002

Cox, Bonnie. The lightbearer. Seattle, Wash. : Black Heron Press, c2003.
BF1031 .C637 2003

The cultic milieu. Walnut Creek : AltaMira Press, c2002.
BP603 .C835 2002

Dreller, Larry. Secrets of a medium. Boston, MA : Weiser Books, 2003.
BF1031 .D69 2003

Duplessis, Yvonne, 1912- Surréalisme et paranormal. Agnières : JMG, 2002.
BF1023 .D87 2002

French, Christopher C. Paranormal perception? London : Institute for Cultural Research, 2001.

Holzer, Hans, 1920- Hans Holzer's the supernatural. Franklin Lakes, NJ : New Page Books, c2003.
BF1031 .H672 2003

Karpenko, M. (Maksim) Vselennaîa razumnaîa = 2. perer. izd. Moskva : MAIK Nauka/Interperiodika, 2001.
BF1036 .K37 2001

LeShan, Lawrence L., 1920- The medium, the mystic, and the physicist. New York : Helios Press, 2003, c1974.
BF1031 .L43 2003

Marks, David. The psychology of the psychic. 2nd ed. Amherst, N.Y. : Prometheus Books, 2000.
BF1042 .M33 2000

Mickaharic, Draja. Spiritual cleansing. York Beach, ME : Red Wheel/Weiser, 2003.

BF1040 .M53 2003

Moody, Raymond A. Life after life. Rev. 25th anniversary ed / with a new preface by Melvin Morse and a foreword by Elisabeth Kübler-Ross. London : Rider, 2001.

Mysterious places. San Diego, CA : Greenhaven Press, 2004.
BF1031 .M96 2004

Occhino, MaryRose. Beyond these four walls. New York : Berkley Books, 2003.
BF1283.O27 A3 2003

Polidoro, Massimo. Secrets of the psychics. Amherst, N.Y. : Prometheus Books, c2003.
BF1031 .P75155 2003

Rogers, Rita. Mysteries. Large print ed. Bath, England : Chivers Press ; Waterville, Me. : Thorndike Press, 2002.
BF1031 .R635 2002

Townsend, John, 1955- Mysteries of body and mind. Chicago, IL : Raintree, 2004.
BF1031 .T65 2004

Twitchell, Paul, 1908-1971. [Stranger by the river. Croation] Stranac na rijeci. Minneapolis, MN : ECKANKAR, c1994.

Wills-Brandon, Carla, 1956- A glimpse of heaven. Avon, MA : Adams Media Corp., c2003.
BF1031 .W68 2003

PARAPSYCHOLOGY AND ANTHROPOLOGY.
Pandian, Jacob. Supernaturalism in human life. New Delhi : Vedams ebooks, [2002]
BF1031.A4-Z+

PARAPSYCHOLOGY AND ARCHAEOLOGY.
Little, Lora. Secrets of the ancient world. Virginia Beach, Va. : A.R.E. Press, c2003.
BF1045.A74 L58 2003

PARAPSYCHOLOGY AND ART - EXHIBITIONS.
Art spirite, mediumnique, visionnaire. [Paris] : Hoëbeke, c1999.
BF1313 .A78 1999

PARAPSYCHOLOGY AND LANGUAGE.
Cherepanova, I. IU. (Irina IUr'evna) Dom koldun'i. Perer., dop. i ispravlennoe izd. Moskva : KSP+, 2001.
BF1156.S8 C53 2001

PARAPSYCHOLOGY AND MEDICINE.
Braud, William. Distant mental influence. Charlottesville, VA : Hampton Roads Pub., c2003.
BF1045.S33 B74 2003

Curcio, Kimberly Panisset. Man of light. 1st ed. New York : SelectBooks, c2002.
BF1045.M44 C87 2002

PARAPSYCHOLOGY AND SCIENCE.
Braud, William. Distant mental influence. Charlottesville, VA : Hampton Roads Pub., c2003.
BF1045.S33 B74 2003

Seymour, Percy. [Paranormal] The third level of reality. New York : Paraview Special Editions, c2003.
BF1045.S33 S48 2003

PARAPSYCHOLOGY - CASE STUDIES.
Nickell, Joe. The mystery chronicles. Lexington, Ky. : University Press of Kentucky, c2004.
BF1031 .N517 2004

Raudive, Konstantins, 1909-1974. [Unhörbares wird hörbar. Latvian] Nedzirdamais kļūst dzirdams. Rīga : Zintnieks, c2003.
BF1029 .R3816 2003

PARAPSYCHOLOGY - ENCYCLOPEDIAS.
Steiger, Brad. The Gale encyclopedia of the unusual and unexplained. Detroit : Thomson/Gale, c2003.
BF1025 .S79 2003

PARAPSYCHOLOGY - IRELAND.
DeFaoîte, Dara. Paranormal Ireland. Ashbourne, Co. Meath : Maverick House, c2002.
BF1031 .D344 2002

deFaoîte, Dara. Paranormal Ireland. Northampton : Maverick House, 2002.

PARAPSYCHOLOGY - JUVENILE LITERATURE.
Townsend, John, 1955- Mysteries of body and mind. Chicago, IL : Raintree, 2004.
BF1031 .T65 2004

PARAPSYCHOLOGY - TEXTBOOKS.
Irwin, H. J. (Harvey J.) An introduction to parapsychology. 4th ed. Jefferson, N.C. : McFarland & Co., 2003.

BF1031 .I79 2003

PARDON. *See* **AMNESTY; FORGIVENESS.**

PARENT-ADULT CHILD RELATIONS. *See* **PARENT AND ADULT CHILD.**

PARENT AND ADULT CHILD.
Jonas, Susan. Friends for life. 1st ed. New York : William Morrow & Co., c1997.
HQ755.85 .J65 1997

PARENT AND ADULT CHILD - UNITED STATES.
McEnroe, Colin. My father's footsteps. New York : Warner Books, c2003.
PS3563.C3615 M9 2003

PARENT AND CHILD. *See also* **ADOPTION; MOTHER AND CHILD; PARENT AND ADULT CHILD; PARENTING.**
Bosco Coletsos, Sandra. La struttura parentale nelle fiabe dei fratelli Grimm. Alessandria : Edizioni dell'Orso, 2001.

Brezak, Dov. Chinuch in turbulent times. 1st ed. Brooklyn, N.Y. : Mesorah Publications, c2002.

Caniato, Benilde Justo. Um testemunho de mãe. 2a. ed. São Paulo : Lato Senso, 2001.
HV901.B6 C36 2001

Children's influence on family dynamics. Mahwah, N.J. : Lawrence Erlbaum Associates, 2003.
HQ518 .C535 2003

Cowen, Lauren. Daughters & mothers. Philadelphia [Penn.] : Courage Books, c1997.
HQ755.85 .C695 1997

Davis, Daniel Leifeld. Your angry child. New York : Haworth Press, c2004.
BF723.A4 D38 2004

Harding, M. Esther (Mary Esther), 1888-1971. The parental image. 3rd ed. Toronto : Inner City Books, c2003.

Nashim, zekenim va-taf. Yerushalayim : Merkaz Zalman Shazar le-toldot Yiśra'el, [2001]

Pierron, Jean-Philippe. On ne choisit pas ses parents. [Paris] : Seuil, c2003.

Rosenberg, Shelley Kapnek. Raising a mensch. 1st ed. Philadelphia : Jewish Publication Society, 2003.
BF723.M54 R68 2003

Wallat, Cynthia. Family-institution interaction. New York : P. Lang, c2002.
HQ755.85 .W35 2002

PARENT AND CHILD (JEWISH LAW).
Yosef, Yitshak. [Yalkut Yosef (Kibud av va-em)] Sefer Yalkut Yosef. Yerushalayim : Mekhon "Hazon 'Ovadyah", 761 [2001]
BM523.5.R4 Y72 2001

PARENT AND CHILD - PSYCHOLOGICAL ASPECTS.
Grolnick, Wendy S. The psychology of parental control. Mahwah, N.J. : L. Erlbaum Associates, 2003.
HQ755.85 .G74 2003

PARENT AND CHILD - UNITED STATES.
Summer, Lauralee, 1976- Learning joy from dogs without collars. New York ; London : Simon & Schuster, c2003.
HV4505 .S86 2003

PARENT AND TEENAGER.
Lhomme-Rigaud, Colette. L'adolescent et ses monstres. Ramonville Saint-Agne : Erès, c2002.

Wiseman, Rosalind, 1969- Queen bees & wannabes. 1st ed. New York : Crown Publishers, c2002.
HQ798 .W544 2002

PARENT BEHAVIOR. *See* **PARENTING.**

PARENT-CHILD RELATIONS. *See* **PARENT AND CHILD.**

PARENT DEATH. *See* **PARENTS - DEATH.**

PARENT-TEACHER RELATIONSHIPS. *See* **HOME AND SCHOOL.**

PARENTAL BEHAVIOR IN HUMANS. *See* **PARENTING.**

PARENTAL DEATH. *See* **PARENTS - DEATH.**

The parental image.
Harding, M. Esther (Mary Esther), 1888-1971. 3rd ed. Toronto : Inner City Books, c2003.

PARENTAL INFLUENCES.
Harding, M. Esther (Mary Esther), 1888-1971. The parental image. 3rd ed. Toronto : Inner City Books, c2003.

PARENTHOOD. *See also* **FATHERHOOD; MOTHERHOOD; PARENTING.**
Pierron, Jean-Philippe. On ne choisit pas ses parents. [Paris] : Seuil, c2003.

Parenti, Christian.
Monkeywrenching the new world order [sound recording]. Oakland, Calif : AK Press : San Francisco, CA : Alternative Tentacles Records, 2001.

PARENTING.
Cronin, W. Jean. Going for the gold. Longmont, CO : Sopris West, c2003.
BF637.B4 C76 2003

Nemeth, Darlyne Gaynor. Helping your angry child. Oakland, Calif. : New Harbinger, c2003.
BF723.A4 N46 2003

PARENTING - PSYCHOLOGICAL ASPECTS.
Grolnick, Wendy S. The psychology of parental control. Mahwah, N.J. : L. Erlbaum Associates, 2003.
HQ755.85 .G74 2003

PARENTING - STUDY AND TEACHING.
Integrating gender and culture in parenting. New York : Haworth Press, 2003.
BF723.P75 I57 2003

PARENTS. *See* **FATHERS; MOTHERS.**

PARENTS AND ADULT CHILDREN. *See* **PARENT AND ADULT CHILD.**

PARENTS AND CHILDREN. *See* **PARENT AND CHILD.**

PARENTS' AND TEACHERS' ASSOCIATIONS. *See* **HOME AND SCHOOL.**

PARENTS - DEATH - PSYCHOLOGICAL ASPECTS.
Lewis, Paddy Greenwall, 1945- Helping children cope with the death of a parent. Westport, Conn. : Praeger, 2004.
BF723.G75 L49 2004

Umberson, Debra. Death of a parent. Cambridge ; New York : Cambridge University Press, 2003.
BF789.D4 U48 2003

PARENTS - EUROPE - PSYCHOLOGY - CASE STUDIES.
Groben, Joseph. Requiem für ein Kind. 2. Aufl. Köln : Dittrich, 2002.
BF575.G7 G76 2002

PARENTS OF CHILDREN WITH DISABILITIES - BIOGRAPHY.
Caniato, Benilde Justo. Um testemunho de mãe. 2a. ed. São Paulo : Lato Senso, 2001.
HV901.B6 C36 2001

PARENTS OF MURDER VICTIMS - CALIFORNIA - INTERVIEWS.
Stetson, Brad. Living victims, stolen lives. Amityville, N.Y. : Baywood Pub., c2003.
HV6533.C2 S73 2003

PARENTS - PSYCHOLOGY.
Grolnick, Wendy S. The psychology of parental control. Mahwah, N.J. : L. Erlbaum Associates, 2003.
HQ755.85 .G74 2003

Parerga and paralipomena.
Schopenhauer, Arthur, 1788-1860. [Parerga and paralipomena. English] Oxford : Clarendon Press ; New York : Oxford University Press, 2000.
B3118.E5 P38 2000

PAREYSON, LUIGI.
Piazza, Giovanni. Sofferenza e senso. Torino : Camilliane, c2002.

Pārika, Kamaleśa.
Bhāvamiśra, 19th cent. [Śṛṅgārasarasī. Hindi & Sanskrit] Śṛṅgārasarasī. Saṃskaraṇa 1. Vrndāvana : Vrndāvana Śodha Saṃsthāna, 2001.
PK2916+

Parker, Elizabeth. Mobile ghosts : Alabama's haunted port city / by Elizabeth Parker 1st ed. Spanish Fort, Ala. : Apparition Pub., c2001. 104 p. : ill. ; 22 cm. ISBN 0-9703385-1-1 DDC 133.1/09761/22
1. Ghosts - Alabama - Mobile. 2. Haunted places - Alabama - Mobile. I. Title.
BF1472.U6 P36 2001

Parker, Lynn M., 1956-.
LePla, F. Joseph, 1955- Brand driven. London : Kogan Page, 2003.

Parkes-Wiener series on Jewish studies
Gender, place, and memory in the modern Jewish experience. London ; Portland, Or. : Vallentine Mitchell, 2003.

DS143 .G36 2003

PARKS. *See also* **PLAYGROUNDS.**
Bruce, Lisa. Math all around me. Chicago, Ill. : Raintree, 2003.
BF294 .B78 2003

Edo-e kara shomotsu made. Tōkyō : Kyūzansha, 1997.
HQ792.J3 N54 1997 v.19

PARKS - WASHINGTON (D.C.). *See* **MALL, THE (WASHINGTON, D.C.).**

PARLIAMENT, MEMBERS OF. *See* **LEGISLATORS.**

A parliament of science : science for the 21st century / edited by Michael Tobias, Teun Timmers, Gill Wright. Albany : State University of New York Press, c2003. 171 p. : ill. ; 23 cm. Includes bibliographical references and index. ISBN 0-7914-5813-X (acid-free paper) ISBN 0-7914-5814-8 (pbk. : acid-free paper) DDC 303.48/3/0905
1. Science - Forecasting. 2. Technological forecasting. 3. Twenty-first century - Forecasts. I. Tobias, Michael. II. Timmers, Teun. III. Wright, Gill.
Q158.5 .P38 2003

Parmenides.
[Nature. English & Greek]
Parmenides of Elea : a verse translation with interpretative essays and commentary to the text / Martin J. Henn. Westport, Conn. : Praeger, 2003. 147 p. ; 25 cm. (Contributions in philosophy, 0084-926X ; no. 88) Includes bibliographical references (p. [143]-144) and index. ISBN 0-275-97933-4 (alk. paper) DDC 182/.3
1. Philosophy. I. Henn, Martin J., 1968- II. Title. III. Series.
B235.P23 N3713 2003

Parmenides of Elea.
Parmenides. [Nature. English & Greek] Westport, Conn. : Praeger, 2003.
B235.P23 N3713 2003

Parnet, Claire.
Deleuze, Gilles. [Dialogues. English] Dialogues II. 2nd ed. New York : Columbia University Press, 2002.
B2430.D453 D4313 2002

PARODY.
Fenomenologiia smekha. Moskva : Rossiĭskiĭ institut kul'turologii, 2002.
PN6149.P3 F45 2002

PAROL EVIDENCE. *See* **EVIDENCE (LAW).**

Le parole dell'etica.
Campanini, Giorgio, 1930- Bologna : EDB, 2002.

Paroles brutes à la recherche d'un trésor / [édité par Guillemette Grobon et Michelle Simian]. Genouilleux : Passe du vent, c2003. 136 p. ; 17 cm. On cover: "Autour de la petite et de la grande histoire entre les femmes et les hommes". "de l'automne 2001 à la fin du printemps 2002"..."Un an de Chantiers de parole autour du socle d'inspiration et de création de Gertrude Productions la petite et la grande Histoire entre les femmes et les hommes"-- Préf. ISBN 2-8456-2057-8 DDC 300
1. Man-woman relationships. I. Grobon, Guillemette. II. Simian, Michelle.

PAROUSIA (PHILOSOPHY). *See* **MIND AND BODY.**

Parrini, Paolo.
Conoscenza e cognizione. 1. ed. Milano : Guerini e associati, 2002.
BJ45.5 .C66 2002

Parrish, Marlene.
Wolke, Robert L. What Einstein told his cook. 1st ed. New York : W.W. Norton & Co., c2002.
TX652 .W643 2002

Parrott, Les. Shoulda, coulda, woulda : live in the present, find your future / Les Parrott. Grand Rapids, Mich. : Zondervan, c2003. p. cm. Includes bibliographical references and index. Table of contents URL: http://www.loc.gov/catdir/toc/ecip047/2003017528.html CONTENTS: Part 1: we all have regrets -- Your future is brighter than you think -- Moving past your past -- Overcoming your if-onlys -- Giving perfectionism the boot -- Part 2: when regret turns toxic -- Getting a grip on the slippery slope of regret -- Dropping the blame game and other self-defeating sports -- Repairing your internal thermostat -- Giving shame a run for its money -- Part 3: living without regret -- The amazing alternative to feeling guilty -- Saying goodbye to false guilt-forever -- Your insurance policy against regret -- Now is the time. ISBN 0-310-22460-8 (alk. paper) DDC 152.4/4
1. Regret. I. Title.
BF575.R33 P37 2004

PARRY, C. HUBERT H. (CHARLES HUBERT HASTINGS), 1848-1918.
Allis, Michael, 1964- Parry's creative process. Aldershot : Ashgate, 2003.

Parry's creative process.
Allis, Michael, 1964- Aldershot : Ashgate, 2003.

Parsai, D. K.
Parsai, K. B. [Predictive astrology] Star guide to predictive astrology. New Delhi : Rupa & Co., c2001.
BF1720.5 .P37 2001

Parsai, K. B.
[Predictive astrology]
Star guide to predictive astrology : bhavas-planets in the 12 houses / K.B. Parsai, D.K. Parsai. New Delhi : Rupa & Co., c2001. xxv, 837 p. : ill. ; 22 cm. ISBN 81-7167-601-4
1. Predictive astrology. 2. Hindu astrology. I. Parsai, D. K. II. Title.
BF1720.5 .P37 2001

Parshev, A. P. (Andreĭ Petrovich) Pochemu Amerika nastupaet / Andreĭ Parshev. Moskva : AST : Astrel', 2002. 370 p. : ill. ; 21 cm. (Velikie protivostoi͡anii͡a) (Amerika protiv Rossii) ISBN 5170165161 (AST) ISBN 5271051854 (Astrel)
1. Russia (Federation) - Foreign economic relations - United States. 2. United States - Foreign economic relations - Russia (Federation) 3. Petroleum industry and trade - Political aspects - Russia (Federation) 4. Russia (Federation) - Foreign relations. 5. Twenty-first century - Forecasts. I. Title. II. Series. III. Series: Amerika protiv Rossii
HF1558.2.Z4 P37 2002

PARSIFAL (LEGENDARY CHARACTER). See **PERCEVAL (LEGENDARY CHARACTER).**

La parte negada de la cultura.
Menéndez, Eduardo L. Barcelona : Edicions Bellaterra, c2002.
HM1121 .M46 2002

Partecipazione e differenza.
Erdas, Franco Epifanio. Roma : Bulzoni, c2002.

PARTIALS (MUSIC). See **HARMONICS (MUSIC).**

PARTICIPATION, POLITICAL. See **POLITICAL PARTICIPATION.**

PARTICLES (NUCLEAR PHYSICS).
Börner, G. The early universe. 4th ed. Berlin : London : Springer, c2003.

PARTICULARS (PHILOSOPHY). See **INDIVIDUATION (PHILOSOPHY).**

PARTIES, POLITICAL. See **POLITICAL PARTIES.**

PARTISANS. See **GUERRILLAS.**

Partners in love and art.
Sarnoff, Irving, 1922- Intimate creativity. Madison, Wis. : University of Wisconsin Press, c2002.
BF411 .S27 2002

PARTNERSHIP. See **STRATEGIC ALLIANCES (BUSINESS).**

Parures d'éros.
Martin, Jean-Clet. Paris : Kimé, 2003.

Parzival.
Perceval = New York : Routledge, 2002.
PN686.P4 P46 2002

PARZIVAL (LEGENDARY CHARACTER). See **PERCEVAL (LEGENDARY CHARACTER).**

Pasaules uzskats jeb cilvēks dabā, sabiedrībā un mūžibā.
Brūžis, Miķelis. Rīga : Jumava, 2002.

PASCAL, BLAISE, 1623-1662. PENSÉES.
Sabalat, Tina. Pascals "Wette". Marburg : Tectum, 2000.

Williams, Jaime Andrés. El argumento de la apuesta de Blaise Pascal. 1. ed. Pamplona : Ediciones Universidad de Navarra, 2002.

Pascalis, Olivier.
The development of face processing in infancy and early childhood. New York : Nova Science, 2003.
BF720.F32 D48 2003

Pascals "Wette".
Sabalat, Tina. Marburg : Tectum, 2000.

Pascarelli, Joseph T.
Global perspectives on mentoring. Greenwich : Information Age Pub., 2004.
BF637.M48 G57 2004

Paschkis, Julie.
Fairchild, Dennis. The fortune telling handbook. 1st ed. Philadelphia, PA : Running Press, c2003.
BF1861 .F35 2003

Pasing, Anton Markus, 1962-.
Unschaerferelationen. Wiesbaden : Nelte, c2002.
BF469 .U5 2002

Pasini, Willy. I nuovi comportamenti amorosi : coppia e trasgressione / Willy Pasini. 2. ed. Milano : Mondadori, 2002. 235 p. ; 23 cm. (Saggi) Includes bibliographical references. ISBN 88-04-50689-X DDC 306
1. Sex customs. 2. Non-monogamous relationships. 3. Sexual deviation. 4. Sex (Psychology) I. Title.

Passagen Orte des Gedächtnisses.
Die Verortung von Gedächtnis. Wien : Passagen, c2001.

Passagen Philosophie
Hübner, Benno. Sinn in Sinn-loser Zeit. Wien : Passagen, c2002.

Maciejewski, Franz. Psychoanalytisches Archiv und jüdisches Gedächtnis. 1. Aufl. Wien : Passagen Verlag, 2002.

Soukup, Johannes. Metaphysik der Zeit oder Wirklichkeit und Wissen. Deutsche 1. Ausg. Wien : Passagen Verlag, c1998.

Tietz, Udo. Ontologie und Dialektik. Wien : Passagen, c2003.
B3279.H49 T54 2003

Passamaneck, Stephen M. Police ethics and the Jewish tradition / by Stephen M. Passamaneck. Springfield, Ill. : C.C. Thomas, c2003. xii, 176 p. ; 26 cm. Includes bibliographical references and index. ISBN 0-398-07421-6 (hard) ISBN 0-398-07422-4 (pbk.) DDC 174/.93632
1. Police ethics. 2. Ethics, Jewish. 3. Law enforcement - Moral and ethical aspects. I. Title.
HV7924 .P37 2003

Passer, Michael W. Psychology : the science of mind and behavior / Michael W. Passer, Ronald E. Smith. 2nd ed. Boston, Mass. : McGraw-Hill, 2003. p. cm. Includes bibliographical references and index. ISBN 0-07-256330-3 DDC 150
1. Psychology. I. Smith, Ronald Edward, 1940- II. Title.
BF121 .P348 2003

Passion and virtue in Descartes / edited by Byron Williston and Andre Gombay. Amherst, N.Y. : Humanity Books, 2003. 348 p. ; 24 cm. Includes bibliographical references (p. 333-341) and index. ISBN 1-59102-005-0 (alk. paper) DDC 128/.37
1. Descartes, Rene, - 1596-1650. - Passions de l'ame. 2. Emotions. 3. Ethics. I. Williston, Byron, 1965- II. Gombay, Andre, 1933-
B1868.P37 P37 2003

The passion for liberty.
Machan, Tibor R. Lanham, Md. : Rowman & Littlefield, c2003.
JC599.U5 M263 2003

Passion play.
Tips, Jack. 1st ed. Austin, Tex. : Apple-A-Day Press, c2002.
BF503 .T56 2002

PASSIONS. See **EMOTIONS.**

Passions du passé : recyclages de la mémoire et usage de l'oubli / sous la direction de Marie-Pascale Huglo, Eric Méchoulan et Walter Moser. Paris : L'Harmattan, c2000. 341 p. ; 22 cm. (Collection L'ouverture philosophique) Includes bibliographical references. ISBN 2-7384-9255-X
1. Memory - Social aspects. 2. Memory - Philosophy. I. Huglo, Marie-Pascale, 1961- II. Méchoulan, Eric. III. Moser, Walter, 1942- IV. Series.
BF378.S65 P37 2000

Passions of the soul.
Olaoye, Elaine H. 2nd ed. Red Bank, N.J. : Northwind Publishers, 2002.

Passivité et création.
Ménasé, Stéphanie. Paris : Presses universitaires de France, c2003.

The past doesn't have a future, but you do.
Baggett, Byrd. Nashville, Tenn. : Cumberland House Pub., c2003.
BF637.S8 B25 2003

Past life memories as a Confederate soldier.
Kent, James H., 1939- Huntsville, AR : Ozark Mountain Publishers, c2003.
BF1156.R45 K45 2003

PAST LIFE REGRESSION THERAPY. See **REINCARNATION THERAPY.**

PAST-LIVES REGRESSION. See **REINCARNATION.**

PAST-LIVES THERAPY. See **REINCARNATION THERAPY.**

Pasternack, Carol Braun.
Gender and difference in the Middle Ages. Minneapolis : University of Minnesota Press, c2003.
HQ1143 .G44 2003

PASTIMES. See **GAMES; SPORTS.**

PASTORAL THEOLOGY. See **CLERGY.**

PASTORS. See **CLERGY; PRIESTS.**

Pastoureau, Michel, 1947- Bleu : histoire d'une couleur / Michel Pastoureau. [Paris] : Seuil, c2000. 215 p. : ill. (chiefly col.) ; 25 cm. Includes bibliographical references (p. 182-191). ISBN 2-02-020475-4 DDC 155.9/1145
1. Blue. 2. Color - Psychological aspects - History. 3. Color - Social aspects - History. 4. Symbolism of colors - History. 5. Blue in art. I. Title.
BF789.C7 P36 2000

PASTRANA ARANGO, ANDRÉS.
Valencia, León. Adiós a la política, bienvenido la guerra. [Bogotá, Colombia?] : Intermedio, c2002.

Yusty, Miguel. Negociar en medio de la guerra. [Cali, Colombia] : Editorial Universidad Santiago de Cali, 2002.

Pataki, Ferenc, 1928- Élettörténet és identitás / Pataki Ferenc. Budapest : Osiris Kiadó, 2001. 425 p. : ill. ; 20 cm. Includes bibliographical references. ISBN 963-389-176-0
1. Identity (Psychology) - Social aspects. 2. Social psychology. 3. Group identity. I. Title.
BF697.5.S65 P38 2001

Patanineru hawatk'ē.
Chiwlean, Eghishē. Venetik ; Halēp : Mkhit'arean Hratarakut'iwn, S. Ghazar, 1998.

Pātañjalayoga evaṃ Jainayoga kā tulanātmaka adhyayana.
Ānanda, Aruṇā, 1957- 1. saṃskaraṇa. Dillī : Motīlāla Banārasīdāsa Pabliśarsa aura Bhogīlāla Leharacanda Bhāratīya Saṃskṛti Saṃsthāna, 2002.
B132.Y6 A496 2002

Patañjali. The Yoga-darshana : comprising the sūtras of Patañjali, with the bhāṣya of Vyāsa / translated into English, with notes, by Gangānātha Jhā. 2nd ed.-- throughly rev. [Fremont, Calif.] : Asian Humanities Press, [2002], 1934. xxviii, 263 p. ; 22 cm. Originally published: Madras, India, Theosophical Publishing House, 1934. Translated from Sanskrit. ISBN 0-89581-951-1 (pbk. : alk. paper) DDC 181/.452
1. Yoga. I. Jha, Ganganatha, Sir, 1871-1941. II. Vyāsa. Sāṃkhyapravacanabhāṣya. English. III. Vācaspatimiśra, fl. 976-1000. Yogatattvavaiśāradī. English. IV. Title.
B132.Y6 P265 2002

YOGASŪTRA.
Ānanda, Aruṇā, 1957- Pātañjalayoga evaṃ Jainayoga kā tulanātmaka adhyayana. 1. saṃskaraṇa. Dillī : Motīlāla Banārasīdāsa Pabliśarsa aura Bhogīlāla Leharacanda Bhāratīya Saṃskṛti Saṃsthāna, 2002.
B132.Y6 A496 2002

Coward, Harold G. Yoga and psychology. Albany : State University of New York Press, 2002.
BF51 .C69 2002

Grinshpon, Yohanan, 1948- Demamah ve-ḥerut ba-yogah ha-Kelasit. [Tel Aviv] : Miśrad ha-biṭaḥon, [2002]

Yogasutra.
The original Yoga. 2nd rev. ed. New Delhi : Munshiram Manoharlal Publishers, 1999.
B132.Y6 O74 1999

YOGASŪTRA.
Rham, Cat de. The spirit of yoga. London : Thorsons, 2001.

A patchwork of comforts.
Wiseman, Carol. Boston, MA : Conari Press, 2004.
BF515 .W57 2004

PATENT LAWS AND LEGISLATION. See **COPYRIGHT.**

Paternoster biblical and theological monographs
McCulloch, Gillian. The deconstruction of dualism in theology. Carlisle : Paternoster Press, 2002.

PATH ANALYSIS. See **FACTOR ANALYSIS.**

PATH in psychology
The life cycle of psychological ideas. New York : Kluwer Academic/Plenum, 2004.

Path of the priestess.
BF38 .L54 2004

Path of the priestess.
Rose, Sharron. Rochester, VT. : Inner Traditions, c2002.
BL625.7 .R67 2002

The path of transformation.
Gawain, Shakti, 1948- Rev. ed. Novato, Calif. : Nataraj Pub., 2000.
BJ1581 .G35 2000

Path to priesthood.
Karade, Akinkugbe. Brooklyn, N.Y. : Kânda Mukûtu Books, c2001.
BL2523.I33 K37 2001

Pāṭhaka, Hariśaṅkara. Jaya.
Vaidyanāthadīkṣita, 15th cent. [Jātakapārijāta] Jātakapārijātaḥ. 1. saṃskaraṇa. Vārāṇasī : Caukhambā Surabhāratī Prakāśana ; Dillī : Caukhambā Saṃskrti Pratiṣṭhāna, 2001.
BF1714.H5 V253 2001

Mantreśvara. Phaladīpikā. 1. saṃskaraṇa. Vārāṇasī : Caukhambā Surabhāratī Prakāśana, 2002.
BF1714.H5+

PATHOGNOMY. *See* **EMOTIONS; FACE; PHRENOLOGY; PHYSIOGNOMY.**

PATHOLOGICAL EATING. *See* **EATING DISORDERS.**

PATHOLOGISTS. *See* **FORENSIC PATHOLOGISTS.**

PATHOLOGY. *See* **DIAGNOSIS, LABORATORY; DISEASES; MEDICINE.**

PATHOLOGY, CLINICAL. *See* **DIAGNOSIS, LABORATORY.**

The pathology of Eurocentrism.
Ephraim, Charles Wm. Trenton, NJ : Africa World Press, c2003.
HT1581 .E64 2003

Paths through life
(v. 4) Bergman, Lars R. Studying individual development in an interindividual context. Mahwah, N.J. : L. Erlbaum Associates, 2003.
BF713 .B464 2003

Pathways to translation.
Kiraly, Donald C., 1953- Kent, Ohio : Kent State University Press, c1995.
P306.5 .K57 1995

Pathy, Dinanath. Art, regional traditions, the Temple of Jagannātha : architecture, sculpture, painting, ritual / Dinanath Pathy. New Delhi : Sundeep Prakashan, 2001. xxvi, 246 p. : ill., maps ; 28 cm. Spine title: Temple of Jagannātha. SUMMARY: With reference to Jagannātha Temple in Dhārākoṭa, Orissa, India. Includes bibliographical reference (p. [179]-183) and index. Includes passages in Oriya (roman). ISBN 81-7574-105-8
1. Jagannātha Temple (Dhārākoṭa, India) 2. Architecture, Hindu. 3. Temples, Hindu - India - Orissa. I. Title. II. Title: Temple of Jagannātha
NA6002 .P37 2001

PATIENCE - RELIGIOUS ASPECTS - BUDDHISM.
Thubten Chodron, 1950- Working with anger. Ithaca, NY : Snow Lion Publication, 2001.
BQ4430.A53 T48 2001

Le patient absent de Jacques Lacan.
Laborie, Philippe. Paris : Harmattan, c2002.

PATIENT AND PSYCHOTHERAPIST. *See* **PSYCHOTHERAPIST AND PATIENT.**

PATIENT CARE RECORDS. *See* **MEDICAL RECORDS.**

PATIENT OUTCOME ASSESSMENT. *See* **OUTCOME ASSESSMENT (MEDICAL CARE).**

PATIENTS. *See* **HIV-POSITIVE PERSONS; PSYCHOTHERAPIST AND PATIENT; SICK.**

Patologías complejas (versión preliminar).
Rodríguez, Luis. [Santiago, Chile] : Corporación de Promoción Universitaria, [1995]

PATRIARCHY. *See also* **FAMILY; PATRILINEAL KINSHIP.**
Thompson, Patricia J. In bed with Procrustes. New York : P. Lang, c2003.
HQ1190 .T52 2002 bk. 2

PATRIARCHY IN LITERATURE.
Göttner-Abendroth, Heide. Die tanzende Göttin. 6. vollst. überarb. Neuaufl. München : Frauenoffensive, 2001, c1982.

PATRILINEAL DESCENT. *See* **PATRILINEAL KINSHIP.**

PATRILINEAL KINSHIP - NIGERIA.
Drews, Annette. Guardians of the society. Leipzig, Germany : Institut für Afrikanistik, Universität Leipzig, 2000.
BF1584.Z33 D44 2000

PATRILINY. *See* **PATRILINEAL KINSHIP.**

Patriot fires.
Lawson, Melinda, 1954- Lawrence : University Press of Kansas, c2002.
E468.9 .L39 2002

PATRIOTISM. *See* **NATIONALISM.**

PATRIOTISM - UNITED STATES.
My America. New York : Scribner, c2002.
E169.1 .M968 2002

PATRIOTISM - UNITED STATES - HISTORY.
Hansen, Jonathan M. The lost promise of patriotism. Chicago : University of Chicago Press, c2003.
E661 .H316 2003

PATRIOTISM - UNITED STATES - HISTORY - 19TH CENTURY.
Lawson, Melinda, 1954- Patriot fires. Lawrence : University Press of Kansas, c2002.
E468.9 .L39 2002

A pattern of madness.
Symington, Neville. London ; New York : Karnac, 2002.

PATTERN PERCEPTION.
Bruce, Lisa. Math all around me. Chicago, Ill. : Raintree, 2003.
BF294 .B78 2003

Burstein, John. Patterns. Milwaukee, WI : Weekly Reader Early Learning Library, 2003.
BF294 .B87 2003

Reed, Janet (Janet C.) Animal patterns. Bloomington, Minn. : Yellow Umbrella Books, c2003.
BF294 .R44 2003

PATTERN PERCEPTION - CONGRESSES.
International Workshop MLDM 2003 (2003 : Leipzig, Germany) Machine learning and data mining in pattern recognition. Berlin ; New York : Springer, c2003.
Q327 .I67 2003

International Workshop on Multiple Classifier Systems (4th : 2003 : Guildford, England) Multiple classifier systems. Berlin ; New York : Springer, c2003.
Q325.5 .I574 2003

PATTERN PERCEPTION - JUVENILE LITERATURE.
Bruce, Lisa. Math all around me. Chicago, Ill. : Raintree, 2003.
BF294 .B78 2003

Burstein, John. Patterns. Milwaukee, WI : Weekly Reader Early Learning Library, 2003.
BF294 .B87 2003

Reed, Janet (Janet C.) Animal patterns. Bloomington, Minn. : Yellow Umbrella Books, c2003.
BF294 .R44 2003

PATTERN RECOGNITION. *See* **PATTERN PERCEPTION.**

Patterns.
Burstein, John. Milwaukee, WI : Weekly Reader Early Learning Library, 2003.
BF294 .B87 2003

Patton, Bobby R., 1935- Decision-making group interaction : achieving quality / Bobby R. Patton and Timothy M. Downs. 4th ed. Boston : Allyn and Bacon, c2003. xii, 180 p. : ill. ; 24 cm. Includes bibliographical references and index. ISBN 0-321-04919-5 DDC 302.3/4
1. Small groups. 2. Group decision making. 3. Social interaction. I. Downs, Timothy M. II. Title.
HM736 .P37 2003

Patzel-Mattern, Katja. Geschichte im Zeichen der Erinnerung : Subjektivität und kulturwissenschaftliche Theoriebildung / Katja Patzel-Mattern. Stuttgart : Franz Steiner, 2002. 339 p. ; 25 cm. (Studien zur Geschichte des Alltags ; Bd. 19) Thesis (Ph. D.)--Universität, Münster, 1998. Includes bibliographical references. ISBN 3-515-08082-1 (hd.bd.)
1. Memory. 2. History - Philosophy. I. Title. II. Series.

Patzig, Günther.
Ethik ohne Dogmen. Paderborn : Mentis, 2001.

Pauer-Studer, Herlinde.
Freiheit, Gleichheit und Autonomie. Wien : Oldenbourg ; Berlin : Akademie Verlag, 2003.
JC575 .F74 2003

Paul Carus lectures
(21st ser.) Danto, Arthur Coleman, 1924- The abuse of beauty. Chicago : Open Court, c2003.
BH39 .D3489 2003

Paul, Jean-Marie.
Le système et le rêve. Paris : Harmattan, c2002.
BF1078 .S97 2002

Pauleen, David, 1957-.
Virtual teams. Hershey, PA ; London : Idea Group Publishing, c2004.
HD66 .V56 2004

Pauley, Penelope J.
Pauley, Thomas L. I'm rich beyond my wildest dreams-- "I am. I am. I am". New York : Berkley Books, 2003.
BF639 .P28 2003

Pauley, Thomas L. I'm rich beyond my wildest dreams-- "I am. I am. I am" : how to get everything you t in life / Thomas L. Pauley and Penelope J. Pauley. New York : Berkley Books, 2003. p. cm. Originally published: Newport Beach, Calif. : Rich Dreams Pub., 1999. ISBN 0-425-19194-X DDC 158.1
1. New Thought. I. Pauley, Penelope J. II. Title.
BF639 .P28 2003

Paulus, Paul B.
Group creativity. Oxford ; New York : Oxford University Press, 2003.
BF408 .G696 2003

PAUPERISM. *See* **POOR.**

Pause philo
Schiffter, Frédéric. Pensées d'un philosophe sous Prozac. [Toulouse] : Milan, c2002.

Pavlicevic, Mercedes. Groups in music : strategies from music therapy / Mercédès Pavlicevic. London ; New York : Jessica Kingsley Publishers, 2003. 252 p. : ill. ; 25 cm. Includes bibliographical references (p. 239-245) and indexes. ISBN 1-84310-081-9 (alk. paper) DDC 615.8/5154
1. Music therapy. 2. Social groups. I. Title.
ML3920 .P2279 2003

The pawprints of history.
Coren, Stanley. New York ; London : Free Press, c2002.

Payne, E. F. J.
Schopenhauer, Arthur, 1788-1860. [Parerga and paralipomena. English] Parerga and paralipomena. Oxford : Clarendon Press ; New York : Oxford University Press, 2000.
B3118.E5 P38 2000

Payr, Sabine, 1956-.
Emotions in humans and artifacts. Cambridge, Mass. : MIT Press, c2002.
BF531 .E517 2002

Le pays de l'écriture.
Baron Supervielle, Silvia. Paris : Seuil, c2002.

Paź, Bogusław. Epistemologiczne założenia ontologii Christiana Wolffa / Bogusław Paź. Wrocław : Wydawn. Uniwersytetu Wrocławskiego, 2002. 311 p. ; 24 cm. (Acta Universitatis Wratislaviensis ; no 2316. Filozofia ; 39) Includes bibliographical references and index. Errata slip inserted. Summary and table of contents in German. ISBN 83-229-2216-7
1. Wolff, Christian, - Freiherr von, - 1679-1754. 2. Ontology. I. Title. II. Series: Acta Universitatis Wratislaviensis ; no 2316. III. Series: Acta Universitatis Wratislaviensis. Filozofia ; 39.

Pazenok, V. S. (Viktor Sergeevich).
Suspil'stvo na porozi XXI stolittia. Kyïv : Ukraïns'kyĭ TSentr dukhovnoï kul'tury, 1999.

PBS Online.
Living with suicide [electronic resource]. [Alexandria, Va.] : PBS Online ; [New York, N.Y.] : Web Lab
BF789.D4

PC (POLITICAL CORRECTNESS). *See* **POLITICAL CORRECTNESS; POLITICAL CORRECTNESS.**

PDMS-2.
Folio, M. Rhonda. 2nd ed. Austin : Pro-Ed, c2000.
BF723.M6 .F65 2000

PEABODY DEVELOPMENTAL MOTOR SCALES-2.

Folio, M. Rhonda. PDMS-2. 2nd ed. Austin : Pro-Ed, c2000.
BF723.M6 .F65 2000

PEACE. *See also* **PEACEFUL CHANGE (INTERNATIONAL RELATIONS); WAR.**
2001, año de las Naciones Unidas del diálogo entre civilizaciones. Guatemala : Fundación Casa de la Reconciliación : MINUGUA, 2001.
JX1952 .A233 2001

Acuerdos de paz y seguridad democrática en Guatemala. 1. ed. [Guatemala] : USAC, DIGI, [2002]

Al oído de Uribe. 1a. ed. Bogotá, Colombia : Editorial Oveja Negra, 2002.

Approaches to peacebuilding. Houndmills, Basingstoke, Hampshire ; New York : Palgrave Macmillan, 2002.
JZ5538 .A675 2002

Barbieri, Katherine, 1965- The liberal illusion. Ann Arbor : University of Michigan Press, c2002.
HF1379 .B363 2002

Boyce, James K. Investing in peace. Oxford : Oxford University Press, 2002.

Christoff, Joseph A. Issues in implementing international peace operations [electronic resource]. [Washington, D.C.] : U.S. General Accounting Office, [2002]

Contemporary peacemaking. Houndmills, Basingstoke ; New York : Palgrave Macmillan, 2003.
JZ6010 .C665 2003

Cotroneo, Girolamo. Le idee del tempo. Soveria Mannelli (Catanzaro) : Rubbettino, c2002.

Le dialogue intercongolais. Bruxelles ; Nairobi : International Crisis Group, [2001]

Dupaigne, Bernard. Afghanistan, rêve de paix. Paris : Buchet-Chastel, 2002.

Ending civil wars. Boulder, Colo. : Lynne Rienner, 2002.
JZ6368 .E53 2002

From Kabila to Kabila. Nairobi ; Brussels : International Crisis Group, 2001.

Globalization and armed conflict. Lanham, Md. : Rowman & Littlefield, c2003.
JZ5538 .G58 2003

Heiwagaku ga wakaru. Tōkyō : Asahi Shinbunsha, 2002.
JZ5534 .H44 2002

Howard, Michael, 1922 Nov. 29- The invention of peace and the reinvention of war. Rev. and extended ed. London : Profile, 2002, c2001.

Idrobo Díaz, Hugo, 1954- La joda de la paz en Colombia. 1. ed. Cali, Colombia : [s.n., 2002?]

Imagine coexistence. 1st ed. San Francisco : Jossey-Bass, c2003.
HM1121 .I42 2003

Kingston, Maxine Hong. The fifth book of peace. 1st ed. New York : Alfred A. Knopf, 2003.
PS3561.I52 F44 2003

Kritik der Gewalt. Wien : Promedia, c2002.
D860 .K75 2002

Kyelem, Apollinaire. L'éventuel et le possible. [Ouagadougou : Presses universitaires de Ouagadougou, 2002]
1. Black author.

Latour, Bruno. War of the worlds. Chicago : Prickly Paradigm Press, c2002.
H61.15 .L38 2002

Lipson, Charles. Reliable partners. Princeton, N.J. : Princeton University Press, c2003.
JC423 .L583 2003

Long, William J., 1956- War and reconciliation. Cambridge, Mass. : MIT Press, c2003.
JZ5597 .L66 2003

Maoz, Zeev. Bound by struggle. Ann Arbor : University of Michigan Press, c2002.
JZ5595 .M366 2002

Masangana Diamaka, Robin, 1962- Dialogue politique. Paris : Editoo.com, 2002.
1. Black author.

Medvedko, Leonid Ivanovich. Rossiía, Zapad, Islam. Zhukovskiĭ ; Moskva : Kuchkovo pole, 2003.

BP173.5 .M44 2003

Naumann, Klaus, 1939- Frieden, der noch nicht erfüllte Auftrag. Hamburg : Mittler & Sohn, c2002.
UA710 .N38 2002

The Nordic peace. Aldershot, England ; Burlington, VT : Ashgate, c2003.
UA646.7 .N672 2003

Ojeda Awad, Alonso. Convivencia y globalización. [1a ed.]. [Bogotá] : Universidad Pedagógica Nacional, [2002]

Order and justice in international relations. Oxford ; New York : Oxford University Press, 2003.
JZ1308 .O73 2003

Panorama estratégico, 2001-2002. [Madrid] : Ministerio de Defensa, 2002.

Peace and conflict resolution. Part 1 [videorecording]. Derry, N.H. : Chip Taylor Communications, 1996.

Peace and conflict resolution. Part 2 [videorecording]. Derry, N.H. : Chip Taylor Communications, 1997.

Peace-building. [Harare] : ACPD, 2002.

Peace, prosperity, and democracy at the cutting edge. New York : Nova Science Publishers, c2003.

Pliskin, Zelig. Harmony with others. 1st ed. Brooklyn, N.Y. : Shaar Press : Distributed by Mesorah Publications, 2002.

Policymaking and peace. Lanham, Md. : Lexington Books, c2003.
JZ5538 .P65 2003

Potorti, David. September 11th Families for Peaceful Tomorrows. New York, NY : RDV Books, c2003.

The power of nonviolence. Boston, Mass. : Beacon Press, c2002.
JZ5538 .P685 2002

Scheunemann, Pam, 1955- Coping with anger. Edina, MN : Abdo Pub., 2004.
BF575.A5 S34 2004

Scheunemann, Pam, 1955- Dealing with bullies. Edina, MN : Abdo Pub., 2004.
BF637.B85 S37 2004

Storm clouds over Sun City. Brussels ; Nairobi : International Crisis Group, 2002.

Téllez, Edgar. Diario íntimo de un fracaso. 1. ed. Bogotá, D.C., Colombia : Planeta, 2002.

La tierra nueva. Río Cuarto, Argentina : Universidad Nacional de Río Cuarto, Facultad de Ciencias Humanas, Centro de Estudios y Actividades para una Cultura de la Paz, 2000.

Valencia, León. Adiós a la política, bienvenido la guerra. [Bogotá, Colombia?] : Intermedio, c2002.

Yusty, Miguel. Negociar en medio de la guerra. [Cali, Colombia] : Editorial Universidad Santiago de Cali, 2002.

Zeitgeschichtliche Hintergründe aktueller Konflikte V. Zürich : Forschungsstelle für Sicherheitspolitik und Konfliktanalyse, Eidgenössische Technische Hochschule, 1995.
JX1952 .Z45 1995

Peace and conflict resolution. Part 1 [videorecording] / a production of Globalvision. Derry, N.H. : Chip Taylor Communications, 1996. 1 videocassette (30 min.) : sd., col. ; 1/2 in. (Rights and wrongs series) VHS. Title from container. Jr.Hi.-Adult. Cast: Charlayne Hunter-Gault. Executive producers, Rory O'Connor, Danny Schechter; director, Eulogio L. Ortiz, Jr. SUMMARY: First segment: Report on the 1995 Tomorrow's Leaders Conference held in Venice, Italy, and sponsored by Nobel Laureate, Elie Wiesel. Young people from Northern Ireland, the former Yugoslavia, Africa, the Middle East and the United States, join seasoned foreign diplomats in discussions about tolerance, dialogue and negotiations. Second segment: An interview with holocaust survivor Eli Wiesel, on the importance of dialogue. Third segment: A visit to elementary school PS 230 in Brooklyn, New York, where students learn conflict resolution techniques in an effort to prevent violence and promote tolerance.
1. Wiesel, Elie, - 1928- - Interviews. 2. Tomorrow's Leaders Conference - (1995 : - Venice, Italy) 3. Conflict management. 4. Conflict management - Study and teaching. 5. Peace. 6. Toleration. 7. Negotiation. 8. Violence - Prevention. 9. Youth - Attitudes. 10. Human rights. I. Hunter-Gault, Charlayne. II. Wiesel, Elie, 1928- III. Ortiz, Eulogio L. IV. Chip Taylor Communications. V. Globalvision, Inc. VI. Series.

Peace and conflict resolution. Part 2 [videorecording] / produced by Globalvision, Inc. Derry, N.H. : Chip Taylor Communications, 1997. 1 videocassette (30 min.) : sd., col. ; 1/2 in. (Rights and wrongs series) VHS. Title from container. Jr.Hi.-Adult. Cast: Charlayne Hunter-Gault. Executive producers, Rory O'Connor, Danny Schechter; director, Eulogio L. Ortiz, Jr. SUMMARY: A profile of three different programs which attempt to heal the conflicts in nations. First segment: Examines, through excerpts from the documentary film "Leap of faith," the creation of an integrated school of Catholics and Protestants established by parents in Northern Ireland to begin the process of religious and political reconciliation. Second segment: Investigates through excerpts from the film "Seas of Peace," a unique summer camp in Maine, where young Israelis and Palestinians learn to understand each other and resolve differences constructively. Third segment: An interview with Archbishop Desmond Tutu about South Africa's Truth and Reconciliation Commission and its mandate to expose the crimes of apartheid and to promote reconciliation.
1. Tutu, Desmond - Interviews. 2. South Africa. - Truth and Reconciliation Commission. 3. Conflict management. 4. Conflict management - Study and teaching. 5. Peace. 6. Toleration. 7. Negotiation. 8. Violence - Prevention. 9. Youth - Northern Ireland - Attitudes. 10. Youth - Israel - Attitudes. 11. Reconciliation (Law) - South Africa. 12. Human rights. I. Ortiz, Eulogio L. II. Hunter-Gault, Charlayne. III. Tutu, Desmond. IV. Chip Taylor Communications. V. Globalvision, Inc. VI. Title: Leap of faith (Motion picture) VII. Title: Seas of peace (Motion picture) VIII. Series.

Peace-building : an introduction for communities. [Harare] : ACPD, 2002. 72 p. : ill. ; 21 cm. "ACPDT"--P. [4] of cover. Includes bibliographical references (p. 69-71).
1. Peace. 2. Conflict management. 3. Mediation. 4. Zimbabwe. I. Africa Community Publishing and Development Trust.

Peace in Croatia - research survey results.
Mir u Hrvatskoj--rezultati istraživanja. Zagreb : Hrvatski Caritas ; Split : Franjevački in-t za kulturu mira, 2001.
HN638.A8 M57 2001

Peace in Croatia - results of research.
Mir u Hrvatskoj--rezultati istraživanja. Zagreb : Hrvatski Caritas ; Split : Franjevački in-t za kulturu mira, 2001.
HN638.A8 M57 2001

PEACE, INNER. *See* **PEACE OF MIND.**

PEACE - JUVENILE LITERATURE.
Scheunemann, Pam, 1955- Coping with anger. Edina, MN : Abdo Pub., 2004.
BF575.A5 S34 2004

Scheunemann, Pam, 1955- Dealing with bullies. Edina, MN : Abdo Pub., 2004.
BF637.B85 S37 2004

PEACE OF MIND.
Borysenko, Joan. Inner peace for busy women. Carlsbad, Calif. : Hay House, 2003.
BF637.P3 B673 2003

Laurel, Alicia Bay, 1949- How to make peace. 1st ed. Layton, Utah : G. Smith, Publisher, c2004.
BF637.P3 L38 2004

O'Hara, Nancy. Serenity in motion. New York : Warner Books, 2003.
BF637.P3 O42 2003

PEACE OF MIND - PROBLEMS, EXERCISES, ETC.
Reeve, Susyn. Choose peace & happiness. Boston, MA : Red Wheel, 2003.
BF637.P3 R44 2003

PEACE (PHILOSOPHY).
Echekwube, A. O. (Anthony Onyebuchi) A metaphysical analysis of the concept of reincarnation. Ekpoma, Nigeria : Ambrose Alli University Publishing House, 2002.
1. Black author.

PEACE PROCESS IN THE MIDDLE EAST. *See* **ARAB-ISRAELI CONFLICT - 1993- - PEACE.**

Peace, prosperity, and democracy at the cutting edge / Stuart Nagel, editor. New York : Nova Science Publishers, c2003. vi, 146 p. ; 24 cm. (Handbook of peace, prosperity and democracy ; v. 1) Includes bibliographical references and index. ISBN 1-59033-205-9
1. Peace. 2. Democracy. 3. Economic development. 4. Economic policy. I. Nagel, Stuart S., 1934- II. Series.

PEACE - PSYCHOLOGICAL ASPECTS.
Grosbard, Ofer, 1954- [Yiśra'el 'al ha-sapah. English] Israel on the couch. Albany : State University of New York Press, c2003.
DS126.5 .G694 2003

Grosbard, Ofer, 1954- Yiśra'el 'al ha-sapah. Tel-Aviv : Yedi'ot aḥaronot : Sifre ḥemed, c2000.

PEACE - RELIGIOUS ASPECTS.
Twyman, James F. Emissary of light. Forres : Findhorn, 2002.

PEACE - RELIGIOUS ASPECTS - JUDAISM.
Pliskin, Zelig. Harmony with others. 1st ed. Brooklyn, N.Y. : Shaar Press : Distributed by Mesorah Publications, 2002.

PEACE - RESEARCH.
Heiwagaku ga wakaru. Tōkyō : Asahi Shinbunsha, 2002.
JZ5534 .H44 2002

PEACE (THEOLOGY). See PEACE - RELIGIOUS ASPECTS.

PEACEFUL CHANGE (INTERNATIONAL RELATIONS).
Searching for peace in Central and South Asia. Boulder, Colo. : Lynne Rienner Publishers, 2002.
JZ5597 .S43 2002

PEACEFUL COEXISTENCE. See INTERNATIONAL RELATIONS; PEACE; WORLD POLITICS - 1945-.

Peaceful passing.
Wood, Robert S. (Robert Snyder), 1930- Sedona, AZ : In Print Pub., c2000.
BF789.D4 W66 2000

PEACEKEEPING FORCES.
Approaches to peacebuilding. Houndmills, Basingstoke, Hampshire ; New York : Palgrave Macmillan, 2002.
JZ5538 .A675 2002

From promise to practice. Boulder ; London : L. Rienner Publishers, 2003.
JZ6368 .S68 2003

PEACEKEEPING FORCES - CONGO (DEMOCRATIC REPUBLIC).
Le dialogue intercongolais. Bruxelles ; Nairobi : International Crisis Group, [2001]

Masangana Diamaka, Robin, 1962- Dialogue politique. Paris : Editoo.com, 2002.
1. Black author.

Peacock, Carol Antoinette. Death and dying / Carol Antoinette Peacock. New York : Franklin Watts, c2004. v. cm. (Life balance) Includes bibliographical references and index. Table of contents URL: http://www.loc.gov/catdir/toc/ecip048/2003019765.html CONTENTS: Grief, a normal response to loss -- The work of grief -- Warm up -- Heavy lifting : expressing the feelings -- Getting extra help -- More heavy lifting : keeping memories alive -- Moving on. ISBN 0-531-12370-7 DDC 155.9/37
1. Grief - Juvenile literature. 2. Bereavement - Juvenile literature. 3. Grief. 4. Bereavement. I. Title. II. Series.
BF575.G7 P3783 2004

Peak experiences.
Marshall, Ian, 1954- Charlottesville : University of Virginia Press, 2003.
PS163 .M37 2003

The peak performance series. Vol. [4] [videorecording] / presented by Pamela Bolling and Karen Hebert ; [taught by] Pamela Bolling and Karen Hebert. Longwood, Fla. : Pamela Bolling Enterprises, c1999. 1 videocassette (VHS, NTSC) (63 min.) : sd., col. ; 1/2 in. Title on cassette label and wrapper: The peak performance video series IV. Special edition. SUMMARY: Instruction in lyrical routines by Pamela Bolling and her mother Karen Hebert, plus an interview. CONTENTS: Karen Hebert's j[unio]r lyrical routine. CONTENTS: Pamela Bolling's classroom lyrical routine. CONTENTS: How yoga is important to dancers / Take 5 interview with Karen Sandler; interviewer, Pamela Bolling. CONTENTS: Pamela Bolling's jazz lyrical routine. CONTENTS: Pamela Bolling's adv[anced] jazz lyrical routine. CONTENTS: Karen Hebert's adv[anced] lyrical routine.
1. Jazz dance - Study and teaching. 2. Ballet - Study and teaching. 3. Yoga. 4. Dance. 5. Instruction. 6. Video. I. Bolling, Pamela. II. Hebert, Karen. III. Sandler, Karen. IV. Title: Peak performance video series IV. Special edition [videorecording]

Peak performance video series IV. Special edition [videorecording].
The peak performance series. Vol. [4] [videorecording]. Longwood, Fla. : Pamela Bolling Enterprises, c1999.

Pearce, John A.
De Kluyver, Cornelis A. Strategy. Upper Saddle River, N.J. : Prentice Hall, c2003.
HD38.2 .D425 2003

Pearce, Joseph Chilton. The crack in the cosmic egg : new constructs of mind and reality / Joseph Chilton Pearce ; foreword by Thom Hartmann. Rochester, Vt. : Park Street Press, c2002. xvii, 205 p. ; 23 cm. Includes bibliographical references (p. 199-205). "Originally published: New York: The Julian Press, Inc., 1971"--T.p. verso. ISBN 0-89281-994-4 DDC 111
1. Reality. 2. Mind and body. 3. Thought and thinking. I. Title.
BD331 .P3915 2002

Pearce, Sharyn.
Youth cultures. Westport, Conn. : Praeger, 2003.
HQ796 .Y59273 2003

Pearlman, Lou. Bands, brands and billions : my top ten rules for success in any business / Lou Pearlman with Les Smith. New York : London : McGraw-Hill, 2002. ix, 256 p. ; 23 cm. Index. ISBN 0-07-138565-7 DDC 658.409
1. Success in business. 2. Entrepreneurship. I. Smith, Wes. II. Title.

Pearsall, Derek Albert. Arthurian romance : a short introduction / Derek Pearsall. Malden, MA : Blackwell Publishers, 2003. viii, 182 p. ; 24 cm. (Blackwell introductions to literature) Includes bibliographical references (p. [168]-172) and index. ISBN 0-631-23319-9 (alk. paper) ISBN 0-631-23320-2 (pbk. : alk. paper) DDC 809/.93351
1. Arthurian romances - History and criticism. I. Title. II. Series.
PN685 .P43 2003

Pearsall, Paul. The Beethoven factor : the new positive psychology of hardiness, happiness, healing, and hope / Paul Pearsall. Charlottesville, VA : Hampton Roads Pub. Co., c2003. xlvi, 257 p. ; 24 cm. Includes bibliographical references (p. 241-250) and index. Table of contents URL: http://www.loc.gov/catdir/toc/ecip044/2003010769.html CONTENTS: Preface: Awakening to a more authentic life -- Introduction: From suffering to savoring -- Thriving through the tough times -- A life fully lived -- Developing your talent for thriving -- An ode to thriving -- Finding meaning in misery -- A course in thriveology -- Conscious acts of creation -- Living a thousand times over -- Testing your thriveability -- Hardiness through the hard times -- Happiness for the sad times -- Healing through the horrible times -- Hoping for all times -- Epilogue: Grandma's recipe for thriving. ISBN 1-57174-397-9 (alk. paper) DDC 158.1
1. Resilience (Personality trait) 2. Self-actualization (Psychology) I. Title.
BF698.35.R47 P43 2003

Pearson, Carol, 1944- PMAI manual : a guide for interpreting the Pearson-Marr Archetype Indicator Instrument / Carol S. Pearson, Hugh K. Marr. Gainesville, FL : Center for Applications of Psychological Type, c2003. p. cm. Includes bibliographical references (p.   ) and index. ISBN 0-935652-74-4 DDC 155.2/8
1. Pearson-Marr Archetype Indicator. I. Marr, Hugh K., 1949- II. Title. III. Title: P.M.A.I. manual
BF698.8.P37 P43 2003

Pearson, Kimberly H., 1970-.
Women's health and psychiatry. Philadelphia, PA : Lippincott Williams & Wilkins, c2002.
RA564.85 .W6652 2002

PEARSON-MARR ARCHETYPE INDICATOR.
Pearson, Carol, 1944- PMAI manual. Gainesville, FL : Center for Applications of Psychological Type, c2003.
BF698.8.P37 P43 2003

PEASANT ART. See FOLK ART.

PEASANTRY. See LAND TENURE.

PEASANTRY - FRANCE - LORRAINE - HISTORY - 16TH CENTURY.
Diedler, Jean-Claude. Le testament de Maître Persin. [Metz] : Editions serpenoise, [2000]
BF1517.F5 D515 2000

PEASANTRY - FRANCE - LORRAINE - HISTORY - 17TH CENTURY.
Diedler, Jean-Claude. Le testament de Maître Persin. [Metz] : Editions serpenoise, [2000]
BF1517.F5 D515 2000

PEASANTS. See PEASANTRY.

Pease, Bob.
Working with men in the human services. Crows Nest, N.S.W. : Allen & Unwin, c2001.

PEDAGOGY. See EDUCATION; TEACHING.

Peddle, David, 1965-.
Philosophy and freedom. Toronto : University of Toronto Press, c2003.

Peden, A. M.
Abbo of Fleury and Ramsay. Oxford ; New York : Oxford University Press, 2002.

PEDIATRIC EMERGENCIES. See CHILDREN - WOUNDS AND INJURIES.

PEDIATRIC NEUROPSYCHOLOGY.
Healy, Jane M. Your child's growing mind. 3rd ed. New York : Broadway Books, 2004.
BF318 .H4 2004

PEDIATRIC TRAUMATOLOGY. See CHILDREN - WOUNDS AND INJURIES.

PEDOLOGY (CHILD STUDY). See CHILDREN.

Pedrick, Cherry.
Claiborn, James. The habit change workbook. Oakland, CA : New Harbinger Publications : Distributed in the U.S.A. by Publishers Group West, c2001.
BF337.B74 C57 2001

Pedroza, Ludim. The ritual of music contemplation : an anthropological study of the solo piano recital as cultural performance genre / by Ludim Pedroza. 2002. v, 119 leaves : ill. ; 28 cm. Thesis (Ph. D.)--Texas Tech University, 2002. Includes bibliographical references (leaves 114-117).
1. Schumann, Clara, - 1819-1896. 2. Liszt, Franz, - 1811-1886. 3. Piano - History - 19th century. 4. Piano - History - 20th century. 5. Music - Performance. 6. Music - Social aspects - 19th century. 7. Music - Social aspects - 20th century. 8. Music - Philosophy and aesthetics. 9. Music - Social aspects. 10. Culture - Philosophy. 11. Performance practice (Music) 12. Music and anthropology. I. Title.

Peer prejudice and discrimination.
Fishbein, Harold D. 2nd ed. Mahwah, N.J. : L. Erlbaum, 2002.
BF723.P75 F57 2002

PEER PRESSURE.
Goals and life lessons support materials [electronic resource]. Greenwood Village, CO : FasTracKids International, [1998]
BF637.S4

Peer rejection.
Bierman, Karen L. New York : Guilford Press, 2004.
BF723.R44 B54 2003

PEERAGE. See NOBILITY.

Peinture et musique : penser la vision, penser l'audition / Catherine Kintzler (éd.). Villeneuve-d'Ascq : Presses universitaires du Septentrion, c2002. 230 p. : ill. ; 22 cm. + 1 computer optical disc (4 3/4 in.). (Esthétique et sciences des arts) Includes bibliographical references. ISBN 2-85939-769-8
1. Art and music. 2. Aesthetics. 3. Picture perception. 4. Auditory perception. 5. Musical perception. I. Kintzler, Catherine.

Peiró, Agustí. Ésser i moral / Agustí Peiró. 1. ed. [Valencia] : Brosquil Edicions, 2002. 92 p. ; 21 cm. (Fora de col·lecció ; 5) ISBN 84-956204-3-X
1. Ethics. 2. Existential ethics. I. Title. II. Series.

Peixoto, Nelson Brissac. Nelson Brissac, Antonio Augusto Arantes : depoimento em 12/08/96. [São Paulo, SP : Fundação Memorial da América Latina, 1997] 39 p. ; 20 cm. (Segundas no Memorial ; 6)
1. Arantes, Antonio Augusto - Interviews. 2. Peixoto, Nelson Brissac - Interviews. 3. Brazil - Social life and customs - 20th century. 4. Popular culture. I. Arantes, Antonio Augusto. II. Title. III. Series.

PEIXOTO, NELSON BRISSAC - INTERVIEWS.
Peixoto, Nelson Brissac. Nelson Brissac, Antonio Augusto Arantes. [São Paulo, SP : Fundação Memorial da América Latina, 1997]

Pelham, Brett W., 1961- Conducting research in psychology : measuring the weight of smoke / Brett W. Pelham, Hart Blanton. 2nd ed. Australia ; Belmont, CA : Thomson/Wadsworth, c2003. xviii, 411 p. : ill. ; 24 cm. Includes bibliographical references (p. 391-401) and indexes. ISBN 0-534-52093-6 DDC 150/.7/2
1. Psychology - Research - Methodology. 2. Psychology, Experimental. I. Blanton, Hart, 1967- II. Title.
BF76.5 .P34 2003

Pellegrini, Anthony D. Observing children in their natural worlds : a methodological primer / Anthony D. Pellegrini, Frank Symons, John Hoch. 2nd ed. Mahwah, N.J. : L. Erlbaum Associates, 2004. p. cm. Includes bibliographical references and indexes. ISBN 0-8058-4689-1 (pbk. : alk. paper) DDC 155.4/07/23
1. Child psychology - Research - Methodology. 2. Observation (Psychology) I. Symons, Frank James, 1967- II. Hoch, John, 1971- III. Title.
BF722 .P45 2004

Pels, Peter.
Magic and modernity. Stanford, Calif. : Stanford University Press, 2003.

GN475.3 .M34 2003

PEMBROKE WELSH CORGI.
Wells, Celia Townsend, 1932- Brood bitch. West Lafayette, Ind. : Purdue University Press, c2003.
SF422.82.W44 A3 2003

PENALTIES (CRIMINAL LAW). See **PUNISHMENT.**

PENANCE. See **REPENTANCE.**

Penczak, Christopher. Gay witchcraft : empowering the tribe / Christopher Penczak. Boston, MA : Weiser Books, 2003. xvii, 265 p. : ill. ; 23 cm. Includes bibliographical references (p. 262-264). ISBN 1-57863-281-1 (pbk.) DDC 133.4/3/08664
1. Witchcraft. 2. Gays - Miscellanea. I. Title.
BF1571.5.G39 P46 2003

Pendragon.
Blake, Steve. London : Rider, 2002.

Pene d'amore.
Pieroni, Osvaldo. Soveria Mannelli : Rubbettino, c2002.

Pene Shabat neḳablah.
Sharir, Avraham Yiśra'el. Yerushalayim : Avraham Kohen-Erez, 763 [2003]
BM670.L44 S527 2003

Penguin classics
Freud, Sigmund, 1856-1939. [Essays. English. Selections] The uncanny. New York : Penguin Books, 2003.
BF109.F75 A25 2003

Freud, Sigmund, 1856-1939. [Zur Psychopathologie des Alltagslebens. English] The psychopathology of everyday life. New York : Penguin Books, 2003.
BF173 .F82513 2003

Penine Avir Ya'aḳov 'al Shir ha-shirim.
Abi-Ḥasira, Jacob ben Masoud, 1808-1880. [Abir Ya'aḳov. Selections. 2002] Sefer Penine Avir Ya'aḳov. Yerushalayim : Hotsa'at ha-Makhon le-hotsa'at sefarim she-'a. y. Yeshivat Ner Yitshak : Mekhon Avraham : Shim'on Abiḥatsira, 763 [2002]
BS1485.X33 A25 2002

Penine Śefat Emet.
Alter, Judah Aryeh Leib, 1847-1905. [Selections. 2000] Ofrah : Mekhon Shovah, [2000?-2003?]
BM198.2 .A55 2000

PENIS - PSYCHOLOGICAL ASPECTS.
Pieroni, Osvaldo. Pene d'amore. Soveria Mannelli : Rubbettino, c2002.

PENITENCE. See **REPENTANCE.**

PENMANSHIP. See **GRAPHOLOGY; WRITING.**

PENNA, ANTONIO GOMES, 1917-.
Figueiredo, Luís Cláudio M. (Luís Cláudio Mendonça), 1945- Antonio Gomes Penna. Brasília, DF : Conselho Federal de Psicologia ; Rio de Janeiro, RJ : Imago, 2002.

PENOLOGY. See **PUNISHMENT.**

Pensées d'un philosophe sous Prozac.
Schifftter, Frédéric. [Toulouse] : Milan, c2002.

Pensées mortelles.
Merdalor, Jean. Port-au-Prince, Haiti : Editions Choucoune, 1999.

Penser avec Whitehead.
Stengers, Isabelle. Paris : Seuil, c2002.

PENTECOSTALISM.
Terrin, Aldo N. (Aldo Natale) Mistiche dell'Occidente. 1. ed. Brescia : Morcelliana, 2001.
BP605.N48 T477 2001

Penz, Otto. Metamorphosen der Schönheit : eine Kulturgeschichte moderner Körperlichkeit / Otto Penz. Wien : Turia + Kant, c2001. 252 p. : ill. ; 20 cm. ISBN 3-85132-314-9 (pbk.)
1. Body, Human - Social aspects. 2. Beauty, Personal. I. Title.
GT495 .P459 2001

Penzenskiĭ gosudarstvennyĭ pedagogicheskiĭ universitet imeni V.G. Belinskogo.
Russkoe slovo. Penza : Izd-vo PGPU, 1998.
PG2026.B66 R88 1998

PEOPLE, MARRIED. See **MARRIED PEOPLE.**

PEOPLE, SINGLE. See **SINGLE PEOPLE.**

PEOPLE, UNMARRIED. See **SINGLE PEOPLE.**

PEOPLE WITH DISABILITIES.
Inclusive design. London ; New York : Springer, c2003.

TA174 .I464 2003
Questions and answers [electronic resource]. [Washington, D.C.] : U.S. Equal Employment Opportunity Commission, [2000?]

PEOPLE WITH DISABILITIES - NIGERIA.
Adekanmbi, Joseph. Disabilities. Ibadan [Nigeria] : Goalim Publishers, 2001.

The peoples of Europe
Snyder, Christopher A. (Christopher Allen), 1966- The Britons. Malden, MA ; Oxford : Blackwell Pub., 2003.
DA140 .S73 2003

Per modo di dire - .
Lurati, Ottavio. Bologna : CLUEB, c2002.

PERCEPTION. See also **AUDITORY PERCEPTION; CONSCIOUSNESS; GEOGRAPHICAL PERCEPTION; HUMAN INFORMATION PROCESSING; MENTAL REPRESENTATION; PATTERN PERCEPTION; PICTURE INTERPRETATION; PICTURE PERCEPTION; SELECTIVITY (PSYCHOLOGY); SELF-PERCEPTION; SIZE PERCEPTION; SOCIAL PERCEPTION; SPACE PERCEPTION; SUBLIMINAL PROJECTION; TIME PERCEPTION; VISUAL PERCEPTION; WHOLE AND PARTS (PSYCHOLOGY).**
Böhme, Gernot. Aisthetik. München : Fink, c2001.
BH39 .B64 2001

Coren, Stanley. Sensation and perception. 6th ed. Hoboken, NJ : J. Wiley & Sons, c2004.
BF233 .C59 2004

Randolph, Joanne. What I look like when I am confused. 1st ed. New York : PowerStart Press, 2004.
BF723.I63 R36 2004

Randolph, Joanne. [What I look like when I am confused. Spanish & English] What I look like when I am confused = 1st ed. New York : Rosen Pub. Group's PowerKids Press, 2004.
BF723.I63 R3618 2004

Wahrnehmung und Medialität. Tübingen : Francke, c2001.
PN2039 .W347 2001

PERCEPTION (CHILD PSYCHOLOGY). See **PERCEPTION IN CHILDREN.**

PERCEPTION - CROSS-CULTURAL STUDIES.
Litvinović, Gorjana. Čovek izmedu istorijskog i ličnog vremena. Beograd : Institut za psihologiju, 2001.
BF697 .L543 2001

PERCEPTION, DISORDERS OF. See **HALLUCINATIONS AND ILLUSIONS.**

PERCEPTION IN CHILDREN.
Saleev, Vadim Alekseevich. Ėsteticheskoe vospriiatie i detskaia fantaziia. Minsk : Natsional'nyĭ in-t obrazovaniia, 1999.
BF723.P36 S25 1999

PERCEPTION IN CHILDREN - JUVENILE LITERATURE.
Randolph, Joanne. What I look like when I am confused. 1st ed. New York : PowerStart Press, 2004.
BF723.I63 R36 2004

Randolph, Joanne. [What I look like when I am confused. Spanish & English] What I look like when I am confused = 1st ed. New York : Rosen Pub. Group's PowerKids Press, 2004.
BF723.I63 R3618 2004

PERCEPTION IN INFANTS.
Early category and concept development. Oxford ; New York : Oxford University Press, 2003.
BF720.C63 E27 2003

Perception, knowledge, and belief.
Dretske, Fred I. Cambridge, U.K. ; New York : Cambridge University Press, 2000.
BD161 .D73 2000

Perception of faces, objects, and scenes : analytic and holistic processes / edited by Mary A. Peterson and Gillian Rhodes. Oxford ; New York : Oxford University Press, 2003. viii, 393 p., [4] p. of plates : ill. (some col.) ; 25 cm. (Advances in visual cognition) Includes bibliographical references and index. CONTENTS: What are the routes to face recognition? / James C. Bartlett, Jean H. Searcy, and Herve Abdi -- The holistic representation of faces / James W. Tanaka and Martha J. Farah -- When is a face not a face? The effects of misorientation on mechanisms of face perception / Janice E. Murray, Gillian Rhodes , and Maria Schuchinsky -- Isolating holistic processes in faces (and perhaps objects) / Elinor McKone, paolo Martini, and Ken Nakayama -- Diagnostic use of scale information for componential and holistic recognition / Philippe G. Schyns and Frederic Gosselin -- Image-based recognition of biological motion, scenes, and objects / Isabelle Bulthoff and Heinrich H. Bullthoff -- Visual object recognition: can a single mechanism suffice? / Michael J. Tarr -- The complementary properties of holistic and analytic representation of shape / John E. Hummel -- Relative dominance of holistic and component properties in the perceptual organization of visual objects / Ruth Kimchi -- Overlapping partial configurations in object memory: an alternative solution to classic problems in perception and recognition / Mary A Peterson -- Neuropsychological approaches to perceptual organization: evidence from visual agnosia / Marlene Behrmann -- Scene perception: what we can learn from visual integration and change detection / Daniel J. Simons, Stephen R. Mitroff, and Steven L. Franconeri -- Eye movements, visual memory, and scene representation / John M. Henderson and Andrew Hollingworth. ISBN 0-19-516538-1 (alk. paper) DDC 152.14
1. Visual perception. 2. Whole and parts (Psychology) I. Peterson, Mary A., 1950- II. Rhodes, Gillian. III. Series.
BF241 .P434 2003

PERCEPTION (PHILOSOPHY).
El buscador de oro. [Madrid] : Lengua de Trapo Ediciones, c2002.

Was kostet den Kopf? Marburg : Tectum Verlag, 2001.

PERCEPTION - PHYSIOLOGY.
Manzotti, Riccardo. Coscienza e realtà. Bologna : Società editrice il mulino, c2001.
BF311 .M35 2001

PERCEPTION, SELECTIVE. See **SELECTIVITY (PSYCHOLOGY).**

PERCEPTUAL CARTOGRAPHY. See **GEOGRAPHICAL PERCEPTION.**

PERCEPTUAL MAPS. See **GEOGRAPHICAL PERCEPTION.**

PERCEPTUAL-MOTOR LEARNING.
Sunbeck, Deborah. The complete Infinity walk . Rochester, N.Y. : Leonardo Foundation Press, c2001-
BF318 .S86 2001

PERCEPTUAL-MOTOR PROCESSES.
Touching for knowing. Amsterdam ; Philadelphia : John Benjamins Pub., c2003.
BF275 .T69 2003

PERCEPTUALLY HANDICAPPED CHILDREN. See **HEARING IMPAIRED CHILDREN.**

PERCEVAL. See **PERCEVAL (LEGENDARY CHARACTER).**

PERCEVAL (LEGENDARY CHARACTER) - ROMANCES - ADAPTATIONS - HISTORY AND CRITICISM.
Perceval = New York : Routledge, 2002.
PN686.P4 P46 2002

PERCEVAL (LEGENDARY CHARACTER) - ROMANCES - HISTORY AND CRITICISM.
Perceval = New York : Routledge, 2002.
PN686.P4 P46 2002

Perceval = Parzival : a casebook / edited with an introduction by Arthur Groos and Norris J. Lacy. New York : Routledge, 2002. viii, 312 p. ; 24 cm. (Arthurian characters and themes) Includes bibliographical references. CONTENTS: Rexque futurus: the anterior order in Le conte du graal / Donald Maddox -- Perlesvaus and the Perceval palimpsest / Norris J. Lacy -- Peredur son of Efrawg -- Brynley F. Roberts -- Dialogic transpositions: the grail hero wins a wife / Arthur Groos -- Parzival's knightly guilt / Wolfgang Mohr -- Parzival's failure (books V and VI) / Dennis Green -- Parzival and Gawan: hero and counterpart / Marianne Wynn -- The grail question in Wolfram and elsewhere / L.P. Johnson -- The saga of Parceval the knight / Marianne E. Kalinke -- Arthurian comedy: the simpleton-hero in Sir Perceval of Galles / Caroline D. Eckhardt -- Malory's Percivale: a case of competing genealogies / Dhira B. Mahoney -- "A very secondary position": Perceval in modern English and American literature / Alan Lupack -- Parsifal / Carl Dahlhaus -- Parsifal and Perceval on film: the reel life of a grail knight / Kevin J. Harty. ISBN 0-8153-0781-0 ISBN 0-8153-0658-X DDC 809/.93351
1. Perceval (Legendary character) - Romances - History and criticism. 2. Perceval (Legendary character) - Romances - Adaptations - History and criticism. 3. Arthurian romances - History and criticism. I. Groos, Arthur. II. Lacy, Norris J. III. Title: Parzival IV. Series.
PN686.P4 P46 2002

Perché la Chiesa.
Giussani, Luigi. PerCorso. Milano : Rizzoli, c1997-

Percheron, René. Matisse : de la couleur à l'architecture / René Percheron, Christian Brouder. Paris : Citadelles & Mazenod, c2002. 381 p. : ill. (some col.) : 33 cm. Includes bibliographical references (p. 380) and indexes. ISBN 2-85088-182-1
1. Matisse, Henri, - 1869-1954 - Criticism and interpretation. 2. Matisse, Henri, - 1869-1954 - Knowledge - Architecture. 3. Color in art. 4. Artists' preparatory studies - France. I. Matisse, Henri, 1869-1954. II. Brouder, Christian. III. Title.
N6853.M33 P47 2002

Percorsi (Bologna, Italy)
Manzotti, Riccardo. Coscienza e realtà. Bologna : Società editrice il mulino, c2001.
BF311 .M35 2001

PerCorso.
Giussani, Luigi. Milano : Rizzoli, c1997-

Le père.
Brodeur, Claude, 1924- Paris : L'Harmattan, 2001.
HQ756 .B76 2001

Peregrinos y vagabundos.
Benítez Torres, Milton. 1. ed. Quito, Ecuador : Ediciones Abya-Yala, 2002.

Pereira, Lygia Maria de França.
Psiquiatria, loucura e arte. São Paulo, SP, Brasil : Edusp, c2002.

The perennial quest for a psychology with a soul.
Vrinte, Joseph, 1949- 1st ed. Delhi : Motilal Banarsidass Publishers, 2002.
BF311+

PERESVETOV, IVAN SEMENOVICH, FL. 1530-1549.
Zaĭtseva, L. I. Russkie providtsy o rossiĭskoĭ gosudarstvennosti. Moskva : In-t ėkonomiki RAN, 1998-
DK49 .Z35 1998

Pérez-Embid Wamba, Javier. Hagiología y sociedad en la España medieval : Castilla y León, siglos 11-13 / Javier Pérez-Embid Wamba. Huelva : Universidad de Huelva, 2002. 390 p. : 24 cm. (Serie Arias Montano ; 59) Includes bibliographical references (p. 375-390). ISBN 84-956994-9-4 (pbk.)
1. Christian saints - Cult - Spain - Castilla y León - History of doctrines - Middle Ages, 600-1500. 2. Christian hagiology - Spain - Castilla y León - History. 3. Hagiography. 4. Castilla y León (Spain) - Church history. I. Pérez-Embid Wamba, Javier. II. Title. III. Title: Castilla y León, siglos 11-13 IV. Series.
BX4659.S8 P47 2002

Pérez-Embid Wamba, Javier. Hagiología y sociedad en la España medieval. Huelva : Universidad de Huelva, 2002.
BX4659.S8 P47 2002

Pérez Jiménez, Aurelio.
Ángeles, demonios y genios en el mundo Mediterráneo. Madrid : Ediciones Clásicas, 2000.

Pérez-Jofre, Ignacio. Huellas y sombras / Ignacio Pérez-Jofre. Sada, A Coruña : Ediciós do Castro, [2001] 124 p. : ill. ; 24 cm. (Arte. Arquitectura) Includes bibliographical references (p. 121-124). ISBN 84-8485-034-X
1. Painting, Modern - 20th century. 2. Visual perception. 3. Shades and shadows in art. I. Title. II. Series: Arte. Arquitectura (Sada, Spain)
ND195 .P368 2001

Perfect, Timothy J.
Applied metacognition. Cambridge, U.K. ; New York : Cambridge University Press, 2002.
BF311 .A638 2002

Perfectionism and contemporary feminist values.
Yuracko, Kimberly A., 1969- Bloomington : Indiana University Press, c2003.
HQ1206 .Y87 2003

PERFECTIONISM (PERSONALITY TRAIT) - RELIGIOUS ASPECTS - JUDAISM.
Miller, Avigdor. [Lev Avigdor] Sefer Lev Avigdor. Bruklin, N.Y. : S. Miller, 762, c2002.
BM538.P4 .M45 2001

PERFORMANCE. *See also* **UNDERACHIEVEMENT.**
Khademian, Anne M., 1961- Working with culture. Washington, D.C. : CQ Press, c2002.
JF1351 .K487 2002

Performance and evolution in the age of Darwin.
Goodall, Jane. London ; New York : Routledge, 2002.
NX180.S3 G66 2002

PERFORMANCE ANXIETY.
Mornell, Adina. Lampenfieber und Angst bei ausübenden Musikern. Frankfurt am Main : P. Lang, 2002.

ML3830 .M67 2002

PERFORMANCE - MEASUREMENT.
Rampersad, Hubert K. Total performance scorecard. Amsterdam ; Boston ; London : Butterworth-Heinemann, c2003.
HD62.15 .R3598 2003

PERFORMANCE PRACTICE (MUSIC).
Pedroza, Ludim. The ritual of music contemplation. 2002.

The performance prism.
Neely, A. D. (Andy D.) London ; New York : Financial Times/Prentice Hall, 2002.
HF5549.5.P35 N44 2002

PERFORMANCE - PSYCHOLOGICAL ASPECTS.
Hays, Kate F. You're on!. 1st ed. Washington, DC : American Psychological Association, c2003.
BF637.C6 H366 2003

PERFORMANCE STANDARDS.
Neely, A. D. (Andy D.) The performance prism. London ; New York : Financial Times/Prentice Hall, 2002.
HF5549.5.P35 N44 2002

PERFORMING ARTS. *See* **DANCE; MOTION PICTURES; PAGEANTS; THEATER.**

Performing emotions.
Tait, Peta, 1953- Aldershot ; Burlington Vt. : Ashgate, c2002.
PG3458.Z9 D774 2002

PERFORMING PRACTICE (MUSIC). *See* **PERFORMANCE PRACTICE (MUSIC).**

Peri, Vittorio. Da oriente ed da occidente : le chiese cristiane dall'impero romano all'Europa moderna / a cura di Mirella Ferrari. Roma : Editrice Antenore, 2002. 2 v. : 25 cm. (Medioevo e umanesimo ; 107, 108) ISBN 88-8455-557-4
1. Church history - Primitive and early church, ca. 30-600. 2. Church history - Middle Ages, 600-1500. 3. Church history - Modern period, 1500- I. Ferrari, Mirella. II. Title. III. Series.
BR162.3 .P475 2002

Perilous planet earth.
Palmer, Trevor, 1944- Cambridge, U.K. ; New York : Cambridge University Press, 2003.
QE506 .P35 2003

PERIODS (MENSTRUATION). *See* **MENSTRUATION.**

PERIPATETICS.
Fortenbaugh, William W. Theophrastean studies. Stuttgart : Steiner, 2003.
B626.T34 F678 2003

PERL (COMPUTER PROGRAM LANGUAGE).
Fraley, R. Chris. How to conduct behavioral research over the internet. New York : Guilford Press, 2005.
BF76.6.I57 F73 2005

Shea, Linchi. Real world SQL server administration with Perl. [Berkeley, CA] : Apress ; New York : Distributed to the book trade in the U.S. by Springer-Verlag, c2003.
QA76.73.S67 S48 2003

Verbruggen, Martien. Graphics programming with Perl. Greenwich : Manning, c2002.
T385 .V465 2002

Perloff, Richard M. The dynamics of persuasion : communication and attitudes in the 21st century / Richard M. Perloff. 2nd ed. Mahwah, N.J. : Lawrence Erlbaum Associates, 2003. xvi, 392 p. : ill. ; 24 cm. Includes bibliographical references (p. 341-378) and indexes. ISBN 0-8058-4087-7 (alk. paper) ISBN 0-8058-4088-5 (pbk. : alk. paper)
1. Persuasion (Psychology) 2. Mass media - Psychological aspects. 3. Attitude change. I. Title.
BF637.P4 .P39 2003

Perry, Laura, 1965- Ancient spellcraft : from the hymns of the Hittites to the carvings of the Celts / by Laura Perry. Franklin Lakes, NJ : New Page Books, c2002. 224 p. : ill. ; 21 cm. Includes bibliographical references (p. 215-218) and index. SUMMARY: Ancient Spellcraft is a practical book of spells and charms derived from a number of ancient pagan cultures, including the Babylonians, Canaanites, Celts, Egyptians and Sumerians. ISBN 1-56414-576-X (pbk.) DDC 133.4/4
1. Magic, Ancient. I. Title.
BF1591 .P47 2002

Perry, Martin. Confidence booster workout : 10 steps to beating self-doubt / Martin Perry. San Diego : Thunder Bay Press, 2004. p. cm. Includes index. ISBN 1-59223-195-0 DDC 158
1. Self-confidence - Problems, exercises, etc. I. Title.

BF575.S39 P48 2004

Perschy, Mary Kelly, 1942- Helping teens work through grief / by Mary Kelly Perschy. 2nd ed. New York : Brunner-Routledge, 2004. p. cm. Includes bibliographical references and index. Table of contents URL: http://www.loc.gov/catdir/toc/ecip048/2003019898.html ISBN 0-415-94696-4 (pbk.) DDC 155.9/37/0835
1. Grief in adolescence. 2. Bereavement in adolescence. 3. Teenagers - Counseling of. 4. Grief therapy. I. Title.
BF724.3.G73 P47 2004

PERSECUTION - EUROPE - HISTORY.
Geschlecht, Magie und Hexenverfolgung. Bielefeld : Verlag für Regionalgeschichte, 2002.

PERSECUTION - EUROPE - HISTORY - ENCYCLOPEDIAS.
Burns, William E., 1959- Witch hunts in Europe and America. Westport, Conn. : Greenwood Press, 2003.
BF1584.E9 B87 2003

PERSECUTION - GERMANY - FRANCONIA - HISTORY - 16TH CENTURY.
Kleinöder-Strobel, Susanne, 1969- Die Verfolgung von Zauberei und Hexerei in den fränkischen Markgraftümern im 16. Jahrhundert. Tübingen : Mohr Siebeck, c2002.
BF1583 .K54 2002

PERSECUTION - HISTORY.
Religion et exclusion, XIIe-XVIIIe siècle. Religion et exclusion, douzième-dix-huitième siècle. Aix-en-Provence : Publications de l'Université de Provence, 2001.
BL238 .R448 2001

PERSECUTION - UNITED STATES - HISTORY - ENCYCLOPEDIAS.
Burns, William E., 1959- Witch hunts in Europe and America. Westport, Conn. : Greenwood Press, 2003.
BF1584.E9 B87 2003

PERSEVERATION (PSYCHOLOGY). *See* **MEMORY.**

The Persistence of religions : essays in honor of Kees W. Bolle / Sara J. Denning-Bolle, Edwin Gerow, editors. Malibu : Undena Publications, 1996. xxi, 444 p. : ill. ; 28 cm. (Other realities ; v. 9) Includes bibliographical references and index. English; 1 paper in German. CONTENTS: Introductory essay. Introduction -- The Persistence of religions. The persistence of religion among jews and in J.-P. Satre / by Seymour Cain ; The Black soldier and World War II / by Jerome H. Long ; The persistence of religious-cultural-socio-political synthesis / by Joseph M. Kitagawa ; Synesius and the persistence of Platonic religiosity / by Jay Bregman ; Pothos and Peitho in Plotinus / by Rein Ferwerda ; Code of behavior and iconographic form / by Karel van Kooij ; The secret in history: an essay on Charles Péguy's Clio / by Annette Aronwicz ; Fusswaschung auf Silbernem Boden / by M. Heerma van Voss / El ciclo de los pastores / Steven Sharbrough ; S. Radhakrishnan, religious tolerance and Advaita Vedānta / by Arvind Sharma ; Ordinary images, extraordinary perceptions / by Patricia North -- Myth. Dead myth patchwork / by Thorkild Jacobsen ; Mesopotamian magic as a mythology and ritual of fate: structural correlations with Biblical religion / by Giorgio Buccellati ; Words of power and why they are considered to be so in primal religions / by Willard Johnson ; Myths and power : four examples / by Cristiano Grottanelli ; When Bhīmasena met Hanumān / by Burt Thorp ; Enthymesis - one source for the creativity and contextuality of mysticism / by Jess Hollenback ; Texts, rituals, and our problems / by Rick Talbott ; Unio mythica : the one that differs in oneness / Wilhelm Dupré -- CONTENTS: Secularization. The later Advaitins' interpretation of 'tat tvan asi' / by Edwin Gerow ; Rebellion and renewal in French romantisism / Lisa Bonoff Raskind ; Myth and the mechanistic universe : a study of religious imagery in the writings of Robert Oppenheimer / by James Eric Lane -- Relgion and politics. The power of the place : the Nebi Musa pilgrimage and the origins of Palestinian nationalism / by Richard Hecht and Roger Friedland ; Religion and polity : reflections on the history of relgions and the analysis of politics - a question of definition / by Ninian Smart ; Kings, rebels, and the left hand / by Bruce Lincoln ; Kings, scholars and texts on the formation of the Avesta / by William Malandra ; The origins of Mithraism : a reconsideration / by Ronald Mellor ; Two notes on the Keret legend / by J. Hoftijzer -- Response essay. Response / by Kees W. Bolle -- Author index.
1. Religion. 2. Religion - History. 3. Religion and politics. 4. Mythology. I. Bolle, Kees W. II. Denning-Bolle, Sara J. III. Gerow, Edwin. IV. Series.

PERSON-NUMBERS. *See* **IDENTIFICATION NUMBERS, PERSONAL.**

PERSON (PHILOSOPHY). *See* **AGENT (PHILOSOPHY).**

PERSON SCHEMAS. *See* **BODY IMAGE.**

La persona e i nomi dell'essere : scritti di filosofia in onore di Virgilio Melchiorre / a cura di Francesco Botturi, Francesco Totaro, Carmelo Vigna. Milano : V&P Università, c2002. 2 v. (xlvi, 1349 p.) ; 22 cm. (Filosofia. Ricerche) Festschrift. "Bibliografia [degli scritti di V. Melchiorre]" (p. [xxiii]-xlvi). Includes bibliographical references. ISBN 88-343-0728-3
1. *Melchiorre, Virgilio.* 2. *Philosophy.* 3. *Philosophy - History.* I. *Melchiorre, Virgilio.* II. *Botturi, Francesco, 1947-* III. *Totaro, Francesco, 1941-* IV. *Vigna, Carmelo, 1940-* V. *Series.*
B29 .P414 2002

PERSONA (LITERATURE). *See* **FIRST PERSON NARRATIVE.**

Personal and moral identity / edited by Albert W. Musschenga ... [et al.]. Dordrecht ; Boston : Kluwer Academic Publishers, c2002. vi, 326 p. ; 25 cm. (Library of ethics and applied philosophy ; v. 11) Includes bibliographical references and indexes. ISBN 1402007647 (alk. paper) DDC 126
1. *Ethics - Congresses.* 2. *Identity (Psychology) - Congresses.* I. *Musschenga, A. W., 1950-* II. *Series.*
BJ45 .P47 2002

PERSONAL BEAUTY. *See* **BEAUTY, PERSONAL.**

PERSONAL COACHING - PRACTICE.
Fairley, Stephen. Getting started in personal and executive coaching. Hoboken, N.J. : J. Wiley & Sons, 2003.
BF637.P36 F35 2003

PERSONAL CONDUCT. *See* **CONDUCT OF LIFE.**

PERSONAL CONSTRUCT PSYCHOLOGY. *See* **PERSONAL CONSTRUCT THEORY.**

PERSONAL CONSTRUCT THEORY.
Butt, Trevor, 1947- Understanding people. New York : Palgrave Macmillan, 2003.
BF698 .B89 2003

PERSONAL CONSTRUCT THEORY - PERIODICALS.
Constructive change. Boise, Idaho : Center for Constructive Change, c1996-
BF698.9.P47 C66

PERSONAL CONSTRUCT THERAPY.
Henehan, Mary Pat. Integrating spirit and psyche. New York ; London : Haworth Pastoral Press, c2003.
RC489.F45 H46 2003

PERSONAL DATA PROTECTION. *See* **DATA PROTECTION.**

PERSONAL DEVELOPMENT. *See* **MATURATION (PSYCHOLOGY); SUCCESS.**

PERSONAL EVANGELISM. *See* **WITNESS BEARING (CHRISTIANITY).**

PERSONAL GROWTH. *See* **MATURATION (PSYCHOLOGY); SELF-ACTUALIZATION (PSYCHOLOGY); SUCCESS.**

PERSONAL HEALTH. *See* **HEALTH.**

PERSONAL HEALTH SERVICES. *See* **MEDICAL CARE.**

PERSONAL IDENTIFICATION NUMBERS. *See* **IDENTIFICATION NUMBERS, PERSONAL.**

Personal illusionism.
Garifullin, Ramil', 1962- Illíuzionizm lichnosti. Kazan' : [s.n.], 1997.
BF491 .G37 1997

PERSONAL INFORMATION MANAGEMENT.
Allen, Kathleen R. Time and information management that really works. Los Angeles, Calif : Affinity Pub., c1995.

PERSONAL LIBERTY. *See* **LIBERTY.**

PERSONAL RELATIONS. *See* **INTERPERSONAL RELATIONS.**

PERSONAL SPACE.
Gendered landscapes. University Park, PA : Center for Studies in Landscape History, c2000.

PERSONALISM. *See* **INDIVIDUALISM.**

PERSONALITY. *See also* **ADAPTABILITY (PSYCHOLOGY); ADJUSTMENT (PSYCHOLOGY); BODY IMAGE; CHARACTER; DETERMINATION (PERSONALITY TRAIT); EGO (PSYCHOLOGY); HUMANISTIC PSYCHOLOGY; IDENTITY (PSYCHOLOGY); MOOD (PSYCHOLOGY); OPPRESSION (PSYCHOLOGY); PERFECTIONISM (PERSONALITY TRAIT);**

PERSONAL CONSTRUCT THEORY; PERSONALITY CHANGE; RESILIENCE (PERSONALITY TRAIT); SELF; TYPOLOGY (PSYCHOLOGY).
Burger, Jerry M. 6th ed. Australia ; Belmont, CA : Thomson/Wadsworth, c2004.
BF698 .B84 2004

Ryckman, Richard M. Theories of personality. 8th ed. Belmont, CA : Thomson/Wadsworth, c2004.
BF698 .R96 2004

PERSONALITY.
Butt, Trevor, 1947- Understanding people. New York : Palgrave Macmillan, 2003.
BF698 .B89 2003

Carver, Charles S. Perspectives on personality. 5th ed. Boston, MA : Allyn and Bacon, 2004.
BF698 .C22 2004

Cloninger, Susan C., 1945- Theories of personality. 4th ed. Upper Saddle River, N.J. : Pearson/Prentice Hall, c2004.
BF698 .C543 2004

Crisand, Ekkehard. Psychologie der Persönlichkeit. 8., durchgesehene Aufl. Heidelberg : I.H. Sauer-Verlag, 2000.
BF698 .C715 2000

Funder, David Charles. The personality puzzle. 3rd ed. New York : Norton, c2004.
BF698 .F84 2004

Gambini, Roberto, 1944- Soul & culture. 1st ed. College Station : Texas A&M University Press, 2003.
BF698.9.C8 G35 2003

Ianitskiĭ, M. S. (Mikhail Sergeevich) Tsennostnye orientatsii lichnosti kak dinamicheskaia sistema. Kemerovo : Kuzbassvuzizdat, 2000.
BF698 .I18 2000

Joines, Vann. Personality adaptations. Nottingham ; Chapel Hill, N.C. : Lifespace, 2002.
BF698.3 .J65 2002

Kaluzniacky, Eugene. Managing psychological factors in information systems work. Hershey PA : Information Science Pub., c2004.
BF576 .K358 2004

Matthews, Gerald. Personality traits. 2nd ed. New York : Cambridge University Press, 2003.
BF698 .M3434 2003

Mischel, Walter. Introduction to personality. 7th ed. Hoboken, NJ : J. Wiley & Sons, c2004.
BF698 .M555 2004

Musek, Janek. Psihološki modeli in teorije osebnosti. Ljubljana : Filozofska fakulteta Univerze v Ljubljani, 1999.
BF698 .M887 1999

Ognev, A. S. (Aleksandr Sergeevich) Teoreticheskie osnovy psikhologii sub"ektogeneza. Voronezh : Izd-vo VF RAGS, 1997.
BF698 .O36 1997

Personality and temperament: genetics, evolution, and structure. Lengerich : Pabst Science Publishers, 2001.
BF698 .P3692 2001

Pieces of the personality puzzle. 3rd ed. New York : Norton, c2004.
BF698 .P525 2004

Romm, M. V. (Mark Valerievich) Adaptatsiia lichnosti v sotsiume. Novosibirsk : "Nauka", 2002.
HM696 .R655 2002

Savchyn, Myroslav, 1950- Dukhovnyĭ potentsial lĭudyny. Ivano-Frankivs'k : Plaĭ, 2001.
BF698 .S288 2001

Slavskaia, A. N. Lichnost' kak sub"ekt interpretatsii. Dubna : "Feniks+", 2002.
BF698 .S54 2002

Tul'chinskiĭ, G. L. (Grigoriĭ L'vovich) Postchelovecheskaia personologiia. Sankt-Peterburg : Aleteiia, 2002.
BD331 .T84 2002

Virtue, vice, and personality. 1st ed. Washington, D.C. : American Psychological Association, c2003.
BF698 .V57 2003

Zeĭgarnik, B. V. (Blíuma Vul'fovna) Psikhologiia lichnosti. Moskva : Moskovskiĭ psikhologo-sotsial'nyĭ in-t, 1998.
BF698 .Z43 1998

Personality adaptations.
Joines, Vann. Nottingham ; Chapel Hill, N.C. : Lifespace, 2002.

BF698.3 .J65 2002

PERSONALITY AND CREATIVE ABILITY.
Bodalev, A. A. Kak stanoviatsia velikimi ili vydaiushchimisia? Moskva : In-t psikhoterapii, 2003.
BF724.5 .B64 2003

Stepanov, S. ÍU. (Sergeĭ ÍUr'evich) Refleksivnaia praktika tvorcheskogo razvitiia cheloveka i organizatsiĭ. Moskva : Nauka, 2000.
BF408 .S75 2000

PERSONALITY AND CULTURE.
Chelovek kak sub"ekt kul'tury. Moskva : Nauka, 2002.

Gambini, Roberto, 1944- Soul & culture. 1st ed. College Station : Texas A&M University Press, 2003.
BF698.9.C8 G35 2003

PERSONALITY AND CULTURE - DICTIONARIES.
Becker, Konrad. Tactical reality dictionary. Vienna : Edition Selene : [s.l.] : Distribution Canada/UK/USA by Autonomedia, 2002.
BF637.P4 B33 2002

PERSONALITY AND EMOTIONS.
Williams, Redford B., 1940- The type E personality. Emmaus, Pa. : Rodale, c2004.
BF576.3 .W55 2004

PERSONALITY AND OCCUPATION.
Personality and organizations. Mahwah, N.J. : Lawrence Erlbaum Associates, 2004.
BF698.9.O3 P46 2004

Personality and work. 1st ed. San Francisco, CA : Jossey-Bass, c2003.
BF698.9.O3 P47 2003

Personality and organizations / edited by Benjamin Schneider, D. Brent Smith. Mahwah, N.J. : Lawrence Erlbaum Associates, 2004. p. cm. (LEA's organization and management series) Includes bibliographical references and indexes. CONTENTS: Introducing personality at work : personality psychology for organizational researchers / Robert Hogan -- Personality and organization : a European perspective on personality assessment in organizations / Adrian Furnham -- Persistent conceptual and methodological issues in personality assessment -- Four lessons learned from the person situation debate : a review and research agenda / Greg L. Stewart and Murray R. Barrick -- Personality, interactional psychology, and person organization fit / Timothy A. Judge and Amy Kristof-Brown -- The implications of impression management for fillreak personality research in organizations / D. Brent Smith and Chet Robie -- The role of personality in work and well-being vocational psychology and personality / W. Bruce Walsh -- The dispositional approach to job attitudes : an empirical and conceptual review / Barry M. Staw -- Personality and work-related distress / Jennifer M. George and Arthur P. Brief -- The role of personality in understanding micro organizational processes -- J-U-S-T-I-F-Y to explain the reasons why : a conditional reasoning approach to understanding motivated behavior / Lawrence R. James and Joan R. Rentsch -- Personality and leadership / William D. Spangler, Robert J. House and Rita Palrecha -- Personality and citizenship behavior in organizations / Dennis W. Organ and Julie Paine -- The role of personality in understanding meso organizational processes : the role of personality in group processes / Lisa M. Moynihan and Randall S. Peterson -- Personality and organizational culture / Benjamin Schneider and D. Brent Smith -- Reflections on personality and organization / Chris Argyris -- Where we've been and where we're going : some conclusions regarding personality and organization / D. Brent Smith and Benjamin Schneider. DDC 158.7
1. *Personality and occupation.* I. *Schneider, Benjamin, 1938-* II. *Smith, D. Brent, 1968-* III. *Series.*
BF698.9.O3 P46 2004

PERSONALITY AND POLITICS.
Comfort, Kenneth Jerold. Power, politics, and the ego. 2nd ed., revised. Cohoes, N.Y. : Public Administration Institute of New York State, 2003.

Personality and temperament: genetics, evolution, and structure / Rainer Riemann, Frank M. Spinath, Fritz Ostendorf, (eds.). Lengerich : Pabst Science Publishers, 2001. ix, 299 p. : ill. ; 23 cm. Includes bibliographical references. ISBN 3-935357-88-5 DDC 155.2
1. *Personality.* 2. *Personality assessment.* 3. *Personality - Physiological aspects.* I. *Riemann, Rainer.* II. *Spinath, Frank M.* III. *Ostendorf, Fritz, 1955-*
BF698 .P3692 2001

Personality and work : reconsidering the role of personality in organizations / Murray R. Barrick, Ann Marie Ryan, editors ; foreword by Neal Schmitt. 1st ed. San Francisco, CA : Jossey-Bass, c2003. xxiii, 365 p. : ill. ; 24 cm. (The organizational frontiers series) Includes bibliographical references and indexes. ISBN 0-7879-6037-3

(alk. paper) DDC 158.7
1. Personality and occupation. 2. Job satisfaction. 3. Achievement motivation. 4. Employees - Attitudes. 5. Corporate culture. I. Barrick, Murray R. II. Ryan, Ann Marie. III. Series.
BF698.9.O3 P47 2003

PERSONALITY ASSESSMENT.
Beutler, Larry E. Integrative assessment of adult personality. 2nd ed. New York : Guilford Press, 2003.
BF698.4 .B42 2003

Big five assessment. Seattle, WA : Hogrefe & Huber Publishers, c2002.
BF698.4 .B52 2002

Offiong, Maria I. The enneagram. [Nigeria] : Modern Business Press, 1998.
1. Black author.

Personality and temperament: genetics, evolution, and structure. Lengerich : Pabst Science Publishers, 2001.
BF698 .P3692 2001

Wiggins, Jerry S. Paradigms of personality assessment. New York : Guilford Press, 2003.
BF698.4 .W525 2003

PERSONALITY CHANGE - STUDY AND TEACHING.
Tayir, Bracha Klein. ha-Manhig she-meʾafsher le-elef peraḥim li-feroaḥ. Tel Aviv : Yediʿot aḥaronot : Sifre ḥemed, c2002.

PERSONALITY - CONGRESSES.
Razvitie lichnosti v kulʾturno-obrazovatelʾnom prostranstve. Tambov : Tambovskiĭ gos. universitet im. G.R. Derzhavina, 2000.
BF698 .R342 2000

Vserossiĭskai͡a konferent͡sii͡a "Mezhdist͡siplinarnyĭ sintez v metodologii gumanitarnykh issledovaniĭ" (2002 : Tomsk, Russia) Lichnostʾ v paradigmakh i metaforakh. Tomsk : Tomskiĭ gos. universitet, 2002.
BF698 .V74 2002

PERSONALITY DEVELOPMENT.
Behavior genetics principles. Washington, DC : American Psychological Association, 2004.
BF698.9.B5 B44 2004

Joines, Vann. Personality adaptations. Nottingham ; Chapel Hill, N.C. : Lifespace, 2002.
BF698.3 .J65 2002

Kozlov, Nikolaĭ (Nikolaĭ Ivanovich) Kniga dli͡a tekh, komu nravitsi͡a zhitʾ, ili, Psikhologii͡a lichnostnogo rosta. Moskva : "AST-Press kniga", 2002.
BF723.P4 K69 2002

Psikhologicheskie i pedagogicheskie problemy samorazvitii͡a lichnosti. Kirov : Vi͡atskiĭ gos. pedagogicheskiĭ universitet, 2002.
BF723.P4 P78 2002

Quaglia, Rocco. Immagini dellʾuomo. Roma : Armando, c2000.

Schwarte, Johannes. Der werdende Mensch. 1. Aufl. Wiesbaden : Westdeutscher Verlag, 2002.

Tromellini, Pina. Un corredo per la vita. Milano : Salani editore, c2002.

PERSONALITY DEVELOPMENT - STUDY AND TEACHING.
Tayir, Bracha Klein. ha-Manhig she-meʾafsher le-elef peraḥim li-feroaḥ. Tel Aviv : Yediʿot aḥaronot : Sifre ḥemed, c2002.

Personality disorder.
Castillo, Heather. London ; Philadelphia : J. Kingsley Pub., 2003.
RC554 .C37 2003

PERSONALITY DISORDERS.
Castillo, Heather. Personality disorder. London ; Philadelphia : J. Kingsley Pub., 2003.
RC554 .C37 2003

St. Clair, Michael, 1940- Object relations and self psychology. 4th ed. Australia ; Belmont, CA : Thomson/Brooks/Cole, c2004.
BF175.5.O24 S7 2004

PERSONALITY - GENETIC ASPECTS.
Behavior genetics principles. Washington, DC : American Psychological Association, 2004.
BF698.9.B5 B44 2004

PERSONALITY IN ADOLESCENCE - RESEARCH - CZECH REPUBLIC.
Utváření a vývoj osobnosti. Vyd. 1. V Brně : Barrister & Principal, 2002.
BF723.P4 U88 2002

PERSONALITY IN CHILDREN - RESEARCH - CZECH REPUBLIC.
Utváření a vývoj osobnosti. Vyd. 1. V Brně : Barrister & Principal, 2002.
BF723.P4 U88 2002

PERSONALITY (LAW). *See also* PRIVACY, RIGHT OF.
Beverley-Smith, Huw. Commercial appropriation of personality. Cambridge, UK ; New York : Cambridge University Press, 2002.
K627 .B48 2002

PERSONALITY - PHILOSOPHY.
Cloninger, Susan C., 1945- Theories of personality. 4th ed. Upper Saddle River, N.J. : Pearson/Prentice Hall, c2004.
BF698 .C543 2004

Monte, Christopher F. Beneath the mask. 7th ed. Hoboken, NJ : J. Wiley & Sons, c2003.
BF698 .M64 2003

PERSONALITY - PHYSIOLOGICAL ASPECTS.
Bryden, Barbara E., 1954- Sundial. Gainesville, FL : Center for Applications of Psychological Type, 2003.
BF698.3 .B79 2003

Personality and temperament: genetics, evolution, and structure. Lengerich : Pabst Science Publishers, 2001.
BF698 .P3692 2001

The personality puzzle.
Funder, David Charles. 3rd ed. New York : Norton, c2004.
BF698 .F84 2004

PERSONALITY TESTS. *See also* CHARACTER TESTS; TAYLOR-JOHNSON TEMPERAMENT ANALYSIS.
Beutler, Larry E. Integrative assessment of adult personality. 2nd ed. New York : Guilford Press, 2003.
BF698.4 .B42 2003

Carter, Philip J. IQ and psychometric tests. London ; Sterling, VA : Kogan Page Ltd., 2004.
BF431.3 .C362 2004

Didato, Salvatore V. The big book of personality tests. New York : Black Dog & Leventhal Publishers, c2003.
BF698.5 .D53 2003

Sadka, Dewey. The Dewey color system. 1st ed. New York : Three Rivers Press, 2004.
BF789.C7 S23 2004

Williams, Andrew N. How do you compare? 1st Perigee ed. New York : Perigee Book, 2004.
BF698.5 .W55 2004

PERSONALITY - TEXTBOOKS.
Burger, Jerry M. Personality. 6th ed. Australia ; Belmont, CA : Thomson/Wadsworth, c2004.
BF698 .B84 2004

Ryckman, Richard M. Theories of personality. 8th ed. Belmont, CA : Thomson/Wadsworth, c2004.
BF698 .R96 2004

PERSONALITY THEORY. *See* PERSONALITY.

PERSONALITY TRAITS. *See also* PERSONALITY.
Matthews, Gerald. 2nd ed. New York : Cambridge University Press, 2003.
BF698 .M3434 2003

PERSONNEL. *See* EMPLOYEES.

PERSONNEL ADMINISTRATION. *See* PERSONNEL MANAGEMENT.

PERSONNEL MANAGEMENT. *See also* EMPLOYEES; INCENTIVES IN INDUSTRY; PSYCHOLOGY, INDUSTRIAL.
Cohen, Allan R. The portable MBA in management. 2nd ed. New York : J. Wiley, c2002.
HD31 .C586 2002

Handbook of organizational performance. New York : Haworth Press, c2001.
HD58.7 .H364 2001

Human resources in the 21st century. Hoboken, N.J. : J. Wiley & Sons, c2003.
HD31 .H81247 2003

Management. Cambridge, Mass. : MIT Press, 2003.
HD31 .M2928 2003

Sweeney, Paul D., 1955- Organizational behavior. Boston : McGraw-Hill Irwin, c2002.
HD58.7 .S953 2002

PERSONNEL MANAGEMENT - NETHERLANDS.
Driekwart eeuw psychotechniek in Nederland. Assen : Van Gorcum, 2001.

HF5548.8 .D73 2001

PERSONOLOGY. *See* PERSONALITY.

PERSONS. *See* ALIENS; ARTISTS; BISEXUALS; CELEBRITIES; DRAFT RESISTERS; EMPLOYEES; FANS (PERSONS); GAYS; GIFTED PERSONS; HEROES; HOMELESS PERSONS; HUMAN BEINGS; IMMIGRANTS; INDIVIDUALISM; INTELLECTUALS; MIDDLE AGED PERSONS; PERSONALITY; PHILOSOPHICAL ANTHROPOLOGY; PSYCHICS; SPOUSES; SUCCESSFUL PEOPLE; TRANSSEXUALS.

PERSONS, MARRIED. *See* MARRIED PEOPLE.

PERSONS, SINGLE. *See* SINGLE PEOPLE.

PERSONS, UNMARRIED. *See* SINGLE PEOPLE.

Perspecta : the Yale archtectural journal
(33) Mining autonomy. Cambridge, Mass. : London : MIT Press, c2002.

PERSPECTIVE. *See* DRAWING.

PERSPECTIVE - CONGRESSES.
Looking into pictures. Cambridge, Mass. : MIT Press, c2003.
BF243 .L66 2003

PERSPECTIVE (PHILOSOPHY).
Baldus, Claus, 1947- Weg im Nicht. Stuttgart : Hatje, c1994.

Perspectives critiques
Schlanger, Jacques. Guide pour un apprenti philosophe. Paris : Presses universitaires de France, 2002.

Perspectives in continental philosophy
(no. 21) Westphal, Merold. Overcoming onto-theology. 1st ed. New York : Fordham University Press, 2001.
BR100 .W47 2001

(no. 24.) Marion, Jean-Luc, 1946- [Prolégomènes à la charité. English] Prolegomena to charity. 1st ed. New York : Fordham University Press, 2002.
BD436 .M3313 2002

Perspectives in linguistics : papers in honor of P.J. Mistry / edited by Ritva Laury ... [et al.]. New Delhi : Indian Institute of Language Studies : Distributed by Creative Books, 2003. 365 p. ; 22 cm. Includes bibliographical references. ISBN 81-86323-12-0
1. Mistry, P. J. 2. Linguistics. 3. Language and languages. I. Laury, Ritva. II. Mistry, P. J. III. Indian Institute of Language Studies.

Perspectives in mentoring
Global perspectives on mentoring. Greenwich : Information Age Pub., 2004.
BF637.M48 G57 2004

Perspectives in neural computing
Kasabov, Nikola K. Evolving connectionist systems. London ; New York : Springer, c2003.
QA76.87 .K39 2003

Perspectives of change in psycholinguistics.
Herdina, Philip. A dynamic model of multilingualism. Clevedon, England Buffalo, N.Y. : Multilingual Matters, 2002.
P115.4 .H47 2002

Perspectives on cognitive psychology / Serge P. Shohov (editor). New York : Nova Science, c2002. 220 p. : ill. ; 26 cm. Includes bibliographical references and index. ISBN 1-59033-361-6 DDC 153
1. Cognitive psychology. I. Shohov, Serge P.
BF201 .P48 2002

Perspectives on Las Américas : a reader in culture, history, and representation / edited and introduced by Matthew C. Gutmann ... [et al.]. Maden, MA : Blackwell Pub., c2003. xv, 461 p. ; 26 cm. (Global perspectives) Includes bibliographical references and index. CONTENTS: Understanding the Américas: insights from Latino/a and Latin American studies / Lynn Stephen ... [et al.] -- Traddutora, traditora: a paradigmatic figure of Chicana feminism / Norma Alarcón -- From the plantation to the plantation (excerpt) / Antonio Benítez-Rojo -- New approaches to the study of peasant rebellion and consciousness: implications of the Andean experience / Steve J. Stern -- The real "new world order": the globalization of racial and ethnic relations in the late twentieth century / Néstor P. Rodríguez -- The Americans: Latin American and Caribbean peoples in the United States / Rubén G. Rumbaut -- "Quién Trabajará?" domestic workers, urban slaves, and the abolition of slavery in Puerto Rico / Félix V. Matos Rodríguez -- A central American genocide: rubber, slavery, nationalism, and the destruction of the Guatusos-Malekus / Marc Edelman -- Transnational labor

process and gender relations: women in fruit and vegetable production in Chile, Brazil and Mexico / Jane I. Collins -- Inequality near and far: international adoption as seen from a Brazilian favela / Claudia Fonseca -- History, culture, and place-making: 'native' status and Maya identity in Belize / Laurie Kroshus Medina -- The carnivalization of the world / Richard Parker -- "Playing with fire": the gendered construction of chicana/Mexicana sexuality / Patricia Zavella -- Returned migration, language, and identity: Puerto Rican bilinguals in dos worlds/two mundos / Ana Celia Zentella -- A place called home: a queer political economy of Mexican immigrant men's family experiences / Lionel Cantú -- Dominican blackness and the modern world / Silvio Torres-Saillant -- Jennifer's butt / Frances Negrón-Muntaner -- La quinceañera: making gender and ethnic identities / Karen Mary Davalos -- Two sides of the same coin: modern gaúcho identity in Brazil / Ruben George Oliven -- The United States, Mexico, and machismo / Américo Paredes -- Spectacular bodies: folklorization and the politics of identity in Ecuadorian beauty pageants / Mark Rogers -- Gender, politics, and the triumph of mestizaje in early 20th-century Nicaragua / Jeffrey Gould -- The construction of indigenous suspects: militarization and the gendered and ethnic dynamics of human rights abuses in southern Mexico / Lynn Stephen -- For whom the Taco Bells toll: popular responses to NAFTA south of the border / Matthew C. Gutmann -- Immigration reform and nativism: the nationalist response to the transnationalist challenge / Leo R. Chavez -- The process of black community organizing in the southern Pacific coast region of Colombia / Libia Grueso, Carlos Rosero, and Arturo Escobar. ISBN 0-631-22295-2 (alk. paper) ISBN 0-631-22296-0 (alk. paper) DDC 980
1. Latin America - History. 2. Hispanic Americans. 3. Latin Americans - United States. 4. Ethnicity. 5. Identity (Psychology) 6. Sex role. 7. Popular culture. 8. Political culture. I. Gutmann, Matthew C., 1953- II. Series.
F1410 .P48 2003

Perspectives on personality.
Carver, Charles S. 5th ed. Boston, MA : Allyn and Bacon, 2004.
BF698 .C22 2004

Perspectives on persuasion, social influence, and compliance gaining / edited by John S. Seiter and Robert H. Gass. Boston, MA : Allyn and Bacon, 2003.
p. cm. ISBN 0-205-33523-3 DDC 153.8/52
1. Persuasion (Psychology) 2. Influence (Psychology) 3. Manipulative behavior. I. Seiter, John S. II. Gass, Robert H.
BF637.P4 P415 2003

Perspectives on social psychology
Self and social identity. Malden, MA : Blackwell Pub., 2003.
BF697.5.S43 S429 2003

Social cognition. Malden, MA : Blackwell Pub., 2003.
BF316.6 .S65 2003

Perspectives on thinking and reasoning : essays in honour of Peter Wason / edited by Stephen E. Newstead and Jonathan St. B.T. Evans. Hove, UK ; Hillsdale : Lawrence Erlbaum Associates, c1995. x, 309 p. : ill. ; 24 cm. Includes bibliographical references and indexes. CONTENTS: Creating a psychology of reasoning: the contribution of Peter Wason / Jonathan St. B.T. Evans and Stephen E. Newstead -- The effects of rule clarification, decision justification, and selection instruction on Wason's abstract selection task / Richard A. Griggs -- Content effects in Wason's selection task / Roger L. Dominowski -- Pragmatic reasoning about human voluntary action: evidence from Wason's selection task / Keith J. Holyoak and Patricia W. Cheng -- Deontic reasoning / Ken I. Manktelow and David E. Over -- Inference and mental models / Philip N. Johnson-Laird -- Relevance and reasoning / Jonathan St. B.T. Evans -- The abstract selection task: thesis, antithesis, and synthesis / David W. Green -- Finding logic in human reasoning requires looking in the right places / David P. O'Brien -- Hypothesis testing / Michael E. Gorman -- Scientific reasoning / Ryan D. Tweney and Susan T. Chitwood -- The THOG problem and its implications for human reasoning / Stephen E. Newstead, Vittorio Girotto, and Paolo Legrenzi -- Creativity in research / Peter Wason. ISBN 0-86377-358-3 DDC 153.4
1. Thought and thinking. 2. Reasoning (Psychology) I. Wason, P. C. (Peter Cathcart) II. Newstead, Stephen E. III. Evans, Jonathan St. B. T., 1948-
BF441 .P48 1995

Die Perspektive der Moral.
Rhonheimer, Martin, 1950- Berlin : Akademie Verlag, c2001.

PERSUASION (PSYCHOLOGY). *See also* **INFLUENCE (PSYCHOLOGY).**
Bauer, Joel, 1960- How to persuade people who don't want to be persuaded. Hoboken, N.J. : John Wiley & Sons, 2004.
BF637.P4 B32 2004

Brenden, Ann E. Persuasive computer presentations. Chicago, Ill. : Law Practice Management Section, American Bar Association, c2001.
KF320.A9 B74 2001

Gardner, Howard. Changing minds. Boston, Mass. : Harvard Business School Press, 2004.
BF637.C4 G37 2004

Grachev, Georgiĭ. Manipulirovanie lichnostʹi͡u. Moskva : Algoritm, 2002.
BF632.5 .G73 2002

Martín Salgado, Lourdes. Marketing político. Barcelona : Paidós, c2002.

Perloff, Richard M. The dynamics of persuasion. 2nd ed. Mahwah, N.J. : Lawrence Erlbaum Associates, 2003.
BF637.P4 .P39 2003

Perspectives on persuasion, social influence, and compliance gaining. Boston, MA : Allyn and Bacon, 2003.
BF637.P4 P415 2003

Walton, Mark S., 1950- Generating buy-in. New York : American Management Association, c2004.
HD30.3 .W35 2004

PERSUASION (PSYCHOLOGY) - COMPUTER PROGRAMS.
Fogg, B. J. Persuasive technology. Amsterdam ; Boston : Morgan Kaufmann Publishers, / c2003.
BF637.P4 F55 2003

PERSUASION (PSYCHOLOGY) - DICTIONARIES.
Becker, Konrad. Tactical reality dictionary. Vienna : Edition Selene ; [s.l.] : Distribution Canada/UK/USA by Autonomedia, 2002.
BF637.P4 B33 2002

PERSUASION (RHETORIC) - DATA PROCESSING.
Visualizing argumentation. London ; New York : Springer, 2003.
QA76.9.H85 V67 2003

Persuasive computer presentations.
Brenden, Ann E. Chicago, Ill. : Law Practice Management Section, American Bar Association, c2001.
KF320.A9 B74 2001

Persuasive technology.
Fogg, B. J. Amsterdam ; Boston : Morgan Kaufmann Publishers, / c2003.
BF637.P4 F55 2003

Perugini, Marco.
Big five assessment. Seattle, WA : Hogrefe & Huber Publishers, c2002.
BF698.4 .B52 2002

Perurim mi-shulḥan gavoah.
Aviner, Shelomoh Ḥayim, ha-Kohen. Yerushalayim : Sifriyat Ḥayah, 762 [2001 or 2002]

Pessanha, Rodolfo Gomes. O irracionalismo--, dos Estados Unidos da América à globalizaçãp / Rodolfo Gomes Pessanha. Niterói : Muiraquitã, c1998. 382 p. ; 21 cm. ISBN 85-85483-51-2
1. National characteristics, American. 2. United States - Civilization. 3. Capitalism - United States. 4. Globalization. I. Title.

PESSIMISM. *See also* **CYNICISM.**
Wolf, Jean-Claude. Ethik und Politik ohne Gewissheiten. Freiburg, Schweiz : Universitätsverlag, c2002.

Pessoa, Fernando, 1888-1935.
[Erostratus. Portuguese & English]
Heróstrato e a busca da imortalidade / Fernando Pessoa ; edição, Richard Zenith ; tradução, Manuela Rocha. Lisboa : Assírio e Alvim, c2000. 267 p. : ill. ; 21 cm. (Obras de Fernando Pessoa ; 14) Includes the original English text and translations into Portuguese of three essays: Erostratus, Impermanence, and Uselessness of criticism. ISBN 972-37-0594-X (pbk.) ISBN 972-37-0595-8 (hard)
1. Fame. 2. Creation (Literary, artistic, etc.) I. Zenith, Richard. II. Rocha, Manuela. III. Pessoa, Fernando, 1888-1935. Impermanence. Portuguese & English. IV. Pessoa, Fernando, 1888-1935. Uselessness of criticism. Portuguese & English. V. Title. VI. Series: Pessoa, Fernando, 1888-1935. Works. 1999 ; 14.

Impermanence. Portuguese & English.
Pessoa, Fernando, 1888-1935. [Erostratus. Portuguese & English] Heróstrato e a busca da imortalidade. Lisboa : Assírio e Alvim, c2000.

Uselessness of criticism. Portuguese & English.
Pessoa, Fernando, 1888-1935. [Erostratus. Portuguese & English] Heróstrato e a busca da imortalidade. Lisboa : Assírio e Alvim, c2000.

Works. 1999
(14.) Pessoa, Fernando, 1888-1935. [Erostratus. Portuguese & English] Heróstrato e a busca da imortalidade. Lisboa : Assírio e Alvim, c2000.

PET OWNERS - PSYCHOLOGY.
Haraway, Donna Jeanne. The companion species manifesto. Chicago, Ill. : Prickly Paradigm ; Bristol : University Presses Marketing, 2003.

Peters, Alan H.
Fisher, Peter S. Industrial incentives. Kalamazoo, Mich. : W.E. Upjohn Institute for Employment Research, 1998.
HF5549.5.I5 F57 1998

Peters, Edward, 1936-.
Jolly, Karen Louise. The Middle Ages. Philadelphia : University of Pennsylvania Press, 2002, 2001. 12 300 xiv, 280 p. ; 24 cm.
BF1593 .J65 2002

Peterson, Christopher, 1950 Feb. 18- Character strengths and virtues : a handbook and classification / Christopher Peterson, Martin E.P. Seligman. New York : Oxford University Press, 2004. p. cm. Includes bibliographical references (p.   ). ISBN 0-19-516701-5 DDC 155.2/32
1. Character - Handbooks, manuals, etc. 2. Virtues - Handbooks, manuals, etc. I. Seligman, Martin E. P. II. Title.
BF818 .P38 2004

Peterson, Gregory R., 1966- Minding God : theology and the cognitive sciences / Gregory R. Peterson. Minneapolis, MN : Fortress Press, c2003. xiii, 252 p. : ill. ; 23 cm. (Theology and the sciences) Includes bibliographical references (p. 235-245) and index. ISBN 0-8006-3498-5 (alk. paper) DDC 261.5/15
1. Religion and Psychology. 2. Cognitive science. I. Title. II. Series.
BL53 .P42 2003

Peterson, Mary A., 1950-.
Perception of faces, objects, and scenes. Oxford ; New York : Oxford University Press, 2003.
BF241 .P434 2003

Petich, Giuseppe, 1869-1953. Divagazioni filosofiche del reverendo Giuseppe Petich tratte dai frammenti del suo "Zibaldone" / a cura di Giuseppe Meo ; saggio introduttivo di Pasquale Di Nunno. Roma : Bulzoni, 2002. 358 p. : ill. (some col.) ; 23 cm. Includes bibliographical references and index. Includes introductory essay (p. 9-94). ISBN 88-8319-744-5 DDC 282
1. Petich, Giuseppe, - 1869-1953 - Diaries. 2. Philosophy. I. Nunno, Pasquale di. II. Meo, Giuseppe. III. Title.

PETICH, GIUSEPPE, 1869-1953 - DIARIES.
Petich, Giuseppe, 1869-1953. Divagazioni filosofiche del reverendo Giuseppe Petich tratte dai frammenti del suo "Zibaldone". Roma : Bulzoni, 2002.

Petit, Philippe.
Babin, Pierre. La fabrique du sexe. Paris : Textuel, [1999]
BF175.5.S48 B23 1999

Petit précis
(10) Vystrecil, Henri. Nostradamus. Portet-sur-Garonne : Loubatières, c2002.

Petitdemange, Guy. Philosophes et philosophies du XXe siècle / Guy Petitdemange. Paris : Seuil, c2003. 504, [1] p. ; 21 cm. (La couleur des idées) Includes bibliographical references (p. 503-[505]). ISBN 2-02-051248-3 DDC 190
1. Philosophy, Modern - 20th century. 2. Philosophers, Modern - Europe. I. Title. II. Series.
B804 .P45 2003

Petitot, Jean, 1944-.
Naturaliser la phénoménologie. Paris : CNRS, c2002.

Petras, Kathryn.
Unusually stupid Americans. 1st ed. New York : Villard, 2003.
BF431 .U65 2003

Petras, Ross.
Unusually stupid Americans. 1st ed. New York : Villard, 2003.
BF431 .U65 2003

Petrill, Stephen A., 1968-.
Nature, nurture, and the transition to early adolescence. Oxford ; New York : Oxford University Press, 2003.
BF341 .N387 2003

PETROGLYPHS - FOUR CORNERS REGION - MISCELLANEA.
Rogers, Barb, 1947- Mystic glyphs. York Beach, ME : Red Wheel/Weiser, 2003.
BF1778.5 .R64 2003

PETROLEUM INDUSTRY AND TRADE - POLITICAL ASPECTS - RUSSIA (FEDERATION).
Parshev, A. P. (Andreĭ Petrovich) Pochemu Amerika nastupaet. Moskva : AST : Astrel', 2002.
HF1558.2.Z4 P37 2002

Petronio, Sandra Sporbert. Boundaries of privacy : dialectics of disclosure / Sandra Petronio. Albany : State University of New York Press, c2002. xix, 268 p. : ill. ; 23 cm. (SUNY series in communication studies) Includes bibliographical references (p. 227-256) and index. ISBN 0-7914-5515-7 (alk. paper) ISBN 0-7914-5516-5 (pbk. : alk. paper) DDC 302.5
1. Self-disclosure. 2. Secrecy. 3. Privacy. 4. Interpersonal communication. I. Title. II. Series.
BF697.5.S427 P48 2002

Petrović, Aleksandar M. Praistorija Srba : razmatranje grade za staru povesnicu / Aleksandar M. Petrović. Beograd : Pešić i sinovi, 2001. 267 p. ; 20 cm. (Biblioteka Tragom Slovena ; knj. 15) Includes bibliographical references. In Serbian (Cyrillic); summaries in English and German. ISBN 86-7540-004-7
1. Serbs - Origin. 2. Serbs - History. 3. Slavs - Origin. 4. Mythology, Slavic. I. Title. II. Series.
DR1953 .P48 2001

Petrovskiĭ, A. V. (Artur Vladimirovich) Psikhologii͡a v Rossii, XX vek / A.V. Petrovskiĭ. Moskva : URAO-- Universitet rossiĭskoĭ akademii obrazovanii͡a, 2000. 309 p. : ill. ; 22 cm. Includes bibliographical references. ISBN 5204002286
1. Psychology - Russia (Federation) - History - 20th century. I. Title. II. Title: Psikhologii͡a v Rossii, 20. vek
BF108.R8 P39 2000

Zapiski psikhologa / Artur Petrovskiĭ. Moskva : Izd-vo URAO, 2001. 463 p. : ill. ; 23 cm. ISBN 5204002456
1. Psychology - Popular works. I. Title.
BF145 .P477 2001

Zapiski psikhologa / Artur Petrovskiĭ. Moskva : Izd-vo URAO, 2001. 463 p. : ill. ; 22 cm. ISBN 5204002456
1. Psychology - Popular works. I. Universitet Rossiĭskoĭ akademii obrazovanii͡a. II. Title.
BF145 .P48 2001

PETS - DEATH.
Kolb, Janice E. M. In corridors of eternal time. Nevada City, Calif. : Blue Dolphin Pub., 2003.
BF1997.K65 A3 2003b

Petta, Paolo, 1963-.
Emotions in humans and artifacts. Cambridge, Mass. : MIT Press, c2002.
BF531 .E517 2002

Pettibone, John W. The ghosts of Hammond castle / John W. Pettibone, John Dandola. Glen Ridge, N.J. : Tory Corner Editions, c2001. 59 p. : ill. ; 22 cm. ISBN 1-87845-230-4 DDC 133.1/297445
1. Haunted castles - Massachusetts - Gloucester. 2. Ghosts - Massachusetts - Gloucester. I. Dandola, John, 1951- II. Title.
BF1474 .P48 2001

Pettit, Philip, 1945- Rules, reasons, and norms : selected essays / Philip Pettit. Oxford : Oxford University Press ; New York : Clarendon Press, 2002. xii, 410 p. ; 24 cm. Includes bibliographical references and index. ISBN 0-19-925187-8 (alk. paper) ISBN 0-19-925186-X (pbk. : alk. paper) DDC 192
1. Thought and thinking. 2. Rules (Philosophy) 3. Decision making - Philosophy. 4. Choice (Psychology) 5. Social norms - Philosophy. I. Title.
B105.T54 P48 2002

Peylet, Gérard.
La fin des temps. Talence : Université Michel de Montaigne, Bordeaux III, L.A.P.R.I.L., 2000-[2001]

Pfaller, Robert. Die Illusionen der anderen : über das Lustprinzip in der Kultur / Robert Pfaller. 1. Aufl. Frankfurt : Suhrkamp, 2002. 342 p. ; 18 cm. (Edition Suhrkamp, 0422-5821 ; 2279) Includes bibliographical references (p. 319-[341]) and index. ISBN 3-518-12279-7 (pbk.)
1. Pleasure principle (Psychology) 2. Sex. 3. Philosophy, German. I. Title. II. Series.

Pfalzgraf, Jochen.
Automated practical reasoning. Wien ; New York : Springer-Verlag, c1995.
QA76.9.A96 A9 1995

Pfitzer, Gregory M. Picturing the past : illustrated histories and the American imagination, 1840-1900 / Gregory M. Pfitzer. Washington [D.C.] : Smithsonian Institution Press, c2002. xviii, 276 p. : ill. ; 24 cm. Includes bibliographical references (p. 245-266) and index. ISBN 1-58834-084-8 (alk. paper) DDC 973/.07/2
1. Illustrated books - United States - History - 19th century. 2. Historiography - Social aspects - United States - History - 19th century. 3. Visual communication - Social aspects - United States - History - 19th century. 4. National characteristics, American. 5. United States - Historiography. I. Title.
E175 .P477 2002

Phaladīpikā.
Mantreśvara. 1. saṃskaraṇa. Vārāṇasī : Caukhambā Surabhāratī Prakāśana, 2002.
BF1714.H5+

Phalen, Richard C., 1937-.
How we have changed. Gretna, La. : Pelican Pub. Co., 2003.
E169.12 .H677 2003

Phalita jyotiṣa mahāgrantha.
[Mānasāgarī. Hindi & Sanskrit.] Mānasāgarī. Saṃskaraṇa 1. Haridvāra : Raṇadhīra Prakāśana, 2000.
BF1714.H5+

PHALLICISM. See **SEX - RELIGIOUS ASPECTS.**

PHALLUS. See **PENIS.**

PHANTASY. See **FANTASY.**

PHANTOMS. See **GHOSTS.**

PHARMACEUTICAL INDUSTRY - UNITED STATES.
United States. Congress. House. Committee on Energy and Commerce. Subcommittee on Health. Examining issues related to competition in the pharmaceutical marketplace. Washington : U.S. G.P.O. : For sale by the Supt. of Docs., U.S. G.P.O. [Congressional Sales Office], 2002.

PHARMACEUTICALS. See **DRUGS.**

PHARMACOLOGY. See **DRUGS.**

PHARMACOPOEIAS. See **DRUGS.**

Pharmacum carthusiense : Medicina, terapie non verbali e mondo monastico / R. Benenzon ... [et al.]. Salzburg, Austria : Institut für Anglistik und Amerikanistik, Universität Salzburg, 2002. 117 p. ; 22 cm. (Analecta Cartusiana ; 205) Includes bibliographical references (p. 115-117). Contributions in Italian and Spanish. ISBN 3-901995-73-0 (pbk.)
1. Medical care. 2. Monastic and religious life. 3. Nonverbal communication. 4. Therapeutics. I. Benenzon, Rolando O. II. Universität Salzburg. Institut für Anglistik und Amerikanistik. III. Series.
BX2435 .P43 2002

PHARMACY. See **DRUGS.**

Pharr, Daniel. The moon & everyday living : use lunar energies to transform your life / Daniel Pharr. 2nd ed. St. Paul, Minn. : LLewellyn, 2002. xiii, 235 p. ; 23 cm. Rev. ed. of: Moon wise, 2000. Includes bibliographical references (p. 225-228) and index. ISBN 0-7387-0184-X (pbk.) DDC 133.5/32
1. Astrology. 2. Human beings - Effect of the moon on. 3. Moon - Miscellanea. I. Pharr, Daniel. Moon wise. II. Title. III. Title: Moon and everyday living
BF1723 .P48 2002

Moon wise.
Pharr, Daniel. The moon & everyday living. 2nd ed. St. Paul, Minn. : LLewellyn, 2002.
BF1723 .P48 2002

PHASES OF THE MOON. See **MOON - PHASES.**

Phelan, Gerald B. (Gerald Bernard), 1892-1965.
Maritain, Jacques, 1882-1973. [Degrés du savoir. English] Distinguish to unite, or, The degrees of knowledge. Notre Dame, Ind. : University of Notre Dame Press, 1998, c1995.
BD162 .M273 1998

PHENOMENA, CRITICAL (PHYSICS). See **CRITICAL PHENOMENA (PHYSICS).**

Le phénomène érotique.
Marion, Jean-Luc, 1946- Paris : Grasset, c2003.
BH301.L65 M37 2003

PHENOMENOLOGICAL PSYCHOLOGY.
Butt, Trevor, 1947- Understanding people. New York : Palgrave Macmillan, 2003.
BF698 .B89 2003

Pracetā Jyoti. Dhātusāmya meṃ manobhāvoṃ kā sthāna. 1. saṃskaraṇa. Nāgapura : Viśvabhāratī Prakāśana, 2001.

BF204.5 .P73 2001

Russon, John Edward, 1960- Human experience. Albany : State University of New York Press, c2003.
BF204.5 .R87 2003

PHENOMENOLOGY.
Barsotti, Bernard. Bachelard critique de Husserl. Paris : Harmattan, c2002.
B2430.B254 B37 2002

Domagala, Edward. L'ermeneutica dell'esperienza dell'amore in Max Scheler. Romae : [s.n.], 2000.

Die erscheinende Welt. Berlin : Duncker & Humblot, c2002.

Grenzen des Verstehens. Göttingen : Vandenhoeck & Ruprecht, c2002.
BD181.5 .G74 2002

Heinamaa, Sara, 1960- Toward a phenomenology of sexual difference. Lanham, Md. ; Oxford : Rowman & Littlefield Publishers, c2003.
HQ1208 .B3523 2003

Husserl's Logical investigations reconsidered. Dordrecht ; Boston : Kluwer Academic Publishers, c2003.
B3279.H93 L64346 2003

Kūle, M. (Maija) Phenomenology and culture. Riga : Institute of Philosophy and Sociology, 2002.

Ledda, Antonio. La fenomelogia tra essenza ed esistenza. 1. ed. Roma : Carocci editore, 2002.

Ménasé, Stéphanie. Passivité et création. Paris : Presses universitaires de France, c2003.

Mensch, James R. Ethics and selfhood. Albany, NY : State University of New York Press, c2003.
B945.M4853 E84 2003

Merleau-Ponty, Maurice, 1908-1961. L'institution dans l'histoire personnelle et publique ; [Paris] : Belin, c2003.
B2430.M3763 I88 2003

Mohanty, Jitendranath, 1928- Explorations in philosophy. New Delhi ; New York : Oxford University Press, c2001-
B131.M54 M63 2001

Naturaliser la phénoménologie. Paris : CNRS, c2002.

Schürmann, Reiner, 1941- [Des hégémonies brisées. English] Broken hegemonies. Bloomington : Indiana University Press, c2003.
BD162 .S48 2003

Schutz, Alfred, 1899-1959. Werkausgabe. Konstanz : UVK, Verlagsgesellschaft, 2003-
BD431 .S284916 2003

Phenomenology and culture.
Kūle, M. (Maija) Riga : Institute of Philosophy and Sociology, 2002.

Phenomenology of spirit.
Hegel's Phenomenology of spirit. Amherst, N.Y. : Humanity Books, 2003.
B2929 .H349 2003

PHENOTYPE.
West-Eberhard, Mary Jane. Developmental plasticity and evolution. Oxford ; New York : Oxford University Press, 2003.
QH546 .W45 2003

PHILANTHROPY. See **SOCIAL SERVICE.**

Philbrick, Nat. Revenge of the whale : the true story of the whaleship Essex / Nathaniel Philbrick. New York : G.P. Putnam, 2002. x, 164 p., [16] p. of plates : ill., maps ; 24 cm. SUMMARY: Recounts the 1820 sinking of the whaleship "Essex" by an enraged sperm whale and how the crew of young men survived against impossible odds. Based on the author's adult book "In the Heart of the Sea." Includes bibliographical references (p. [161]) and index. ISBN 0-399-23795-X DDC 910/.9164
1. Essex (Whaleship) - Juvenile literature. 2. Shipwrecks - Pacific Ocean - Juvenile literature. 3. Whaling. 4. Survival. I. Title.
G530.E77 P454 2002

Philip, Cynthia Owen. Wilderstein and the Suckleys : a Hudson River legacy / by Cynthia Owen Philip ; introduction by Geoffrey C. Ward. Rhinebeck, N.Y. : Wilderstein Preservation, 2001. 127 p. : ill. (some col.), map ; 23 cm. ISBN 0-9706846-0-6 DDC 920.0747/3
1. Suckley family. 2. Wilderstein (N.Y.) 3. Hudson River Valley (N.Y. and N.J.) - Biography. 4. Hudson River Valley (N.Y. and N.J.) - Social life and customs. I. Wilderstein Preservation. II. Title.
F129.W747 P48 2001

Philip, Neil. The little people : stories of fairies, pixies and other small folk / Neil Philip. New York ; London : Harry N. Abrams, 2002. 115 p. : ill. (chiefly col.) ; 27 cm. Includes bibliographical references (p. 112). SUMMARY: Describes the origins, physical characteristics, dwelling places, activities, and special powers of different types of fairy folk from around the world. Illustrative traditional stories from various cultures are interspersed throughout the text. CONTENTS: World of the fairies -- Fairy folk -- Fairy neighbors -- Fairy helpers -- Mischievous fairies -- Fairy treasure -- Fairy frolics -- Fairylands. ISBN 0-8109-0570-1 DDC 398.2
1. *Fairies - Juvenile literature.* 2. *Folklore - Juvenile literature.* 3. *Fairy tales - Juvenile literature.* I. Title.

Philipp Melanchthon.
Kuropka, Nicole. Tübingen : Mohr Siebeck, c2002.
BR339 .K86 2002

PHILIPPINE LITERATURE - BIO-BIBLIOGRAPHY.
Feminine voices. [Manila?] : NCCA, c2001-

PHILIPPINE LITERATURE - WOMEN AUTHORS - BIOGRAPHY.
Feminine voices. [Manila?] : NCCA, c2001-

PHILIPPINES - FOREIGN RELATIONS - UNITED STATES.
Vestiges of war. New York : New York University Press, 2000.
DS679 .V47 2000

PHILIPPINES - HISTORY - PHILIPPINE AMERICAN WAR, 1899-1902.
Vestiges of war. New York : New York University Press, 2000.
DS679 .V47 2000

PHILIPPINES - LITERATURES. *See* **PHILIPPINE LITERATURE.**

PHILIPPINOS. *See* **FILIPINOS.**

Philippot, Pierre, 1960- .
Nonverbal behavior in clinical settings. Oxford ; New York : Oxford University Press, 2003.
RC489.N65 N66 2003

The regulation of emotion. Mahwah, NJ : Lawrence Erlbaum, 2003.
BF531 .R45 2003

Phillips, Donald T. (Donald Thomas), 1952- Character in action : the U.S. Coast Guard on leadership / Donald T. Phillips with James M. Loy. Annapolis, Md. : Naval Institute Press, c2003. xi, 178 p. ; 24 cm. Includes index. CONTENTS: Pt. 1. Set the foundation: Define the culture and live the values -- Select the best -- Promote team over self -- Instill a commitment to excellence -- pt. 2. Focus on people: Eliminate the frozen middle -- Cultivate caring relationships -- Build strong alliances -- Create an effective communication system -- pt. 3. Instill a bias for action: Make change the norm -- Encourage decisiveness -- Empower the young -- Give the field priority -- pt. 4. Ensure the future: Leverage resources -- Sponsor continual learning -- Spotlight excellence -- Honor history and tradition. ISBN 1-59114-672-0 (alk. paper) DDC 658.4/092
1. *United States. - Coast Guard.* 2. *Leadership.* I. Loy, James M., 1942- II. Title.
VG53 .P49 2003

Phillips, Graham.
[Search for the Grail]
The chalice of Magdalene : the search for the cup that held the blood of Christ / Graham Phillips. Rochester, Vt. : Bear & Company, 2004. p. cm. Originally published: The search for the Grail. United Kingdom : Arrow Books Ltd., 1996. Includes bibliographical references and index. CONTENTS: The Arthurian romances -- The original tales -- Historical manuscripts -- The Arthurian era -- Prelude to Badon -- Arthur of Britons -- Tracking the Bear King -- Isle of Ava Ion -- The Grail romances -- The history of the White Land -- The emperor king -- The heirs of Arthur -- Perceval -- Mystery of the tarot -- The secret Gospel -- Robin and Marian. ISBN 1-59143-038-0 (pbk.) DDC 001.94
1. *Grail.* 2. *Arthurian romances - Miscellanea.* I. Title.
BF1442.G73 P48 2004

Phillips, James, 1938- .
Imagination and its pathologies. Cambridge, Mass. : MIT Press, c2003.
BF408 .I455 2003

Phillips, Nicola. The big difference : life works when you choose it / Nicola Phillips. Cambridge, MA : Perseus Pub., c2001. 203 p. ; 21 cm. ISBN 0-7382-0654-7 (pbk.) DDC 158.1
1. *Commitment (Psychology)* 2. *Choice (Psychology)* 3. *Decision making - Psychological aspects.* 4. *Self-actualization (Psychology)* 5. *Success - Psychological aspects.* I. Title.

BF619 .P48 2001

Phillips, Osborne.
Denning, Melita. Mysteria magica. 3rd ed. St. Paul, Minn. : Llewellyn Publications, 2004.
BF1611 .D395 2004

Phillips, Sara. Dream symbols / by Sara Phillips. Philadelphia, Pa. : Courage Books, c2002. 127 p. : col. ill. ; 29 cm. ISBN 0-7624-1394-8 DDC 154.6/3
1. *Dream interpretation - Dictionaries.* 2. *Symbolism (Psychology) - Dictionaries.* I. Title.
BF1091 .P46 2002

PHILOLOGIANS. *See* **PHILOLOGISTS.**

Philologies old and new : Essays in honor of Peter Florian Dembowski / edited by Joan Tasker Grimbert and Carol J. Chase. Princeton : The Edward C. Armstrong Monographs, 2001. xxx, 354 p. ; 23 cm. (The Edward C. Armstrong monographs on medieval literature.) (E.C.A.M.M.L. ; 12) Includes bibliographical references. "Publications of Peter F. Dembowski"--P. xvii-xxx. English and French. CONTENTS: Peter F. Dembowski / Michael Murrin -- Peter F. Dembowski's contribution to medieval studies / Keith Busby -- Publications of Peter F. Dembowski -- The Spanish 'Santiago' and Latin Europe / Karl D. Utti -- What is a legendary? / Duncan Robertson -- The legend of Saint Mary of Egypt in Petrus Calò's 'Legendæ de sanctis' -- Le Chansonnier N2 occitan et son rapport avec les chansonniers I et K / Hans-Erich Keller -- 'Peregrinatio': Joïe, Constance and the tale(s) / Barbara N. Sargent-Baur -- Le sort de Roland est-il tragique? / Don A. Monson -- Formulaic diction from orality to writing: evidence from the Old French 'Charroi de Nîmes' in Manuscript D / William D. Paden -- Le Sens du terme 'cortois' dans le premiers poèmes du Cycle de Guillaume d'Orange / Rupert T. Pickens -- Charlemagne in the 'Encyclopédie / Robert Morrissey -- "Des 'bacons' comme s'il en pleuvait..." Le pathétique dans un extrait des 'Quatre fils Aymon' à la fin du dix-neuvième siècle / Bernard Guidot -- Liturgical citation in French medieval epic and romance / Evelyn Birge Vitz -- Wrapping memory around the metaphor in Marie de France's 'Chievrefoil' / SunHee Gertz -- The birth of the hero in Thomas' 'Tristan' / Gerard J. Brault -- Chrétien, the troubadours and the Tristan legend: the rhetoric of passionate love in 'D'amors, qui m'a tolu a moi / Joan Tasker Grimbert -- "Wild oats" : The parable of the sower in the prologue to Chrétien de Troyes' 'Conte du graal / Jeff Rider -- The 'Chastelaine de vergi' at the crossroads of courtly, moral, and devotional literature / Sylvia Huot -- Jealousy, fidelity, and form in the 'Livre de Caradoc / Norris J. Lacy -- The vision of the grail in the 'Estoire de saint graal' / Carol J. Chase -- When women learn to write Old French prose romance / Michael N. Salada -- Power and worth in 'The knight of the two swords' / Noel Corbett -- 'L'Orloge amoureus' di Jean Froissart / Paolo Cherchi. ISBN 0-9707991-0-1 (pbk).
1. *Dembowski, Peter F. - (Peter Florian), - 1925-* 2. *Arthurian romances - History and criticism.* 3. *Knights and knighthood in literature.* I. Chase, Carol J. II. Grimbert, Joan T. III. Title: *Essays in honor of Peter Florian Dembowski* IV. Series: *Edward C. Armstrong monographs on medieval literature ; 12.*

PHILOLOGISTS - GREAT BRITAIN - BIOGRAPHY.
Read, Malcolm K. (Malcolm Kevin), 1945- Educating the educators. 1st American ed. Newark : University of Delaware Press ; Cranbury, NJ : Associated University Presses, 2003.
PC4064.R43 A3 2003

PHILOLOGY. *See also* **GRAMMAR, COMPARATIVE AND GENERAL; LANGUAGE AND LANGUAGES; LITERATURE; LITERATURE, COMPARATIVE.**
Svobodnyĭ vzgli͡ad na literaturu. Moskva : Nauka, 2002.

PHILOSEMITISM. *See* **ANTISEMITISM.**

The philosopher queen.
Cuomo, Chris J. Lanham, Md. ; Oxford : Rowman & Littlefield, c2003.
HQ1190 .C866 2003

PHILOSOPHERS. *See also* **PLATONISTS.**
The world's great philosophers. Malden, MA : Blackwell Pub., 2003.
B29 .W69 2003

PHILOSOPHERS, ANCIENT.
Burlaeus, Gualterus, 1275-1345? [De vita et moribus philosophorum. Spanish] Vida y costumbres de los viejos filósofos. Madrid : Iberoamericana ; Frankfurt : Vervuert, 2002.

Eslin, Jean-Claude, 1935- Saint Augustin. Paris : Michalon, c2002.

PHILOSOPHERS - ATTITUDES.
Le Dœuff, Michèle. The philosophical imaginary. London : Continuum, 2002.

The philosopher's autobiography.
Schuster, Shlomit C., 1951- Westport, Conn. ; London : Praeger, 2003.
B52.7 .S38 2003

PHILOSOPHERS - BIOGRAPHY - HISTORY AND CRITICISM.
Schuster, Shlomit C., 1951- The philosopher's autobiography. Westport, Conn. ; London : Praeger, 2003.
B52.7 .S38 2003

PHILOSOPHERS' EGG. *See* **ALCHEMY.**

PHILOSOPHERS - EUROPE - ATTITUDES.
Race and racism in continental philosophy. Bloomington : Indiana University Press, c2003.
HT1523 .R2514 2003

PHILOSOPHERS - FRANCE.
Fox, Nik Farrell. The new Sartre. New York ; London : Continuum, 2003.

PHILOSOPHERS - FRANCE - BIOGRAPHY.
Schiffter, Frédéric. Pensées d'un philosophe sous Prozac. [Toulouse] : Milan, c2002.

PHILOSOPHERS - FRANCE - INTERVIEWS.
Changeux, Jean-Pierre. [Ce qui nous fait penser. English] What makes us think? Princeton, N.J. : Princeton University Press, c2000.
BJ45 .C4313 2000

Philosophers' hobbies and other essays.
Teichman, Jenny. Carlton, Vic. : Black Jack Press, 2003.

PHILOSOPHERS, MODERN - BELGIUM - INTERVIEWS.
Hottois, Gilbert, 1946- Species technica ; Paris : Vrin, 2002.

PHILOSOPHERS, MODERN - EUROPE.
Petitdemange, Guy. Philosophes et philosophies du XXe siècle. Paris : Seuil, c2003.
B804 .P45 2003

PHILOSOPHERS - RELATIONS WITH WOMEN - PSYCHOLOGICAL ASPECTS.
Le Dœuff, Michèle. The philosophical imaginary. London : Continuum, 2002.

PHILOSOPHERS - RELATIONSHIP WITH WOMEN. *See* **PHILOSOPHERS - RELATIONS WITH WOMEN.**

PHILOSOPHERS - RUSSIA - BIOGRAPHY.
Zaĭtseva, L. I. Russkie providt͡sy o rossiĭskoĭ gosudarstvennosti. Moskva : In-t ėkonomiki RAN, 1998-
DK49 .Z35 1998

PHILOSOPHERS - SPAIN - BIOGRAPHY.
Vega, Amador. Ramon Llull y el secreto de la vida. Madrid : Siruela, 2002.

PHILOSOPHERS' STONE. *See* **ALCHEMY.**

The philosopher's toolkit.
Baggini, Julian. Malden, MA : Blackwell Publishers, 2003.
BC177 .B19 2003

Philosophes et philosophies du XXe siècle.
Petitdemange, Guy. Paris : Seuil, c2003.
B804 .P45 2003

"Philosophi" e "logici".
Zerbi, Piero. Roma : Istituto storico italiano per il Medio Evo ; Milano : Vita e pensiero, 2002.
B765.A24 Z473 2002

Philosophical accounts of self-knowledge.
Privileged access. Aldershot ; Burlington, VT : Ashgate, c2003.

PHILOSOPHICAL ANALYSIS. *See* **ANALYSIS (PHILOSOPHY).**

PHILOSOPHICAL ANTHROPOLOGY. *See also* **FEMININITY (PHILOSOPHY); HUMANISM; MIND AND BODY; PHILOSOPHY OF MIND; SOUL.**
Antropología e interpretación. Tucumán, Argentina : Instituto de Estudios Antropológicos y Filosofía de la Religión, Facultad de Filosofía y Letras, Universidad Nacional de Tucumán, c2001.
BD450 .A564 2001

Bodei, Remo, 1938- Destini personali. Milano : Feltrinelli, 2002.

Bronowski, Jacob, 1908-1974. The identity of man. Amherst, N.Y. : Prometheus Books, 2002.
BD450 .B653 2002

Collen, Lindsey. Natir imin. Port Louis, Mauritius : Ledikasyon pu travayer, [2000]

Philosophical anthropology

Dei, Héctor Daniel. The human being in history. Lanham, Md. : Lexington Books, c2003.
BD450 .D395 2003

Kämpf, Heike. Helmuth Plessner. 1. Aufl. Düsseldorf : Parerga, 2001.
B3323.P564 K36 2001

Krasikov, V. I. (Vladimir Ivanovich) Sindrom sushchestvovaniiã. Tomsk : [s.n.], 2002.

Rapport, Nigel, 1956- I am dynamite. London ; New York : Routledge, 2003.

Rogers, W. Kim. Reason and life. Lanham, Md. : University Press of America, c2003.
BD431 .R5515 2003

Spoerri, Hubert M. Mensch und Kunst. München : Scaneg, c2002.

PHILOSOPHICAL ANTHROPOLOGY - EARLY WORKS TO 1800.

Jean, de la Rochelle, d. 1245. Summa de anima. Paris : J. Vrin, 1995.
BD420 .J43 1995

PHILOSOPHICAL COUNSELING. See CONDUCT OF LIFE.

PHILOSOPHICAL GRAMMAR. See GRAMMAR, COMPARATIVE AND GENERAL.

The philosophical imaginary.
Le Doeuff, Michèle. London : Continuum, 2002.

The philosophical poetics of Alfarabi, Avicenna and Averroes.
Kemal, Salim. London ; New York : RoutledgeCurzon, 2003.

Philosophical studies series
(v. 89) Vallicella, William F. A paradigm theory of existence. Dordrecht ; Boston : Kluwer Academic, c2002.
BD331 .V36 2002

(v. 91) Philosophy, psychology, and psychologism. Dordrecht ; Boston : Kluwer Academic Publishers, c2003.
BF41 .P553 2003

(v. 93) De Muijnck, Wim. Dependencies, connections, and other relations. Dordrecht ; Boston : Kluwer Academic Publishers, c2003.
BD418.3 .D4 2003

PHILOSOPHICAL THEOLOGY.

Gibson, Arthur, 1943- Metaphysics and transcendence. London ; New York : Routledge, 2003.
BT40 .G53 2003

PHILOSOPHICAL THEOLOGY - HISTORY.

The medieval heritage in early modern metaphysics and modal theory, 1400-1700. Dordrecht ; Boston : Kluwer Academic Publishers, c2003.
BD111 .M47 2003

PHILOSOPHICAL THEOLOGY - METHODOLOGY.

Sabalat, Tina. Pascals "Wette". Marburg : Tectum, 2000.

Williams, Jaime Andrés. El argumento de la apuesta de Blaise Pascal. 1. ed. Pamplona : Ediciones Universidad de Navarra, 2002.

Philosophie der Antike
(Bd. 17) Fortenbaugh, William W. Theophrastean studies. Stuttgart : Steiner, 2003.
B626.T34 F678 2003

Philosophie der natürlichen Mitwelt : Grundlagen, Probleme, Perspektiven ; Festschrift für Klaus Michael Meyer-Abich / Hans Werner Ingensiep, Anne Eusterschulte (Hrsg.). Würzburg : Königshausen & Neumann, 2002. 455 p. : port., ill. ; 24 cm. Includes bibliographical references (p. 409-434) and Schriftenverzeichnis of Klaus Michael Meyer-Abich (p. 436-454). ISBN 3-8260-2329-3 (hd. bd.)
1. Ethics. 2. Philosophy of nature. 3. Ecology - Philosophy. I. Ingensiep, Hans Werner, 1953- II. Eusterschulte, Anne. III. Meyer-Abich, Klaus Michael, 1936-

Philosophie d'Ernst Cassirer : une épistémologie de la troisième voie?.
Janz, Nathalie. Globus symbolicus. [Lausanne : Université de Lausanne, 1999]

Philosophie (Desclée De Brouwer (Firm))
Tiberghien, Gilles A., 1953- Amitier. Paris : Desclée de Brouwer, c2002.

Philosophie en commun.
Jouffroy, Théodore, 1796-1842. [Selections] La psychologie de Th. Jouffroy. Paris : L'Harmattan, c2003.

La philosophie en commun
Levent, Jean-Marc. Les ânes rouges. Paris : Harmattan, 2003.

Philosophie en commun.
Moulinier, Didier. Dictionnaire de la jouissance. Paris : L'Harmattan, c1999.
BF575.H27 M68 1999

La philosophie en commun
Renouvier, Charles, 1815-1903. Sur le peuple, l'église et la république. Paris : Harmattan, c2002.

Philosophie im Kontext
(Bd. 8) Anders, Martin. Präsenz zu denken--. St. Augustin : Gardez!, c2002.
B3303 .A53 2002

Philosophie in Aktion : Demokratie - Rassismus - Österreich / hg. von Silvia Stoller, Elisabeth Nemeth, Gerhard Unterthurner. Wien : Turia + Kant, 2000. 156 p. ; 20 cm. Collected essays written on the occasion of an 'Aktionswoche' at the Universität Wien, March 23 to 29, 2000. Includes bibliographical references. ISBN 3-85132-275-4 (corrected : pbk.)
1. Philosophy. 2. Philosophy, Modern. 3. Austria - Civilization - Congresses. 4. Austria - Politics and government - 1945- I. Stoller, Silvia. II. Nemeth, Elisabeth. III. Unterthurner, Gerhard.

Philosophie in der Blauen Eule
(Bd. 51) Krollmann, Fritz-Peter, 1963- Ethik und Ästhetik. Essen : Blaue Eule, 2002.

Philosophie und andere Künste
Kämpf, Heike. Helmuth Plessner. 1. Aufl. Düsseldorf : Parerga, 2001.
B3323.P564 K36 2001

Philosophie und Geschichte der Wissenschaften
(Bd. 43) Hong, Joon-kee, 1962- Der Subjektbegriff bei Lacan und Althusser. Frankfurt am Main ; New York : Peter Lang , c2000.
BF109.L28 H66 2000

Philosophie und Öffentlichkeit.
Hösle, Vittorio, 1960- Würzburg : Königshausen & Neumann, c2003.

Philosophie und Ökonomik
(Bd. 4) Grundherr, Michael von. Kants Ethik in modernen Gesellschaften. Hamburg : Lit, 2003.

Philosophieren.
Reiner, Hans, 1896- Oberried bei Freiburg i. Br. : PAIS-Verlag, c2002.

Philosophieren aus dem Diskurs : Beiträge zur Diskurspragmatik / im Auftrag des Hans-Jonas-Zentrums e.V. herausgegeben von Holger Burckhart, Horst Gronke ; Redaktion, Jens Peter Brune. Würzburg : Königshausen & Neumann, c2002. 763 p. ; 24 cm. Issued in honor of Dietrich Böhler's 60th birthday. Includes bibliographical references. German and English. ISBN 3-8260-2334-X (pbk.)
1. Reason. 2. Philosophy, Modern - 20th century. I. Böhler, Dietrich. II. Burckhart, Holger. III. Gronke, Horst. IV. Brune, Jens Peter. V. Hans Jonas-Zentrum e.V.

Philosophies
(158) Moreau, Pierre-François, 1948- Lucrèce. 1. ed. Paris : Presses universitaires de France, 2002.

Philosophische Abhandlungen
(Bd. 87) Willaschek, Marcus. Der mentale Zugang zur Welt. Frankfurt am Main : Klostermann, 2003.
B835 .W55 2003

Philosophische Schriften
(Bd. 47) Aufklärungen. Berlin : Duncker und Humblot, c2002.

(Bd. 49) Die erscheinende Welt. Berlin : Duncker & Humblot, c2002.

(Bd. 50) Societas rationis. Berlin : Duncker & Humblot, c2002.
B29 .S633 2002

Philosophische Texte und Studien
(Bd. 66) Erkennen und Leben. Hildesheim [Germany] ; New York : Olms, 2002.
BD435 .E75 2002

PHILOSOPHY. See also ABSURD (PHILOSOPHY); ACCIDENTS (PHILOSOPHY); ACT (PHILOSOPHY); AESTHETICS; AGENT (PHILOSOPHY); ALIENATION (PHILOSOPHY); ANALYSIS (PHILOSOPHY); AUTHENTICITY (PHILOSOPHY); AUTONOMY (PHILOSOPHY); BECOMING (PHILOSOPHY); BODY, HUMAN (PHILOSOPHY); COMPLEXITY (PHILOSOPHY); COMPREHENSION (THEORY OF KNOWLEDGE); CONSCIOUSNESS; CONSTRUCTIVISM (PHILOSOPHY); CONTINGENCY (PHILOSOPHY); CRITICISM (PHILOSOPHY); CYNICISM; DESIRE (PHILOSOPHY); DETERMINISM (PHILOSOPHY); DIFFERENCE (PHILOSOPHY); DISPOSITION (PHILOSOPHY); EMOTIONS (PHILOSOPHY); ETHICS; EXPECTATION (PHILOSOPHY); EXPRESSION (PHILOSOPHY); FACTS (PHILOSOPHY); FATE AND FATALISM; FEMININITY (PHILOSOPHY); GOOD AND EVIL; HARMONY (PHILOSOPHY); HUMANISM; IDEOLOGY; IMAGE (PHILOSOPHY); IMAGINATION (PHILOSOPHY); IMMORTALITY (PHILOSOPHY); INDIAN PHILOSOPHY; INDIVIDUATION (PHILOSOPHY); INTENTIONALITY (PHILOSOPHY); INTERPRETATION (PHILOSOPHY); KNOWLEDGE, THEORY OF; LOGIC; MATERIALISM; MEANING (PHILOSOPHY); MEMORY (PHILOSOPHY); METAPHYSICS; NATURALISM; NIHILISM (PHILOSOPHY); NORM (PHILOSOPHY); ORIGIN (PHILOSOPHY); PEACE (PHILOSOPHY); PERCEPTION; PERCEPTION (PHILOSOPHY); PERSPECTIVE (PHILOSOPHY); PHILOSOPHY OF MIND; PLACE (PHILOSOPHY); PLAY (PHILOSOPHY); POWER (PHILOSOPHY); PSYCHOANALYSIS AND PHILOSOPHY; PSYCHOLOGY; PSYCHOLOGY AND PHILOSOPHY; RECOGNITION (PHILOSOPHY); REFERENCE (PHILOSOPHY); RENUNCIATION (PHILOSOPHY); REPRESENTATION (PHILOSOPHY); RULES (PHILOSOPHY); SELF (PHILOSOPHY); SILENCE (PHILOSOPHY); SPIRITUALISM (PHILOSOPHY); SUBJECT (PHILOSOPHY); THEORY (PHILOSOPHY); THOUGHT AND THINKING; TRADITION (PHILOSOPHY); TRANSCENDENCE (PHILOSOPHY); TRANSCENDENTALISM; TRUTH; WAR (PHILOSOPHY); WILL; WOMAN (PHILOSOPHY).

Adorno, Theodor W., 1903-1969. [Ob nach Auschwitz noch sich leben lasse. English] Can one live after Auschwitz? Stanford, Calif. : Stanford University Press, 2003.
B3199.A33 O213 2003

Albert, Hans, 1921- Lesebuch. Tübingen : Mohr Siebeck, 2001.

Aufklärungen. Berlin : Duncker und Humblot, c2002.

Bahnñuk, Anatoliĭ. Filosofiă. Rivne : [s.n.], 1997.

Beelmann, Axel. Theoretische Philosophiegeschichte. Basel : Schwabe, c2001.

Bencivenga, Ermanno, 1950- Exercises in constructive imagination. Dordrecht ; Boston : Kluwer Academic Publishers, c2001.
B3613.B3853 E93 2001

Between philosophy and poetry. New York : Continuum, 2002.
B66 .B48 2002

Bibler, V. S. (Vladimir Solomonovich), 1918- Zamysly. Moskva : Rossiĭskiĭ gos. gumanitarnyĭ universitet, 2002.
B99.R9 B53 2002

Bodei, Remo, 1938- Destini personali. Milano : Feltrinelli, 2002.

Burke, Kenneth, 1897- On human nature. Berkeley : University of California Press, c2003.
B945.B771 R84 2003

Cahn, Steven M. Puzzles & perplexities. Lanham, Md. ; Oxford : Rowman & Littlefield, c2002.
BD41 .C26 2002

Châtelet, Gilles. [Enjeux du mobile. English] Figuring space. Dordrecht ; Boston : Kluwer, c2000.
B67 .C4313 2000

Chukwu, Cletus N. Introduction to philosophy in an African perspective. Eldoret, Kenya : Zapf Chancery, 2002.
1. Black author.

Cioran, E. M. (Emile M.), 1911- [Précis de décomposition. Romanian] Tratat de descompunere. Bucureşti : Humanitas, 2002, c1996.

Cohen, Hermann, 1842-1918. [Works. 1977. Supplementa] Werke. Supplementa. Hildesheim : G. Olms, 2000-

Dagognet, François. Changement de perspective. Paris : Table ronde, c2002.

Deleuze, Gilles. [Dialogues. English] Dialogues II. 2nd ed. New York : Columbia University Press, 2002.
B2430.D453 D4313 2002

Dépayser la pensée. Paris : Empêcheurs de penser en rond, 2003.

Dobeneck, Holger von. Das Sloterdijk Alphabet. Würzburg : Königshausen & Neumann, c2002.

Dornseiff, Johannes. Tractatus absolutus. 1. Aufl. Berlin : Frieling, 2000.

Elzenberg, Henryk, 1887-1967. Kłopot z istnieniem. Wyd. 1., popr. i uzup. Toruń : Wydawn. Uniwersytetu Mikołaja Kopernika, 2002.

Die erscheinende Welt. Berlin : Duncker & Humblot, c2002.

Ferry, Luc. Qu'est-ce qu'une vie réussie? Paris : Grasset, c2002.
BJ1612 .F47 2002

Filosofía, retórica e interpretación. México, D.F. : Universidad Nacional Autónoma de México, 2000.

Froment Meurice, Marc. Incitations. Paris : Galilée, c2002.

Gawor, Leszek. Katastrofizm konsekwentny. Lublin : Wydawn. Uniwersytetu Marii Curie Skłodowskiej, 1998.
B4691.Z384 G38 1998

Gellner, Ernest. [Essays. Selections] Ernest Gellner. London ; New York : Routledge, 2003.
B1626.G441 G76 2003

German 20th century philosophical writings. New York : Continuum, 2003.
B29 .G397 2003

Gloyna, Tanja. Kosmos und System. Stuttgart-Bad Cannstatt : Frommann-Holzboog, c2002.
B2898 .G56 2002

Goñi Zubieta, Carlos. Futbolsofía. Madrid : Ediciones del Laberinto, [2002]

Grünewald, Lars. Zwölf Weltanschauungen. 1. Aufl. Borchen : Ch. Möllmann, 2001.

Habermas, Jürgen. [Wahrheit und Rechtfertigung. English] Truth and justification. Cambridge, Mass. : MIT Press, c2003.
B3258.H323 W3413 2003

Heidegger, Martin, 1889-1976. [Essays. English. Selections] Supplements. Albany : State University of New York Press, c2002.
B3279.H47 E5 2002d

Huang, Kejian. [Selections. 1998] Huang Kejian zi xuan ji. Di 1 ban. Guilin Shi : Guangxi shi fan da xue chu ban she, 1998.
B99.C52 H765 1998

Interpretation und Argument. Würzburg : Königshausen & Neumann, c2002.

James, William, 1842-1910. [Pragmatism. German] Pragmatismus. Berlin : Akademie Verlag, c2000.

Jannoud, Claude. La crise de l'esprit. Lausanne, Suisse : Age d'homme, c2001.

Kāviyānī, Shīvā. Farzānagī dar āyinah-i zamān. Tihrān : Nigāh, 2001.

Kingwell, Mark, 1963- Practical judgments. Toronto : University of Toronto Press, c2002.

Kriza i perspektive filozofije. 1. izd. Beograd : Tersit, 1995.
B99.S462 K75 1995

Kuno Akira Kyōju kanreki kinen tetsugaku ronbunshū. Tōkyō : Ibunsha, 1995.
B29 .K826 1995 <Orien Japan>

Le Dœuff, Michèle. The philosophical imaginary. London : Continuum, 2002.

Le leggi del pensiero tra logica, ontologia e psicologia. Milano : UNICOPLI, 2002.

Leibniz, Gottfried Wilhelm, Freiherr von, 1646-1716. [Selections. English & Latin. 2001] The labyrinth of the continuum. New Haven : Yale University Press, c2001.

B2558 .A78 2001

Li, Zehou. Tan xun yu sui. Di 1 ban. Shanghai : Shanghai wen yi chu ban she, 2000.
B126 .L532 2000

Lin, Jian. Ren di zi you di zhe xue si suo. Di 1 ban. Beijing : Zhongguo ren min da xue chu ban she : Jing xiao xin hua shu dian, 1996.
B99.C52 L55 1996 <Orien China>

Liu, Shuxian, 1934- Li yi fen shu. Di 1 ban. Shanghai : Shanghai wen yi chu ban she, 2000.
B29 .L68 2000

Ludwig Wittgenstein, Tractatus logico-philosophicus. Berlin : Akademie Verlag, 2001.

Maiorescu, Toma George, 1928- Îmblâzirea fiarei din om sau ecosofia. 3a ediția revăzută și completată. București : Lumina Lex, 2002.

The many faces of philosophy. Oxford ; New York : Oxford University Press, 2003.
B72 .M346 2003

Manzoni, Alessandro, 1785-1873. Postille. Milano : Centro nazionale studi manzoniani, 2002.

Merleau-Ponty. Paris : Vrin ; Milano : Mimesis, 2001.

Mersmann, Paul. Kaleidoskopische Schriften. Hamburg : Maximilian-Gesellschaft, 2002.

Metáfora y discurso filosófico. Madrid : Tecnos, 2000.

Mićunović, Dragoljub. Filozofija minima. Beograd : "Filip Višnjić", 2001.
H61.15 .M5 2001

Midgley, Mary, 1919- The myths we live by. London ; New York : Routledge, 2003.
BL304 .M53 2003

Mohanty, Jitendranath, 1928- Explorations in philosophy. New Delhi ; New York : Oxford University Press, c2001-
B131.M54 M63 2001

Nietzsche, Friedrich Wilhelm, 1844-1900. [Selections. English. 2003] Writings from the late notebooks. Cambridge, UK ; New York : Cambridge University Press, c2003.
B3312.E5 B58 2003

Parmenides. [Nature. English & Greek] Parmenides of Elea. Westport, Conn. : Praeger, 2003.
B235.P23 N3713 2003

La persona e i nomi dell'essere. Milano : V&P Università, c2002.
B29 .P414 2002

Petich, Giuseppe, 1869-1953. Divagazioni filosofiche del reverendo Giuseppe Petich tratte dai frammenti del suo "Zibaldone". Roma : Bulzoni, 2002.

Philosophie in Aktion. Wien : Turia + Kant, 2000.

The philosophy of Marjorie Grene. Chicago : Open Court, c2002.
B945.G734 P47 2002

Przybylak, Feliks. Inskrypcje ulotności. Wrocław : Oficyna Wydawnicza ATUT-Wrocławskie Wydawn. Oświatowe, 2002.
PN56.C69 P79 2002

Rée, Paul, 1849-1901. [Ursprung der moralischen Empfindungen. English] Basic writings. Urbana : University of Illinois Press, c2003.
B3323.R343 U67 2003

Reiner, Hans, 1896- Philosophieren. Oberried bei Freiburg i. Br. : PAIS-Verlag, c2002.

Reinhold, Karl Leonhard, 1757-1823. [Ueber den Begriff der Philosophie. Italian] Concetto e fondamento della filosofia. Roma : Edizioni di storia e letteratura, 2002.

Renouvier, Charles, 1815-1903. Sur le peuple, l'église et la république. Paris : Harmattan, c2002.

Roche, Christian. Le bestiaire des philosophes. [Paris] : Seuil, c2001.

Rothenberg, David, 1962- Always the mountains. Athens : University of Georgia Press, c2002.
GF21 .R68 2002

Salamucha, Jan. [Selections. English. 2003] Knowledge and faith. Amsterdam ; New York, NY : Rodopi, 2003.

Schiffter, Frédéric. Pensées d'un philosophe sous Prozac. [Toulouse] : Milan, c2002.

Schlanger, Jacques. Guide pour un apprenti philosophe. Paris : Presses universitaires de France, 2002.

Schopenhauer, Arthur, 1788-1860. [Parerga und paralipomena. English] Parerga and paralipomena. Oxford : Clarendon Press ; New York : Oxford University Press, 2000.
B3118.E5 P38 2000

Schweitzer, Albert, 1875-1965. Vorträge, Vorlesungen, Aufsätze. München : C.H. Beck, c2003.

The search for a holistic approach to human existence and development. [Nigeria?] : Osigwe Anyiam-Osigwe Foundation, [1999?]
B53 .E46 1999

Serres, Michel. L'incandescent. [Paris] : Pommier, c2003.

Shoemaker, Sydney. Identity, cause, and mind. Expanded ed. Oxford : Clarendon Press ; New York : Oxford University Press, c2003.
B29 .S5135 2003

Societas rationis. Berlin : Duncker & Humblot, c2002.
B29 .S633 2002

Sporiș, Mihai, 1951- Spiritul civic. Râmnicu Vâlcea : Editura Adrianso, 1999-

Svobodnyĭ vzgli͡ad na literaturu. Moskva : Nauka, 2002.

Le système et le rêve. Paris : Harmattan, c2002.
BF1078 .S97 2002

Tang, Yongtong, 1893-1964. [Works. 2000] Tang Yongtong quan ji. Di 1 ban. Shijiazhuang Shi : Hebei ren min chu ban she, 2000.
BQ626 .T37 2000

Tapergi, Fausto, 1909- La filosofia come scienza della vita. 1a ed. Milano : Spirali, 2001.

Teichman, Jenny. Philosophers' hobbies and other essays. Carlton, Vic. : Black Jack Press, 2003.

Tiberghien, Gilles A., 1953- Amitier. Paris : Desclée de Brouwer, c2002.

Tshe-riṅ-rdo-rje, 'Broṅ-bu. Nub phyogs śer rtogs rig pa'i tshig bum. Par theṅs 1. Pe-cin : Mi rigs dpe skrun khaṅ, 1995.

Tu, Wei-ming. [Selections. 2002] Du Weiming wen ji. Wuhan Shi : Wuhan chu ban she, 2002.
B5233.C6 T813 2002

Tugendhat, Ernst. Aufsätze 1992-2000. 1. Aufl. Frankfurt : Suhrkamp, 2001.

Unger, Roberto Mangabeira. False necessity--antinecessitarian social theory in the service of radical democracy. New ed. London ; New York : Verso, 2001.

Vallega-Neu, Daniela, 1966- Heidegger's contributions to philosophy. Bloomington, IN : Indiana University Press, c2003.
B3279.H48 B454 2003

Verene, Donald Phillip, 1937- Knowledge of things human and divine. New Haven, Conn. : Yale University Press, c2003.
B3581.P73 V47 2003

Verna, Arturo. Letture filosofiche. Padova : Unipress, 2002.

Werder, Lutz von. Lehrbuch der philosophischen Lebenskunst für das 21. Jahrhundert. Berlin : Schibri-Verlag, c2000.

Willaschek, Marcus. Der mentale Zugang zur Welt. Frankfurt am Main : Klostermann, 2003.
B835 .W55 2003

The world's great philosophers. Malden, MA : Blackwell Pub., 2003.
B29 .W69 2003

Zambrano, María. De la aurora. Córdoba, Argentina : Alción Editora, c1999.

PHILOSOPHY - AFRICA.
Chukwu, Cletus N. Introduction to philosophy in an African perspective. Eldoret, Kenya : Zapf Chancery, 2002.
1. Black author.

Philosophy after postmodernism.
Crowther, Paul. London ; New York : Routledge, 2003.
B831.2 .C76 2003

PHILOSOPHY, ANALYTICAL. See ANALYSIS (PHILOSOPHY).

PHILOSOPHY, ANCIENT. See also EPICUREANS (GREEK PHILOSOPHY); PLATONISTS.
Alonso-Nuñez, José Miguel. The idea of universal history in Greece. Amsterdam : J.C. Gieben, 2002.

D13.5.G8 A46 2002
Ammonius, Hermiae. Commentaria in quinque voces Porphyrii. Stuttgart : Frommann-Holzboog, 2002.

Basov, R. A. Istoriia drevnegrecheskoĭ filosofii ot Falesa do Aristotelia. Moskva : Letopis' XXI, 2002.
B175.R9 B37 2002

Beare, John I. (John Isaac), d. 1918 Greek theories of elementary cognition. Mansfield Centre, Conn. : Martino Pub., 2004.
BF91.B3 2004

The Blackwell guide to ancient philosophy. Malden, MA ; Oxford : Blackwell Pub., 2003.
B171.B65 2003

Burlaeus, Gualterus, 1275-1345? [De vita et moribus philosophorum. Spanish] Vida y costumbres de los viejos filósofos. Madrid : Iberoamericana ; Frankfurt : Vervuert, 2002.
B173.B8 2000

The Cambridge companion to Greek and Roman philosophy. Cambridge, U.K. ; New York : Cambridge University Press, 2003.
B111.C36 2003

Catrysse, Andrée. Les grecs et la vieillesse. Paris : L'Harmattan, c2003.

Couprie, Dirk, 1940- Anaximander in context. Albany : State University of New York Press, c2003.
B208.Z7 C68 2003

Dillon, John M. The heirs of Plato. Oxford : Clarendon Press ; New York : Oxford University Press, 2003.
B517.D536 2003

Dixsaut, Monique. Métamorphoses de la dialectique dans les dialogues de Platon. Paris : Vrin, c2001.
B398.D5 D598 2001

Droit, Roger-Pol. Fous comme des sages. Paris : Seuil, c2002.

Eslin, Jean-Claude, 1935- Saint Augustin. Paris : Michalon, c2002.

Ferguson, Everett, 1933- Backgrounds of early Christianity. 3rd ed. Grand Rapids, Mich. : W.B. Eerdmans, c2003.

Fortenbaugh, William W. Theophrastean studies. Stuttgart : Steiner, 2003.
B626.T34 F678 2003

Gelehrte in der Antike. Köln : Böhlau, c2002.

Grammatical theory and philosophy of language in antiquity. Leuven ; Sterling, Va. : Peeters, 2002.
P63.G73 2002

Green, Christopher D. Early psychological thought. Westport, Conn. ; London : Praeger, 2003.
BF91.G74 2003

Klatt, Norbert. Die Rivalin Gottes. Göttingen : N. Klatt, 2000.

Lloyd, G. E. R. (Geoffrey Ernest Richard), 1933- In the grip of disease. Oxford ; New York : Oxford University Press, 2003.
B187.M4 L56 2003

McEvilley, Thomas, 1939- The shape of ancient thought. New York : Allworth Press : School of Visual Arts, c2002.
B165.M22 2002

Moreau, Pierre-François, 1948- Lucrèce. 1. ed. Paris : Presses universitaires de France, 2002.

Muñoz Llamosas, Virginia. La intervención divina en el hombre a través de la literatura griega de época arcaica y clásica. Amsterdam : Hakkert, 2002.
PA3015.R5 M87 2002

Plato. [Selections. Latvian] Platons dialogi un vēstules = [Rīga] : Zinātne, c1999.

Pradeau, Jean-François. Plato and the city. Exeter, UK : University of Exeter Press, 2002.
B395.P7313 2002

Presocratic philosophy. Aldershot, Hants, England ; Burlington, VT : Ashgate, 2002.
B187.5.P743 2002

Protopapas-Marneli, Maria. La rhétorique des stoïciens. Paris : Harmattan, c2002.

Radford, Robert T. Cicero. Amsterdam ; New York, NY : Rodopi, 2002.
DG260.C5 R33 2002

Ricot, Jacques. Leçon sur L'éthique à Nicomaque, d'Aristote. 1re ed. Paris : Presses universitaires de France, c2001.

B430.R536 2001
Sichirollo, Livio. Filosofia, storia, istituzioni. Nuova ed. [Urbino] : Università degli studi di Urbino, [2001]

Songe-Möller, Vigdis. Philosophy without women. London : Continuum, c2002.

Thinking about the environment. Lanham, Md. : Lexington Books, c2002.
GE50.T48 2002

Torre, Francisco Javier de la. Aproximación a las fuentes clásicas latinas de Hannah Arendt. Málaga : Universidad de Málaga, 2002.

Trabattoni, Franco. La filosofia antica. 1a ed. Roma : Carocci, 2002.

Tyrannis und Verführung. Wien : Turia + Kant, 2000.
JC381.T973 2000

Walde, Christine, 1960- Antike Traumdeutung und moderne Traumforschung. Düsseldorf : Artemis & Winkler, c2001.

PHILOSOPHY AND CIVILIZATION. See **CIVILIZATION - PHILOSOPHY.**

Philosophy and freedom : the legacy of James Doull / edited with an introduction by David G. Peddle and Neil G. Robertson. Toronto : University of Toronto Press, c2003. xxix, 520 p. : ill., port. ; 24 cm. Includes bibliographical references (p. [505]-507) and index. ISBN 0-8020-3698-8 DDC 123/.5
1. Doull, James - Contributions in the philosophy of liberty. 2. Liberty - Philosophy. 3. Liberty. I. Peddle, David, 1965- II. Robertson, Neil G.

PHILOSOPHY AND PSYCHOANALYSIS. See **PSYCHOANALYSIS AND PHILOSOPHY.**

PHILOSOPHY AND PSYCHOLOGY. See **PSYCHOLOGY AND PHILOSOPHY.**

PHILOSOPHY AND RELIGION. See also **PHILOSOPHICAL THEOLOGY.**
Boethius, d. 524. [De consolatione philosophiae. English] Consolation of philosophy. Indianapolis, IN : Hackett Pub. Co., c2001.
B659.C2 E52 2001

Kunin, Seth Daniel. Religion. Baltimore : Johns Hopkins University Press, 2003.

Renouvier, Charles, 1815-1903. Sur le peuple, l'église et la république. Paris : Harmattan, c2002.

Salamucha, Jan. [Selections. English. 2003] Knowledge and faith. Amsterdam ; New York, NY : Rodopi, 2003.

The search for a holistic approach to human existence and development. [Nigeria?] : Osigwe Anyiam-Osigwe Foundation, [1999?]
B53.E46 1999

Transcendence in philosophy and religion. Bloomington, IN : Indiana University Press, c2003.
B56.T73 2003

PHILOSOPHY AND SCIENCE. See also **SCIENCE - PHILOSOPHY.**
Castagnino, M. (Mario) Tempo e universo. Roma : Armando, c2000.
BD632.C37 2000

Kultur, Handlung, Wissenschaft. 1. Aufl. Weilerswist : Velbrück Wissenschaft, 2002.
B67.K853 2002

Mind, matter, and mystery. New Delhi : Scientia, 2001.
BD418.3.M5556 2001

Sciences et archétypes. Paris : Dervy, 2002.

PHILOSOPHY, ARAB. See **PHILOSOPHY, ISLAMIC.**

PHILOSOPHY, ARABIC. See **PHILOSOPHY, ISLAMIC.**

PHILOSOPHY, ASIAN.
Merlo Lillo, Vicente. La fascinación de Oriente. 1. ed. Barcelona : Editorial Kairós, 2002.

PHILOSOPHY - AUTHORSHIP.
Schuster, Shlomit C., 1951- The philosopher's autobiography. Westport, Conn. ; London : Praeger, 2003.
B52.7.S38 2003

PHILOSOPHY - BIOGRAPHY. See **PHILOSOPHERS.**

PHILOSOPHY, BRITISH - 19TH CENTURY.
Carter, Matt. T.H. Green and the development of ethical socialism. Thorverton : Imprint Academic, 2003.

B1638.E8 C37 2003
PHILOSOPHY, CHINESE.
Huang, Kejian. [Selections. 1998] Huang Kejian zi xuan ji. Di 1 ban. Guilin Shi : Guangxi shi fan da xue chu ban she, 1998.
B99.C52 H765 1998

Li, Zehou. Tan xun yu sui. Di 1 ban. Shanghai : Shanghai wen yi chu ban she, 2000.
B126.L532 2000

Liu, Shuxian, 1934- Li yi fen shu. Di 1 ban. Shanghai : Shanghai wen yi chu ban she, 2000.
B29.L68 2000

Tang, Yijie. Xi bu zhi jin. Di 1 ban. Shanghai : Shanghai wen yi chu ban she, 1999.
B126.T1965 1999

Tang, Yongtong, 1893-1964. [Works. 2000] Tang Yongtong quan ji. Di 1 ban. Shijiazhuang Shi : Hebei ren min chu ban she, 2000.
BQ626.T37 2000

Tu, Wei-ming. [Selections. 2002] Du Weiming wen ji. Di 1 ban. Wuhan shi : Wuhan chu ban she, 2002.
B5233.C6 T813 2002

Xu, Fancheng. Xu Fancheng ji. Di 1 ban. Beijing : Zhongguo she hui ke xue chu ban she, 2001.
PL2262.2.X84 2001

Zhang, Shunhui. Zhang Shunhui xue shu wen hua sui bi. Beijing di 1 ban. Beijing : Zhongguo qing nian chu ban she, 2001.
PL2272.5.Z427 2001

PHILOSOPHY, CHINESE - 221 B.C.-960 A.D.
Wagner, Rudolf G. Language, ontology, and political philosophy in China. Albany : State University of New York Press, c2003.
B126.W284 2003

PHILOSOPHY, CHINESE - CHINA.
Xue lin chun qiu. Di 1 ban. Beijing : Chao hua chu ban she, 1999.
PL2272.5.X846 1999

PHILOSOPHY, COMPARATIVE.
McEvilley, Thomas, 1939- The shape of ancient thought. New York : Allworth Press : School of Visual Arts, c2002.
B165.M22 2002

PHILOSOPHY, CONFUCIAN.
Tu, Wei-ming. [Selections. 2002] Du Weiming wen ji. Wuhan Shi : Wuhan chu ban she, 2002.
B5233.C6 T813 2002

PHILOSOPHY, CONTINENTAL. See **PHILOSOPHY, EUROPEAN.**

Philosophy, culture, and religion
Matilal, Bimal Krishna. Ethics and epics. New Delhi ; New York : Oxford University Press, 2002.
B131.M398 2002b

PHILOSOPHY, ENGLISH. See **PHILOSOPHY, BRITISH.**

PHILOSOPHY, EUROPEAN.
Race and racism in continental philosophy. Bloomington : Indiana University Press, c2003.
HT1523.R2514 2003

PHILOSOPHY, EUROPEAN - 20TH CENTURY.
Merleau-Ponty. Paris : Vrin : Milano : Mimesis, 2001.

PHILOSOPHY, FRENCH.
Froment Meurice, Marc. Incitations. Paris : Galilée, c2002.

PHILOSOPHY, FRENCH - 20TH CENTURY.
Levent, Jean-Marc. Les ânes rouges. Paris : Harmattan, 2003.

PHILOSOPHY, GERMAN.
Pfaller, Robert. Die Illusionen der anderen. 1. Aufl. Frankfurt : Suhrkamp, 2002.

PHILOSOPHY, GERMAN - HISTORY - 20TH CENTURY.
Sagnol, Marc, 1956- Tragique et tristesse. Paris : Cerf, 2003.

PHILOSOPHY, HINDU. See also **KNOWLEDGE, THEORY OF (HINDUISM); YOGA.**
Tagore, Rabindranath, 1861-1941. [Sādhanā. Marathi] Sādhanā. Kolhāpūra : Mahārāṣṭra Grantha Bhāṇḍāra, 2000.
B131.T28 2000

PHILOSOPHY - HISTORIOGRAPHY.
Beelmann, Axel. Theoretische Philosophiegeschichte. Basel : Schwabe, c2001.

PHILOSOPHY - HISTORY.
Ambjörnsson, Ronny, 1936- Tankens pilgrimer. Stockholm : Natur och Kultur, c2002.

Beelmann, Axel. Theoretische Philosophiegeschichte. Basel : Schwabe, c2001.

Karl Jaspers on philosophy of history and history of philosophy. Amherst, N.Y. : Humanity Books, 2003.
B3279.J34 K292 2003

La persona e i nomi dell'essere. Milano : V&P Università, c2002.
B29 .P414 2002

Schürmann, Reiner, 1941- [Des hégémonies brisées. English] Broken hegemonies. Bloomington : Indiana University Press, c2003.
BD162 .S48 2003

Sichirollo, Livio. Filosofia, storia, istituzioni. Nuova ed. [Urbino] : Università degli studi di Urbino, [2001]

Songe-Möller, Vigdis. Philosophy without women. London : Continuum, c2002.

Philosophy in a time of crisis.
Feldman, Seymour. London ; New York : RoutledgeCurzon, 2003.
BM755.A25 F45 2003

Philosophy in an African perspective.
Chukwu, Cletus N. Introduction to philosophy in an African perspective. Eldoret, Kenya : Zapf Chancery, 2002.
1. Black author.

PHILOSOPHY IN LITERATURE.
Carmona Fernández, Fernando. La mentalidad literaria medieval. 1. ed. Murcia : Universidad de Murcia, Servicio de Publicaciones, 2001.

Philosophy in the age of science and capital.
Adamson, Gregory Dale, 1966- London ; New York : Continuum, 2002.
B804 .A33 2002

PHILOSOPHY, INDIAN. See INDIAN PHILOSOPHY.

PHILOSOPHY, INDIC.
Bhāratīya darśana paribhāṣā kośa = Naī Dillī : Vaijñānika tathā Takanīkī Śabdāvalī Āyoga, Mānava Saṃsādhana Vikāsa Mantrālaya, Śikṣā Vibhāga, Bhārata Sarakāra, 1999-
B131 .B498 1999

Caturvedī, Saccidānanda. Vairāgya. Itanagar : Himālayana Pabliśarsa, 2000.
BL1239.5.A82 C28 2000

Chatterjea, Tara, 1937- Knowledge and freedom in Indian philosophy. Lanham, Md. ; Oxford : Lexington Books, 2002.
B131 .C518 2002

Gupta, Bina, 1947- CIT consciousness. New Delhi ; New York : Oxford University Press, 2003.
BF311+

Jośī, Gajānana Nārāyaṇa. Bhāratīya tattvajñānācā brhad itihāsa. 1. āvrttī. Puṇe : Marāṭhī Tattvajñāna-Mahākośa Maṇḍala yāñce karitā Śubhadā-Sārasvata Prakāśana, 1994.
B131 .J674 1994

Krishna, Daya. Developments in Indian philosophy from Eighteenth century onwards. New Delhi : Project of History of Indian Science, Philosophy, and Culture : Centre for Studies in Civilizations : Distributed by Motilal Banarsidass, 2002.
B131+

Matilal, Bimal Krishna. Ethics and epics. New Delhi ; New York : Oxford University Press, 2002.
B131 .M398 2002b

McEvilley, Thomas, 1939- The shape of ancient thought. New York : Allworth Press : School of Visual Arts, c2002.
B165 .M22 2002

Merlo Lillo, Vicente. La fascinación de Oriente. 1. ed. Barcelona : Editorial Kairós, 2002.

Miśra, Ānanda, lecturer. Saṃvitprakāśavāda. 1. saṃskaraṇa. Dillī : Bhāratīya Vidyā Prakāśana, 2002.
B132.K6 M58 2002

Mohanty, Jitendranath, 1928- Explorations in philosophy. New Delhi ; New York : Oxford University Press, c2001-
B131.M54 M63 2001

Olson, Carl. Indian philosophers and postmodern thinkers. New Delhi ; New York : Oxford University Press, 2002.

B131 .O57 2002

Shastri, L. C., 1933- Indian philosophy of knowledge. 1st ed. Delhi, India : Global Vision Pub. House, 2002.
B132.K6 S48 2002

Siṃha, Kīrti Kumāra. Bhāratīya darśana meṃ duḥkha aura mukti. 1. saṃskaraṇa. Ilāhābāda : Śekhara Prakāśana, 2001.
B132.M64 S56 2001

Tang, Yongtong, 1893-1964. [Works. 2000] Tang Yongtong quan ji. Di 1 ban. Shijiazhuang Shi : Hebei ren min chu ban she, 2000.
BQ626 .T37 2000

PHILOSOPHY, IRANIAN.
Tabatabai, Sayyid Muhammad Husayn. The elements of Islamic metaphysics (Bidāyat al-Ḥikmah). London : ICAS, 2003.

PHILOSOPHY, ISLAMIC.
Arnaldez, Roger. Fakhr al-Dîn al-Râzî. Paris : J. Vrin, 2002.

Tabatabai, Sayyid Muhammad Husayn. The elements of Islamic metaphysics (Bidāyat al-Ḥikmah). London : ICAS, 2003.

PHILOSOPHY, ISLAMIC - GREEK INFLUENCES.
Jambet, Christian. L'acte d'être. [Paris] : Fayard, c2002.

PHILOSOPHY, ITALIAN.
De Pace, Anna. La scepsi, il sapere e l'anima. Milano : LED, c2002.

Early studies of Giordano Bruno. Bristol : Thoemmes, 2000.

PHILOSOPHY, ITALIAN - 19TH CENTURY.
Cospito, Giuseppe, 1966- Il "gran Vico". Genova : Name, c2002.

PHILOSOPHY, JEWISH.
The Cambridge companion to medieval Jewish philosophy. Cambridge, UK ; New York : Cambridge University Press, 2003.
B755 .C36 2003

Cohen, Hermann, 1842-1918. [Works. 1977. Supplementa] Werke. Supplementa. Hildesheim : G. Olms, 2000-

Dorff, Elliot N. Love your neighbor and yourself. 1st ed. Philadelphia, PA : Jewish Publication Society, 2003.
BJ1285 .D67 2003

Feldman, Seymour. Philosophy in a time of crisis. London ; New York : RoutledgeCurzon, 2003.
BM755.A25 F45 2003

Halbertal, Moshe. Ben Torah le-ḥokhmah. Yerushalayim : Hotsa'at sefarim 'a. sh. Y. L. Magnes, ha-Universiṭah ha-'Ivrit, 760, 2000.
BM755.M54 H35 2000

Maimonides, Moses, 1135-1204. [Selections] Sefer Musarim ve-de'ot leha-Rambam. Bene Beraḳ : [ḥ. mo. l], 761 [2000 or 2001]

Portaleone, Abraham ben David, 1542-1612. [Shilṭe Ha Gibborim. German] Die Heldenschilde. Frankfurt am Main : Lang, 2002.

PHILOSOPHY, MARXIST.
Read, Jason. The micro-politics of capital. Albany : State University of New York Press, c2003.
HB97.5 .R42 2003

PHILOSOPHY, MEDIEVAL.
Abbo of Fleury and Ramsay. Oxford ; New York : Oxford University Press, 2002.

Ambjörnsson, Ronny, 1936- Tankens pilgrimer. Stockholm : Natur och Kultur, c2002.

Anselm, Saint, Archbishop of Canterbury, 1033-1109. [Dialogues. English. Selections] Three philosophical dialogues. Indianapolis, IN : Hackett Pub., c2002.
B765.A81 .A2513 2002

Arnaldez, Roger. Fakhr al-Dîn al-Râzî. Paris : J. Vrin, 2002.

Boethius, d. 524. [De consolatione philosophiae. French] La consolation de philosophie. Paris : Belles lettres, 2002.

The Cambridge companion to medieval Jewish philosophy. Cambridge, UK ; New York : Cambridge University Press, 2003.
B755 .C36 2003

The Cambridge companion to medieval philosophy. Cambridge ; New York : Cambridge University Press, 2003.

B721 .C36 2003

Canning, Joseph. [History of medieval political thought, 300-1450. French] Histoire de la pensée politique médiévale (300-1450). Fribourg, Suisse : Éditions universitaires ; Paris : Cerf, [2003]

Carmona Fernández, Fernando. La mentalidad literaria medieval. 1. ed. Murcia : Universidad de Murcia, Servicio de Publicaciones, 2001.

Cohen, Jeffrey Jerome. Medieval identity machines. Minneapolis : University of Minnesota Press, c2003.
CB353 .C64 2003

Curiositas. Göttingen : Wallstein, c2002.
BF323.C8 C872 2002

Feldman, Seymour. Philosophy in a time of crisis. London ; New York : RoutledgeCurzon, 2003.
BM755.A25 F45 2003

La filosofía medieval. Madrid : Trotta, 2002.
B721 .F47 2002

Fumagalli Beonio Brocchieri, Mariateresa, 1933- Profilo del pensiero medievale. 1. ed. Roma : Laterza, 2002.

Gill, Harjeet Singh, 1935- Signification in Buddhist and French traditions. New Delhi : Harman Pub. House, 2001.
BC25 .G55 2001

González, Angel Luis. Ser y participación. 3. ed. revisada y ampliada. Pamplona : Ediciones Universidad de Navarra, c2001.
BX4700.T6 G66 2001

Halbertal, Moshe. Ben Torah le-ḥokhmah. Yerushalayim : Hotsa'at sefarim 'a. sh. Y. L. Magnes, ha-Universitah ha-'Ivrit, 760, 2000.
BM755.M54 H35 2000

Hehle, Christine. Boethius in St. Gallen. Tübingen : Niemeyer, 2002.

Jean, de la Rochelle, d. 1245. Summa de anima. Paris : J. Vrin, 1995.
BD420 .J43 1995

The medieval heritage in early modern metaphysics and modal theory, 1400-1700. Dordrecht ; Boston : Kluwer Academic Publishers, c2003.
BD111 .M47 2003

Medieval philosophy and the classical tradition. London ; New York : Curzon, c2002.
B721 .M4535 2002

The Platonic tradition in the Middle Ages. Berlin ; New York : W. de Gruyter, 2002.

Portaleone, Abraham ben David, 1542-1612. [Shilṭe Ha Gibborim. German] Die Heldenschilde. Frankfurt am Main : Lang, 2002.

Progrès, réaction, décadence dans l'Occident médiéval. Genève : Droz, 2003.
PN681 .P764 2003

Prudentia und Contemplatio. Paderborn : Ferdinand Schöningh, 2002.

Reina, Maria Elena. Hoc hic et nunc. [Firenze] : Leo S. Olschki, 2002.

Rousselot, Pierre, 1878-1915. [Pour l'histoire du problème de l'amour au moyen âge. English] The problem of love in the Middle Ages. Milwaukee : Marquette University Press, [2001?]
B738.L68 R68 2001

Salamucha, Jan. [Selections. English. 2003] Knowledge and faith. Amsterdam ; New York, NY : Rodopi, 2003.

The sciences in enlightened Europe. Chicago : University of Chicago Press, 1999.
Q127.E8 S356 1999

La servante et la consolatrice. Paris : Vrin, 2002.
B721 .S479 2002

Thinking about the environment. Lanham, Md. : Lexington Books, c2002.
GE50 .T48 2002

Vega, Amador. Ramon Llull y el secreto de la vida. Madrid : Siruela, 2002.

Vizantijska filozofija u srednjevekovnoj Srbiji. Beograd : Stubovi kulture, 2002.

Zerbi, Piero. "Philosophi" e "logici". Roma : Istituto storico italiano per il Medio Evo ; Milano : Vita e pensiero, 2002.

Philosophy, Medieval.

B765.A24 Z473 2002

PHILOSOPHY, MEDIEVAL - CONGRESSES.
Internationales Eriugena-Colloquium (10th : Maynooth and Dublin : 2002) History and eschatology in John Scottus Eriugena and his time. Leuven : University Press, 2002.

PHILOSOPHY, MEDIEVAL, IN LITERATURE.
Fumagalli Beonio Brocchieri, Mariateresa, 1933- Profilo del pensiero medievale. 1. ed. Roma : Laterza, 2002.

PHILOSOPHY, MODERN. See also SEMANTICS (PHILOSOPHY); TRANSCENDENTALISM.
Bewes, Timothy. Reification, or, The anxiety of late capitalism. London ; New York : Verso, 2002.
HM449 .B49 2002

Cumpeta, Silvio. I dialoghi dell'ego. Gorizia : Biblioteca statale isontina, c2001.

Genuss und Egoismus. Berlin : Akademie Verlag, c2002.

Holismus in der Philosophie. 1. Aufl. Weilerswist : Velbrück Wissenschaft, c2002.

Krishna, Daya. Developments in Indian philosophy from Eighteenth century onwards. New Delhi : Project of History of Indian Science, Philosophy, and Culture : Centre for Studies in Civilizations : Distributed by Motilal Banarsidass, 2002.
B131+

The medieval heritage in early modern metaphysics and modal theory, 1400-1700. Dordrecht ; Boston : Kluwer Academic Publishers, c2003.
BD111 .M47 2003

Philosophie in Aktion. Wien : Turia + Kant, 2000.

Sepúlveda, Jesús. El jardín de las peculiaridades. Buenos Aires : Ediciones del Leopardo, [2002]

Sichirollo, Livio. Filosofia, storia, istituzioni. Nuova ed. [Urbino] : Università degli studi di Urbino, [2001]

Zima, P. V. Theorie des Subjekts. Tübingen : A. Francke, c2000.
BD223 .Z56 2000

PHILOSOPHY, MODERN - 17TH CENTURY.
Broad, Jacqueline. Women philosophers of the seventeenth century. Cambridge, UK ; New York : Cambridge University Press, 2002.
B105.W6 B76 2002

Curiositas. Göttingen : Wallstein, c2002.
BF323.C8 C872 2002

Orio de Miguel, Bernardino, 1936- Leibniz y el pensamiento hermético. Valencia : Universidad Politécnica de Valéncia, Editorial U.P.V., [2002]

Renaissance and early modern philosophy. Malden, MA ; Oxford : Blackwell Pub., c2002.
B775 .R46 2002

Silhon, sieur de (Jean), 1596?-1667. De la certitude des connaissances humaines. [Paris] : Fayard, c2002.

PHILOSOPHY, MODERN - 18TH CENTURY.
Protsenko, Oleh. Konservatyzm. Kyïv : "Smoloskyp", 1998.

PHILOSOPHY, MODERN - 19TH CENTURY.
Merleau-Ponty, Maurice, 1908-1961. L'institution dans l'histoire personnelle et publique : [Paris] : Belin, c2003.
B2430.M3763 I88 2003

Protsenko, Oleh. Konservatyzm. Kyïv : "Smoloskyp", 1998.

PHILOSOPHY, MODERN - 20TH CENTURY. *See also* **POSTMODERNISM.**
Adamson, Gregory Dale, 1966- Philosophy in the age of science and capital. London ; New York : Continuum, 2002.
B804 .A33 2002

Alemán, Jorge. Lacan en la razón posmoderna. Málaga : Miguel Gómez Ediciones, c2000.
BF109.L28 A44 2000

Arthurs, Jane. Crash cultures. Bristol, UK ; Portland, OR : Intellect, 2002.

Bardy, Jean. Regard sur "l'évolution créatrice". Paris : Harmattan, c2003.

Bošković, Hijacint. Filozofski izvori fašizma i nacionalnog socijalizma. 2. izd. Zagreb : Dom i svijet, 2000.
B804 .B66 2000

Civilisation et barbarie. 1re éd. Paris : Presses universitaires de France, c2002.

Clair, André. Sens de l'existence. Paris : Armand Colin, c2002.

Conche, Marcel. Confession d'un philosophe. Paris : Albin Michel, c2003.
B804 .C66 2003

Del Bufalo, Erik. Deleuze et Laruelle. Paris : Kimé, 2003.

Foucault au Collège de France. Pessac : Presses universitaires de Bordeaux, c2003.
B2430.F724 F6855 2003

Gadamer, Hans Georg, 1900- Die Lektion des Jahrhunderts. Münster : Lit, [2002]

Gendai tetsugaku ga wakaru. Tōkyō : Asahi Shinbunsha, 2002.
B804 .G43 2002

Günzel, Stephan, 1971- Anteile. Weimar : Verlag und Datenbank für Geisteswissenschaften, 2002.

Habermas, Jürgen. Kommunikatives Handeln und detranszendentalisierte Vernunft. Stuttgart : Reclam, c2001.
P91 .H33 2001

Hösle, Vittorio, 1960- Philosophie und Öffentlichkeit. Würzburg : Königshausen & Neumann, c2003.

Hottois, Gilbert, 1946- Species technica ; Paris : Vrin, 2002.

Kämpf, Heike. Helmuth Plessner. 1. Aufl. Düsseldorf : Parerga, 2001.
B3323.P564 K36 2001

Kneer, Markus, 1972- Die dunkle Spur im Denken. Paderborn : Schöningh, 2003.
DS145 .K64 2003

Köhler, Manfred. Apokalypse oder Umkehr? Marburg : Tectum, 2000.

Lefter, Ion Bogdan. Postmodernism. Pitești : Editura Paralela 45, 2000.

Lenger, Hans-Joachim. Vom Abschied. Bielefeld : Transcript, c2001.
B105.D5 L46 2001

Levent, Jean-Marc. Les ânes rouges. Paris : Harmattan, 2003.

Li, Xiaobing. Wo zai, wo si. Di 1 ban. Beijing : Dong fang chu ban she : Xin hua shu dian jing xiao, 1996.
CB425 .L39 1996 <Orien China>

Lobkowicz, Nikolaus. Czas kryzysu, czas prezełomu. Kraków : Wydawnictwo WAM : Znak, 1996.

Marías, Julián, 1914- Entre dos siglos. Madrid : Alianza Editorial, c2002.
PQ6663.A72183 E68 2002

Merleau-Ponty, Maurice, 1908-1961. L'institution dans l'histoire personnelle et publique : [Paris] : Belin, c2003.
B2430.M3763 I88 2003

Merleau-Ponty. Paris : Vrin ; Milano : Mimesis, 2001.

Mires, Fernando. Crítica de la razón científica. 1a ed. Caracas : Editorial Nueva Sociedad, 2002.

Nazarchuk, A. V. (Aleksandr Viktorovich) Ėtika globaliziruiushchegosia obshchestva. Moskva : DirectMedia Pablishing, 2002.
B3199.A634 N39 2002

Pabón, Carlos. Nación postmortem. 1. ed. San Juan, P.R. : Ediciones Callejón, 2002.

Petitdemange, Guy. Philosophes et philosophies du XXe siècle. Paris : Seuil, c2003.
B804 .P45 2003

Philosophieren aus dem Diskurs. Würzburg : Königshausen & Neumann, c2002.

Poitevin, Michel. Georges Dumézil, un naturel comparatiste. Paris : Harmattan, c2002.

Powell, Jim, 1946- Postmodernism for beginners. New York : Writers and Readers Pub., c1998.

Protsenko, Oleh. Konservatyzm. Kyïv : "Smoloskyp", 1998.

Schulz, Walter, 1912- Prüfendes Denken. Tübingen : Klöpfer & Meyer, c2002.

Simone Weil, la passion de la raison. Paris : Harmattan, c2003.
B2430.W474 S55 2003

Stengers, Isabelle. Penser avec Whitehead. Paris : Seuil, c2002.

Stróżewski, Władysław. Wokół piękna. Kraków : Universitas, c2002.

Suspil'stvo na porozi XXI stolittia. Kyïv : Ukraïns'kyï TSentr dukhovnoï kul'tury, 1999.

Tabatabai, Sayyid Muhammad Husayn. The elements of Islamic metaphysics (Bidāyat al-Ḥikmah). London : ICAS, 2003.

Zons, Raimar. Die Zeit des Menschen. 1. Aufl., Originalausg. Frankfurt : Suhrkamp, c2001.

PHILOSOPHY, MODERN - CONGRESSES.
Der Grund, die Not und die Freude des Bewusstseins. Würzburg : Königshausen & Neumann, c2002.
B808.9 .G78 2002

PHILOSOPHY, MORAL. *See* **ETHICS.**

Philosophy, music and emotion.
Madell, Geoffrey. Edinburgh : Edinburgh University Press, c2002.

PHILOSOPHY, MUSLIM. *See* **PHILOSOPHY, ISLAMIC.**

PHILOSOPHY, NATURAL. *See* **PHYSICS.**

Philosophy of being.
Blanchette, Oliva. Washington, D.C. : Catholic University of America Press, c2003.
BD331 .B565 2003

A philosophy of culture.
White, Morton Gabriel, 1917- Princeton, N.J. : Princeton University Press, c2002.
B945.W453 P48 2002

Philosophy of economics : stepping forward from the philosophy of history to the philosophy of economics.
Zhang, Xiong, 1953- Jing ji zhe xue. Di 1 ban. [Kunming] : Yunnan ren min chu ban she, 2002.
D16.8 .Z536 2002

Philosophy of history : the philosophical interpretation of historicity.
Han, Zhen. Li shi zhe xue. Di 1 ban. Kunming : Yunnan ren min chu ban she, 2002.
D16.8 .H3597 2002

The philosophy of Keynes' economics : probability, uncertainty and convention / edited by Jochen Runde and Sohei Mizuhara. London ; New York : Routledge, 2003. xiii, 274 p. : ill. ; 24 cm. (Economics as social theory) Includes bibliographical references (p. [252]-263) and index. ISBN 0-415-28153-9 ISBN 0-415-31244-2 (pbk.) DDC 330.15/6
1. Keynesian economics. 2. Probabilities. 3. Uncertainty. I. Runde, Jochen, 1959- II. Mizuhara, Sohei, 1969- III. Series.
HB99.7 .P45 2003

The philosophy of Marjorie Grene / edited by Randall E. Auxier and Lewis Edwin Hahn. Chicago : Open Court, c2002. xx, 594 p. ; 24 cm. (The library of living philosophers ; v. 29) Includes bibliographical references (p. [569]-579) and index. ISBN 0-8126-9527-5 (trade) ISBN 0-8126-9526-7 (cloth) DDC 191
1. Grene, Marjorie Glicksman, - 1910- 2. Philosophy. I. Grene, Marjorie Glicksman, 1910- II. Auxier, Randall E., 1961- III. Hahn, Lewis Edwin, 1908- IV. Series.
B945.G734 P47 2002

PHILOSOPHY OF MIND. *See also* **COGNITIVE SCIENCE; METAPHYSICS; PHILOSOPHICAL ANTHROPOLOGY.**
The Blackwell guide to philosophy of mind. Malden, MA ; Oxford : Blackwell Pub., 2003.
BD418.3 .B57 2003

PHILOSOPHY OF MIND.
Bermudez, Jose Luis. Thinking without words. Oxford ; New York : Oxford University Press, 2003.
BD418.3 .B47 2003

Birtchnell, John. The two of me. Hove, East Sussex [England] ; New York : Routledge, 2003.
BF311 .B533 2003

The Blackwell guide to philosophy of mind. Malden, MA ; Oxford : Blackwell Pub., 2003.
BD418.3 .B57 2003

Clarke, Desmond M. Descartes's theory of mind. Oxford ; New York : Oxford University Press, 2003.

Collette, Bernard. Dialectique et hénologie chez Plotin. Bruxelles : Ousia, c2002.
B693.Z7 C655 2002

Conoscenza e cognizione. 1. ed. Milano : Guerini e associati, 2002.
BJ45.5 .C66 2002

Damiani, Anthony, 1922-1984. Astronoesis. Burdett, N.Y. : Published for Wisdom's Goldenrod, Ltd. by Larson Publications, c2000.
BD418.3 .D347 2000

De Muijnck, Wim. Dependencies, connections, and other relations. Dordrecht ; Boston : Kluwer Academic Publishers, c2003.
BD418.3 .D4 2003

Dretske, Fred I. Perception, knowledge, and belief. Cambridge, U.K. ; New York : Cambridge University Press, 2000.
BD161 .D73 2000

Dupouey, Patrick. Est-ce le cerveau qui pense? Nantes : Pleins feux, [2002].

Esfeld, Michael. Holism in philosophy of mind and philosophy of physics. Dordrecht ; Boston : Kluwer Academic Publishers, c2001.
B818 .E74 2001

Fodor, Jerry A. Hume variations. Oxford : Clarendon Press ; New York : Oxford University Press, 2003.
B1489 .F63 2003

Hinterhuber, H. (Hartmann) Die Seele. Wien ; New York : Springer, c2001.

Landucci, Sergio, 1938- La mente in Cartesio. Milano : FrancoAngeli, c2002.

McCulloch, Gregory. The life of the mind. London ; New York : Routledge, 2003.
BD418.3 .M363 2003

Mental causation and the metaphysics of mind. Peterborough, Ont. : Broadview Press, c2003.

Mind, matter, and mystery. New Delhi : Scientia, 2001.
BD418.3 .M5556 2001

Naturalism, evolution, and intentionality. Calgary, Alta., Canada : University of Calgary Press, c2001.
BD418.3 .N35 2001

Nichols, Shaun. Mindreading. Oxford : Clarendon Press ; New York : Oxford University Press, 2003.

Papineau, David, 1947- The roots of reason. Oxford : Clarendon Press ; New York : Oxford University Press, 2003.
BD418.3 .P35 2003

Physicalism and mental causation. Exeter, UK ; Charlottesville, VA : Imprint Academic, c2003.
B825 .P494 2003

Rowlands, Mark. The body in mind. Cambridge, U.K. ; New York : Cambridge University Press, 1999.
BD418.3 .R78 1999

Schiffer, Stephen R. The things we mean. Oxford ; New York : Clarendon, 2003.

Tallis, Raymond. The hand. Edinburgh : Edinburgh University Press, c2003.
BF908 .T35 2003

Weed, Laura E. The structure of thinking. Exeter : Imprint Academic, c2003.

Wilkens, Sander. Die Konvertibilität des Bewusstseins. 1. Aufl. Würzburg ; Boston : Deutscher Wissenschafts-Verlag (DWV), c2002.
BD163 .E45 2001

Zoglauer, Thomas. Geist und Gehirn. Göttingen : Vandenhoeck & Ruprecht, 1998.
BF163 .Z64 1998

PHILOSOPHY OF MIND - HISTORY.
Green, Christopher D. Early psychological thought. Westport, Conn. ; London : Praeger, 2003.
BF91 .G74 2003

MacDonald, Paul S., 1951- History of the concept of mind. Aldershot ; Burlington, VT : Ashgate, c2003.

PHILOSOPHY OF MIND IN CHILDREN.
Individual differences in theory of mind. New York : Psychology Press, 2003.
BF723.P48 I53 2003

Philosophy of mind series
Bermudez, Jose Luis. Thinking without words. Oxford ; New York : Oxford University Press, 2003.
BD418.3 .B47 2003

PHILOSOPHY OF NATURE.
Maritain, Jacques, 1882-1973. [Degrés du savoir. English] Distinguish to unite, or, The degrees of knowledge. Notre Dame, Ind. : University of Notre Dame Press, 1998, c1995.
BD162 .M273 1998

Philosophie der natürlichen Mitwelt. Würzburg : Königshausen & Neumann, 2002.

Roach, Catherine M., 1965- Mother/nature. Bloomington, IN : Indiana University Press, c2003.
BD581 .R59 2003

Seeing nature through gender. Lawrence : University Press of Kansas, c2003.
GF21 .S44 2003

PHILOSOPHY, POLISH.
Przełęcki, Marian, 1923- O rozumności i dobroci. Warszawa : "Semper", 2002.
B833 .P79 2002

Salamucha, Jan. [Selections. English. 2003] Knowledge and faith. Amsterdam ; New York, NY : Rodopi, 2003.

PHILOSOPHY, POLISH - 20TH CENTURY.
Jadacki, Jacek Juliusz. From the viewpoint of the Lvov-Warsaw school. Amsterdam ; New York, NY : Rodopi, 2003.

PHILOSOPHY, PORTUGUESE.
Chacon, Vamireh. O humanismo ibérico. [Lisboa?] : Imprensa Nacional-Casa da Moeda, [1998]
B821 .C43 1998

Philosophy, psychology, and psychologism : critical and historical readings on the psychological turn in philosophy / edited by Dale Jacquette. Dordrecht ; Boston : Kluwer Academic Publishers, c2003. xiii, 339 p. : ill. ; 25 cm. (Philosophical studies series ; v. 91) Includes bibliographical references and index. ISBN 140201337X (acid-free paper) DDC 149
  1. Psychologism. 2. Psychology - Philosophy. I. Jacquette, Dale. II. Series.
BF41 .P553 2003

PHILOSOPHY, RENAISSANCE.
De Pace, Anna. La scepsi, il sapere e l'anima. Milano : LED, c2002.

Early studies of Giordano Bruno. Bristol : Thoemmes, 2000.

Das Ende des Hermetismus. Tübingen : Mohr Siebeck, c2002.
BF1587 .E53 2002

Hankins, James. Humanism and platonism in the Italian Renaissance. Roma : Edizioni di storia e letteratura, 2003-

Renaissance and early modern philosophy. Malden, MA : Oxford : Blackwell Pub., c2002.
B775 .R46 2002

Sacerdoti, Gilberto, 1952- Sacrificio e sovranità. Torino : Einaudi, 2002.

Scazzola, Andrea. Giovanni Gentile e il Rinascimento. Napoli : Vivarium, 2002.

Vecchiotti, Icilio. Introduzione alla filosofia di Giordano Bruno. Urbino : QuattroVenti, c2000.
B783.Z7 V43 2000

PHILOSOPHY - RUSSIA - HISTORY.
Domnikov, S. D. (Sergeĭ Dmitrievich) Matʹ-zemli︠a︡ i TSarʹ-gorod. Moskva : Alete︠ĭ︡a, 2002.
B4235.H57 D65 2002

PHILOSOPHY, RUSSIAN.
Afanasʹev, Valeri, 1963- Russische Geschichtsphilosophie auf dem Prüfstand. Münster : Lit, [2002]

Florovsky, Georges, 1893-1979. [Selections. Russian. 2002] Vera i kulʹtura. Sankt-Peterburg : Izd-vo Russkogo Khristianskogo gumanitarnogo instituta, 2002.
BX260 .F552 2002

Gidirinskiĭ, V. I. (Viktor Ilʹich) Vvedenie v russkui︠u︡ filosofii︠u︡. Moskva : Russkoe slovo, 2003.
B4201 .G536 2003

Maler, Arkadiĭ. Strategii sakralʹnogo smysla. Moskva : Parad izdatelʹskiĭ dom, 2003.

Mamleev, I︠U︡riĭ. Rossii︠a︡ vechnai︠a︡. Moskva : AiF-Print, 2002.
DK32 .M355 2002

Menʹshikov, Alekseĭ. Durilka. Moskva : "Kraft+", 2003.

Trufanov, A. A. (Andreĭ Andreevich) Osnovy teorii intelligentnosti. Kazanʹ : ZAO "Novoe znanie", 2002.
BF431 .T78 2002

TSiolkovskiĭ, K. (Konstantin), 1857-1935. Geniĭ sredi li︠u︡deĭ. Moskva : Myslʹ, 2002.

TL781.85.T84 A25 2002

Zaĭtseva, L. I. Russkie providt︠s︡y o rossiĭskoĭ gosudarstvennosti. Moskva : In-t ėkonomiki RAN, 1998-
DK49 .Z35 1998

Zamaleev, A. F. (Aleksandr Fazlaevich) Idei i napravlenii︠a︡ otechestvennogo li︠u︡bomudrii︠a︡. Sankt-Peterburg : Izdatelʹsko-torgovyĭ dom "Letniĭ sad", 2003.
B4201 .Z33 2003

PHILOSOPHY, RUSSIAN - HISTORY.
Ionov, I. N. (Igorʹ Nikolaevich) Teorii︠a︡ t︠s︡ivilizat︠s︡iĭ. Sankt-Peterburg : Alete︠ĭ︡a, 2002.
CB19 .I656 2002

PHILOSOPHY, RUSSIAN - STUDY AND TEACHING (HIGHER) - RUSSIA (FEDERATION).
Gidirinskiĭ, V. I. (Viktor Ilʹich) Vvedenie v russkui︠u︡ filosofii︠u︡. Moskva : Russkoe slovo, 2003.
B4201 .G536 2003

PHILOSOPHY, SPANISH - HISTORY.
La filosofía medieval. Madrid : Trotta, 2002.
B721 .F47 2002

Philosophy without women.
Songe-Möller, Vigdis. London : Continuum, c2002.

Phiri, Isabel Aphawo.
Her-stories. Pietermaritzburg, South Africa : Cluster, 2002.

PHONETICS. See also SPEECH; VOICE.
Phonetics, phonology, and cognition. Oxford : Oxford University Press, 2002.
P221 .P475 2002

Phonetics, phonology, and cognition / edited by Jacques Durand and Bernard Laks. Oxford : Oxford University Press, 2002. xiii, 338 p. : ill. ; 24 cm. (Oxford studies in theoretical linguistics ; 3) (Oxford linguistics) Includes bibliographical references (p. [281]-323) and indexes. Table of contents URL: http://www.loc.gov/catdir/toc/fy033/2002512788.html ISBN 0-19-829984-2 ISBN 0-19-829983-4 (CASED) DDC 414/.8
  1. Phonetics. 2. Grammar, Comparative and general - Phonology. 3. Cognition. I. Durand, Jacques, 1947- II. Laks, Bernard. III. Series. IV. Series: Oxford linguistics
P221 .P475 2002

PHONODISCS. See SOUND RECORDINGS.

PHONOGRAPH RECORDS. See SOUND RECORDINGS.

PHONORECORDS. See SOUND RECORDINGS.

PHOTO JOURNALISM. See PHOTOJOURNALISM.

PHOTOGRAPHERS - UNITED STATES - BIOGRAPHY.
Gallop, Jane, 1952- Living with his camera. Durham : Duke University Press, 2003.
TR140.B517 G35 2003

PHOTOGRAPHY, ARTISTIC.
Kiefer, Anselm, 1945- Merkaba. New York : Gagosian Gallery, c2002.
N6888.K43 A4 2002

PHOTOGRAPHY, COMBAT. See WAR PHOTOGRAPHY.

PHOTOGRAPHY FOR THE PRESS. See PHOTOJOURNALISM.

PHOTOGRAPHY, JOURNALISTIC. See PHOTOJOURNALISM.

PHOTOGRAPHY OF FAMILIES.
Kuhn, Annette. Family secrets. New ed. London ; New York : Verso, 2002.
CT274 .K84 2002

PHOTOGRAPHY - PHILOSOPHY.
Friday, Jonathan. Aesthetics and photography. Aldershot, England ; Burlington, VT : Ashgate, c2002.
TR183 .F75 2002

PHOTOGRAPHY, WAR. See WAR PHOTOGRAPHY.

PHOTOJOURNALISM. See WAR PHOTOGRAPHY.

PHOTOJOURNALISM - SOCIAL ASPECTS.
Sontag, Susan, 1933- Regarding the pain of others. 1st ed. New York : Farrar, Straus and Giroux, 2003.
HM554 .S65 2003

PHOTOMONTAGE.
Okanoue, Toshiko. Drop of dreams. Tucson, AZ : Nazraeli Press, c2002.

PHOTORECEPTORS. *See* **EYE.**

PHRENOLOGY. *See* **MIND AND BODY; PHYSIOGNOMY.**

Phrenology and the origins of Victorian scientific naturalism.
Van Wyhe, John, 1971- Burlington, VT : Ashgate, c2003.
BF879 .V36 2003

PHRENOLOGY - GREAT BRITAIN - HISTORY - 19TH CENTURY.
Van Wyhe, John, 1971- Phrenology and the origins of Victorian scientific naturalism. Burlington, VT : Ashgate, c2003.
BF879 .V36 2003

PHYLOGENY. *See* **EVOLUTION (BIOLOGY).**

PHYSICAL ANTHROPOLOGY. *See also* **ANTHROPOMETRY; HUMAN BEHAVIOR; HUMAN EVOLUTION; RACE.**
Russkaia rasovaia teoriia do 1917 goda. Moskva : Feri-V, 2002.

PHYSICAL ANTHROPOLOGY - PHILOSOPHY.
Kessidi, F. Kh. Filosofskie i ėticheskie problemy genetiki cheloveka. Moskva : Martis, 1994.
BF341 .K45 1994

PHYSICAL ANTHROPOLOGY - RUSSIA.
Russkaia rasovaia teoriia do 1917 goda. Moskva : Feri-V, 2002.

PHYSICAL EDUCATION AND TRAINING. *See also* **GAMES; MOTOR LEARNING; MOVEMENT EDUCATION; SPORTS.**
Silva, Ana Márcia. Corpo, ciência e mercado. Campinas : Editora da UFSC : Editora Autores Associados, 2001.
GT495 .S55 2001

PHYSICAL EDUCATION FOR CHILDREN. *See* **MOVEMENT EDUCATION.**

PHYSICAL SCIENCES. *See* **ASTRONOMY; CHEMISTRY; PHYSICS.**

PHYSICAL SCIENCES - EXPERIMENTS - COMPUTER SIMULATION.
Santner, Thomas J., 1947- The design and analysis of computer experiments. New York : Springer, 2003.
QA279 .S235 2003

PHYSICAL SCIENTISTS. *See* **PHYSICISTS.**

PHYSICALISM. *See* **MATERIALISM.**

Physicalism and mental causation : the metaphysics of mind and action / edited by Sven Walter, Heinz-Dieter Heckmann. Exeter, UK ; Charlottesville, VA : Imprint Academic, c2003. vii, 362 p. : ill. ; 24 cm. Includes bibliographical references (p. [342]-353) and indexes. ISBN 0-907845-46-0 (pbk.) ISBN 0-907845-47-9 (hbk) DDC 128.2
1. Materialism. 2. Philosophy of mind. I. Walter, Sven, 1974- II. Heckmann, Heinz-Dieter.
B825 .P494 2003

PHYSICIANS. *See* **MEDICINE; PSYCHIATRISTS; WOMEN PHYSICIANS.**

PHYSICIANS - PSYCHOLOGY.
Mironova, T. L. (Tat′iana L′vovna) Samosoznanie professionala. Ulan-Udė: Izd-vo Buriatskogo gosuniversiteta, 1999.
BF697.5.S43 M57 1999

PHYSICIANS - UNITED STATES - PERSONAL NARRATIVES.
Davis, Sampson. The pact. Waterville, ME : Thorndike Press, 2002.
1. Black author.

PHYSICISTS - UNITED STATES.
Schrieffer, J. R. (John Robert), 1931- [Papers. Selections] Selected papers of J. Robert Schrieffer. River Edge, NJ : World Scientific, c2002.
QC21.3 .S37 2002

PHYSICS. *See also* **CRITICAL PHENOMENA (PHYSICS); FORCE AND ENERGY; OPEN SYSTEMS (PHYSICS); SOUND.**
Di Silvestre, Ettore. I concetti della fisica attraverso il tempo. Pisa : ETS, 2000.

Haché, Alain, 1970- The physics of hockey. Baltimore : Johns Hopkins University Press, 2002.
QC28 .H23 2002

On the shoulders of giants. Philadelphia : Running Press, c2002.

QC6.2 .O5 2002
Piaget, Jean, 1896- [Développement des quantités chez l'enfant. English] The child's construction of quantities. London ; New York : Routledge, 1997.
BF723.P5 P5 1997

Schrieffer, J. R. (John Robert), 1931- [Papers. Selections] Selected papers of J. Robert Schrieffer. River Edge, NJ : World Scientific, c2002.
QC21.3 .S37 2002

Tipler, Paul Allen, 1933- Modern physics. 4th ed. New York : W.H. Freeman, 2002 printing, c2003.
QC21.3 .T56 2003

The physics of hockey.
Haché, Alain, 1970- Baltimore : Johns Hopkins University Press, 2002.
QC28 .H23 2002

PHYSICS - PHILOSOPHY.
Châtelet, Gilles. [Enjeux du mobile. English] Figuring space. Dordrecht ; Boston : Kluwer, c2000.
B67 .C4313 2000

PHYSIOGNOMY. *See also* **FACE; PHRENOLOGY.**
Bridges, Lillian. Face reading in Chinese medicine. St. Louis, MO : Churchill Livingstone, 2003.
BF851 .B69 2003

Sertori, J. M. Face reading. London : Hodder & Stoughton, 2000.

PHYSIOGNOMY - CHINA.
De Mente, Boye. Asian face reading. Boston, MA : Tuttle Pub., 2003.
BF851 .D37 2003

Henning, Hai Lee Yang. Mian xiang. London : Vega, 2001.
BF851 .H46 2001

PHYSIOGNOMY - GERMANY - HISTORY.
Gray, Richard T. About face. Detroit : Wayne State University Press, c2004.
BF851 .G73 2004

PHYSIOGNOMY - HISTORY - CONGRESSES.
Der exzentrische Blick. Berlin : Akademie Verlag, 1996.
BF853 .E98 1996

PHYSIOGNOMY - JAPAN.
De Mente, Boye. Asian face reading. Boston, MA : Tuttle Pub., 2003.
BF851 .D37 2003

PHYSIOLOGICAL ASPECTS OF LEARNING. *See* **LEARNING - PHYSIOLOGICAL ASPECTS.**

PHYSIOLOGICAL STRESS. *See* **STRESS (PHYSIOLOGY).**

PHYSIOLOGY. *See* **CLIMACTERIC; HEALTH; ORIENTATION (PHYSIOLOGY).**

PHYSIOLOGY - MATHEMATICAL MODELS.
Westwick, D. T. (David T.) Identification of nonlinear physiological systems. Piscataway, NJ : IEEE Press ; Hoboken, NJ : Wiley-Interscience, c2003.
QP33.6.M36 W475 2003

PHYSIOLOGY - MISCELLANEA.
King, Joan C. Cellular wisdom. Berkeley : Celestial Arts, 2003.
BF637.S4 K548 2003

PHYSIOPHILOSOPHY. *See* **NATURAL HISTORY.**

Piaget, Jean, 1896-
[Développement des quantités chez l'enfant. English]
The child's construction of quantities : conservation and atomism / Jean Piaget and Bärbel Inhelder ; translated by Arnold J. Pomerans. London ; New York : Routledge, 1997. viii, 285 p. ; 23 cm. (Selected works ; v. 8) Includes bibliographical references and index. ISBN 0-415-16891-0 ISBN 0-415-16886-4 (Set) DDC 155.4/13
1. Child psychology. 2. Physics. I. Inhelder, Bärbel. II. Title. III. Series: Piaget, Jean, 1896- Selections. English. 1997 ; v. 8.
BF723.P5 P5 1997

Selections. English. 1997
(v. 8.) Piaget, Jean, 1896- [Développement des quantités chez l'enfant. English] The child's construction of quantities. London ; New York : Routledge, 1997.
BF723.P5 P5 1997

PIAGET, JEAN, 1896-.
Ducret, Jean-Jacques, 1946- Jean Piaget, 1868-1979. Genève, Switzerland : Service de la recherche en éducation, c2000.

BF311 .D813 2000
PIANO - HISTORY - 19TH CENTURY.
Pedroza, Ludim. The ritual of music contemplation. 2002.

PIANO - HISTORY - 20TH CENTURY.
Pedroza, Ludim. The ritual of music contemplation. 2002.

Piazza, Giovanni. Sofferenza e senso : l'ermeneutica del male e del dolore in Ricoeur e Pareyson / Giovanni Piazza ; presentazione di Giuseppe Riconda. Torino : Camilliane, c2002. 155 p. ; 21 cm. (Salute e salvezza ; 19) Includes bibliographical references. ISBN 88-8257-083-5 DDC 121
1. Ricœur, Paul. 2. Pareyson, Luigi. 3. Hermeneutics. 4. Good and evil. I. Title. II. Series.

Piccola biblioteca delle religioni
(20) Prandi, Carlo. La religione popolare fra tradizione e modernità. Brescia : Queriniana, c2002.

Pichot, Daniel.
Religion et mentalités au Moyen Age. Rennes : Presses universitaires de Rennes, c2003.
BR141 .R45 2003

Pick, Daniel.
Dreams and history. 1st ed. New York, NY : Brunner-Routledge, 2003.
BF1078 .D735 2003

Pickover, Clifford A. Chaos in Wonderland : visual adventures in a fractal world / Clifford A. Pickover. 1st ed. New York : St. Martin's Press, 1994. xv, 302 p., [8] p. of plates : ill. (some col.), map ; 25 cm. Includes bibliographical references and index. CONTENTS: The ancient Latoocarfian Civilization -- Modern history -- Biology of the Latoocarfians -- Interlude: graphics and mathematics -- The King -- Interlude: chaos and dynamica systems -- Research at the King's Fractal Palace -- Latoocarfian classes -- Interlude: what is interation? -- The dreams of the Lords -- Interlude: where is the beauty? -- The dreams of the villeins and serfs -- Interlude: lyapunov logomania -- The dreams of the crofters and cotters -- Interlude: rendering ratiocination -- Latoocarfian cosmology -- Flavor enhancers -- Inside-out universe -- CONTENTS: Ganymedean blood and biology -- Conflict on Callisto -- Arrival -- Fractal spiders -- Kalinda -- Prelude to battle -- Battle -- Brain parasites and polyp men -- Pipe world -- The Navanax people -- The underground association -- The water beings -- The imaginarium -- The leapers -- The Fractal Palace of Ice -- The glass girls of Ganymede -- Death-fungi and zine ants -- Starfish soup -- Attack of the attractors. ISBN 0-312-10743-9 DDC 003/.7
1. Chaotic behavior in systems. 2. Fractals. 3. Computer graphics. 4. Visualization. I. Title.
Q172.5.C45 P53 1994

PICO DELLA MIRANDOLA, GIOVANNI, 1463-1494 - CRITICISM AND INTERPRETATION.
De Pace, Anna. La scepsi, il sapere e l'anima. Milano : LED, c2002.

Picot, Nicole.
Arts en bibliothèques. Paris : Editions du Cercle de la Librairie, c2003.
Z675.A85 A78 2003

Picq, Pascal G. A la recherche de l'homme / Pascal Picq, Laurent Lemire. Paris : Nil, c2002. 317 p. ; 23 cm. Includes bibliographical references (p. 305-[308]) and index. ISBN 2-8411-1227-6
1. Human evolution. I. Lemire, Laurent. II. Title.
GN281 .P48 2002

PICTORIAL COMMUNICATION. *See* **VISUAL COMMUNICATION.**

PICTURE BOOKS FOR CHILDREN - FRANCE.
Beguery, Jocelyne. Une esthétique contemporaine de l'album de jeunesse. Paris : Harmattan, c2002.

PICTURE BOOKS FOR CHILDREN - PUBLISHING - FRANCE.
Beguery, Jocelyne. Une esthétique contemporaine de l'album de jeunesse. Paris : Harmattan, c2002.

PICTURE-GALLERIES. *See* **ART MUSEUMS.**

PICTURE INTERPRETATION - CONGRESSES.
Looking into pictures. Cambridge, Mass. : MIT Press, c2003.
BF243 .L66 2003

PICTURE PERCEPTION. *See also* **PICTURE INTERPRETATION.**
Peinture et musique. Villeneuve-d'Ascq : Presses universitaires du Septentrion, c2002.

Salber, Wilhelm. Psychästhetik. Köln : König, c2002.

PICTURE PERCEPTION - CONGRESSES.
Looking into pictures. Cambridge, Mass. : MIT Press, c2003.
BF243 .L66 2003

PICTURE-WRITING. *See* **PETROGLYPHS.**

PICTURES. *See also* **ILLUSTRATION OF BOOKS.**
Die Unvermeidlichkeit der Bilder. Tübingen : G. Narr, c2001.
N72.A56 U58 2001x

Pictures from the heart.
Thomson, Sandra A. 1st ed. New York : St. Martin's Press, c2003.
BF1879.T2 T52 2003

Picturing extraterrestrials.
Moffitt, John F. (John Francis), 1940- Amherst, N.Y. : Prometheus Press, c2003.
BF2050 .M64 2003

Picturing the past.
Pfitzer, Gregory M. Washington [D.C.] : Smithsonian Institution Press, c2002.
E175 .P477 2002

Pieces of the personality puzzle : readings in theory and research / [edited by] David C. Funder, Daniel J. Ozer. 3rd ed. New York : Norton, c2004. p. cm. Includes bibliographical references. ISBN 0-393-97997-0 (pbk.) DDC 155.2
1. Personality. I. Funder, David Charles. II. Ozer, Daniel J.
BF698 .P525 2004

Piel que habla : viaje a través de los cuerpos femeninos / M. Azpeitia ... [et al.], eds. Barcelona : Icaria, [2001] 293 p. : ill. ; 22 cm. (Akadēmeia ; 7) (Mujeres y culturas) Includes bibliographical references. ISBN 84-7426-514-2
1. Body image in women. I. Azpeitia Gimeno, Marta. II. Series. III. Series: Mujeres y culturas
BF697.5.B63 P54 2001

Pierce, W. David. Behavior analysis and learning / W. David Pierce, Carl D. Cheney. 3rd ed. Mahwah, N.J. : L. Erlbaum Associates, 2004. xviii, 509 p. : ill. ; 26 cm. Includes bibliographical references (p. 449-484) and indexes. ISBN 0-8058-4489-9 (alk. paper) DDC 150.19/434
1. Behaviorism (Psychology) 2. Learning, Psychology of. I. Cheney, Carl D. II. Title.
BF199 .P54 2004

Pieroni, Osvaldo. Pene d'amore : alla ricerca del pene perduto : maschi, ambiente e società / Osvaldo Pieroni. Soveria Mannelli : Rubbettino, c2002. 231 p. : ill. ; 21 cm. (Altera ; 3) Includes bibliographical references. ISBN 88-498-0324-9 DDC 305
1. Penis - Psychological aspects. 2. Men - Psychology. 3. Sex (Psychology) 4. Castration anxiety. 5. Masculinity. I. Title. II. Series.

Pierron, Jean-Philippe. On ne choisit pas ses parents : comment penser l'adoption et la filiation? / Jean-Philippe Pierron. [Paris] : Seuil, c2003. 217 p. ; 22 cm. Includes bibliographical references. ISBN 2-02-057339-3 DDC 194
1. Adoption. 2. Parent and child. 3. Parenthood. 4. Adopted children. 5. Adoptive parents. I. Title.

Pierssens, Michel.
Colloque des Invalides (5th : 2001 : Hôtel des invalides) Ce que je ne sais pas. Tusson, Charente : Du Lérot, [2002?]
PQ145 .C65 2001

Pievani, Telmo. Homo sapiens e altre catastrofi : per un'archeologia della globalizzazione / Telmo Pievani ; prefazione di Niles Eldredge. Roma : Meltemi, c2002. 404, [1] p. : 19 cm. (Mutazioni ; 8) (Ai margini del caos ; 1) Includes bibliographical references (p. [383]-[405]). ISBN 88-8353-195-7 DDC 573
1. Nature - Effect of human beings on. 2. Human evolution. 3. Human ecology. 4. Fossil hominids. I. Title. II. Series.

Pigmalion naiznanku.
Bernshteĭn, Boris Moiseevich. Moskva : I︠A︡zyki slavi︠a︡nskoĭ kul'tury, 2002.
N5300 .B614 2002

Piirto, Jane, 1941- Understanding creativity / by Jane Piirto. Scottsdale, Ar. : Great Potential Press : 2004. p. cm. Rev. ed. of: Understanding those who create. 2nd ed. 1998. Includes bibliographical references and index. Table of contents URL: http://www.loc.gov/catdir/toc/ecip048/2003019982.html ISBN 0-910707-58-8 (pbk.) DDC 153.3/5
1. Creative ability. I. Piirto, Jane, 1941- Understanding those who create. II. Title.
BF408 .P87 2004

Understanding those who create.
Piirto, Jane, 1941- Understanding creativity. Scottsdale, Ar. : Great Potential Press : 2004.
BF408 .P87 2004

Pike, Diane Kennedy. Awakening to wisdom / by Mariamne Paulus. Scottsdale, AZ : LP Publications, c2003. iv, 173 p. ; 22 cm. Includes bibliographical references and index. Table of contents URL: http://www.loc.gov/catdir/toc/ecip042/2003008172.html ISBN 0-916192-48-2 (pbk.) DDC 299/.93
1. Self-actualization (Psychology) - Miscellanea. 2. Religious awakening - Miscellanea. 3. Consciousness - Miscellanea. I. Title.
BF1999 .P5485 2003

A pilgrim's digress.
Spalding, John D. 1st ed. New York : Harmony Books, c2003.
BL50 .S627 2003

PILIPINOS. *See* **FILIPINOS.**

Pillo, Cary, ill.
Shuman, Carol. Jenny is scared. Washington, DC : Magination Press, c2003.
BF723.F4 S58 2003

Pimental-Habib, Richard L. The power of a partner : creating and maintaining healthy gay and lesbian relationships / Richard L. Pimental-Habib. 1st ed. Los Angeles, CA : Alyson Books, 2002. 229 p. ; 21 cm. ISBN 1-55583-632-1 (pbk. : alk. paper) DDC 306.76/6
1. Gay couples. 2. Interpersonal relations. 3. Gay couples - Counseling of. I. Title.
HQ76.25 .P56 2002

Pinch, Geraldine. Magic in ancient Egypt / Geraldine Pinch. London : British Museum Press, c1994. 191 p. : ill. ; 24 cm. Includes bibliographical references (p. 183-185) and index. ISBN 0-7141-0971-1
1. Magic, Ancient. 2. Magic, Egyptian. 3. Egypt - Antiquities. I. Title.

Pinchbeck, Daniel. Breaking open the head : a psychedelic journey into the heart of contemporary shamanism / Daniel Pinchbeck. 1st ed. New York : Broadway Books, 2002. 322 p. ; 22 cm. Includes bibliographical references (p. 299-305) and index. ISBN 0-7679-0742-6 DDC 299.9
1. Shamanism. 2. Spiritual life - New Age movement. I. Title.
BF1621 .P56 2002

The Pine Forge Press series in research methods and statistics
Frankfort-Nachmias, Chava. Social statistics for a diverse society. 3rd ed. Thousand Oaks, Calif. : Pine Forge Press, c2002.
HA29 .N25 2002

Pinḥasi, Raḥamim. Sefer Ḥesed ye-raḥamim : ḳovets śiḥot musar ... 'al parashiyot ha-shavu'a u-śemaḥot / Raḥamim Pinḥasi. Yerushalayim : R. Pinḥasi, 762 [2001 or 2002] 398 p. ; 24 cm. Running title: Ḥesed ye-raḥamim.
1. Bible - O.T. - Pentateuch - Commentaries. 2. Ethics, Jewish. I. Title. II. Title: Ḥesed ye-raḥamim

Pinheiro, José Moura. Mitos atuais : influências no mercado e na cultura contemporânea / José Moura Pinheiro. Salvador : Secretaria da Cultura e Turismo : Fundação Cultural do Estado da Bahia : Empresa Gráfoca da Bahia, 2001. 117, [1] p. ; 22 cm. (Coleção Selo Editorial Letras da Bahia ; 66) Includes bibliographical references (p. 115-[118]). ISBN 85-7505-011-7
1. Myth. 2. Mythology. 3. Mass media and culture. 4. Mass media and folklore. I. Title. II. Series.

Pinker, Steven, 1954- The blank slate : the modern denial of human nature / Steven Pinker. New York : Viking, 2002. xvi, 509 p. : ill. ; 25 cm. Includes bibliographical references (p.461-489) and index. CONTENTS: pt. 1. The blank slate, the noble savage, and the ghost in the machine -- The official theory -- Silly putty -- The last wall to fall -- Culture vultures -- The slate's last stand -- pt. 2. Fear and loathing -- Political scientists -- The holy trinity -- pt. 3. Human nature with a human face -- The fear of inequality -- The fear of imperfectibility -- The fear of determinism -- The fear of nihilism -- pt 4. Know thyself -- In touch with reality -- Out of our depths -- The many roots of our suffering -- The sanctimonious animal -- pt. 5. Hot buttons -- Politics -- Violence -- Gender -- Children -- The arts -- pt. 6. The voice of the species -- Appendix: Donald E. Brown's list of human universals. ISBN 0-670-03151-8 (alk. paper) DDC 155.2/34
1. Nature and nurture. I. Title.
BF341 .P47 2002

Pinkerton, Steven D.
Abramson, Paul R., 1949- With pleasure. Rev. ed. Oxford ; New York : Oxford University Press, 2002.
HQ23 .A25 2002

Pinkney, Andrea Marion.
[Kāmasūtra. English.]
The Kama Sutra illuminated / text by Andrea Pinkney ; photo editor, Lance Dane. New York, N.Y. : Abrams, c2002. 256 p. : ill. (some col.) ; 36 cm. Includes Sanskrit verses, commentaries and excerpts from the Burton translation. Text in English with Sanskrit verses and ancient commentaries. ISBN 0-8109-3532-5
1. Vātsyāyana. - Kāmasūtra. 2. Erotic literature. 3. Erotic art - India. 4. Love - Early works to 1800. 5. Sex instruction - India - Early works to 1800. 6. Sex customs - India - Early works to 1800. I. Vātsyāyana. II. Dane, Lance. III. Burton, Richard Francis, Sir, 1821-1890. IV. Title.

Pino, Fermín del., coord.
Demonio, religión y sociedad entre España y América. Madrid : Consejo Superior de Investigaciones Científicas, 2002.

Pinos nuevos. Divulgación científico-técnica
Reyes, Arnoldo Juan. Una alternativa para ser feliz. Ciudad de La Habana, Cuba : Editorial Científico-Técnica, 2001, c2000.

Pinotti, Roberto, 1944- Oltre : dal SETI agli UFO : viaggio tra i fenomeni non classificati alla ricerca del pensiero alieno / Roberto Pinotti, Maurizio Blondet ; con un saggio di Massimo Teodorani. Firenze : Olimpia, c2002. 319 p. : ill. (some col.) ; 21 cm. Includes bibliographical references. DDC 001
1. Extraterrestrial beings. 2. Life on other planets. 3. Unidentified flying objects. I. Blondet, Maurizio, 1944- II. Teodorani, Massimo. III. Title.

Pint, A. A. (Aleksandr Aleksandrovich) Nas mnogo, no my odno / A.A. Pint. Moskva : Shkola kholisticheskoĭ psikhologii, 2003. 280 p. ; 22 cm. (Proryv v chetvertoe izmerenie) ISBN 5899390921
1. Whole and parts (Psychology) 2. Holism. 3. Transpersonal psychology. I. Title. II. Series.
BF202 .P56 2003

Pinter, Leib. Sefer 'Aśarah nisyonot : meyusad 'al 'aśarah nisyonotav shel Avraham li-lemod ule-lamed Bene Yehudah ḳeshet : ekh le-hitmoded 'im nisyonot u-matsavim ḳashim be-ḥaye ha-adam / El'azar Yehudah Leyb Pinṭer. Brooklyn, N.Y. : E.Y.L. Pinṭer, c[2002?] 15, 658 p. ; 24 cm. Running title: 'Aśarah nisyonot.
1. Abraham - (Biblical patriarch) 2. Ordeal - Religious aspects - Judaism. 3. Faith (Judaism) 4. God (Judaism) 5. Ethics, Jewish. I. Title. II. Title: 'Aśarah nisyonot

Pinto Cañón, Ramiro. Grupos gnósticos : secretos y mentiras : el fanatismo dentro de nuestra sociedad / Ramiro Pinto Cañón, Pepa Sanz Bisbal. Madrid : Entinema, 2002. 351 p. : ill. ; 24 cm. "Basado en los texto de Víctor M. Gómez Rodríguez - Samael Aun Weor"--cover. Includes bibliographical references (p. 347-351). ISBN 84-8198-398-5
1. Gnosticism. 2. Sects. 3. Cults. I. Sanz Bisbal, Pepa. II. Title. III. Title: Fanatismo dentro de nuestra sociedad

PIONEER LIFE. *See* **FRONTIER AND PIONEER LIFE.**

PIONEERS. *See* **FRONTIER AND PIONEER LIFE.**

Pipek, Volkmar.
Sharing expertise. Cambridge, Mass. : MIT Press, c2003.
HD30.2 .S53 2003

Piper, Steen.
Haugen Sørensen, Arne, 1932- Samtaler på en bjergtop. 1. oplag. Højbjerg : Hovedland, c2002.

Pippin, Robert B., 1948-.
Raz, Joseph. The practice of value. Oxford ; New York : Oxford University Press, 2003.
BD232 .R255 2003

Pircher, Wolfgang, 1946-.
Tyrannis und Verführung. Wien : Turia + Kant, 2000.
JC381 .T973 2000

PISA (ITALY) - BUILDINGS, STRUCTURES, ETC.
Gianfaldoni, Paolo. Benvenuto a Pisa. [Fornacette, Pisa] : CLD iniziative speciali, c2000.

PISA (ITALY) - CIVILIZATION.
Gianfaldoni, Paolo. Benvenuto a Pisa. [Fornacette, Pisa] : CLD iniziative speciali, c2000.

Pisacreta, Richard.
Kellogg, Ronald Thomas. The best test preparation for the Graduate Record Examination, GRE psychology. Piscataway, N.J. : Research and Education Association, [2000]
BF78 .K45 2000

PISCES. *See* **FISHES.**

Piscitelli, Alejandro. Meta-cultura : el eclipse de los medios masivos en la era de la internet / Alejandro Piscitelli. Buenos Aires : La Crujía, 2002. 271 p. ; 20 cm. (Colección Inclusiones. Serie Categorías) Includes bibliografíon references (p. [227]-271). ISBN 9871004133

Píslarsaga

1. Mass media and technology. 2. Computers and civilization. 3. Artificial intelligence. 4. Internet. I. Title. II. Series.
P96.T42 P575

Píslarsaga.
Jón Magnússon, 1610-1696. Píslarsaga séra Jóns Magnússonar. Reykjavík : Mál og menning, 2001.
BF1584.I2 J66 2001

Píslarsaga séra Jóns Magnússonar.
Jón Magnússon, 1610-1696. Reykjavík : Mál og menning, 2001.
BF1584.I2 J66 2001

Pisma filozoficzne
(t. 84) Dobosz, Artur. Tożsamość metamorficzna a komunikacja językowa. Poznań : Wydawn. Naukowe Instytutu Filozofii Uniwersytetu im. Adama Mickiewicza w Poznaniu, 2002.

Pistes didactiques et chemins historiques : Textes offerts à Henri Moniot / recueillis et édités par Marie-Christine Baques, Annie Bruter, Nicole Tutiaux-Guillon. Paris : Harmattan, 2003. 380 p. ; 22 cm. (Collection Logiques historiques) Includes bibliographical references. ISBN 2-7475-3879-6 DDC 901
1. History - Philosophy. I. Bacques, Marie-Christine. II. Moniot, Henri. III. Series.

Pitkin, David J. Ghosts of the Northeast / David J. Pitkin ; illustrated by Linda C. Setchfield. Salem, NY : Aurora Publications, c2002. x, 396 p. : ill. ; 22 cm. Includes index. ISBN 0-9663925-2-3 DDC 133.1/0974
1. Ghosts - New England. 2. Haunted places - New England. I. Title.
BF1472.U6 P57 2002

Piven, Jerry S.
The psychology of death in fantasy and history. Westport, CT : Praeger, 2004.
BF789.D4 P79 2004

Piven, Joshua. As luck would have it : incredible stories, from lottery wins to lightning strikes / Joshua Piven. 1st ed. New York : Villard, c2003. xx, 199 p. ; 19 cm. Includes bibliographical references (p. [185]-199). ISBN 1400060559 (alk. paper) DDC 123/.3
1. Fortune. I. Title.
BF1778 .P58 2003

PIYUTIM.
Naphtali ben Isaac, ha-Kohen, 1649-1719. Sefer Bet Rahel. Yerushalayim : Ahavat Shalom, 761 [2001]
BM665 .N257 2001

The PK man.
Mishlove, Jeffrey, 1946- Charlottesville, VA : Hampton Roads, [c2000]
BF1027.O94 M57 2000

The place of enchantment.
Owen, Alex, 1948- Chicago, Ill. : University of Chicago Press, c2004.
BF1429 .O94 2004

PLACE (PHILOSOPHY).
Bonesio, Luisa, 1950- Oltre il paesaggio. 1. ed. Casalecchio (Bologna) : Arianna, 2002.

Brosman, Catharine Savage, 1934- Finding higher ground. Reno : University of Nevada Press, c2003.
F787 .B76 2003

Place, Robert Michael. The Buddha tarot companion : a mandala of cards / Robert M. Place. St. Paul, Minn. : Llewellyn, 2004. p. cm. Includes bibliographical references and index. ISBN 1-56718-529-0 DDC 133.3/2424
1. Tarot. 2. Buddhism - Miscellanea. I. Title.
BF1879.T2 P547 2004

[Gnostic book of saints. Spanish]
El mensaje de los santos / Robert M. Place ; traducido por Héctor Ramírez, Edgar Rojas. St. Paul, Minn. : Llewellyn Español, 2003. xv, 248 p. : ill. ; 24 cm. Includes bibliographical references (p. 239-242) and index. ISBN 0-7387-0117-3 DDC 33.3/2424
1. Tarot. 2. Saints - Miscellanea. I. Title.
BF1879.T2 P5518 2003

A place to land.
Manning, Martha. 1st ed. New York : Ballantine Books, 2003.
BF575.F66 M26 2003

PLACEBO (MEDICINE).
Moerman, Daniel E. Meaning, medicine, and the "placebo effect". Cambridge ; New York : Cambridge University Press, 2002.
R726.5 .M645 2002

PLACES, HAUNTED. *See* **HAUNTED PLACES.**

PLACES, SACRED. *See* **SACRED SPACE.**

Le plaisir.
Marguier, Florence. Paris : Oxus, c2003.

PLANE CRASHES. *See* **AIRCRAFT ACCIDENTS.**

Planet two.
Grabhorn, Lynn, 1931- Charlottesville, VA : Hampton Roads Pub. Co., 2004.
BF1999 .G678 2004

PLANETOIDS. *See* **ASTEROIDS.**

PLANETS. *See also* **LIFE ON OTHER PLANETS.**
Behari, Bepin. The timing of events. 1st ed. Delhi : Motilal Banarsidass Publishers, 2002.
BF1720.5+

PLANETS, MINOR. *See* **ASTEROIDS.**

PLANETS - OBSERVATIONS - HISTORY.
Brown, David, 1968- Mesopotamian planetary astronomy-astrology. Groningen : Styx, 2000.
BF1714.A86 B76 2000

PLANNING. *See also* **CITY PLANNING; POLITICAL PLANNING; STRATEGIC PLANNING.**
Gordon, Andrew S. Strategy representation. Mahwah, NJ. : L. Erlbaum, 2003.
BF316.6 .G67 2003

PLANNING IN POLITICS. *See* **POLITICAL PLANNING.**

PLANNING - JUVENILE LITERATURE.
Silverman, Robin Landew. Reaching your goals. New York : F. Watts, 2003.
BF505.G6 S57 2003

PLANNING - PSYCHOLOGICAL ASPECTS.
Dahl, Bernhoff A., 1938- Optimize your life with the one-page strategic planner. Bangor, Me. : Wind-Breaker Press, c2003.
BF637.S8 D26 2003

PLANNING, STRATEGIC. *See* **STRATEGIC PLANNING.**

Plantinga, Alvin. Essays in the metaphysics of modality / Alvin Plantinga ; edited by Matthew Davidson. Oxford ; New York : Oxford University Press, 2003. vi, 239 p. ; 25 cm. A collection of previously published articles from 1969 to 1993. Includes bibliographical references and index. ISBN 0-19-510376-9 (alk. paper) ISBN 0-19-510377-7 (pbk. alk. paper) DDC 110
1. Modality (Logic) 2. Metaphysics. I. Davidson, Matthew, 1972- II. Title.
B945.P553 M48 2003

PLANTS. *See* **TREES.**

PLANTS, USEFUL. *See* **HERBS.**

Plaquetas da Oficina
(1) Candido, Antonio. O nobre. São Paulo : Imprensa Oficial do Estado, 2002.
BJ1533.N6 C36 2002

(55) Jackson, Holbrook, 1874-1948. [Anatomy of bibliomania. Portuguese. Selections] O tato. São Paulo : Imprensa Oficial do Estado, 2002.
Z992 .J33 2002

PLASTIC SURGEONS. *See* **SURGERY, PLASTIC.**

PLASTIC SURGERY. *See* **SURGERY, PLASTIC.**

PLASTICITY (PHYSIOLOGY). *See* **ADAPTATION (PHYSIOLOGY).**

Plastino, Carlos Alberto.
Transgressões. Rio de Janeiro, RJ : Espaço Brasileiro de Estudos Psicanalíticos : Contra Capa, 2002.

PLATO.
DIALOGUES.
Ackeren, Marcel van. Das Wissen vom Guten. Amsterdam ; Philadelphia : B.R. Gruner, c2003.
B398.V57 A33 2003

Dixsaut, Monique. Métamorphoses de la dialectique dans les dialogues de Platon. Paris : Vrin, c2001.
B398.D5 D598 2001

LYSIS.
Geier, Alfred, 1930- Plato's erotic thought. Rochester, NY : University of Rochester Press, 2002.
B398.L9 G45 2002

PHAEDRUS.
Geier, Alfred, 1930- Plato's erotic thought. Rochester, NY : University of Rochester Press, 2002.
B398.L9 G45 2002

[Selections. Latvian]
Platons dialogi un vēstules = Platōnos / no sengrieķu valodas tulkojis Ābrams Feldhūns. [Rīga] : Zinātne, c1999. 273 p. ; 21 cm. Includes bibliographical references. Translated from the ancient Greek. CONTENTS: Protagors = Prōtagoras -- Hipijs lielākais = Ippias meizōn -- Faidrs = Phaidros -- Septītā vēstule = Epistolē 7 -- Astotā vēstule = Epistolē 8. ISBN 5796612433
1. Plato - Translations into Latvian. 2. Socrates. 3. Plato - Correspondence. 4. Philosophy, Ancient. I. Feldhūns, Ā. (Ābrams) II. Title. III. Title: Platōnos IV. Title: Dialogi un vēstules

SYMPOSIUM.
Geier, Alfred, 1930- Plato's erotic thought. Rochester, NY : University of Rochester Press, 2002.
B398.L9 G45 2002

PLATO.
Rhodes, James M. Eros, wisdom, and silence. Columbia, Mo. : University of Missouri Press, c2003.
B398.L9 .R46 2003

Plato and the city.
Pradeau, Jean-François. Exeter, UK : University of Exeter Press, 2002.
B395 .P7313 2002

PLATO - CONTRIBUTIONS IN CONCEPT OF LOVE.
Geier, Alfred, 1930- Plato's erotic thought. Rochester, NY : University of Rochester Press, 2002.
B398.L9 G45 2002

PLATO - CORRESPONDENCE.
Plato. [Selections. Latvian] Platons dialogi un vēstules = [Rīga] : Zinātne, c1999.

PLATO - CRITICISM AND INTERPRETATION.
Binayemotlagh, Saïd. Etre et liberté selon Platon. Paris : Harmattan, 2002.
B395 .B553 2002

Pradeau, Jean-François. Plato and the city. Exeter, UK : University of Exeter Press, 2002.
B395 .P7313 2002

PLATO - INFLUENCE.
The Platonic tradition in the Middle Ages. Berlin ; New York : W. de Gruyter, 2002.

PLATO - TRANSLATIONS INTO LATVIAN.
Plato. [Selections. Latvian] Platons dialogi un vēstules = [Rīga] : Zinātne, c1999.

PLATO - VIEWS ON LOVE.
Gučetić, Nikola Vitov, 1549-1610. [Dialogo della bellezza. Serbo-Croatian & Italian] Dijalog o ljepoti = Dvojezično izd. Zagreb : Društvo hrvatskih književnika, 1995.
BH301.L65 G8318 1995

The Platonic tradition in the Middle Ages : a doxographic approach / edited by Stephen Gersh and Maarten J.F.M. Hoenen ; with the assistance of Pieter Th. van Wingerden. Berlin ; New York : W. de Gruyter, 2002. viii, 466 p. : ill. ; 24 cm. Includes bibliographical references (p. [417]-451) and indexes. CONTENTS: The Medieval legacy from ancient platonism / Stephen Gersh -- Plato arabico-latinus : philosophy, wisdom literature, occult sciences / Dag Nikolaus Hasse -- Platonism, a doxographic approach : the early middle ages / John Marenbon -- Simmistes veri : das Bild Platons in der Theologie des zwölften Jahrhunderts / Frank Bezner -- Plato im zwölften Jahrhundert : einige Hinweise zu seinem Verschwinden / Thomas Ricklin -- "Magis sit Platonicus quam Aristotelicus" : interpretations of Boethius's platonism in the Consolatio Philosophiae from the twelfth to the seventeenth century / Lodi Nauta -- Die platonische Tradition bei Albertus Magnus : eine Hinführung / Henryk Anzulewicz -- Aquinas and the platonists / Wayne J. Hankey -- 'Modus loquendi platonicorum' : Johannes Gerson und seine Kritik an Platon und den Platonisten / Maarten J.F.M. Hoenen -- Cusanus Platonicus : references to the term 'Platonici' in Nicholas of Cusa / Markus L. Fuehrer -- Medieval visual images of Plato / David Knipp. ISBN 3-11-016844-8
1. Plato - Influence. 2. Philosophy, Medieval. I. Gersh, Stephen. II. Hoenen, M. J. F. M., 1957-

PLATONISM. *See* **PLATONISTS.**

Platonismo, marxismo y comunicación social.
Vazeilles, José Gabriel. Buenos Aires : Editorial Biblos, c2002.

PLATONISTS.
Vazeilles, José Gabriel. Platonismo, marxismo y comunicación social. Buenos Aires : Editorial Biblos, c2002.

PLATONISTS - HISTORY.
Dillon, John M. The heirs of Plato. Oxford : Clarendon Press ; New York : Oxford University Press, 2003.

B517 .D536 2003
PLATONISTS - ITALY - HISTORY.
Hankins, James. Humanism and platonism in the Italian Renaissance. Roma : Edizioni di storia e letteratura, 2003-

Platōnos.
Plato. [Selections. Latvian] Platons dialogi un vēstules = [Rīga] : Zinātne, c1999.

PLATONOV, KONSTANTIN KONSTANTINOVICH.
Kazakova, N. E. (Natal'ia Evgen'evna) Poliprofessionalizm deiatel'nosti vydaiushchegosia psikhologa - akmeologa K.K. Platonova. Shuia : Vest', 2002.
BF109.P56 K39 2002

Platons dialogi un vēstules.
Plato. [Selections. Latvian] [Rīga] : Zinātne, c1999.

Plato's erotic thought.
Geier, Alfred, 1930- Rochester, NY : University of Rochester Press, 2002.
B398.L9 G45 2002

Platvoet, Jan.
Modern societies & the science of religions. Leiden ; Boston : Brill, 2002.
BL48 .M542 2002

Plavinskaia, Elizaveta.
Klimov, R. B. Teoriia stadial'nogo razvitiia iskusstva i stat'i. Moskva : O.G.I., 2002.
N5300 .K55 2002

Plavinskaia, Mariia.
Klimov, R. B. Teoriia stadial'nogo razvitiia iskusstva i stat'i. Moskva : O.G.I., 2002.
N5300 .K55 2002

PLAY. See **GAMES.**

PLAY CENTERS. See **PLAYGROUNDS.**

PLAY ENVIRONMENTS. See **PLAYGROUNDS.**

PLAY (PHILOSOPHY).
Auffret, Séverine. Des blessures et des jeux. Arles : Actes sud, c2003.

PLAY - PSYCHOLOGICAL ASPECTS.
The child's right to play. Westport, Conn. : Praeger, 2003.
BF717 .C44 2003

Hartley, Ruth E. (Ruth Edith), b.1909 Understanding children's play. London : Routledge, 2000.
BF717 .H3 2000

PLAYERS, MUSICAL INSTRUMENT. See MUSICIANS.

PLAYGROUNDS - BARRIER-FREE DESIGN - UNITED STATES.
Barzach, Amy Jaffe. Accidental courage, boundless dreams. 1st ed. West Hartford, CT : Aurora Pub., c2001.
BF575.G7 B375 2001

The playing card oracles.
Cortez, Ana. Denver, CO : Two Sisters Press, c2002.
BF1778.5 .C67 2002

PLAYS. See **DRAMA.**

Please God by you = BekarovEtzlech : choosing a spouse & a guide to dating.
Gorfine, Yehudit. Be-karov etslekh. Petah Tikvah : Mar'ot, 2002.

PLEASURE. See also HAPPINESS; PAIN.
Abramson, Paul R., 1949- With pleasure. Rev. ed. Oxford ; New York : Oxford University Press, 2002.
HQ23 .A25 2002

Frey, Jean-Marie. Le corps peut-il nous rendre heureux? Nantes : Pleins feux, [2002]

Marguier, Florence. Le plaisir. Paris : Oxus, c2003.

Thomashauer, Regena. Mama Gena's School of Womanly Arts. New York : Simon & Schuster, c2002.
HQ1206 .T4673 2002

Wiseman, Carol. A patchwork of comforts. Boston, MA : Conari Press, 2004.
BF515 .W57 2004

Zupančič, Alenka. Esthétique du désir, éthique de la jouissance. Lecques : Théétète, c2002.

PLEASURE - PHILOSOPHY.
Bard, Xavier, 1935- Du plaisir, de la douleur et de quelques autres. Paris, France : Harmattan, c2002.

Zupančič, Alenka. Esthétique du désir, éthique de la jouissance. Lecques : Théétète, c2002.

PLEASURE PRINCIPLE (PSYCHOLOGY).
Pfaller, Robert. Die Illusionen der anderen. 1. Aufl. Frankfurt : Suhrkamp, 2002.

PLEBISCITE. See **MINORITIES; SELF-DETERMINATION, NATIONAL.**

PLECH (GERMANY) - CHURCH HISTORY - TO 1500.
Stark, Heinz. Plecher Kirchengeschichte im Mittelalter. Simmelsdorf : Altnürnberger Landschaft, 2002.

Plecher Kirchengeschichte im Mittelalter.
Stark, Heinz. Simmelsdorf : Altnürnberger Landschaft, 2002.

PLEIADES - MISCELLANEA.
Clow, Barbara Hand, 1943- Catastrophobia. Rochester, Vt. : Bear & Company, c2001.
BF1999 .C587 2001

Pleij, Herman.
[Dromen van Cocagne. English]
Dreaming of Cockaigne : medieval fantasies of the perfect life / Herman Pleij ; translated by Diane Webb. New York : Columbia University Press, c2001. ix, 533 p. : ill. ; 24 cm. Includes bibliographical references (p. 489-514) and index. CONTENTS: Pt. 1. The forfeiture of happiness, the beginning: Paradise lost -- Contours of a book -- The power of literature -- pt.2. Texts as maps: Rhyming Texts L and B, Prose Text G -- The two rhyming texts on the land of Cockaigne -- Recitation and writing -- Oral structures in writing -- The existing potential -- The prose text of Luilekkerland -- pt. 3. Eating to forget: Eating habits -- Hunger and scarcity -- The topos of hunger -- The intoxicating effect of fasting -- Gorging in self-defense -- Food in motion -- Literary refreshment -- pt. 4. Paradise refurbished: The land of Cockaigne as paradise -- Never say die -- Heavenly rewards -- Other paradises -- Lovely places, golden ages -- Wonder gardens and pleasure parks -- Dreams of immortality -- pt. 5. The imagination journeys forth: Geographical musings -- Real dreamworlds -- Wonders of east and west -- Fanciful destinations -- Virtual dreamlands -- pt. 6. Heretical excesses: The thousand-year reign of peace and prosperity -- Heresies of the free spirit -- Sex Adam-and-Eve style -- Low-country heterodoxy -- pt. 7. Learning as a matter of survival: Didactic differences -- Topsy-turvy worlds -- Hard times -- Moderation, ambition, and decorum -- Lessons in pragmatism -- pt. 8. Dreaming of Cockaigne, the end: The name Cockaigne -- A depreciated cultural asset -- From countryside to town -- The necessity of fiction. ISBN 0-231-11702-7 (cloth : alk. paper) DDC 398/.42/0940902
1. Cockaigne. 2. Civilization, Medieval. 3. Social history - Medieval, 500-1500. 4. Literature, Medieval. 5. Cockaigne in literature. I. Webb, Diane. II. Title.
CB353 .P5413 2001

Kleuren van de Middeleeuwen.
Pleij, Herman. Van karmijn, purper en blauw. Amsterdam : Prometheus, 2002.

[Van karmijn, purper en blauw. English]
Colors demonic and divine : shades of meaning in the Middle Ages and after / Herman Pleij ; translated by Diane Webb. New York : Columbia University Press, 2004. p. cm. Includes bibliographical references and index. ISBN 0-231-13022-8 (alk. paper) DDC 155.9/1145/09
1. Color - Psychological aspects - History. I. Title.
BF789.C7 P5713 2004

Van karmijn, purper en blauw : over kleuren van de Middeleeuwen en daarna / Herman Pleij. Amsterdam : Prometheus, 2002. 170 p., 20 p. of plates : col. ill. ; 21 cm. Based on the author's earlier work, Kleuren van de Middeleeuwen. Includes bibliographical references (p. 153-164) and index. ISBN 90-446-0100-8
1. Color - Psychological aspects - History. 2. Color in art. I. Pleij, Herman. Kleuren van de Middeleeuwen. II. Title.

The Plenum series in adult development and aging
Lindauer, Martin S. Aging, creativity, and art. New York : Kluwer Academic/Plenum Publishers, c2003.
BF724.85.C73 L56 2003

Plessner, Helmuth, 1892- Elemente der Metaphysik : eine Vorlesung aus dem Wintersemester 1931/32 / Helmuth Plessner ; herausgegeben von Hans-Ulrich Lessing. Berlin : Akademie, 2002. 196 p. : ill. ; 25 cm. Includes bibliographical references and index. ISBN 3-05-003708-3 DDC 110
1. Metaphysics. I. Lessing, Hans-Ulrich, 1953- II. Title.
BD113 .P56 2002

PLESSNER, HELMUTH, 1892-.
Kämpf, Heike. Helmuth Plessner. 1. Aufl. Düsseldorf : Parerga, 2001.
B3323.P564 K36 2001

Pliskin, Zelig. Enthusiasm! : formulas, stories and insights / Zelig Pliskin. 1st ed. Brooklyn, N.Y. : Shaar Press : Distributed by Mesorah Publications, 2002. 237 p. ; 17 cm. (A Pocketscroll book) Includes bibliographical references. ISBN 1-57819-765-1
1. Enthusiasm. 2. Enthusiasm - Religious aspects - Judaism. 3. Self-actualization (Psychology) I. Title. II. Series: Pocketscroll series.

Harmony with others : formulas, stories and insights / Zelig Pliskin. 1st ed. Brooklyn, N.Y. : Shaar Press : Distributed by Mesorah Publications, 2002. 228 p. ; 17 cm. (A Pocketscroll book) Includes bibliographical references. ISBN 1-57819-711-2
1. Peace. 2. Peace - Religious aspects - Judaism. 3. Harmony (Philosophy) 4. Harmony (Philosophy) - Religious aspects. 5. Self-actualization (Psychology) 6. Self-actualization (Psychology) - Religious aspects - Judaism. I. Title. II. Series: Pocketscroll series.

Pliszka, Steven R. Neuroscience for the mental health clinician / Steven R. Pliszka. New York : Guilford Press, c2003. vii, 280 p., [2] p. of plates : ill. (some col.) ; 24 cm. Includes bibliographical references and index. ISBN 1-57230-811-7 (alk. paper) DDC 616.89
1. Neurosciences. I. Title.
RC341 .P58 2003

PLOTINUS - CONTRIBUTIONS IN CONCEPT OF SOUL.
Yhap, Jennifer. Plotinus on the soul. Selinsgrove : Susquehanna University Press ; London : Associated University Presses, c2003.
B693.Z7 Y43 2003

PLOTINUS - CRITICISM AND INTERPRETATION.
Collette, Bernard. Dialectique et hénologie chez Plotin. Bruxelles : Ousia, c2002.
B693.Z7 C655 2002

Plotinus on the soul.
Yhap, Jennifer. Selinsgrove : Susquehanna University Press ; London : Associated University Presses, c2003.
B693.Z7 Y43 2003

Plotkin, Bill, 1950- Soulcraft : crossing into the mysteries of nature and psyche / Bill Plotkin. Novato, Calif. : New World Library, c2003. p. cm. Includes bibliographical references and index. Table of contents URL: http://www.loc.gov/catdir/toc/ecip043/2003010036.html ISBN 1-57731-422-0 DDC 158.1
1. Self-actualization (Psychology) 2. Soul - Psychological aspects. 3. Vision quests. I. Title.
BF637.S4 P58 2003

Plug, Cornelis.
Ross, Helen Elizabeth, 1935- The mystery of the moon illusion. Oxford ; New York : Oxford University Press, 2002.
QP495 .R67 2002

Pluháček, Stephen.
Irigaray, Luce. [Voie de l'amour. English] The way of love. London ; New York : Continuum, 2002.
BF575.L8 I7513 2002

Irigaray, Luce. The way of love. London ; New York : Continuum, 2002.

Plung, Daniel L. Professional communication : the corporate insider's approach / Daniel L. Plung, Tracy T. Montgomery. Mason, Ohio : Thomson/South-Western, c2004. xxiii, 504 p. : ill., forms ; 25 cm. Includes bibliographical references and index. ISBN 0-324-15981-1 (alk. paper) DDC 651.7
1. Business communication. 2. Interpersonal communication. I. Montgomery, Tracy T. II. Title.
HF5718 .P58 2004

PLURALISM.
Nemoianu, Virgil. Tradiție și libertate. București : Curtea Veche, 2001.
JC585 .N42 2001

PLURALISM (SOCIAL SCIENCES). See also MULTICULTURALISM.
Baritono, Raffaella. La democrazia vissuta. Torino : La Rosa, c2001.

Bilbeny, Norbert. Por una causa común. 1. ed. Barcelona : Gedisa Editorial, c2002.
HM1271 .B553 2002

Erdas, Franco Epifanio. Partecipazione e differenza. Roma : Bulzoni, c2002.

Making sense of collectivity. London ; Sterling, Va. : Pluto Press, 2002.
HM753 .M35 2002

Shweder, Richard A. Why do men barbecue? Cambridge, Mass. : Harvard University Press, 2003.

Pluralism (Social sciences)

GN502 .S59 2003

PLURALISM (SOCIAL SCIENCES) - UNITED STATES.
The fractious nation? Berkeley : University of California Press, c2003.
E169.12 .F69 2003

PLURILINGUALISM. *See* **MULTILINGUALISM.**

PMAI manual.
Pearson, Carol, 1944- Gainesville, FL : Center for Applications of Psychological Type, c2003.
BF698.8.P37 P43 2003

Pearson, Carol, 1944- PMAI manual. Gainesville, FL : Center for Applications of Psychological Type, c2003.
BF698.8.P37 P43 2003

PNEUMA. *See* **SOUL.**

PNEUMATICS. *See* **SOUND.**

PNEUMATOLOGY (THEOLOGY). *See* **HOLY SPIRIT.**

Po toï bik bezodni.
Andrushkiv, Bohdan, 1947- Po toï bik bezodni, abo, Mertvi pro vartist' zhyttia ne rozkazhut'. Ternopil' : "Pidruchnyky & posibnyky", 1997.
HV6545 .A616 1997

Po toï bik bezodni, abo, Mertvi pro vartist' zhyttia ne rozkazhut'
Andrushkiv, Bohdan, 1947- Ternopil' : "Pidruchnyky & posibnyky", 1997.
HV6545 .A616 1997

POCAHONTAS, D. 1617.
Price, David, 1961- Love and hate in Jamestown. 1st ed. New York : Alfred A. Knopf : Distributed by Random House, 2003.
F234.J3 P68 2003

Pochemu Amerika nastupaet.
Parshev, A. P. (Andreĭ Petrovich) Moskva : AST : Astrel', 2002.
HF1558.2.Z4 P37 2002

The pocket spell creator.
Connor, Kerri, 1970- Franklin Lakes, N.J. : New Page Books, c2003.
BF1611 .C724 2003

Pocketscroll series.
Pliskin, Zelig. Enthusiasm!. 1st ed. Brooklyn, N.Y. : Shaar Press : Distributed by Mesorah Publications, 2002.

Pliskin, Zelig. Harmony with others. 1st ed. Brooklyn, N.Y. : Shaar Press : Distributed by Mesorah Publications, 2002.

Podróże z moją kotką.
Ziolkowska, Aleksandra. Wyd. 1. Warszawa : Wydawn. Nowy Świat, 2002.

Poèmes.
Jouffroy, Alain, 1928- [Mots et moi] Les mots et moi ; Nantes : Pleins feux, c2002.

POEMS. *See* **POETRY.**

Poerksen, Bernhard.
Von Foerster, Heinz, 1911- Understanding systems. New York : Kluwer Academic/Plenum Publishers ; Heidelberg : Carl-Auer-Systeme Verlag, c2002.

Una poetica dell'analisi.
Donfrancesco, Francesco. Bergamo : Moretti & Vitali, 2000.

Poėticheskaia ėnergiia slova.
Alefirenko, M. F. Moskva : Academia, 2002.
P35 .A544 2002

POETICS.
Dobyns, Stephen, 1941- Best words, best order. 2nd ed. New York : Palgrave Macmillan, 2003.

Poétique du désastre.
Makeieff, Macha. Arles : Actes sud, c2001.

POETRY.
Between philosophy and poetry. New York : Continuum, 2002.
B66 .B48 2002

Dobyns, Stephen, 1941- Best words, best order. 2nd ed. New York : Palgrave Macmillan, 2003.

Luft, Sandra Rudnick, 1934- Vico's uncanny humanism. Ithaca, N.Y. : Cornell University Press, 2003.
B3581.P73 L84 2003

POETRY, AMERICAN - AFRICAN AMERICAN AUTHORS.
Olaoye, Elaine H. Passions of the soul. 2nd ed. Red Bank, N.J. : Northwind Publishers, 2002.
1. Black author.

POETRY AND HISTORY. *See* **LITERATURE AND HISTORY.**

POETRY - PHILOSOPHY. *See* **POETRY.**

POETRY - THERAPEUTIC USE.
Mazza, Nicholas. Poetry therapy. Boca Raton, Fla : CRC Press, 1999.
RC489.P6 M39 1999

Poetry therapy.
Mazza, Nicholas. Boca Raton, Fla : CRC Press, 1999.
RC489.P6 M39 1999

POETRY - WOMEN AUTHORS.
Olaoye, Elaine H. Passions of the soul. 2nd ed. Red Bank, N.J. : Northwind Publishers, 2002.
1. Black author.

POETS, ISRAELI.
Me-ayin nahalti et shiri. Tel Aviv : Yedi'ot aharonot : Sifre hemed, c2002.

Poggi, Stefano.
Le leggi del pensiero tra logica, ontologia e psicologia. Milano : UNICOPLI, 2002.

Poggio, Rosauta Maria Galvão Fagundes. Processos de gramaticalização de preposições do Latim ao Português : uma abordagem funcionalista / Rosauta maria Galvão Fagundes Poggio. Salvador : EDUFBA, 2002. 302 p. ; 24 cm. Includes bibliographical references (p. 289-302). ISBN 85-232-0269-2
1. Historical linguistics. 2. Grammar, Comparative and general - Prepositions. 3. Functionalism (Linguistics) 4. Portuguese language - Prepositions. 5. Latin language - Prepositions. I. Title.

Poĭas mira.
Kanygin, I︠U︡riĭ Mikhaĭlovich. Kiev : MAUP, 2001.

POINCARÉ, HENRI, 1854-1912.
Galison, Peter Louis. Einstein's clocks, Poincaré's maps. 1st ed. New York : W.W. Norton, c2003.
QB209 .G35 2003

Point hors ligne
Croix, Laurence. La douleur en soi. Ramonville Saint-Agne (France) : Erès, c2002.

Yankelevich, Héctor, 1946- Du père à la lettre. Ramonville Saint-Agne : Erès, c2003.

POINT OF VIEW (LITERATURE). *See* **FIRST PERSON NARRATIVE.**

Poitevin, Michel. Georges Dumézil, un naturel comparatiste / Michel Poitevin. Paris : Harmattan, c2002. 209 p. ; 22 cm. (Collection Ouverture philosophique) Includes bibliographical references (p. 195-204). ISBN 2-7475-2897-9 DDC 194
1. Dumézil, Georges, - 1898- 2. Mythology. 3. Philosophy, Modern - 20th century. I. Title. II. Series: Collection L'ouverture philosophique.

Pokrovsky, Gleb, 1954-.
The way of a pilgrim. London : Darton Longman & Todd, 2003, c2001.

Polacy i niemcy : historia, kultura, polityka / redakcja Andreas Lawaty, Hubert Orłowski. òznań : Wydawn. Poznańskie, 2003. 711 p. ; 21 cm. (Poznańska biblioteka niemiecka ; 17) Includes bibliographical references and index. ISBN 83-7177-175-4
1. National characteristics, Polish. 2. National characteristics, German. 3. Poland - Relations - Germany. 4. Germany - Relations - Poland. I. Lawaty, Andreas, 1953- II. Orłowski, Hubert. III. Series: Poznańska biblioteka niemiecka ; 17.
DK4121 .P65 2003

POLAND - CHURCH HISTORY.
Radzimiński, Andrzej. Życie i obyczajowość średniowiecznego duchowieństwa. Warszawa : Wydawn. DiG, 2002.
BX1565 .R32 2002

Poland, Fiona.
Women's minds, women's bodies. Basingstoke ; New York : Palgrave Macmillan, 2003.
RA778 .P724 2003

POLAND - RELATIONS - GERMANY.
Polacy i niemcy. òznań : Wydawn. Poznańskie, 2003.
DK4121 .P65 2003

POLARITY. *See* **GOOD AND EVIL.**

Polarity magic.
Berg, Wendy, 1951- St. Paul, Minn. : Llewellyn Publications, 2003.

BF1589 .B47 2003

Polcz, Alaine. Gyermek a halál kapujában / Polcz Alaine. Budapest : PONT, c2001. 123 p. ; 20 cm. (Fordulópont könyvek, 1585-5503) ISBN 9639312231
1. Children - Death - Psychological aspects - Case studies. 2. Death - Psychological aspects - Case studies. 3. Terminally ill children - Psychology - Case studies. 4. Terminally ill children - Family relationships - Case studies. I. Title. II. Series.
BF723.D3 P65 2001

Poli︠a︡kov, G. I. (Grigoriĭ Izraĭlevich).
Spivak, M. L. Posmertnai︠a︡ diagnostika genial'nosti. Moskva : Agraf, 2001.
BF416.A1 S68 2001

POLICE ETHICS.
Passamaneck, Stephen M. Police ethics and the Jewish tradition. Springfield, Ill. : C.C. Thomas, c2003.
HV7924 .P37 2003

Police ethics and the Jewish tradition.
Passamaneck, Stephen M. Springfield, Ill. : C.C. Thomas, c2003.
HV7924 .P37 2003

POLICE INTERROGATION. *See* **POLICE QUESTIONING.**

POLICE QUESTIONING - FICTION.
Cook, Thomas H. The interrogation. Rockland, MA : Wheeler Pub., 2002.
PS3553.O55465 I58 2002

Polich, Judith Bluestone, 1948- Return of the children of light : Incan and Mayan prophecies for a new world / Judith Bluestone Polich. Santa Fe, N.M. : Linkage Publications, c1999. xviii, 155 p. ; 23 cm. Includes bibliographical references (p. 149-150) and index. ISBN 0-9671775-0-2
1. Incas - Religion - Miscellanea. 2. Prophecies (Occultism) - Peru. 3. Mayas - Religion - Miscellanea. 4. Prophecies (Occultism) - Mexico. 5. Spiritual life - Miscellanea. I. Title.
BF1812.P4 P65 1999

POLICY, MEDICAL. *See* **MEDICAL POLICY.**

Policy papers (Merkaz Ari'el le-meḥkere mediniyut) (144.) Eidelberg, Paul. Clash of two decadent civilizations. Shaarei Tikva, Israel : ACPR Publications, 2002.
BM537 .E53 2002

POLICY SCIENCES. *See also* **POLITICAL PLANNING.**
Policymaking and peace. Lanham, Md. : Lexington Books, c2003.
JZ5538 .P65 2003

Policymaking and peace : a multinational anthology / edited by Stuart Nagel. Lanham, Md. : Lexington Books, c2003. xiii, 376 p. : ill. ; 24 cm. (Studies in public policy) Includes bibliographical references and index. CONTENTS: Policy and peace : prospects and prejudices / Paul J. Rich -- Politics of the 'state' in the Cold War / Richard Saull -- Reforming the United Nations Security Council : a decision-making analysis / Courtney B. Smith -- UN rapid deployment capability : exploring an instrument of conflict prevention / H. Peter Langille -- Chinese perspectives on multilateralism : implications for cooperative security in Asia Pacific / Jing-dong Yuan -- Participatory management of the commons / A.W. Harris -- Contemporary diplomacy and conflict resolution : the intertwining / John D. Stempel -- Yugo-nostalgia, pragmatism, and reality : prospects for inter-republic cooperation / James H. Seroka -- Dunblane and the international politics of gun control / Aaron Karp -- Domination, quiescence, and war crimes / John Braithwaite -- The threat of terrorist exploitation of nuclear smuggling / Gavin Cameron -- International legal harmonization : peace, prosperity, and democracy? / Jarrod Wiener -- Lawyers as a commodity in international trade / Timothy J. O'Neill -- Violent conflict, security, and development / Yannis A. Stivachtis -- Democracy, diversion, and the news media / Douglas A. Van Belle -- Institutional constraints, political opposition, and interstate dispute escalation : evidence from parliamentary systems, 1946-89 / Brandon C. Prins and Christopher Sprecher. ISBN 0-7391-0461-6 (hardcover : alk. paper) DDC 327.1/72
1. Peace. 2. Conflict management. 3. International relations. 4. Policy sciences. I. Nagel, Stuart S., 1934- II. Series: Studies in public policy (Lanham, Md.)
JZ5538 .P65 2003

Polidoro, Massimo. Secrets of the psychics : investigating the paranormal claims / by Massimo Polidoro. Amherst, N.Y. : Prometheus Books, c2003. p. cm. Includes bibliographical references. Table of contents URL: http://www.loc.gov/catdir/toc/ecip043/2003010023.html CONTENTS: It's all in the mind : on the mechanisms of deception in psychic fraud -- When I was a psychic for an

hour -- Eusapia's sapient foot : a new examination of the Feilding report -- The case of Anna Eva Fay : the medium that baffled Sir William Crookes -- Houdini and Conan Doyle : the story of a strange friendship -- Houdini vs. Margery : when the magician met the blond witch of Lime Street -- Houdini's last miracle : submerged under water! -- Investigating spirit moulds -- Chemistry of "supernatural" substances -- There be poltergeists! -- Roll up for the mystery tour -- Secrets of a russian psychic -- The mystery of the watch that was "alive" -- Miraculous oil inside a glass tube? -- The girl with the x-ray eyes -- An experiment in clairvoyance -- The strange case of the creeping doors -- Investigating table-tipping -- The case of the human magnets. ISBN 1-59102-086-7 (alk. paper) DDC 133
1. Parapsychology I. Title.
BF1031 .P75155 2003

Poliprofessionalizm deiatel'nosti vydaiushchegosia psikhologa - akmeologa K.K. Platonova.
Kazakova, N. E. (Natal'ia Evgen'evna) Shuia : Vest', 2002.
BF109.P56 K39 2002

Polish analytical philosophy
(v. 4) Salamucha, Jan. [Selections. English. 2003] Knowledge and faith. Amsterdam ; New York, NY : Rodopi, 2003.

POLISH PHILOSOPHY. *See* **PHILOSOPHY, POLISH.**

Polish studies in English language and literature
(v. 5.) Language function, structure, and change. Frankfurt am Main ; New York : Lang, c2002.
P125 .L36 2002

Politeia (Florence, Italy)
(5.) Valente, Michaela, 1972- Bodin in Italia. Firenze : Centro editoriale toscano, c1999.
BF1602.B633 V35 1999

POLITICAL ACTIVISTS. *See* **POLITICAL PARTICIPATION.**

POLITICAL ACTIVISTS - UNITED STATES - HISTORY.
Hansen, Jonathan M. The lost promise of patriotism. Chicago : University of Chicago Press, c2003.
E661 .H316 2003

POLITICAL ACTIVITY. *See* **POLITICAL PARTICIPATION.**

POLITICAL ALIENATION.
Zournazi, Mary. Hope. Annandale, N.S.W. : Pluto Press, 2002.

POLITICAL ANTHROPOLOGY. *See* **CHIEFDOMS.**

POLITICAL BEHAVIOR. *See* **POLITICAL PARTICIPATION.**

POLITICAL CAMPAIGNS.
Brettschneider, Frank. Spitzenkandidaten und Wahlerfolg. 1. Aufl. Wiesbaden : Westdeutscher Verlag, 2002.

Martín Salgado, Lourdes. Marketing político. Barcelona : Paidós, c2002.

POLITICAL CANDIDATES - PSYCHOLOGY.
Brettschneider, Frank. Spitzenkandidaten und Wahlerfolg. 1. Aufl. Wiesbaden : Westdeutscher Verlag, 2002.

POLITICAL CANDIDATES - SOCIAL ASPECTS.
Brettschneider, Frank. Spitzenkandidaten und Wahlerfolg. 1. Aufl. Wiesbaden : Westdeutscher Verlag, 2002.

POLITICAL COMMUNICATION. *See* **COMMUNICATION IN POLITICS.**

Political communications in greater China : the construction and reflection of identity / edited by Gary D. Rawnsley and Ming-Yeh T. Rawnsley. London ; New York : RoutledgeCurzon, 2003. xi, 326 p. : ill. : 25 cm. Includes bibliographical references and index. ISBN 0-7007-1734-X (alk. paper) DDC 324.951/001/4
1. Communication in politics - China. 2. Communication in politics - Taiwan. 3. Communication in politics - Hong Kong (China) 4. Group identity. I. Rawnsley, Gary D. II. Rawnsley, Ming-Yeh T.
JF1525.C59 P65 2003

POLITICAL CONVENTIONS. *See* **POLITICAL PARTIES.**

POLITICAL CORRECTNESS.
Valle, Alexandre del. Le totalitarisme islamiste à l'assaut des démocraties. Paris : Syrtes, c2002.

POLITICAL CORRECTNESS - EUROPE.
Lurati, Ottavio. Per modo di dire--. Bologna : CLUEB, c2002.

POLITICAL CORRUPTION.
Simonetti, José María, 1942- El fin de la inocencia. Bernal, Argentina : Universidad Nacional de Quilmes, 2002.
JF1081 S57 2002

POLITICAL CRIMES AND OFFENSES. *See* **INSURGENCY; POLITICAL VIOLENCE; TERRORISM.**

POLITICAL CULTURE.
Perspectives on Las Américas. Maden, MA : Blackwell Pub., c2003.
F1410 .P48 2003

Smith, Rogers M., 1953- Stories of peoplehood. Cambridge ; New York : Cambridge University Press, 2003.
JA75.7 .S65 2003

Zournazi, Mary. Hope. Annandale, N.S.W. : Pluto Press, 2002.

POLITICAL CULTURE - NORTHEASTERN STATES - HISTORY - 19TH CENTURY.
Lawson, Melinda, 1954- Patriot fires. Lawrence : University Press of Kansas, c2002.
E468.9 .L39 2002

POLITICAL CULTURE - RUSSIA (FEDERATION).
Denisovskiĭ, G. M. Politicheskaia tolerantnost' v reformiruemom rossiĭskom obshchestve vtoroĭ poloviny 90-kh godov. Moskva : TSentr obshchechelovecheskikh tsennosteĭ, 2002.
JN6699.A15 D46 2002

Ol'shanskiĭ, D. V. (Dmitriĭ Vadimovich) Psikhologiia sovremennoĭ rossiĭskoĭ politiki. Moskva : Akademicheskiĭ proekt, 2001.
JN6699.A15 O46 2001

POLITICAL CULTURE - UNITED STATES.
The fractious nation? Berkeley : University of California Press, c2003.
E169.12 .F69 2003

Gutfeld, Arnon. American exceptionalism. Brighton [England] ; Portland, Or. : Sussex Academic Press, 2002.
E169.1 .G956 2002

POLITICAL CULTURE - UNITED STATES - HISTORY.
Hansen, Jonathan M. The lost promise of patriotism. Chicago : University of Chicago Press, c2003.
E661 .H316 2003

POLITICAL CULTURE - UNITED STATES - HISTORY - 18TH CENTURY.
Trees, Andrew S., 1968- The founding fathers and the politics of character. Princeton, N.J. : Princeton University Press, c2004.
E302.1 .T74 2004

POLITICAL CULTURE - UNITED STATES - HISTORY - 19TH CENTURY.
Lawson, Melinda, 1954- Patriot fires. Lawrence : University Press of Kansas, c2002.
E468.9 .L39 2002

Skeen, Carl Edward. 1816. Lexington : University Press of Kentucky, c2003.
E341 .S57 2003

Winger, Stewart Lance. Lincoln, religion, and romantic cultural politics. DeKalb : Northern Illinois University Press, c2003.
E457.2 .W77 2003

POLITICAL CULTURE - UNITED STATES - HISTORY - 20TH CENTURY.
The achievement of American liberalism. New York : Columbia University Press, c2003.
E806 .M63 2003

Barber, Lucy G. (Lucy Grace), 1964- Marching on Washington. Berkeley : University of California Press, c2002.
E743 .B338 2002

POLITICAL DEVELOPMENT.
Norton, Anne. Bloodrites of the post-structuralists. New York : Routledge, 2002.
HM626 .N6785 2002

POLITICAL ECONOMY. *See* **ECONOMICS.**

POLITICAL ETHICS.
Celli, Pier Luigi. Breviario di cinismo ben temperato. 1. ed. Roma : Fazi, 2002.

Dilemmas of reconciliation. Waterloo, Ont. : Wilfrid Laurier University Press, 2003.

Politique et responsabilité, enjeux partagés. Paris : Harmattan ; Lille : Université des sciences et technologies de Lille, 2003.

Reemtsma, Jan Philipp. Wie hätte ich mich verhalten? München : Beck, c2001.
HM216 .R38 2001

POLITICAL HISTORY. *See* **WORLD POLITICS.**

POLITICAL LEADERSHIP.
Elite configurations at the apex of power. Leiden ; Boston : Brill, 2003.
JC330.3 .E45 2003

Roberts, Andrew, 1963- Hitler and Churchill. London : Weidenfeld & Nicolson, 2003.

POLITICAL MESSIANISM. *See* **MESSIANISM, POLITICAL.**

POLITICAL NOMINEES. *See* **POLITICAL CANDIDATES.**

POLITICAL OBLIGATION.
Lister, Ruth, 1949- Citizenship. 2nd ed. Basingstoke, Hampshire ; New York : Palgrave Macmillan, 2003.
HQ1236 .L57 2003

POLITICAL PARTICIPATION. *See also* **POLITICAL ACTIVISTS.**
Campos, Edemilson Antunes de. A tirania de Narciso. 1. ed. São Paulo, SP, Brasil : Annablume/FAPESP, 2001.

Smith, Rogers M., 1953- Stories of peoplehood. Cambridge ; New York : Cambridge University Press, 2003.
JA75.7 .S65 2003

POLITICAL PARTICIPATION - UNITED STATES.
Shafer, Byron E. The two majorities and the puzzle of modern American politics. Lawrence, Kan. : University Press of Kansas, c2003.
JK2261 .S4298 2003

POLITICAL PARTICIPATION - UNITED STATES - HISTORY - 20TH CENTURY.
Barber, Lucy G. (Lucy Grace), 1964- Marching on Washington. Berkeley : University of California Press, c2002.
E743 .B338 2002

POLITICAL PARTIES - UNITED STATES.
Shafer, Byron E. The two majorities and the puzzle of modern American politics. Lawrence, Kan. : University Press of Kansas, c2003.
JK2261 .S4298 2003

POLITICAL PERSECUTION. *See* **CIVIL RIGHTS.**

POLITICAL PLANNING.
Public policy in knowledge-based economies. Cheltenham, UK ; Northampton, MA : Edward Elgar, c2003.
HC79.I55 P83 2003

Rescher, Nicholas. Sensible decisions. Lanham, Md. ; Oxford : Rowman & Littlefield Publishers, c2003.
B945.R453 S46 2003

Zahariadis, Nikolaos, 1961- Ambiguity and choice in public policy. Washington, D.C. : Georgetown University Press, c2003.
H97 .Z34 2003

POLITICAL PLANNING - CANADA.
Helliwell, John F. Globalization and well-being. Vancouver : UBC Press, 2002.
HF1359 .H43 2002

POLITICAL POWER. *See* **POWER (SOCIAL SCIENCES).**

POLITICAL PRISONERS - PSYCHOLOGY.
Oron, Israel. Mavet, almavet ve-ide'ologyah. [Israel] : Miśrad ha-biṭaḥon, [2002]

POLITICAL PSYCHOLOGY. *See also* **PUBLIC OPINION.**
Brettschneider, Frank. Spitzenkandidaten und Wahlerfolg. 1. Aufl. Wiesbaden : Westdeutscher Verlag, 2002.

Cheng zhang de Zhongguo. Di 1 ban. Beijing : Ren min chu ban she, 2002.
HQ799.2.P6 C449 2002

Comfort, Kenneth Jerold. The ego and the social order. Cohoes, N.Y. : Public Administration Institute of New York State, 2000.
BF175.5.E35 C65 2000

Comfort, Kenneth Jerold. Power, politics, and the ego. 2nd ed., revised. Cohoes, N.Y. : Public Administration Institute of New York State, 2003.

Political psychology

Denisovskiĭ, G. M. Politicheskaia tolerantnost' v reformiruemom rossiĭskom obshchestve vtoroĭ poloviny 90-kh godov. Moskva : TSentr obshchechelovecheskikh tsennosteĭ, 2002.
JN6699.A15 D46 2002

Donchenko, E. A. (Elena Andreevna) Arkhetypy sotsial'noho zhyttia i polityka. Kyïv : Lybid', 2001.
JA74.5 .D65 2001

Grosbard, Ofer, 1954- [Yiśra'el 'al ha-sapah. English] Israel on the couch. Albany : State University of New York Press, c2003.
DS126.5 .G694 2003

Katznelson, Ira. Desolation and enlightenment. New York : Columbia University Press, c2003.
JA71 .K35 2003

Lamizet, Bernard. Politique et identité. Lyon : Presses universitaires de Lyon, 2002.

Meyer, Gerd. Freiheit wovon, Freiheit wozu? Opladen : Leske + Budrich, 2002.

Moreno-Riaño, Gerson, 1971- Political tolerance, culture, and the individual. Lewiston, N.Y. : E. Mellen Press, c2002.
JA74.5 .M653 2002

Ol'shanskiĭ, D. V. (Dmitriĭ Vadimovich) Psikhologiia sovremennoĭ rossiĭskoĭ politiki. Moskva : Akademicheskiĭ proekt, 2001.
JN6699.A15 O46 2001

Oxford handbook of political psychology. Oxford ; New York : Oxford University Press, 2003.
JA74.5 .H355 2003

Roazen, Paul, 1936- Cultural foundations of political psychology. New Brunswick, N.J. : Transaction Publishers, c2003.
JA74.5 .R63 2003

Rowland, Robert C., 1954- Shared land/conflicting identity. East lansing : Michigan State University Press, 2002.
DS119.7 .R685 2003

Sayyid, 'Azīzah Muḥammad. al-Sulūk al-siyāsī. al-Ṭab'ah 1. [Cairo] : Dār al-Ma'ārif, 1994.
JA74.5 .S29 1994

Smith, Rogers M., 1953- Stories of peoplehood. Cambridge ; New York : Cambridge University Press, 2003.
JA75.7 .S65 2003

POLITICAL REHABILITATION. See **AMNESTY.**

POLITICAL RIGHTS. See **CITIZENSHIP; POLITICAL PARTICIPATION.**

POLITICAL SCIENCE. See also **AUTHORITY; CITIZENSHIP; COMMUNICATION IN POLITICS; CONSERVATISM; GOVERNMENT, RESISTANCE TO; IDEOLOGY; IMPERIALISM; INDIVIDUALISM; ISLAM AND POLITICS; LIBERALISM; LIBERTY; NATIONALISM; POLITICAL PARTIES; POWER (SOCIAL SCIENCES); PUBLIC ADMINISTRATION; PUBLIC OPINION; RELIGION AND POLITICS; SOVEREIGNTY; UTOPIAS; WORLD POLITICS.**
Adeleke, Veronica I. Concept of gender equality as a paradox in Nigeria's democratic experience. Ikeja [Nigeria] : Dept. of Political Science and Sociology, Babcock University, 2002.
1. Black author.

Mykytenko, Svitlana. Enihma lidera, abo, Shcho mozhe obitsiaty polytychna kar'iera poriadnii liudyni, okrim vtraty poriadnosti. Kyïv : Vyd-vo "Molod'", 2001.
JC330.3 .M95 2001

Pradeau, Jean-François. Plato and the city. Exeter, UK : University of Exeter Press, 2002.
B395 .P7313 2002

Protsenko, Oleh. Konservatyzm. Kyïv : "Smoloskyp", 1998.

Roazen, Paul, 1936- Cultural foundations of political psychology. New Brunswick, N.J. : Transaction Publishers, c2003.
JA74.5 .R63 2003

Rosen, Stanley, 1929- Hermeneutics as politics. 2nd ed. New Haven, Conn. : Yale University Press, 2003.
BD241 .R81 2003

Stoppino, Mario. Potere e teoria politica. 3. ed. riv. e accresciuta. Milano : Giuffrè, 2001.

Toshchenko, Zhan Terent'evich. Tri osobennykh lika vlasti. Moskva : RGGU, 2002.
JC330 .T674 2002

Unger, Roberto Mangabeira. False necessity--anti-necessitarian social theory in the service of radical democracy. New ed. London ; New York : Verso, 2001.

POLITICAL SCIENCE - CHINA.
Shi, Sheng. Fan Zhongyan li shen xing shi jiu ju fang lüe. Di 1 ban. Beijing : Zhongguo xi ju chu ban she, 2001.
DS751.6.F3 S5 2001

POLITICAL SCIENCE - HISTORY.
Canning, Joseph. [History of medieval political thought, 300-1450. French] Histoire de la pensée politique médiévale (300-1450). Fribourg, Suisse : Editions universitaires ; Paris : Cerf, [2003]

Klosko, George. Jacobins and utopians. Notre Dame, Ind. : University of Notre Dame Press, c2003.
JC491 .K54 2003

POLITICAL SCIENCE - HISTORY - 18TH CENTURY.
Barnard, Frederick M., 1921- Herder on nationality, humanity, and history. Montreal : McGill-Queen's University Press, c2003.

POLITICAL SCIENCE - PHILOSOPHY.
Canto-Sperber, Monique. Les règles de la liberté. [Paris] : Plon, c2003.

Collen, Lindsey. Natir imin. Port Louis, Mauritius : Ledikasyon pu travayer, [2000]

Connolly, William E. Identity/difference. Expanded ed. Minneapolis : University of Minnesota Press, c2002.
JA74 .C659 2002

Cultivating citizens. Lanham : Lexington Books, c2002.
JK1759 .C85 2002

Essays in honor of Burleigh Wilkins. New York : Peter Lang, c2001.
JA71 .E694 2001

Extreme beauty. London ; New York : Continuum, 2002.
BH39 .E98 2002

Gellner, Ernest. [Essays. Selections] Ernest Gellner. London ; New York : Routledge, 2003.
B1626.G441 G76 2003

Hösle, Vittorio, 1960- Philosophie und Öffentlichkeit. Würzburg : Königshausen & Neumann, c2003.

Katznelson, Ira. Desolation and enlightenment. New York : Columbia University Press, c2003.
JA71 .K35 2003

Mićunović, Dragoljub. Filozofija minima. Beograd : "Filip Višnjić", 2001.
H61.15 .M5 2001

Politique et responsabilité, enjeux partagés. Paris : Harmattan ; Lille : Université des sciences et technologies de Lille, 2003.

Silhon, sieur de (Jean), 1596?-1667. De la certitude des connaissances humaines. [Paris] : Fayard, c2002.

Tucci, Antonio. Individualità e politica. Napoli : Edizioni scientifiche italiane, 2002.

Zakaria, Fareed. The future of freedom. 1st ed. New York : W.W. Norton, c2003.
JC423 .Z35 2003

Zournazi, Mary. Hope. Annandale, N.S.W. : Pluto Press, 2002.

POLITICAL SCIENCE - RELIGIOUS ASPECTS. See **RELIGION AND POLITICS.**

POLITICAL SOCIOLOGY.
Aux frontières des attitudes. Paris, France : Harmattan, c2002.

Katznelson, Ira. Desolation and enlightenment. New York : Columbia University Press, c2003.
JA71 .K35 2003

Lamizet, Bernard. Politique et identité. Lyon : Presses universitaires de Lyon, 2002.

Nelson, Phillip J., 1929- Signaling goodness. Ann Arbor : University of Michigan Press, c2003.
HV31 .N45 2003

Smith, Rogers M., 1953- Stories of peoplehood. Cambridge ; New York : Cambridge University Press, 2003.

JA75.7 .S65 2003

Stoppino, Mario. Potere e teoria politica. 3. ed. riv. e accresciuta. Milano : Giuffrè, 2001.

POLITICAL THEORY. See **POLITICAL SCIENCE.**

POLITICAL THOUGHT. See **POLITICAL SCIENCE.**

Political tolerance, culture, and the individual.
Moreno-Riaño, Gerson, 1971- Lewiston, N.Y. : E. Mellen Press, c2002.
JA74.5 .M653 2002

POLITICAL VIOLENCE. See also **GOVERNMENT, RESISTANCE TO; TERRORISM.**
Imagine coexistence. 1st ed. San Francisco : Jossey-Bass, c2003.
HM1121 .I42 2003

POLITICAL VIOLENCE - COLOMBIA.
Al oído de Uribe. 1a. ed. Bogotá, Colombia : Editorial Oveja Negra, 2002.

Téllez, Edgar. Diario íntimo de un fracaso. 1. ed. Bogotá, D.C., Colombia : Planeta, 2002.

Políticas sociales y modelos de atención integral a la infancia.
Amar Amar, José Juan. Barranquilla, Colombia : Ediciones Uninorte, 2001.

Politicheskaia tolerantnost' v reformiruemom rossiĭskom obshchestve vtoroĭ poloviny 90-kh godov.
Denisovskiĭ, G. M. Moskva : TSentr obshchechelovecheskikh tsennosteĭ, 2002.
JN6699.A15 D46 2002

POLITICIANS. See **POLITICAL CANDIDATES.**

POLITICS. See **POLITICAL SCIENCE.**

POLITICS AND ARCHITECTURE. See **ARCHITECTURE AND STATE.**

POLITICS AND BUSINESS. See **BUSINESS AND POLITICS.**

POLITICS AND COMMUNICATION. See **COMMUNICATION - POLITICAL ASPECTS.**

POLITICS AND CULTURE. See also **POLITICS AND LITERATURE.**
Kul'tura i vlast' v usloviiakh kommunikatsionnoĭ revoliutsii XX veka. Moskva : "AIRO-XX", 2002.
HM621 .K858 2002

POLITICS AND CULTURE - CHINA.
Excursions in Chinese culture. Hong Kong : Chinese University Press, c2002.

Politics and culture (London, England)
Abbinnett, Ross. Culture and identity. London ; Thousand Oaks, Ca. : SAGE, 2003.
HM621 .A23 2003

POLITICS AND ISLAM. See **ISLAM AND POLITICS.**

POLITICS AND LITERATURE. See **RHETORIC - POLITICAL ASPECTS.**

POLITICS AND LITERATURE - ENGLAND - HISTORY - TO 1500.
Heng, Geraldine. Empire of magic. New York : Columbia University Press, c2003.
PR321 .H46 2003

POLITICS AND RELIGION. See **RELIGION AND POLITICS.**

POLITICS AND THE PRESS. See **PRESS AND POLITICS.**

The politics of fortune.
Garten, Jeffrey E., 1946- Boston : Harvard Business School Press, c2002.
HD57.7 .G377 2002

The politics of memory : truth, healing, and social justice / edited by Ifi Amadiume and Abdullahi An-Na'im. London ; New York : Zed Books, c2000. xii, 207 p. ; 23 cm. Includes bibliographical references and index. CONTENTS: Memory, truth, and healing / Wole Soyinka -- The politics of memory : Biafra and intellectual responsibility / Ifi Amadiume -- Biafran war literature and Africa's search for social justice / Akachi Ezeigbo -- Social movements revisited / Abdullahi An-Na'im and Svetlana Peshkova -- Post-Biafran marginalization of the Igbo in Nigeria / Nnaemeka Ikpeze -- Towards a social history of warfare and reconstruction : the Nigerian/Biafran case / Axel Harneit-Sievers and Sydney Emezue -- Latin American experiences of accountability / Juan E. Méndez -- Truth in a box : the limits of justice through judicial mechanisms / Julie Mertus -- Justice for women

victims of violence : Rwanda after the 1994 genocide / Binaifer Nowrojee and Regan Ralph -- The truth according to the TRC / Mahmood Mamdani -- Conclusion : the cause of justice behind civil wars / Francis M. Deng. ISBN 1-85649-842-5 (cloth) ISBN 1-85649-843-3 (pbk.) DDC 323.1
1. Human rights. 2. Reconciliation. 3. Social justice. I. Amadiume, Ifi, 1947- II. Na'īm, 'Abd Allāh Aḥmad, 1946-
JC571 .P642 2000

POLITICS, PRACTICAL. See also **BUSINESS AND POLITICS; POLITICAL PARTICIPATION; POLITICAL PLANNING; WOMEN IN POLITICS.**
Palonen, Kari, 1947- Eine Lobrede für Politiker. Opladen : Leske + Budrich, 2002.
JF2051.W43 J35 2002

POLITICS, PRACTICAL - RELIGIOUS ASPECTS. See **RELIGION AND POLITICS.**

Die Politik der Massenmedien : Heribert Schatz zum 65. Geburtstag / Frank Marcinkowski (Hrsg.). Köln : Halem, 2001. 256 p : ill. ; 22 cm. Includes bibliographical references. ISBN 3-931606-46-5
1. Mass media - Political aspects - Germany. 2. Communication in politics - Germany. 3. Telecommunication - Germany. 4. Communication. I. Marcinkowski, Frank. II. Schatz, Heribert.

Politique et identité.
Lamizet, Bernard. Lyon : Presses universitaires de Lyon, 2002.

Politique et responsabilité, enjeux partagés / sous la direction de Nabil el Haggar et Jean-François Rey ; Jean-Marie Breuvart ... [et al.]. Paris : Harmattan ; Lille : Université des sciences et technologies de Lille, 2003. 431 p. ; 22 cm. (Les rendez-vous d'Archimède) Includes bibliographical references. ISBN 2-7475-3869-9 DDC 194
1. Political ethics. 2. Political science - Philosophy. 3. Responsibility. 4. Common good. I. Series.

Die politische Religion des Nationalsozialismus.
Bärsch, Claus-Ekkehard. 2., vollst. überarb. Aufl. München : W. Fink, c2002.

Politische Soziologie
(Bd. 17) Heck, Alexander. Auf der Suche nach Anerkennung. Münster : Lit, c2003.

POLIZIANO, ANGELO, 1454-1494 - CRITICISM AND INTERPRETATION.
De Pace, Anna. La scepsi, il sapere e l'anima. Milano : LED, c2002.

Polk, Thad A.
Cognitive modeling. Cambridge, Mass. : MIT Press, c2002.
BF311 .C55175 2002

Pollack, H. N. Uncertain science-- uncertain world / Henry N. Pollack. Cambridge, U.K. ; New York : Cambridge University Press, 2003. xii, 243 p. ; 24 cm. Includes bibliographical references and index. Publisher description URL: http://www.loc.gov/catdir/description/cam031/2002031200.html Table of contents URL: http://www.loc.gov/catdir/toc/cam031/2002031200.html ISBN 0-521-78188-4 DDC 501
1. Science - Philosophy. 2. Uncertainty. I. Title.
Q175 .P835 2003

Pollard, Irina. Life, love and children : a practical introduction to bioscience ethics and bioethics / Irina Pollard. Boston : Kluwer Academic Publishers, c2002. xvi, 269 p. : ill. ; 25 cm. Includes bibliographical references (p. [223]-244) and index. ISBN 1402072945 (alk. paper) DDC 174/.2
1. Medical ethics. 2. Bioethics. 3. Life. 4. Love. I. Title.
R725.5 .P655 2002

Poller, Nidra.
Lévinas, Emmanuel. [Humanisme de l'autre homme. English] Humanism of the other. Urbana : University of Illinois Press, c2003.
B2430.L48 H8413 2003

Pollock, George H.
Friends and friendship. Madison, Conn. : Psychosocial Press, 2003.
BF575.F66 F695 2003

POLTERGEISTS.
Vinokurov, Igor'. Ne smotrite im v glaza!. Moskva : AiF-Print, 2001.
BF1466 .V56 2001

POLTERGEISTS - JUVENILE LITERATURE.
Netzley, Patricia D. Haunted houses. San Diego, Calif. : Lucent Books, c2000.
BF1461 .N48 2000

Pöltner, Günther.
Orte des Schönen. Würzburg : Königshausen & Neumann, c2003.
BH23 .O78 2003

POLYGLOTTISM. See **MULTILINGUALISM.**
POLYTHEISM. See **MONOTHEISM.**

Pompeo Faracovi, Ornella. Scritto negli astri : l'astrologia nella cultura dell'Occidente / Ornella Pompeo Faracovi. Venezia : Marsilio, c1996. 297 p. : ill. (some col.) ; 22 cm. (Saggi Marsilio) Includes bibliographical references (p. 281-288) and index. ISBN 88-317-6430-6
1. Astrology - History. I. Title.
BF1671 .P66 1996x

Pompeo, Francesco. Il mondo è poco : un tragitto antropologico nell'interculturalità / Francesco Pompeo. Roma : Meltemi, c2002. 191 p. ; 19 cm. (Ricerche ; 21) Includes bibliographical references (p. [175]-191). ISBN 88-8353-139-6 DDC 305.8
1. Ethnicity. 2. Intercultural communication. 3. Globalization. 4. Multiculturalism. I. Title. II. Series: Ricerche (Meltemi editore) ; 21.
GN495.6 .P66 2002

PONGIDAE. See **APES.**

Ponomarenko, V. A. (Vladimir Aleksandrovich)
Sozidatel'naia psikhologiia / V.A. Ponomarenko. Moskva : Moskovskiĭ psikhologo-sotsial'nyĭ institut ; Voronezh : Izd-vo NPO "MODEK", 2000. 841, [1] p. : ill. ; 21 cm. (Psikhologi otechestva: izbrannye psikhologicheskie trudy v 70-ti tomakh) At head of title: Rossiĭskaia akademiia obrazovaniia. Moskovskiĭ psikhologo-sotsial'nyĭ institut. Includes bibliographical references (p. 820-[842]). ISBN 5895021670
1. Creative ability. I. Rossiĭskaia akademiia obrazovaniia. II. Moskovskiĭ psikhologo-sotsial'nyĭ institut III. Title. IV. Series: Psikhologi otechestva.
BF408 .P572 2000

Pontificia Studiorum Universitas a Sancto Thoma Aquinate in Urbe.
Domagala, Edward. L'ermeneutica dell'esperienza dell'amore in Max Scheler. Romae : [s.n.], 2000.

Pontifícia Universidade Católica de Minas Gerais. Instituto de Psicologia.
Psicologia em revista. Belo Horizonte : Editora PUC Minas, 2000-
BF5 .C24

POOH BEAR (FICTITIOUS CHARACTER). See **WINNIE-THE-POOH (FICTITIOUS CHARACTER).**
POOR. See **POOR CHILDREN.**
POOR CHILDREN - ECONOMIC CONDITIONS. See **POOR CHILDREN.**

POOR CHILDREN - UNITED STATES.
Rector, Robert. The effects of marriage and maternal education in reducing child poverty. Washington, D.C. : Heritage Foundation, 2002.

POOR - ECONOMIC CONDITIONS. See **POOR.**

POOR - EGYPT - CAIRO.
El-Kholy, Heba Aziz. Defiance and compliance. New York : Berghahn Books, 2002.
HQ1793.Z9 C353 2002

Poortinga, Ype H., 1939-.
Between culture and biology. Cambridge, U.K. ; New York : Cambridge University Press, 2002.
BF721 .B4138 2002

POP ART.
Pop unlimited? Wien : Turia + Kant, 2001.
NX456.5.P6 P67 2001

POP CULTURE. See **POPULAR CULTURE.**

Pop unlimited? : Imagetransfers in der aktuellen Popkultur / herausgegeben von Christian Höller. Wien : Turia + Kant, 2001. 173 p. : ill. ; 24 cm. Includes bibliographical references. ISBN 3-85132-280-0
1. Pop art. 2. Popular culture. I. Höller, Christian, 1966-
NX456.5.P6 P67 2001

Pope-Davis, Donald B.
Handbook of multicultural competencies in counseling & psychology. Thousand Oaks, Calif. : Sage Publications, c2003.
BF637.C6 H3173 2003

Pope, Stephanie.
Vint/age 2001 conference : [videorecording]. New York, c2001.

POPE, STEPHANIE.
Vint/age 2001 conference : [videorecording]. New York, c2001.

Popoli dell'Italia antica
Antico Gallina, Mariavittoria. I romani. Cinisello Balsamo (Milano) : Silvana, 1998.

Popović, Velimir B. O duši i bogovima : teorija i praksa arhetipske psihologije / Velimir B. Popović. Niš : Prosveta, 2001. 274 p. ; 20 cm. (Biblioteka Duša i kultura) Includes bibliographical references. ISBN 86-7455-502-0
1. Archetype (Psychology) I. Title. II. Series.
BF175.5.A72 P67 2001

Popper, Arthur N.
Eaton, Robert C. The octavolateralis system and Mauthner cell interactions and questions [microform]. [Washington, D.C. : National Aeronautics and Space Administration, 1997]

Popper, Steven W., 1953-.
Lempert, Robert J. Shaping the next one hundred years. Santa Monica, CA : RAND, 2003.
T57.6 .L46 2003

POPULAR ARTS. See **POPULAR CULTURE.**

POPULAR CULTURE.
Bloom, Michelle E. Waxworks. Minneapolis : University of Minnesota Press, c2003.
GV1836 .B56 2003

Bonz, Jochen. Der Welt-Automat von Malcolm McLaren. Wien : Turia + Kant, [2002]

Britto García, Luis. Conciencia de América Latina. 1. ed. Caracas, Venezuela : Editorial Nueva Sociedad, [2002]

Les cultes médiatiques. Rennes : Presses universitaires de Rennes, [2002]

Danesi, Marcel, 1946- Forever young. Toronto : University of Toronto Press, c2003.

Digging holes in popular culture. Oxford : Oxbow, 2002.
PN3433.6 .D54 2002

The feminism and visual culture reader. London ; New York : Routledge, 2003.
HQ1121 .F46 2003

Frederiksen, Bodil Folke, 1943- Popular culture, family relations, and issues of everyday democracy. [Nairobi] : Institute for Development Studies, University of Nairobi, [2000]
HQ799.K42 N354 2000

Freedman, Carl Howard. The incomplete projects. Middletown, Conn. : Wesleyan University Press, c2002.
HX523 .F74 2002

Genis, Aleksandr, 1953- Ivan Petrovich umer. Moskva : Novoe literaturnoe obozrenie, 1999.
PG3021 .G46 1999

La (indi)gestión cultural. 1. ed. Bs. As., Argentina : Ediciones Ciccus-La Crujía, 2002.
HM621 .I535 2002

Moffitt, John F. (John Francis), 1940- Picturing extraterrestrials. Amherst, N.Y. : Prometheus Press, c2003.
BF2050 .M64 2003

Peixoto, Nelson Brissac. Nelson Brissac, Antonio Augusto Arantes. [São Paulo, SP : Fundação Memorial da América Latina, 1997]

Perspectives on Las Américas. Maden, MA : Blackwell Pub., c2003.
F1410 .P48 2003

Pop unlimited? Wien : Turia + Kant, 2001.
NX456.5.P6 P67 2001

Popvisionen. Frankfurt : Suhrkamp, 2003.
ML3470 .P69 2003

Ries, Marc, 1956- Medienkulturen. Wien : Sonderzahl, c2002.
P94.6 .R54 2002

Roach, Catherine M., 1965- Mother/nature. Bloomington, IN : Indiana University Press, c2003.
BD581 .R59 2003

Shakespeare, the movie, II: popularizing the plays on film, TV, video, and DVD. London ; New York : Routledge, 2003.
PR3093 .S543 2003

Sterne, Jonathan, 1970- The audible past. Durham : Duke University Press, 2003.
TK7881.4 .S733 2003

Storey, John, 1950- Inventing popular culture. Malden, MA : Blackwell Pub., 2003.

CB19 .S7455 2003

Strategies for theory. Albany : State University of New York Press, c2003.
B842 .S77 2003

Walker, John Albert, 1938- Art and celebrity. London ; Sterling, Va. : Pluto Press, 2003.
NX180.S6 W35 2003

Witkin, Robert W. (Robert Winston) Adorno on popular culture. London ; New York : Routledge, 2003.
B3199.A34 W58 2003

Xu, Fen. Zou xiang hou xian dai yu hou zhi min. Di 1 ban. Beijing : Zhongguo she hui ke xue chu ban she : Xin hua shu dian jing xiao, 1996.
PN81 .H76 1996 <Asian China>

Youth cultures. Westport, Conn. : Praeger, 2003.
HQ796 .Y59273 2003

POPULAR CULTURE - EUROPE - HISTORY - 20TH CENTURY.
Kazaaam! splat! ploof!. Lanham, Md. ; Oxford : Rowman & Littlefield, c2003.
D1055 .K39 2003

POPULAR CULTURE - EUROPE - RELIGIOUS ASPECTS - CHRISTIANITY.
Marvels, monsters, and miracles. Kalamazoo, Mich. : Medieval Institute Publications, 2002.
GR825 .M218 2002

Popular culture, family relations, and issues of everyday democracy.
Frederiksen, Bodil Folke, 1943- [Nairobi] : Institute for Development Studies, University of Nairobi, [2000]
HQ799.K42 N354 2000

POPULAR CULTURE - HISTORY.
Chlada, Marvin, 1970- Klangmaschine. 2., überarbeitete und erw. Aufl. Aschaffenburg : Alibri ; [Stuttgart] : Lautsprecher, 2001.
ML3470 .C55 2001

POPULAR CULTURE - LATIN AMERICA.
García Canclini, Néstor. Culturas híbridas. Nueva edición actualizada. Buenos Aires : Paidós, 2001.

POPULAR CULTURE - PHILOSOPHY.
Storey, John, 1950- Inventing popular culture. Malden, MA : Blackwell Pub., 2003.
CB19 .S7455 2003

POPULAR CULTURE - RELIGIOUS ASPECTS.
Ostwalt, Conrad Eugene, 1959- Secular steeples. Harrisburg, PA : Trinity Press International, c2003.
BL65.C8 O88 2003

Prandi, Carlo. La religione popolare fra tradizione e modernità. Brescia : Queriniana, c2002.

POPULAR CULTURE - RUSSIA (FEDERATION).
Genis, Aleksandr, 1953- Ivan Petrovich umer. Moskva : Novoe literaturnoe obozrenie, 1999.
PG3021 .G46 1999

POPULAR CULTURE - SOVIET UNION.
Genis, Aleksandr, 1953- Ivan Petrovich umer. Moskva : Novoe literaturnoe obozrenie, 1999.
PG3021 .G46 1999

POPULAR CULTURE - UNITED STATES. See also **HIP-HOP.**
Dyson, Anne Haas. The brothers and sisters learn to write. New York : Teachers College Press, c2003.
LB1139.L3 D97 2003

POPULAR CULTURE - UNITED STATES - HISTORY - 19TH CENTURY.
Kaplan, Amy. The anarchy of empire in the making of U.S. culture. Cambridge, Mass. : Harvard University Press, 2002.
E661.7 .K37 2002

POPULAR CULTURE - UNITED STATES - HISTORY - 20TH CENTURY.
Kaplan, Amy. The anarchy of empire in the making of U.S. culture. Cambridge, Mass. : Harvard University Press, 2002.
E661.7 .K37 2002

Macdonald, Dwight. Interviews with Dwight Macdonald. Jackson : University Press of Mississippi, c2003.
E169.1 .M1363 2003

Popular herbs in the U.S. market.
Blumenthal, Mark. Austin : American Botanical Council, 1997.

Popular magic in English history.
Davies, Owen, 1969- Cunning-folk. London ; New York : Hambledon and London, 2003.

BF1622.G7 D385 2002

POPULAR MUSIC. See also **COUNTRY MUSIC; ROCK MUSIC.**
Bonz, Jochen. Der Welt-Automat von Malcolm McLaren. Wien : Turia + Kant, [2002]

POPULAR MUSIC FANS. See **ROCK MUSIC FANS.**

POPULAR MUSIC - HISTORY AND CRITICISM.
Chlada, Marvin, 1970- Klangmaschine. 2., überarbeitete und erw. Aufl. Aschaffenburg : Alibri ; [Stuttgart] : Lautsprecher, 2001.
ML3470 .C55 2001

Popvisionen. Frankfurt : Suhrkamp, 2003.
ML3470 .P69 2003

POPULAR MUSIC - PSYCHOLOGICAL ASPECTS.
Hemming, Jan. Begabung und Selbstkonzept. Münster : Lit, [2002?]
ML3838 .H46 2002

POPULAR MUSIC RECORD INDUSTRY. See **SOUND RECORDING INDUSTRY.**

POPULAR MUSIC - SOCIAL ASPECTS.
Popvisionen. Frankfurt : Suhrkamp, 2003.
ML3470 .P69 2003

POPULAR SONGS. See **POPULAR MUSIC.**

POPULAR VOCAL MUSIC. See **POPULAR MUSIC.**

POPULATION. See **BABY BOOM GENERATION; HOUSEHOLDS.**

POPULATION BIOLOGY. See **ECOLOGY.**

POPULATION FORECASTING.
Riding the next wave. Indianapolis, Ind. : Hudson Institute ; [Washington, DC : Distributed by the Brookings Institution Press], c2001.
HM901 .R43 2001

Some significant 21st century trends and issues. Islamabad : Pakistan Futuristics Foundation & Institute, 1998.
CB161 .S62 1998

POPULATION GEOGRAPHY. See **EMIGRATION AND IMMIGRATION.**

Poputnye mysli.
Esin, Sergeĭ. Moskva : Literaturnyĭ in-t im. A. M. Gor'kogo, 2002.
PN145 .E755 2002

Popvisionen : Links in die Zukunft / herausgegeben von Klaus Neumann-Braun, Axel Schmidt und Manfred Mai. Frankfurt : Suhrkamp, 2003. 276 p. ; 18 cm. Includes bibliographical references and index. ISBN 3-518-12257-6 (pbk.)
  1. Popular music - History and criticism. 2. Popular music - Social aspects. 3. Music and technology. 4. Popular culture. I. Neumann-Braun, Klaus. II. Schmidt, Axel, 1968- III. Mai, Manfred, 1953-
ML3470 .P69 2003

Por la vereda digital.
Malvido Arriaga, Adriana. 1. ed. México : CONACULTA (Consejo Nacional para la Cultura y las Artes), 1999.
QA76.9.C66 M35 1999

Por qué merece la pena luchar por el legado cristiano?.
Žižek, Slavoj, 1949- [Fragile absolute. Spanish] El frágil absoluto, o, Por qué merece la pena luchar por el legado cristiano? 1. ed. Valencia : Pre-Textos, 2002.
BT1102 .Z58

Por qué se maltrata al más íntimo?.
López Díaz, Yolanda. 1. ed. [Bogota] : Universidad Nacional de Colombia, Sede Bogota, 2002.

Por una causa común.
Bilbeny, Norbert. 1. ed. Barcelona : Gedisa Editorial, c2002.
HM1271 .B553 2002

PORNOGRAPHY. See also **EROTICA.**
Bonnet, Gérard. Défi à la pudeur. Paris : Albin Michel, c2003.
HQ784.S45 .B66 2003

The portable MBA in management.
Cohen, Allan R. 2nd ed. New York : J. Wiley, c2002.
HD31 .C586 2002

The portable MBA series
Cohen, Allan R. The portable MBA in management. 2nd ed. New York : J. Wiley, c2002.

HD31 .C586 2002

The portable postmodernist.
Berger, Arthur Asa, 1933- Walnut Creek, CA ; Oxford : Altamira Press, c2003.
B831.2 .B465 2003

Portaleone, Abraham ben David, 1542-1612. [Shilṭe Ha Gibborim. German]
Die Heldenschilde / Abraham Ben David Portaleone ; vom Hebräischen ins Deutsche übersetzt und kommentiert von Gianfranco Miletto. Frankfurt am Main : Lang, 2002. 2 v. (883 p.) : ill. ; 21 cm. (Judentum und Umwelt ; Bd. 74 = Realms of Judaism ; Bd. 74, 0721-3131) Includes bibliographical references and indexes. ISBN 3-631-38890-X (2-v. set : pbk.) DDC 296.491
  1. Philosophy, Jewish. 2. Philosophy, Medieval. 3. Judaism - Works to 1900. I. Miletto, Gianfranco, 1960- II. Title.

Le porte del cielo.
Vlora, Nedim R., 1943- Bari : M. Adda, c2001.
BF1674 .V56 2001

PORTENTS. See **OMENS.**

Porter, Norman, 1952- The elusive quest : reconciliation in Northern Ireland / Norman Porter. Belfast : Blackstaff, 2003. 290 p. ; 21 cm. Includes bibliographical references and index. ISBN 0-85640-730-5 DDC 320.9416
  1. Conflict management. 2. Northern Ireland - Politics and government - 1994- I. Title.

Portera Sánchez, Alberto.
Envejecimiento y cultura. [Madrid] : Instituto de España, c2001.

Portinaro, Pier Paolo, 1953-.
I concetti del male. Torino : Einaudi, c2002.

Portmann, John. The lure of self-harm / John Portmann. Boston : Beacon Press, 2004. p. cm. Includes bibliographical references and index. ISBN 0-8070-1618-7 (cloth : alk. paper) DDC 155.2
  1. Self-defeating behavior. I. Title.
BF637.S37 P67 2004

Portrait de l'artiste en travailleur.
Menger, Pierre-Michel. Paris : Seuil, c2002.

Portrait of America.
Hirsch, Jerrold, 1948- Chapel Hill : University of North Carolina Press, c2003.
E175.4.W9 H57 2003

Portrait of the mother-artist.
Gerber, Nancy, 1956- Lanham, Md. : Lexington Books, c2003.
PS374.M547 G47 2003

PORTUGAL - CIVILIZATION - 21ST CENTURY.
Arenas, Fernando, 1963- Utopias of otherness. Minneapolis : University of Minnesota Press, c2003.
DP681 .A74 2003

PORTUGUESE FICTION - 20TH CENTURY - CRITICISM AND INTERPRETATION.
Arenas, Fernando, 1963- Utopias of otherness. Minneapolis : University of Minnesota Press, c2003.
DP681 .A74 2003

PORTUGUESE LANGUAGE - PREPOSITIONS.
Poggio, Rosauta Maria Galvão Fagundes. Processos de gramaticalização de preposições do Latim ao Português. Salvador : EDUFBA, 2002.

PORTUGUESE LITERATURE. See **PORTUGUESE FICTION.**

Porus, V. N. Ratsional'nost', nauka, kul'tura / V.N. Porus. Moskva : Universitet Rossiĭskoĭ akademii obrazovaniia̐, Kafedra filosofii, 2002. 351 p. : port. ; 23 cm. Includes bibliographical references. ISBN 581250251X
  1. Science - Philosophy. 2. Knowledge, Theory of. 3. Rationalism. 4. Science and civilization. 5. Civilization - Philosophy. I. Title.
Q175.32.K45 P678 2002

Poser, Hans.
Neuzeitliches Denken. Berlin ; New York : De Gruyter, 2002.

Positions (Durham, N.C.). Vol. 11, no. 1, spring 2003.
The afro-asian century. Durham, N.C. : Duke University Press, 2003.

Positions east asia cultures critique.
The afro-asian century. Durham, N.C. : Duke University Press, 2003.

Positive magic.
Weinstein, Marion. Rev. ed. Franklin Lakes, NJ : New Page Books, c2002.
BF1411 .W393 2002

Positive psychology.
Carr, Alan, Dr. London ; New York : Brunner-Routledge, 2004.
BF121 .C355 2004

POSITIVISM. *See* **MATERIALISM; NATURALISM.**

Posmertnaia diagnostika genial'nosti.
Spivak, M. L. Moskva : Agraf, 2001.
BF416.A1 S68 2001

POSSESSION, DEMONIAC. *See* **DEMONIAC POSSESSION.**

POSSESSION (LAW). *See* **PROPERTY.**

POSSESSION, SPIRIT. *See* **SPIRIT POSSESSION.**

Possessions.
Richardson, Judith. Cambridge, Mass. : Harvard University Press, 2003.
BF1472.U6 R54 2003

Possessions and exorcisms / Tom Head, book editor. San Diego, Calif. : Greenhaven Press, 2004. p. cm. (Fact or fiction) Includes bibliographical references and index. ISBN 0-7377-1645-2 (lib. : alk. paper) ISBN 0-7377-1646-0 (pbk. : alk. paper) DDC 133.4/26
1. Demoniac possession. 2. Exorcism. I. Head, Tom. II. Series: Fact or fiction (Greenhaven Press)
BF1555 .P68 2004

POSSIBILITY.
Hüntelmann, Rafael. Existenz und Modalität. Frankfurt a. M. ; New York : Hänsel-Hohenhausen, c2002.
BD331 .H86 2002

Stalnaker, Robert. Ways a world might be. Oxford : Clarendon ; New York : Oxford University Press, 2003.
BD111 .S73 2003

POST-COMMUNISM. *See also* **COMMUNISM.**
Read, Jason. The micro-politics of capital. Albany : State University of New York Press, c2003.
HB97.5 .R42 2003

Post-contemporary interventions
Khanna, Ranjana, 1966- Dark continents. Durham, NC : Duke University Press, 2003.
BF175.4.S65 K43 2003

Sánchez-Pardo, Esther. Cultures of the death drive. Durham [N.C.] : Duke University Press, c2003.
BF175.5.D4 S26 2003

Post Keynesian econometrics, microeconomics and the theory of the firm.
Beyond Keynes. Cheltenham ; Northampton, Mass. : Edward Elgar, c2002.

Post-Keynesian Economics Study Group.
Beyond Keynes. Cheltenham ; Northampton, Mass. : Edward Elgar, c2002.

Post-Keynesian Economics Study Group (Series)
Beyond Keynes. Cheltenham ; Northampton, Mass. : Edward Elgar, c2002.

POST-MODERNISM. *See* **POSTMODERNISM.**

Post-modernism for psychotherapists.
Loewenthal, Del, 1947- Hove, East Sussex ; New York : Brunner-Routledge, 2003.
BF41 .L64 2003

POST-MORTEM EXAMINERS. *See* **MEDICAL EXAMINERS (LAW).**

POST-TRAUMATIC STRESS DISORDER.
Kitaev-Smyk, L. A. (Leonid Aleksandrovich) Stress voĭny. Moskva : Ministerstvo kul'tury RF : Rossiĭskiĭ in-t kul'turologii, 2001.

McNally, Richard J. Remembering trauma. Cambridge, Mass. : Belknap Press of Harvard University Press, 2003.
RC552.P67 M396 2003

Shay, Jonathan. Odysseus in America. New York : Scribner, c2002.
RC550 .S533 2002

POST-TRAUMATIC STRESS DISORDER - PATIENTS - REHABILITATION.
Terrorism and disaster. Cambridge, UK ; New York : Cambridge University Press, 2003.
RC552.P67 T476 2003

POST-WAR GENERATION. *See* **BABY BOOM GENERATION.**

POSTAL ADDRESSES. *See* **STREET ADDRESSES.**

Postchelovecheskaia personologiia.
Tul'chinskiĭ, G. L. (Grigoriĭ L'vovich) Sankt-Peterburg : Aleteĭia, 2002.
BD331 .T84 2002

POSTCOLONIALISM. *See also* **DECOLONIZATION.**
Power, postcolonialism, and international relations. London ; New York : Routledge, 2002.
JV51 .P69 2002

Radhakrishnan, R. (Rajagopalan) Theory in an uneven world. Oxford ; Malden, MA : Blackwell, 2003.

POSTERS. *See* **COMMERCIAL ART; SIGNS AND SIGNBOARDS.**

Postille.
Manzoni, Alessandro, 1785-1873. Milano : Centro nazionale studi manzoniani, 2002.

Postmoderne auf dem Bildschirm, auf der Leinwand.
Bühler, Gerhard, 1959- Sankt Augustin : Gardez!, c2002.

Postmodernism.
Butler, Christopher, 1940- Oxford ; New York : Oxford University Press, 2002.
NX456.5.P66 B88 2002

Lefter, Ion Bogdan. Pitești : Editura Paralela 45, 2000.

POSTMODERNISM.
Abbinnett, Ross. Culture and identity. London ; Thousand Oaks, Ca. : SAGE, 2003.
HM621 .A23 2003

Altomare, Vincenzo. Alla ricerca dell'uomo tra Bibbia e modernità. 1. ed. Cosenza : Progetto 2000, c2000.

Berger, Arthur Asa, 1933- The portable postmodernist. Walnut Creek, CA ; Oxford : Altamira Press, c2003.
B831.2 .B465 2003

Bühler, Gerhard, 1959- Postmoderne auf dem Bildschirm, auf der Leinwand. Sankt Augustin : Gardez!, c2002.

Butler, Christopher, 1940- Postmodernism. Oxford ; New York : Oxford University Press, 2002.
NX456.5.P66 B88 2002

Caballero, Rufo, 1966- Sedición en la pasarela. La Habana, Cuba : Editorial Arte y Literatura, c2001.

Carter, Michael, 1950 Aug. 8- Where writing begins. Carbondale : Southern Illinois University Press, c2003.
P301 .C29 2003

Chlada, Marvin, 1970- Klangmaschine. 2., überarbeitete und erw. Aufl. Aschaffenburg : Alibri ; [Stuttgart] : Lautsprecher, 2001.
ML3470 .C55 2001

Clark, J. C. D. Our shadowed present. London : Atlantic, 2003.

Crowther, Paul. Philosophy after postmodernism. London ; New York : Routledge, 2003.
B831.2 .C76 2003

Deely, John N. The impact on philosophy of semiotics. South Bend, Ind. : St. Augustine's Press, 2003.
B831.2 .D437 2003

Dei, Héctor Daniel. The human being in history. Lanham, Md. : Lexington Books, c2003.
BD450 .D395 2003

Edgeworth, Brendan. Law, modernity, postmodernity. Aldershot, England ; Burlington, VT : Ashgate/Dartmouth, c2003.
K370 .E34 2003

El-Ojeili, Chamsy. From left communism to post-modernism. Lanham, Md. ; Oxford : University Press of America, c2003.
HX44.5 .E46 2003

The end of everything. Cambridge : Icon, 2003.

Facetas das pós-modernidade. São Paulo : Universidade de São Paulo, Faculdade De Filosofia Letras e Ciências Humanas, 1996.

Fox, Nik Farrell. The new Sartre. New York ; London : Continuum, 2003.

García Canclini, Néstor. Culturas híbridas. Nueva edición actualizada. Buenos Aires : Paidós, 2001.

Grasskamp, Walter. Ist die Moderne eine Epoche? München : C.H. Beck, c2002.

International relations and the "third debate". Westport, Conn. : Praeger, 2002.

JZ1306 .I577 2002

Jameson, Fredric. A singular modernity. London ; New York : Verso, 2002.
CB358 .J348 2002

Janaszek-Ivaničková, Halina. Nowa twarz postmodernizmu. Wyd. 1. Katowice : Wydawn. Uniwersytetu Śląskiego, 2002.

Kropotov, S. L. (Sergeĭ Leonidovich) Ėkonomika teksta v neklassicheskoĭ filosofii iskusstva. Ekaterinburg : Gumanitarnyĭ universitet, 1999.
B831.2 .K76 1999

Kuz'menko, Volodymyr. Na porozi nadt͡syvilizat͡siï. L'viv : "Universum", 1998.
HM901 .K89 1998

Latin America writes back. New York : Routledge, 2002.
PQ7081.A1 L336 2002

Li, Yi. Zou xiang he chu. Di 1 ban. Beijing : Zhongguo she hui chu ban she : Xin hua shu dian Beijing fa xing suo jing xiao, 1994.
ND196.P66 L5 1994 <Orien China>

Loewenthal, Del, 1947- Post-modernism for psychotherapists. Hove, East Sussex ; New York : Brunner-Routledge, 2003.
BF41 .L64 2003

Lyotard. New York ; London : Routledge, 2002.

Ma, Wenqi. Shui yue jing hua. Di 1 ban. Beijing : Zhongguo she hui chu ban she, 1994.
PN2039 .M28 1994 <Orien China>

Milner, Andrew, 1950- Contemporary cultural theory. 3rd ed. Crows Nest, N.S.W. : Allen & Unwin, 2002.

La modernité après le post-moderne. Paris : Maisonneuve & Larose, [2002]

Moulinier, Didier. Dictionnaire de la jouissance. Paris : L'Harmattan, c1999.
BF575.H27 M68 1999

Olson, Carl. Indian philosophers and postmodern thinkers. New Delhi ; New York : Oxford University Press, 2002.
B131 .O57 2002

Postmodernism and the postsocialist condition. Berkeley : University of California Press, c2003.
N6494.P66 P684 2003

Powell, Jim, 1946- Postmodernism for beginners. New York : Writers and Readers Pub., c1998.

Radhakrishnan, R. (Rajagopalan) Theory in an uneven world. Oxford ; Malden, MA : Blackwell, 2003.

Read, Jason. The micro-politics of capital. Albany : State University of New York Press, c2003.
HB97.5 .R42 2003

Religious experience and the end of metaphysics. Bloomington, Ind. : Indiana University Press, c2003.
BL53 .R444 2003

Sardar, Ziauddin. The A-Z of postmodern life. London : Vision, c2002.

Strategies for theory. Albany : State University of New York Press, c2003.
B842 .S77 2003

Venne, Jean-François, 1972- Le lien social dans le modèle de l'individualisme privé. Paris : L'Harmattan, c2002.

Zima, P. V. Theorie des Subjekts. Tübingen : A. Francke, c2000.
BD223 .Z56 2000

Žižek, Slavoj, 1949- [Fragile absolute. Spanish] El frágil absoluto, o, Por qué merece la pena luchar por el legado cristiano? 1. ed. Valencia : Pre-Textos, 2002.
BT1102 .Z58

Zons, Raimar. Die Zeit des Menschen. 1. Aufl., Originalausg. Frankfurt : Suhrkamp, c2001.

Postmodernism and the postsocialist condition : politicized art under late socialism / edited by Aleš Erjavec ; with a foreword by Martin Jay and contributions by Boris Groys ... [et al.]. Berkeley : University of California Press, c2003. xix, 297 p. : ill. (some col.) ; 26 cm. Includes bibliographical references and index. CONTENTS: The other gaze: Russian unofficial art's view of the Soviet world / Boris Groys -- Art as a political machine: fragments on the late socialist and postsocialist art of Mitteleuropa and the Balkans / Miško Šuvaković -- Neue Slowenische kunst - new Slovenian art: Slovenia, Yugoslavia, self-management, and the 1980s / Aleš Erjavec -- Hungarian marginal art in the late period of state socialism / Péter

György -- The new Cuban art / Gerardo Mosquera -- Post-utopian avant-garde art in China / Gao Minglu. ISBN 0-520-23334-4 (alk. paper) DDC 709/.171/709049
1. Postmodernism. 2. Socialism and art. 3. Art - Political aspects. I. Erjavec, Aleš. II. Groĭs, Boris.
N6494.P66 P684 2003

POSTMODERNISM - CHINA.
Li, Yi. Zou xiang he chu. Di 1 ban. Beijing : Zhongguo she hui chu ban she : Xin hua shu dian Beijing fa xing suo jing xiao, 1994.
ND196.P66 L5 1994 <Orien China>

Postmodernism for beginners.
Powell, Jim, 1946- New York : Writers and Readers Pub., c1998.

POSTMODERNISM (LITERATURE). *See also* **MODERNISM (LITERATURE).**
Janaszek-Ivaničková, Halina. Nowa twarz postmodernizmu. Wyd. 1. Katowice : Wydawn. Uniwersytetu Śląskiego, 2002.

Xu, Fen. Zou xiang hou xian dai yu hou zhi min. Di 1 ban. Beijing : Zhongguo she hui ke xue chu ban she : Xin hua shu dian jing xiao, 1996.
PN81 .H76 1996 <Asian China>

POSTMODERNISM (PHILOSOPHY). *See* **POSTMODERNISM.**

POSTMODERNISM - PSYCHOLOGICAL ASPECTS.
Habitar la tierra. Buenos Aires : Grupo Editor Altamira, 2002.
CB358 .H32 2002

Understanding experience. London ; New York : Routledge, 2003.
B105.E9 U53 2003

POSTMODERNISM - PUERTO RICO.
Pabón, Carlos. Nación postmortem. 1. ed. San Juan, P.R. : Ediciones Callejón, 2002.

POSTMODERNISM - RELIGIOUS ASPECTS.
Habitar la tierra. Buenos Aires : Grupo Editor Altamira, 2002.
CB358 .H32 2002

Jannoud, Claude. La crise de l'esprit. Lausanne, Suisse : Age d'homme, c2001.

POSTMODERNISM - RELIGIOUS ASPECTS - CHRISTIANITY.
2000 years and beyond. London ; New York : Routledge, 2003.
BR53 .T86 2003

Westphal, Merold. Overcoming onto-theology. 1st ed. New York : Fordham University Press, 2001.
BR100 .W47 2001

POSTMODERNISM - ROMANIA.
Lefter, Ion Bogdan. Postmodernism. Pitești : Editura Paralela 45, 2000.

POSTMODERNISM - SOCIAL ASPECTS.
Bewes, Timothy. Reification, or, The anxiety of late capitalism. London ; New York : Verso, 2002.
HM449 .B49 2002

Breisach, Ernst. On the future of history. Chicago : University of Chicago Press, c2003.
HM449 .B74 2003

Luhmann, Niklas. [Beobachtungen der Moderne. English] Observations on modernity. Stanford, CA : Stanford University Press, 1998.
HM24 .L88813 1998

Rosseel, Eric. Het onschatbare subject. Brussel : VUBPress, c2001.
BF697.5.S65 R67 2001

POSTMORTEM EXAMINERS. *See* **MEDICAL EXAMINERS (LAW).**

Postrel, Virginia I., 1960- The substance of style : how the rise of aesthetic value is remaking commerce, culture, and consciousness / Virginia Postrel. 1st ed. New York : HarperCollins, c2003. xv, 237 p. ; 237 cm. Includes bibliographical references (p. [193]-227) and index. ISBN 0-06-018632-1 DDC 111/.85
1. Aesthetics. I. Title.
BH39 .P6692 2003

POSTSTRUCTURALISM.
Radhakrishnan, R. (Rajagopalan) Theory in an uneven world. Oxford ; Malden, MA : Blackwell, 2003.

Strategies for theory. Albany : State University of New York Press, c2003.
B842 .S77 2003

POSTTRAUMATIC STRESS DISORDER. *See* **POST-TRAUMATIC STRESS DISORDER.**

POSTURE.
The Alexander technique [videorecording]. New York, N.Y. : Wellspring Media, c1999.

POSTURE, BIPEDAL. *See* **BIPEDALISM.**

POSTWAR GENERATION. *See* **BABY BOOM GENERATION.**

POTABLE LIQUIDS. *See* **BEVERAGES.**

POTABLES. *See* **BEVERAGES.**

A potent spell.
Smith, Janna Malamud. Boston : Houghton Mifflin, 2003.
HQ759 .S618 2003

Potere e teoria politica.
Stoppino, Mario. 3. ed. riv. e accresciuta. Milano : Giuffrè, 2001.

Potkonjak, Miodrag.
Qu, Gang, 1969- Intellectual property protection in VLSI designs. Boston, Mass. : London : Kluwer Academic, c2003.

Potorti, David. September 11th Families for Peaceful Tomorrows : turning our grief into action for peace / by David Potorti, with Peaceful Tomorrows. New York, NY : RDV Books, c2003. 246 p. : ill. ; 21 cm. ISBN 0-9719206-4-8 DDC 973.931
1. September 11 Terrorist Attacks, 2001. 2. Terrorism - Prevention. 3. Nonviolence. 4. Peace. I. September 11th Families for Peaceful Tomorrows. II. Title: September Eleventh Families for Peaceful Tomorrows

POTTER, HARRY (FICTITIOUS CHARACTER).
Gupta, Suman, 1966- Re-reading Harry Potter. Houndmills, Basingstoke ; New York : Palgrave Macmillan, 2003.
PR6068.O93 Z68 2003

Harry Potter's world. New York ; London : RoutledgeFalmer, 2003.
PR6068.O93 Z73 2003

The ivory tower and Harry Potter. Columbia : University of Missouri Press, 2002.
PR6068.O93 Z734 2002

Reading Harry Potter. Westport, Conn. ; London : Praeger Publishers, 2003.
PR6068.O93 Z84 2003

Potter, Nancy Nyquist, 1954- How can I be trusted? : a virtue theory of trustworthiness / Nancy Nyquist Potter. Lanham, Md. : Oxford : Rowman & Littlefield, c2002. xviii, 194 p. ; 24 cm. (Feminist constructions) Includes bibliographical references (p. 181-187) and index. CONTENTS: A virtue theory of trustworthiness -- Justified lies and broken trust -- When relations of trust pull us in different directions -- The trustworthy teacher -- Trustworthy relations among intimates -- Giving uptake and its relation to trustworthiness. ISBN 0-7425-1150-2 (hbk. : alk. paper) ISBN 0-7425-1151-0 (pbk. : alk. paper) DDC 179/.9
1. Trust. 2. Reliability. I. Title. II. Series.
BJ1500.T78 P68 2002

POTTERY. *See* **INDIAN POTTERY.**

POTTERY, ANCIENT.
La céramique. Paris : Editions Errance, c2003.

POTTERY - CLASSIFICATION.
La céramique. Paris : Editions Errance, c2003.

POTTERY - HISTORY.
La céramique. Paris : Editions Errance, c2003.

POTTERY, INDIAN. *See* **INDIAN POTTERY.**

POTTERY, PREHISTORIC.
La céramique. Paris : Editions Errance, c2003.

POTTERY, PRIMITIVE. *See* **POTTERY.**

Pound, Linda. Supporting musical development in the early years / Linda Pound and Chris Harrison. Buckingham ; Philadelphia : Open University Press, 2003. ix, 156 p. : ill. ; 23 cm. (Supporting early learning) Includes bibliographical references (p. [145]-150) and index. ISBN 0-335-21225-5 ISBN 0-335-21224-7 (pbk.) DDC 372.87/049
1. Music - Instruction and study - Juvenile. 2. Child development. 3. Education, Elementary. I. Harrison, Chris. II. Title. III. Series.
MT1 .P66 2003

Pour demain
Hottois, Gilbert, 1946- Species technica ; Paris : Vrin, 2002.

Pour un plein accès à l'acte d'être avec Thomas d'Aquin et Aristote.
Balmès, Marc. Paris : Harmattan, c2003.

Poussou, Jean-Pierre.
La renaissance. [Paris] : Sedes, 2002.

POVERTY. *See also* **POOR.**
Abrahamsson, Hans, 1949- Understanding world order and structural change. Basingstoke, Hampshire : New York : Palgrave Macmillan, 2003.
HF1359 .A24 2003

Wagner de Reyna, Alberto. El privilegio de ser latinoamericano. 1. ed. Córdoba, Argentina : Editorial Alejandro Korn, c2002.
F1408.3 .W35 2002

POWDERS. *See* **CRYSTALS.**

POWELL FAMILY.
Nanteos. Llandysul, Wales : Gomer, [2001]
DA738.N36 N36 2001

POWELL, JANE, 1929-.
Vint/age 2001 conference : [videorecording]. New York, c2001.

Powell, Jane, 1929- panelist.
Vint/age 2001 conference : [videorecording]. New York, c2001.

Powell, Jim, 1946- Postmodernism for beginners / by James N. Powell. New York : Writers and Readers Pub., c1998. 163 p. : ill. ; 24 cm. Includes bibliographical references and index.
1. Postmodernism. 2. Philosophy, Modern - 20th century. 3. Arts, Modern - 20th century. I. Title.

POWER, BALANCE OF. *See* **BALANCE OF POWER.**

Power, gender, and Christian mysticism.
Jantzen, Grace. Cambridge ; New York : Cambridge University Press, 1995.
BV5083 .J36 1995

The power of a partner.
Pimental-Habib, Richard L. 1st ed. Los Angeles, CA : Alyson Books, 2002.
HQ76.25 .P56 2002

The power of appreciation.
Nelson, Noelle C. Hillsboro, Or. : Beyond Words Pub., c2003.
BF575.G68 N45 2003

Power of darkness revealed : an eye witness of demons in the temple.
Aluko, Jonathan O. The spirit of this age. [[Akure, Nigeria : Christ Liberation Publications, c1996]
BL480 .A494 1996
1. Black author.

The power of intention.
Dyer, Wayne W. Carlsbad, Calif. : Hay House, c2004.
BF619.5 .D94 2004

The power of legitimacy.
Gelpi, Christopher, 1966- Princeton, N.J. : Princeton University Press, c2003.
JZ5595.5 .G45 2003

The power of management capital.
Feigenbaum, A. V. (Armand Vallin) New York ; Toronto : McGraw-Hill, c2003.
HD31 .F45 2003

The power of nonviolence : writings by advocates of peace / introduction by Howard Zinn ; [authors, Howard Zinn ... et al.]. Boston, Mass. : Beacon Press, c2002. x, 202 p. ; 21 cm. Originally published: Instead of violence / edited with notes and introductions by Arthur and Lila Weinberg. New York : Grossman Publishers, 1963. ISBN 0-8070-1407-9 (pbk. : alk. paper) DDC 327.1/72
1. Peace. 2. Pacifism. 3. Nonviolence. I. Zinn, Howard, 1922-
JZ5538 .P685 2002

The power of oneness.
Brossman, Sandra C. Boston, MA : Red Wheel, 2003.
BF637.S4 B8 2003

The power of positive habits.
Robey, Dan. Miami, Fla. : Abritt Pub. Group, c2003.
BF335 .R56 2003

The power of positive talk.
Bloch, Douglas, 1949- Rev. and updated ed. Minneapolis, Minn. : Free Spirit Pub., 2003.
BF723.S3 B56 2003

The power of relaxation.
Thomas, Patrice Olympus. 1st U.S. ed. St. Paul, MN : Redleaf Press, 2003.
BF723.S75 T48 2003

The power of resilience.
Brooks, Robert B. Chicago : Contemporary Books, c2004.
BF698.35.R47 B76 2004

The power of whiteness.
Goudge, Paulette. London : Lawrence & Wishart, 2003.

POWER (PHILOSOPHY).
Dei, Héctor Daniel. The human being in history. Lanham, Md. : Lexington Books, c2003.
BD450 .D395 2003

Molnar, George, d. 1999. Powers. Oxford ; New York : Oxford University Press, 2003.
BD541 .M54 2003

POWER PLANTS, NUCLEAR. *See* **NUCLEAR POWER PLANTS.**

POWER POLITICS. *See* **BALANCE OF POWER.**

Power, politics, and the ego.
Comfort, Kenneth Jerold. 2nd ed., revised. Cohoes, N.Y. : Public Administration Institute of New York State, 2003.

Power, postcolonialism, and international relations : reading race, gender, and class / edited by Geeta Chowdhry and Sheila Nair. London ; New York : Routledge, 2002. xii, 324 p. ; 25 cm. (Routledge advances in international relations and global politics ; 16) Includes bibliographical references (p. 285-311) and index. ISBN 0-415-27160-6 (hardbound) DDC 327.1/01
1. Postcolonialism. 2. Power (Social sciences) 3. International relations. I. Chowdhry, Geeta, 1956- II. Nair, Sheila, 1959- III. Series: Routledge advances in international relations and politics ; 16.
JV51 .P69 2002

POWER (PSYCHOLOGY). *See* **CONTROL (PSYCHOLOGY).**

POWER RESOURCES. *See* **ELECTRIC POWER.**

POWER (SOCIAL SCIENCES). *See also* **ELITE (SOCIAL SCIENCES).**

Allen, John, 1951- Lost geographies of power. Malden, MA ; Oxford : Blackwell Pub., 2003.
GF50 .A453 2003

Barrett, Stanley R. Culture meets power. Westport, Conn. ; London : Praeger, 2002.
HM1256 .B27 2002

Benitez, Juan Carlos. El concepto de poder en Alain Touraine. Buenos Aires : Editorial de Belgrano, 2002.
HM479.T6 B455 2002

Broom, Michael F. The infinite organization. 1st ed. Palo Alto, Calif. : Davies-Black, c2002.
HD58.7 .B755 2002

Brush, Lisa Diane. Gender and governance. Walnut Creek, CA ; Oxford : AltaMira Press, c2003.
JC330 .B75 2003

Davydov, IU. P. (IUriĭ Pavlovich) Norma protiv sily. Moskva : Nauka, 2002.

Elite configurations at the apex of power. Leiden ; Boston : Brill, 2003.
JC330.3 .E45 2003

Foucault, cultural studies, and governmentality. Albany : State University of New York Press, c2003.
JC330 .F63 2003

García de León, María Antonia. Herederas y heridas. 1a ed. [Madrid] : Ediciones Cátedra, Universitat de València, Instituto de la Mujer, 2002.
HD6054.2.S7 G37 2002

Gendering the master narrative. Ithaca : Cornell University Press, c2003.
HQ1143 .G46 2003

Guerra Manzo, Enrique. Caciquismo y orden público en Michoacán, 1920-1940. 1. ed. México : El Colegio de México, Centro de Estudios Sociológicos, c2002.
F1219.3.P7 G84 2002

Habitar la tierra. Buenos Aires : Grupo Editor Altamira, 2002.
CB358 .H32 2002

John, Mary. Children's rights and power. London ; New York : Jessica Kingsley Publishers, 2003.
HQ789 .J64 2003

Klosko, George. Jacobins and utopians. Notre Dame, Ind. : University of Notre Dame Press, c2003.
JC491 .K54 2003

Kul'tura i vlast' v uslovii͡akh kommunikat͡sionnoĭ revoli͡ut͡sii XX veka. Moskva : "AIRO-XX", 2002.

HM621 .K858 2002

La Branche, Stéphane. Mondialisation et terrorisme identitaire, ou, Comment l'Occident tente de transformer le monde. Paris : Harmattan, c2003.
JC330 .L2 2003

Lichev, Valeri. T͡Sinichnoto, ili, Igrata na vlast i udovolstvie. Sofii͡a : EON-2000, 2000.
B809.5 .L53 2000

Lukowski, Jerzy. The European nobility in the eighteenth century. Houndmills [England] ; New York : Palgrave Macmillan, 2003.
HT653.E9 L85 2003

Maset, Michael. Diskurs, Macht und Geschichte. Frankfurt/Main ; New York : Campus, c2002.
BF24.30.F724 M37 2002

Norton, Anne. Bloodrites of the post-structuralists. New York : Routledge, 2002.
HM626 .N6785 2002

Oakley, Ann. Gender on planet Earth. Oxford : Polity, 2002.

Palais et pouvoir. Vincennes : Presses universitaires de Vincennes, c2003.

Papcke, Sven, 1939- Gesellschaft der Eliten. 1. Aufl. Münster : Westfälisches Dampfboot, 2001.
HM821 .P37 2001

Power, postcolonialism, and international relations. London ; New York : Routledge, 2002.
JV51 .P69 2002

Race, nature, and the politics of difference. Durham : Duke University Press, c2003.
HT1521 .R2355 2003

Rosero Garcés, F. (Fernando) Líderes sociales en el siglo XXI. Quito : Ediciones Abya-Yala, 2002.

Simonetti, José María, 1942- El fin de la inocencia. Bernal, Argentina : Universidad Nacional de Quilmes, 2002.
JF1081 S57 2002

Stoppino, Mario. Potere e teoria politica. 3. ed. riv. e accresciuta. Milano : Giuffrè, 2001.

Tew, Jerry, 1955- Social theory, power and practice. Houndmills [England] ; New York : Palgrave, 2002.
HN49.P6 T49 2002

Topographies of power in the early Middle Ages. Leiden ; Boston : Brill, 2001.
D117 .T67 2001

Toshchenko, Zhan Terent'evich. Tri osobennykh lika vlasti. Moskva : RGGU, 2002.
JC330 .T674 2002

Translation and power. Amherst : University of Massachusetts Press, 2002.
P306.97.S63 T7 2002

Transparency and conspiracy. Durham : Duke University Press, 2003.
JC330 .T73 2003

POWER (SOCIAL SCIENCES) - BENIN.
Vallier, Gilles-Félix. La logique de l'éternité. 1998.

POWER (SOCIAL SCIENCES) - EUROPE.
A companion to the worlds of the Renaissance. Malden, MA : Blackwell Publishers, 2002.
CB367 .C65 2002

POWER (SOCIAL SCIENCES) - HISTORY - TO 500.
Ancient queens. Walnut Creek, Calif. ; Oxford : AltaMira Press, c2003.
HQ1127 .A53 2003

POWER (SOCIAL SCIENCES) IN ART.
Palais et pouvoir. Vincennes : Presses universitaires de Vincennes, c2003.

POWER (SOCIAL SCIENCES) - ITALY.
A companion to the worlds of the Renaissance. Malden, MA : Blackwell Publishers, 2002.
CB367 .C65 2002

POWER (SOCIAL SCIENCES) - MORAL AND ETHICAL ASPECTS.
Luz, Ehud. [Ma'avak be-nahal Yabok. English] Wrestling with an angel. New Haven : Yale University Press, c2003.
DS143 .L8913 2003

POWER SUPPLY, ELECTRIC. *See* **ELECTRIC POWER.**

Power tools for women.
Daniels, Joni T. 1st ed. New York : Three Rivers Press, c2002.

HQ1221 .D26 2002

Powers.
Molnar, George, d. 1999. Oxford ; New York : Oxford University Press, 2003.
BD541 .M54 2003

POWERS (CHRISTIAN THEOLOGY). *See* **SPIRITS.**

Powers, Marilyn. The bridge between two lifetimes : a midlife map shaping our future / by Marilyn Powers, with Sherry Folb. Phoenix, AZ : Sophia Publications, c1999. 147 p. ; 23 cm. ISBN 0-9670495-0-4 (pbk.) DDC 158.1/084/4
1. Middle age - Psychological aspects. 2. Middle aged persons - Psychology. 3. Midlife crisis. I. Folb, Sherry. II. Title.
BF724.6 .P68 1999

POWHATAN INDIANS - ANTIQUITIES.
Gallivan, Martin D., 1968- James River chiefdoms. Lincoln : University of Nebraska Press, c2003.
E99.P85 G35 2003

POWHATAN INDIANS - FIRST CONTACT WITH EUROPEANS.
Gallivan, Martin D., 1968- James River chiefdoms. Lincoln : University of Nebraska Press, c2003.
E99.P85 G35 2003

POWHATAN INDIANS - KINGS AND RULERS.
Gallivan, Martin D., 1968- James River chiefdoms. Lincoln : University of Nebraska Press, c2003.
E99.P85 G35 2003

POWHATAN INDIANS - VIRGINIA - JAMESTOWN - HISTORY - 17TH CENTURY.
Price, David, 1961- Love and hate in Jamestown. 1st ed. New York : Alfred A. Knopf : Distributed by Random House, 2003.
F234.J3 P68 2003

Poznań studies in the philosophy of the sciences and the humanities
(v. 77) Salamucha, Jan. [Selections. English. 2003] Knowledge and faith. Amsterdam ; New York, NY : Rodopi, 2003.

(v. 78) Jadacki, Jacek Juliusz. From the viewpoint of the Lvov-Warsaw school. Amsterdam ; New York, NY : Rodopi, 2003.

Poznańska biblioteka niemiecka
(17.) Polacy i niemcy. òznań : Wydawn. Poznańskie, 2003.
DK4121 .P65 2003

Pozner, Vladimir.
Slutskiĭ, O. I. (Oleg Isaakovich) Chto posle ill͡iuzii? Moskva : Veche, 2002.
BV4509.R8 S58 2002

Prace Komisji Historii Sztuki
(t. 32.) Marmur dziejowy. Poznań : Wydawnictwo Poznańskiego Towarzystwa Przyjaciól Nauk, 2002.

Prace Komitetu Nauk Etnologicznych PAN
(v. 11) Between tradition and postmodernity. Warsaw : Wydawnictwo DiG, 2003.

Prace naukowe Uniwersytetu Śląskiego w Katowicach
(nr. 2025) Janaszek-Ivaničková, Halina. Nowa twarz postmodernizmu. Wyd. 1. Katowice : Wydawn. Uniwersytetu Śląskiego, 2002.

(nr. 2070) Dołęga, Zofia. Samotność młodzieży. Wyd. 1. Katowice : Wydawn. Uniwersytetu Śląskiego, 2003.
BF724.3.L64 D65 2003

Prace psychologiczne
(55) Szkice psychologiczne. Wrocław : Wydawn. Uniwersytetu Wrocławskiego, 2002.
BF76.5 .S97 2002

Praceta Jyoti. Dhātusāmya mem̐ manobhāvom̐ kā sthāna / Pracetā Jyoti. 1. samskaraṇa. Nāgapura : Viśvabhāratī Prakāśana, 2001. 360 p. : ill. ; 22 cm. + 4 folded tables. SUMMARY: Study of psychology with references to Ayurveda. Includes bibliographical references (p. 356-360). Includes statistical tables. In Hindi.
1. Phenomenological psychology. 2. Medicine, Ayurveda. 3. Psychology - Philosophy. I. Title.
BF204.5 .P73 2001

Practical ethics.
The Oxford handbook of practical ethics. Oxford ; New York : Oxford University Press, 2003.
BJ1031 .O94 2003

A practical guide to witchcraft and magick spells.
Eason, Cassandra. London ; New York : Quantum, c2001.

Practical judgments.
Kingwell, Mark, 1963- Toronto : University of Toronto Press, c2002.

The practical pagan.
Eilers, Dana D. Franklin Lakes, NJ : New Page Books, c2002.
BF1411 .E34 2002

PRACTICAL REASON.
Automated practical reasoning. Wien ; New York : Springer-Verlag, c1995.
QA76.9.A96 A9 1995

Sabalat, Tina. Pascals "Wette". Marburg : Tectum, 2000.

Schueler, G. F. Reasons and purposes. Oxford : Oxford University Press, 2003.

Vogler, Candace A. Reasonably vicious. Cambridge, Mass. : Harvard University Press, 2002.
BJ1031 .V64 2002

PRACTICE OF LAW. *See* **TRIAL PRACTICE.**

PRACTICE OF LAW - UNITED STATES - AUTOMATION.
Brenden, Ann E. Persuasive computer presentations. Chicago, Ill. : Law Practice Management Section, American Bar Association, c2001.
KF320.A9 B74 2001

The practice of value.
Raz, Joseph. Oxford ; New York : Oxford University Press, 2003.
BD232 .R255 2003

Practicing beauty.
Mustafa, Huda Nura. 1997.

Practicing multiculturalism : affirming diversity in counseling and psychology / edited by Timothy B. Smith. Boston, MA : Allyn and Bacon, c2004. xv, 341 p. : ill. ; 24 cm. Includes bibliographical references and index. ISBN 0-205-33640-X (pbk.) DDC 158/.3
1. Cross-cultural counseling. I. Smith, Timothy B.
BF637.C6 P7 2004

Pradeau, Jean-François. Plato and the city : a new introduction to Plato's political thought / Jean-François Pradeau ; translated by Janet Lloyd ; with a foreword by Christopher Gill. Exeter, UK : University of Exeter Press, 2002. xvii, 181 p. ; 22 cm. "First published in 1997 in French as Platon et la cité by Presses Universitaires de France"--T.p. verso. Includes bibliographical references (p. 169-175) and index. ISBN 0-85989-653-6 ISBN 0-85989-654-4 (PBK.) DDC 184
1. Plato - Criticism and interpretation. 2. Political science. 3. Philosophy, Ancient. I. Pradeau, Jean-François. Platon et la cité. II. Title.
B395 .P7313 2002

Platon et la cite.
Pradeau, Jean-François. Plato and the city. Exeter, UK : University of Exeter Press, 2002.
B395 .P7313 2002

Prager, Carol A. L. (Anne Leuchs), 1939-.
Dilemmas of reconciliation. Waterloo, Ont. : Wilfrid Laurier University Press, 2003.

Pragier, Georges.
Freud, le sujet social. 1re éd. Paris : Presses universitaires de France, 2002.

PRAGMATICS.
Huls, Erica. Dilemma's in menselijke interactie. Utrecht : Lemma, 2001.

Prepositions in their syntactic, semantic, and pragmatic context. Amsterdam ; Philadelphia, PA : J. Benjamins Pub., c2002.
P285 .P74 2002

Problemy interpretatsionnoĭ lingvistiki. Novosibirsk : Novosibirskiĭ gos. pedagog. universitet, 2001.
P128.E95 P762 2001

Wort und (Kon)text. Frankfurt : Lang, 2001.
P325.5.C65 W678 2001

Pragmatics & beyond
(new ser. v. 98.) Us and others. Amsterdam ; Philadelphia : John Benjamins Pub., c2002.
HM753 .U72 2002

Pragmatika kul'tury.
Dolgin, Aleksandr. Moskva : Fond nauchnykh issledovaniĭ "Pragmatika kul'tury", 2002.

PRAGMATISM. *See also* **TRUTH.**
Fesmire, Steven, 1967- John Dewey and moral imagination. Bloomington, IN : Indiana University Press, c2003.

BJ1031 .F47 2003

James, William, 1842-1910. [Pragmatism. German] Pragmatismus. Berlin : Akademie Verlag, c2000.

Lekan, Todd, 1967- Making morality. 1st ed. Nashville, TN : Vanderbilt University Press, 2003.
BJ1031 .L45 2003

White, Morton Gabriel, 1917- A philosophy of culture. Princeton, N.J. : Princeton University Press, c2002.
B945.W453 P48 2002

Pragmatismus.
James, William, 1842-1910. [Pragmatism. German] Berlin : Akademie Verlag, c2000.

Prairie, Arleen.
Butterfield, Perry M., 1932- Emotional connections. Washington, DC : Zero To Three, 2004.
BF720.E45 B879 2004

Butterfield, Perry M., 1932- Emotional connections. 1st ed. Washington, DC : Zero To Three Press, c2003.
BF720.E45 B88 2003

Praistorija Srba.
Petrović, Aleksandar M. Beograd : Pešić i sinovi, 2001.
DR1953 .P48 2001

Prakāśa, Priyadarśī.
Asalī prācīna Vaidika vāstu śāstra. 1. saṃskaraṇa. Dillī : Manoja Pōketa Buksa, [2002?]
BF1729.A7 A83 2002

Prakticheskaia psikhologiia (Astrel' (Firm))
Prakticheskaia psikhologiia v testakh, ili, Kak nauchit'sia ponimat' sebia i drugikh. Moskva : AST-Press kniga, 2003.
BF176 .P73 2003

Prakticheskaia psikhologiia v testakh, ili, Kak nauchit'sia ponimat' sebia i drugikh / [sostaviteli R. Rimskaia, S. Rimskiĭ]. Moskva : AST-Press kniga, 2003. 393, [1] p. : ill. (some col.) ; 22 cm. (Prakticheskaia psikhologiia) Includes bibliographical references (p. [394]). ISBN 5780502943
1. Psychological tests. I. Rimskaia, R. II. Rimskiĭ, S. III. Title: Kak nauchit'sia ponimat' sebia i drugikh IV. Series: Prakticheskaia psikhologiia (Astrel' (Firm))
BF176 .P73 2003

Praktikum po psikhodiagnostike
Kostina, L. M. (Liubov' Mikhaĭlovna) Metody diagnostiki trevozhnosti. Sankt-Peterburg : Rech', 2002.
BF575.A6 K65 2002

Prandi, Carlo. La religione popolare fra tradizione e modernità / Carlo Prandi. Brescia : Queriniana, c2002. 171 p. ; 19 cm. (Piccola biblioteca delle religioni ; 20) Includes bibliographical references. ISBN 88-399-1190-1 DDC 306
1. Religious life and customs. 2. Religion. 3. Popular culture - Religious aspects. I. Title. II. Series.

Präsenz zu denken - .
Anders, Martin. St. Augustin : Gardez!, c2002.
B3303 .A53 2002

Prather, Hugh. Standing on my head : life lessons in contradictions / Hugh Prather. Boston, MA : Conari Press, 2004. p. cm. ISBN 1-57324-918-1 DDC 158.1
1. Conduct of life. I. Title.
BF637.C5 P82 2004

Pratiques théoriques
Ménasé, Stéphanie. Passivité et création. Paris : Presses universitaires de France, c2003.

PRAYER. *See also* **MEDITATION.**
Aransiola, Moses Olanrewaju. The roots and solutions to peculiar problems (dealing with bad luck, lost opportunities and failure). 1st ed.
1. Black author.

The Book of prayer. New Delhi ; New York, USA : Viking, 2001.
BL560 .B625 2001

Nwokogba, Isaac E. Seeds of luck. Cranston, R.I. : Writers' Collective, 2003.
BF1778 .N96 2003

Ofori Onwona, Samuel. Shadows come to light. Achimota, Ghana : Africa Christian Press, 2000.
BV215 .O46 2000

PRAYER BOOKS AND DEVOTIONS.
What can happen when we pray. Minneapolis : Augsburg Fortress, c2001.

PRAYER - CHRISTIANITY.
Ofori Onwona, Samuel. Shadows come to light. Achimota, Ghana : Africa Christian Press, 2000.

BV215 .O46 2000

Prayer, magic, and the stars in the ancient and late antique world / edited by Scott Noegel, Joel Walker, and Brannon Wheeler. University Park, Pa. : Pennsylvania State University Press, 2003. p. cm. (Magic in history) Includes bibliographical references and index. Table of contents URL: http://www.loc.gov/catdir/toc/ecip043/2003009823.html ISBN 0-271-02257-4 (alk. paper) ISBN 0-271-02258-2 (pbk. : alk. paper) DDC 200/.93
1. Magic, Ancient - Congresses. 2. Magic - Religious aspects - History - Congresses. 3. Dreams - Religious aspects - History - Congresses. 4. Stars - Religious aspects - History - Congresses. 5. Divination - History - Congresses. I. Noegel, Scott B. II. Walker, Joel Thomas, 1968- III. Wheeler, Brannon M., 1965- IV. Series.
BF1591 .P73 2003

PRAYER, MENTAL. *See* **MEDITATION.**

PRAYER - ORTHODOX EASTERN CHURCH.
The way of a pilgrim. London : Darton Longman & Todd, 2003, c2001.

PRAYER - PSYCHOLOGY.
Ofori Onwona, Samuel. Shadows come to light. Achimota, Ghana : Africa Christian Press, 2000.
BV215 .O46 2000

PRAYERS. *See* **CONFESSION (PRAYER); PRAYER.**

PRAYERS FOR PEACE. *See* **PEACE - RELIGIOUS ASPECTS.**

PRE-COLUMBIAN INDIANS. *See* **INDIANS.**

PRE-EXISTENCE. *See also* **REINCARNATION.**
Bongard, Jerry. The near birth experience. New York : Marlowe & Co. ; [Emeryville, CA?] : Distributed by Publishers Group West, c2000.
BF1156.R45 B66 2000

PRE-SOCRATIC PHILOSOPHERS.
Presocratic philosophy. Aldershot, Hants, England ; Burlington, VT : Ashgate, 2002.
B187.5 .P743 2002

PRE-TEENS. *See* **PRETEENS.**

Pre-textos. Ensayo
(579) Žižek, Slavoj, 1949- [Fragile absolute. Spanish] El frágil absoluto, o, Por qué merece la pena luchar por el legado cristiano? 1. ed. Valencia : Pre-Textos, 2002.
BT1102 .Z58

PREADOLESCENTS. *See* **PRETEENS.**

PRECEPTS, SIX HUNDRED AND THIRTEEN. *See* **COMMANDMENTS, SIX HUNDRED AND THIRTEEN.**

PRECIOUS STONES. *See* **GEMS.**

PRECIOUS STONES - MISCELLANEA.
Gillotte, Galen, 1952- Sacred stones of the goddess. 1st ed. St. Paul, Minn. : Llewellyn Publications, 2003.
BF1611 .G55 2003

PRECIOUS STONES - PSYCHIC ASPECTS.
Dunwich, Gerina. Dunwich's guide to gemstone sorcery. Franklin Lakes, NJ : New Page Books, c2003.
BF1442.P74 D86 2003

Knight, Brenda, 1958- Gem magic. Gloucester, MA : Fair Winds Press, 2003.
BF1442.P74 K65 2004

Precision journalism.
Meyer, Philip. 4th ed. Lanham, Md. : Rowman & Littlefield Publishers, c2002.
PN4775 .M48 2002

PRECOLUMBIAN INDIANS. *See* **INDIANS.**

Precursors of functional literacy / edited by Ludo Verhoeven ; Carsten Elbro, Pieter Reitsma. Amsterdam ; Philadelphia : J. Benjamins Pub., c2002. vi, 359 p. : ill. ; 23 cm. (Studies in written language and literacy ; v. 11) Includes bibliographical references and index. ISBN 1-58811-228-4 (alk. paper) ISBN 90-272-1806-4 (Amsterdam : hd.bd.) DDC 302.2/244
1. Language acquisition. 2. Literacy. 3. Language awareness in children. I. Verhoeven, Ludo Th. II. Elbro, Carsten. III. Reitsma, P. (Pieter) IV. Series.
P118.7 .P74 2002

PREDESTINATION. *See* **ELECTION (THEOLOGY).**

PREDICAMENTS (CATEGORIES). *See* **CATEGORIES (PHILOSOPHY).**

PREDICATE (LOGIC). *See* **CATEGORIES (PHILOSOPHY).**

PREDICTION OF OCCUPATIONAL SUCCESS. See SUCCESS IN BUSINESS.

PREDICTIONS. See PROPHECIES.

Predictive astrology.
Rushman, Carol. The art of predictive astrology. 1st ed. St. Paul, Minn. : Llewellyn Publications, 2003, c2002.
BF1720.5 .R87 2002

PREDICTIVE ASTROLOGY.
Behari, Bepin. The timing of events. 1st ed. Delhi : Motilal Banarsidass Publishers, 2002.
BF1720.5+

Parsai, K. B. [Predictive astrology] Star guide to predictive astrology. New Delhi : Rupa & Co., c2001.
BF1720.5 .P37 2001

Rushman, Carol. The art of predictive astrology. 1st ed. St. Paul, Minn. : Llewellyn Publications, 2003, c2002.
BF1720.5 .R87 2002

PREGNANCY.
Bowers, Keri. Single pregnancy - single parenting. Pleasant Hill, CA : Park Alexander Press, c1996.
HQ759.45 .B68 1996

PREGNANT WOMEN. See MOTHERS.

Pregosin, Ann. The dogs who grew me : a tribute to the six dogs who taught me what really matters in life / Ann Pregosin. Sterling, Va. : Capital Books, c2002. xiii, 205 p. ; 24 cm. ISBN 1-89212-362-2 (alk. paper) DDC 636.7
1. Pregosin, Ann. 2. Dogs. 3. Dogs - Anecdotes. 4. Human-animal relationships. I. Title.
SF426.2 .P74 2002

PREGOSIN, ANN.
Pregosin, Ann. The dogs who grew me. Sterling, Va. : Capital Books, c2002.
SF426.2 .P74 2002

PREHISTORIC ARCHAEOLOGY. See PREHISTORIC PEOPLES.

PREHISTORIC HUMAN BEINGS. See PREHISTORIC PEOPLES.

PREHISTORIC HUMANS. See PREHISTORIC PEOPLES.

PREHISTORIC PEOPLES - SOCIAL CONDITIONS.
Mithen, Steven J. After the ice. London : Weidenfeld & Nicolson, 2003.

PREHISTORIC PEOPLES - SOCIAL LIFE AND CUSTOMS.
Mithen, Steven J. After the ice. London : Weidenfeld & Nicolson, 2003.

PREHISTORIC RELIGION. See RELIGION, PREHISTORIC.

PREHISTORY. See also PREHISTORIC PEOPLES.
Gosden, Chris, 1955- Oxford ; New York : Oxford University Press, 2003.

PREJUDGMENTS. See PREJUDICES.

PREJUDICE. See also PREJUDICES.
Davidson, Tish. New York : Franklin Watts, c2003.
BF575.P9 D38 2003

PREJUDICE - GREAT BRITAIN.
Hadikin, Ruth. The bullying culture. Oxford ; Boston : Books for Midwives, 2000.
BF637.B85 H33 2000

PREJUDICES. See also AGEISM; ANTISEMITISM; ETHNOCENTRISM; RACISM; SEXISM.
Alexander, Jeffrey C. The meanings of social life. New York : Oxford University Press, 2003.
HM585 .A5 2003

Borges, Edson. Racismo, preconceito e intolerancia. [São Paulo, Brazil] : Atual, c2002.

Brashears, Deya. Challenging biases-- facing our fears. Dubuque, Iowa : Kendall/Hunt Pub., c1999.
BF575.P9 B735 1999

Culture of prejudice. Peterborough, Ont. : Broadview Press, 2003.

Ensaios sobre a intolerância. São Paulo, SP, Brasil : Humanitas, FFLCH/USP : FAPESP : LEI-Laboratório de Estudos sobre a Intolerância, 2002.

Fishbein, Harold D. Peer prejudice and discrimination. 2nd ed. Mahwah, N.J. : L. Erlbaum, 2002.

BF723.P75 F57 2002

PREJUDICES AND ANTIPATHIES. See PREJUDICES.

PREJUDICES AND ANTIPATHIES (CHILD PSYCHOLOGY). See PREJUDICES IN CHILDREN.

PREJUDICES - BRAZIL.
Borges, Edson. Racismo, preconceito e intolerancia. [São Paulo, Brazil] : Atual, c2002.

PREJUDICES IN CHILDREN.
Fishbein, Harold D. Peer prejudice and discrimination. 2nd ed. Mahwah, N.J. : L. Erlbaum, 2002.
BF723.P75 F57 2002

PREJUDICES IN CHILDREN - PREVENTION.
Fishbein, Harold D. Peer prejudice and discrimination. 2nd ed. Mahwah, N.J. : L. Erlbaum, 2002.
BF723.P75 F57 2002

Integrating gender and culture in parenting. New York : Haworth Press, 2003.
BF723.P75 I57 2003

PREJUDICES - JUVENILE LITERATURE.
Davidson, Tish. Prejudice. New York : Franklin Watts, c2003.
BF575.P9 D38 2003

Preliminary paper (University of Delaware. Disaster Research Center)
(no. 313.) Monahan, Brian. From ground zero to ground hero. [Newark, Del.?] : Disaster Research Center, University of Delaware, 2001.

(no. 318.) Kendra, James M. Elements of community resilience in the World Trade Center attack. [Newark, Del.?] : Disaster Research Center, University of Delaware, 2001.

PRELIMINARY SKETCHES (ART). See ARTISTS' PREPARATORY STUDIES.

Premier matin.
Kaufmann, Jean-Claude. Paris : Colin, 2002.

PREMIERS. See PRIME MINISTERS.

Premoli De Marchi, Paola. Etica dell'assenso : se accettare i principi morali sia un problema della volontà / Paola Premoli De Marchi. Milano : FrancoAngeli, c2002. 312 p. ; 23 cm. (Collana di filosofia ; 76) Includes bibliographical references and indexes. ISBN 88-464-3963-5 DDC 121
1. Ethics. 2. Choice - Philosophy. I. Title. II. Series: Collana di filosofia (Milan, Italy) ; 75.

PREPARATORY STUDIES (ART). See ARTISTS' PREPARATORY STUDIES.

Prepositions in their syntactic, semantic, and pragmatic context / edited by Susanne Feigenbaum, Dennis Kurzon. Amsterdam ; Philadelphia, PA : J. Benjamins Pub., c2002. vi, 302 p. : ill. ; 23 cm. (Typological studies in language ; v. 50) Includes bibliographical references and index. ISBN 1-58811-172-5 (US hb : alk. paper) ISBN 90-272-2956-2 (Eur) DDC 415
1. Grammar, Comparative and general - Prepositions. 2. Grammar, Comparative and general - Syntax. 3. Semantics. 4. Pragmatics. I. Feigenbaum, Susanne. II. Kurzon, Dennis. III. Series.
P285 .P74 2002

PRESCHOOL READERS. See READERS.

Present pasts.
Huyssen, Andreas. Stanford, Calif. : Stanford University Press, 2003.
BD181.7 .H89 2003

PRESENTATION DRAWINGS (ART). See ARTISTS' PREPARATORY STUDIES.

PRESENTS. See GIFTS.

PRESERVATION OF HISTORICAL RECORDS. See ARCHIVES.

PRESIDENCY. See PRESIDENTS.

PRESIDENTS - UNITED STATES - BIOGRAPHY.
Abraham Lincoln's daily treasure. Grand Rapids, Mich. : F.H. Revell, c2002.
E457.2 .F787 2002

Gould, Lewis L. The modern American presidency. Lawrence : University Press of Kansas, c2003.
E176.1 .G68 2003

PRESIDENTS - UNITED STATES - HISTORY - 20TH CENTURY.
Gould, Lewis L. The modern American presidency. Lawrence : University Press of Kansas, c2003.
E176.1 .G68 2003

Presocratic philosophy : essays in honour of Alexander Mourelatos / edited by Victor Caston and Daniel W. Graham. Aldershot, Hants, England ; Burlington, VT : Ashgate, 2002. xv, 346 p. ; 25 cm. Festschrift for Alexander Mourelatos. Includes bibliographical references and indexes. CONTENTS: Thales and the stars / Stephen White -- Greek law and the presocratics / Michael Gagarin -- Heraclitus and Parmenides / Daniel W. Graham -- Parmenidean being, Heraclitean fire / Alexander Nehamas -- Parmenides and the metaphysics of changelessness / R.J. Hankinson -- Parmenides and Plato / Charles H. Kahn -- Parmenides, double-negation, and dialectic / Scott Austin -- The cosmology of mortals / Herbert Granger -- Anaxagoras, Plato and the naming of parts / David Furley -- Reading the readings : on the first person plurals in the Strasburg Empedocles / André Laks -- The metaphysics of physics : mixture and separation in Empedocles and Anaxagoras / Patricia Curd -- Democritus and Xeniades / Jacques Brunschwig -- Democritus and eudaimonism / Julia Annas -- Democritus and the explanatory power of the void / Sylvia Berryman -- Natural justice? / Paul Woodruff -- Gorgias on thought and its objects / Victor Caston -- To tell the truth : Dissoi logoi 4 and Aristotle's responses / Owen Goldin -- Archytas and the Sophists / Carl Huffman -- Aetius, Aristotle and others on coming to be and passing away / Jaap Mansfeld -- The pervasiveness of being / Paul Thom -- Three philosophers look at the stars / Sarah Broadie -- Protagoras' Great speech and Plato's defense of Athenian democracy / William Prior. ISBN 0-7546-0502-7 DDC 182
1. Philosophy, Ancient. 2. Pre-Socratic philosophers. I. Mourelatos, Alexander P. D., 1936- II. Caston, Victor Miles, 1963- III. Graham, Daniel W.
B187.5 .P743 2002

PRESS. See PUBLIC OPINION.

PRESS AND POLITICS - UNITED STATES - HISTORY - 20TH CENTURY.
Elfenbein, Stefan W., 1964- Die veränderte Rolle der New York Times. Frankfurt am Main ; New York : P. Lang, c1996.
PN4899.N42 N375 1996

PRESS LAW. See LIBEL AND SLANDER; PRIVACY, RIGHT OF.

PRESS PHOTOGRAPHY. See PHOTOJOURNALISM.

PRESS - SOCIAL ASPECTS. See JOURNALISM - SOCIAL ASPECTS.

Pressfield, Steven. The war of art : break through the blocks and win your inner creative battles / Steven Pressfield. Warner Books ed. New York : Warner Books, c2002, (2003 printing). 165 p. ; 21 cm. ISBN 0-446-69143-7 (pbk.) DDC 153.3/5
1. Creation (Literary, artistic, etc.) 2. Creative thinking. 3. Resistance (Psychoanalysis) 4. Procrastination. 5. Inhibition. 6. Pressfield, Steven. I. Title. II. Title: Break through the blocks and win your inner creative battles
BF408 .P69 2003

PRESSFIELD, STEVEN.
Pressfield, Steven. The war of art. Warner Books ed. New York : Warner Books, c2002, (2003 printing).
BF408 .P69 2003

PRESSURE GROUPS. See also SOCIAL CONTROL.
Gutmann, Amy. Identity in democracy. Princeton, N.J. : Princeton University Press, c2003.
JF529 .G886 2003

Prester, Thomas A.
Psychology of adolescents. Hauppauge, N.Y. : Nova Science, c2003.
BF724 .P783 2003

PRESTIGE. See also SOCIAL INFLUENCE.
Monahan, Brian. From ground zero to ground hero. [Newark, Del.?] : Disaster Research Center, University of Delaware, 2001.

Preston, Christopher J. Grounding knowledge : environmental philosophy, epistemology, and place / Christopher J. Preston. Athens, Ga. : University of Georgia Press, c2003. xvi, 161 p. ; 24 cm. Includes bibliographical references (p. 147-154) and index. CONTENTS: Unnatural knowledge -- Grounding knowledge -- Organisms and environments -- Active landscapes -- Making place matter -- Preserving place and mind. ISBN 0-8203-2450-7 (alk. paper) DDC 121
1. Knowledge, Theory of. 2. Environmentalism - Philosophy. I. Title.
BD161 .P746 2003

PRETEENAGERS. See PRETEENS.

PRETEENS - PSYCHOLOGY.
Scales, Peter, 1949- Coming into their own. Minneapolis, MN : Search Institute, c2004.
BF721 .S347 2004

Preventive detention and individual liberty. New Delhi : South Asia Human Rights Documentation Centre, 2000. ii, 41 p. ; 22 cm. "SAHRDC's subbmission to the National Commission for the Review of the Working of the Constitution." SUMMARY: With reference to India. Includes bibliographical references (p. 30-41). ISBN 81-87379-03-0
1. Preventive detention - India. 2. Civil rights - India. 3. Liberty. 4. Constitutional law - India. I. South Asia Human Rights Documentation Centre.
KNS4654 .P74 2000

PREVENTIVE DETENTION - INDIA.
Preventive detention and individual liberty. New Delhi : South Asia Human Rights Documentation Centre, 2000.
KNS4654 .P74 2000

Prez vremeto i prostranstvoto.
Nicheva, Nina. [Bulgaria] : Gutoranov i sin, [1998?]
BF1999 .N46 1998

Prezicerile în Câmpia Transylvaniei.
Keszeg, Vilmos. Jóslások a mezőségen. Sepsiszentgyörgy : BON AMI, 1997.
BF1868.H8 K47 1997

Preziosi, Donald, 1941- Brain of the earth's body : art, museums, and the phantasms of modernity / Donald Preziosi. Minneapolis : University of Minnesota Press, c2003. xii, 175 p. : ill. ; 23 cm. "The 2001 Slade Lectures in the Fine Arts, Oxford University." Includes bibliographical references (p. 153-164) and index. ISBN 0-8166-3357-6 ISBN 0-8166-3358-4 (pbk.) DDC 700/.1
1. Art - Historiography. 2. Aesthetics. 3. Art museums - Philosophy. I. Title. II. Title: Art, museums, and the phantasms of modernity
N380 .P67 2003

Price, David, 1961- Love and hate in Jamestown : John Smith, Pocahontas, and the heart of a new nation / David A. Price. 1st ed. New York : Alfred A. Knopf : Distributed by Random House, 2003. 305 p. : maps ; 25 cm. Includes bibliographical references (p. 283-290) and index. ISBN 0-375-41541-6 DDC 975.5/425101
1. Smith, John, - 1580-1531. 2. Pocahontas, - d. 1617. 3. Jamestown (Va.) - History. 4. Indians of North America - First contact with Europeans - Virginia - Jamestown. 5. Jamestown (Va.) - Biography. 6. Powhatan Indians - Virginia - Jamestown - History - 17th century. 7. Virginia - History - Colonial period, ca. 1600-1775. I. Title.
F234.J3 P68 2003

Prichard, H. A. (Harold Arthur), 1871-1947. Moral writings / H.A. Prichard ; edited by Jim MacAdam. Oxford : Clarendon Press ; New York : Oxford University Press, 2002. xx, 298 p. ; 24 cm. (British moral philosophers ; no. 3) Includes bibliographical references (p. 288-293) and index. ISBN 0-19-925018-9 ISBN 0-19-925019-7 (pbk.)
1. Ethics. I. MacAdam, Jim. II. Title. III. Series.

PRICING.
McAfee, R. Preston. Competitive solutions. Princeton, N.J. : Princeton University Press, c2002.
HD30.28 .M3815 2002

PRIESTHOOD. *See* **PRIESTS.**

PRIESTS - BIOGRAPHY.
Karade, Akinkugbe. Path to priesthood. Brooklyn, N.Y. : Kânda Mukûtu Books, c2001.
BL2523.I33 K37 2001
1. Black author.

PRIESTS, BUDDHIST. *See* **LAMAS.**

Prima degli etruschi.
Feo, Giovanni. Roma : Stampa alternativa, 2001.
BL813.E8 F46 2001

Primary sources in psychology / [edited by] Spencer A. Rathus. Orlando, FL : Harcourt, c2000. xii, 415 p. : ill. ; 28 cm. Includes bibliographical references. ISBN 0-15-507461-X DDC 150
1. Psychology - Textbooks. I. Rathus, Spencer A.
BF121 .P69 2000

Primate psychology / edited by Dario Maestripieri. Cambridge, MA : Harvard University Press, 2003. p. cm. Includes bibliographical references and index. ISBN 0-674-01152-X DDC 156
1. Psychology, Comparative. I. Maestripieri, Dario.
BF671 .P75 2003

PRIMATES. *See* **APES.**

PRIME MINISTERS - GREAT BRITAIN - BIOGRAPHY.
Sandys, Celia. We shall not fail. New York : Portfolio ; London : Penguin Books, 2003.
DA566.9.C5 S266 2003

Primitive Features Inc.
McLuhan's wake [videorecording]. [Montreal, Quebec] : Primitive Entertainment/National Film Board of Canada, c2002.

PRIMITIVE GAMES. *See* **GAMES.**

PRIMITIVE MEDICINE. *See* **TRADITIONAL MEDICINE.**

PRIMITIVE SOCIETIES.
Pulman, Bertrand. Anthropologie et psychanalyse. Paris : Presses universitaires de France, 2002.
GN502 .P85 2002

PRIMITIVE SOCIETIES - HISTORY.
Mithen, Steven J. After the ice. London : Weidenfeld & Nicolson, 2003.

PRIMITIVE SOCIETY. *See* **PRIMITIVE SOCIETIES.**

PRINCES.
Callières, Monsieur de (François), 1645-1717. De la manière de négocier avec les souverains. Genève : Droz, c2002.

PRINCESSES - FRANCE - CORRESPONDENCE.
Montpensier, Anne-Marie-Louise d'Orléans, duchesse de, 1627-1693. [Correspondence. English & French] Against marriage. Chicago : University of Chicago Press, 2002.
DC130.M8 A4 2002

Principle of hope.
Takahashi, Keiko, 1956- Kibō no genri = Tōkyō : Sanpō Shuppan, 1997.
BD216 .T35 1997

Principles of behavior.
Malott, Richard W. 5th ed. Upper Saddle River, N.J. : Pearson/Prentice Hall, 2003.
BF319.5.O6 M34 2003

Prinstein, Mitchell J., 1970-.
Internships in psychology. Washington, D.C. : American Psychological Association, c2004.
BF77 .I67 2004

Printed commonplace-books and the structuring of Renaissance thought.
Moss, Ann, 1938- Oxford : Clarendon Press ; New York : Oxford University Press, 1996.
PA2047 .M67 1996

PRINTING - HISTORY.
Tagle Frías de Cuenca, Matilde. Notas sobre historia del libro. Córdoba, República Argentina : Ediciones del Copista, c1997.
Z4

PRINTING, PRACTICAL. *See* **PRINTING.**

Prinz, Wolfgang, 1942-.
Voluntary action. Oxford ; New York : Oxford University Press, 2003.
BF621 .V658 2003

Priroda khudozhestvennogo talanta.
Drankov, V. L. (Vladimir L'vovich) Sankt-Peterburg : Sankt-Peterburgskiĭ gos. universitet kul'tury i iskusstv, 2001.
BF408 .D66 2001

Drankov, V. L. (Vladimir L'vovich) Sankt-Peterburg : Sankt-Peterburgskiĭ gosudarstvennyĭ universitet kul'tury i iskusstv, 2001.

PRISON INDUSTRIES - LAW AND LEGISLATION - UNITED STATES.
United States. Congress. House. Committee on the Judiciary. Federal Prison Industries Competition in Contracting Act of 2003. [Washington, D.C. : U.S. G.P.O., 2003]

PRISONERS. *See* **DEATH ROW INMATES; POLITICAL PRISONERS.**

PRISONERS OF CONSCIENCE. *See* **POLITICAL PRISONERS.**

PRIVACY.
Cladis, Mark Sydney. Public vision, private lives. Oxford ; New York : Oxford University Press, 2003.
JC179.R9 C53 2003

Petronio, Sandra Sporbert. Boundaries of privacy. Albany : State University of New York Press, c2002.
BF697.5.S427 P48 2002

Privacy and disclosure of HIV in interpersonal relationships. Mahwah, N.J. : Lawrence Erlbaum Associates, 2003.
RA643.8 .P755 2003

Privacy [electronic resource]. [Washington, D.C.] : Federal Trade Commission, Bureau of Consumer Protection, Office of Consumer and Business Education, [2002]

Privacy [electronic resource]. [Washington, D.C.] : Federal Trade Commission, Bureau of Consumer Protection, Office of Consumer and Business Education, [2002]

Privacy [electronic resource]. [Washington, D.C.] : Federal Trade Commission, Bureau of Consumer Protection, Office of Consumer and Business Education, [2002]

Rössler, Beate. Der Wert des Privaten. 1. Aufl. Frankfurt am Main : Suhrkamp, 2001.

Privacy and disclosure of HIV in interpersonal relationships : a sourcebook for researchers and practitioners / Kathryn Greene ... [et al.]. Mahwah, N.J. : Lawrence Erlbaum Associates, 2003. xv, 265 p. : ill. ; 24 cm. (LEA's communication series) Includes bibliographical references (p. 225-249) and indexes. Table of contents URL: http://www.loc.gov/catdir/toc/fy038/2002192838.html ISBN 0-8058-3694-2 (alk. paper) ISBN 0-8058-3695-0 (pbk. : alk. paper) DDC 362.1/969792
1. AIDS (Disease) - Reporting. 2. Privacy. 3. HIV-positive persons. 4. AIDS (Disease) - Social aspects. I. Greene, Kathryn. II. Series.
RA643.8 .P755 2003

Privacy [electronic resource] : tips for protecting your personal information. [Washington, D.C.] : Federal Trade Commission, Bureau of Consumer Protection, Office of Consumer and Business Education, [2002] (FTC consumer alert) Mode of access: Internet from the FTC web site. Address as of 11/22/03: http://www.ftc.gov/bcp/conline/pubs/alerts/privtipsalrt.pdf; current access is available via PURL. Title from title screen (viewed on Nov. 22, 2003). "January 2002." URL: http://purl.access.gpo.gov/GPO/LPS40369 DDC 929.9 DDC 070.5797 DDC 011.53 DDC 640.73 DDC 323.448
1. False personation - United States - Prevention. 2. Privacy, Right of - United States. 3. Identification numbers, Personal - United States. 4. Consumer protection - United States. 5. Identification numbers, Personal. 6. Electronic publications. 7. Government publications. 8. Consumer education. 9. Privacy. I. United States. Federal Trade Commission. Office of Consumer and Business Education. II. Title: Tips for protecting your personal information III. Series.

Privacy [electronic resource] : tips for protecting your personal information. [Washington, D.C.] : Federal Trade Commission, Bureau of Consumer Protection, Office of Consumer and Business Education, [2002] (FTC consumer alert) World Wide Web Resource. System requirements: Adobe Acrobat Reader. Mode of access: Internet from the FTC web site. Address as of 4/3/03: http://www.ftc.gov/bcp/conline/pubs/alerts/privtipsalrt.pdf; current access is available via PURL. Title from title screen (viewed on Apr. 3, 2003). SUMMARY: The U.S. Federal Trade Commission (FTC) Bureau of Consumer Protection presents the January 2002 consumer alert "Privacy: Tips for Protecting Your Personal Information" in PDF format. The alert offers suggestions for helping consumers manage their personal information and minimize its misuse. URL: http://purl.access.gpo.gov/GPO/LPS29266 DDC 929.9 DDC 070.5797 DDC 011.53 DDC 640.73 DDC 323.448
1. United States. Federal Trade Commission. Bureau of Consumer Protection. 2. Identification numbers, Personal - United States. 3. Privacy, Right of - United States. 4. Data protection - United States. 5. False personation - United States - Prevention. 6. Identification numbers, Personal. 7. Electronic publications. 8. Government publications. 9. Consumer education. 10. Privacy. I. United States. Federal Trade Commission. Office of Consumer and Business Education. II. Series.

Privacy [electronic resource] : what you do know can protect you. [Washington, D.C.] : Federal Trade Commission, Bureau of Consumer Protection, Office of Consumer and Business Education, [2002] (FTC consumer alert) World Wide Web Resource. System requirements: Adobe Acrobat Reader. Mode of access: Internet from the FTC web site. Address as of 12/13/02: http://www.ftc.gov/bcp/conline/pubs/alerts/privprotalrt.pdf; current access is available via PURL. Title from title screen (viewed on Dec. 13, 2002). SUMMARY: The U.S. Federal Trade Commission (FTC) Bureau of Consumer Protection presents the January 2002 consumer alert "Privacy: What You Do Know Can Protect You" in PDF format. The alert offers contact information for agencies that can help consumers protect their personal information. The office provides this information for credit bureaus, state departments of motor vehicles, direct marketers, and others. URL: http://purl.access.gpo.gov/GPO/LPS24982 DDC 929.9 DDC 070.5797 DDC 011.53 DDC 640.73 DDC 323.448
1. United States. Federal Trade Commission. Bureau of Consumer Protection. 2. Consumers - Information services - Access control - United States. 3. Infomediaries - United States. 4. Identification numbers, Personal. 5. Electronic

publications. 6. Government publications. 7. Consumer education. 8. Privacy. I. United States. Federal Trade Commission. Office of Consumer and Business Education. II. Series.

PRIVACY, RIGHT OF.
Rössler, Beate. Der Wert des Privaten. 1. Aufl. Frankfurt am Main : Suhrkamp, 2001.

PRIVACY, RIGHT OF - UNITED STATES.
Privacy [electronic resource]. [Washington, D.C.] : Federal Trade Commission, Bureau of Consumer Protection, Office of Consumer and Business Education, [2002]

Privacy [electronic resource]. [Washington, D.C.] : Federal Trade Commission, Bureau of Consumer Protection, Office of Consumer and Business Education, [2002]

PRIVATE ENTERPRISE. See **FREE ENTERPRISE.**

PRIVATE REVELATIONS.
Adam, of Eynsham, fl. 1196-1232. [Visio Monachi de Eynsham. English (Middle English) & Latin] The revelation of the Monk of Eynsham. Oxford : Published for the Early English Text Society by the Oxford University Press, 2002.

Buxani, Shyam D. Salam. 1st ed. New York : SAU Salam Foundation, c2003.

Callahan, Sidney Cornelia. Women who hear voices. New York : Paulist Press, 2003.
BV5091.R4 C35 2003

Johnson, Deborah L., 1956- Letters from the Infinite. Aptos, CA : New Brighton Books, c2002-
BF1301 .J575 2002
1. Black author.

Sartorio, Ugo. Credere in dialogo. Padova : Edizioni Messaggero, 2002.

Privileged access : philosophical accounts of self-knowledge / edited by Brie Gertler. Aldershot ; Burlington, VT : Ashgate, c2003. xxii, 266 p ; 24 cm. (Ashgate epistemology and mind series) Includes bibliographical references and index. ISBN 0-7546-1647-9 (hbk.) ISBN 0-7546-1648-7 (pbk.) DDC 126
1. Self (Philosophy) 2. Self-knowledge, Theory of. I. Gertler, Brie. II. Title: Philosophical accounts of self-knowledge III. Series.

El privilegio de ser latinoamericano.
Wagner de Reyna, Alberto. 1. ed. Córdoba, Argentina : Editorial Alejandro Korn, c2002.
F1408.3 .W35 2002

"Pro exoneratione sua propria coscientia".
Ferraiuolo, Augusto. Milano : F. Angeli, c2000.
BF1584.I8 F44 2000

Pro Oriente (Frankfurt am Main, Germany)
(Bd. 1.) 'Gottes auserwählte Völker'. Frankfurt am Main ; New York : Lang, c2001.
BT810.2 .G65 2001

PROBABILITIES.
The philosophy of Keynes' economics. London ; New York : Routledge, 2003.
HB99.7 .P45 2003

Vernes, Jean-René. The existence of the external world. Ottawa : University of Ottawa Press, c2000.

Vind, Karl. Independence, additivity, uncertainty. Berlin ; New York : Springer, c2003.
HB135 .V56 2003

PROBATE LAW AND PRACTICE. See **EXECUTORS AND ADMINISTRATORS.**

PROBLEM CHILDREN - EDUCATION. See **TEACHERS OF PROBLEM CHILDREN.**

PROBLEM CHILDREN - EDUCATION - UNITED STATES.
Lampert, Khen. Compassionate education. Lanham, Md. : University Press of America, c2003.

PROBLEM CHILDREN, TEACHERS OF. See **TEACHERS OF PROBLEM CHILDREN.**

Das Problem des historischen Bewusstseins.
Gadamer, Hans Georg, 1900- [Problème de la conscience historique. German] Tübingen : Mohr Siebeck, 2001.

PROBLEM DRINKERS. See **ALCOHOLICS.**

The problem of existence.
Witherall, Arthur, 1966- Aldershot, England ; Brookfield, VT : Ashgate, c2002.
BD331 .W58 2002

The problem of love in the Middle Ages.
Rousselot, Pierre, 1878-1915. [Pour l'histoire du problème de l'amour au moyen âge. English] Milwaukee : Marquette University Press, [2001?]
B738.L68 R68 2001

PROBLEM SOLVING. See also **CONFLICT MANAGEMENT; INSIGHT.**
Eppler, Mark, 1946- The Wright way. New York : AMACOM, c2004.
TL540.W7 E64 2004

Gordon, Barry, M.D. Intelligent memory. New York : Viking, 2003.
BF371 .G66 2003

Koberg, Don, 1930- The universal traveler. 4th ed. Menlo Park, Calif. : Crisp Learning, c2003.
BF441 .K55 2003

Miller, John G., 1958- QBQ!. Denver, CO : Denver Press, c2001.
BF611 .M55 2001

Taylor, Scott L., 1964- The opportunity in every problem. 1st ed. Salt Lake City : Gibbs Smith, c2003.
BF637.S8 T285 2003

PROBLEM SOLVING - GRAPHIC METHODS.
Hugl, Ulrike. Qualitative Inhaltsanalyse und Mind-Mapping. Wiesbaden : Gabler, 1995.

PROBLEM SOLVING IN CHILDREN.
Garton, Alison, 1950- Exploring cognitive development. 1st ed. Oxford, UK ; Malden, MA : Blackwell Pub., 2004.
BF723.P8 G37 2004

PROBLEM SOLVING - METHODOLOGY.
Rantanen, Kalevi. Simplified TRIZ. Boca Raton : St. Lucie Press, c2002.
TA153 .R26 2002

PROBLEM SOLVING - MISCELLANEA.
Maisel, Eric, 1947- Sleep thinking. Holbrook, Mass. : Adams Media Corp., c2000.
BF1099.P75 M35 2000

The problem with the past.
Adediran, A. A. Ile-Ife, Nigeria : Obafemi Awolowo University Press, c2002.

Problema soznaniia v psikhologii.
Akopov, G. V. Samara : Samarskiĭ gos. pedagog. universitet, 2002.
BF311 .A44 2002

Problème de la passivité, le sommeil, l'inconscient, la mémoire.
Merleau-Ponty, Maurice, 1908-1961. L'institution dans l'histoire personnelle et publique ; [Paris] : Belin, c2003.
B2430.M3763 I88 2003

Probleme der Semiotik
(Bd. 20.) Schmauks, Dagmar. Orientierung im Raum. Tübingen : Stauffenburg, c2002.
QP443 .S363 2002

Problemy interpretatsionnoĭ lingvistiki : avtor, tekst, adresat : sbornik nauchnykh trudov / pod redaktsieĭ T.A. Tripol'skoĭ. Novosibirsk : Novosibirskiĭ gos. pedagog. universitet, 2001. 166 p. ; 20 cm. ISBN 5859212526
1. Explanation (Linguistics) 2. Discourse analysis - Psychological aspects. 3. Semantics. 4. Pragmatics. I. Tripol'skaia, T. A. II. Novosibirskiĭ gosudarstvennyĭ pedagogicheskiĭ universitet.
P128.E95 P762 2001

Problemy obshcheĭ akmeologii / pod redaktsieĭ A.A. Reana. S.-Peterburg : Izd-vo Sankt-Peterburgskogo universiteta, 2000. 154, [1] p. : ill. ; 20 cm. Includes bibliographical references (p. 147-[155]). ISBN 528801826X
1. Adulthood - Psychological aspects. I. Rean, A. A.
BF724.5 .P76 2000

Problemy psikhologii razvitiia.
Mezhdunarodnaia psikhologicheskaia konferentsiia "Psikhicheskoe razvitie v ontogeneze-- zakonomernosti i vozmozhnye periodizatsii" (1999 : Moscow, Russia) Moskva : RGGU, 2000.
BF712.5 .M49 2000

Proceedings of the inaugural session Emmanuel Onyechere Osigwe Anyiam-Osigwe Memorial Lecture Series, 1999.
The search for a holistic approach to human existence and development. [Nigeria?] : Osigwe Anyiam-Osigwe Foundation, [1999?]
B53 .E46 1999

Proceedings of the International Conference on Simulation and Multimedia in Engineering Education & Virtual Worlds and Simulation.
International Conference on Simulation in Engineering Education (2001 : Phoenix, Ariz.) San Diego, CA : Society for Computer Simulation International, c2001.

Proceedings of the International Conference on Virtual Worlds and Simulation.
International Conference on Simulation in Engineering Education (2001 : Phoenix, Ariz.) Proceedings of the International Conference on Simulation and Multimedia in Engineering Education & Virtual Worlds and Simulation. San Diego, CA : Society for Computer Simulation International, c2001.

Proceedings volume in the Santa Fe Institute studies in the sciences of complexity.
Evolutionary dynamics. Oxford ; New York : Oxford University Press, 2003.
QH366.2 .E867 2003

PROCESS CONTROL.
Process management. Springer-verlag, Berlin, Heidelberg ; New York : Springer, c2003.
HD31 .P756 2003

Process management : a guide for the design of business processes / Jörg Becker, Martin Kugler, Michael Rosemann, editors. Springer-verlag, Berlin, Heidelberg ; New York : Springer, c2003. xv, 337 p. : ill. ; 24 cm. Includes bibliographical references (p. [311]-319) and index. ISBN 3-540-43499-2 (alk. paper) DDC 658.5
1. Industrial management. 2. Information resources management. 3. Industrial engineering. 4. Process control. 5. Management. I. Becker, Jörg, 1959- II. Kugeler, Martin, 1971- III. Rosemann, Michael, 1967-
HD31 .P756 2003

PROCESS PHILOSOPHY. See also **BECOMING (PHILOSOPHY).**
Christ, Carol P. She who changes. 1st ed. New York ; Houndmills, England : Palgrave Macmillan, 2003.
BD372 .C48 2003

PROCESSIONS. See **FESTIVALS; PAGEANTS.**

Processos de gramaticalização de preposições do Latim ao Português.
Poggio, Rosauta Maria Galvão Fagundes. Salvador : EDUFBA, 2002.

PROCRASTINATION.
Davidson, Jeffrey P. The 60 second procrastinator. Avon, MA : Adams Media Corp., c2003.
BF637.P76 D38 2003

Knaus, William J. The procrastination workbook. Oakland, Calif. : New Harbinger, 2002.
BF637.P76 K55 2002

Pressfield, Steven. The war of art. Warner Books ed. New York : Warner Books, c2002, (2003 printing).
BF408 .P69 2003

PROCRASTINATION - PROBLEMS, EXERCISES, ETC.
Knaus, William J. The procrastination workbook. Oakland, Calif. : New Harbinger, 2002.
BF637.P76 K55 2002

The procrastination workbook.
Knaus, William J. Oakland, Calif. : New Harbinger, 2002.
BF637.P76 K55 2002

Proctor, Robert W.
Johnson, Addie. Attention. Thousand Oaks, Calif. : Sage Publications, c2004.
BF321 .J56 2004

Proctor, Russell F.
Adler, Ronald B. (Ronald Brian), 1946- Interplay. New York : Oxford University Press, 2004. 9th ed.
BF637.C45 A33 2004

PROCUREMENT, GOVERNMENT. See **GOVERNMENT PURCHASING.**

PRODIGIES (OMENS). See **OMENS.**

PRODIGIES (PERSONS). See **GIFTED PERSONS.**

PRODUCT DEVELOPMENT. See **NEW PRODUCTS.**

PRODUCT MANAGEMENT. See **NEW PRODUCTS.**

PRODUCTION (ECONOMIC THEORY).
Read, Jason. The micro-politics of capital. Albany : State University of New York Press, c2003.
HB97.5 .R42 2003

PRODUCTION ECONOMICS, AGRICULTURAL.
See **AGRICULTURE - ECONOMIC ASPECTS.**

Production methods : behind the scenes of virtual inhabited 3D worlds / Kim Halskov Madsen (ed.). London ; New York : Springer, c2003. viii, 271 p. : ill. ; 24 cm. + 1 CD-ROM (4 3/4 in.). Includes bibliographical references and index. Table of contents URL: http://www.loc.gov/catdir/toc/fy033/2002070459.html ISBN 1-85233-612-9 (alk. paper) DDC 006.7
  1. Interactive multimedia. 2. Virtual reality. I. Madsen, Kim Halskov, 1956-
  QA76.76.I59 P76 2003

PRODUCTS, NEW. *See* **NEW PRODUCTS.**

Proektivnye metody.
  Burlakova, N. S. Moskva : In-t obshchegumanitarnykh issledovaniĭ, 2001.
  BF698.7 .B87 2001

Professional communication.
  Plung, Daniel L. Mason, Ohio : Thomson/South-Western, c2004.
  HF5718 .P58 2004

Professional concerns arising from twenty years of counselling practice in Nigeria / editors, Ibrahim A. Kolo, Festus D Kolo, and Adeyemi I. Idowu ; with forward [i.e. foreword] by P.F.C. Carew. Garki, Abuja, Nigeria : Official Printers, Jayawahs Communications, 1996. iv, 283 p. ; 21 cm. Spine title: Professional concerns from counselling practice in Nigeria. "A book of the Counselling Association of Nigeria (CASSON) 1996". "Series 2"--Cover. Includes bibliographical references.
  1. Counseling - Nigeria. I. Kolo, Ibrahim A. II. Kolo, Festus D. III. Idowu, Adeyemi I. IV. Counselling Association of Nigeria. V. Title: Professional concerns from counselling practice in Nigeria
  BF637.C6 P775 1996

Professional concerns from counselling practice in Nigeria.
  Professional concerns arising from twenty years of counselling practice in Nigeria. Garki, Abuja, Nigeria : Official Printers, Jayawahs Communications, 1996.
  BF637.C6 P775 1996

The professional counselor.
  Engels, Dennis W. 3d ed. / Dennis W. Engels and associates. Alexandria, VA : American Counseling Association, c2004.
  BF637.C6 P78 2004

Professional counselor.
  Engels, Dennis W. The professional counselor. 3d ed. / Dennis W. Engels and associates. Alexandria, VA : American Counseling Association, c2004.
  BF637.C6 P78 2004

PROFESSIONAL EMPLOYEES. *See* **BUSINESSPEOPLE.**

PROFESSIONAL EMPLOYEES IN GOVERNMENT. *See* **GOVERNMENT INVESTIGATORS.**

PROFESSIONAL EMPLOYEES - PSYCHOLOGY.
  Mironova, T. L. (Tat'ĭana L'vovna) Samosoznanie professionala. Ulan-Udė: Izd-vo Burĭatskogo gosuniversiteta, 1999.
  BF697.5.S43 M57 1999

PROFESSIONAL ETHICS. *See also* **MEDICAL ETHICS.**
  Celli, Pier Luigi. Breviario di cinismo ben temperato. 1. ed. Roma : Fazi, 2002.

PROFESSIONAL SERVICES. *See* **PROFESSIONS.**

Professional skills for counsellors
  Anti-discriminatory counselling practice. London ; Thousand Oaks, Calif. : SAGE Publications, 2003.
  BF637.C6 A49 2003

Professional tarot.
  Jette, Christine, 1953- 1st ed. St. Paul, Minn. : Llewellyn Publications, 2003.
  BF1879.T2 J475 2003

PROFESSIONALS. *See* **PROFESSIONAL EMPLOYEES.**

The professional's guide to mining the Internet.
  Clegg, Brian. 2nd ed. London : Kogan Page ; Sterling, VA : Stylus Pub., 2001.
  ZA4230 .C56 2001

PROFESSIONS. *See* **WOMEN IN THE PROFESSIONS.**

PROFESSIONS - FRANCE - SOCIOLOGICAL ASPECTS.
  Osty, Florence. Le désir de métier. Rennes [France] : Presses universitaires de Rennes, [2003]

Profiles of the 16 personality types.
  Jeffries, William C. Noblesville, IN : Buttermilk Ridge Pub. ; Zionsville, Ind. : Distributed by Executive Strategies International, c2002.
  BF698.8.M94 J43 2002

Profiles of the sixteen personality types.
  Jeffries, William C. Profiles of the 16 personality types. Noblesville, IN : Buttermilk Ridge Pub. ; Zionsville, Ind. : Distributed by Executive Strategies International, c2002.
  BF698.8.M94 J43 2002

Profiles, probabilities, and stereotypes.
  Schauer, Frederick F. Cambridge, Mass. : Belknap Press of Harvard University Press, 2003.
  HM1096 .S34 2003

Profilo del pensiero medievale.
  Fumagalli Beonio Brocchieri, Mariateresa, 1933- 1. ed. Roma : Laterza, 2002.

PROFIT. *See* **CAPITALISM.**

PROGRAMMING (ELECTRONIC COMPUTERS). *See* **COMPUTER SOFTWARE.**

PROGRAMMING LANGUAGES (ELECTRONIC COMPUTERS). *See* **PERL (COMPUTER PROGRAM LANGUAGE).**

PROGRAMS, TWELVE-STEP. *See* **TWELVE-STEP PROGRAMS.**

Progrès, réaction, décadence dans l'Occident médiéval / 'etudes recueillies par Emmanuèle Baumgartner et Laurence Harf-Lancner. Genève : Droz, 2003. 274 p. ; 23 cm. (Publications romanes et françaises, 0079-7812 ; 231) Includes bibliographical references and index. ISBN 2-600-00831-4 (pbk.) DDC 940
  1. Literature, Medieval - History and criticism. 2. Progress in literature. 3. Philosophy, Medieval. 4. History - Philosophy. I. Baumgartner, Emmanuèle. II. Harf-Lancner, Laurence. III. Series.
  PN681 .P764 2003

PROGRESS - FORECASTING.
  Riding the next wave. Indianapolis, Ind. : Hudson Institute ; [Washington, DC : Distributed by the Brookings Institution Press], c2001.
  HM901 .R43 2001

PROGRESS IN LITERATURE.
  Progrès, réaction, décadence dans l'Occident médiéval. Genève : Droz, 2003.
  PN681 .P764 2003

Progressive witchcraft.
  Farrar, Janet. Franklin Lakes, NJ : New Page Books, 2004.
  BF1571 .F346 2004

PROHIBITED EXPORTS AND IMPORTS. *See* **FOREIGN TRADE REGULATION.**

Proja, Giovanni Battista. Uomini, diavoli, esorcismi : la verità sul mondo dell'occulto / Giovanni Battista Proja. Roma : Città nuova, 2002. 172 p. : ill. (some col.) ; 20 cm. Includes appendices (p. 125-167) and notes. ISBN 88-311-3973-8 DDC 133
  1. Occultism - Religious aspects - Christianity. 2. Exorcism. 3. Demonology - Catholic Church. 4. Demonology in the Bible. I. Title.

Project management.
  Moore, David (David R.) Oxford, [Eng.] ; Malden, MA : Blackwell Science, c2002.

PROJECT MANAGEMENT.
  Kliem, Ralph L. The organizational engineering approach to project management. Boca Raton : St. Lucie Press, c2003.
  HD66 .K585 2003

  Moore, David (David R.) Project management. Oxford, [Eng.] ; Malden, MA : Blackwell Science, c2002.

Project Muse.
  [Journal for the psychoanalysis of culture & society (Online)] Journal for the psychoanalysis of culture and society [electronic resource]. Columbus, Ohio : Ohio State University Press
  BF175.4.C84

Project of History of Indian Science, Philosophy, and Culture.
  Krishna, Daya. Developments in Indian philosophy from Eighteenth century onwards. New Delhi : Project of History of Indian Science, Philosophy, and Culture : Centre for Studies in Civilizations : Distributed by Motilal Banarsidass, 2002.
  B131+

PROJECTION. *See* **PERSPECTIVE.**

PROJECTION, SUBLIMINAL. *See* **SUBLIMINAL PROJECTION.**

PROJECTIVE TECHNIQUES.
  Burlakova, N. S. Proektivnye metody. Moskva : In-t obshchegumanitarnykh issledovaniĭ, 2001.
  BF698.7 .B87 2001

Prokofieff, Sergei O., 1954-.
  Die Grundsteinmeditation als Schulungsweg. Dornach : Verlag am Goetheanum, c2002.

Prolegomena to charity.
  Marion, Jean-Luc, 1946- [Prolégomènes à la charité. English] 1st ed. New York : Fordham University Press, 2002.
  BD436 .M3313 2002

Promenade
  Schulz, Walter, 1912- Prüfendes Denken. Tübingen : Klöpfer & Meyer, c2002.

Promise and peril : the paradox of religion as resource and threat / edited by Anna Lännström. Notre Dame, Ind. : University of Notre Dame Press, c2003. xv, 128 p. ; 24 cm. (Boston University studies in philosophy and religion ; v. 24) Includes bibliographical references and indexes. CONTENTS: What is fundamentalism? / Karen Armstrong -- Jewish Islamic negotiations in Israel and Palestine : a participant observer's critical analysis / Marc Gopin -- Nuclearization in the South Asian region : interactions between Pakistan and India / Gerald James Larson -- State-religion partnership : boon or curse? / Bhikhu Parekh -- Awe as promise and peril : the entheogenic evidence / Huston Smith -- Killing for salvation : Aum Shinrikyō and the perils of religion / Ian Reader -- Moral paradoxes in Hinduism / Wendy Doniger. ISBN 0-268-03825-2 (cloth : alk. paper) DDC 291.1/78
  1. Religion. 2. Violence - Religious aspects. I. Lännström, Anna. II. Series.
  BL50 .P65 2003

Promising practies in the field of caregiving
  [electronic resource]. [Washington, D.C.] : U.S. Dept. of Health and Human Services, Administration on Aging, [2003?] System requirements: Adobe Acrobat Reader. Mode of access: Internet from the AOA web site. Address as of 10/15/03: http://www.aoa.gov/prof/aoaprog/caregiver/carepmf/nfcsp%5Fprojects/PromisingPractices.pdf; current access is available via PURL. Title from title screen (viewed on Oct. 15, 2003). URL: http://purl.access.gpo.gov/GPO/LPS37515
  1. Aged - Care. 2. Caregivers. 3. Medical personnel-caregiver relationships. I. United States. Administration on Aging.

Promoting peace : the role of civilian conflict resolution / Günther Baechler, ed. Berne, Switzerland : Staempfli, 2002. 150 p. : ill. ; 23 cm. Includes bibliographical references. ISBN 3-7272-9033-1
  1. Pacific settlement of international disputes. 2. Mediation, International. 3. Conflict management. I. Baechler, Günther.

PROPAGANDA. *See* **ADVERTISING; PERSUASION (PSYCHOLOGY); PUBLIC OPINION.**

PROPAGANDA, ARAB - HISTORY - 20TH CENTURY.
  Rowland, Robert C., 1954- Shared land/conflicting identity. East lansing : Michigan State University Press, 2002.
  DS119.7 .R685 2003

PROPAGANDA, ARABIC. *See* **PROPAGANDA, ARAB.**

PROPAGANDA, ZIONIST - HISTORY - 20TH CENTURY.
  Rowland, Robert C., 1954- Shared land/conflicting identity. East lansing : Michigan State University Press, 2002.
  DS119.7 .R685 2003

PROPERTY. *See also* **CULTURAL PROPERTY.**
  Anderson, Terry Lee, 1946- Property rights. Stanford, Calif. : Hoover Institution Press, c2003.
  HB701 .A44 2003

PROPERTY, LITERARY. *See* **COPYRIGHT.**

Property rights.
  Anderson, Terry Lee, 1946- Stanford, Calif. : Hoover Institution Press, c2003.
  HB701 .A44 2003

PROPERTY - SEX DIFFERENCES.
  Gender perspectives on property and inheritance. Oxford : Oxfam, c2001.
  HB715 .G45 2001

PROPHECIES.
  Expecting Armageddon. New York : Routledge, 2000.

BL503 .E97 2000

PROPHECIES - CONGRESSES.
Colloque de Strasbourg (14th : 1995) Oracles et prophéties dans l'Antiquité. Strasbourg : Publications de l'Université de Strasbourg II, 1997.
BF1761 .C65 1995

PROPHECIES (OCCULT SCIENCES). *See* **PROPHECIES (OCCULTISM).**

PROPHECIES (OCCULTISM).
Free, Wynn, 1946- The reincarnation of Edgar Cayce? Berkeley, Calif. : Frog, 2004.
BF1815.W49 F74 2004

Tolsdorf, Samuel, 1926- The theory of reality. Vancouver, B.C. : Leumas Publications, [1998]
BF1999 .T62 1998

Van Auken, John. The end times. New York : Signet Book, c2001. [Updated ed.].
BF1791 .V36 2001

Welch, R. W., 1929- Comet of Nostradamus. 1st ed. St. Paul, Minn. : Llewellyn Publications, 2000 (2001 printing)
BF1815.N8 A269 2000

Wilson, Ian, 1941- Nostradamus. 1st U.S. ed. New York : St. Martin's Press, 2003.
BF1815.N8 W56 2003

PROPHECIES (OCCULTISM) - FRANCE - HENDAYE - HISTORY - 17TH CENTURY.
Weidner, Jay. The mysteries of the great cross of Hendaye. Rochester, Vt. : Destiny Books, 2003.
BF1999 .W435 2003

PROPHECIES (OCCULTISM) - HISTORY.
Konstantinovskai͡a, L. V. (Li͡udmila Vasil'evna) Kogda prikhodi͡at proroki. Moskva : Klassiks Stil', 2002.
BF1796 .K66 2002

PROPHECIES (OCCULTISM) - MEXICO.
Polich, Judith Bluestone, 1948- Return of the children of light. Santa Fe, N.M. : Linkage Publications, c1999.
BF1812.P4 P65 1999

PROPHECIES (OCCULTISM) - PERU.
Polich, Judith Bluestone, 1948- Return of the children of light. Santa Fe, N.M. : Linkage Publications, c1999.
BF1812.P4 P65 1999

PROPHECY.
Brenneman, James E., 1954- Canons in conflict. New York : Oxford University Press, 1997.
BS465 .B74 1997

Keszeg, Vilmos. Jóslások a mezőségen. Sepsiszentgyörgy : BON AMI, 1997.
BF1868.H8 K47 1997

Mould, Tom, 1969- Choctaw prophecy. Tuscaloosa : University of Alabama Press, c2003.
E99.C8 M68 2003

PROPHECY - HISTORY.
Nissinen, Martti. Prophets and prophecy in the ancient Near East. Atlanta, GA : Society of Biblical Literature, c2003.
BF1762 .N58 2003b

Nissinen, Martti. Prophets and prophecy in the ancient Near East. Leiden ; Boston : Brill, 2003.
BF1762 .N58 2003

PROPHECY IN LITERATURE.
Wickham-Crowley, Kelley M. Writing the future. Cardiff : University of Wales Press, 2002.

PROPHETHOOD. *See* **PROPHETS.**

Prophets and prophecy in the ancient Near East.
Nissinen, Martti. Atlanta, GA : Society of Biblical Literature, c2003.
BF1762 .N58 2003b

Nissinen, Martti. Leiden ; Boston : Brill, 2003.
BF1762 .N58 2003

PROPHETS - FRANCE - BIOGRAPHY.
Vystrecil, Henri. Nostradamus. Portet-sur-Garonne : Loubatières, c2002.

Wilson, Ian, 1941- Nostradamus. 1st U.S. ed. New York : St. Martin's Press, 2003.
BF1815.N8 W56 2003

PROPHETS - HISTORY.
Konstantinovskai͡a, L. V. (Li͡udmila Vasil'evna) Kogda prikhodi͡at proroki. Moskva : Klassiks Stil', 2002.
BF1796 .K66 2002

PROPHETS - MIDDLE EAST - HISTORY.
Nissinen, Martti. Prophets and prophecy in the ancient Near East. Atlanta, GA : Society of Biblical Literature, c2003.
BF1762 .N58 2003b

Nissinen, Martti. Prophets and prophecy in the ancient Near East. Leiden ; Boston : Brill, 2003.
BF1762 .N58 2003

PROPHETS - RUSSIA - BIOGRAPHY.
Zaĭtseva, L. I. Russkie providt͡sy o rossiĭskoĭ gosudarstvennosti. Moskva : In-t ėkonomiki RAN, 1998-
DK49 .Z35 1998

PROPORTION. *See* **AESTHETICS.**

PROPORTION (ART). *See* **COMPOSITION (ART); PERSPECTIVE.**

Le propre de l'homme : psychanalyse et préhistoire / sous la direction de François Sacco, Georges Sauvet. Lausanne : Delachaux et Niestlé, c1998. 213 p. : ill. (some col.) ; 21 cm. (Champs psychanalytiques) Includes bibliographical references (p. [203]-213). ISBN 2-603-01085-9
1. Psychoanalysis - History. 2. Archaeology. 3. Art - History. I. Sacco, François. II. Sauvet, Georges. III. Series.
BF175 .P69 1998

PROPRIETARY RIGHTS. *See* **INTELLECTUAL PROPERTY.**

PROPRIOCEPTION. *See* **ORIENTATION (PHYSIOLOGY).**

Proryv v chetvertoe izmerenie
Pint, A. A. (Aleksandr Aleksandrovich) Nas mnogo, no my odno. Moskva : Shkola kholisticheskoĭ psikhologii, 2003.
BF202 .P56 2003

PROSE LITERATURE. *See* **FICTION.**

PROSE LITERATURE - WOMEN AUTHORS - HISTORY AND CRITICISM.
Ingram, Susan. Zarathustra's sisters. Toronto ; Buffalo : University of Toronto Press, c2003.
PN471 .I537 2003

PROSPECTING - GEOPHYSICAL METHODS.
Neubauer, Wolfgang, 1963- Magnetische Prospektion in der Archäologie. Wien : Verlag der Österreichischen Akademie der Wissenschaften, 2001.

Prospects for immortality.
Adams, J. Robert. Amityville, N.Y. : Baywood Pub., c2003.
BD421 .A33 2003

Prosperity.
Palmer, Lynne. Las Vegas : Star Bright Publishers, [c2001]
BF1729.F48 P35 2001

PROSTITUTION. *See* **SEX CRIMES.**

Os protagonistas anônimos da história.
Vainfas, Ronaldo. Rio de Janeiro : Editora Campus, 2002.
D16 .V35 2002

PROTECTION, DATA. *See* **DATA PROTECTION.**

PROTECTION OF CHILDREN. *See* **CHILD WELFARE.**

PROTECTION OF NATURE. *See* **NATURE CONSERVATION.**

PROTECTION OF SOFTWARE. *See* **SOFTWARE PROTECTION.**

Protest-Inszenierungen.
Fahlenbrach, Kathrin. 1. Aufl. Wiesbaden : Westdeutscher Verlag, 2002.

PROTEST MOVEMENTS.
Fahlenbrach, Kathrin. Protest-Inszenierungen. 1. Aufl. Wiesbaden : Westdeutscher Verlag, 2002.

PROTEST MOVEMENTS (CIVIL RIGHTS). *See* **CIVIL RIGHTS MOVEMENTS.**

Proto, Antonino, 1925- Ermete Trismegisto : gli inni : le preghiere di un santo pagano / Antonino Proto. Milano : Mimesis, 2000. 178 p. ; 21 cm. (Mimesis) Includes bibliographical references and index. ISBN 88-87231-98-2
1. Corpus Hermeticum. 2. Hermes, - Trismegistus. 3. Hermetism in literature. I. Title. II. Series: Collana Mimesis.
BF1598.H6 P76 2000

Protopapas-Marneli, Maria. La rhétorique des stoïciens : thèse de doctorat / Maria Protopapas-Marneli ; sous la direction de Gilbert Romeyer Dherbey. Paris : Harmattan, c2002. 222 p. ; 22 cm. (L'ouverture philosophique) Thesis (Ph. D.)--Université de Paris Sorbonne, 2002. Includes bibliographical references (p. 179-206) and indexes. ISBN 2-7475-2817-0 DDC 188
1. Stoics. 2. Philosophy, Ancient. 3. Classical poetry - History and criticism. I. Romeyer-Dherbey, Gilbert. II. Title. III. Series: Collection L'ouverture philosophique.

Protsenko, Oleh. Konservatyzm : antolohii͡a / Uporiadnyky: Oleh Protsenko, Vasyl' Lisovyĭ. Kyïv : "Smoloskyp", 1998. 596 p. : ports. ; 24 cm. At head of title: Naukove tovarystvo im. Vi͡acheslava Lypyns'koho. Includes bibliographical references and index.
1. Conservatism. 2. Political science. 3. Philosophy, Modern - 18th century. 4. Philosophy, Modern - 19th century. 5. Philosophy, Modern - 20th century. I. Lisovyĭ, Vasyl'. II. Title.

The proverbial Cracker Jack.
Henry, Dale. Hagerstown, Md. : Autumn House Pub., c2002.
BF637.S4 H857 2002

PROVERBS. *See* **APHORISMS AND APOTHEGMS; MAXIMS.**

PROVERBS, ENGLISH - HISTORY AND CRITICISM.
Hoggart, Richard, 1918- Everyday language & everyday life. New Brunswick, N.J. ; London : Transaction Publishers, c2003.
PE1074.8 .H64 2003

PROVIDENCE AND GOVERNMENT OF GOD IN LITERATURE.
Muñoz Llamosas, Virginia. La intervención divina en el hombre a través de la literatura griega de época arcaica y clásica. Amsterdam : Hakkert, 2002.
PA3015.R5 M87 2002

PROXEMIC BEHAVIOR. *See* **SPATIAL BEHAVIOR.**

Prthuyaśas. Saṭpañcāśikā / Daivaijñaprthuyaśo viracitā ; "Bhaṭṭotpalīya" Saṃskṛta evaṃ "Saralā" Hindī ṭīkā sahita ; Hindī ṭīkākāra Guruprasāda Gauṛa. 1. saṃskaraṇa. Vārāṇasī : Caukhambā Surabhāratī Prakāśana ; Dillī : Caukhambā Saṃskṛta Pratiṣṭhāna, 2002. 9, 88 p. ; 18 cm. (Caukhambā Surabhāratī granthamālā ; 350) In Sanskrit; commentaries in Hindi and Sanskrit. SUMMARY: Treatise on Hindu astrology. Includes index.
1. Hindu astrology - Early works to 1800. I. Bhaṭṭotpala, 12th cent. II. Gaura, Guruprasada. III. Title. IV. Series.
BF1714.H5 P7 2002

Prudentia und Contemplatio : Ethik und Metaphysik im Mittelalter : Festschrift für Georg Wieland zum 65. Geburtstag / herausgegeben von Johannes Brachtendorf. Paderborn : Ferdinand Schöningh, 2002. 322 p. ; 24 cm. Includes bibliographical references and index. ISBN 3-506-71402-3
1. Ethics. 2. Metaphysics. 3. Philosophy, Medieval. I. Wieland, Georg, 1937- II. Brachtendorf, Johannes.

Prüfendes Denken.
Schulz, Walter, 1912- Tübingen : Klöpfer & Meyer, c2002.

Prusak, Laurence.
Davenport, Thomas H. What's the big idea? Boston, Mass. : Harvard Business School Press, c2003.
HD53 .D38 2003

Prusse, Rachelle.
Critical incidents in group counseling. Alexandria, VA : American Counseling Association, 2004.
BF637.C6 C72 2004

Pryor, Karen, 1932- On behavior : essays & research / Karen Pryor. 1st ed. North Bend, Wash. : Sunshine Books, c1995. xxiii, 405 p. : ill. ; 21 cm. Includes bibliographical references (p. 387-394) and index. ISBN 0-9624017-1-4 DDC 150
1. Behavior modification. 2. Reinforcement (Psychology) 3. Conditioned response. I. Title.
BF637.B4 P68 1995

Przełęcki, Marian, 1923- O rozumności i dobroci : propozycje i morały / Marian Przełęcki. Warszawa : "Semper", 2002. 274 p. ; 25 cm. Includes bibliographical references and index. ISBN 83-89100-15-0
1. Rationalism. 2. Values. 3. Ethics. 4. Philosophy, Polish. I. Title.
B833 .P79 2002

Przesmycki, Piotr, 1965- W stronę Bogoczłowieczeństwa : teologicznomoralne studium myśli Nikołaja Bierdiajewa / Piotr Przesmycki. Łódź : "Ibidem", 2002. 220 p. ; 23 cm. (Idee w Rosji) At head of title: Interdyscyplinarny Zespół Badań Sowietologicznych Uniwersytetu Łódzkiego. Includes bibliographical references (p. [191]-208) and index. Summary in French and Russian. ISBN 83-88679-24-4
1. Berdi͡aev, Nikolaĭ, - 1874-1948. 2. Man (Christian theology) 3. Ethics. I. Title. II. Series.

Przybylak, Feliks.
B4238.B44 P79 2002

Przybylak, Feliks. Inskrypcje ulotności : przemiany w polu tworzenia / Feliks Przybylak. Wrocław : Oficyna Wydawnicza ATUT-Wrocławskie Wydawn. Oświatowe, 2002. 230 p. ; 20 cm. Includes bibliographical references (p. 227-[229]) and index. ISBN 83-89247-12-7
1. Creation (Literary, artistic, etc.) 2. Literature - Philosophy. 3. Philosophy. I. Title.
PN56.C69 P79 2002

PRZYWARA, ERICH, 1889-1972.
Luciani Rivero, Rafael Francisco. El misterio de la diferencia. Roma : Pontificia università gregoriana, 2001.

Pseudo-Dionysius, the Areopagite.
De mystica theologia. Serbian.
Vizantijska filozofija u srednjevekovnoj Srbiji. Beograd : Stubovi kulture, 2002.

PSEUDO-ROMANTICISM. *See* **ROMANTICISM.**

PSI (PARAPSYCHOLOGY). *See* **PARAPSYCHOLOGY.**

"Psiche è una parola greca - ".
Traverso, Paola. Genova, Italy : Compagnia dei librai, 2000.
BF109.F74 T73 2000

Psicoanalisi contemporanea. Sez. 4, Studi interdisciplinari
(1.) L'inconscio antinomico. Milano : F. Angeli, c1999.
BF315 .I56 1999

Psicoanálisis psicosomática ida y atleuv [sic.].
D'Alvia, Rodolfo. Buenos Aires : Editorial Dunken, 2002.

Psicoanálisis psicosomática ida y vuelta.
D'Alvia, Rodolfo. Psicoanálisis psicosomática ida y atleuv [sic.]. Buenos Aires : Editorial Dunken, 2002.

Psicodebate : revista de la Facultad de Humanidades y Ciencias Sociales, Universidad de Palermo. Buenos Aires, Argentina : Universidad de Palermo, Facultad de Humanidades y Ciencias Sociales, [2000]- v. : ill. ; 30 cm. Frequency: Semiannual. Año 2000, no. 1 (jul. 2000)- . Chiefly in Spanish, some in English and Portuguese. ISSN 1515-2251
1. Psychology - Periodicals 2. Psychology - Argentina - Periodicals. I. Universidad de Palermo (Palermo, Buenos Aires, Argentina). Facultad de Humanidades y Ciencias Sociales.
BF5 .P+

La psicología.
Jáidar, Isabel. 1. ed. México, D.F. : Universidad Autónoma Metropolitana, Unidad Xochimilco, División de Ciencias Sociales y Humanidades, 2002.

Psicologia em revista. Belo Horizonte : Editora PUC Minas, 2000- v. ; 26 cm. Frequency: Semiannual. V. 1, n. 10 (jul. 2000)- . Latest issue consulted: vol. 8, n. 11 (junho de 2002). Issued by: PUC Minas, Instituto de Psicologia. Continues: Cadernos de psicologia (Belo Horizonte, Brazil : 1993) (DLC) 94648875 (OCoLC)29901000. ISSN 1677-1168
1. Psychology - Periodicals. I. Pontifícia Universidade Católica de Minas Gerais. Instituto de Psicologia. II. Title: Cadernos de psicologia (Belo Horizonte, Brazil : 1993)
BF5 .C24

La psicologia filosofica in Italia.
Sava, Gabriella. Galatina (Lecce) : Congedo, 2000.
BF38 .S235 2000

Psicologia social nos estudos culturais : perspectivas e desafios para uma nova psicologia social / Nueza Maria de Fátima Guareschi, Michel Euclides Bruschi, orgs. Petrópolis : Editora Voces, c2003. 319 p. : ill. ; 21 cm. (Coleção Psicologia social) Includes bibliographical references. ISBN 85-326-2819-2
1. Social psychology. 2. Culture - Study and teaching. 3. Brazil - Civilization - 20th century. I. Guareschi, Nueza Maria de Fátima. II. Bruschi, Michel Euclides. III. Series.
HM1033 .P75 2003

Psihološke monografije
(7) Litvinović, Gorjana. Čovek izmedu istorijskog i ličnog vremena. Beograd : Institut za psihologiju, 2001.
BF697 .L543 2001

Psihološki modeli in teorije osebnosti.
Musek, Janek. Ljubljana : Filozofska fakulteta Univerze v Ljubljani, 1999.
BF698 .M887 1999

Psikhologi otechestva.
Ponomarenko, V. A. (Vladimir Aleksandrovich) Sozidatel'naia psikhologiia. Moskva : Moskovskiĭ psikhologo-sotsial'nyĭ institut ; Voronezh : Izd-vo NPO "MODEK", 2000.

BF408 .P572 2000
Shadrikov, V. D. (Vladimir Dmitrievich) Sposobnosti cheloveka. Moskva : In-t prakticheskoĭ psikhologii ; Voronezh : NPO "MODEK", 1997.
BF431 .S46512 1997

Zeĭgarnik, B. V. (Blĭuma Vul'fovna) Psikhologiia lichnosti. Moskva : Moskovskiĭ psikhologo-sotsial'nyĭ in-t, 1998.
BF698.Z43 1998

Psikhologicheskaia sluzhba v obshchestve : problemy i perspektivy razvitiia : materialy Vserossiĭskoĭ nauchno-prakticheskoĭ konferentsii, g. Komsomol'sk-na-Amure, 27-28 noiabria 2001 g. : v 3-kh chastiakh / [nauchnyĭ redaktor Opelvalova Ekaterina Vasil'evna]. Komsomol'sk-na-Amure : Komsomol'skiĭ-na-Amure gos. pedagogicheskiĭ universitet, 2002. 3 v. : ill. ; 21 cm. Description based on: v. 2, published in 2002. Includes bibliographical references. ISBN 5850942165
1. Psychology - Congresses. I. Opevalova, E. V. (Ekaterina Vasil'evna) II. Komsomol'skiĭ-na-Amure gosudarstvennyĭ pedagogicheskiĭ universitet.
BF20 .P743 2002

Psikhologicheskie i pedagogicheskie problemy samorazvitiia lichnosti : materialy Vserossiĭskoĭ nauchno-prakticheskoĭ konferentsii : [v 2 chastiakh] / [redaktory, T. Kotel'nikova, O. Korobkova, IU. Boldyreva]. Kirov : Viatskiĭ gos. pedagogicheskiĭ universitet, 2002. 2 v. : 20 cm. (Seriia "Nauchnye konferentsii Instituta psikhologii i pedagogiki Viatskogo gosudarstvennogo pedagogicheskogo universiteta") "Nauchnoe izdanie"--Colophon. Includes bibliographical references. ISBN 5938250196
1. Personality development. I. Kotel'nikova, T. II. Series.
BF723.P4 P78 2002

Psikhologicheskie issledovaniia.
Morozov, S. M. (Stanislav Mikhaĭlovich) Dialektika Vygotskogo. Moskva : Smysl, 2002.
BF109.V95 M67 2002

Sovremennaia psikhologiia motivatsii. Moskva : Smysl, 2002.
BF503 .S68 2002

Tvorogova, N. D. (Nadezhda Tvorogova) Obshchenie. Moskva : Smysl, 2002.
BF637.C45 T88 2002

Ulybina, E. V. Psikhologiia obydennogo soznaniia. Moskva : Smysl, 2001.
BF311 .U52 2001

Psikhologicheskie mekhanizmy volevoĭ reguliatsii.
Ivannikov, V. A. (Viacheslav Andreevich) [2. izd.]. Moskva : Izd-vo URAO, 1998.
BF616 .I93 1998

Psikhologicheskie osobennosti preodoleniia ėkstremal'nykh i ėmotsiogennykh situatsiĭ v podrostkovo-iunosheskom vozraste.
Mezhregional'naia Rossiĭskaia nauchno-prakticheskaia konferentsiia "Psikhologicheskie osobennosti preodoleniia ėkstremal'nykh i ėmotsiogennykh situatsiĭ v podrostkovo-iunosheskom vozraste" (2002 : Syktyvkar, Russia) Syktyvkar : Syktyvkarskiĭ gos. universitet, 2002.
BF724 .M48 2002

Psikhologicheskie osobennosti tvorcheskogo povedeniia.
Galin, A. L. (Aleksandr Latypovich) Novosibirsk : Novosibirskiĭ gos. universitet, 2001.
BF408 .G315 2001

Psikhologicheskie problemy bytiia cheloveka v sovremennom obshchestve : problema gumanizatsii protsessa obucheniia i vospitaniia : materialy mezhvuzovskoĭ nauchno-prakticheskoĭ konferentsii, 16-17 fevralia 2001 g. / pod red. E.M. Razumovoĭ]. Magnitogorsk : Magnitogorskiĭ gos. universitet, 2001. 210 p. ; 21 cm. Includes bibliographical references. ISBN 5867811239
1. Psychology - Congresses. I. Razumova, E. M. II. Magnitogorskiĭ gosudarstvennyĭ pedagogicheskiĭ institut.
BF20 .P744 2001

Psikhologicheskie problemy priniatiia resheniia : sbornik nauchnykh trudov. IAroslavl' : IAroslavskiĭ gos. universitet, 2001. 91 p. : ill. ; 21 cm. Includes bibliographical references. ISBN 5839701661
1. Decision making. I. IAroslavskiĭ gosudarstvennyĭ universitet im. P.G. Demidova.
BF448 .P78 2001

Psikhologiia bytovogo shrifta.
Florenskaia, O. Sankt-Peterburg : Krasnyĭ matros, 2001.

BF896 .F66 2001
Psikhologiia chuvstvennogo poznaniia.
Anan'ev, Boris Gerasimovich. Moskva : "Nauka", 2001.
BF233 .A5 2001

Psikhologiia i religiia.
Zen'ko, IU. M. Sankt-Peterburg : Aleteiia, 2002.
BF51 .Z46 2002

Psikhologiia khudozhestvennogo deĭstviia sub"ekta.
Ivanov, S. P. (Sergeĭ Petrovich) Moskva : Moskovskiĭ psikhologo-sotsial'nyĭ institut ; Voronezh : Izd-vo NPO "MODEK", 2002.
BF408 .I93 2002

Psikhologiia lichnosti.
Zeĭgarnik, B. V. (Blĭuma Vul'fovna) Moskva : Moskovskiĭ psikhologo-sotsial'nyĭ in-t, 1998.
BF698.Z43 1998

Psikhologiia lichnostnogo rosta.
Kozlov, Nikolaĭ (Nikolaĭ Ivanovich) Kniga dlia tekh, komu nravitsia zhit', ili, Psikhologiia lichnostnogo rosta. Moskva : "AST-Press kniga", 2002.
BF723.P4 K69 2002

Psikhologiia mezhkul'turnykh razlichiĭ.
Kochetkov, V. V. (Vladimir Viktorovich) Moskva : PER SE, 2002.
GN502 .K6 2002

Psikhologiia na razgovora.
Iliev, Vladimir. 1. izd. Pleven : Lege Artis, 2002.
BF637.C45 I45 2002

Psikhologiia obydennogo soznaniia.
Ulybina, E. V. Moskva : Smysl, 2001.
BF311 .U52 2001

Psikhologiia ot pervogo litsa.
Artamonov, V. I. (Vladimir Ivanovich) Moskva : Academia, 2003.
BF109.A1 A78 2003

Psikhologiia otnosheniĭ : materialy regional'noĭ nauchno-prakticheskoĭ konferentsii / [otvetstvennyĭ redaktor V.A. Zobkov]. Vladimir : Vladimirskiĭ gos. pedagogicheskiĭ universitet, 2001. 270 p. ; 21 cm. ISBN 5878462532
1. Interpersonal communication - Congresses. 2. Interpersonal relations - Congresses. 3. Social psychology - Congresses. I. Zobkov, V. A. II. Vladimirskiĭ gosudarstvennyĭ pedagogicheskiĭ universitet.
BF637.C45 P74 2001

Psikhologiia razvitiia i vozrastnaia psikhologiia : khrestomatiia. Moskva : Izd-vo MNEPU, 2001- v. <1 > ; 21 cm. Includes bibliographical references. PARTIAL CONTENTS: ch. 1. Problemy razvitiia psikhiki ISBN 573830179X
1. Developmental psychology - Congresses. I. Mezhdunarodnyĭ nezavisimyĭ ėkologo-politologicheskiĭ universitet.
BF712.5 .P75 2001

Psikhologiia razvitiia tvorcheskogo potentsiala lichnosti.
IAkovleva, E. L. (Evgeniia Leonovna) Moskva : Moskovskiĭ psikhologo-sotsial'nyĭ institut : Izd-vo "Flinta" / 1997.
BF408 .I15 1997

Psikhologiia snovideniĭ.
Smirnov, Terentiĭ. Moskva : "KSP+", 2001.
BF175.5.D74 S5 2001

Psikhologiia sovremennoĭ rossiĭskoĭ politiki.
Ol'shanskiĭ, D. V. (Dmitriĭ Vadimovich) Moskva : Akademicheskiĭ proekt, 2001.
JN6699.A15 O46 2001

Psikhologiia sub"ektnosti : chelovek kak avtor zhizni : materialy mezhregional'noĭ nauchno-prakticheskoĭ konferentsii / [nauchnye redaktory N.N Ershova, N.A. Nizovskikh]. Kirov : Viatskiĭ gos. pedagog. universitet, 2001. 151 p. : ill. ; 20 cm. "Nauchnoe izdanie"--Colophon. At head of title: Departament obrazovaniia administratsii Kirovskoĭ oblasti ... Includes bibliographical references.
1. Self psychology - Congresses. I. Ershova, N. N. II. Nizovskikh, N. A. (Nina Arkad'evna) III. Title: Chelovek kak avtor zhizni
BF697.P75 2001

Psikhologiia transtsendirovaniia.
Ageev, Valentin. Almaty: "Qazaq Universitetĭ", 2002.
BF713 .A34 1998

Psikhologiia v litsakh.
Stepanov, S. S. (Sergeĭ Sergeevich) Moskva : EKSMO-Press, 2001.
BF109.A1 S74 2001

Psikhologīiā v Rossii, 20. vek.
Petrovskiĭ, A. V. (Artur Vladimirovich) Psikhologīiā v Rossii, XX vek. Moskva : URAO-- Universitet rossiĭskoĭ akademii obrazovaniiā, 2000.
BF108.R8 P39 2000

Psikhologīiā v Rossii, XX vek.
Petrovskiĭ, A. V. (Artur Vladimirovich) Moskva : URAO-- Universitet rossiĭskoĭ akademii obrazovaniiā, 2000.
BF108.R8 P39 2000

Psikhologyah shel tahalikh ha-shalom.
Grosbard, Ofer, 1954- Yiśra'el 'al ha-sapah. Tel-Aviv : Yedi'ot aḥaronot : Sifre ḥemed, c2000.

Psiquiatria, loucura e arte : fragmentos de história brasileira / Eleonora Haddad Antunes, Lúcia Helena Siqueira Barbosa, Lygia Maria de França Pereira (organizadoras). São Paulo, SP, Brasil : Edusp, c2002. 166 p. : ill. (some col.) ; 25 cm. (Estante USP--Brasil 500 anos ; no. 6) Includes bibliographical references. CONTENTS: Apresentação / Moisés Goldbaum -- História e arte no Programa de Saúde Mental / Eleonora Haddad Antunes, Lúcia Helena Siqueira Barbosa e Lygia Maria de França Pereira -- Os primeiros sessenta anos da terapêutica psiquiátrica no estado de São Paulo / Lygia Maria de França Pereira -- Casas de orates / Hugo Segawa -- Raça de gigantes : a higiene mental e a imigração no Brasil / Eleonora Haddad Antunes -- Literatura e loucura / Cecília Lara -- "Pequenos psicopatas" : infância, criminalidade e loucura na Primeira República / Judith Zuquim -- A arte não revela a verdade da loucura, a loucura não detém a verdade da arte / Teixeira Coelho. ISBN 85-314-0662-5
1. Mental health services - Brazil - History. 2. Mental illness - Brazil - History. 3. Psychiatry - Brazil - History. 4. Psychiatric hospitals - Brazil - History. 5. Art and mental illness - Brazil. I. Antunes, Eleonora Haddad. II. Barbosa, Lúcia Helena Siqueira. III. Pereira, Lygia Maria de França. IV. Series.

PSYCHAGOGY. *See* **PSYCHOLOGY, APPLIED; PSYCHOTHERAPY.**

Psychanalyse
Delrieu, Alain. Sigmund Freud. 2e éd. rev., augm. et mise à jour. Paris : Anthropos : Diffusion Economica, c2001.
BF109.F74 D45 2001

Psychanalyse &
Soler, Colette. L'inconscient à ciel ouvert de la psychose. Toulouse : Presses universitaires du Mirail, c2002.

Psychanalyse & (Toulouse, France)
Soler, Colette. L'inconscient à ciel ouvert de la psychose. Toulouse : Presses universitaires du Mirail, c2002.

Psychanalyse d'un choc esthétique.
Hachet, Pascal. Paris, France : Harmattan, c2002.

Psychanalyse et civilisations
Charles, Monique. Borges, ou, L'étrangeté apprivoisée. Paris : Harmattan, c2002.

Lefèvre, Alain, 1947- De la paternité et des psychoses. Paris : Harmattan, c2002-

Psychanalyse et décolonisation. Paris : L'Harmattan, c1999.
BF175.4.C84 P76 1999

Psychanalyse et civilisations. Série Trouvailles et retrouvailles.
Bolzinger, André. La réception de Freud en France. Paris : L'Harmattan, c1999.
BF175 .B575 1999

Brodeur, Claude, 1924- Le père. Paris : L'Harmattan, 2001.
HQ756 .B76 2001

Hachet, Pascal. Psychanalyse d'un choc esthétique. Paris, France : Harmattan, c2002.

Rhodes, Henry T. F. (Henry Taylor Fowkes), b. 1892. Le génie et le crime. Paris, France : Harmattan, c2002.

Psychanalyse et civilisations. Trouvailles et retrouvailles.
Laborie, Philippe. Le patient absent de Jacques Lacan. Paris : Harmattan, c2002.

Psychanalyse et décolonisation : hommage à Octave Mannoni / sous la direction d'Anny Combrichon ; avec la collaboration de Véronique Collomb. Paris : L'Harmattan, c1999. 223 p. : ill. ; 22 cm. (Psychanalyse et civilisations) Papers originally presented at conferences held in Antananarivo, Madagascar, in Dec. 1997, and in Paris, France, in Feb. 1998. Includes bibliographical references. ISBN 2-7384-8078-0 DDC 150.19/5
1. Psychoanalysis and culture - Developing countries - Congresses. 2. Decolonization - Psychological aspects - Congresses. 3. Mannoni, Octave. 4. Psychoanalysis - Congresses. 5. Colonialism - history - Congresses. 6. Developing Countries - history - Congresses. I. Mannoni, Octave. II. Combrichon, Anny. III. Collomb, Véronique. IV. Series.
BF175.4.C84 P76 1999

La psychanalyse prise au mot
Depuis Lacan. Paris : Aubier, c2000.
BF173 .D44 2000

Psychanalyse prise au mot.
Lévesque, Claude, 1927- Par-delà le masculin et le féminin. Paris : Aubier, 2002.

Psychästhetik.
Salber, Wilhelm. Köln : König, c2002.

Psyche and death.
Herzog, Edgar. [Psyche und Tod. English] New ed. / edited and designed by C.L. Sebrell. Woodstock, Conn. : Spring Publications, c2000.

La psyché humaine.
Safty, Essam. Paris : Harmattan, c2003.
B528 .S34 2003

Psyché (Prague, Czech Republic)
Holá, Lenka. Mediace. Vyd. 1. Praha : Grada Pub., 2003.
BF637.I48 H63 2003

Psyche's child.
Bolich, Gregory G. Dubuque, Iowa : Kendall/Hunt Pub., c2000.
BF121 .B57 2000

PSYCHIATRIC CARE. *See* **MENTAL HEALTH SERVICES.**

PSYCHIATRIC HOSPITALS - BRAZIL - HISTORY.
Psiquiatria, loucura e arte. São Paulo, SP, Brasil : Edusp, c2002.

PSYCHIATRIC PATIENTS. *See* **PSYCHOTHERAPY PATIENTS.**

PSYCHIATRIC SERVICES. *See* **MENTAL HEALTH SERVICES.**

PSYCHIATRISTS. *See* **PSYCHOANALYSTS.**

PSYCHIATRISTS - ATTITUDES.
Creating racism. Los Angeles, CA : Citizens Commission on Human Rights, 1995.
RC455.4.E8 C74x 1995

PSYCHIATRISTS - SPAIN - INTERVIEWS.
Cruz, Mariano de la, 1921-1999. Mens sana in corpore insepulto. 1. ed. Barcelona : Edicions 62, 2002.

PSYCHIATRY. *See also* **MENTAL HEALTH; MENTAL ILLNESS; PSYCHOTHERAPY.**
Breathing spaces. New York : Columbia University Press, c2003.
RA781.8 .B73 2003

Cruz, Mariano de la, 1921-1999. Mens sana in corpore insepulto. 1. ed. Barcelona : Edicions 62, 2002.

Jerotić, Vladeta. [Selections 2000] Izabrani ogledi. Beograd: Srpska književna zadruga, 2000.
BF109.J47 A25 2000

Memory and emotion. Oxford University Press : New York, 2003.
BF378.A87 M46 2003

PSYCHIATRY AND ART. *See* **ART AND MENTAL ILLNESS.**

PSYCHIATRY AND RELIGION.
Frankl, Viktor Emil. Man's search for ultimate meaning. Cambridge, Mass. : Perseus Pub., c2000.
RC455.4.R4 F7 2000

PSYCHIATRY - BRAZIL - HISTORY.
Psiquiatria, loucura e arte. São Paulo, SP, Brasil : Edusp, c2002.

Russo, Jane. O mundo psi no Brasil. Rio de Janeiro : Jorge Zahar Editor, c2002.
BF173 .R877 2002

PSYCHIATRY - FRANCE - HISTORY.
Huteau, Michel. Psychologie, psychiatrie et société sous la troisième république. Paris : Harmattan, c2002.

PSYCHIATRY IN GENERAL HOSPITALS. *See* **PSYCHIATRIC HOSPITALS.**

PSYCHIATRY - PATIENTS. *See* **PSYCHOTHERAPY PATIENTS.**

PSYCHIATRY - PHILOSOPHY.
Imagination and its pathologies. Cambridge, Mass. : MIT Press, c2003.
BF408 .I455 2003

PSYCHIATRY, TRANSCULTURAL.
Multicultural counseling competencies 2003. Alexandria, VA : Association for Multicultural Counseling and Development, 2003.
BF637.C6 M8367 2003

Psychiatry's betrayal in the guise of help.
Creating racism. Los Angeles, CA : Citizens Commission on Human Rights, 1995.
RC455.4.E8 C74x 1995

PSYCHIC ABILITY.
Byrd, Da Juana. Ghosts talk. 1st ed. Cedar Hills, Tex. : Byrd Pub., c2002.
BF1031 .B97 2002

Cox, Bonnie. The lightbearer. Seattle, Wash. : Black Heron Press, c2003.
BF1031 .C637 2003

Davis, Audrey Craft. Metaphysical techniques that really work. Nevada City, CA : Blue Dolphin Pub., 2004.
BF1411 .D38 2004

Fenton, Sasha. How to be psychic. New York : Sterling Pub., c2003.
BF1031 .F46 2003

Hathaway, Michael R. The everything psychic book. Avon, Mass. : Adams Media Corp., c2003.
BF1031 .H2955 2003

Soskin, Julie. Are you psychic? London : Carroll & Brown, 2002.
BF1031 .S674 2002

PSYCHIC ABILITY - PROBLEMS, EXERCISES, ETC.
Eason, Cassandra. The complete guide to psychic development. Berkeley, Calif. : Crossing Press, c2003.
BF1031 .E295 2003

PSYCHIC ART. *See* **SPIRIT ART.**

Psychic development.
Eason, Cassandra. The complete guide to psychic development. Berkeley, Calif. : Crossing Press, c2003.
BF1031 .E295 2003

Psychic diaries.
Moskowitz-Mateu, Lysa. New York : Harper Entertainment, 2003.
BF1283.M66 A3 2003

PSYCHIC HEALERS. *See* **HEALERS.**

PSYCHIC PHENOMENA. *See* **PARAPSYCHOLOGY.**

PSYCHIC READINGS - CASE STUDIES.
Hite, Sheilaa, 1958- Secrets of a psychic counselor. Needham, Mass. : Moment Point Press ; [Oakland, Calif.] : Distributed to the trade by Words Distributing Co., c2003.
BF1045.R43 H58 2003

PSYCHIC RESEARCHERS. *See* **PARAPSYCHOLOGISTS.**

PSYCHIC TRAUMA.
Castillo, Heather. Personality disorder. London ; Philadelphia : J. Kingsley Pub., 2003.
RC554 .C37 2003

Edkins, Jenny. Trauma and the memory of politics. Cambridge ; New York : Cambridge University Press, 2003.
BF175.5.P75 E35 2003

McNally, Richard J. Remembering trauma. Cambridge, Mass. : Belknap Press of Harvard University Press, 2003.
RC552.P67 M396 2003

Ross, Gina, 1947- Beyond the trauma vortex. Berkeley, Calif. : North Atlantic Books, c2003.
PN4784.D57 R67 2003

Understanding terrorism. 1st ed. Washington, DC : American Psychological Association, 2004.
HV6431 .U35 2004

PSYCHIC TRAUMA - CROSS-CULTURAL STUDIES.
Cvetkovich, Ann, 1957- An archive of feelings. Durham : Duke University Press, 2003.
HQ75.5 .C89 2003

PSYCHIC TRAUMA - TREATMENT.
Terrorism and disaster. Cambridge, UK ; New York : Cambridge University Press, 2003.
RC552.P67 T476 2003

Psychic vampires.
Slate, Joe H. 1st ed. St. Paul, Minn. : Llewellyn Publications, 2002.
BF1045.S46 S53 2002

PSYCHICAL RESEARCH. *See* **PARAPSYCHOLOGY.**

PSYCHICS. *See* **CLAIRVOYANTS.**

PSYCHICS - BIOGRAPHY.
Mishlove, Jeffrey, 1946- The PK man. Charlottesville, VA : Hampton Roads, [c2000]
BF1027.O94 M57 2000

PSYCHICS - GREAT BRITAIN - BIOGRAPHY.
Dolan, Mia. I know why we're here. 1st U.S. ed. New York : Harmony Books, 2004.
BF1283.D485 A3 2004

PSYCHICS - SOVIET UNION - BIOGRAPHY.
Küppers, Topsy, 1931- Wolf Messing. München : Langen Müller, c2002.
BF1027.M47 K87 2002

PSYCHICS - UNITED STATES - BIOGRAPHY.
Moskowitz-Mateu, Lysa. Psychic diaries. New York : Harper Entertainment, 2003.
BF1283.M66 A3 2003

Sugrue, Thomas, 1907- There is a river. Virginia Beach, Va. : A.R.E. Press, c2003.
BF1027.C3 S8 2003

Psychische Energien bildender Kunst : Festschrift Klaus Herding / Henry Keazor (Hg.). 1. Aufl. Köln : DuMont, 2002. 277 p. : ill. ; 21 cm. Includes bibliographical references. 1 English contribution. ISBN 3-8321-7225-4 (pbk.) 1. Art - Psychology. 2. Art - History. I. Herding, Klaus. II. Keazor, Henry.

Psychismes
Bergeret, Jean. La sexualité infantile et ses mythes. Paris : Dunod, c2001.

Célérier, Marie-Claire. Repenser la cure psychanalytique. Paris : Dunod, c2002.
RC504 .C454 2002

Mijolla-Mellor, Sophie de. Le besoin de savoir. Paris : Dunod, c2002.
BF723.S4 M556 2002

Psycho-logiques
Xypas, Constantin. Les stades du développement affectif selon Piaget. Paris : Harmattan, c2001.

Psychoanalyse und Sozialpsychologie.
Kaus, Rainer J. Heidelberg : C. Winter, c1999.
BF109.F74 K38 1999

PSYCHOANALYSIS. *See also* **ARCHETYPE (PSYCHOLOGY); EGO (PSYCHOLOGY); JUNGIAN PSYCHOLOGY; OBJECT RELATIONS (PSYCHOANALYSIS); PLEASURE PRINCIPLE (PSYCHOLOGY); RESISTANCE (PSYCHOANALYSIS); SHADOW (PSYCHOANALYSIS); SOCIAL SCIENCES AND PSYCHOANALYSIS; SYMBOLISM (PSYCHOLOGY); WOMEN AND PSYCHOANALYSIS.**
Abelhauser, Alain, 1954- Le sexe et le signifiant. Paris : Seuil, c2002.
BF175.5.S48 A24 2002

Alford, C. Fred. Levinas, the Frankfurt school and psychoanalysis. 1st US ed. Middletown, CT : Wesleyan University Press, c2002.

Ayers, Mary, 1960- The eyes of shame. 1st ed. Hove, East Sussex ; New York : Brunner-Routledge, 2003.
BF175.5.O24 A94 2003

Babin, Pierre. La fabrique du sexe. Paris : Textuel, [1999]
BF175.5.S48 B23 1999

Berg, Henk de, 1963- Freud's theory and its use in literary and cultural studies. Rochester, NY : Camden House, 2003.
PN56.P92 B36 2003

Bergeret, Jean. La sexualité infantile et ses mythes. Paris : Dunod, c2001.

Brickman, Celia. Aboriginal populations in the mind. New York : Columbia University Press, c2003.
BF173 .B79 2003

Britton, Celia. Race and the unconscious. Oxford : Legenda, 2002.

Cabot, Catharine Rush. Jung, my mother and I. Einsiedeln : Daimon, 2001.

Campos, Edemilson Antunes de. A tirania de Narciso. 1. ed. São Paulo, SP, Brasil : Annablume/FAPESP, 2001.

Cannac, Edith. Caïn ou le détournement du sens. [Paris] : Plon, c2002.

Célérier, Marie-Claire. Repenser la cure psychanalytique. Paris : Dunod, c2002.
RC504 .C454 2002

Chebili, Saïd. La tâche civilisatrice de la psychanalyse selon Freud. Paris : L'Harmattan, c2002.

Creative dissent. Westport, Conn. : Praeger Publishers, 2003.
BF173 .C794 2003

D'Alvia, Rodolfo. Psicoanálisis psicosomática ida y atleuv [sic.]. Buenos Aires : Editorial Dunken, 2002.

Delaisi de Parseval, Geneviève. Le Roman familial d'Isadora D.. Paris : Odile Jacob, c2002.

Depuis Lacan. Paris : Aubier, c2000.
BF173 .D44 2000

Dilemmas in the consulting room. London ; New York : Karnac, 2002.

Dufourmantelle, Anne. La sauvagerie maternelle. Paris : Calmann-Lévy, c2001.

Elliott, Anthony. Psychoanalytic theory. 2nd ed. Durham, NC : Duke University Press, 2002.
BF173 .E63 2002

Fantasm. Melbourne : Freudian School of Melbourne, 2000.

Fekete, Mária. Pszichológia és pszichopatológia jogászoknak. Budapest : HVG-ORAC, c2002.
BF173 .F349 2002

Femenilidades. Rio de Janeiro : Espaço Brasileiro de Estudos Psicanalíticos : Contra Capa, c2002.

Fierens, Christian. Lecture de l'étourdit. Paris : Harmattan, c2002.
BF109.L28 F53 2002

Fink, Bruce, 1956- Lacan to the letter. Minneapolis, MN : University of Minnesota Press, c2004.
BF173 .L1434 2004

Flem, Lydia. La voix des amants. [Paris] : Seuil, c2002.

Freud [electronic resource]. Washington, DC : Library of Congress
BF173

Freud, le sujet social. 1re éd. Paris : Presses universitaires de France, 2002.

Freud, Sigmund, 1856-1939. [Essays. English. Selections] The uncanny. New York : Penguin Books, 2003.
BF109.F75 A25 2003

Freud, Sigmund, 1856-1939. [Zur Psychopathologie des Alltagslebens. English] The psychopathology of everyday life. New York : Penguin Books, 2003.
BF173 .F82513 2003

Frosh, Stephen. Key concepts in psychoanalysis. London : British Library, 2002.
BF173 .F898 2002

Frosh, Stephen. Key concepts in psychoanalysis. New York : New York University Press, 2003.
BF173 .F898 2003

Die Gegenwart der Psychoanalyse, die Psychoanalyse der Gegenwart. 2. Aufl. Stuttgart : Klett-Cotta, 2002.

Gilbert, Muriel. L'identité narrative. Genève : Labor et Fides, c2001.

Goldberg, Arnold, 1929- Misunderstanding Freud. New York : Other Press, 2004.
BF173 .G59 2004

Guillerault, Gérard. Les deux corps du moi. Paris : Gallimard, c1996.
BF175.5.B64 G86 1996

Haddad, Gérard. Le jour où Lacan m'a adopté. Paris : Bernard Grasset, c2002.

Hating in the first person plural. New York : Other Press, c2003.
RC506 .H285 2003

Hurson, Didier. Alexander Mitscherlich, 1908-1982. Paris : Presses de l'Université de Paris-Sorbonne, 2002.

Kaus, Rainer J. Psychoanalyse und Sozialpsychologie. Heidelberg : C. Winter, c1999.
BF109.F74 K38 1999

Kaus, Rainer J. Psychoanalyse und Sozialpsychologie. Heidelberg : C. Winter, c1999.
BF109.F74 K38 1999

Khasnabish, Ashmita, 1959- Jouissance as ānanda. Lanham, Md. : Lexington Books, c2003.
BF173 .K427 2003

Laborie, Philippe. Le patient absent de Jacques Lacan. Paris : Harmattan, c2002.

Lawrence, D. H. (David Herbert), 1885-1930. [Psychoanalysis and the unconscious] Psychoanalysis and the unconscious; New York : Cambridge, 2003.
BF173 .L28 2003

Lear, Jonathan. Therapeutic action. New York : Other Press, c2003.
BF175.4.C68 L43 2003

Lefèvre, Alain, 1947- De la paternité et des psychoses. Paris : Harmattan, c2002-

Lévy, Ghyslain. Au-delà du malaise. Ramonville Saint-Agne : Erès, c2000.
BF175 .L487 2000

Liaudet, Jean-Claude. Telle fille, quel père? Paris : Archipel, c2002.

Lichtenberg, Joseph D. A spirit of inquiry. Hillsdale, NJ : Analytic Press, 2002.
RC506 .L5238 2002

Loch, Wolfgang. "Mit Freud über Freud hinaus". Tübingen : Edition Diskord, c2001.
BF173 .L554 2001

Loch, Wolfgang. "Mit Freud über Freud hinaus". Tübingen : Edition Diskord, c2001.
BF173 .L554 2001

López Díaz, Yolanda. Por qué se maltrata al más íntimo? 1. ed. [Bogota] : Universidad Nacional de Colombia, Sede Bogota, 2002.

Lowenkopf, Eugene L. The almighty dollar. New York : iUniverse, Inc., c2003.

Małyszek, Tomasz, 1971- Romans Freuda i Gradivy. Wrocław : Wydawn. Uniwersytetu Wrocławskiego, 2002.
BF173.F85 M255 2002

Matheus, Tiago Corbisier. Ideais na adolescência. 1a ed. São Paulo, SP : Annablume, 2002.

Meadow, Phyllis W., 1924- The new psychoanalysis. Lanham, Md. : Rowman & Littlefield, c2003.
BF173 .M3585 2003

Menzhulin, V. (Vadim), 1968- Raskoldovyvaia︠ ︡ IUnga. Kiev : Izd-vo "Sfera", 2002.
BF173.J85 M46 2002

Mitchell, Juliet, 1940- Siblings. Cambridge, UK : Polity Press, c2003.
BF723.S43 M58 2003

Moulinier, Didier. Dictionnaire de la jouissance. Paris : L'Harmattan, c1999.
BF575.H27 M68 1999

Nasio, Juan-David. [Livre de la douleur et de l'amour. English] The book of love and pain. Albany : State University of New York, 2003.
BF515 .N3713 2003

Psychoanalytic knowledge. New York : Palgrave Macmillan, 2003.
BF173 .P7763 2003

Pulman, Bertrand. Anthropologie et psychanalyse. Paris : Presses universitaires de France, 2002.
GN502 .P85 2002

Quaglia, Rocco. Immagini dell'uomo. Roma : Armando, c2000.

Ranchan, Som P., 1932- Aurotherapy. Delhi : Indian Publishers Distributors, 2001.
BF173.A25 R36 2001

Rizzuto, Ana-María. The dynamics of human aggression. New York, NY : Brunner-Routledge, 2003.
BF175.5.A36 R59 2003

Rubin, Gabrielle, 1921- Le roman familial de Freud. Paris : Payot, 2002.

Rudnytsky, Peter L. Reading psychoanalysis. Ithaca : Cornell University Press, 2002.

BF173 .R794 2002

Rufo, Marcel. Frères et soeurs une maladie d'amour. Paris : Fayard, 2002.

Safouan, Moustafa. Four lessons of psychoanalysis. New York : Other Press, c2004.
BF175 .S19 2004

Sánchez-Pardo, Esther. Cultures of the death drive. Durham [N.C.] : Duke University Press, c2003.
BF175.5.D4 S26 2003

Sayers, Janet. Divine therapy. Oxford ; New York : Oxford University Press, 2003.
BF175.4.R44 S28 2003

Schafer, Roy. Insight and interpretation. New York : Other Press, c2003.
BF173 .S3277 2003

Sexual faces. Madison, Conn. : International Universities Press, c2002.
BF175.5.S48 S47 2002

Shamdasani, Sonu, 1962- C.G. Jung and the making of modern psychology. Cambridge, UK ; New York : Cambridge University Press, 2003.
BF173 .S485 2003

The Ship of thought. London : Karnac, 2002.

Smith, David Livingston, 1953- Psychoanalysis in focus. London ; Thousand Oaks, Calif. : SAGE Publications, 2003.
BF173 .S569 2003

Strenger, Carlo. The quest for voice in contemporary psychoanalysis. Madison, Conn. : International Universities Press, c2002.
RC506 .S773 2002

Symington, Neville. A pattern of madness. London ; New York : Karnac, 2002.

Veličková, Helena. Grafologie, cesta do hlubin duše. Vyd. 1. Praha : Academia, 2002.
BF896 .V45 2002

The vitality of objects. 1st US ed. Middletown, Conn. : Wesleyan University Press, 2002.
BF173 .V55 2002

Yankelevich, Héctor, 1946- Du père à la lettre. Ramonville Saint-Agne : Erès, c2003.

Young-Bruehl, Elisabeth. Where do we fall when we fall in love? New York : Other Press, c2003.
BF173 .Y68 2003

Psychoanalysis & women series
Studies on femininity. London ; New York : Karnac, 2003.

PSYCHOANALYSIS AND ART.
Didier-Weill, Alain. Lila et la lumière de Vermeer. Paris : Denoël, c2003.

Donfrancesco, Francesco. Una poetica dell'analisi. Bergamo : Moretti & Vitali, 2000.

Hachet, Pascal. Psychanalyse d'un choc esthétique. Paris, France : Harmattan, c2002.

Newton, Stephen J. Painting, psychoanalysis, and spirituality. New York : Cambridge University Press, 2001.
ND1158.P74 N48 2001

Roland, Alan, 1930- Dreams and drama. 1st US ed. Middletown, CT : Wesleyan University Press, 2003.
BF408 .R65 2003

Roland, Alan, 1930- Dreams and drama. 1st US ed. Middletown, CT : Wesleyan University Press, 2003.
BF408 .R65 2003

Sentieri della mente. 1. ed. Torino : Bollati Boringhieri, 2001.

Psychoanalysis and Buddhism : an unfolding dialogue / edited by Jeremy D. Safran. 1st ed. Boston : Wisdom Publications, c2003. xvii, 443 p. ; 23 cm. Includes bibliographical references and index. ISBN 0-86171-342-7 (pbk. : alk. paper) DDC 294.3/375
1. Buddhism and psychoanalysis. 2. Buddhism - Psychology. I. Safran, Jeremy D.
BF175.4.R44 P785 2003

PSYCHOANALYSIS AND CULTURE.
Gambini, Roberto, 1944- Soul & culture. 1st ed. College Station : Texas A&M University Press, 2003.
BF698.9.C8 G35 2003

McGowan, Todd. The end of dissatisfaction? Albany : State University of New York Press, c2004.
BF175.4.C84 M4 2004

Melman, Charles, 1931- L'homme sans gravité. Paris : Denoël, c2002.

Paquette, Didier. La mascarade interculturelle. Paris : Harmattan, c2002.

Randolph, Jeanne, 1943- Why stoics box. Toronto : YYZ Books, 2003.

PSYCHOANALYSIS AND CULTURE - DEVELOPING COUNTRIES - CONGRESSES.
Psychanalyse et décolonisation. Paris : LHarmattan, c1999.
BF175.4.C84 P76 1999

PSYCHOANALYSIS AND CULTURE - FRANCE.
Bolzinger, André. La réception de Freud en France. Paris : L'Harmattan, c1999.
BF175 .B575 1999

PSYCHOANALYSIS AND CULTURE - INDIA.
Vishnu on Freud's desk. Delhi ; Oxford : Oxford University Press, 1999 (2002 [printing])

PSYCHOANALYSIS AND CULTURE - PERIODICALS.
Espectros del psicoanalisis. Mexico, D.F. : Editorial la Tinta en el Divan, 1997-
BF173.A2 E75

[Journal for the psychoanalysis of culture & society (Online)] Journal for the psychoanalysis of culture and society [electronic resource]. Columbus, Ohio : Ohio State University Press
BF175.4.C84

PSYCHOANALYSIS AND CULTURE - RUSSIA (FEDERATION).
Russian Imago 2001. Nauchnoe izd. Sankt-Peterburg : Izd-vo "Aleteĭia", 2002.
BF175.4.C84 R87 2002

PSYCHOANALYSIS AND FEMINISM.
Burack, Cynthia, 1958- Healing identities. Ithaca : Cornell University Press, 2004.
BF175.4.F45 B87 2004

Campbell, Kirsten, 1969- Jacques Lacan and feminist epistemology. New York, NY : Routledge, 2004.
BF175.4.F45 .C37 2004

Musachi, Graciela. Mujeres en movimiento. Argentina : Fondo de Cultura Económica / Argentina, 2001.

Rowland, Susan, 1962- Jung. Cambridge, UK : Polity ; Malden, MA : Blackwell, 2002.
BF175.4.F45 R69 2002

Therapies with women in transition. Madison, Conn. : International Universities Press, c2003.
RC451.4.W6 T46 2003

Weiler, Gerda, 1921- Der enteignete Mythos. Königstein : Helmer, [1996]

PSYCHOANALYSIS AND FEMINISM - CONGRESSES.
Konferentsiia "Gerndernyĭ podkhod v psikhologicheskom konsul'tirovanii" (2002 : Evropeĭskiĭ Gumanitarnyĭ Universitet) Gerndernyĭ podkhod v psikhologicheskikh issledovaniiakh i konsul'tirovanii. Minsk : Evropeĭskiĭ Gumanitarnyĭ Universitet, 2002.
BF201.4 .K66 2002

PSYCHOANALYSIS AND LITERATURE.
Berg, Henk de, 1963- Freud's theory and its use in literary and cultural studies. Rochester, NY : Camden House, 2003.
PN56.P92 B36 2003

Charles, Monique. Borges, ou, L'étrangeté apprivoisée. Paris : Harmattan, c2002.

D'Cruz, Doreen, 1950- Loving subjects. New York : P. Lang, c2002.
PR888.W6 D39 2002

Halpern, Richard, 1954- Shakespeare's perfume. Philadelphia : University of Pennsylvania Press, c2002.
PR2848 .H25 2002

Keller, John Robert. Samuel Beckett and the primacy of love. Manchester : Manchester University Press, 2002.

Kristeva, Julia, 1941- [Révolte intime. English] Intimate revolt. New York : Columbia University Press, c2002.
PN56.P92 K7513 2002

Liddelow, Eden. After Electra. Melbourne : Australian Scholarly, 2002, c2001.

Literature, science, psychoanalysis, 1830-1970. Oxford ; New York : Oxford University Press, 2003.

PN55 .L58 2003

Małyszek, Tomasz, 1971- Ästhetik der Psychoanalyse. Wrocław : Wydawn. Uniwersytetu Wrocławskiego, 2000.

Matt, Peter von. Literaturwissenschaft und Psychoanalyse. Stuttgart : Reclam, c2001.

Milmaniene, José E. Clínica del texto. [1. ed.]. Buenos Aires : Editorial Biblos, c2002.

Roland, Alan, 1930- Dreams and drama. 1st US ed. Middletown, CT : Wesleyan University Press, 2003.
BF408 .R65 2003

Roland, Alan, 1930- Dreams and drama. 1st US ed. Middletown, CT : Wesleyan University Press, 2003.
BF408 .R65 2003

Royle, Nicholas, 1963- The uncanny. Manchester (UK) ; New York : Manchester University Press, 2003.
PN49 .R75 2002

Sentieri della mente. 1. ed. Torino : Bollati Boringhieri, 2001.

Starobinski, Jean. La relation critique. Ed. rev. et augm. [Paris] : Gallimard, c2001.
PN81 .S69 2001

Villari, Rafael Andrés. Literatura e psicanálise. Florianópolis : Editora da UFSC, 2002.

Vinet, Dominique. Romanesque britannique et psyché. Paris : L'Harmattan, c2003.

Wortham, Simon. Samuel Weber. Aldershot, England ; Burlington, VT : Ashgate, c2003.
PN81 .W64 2003

Yankelevich, Héctor, 1946- Du père à la lettre. Ramonville Saint-Agne : Erès, c2003.

PSYCHOANALYSIS AND LITERATURE - PERIODICALS.
(Re)-turn. Columbia, Mo. : University of Missouri Press, 2003-
BF173.L15 R48

Psychoanalysis and management / Michael Hofmann, Monika List, (eds.) ; with contributions by S. Allcorn ... [et al.]. Heidelberg : Physica-Verlag, c1994. xii, 392 p. : ill. ; 24 cm. (Contributions to management science) Includes bibliographical references. ISBN 3-7908-0795-8 (alk. paper)
1. Social sciences and psychoanalysis. 2. Management - Psychological aspects. 3. Organizational behavior. I. Hofmann, Michael, 1932- II. List, Monika. III. Allcorn, Seth. IV. Series.
BF175.4.S65 P777 1994

PSYCHOANALYSIS AND MUSIC.
Didier-Weill, Alain. Lila et la lumière de Vermeer. Paris : Denoël, c2003.

Sentieri della mente. 1. ed. Torino : Bollati Boringhieri, 2001.

PSYCHOANALYSIS AND PHILOSOPHY.
Barris, Jeremy. Paradox and the possibility of knowledge. Selinsgrove : Susquehanna University Press, c2003.
BF175.4.P45 B37 2003

Cathelineau, Pierre-Christophe, 1961- Lacan, lecteur d'Aristote. 2. éd., rev. et corr. Paris : Éditions de l'Association freudienne internationale, c2001 (2002 printing)

Chapelle, Daniel, 1951- The soul in everyday life. Albany, NY : State University of New York Press, c2003.
BF175.4.P45 C48 2003

Deleuze, Gilles. [Dialogues. English] Dialogues II. 2nd ed. New York : Columbia University Press, 2002.
B2430.D453 D4313 2002

Green, André. Time in psychoanalysis. London ; New York : Free Association Books, 2002.
BF468 .G6713 2002

Kristeva, Julia, 1941- [Révolte intime. English] Intimate revolt. New York : Columbia University Press, c2002.
PN56.P92 K7513 2002

Rereading Freud. Albany : State University of New York Press, 2004.
BF109.F74 R47 2004

Schuster, Shlomit C., 1951- The philosopher's autobiography. Westport, Conn. ; London : Praeger, 2003.

Psychoanalysis and philosophy.

B52.7 .S38 2003

Sentieri della mente. 1. ed. Torino : Bollati Boringhieri, 2001.

Strenger, Carlo. The quest for voice in contemporary psychoanalysis. Madison, Conn. : International Universities Press, c2002.
RC506 .S773 2002

Understanding experience. London ; New York : Routledge, 2003.
B105.E9 U53 2003

PSYCHOANALYSIS AND PHILOSOPHY - HISTORY.
Berto, G. (Graziella) Freud, Heidegger. Milano : Bompiani, c1998.
BF175.4.P45 B46 1998

PSYCHOANALYSIS AND RACISM.
Clarke, Simon, 1962- Social theory, psychoanalysis, and racism. New York : Palgrave Macmillan, 2003.
BF175.4.R34 C58 2003

Dalal, Farhad. Race, colour and the process of racialization. Hove, [England] ; New York : Brunner-Routledge, 2002.
BF175.4.R34 D35 2002

PSYCHOANALYSIS AND RELIGION.
Bingaman, Kirk A. Freud and faith. Albany, NY : State University of New York Press, c2003.
BF175.4.R44 B56 2003

Clément, Catherine, 1939- Le divan et le grigri. Paris : Jacob, c2002.

Lioger, Richard. La folie du chaman. Paris : Presses universitaires de France, c2002.

Quaglia, Rocco. I sogni della Bibbia. Roma : Borla, c2002.

Ryan, Robert E. Shamanism and the psychology of C.G. Jung. London : Vega, 2002.
BF175.4.R44 R93 2002

Sorenson, Randall Lehmann, 1954- Minding spirituality. Hillsdale, NJ : Analytic Press, 2003.
BF175.4.R44 S67 2003

PSYCHOANALYSIS AND RELIGION - INDIA.
Vishnu on Freud's desk. Delhi ; Oxford : Oxford University Press, 1999 (2002 [printing])

PSYCHOANALYSIS AND SOCIAL SCIENCES.
See **SOCIAL SCIENCES AND PSYCHOANALYSIS.**

Psychoanalysis and social theory
Burack, Cynthia, 1958- Healing identities. Ithaca : Cornell University Press, 2004.
BF175.4.F45 B87 2004

PSYCHOANALYSIS AND THE ARTS.
Randolph, Jeanne, 1943- Why stoics box. Toronto : YYZ Books, 2003.

Psychoanalysis and the unconscious.
Lawrence, D. H. (David Herbert), 1885-1930. [Psychoanalysis and the unconscious] New York : Cambridge, 2003.
BF173 .L28 2003

PSYCHOANALYSIS AND WOMEN. *See* **WOMEN AND PSYCHOANALYSIS.**

Psychoanalysis at the limit : epistemology, mind, and the question of science / [edited by] Jon Mills. Albany : State University of New York Press, 2004. p. cm. Includes bibliographical references and index. ISBN 0-7914-6065-7 (alk. paper) ISBN 0-7914-6066-5 (pbk. : alk. paper) DDC 150.19/5
1. Psychoanalysis - Philosophy. I. Mills, Jon, 1964-
BF173 .P7753 2004

PSYCHOANALYSIS - BIBLIOGRAPHY.
Stock, Karl F. Freud-Bibliographien. Graz : Stock & Stock, 1998.
BF109.F73 S76 1998

PSYCHOANALYSIS - BRAZIL - HISTORY.
Russo, Jane. O mundo psi no Brasil. Rio de Janeiro : Jorge Zahar Editor, c2002.
BF173 .R877 2002

PSYCHOANALYSIS - CONGRESSES.
Psychanalyse et décolonisation. Paris : LHarmattan, c1999.
BF175.4.C84 P76 1999

Transgressões. Rio de Janeiro, RJ : Espaço Brasileiro de Estudos Psicanalíticos : Contra Capa, 2002.

PSYCHOANALYSIS - FRANCE - HISTORY.
Bolzinger, André. La réception de Freud en France. Paris : L'Harmattan, c1999.

BF175 .B575 1999

PSYCHOANALYSIS - GERMANY - HISTORY.
Rickels, Laurence A. Nazi psychoanalysis. Minneapolis : University of Minnesota Press, c2002-
BF173 .R49 2002

PSYCHOANALYSIS - HISTORY.
Creative dissent. Westport, Conn. : Praeger Publishers, 2003.
BF173 .C794 2003

Flem, Lydia. [Homme Freud. English] Freud the man. New York : Other Press, c2003.
BF109.F74 F4813 2003

Freud [electronic resource]. Washington, DC : Library of Congress
BF173

Marinelli, Lydia. Dreaming by the book. New York : Other Press, c2003.
BF175.5.D74 F7436 2003

Marinelli, Lydia. Träume nach Freud. Wien : Turia + Kant, c2002.

Masson, J. Moussaieff (Jeffrey Moussaieff), 1941- The assault on truth. 1st Ballantine Books ed. New York : Ballantine Books, 2003.
BF109.F74 M38 2003

Le propre de l'homme. Lausanne : Delachaux et Niestlé, c1998.
BF175 .P69 1998

Zaretsky, Eli. Secrets of the soul. 1st ed. New York : A.A. Knopf, 2004.
BF173 .Z37 2004

PSYCHOANALYSIS - HISTORY - 19TH CENTURY.
Bolzinger, André. La réception de Freud en France. Paris : L'Harmattan, c1999.
BF175 .B575 1999

Psychoanalysis in focus.
Smith, David Livingston, 1953- London ; Thousand Oaks, Calif. : SAGE Publications, 2003.
BF173 .S569 2003

PSYCHOANALYSIS IN LITERATURE.
Kristeva, Julia, 1941- [Révolte intime. English] Intimate revolt. New York : Columbia University Press, c2002.
PN56.P92 K7513 2002

Literature, science, psychoanalysis, 1830-1970. Oxford ; New York : Oxford University Press, 2003.
PN55 .L58 2003

PSYCHOANALYSIS - MORAL AND ETHICAL ASPECTS.
Meissner, W. W. (William W.), 1931- The ethical dimension of psychoanalysis. Albany : State University of New York Press, c2003.
BF173 .M3592 2003

PSYCHOANALYSIS PATIENTS. *See* **ANALYSANDS.**

PSYCHOANALYSIS - PERIODICALS.
Espectros del psicoanalisis. Mexico, D.F. : Editorial la Tinta en el Divan, 1997-
BF173.A2 E75

[Journal for the psychoanalysis of culture & society (Online)] Journal for the psychoanalysis of culture and society [electronic resource]. Columbus, Ohio : Ohio State University Press
BF175.4.C84

[Pubblic/azione (Troina, Italy)] Pubblic/azione. Troina (Enna) : Oasi editrice, 2002-

(Re)-turn. Columbia, Mo. : University of Missouri Press, 2003-
BF173.L15 R48

PSYCHOANALYSIS - PHILOSOPHY.
Psychoanalysis at the limit. Albany : State University of New York Press, 2004.
BF173 .P7753 2004

PSYCHOANALYSIS - POLITICAL ASPECTS - GERMANY - HISTORY.
Rickels, Laurence A. Nazi psychoanalysis. Minneapolis : University of Minnesota Press, c2002-
BF173 .R49 2002

PSYCHOANALYSIS - PRACTICE.
Apollon, Willy. After Lacan. Albany : State University of New York Press, 2002.
RC506 .A65 2002

PSYCHOANALYSIS - SOCIAL ASPECTS - HISTORY.

Zaretsky, Eli. Secrets of the soul. 1st ed. New York : A.A. Knopf, 2004.
BF173 .Z37 2004

PSYCHOANALYST AND PATIENT. *See* **PSYCHOTHERAPIST AND PATIENT.**

PSYCHOANALYSTS - AUSTRIA - BIOGRAPHY.
Flem, Lydia. [Homme Freud. English] Freud the man. New York : Other Press, c2003.
BF109.F74 F4813 2003

PSYCHOANALYSTS - AUSTRIA - CORRESPONDENCE.
Analyzing Freud. New York : New Directions, c2002.
BF109.F74 A845 2002

PSYCHOANALYSTS - ENGLAND - BIOGRAPHY.
Hubback, Judith. From dawn to dusk. Wilmette, Ill. : Chiron Publications, 2003.
BF109.H77 A3 2003

PSYCHOANALYSTS - FRANCE - INTERVIEWS.
Babin, Pierre. La fabrique du sexe. Paris : Textuel, [1999]
BF175.5.S48 B23 1999

PSYCHOANALYSTS - GERMANY - BIOGRAPHY.
Hurson, Didier. Alexander Mitscherlich, 1908-1982. Paris : Presses de l'Université de Paris-Sorbonne, 2002.

PSYCHOANALYSTS - SWITZERLAND - BIOGRAPHY.
Bair, Deirdre. Jung. Boston : Little, Brown, 2003.
BF109.J8 B35 2003

PSYCHOANALYSTS - UNITED STATES - BIOGRAPHY.
Corrington, Robert S., 1950- Wilhelm Reich. 1st ed. New York : Farrar, Straus and Giroux, 2003.
BF109.R38 C67 2003

Strozier, Charles B. Heinz Kohut. 1st pbk. ed. New York : Other Press, 2004.
BF109.K6 S77 2004

PSYCHOANALYTIC COUNSELING.
Lear, Jonathan. Therapeutic action. New York : Other Press, c2003.
BF175.4.C68 L43 2003

Smith, David Livingston, 1953- Psychoanalysis in focus. London ; Thousand Oaks, Calif. : SAGE Publications, 2003.
BF173 .S569 2003

PSYCHOANALYTIC COUNSELING - BIBLIOGRAPHY.
Stock, Karl F. Freud-Bibliographien. Graz : Stock & Stock, 1998.
BF109.F73 S76 1998

Psychoanalytic inquiry book series
(v. 19) Lichtenberg, Joseph D. A spirit of inquiry. Hillsdale, NJ : Analytic Press, 2002.
RC506 .L5238 2002

PSYCHOANALYTIC INTERPRETATION.
Dandyk, Alfred. Unaufrichtigkeit. Würzburg : Königshausen & Neumann, c2002.

Gambini, Roberto, 1944- Soul & culture. 1st ed. College Station : Texas A&M University Press, 2003.
BF698.9.C8 G35 2003

Zeichen des Todes in der psychoanalytischen Erfahrung. Tübingen : Edition Diskord, c2000.

Psychoanalytic knowledge / edited by Man Cheung Chung & Colin Feltham. New York : Palgrave Macmillan, 2003. p. cm. Includes bibliographical references and index. ISBN 0-333-97391-7 DDC 150.19/6
1. Psychoanalysis. 2. Freud, Sigmund, - 1856-1939 I. Chung, Man Cheung, 1962- II. Feltham, Colin, 1950-
BF173 .P7763 2003

PSYCHOANALYTIC LITERARY CRITICISM.
See **PSYCHOANALYSIS AND LITERATURE.**

Psychoanalytic theory.
Elliott, Anthony. 2nd ed. Durham, NC : Duke University Press, 2002.
BF173 .E63 2002

PSYCHOANALYTIC THEORY.
Fink, Bruce, 1956- Lacan to the letter. Minneapolis, MN : University of Minnesota Press, c2004.
BF173 .L1434 2004

(Re)-turn. Columbia, Mo. : University of Missouri Press, 2003-
BF173.L15 R48

Reeder, Jurgen, 1947- [Tolkandets gränser. English] Reflecting psychoanalysis. London ; New York : Karnac Books, 2002.

Rizzuto, Ana-María. The dynamics of human aggression. New York, NY : Brunner-Routledge, 2003.
BF175.5.A36 R59 2003

Sayers, Janet. Divine therapy. Oxford ; New York : Oxford University Press, 2003.
BF175.4.R44 S28 2003

PSYCHOANALYTIC THEORY - BIBLIOGRAPHY.
Stock, Karl F. Freud-Bibliographien. Graz : Stock & Stock, 1998.
BF109.F73 S76 1998

PSYCHOANALYTIC THERAPY - BIBLIOGRAPHY.
Stock, Karl F. Freud-Bibliographien. Graz : Stock & Stock, 1998.
BF109.F73 S76 1998

Psychoanalytisches Archiv und jüdisches Gedächtnis. Maciejewski, Franz. 1. Aufl. Wien : Passagen Verlag, 2002.

PSYCHOBIOLOGY.
Biologische Grundlagen der Psychologie. Göttingen ; Seattle : Hogrefe, 2001.
QP360.B565 2001

Marcus, Gary F. (Gary Fred) The birth of the mind. New York : Basic Books, 2004.
BF701.M32 2004

PSYCHODIAGNOSTICS.
Kostina, L. M. (Lîubov' Mikhaĭlovna) Metody diagnostiki trevozhnosti. Sankt-Peterburg : Rech', 2002.
BF575.A6 K65 2002

PSYCHODRAMA.
Edgar, Iain R. Guide to imagework. London ; New York : Routledge, 2004.
BF367.E34 2004

PSYCHODYNAMIC PSYCHOTHERAPY.
Quaglia, Rocco. I sogni della Bibbia. Roma : Borla, c2002.

PSYCHOGENIC NEEDS. See NEED (PSYCHOLOGY).

Die Psychohistorie des Erlebens / Ralph Frenken, Martin Rheinheimer (Hrsg.). Kiel : Oetker-Voges, c2000. 361 p. : ill. ; 21 cm. (PsychoHistorische Forschungen ; Bd. 2) Includes bibliographical references. ISBN 3-9804322-8-9 (pbk.)
1. History - Psychological aspects. 2. Psychohistory. I. Frenken, Ralph, 1965- II. Rheinheimer, Martin. III. Series.

PsychoHistorische Forschungen
(Bd. 2) Die Psychohistorie des Erlebens. Kiel : Oetker-Voges, c2000.

PSYCHOHISTORY.
Oron, Israel. Mayet, almayet ye-ide'ologyah. [Israel] : Miśrad ha-biṭaḥon, [2002]

Die Psychohistorie des Erlebens. Kiel : Oetker-Voges, c2000.

PSYCHOKINESIS. See also LEVITATION.
Karpenko, M. (Maksim) Vselennaîa razumnaîa = 2. perer. izd. Moskva : MAIK Nauka/Interperiodika, 2001.
BF1036.K37 2001

Mishlove, Jeffrey, 1946- The PK man. Charlottesville, VA : Hampton Roads, [c2000]
BF1027.O94 M57 2000

PSYCHOLINGUISTICS. See also LANGUAGE ACQUISITION; THOUGHT AND THINKING.
Alefirenko, M. F. Poėticheskaîa ėnergiîa slova. Moskva : Academia, 2002.
P35.A544 2002

Aventuras do sentido. Porto Alegre : EDIPUCRS, 2002.

Chipere, Ngoni, 1965- Understanding complex sentences. New York : Palgrave Macmillan, 2003.
P295.C485 2003

Costes, Alain. Lacan, le fourvoiement linguistique. Paris : Presses universitaires de France, 2003.

Fernández, Eva M. Bilingual sentence processing. Amsterdam ; Philadelphia : J. Benjamins Pub., 2003.
P115.4.F47 2003

Giora, Rachel, 1945- On our mind. New York : Oxford University Press, c2003.
BF455.G525 2003

Harley, Trevor A. The psychology of language. Hove, East Sussex, UK : Erlbaum (UK) Taylor & Francis, c1995.

Herdina, Philip. A dynamic model of multilingualism. Clevedon, England Buffalo, N.Y. : Multilingual Matters, 2002.
P115.4.H47 2002

Hochman, Judith. Image and word in Ahsen's image psychology. New York : Brandon House, c2000.
BF367.H63 2000

Jusczyk, Peter W. The discovery of spoken language. 1st MIT Press pbk. ed. Cambridge, Mass. : MIT Press, 2000.
BF720.S67 J87 2000

Kessler, Klaus. Raumkognition und Lokalisationsäusserungen. Wiesbaden : Deutscher Universitäts-Verlag, 2000.
BF469.K47 2000

Kiraly, Donald C., 1953- Pathways to translation. Kent, Ohio : Kent State University Press, c1995.
P306.5.K57 1995

Language in mind. Cambridge, Mass. : MIT Press, c2003.
P37.L357 2003

El lenguaje y la mente humana. 1. ed. Barcelona : Ariel Editorial, 2002.

Psycholinguistik. Berlin : W. de Gruyter, c2003.

Raĭnov, Vasil G. Za psikhosemantichnata spetsifika na ezikovoto vŭzpriîatie. Sofiîa : Akademichno izd-vo "Prof. Marin Drinov", 1998.
P37.R27 1998

Reading complex words. New York : Kluwer Academic/Plenum Publishers, c2003.
P37.5.R42 R43 2003

Schröder, Jürgen. Die Sprache des Denkens. Würzburg : Königshausen & Neumann, c2001.

Sprache, Sinn und Situation. 1. Aufl. Wiesbaden : Deutscher Universitäts-Verlag, 2001.

Vasishth, Shravan, 1964- Working memory in sentence comprehension. New York ; London : Routledge, 2003.
PK1933.V28 2003

Word order and scrambling. Malden, MA : Blackwell Pub., 2003.
P295.W65 2003

Psycholinguistics : an international handbook.
Psycholinguistik. Berlin : W. de Gruyter, c2003.

PSYCHOLINGUISTICS, DEVELOPMENTAL. See LANGUAGE ACQUISITION.

Psycholinguistik : ein internationales Handbuch / herausgegeben von Gert Rickheit, Theo Herrmann, Werner Deutsch = Psycholinguistics : an international handbook / edited by Gert Rickheit, Theo Herrmann, Werner Deutsch. Berlin : W. de Gruyter, c2003. xi, 947 p. : ill. ; 28 cm. (Handbücher zur Sprach- und Kommunikationswissenschaft ; Bd. 24 = Handbooks of linguistics and communication science = Manuels de linguistique et des sciences de communication) Includes bibliographical references and index. Chiefly in German; some English. ISBN 3-11-011424-0 (cl.)
1. Psycholinguistics. I. Rickheit, Gert. II. Herrmann, Theo. III. Deutsch, Werner. IV. Herrmann, Theo. V. Title: Psycholinguistics : an international handbook VI. Series: Handbücher zur Sprach- und Kommunikationswissenschaft ; Bd. 24.

Psychologia nie tylko dla psychologów : praca zbiorowa / pod redakcją Jana Bieleckiego. Warszawa : Uniwersytet Kardynała Stefana Wyszyńskiego, 2002. 415 p. ; 21 cm. Includes bibliographical references. ISBN 83-7072-245-8
1. Psychology. I. Bielecki, Jan, OMI.
BF126.P749 2002

Psychologia universalis
(neue Reihe, Bd. 19) Kray, Jutta. Adult age differences in task switching. Lengerich : Pabst Science Publishers, 2000.
BF724.55.C63 K73 2000

Psychologia w obliczu zachodzących przemian społeczno-kulturowych / pod red. naukową Jerzego Brzezińskiego i Heleny Sęk. Warszawa : Instytut Psychologii PAN, 2002. 282 p. : ill. ; 24 cm. (Kolokwia psychologiczne ; t. 10) Includes bibliographical references. Summaries in English. ISBN 83-85459-59-6
1. Psychology - Congresses. 2. Social change - Psychological aspects - Congresses. 3. Social change - Poland - Congresses. I. Brzeziński, Jerzy. II. Sęk, Helena. III. Series.
BF20.P79 2002

PSYCHOLOGICAL ABUSE.
Engel, Beverly. The emotionally abusive relationship. New Jersey : J. Wiley, c2002.

PSYCHOLOGICAL ANTHROPOLOGY. See ETHNOPSYCHOLOGY.

PSYCHOLOGICAL ASSESSMENT. See PSYCHOLOGICAL TESTS.

Psychological Association of the Philippines.
Forty years of Philippine psychology. Diliman, Quezon City, Philippines : Psychological Association of the Philippines, c2002.
BF108.F67 2002

The psychological development of girls and women.
Greene, Sheila, 1946- London ; New York : Routledge, 2003.
HQ1206.G767 2003

Psychological dimensions to war and peace
Evolutionary psychology and violence. Westport, Conn. : Praeger, 2003.
HM1116.E96 2003

Kraft, Robert Nathaniel. Memory perceived. Westport, Conn. : Praeger, 2002.
D804.195.K73 2002

The psychology of terrorism. Westport, CT : Praeger, 2002.
HV6431.P798 2002

PSYCHOLOGICAL FICTION - HISTORY AND CRITICISM.
D'Cruz, Doreen, 1950- Loving subjects. New York : P. Lang, c2002.
PR888.W6 D39 2002

PSYCHOLOGICAL LITERATURE. See also PSYCHOLOGY - BIBLIOGRAPHY.
Sternberg, Robert J. The psychologist's companion. 4th ed. Cambridge, U.K. ; New York : Cambridge University Press, 2003.
BF76.8.S73 2003

PSYCHOLOGICAL LITERATURE - PUBLISHING - HANDBOOKS, MANUALS, ETC.
Publication manual of the American Psychological Association. 4th ed. Washington, DC : American Psychological Association, 1994.
BF76.7.P82 1994

Publication manual of the American Psychological Association. 5th ed. Washington, DC : American Psychological Association, c2001.
BF76.7.P83 2001

PSYCHOLOGICAL MEASUREMENT. See PSYCHOMETRICS.

Psychological Publications, Inc.
T-JTA scoring program [electronic resource]. Windows version 2.0. Thousand Oaks, CA : Psychological Pub., c2002.
BF698.8.T35

PSYCHOLOGICAL RESEARCH. See PSYCHOLOGY - RESEARCH.

PSYCHOLOGICAL SCALING. See PSYCHOMETRICS.

PSYCHOLOGICAL SCHEMAS. See SCHEMAS (PSYCHOLOGY).

PSYCHOLOGICAL STATISTICS. See PSYCHOMETRICS.

PSYCHOLOGICAL STRESS. See STRESS (PSYCHOLOGY).

Psychological testing.
Gregory, Robert J., 1943- 4th ed. Boston, MA : Allyn and Bacon, 2004.
BF176.G74 2004

PSYCHOLOGICAL TESTS. See also CHARACTER TESTS; INTELLIGENCE TESTS; PSYCHOMETRICS.
Drummond, Robert J. Appraisal procedures for counselors and helping professionals. 5th ed. Upper Saddle River, N.J. : Merrill/Prentice Hall, 2003.
BF176.D78 2003

Gregory, Robert J., 1943- Psychological testing. 4th ed. Boston, MA : Allyn and Bacon, 2004.
BF176.G74 2004

Prakticheskaîa psikhologiîa v testakh, ili, Kak nauchit' sîa ponimat' sebîa i drugikh. Moskva : AST-Press kniga, 2003.
BF176.P73 2003

PSYCHOLOGICAL TESTS - ENCYCLOPEDIAS.
Encyclopedia of psychological assessment. London ; Thousand Oaks, Calif. : SAGE Publications, 2003.
BF39 .E497 2003

PSYCHOLOGICAL TESTS FOR CHILDREN.
Handbook of psychological and educational assessment of children. 2nd ed. New York, N.Y. : Guilford Press, 2003.
BF722 .H33 2003

Handbook of psychological and educational assessment of children. 2nd ed. New York : Guilford Press, 2003.
BF722 .H33 2003b

PSYCHOLOGICAL TESTS - HISTORY.
Gregory, Robert J., 1943- Psychological testing. 4th ed. Boston, MA : Allyn and Bacon, 2004.
BF176 .G74 2004

PSYCHOLOGICAL TESTS - PROBLEMS, EXERCISES, ETC.
Condon, Margaret E. Exercises in psychological testing. Boston : Allyn and Bacon, c2002.
BF176 .T47 2002

PSYCHOLOGICAL TESTS - SOUTH AFRICA.
An introduction to psychological assessment in the South African context. Cape Town, South Africa : Oxford University Press Southern Africa, 2001.
BF39 .I58 2001

PSYCHOLOGICAL TESTS - STATISTICAL METHODS.
Cliff, Norman, 1930- Ordinal measurement in the behavioral sciences. Mahwah, N.J. : Lawrence Erlbaum Associates, 2003.
BF39 .C525 2003

Psychological theories for environmental issues / edited by Mirilia Bonnes, Terence Lee and Marino Bonaiuto. Aldershot, Hants, England ; Burlington, VT : Ashgate, 2003. [ix], 284 p. ; 22 cm. (Ethnoscapes) Includes bibliographical references and indexes. ISBN 0-7546-1888-9 (alk. paper) DDC 155.9
 1. Environmental psychology. I. Bonnes, Mirilia. II. Lee, Terence, 1924- III. Bonaiuto, Marino. IV. Series.
BF353 .P774 2003

PSYCHOLOGICAL TYPES. See **TYPOLOGY (PSYCHOLOGY).**

PSYCHOLOGICAL WARFARE. See **BRAINWASHING.**

La psychologie de Th. Jouffroy.
Jouffroy, Théodore, 1796-1842. [Selections] Paris : L'Harmattan, c2003.

Psychologie der Persönlichkeit.
Crisand, Ekkehard. 8., durchgesehene Aufl. Heidelberg : I.H. Sauer-Verlag, 2000.
BF698 .C715 2000

Psychologie des Internet / Peter Vitouch (Hg.). Wien : WUV, Universitätsverlag, 2001. 241 p. : ill. ; 23 cm. Includes bibliographical references. ISBN 3-85114-568-2
 1. Communication - Psychological aspects. 2. Internet - Psychological aspects. 3. Computer networks - Psychological aspects. I. Vitouch, Peter.
BF637.C45 P759 2001

Psychologie (Desclée De Brouwer (Firm))
Canault, Nina. Comment le désir de naître vient au foetus. Paris : Desclée de Brouwer, c2001.

Psychologie et révélation.
Emtcheu, André. Yaoundé, Cameroun : Editions SHERPA, c2001.

Psychologie : Fühlen, Denken und Verhalten verstehen.
Der Brockhaus Psychologie. Mannheim : Brockhaus, c2001.

Psychologie, psychiatrie et société sous la troisième république.
Huteau, Michel. Paris : Harmattan, c2002.

Psychologische Beiträge.
Psychology science. Lengereich [Germany] : Pabst Science Publishers, 2003-
BF3 .P64

Psychologische Schriften.
Benussi, V. (Vittorio) [Selections. 2002] Amsterdam ; New York : Rodopi, 2002.

PSYCHOLOGISM.
Philosophy, psychology, and psychologism. Dordrecht ; Boston : Kluwer Academic Publishers, c2003.
BF41 .P553 2003

Psychologist.
Brinkerhoff, Shirley. Broomall, Pa. : Mason Crest Publishers, c2003.
BF76 .B75 2003

PSYCHOLOGISTS. See **MINORITY PSYCHOLOGISTS.**

PSYCHOLOGISTS - BIOGRAPHY.
Stepanov, S. S. (Sergeĭ Sergeevich) Psikhologii︠a︡ v litsakh. Moskva : ĖKSMO-Press, 2001.
BF109.A1 S74 2001

Stepanov, S. S. (Sergeĭ Sergeevich) Vek psikhologii. Izd. 2., ispr. i dop. Moskva : ĖKSMO, 2002.
BF109.A1 S75 2002

PSYCHOLOGISTS - BIOGRAPHY - ENCYCLOPEDIAS.
Sheehy, Noel, 1955- Fifty key thinkers in psychology. London ; New York : Routledge, 2003.
BF109.A1 S49 2003

The psychologist's companion.
Sternberg, Robert J. 4th ed. Cambridge, U.K. ; New York : Cambridge University Press, 2003.
BF76.8 .S73 2003

PSYCHOLOGISTS - FRANCE - HISTORY.
Nicolas, Serge. Histoire de la psychologie française. Paris : In press, c2002.
BF108.F8 N536 2002

PSYCHOLOGISTS - LEGAL STATUS, LAWS, ETC. - UNITED STATES.
Lipinski, Barbara. The tao of integrity. San Buenaventura, CA : Pacific Meridian Publications, c2001.
BF75 .L655 2001

PSYCHOLOGISTS, MINORITY. See **MINORITY PSYCHOLOGISTS.**

PSYCHOLOGISTS - OKLAHOMA - HISTORY.
Oklahoma psychology in the twentieth century. [Oklahoma City, OK : Oklahoma Psychological Association, 2003?]
BF77 .O35 2003

PSYCHOLOGISTS - PROFESSIONAL ETHICS.
Ethical conflicts in psychology. 3rd ed. Washington, DC : American Psychological Association, c2003.
BF76.4 .E814 2003

Fisher, Celia B. Decoding the ethics code. Thousand Oaks, Calif. : Sage Publications, c2003.
BF76.4 .F57 2003

PSYCHOLOGISTS - PROFESSIONAL ETHICS - UNITED STATES.
Lipinski, Barbara. The tao of integrity. San Buenaventura, CA : Pacific Meridian Publications, c2001.
BF75 .L655 2001

PSYCHOLOGISTS - RUSSIA (FEDERATION) - BIOGRAPHY.
Artamonov, V. I. (Vladimir Ivanovich) Psikhologii︠a︡ ot pervogo litsa. Moskva : Academia, 2003.
BF109.A1 A78 2003

Kitaev-Smyk, L. A. (Leonid Aleksandrovich) Stress voĭny. Moskva : Ministerstvo kul'tury RF : Rossiĭskiĭ in-t kul'turologii, 2001.

Shchedrovit︠s︡kiĭ, G. P. (Georgiĭ Petrovich), 1929-1994. I︠A︡ vsegda byl idealistom--. Moskva : Put', 2001.
BF109.S44 A3 2001

PSYCHOLOGISTS - RUSSIA (FEDERATION) - INTERVIEWS.
Artamonov, V. I. (Vladimir Ivanovich) Psikhologii︠a︡ ot pervogo litsa. Moskva : Academia, 2003.
BF109.A1 A78 2003

PSYCHOLOGISTS - UNITED STATES - BIOGRAPHY.
Cohen, David, 1946- Carl Rogers. London : Constable, 1997.
BF109.R63 C64 1997

PSYCHOLOGY. See also **ADJUSTMENT (PSYCHOLOGY); ADOLESCENT PSYCHOLOGY; AFFECT (PSYCHOLOGY); ATTITUDE (PSYCHOLOGY); BEHAVIORISM (PSYCHOLOGY); CHANGE (PSYCHOLOGY); CHILD PSYCHOLOGY; CHOICE (PSYCHOLOGY); COGNITION; COGNITIVE PSYCHOLOGY; COMMUNICATION IN PSYCHOLOGY; COMMUNISM AND PSYCHOLOGY; CONSCIOUSNESS; CONSTRUCTIVISM (PSYCHOLOGY); CONTROL (PSYCHOLOGY); CRIMINAL PSYCHOLOGY; CYNICISM; DEVELOPMENTAL PSYCHOLOGY; DIFFERENCE (PSYCHOLOGY); EDUCATIONAL PSYCHOLOGY; EGO (PSYCHOLOGY); EMOTIONS; ETHNOPSYCHOLOGY; FAILURE (PSYCHOLOGY); FEMINIST PSYCHOLOGY; FIGHTING (PSYCHOLOGY); GENETIC PSYCHOLOGY; HOSTILITY (PSYCHOLOGY); HUMAN BEHAVIOR; HUMANISTIC PSYCHOLOGY; IDEOLOGY; INDIVIDUATION (PSYCHOLOGY); INFLUENCE (PSYCHOLOGY); INTELLECT; KNOWLEDGE, THEORY OF; LEFT AND RIGHT (PSYCHOLOGY); LOGIC; LOSS (PSYCHOLOGY); MATURATION (PSYCHOLOGY); MEANING (PSYCHOLOGY); MEMORY; MENTAL HEALTH; MOTIVATION (PSYCHOLOGY); OBSERVATION (PSYCHOLOGY); OPPRESSION (PSYCHOLOGY); PARAPSYCHOLOGY; PERCEPTION; PERSONAL CONSTRUCT THEORY; PERSONALITY; PHRENOLOGY; PHYSIOGNOMY; PROBLEM SOLVING; PSYCHOANALYSIS; PSYCHOLOGY, APPLIED; RACISM IN PSYCHOLOGY; SELF PSYCHOLOGY; SELF-ACCEPTANCE; SOCIAL INTERACTION; SOCIAL PSYCHOLOGY; SPATIAL BEHAVIOR; STRESS (PSYCHOLOGY); SUBCONSCIOUSNESS; SYMBOLISM (PSYCHOLOGY); THOUGHT AND THINKING; THREAT (PSYCHOLOGY); TYPOLOGY (PSYCHOLOGY); VALUES; WHOLE AND PARTS (PSYCHOLOGY); WILL.**

Bruno, Frank Joe, 1930- New York : John Wiley & Sons, c2002.
BF77 .B78 2002

Cardwell, Mike. Schaum's A-Z psychology. New York : McGraw-Hill, 2003.
BF31 .C29 2003

Franzoi, Stephen L. Cincinnati, Ohio : Atomic Dog Pub., c2002.
BF121 .F67 2002

Franzoi, Stephen L. Cincinnati, Ohio : Atomic Dog Pub., c2003.
BF121 .F675 2003

Gleitman, Henry. 6th ed. New York : W.W. Norton, c2004.
BF121 .G58 2004

Hockenbury, Don H. 3rd ed. New York : Worth Publishers , c2003.
BF121 .H59 2003

Johnston, Joni E., 1960- The complete idiot's guide to psychology. 2nd ed. Indianapolis, IN : Alpha Books, c2003.
BF121 .J64 2003

Kagan, Jerome. Kagan & Segal's psychology. 9th ed. Belmont, CA : Thomson/Wadsworth, c2004.
BF121 .K22 2004

Kassin, Saul M. 4th ed. Upper Saddle River, NJ : Pearson/Prentice Hall, 2003.
BF121 .K34 2003

Kelly, Brian, 1956- iSearch. Boston, MA : Allyn and Bacon, c2003.
BF76.78 .K45 2003

Kosslyn, Stephen Michael, 1948- 2nd ed. Boston, MA : Allyn and Bacon, 2004.
BF121 .K59 2004

Nevid, Jeffrey S. Boston, MA : Houghton Mifflin, c2003.
BF121 .N42 2003

Passer, Michael W. 2nd ed. Boston, Mass. : McGraw-Hill, 2003.
BF121 .P348 2003

Santrock, John W. 2nd ed. Boston : McGraw-Hill, c2003.
BF121 .S2642 2003

Santrock, John W. Updated 2nd ed. Boston, Mass. : McGraw-Hill, 2004.
BF121 .S2642 2004

Santrock, John W. Updated 7th ed. Boston : McGraw-Hill, c2005.

BF121 .S265 2005
Sternberg, Robert J. 4th ed. Belmont, CA : Thomson/ Wadsworth, c2004.
BF121 .S84 2004
Weiten, Wayne, 1950- 6th ed. Australia ; Belmont, CA : Thomson/Wadsworth, c2004.
BF121 .W38 2004

PSYCHOLOGY.
Az Általánostól a különösig. [Budapest] : Gondolat : MTA Pszichológiai Kutatóintézet, c2002.
BF128.H8 A44 2002

Atkinson & Hilgard's introduction to psychology. 14th ed. Australia ; Belmont, CA : Wadworth/ Thomson Learning, c2003.
BF121 .I57 2003

Benussi, V. (Vittorio) [Selections. 2002] Psychologische Schriften. Amsterdam ; New York : Rodopi, 2002.

Bolich, Gregory G. Psyche's child. Dubuque, Iowa : Kendall/Hunt Pub., c2000.
BF121 .B57 2000

Carr, Alan, Dr. Positive psychology. London ; New York : Brunner-Routledge, 2004.
BF121 .C355 2004

Coon, Dennis. Essentials of psychology. 9th ed. Australia ; Belmont, CA : Thoomson Learning/ Wadsworth, c2003.
BF121 .C624 2003

Evolutionary economics and human nature. Cheltenham : Edward Elgar, c2003.

Franzoi, Stephen L. Psychology. Cincinnati, Ohio : Atomic Dog Pub., c2002.
BF121 .F67 2002

Franzoi, Stephen L. Psychology. Cincinnati, Ohio : Atomic Dog Pub., c2003.
BF121 .F675 2003

Gleitman, Henry. Psychology. 6th ed. New York : W.W. Norton, c2004.
BF121 .G58 2004

Handbook of psychology. Hoboken, N.J. : John Wiley, c2003.
BF121 .H1955 2003

Harkai Schiller, Pál, 1908-1949. A lélektan feladata. Budapest : Osiris Kiadó, 2002.
BF128.H8 H37 2002

Hobfoll, Stevan E. [Work won't love you back. Chinese] Top shuang xin jia ting. Chu ban. Taibei Shi : Ye qiang chu ban she, 1997.

Huffman, Karen. Psychology in action. 7th ed. Hoboken, NJ : John Wiley & Sons, c2004.
BF121 .H78 2004

Humphrey, Nicholas. The mind made flesh. Oxford ; New York : Oxford University Press, 2002.
BF701 .H86 2002

James, William, 1842-1910. [Pragmatism. German] Pragmatismus. Berlin : Akademie Verlag, c2000.

Johnston, Joni E., 1960- The complete idiot's guide to psychology. 2nd ed. Indianapolis, IN : Alpha Books, c2003.
BF121 .J64 2003

Kagan, Jerome. Kagan & Segal's psychology. 9th ed. Belmont, CA : Thomson/Wadsworth, c2004.
BF121 .K22 2004

Kassin, Saul M. Psychology. 4th ed. Upper Saddle River, NJ : Pearson/Prentice Hall, 2003.
BF121 .K34 2003

Khurmetbek, Khalikiĭn. Ŭl bichigdmėlůůd. Ulaanbaatar : "Monsudar" Khėvlėliĭn Gazar, 2001.
QA465 .K48 2001

Kohn, Arthur J. The integrator for Introductory psychology 2.0 [electronic resource]. Pacific Grove, Calif. : Brooks/Cole, c1998.
BF121

Kosslyn, Stephen Michael, 1948- Psychology. 2nd ed. Boston, MA : Allyn and Bacon, 2004.
BF121 .K59 2004

Le leggi del pensiero tra logica, ontologia e psicologia. Milano : UNICOPLI, 2002.

Malott, Richard W. Principles of behavior. 5th ed. Upper Saddle River, N.J. : Pearson/Prentice Hall, 2003.

BF319.5.O6 M34 2003
Matheus, Tiago Corbisier. Ideais na adolescência. 1a ed. São Paulo, SP : Annablume, 2002.

Melucci, Nancy J. Psychology the easy way. Hauppauge, N.Y. : Barron's Educational Series, c2004.
BF121 .M45 2004

Mongeau, Pierre, 1954- Survivre. Sainte-Foy : Presses de l'Université du Québec, 2002.
BF122 .M66 2002

Nevid, Jeffrey S. Psychology and the challenges of life. 9th ed. Hoboken, NJ : Wiley, c2005.
BF335 .N475 2005

Nevid, Jeffrey S. Psychology. Boston, MA : Houghton Mifflin, c2003.
BF121 .N42 2003

Passer, Michael W. Psychology. 2nd ed. Boston, Mass. : McGraw-Hill, 2003.
BF121 .P348 2003

Psychologia nie tylko dla psychologów. Warszawa : Uniwersytet Kardynała Stefana Wyszyńskiego, 2002.
BF126 .P749 2002

Psychology. 6th ed. Boston : Houghton Mifflin Co., c2003.
BF121 .P794 2003

Robinson, Daniel N., 1937- A student's guide to psychology. 1st ed. Wilmington, Del. : ISI Books, c2002.
BF121 .R598 2002

Shaffer, Lary. Research stories for introductory psychology. 2nd ed. Boston, MA : Allyn and Bacon, c2004.
BF76.5 .S43 2004

Shinpan shinrigaku ga wakaru. Tōkyō : Asahi Shinbunsha, 2003.
BF108.J3 S55 2003

Shoemaker, Sydney. Identity, cause, and mind. Expanded ed. Oxford : Clarendon Press ; New York : Oxford University Press, 2003.
B29 .S5135 2003

A small matter of proof. Reno, NV : Context Press, c2003.
BF121 .S545 2003

Sternberg, Robert J. Psychology. 4th ed. Belmont, CA : Thomson/Wadsworth, c2004.
BF121 .S84 2004

Toomela, Aaro. Cultural-historical psychology. Tartu : Tartu University Press, c2000.
BF109.V95 T66 2000

Toševski, Jovo. Nerazumna mreža. Novi Sad : Prometej ; [Kragujevac] : Jefimija, c2002.

Weiten, Wayne, 1950- Psychology. 6th ed. Australia ; Belmont, CA : Thomson/Wadsworth, c2004.
BF121 .W38 2004

Wood, Samuel E. Mastering the world of psychology. Boston : Pearson/Allyn and Bacon, c2004.
BF121 .W656 2004

Psychology & evolution.
Bridgeman, Bruce. Thousand Oaks, Calif. : SAGE Publications, c2003.
BF698.95 .B75 2003

Psychology 101 1/2.
Sternberg, Robert J. Washington, DC : American Psychological Association, 2004.
BF77 .S68 2004

PSYCHOLOGY AND ART.
Duplessis, Yvonne, 1912- Surréalisme et paranormal. Agnières : JMG, 2002.
BF1023 .D87 2002

Matière à symbolisation. Lausanne : Delachaux et Niestlé, c1998.
BF458 .M38 1998

Psychology and Buddhism : from individual to global community / edited by Kathleen H. Dockett, G. Rita Dudley-Grant, C. Peter Bankart. New York : Kluwer Academic/Plenum Publishers, c2003. xv, 308 p. ; 24 cm. (International and cultural psychology series) Includes bibliographical references and indexes. ISBN 0-306-47412-3 DDC 294.3/375
1. *Psychotherapy - Religious aspects - Buddhism. 2. Healing - Religious aspects - Buddhism. 3. Buddhism - Psychology.* I. *Dockett, Kathleen H., 1942-* II. *Dudley-Grant, G. Rita, 1951-* III. *Bankart, C. Peter, 1946-* IV. *Series.*
BQ4570.P76 P78 2003

PSYCHOLOGY AND COMMUNISM. *See* **COMMUNISM AND PSYCHOLOGY.**

Psychology and consumer culture : the struggle for a good life in a materialistic world / edited by Tim Kasser and Allen D. Kanner. 1st ed. Washington, DC : American Psychological Association, c2004. xi, 297 p. ; 26 cm. Includes bibliographical references and indexes. ISBN 1-59147-046-3 DDC 306.3
1. *Consumption (Economics) - United States - Psychological aspects. 2. Materialism - Psychological aspects. 3. Acquisitiveness. 4. Identity (Psychology) 5. Consumers - Psychology.* I. *Kasser, Tim.* II. *Kanner, Allen.*
HC110.C6 P76 2004

Psychology and evolution.
Bridgeman, Bruce. Psychology & evolution. Thousand Oaks, Calif. : SAGE Publications, c2003.
BF698.95 .B75 2003

PSYCHOLOGY AND LITERATURE.
Heuscher, Julius E. (Julius Ernest), 1918- Psychology, folklore, creativity, and the human dilemma. Springfield, Ill. : Charles C Thomas Publisher, c2003.
BF637.C5 H475 2003

PSYCHOLOGY AND MEDICINE. *See* **MEDICINE AND PSYCHOLOGY.**

PSYCHOLOGY AND PHILOSOPHY.
Arpaly, Nomy. Unprincipled virtue. Oxford ; New York : Oxford University Press, 2003.
BJ45 .A76 2003

Loewenthal, Del, 1947- Post-modernism for psychotherapists. Hove, East Sussex ; New York : Brunner-Routledge, 2003.
BF41 .L64 2003

Moravia, Sergio, 1940- L'esistenza ferita. 1. ed. in "Campi del sapere.". Milano : Feltrinelli, 1999.
BF41 .M67 1999

PSYCHOLOGY AND PHILOSOPHY - HISTORY.
Rossi, Paolo, 1923- Bambini, sogni, furori. 1. ed. in "Campi del sapere.". Milano : Feltrinelli, 2001.
BF41 .R67 2001

PSYCHOLOGY AND PHILOSOPHY - ITALY - HISTORY.
Sava, Gabriella. La psicologia filosofica in Italia. Galatina (Lecce) : Congedo, 2000.
BF38 .S235 2000

PSYCHOLOGY AND RELIGION.
Bond, D. Stephenson. The archetype of renewal. Toronto : Inner City Books, c2003.

Coward, Harold G. Yoga and psychology. Albany : State University of New York Press, 2002.
BF51 .C69 2002

Frame, Marsha Wiggins. Integrating religion and spirituality into counseling. Australia ; Pacific Grove, CA : Thomson/Brooks/Cole, c2003.
BF637.C6 F64 2003

Goleman, Daniel. Destructive emotions. New York : Bantam Books, c2003.
BL65.E46 G65 2003

Hinterhuber, H. (Hartmann) Die Seele. Wien ; New York : Springer, c2001.

Romanova, A. P. (Anna Petrovna) Stanovlenie religioznogo kompleksa. Astrakhan : Izd-vo Astrakhanskogo pedagog. universiteta, 1999.
BF51 .R66 1999

Zen'ko, I͡U. M. Psikhologii͡a i religii͡a. Sankt-Peterburg : Aletei͡a, 2002.
BF51 .Z46 2002

Psychology and the challenges of life.
Nevid, Jeffrey S. 9th ed. Hoboken, NJ : Wiley, c2005.
BF335 .N475 2005

Psychology and the Internet : intrapersonal, interpersonal, and transpersonal implications / edited by Jayne Gackenbach. San Diego, Calif. : Academic Press, c1998. xix, 369 p. : ill. ; 23 cm. Includes bibliographical references and indexes. Publisher description URL: http://www.loc.gov/catdir/description/els033/98085527.html Table of contents URL: http://www.loc.gov/catdir/toc/els032/98085527.html CONTENTS: Introduction to psychological aspects of Internet use / Jayne Gackenbach and Evelyn Ellerman -- The intrapersonal : statistically "normal" and "deviant" aspects of the self -- The self and the Internet : variations on the illusion of one self / Elizabeth Reid -- Causes and implications of disinhibited behavior on the Internet / Adam Joinson -- Internet addiction : does it really exist? / Mark Griffiths -- Internet therapy and self-help groups : the pros and cons / Storm A. King and Danielle Moreggi -- Future clinical directions : professional development, pathology, and psychotherapy on-line / John M. Grohol -- The interpersonal :

from close to distant relationships -- The psychology of sex : a mirror from the Internet / Raymond J. Noonan -- Males, females, and the Internet / Janet Morahan-Martin -- Work and community via computer-mediated communication / Caroline Haythornthwaite, Barry Wellman, and Laura Garton -- Virtual societies : their prospects and dilemmas / Magid Igbaria, Conrad Shayo, and Lorne Olfman -- The transpersonal : on the net and the net itself -- From mediated environments to the development of consciousness / Joan M. Preston -- World wide brain : self-organizing Internet intelligence as the actualization of the collective unconscious / Ben Goertzel -- The coevolution of technology and consciousness / Jayne Gackenbach, Greg Guthrie, and Jim Karpen. ISBN 0-12-271950-6 (alk. paper) DDC 150/.285/4678
1. Communication - Psychological aspects. 2. Internet - Psychological aspects. 3. Computer networks - Psychological aspects. I. Gackenbach, Jayne, 1946-
BF637.C45 P79 1998

Psychology and the question of agency.
Martin, Jack, 1950- Albany : State University of New York Press, c2003.
BF575.A88 M37 2003

PSYCHOLOGY, APPLIED. *See also* **COUNSELING; INTERVIEWING; MEDICINE AND PSYCHOLOGY; NEGOTIATION; PEACE OF MIND; PERSUASION (PSYCHOLOGY); PSYCHOLOGY, INDUSTRIAL; PSYCHOLOGY, MILITARY; SCHOOL PSYCHOLOGY; SECURITY (PSYCHOLOGY); SELF-HELP TECHNIQUES.**
Applied psychology. London ; Thousand Oaks, Calif. : SAGE Publications, 2003.
BF636.A62 2003

Chagas, Arnaldo Sousa das Chagas. O sujeito imaginário no discurso de auto-ajuda. Rio Grande do Sul : Editora UNIJUÍ, 2002.

Kozlov, Nikolaĭ (Nikolaĭ Ivanovich) Kniga dlia tekh, komu nravitsia zhit', ili, Psikhologiia lichnostnogo rosta. Moskva : "AST-Press kniga", 2002.
BF723.P4 K69 2002

Milmaniene, José E. Clínica del texto. [1. ed.]. Buenos Aires : Editorial Biblos, c2002.

Olaoye, Elaine H. Passions of the soul. 2nd ed. Red Bank, N.J. : Northwind Publishers, 2002.
1. Black author.

Spelman, Elizabeth V. Repair. Boston : Beacon Press, c2002.
BF636.S689 2002

PSYCHOLOGY, APPLIED - METHODS.
Carr, Alan, Dr. Positive psychology. London ; New York : Brunner-Routledge, 2004.
BF121.C355 2004

PSYCHOLOGY - ARGENTINA - PERIODICALS.
Psicodebate. Buenos Aires, Argentina : Universidad de Palermo, Facultad de Humanidades y Ciencias Sociales, [2000]-
BF5.P+

PSYCHOLOGY - AUTHORSHIP.
Dunn, Dana. A short guide to writing about psychology. Upper Saddle River, NJ : Pearson/Longman, 2003.
BF76.8.D86 2003

Mitchell, Mark L. Writing for psychology. 1st ed. Australia ; Belmont, CA : Wadsworth/Thomson, 2004.
BF76.7.M58 2004

PSYCHOLOGY - AUTHORSHIP - HANDBOOKS, MANUALS, ETC.
Publication manual of the American Psychological Association. 4th ed. Washington, DC : American Psychological Association, 1994.
BF76.7.P82 1994

Publication manual of the American Psychological Association. 5th ed. Washington, DC : American Psychological Association, c2001.
BF76.7.P83 2001

PSYCHOLOGY - BIBLIOGRAPHY. *See* **PSYCHOLOGICAL LITERATURE.**

PSYCHOLOGY - BIBLIOGRAPHY - DATABASES.
Psychology, IUPsyS global resource [electronic resource]. Hove, East Sussex, UK : published on behalf of the international Union of Psychological Science by Psychology Press Ltd., 2000-
BF76.5.P79

PSYCHOLOGY - BRAZIL - HISTORY.
Figueiredo, Luís Cláudio M. (Luís Cláudio Mendonça), 1945- Antonio Gomes Penna. Brasília, DF : Conselho Federal de Psicologia ; Rio de Janeiro, RJ : Imago, 2002.

Russo, Jane. O mundo psi no Brasil. Rio de Janeiro : Jorge Zahar Editor, c2002.
BF173.R877 2002

Stubbe, Hannes, 1941- Kultur und Psychologie in Brasilien. Bonn : Holos, 2001.
BF108.B6 S783 2001

PSYCHOLOGY - BULGARIA - HISTORY - 20TH CENTURY.
Antologiia. 1. izd. Veliko Tŭrnovo : Izd-vo PAN-VT, 2001.
BF108.B9 A58 2001

PSYCHOLOGY, CHILD. *See* **CHILD PSYCHOLOGY.**

PSYCHOLOGY - CHILE.
Retroprospectivas psicológicas. Santiago : Ediciones UCSH, [2002]
BF75.R48 2002

PSYCHOLOGY, COGNITIVE. *See* **COGNITIVE PSYCHOLOGY.**

PSYCHOLOGY, COMPARATIVE. *See also* **HUMAN BEHAVIOR.**
Cimatti, Felice. La mente silenziosa. 1. ed. Roma : Editori riuniti, 2002.

Primate psychology. Cambridge, MA : Harvard University Press, 2003.
BF671.P75 2003

Rumbaugh, Duane M., 1929- Intelligence of apes and other rational beings. New Haven : Yale University Press, c2003.
QL737.P96 R855 2003

PSYCHOLOGY, COMPARATIVE - CONGRESSES.
Nebraska Symposium on Motivation (2001) Evolutionary psychology and motivation. Lincoln, Neb. ; London : University of Nebraska Press, c2001.
BF701.N43 2001

PSYCHOLOGY - COMPUTER NETWORK RESOURCES - DIRECTORIES.
Kelly, Brian, 1956- iSearch. Boston, MA : Allyn and Bacon, c2003.
BF76.78.K45 2003

PSYCHOLOGY - CONGRESSES.
Aktual'nye voprosy obshcheĭ, vozrastnoĭ i sotsial'noĭ psikhologii. Tver' : Tverskoĭ gos. universitet, 2001.
BF20.A46 2001

Fundamental'nye problemy psikhologii. Sankt-Peterburg : Izd-vo S.-Peterburgskogo universiteta, 2002.
BF20.F86 2002

Innovatsii v psikhologii. Biĭsk : Nauchno-izdatel'skiĭ tsentr Biĭskogo pedagog. gos. universiteta, 2001-
BF20.I45 2001

Psikhologicheskaia sluzhba v obshchestve. Komsomol'sk-na-Amure : Komsomol'skiĭ-na-Amure gos. pedagogicheskiĭ universitet, 2002.
BF20.P743 2002

Psikhologicheskie problemy bytiia cheloveka v sovremennom obshchestve. Magnitogorsk : Magnitogorskiĭ gos. universitet, 2001.
BF20.P744 2001

Psychologia w obliczu zachodzących przemian społeczno-kulturowych. Warszawa : Instytut Psychologii PAN, 2002.
BF20.P79 2002

Sovremennaia psikhologiia. Moskva : In-t psikhologii RAN, 2002.
BF20.S64 2002

Transgressões. Rio de Janeiro, RJ : Espaço Brasileiro de Estudos Psicanalíticos : Contra Capa, 2002.

PSYCHOLOGY, CRIMINAL. *See* **CRIMINAL PSYCHOLOGY.**

PSYCHOLOGY, CRITICAL. *See* **CRITICAL PSYCHOLOGY.**

PSYCHOLOGY, CROSS-CULTURAL. *See* **ETHNOPSYCHOLOGY.**

PSYCHOLOGY - DATABASES.
Psychology, IUPsyS global resource [electronic resource]. Hove, East Sussex, UK : published on behalf of the international Union of Psychological Science by Psychology Press Ltd., 2000-
BF76.5.P79

PSYCHOLOGY - DICTIONARIES.
Cardwell, Mike. Schaum's A-Z psychology. New York : McGraw-Hill, 2003.
BF31.C29 2003

Mansūrī, Jī. Āra. Manovijñānano śabdakośa. Āvrtti 1. Amadāvāda : Mayūra Prakāśana, 2003.
BF31+

Statt, David A., 1942- A students dictionary of psychology. 1st ed. Hove, UK ; New York : Psychology Press, 2003.
BF31.S64 2003

PSYCHOLOGY - DICTIONARIES - FRENCH.
Sillamy, Norbert. Dictionnaire de psychologie. [Nouv. éd.]. Paris : Larousse, 2003.
BF31.S5 2003

PSYCHOLOGY, DIFFERENTIAL. *See* **DIFFERENCE (PSYCHOLOGY).**

PSYCHOLOGY - DIRECTORIES.
American Psychological Association. The directory of ethnic minority professionals in psychology. 4th ed. Washington, D.C. : American Psychological Association, c2001.
BF30.A493 2001

Psychology / Douglas A. Bernstein ... [et al.]. 6th ed. Boston : Houghton Mifflin Co., c2003. xx, 718 [149] p. : ill. (chiefly col.) ; 29 cm. Includes bibliographical references (p. R-1-R-78) and indexes. ISBN 0-618-21990-0 (instructor's annotated ed.) ISBN 0-618-21374-0 (student ed.) DDC 150
1. Psychology. I. Bernstein, Douglas A.
BF121.P794 2003

PSYCHOLOGY, EDUCATIONAL. *See* **EDUCATIONAL PSYCHOLOGY.**

PSYCHOLOGY - ENCYCLOPEDIAS.
Der Brockhaus Psychologie. Mannheim : Brockhaus, c2001.

The concise Corsini encyclopedia of psychology and behavioral science. 3rd ed. Hoboken, NJ : John Wiley & Sons, 2004.
BF31.E52 2004

PSYCHOLOGY, ETHNIC. *See* **ETHNOPSYCHOLOGY.**

Psychology, evolution & gender.
Sexualities, evolution & gender. Sheffield, England : BrunnerRoutledge, 2003-
BF309.P78

PSYCHOLOGY - EXAMINATIONS, QUESTIONS, ETC.
The best test preparation for the Advanced Placement Examination. Piscataway, N.J. : Research & Education Association, c2003.
BF78.B48 2003

Kellogg, Ronald Thomas. The best test preparation for the Graduate Record Examination, GRE psychology. Piscataway, N.J. : Research and Education Association, [2000]
BF78.K45 2000

McEntarffer, Robert. Barron's how to prepare for the AP pscyhology advanced placement examination. Hauppauge, N.Y. : Barron's, c2004.
BF78.M34 2004

PSYCHOLOGY - EXAMINATIONS - STUDY GUIDES.
The best test preparation for the Advanced Placement Examination. Piscataway, N.J. : Research & Education Association, c2003.
BF78.B48 2003

Kellogg, Ronald Thomas. The best test preparation for the Graduate Record Examination, GRE psychology. Piscataway, N.J. : Research and Education Association, [2000]
BF78.K45 2000

McEntarffer, Robert. Barron's how to prepare for the AP pscyhology advanced placement examination. Hauppauge, N.Y. : Barron's, c2004.
BF78.M34 2004

PSYCHOLOGY, EXPERIMENTAL. *See also* **PSYCHOLOGY - EXPERIMENTS.**
Christensen, Larry B., 1941- Experimental methodology. 9th ed. Boston, MA : Allyn and Bacon, 2004.
BF181.C48 2004

Pelham, Brett W., 1961- Conducting research in psychology. 2nd ed. Australia ; Belmont, CA : Thomson/Wadsworth, c2003.

BF76.5 .P34 2003
PSYCHOLOGY, EXPERIMENTAL - PERIODICALS.
[Experimental psychology (Online)] Experimental psychology [electronic resource]. Göttingen, Germany : Hogrefe & Huber, c2002-
BF3

PSYCHOLOGY, EXPERIMENTAL - RESEARCH - METHODOLOGY.
Handbook of research methods in experimental psychology. Malden, MA ; Oxford : Blackwell Pub., 2003.
BF76.5 .H35 2003

PSYCHOLOGY - EXPERIMENTS. *See also* **PSYCHOLOGY, EXPERIMENTAL.**
Christensen, Larry B., 1941- Experimental methodology. 9th ed. Boston, MA : Allyn and Bacon, 2004.
BF181 .C48 2004

PSYCHOLOGY - EXPERIMENTS - HISTORY - 20TH CENTURY.
Slater, Lauren. Opening Skinner's box. 1st ed. New York : W.W. Norton, c2004.
BF198.7 .S57 2004

Psychology, folklore, creativity, and the human dilemma.
Heuscher, Julius E. (Julius Ernest), 1918- Springfield, Ill. : Charles C Thomas Publisher, c2003.
BF637.C5 H475 2003

PSYCHOLOGY - FRANCE - HISTORY.
Huteau, Michel. Psychologie, psychiatrie et société sous la troisième république. Paris : Harmattan, c2002.

Nicolas, Serge. Histoire de la psychologie française. Paris : In press, c2002.
BF108.F8 N536 2002

PSYCHOLOGY - GHANA - PERIODICALS.
Ghana journal of psychology. Legon : The Ghana Psychological Association, 2001-

PSYCHOLOGY - HISTORIOGRAPHY.
Thick description and fine texture. 1st ed. Akron, Ohio : University of Akron Press, 2003.
BF81 .T47 2003

PSYCHOLOGY - HISTORY.
Defining difference. 1st ed. Washington, DC : American Psychological Association, c2004.
BF76.45 .D44 2004

Green, Christopher D. Early psychological thought. Westport, Conn. ; London : Praeger, 2003.
BF91 .G74 2003

Guthrie, Robert V. Even the rat was white a historical view of psychology. Classic ed., 2nd ed. Boston, MA : Allyn and Bacon, 2004.
BF105 .G87 2004

Hothersall, David. History of psychology. 4th ed. Boston : McGraw-Hill, c2004.
BF95 .H67 2004

Jáidar, Isabel. La psicología. 1. ed. México, D.F. : Universidad Autónoma Metropolitana, Unidad Xochimilco, División de Ciencias Sociales y Humanidades, 2002.

Leahey, Thomas Hardy. A history of psychology. 6th ed. Upper Saddle River, N.J. : Prentice Hall, 2004.
BF81 .L4 2004

The life cycle of psychological ideas. New York : Kluwer Academic/Plenum, 2004.
BF38 .L54 2004

Stepanov, S. S. (Sergeĭ Sergeevich) Psikhologiia v litsakh. Moskva : ÉKSMO-Press, 2001.
BF109.A1 S74 2001

Stepanov, S. S. (Sergeĭ Sergeevich) Vek psikhologii. Izd. 2., ispr. i dop. Moskva : ÉKSMO, 2002.
BF109.A1 S75 2002

PSYCHOLOGY - HISTORY - 19TH CENTURY.
Lamiell, James T. Beyond individual and group differences. Thousand Oaks, Calif. : Sage Publications, c2003.
BF105 .L36 2003

PSYCHOLOGY - HISTORY - 20TH CENTURY.
Lamiell, James T. Beyond individual and group differences. Thousand Oaks, Calif. : Sage Publications, c2003.
BF105 .L36 2003

Romenets, V. A. (Vladimir Andreevich) Istoriia psykholohii XX stolittia. Kyïv : "Lebid'", 1998.

BF105 .R66 1998
PSYCHOLOGY - HISTORY - ENCYCLOPEDIAS.
Sheehy, Noel, 1955- Fifty key thinkers in psychology. London ; New York : Routledge, 2003.
BF109.A1 S49 2003

PSYCHOLOGY - HISTORY - TEXTBOOKS.
Schultz, Duane P. A history of modern psychology. 8th ed. Belmont, CA : Thomson/Wadsworth, c2004.
BF95 .S35 2004

PSYCHOLOGY - HISTORY - TO 1500.
Beare, John I. (John Isaac), d. 1918 Greek theories of elementary cognition. Mansfield Centre, Conn. : Martino Pub., 2004.
BF91 .B3 2004

Psychology in action.
Huffman, Karen. 7th ed. Hoboken, NJ : John Wiley & Sons, c2004.
BF121 .H78 2004

PSYCHOLOGY IN ART.
Hogan, Patrick Colm. Cognitive science, literature, and the arts. New York ; London : Routledge, 2003.
PN56.P93 H64 2003

PSYCHOLOGY IN LITERATURE. *See also* **PSYCHOLOGICAL FICTION.**
Hogan, Patrick Colm. Cognitive science, literature, and the arts. New York ; London : Routledge, 2003.
PN56.P93 H64 2003

Marshall, Ian, 1954- Peak experiences. Charlottesville : University of Virginia Press, 2003.
PS163 .M37 2003

Tucker, Kenneth. Shakespeare and Jungian typology. Jefferson, N.C. ; London : McFarland & Co., c2003.
PR3065 .T83 2003

PSYCHOLOGY, INDUSTRIAL. *See also* **JOB STRESS; ORGANIZATIONAL BEHAVIOR.**
Frost, Peter J. Toxic emotions at work. Boston : Harvard Business School Press, c2003.
HD42 .F76 2003

The new workplace. Chichester, UK ; Hoboken, NJ : Wiley, c2003.
HD6955 .N495 2003

Tonn, Joan C. Mary P. Follett. New Haven [Conn.] : Yale University Press, 2003.
HN57 .T695 2003

The trust process in organizations. Cheltenham, UK ; Northampton, MA : Edward Elgar, c2003.
HD58.7 .T744 2003

PSYCHOLOGY, INDUSTRIAL - NETHERLANDS.
Driekwart eeuw psychotechniek in Nederland. Assen : Van Gorcum, 2001.
HF5548.8 .D73 2001

Psychology, IUPsyS global resource [electronic resource] / edited by J. Bruce Overmier & Judith A. Overmier. Hove, East Sussex, UK : published on behalf of the international Union of Psychological Science by Psychology Press Ltd., 2000- computer optical discs ; 4 3/4 in. Frequency: Annual. Ed. 2000- . Title from opening screen. Latest issue consulted: Ed. 2003. System requirements: IBM compatible PC; Windows 95 or higher. SUMMARY: An integrated set of searchable resources organized as separate information files and databases. Contains directories, bibliographies, surveys, historical records, and descriptive texts, including: Worldwide directory of psychology departments and research institutes, National survey and reports on status of psychology, Bibliography on psychology nationally and worldwide, Directory of international psychological organizations, International Congress of Psychology, Directory of child-family research centres in developing countries and Eastern Europe, Directory of health psychology in Latin America, International survey on ethics codes in psychology, and: International survey on cognitive science. Interactive CD-Rom launched by: the International Union of Psychological Science. Distributed to all libraries subscribing to: the International Journal of Psychology International journal of psychology ISSN: 0020-7594 (DLC) 66009906 (OCoLC)1753586.
1. International Union of Psychological Science. 2. Psychology - Databases. 3. Psychology - Societies, etc. - Databases. 4. Psychology - Bibliography - Databases. I. Overmier, J. Bruce. II. Overmier, Judith A., 1939- III. International Union of Psychological Science. IV. International Congress of Psychology. V. Title: International Journal of Psychology. VI. Title: Worldwide directory of psychology departments and research institutes. VII. Title: National survey and reports on status of psychology. VIII. Title: Bibliography on psychology nationally and worldwide. IX. Title: Directory of international psychological organizations. X. Title: Directory of child-family research centres in developing countries and Eastern Europe. XI. Title:

Directory of health psychology in Latin America. XII. Title: International survey on ethics codes in psychology. XIII. Title: International survey on cognitive science. XIV. Title: IUPsyS global resource XV. Title: International journal of psychology
BF76.5 .P79

PSYCHOLOGY - JAPAN.
Shinpan shinrigaku ga wakaru. Tōkyō : Asahi Shinbunsha, 2003.
BF108.J3 S55 2003

PSYCHOLOGY LITERATURE. *See* **PSYCHOLOGICAL LITERATURE.**

PSYCHOLOGY - MATHEMATICAL MODELS.
Cliff, Norman, 1930- Ordinal measurement in the behavioral sciences. Mahwah, N.J. : Lawrence Erlbaum Associates, 2003.
BF39 .C525 2003

PSYCHOLOGY - MEASUREMENT. *See* **PSYCHOMETRICS.**

PSYCHOLOGY - METHODOLOGY. *See also* **PSYCHOLOGICAL TESTS; PSYCHOMETRICS.**
Kostina, L. M. (Liubov' Mikhaĭlovna) Metody diagnostiki trevozhnosti. Sankt-Peterburg : Rech', 2002.
BF575.A6 K65 2002

Uttal, William R. Psychomythics. Mahwah, N.J. : L. Erlbaum Associates, 2003.
BF38.5 .U88 2003

PSYCHOLOGY - METHODOLOGY - CONGRESSES.
International Society for Theoretical Psychology. Conference (9th : 2001 : Calgary, Alta.) Theoretical psychology. Concord, Ont. : Captus Press, c2003.

PSYCHOLOGY - MEXICO - HISOTRY.
Jáidar, Isabel. La psicología. 1. ed. México, D.F. : Universidad Autónoma Metropolitana, Unidad Xochimilco, División de Ciencias Sociales y Humanidades, 2002.

PSYCHOLOGY, MILITARY. *See* **MORALE.**

PSYCHOLOGY, MILITARY - STUDY AND TEACHING - RUSSIA (FEDERATION) - TVERSKAIA OBLAST' - HISTORY.
Shikun, A. A. (Alekseĭ Alekseevich) Istoriia i razvitie psikhologicheskogo obrazovaniia v gorode Tveri i oblasti. Tver' : Tverskoĭ gos. universitet : Mezhdunarodnaia akademiia psikhologicheskikh nauk, 1999.
BF80.7.R8 S55 1999

PSYCHOLOGY - MISCELLANEA.
Bô Yin Râ, 1876-1943. [Buch vom Menschen. English] The book on human nature. Berkeley, Calif. : Kober Press, c2000.
BF1999 .B6516713 2000

PSYCHOLOGY - MORAL AND ETHICAL ASPECTS.
Ethical conflicts in psychology. 3rd ed. Washington, DC : American Psychological Association, c2003.
BF76.4 .E814 2003

Fisher, Celia B. Decoding the ethics code. Thousand Oaks, Calif. : Sage Publications, c2003.
BF76.4 .F57 2003

PSYCHOLOGY, NATIONAL. *See* **ETHNOPSYCHOLOGY.**

Psychology of adolescents / Thomas A. Prester, editor. Hauppauge, N.Y. : Nova Science, c2003. vi, 191 p. : ill. ; 26 cm. Includes bibliographical references and index. CONTENTS: Adolescent addiction and recovery : a study in extremes / Courtney Vaughn and Wesley Long -- Family functioning and psychological well-being, school adjustment and substance abuse in Chinese adolescents : are findings based on multiple studies consistent? / Daniel T.L. Shek -- Conditional associations between interparental conflict and adolescent problems : a search for personality-environment interactions / Brian P. O'Connor and Troy Dvorak -- The relation of social influences and social relationships to prosocial and antisocial behavior in Hong Kong Chinese adolescents / Hing Keung Ma, Daniel T.L. Shek and Ping Chung Cheung -- Self-concept, weight issues and body image in children and adolescents / Jennifer A. O'Dea -- The stability and correlates of a negative coping self among adolescents / Eila Laukkanen ... [et. al.] -- Autonomic substrates of heart rate reactivity in adolescent males with conduct disorder and/or attention-deficit/hyperactivity disorder / Theodore P. Beauchaine -- Counting in mentally retarded adolescents / V. Camos and F. Freeman -- Meaning of life and adjustment among Chinese adolescents with and without economic disadvantage / Daniel T.L. Shek ... [et al.]. ISBN 1-59033-727-1
1. Adolescent psychology. I. Prester, Thomas A.

BF724 .P783 2003

The psychology of art and the evolution of the conscious brain.
Solso, Robert L., 1933- Cambridge, Mass. : MIT Press, 2003.
BF311 .S652 2003

The psychology of bulimia nervosa.
Cooper, Myra, 1957- Oxford ; New York : Oxford University Press, 2003.
RC552.B84 C66 2003

The psychology of death in fantasy and history / edited by Jerry S. Piven. Westport, CT : Praeger, 2004. p. cm. Includes bibliographical references and index. ISBN 0-275-98178-9 (alk. paper) DDC 155.9/37
1. Death - Psychological aspects - History. 2. Fantasy - History. I. Piven, Jerry S.
BF789.D4 P79 2004

The psychology of economic decisions / edited by Isabelle Brocas and Juan D. Carrillo. Oxford [England] ; New York : Oxford University Press, 2003- v. : ill. ; 24 cm. "Center for Economic Policy Research"--P. [ii]. Includes bibliographical references and index. PARTIAL CONTENTS: v. 1. Rationality and well-being. ISBN 0-19-925106-1 ISBN 0-19-925108-8 (pbk.) DDC 330/.01/9
1. Economics - Psychological aspects. 2. Decision making - Psychological aspects. I. Brocas, Isabelle. II. Carrillo, Juan D. III. Centre for Economic Policy Research (Great Britain)
HB74.P8 P725 2003

Psychology of fear / Paul L. Gower, editor. New York : Nova Science Publishers, 2003. p. cm. Includes bibliographical references and index. Table of contents URL: http://www.loc.gov/catdir/toc/ecip045/2003014367.html ISBN 1-59033-786-7 DDC 152.4/6
1. Fear. I. Gower, Paul L.
BF575.F2 P79 2003

The psychology of gender and sexuality.
Stainton Rogers, Wendy. Philadelphia : Open University Press, 2001.
BF692 .S72 2001

The psychology of gender / edited by Alice H. Eagly, Anne E. Beall, Robert J. Sternberg. 2nd ed. New York : Guilford Press, 2004. p. cm. Includes bibliographical references and index. ISBN 1-57230-983-0 (hardcover : alk. paper) DDC 155.3/3
1. Sex differences (Psychology) - Textbooks. I. Eagly, Alice Hendrickson. II. Beall, Anne E. III. Sternberg, Robert J.
BF692.2 .P764 2004

The psychology of gratitude / edited by Robert A. Emmons and Michael E. McCullough. New York : Oxford University Press, 2004. p. cm. Includes bibliographical references and index. Table of contents URL: http://www.loc.gov/catdir/toc/ecip041/2003005497.html CONTENTS: The psychology of gratitude / Robert A. Emmons -- Part I: Philosophical and theological foundations -- Gratitude in the history of ideas / Edward Harpham -- Gratitude in Judaism / Solomon Schimmel -- The blessings of gratitude : a conceptual analysis / Robert C. Roberts -- Part II: Social, personality and developmental approaches to gratitude -- Gratitude in modern life : its manifestations and development / Dan P. McAdams and Jack Bauer -- The gratitude of exchange and the gratitude of caring : a developmental interactionist perspective of moral emotions / Ross Buck -- Parent of the virtues? the prosocial contours of gratitude / Michael E. McCullough and Jo-Ann Tsang -- Part III: Perspectives from emotion theory -- Gratitude (like other positive emotions) broadens and builds / Barbara L. Fredrickson -- Gratitude and subjective well-being / Philip Watkins -- Part IV: Perspectives from anthropology and biology -- Gratitude and gift exchange / Aafke Komter -- Primate social reciprocity and the origin of gratitude / Kristin Bonnie and Frans de Waal -- Gratitude and the heart : the psychophysiology of appreciation / Rollin McCraty and Doc Childre -- Part V: Discussion and conclusions -- Gratitude : considerations from a moral perspective / Charles Shelton -- Gratitude as thankfulness and as gratefulness / Brother David Steindl-Rast. ISBN 0-19-515010-4 (cloth : alk. paper) DDC 155.2/32
1. Gratitude. I. Emmons, Robert A. II. McCullough, Michael E.
BF575.G68 P79 2003

Psychology of intercultural differences.
Kochetkov, V. V. (Vladimir Viktorovich) Psikhologiia mezhkul'turnykh razlichiĭ. Moskva : PER SĖ, 2002.
GN502 .K6 2002

The psychology of language.
Harley, Trevor A. Hove, East Sussex, UK : Erlbaum (UK) Taylor & Francis, c1995.

PSYCHOLOGY OF LEARNING. See **LEARNING, PSYCHOLOGY OF.**

The psychology of learning.
Machado, Armando. Upper Saddle River, NJ : Prentice Hall, 2003.
BF318 .M29 2003

The psychology of parental control.
Grolnick, Wendy S. Mahwah, N.J. : L. Erlbaum Associates, 2003.
HQ755.85 .G74 2003

The psychology of social movements.
Cantril, Hadley, 1906-1969. New Brunswick, [N.J.] : Transaction Publishers, c2002.
HM881 .C36 2002

The psychology of stereotyping.
Schneider, David J., 1940- New York : Guilford Press, c2004.
BF323.S63 S36 2003

Psychology of success.
Waitley, Denis. 4th ed. Boston : McGraw-Hill Higher Education, c2004.
BF637.S8 W269 2004

The psychology of terrorism / edited by Chris E. Stout ; foreword by Klaus Schwab. Westport, CT : Praeger, 2002. 4 v. : ill. ; 24 cm. (Psychological dimensions to war and peace, 1540-5265) Includes bibliographical references and index. CONTENTS: v. 1. A public understanding -- v. 2. Clinical aspects and responses -- v. 3. Theoretical understandings and perspectives -- v. 4. Programs and practices in response and prevention. ISBN 0-275-97771-4 (set) ISBN 0-275-97865-6 (vol. I) ISBN 0-275-97866-4 (vol. II) ISBN 0-275-97867-2 (vol. III) ISBN 0-275-97868-0 (vol. IV) DDC 303.6/25
1. Terrorism - Psychological aspects. 2. Terrorists - Psychology. 3. Terrorism - Prevention. I. Stout, Chris E. II. Series.
HV6431 .P798 2002

Psychology of the peace process.
Grosbard, Ofer, 1954- Yiśra'el 'al ha-sapah. Tel-Aviv : Yedi'ot aḥaronot : Sifre ḥemed, c2000.

The psychology of the psychic.
Marks, David. 2nd ed. Amherst, N.Y. : Prometheus Books, 2000.
BF1042 .M33 2000

Psychology of women book series
Feminist family therapy. 1st ed. Washington, DC : American Psychological Association, c2003.
RC488.5 .F453 2003

PSYCHOLOGY - OKLAHOMA - HISTORY.
Oklahoma psychology in the twentieth century. [Oklahoma City, OK : Oklahoma Psychological Association, 2003?]
BF77 .O35 2003

Psychology one hundred and one and a half.
Sternberg, Robert J. Psychology 101 1/2. Washington, DC : American Psychological Association, 2004.
BF77 .S68 2004

Psychology one hundred one and a half.
Sternberg, Robert J. Psychology 101 1/2. Washington, DC : American Psychological Association, 2004.
BF77 .S68 2004

PSYCHOLOGY, PATHOLOGICAL. See also **BRAIN DAMAGE; CRIMINAL PSYCHOLOGY; DOUBLE BIND (PSYCHOLOGY); EATING DISORDERS; MENTAL HEALTH; MENTAL ILLNESS; NARCISSISM; PANIC DISORDERS; PSYCHIATRY; PSYCHIC TRAUMA; PSYCHOANALYSIS.**
Behavior genetics principles. Washington, DC : American Psychological Association, 2004.
BF698.9.B5 B44 2004

Fekete, Mária. Pszichológia és pszichopatológia jogászoknak. Budapest : HVG-ORAC, c2002.
BF173 .F349 2002

Lhomme-Rigaud, Colette. L'adolescent et ses monstres. Ramonville Saint-Agne : Erès, c2002.

Rodríguez, Luis. Patologías complejas (versión preliminar). [Santiago, Chile] : Corporación de Promoción Universitaria, [1995]

Symington, Neville. A pattern of madness. London ; New York : Karnac, 2002.

Upādhyāya, Govindaprasāda. Āyurvedīya mānasaroga cikitsā. 1. saṃskaraṇa. Vārāṇasī : Caukhabā Surabhāratī Prakāśana ; Dillī : Anya Prāptisthāna Caukhambā Saṃskṛta Pratishṭhāna, 2000.
R605 .U67 2000

PSYCHOLOGY - PERIODICALS.
Aktual'ni problemy psykholohiĭ. Kyïv : In-tyt psykholohiĭ im. H.S. Kostiuka, 2001-
BF8.U38 A38

Escrita psi. Natal/RN : Universidade Potiguar, 2002-
BF5 .E83

[Experimental psychology (Online)] Experimental psychology [electronic resource]. Göttingen, Germany : Hogrefe & Huber, c2002-
BF3

Ghana journal of psychology. Legon : The Ghana Psychological Association, 2001-

Psicodebate. Buenos Aires, Argentina : Universidad de Palermo, Facultad de Humanidades y Ciencias Sociales, [2000]-
BF5 .P+

Psicologia em revista. Belo Horizonte : Editora PUC Minas, 2000-
BF5 .C24

Psychology science. Lengereich [Germany] : Pabst Science Publishers, 2003-
BF3 .P64

PSYCHOLOGY - PHILIPPINES.
Forty years of Philippine psychology. Diliman, Quezon City, Philippines : Psychological Association of the Philippines, c2002.
BF108 .F67 2002

PSYCHOLOGY - PHILOSOPHY.
About psychology. Albany : State University of New York Press, c2003.
BF38 .A28 2003

Bottenberg, Ernst Heinrich. Seele im Lichtzwang, im Lichtzwang der Seele. 1. Aufl. Sankt Augustin : Academia, 1994.
BF38 .B625 1994

Jouffroy, Théodore, 1796-1842. [Selections] La psychologie de Th. Jouffroy. Paris : L'Harmattan, c2003.

Loewenthal, Del, 1947- Post-modernism for psychotherapists. Hove, East Sussex ; New York : Brunner-Routledge, 2003.
BF41 .L64 2003

Philosophy, psychology, and psychologism. Dordrecht ; Boston : Kluwer Academic Publishers, c2003.
BF41 .P553 2003

Pracetā Jyoti. Dhātusāmya meṃ manobhāvoṃ kā sthāna. 1. saṃskaraṇa. Nāgapura : Viśvabhāratī Prakāśana, 2001.
BF204.5 .P73 2001

Retroprospectivas psicológicas. Santiago : Ediciones UCSH, [2002]
BF75 .R48 2002

Ruben, David-Hillel. Action and its explanation. 1st ed. Oxford : Clarendon Press, 2003.
BF38 .R83 2003

Sanguineti, Vincenzo R. A rosetta stone to the human mind. Madison, Conn. : PsychoSocial Press, 2003.
BF38 .S225 2003

Sergeev, K. K. (Konstantin Konstantinovich) Filosofskaia psikhologiia. Tol'iatti : "Sovremennik", 1999.
BF38 .S47 1999

Uttal, William R. Psychomythics. Mahwah, N.J. : L. Erlbaum Associates, 2003.
BF38.5 .U88 2003

Wolinsky, Stephen. The beginner's guide to quantum psychology. Capitola, Calif. : S.H. Wolinsky, c2000.
BF38 .W7677 2000

PSYCHOLOGY - PHILOSOPHY - CONGRESSES.
The embodiment of mind. Delft : Eburon, c1998.
BF161 .E43 1998

International Society for Theoretical Psychology. Conference (9th : 2001 : Calgary, Alta.) Theoretical psychology. Concord, Ont. : Captus Press, c2003.

Nosov, N. A. Ne-virtualistika. Moskva : Gumanitariĭ, 2001.
BF38 .N67 2001

PSYCHOLOGY - PHILOSOPHY - HISTORY.
The life cycle of psychological ideas. New York : Kluwer Academic/Plenum, 2004.
BF38 .L54 2004

Psychology - Study and teaching

PSYCHOLOGY - PHYSIOLOGICAL ASPECTS.
Biologische Grundlagen der Psychologie. Göttingen ; Seattle : Hogrefe, 2001.
QP360 .B565 2001

PSYCHOLOGY - POLAND - HISTORY - 20TH CENTURY.
Rzepa, Teresa. O interpretowaniu psychologicznym w kręgu szkoły lwowsko-warszawskiej. Warszawa : Polskie Tow. Semiotyczne, 2002.
BF108.P7 R94 2002

PSYCHOLOGY - POPULAR WORKS.
Petrovskiĭ, A. V. (Artur Vladimirovich) Zapiski psikhologa. Moskva : Izd-vo URAO, 2001.
BF145 .P477 2001

Petrovskiĭ, A. V. (Artur Vladimirovich) Zapiski psikhologa. Moskva : Izd-vo URAO, 2001.
BF145 .P48 2001

PSYCHOLOGY, PRACTICAL. See **PSYCHOLOGY, APPLIED.**

PSYCHOLOGY - PRACTICE.
Retroprospectivas psicológicas. Santiago : Ediciones UCSH, [2002]
BF75 .R48 2002

PSYCHOLOGY - PRACTICE - UNITED STATES.
Lipinski, Barbara. The tao of integrity. San Buenaventura, CA : Pacific Meridian Publications, c2001.
BF75 .L655 2001

PSYCHOLOGY, RACIAL. See **ETHNOPSYCHOLOGY.**

Psychology, religion, and spirituality.
Fontana, David. Malden, MA : BPS Blackwell, 2003.
BL53 .F57 2003

PSYCHOLOGY, RELIGIOUS. See also **EXPERIENCE (RELIGION).**
Atran, Scott, 1952- In gods we trust. Oxford ; New York : Oxford University Press, 2002.
BL53 .A88 2002

Cuevas Sosa, Andrés Alejandro, 1939- How do religious figures induce the establishment of sects? 2nd ed. Leicestershire : Upfront Pub., 2002.
BF1272 .C84 2002

Emtcheu, André. Psychologie et révélation. Yaoundé, Cameroun : Editions SHERPA, c2001.
1. Black author.

Fontana, David. Psychology, religion, and spirituality. Malden, MA : BPS Blackwell, 2003.
BL53 .F57 2003

Hood, Ralph W. Dimensions of mystical experiences. Amsterdam ; New York, NY : Rodopi, 2001.

Lewis, James R. Legitimating new religions. New Brunswick, N.J. : Rutgers University Press, c2003.
BP603 .L49 2003

Moore, Thomas, 1940- Original self. 1st ed. New York : HarperCollins, c2000.
BL624 .M6643 2000

Mustakova-Possardt, Elena, 1960- Critical consciousness. Westport, Conn. ; London : Praeger, 2003.
BL53 .M98 2003

Pyysiäinen, Ilkka. How religion works. Leiden ; Boston : Brill, 2001.
BL53 .P98 2001

Simonetta, Catherine. Renoncement et narcissisme chez Maurice Zundel. Saint-Maurice : Editions Saint-Augustin, c2002.

Stolz, Fritz. Weltbilder der Religionen. Zürich : Pano Verlag, c2001.

Washburn, Michael, 1943- Embodied spirituality in a sacred world. Albany : State University of New York Press, 2003.
BF204.7 .W372 2003

Zen'ko, I͡U. M. Psikhologii͡a i religii͡a. Sankt-Peterburg : Alete͡ii͡a, 2002.
BF51 .Z46 2002

Zweig, Connie. The holy longing. New York : Jeremy P. Tarcher/Putnam, c2003.
BL53 .Z84 2003

PSYCHOLOGY - RESEARCH. See also **PSYCHOLOGY, EXPERIMENTAL.**
Szkice psychologiczne. Wrocław : Wydawn. Uniwersytetu Wrocławskiego, 2002.
BF76.5 .S97 2002

PSYCHOLOGY - RESEARCH - DATA PROCESSING.
Fraley, R. Chris. How to conduct behavioral research over the internet. New York : Guilford Press, 2005.
BF76.6.I57 F73 2005

PSYCHOLOGY - RESEARCH - METHODOLOGY.
Auerbach, Carl F. Qualitative data. New York : New York University Press, c2003.
BF76.5 .A95 2003

Beins, Bernard. Research methods. Boston : Pearson/Allyn and Bacon, 2003.
BF76.5 .B439 2003

Coolican, Hugh. Introduction to research methods and statistics in psychology. 2nd ed. London : Hodder & Stoughton, c1996.
BF76.5 .C663 1996

Coolican, Hugh. Research methods and statistics in psychology. 3rd ed. London : Hodder & Stoughton, 1999.
BF76.5 .C664 1999

Cozby, Paul C. Methods in behavioral research. 8th ed. Boston : McGraw-Hill, c2004.
BF76.5 .C67 2004

Fraley, R. Chris. How to conduct behavioral research over the internet. New York : Guilford Press, 2005.
BF76.6.I57 F73 2005

Gravetter, Frederick J. Research methods for the behavioral sciences. Belmont, CA : Wadsworth, c2003.
BF76.5 .G73 2003

Handbook of research methods in experimental psychology. Malden, MA ; Oxford : Blackwell Pub., 2003.
BF76.5 .H35 2003

Jackson, Sherri L., 1962- Research methods and statistics. Australia ; Belmont, CA : Thomson/Wadsworth, c2003.
BF76.5 .J29 2003

Leary, Mark R. Introduction to behavioral research methods. 4th ed. Boston, MA : Allyn and Bacon, 2004.
BF76.5 .L39 2004

Mixing methods in psychology. New York : Psychology Press, 2004.
BF76.5 .M59 2004

Pelham, Brett W., 1961- Conducting research in psychology. 2nd ed. Australia ; Belmont, CA : Thomson/Wadsworth, c2003.
BF76.5 .P34 2003

Shaffer, Lary. Research stories for introductory psychology. 2nd ed. Boston, MA : Allyn and Bacon, c2004.
BF76.5 .S43 2004

Spata, Andrea. Research methods. New York : John Wiley & Sons, Inc., c2003.
BF76.5 .S63 2003

Stanovich, Keith E., 1950- How to think straight about psychology. 7th ed. Boston, MA : Allyn and Bacon, 2004.
BF76.5 .S68 2004

PSYCHOLOGY - RESEARCH - METHODOLOGY - SOFTWARE.
Dixon, Mark R., 1970- Visual Basic for behavioral psychologists. Reno, NV : Context Press, c2003.
BF76.5 .D59 2003

PSYCHOLOGY - RESEARCH - METHODOLOGY - TEXTBOOKS.
Clark-Carter, David. Quantitative psychological research. 2nd ed. New York, NY : Taylor & Francis, 2004.
BF76.5 .C53 2004

Qualitative psychology. London : Thousand Oaks, Calif. : SAGE Publications, 2003.
BF76.5 .Q3375 2003

PSYCHOLOGY - RUSSIA (FEDERATION).
Akopov, G. V. Mentalistika. Samara : Samarskiĭ gos. pedagog. universitet, 2001.
BF108.R8 A478 2001

PSYCHOLOGY - RUSSIA (FEDERATION) - HISTORY - 20TH CENTURY.
Artamonov, V. I. (Vladimir Ivanovich) Psikhologii͡a ot pervogo litsa. Moskva : Academia, 2003.
BF109.A1 A78 2003

Petrovskiĭ, A. V. (Artur Vladimirovich) Psikhologii͡a v Rossii, XX vek. Moskva : URAO-- Universitet rossiĭskoĭ akademii obrazovanii͡a, 2000.
BF108.R8 P39 2000

PSYCHOLOGY - RUSSIA (FEDERATION) - SIBERIA - CONGRESSES.
Sibirskai͡a psikhologii͡a segodni͡a. Kemerovo : Kemerovskiĭ gos. universitet, 2002.
BF20 .S53 2002

PSYCHOLOGY - SCALING. See **PSYCHOMETRICS.**

PSYCHOLOGY, SCHOOL. See **SCHOOL PSYCHOLOGY.**

Psychology science. Lengerich [Germany] : Pabst Science Publishers, 2003- Frequency: Six issues per year. Vol. 45, suppl. 1 (2003)- . Each issue has topical focus. Title from cover. Latest issue consulted: Vol. 45, suppl. 2 (2003). Continues: Psychologische Beiträge ISSN: 0033-3018 (DLC) 67051016 (OCoLC)2001918.
1. Psychology - Periodicals. I. Title: Psychologische Beiträge
BF3 .P64

PSYCHOLOGY, SEXUAL. See **SEX (PSYCHOLOGY).**

PSYCHOLOGY, SOCIAL. See also **SOCIAL PSYCHOLOGY.**
Kaus, Rainer J. Psychoanalyse und Sozialpsychologie. Heidelberg : C. Winter, c1999.
BF109.F74 K38 1999

PSYCHOLOGY - SOCIAL ASPECTS.
Retroprospectivas psicológicas. Santiago : Ediciones UCSH, [2002]
BF75 .R48 2002

PSYCHOLOGY - SOCIETIES, ETC. - DATABASES.
Psychology, IUPsyS global resource [electronic resource]. Hove, East Sussex, UK : published on behalf of the international Union of Psychological Science by Psychology Press Ltd., 2000-
BF76.5 .P79

PSYCHOLOGY - SOVIET UNION - HISTORY.
Morozov, S. M. (Stanislav Mikhaĭlovich) Dialektika Vygotskogo. Moskva : Smysl, 2002.
BF109.V95 M67 2002

PSYCHOLOGY - STANDARDS - UNITED STATES.
Lipinski, Barbara. The tao of integrity. San Buenaventura, CA : Pacific Meridian Publications, c2001.
BF75 .L655 2001

PSYCHOLOGY - STATISTICAL METHODS.
Brace, Nicola. SPSS for psychologists. 2nd ed. Mahwah, NJ : Lawrence Erlbaum Associates, 2003.
BF39 .K447 2003

PSYCHOLOGY - STATISTICAL METHODS - COMPUTER PROGRAMS.
SPSS explained. London ; New York : Routledge, 2004.
BF39 .S68 2004

PSYCHOLOGY - STATISTICS. See **PSYCHOMETRICS.**

PSYCHOLOGY - STUDY AND TEACHING.
Bruno, Frank Joe, 1930- Psychology. New York : John Wiley & Sons, c2002.
BF77 .B78 2002

PSYCHOLOGY - STUDY AND TEACHING (GRADUATE).
Kuther, Tara L. Graduate study in psychology. Springfield, Ill. : Charles C. Thomas, 2004.
BF77 .K85 2004

Sternberg, Robert J. Psychology 101 1/2. Washington, DC : American Psychological Association, 2004.
BF77 .S68 2004

PSYCHOLOGY - STUDY AND TEACHING (GRADUATE) - UNITED STATES - HISTORY.
Setting standards in graduate education. 1st ed. Washington, DC : American Psychological Association, c2003.
BF80.7.U6 S48 2003

PSYCHOLOGY - STUDY AND TEACHING (HIGHER).
Sternberg, Robert J. Psychology 101 1/2. Washington, DC : American Psychological Association, 2004.
BF77 .S68 2004

PSYCHOLOGY - STUDY AND TEACHING (HIGHER) - OKLAHOMA - HISTORY.
Oklahoma psychology in the twentieth century.

[Oklahoma City, OK : Oklahoma Psychological Association, 2003?]
BF77 .O35 2003

PSYCHOLOGY - STUDY AND TEACHING (HIGHER) - TEXAS - AUSTIN - HISTORY.
Texas psychology. Austin : The University of Texas at Austin, c2002.
BF80.7.U62 T48 2002

PSYCHOLOGY - STUDY AND TEACHING (INTERNSHIP).
Internships in psychology. Washington, D.C. : American Psychological Association, c2004.
BF77 .I67 2004

PSYCHOLOGY - STUDY AND TEACHING - RUSSIA (FEDERATION) - TVERSKAĬA OBLAST' - HISTORY.
Shikun, A. A. (Alekseĭ Alekseevich) Istoriia i razvitie psikhologicheskogo obrazovaniia v gorode Tveri i oblasti. Tver' : Tverskoĭ gos. universitet : Mezhdunarodnaia akademiia psikhologicheskikh nauk, 1999.
BF80.7.R8 S55 1999

PSYCHOLOGY - TEXTBOOKS.
Hockenbury, Don H. Discovering psychology. 3rd ed. New York : Worth Publishers, c2004.
BF121 .H587 2003

Hockenbury, Don H. Psychology. 3rd ed. New York : Worth Publishers , c2003.
BF121 .H59 2003

Kassin, Saul M. Essentials of psychology. 1st ed. Upper Saddle River, NJ : Prentice Hall, 2003.
BF121 .K335 2003

Kosslyn, Stephen Michael, 1948- Fundamentals of psychology. 2nd ed. Boston : Allyn and Bacon, c2005.
BF121 .K585 2005

Primary sources in psychology. Orlando, FL : Harcourt, c2000.
BF121 .P69 2000

Santrock, John W. Psychology. 2nd ed. Boston : McGraw-Hill, c2003.
BF121 .S2642 2003

Santrock, John W. Psychology. Updated 2nd ed. Boston, Mass. : McGraw-Hill, 2004.
BF121 .S2642 2004

Santrock, John W. Psychology. Updated 7th ed. Boston : McGraw-Hill, c2005.
BF121 .S265 2005

Wade, Carole. Invitation to psychology. 3rd ed. Upper Saddle River, NJ : Pearson/Prentice Hall, 2004.
BF121 .W265 2004

Psychology the easy way.
Melucci, Nancy J. Hauppauge, N.Y. : Barron's Educational Series, c2004.
BF121 .M45 2004

PSYCHOLOGY - UNITED STATES - DIRECTORIES.
American Psychological Association. The directory of ethnic minority professionals in psychology. 4th ed. Washington, D.C. : American Psychological Association, c2001.
BF30 .A493 2001

PSYCHOLOGY - UNITED STATES - HISTORY.
Defining difference. 1st ed. Washington, DC : American Psychological Association, c2004.
BF76.45 .D44 2004

PSYCHOLOGY - UNITED STATES - HISTORY - 20TH CENTURY.
Pandora, Katherine, 1958- Rebels within the ranks. Cambridge ; New York : Cambridge University Press, 1997.
BF105 .P36 1997

PSYCHOLOGY - VOCATIONAL GUIDANCE.
Brinkerhoff, Shirley. Psychologist. Broomall, Pa. : Mason Crest Publishers, c2003.
BF76 .B75 2003

PSYCHOLOGY - VOCATIONAL GUIDANCE - JUVENILE LITERATURE.
Brinkerhoff, Shirley. Psychologist. Broomall, Pa. : Mason Crest Publishers, c2003.
BF76 .B75 2003

Clayton, Lawrence, Ph. D. Careers in behavioral science. [2nd ed.]. Oklahoma City, Okla. : Transcontinental Pub., 2001.
BF76 .C64 2001

PSYCHOLOSGISTS - BRAZIL - BIOGRAPHY.
Figueiredo, Luís Cláudio M. (Luís Cláudio Mendonça), 1945- Antonio Gomes Penna. Brasília, DF : Conselho Federal de Psicologia ; Rio de Janeiro, RJ : Imago, 2002.

PSYCHOMETRICS. See also FACTOR ANALYSIS; SCALE ANALYSIS (PSYCHOLOGY).
Brace, Nicola. SPSS for psychologists. 2nd ed. Mahwah, NJ : Lawrence Erlbaum Associates, 2003.
BF39 .K447 2003

Coolican, Hugh. Introduction to research methods and statistics in psychology. 2nd ed. London : Hodder & Stoughton, c1996.
BF76.5 .C663 1996

Coolican, Hugh. Research methods and statistics in psychology. 3rd ed. London : Hodder & Stoughton, 1999.
BF76.5 .C664 1999

Jackson, Sherri L., 1962- Research methods and statistics. Australia ; Belmont, CA : Thomson/Wadsworth, c2003.
BF76.5 .J29 2003

Jensen, Arthur Robert. Intelligence, race, and genetics. Boulder, Colo. : Westview, 2002.

Russo, Riccardo. Statistics for the behavioural sciences. 1st ed. Hove, East Sussex ; New York, N.Y. : Psychology Press, 2003.
BF39 .R82 2003

Spata, Andrea. Research methods. New York : John Wiley & Sons, Inc., c2003.
BF76.5 .S63 2003

PSYCHOMETRICS - ENCYCLOPEDIAS.
Encyclopedia of psychological assessment. London ; Thousand Oaks, Calif. : SAGE Publications, 2003.
BF39 .E497 2003

PSYCHOMETRICS - SOUTH AFRICA.
An introduction to psychological assessment in the South African context. Cape Town, South Africa : Oxford University Press Southern Africa, 2001.
BF39 .I58 2001

PSYCHOMETRICS - TEXTBOOKS.
Hinton, Perry R. (Perry Roy), 1954- Statistics explained. 2nd ed. New York : Routledge, 2004.
BF39 .H54 2004

Kline, Rex B. Beyond significance testing: reforming data analysis methods in behavioral research. 1st ed. Washington, DC : American Psychological Association, c2004.
BF39 .K59 2004

PSYCHOMETRY (PSYCHOPHYSICS). See PSYCHOMETRICS.

Psychomythics.
Uttal, William R. Mahwah, N.J. : L. Erlbaum Associates, 2003.
BF38.5 .U88 2003

PSYCHOPATHOLOGISTS. See PSYCHIATRISTS.

The psychopathology of everyday life.
Freud, Sigmund, 1856-1939. [Zur Psychopathologie des Alltagslebens. English] New York : Penguin Books, 2003.
BF173 .F82513 2003

PSYCHOPHYSICS.
Solodin, A. I. Strategiia ontologicheskoĭ igry. Sankt-Peterburg : Aleteĭia, 2002.
BF237 .S6 2002

PSYCHOPHYSIOLOGY. See also MIND AND BODY.
Darlington, Cynthia L. The female brain. London ; New York : Taylor & Francis, c2002.
QP402 .D366 2002

Memory and emotion. Oxford University Press : New York, 2003.
BF378.A87 M46 2003

Psychosemantics and language perception.
Raĭnov, Vasil G. Za psikhosemantichnata spetsifika na ezikovoto vŭzpriiatie. Sofiia : Akademichno izd-vo "Prof. Marin Drinov", 1998.
P37 .R27 1998

PSYCHOSES.
Lefèvre, Alain, 1947- De la paternité et des psychoses. Paris : Harmattan, c2002-

Soler, Colette. L'inconscient à ciel ouvert de la psychose. Toulouse : Presses universitaires du Mirail, c2002.

PSYCHOSEXUAL DEVELOPMENT.
Dacquino, Giacomo, 1930- Bisogno d'amore. 1. ed. Milano : Mondadori, 2002.
BF697.5.S43 D33 2002

Lhomme-Rigaud, Colette. L'adolescent et ses monstres. Ramonville Saint-Agne : Erès, c2002.

PSYCHOSEXUAL DEVELOPMENT - CONGRESSES.
Sexual development in childhood. Bloomington : Indiana University Press, 2003.
BF723.S4 S47 2003

PSYCHOTECHNICS. See PSYCHOLOGY, INDUSTRIAL.

PSYCHOTHERAPIST AND PATIENT.
Lichtenberg, Joseph D. A spirit of inquiry. Hillsdale, NJ : Analytic Press, 2002.
RC506 .L5238 2002

PSYCHOTHERAPIST AND PATIENT - SWITZERLAND - ZURICH.
Cabot, Catharine Rush. Jung, my mother and I. Einsiedeln : Daimon, 2001.

PSYCHOTHERAPY. See also GRIEF THERAPY; REINCARNATION THERAPY; RESISTANCE (PSYCHOANALYSIS).
Adlerian, cognitive, and constructivist therapies. New York : Springer Pub., c2003.
BF637.C6 A335 2003

Cuevas Sosa, Andrés Alejandro, 1939- How do religious figures induce the establishment of sects? 2nd ed. Leicestershire : Upfront Pub., 2002.
BF1272 .C84 2002

Fall, Kevin A. Theoretical models of counseling and psychotherapy. New York : Brunner-Routledge, 2003.
BF637.C6 F324 2003

Frankl, Viktor Emil. Man's search for ultimate meaning. Cambridge, Mass. : Perseus Pub., c2000.
RC455.4.R4 F7 2000

Handbook of counseling women. Thousand Oaks, Calif. ; London : Sage Publications, c2003.
RC451.4.W6 H36 2003

Handbook of motivational counseling. Chichester, West Sussex, England ; Hoboken, NJ : J. Wiley, c2004.
BF637.C6 H3172 2004

Jerotić, Vladeta. [Selections 2000] Izabrani ogledi. Beograd: Srpska književna zadruga, 2000.
BF109.J47 A25 2000

Mazza, Nicholas. Poetry therapy. Boca Raton, Fla : CRC Press, 1999.
RC489.P6 M39 1999

Moravia, Sergio, 1940- L'esistenza ferita. 1. ed. in "Campi del sapere.". Milano : Feltrinelli, 1999.
BF41 .M67 1999

Murdock, Nancy L. Theories of counseling and psychotherapy. Upper Saddle River, N.J. : Merrill/Prentice Hall, 2004.
BF637.C6 M846 2004

Nonverbal behavior in clinical settings. Oxford ; New York : Oxford University Press, 2003.
RC489.N65 N66 2003

Ritter, Kathleen. Handbook of affirmative psychotherapy with lesbians and gay men. New York : Guilford Press, c2002.
RC451.4.G39 R55 2002

Sommers-Flanagan, John, 1957- Counseling and psychotherapy. Hoboken, NJ : John Wiley & Sons, 2004.
BF637.C6 S69 2004

Spiegel, Josef. Sexual abuse of males. New York : Brunner-Routledge, 2003.
RC569.5.A28 S65 2003

Strean, Herbert S. Psychotherapy with the unattached. Northvale, N.J. : Jason Aronson Inc., 1995.
RC451.4.S55 S77 1995

Tuckwell, Gill, 1948- Racial identity, White counsellors and therapists. Buckingham ; Philadelphia : Open University Press, 2002.
BF637.C6 T84 2002

Verführung, Trauma, Missbrauch. [2. Aufl.]. Giessen : Psychosozial-Verlag, c2002.

What's the good of counselling & psychotherapy? London ; Thousand Oaks, Calif. : SAGE Publications, 2002.

BF637.C6 W465 2002

PSYCHOTHERAPY - CASE STUDIES.
Eigen, Michael. Rage. Middletown, Conn. : Wesleyan University Press, c2002.
RC569.5.A53 E38 2002

Friedman, Bonnie, 1958- The thief of happiness. Boston, Mass. : Beacon Press, 2002.
RC464.F75 A3 2002

Murdock, Nancy L. Theories of counseling and psychotherapy. Upper Saddle River, N.J. : Merrill/Prentice Hall, 2004.
BF637.C6 M846 2004

Rabinor, Judith Ruskay, 1942- A starving madness. Carlsbad, CA : Gurze Books, c2002.
RC552.E18 R33 2001

PSYCHOTHERAPY - COMPUTER NETWORK RESOURCES.
Technology in counselling and psychotherapy. New York : Palgrave Macmillan, 2003.
BF637.C6 T467 2003

Tyler, J. Michael. Using technology to improve counseling practice. Alexandria, VA : American Counseling Association, 2003.
BF637.C6 T89 2003

PSYCHOTHERAPY - COMPUTER PROGRAMS.
Technology in counselling and psychotherapy. New York : Palgrave Macmillan, 2003.
BF637.C6 T467 2003

Tyler, J. Michael. Using technology to improve counseling practice. Alexandria, VA : American Counseling Association, 2003.
BF637.C6 T89 2003

PSYCHOTHERAPY - CONGRESSES.
[Nuevos paradigmas. English.] New paradigms, culture, and subjectivity. Cresskill, N.J. : Hampton Press, c2002.
BD161.N8413 2002

PSYCHOTHERAPY - HISTORY.
Jacobs, Michael, 1941-. Sigmund Freud. 2nd ed. London ; Thousand Oaks, Calif. : SAGE Publications, 2003.
BF109.F74 J33 2003

PSYCHOTHERAPY PATIENTS. *See* **ANALYSANDS.**

PSYCHOTHERAPY PATIENTS - SWITZERLAND - ZURICH - DIARIES.
Cabot, Catharine Rush. Jung, my mother and I. Einsiedeln : Daimon, 2001.

PSYCHOTHERAPY - PHILOSOPHY.
Schafer, Roy. Insight and interpretation. New York : Other Press, c2003.
BF173.S3277 2003

Understanding experience. London ; New York : Routledge, 2003.
B105.E9 U53 2003

PSYCHOTHERAPY - RELIGIOUS ASPECTS - BUDDHISM.
Encountering Buddhism. Albany : State University of New York Press, 2003.
BQ4570.P755 E62 2003

Psychology and Buddhism. New York : Kluwer Academic/Plenum Publishers, c2003.
BQ4570.P76 P78 2003

PSYCHOTHERAPY - RELIGIOUS ASPECTS - ZEN BUDDHISM.
Magid, Barry. Ordinary mind. Boston : Wisdom, c2002.
BQ9286.M34 2002

Psychotherapy with the unattached.
Strean, Herbert S. Northvale, N.J. : Jason Aronson Inc., 1995.
RC451.4.S55 S77 1995

PSYCHOTIC ART. *See* **ART AND MENTAL ILLNESS.**

Psykholohiia IA-kontseptsii.
Humeniuk, O. IE. (Oksana IEvstakhivna) Ternopil' : Ekononichna dumka, 2002.
BF697.5.S43 H84 2002

Psykholohiia potaiemnoho "IA".
Manokha, I. P. (Iryna Petrivna) Kyïv : "Polihrafknyha", 2001.
BF637.S4 M338 2001

Psykholohiia rozvytku intelektu.
Smul'son, M. L. (Maryna Lazarivna) Kyïv : Instytut psykholohiï im. H.S. Kostiuka APN Ukraïny, 2001.

BF431.S68 2001

Pszichológia és pszichopatológia jogászoknak.
Fekete, Mária. Budapest : HVG-ORAC, c2002.
BF173.F349 2002

PTOLEMY, 2ND CENT.
Sela, Shlomo. Abraham Ibn Ezra and the rise of medieval Hebrew science. Leiden ; Boston, MA : Brill, 2003.
BM538.S3 S45 2003

PTSD (PSYCHIATRY). *See* **POST-TRAUMATIC STRESS DISORDER.**

[Pubblic/azione (Troina, Italy)] Pubblic/azione : rivista semestrale interdisciplinare sulla pensabilità. Troina (Enna) : Oasi editrice, 2002- v. : col. ill. ; 24 cm. Frequency: Semiannual. Anno 1, n. 1 (genn.-giugno 2002)- . Title from cover. Each issue also has a distinctive theme title.
1. Psychoanalysis - Periodicals. 2. Social sciences and psychoanalysis - Periodicals. I. Title: Pubblicazione

Pubblicazione.
[Pubblic/azione (Troina, Italy)] Pubblic/azione. Troina (Enna) : Oasi editrice, 2002-

Pubblicazioni del D.AR.FI.CL.ET.
(nuova ser., 194.) Traverso, Paola. "Psiche è una parola greca--". Genova, Italy : Compagnia dei librai, 2000.
BF109.F74 T73 2000

Pubblicazioni della Facoltà teologica dell'Italia settentrionale. Sezione di Padova
Sartorio, Ugo. Credere in dialogo. Padova : Edizioni Messaggero, 2002.

Pubblicazioni dell'Università di Urbino. Scienze umane. Serie di filosofia pedagogia psicologia
(9) Sichirollo, Livio. Filosofia, storia, istituzioni. Nuova ed. [Urbino] : Università degli studi di Urbino, [2001]

PUBERTY. *See* **ADOLESCENCE.**

PUBLIC-ACCESS TELEVISION. *See* **CABLE TELEVISION.**

PUBLIC ADMINISTRATION. *See also* **PERSONNEL MANAGEMENT; POLITICAL PLANNING.**
Government reformed. Aldershot, England ; Burlington, VT : Ashgate, c2003.
JF1525.O73 G686 2003

Khademian, Anne M., 1961- Working with culture. Washington, D.C. : CQ Press, c2002.
JF1351.K487 2002

Terry, Larry D. Leadership of public bureaucracies. 2nd ed. Armonk, N.Y. : M.E. Sharpe, c2003.
JF1525.L4 .T47 2003

PUBLIC ADMINISTRATION - ISRAEL.
Frankenburg, Reuven. Revadim 'elyonim ba-minhal ha-tsiburi ha-Yiśre'eli. [Israel : ḥ. mo. l., 1999?]

Public affairs and policy administration series
Khademian, Anne M., 1961- Working with culture. Washington, D.C. : CQ Press, c2002.
JF1351.K487 2002

Public Broadcasting Service (U.S.)
With eyes open [electronic resource]. San Francisco : KQED ; [Alexandria, Va.] : PBS
BF789.D4

Young Dr. Freud [electronic resource]. [Alexandria, Va.?] : PBS, 2002.
BF109.F74

PUBLIC CONTRACTS - LAW AND LEGISLATION. *See* **PUBLIC CONTRACTS.**

PUBLIC CONTRACTS - UNITED STATES.
United States. Congress. House. Committee on the Judiciary. Federal Prison Industries Competition in Contracting Act of 2003. [Washington, D.C. : U.S. G.P.O., 2003]

PUBLIC CORPORATIONS. *See* **CORPORATIONS.**

PUBLIC DEMONSTRATIONS. *See* **DEMONSTRATIONS.**

PUBLIC DOMAIN. *See* **PUBLIC LANDS.**

The public emotions.
Little, Graham. Sydney : ABC Books for the Australian Broadcasting Corporation, 1999.
BF531.L58 1999

PUBLIC HEALTH. *See* **HEALTH FACILITIES; MEDICAL CARE; MENTAL HEALTH; SOCIAL MEDICINE.**

PUBLIC HEALTH - GOVERNMENT POLICY. *See* **MEDICAL POLICY.**

PUBLIC INSTITUTIONS. *See* **MUSEUMS; UNIVERSITIES AND COLLEGES.**

PUBLIC INTEREST.
Archives and the public good. Westport, Conn. ; London : Quorum Books, 2002.

Cladis, Mark Sydney. Public vision, private lives. Oxford ; New York : Oxford University Press, 2003.
JC179.R9 C53 2003

Nelson, Phillip J., 1929- Signaling goodness. Ann Arbor : University of Michigan Press, c2003.
HV31.N45 2003

PUBLIC LANDS - UNITED STATES - HISTORY.
Linklater, Andro. Measuring America. New York : Walker & Co., 2002.
E161.3.L46 2002

PUBLIC LAW. *See* **CITIZENSHIP; CONSTITUTIONAL LAW.**

Public lecture series (Ledikasyon pu travayer)
Collen, Lindsey. Natir imin. Port Louis, Mauritius : Ledikasyon pu travayer, [2000]

PUBLIC LIMITED COMPANIES. *See* **CORPORATIONS.**

PUBLIC MANAGEMENT. *See* **PUBLIC ADMINISTRATION.**

PUBLIC MEETINGS. *See* **DEMONSTRATIONS.**

PUBLIC OFFICERS. *See* **GOVERNMENT EXECUTIVES; MEDICAL EXAMINERS (LAW); PUBLIC ADMINISTRATION.**

PUBLIC OPINION. *See also* **ATTITUDE (PSYCHOLOGY); SCALE ANALYSIS (PSYCHOLOGY).**
Looking at the other. Oulu, Finland : University of Oulu, 2002.

PUBLIC OPINION - UNITED STATES.
Wernitznig, Dagmar. Going native or going naive? Lanham, MD : University Press of America, c2003.
E98.P99 W47 2003

PUBLIC OPINION - UNITED STATES - HISTORY - 20TH CENTURY.
Horowitz, David A. America's political class under fire. New York ; London : Routledge, 2003.
HN90.S6 H67 2003

PUBLIC PLAYGROUNDS. *See* **PLAYGROUNDS.**

PUBLIC POLICY. *See* **POLITICAL PLANNING.**

Public policy in knowledge-based economies : foundations and frameworks / David Rooney ... [et al.]. Cheltenham, UK ; Northampton, MA : Edward Elgar, c2003. xxv, 181 p. : ill. ; 25 cm. (New horizons in public policy) Includes bibliographical references (p 157-173) and index. ISBN 1-84064-340-4 DDC 306.4/2
1. Information policy - Economic aspects. 2. Knowledge, Sociology of. 3. Political planning. 4. Information society. 5. Knowledge management. I. Rooney, David, 1959- II. Series.
HC79.I55 P83 2003

PUBLIC PROCUREMENT. *See* **GOVERNMENT PURCHASING.**

PUBLIC PURCHASING. *See* **GOVERNMENT PURCHASING.**

PUBLIC RECORDS. *See* **ARCHIVES.**

PUBLIC RECORDS - PRESERVATION. *See* **ARCHIVES.**

PUBLIC RELATIONS. *See* **ADVERTISING; CUSTOMER RELATIONS; PUBLIC OPINION.**

PUBLIC SCULPTURE. *See* **MONUMENTS.**

PUBLIC SECTOR MANAGEMENT. *See* **PUBLIC ADMINISTRATION.**

PUBLIC SPACES.
Ilardi, Massimo. In nome della strada. Roma : Meltemi, c2002.

PUBLIC SPEAKING. *See* **EXPRESSION.**

PUBLIC UTILITIES. *See* **CORPORATIONS.**

Public vision, private lives.
Cladis, Mark Sydney. Oxford ; New York : Oxford University Press, 2003.
JC179.R9 C53 2003

PUBLIC WELFARE. *See* **CHILD WELFARE; FAMILY POLICY; INTERNATIONAL RELIEF; SOCIAL MEDICINE.**

Publicação (Biblioteca do Exército (Brazil))
(714.) Gaulle, Charles de, 1890-1970. [Fil de l'épée. Portuguese] O fio da espada. Rio de Janeiro : Biblioteca do Exército Editora, 2001.

Publication manual of the American Psychological Association. 4th ed. Washington, DC : American Psychological Association, 1994. xxxii, 368 p. : ill. ; 26 cm. Includes bibliographical references (p. 319-330) and index. ISBN 1-55798-243-0 (alk. paper) ISBN 1-55798-241-4 (pbk. : alk. paper) DDC 808/.06615
1. Psychology - Authorship - Handbooks, manuals, etc. 2. Social sciences - Authorship - Handbooks, manuals, etc. 3. Psychological literature - Publishing - Handbooks, manuals, etc. 4. Social science literature - Publishing - Handbooks, manuals, etc. I. American Psychological Association.
BF76.7 .P82 1994

Publication manual of the American Psychological Association. 5th ed. Washington, DC : American Psychological Association, c2001. xxviii, 439 p. : ill. ; 27 cm. Includes bibliographical references (p. 363-377) and index. CONTENTS: Content and organization of a manuscript -- Expressing ideas and reducing bias in language -- APA editorial style -- Reference list -- Manuscript preparation and sample papers to be submitted for publication -- Material other than journal articles -- Manuscript acceptance and production -- Journals program of the American Psychological Association -- Appendix A: Checklist for manuscript submission -- Appendix B: Checklist for transmitting accepted manuscripts for electronic production -- Appendix C: Ethical standards for the reporting and publishing of scientific information -- Appendix D: References to legal materials -- Appendix E: Sample cover letter. ISBN 1-55798-810-2 (alk. paper) ISBN 1-55798-791-2 (pbk.) ISBN 1-55798-790-4 (VARIANT) DDC 808/.06615
1. Psychology - Authorship - Handbooks, manuals, etc. 2. Social sciences - Authorship - Handbooks, manuals, etc. 3. Psychological literature - Publishing - Handbooks, manuals, etc. 4. Social science literature - Publishing - Handbooks, manuals, etc. I. American Psychological Association.
BF76.7 .P83 2001

Publications in creativity research
Sawyer, R. Keith (Robert Keith) Improvised dialogues. Westport, Conn. : Ablex Pub., 2003.
P95.45 .S3 2003

Publications in medieval studies (Unnumbered)
Keefe, Susan A. Water and the Word. Notre Dame, Ind. : University of Notre Dame Press, c2002.
BR200 .K44 2002

Publications romanes et françaises
(231) Progrès, réaction, décadence dans l'Occident médiéval. Genève : Droz, 2003.
PN681 .P764 2003

PUBLICITY. See **ADVERTISING; JOURNALISM; PUBLIC OPINION.**

PUBLICITY (LAW).
Beverley-Smith, Huw. Commercial appropriation of personality. Cambridge, UK ; New York : Cambridge University Press, 2002.
K627 .B48 2002

PUBLISHERS AND PUBLISHING. See **BOOKSELLERS AND BOOKSELLING.**

PUBLISHERS AND PUBLISHING - UGANDA - PERIODICALS.
Uganda book news. Kampala, Uganda : UPABA, 1996-
Z467.U337 U34

PUERTO RICO - INTELLECTUAL LIFE - 20TH CENTURY.
Pabón, Carlos. Nación postmortem. 1. ed. San Juan, P.R. : Ediciones Callejón, 2002.

Pufendorf, Samuel, Freiherr von, 1632-1694.
[De officio hominis et civis. English]
The whole duty of man, according to the law of nature / Samuel Pufendorf ; translated by Andrew Tooke, 1691 ; edited and with an introduction by Ian Hunter and David Saunders. Two discourses and a commentary / by Jean Barbeyrac ; translated by David Saunders. Indianapolis, Ind. : Liberty Fund, c2003. xviii, 381 p. ; 23 cm. (Natural law and enlightenment classics) Includes bibliographical references and indexes. Works by Jean Barbeyrac translated from the French. ISBN 0-86597-374-1 (hardcover : alk. paper) ISBN 0-86597-375-X (pbk. : alk. paper) DDC 340/.112
1. Natural law. 2. Ethics. 3. State, The. I. Hunter, Ian, 1949- II. Saunders, David, 1940- III. Barbeyrac, Jean, 1674-1744. Two discourses and a commentary. IV. Title. V. Title: Two discourses and a commentary. VI. Series.
K457.P8 D4313 2003

Pugguil' thū" myā" nhaṅ'' gambhīra laṃ'" mha phyac' rap' chan'" myā".
'Arindamā, Cha rā krī". Ran' kun' : Cin' Pan'" Mruiṅ' Cā pe : [Phran'' khyi re"], Cui" Cā pe, 2002-
BF1281 .A756 2002

Pugh, David G. (David George), 1944-.
Bacon, Terry R. Winning behavior. New York : AMACOM, c2003.
HD58.7 .B3423 2003

PUGNACITY. See **FIGHTING (PSYCHOLOGY).**

Pūjyapāda Svāmī Ānandānanda janma śatī, 29 Janavarī, 2001.
Smārikā. Jayapura : Yoga Sādhanā Āśrama, 2001.
BL1175.A4955 S62 2001

Pulman, Bertrand. Anthropologie et psychanalyse : Malinowski contre Freud / Bertrand Pulman. Paris : Presses universitaires de France, 2002. vi, 235 p. ; 22 cm. (Sociologie d'aujourd'hui) Includes bibliographical references (p. [229]-235). ISBN 2-13-052377-3 DDC 300
1. Malinowski, Bronislaw, - 1884-1942. 2. Freud, Sigmund, - 1856-1939. 3. Primitive societies. 4. Sex customs. 5. Anthropology. 6. Psychoanalysis. I. Title. II. Series.
GN502 .P85 2002

Punctum
(16) Spoerri, Hubert M. Mensch und Kunst. München : Scaneg, c2002.

PUNISHMENT. See also **REPARATION.**
Corlett, J. Angelo, 1958- Responsibility and punishment. Dordrecht ; Boston : Kluwer Academic Publishers, c2001.
BJ1451 .C67 2001

PUNISHMENT - EUROPE - HISTORY - TO 1500.
Jones, Malcolm, 1953- The secret middle ages. Stroud : Sutton, 2002.

PUNK ROCK MUSICIANS. See **ROCK MUSICIANS.**

Puñña, Ca le Ū", 1802 or 3-1866 or 7.
Mraṅ'' Svaṅ', Ū". Ca le cha rā krī" Ū" Puñña bedaṅ' 'a ho te" thap' 'a phvaṅ' kyaṃ'". Ran' kun' : Khyui Te" Saṃ Cā pe : [Phran'' khyi re"], Paññā Rvhe Toṅ' Cā 'up' Tuik', 2002.
BF1714.B8 M73 2002

PUPPET OPERAS. See **OPERAS.**

PURANAS. BHĀGAVATAPURĀṆA - CRITICISM, INTERPRETATION, ETC.
Karṇāṭaka, Vimalā. Śrīmadbhāgavata meṃ Sāṅkhyayoga ke tattva. 1. saṃskaraṇa. Vārāṇasī : Sampūrṇānanda Saṃskṛta Viśvavidyālaya, 2001.
BL1140.4.B437 K27 2001

PURCHASING. See **GOVERNMENT PURCHASING.**

PURCHASING, GOVERNMENT. See **GOVERNMENT PURCHASING.**

PURGATORY.
Adam, of Eynsham, fl. 1196-1232. [Visio Monachi de Eynsham. English (Middle English) & Latin] The revelation of the Monk of Eynsham. Oxford : Published for the Early English Text Society by the Oxford University Press, 2002.

PURIM.
Leṿin, Yitsḥaḳ, 1938- Sefer Netivot Yitsḥaḳ. [Bene Beraḳ] : Y. Leṿin, [2000-

PURPOSES, EDUCATIONAL. See **EDUCATION - AIMS AND OBJECTIVES.**

The pursuit of happiness in times of war.
Cannon, Carl M. Lanham, MD : Oxford : Rowman & Littlefield ; [Lanham, Md.] : Distributed by National Book Network, c2004.
E183 .C25 2004

PUSHKIN, ALEKSANDR SERGEEVICH, 1799-1837.
Drankov, V. L. (Vladimir L'vovich) Priroda khudozhestvennogo talanta. Sankt-Peterburg : Sankt-Peterburgskiĭ gos. universitet kul'tury i iskusstv, 2001.
BF408 .D66 2001

PUSHKIN, ALEKSANDR SERGEEVICH, 1799-1837 - CRITICISM AND INTERPRETATION.
Drankov, V. L. (Vladimir L'vovich) Priroda khudozhestvennogo talanta. Sankt-Peterburg : Sankt-Peterburgskiĭ gosudarstvennyĭ universitet kul'tury i iskusstv, 2001.

Put' okkul'tizma.
Karasev, Nikolaĭ, iereĭ. Moskva : Izd-vo "Prensa", 2003.
BF1416 .K37 2003

Putnam, Hilary. The collapse of the fact/value dichotomy and other essays / Hilary Putnam. Cambridge, MA : Harvard University Press, 2002. ix, 190 p. ; 22 cm. Includes bibliographical references (p. [147]-181) and index. CONTENTS: I. Collapse of the fact/value dichotomy -- Empiricist background -- Entanglement of fact and value -- Fact and value in the world of Amartya Sen -- II. Rationality and value -- Sen's "prescriptivist" beginnings -- On the rationality of preferences -- Are values made or discovered? -- Values and norms -- Philosophers of science's evasion of values. ISBN 0-674-00905-3 DDC 121/.8
1. Sen, Amartya Kumar. 2. Values. 3. Facts (Philosophy) 4. Welfare economics. I. Title.
B945.P873 C65 2002

Putting the tarot to work.
McElroy, Mark, 1964- 1st ed. St. Paul, Minn. : Llewellyn Publications, 2004.
BF1879.T2 M43 2004

PUZZLES.
Brecher, Erwin. Hocus-pocus. London : Panacea Press, 2001.
GV1282.3 .B725 2001

Carter, Philip J. Maximize your brainpower. West Sussex, England ; New York : John Wiley & Sons, Ltd, 2002.
BF431.3 .C3647 2002

Cohn, Arthur, 1910- Musical puzzlemania. Mew York, NY : Carl Fischer, c1998.

Puzzles & perplexities.
Cahn, Steven M. Lanham, Md. ; Oxford : Rowman & Littlefield, c2002.
BD41 .C26 2002

Puzzles and perplexities.
Cahn, Steven M. Puzzles & perplexities. Lanham, Md. ; Oxford : Rowman & Littlefield, c2002.
BD41 .C26 2002

Py, Luiz Alberto. Olhar acima do horizonte : aprendendo com as coisas simples da vida / Luiz Alberto Py. Rio de Janeiro : Rocco, 2002. 177 p. ; 21 cm. ISBN 85-325-1442-1
1. Self-realization. 2. Change (Psychology) I. Title.

Pylyshyn, Zenon W., 1937- Seeing and visualizing : it's not what you think / Zenon Pylyshyn. Cambridge, Mass. : MIT Press, 2003. p. cm. (Life and mind) "A Bradford book". Includes bibliographical references and index. ISBN 0-262-16217-2 (hc. : alk. paper) DDC 152.4
1. Visual perception. 2. Visualization. 3. Mental representation. 4. Recognition (Psychology) 5. Categorization (Psychology) 6. Cognitive science. I. Title. II. Series.
BF241 .P95 2003

The pyramid discourses.
Re-Cord-El, 1943- Columbus, OH : Howie Pub., 2003.
BF1999 .R3956 2003

PYRAMID TEXTS.
Eyre, Christopher. The cannibal hymn. Liverpool : Liverpool University Press, 2002.

PYSCHOLOGY - POPULAR WORKS.
Bu ping ze ming. Di 2 ban. Beijing : Zhongguo cheng shi chu ban she, 2001.

Pyszczynski, Thomas A. In the wake of 9/11 : the psychology of terror / Tom Pyszczynski, Jeff Greenberg, Sheldon Solomon. Washington, DC : American Psychological Association, c2003. xiv, 227 p. ; 26 cm. Includes bibliographical references (p. 199-215) and index. ISBN 1-55798-954-0 (alk. paper) DDC 155.9/35
1. September 11 Terrorist Attacks, 2001 - Psychological aspects. 2. Terrorism - United States - Psychological aspects. 3. Terrorism - Psychological aspects. 4. Terror. 5. Fear of death. I. Greenberg, Jeff, 1954- II. Solomon, Sheldon. III. Title.
HV6432 .P97 2003

PYTHAGORAS AND PYTHAGOREAN SCHOOL.
Tokar, David A. Hans Kayser's Lehrbuch der Harmonik. 2002.

Pyysiäinen, Ilkka. How religion works : towards a new cognitive science of religion / Ilkka Pyysiäinen. Leiden ; Boston : Brill, 2001. xi, 272 p. : ill. ; 25 cm. (Cognition and culture book series ; v. 1) Includes bibliographical references (p. [237]-266) and indexes. ISBN 90-04-12319-9 (cloth : alk. paper) DDC 200/.1/9
1. Psychology, Religious. I. Title. II. Series.
BL53 .P98 2001

Qanāzi', Jūrj.
Shayzarī, 'Abd al-Raḥmān ibn Naṣr, 12th cent. Rawḍat al-qulūb wa-nuzhat al-muḥibb wa-al-maḥbūb. Wiesbaden : Harrassowitz, 2003.

Qarn-i rawshanfikrān.
Qizilsaflī, Muḥammad Taqī. Chāp-i 1. Tihrān : Markaz-i Bayn al-Milalī-i Guftugū-yi Tamaddun'hā : Hirmis, 1380 [2001]

QBQ!.
Miller, John G., 1958- Denver, CO : Denver Press, c2001.
BF611 .M55 2001

QI (CHINESE PHILOSOPHY).
Cho, Hyeon-Kweon Stephan, 1962- Heiliger Geist als Lebenskraft in Kirche und Menschheit. Frankfurt am Main ; New York : Peter Lang, c2002.
BT121.3 .C56 2002

QI GONG.
Breathing spaces. New York : Columbia University Press, c2003.
RA781.8 .B73 2003

QI GONG - POLITICAL ASPECTS.
Breathing spaces. New York : Columbia University Press, c2003.
RA781.8 .B73 2003

QI GONG - SOCIAL ASPECTS.
Breathing spaces. New York : Columbia University Press, c2003.
RA781.8 .B73 2003

Qi, Zhixiang. Fo jiao mei xue / Qi Zhixiang zhu. Di 1 ban. Shanghai : Shanghai ren min chu ban she : Xin hua shu dian Shanghai fa xing suo jing xiao, 1997. 3, 9, 294 p. ; 21 cm. Includes bibliographical references (p. 291-292). ISBN 7-208-02430-8
1. Buddhism and the arts. 2. Aesthetics. I. Title.
BQ4570.A72 C45 1997 <Asian China>

Qian, Wenzhong.
Tang, Yijie. Xi bu zhi jin. Di 1 ban. Shanghai : Shanghai wen yi chu ban she, 1999.
B126 .T1965 1999

Qian, Zhongshu, 1910-.
Guan zhui bian. 1998.
Motsch, Monika, 1942- [Mit Bambusrohr und Ahle von Qian Zhongshus Guanzhuibian zu einer Neubetrachtung Du Fus. Chinese] "Guan zhui bian" yu Du Fu xin jie. Di 1 ban. Shijiazhuang Shi : Hebei jiao yu chu ban she, 1997 (2002 printing)
PL2749.C8 Z85 1997

Qian Zhongshu yan jiu cong shu
Motsch, Monika, 1942- [Mit Bambusrohr und Ahle von Qian Zhongshus Guanzhuibian zu einer Neubetrachtung Du Fus. Chinese] "Guan zhui bian" yu Du Fu xin jie. Di 1 ban. Shijiazhuang Shi : Hebei jiao yu chu ban she, 1997 (2002 printing)
PL2749.C8 Z85 1997

Qiao, Zhihang.
Wen, Yiduo, 1899-1946. Wen Yiduo xue shu wen hua sui bi. Beijing di 1 ban. Beijing : Zhongguo qing nian chu ban she, 2001.
PL2272.5 .W46 2001

Qigong, psychiatry, and healing in China.
Breathing spaces. New York : Columbia University Press, c2003.
RA781.8 .B73 2003

Qing hua Bei da xue bu dao.
Yazi. Di 1 ban. Beijing : Xin hua chu ban she, 2002.
BJ1618.C5 Y38 2002

Qing, Shan.
Liang Qichao, Zhang Taiyan jie du Zhonghua wen hua jing dian. Di 1 ban. Shenyang Shi : Liao Hai chu ban she, 2003.
PL2262.2 .L54 2003

Qizilsaflī, Muḥammad Taqī. Qarn-i rawshanfikrān / Muḥammad Taqī Qizilsaflī. Chāp-i 1. Tihrān : Markaz-i Bayn al-Milalī-i Guftugū-yi Tamaddun'hā : Hirmis, 1380 [2001] 6, 355 p. ; 23 cm. Includes bibliographical references. In Persian. ISBN 9643630064
1. Intellectuals - Iran - Interviews. 2. Iran - Intellectual life - 20th century. 3. Culture - Philosophy. I. Title.

Qu, Gang, 1969- Intellectual property protection in VLSI designs : theory and practice / by Gang Qu and Miodrag Potkonjak. Boston, Mass. : London : Kluwer Academic, c2003. xix, 183 p. : ill. ; 25 cm. Includes bibliographical references. ISBN 1402073208 DDC 005.8
1. Intellectual property. 2. Integrated circuits - Very large scale integration. I. Potkonjak, Miodrag. II. Title.

Qu, Ming'an.
Zhongguo xiang zheng wen hua. Di 1 ban. Shanghai : Shanghai ren min chu ban she : Xin hua shu dian Shanghai fa xing suo jing xiao, 2001.
DS721 .Z4985 2001

Quaderni della Rassegna (Florence, Italy)
(22.) Il sacro nel Rinascimento. Firenze : F. Cesati, c2002.
PN49 .S337 2002

Quaderni di Acme
(50) Tra IV e V secolo. Milano : Cisalpino, 2002.

I quaderni di Storia verità
(9) Franchi, Franco. La libertà nel fascismo. Roma : Europa : Settimo sigillo, c2002.

Quadrio, Assunto.
La comunicazione nei processi sociali e organizzativi. Nuova ed. aggiornata. Milano, Italy : FrancoAngeli, [2001?], c1997.

Quaestiones
(15) Schröder, Winfried, Dr. phil. Moralischer Nihilismus. Stuttgart-Bad Canstatt : Frommann-Holzboog, c2002.

Quaglia, Rocco. Immagini dell'uomo : costruzione di sé e del mondo / Rocco Quaglia. Roma : Armando, c2000. 188 p. ; 22 cm. (Scaffale aperto. Psicologia) Includes bibliographical references. ISBN 88-8358-104-0 DDC 155
1. Psychoanalysis. 2. Personality development. 3. Self-perception. 4. Family - Psychological aspects. I. Title. II. Series.

I sogni della Bibbia : un'interpretazione psicodinamica e altri scritti / Rocco Quaglia. Roma : Borla, c2002. 113 p. ; 21 cm. Includes bibliographical references. ISBN 88-263-1434-9 DDC 220
1. Bible. - O.T. - Criticism, interpretation, etc. 2. Dreams in the Bible. 3. Psychoanalysis and religion. 4. Psychodynamic psychotherapy. I. Title.

Il "valore" del padre. Torino : UTET libreria, 2001.
BF723.P25 V35 2001

Qualitative data.
Auerbach, Carl F. New York : New York University Press, c2003.
BF76.5 .A95 2003

Qualitative Inhaltsanalyse und Mind-Mapping.
Hugl, Ulrike. Wiesbaden : Gabler, 1995.

Qualitative methods and health policy research.
Murphy, Elizabeth. Hawthorne, N.Y. : Aldine de Gruyter, c2003.
RA394 .M87 2003

Qualitative psychology : a practical guide to research methods / edited by Jonathan A. Smith. London ; Thousand Oaks, Calif. : SAGE Publications, 2003. ix, 258 p. : ill. ; 25 cm. Includes bibliographical references (p. 236-250) and index. ISBN 0-7619-7231-5 (pbk.) ISBN 0-7619-7230-7 DDC 150/.72
1. Psychology - Research - Methodology - Textbooks. 2. Qualitative research - Textbooks. I. Smith, Jonathan A.
BF76.5 .Q3375 2003

QUALITATIVE REASONING.
Collecting and interpreting qualitative materials. 2nd ed. Thousand Oaks, Calif. : Sage, c2003.
H62 .C566 2003

Janesick, Valerie J. "Stretching" exercises for qualitative researchers. 2nd ed. Thousand Oaks, Calif. : Sage Publications, c2004.
H62 .J346 2004

Rossman, Gretchen B. Learning in the field. 2nd ed. Thousand Oaks, Calif. ; London : Sage Publications, c2003.
H62 .R667 2003

QUALITATIVE RESEARCH.
Auerbach, Carl F. Qualitative data. New York : New York University Press, c2003.
BF76.5 .A95 2003

Expressions of ethnography. Albany, NY : State University of New York Press, c2003.
GN33 .E97 2003

Givens, Gretchen Zita. Black women in the field. Cresskill, N.J. : Hampton Press, c2003.
LC2781.5 .G58 2003

Murphy, Elizabeth. Qualitative methods and health policy research. Hawthorne, N.Y. : Aldine de Gruyter, c2003.
RA394 .M87 2003

Using qualitative research in advertising: strategies, techniques, and applications. Thousand Oaks, Calif. : Sage, c2002.
HF5814 .U78 2002

Writing in the dark : phenomenological studies in interpretive inquiry. London, Ont. : Althouse Press, 2002.

B829.5 .W75 2002

QUALITATIVE RESEARCH - TEXTBOOKS.
Qualitative psychology. London ; Thousand Oaks, Calif. : SAGE Publications, 2003.
BF76.5 .Q3375 2003

Qualitative studies in psychology
Auerbach, Carl F. Qualitative data. New York : New York University Press, c2003.
BF76.5 .A95 2003

Quality Air Force in an emergency [electronic resource].
Bird, David F. Maxwell Air Force Base, Ala. : Air War College, Air University, [1996]

QUALITY ASSURANCE. See **QUALITY CONTROL.**

QUALITY CONTROL - STATISTICAL METHODS.
Yang, Kai. Design for Six Sigma. New York ; London : McGraw-Hill, c2003.
TS156 .Y33 2003

The quality of courage.
Mantle, Mickey, 1931- Lincoln : University of Nebraska Press, [1999]
GV865.A1 M317 1999

The quality of freedom.
Kramer, Matthew H., 1959- Oxford ; New York : Oxford University Press, 2003.
JC585 .K74 2003

QUALITY OF LIFE.
Children in the city. London : Routledge/Falmer, 2003.

Crouch, Chris. Simple works. Memphis, TN : Black Pants Pub., c2001.
BF637.C5 C78 2001

Giardina, Ric. Become a life balance master. Hillsboro, Or. : Beyond Words Pub., 2003.
BF637.S4 G486 2003

Helliwell, John F. Globalization and well-being. Vancouver : UBC Press, 2002.
HF1359 .H43 2002

McCulloch, Douglas, 1950- Valuing health in practice. Aldershot, Hampshire, England ; Burlington, VT : Ashgate, c2003.
RA410.5 .M37 2002

El milagro y el valor de la vida. 1. ed. Buenos Aires : Patria Grande, 2000.

Saúde e ambiente sustentável. Rio de Janeiro, RJ : Editora Fiocruz : Abrasco, 2002.

[Wohlstand entschleiern. English] Unveiling wealth. Dordrecht ; Boston : Kluwer, c2002.
HD75.6 .U58 2002

QUALITY OF LIFE - MISCELLANEA.
MacGregor, Cynthia. Little indulgences. York Beach, ME : Conari Press, 2003.
BF637.C5 M32 2003

QUALITY OF PRODUCTS. See **QUALITY CONTROL.**

QUALITY OF WORK LIFE.
The new workplace. Chichester, UK ; Hoboken, NJ : Wiley, c2003.
HD6955 .N495 2003

Quantitative psychological research.
Clark-Carter, David. 2nd ed. New York, NY : Taylor & Francis, 2004.
BF76.5 .C53 2004

Quantum leap thinking.
Mapes, James J., 1945- Naperville, Ill. : Sourcebooks, c2003.
BF441 .M265 2003

QUANTUM THEORY.
Esfeld, Michael. Holism in philosophy of mind and philosophy of physics. Dordrecht ; Boston : Kluwer Academic Publishers, c2001.
B818 .E74 2001

QUARRELING. See also **VERBAL SELF-DEFENSE.**
Johnston, Marianne. [Dealing with fighting. Spanish] Como tratar las peleas. New York : PowerKids Press, 2005.
BF637.I48 J6418 2005

QUARRELING - JUVENILE LITERATURE.
Johnston, Marianne. [Dealing with fighting. Spanish] Como tratar las peleas. New York : PowerKids Press, 2005.

QuasiBook edition

BF637.I48 J6418 2005

QuasiBook edition
The occult Webb. Toronto : Colombo & Co., c1999.
BF1408.2.W42 O33 1999

Que busca encuentra.
Morales Tomas, Marco Antonio. El que busca encuentra = Guatemala : ESEDIR : Editorial Saqil Tzij, 1999.

Que no le cuenten cuentos.
Valle Bonilla, Otto René. Guatemala : ESEDIR : Editorial Saqil Tzij, 1999.

Qué quiere decir género?.
Burggraf, Jutta. 1. ed. San Jose, Costa Rica : Promesa, 2001.

Queen bees & wannabes.
Wiseman, Rosalind, 1969- 1st ed. New York : Crown Publishers, c2002.
HQ798 .W544 2002

Queen bees and wannabes.
Wiseman, Rosalind, 1969- Queen bees & wannabes. 1st ed. New York : Crown Publishers, c2002.
HQ798 .W544 2002

Queen Elizabeth House series in development studies
Group behaviour and development. Oxford ; New York : Oxford University Press, 2002.
HD58.7 .G76 2002

QUEENS. See **LADIES-IN-WAITING.**

QUEENS - BIOGRAPHY.
Ancient queens. Walnut Creek, Calif. ; Oxford : AltaMira Press, c2003.
HQ1127 .A53 2003

Queer counselling and narrative practice / edited by David Denborough. Adelaide : Dulwich Centre Publications, c2002. 279 p. ; 21 cm. Includes bibliographical references. ISBN 0-9577929-6-4 (pbk.)
1. Homosexuality. 2. Bisexuality. 3. Transsexualism. 4. Gays - Counseling of. 5. Bisexuals - Counseling of. 6. Transsexuals - Counseling of. I. Denborough, David. II. Title.

Queer mixture : gender perspectives on minority sexual identities.
Odmiany odmieńca. Katowice : "Śląsk", 2002.
HQ23 .O36 2002

Quellen und Forschungen zur höchsten Gerichtsbarkeit im alten Reich
(Bd. 43) Westphal, Siegrid, 1963- Kaiserliche Rechtsprechung und herrschaftliche Stabilisierung. Köln : Böhlau, 2002.

Quellen und Studien zur Geschichte des Deutschen Ordens
(Bd. 57) Sankt Georg und sęin Bilderzyklus in Neuhaus/Böhmen (Jindřichuv Hradec). Marburg : N.G. Elwert, c2002.
BR1720.G4 S26 2002

Quellen und Studien zur Philosophie
(Bd. 58) Araujo, Marcelo de. Scepticism, freedom and autonomy. Berlin : De Gruyter, 2003.

Qu'est-ce-donc qu'apprendre? / sous la direction de J.-D. de Lannoy et P. Feyereisen ; A. Bandura ... [et al.]. Lausanne : Delachaux et Niestlé, 1999. 255 p. : ill. ; 21 cm. (Textes de base en psychologie). Includes bibliographical references (p. [239]-255). ISBN 2-603-01160-X
1. Learning, Psychology of. 2. Cognitive psychology. I. Lannoy, Jacques-Dominique de. II. Feyereisen, Pierre. III. Bandura, Albert, 1925- IV. Series.
BF318 .Q84 1999

Qu'est-ce que la société féodale?.
Duby, Georges. Paris : Flammarion, c2002.

Qu'est-ce qu'une vie réussie?.
Ferry, Luc. Paris : Grasset, c2002.
BJ1612 .F47 2002

The quest for the phoenix.
Tilton, Hereward. Berlin ; New York : Walter de Gruyter, 2003.
QD24.M3 T558 2003

The quest for voice in contemporary psychoanalysis.
Strenger, Carlo. Madison, Conn. : International Universities Press, c2002.
RC506 .S773 2002

Quest (Lusaka, Zambia). Special issue.
Language & culture. Lusaka, Zambia : Quest, 1999.

Questão da modernidade
(caderno 2) Facetas das pós-modernidade. São Paulo : Universidade de São Paulo, Faculdade De Filosofia Letras e Ciências Humanas, 1996.

Question behind the question.
Miller, John G., 1958- QBQ!. Denver, CO : Denver Press, c2001.
BF611 .M55 2001

QUESTIONING. See also **INTERVIEWING; POLICE QUESTIONING.**
Flage, Daniel E., 1951- The art of questioning. Upper Saddle River, N.J. : Pearson/Prentice Hall, c2004.
BF441 .F55 2004

QUESTIONS AND ANSWERS.
Brian, Sarah Jane. The quiz book 2. Middleton, Wis. : Pleasant Co. , c2001.
BF831 .B75 2001

Questions and answers about disability and service retirement plans under the Americans with Disabilities Act (ADA) [electronic resource]. [Washington, D.C.] : U.S. Equal Employment Opportunity Commission, [1995]

Questions and answers [electronic resource]. [Washington, D.C.] : U.S. Equal Employment Opportunity Commission, [2000?]

Questions and answers about disability and service retirement plans under the Americans with Disabilities Act (ADA) [electronic resource]. [Washington, D.C.] : U.S. Equal Employment Opportunity Commission, [1995] (EEOC notice ; no. 915.002) World Wide Web Resource Mode of access: Internet from the EEOC web site. Address as of 4/10/03: http://www.eeoc.gov/docs/qadsre.html; current access is available via PURL. Title from title screen (viewed on Apr. 10, 2003). SUMMARY: The U.S. Equal Employment Opportunity Commission (EEOC) presents questions and answers regarding disability and service retirement plans under the Americans with Disabilities Act (ADA). The questions and answers are provided to assist EEOC field offices that are dealing with discrimination charges and informal inquiries concerning the application of the ADA to disability and service retirement plans. URL: http://purl.access.gpo.gov/GPO/LPS29473 DDC 344.07911026 DDC 331.133026 DDC 011.53 DDC 030 DDC 306.38
1. United States. Equal Employment Opportunity Commission. 2. Disability retirement - Law and legislation - United States - Miscellanea. 3. Discrimination against the handicapped - Prevention - Law and legislation. 4. Discrimination in employment - Prevention - Law and legislation. 5. Government publications. 6. Questions and answers. 7. Retirement. 8. United States. I. United States. Equal Employment Opportunity Commission. II. Series: United States. Equal Employment Opportunity Commission. Notice ; 915.002.

Questions and answers [electronic resource] : enforcement guidance on disability-related inquiries and medical examinations of employees under the Americans with Disabilities Act (ADA). [Washington, D.C.] : U.S. Equal Employment Opportunity Commission, [2000?] World Wide Web Resource Mode of access: Internet from the EEOC web site. Address as of 4/10/03: http://www.eeoc.gov/docs/qanda-inquiries.html; current access is available via PURL. Title from title screen (viewed on Apr. 10, 2003). SUMMARY: The U.S. Equal Employment Opportunity Commission (EEOC) presents questions and answers regarding "Enforcement Guidance on Disability-Related Inquiries and Medical Examinations of Employees Under the Americans with Disabilities Act (ADA)." The publication focuses on the ADA's limitation on disability-related inquiries and medical examinations during employment. URL: http://purl.access.gpo.gov/GPO/LPS29474 DDC 331.133026 DDC 351 DDC 030 DDC 305.90816
1. United States. Equal Employment Opportunity Commission. 2. Employees - Medical examinations - Law and legislation - United States - Miscellanea. 3. Medical records - Access control - United States - Miscellanea. 4. Discrimination in employment - Prevention - Law and legislation. 5. Administrative agencies. 6. Questions and answers. 7. People with disabilities. 8. United States. I. United States. Equal Employment Opportunity Commission. II. Title: Enforcement guidance on disability-related inquiries and medical examinations of employees under the Americans with Disabilities Act (ADA)

Quevedo Torrientes, Elena.
Desarrollo de los valores en las instituciones educativas. Bilbao : Mensajero, 2001.

Quiet rumours : an anarcha-feminist reader. Edinburgh ; San Francisco : AK Press/Dark Star, 2002. 119 p. : ill. ; 21 cm. On cover: "Texts collected by Dark Star." Includes bibliographical references. ISBN 1-902593-40-5
1. Feminism. 2. Anarchism. 3. Anarchists. I. Dark Star (Firm)

QUIMBANDA (CULT). See **UMBANDA (CULT).**

Quindlen, Anna. Blessings : a novel / Anna Quindlen. 1st large print ed. New York : Random House Large Print, c2002. 387 p. (large print) ; 25 cm. ISBN 0-375-43184-5 DDC 813/.54
1. Large type books. 2. Foundlings - Fiction. 3. Administration of estates - Fiction. 4. Women landowners - Fiction. I. Title.
PS3567.U336 B59 2002b

Quinlan, Mary Kay.
Sommer, Barbara W. The oral history manual. Walnut Creek, CA ; Oxford : Altamira Press, c2002.
D16.14 .S69 2002

Quinze cartas sobre moralidade & ciência.
Ramos, João Baptista. Brasilia : Thesaurus, 2000.

Quiromancia para principiantes.
Webster, Richard, 1946- [Palm reading for beginners. Spanish] 1. ed. St. Paul, Minn. : Llewellyn Español, 2003.
BF921 .W418 2003

The quiz book 2.
Brian, Sarah Jane. Middleton, Wis. : Pleasant Co. , c2001.
BF831 .B75 2001

Quiz book two.
Brian, Sarah Jane. The quiz book 2. Middleton, Wis. : Pleasant Co. , c2001.
BF831 .B75 2001

QUOTATIONS. See also **APHORISMS AND APOTHEGMS; MAXIMS.**
Morales Villaroel, Oscar. Huellas y relatos. Caracas : [s.n.], 2001.

QUOTATIONS, ENGLISH - MISCELLANEA.
Bolt, Carol, 1963- Mom's book of answers. New York : Stewart, Tabori & Chang, 2004.
BF1891.B66 B649 2004

QUOTATIONS, LATIN - STUDY AND TEACHING - EUROPE - HISTORY.
Moss, Ann, 1938- Printed commonplace-books and the structuring of Renaissance thought. Oxford : Clarendon Press ; New York : Oxford University Press, 1996.
PA2047 .M67 1996

RA (EGYPTIAN DEITY).
Görg, Manfred. Die Barke der Sonne. Freiburg im Breisgau : Herder, 2001.
BL2450.R2 G647 2001

RA (SPIRIT).
Free, Wynn, 1946- The reincarnation of Edgar Cayce? Berkeley, Calif. : Frog, 2004.
BF1815.W49 F74 2004

Raad, Boele de.
Big five assessment. Seattle, WA : Hogrefe & Huber Publishers, c2002.
BF698.4 .B52 2002

Raam, Gabriel. Omanut ha-śihah : mi-lahag u-fitpuṭ 'ad hidabrut ye-di'alog / Gavri'el Ra'am. Tel-Aviv : Yedi'ot aharonot : Sifre ḥemed, c2003. 336 p. ; 24 cm. Title on t.p. verso: Art of conversation. Includes bibliographical references (p. 330-336).
1. Conversation. 2. Oral communication. 3. Interpersonal communication. I. Title. II. Title: Art of conversation
P95.45 .R33 2003

Raayonot umssarim lhaftarot hashavua.
Koll, Shmuel, 1938- Sefer Ra'yonot u-mesarim. Yerushalayim : S. Kol, 761- [2001-

Rábago, Jesús. Le sens de bâtir : architecture et philosophie / Jesús Rábago. Lecques : Théétète, c2000. 181 p. ; 21 cm. (Collection Des lieux et des espaces) Includes bibliographical references and index. ISBN 2-912860-15-6
1. Architecture - Philosophy. I. Title. II. Series.
NA2500 .R29 2000

RABBINICAL LITERATURE. See **AGGADA; MIDRASH.**

RABBINICAL LITERATURE - HISTORY AND CRITICISM.
Neusner, Jacob, 1932- Analysis and argumentation in Rabbinic Judaism. Lanham, Md. : University Press of America, c2003.
BM496.5 .N4775 2003

RABBIS.
Adler, Yitshaḳ Eliyahu, ha-Kohen. Sefer Kibud ye-hidur. Ofaḳim : Y.E. ha-Kohen Adler, 754 [1994]

RABBIS - BIOGRAPHY.
Shtern, Shemu'el Eli'ezer. Sefer Sene bo'er ba-esh. Bene Beraḳ : Mekhon "Mayim ḥayim", 762 [2002]

Vital, Ḥayyim ben Joseph, 1542 or 3-1620. 'Ets ha-da'at ṭov. Yerushalayim : Hotsa'at Ahavat shalom, 761 [2000 or 2001]

RABBIS - JERUSALEM - BIOGRAPHY.
Mar'eh Kohen. Yerushalayim : Makhon le-ḥeker mishnat ha-Re'iyah Ḳuḳ be-shituf 'im "Bet ha-Rav", c762 [2001 or 2002]

RABBIS - SLOVAKIA - BRATISLAVA - BIOGRAPHY.
Shṭern, Shemu'el Eli'ezer. Sefer Sene bo'er ba-esh. Bene Beraḳ : Mekhon "Mayim ḥayim", 762 [2002]

Rabinor, Judith Ruskay, 1942- A starving madness : tales of hunger, hope & healing in psychotherapy / Judith Ruskay Rabinor. Carlsbad, CA : Gurze Books, c2002. xviii, 212 p. ; 25 cm. Includes bibliographical references and index. ISBN 0-936077-41-7 DDC 616.85/260651
1. Eating disorders - Adjuvant treatment - Case studies. 2. Psychotherapy - Case studies. I. Title.
RC552.E18 R33 2001

RACE. See also ETHNOCENTRISM.
Corlett, J. Angelo, 1958- Race, racism, & reparations. Ithaca : Cornell University Press, c2003.
HT1523 .C67 2003

Nagel, Joane. Race, ethnicity, and sexuality. New York : Oxford University Press, 2003.
HQ21 .N195 2003

Race and IQ. Expanded ed. New York : Oxford University Press, 1999.
BF432.A1 R3 1999

Race and racism in continental philosophy. Bloomington : Indiana University Press, c2003.
HT1523 .R2514 2003

Russkaia rasovaia teoriia do 1917 goda. Moskva : Feri-V, 2002.

Yanow, Dvora. Constructing "race" and "ethnicity" in America. Armonk, N.Y. : M.E. Sharpe, c2003.
HM753 .Y36 2003

Race and ethnicity in psychology
Collins, Catherine Fisher. Sources of stress and relief for African American women. Westport, Conn. ; London : Praeger, 2003.
BF575.S75 C57 2003

Race and IQ / edited by Ashley Montagu. Expanded ed. New York : Oxford University Press, 1999. viii, 486 p. : ill. ; 22 cm. Includes bibliographical references. CONTENTS: Natural selection and the mental capacities of mankind / Th. Dobzhansky and Ashley Montagu -- The IQ mythology / Ashley Montagu -- The debate over race: thirty years and two centuries later / Leonard Lieberman, with Alice Littlefield and Larry T. Reynolds -- What can biologists solve? / S.E. Luria -- The magical aura of the IQ / Jerome Kagan -- An examination of Jensen's theory concerning educability, heritability, and population differences / S. Biesheuvel -- An affluent society's excuses for inequality: developmental, economic, and educational / Edmund W. Gordon with Derek Green -- Nature with nurture: a reinterpretation of the evidence / Urie Bronfenbrenner -- Racist arguments and IQ / Stephen Jay Gould -- Intelligence, IQ, and race / Ashley Montagu -- On creeping Jensenism / C. Loring Brace and Frank B. Livingstone -- Race and intelligence / Richard C. Lewontin -- Heritability analyses of IQ scores: science or numerology? / David Layzer -- On the causes of IQ differences between groups and implications for social policy / Peggy R. Sanday -- Race and IQ: the genetic background / W.F. Bodmer -- Is early intervention effective? Some studies of early education in familial and extra-familial settings / Urie Bronfenbrenner -- Bad science, worse politics / Alan Ryan -- Behind the curve / Leon J. Kamin -- The tainted sources of the bell curve / Charles Lane -- "Science" in the service of racism / C. Loring Brace -- How heritability misleads about race / Ned Block. ISBN 0-19-510220-7 ISBN 0-19-510221-5 (pbk.) DDC 155.8/2
1. Intelligence tests. 2. Race. 3. Nature and nurture. 4. Racism in psychology. I. Montagu, Ashley, 1905-
BF432.A1 R3 1999

Race and racism in continental philosophy / edited by Robert Bernasconi ; with Sybol Cook. Bloomington : Indiana University Press, c2003. vii, 316 p. ; 25 cm. (Studies in Continental thought) Includes bibliographical references and index. CONTENTS: Acknowledgments -- Introduction / Robert Bernasconi -- Negroes / Alain David -- "One far off divine event" : "race" and a future history in Du Bois / Kevin Thomas Miles -- Douglass and Du Bois's der schwartze Volksgeist / Ronald R. Sundstrom -- On the use and abuse of race in philosophy : Nietzsche, Jews, and race / Jacqueline Scott -- Heidegger and race / Sonia Sikka -- Ethos and ethnos : an introduction to Eric Voegelin's critique of European racism / David J. Levy -- Tropiques and Suzanne Césaire : the expanse of negritude and surrealism / T. Denean Sharpley-Whiting -- Losing sight of the real : recasting Merleau-Ponty in Fanon's critique of Mannoni / Nigel Gibson -- Fanon reading (W)right, the (W)right reading of Fanon : race, modernity, and the fate of humanism / Lou Turner -- Alienation and its double; or, The secretion of race / Kelly Oliver -- (Anti-semitic) subject, liberal in/tolerance, universal politics : Sartre re-petitioned / Erik Vogt -- Sartre and the social construction of race / Donna Marcano -- The interventions of culture : Claude Lévi-Strauss, race, and the critique of historical time / Kamala Visweswaran -- All power to the people! Hannah Arendt's theory of communicative action in a racialized democracy / Joy James -- Beyond Black Orpheus : preliminary thoughts on the good of African philosophy / Jason W. Wirth -- Appendix: what the black man contributes / Léopold Sédar Senghor -- Contributors -- Index. ISBN 0-253-34223-6 (cloth : alk. paper) ISBN 0-253-21590-0 (pbk. : alk. paper) DDC 305.8
1. Racism. 2. Race. 3. Philosophy, European. 4. Philosophers - Europe - Attitudes. I. Bernasconi, Robert. II. Cook, Sybol. III. Series.
HT1523 .R2514 2003

Race and the cosmos.
Holmes, Barbara Ann, 1943- Harrisburg, Pa. : Trinity Press International, c2002.
BR563.N4 H654 2002

Race and the unconscious.
Britton, Celia. Oxford : Legenda, 2002.

RACE AWARENESS. See also BLACKS - RACE IDENTITY; ETHNIC ATTITUDES.
Clarke, Simon, 1962- Social theory, psychoanalysis, and racism. New York : Palgrave Macmillan, 2003.
BF175.4.R34 C58 2003

Dalal, Farhad. Race, colour and the process of racialization. Hove, [England] ; New York : Brunner-Routledge, 2002.
BF175.4.R34 D35 2002

Katz, Judy H., 1950- White awareness. 2nd ed., rev. Norman : University of Oklahoma Press, c2003.
HT1523 .K37 2003

Song, Miri, 1964- Choosing ethnic identity. Cambridge, UK : Polity Press : Oxford ; Malden, MA : Blackwell Publishing, 2003.
GN495.6 .S65 2003

Tuckwell, Gill, 1948- Racial identity, White counsellors and therapists. Buckingham ; Philadelphia : Open University Press, 2002.
BF637.C6 T84 2002

RACE AWARENESS - CARIBBEAN, FRENCH-SPEAKING.
Britton, Celia. Race and the unconscious. Oxford : Legenda, 2002.

RACE AWARENESS IN ADOLESCENCE - UNITED STATES.
Cornbleth, Catherine. Hearing America's youth. New York : P. Lang, c2003.
BF724.3.13 .C67 2003

RACE AWARENESS - POLITICAL ASPECTS.
Amódélé, Jons. The new Jews. Banjul, The Gambia : Vinasha Publishing, 2000.
1. Black author.

RACE BIAS. See RACE DISCRIMINATION; RACISM.

Race, colour and the process of racialization.
Dalal, Farhad. Hove, [England] ; New York : Brunner-Routledge, 2002.
BF175.4.R34 D35 2002

RACE DISCRIMINATION.
Borges, Edson. Racismo, preconceito e intolerancia. [São Paulo, Brazil] : Atual, c2002.

RACE DISCRIMINATION - BRAZIL.
Borges, Edson. Racismo, preconceito e intolerancia. [São Paulo, Brazil] : Atual, c2002.

RACE DISCRIMINATION IN EMPLOYMENT. See DISCRIMINATION IN EMPLOYMENT.

RACE DISCRIMINATION - PSYCHOLOGICAL ASPECTS.
Katz, Judy H., 1950- White awareness. 2nd ed., rev. Norman : University of Oklahoma Press, c2003.
HT1523 .K37 2003

Race, ethnicity, and sexuality.
Nagel, Joane. New York : Oxford University Press, 2003.
HQ21 .N195 2003

RACE IMPROVEMENT. See EUGENICS.

Race, nature, and the politics of difference / edited by Donald S. Moore, Jake Kosek & Anand Pandian. Durham : Duke University Press, c2003. viii, 475 p. ; 24 cm. Includes bibliographical references (p. [407]-460) and index. CONTENTS: After the great white error...the great black mirage / Paul Gilroy -- Simians, savages, skulls, and sex: science and colonial militarism in nineteenth-century South Africa / Zine Magubane -- "The more you kill the more you will live": the Maya, "race," and biopolitical hopes for peace in Guatemala / Diane M. Nelson -- "There is a land where everything is pure": linguistic nationalism and identity politics in Germany / Uli Linke -- "On the raggedy edge of risk": articulations of race and nature after biology / Bruce Braun -- Beyond ecoliberal "common futures": environmental justice, toxic touring, and a transcommunal politics of place / Giovanna di Chiro -- Inventing the heterozygote: molecular biology, racial identity, and the narratives of sickle-cell disease, Tay-Sachs, and cystic fibrosis / Keith Wailoo -- For the love of a good dog: webs of action in the world of dog genetics / Donna Haraway -- Intimate publics: race, property, and personhood / Robyn Wiegman -- Men in paradise: sex tourism and the political economy of masculinity / Steven Gregory -- Pulp fictions of indigenism / Alcida Ramos -- Masyarakat adat, difference, and the limits of recognition in Indonesia's forest zone / Tania Murray Li. ISBN 0-8223-3079-2 (alk. paper) ISBN 0-8223-3091-1 (pbk. : alk. paper) DDC 305.8
1. Race relations. 2. Ethnic relations. 3. Group identity. 4. Nature - Political aspects. 5. Power (Social sciences) I. Moore, Donald S., 1963- II. Kosek, Jake. III. Pandian, Anand.
HT1521 .R2355 2003

RACE PREJUDICE. See RACISM.

RACE PROBLEMS. See RACE RELATIONS.

RACE - PSYCHOLOGICAL ASPECTS.
Amódélé, Jons. The new Jews. Banjul, The Gambia : Vinasha Publishing, 2000.
1. Black author.

Clarke, Simon, 1962- Social theory, psychoanalysis, and racism. New York : Palgrave Macmillan, 2003.
BF175.4.R34 C58 2003

Dalal, Farhad. Race, colour and the process of racialization. Hove, [England] ; New York : Brunner-Routledge, 2002.
BF175.4.R34 D35 2002

RACE PSYCHOLOGY. See ETHNOPSYCHOLOGY.

RACE QUESTION. See RACE RELATIONS.

Race, racism, & reparations.
Corlett, J. Angelo, 1958- Ithaca : Cornell University Press, c2003.
HT1523 .C67 2003

Race, racism, and reparations.
Corlett, J. Angelo, 1958- Race, racism, & reparations. Ithaca : Cornell University Press, c2003.
HT1523 .C67 2003

RACE RELATIONS. See also ANTISEMITISM; MINORITIES; RACISM.
Borges, Edson. Racismo, preconceito e intolerancia. [São Paulo, Brazil] : Atual, c2002.

Fenton, Steve, 1942- Ethnicity. Cambridge : Polity ; Oxford ; Malden, MA : Blackwell, c2003.
GN495.6 .F46 2003

Race, nature, and the politics of difference. Durham : Duke University Press, c2003.
HT1521 .R2355 2003

RACE RELATIONS - HISTORY.
Antinomies of modernity. Durham : Duke University Press, 2003.
CB358 .A59 2003

Racism. Armonk, N.Y. : M.E. Sharpe, c2003.
HT1521 .R323 2003

RACE RELATIONS - POLITICAL ASPECTS.
Violence and the body. Bloomington : Indiana University Press, c2003.
HM1116 .V557 2003

RACE - RELIGIOUS ASPECTS - CHRISTIANITY.
Holmes, Barbara Ann, 1943- Race and the cosmos. Harrisburg, Pa. : Trinity Press International, c2002.
BR563.N4 H654 2002
1. Black author.

RACES OF MAN. See ETHNOLOGY.

RACIAL BIAS. See RACE DISCRIMINATION; RACISM.

RACIAL DISCRIMINATION. See RACE DISCRIMINATION.

RACIAL IDENTITY OF BLACKS. See BLACKS - RACE IDENTITY.

Racial identity, White counsellors and therapists.
Tuckwell, Gill, 1948- Buckingham ; Philadelphia : Open University Press, 2002.
BF637.C6 T84 2002

RACIALLY MIXED PEOPLE - ETHNIC IDENTITY.
Song, Miri, 1964- Choosing ethnic identity.

Cambridge, UK : Polity Press ; Oxford ; Malden, MA : Blackwell Publishing, 2003.
GN495.6 .S65 2003

RACISM. *See also* **ANTISEMITISM; RACE RELATIONS.**
Avdeev, V. B. (Vladimir Borisovich) Metafizicheskaia antropologiia. Moskva : Belye al'vy, 2002.
DK510.763 .A93 2002

Borges, Edson. Racismo, preconceito e intolerancia. [São Paulo, Brazil] : Atual, c2002.

Corlett, J. Angelo, 1958- Race, racism, & reparations. Ithaca : Cornell University Press, c2003.
HT1523 .C67 2003

Creating racism. Los Angeles, CA : Citizens Commission on Human Rights, 1995.
RC455.4.E8 C74x 1995

Dalal, Farhad. Race, colour and the process of racialization. Hove, [England] ; New York : Brunner-Routledge, 2002.
BF175.4.R34 D35 2002

Ephraim, Charles Wm. The pathology of Eurocentrism. Trenton, NJ : Africa World Press, c2003.
HT1581 .E64 2003

Gibson, Nigel C. Fanon. Cambridge, U.K. : Polity Press in association with Blackwell Pub. ; Malden, MA : Distributed in the USA by Blackwell Pub., 2003.
CT2628.F35 G53 2003

Goudge, Paulette. The power of whiteness. London : Lawrence & Wishart, 2003.

Hating in the first person plural. New York : Other Press, c2003.
RC506 .H285 2003

Howard, Bradley Reed. Indigenous peoples and the state. DeKalb : Northern Illinois University Press, c2003.
GN380 .H68 2003

Katz, Judy H., 1950- White awareness. 2nd ed., rev. Norman : University of Oklahoma Press, c2003.
HT1523 .K37 2003

Menéndez, Eduardo L. La parte negada de la cultura. Barcelona : Edicions Bellaterra, c2002.
HM1121 .M46 2002

Race and racism in continental philosophy. Bloomington : Indiana University Press, c2003.
HT1523 .R2514 2003

Racism. Armonk, N.Y. : M.E. Sharpe, c2003.
HT1521 .R323 2003

Segrest, Mab, 1949- Born to belonging. New Brunswick, NJ : Rutgers University Press, c2002.
HQ75.25 .S44 2002

Racism : a global reader / edited by Kevin Reilly, Stephen Kaufman, and Angela Bodino. Armonk, N.Y. : M.E. Sharpe, c2003. xiv, 400 p. : ill., maps ; 24 cm. (Sources and studies in world history) Includes bibliographical references and index. ISBN 0-7656-1059-0 (alk. paper) DDC 305.8
1. Racism. 2. Racism - History. 3. Race relations - History. 4. Colonies. I. Reilly, Kevin, 1941- II. Kaufman, Stephen, 1946- III. Bodino, Angela, 1940- IV. Series.
HT1521 .R323 2003

RACISM - BRAZIL.
Borges, Edson. Racismo, preconceito e intolerancia. [São Paulo, Brazil] : Atual, c2002.

RACISM - HISTORY.
Racism. Armonk, N.Y. : M.E. Sharpe, c2003.
HT1521 .R323 2003

RACISM IN ANTHROPOLOGY.
Avdeev, V. B. (Vladimir Borisovich) Metafizicheskaia antropologiia. Moskva : Belye al'vy, 2002.
DK510.763 .A93 2002

RACISM IN PSYCHOLOGY.
Jensen, Arthur Robert. Intelligence, race, and genetics. Boulder, Colo. : Westview, 2002.

Race and IQ. Expanded ed. New York : Oxford University Press, 1999.
BF432.A1 R3 1999

RACISM IN PSYCHOLOGY - HISTORY.
Defining difference. 1st ed. Washington, DC : American Psychological Association, c2004.
BF76.45 .D44 2004

RACISM IN PSYCHOLOGY - UNITED STATES - HISTORY.
Defining difference. 1st ed. Washington, DC : American Psychological Association, c2004.
BF76.45 .D44 2004

RACISM - PSYCHOLOGICAL ASPECTS.
Clarke, Simon, 1962- Social theory, psychoanalysis, and racism. New York : Palgrave Macmillan, 2003.
BF175.4.R34 C58 2003

RACISM - RELIGIOUS ASPECTS - CHRISTIANITY.
Locke, Hubert G. Searching for God in godforsaken times and places. Grand Rapids, Mich. : W.B. Eerdmans Pub., c2003.
BT774 .L63 2003
1. Black author.

RACISM - UNITED STATES.
Katz, Judy H., 1950- White awareness. 2nd ed., rev. Norman : University of Oklahoma Press, c2003.
HT1523 .K37 2003

RACISM - UNITED STATES - PSYCHOLOGICAL ASPECTS.
Jones, Charisse. Shifting. 1st ed. New York : HarperCollins, c2003.
E185.625 .J657 2003

Longing to tell. 1st ed. New York : Farrar, Straus and Giroux, 2003.
E185.625 .L66 2003

Racismo, preconceito e intolerancia.
Borges, Edson. [São Paulo, Brazil] : Atual, c2002.

Radford, Robert T. Cicero : a study in the origins of republican philosophy / Robert T. Radford. Amsterdam ; New York, NY : Rodopi, 2002. x, 142 p. : 23 cm. (Value inquiry book series ; v. 117) (Studies in the history of western philosophy) Includes bibliographical references (p. [109]-125) and index. ISBN 90-420-1467-9
1. Cicero, Marcus Tullius. 2. Statesmen - Rome - Biography. 3. Authors, Latin - Biography. 4. Philosophy, Ancient. I. Title. II. Series. III. Series: Value inquiry book series. Studies in the history of western philosophy.
DG260.C5 R33 2002

Radhakrishnan, R. (Rajagopalan) Theory in an uneven world / R. Radhakrishnan. Oxford ; Malden, MA : Blackwell, 2003. xv, 217 p. ; 23 cm. Includes bibliographical references and index. ISBN 0-631-17537-7 ISBN 0-631-17538-5 (PBK.) DDC 801.95
1. Theory (Philosophy) 2. Postmodernism. 3. Poststructuralism. 4. Postcolonialism. 5. Criticism. I. Title.

The radiance of being.
Combs, Allan, 1942- 2nd ed. St. Paul, Minn. : Paragon House, 2002.
BF311 .C575 2002

RADIATION. *See* **SOUND.**

RADICAL ECONOMICS.
Glendinning, Chellis. Off the map. Gabriola Island, BC : New Society Publishers, c2002.
HF1414 .G553 2002

Radical forgiveness.
Tipping, Colin C. Atlanta, GA : GOLDENeight Publishers, c1997.
BF637.F67 T57 1997

Radical simplicity.
Hayes-Roth, Frederick, 1947- Upper Saddle River, N.J. ; London : Prentice Hall PTR, 2003.

RADIO PLAYS. *See* **SOAP OPERAS.**

RADIO SERIALS. *See* **SOAP OPERAS.**

RADIO VISION. *See* **TELEVISION.**

Radiografía social de América Hispana.
Idrobo Díaz, Hugo, 1954- La joda de la paz en Colombia. 1. ed. Cali, Colombia : [s.n., 2002?]

Radstone, Susannah.
Contested pasts. London ; New York : Routledge, 2003.
BF378.S65 C665 2003

Radulescu, Raluca, 1974- The gentry context for Malory's Morte Darthur / Raluca L. Radulescu. Cambridge [England] ; Rochester, NY : D.S. Brewer, 2003. 165 p. ; 23 cm. (Arthurian studies, 0261-9814 ; 55) Includes bibliographical references (p. [149]-159) and index. ISBN 0-85991-785-1 (alk. paper) DDC 823/.2
1. Malory, Thomas, - Sir, - 15th cent. - Morte d'Arthur. 2. Malory, Thomas, - Sir, - 15th cent. - Political and social views. 3. Literature and society - England - History - To 1500. 4. England - Social life and customs - 1066-1485. 5. Arthurian romances - History and criticism. 6. Gentry - England - History - To 1500. 7. Social classes in literature. 8. Gentry in literature. I. Title. II. Series.

PR2047 .R33 2003

Radzimiński, Andrzej. Życie i obyczajowość średniowiecznego duchowieństwa / Andrzej Radzimiński. Warszawa : Wydawn. DiG, 2002. 191 p. : ill. ; 17 cm. (Człowiek - symbol - historia) At head of title: Towarzystwo Miłośników Historii. Errata slip inserted. Includes bibliographical references (p. [171]-174) and index. ISBN 83-7181-243-4
1. Catholic Church - Poland - History. 2. Catholic Church - Poland - Clergy - History. 3. Church history - Middle Ages, 600-1500. 4. Poland - Church history. I. Title. II. Series.
BX1565 .R32 2002

Rael, Elsa.
Vint/age 2001 conference : [videorecording]. New York, c2001.

RAEL, ELSA.
Vint/age 2001 conference : [videorecording]. New York, c2001.

Raelin, Joseph A., 1948- Creating leaderful organizations : how to bring out leadership in everyone / Joseph A. Raelin. 1st ed. San Francisco : Berrett-Koehler, c2003. xvii, 289 p. : ill. ; 23 cm. Includes bibliographical references (p. 253-276) and indexes. ISBN 1-57675-233-X DDC 658.4/092
1. Leadership. I. Title.
HD57.7 .R34 2003

RAG TRADE. *See* **CLOTHING TRADE.**

RAGE. *See also* **ANGER.**
Eigen, Michael. Middletown, Conn. : Wesleyan University Press, c2002.
RC569.5.A53 E38 2002

Rahbar'zādah, Ḥasan. Shinākht-i rūḥ / nivīsandah, Ḥasan Rahbar'zādah. Chāp-i 1. Tihrān : Nashr-i Pārsā, 1380 [2001 04 2002] 2 v. ; 25 cm. In Persian.
1. Spirits. 2. Occultism. I. Title.

Rahnasto, Ilkka. Intellectual property rights, external effects, and antitrust law : leveraging IPRs in the communications industry / Ilkka Rahnasto. Oxford ; New York : Oxford University Press, 2003. xx, 234 p. : ill. ; 25 cm. Includes bibliographical references and index. ISBN 0-19-925428-1 DDC 343.099
1. Intellectual property. 2. Communication and traffic - Law and legislation. 3. Antitrust law. I. Title.

Raiffa, Howard, 1924- Negotiation analysis : the science and art of collaborative decision making / Howard Raiffa with John Richardson, David Metcalfe. Cambridge, MA : Belknap Press of Harvard University Press, 2002. xiv, 548 p. : ill. ; 26 cm. Includes bibliographical references (p. [523]-530) and index. ISBN 0-674-00890-1 (alk. paper) DDC 658.4/052
1. Negotiation in business. 2. Negotiation. 3. Decision making. 4. Game theory. I. Richardson, John, 1966- II. Metcalfe, David. III. Title.
HD58.6 .R342 2002

Raĭgorodskiĭ, D. IA.
Reklama. Moskva : Izd-vo Dom "Bakhrakh-M", 2001.

Raĭkov, V. L. (Vladimir Leonidovich), 1934- Soznanie i poznanie III tysiachelet︠i︡i︠a︡ / V.L. Raĭkov. Moskva : [s.n.], 1999. 161 p. ; 21 cm. Includes bibliographical references (p. 161). ISBN 5785601222
1. Cognition and culture. 2. Cognitive psychology. 3. Consciousness. I. Title. II. Title: Soznanie i poznanie 3. tysi︠a︡chelet︠i︡i︠a︡ III. Title: Soznanie i poznanie tret'ego tysi︠a︡chelet︠i︡i︠a︡
BF311 .R26 1999

Railton, Peter Albert. Facts, values, and norms : essays toward a morality of consequence / Peter Railton. Cambridge, U.K. ; New York : Cambridge University Press, 2003. xx, 388 p. ; 24 cm. (Cambridge studies in philosophy) Includes bibliographical references and index. CONTENTS: Moral realism -- Facts and values -- Noncognitivism about rationality -- Aesthetic value, moral value, and the ambitions of naturalism -- Red, bitter, good -- Alienation, consequentialism, and the demands of morality -- Locke, stock, and peril -- How thinking about character and utilitarianism might lead to rethinking the character of utilitarianism -- Pluralism, dilemma, and the expression of moral conflict -- On the hypothetical and non-hypothetical in reasoning about thought and action -- Normative force and normative freedom -- Morality, ideology, and reflection, or, the duck sits yet. ISBN 0-521-41697-3 ISBN 0-521-42693-6 (pbk.) DDC 170
1. Ethics. I. Title. II. Series.
BJ1012 .R33 2003

Rainieri, Caelum. The Nahualli animal oracle / Caelum Rainieri and Ivory Andersen ; illustrated by Raphael Montoliu. Rochester, Vt. : Bear & Co., 2003. n.m. Includes bibliographical references. Table of contents URL: http://www.loc.gov/catdir/toc/ecip043/2003010438.html ISBN 1-59143-017-8 DDC 133.3/248

1. Oracles. 2. Aztecs - Miscellanea. 3. Animals - Miscellanea.
I. Andersen, Ivory. II. Title.
BF1773 .R35 2003

Raino, Lynda.
Big Dance [videorecording]. Buffalo, N.Y. :
Kineticvideo.com, c1998.

Raĭnov, Vasil G. Za psikhosemantichnata spetsifika na ezikovoto vŭzpriĭatie / Vasil Raĭnov. Sofiia : Akademichno izd-vo "Prof. Marin Drinov", 1998. 94 p. ; 20 cm. Title on leaf facing t.p.: Psychosemantics and language perception. Includes bibliographical references (p. 92-93). ISBN 9544304959
1. Psycholinguistics. 2. Dyslexia. 3. Language disorders. 4. Neurolinguistics. I. Title. II. Title: Psychosemantics and language perception
P37 .R27 1998

Raising a mensch.
Rosenberg, Shelley Kapnek. 1st ed. Philadelphia : Jewish Publication Society, 2003.
BF723.M54 R68 2003

RAISING OF CHILDREN. See **CHILD REARING.**

Rakison, David H., 1969-.
Early category and concept development. Oxford ; New York : Oxford University Press, 2003.
BF720.C63 E27 2003

Rallis, Sharon F.
Rossman, Gretchen B. Learning in the field. 2nd ed. Thousand Oaks, Calif. ; London : Sage Publications, c2003.
H62 .R667 2003

Rāmabhadrācārya.
Veṅkaṭanāthārya. [Daśanirṇayī] Vaidikasārvabhaumanāmnā suprasiddhaiḥ Veṅkaṭanāthāryaiḥ Vaidikakarmānuṣṭhānasaukaryāya viracitā Daśanirṇayī. 1st ed. Mumbai : Śrīmadahobilamathena, 1998.
BL1226.72 .V36 1998

Ramet, Sabrina P., 1949-.
Kazaaam! splat! ploof!. Lanham, Md. ; Oxford : Rowman & Littlefield, c2003.
D1055 .K39 2003

RAMÍREZ, SANTIAGO MARÍA, 1891-1967.
Gambra, José Miguel. La analogía en general. 1. ed. Pamplona : EUNSA, 2002.

Ramon Llull y el secreto de la vida.
Vega, Amador. Madrid : Siruela, 2002.

Ramos, João Baptista. Quinze cartas sobre moralidade & ciência / João Baptista Ramos. Brasília : Thesaurus, 2000. 219 p. : ill. ; 22 cm. ISBN 85-7062-231-7
1. Knowledge, Theory of. 2. Science - Philosophy. I. Title.

Rampersad, Hubert K. Total performance scorecard : redefining management to achieve performance with integrity / Hubert K. Rampersad ; with a foreword by Dorothy A Leonard. Amsterdam ; Boston ; London : Butterworth-Heinemann, c2003. xx, 332 p. ; 24 cm. Includes bibliographical references (p. 313-317) and index. ISBN 0-7506-7714-7 (alk. paper) DDC 658.4/013
1. Total quality management. 2. Performance - Measurement. 3. Employee motivation. 4. Organizational learning. I. Title.
HD62.15 .R3598 2003

Ramsay, Chevalier (Andrew Michael), 1686-1743. Discours sur la mythologie. 2002.
Ramsay, Chevalier (Andrew Michael), 1686-1743. Les voyages de Cyrus. Paris : Champion, 2002.

Ramsay, Chevalier (Andrew Michael), 1686-1743.
Les voyages de Cyrus : avec un discours sur la mythologie / Andrew Michael Ramsay ; édition critique établie par Georges Lamoine. Paris : Champion, 2002. 234 p. ; 23 cm. (L'âge des lumières, 1278-3862 ; 17) Includes bibliographical references and index. ISBN 2-7453-0603-0 DDC 843
1. Voyages, Imaginary. 2. Mythology. 3. Religions - Fiction. I. Lamoine, Georges. II. Ramsay, Chevalier (Andrew Michael), 1686-1743. Discours sur la mythologie. 2002. III. Title. IV. Series.

Ranchan, Som P., 1932- Aurotherapy : an alternate therapy system / Som P. Ranchan. Delhi : Indian Publishers Distributors, 2001. 313, [2] p. ; 22 cm. Includes bibliographical references and index. ISBN 81-7341-215-4
1. Ghose, Aurobindo, - 1872-1950. 2. Psychoanalysis. 3. Yoga - Therapeutic use. I. Title.
BF173.A25 R36 2001

Rand Corporation.
Leed, Maren. Keeping the warfighting edge. Santa Monica, CA : RAND, 2002.

UB413 .L386 2002

Randolph, Jeanne, 1943- Why stoics box : essays on art and society / by Jeanne Randolph ; Bruce Grenville, editor. Toronto : YYZ Books, 2003. 157 p. : ill., ports. ; 23 cm. Includes bibliographical references. ISBN 0-920397-81-6 (pbk.) DDC 700/.1/9
1. Psychoanalysis and the arts. 2. Psychoanalysis and culture. 3. Arts and society. I. Grenville, Bruce. II. Title.

Randolph, Joanne. What I look like when I am confused / Joanne Randolph. 1st ed. New York : PowerStart Press, 2004. 24 p. : col. ill. ; 21 cm. (Let's look at feelings) Includes index. SUMMARY: Describes how different parts of a face look when a person is confused. Table of contents URL: http://www.loc.gov/catdir/toc/ecip043/2003009109.html CONTENTS: I am confused -- My face. ISBN 1404225102 DDC 152.4
1. Human information processing in children - Juvenile literature. 2. Perception in children - Juvenile literature. 3. Perception. 4. Miscommunication. 5. Facial expression. 6. Emotions. I. Title. II. Series.
BF723.I63 R36 2004

[What I look like when I am confused. Spanish & English]
What I look like when I am confused = Cómo me veo cuando estoy confundido / Joanne Randolph ; translated by Maria Cristina Brusca. 1st ed. New York : Rosen Pub. Group's PowerKids Press, 2004. p. cm. (Let's look at feelings) SUMMARY: Describes how the parts of the face look when a person is confused. Spanish and English. Includes bibliographical references and index. CONTENTS: Confused -- My eyes -- My cheeks -- My eyebrows -- My forehead -- My mouth -- My face -- Words to know. ISBN 140427510X (library binding) DDC 152.4
1. Human information processing in children - Juvenile literature. 2. Perception in children - Juvenile literature. 3. Perception. 4. Miscommunication. 5. Facial expression. 6. Emotions. 7. Spanish language materials - Bilingual. I. Title. II. Title: Cómo me veo cuando estoy confundido III. Series.
BF723.I63 R3618 2004

What I look like when I am sad / Joanne Randolph. 1st ed. New York : PowerStart Press, 2004. 24 p. : col. ill. ; 21 cm. (Let's look at feelings) SUMMARY: Describes what different parts of a face look like when a person is sad. Table of contents URL: http://www.loc.gov/catdir/toc/ecip043/2003009072.html CONTENTS: When I am sad -- My head -- My mouth -- My eyebrows -- My eyes -- My face -- Words to know (picture glossary). ISBN 1404225072 DDC 152.4
1. Sadness in children - Juvenile literature. 2. Sadness. 3. Facial expression. 4. Emotions. I. Title. II. Series.
BF723.S15 R36 2004

[What I look like when I am sad. Spanish & English]
What I look like when I am sad = Cómo me veo cuando estoy triste / Joanne Randolph ; traducción al español: Maria Cristina Brusca. 1st ed. New York : Rosen Pub. Group's PowerKids Press, 2004. 24 p. : col. ill. ; 22 cm. (Let's look at feelings) SUMMARY: Describes how the parts of the face look when a person is sad. English and Spanish. Includes index. CONTENTS: When I am sad -- My face -- Words to know. ISBN 140427507X (lib. bdg.) DDC 152.4
1. Sadness in children - Juvenile literature. 2. Sadness. 3. Facial expression. 4. Emotions. 5. Spanish language materials - Bilingual. I. Title. II. Title: Cómo me veo cuando estoy triste III. Series.
BF723.S15 R3618 2004

Randolph, Paschal Beverly, 1825-1874.
Hermes, Trismegistus. Divine Pymander. Rev. ed. Quakertown, PA : Philosophical Pub. Co., 2001.
BF1598.H5 E5 2001

RANDOM SAMPLING. See **SAMPLING (STATISTICS).**

RANGE MANAGEMENT. See **LIVESTOCK.**

RANGELANDS. See **LIVESTOCK.**

RANK. See **SOCIAL CLASSES.**

Ransley, Cynthia.
Forgiveness and the healing process. Hove, East Sussex ; New York : Brunner-Routledge, c2003.
BF637.F67 F66 2003

Rantanen, Kalevi. Simplified TRIZ : new problem-solving applications for engineers and manufacturing professionals / Kalevi Rantanen and Ellen Domb. Boca Raton : St. Lucie Press, c2002. 262 p. : ill. ; 25 cm. Includes bibliographical references and index. Table of contents URL: http://www.loc.gov/catdir/toc/fy034/2002019233.html ISBN 1-57444-323-2 (alk. paper) DDC 620/.0076
1. Engineering - Methodology. 2. Problem solving -

Methodology. 3. Creative thinking. 4. Technological innovations. I. Domb, Ellen. II. Title.
TA153 .R26 2002

RAPE.
Evolution, gender, and rape. Cambridge, Mass. : MIT Press, c2003.
HV6558 .E92 2003

Rapp-Paglicci, Lisa A.
Handbook of violence. New York : Wiley, c2002.
HM1116 .H36 2002

Rapport, Nigel, 1956- I am dynamite : an Andean anthropology of power / Nigel Rapport. London ; New York : Routledge, 2003. 283 p. : ill. ; 24 cm. Includes bibliographical references and index. ISBN 0-415-25862-6 ISBN 0-415-25863-4 (PBK.) DDC 141.4
1. Individualism. 2. Philosophical anthropology. 3. Individualism - Case studies. I. Title.

Rasario, Giovanni Battista, 1517-1578.
Ammonius, Hermiae. Commentaria in quinque voces Porphyrii. Stuttgart : Frommann-Holzboog, 2002.

Raskoldovyvaĭa ĪUnga.
Menzhulin, V. (Vadim), 1968- Kiev : Izd-vo "Sfera", 2002.
BF173.J85 M46 2002

Rassa shastra.
Inayat Khan, 1882-1927. Berwick, ME : Ibis Press ; York Beach, ME : distributed to the trade by Red Wheel/Weiser, 2003.
BF692 .I5 2003

Rastiannikov, A. V. Refleksivnoe razvitie kompetentnosti v sovmestnom tvorchestve / A.V. Rastiannikov, S.ĪU. Stepanov, D.V. Ushakov. Moskva : PER SĖ, 2002. 319 p. ; 21 cm. Includes bibliographical references (p. 298-316). ISBN 5929200661
1. Creation (Literary, artistic, etc.) - Psychological aspects. 2. Reflexes. I. Stepanov, S. ĪU. (Sergeĭ ĪUr'evich) II. Ushakov, D. V. III. Title.
BF408 .R235 2002

Rastier, François.
Une introduction aux sciences de la culture. 1. ed. Paris : Presses universitaires de France ; [Paris] : Institut Ferdinand-de-Saussure, 2002.

Rathkey, Julia Wilcox. What children need when they grieve : the four essentials : routine, love, honesty, and security / Julia Wilcox Rathkey ; foreword by Barbara Bush ; introduction by Cynthia R. Pfeffer. 1st ed. New York : Three Rivers Press, 2004. p. cm. Table of contents URL: http://www.loc.gov/catdir/toc/ecip048/2003019687.html ISBN 1400051169 (pbk.) DDC 155.9/37/083
1. Grief in children. 2. Bereavement in children. 3. Loss (Psychology) in children. 4. Child rearing. I. Title.
BF723.G75 R38 2004

Rathus, Spencer A.
Nevid, Jeffrey S. Psychology and the challenges of life. 9th ed. Hoboken, NJ : Wiley, c2005.
BF335 .N475 2005

Primary sources in psychology. Orlando, FL : Harcourt, c2000.
BF121 .P69 2000

Psychology and the challenges of life.
Nevid, Jeffrey S. Psychology and the challenges of life. 9th ed. Hoboken, NJ : Wiley, c2005.
BF335 .N475 2005

RATIOCINATION. See **REASONING.**

RATIONAL CHOICE THEORY.
Sen, Amartya Kumar. Rationality and freedom. Cambridge, Mass. : Belknap Press of Harvard University Press, 2002.
HB846.8 .S466 2002

Rational mysticism.
Horgan, John, 1953- Boston : Houghton Mifflin, 2003.
BL625 .H67 2003

RATIONALISM. See also **REASON.**
Kneer, Markus, 1972- Die dunkle Spur im Denken. Paderborn : Schöningh, 2003.
DS145 .K64 2003

Porus, V. N. Ratsional'nost', nauka, kul'tura. Moskva : Universitet Rossiĭskoĭ akademii obrazovaniĭa, Kafedra filosofii, 2002.
Q175.32.K45 P678 2002

Przełęcki, Marian, 1923- O rozumności i dobroci. Warszawa : "Semper", 2002.
B833 .P79 2002

Singer, Marcus George, 1926- The ideal of a rational morality. Oxford : Clarendon Press ; Oxford ; New York : Oxford University Press, 2002.

BJ1012 .S48 2002

Sub"ekt, poznanie, deĭatel'nost'. Moskva : Kanon+, 2002.
BD166 .S84 2002

Tul'chinskiĭ, G. L. (Grigoriĭ L'vovich) Postchelovecheskaia personologiia. Sankt-Peterburg : Aleteĭia, 2002.
BD331 .T84 2002

Rationality and freedom.
Sen, Amartya Kumar. Cambridge, Mass. : Belknap Press of Harvard University Press, 2002.
HB846.8 .S466 2002

RATIONALIZATION OF INDUSTRY. *See* **INDUSTRIAL MANAGEMENT.**

Ratnasingam, Pauline. Inter-organizational trust in business-to-business e-commerce / Pauline Ratnasingam. Hershey, PA : IRM Press, c2003. x, 209 p. : ill. ; 26 cm. Cover title: Inter-organizational trust for business-to-business e-commerce. Available also in electronic form. Includes bibliographical references (p. 159-182) and index. ISBN 1-931777-75-6 (soft cover) DDC 658.8/4
1. Electronic commerce - Psychological aspects. 2. Electronic commerce - Psychological aspects - Case studies. 3. Trust. 4. Interorganizational relations. I. Title. II. Title: Interorganizational trust for business-to-business e-commerce
HF5548.32 .R378 2003

Das Rätsel von Leib und Seele : der Mensch zwischen Geist und Materie / herausgegeben von Reinhard Breuer ; mit Beiträgen von Hubertus Breuer ... [et al.]. Herne : Heitkamp, c1997. 233 p. : ill. (some col.) ; 27 cm. (Wir in unserer Welt) Includes bibliographical references (p. 230-231). ISBN 3-421-02773-0
1. Mind and body. 2. Brain - Psychophysiology. 3. Soul. I. Breuer, Reinhard A., 1946- II. Breuer, Hubertus. III. Series.
BF163 .R28 1997

Ratsional'nost', nauka, kul'tura.
Porus, V. N. Moskva : Universitet Rossiĭskoĭ akademii obrazovaniia, Kafedra filosofii, 2002.
Q175.32.K45 P678 2002

Raudive, Konstantins, 1909-1974.
[Unhörbares wird hörbar. Latvian]
Nedzirdamais kļūst dzirdams : garu pasaules pēdās : pētījums eksperimentālajā parapsiholoģijā / Konstantins Raudive. Rīgā : Zintnieks, c2003. 446 p. : 20 cm. ISBN 9984739058
1. Parapsychology - Case studies. I. Title.
BF1029 .R3816 2003

Raudvere, Catharina.
Jolly, Karen Louise. The Middle Ages. Philadelphia : University of Pennsylvania Press, 2002, 2001. 12 300 xiv, 280 p. ; 24 cm.
BF1593 .J65 2002

Raulet, Gérard.
Vom Parergon zum Labyrinth. Wien : Böhlau, c2001.
NK1505 .V65 2001

Raumkognition und Lokalisationsäusserungen.
Kessler, Klaus. Wiesbaden : Deutscher Universitäts-Verlag, 2000.
BF469 .K47 2000

Rauschen : seine Phänomenologie und Semantik zwischen Sinn und Störung / herausgegeben von Andreas Hiepko, Katja Stopka. Würzburg : Königshausen & Neumann, c2001. 287 p. : ill. ; 24 cm. Includes bibliographical references. ISBN 3-8260-1989-X
1. German literature - History and criticism. 2. Aesthetics. 3. German language - Semantics. 4. Art criticism. I. Hiepko, Andreas. II. Stopka, Katja.

Rauschenbach, Sina.
Denkwelten um 1700. Köln : Böhlau, 2002.
BF441 .D46 2002

Rauscher, William V. The mind readers : masters of deception / William V. Rauscher ; with a foreword by Cyprian Murray. Woodbury, N.J. : Mystic Light Press, c2002. iv, 172 p. : ill. ; 29 cm. Includes index. DDC 792.7
1. Telepathy. 2. Clairvoyance. I. Title.
BF1171 .R28 2002

Raushenbakh, Boris Viktorovich.
Artamonov, V. I. (Vladimir Ivanovich) Psikhologiia ot pervogo litsa. Moskva : Academia, 2003.
BF109.A1 A78 2003

Ravdin, Boris.
Rīgas gaišregis Eižens Finks. Jauns papildināts izdevums. [Rīga] : Jumava, c2002.
BF1283.F55 R66 2002

Rīgas gaišregis Eižens Finks. Rīgā : Jumava, c2002.

BF1997.F56 R54 2002

Ravenscroft, Ian.
Currie, Gregory. Recreative minds. Oxford : Clarendon Press ; New York : Oxford University Press, 2002.
BH301.I53 C87 2002

Rawḍat al-qulūb wa-nuzhat al-muḥibb wa-al-maḥbūb.
Shayzarī, ʻAbd al-Raḥmān ibn Naṣr, 12th cent. Wiesbaden : Harrassowitz, 2003.

Rawḍat al qulūb wa-nuzhat al-muḥibb wal-maḥbūb.
Shayzarī, ʻAbd al-Raḥmān ibn Naṣr, 12th cent. Rawḍat al-qulūb wa-nuzhat al-muḥibb wa-al-maḥbūb. Wiesbaden : Harrassowitz, 2003.

Rawnsley, Gary D.
Political communications in greater China. London ; New York : RoutledgeCurzon, 2003.
JF1525.C59 P65 2003

Rawnsley, Ming-Yeh T.
Political communications in greater China. London ; New York : RoutledgeCurzon, 2003.
JF1525.C59 P65 2003

Ray, Kelly Paulk.
Nemeth, Darlyne Gaynor. Helping your angry child. Oakland, Calif. : New Harbinger, c2003.
BF723.A4 N46 2003

Raynor, Michael E.
Christensen, Clayton M. The innovator's solution. Boston, Mass. : Harvard Business School Press, c2003.

Raʻyonot u-mesarim.
Koll, Shmuel, 1938- Sefer Raʻyonot u-mesarim. Yerushalayim : S. Kol, 761- [2001-

Raz, Joseph. The practice of value / Joseph Raz ; with commentaries by Christine M. Korsgaard, Robert Pippin, Bernard Williams ; edited and introduced by R. Jay Wallace. Oxford ; New York : Oxford University Press, 2003. viii, 161 p. ; 21 cm. (The Berkeley Tanner lectures) Includes bibliographical references and index. ISBN 0-19-926147-4 (alk. paper) DDC 121/.8
1. Values. I. Korsgaard, Christine M. (Christine Marion) II. Pippin, Robert B., 1948- III. Williams, Bernard Arthur Owen. IV. Wallace, R. Jay. V. Title. VI. Series.
BD232 .R255 2003

RĀZĪ, FAKHR AL-DĪN MUḤAMMAD IBN ʻUMAR, 1149 OR 50-1210.
Arnaldez, Roger. Fakhr al-Dîn al-Râzî. Paris : J. Vrin, 2002.

Razumova, E. M.
Psikhologicheskie problemy bytiia cheloveka v sovremennom obshchestve. Magnitogorsk : Magnitogorskiĭ gos. universitet, 2001.
BF20 .P744 2001

Razvitie individual'nosti lichnosti v sovremennykh usloviiakh.
Viatkina, G. V. Moskva : In-t molodezhi, 1997.
BF697.V52 1997

Razvitie lichnosti v kul'turno-obrazovatel'nom prostranstve : sbornik stateĭ po materialam regional'noĭ konferentsii (aprel' 2000 g.) / [otvetstvennyĭ redaktor N.A. Koval']. Tambov : Tambovskiĭ gos. universitet im. G.R. Derzhavina, 2000. 101 p. : ill. ; 21 cm. Includes bibliographical references.
1. Personality - Congresses. 2. Social influence - Congresses. 3. Social psychology - Congresses. I. Koval', N. A. II. Tambovskiĭ gosudarstvennyĭ universitet imeni G.R. Derzhavina.
BF698 .R342 2000

Razvitie natsional'noĭ, ėtnolingvisticheskoĭ i religioznoĭ identichnosti u deteĭ i podrostkov = Development of national, ethnolinguistic and religious identities in children and adolescents / pod red. Martina Barretta, Tatʻiany Riazanovoĭ, Margarity Volovikovoĭ. Moskva : In-t psikhologii RAN, 2001. 196 p. : ill. ; 20 cm. Cover title: Development of national, ethnolinguistic and religious identities in children and adolescents. In Russian and English. Includes bibliographical references. ISBN 5927000223
1. Cognition in children. 2. Cognition in adolescence. 3. Anthropological linguistics. 4. Ethnopsychology. 5. Ethnicity. I. Barrett, Martin. II. Riazanova, Tatʻiana. III. Volovikova, M. IV. Institut psikhologii (Rossiĭskaia akademiia nauk) V. Title: Development of national, ethnolinguistic and religious identities in children and adolescents
BF723.C5 R39 2001

Re-Cord-El, 1943- The pyramid discourses : messages to the seeker for the journey back to God / received by Re-Cord-El. Columbus, OH : Howie Pub., 2003. p. cm. Includes index. ISBN 1-88527-511-0 (pbk. : alk. paper) DDC

291.4/35
1. Meditations. I. Title.
BF1999 .R3956 2003

RE (EGYPTIAN DEITY). *See* **RA (EGYPTIAN DEITY).**

RE-ENGINEERING (MANAGEMENT). *See* **REENGINEERING (MANAGEMENT).**

Re-membering lives.
Hedtke, Lorraine, 1957- Amityville, N.Y. : Baywood Pub. Co., 2004.
BF789.D4 H4 2004

Re-reading Harry Potter.
Gupta, Suman, 1966- Houndmills, Basingstoke ; New York : Palgrave Macmillan, 2003.
PR6068.O93 Z68 2003

(Re)-turn. Columbia, Mo. : University of Missouri Press, 2003- v. Frequency: Annual. Vol. 1 (winter 2003)- . Title from cover. Some issues have distinctive titles. Available also online. URL: http://www.missouri.edu/%7Eraglande/Lacan/home.html
1. Psychoanalysis - Periodicals. 2. Psychoanalysis and literature - Periodicals. 3. Lacan, Jacques, - 1901- - Periodicals. 4. Lacan, Jacques, - 1901- 5. Psychoanalytic Theory I. Title: Return
BF173.L15 R48

Re-Visionen : zur Aktualität von Kunstgeschichte / herausgegeben von Barbara Hüttel, Richard Hüttel und Jeanette Kohl. Berlin : Akademie Verlag, c2002. vi, 288 p. : ill. (some col.) ; 25 cm. Includes bibliographical references and index. ISBN 3-05-003597-8 (hd.bd.)
1. Art - History. I. Hüttel, Barbara. II. Huttel, Richard. III. Kohl, Jeanette.

Re-writing histories.
The Renaissance. London ; New York : Routledge, 2003.
DG445 .R565 2003

Rea, Michael C. (Michael Cannon), 1968- World without design : the ontological consequence of naturalism / Michael C. Rea. Oxford : Clarendon Press ; New York : Oxford University Press, 2002. viii, 245 p. ; 23 cm. Includes bibliographical references (p. [227]-240) and index. ISBN 0-19-924760-9 DDC 146
1. Naturalism. 2. Ontology. I. Title.
B828.2 .R43 2003

Reaching your goals.
Silverman, Robin Landew. New York : F. Watts, 2003.
BF505.G6 S57 2003

Read 180. Stage C
Survivors. New York : Scholastic, c2002.
BF637.S8 S8317 2002

Read, Jason. The micro-politics of capital : Marx and the prehistory of the present / Jason Read. Albany : State University of New York Press, c2003. ix, 213 p. ; 24 cm. Includes bibliographical references (p. 163-208) and index. ISBN 0-7914-5843-1 (alk. paper) ISBN 0-7914-5844-X (pbk. : alk. paper) DDC 335.4/12
1. Althusser, Louis. 2. Marxian economics. 3. Philosophy, Marxist. 4. Economics - Philosophy. 5. Capitalism - Political aspects. 6. Intellectual capital. 7. Production (Economic theory) 8. Post-communism. 9. Postmodernism. 10. Subjectivity. 11. Marx, Karl, - 1818-1883. I. Title.
HB97.5 .R42 2003

Read, Malcolm K. (Malcolm Kevin), 1945- Educating the educators : Hispanism and its institutions / Malcolm K. Read. 1st American ed. Newark : University of Delaware Press ; Cranbury, NJ : Associated University Presses, 2003. viii, 172 p. ; 24 cm. (Monash romance studies) Includes bibliographical references (p. 165-170). CONTENTS: Traveling south : ideology and Hispanism -- Allison Peers : for God, king and country -- The making of a Hispanist -- Writing in the institution : Malcolm K. Read and Paul Julian Smith -- Who walked a crooked mile -- In the meantime : British Hispanism and the rise of cultural studies -- Placing changes. ISBN 0-87413-840-X (alk. paper) DDC 860/.71/041
1. Read, Malcolm K. - (Malcolm Kevin), - 1945- 2. Spanish literature - Study and teaching - Great Britain. 3. Education - Social aspects - Great Britain. 4. Education - Economic aspects - Great Britain. 5. Identity (Psychology) 6. Hispanists - Great Britain - Biography. 7. Philologists - Great Britain - Biography. I. Title. II. Series: Monash romance studies (Newark, Del.)
PC4064.R43 A3 2003

READ, MALCOLM K. (MALCOLM KEVIN), 1945-.
Read, Malcolm K. (Malcolm Kevin), 1945- Educating the educators. 1st American ed. Newark : University of Delaware Press ; Cranbury, NJ : Associated University Presses, 2003.

PC4064.R43 A3 2003

Reader, Will.
Workman, Lance. Evolutionary psychology. New York : Cambridge University Press, 2004.
BF698.95 .W67 2004

READERS AND AUTHORS. See **AUTHORS AND READERS.**

READERS - SOCIAL SCIENCES.
Writing in the dark : phenomenological studies in interpretive inquiry. London, Ont. : Althouse Press, 2002.
B829.5 .W75 2002

READING. See **EXPRESSION.**

Reading, Anna. The social inheritance of the Holocaust : gender, culture and memory / Anna Reading. Houndmills [England] ; New York : Palgrave Macmillan, 2002. xv, 223 p. ; 23 cm. Includes bibliographical references (p. 194-211) and index. ISBN 0-333-76147-2 (hbk.) DDC 940.53/18
1. Holocaust, Jewish (1939-1945) - Influence. 2. Memory - Social aspects. 3. Memory - Psychological aspects. 4. Women. I. Title.
D804.3 .R42 2002

Reading complex words : cross-language studies / edited by Egbert M.H. Assink, Dominiek Sandra. New York : Kluwer Academic/Plenum Publishers, c2003. xxii, 338 p. : ill. ; 25 cm. (Neuropsychology and cognition ; 22) Includes bibliographical references and index. ISBN 0-306-47707-6 DDC 401/.9
1. Psycholinguistics. 2. Reading, Psychology of. 3. Grammar, Comparative and general - Morphology. I. Assink, E., 1944- II. Sandra, Dominiek, 1960- III. Series.
P37.5.R42 R43 2003

READING DISABILITIES. See **READING DISABILITY.**

READING DISABILITY - PHYSIOLOGICAL ASPECTS.
Dyslexia, fluency, and the brain. Timonium, Md. : York Press, 2001.
RC394.W6 D958 2001

Reading Harry Potter : critical essays / edited by Giselle Liza Anatol. Westport, Conn. ; London : Praeger Publishers, 2003. xxv, 217 p. ; 25 cm. (Contributions to the study of popular culture, 0198-9871 ; no. 78) Includes bibliographical references (p. [207]-209) and index. ISBN 0-313-32067-5 (alk. paper) DDC 823/.914
1. Rowling, J. K. - Criticism and interpretation. 2. Rowling, J. K. - Characters - Harry Potter. 3. Children - Books and reading - English-speaking countries. 4. Children's stories, English - History and criticism. 5. Fantasy fiction, English - History and criticism. 6. Potter, Harry (Fictitious character) 7. Wizards in literature. 8. Magic in literature. I. Anatol, Giselle Liza, 1970- II. Series.
PR6068.O93 Z84 2003

READING INTERESTS OF CHILDREN. See **CHILDREN - BOOKS AND READING.**

Reading psychoanalysis.
Rudnytsky, Peter L. Ithaca : Cornell University Press, 2002.
BF173 .R794 2002

READING, PSYCHOLOGY OF.
Reading complex words. New York : Kluwer Academic/Plenum Publishers, c2003.
P37.5.R42 R43 2003

READING READINESS.
Gemmen, Heather. Dreams from God. Colorado Springs, Colo. : Faith Kidz, 2003.
BF1099.B5 G46 2003

READING RETARDATION. See **READING DISABILITY.**

Readings in cognitive psychology : applications, connections, and individual differences / [edited by] Bridget Robinson-Riegler, Gregory Robinson-Riegler. Boston, Mass. : Pearson Allyn & Bacon, 2003. p. cm. Includes bibliographical references and index. ISBN 0-205-35867-5 DDC 153
1. Cognitive psychology - Textbooks. I. Robinson-Riegler, Bridget. II. Robinson-Riegler, Gregory.
BF201 .R425 2003

Readings in evolutionary psychology / [edited by] Douglas T. Kenrick, Carol L. Luce. Boston : Pearson/Allyn and Bacon, c2004. p. cm. Includes bibliographical references. ISBN 0-205-34409-7 (alk. paper) DDC 155.7
1. Evolutionary psychology. I. Kenrick, Douglas T. II. Luce, Carol L.
BF698.95 .R43 2004

READINGS (PARAPSYCHOLOGY). See **PSYCHIC READINGS.**

READINGS, PSYCHIC. See **PSYCHIC READINGS.**

Ready for anything.
Allen, David, 1945 Dec. 28- New York : Viking, 2003.
BF637.T5 A46 2003

Real kids come in all sizes.
Kater, Kathy. New York : Broadway Books, 2004.
BF723.B6 K38 2004

Real metaphysics : essays in honour of D.H. Mellor / edited by Hallvard Lillehammer and Gonzalo Rodriguez-Pereyra. London ; New York : Routledge, 2003. viii, 248 p. ; 24 cm. (Routledge studies in twentieth century philosophy ; 14) Includes bibliographical references and index. ISBN 0-415-24981-3 DDC 110
1. Metaphysics. I. Mellor, D. H. II. Lillehammer, Hallvard, 1970- III. Rodriguez Pereyra, Gonzalo. IV. Series.
BD111 .R227 2003

REAL PROPERTY. See also **ADMINISTRATION OF ESTATES; INHERITANCE AND SUCCESSION; LAND TENURE.**
Anderson, Terry Lee, 1946- Property rights. Stanford, Calif. : Hoover Institution Press, c2003.
HB701 .A44 2003

Real spaces.
Summers, David, 1941- London : Phaidon, c2003.

The real Warren Buffett.
O'Loughlin, James. London ; Yarmouth, ME : Nicholas Brealey, 2003.

Real world SQL server administration with Perl.
Shea, Linchi. [Berkeley, CA] : Apress ; New York : Distributed to the book trade in the U.S. by Springer-Verlag, c2003.
QA76.73.S67 S48 2003

REALISM. See also **MATERIALISM.**
Cruickshank, Justin, 1969- Realism and sociology. London ; New York : Routledge, 2003.
HM511 .C78 2003

Deely, John N. The impact on philosophy of semiotics. South Bend, Ind. : St. Augustine's Press, 2003.
B831.2 .D437 2003

Willaschek, Marcus. Der mentale Zugang zur Welt. Frankfurt am Main : Klostermann, 2003.
B835 .W55 2003

Realism and sociology.
Cruickshank, Justin, 1969- London ; New York : Routledge, 2003.
HM511 .C78 2003

REALITY. See also **KNOWLEDGE, THEORY OF; SUBSTANCE (PHILOSOPHY); VIRTUAL REALITY.**
Arthurs, Jane. Crash cultures. Bristol, UK ; Portland, OR : Intellect, 2002.

Bewes, Timothy. Reification, or, The anxiety of late capitalism. London ; New York : Verso, 2002.
HM449 .B49 2002

Pearce, Joseph Chilton. The crack in the cosmic egg. Rochester, Vt. : Park Street Press, c2002.
BD331 .P3915 2002

Soukup, Johannes. Metaphysik der Zeit oder Wirklichkeit und Wissen. Deutsche 1. Ausg. Wien : Passagen Verlag, c1998.

Realms of impossibility. Ground.
Lim, C. J. Chichester : Wiley-Academy, 2002.

Rean, A. A.
Problemy obshcheĭ akmeologii. S.-Peterburg : Izd-vo Sankt-Peterburgskogo universiteta, 2000.
BF724.5 .P76 2000

REARING OF CHILDREN. See **CHILD REARING.**

REASON. See also **FAITH AND REASON; REASONING.**
Ameriks, Karl, 1947- Interpreting Kant's critiques. Oxford : Clarendon Press ; New York : Oxford University Press, 2003.
B2779 .A64 2003

Fogelin, Robert J. Walking the tightrope of reason. Oxford ; New York : Oxford University Press, 2003.
BC177 .F64 2003

Holt, Lynn, 1959- Apprehension. Aldershot, Hants, England ; Burlington, VT : Ashgate, c2002.

BC177 .H655 2002

Mires, Fernando. Crítica de la razón científica. 1a ed. Caracas : Editorial Nueva Sociedad, 2002.

Papineau, David, 1947- The roots of reason. Oxford : Clarendon Press ; New York : Oxford University Press, 2003.
BD418.3 .P35 2003

Philosophieren aus dem Diskurs. Würzburg : Königshausen & Neumann, c2002.

Rogers, W. Kim. Reason and life. Lanham, Md. : University Press of America, c2003.
BD431 .R5515 2003

Vernes, Jean-René. The existence of the external world. Ottawa : University of Ottawa Press, c2000.

REASON AND FAITH. See **FAITH AND REASON.**

Reason and life.
Rogers, W. Kim. Lanham, Md. : University Press of America, c2003.
BD431 .R5515 2003

REASON - PHILOSOPHY.
Materiali per un lessico della ragione. Pisa : Edizioni ETS, c2001.

Reasonably vicious.
Vogler, Candace A. Cambridge, Mass. : Harvard University Press, 2002.
BJ1031 .V64 2002

REASONING. See also **FALLACIES (LOGIC); INDUCTION (LOGIC); JUDGMENT (LOGIC); LOGIC.**
Automated practical reasoning. Wien ; New York : Springer-Verlag, c1995.
QA76.9.A96 A9 1995

Baggini, Julian. The philosopher's toolkit. Malden, MA : Blackwell Publishers, 2003.
BC177 .B19 2003

Descartes, René, 1596-1650. [Regulae ad directionem ingenii. French] Règles pour la direction de l'esprit. Paris : Librairie générale française, c2002.

Enç, Berent. How we act. Oxford : Clarendon Press ; New York : Oxford University Press, 2003.
B105.A35 E63 2003

Faith in the age of uncertainty. New Delhi : Published by Indialog Publications in association with the India International Centre, 2002.
BL626.3+

Löffelmann, Markus. Das Urteil. Würzburg : Königshausen & Neumann, c2002.
BC181 .L64 2002

Materiali per un lessico della ragione. Pisa : Edizioni ETS, c2001.

Neusner, Jacob, 1932- Analysis and argumentation in Rabbinic Judaism. Lanham, Md. : University Press of America, c2003.
BM496.5 .N4775 2003

Schreiber, Scott G. (Scott Gregory), 1952- Aristotle on false reasoning. Albany : State University of New York Press, 2003.
B491.R4 S37 2003

Stenning, Keith. Seeing reason. Oxford ; New York : Oxford University Press, 2002.
BF441 .S775 2002

Wagman, Morton. Logical processes in humans and computers. Westport, Conn. : Praeger, 2003.
BF311 .W26566 2003

REASONING - ABILITY TESTING.
Mangieri, John N. Yale Assessment of Thinking. San Francisco : Jossey-Bass, c2003.
BF442 .M34 2003

REASONING (CHILD PSYCHOLOGY). See **REASONING IN CHILDREN.**

REASONING - DATA PROCESSING.
Visualizing argumentation. London ; New York : Springer, 2003.
QA76.9.H85 V67 2003

REASONING IN CHILDREN - JUVENILE LITERATURE.
Berry, Joy Wilt. Saying no. New York : Scholastic, c2001.
BF723.R4 B37 2001

REASONING (PSYCHOLOGY).
Artman, Lavee. ha-Nisayon ha-yomyomi u-fitron heseke tenai ya-hakhalah lo-tekefim. [Israel : h. mo. l., 1999?]

Reasoning (Psychology)

Gordon, Andrew S. Strategy representation. Mahwah, NJ. : L. Erlbaum, 2003.
BF316.6 .G67 2003

The nature of reasoning. Cambridge, U.K. ; New York : Cambridge University Press, 2003.
BF442 .N38 2003

Perspectives on thinking and reasoning. Hove, UK ; Hillsdale : Lawrence Erlbaum Associates, c1995.
BF441 .P48 1995

Thinking. Hoboken, NJ : Wiley, c2003.
BF441 .T466 2003

REASONING (PSYCHOLOGY) - EXAMINATIONS, QUESTIONS, ETC.
Wiesen, Joel P. (Joel Peter) How to prepare for mechanical aptitude & spatial relations tests. Hauppauge, NY : Barron's, 2003.
BF433.M4 W535 2003

Reasons and purposes.
Schueler, G. F. Oxford : Oxford University Press, 2003.

REBELLIONS. See CIVIL WAR; INSURGENCY.

REBELS (SOCIAL PSYCHOLOGY). See CONFORMITY.

Rebels within the ranks.
Pandora, Katherine, 1958- Cambridge ; New York : Cambridge University Press, 1997.
BF105 .P36 1997

REBIRTH. See REINCARNATION.

Rebuilding society on feminine principles.
Longstaff, Bill, 1934- Confessions of a matriarchist. Calgary : Ballot Pub., 2003.

Recalcati, Massimo.
Di Ciaccia, Antonio. Jacques Lacan. Milano : B. Mondadori, 2000.
BF109.L28 D53 2000

RECALL (PSYCHOLOGY). See RECOLLECTION (PSYCHOLOGY).

Recasting German identity : culture, politics, and literature in the Berlin Republic / edited by Stuart Taberner and Frank Finlay. Rochester, NY : Camden House, 2002. vi, 276 p. ; 24 cm. (Studies in German literature, linguistics, and culture) Includes bibliographical references and index. ISBN 1-57113-244-9 (alk. paper) DDC 305.8/00943
1. Germany - Intellectual life - 20th century. 2. Germany - Ethnic relations. 3. National characteristics, German. 4. Holocaust, Jewish (1939-1945) - Psychological aspects. 5. German literature - 20th century - History and criticism. I. Taberner, Stuart. II. Finlay, Frank. III. Series: Studies in German literature, linguistics, and culture (Unnumbered)
DD239 .R43 2002

Recent advances in psychology and aging / edited by Paul Costa. Amsterdam ; Boston : Elsevier, 2003. p. cm. (Advances in cell aging and gerontology ; v. 15) Includes bibliographical references and index. ISBN 0-444-51495-3 DDC 155.67
1. Aged - Psychology. 2. Aging - Psychological aspects. I. Costa, Paul T. II. Series.
BF724.8 .R43 2003

La réception de Freud en France.
Bolzinger, André. Paris : L'Harmattan, c1999.
BF175 .B575 1999

Recharge in minutes.
Zoglio, Suzanne Willis. 1st ed. Doylestown, PA : Tower Hill Press, c2003.
BF632 .Z64 2003

Reck, H. U. Mythos Medienkunst / Hans Ulrich Reck. Köln : König, c2002. 100 p. ; 23 cm. (Kunstwissenschaftliche Bibliothek ; Bd. 20) Includes bibliographical references. ISBN 3-88375-558-3 (pbk.)
1. Digital art. 2. Computer art. 3. Multimedia (Art) 4. Aesthetics. I. Title. II. Series.

Reckhardt, Carsten.
Oldenburger Symposion zur Psychologischen Akustik (8th : 2000) Contributions to psychological acoustics. 1. ed. Oldenburg : BIS, Bibliotheks- und Informationssystem der Universität Oldenburg, 2000.
BF251 .O44 2000

RECLAIMING COLLECTIVE (SAN FRANCISCO, CALIF.).
Salomonsen, Jone, 1956- Enchanted feminism. London ; New York : Routledge, 2002.
BF1577.C2 S25 2002

Reclam-Bibliothek
(20015) Brenner, Andreas. Lexikon der Lebenskunst. Leipzig : Reclam-Verlag, 2002.

RECOGNITION (PHILOSOPHY).
Heck, Alexander. Auf der Suche nach Anerkennung. Münster : Lit, c2003.

Markell, Patchen, 1969- Bound by recognition. Princeton, N.J. : Princeton University Press, c2003.
JC575 .M37 2003

RECOGNITION (PSYCHOLOGY). See also RECOLLECTION (PSYCHOLOGY).
Pylyshyn, Zenon W., 1937- Seeing and visualizing. Cambridge, Mass. : MIT Press, 2003.
BF241 .P95 2003

RECOLLECTION (PSYCHOLOGY).
Tadié, Jean-Yves, 1936- Le sens de la mémoire. Paris : Gallimard, c1999.
BF371 .T32 1999

RECONCILIATION.
Burying the past. Expanded and updated. Washington, D.C. : Georgetown University Press, c2003.
JC578 .B49 2003

Christoff, Joseph A. Issues in implementing international peace operations [electronic resource]. [Washington, D.C.] : U.S. General Accounting Office, [2002]

Dilemmas of reconciliation. Waterloo, Ont. : Wilfrid Laurier University Press, 2003.

Long, William J., 1956- War and reconciliation. Cambridge, Mass. : MIT Press, c2003.
JZ5597 .L66 2003

Loveman, Brian. El espejismo de la reconciliación política. 1. ed. Santiago : LOM Ediciones : DIBAM, 2002.

Mir u Hrvatskoj--resultati istraživanja. Zagreb : Hrvatski Caritas ; Split : Franjevački in-t za kulturu mira, 2001.
HN638.A8 M57 2001

The politics of memory. London ; New York : Zed Books, c2000.
JC571 .P642 2000

Searching for peace in Central and South Asia. Boulder, Colo. : Lynne Rienner Publishers, 2002.
JZ5597 .S43 2002

Truth v. justice. Princeton, N.J. : Princeton University Press, c2000.
DT1945 .T78 2000

Worthington, Everett L., 1946- Forgiving and reconciling. Rev. ed. Downers Grove, Ill. : InterVarsity Press, c2003.
BF637.F67 W67 2003

RECONCILIATION (LAW) - SOUTH AFRICA.
Peace and conflict resolution. Part 2 [videorecording]. Derry, N.H. : Chip Taylor Communications, 1997.

Reconstructing economic theory.
Oakley, Allen. Cheltenham, UK ; Northampton, MA, USA : E. Elgar Pub., c2002.
HB74.P8 O15 2002

RECONSTRUCTION (1914-1939). See PEACE.

RECONSTRUCTIVE SURGERY. See SURGERY, PLASTIC.

RECORD COMPANIES. See SOUND RECORDING INDUSTRY.

RECORD INDUSTRY. See SOUND RECORDING INDUSTRY.

RECORDED MUSIC INDUSTRY. See SOUND RECORDING INDUSTRY.

RECORDING INDUSTRY. See SOUND RECORDING INDUSTRY.

RECORDING OF SOUND. See SOUND - RECORDING AND REPRODUCING.

RECORDINGS, SOUND. See SOUND RECORDINGS.

RECORDS. See ARCHIVES.

RECORDS MANAGEMENT. See RECORDS - MANAGEMENT.

RECORDS - MANAGEMENT - CASE STUDIES.
Archives and the public good. Westport, Conn. ; London : Quorum Books, 2002.

Records of Yoga.
Ghose, Aurobindo, 1872-1950. 1st ed. Pondicherry : Sri Aurobindo Ashram, 2001.
B132.Y6+

RECORDS, PHONOGRAPH. See SOUND RECORDINGS.

RECORDS, SOUND. See SOUND RECORDINGS.

RECOVERED MEMORY.
McNally, Richard J. Remembering trauma. Cambridge, Mass. : Belknap Press of Harvard University Press, 2003.
RC552.P67 M396 2003

Recreating strategy.
Cummings, Stephen. London ; Thousand Oaks : Sage Publications, 2002.
HD30.28 .C855 2002

RECREATION. See PLAY; POPULAR CULTURE; SPORTS.

RECREATIONAL FISHING. See FISHING.

RECREATIONS. See GAMES; PLAY; SPORTS.

Recreative minds.
Currie, Gregory. Oxford : Clarendon Press ; New York : Oxford University Press, 2002.
BH301.I53 C87 2002

Rectifying the state of Israel.
Ginzburg, Yitshak. 1st ed. Jerusalem : Gal Einai ; Cedarhurst, NY : For information address, Gal Einai Institute, c2002.

Rector, Robert. The effects of marriage and maternal education in reducing child poverty / Robert Rector and Kirk A. Johnson. Washington, D.C. : Heritage Foundation, 2002. 12 p. ; 28 cm. "A report of the Heritage Center for Data Analysis". Includes bibliographical references.
1. Poor children - United States. 2. Mother and child. I. Johnson, Kirk A. II. Title.

RECTORS. See CLERGY.

Los recuerdos robados a las estrellas muertas.
Papalotzin, Itzcoatl. Barcelona : Mtm editor.es, c2002.

Recurring dream symbols.
Sullivan, Kathleen, 1941- New York : Paulist Press, c2004.
BF1091 .S813 2004

Red square & green squigglies.
Bagley, Michael T. Woodcliff Lake, NJ : Green Squiggliess Press, c1996.
BF408 .B327 1996

Red square and green squigglies.
Bagley, Michael T. Red square & green squigglies. Woodcliff Lake, NJ : Green Squiggliess Press, c1996.
BF408 .B327 1996

Red Star, Nancy, 1950-.
Legends of the star ancestors. Rochester, Vt. : Bear & Co., c2002.
BF2050 .L44 2002

REDEVELOPMENT, URBAN. See CITY PLANNING.

Redfield, James. God and the evolving universe : the next step in personal evolution / James Redfield, Michael Murphy, Sylvia Timbers. New York : Jeremy P. Tarcher/Putnam, c2002. 321 p. ; 23 cm. Includes bibliographical references (p. [249]-315) and index.. ISBN 1-58542-137-5 (alk. paper) DDC 110
1. Teleology. 2. Cosmology. 3. Evolution. 4. Human beings. 5. Consciousness. I. Murphy, Michael, 1930 Sept. 3- II. Timbers, Sylvia, 1955- III. Title.
BD541 .R43 2002

Miller, Larry, 1947- Exploring the "zone". Gretna, La. : Pelican, 2001.
BF1045.S83 M55 2001

Redmon, William K.
Handbook of organizational performance. New York : Haworth Press, c2001.
HD58.7 .H364 2001

Redmond, Mark V., 1949-.
Beebe, Steven A., 1950- Interpersonal communication. 4th ed. Boston, MA : Allyn and Bacon, 2004.
BF637.C45 B43 2004

Rée, Paul, 1849-1901.
Psychologische beobachtungen aus dem Empfindungen. English.
Rée, Paul, 1849-1901. [Ursprung der moralischen Empfindungen. English] Basic writings. Urbana : University of Illinois Press, c2003.
B3323.R343 U67 2003

[Ursprung der moralischen Empfindungen. English]
Basic writings / Paul Rée ; translated from the German and edited by Robin Small. Urbana :

University of Illinois Press, c2003. liii, 178 p. ; 24 cm. (International Nietzsche studies) Includes bibliographical references (p. [169]-173) and index. CONTENTS: On books and authors -- On human actions and their motives -- On women, love, and marriage -- Mixed thoughts -- On religious things -- On happiness and unhappiness -- Essay on vanity -- The origin of the concepts "good" and"evil" -- The origin of conscience -- Responsibility and freedom of the will -- The origin of punishment and the feeling of justice : on deterrence and retribution -- The origin of vanity -- Moral progress -- The relation of goodness to happiness. ISBN 0-252-02818-X (alk. paper) DDC 193
1. Philosophy. I. Rée, Paul, 1849-1901. Psychologische beobachtungen aus dem Empfindungen. English. II. Small, Robin, 1944- III. Title. IV. Series.
B3323.R343 U67 2003

Reed, Bob, 1942- Master your whole life : foundation for an art, science and technology of human development / Bob Reed. 1st ed. Toronto, Ont. : New Vision Pub., 2000. 124 p. ; 22 cm. Includes index. ISBN 0-9686390-0-3 DDC 158.1
1. Self-actualization (Psychology) I. Title.
BF637.S4 R44 2000

Reed, Janet (Janet C.) Animal patterns / by Janet Reed. Bloomington, Minn. : Yellow Umbrella Books, c2003. p. cm. SUMMARY: An introduction to the concept of patterns, using examples from the coats and feathers of animals as well as the designs some make. ISBN 0-7368-2914-8 (hardcover) ISBN 0-7368-2873-7 (softcover) DDC 152.14/23
1. Pattern perception - Juvenile literature. 2. Animals - Juvenile literature. 3. Pattern perception. 4. Animals. I. Title.
BF294 .R44 2003

Reed, Peter J.
Adair, John Eric, 1934- Not bosses but leaders. 3rd ed. / John Adair with Peter Reed. London ; Sterling, VA : Kogan Page, 2003.

Reed, Stephen K. Cognition : theory and applications / Stephen K. Reed. 6th ed. Australia ; Belmont, CA : Wadsworth/Thomson c2004. xiv, 418 p. : ill. ; 24 cm. Includes bibliographical references (p. 381-409) and indexes. ISBN 0-534-60867-1 (alk. paper)
1. Cognition. 2. Cognitive psychology. I. Title.
BF311 .R357 2004

Reeder, Jurgen, 1947-
[Tolkandets gränser. English]
Reflecting psychoanalysis : narrative and resolve in the psychoanalytic experience / Jurgen Reeder. London ; New York : Karnac Books, 2002. vi, 284 p. : ill. Includes bibliographical references (p. 269-277) and index. ISBN 1-85575-284-0
1. Psychoanalytic Theory. I. Title.

Reemtsma, Jan Philipp. Wie hätte ich mich verhalten? : und andere nicht nur deutsche Fragen : Reden und Aufsätze / Jan Philipp Reemtsma. München : Beck, c2001. 217 p. ; 21 cm. Includes bibliographical references. ISBN 3-406-47398-9 (acid-free paper)
1. Political ethics. 2. Social ethics. 3. Responsibility. 4. Germany - History - Historiography. 5. National socialism. I. Title.
HM216 .R38 2001

REENGINEERING (MANAGEMENT).
Harmon, Paul, 1942- Business process change. Amsterdam ; Boston : Morgan Kaufmann, c2003.
HD58.8 .H37 2003

Tsai, Hui-Liang. Information technology and business process reengineering. Westport, Conn. : Praeger, 2003.
HD58.87 .T73 2003

Reenkola, Elina M. The veiled female core / Elina M. Reenkola ; translated by Kimmo Absetz and Nely Keinanen. New York : Other Press, c2002. xv, 156 p. ; 21 cm. Includes bibliographical references (p. [141]-146) and index. Translated from Finnish. ISBN 1-89274-686-7 DDC 155.3/33
1. Women and psychoanalysis. 2. Women - Psychology. I. Title.
BF173 .R368 2002

Reeve, Susyn. Choose peace & happiness : a 52-week guide / Susyn Reeve. Boston, MA : Red Wheel, 2003. xvi, 191 p. ; 23 cm. Table of contents URL: http://www.loc.gov/catdir/toc/ecip042/2003008573.html CONTENTS: Week 1 : use the law of attraction -- Week 2 : acknowledge accomplishments -- Week 3 : journal -- Week 4 : be grateful -- Week 5 : use the creative power of your word -- Week 6 : breathe -- Week 7 : use virtual reality -- Week 8 : be kind -- Week 9 : pamper yourself -- Week 10 : read inspiring words -- Week 11 : eliminate gossip -- Week 12 : forgive -- Week 13 : spend time with a pet -- Week 14 : express your love -- Week 15 : listen to music -- Week 16 : give compliments -- Week 17 : use the good dishes -- Week 18 : seize the moment -- Be here now -- Week 19 : meditate -- Week 20 : go on a media diet -- Week 21: wear your favorite outfit -- Week 22 : smell the flowers -- Week 23 : be silent -- Week 24 : do your best -- Week 25 : faith -- Week 26 : imagine -- Week 27 : listen to and follow the still small voice -- Week 28 : spend time with a child -- Week 29 : pray -- Week 30 : be a visitor in your town -- Week 31 : exercise -- Week 32 : use your feelings as your guide -- Week 33 : take a new path -- Week 34 : ask for help -- Week 35 : take a vacation -- Week 36 : eat dessert first -- Week 37 : massage -- Week 38 : have a new thought -- Week 39 : live abundantly -- Week 40 : hug -- Week 41 : detach and let go -- Week 42 : smile -- Week 43 : spend time with a friend -- Week 44 : take a risk -- Week 45 : go to the movies -- Week 46 : live your dreams -- Week 47 : focus on success -- Week 48 : sing -- Week 49 : be the world's greatest lover -- Week 50 : create a bag of tricks -- Week 51 : write your obituary -- Week 52 : create a spiritual practice. ISBN 1-59003-059-1 DDC 646.7
1. Peace of mind - Problems, exercises, etc. 2. Happiness - Problems, exercises, etc. I. Title. II. Title: Choose peace and happiness
BF637.P3 R44 2003

Refa'el ben Zekharyah, mi-ḳ.ḳ. Yampola, 18th cent.
Marpe la nefesh.
Bahya ben Joseph ibn Pakuda, 11th cent. [Hidāyah ilá farā'id al-qulūb] Torat hovat ha-levavot ha-mefo'ar. Nyu York : Y. Vais : Star Kompozishan : [Hotsa'at Ateret], 760 [2000]

Reference and consciousness.
Campbell, John, 1956- Oxford : Clarendon Press ; New York : Oxford University Press, 2002.
BF321 .C36 2002

REFERENCE BOOKS. *See* **ENCYCLOPEDIAS AND DICTIONARIES.**

REFERENCE (LINGUISTICS).
Campbell, John, 1956- Reference and consciousness. Oxford : Clarendon Press ; New York : Oxford University Press, 2002.
BF321 .C36 2002

Grounding. Berlin ; Hawthorne, N.Y. : M. de Gruyter, 2002.
P165 .G76 2002

Indexikalität und sprachlicher Weltbezug. Paderborn : Mentis, c2002.

Shi, Yili. Discourse analysis of Chinese referring expressions. Lewiston, N.Y. : E. Mellen Press, c2002.
P325.5.R44 S53 2002

REFERENCE (PHILOSOPHY).
Indexikalität und sprachlicher Weltbezug. Paderborn : Mentis, c2002.

Références Maisonneuve et Larose
Hurbon, Laënnec. Dieu dans le vaudou haïtien. Nouv. éd. Paris : Maisonneuve et Larose, 2002.

REFERRING, THEORY OF. *See* **REFERENCE (PHILOSOPHY).**

Refiguring history.
Jenkins, Keith, 1943- London : New York : Routledge, 2003 .
D16.8 .J385 2003

Reflecting psychoanalysis.
Reeder, Jurgen, 1947- [Tolkandets gränser. English] London ; New York : Karnac Books, 2002.

Reflection and theory in the study of religion
Styers, Randall. Making magic. New York : Oxford University Press, 2003.
BF1611 .S855 2003

Reflections from the journey of life.
Bstan-'dzin-rgya-mtsho, Dalai Lama XIV, 1935- Berkeley, Calif. : North Atlantic Books, c2002.
BQ5670 .B76 2002

Reflections in the light.
Gawain, Shakti, 1948- Rev. ed. Novato, Calif. : Nataraj Pub., c2003.
BF637.S4 G393 2003

Reflections on death, dying, and bereavement.
Smith, William A. (William Aloysius), 1929- Amityville, N.Y. : Baywood Pub., c2003.
BD444 .S57 2003

Refleksivnaia praktika tvorcheskogo razvitiia cheloveka i organizatsii.
Stepanov, S. IU. (Sergeĭ IUr'evich) Moskva : Nauka, 2000.
BF408 .S75 2000

Refleksivnoe razvitie kompetentnosti v sovmestnom tvorchestve.
Rastiannikov, A. V. Moskva : PER SĖ, 2002.
BF408 .R235 2002

REFLEXES.
Rastiannikov, A. V. Refleksivnoe razvitie kompetentnosti v sovmestnom tvorchestve. Moskva : PER SĖ, 2002.
BF408 .R235 2002

REFORM, SOCIAL. *See* **SOCIAL PROBLEMS.**

REFORMATION. *See also* **EUROPE - HISTORY - 1517-1648.**
The European Renaissance and Reformation, 1350-1600. Detroit, MI : Gale Group, 2001.
CB359 .W67 2001

Stark, Rodney. For the glory of God. Princeton, N.J. : Princeton University Press, c2003.
BL221 .S747 2003

REFORMED OGBONI FRATERNITY (NIGERIA).
Kómoláfé, Kóláwolé. African traditional religion. Lagos : Ifa-Òrúnmìlà Organisation, 1995.
BL2480.Y6 K65 1995

REFORMERS. *See* **SOCIAL REFORMERS.**

Refractions of violence.
Jay, Martin, 1944- New York ; London : Routledge, 2003.
HM1116 .J39 2003

REFUGEES.
Beyond integration. Lund, Sweden : Nordic Academic Press, c2001.
JV6225 .B49 2001

REFUGEES, POLITICAL - LEGAL STATUS, LAWS, ETC. *See* **EMIGRATION AND IMMIGRATION LAW.**

Réfutation inédite de Spinoza.
Leibniz, Gottfried Wilhelm, Freiherr von, 1646-1716. Arles [France] : Actes Sud ; [Montréal] : Leméac, 1999.

REGALIA. *See* **PUBLIC LANDS.**

Regard sur "l'évolution créatrice".
Bardy, Jean. Paris : Harmattan, c2003.

Regarding the pain of others.
Sontag, Susan, 1933- 1st ed. New York : Farrar, Straus and Giroux, 2003.
HM554 .S65 2003

Regards sur l'histoire. Histoire moderne
La renaissance. [Paris] : Sedes, 2002.

REGENERATION (THEOLOGY). *See* **CONVERSION.**

Regensburger Studien zur Theologie
(Bd. 62) Cho, Hyeon-Kweon Stephan, 1962- Heiliger Geist als Lebenskraft in Kirche und Menschheit. Frankfurt am Main ; New York : Peter Lang, c2002.
BT121.3 .C56 2002

Regional conflict management / edited by Paul F. Diehl and Joseph Lepgold. Lanham, Md. : Rowman & Littlefield, c2003. xvi, 291 p. ; 23 cm. Includes bibliographical references and index. ISBN 0-7425-1901-5 (cloth : alk. paper) ISBN 0-7425-1902-3 (pbk. : alk. paper) DDC 327.1/7
1. Regionalism. 2. Conflict management. 3. Security, International. I. Diehl, Paul F. (Paul Francis) II. Lepgold, Joseph.
JZ5330 .R437 2003

REGIONAL PLANNING. *See* **CITY PLANNING.**

REGIONALISM.
Brosman, Catharine Savage, 1934- Finding higher ground. Reno : University of Nevada Press, c2003.
F787 .B76 2003

Regional conflict management. Lanham, Md. : Rowman & Littlefield, c2003.
JZ5330 .R437 2003

Les règles de la liberté.
Canto-Sperber, Monique. [Paris] : Plon, c2003.

Règles pour la direction de l'esprit.
Descartes, René, 1596-1650. [Regulae ad directionem ingenii. French] Paris : Librairie générale française, c2002.

REGRESSION ANALYSIS.
Jaccard, James. Interaction effects in multiple regression. 2nd ed. Thousand Oaks, Calif. : Sage Publications, c2003.
HA31.3 .J33 2003

REGRESSION (CIVILIZATION). *See* **PROGRESS.**

REGRESSION, HYPNOTIC AGE. *See* **HYPNOTIC AGE REGRESSION.**

REGRESSION, PAST-LIVES. *See* **REINCARNATION.**

Regression periods in human infancy / edited by Mikael Heimann. Mahwah, N.J. : Lawrence Erlbaum Associates, 2003. xiv, 220 p. : ill. ; 24 cm. Includes bibliographical references and indexes. ISBN 0-8058-4098-2 (alk. paper) DDC 155.42/28
 1. *Regression (Psychology) in infants - Cross-cultural studies.* 2. *Mother and infant - Cross-cultural studies.* 3. *Attachment behavior in infants - Cross-cultural studies.* I. *Heimann, Mikael.*
 BF720.R43 R44 2003

REGRESSION (PSYCHOLOGY). *See* **HYPNOTIC AGE REGRESSION.**

REGRESSION (PSYCHOLOGY) IN INFANTS - CROSS-CULTURAL STUDIES.
 Regression periods in human infancy. Mahwah, N.J. : Lawrence Erlbaum Associates, 2003.
 BF720.R43 R44 2003

REGRET.
 Beazley, Hamilton, 1943- No regrets. Hoboken, N.J. : John Wiley & Sons, c2004.
 BF575.R33 B43 2004

 Parrott, Les. Shoulda, coulda, woulda. Grand Rapids, Mich. : Zondervan, c2003.
 BF575.R33 P37 2004

The regulation of emotion / edited by Pierre Philippot, Robert S. Feldman. Mahwah, NJ : Lawrence Erlbaum, 2003. p. cm. Includes bibliographical references and index. ISBN 0-8058-4201-2 (alk. paper) DDC 152.4
 1. *Emotions.* 2. *Self-control.* 3. *Emotions - Social aspects.* I. *Philippot, Pierre, 1960-* II. *Feldman, Robert S. (Robert Stephen), 1947-*
 BF531 .R45 2003

Rehm, Ulrich. Stumme Sprache der Bilder : Gestik als Mittel neuzeitlicher Bilderzählung / Ulrich Rehm. München : Deutscher Kunstverlag, 2002. 439 p. : ill. ; 24 cm. (Kunstwissenschaftliche Studien ; Bd. 106) Includes bibliographical references (p. 394-434) and index. Originally published as the author's Habilitation--Rheinische Friedrich Wilhelms-Universität, Bonn, 2000. ISBN 3-422-06398-6 (pbk.)
 1. *Narrative art.* 2. *Gesture in art.* 3. *Symbolism in art.* 4. *Symbolism in communication.* 5. *Sign language.* I. *Title.* II. *Series: Kunstwissenschaftliche Studien (Deutscher Kunstverlag) ; Bd. 106.*

REICH, WILHELM, 1897-1957.
 Corrington, Robert S., 1950- Wilhelm Reich. 1st ed. New York : Farrar, Straus and Giroux, 2003.
 BF109.R38 C67 2003

Reichholf, Josef. Warum wir siegen wollen : der sportliche Ehrgeiz als Triebkraft in der Evolution des Menschen / Josef H. Reichholf. München : Deutscher Taschenbuch, c2001. 260 p. ; 21 cm. Includes bibliographical references and index. ISBN 3-423-24271-X (pbk.)
 1. *Sports - Psychological aspects.* 2. *Competition (Psychology)* 3. *Evolution (Biology)* I. *Title.*

Reid, Howard. In search of the immortals : mummies, death and the afterlife / Howard Reid. London : Headline, 1999. ix, 307 p. : col. ill. ; 24 cm. Includes bibliographical references (p. 291-298) and index. ISBN 0-7472-7555-6 DDC 393.3
 1. *Death.* 2. *Mummies.* 3. *Future life.* I. *Title.*

Reid, Jennifer, 1962-.
 Religion and global culture. Lanham, MD ; Oxford : Lexington Books, c2003.
 BL65.C8 R444 2003

Reification.
 Bewes, Timothy. Reification, or, The anxiety of late capitalism. London ; New York : Verso, 2002.
 HM449 .B49 2002

Reification, or, The anxiety of late capitalism.
 Bewes, Timothy. London ; New York : Verso, 2002.
 HM449 .B49 2002

Reig, Ramón. El éxtasis cibernético : comunicación, democracia y neototalitarismo a comienzos del siglo XXI / Ramón Reig. 1. ed. Madrid : Ediciones Libertarias, 2001. 313 p. : ill. ; 20 cm. (Ensayo / Ediciones Libertarias ; 129) Includes bibliographical references (p. 303-313). ISBN 84-7954-606-9 (pbk.)
 1. *Communication.* 2. *Cybernetics.* 3. *Electronic commerce.* 4. *Twenty-first century.* I. *Title.* II. *Title: Comunicación, democracia y neototalitarismo a comienzos del siglo XXI* III. *Series: Ensayo (Ediciones Libertarias) ; 129.*

Reihe Frauenforschung
 (Bd. 38) Ernst, Waltraud, 1964- Diskurspiratinnen. Wien : Milena, c1999.

 HQ1154 .E7 1999
Reihe Geschichtswissenschaft
 (Bd. 50) Kiesewetter, Hubert, 1939- Irreale oder reale Geschichte? Herbolzheim : Centaurus, 2002.

Reihe Historische Anthropologie
 (Sonderband) Logik und Leidenschaft. Berlin : D. Reimer Verlag, c2002.

Reihe "Politik der Geschlechterverhältnisse"
 (Bd. 19) Gewalt-Verhältnisse. Frankfurt ; New York : Campus, c2002.

 (Bd. 20) Engel, Antke. Wider die Eindeutigkeit. Frankfurt/Main ; New York : Campus, c2002.

Reihe Studien zur politischen Gesellschaft
 (Bd. 4.) Palonen, Kari, 1947- Eine Lobrede für Politiker. Opladen : Leske + Budrich, 2002.
 JF2051.W43 J35 2002

Reilly, Kevin, 1941-.
 Racism. Armonk, N.Y. : M.E. Sharpe, c2003.
 HT1521 .R323 2003

Reimitz, Helmut.
 The construction of communities in the early Middle Ages. Leiden ; Boston : Brill, 2003.
 HN11 .C66 2003

Reina, Maria Elena. Hoc hic et nunc : Buridano, Marsilio di Inghen e la conoscenza del singolare / Maria Elena Reina. [Firenze] : Leo S. Olschki, 2002. xii, 416 p. ; 24 cm. Includes bibliographical references (p. 385-409) and indexes. ISBN 88-222-5085-0 DDC 189
 1. *Buridan, Jean, -1300-1358.* 2. *Marsilius, of Inghen, -d. 1396.* 3. *Philosophy, Medieval.* I. *Title.* II. *Title: Buridano, Marsilio di Inghen e la conoscenza del singolare*

REINCARNATION.
 Cai, Zhichun. Huo fo zhuan shi. Di 1 ban. Beijing : Hua wen chu ban she : Xin hua shu dian jing xiao, 2000.
 BL515 .C345 2000

 Echekwube, A. O. (Anthony Onyebuchi) A metaphysical analysis of the concept of reincarnation. Ekpoma, Nigeria : Ambrose Alli University Publishing House, 2002.
 1. *Black author.*

 Hubaut, Michel. Dieu, l'homme et la réincarnation. Paris : Desclée de Brouwer, c1998.

 Nwokogba, Isaac, 1957- Voices from beyond. Cranston, R.I. : Writers' Collective, 2003.
 BF1261.2 .N96 2003

REINCARNATION AND PSYCHOTHERAPY. *See* **REINCARNATION THERAPY.**

REINCARNATION - CASE STUDIES.
 Kent, James H., 1939- Past life memories as a Confederate soldier. Huntsville, AR : Ozark Mountain Publishers, c2003.
 BF1156.R45 K45 2003

 Moody, Raymond A. Life after life. Rev. 25th anniversary ed / with a new preface by Melvin Morse and a foreword by Elisabeth Kübler-Ross. London : Rider, 2001.

 Nissanka, H. S. S. [Năvata upan dăriya. English] The girl who was reborn. Colombo : S. Godage Brothers, 2001.
 BL515+

REINCARNATION - CHRISTIANITY.
 Meier, Jürgen. Karma und Christentum. Dornach : Verlag am Goetheanum, c2001.

The reincarnation of Edgar Cayce?.
 Free, Wynn, 1946- Berkeley, Calif. : Frog, 2004.
 BF1815.W49 F74 2004

REINCARNATION THERAPY - CASE STUDIES.
 Moody, Raymond A. Life after life. Rev. 25th anniversary ed / with a new preface by Melvin Morse and a foreword by Elisabeth Kübler-Ross. London : Rider, 2001.

Reiner, Hans, 1896- Philosophieren : eine Einleitung in die Philosophie / Hans Reiner ; bearbeitet von Jörg-Johannes Lechner. Oberried bei Freiburg i. Br. : PAIS-Verlag, c2002. 166 p. ; 21 cm. (Hans-Reiner-Gesamtwerk) ISBN 3-931992-15-2
 1. *Philosophy.* I. *Lechner, Jörg-Johannes, 1966-* II. *Title.* III. *Series: Reiner, Hans, 1896- Works. 2002.*

Works. 2002.
 Reiner, Hans, 1896- Philosophieren. Oberried bei Freiburg i. Br. : PAIS-Verlag, c2002.

REINFORCEMENT (PSYCHOLOGY).
 Pryor, Karen, 1932- On behavior. 1st ed. North Bend, Wash. : Sunshine Books, c1995.

 BF637.B4 P68 1995
Reinhardt, Gregory A.
 Many faces of gender. Boulder : University Press of Colorado ; Calgary, Alta., Canada : University of Calgary Press, c2002.
 E98.P95 M35 2002

Reinhold, Karl Leonhard, 1757-1823.
 Ueber das Fundament des philosophischen Wissens. Italian.
 Reinhold, Karl Leonhard, 1757-1823. [Ueber den Begriff der Philosophie. Italian] Concetto e fondamento della filosofia. Roma : Edizioni di storia e letteratura, 2002.

 [Ueber den Begriff der Philosophie. Italian]
 Concetto e fondamento della filosofia / Karl Leonhard Reinhold ; a cura di Faustino Fabbianelli. Roma : Edizioni di storia e letteratura, 2002. xxxvii, 144 p. ; 24 cm. (Temi e testi ; 44) Includes bibliographical references and index. ISBN 88-8498-069-0 DDC 193
 1. *Philosophy.* I. *Reinhold, Karl Leonhard, 1757-1823. Ueber das Fundament des philosophischen Wissens. Italian.* II. *Fabbianelli, Faustino.* III. *Title.* IV. *Series.*

Reis, Donna. Seeking ghosts in the Warwick Valley : 60 personal accounts / Donna Reis. Atglen, PA : Schiffer Pub., c2002. 159 p. : ill. ; 23 cm. ISBN 0-7643-1740-7 DDC 133.1/09747/31
 1. *Ghosts - New York (State) - Warwick.* 2. *Haunted places - New York (State) - Warwick.* I. *Title.*
 BF1472.U6 R45 2002

Reisberg, Daniel.
 Gleitman, Henry. Psychology. 6th ed. New York : W.W. Norton, c2004.
 BF121 .G58 2004

 Memory and emotion. Oxford University Press : New York, 2003.
 BF378.A87 M46 2003

Reischuk, Rüdiger.
 ALT 2002 (2002 : Lübeck, Germany) Algorithmic learning theory. Berlin ; New York : Springer, c2002.
 QA76.9.A43 A48 2002

Reiss-Schimmel, Ilana.
 Freud, le sujet social. 1re éd. Paris : Presses universitaires de France, 2002.

Reiter, Mark.
 Tharp, Twyla. The creative habit. New York : Simon & Schuster, c2003.
 BF408 .T415 2003

Reitsma, P. (Pieter).
 Precursors of functional literacy. Amsterdam ; Philadelphia : J. Benjamins Pub., 2002.
 P118.7 .P74 2002

REJECTION (PSYCHOLOGY).
 Anderson, Susan, C.S.W. Black swan. Huntington, N.Y. : Rock Foundations Press, c1999.
 BF575.R35 A52 1999

 Anderson, Susan, C.S.W. The journey from heartbreak to connection. Berkley trade pbk. ed. New York : Berkley Books, 2003.
 BF575.R35 A533 2003

REJECTION (PSYCHOLOGY) IN CHILDREN.
 Bierman, Karen L. Peer rejection. New York : Guilford Press, 2004.
 BF723.R44 B54 2003

Reklama : vnushenie i manipuliatsiia : media-orientirovannyĭ podkhod / [redaktor-sostavitel' D. IA. Raĭgorodskiĭ]. Moskva : Izd-vo Dom "Bakhrakh-M", 2001. 751 p. : ill. ; 21 cm. "Media-orientirovannyĭ podkhod, psikhologicheskie éffekty SMI, Kommunikatsiia, vnushenie, stereotipy, mify, imidzh, pablik rileĭshn, psikhologiia vozdeĭstviia rechi i tsveta, obman, manipulirovanie"--Cover. ISBN 5895700209
 1. *Mass media - Psychological aspects.* 2. *Advertising - Psychological aspects.* I. *Raĭgorodskiĭ, D. IA.*

Rekonstruktsiia vseobshcheĭ istorii.
 Nosovskiĭ, G. V. (Gleb Vladimirovich), 1958- Moskva : FID "Delovoĭ ékspress", 2002.
 DK38 .N68 2002

Relaciones hombre-fauna : una zona interdisciplinaria de estudio / Eduardo Corona-M., Joaquín Arroyo-Cabrales (coordinadores). México, D.F. : CONACULTA, INAH ; Plaza y Valdes, 2002. 229 p. : ill. ; 24 cm. (Arqueología) Includes bibliographical references. ISBN 9701883098 (INAH) ISBN 9707220880 (Plaza y Valdes)
 1. *Human-animal relationships.* 2. *Paleoecology.* 3. *Paleontology.* I. *Corona M., Eduardo.* II. *Arroyo-Cabrales, Joaquín.* III. *Series: Serie Arqueología (Mexico City, Mexico)*

QL85 .R453 2002

La relation à l'autre.
Germain-Thiant, Myriam. Lyon : Chronique sociale, [2002]

La relation critique.
Starobinski, Jean. Ed. rev. et augm. [Paris] : Gallimard, c2001.
PN81 .S69 2001

Relational perspectives book series
(v. 22) Dimen, Muriel. Sexuality, intimacy, power. Hillsdale, NJ : Analytic Press, 2003.
BF201.4 .D556 2003

(v. 24) Sorenson, Randall Lehmann, 1954- Minding spirituality. Hillsdale, NJ : Analytic Press, 2003.
BF175.4.R44 S67 2003

Relational remembering.
Campbell, Sue, 1956- Lanham, Md. ; Oxford : Rowman & Littlefield, c2003.
BF378.A87 C36 2003

RELATIONS, INTERGENERATIONAL. *See* **INTERGENERATIONAL RELATIONS.**

RELATIONS, INTERGROUP. *See* **INTERGROUP RELATIONS.**

RELATIONS, INTERPERSONAL. *See* **INTERPERSONAL RELATIONS.**

RELATIONS, RACE. *See* **RACE RELATIONS.**

The relationship among voice onset, voice quality and fundamental frequency.
Steinhauer, Kimberly Marie. 2000.

RELATIONSHIP MARKETING. *See* **CUSTOMER RELATIONS.**

RELATIONSHIPS, HUMAN-ANIMAL. *See* **HUMAN-ANIMAL RELATIONSHIPS.**

RELATIONSHIPS, INTERPERSONAL. *See* **INTERPERSONAL RELATIONS.**

RELATIONSHIPS, MAN-WOMAN. *See* **MAN-WOMAN RELATIONSHIPS.**

RELATIVITY. *See* **SUBJECTIVITY.**

RELATIVITY (PHYSICS).
Galison, Peter Louis. Einstein's clocks, Poincaré's maps. 1st ed. New York : W.W. Norton, c2003.
QB209 .G35 2003

Relatos de la pareja.
Bianchi, Carlos J. (Carlos Juan) Buenos Aires : Corregidor, c2001.

RELAXATION.
McKay, Matthew. The self-nourishment companion. Oakland, CA : New Harbinger Publications, c2001.
BF637.S4 M3925 2001

RELIABILITY.
Golin, Al, 1929- Trust or consequences. New York : American Management Association, c2004.
HF5387 .G65 2004

Potter, Nancy Nyquist, 1954- How can I be trusted? Lanham, Md. ; Oxford : Rowman & Littlefield, c2002.
BJ1500.T78 P68 2002

RELIABILITY (ENGINEERING). *See* **QUALITY CONTROL.**

Reliable partners.
Lipson, Charles. Princeton, N.J. : Princeton University Press, c2003.
JC423 .L583 2003

RELICS AND RELIQUARIES. *See* **RELIQUARIES.**

RELIEF (AID). *See* **INTERNATIONAL RELIEF.**

RELIEF, INTERNATIONAL. *See* **INTERNATIONAL RELIEF.**

RELIEF STATIONS (FOR THE POOR). *See* **SOCIAL SERVICE.**

RELIGION. *See also* **DUALISM (RELIGION); GOD; HOLY, THE; INDIFFERENTISM (RELIGION); KARMA; MONOTHEISM; MYSTERIES, RELIGIOUS; MYTH; MYTHOLOGY; PSYCHOANALYSIS AND RELIGION; RELIGIONS; RELIGIOUS AWAKENING; RELIGIOUS FUNDAMENTALISM; RELIGIOUS THOUGHT; SUPERNATURAL; SUPERSTITION; THEOLOGY; WOMEN AND RELIGION.**
Kunin, Seth Daniel. Baltimore : Johns Hopkins University Press, 2003.

RELIGION.
2000 years and beyond. London ; New York : Routledge, 2003.
BR53 .T86 2003

Billington, Ray. Religion without God. London ; New York : Routledge, 2002.
BL2747.3 .B55 2002

Bolle, Kees W. The enticement of religion. Notre Dame, Ind. : University of Notre Dame Press, c2002.
BL48 .B585 2002

Clément, Catherine, 1939- Le divan et le grigri. Paris : Jacob, c2002.

Crawford, Robert G. (Robert George), 1927- What is religion? London ; New York : Routledge, 2002.
BL48 .C722 2002

Devout sceptics. London : Hodder & Stoughton, 2003.

Giussani, Luigi. PerCorso. Milano : Rizzoli, c1997-

Haldane, John. An intelligent person's guide to religion. London : Duckworth, 2003.

Kunin, Seth Daniel. Religion. Baltimore : Johns Hopkins University Press, 2003.

Modern societies & the science of religions. Leiden ; Boston : Brill, 2002.
BL48 .M542 2002

Muller, F. Max (Friedrich Max), 1823-1900. The essential Max Muller. 1st ed. New York ; Houndmills, England : Palgrave Macmillan, 2002.
BL50 .M785 2002

The Persistence of religions. Malibu : Undena Publications, 1996.

Prandi, Carlo. La religione popolare fra tradizione e modernità. Brescia : Queriniana, c2002.

Promise and peril. Notre Dame, Ind. : University of Notre Dame Press, c2003.
BL50 .P65 2003

Romanova, A. P. (Anna Petrovna) Stanovlenie religioznogo kompleksa. Astrakhan : Izd-vo Astrakhanskogo pedagog. universiteta, 1999.
BF51 .R66 1999

Smith, Huston. The way things are. Berkeley : University of California Press, 2003.
BL43.S64 A5 2003

Smullyan, Raymond M. Who knows? Bloomington : Indiana University Press, 2003.
BL50 .S59 2003

Spalding, John D. A pilgrim's digress. 1st ed. New York : Harmony Books, c2003.
BL50 .S627 2003

Tijan Bangura, Abubakar. The truth can be discovered in the Qur'an. [Freetown, Sierra Leone : s.n., 2002]
1. Black author.

Ward, Graham. True religion. Malden, MA ; Oxford : Blackwell Pub., 2003.
BL48 .W189 2003

Xie jiao zhen xiang. Di 1 ban. Beijing : Dang dai shi jie chu ban she, 2001.
BT1315.2 .X54 2001

RELIGION AND CAPITALISM. *See* **CAPITALISM - RELIGIOUS ASPECTS.**

Religion and civil society.
Herbert, David, 1939- Aldershot, Hampshire, England ; Burlington, VT : Ashgate, c2003.
BL60 .H457 2003

RELIGION AND CULTURE.
Beauperin, Yves. Anthropologie du geste symbolique. Paris : Harmattan, c2002.
BL60 .B339 2002

Herbert, David, 1939- Religion and civil society. Aldershot, Hampshire, England ; Burlington, VT : Ashgate, c2003.
BL60 .H457 2003

Lewis, Richard D. The cultural imperative. Yarmouth, Me. : Intercultural Press, c2003.
GN357 .L49 2003

Lincoln, Bruce. Holy terrors. Chicago : University of Chicago Press, 2003.
BL65.T47 L56 2003

Lozito, Vito. Agiografia, magia, superstizione. Bari : Levante, [1999]
BF1775 .L69 1999

Ostwalt, Conrad Eugene, 1959- Secular steeples. Harrisburg, PA : Trinity Press International, c2003.

BL65.C8 O88 2003

Religion and global culture. Lanham, MD : Oxford : Lexington Books, c2003.
BL65.C8 R444 2003

Rosen, Lawrence, 1941- The culture of Islam. Chicago : University of Chicago Press, 2002.
DT312 R64 2002

RELIGION AND CULTURE - EUROPE - HISTORY.
The European Renaissance and Reformation, 1350-1600. Detroit, MI : Gale Group, 2001.
CB359 .W67 2001

RELIGION AND CULTURE - NIGERIA.
Babalola, E. O. African cultural revolution of Islam and Christianity in Yoruba land. Ipaja-Lagos : Eternal Communications, 2002.
1. Black author.

RELIGION AND ECONOMICS. *See* **ECONOMICS - RELIGIOUS ASPECTS.**

RELIGION AND ETHICS.
Lāla, Mukuṭa Bihārī. [Sāmyayogamīmāṃsā. Hindi & Sanskrit] Sāmyayogamīmāṃsā. 1. saṃskaraṇa. Vārāṇasī : Śaivabhāratī Śodhapratiṣṭhānam, 2001.
BL1237.32+

Religion and gender
Salomonsen, Jone, 1956- Enchanted feminism. London ; New York : Routledge, 2002.
BF1577.C2 S25 2002

RELIGION AND GEOGRAPHY. *See* **SACRED SPACE.**

Religion and global culture : new terrain in the study of religion and the work of Charles H. Long / edited by Jennifer I.M. Reid. Lanham, MD : Oxford : Lexington Books, c2003. x, 202 p. ; 24 cm. Based on a conference held Apr. 5-7, 2001 at the University of Maine at Farmington. Includes bibliographical references (p. 181-195) and index. ISBN 0-7391-0552-3 (cloth : alk. paper) DDC 200/.9
1. Long, Charles H. 2. Globalization - Religious aspects. 3. Religion and culture. I. Reid, Jennifer, 1962-
BL65.C8 R444 2003

RELIGION AND LAW.
On interpretation. Madison, Wis. : University of Wisconsin Press for the University of Wisconsin Law School, c2002.

RELIGION AND LITERATURE - GREECE.
Muñoz Llamosas, Virginia. La intervención divina en el hombre a través de la literatura griega de época arcaica y clásica. Amsterdam : Hakkert, 2002.
PA3015.R5 M87 2002

Religion and magic in ancient Egypt.
David, A. Rosalie (Ann Rosalie) London : Penguin, 2002.

RELIGION AND PEACE. *See* **PEACE - RELIGIOUS ASPECTS.**

RELIGION AND POLITICS.
Davis, Charles, 1923- Religion and the making of society. New York, NY, USA : Cambridge University Press, 1994.
BT738 .D36 1994

The Persistence of religions. Malibu : Undena Publications, 1996.

Van de Weyer, Robert. The shared well. 1st ed. Washington, D.C. : Brassey's, c2002.
BL65.P7 V36 2002

RELIGION AND POLITICS - EUROPE - HISTORY - 16TH CENTURY.
Sacerdoti, Gilberto, 1952- Sacrificio e sovranità. Torino : Einaudi, 2002.

RELIGION AND POLITICS - MOROCCO.
Rosen, Lawrence, 1941- The culture of Islam. Chicago : University of Chicago Press, 2002.
DT312 R64 2002

RELIGION AND POLITICS - NIGERIA.
Babalola, E. O. African cultural revolution of Islam and Christianity in Yoruba land. Ipaja-Lagos : Eternal Communications, 2002.
1. Black author.

RELIGION AND POLITICS - UNITED STATES.
Barrios, Luis. Josconiando. 1st ed. New York : Editorial Aguiar, 2000.

RELIGION AND POLITICS - UNITED STATES - HISTORY - 19TH CENTURY.
Winger, Stewart Lance. Lincoln, religion, and romantic cultural politics. DeKalb : Northern Illinois University Press, c2003.

Religion and psychoanalysis

E457.2 .W77 2003

RELIGION AND PSYCHOANALYSIS. *See* **PSYCHOANALYSIS AND RELIGION.**

RELIGION AND PSYCHOLOGY.
Peterson, Gregory R., 1966- Minding God. Minneapolis, MN : Fortress Press, c2003.
BL53 .P42 2003

RELIGION AND RACE. *See* **RACE - RELIGIOUS ASPECTS.**

RELIGION AND SCIENCE.
Giberson, Karl. Species of origins. Lanham, Md. : Rowman & Littlefield, c2002.
BL240.3 .G53 2002

Holmes, Barbara Ann, 1943- Race and the cosmos. Harrisburg, Pa. : Trinity Press International, c2002.
BR563.N4 H654 2002
1. Black author.

Horgan, John, 1953- Rational mysticism. Boston : Houghton Mifflin, 2003.
BL625 .H67 2003

Smith, Huston. The way things are. Berkeley : University of California Press, c2003.
BL43.S64 A5 2003

RELIGION AND SCIENCE - HISTORY.
Stark, Rodney. For the glory of God. Princeton, N.J. : Princeton University Press, c2003.
BL221 .S747 2003

RELIGION AND SOCIETY. *See* **RELIGION AND SOCIOLOGY.**

RELIGION AND SOCIOLOGY.
Aux frontières des attitudes. Paris, France : Harmattan, c2002.

Barrios, Luis. Josconiando. 1st ed. New York : Editorial Aguiar, 2000.

Bastide, Roger, 1898-1974. [Eléments de sociologie religieuse. English] Social origins of religion. Minneapolis : University of Minnesota Press, c2003.
BL60 .B313 2003

Beauperin, Yves. Anthropologie du geste symbolique. Paris : Harmattan, c2002.
BL60 .B339 2002

Beckford, James A. Social theory and religion. Cambridge, U.K. ; New York : Cambridge University Press, 2003.
BL60 .B34 2003

The Blackwell companion to sociology of religion. Oxford, UK ; Malden, Mass. : Blackwell Publishers, 2001.
BL60 .B53 2001

Caillois, Roger, 1913- The edge of surrealism. Durham : Duke University Press, 2003.
HM590 .C35 2003

Challenging religion. London ; New York : Routledge, 2003.
BL60 .C437 2003

Christiano, Kevin J. Sociology of religion. Walnut Creek, CA : AltaMira Press, c2002.
BL60 .C465 2002

Davis, Charles, 1923- Religion and the making of society. New York, NY, USA : Cambridge University Press, 1994.
BT738 .D36 1994

Herbert, David, 1939- Religion and civil society. Aldershot, Hampshire, England ; Burlington, VT : Ashgate, c2003.
BL60 .H457 2003

Hunt, Stephen, 1954- Alternative religions. Aldershot, Hampshire, England ; Burlington, VT : Ashgate, c2003.
BP603 .H87 2003

King, Ursula. Mysticism and contemporary society. [Lewisburg, Pa.] : American Teilhard Association, c2002.
B2430.T374 A18 no.44

Lāla, Mukuṭa Bihārī. [Sāmyayogamīmāṃsā. Hindi & Sanskrit] Sāmyayogamīmāṃsā. 1. saṃskaraṇa. Vārāṇasī : Śaivabhāratī Śodhapratiṣṭhānam, 2001.
BL1237.32+

Lewis, I. M. Ecstatic religion. 3rd ed. London ; New York : Routledge, 2003.
BL626 .L48 2003

Lowman, Pete. A long way east of Eden. Carlisle : Paternoster, 2002.

Modern societies & the science of religions. Leiden ; Boston : Brill, 2002.
BL48 .M542 2002

Pandian, Jacob. Supernaturalism in human life. New Delhi : Vedams ebooks, [2002]
BF1031.A4-Z+

RELIGION AND SOCIOLOGY - NIGERIA.
Studies in the theology and sociology of Yoruba indigenous religion. Lagos, Nigeria : Concept Publications (Nig.), 2002.

RELIGION AND STATE - BENIN.
Vallier, Gilles-Félix. La logique de l'éternité. 1998.

RELIGION AND STATE - UNITED STATES.
Barrios, Luis. Josconiando. 1st ed. New York : Editorial Aguiar, 2000.

Religion and the making of society.
Davis, Charles, 1923- New York, NY, USA : Cambridge University Press, 1994.
BT738 .D36 1994

RELIGION, COMPARATIVE. *See* **RELIGIONS.**

Religion et exclusion, 12e-18e siècle.
Religion et exclusion, XIIe-XVIIIe siècle. Religion et exclusion, douzième-dix-huitième siècle. Aix-en-Provence : Publications de l'Université de Provence, 2001.
BL238 .R448 2001

Religion et exclusion, XIIe-XVIIIe siècle / sous la direction de Gabriel Audisio. Religion et exclusion, douzième-dix-huitième siècle. Aix-en-Provence : Publications de l'Université de Provence, 2001. 216 p. ; 21 cm. (Collection Le temps de l'histoire) Includes bibliographical references (p. [207]-214). ISBN 2-85399-491-0
1. Religious fundamentalism - History. 2. Religious minorities - History. 3. Persecution - History. 4. Fanaticism - History. 5. Sects - History. I. Audisio, Gabriel. II. Title: Religion et exclusion, 12e-18e siècle III. Series.
BL238 .R448 2001

Religion et mentalités au Moyen Age : mélanges en l'honneur d'Hervé Martin / sous la direction de Sophie Cassagnes-Brouquet, Amaury Chauou, Daniel Pichot ... [et al.]. Rennes : Presses universitaires de Rennes, c2003. 604 p., [8] p. of plates : col. ill. ; 24 cm. (Collection "Histoire") Includes bibliographical references. ISBN 2-86847-802-6 DDC 940
1. Church history - Middle Ages, 600-1500. 2. Historiography - France. 3. Europe - Social life and customs. I. Cassagnes-Brouquet, Sophie, 1957- II. Pichot, Daniel. III. Martin, Hervé, 1940- IV. Series: Collection "Histoire" (Rennes, France)
BR141 .R45 2003

Religion et piété à Rome.
Scheid, John. [2e éd.]. Paris : Albin Michel, 2001.

RELIGION HISTORIANS - UNITED STATES - INTERVIEWS.
Smith, Huston. The way things are. Berkeley : University of California Press, c2003.
BL43.S64 A5 2003

RELIGION - HISTORIOGRAPHY. *See* **RELIGION HISTORIANS.**

RELIGION - HISTORY.
The Persistence of religions. Malibu : Undena Publications, 1996.

Rozanov, V. V. (Vasiliĭ Vasil'evich), 1856-1919. Vo dvore i͡azychnikov. Moskva : Izd-vo "Respublika", 1999.
BL96 .R69 1999

RELIGION - HUMOR.
Gotz, Ignacio L. Faith, humor, and paradox. Westport, Conn. : Praeger, 2002.
BL51 .G6854 2002

RELIGION IN LITERATURE.
Muñoz Llamosas, Virginia. La intervención divina en el hombre a través de la literatura griega de época arcaica y clásica. Amsterdam : Hakkert, 2002.
PA3015.R5 M87 2002

Vadillo, Alicia E. Santería y Vodú. Madrid : Biblioteca Nueva, c2002.
PQ7372 .V33 2002

RELIGION - INDIA - HISTORY.
Jośī, Gajānana Nārāyaṇa. Bhāratīya tattvajñānācā br̥had itihāsa. 1. āvr̥ttī. Puṇe : Marāṭhī Tattvajñāna-Mahākośa Maṇḍaḷa yāñce karitā Śubhadā-Sārasvata Prakāśana, 1994.
B131 .J674 1994

RELIGION - INDIA - MAHARASHTRA - HISTORY.
Jośī, Gajānana Nārāyaṇa. Bhāratīya tattvajñānācā br̥had itihāsa. 1. āvr̥ttī. Puṇe : Marāṭhī Tattvajñāna-Mahākośa Maṇḍaḷa yāñce karitā Śubhadā-Sārasvata Prakāśana, 1994.
B131 .J674 1994

RELIGION - MISCELLANEA.
Charlton-Davis, Mark K. Thoughts from the underworld. Los Angeles, Calif. : Amen-Ra Theological Seminary Press, c2001 (Kearney, NE : Morris Pub.)
BF1999 .C5145 2001

RELIGION - PHILOSOPHY. *See also* **KNOWLEDGE, THEORY OF (RELIGION).**
Cohen, Hermann, 1842-1918. [Works. 1977. Supplementa] Werke. Supplementa. Hildesheim : G. Olms, 2000-

Gotz, Ignacio L. Faith, humor, and paradox. Westport, Conn. : Praeger, 2002.
BL51 .G6854 2002

Kunin, Seth Daniel. Religion. Baltimore : Johns Hopkins University Press, 2003.

Lincoln, Bruce. Holy terrors. Chicago : University of Chicago Press, 2003.
BL65.T47 L56 2003

Religious experience and the end of metaphysics. Bloomington, Ind. : Indiana University Press, c2003.
BL53 .R444 2003

Silhon, sieur de (Jean), 1596?-1667. De la certitude des connaissances humaines. [Paris] : Fayard, c2002.

RELIGION - POLITICAL ASPECTS. *See* **RELIGION AND POLITICS.**

Religion, politics, and society in the new millennium
Gregg, Samuel, 1969- On ordered liberty. Lanham, MD : Lexington Books, c2003.
JC585 .G744 2003

RELIGION, PREHISTORIC. *See also* **MEGALITHIC MONUMENTS.**
Sermonti, Giuseppe. Il mito della grande madre. Milano : Mimesis, c2002.

RELIGION, PREHISTORIC - TURKEY.
Sermonti, Giuseppe. Il mito della grande madre. Milano : Mimesis, c2002.

RELIGION, PRIMITIVE. *See* **RELIGION.**

RELIGION - SOCIOLOGICAL ASPECTS.
Kunin, Seth Daniel. Religion. Baltimore : Johns Hopkins University Press, 2003.

Religion und Aufklärung
(Bd. 9) Das Ende des Hermetismus. Tübingen : Mohr Siebeck, c2002.
BF1587 .E53 2002

Religion without God.
Billington, Ray. London ; New York : Routledge, 2002.
BL2747.3 .B55 2002

La religione popolare fra tradizione e modernità.
Prandi, Carlo. Brescia : Queriniana, c2002.

RELIGIONS. *See also* **BUDDHISM; CHRISTIANITY; CHRISTIANITY AND OTHER RELIGIONS; CULTS; DRUIDS AND DRUIDISM; GODS; HINDUISM; ISLAM; JAINISM; JUDAISM; MYTHOLOGY; NEOPAGANISM; OCCULTISM; PAGANISM; RELIGION; SECTS; SHAMANISM.**
Harvey, Andrew, 1952- A walk with four spiritual guides. Woodstock, VT : SkyLight Paths Pub., c2003.
BL624 .H3445 2003

Hunt, Stephen, 1954- Alternative religions. Aldershot, Hampshire, England ; Burlington, VT : Ashgate, c2003.
BP603 .H87 2003

Lattin, Don. Following our bliss. 1st ed. New York : HarperCollins, c2003.

Modern societies & the science of religions. Leiden ; Boston : Brill, 2002.
BL48 .M542 2002

New religious movements. London ; New York : Routledge in association with the Institute of Oriental Philosophy European Centre, 1999.
BL80.2 .N397 1999

York, Michael, 1939- Pagan theology. New York ; London : New York University Press, c2003.
BL85 .Y67 2003

RELIGIONS, COMPARATIVE. *See* **RELIGIONS.**

RELIGIONS - FICTION.
Ramsay, Chevalier (Andrew Michael), 1686-1743. Les voyages de Cyrus. Paris : Champion, 2002.

RELIGIONS - HISTORY.
Rozanov, V. V. (Vasiliĭ Vasil'evich), 1856-1919. Vo dvore iazychnikov. Moskva : Izd-vo "Respublika", 1999.
BL96 .R69 1999

RELIGIONS, MODERN. *See* **CULTS; SECTS.**

RELIGIONS - POLITICAL ASPECTS. *See* **RELIGION AND POLITICS.**

RELIGIOUS ARCHITECTURE. *See* **CHURCH ARCHITECTURE.**

RELIGIOUS ARTICLES. *See* **RELIQUARIES.**

RELIGIOUS AWAKENING.
Anderson, Walt, 1933- The next enlightenment. 1st ed. New York : St. Martin's Press, 2003.
BL476 .A53 2003

RELIGIOUS AWAKENING - ISLAM. *See* **ISLAMIC RENEWAL.**

RELIGIOUS AWAKENING - MISCELLANEA.
Pike, Diane Kennedy. Awakening to wisdom. Scottsdale, AZ : LP Publications, c2003.
BF1999 .P5485 2003

RELIGIOUS BIOGRAPHY. *See* **MYSTICS; PROPHETS; SAINTS.**

RELIGIOUS CALENDARS - ROME.
Bernstein, Frances. Classical living. 1st ed. San Francisco : HarperSanFrancisco, 2000.
BL808 .B47 2000

RELIGIOUS CEREMONIES. *See* **RITES AND CEREMONIES.**

RELIGIOUS COMMUNITIES.
Twyman, James F. Emissary of light. Forres : Findhorn, 2002.

RELIGIOUS DENOMINATIONS. *See* **RELIGIONS; SECTS.**

RELIGIOUS EDUCATION. *See* **MORAL EDUCATION.**

RELIGIOUS EDUCATION - PHILOSOPHY.
Spirituality, philosophy and education. London ; New York : RoutledgeFalmer, 2003.
BV4501.3 .S65 2003

RELIGIOUS ETHICS. *See* **CHRISTIAN ETHICS.**

RELIGIOUS EXPERIENCE. *See* **EXPERIENCE (RELIGION).**

Religious experience and the end of metaphysics / edited by Jeffrey Bloechl. Bloomington, Ind. : Indiana University Press, c2003. x, 209 p. ; 25 cm. (Indiana series in the philosophy of religion) Includes bibliographical references and index. CONTENTS: The disappearance of philosophical theology in hermeneutic philosophy : historicizing and hermeneuticizing the philosophical idea of God / Ben Vedder -- Rethinking God : Heidegger in the light of absolute nothing, Nishida in the shadow of onto-theology / John C. Maraldo -- Light and shadows from the Heideggerian interpretation of the sacred / Emilio Brito -- The work and complement of appearing / Jean-Yves Lacoste -- Affective theology, theological affectivity / Adriaan Peperzak -- Immanent transcendence as way to "God" : between Heidegger and Marion / Ignace Verhack -- Derrida and Marion : two Husserlian revolutions / John D. Caputo -- The universal in Jewish particularism : Benamozegh and Levinas / Richard A. Cohen -- The kingdom and the Trinity / Kevin Hart -- Ultimacy and conventionality in religious experience / Joseph S. O'Leary. ISBN 0-253-34226-0 (alk. paper) ISBN 0-253-21592-7 (pbk. : alk. paper) DDC 291.4/2
1. Experience (Religion) 2. Religion - Philosophy. 3. Postmodernism. I. Bloechl, Jeffrey, 1966- II. Series.
BL53 .R444 2003

RELIGIOUS FESTIVALS. *See* **FASTS AND FEASTS.**

RELIGIOUS FUNDAMENTALISM. *See* **ISLAMIC FUNDAMENTALISM.**

RELIGIOUS FUNDAMENTALISM - HISTORY.
Religion et exclusion, XIIe-XVIIIe siècle. Religion et exclusion, douzième-dix-huitième siècle. Aix-en-Provence : Publications de l'Université de Provence, 2001.
BL238 .R448 2001

RELIGIOUS HISTORIANS. *See* **RELIGION HISTORIANS.**

RELIGIOUS INDIFFERENCE. *See* **INDIFFERENTISM (RELIGION).**

RELIGIOUS KNOWLEDGE, THEORY OF. *See* **KNOWLEDGE, THEORY OF (RELIGION).**

RELIGIOUS LIFE. *See* **SPIRITUAL LIFE.**

RELIGIOUS LIFE AND CUSTOMS.
Prandi, Carlo. La religione popolare fra tradizione e modernità. Brescia : Queriniana, c2002.

RELIGIOUS LIFE - BUDDHISM.
Glickman, Marshall. Beyond the breath. 1st ed. Boston : Journey Editions ; North Clarendon, VT : Distributed by Tuttle Pub., 2002.
BQ5630.V5 G54 2002

Thubten Chodron, 1950- Working with anger. Ithaca, NY : Snow Lion Publication, 2001.
BQ4430.A53 T48 2001

RELIGIOUS LIFE - TANTRIC BUDDHISM.
Osho, 1931-1990. Tantra, the supreme understanding. Delhi : Full Circle, 1999.
BP605.R34 T367 1999

RELIGIOUS LIFE - ZEN BUDDHISM.
Magid, Barry. Ordinary mind. Boston : Wisdom, c2002.
BQ9286 .M34 2002

RELIGIOUS LITERATURE. *See* **HINDU LITERATURE.**

RELIGIOUS LITERATURE, TAMIL - TRANSLATIONS INTO ENGLISH.
Robinson, Edward Jewitt. Tamil wisdom. New Delhi : Asian Educational Services, 2001.
BJ1571 .R63 2001

RELIGIOUS MINORITIES - HISTORY.
Religion et exclusion, XIIe-XVIIIe siècle. Religion et exclusion, douzième-dix-huitième siècle. Aix-en-Provence : Publications de l'Université de Provence, 2001.
BL238 .R448 2001

RELIGIOUS MYSTERIES. *See* **MYSTERIES, RELIGIOUS.**

Religious organizations in community services : a social work perspective / Terry Tirrito, Toni Cascio, editors. New York : Springer Pub., 2003. xii, 202 p. ; 24 cm. Includes bibliographical references and index. ISBN 0-8261-1548-9 DDC 361.7/5
1. Social service - Religious aspects - History. 2. Social service - United States - Religious aspects. 3. Social workers - Religious life - United States. 4. Spiritual life. 5. Church and social problems - United States. I. Tirrito, Terry, 1945- II. Cascio, Toni.
HV530 .R25 2003

RELIGIOUS PERSECUTION. *See* **PERSECUTION.**

RELIGIOUS RITES. *See* **RITES AND CEREMONIES.**

RELIGIOUS SOCIOLOGY. *See* **RELIGION AND SOCIOLOGY.**

RELIGIOUS THOUGHT. *See* **ESCHATOLOGY; GOOD AND EVIL.**

RELIGIOUS THOUGHT - HISTORY.
Botschaften aus dem Jenseits. [Düsseldorf] : Droste, c2002.

RELIGIOUS TOLERANCE - CHRISTIANITY.
Sartorio, Ugo. Credere in dialogo. Padova : Edizioni Messaggero, 2002.

RELIGIOUS LEADERS.
Tayir, Bracha Klein. ha-Manhig she-me'afsher le-elef peraḥim li-feroaḥ. Tel Aviv : Yedi'ot aḥaronot : Sifre ḥemed, c2002.

Relihan, Joel C.
Boethius, d. 524. [De consolatione philosophiae. English] Consolation of philosophy. Indianapolis, IN : Hackett Pub. Co., c2001.
B659.C2 E52 2001

RELIQUARIES - ITALY - TURIN - DESIGNS AND PLANS.
Scott, John Beldon, 1946- Architecture for the shroud. Chicago : University of Chicago Press, c2003.
NA5621.T823 S36 2003

RELOCATION (HOUSEHOLD MOVING). *See* **MOVING, HOUSEHOLD.**

REMARRIAGE. *See* **MATE SELECTION.**

Remedial genius.
Cabrera, Derek. 1st ed. Loveland, Colo. : Project N Press, 2001.
BF441 .C23 2001

Remembering Africa / edited by Elisabeth Mudimbe-Boyi. Portsmouth, NH : Heinemann, c2002. xx, 339 p. : ill. ; 24 cm. (Studies in African literature, 1351-5713) Includes bibliographical references and index. ISBN 0-325-07072-5 (alk. paper) ISBN 0-325-07071-7 (pbk. : alk. paper) DDC 303.48/2601821
1. Africa - Civilization - Western influences. 2. Civilization, Western - African influences. 3. Memory - Social aspects. 4. Africa - In mass media. 5. Africa - Colonial influence. 6. Imperialism in literature. I. Mudimbe-boyi, M. Elisabeth. II. Series.
DT14 .R46 2002

Remembering lives.
Hedtke, Lorraine. 1957- Re-membering lives. Amityville, N.Y. : Baywood Pub. Co., 2004.
BF789.D4 H4 2004

Remembering trauma.
McNally, Richard J. Cambridge, Mass. : Belknap Press of Harvard University Press, 2003.
RC552.P67 M396 2003

REMINISCING.
Edgar, Robin A. In my mother's kitchen. 2nd ed. Charlotte, N.C. : Tree House Enterprises, 2003.
BF378.R44 E34 2003

Rémond-Dalyac, Emmanuelle.
Contes de l'Egypte ancienne. Paris : Flammarion, c2002.

REMORSE.
Tudor, Steven. Compassion and remorse. Leuven ; Sterling, Va. : Peeters, 2001.
BJ1475 .T84 2001

Remote viewing.
Rifat, Tim, 1957- London : Vision, 2001.

REMOTE VIEWING (PARAPSYCHOLOGY).
Rifat, Tim, 1957- Remote viewing. London : Vision, 2001.

Targ, Russell. Limitless mind. Novato, Calif. : New World Library, c2004.
BF1389.R45 T37 2004

Ren di zi you di zhe xue si suo.
Lin, Jian. Di 1 ban. Beijing : Zhongguo ren min da xue chu ban she : Jing xiao xin hua shu dian, 1996.
B99.C52 L55 1996 <Orien China>

Ren lei she hui zi wo ren shi zhi mi de zhe xue tan suo.
Ouyang, Kang, 1953- She hui ren shi lun. Di 1 ban. [Kunming] : Yunnan ren min chu ban she, 2002.
BF323.S63 O93 2002

RENAISSANCE. *See* **CIVILIZATION, MEDIEVAL; CIVILIZATION, MODERN; HUMANISM; MIDDLE AGES.**

The Renaissance.
Lee-Browne, Patrick. New York : Facts on File, c2003.

RENAISSANCE.
Antiquity renewed. Leuven, Netherlands ; Dudley, MA : Peeters, 2003.
CB365 .A58 2003

Bastl, Beatrix, 1954- Europas Aufbruch in die Neuzeit 1450-1650. Darmstadt : Primus, c2002.
D208 .B37 2002

Cité des hommes, cité de Dieu. Genève : Droz, 2003.
PN723 .C584 2003

A companion to the worlds of the Renaissance. Malden, MA : Blackwell Publishers, 2002.
CB367 .C65 2002

Court festivals of the European Renaissance. Aldershot ; Burlington, VT : Ashgate, c2002.

The European Renaissance and Reformation, 1350-1600. Detroit, MI : Gale Group, 2001.
CB359 .W67 2001

Intellektuelle in der Frühen Neuzeit. München : Fink, c2002.

Kalisch, Eleonore. Konfigurationen der Renaissance. Berlin : Vistas, c2002.

Lee-Browne, Patrick. The Renaissance. New York : Facts on File, c2003.

Mauriès, Patrick, 1952- Cabinets of curiosities. New York : Thames & Hudson, c2002.
AM221 .M38 2002

Moss, Ann, 1938- Printed commonplace-books and the structuring of Renaissance thought. Oxford : Clarendon Press ; New York : Oxford University Press, 1996.
PA2047 .M67 1996

Renaissance der Kulturgeschichte? Dresden : Verlag der Kunst, 2001.

Renaissance.

AM101.B4856 R36 2001

La renaissance. [Paris] : Sedes, 2002.

The Renaissance. London ; New York : Routledge, 2003.
DG445 .R565 2003

Speck, Paul. [Selections. English. 1999]
Understanding Byzantium. Aldershot, Great Britain ; Burlington, Vt. : Ashgate/Variorum, c2003.
DF503 .S742513 2003

Szőnyi, György Endre. John Dee's occultism. Albany : State University of New York Press, 2004.
BF1598.D5 S98 2004

West, William. Theatres and encyclopedias in early modern Europe. Cambridge : Cambridge University Press, 2002.

La Renaissance : actes du colloque de 2002 / [Association des historiens modernistes des universités ; préface, Jean-Marie Constant ; contributions de Arlette Jouanna ... [et al.]]. Paris : Presses de l'université de Paris-Sorbonne, 2003. 173 p. : ill. ; 24 cm. (Bulletin / Association des historiens modernistes des universités, 0221-3486 ; no 28) Includes bibliographical references. ISBN 2-8405-0278-X DDC 940
1. Renaissance - Congresses. 2. Europe - Intellectual life - 16th century - Congresses. 3. Europe - History - 1492-1517 - Congresses. 4. Europe - History - 1517-1648 - Congresses. I. Jouanna, Arlette. II. Association des historiens modernistes des universités (France) III. Series: Bulletin (Association des historiens modernistes des universités (France)) ; no 28.

Renaissance and early modern philosophy / editors, Peter A. French, Howard K. Wettstein and Bruce Silver. Malden, MA ; Oxford : Blackwell Pub., c2002. 306 p. ; 24 cm. (Midwest studies in philosophy ; v. 26) Includes bibliographical references. CONTENTS: "Always to do ladies, damosels, and gentlewomen succour": women and the chivalric code in Malory's "Morte Darthur" / Felicia Ackerman -- Nicholas of Cusa (1401-1464): first modern philosopher? / Jasper Hopkins -- Marsilio Ficino on "Significatio" / Michael J.B. Allen -- Pomponazzi: moral virtue in a deterministic universe / John L. Treloar -- The secret of Pico's "Oration": Cabala and renaissance / Brian P. Copenhaver -- Between republic and monarchy? Liberty, security, and the Kingdom of France in Machiavelli / Cary Nederman and Tatiana V. Gomez -- Montaigne, "An apology for Raymond Sebond": happiness and the poverty of reason / Bruce Silver -- The natural philosophy of Giordano Bruno / Hilary Gatti -- Francis Bacon ahd the humanistic aspects of modernity / Rose-Mary Sargent -- Hobbes's atheism? / Douglas M. Jesseph -- New wine in old bottles: Gassendi and the Aristotelian origin of physics / Margaret J. Oster -- Descartes. mechanics and the mechanical philosophy / Daniel Garber -- "Presence" and "Likeness" in Arnauld's critique of Malebranche / Nancy Kendrick -- Pascal's wagers / Jeff Jordan -- Eternity and immortality in Spinoza's "Ethics" / Steven Nadler -- Occasionalism and efficacious laws in Malebranche / Micholas Jolley -- What kind of a skeptic was Bayle? / Thomas M. Lennon -- From Locke's "Letter" to Montesquieu's "Lettres" / Edwin Curley. ISBN 0-631-23381-4 ISBN 0-631-23382-2 (pbk.) DDC 109.031
1. Philosophy, Modern - 17th century. 2. Philosophy, Renaissance. I. French, Peter A. II. Wettstein, Howard K. III. Silver, Bruce. IV. Series.
B775 .R46 2002

RENAISSANCE ART. See **ART, RENAISSANCE.**

RENAISSANCE - CONGRESSES.
Antike Weisheit und kulturelle Praxis. Göttingen : Vandenhoeck & Ruprecht, 2001.
BF1586 .A58 2001

Komik der Renaissance, Renaissance der Komik. Frankfurt am Main ; New York : P. Lang, c2000.
BH301.C7 .K63 2000

La Renaissance. Paris : Presses de l'université de Paris-Sorbonne, 2003.

Il sacro nel Rinascimento. Firenze : F. Cesati, c2002.
PN49 .S337 2002

Renaissance der Komik.
Komik der Renaissance, Renaissance der Komik. Frankfurt am Main ; New York : P. Lang, c2000.
BH301.C7 .K63 2000

Renaissance der Kulturgeschichte? : die Wiederentdeckung des Märkischen Museums in Berlin aus einer europäischen Pespektive / herausgegeben im Auftrag der Richard-Schöne-Gesellschaft für Museumsgeschichte e.V. und der Stiftung Stadtmuseum Berlin von Alexis Joachimides und Sven Kuhrau. Dresden : Verlag der Kunst, 2001. 304 p. ; 79 ill. ; 21 cm. ISBN 3-364-00381-5 (pbk.) DDC 907/.4/431552

1. Märkisches Museum - History. 2. Renaissance - Germany. 3. Renaissance. 4. Germany - Civilization - 19th century.
AM101.B4856 R36 2001

La renaissance : des années 1470 aux années 1560 / Jean-Pierre Poussou ... [et al.]. [Paris] : Sedes, 2002. 318 p. ; 24 cm. (Regards sur l'histoire. Histoire moderne) Includes bibliographical references. ISBN 2-7181-9438-3 DDC 940
1. Renaissance. 2. Europe - Civilization - 16th century. 3. Europe - History - 15th century. 4. Europe - History - 16th century. I. Poussou, Jean-Pierre. II. Series

RENAISSANCE - ENGLAND.
Cockcroft, Robert, 1939- Rhetorical affect in early modern writing. New York : Palgrave Macmillan, 2003.
PR428.E56 C63 2003

RENAISSANCE - EUROPE. See **RENAISSANCE.**

RENAISSANCE - GERMANY.
Renaissance der Kulturgeschichte? Dresden : Verlag der Kunst, 2001.
AM101.B4856 R36 2001

RENAISSANCE - HISTORY. See **RENAISSANCE.**

RENAISSANCE - ITALY.
A companion to the worlds of the Renaissance. Malden, MA : Blackwell Publishers, 2002.
CB367 .C65 2002

Hankins, James. Humanism and platonism in the Italian Renaissance. Roma : Edizioni di storia e letteratura, 2003-

The Renaissance. London ; New York : Routledge, 2003.
DG445 .R565 2003

The Renaissance : Italy and abroad / edited by John Jeffries Martin. London ; New York : Routledge, 2003. xxiii, 328 p. : ill. ; 24 cm. (Rewriting histories) Includes bibliographical references (p. 317-320) and index. ISBN 0-415-26062-0 (hbk. : alk. paper) ISBN 0-415-26063-9 (pbk. : alk. paper) DDC 945/.05
1. Renaissance - Italy. 2. Renaissance. 3. Italy - Civilization - 1268-1559. I. Martin, John Jeffries, 1951- II. Series: Re-writing histories.
DG445 .R565 2003

RENAISSANCE LITERATURE. See **EUROPEAN LITERATURE - RENAISSANCE, 1450-1600.**

Renaissance rivals.
Goffen, Rona, 1944- New Haven : University Press, c2002.
N6915 .G54 2002

Les rendez-vous d'Archimède
Les dons de l'image. Paris : Harmattan, 2003.

Politique et responsabilité, enjeux partagés. Paris : Harmattan ; Lille : Université des sciences et technologies de Lille, 2003.

Renesch, John, 1937-.
Leadership in a new era. New York : Paraview Special Editions, c2002.
BF637.L4 .L395 2002

Renfrew, Colin.
Archaeology. Oxford : Published for The British Academy by Oxford University Press, c2002.

Rengarajan, T., 1962- Dictionary on Indian religions / T. Rengarajan. Delhi : Eastern Book Linkers, 2003. 2 v. ; 25 cm. ISBN 81-7854-023-1 (v. 1) ISBN 81-7854-024-X (v. 2) ISBN 81-7854-022-3 (set)
1. India - Religion - Dictionaries. I. Title.
BL2001.2 .R46 2003

RENNES-LE-CHÂTEAU (FRANCE) - HISTORY - MISCELLANEA.
Douzet, André. Nouvelles lumières sur Rennes-le-Château. Chêne-Bourg (Suisse) : Acquarius, c1998-
BF1434.F8 D69 1998

Rennie Peyton, Pauline, 1952- Dignity at work : eliminate bullying and create a positive working environment / Pauline Rennie Peyton. 1st ed. Hove, East Sussex ; New York : Brunner-Routledge, 2003. p. cm. Includes bibliographical references and index. Table of contents URL: http://www.loc.gov/catdir/toc/ecip044/2003011070.html ISBN 1-58391-237-1 (hbk) ISBN 1-58391-238-X (pbk.) DDC 658.3/82
1. Bullying. 2. Bullying in the workplace. I. Title.
BF637.B85 R46 2003

Renoncement et narcissisme chez Maurice Zundel.
Simonetta, Catherine. Saint-Maurice : Editions Saint-Augustin, c2002.

Renouvier, Charles, 1815-1903.
Memento retrouve. 2002.
Renouvier, Charles, 1815-1903. Sur le peuple, l'église et la république. Paris : Harmattan, c2002.

Sur le peuple, l'église et la république : articles de 1850-1851 / Charles Renouvier ; texte établi et commenté par Laurent Fedi et Raymond Huard. Suivi du, Mémento retrouvé / [Charles Renouvier] ; texte inédit, établi et annoté par Roland Andréani, Laurent Fedi et Jean-Claude Richard. Paris : Harmattan, c2002. 304 p. ; 22 cm. (La philosophie en commun) Includes bibliographical references (p. 289-294). ISBN 2-7475-3700-5 DDC 194
1. Philosophy. 2. Philosophy and religion. I. Fedi, Laurent. II. Andreani, Roland. III. Huard, Raymond. IV. Richard, Jean-Claude. V. Renouvier, Charles, 1815-1903. Mémento retrouvé. 2002. VI. Title. VII. Title: Mémento retrouvé. VIII. Series.

RENOWN. See **FAME.**

RENUNCIATION (PHILOSOPHY).
Caturvedī, Saccidānanda. Vairāgya. Itanagar : Himālayana Pablisārsa, 2000.
BL1239.5.A82 C28 2000

REORGANIZATION OF CORPORATIONS. See **CORPORATE REORGANIZATIONS.**

Repacholi, Betty.
Individual differences in theory of mind. New York : Psychology Press, 2003.
BF723.P48 I53 2003

Repair.
Spelman, Elizabeth V. Boston : Beacon Press, c2002.
BF636 .S689 2002

REPAIR SHOPS, AUTOMOBILE. See **AUTOMOBILE REPAIR SHOPS.**

REPAIRING - PSYCHOLOGICAL ASPECTS.
Spelman, Elizabeth V. Repair. Boston : Beacon Press, c2002.
BF636 .S689 2002

REPARATION - UNITED STATES.
Corlett, J. Angelo, 1958- Race, racism, & reparations. Ithaca : Cornell University Press, c2003.
HT1523 .C67 2003

Le repas du grand homme.
Derroudida, Jacques. Paris : Harmattan, 2002.

Repenser la cure psychanalytique.
Célérier, Marie-Claire. Paris : Dunod, c2002.
RC504 .C454 2002

REPENTANCE.
Schimmel, Solomon. Wounds not healed by time. Oxford ; New York : Oxford University Press, 2002.
BJ1476 .S34 2002

REPENTANCE - JUDAISM.
Cordovero, Moses ben Jacob, 1522-1570. Sefer Mesilot teshuvah. Bene Berak : Daʻat ḳedoshim, 762 [2002]
BM645.R45 C67 2002

Levin, Yitshaḳ, 1938- Sefer Netivot Yitshaḳ. [Bene Beraḳ] : Y. Leyin, [2000-

Lugasi, Yaʻaḳov Yiśraʼel. Mishpete Yiśraʼel. Mahadurah ḥadashah be-tosefet le-ḥag ha-Pesaḥ. Yerushalayim : Y. Y. Lugasi, 761 [2001]

Sefer Shaʻagat Aryeh. Yerushalayim : Yerid ha-sefarim, 761 [2000 or 2001]

Tamari, Meir. Maśa u-matan be-emunah. Yerushalayim : Śimḥonim, [761, 2001]

REPERTORY GRID TECHNIQUE. See also **PERSONAL CONSTRUCT THEORY.**
Fransella, Fay. A manual for repertory grid technique. 2nd ed. Hoboken, NJ : Wiley, c2004.
BF698.8.R38 F72 2004

Jankowicz, Devi. The easy guide to repertory grids. Chichester, West Sussex, England ; Hoboken, N.J. : Wiley, 2003.
BF698.8.R38 J36 2003

REPETITIVE HOMICIDE. See **SERIAL MURDERS.**

Report (Stanford University. Computer Science Dept.)
(no. STAN-CS-93-1482.) Levy, Alon Y. (Alon Yitzchak) Irrelevance reasoning in knowledge based systems [miroform]. [Washington, DC : National Aeronautics and Space Administration] ; Springfield, VA : Available from the National Technical Information Service, [1998]

(STAN- CS-TR-94-1512.) Washington, Richard. Abstraction planning in real time [microform].

Stanford, Calif. : Stanford University, Dept. of Computer Science, [1994] (Springfield, Va. : U.S. Dept. of Commerce, National Technical Information Service).

REPORT WRITING.
Duitch, Suri. The big idea. New York : City Limits Community Information Service, c2002.

Dunn, Dana. A short guide to writing about psychology. Upper Saddle River, NJ : Pearson/Longman, 2003.
BF76.8 .D86 2003

Lanham, Richard A. Analyzing prose. 2nd ed. London ; New York : Continuum, 2003.
PE1421 .L295 2003

Stafford, Kim Robert. The muses among us. Athens : University of Georgia Press, c2003.
PE1408 .S6667 2003

Sternberg, Robert J. The psychologist's companion. 4th ed. Cambridge, U.K. ; New York : Cambridge University Press, 2003.
BF76.8 .S73 2003

REPORT WRITING - STUDY AND TEACHING (HIGHER).
Directed self-placement. Cresskill, N.J. : Hampton Press, c2003.
PE1404 .D57 2003

Reporting discourse, tense, and cognition. Sakita, Tomoko I. 1st ed. Amsterdam ; Boston : Elsevier, 2002.
P301.5.I53 S25 2002

REPRESENTATION IN ADMINISTRATIVE PROCEEDINGS. See **LAWYERS**.

REPRESENTATION, MENTAL. See **MENTAL REPRESENTATION**.

REPRESENTATION OF KNOWLEDGE (INFORMATION THEORY). See **KNOWLEDGE REPRESENTATION (INFORMATION THEORY)**.

REPRESENTATION (PHILOSOPHY).
Hayat, Michaël. Dynamique des formes et représentations. Paris : Harmattan, c2002.
B105.R4 H392 2002

REPRESENTATIONALISM (PHILOSOPHY). See **REPRESENTATION (PHILOSOPHY)**.

REPRESENTATIONISM (PHILOSOPHY). See **REPRESENTATION (PHILOSOPHY)**.

Les représentations des groupes dominants et dominés.
Lorenzi-Cioldi, Fabio, 1955- Grenoble : Presses universitaires de Grenoble, c2002.
HM716 .L674 2002

REPRESENTATIVES IN CONGRESS (UNITED STATES). See **LEGISLATORS - UNITED STATES**.

Representing animals / Nigel Rothfels, editor. Bloomington : Indiana University Press, c2002. xv, 235 p. : ill. ; 25 cm. (Theories of contemporary culture ; v. 26) Includes bibliographical references and index. CONTENTS: A left-handed blow: writing the history of animals / Erica Fudge -- Animals and ideology: the politics of animal protection in Europe / Kathleen Kete -- Dog years, human years / Teresa Mangum -- The moral ecology of wildlife / Andrew C. Isenberg -- What does becoming-animal look like? / Steve Baker -- Watching eyes, seeing dreams, knowing lives / Marcus Bullock -- From wild technology to electric animal / Akira Mizuta Lippit -- Unspeakability, inedibility, and the structures of pursuit in the English foxhunt / Garry Marvin -- Displaying death, animating life: changing fictions of "liveness" from taxidermy to animatronics / Jane Desmond -- Bitches from brazil: cloning and owning dogs through the missyplicity project / Susan McHugh -- Immersed with animals / Nigel Rothfels. ISBN 0-253-34154-X (cloth : alk. paper) ISBN 0-253-21551-X (pbk. : alk. paper) DDC 306.4
1. Human-animal relationships. 2. Animals - Psychological aspects. I. Rothfels, Nigel. II. Series.
QL85 .R46 2002

REPRESSION (PSYCHOLOGY).
Freud, Sigmund, 1856-1939. [Zur Psychopathologie des Alltagslebens. English] The psychopathology of everyday life. New York : Penguin Books, 2003.
BF173 .F82513 2003

REPRODUCING OF SOUND. See **SOUND - RECORDING AND REPRODUCING**.

REPRODUCTION. See **HUMAN REPRODUCTION**.

REPRODUCTION (PSYCHOLOGY). See **MEMORY; MNEMONICS**.

REPRODUCTIVE TECHNOLOGY. See **HUMAN REPRODUCTIVE TECHNOLOGY**.

La république des idées
Menger, Pierre-Michel. Portrait de l'artiste en travailleur. Paris : Seuil, c2002.

REPUGNANCE. See **AVERSION**.

Requiem für ein Kind.
Groben, Joseph. 2. Aufl. Köln : Dittrich, 2002.
BF575.G7 G76 2002

Rereading Freud : psychoanalysis through philosophy / [edited by] Jon Mills. Albany : State University of New York Press, 2004. p. cm. Includes bibliographical references and index. ISBN 0-7914-6047-9 (alk. paper) ISBN 0-7914-6048-7 (pbk. : alk. paper) DDC 150.19/52/092
1. Freud, Sigmund, - 1856-1939. 2. Psychoanalysis and philosophy. I. Mills, Jon, 1964-
BF109.F74 R47 2004

Rescher, Nicholas. Epistemology : an introduction to the theory of knowledge / Nicholas Rescher. Albany : State University of New York Press, c2003. xvii, 406 p. : ill. ; 23 cm. (SUNY series in philosophy) Includes bibliographical references (p. 369-401) and index. ISBN 0-7914-5811-3 (alk. paper) ISBN 0-7914-5812-1 (pbk. : alk. paper) DDC 121
1. Knowledge, Theory of. I. Title. II. Series.
BD161 .R477 2003

Sensible decisions : issues of rational decision in personal choice and public policy / Nicholas Rescher. Lanham, Md. ; Oxford : Rowman & Littlefield Publishers, c2003. ix, 147 p. : ill. ; 24 cm. Includes bibliographical references (p. 141-143) and index. CONTENTS: Homo optans : on the human condition and the burden of choice -- Why be rational? (on the rationale of rationality) -- Is reasoning about values viciously circular? -- Deliberative conservatism -- Predictive incapacity and rational decision -- Dismissing extremely remote possibilities -- Nomic hierarchies and problems of relativism -- Technology, complexity, and social decision -- Is consensus required for a rational social order? -- Risking democracy (some reflections on contemporary problems of political decision) -- Collective responsibility. ISBN 0-7425-1490-0 (cloth : alk. paper) DDC 128/.4
1. Decision making. 2. Political planning. I. Title.
B945.R453 S46 2003

Reschke, Renate.
Asthetik. Hamburg : Kovač, c2002.

RESEARCH. See **LEARNING AND SCHOLARSHIP; MARKETING RESEARCH**.

Research and Education Association.
The best test preparation for the Advanced Placement Examination. Piscataway, N.J. : Research & Education Association, c2003.
BF78 .B48 2003

The best test preparation for the CLEP, College-Level Examination Program, human growth & development. Piscataway, N.J. : Research & Education Association, c2003.
BF713 .B49 2003

Research and teaching in rhetoric and composition Directed self-placement. Cresskill, N.J. : Hampton Press, c2003.
PE1404 .D57 2003

Research in management.
Leadership. Greenwich, Conn. : Information Age Pub., c2002.
HD57.7 .L4313 2002

Research in multi-level issues
(v. 2) Multi-level issues in organizational behavior and strategy. Amsterdam : London : JAI, 2003.

RESEARCH, INDUSTRIAL. See **MARKETING RESEARCH; NEW PRODUCTS; TECHNOLOGICAL INNOVATIONS**.

Research manual in child development.
Nadelman, Lorraine, 1924- 2nd ed. Mahwah, N.J. : Lawrence Erlbaum Associates, Publishers, 2004.
BF722 .N32 2004

RESEARCH - METHODOLOGY.
Morales Tomas, Marco Antonio. El que busca encuentra = Guatemala : ESEDIR : Editorial Saqil Tzij, 1999.

Valle Bonilla, Otto René. Que no le cuenten cuentos = Guatemala : ESEDIR : Editorial Saqil Tzij, 1999.

Research methods.
Beins, Bernard. Boston : Pearson/Allyn and Bacon, 2003.

BF76.5 .B439 2003
Spata, Andrea. New York : John Wiley & Sons, Inc., c2003.
BF76.5 .S63 2003

Research methods and statistics.
Jackson, Sherri L., 1962- Australia ; Belmont, CA : Thomson/Wadsworth, c2003.
BF76.5 .J29 2003

Research methods and statistics in psychology.
Coolican, Hugh. 3rd ed. London : Hodder & Stoughton, 1999.
BF76.5 .C664 1999

Research methods for the behavioral sciences.
Gravetter, Frederick J. Belmont, CA : Wadsworth, c2003.
BF76.5 .G73 2003

Research monographs in French studies
(12) Britton, Celia. Race and the unconscious. Oxford : Legenda, 2002.

RESEARCH PAPER WRITING. See **REPORT WRITING**.

Research practice for cultural studies.
Gray, Ann, 1946- London ; Thousand Oaks, Calif. : SAGE, 2003.
H62 .G73 2003

Research stories for introductory psychology.
Shaffer, Lary. 2nd ed. Boston, MA : Allyn and Bacon, c2004.
BF76.5 .S43 2004

RESEARCH TEAMS. See **RESEARCH**.

Research to practice
(v. 1) Creativity and music education. Edmonton, Canada : Canadian Music Educators' Association, c2002.

RESEARCHERS, PSYCHIC. See **PARAPSYCHOLOGISTS**.

RESETTLEMENT. See **LAND SETTLEMENT**.

Reshenie problemy kak poisk smyslov.
Matiushkina, A. A. (Anna Alekseevna) Moskva : Izdatel'skiĭ tsentr GUU, 2003.
BF463.M4 M33 2003

RESIDENCES. See **ARCHITECTURE, DOMESTIC; DWELLINGS**.

RESIDENT ALIENS. See **ALIENS**.

RESIDENTIAL BUILDINGS. See **DWELLINGS**.

Resilience.
Deveson, Anne. Crows Nest, NSW : Allen & Unwin, 2003.

Resilience for today : gaining strength from adversity / edited by Edith Henderson Grotberg. Westport, CT : Praeger, 2003. p. cm. (Contemporary psychology) Includes bibliographical references and index. ISBN 0-275-97984-9 (alk. paper) DDC 155.2/32
1. Resilience (Personality trait) I. Grotberg, Edith Henderson, 1928- II. Series: Contemporary psychology (Praeger Publishers)
BF698.35.R47 R47 2003

The resilience of language.
Goldin-Meadow, Susan. New York ; Hove [England] : Psychology Press, 2003.
P118 .G57 2003

RESILIENCE (PERSONALITY TRAIT).
Brooks, Robert B. The power of resilience. Chicago : Contemporary Books, c2004.
BF698.35.R47 B76 2004

Deveson, Anne. Resilience. Crows Nest, NSW : Allen & Unwin, 2003.

Pearsall, Paul. The Beethoven factor. Charlottesville, VA : Hampton Roads Pub. Co., c2003.
BF698.35.R47 P43 2003

Resilience for today. Westport, CT : Praeger, 2003.
BF698.35.R47 R47 2003

RESILIENCE (PERSONALITY TRAIT) - PROBLEMS, EXERCISES, ETC.
Brooks, Robert B. The power of resilience. Chicago : Contemporary Books, c2004.
BF698.35.R47 B76 2004

RESILIENCY (PERSONALITY TRAIT). See **RESILIENCE (PERSONALITY TRAIT)**.

Résistance au chaos.
Vidal, Jordi. Paris : Allia, 2002.

Resistance (Psychoanalysis)

RESISTANCE (PSYCHOANALYSIS).
Pressfield, Steven. The war of art. Warner Books ed. New York : Warner Books, c2002, (2003 printing).
BF408 .P69 2003

RESISTANCE TO GOVERNMENT. *See* **GOVERNMENT, RESISTANCE TO.**

RESISTERS, DRAFT. *See* **DRAFT RESISTERS.**

RESOLUTENESS (PERSONALITY TRAIT). *See* **DETERMINATION (PERSONALITY TRAIT).**

RESOUNDING VASES. *See* **VASES, ACOUSTIC.**

RESPECT FOR PERSONS. *See* **SELF-ESTEEM.**

RESPECT FOR PERSONS (JEWISH LAW).
Adler, Yitshak Eliyahu, ha-Kohen. Sefer Kibud ve-hidur. Ofakim : Y.E. ha-Kohen Adler, 754 [1994]

Respondents, operants, and emergents [microform].
Rumbaugh, Duane M., 1929- [Washington, D.C. : National Aeronautics and Space Administration, 1997]

RESPONSA - 1900-.
Rozner, Shelomoh. Sh. u-t. La-hafets be-hayim. Mahad. 3, be-tosefet 13 she'elot be-helek 3. Yerushalayim : Kolel shemirat ha-lashon : le-hasig, Sh. Rozner, 762 [2001 or 2002]

La responsabilidad de los medios de comunicación.
Fernández Christlieb, Fátima. 1a. ed. México : Paidós, 2002.

The response of discourse ethics to the moral challenge of the human situation as such and especially today.
Apel, Karl-Otto. Leuven : Peeters, 2001.
BJ1012 .A64 2001

RESPONSIBILITY.
Archives and the public good. Westport, Conn. ; London : Quorum Books, 2002.

Corlett, J. Angelo, 1958- Responsibility and punishment. Dordrecht ; Boston : Kluwer Academic Publishers, c2001.
BJ1451 .C67 2001

Fernández Christlieb, Fátima. La responsabilidad de los medios de comunicación. 1a. ed. México : Paidós, 2002.

Hurley, S. L. (Susan L.) Justice, luck, and knowledge. Cambridge, Mass. : Harvard University Press, 2003.
BJ1451 .H87 2003

Mark, Shelomoh Zalman ben Nehemyah. Sefer Ma'aseh uman. Yerushalayim : Nahalat kolel "Bet ulpana de-rabenu Yohanan, 763 [2002 or 2003]

Miller, John G., 1958- QBQ!. Denver, CO : Denver Press, c2001.
BF611 .M55 2001

Moral responsibility and alternative possibilities. Aldershot, England ; Burlington, VT : Ashgate, c2003.
BJ1451 .M6472 2003

Politique et responsabilité, enjeux partagés. Paris : Harmattan ; Lille : Université des sciences et technologies de Lille, 2003.

Reemtsma, Jan Philipp. Wie hätte ich mich verhalten? München : Beck, c2001.
HM216 .R38 2001

Responsibility and punishment.
Corlett, J. Angelo, 1958- Dordrecht ; Boston : Kluwer Academic Publishers, c2001.
BJ1451 .C67 2001

Ressler, Paula. Dramatic changes : talking about sexual orientation and gender identity with high school students through drama / Paula Ressler. Portsmouth, NH : Heinemann, c2002. xi, 124 p. : ill. ; 23 cm. Includes bibliographical references (p. 119-124). CONTENTS: Introduction -- Role plays -- Scripted dramas -- Multi-faceted and extended dramas -- Socially critical drama approaches. ISBN 0-325-00414-5 (acid-free paper) DDC 306.76/6/0712 1. Drama in education. 2. Homosexuality and education. 3. Gender identity. 4. Role playing. I. Title. II. Title: Talking about sexual orientation and gender identity with high school students through drama
PN3171 .R47 2002

Restall, Matthew, 1964- Seven myths of the Spanish conquest / Matthew Restall. Oxford ; New York : Oxford University Press, 2003. xix, 218 p. : ill., maps 25 cm. Includes bibliographical references (p. 161-207) and index. ISBN 0-19-516077-0 DDC 980/.013/072 1. Mexico - History - Conquest, 1519-1540 - Historiography. 2. Spaniards - America - Historiography. 3. Latin America - History - Errors, inventions, etc. 4. Myth. I. Title.

F1230 .R47 2003

RESTITUTION (CRIMINAL PROCEDURE). *See* **REPARATION.**

RESTITUTION FOR VICTIMS OF CRIME. *See* **REPARATION.**

RESTORATIVE JUSTICE.
Burying the past. Expanded and updated. Washington, D.C. : Georgetown University Press, c2003.
JC578 .B49 2003

Restore your magnificence.
Rubino, Joe. 1st ed. Boxford, Mass. : Vision Works Pub., c2003.
BF697.5.S46 R83 2003

RESURRECTION.
Babarinde, A. O. The end of man. Lagos, Nigeria : Christ Foundation Baptist Church, 2001.
1. Black author.

RETAIL ADVERTISING. *See* **ADVERTISING.**

RETAIL MARKETING. *See* **MARKETING.**

RETAIL TRADE. *See* **ADVERTISING.**

RETAIL TRADE - MARKETING. *See* **MARKETING.**

RETAIL TRADE - UNITED STATES.
United States. General Accounting Office. Federal Trade Commission [electronic resource]. [Washington, D.C.] : U.S. General Accounting Office, [2002]

RETAILING. *See* **RETAIL TRADE.**

RETARDED READERS. *See* **READING DISABILITY.**

RETENTION (PSYCHOLOGY). *See* **MEMORY.**

Rethinking implicit memory / edited by Jeffrey S. Bowers and Chad J. Marsolek. Oxford ; New York : Oxford University Press, c2003. xii, 350 p. : ill. ; 25 cm. Includes bibliographical references and index. Table of contents URL: http://www.loc.gov/catdir/toc/fy035/2002075722.html ISBN 0-19-263233-7 (hbk. : alk. paper) ISBN 0-19-263232-9 (pbk. : alk. paper) DDC 616.8/4 1. Memory disorders. 2. Memory. I. Bowers, Jeffrey S. II. Marsolek, Chad J.
RC394.M46 R485 2003

Rethinking the Western tradition
Mill, John Stuart, 1806-1873. On liberty. New Haven : Yale University Press, c2003.
JC585 .M76 2003

Retire your family karma.
Bedi, Ashok. Berwick, Me. : Nicolas-Hays, 2003.
BF637.S4 B423 2003

RETIRED MILITARY PERSONNEL. *See* **VETERANS.**

RETIREMENT. *See also* **DISABILITY RETIREMENT.**
Questions and answers about disability and service retirement plans under the Americans with Disabilities Act (ADA) [electronic resource]. [Washington, D.C.] : U.S. Equal Employment Opportunity Commission, [1995]

RETIREMENT, DISABILITY. *See* **DISABILITY RETIREMENT.**

Retomemos la palabra - .
Guoron Ajquijay, Pedro. Guatemala, Guatemala : Editorial Saqil Tzij, 1995.

RETRIBUTION. *See also* **PUNISHMENT; REVENGE.**
Corlett, J. Angelo, 1958- Responsibility and punishment. Dordrecht ; Boston : Kluwer Academic Publishers, c2001.
BJ1451 .C67 2001

Retroprospectivas psicológicas : desafíos disciplinarios frente a la realidad social contemporánea / Marcela Rivera Hutinel, ed. ; Jean de Munck ... [et al.]. Santiago : Ediciones UCSH, [2002] 103 p. ; 22 cm. (Colección Monografías y textos) Includes bibliographical references (p. 103). ISBN 9567947023 1. Psychology - Practice. 2. Psychology - Social aspects. 3. Psychology - Philosophy. 4. Psychology - Chile. I. Rivera Hutinel, Marcela. II. Munck, Jean de. III. Series: Colección Monografías y textos.
BF75 .R48 2002

Return.
(Re)-turn. Columbia, Mo. : University of Missouri Press, 2003-
BF173.L15 R48

The return of King Arthur.
Durham, Diana. New York : Jeremy P. Tarcher/Penguin, 2004.
BF637.S4 D88 2004

Return of the children of light.
Polich, Judith Bluestone, 1948- Santa Fe, N.M. : Linkage Publications, c1999.
BF1812.P4 P65 1999

Reunion.
Ezell, Jessica. Walpole, NH : Stillpoint Pub., c1996.
BF1283.E94 A3 1996

Revadim 'elyonim ba-minhal ha-tsiburi ha-Yiśre'eli.
Frankenburg, Reuven. [Israel : h. mo. l., 1999?]

Revah, Frédéric.
Klarsfeld, André. [Biologie de la mort. English] The biology of death. Ithaca, NY : Comstock Pub. Associates/Cornell University Press, 2004.
QH530 .K5613 2004

Revealing the inner worlds of young children : the MacArthur story stem battery and parent-child narratives / edited by Robert N. Emde, Dennis P. Wolf, David Oppenheim. New York : Oxford University Press, 2003. viii, 407 p. : ill. ; 24 cm. Includes bibliographical references and index. CONTENTS: Early narratives : a window to the child's inner world / Robert N. Emde -- Making meaning from emotional exprience in early narratives / Dennis Palmer Wolf -- The MacArthur story stem battery : development, administration, reliability, validity, and reflections about meaning / Inge Bretherton and David Oppenheim -- The MacArthur narrative coding system : one approach to highlighting affective meaning making in the MacArthur story stem battery / JoAnn L. Robinson and Linda Mantz-Simmons -- Narrative emotion coding system (NEC) / Susan L. Warren -- The structure of 5-year-old children's play narratives within the MacArthur story stem methodology / Kai von Klitzing, Kim Kelsay, and Robert N. Emde -- Temperament and guilt representations in children's narratives / Nazan Aksan and H.H. Goldsmith -- Children's emotional resolution of MSSB narratives : relations with child behavior problems and parental psychological distress / David Oppenheim -- An attachment perspective on children's emotion narratives : links across generations / Miriam Steele ... [et al.] -- Emotional apprenticeships : the development of affect regulation during the preschool years / Eva Appelman and Dennie Palmer Wolf -- Portrayals in maltreated children's play narratives : representations or emotion regulation? / Robert B. Clyman -- Narratives in risk and clinical populations / Susan L. Warren -- Mental representations and defences in severely maltreated children : a story stem battery and rating system for clinical assessment and research applications / Jill Hodges ... [et al.] -- The mother-child co-construction of an event lived by the preschool child : the role of the mother's knowledge of "what happened" / Christine Gertsch Bettens, Nicolas Favez, and Daniel N. Stern -- Patterns of maternal affect regulation during the co-construction of preschoolers' autobiographical narratives / Nicolas Favez -- Relationships and interactions of mothers and metaplot with 3-year-old kibbutz children in two functional contexts / R. Landau ... [et al.] -- Dialogues of 7-year-olds with their mothers about emotional events : development of a typology / Nina Koren-Karie ... [et al.] -- Affective meaning making among young peers in narrative co-constructions / Ora Aviezer. ISBN 0-19-515404-5 (cloth : alk. paper) DDC 155.4/13 1. Storytelling ability in children. 2. Cognition in children. 3. Children - Language. I. Emde, Robert N. II. Wolf, Dennie. III. Oppenheim, David.
BF723.S74 A37 2003

REVELATION OF SELF. *See* **SELF-DISCLOSURE.**

The revelation of the Monk of Eynsham.
Adam, of Eynsham, fl. 1196-1232. [Visio Monachi de Eynsham. English (Middle English) & Latin] Oxford : Published for the Early English Text Society by the Oxford University Press, 2002.

REVENGE - HUMOR.
Shulman, Mark, 1962- The voodoo revenge book. New York : Main Street, c2002.
BF637.R48 S55 2002

REVENGE - MISCELLANEA.
Silverman, Stephen M. Envy, anger & sweet revenge. New York : Red Rock Press, c2002.
BF575.E65 S55 2002

Revenge of the whale.
Philbrick, Nat. New York : G.P. Putnam, 2002.
G530.E77 P454 2002

Reverse ritual.
Steiner, Rudolf, 1861-1925. Great Barrington, MA : Anthroposophic Press, c2001.
BP595.S894 R48 2001

Revised manual and handbook of interpretations for the Comrey Personality Scales.
Comrey, Andrew Laurence. San Diego, Calif. : EdITS, c1995.
BF698.8.C66 C66 1995

Revisions.
Adkins, Lisa, 1966- Buckingham [UK] ; Philadelphia : Open University Press, 2002.
HQ1075 .A24 2002

REVIVAL OF LETTERS. See **RENAISSANCE.**

Revoir, Katherine Q. Spiritual doodles & mental leapfrogs : a playbook for unleashing spiritual self-expression / Katherine Q. Revoir. Boston, MA : Red Wheel, 2002. vii, 150 p. : ill. ; 25 cm. ISBN 1-59003-029-X (alk. paper)
1. Self-disclosure - Problems, exercises, etc. 2. Drawing - Psychological aspects. 3. Spiritual exercises. I. Title. II. Title: Spiritual doodles and mental leapfrogs
BF697.5.S427 R48 2002

REVOLUTION, AMERICAN. See **UNITED STATES - HISTORY - REVOLUTION, 1775-1783.**

REVOLUTIONARY WAR, AMERICAN. See **UNITED STATES - HISTORY - REVOLUTION, 1775-1783.**

REVOLUTIONS. See also **CIVIL WAR; GOVERNMENT, RESISTANCE TO; INSURGENCY.**
Klosko, George. Jacobins and utopians. Notre Dame, Ind. : University of Notre Dame Press, c2003.
JC491 .K54 2003

Les révolutions et les cycles.
Ikhwān al-Ṣafā'. [Rasā'il. 36. French & Arabic] Louvain-la-Neuve : Bruylant-Academia ; Beyrouth : Al-Bouraq Editions, 1996.

Revzin, G. I. (Grigoriĭ I.) Ocherki po filosofii arkhitekturnoĭ formy / G. Revzin. Moskva : O.G.I., 2002. 141 p. ; 22 cm. Includes bibliographical references. ISBN 594182083X
1. Architecture - Philosophy. I. Title.
NA2500 .R464 2002

Reyes, Arnoldo Juan. Una alternativa para ser feliz / Arnoldo Juan Reyes. Ciudad de La Habana, Cuba : Editorial Científico-Técnica, 2001, c2000. 85 p. ; 18 cm. (Pinos nuevos. Divulgación científico-técnica) Series statement from cover. ISBN 9590502652
1. Interpersonal relations. 2. Self-realization. 3. Happiness. I. Title. II. Series.

Reynolds, Cecil R., 1952-.
Handbook of psychological and educational assessment of children. 2nd ed. New York, N.Y. : Guilford Press, 2003.
BF722 .H33 2003

Handbook of psychological and educational assessment of children. 2nd ed. New York : Guilford Press, 2003.
BF722 .H33 2003b

Reynolds, David K. A handbook for constructive living / David K. Reynolds. Honolulu : University of Hawaii Press, 2002. xx, 293 p. ; 22 cm. Originally published: New York : W. Morrow, 1995. Includes bibliographical references (p. [281]-284) and index. ISBN 0-8248-2600-0 (pbk. : alk. paper) DDC 158.1
1. Morita psychotherapy. 2. Naikan psychotherapy. 3. Conduct of life. I. Title.
RC489.M65 R438 2002

RGS-IBG book series
Allen, John, 1951- Lost geographies of power. Malden, MA ; Oxford : Blackwell Pub., 2003.
GF50 .A453 2003

Rham, Cat de. The spirit of yoga / by Cat de Rham & Michèle Gill. London : Thorsons, 2001. xv, 208 p. : ill. ; 21 cm. Includes bibliographical references. ISBN 0-00-710882-6 DDC 181.452
1. Patañjali. - Yogasūtra. 2. Yoga. I. Gill, Michèle. II. Title.

Rheinheimer, Martin.
Die Psychohistorie des Erlebens. Kiel : Oetker-Voges, c2000.

RHETORIC. See also **CRITICISM; EXPRESSION; NARRATION (RHETORIC); PERSUASION (RHETORIC).**
Filosofía, retórica e interpretación. México, D.F. : Universidad Nacional Autónoma de México, 2000.

Rhetoric and public affairs series
Rowland, Robert C., 1954- Shared land/conflicting identity. East lansing : Michigan State University Press, 2002.

DS119.7 .R685 2003

RHETORIC, MEDIEVAL.
Gendering the master narrative. Ithaca : Cornell University Press, c2003.
HQ1143 .G46 2003

Thompson, Anne Booth. Everyday saints and the art of narrative in the South English legendary. Aldershot, England ; Burlington, Vt. : Ashgate, c2003.
PR2143.S543 T48 2003

RHETORIC - PHILOSOPHY.
Carter, Michael, 1950 Aug. 8- Where writing begins. Carbondale : Southern Illinois University Press, c2003.
P301 .C29 2003

RHETORIC - POLITICAL ASPECTS - UNITED STATES - HISTORY - 18TH CENTURY.
Trees, Andrew S., 1968- The founding fathers and the politics of character. Princeton, N.J. : Princeton University Press, c2004.
E302.1 .T74 2004

RHETORIC - STUDY AND TEACHING.
Carter, Michael, 1950 Aug. 8- Where writing begins. Carbondale : Southern Illinois University Press, c2003.
P301 .C29 2003

Rhetorical affect in early modern writing.
Cockcroft, Robert, 1939- New York : Palgrave Macmillan, 2003.
PR428.E56 C63 2003

Rhetorical philosophy and theory
Carter, Michael, 1950 Aug. 8- Where writing begins. Carbondale : Southern Illinois University Press, c2003.
P301 .C29 2003

La rhétorique des stoïciens.
Protopapas-Marneli, Maria. Paris : Harmattan, c2002.

Rhijn, Carine van.
Topographies of power in the early Middle Ages. Leiden ; Boston : Brill, 2001.
D117 .T67 2001

Rhodes, Gillian.
Perception of faces, objects, and scenes. Oxford ; New York : Oxford University Press, 2003.
BF241 .P434 2003

Rhodes, Henry T. F. (Henry Taylor Fowkes), b. 1892.
Le génie et le crime / Henry T.-F. Rhodes. Paris, France : Harmattan, c2002. 220 p. ; 22 cm. (Collection Psychanalyse et civilisations. Série Trouvailles et retrouvailles) ISBN 2-7475-3355-7 DDC 364
1. Genius. 2. Criminals. 3. Criminal psychology. 4. Genius and mental illness. I. Title. II. Series. III. Series: Psychanalyse et civilisations. Série Trouvailles et retrouvailles.

Rhodes, James M. Eros, wisdom, and silence : Plato's erotic dialogues / James M. Rhodes. Columbia, Mo. : University of Missouri Press, c2003. xiv, 573 p. ; 25 cm. (Eric Voegelin Institute series in political philosophy) Includes bibliographical references (p. 549-558) and indexes. ISBN 0-8262-1459-2 (alk. paper) DDC 177/.7
1. Plato. 2. Love. 3. Silence (Philosophy) I. Title. II. Series.
B398.L9 .R46 2003

Rhodes, Jewell Parker. Douglass' women : a novel / Jewell Parker Rhodes. New York, NY : Atria Books, c2002. 358 p. ; 25 cm. Includes bibliographical references (p. [357]-358). ISBN 0-7434-1009-2
1. Douglass, Frederick, - 1818-1895 - Fiction. 2. Douglass, Anna Murray, - d. 1882 - Fiction. 3. Assing, Ottilie - Fiction. 4. Man-woman relationships. 5. American fiction - African American authors. 6. Autobiographical fiction. 7. Black author. I. Title.

Rhodes, Nancy.
Vint/age 2001 conference : [videorecording]. New York, c2001.

Rhonheimer, Martin, 1950- Die Perspektive der Moral : philosophische Grundlagen der Tugendethik / Martin Rhonheimer. Berlin : Akademie Verlag, c2001. 398 p. ; 25 cm. The first edition of this book was published 1994 translated into Italian under the title "La prospettiva della morale" by Armando ; the second version was published 2000 in a Spanish translation. This title presents the German original in an updated and extended version. Includes bibliographical references (p. [369]-382) and index. ISBN 3-05-003629-X (hd.bd.)
1. Thomas, - Aquinas, Saint, - 1225?-1274 - Ethics. 2. Aristotle - Ethics. 3. Ethics. I. Rhonheimer, Martin, 1950- Prospettiva della morale. II. Title.

Prospettiva della morale.
Rhonheimer, Martin, 1950- Die Perspektive der Moral. Berlin : Akademie Verlag, c2001.

Ri͡azanova, T͡atʹi͡ana.
Razvitie natsionalʹnoĭ, ėtnolingvisticheskoĭ i religioznoĭ identichnosti u deteĭ i podrostkov = Moskva : In-t psikhologii RAN, 2001.
BF723.C5 R39 2001

Ricciardi, Alessia. The ends of mourning : psychoanalysis, literature, film / Alessia Ricciardi. Stanford, Calif. : Stanford University Press, 2003. x, 266 p. ; 23 cm. (Cultural memory in the present) Includes bibliographical references (p. [207]-257) and index. ISBN 0-8047-4776-8 (cloth : alk. paper) ISBN 0-8047-4777-6 (pbk. : alk. paper) DDC 809/.933548
1. Death in literature. 2. Literature, Modern - History and criticism. 3. Death in motion pictures. 4. Death - Psychological aspects. 5. Bereavement - Psychological aspects. I. Title. II. Series.
PN56.D4 R53 2003

Ricerche (Carocci editore)
(114.) Ledda, Antonio. La fenomenologia tra essenza ed esistenza. 1. ed. Roma : Carocci editore, 2002.

Ricerche (Carocci editore). Filosofia.
Ledda, Antonio. La fenomenologia tra essenza ed esistenza. 1. ed. Roma : Carocci editore, 2002.

Ricerche (Meltemi editore)
(21.) Pompeo, Francesco. Il mondo è poco. Roma : Meltemi, c2002.
GN495.6 .P66 2002

Rich, Cynthia.
Macdonald, Barbara, 1913- Look me in the eye. New, expanded ed. Denver, CO : Spinsters Ink Books, 2001.

RICH PEOPLE. See **MILLIONAIRES.**

Richard, Jean-Claude.
Renouvier, Charles, 1815-1903. Sur le peuple, l'église et la république. Paris : Harmattan, c2002.

Richards, P. M., 1962-.
Madigan, M. A., 1962- Symbols of the craft. 1st ed. St. Paul, Minn. : Llewellyn Publications, 2003.
BF1773 .M29 2003

Richards, Rand, 1949-.
Haunted San Francisco. 1st ed. San Francisco : Heritage House Publishers, 2004.
BF1472.U6 H385 2004

Richardson, Denise.
Vint/age 2001 conference : [videorecording]. New York, c2001.

RICHARDSON, DENISE.
Vint/age 2001 conference : [videorecording]. New York, c2001.

Richardson, James T., 1941-.
Challenging religion. London ; New York : Routledge, 2003.
BL60 .C437 2003

Richardson, John, 1966-.
Raiffa, Howard, 1924- Negotiation analysis. Cambridge, MA : Belknap Press of Harvard University Press, 2002.
HD58.6 .R342 2002

Richardson, Judith. Possessions : the history and uses of haunting in the Hudson Valley / Judith Richardson. Cambridge, Mass. : Harvard University Press, 2003. xi, 296 p. : ill., maps ; 23 cm. Includes bibliographical references (p. 211-286) and index. ISBN 0-674-01161-9 (alk. paper) DDC 133.1/09747/7
1. Ghosts - Hudson River Valley (N.Y. and N.J.) 2. Haunted places - Hudson River Valley (N.Y. and N.J.) 3. Ghosts in literature. 4. Hudson River Valley (N.Y. and N.J.) - Social life and customs. I. Title.
BF1472.U6 R54 2003

Richardson, S. Cheryl. Magicka formularia : a study in formulary magick / S. Cheryl Richardson. [Miami, Fla.] : S.C. Richardson, c2001. xvi, 137 p. : ill. ; 28 cm. Includes bibliographical references (p. 134) and index.
1. Magic. 2. Witchcraft. 3. Charms. I. Title.
BF1611 .R53 2001

Richmond, Virginia P., 1949- Nonverbal behavior in interpersonal relations / Virginia P. Richmond, James C. McCroskey. 5th ed. Boston, Mass. : Pearson, 2004. p. cm. Includes bibliographical references and index. ISBN 0-205-37246-5 (alk. paper) DDC 153.6/9
1. Body language. 2. Interpersonal relations. I. McCroskey, James C. II. Title.
BF637.N66 R53 2004

Richter-Appelt, Hertha.
Verführung, Trauma, Missbrauch. [2. Aufl.]. Giessen : Psychosozial-Verlag, c2002.

Richter, Helmut, 1935-.
Botschaften verstehen. Frankfurt am Main ; New York : P. Lang, c2000.
P91.25 .B688 2000

Rickels, Laurence A. Nazi psychoanalysis / Laurence A. Rickels ; foreword by Benjamin Bennett. Minneapolis : University of Minnesota Press, c2002- 3 v. : ill. ; 24 cm. "Three-volume project"--Foreword. Includes bibliographical references and index. Includes filmography. PARTIAL CONTENTS: v. 1. Only psychoanalysis won the war -- v. 2. Crypto-fetishism -- v. 3. Psy fi. ISBN 0-8166-3697-4 (pbk. : alk. paper : v. 1) ISBN 0-8166-3696-6 (alk. paper : v. 1) ISBN 0-8166-3699-0 (pbk. : v. 2) ISBN 0-8166-3698-2 (cloth : v. 2) ISBN 0-8166-3701-6 (paper : v. 3) ISBN 0-8166-3700-8 (cloth : v. 3) DDC 150.19/5/0943
1. Psychoanalysis - Germany - History. 2. Psychoanalysis - Political aspects - Germany - History. 3. National socialism - History. I. Title.
BF173 .R49 2002

Ricketson, Sam.
Monotti, Ann Louise. Universities and intellectual property. Oxford ; New York : Oxford University Press, 2003.
KF4225.U55 M66 2003

Rickheit, Gert.
Psycholinguistik. Berlin : W. de Gruyter, c2003.

Sprache, Sinn und Situation. 1. Aufl. Wiesbaden : Deutscher Universitäts-Verlag, 2001.

Ricklef, James, 1954- Tarot tells the tale : explore three-card readings through familiar stories / James Ricklef. St. Paul, Minn. : Llewellyn Publications, 2003. p. cm. Includes bibliographical references. ISBN 0-7387-0272-2 DDC 133.3/2424
1. Tarot. I. Title.
BF1879.T2 R53 2003

Ricœur, Paul.
Changeux, Jean-Pierre. [Ce qui nous fait penser. English] What makes us think? Princeton, N.J. : Princeton University Press, c2000.
BJ45 .C4313 2000

RICŒUR, PAUL.
Gilbert, Muriel. L'identité narrative. Genève : Labor et Fides, c2001.

Piazza, Giovanni. Sofferenza e senso. Torino : Camilliane, c2002.

RICŒUR, PAUL - INFLUENCE.
Gavalchin, John. Temporality in music. 2000.

RICŒUR, PAUL - INTERVIEWS.
Changeux, Jean-Pierre. [Ce qui nous fait penser. English] What makes us think? Princeton, N.J. : Princeton University Press, c2000.
BJ45 .C4313 2000

Ricot, Jacques. Leçon sur L'éthique à Nicomaque, d'Aristote : livres sur l'amitié / par Jacques Ricot. 1re ed. Paris : Presses universitaires de France, c2001. 131 p. ; 17 cm. (Collection Major) ISBN 2-13-052100-2 DDC 100
1. Aristotle. - Nicomachean ethics. 2. Philosophy, Ancient. I. Title. II. Series.
B430 .R536 2001

Ridder, Klaus.
Kunst und Erinnerung. Köln : Böhlau, 2003.
PN674 .K86 2003

Ridderschap in Holland.
Janse, A. Hilversum : Verloren, 2001.
DJ152 .J26 2001

Rider, Elizabeth A. Our voices : psychology of women / Elizabeth A. Rider. Belmont, CA : Wadsworth, c2000. xv, 608 p. : ill. ; 23 cm. Includes bibliographical references (p. [559]-591) and indexes. ISBN 0-534-34681-2 DDC 305.4
1. Women - Psychology. 2. Women - Social conditions - Psychological aspects. 3. Sex role - Psychological aspects. 4. Feminist psychology. I. Title.
HQ1206 .R54 2000

RIDICULOUS, THE. See COMIC, THE; WIT AND HUMOR.

Riding the next wave : why this century will be a golden age for workers, the environment, and developing countries / edited by Thomas J. Duesterberg and Herbert I. London. Indianapolis, Ind. : Hudson Institute ; [Washington, DC : Distributed by the Brookings Institution Press], c2001. ix, 238 p. : ill. ; 24 cm. Includes bibliographical references (p. 211-233). CONTENTS: The great transition and the long term perspective / Thomas J. Duesterberg and Herbert I. London -- World population prospects to the year 2025 : declining fertility, aging societies, and health setbacks / Nicholas Eberstadt -- The biotech breakthrough / Michael Fumento -- High-tech help for the environment / Dennis T. Avery -- The future of space exploration / James C. Bennett -- Prairies with lampposts or centers of civil society? : the future of the city--if any / John C. Weicher -- The future of the state / Robert Dujarric -- How values shape the future / Herbert I. London. ISBN 1-55813-090-X DDC 303.49
1. Social prediction. 2. Economic forecasting. 3. Twenty-first century - Forecasts. 4. Population forecasting. 5. Sustainable development. 6. Progress - Forecasting. 7. Developing countries - Forecasting. 8. Social values. I. Duesterberg, Thomas James, 1950- II. London, Herbert Ira. III. Hudson Institute. IV. Title: Why this century will be a golden age for workers, the environment, and developing countries
HM901 .R43 2001

Ridley, Matt. Nature via nurture : genes, experience, and what makes us human / Matt Ridley. 1st ed. New York : HarperCollins, c2003. 326 p. ; 24 cm. Includes bibliographical references (p. [283]-306) and index. ISBN 0-06-000678-1 DDC 155.7
1. Nature and nurture. 2. Human genetics. I. Title.
QH438.5 .R535 2003

Rieber, Arnulf, 1935-.
Roehle, Friedrich, 1916-1995. Die Struktur des Bewusstseins. Frankfurt am Main ; New York : Peter Lang, c2001.

Rieder, Jonathan.
The fractious nation? Berkeley : University of California Press, c2003.
E169.12 .F69 2003

Rieger, Stefan.
Die Unvermeidlichkeit der Bilder. Tübingen : G. Narr, c2001.
N72.A56 U58 2001x

Riegler, Alexander.
Virtual reality. Frankfurt am Main ; New York : P. Lang, c2001.
QA76.9.H85 V5815 2001

Riemann, Rainer.
Personality and temperament: genetics, evolution, and structure. Lengerich : Pabst Science Publishers, 2001.
BF698 .P3692 2001

Ries, Marc, 1956- Medienkulturen / Marc Ries. Wien : Sonderzahl, c2002. 271 p. ; 21 cm. Includes bibliographical references. ISBN 3-85449-203-0 (pbk.)
1. Mass media and culture. 2. Popular culture. I. Title.
P94.6 .R54 2002

Rifat, Tim, 1957- Remote viewing : what it is, who uses it and how to do it / Tim Rifat. London : Vision, 2001. ix, 278 p. ; 22 cm. Includes bibliographical references (p. 258-267) and index. ISBN 1-901250-96-2 DDC 133.8
1. Remote viewing (Parapsychology) I. Title.

Rifkin, June.
Imberman, Arlyn. Signature for success. Kansas City, Mo. : Andrews McMeel Pub., 2003.
BF891 .I46 2003

Rīgas gaišregis Eižens Finks : raksti par viņu, dokumenti, materiāli / [sastādītājs Boriss Ravdins]. Jauns papildināts izdevums. [Rīga] : Jumava, c2002. 364 p. : ill. ; 21 cm. Includes bibliographical references and index. ISBN 9984055140
1. Finks, Eižens, - 1885-1958. 2. Clairvoyants - Latvia - Biography. 3. Telepathy - Latvia. I. Ravdin, Boris.
BF1283.F55 R66 2002

Rīgas gaišregis Eižens Finks : raksti par viņu, dokumenti, materiāli / [sastādītājs Boriss Ravdins], piedaloties Silvijai Apinei un Jānim Zālītim]. Rīgā : Jumava, c2002. 364 p. : ill. ; 21 cm. Includes index. ISBN 9984055140
1. Finks, Eižens, - 1885-1958. 2. Fortune-tellers - Latvia - Biography. I. Ravdin, Boris. II. Title: Eižens finks
BF1997.F56 R54 2002

Riggins, Chance W.
Blumenthal, Mark. Popular herbs in the U.S. market. Austin : American Botanical Council, 1997.

Riggs-Bergesen, Catherine. Candle therapy : a magical guide to life enhancement / Catherine Riggs-Bergesen. Kansas City, Mo. : Andrews McMeel Pub., c2003. xi, 221 p. : ill. ; 23 cm. Includes bibliographical references. ISBN 0-7407-3855-0 (pbk.) DDC 133.4/3
1. Candles and lights - Miscellanea. 2. Magic. I. Title.
BF1623.C26 R54 2003

RIGHT OF PRIVACY. See PRIVACY, RIGHT OF.

RIGHT OF PROPERTY.
Anderson, Terry Lee, 1946- Property rights. Stanford, Calif. : Hoover Institution Press, c2003.
HB701 .A44 2003

RIGHT (POLITICAL SCIENCE). See CONSERVATISM.

Right risk.
Treasurer, Bill, 1962- San Francisco : Berrett-Koehler, c2003.
BF637.R57 T74 2003

RIGHT TO DIE.
Nosmas, Alma. La mort élégante. Paris : Horay, c2003.

The right words at the right time / Marlo Thomas [editor], and friends. New York : Atria Books, c2002. xv, 381 p. : ill. ; 23 cm. SUMMARY: "For everyone who needs a hero or loves a good story, here is an inspiring collection of personal revelations from more than 100 remarkable men and women who share a moment when words changed their lives"--Jacket. "Marlo Thomas and friends have contributed their stories and royalties ... to St. Jude Children's Research Hospital"--Jacket. Publisher description URL: http://www.loc.gov/catdir/desc ription/simon033/2002510322.html PARTIAL CONTENTS: Contributors: Muhammad Ali, Christine Amanpour, Stephen Ambrose, Jennifer Aniston, Lance Armstrong, Candice Bergen, Jeff Bezos, David Boies, Tom Brokaw, Mel Brooks, Barbara Bush, Laura Bush, President Jimmy Carter, Hillary Rodham Clinton, Chuck Close, Kenneth Cole, Bill Cosby, Katie Couric, Cindy Crarford, Walter Cronkite, Cameron Crowe, Billy Crystal, Ellen DeGeneres, Barry Diller, Peter Doherty, Phil Donahue, Michael Eisner, Daniel Ellsberg, Betty Ford, Diane von Furstenberg, Frank Gehry, Richard Gephardt, Ruth Bader Ginsburg, Rudolph Giuliani, Whoopie Goldberg, William Goldman, Doris Kearns Goodwin, Matt Groening, Uta Hagen, Scott Hamilton, Mia Hamm, David Ho, Ariana Huffington, James Jeffords, Philip Johnson, Quincy Jones, Andrea Jung, David E. Kelley, Billie Jean King, Ted Koppel, Ralph Lauren, Ang Lee, John Leguizamo, Jay Leno, Maya Lin, PARTIAL CONTENTS: David Mamet, Wilma Mankiller, Mary Matalin, Dave Matthews, John McCain, Paul McCartney, Dennis Miller, Toni Morrison, Ralph Nader, Willie Nelson, Paul Newman, Mice Nichols, Jack Nicholson, Conan O'Brien, Rosie O'Donnell, Shaquille O'Neal, Al Pacino, Gwyneth Paltrow, Sarah Jessica Parker, Sean Penn, Itzhak Perlman, Bob Pittman, Sidney Poitier, Vladimir Pozner, Anna Quindlen, Cal Ripken Jr., Dennis Rivers, Chris Rock, Ray Romano, Carlos Santana, Diane Sawyer, Martin Sheen, Ruth Simmons, Carly Simon, Sammy Sosa, Steven Spielberg, George Steinbrenner, Gloria Steinem, Marthha Stewart, Amy Tan, Julie Taymor, Twyla Tharp, Ted Turner, Mike Wallace, Vera Wang, Wendy Wasserstein, Maxine Waters, Venus Williams, Oprah Winfrey, Tom Wolfe, and the Dalai Lama. ISBN 0-7434-4649-6 DDC 170/.44
1. Success. 2. Celebrities - United States. I. Thomas, Marlo.
BJ1611.2 .R52 2002

Rights and wrongs series
Children and human rights. Part 1 [videorecording]. Derry, N.H. : Chip Taylor Communications, 1995.

Peace and conflict resolution. Part 1 [videorecording]. Derry, N.H. : Chip Taylor Communications, 1996.

Peace and conflict resolution. Part 2 [videorecording]. Derry, N.H. : Chip Taylor Communications, 1997.

RIGHTS, CIVIL. See CIVIL RIGHTS.

RIGHTS, HUMAN. See HUMAN RIGHTS.

RIGHTS OF CHILDREN. See CHILDREN'S RIGHTS.

RIGHTS OF MAN. See HUMAN RIGHTS.

RIGHTS OF WOMEN. See WOMEN'S RIGHTS.

RIGHTS, PROPRIETARY. See INTELLECTUAL PROPERTY.

RIGIDITY (PSYCHOLOGY). See STEREOTYPE (PSYCHOLOGY).

RIGNANO, EUGENIO, 1870-1930.
Sava, Gabriella. La psicologia filosofica in Italia. Galatina (Lecce) : Congedo, 2000.
BF38 .S235 2000

Rihani, Samir, 1938- Complex systems theory and development practice : understanding non-linear realities / Samir Rihani ; with a foreword by Hernando de Soto. London ; New York : Zed Books, 2002. xvi, 280 p. ; 23 cm. Includes bibliographical references (p. [264]-270) and index. ISBN 1-84277-046-2 (hb) ISBN 1-84277-047-0 (pbk.) DDC 338.9
1. Economics. 2. Economic development. 3. Economic history. 4. System theory. 5. Complexity (Philosophy) I. Title.
HB71 .R485 2002

Rimskaia, R.
Prakticheskaia psikhologiia v testakh, ili, Kak nauchit'sia ponimat' sebia i drugikh. Moskva : AST-Press kniga, 2003.

BF176 .P73 2003

Rimskiĭ, S.
Prakticheskaia psikhologiia v testakh, ili, Kak nauchit'sia ponimat' sebia i drugikh. Moskva : AST-Press kniga, 2003.
BF176 .P73 2003

Rind, Patricia. Women's best friendships : beyond Betty, Veronica, Thelma, and Louise / Patricia Rind. New York : Haworth Press, c2002. xvi, 183 p. ; 23 cm. Includes bibliographical references (p. 175-179) and index. ISBN 0-7890-1539-0 (alk. paper) ISBN 0-7890-1540-4 (pbk. : alk. paper) DDC 158.2/5/082
1. Female friendship. I. Title.
BF575.F66 R56 2002

Ring, Susan. Needs and wants / by Susan Ring. Mankato, Minn. : Yellow Umbrella Books, c2003. 17 p. : col. ill. ; 21 cm. Includes index. SUMMARY: Presents the things that everyone needs, as well as things some people want, and invites the reader to consider his or her own wants and needs. ISBN 0-7368-2028-0 (hardcover : alk. paper) DDC 153.8
1. Motivation (Psychology) in children - Juvenile literature. 2. Need (Psychology) - Juvenile literature. 3. Desire - Juvenile literature. 4. Motivation (Psychology) 5. Need (Psychology). 6. Desire. I. Title.
BF723.M56 R56 2003

RIOTS. See **DEMONSTRATIONS.**

RIPLEY'S BELIEVE IT OR NOT (NEW YORK : 1965).
Mooney, Julie. The world of Ripley's believe it or not!. New York : Black Dog & Leventhal, c1999.
AG243 .M653 1999

Mooney, Julie. The world of Ripley's believe it or not!. New York : Black Dog & Leventhal, c1999.
AG243 .M653 1999

Rippe, Klaus Peter, 1959-.
Ethik ohne Dogmen. Paderborn : Mentis, 2001.

RIS-MED (LAMAISM). See **BUDDHISM.**

The rise of Western Christendom.
Brown, Peter Robert Lamont. 2nd ed. Malden, MA ; Oxford : Blackwell Publishing, 2003.
BR162.3 .B76 2003

Rishoi, Christy, 1958- From girl to woman : American women's coming-of-age narratives / by Christy Rishoi. Albany : State University of New York Press, c2003. xi, 201 p. ; 23 cm. (SUNY series in feminist criticism and theory) (SUNY series in postmodern culture) Includes bibliographical references (p. 177-190) and index. ISBN 0-7914-5721-4 (alk. paper) ISBN 0-7914-5722-2 (pbk. : alk. paper) DDC 305.42
1. Women's studies - United States - Biographical methods. 2. Women - Identity. 3. Social role. 4. Maturation (Psychology) 5. Self-realization. 6. Autobiography - Women authors. 7. Feminist criticism. I. Title. II. Series. III. Series: SUNY series in postmodern culture
HQ1186.A9 R57 2003

RISING SIGN (ASTROLOGY). See **ASCENDANT (ASTROLOGY).**

RISK.
DiMatteo, Larry A. The law of international business transactions. Mason, OH : Thomson/South-Western West, c2003.
KF915 .D56 2003

Füredi, Frank, 1947- Culture of fear. Rev. ed. London ; New York : Continuum, 2002.
BF575.F2 F86 2002

Gilad, Benjamin. Early warning. New York, NY : American Management Association, c2003.
HD61 .G533 2003

The handbook of risk. Hoboken, N.J. : Wiley, c2003.
HB615 .H266 2003

RISK ASSESSMENT.
Borge, Dan. The book of risk. New York : Wiley, c2001.
HD61 .B647 2001

Greenway, A. Roger. Risk management planning handbook. 2nd ed. Rockville, MD : ABS Consulting, Government Institutes, c2002.
HD61 .G733 2002

RISK BEHAVIOR. See **RISK-TAKING (PSYCHOLOGY).**

RISK MANAGEMENT.
Borge, Dan. The book of risk. New York : Wiley, c2001.
HD61 .B647 2001

Gilad, Benjamin. Early warning. New York, NY : American Management Association, c2003.
HD61 .G533 2003

Greenway, A. Roger. Risk management planning handbook. 2nd ed. Rockville, MD : ABS Consulting, Government Institutes, c2002.
HD61 .G733 2002

The handbook of risk. Hoboken, N.J. : Wiley, c2003.
HB615 .H266 2003

Risk management planning handbook.
Greenway, A. Roger. 2nd ed. Rockville, MD : ABS Consulting, Government Institutes, c2002.
HD61 .G733 2002

RISK-TAKING (PSYCHOLOGY).
Borge, Dan. The book of risk. New York : Wiley, c2001.
HD61 .B647 2001

From child sexual abuse to adult sexual risk. 1st ed. Washington, DC : American Psychological Association, c2004.
RC569.5.A28 F76 2004

Sabalat, Tina. Pascals "Wette". Marburg : Tectum, 2000.

Treasurer, Bill, 1962- Right risk. San Francisco : Berrett-Koehler, c2003.
BF637.R57 T74 2003

Wowisms. 1st ed. New York : Newmarket Press, c2003.
BF637.S8 W7 2003

RISK-TAKING (PSYCHOLOGY) IN ADOLESCENCE - AUSTRALIA - NEW SOUTH WALES.
Suicide & risk-taking deaths of children & young people. Surry Hills, NSW : The Commission, c2003.

RISK-TAKING (PSYCHOLOGY) IN CHILDREN - AUSTRALIA - NEW SOUTH WALES.
Suicide & risk-taking deaths of children & young people. Surry Hills, NSW : The Commission, c2003.

RISK-TAKING (PSYCHOLOGY) - RELIGIOUS ASPECTS - CHRISTIANITY.
Williams, Jaime Andrés. El argumento de la apuesta de Blaise Pascal. 1. ed. Pamplona : Ediciones Universidad de Navarra, 2002.

RISKY BEHAVIOR. See **RISK-TAKING (PSYCHOLOGY).**

Ritchie, Donald A., 1945- Doing oral history : a practical guide / Donald A. Ritchie. 2nd ed. Oxford ; New York : Oxford University Press, c2003. 318 p. ; 24 cm. Includes bibliographical references (p. [261]-303) and index. Includes web resources. CONTENTS: An oral history of our time -- Setting up an oral history project -- Conducting interviews -- Using oral history in research and writing -- Videotaping oral history -- Preserving oral history in archives and libraries -- Teaching oral history -- Presenting oral history. ISBN 0-19-515433-9 (hbk. : alk. paper) ISBN 0-19-515434-7 (pbk. : alk. paper) DDC 907/.2
1. Oral history. 2. Oral history - Methodology. 3. Historiography. I. Title.
D16.14 .R57 2003

RITES AND CEREMONIES. See also **CEREMONIAL EXCHANGE; EXORCISM; FASTS AND FEASTS; FUNERAL RITES AND CEREMONIES; MYSTERIES, RELIGIOUS; SACRAMENTS.**
Aveni, Anthony F. The book of the year. Oxford ; New York : Oxford University Press, 2003.
GT3930 .A94 2003

Caillois, Roger, 1913- The edge of surrealism. Durham : Duke University Press, 2003.
HM590 .C35 2003

Spiraldancer. Moon rites. South Melbourne : [Great Britain] : Lothian, 2002.

RITES AND CEREMONIES - BELARUS.
Kazakova, I. V. (Iryna Valer'eŭna) Mifalahemy i mahiia ŭ belaruskim abradavym fal'klory. Minsk : "BOFF", 1997.
GR203.4 .K39 1997

RITES AND CEREMONIES - CUBA.
Oricha. 1. ed. Barcelona : Editorial Humanitas, 2003.

RITES AND CEREMONIES - GREECE.
Burkert, Walter, 1931- [Wilder Ursprung. English] Savage energies. Chicago : University of Chicago Press, c2001.
BL785 .B8513 2001

RITES AND CEREMONIES - ITALY - TURIN.
Scott, John Beldon, 1946- Architecture for the shroud. Chicago : University of Chicago Press, c2003.
NA5621.T823 S36 2003

RITES AND CEREMONIES - ROME.
Bernstein, Frances. Classical living. 1st ed. San Francisco : HarperSanFrancisco, 2000.
BL808 .B47 2000

RITES OF PASSAGE. See **RITES AND CEREMONIES.**

Ritner, Robert Kriech, 1953-.
Nissinen, Martti. Prophets and prophecy in the ancient Near East. Atlanta, GA : Society of Biblical Literature, c2003.
BF1762 .N58 2003b

Ritter, Kathleen. Handbook of affirmative psychotherapy with lesbians and gay men / Kathleen Y. Ritter, Anthony I. Terndrup ; foreword by Sari H. Dworkin. New York : Guilford Press, c2002. xvi, 493 p. : ill. ; 26 cm. Includes bibliographical references (p. 413-475) and index. CONTENTS: Heterosexism : a fundamental reality -- Concepts of sexual orientation -- Sexual orientations : origins and influences -- Sexual orientation and the law -- Theories of gay, lesbian, and bisexual identity formation -- Issues for sexual minority adolescents -- Midlife and later-life issues for sexual minority adults -- Psychodiagnostic considerations -- Psychotherapeutic applications for identity formation -- Sexual minorities within other minority populations -- Career choice and development with sexual minority clients -- Health and medical concerns -- Religious concerns and spiritual development -- families of origin and coming-out issues -- Understanding same-sex couples -- Sex therapy with gay and lesbian couples -- Families with a gay, lesbian, and bisexual parent. ISBN 1-57230-714-5 (hardcover) DDC 616.89/14/08664
1. Gays - Mental health. 2. Lesbians - Mental health. 3. Psychotherapy. 4. Gays - Mental health services. I. Terndrup, Anthony I. II. Title.
RC451.4.G39 R55 2002

RITUAL. See also **RITES AND CEREMONIES.**
Aoumiel. Grimoire for the green witch. 1st ed. St. Paul, Minn. : Llewellyn Publications, c2003.
BF1572.P43 A583 2003

Conway, D. J. (Deanna J.) Magickal, mystical creatures. 2nd ed. St. Paul, Minn. : Llewellyn Publications, 2003.
BF1623.A55 C67 2003

Cunningham, Scott, 1956- [Wicca. Spanish] Wicca. 1. ed. St. Paul, Minn. : Llewellyn Español, 2003.
BF1566 .C8618 2003

Gruenwald, Ithamar. Rituals and ritual theory in ancient Israel. Leiden ; Boston : Brill, 2003.
BM660 .G78 2003

Sophia, 1955- The ultimate guide to goddess empowerment. Kansas City : Andrews McMeel Pub., c2003.
BF1621 .S67 2003

RITUAL CALENDARS. See **RELIGIOUS CALENDARS.**

The ritual of music contemplation.
Pedroza, Ludim. 2002.

RITUALISM. See **RITES AND CEREMONIES.**

Rituals and ritual theory in ancient Israel.
Gruenwald, Ithamar. Leiden ; Boston : Brill, 2003.
BM660 .G78 2003

Rivalidad y complicidad entre mujeres.
Alborch Bataller, Carmen. Malas. 3. ed. [Madrid] : Aguilar, 2002.

Die Rivalin Gottes.
Klatt, Norbert. Göttingen : N. Klatt, 2000.

River of words : images and poetry in praise of water / edited by Pamela Michael ; introductory essays by Robert Hass and Thacher Hurd. Berkeley, Calif. : Heyday Books, c2003. xviii, 77 p. : col. ill. ; 21 cm. ISBN 1-89077-165-1 (pbk. : alk. paper) DDC 808.81/936
1. Water - Poetry. 2. Children's writings, American. 3. Youths' writings, American. 4. Children's writings. 5. Youths' writings. 6. Water in art. I. Michael, Pamela.
PS595.W374 R58 2003

Rivera Hutinel, Marcela.
Retroprospectivas psicológicas. Santiago : Ediciones UCSH, [2002]
BF75 .R48 2002

Rix, Helmut, 1926- Kleine Schriften : Festgabe für Helmut Rix zum 75. Geburtstag / Helmut Rix ; ausgewählt und herausgegeben von Gerhard Meiser. Bremen : Hempen, 2001. xxv, 402 p. ; 25 cm. Includes

Rizzuto, Ana-María.
bibliographical references and index. 13 German, 1 English, 6 Italian contributions. ISBN 3-934106-17-X (cl.)
1. Language and languages. 2. Linguistics. I. Meiser, Gerhard. II. Title.

Rizzuto, Ana-María. The dynamics of human aggression : theoretical foundations, clinical applications / by Ana-Maria Rizzuto, W.W. Meissner, and Dan H. Buie. New York, NY : Brunner-Routledge, 2003. p. ; cm. Includes bibliographical references and index. Table of contents URL: http://www.loc.gov/catdir/toc/ecip043/2003009528.html CONTENTS: Aggression in psychoanalysis : paradigm shift from drive to motivational theory -- Other theories -- A case of aggression in analysis -- "I always hurt the one I love, and like it" -- The agent of aggressive action -- Aggression as motivation -- Affects and aggression -- Developmental perspectives on aggression -- Aggression in phobic states -- The role of aggression in sadomasochism -- Aggression in the analysis of male hysteria -- Intensive psychotherapy of aggression in a borderline personality -- Aggression in the analytic process : technical considerations. ISBN 0-415-94591-7 (hardcover : alk. paper) DDC 155.2/32
1. Aggressiveness. 2. Psychoanalysis. 3. Aggression - psychology. 4. Psychoanalytic Theory. I. Meissner, W. W. (William W.), 1931- II. Buie, Dan H. III. Title.
BF175.5.A36 R59 2003

Roach, Catherine M., 1965- Mother/nature : popular culture and environmental ethics / Catherine M. Roach. Bloomington, IN : Indiana University Press, c2003. xvi, 221 p. : ill. ; 24 cm. Includes bibliographical references (p. 201-214) and index. ISBN 0-253-34178-7 (alk. paper) ISBN 0-253-21562-5 (pbk. : alk. paper) DDC 304.2
1. Philosophy of nature. 2. Ecology - Philosophy. 3. Popular culture. 4. Environmental ethics. I. Title.
BD581 .R59 2003

Roach, Marilynne K. The Salem witch trials : a day-by-day chronicle of a community under siege / Marilynne K. Roach. 1st Cooper Square Press ed. New York : Cooper Square Press : Distributed by National Book Network, 2002. xlvii, 688 p., [12] p. of plates : ill., maps ; 24 cm. Includes bibliographical references (p. [661]-673) and index. ISBN 0-8154-1221-5 (cloth : alk. paper) DDC 133.4/3/097445
1. Witchcraft - Massachusetts - Salem - History - 17th century. 2. Salem (Mass.) - Social conditions. 3. Trials (Witchcraft) - Massachusetts - Salem. I. Title.
BF1575 .R63 2002

The road to Delphi.
Wood, Michael, 1936- 1st ed. New York : Farrar, Straus and Giroux, 2003.
PN56.O63 W66 2003

The road to Malpsychia.
Milton, Joyce. 1st ed. San Francisco : Encounter Books, 2002.
BF204 .M54 2002

Roads, Michael J. The magic formula : it works! / Michael J. Roads. 1st ed. Cleveland : SilverRoads Pub., 2003. 131 p. ; 22 cm. ISBN 0-9729145-1-X (pbk.) DDC 158
1. Self-actualization (Psychology) - Miscellanea. 2. Self-actualization (Psychology) - Religious aspects. 3. New Age movement. I. Title.
BF637.S4 R575 2003

Roads to recovery : inspiring stories from survivors of illness, accident, and loss / [edited by] Pamela Traynor. St. Leonards, NSW : Allen & Unwin, 1997. xii, 270 p. : ports. ; 20 cm. ISBN 1-86448-195-1 DDC 155.9
1. Determination (Personality trait) 2. Sick - Psychology. 3. Accidents - Psychological aspects. 4. Loss (Psychology) I. Traynor, Pamela, 1941-
BF698.35.D48 R63 1997

Roadways to success.
Williamson, James C. 3rd ed. Upper Saddle River, NJ : Pearson/ Prentice Hall, 2004.
BF637.S8 W5216 2004

Roazen, Paul, 1936- Cultural foundations of political psychology / Paul Roazen. New Brunswick, N.J. : Transaction Publishers, c2003. xv, 295 p. ; 24 cm. Includes bibliographical references and index. ISBN 0-7658-0182-5 (alk. paper) DDC 320/.01/9
1. Political psychology. 2. Political science. 3. Culture. I. Title.
JA74.5 .R63 2003

Robbins, Ken, 1945-.
Caspari, Elizabeth, 1926- Animal life in nature, myth and dreams. Wilmette, Ill. : Chiron Publications, c2003.
BF458 .C37 2003

Robbins, Stephen P., 1943- Decide & conquer : a guide to helping you make better decisions and improve your life and work / Stephen P. Robbins. Upper Saddle River : Prentice Hall Financial Times, 2003. p. cm. Includes bibliographical references and index. ISBN 0-13-142501-3 DDC 658.4/03
1. Decision making. I. Title. II. Title: Decide and conquer
BF448 .R63 2003

Robbins, Trina. Eternally bad : goddesses with attitude / Trina Robbins ; forwarded by Rachael Pollack. Berkeley, Calif. : Conari Press, c2001. xiii, 203 p. : ill. ; 18 cm. Includes bibliographical references (p. [201]-203) and index. ISBN 1-57324-550-X (alk. paper) DDC 291.2/114
1. Goddesses - Miscellanea. I. Title.
BF1623.G63 .R63 2001

Robert, Raymonde.
Texte et théâtralité. Nancy : Presses universitaires de Nancy, 2000.

Roberto, Ned.
Kotler, Philip. Social marketing. 2nd ed. Thousand Oaks, Calif. ; London : Sage Publications, c2002.
HF5414 .K67 2002

Roberts, Albert R.
Handbook of violence. New York : Wiley, c2002.
HM1116 .H36 2002

Roberts, Andrew, 1963- Hitler and Churchill : secrets of leadership / Andrew Roberts. London : Weidenfeld & Nicolson, 2003. xxxiii, 202 p., [24] p. of plates : ill. ; 24 cm. TV tie-in. Includes bibliographical references (p. 185-189) and index. ISBN 0-297-84330-3 DDC 320.922
1. Hitler, Adolf, - 1889-1945. 2. Churchill, Winston S. - (Winston Spencer), - 1874-1965. 3. Leadership. 4. Political leadership. I. Title.

Roberts, Courtney, 1957- Visions of the Virgin Mary : an astrological analysis of divine intercession / Courtney Roberts. St. Paul, Minn. : Llewellyn, 2004. p. cm. Includes bibliographical references. ISBN 0-7387-0503-9 DDC 133.5/8230917
1. Astrology. 2. Mary, Blessed Virgin, Saint - Apparitions and miracles - History - Miscellanea. I. Title.
BF1729.R4 R63 2004

Roberts, Mark S.
High culture. Albany : State University of New York Press, c2003.
HV4998 .H544 2003

Roberts, Nancy, 1924- Georgia ghosts / by Nancy Roberts. Winston-Salem N.C. : John F. Blair, Publisher, c1997, 2002. xi, 267 p. : ill. ; 21 cm. ISBN 0-89587-172-6 (alk. paper) DDC 133.1/09758
1. Ghosts - Georgia. 2. Haunted houses - Georgia. 3. Haunted hotels - Georgia. I. Title.
BF1472.U6 R6318 1997

Roberts, Richard D.
Matthews, Gerald. Emotional intelligence. Cambridge, Mass. : MIT Press, c2002.
BF576 .M28 2002

Robertson, James I.
Jackson, Stonewall, 1824-1863. Stonewall Jackson's book of maxims. Nashville, Tenn. : Cumberland House, 2002.
E467.1.J15 J17 2002

Robertson, Linda R. (Linda Raine), 1946- The dream of civilized warfare : World War I flying aces and the American imagination / Linda R. Robertson. Minneapolis : University of Minnesota Press, c2003. xx, 481 p. : ill. ; 24 cm. Includes bibliographical references (p. 459-472) and index. ISBN 0-8166-4270-2 (hard. : alk. paper) DDC 940.4/4973
1. World War, 1914-1918 - Aerial operations, American. 2. World War, 1914-1918 - Campaigns - Western Front. 3. Heroes. 4. Fighter pilots. 5. World War, 1914-1918 - Social aspects - United States. 6. War and society - United States. I. Title.
D606 .R63 2003

Robertson, Neil G.
Philosophy and freedom. Toronto : University of Toronto Press, c2003.

Robey, Dan. The power of positive habits : put your mind and body on autopilot in 21 days and reach your goals automatically! / Dan Robey. Miami, Fla. : Abritt Pub. Group, c2003. v, 197 p. ; 22 cm. Includes bibliographical references (p. 159-168) and indexes. ISBN 0-9725219-7-6 (pbk.) DDC 646.7
1. Habit. I. Title.
BF335 .R56 2003

Robin, Régine, 1936- La mémoire saturée / Régine Robin. Paris : Stock, 2003. 524 p. ; 22 cm. (Ordre d'idées) Includes bibliographical references (p. 501-[525]) ISBN 2-234-05568-7 DDC 900
1. History - Philosophy. I. Title. II. Series.

D16.8 .R59 2003

Robinson, Daniel N., 1937- A student's guide to psychology / Daniel N. Robinson. 1st ed. Wilmington, Del. : ISI Books, c2002. 70 p. ; 21 cm. (ISI guides to the major disciplines) Includes bibliographical references. ISBN 1-88292-695-1 DDC 150
1. Psychology. I. Title. II. Series.
BF121 .R598 2002

Robinson, Edward Jewitt. Tamil wisdom : traditions concerning Hindu sages and selections from their writings / Edward Jewitt Robinson; with an introduction by Elijah Hoole. New Delhi : Asian Educational Services, 2001. x, 140 p. ; 19 cm. Originally published: London : Wesleyan Conference Office, 1873. ISBN 81-206-1587-5 DDC 294.5/4
1. Conduct of life. 2. Hindu literature - Translations into English. 3. Religious literature, Tamil - Translations into English. I. Title.
BJ1571 .R63 2001

Robinson-Riegler, Bridget.
Readings in cognitive psychology. Boston, Mass. : Pearson Allyn & Bacon, 2003.
BF201 .R425 2003

Robinson-Riegler, Gregory. Cognitive psychology. Boston : Allyn and Bacon, c2004.
BF201 .R63 2004

Robinson-Riegler, Gregory. Cognitive psychology : applying the science of the mind / Gregory Robinson-Riegler, Bridget Robinson-Riegler. Boston : Allyn and Bacon, c2004. p. cm. Includes bibliographical references and index. ISBN 0-205-32763-X DDC 153
1. Cognitive psychology. I. Robinson-Riegler, Bridget. II. Title.
BF201 .R63 2004

Readings in cognitive psychology. Boston, Mass. : Pearson Allyn & Bacon, 2003.
BF201 .R425 2003

Robinson, T. M.
Thinking about the environment. Lanham, Md. : Lexington Books, c2002.
GE50 .T48 2002

ROBOTICS. See **ROBOTS.**

ROBOTS - DESIGN AND CONSTRUCTION.
Breazeal, Cynthia L. Designing sociable robots. Cambridge, Mass. : MIT Press, c2002.
TA167 .B74 2002

ROBOTS - DESIGN AND CONSTRUCTION - HISTORY.
Wood, Gaby. Edison's Eve. 1st American ed. New York : A.A. Knopf, 2002.
TJ211 .W65 2002

Roccatagliata Orsini, Susana. Un hijo no puede morir : la experiencia de seguir viviendo / Susana Roccatagliata Orsini. 3. ed. Santiago de Chile : Grijalbo, 2000. 254 p. : ill. ; 23 cm. Includes bibliographical references (p. 249). ISBN 9562581098 (pbk.). DDC 155.9/37
1. Children - Death. 2. Bereavement - Psychological aspects. I. Title.
BF723.D3 R6 2000

Rocha, Manuela.
Pessoa, Fernando, 1888-1935. [Erostratus. Portuguese & English] Heróstrato e a busca da imortalidade. Lisboa : Assírio e Alvim, c2000.

Roche, Christian. Le bestiaire des philosophes / Christian Roche, Jean-Jacques Barrère ; [illustrations, Joëlle Jolivet]. [Paris] : Seuil, c2001. 143 p. : ill. ; 19 cm. Includes bibliographical references (p. 127-140). ISBN 2-02-036356-9 DDC 100
1. Animals (Philosophy) 2. Animals, Mythical. 3. Bestiaries. 4. Philosophy. I. Barrère, Jean-Jacques. II. Jolivet, Joëlle. III. Title.

Rochester studies in historiography
Turning points in historiography. Rochester, NY : University of Rochester Press, 2002.
D13 .T87 2002

Rochester studies in philosophy
(3) Geier, Alfred, 1930- Plato's erotic thought. Rochester, NY : University of Rochester Press, 2002.
B398.L9 G45 2002

ROCK AND ROLL MUSIC. See **ROCK MUSIC.**
ROCK CARVINGS. See **PETROGLYPHS.**
ROCK ENGRAVINGS. See **PETROGLYPHS.**
ROCK GROUPS. See **ROCK MUSICIANS.**
ROCK MUSIC. See **GRUNGE MUSIC.**

ROCK MUSIC - FANS. *See* **ROCK MUSIC FANS.**

ROCK MUSIC FANS - UNITED STATES.
Fletcher, John Wright. A hermeneutic study of generational music. 2002.

ROCK MUSIC - SOCIAL ASPECTS - UNITED STATES.
Fletcher, John Wright. A hermeneutic study of generational music. 2002.

ROCK MUSICIANS - PSYCHOLOGY.
Hemming, Jan. Begabung und Selbstkonzept. Münster : Lit, [2002?]
ML3838 .H46 2002

Rock my soul.
Hooks, Bell. New York, NY : Atria Books, c2003.

ROCK-N-ROLL MUSIC. *See* **ROCK MUSIC.**

ROCK PAINTINGS. *See* **PETROGLYPHS.**

ROCKETRY - BIOGRAPHY.
TSiolkovskiĭ, K. (Konstantin), 1857-1935. Geniĭ sredi liudeĭ. Moskva : Mysl', 2002.
TL781.85.T84 A25 2002

Rocking the goddess.
Paige, Anthony. New York : Citadel Press, c2002.
BF1571.5.C64 P35 2002

Roderick, Timothy, 1963- Dark moon mysteries : wisdom, power, and magic of the shadow world / Timothy Roderick. Aptos, Calif. : New Brighton Books, 2003. p. cm. Originally published: St. Paul, Minn. : Llewellyn Publications, 1996. Includes bibliographical references. ISBN 0-9718377-2-4 DDC 133.4/3
1. Magic. 2. New moon - Miscellanea. 3. Goddess religion. 4. New moon - Religious aspects. I. Title.
BF1623.M66 R63 2003

Rodríguez, Luis. Patologías complejas (versión preliminar) / Luis Rodríguez. [Santiago, Chile] : Corporación de Promoción Universitaria, [1995] 23 l. : 27 cm. (Documento de trabajo ; no. 11/95)
1. Psychology, Pathological. 2. Diagnosis, Laboratory - Chile. I. Title. II. Series: Serie Documentos de trabajo C.P.U. ; no. 95/11.

Rodríguez Mampaso, Ma. José (María José).
Jornadas de Roles Sexuales y de Género (2nd : 1995 : Madrid, Spain) Mujer, ideología y población. 1. ed. Madrid : Ediciones Clásicas, 1998.
HQ1075 .J67 1995

Rodriguez Pereyra, Gonzalo.
Real metaphysics. London ; New York : Routledge, 2003.
BD111 .R227 2003

Roehle, Friedrich, 1916-1995. Die Struktur des Bewusstseins / Friedrich Roehle ; bearbeitet, ergänzt und herausgegeben von Arnulf Rieber. Frankfurt am Main ; New York : Peter Lang, c2001. 407 p. ; ill. (5 folded) ; 21 cm. (Schriften zur Triadik und Ontodynamik, 0932-2434 ; Bd. 20) Includes bibliographical references (p. 333-361) and index. ISBN 3-631-38415-7 (pbk.)
1. Knowledge, Theory of. 2. Awareness. 3. Communication - Philosophy. I. Rieber, Arnulf, 1935- II. Title. III. Series.

Roelcke, Thorsten. Kommunikative Effizienz : eine Modellskizze / Thorsten Roelcke. Heidelberg : Winter, c2002. 139 p. ; 21 cm. (Sprache, Literatur und Geschichte ; Bd. 23) Includes bibliographical references (p. 131-139). ISBN 3-8253-1353-0 (pbk.)
1. Communication. 2. Written communication. 3. Oral communication. I. Title. II. Series.

Roeper, Richard, 1959- 10 sure signs a movie character is doomed, and other surprising movie lists / Richard Roeper. 1st ed. New York : Hyperion, c2003. xi, 289, [2] p. ; 21 cm. Includes bibliographical references (p. [291]). ISBN 0-7868-8830-X DDC 791.43/02/907
1. Motion pictures - Miscellanea. I. Title. II. Title: Ten sure signs a movie character is doomed, and other surprising movie lists
PN1998 .R568 2003

Roessler, Johannes.
Agency and self-awareness. Oxford : Clarendon Press ; New York : Oxford University Press, 2003.

Rogers, Barb, 1947- Mystic glyphs : an oracle based on Native American symbols / Barb Rogers. York Beach, ME : Red Wheel/Weiser, 2003. p. cm. Table of contents URL: http://www.loc.gov/catdir/toc/ecip043/2003009717.html ISBN 1-59003-047-8 DDC 133.3/3
1. Divination cards. 2. Petroglyphs - Four Corners Region - Miscellanea. I. Title.
BF1778.5 .R64 2003

ROGERS, CARL R. (CARL RANSOM), 1902-.
Cohen, David, 1946- Carl Rogers. London : Constable, 1997.

BF109.R63 C64 1997

Rogers, Rita. Mysteries : Rita Rogers' first-hand accounts of the amazing world of the unexplained / Rita Rogers. Large print ed. Bath, England : Chivers Press ; Waterville, Me. : Thorndike Press, 2002. xvii, 213 p. ; 22 cm. ISBN 0-7862-4233-7 (US : softcover : alk. paper : Chivers lg. print) ISBN 0-7540-4885-3 (UK : hardcover : alk. paper : Chivers lg. print ISBN 0-7540-4886-1 (UK : softcover : alk. paper : Camden lg. print)
1. Parapsychology. 2. Occultism. 3. Large type books. I. Title.
BF1031 .R635 2002

Rogers, W. Kim. Reason and life : an introduction to an ecological approach in philosophy / W. Kim Rogers. Lanham, Md. : University Press of America, c2003. xi, 246 p. ; 22 cm. Includes bibliographical references (p. [227]-238) and index. ISBN 0-7618-2541-X (pbk. : alk. paper) DDC 113.8
1. Life. 2. Reason. 3. Philosophical anthropology. I. Title.
BD431 .R5515 2003

Rogoff, Barbara. The cultural nature of human development / Barbara Rogoff. Oxford ; New York : Oxford University Press, 2003. xiii, 434 p. : ill. ; 24 cm. Includes bibliographical references (p. 371-411) and index. ISBN 0-19-513133-9 (hardcover : alk. paper) DDC 305.231
1. Socialization. 2. Child development. 3. Cognition and culture. 4. Developmental psychology. I. Title.
HM686 .R64 2003

Rohrbach, Rudolf.
Augustine, Saint, Bishop of Hippo. De magistro = Paderborn : F. Schöningh, 2002.
BR65.A5 G4 2002

Roić, Sanja, 1953-.
Gučetić, Nikola Vitov, 1549-1610. [Dialogo della bellezza. Serbo-Croatian & Italian] Dijalog o ljepoti = Dvojezično izd. Zagreb : Društvo hrvatskih književnika, 1995.
BH301.L65 G8318 1995

Roid, Gale H. S-BIT, Stoelting Brief Nonverbal Intelligence Test : examiner's manual for the Stoelting Brief Nonverbal Intelligence Test / Gale H. Roid, Lucy J. Miller. Wood Dale, IL : Stoelting Co., c1999. 1 v. (various pagings) : ill. ; 28 cm. Includes bibliographical references.
1. Stoelting Brief Nonverbal Intelligence Test. I. Miller, Lucy J. II. Title. III. Title: Examiner's manual for the Stoelting Brief Nonverbal Intelligence Test
BF432.5.S85 R65 1999

Rojas Marcos, Luis, 1943- Más allá del 11 de septiembre : la superación del trauma / Luis Rojas Marcos. [Madrid] : Espasa, c2002. 156 p. ; 22 cm. (Espasa hoy) Includes bibliographical references (p. 149-154) and index. ISBN 84-670-0170-4 DDC 974.7/1044
1. September 11 Terrorist Attacks, 2001 - Psychological aspects. 2. Terrorism - Psychological aspects. I. Title. II. Series.
HV6432.7 .R64 2002

Rojas Nieto, Cecilia.
La Adquisición de la lengua materna. México : Universidad Nacional Autónoma de México : Centro de Investigaciones y Estudios Superiores en Antropología Social, 2001.
P118 .A227 2001

Rojek, Chris. Stuart Hall / Chris Rojek. Cambridge, UK : Polity in association with Blackwell, 2003. xi, 230 p. ; 24 cm. (Key contemporary thinkers) Includes bibliographical references (p. [212]-225) and index. ISBN 0-7456-2480-4 (hbk : alk. paper) ISBN 0-7456-2481-2 (pbk : alk. paper) DDC 306/.01
1. Hall, Stuart. 2. Culture - Philosophy. I. Title. II. Series.
HM621 .R64 2003

Roland, Alan, 1930-.
Creative dissent. Westport, Conn. : Praeger Publishers, 2003.
BF173 .C794 2003

Dreams and drama : psychoanalytic criticism, creativity and the artist / Alan Roland. 1st US ed. Middletown, CT : Wesleyan University Press, 2003. 170 p. ; 24 cm. (Disseminations : psychoanalysis in contexts) Includes bibliographical references (p. [153]-161) and index. ISBN 0-8195-6601-2 (pbk.) ISBN 0-8195-6600-4 (cloth) DDC 153.3/5
1. Creation (Literary, artistic, etc.) 2. Drama - History and criticism. 3. Psychoanalysis and art. 4. Psychoanalysis and literature. I. Title. II. Series: Disseminations.
BF408 .R65 2003

Dreams and drama : psychoanalytic criticism, creativity and the artist / Alan Roland. 1st US ed. Middletown, CT : Wesleyan University Press, 2003. 170 p. ; 24 cm. (Disseminations : psychoanalysis in contexts) Includes bibliographical references (p. [153]-161) and index.

ISBN 0-8195-6600-4 (cloth) ISBN 0-8195-6601-2 (pbk.)
1. Creation (Literary, artistic, etc.) 2. Drama - History and criticism. 3. Psychoanalysis and art. 4. Psychoanalysis and literature. I. Title. II. Series: Disseminations.
BF408 .R65 2003

Roland, Alex, 1944- Strategic computing : DARPA and the quest for machine intelligence, 1983-1993 / Alex Roland with Philip Shiman. Cambridge, Mass. : MIT Press, c2002. xxvi, 427 p. : ill. ; 24 cm. (History of computing) Includes bibliographical references (p. [333]-396) and index. Table of contents URL: http://www.loc.gov/catdir/toc/fy033/2001056252.html ISBN 0-262-18226-2 (hc. : alk. paper) DDC 004.3
1. High performance computing. 2. Artificial intelligence. I. Shiman, Philip. II. Title. III. Series.
QA76.88 .R65 2002

ROLE MODELS.
Mantle, Mickey, 1931- The quality of courage. Lincoln : University of Nebraska Press, [1999]
GV865.A1 M317 1999

ROLE PLAYING.
Broich, Josef, 1948- Körper- und Bewegungsspiele. 1. Aufl. 1999. Köln : Maternus, 1999.

Capp, Ray, 1953- When you mean business about yourself. Nashville, Tenn. : Rutledge Hill Press, c2002.
BF637.S8 C37 2002

Ressler, Paula. Dramatic changes. Portsmouth, NH : Heinemann, c2002.
PN3171 .R47 2002

Le rôle social de l'historien.
Dumoulin, Olivier. Paris : Albin Michel, 2002, c2003.
D13.2 .D85 2002

Roli, Fabio, 1962-.
International Workshop on Multiple Classifier Systems (4th : 2003 : Guildford, England) Multiple classifier systems. Berlin ; New York : Springer, c2003.
Q325.5 .I574 2003

Rolland, Romain, 1866-1944. Le théâtre du peuple / Romain Rolland ; édition préfacée et annotée par Chantal Meyer-Plantureux. Nouvelle éd. Bruxelles : Complexe, c2003. 191 p. ; 22 cm. (Le théâtre en question) Includes bibliographical references (p. 181-[184]). ISBN 2-87027-958-2 DDC 809
1. Drama - History and criticism. 2. Theater. 3. French drama - History and criticism. I. Meyer-Plantureux, Chantal. II. Title. III. Series.
PN1655 .R68 2003

Die Rolle des Vaters in der Familie.
Fthenakis, Wassilios E. Stuttgart : Kohlhammer, 2002.

ROMAN ALPHABET. *See* **ALPHABET.**

ROMAN AUTHORS. *See* **AUTHORS, LATIN.**

Le roman familial de Freud.
Rubin, Gabrielle, 1921- Paris : Payot, 2002.

Le Roman familial d'Isadora D.
Delaisi de Parseval, Geneviève. Paris : Odile Jacob, c2002.

The Roman gaze : vision, power, and the body / edited by David Fredrick. Baltimore : Johns Hopkins University Press, 2002. x, 334 p. : ill. ; 24 cm. (Arethusa books) Includes bibliographical references (p. [297]-322) and index. CONTENTS: Split vision : the politics of the gaze in Seneca's Troades / Cindy Benton -- This ship of fools : epic vision in Lucan's Vulteius episode / Katherine Owen Eldred -- Some unseen monster : rereading Lucretius on sex / Pamela Gordon -- Reading programs in Greco-Roman art : reflections on the Spada reliefs / Zahra Newby -- Look who's laughing at sex : men and women viewers in the Apodyterium of the suburban baths at Pompeii / John R. Clarke -- Political movement : walking and ideology in republican Rome / Anthony Corbeill -- Being in the eyes : shame and sight in ancient Rome / Carlin Barton -- Mapping penetrability in late republican and early imperial Rome / David Fredrick -- Looking at looking : can you resist a reading? / Alison R. Sharrock. ISBN 0-8018-6961-7 DDC 937
1. Gaze - Psychological aspects. 2. Rome - Civilization. I. Fredrick, David, 1959- II. Series.
BF637.C45 R64 2002

ROMAN LITERATURE. *See* **LATIN LITERATURE.**

ROMANCES. *See* **ARTHURIAN ROMANCES.**

ROMANCES, ENGLISH - HISTORY AND CRITICISM.
Heng, Geraldine. Empire of magic. New York : Columbia University Press, c2003.
PR321 .H46 2003

ROMANCES, GERMAN - HISTORY AND CRITICISM.
Hübner, Gert. Erzählform im höfischen Roman. Tübingen : Francke, 2003.

Romanchuk, Oleh.
Kuz'menko, Volodymyr. Na porozi nadtsyvilizatsii. L'viv : "Universum", 1998.
HM901 .K89 1998

Romanenko, I͡Uriĭ.
Donchenko, E. A. (Elena Andreevna) Arkhetypy sotsial'noho zhyttia i polityka. Kyiv : Lybid', 2001.
JA74.5 .D65 2001

Romanesque britannique et psyché.
Vinet, Dominique. Paris : L'Harmattan, c2003.

I romani.
Antico Gallina, Mariavittoria. Cinisello Balsamo (Milano) : Silvana, 1998.

ROMANIES.
Buckland, Raymond. Gypsy witchcraft & magic. 1st ed. St. Paul, Minn. : Llewellyn Publications, 2001, c1998.

Romanov, V. N. (Vladimir Nikolaevich) Istoricheskoe razvitie kul'tury : psikhologo-tipologicheskiĭ aspekt / V.N. Romanov. Moskva : Savin, 2003. 447 p. ; 22 cm. ISBN 5902121035
1. Civilization - Philosophy. 2. Civilization - History. I. Title.
CB19 .R65 2003

Romanova, A. P. (Anna Petrovna) Stanovlenie religioznogo kompleksa : monografiia / A.P. Romanova. Astrakhan : Izd-vo Astrakhanskogo pedagog. universiteta, 1999. 148 p. ; 21 cm. At head of title: Ministerstvo obrazovaniia Rossiĭskoĭ Federatsii. Astrakhanskiĭ gos. pedagog. universitet. Includes bibliographical references (p. 143-148). ISBN 5882003717
1. Psychology and religion. 2. Existential psychology. 3. Religion. I. Astrakhanskiĭ gosudarstvennyĭ pedagogicheskiĭ universitet. II. Title.
BF51 .R66 1999

Romans Freuda i Gradivy.
Małyszek, Tomasz, 1971- Wrocław : Wydawn. Uniwersytetu Wrocławskiego, 2002.
BF173.F85 M255 2002

ROMANS - ITALY.
Antico Gallina, Mariavittoria. I romani. Cinisello Balsamo (Milano) : Silvana, 1998.

ROMANTICISM IN LITERATURE. See ROMANTICISM.

ROMANTICISM - POLITICAL ASPECTS - UNITED STATES - HISTORY - 19TH CENTURY.
Winger, Stewart Lance. Lincoln, religion, and romantic cultural politics. DeKalb : Northern Illinois University Press, c2003.
E457.2 .W77 2003

Romberg, Raquel. Witchcraft and welfare : spritual capital and the business of magic in modern Puerto Rico / Raquel Romberg. 1st ed. Austin : University of Texas Press, c2003. xviii, 315 p. : ill. ; 24 cm. Includes bibliographical references (p. 289-303) and index. ISBN 0-292-77123-1 (alk. paper) ISBN 0-292-77126-6 (pbk. : alk. paper) DDC 133.4/3/097295
1. Witchcraft - Puerto Rico. 2. Magic - Puerto Rico. I. Title. II. Title: Spritual capital and the business of magic in modern Puerto Rico
BF1584.P9 R66 2003

ROME. See ROMANS.

ROME - CIVILIZATION.
Alföldi, Maria R.- Gloria romanorum. Stuttgart : Franz Steiner Verlag, 2001.
DG78 .A546 2001

Antico Gallina, Mariavittoria. I romani. Cinisello Balsamo (Milano) : Silvana, 1998.

The Roman gaze. Baltimore : Johns Hopkins University Press, 2002.
BF637.C45 R64 2002

Scheid, John. Religion et piété à Rome. [2e éd.]. Paris : Albin Michel, 2001.

Studien zu antiken Identitäten. Würzburg : Ergon Verlag, c2001.
DG78 .S78 2001

Tra IV e V secolo. Milano : Cisalpino, 2002.

Wisdom, Stephen. Gladiators 100 BC-AD 200. Oxford : Osprey, 2001 (2002 printing)

ROME - CIVILIZATION - CHRISTIAN INFLUENCES.
Antiquity renewed. Leuven, Netherlands ; Dudley, MA : Peeters, 2003.
CB365 .A58 2003

ROME - HISTORY.
Alföldi, Maria R.- Gloria romanorum. Stuttgart : Franz Steiner Verlag, 2001.
DG78 .A546 2001

ROME - HISTORY - 53-44 B.C.
Caesar against liberty? Cambridge : Francis Cairns, c2003.

ROME - HISTORY - REPUBLIC, 510-30 B.C.
Ferguson, Everett, 1933- Backgrounds of early Christianity. 3rd ed. Grand Rapids, Mich. : W.B. Eerdmans, c2003.

ROME - RELIGION.
Bernstein, Frances. Classical living. 1st ed. San Francisco : HarperSanFrancisco, 2000.
BL808 .B47 2000

Scheid, John. Religion et piété à Rome. [2e éd.]. Paris : Albin Michel, 2001.

Studien zu antiken Identitäten. Würzburg : Ergon Verlag, c2001.
DG78 .S78 2001

ROME - RELIGION - CONGRESSES.
Divination and portents in the Roman world. Odense : Odense University Press, c2000.
BF1768 .D57 2000

ROME - RELIGIOUS LIFE AND CUSTOMS.
Bernstein, Frances. Classical living. 1st ed. San Francisco : HarperSanFrancisco, 2000.
BL808 .B47 2000

Scheid, John. Religion et piété à Rome. [2e éd.]. Paris : Albin Michel, 2001.

Romenet͡s, V. A. (Vladimir Andreevich) Istoriia psykholohii XX stolittia / V.A. Romenets'. Kyiv : "Lebid'", 1998. 988 p. ; 21 cm. Authorized for instructional purposes. Includes bibliographical references (p.962-[964]) and index. Gift of Victor Kamkin, Inc. March 2002 ISBN 9660601166
1. Psychology - History - 20th century. I. Title. II. Title: Istoriia psykholohii dvadtsiatoho stolittia
BF105 .R66 1998

Romero, Pedro G., 1964- En el ojo de la batalla : estudios sobre iconoclastia e iconodulia : historia del arte y vanguardia moderna : guerra y economía : estética y política : sociología sagrada y antropología materialista / Pedro G. Romero ; [escritos por Teresa Grandas, Horacio Fernández y Nicolás Sánchez Durá]. Valencia : Universitat de València, 2002. 238 p. : ill. (chiefly col.) ; 24 cm. Includes bibliographical references. ISBN 84-370-5347-1
1. Aesthetics. 2. Symbolism in art. 3. Art and society. 4. Art, Modern - 20th century - History. I. Grandas, Teresa. II. Fernández, Horacio. III. Sánchez Durá, Nicolás. IV. Title.

Romeyer-Dherbey, Gilbert.
Protopapas-Marneli, Maria. La rhétorique des stoïciens. Paris : Harmattan, c2002.

Romm, M. V. (Mark Valerievich) Adaptatsiia lichnosti v sotsiume : teoretiko-metodologicheskiĭ aspekt / M. V. Romm. Novosibirsk : "Nauka", 2002. 268 p. : ill. ; 20 cm. Added title page title: Adaptation of a person in a society. At head of title: Ministerstvo obrazovaniia Rossiĭskoĭ ederatsii. Novosibirskiĭ gosudarstvennyĭ tekhnicheskiĭ universitet. Includes bibliographical references (p. 249-265) and index. Summary and addded table of contents in English. ISBN 5020318620
1. Social adjustment. 2. Adaptability (Psychology) 3. Personality. 4. Social psychology. I. Title. II. Title: Adaptation of a person in a society
HM696 .R655 2002

Roṅ' pran' lak' choṅ' / Moṅ' Moṅ' Mraṅ'' 'E'' cī cañ' mvam'' mam taññ'''' phrat' saññ'. Raṅ' kun' : 'Aruṇ' Ū'' Cā pe : Phraṅ'' khyi re", Lābh' Mui'' Cve Cā pe, 2001. 111 p. : ill. ; 25 cm. In Burmese. Cover title. SUMMARY: Occultism as practiced in Burma; articles.
1. Occultism - Burma. I. Moṅ' Moṅ' Mraṅ'' 'E''.
BF1434.B+

Roncal Martínez, Federico.
Guoron Ajquijay, Pedro. Retomemos la palabra--. Guatemala, Guatemala : Editorial Saqil Tzij, 1995.

Rong, Ziyou.
Li, Tianming, 1945- Li Tianming di si kao yi shu. Beijing di 1 ban. Beijing : Sheng huo, du shu, xin zhi san lian shu dian, 1996.

ROOD-LOFTS. See CHURCH ARCHITECTURE.

Roodt, G.
An introduction to psychological assessment in the South African context. Cape Town, South Africa : Oxford University Press Southern Africa, 2001.
BF39 .I58 2001

Rooney, David, 1959-.
Public policy in knowledge-based economies. Cheltenham, UK ; Northampton, MA : Edward Elgar, c2003.
HC79.I55 P83 2003

The roots and solutions to peculiar problems (dealing with bad luck, lost opportunities and failure).
Aransiola, Moses Olanrewaju. 1st ed.

The roots of reason.
Papineau, David, 1947- Oxford : Clarendon Press ; New York : Oxford University Press, 2003.
BD418.3 .P35 2003

Rootwork.
McQuillar, Tayannah Lee, 1977- New York : Simon & Schuster, c2003.
BF1622.A34 M37 2003

Roper, Lyndal.
Dreams and history. 1st ed. New York, NY : Brunner-Routledge, 2003.
BF1078 .D735 2003

Rorty, Amélie.
The many faces of philosophy. Oxford ; New York : Oxford University Press, 2003.
B72 .M346 2003

ROSAECRUCIANS. See ROSICRUCIANS.

Rose, Kenneth, 1924- Elusive Rothschild : the life of Victor, third baron / Kenneth Rose. London : Weidenfeld & Nicolson, 2003. xi, 338 p., [16] p. of plates : ill. ; 24 cm. Includes bibliographical references (p. 320-324) and index. ISBN 0-297-81229-7 DDC 941.082092
1. Rothschild, Nathaniel Mayer Victor Rothschild, - Baron, - 1910- 2. Rothschild, Nathaniel Mayer Victor Rothschild, - Baron, - 1910- - Friends and associates. 3. Businessmen - Great Britain - Biography. 4. Great Britain - Biography. I. Title.

Rose, Sharron. Path of the priestess : a guidebook for awakening the divine feminine / Sharron Rose. Rochester, VT. : Inner Traditions, c2002. xii, 291 p. : ill. ; 26 cm. Includes bibliographical references (p. 272-287) and index. ISBN 0-89281-964-2 (pbk.) DDC 291.4/4/082
1. Women - Religious life. 2. Goddess religion. I. Title.
BL625.7 .R67 2002

Rose, Tricia.
Longing to tell. 1st ed. New York : Farrar, Straus and Giroux, 2003.
E185.625 .L66 2003

Rosemann, Michael, 1967-.
Process management. Springer-verlag, Berlin, Heidelberg ; New York : Springer, c2003.
HD31 .P756 2003

Rosén, Ingrid. Glas i konsten : från antiken till våra dagar / Ingrid Rosén. Stockholm : Carlssons, c2000. 155 p. : ill. (some col.) ; 23 cm. Includes bibliographical references and index. ISBN 91-7203-975-2
1. Glassware in art. 2. Art - History. I. Title.

Rosen, Lawrence, 1941- The culture of Islam : changing aspects of contemporary Muslim life / Lawrence Rosen. Chicago : University of Chicago Press, 2002. xvii, 230 p. ; 24 cm. Includes bibliographical references (p. 211-228) and index. CONTENTS: Ambivalent culture. The circle of beneficence : narrating coherence in a world of corruption -- Ambivalence towards power : approaches to authority in postcolonial Morocco -- What is a tribe, and why does it matter? -- Constructing institutions in a political culture of personalism -- Memory worlds, plausible worlds. Contesting sainthood -- Memory in Morocco -- Have the Arabs changed their mind? -- Shifting concepts, Discerning change. Marriage stories : crossing the boundaries of nation, gender, and law -- Euro-Islam -- Never in doubt : Salman Rushdie's deeper challenge to Islam. ISBN 0-226-72613-4 (cloth : alk. paper) DDC 306/.0964
1. Morocco - Social life and customs. 2. Civilization, Islamic. 3. East and West. 4. Ethnology - Morocco. 5. Religion and culture. 6. Religion and politics - Morocco. I. Title.
DT312 R64 2002

Rosen, Stanley, 1929- Hermeneutics as politics / Stanley Rosen with a foreword by Robert B. Pippin. 2nd ed. New Haven, Conn. : Yale University Press, 2003. xiii, 213 p. ; 21 cm. Includes bibliographical references (p. 194-208) and index. ISBN 0-300-09987-8
1. Hermeneutics. 2. Political science. I. Title.
BD241 .R81 2003

Rosenau, Pauline Vaillancourt. The competition paradigm : America's romance with conflict, contest, and commerce / Pauline Vaillancourt Rosenau. Lanham, Md. ; Oxford : Rowman & Littlefield, c2003. xiv, 237 p. : ill. ; 24 cm. Includes bibliographical references and index. ISBN 0-7425-2037-4 (hbk : alk. paper) ISBN 0-7425-2038-2 (pbk. : alk. paper) DDC 320/.14
1. Competition (Psychology) 2. Competition - United States. 3. Competition, International - United States. I. Title.
BF637.C47 R67 2003

Rosenbaum, J. F. (Jerrold F.).
Women's health and psychiatry. Philadelphia, PA : Lippincott Williams & Wilkins, c2002.
RA564.85 .W6652 2002

ROSENBERG, ALFRED, 1893-1946.
Bärsch, Claus-Ekkehard. Die politische Religion des Nationalsozialismus. 2., vollst. überarb. Aufl. München : W. Fink, c2002.

Rosenberg, Jay F. Thinking about knowing / Jay F. Rosenberg. Oxford : Clarendon Press ; New York : Oxford University Press, 2002. viii, 257 p. ; 24 cm. Includes bibliographical references (p. [249]-254) and index. ISBN 0-19-925133-9 (alk. paper) DDC 121
1. Knowledge, Theory of. I. Title.
BD161 .R65 2002

Rosenberg, Marshall B. Nonviolent communication : a language of life / by Marshall B. Rosenberg. 2nd ed. Encinitas, CA : PuddleDancer Press, 2003. p. cm. Includes bibliographical references and index. CONTENTS: Giving from the heart : the heart of nonviolent communication -- Communication that blocks compassion -- Observing without evaluating -- Identifying and expressing feelings -- Taking responsibility for our feelings -- Requesting that which would enrich life -- Receiving empathically -- The power of empathy -- Connecting compassionately with ourselves -- Expressing anger fully -- The protective use of force -- Liberating ourselves and counseling others -- Expressing appreciation in nonviolent communication. ISBN 1-89200-503-4 DDC 153.6
1. Interpersonal communication. 2. Interpersonal relations. I. Title.
BF637.C45 R645 2003

Rosenberg, Robin S.
Kosslyn, Stephen Michael, 1948- Fundamentals of psychology. 2nd ed. Boston : Allyn and Bacon, c2005.
BF121 .K585 2005

Rosenberg, Shelley Kapnek. Raising a mensch : [how to bring up ethical children in today's world] / Shelley Kapnek Rosenberg. 1st ed. Philadelphia : Jewish Publication Society, 2003. xxii, 176 p. ; 23 cm. Subtitle from cover. Includes bibliographical references (p. [167]-170) and index. ISBN 0-8276-0754-7 DDC 296.7/4
1. Moral development. 2. Parent and child. 3. Child rearing. 4. Ethics, Jewish. I. Title.
BF723.M54 R68 2003

Rosenfeld, Lawrence B.
Adler, Ronald B. (Ronald Brian), 1946- Interplay. New York : Oxford University Press, 2004. 9th ed.
BF637.C45 A33 2004

Rosenfield, Denis L. (Denis Lerrer), 1950-.
Civilisation et barbarie. 1re éd. Paris : Presses universitaires de France, c2002.

Rosental, Claude. La trame de l'évidence : sociologie de la démonstration en logique / Claude Rosental. 1 éd. Paris : Presses universitaires de France, c2003. 367 p. ; 22 cm. (Collection Sciences, modernités, philosophies) Includes bibliographical references and indexes. ISBN 2-13-053330-2 DDC 300
1. Artificial intelligence. 2. Sociology. 3. Logic. I. Title. II. Series.

Rosenthal, Don. Intimacy : the noble adventure / Don & Martha Rosenthal. Doughcloyne, Wilton, Cork : Collins Press, 1999. vi, 220 p. ; 22 cm. ISBN 1-89825-677-2 DDC 158.2
1. Intimacy (Psychology) I. Rosenthal, Martha. II. Title.
BF575.I5 R67 1999

Rosenthal, Martha.
Rosenthal, Don. Intimacy. Doughcloyne, Wilton, Cork : Collins Press, 1999.
BF575.I5 R67 1999

Rosero Garcés, F. (Fernando) Líderes sociales en el siglo XXI : desafíos y propuestas / Fernando Rosero Garcés, Sebastián Betancourt. Quito : Ediciones Abya-Yala, 2002. 128 p. ; 20 cm. Includes bibliographical references ([127]-128). ISBN 9978221972
1. Leadership. 2. Elite (Social sciences) 3. Power (Social sciences) I. Betancourt, Sebastián. II. Title.

Rosett, Marianna.
The Alexander technique [videorecording]. New York, N.Y. : Wellspring Media, c1999.

A rosetta stone to the human mind.
Sanguineti, Vincenzo R. Madison, Conn. : PsychoSocial Press, 2003.
BF38 .S225 2003

ROSICRUCIANS - HISTORY.
Tilton, Hereward. The quest for the phoenix. Berlin ; New York : Walter de Gruyter, 2003.
QD24.M3 T558 2003

Roskos-Ewoldsen, David R.
Communication and emotion. Mahwah, N.J. ; London : Lawrence Erlbaum, c2003.
BF637.C45 C6375 2003

ROSLYN (SCOTLAND).
Sinclair, Andrew, 1935- The secret scroll. Edinburgh : Birlinn, 2002.

Ross, Brian H.
Medin, Douglas L. Cognitive psychology. 4th ed. Hoboken, NJ : John Wiley & Sons, 2004.
BF201 .M43 2004

Ross, Gina, 1947- Beyond the trauma vortex : the media's role in healing fear, terror, and violence / Gina Ross ; [foreword by Peter A. Levine]. Berkeley, Calif. : North Atlantic Books, c2003. xviii, 210 p. ; 23 cm. Includes bibliographical references. CONTENTS: What everyone should know about trauma -- The trauma vortex -- Trauma is a root cause of violence -- The role of the trauma vortex in international conflicts -- Second hand trauma -- The role of the news media in transmitting trauma -- The healing vortex -- The role of the entertainment industry in transmitting trauma -- Engaging the healing vortex in entertainment -- Trauma is curable -- Breakthroughs in treatment -- Fast forward to a better world. ISBN 1-55643-446-4 (pbk.) DDC 303.6
1. Disasters - Press coverage. 2. Violence - Press coverage. 3. War - Press coverage. 4. Psychic trauma. I. Title.
PN4784.D57 R67 2003

Ross, Helen Elizabeth, 1935- The mystery of the moon illusion : exploring size perception / Helen E. Ross, Cornelis Plug. Oxford ; New York : Oxford University Press, 2002. viii, 277 p. : ill. ; 24 cm. Includes bibliographical references (p. [236]-265) and indexes. Table of contents URL: http://www.loc.gov/catdir/toc/fy033/2002072659.html ISBN 0-19-850862-X DDC 152.14/8
1. Optical illusions. 2. Size perception. 3. Moon. I. Plug, Cornelis. II. Title.
QP495 .R67 2002

Ross, Norbert. Culture and cognition : implications for theory and method / by Norbert Ross. Thousand Oaks, CA : Sage Publications, c2004. p. cm. Includes bibliographical references and index. ISBN 0-7619-2906-1 ISBN 0-7619-2907-X (paper) DDC 306.4/2
1. Cognition and culture. I. Title.
BF311 .R6542 2004

Rosseel, Eric. Het onschatbare subject : aspecten van het postmoderne Zelf / Eric Rosseel. Brussel : VUBPress, c2001. 214 p. ; 24 cm. Includes bibliographical references (p. 207-214). ISBN 90-5487-283-7
1. Self - Social aspects. 2. Postmodernism - Social aspects. I. Title.
BF697.5.S65 R67 2001

Rossi, Paolo, 1923- Bambini, sogni, furori : tre lezioni di storia delle idee / Paolo Rossi. 1. ed. in "Campi del sapere.". Milano : Feltrinelli, 2001. 167 p. ; 22 cm. (Campi del sapere. Filosofia) Includes bibliographical references and index. ISBN 88-07-10310-9
1. Psychology and philosophy - History. 2. Child psychology - Philosophy - History. 3. Dreams - History. 4. Fanaticism - History. I. Title. II. Series.
BF41 .R67 2001

Rossiia kak traditsionnoe obshchestvo.
Domnikov, S. D. (Sergeĭ Dmitrievich) Mat'-zemli︠a︡ i TSar'-gorod. Moskva : Aleteĭi︠a︡, 2002.
B4235.H57 D65 2002

Rossiia vechnai͡a.
Mamleev, IUriĭ. Moskva : AiF-Print, 2002.
DK32 .M355 2002

Rossiia zabytai͡a i neizvestnai͡a
Akif'ev, A. P. Genetika i sud'by. Moskva : TSentrpoligraf, 2001.
GN281 .A45 2001

Rossiia, Zapad, Islam.
Medvedko, Leonid Ivanovich. Zhukovskiĭ ; Moskva : Kuchkovo pole, 2003.
BP173.5 .M44 2003

Rossiĭskai͡a akademii͡a nauk. Otdelenie literatury i iskusstva.
Alefirenko, M. F. Poėticheskai͡a ėnergii͡a slova. Moskva : Academia, 2002.

P35 .A544 2002

Rossiĭskai͡a akademii͡a nauk. Samarskiĭ nauchnyĭ tsentr.
Akopov, G. V. Mentalistika. Samara : Samarskiĭ gos. pedagog. universitet, 2001.
BF108.R8 A478 2001

Rossiĭskai͡a akademii͡a obrazovanii͡a.
Ivanov, S. P. (Sergeĭ Petrovich) Psikhologii͡a khudozhestvennogo deĭstvii͡a sub"ekta. Moskva : Moskovskiĭ psikhologo-sotsial'nyĭ institut ; Voronezh : Izd-vo NPO "MODĖK", 2002.
BF408 .I93 2002

Ponomarenko, V. A. (Vladimir Aleksandrovich) Sozidatel'nai͡a psikhologii͡a. Moskva : Moskovskiĭ psikhologo-sotsial'nyĭ institut ; Voronezh : Izd-vo NPO "MODĖK", 2000.
BF408 .P572 2000

Rossiĭskiĭ gosudarstvennyĭ gumanitarnyĭ universitet.
International Conference on Motivation (8th : 2002 Moscow, Russia) 8th International Conference on Motivation. Moscow : Russian State University for Humanities, 2002.
BF501.5 .I58 2002

Rossiĭskiĭ gosudarstvennyĭ gumanitarnyĭ universitet. Institut psikhologii im. L.S. Vygotskogo.
Issledovanii͡a obuchenii͡a i razvitii͡a v kontekste kul'turno-istoricheskogo podkhoda. Moskva : Smysl, 2002.
BF712.5 .I88 2002

Rossiĭskoe pedagogicheskoe obshchestvo.
Slovar'-spravochnik po vozrastnoĭ i pedagogicheskoĭ psikhologii. Moskva : Pedagog. ob-vo Rossii, 2001.
BF712.7 .S56 2001

Rossiĭskoe psikhologicheskoe obshchestvo. Altaĭskoe otdelenie.
Innovatsii v psikhologii. Biĭsk : Nauchno-izdatel'skiĭ tsentr Biĭskogo pedagog. gos. universiteta, 2001-
BF20 .I45 2001

Rössler, Beate. Der Wert des Privaten / Beate Rössler. 1. Aufl. Frankfurt am Main : Suhrkamp, 2001. 379 p. ; 18 cm. (Suhrkamp Taschenbuch Wissenschaft ; 1530) Includes bibliographical references and index. ISBN 3-518-29130-0 (pbk.)
1. Privacy. 2. Privacy, Right of. I. Title. II. Series.

Rossman, Gretchen B. Learning in the field : an introduction to qualitative research / Gretchen B. Rossman, Sharon F. Rallis. 2nd ed. Thousand Oaks, Calif. ; London : Sage Publications, c2003. xix, 369 p. : ill. ; 24 cm. Includes bibliographical references (p. 353-359) and indexes. ISBN 0-7619-2651-8 (P) DDC 300/.7/2
1. Social sciences - Research - Methodology. 2. Qualitative reasoning. I. Rallis, Sharon F. II. Title.
H62 .R667 2003

"Röstigraben".
Büchi, Christophe. 2. aufl. Zürich : NZZ, c2001.

Rot, Eliyahu.
Otsrot ha melekh.
Maimonides, Moses, 1135-1204. [Selections] Sefer Musarim ve-de'ot leha-Rambam. Bene Berak : [h. mo. l], 761 [2000 or 2001]

Rotberg, Robert I.
Truth v. justice. Princeton, N.J. : Princeton University Press, c2000.
DT1945 .T78 2000

Roth, Gerhard, 1942 Aug. 15-.
Voluntary action. Oxford ; New York : Oxford University Press, 2003.
BF621 .V658 2003

Roth, Michael S., 1957-.
Freud [electronic resource]. Washington, DC : Library of Congress
BF173

Rothchild, Donald S.
Ending civil wars. Boulder, Colo. : Lynne Rienner, 2002.
JZ6368 .E53 2002

Rothenberg, David, 1962- Always the mountains / David Rothenberg. Athens : University of Georgia Press, c2002. ix, 281 p. ; 24 cm. Includes bibliographical references (p. 263-271) and index. ISBN 0-8203-2454-X (hardcover : alk. paper) DDC 304.2
1. Human ecology - Philosophy. 2. Philosophy. 3. Nature conservation - Philosophy. 4. Environment (Aesthetics) I. Title.
GF21 .R68 2002

Rothfels, Nigel.
Representing animals. Bloomington : Indiana University Press, c2002.

Rothschild, Max Frederick, 1952-.
Intellectual property rights in animal breeding and genetics. Wallingford ; New York : CABI, c2002.
QL85 .R46 2002

ROTHSCHILD, NATHANIEL MAYER VICTOR ROTHSCHILD, BARON, 1910-.
Rose, Kenneth, 1924- Elusive Rothschild. London : Weidenfeld & Nicolson, 2003.

ROTHSCHILD, NATHANIEL MAYER VICTOR ROTHSCHILD, BARON, 1910- - FRIENDS AND ASSOCIATES.
Rose, Kenneth, 1924- Elusive Rothschild. London : Weidenfeld & Nicolson, 2003.

Rotner, Shelley. Lots of feelings / Shelley Rotner. Brookfield, Conn. : Millbrook Press, c2003. p. cm. SUMMARY: Simple text and photographs introduce basic emotions--happy, grumpy, thoughtful, and more--and how people express them. ISBN 0-7613-2896-3 (lib. bdg.) ISBN 0-7613-2377-5 (trade pbk.) DDC 152.4
1. Emotions in children - Juvenile literature. 2. Emotions. I. Title.
BF723.E6 R68 2003

ROUDINESCO, EIZABETH, 1944-.
Derroudida, Jacques. Le repas du grand homme. Paris : Harmattan, 2002.

La roue à livres
(43. v) Boethius, d. 524. [De consolatione philosophiae. French] La consolation de philosophie. Paris : Belles lettres, 2002.

The round art of astrology.
Mann, A. T., 1943- [Round art] London : Vega, c2003.
BF1708.1 .M36 2003

Roundtree, Kathryn. Embracing the witch and the goddess : feminist ritual-makers in New Zealand / Kathryn Roundtree. London ; New York : Routledge, 2003. p. cm. Includes bibliographical references and index. ISBN 0-415-30358-3 ISBN 0-415-30360-5 (pbk.) DDC 133.4/3/0993
1. Witchcraft - New Zealand. 2. Magic - New Zealand. 3. Goddess religion - New Zealand. 4. Neopaganism - New Zealand. I. Title.
BF1584.N45 R68 2003

Roush, Sherry. Hermes' lyre : Italian poetic self-commentary from Dante to Tommasco Campanella / Sherry Roush. Toronto : University of Toronto Press, c2002. ix, 249 p. ; 24 cm. (Toronto Italian studies) Includes bibliographical references (p. [217]-238) and index. ISBN 0-8020-3712-7 DDC 851.009
1. Italian poetry - History and criticism. 2. Hermeneutics. I. Title. II. Series.

ROUSSEAU, JEAN-JACQUES, 1712-1778.
Campos, Edemilson Antunes de. A tirania de Narciso. 1. ed. São Paulo, SP, Brasil : Annablume/FAPESP, 2001.

ROUSSEAU, JEAN-JACQUES, 1712-1778 - CONTRIBUTIONS IN POLITICAL SCIENCE.
Cladis, Mark Sydney. Public vision, private lives. Oxford ; New York : Oxford University Press, 2003.
JC179.R9 C53 2003

ROUSSEAU, JEAN-JACQUES, 1712-1778 - RELIGION.
Cladis, Mark Sydney. Public vision, private lives. Oxford ; New York : Oxford University Press, 2003.
JC179.R9 C53 2003

Rousselot, Pierre, 1878-1915.
[Pour l'histoire du problème de l'amour au moyen âge. English]
The problem of love in the Middle Ages : a historical contribution / by Pierre Rousselot ; translated and with an introdction by Alan Vincelette ; reviewed and corrected by Pol Vandevelde. Milwaukee : Marquette University Press, [2001?] 277 p. ; 22 cm. (Marquette studies in philosophy ; no. 24) (Collected philosophical works of Pierre Rousselot ; v. 2) Includes bibliographical references (p. [254]-263) and indexes. CONTENTS: Thomist solution to the problem of love -- Remarks on the elements of the Thomist solution in Greek and medieval thought -- Two medieval sketches of the physical theory -- First characteristic : duality of the lover and the beloved -- Second characteristic : the violence of love -- Third characteristic : irrational love -- Fourth characteristic : love as the final end -- Appendix 1: The postulation of the problem of love in the first scholastics -- Appendix 2: The formal identification of love and understanding in William of St. Thierry. ISBN 0-87462-623-4 (pbk. : alk. paper) DDC 177/.7
1. Philosophy, Medieval. 2. Love - History - To 1500. 3. Love - Religious aspects - Christianity - History of doctrines - Middle Ages, 600-1500. I. Vandevelde, Pol. II. Title. III. Series: Rousselot, Pierre, 1878-1915. Selections. English. 1998 ; v. 2. IV. Series: Marquette studies in philosophy ; #24.
B738.L68 R68 2001

Selections. English. 1998
(v. 2.) Rousselot, Pierre, 1878-1915. [Pour l'histoire du problème de l'amour au moyen âge. English] The problem of love in the Middle Ages. Milwaukee : Marquette University Press, [2001?]
B738.L68 R68 2001

Routledge advances in international relations and politics
(16.) Power, postcolonialism, and international relations. London ; New York : Routledge, 2002.
JV51 .P69 2002

Routledge key guides
Sheehy, Noel, 1955- Fifty key thinkers in psychology. London ; New York : Routledge, 2003.
BF109.A1 S49 2003

Routledge modular psychology.
Gorman, Phil, 1965- Motivation and emotion. 1st ed. New York : Routledge, 2003.
BF503 .G67 2003

Oakley, Lisa. Cognitive development. New York : Psychology Press, 2004.
BF311 .O12 2004

Routledge research international series in social psychology
Doise, Willem, 1935- Human rights as social representations. London ; New York : Routledge, 2002.
JC571 .D65 2002

Routledge student readers
Gender. London ; New York : Routledge, 2002.
HQ1075 .G426 2002

Routledge studies in critical realism
(5) Cruickshank, Justin, 1969- Realism and sociology. London ; New York : Routledge, 2003.
HM511 .C78 2003

Routledge studies in human resource development
(4) Interpreting the maternal organisation. London ; New York : Routledge, 2003.
HM786 .I58 2003

Routledge studies in memory and narrative
Contested pasts. London ; New York : Routledge, 2003.
BF378.S65 C665 2003

Routledge studies in religion
(5) Gibson, Arthur, 1943- Metaphysics and transcendence. London ; New York : Routledge, 2003.
BT40 .G53 2003

Routledge studies in social and political thought
(37) Infantino, Lorenzo, 1948- [Ignoranza e libertà. English] Ignorance and liberty. London ; New York : Routledge, 2003.
HB95 .I4913 2003

Routledge studies in twentieth-century philosophy
(13) D'Oro, Giuseppina, 1964- Collingwood and the metaphysics of experience. London ; New York : Routledge, 2002.
B1618.C74 D67 2002

Routledge studies in twentieth century philosophy
(14) Real metaphysics. London ; New York : Routledge, 2003.
BD111 .R227 2003

(16.) Crowther, Paul. Philosophy after postmodernism. London ; New York : Routledge, 2003.
B831.2 .C76 2003

Rowan, Leonie, 1966-.
Boys, literacies, and schooling. Buckingham [England] ; Philadelphia : Open University Press, 2002.
LC1390 .B69 2002

Rowland, Robert C., 1954- Shared land/conflicting identity : trajectories of Israeli and Palestinian symbol use / Robert C. Rowland and David A. Frank. East lansing : Michigan State University Press, 2002. 406 p. ; 24 cm. (Rhetoric and public affairs series) Includes bibliographical references (p. 379-398) and index. ISBN 0-87013-635-6 (cloth : alk. paper) DDC 956.9405
1. Arab-Israeli conflict - Psychological aspects. 2. National characteristics, Israeli - Psychological aspects. 3. National characteristics, Arab - Psychological aspects. 4. Symbolism in politics. 5. Communication - Political aspects - Israel. 6. Group identity - Political aspects - Israel. 7. Signs and symbols - Israel - History - 20th century. 8. Propaganda, Zionist - History - 20th century. 9. Propaganda, Arab - History - 20th century. 10. Political psychology. I. Frank, David A. II. Title. III. Title: Conflicting identity IV. Series.
DS119.7 .R685 2003

Rowland, Susan, 1962- Jung : a feminist revision / Susan Rowland. Cambridge, UK : Polity ; Malden, MA : Blackwell, 2002. xii, 186 p. ; 24 cm. Includes bibliographical references and index. ISBN 0-7456-2516-9 (HB : alk. paper) ISBN 0-7456-2517-7 (pbk. : alk. paper)
1. Psychoanalysis and feminism. 2. Jung, C. G. - (Carl Gustav), - 1875-1961. 3. Jungian psychology. 4. Jung, C. G. - (Carl Gustav), - 1875-1961. 5. Feminism. 6. Jungian Theory. I. Title.
BF175.4.F45 R69 2002

Rowlands, Alison. Witchcraft narratives in Germany : Rothenburg 1561-1652 / Alison Rowlands. Manchester, UK ; New York : Manchester University Press ; New York : Distributed exclusively in the USA by Palgrave, 2003. 248 p. : 1 map ; 24 cm. (Studies in early modern European history) Includes bibliographical references (p. [229]-238 and index. ISBN 0-7190-5259-9 DDC 133.4/3/094332
1. Witchcraft - Germany - Rothenburg ob der Tauber - History - 16th century. 2. Witchcraft - Germany - Rothenburg ob der Tauber - History - 17th century. I. Title. II. Series.
BF1583 .R69 2003

Rowlands, Mark. The body in mind : understanding cognitive processes / Mark Rowlands. Cambridge, U.K. ; New York : Cambridge University Press, 1999. x, 270 p. ; 23 cm. (Cambridge studies in philosophy) Includes bibliographical references (p. 258-266) and index. Sample text URL: http://www.loc.gov/catdir/samples/cam032/98045620.html Table of contents URL: http://www.loc.gov/catdir/toc/cam024/98045620.html Publisher description URL: http://www.loc.gov/catdir/description/cam029/98045620.html ISBN 0-521-65274-X (hb) DDC 128/.2
1. Philosophy of mind. 2. Mind and body. 3. Cognition. 4. Externalism (Philosophy of mind) I. Title. II. Series.
BD418.3 .R78 1999

ROWLING, J. K. - CHARACTERS - HARRY POTTER.
Gupta, Suman, 1966- Re-reading Harry Potter. Houndmills, Basingstoke ; New York : Palgrave Macmillan, 2003.
PR6068.O93 Z68 2003

Harry Potter's world. New York ; London : RoutledgeFalmer, 2003.
PR6068.O93 Z73 2003

The ivory tower and Harry Potter. Columbia : University of Missouri Press, 2002.
PR6068.O93 Z734 2002

Reading Harry Potter. Westport, Conn. ; London : Praeger Publishers, 2003.
PR6068.O93 Z84 2003

ROWLING, J. K. - CRITICISM AND INTERPRETATION.
Gupta, Suman, 1966- Re-reading Harry Potter. Houndmills, Basingstoke ; New York : Palgrave Macmillan, 2003.
PR6068.O93 Z68 2003

Harry Potter's world. New York ; London : RoutledgeFalmer, 2003.
PR6068.O93 Z73 2003

Reading Harry Potter. Westport, Conn. ; London : Praeger Publishers, 2003.
PR6068.O93 Z84 2003

Rowsell, Lorna V., 1933-.
Sutcliffe, Eileen, 1934- Eve returns Adam's rib. Calgary : Loraleen Enterprises, c2002.

ROYALTY. *See* **PRINCESSES; QUEENS.**

Royer, Daniel.
Directed self-placement. Cresskill, N.J. : Hampton Press, c2003.
PE1404 .D57 2003

Royle, Nicholas, 1963- The uncanny / Nicholas Royle. Manchester (UK) ; New York : Manchester University Press, 2003. x, 340 p. : ill. ; 24 cm. Includes bibliographical references and index. ISBN 0-7190-5560-1 (hc.) ISBN 0-7190-5561-X (pbk.) DDC 809/.93353
1. Literature - Philosophy. 2. Psychoanalysis and literature. 3. Curiosities and wonders in literature. 4. Supernatural in literature. I. Title.
PN49 .R75 2002

Roysircar, Gargi.
Multicultural counseling competencies 2003. Alexandria, VA : Association for Multicultural Counseling and Development, 2003.
BF637.C6 M8367 2003

Rozanov, V. V. (Vasiliĭ Vasil'evich), 1856-1919. Apokalipsicheskaia sekta.
Rozanov, V. V. (Vasiliĭ Vasil'evich), 1856-1919. Vozrozhdaiushchiĭsia Egipet. Moskva : Izd-vo "Respublika", 2002.

Vo dvore iazychnikov : sobranie sochineniĭ / V.V. Rozanov ; pod obshcheĭ redaktsieĭ A.N. Nikoliukina. Moskva : Izd-vo "Respublika", 1999. 462 p. : ill., port. ; 21 cm. (Sobranie sochineniĭ / V.V. Rozanov ; [t. 10]) ISBN 5250027377
1. Religion - History. 2. Religions - History. 3. Mythology. 4. Civilization, Ancient. I. Nikoliukin, Aleksandr Nikolaevich. II. Title. III. Series: Rozanov, V. V. (Vasiliĭ Vasil'evich), 1856-1919. Works. 1994. Respublika ; t. 10.
BL96 .R69 1999

Vozrozhdaiushchiĭsia Egipet / sobranie sochineniĭ pod obshcheĭ red. A.N. Nikoliukina. Moskva : Izd-vo "Respublika", 2002. 525 p. : ill. ; 21 cm. Includes bibliographical references and index. CONTENTS: Vozrozhdaiushchiĭsia Egipet -- Apokalipsicheskaia sekta (Khlysty i skoptsy) -- Malye proizvedeniia 1909-1914 godov: Bibleĭskaia poeziia ; V sosedstve Sodoma (Istoki Izrailia) ; "Angel Iegovy" u evreev (Istoki Izrailia) ; Evropa i evrei -- Sokrovennyĭ trud Rozanova / S. Fediakin -- Kommentarii. ISBN 5250018408
1. Egypt - Civilization - To 332 B.C. 2. Egypt - Religion. 3. Sex role - Religious aspects. 4. Khlysty. 5. Skoptsy. 6. Christian sects - Russia. 7. Jews - Civilization. I. Nikoliukin, Aleksandr Nikolaevich. II. Rozanov, V. V. (Vasiliĭ Vasil'evich), 1856-1919. Apokalipsicheskaia sekta. III. Title. IV. Series: Rozanov, V. V. (Vasiliĭ Vasil'evich), 1856-1919. Works. 1994. Respublika ; t. 14.

Works. 1994. Respublika
(t. 10.) Rozanov, V. V. (Vasiliĭ Vasil'evich), 1856-1919. Vo dvore iazychnikov. Moskva : Izd-vo "Respublika", 1999.
BL96 .R69 1999

(t. 14.) Rozanov, V. V. (Vasiliĭ Vasil'evich), 1856-1919. Vozrozhdaiushchiĭsia Egipet. Moskva : Izd-vo "Respublika", 2002.

Rozenzweig, Mark R.
International Union of Psychological Science. History of the International Union of Psychological Science (IUPsyS). Hove, East Sussex ; Philadelphia, PA : Psychology Press, c2000.
BF11 .I62 2000

Rozin, V. M. Liubov' i seksual'nost' v kul'ture, sem'e i vzgliadakh na polovoe vospitanie : [uchebnoe posobie] / V.M. Rozin. Moskva : Logos : Vysshaia shkola, 1999. 207 p. ; 22 cm. Authorized for instructional purposes. "Uchebnoe izdanie"--Colophon. Includes bibliographical references. ISBN 5884390963
1. Love. 2. Sex. 3. Family. 4. Interpersonal relations. I. Title.
BF575.L8 R69 1999

Rozman, Deborah.
Childre, Doc Lew, 1945- Transforming anger. Oakland, Calif. : New Harbinger ; London : Hi Marketing, 2003.
BF575.A5 C45 2003

Rozner, Shelomoh. Sh. u-t. La-ḥafets be-ḥayim : libun she'elot metsuyot be-hilkhot leshon ha-ra' / 'arukh 'a. y. Shelomoh Rozner. Mahad. 3, be-tosefet 13 she'elot be-ḥelek 3. Yerushalayim : Kolel shemirat ha-lashon : le-hasig, Sh. Rozner, 762 [2001 or 2002] 260 p. ; 24 cm.
1. Libel and slander - Religious aspects - Judaism. 2. Gossip. 3. Ethics, Jewish. 4. Responsa - 1900- I. Title. II. Title: La-ḥafets be-ḥayim

Rozov, N. S. (Nikolaĭ Sergeevich) Filosofiia i teoriia istorii / N.S. Rozov. Moskva : Logos, 2002- v. ; 22 cm. At head of title: Federal'naia t︠s︡elevaia programma "Gosudarstvennaia t︠s︡elevaia podderzhka integrat︠s︡ii vysshego obrazovaniia i fundamental'noĭ nauki na 1997-2000 gody" Includes bibliographical references. PARTIAL CONTENTS: Kn. 1. Prolegomeny ISBN 5940101275
1. History - Philosophy. 2. History - Methodology. I. Title.
D16.8 .R873 2002

Rozprawa habilitacyjna (Katolicki Uniwersytet Lubelski. Wydział Nauk Społecznych)
Śliwak, Jacek. Osobowość altruistyczna. Wyd. 1. Lublin : Red. Wydawnictw Katolickiego Uniwersytetu Lubelskiego, 2001.
BF637.H4 S58 2001

Rozvorozhuiuchy Iunga.
Menzhulin, V. (Vadim), 1968- Raskoldovyvaia Iunga. Kiev : Izd-vo "Sfera", 2002.
BF173.J85 M46 2002

Rozvytok psykhiky v ontohenezi.
Maksymenko, S. D. (Serhiĭ Dmytrovych) Kyïv : "Forum", 2002.

BF706 .M34 2002

Ru jie cai gen tan.
Hong, Zicheng, fl. 1596. [Cai gen tan] Di 1 ban. Beijing Shi : Zong jiao wen hua chu ban she, 1996 (1997 printing)
BJ1558.C5 H85 1996b <Asian China>

Ruben, David-Hillel. Action and its explanation / David-Hillel Ruben. 1st ed. Oxford : Clarendon Press, 2003. vii, 240 p. .: 25 cm. Includes bibliographical references (p. [230]-238) and index. Includes "Appendix on the epistemology of action: certain and basic physical action." ISBN 0-19-823588-7 DDC 128.4
1. Psychology - Philosophy. 2. Knowledge, Theory of. I. Title.
BF38 .R83 2003

Rubin, Gabrielle, 1921- Le roman familial de Freud / Gabrielle Rubin. Paris : Payot, 2002. 198 p. ; 23 cm. Includes bibliographical references (p. [195]-196). ISBN 2-228-89622-5 DDC 150
1. Freud, Sigmund, - 1856-1939. 2. Family. 3. Psychoanalysis. I. Title.

Rubin, Ron.
Wowisms. 1st ed. New York : Newmarket Press, c2003.
BF637.S8 W7 2003

Rubino, Joe. Restore your magnificence : a life-changing guide to reclaiming your self-esteem : complete your past, assess your present, design your future / Joe Rubino. 1st ed. Boxford, Mass. : Vision Works Pub., c2003. 194 p. : ill. ; 21 cm. "Includes: The 12 steps to restoring your self-esteem." Includes index. ISBN 0-9678529-9-4 (pbk.)
1. Self-esteem. I. Title.
BF697.5.S46 R83 2003

Rudkevich, L. A. (Lev Aleksandrovich).
Bodalev, A. A. Kak stanoviatsia velikimi ili vydaiushchimisia? Moskva : In-t psikhoterapii, 2003.
BF724.5 .B64 2003

Rudnytsky, Peter L. Reading psychoanalysis : Freud, Rank, Ferenczi, Groddeck / Peter L. Rudnytsky. Ithaca : Cornell University Press, 2002. xviii, 312 p. ; 23 cm. (Cornell studies in the history of psychiatry) Includes bibliographical references (p. 285-302) and index. ISBN 0-8014-3777-6 (cloth) ISBN 0-8014-8825-7 (pbk.) DDC 150.19/5
1. Psychoanalysis. I. Title. II. Series.
BF173 .R794 2002

Rueckert, William H. (William Howe), 1926-.
Burke, Kenneth, 1897- On human nature. Berkeley : University of California Press, c2003.
B945.B771 R84 2003

Rueschemeyer, Dietrich.
Comparative historical analysis in the social sciences. Cambridge, U.K. ; New York : Cambridge University Press, 2003.
H61 .C524 2003

Ruffinengo, Pier Paolo, 1937- Ontonèesis : introduzione alla metafisica : per un amico pasticciere / Pier Paolo Ruffinengo. 1. ed. Genova : Marietti, 2002. 253 p. ; 21 cm. Includes bibliographical references. ISBN 88-211-8687-3 DDC 110
1. Metaphysics. I. Title.

Rufo, Marcel. Frères et soeurs une maladie d'amour / Marcel Rufo ; avec la collaboration de Christine Schilte. Paris : Fayard, 2002. 306 p. ; 22 cm. Includes bibliographical references. ISBN 2-213-61103-3 DDC 150
1. Brothers and sisters. 2. Psychoanalysis. I. Schilte, Christine. II. Title.

Ruge, Kenneth. The Othello response : dealing with jealousy, suspicion, and rage in your relationship / Kenneth C. Ruge ; with Barry Lenson. New York : Marlowe & Co., 2003. p. cm. Includes bibliographical references and index. ISBN 1-56924-503-7 DDC 152.4/8
1. Jealousy. I. Lenson, Barry. II. Title.
BF575.J4 R84 2003

Ruggiero, Fabio. La follia dei cristiani : la reazione pagana al cristianesimo nei secoli I-V / Fabio Ruggiero ; prefazione di Manlio Simonetti. Roma : Città nuova, c2002. 260 p. ; 20 cm. (I volti della storia ; 11) Includes bibliographical references (p. 213-251) and index. ISBN 88-311-0335-0 DDC 270
1. Church history - Primitive and early church, ca. 30-600. 2. Paganism - History. 3. Christianity and other religions. I. Title. II. Series: Volti della storia (Città nuova editrice) ; 11.
BR166 .R84 2002

Ruggiero, Guido, 1944-.
A companion to the worlds of the Renaissance. Malden, MA : Blackwell Publishers, 2002.
CB367 .C65 2002

Ruggiero, Vincent Ryan. The art of thinking : a guide to critical and creative thought / Vincent Ryan Ruggiero. 7th ed. New York : Pearson/Longman, c2004. p. cm. Includes bibliographical references (p.   ) and index. ISBN 0-321-16332-X (pbk.) DDC 153.4/2
1. Thought and thinking. 2. Critical thinking. 3. Creative thinking. 4. Thought and thinking - Problems, exercises, etc. I. Title.
BF441 .R84 2004

Making your mind matter : strategies for increasing practical intelligence / Vincent Ryan Ruggiero. Lanham, Md. : Rowman & Littlefield, c2003. xxii, 119 p. ; 24 cm. Includes bibliographical references (p. 109-111) and index. Table of contents URL: http://www.loc.gov/catdir/toc/ecip042/2003008107.html ISBN 0-7425-1462-5 (hardcover : alk. paper) ISBN 0-7425-1463-3 (pbk. : alk. paper) DDC 153.9
1. Intellect. I. Title.
BF431 .R78 2003

Rui, Yong.
Zhou, Xiang Sean. Exploration of visual data. Boston ; London : Kluwer Academic Publishers, c2003.
T385 .Z55 2003

RUINS. See EXCAVATIONS (ARCHAEOLOGY).

Rukmini Bhaya Nair. Narrative gravity : conversation, cognition, culture / Rukmini Bhaya Nair. New Delhi ; New York : Oxford University Press, 2002. xi, 425 p. ; 23 cm. Includes bibliographical references (p. [399]-417) and index. ISBN 0-19-565700-4 DDC 401/.41
1. Discourse analysis, Narrative. 2. Discourse analysis - Psychological aspects. I. Title.
P302.7 .R85 2002

Narrative gravity : conversation, cognition, culture / Rukmini Bhaya Nair. London ; New York : Routledge, 2003. xi, 425 p. ; 23 cm. Includes bibliographical references (p. [399]-417) and index. ISBN 0-415-30735-X DDC 401/.41
1. Discourse analysis, Narrative. 2. Discourse analysis - Psychological aspects. I. Title.
P302.7 .R85 2003

The rule of freedom.
Joyce, Patrick, 1945- London : Verso, 2003.
JC585 .J69 2003

RULE OF LAW.
Davydov, IU. P. (IUriĭ Pavlovich) Norma protiv sily. Moskva : Nauka, 2002.

RULERS. See QUEENS.

Rulers, leaders, and people.
Karauri, Mathew Adams, 1947- Nairobi : Karma Pub. Co., 2001.

Rules for getting it right - now, and no matter what!.
Marcum, Dave. BusinessThink. New York : Wiley, c2002.
HF5386 .M3087 2002

RULES (PHILOSOPHY).
Pettit, Philip, 1945- Rules, reasons, and norms. Oxford : Oxford University Press ; New York : Clarendon Press, 2002.
B105.T54 P48 2002

Rules, reasons, and norms.
Pettit, Philip, 1945- Oxford : Oxford University Press ; New York : Clarendon Press, 2002.
B105.T54 P48 2002

RULES, SOCIAL. See SOCIAL NORMS.

Rumbaugh, Duane M., 1929- Intelligence of apes and other rational beings / Duane M. Rumbaugh and David A. Washburn. New Haven : Yale University Press, c2003. xvii, 326 p. : ill. ; 25 cm. (Current perspectives in psychology) Includes bibliographical references (p. 291-316) and index. ISBN 0-300-09983-5 (cloth : alk. paper) DDC 156
1. Apes - Psychology. 2. Animal intelligence. 3. Psychology, Comparative. I. Washburn, David A., 1961- II. Title. III. Series.
QL737.P96 R855 2003

Respondents, operants, and emergents [microform] : toward an integrated perspective on behavior / Duane M. Rumbaugh, David A. Washburn, William A. Hillix. [Washington, D.C. : National Aeronautics and Space Administration, 1997] 8 p. ([NASA contractor report] : NASA-CR-204798) Caption title. Shipping list no.: 98-0317-M. Originally published: [Mahwah, N.J.] : Lawrence Erlbaum Associates, 1996. Includes bibliographical references (p. 8). Microfiche. [Washington, D.C. : National Aeronautics and Space Administration, 1997] 1 microfiche ; negative.
1. Learning, Psychology of. 2. Operant behavior. I. Washburn, David A. II. Hillix, William A. (William Allen), 1927- III. United States. National Aeronautics and Space Administration.

IV. Title. V. Title: Learning as a Self-Organization. 1996. VI. Title: Toward an integrated perspective on behavior VII. Series: NASA contractor report ; NASA CR-204798.

RUMSFELD, DONALD, 1932-.
Krames, Jeffrey A. The Rumsfeld way. 1st ed. New York : McGraw-Hill, c2002.
UB210 .K73 2002

The Rumsfeld way.
Krames, Jeffrey A. 1st ed. New York : McGraw-Hill, c2002.
UB210 .K73 2002

Rumstuckle, Cornelius, 1940- The book of wizardry : the apprentice's guide to the secrets of the wizard's guild / Cornelius Rumstuckle. 1st ed. St. Paul, Minn. : Llewellyn Publications, 2003. x, 325 p. : ill. ; 21 cm. SUMMARY: Gives the twenty-two secrets for becoming a Wizard, including how to make a wand, read an oracle, and achieve member status in the Wizards' Guild. ISBN 0-7387-0165-3 DDC 133.4/3
1. Magic - Juvenile literature. 2. Magic. 3. Wizards. I. Title.
BF1611 .R85 2003

Runde, Jochen, 1959-.
The philosophy of Keynes' economics. London ; New York : Routledge, 2003.
HB99.7 .P45 2003

RUNES.
Hathaway, Robert A. Runes from the New World. 2nd ed. [San Diego, Calif.?] : R.A. Hathaway, c2002.
BF1891.R85 H38 2002

Runica, Germanica, Mediaevalia. Berlin : W. de Gruyter, 2003.

Runes from the New World.
Hathaway, Robert A. 2nd ed. [San Diego, Calif.?] : R.A. Hathaway, c2002.
BF1891.R85 H38 2002

RUNES - MISCELLANEA.
Aswynn, Freya, 1949- Northern mysteries & magick. 2nd ed. St. Paul, Minn. : Llewellyn Publications, 1998 (2002 printing)
BF1623.R89 A78 1998

Melville, Francis. The book of runes. 1st ed. Hauppauge, NY : Barrons, c2003.
BF1891.R85 M45 2003

Mountfort, Paul Rhys. Nordic runes. Rochester, Vt. : Destiny Books, 2003.
BF1779.R86 M68 2003

Thorsson, Edred. The truth about Teutonic magick. 2nd ed. Saint Paul, MN : Llewellyn Publications, 1994.
BF1622.G3 T488 1994

RUNIC ALPHABETS. *See* **RUNES.**

The runic oracle.
Seachrist, Brian. Riverview, FL : Green Warden Foundation, c1999.
BF1891.R85 S43 1999

Runica, Germanica, Mediaevalia / herausgegeben von Wilhelm Heizmann and Astrid van Nahl. Berlin : W. de Gruyter, 2003. xv, 1024 p. : ill., maps ; 25 cm. (Ergänzungsbände zum Reallexikon der germanischen Altertumskunde ; Bd. 37) Contributions in German, English, Norwegian, Swedish, and French. Includes bibliographical references. ISBN 3-11-017778-1 (alk. paper)
1. Inscriptions, Runic. 2. Runes. 3. Germanic literature - History and criticism. 4. Germanic languages. 5. Scandanavia - History. 6. Germany - History. I. Heinzmann, Wilhelm. II. Nahl, Astrid van, 1951- III. Series.

The Running Press pocket guide
MacGregor, Rob. Dreams. Philadelphia, Pa. : Running Press, c2002.
BF1091 .M314 2002

Ruotsala, Helena.
Making and breaking of borders. Helsinki : Finnish Literature Society, 2003.
JC323 .M35 2003

RURAL ARCHITECTURE. *See* **ARCHITECTURE, DOMESTIC.**

RURAL POPULATION. *See* **PEASANTRY.**

RURAL-URBAN MIGRATION. *See* **URBANIZATION.**

Rus' mnogolikaia
Mamleev, IUrii. Rossiia vechnaia. Moskva : AiF-Print, 2002.
DK32 .M355 2002

Rüsen, Jörn. Geschichte im Kulturprozess / Jörn Rüsen. Köln : Böhlau, c2002. x, 298 p. ; 23 cm. Includes bibliographical references (p. [269]-291) and index. ISBN 3-412-06002-X (pbk.)
1. History - Philosophy. 2. Historiography. 3. Intercultural communication. I. Title.
D16.8 .R913 2002

Western historical thinking. New York : Berghahn Books, 2002.
D16.9 .W454 2002

Rushman, Carol. The art of predictive astrology : forecasting your life events / Carol Rushman. 1st ed. St. Paul, Minn. : Llewellyn Publications, 2003, c2002. xiv, 272 p. : ill. ; 23 cm. Includes bibliographical references (p. 269-270) and index. ISBN 0-7387-0164-5 DDC 133.5
1. Predictive astrology. I. Title. II. Title: Forecasting your life events III. Title: Predictive astrology
BF1720.5 .R87 2002

Russell, Bertrand, 1872-1970. Russell on metaphysics : selections from the writings of Bertrand Russell / edited by Stephen Mumford. London ; New York : Routledge, 2003. viii, 256 p. ; 23 cm. Includes bibliographical references (p. 248-250) and index. ISBN 0-415-27744-2 (hbk.) ISBN 0-415-27745-0 (pbk.) DDC 110
1. Metaphysics. I. Mumford, Stephen. II. Title.
B1649.R91 M86 2003

Russell, Kenneth, 1928- The Times book of IQ tests. Book 1 / top UK Mensa puzzle editors Ken Russell and Philip Carter. London : Kogan Page, 2001. 193 p. : ill. ; 22 cm. Published in association with The Times. ISBN 0-7494-3473-2 DDC 153.93
1. Intelligence tests. I. Carter, Philip J. II. Title.

The Times book of IQ tests. Book 2 / Ken Russell and Philip Carter. London ; Milford, CT : Kogan Page, 2002. 195 p. : ill. ; 22 cm. ISBN 0-7494-3733-2 DDC 153.93
1. Intelligence tests. 2. Self-evaluation. I. Carter, Philip J. II. Times Newspapers. III. Title. IV. Title: Book of IQ tests.

Russell, Kenneth A.
Carter, Philip J. Maximize your brainpower. West Sussex, England ; New York : John Wiley & Sons, Ltd, 2002.
BF431.3 .C3647 2002

Carter, Philip J. More IQ testing. Chichester, West Sussex, England ; New York : John Wiley & Sons, Ltd, 2002.
BF431.3 .C367 2002

The Times book of IQ tests. Book 3 / Ken Russell and Philip Carter. London ; Sterling, VA : Kogan Page Ltd., 2003. 199 p. : ill. ; 22 cm. Includes bibliographical references. ISBN 0-7494-3959-9 (pbk.) DDC 153.9/32
1. Intelligence tests. 2. Self-evaluation. I. Carter, Philip J. II. Title.
BF431.3 .R87 2003

Russell, Mary T. The 16PF fifth edition administrator's manual : with updated norms / Mary T. Russell and Darcie L. Karol. 3rd ed. Champaign, Ill. : Institute for Personality and Ability Testing, 2002. xiv, 162 p. : ill. ; 28 cm. Includes bibliographical references (p. 145-149) and indexes. ISBN 0-918296-21-8 DDC 155.2/83
1. Sixteen Personality Factor Questionnaire. I. Karol, Darcie L. II. Institute for Personality and Ability Testing. III. Title. IV. Title: Sixteen personality factor fifth edition administrator's manual
BF698.8.S5 A37 2002

Russell, Miles.
Digging holes in popular culture. Oxford : Oxbow, 2002.
PN3433.6 .D54 2002

Russell on metaphysics.
Russell, Bertrand, 1872-1970. London ; New York : Routledge, 2003.
B1649.R91 M86 2003

Russell Sage Foundation series on trust
(v. 6) Distrust. New York : Russell Sage Foundation, 2004.
BF575.T7 D57 2004

RUSSIA - CIVILIZATION.
Lichev, Aleksandŭr. Russland verstehen. 1. Aufl. Düsseldorf : Grupello, 2001.

Meniailov, Aleksei. Durilka. Moskva : "Kraft+", 2003.

RUSSIA (FEDERATION) - CIVILIZATION.
Beliaev, G. G. Dukhovnye korni russkogo naroda. Moskva : Bylina, 2002.
DK32 .B358 2002

Mamleev, IUrii. Rossiia vechnaia. Moskva : AiF-Print, 2002.
DK32 .M355 2002

V'iunov, IU. A. Slovo o russkikh. Moskva : Izd-vo IKAR, c2002.

RUSSIA (FEDERATION) - ECONOMIC CONDITIONS.
Tumusov, F. S. (Fedot Semenovich) Budushchee mira i Rossii. Moskva : "Mysl'", 2000.
HC340.12.Z7 S2357 2000

RUSSIA (FEDERATION) - FOREIGN ECONOMIC RELATIONS - UNITED STATES.
Parshev, A. P. (Andreĭ Petrovich) Pochemu Amerika nastupaet. Moskva : AST : Astrel', 2002.
HF1558.2.Z4 P37 2002

RUSSIA (FEDERATION) - FOREIGN RELATIONS.
Parshev, A. P. (Andreĭ Petrovich) Pochemu Amerika nastupaet. Moskva : AST : Astrel', 2002.
HF1558.2.Z4 P37 2002

RUSSIA (FEDERATION) - HISTORY - PHILOSOPHY.
Mamleev, IUrii. Rossiia vechnaia. Moskva : AiF-Print, 2002.
DK32 .M355 2002

Shakhmagonov, N. (Nikolaĭ) Somknem riady, chtoby zhila Rossiia. Moskva : Ispo-Servis, 1999.

RUSSIA (FEDERATION) - INTELLECTUAL LIFE.
Beliaev, G. G. Dukhovnye korni russkogo naroda. Moskva : Bylina, 2002.
DK32 .B358 2002

Russia (Federation). Ministerstvo kul'tury.
Drankov, V. L. (Vladimir L'vovich) Priroda khudozhestvennogo talanta. Sankt-Peterburg : Sankt-Peterburgskiĭ gosudarstvennyĭ universitet kul'tury i iskusstv, 2001.

RUSSIA (FEDERATION) - POLITICS AND GOVERNMENT - 1991-.
Denisovskiĭ, G. M. Politicheskaia tolerantnost' v reformiruemom rossiĭskom obshchestve vtoroĭ poloviny 90-kh godov. Moskva : TSentr obshchechelovecheskikh tsennosteĭ, 2002.
JN6699.A15 D46 2002

Ol'shanskiĭ, D. V. (Dmitriĭ Vadimovich) Psikhologiia sovremennoĭ rossiĭskoĭ politiki. Moskva : Akademicheskiĭ proekt, 2001.
JN6699.A15 O46 2001

RUSSIA (FEDERATION) - RELIGION.
Balagushkin, E. G. (Evgeniĭ Gennad'evich) Netraditsionnye religii v sovremennoĭ Rossii. Moskva : Rossiĭskaia akademiia nauk, Institut filosofii, 1999-2002.
BL980.R8 B35 1999

Beliaev, G. G. Dukhovnye korni russkogo naroda. Moskva : Bylina, 2002.
DK32 .B358 2002

RUSSIA - FORECASTING.
Moiseev, N. N. (Nikita Nikolaevich) Kak daleko do zavtrashnego dnia--. Moskva : Taĭdeks Ko, 2002.
DK49 .M64 2002

RUSSIA - HISTORY - PHILOSOPHY.
Moiseev, N. N. (Nikita Nikolaevich) Kak daleko do zavtrashnego dnia--. Moskva : Taĭdeks Ko, 2002.
DK49 .M64 2002

Shakhmagonov, N. (Nikolaĭ) Somknem riady, chtoby zhila Rossiia. Moskva : Ispo-Servis, 1999.

RUSSIA - HISTORY - PROPHECIES.
Zaĭtseva, L. I. Russkie providtsy o rossiĭskoĭ gosudarstvennosti. Moskva : In-t ėkonomiki RAN, 1998-
DK49 .Z35 1998

RUSSIA - POETRY.
Mamleev, IUrii. Rossiia vechnaia. Moskva : AiF-Print, 2002.
DK32 .M355 2002

Russian Imago 2001 : issledovaniia po psikhoanalizu kul'tury : sbornik stateĭ / [glavnyĭ redaktor V.A. Medvedev]. Nauchnoe izd. Sankt-Peterburg : Izd-vo "Aleteĭia", 2002. 559 p. : ill. ; 22 cm. Includes bibliographical references. ISBN 5893294912
1. Psychoanalysis and culture - Russia (Federation) I. Medvedev, V. A. (Vladimir Aleksandrovich) II. Title: Russian Imago two thousand and one
BF175.4.C84 R87 2002

Russian Imago two thousand and one.
Russian Imago 2001. Nauchnoe izd. Sankt-Peterburg : Izd-vo "Aleteĭia", 2002.
BF175.4.C84 R87 2002

RUSSIAN LANGUAGE.
Russkoe slovo. Penza : Izd-vo PGPU, 1998.

PG2026.B66 R88 1998

Zhuravlev, V. K. (Vladimir Konstantinovich) Russkiĭ iazyk i russkiĭ kharakter. Moskva : Moskovskiĭ patriarkhat, 2002.
PG2095 .Z48 2002

RUSSIAN LITERATURE - 19TH CENTURY - HISTORY AND CRITICISM.
Esin, A. B. (Andreĭ Borisovich) Literaturovedenie. Kulturologiia. Moskva : Flinta ; Nauka, 2002.

RUSSIAN LITERATURE - 20TH CENTURY - HISTORY AND CRITICISM.
Esin, A. B. (Andreĭ Borisovich) Literaturovedenie. Kulturologiia. Moskva : Flinta ; Nauka, 2002.

Genis, Aleksandr, 1953- Ivan Petrovich umer. Moskva : Novoe literaturnoe obozrenie, 1999.
PG3021 .G46 1999

RUSSIAN LITERATURE - HISTORY AND CRITICISM.
Individualitätskonzepte in der russischen Kultur. Berlin : Berlin Verlag Arno Spitz, c2002.
PG2987.I48 .I53 2002

Kurganov, E. Anekdot, simvol, mif. Sankt-Peterburg : Izd-vo zhurnala "Zvezda", 2002.

Mamleev, IUriĭ. Rossiia vechnaia. Moskva : AiF-Print, 2002.
DK32 .M355 2002

RUSSIAN PHILOSOPHY. See **PHILOSOPHY, RUSSIAN.**

RUSSIAN WIT AND HUMOR, PICTORIAL.
Fenomenologiia smekha. Moskva : Rossiĭskiĭ institut kul'turologii, 2002.
PN6149.P3 F45 2002

RUSSIANS - ETHNIC IDENTITY.
Shcheglov, A. (Alekseĭ IAzycheskaia zaria. Moskva : [Izdatel'stvo "PROBEL-2000"], 2002.
BL980.R5 S53 2002

V'iunov, IU. A. Slovo o russkikh. Moskva : Izd-vo IKAR, c2002.

Russische Geschichtsphilosophie auf dem Prüfstand.
Afanasjev, Valeri, 1963- Munster : Lit, [2002]

RUSSKAIA PRAVOSLAVNAIA TSERKOV' - DOCTRINES.
Maler, Arkadiĭ. Strategii sakral'nogo smysla. Moskva : Parad izdatel'skiĭ dom, 2003.

Russkaia pravoslavnaia tserkov'. Moskovskaia patriarkhiia. Missionerskiĭ otdel.
Novye religioznye ob"edineniia Rossii destruktivnogo i okkul'tnogo kharaktera. Izd. 3-e, dop. Belgorod : Missionerskiĭ otdel Moskovskogo Patriarkhata Russkoĭ Pravoslavnoĭ TSerkvi, 2002.
BF1434.R8 N67 2002

Russkaia rasovaia teoriia do 1917 goda / sbornik original'nykh rabot russkikh klassikov pod redaktsieĭ V.B. Avdeeva. Moskva : Feri-V, 2002. 679 p. : ill. ; 25 cm. Includes bibliographical references. CONTENTS: Russkaia rasovaia teoriia do 1917 goda / V.B. Avdeev -- O znachenii ras v istorii / S.V. Eshevskiĭ -- Antropologicheskaia fiziognomika / A.P. Bogdanov -- Skreshchivanie i metisy / A.P. Bogdanov -- Velikorussy: ocherk fizicheskogo tipa / V.V. Vorob'ev -- O velikorusskom plemeni / I.D. Beliaev -- Rasy i natsional'nosti s psikhologicheskoĭ tochki zreniia / N.I. Karecv -- Cherty iz psikhologii slavian / I.A. Sikorskiĭ -- Dannye iz antropologii / I.A. Sikorskiĭ -- Russkie i ukraintsy / I.A. Sikorskiĭ -- Kharakteristika chernoĭ, zheltoĭ i beloĭ ras v sviazi s voprosami russko-iaponskoĭ voĭny / I.A. Sikorskiĭ -- Antropologicheskaia i psikhologicheskaia genealogiia Pushkina / I.A. Sikorskiĭ -- Ėkspertiza po delu ob ubiĭstve Andriushi IUshchinskogo / I.A. Sikorskiĭ -- Znaki vyrozhdeniia / I.A. Sikorskiĭ -- Fizicheskie priznaki psikhicheskoĭ degeneratsii / S.S. Korsakov -- Variatsii v skelete sovremennogo chelovechestva i ikh znachenie dlia resheniia voprosa o proiskhozhdenii i obrazovanii ras / K.A. Bari -- Znachenie antropologii v meditsine / P.A. Minakov -- Bor'ba za sushchesvovanie / I.I. Mechnikov -- Slavianskiĭ mir / A.F. Rittikh -- Novaia teoriia proiskhozhdeniia cheloveka i ego vyrozhdeniia / V.A. Moshkov -- Mekhanika vyrozhdeniia / V.A. Moshkov. ISBN 5941380178
1. Race. 2. Physical anthropology. 3. Physical anthropology - Russia. 4. Slavs. I. Avdeev, V. B. (Vladimir Borisovich) II. Sikorskiĭ, I. A. (Ivan Alekseevich), 1842-1919. Selections. 2002. III. Bogdanov, A. P. (Valentin Alekseevich). Selections. 2002. IV. Bogdanov, Anatoliĭ Petrovich, 1834-1896. Selections. 2002. V. Eshevskiĭ, S. V. (Stepan Vasil'evich). Selections. 2002. VI. Metchnikoff, Elie, 1845-1916. Selections. 2002.

Russkie providtsy o rossiĭskoĭ gosudarstvennosti.
Zaĭtsova, L. I. Moskva : In-t ėkonomiki RAN, 1998-
DK49 .Z35 1998

Russkiĭ iazyk i russkiĭ kharakter.
Zhuravlev, V. K. (Vladimir Konstantinovich) Moskva : Moskovskiĭ patriarkhat, 2002.
PG2095 .Z48 2002

Russkoe slovo : 70-letiiu professora V.D. Bondaletova posviashchaetsia : mezhvuzovskiĭ sbornik nauchnykh trudov / [redaktsionnaia kollegiia, E.S. Skoblikova (sostavitel' i otvetstvennyĭ redaktor) ... et al.]. Penza : Izd-vo PGPU, 1998. 232 p. : ill. ; 21 cm. Includes bibliographical references.
1. Russian language. 2. Language and languages. I. Bondaletov, V. D. II. Skoblikova, E. S. (Elena Sergeevna) III. Penzenskiĭ gosudarstvennyĭ pedagogicheskiĭ universitet imeni V.G. Belinskogo.
PG2026.B66 R88 1998

Russland verstehen.
Lichev, Aleksandŭr. 1. Aufl. Düsseldorf : Grupello, 2001.

Russo, Jane. O mundo psi no Brasil / Jane Russo. Rio de Janeiro : Jorge Zahar Editor, c2002. 89 p., [4] p. of plates : ill., facsims., ports. ; 18 cm. (Descobrindo o Brasil) Includes bibliographical references (p. 84-87). ISBN 85-7110-648-7
1. Psychoanalysis - Brazil - History. 2. Psychiatry - Brazil - History. 3. Psychology - Brazil - History. I. Title. II. Series.
BF173 .R877 2002

Russo, Riccardo. Statistics for the behavioural sciences : an introduction / Riccardo Russo. 1st ed. Hove, East Sussex ; New York, N.Y. : Psychology Press, 2003. p. cm. Includes bibliographical references and index. Table of contents URL: http://www.loc.gov/catdir/toc/ecip043/2003009699.html ISBN 1-84169-319-7 ISBN 1-84169-320-0 (pbk.) DDC 150/.1/5195
1. Psychometrics. I. Title.
BF39 .R82 2003

Russon, John Edward, 1960- Human experience : philosophy, neurosis, and the elements of everyday life / John Russon. Albany : State University of New York Press, c2003. viii, 162 p. ; 23 cm. (SUNY series in contemporary continental philosophy) Includes bibliographical references (p. 149-156) and index. ISBN 0-7914-5754-0 (pbk. : alk. paper) ISBN 0-7914-5753-2 (alk. paper) DDC 128/.4
1. Phenomenological psychology. 2. Neuroses. I. Title. II. Series.
BF204.5 .R87 2002

Rutgers series on self and social identity
(v. 2) Self, social identity, and physical health. New York : Oxford University Press, 1999.
R726.5 .S46 1999

Rutgers Symposium on Self and Social Identity (2nd : 1977).
Self, social identity, and physical health. New York : Oxford University Press, 1999.
R726.5 .S46 1999

Rutgers University Press.
Steedman, Carolyn. Dust. New Brunswick, N.J. : Rutgers University Press, 2002, c2001.
CD947 .S73 2002

Ruthven, Malise, 1942- A fury for God : the Islamist attack on America / Malise Ruthven. London ; New York : Granta, 2002. xxii, 324 p. ; 24 cm. Includes bibliographical references and index. ISBN 1-86207-540-9 DDC 322.10917671
1. Islamic fundamentalism. 2. Culture conflict. 3. Terrorism - United States. I. Title.
HV6432 .R87 2002

Ruthven, Suzanne. What you call time : a practical guide to modern witchcraft and western ritual magic / Suzanne Ruthven. London : Ignotus Press, c1998. 275 p. ; 21 cm. Includes bibliographical references and index. ISBN 0-9522689-3-0 DDC 133.43
1. Witchcraft. I. Title.

Rutledge, Thom. Embracing fear : and finding the courage to live your life / Thom Rutledge. 1st ed. [San Francisco] : HarperSanFrancisco, c2002. xi, 206 p. ; 22 cm. Publisher description URL: http://www.loc.gov/catdir/description/hc041/2002512662.html ISBN 0-06-251774-0 DDC 152.4/6
1. Fear. 2. Conduct of life. I. Title.
BF575.F2 R88 2002

Rutlen, Carmen Richardson, 1948- Dancing naked-- in fuzzy red slippers / by Carmen Richardson Rutlen. 1st ed. Fort Bragg, CA : Cypress House, c2003. p. cm. ISBN 1-87938-453-1 (alk. paper) DDC 158
1. Self-actualization (Psychology) 2. Conduct of life. Elie. I. Title.
BF637.S4 R877 2003

Rutsky, R. L.
Strategies for theory. Albany : State University of New York Press, c2003.

B842 .S77 2003

Ruxton, Graeme D. Elementary experimental design for the life sciences / Graeme D. Ruxton, Nick Colegrave. Oxford : Oxford University Press, 2003. xviii, 114 p. : ill. ; 25 cm. Includes bibliographical references (p. 110-112) and index. ISBN 0-19-925232-7 DDC 570.724
1. Life sciences - Experiments. 2. Experimental design. I. Colegrave, Nick. II. Title.

Ryan, Ann Marie.
Personality and work. 1st ed. San Francisco, CA : Jossey-Bass, c2003.
BF698.9.O3 P47 2003

Ryan, M. J. (Mary Jane), 1952- Trusting yourself : how to stop feeling overwhelmed and live more happily with less effort / M.J. Ryan. New York : Broadway Books, 2004. p. cm. Includes bibliographical references. ISBN 0-7679-1490-2 (alk. paper) DDC 158.1
1. Self-confidence. 2. Self-actualization (Psychology) I. Title.
BF575.S39 R93 2004

Ryan, Richard M.
Handbook of self-determination research. Soft cover ed. Rochester, NY : University of Rochester Press, 2004.
BF575.A88 H36 2004

Ryan, Robert E. Shamanism and the psychology of C.G. Jung : the great circle / Robert E. Ryan. London : Vega, 2002. 272 p. : ill. ; 24 cm. Includes bibliographical references (p. [261]-266) and index. Publisher description URL: http://www.loc.gov/catdir/description/ste031/2002489211.html ISBN 1-84333-588-3 DDC 150.19/54
1. Psychoanalysis and religion. 2. Shamanism - Psychology. 3. Jungian psychology. 4. Jung, C. G. - (Carl Gustav), - 1875-1961. I. Title.
BF175.4.R44 R93 2002

Ryckman, Richard M. Theories of personality / Richard M. Ryckman. 8th ed. Belmont, CA : Thomson/Wadsworth, c2004. 698 p. ; 25 cm. Includes bibliographical references and indexes. ISBN 0-534-61983-5
1. Personality - Textbooks. I. Title. II. Title: Personality
BF698 .R96 2004

Ryff, Carol D.
How healthy are we? Chicago, Ill. : University of Chicago Press, c2003.
BF724.6 .H69 2003

Rymes, Betsy.
Linguistic anthropology of education. Westport, Conn. ; London : Praeger, 2003.
P40.8 .L55 2003

Rymut, Kazimierz.
Język w przestrzeni społecznej. Opole : Uniwersytet Opolski, 2002.
P40 .J492 2002

Rysev, Sergeĭ. Vyshe kryshi : popurri na ėzotericheskie temy / S. Rysev. Sankt-Peterburg : Gelikon Plius, 2001. 234 p. ; 20 cm. Includes bibliographical references (p. 230-[232]) and index. ISBN 5936820610
1. Complexity (Philosophy) 2. New Age movement. I. Title.
B105.C473 R97 2001

Ryter, Jon Christian. Whatever happened to America? / by Jon Christian Ryter. Tampa, FL : Hallberg Pub., 2001, c2000. vi, 551 p. ; 24 cm. Includes bibliographical references and index. ISBN 0-87319-049-1 DDC 973.91
1. United States - Politics and government - 20th century. 2. Constitutional history - United States. 3. Self-determination, National - United States. 4. Sovereignty. I. Title.
E743 .R98 2001

Rzepa, Teresa. O interpretowaniu psychologicznym w kręgu szkoły lwowsko-warszawskiej / Teresa Rzepa. Warszawa : Polskie Tow. Semiotyczne, 2002. 150 p. ; 24 cm. (Biblioteka myśli semiotycznej, 0867-2261 ; 47) On t.p.: Znak-Język-Rzeczywistość. Includes bibliographical references (p. [141]-146). ISBN 83-85372-36-9
1. Psychology - Poland - History - 20th century. 2. Twardowski, Kazimierz, - 1866-1938. 3. Witwicki, Władysław, - 1878-1948. I. Title. II. Series.
BF108.P7 R94 2002

S-BIT, Stoelting Brief Nonverbal Intelligence Test.
Roid, Gale H. Wood Dale, IL : Stoelting Co., c1999.
BF432.5.S85 R65 1999

Saar, Martin.
Kontexte und Kulturen des Erinnerns. Konstanz : UVK Verlagsgesellschaft, 2002.
BF378.S65 K65 2002

Sabalat, Tina. Pascals "Wette" : ein Spiel um das ewige Leben : das Fragment 233 der "Pensées" Blaise Pascals / von Tina Sabalat. Marburg : Tectum, 2000. vii, 125 p. ; 21 cm. Includes bibliographical references (p. 121-125). ISBN 3-8288-8173-4 (pbk.)

1. Pascal, Blaise, - 1623-1662. - Pensées. 2. God - Proof. 3. Philosophical theology - Methodology. 4. Practical reason. 5. Risk-taking (Psychology) 6. Faith. 7. God - Knowableness. I. Title.

SÁBATO, ERNESTO R. - CRITICISM AND INTERPRETATION.
Villari, Rafael Andrés. Literatura e psicanálise. Florianópolis : Editora da UFSC, 2002.

Sabelis, Ida, 1954-.
Making time. Oxford ; New York : Oxford University Press, 2002.
HD69.T54 M34 2002

Sabella, Russell A., 1965-.
Tyler, J. Michael. Using technology to improve counseling practice. Alexandria, VA : American Counseling Association, 2003.
BF637.C6 T89 2003

Saber ambiental.
Leff, Enrique. 3a ed. correg. y aument. México : PNUMA ; Siglo Veintiuno, 2002.

Saberi, Reza, 1941- Insights and intuitions : reflections on the nature of existence / Reza Saberi. Lanham, Md. : University Press of America, c2003. 303 p. ; 22 cm. ISBN 0-7618-2507-X (pbk. : alk. paper) DDC 181/.5
1. Saberi, Reza, - 1941- - Diaries. 2. Life - Miscellanea. I. Title.
BF1999 .S225 2003

SABERI, REZA, 1941- - DIARIES.
Saberi, Reza, 1941- Insights and intuitions. Lanham, Md. : University Press of America, c2003.
BF1999 .S225 2003

Sabourin, Teresa Chandler. The contemporary American family : a dialectical perspective on communication and relationships / Teresa Chandler Sabourin. Thousand Oaks, Calif. : Sage Publications, c2003. xiii, 171 p. ; 24 cm. Includes bibliographical references (p. 157-163) and index. ISBN 0-7619-2445-0 ISBN 0-7619-2446-9 (pbk.) DDC 306.85/0973
1. Family - United States. 2. Change (Psychology) I. Title.
HQ536 .S213 2003

Sabrina, Lady. Celebrating Wiccan spirituality : spells, sacred rites, and folklore for each day of the year / by Lady Sabrina. Franklin Lakes, NJ : New Page Books, 2003. 379 p. : ill. ; 21 cm. Includes bibliographical references (p. 309-311) and index. ISBN 1-56414-593-X (pbk.) DDC 299
1. Witchcraft - Calendars. I. Title.
BF1572.F37 S23 2003

Exploring Wicca : the beliefs, rites, and rituals of the Wiccan religion / by Lady Sabrina. Franklin Lakes, NJ : New Page Books, c2001. 221 p. : ill. ; 21 cm. Includes bibliographical references (p. 205-214) and index. ISBN 1-56414-481-X
1. Witchcraft. I. Title.

Sacco, François.
Le propre de l'homme. Lausanne : Delachaux et Niestlé, c1998.
BF175 .P69 1998

Sacerdoti, Gilberto, 1952- Sacrificio e sovranità : teologia e politica nell'Europa di Shakespeare e Bruno / Gilberto Sacerdoti. Torino : Einaudi, 2002. vi, 378 p. : ill. ; 21 cm. (Biblioteca Einaudi ; 139) Includes bibliographical references and index. ISBN 88-06-15423-0 DDC 320
1. Bruno, Giordano, - 1548-1600. 2. Sovereignty. 3. Theology - History - 16th century. 4. Philosophy, Renaissance. 5. Religion and politics - Europe - History - 16th century. I. Title. II. Series.

SACHMET (EGYPTIAN DEITY). See **SEKHMET (EGYPTIAN DEITY).**

Sack, Bracha, 1933- Shomer ha-pardes : ha-mekubal Rabi Shabtai Sheftl Horovits mi-Prag / Berakhah Zak. Be'er Sheva' : Universiṭat Ben-Guryon ba-Negev, c2002. 240 p. ; 23 cm. Title on verso of t.p.: Shomer ha-Pardes : the Kabbalist Rabbi Shabbetai Sheftel Horowitz of Prague. Includes bibliographical references and indexes. ISBN 9653428357
1. Horowitz, Shabbetai Sheftel ben Akiva, - d. 1619. 2. Cordovero, Moses ben Jacob, - 1522-1570 - Influence. 3. Cabala. 4. God (Judaism) I. Title. II. Title: Shomer ha-Pardes : the Kabbalist Rabbi Shabbetai Sheftel Horowitz of Prague III. Title: Kabbalist Rabbi Shabbetai Sheftel Horowitz of Prague

SACRAMENTALS. See **CANDLES AND LIGHTS.**

SACRAMENTS. See **BAPTISM; MARRIAGE.**

SACRAMENTS - CATHOLIC CHURCH.
Chauvet, Louis Marie. [Symbole et sacrement. English] Symbol and sacrament. Collegeville, Minn. : Liturgical Press, c1995.

BV800 .C5213 1995

The sacred and the profane : contemporary demands on hermeneutics / edited by Jeffrey F. Keuss. Aldershot, Hants, England ; Burlington, VT : Ashgate, c2003. vii, 133 p. ; 25 cm. Includes bibliographical references (p. 127-130) and index. ISBN 0-7546-0767-4 (alk. paper) DDC 121/.686
1. Hermeneutics. 2. Hermeneutics - Religious aspects. I. Keuss, Jeffrey F., 1965-
BD241 .S312 2003

SACRED CANTATAS. See **CANTATAS, SACRED.**

The sacred magic of ancient Egypt.
Clark, Rosemary, 1948- 1st ed. St. Paul, Minn. : Llewellyn Publications, 2003.
BF1591 .C52 2003

SACRED MEALS. See **FASTS AND FEASTS.**

SACRED NUMBERS. See **SYMBOLISM OF NUMBERS.**

SACRED PLACES. See **SACRED SPACE.**

SACRED SPACE - ENCYCLOPEDIAS.
Franklin, Anna. The illustrated encyclopedia of fairies. London : Vega, 2002.
GR549 .F73 2002

SACRED SPACE - MISCELLANEA.
Alexander, Jane. The smudging and blessings book. New York: Sterling Pub., 2001.
BF1999 .A6329 2001

SACRED SPACES. See **SACRED SPACE.**

Sacred stones of the goddess.
Gillotte, Galen, 1952- 1st ed. St. Paul, Minn. : Llewellyn Publications, 2003.
BF1611 .G55 2003

SACRED, THE. See **HOLY, THE.**

SACRED VOCAL MUSIC. See **CANTATAS, SACRED.**

SACRIFICE. See also **ANIMAL SACRIFICE; SELF-SACRIFICE.**
Frantzen, Allen J., 1947- Bloody good. Chicago : University of Chicago Press, 2004.
D523 .F722 2004

Sacrificio e sovranità.
Sacerdoti, Gilberto, 1952- Torino : Einaudi, 2002.

Il sacro nel Rinascimento : atti del XII convegno internazionale : Chianciano-Pienza, 17-20 luglio 2000 / [a cura di Luisa Secchi Tarugi]. Firenze : F. Cesati, c2002. 778 p. : ill. ; 23 cm. (Quaderni della Rassegna ; 22) Includes bibliographical references and index. Texts in English, French or Italian. ISBN 88-7667-116-1 DDC 200
1. Holy, The, in literature - Congresses. 2. Renaissance - Congresses. 3. Holy, The - Congresses. I. Secchi Tarugi, Luisa Rotondi, 1943- II. Series: Quaderni della Rassegna (Florence, Italy) ; 22.
PN49 .S337 2002

Sad.
Nelson, Robin, 1971- Minneapolis, MN : Lerner Publications Co., c2004.
BF723.S15 N45 2004

SADE, MARQUIS DE, 1740-1814 - CRITICISM AND INTERPRETATION - BIOGRAPHY.
Stobbe, Heinz-Günther, 1948- Vom Geist der Übertretung und Vernichtung. Regensburg : Friedrich Pustet, c2002.

Sādhanā.
Tagore, Rabindranath, 1861-1941. [Sādhanā. Marathi] Kolhāpūra : Mahārāshṭra Grantha Bhāṇḍāra, 2000.
B131 .T28 2000

Sādhanamālā, Avalokiteśvara section.
[Aids to Sadhana series. Tibetan & Sanskrit. Selections.] Delhi : Adroit Publishers ; New Delhi : Distributors, Akhil Book Distributors, 2002.
BQ8915 .S23 2002

Sadka, Dewey. The Dewey color system : choose your colors, change your life / Dewey Sadka. 1st ed. New York : Three Rivers Press, 2004. p. cm. Table of contents URL: http://www.loc.gov/catdir/toc/ecip048/2003018421.html ISBN 1400050626 (Trade paperback) DDC 155.2/84
1. Color - Psychological aspects. 2. Personality tests. 3. Self-evaluation. I. Title.
BF789.C7 S23 2004

Sadler, Philip, 1930- Leadership / Philip Sadler. 2nd ed. London ; Sterling, VA : Kogan Page Ltd., 2003. vii, 195 p. : ill. ; 23 cm. (MBA masterclass series) Includes bibliographical references (p. [181]-186) and index. ISBN 0-7494-3919-X (pbk.) DDC 658.4/092
1. Leadership. I. Title. II. Series.

HD57.7 .S227 2003

SADNESS. See also **MELANCHOLY.**
Leonard, Marcia. I feel sad. Nashville, Tenn. : CandyCane Press, 2003.
BF575.S23 L46 2003

Nelson, Robin, 1971- Sad. Minneapolis, MN : Lerner Publications Co., c2004.
BF723.S15 N45 2004

Niẓām al-Dīn, 'Irfān. Lā lil-ikti'āb na'am lil-farh!!? al-Ṭab'ah 1. [Beirut?] : al-Mu'assasah al-'Arabīyah-al-Urūbbīyah lil-Ṣiḥāfah wa-al-Nashr, 2001.

Randolph, Joanne. What I look like when I am sad. 1st ed. New York : PowerStart Press, 2004.
BF723.S15 R36 2004

Randolph, Joanne. [What I look like when I am sad. Spanish & English] What I look like when I am sad = 1st ed. New York : Rosen Pub. Group's PowerKids Press, 2004.
BF723.S15 R3618 2004

Sagnol, Marc, 1956- Tragique et tristesse. Paris : Cerf, 2003.

SADNESS IN CHILDREN - JUVENILE LITERATURE.
Nelson, Robin, 1971- Sad. Minneapolis, MN : Lerner Publications Co., c2004.
BF723.S15 N45 2004

Randolph, Joanne. What I look like when I am sad. 1st ed. New York : PowerStart Press, 2004.
BF723.S15 R36 2004

Randolph, Joanne. [What I look like when I am sad. Spanish & English] What I look like when I am sad = 1st ed. New York : Rosen Pub. Group's PowerKids Press, 2004.
BF723.S15 R3618 2004

SADNESS - JUVENILE LITERATURE.
Leonard, Marcia. I feel sad. Nashville, Tenn. : CandyCane Press, 2003.
BF575.S23 L46 2003

SADOMASOCHISM.
Califia-Rice, Patrick, 1954- Speaking sex to power. 1st ed. San Francisco : Cleis Press, c2002.
HQ76.25 .C32 2002

ṢADR AL-DĪN SHĪRĀZĪ, MUḤAMMAD IBN IBRĀHĪM, D. 1641.
Jambet, Christian. L'acte d'être. [Paris] : Fayard, c2002.

Safari, J. F. The new art of leadership for Africa 2000 : analysis of the social and intellectual qualities of good leadership in politics and organizations / by Safari, Joseph F. Safari. Peramiho, Tanzania : Benedictine Publications Ndanda, 1996. 117 p. ; 21 cm. Includes bibliographical references (p. 114-117). ISBN 9976-63-431-5
1. Leadership. 2. Leadership - Africa. 3. Black author. I. Title. II. Title: Analysis of the social and intellectual qualities of good leadership in politics and organizations
HM1261 .S35 1996

SAFARIS. See **HUNTING.**

SAFETY.
Leaney, Cindy. Long walk to school. Vero Beach, Fla. : Rourke Pub., 2003.
BF637.B85 L43 2003

Safouan, Moustafa. Four lessons of psychoanalysis / by Moustafa Safouan ; edited by Anna Shane. New York : Other Press, c2004. p. cm. CONTENTS: Lesson 1 -- Lesson 2 -- Lesson 3 -- Lesson 4. ISBN 1-59051-087-9 (pbk. : alk. paper) DDC 150.19/5
1. Psychoanalysis. 2. Lacan, Jacques, - 1901- 3. Freud, Sigmund, - 1856-1939. I. Shane, Anna. II. Title.
BF175 .S19 2004

Safran, Jeremy D.
Psychoanalysis and Buddhism. 1st ed. Boston : Wisdom Publications, c2003.
BF175.4.R44 P785 2003

Safty, Essam. La psyché humaine : conceptions populaires, religieuses et philosophiques en Grèce, des origines à l'ancien stoïcisme / Essam Safty. Paris : Harmattan, c2003. 384 p. ; 22 cm. (Collection Ouverture philosophique) Includes bibliographical references (p. [363]-380) and indexes. ISBN 2-7475-3896-6 DDC 180
1. Stoics. 2. Soul. I. Title. II. Series: Collection L'ouverture philosophique.
B528 .S34 2003

Sage university papers series. Quantitative applications in the social sciences
(no. 07-072.) Jaccard, James. Interaction effects in multiple regression. 2nd ed. Thousand Oaks, Calif. : Sage Publications, c2003.

HA31.3 .J33 2003

(no. 07-140.) Smithson, Michael. Confidence intervals. Thousand Oaks, Calif. : Sage Publications, c2003.
HA31.2 .S59 2003

Sagesses musulmanes
(3) Ikhwān al-Ṣafā'. [Rasā'il. 36. French & Arabic] Les révolutions et les cycles . Louvain-la-Neuve : Bruylant-Academia ; Beyrouth : Al-Bouraq Editions, 1996.

SAGGERS. *See* **POTTERY.**

Saggi (Arnoldo Mondadori editore)
Dacquino, Giacomo, 1930- Bisogno d'amore. 1. ed. Milano : Mondadori, 2002.
BF697.5.S43 D33 2002

Saggi (Bollati Boringhieri (Firm)). Storia, filosofia e scienze sociali.
De Martino, Ernesto, 1908-1965. Il mondo magico. 1. ed. Torino : Bollati Boringhieri, 1997.
BF1589 .D46 1997

Saggi e ricerche (Istituto italiano per gli studi filosofici)
(8.) Scazzola, Andrea. Giovanni Gentile e il Rinascimento. Napoli : Vivarium, 2002.

Saggi filosofici (Padua, Italy)
Verna, Arturo. Letture filosofiche. Padova : Unipress, 2002.

Saggi. Scienza e filosofia
Braidotti, Rosi. [Nomadic subjects. Italian] Soggetto nomade. Roma : Donzelli, 1995.

Saggi (Soveria Mannelli, Italy)
(99.) Cotroneo, Girolamo. Le idee del tempo. Soveria Mannelli (Catanzaro) : Rubbettino, c2002.

Saggistica (Antonio Stango editore)
Giachery, Emerico. L'avventura del sogno. Roma : A. Stango, 2002.

Sagnol, Marc, 1956- Tragique et tristesse : Walter Benjamin, archéologue de la modernité / Marc Sagnol ; préface par Stéphane Mosès. Paris : Cerf, 2003. 240 p. ; 24 cm. (Passages, 0298-9972) Includes bibliographical references (p. [231]-238). ISBN 2-204-07026-2 DDC 193
1. Benjamin, Walter, - 1892-1940. 2. Tragic, The. 3. Sadness. 4. Philosophy, German - History - 20th century. 5. Aesthetics, Modern - 20th century. I. Title.

Sahlin-Andersson, Kerstin.
The expansion of management knowledge. Stanford, Calif. : Stanford Business Books, c2002.
HD31 .E873 2002

ṢAḤWAH (ISLAM). *See* **ISLAMIC RENEWAL.**

Saída de Iaô.
Verger, Pierre. Sao Paulo : Fundação Pierre Verger : Axis Mundi Editora, 2002.

Saĭko, Ė. V. (Ėdi Viktorovna).
Chelovek kak sub"ekt kul'tury. Moskva : Nauka, 2002.

Saint Augustin.
Eslin, Jean-Claude, 1935- Paris : Michalon, c2002.

Saint-Germain, Jon, 1960- Karmic palmistry : explore past lives, soul mates & karma / Jon Saint-Germain ; foreword by Richard Webster. 1st ed. St. Paul, Minn. : Llewellyn Publications, 2003. xvi, 236 p. : ill. ; 24 cm. Includes bibliographical references (p. 231-2232) and index. Table of contents URL: http://www.loc.gov/catdir/toc/fy038/2002043479.html ISBN 0-7387-0317-6 (pbk.) DDC 133.6
1. Palmistry. 2. Karma. I. Title.
BF921 .S215 2003

Saint-Saëns, Camille, 1835-1921.
Operas. Selections.
Malaniuk, Ira. Arien und Lieder [sound recording]. [Germany] : Preiser Records, p2000.

SAINTS. *See* **CHRISTIAN SAINTS.**

SAINTS - INDIA.
Glener, Doug. Wisdom's blossoms. Boston, Mass. : Shambhala, 2002.
BL2003 .G64 2002

SAINTS - INDIA - MAHARASHTRA.
Jośī, Gajānana Nārāyaṇa. Bhāratīya tattvajñānācā brhad itihāsa. 1. āvṛttī. Puṇe : Marāṭhī Tattvajñāna-Mahākośa Maṇḍala yāñce karitā Śubhadā-Sārasvata Prakāśana, 1994.
B131 .J674 1994

SAINTS - MISCELLANEA.
Place, Robert Michael. [Gnostic book of saints.

Spanish] El mensaje de los santos. St. Paul, Minn. : Llewellyn Español, 2003.
BF1879.T2 P5518 2003

Śaivabhāratī-Śodhapratiṣṭhāna.
Lāla, Mukuṭa Bihārī. [Sāmyayogamīmāṃsā. Hindi & Sanskrit] Sāmyayogamīmāṃsā. 1. saṃskaraṇa. Vārāṇasī : Śaivabhāratī Śodhapratiṣṭhānam, 2001.
BL1237.32+

SAKHA (RUSSIA) - ECONOMIC CONDITIONS.
Tumusov, F. S. (Fedot Semenovich) Budushchee mira i Rossii. Moskva : "Mysl'", 2000.
HC340.12.Z7 S2357 2000

SAKHMET (EGYPTIAN DEITY). *See* **SEKHMET (EGYPTIAN DEITY).**

Sakita, Tomoko I. Reporting discourse, tense, and cognition / by Tomoko I Sakita. 1st ed. Amsterdam ; Boston : Elsevier, 2002. xiii, 290 p. : ill. ; 24 cm. Includes bibliographical references (p. [259]-282) and indexes. ISBN 0-08-044041-X (alk. paper) DDC 415
1. Grammar, Comparative and general - Indirect discourse. 2. Grammar, Comparative and general - Tense. 3. Discourse analysis - Psychological aspects. 4. Language and languages - Style. I. Title.
P301.5.I53 S25 2002

Sakuma, Ruriko.
[Aids to Sadhana series. Tibetan & Sanskrit. Selections.] Sādhanamālā, Avalokiteśvara section. Delhi : Adroit Publishers ; New Delhi : Distributors, Akhil Book Distributors, 2002.
BQ8915 .S23 2002

Salam.
Buxani, Shyam D. 1st ed. New York : SAU Salam Foundation, c2003.

Salamucha, Jan.
[Selections. English. 2003]
Knowledge and faith / Jan Salamucha ; edited by Kordula Świętorzecka and Jacek Juliusz Jadacki. Amsterdam ; New York, NY : Rodopi, 2003. 419 p. ; 23 cm. (Polish analytical philosophy ; v. 4) (Poznań studies in the philosophy of the sciences and the humanities ; v. 77) Includes bibliographical references (p. [395]-419). A collection of previously published articles by Salamucha. "Comments and discussions" (p. 311-393) comprises reviews and comments by various authors. ISBN 90-420-0894-6
1. Salamucha, Jan. 2. Philosophy. 3. Logic - History. 4. Philosophy and religion. 5. Christian ethics. 6. God - Proof. 7. Philosophy, Medieval. 8. Faith and reason - Christianity. 9. Metaphysics. 10. Analysis (Philosophy) 11. Philosophy, Polish. I. Świętorzecka, Kordula. II. Jadacki, Jacek Juliusz. III. Title. IV. Title: Jan Salamucha, knowledge and faith V. Series. VI. Series: Poznań studies in the philosophy of the sciences and the humanities ; v. 77

SALAMUCHA, JAN.
Salamucha, Jan. [Selections. English. 2003] Knowledge and faith. Amsterdam ; New York, NY : Rodopi, 2003.

Salanter, Israel, 1810-1883. Sefer Torat rabi Yiśra'el mi-Salant : leket mi-divre ... Yiśra'el Lipkin ... / kines ve-'arakh ... Ḥayim Yitsḥak Lipkin. Yerushalayim : [ḥ. mo. l], 763 [2003] 296 p. ; 24 cm.
1. Salanter, Israel, - 1810-1883. 2. Ethics, Jewish. I. Title. II. Title: Torat rabi Yiśra'el mi-Salanṭ

SALANTER, ISRAEL, 1810-1883.
Salanter, Israel, 1810-1883. Sefer Torat rabi Yiśra'el mi-Salanṭ. Yerushalayim : [ḥ. mo. l], 763 [2003]

Salber, Wilhelm. Psychästhetik / Wilhelm Salber. Köln : König, c2002. 139 p. : ill. ; 23 cm. (Kunstwissenschaftliche Bibliothek ; Bd. 17. Pamphlet) Includes bibliographical references. ISBN 3-88375-523-0 (pbk.)
1. Aesthetics - Psychological aspects. 2. Gestalt psychology. 3. Picture perception. 4. Art - Psychological aspects. I. Title. II. Series: Kunstwissenschaftliche Bibliothek ; Bd. 17. III. Series: Kunstwissenschaftliche Bibliothek. Pamphlet.

Saldarriaga Roa, Alberto. La Arquitectura como experiencia : espacio, cuerpo y sensibilidad / Alberto Saldarriaga Roa. 1. ed. Bogotá : Villegas Editores : Universidad Nacional de Colombia, Facultad de Artes, c2002. 319 p. : ill. ; 21 cm. Includes bibliographical references (p. [309]-311) ISBN 958-816-024-3
1. Space (Architecture) 2. Architecture - Philosophy. 3. Aesthetics. I. Title.
NA2765 .S36 2002

Salecl, Renata, 1962- On anxiety / Renata Salecl. 1st ed. London ; New York : Routledge, 2004. p. cm. (Thinking in action) CONTENTS: Anxiety at times of war -- Anxiety and fear -- Fantasy as a defense from anxiety -- Anxiety and the desire of the other -- Mourning and suicide -- Fantasy of Bayonet killing -- Anxiety-free wars -- Arts and death --

Success in failure or how hypercapitalism relies on peoples feeling of inadequacy -- Anxiety between desire and jouissance -- Anxiety and the new imaginary -- The horror of poverty -- Against contingency -- Love anxieties -- Love letters or what does a hysteric want -- Cyrano de Bergerac or obsessional desire -- Law of desire or the perverts trap -- Anxiety of motherhood -- Psychoanalysis and crime -- Infanticide as a way to discover a woman behind a mother -- Religion and psychosis -- Psychotic love -- Paranoid parenting -- Telling it all -- Can testimony offer a cure for anxiety? -- Father don't you hear me? -- Son's liberation through father's sacrifice. ISBN 0-415-31276-0 (pbk. : alk. paper) ISBN 0-415-31275-2 (hardcover : alk. paper) DDC 152.4/6
1. Anxiety. I. Title. II. Series.
BF575.A6 S25 2004

Saleev, Vadim Alekseevich. Ėsteticheskoe vospriiatie i detskaia fantaziia / V.A. Saleev, O.V. Ivashkevich. Minsk : Natsional'nyĭ in-t obrazovaniia, 1999. 125 p. : ill. ; 20 cm. Includes bibliographical references (p. 95-101). ISBN 9856510147
1. Perception in children. 2. Aesthetics. 3. Child psychology. I. Ivashkevich, O. V. (Ol'ga Vladimirovna) II. Title.
BF723.P36 S25 1999

SALEM (MASS.) - SOCIAL CONDITIONS.
Roach, Marilynne K. The Salem witch trials. 1st Cooper Square Press ed. New York : Cooper Square Press : Distributed by National Book Network, 2002.
BF1575 .R63 2002

The Salem witch trials.
Roach, Marilynne K. 1st Cooper Square Press ed. New York : Cooper Square Press : Distributed by National Book Network, 2002.
BF1575 .R63 2002

SALES. *See* **EXPORT SALES CONTRACTS.**

SALES, EXPORT. *See* **EXPORT SALES CONTRACTS.**

SALES, INTERNATIONAL. *See* **EXPORT SALES CONTRACTS.**

SALES PERSONNEL.
Trainor, Norm, 1946- The eight best practices of high-performing salespeople. Toronto ; New York : Wiley, c2000.
HF5438.25 .T72 2000

SALES PROMOTION. *See* **ADVERTISING.**

Sales, Véronique.
Les historiens. Paris : A. Colin, 2003.
D14 .H523 2003

Saliba, John A. Understanding new religious movements / John A, Saliba. 2nd ed. Walnut Creek, CA ; Oxford : Altamira Press, c2003. xvi, 293 p. ; 24 cm. Includes bibliographical references and index. ISBN 0-7591-0355-0 (hbk. : alk. paper) ISBN 0-7591-0356-9 (pbk. : alk. paper) DDC 200/.9/04
1. Cults. 2. Sects. I. Title.
BP603 .S25 2003

Salisse, John.
Davenport, Anne Ashley. St. George's Hall. Pasadena : Mike Caveney's Magic Words, c2001.
BF1623 .D38 2001

Salkind, Neil J. An introduction to theories of human development / Neil J. Salkind. Thousand Oaks, Calif. : Sage Publications, c2004. p. cm. Includes bibliographical references and index. Table of contents URL: http://www.loc.gov/catdir/toc/ecip047/2003017477.html CONTENTS: An introduction and important ideas -- An introduction to the study of human development -- Trends and issues in human development -- The maturational and biological approaches -- Arnold Gesell and the maturational model -- The importance of biology : sociobiology and ethology -- The psychodynamic approach -- Sigmund Freud's psychosexual theory -- Erik Erickson's focus on psychosocial development -- The behavioral perspective -- The behavioral models of development -- Social learning theory -- The cognitive developmental view -- Jean Piaget's cognitive model -- Lev Vygotsky's sociocultural theory of development -- A comparative analysis -- Comparing theories of human development. ISBN 0-7619-2639-9 (pbk.) DDC 155
1. Developmental psychology - Philosophy. I. Title.
BF713 .S245 2004

Salles, Alexandre de. Esù ou Exu? : da domonização ao resgate da identidade / Alexandre de Salles. Rio de Janeiro : Ilú Aiye, 2001. 193 p. : ill. ; 21 cm. Includes bibliographical references (p. [189]-193). ISBN 85-902165-1-9
1. Brazil - Religion - African influences. 2. Brazil - Popular culture - African influences. 3. Candomblé (Religion) 4. Yoruba (African people) - Religion. 5. Afro-Brazilian cults. 6. Blacks - Race identity - Brazil. 7. Black author. I. Title.

Salmon, Catherine.
Evolutionary psychology, public policy, and personal decisions. Mahwah, N.J. : Lawrence Erlbaum Associates, 2004.
BF698.95 .E96 2004

Salmon, Rosemary.
Salmon, William A. The mid-career tune-up. New York : Amacom, c2000.
HF5381 .S256 2000

Salmon, William A. The mid-career tune-up : 10 new habits for keeping your edge in today's fast-paced workplace / William A. Salmon and Rosemary T. Salmon. New York : Amacom, c2000. ix, 214 p. : ill. ; 23 cm. Includes index. ISBN 0-8144-0523-1 DDC 650.14
1. Career development. 2. Success in business. 3. Job satisfaction. 4. Job security. I. Salmon, Rosemary. II. Title.
HF5381 .S256 2000

Salomonsen, Jone, 1956- Enchanted feminism : ritual, gender and divinity among the reclaiming witches of San Francisco / Jone Salomonsen. London ; New York : Routledge, 2002. x, 318 p. : ill. ; 24 cm. (Religion and gender) Includes bibliographical references (p. [303]-312) and index. ISBN 0-415-22392-X ISBN 0-415-22393-8 (pbk.) DDC 299
1. Reclaiming Collective (San Francisco, Calif.) I. Title. II. Series.
BF1577.C2 S25 2002

Salon.com (Firm).
Life as we know it. 1st Washington Square Press trade pbk. ed. New York : Washington Square Press, 2003.

Saltz, Gail. Becoming real : overcoming the stories we tell ourselves that hold us back / by Gail Saltz. New York: Riverhead Books, 2004. p. cm. Includes index. ISBN 1-57322-279-8 DDC 158.1
1. Self-actualization (Psychology) 2. Self-defeating behavior. 3. Schemas (Psychology) I. Title.
BF637.S4 S245 2004

Salute e salvezza
(19) Piazza, Giovanni. Sofferenza e senso. Torino : Camilliane, c2002.

SALVATION. See CONVERSION; ELECTION (THEOLOGY).

Samarskiĭ gosudarstvennyĭ pedagogicheskiĭ universitet.
Akopov, G. V. Mentalistika. Samara : Samarskiĭ gos. pedagog. universitet, 2001.
BF108.R8 A478 2001

Samosoznanie professionala.
Mironova, T. L. (Tatʹiana Lʹvovna) Ulan-Udė: Izd-vo Burĭatskogo gosuniversiteta, 1999.
BF697.5.S43 M57 1999

Samotność młodzieży.
Dołęga, Zofia. Wyd. 1. Katowice : Wydawn. Uniwersytetu Śląskiego, 2003.
BF724.3.L64 D65 2003

Sampaio, Luiz Sergio Coelho de, 1933- Filosofia da cultura : Brasil--luxo ou originalidade / Luiz Sergio Coelho de Sampaio. Rio de Janeiro : Editora Agora da Ilha, 2002. 377 p. : ill. ; 21 cm. Includes bibliographical references. ISBN 85-86854-91-3
1. Brazil - Civilization. 2. Culture - Philosophy. 3. Civilization - Philosophy. I. Title.

SAMPLING (STATISTICS). See also QUALITY CONTROL.
Nardi, Peter M. Doing survey research. Boston ; London : Allyn and Bacon, c2003.
HN29 .N25 2003

Sampūrṇānanda Saṃskr̥ta Viśvavidyālaya.
Karṇāṭaka, Vimalā. Śrīmadbhāgavata meṃ Sāṅkhyayoga ke tattva. 1. saṃskaraṇa. Vārāṇasī : Sampūrṇānanda Saṃskr̥ta Viśvavidyālaya, 2001.
BL1140.4.B437 K27 2001

Śukla, Kamalākānta, 1911- Vāstusārasaṅgrahaḥ. 1. saṃskaraṇam. Vārāṇasī : Sampūrṇānanda Saṃskr̥ta Viśvavidyālaye, 2002.
BF1729.A7+

Varāhamihira, 505-587. Br̥hatsaṃhitā. 1. saṃskaraṇam. Vārāṇasī : Sampūrṇānanda Saṃskr̥ta Viśvavidyālaye, 2002-
BF1714.H5+

Samtaler på en bjergtop.
Haugen Sørensen, Arne, 1932- 1. oplag. Højbjerg : Hovedland, c2002.

Samuel Beckett and the primacy of love.
Keller, John Robert. Manchester : Manchester University Press, 2002.

Samuel Falk, the Baal Shem of London.
Oron, Michal. Mi-'Ba'al shed' le-'Ba'al Shem'. Yerushalayim : Mosad Byaliḳ : Bet ha-sefer le-mada'e ha-Yahadut 'a. sh. Ḥayim Rozenberg, Universiṭat Tel-Aviv, c763 [2002]

Samuel, Geoffrey, 1947- Epistemology and method in law / Geoffrey Samuel. Aldershot, Hampshire, England : Burlington, VT : Ashgate, c2003. xxvi, 384 p. ; 25 cm. (Applied legal philosophy) Includes bibliographical references (p. 343-363) and index. ISBN 1-85521-599-3 DDC 340/.14
1. Semantics (Law) 2. Law - Methodology. 3. Knowledge, Theory of. I. Title. II. Series.
K213 .S259 2003

Samuel Weber.
Wortham, Simon. Aldershot, England ; Burlington, VT : Ashgate, c2003.
PN81 .W64 2003

Samul, A. L. Wisdom in the cards / by A.L. Samul. 1st ed. Stamford, CT : U.S. Games Systems, c2002. 300 p. : ill. ; 18 cm. Includes bibliographical references (p. 297-299). ISBN 1-57281-335-0 DDC 133.3/2424
1. Tarot. I. Title.
BF1879.T2 S26 2002

Saṃvit prakāśavāda.
Miśra, Ānanda, lecturer. Saṃvitprakāśavāda. 1. saṃskaraṇa. Dillī : Bhāratīya Vidyā Prakāśana, 2002.
B132.K6 M58 2002

Saṃvitprakāśavāda.
Miśra, Ānanda, lecturer. 1. saṃskaraṇa. Dillī : Bhāratīya Vidyā Prakāśana, 2002.
B132.K6 M58 2002

Sāṃyayogamīmāṃsā.
Lāla, Mukuṭa Bihārī. [Sāṃyayogamīmāṃsā. Hindi & Sanskrit] 1. saṃskaraṇa. Vārāṇasī : Śaivabhāratī Śodhapratiṣṭhānam, 2001.
BL1237.32+

Sāṃyayogamīmāṃsā : with Hindi translation.
Lāla, Mukuṭa Bihārī. [Sāṃyayogamīmāṃsā. Hindi & Sanskrit] Sāṃyayogamīmāṃsā. 1. saṃskaraṇa. Vārāṇasī : Śaivabhāratī Śodhapratiṣṭhānam, 2001.
BL1237.32+

San zu wu wen cong
Xing, Li. Guanyin. Beijing di 2 ban. Beijing : Xue yuan chu ban she, 2001.
BQ4710.A8 X564 2001

Sánchez Durá, Nicolás.
Romero, Pedro G., 1964- En el ojo de la batalla. Valencia : Universitat de València, 2002.

Sánchez-Pardo, Esther. Cultures of the death drive : Melanie Klein and modernist melancholia / Esther Sánchez-Pardo. Durham [N.C.] : Duke University Press, c2003. xi, 490 p. : ill. ; 25 cm. (Post-contemporary interventions) Includes bibliographical references (p. [395]-474) and index. CONTENTS: Itineraries -- Kleinian metapsychology -- Femininities : melancholia, masquerade, and the paternal superego -- Masculinities : anxiety, sadism and the intricacies of object-love -- Kleinian melancholia -- The death drive and aggression -- The setting (up) of phantasy -- Modernist cultures of the death drive -- Framing the fetish : To the Lighthouse : ceci n'est pas un roman -- Funereal rites : melancholia, masquerade, and the art of biography in Lytton Strachey -- Melancholia reborn : Djuna Barne's styles of grief -- Melancholia, the new Negro, and the fear of modernity : forms sublime and denigrated in Countee Cullen's writings -- Afterword : modern(ist) cultures of the death drive and the melancholic apparatus. ISBN 0-8223-3009-1 (cloth : alk. paper) ISBN 0-8223-3045-8 (pbk. : alk. paper) DDC 150.19/5/092
1. Klein, Melanie. 2. Death instinct. 3. Psychoanalysis. I. Title. II. Series.
BF175.5.D4 S26 2003

SANCTIONS, ECONOMIC. See ECONOMIC SANCTIONS.

SANCTIONS (INTERNATIONAL LAW). See ECONOMIC SANCTIONS.

Sandbothe, Mike, 1961-
[Verzeitlichung der Zeit. English]
The temporalization of time : basic tendencies in modern debate on time in philosophy and science / Mike Sandbothe ; translated by Andrew Inkpin. Lanham, MD : Rowman & Littlefield, c2001. vii, 129 p. ; 24 cm. Includes bibliographical references (p. 113-124) and index. ISBN 0-7425-1289-4 (alk. paper) ISBN 0-7425-1290-8 (pbk. : alk. paper) DDC 115
1. Time. I. Title.
BD638 .S27 2001

Sanders, Mark D. I hope you dance! / by Mark D. Sanders & Tia Sillers ; pictures by Buddy Jackson & Karinne Caulkins. Nashville, Tenn. : Rutledge Hill Press, 2003. 1 v. (unpaged) : col. ill. ; 27 cm. SUMMARY: An illustrated version of the country music song that encourages one to enjoy life, no matter what comes along. ISBN 1401601278 DDC 782.421642/0268
1. Inspiration - Songs and music - Juvenile literature. 2. Country music - 1991-2000 - Juvenile literature. 3. Happiness - Songs and music. 4. Self-actualization (Psychology) - Songs and music. 5. Songs. I. Sillers, Tia. II. Jackson, Buddy, ill. III. Caulkins, Karinne, ill. IV. Title.
BF410 .S26 2003

Sanders, Robert, 1946- Sibling relationships : theory and issues for practice / Robert Sanders ; consultant editor, Jo Campling. New York : Palgrave Macmillan, 2004. p. cm. Includes bibliographical references and index. ISBN 0-333-96410-1 (cloth) ISBN 0-333-96411-X (pbk.) DDC 306.875
1. Brothers and sisters. 2. Developmental psychology. I. Campling, Jo. II. Title.
BF723.S43 S159 2004

Sanders, Todd, 1965-.
Transparency and conspiracy. Durham : Duke University Press, 2003.
JC330 .T73 2003

Sandifer, Jon. Feng shui / Jon Sandifer. London : Piatkus, 1999. 150 p. : ill. ; 20 cm. (Piatkus guides) Includes index. ISBN 0-7499-1870-5 DDC 133.3337
1. Feng shui. I. Title.

Sandler, Karen.
The peak performance series. Vol. [4] [videorecording]. Longwood, Fla. : Pamela Bolling Enterprises, c1999.

Sandra, Dominiek, 1960-.
Reading complex words. New York : Kluwer Academic/Plenum Publishers, c2003.
P37.5.R42 R43 2003

Sandvoss, Ernst. Vom homo sapiens zum homo spaciens : eine Sinnperspektive der Menschheitsentwicklung / [Ernst Sandvoss]. Berlin : Logos, c2002. xii, 289 p. ; 21 cm. Includes bibliographical references and index. ISBN 3-8325-0030-8 (pbk.)
1. Human evolution. 2. Astronautics and civilization. I. Title.

Sandys, Celia. We shall not fail : the inspiring leadership of Winston Churchill / Celia Sandys and Jonathan Littman. New York : Portfolio ; London : Penguin Books, 2003. xvii, 283 p. : ill., facsims. ; 22 cm. Includes index. ISBN 1-59184-015-5 DDC 941.084/092
1. Churchill, Winston, - Sir, - 1874-1965. 2. Churchill, Winston, - Sir, - 1874-1965 - Views on leadership. 3. Great Britain - Politics and government - 20th century. 4. Prime ministers - Great Britain - Biography. 5. Leadership. I. Littman, Jonathan, 1958- II. Title.
DA566.9.C5 S266 2003

Sanguineti, Juan José.
Castagnino, M. (Mario) Tempo e universo. Roma : Armando, c2000.
BD632 .C37 2000

Sanguineti, Vincenzo R. A rosetta stone to the human mind : three alphabets to decipher psyche / Vincenzo R. Sanguineti. Madison, Conn. : PsychoSocial Press, 2003. p. cm. Includes bibliographical references. ISBN 1-88784-160-1 DDC 150/.1
1. Psychology - Philosophy. I. Title.
BF38 .S225 2003

Sani, Fabio, 1961-.
The development of the social self. 1st ed. London ; New York : Psychology Press, 2003.
BF723.S24 D48 2003

Śaṅkarācārya.
[Bhajagovinda. Gujarati & Sanskrit]
Mohamudgarastotram : prastāvanā, śloka, anvaya, anuvāda, abhyāsanondha sahita / sampādikā Punitā Nāgarajī Desāī. Adyatana āvr̥tti. Amadāvāda : Sarasvatī Pustaka Bhaṇḍāra, 1998/99 [i.e. 1999] 83 p. ; 22 cm. SUMMARY: Sanskrit text with Gujarati translation on Advaita approach to self-realization. Sanskrit and Gujarati.
1. Self-realization. 2. Advaita. I. Desāī, Punitā Nāgarajī. II. Title.
B133.S463 B5315 1998

Sankey, Melissa.
Suicide & risk-taking deaths of children & young people. Surry Hills, NSW : The Commission, c2003.

SANKHYA.
Karṇāṭaka, Vimalā. Śrīmadbhāgavata meṃ Sāṅkhyayoga ke tattva. 1. saṃskaraṇa. Vārāṇasī : Sampūrṇānanda Saṃskr̥ta Viśvavidyālaya, 2001.

BL1140.4.B437 K27 2001

Saṅkhyāparaka śabda kośa / sampādaka Śāligrāma Gupta. 1. saṃskaraṇa. Ilāhābāda : Sāhitya Bhavana, 2002. 474 p. ; 22 cm. In Hindi; includes passages in Sanskrit. SUMMARY: Dictionary of symbolic numbers used in different religions in India.
1. Symbolism of numbers - Dictionaries. 2. Indology - Dictionaries. 3. India - Religion - Dictionaries. I. Gupta, Śāligrāma.
BF1623.P9+

Sankt Georg und sein Bilderzyklus in Neuhaus/ Böhmen (Jindřichův Hradec) : historische, kunsthistorische und theologische Beiträge / herausgegeben von Ewald Volgger ; [Bernhard Demel ... et al.]. Marburg : N.G. Elwert, c2002. ix, 182 p., [39] p. of plates : ill. (some col.) ; 30 cm. (Quellen und Studien zur Geschichte des Deutschen Ordens ; Bd. 57) Includes bibliographical references and index. ISBN 3-7708-1212-3 (cl.) DDC 270.1/092
1. George, - Saint, - d. 303 - Cult - Czech Republic - Jindřichův Hradec. 2. George, - Saint, - d. 303 - Art. 3. Schloss Neuhaus (Jindřichův Hradec, Czech Republic) 4. Teutonic Knights. - Ballei Böhmen - History - To 1500. 5. Mural painting and decoration - Czech Republic - Jindřichův Hradec. 6. Church history - Middle Ages, 600-1500. 7. Jindřichův Hradec (Czech Republic) - Church history. I. Volgger, Ewald. II. Demel, Bernhard. III. Series.
BR1720.G4 S26 2002

Sanna, Lawrence J.
Virtue, vice, and personality. 1st ed. Washington, D.C. : American Psychological Association, c2003.
BF698 .V57 2003

Sanna, Manuela. La "fantasia, che è l'occhio dell'ingegno" : la questione della verità e della sua rappresentazione in Vico / Manuela Sanna. Napoli : A. Guida editore, c2001. 130 p. ; 21 cm. (Studi vichiani ; 34) Includes bibliographical references and index. ISBN 88-7188-538-4 DDC 121
1. Vico, Giambattista, - 1668-1744. 2. Metaphysics. I. Title. II. Series.
B3583 .S26 2001

SANSKRIT LANGUAGE - GRAMMAR.
Alackapally, Sebastian, 1961- Being and meaning. 1st ed. Delhi : Motilal Banarsidass Publishers, 2002.
PK541.B48 A43 2002

SANSKRIT LITERATURE. *See* **SANSKRIT POETRY.**

SANSKRIT POETRY - HISTORY AND CRITICISM.
Bhāvamiśra, 19th cent. [Śṛṅgārasarasī. Hindi & Sanskrit] Śṛṅgārasarasī. Saṃskaraṇa 1. Vṛndāvana : Vṛndāvana Śodha Saṃsthāna, 2001.
PK2916+

Sant Baba Ishar Singh Ji : guru, gurmantar, gobind : spiritual experiences of an unknown author. Hardwar : Nanak-Dar Sant Baba Nand Singh Sant Baba Ishar Singh Spiritual Mission, 2002. iii, 69 p. : col. ill. ; 29 cm.
1. Īshara Siṅgha, - 1905-1975. 2. Spiritualism. 3. Gurus. I. Nanak-Dar Sant Baba Nand Singh Sant Baba Ishar Singh Spiritual Mission (Haridwār, India)
BL2017.9.I84 S27 2002

Santangelo, Paolo. Sentimental education in Chinese history : an interdisciplinary textual research on Ming and Qing sources / by Paolo Santangelo. Leiden ; Boston : Brill, 2003. x, 606 p. ; 25 cm. (Sinica Leidensia ; v. 60) Includes bibliographical references (p. [468]-533) and index. ISBN 90-04-12360-1 DDC 152.4/0951
1. Emotions. 2. Emotions in literature. 3. Chinese literature - History and criticism. I. Title. II. Series.
BF538.C48 S25 2003

SANTERIA IN LITERATURE.
Vadillo, Alicia E. Santería y Vodú. Madrid : Biblioteca Nueva, c2002.
PQ7372 .V33 2002

Santería y Vodú.
Vadillo, Alicia E. Madrid : Biblioteca Nueva, c2002.
PQ7372 .V33 2002

Santner, Thomas J., 1947- The design and analysis of computer experiments / Thomas J. Santner, Brian J. Williams, William I. Notz. New York : Springer, 2003. xii, 283 p. : ill. ; 24 cm. (Springer series in statistics) Includes bibliographical references (p. [251]-271) and indexes. ISBN 0-387-95420-1 (alk. paper) DDC 519.5
1. Experimental design. 2. Physical sciences - Experiments - Computer simulation. I. Williams, Brian J. II. Notz, William. III. Title. IV. Series.
QA279 .S235 2003

Santoni, Ronald E. Sartre on violence--curiously ambivalent / Ronald E. Santoni. University Park, Pa. : Pennsylvania State University Press, c2003. xx, 179 p. ; 24 cm. Includes bibliographical references and index. CONTENTS: Theoretical underpinnings -- "Violence" in the Notebooks for an ethics -- "Violence" in the Critique of dialectical reason, volume I -- "Violence" in the Critique of dialectical reason, volume II -- "Violence" in Sartre's preface to The wretched of the earth -- "Violence" in Hope now : the 1980 interviews -- Background to the confrontation -- The confrontation -- The 1964 "Rome lecture" -- Justificational ambivalence : problematic interpretation. ISBN 0-271-02300-7 (alk. paper) DDC 303.6
1. Sartre, Jean Paul, - 1905- 2. Violence. I. Title.
B2430.S34 S315 2003

Santos do povo brasileiro.
Megale, Nilza Botelho. Petrópolis : Editora Vozes, 2002.

Santos, Robson Pinheiro, 1961- Tambores de Angola : helo espírito Angelo Inácio / [ditado pelo espírito Angelo Inácio ; Robson Pinheiro Santos, do sirrum. Contagem [Brazil] : Casa dos Espíritos, 2002. 174 p. ill., 18 cm. ISBN 85-87781-05-7
1. Spirit writings. 2. Umbanda (Cult) 3. Black author. I. Angelo Inácio, (Spirit) II. Title.

Santrock, John W. Psychology : essentials / John W. Santrock. 2nd ed. Boston : McGraw-Hill, c2003. xviii, 547, [57] p. : ill. (chiefly col.) ; 28 cm. + 1 computer laser optical disc (4 3/4 in.). Includes bibliographical references (p. R-1-R-32) and indexes. System requirements for accompanying computer disc: Windows 98 or higher; Mac OS 8.6 or higher; with 48 MB RAM, 4X CD-ROM drive; Netscape Navigator 4.7 or higher; Microsoft Internet Explorer 5.0 or higher. The CD-ROM disc "gives students more pretice review tests and a learning style assessment in an easy-to-use format". URL: http://www.mhhe.com/santrockep2(thebook'sOnlineLearningCenter) ISBN 0-07-256201-3 (alk. paper) ISBN 0-07-256208-0 (CD) DDC 150
1. Psychology - Textbooks. I. Title.
BF121 .S2642 2003

Psychology : essentials / John W. Santrock. Updated 2nd ed. Boston, Mass. : McGraw-Hill, 2004. p. cm. Includes bibliographical references and index. ISBN 0-07-293762-9 DDC 150
1. Psychology - Textbooks. I. Title.
BF121 .S2642 2004

Psychology / John W. Santrock. Updated 7th ed. Boston : McGraw-Hill, c2005. p. cm. Includes bibliographical references and indexes. ISBN 0-07-293776-9 (alk. paper) DDC 150
1. Psychology - Textbooks. I. Title.
BF121 .S265 2005

San" Ū", Sutagavesī. Mran' mā' rui" rā 'im' khraṃ mre naññ'" paññā / Sutagavesī San'" Ū". Ran' kun' : Rvhe Pu ra puid' Cā pe : Phran'' khyi re", Sa mī" Jotika Cā pe, 2000. 136 p. ; 17 cm. In Burmese. SUMMARY: Ancient wisdom on architecture of the Burmese people to achieve harmony with the spiritual forces perceived in enviroment. Includes bibliographical references (p. 136).
1. Occultism - Burma. 2. Architecture - Burma. I. Title.
BF1773.2.B93 S26 2000

Sanz Bisbal, Pepa.
Pinto Cañon, Ramiro. Grupos gnósticos. Madrid : Entinema, 2002.

Sapadin, Linda. Master your fears : how to triumph over your worries and get on with your life / Linda Sapadi. Hoboken, N.J. : John Wiley & Sons, 2004. p. cm. Includes bibliographical references and index. Table of contents URL: http://www.loc.gov/catdir/toc/wiley032/2003017782.html ISBN 0-471-27272-8 (Cloth) DDC 152.4/6
1. Fear. 2. Self-actualization (Psychology) I. Title.
BF575.F2 S26 2004

Saraswati, T. S.
Cross-cultural perspectives in human development. New Delhi ; Thousand Oaks, Calif. : Sage Publications, 2003.
BF713.5 .C76 2003

Saratovskiĭ gosudarstvennyĭ tekhnicheskiĭ universitet.
Gender, vlast', kul'tura. Saratov : Saratovskiĭ gos. tekhn. universitet, 2000.
HQ1075 .G4667 2000

Saraydarian, Torkom. Aura : shield of protection & glory / Torkom Saraydarian. Cave Creek, Ariz. : T.S.G. Pub. Foundation, 1999. 219 p. ; 22 cm. Includes bibliographical references and index. ISBN 0-929874-06-4 DDC 133.8/92
1. Aura. 2. Spiritualism. I. Title.
BF1389.A8 S35 1999

Dynamics of the soul / Torkom Saraydarian. Cave Creek, Ariz. : T.S.G. Pub., c2001. 344 p. ; 22 cm. Includes bibliographical references and index. ISBN 0-929874-01-3
1. Spiritual life. 2. Soul. 3. Occultism. I. Title.
BF1999 .S3352 2001

Sardar, Ziauddin. The A-Z of postmodern life : essays on global culture in the noughties / Ziauddin Sardar. London : Vision, c2002. vi, 278 p. ; 24 cm. Includes bibliographic references. ISBN 1-904132-03-0 DDC 909.83
1. Civilization, Modern - 21st century. 2. Postmodernism. I. Title.

Sardello, Robert J., 1942- Facing the world with soul : the reimagination of modern life / Robert Sardello. 2nd ed. Great Barrington, MA : Lindisfarne Books, c2003. p. cm. (Studies in imagination) Includes bibliographical references. Table of contents URL: http://www.loc.gov/catdir/toc/ecip048/2003020149.html CONTENTS: The soul of the world -- House and city -- Learning through soul -- Disease -- Economics and money -- Technology -- Things -- Violence and the longing for beauty -- Food, a case history -- World, soul, and hermetic consciousness. ISBN 1-58420-014-6 DDC 158/.1
1. Conduct of life. I. Title. II. Series.
BF637.C5 S27 2003

Sargent, Denny, 1956- Your guardian angel and you / Denny Sargent. York Beach, ME : Red Wheel/Weiser, 2004. p. cm. Includes bibliographical references. Table of contents URL: http://www.loc.gov/catdir/toc/ecip048/2003019492.html CONTENTS: A brief history of the holy guardian angel -- Preparing to meet your guardian angel -- Contacting your guardian angel -- Nurturing your angelic connection -- Expanding your relationship with your guardian angel -- Balancing your relationship with your guardian angel -- Your guardian angel and your shadow -- Knowledge and conversation of the holy guardian angel -- Merging with your guardian angel. ISBN 1-57863-275-7 DDC 202/.15
1. Guides (Spiritualism) 2. Guardian angels. I. Title.
BF1275.G85 S27 2004

Sarker, Ruhul A.
Data mining. Hershey : Idea Group, c2002.
QA76.9.D343 D36 2002

Śarmā, Kisanalāla. Lāla kitāba : Bhāratīya jyotisha ke pariprekshya meṃ Lāla kitāba kā bebāka vivecana saikaroṃ upāyoṃ aura ṭoṭakoṃ ke sātha / Kisanalāla Śarmā ; sampādana, Rājīva Tivārī. 1. saṃskaraṇa. Dillī : Manoja Pôketa Buksa, [2000?] 397 p. : ill. ; 23 cm. Cover title: Asalī prācīna Lāla kitāba. SUMMARY: On Hindu astrology. In Hindi.
1. Hindu astrology. I. Tivārī, Rājīva. II. Title. III. Title: Asalī prācīna Lāla kitāba
BF1714.H5+

Śarmā, Madhusūdana.
Asalī prācīna Vaidika vāstu śāstra. 1. saṃskaraṇa. Dillī : Manoja Pôketa Buksa, [2002?]
BF1729.A7 A83 2002

Sarnoff, Irving, 1922- Intimate creativity : partners in love and art / Irving and Suzanne Sarnoff. Madison, Wis. : University of Wisconsin Press, c2002. xii, 255 p. : ill., ports. ; 24 cm. Includes bibliographical references (p. 233-245) and index. CONTENTS: Introduction: Exploring intimate creativity -- Relating and creating -- Transcending the culture of individualism -- Embracing a collective identity -- The unending conversation -- From inspiration to implementation -- The harmony of equals -- Making art/making love -- Couple and community -- Epilogue: The composite picture. ISBN 0-299-18050-6 (cloth : alk. paper) ISBN 0-299-18054-9 (pbk.) DDC 153.3/5
1. Creation (Literary, artistic, etc.) 2. Man-woman relationships. 3. Intimacy (Psychology) 4. Love. I. Sarnoff, Suzanne. II. Title. III. Title: Partners in love and art
BF411 .S27 2002

Sarnoff, Suzanne.
Sarnoff, Irving, 1922- Intimate creativity. Madison, Wis. : University of Wisconsin Press, c2002.
BF411 .S27 2002

Sartorio, Ugo. Credere in dialogo : percorsi di fede e di annuncio / Ugo Sartorio. Padova : Edizioni Messaggero, 2002. 223 p. ; 21 cm. (Pubblicazioni della Facoltà teologica dell'Italia settentrionale. Sezione di Padova) (La croce di Aquileia. Percorsi teologici ; 3) Includes bibliographical references and index. ISBN 88-250-1196-2 DDC 234
1. Christianity - 20th century. 2. Faith. 3. Religious tolerance - Christianity. 4. Evangelistic work. 5. Private revelations. I. Title. II. Series.

Sartre, Jean Paul, 1905-
[Imaginaire. English]
The imaginary : a phenomenological psychology of the imagination / Jean-Paul Sartre ; revised by Arlette Elkaïm Sartre ; translated and with an introduction by Jonathan Webber. London ; New York : Routledge, 2003. p. cm. Includes bibliographical references and index. Table of contents URL: http://

www.loc.gov/catdir/toc/ecip044/2003012478.html ISBN 0-415-28754-5 ISBN 0-415-28755-3 (pbk.) DDC 128/.3
1. Imagination. I. Elkaïm-Sartre, Arlette. II. Title.
BF408 .S263 2003

SARTRE, JEAN PAUL, 1905-.
Dandyk, Alfred. Unaufrichtigkeit. Würzburg : Königshausen & Neumann, c2002.

Fox, Nik Farrell. The new Sartre. New York ; London : Continuum, 2003.

Santoni, Ronald E. Sartre on violence--curiously ambivalent. University Park, Pa. : Pennsylvania State University Press, c2003.
B2430.S34 S315 2003

SARTRE, JEAN PAUL, 1905- - ONTOLOGY.
Mavouangui, David, 1953- Jean-Paul Sartre. Paris : Paari, [2002], c2001.

Sartre on violence - curiously ambivalent.
Santoni, Ronald E. University Park, Pa. : Pennsylvania State University Press, c2003.
B2430.S34 S315 2003

Sashkin, Marshall, 1944- Leadership that matters : the critical factors for making a difference in people's lives and organizations' success / Marshall Sashkin, Molly G. Sashkin. 1st ed. San Francisco : Berrett-Koehler, c2003. xi, 241 p. ; 23 cm. Includes bibliographical references (p. 211-230) and index. ISBN 1-57675-193-7 DDC 658.4/092
1. Leadership. I. Sashkin, Molly G. II. Title.
HD57.7 .S27 2003

Sashkin, Molly G.
Sashkin, Marshall, 1944- Leadership that matters. 1st ed. San Francisco : Berrett-Koehler, c2003.
HD57.7 .S27 2003

Sasso, Gennaro. Il guardiano della storiografia : profilo di Federico Chabod e altri saggi / Gennaro Sasso. 2. ed. [Bologna] : Società editrice il Mulino, c2002. x, 594 p. ; 25 cm. (Istituto italiano per gli studi storici in Napoli) Includes bibliographical references and index. ISBN 88-15-08743-5 DDC 907
1. Chabod, Federico. 2. Historiography. 3. Historians - Europe. I. Title. II. Series: Istituto italiano per gli studi storici (Series)

Sasson, Gahl. A wish can change your life : unlocking mysteries of the Kabbalah to make your dreams come true / Gahl Sasson and Steve Weinstein. New York : Simon & Schuster, 2003. p. cm. Includes bibliographical references. ISBN 0-7432-4505-9 DDC 135/.47
1. Cabala. 2. Tree of life. 3. Self-actualization (Psychology) I. Weinstein, Steve, 1960- II. Title.
BF1623.C2 S27 2003

Sastre, Juan Carlos.
Arsuaga, Juan Luis de. [Collar del neandertal. English] The Neanderthal's necklace. New York : Four Walls Eight Windows, c2002.
GN285 .A7713 2002

Śāstrī, Girijā Śaṅkara. Ācārya Varāhamihira / Girijā Śaṅkara Śāstrī. 1. saṃskaraṇa. Ilāhābāda : Jyotiṣa Karmakāṇḍa evaṃ Adhyātma Śodha Saṃsthāna, 2001. 184 p. ; 22 cm. SUMMARY: On the life and works of Varāhamihira, 505-587, ancient Hindu astrologer. Includes bibliographical references (p. [180]-184). In Hindi; includes passages in Sanskrit.
1. Varāhamihira, - 505-587. 2. Astrologers - India - Biography. 3. Hindu astrology. I. Title.
BF1679.8.V37 S27 2001

Bhāratīya Kuṇḍalī-vimarśa / Girijā Śaṅkara Śāstrī. 1. saṃskaraṇa. Ilāhābāda : Jyotiṣa Karmakāṇḍa evaṃ Adhyātma Śodha Saṃsthāna, 2002. 262 p. ; 22 cm. In Hindi; includes passages in Sanskrit. SUMMARY: On the fundamentals of astrological calculations according to Hindu Calendar.
1. Hindu astrology. 2. Calendar, Hindu. I. Title.
BF1714.H5+

Jyotisha tattva-viveka / Girijā Śaṅkara Śāstrī. 1. saṃskaraṇa. Ilāhābāda : Jyotiṣa Karmakāṇḍa evaṃ Adhyātma Śodha Saṃsthāna, 2001. 240 p. ; 22 cm. SUMMARY: On the fundamentals of Hindu astrology. In Hindi; includes passages in Sanskrit.
1. Hindu astrology - History. I. Title.
BF1714.H5 S277 2001

Lomaśa, Maharṣi. [Lomaśa saṃhitā. Hindi & Sanskrit] Lomaśa saṃhitā. Saṃskaraṇa 1. Ilāhābāda : Hindī Sāhitya Sammelana, Prayāga, 2002.
BF1714.H5+

Śāstrī, Umeśa. Vyāsasūtram / Ācārya Umeśa Śāstrī. Jayapura : Yūnika Ṭreḍarsa, 2002. 232 p. ; 22 cm. Added title page title: Vyas-sutram. SUMMARY: On Hindu astrology. In Sanskrit; introduction in Hindi.
1. Hindu astrology. I. Title. II. Title: Vyas-sutram

BF1714.H5 S287 2002

Śāstrī, Vinoda, 1959- Jyotisha-vijñāna-nirjharī / Vinoda Śāstrī ; [pradhāna-sampādana, Harirāma Ācārya]. Jayapura : Rājasthāna Saṃskṛta Akādamī, [2002?] [12], 280 p. : ill. ; 25 cm. SUMMARY: Articles on various aspects of Hindu astrology and omens. In Hindi; includes passages in Sanskrit.
1. Hindu astrology. 2. Omens. I. Ācārya, Harirāma, 1936- II. Title.
BF1714.H5 S288 2002

SATAN. *See* **DEVIL.**

SATANIC CULTS. *See* **SATANISM.**

SATANISM.
Ellis, Bill, 1950- Lucifer ascending. Lexington : University Press of Kentucky, c2003.
BF1548 .E44 2003

Ofoegbu, Mike. Exposing satanic manipulations. [Lagos, Nigeria : Holy Ghost Anointed Books Ministries, c1998]
1. Black author.

Olorunfemi, Samuel Jimson. Breaking the evil blood covenant. Ibadan, Oyo State, Nigeria : Triumphant Faith Publications, 2001.
1. Black author.

Tsiakkas, Christophoros A. Mageia-satanismos. 3 ekd. Leukōsia : Ekdosē Hieras Monēs Trooditissēs, 2001.
BF1550 .T73 2001

SATANISM - ENCYCLOPEDIAS.
Lewis, James R. Satanism today. Santa Barbara, Calif. : ABC-CLIO, c2001.
BF1548 .L49 2001

SATANISM - FRANCE - HISTORY.
Waite, Arthur Edward, 1857-1942. Devil-worship in France with Diana Vaughan and the question of modern palladism. Boston, MA : Weiser Books, 2003.
BF1548 .W2 2003

SATANISM - HISTORY - 20TH CENTURY.
Newton, Toyne. The dark worship. London : Vega, 2002.
BF1531 .N49 2002

Satanism today.
Lewis, James R. Santa Barbara, Calif. : ABC-CLIO, c2001.
BF1548 .L49 2001

Satan's conspiracy.
Maxwell-Stuart, P. G. East Linton, Scotland : Tuckwell Press, 2001.
BF1622.S38 .M39 2001

SATELLITE TELEVISION, DIRECT BROADCAST. *See* **DIRECT BROADCAST SATELLITE TELEVISION.**

SATELLITE TELEVISION, HOME. *See* **DIRECT BROADCAST SATELLITE TELEVISION.**

SATELLITES. *See* **MOON.**

Sathe, Vijay. Corporate entrepreneurship : top managers and new business creation / Vijay Sathe ; foreword by Peter F. Drucker. Cambridge : Cambridge University Press, 2003. xvii, 387 p. : ill. ; 24 cm. Includes bibliographical references (p. 359-375) and index. ISBN 0-521-82499-0 ISBN 0-521-53197-7 (PBK.) DDC 658.4063
1. Entrepreneurship. 2. Creative ability in business. 3. Executive ability. I. Title.

SATIRE. *See* **INVECTIVE.**

SATISFACTION. *See* **SELF-REALIZATION.**

Ṣaṭpañcāśikā.
Pṛthuyaśas. 1. saṃskaraṇa. Vārāṇasī : Caukhambā Surabhāratī Prakāśana ; Dillī : Caukhambā Saṃskṛta Pratiṣṭhāna, 2002.
BF1714.H5 P7 2002

SAU Salam Foundation.
Buxani, Shyam D. Salam. 1st ed. New York : SAU Salam Foundation, c2003.

SAUCERS, FLYING. *See* **UNIDENTIFIED FLYING OBJECTS.**

Saúde e ambiente sustentável : estreitando nós / Maria Cecília de Souza Minayo, Ary Carvalho de Miranda, organizadores. Rio de Janeiro, RJ : Editora Fiocruz : Abrasco, 2002. 343 p. : ill. ; 23 cm. Includes bibliographical references. ISBN 85-7541-013-X
1. Environmental health. 2. Environmental policy. 3. Sustainable development. 4. Environmental risk assessment. 5. Quality of life. I. Minayo, Maria Cecília de Souza. II. Miranda, Ary Carvalho de.

Sauer, Tim.
Coping with chaos. New York : J. Wiley, c1994.
Q172.5.C45 C67 1994

Sauerländer, Willibald. Die Luft auf der Spitze des Pinsels : kritische Spaziergänge durch Bildersäle / Willibald Sauerländer. München : Hanser, 2002. 163 p. ; 20 cm. (Edition Akzente) Reviews on various exhibitions published previously in Süddeutsche Zeitung. ISBN 3-446-20228-5 (pbk.)
1. Art - Exhibitions. 2. Art - History. I. Title. II. Series.

Saunders, David, 1940-.
Pufendorf, Samuel, Freiherr von, 1632-1694. [De officio hominis et civis. English] The whole duty of man, according to the law of nature. Indianapolis, Ind. : Liberty Fund, c2003.
K457.P8 D4313 2003

SAUNIÈRE, BÉRENGER, 1852-1917.
Douzet, André. Nouvelles lumières sur Rennes-le-Château. Chêne-Bourg (Suisse) : Acquarius, c1998-
BF1434.F8 D69 1998

La sauvagerie maternelle.
Dufourmantelle, Anne. Paris : Calmann-Lévy, c2001.

Sauvet, Georges.
Le propre de l'homme. Lausanne : Delachaux et Niestlé, c1998.
BF175 .P69 1998

Sava, Gabriella. La psicologia filosofica in Italia : studi su Francesco De Sarlo, Antonio Aliotta, Eugenio Rignano / Gabriella Sava. Galatina (Lecce) : Congedo, 2000. 234 p. ; 24 cm. (Testi e saggi / Università degli studi di Lecce, Facoltà di lettere e filosofia, Dipartimento di filologia classica e di scienze filosofiche ; 24) Includes bibliographical references and index. ISBN 88-8086-345-2 DDC 150
1. De Sarlo, Francesco, - 1864-1937. 2. Aliotta, Antonio, - 1881-1964. 3. Rignano, Eugenio, - 1870-1930. 4. Psychology and philosophy - Italy - History. I. Title. II. Series: Testi e saggi (Università degli studi di Lecce. Dipartimento di filologia classica e di scienze filosofiche) ; 24.
BF38 .S235 2000

Savage energies.
Burkert, Walter, 1931- [Wilder Ursprung. English] Chicago : University of Chicago Press, c2001.
BL785 .B8513 2001

Savater, Fernando. El contenido de la felicidad / Fernando Savater. 1. ed. Madrid : Santillana, 2002. 203 p. ; 24 cm. ISBN 84-03-09311-X
1. Ethics. 2. Happiness. I. Title.

Savchyn, Myroslav, 1950- Dukhovnyĭ potentsial li︠u︡dyny : monohrafii︠a︡ / Myroslav Savchyn. Ivano-Frankivsʹk : Plaĭ, 2001. 202 p. ; 20 cm. Table of contents also in English. "Naukove vydannia︡"--Colophon. Includes bibliographical references (p. 186-193). ISBN 9666400170
1. Personality. 2. Spirituality. I. Title.
BF698 .S288 2001

Savoir communiquer
Germain-Thiant, Myriam. La relation à l'autre. Lyon : Chronique sociale, [2002]

Le savoir et l'ordinateur.
Berthier, Denis. Paris : Harmattan, c2002.

Savoy, Lauret E.
The colors of nature. 1st ed. Minneapolis, Minn. : Milkweed Editions, 2002.
QH81 .C663 2002

Sawyer, R. Keith (Robert Keith).
Creativity and development. New York : Oxford University Press, 2003.
BF408 .C7545 2003

Group creativity : music, theater, collaboration / R. Keith Sawyer. Mahwah, N.J. : L. Erlbaum Associates, 2003. ix, 214 p. : ill. ; 24 cm. Includes bibliographical references (p. 190-204) and indexes. ISBN 0-8058-4435-X (alk. paper) ISBN 0-8058-4436-8 (pbk. : alk. paper) DDC 302.3/4
1. Creative thinking - Social aspects. 2. Creation (Literary, artistic, etc.) - Social aspects. 3. Group problem solving. I. Title.
BF408 .S285 2003

Improvised dialogues : emergence and creativity in conversation / R. Keith Sawyer ; foreword by Michael Silverstein. Westport, Conn. : Ablex Pub., 2003. x, 262 p. : ill. ; 25 cm. (Publications in creativity research) Includes bibliographical references (p. [243]-253) and index. ISBN 1-56750-677-1 (alk. paper) DDC 302.3/46
1. Conversation analysis. 2. Improvisation (Acting) 3. Creation (Literary, artistic, etc.) I. Title. II. Series.
P95.45 .S3 2003

Saxena, D. P. (Dayal Prasad), 1929-.
Nīlakaṇṭha, 16th cent. [Tājikanīlakaṇṭhī. English & Sanskrit] Tajik Nilkanthi = 1st ed. New Delhi : Ranjan Publications, 2001.
BF1714.H5 N4813 2001

Sayers, Janet. Divine therapy : love, mysticism, and psychoanalysis / Janet Sayers. Oxford ; New York : Oxford University Press, 2003. 250 p. : ill. ; 24 cm. (Oxford medical publications) Includes bibliographical references and index. ISBN 0-19-850981-2 (alk. paper) DDC 615.852
1. Psychoanalytic Theory. 2. Love. 3. Mental Healing. 4. Mysticism. 5. Spiritual healing. 6. Mental healing. 7. Psychoanalysis. 8. Love - Health aspects. I. Title. II. Series.
BF175.4.R44 S28 2003

Saying no.
Berry, Joy Wilt. New York : Scholastic, c2001.
BF723.R4 B37 2001

SAYINGS. See **APHORISMS AND APOTHEGMS; MAXIMS.**

Sayyid, 'Azīzah Muḥammad. al-Sulūk al-siyāsī : al-naẓarīyah wa-al-wāqi' : dirāsah fī 'ilm al-nafs al-siyāsī / 'Azīzah Muḥammad al-Sayyid, al-Ṭab'ah 1. [Cairo] : Dār al-Ma'ārif, 1994. 112 p. : ill. 24 cm. Includes bibliographical references (p. 102-106) In Arabic. ISBN 9770245224
1. Political psychology. I. Title.
JA74.5 .S29 1994

Sazont'ev, B. A.
Aktual'nye voprosy obshcheĭ, vozrastnoĭ i sot︠s︡ial'noĭ psikhologii. Tver' : Tverskoĭ gos. universitet, 2001.
BF20 .A46 2001

Scaffale aperto. Psicologia
Quaglia, Rocco. Immagini dell'uomo. Roma : Armando, c2000.

SCALE ANALYSIS (PSYCHOLOGY).
Scaling methods. 2nd ed. / Peter Dunn-Rankin ... [et al.]. Mahwah, N.J. : L. Erlbaum Associates, 2004.
BF39.2.S34 S33 2004

Scales, Peter, 1949- Coming into their own : how developmental assets promote positive growth in middle childhood / Peter C. Scales, Arturo Sesma, and Brent Bolstrom. Minneapolis, MN : Search Institute, c2004. p. cm. Includes bibliographical references and index. ISBN 1-57482-431-7 DDC 155.42/4
1. Child psychology. 2. Preteens - Psychology. I. Sesma, Arturo. II. Bolstrom, Brent. III. Title.
BF721 .S347 2004

Scalia, Joseph.
The vitality of objects. 1st US ed. Middletown, Conn. : Wesleyan University Press, 2002.
BF173 .V55 2002

Scaling methods. 2nd ed. / Peter Dunn-Rankin ... [et al.]. Mahwah, N.J. : L. Erlbaum Associates, 2004. p. cm. Rev. ed. of: Scaling methods / Peter Dunn-Rankin. Includes bibliographical references (p.   ) and index. ISBN 0-8058-1802-2 DDC 150/.28/7
1. Scale analysis (Psychology) I. Dunn-Rankin, Peter. II. Dunn-Rankin, Peter. Scaling methods.
BF39.2.S34 S33 2004

SCALING, PSYCHOLOGICAL. See **PSYCHOMETRICS.**

SCALING (SOCIAL SCIENCES). See **PSYCHOMETRICS; SCALE ANALYSIS (PSYCHOLOGY).**

Scalzi, John, 1969- Uncle John's presents Book of the dumb / John Scalzi. San Diego, CA : Portable Press, 2003. p. cm. On t.p. "b" in "dumb" is presented backwards. ISBN 1-59223-149-7 (pbk.) DDC 081
1. Stupidity - Anecdotes. 2. Insight - Anecdotes. 3. Stupidity - Humor. 4. Insight - Humor. I. Title. II. Title: Book of dumb
BF431 .S273 2003

SCANDANAVIA - HISTORY.
Runica, Germanica, Mediaevalia. Berlin : W. de Gruyter, 2003.

SCANDINAVIA - ETHNIC RELATIONS.
The Nordic peace. Aldershot, England ; Burlington, VT : Ashgate, c2003.
UA646.7 .N672 2003

SCANDINAVIA - STRATEGIC ASPECTS.
The Nordic peace. Aldershot, England ; Burlington, VT : Ashgate, c2003.
UA646.7 .N672 2003

Scandinavian Summer University.
Moulding masculinities. Aldershot, Hants, England ; Burlington, VT : Ashgate, c2003.
BF692.5 .M68 2003

Scars of the spirit.
Hartman, Geoffrey H. New York ; Houndmills, England : Palgrave, 2002.
B105.A8 H37 2002

Scazzola, Andrea. Giovanni Gentile e il Rinascimento / Andrea Scazzola. Napoli : Vivarium, 2002. xvi, 291 p., [17] p. of plates : ill. ; 24 cm. (Saggi e ricerche / Istituto italiano per gli studi filosofici ; 8) Includes bibliographical references. ISBN 88-85239-72-2 DDC 195
1. Gentile, Giovanni, - 1875-1944. 2. Philosophy, Renaissance. I. Title. II. Series: Saggi e ricerche (Istituto italiano per gli studi filosofici) ; 8.

Scenario planning.
Lindgren, Mats, 1959- Houndmills [England] ; New York : Palgrave Macmillan, 2002.
HD30.28 .L543 2002

La scepsi, il sapere e l'anima.
De Pace, Anna. Milano : LED, c2002.

Scepticism, freedom and autonomy.
Araujo, Marcelo de. Berlin : De Gruyter, 2003.

Schäfer, Reinhild.
Gewalt-Verhältnisse. Frankfurt ; New York : Campus, c2002.

Schafer, Roy. Insight and interpretation : the essential tools of psychoanalysis / Roy Schafer. New York : Other Press, c2003. xv, 165 p. ; 24 cm. Includes bibliographical references (p. [153]-158) and index. Table of contents URL: http://www.loc.gov/catdir/toc/ecip042/2003007776.html CONTENTS: Insight and its vicissitudes -- Insight into insight -- Insight for whom? -- Insight : seeing or telling? -- Remembering in the countertransference -- Intimate neutrality -- Applications -- Interpreting sex -- Psychoanalytic discourse on male non-normative sexuality -- Gender jokes/sexual politics -- An overview -- Knowing another person psychoanalytically. ISBN 1-59051-047-X (alk. paper) DDC 150.19/5
1. Psychoanalysis. 2. Sex (Psychology) 3. Psychotherapy - Philosophy. 4. Freud, Sigmund, - 1856-1939. I. Title.
BF173 .S3277 2003

Schaffer, H. Rudolph. Introducing child psychology / H. Rudolph Schaffer. Malden, MA : Blackwell Pub. Ltd., 2004. p. cm. Includes bibliographical references and index. ISBN 0-631-21627-8 (hardcover) ISBN 0-631-21628-6 (pbk.) DDC 155.4
1. Child psychology. 2. Child development. I. Title.
BF721 .S349 2004

Schäffer, Margareth.
Aventuras do sentido. Porto Alegre : EDIPUCRS, 2002.

Schaffer, Simon, 1955-.
The sciences in enlightened Europe. Chicago : University of Chicago Press, 1999.
Q127.E8 S356 1999

Schaie, K. Warner (Klaus Warner), 1928-
Developmental influences on adult intelligence : the Seattle longitudinal study / K. Warner Schaie. [Update]. New York : Oxford University Press, 2004. p. cm. Rev. ed. of: Intellectual development in adulthood. Includes bibliographical references (p.   ) and indexes. ISBN 0-19-515673-0 (cloth : alk. paper) DDC 155.6
1. Cognition - Age factors - Longitudinal studies. 2. Adulthood - Psychological aspects - Longitudinal studies. 3. Aging - Psychological aspects - Longitudinal studies. I. Schaie, K. Warner (Klaus Warner), 1928- Intellectual development in adulthood. II. Title.
BF724.55.C63 S32 2004

Intellectual development in adulthood.
Schaie, K. Warner (Klaus Warner), 1928- Developmental influences on adult intelligence. [Update]. New York : Oxford University Press, 2004.
BF724.55.C63 S32 2004

Schaller, Helmut Wilhelm, 1940- Der Nationalsozialismus und die slawische Welt / Helmut Schaller. Regensburg : Pustet, c2002. 320 p. : ill., ports. ; 24 cm. Includes bibliographical references (p. 292-318) and index. ISBN 3-7917-1820-7
1. National socialism - History. 2. Germany - Politics and government - 1933-1945. 3. Slavs - History - 20th century. 4. Europe, Eastern - History - 1918-1945. 5. World War, 1939-1945 - Occupied territories. I. Title.
DD256.5 .S259 2002

Scharff, Virginia.
Seeing nature through gender. Lawrence : University Press of Kansas, c2003.
GF21 .S44 2003

Schatz, Heribert.
Die Politik der Massenmedien. Köln : Halem, 2001.

Schaub, Bonney Gulino. Dante's path : a practical approach to achieving inner wisdom / Bonney Gulino Schaub, and Richard Schaub. New York, N.Y. : Gotham Books, 2003. p. cm. Includes bibliographical references and index. Table of contents URL: http://www.loc.gov/catdir/toc/ecip042/2003008515.html CONTENTS: The experience of more -- Maps and guides -- The problem and the promise -- Hell-the sea of pain -- Learning to move out of hell -- Climbing the mountain of transformation -- First contact with wisdom -- Developing a relationship with your wisdom mind -- Experiences in higher consciousness -- The candle for its flame prepared -- Epilogue: Michelangelo's eyes. ISBN 1-59240-029-9 (alk. paper) DDC 158
1. Transpersonal psychology. I. Schaub, Richard, Ph. D. II. Title.
BF204.7 .S33 2003

Schaub, Richard, Ph. D.
Schaub, Bonney Gulino. Dante's path. New York, N.Y. : Gotham Books, 2003.
BF204.7 .S33 2003

Schauer, Frederick F. Profiles, probabilities, and stereotypes / Frederick Schauer. Cambridge, Mass. : Belknap Press of Harvard University Press, 2003. xiii, 359 p. ; 22 cm. Includes bibliographical references (p. 301-353) and index. ISBN 0-674-01186-4 (alk. paper) DDC 303.3/85
1. Stereotype (Psychology) 2. Decision making. 3. Judgment. 4. Forecasting. 5. Justice. I. Title.
HM1096 .S34 2003

Schaum's A-Z psychology.
Cardwell, Mike. New York : McGraw-Hill, 2003.
BF31 .C29 2003

Schaum's A-Z series
Cardwell, Mike. Schaum's A-Z psychology. New York : McGraw-Hill, 2003.
BF31 .C29 2003

SCHEDULED AIRLINES. See **AIRLINES.**

Scheid, John. Religion et piété à Rome / John Scheid. [2e éd.]. Paris : Albin Michel, 2001. 189 p. : ill. ; 23 cm. (Sciences des religions) Includes bibliographical references (p. [181]-186) and index. ISBN 2-226-12134-X
1. Rome - Religion. 2. Rome - Religious life and customs. 3. Rome - Civilization. I. Title. II. Series.

Scheier, Michael.
Carver, Charles S. Perspectives on personality. 5th ed. Boston, MA : Allyn and Bacon, 2004.
BF698 .C22 2004

Scheiner, Joachim Alfred P.
Bradler, Christine M. [Feng Shui Symbole des Ostens. English] Feng shui symbols. New York : Sterling Pub., c2001.
BF1779.F4 .B7313 2001

SCHELER, MAX, 1874-1928.
Domagala, Edward. L'ermeneutica dell'esperienza dell'amore in Max Scheler. Romae : [s.n.], 2000.

SCHELLING, FRIEDRICH WILHELM JOSEPH VON, 1775-1854.
Gloyna, Tanja. Kosmos und System. Stuttgart-Bad Cannstatt : Frommann-Holzboog, c2002.
B2898 .G56 2002

Schellingiana
(Bd. 15) Gloyna, Tanja. Kosmos und System. Stuttgart-Bad Cannstatt : Frommann-Holzboog, c2002.
B2898 .G56 2002

SCHEMAS (PSYCHOLOGY).
Estivals, Robert. Théorie générale de la schématisation. Paris : Harmattan, c2002-

Saltz, Gail. Becoming real. New York: Riverhead Books, 2004.
BF637.S4 S245 2004

SCHEMATA (COGNITION). See **SCHEMAS (PSYCHOLOGY).**

SCHEMATA (PSYCHOLOGY). See **SCHEMAS (PSYCHOLOGY).**

Schendel, Willem van.
Time matters. Amsterdam : VU University Press, 2001.
BF468 .T555 2001

Scherer, Klaus R.
Handbook of affective sciences. Oxford ; New York : Oxford University Press, 2003.
BF511 .H35 2003

Scheunemann, Pam, 1955- Coping with anger / Pam Scheunemann. Edina, MN : Abdo Pub., 2004. p. cm. (Keeping the peace) Includes index. SUMMARY: Describes

ways of coping with anger that help to maintain the peace.
ISBN 1-59197-559-X DDC 152.4/7
1. Anger - Juvenile literature. 2. Conduct of life - Juvenile literature. 3. Peace - Juvenile literature. 4. Anger. 5. Peace. I. Title. II. Series: Scheunemann, Pam, 1955- Keeping the peace.
BF575.A5 S34 2004

Dealing with bullies / Pam Scheunemann. Edina, MN : Abdo Pub., 2004. p. cm. Includes index.
SUMMARY: Describes different ways that bullies hurt others, physically or emotionally, and how to deal with these actions.
ISBN 1-59197-560-3 DDC 303.6/*
1. Bullying - Juvenile literature. 2. Conduct of life - Juvenile literature. 3. Peace - Juvenile literature. 4. Bullying. 5. Conduct of life. 6. Peace. I. Title. II. Series: Scheunemann, Pam, 1955- Keeping the peace.
BF637.B85 S37 2004

Keeping the peace.
Scheunemann, Pam, 1955- Coping with anger. Edina, MN : Abdo Pub., 2004.
BF575.A5 S34 2004

Scheunemann, Pam, 1955- Dealing with bullies. Edina, MN : Abdo Pub., 2004.
BF637.B85 S37 2004

Scheutz, Matthias.
Computationalism. Cambridge, MA : MIT Press, c2002.

Schexnayder, Máydel Morín.
Nemeth, Darlyne Gaynor. Helping your angry child. Oakland, Calif. : New Harbinger, c2003.
BF723.A4 N46 2003

Schick, August.
Oldenburger Symposion zur Psychologischen Akustik (8th : 2000) Contributions to psychological acoustics. 1. ed. Oldenburg : BIS, Bibliotheks- und Informationssystem der Universität Oldenburg, 2000.
BF251 .O44 2000

Schiffer, Stephen R. The things we mean / Stephen Schiffer. Oxford ; New York : Clarendon, 2003. 362 p. ; 22 cm. Includes bibliographical references (p. [351]-358) and index. ISBN 0-19-824108-9 ISBN 0-19-925776-0 (PBK.) DDC 121.68
1. Meaning (Philosophy) 2. Philosophy of mind. I. Title.

Schiffter, Frédéric. Pensées d'un philosophe sous Prozac / Frédéric Schiffter. [Toulouse] : Milan, c2002. 99 p. ; 20 cm. (Pause philo) ISBN 2-7459-0758-1 DDC 844
1. Schiffter, Frédéric. 2. Philosophers - France - Biography. 3. Philosophy. I. Title. II. Series.

SCHIFFTER, FRÉDÉRIC.
Schiffter, Frédéric. Pensées d'un philosophe sous Prozac. [Toulouse] : Milan, c2002.

Schiller, Norbert.
Be thou there. Cairo ; New York : American University in Cairo Press, c2001.

Schilling, Dennis R. Spruch und Zahl : die chinesischen Orakelbücher "Kanon des Höchsten Geheimen" (Taixuanjing) und "Wald der Wandlungen" (Yilin) aus der Han-Zeit : mit einer Studie über die Entwicklung, Nachahmung und Neuschaffung des "Buches der Wandlungen" (Yijing) von den Anfängen bis zur Ming-Zeit / Dennis R. Schilling. Aalen : Scientia, 1998. xi, 692 p. : ill. ; 24 cm. Errata slip inserted. A revision of the author's thesis (doctoral)--Universität München, 1995. Includes bibliographical references and index. ISBN 3-511-09235-3
1. Yi jing. 2. Divination - China. 3. Oracles. I. Title.
BF1770.C5 S42 1998

Schilling, Willy.
Jonscher, Reinhard. Kleine thüringische Geschichte. 3., überarb. und erw. Aufl. Jena : Jenzig-Verlag Köhler, 2001.
DD801.T44 J658 2001

Schilte, Christine.
Rufo, Marcel. Frères et soeurs une maladie d'amour. Paris : Fayard, 2002.

Schimmel, Solomon. Wounds not healed by time : the power of repentance and forgiveness / Solomon Schimmel. Oxford ; New York : Oxford University Press, 2002. xi, 265 p. ; 24 cm. Includes bibliographical references (p. 251-257) and indexes. SUMMARY: How should we respond to injuries done to us and to the hurts that we inflict on others? In this book Solomon Schimmel guides us through the meanings of justice, forgiveness, repentance, and reconciliation. In doing so, he probes to the core of the human encounter with evil, drawing on religious traditions, psychology, philosophy, and the personal experiences of both perpetrators and of victims. Christianity, Judaism and Islam call for forgiveness and repentance in our relations with others. Yet, as Schimmel points out, there are significant differences between us as to when and whom to forgive. Is forgiving always more moral than refusing to forgive? Is it ever immoral to forgive? When is repentance a pre-condition for forgiveness, and what does repentance entail? Schimmel explores these questions in diverse contexts, ranging from conflicts in a marriage and personal slights we experience every day to enormous crimes such as the Holocaust. He applies insights on forgiveness and repentance to the Middle East, post-apartheid South Africa, inter-religious relationships, and the criminal justice system. Schimmel also provides practical strategies to help us forgive and repent, preparing the way for healing and reconciliation between individuals and groups. ISBN 0-19-512841-9 (alk. paper) DDC 179/.9
1. Forgiveness. 2. Repentance. I. Title.
BJ1476 .S34 2002

Schindewolf, Dorrit. Weltbild und Wirklichkeit : ein Überblick der Geschichte der Hochkulturen ; die weltanschaulichen und politischen Erfahrungen aus fünf Jahrtausenden / Dorrit Schindewolf. [S.l.] : Schindewolf, [1999] 662 p. ; 21 cm. Includes bibliographical references and indexes. ISBN 3-89811-027-3 (pbk.) DDC 909
1. Civilization - History. I. Title.
CB88 .S35 1999

Schipper, Kristofer Marinus.
Condordance du Dao zang.
Schipper, Kristofer Marinus. Dao zang suo yin. Di 1 ban. Shanghai : Shanghai shu dian chu ban she : Xin hua shu dian Shanghai fa xing suo fa xin, 1996.
BL1900.T387 S35 1996 <Orien China>

Dao zang suo yin : wu zhong ban ben Dao zang tong jian / Shi Zhouren yuan bian ; Chen Yaoting gai ban. Di 1 ban. Shanghai : Shanghai shu dian chu ban she : Xin hua shu dian Shanghai fa xing suo fa xin, 1996. 6, 24, 363 p. ; 27 cm. Based on: Concordance du Tao-Tsang / Kristofer Marinus Schipper. Includes bibliographical references and index. ISBN 7-80622-012-7
1. Dao zang - Concordances. 2. Taoism. I. Chen, Yaoting. II. Schipper, Kristofer Marinus. Condordance du Dao zang. III. Title. IV. Title: Wu zhong ban ben Dao zang tong jian
BL1900.T387 S35 1996 <Orien China>

Schirmacher, Wolfgang.
German 20th century philosophical writings. New York : Continuum, 2003.
B29 .G397 2003

Schlafly, Phyllis. Feminist fantasies / Phyllis Schlafly ; foreword by Ann Coulter. Dallas : Spence Publishing Co., 2003. xx, 262 p. ; 24 cm. Includes index. ISBN 1-89062-646-5 DDC 305.42
1. Anti-feminism. 2. Feminism. 3. Sex role. I. Title.
HQ1150 .S34 2003

Schlange-Schöningen, Heinrich, 1960-.
Gelehrte in der Antike. Köln : Böhlau, c2002.

Schlanger, Jacques. Guide pour un apprenti philosophe / Jacques Schlanger. Paris : Presses universitaires de France, 2002. 253 p. ; 20 cm. (Perspectives critiques) ISBN 2-13-052410-9 DDC 194
1. Philosophy. I. Title. II. Series.

Schleiermacher, Friedrich, 1768-1834. Lectures on philosophical ethics / Friedrich Schleiermacher ; edited by Robert B. Louden ; translated by Louise Adey Huish. Cambridge ; New York : Cambridge University Press, 2002. xl, 253 p. ; 24 cm. (Cambridge texts in the history of philosophy) Includes bibliographical references and index. Translation based on the German edition: Ethik (1812/13) / edited by Hans-Joachim Birkner. Hamburg : Meiner, 1981. ISBN 0-521-80982-7
1. Ethics. I. Louden, Robert B., 1953- II. Title. III. Series.

Schlein, Alan M. Find it online : the complete guide to online research / [by Alan M. Schlein ; edited by J.J. Newby and Peter J. Weber]. 3rd ed. Tempe, AZ : Facts on Demand Press, c2003. xii, 547 p. : ill. ; 24 cm. "Fully revised"--Cover. Includes bibliographical references and index.
1. Internet addresses - Directories. 2. Web sites - Directories. 3. Street addresses - Directories. 4. Database searching. I. Title.

Schlenger, Sunny. Organizing for the spirit : making the details of your life meaningful and manageable / Sunny Schlenger ; foreword by Harriet Schecter. 1st ed. San Francisco : Jossey-Bass, c2004. p. cm. CONTENTS: Begin at the beginning -- Play detective -- Be who you are -- Be where you are -- Enjoy your life -- Give back -- Conclusion: The end of one story. ISBN 0-7879-6759-9 (alk. paper) DDC 646.7
1. Self-actualization (Psychology) I. Title.
BF637.S4 S345 2004

SCHLOSS NEUHAUS (JINDŘICHŮV HRADEC, CZECH REPUBLIC).
Sankt Georg und sein Bilderzyklus in Neuhaus/Böhmen (Jindřichuv Hradec). Marburg : N.G. Elwert, c2002.
BR1720.G4 S26 2002

Schlosser, Herta. Der Mensch als Wesen der Freiheit / Herta Schlosser. Vallendar-Schönstatt : Patris Verlag, 2002. 125 p. ; 21 cm. (Beiträge zu einer christlichen Kultur ; Bd. 3) Includes bibliographical references. ISBN 3-87620-243-4 (pbk.)
1. Kentenich, Joseph. 2. Free will and determinism. 3. Liberty. I. Title. II. Series.

Schmalensee, Richard.
Management. Cambridge, Mass. : MIT Press, 2003.
HD31 .M2928 2003

Schmauder, Andreas.
Frühe Hexenverfolgung in Ravensburg und am Bodensee. Konstanz : UVK Verlagsgesellschaft, c2001.
BF1583 .F784 2001

Schmauks, Dagmar. Orientierung im Raum : Zeichen für die Fortbewegung / Dagmar Schmauks. Tübingen : Stauffenburg, c2002. xiv, 144 p. : ill. ; 23 cm. (Probleme der Semiotik, 0933-4483 ; Bd. 20 = Problems in semiotics) Includes bibliographical references (p. 134-144). ISBN 3-86057-096-X (pbk.)
1. Orientation (Physiology) 2. Space perception. 3. Cognition. 4. Signs and signboards. 5. Space and time in language. I. Title. II. Series: Probleme der Semiotik ; Bd. 20.
QP443 .S363 2002

Schmerl, Christiane.
Sexuelle Szenen. Opladen : Leske + Budrich, 2000.
HQ16 .S474 2000

Schmid, U. (Ute) Inductive synthesis of functional programs : universal planning, folding of finite programs, and schema abstraction by analogical reasoning / Ute Schmid. Berlin ; New York : Springer, c2003. xxii, 398 p. : ill. ; 24 cm. (Lecture notes in computer science ; 2654. Lecture notes in artificial intelligence) Includes bibliographical references (p. [327]-340) and index. ISBN 3-540-40174-1 (softcover : alk. paper) DDC 005.1
1. Computer programming. 2. Software engineering. 3. Artificial intelligence. I. Title. II. Series: Lecture notes in computer science ; 2654. III. Series: Lecture notes in computer science. Lecture notes in artificial intelligence.
QA76.6 .S3855 2003

Schmidt, Axel, 1968-.
Popvisionen. Frankfurt : Suhrkamp, 2003.
ML3470 .P69 2003

Schmidt, Burghart, 1942-.
Vom Parergon zum Labyrinth. Wien : Böhlau, c2001.
NK1505 .V65 2001

Schmidt, Richard A., 1941- Motor learning and performance / Richard A. Schmidt, Craig A. Wrisberg. 3rd ed. Champaign, IL : Human Kinetics, 2004. p. cm. Includes bibliographical references and index. ISBN 0-7360-4566-X (hardcover) DDC 152.3/34
1. Motor learning - Textbooks. I. Wrisberg, Craig A. II. Title.
BF295 .S249 2004

Schmidt, Victor Michael.
Antiquity renewed. Leuven, Netherlands ; Dudley, MA : Peeters, 2003.
CB365 .A58 2003

Schmitz, H. Walter.
Botschaften verstehen. Frankfurt am Main ; New York : P. Lang, c2000.
P91.25 .B688 2000

Schmölders, Claudia.
Der exzentrische Blick. Berlin : Akademie Verlag, 1996.
BF853 .E98 1996

Schnall, Maxine. What doesn't kill you makes you stronger : turning bad breaks into blessings / Maxine Schnall. Cambridge, MA : Perseus Pub., c2002. xi, 243 p. ; 22 cm. Includes bibliographical references (p. 241-243). Table of contents URL: http://www.loc.gov/catdir/toc/fy038/2002112391.html ISBN 0-7382-0732-2 DDC 155.9/3
1. Loss (Psychology) 2. Grief. I. Title.
BF575.D35 S36 2002

Schnapp, Alain, 1946-.
Arts en bibliothèques. Paris : Editions du Cercle de la Librairie, c2003.
Z675.A85 A78 2003

Schneider, Benjamin, 1938-.
Personality and organizations. Mahwah, N.J. : Lawrence Erlbaum Associates, 2004.
BF698.9.O3 P46 2004

Schneider, David J., 1940- The psychology of stereotyping / by David J. Schneider. New York : Guilford Press, c2004. p. cm. (Distinguished contributions in psychology) Includes bibliographical references and index. Table of contents URL: http://www.loc.gov/catdir/toc/

ecip043/2003008819.html CONTENTS: Introduction -- Methods -- Categories and categorization -- Schema theories -- Stereotype structure and implicit personality theory -- Stereotypes as hypotheses -- Ingroups and outgroups -- Prejudice and discrimination -- The development of stereotypes -- Change of stereotypes and prejudice -- Content of stereotypes : gender, race, and age -- Content of stereotypes : the stigmatized -- Content of stereotypes : other groups -- Stereotype content and features. ISBN 1-57230-929-6 (alk. paper) DDC 303.3/85
1. *Stereotype (Psychology)* I. Title. II. Series.
BF323.S63 S36 2003

Schneider, Gerald, 1962-.
Globalization and armed conflict. Lanham, Md. : Rowman & Littlefield, c2003.
JZ5538 .G58 2003

Schneider, Jennifer P.
Corley, M. Deborah. Embracing recovery from chemical dependency. Sottsdale, AZ : Gentle Path Press, c2003.
BF632 .C63 2003

Schneidewind, Ulrike.
Mörschel, Thomas. Die Historia vom heiligen Gral. Saarbrücken : Logos, 1994-

Schnitman, Jorge.
[Nuevos paradigmas. English.] New paradigms, culture, and subjectivity. Cresskill, N.J. : Hampton Press, c2002.
BD161 .N8413 2002

SCHOLARS. See **HISTORIANS; PHILOLOGISTS; PHILOSOPHERS.**

Scholars and courtiers : intellectuals and society in the medieval West / [collected by] C. Stephen Jaeger. Aldershot ; Burlington, Vt. : Ashgate/Variorum, c2002. 1 v. (various pagings) : port. ; 24 cm. (Variorum collected studies series) Includes bibliographical references and index. ISBN 0-86078-879-2 (alk. paper) DDC 305.5/52/094
1. *Europe - Intellectual life.* 2. *Europe - Court and courtiers.* 3. *Scholars - Europe.* 4. *Civilization, Medieval.* I. Jaeger, C. Stephen. II. Series: Collected studies.
AZ183.E8 S36 2002

SCHOLARS - CHINA - BIO-BIBLIOGRAPHY.
Nielsen, Bent. A companion to Yi jing numerology and cosmology. London ; New York : RoutledgeCurzon, 2003.

SCHOLARS - EUROPE.
Scholars and courtiers. Aldershot ; Burlington, Vt. : Ashgate/Variorum, c2002.
AZ183.E8 S36 2002

SCHOLARSHIP. See **LEARNING AND SCHOLARSHIP.**

SCHOLASTIC ACHIEVEMENT. See **ACADEMIC ACHIEVEMENT.**

SCHOLASTIC SUCCESS. See **ACADEMIC ACHIEVEMENT.**

SCHOLASTICISM. See **PHILOSOPHY, MEDIEVAL.**

Schölkopf, Bernhard.
Conference on Computational Learning Theory (16th : 2003 : Washington, D.C.) Learning theory and Kernel machines. Berlin ; New York : Springer, c2003.
Q325.5 .C654 2003

Schölmerich, Axel.
Between culture and biology. Cambridge, U.K. ; New York : Cambridge University Press, 2002.
BF721 .B4138 2002

Scholtz, Gunter.
Grenzen des Verstehens. Göttingen : Vandenhoeck & Ruprecht, c2002.
BD181.5 .G74 2002

Scholz, Piotr O. Die Sehnsucht nach Tausendundeiner Nacht : Begegnung von Orient und Okzident / Piotr O. Scholz. Stuttgart : Thorbecke, 2002. 191 p. : ill. ; 22 cm. Includes bibliographical references. ISBN 3-7995-0107-X (hd.bd.)
1. *Arabian nights.* 2. *East and West.* I. Title.

Schomburg Children's Collection.
Morrison, Toni. The book of mean people. 1st ed. New York : Hyperion Books for Children, c2002.
1. *Black authors.*

SCHOOL AND HOME. See **HOME AND SCHOOL.**

SCHOOL CREDITS. See **ADVANCED PLACEMENT PROGRAMS (EDUCATION).**

SCHOOL ENVIRONMENT - UNITED STATES.
Lampert, Khen. Compassionate education. Lanham, Md. : University Press of America, c2003.

SCHOOL FACILITIES. See **LYCEUMS.**

SCHOOL GRADE PLACEMENT. See **ADVANCED PLACEMENT PROGRAMS (EDUCATION).**

SCHOOL PERSONNEL MANAGEMENT.
Conflict resolution for school personnel [electronic resource]. [Washington, D.C.?] : U.S. Dept. of Justice, Office of Justice Programs, National Institute of Justice, c1999.

SCHOOL PLAYGROUNDS. See **PLAYGROUNDS.**

SCHOOL PSYCHOLOGY.
Elias, Maurice J. Bullying, peer harassment, and victimization in the schools. New York : Haworth Press, 2003.
BF637.B85 E45 2003

Montagner, Hubert. L'enfant, la vraie question de l'école. Paris : Jacob, c2002.

SCHOOL PSYCHOLOGY - SPAIN - HISTORY.
Cerezo Manrique, Miguel Ángel. Los comienzos de la psicopedagogía en España, 1882-1936. Madrid : Biblioteca Nueva, c2001.

SCHOOL TEACHING. See **TEACHING.**

SCHOOL VANDALISM. See **SCHOOL VIOLENCE.**

SCHOOL VIOLENCE - PREVENTION.
Conflict resolution for school personnel [electronic resource]. [Washington, D.C.?] : U.S. Dept. of Justice, Office of Justice Programs, National Institute of Justice, c1999.

Schooling, the Puritan imperative, and the molding of an American national identity.
McKnight, Douglas. Mahwah, N.J. ; London : L. Erlbaum Associates, 2003.
LC311 .M24 2003

SCHOOLS. See also **EDUCATION; UNIVERSITIES AND COLLEGES.**
Bruce, Lisa. Sizes at school. Chicago, IL : Raintree, c2003.
BF299.S5 B78 2003

SCHOOLTEACHING. See **TEACHING.**

Schopenhauer, Arthur, 1788-1860.
[Parerga and paralipomena. English]
Parerga and paralipomena : short philosophical essays / by Arthur Schopenhauer ; translated from the German by E.F.J. Payne. Oxford : Clarendon Press ; New York : Oxford University Press, 2000. 2 v. : port. ; 22 cm. Includes bibliographical references (v. 2, p. [659]-660) and index. First published 1974, reissued 2000. ISBN 0-19-924220-8 ISBN 0-19-924221-6 DDC 193
1. *Philosophy.* I. Payne, E. F. J. II. Title.
B3118.E5 P38 2000

Die Schöpfung in der bildenden Kunst.
Kupka, František, 1871-1957. [Création dans les arts plastiques. Czech. German] Ostfildern-Ruit : Hatje Cantz, c2001.

Schostak, Sherene. Surviving saturn's return : vital lessons for overcoming life's most tumultuous cycle / Sherene Schostak, Stefanie Iris Weiss. 1st ed. New York : McGraw-Hill, 2004. p. cm. Table of contents URL: http://www.loc.gov/catdir/toc/ecip045/2003014508.html Publisher description URL: http://www.loc.gov/catdir/description/mh031/2003014508.html CONTENTS: Self -- Attachment -- The mind -- Home -- Creativity -- Purification -- The other -- Transformation -- Higher mind -- The world -- Community -- The source. ISBN 0-07-142196-3 (pbk. : alk. paper) DDC 133.5/37/08422
1. *Human beings - Effect of Saturn on.* 2. *Astrology.* I. Weiss, Stefanie Iris. II. Title.
BF1724.2.S3 S36 2004

Schreck, Jorg. Security and privacy in user modeling / by Jorg Schreck. Dordrecht ; Boston ; London : Kluwer Academic Publishers, c2003. xxi, 210 p. : ill. ; 25 cm. (Human computer interaction series ; v. 2) Includes bibliographical references (p. 187-206) and index. ISBN 140201130X (alk. paper) DDC 005.8
1. *Computer security.* 2. *Human-computer interaction.* 3. *User interfaces (Computer systems)* I. Title. II. Series: Kluwer international series on HCI ; v. 2.
QA76.9.A25 S353 2003

Schreiber, Scott G. (Scott Gregory), 1952- Aristotle on false reasoning : language and the world in the Sophistical refutations / Scott G. Schreiber. Albany : State University of New York Press, 2003. xv, 248 p. ; 23 cm. (SUNY series in ancient Greek philosophy) Includes bibliographical references (p. 233-240) and indexes. ISBN 0-7914-5659-5 (alk. paper) ISBN 0-7914-5660-9 (pbk. : alk. paper) DDC 185
1. *Aristotle.* 2. *Reasoning.* 3. *Fallacies (Logic)* I. Title. II. Series.
B491.R4 S37 2003

Schreiner, Klaus.
Frömmigkeit im Mittelalter. München : Fink, c2002.

Schrieffer, J. R. (John Robert), 1931-
[Papers. Selections]
Selected papers of J. Robert Schrieffer : in celebration of his 70th birthday / editors, N.E. Bonesteel. L.P. Gor'kov. River Edge, NJ : World Scientific, c2002. xiii, 509 p. : ill. ; 27 cm. (World Scientific series in 20th century physics ; v. 30) Includes bibliographical references. ISBN 981-238-078-7 ISBN 981-238-079-5 (pbk) DDC 530
1. *Schrieffer, J. R. - (John Robert), - 1931-* 2. *Physics.* 3. *Physicists - United States.* I. Bonesteel, N. E. II. Gor'kov, L. P. (Lev Petrovich) III. Title. IV. Series.
QC21.3 .S37 2002

SCHRIEFFER, J. R. (JOHN ROBERT), 1931-.
Schrieffer, J. R. (John Robert), 1931- [Papers. Selections] Selected papers of J. Robert Schrieffer. River Edge, NJ : World Scientific, c2002.
QC21.3 .S37 2002

Schriesheim, Chester.
Leadership. Greenwich, Conn. : Information Age Pub., c2002.
HD57.7 .L4313 2002

Schriften der Philosophischen Fakultäten der Universität Augsburg. Philosophisch-erziehungswissenschaftliche Reihe
(Nr. 67) Arnold, Margret. Aspekte einer modernen Neurodidaktik. München : Ernst Vögel, 2002.

Schriften zu Psychopathologie, Kunst und Literatur
(7) Ekel. 1. Aufl. Hürtgenwald : G. Pressler, c2003.
BF575.A886 E34 2003

Schriften zur Musikpsychologie und Musikästhetik
(Bd. 14.) Mornell, Adina. Lampenfieber und Angst bei ausübenden Musikern. Frankfurt am Main : P. Lang, 2002.
ML3830 .M67 2002

Schriften zur Triadik und Ontodynamik
(Bd. 20) Roehle, Friedrich, 1916-1995. Die Struktur des Bewusstseins. Frankfurt am Main ; New York : Peter Lang, c2001.

Schriftenreihe Boethiana
(Bd. 54) Ästhetik. Hamburg : Kovač, c2002.

Schriftenreihe der Universität Dortmund
(Bd. 46.) Markt - Medien - Moral. Bochum : Projekt-Verlag, 2001.

Schriftenreihe der Universität Dortmund. Studium generale
(Bd. 10.) Markt - Medien - Moral. Bochum : Projekt-Verlag, 2001.

Schriftenreihe des Bundesministeriums für Familie, Senioren, Frauen und Jugend
(Bd. 213) Fthenakis, Wassilios E. Die Rolle des Vaters in der Familie. Stuttgart : Kohlhammer, 2002.

Schröder, Jürgen. Die Sprache des Denkens / Jürgen Schröder. Würzburg : Königshausen & Neumann, c2001. iii, 249 p. ; 24 cm. ISBN 3-8260-2128-2 (pbk.)
1. *Language and languages - Philosophy.* 2. *Thought and thinking.* 3. *Cognitive grammar.* 4. *Psycholinguistics.* I. Title.

Schröder, Winfried, Dr. phil. Moralischer Nihilismus : Typen radikaler Moralkritik von den Sophisten bis Nietzsche / Winfried Schröder. Stuttgart-Bad Canstatt : Frommann-Holzboog, c2002. 283 p. : 25 cm. (Quaestiones ; 15) Errata slip inserted. Includes bibliographical references (p. [255]-270) and indexes. ISBN 3-7728-2190-1 ISBN 3-7728-2232-0 (corrected : cl.)
1. *Ethics.* I. Title. II. Series.

Schröger, Erich.
Working on working memory. Leipzig : Leipziger Universitätsverlag, 2000.
BF378.S54 W675 2000

Schueler, G. F. Reasons and purposes : human rationality and the teleological explanation of action / G.F. Schueler. Oxford : Oxford University Press, 2003. xii, 174 p. ; 23 cm. Includes bibliographical references and index. ISBN 0-19-925507-5 DDC 128.4
1. *Intentionality (Philosophy)* 2. *Practical reason.* I. Title.

Schuerger, James M.
Cattell, Heather Birkett. Essentials of 16PF assessment. Hoboken, NJ : John Wiley & Sons, 2003.

Schulman, Martin A.
Sexual faces. Madison, Conn. : International Universities Press, c2002.
BF175.5.S48 S47 2002

Schulman, Rita.
Friends and friendship. Madison, Conn. : Psychosocial Press, 2003.
BF575.F66 F695 2003

Schulte Nordholt, Henk, 1953-.
Time matters. Amsterdam : VU University Press, 2001.
BF468 .T555 2001

Schulthess, Peter, Dr. phil.
Augustine, Saint, Bishop of Hippo. De magistro = Paderborn : F. Schöningh, 2002.
BR65.A5 G4 2002

Schultz, Duane P. A history of modern psychology / Duane P. Schultz, Sydney Ellen Schultz. 8th ed. Belmont, CA : Thomson/Wadsworth, c2004. xviii, 534 p. : ill. ; 25 cm. Includes bibliographical references (p. 510-525) and indexes. ISBN 0-534-55775-9 (alk. paper)
1. Psychology - History - Textbooks. I. Schultz, Sydney Ellen. II. Title.
BF95 .S35 2004

Schultz, Katherine. Listening : a framework for teaching across differences / Katherine Schultz ; foreword by Frederick Erickson. New York : Teachers College Press, c2003. xv, 197 p. : ill. ; 23 cm. Includes bibliographical references (p. 175-185) and index. ISBN 0-8077-4377-1 (pbk. : alk. paper) ISBN 0-8077-4378-X (cloth : alk. paper) DDC 371.39
1. Effective teaching. 2. Listening. 3. Teacher-student relationships. I. Title. II. Title: Framework for teaching across differences
LB1027 .S36638 2003

Schultz, Sydney Ellen.
Schultz, Duane P. A history of modern psychology. 8th ed. Belmont, CA : Thomson/Wadsworth, c2004.
BF95 .S35 2004

Schultz, William, 1925-.
Excursions in Chinese culture. Hong Kong : Chinese University Press, c2002.

SCHULTZ, WILLIAM, 1925-.
Excursions in Chinese culture. Hong Kong : Chinese University Press, c2002.

Schulz, Andreas.
Generationswechsel und historischer Wandel. München : Oldenbourg, 2003.

Schulz, Walter, 1912- Prüfendes Denken : Essays zur Wiederbelebung der Philosophie / von Walter Schulz. Tübingen : Klöpfer & Meyer, c2003. 230 p. : ill. ; 20 cm. (Promenade) Collection of texts published previously. ISBN 3-421-05741-9
1. Philosophy, Modern - 20th century. I. Title. II. Series.

Schulze, Winfried.
Wahrheit, Wissen, Erinnerung. Münster : Lit, [2002]

Schumacher, Frank, 1965-.
Culture and international history. New York : Berghahn Books, 2003.
JZ1251 .C84 2003

SCHUMANN, CLARA, 1819-1896.
Pedroza, Ludim. The ritual of music contemplation. 2002.

SCHUMPETER, JOSEPH ALOIS, 1883-1950.
Mezias, Stephen J. Organizational dynamics of creative destruction. Houndmills [England] ; New York : Palgrave Macmillan, 2002.
HB615 .M49 2002

Schürmann, Reiner, 1941-
[Des hégémonies brisées. English]
Broken hegemonies / by Reiner Schürmann ; translated by Reginald Lilly. Bloomington : Indiana University Press, c2003. xii, 692 p. ; 24 cm. (Studies in Continental thought) Includes bibliographical references (p. [633]-680) and indexes. ISBN 0-253-34144-2 (alk. paper) ISBN 0-253-21547-1 (pbk. : alk. paper) DDC 190
1. Knowledge, Theory of. 2. Phenomenology. 3. Norm (Philosophy) 4. Philosophy - History. I. Lilly, Reginald. II. Title. III. Series.
BD162 .S48 2003

Schuster, Peter, 1939-.
Evolutionary dynamics. Oxford ; New York : Oxford University Press, 2003.
QH366.2 .E867 2003

Schuster, Shlomit C., 1951- The philosopher's autobiography : a qualitative study / Shlomit C. Schuster ; foreword by Maurice Friedman. Westport, Conn. ; London : Praeger, 2003. x, 244 p. ; 25 cm. Includes bibliographical references (p. [219]-229) and index. ISBN 0-275-97789-7 (alk. paper) DDC 190
1. Philosophy - Authorship. 2. Philosophers - Biography - History and criticism. 3. Autobiography. 4. Psychoanalysis and philosophy. I. Title.
B52.7 .S38 2003

Schutz, Alfred, 1899-1959. Werkausgabe : ASW / Alfred Schütz ; herausgegeben von Richard Grathoff, Hans-Georg Soeffner und Ilja Srubar ; Redaktion: Martin Endress. Konstanz : UVK, Verlagsgesellschaft, 2003- v. ; 22 cm. PARTIAL CONTENTS: Bd. 5. Theorie der Lebenswelt. [T.] 1. Die pragmatische Schichtung der Lebenswelt / herausgegeben von M. Endress und I. Srubar. ISBN 3-89669-738-2 (12-v.set) ISBN 3-89669-774-9 (v. 5,1)
1. Life. 2. Knowledge, Sociology of. 3. Phenomenology. I. Grathoff, Richard, 1934- II. Soeffner, Hans-Georg. III. Srubar, Ilja. IV. Title. V. Title: ASW
BD431 .S284916 2003

Schwader, Marilyn.
A guide to getting it. 1st ed. Portland, Or. : Clarity of Vision Pub., 2002.
BF637.S8 G84 2002

Schwandner-Sievers, Stephanie.
Albanian identities. Bloomington : Indiana University Press, 2002.
DR950 .A385 2002

Schwarte, Johannes. Der werdende Mensch : Persönlichkeitsentwicklung und Gesellschaft heute / Johannes Schwarte. 1. Aufl. Wiesbaden : Westdeutscher Verlag, 2002. 556 p. : ill. ; 23 cm. Includes bibliographical references (p. [547]-556). ISBN 3-531-13870-7 (pbk.)
1. Personality development. 2. Socialization. I. Title.

Schwartz, Barry, 1946- The tyranny of choice / Barry Schwartz. 1st ed. New York : ECCO, 2004. p. cm. Includes index. Publisher description URL: http://www.loc.gov/catdir/description/hc043/2003053138.html ISBN 0-06-000568-8 DDC 153.8/3
1. Choice (Psychology) 2. Decision making. I. Title.
BF611 .S38 2004

Schwartz, Bennett L.
Applied metacognition. Cambridge, U.K. ; New York : Cambridge University Press, 2002.
BF311 .A638 2002

Schwartz, Charlotte, 1928-.
Sexual faces. Madison, Conn. : International Universities Press, c2002.
BF175.5.S48 S47 2002

Schwartz, Robert, 1940-.
Looking into pictures. Cambridge, Mass. : MIT Press, c2003.
BF243 .L66 2003

Schwarzkopf & Schwarzkopf Debatte
Hoffmann, Arne. Sind Frauen bessere Menschen? Berlin : Schwarzkopf & Schwarzkopf, 2001.
HQ1075 .H64 2001

Schweidler, Walter, 1957-.
Markt - Medien - Moral. Bochum : Projekt-Verlag, 2001.

Schweitzer, Albert, 1875-1965.
Selections. 1995.
Schweitzer, Albert, 1875-1965. Vorträge, Vorlesungen, Aufsätze. München : C.H. Beck, c2003.

Vorträge, Vorlesungen, Aufsätze / Albert Schweitzer ; herausgegeben von Claus Günzler, Ulrich Luz und Johann Zürcher. München : C.H. Beck, c2003. 421 p. ; 23 cm. (Werke aus dem Nachlass / Albert Schweitzer) Includes bibliographical references and index. Primarily in German; a few documents in French. CONTENTS: Zur Edition / von Johann Zürcher -- I. Philosophische Texte -- II. Theologische Texte -- III. Kleine Texte aus dem Alltag. ISBN 3-406-50165-6 ISBN 3-406-39130-3 (set)
1. Schweitzer, Albert, 1875-1965. 2. Philosophy. 3. Theology. 4. Ethics, Modern. I. Günzler, Claus, 1937- II. Luz, Ulrich. III. Zürcher, Johann, 1926- IV. Title. V. Series: Schweitzer, Albert, 1875-1965. Selections. 1995.

SCHWEITZER, ALBERT, 1875-1965.
Schweitzer, Albert, 1875-1965. Vorträge, Vorlesungen, Aufsätze. München : C.H. Beck, c2003.

Schweizer, Andreas, 1946- Seelenführer durch den verborgenen Raum : das ägyptische Unterweltsbuch Amduat / Andreas Schweizer ; mit einem Vorwort von Erik Hornung. München : Kösel, 1994. 239 p., 8 leaves of plates : ill. (8 col.) ; 22 cm. Includes bibliographical references (p. 236-237) ISBN 3-466-36411-6
1. Book of that which is in the nether world. 2. Egypt - Religion. I. Hornung, Erik. II. Title.

Schweppenhäuser, Gerhard. Die Fluchtbahn des Subjekts : Beiträge zu Ästhetik und Kulturphilosophie / Gerhard Schweppenhäuser. Münster : Lit, 2001. 237 p. : ill. ; 24 cm. (Ästhetik und Kulturphilosophie ; Bd. 1) Includes bibliographical references. ISBN 3-8258-4974-0 (pbk.) DDC 306.01
1. Aesthetics. 2. Culture - Philosophy. I. Title. II. Series.

Schwickert, Eva-Maria. Feminismus und Gerechtigkeit : über eine Ethik von Verantwortung und Diskurs / Eva-Maria Schwickert. Berlin : Akademie Verlag, c2000. 210 p. ; 25 cm. Originally presented as the author's thesis (doctoral)--Freie Universität Berlin, 1999. Includes bibliographical references (p. [193]-207) and index. ISBN 3-05-003537-4 (hd. bd.)
1. Gilligan, Carol, - 1936- - Contributions in psychology of femininity. 2. Kohlberg, Lawrence, - 1927- - Contributions in moral philosophy. 3. Feminist ethics. 4. Sexual ethics for women. 5. Moral development. I. Title.

Sci-Fi Channel true life encounters.
Spencer, John, 1954- Mysteries and magic. London : Orion, 2000.

SCIENCE. *See also* **COGNITIVE SCIENCE; JUDAISM AND SCIENCE; LIFE SCIENCES; MATHEMATICS; NATURAL HISTORY; PHYSICAL SCIENCES; RELIGION AND SCIENCE; TECHNOLOGY.**
Fonseca, Eduardo Giannetti da, 1957- Nada é tudo. Rio de Janeiro, RJ, Brasil : Editora Campus, c2000.
F2521 .F64 2000

Science & technology education library
(v. 18) Lawson, Anton E. The neurological basis of learning, development, and discovery. Dordrecht ; Boston : Kluwer Academic Publishers, c2003.
BF318 .L365 2003

SCIENCE AND ASTROLOGY.
Seymour, Percy. [Paranormal] The third level of reality. New York : Paraview Special Editions, c2003.
BF1045.S33 S48 2003

SCIENCE AND CIVILIZATION.
Porus, V. N. Ratsional'nost', nauka, kul'tura. Moskva : Universitet Rossiĭskoĭ akademii obrazovaniia, Kafedra filosofii, 2002.
Q175.32.K45 P678 2002

SCIENCE AND JUDAISM. *See* **JUDAISM AND SCIENCE.**

Science and philosophy
(8.) Châtelet, Gilles. [Enjeux du mobile. English] Figuring space. Dordrecht ; Boston : Kluwer, c2000.
B67 .C4313 2000

SCIENCE AND RELIGION. *See* **RELIGION AND SCIENCE.**

SCIENCE AND STATE. *See* **MEDICAL POLICY.**

SCIENCE AND THE ARTS - HISTORY - 19TH CENTURY.
Goodall, Jane. Performance and evolution in the age of Darwin. London ; New York : Routledge, 2002.
NX180.S3 G66 2002

SCIENCE, APPLIED. *See* **TECHNOLOGY.**

SCIENCE - CONGRESSES.
[Nuevos paradigmas. English.] New paradigms, culture, and subjectivity. Cresskill, N.J. : Hampton Press, c2002.
BD161 .N8413 2002

SCIENCE - EARLY WORKS TO 1800.
Dee, John, 1527-1608. [Selections. 2003] John Dee. Berkeley, Calif. : North Atlantic Books, c2003.
BF1598.D5 A25 2003

Ikhwān al-Ṣafā'. [Rasā'il. 36. French & Arabic] Les révolutions et les cycles . Louvain-la-Neuve : Bruylant-Academia ; Beyrouth : Al-Bouraq Editions, 1996.

Leonardo, da Vinci, 1452-1519. [Selections. English. 1999] The manuscripts of Leonardo da Vinci in the Institut de France. Milano : Ente raccolta vinciana, 1999-
Q113 .L3513 1999

SCIENCE - ENGLAND - MANCHESTER - HISTORY - 19TH CENTURY.
Cardwell, D. S. L. (Donald Stephen Lowell) The development of science and technology in nineteenth-century Britain. Aldershot, Great Britain ; Burlington, VT : Ashgate/Variorum, c2003.

Q127.G4 C37 2003

SCIENCE - EUROPE - HISTORY - 18TH CENTURY.
The sciences in enlightened Europe. Chicago : University of Chicago Press, 1999.
Q127.E8 S356 1999

SCIENCE FICTION.
Aveni, Anthony F. Conversing with the planets. Rev. ed. Boulder, Colo. : University Press of Colorado, c2002.
QB981 .A99 2002

A science for the soul.
Treitel, Corinna. Baltimore : Johns Hopkins University Press, 2004.
BF1434.G5 T74 2004

SCIENCE - FORECASTING.
A parliament of science. Albany : State University of New York Press, c2003.
Q158.5 .P38 2003

SCIENCE - GREAT BRITAIN - HISTORY - 19TH CENTURY.
Cardwell, D. S. L. (Donald Stephen Lowell) The development of science and technology in nineteenth-century Britain. Aldershot, Great Britain ; Burlington, VT : Ashgate/Variorum, c2003.
Q127.G4 C37 2003

Van Wyhe, John, 1971- Phrenology and the origins of Victorian scientific naturalism. Burlington, VT : Ashgate, c2003.
BF879 .V36 2003

SCIENCE - HISTORY.
Sciences et archétypes. Paris : Dervy, 2002.

SCIENCE - HISTORY - 19TH CENTURY.
Literature, science, psychoanalysis, 1830-1970. Oxford ; New York : Oxford University Press, 2003.
PN55 .L58 2003

SCIENCE - HISTORY - 20TH CENTURY.
Literature, science, psychoanalysis, 1830-1970. Oxford ; New York : Oxford University Press, 2003.
PN55 .L58 2003

SCIENCE IN LITERATURE.
Literature, science, psychoanalysis, 1830-1970. Oxford ; New York : Oxford University Press, 2003.
PN55 .L58 2003

SCIENCE, MENTAL. See PSYCHOLOGY.

SCIENCE - METHODOLOGY. See also LOGIC.
Descartes, René, 1596-1650. [Regulae ad directionem ingenii. French] Règles pour la direction de l'esprit. Paris : Librairie générale française, c2002.

Morales Tomas, Marco Antonio. El que busca encuentra = Guatemala : ESEDIR : Editorial Saqil Tzij, 1999.

Valle Bonilla, Otto René. Que no le cuenten cuentos = Guatemala : ESEDIR : Editorial Saqil Tzij, 1999.

SCIENCE - MISCELLANEA.
Townsend, John. Mysterious encounters. Chicago, IL : Raintree, 2004.
BF2050 .T69 2004

Wolke, Robert L. What Einstein told his cook. 1st ed. New York : W.W. Norton & Co., c2002.
TX652 .W643 2002

SCIENCE, MORAL. See ETHICS.

SCIENCE - MORAL AND ETHICAL ASPECTS.
Leibowitz, Yeshayahu, 1903- Ben mada' le-filosofyah. Yerushalayim : Aḳademon, 762 [2002]

SCIENCE OF LANGUAGE. See LINGUISTICS.

The science of romance.
Barber, Nigel, 1955- Amherst, N.Y. : Prometheus Books, 2002.
HQ21 .B184 2002

SCIENCE OF SCIENCE. See SCIENCE.

Science of the soul.
Edinger, Edward F. Toronto, Ont. : Inner City Books, c2002.
BF173 .E27 2002

SCIENCE - PHILOSOPHY. See also NATURALISM.
Appraising Lakatos. Dordrecht ; Boston : Kluwer Academic, c2002.
Q175 .A685 2002

Bachelard, Gaston. [Formation de l'esprit scientifique. English] The formation of the scientific mind. Manchester : Clinamen, c2002.

Bronowski, Jacob, 1908-1974. The identity of man. Amherst, N.Y. : Prometheus Books, 2002.
BD450 .B653 2002

Casti, J. L. The one true platonic heaven. Washington, D.C. : Joseph Henry Press, c2003.
Q175 .C4339 2003

Dufour, Adrian. Ciencia y logica de mundos posibles. Bern : Lang, 2001.

Dugin, Aleksandr. Evoliutsiia paradigmal'nykh osnovaniĭ nauki. Moskva : Arktogeia, 2002.
Q174.8 .D845 2002

Hawking, S. W. (Stephen W.). [Cambridge lectures] The theory of everything. Beverly Hills, CA : New Millennium Press, c2002, 1996.
QB985 .H39 2002

Laszlo, Ervin, 1932- The connectivity hypothesis. Albany : State University of New York Press, c2003.
Q175 .L2854 2003

Leibowitz, Yeshayahu, 1903- Ben mada' le-filosofyah. Yerushalayim : Aḳademon, 762 [2002]

Mires, Fernando. Crítica de la razón científica. 1a ed. Caracas : Editorial Nueva Sociedad, 2002.

Motycka, Alina. Nauka o nieświadomośc. Wrocław : Leopoldinum, 1998.

Nietzsche and the sciences. Dordrecht ; Boston : Kluwer Academic Publishers, c1999-
B3318.K7 N54 1999

Paál, Gábor. Was ist schön? Würzburg : Königshausen & Neumann, c2003.
BH39 .P33 2003

Pollack, H. N. Uncertain science-- uncertain world. Cambridge, U.K. ; New York : Cambridge University Press, 2003.
Q175 .P835 2003

Porus, V. N. Ratsional'nost', nauka, kul'tura. Moskva : Universitet Rossiĭskoĭ akademii obrazovaniia, Kafedra filosofii, 2002.
Q175.32.K45 P678 2002

Ramos, João Baptista. Quinze cartas sobre moralidade & ciência. Brasilia : Thesaurus, 2000.

Sciences et archétypes. Paris : Dervy, 2002.

Sub"ekt, poznanie, deiatel'nost'. Moskva : Kanon+, 2002.
BD166 .S84 2002

SCIENCE - PHILOSOPHY - CONGRESSES.
Collège de France. Symposium annuel. La vérité dans les sciences. Paris : Jacob, c2003.

SCIENCE - PHILOSOPHY - HISTORY - 16TH CENTURY.
Das Ende des Hermetismus. Tübingen : Mohr Siebeck, c2002.
BF1587 .E53 2002

SCIENCE, POLITICAL. See POLITICAL SCIENCE.

SCIENCE - POLITICAL ASPECTS.
Turner, Stephen P., 1951- Liberal democracy 3.0. London ; Thousand Oaks, Calif. : SAGE Publications, 2003.
JC423 .T87 2003

SCIENCE - RESEARCH. See RESEARCH.
SCIENCE RESEARCH. See RESEARCH.

Science, technology, and culture, 1700-1945
Van Wyhe, John, 1971- Phrenology and the origins of Victorian scientific naturalism. Burlington, VT : Ashgate, c2003.
BF879 .V36 2003

SCIENCES. See SCIENCE.

Sciences & archétypes.
Sciences et archétypes. Paris : Dervy, 2002.

Sciences cognitives et cerveau.
Jeannerod, Marc. La nature de l'esprit. Paris : Odile Jacob, c2002.
BF311 .J435 2002

Sciences des religions
Scheid, John. Religion et piété à Rome. [2e éd.]. Paris : Albin Michel, 2001.

Sciences (Editions Odile Jacob)
Jeannerod, Marc. La nature de l'esprit. Paris : Odile Jacob, c2002.
BF311 .J435 2002

Sciences et archétypes : fragments philosophiques pour un réenchantement du monde : hommage au professeur Gilbert Durand / sous la direction de Mohammed Taleb ; avec les contributions de Michel Cazenave ... [et al.]. Paris : Dervy, 2002. 426 p. ; 24 cm. Includes bibliographical references and indexes. ISBN 2-8445-4149-6 DDC 194
1. Science - History. 2. Archetype (Psychology) 3. Philosophy and science. 4. Science - Philosophy. 5. Myth. I. Durand, Gilbert, 1921- II. Cazenave, Michel. III. Taleb, Mohammed. IV. Title: Sciences & archétypes

The sciences in enlightened Europe / edited by William Clark, Jan Golinski, and Simon Schaffer. Chicago : University of Chicago Press, 1999. xi, 566 p. : ill. ; 24 cm. Includes bibliographical references (p. [505]-538) and index. ISBN 0-226-10939-9 (cloth : acid-free paper) ISBN 0-226-10940-2 (pbk. : acid-free paper) DDC 509.4/09033
1. Foucault, Michel - Influence. 2. Science - Europe - History - 18th century. 3. Philosophy, Medieval. I. Clark, William, 1953- II. Golinski, Jan. III. Schaffer, Simon, 1955-
Q127.E8 S356 1999

SCIENCES, LIFE. See LIFE SCIENCES.
SCIENCES, SOCIAL. See SOCIAL SCIENCES.

Sciences sociales et sociétés
Flamant, Nicolas. Une anthropologie des managers. Paris : Presses universitaires de France, c2002.
HD33 .F525 2002

Scientia nova
Lenk, Hans. Das Denken und sein Gehalt. München : Oldenbourg, 2001.
BF441 .L455 2001

Lenk, Hans. Das Denken und sein Gehalt. München : Oldenbourg, 2001.

SCIENTIFIC MANAGEMENT. See INDUSTRIAL MANAGEMENT.
SCIENTIFIC RESEARCH. See RESEARCH.

The scientific study of general intelligence : tribute to Arthur R. Jensen / edited by Helmuth Nyborg. 1st ed. Amsterdam ; Boston : Pergamon, 2003. xxvi, 642 p. : ill. ; 25 cm. Includes bibliographical references and indexes. ISBN 0-08-043793-1 (alk. paper) DDC 153.9
1. General factor (Psychology) 2. Intellect. I. Jensen, Arthur Robert. II. Nyborg, Helmuth.
BF433.G45 S35 2003

SCIENTISTS. See NATURALISTS; PARAPSYCHOLOGISTS; WOMEN SCIENTISTS.

Scienze umane (Brescia, Italy)
Terrin, Aldo N. (Aldo Natale) Mistiche dell'Occidente. 1. ed. Brescia : Morcelliana, 2001.
BP605.N48 T477 2001

Scigliano, Eric, 1953- Love, war, and circuses : the age-old relationship between elephants and humans / Eric Scigliano. Boston : Houghton Mifflin, 2002. x, 358 p. ; 22 cm. Includes bibliographical references (p. [330]-345). ISBN 0-618-01583-3 DDC 599.67
1. Elephants. 2. Human-animal relationships. I. Title.
QL737.P98 S42 2002

Scola, Angelo. Uomo-donna : il "caso serio" dell'amore / Angelo Scola. 1. ed. italiana. Genova : Marietti, c2002. 118 p. ; 21 cm. Includes bibliographical references. ISBN 88-211-6820-4 DDC 261
1. Love. 2. Man-woman relationships. I. Title.

The scope magazine / Law Development Centre. Kampala, Uganda : LDC Publishers, [2001- v. : ill. ; 30 cm. Vol. 1, no. 1 (Feb. 2001)- . Title from cover.
1. Law - Uganda - Periodicals. 2. Uganda - Periodicals. I. Law Development Centre.
K23 .C665

Scott, Christopher, 1946- Beyond death : confronting the ultimate mystery / Christopher Scott. Nevada City, CA : Blue Dolphin Pub., 2001. xix, 223 p. : ill. ; 23 cm. Includes bibliographical references (p. 214-215) and index. ISBN 1-57733-077-3 (pbk.) DDC 133.9
1. Spiritualism. I. Title.
BF1261 .S45 2001

Scott, John Beldon, 1946- Architecture for the shroud : relic and ritual in Turin / John Beldon Scott. Chicago : University of Chicago Press, c2003. xxxi, 443 p., 16 p. of plates : ill. (some col.), maps ; 31 cm. Includes bibliographical references (p. 405-428) and index. CONTENTS: Architecture and relic -- Peregrinations -- Relic and kingship -- Shroud of Chambéry: Sainte-Chapelle -- A new capital and its relic -- "Terror of architecture": Guarino Guarini and the Chapel of the Holy Shroud -- Seeing the shroud: Guarini's sacred theater -- Faith in geometry -- Imagery of devotion and dynasty -- Illusion of meaning/meaning of illusion -- Relic and monarchy

in the urban setting -- Cultic urbanism: ritual in the public theater of ostension -- Dynastic pantheon: revolution and Risorgimento -- Shroud and architecture in the Italian state -- Ritual architecture and power. ISBN 0-226-74316-0 (alk. paper) DDC 232.96/6
1. Guarini, Guarino, - 1624-1683 - Criticism and interpretation. 2. Cappella della Sindone (Duomo di Torino) 3. Church architecture - Italy - Turin. 4. Holy Shroud. 5. Reliquaries - Italy - Turin - Designs and plans. 6. Rites and ceremonies - Italy - Turin. 7. Turin (Italy) - Buildings, structures, etc. I. Title.
NA5621.T823 S36 2003

Scott, Steve, 1948- Mentored by a millionaire / Steven K. Scott. Hoboken, N.J. : J. Wiley & Sons, 2004. p. cm. Includes index. Table of contents URL: http://www.loc.gov/catdir/toc/ecip048/2003018876.html Publisher description URL: http://www.loc.gov/catdir/desc ription/wiley039/2003018876.html ISBN 0-471-46763-4 DDC 158.1
1. Success - Psychological aspects. I. Title.
BF637.S8 S388 2004

Scott, Sue.
Gender. London ; New York : Routledge, 2002.
HQ1075 .G426 2002

SCREENS (PLANTS). *See* **HEDGES.**

Scrinium (San Mauro Torinese, Italy)
(20.) Casoni, Guido, 1561-1642. Della magia d'amore. Torino : Res, 2002.
BF575.L8 C3 2002

SCRIPTS (PSYCHOLOGY). *See* **SCHEMAS (PSYCHOLOGY).**

Scritto negli astri.
Pompeo Faracovi, Ornella. Venezia : Marsilio, c1996.
BF1671 .P66 1996x

La scrittura e il debito.
Sini, Carlo, 1933- Milano : Jaca book, 2002.

Scully, Nicki, 1943- Alchemical healing : a guide to spiritual, physical, and transformational medicine / Nicki Scully. Rochester, Vt. : Bear & Co., 2003. p. cm. Includes index. ISBN 1-59143-015-1 DDC 299/.93
1. Healing - Miscellanea. 2. Spiritual healing - Miscellanea. 3. Occultism. I. Title.
BF1999 .S369 2003

SCULPTURE. *See* **MONUMENTS.**

Scuto, Giuseppe. Epistemologica : una teoria del conoscere e del significare / Giuseppe Scuto ; prefazione di Miranda Alberti Rappmannsberger. Milano : FrancoAngeli, c2002. 120 p. ; 23 cm. Includes bibliographical references (p. 115-116) and index. ISBN 88-464-3878-7 DDC 121
1. Knowledge, Theory of. I. Title.

Seachrist, Brian. The runic oracle / by Brian Seachrist. Riverview, FL : Green Warden Foundation, c1999. 36 p. ; 22 cm. Cover title. Page 36 is on p. 4 of cover. Includes bibliographical references (p. 35-36).
1. Fortune-telling by runes. I. Title.
BF1891.R85 S43 1999

The search for a holistic approach to human existence and development : proceedings of the inaugural session Emmanuel Onyechere Osigwe Anyiam-Osigwe Memorial Lecture Series, 1999 / editors, Charles Anyiam-Osigwe, Davy Ozurumba, Peace Anyiam-Fiberesima. [Nigeria?] : Osigwe Anyiam-Osigwe Foundation, [1999?] 95 p. ; 25 cm. (Onyechere Osigwe Anyiam-Osigwe memorial lecture series ; 1999) Includes bibliographical references. "Memorial lecture series on 24th Novemember, 1999 at the Nigerian Institute of International Affairs ..., Victoria Island, Lagos ..."--P. 11. CONTENTS: The Onto-theistic destiny of creation (The 'Chi' dynamic in the essential determination of the cosmos and man) / Anthony J.V. Obinna, Innocent Maduakolam Osuagwu -- People and development: Towards participatory sustainable human development / Emmanuel Olukayode Oladipo -- Topical issues on democracy and governance / S.B. Awoniyi.
1. Philosophy. 2. Humanism - 20th century. 3. Philosophy and religion. 4. Conduct of life. 5. Human beings - Spiritual aspects. 6. Ethics. I. Anyiam-Osigwe, Charles O. II. Ozurumba, Davy. III. Anyiam-Fiberesima, Peace. IV. Title: Proceedings of the inaugural session Emmanuel Onyechere Osigwe Anyiam-Osigwe Memorial Lecture Series, 1999 V. Series.
B53 .E46 1999

Searching for God in godforsaken times and places.
Locke, Hubert G. Grand Rapids, Mich. : W.B. Eerdmans Pub., c2003.
BT774 .L63 2003

Searching for peace in Central and South Asia : an overview of conflict prevention and peacebuilding activities / edited by Monique Mekenkamp, Paul van Tongeren, and Hans van de Veen. Boulder, Colo. : Lynne Rienner Publishers, 2002. xiv, 665 p. : ill., maps (some col.) ; 24 cm. "A project of European Centre for Conflict Prevention." Includes bibliographical references 9p. 629-638) and index. ISBN 1-58826-096-8 (hc : alk. paper) ISBN 1-58826-072-0 (pbk. : alk. paper) DDC 327.1/72
1. Pacific settlement of international disputes. 2. Peaceful change (International relations) 3. Confidence and security building measures (International relations) 4. Reconciliation. 5. Conflict management. 6. Asia, Central - Politics and government. 7. South Asia - Politics and government. I. Mekenkamp, Monique. II. Tongeren, Paul van. III. Veen, Hans van de.
JZ5597 .S43 2002

Sears, David O.
Oxford handbook of political psychology. Oxford ; New York : Oxford University Press, 2003.
JA74.5 .H355 2003

Seas of peace (Motion picture).
Peace and conflict resolution. Part 2 [videorecording]. Derry, N.H. : Chip Taylor Communications, 1997.

SEASONS - MYTHOLOGY.
Hardie, Titania. Titania's book of hours. London : Quadrille, 2002.

Sebrell, C. L.
Herzog, Edgar. [Psyche und Tod. English] Psyche and death. New ed. / edited and designed by C.L. Sebrell. Woodstock, Conn. : Spring Publications, c2000.

Secchi Tarugi, Luisa Rotondi, 1943-.
Il sacro nel Rinascimento. Firenze : F. Cesati, c2002.
PN49 .S337 2002

SECOND LANGUAGE ACQUISITION.
Herdina, Philip. A dynamic model of multilingualism. Clevedon, England Buffalo, N.Y. : Multilingual Matters, 2002.
P115.4 .H47 2002

Kecskés, István. Situation-bound utterances in L1 and L2. Berlin ; New York : Mouton de Gruyter, 2002.
P95.45 .K4 2002

SECOND LANGUAGE ACQUISITION - METHODOLOGY.
Toda, Takako. Second language speech perception and production. Lanham, Md. ; Oxford : University Press of America, c2003.
PL541 .T63 2003

SECOND LANGUAGE LEARNING. *See* **SECOND LANGUAGE ACQUISITION.**

Second language speech perception and production.
Toda, Takako. Lanham, Md. ; Oxford : University Press of America, c2003.
PL541 .T63 2003

SECRECY.
Petronio, Sandra Sporbert. Boundaries of privacy. Albany : State University of New York Press, c2002.
BF697.5.S427 P48 2002

SECRECY - LAW AND LEGISLATION. *See* **PRIVACY, RIGHT OF.**

The secret architecture of our nation's capital.
Ovason, David. [Secret zodiacs of Washington DC] 1st Perennial ed. New York, NY : Perennial, 2002.

A secret history of consciousness.
Lachman, Gary, 1955- Great Barrington, MA : Lindisfarne Books, 2003.
BF311 .L19 2003

The secret life of dreams.
Gibson, Clare K., 1964- San Diego, Calif. : Thunder Bay Press, 2004.
BF1091 .G49 2004

The secret middle ages.
Jones, Malcolm, 1953- Stroud : Sutton, 2002.

The secret science of numerology.
Lawrence, Shirley Blackwell. Franklin Lakes, NJ : New Page Books, c2001.
BF1623.P9 L38 2001

The secret scroll.
Sinclair, Andrew, 1935- Edinburgh : Birlinn, 2002.

SECRET SOCIETIES. *See also* **MYSTERIES, RELIGIOUS.**
Hall, Manly Palmer, 1901- The secret teachings of all ages. Reader's ed. New York : Jeremy P. Tarcher/Putnam, 2003.
BF1411 .H3 2003

The secret teachings of all ages.
Hall, Manly Palmer, 1901- Reader's ed. New York : Jeremy P. Tarcher/Putnam, 2003.
BF1411 .H3 2003

Secretos de un malogrado proceso de paz.
Valencia, León. Adiós a la política, bienvenido la guerra. [Bogotá, Colombia?] : Intermedio, c2002.

Secrets & mysteries.
Linn, Denise. Carlsbad, Calif. : Hay House, c2002.
HQ1206 .L513 2002

Secrets & mysteries of the world.
Browne, Sylvia. Carlsbad, Calif. : Hay House, c2005.
BF1411 .B78 2005

Secrets and mysteries.
Linn, Denise. Secrets & mysteries. Carlsbad, Calif. : Hay House, c2002.
HQ1206 .L513 2002

Secrets and mysteries of the world.
Browne, Sylvia. Secrets & mysteries of the world. Carlsbad, Calif. : Hay House, c2005.
BF1411 .B78 2005

Secrets of a dream catcher.
Chaplin, Nikki. Hallandale Beach, Fla. : Aglob Pub., 2003.
BF637.S4 C492 2003

Secrets of a medium.
Dreller, Larry. Boston, MA : Weiser Books, 2003.
BF1031 .D69 2003

Secrets of a psychic counselor.
Hite, Sheilaa, 1958- Needham, Mass. : Moment Point Press ; [Oakland, Calif.] : Distributed to the trade by Words Distributing Co., c2003.
BF1045.R43 H58 2003

Secrets of comfort and joy.
Walters, J. Donald. [Nevada City, CA] : Crystal Clarity, 2000.
BF575.H27 W362 2000

Secrets of friendship.
Walters, J. Donald. Nevada City, CA : Crystal Clarity Publishers, c2001.
BF575.F66 WW355 2001

Secrets of power conversation.
Bjornson, Lawrence E. [S.l.] : L.E. Bjornson, c2002.
BF637.C45 B575 2002

The secrets of self-esteem.
Cleghorn, Patricia. London : Vega, c2002.
BF697.5.S46 C55 2002

Secrets of the Amazon shamans.
Langevin, Michael Peter, 1952- Franklin Lakes, NJ : New Page Books, c2003.
BF1622.S63 L36 2003

Secrets of the ancient world.
Little, Lora. Virginia Beach, Va. : A.R.E. Press, c2003.
BF1045.A74 L58 2003

Secrets of the psychics.
Polidoro, Massimo. Amherst, N.Y. : Prometheus Books, c2003.
BF1031 .P75155 2003

Secrets of the soul.
Zaretsky, Eli. 1st ed. New York : A.A. Knopf, 2004.
BF173 .Z37 2004

The secrets of the vaulted sky.
Berlinski, David, 1942- 1st U.S. ed. Orlando, Fla. : Harcourt, c2003.
BF1674 .B47 2003

Secrets of the young & successful.
Kushell, Jennifer. New York : Simon & Schuster, c2003.
BF637.S8 K875 2003

Secrets of the young and successful.
Kushell, Jennifer. Secrets of the young & successful. New York : Simon & Schuster, c2003.
BF637.S8 K875 2003

The secrets of your handwriting.
Gullan-Whur, Margaret. [New ed.]. London : Thorsons, 1998.
BF891 .G846 1998

The secrets of your rising sign.
Lamb, William, 1944 Apr. 22- Gloucester, MA : Fair Winds Press, 2004.
BF1717 .L36 2004

Secrets you keep from yourself.
Neuharth, Dan. 1st U.S. ed. New York : St. Martins Press, 2004.
BF637.S37 N48 2004

SECTS. *See also* **CHRISTIAN SECTS; CULTS.**
Cuevas Sosa, Andrés Alejandro, 1939- How do

religious figures induce the establishment of sects? 2nd ed. Leicestershire : Upfront Pub., 2002.
BF1272 .C84 2002

Galovic, Jelena. Los grupos místico-espirituales de la actualidad. México : Plaza y Valdés, 2002.
BL625 .G346 2002

Hunt, Stephen, 1954- Alternative religions. Aldershot, Hampshire, England ; Burlington, VT : Ashgate, c2003.
BP603 .H87 2003

New religious movements. London ; New York : Routledge in association with the Institute of Oriental Philosophy European Centre, 1999.
BL80.2 .N397 1999

Pinto Cañon, Ramiro. Grupos gnósticos. Madrid : Entinema, 2002.

Saliba, John A. Understanding new religious movements. 2nd ed. Walnut Creek, CA ; Oxford : Altamira Press, c2003.
BP603 .S25 2003

SECTS, CHRISTIAN. See **CHRISTIAN SECTS.**

SECTS - FICTION.
Kava, Alex. The soul catcher. Waterville, Me. : Thorndike Press, 2003, 2002.
PS3561.A8682 S6 2003

SECTS - HISTORY.
Religion et exclusion, XIIe-XVIIIe siècle. Religion et exclusion, douzième-dix-huitième siècle. Aix-en-Provence : Publications de l'Université de Provence, 2001.
BL238 .R448 2001

SECTS - RUSSIA (FEDERATION).
Balagushkin, E. G. (Evgeniĭ Gennadʹevich) Netraditsionnye religii v sovremennoĭ Rossii. Moskva : Rossiĭskai͡a akademii͡a nauk, Institut filosofii, 1999-2002.
BL980.R8 B35 1999

Novye religioznye ob"edineniia Rossii destruktivnogo i okkul'tnogo kharaktera. Izd. 3-e, dop. Belgorod : Missionerskiĭ otdel Moskovskogo Patriarkhata Russkoĭ Pravoslavnoĭ TSerkvi, 2002.
BF1434.R8 N67 2002

Secular steeples.
Ostwalt, Conrad Eugene, 1959- Harrisburg, PA : Trinity Press International, c2003.
BL65.C8 O88 2003

SECULARISM.
Ostwalt, Conrad Eugene, 1959- Secular steeples. Harrisburg, PA : Trinity Press International, c2003.
BL65.C8 O88 2003

Secunda, Al. The 15-second principle : short, simple steps to achieving long-term goals / by Al Secunda. Franklin Lakes, NJ : Career Press, 2004. p. cm. Includes index. ISBN 1-56414-738-X DDC 158.1
1. Self-actualization (Psychology) 2. Success - Psychological aspects. 3. Goal (Psychology) I. Title. II. Title: Fifteen-second principle
BF637.S4 S43 2004

SECURITIES. See **STOCKS.**

SECURITIES EXCHANGES. See **STOCK EXCHANGES.**

Security and privacy in user modeling.
Schreck, Jorg. Dordrecht ; Boston ; London : Kluwer Academic Publishers, c2003.
QA76.9.A25 S353 2003

SECURITY, INTERNATIONAL. See also **PEACE.**
Christoff, Joseph A. Issues in implementing international peace operations [electronic resource]. [Washington, D.C.] : U.S. General Accounting Office, [2002]

Gelpi, Christopher, 1966- The power of legitimacy. Princeton, N.J. : Princeton University Press, c2003.
JZ5595.5 .G45 2003

Global security concerns [electronic resource]. Maxwell Air Force Base, Ala. : Air University Press, [1996]

Globalization and armed conflict. Lanham, Md. : Rowman & Littlefield, c2003.
JZ5538 .G58 2003

Howard, Michael, 1922 Nov. 29- The invention of peace and the reinvention of war. Rev. and extended ed. London : Profile, 2002, c2001.

Order and justice in international relations. Oxford ; New York : Oxford University Press, 2003.

JZ1308 .O73 2003

Panorama estratégico, 2001-2002. [Madrid] : Ministerio de Defensa, 2002.

Regional conflict management. Lanham, Md. : Rowman & Littlefield, c2003.
JZ5330 .R437 2003

Zeitgeschichtliche Hintergründe aktueller Konflikte V. Zürich : Forschungsstelle für Sicherheitspolitik und Konfliktanalyse, Eidgenössische Technische Hochschule, 1995.
JX1952 .Z45 1995

SECURITY (PSYCHOLOGY).
Boughton, Harold "Bud" The missing piece. [Lancaster, Ohio] : Lucky Press, c2003.
BF575.S35 B68 2003

Security sector reform.
Chanaa, Jane. Oxford ; New York : Oxford University Press for the International Institute for Strategic Studies, 2002.
HV6419 .C52 2002

Sedición en la pasarela.
Caballero, Rufo, 1966- La Habana, Cuba : Editorial Arte y Literatura, c2001.

SEDLAR, JERI.
Vint/age 2001 conference : [videorecording]. New York, c2001.

Sedlar, Jeri, panelist.
Vint/age 2001 conference : [videorecording]. New York, c2001.

Sedley, D. N.
The Cambridge companion to Greek and Roman philosophy. Cambridge, U.K. ; New York : Cambridge University Press, 2003.
B111 .C36 2003

Sedlmeier, Peter.
Etc. frequency processing and cognition. Oxford ; New York : Oxford University Press, c2002.
BF448 .E83 2002

SEDUCTION - PSYCHOLOGICAL ASPECTS - HISTORY.
Masson, J. Moussaieff (Jeffrey Moussaieff), 1941- The assault on truth. 1st Ballantine Books ed. New York : Ballantine Books, 2003.
BF109.F74 M38 2003

Seeber, Ronald Leroy.
Lipsky, David B., 1939- Emerging systems for managing workplace conflict. 1st ed. San Francisco : Jossey-Bass, c2003.
HD42 .L564 2003

Seeds of luck.
Nwokogba, Isaac E. Cranston, R.I. : Writers' Collective, 2003.
BF1778 .N96 2003

Seeing and visualizing.
Pylyshyn, Zenon W., 1937- Cambridge, Mass. : MIT Press, 2003.
BF241 .P95 2003

Seeing nature through gender / edited by Virginia J. Scharff. Lawrence : University Press of Kansas, c2003. xxii, 345 p. : ill. : 24 cm. (Development of western resources) Includes bibliographical references and indexes. ISBN 0-7006-1284-X (cloth : alk. paper) ISBN 0-7006-1285-8 (pbk. : alk. paper) DDC 304.2
1. Human ecology - Philosophy. 2. Philosophy of nature. 3. Sex role - History. 4. Sex role - Environmental aspects. 5. Body, Human - Social aspects. I. Scharff, Virginia. II. Series.
GF21 .S44 2003

Seeing reason.
Stenning, Keith. Oxford ; New York : Oxford University Press, 2002.
BF441 .S775 2002

Seeking ghosts in the Warwick Valley.
Reis, Donna. Atglen, PA : Schiffer Pub., c2002.
BF1472.U6 R45 2002

Seel, Gerhard, 1940-.
Interpretation und Argument. Würzburg : Königshausen & Neumann, c2002.

Die Seele.
Hinterhuber, H. (Hartmann) Wien ; New York : Springer, c2001.

Seele im Lichtzwang, im Lichtzwang der Seele.
Bottenberg, Ernst Heinrich. 1. Aufl. Sankt Augustin : Academia, 1994.
BF38 .B625 1994

Seelenführer durch den verborgenen Raum.
Schweizer, Andreas, 1946- München : Kösel, 1994.

Seelenmaschinen : Gattungstraditionen, Funktionen, und Leistungsgrenzen der Mnemotechniken vom späten Mittelalter bis zum Beginn der Moderne / herausgegeben von Jörg Jochen Berns und Wolfgang Neuber. Wien : Böhlau Verlag, c2000. 800 p. : ill. ; 25 cm. (Frühneuzeit-Studien ; n.F. 2) Based on a colloquium held Nov. 29-Dec. 2, 1995 in Vienna, Austria. Includes bibliographical references and indexes. ISBN 3-205-99148-6
1. Mnemonics - History - to 1500 - Congresses. I. Berns, Jörg Jochen. II. Neuber, Wolfgang. III. Series.
BF381 .S44 2000

SEERS. See **PROPHETS.**

Śefat emet likutim.
Alter, Judah Aryeh Leib, 1847-1905. [Śefat emet (Torah). Selections] Sefer Śefat emet. Yerushalayim : Mir, 762 [2001 or 2002]

Sefer Aḥat sha'alti.
Karelits, Ḥayim Sha'ul ben Me'ir. Bene Beraḳ : Mish. Karelits, 762 [2002]

Sefer Ahavat 'olam.
Algazi, Solomon ben Abraham, 1610?-ca. 1683. Bruḳlin : Sifre Algazi, 760 [2000]

Sefer Ahavat shalom.
Hilel, Ya'aḳov Mosheh. [Hotsa'ah 2], 'im hosafot rabot. Yerushala[y]im : ha-Makhon le-hotsa'at sefarim ye-khitve yad "Ahavat Shalom", 762 [2002]

Sefer Ahavat Yiśra'el.
Mosheh ben Ḥayim, Koznitser, d. 1874. Yotse le-or me-ḥadash. Yerushalayim : Mekhon Sod yesharim, 760 [2000]

Sefer 'Ahavat Yiśra'el.
Mosheh ben Ḥayim, Koznitser, d. 1874. Bruḳlin : [Yehoshu'a Pinḥas Bukhinger], 762 [2001]

Sefer 'Amude ha-Ḳabalah : kinus shel ḥiburim ḳadmonim ... Yerushalayim : Nezer Sheraga, 761 [2001] 12, 60, 80, 154, 225, 75 p. ; 25 cm. Includes bibliographical references. CONTENTS: Sefer Keter Shem ṭov / le-rabi Avraham ben Aleksander mi-Kolonya -- Sefer Sheḳel ha-ḳodesh / le-rabi Mosheh ben Shem Ṭov mi-Le'on -- Sefer Keter Shem ṭov / le-rabi Shem Ṭov ben Avraham Ga'on -- Sefer Bade ha-aron, ye-niḳra gam Migdal Ḥanan'el / le-rabi Shem Ṭov ben Avraham Ga'on -- Sefer ha-Emunot / ... Shem Ṭov ben rabi Shem Ṭov -- Sefer Torat ha-sefirot / ... Shem Ṭov ben rabi Shem Ṭov.
1. Cabala. 2. God (Judaism) - Name - Early works to 1800. 3. Sefirot (Cabala) I. Abraham ben Alexander, of Cologne, 13th cent. Keter Shem Tov. II. Moses ben Shem Tov, de Leon, d. 1305. Shekel ha-kodesh. III. Ibn Gaon, Shem Tov ben Abraham, 13th/14th cent. Keter Shem Tov. IV. Ibn Gaon, Shem Tov ben Abraham, 13th/14th cent. Bade ha-aron. V. Ibn Shem Tov, Shem Tov ben Joseph ben Shem Tov, 15th cent. Emunot. VI. Ibn Shem Tov, Shem Tov ben Joseph ben Shem Tov, 15th cent. Torat ha-sefirot. VII. Title: Migdal Ḥanan'el. VIII. Title: 'Amude ha-ḳabalah

Sefer 'Aśarah nisyonot.
Pinter, Leib. Brooklyn, N.Y. : E.Y.L. Pinter, c[2002?]

Sefer Asefat divre ḥakhamim.
Ḥayim Yeroḥam ben Shimshon Meshulam Feybish, mi-Snatin. Yerushalayim : Mekhon Sod yesharim, 761 [2001]

Sefer 'Avodat 'avodah.
Admur ha-Ḳ. ha-Ḳ., Shelita. ['Avodat 'avodah (Torah)] Ḳiryat Ṭohsh, Ḳanada : N. M. Hershḳoyiṭsh, 763 [2002 or 2003]

Sefer Bet ginze.
[Mishnah. Avot. 2001.] Yerushalayim : R. M. Lurya, 762 [2001 or 2002]

Sefer Bet Raḥel.
Naphtali ben Isaac, ha-Kohen, 1649-1719. Yerushalayim : Ahavat Shalom, 761 [2001]
BM665 .N257 2001

Sefer Birkat Me'ir.
Medan, Barukh. Netivot : Barukh Medan, 763 [2002 or 2003]

Sefer Darkhe tsedeḳ.
Gantsersḳi, Betsal'el Shelomoh, ha-Levi. Tifraḥ : Mishp. Gantsersḳi, 762 [2001 or 2002]

Sefer Dibrot Tsevi.
Vaisfish, Tsevi ben Shemu'el A. L. Yerushalayim : Makhon le-hotsa'at sefarim 'a. sh. Rabi Naḥum mi-Shadiḳ, 762- [2002-

Sefer Doreshe Tsevi.
Segal, Yehudah Zeraḥyah, ha-Levi. Tel-Aviv : Talmiday ye-shmom'e liḳho, 763 [2003]

Sefer Dover mesharim.
BJ1287.S43 D66 2003

Sefer Dover mesharim.
Mermelshtain, Avraham Yitshak David. Kuntres Dover mesharim. Hotsa'ah 2. [Brooklyn] : A.Y.D. Mermelshtain, 762 [2001]

Sefer 'Ets ha-da'at tov.
Vital, Hayyim ben Joseph, 1542 or 3-1620. 'Ets ha-da'at tov. Yerushalayim : Hotsa'at Ahavat shalom, 761 [2000 or 2001]

Sefer Even shetiyah.
Milshtein, Mosheh. Bruklin : [Lee Printing corp.], 758- [1998-

Sefer Ginze Armoni.
Armoni, Mosheh Hayim. Yerushalayim : 'Amutat "Nahalat-Rahel", 762 [2002]
BM670.S5 A756 2002

Sefer ha-Hayim.
Mosheh ben Hayim, Koznitser, d. 1874. Sefer 'Ahavat Yiśra'el. Bruklin : [Yehoshu'a Pinhas Bukhinger], 762 [2001]

Sefer ha-hinukh.
Globerman, Daniyel Aharon. Yalkut Sefer ha-Hinukh. Modi'in 'Ilit : D. A. Globerman, Kolel "Libo hafets", 761 [2000 or 2001]
BM520.8.A32 G4 2001

Sefer ha-kadosh Zohar hadash 'im perush Matok mo-devash.
[Zohar hadash.] Sefer Zohar hadash. Yerushalayim : Mekhon Da'at Yosef ; Brooklyn, N.Y. (225 Division Ave., Brooklyn 11211) : Le-haśig, B. Daskal, 760- [1999 or 2000-
BM525.A6 Z6+

Sefer ha-Neshamah ba-guf.
Golan, Mor Yosef. Itamar : M.Y. Golan, 762 [2001 or 2002]

Sefer ha-Nistarot yeha-niglot.
Ben Ratson-Lahat, Tsiyon. [Israel? : h. mo. l.], 761 i.e. 2001?]

Sefer Hesed ye-rahamim.
Pinhasi, Rahamim. Yerushalayim : R. Pinhasi, 762 [2001 or 2002]

Sefer Ka-sheleg yalbinu.
Va'eknin, Yosef ben Avraham. Yerushalayim : Y. Va'eknin, 763 [2002 or 2003]

Sefer Kedushat ha-dibur / nilkat 'a. y. Yehudah Yosef ha-Levi Gruber (Hefer) Bene Berak : Yehudah Yosef Ha-levi Gruber, 761- [2001-] v. (321-632 p.) ; 25 cm. Running title: Kedushat ha-dibur. PARTIAL CONTENTS: helek 2. bc-Ma'alat ha-shetikah, nekiyut ha-dibur, kitsur be-dibur ye-himan'ut mi-diburim asurim.
1. Silence - Religious aspects - Judaism. 2. Oral communication - Religious aspects - Judaism. 3. Ethics, Jewish. I. Gruber, Yehudah Yosef, ha-Levi. II. Title: Kedushat ha-dibur

Sefer Kerem Shelomoh.
Eliyahu, Saliman. Yerushala[y]im : Hevrat Ahavat shalom, 762 [2001 or 2002]

Sefer Kibud ye-hidur.
Adler, Yitshak Eliyahu, ha-Kohen. Ofakim : Y.E. ha-Kohen Adler, 754 [1994]

Sefer Kitve paz.
Goldberg, Avraham Yehoshu'a, 1856-1921. Yerushalayim : ha-Mishpahah, 763, c2003.

Sefer Lev Avigdor.
Miller, Avigdor. [Lev Avigdor] Bruklin, N.Y. : S. Miller, 762, c2002.
BM538.P4 .M45 2001

Sefer Likute u-ferushe niglot Leshem shevo ye-ahlamah.
Shelomoh ben Hayim Haikel. Kiryat Sefer : Mosheh Vais, 762 [2002]
BM525 .H4332 2002

Sefer Ma'aśeh uman.
Mark, Shelomoh Zalman ben Nehemyah. Yerushalayim : Nahalat kolel "Bet ulpana de-rabenu Yohanan, 763 [2002 or 2003]

Sefer Madregat ha-adam.
Hurwitz, Joseph, d. 1919. Hotsa'ah hadashah mefo'eret menukedet u-metukenet. Yerushalayim : Yeshivat Ner Shemu'el, 762 [2002]

Sefer Masekhet ha-hayim.
Hayun, Yehudah ben Mordekhai. Masekhet ha-hayim. Bene Berak : Y. Hayun, 762 [2001 or 2002]

Sefer Mesilot teshuvah.
Cordovero, Moses ben Jacob, 1522-1570. Bene Berak : Da'at kedoshim, 762 [2002]

BM645.R45 C67 2002

Sefer Mi-torato de-rabi El'azar.
Shakh, El'azar Menahem Man. [Bene Berak] : le-haśig mishpahat Kohen, [763 i.e. 2003]

Sefer Mishnat avot.
Vaserman, Asher ben Avraham Betsal'el. Bene Berak : A. Vaserman, 760- [2000-

Sefer Musarim ye-de'ot leha-Rambam.
Maimonides, Moses, 1135-1204. [Selections] Bene Berak : [h. mo. l], 761 [2000 or 2001]

Sefer Netivot Yitshak.
Levin, Yitshak, 1938- [Bene Berak] : Y. Levin, [2000-

Sefer No'am ha-musar.
Vakhtfoigel, Nathan. Laikyud : [h. mo. l.], 762 [2001 or 2002]
BJ1285 .V35 2001

Sefer 'Olamot shel tohar.
Sofer, Mikha'el Uri. Mahad. 2. Bene Berak : M.U. Sofer, 761 [2000 or 2001]
BM726 .S633 2000

Sefer Or ha-da'at.
Vainshtok, Bentsiyon Mosheh Ya'ir ben Mordekhai David. Yerushalayim : ha-Makhon le-hotsa'at sifre ha-g. R. M.Y. Vainshtok, 762 [2001 or 2002]

Sefer 'Orot ha-Alshekh.
Alshekh, Moses, 16th cent. [Torat Mosheh. Selections] Yerushalayim : [h. mo. l.], 763 [2002 or 2003]

Sefer Otsrot av.
Bardah, Asher. [Bene Berak?] : A. Bardah, 762- [2001 or 2002-
BS1225.54 .B37 2001

Sefer Otsrot ha-musar.
Tsuri'el, Mosheh Yehi'el. Otsrot ha-musar. Yerushalayim : Yerid ha-sefarim, 763, 2002.

Sefer Penine Avir Ya'akov.
Abi-Hasira, Jacob ben Masoud, 1808-1880. [Abir Ya'akov. Selections. 2002] Yerushalayim : Hotsa'at ha-Makhon le-hotsa'at sefarim she-'a. y. Yeshivat Ner Yitshak : Mekhon Avraham : Shim'on Abihatsira, 763 [2002]
BS1485.X33 A25 2002

Sefer Ra'yonot u-mesarim.
Koll, Shmuel, 1938- Yerushalayim : S. Kol, 761- [2001-

Sefer Śefat emet.
Alter, Judah Aryeh Leib, 1847-1905. [Śefat emet (Torah). Selections] Yerushalayim : Mir, 762 [2001 or 2002]

Sefer Śefat emet Tikune ha-Zohar.
Alter, Judah Aryeh Leib, 1847-1905. [Śefat emet (Torah). Selections] Sefer Śefat emet. Yerushalayim : Mir, 762 [2001 or 2002]

Sefer Sene bo'er ba-esh.
Shtern, Shemu'el Eli'ezer. Bene Berak : Mekhon "Mayim hayim", 762 [2002]

Sefer Sha'agat Aryeh : kolel divre rabotenu ha-kedoshim ba-Talmud uva-midrashim 'al keruv levavot le-haye Torah ye-kiyum ha-mitsyot ye-'al devarim ha-'omdim 'al ha-perek bi-tekufatenu ... / ne'erakh 'a. y. talmide hakhamim shelita le-keruv ge'ulat Yiśra'el. Yerushalayim : Yerid ha-sefarim, 761 [2000 or 2001] 158 p. : ill. ; 18 cm.
1. Dery, Arie, - 1959- 2. Shas (Political party : Israel) 3. Ethics, Jewish. 4. Repentance - Judaism. I. Title: Sha'agat ariyeh

Sefer Shi'ure da'at.
Blokh, Avraham Yitshak ben Y. L. (Avraham Yitshak ben Yosef Leyb), d. 1941. Yerushalayim : Feldhaim ; Wickliffe, Ohio : Peninei Daas Publications, 761 [2001]

Sefer Shorshe ha-Yam.
Hilel, Ya'akov Mosheh. Yerushalayim : ha-Makhon le-hotsa'at sefarim "Ahavat shalom", 759- [1999-
BM525.V532 H5 1999

Sefer Śifte hayim.
Fridlander, Hayim ben Mosheh. Bene-Berak : ha-Rabanit Fridlander, 763- [2002 or 2003-

Sefer Śifte tsedek.
Eliyahu, Mordekhai. Rekhasim : M. Eliyahu, 762 [2002]

Sefer Śihot musar.
Shemu'elevits, Hayim, 1901-1979. Mahad. hadashah u-metukenet. Yerushalayim : Bene va-hatane ha-mehaber, 762, c2002.

BJ1287.S56 S5 2002

Sefer Sode razaya ...
Eleazar ben Judah, of Worms, 1176 (ca.)-1238. Bene-Berak : Korah, 759 [1998 or 1999]
BM525 .E432 1999

Sefer Torat Avigdor.
Miler, Avigdor Hakohen. Bene Brak : [h. mo. l], 762- [2001 or 2002-

Sefer Torat rabi Yiśra'el mi-Salant.
Salanter, Israel, 1810-1883. Yerushalayim : [h. mo. l], 763 [2003]

Sefer Yalkut Yosef.
Yosef, Yitshak. [Yalkut Yosef (Kibud av va-em)] Yerushalayim : Mekhon "Hazon 'Ovadyah", 761 [2001]
BM523.5.R4 Y72 2001

Sefer Yede Mosheh ye-Torah or.
Mosheh ben Shelomoh El'azar. Bene Berak : Sifre Or ha-hayim, [760 i.e. 2000]

Sefer Zohar hadash.
[Zohar hadash.] Yerushalayim : Mekhon Da'at Yosef ; Brooklyn, N.Y. (225 Division Ave., Brooklyn 11211) : Le-haśig, B. Daskal, 760- [1999 or 2000-
BM525.A6 Z6+

SEFIRA (CABALA). *See* **SEFIROT (CABALA).**

SEFIRAH (CABALA). *See* **SEFIROT (CABALA).**

SEFIROT (CABALA).
Mantovani, Massimo. Meditazioni sull'albero della cabala. Milano : Xenia, 2002.

Sefer 'Amude ha-Kabalah. Yerushalayim : Nezer Sheraga, 761 [2001]

SEG.
Sexualities, evolution & gender. Sheffield, England : BrunnerRoutledge, 2003-
BF309 .P78

Segal, Julius, 1924-.
Kagan, Jerome. Kagan & Segal's psychology. 9th ed. Belmont, CA : Thomson/Wadsworth, c2004.
BF121 .K22 2004

Segal, Yehudah Zerahyah, ha-Levi. Sefer Doreshe H. : sheloshah sefarim ... / me-otsrotav umi-peri ruho shel Yehudah Zerahyah Segal. Ne'erakh ye-yotse la-or 'a[l] ye[de] talmiday ye-shom'e likho. Tel-Aviv : Talmiday ye-shmom'e likho, 763 [2003] 242 p. ; 25 cm. Added title page title: Derekh la-'aliyah. Added title page title: Bi-shevile ha-'avodah. Added title page title: Doreshe H. Each pt. has sep. t.p.
1. Jewish way of life. 2. Ethics, Jewish. 3. Hasidism. I. Title. II. Title: Kuntres ha-Derekh la-'aliyah : tsiyune derekh ba-'avodat D. : kovets śihot ya-hagigim .... III. Title: Kuntres Bi-shevile ha-'avodah. IV. Title: Derekh la-'aliyah V. Title: Bi-shevile ha-'avodah VI. Title: Doreshe H. VII. Title: Doreshe Ha-shem
BJ1287.S43 D66 2003

Segall, Seth Robert.
Encountering Buddhism. Albany : State University of New York Press, 2003.
BQ4570.P755 E62 2003

Segalove, Ilene, 1950- Snap out of it : 101 ways to get out of your rut and into your groove / Ilene Segalove. Boston, MA : Conari Press, 2004. p. cm. Includes index. Table of contents URL: http://www.loc.gov/catdir/toc/ecip046/2003015357.html CONTENTS: Twist and shout -- All ears -- The eyes have it -- Heartfelt gestures -- Daily grind -- Make your mark -- Jump on your bed. ISBN 1-59003-061-3 (alk. paper) DDC 158.1
1. Self-actualization (Psychology) 2. Self-actualization (Psychology) - Problems, exercises, etc. I. Title.
BF637.S4 S438 2004

SEGREGATION. *See* **APARTHEID; MINORITIES.**

Segrest, Mab, 1949- Born to belonging : writings on spirit and justice / Mab Segrest. New Brunswick, NJ : Rutgers University Press, c2002. xii, 263 p. ; 24 cm. Includes bibliographical references and index. ISBN 0-8135-3100-4 (alk. paper) ISBN 0-8135-3101-2 (pbk. : alk. paper) DDC 305.48/9664
1. Segrest, Mab, - 1949- - Travel. 2. Lesbian activists - Travel. 3. Capitalism. 4. Heterosexism. 5. Racism. I. Title.
HQ75.25 .S44 2002

SEGREST, MAB, 1949- - TRAVEL.
Segrest, Mab, 1949- Born to belonging. New Brunswick, NJ : Rutgers University Press, c2002.
HQ75.25 .S44 2002

Segulot.
Tsuri'el, Mosheh Yehi'el. Otsrot ha-musar. Yerushalayim : Yerid ha-sefarim, 763, 2002.

Segundas no Memorial
(6) Peixoto, Nelson Brissac. Nelson Brissac, Antonio Augusto Arantes. [São Paulo, SP : Fundação Memorial da América Latina, 1997]

Die Sehnsucht nach Tausendundeiner Nacht.
Scholz, Piotr O. Stuttgart : Thorbecke, c2002.

Seidl, Horst, 1938-.
Erkennen und Leben. Hildesheim [Germany] ; New York : Olms, 2002.
BD435 .E75 2002

Seidman, Richard. The oracle of Kabbalah : mystical teachings of the Hebrew letters / Richard Seidman. 1st ed. New York : St. Martin's Press, 2001. xviii, 190 p. : 18 cm. + 1 box of tarot cards. Accompanied by one box of tarot cards. Includes bibliographical references (p. 178-189). ISBN 0-312-24173-9 DDC 135/.47
1. Hebrew language - Alphabet - Religious aspects - Judaism. 2. Cabala. 3. Spiritual life - Judaism. 4. Tarot. I. Title.
PJ4589 .S42 2001

Seifert, Colleen M.
Cognitive modeling. Cambridge, Mass. : MIT Press, c2002.
BF311 .C55175 2002

Seigfried, Charlene Haddock, 1943-.
Addams, Jane, 1860-1935. The long road of woman's memory. Urbana : University of Illinois Press, 2002.
HQ1206 .A25 2002

Seine letzten Aufnahmen.
Hann, Georg. Georg Hann [sound recording]. [Germany] : Preiser Records, p2001.

Seiter, John S.
Perspectives on persuasion, social influence, and compliance gaining. Boston, MA : Allyn and Bacon, 2003.
BF637.P4 P415 2003

Sęk, Helena.
Psychologia w obliczu zachodzących przemian społeczno-kulturowych. Warszawa : Instytut Psychologii PAN, 2002.
BF20 .P79 2002

SEKHET (EGYPTIAN DEITY). See **SEKHMET (EGYPTIAN DEITY).**

SEKHMET (EGYPTIAN DEITY).
Constantine, Storm. Bast and Sekhmet. London : R. Hale, c1999.

Sekrety prirody
Turovich, V. (Vasiliĭ) 1000 primet pogody. Perm' : Izd-vo "Poligrafist", 1997.
BF1777 .T87 1997

Sela, Shlomo. Abraham Ibn Ezra and the rise of medieval Hebrew science / by Shlomo Sela. Leiden ; Boston, MA : Brill, 2003. ix, 422 p. ; 25 cm. (Brill's series in Jewish studies ; v. 32) Includes bibliographical references (p. [387]-402) and index. ISBN 90-04-12973-1 DDC 181/.06
1. Ibn Ezra, Abraham ben Meir, - 1092-1167 - Contributions in science. 2. Ptolemy, - 2nd cent. 3. Judaism and science - History. 4. Jewish astrology. I. Title. II. Series.
BM538.S3 S45 2003

Selbstkritik der Moderne.
Bruyn, Gerd de. Fisch und Frosch, oder, Die Selbstkritik der Moderne. Gütersloh ; Berlin : Bertelsmann Fachzeitschriften ; Basel ; Boston ; Berlin : Birkhäuser, c2001.

Selbstliebe.
Hoffmann, Monika, 1972- Paderborn : Schöningh, c2002.
BF575.S37 H66 2002

Selected papers of J. Robert Schrieffer.
Schrieffer, J. R. (John Robert), 1931- [Papers. Selections] River Edge, NJ : World Scientific, c2002.
QC21.3 .S37 2002

Selected philosophical themes.
Gellner, Ernest. [Essays. Selections] Ernest Gellner. London ; New York : Routledge, 2003.
B1626.G441 G76 2003

SELECTIVITY (PSYCHOLOGY).
Heijden, A. H. C. van der. Attention in vision. 1st ed. New York : Psychology Press, 2003.
BF241 .H42 2003

SELENOLOGY. See **MOON.**

SELF. See also **BODY, HUMAN; CONSCIOUSNESS; EGO (PSYCHOLOGY); IDENTITY (PSYCHOLOGY); MIND AND BODY; PERSONALITY; THOUGHT AND THINKING; WILL.**
Bertelsen, Preben. Free will, consciousness, and the self. New York : Berghahn Books, 2003.

BF621 .B47 2003
Cottle, Thomas J. Beyond self-esteem. New York : P. Lang, c2003.
BF697 .C675 2003

Dreaming and the self. Albany : State University of New York Press, c2003.
BF1091 .D735 2003

Eberlein, Undine. Einzigartigkeit. Frankfurt ; New York : Campus, c2000.
BF697 .E463 2000

Hochschild, Arlie Russell, 1940- The commercialization of intimate life. Berkeley : University of California Press, 2003.
HM1106 .H63 2003

Humphrey, Nicholas. The mind made flesh. Oxford ; New York : Oxford University Press, 2002.
BF701 .H86 2002

Humphrey, Nicholas. The mind made flesh. Oxford ; New York : Oxford University Press, 2002.

International advances in self research. Greenwich, CT : Information Age Pub., 2003.
BF697 .I675 2003

Leary, Mark R. The curse of the self. New York : Oxford University Press, 2004.
BF697 .L33 2004

Models of the self. Thorverton, UK : Imprint Academic, c1999.
BF697 .M568 1999

Napier, A. David. The age of immunology. Chicago : University of Chicago Press, 2003.
GN345 .N36 2003

Zlatanović, Ljubiša, 1958- Jung, jastvo i individuacija. 1. izd. Niš : Studenski informativno-izdavački centar Niš, 2001.
BF109.J8 Z53 2001

SELF-ACCEPTANCE.
Walker, Jamie. 101 ways black women can learn to love themselves. Washington, D.C. : J.D. Publishing, c2002.
1. Black author.

SELF-ACCEPTANCE - RELIGIOUS ASPECTS - CHRISTIANITY.
Hoffmann, Monika, 1972- Selbstliebe. Paderborn : Schöningh, c2002.
BF575.S37 H66 2002

Manning, Brennan. A glimpse of Jesus. 1st ed. [San Francisco] : HarperSanFrancisco, c2003.
BV4647.S43 M36 2003

Self actualization.
Edward, J. J. [S.l. : s.n., 1998?] (Islamabad : Shahkar Publications)
BF637.S4 E39 1998

SELF-ACTUALIZATION.
Walker, Jamie. 101 ways black women can learn to love themselves. Washington, D.C. : J.D. Publishing, c2002.
1. Black author.

SELF-ACTUALIZATION - JUVENILE LITERATURE.
Mawi Asgedom. The code. New York : Little, Brown, 2003.
BF724.3.S9 M34 2003

SELF-ACTUALIZATION (PSYCHOLOGY).
Austin, Linda S., 1951- Heart of the matter. New York : Atria Books, c2003.
BF575.L8 A97 2003

Ball, Pamela, 1940- A woman's way to wisdom. London ; New York : Quantum, 2002.

Beavers, Brett. Something worth leaving behind. Nashville, Tenn. : Rutledge Hill Press, c2002.
BF637.S8 B383 2002

Bedi, Ashok. Retire your family karma. Berwick, Me. : Nicolas-Hays, 2003.
BF637.S4 B423 2003

Braham, Barbara J. Finding your purpose. Rev. ed. Menlo Park, CA : Crisp Publications, c2003.
BF637.S4 B67 2003

Breslin, Dawn, 1969- Zest for life. Carlsbad, Calif. : Hay House, 2004.
BF637.S4 B735 2004

Bridges, William, 1933- The way of transition. Cambridge, Mass. : Perseus Pub., c2001.

BF335 .B717 2001
Bronson, Po, 1964- What should I do with my life? . Waterville, Me. : Thorndike Press, 2003.
BF637.S4 B79 2003

Brossman, Sandra C. The power of oneness. Boston, MA : Red Wheel, 2003.
BF637.S4 B8 2003

Bruce, Anne, 1952- Discover true north. New York : McGraw-Hill, c2004.
BF637.S4 B82 2004

Caliandro, Arthur. Lost and found. 1st ed. New York : McGraw-Hill, 2003.
BF637.S4 .C32 2003

Cameron, Julia. The sound of paper. New York : Jeremy P. Tarcher, 2004.
BF408 .C1758 2004

Chaplin, Nikki. Secrets of a dream catcher. Hallandale Beach, Fla. : Aglob Pub., 2003.
BF637.S4 C492 2003

Chiodi, Michael. The art of building people. 1st ed. St. Paul, Minn. : Chiberry Press, c2003.
BF637.S4 C497 2003

Chopra, Deepak. The spontaneous fulfillment of desire. 1st ed. New York : Harmony Books, c2003.
BF1175 .C48 2003

Chopra, Deepak. The spontaneous fulfillment of desire. New York : Random House Large Print, 2003.
BF1175 .C48 2003b

Cleghorn, Patricia. The secrets of self-esteem. London : Vega, c2002.
BF697.5.S46 C55 2002

Cole, Harriette. Choosing truth. New York : Simon & Schuster, c2003.
BF637.S4 C652 2003
1. Black author.

Comstock, Kani. Journey into love. Ashland, OR : Willow Press, c2000.
BF575.L8 C647 2002

Denise, Jan. Naked relationships. Charlottesville, VA : Hampton Roads Pub., c2002.
BF575.I5 D46 2002

Dooley, Deborah. Journeying into wholeness with map & skills. [Meno Park, Calif. : Delphi Press, c2003]
BF710 .D64 2003

Durham, Diana. The return of King Arthur. New York : Jeremy P. Tarcher/Penguin, 2004.
BF637.S4 D88 2004

Eckblad, John. If your life were a business, would you invest in it? New York : McGraw-Hill, c2003.
BF637.S4 E38 2003

Edward, J. J. Self actualization. [S.l. : s.n., 1998?] (Islamabad : Shahkar Publications)
BF637.S4 E39 1998

Edwards, Jaroldeen. The daffodil principle. Salt Lake City, Utah : Shadow Mountain, 2004.
BF637.S4 E4 2004

SELF ACTUALIZATION (PSYCHOLOGY).
Fischer, Norman, 1946- Taking our places. 1st ed. San Francisco : HarperSanFrancisco, c2003.
BF710 .F57 2003

SELF-ACTUALIZATION (PSYCHOLOGY).
Flickstein, Matthew. Journey to the center. Somerville, MA : Wisdom Publications, c1998.
BF637.S4 F58 1998

Fralix, Philip. How to thrive in spite of mess, stress and less!. 1st ed. Raleigh, NC : Triunity Publishers, c2002.
BF637.S4 F72 2002

Fritz, Robert, 1943- Your life as art. 1st ed. Newfane, VT : Newfane Press, c2003.
BF637.S4 F753 2003

Funes, Mariana. Laughing matters. Dublin : Newleaf, 2000.

Gawain, Shakti, 1948- Creative visualization. [Rev. ed.]. Navato, Calif. : Nataraj Pub./New World Library, c2002.
BF367 .G34 2002

Gawain, Shakti, 1948- Reflections in the light. Rev. ed. Navato, Calif. : Nataraj Pub., c2003.
BF637.S4 G393 2003

Giardina, Ric. Become a life balance master. Hillsboro, Or. : Beyond Words Pub., 2003.

Self-actualization (Psychology)

BF637.S4 G486 2003
Goals and life lessons support materials [electronic resource]. Greenwood Village, CO : FasTracKids International, [1998]
BF637.S4

Goodier, Steve. A life that makes a difference. 1st ed. Divide, CO : Life Support System Pub., c2002.
BF637.C5 G68 2002

SELF-ACTUALIZATION (PSYCHOLOGY).
Gōpālakrṣṇa, Pi. Es. Migurinci mikutelusā? Hyderabad : Media House Publications, 2002.
BF637.S4 G655 2002

SELF-ACTUALIZATION (PSYCHOLOGY).
Hall, Judy, 1943- The intuition handbook. London : Vega, 2003.
BF315.5 .H35 2003

Hamel, Jean-Marie. Living from the inside out. 1st ed. New York : Harmony Books, 2004.
BF637.S4 H34 2004

Harry, Lou, 1963- The game of life. Philadelphia : Running Press, c2003.
BF637.S4 H357 2003

Henry, Dale. The proverbial Cracker Jack. Hagerstown, Md. : Autumn House Pub., c2002.
BF637.S4 H857 2002

Hinz, Michael. Learn to balance your life. San Francisco : Chronicle Books, 2004.
BF637.S4 H55 2004

Hurley, Jessica, 1970- Burn this book--. Kansas City, Mo. : Andrews McMeel, c2002.
BF637.S4 H87 2002

Johnston, Daniel H. Lessons for living. 1st ed. Macon, Ga. : Dagali Press, c2001.
BF637.S4 J65 2001

Judd, Naomi. Naomi's breakthrough guide. New York : Simon & Schuster, 2004.
BF637.S4 J84 2004

Kaufman, Ronald A. Anatomy of success. Dubuque, Iowa : Kendall/Hunt Pub., c1999.
BF637.S8 .K379 1999

King, Joan C. Cellular wisdom. Berkeley : Celestial Arts, 2003.
BF637.S4 K548 2003

Krauss, Sandy. Set yourself free. North Royalton, Ohio : Success Talks Pub., c1999.
BF637.S4 K73 1999

Levine, Leslie. Wish it, dream it, do it. New York : Simon & Schuster, c2004.
BF637.S8 L449 2004

Mandel, Robert Steven, 1943- 9 journeys home. Berkeley : Celestial Arts, c2003.
BF575.S4 M36 2003

Mandell, Faye. Self-powerment. New York : Dutton, c2003.
BF637.S4 M337 2003

Manokha, I. P. (Iryna Petrivna) Psykholohiia potaiemnoho "IA". Kyiv : "Polihrafknyha", 2001.
BF637.S4 M338 2001

McCain, Marian Van Eyk. Elderwoman. Forres : Findhorn Press, 2002.

McKay, Matthew. The self-nourishment companion. Oakland, CA : New Harbinger Publications, c2001.
BF637.S4 M3925 2001

McWilliam, Erica. What about Uranus? Sydney, NSW, Australia : UNSW Press, 2002.
BF637.S4 M397 2002

McWilliam, Erica. What about Uranus? Sydney : UNSW Press, 2002.

Miller, Scott D. Staying on top and keeping the sand out of your pants. Deerfield Beach, Fla. : Health Communications, c2003.
BF637.S8 M565 2003

Neuharth, Dan. Secrets you keep from yourself. 1st U.S. ed. New York : St. Martins Press, 2004.
BF637.S37 N48 2004

O'Hanlon, William Hudson. Thriving through crisis. 1st Perigee ed. New York : Perigee, 2004.
BF789.S8 O35 2004

Oracle (Writer) The Oracle teachings. 1st ed. Kaua'i, Hawai'i : Oracle Productions, c1996.
BF637.S4 O72 1996

Pearsall, Paul. The Beethoven factor. Charlottesville, VA : Hampton Roads Pub. Co., c2003.

BF698.35.R47 P43 2003
Phillips, Nicola. The big difference. Cambridge, MA : Perseus Pub., c2001.
BF619 .P48 2001

Pliskin, Zelig. Enthusiasm!. 1st ed. Brooklyn, N.Y. : Shaar Press : Distributed by Mesorah Publications, 2002.

Pliskin, Zelig. Harmony with others. 1st ed. Brooklyn, N.Y. : Shaar Press : Distributed by Mesorah Publications, 2002.

Plotkin, Bill, 1950- Soulcraft. Novato, Calif. : New World Library, c2003.
BF637.S4 P58 2003

Reed, Bob, 1942- Master your whole life. 1st ed. Toronto, Ont. : New Vision Pub., 2000.
BF637.S4 R44 2000

Rutlen, Carmen Richardson, 1948- Dancing naked-- in fuzzy red slippers. 1st ed. Fort Bragg, CA : Cypress House, c2003.
BF637.S4 R877 2003

Ryan, M. J. (Mary Jane), 1952- Trusting yourself. New York : Broadway Books, 2004.
BF575.S39 R93 2004

Saltz, Gail. Becoming real. New York: Riverhead Books, 2004.
BF637.S4 S245 2004

Sapadin, Linda. Master your fears. Hoboken, N.J. : John Wiley & Sons, 2004.
BF575.F2 S26 2004

Sasson, Gahl. A wish can change your life. New York : Simon & Schuster, 2003.
BF1623.C2 S27 2003

Schlenger, Sunny. Organizing for the spirit. 1st ed. San Francisco : Jossey-Bass, c2004.
BF637.S4 S345 2004

Secunda, Al. The 15-second principle. Franklin Lakes, NJ : Career Press, 2004.
BF637.S4 S43 2004

Segalove, Ilene, 1950- Snap out of it. Boston, MA : Conari Press, 2004.
BF637.S4 S438 2004

Shabazz, David L. Discover your gold mind. Clinton, S.C. : Awesome Records, c2001.
BF637.S8 S428 2001

Sherfield, Robert M. The everything self-esteem book. Avon, MA : Adams Media Corp., c2004.
BF697.5.S46 S52

Sills, Judith. If the horse is dead, get off!. New York : Viking, 2004.
BF637.S38 S55 2004

Summer, Lauralee, 1976- Learning joy from dogs without collars. New York ; London : Simon & Schuster, c2003.
HV4505 .S86 2003

Ventrella, Tony, 1944- Smile in the mirror. 1st ed. Sammamish, WA : Positive Energy Productions, c2001.
BF637.S4 V46 2001

Whalen, Charles E., Jr. The gift of renewal. 1st ed. Gainesville, GA : Warren Featherbone Foundation, c2003 (Gainesville, GA : Matthews Print.)
BF637.S4 W47 2003

What makes a champion!. Camberwell, Vic., Australia ; New York : Penguin Books, 2002.
BF637.S8 W45 2002

Wilde, Liz. Unlock your potential. New York : Ryland Peters & Small, 2004.
BF637.S4 W488 2004

SELF-ACTUALIZATION (PSYCHOLOGY) IN MIDDLE AGE.
Zoglio, Suzanne Willis. Create a life that tickles your soul. Doylestown, Pa. : Tower Hill Press, c1999.
BF724.65.S44 Z65 1999

SELF-ACTUALIZATION (PSYCHOLOGY) - MISCELLANEA.
Miller, D. Patrick, 1953- News of a new human nature. 1st ed. Berkeley, Calif. : Fearless Books, 2002.
BF637.S4 M547 2002

Pike, Diane Kennedy. Awakening to wisdom. Scottsdale, AZ : LP Publications, c2003.
BF1999 .P5485 2003

Roads, Michael J. The magic formula. 1st ed. Cleveland : SilverRoads Pub., 2003.

BF637.S4 R575 2003
Todeschi, Kevin J. Soul signs. Virginia Beach, Va. : A.R.E. Press, c2003.
BF1045.S44 T63 2003

Varnum, Keith. Inner coach, outer power. Phoenix, Ariz. : New Dimensions Pub., c2002.
BF1999 .V36 2002

SELF-ACTUALIZATION (PSYCHOLOGY) - PROBLEMS, EXERCISES, ETC.
Linn, Denise. Soul coaching. Carlsbad, CA : Hay House, 2003.
BF637.S4 L565 2003

Segalove, Ilene, 1950- Snap out of it. Boston, MA : Conari Press, 2004.
BF637.S4 S438 2004

SELF-ACTUALIZATION (PSYCHOLOGY) - RELIGIOUS ASPECTS.
Roads, Michael J. The magic formula. 1st ed. Cleveland : SilverRoads Pub., 2003.
BF637.S4 R575 2003

Solodin, A. I. Strategiia ontologicheskoĭ igry. Sankt-Peterburg : Aleteĭa, 2002.

SELF-ACTUALIZATION (PSYCHOLOGY) - RELIGIOUS ASPECTS - JUDAISM.
Pliskin, Zelig. Harmony with others. 1st ed. Brooklyn, N.Y. : Shaar Press : Distributed by Mesorah Publications, 2002.

SELF-ACTUALIZATION (PSYCHOLOGY) - SOCIAL ASPECTS.
Kliuchnikov, Sergeĭ. Master zhizni. Moskva : Belovod'e, 2001.
BF637.S4 K556 2001

SELF-ACTUALIZATION (PSYCHOLOGY) - SONGS AND MUSIC.
Sanders, Mark D. I hope you dance!. Nashville, Tenn. : Rutledge Hill Press, 2003.
BF410 .S26 2003

Self and social identity / edited by Marilynn Brewer and Miles Hewstone. Malden, MA : Blackwell Pub., 2003. p. cm. (Perspectives on social psychology) Includes bibliographical references and index. CONTENTS: Self-concept and identity / Daphna Oyserman -- Identity through time : constructing personal pasts and futures / Michael Ross and Roger Buchler -- An evolutionary-psychological approach to self-esteem : multiple domains and multiple functions / Lee A. Kirkpatrick and Bruce J. Ellis -- Is loving the self necessary for loving another? An examination of identity and intimacy / W. Keith Campbell and Roy F. Baumeister -- Self-expansion model of motivation and cognition in close relationships and beyond / Arther Aron, Elaine N. Aron, and Christina Norman -- Psychological consequences of devalued identities / Jennifer Crocker and Diane M. Quinn -- Collective identity : group membership and self-conception / Dominic Abrams and Michael A. Hogg -- It takes two to tango : relating group identity to individual identity within the framework of group development / Stephen Worchel and Dawna Coutant -- Social categorization, depersonalization, and group behavior / Michael A. Hogg -- The psychology of crowd dynamics / Stephen Reicher -- The social identity perspective in intergroup relations : theories, themes, and controversies / John C. Turner and Katherine J. Reynolds -- The social psychology of minority-majority relations / Bernd Simon, Birgit Aufderheide, and Claudia Kampmeier -- Toward reduction of prejudice : intergroup contact and social categorization / Marilynn B. Brewer and Samuel L. Gaertner. ISBN 1405110694 (pbk. : alk. paper) DDC 302/.1
1. Self-perception. 2. Self-perception - Social aspects. 3. Identity (Psychology) 4. Group identity. I. Brewer, Marilynn B., 1942- II. Hewstone, Miles. III. Series.
BF697.5.S43 S429 2003

SELF-ASSURANCE. See **SELF-CONFIDENCE.**

SELF-AWARENESS. See **SELF-PERCEPTION.**

SELF-CARE, HEALTH.
Markham, Ursula. The beginner's guide to self-hypnosis. London : Vega, 2002.
BF1141 .M36 2002

SELF-CARE, HEALTH - MISCELLANEA.
Alexander, Jane. The smudging and blessings book. New York: Sterling Pub., 2001.
BF1999 .A6329 2001

SELF-CARE, MEDICAL. See **SELF-CARE, HEALTH.**

SELF-CHANGE TECHNIQUES. See **SELF-HELP TECHNIQUES.**

SELF-CONCEPT. See **SELF-PERCEPTION.**

SELF-CONFIDENCE.
Bucay, Jorge, 1949- Hojas de ruta. 1a ed. Buenos Aires : Editorial Sudamericana : Editorial Del nuevo extremo, 2001.

Danzig, Robert J., 1932- Every child deserves a champion. Washington, DC : Child & Family Press, c2003.
BF637.E53 D36 2003

Darbo, Patrika. 365 glorious nights of love and romance. 1st ed. New York : ReganBooks, c2002.
HQ46 .D35 2002

Hagberg, Karen A., 1943- Stage presence from head to toe. Lanham, Md. : Scarecrow Press, 2003.
ML3795 .H13 2003

Ryan, M. J. (Mary Jane), 1952- Trusting yourself. New York : Broadway Books, 2004.
BF575.S39 R93 2004

Waitley, Denis. Psychology of success. 4th ed. Boston : McGraw-Hill Higher Education, c2004.
BF637.S8 W269 2004

Webb, Wyatt. Five steps for overcoming fear and self-doubt. Carlsbad, Calif. : Hay House, 2004.
BF575.F2 W42 2004

SELF-CONFIDENCE - PROBLEMS, EXERCISES, ETC.
Perry, Martin. Confidence booster workout. San Diego : Thunder Bay Press, 2004.
BF575.S39 P48 2004

SELF - CONGRESSES.
Jean Piaget Society. Meeting (30th : 2000 : Montréal, Québec) Changing conceptions of psychological life. Mahwah, N.J. : L. Erlbaum Associates, 2004.
BF697.J36 2004

The self. New York : New York Academy of Sciences, 2003.
BF697

Self, social identity, and physical health. New York : Oxford University Press, 1999.
R726.5 .S46 1999

SELF-CONSCIOUSNESS. See EMBARRASSMENT.

SELF-CONTROL. See also HABIT BREAKING; METACOGNITION.
Handbook of self-regulation. New York : Guilford Press, 2004.
BF632 .H262 2004

The regulation of emotion. Mahwah, NJ : Lawrence Erlbaum, 2003.
BF531 .R45 2003

SELF-CULTURE. See also MNEMONICS.
Olaoye, Elaine H. Passions of the soul. 2nd ed. Red Bank, N.J. : Northwind Publishers, 2002.
1. Black author.

SELF-DEFEATING BEHAVIOR.
Neuharth, Dan. Secrets you keep from yourself. 1st U.S. ed. New York : St. Martins Press, 2004.
BF637.S37 N48 2004

Portmann, John. The lure of self-harm. Boston : Beacon Press, 2004.
BF637.S37 P67 2004

Saltz, Gail. Becoming real. New York : Riverhead Books, 2004.
BF637.S4 S245 2004

SELF-DEFENSE. See also VERBAL SELF-DEFENSE.
Johnston, Marianne. [Dealing with insults. Spanish] Como tratar los insultos. New York : PowerKids Press, 2005.
BF637.V47 J6418 2005

Kli͡uchnikov, Sergeĭ. Master zhizni. Moskva : Belovodʹe, 2001.
BF637.S4 K556 2001

SELF-DEFENSE - PSYCHIC ASPECTS.
Slate, Joe H. Psychic vampires. 1st ed. St. Paul, Minn. : Llewellyn Publications, 2002.
BF1045.S46 S53 2002

SELF-DEFENSE - PSYCHOLOGICAL ASPECTS.
Webster-Doyle, Terrence, 1940- One encounter, one chance. 1st Weatherhill ed. Trumbull, CT : Weatherhill, 2000.
GV1114.3 .W43 2000

SELF-DENIAL.
Simonetta, Catherine. Renoncement et narcissisme chez Maurice Zundel. Saint-Maurice : Editions Saint-Augustin, c2002.

SELF-DETERMINATION, NATIONAL. See also SOVEREIGNTY.
Howard, Bradley Reed. Indigenous peoples and the state. DeKalb : Northern Illinois University Press, c2003.
GN380 .H68 2003

Toshchenko, Zhan Terentʹevich. Tri osobennykh lika vlasti. Moskva : RGGU, 2002.
JC330 .T674 2002

SELF-DETERMINATION, NATIONAL - UNITED STATES.
Ryter, Jon Christian. Whatever happened to America? Tampa, FL : Hallberg Pub., 2001, c2000.
E743 .R98 2001

SELF-DETERMINATION (PSYCHOLOGY). See AUTONOMY (PSYCHOLOGY).

SELF-DIRECTED CHANGE. See SELF-HELP TECHNIQUES.

SELF-DIRECTION (PSYCHOLOGY). See AUTONOMY (PSYCHOLOGY).

SELF-DISCLOSING BEHAVIOR. See SELF-DISCLOSURE.

SELF-DISCLOSURE.
Klitzman, Robert. Mortal secrets. Baltimore : Johns Hopkins University Press, 2003.
RA643.8 .K56 2003

Petronio, Sandra Sporbert. Boundaries of privacy. Albany : State University of New York Press, c2002.
BF697.5.S427 P48 2002

SELF-DISCLOSURE - PROBLEMS, EXERCISES, ETC.
Revoir, Katherine Q. Spiritual doodles & mental leapfrogs. Boston, MA : Red Wheel, 2002.
BF697.5.S427 R48 2002

SELF-DOUBT.
Miller, William Ian, 1946- Faking it. Cambridge ; New York : Cambridge University Press, 2003.
BF697 .M525 2003

Webb, Wyatt. Five steps for overcoming fear and self-doubt. Carlsbad, Calif. : Hay House, 2004.
BF575.F2 W42 2004

SELF-EFFICACY.
Sills, Judith. If the horse is dead, get off!. New York : Viking, 2004.
BF637.S38 S55 2004

SELF-ESTEEM.
Cleghorn, Patricia. The secrets of self-esteem. London : Vega, c2002.
BF697.5.S46 C55 2002

Cottle, Thomas J. Beyond self-esteem. New York : P. Lang, c2003.
BF697 .C675 2003

Farber, Barry J. Diamond in the rough. New York : Berkley Books, c1995.
BF637.S8 F34 1995

Hooks, Bell. Rock my soul. New York, NY : Atria Books, c2003.
1. Black author.

Krauss, Sandy. Set yourself free. North Royalton, Ohio : Success Talks Pub., c1999.
BF637.S4 K73 1999

Rubino, Joe. Restore your magnificence. 1st ed. Boxford, Mass. : Vision Works Pub., c2003.
BF697.5.S46 R83 2003

Sherfield, Robert M. The everything self-esteem book. Avon, MA : Adams Media Corp., c2004.
BF697.5.S46 S52

Waitley, Denis. Psychology of success. 4th ed. Boston : McGraw-Hill Higher Education, c2004.
BF637.S8 W269 2004

Woods, Earl, 1932- Start something. New York : Simon & Schuster, c2000.
BJ1631 .W726 2000

SELF-ESTEEM IN CHILDREN.
Bloch, Douglas, 1949- The power of positive talk. Rev. and updated ed. Minneapolis, Minn. : Free Spirit Pub., 2003.
BF723.S3 B56 2003

Dobson, James C., 1936- The new hide or seek. Pbk. ed. Grand Rapids, Mich. : F.H. Revell, 2001.
BF723.S3 D6 2001

Kater, Kathy. Real kids come in all sizes. New York : Broadway Books, 2004.
BF723.B6 K38 2004

Kunjufu, Jawanza. Black students-Middle class teachers. Chicago, Ill. : African American Images, c2002.
1. Black author.

Losquadro-Liddle, Tara. Why motor skills matter. Chicago : Contemporary Books, c2004.
BF723.M6 L67 2004

SELF-ESTEEM IN WOMEN.
Big Dance [videorecording]. Buffalo, N.Y. : Kineticvideo.com, c1998.

Dyson, Michael Eric. Why I love black women. New York : Basic Civitas Books, c2003.

Freedman, Rita Jackaway. Bodylove. Updated ed. Carlsbad, CA : Gürze Books, c2002.
BF697.5.B63 F74 2002

Lee, Michelle. Fashion victim. 1st ed. New York : Broadway Books, 2003.
GT524 .L44 2003

Sutcliffe, Eileen, 1934- Eve returns Adam's rib. Calgary : Loraleen Enterprises, c2002.

Walker, Jamie. 101 ways black women can learn to love themselves. Washington, D.C. : J.D. Publishing, c2002.
1. Black author.

SELF-ESTEEM - JUVENILE LITERATURE.
Mawi Asgedom. The code. New York : Little, Brown, 2003.
BF724.3.S9 M34 2003

The self-esteem program.
Liptak, John J. Plainview, NY : Wellness Reproductions & Pub., c2002.
BF697.5.S46 L57 2002

SELF-ESTEEM - STUDY AND TEACHING.
Liptak, John J. The self-esteem program. Plainview, NY : Wellness Reproductions & Pub., c2002.
BF697.5.S46 L57 2002

SELF-EVALUATION. See also SELF-PERCEPTION.
Carter, Philip J. IQ and psychometric tests. London ; Sterling, VA : Kogan Page Ltd., 2004.
BF431.3 .C362 2004

Carter, Philip J. More IQ testing. Chichester, West Sussex, England ; New York : John Wiley & Sons, Ltd, 2002.
BF431.3 .C367 2002

Directed self-placement. Cresskill, N.J. : Hampton Press, c2003.
PE1404 .D57 2003

Mangieri, John N. Yale Assessment of Thinking. San Francisco : Jossey-Bass, c2003.
BF442 .M34 2003

Russell, Kenneth, 1928- The Times book of IQ tests. Book 2. London : Milford, CT : Kogan Page, 2002.

Russell, Kenneth A. The Times book of IQ tests. Book 3. London ; Sterling, VA : Kogan Page Ltd., 2003.
BF431.3 .R87 2003

Sadka, Dewey. The Dewey color system. 1st ed. New York : Three Rivers Press, 2004.
BF789.C7 S23 2004

Williams, Andrew N. How do you compare? 1st Perigee ed. New York : Perigee Book, 2004.
BF698.5 .W55 2004

The self : from soul to brain / edited by Joseph LeDoux, Jacek Debiec, and Henry Moss. New York : New York Academy of Sciences, 2003. p. cm. (Annals of the New York Academy of Sciences ; v. 1001) Includes bibliographical references and index. Table of contents URL: http://www.loc.gov/catdir/toc/ecip047/2003018198.html ISBN 1-57331-450-1 (cloth : alk. paper) ISBN 1-57331-451-X (pbk. : alk. paper) DDC 500 s; 155.2
1. Self - Congresses. I. LeDoux, Joseph E. II. Debiec, Jacek. III. Moss, Henry, 1948- IV. Series.
BF697

SELF-FULFILLMENT. See SELF-REALIZATION.

SELF HEALTH CARE. See SELF-CARE, HEALTH.

SELF-HELP, HEALTH. See SELF-CARE, HEALTH.

SELF-HELP TECHNIQUES. See also SELF-MANAGEMENT (PSYCHOLOGY); TWELVE-STEP PROGRAMS.

Self-help techniques

Bourne, Edmund J. Coping with anxiety. Oakland, CA : New Harbinger, c2003.
BF575.A6 B68 2003

Chagas, Arnaldo Sousa das Chagas. O sujeito imaginário no discurso de auto-ajuda. Rio Grande do Sul : Editora UNIJUÍ, 2002.

Cleghorn, Patricia. The secrets of self-esteem. London : Vega, c2002.
BF697.5.S46 C55 2002

Gross, Esther. You are not alone. Jerusalem, Israel ; Nanuet, NY : Feldheim, 2002.

Johnston, Daniel H. Lessons for living. 1st ed. Macon, Ga. : Dagali Press, c2001.
BF637.S4 J65 2001

Markham, Ursula. The beginner's guide to self-hypnosis. London : Vega, 2002.
BF1141 .M36 2002

Sutcliffe, Eileen, 1934- Eve returns Adam's rib. Calgary : Loraleen Enterprises, c2002.

Wilde, Liz. Unlock your potential. New York : Ryland Peters & Small, 2004.
BF637.S4 W488 2004

Zoglio, Suzanne Willis. Recharge in minutes. 1st ed. Doylestown, PA : Tower Hill Press, c2003.
BF632 .Z64 2003

SELF-HELP TECHNIQUES - MISCELLANEA.
Miller, D. Patrick, 1953- News of a new human nature. 1st ed. Berkeley, Calif. : Fearless Books, 2002.
BF637.S4 M547 2002

Self-hypnosis.
Goldberg, Bruce, 1948- Franklin Lakes, NJ : New Page Books, c2001.
BF1156.S8 G65 2001

SELF IMAGE. See SELF-PERCEPTION.

SELF-IMPROVEMENT. See SELF-ACTUALIZATION (PSYCHOLOGY); SUCCESS.

SELF IN CHILDREN.
The development of the social self. 1st ed. London ; New York : Psychology Press, 2003.
BF723.S24 D48 2003

SELF IN LITERATURE.
Individualitätskonzepte in der russischen Kultur. Berlin : Berlin Verlag Arno Spitz, c2002.
PG2987.I48 .I53 2002

Liddelow, Eden. After Electra. Melbourne : Australian Scholarly, 2002, c2001.

Self-initiation for the solitary witch.
Shanddaramon, 1959- Franklin Lakes, NJ : New Page Books, c2004.
BF1566 .S44 2004

SELF-INTEREST. See INDIVIDUALISM.

SELF-KNOWLEDGE, THEORY OF.
Archer, Margaret Scotford. Structure, agency and the internal conversation. Cambridge, U.K. ; New York : Cambridge University Press, 2003.
HM708 .A73 2003

Flahault, François, 1943- Le sentiment d'exister. Paris : Descartes & Cie, c2002.
BD438.5 .F54 2002

New essays on semantic externalism and self-knowledge. Cambridge, Mass. : MIT Press, c2003.
BD418.3 .N49 2003

Privileged access. Aldershot ; Burlington, VT : Ashgate, c2003.

Stepanov, S. IU. (Sergeĭ IUr'evich) Refleksivnaia praktika tvorcheskogo razvitiia cheloveka i organizatsiĭ. Moskva : Nauka, 2000.
BF408 .S75 2000

Sullivan, Karen. Finding the inner you. 1st ed. Hauppauge, N.Y. : Barrons Educational Series, 2003.
BF697.5.S43 S95 2003

Webster-Doyle, Terrence, 1940- One encounter, one chance. 1st Weatherhill ed. Trumbull, CT : Weatherhill, 2000.
GV1114.3 .W43 2000

SELF-LOVE (PSYCHOLOGY). See SELF-ACCEPTANCE; SELF-ESTEEM.

SELF-MANAGEMENT (PSYCHOLOGY).
Allen, David, 1945 Dec. 28- Ready for anything. New York : Viking, 2003.
BF637.T5 A46 2003

Handy, Charles B. 21 ideas for managers. 1st ed. San Francisco : Jossey-Bass, c2000.
HD31 .H31259 2000

SELF-MANAGEMENT (PSYCHOLOGY) FOR CHILDREN.
Dawson, Peg. Executive skills in children and adolescents. New York : Guilford Press, 2004.
BF723.E93 D39 2004

SELF-MANAGEMENT (PSYCHOLOGY) FOR TEENAGERS.
Dawson, Peg. Executive skills in children and adolescents. New York : Guilford Press, 2004.
BF723.E93 D39 2004

The self-nourishment companion.
McKay, Matthew. Oakland, CA : New Harbinger Publications, c2001.
BF637.S4 M3925 2001

SELF-ORGANIZING SYSTEMS. See ADAPTATION (BIOLOGY); ARTIFICIAL INTELLIGENCE.

SELF-PERCEPTION. See also BODY IMAGE; METACOGNITION.
Agency and self-awareness. Oxford : Clarendon Press ; New York : Oxford University Press, 2003.

Breslin, Dawn, 1969- Zest for life. Carlsbad, Calif. : Hay House, 2004.
BF637.S4 B735 2004

El buscador de oro. [Madrid] : Lengua de Trapo Ediciones, c2002.

Carson, Richard David. Taming your gremlin. Rev. ed. New York : Quill, 2003.
BF575.H27 C38 2003

Chagas, Arnaldo Sousa das Chagas. O sujeito imaginário no discurso de auto-ajuda. Rio Grande do Sul : Editora UNIJUÍ, 2002.

Dacquino, Giacomo, 1930- Bisogno d'amore. 1. ed. Milano : Mondadori, 2002.
BF697.5.S43 D33 2002

Demmin, Herbert S., 1959- The ghosts of consciousness. St. Paul, Minn. : Paragon House, c2003.
BF441 .D395 2003

Ford, Loren. Human relations. 3rd ed. Upper Saddle River, N.J. : Pearson/Prentice Hall, c2004.
BF335 .F67 2004

Hemming, Jan. Begabung und Selbstkonzept. Münster : Lit, [2002?]
ML3838 .H46 2002

Hollis, James, 1940- On this journey we call our life. Toronto, Ont. : Inner City Books, c2003.
BF697.5.S43 H65 2003

Hollis, James, 1940- On this journey we call our life. Toronto : Inner City Books, c2003.

Humeniuk, O. IE. (Oksana IEvstakhïvna) Psykholohiia IA-kontseptsii. Ternopil' : Ekononichna dumka, 2002.
BF697.5.S43 H84 2002

Lord, Robert G. (Robert George), 1946- Leadership processes and follower self-identity. Mahwah, N.J. ; London : Lawrence Erlbaum, 2004.
HM1261 .L67 2004

Mandell, Faye. Self-powerment. New York : Dutton, c2003.
BF637.S4 M337 2003

Mironova, T. L. (Tat'iana L'vovna) Samosoznanie professionala. Ulan-Udè: Izd-vo Buriatskogo gosuniversiteta, 1999.
BF697.5.S43 M57 1999

Moessinger, Pierre Le jeu de l'identité. 1re éd. Paris : Presses universitaires de France, 2000.
BF697.5.S43 M634 2000

Quaglia, Rocco. Immagini dell'uomo. Roma : Armando, c2000.

Self and social identity. Malden, MA : Blackwell Pub., 2003.
BF697.5.S43 S429 2003

Sullivan, Karen. Finding the inner you. 1st ed. Hauppauge, N.Y. : Barrons Educational Series, 2003.
BF697.5.S43 S95 2003

Too, Lillian. Discover yourself. Carlsbad, Calif. : Hay House, c2002 (2003 printing)
BF697.5.S43 T66 2002

Western eyes [videorecording]. New York, NY : First Run/Icarus Films, 2000.

SELF-PERCEPTION IN CHILDREN.
Korepanova, M. V. (Marina Vasil'evna) Teoriia i praktika stanovleniia i razvitiia obraza IA doshkol'nika. Volgograd : Peremena, 2001.
BF723.S28 K66 2001

SELF-PERCEPTION IN WOMEN.
Género, desarrollo psicosocial y trastornos de la imagen corporal. Madrid : Instituto de la Mujer, 2001.

SELF-PERCEPTION - SOCIAL ASPECTS.
Self and social identity. Malden, MA : Blackwell Pub., 2003.
BF697.5.S43 S429 2003

SELF-PERCEPTION - STUDY AND TEACHING (ELEMENTARY).
Self-science. 2nd ed., rev. and updated. San Mateo, Calif. : Six Seconds, c1998.
BF697 .S84 1998

SELF-PERCEPTION - STUDY AND TEACHING (PRESCHOOL).
Korepanova, M. V. (Marina Vasil'evna) Teoriia i praktika stanovleniia i razvitiia obraza IA doshkol'nika. Volgograd : Peremena, 2001.
BF723.S28 K66 2001

SELF-PERCEPTION - TESTING.
Mangieri, John N. Yale Assessment of Thinking. San Francisco : Jossey-Bass, c2003.
BF442 .M34 2003

SELF (PHILOSOPHY).
Agency and self-awareness. Oxford : Clarendon Press ; New York : Oxford University Press, 2003.

Baldus, Claus, 1947- Weg im Nicht. Stuttgart : Hatje, c1994.

Bronowski, Jacob, 1908-1974. The identity of man. Amherst, N.Y. : Prometheus Books, 2002.
BD450 .B653 2002

Farago, France. Sören Kierkegaard. 1. éd. Paris : Houdiard, c2002.

Gray, John, 1948- Straw dogs. London : Granta, 2002.

Mensch, James R. Ethics and selfhood. Albany, NY : State University of New York Press, c2003.
B945.M4853 E84 2003

Privileged access. Aldershot ; Burlington, VT : Ashgate, c2003.

Sullivan, Karen. Finding the inner you. 1st ed. Hauppauge, N.Y. : Barrons Educational Series, 2003.
BF697.5.S43 S95 2003

SELF (PHILOSOPHY) IN LITERATURE.
Jouffroy, Alain, 1928- [Mots et moi] Les mots et moi ; Nantes : Pleins feux, c2002.

Self-powerment.
Mandell, Faye. New York : Dutton, c2003.
BF637.S4 M337 2003

SELF PSYCHOLOGY.
Goldberg, Arnold, 1929- Misunderstanding Freud. New York : Other Press, 2004.
BF173 .G59 2004

Ivanov, S. P. (Sergeĭ Petrovich) Psikhologiia khudozhestvennogo deĭstviia sub"ekta. Moskva : Moskovskiĭ psikhologo-sotsial'nyĭ institut ; Voronezh : Izd-vo NPO "MODÈK", 2002.
BF408 .I93 2002

St. Clair, Michael, 1940- Object relations and self psychology. 4th ed. Australia ; Belmont, CA : Thomson/Brooks/Cole, c2004.
BF175.5.O24 S7 2004

SELF PSYCHOLOGY - CONGRESSES.
Psikhologiia sub"ektnosti. Kirov : Viatskiĭ gos. pedagog. universitet, 2001.
BF697 .P75 2001

SELF-REALIZATION.
Broqueville, Paulette Renée. Unraveling your past to get into the present. Rev. ed. Costa Mesa, Calif. : Broqueville Pub., c2002-
BF315 .B76 2002

Demo, Pedro. Dialética da felicidade. Petrópolis : Editora Vozes, 2001.

Gilbert, Toni. Messages from the archetypes. Ashland, Or. : White Cloud Press, c2003.
BF1879.T2 G53 2003

Guiley, Rosemary. The dreamer's way. New York : Berkley Books, 2004.
BF1099.S36 G85 2004

Linn, Denise. Secrets & mysteries. Carlsbad, Calif. : Hay House, c2002.

HQ1206 .L513 2002

Mazumdar, Krishna, 1949- Determinants of human well-being. New York : Nova Science Publishers, c2003.
HB171 .M462 2003

Obley, Carole J. Embracing the ties that bind. [Philadelphia] : Xlibris, c2003.
BF1275.S44 O25 2003

Oracle (Writer) The Oracle teachings. 1st ed. Kaua'i, Hawai'i : Oracle Productions, c1996.
BF637.S4 O72 1996

Py, Luiz Alberto. Olhar acima do horizonte. Rio de Janeiro : Rocco, 2002.

Reyes, Arnoldo Juan. Una alternativa para ser feliz. Ciudad de La Habana, Cuba : Editorial Científico-Técnica, 2001, c2000.

Rishoi, Christy, 1958- From girl to woman. Albany : State University of New York Press, c2003.
HQ1186.A9 R57 2003

Śaṅkarācārya. [Bhajagovinda. Gujarati & Sanskrit] Mohamvdgarastotram. Adyatana āvrtti. Amadāvāda : Sarasvatī Pustaka Bhaṇḍāra, 1998/99 [i.e. 1999]
B133.S463 B5315 1998

Sullivan, Kathleen, 1941- Recurring dream symbols. New York : Paulist Press, c2004.
BF1091 .S813 2004

Thomashauer, Regena. Mama Gena's School of Womanly Arts. New York : Simon & Schuster, c2002.
HQ1206 .T4673 2002

SELF-REALIZATION - MISCELLANEA.
Harris, Maxine. The twenty-four carat Buddha and other fables. Baltimore, Md. : Sidran Institute Press, 2003.
BF637.S4 H355 2003

Hite, Sheilaa, 1958- Secrets of a psychic counselor. Needham, Mass. : Moment Point Press ; [Oakland, Calif.] : Distributed to the trade by Words Distributing Co., c2003.
BF1045.R43 H58 2003

SELF-REALIZATION (PSYCHOLOGY). See **SELF-ACTUALIZATION (PSYCHOLOGY).**

SELF-REALIZATION - RELIGIOUS ASPECTS.
Cuin, Joao. A luz de um novo dia. Sao Paulo : DPL, c2001.

Guiley, Rosemary. The dreamer's way. New York : Berkley Books, 2004.
BF1099.S36 G85 2004

Vieira, Anselmo, 1923- Ser ou não ter. Lisboa : Roma Editora, [2002]-

SELF-RELIANCE. See also **SELF-CONFIDENCE.**
Bucay, Jorge, 1949- Hojas de ruta. 1a ed. Buenos Aires : Editorial Sudamericana : Editorial Del nuevo extremo, 2001.

SELF-RESPECT. See **SELF-ESTEEM.**

SELF-REVELATION. See **SELF-DISCLOSURE.**

SELF-SACRIFICE.
Berry, Carmen Renee. When helping you is hurting me. Revised and updated ed. New York : Crossroad Pub. Co., c2003.
BF637.S42 B47 2003

SELF-SACRIFICE - CASE STUDIES.
Berry, Carmen Renee. When helping you is hurting me. Revised and updated ed. New York : Crossroad Pub. Co., c2003.
BF637.S42 B47 2003

Self-science : the emotional intelligence curriculum / Karen Stone-McCown ... [et al.]. 2nd ed., rev. and updated. San Mateo, Calif. : Six Seconds, c1998. xiv, 165 p. : ill. ; 28 cm. Includes bibliographical references. ISBN 0-9629123-4-4 DDC 372.1/1/2
1. Self-perception - Study and teaching (Elementary) 2. Emotional intelligence - Study and teaching (Elementary) I. Stone-McCown, Karen.
BF697 .S84 1998

SELF - SOCIAL ASPECTS.
Cottle, Thomas J. Beyond self-esteem. New York : P. Lang, c2003.
BF697 .C675 2003

De Munck, Victor C. Culture, self, and meaning. Prospect Heights, Ill. : Waveland Press, c2000.
BF697.5.S65 M86 2000

The development of the social self. 1st ed. London ; New York : Psychology Press, 2003.

BF723.S24 D48 2003

Rosseel, Eric. Het onschatbare subject. Brussel : VUBPress, c2001.
BF697.5.S65 R67 2001

Vi͡atkina, G. V. Razvitie individual'nosti lichnosti v sovremennykh uslovii͡akh. Moskva : In-t molodezhi, 1997.
BF697 .V52 1997

Woodward, Gary C. The idea of identification. Albany : State University of New York Press, c2003.
BF697.5.S65 W66 2003

SELF - SOCIAL ASPECTS - HISTORY.
Mozzhilin, S. I. (Sergeĭ Ivanovich) Obretenie I͡A i vozniknovenie rannikh form sotsial'nosti. Saratov : Saratovskiĭ gos. sotsial'no-ėkonomicheskiĭ universitet, 2002.
BF697.5.S65 M69 2002

Self, social identity, and physical health : interdisciplinary explorations / edited by Richard J. Contrada, Richard D. Ashmore. New York : Oxford University Press, 1999. xxiv, 269 p. : ill. :24 cm. (Rutgers series on self and social identity ; v. 2) Papers from the Second Rutgers Symposium on Self and Social Identity held in 1997. Includes bibliographical references and index. CONTENTS: Self and social identity : key to understanding social and behavioral aspects of physical health and disease? / Richard J. Contrada, Richard D. Ashmore -- Self, sickness, somatization, and systems of care / John F. Kihlstrom, Lucy Canter Kihlstrom -- Politics of health, identity, and culture / Margaret Lock -- Race, stress, and physical health : the role of group identity / David R. Williams, Michael S. Spencer, James S. Jackson -- Revealing, organizing, and reorganizing the self in response to stress and emotion / James W. Pennebaker, Kelli A. Keough -- Relationship between personality and health : what self and identity have to do with it / Suzanne C. Ouellette -- What's sex got to do with it? the development of sexual identities during adolescence / Jeanne Brooks-Gunn, Julia A. Graber -- Impact of chronic illness on the self system / Howard Leventhal, Ellen L. Adler, Elaine A. Leventhal -- From the "sick role" to stories of self : understanding the self in illness / Kathy Charmuz -- Self, social identity, and the analysis of social and behavioral aspects of physical health and disease / Richard D. Ashmore, Richard J. Contrada. ISBN 0-19-512730-7 (hardcover : alk. paper) ISBN 0-19-512731-5 (pbk. : alk. paper) DDC 610/.1/9
1. Medicine and psychology - Congresses. 2. Health behavior - Congresses. 3. Self - Congresses. 4. Identity (Psychology) - Congresses. I. Contrada, Richard J. II. Ashmore, Richard D. III. Rutgers Symposium on Self and Social Identity (2nd : 1977) IV. Series.
R726.5 .S46 1999

SELF-TALK.
Decker, Dru Scott, 1942- Stress that motivates. Rev. ed. Menlo Park, CA : Crisp Publications, c2002.
BF575.S75 D38 2002

Hay, Louise L. I can do it!. Carlsbad, CA : Hay House, c2004.
BF697.5.S47 H388 2004

Wilde, Liz. Unlock your potential. New York : Ryland Peters & Small, 2004.
BF637.S4 W488 2004

SELF-TALK IN CHILDREN.
Bloch, Douglas, 1949- The power of positive talk. Rev. and updated ed. Minneapolis, Minn. : Free Spirit Pub., 2003.
BF723.S3 B56 2003

Self-teaching guide.
Bruno, Frank Joe, 1930- Psychology. New York : John Wiley & Sons, c2002.
BF77 .B78 2002

Self-trust and reproductive autonomy.
McLeod, Carolyn. Cambridge, Mass. : MIT Press, c2002.
RG133.5 .M39 2002

SELF-UNDERSTANDING. See **SELF-PERCEPTION.**

SELF-WORTH. See **SELF-ESTEEM.**

Seligman, Martin E. P.
Peterson, Christopher, 1950 Feb. 18- Character strengths and virtues. New York : Oxford University Press, 2004.
BF818 .P38 2004

Selihot.
Naphtali ben Isaac, ha-Kohen, 1649-1719. Sefer Bet Rahel. Yerushalayim : Ahavat Shalom, 761 [2001]
BM665 .N257 2001

SELLING. See also **ADVERTISING; MARKETING.**
Trainor, Norm, 1946- The eight best practices of high-performing salespeople. Toronto ; New York : Wiley, c2000.
HF5438.25 .T72 2000

Selmi, Elisabetta.
Casoni, Guido, 1561-1642. Della magia d'amore. Torino : Res, 2002.
BF575.L8 C3 2002

Selo universidade
(195.) Matheus, Tiago Corbisier. Ideais na adolescência. 1a ed. São Paulo, SP : Annablume, 2002.

(v. 156) Campos, Edemilson Antunes de. A tirania de Narciso. 1. ed. São Paulo, SP, Brasil : Annablume/FAPESP, 2001.

Selo universidade. Psicologia.
Matheus, Tiago Corbisier. Ideais na adolescência. 1a ed. São Paulo, SP : Annablume, 2002.

SEMANTIC WEB.
Towards the semantic web. Chichester, England ; Hoboken, N.J. : J. Wiley, c2003.
TK5105.88815 .T68 2003

SEMANTIC WEB.
Visualizing the semantic Web. London ; [New York] : Springer, c2003.
TK5105.888 .V55 2003

SEMANTICS. See also **DISCOURSE ANALYSIS; INDEXICALS (SEMANTICS); REFERENCE (LINGUISTICS).**
Alefirenko, M. F. Poėticheskai͡a ėnergii͡a slova. Moskva : Academia, 2002.
P35 .A544 2002

Levkievskai͡a, E. E. (Elena Evgen'evna) Slavi͡anskiĭ obereg. Moskva : Indrik, 2002.
BL480 .L38 2002

Prepositions in their syntactic, semantic, and pragmatic context. Amsterdam ; Philadelphia, PA : J. Benjamins Pub., c2002.
P285 .P74 2002

Problemy interpretatsionnoĭ lingvistiki. Novosibirsk : Novosibirskiĭ gos. pedagog. universitet, 2001.
P128.E95 P762 2001

Wort und (Kon)text. Frankfurt : Lang, 2001.
P325.5.C65 W678 2001

SEMANTICS (LAW).
Samuel, Geoffrey, 1947- Epistemology and method in law. Aldershot, Hampshire, England : Burlington, VT : Ashgate, c2003.
K213 .S259 2003

SEMANTICS (LOGIC). See **SEMANTICS (PHILOSOPHY).**

SEMANTICS (PHILOSOPHY). See also **ANALYSIS (PHILOSOPHY); INDEXICALS (SEMANTICS); MEANING (PHILOSOPHY); SPEECH ACTS (LINGUISTICS).**
Barbieri, Marcello. The organic codes. Cambridge, UK. ; New York : Cambridge University Press, 2003.
QH331 .B247 2003

SEMEIOTICS. See **SEMANTICS (PHILOSOPHY); SIGNS AND SYMBOLS.**

Semel, Eleanor Messing. Following directions [electronic resource] : left & right / Eleanor Semel. Macintosh/Windows version. Winooski, VT : Laureate Learning Systems, c2000. 1 CD-ROM : col. ; 4 3/4 in. + 1 user's manual (loose-leaf) + 1 sample goals & objectives sheet. System requirements for Windows: 486/66MHz PC or above; 8MB RAM; Windows 95; hard drive; CD-ROM drive; SVGA graphics (640 x 480 pixels, 256-color screen display); Windows compatible sound card. System requirements for Macintosh: Macintosh LC (or above); 4MB RAM; System 7; hard drive; CD-ROM drive; twelve-inch color monitor. Title from disc label. SUMMARY: Designed to help students improve their ability to follow directions by reinforcing comprehension skills of left-right discrimination concepts. ISBN 1-56405-184-6 (Windows ver.; manual) ISBN 1-56405-228-1 (Macintosh ver.; manual) DDC 152.3
1. Left and right (Psychology) - Study and teaching (Preschool) - Activity programs. I. Laureate Learning Systems. II. Title.
BF637.L36

SEMI-PRECIOUS STONES. See **PRECIOUS STONES.**

Seminar "Adolescencija: kontinuitet i/ili discontinuitet u razvoju" (1997 : Belgrade, Serbia)
Adolescencija : revolucija i evolucija u razvoju /

priredio Vojislav Ćurčić. Beograd : KBC "Dr Dragiša Mišović", 1997. 215 p. ; 24 cm. In Serbian (Roman). Includes bibliographical references.
1. Adolescent psychology - Congresses. 2. Adolescence - Congresses. I. Ćurčić, Vojislav. II. Title.
BF724 .S399 1997

SEMIOTICS. *See also* **DISCOURSE ANALYSIS; SEMANTICS (PHILOSOPHY); SIGNS AND SYMBOLS.**
Chagas, Arnaldo Sousa das Chagas. O sujeito imaginário no discurso de auto-ajuda. Rio Grande do Sul : Editora UNIJUÍ, 2002.

Deely, John N. The impact on philosophy of semiotics. South Bend, Ind. : St. Augustine's Press, 2003.
B831.2 .D437 2003

Dyson, Anne Haas. The brothers and sisters learn to write. New York : Teachers College Press, c2003.
LB1139.L3 D97 2003

Une introduction aux sciences de la culture. 1. ed. Paris : Presses universitaires de France ; [Paris] : Institut Ferdinand-de-Saussure, 2002.

McLuhan's wake [videorecording]. [Montreal, Quebec] : Primitive Entertainment/National Film Board of Canada, c2002.

Medien, Texte und Maschinen. 1. Aufl. Wiesbaden : Westdeutscher Verlag, c2001.

Meo, Oscar. Mondi possibili. Genova : Il melangolo, c2002.
N68.3 .M46 2002

Merrell, Floyd, 1937- Sensing corporeally. Toronto ; Buffalo : University of Toronto Press, c2003.
P99 .M477 2003

SEMITES. *See* **JEWS.**

SEMITES - RELIGION. *See* **JUDAISM.**

SEMITIC LANGUAGES. *See also* **ARABIC LANGUAGE.**
Mélanges David Cohen. Paris : Maisonneuve et Larose, 2003.

SEMITIC LANGUAGES, NORTHWEST. *See* **HEBREW LANGUAGE.**

SEMITIC PHILOLOGY.
Mélanges David Cohen. Paris : Maisonneuve et Larose, 2003.

Sen, Amartya Kumar. Rationality and freedom / Amartya Sen. Cambridge, Mass. : Belknap Press of Harvard University Press, 2002. ix, 736 p. ; 24 cm. Includes bibliographical references and indexes. ISBN 0-674-00947-9 (alk. paper) DDC 302.1/3
1. Social choice. 2. Rational choice theory. 3. Decision making. 4. Liberty. I. Title.
HB846.8 .S466 2002

Putnam, Hilary. The collapse of the fact/value dichotomy and other essays. Cambridge, MA : Harvard University Press, 2002.
B945.P873 C65 2002

Sen, Asim, 1935- Democratic management : the path to total quality with total liberty and equality / Asim Sen. Lanham, Md. ; Oxford : University Press of America, c2003. xvi, 235 p. : ill. ; 23 cm. Includes bibliographical references (p. [197]-221) and index. ISBN 0-7618-2612-2 (pbk. : alk. paper) DDC 658.4/013
1. Management by objectives. 2. Total quality management. 3. Liberty. 4. Equality. I. Title.
HD30.65 .S46 2003

SENATORS (UNITED STATES). *See* **LEGISLATORS - UNITED STATES.**

Sene boʻer ba-esh.
Shtern, Shemuʼel Eliʻezer. Sefer Sene boʻer ba-esh. Bene Beraḳ : Mekhon "Mayim ḥayim", 762 [2002]

SENECA, LUCIUS ANNAEUS, CA. 4 B.C.-65 A.D. - CRITICISM AND INTERPRETATION.
Zöller, Rainer. Die Vorstellung vom Willen in der Morallehre Senecas. Leipzig : K.G. Saur, 2003.
PA6686 .Z65 2003

Sened, Alexander.
Korczak, Janusz, 1878-1942. [Works. Hebrew. 1996] Ketavim. [Tel Aviv] : Yad va-shem : ha-Agudah ʻa. sh. Yanush Ḳortsʼaḳ be-Yiśraʼel : Bet Loḥame ha-geṭaʼot ʻa. sh. Yitshaḳ Ḳatsenelson : ha-Ḳibuts ha-meʼuḥad, [1996-
LB775.K627 K48 1996 <Hebr>

Sened, Yonat.
Korczak, Janusz, 1878-1942. [Works. Hebrew. 1996] Ketavim. [Tel Aviv] : Yad va-shem : ha-Agudah ʻa. sh. Yanush Ḳortsʼaḳ be-Yiśraʼel : Bet Loḥame ha-geṭaʼot ʻa. sh. Yitshaḳ Ḳatsenelson : ha-Ḳibuts ha-meʼuḥad, [1996-
LB775.K627 K48 1996 <Hebr>

SENEGAL - ECONOMIC CONDITIONS.
Mustafa, Huda Nura. Practicing beauty. 1997.

SENESCENCE. *See* **AGING; OLD AGE.**

Sengers, Gerda. Vrouwen en demonen : zar en korangenezing in hedendaags Egypte / Gerda Sengers. Amsterdam : Het Spinhuis, 2000. 262 p. ; 23 cm. Originally presented as the author's thesis (doctoral)--Rotterdam, 2000. Includes bibliographical references (p. [247]-262). ISBN 90-5589-165-7
1. Spiritual healing - Egypt. 2. Healing - Religious aspects - Islam. 3. Zār - Egypt. 4. Women - Egypt - Social conditions. I. Title.
BF1275.F3 S46 2000

Women and demons : cult healing in Islamic Egypt / by Gerda Sengers. Leiden ; Boston : Brill, 2003. viii, 302 p. ; 25 cm. (International studies in sociology and social anthropology, 0074-8684 ; v. 86) Includes bibliographical references (p. [280]-294) and indexes. ISBN 90-04-12771-2 DDC 297.3/9
1. Spiritual healing - Egypt. 2. Healing - Religious aspects - Islam. 3. Zār - Egypt. 4. Women - Egypt - Cairo - Social conditions. I. Title. II. Series.
BF1275.F3 S463 2003

Senie latviešu sapņu skaidrojumi. [Rīga] : Tapals, 2002. 157 p. ; 22 cm. Based on Latviešu tautas sapņu iztulkošana / Arvīds Aizsils. Rīga : Latviešu folkloras krātuves izdevums, 1939. Includes bibliographical references (p. 44). ISBN 9984720128
1. Dream interpretation - Dictionaries - Latvian. 2. Folklore - Latvia - Dictionaries - Latvian. I. Aizsils, Arvīds, 1904-1940. Latviešu tautas sapņu iztulkošana.
BF1098.L35 S46 2002

SENIOR CITIZENS. *See* **AGED.**

SENIORS (OLDER PERSONS). *See* **AGED.**

Le sens de bâtir.
Rábago, Jesús. Lecques : Théétète, c2000.
NA2500 .R29 2000

Le sens de la mémoire.
Tadié, Jean-Yves, 1936- Paris : Gallimard, c1999.
BF371 .T32 1999

Sens de l'existence.
Clair, André. Paris : Armand Colin, c2002.

Sens social (Rennes, France)
Les cultes médiatiques. Rennes : Presses universitaires de Rennes, [2002]

Sensation and perception.
Coren, Stanley. 6th ed. Hoboken, NJ : J. Wiley & Sons, c2004.
BF233 .C59 2004

Sense & nonsense.
Laland, Kevin N. Sense and nonsense. Oxford ; New York : Oxford University Press, 2002.
BF701 .L34 2002

Sense and nonsense.
Laland, Kevin N. Oxford ; New York : Oxford University Press, 2002.
BF701 .L34 2002

A sense of self.
Cottle, Thomas J. Amherst : University of Massachusetts Press, c2003.
BF697 .C68 2003

SENSES AND SENSATION. *See also* **CONTROL (PSYCHOLOGY); ORIENTATION (PHYSIOLOGY); PAIN; PERCEPTION; PLEASURE; SEXUAL EXCITEMENT.**
Ananʼev, Boris Gerasimovich. Psikhologiia chuvstvennogo poznaniia. Moskva : "Nauka", 2001.
BF233 .A5 2001

Coren, Stanley. Sensation and perception. 6th ed. Hoboken, NJ : J. Wiley & Sons, c2004.
BF233 .C59 2004

Jackson, Holbrook, 1874-1948. [Anatomy of bibliomania. Portuguese. Selections] O tato. São Paulo : Imprensa Oficial do Estado, 2002.
Z992 .J33 2002

Sensible flesh. Philadelphia, PA : University of Pennsylvania Press, 2003.
BF275 .S46 2003

SENSES AND SENSATION IN CHILDREN. *See* **PERCEPTION IN CHILDREN.**

Sensible decisions.
Rescher, Nicholas. Lanham, Md. ; Oxford : Rowman & Littlefield Publishers, c2003.
B945.R453 S46 2003

Sensible flesh : on touch in early modern culture / edited by Elizabeth D. Harvey. Philadelphia, PA : University of Pennsylvania Press, 2003. vi, 320 p. : ill. ; 24 cm. Includes bibliographical references (p. [255]-307) and index. CONTENTS: Introduction: The "Sense of all senses" / Elizabeth D. Harvey -- Anxious and fatal contacts: taming the contagious touch / Margaret Healy -- "Handling soft the hurts": sexual healing and manual contact in Orlando Furioso Queene, The Faerie Queene, and All's well that ends well / Sujata Iyengar -- The subject of touch: medical authority in early modern midwifery / Eve Keller -- The touching organ: allegory, anatomy, and the renaissance skin envelope / Elizabeth D. Harvey -- As long as a Swan's neck? The significance of the "enlarged" clitoris for early modern anatomy / Bettina Mathes -- New world contacts and the trope of the "naked savage" / Scott Manning Stevens -- Noli me tangere: colonialist imperatives and enclosure acts in early modern England / Elizabeth Sauer and Lisa M. Smith -- Acting with tact: touch and theater in the Renaissance / Carla Mazzio -- Living in a material world: Margaret Cavendish's The convent of pleasure / Misty G. Anderson -- Touch in the Hypnerotomachia Poliphili: the sensual ethics of architecture / Rebekah Smick -- The touch of the blind man: the phenomenology of vividness in Italian Renaissance Art / Jodi Cranston -- Afterword: touching rhetoric / Lynn Enterline. ISBN 0-8122-3693-9 (cloth : alk. paper) ISBN 0-8122-1829-9 (pbk. : alk. paper) DDC 152/.82
1. Touch. 2. Senses and sensation. I. Harvey, Elizabeth D.
BF275 .S46 2003

Sensing corporeally.
Merrell, Floyd, 1937- Toronto ; Buffalo : University of Toronto Press, c2003.
P99 .M477 2003

SENSITIVES (PSYCHICS). *See* **PSYCHICS.**

Senso religioso.
Giussani, Luigi. PerCorso. Milano : Rizzoli, c1997-

SENSUALITY. *See* **SEX (PSYCHOLOGY).**

SENTENCES (GRAMMAR). *See* **GRAMMAR, COMPARATIVE AND GENERAL - SENTENCES.**

Sentieri della mente : filosofia, letteratura, arte e musica in dialogo con la psicoanalisi / a cura di Luigi Longhin, Mauro Mancia ; scritti di: Gabriella Baldissera ... [et al.]. 1. ed. Torino : Bollati Boringhieri, 2001. 357 p. : music ; 24 cm. (Manuali di psicologia, psichiatria, psicoterapia) Includes bibliographical references and index. ISBN 88-339-5671-7 DDC 150
1. Psychoanalysis and art. 2. Psychoanalysis and literature. 3. Psychoanalysis and philosophy. 4. Psychoanalysis and music. I. Longhin, Luigi. II. Mancia, Mauro. III. Baldissera, Gabriella. IV. Series.

Le sentiment d'exister.
Flahault, François, 1943- Paris : Descartes & Cie, c2002.
BD438.5 .F54 2002

Sentimental education in Chinese history.
Santangelo, Paolo. Leiden ; Boston : Brill, 2003.
BF538.C48 S25 2003

SENTIMENTALISM IN LITERATURE.
Fichtelberg, Joseph. Critical fictions. Athens : University of Georgia Press, c2003.
PS366.S35 F53 2003

Seow, C. L. (Choon Leong).
Nissinen, Martti. Prophets and prophecy in the ancient Near East. Atlanta, GA : Society of Biblical Literature, c2003.
BF1762 .N58 2003b

SEPARATE DEVELOPMENT (RACE RELATIONS). *See* **APARTHEID.**

Separation of powers : documents and commentary / edited by Katy J. Harriger. Washington, D.C. : CQ Press, a division of Congressional Quarterly Inc., c2003. xv, 420 p. : ill. ; 24 cm. (Understanding constitutional principles) Includes bibliographical references and an index CONTENTS: Understanding the separation of powers doctrine. The separation of powers at the founding / Keith E. Whittington. The separation of powers in the modern context / Katy J. Harriger -- Core functions of the branches. The lawmaking power / Richard A. Baker. The evolution of presidential power / William E. Leuchtenburg. The law and politics of judicial review / Mark A. Graber -- Boundary struggles between the branches. The power to make war / Nancy Kassop. Emergency powers / Harold C. Relyea. Understanding the impeachment power : lessons from the Clinton case / Michael J. Gerhardt. The debate about the delegation of lawmaking power to the Executive Branch / Thomas O. Sargentich. Congressional power vis-?-vis the states : the context and consequences of the U.S. Supreme Court's decisions / John Dinan. Executive privilege and

congressional and independent investigations / Neal Devins. The Supreme Court and constitutional dialogue / Louis Fisher. ISBN 1-56802-727-3 (hardcover : alk. paper) DDC 320.473/04
1. Separation of powers - United States. 2. United States - Politics and government - 20th century. I. Harriger, Katy J. (Katy Jean) II. Series.
JK305 .S465 2003

SEPARATION OF POWERS - UNITED STATES.
Separation of powers. Washington, D.C. : CQ Press, a division of Congressional Quarterly Inc., c2003.
JK305 .S465 2003

SEPARATION (PSYCHOLOGY).
Anderson, Susan, C.S.W. Black swan. Huntington, N.Y. : Rock Foundations Press, c1999.
BF575.R35 A52 1999

Anderson, Susan, C.S.W. The journey from heartbreak to connection. Berkley trade pbk. ed. New York : Berkley Books, 2003.
BF575.R35 A533 2003

SEPARATION (PSYCHOLOGY) - CASE STUDIES.
Hell hath no fury. 1st Carroll & Graf ed. New York : Carroll & Graf Publishers, 2002.
HQ801 .H45 2002

SEPHIRA (CABALA). *See* **SEFIROT (CABALA).**

SEPHIROT (CABALA). *See* **SEFIROT (CABALA).**

SEPHIROTH (CABALA). *See* **SEFIROT (CABALA).**

SEPTEMBER 11 TERRORIST ATTACKS, 2001.
Baudrillard, Jean. [Esprit du terrorisme. English] The spirit of terrorism and requiem for the Twin Towers. London : Verso, 2002.
HV6431 .B38 2002

Giuliani, Rudolph W. Leadership. London : Little, Brown, 2002.

L'incubo globale. Bergamo : Moretti & Vitali, c2002.

Kendra, James M. Elements of community resilience in the World Trade Center attack. [Newark, Del.?] : Disaster Research Center, University of Delaware, 2001.

Lincoln, Bruce. Holy terrors. Chicago : University of Chicago Press, 2003.
BL65.T47 L56 2003

Noonan, Peggy, 1950- A heart, a cross & a flag. New York : Free Press, c2003.
E903 .N66 2003

Potorti, David. September 11th Families for Peaceful Tomorrows. New York, NY : RDV Books, c2003.

Van de Weyer, Robert. The shared well. 1st ed. Washington, D.C. : Brassey's, c2002.
BL65.P7 V36 2002

Vint/age 2001 conference : [videorecording]. New York, c2001.

SEPTEMBER 11 TERRORIST ATTACKS, 2001 - BIBLICAL TEACHING.
Glazerson, Matityahu. Migdele ha-te'omim be-diluge otiyot ba-Torah. Yerushalayim : Yerid ha-sefarim, 2002.

SEPTEMBER 11 TERRORIST ATTACKS, 2001 - CAUSES.
Crockatt, Richard. America embattled. London ; New York : Routledge, 2003.
E902 .C76 2003

SEPTEMBER 11 TERRORIST ATTACKS, 2001 - INFLUENCE.
Crockatt, Richard. America embattled. London ; New York : Routledge, 2003.
E902 .C76 2003

SEPTEMBER 11 TERRORIST ATTACKS, 2001 - MISCELLANEA.
9-11 in American culture. Walnut Creek ; Oxford : AltaMira Press, c2003.
HV6432.7 .A13 2003

Civilization under attack. 1st ed. St. Paul, Minn. : Llewellyn Publications, 2001.
BF1729.U5 C57 2001

SEPTEMBER 11 TERRORIST ATTACKS, 2001 - PSYCHOLOGICAL ASPECTS.
The day our world changed. New York : Harry N. Abrams Inc., 2002.

Pyszczynski, Thomas A. In the wake of 9/11. Washington, DC : American Psychological Association, c2003.

HV6432 .P97 2003
Rojas Marcos, Luis, 1943- Más allá del 11 de septiembre. [Madrid] : Espasa, c2002.
HV6432.7 .R64 2002

Vint/age 2001 conference : [videorecording]. New York, c2001.

SEPTEMBER 11 TERRORIST ATTACKS, 2001 - RELIGIOUS ASPECTS - JUDAISM.
Glazerson, Matityahu. Migdele ha-te'omim be-diluge otiyot ba-Torah. Yerushalayim : Yerid ha-sefarim, 2002.

SEPTEMBER 11 TERRORIST ATTACKS, 2001 - SOCIAL ASPECTS.
Monahan, Brian. From ground zero to ground hero. [Newark, Del.?] : Disaster Research Center, University of Delaware, 2001.

September 11th Families for Peaceful Tomorrows.
Potorti, David. September 11th Families for Peaceful Tomorrows. New York, NY : RDV Books, c2003.

September Eleventh Families for Peaceful Tomorrows.
Potorti, David. September 11th Families for Peaceful Tomorrows. New York, NY : RDV Books, c2003.

Sepúlveda, Jesús. El jardín de las peculiaridades / Jesús Sepúlveda. Buenos Aires : Ediciones del Leopardo, [2002] 119 p. ; 20 cm. ISBN 9879891139
1. Humanism - 20th century. 2. Philosophy, Modern. 3. Knowledge, Theory of. I. Title.

Sequeri, Pier Angelo. L'umano alla prova : soggetto, identità, limite / Pierangelo Sequeri. Milano : V & P Università, c2002. 159 p. ; 22 cm. (Filosofia. Ricerche)
Includes bibliographical references. ISBN 88-343-0792-5 DDC 128
1. Subjectivity. 2. Identity (Philosophical concept) 3. Ethics. I. Title. II. Series: Filosofia. Ricerche.
BD222.S47 U6 2002

Ser ou não ter.
Vieira, Anselmo, 1923- Lisboa : Roma Editora, [2002]-

Ser y participación.
González, Angel Luis. 3. ed. revisada y ampliada. Pamplona : Ediciones Universidad de Navarra, c2001.
BX4700.T6 G66 2001

SERAPHIM. *See* **ANGELS.**

SERBIA - CIVILIZATION - BYZANTINE INFLUENCES.
Vizantijska filozofija u srednjevekovnoj Srbiji. Beograd : Stubovi kulture, 2002.

SERBIAN LITERATURE - HISTORY AND CRITICISM.
Biserje. 3., dop. izd. Sarajevo : Ljiljan, 1998.

Deretić, Jovan. Kratka istorija srpske književnosti. 3., prerađeno i dop. izd. Novi Sad : Svetovi, 2001.

Jerotić, Vladeta. [Selections 2000] Izabrani ogledi. Beograd: Srpska književna zadruga, 2000.
BF109.J47 A25 2000

Lis, Izabela. Śmierć w literaturze staroserbskiej. Poznań : Wydawn. Nauk. Uniwersytetu im. Adama Mickiewicza w Poznaniu, 2003.
PG1406 .L59 2003

SERBIAN LITERATURE - PSYCHOLOGICAL ASPECTS.
Jerotić, Vladeta. [Selections 2000] Izabrani ogledi. Beograd: Srpska književna zadruga, 2000.
BF109.J47 A25 2000

SERBIANS. *See* **SERBS.**

SERBO-CROATIANS. *See* **SERBS.**

SERBS - HISTORY.
Petrović, Aleksandar M. Praistorija Srba. Beograd : Pešić i sinovi, 2001.
DR1953 .P48 2001

SERBS - ORIGIN.
Petrović, Aleksandar M. Praistorija Srba. Beograd : Pešić i sinovi, 2001.
DR1953 .P48 2001

Serenity in motion.
O'Hara, Nancy. New York : Warner Books, 2003.
BF637.P3 O42 2003

SERFDOM. *See* **LAND TENURE; SLAVERY.**

Sergeev, K. K. (Konstantin Konstantinovich)
Filosofskaia psikhologiia / K.K. Sergeev. Tol'iatti : "Sovremennik", 1999. 142 p. ; 20 cm. ISBN 5852341045
1. Psychology - Philosophy. I. Title.

BF38 .S47 1999
Seria Filologia słowiańska
(nr 9) Lis, Izabela. Śmierć w literaturze staroserbskiej. Poznań : Wydawn. Nauk. Uniwersytetu im. Adama Mickiewicza w Poznaniu, 2003.
PG1406 .L59 2003

SERIAL KILLING. *See* **SERIAL MURDERS.**

SERIAL KILLINGS. *See* **SERIAL MURDERS.**

SERIAL MURDERS - FICTION.
Kava, Alex. The soul catcher. Waterville, Me. : Thorndike Press, 2003, 2002.
PS3561.A8682 S6 2003

Serie Antropología (San José, Costa Rica)
Burggraf, Jutta. Qué quiere decir género? 1. ed. San Jose, Costa Rica : Promesa, 2001.

Serie Arias Montano
(59) Pérez-Embid Wamba, Javier. Hagiología y sociedad en la España medieval. Huelva : Universidad de Huelva, 2002.
BX4659.S8 P47 2002

Serie Arqueología (Mexico City, Mexico)
Relaciones hombre-fauna. México, D.F. : CONACULTA, INAH ; Plaza y Valdes, 2002.
QL85 .R453 2002

Serie Breves (Fondo de Cultura Económica (Mexico))
Cornblit, Oscar. Violencia social, genocidio y terrorismo. 1. ed. México, D.F. : Fondo de Cultura Económica, 2002.
HM886 .C67 2002

Serie di psicologia (Franco Angeli editore)
(136.) La comunicazione nei processi sociali e organizzativi. Nuova ed. aggiornata. Milano, Italy : FrancoAngeli, [2001?], c1997.

Serie Documentos de trabajo C.P.U.
(no. 95/11.) Rodríguez, Luis. Patologías complejas (versión preliminar). [Santiago, Chile] : Corporación de Promoción Universitaria, [1995]

Serie "Estudios" (Instituto de la Mujer (Spain))
(71.) Género, desarrollo psicosocial y trastornos de la imagen corporal. Madrid : Instituto de la Mujer, 2001.

Serie General universitaria
(16) Menéndez, Eduardo L. La parte negada de la cultura. Barcelona : Edicions Bellaterra, c2002.
HM1121 .M46 2002

Serie Poesía (Biblioteca Nacional (Dominican Republic))
La palabra como cuerpo del delito. Santo Domingo, República Dominicana : Biblioteca Nacional "Dr. Pedro Henríquez Ureña", 2001.

Serie Reflexiones en el Museo
(no. 2) Krebs, Víctor J., 1957- Del alma y el arte. Caracas, Venezuela : Museo de Bellas Artes, 1997.
N70 .K74 1997

Série V.O.
Cyrulnik, Boris. Dialogue sur la nature humaine. La Tour d'Aigues : Editions de l'Aube, c2000.
BF57 .C97 2000

Series in affective science
Handbook of affective sciences. Oxford ; New York : Oxford University Press, 2003.
BF511 .H35 2003

Memory and emotion. Oxford University Press : New York, 2003.
BF378.A87 M46 2003

Nonverbal behavior in clinical settings. Oxford ; New York : Oxford University Press, 2003.
RC489.N65 N66 2003

Series in applied psychology
Cohen, Aaron, 1952- Multiple commitments in the workplace. Mahwah, New Jersey : Lawrence Erlbaum Associates, 2003.
HD58.7 .C6213 2003

Vardi, Yoav, 1944- Misbehavior in organizations. Mahwah, NJ ; London : Lawrence Erlbaum, 2004.
HD58.7 .V367 2004

Series on innovative intelligence
(v.3) Internet-based intelligent information processing systems. Singapore ; River Edge, NJ : World Scientific, 2003.

The series on school reform
Goodman, Steven. Teaching youth media. New York : Teachers College Press, c2003.

LB1043 .G59 2003

Series Q
Cvetkovich, Ann, 1957- An archive of feelings.
Durham : Duke University Press, 2003.
HQ75.5 .C89 2003

Seriia "Filosofska antropologiia"
Lichev, Valeri. TSinichnoto, ili, Igrata na vlast i udovolstvie. Sofiia : EON-2000, 2000.
B809.5 .L53 2000

Seriia "Grani nashego mira"
Vinokurov, Igor' Charodei ponevole. Moskva : AiF-Print, 2003.
BF1288 .V55 2003

Seriia "Kniga Sitarkhisa"
Ul'rikh, I. V. Zhizn' cheloveka. Moskva : Izd-vo "Litan", 1999.

Seriia "Nauchnye konferentsii Instituta psikhologii i pedagogiki Viatskogo gosudarstvennogo pedagogicheskogo universiteta"
Psikhologicheskie i pedagogicheskie problemy samorazvitiia lichnosti. Kirov : Viatskiĭ gos. pedagogicheskiĭ universitet, 2002.
BF723.P4 P78 2002

Seriia Neĭro-lingvisticheskoe programmirovanie
(vyp. 2) Koleda, Sergeĭ. Modelirovanie bessoznatel'nogo. Moskva : In-t obshchegumanitarnykh issledovaniĭ, 2000.
BF637.N46 K65 2000

Seriia "Sotsial'nye i gumanitarnye nauki v XX veke"
XX vek. Moskva : INION RAN, 2001-
XX vek. Moskva : INION RAN, 2001-

Seriia Tela mysli
Tul'chinskiĭ, G. L. (Grigoriĭ L'vovich) Postchelovecheskaia personologiia. Sankt-Peterburg : Aleteĭa, 2002.
BD331 .T84 2002

Seriia Uchebniki psikhoterapii
(vyp. 1) Burlakova, N. S. Proektivnye metody. Moskva : In-t obshchegumanitarnykh issledovaniĭ, 2001.
BF698.7 .B87 2001

Seriia "Zemnye fenomeny"
Karpenko, M. (Maksim) Vselennaia razumnaia = 2. perer. izd. Moskva : MAIK Nauka/Interperiodika, 2001.
BF1036 .K37 2001

Sermonti, Giuseppe. Il mito della grande madre : dalle amigdale a Çatal Hüyük / Giuseppe Sermonti. Milano : Mimesis, c2002. 151 p. : ill. ; 21 cm. (Collana Mimesis) (Airesis) Includes bibliographical references and index. ISBN 88-8483-082-6 DDC 291
1. Çatal Mound (Turkey) 2. Goddess religion - Turkey. 3. Religion, Prehistoric - Turkey. 4. Goddess religion. 5. Religion, Prehistoric. I. Title. II. Series. III. Series: Airesis

SEROTONIN - ANTAGONISTS. *See* **LSD (DRUG).**

Serres, Michel. L'incandescent / Michel Serres. [Paris] : Pommier, c2003. 351 p. ; 21 cm. (Essais) ISBN 2-7465-0065-5 DDC 194
1. Philosophy. I. Title. II. Series: Dolto, Françoise. Essais.

Serret, Estela. Identidad femenina y proyecto ético / Estela Serret. 1. ed. México : UNAM, PUEG : Universidad Autónoma Metropolitana, Azcapotzalco : M.A. Porrúa, 2002. 301 p. ; 21 cm. (Las Ciencias sociales. Estudios de género) Includes bibliographical references (p. 291-301). ISBN 9707012528
1. Women - Identity. 2. Women - Psychology. 3. Femeninsm. I. Title. II. Series: Colección Las Ciencias sociales. Estudios de género.

Sertillanges, Thomas.
Chouchena, Emmanuel. L'homme, espoir de dieu. Paris : Trajectoire, 2001.

Sertori, J. M. Face reading : a beginner's guide / J. M. Sertori. London : Hodder & Stoughton, 2000. 90 p. : ill. ; 20 cm. Includes bibliographical references (p. 90). ISBN 0-340-77228-X DDC 138
1. Physiognomy. I. Title.

La servante et la consolatrice : la philosophie dans ses rapports avec la théologie au Moyen Age / études réunies par Jean-Luc Solère et Zénon Kaluza. Paris : Vrin, 2002. xv, 258 p. ; 24 cm. (Textes et traditions ; 3) Includes bibliographical references and indexes. ISBN 2-7116-1563-4 DDC 100
1. Philosophy, Medieval. 2. Theology, Doctrinal - History - Middle Ages, 600-1500. I. Solère, J.-L. (Jean-Luc) II. Kałuża, Zenon. III. Series.
B721 .S479 2002

SERVIANS. *See* **SERBS.**

Service de la recherche en éducation (Geneva, Switzerland).
Ducret, Jean-Jacques, 1946- Jean Piaget, 1868-1979. Genève, Switzerland : Service de la recherche en éducation, c2000.
BF311 .D813 2000

SERVICE INDUSTRIES. *See* **UNDERTAKERS AND UNDERTAKING.**

SERVICE STATIONS. *See* **AUTOMOBILE REPAIR SHOPS.**

SERVICEMEN, MILITARY. *See* **SOLDIERS.**

SERVICES, HUMAN. *See* **HUMAN SERVICES.**

SERVITUDE. *See* **SLAVERY.**

Seryĭ, A. V.
Sibirskaia psikhologiia segodnia. Kemerovo : Kemerovskiĭ gos. universitet, 2002.
BF20 .S53 2002

Sesma, Arturo.
Scales, Peter, 1949- Coming into their own. Minneapolis, MN : Search Institute, c2004.
BF721 .S347 2004

SET THEORY. *See* **LOGIC, SYMBOLIC AND MATHEMATICAL.**

Set yourself free.
Krauss, Sandy. North Royalton, Ohio : Success Talks Pub., c1999.
BF637.S4 K73 1999

Sethi, S. Prakash. Setting global standards : guidelines for creating codes of conduct in multinational corporations / S. Prakash Sethi. Hoboken, N.J. : J. Wiley, c2003. xiii, 306 p. : ill. ; 24 cm. Includes bibliographical references (p. 291-298) and index. ISBN 0-471-41455-7 (cloth) DDC 658.3/14
1. International business enterprises - Management. 2. Business etiquette. 3. Corporate culture. I. Title.
HD62.4 .S48 2003

Settersten, Richard A.
Invitation to the life course. Amityville, N.Y. : Baywood Pub. Co., c2003.
HQ1061 .I584 2003

Setti, Nadia.
Simone Weil, la passion de la raison. Paris : Harmattan, c2003.
B2430.W474 S55 2003

Settineri, Franciso Franke.
Aventuras do sentido. Porto Alegre : EDIPUCRS, 2002.

Setting global standards.
Sethi, S. Prakash. Hoboken, N.J. : J. Wiley, c2003.
HD62.4 .S48 2003

Setting standards in graduate education : psychology's commitment to excellence in accreditation / edited by Elizabeth M. Altmaier. 1st ed. Washington, DC : American Psychological Association, c2003. x, 191 p. ; 26 cm. Includes bibliographical references and index. Table of contents URL: http://www.loc.gov/catdir/toc/ecip041/2003005129.html CONTENTS: Introduction in psychology and public accountability / Paul D. Nelson and Laura C. Messenger -- The history of accreditation of doctoral programs in psychology / Elizabeth M. Altmaier -- The history of accreditation of internship programs and postdoctoral residencies / Cynthia D. Belar and Nadine Kaslow -- The impact of accreditation on the practice of professional psychology / Tommy T. Stigall -- The future of accreditation / Deborah C. Beidel, Susan D. Phillips, and Susan Zlotlow. ISBN 1-59147-009-9 (pbk.) DDC 150/.71/73
1. Psychology - Study and teaching (Graduate) - United States - History. I. Altmaier, Elizabeth M.
BF80.7.U6 S48 2003

SETTLEMENT OF LAND. *See* **LAND SETTLEMENT.**

SEVEN CAPITAL SINS. *See* **DEADLY SINS.**

Seven choices.
Neeld, Elizabeth Harper, 1940- New York : Warner Books, c2003.
BF575.G7 N44 2003

SEVEN DEADLY SINS. *See* **DEADLY SINS.**

Seven heavens.
Meier, Levi. [S.l.] : Devora Publishing, c2002.
BF789.D4 M39 2002

Seven myths of the Spanish conquest.
Restall, Matthew, 1964- Oxford ; New York : Oxford University Press, 2003.
F1230 .R47 2003

Seven steps to heaven.
Keller, Joyce (Joyce E.) New York : Simon & Schuster, 2003.
BF1261.2 .K45 2003

Sévérac, Pascal.
Fortitude et servitude. Paris : Kimé, c2003.

Sevilla Fernández, José M.
Metáfora y discurso filosófico. Madrid : Tecnos, 2000.

SEX. *See also* **SEX (BIOLOGY); SEX INSTRUCTION.**
Abramson, Paul R., 1949- With pleasure. Rev. ed. Oxford ; New York : Oxford University Press, 2002.
HQ23 .A25 2002

Barber, Nigel, 1955- The science of romance. Amherst, N.Y. : Prometheus Books, 2002.
HQ21 .B184 2002

Bhattacharyya, Gargi, 1964- Sexuality and society. London ; New York : Routledge, 2002.
HQ21 .B6185 2002

Brenot, Philippe. Le sexe et l'amour. Paris : Jacob, c2003.

Buss, David M. The evolution of desire. Rev. ed. New York : BasicBooks, c2003.

Cvetkovich, Ann, 1957- An archive of feelings. Durham : Duke University Press, 2003.
HQ75.5 .C89 2003

Dacquino, Giacomo, 1930- Bisogno d'amore. 1. ed. Milano : Mondadori, 2002.
BF697.5.S43 D33 2002

Dīkṣita, Mathurā Prasāda, 1878-1978. [Kelikutūhala. Hindi & Sanskrit] Kelikutūhalam. Vārāṇasī : Krshadāsa Akādamī, 2002.
HQ470.S3 D55155 2002

Fisher, Helen E. Why we love. 1st ed. New York : Henry Holt and Company, 2004.
BF575.L8 F53 2004

Francis, Richard C., 1953- Why men won't ask for directions. Princeton, N.J. : Princeton University Press, 2004.
BF698.95 .F73 2004

Gendered sexualities. New York : JAI, 2002.
HQ1075.A27 vol. 6

Judson, Olivia. Dr. Tatiana's sex advice to all creation. 1st ed. New York : Metropolitan Books, 2002.
HQ25 .J83 2002

Lichev, Valeri. TSinichnoto, ili, Igrata na vlast i udovolstvie. Sofiia : EON-2000, 2000.
B809.5 .L53 2000

Moreno, María, 1947- El fin del sexo y otras mentiras. Buenos Aires : Editorial Sudamericana, c2002.

Moser, Antônio. O enigma da esfinge. 3a ed. Petrópolis : Editora Vozes, 2002, c2001.

Nāgārjuna, Siddha. [Ratiśāstra. English & Sanskrit] Conjugal love in India. Leiden Boston, MA : Brill, 2002.
HQ470.S3 N3413 2002

Nagel, Joane. Race, ethnicity, and sexuality. New York : Oxford University Press, 2003.
HQ21 .N195 2003

Pfaller, Robert. Die Illusionen der anderen. 1. Aufl. Frankfurt : Suhrkamp, 2002.

Rozin, V. M. Liubov' i seksual'nost' v kul'ture, sem'e i vzgliadakh na polovoe vospitanie. Moskva : Logos : Vysshaia shkola, 1999.
BF575.L8 R69 1999

Sexuelle Szenen. Opladen : Leske + Budrich, 2000.
HQ16 .S474 2000

Stainton Rogers, Wendy. The psychology of gender and sexuality. Philadelphia : Open University Press, 2001.
BF692 .S72 2001

Zwang, Gérard. Aux origines de la sexualité humaine. 1re éd. Paris : Presses universitaires de France, 2002.
HQ21 .Z935 2002

Sex advice to all creation.
Judson, Olivia. Dr. Tatiana's sex advice to all creation. 1st ed. New York : Metropolitan Books, 2002.
HQ25 .J83 2002

SEX AND LAW. *See* **SEX CRIMES; STERILIZATION, EUGENIC.**

SEX AND RELIGION. *See* **SEX - RELIGIOUS ASPECTS.**

SEX BIAS. *See* **SEXISM.**

SEX (BIOLOGY). *See also* **SEXUAL EXCITEMENT.**
Shlain, Leonard. Sex, time, and power. New York ; London : Viking, 2003.
HQ23 .S45 2003

Zwang, Gérard. Aux origines de la sexualité humaine. 1re éd. Paris : Presses universitaires de France, 2002.
HQ21 .Z935 2002

SEX CHROMOSOMES. *See* **Y CHROMOSOME.**

SEX COUNSELING. *See* **SEX INSTRUCTION.**

SEX CRIMES. *See* **CHILD SEXUAL ABUSE; SEDUCTION.**

SEX CRIMES - PSYCHOLOGICAL ASPECTS.
Verführung, Trauma, Missbrauch. [2. Aufl.]. Giessen : Psychosozial-Verlag, c2002.

SEX CUSTOMS.
Pasini, Willy. I nuovi comportamenti amorosi. 2. ed. Milano : Mondadori, 2002.

Pulman, Bertrand. Anthropologie et psychanalyse. Paris : Presses universitaires de France, 2002.
GN502 .P85 2002

SEX CUSTOMS - INDIA - EARLY WORKS TO 1800.
Pinkney, Andrea Marion. [Kāmasūtra. English.] The Kama Sutra illuminated. New York, N.Y. : Abrams, c2002.

SEX DIFFERENCES.
Braidotti, Rosi. [Nomadic subjects. Italian] Soggetto nomade. Roma : Donzelli, 1995.

Fisher, Helen E. Why we love. 1st ed. New York : Henry Holt and Company, 2004.
BF575.L8 F53 2004

Francis, Richard C., 1953- Why men won't ask for directions. Princeton, N.J. : Princeton University Press, 2004.
BF698.95 .F73 2004

Gênero em matizes. Bragança Paulista, SP : EDUSF, [2002]

Irigaray, Luce. [Voie de l'amour. English] The way of love. London ; New York : Continuum, 2002.
BF575.L8 I7513 2002

Irigaray, Luce. The way of love. London ; New York : Continuum, 2002.

Judson, Olivia. Dr. Tatiana's sex advice to all creation. 1st ed. New York : Metropolitan Books, 2002.
HQ25 .J83 2002

Kītā, Va. Gender. Calcutta : Stree, 2002.
HQ1075 .K576 2002

Kōvintan, Ka. Tamiḻt tiraippaṭaṅkaḷil āṇ-peṇ pāl pēṭam. 1. patippu. Ceṉṉai : Kumaraṉ Papḷiṣars, 2001.
BF692.2 .K68 2001

Many faces of gender. Boulder : University Press of Colorado ; Calgary, Alta., Canada : University of Calgary Press, c2002.
E98.P95 M35 2002

SEX DIFFERENCES IN EDUCATION.
Tooley, James. The miseducation of women. London ; New York : Continuum, 2002.
HQ1154 .T64 2002

SEX DIFFERENCES IN EDUCATION - SOCIAL ASPECTS.
Boys, literacies, and schooling. Buckingham [England] ; Philadelphia : Open University Press, 2002.
LC1390 .B69 2002

SEX DIFFERENCES - PHILOSOPHY.
Heinamaa, Sara, 1960- Toward a phenomenology of sexual difference. Lanham, Md. ; Oxford : Rowman & Littlefield Publishers, c2003.
HQ1208 .B3523 2003

SEX DIFFERENCES - PHILOSOPHY - HISTORY.
Gender and difference in the Middle Ages. Minneapolis : University of Minnesota Press, c2003.
HQ1143 .G44 2003

SEX DIFFERENCES (PSYCHOLOGY). *See also* **SEX ROLE.**

Barber, Nigel, 1955- The science of romance. Amherst, N.Y. : Prometheus Books, 2002.
HQ21 .B184 2002

Continental feminism reader. Lanham, Md. : Rowman & Littlefield Publishers, c2003.
HQ1075 .C668 2003

Darlington, Cynthia L. The female brain. London ; New York : Taylor & Francis, c2002.
QP402 .D366 2002

Eller, Cynthia (Cynthia Lorraine) Am I a woman? Boston : Beacon Press, c2003.
HQ1190 .E424 2003

Giuffrida, Angela, 1943- Il corpo pensa. Roma : Prospettiva, c2002.

Hoffmann, Arne. Sind Frauen bessere Menschen? Berlin : Schwarzkopf & Schwarzkopf, 2001.
HQ1075 .H64 2001

Kimmel, Michael S. The gendered society. 2nd ed. New York : Oxford University Press, 2004.
HQ1075 .K547 2004

Korsström, Tuva. Kan kvinnor tänka? Stockholm/ Stehag : Symposion, 2002.

Lévesque, Claude, 1927- Par-delà le masculin et le féminin. Paris : Aubier, 2002.

Muraro, Rose Marie. Feminino e masculino. Rio de Janeiro : Sextante, 2002.
HQ801 .M87 2002

Paquette, Didier. La mascarade interculturelle. Paris : Harmattan, c2002.

Stainton Rogers, Wendy. The psychology of gender and sexuality. Philadelphia : Open University Press, 2001.
BF692 .S72 2001

SEX DIFFERENCES (PSYCHOLOGY) - CONGRESSES.
Gender, vlast', kul'tura. Saratov : Saratovskiĭ gos. tekhn. universitet, 2000.
HQ1075 .G4667 2000

Konferent︠s︡i︠a︡ "Gendernyĭ podkhod v psikhologicheskom konsul'tirovanii" (2002 : Evropeĭskiĭ Gumanitarnyĭ Universitet) Gendernyĭ podkhod v psikhologicheskikh issledovani︠i︡akh i konsul'tirovanii. Minsk : Evropeĭskiĭ Gumanitarnyĭ Universitet, 2002.
BF201.4 .K66 2002

SEX DIFFERENCES (PSYCHOLOGY) - HISTORY.
Storkey, Elaine, 1943- Created or constructed? Carlisle [Eng.] : Paternoster Press, 2000.

SEX DIFFERENCES (PSYCHOLOGY) - TEXTBOOKS.
The psychology of gender. 2nd ed. New York : Guilford Press, 2004.
BF692.2 .P764 2004

SEX DIFFERENTIATION. *See* **SEX DIFFERENCES.**

SEX DISCRIMINATION.
Kimmel, Michael S. The gendered society. 2nd ed. New York : Oxford University Press, 2004.
HQ1075 .K547 2004

Oakley, Ann. Gender on planet Earth. Oxford : Polity, 2002.

SEX DISCRIMINATION IN EMPLOYMENT.
Hearn, Jeff. Gender, sexuality and violence in organizations. London ; Thousand Oaks : SAGE, 2001.

SEX EDUCATION. *See* **SEX INSTRUCTION.**

SEX (GENDER). *See* **SEX.**

SEX IDENTITY (GENDER IDENTITY). *See* **GENDER IDENTITY.**

SEX IN ART. *See* **EROTIC ART.**

SEX IN MARRIAGE.
Nāgārjuna, Siddha. [Ratiśāstra. English & Sanskrit] Conjugal love in India. Leiden Boston, MA : Brill, 2002.
HQ470.S3 N3413 2002

SEX (IN RELIGION, FOLKLORE, ETC.). *See* **SEX - RELIGIOUS ASPECTS.**

SEX INSTRUCTION FOR WOMEN.
Darbo, Patrika. 365 glorious nights of love and romance. 1st ed. New York : ReganBooks, c2002.
HQ46 .D35 2002

SEX INSTRUCTION - INDIA - EARLY WORKS TO 1800.
Pinkney, Andrea Marion. [Kāmasūtra. English.] The Kama Sutra illuminated. New York, N.Y. : Abrams, c2002.

SEX - MISCELLANEA.
Ashley, Leonard R. N. The complete book of sex magic. Fort Lee, NJ : Barricade Books, 2003.
BF1623.S4 A85 2002

Kosarin, Jenni. The everything love signs book. Avon, MA : Adams Media, c2004.
BF1729.L6 K67 2004

SEX OFFENSES. *See* **SEX CRIMES.**

SEX - PHYSIOLOGICAL ASPECTS. *See* **SEX (BIOLOGY).**

SEX (PHYSIOLOGY). *See* **SEX (BIOLOGY).**

SEX - PSYCHOLOGICAL ASPECTS. *See* **SEX (PSYCHOLOGY).**

SEX (PSYCHOLOGY). *See also* **GENDER IDENTITY; MASCULINITY; PSYCHOSEXUAL DEVELOPMENT; SEX DIFFERENCES (PSYCHOLOGY); SEX ROLE; SEXISM; SEXUAL EXCITEMENT; SEXUAL ORIENTATION.**
Abelhauser, Alain, 1954- Le sexe et le signifiant. Paris : Seuil, c2002.
BF175.5.S48 A24 2002

Babin, Pierre. La fabrique du sexe. Paris : Textuel, [1999]
BF175.5.S48 B23 1999

Barber, Nigel, 1955- The science of romance. Amherst, N.Y. : Prometheus Books, 2002.
HQ21 .B184 2002

Burggraf, Jutta. Qué quiere decir género? 1. ed. San Jose, Costa Rica : Promesa, 2001.

Buss, David M. The evolution of desire. Rev. ed. New York : BasicBooks, c2003.

Galende, Emiliano. Sexo y amor. 1a ed. Buenos Aires : Paidós, 2001.

Inayat Khan, 1882-1927. Rassa shastra. Berwick, ME : Ibis Press ; York Beach, ME : distributed to the trade by Red Wheel/Weiser, 2003.
BF692 .I5 2003

Lévesque, Claude, 1927- Par-delà le masculin et le féminin. Paris : Aubier, 2002.

Mijolla-Mellor, Sophie de. Le besoin de savoir. Paris : Dunod, c2002.
BF723.S4 M556 2002

Mitchell, Juliet, 1940- Siblings. Cambridge, UK : Polity Press, c2003.
BF723.S43 M58 2003

Pasini, Willy. I nuovi comportamenti amorosi. 2. ed. Milano : Mondadori, 2002.

Pieroni, Osvaldo. Pene d'amore. Soveria Mannelli : Rubbettino, c2002.

Schafer, Roy. Insight and interpretation. New York : Other Press, c2003.
BF173 .S3277 2003

Sexual faces. Madison, Conn. : International Universities Press, c2002.
BF175.5.S48 S47 2002

Stainton Rogers, Wendy. The psychology of gender and sexuality. Philadelphia : Open University Press, 2001.
BF692 .S72 2001

Studies on femininity. London ; New York : Karnac, 2003.

SEX - RELIGIOUS ASPECTS - CHRISTIANITY.
Jantzen, Grace. Power, gender, and Christian mysticism. Cambridge ; New York : Cambridge University Press, 1995.
BV5083 .J36 1995

Moser, Antônio. O enigma da esfinge. 3a ed. Petrópolis : Editora Vozes, 2002, c2001.

SEX ROLE. *See also* **SEXISM.**
Adkins, Lisa, 1966- Revisions. Buckingham [UK] ; Philadelphia : Open University Press, 2002.
HQ1075 .A24 2002

Balancing the scales. Lanham, Md. ; Oxford : University Press of America, c2003.
HQ1075 .B3417 2003

Cealey Harrison, Wendy. Beyond sex and gender. London ; Thousand Oaks, Calif. : SAGE, 2002.

Sex role

HQ1075 .C43 2002

Eller, Cynthia (Cynthia Lorraine) Am I a woman? Boston : Beacon Press, c2003.
HQ1190 .E424 2003

Fthenakis, Wassilios E. Die Rolle des Vaters in der Familie. Stuttgart : Kohlhammer, 2002.

Gender. London ; New York : Routledge, 2002.
HQ1075 .G426 2002

Gender identity and discourse analysis. Amsterdam ; Philadelphia : John Benjamins Pub., c2002.
HQ1075 .G428 2002

Gender nonconformity, race, and sexuality. Madison : University of Wisconsin Press, [2002]
HQ1075 .G4645 2002

Gendered landscapes. University Park, PA : Center for Studies in Landscape History, c2000.

Gendered sexualities. New York : JAI, 2002.
HQ1075.A27 vol. 6

Hoffmann, Arne. Sind Frauen bessere Menschen? Berlin : Schwarzkopf & Schwarzkopf, 2001.
HQ1075 .H64 2001

Hopper, Robert. Gendering talk. East Lansing : Michigan State University Press, c2003.
HQ1075 .H67 2003

Kimmel, Michael S. The gendered society. 2nd ed. New York : Oxford University Press, 2004.
HQ1075 .K547 2004

Kītā, Va. Gender. Calcutta : Stree, 2002.
HQ1075 .K576 2002

Longstaff, Bill, 1934- Confessions of a matriarchist. Calgary : Ballot Pub., 2003.

Montpensier, Anne-Marie-Louise d'Orléans, duchesse de, 1627-1693. [Correspondence. English & French] Against marriage. Chicago : University of Chicago Press, 2002.
DC130.M8 A4 2002

Oakley, Ann. Gender on planet Earth. Oxford : Polity, 2002.

Perspectives on Las Américas. Maden, MA : Blackwell Pub., c2003.
F1410 .P48 2003

Schlafly, Phyllis. Feminist fantasies. Dallas : Spence Publishing Co., 2003.
HQ1150 .S34 2003

Sexuelle Szenen. Opladen : Leske + Budrich, 2000.
HQ16 .S474 2000

Tyler, Carole-Anne. Female impersonation. New York : Routledge, c2003.
HQ1190 .T95 2003

SEX ROLE - BRAZIL.
Gênero em matizes. Bragança Paulista, SP : EDUSF, [2002]

SEX ROLE - CONGRESSES.
Gender, vlast', kul'tura. Saratov : Saratovskiĭ gos. tekhn. universitet, 2000.
HQ1075 .G4667 2000

Jornadas de Roles Sexuales y de Género (2nd : 1995 : Madrid, Spain) Mujer, ideología y población. 1. ed. Madrid : Ediciones Clásicas, 1998.
HQ1075 .J67 1995

Konferentsiia̐ "Gendernyĭ podkhod v psikhologicheskom konsul'tirovanii" (2002 : Evropeĭskiĭ Gumanitarnyĭ Universitet) Gendernyĭ podkhod v psikhologicheskikh issledovaniiakh i konsul'tirovanii. Minsk : Evropeĭskiĭ Gumanitarnyĭ Universitet, 2002.
BF201.4 .K66 2002

The silent revolution. Bad Homburg v.d. Höhe : Herbert Quandt Foundation, 2000.
HQ1075 .S55 2000

Wissen Macht Geschlecht. Zürich : Chronos, c2002.

SEX ROLE - CROSS-CULTURAL STUDIES.
Feminist futures. London ; New York : Zed Books ; New York : Distributed in the USA exclusively by Palgrave, c2003.
HQ1161 .F455 2003

SEX ROLE - DEVELOPED COUNTRIES - CONGRESSES.
The silent revolution. Bad Homburg v.d. Höhe : Herbert Quandt Foundation, 2000.
HQ1075 .S55 2000

SEX ROLE - ECONOMIC ASPECTS.
Gender, development and money. Oxford : Oxfam, 2001.

SEX ROLE - ECUADOR - CONGRESSES.
Masculinidades en Ecuador. Quito, Ecuador : FLACSO ; [S.l.] : UNFPA, 2001.
BF692.5 .M388 2001

Masculinidades en Ecuador. Quito, Ecuador : FLACSO ; [s.l.] : UNFPA, 2001.
BF692.5 .M37 2001

SEX ROLE - EGYPT - CAIRO.
El-Kholy, Heba Aziz. Defiance and compliance. New York : Berghahn Books, 2002.
HQ1793.Z9 C353 2002

SEX ROLE - ENVIRONMENTAL ASPECTS.
Seeing nature through gender. Lawrence : University Press of Kansas, c2003.
GF21 .S44 2003

SEX ROLE - HISTORY.
Ancient queens. Walnut Creek, Calif. ; Oxford : AltaMira Press, c2003.
HQ1127 .A53 2003

French, Marilyn, 1929- From Eve to dawn. Toronto : McArthur, 2002-

Hirdman, Yvonne, 1943- Genus. 1. uppl. Malmö : Liber, 2001.

Mozzhilin, S. I. (Sergeĭ Ivanovich) Obretenie IA i vozniknovenie rannikh form sotsial'nosti. Saratov : Saratovskiĭ gos. sotsial'no-ėkonomicheskiĭ universitet, 2002.
BF697.5.S65 M69 2002

Seeing nature through gender. Lawrence : University Press of Kansas, c2003.
GF21 .S44 2003

Stikker, Allerd, 1928- Closing the gap. Amsterdam : Amsterdam University Press : Salomé, c2002.

Storkey, Elaine, 1943- Created or constructed? Carlisle [Eng.] : Paternoster Press, 2000.

SEX ROLE - HISTORY - TO 1500.
Gender and difference in the Middle Ages. Minneapolis : University of Minnesota Press, c2003.
HQ1143 .G44 2003

SEX ROLE IN THE WORK ENVIRONMENT.
Adkins, Lisa, 1966- Revisions. Buckingham [UK] ; Philadelphia : Open University Press, 2002.
HQ1075 .A24 2002

Hearn, Jeff. Gender, sexuality and violence in organizations. London ; Thousand Oaks : SAGE, 2001.

Interpreting the maternal organisation. London ; New York : Routledge, 2003.
HM786 .I58 2003

SEX ROLE - NORTH AMERICA.
Many faces of gender. Boulder : University Press of Colorado ; Calgary, Alta., Canada : University of Calgary Press, c2002.
E98.P95 M35 2002

SEX ROLE - PHILOSOPHY.
Thompson, Patricia J. In bed with Procrustes. New York : P. Lang, c2003.
HQ1190 .T52 2002 bk. 2

SEX ROLE - PSYCHOLOGICAL ASPECTS.
Rider, Elizabeth A. Our voices. Belmont, CA : Wadsworth, c2000.
HQ1206 .R54 2000

SEX ROLE - RELIGIOUS ASPECTS.
Rozanov, V. V. (Vasiliĭ Vasil'evich), 1856-1919. Vozrozhdaiushchiisia Egipet. Moskva : Izd-vo "Respublika", 2002.

SEX ROLE - SWEDEN - HISTORY.
Hirdman, Yvonne, 1943- Genus. 1. uppl. Malmö : Liber, 2001.

SEX ROLE - UNITED STATES.
Longing to tell. 1st ed. New York : Farrar, Straus and Giroux, 2003.
E185.625 .L66 2003

SEX - SOCIAL ASPECTS.
Gender. London ; New York : Routledge, 2002.
HQ1075 .G426 2002

SEX - STUDY AND TEACHING. *See* **SEX INSTRUCTION.**

Sex, time, and power.
Shlain, Leonard. New York ; London : Viking, 2003.

HQ23 .S45 2003

Le sexe et l'amour.
Brenot, Philippe. Paris : Jacob, c2003.

Le sexe et le signifiant.
Abelhauser, Alain, 1954- Paris : Seuil, c2002.
BF175.5.S48 A24 2002

SEXISM. *See also* **SEX ROLE.**
Balancing the scales. Lanham, Md. ; Oxford : University Press of America, c2003.
HQ1075 .B3417 2003

Hoffmann, Arne. Sind Frauen bessere Menschen? Berlin : Schwarzkopf & Schwarzkopf, 2001.
HQ1075 .H64 2001

Violence and the body. Bloomington : Indiana University Press, c2003.
HM1116 .V557 2003

SEXISM IN RELIGION. *See also* **WOMEN AND RELIGION.**
Balancing the scales. Lanham, Md. ; Oxford : University Press of America, c2003.
HQ1075 .B3417 2003

SEXISM - UNITED STATES.
Vint/age 2001 conference : [videorecording]. New York, c2001.

Sexo y amor.
Galende, Emiliano. 1a ed. Buenos Aires : Paidós, 2001.

SEXOLOGY. *See* **SEX.**

SEXUAL ABUSE. *See* **SEX CRIMES.**

SEXUAL ABUSE OF CHILDREN. *See* **CHILD SEXUAL ABUSE.**

Sexual abuse of males.
Spiegel, Josef. New York : Brunner-Routledge, 2003.
RC569.5.A28 S65 2003

SEXUAL ABUSE VICTIMS. *See* **ADULT CHILD SEXUAL ABUSE VICTIMS; MALE SEXUAL ABUSE VICTIMS; SEXUALLY ABUSED CHILDREN.**

SEXUAL ABUSE VICTIMS - PSYCHOLOGY.
Verführung, Trauma, Missbrauch. [2. Aufl.]. Giessen : Psychosozial-Verlag, c2002.

SEXUAL ANIMOSITY.
Champion, David R. Narcissism and entitlement. New York : LFB Scholarly Pub. LLC, c2003.
BF692.15 .C47 2003

SEXUAL AROUSAL. *See* **SEXUAL EXCITEMENT.**

SEXUAL ATTRACTION.
Buss, David M. The evolution of desire. Rev. ed. New York : BasicBooks, c2003.

Darbo, Patrika. 365 glorious nights of love and romance. 1st ed. New York : ReganBooks, c2002.
HQ46 .D35 2002

Shlain, Leonard. Sex, time, and power. New York ; London : Viking, 2003.
HQ23 .S45 2003

SEXUAL BEHAVIOR. *See* **SEX; SEX CUSTOMS.**

SEXUAL BEHAVIOR IN ANIMALS.
Judson, Olivia. Dr. Tatiana's sex advice to all creation. 1st ed. New York : Metropolitan Books, 2002.
HQ25 .J83 2002

SEXUAL BEHAVIOR, PSYCHOLOGY OF. *See* **SEX (PSYCHOLOGY).**

SEXUAL CHILD ABUSE. *See* **CHILD SEXUAL ABUSE.**

SEXUAL CRIMES. *See* **SEX CRIMES.**

SEXUAL DELINQUENCY. *See* **SEX CRIMES.**

Sexual development in childhood / edited by John Bancroft. Bloomington : Indiana University Press, 2003. p. cm. (The Kinsey Institute series ; v. 7) Includes bibliographical references and index. ISBN 0-253-34243-0 (alk. paper) DDC 306.7/083
1. Psychosexual development - Congresses. 2. Children - Sexual behavior - Congresses. 3. Teenagers - Sexual behavior - Congresses. I. Bancroft, John. II. Series.
BF723.S4 S47 2003

SEXUAL DEVIATION.
Pasini, Willy. I nuovi comportamenti amorosi. 2. ed. Milano : Mondadori, 2002.

SEXUAL DIMORPHISM IN HUMANS. *See* **SEX DIFFERENCES.**

SEXUAL DISEASES. *See* **SEXUALLY TRANSMITTED DISEASES.**

SEXUAL DIVISION OF LABOR.
Hearn, Jeff. Gender, sexuality and violence in organizations. London ; Thousand Oaks : SAGE, 2001.

Hirata, Helena Sumiko. [División sexual del trabajo. Portuguese] Nova divisão sexual do trabalho? 1a ed. São Paulo : Boitempo, 2002.
HD6060.6 .H5717 2002

Sexual ecstasy & the divine.
Galenorn, Yasmine, 1961- Berkeley, Calif. : Crossing Press, c2003.
BF1572.S4 G35 2003

Sexual ecstasy and the divine.
Galenorn, Yasmine, 1961- Sexual ecstasy & the divine. Berkeley, Calif. : Crossing Press, c2003.
BF1572.S4 G35 2003

SEXUAL ETHICS.
Moser, Antônio. O enigma da esfinge. 3a ed. Petrópolis : Editora Vozes, 2002, c2001.

Sofer, Mikha'el Uri. Sefer 'Olamot shel ṭohar. Mahad. 2. Bene Beraḳ : M.U. Sofer, 761 [2000 or 2001]
BM726 .S633 2000

SEXUAL ETHICS FOR WOMEN.
Schwickert, Eva-Maria. Feminismus und Gerechtigkeit. Berlin : Akademie Verlag, c2000.

SEXUAL EXCITEMENT.
Abramson, Paul R., 1949- With pleasure. Rev. ed. Oxford ; New York : Oxford University Press, 2002.
HQ23 .A25 2002

SEXUAL EXCITEMENT - PHILOSOPHY.
Martin, Jean-Clet. Parures d'éros. Paris : Kimé, 2003.

Sexual faces / edited by Charlotte Schwartz, Martin A. Schulman. Madison, Conn. : International Universities Press, c2002. xvi, 281 p. ; 23 cm. Includes bibliographical references and indexes. ISBN 0-8236-6066-4 DDC 155.3
1. Sex (Psychology) 2. Psychoanalysis. 3. Homosexuality. 4. Gender identity. I. Schwartz, Charlotte, 1928- II. Schulman, Martin A.
BF175.5.S48 S47 2002

SEXUAL HARASSMENT OF WOMEN.
Hearn, Jeff. Gender, sexuality and violence in organizations. London ; Thousand Oaks : SAGE, 2001.

SEXUAL IDENTITY (GENDER IDENTITY). *See* **GENDER IDENTITY.**

SEXUAL INTERCOURSE.
Dīkṣita, Mathurā Prasāda, 1878-1978. [Kelikutūhala. Hindi & Sanskrit] Kelikutūhalam. Vārāṇasī : Krshadāsa Akādamī, 2002.
HQ470.S3 D55155 2002

SEXUAL OFFENSES. *See* **SEX CRIMES.**

SEXUAL ORIENTATION. *See also* **HOMOSEXUALITY.**
Engel, Antke. Wider die Eindeutigkeit. Frankfurt/Main ; New York : Campus, c2002.

Odmiany odmieńca. Katowice : "Śląsk", 2002.
HQ23 .O36 2002

SEXUAL ORIENTATION - PSYCHOLOGICAL ASPECTS.
Bailey, J. Michael. The man who would be queen. Washington, D.C. : Joseph Henry Press, c2003.
HQ76.2.U5 B35 2003

SEXUAL PREFERENCE. *See* **SEXUAL ORIENTATION.**

SEXUAL PSYCHOLOGY. *See* **SEX (PSYCHOLOGY).**

SEXUAL VIOLENCE VICTIMS. *See* **SEXUAL ABUSE VICTIMS.**

La sexualité infantile et ses mythes.
Bergeret, Jean. Paris : Dunod, c2001.

Sexualities, evolution & gender : SEG Sheffield, England : BrunnerRoutledge, 2003- v. ; 23 cm. Frequency: Three times a year. Vol. 5, no. 1 (Apr. 2003)- . Title from cover. "An international journal of feminist and evolutionary standpoints." Continues: Psychology, evolution & gender ISSN: 1461-6661 (DLC)sn 99044513 (OCoLC)42439793. ISSN 1479-2508
1. Genetic psychology - Periodicals. 2. Gender identity - Periodicals. I. Title: Sexualities, evolution and gender II. Title: SEG III. Title: Psychology, evolution & gender
BF309 .P78

Sexualities, evolution and gender.
Sexualities, evolution & gender. Sheffield, England : BrunnerRoutledge, 2003-
BF309 .P78

SEXUALITY. *See* **SEX.**

Sexuality and society.
Bhattacharyya, Gargi, 1964- London ; New York : Routledge, 2002.
HQ21 .B6185 2002

Sexuality, intimacy, power.
Dimen, Muriel. Hillsdale, NJ : Analytic Press, 2003.
BF201.4 .D556 2003

SEXUALLY ABUSED CHILDREN. *See* **ADULT CHILD SEXUAL ABUSE VICTIMS.**

SEXUALLY ABUSED CHILDREN - MENTAL HEALTH.
Spiegel, Josef. Sexual abuse of males. New York : Brunner-Routledge, 2003.
RC569.5.A28 S65 2003

SEXUALLY ABUSED CHILDREN - MENTAL HEALTH - HISTORY.
Masson, J. Moussaieff (Jeffrey Moussaieff), 1941- The assault on truth. 1st Ballantine Books ed. New York : Ballantine Books, 2003.
BF109.F74 M38 2003

SEXUALLY TRANSMITTED DISEASES - PSYCHOLOGICAL ASPECTS.
From child sexual abuse to adult sexual risk. 1st ed. Washington, DC : American Psychological Association, c2004.
RC569.5.A28 F76 2004

Sexuelle Szenen : Inszenierungen von Geschlecht und Sexualität in modernen Gesellschaften / Christiane Schmerl ... [et al.] (Hrsg.). Opladen : Leske + Budrich, 2000. 283 p. ; 21 cm. Includes bibliographical references. ISBN 3-8100-2893-2 (pbk.)
1. Sex. 2. Sex role. I. Schmerl, Christiane.
HQ16 .S474 2000

Seymour, Percy.
[Paranormal]
The third level of reality : a unified theory of the paranormal / Percy Seymour. New York : Paraview Special Editions, c2003. 187 p. : ill. ; 21 cm. Originally published: The paranormal. London ; New York : Arkana, 1992. Includes bibliographical references (p. [177]-179) and index. ISBN 1-931044-47-3
1. Parapsychology and science. 2. Science and astrology. I. Title.
BF1045.S33 S48 2003

Sh. u-t. La-ḥafets be-ḥayim.
Rozner, Shelomoh. Mahad. 3, be-tosefet 13 she'elot be-ḥeleḳ 3. Yerushalayim : Kolel shemirat ha-lashon : le-haśig, Sh. Rozner, 762 [2001 or 2002]

Sha'agat aryeh.
Sefer Sha'agat Aryeh. Yerushalayim : Yerid ha-sefarim, 761 [2000 or 2001]

Sha'are Ḥayim.
Shemu'elevits, Ḥayim, 1901-1979. Sefer Śiḥot musar. Mahad. ḥadashah u-metuḳenet. Yerushalayim : Bene ya-hatane ha-mehaber, 762, c2002.
BJ1287.S56 S5 2002

Shabazz, David L. Discover your gold mind / David L. Shabazz. Clinton, S.C. : Awesome Records, c2001. 147 p. : ill. ; 22 cm. ISBN 1-89368-004-5 DDC 158.1
1. Success - Psychological aspects. 2. Self-actualization (Psychology) I. Title.
BF637.S8 S428 2001

SHADES AND SHADOWS. *See* **PERSPECTIVE.**

SHADES AND SHADOWS IN ART.
Pérez-Jofre, Ignacio. Huellas y sombras. Sada, A Coruña : Edicios do Castro, [2001]
ND195 .P368 2001

SHADOW (PSYCHOANALYSIS) - MISCELLANEA.
Akron, 1948- H.R. Giger tarot. Köln : Evergreen, c2000.

Shadows come to light.
Ofori Onwona, Samuel. Achimota, Ghana : Africa Christian Press, 2000.
BV215 .O46 2000

Shadrikov, V. D. (Vladimir Dmitrievich) Sposobnosti cheloveka / V.D. Shadrikov. Moskva : In-t prakticheskoĭ psikhologii ; Voronezh : NPO "MODEK", 1997. 285, [1] p. : ill. ; 21 cm. (Psikhologi otechestva) Includes bibliographical references (p. 274-[286]).

ISBN 5893950283
1. Ability. I. Title. II. Series.
BF431 .S46512 1997

Shafer, Byron E. The two majorities and the puzzle of modern American politics / Byron E. Shafer. Lawrence, Kan. : University Press of Kansas, c2003. xiv, 356 p. : ill. ; 24 cm. Includes bibliographical references (p. 321-342) and index. CONTENTS: Part 1. In our time -- Economic development, issue evolution, and divided government, 1955-2000 -- The search for a new center -- Are there any new Democrats? : and by the way, was there a Republican revolution? -- We are all Southern Democrats now -- The changing structure of American politics -- Part 2. Our time in perspective -- The circulation of elites, 1946-1996 -- Reform in the American experience -- From social welfare to cultural values in Anglo-America -- Issue evolution, institutional structure, and public preferences in the G-7 -- What is the American way? : four themes in search of their next incarnation. ISBN 0-7006-1235-1 (cloth : alk. paper) ISBN 0-7006-1236-X (pbk. : alk. paper) DDC 320.973
1. Political parties - United States. 2. Political participation - United States. 3. United States - Politics and government - 20th century. I. Title.
JK2261 .S4298 2003

Shafer-Landau, Russ. Whatever happened to good and evil? / Russ Shafer-Landau. New York ; Oxford : Oxford University Press, 2004. x, 150 p. ; 21 cm. Includes index. ISBN 0-19-516873-9 (pbk. : alk. paper) DDC 170
1. Good and evil. 2. Ethics. I. Title.
BJ1401 .S46 2004

Shaffer, Lary. Research stories for introductory psychology / Lary Shaffer, Matthew R. Merrens. 2nd ed. Boston, MA : Allyn and Bacon, c2004. xvii, 331 p. : ill. ; 23 cm. Includes bibliographical references and indexes. ISBN 0-205-38586-9 (alk. paper) DDC 150/.7/2
1. Psychology - Research - Methodology. 2. Psychology. I. Merrens, Matthew R. II. Title.
BF76.5 .S43 2004

Shaffer, Leigh S.
Berger, Helen A., 1949- Voices from the pagan census. Columbia, S.C. : University of South Carolina Press, c2003.
BF1573 .B48 2003

SHAHAR, SHULAMITH - BIBLIOGRAPHY.
Nashim, zeḳenim va-taf. Yerushalayim : Merkaz Zalman Shazar le-toldot Yiśra'el, [2001]

Shahryari, Kazem.
La figure des héros dans la création contemporaine. Paris : Harmattan, c2002.

Shakespeare and Jungian typology.
Tucker, Kenneth. Jefferson, N.C. ; London : McFarland & Co., c2003.
PR3065 .T83 2003

Shakespeare oracle.
Llewellyn, A. Bronwyn (Anita Bronwyn) Gloucester, Mass. : Fair Winds Press, 2003.
BF1879.T2 L59 2003

Shakespeare, the movie, II: popularizing the plays on film, TV, video, and DVD / edited by Richard Burt and Lynda E. Boose. London ; New York : Routledge, 2003. xi, 340 p. : ill. ; 24 cm. Includes bibliographical references (p. 304-322) and index. Includes filmography. ISBN 0-415-28298-5 (hbk. : alk. paper) ISBN 0-415-28299-3 (pbk. : alk. paper) DDC 791.43/6
1. Shakespeare, William, - 1564-1616 - Film and video adaptations. 2. English drama - Film and video adaptations. 3. Film adaptations. 4. Popular culture. I. Burt, Richard, 1954- II. Boose, Lynda E., 1943-
PR3093 .S543 2003

SHAKESPEARE, WILLIAM, 1564-1616. SONNETS.
Halpern, Richard, 1954- Shakespeare's perfume. Philadelphia : University of Pennsylvania Press, c2002.
PR2848 .H25 2002

SHAKESPEARE, WILLIAM, 1564-1616.
Llewellyn, A. Bronwyn (Anita Bronwyn) Shakespeare oracle. Gloucester, Mass. : Fair Winds Press, 2003.
BF1879.T2 L59 2003

SHAKESPEARE, WILLIAM, 1564-1616 - CHARACTERS.
Tucker, Kenneth. Shakespeare and Jungian typology. Jefferson, N.C. ; London : McFarland & Co., c2003.
PR3065 .T83 2003

SHAKESPEARE, WILLIAM, 1564-1616 - FILM AND VIDEO ADAPTATIONS.
Shakespeare, the movie, II: popularizing the plays on film, TV, video, and DVD. London ; New York : Routledge, 2003.

Shakespeare, William, 1564-1616 - In literature.

PR3093 .S543 2003

SHAKESPEARE, WILLIAM, 1564-1616 - IN LITERATURE.
Halpern, Richard, 1954- Shakespeare's perfume. Philadelphia : University of Pennsylvania Press, c2002.
PR2848 .H25 2002

SHAKESPEARE, WILLIAM, 1564-1616 - KNOWLEDGE - PSYCHOLOGY.
Tucker, Kenneth. Shakespeare and Jungian typology. Jefferson, N.C. ; London : McFarland & Co., c2003.
PR3065 .T83 2003

Shakespeare's perfume.
Halpern, Richard, 1954- Philadelphia : University of Pennsylvania Press, c2002.
PR2848 .H25 2002

Shakh, El'azar Menaḥem Man. Sefer Mi-torato de-rabi El'azar : 'uvdot hanhagot ye-amarot tohorot / me-rabenu ... El'azar Menaḥem Man Shakh ... mi-pi ... Yeḥi'el Mikha'el Shlezinger ... nikhtav 'a. y. ... Ya'aḳov Yiśra'el Kohen ... [Bene Berak] : le-haśig mishpaḥat Kohen, [763 i.e. 2003] 242 p. ; 25 cm. Cover title: Mi-torato de-rabi El'azar.
1. Ethics, Jewish. I. Shlezinger, Yeḥi'el Mikha'el. II. Kohen, Ya'aḳov Yiśra'el. III. Title. IV. Title: Mi-torato de-rabi El'azar

Shakhmagonov, N. (Nikolaĭ) Somknem rĭady, chtoby zhila Rossiĭa : opyt sozdaniĭa katekhiziza Velikorossa / Nikolaĭ Shakhmagonov. Moskva : Ispo-Servis, 1999. 76 p. ; 21 cm. (Narodnaĭa bibliotechka. Seriĭa "Velikorossy") Limited edition. Library has copy no. 314. Autographed by the author.
1. Nationalism - Russia (Federation) 2. National characteristics, Russian. 3. Russia (Federation) - History - Philosophy. 4. Russia - History - Philosophy. I. Title. II. Series.

Shamanism.
Stutley, Margaret, 1917- London ; New York : Routledge, 2003.
BL2370.S5 S88 2003

SHAMANISM.
Kottler, Jeffrey A. American shaman. New York : Brunner-Routledge, 2004.
BF1598.K43 K68 2004

Lewis, I. M. Ecstatic religion. 3rd ed. London ; New York : Routledge, 2003.
BL626 .L48 2003

Papalotzin, Itzcoatl. Los recuerdos robados a las estrellas muertas. Barcelona : Mtm editor.es, c2002.

Pinchbeck, Daniel. Breaking open the head. 1st ed. New York : Broadway Books, 2002.
BF1621 .P56 2002

Stutley, Margaret, 1917- Shamanism. London ; New York : Routledge, 2003.
BL2370.S5 S88 2003

Shamanism and the psychology of C.G. Jung.
Ryan, Robert E. London : Vega, 2002.
BF175.4.R44 R93 2002

SHAMANISM - HAWAII. See **HUNA.**

SHAMANISM - PSYCHOLOGY.
Lioger, Richard. La folie du chaman. Paris : Presses universitaires de France, c2002.
Ryan, Robert E. Shamanism and the psychology of C.G. Jung. London : Vega, 2002.
BF175.4.R44 R93 2002

SHAMANISM - SOUTH AMERICA.
Langevin, Michael Peter, 1952- Secrets of the Amazon shamans. Franklin Lakes, NJ : New Page Books, c2003.
BF1622.S63 L36 2003

SHAMANISM - UNITED STATES.
Wernitznig, Dagmar. Going native or going naive? Lanham, MD : University Press of America, c2003.
E98.P99 W47 2003

Shamdasani, Sonu, 1962- C.G. Jung and the making of modern psychology : the dream of a science / Sonu Shamdasani. Cambridge, UK ; New York : Cambridge University Press, 2003. p. cm. Includes bibliographical references and index. Publisher description URL: http://www.loc.gov/catdir/description/cam032/2003048562.html Table of contents URL: http://www.loc.gov/catdir/toc/cam032/2003048562.html ISBN 0-521-83145-8 ISBN 0-521-53909-9 (pbk.) DDC 150.19/54/092
1. Psychoanalysis. 2. Jungian psychology. 3. Jung, C. G. - (Carl Gustav), - 1875-1961. I. Title.
BF173 .S485 2003

SHAME.
Ayers, Mary, 1960- The eyes of shame. 1st ed. Hove, East Sussex ; New York : Brunner-Routledge, 2003.

BF175.5.O24 A94 2003

Ogien, Ruwen. La honte est-elle immorale? Paris : Bayard, c2002.

Shanddaramon, 1959- Self-initiation for the solitary witch : attaining higher spirituality through a five-degree system / by Shanddaramon. Franklin Lakes, NJ : New Page Books, c2004. p. cm. Includes bibliographical references (p.   ) and index. ISBN 1-56414-726-6 (pbk.) DDC 133.4/3
1. Witchcraft. I. Title.
BF1566 .S44 2004

Shane, Anna.
Safouan, Moustafa. Four lessons of psychoanalysis. New York : Other Press, c2004.
BF175 .S19 2004

Shanghai san lian wen ku
Pan, Zhichang, 1956- Shi yu si di dui hua. Di 1 ban. Shanghai Shi : Shanghai san lian shu dian : Fa xing Xin hua shu dian Shanghai fa xing suo, 1997.
BH39 .P2286 1997<Asian China>

Shanghai san lian wen ku. Xue shu xi lie
Pan, Zhichang, 1956- Shi yu si di dui hua. Di 1 ban. Shanghai Shi : Shanghai san lian shu dian : Fa xing Xin hua shu dian Shanghai fa xing suo, 1997.
BH39 .P2286 1997<Asian China>

Shanon, Benny. The antipodes of the mind : charting the phenomenology of the Ayahuasca experience / Benny Shanon. Oxford ; New York : Oxford University Press, 2002. vi, 475 p. : ill. ; 24 cm. Includes bibliographical references (p. [435]-452) and index. ISBN 0-19-925292-0 (hbk. : alk. paper) ISBN 0-19-925293-9 (pbk. : alk. paper) DDC 615/.7883
1. Ayahuasca - Psychotropic effects. I. Title.
BF209.A93 S53 2002

SHAPE.
Bruce, Lisa. Math all around me. Chicago, Ill. : Raintree, 2003.
BF294 .B78 2003

The shape of ancient thought.
McEvilley, Thomas, 1939- New York : Allworth Press : School of Visual Arts, c2002.
B165 .M22 2002

Shapesville.
Mills, Andy, 1979- 1st ed. Carlsbad, CA : Gurze Books, 2003.
BF723.B6 M55 2003

Shaping the next one hundred years.
Lempert, Robert J. Santa Monica, CA : RAND, 2003.
T57.6 .L46 2003

Shapira, Mosheh.
Alter, Judah Aryeh Leib, 1847-1905. [Selections. 2000] Penine Śefat Emet. Ofrah : Mekhon Shovah, [2000?-2003?]
BM198.2 .A55 2000

Shapiro, Lawrence A. The mind incarnate / Lawrence A. Shapiro. Cambridge, Mass. : MIT Press, 2004. p. cm. (Life and mind) Includes bibliographical references and index. ISBN 0-262-19496-1 (alk. paper) DDC 128/.2
1. Mind and body. I. Title. II. Series.
BF161 .S435 2004

Sharabi, Shalom, 1720-1777.
['Ets ha-tidhar.] Sidur kayanot 'Ets ha-tidhar. Yerushalayim : Kolel Shemen śaśon, [1998?]
1. Ḳeri'at shema 'al ha-miṭah.

SHARABI, SHALOM, 1720-1777.
Hilel, Ya'aḳov Mosheh. Sefer Ahavat shalom. [Hotsa'ah 2], 'im hosafot rabot. Yerushala[y]im : ha-Makhon le-hotsa'at sefarim ye-khitve yad "Ahavat Shalom", 762 [2002]

Shared experiences and voices of loss.
Living with suicide [electronic resource]. [Alexandria, Va.] : PBS Online ; [New York, N.Y.] : Web Lab
BF789.D4

Shared land/conflicting identity.
Rowland, Robert C., 1954- East lansing : Michigan State University Press, 2002.
DS119.7 .R685 2003

The shared well.
Van de Weyer, Robert. 1st ed. Washington, D.C. : Brassey's, c2002.
BL65.P7 V36 2002

SHARES OF STOCK. See **STOCKS.**

SHARING.
Honey from my heart for you. Nashville, Tenn. : J. Countryman, c2002.
BF575.F66 H66 2002

Jordan, Denise. Your fair share. Chicago, Ill. : Heinemann Library, 2003.
BF723.S428 J67 2003

Jordan, Denise. [Your fair share. Spanish] A partes iguales. Chicago : Heinemann Library, c2004.
BF723.S428 J6718 2003

Sharing expertise : beyond knowledge management / edited by Mark S. Ackerman, Volkmar Pipek, and Volker Wulf. Cambridge, Mass. : MIT Press, c2003. xx, 418 p. : ill. ; 24 cm. Includes bibliographical references and index. CONTENTS: I. Overview and background -- Why organizations don't "know what they know": cognitive and motivational factors affecting the transfer of expertise / Pamela J. Hinds and Jeffrey Pfeffer -- Critical evaluation of knowledge management practices / Marleen Huysman, Kirk de Wit -- Coming to the crossroads of knowledge, learning, and technology: integrating knowledge management and workplace learning / Bill Penuel, Andrew Cohen -- II. Studies of expertise sharing in organizations -- Emergent expertise sharing in a new community / Geraldine Fitzpatrick -- Sharing expertise: challenges for technical support / Volkmar Pipek, Joachim Hinrichs, Volker Wulf -- Locating expertise: design issues for an expertise locator system / Kate Ehrlich -- Who's there? The knowledge-mapping approximation project / Mark S. Ackerman... [et al.] -- Enabling communities of practice at EADS Airbus / Roland Haas, Wilfried Aulbur, Sunil Thakar -- III. Exploring technology for sharing expertise -- Using a room metaphor to ease transitions in groupware / Saul Greenberg and Mark Roseman -- NewsMate: Providing timely knowledge to mobile and distributed news journalists / Henrik Fagrell -- Supporting informal communities of practice within organization / R.T. Jim Eales -- Knowledge communities: online environments for supporting knowledge management and its social context / Thomas Erickson, Wendy A. Kellogg -- Expert-finding systems for organizations: problem and domain analysis and the DEMOIR approach / Dawit Yimam-Seid, Alfred Kobsa -- Automated discovery and mapping of expertise / Mark Maybury, Ray D'Amore, David House -- OWL: a system for the automated sharing of expertise / Frank Linton. ISBN 0-262-01195-6 (hc. : alk. paper) DDC 658.4/038
1. Knowledge management. 2. Organizational learning - Management. 3. Information technology - Management. 4. Human-computer interaction. I. Ackerman, Mark S. II. Pipek, Volkmar. III. Wulf, Volker.
HD30.2 .S53 2003

SHARING IN CHILDREN - JUVENILE LITERATURE.
Jordan, Denise. Your fair share. Chicago, Ill. : Heinemann Library, 2003.
BF723.S428 J67 2003

Jordan, Denise. [Your fair share. Spanish] A partes iguales. Chicago : Heinemann Library, c2004.
BF723.S428 J6718 2003

Sharir, Avraham Yiśra'el. Pene Shabat neḳablah : le-ve'uram shel mizmore Ḳabalat Shabat / Avraham Yiśra'el Sharir. Yerushalayim : Avraham Kohen-Erez, 763 [2003] 319 p. ; 25 cm. Partly printed in polychrome. ISBN 9657139171
1. Alḳabeẓ, Solomon ben Moses, - ha-Levi, - ca. 1505-1576. - Lekha Dodi. 2. Bible. - O.T. - Psalms XXIX, XCII, XCIII, VC-C - Commentaries. 3. Cabala. 4. Judaism - Liturgy - Sabbath prayers. I. Title.
BM670.L44 S527 2003

Sharma, Kalpana, 1947-.
Terror, counter-terror. London ; New York : Zed Books ; New Delhi : Kali for Women ; New York : Distributed in the U.S. exclusively by Palgrave, 2003.
HQ1236 .T47 2003

Sharma, Sima.
Faith in the age of uncertainty. New Delhi : Published by Indialog Publications in association with the India International Centre, 2002.
BL626.3+

Sharman-Burke, Juliet. Beginner's guide to tarot / Juliet Sharman-Burke ; with cards illustrated by Giovanni Caselli. 1st St. Martin's Griffin ed. New York : St. Martin's Griffin, 2001. 192 p. : ill. ; 18 cm. + (2 deck of cards). Includes two pack (78 cards) of tarot cards. Publisher description URL: http://www.loc.gov/catdir/description/hol032/2002726609.html ISBN 0-312-28482-9 (pbk.) DDC 133.32424
1. Tarot. I. Title.
BF1879.T2 S52 2001

Sharp, Daryl, 1936-.
Edinger, Edward F. Science of the soul. Toronto, Ont. : Inner City Books, c2002.
BF173 .E27 2002

Harding, M. Esther (Mary Esther), 1888-1971. The parental image. 3rd ed. Toronto : Inner City Books, c2003.

SHAS (POLITICAL PARTY : ISRAEL).
Sefer Sha'agat Aryeh. Yerushalayim : Yerid ha-sefarim, 761 [2000 or 2001]

Shastri, L. C., 1933- Indian philosophy of knowledge : comparative study / L.C. Shastri. 1st ed. Delhi, India : Global Vision Pub. House, 2002. vi, 210 p. ; 22 cm. Includes bibliographical references (p. [177]-198) and index. ISBN 81-87746-38-6
1. Knowledge, Theory of (Hinduism) 2. Philosophy, Indic. I. Title.
B132.K6 S48 2002

Shattered past.
Jarausch, Konrad Hugo. Princeton, N.J. : Princeton University Press, c2003.
DD86 .J253 2003

Shavell, Steven, 1946-.
Kaplow, Louis. Fairness versus welfare. Cambridge, MA : Harvard University Press, 2002.
K247 .K37 2002

Shavinina, Larisa V.
Beyond knowledge. Mahwah, N.J. : L. Erlbaum Associates, 2003.
BF412 .B44 2003

Shaw, Angel Velasco.
Vestiges of war. New York : New York University Press, 2000.
DS679 .V47 2000

Shaw, Maria, 1963- Maria Shaw's star gazer : your soul searching, dream seeking, make something happen guide to the future. 1st ed. St. Paul, Minn. : Llewellyn Publications, 2003. xvi, 308 p. : ill. ; 24 cm. Includes bibliographical references (p. 305) and index. ISBN 0-7387-0422-9 (pbk. : alk. paper) DDC 133
1. Occultism - Juvenile literature. 2. Occultism. 3. Fortune telling. 4. Astrology. 5. Numerology. I. Title. II. Title: Star gazer
BF1411 .S52 2003

Shaw, Mary Ann. Your anxious child : raising a healthy child in a frightening world / Mary Ann Shaw. 2nd ed. Irving, Tex. : Tapestry Press, c2003. xvi, 223 p. ; 22 cm. Includes bibliographical references (p. 215-216) and index. Table of contents URL: http://www.loc.gov/catdir/toc/ecip041/2003005505.html CONTENTS: Part I: Recognizing anxiety in your child -- Our anxious society : why it's so hard to raise carefree children -- Anxiety and temperament : when to push and when not to push -- Anxiety and your child's health : recognizing physical problems -- Part II: The common varieties of anxiety -- Performance anxiety : conquering your child's fear of failure -- Separation anxiety : raising inendent children -- Trauma-induced anxiety : hen bad things happen to little people -- Anxiety and sibling rivalry : managing competition and conflict -- Part III: The tough stuff -- Anxiety and the special needs child : building security with freedom -- Phobias, panic, and obsessive-compulsive disorders : a need for order in chaotic lives -- Anxiety and divorce : keeping families together when parents part -- Anxiety and parenting skills : altering your own behavior and expectations. ISBN 1-930819-17-X (alk. paper) DDC 649/.154
1. Anxiety in children. 2. Child rearing. I. Title.
BF723.A5 S43 2003

Shay, Jonathan. Odysseus in America : combat trauma and the trials of homecoming / Jonathan Shay ; foreword by Max Cleland and John McCain. New York : Scribner, c2002. xvi, 329 p. ; 24 cm. Includes bibliographical references (p. 303-312) and index. ISBN 0-7432-1156-1 DDC 616.85/212
1. Homer. - Odyssey. 2. War neuroses. 3. Vietnamese Conflict, 1961-1975 - Veterans - Mental health - United States. 4. Post-traumatic stress disorder. 5. Vietnamese Conflict, 1961-1975 - Psychological aspects. 6. Veterans - Mental health - United States. 7. War - Psychological aspects. I. Title.
RC550 .S533 2002

Shayegan, Darius. La lumière vient de l'Occident : le réenchantement du monde et la pensée nomade / Daryush Shayegan. [La Tour-d'Aigues] : Éditions de l'Aube, c2001. 268 p. ; 25 cm. (Monde en cours) Includes bibliographical references. ISBN 2-87678-656-7 DDC 190
1. Civilization, Modern - 1950- 2. East and West. 3. Values. I. Title. II. Series.
CB 430

Shayzarī, 'Abd al-Raḥmān ibn Naṣr, 12th cent.
Rawḍat al-qulūb wa-nuzhat al-muḥibb wa-al-maḥbūb / li-Abī al-Faraj 'Abd al-Raḥmān ibn Naṣr al-Shayzarī ; bada'a al-taḥqīq Dāfid Šīmah ; atamma al-'amal wa-a'adda al-kitāb lil-ṭab' Jūrj Qanāzī. Wiesbaden : Harrassowitz, 2003. xlvi, [5] p. of plates, 381, 25 p. : facsims. ; 25 cm. (Codices Arabici antiqui, 0340-6393 ; Bd. 8) Includes bibliographical references and indexes. On t.p.: ... edition initiated by David Semah ; completed and brought to press by George J. Kanazi. Arabic with introduction also in English. ISBN 3-447-04720-8 (hd.bd.)
1. Love - Early works to 1800. I. Qanāzī', Jūrj. II. Šīmah, Dāvīd III. Title. IV. Title: Rawḍat al qulūb wa-nuzhat al-muḥibb wal-maḥbūb V. Series.

Shchedrovit͡skiĭ, G. P. (Georgiĭ Petrovich), 1929-1994.
I͡A vsegda byl idealistom-- / G.P. Shchedrovit͡skiĭ. Moskva : Put', 2001. 365 p. : ill. ; 17 cm. ISBN 5937330102
1. Shchedrovit͡skiĭ, G. P. - (Georgiĭ Petrovich) - 1929-1994. 2. Psychologists - Russia (Federation) - Biography. I. Title.
BF109.S44 A3 2001

SHCHEDROVIT͡SKIĬ, G. P. (GEORGIĬ PETROVICH), 1929-1994.
Shchedrovit͡skiĭ, G. P. (Georgiĭ Petrovich), 1929-1994. I͡A vsegda byl idealistom--. Moskva : Put', 2001.
BF109.S44 A3 2001

Shcheglov, A. (Alekseĭ) I͡Azycheskai͡a zari͡a : perspektivy i͡azycheskogo dvizhenii͡a / A. Shcheglov. Moskva : [Izdatel'stvo "PROBEL-2000"], 2002. 67 p. : ill. ; 20 cm. On p. 2 of cover, "Formuli͡arnyĭ spisok o sluzhbe arkhivarusa Penzenskogo okruzhnogo suda nadvornogo svetnika Ivana Aleksandrovicha Anirova. Sostavlen mai͡a 2 dni͡a 1880 goda." Includes bibliographical references. ISBN 5901683269
1. Neopaganism - Russia (Federation) - Political aspects. 2. Paganism - Russia - Political aspects. 3. National characteristics, Russian. 4. Russians - Ethnic identity. I. Title.
BL980.R5 S53 2002

Shcho mozhe obit͡si͡aty politychna kar'i͡era pori͡adniĭ li͡udyni, okrim vtraty pori͡adnosti.
Mykytenko, Svitlana. Eniḣma lidera, abo, Shcho mozhe obit͡si͡aty politychna kar'i͡era pori͡adniĭ li͡udyni, okrim vtraty pori͡adnosti. Kyïv : Vyd-vo "Molod'", 2001.
JC330.3 .M95 2001

She hui mao dun yu jin dai Zhongguo.
Liu, Peiping. Di 1 ban. Jinan Shi : Shandong jiao yu chu ban she, 2000.
HN733 .L569 2000

She hui ping jia lun.
Chen, Xinhan. Di 1 ban. Shanghai : Shanghai she hui ke xue yuan chu ban she : Xin hua shu dian Shanghai fa xing suo fa xing, 1997.
HM131 .C7135 1997 <Asian China>

She hui ren shi lun.
Ouyang, Kang, 1953- Di 1 ban. [Kunming] : Yunnan ren min chu ban she, 2002.
BF323.S63 O93 2002

She hui si wei xue.
Zeng, Jie. Di 1 ban. Beijing : Ren min chu ban she : Xin hua shu dian jing xiao, 1996.
BF323.S63 T75 1996 <Asian China>

She jiao jin yao shi cong shu.
Bu ping ze ming. Di 2 ban. Beijing : Zhongguo cheng shi chu ban she, 2001.

She who changes.
Christ, Carol P. 1st ed. New York ; Houndmills, England : Palgrave Macmillan, 2003.
BD372 .C48 2003

She who dreams.
Burch, Wanda Easter, 1947- Novato, Calif. : New World Library, c2003.
BF1099.W65 B87 2003

Shea, Linchi. Real world SQL server administration with Perl / Linchi Shea. [Berkeley, CA] : Apress ; New York : Distributed to the book trade in the U.S. by Springer-Verlag, c2003. xxxi, 798 p. : ill. ; 24 cm. (Books for professionals by professionals) "The Author's Press"--Cover. Includes bibliographical references and index. ISBN 1-59059-097-X DDC 005.7585
1. SQL server. 2. Perl (Computer program language) I. Title. II. Title: SQL server administration with Perl III. Series.
QA76.73.S67 S48 2003

Shear, J. (Jonathan).
Models of the self. Thorverton, UK : Imprint Academic, c1999.
BF697 .M568 1999

The view from within. Thorverton, UK : Bowling Green, OH : Imprint Academic, 2000.
BF311 .V512 2000

Sheehy, Noel, 1955- Fifty key thinkers in psychology / Noel Sheehy. London ; New York : Routledge, 2003. p. cm. (Routledge key guides) Includes bibliographical references and index. Table of contents URL: http://www.loc.gov/catdir/toc/ecip042/2003007402.html ISBN 0-415-16774-4 (hardback) ISBN 0-415-16775-2 (pbk.) DDC 150/.92/2
1. Psychologists - Biography - Encyclopedias. 2. Psychology - History - Encyclopedias. I. Title. II. Series.

BF109.A1 S49 2003

SHE'ELOT U-TESHUVOT. See **RESPONSA.**

SHE'ELOTH U-TESHUVOTH. See **RESPONSA.**

Sheffield, Gary, 1961-.
The challenges of high command. Houndmills, Basingstoke ; New York : Palgrave Macmillan, 2003.
UB210 .C477 2003

Shehui maodun yu jindai Zhongguo.
Liu, Peiping. She hui mao dun yu jin dai Zhongguo. Di 1 ban. Jinan Shi : Shandong jiao yu chu ban she, 2000.
HN733 .L569 2000

Shehui siwei xue.
Zeng, Jie. She hui si wei xue. Di 1 ban. Beijing : Ren min chu ban she : Xin hua shu dian jing xiao, 1996.
BF323.S63 T75 1996 <Asian China>

Sheḳalim, Rami. Torat ha-ḥalom ba-Yahadut / Dr. Rami Sheḳalim. Tel Aviv : R. Sheḳalim, 762, 2002. 2 v. ; 24 cm.
1. Dreams in the Bible. 2. Dreams - Religious aspects - Judaism. 3. Dream interpretation in rabbinical literature. I. Title.

Shelomoh ben Ḥayim Haiḳel. Sefer Liḳuṭe u-ferushe niglot Leshem shevo ye-aḥlamah / Shelomoh Elyashiv. Kiryat Sefer : Mosheh Vais, 762 [2002] 131. [6] p. ; 25 cm. Cover title: Liḳuṭe niglot Leshem shevo ye-aḥlamah. Running title: Liḳuṭe Leshem shevo ye-aḥlamah.
1. Bible. - O.T. - Pentateuch - Commentaries. 2. Talmud - Commentaries. 3. Cabala. I. Title. II. Title: Liḳuṭe niglot Leshem shevo ye-aḥlamah III. Title: Liḳuṭe Leshem shevo ye-aḥlamah
BM525 .H4332 2002

Shelton, Christine.
Women on power. Boston : Northeastern University Press, c2001.
HQ1233 .W597 2001

Shemu'elevits, Ḥayim, 1901-1979. Sefer Śiḥot musar : Sha'are Ḥayim / Ḥayim Leyb ha-Levi Shemu'elevits. Mahad. ḥadashah u-metuḳenet. Yerushalayim : Bene ya-hatane ha-meḥaber, 762, c2002. 501 p. ; 25 cm. Other title: Sha'are Ḥayim. Running title: Śiḥot musar. Includes indexes. "Derekh ḥayim tokhaḥot musar she-hinḥil le-rabim ba-yeshivah ha-ḳedoshah Yerushalayim t. y., ba-shanim 731-733". "Ne'erakh meḥadash lefi seder parashiyot ha-Torah, 'im tiḳunim ye-hosafot".
1. Bible. - O.T. - Pentateuch - Sermons. 2. Ethics, Jewish. 3. Jewish sermons, Hebrew - Israel. I. Title. II. Title: Sha'are Ḥayim III. Title: Śiḥot musar
BJ1287.S56 S5 2002

Shen mei huo dong de ben ti lun nei han ji qi xian dai chan shi.
Pan, Zhichang, 1956- Shi yu si di dui hua. Di 1 ban. Shanghai Shi : Shanghai san lian shu dian : Fa xing Xin hua shu dian Shanghai fa xing suo, 1997.
BH39 .P2286 1997<Asian China>

Shen mei shi dai di wen hua li lun.
Xiao, Ying. Xing xiang yu sheng cun. Beijing di 1 ban. Beijing : Zuo jia chu ban she : Jing xiao Xin hua shu dian Beijing fa xing suo, 1996.
NX583.A1 H756 1996 <Asian China>

Sheng yu xiang jie / [Liang Yannian ji]. Di 1 ban. [Peking] : Xian zhuang shu ju, 1995. 10 v. : ill. ; 27 cm. Annotations, with illustrations, of 16 codes of conduct proclaimed by emperor Kangxi. Reprint of 1887 ed. On double leaves, oriental style, in case. ISBN 7-80106-020-2 (set)
1. Ethics - China. 2. Conduct of life. 3. China - History - Anecdotes. I. Kangxi, Emperor of China, 1654-1722. II. Liang, Yannian, fl. 1673-1681.
BJ117 .S486 1995 <Orien China>

Shenot Ḥayim.
Vital, Ḥayyim ben Joseph, 1542 or 3-1620. 'Ets ha-da'at tov. Yerushalayim : Hotsa'at Ahavat shalom, 761 [2000 or 2001]

Shepard, Ernest H. (Ernest Howard), 1879-1976.
Winnie-the-Pooh's little book of feng shui. London : Methuen Children's, 1999.

Shepard, Florence R.
Shepard, Paul, 1925- Where we belong. Athens : University of Georgia Press, c2003.
GF21 .S524 2003

Shepard, Paul, 1925- Where we belong : beyond abstraction in perceiving nature / Paul Shepard ; edited by Florence Rose Shepard. Athens : University of Georgia Press, c2003. xxiii, 255 p. : ill. ; 24 cm. Includes bibliographical references (p. 235-242) and index. ISBN 0-8203-2420-5 (hardcover : alk. paper) DDC 304.2
1. Human ecology - Philosophy. 2. Nature (Aesthetics) 3.

Shepard, Rita S.
Landscape assessment. 4. Human-animal relationships. I. Shepard, Florence R. II. Title.
GF21 .S524 2003

Shepard, Rita S.
Many faces of gender. Boulder : University Press of Colorado ; Calgary, Alta., Canada : University of Calgary Press, c2002.
E98.P95 M35 2002

Shepherd, Joanne. What I look like when I am scared / Joanne Shepherd. New York : Rosen Pub. Group's PowerStart Press, 2004. 24 p. : col. ill. ; 21 cm. (Let's look at feelings) SUMMARY: Describes how different parts of a face may look when a person is scared. Includes index. Table of contents URL: http://www.loc.gov/catdir/toc/ecip041/2003005992.html ISBN 1404225099 DDC 152.4/6
1. Fear in children - Juvenile literature. 2. Fear. 3. Facial expression. 4. Emotions. I. Title. II. Series.
BF723.F4 S54 2004

[What I look like when I am scared. Spanish & English]
What I look like when I am scared = Cómo me veo cuando estoy asustado / Joanne Shepherd ; translated by Maria Cristina Brusca. 1st ed. New York : Rosen Pub. Group's PowerKids Press, 2004. p. cm. (Let's look at feelings) Spanish and English. SUMMARY: Describes what different parts of the face look like when a person is frightened. Includes and index. ISBN 1404275096 (library binding) DDC 152.4/6
1. Fear in children - Juvenile literature. 2. Fear. 3. Facial expression. 4. Emotions. 5. Spanish language materials - Bilingual. I. Title. II. Title: Cómo me veo cuando estoy asustado III. Series.
BF723.F4 S5418 2004

What I look like when I am surprised / Joanne Shepherd. 1st ed. New York : Rosen Pub. Group's PowerStart Press, 2004. 24 p. : col. ill. ; 21 cm. (Let's look at feelings) SUMMARY: Describes what different parts of the face look when a person is surprised. Includes index. Table of contents URL: http://www.loc.gov/catdir/toc/ecip041/2003005471.html ISBN 1404225110 DDC 152.4
1. Surprise in children - Juvenile literature. 2. Surprise. 3. Facial expression. 4. Emotions. I. Title. II. Series.
BF723.S87 S44 2004

[What I look like when I am surprised. Spanish & English]
What I look like when I am surprised = Cómo me veo cuando estoy sorprendido / Joanne Shepherd ; translated by Maria Cristina Brusca. 1st ed. New York : Rosen Pub. Group's PowerKids Press, 2004. p. cm. (Let's look at feelings) Spanish and English. SUMMARY: Describes what different parts of the face look like when a person is surprised. Includes index. Table of contents URL: http://www.loc.gov/catdir/toc/ecip043/2003009147.html ISBN 1404275118 (library binding) DDC 152.4
1. Surprise in children - Juvenile literature. 2. Surprise. 3. Facial expression. 4. Emotions. 5. Spanish language materials - Bilingual. I. Title. II. Series.
BF723.S87 S4418 2004

Shepherd, Rowena. 1000 symbols / Rowena & Rupert Shepherd. New York : Thames & Hudson, 2002. 352 p. : ill. ; 24 cm. Includes bibliographical references (p. 351-352). ISBN 0-500-28351-6 DDC 302.2/223
1. Symbolism (Psychology) - Dictionaries. I. Shepherd, Rupert. II. Title. III. Title: One thousand symbols
BF458 .S63 2002

Shepherd, Rupert.
Shepherd, Rowena. 1000 symbols. New York : Thames & Hudson, 2002.
BF458 .S63 2002

Shepherd, S. H. A.
Malory, Thomas, Sir, 15th cent. [Morte d'Arthur] Le morte Darthur, or, The hoole book of Kyng Arthur and of his noble knyghtes of the Rounde Table. 1st ed. New York ; London : Norton, c2004.
PR2041 .M37 2004

Sherfield, Robert M. The everything self-esteem book / Robert M. Sherfield. Avon, MA : Adams Media Corp., c2004. p. cm. (An everything series book) Table of contents URL: http://www.loc.gov/catdir/toc/ecip047/2003017008.html ISBN 1-58062-976-8 DDC 158.1
1. Self-esteem. 2. Self-actualization (Psychology) I. Title. II. Series: Everything series.
BF697.5.S46 S52

Sherman, Harold Morrow, 1898-.
Wilkins, George H. (George Hubert), Sir, 1888-1958. Thoughts through space. Charlottesville, VA : Hampton Roads Pub. Co., 2004.
BF1171 .W49 2004

Sherwood, Dyane N.
Henderson, Joseph L. (Joseph Lewis), 1903- Transformation of the psyche. New York : Brunner-Routledge, 2003.
BF173 .H4346 2003

Sherwood, Nancy E. The MMPI-A content component scales : development, psychometric characteristics, and clinical application / Nancy E. Sherwood, Yossef S. Ben-Porath, Carolyn L. Williams. Minneapolis : University of Minnesota Press, c1997. 58 p. ; 28 cm. (MMPI-2/MMPI-A test reports ; 3) Includes bibliographical references (p. 41). ISBN 0-8166-3071-2 DDC 155.2/83
1. Minnesota Multiphasic Personality Inventory. 2. MMPI. I. Ben-Porath, Yossef S. II. Williams, Carolyn L., 1951- III. Title. IV. Series.
BF698.8.M5 S54 1997

Shestakov, Vi͡acheslav Pavlovich.
Fenomenologii͡a smekha. Moskva : Rossiĭskiĭ institut kul'turologii, 2002.
PN6149.P3 F45 2002

SHESTOV, LEV, 1866-1938.
Fotiade, Ramona. Conceptions of the absurd. Oxford : Legenda, 2001.

Shi ji mo she hui si chao yu Lu Xun.
Wang, Furen. Tu po mang dian. Di 1 ban. Beijing Shi : Zhongguo wen lian chu ban she, 2001.
PL2754.S5 Z89 2001

Shi ji zhi jiao de dui hua : Gu dian wen xue yan jiu de hui gu yu zhan wang / "Wen xue yi chan" bian ji bu bian. Di 1 ban. Shanghai : Shanghai gu ji chu ban she : Xin hua shu dian Shanghai fa xing suo fa xing, 2000. 309 p. ; 21 cm. ISBN 7-5325-2814-6
1. Chinese literature. 2. Chinese literature - History and criticism. I. "Wen xue yi chan" bian ji bu. II. Title: Gu dian wen xue yan jiu de hui gu yu zhan wang

Shi ji zhi jiao di wen hua yu zhe xue.
Li, Xiaobing. Wo zai, wo si. Di 1 ban. Beijing : Dong fang chu ban she : Xin hua shu dian jing xiao, 1996.
CB425 .L39 1996 <Orien China>

Shi, Lin. Zhi xin jing / Zeng Guofan zhu ; Shi Lin zhu yi. Di 1 ban. Beijing : Zhongguo yan shi chu ban she, 1999. 5, 8, 518 p. ; 22 cm. Cover title: Zhixinjing. ISBN 7-80128-212-4
1. Zeng, Guofan, - 1811-1872. 2. Conduct of life. I. Zeng, Guofan, 1811-1872. Selections. 1999. II. Title. III. Title: Zhixinjing
DS758.23.T74 S522 1999

Shi, Sheng. Fan Zhongyan li shen xing shi jiu jiu fang lüe / Shi Sheng, Deng Minxuan bian zhu. Di 1 ban. Beijing : Zhongguo xi ju chu ban she, 2001. 8, 13, 449 p. ; 20 cm. Can kao wen xian (p. 449) ISBN 7-104-01404-7
1. Fan, Zhongyan, - 989-1052. 2. Statesmen - China. 3. Conduct of life. 4. Political science - China. 5. China - History - Song dynasty, 960-1279. I. Deng, Minxuan. II. Title.
DS751.6.F3 S5 2001

Shi, Yili. Discourse analysis of Chinese referring expressions : an application of Gundel, Hedberg, and Zacharski's givenness heirarchy / Yili Shi. Lewiston, N.Y. : E. Mellen Press, c2002. xxi, 240 p. ; 24 cm. (Chinese studies ; v. 26) Includes bibliographical references (p. [225]-233) and index. ISBN 0-7734-7015-8 (v. 26) ISBN 0-88964-076-0 (ChS series) DDC 495.1/5
1. Reference (Linguistics) 2. Chinese language. I. Title. II. Series.
P325.5.R44 S53 2002

Shi yu si di dui hua.
Pan, Zhichang, 1956- Di 1 ban. Shanghai Shi : Shanghai san lian shu dian : Fa xing Xin hua shu dian Shanghai fa xing suo, 1997.
BH39 .P2286 1997<Asian China>

Shi, Zhecun. Beishan si chuang / Shi Zhecun [zhu] ; Liu Ling bian. Di 1 ban. Shanghai : Shanghai wen yi chu ban she : Xin hua shu dian jing xiao, 2000. 8, 1, 461 p. : col. ill. ; 21 cm. (Xue yuan ying hua) Cover title: Beishan sichuang. ISBN 7-5321-1969-6
1. Chinese literature - History and criticism. I. Liu, Ling. II. Title. III. Title: Beishan sichuang IV. Series.
PL2272.5 .S543 2000

SHĪ'AH.
Jambet, Christian. L'acte d'être. [Paris] : Fayard, c2002.

Shields, Christopher John.
The Blackwell guide to ancient philosophy. Malden, MA ; Oxford : Blackwell Pub., 2003.
B171 .B65 2003

Shields, Stephanie A. Speaking from the heart : gender and the social meaning of emotion / Stephanie A. Shields. Cambridge, U.K. ; New York : Cambridge University Press, 2002. xiii, 214 p. ; 24 cm. (Studies in emotion and social interaction. Second series) Includes bibliographical references (p. 188-207) and index. CONTENTS: That 'vivid, unforgettable condition' -- When does gender matter? -- Doing emotion/doing gender: practising in order to 'get it right' -- Sentiment, sympathy, and passion in the late nineteenth century -- The education of the emotions -- Ideal emotion and the fallacy of the inexpressive male -- Emotional [equals] female, angry [equals] male? -- Speaking from the heart. ISBN 0-521-80297-0 ISBN 0-521-00449-7 (pbk.) DDC 152.4
1. Emotions - Social aspects. 2. Emotions - Sex differences. I. Title. II. Series.
BF531 .S55 2002

Shifting.
Jones, Charisse. 1st ed. New York : HarperCollins, c2003.
E185.625 .J657 2003

Shikun, A. A. (Alekseĭ Alekseevich) Istorii͡a i razvitie psikhologicheskogo obrazovanii͡a v gorode Tveri i oblasti / Shikun A.A. Tver' : Tverskoĭ gos. universitet : Mezhdunarodnai͡a akademii͡a psikhologicheskikh nauk, 1999. 206 p. : ill., facsims. ; 21 cm. Includes bibliographical references (p. 154-[162]). ISBN 5894170222
1. Psychology - Study and teaching - Russia (Federation) - Tverskai͡a oblast' - History. 2. Human engineering - Study and teaching - Russia (Federation) - Tverskai͡a oblast' - History. 3. Psychology, Military - Study and teaching - Russia (Federation) - Tverskai͡a oblast' - History. I. Title.
BF80.7.R8 S55 1999

Shikun, A. F.
Aktual'nye voprosy obshcheĭ, vozrastnoĭ i sotsial'noĭ psikhologii. Tver' : Tverskoĭ gos. universitet, 2001.
BF20 .A46 2001

Shilony, Tamar. Model mentali shel morim menusim ve-tironim be-miktso'ot mada'iyim ve-humaniyim le-gabe lemidah be-kerev yeladim / mugeshet 'al-yede Tamar Shiloni. [Israel : h. mo. l., 1994?] 5, 275, iii leaves ; 28 cm. Added title page title: Mental model of teachers with different teaching experience who teach different subject matter about the structure of children's minds and its functioning in learning. Thesis (M.A.)--Universitat Tel-Aviv, 1994. Includes bibliographical references (leaves 187-198). Abstract also in English.
1. Education, Secondary. 2. Educational psychology. 3. High school teachers. 4. Teacher effectiveness. I. Title. II. Title: Mental model of teachers with different teaching experience who teach different subject matter about the structure of children's minds and its functioning in learning

Shiman, Philip.
Roland, Alex, 1944- Strategic computing. Cambridge, Mass. : MIT Press, c2002.
QA76.88 .R65 2002

Shin, Ann.
Western eyes [videorecording]. New York, NY : First Run/Icarus Films, 2000.

Shinākht-i rūḥ.
Rahbar'zādah, Hasan. Chāp-i 1. Tihrān : Nashr-i Pārsā, 1380 [2001 04 2002]

Shine, Betty, 1929- A free spirit : gives you the right to make choices / Betty Shine. London : HarperCollinsPublishers, 2001. 305 p. ; 20 cm. ISBN 0-00-257162-5 DDC 133.91092
1. Shine, Betty, - 1929- 2. Women mediums - Great Britain - Biography. 3. Spiritualism. 4. Human-animal communication. 5. Mediums - Great Britain - Biography. I. Title.

SHINE, BETTY, 1929-.
Shine, Betty, 1929- A free spirit. London : HarperCollinsPublishers, 2001.

Shine forth.
Meader, William A., 1955- Mariposa, Calif. : Source Publications, c2004.
BF1611 .M412 2004

Shinpan shinrigaku ga wakaru. Tōkyō : Asahi Shinbunsha, 2003. 176 p. : ill. ; 26 cm. (AERA Mook ; no. 89) Cover title. "Asahi Shimbun extra report & analysis special number 89, 2003"--Cover. Includes lists of universities and graduate schools in Japan which offer psychology (p. 91-96). Includes bibliographical references. "Shinrigaku o yomu": p. 162-175. ISBN 4-02-274139-2
1. Psychology. 2. Psychology - Japan. I. Title: Aera (Tokyo, Japan) II. Title: Shinrigaku ga wakaru III. Series.
BF108.J3 S55 2003

Shinrigaku ga wakaru.
Shinpan shinrigaku ga wakaru. Tōkyō : Asahi Shinbunsha, 2003.
BF108.J3 S55 2003

The Ship of thought : essays on psychoanalysis and learning / edited by Duncan Barford. London : Karnac, 2002. 247 p. ; 23 cm. (Encyclopaedia of

psychoanalysis ; 4) Includes bibliographical references (p. [230]-239) and index. ISBN 1-85575-286-7
1. Psychoanalysis. 2. Learning, Psychology of. I. Bradford, Duncan. II. Series.

SHIPWRECKS - PACIFIC OCEAN - JUVENILE LITERATURE.
Philbrick, Nat. Revenge of the whale. New York : G.P. Putnam, 2002.
G530.E77 P454 2002

Shir ha-shirim.
Halfon, Eliyahu ben Hayim. [Israel] : Or tsah hadpasah ve-hafatsah shel sipre Yahadut, [2001]

Shi'ure da'at.
Blokh, Avraham Yitshak ben Y. L. (Avraham Yitshak ben Yosef Leyb), d. 1941. Sefer Shi'ure da'at. Yerushalayim : Feldhaim ; Wickliffe, Ohio : Peninei Daas Publications, 761 [2001]

Shiva, Vandana.
Monkeywrenching the new world order [sound recording]. Oakland, Calif : AK Press ; San Francisco, CA : Alternative Tentacles Records, 2001.

Shlain, Leonard.
Sex, time, and power : how women's sexuality shaped human evolution / Leonard Shlain. New York ; London : Viking, 2003. xx, 420 p. : ill. ; 24 cm. Includes bibliographical references (p. [371]-402) and index. ISBN 0-670-03233-6 (alk. paper) DDC 306.7
1. Sexual attraction. 2. Mate selection. 3. Human evolution. 4. Social evolution. 5. Sex (Biology) 6. Evolution (Biology) I. Title.
HQ23 .S45 2003

Shlezinger, Yehi'el Mikha'el.
Shakh, El'azar Menahem Man. Sefer Mi-torato de-rabi El'azar. [Bene Berak] : le-haśig mishpahat Kohen, [763 i.e. 2003]

Shneiderman, Ben, 1947-.
Bederson, Benjamin. The craft of information visualization. San Francisco, Calif. : Morgan Kaufmann ; Oxford : Elsevier Science, 2003.

SHNEUR ZALMAN, OF LYADY, 1745-1813. LIKUTE AMARIM.
Steinsaltz, Adin. [Be'ur Tanya. English] Opening the Tanya. 1st ed. San Francisco : Jossey-Bass, c2003.
BM198.2.S563 S7413 2003

Likute amarim. English.
Steinsaltz, Adin. [Be'ur Tanya. English] Opening the Tanya. 1st ed. San Francisco : Jossey-Bass, c2003.
BM198.2.S563 S7413 2003

SHO'AH (1939-1945). See HOLOCAUST, JEWISH (1939-1945).

Shoemaker, Sydney.
Identity, cause, and mind : philosophical essays / Sydney Shoemaker. Expanded ed. Oxford : Clarendon Press ; New York : Oxford University Press, c2003. xii, 461 p. ; 24 cm. Includes bibliographical references (p. [452]-458) and index. ISBN 0-19-926470-8 (pbk. : alk. paper) ISBN 0-19-926469-4 (alk. paper) DDC 110
1. Philosophy. 2. Psychology. I. Title.
B29 .S5135 2003

SHOFAR CALLS.
He lakhem hamishah sefari.. [Brooklyn, NY : Renaissance Hebraica, 2000?]

Shoham, S. Giora, 1929-
Art, crime, and madness : Gesualdo, Caravaggio, Genet, Van Gogh, Artaud / Shlomo Giora Shoham. Brighton [England] ; Portland, Or. : Sussex Academic Press, 2002, c2003. ix, 209 p. ; 23 cm. Includes bibliographical references (p. [190]-200) and index. ISBN 1-903900-05-0 (alk. paper) ISBN 1-903900-06-9 (pbk.) DDC 700/.1/9
1. Art and mental illness. 2. Artists - Psychology. 3. Creative ability. I. Title.
N71.5 .S53 2003

Teruf, setiyah vi-yetsirah / Shelomoh Giyorah Shoham. [Israel] : Miśrad ha-bitahon, [2002] 283 p., [8] leaves of plates : ill. (some col.) ; 21 cm. (Siriyat "universitah meshuderet") Title on verso of t.p.: Madness, deviance and creativity. Includes bibliographical references. ISBN 9650511377
1. Gesualdo, Carlo, - principe di Venosa, - 1560 (ca.)-1613. 2. Caravaggio, Michelangelo Merisi da, 1573-1610. 3. Gogh, Vincent van, 1853-1890. 4. Genet, Jean, - 1910- 5. Astraud Antonin, - 1896-1948. 6. Artists - Psychology. 7. Art and mental illness. 8. Genius and mental illness. 9. Deviant behavior. 10. Creative ability. I. Title. II. Title: Madness, deviance and creativity

Shohov, Serge P.
Perspectives on cognitive psychology. New York : Nova Science, c2002.
BF201 .P48 2002

Topics in cognitive psychology. New York : Nova Science Publishers, 2003.
BF201 .T67 2003

Trends in cognitive psychology. New York : Nova Science Publishers, c2002.
BF311 .T723 2002

Shōkokumin bunka shinsho
(2.) Edo-e kara shomotsu made. Tōkyō : Kyūzansha, 1997.
HQ792.J3 N54 1997 v.19

Shomer ha-pardes.
Sack, Bracha, 1933- Be'er Sheva' : Universitat Ben-Guryon ba-Negev, c2002.

Shomer ha-Pardes : the Kabbalist Rabbi Shabbetai Sheftel Horowitz of Prague.
Sack, Bracha, 1933- Shomer ha-pardes. Be'er Sheva' : Universitat Ben-Guryon ba-Negev, c2002.

Shooter, Jonathan.
The wisdom within : a parashah companion / Jonathan Shooter. Southfield, MI : Targum Press ; Nanuet, NY : Distributed by Feldheim Publishers, 2002. 345 p. ; 24 cm. Includes bibliographical references (p. [337]-345). ISBN 1-56871-223-5
1. Bible. - O.T. - Pentateuch - Sermons. 2. Bible. - O.T. - Pentateuch - Meditations. 3. Ethics, Jewish. 4. Jewish way of life. I. Title.

SHOOTING. See FIREARMS.
SHOPPING CENTERS. See RETAIL TRADE.

Shore, Hennie.
The you & me scriptbook / by Hennie Shore. [United States] : Childswork Childsplay, c2002. 1 c. (various pagings) ; 28 cm. ISBN 1-58815-054-2 DDC 155.4/18
1. Social skills in children. 2. Socialization. I. Title. II. Title: You and me scriptbook
BF723.S62 S46 2002

Shorshe ha-Yam.
Hilel, Ya'akov Mosheh. Sefer Shorshe ha-Yam. Yerushalayim : ha-Makhon le-hotsa'at sefarim "Ahavat shalom", 759- [1999-
BM525.V532 H5 1999

Hilel, Ya'akov Mosheh. Sefer Shorshe ha-Yam. Yerushalayim : ha-Makhon le-hotsa'at sefarim "Ahavat shalom", 759- [1999-
BM525.V532 H5 1999

A short guide to writing about psychology.
Dunn, Dana. Upper Saddle River, NJ : Pearson/Longman, 2003.
BF76.8 .D86 2003

SHORT-TERM MEMORY - CONGRESSES.
Working on working memory. Leipzig : Leipziger Universitätsverlag, 2000.
BF378.S54 W675 2000

SHORT VACATIONS.
Laing, Kathleen. Girlfriends' getaway. 1st ed. Colorado Springs, Colo. : WaterBrook Press, 2002.
BF575.F66 L35 2002

Shorter-Gooden, Kumea.
Jones, Charisse. Shifting. 1st ed. New York : HarperCollins, c2003.
E185.625 .J657 2003

Should we worry about family change?.
Lewis, Jane (Jane E.) Toronto : University of Toronto Press, c2003.

Shoulda, coulda, woulda.
Parrott, Les. Grand Rapids, Mich. : Zondervan, c2003.
BF575.R33 P37 2004

SHRINES. See CHRISTIAN SHRINES; RELIQUARIES.
SHRINES, CHRISTIAN. See CHRISTIAN SHRINES.

Shrinking violets and Caspar Milquetoasts.
McDaniel, Patricia (Patricia A.) New York : New York University Press, 2003.
BF575.B3 M34 2003

SHRUBS. See HEDGES.

Shtayn, Moysheh Yitshok.
Fridman, Aharon (Aharon ben Yehoshu'a) [Gam atah yakhol. Yiddish] Du kenst oykh!. Nyu York : Lev Yiśroel, 762, 2002.

Shtern, Shemu'el Eli'ezer.
Sefer Sene bo'er ba-esh : perakim be-mishnat maran "ha-Hatam Sofer" ... / me-et ha-rav Shemu'el Eli'ezer Shtern. Bene Berak : Mekhon "Mayim hayim", 762 [2002] 419 p. : facsim. ; 24 cm. Running title: Sene bo'er ba-esh. On cover : "Orhot hayay, hashkafato u-mishnato shel maran ha-Hatam Sofer ..."

Includes bibliographical references.
1. Sofer, Moses, - 1762-1839. 2. Rabbis - Slovakia - Bratislava - Biography. 3. Rabbis - Biography. 4. Ethics, Jewish. I. Title. II. Title: Sene bo'er ba-esh

Shu shu cong shu (Zhongguo zhe xue wen hua xie jin hui)
Tai ji wen hua. Xianggang : Zhongguo zhe xue wen hua xie jin hui, [2001-
BF1770.C5 T35

Shu yuan si xu.
Liu, Zaifu, 1941- Xianggang : Tian di tu shu you xian gong si, 2002.
PL2879.T653 S58 2002

Shuang xin jia ting.
Hobfoll, Stevan E. [Work won't love you back. Chinese] Top shuang xin jia ting. Chu ban. Taibei Shi : Ye qiang chu ban she, 1997.

Shubniakov, B. P.
Svoboda kak sotsial'nyi i dukhovno-psikhicheskii fenomen / B.P. Shubniakov, G.M. Nazhmudinov. IAroslavl' : DIA-press, 2000. 155 p. ; 21 cm. Includes bibliographical references.
1. Free will and determinism. 2. Liberty. I. Nazhmudinov, G. M. II. Title.

Shui yue jing hua.
Ma, Wenqi. Di 1 ban. Beijing : Zhongguo she hui chu ban she, 1994.
PN2039 .M28 1994 <Orien China>

Shulman, Mark, 1962-
The voodoo revenge book : an anger management program you can really stick with / by Mark Shulman ; illustrated by Joe Bartos. New York : Main Street, c2002. 96 p. : ill. ; 24 cm. Includes index. Publisher description URL: http://www.loc.gov/catdir/description/ste031/2003268615.html ISBN 1402700520 (hbk.) DDC 818/.602
1. Revenge - Humor. 2. Voodooism - Humor. 3. Stress management - Humor. 4. Anger - Humor. I. Bartos, Joe. II. Title.
BF637.R48 S55 2002

Shultz, Thomas R.
Computational developmental psychology / Thomas R. Shultz. Cambridge, Mass. : MIT Press, c2003. xiv, 322 p. : ill. ; 24 cm. "A Bradford book". Includes bibliographical references (p. [293]-315) and index. ISBN 0-262-19483-X (alk. paper) DDC 155
1. Developmental psychology. 2. Cognitive science. I. Title.
BF713 .S35 2003

Shuman, Carol.
Jenny is scared : when sad things happen in the world / by Carol Shuman ; illustrated by Cary Pillo. Washington, DC : Magination Press, c2003. p. cm. SUMMARY: When Jenny and her brother are frightened by events in the world, their parents help them talk about their fears and feel better. ISBN 1-59147-003-X (pbk. : alk. paper) ISBN 1-59147-002-1 (alk. paper) DDC 152.4/6
1. Fear in children - Juvenile literature. 2. Fear. 3. Emotions. I. Pillo, Cary, ill. II. Title.
BF723.F4 S58 2003

Shumway, David R.
Modern love : romance, intimacy, and the marriage crisis / David R. Shumway. New York : New York University Press, c2003. xi, 269 p. : ill. ; 24 cm. Includes bibliographical references and index. ISBN 0-8147-9830-6 (cloth : alk. paper) ISBN 0-8147-9831-4 (pbk. : alk. paper) DDC 306.81
1. Marriage. 2. Marriage in popular culture. 3. Marriage in literature. 4. Marriage in motion pictures. I. Title.
HQ503 .S54 2003

Shupe, Anson D.
Iadicola, Peter. Violence, inequality, and human freedom. 2nd ed. Lanham, Md. ; Oxford : Rowman & Littlefield Publishers, Inc., c2003.
HM886 .I18 2003

Shweder, Richard A.
Why do men barbecue? : recipes for cultural psychology / Richard A. Shweder. Cambridge, Mass. : Harvard University Press, 2003. viii, 419 p. ; 22 cm. Includes bibliographical references (p. 369-400) and index. ISBN 0-674-01057-4 (cloth : alk. paper) ISBN 0-674-01135-X (paper : alk. paper) DDC 155.82
1. Ethnopsychology. 2. Pluralism (Social sciences) 3. Multiculturalism. I. Title.
GN502 .S59 2003

Shyles, Leonard, 1948-.
Deciphering cyberspace. Thousand Oaks, Calif. : Sage Publications, c2003.
TK5102.2 .D43 2003

SHYNESS. See BASHFULNESS.

The shyness breakthrough.
Carducci, Bernardo J. [Emmaus, Pa.] : Rodale, c2003.
BF723.B3 C37 2003

Si wang mei xue.
Yan, Xianglin, 1960- Di 1 ban. Shanghai : Xue lin chu ban she, 1998.

Si xiang xue shu sheng huo
Jiang, Yin. Xue shu de nian lun. Di 1 ban. [Beijing] : Zhongguo wen lian chu ban she, 2000.
PL2262 .J536 2000

Sibirskaia psikhologiia segodnia : sbornik nauchnykh trudov / [redaktsionnaia kollegiia, M.M. Gorbatova, A.V. Seryĭ, M.S. IAnitskiĭ (otv. redaktor)]. Kemerovo : Kemerovskiĭ gos. universitet, 2002. 334 p. : ill. ; 21 cm. Includes bibliographical references. ISBN 5202005555
1. Psychology - Russia (Federation) - Siberia - Congresses. I. Gorbatova, M. M. II. Seryĭ, A. V. III. IAnitskiĭ, M. S. (Mikhail Sergeevich) IV. Kemerovskiĭ gosudarstvennyĭ universitet.
BF20 .S53 2002

SIBLING ABUSE. See **BROTHERS AND SISTERS.**

SIBLING RELATIONS. See **BROTHERS AND SISTERS.**

Sibling relationships.
Sanders, Robert, 1946- New York : Palgrave Macmillan, 2004.
BF723.S43 S159 2004

SIBLING RIVALRY.
Wolf, Anthony E. "Mom, Jason's breathing on me!". 1st ed. New York : Ballantine Books, 2003.
BF723.S43 W65 2003

SIBLINGS. See also **BROTHERS AND SISTERS.**
Mitchell, Juliet, 1940- Cambridge, UK : Polity Press, c2003.
BF723.S43 M58 2003

Sichelschmidt, Lorenz.
Sprache, Sinn und Situation. 1. Aufl. Wiesbaden : Deutscher Universitäts-Verlag, 2001.

Sichirollo, Livio. Filosofia, storia, istituzioni / Livio Sichirollo. Nuova ed. [Urbino] : Università degli studi di Urbino, [2001] 346 p. ; 22 cm. (Pubblicazioni dell'Università di Urbino. Scienze umane. Serie di filosofia pedagogia psicologia ; 9) Originally published 1990, now enlarged. Includes bibliographical references and index. ISBN 88-392-0576-4 DDC 190
1. Philosophy - History. 2. Philosophy, Ancient. 3. Philosophy, Modern. I. Title. II. Series.

SICK. See **DISEASES; MENTALLY ILL.**

SICK - PRAYER-BOOKS AND DEVOTIONS, JEWISH.
Naphtali ben Isaac, ha-Kohen, 1649-1719. Sefer Bet Raḥel. Yerushalayim : Ahavat Shalom, 761 [2001]
BM665 .N257 2001

SICK - PSYCHOLOGY.
Dahlin, Olov, 1962- Zvinorwadza. Frankfurt am Main ; New York : P. Lang, c2002.
R726.5 .D34 2002

Keppe, Norberto R. [Origem Das Enfermidades. English] The origin of illness. 1st American ed. Englewood Cliffs, N.J. : Campbell Hall Press, 2002.
RC460 .K4713 2002

Roads to recovery. St. Leonards, NSW : Allen & Unwin, 1997.
BF698.35.O48 R63 1997

Woolf, Virginia, 1882-1941. On being ill. Ashfield, Mass. : Paris Press, 2002.
PR6045.O72 O5 2002

SICKNESS. See **DISEASES.**

SICKNESSES. See **DISEASES.**

SIDEREAL SYSTEM. See **STARS.**

Sidrat "universiṭah meshuderet"
Grinshpon, Yoḥanan, 1948- Demamah ve-ḥerut ba-yogah ha-Kelasit. [Tel Aviv] : Misrad ha-biṭaḥon, [2002]

Sieff, Paris, ill.
Johnson, Marvin. Where's Jess? Rev. Omaha, NE : Centering Corp. Resource, 2003.
BF723.G75 J645 2003

Šifler-Premec, Ljerka, 1941-.
Gučetić, Nikola Vitov, 1549-1610. [Dialogo della bellezza. Serbo-Croatian & Italian] Dijalog o ljepoti = Dvojezično izd. Zagreb : Društvo hrvatskih književnika, 1995.
BH301.L65 G8318 1995

Sifre Mekhon "Ahavat shalom" Yerushalayim.
Eliyahu, Saliman. Sefer Kerem Shelomoh. Yerushala[y]im : Ḥevrat Ahavat shalom, 762 [2001 or 2002]

Sifre Mekhon "Ahavat Shalom" Yerushalayim
(278) Vital, Ḥayyim ben Joseph, 1542 or 3-1620.
'Ets ha-da'at tov. Yerushalayim : Hotsa'at Ahavat shalom, 761 [2000 or 2001]

Sifre Mekhon "Ahavat shalom" Yerushalayim
(281) Naphtali ben Isaac, ha-Kohen, 1649-1719. Sefer Bet Raḥel. Yerushalayim : Ahavat Shalom, 761 [2001]
BM665 .N257 2001

(300) Hilel, Ya'aḳov Mosheh. Sefer Ahavat shalom. [Hotsa'ah 2], 'im hosafot rabot. Yerushala[y]im : ha-Makhon le-hotsa'at sefarim ve-khitve yad "Ahavat Shalom", 762 [2002]

Sifriyat "Ḥelal Ben-Ḥayim"
Ta-Shma, Israel M. ha-Nigleh sheba-nistar. Nusaḥ murḥav. [Tel Aviv] : ha-Ḳibuts ha-me'uḥad, c2001.

Sifriyat "Universiṭah meshuderet"
Elior, Rachel. Ḥerut 'al ha-luḥot. [Tel Aviv] : Misrad ha-biṭaḥon, [1999]

Śifte ḥayim.
Fridlander, Ḥayim ben Mosheh. Sefer Śifte ḥayim. Bene-Beraḳ : ha-Rabanit Fridlander, 763- [2002 or 2003-

Śifte tsedeḳ.
Eliyahu, Mordekhai. Sefer Śifte tsedeḳ. Rekhasim : M. Eliyahu, 762 [2002]

Sigaud, Olivier.
Workshop on Adaptive Behavior in Anticipatory Learning Systems (1st : 2002 : Edinburgh, Scotland) Anticipatory behavior in adaptive learning systems. Berlin ; New York : Springer, c2003.
Q325.5 .W65 2003

SIGHTINGS OF UNIDENTIFIED FLYING OBJECTS. See **UNIDENTIFIED FLYING OBJECTS - SIGHTINGS AND ENCOUNTERS.**

Sigmund Freud.
Bocock, Robert. Rev. ed. London ; New York : Routledge, 2002.
BF173.F85 B63 2002

Delrieu, Alain. 2e éd. rev., augm. et mise à jour. Paris : Anthropos : Diffusion Economica, c2001.
BF109.F74 D45 2001

Freud [electronic resource]. Washington, DC : Library of Congress
BF173

Jacobs, Michael, 1941-. 2nd ed. London ; Thousand Oaks, Calif. : SAGE Publications, 2003.
BF109.F74 J33 2003

SIGN-BOARDS. See **SIGNS AND SIGNBOARDS.**

SIGN LANGUAGE. See also **GESTURE; SIGNS AND SYMBOLS.**
Acredolo, Linda P. My first baby signs. [New York] : HarperFestival, c2002.
BF720.C65 A27 2002

Oxford handbook of deaf studies, language, and education. Oxford ; New York : Oxford University Press, c2003.
HV2380 .O88 2003

Rehm, Ulrich. Stumme Sprache der Bilder. München : Deutscher Kunstverlag, 2002.

SIGNAGE. See **SIGNS AND SIGNBOARDS.**

Signaling goodness.
Nelson, Phillip J., 1929- Ann Arbor : University of Michigan Press, c2003.
HV31 .N45 2003

Signature for success.
Imberman, Arlyn. Kansas City, Mo. : Andrews McMeel Pub., 2003.
BF891 .I46 2003

SIGNBOARDS. See **SIGNS AND SIGNBOARDS.**

SIGNIFICANCE LOGIC. See **SIGNIFICATION (LOGIC).**

Signification in Buddhist and French traditions.
Gill, Harjeet Singh, 1935- New Delhi : Harman Pub. House, 2001.
BC25 .G55 2001

SIGNIFICATION (LINGUISTICS). See **REFERENCE (LINGUISTICS).**

SIGNIFICATION (LOGIC).
Gill, Harjeet Singh, 1935- Signification in Buddhist and French traditions. New Delhi : Harman Pub. House, 2001.
BC25 .G55 2001

SIGNIFICS. See **SEMANTICS (PHILOSOPHY).**

Signos de identidad histórica para Navarra / dirección científica, Angel Martín Duque ; adjunto, Javier Martínez de Aguirre ; dirección editorial, Arturo Navallas Rebolé ; adjunto, Roldán Jimeno Aranguren. Pamplona : Caja de Ahorros de Navarra, 1996. 2 v. : ill., maps (some col.) ; 28 cm. (Biblioteca Caja de Ahorros de Navarra ; 5) Includes bibliographical references. ISBN 84-87120-30-X (obra completa) ISBN 84-87120-31-8 (v. 1) ISBN 84-87120-32-6 (v. 2)
1. Navarre (Spain) - Civilization. 2. Symbolism. 3. Signs and symbols. I. Series.
DP302.N267 S54 1996

SIGNS. See **SIGNS AND SIGNBOARDS; SIGNS AND SYMBOLS.**

SIGNS (ADVERTISING). See **SIGNS AND SIGNBOARDS.**

SIGNS AND SIGN-BOARDS. See **SIGNS AND SIGNBOARDS.**

SIGNS AND SIGNBOARDS.
Schmauks, Dagmar. Orientierung im Raum. Tübingen : Stauffenburg, c2002.
QP443 .S363 2002

SIGNS AND SIGNBOARDS - RUSSIA (FEDERATION) - LETTERING.
Florenskaia, O. Psikhologiia bytovogo shrifta. Sankt-Peterburg : Krasnyĭ matros, 2001.
BF896 .F66 2001

SIGNS AND SYMBOLS. See also **EMBLEMS; OMENS; SEMANTICS (PHILOSOPHY).**
A che servono i simboli? Milano : FrancoAngeli, c2002.

Signos de identidad histórica para Navarra. Pamplona : Caja de Ahorros de Navarra, 1996.
DP302.N267 S54 1996

SIGNS AND SYMBOLS - GERMANY - HISTORY - 17TH CENTURY.
Strasser, Gerhard F. Emblematik und Mnemonik der frühen Neuzeit im Zusammenspiel Johannes Buno und Johann Justus Winckelmann. Wiesbaden : Harrassowitz Wolfenbüttel : Herzog August Bibliothek, c2000.
PN6348.5 .S873 2000

SIGNS AND SYMBOLS IN ARCHITECTURE. See **SYMBOLISM IN ARCHITECTURE.**

SIGNS AND SYMBOLS IN ART. See **SYMBOLISM IN ART.**

SIGNS AND SYMBOLS - ISRAEL - HISTORY - 20TH CENTURY.
Rowland, Robert C., 1954- Shared land/conflicting identity. East lansing : Michigan State University Press, 2002.
DS119.7 .R685 2003

SIGNS AND SYMBOLS - PHILOSOPHY.
Janz, Nathalie. Globus symbolicus. [Lausanne : Université de Lausanne, 1999]

SIGNS AND SYMBOLS - UNITED STATES.
Azoulay, Paul. Uncle Sam. Anglet : Atlantica, c2002.

Signs of the times.
Erlanger, Gad. [Mazalot, ha-Yahadut va-ani. English] Jerusalem ; New York : Feldheim Pub., 2000.
BF1714.J4 E74 2001

SIGNS (OMENS). See **OMENS.**

Signs, symbols & omens.
Buckland, Raymond. 1st ed. St. Paul, Minn. : Llewellyn Publications, 2003.
BF1623.S9 B83 2003

Signs, symbols, and omens.
Buckland, Raymond. Signs, symbols & omens. 1st ed. St. Paul, Minn. : Llewellyn Publications, 2003.
BF1623.S9 B83 2003

Śiḥot musar.
Shemu'elevits, Ḥayim, 1901-1979. Sefer Śiḥot musar. Mahad. ḥadashah u-metukenet. Yerushalayim : Bene va-hatane ha-meḥaber, 762, c2002.
BJ1287.S56 S5 2002

Śiḥot musar Da'at u-tevunah : be-'inyene emunah, hashkafah ve-tiḳun ha-midot : she-ne'emru ben kotle Yeshivat Da'at u-tevunah ... / liḳeṭ ve-'arakh ... Shimshon b.R. Eliyahu Bamnolḳer (Ben Raḥamim). Ashdod : Sh. ben E. Bamnolḳer, 761 [2001] 208 p. ; 25 cm. Running title: Da'at u-tevunah.
1. Bible. - O.T. - Pentateuch - Sermons. 2. Ethics, Jewish. I. Bamnolḳer, Shimshon ben Eliyahu. II. Yeshivat Da'at u-tevunah (Ashdod, Israel) III. Title: Da'at u-tevunah

BJ1280 .B34 2001

Šik, Miroslav. Altneue Gedanken : Texte und Gespräche, 1987-2001 / Miroslav Šik ; [Herausgeber, Heinz Wirz]. Luzern : Quart, c2002. 175 p. : ill. ; 23 cm. (Bibliotheca ; Bd. 3) Includes bibliographical references. ISBN 3-907631-13-7 (pbk.)
1. Aesthetics. 2. Art. 3. Architecture. I. Wirz, Heinz. II. Title. III. Series: Bibliotheca (Lucerne, Switzerland) ; Bd. 3.

Sikora, Mario, 1963-.
Tallon, Robert, 1947- From awareness to action. Scranton, Pa. : University of Scranton Press, 2003.
BF698.35.E54 T35 2003

Sikora, Tomasz.
Odmiany odmieńca. Katowice : "Śląsk", 2002.
HQ23 .O36 2002

Sikorskiĭ, I. A. (Ivan Alekseevich), 1842-1919. Selections. 2002.
Russkaia rasovaia teoriia do 1917 goda. Moskva : Feri-V, 2002.

Silber, Gus.
Grulke, Wolfgang. Lessons in radical innovation. International ed. London : Financial Times Prentice Hall, 2002.

Silber, Lee T. Aim first! : get focused and fired up to follow through on your goals / Lee T. Silber. Mission, Kan. : SkillPath Publications, c1999. x, 130 p. ; 23 cm. (SkillPath self-study sourcebook) ISBN 1-57294-071-9 DDC 153.8
1. Goal (Psychology) - Problems, exercises, etc. I. Title. II. Series.
BF505.G6 S55 1999

SILENCE. See NOISE.

Silence and liberation in Classical Yoga.
Grinshpon, Yohanan, 1948- Demamah ve-ḥerut ba-yogah ha-Kelasit. [Tel Aviv] : Miśrad ha-biṭaḥon, [2002]

SILENCE (PHILOSOPHY).
Jadacki, Jacek Juliusz. From the viewpoint of the Lvov-Warsaw school. Amsterdam ; New York, NY : Rodopi, 2003.

Rhodes, James M. Eros, wisdom, and silence. Columbia, Mo. : University of Missouri Press, c2003.
B398.L9 .R46 2003

SILENCE - RELIGIOUS ASPECTS - JUDAISM.
Sefer Ḳedushat ha-dibur. Bene Beraḳ : Yehudah Yosef Ha-leyi Gruber, 761- [2001-]

The silent psalms of our son.
Jarashow, Jonathan. Jerusalem, Israel : Feldheim Publishers, c2001.

The silent revolution : the change of gender roles : 14th Sinclair House Debate, April 7-8, 2000. Bad Homburg v.d. Höhe : Herbert Quandt Foundation, 2000. 107 p. : ill. ; 26 cm. (Sinclair House Debate, 1438-7885 ; 14) ISBN 3-00-006332-3 (pbk.)
1. Sex role - Congresses. 2. Sex role - Developed countries - Congresses. 3. Women - Social conditions - Congresses. 4. Women - Developed countries - Social conditions - Congresses. I. Herbert Quandt Stiftung. II. Series.
HQ1075 .S55 2000

Silhon, sieur de (Jean), 1596?-1667. De la certitude des connaissances humaines / Jean de Silhon. [Paris] : Fayard, c2002. 368 p. ; 22 cm. (Corpus des œuvres de philosophie en langue française) Originally published: Amsterdam : A. Michiels, 1662. ISBN 2-213-61177-7 DDC 194
1. Political science - Philosophy. 2. Religion - Philosophy. 3. Philosophy, Modern - 17th century. I. Title. II. Series.

Sillamy, Norbert. Dictionnaire de psychologie / Norbert Sillamy. [Nouv. éd.]. Paris : Larousse, 2003. 281 p. : ill. ; 21 cm. (In extenso) ISBN 2-03-575086-5
1. Psychology - Dictionaries - French. I. Title. II. Series: In extenso (Larousse (Firm))
BF31 .S5 2003

Sillers, Tia.
Sanders, Mark D. I hope you dance!. Nashville, Tenn. : Rutledge Hill Press, 2003.
BF410 .S26 2003

Sills, Judith. If the horse is dead, get off! : creating change when you're stuck in your comfort zone / Judith Sills. New York : Viking, 2004. p. cm. Includes index. ISBN 0-670-85847-1 DDC 158.1
1. Self-efficacy. 2. Change (Psychology) 3. Self-actualization (Psychology) I. Title.
BF637.S38 S55 2004

Śilpa-śāstram.
[Śilpaśāstra. English & Sanskrit.] Vāstu-śāstram. Calcutta : Sanskrit Pustak Bhandar, 2001.

NA7427 .M34 2001

Śilpaśāstra.
Khadiratna, Dayanidhi. Brhat śilpaśāstra, bā, Gṛhabandha bijñāna ; Gṛhabandha gaṇanā o śubhastambhāropaṇa bicāra. Kaṭaka : Dharmagrantha Shtora, [1995?]
TH4809.14 K48 1995

[Śilpaśāstra. English & Sanskrit.] Vāstu-śāstram : Śilpa-śāstram : a Sanskrit treatise on ancient Indian architecture / by Bāuri Mahārāṇā ; translated in English by Prof. P.N. Bose ; edited by Manabendu Banerjee. Calcutta : Sanskrit Pustak Bhandar, 2001. xxviii, 58 p. ; 21 cm. Authorship acribed to: Bāurī Mahārāṇā. SUMMARY: Verse work on domestic architecture with special reference to Hindu astrology. Includes bibliographical references (p. [57]-58). English and Sanskrit.
1. Architecture, Domestic - India. 2. Architecture, Hindu. 3. Astrology and architecture - India. I. Bāurī Mahārāṇa. II. Banerjee, Manabendu. III. Title. IV. Title: Śilpa-śāstram
NA7427 .M34 2001

Silva, Ana Márcia. Corpo, ciência e mercado : reflexões acerca da gestação de um novo arquetipo da felicidade / Ana Márcia Silva. Campinas : Editora da UFSC : Editora Autores Associados, 2001. 144 p. ; 21 cm. (Coleção Educação física e esportes) Includes bibliographical references. ISBN 85-7496-013-6
1. Body, Human - Social aspects. 2. Body, Human (Philosophy) 3. Physical education and training. I. Title. II. Series.
GT495 .S55 2001

Silva, Francisco J.
Machado, Armando. The psychology of learning. Upper Saddle River, NJ : Prentice Hall, 2003.
BF318 .M29 2003

Silva, Lina Gorenstein Ferreira da, 1951-.
Ensaios sobre a intolerância. São Paulo, SP, Brasil : Humanitas, FFLCH/USP : FAPESP : LEI-Laboratório de Estudos sobre a Intolerância, 2002.

Silva, Vagner Gonçalves da.
Verger, Pierre. Saída de Iaô. Sao Paulo : Fundação Pierre Verger : Axis Mundi Editora, 2002.

Silva, W. W. da Matta e (Woodrow Wilson da Matta e), 1917- Mistérios e práticas da lei de Umbanda / W.W. da Matta e Silva (Mestre Yapacani). Sao Paulo : Icone Editora, c1999. 224 p. : ill. ; 23 cm. ISBN 85-274-0585-7
1. Umbanda (Cult) 2. Spiritualism. I. Title.

SILVER. See MONEY.

Silver, Bruce.
Renaissance and early modern philosophy. Malden, MA : Oxford : Blackwell Pub., c2002.
B775 .R46 2002

SILVER, MARK.
Vint/age 2001 conference : [videorecording]. New York, c2001.

Silver, Mark, panelist.
Vint/age 2001 conference : [videorecording]. New York, c2001.

SILVER QUESTION. See MONEY.

Silverman, Bynjamin, Dr.
Koll, Shmuel, 1938- Sefer Raʻyonot u-mesarim. Yerushalayim : S. Kol, 761- [2001-

Silverman, Hugh J.
Lyotard. New York ; London : Routledge, 2002.

Silverman, Robin Landew. Reaching your goals / Robin Silverman. New York : F. Watts, 2003. p. cm. (Life balance) SUMMARY: Examines how to use imagination, thought, determination, and other abilities to transform a wish into a goal, visualize achieving it, plan how to reach it, and ultimately find success. Includes bibliographical references and index. Table of contents URL: http://www.loc.gov/catdir/toc/ecip046/2003014720.html CONTENTS: Imagine that! -- What are you thinking about? -- Who do you want to be? -- What's your problem? -- Happy endings -- Plan it! -- Get started today -- Making it happen. ISBN 0-531-12342-1 DDC 153.8
1. Goal (Psychology) - Juvenile literature. 2. Planning - Juvenile literature. 3. Goal (Psychology) 4. Success. I. Title. II. Series.
BF505.G6 S57 2003

Silverman, Stephen M. Envy, anger & sweet revenge : hey, it works in Hollywood! / Stephen M. Siverman. New York : Red Rock Press, c2002. 126 p. : ill. (some col.) ; 20 cm. (Sin series ; v. 5) ISBN 0-9669573-5-0 DDC 152.4/8
1. Envy - Miscellanea. 2. Anger - Miscellanea. 3. Revenge - Miscellanea. 4. Motion pictures - Miscellanea. I. Title. II. Title: Envy, anger, and sweet revenge III. Series.
BF575.E65 S55 2002

Silvers, Terry.
Francis-Cheung, Theresa. Teen tarot. Avon, MA : Adams Media Corp., 2003.
BF1879.T2 F7 2003

Silverstein, Louise B.
Auerbach, Carl F. Qualitative data. New York : New York University Press, c2003.
BF76.5 .A95 2003

Feminist family therapy. 1st ed. Washington, DC : American Psychological Association, c2003.
RC488.5 .F453 2003

SIL'VESTR, D. CA. 1566.
Zaĭtseva, L. I. Russkie providt͡sy o rossiĭskoĭ gosudarstvennosti. Moskva : In-t ėkonomiki RAN, 1998-
DK49 .Z35 1998

Sima, Lieren. Tong jing : Zeng Guofan ba shi yi ge zhong gao / Zeng Guofan yuan dian ; Sima Lieren jie yi. Di 1 ban. Beijing : Zhongguo hua qiao chu ban she, 2002. 4, 14, 385 p. ; 21 cm. ISBN 7-80120-583-9 DDC 951.03092
1. Zeng, Guofan, - 1811-1872 - Philosophy. 2. Statesmen - China - Biography. 3. Conduct of life. I. Zeng, Guofan, 1811-1872. II. Title. III. Title: Zeng Guofan ba shi yi ge zhong gao
DS758.23.T74 S575 2002

Ṣīmaḥ, Dāvīd.
Shayzarī, ʻAbd al-Raḥmān ibn Naṣr, 12th cent. Rawdat al-qulūb wa-nuzhat al-muḥibb wa-al-maḥbūb. Wiesbaden : Harrassowitz, 2003.

Simard-Laflamme, Carole. Habit Habitat Habitus / Carole Simard-Laflamme. Trois-Rivières, Québec, Canada : Editions d'art Le Sabord, [2002] 145 p. : ill. (some col.) ; 24 cm. Cover title. Includes bibliographical references (p. 136-137). ISBN 2922685136 DDC 746.9/2
1. Costume design. 2. Textile fabrics. 3. Aesthetics. 4. Clothing and dress - Psychological aspects. 5. Costume - Psychological aspects. I. Title.
TT507 .S653 2002

Simeon bar Yoḥai, 2nd cent.
[Zohar ḥadash.] Sefer Zohar ḥadash. Yerushalayim : Mekhon Daʻat Yosef ; Brooklyn, N.Y. (225 Division Ave., Brooklyn 11211) : Le-haśig, B. Daskal, 760- [1999 or 2000-
BM525.A6 Z6+

[Zohar ḥadash. Lamentations. 2000.] Zohar ḥadash Megilat Ekhah. "Hotsaʼah meyuhedet li-yeme ben ha-metsarim". Yerushalayim : Mekhon Daʻat Yosef, 761 [2000 or 2001]
BM525.A6 Z6 2001

Siṃha, Kīrti Kumāra. Bhāratīya darśana meṃ duḥkha aura mukti / lekhaka, Kīrti Kumāra Siṃha. 1. saṃskaraṇa. Ilāhābāda : Śekhara Prakāśana, 2001. 267 p. ; 22 cm. Title on t.p. verso: Bharateey darshan men dukha aur mukti. Includes bibliographical references. In Hindi; includes passages in Sanskrit.
1. Suffering - Religious aspects. 2. Mokṣa. 3. Philosophy, Indic. I. Title. II. Title: Bharateey darshan men dukha aur mukti
B132.M64 S56 2001

Simian, Michelle.
Paroles brutes à la recherche d'un trésor. Genouilleux : Passe du vent, c2003.

SIMKIN, MARGERY.
Vint/age 2001 conference : [videorecording]. New York, c2001.

Simkin, Margery, panelist.
Vint/age 2001 conference : [videorecording]. New York, c2001.

Simon, Bernd. Identity in modern society : a social psychological perspective / Bernd Simon. Oxford, UK ; Malden, MA : Blackwell Pub., 2004. p. cm. Includes bibliographical references and index. Table of contents URL: http://www.loc.gov/catdir/toc/ecip042/2003007537.html ISBN 0-631-22746-6 (alk. paper) ISBN 0-631-22747-4 (pbk. : alk. paper) DDC 302.5
1. Identity (Psychology) 2. Identity (Psychology) - Social aspects. I. Title.
BF697 .S546 2004

Simon, Jack. This book is for all kids, but especially my sister Libby, Libby died. / by Jack Simon ; illustrated by Annette Simon. Kansas City, Mo. : Andrews McMeel Pub., c2002. 1 v. (unpaged) : col. ill. ; 24 cm. ISBN 0-7407-2952-7
1. Children and death - Juvenile literature. 2. Brothers and sisters - Death - Psychological aspects - Juvenile literature. 3. Children's writings. I. Title.
BF723.D3 S59 2002

Simon, Jürgen, 1966- Kriminalbiologie und Zwangssterilisation : eugenischer Rassismus 1920-1945 / Jürgen Simon. Münster ; New York :

Simon, Rita James.
Waxmann, c2001. 355 p. ; 21 cm. (Internationale Hochschulschriften, 0932-4763 ; Bd. 372) Originally presented as the author's thesis (doctoral)--Universität Münster, 2000. Includes bibliographical references (p. [321]-355). ISBN 3-8309-1063-0 (pbk.)
1. Criminal anthropology - History. 2. Eugenics - Germany - History - 20th century. 3. Sterilization, Eugenic - Germany - History - 20th century. 4. Criminology - Germany - History - 20th century. 5. National socialism - History. I. Title. II. Series.

Simon, Rita James. Global perspectives on social issues : marriage and divorce / Rita J. Simon and Howard Altstein. Lanham : Lexington Books, c2003. vi, 139 p. ; 24 cm. Includes bibliographical references and index. CONTENTS: A brief background on the history of marriage and divorce -- Gay marriages -- Overall summary of marriage and divorce rates and legal and mean ages of marriage -- United States of America -- Canada -- Chile -- Colombia -- United kingdom -- Ireland -- France -- Germany -- Sweden -- Russia -- Poland -- Romania -- Hungary -- Israel -- Egypt -- Iran -- Syria -- South africa -- Kenya -- Ghana -- Nigeria -- India -- China -- Japan -- Australia. ISBN 0-7391-0588-4 (hardcover : alk. paper) DDC 306.81
1. Marriage. 2. Divorce. 3. Marriage - Government policy. 4. Divorce - Government policy. 5. Marriage - Social aspects. 6. Divorce - Social aspects. I. Altstein, Howard. II. Title.
HQ503 .S56 2003

Simon, Yves René Marie, 1903-1961.
[Critique de la connaissance morale. English]
A critique of moral knowledge / by Yves R. Simon ; translated with an introduction by Ralph McInerny. New York : Fordham University Press, 2002. xix, 98 p. : ill. ; 23 cm. Includes bibliographical references (p. [89]-91) and index. ISBN 0-8232-2103-2 ISBN 0-8232-2104-0 (pbk.) DDC 170
1. Christian ethics - Catholic authors. 2. Knowledge, Theory of. I. Title.
BJ1249 .S4513 2002

Simone Weil, la passion de la raison / textes réunis et présentés par Mireille Calle et Eberhard Gruber ; avec la collaboration de Nadia Setti. Paris : Harmattan, c2003. 258 p. : ill. ; 22 cm. (Collection Trait d'union) Includes bibliographical references and index. ISBN 2-7475-3995-4 DDC 194
1. Weil, Simone, - 1909-1943. 2. Philosophy, Modern - 20th century. I. Calle-Gruber, Mireille, 1945- II. Gruber, Eberhard. III. Setti, Nadia. IV. Series.
B2430.W474 S55 2003

Simonetta, Catherine. Renoncement et narcissisme chez Maurice Zundel / Catherine Simonetta. Saint-Maurice : Editions Saint-Augustin, c2002. 175 p. ; 24 cm. Includes bibliographical references (p. [167]-171). ISBN 2-88011-265-6 DDC 150
1. Zundel, Maurice. 2. Self-denial. 3. Narcissism - Religious aspects. 4. Psychology, Religious. I. Title.

Simonetti, José María, 1942- El fin de la inocencia : ensayos sobre la corrupción y la ilegalidad del poder / José M. Simonetti ; prólogo Rafael Bielsa. Bernal, Argentina : Universidad Nacional de Quilmes, 2002. 273 p. ; 20 cm. (Colección Documentos) Includes bibliographical references. ISBN 987917383X
1. Political corruption. 2. Power (Social sciences) I. Title. II. Title: Ensayos sobre la corrupción y la ilegalidad del poder III. Series: Documentos (Universidad Nacional de Quilmes)
JF1081 S57 2002

Simple feng shui.
Mitchell, Shawne, 1958- [Exploring feng shui] New York : Gramercy Books, 2004.
BF1779.F4 M58 2004

Simple joys : a reminder to slow down and enjoy the little things in life / edited by Diane Mastromarino. Boulder, Colo. : Blue Mountain Arts, Inc., c2003. 64 p. : col. ill. ; 22 cm. "A Blue Mountain Arts collection". Table of contents URL: http://www.loc.gov/catdir/toc/ecip043/2003009864.html ISBN 0-88396-766-9 (alk. paper) DDC 170/.44
1. Conduct of life. I. Mastromarino, Diane, 1978-
BF637.C5 S5443 2003

Simple works.
Crouch, Chris. Memphis, TN : Black Pants Pub., c2001.
BF637.C5 C78 2001

SIMPLICITY.
Lippe, Toinette, 1939- Nothing left over. New York : J.P. Tarcher/Putnam, c2002.
BJ1496 .L57 2002

Simplicius, of Cilicia.
[Commentarius in Enchiridion Epicteti. 1-26. English]
On Epictetus' "Handbook 1-26" / Simplicius ; translated by Charles Brittain & Tad Brennan. Ithaca, N.Y. : Cornell University Press, 2002. viii,

184 p. ; 25 cm. ([The ancient commentators on Aristotle]) Series from jacket. Includes bibliographical references (p. [140]-142) and indexes. ISBN 0-8014-3904-3 DDC 188
1. Epictetus. - Manual - 1-26. 2. Ethics. 3. Conduct of life. I. Brittain, Charles. II. Brennan, Tad, 1962- III. Title. IV. Series.
B561.M523 S5613 2002

Simplified TRIZ.
Rantanen, Kalevi. Boca Raton : St. Lucie Press, c2002.
TA153 .R26 2002

Sims, Robert Vincent. Lifting the mind fog / Robert Vincent Sims. [S.l.] : Garden Rebel Books, c1996. 130 p. ; 22 cm. ISBN 1-88930-412-3 (pbk.)
1. Conduct of life. I. Title.
BF637.C5 S5444 1996

SIMULATION METHODS. *See* **ARTIFICIAL INTELLIGENCE.**

Simulation series
(v. 33, no. 2) International Conference on Simulation in Engineering Education (2001 : Phoenix, Ariz.) Proceedings of the International Conference on Simulation and Multimedia in Engineering Education & Virtual Worlds and Simulation. San Diego, CA : Society for Computer Simulation International, c2001.

SIMULTANEOUSNESS. *See* **COINCIDENCE.**

SIN. *See* **REPENTANCE.**

SIN, MORTAL. *See* **DEADLY SINS.**

Sin series
(v. 5) Silverman, Stephen M. Envy, anger & sweet revenge. New York : Red Rock Press, c2002.
BF575.E65 S55 2002

Sinclair, Andrew, 1935- The secret scroll / Andrew Sinclair. Edinburgh : Birlinn, 2002. 218 p., [16] p. of plates : ill. (some col.), facsims. (some col.), maps, plan ; 24 cm. Originally published: London: Sinclair-Stevenson, 2001. Includes bibliographical references. ISBN 1-84158-219-0 DDC 271.7913
1. Knights Templar (Masonic order) - History. 2. Grail. 3. Crusades. 4. Roslyn (Scotland) I. Title.

Sinclair House Debate
(14) The silent revolution. Bad Homburg v.d. Höhe : Herbert Quandt Foundation, 2000.
HQ1075 .S55 2000

Sind Frauen bessere Menschen?.
Hoffmann, Arne. Berlin : Schwarzkopf & Schwarzkopf, 2001.
HQ1075 .H64 2001

Sindrom sushchestvovaniia.
Krasikov, V. I. (Vladimir Ivanovich) Tomsk : [s.n.], 2002.

Singer, Alan, 1948- Aesthetic reason : artworks and the deliberative ethos / Alan Singer. University Park, Pa. : Pennsylvania State University Press, c2003. viii, 302 p. : ill. ; 24 cm. (Literature and philosophy) Includes bibliographical references (p. [289]-295) and index. CONTENTS: The adequacy of the aesthetic -- Aesthetic community: recognition as an other sense of Sensus communis -- Acting in the space of appearance: incontinent will and the pathos of aesthetic representation -- Beautiful errors: aesthetics and the art of contextualization -- Aesthetic corrigibility: Bartleby and the character of the aesthetic -- From tragedy to deliberative heroics -- Living in aesthetic community: art and the bonds of productive agency. ISBN 0-271-02312-0 (alk. paper) DDC 111/.85
1. Aesthetics. I. Title. II. Series.
BH91 .S56 2003

Singer, Jerome L.
Creativity. 1st ed. Washington, DC : American Psychological Association, c2004.
BF408 .C7548 2004

Singer, Marcus George, 1926- The ideal of a rational morality : philosophical compositions / Marcus George Singer. Oxford : Clarendon Press ; Oxford ; New York : Oxford University Press, 2002. xix, 333 p. ; 24 cm. Includes bibliographical references and index. ISBN 0-19-825021-5 (alk. paper) DDC 171/.2
1. Ethics. 2. Rationalism. I. Title.
BJ1012 .S48 2002

Singer, Margaret Thaler. Cults in our midst / Margaret Thaler Singer ; foreword by Robert Jay Lifton. Rev. ed. San Francisco : Jossey-Bass, c2003. xxviii, 397 p. ; 23 cm. Cover title: Cults in our midst : the continuing fight against their hidden menace. Includes bibliographical references (p. 357-384) and index. ISBN 0-7879-6741-6 DDC 291.9
1. Cults - Psychology. 2. Brainwashing. 3. Cults - United States - Psychology. 4. Brainwashing - United States. I. Title.

II. Title: Cults in our midst : the continuing fight against their hidden menace
BP603 .S56 2003

Singer, Peter, 1946- One world : the ethics of globalization / Peter Singer. New Haven, Conn. : London : Yale University Press, 2002. xiii, 235 p. : ill. ; 22 cm. (The Terry lectures) Includes bibliographical references and index. ISBN 0-300-09686-0 DDC 179.1
1. Globalization - Moral and ethical aspects. 2. Climatic changes - Moral and ethical aspects. 3. Trade regulation - Moral and ethical aspects. 4. Ethics. I. Title. II. Series.

SINGERS - MEXICO - BIOGRAPHY.
Trevi, Gloria. Gloria. México, D.F. : Planeta, c2002.
ML420.T725 A3 2002

SINGING. *See also* **VOICE.**
Steinhauer, Kimberly Marie. The relationship among voice onset, voice quality and fundamental frequency. 2000.

Singing mother home.
Davenport, Donna S. Denton, Tex. : University of North Texas Press, c2002.
BF575.G7 D365 2002

SINGLE-PARENT FAMILY. *See* **WIDOWS.**

SINGLE PEOPLE. *See* **SINGLE WOMEN.**

SINGLE PEOPLE - MENTAL HEALTH.
Strean, Herbert S. Psychotherapy with the unattached. Northvale, N.J. : Jason Aronson Inc., 1995.
RC451.4.S55 S77 1995

SINGLE PERSONS. *See* **SINGLE PEOPLE.**

Single pregnancy - single parenting.
Bowers, Keri. Pleasant Hill, CA : Park Alexander Press, c1996.
HQ759.45 .B68 1996

SINGLE WOMEN - CHINA.
Dan shen gao bai. Di 1 ban. Beijing : Beijing chu ban she, 2001.
HQ800.2 .D36 2001

Hu, Liuming, 1950- Dan shen gui zu. Di 1 ban. [Wuhan Shi] : Chang jiang wen yi chu ban she, [2000]
PL2863.L58 D365 2000

SINGLE WOMEN - PSYCHOLOGY.
Meeks, James T., 1956- Life changing relationships. Chicago, Ill. : Moody Press, c2002.
HQ801 .M515 2002
1. Black author.

SINGLES (PERSONS). *See* **SINGLE PEOPLE.**

SINGSPIELS. *See* **OPERAS.**

A singular modernity.
Jameson, Fredric. London ; New York : Verso, 2002.
CB358 .J348 2002

The singular objects of architecture.
Baudrillard, Jean. [Objets singuliers. English] Minneapolis : University of Minnesota Press, c2002.
NA2500 .B3413 2002

Sini, Carlo, 1933- La scrittura e il debito : conflitto tra culture e antropologia / Carlo Sini. Milano : Jaca book, 2002. 95 p. ; 23 cm. (Di fronte e attraverso ; 581) (Lo spoglio dell'occidente ; 17. Saggi) Includes bibliographical references. ISBN 88-16-40581-3 DDC 121
1. Writing - History. 2. Writing - Philosophy. I. Title. II. Series. III. Series: Spoglio dell'occidente ; 17. IV. Series: Spoglio dell'occidente. Saggi.

Sinica Leidensia
(v. 60) Santangelo, Paolo. Sentimental education in Chinese history. Leiden ; Boston : Brill, 2003.
BF538.C48 S25 2003

Sinkler, Lorraine.
Goldsmith, Joel S., 1892-1964. Spiritual discernment. Atlanta, Ga. : Acropolis Books, c2002.
BF639.G56886 2002

Sinn in Sinn-loser Zeit.
Hübner, Benno. Wien : Passagen, c2002.

SINO-TIBETAN LANGUAGES. *See* **CHINESE LANGUAGE.**

SINS. *See* **DEADLY SINS.**

SINS, CAPITAL. *See* **DEADLY SINS.**

SINS, DEADLY. *See* **DEADLY SINS.**

Sipilä, Jorma.
The young, the old, and the state. Cheltenham, UK ; Northhampton, MA : E. Elgar Pub., c2003.
HQ778.5 .Y69 2003

Sir George Trevelyan and the new spiritual awakening.
Farrer, Frances, 1950- Edinburgh : Floris, 2002.

Sir Henry Wellcome Asian studies
(v. 1) Nāgārjuna, Siddha. [Ratiśāstra. English & Sanskrit] Conjugal love in India. Leiden Boston, MA : Brill, 2002.
HQ470.S3 N3413 2002

Sistering.
Mauthner, Melanie L., 1964- New York : Palgrave Macmillan, 2002.
BF723.S43 M385 2002

SISTERS.
Chicken soup for the soul celebrates sisters. Deerfield Beach, Fla. : Health Communications, 2004.
BF723.S43 C43 2004

Mauthner, Melanie L., 1964- Sistering. New York : Palgrave Macmillan, 2002.
BF723.S43 M385 2002

SISTERS AND BROTHERS. See **BROTHERS AND SISTERS.**

SISTERS - FAMILY RELATIONSHIPS.
Chicken soup for the soul celebrates sisters. Deerfield Beach, Fla. : Health Communications, 2004.
BF723.S43 C43 2004

Mauthner, Melanie L., 1964- Sistering. New York : Palgrave Macmillan, 2002.
BF723.S43 M385 2002

SITES, EXCAVATION (ARCHAEOLOGY). See **EXCAVATIONS (ARCHAEOLOGY).**

Situation-bound utterances in L1 and L2.
Kecskés, István. Berlin ; New York : Mouton de Gruyter, 2002.
P95.45 .K4 2002

SITUATION (LINGUISTICS). See **CONTEXT (LINGUISTICS).**

The situational mentor : an international review of competencies and capabilities in mentoring / edited by David Clutterbuck and Gill Lane. Burlington, VT : Gower, 2004. p. cm. Includes bibliographical references (p.   ) and index. ISBN 0-566-08543-7 (alk. paper) DDC 158/.3
1. Mentoring. I. Clutterbuck, David. II. Lane, Gill.
BF637.M48 S56 2004

Sivananda, Swami. Thought power / Sri Swami Sivananda. 13th ed. Uttaranchal, Himalayas, India : Divine Life Society, 2002. xvi, 118 p. : port. ; 18 cm. ISBN 81-7052-017-7
1. Mental discipline. 2. Spiritual life - Hinduism. I. Title.

Śivasaṃhitā. English & Sanskrit.
The original Yoga. 2nd rev. ed. New Delhi : Munshiram Manoharlal Publishers, 1999.
B132.Y6 O74 1999

Six, Frederique, 1962-.
The trust process in organizations. Cheltenham, UK ; Northampton, MA : Edward Elgar, c2003.
HD58.7 .T744 2003

SIX HUNDRED AND THIRTEEN COMMANDMENTS. See **COMMANDMENTS, SIX HUNDRED AND THIRTEEN.**

Six, Jean François. Médiation : essai / Jean-François Six et Véronique Mussaud ; préface de Raymond Barre et Michel Rocard. Paris : Editions du Seuil, c2002. 341 p. ; 21 cm. Includes bibliographical references and index. ISBN 2-02-051669-1
1. Mediation. I. Mussaud, Véronique. II. Title.
HM1126 .S59 2002

Sixteen personality factor fifth edition administrator's manual.
Russell, Mary T. The 16PF fifth edition administrator's manual. 3rd ed. Champaign, Ill. : Institute for Personality and Ability Testing, 2002.
BF698.8.S5 A37 2002

SIXTEEN PERSONALITY FACTOR QUESTIONNAIRE.
Cattell, Heather Birkett. Essentials of 16PF assessment. Hoboken, NJ : John Wiley & Sons, 2003.
BF698.8.S5 C265 2003

Russell, Mary T. The 16PF fifth edition administrator's manual. 3rd ed. Champaign, Ill. : Institute for Personality and Ability Testing, 2002.
BF698.8.S5 A37 2002

SIXTEENTH CENTURY.
The 1500s. San Diego, Calif : Greenhaven Press, c2001.
CB367 .A165 2001

Sixteenth century essays & studies
(v. 62) Werewolves, witches, and wandering spirits. Kirksville, MO : Truman State University Press, c2002.
GR135 .W47 2002

Sixty second procrastinator.
Davidson, Jeffrey P. The 60 second procrastinator. Avon, MA : Adams Media Corp., c2003.
BF637.P76 D38 2003

SIZE.
Bruce, Lisa. Sizes at school. Chicago, IL : Raintree, c2003.
BF299.S5 B78 2003

Gordon, Sharon. Big - small. New York : Benchmark Books, 2003.
BF299.S5 G67 2003

Harris, Nicholas, 1956- How big? San Diego, CA : Blackbirch Press, 2004.
BF299.S5 H37 2004

SIZE JUDGMENT - JUVENILE LITERATURE.
Bruce, Lisa. Sizes at school. Chicago, IL : Raintree, c2003.
BF299.S5 B78 2003

Gordon, Sharon. Big - small. New York : Benchmark Books, 2003.
BF299.S5 G67 2003

Harris, Nicholas, 1956- How big? San Diego, CA : Blackbirch Press, 2004.
BF299.S5 H37 2004

SIZE PERCEPTION. See also **SIZE JUDGMENT.**
Bruce, Lisa. Sizes at school. Chicago, IL : Raintree, c2003.
BF299.S5 B78 2003

Ross, Helen Elizabeth, 1935- The mystery of the moon illusion. Oxford ; New York : Oxford University Press, 2002.
QP495 .R67 2002

SIZE PERCEPTION - JUVENILE LITERATURE.
Bruce, Lisa. Sizes at school. Chicago, IL : Raintree, c2003.
BF299.S5 B78 2003

Gordon, Sharon. Big - small. New York : Benchmark Books, 2003.
BF299.S5 G67 2003

Harris, Nicholas, 1956- How big? San Diego, CA : Blackbirch Press, 2004.
BF299.S5 H37 2004

Sizes at school.
Bruce, Lisa. Chicago, IL : Raintree, c2003.
BF299.S5 B78 2003

Skeen, Carl Edward. 1816 : America rising / C. Edward Skeen. Lexington : University Press of Kentucky, c2003. xvi, 299 p. : ports. ; 24 cm. Includes bibliographical references (p. [237]-289) and index. ISBN 0-8131-2271-6 (acid-free paper) DDC 973.5/1
1. United States - History - 1809-1817. 2. United States - Politics and government - 1809-1817. 3. United States - History - War of 1812 - Influence. 4. Political culture - United States - History - 19th century. 5. National characteristics, American. I. Title.
E341 .S57 2003

SKELETAL REMAINS. See **ANTHROPOMETRY.**
SKEPTICISM. See also **CYNICISM; TRUTH.**
Araujo, Marcelo de. Scepticism, freedom and autonomy. Berlin : De Gruyter, 2003.

Baldus, Claus, 1947- Weg im Nicht. Stuttgart : Hatje, c1994.

Devout sceptics. London : Hodder & Stoughton, 2003.

Epstein, Richard A. Skepticism and freedom. Chicago : University of Chicago Press, c2003.
K487.L5 E67 2003

Fogelin, Robert J. Walking the tightrope of reason. Oxford ; New York : Oxford University Press, 2003.
BC177 .F64 2003

Holl, Adolf, 1930- Brief an die gottlosen Frauen. Wien : Zsolnay, 2002.

Skepticism and freedom.
Epstein, Richard A. Chicago : University of Chicago Press, c2003.
K487.L5 E67 2003

SKETCHES, PREPARATORY (ART). See **ARTISTS' PREPARATORY STUDIES.**

SKETCHING. See **DRAWING.**

Skidmore, Warren. Lord Dunmore's little war of 1774 : his captains and their men who opened up Kentucky & the West to American settlement / by Warren Skidmore with Donna Kaminsky. Bowie, Md. : Heritage Books, 2002. xvi, 283 p. ; 28 cm. Includes bibliographical references and index. ISBN 0-7884-2271-5
1. Dunmore, John Murray, - Earl of, - 1732-1809. 2. Lord Dunmore's War, 1774. 3. Lord Dunmore's War, 1774 - Registers. 4. Kentucky - History - To 1792. 5. Virginia - History - Colonial period, ca. 1600-1775. 6. Virginia - Genealogy. 7. Kentucky - Genealogy. I. Kaminsky, Donna. II. Title.

Skiffington, Jeannie. Winning is contagious : 101 practical lessons to help you win at the game of life / by Jeannie Skiffington. 1st ed. East Amherst, N.Y. : Winning Track Press, c2002. 272 p. : ill. ; 22 cm. ISBN 0-9722033-0-3 DDC 158.1
1. Success - Psychological aspects. I. Title.
BF637.S8 S548 2002

SkillPath self-study sourcebook
Silber, Lee T. Aim first!. Mission, Kan. : SkillPath Publications, c1999.
BF505.G6 S55 1999

SKINHEADS. See **WHITE SUPREMACY MOVEMENTS.**

Skloot, Floyd. In the shadow of memory / Floyd Skloot. Lincoln : University of Nebraska Press, c2003. xv, 243 p. ; 24 cm. (American lives) ISBN 0-8032-4297-2 (cloth : alk. paper) DDC 362.1/97481/092
1. Skloot, Floyd. 2. Authors, American - 20th century - Biography. 3. Brain damage - Patients - Biography. 4. Creative ability. I. Title. II. Series.
PS3569.K577 Z47 2003

SKLOOT, FLOYD.
Skloot, Floyd. In the shadow of memory. Lincoln : University of Nebraska Press, c2003.
PS3569.K577 Z47 2003

Skoblikova, E. S. (Elena Sergeevna).
Russkoe slovo. Penza : Izd-vo PGPU, 1998.
PG2026.B66 R88 1998

SKOPTSY.
Rozanov, V. V. (Vasiliĭ Vasil'evich), 1856-1919. Vozrozhdaiushchiĭsi͡a Egipet. Moskva : Izd-vo "Respublika", 2002.

SLANDER. See **LIBEL AND SLANDER.**
SLANG.
Lichev, Valeri. TSinichnoto, ili, Igrata na vlast i udovolstvie. Sofii͡a : EON-2000, 2000.
B809.5 .L53 2000

Slate, Joe H. Psychic vampires : protection from energy predators & parasites / Joe H. Slate. St. Paul, Minn. : Llewellyn Publications, 2002. xv, 243 p. : ill. ; 23 cm. Includes bibliographical references (p. 235-237) and index. ISBN 0-7387-0191-2 (pbk.) DDC 133.8
1. Self-defense - Psychic aspects. 2. Vital force. 3. Vampires - Psychology. I. Title.
BF1045.S46 S53 2002

Slater, Alan.
The development of face processing in infancy and early childhood. New York : Nova Science, 2003.
BF720.F32 D48 2003

Slater, Lauren.
The complete guide to mental health for women. 1st ed. Boston : Beacon Press, c2003.
RC451.4.W6 C65 2003

Opening Skinner's box : great psychological experiments of the twentieth century / Lauren Slater. 1st ed. New York : W.W. Norton, c2004. p. cm. Includes bibliographical references and index. Table of contents URL: http://www.loc.gov/catdir/toc/ecip047/2003018199.html CONTENTS: Opening Skinner's box -- Obscura : Stanley Milgram and obedience to authority -- On being sane in insane places -- In the unlikely event of a water landing : Darley and Latane's training manual -- Quieting the mind : the experiments of Leon Festinger -- Monkey love : Harry Harlow's primates -- Rat park : the radical addiction experiment -- Lost in the mall : the false memory experiment -- Memory Inc : Eric Kandel's sea slug experiment -- Chipped : this century's most radical mind cures. ISBN 0-393-05095-5 DDC 150/.7/2
1. Psychology - Experiments - History - 20th century. I. Title.
BF198.7 .S57 2004

Slaughter, Virginia.
Individual differences in theory of mind. New York : Psychology Press, 2003.
BF723.P48 I53 2003

SLAVE KEEPING. *See* **SLAVERY.**

SLAVERY - RELIGIOUS ASPECTS - HISTORY.
Stark, Rodney. For the glory of God. Princeton, N.J. : Princeton University Press, c2003.
BL221 .S747 2003

Slavianskaia astrologiia.
Asov, A. I. (Aleksandr Igorevich) Moskva : Fair-Press : Grand, 2001.
BF1714.S58 A86 2001

Asov, A. I. (Aleksandr Igorevich) Moskva : FAIR-PRESS, 2001.

Slavianskie drevnosti
Domnikov, S. D. (Sergeĭ Dmitrievich) Mat'-zemliā i TSar'-gorod. Moskva : Aleteĭā, 2002.
B4235.H57 D65 2002

Slavianskiĭ obereg.
Levkievskaia, E. E. (Elena Evgen'evna) Moskva : Indrik, 2002.
BL480 .L38 2002

SLAVIC COUNTRIES. *See* **SLAVS.**

SLAVIC COUNTRIES - SOCIAL LIFE AND CUSTOMS.
Asov, A. I. (Aleksandr Igorevich) Slaviānskaia astrologiia. Moskva : Fair-Press : Grand, 2001.
BF1714.S58 A86 2001

Asov, A. I. (Aleksandr Igorevich) Slaviānskaia astrologiia. Moskva : FAIR-PRESS, 2001.

Levkievskaia, E. E. (Elena Evgen'evna) Slaviānskiĭ obereg. Moskva : Indrik, 2002.
BL480 .L38 2002

SLAVIC RACE. *See* **SLAVS.**

SLAVS. *See also* **PANSLAVISM; SLAVIC COUNTRIES.**
Russkaia rasovaia teoriia do 1917 goda. Moskva : Feri-V, 2002.

SLAVS, EASTERN. *See* **RUSSIANS.**

SLAVS - FOLKLORE.
Levkievskaia, E. E. (Elena Evgen'evna) Slaviānskiĭ obereg. Moskva : Indrik, 2002.
BL480 .L38 2002

SLAVS - HISTORY.
Asov, A. I. (Aleksandr Igorevich) Sviashchennye prarodiny slaviān. Moskva : Veche, 2002.
BL930 .A863 2002

V'iunov, IU. A. Slovo o russkikh. Moskva : Izd-vo IKAR, c2002.

SLAVS - HISTORY - 20TH CENTURY.
Schaller, Helmut Wilhelm, 1940- Der Nationalsozialismus und die slawische Welt. Regensburg : Pustet, c2002.
DD256.5 .S259 2002

SLAVS - ORIGIN.
Petrović, Aleksandar M. Praistorija Srba. Beograd : Pešić i sinovi, 2001.
DR1953 .P48 2001

SLAVS - RELIGION.
Asov, A. I. (Aleksandr Igorevich) Sviashchennye prarodiny slaviān. Moskva : Veche, 2002.
BL930 .A863 2002

Domnikov, S. D. (Sergeĭ Dmitrievich) Mat'-zemliā i TSar'-gorod. Moskva : Aleteĭā, 2002.
B4235.H57 D65 2002

Gavrilov, D. A. Bogi slaviān, iāzychestvo, traditsiiā. [Moskva] : Refl-buk, 2002.
BL930 .G38 2002

Levkievskaia, E. E. (Elena Evgen'evna) Slaviānskiĭ obereg. Moskva : Indrik, 2002.
BL480 .L38 2002

Slavskaiā, A. N. Lichnost' kak sub"ekt interpretatsii / A.N. Slavskaiā. Dubna : "Feniks+", 2002. 239 p. ; 22 cm. Includes bibliographical references (p. [230]-239). ISBN 5927900232
1. Personality. 2. Hermeneutics. I. Title.
BF698 .S54 2002

SLEEP. *See* **DREAMS.**

Sleep and dreams.
Steiner, Rudolf, 1861-1925. [Lectures. English. Selections] 1st ed. Great Barrington, MA : SteinerBooks, 2003.
BF1091 .S715213 2003

SLEEP CUSTOMS. *See* **SLEEPING CUSTOMS.**

Sleep thinking.
Maisel, Eric, 1947- Holbrook, Mass. : Adams Media Corp., c2000.
BF1099.P75 M35 2000

Sleeping.
Kennedy, Michelle. Hauppauge, N.Y. : Barron's, c2003.
BF723.S45 .K46 2003

SLEEPING CUSTOMS - HISTORY.
Verdon, Jean. [Nuit au Moyen Age. English] Night in the Middle Ages. Notre Dame, Ind. : University of Notre Dame Press, c2002.
HM1033 .V4713 2002

Sleinis, E. E. (Edgar Evalt), 1943- Art and freedom / E.E. Sleinis. Urbana : University of Illinois Press, c2003. 235 p. ; 22 cm. Includes bibliographical references (p. 225-229) and index. ISBN 0-252-02777-9 (cloth : alk. paper) DDC 701/.17
1. Aesthetics. 2. Arts - Philosophy. 3. Liberty. I. Title.
BH39 .S5518 2003

Slinger, Penny.
Douglas, Nik. The Tantric Dakini oracle. Rochester, Vt. : Destiny Books, 2003.
BF1879.T2 D695 2003

Śliwak, Jacek. Osobowość altruistyczna : osobowościowe korelaty altruizmu : psychologiczne badania empiryczne / Jacek Śliwak. Wyd. 1. Lublin : Red. Wydawnictw Katolickiego Uniwersytetu Lubelskiego, 2001. 342 p. : ill. ; 24 cm. (Rozprawa habilitacyjna / Katolicki Uniwersytet Lubelski. Wydział Nauk Społecznych) Summary in English. Includes bibliographical references (p. [269]-296). ISBN 83-228-0914-X
1. Altruism. 2. Helping behavior. I. Title. II. Series: Rozprawa habilitacyjna (Katolicki Uniwersytet Lubelski. Wydział Nauk Społecznych)
BF637.H4 S58 2001

Sloan School of Management.
Management. Cambridge, Mass. : MIT Press, 2003.
HD31 .M2928 2003

Slocum, Terry A. Thematic cartography and visualization / Terry A. Slocum. Upper Saddle River, N.J. : Prentice Hall, c1999. x, 293 p., 32 p. of plates : ill. (some col.), maps (some col.) ; 29 cm. Includes bibliographical references (p. 274-287) and index. ISBN 0-13-209776-1 DDC 526
1. Cartography. 2. Visualization. I. Title.
GA108.7 .S58 1999

Das Sloterdijk Alphabet.
Dobeneck, Holger von. Würzburg : Königshausen & Neumann, c2002.

Sloterdijk, Peter, 1947-.
Neues Bewusstsein. Wien : Edition Selene, 1999.

SLOTERDIJK, PETER, 1947- - LANGUAGE - GLOSSARIES, ETC.
Dobeneck, Holger von. Das Sloterdijk Alphabet. Würzburg : Königshausen & Neumann, c2002.

Slovar'-spravochnik po vozrastnoĭ i pedagogicheskoĭ psikhologii / pod redaktsieĭ Gamezo M.V. Moskva : Pedagog. ob-vo Rossii, 2001. 127 p. ; 20 cm. ISBN 5931341390
1. Developmental psychology - Dictionaries - Russian. 2. Educational psychology - Dictionaries - Russian. I. Gamezo, M. V. (Mikhail Viktorovich) II. Rossiĭskoe pedagogicheskoe obshchestvo.
BF712.7 .S56 2001

Slovo o russkikh.
V'iunov, IU. A. Moskva : Izd-vo IKAR, c2002.

SLUM CLEARANCE. *See* **CITY PLANNING.**

Slutskiĭ, O. I. (Oleg Isaakovich) Chto posle illiuzii? : konets nasheĭ ėry / O.I. Slutskiĭ. Moskva : Veche, 2002. 523 p. ; 23 cm. Includes index. "Izdano pri sodeĭstvii V.V. Poznera." ISBN 594538089X
1. Spiritual life. 2. Life. I. Pozner, Vladimir. II. Title.
BV4509.R8 S58 2002

Šmahel, František.
Člověk českého středověku. Vyd. 1. Praha : Argo, 2002.

SMALL AND MEDIUM-SIZED BUSINESS. *See* **SMALL BUSINESS.**

SMALL AND MEDIUM-SIZED ENTERPRISES. *See* **SMALL BUSINESS.**

SMALL ARMS. *See* **FIREARMS.**

SMALL BUSINESS - INDIA - FORECASTING..
Millennium projects. 1st ed. New Delhi : Small Scale Industries, Ministry of Small Scale Industries, Agro & Rural Industries, Govt. of India, 2000-
HD2346.I5 M45 2000

Small business solutions
Allen, Kathleen R. Time and information management that really works. Los Angeles, Calif : Affinity Pub., c1995.

SMALL GROUPS.
Corey, Gerald. Theory and practice of group counseling. 6th ed. Australia ; Belmont, CA : Thomson/Brooks/Cole, c2004.
BF637.C6 C576 2004

Patton, Bobby R., 1935- Decision-making group interaction. 4th ed. Boston : Allyn and Bacon, c2003.
HM736 .P37 2003

SMALL GROUPS - RELIGIOUS ASPECTS.
Grainger, Roger. Group spirituality. Hove, East Sussex ; New York : Brunner-Routledge, 2003.
BL628.4 .G73 2003

Small, Helen.
Literature, science, psychoanalysis, 1830-1970. Oxford ; New York : Oxford University Press, 2003.
PN55 .L58 2003

A small matter of proof : the legacy of Donald M. Baer / edited by Karen S. Budd, Trevor Stokes ; foreword by Barbara C. Etzel. Reno, NV : Context Press, c2003. xv, 328 p. : ill. ; 23 cm. Includes bibliographical references. Table of contents URL: http://www.loc.gov/catdir/toc/ecip042/2003008014.html ISBN 1-87897-843-8 DDC 150.19/43/092
1. Psychology. 2. Baer, Donald Merle, - 1931- - Career in psychology. I. Budd, Karen S. II. Stokes, Trevor, 1951-
BF121 .S545 2003

Small, Robin, 1944-.
Rée, Paul, 1849-1901. [Ursprung der moralischen Empfindungen. English] Basic writings. Urbana : University of Illinois Press, c2003.
B3323.R343 U67 2003

SMALL TOWNS. *See* **CITIES AND TOWNS.**

Sman-bla Don-grub, 15th cent.
Rulai fo shen liang ming xi bao lun. Xizang fo jiao cai hui cai su yi shu. Di 1 ban. Beijing : Zhongguo Zang xue chu ban she : Xin hua shu dian Beijing fa xing suo fa xing, 1997.
ND1489 .X593 1997

Smaragdine table.
Hermes, Trismegistus. Divine Pymander. Rev. ed. Quakertown, PA : Philosophical Pub. Co., 2001.
BF1598.H5 E5 2001

Smārikā : Svāmī Ānandānanda janma śatī, 29 Janavarī, 2001 / [sampādaka Pushpalatā Garga]. Jayapura : Yoga Sādhanā Āśrama, 2001. iv, 100 p. : ports. ; 25 cm. Cover title: Pūjyapāda Svāmī Ānandānanda janma śatī, 29 Janavarī, 2001. Articles in Hindi or English.
1. Ānandānanda, - Swami, - 1902-1991. 2. Yoga - Therapeutic use. 3. Yogis - India - Biography. I. Ānandānanda, Swami, 1902-1991. II. Garga, Pushpalatā. III. Yoga Sādhana Āśrama. IV. Title: Pūjyapāda Svāmī Ānandānanda janma śatī, 29 Janavarī, 2001
BL1175.A4955 S62 2001

The smart spot.
North, Dia. Boston, MA : Red Wheel, 2003.
BF637.S8 N655 2003

Smarter companies after the technology shakeout.
Burke, Dan, 1965- Business @ the speed of stupid. Cambridge, MA : Perseus Pub., c2001.
HD45 .B7995 2001

Smékal, Vladimír.
Utváření a vývoj osobnosti. Vyd. 1. V Brně : Barrister & Principal, 2002.
BF723.P4 U88 2002

Smereka, Vira, 1923- Vichnyĭ vohon' / Vira Smereka. L'viv : Vyd-vo "Spolom", 2000. 380 p. : ill. ; 24 cm. ISBN 9667445739
1. Christian life. I. Title.
PG3949.29.M4 V5 2000

SMES (SMALL BUSINESS). *See* **SMALL BUSINESS.**

Smetanka, Z. Archeologické etudy : osmnáct kapitol o poznávání středověku / Zdeněk Smetánka. Praha : [Lidové noviny], 2003. 216 p. : ill. ; 19 cm. (Knižnice Dějin a současnosti ; 19) Includes bibliographical references and index. ISBN 80-7106-506-4 (brož.)
1. Archaeology. 2. Archaeology, Medieval. I. Title. II. Series: Knižnice dějin a současnosti ; sv. 19.

Śmierć w literaturze staroserbskiej.
Lis, Izabela. Poznań : Wydawn. Nauk. Uniwersytetu im. Adama Mickiewicza w Poznaniu, 2003.

PG1406 .L59 2003

Smile in the mirror.
Ventrella, Tony, 1944- 1st ed. Sammamish, WA : Positive Energy Productions, c2001.
BF637.S4 V46 2001

Smirnov, Terentiĭ. Psikhologiia snovideniĭ / Terentiĭ Smirnov. Moskva : "KSP+", 2001. 190 p. : ill. ; 20 cm. (Osoznannye snovideniia) "Nauchno-populiarnoe izdanie"-- Colophon. Includes bibliographical references (p. 187-190). ISBN 5896920938
1. Dreams. 2. Dream interpretation. I. Title. II. Series.
BF175.5.D74 S5 2001

Smith, Alison, 1968- Name all the animals : a memoir / Alison Smith. New York : Scribner, c2004. p. cm. ISBN 0-7432-5522-4 DDC 155.9/37/092
1. Smith, Alison, - 1968- 2. Bereavement - Psychological aspects. 3. Brothers - Death - Psychological aspects. I. Title.
BF575.G7 S58 2004

SMITH, ALISON, 1968-.
Smith, Alison, 1968- Name all the animals. New York : Scribner, c2004.
BF575.G7 S58 2004

Smith, Barbara, 1947- Canadian ghost stories / Barbara Smith ; illustrations by Arlana Anderson-Hale. Edmonton, Alta. : Lone Pine Pub., 2001. 248 p. : ill. ; 21 cm. ISBN 1-55105-302-0 DDC 133.1/0971
1. Ghosts - Canada. I. Title.
BF1472.C3 S533 2001

Smith, Barbara, 1955-.
Anti-discriminatory counselling practice. London ; Thousand Oaks, Calif. : SAGE Publications, 2003.
BF637.C6 A49 2003

Smith, Carolyn D.
Kagan, Jerome. Kagan & Segal's psychology. 9th ed. Belmont, CA : Thomson/Wadsworth, c2004.
BF121 .K22 2004

Smith, D. Brent, 1968-.
Personality and organizations. Mahwah, N.J. : Lawrence Erlbaum Associates, 2004.
BF698.9.O3 P46 2004

Smith, David Livingstone, 1953- Psychoanalysis in focus / David Livingstone Smith. London ; Thousand Oaks, Calif. : SAGE Publications, 2003. 157 p. ; 22 cm. (Counselling & psychotherapy in focus) Includes bibliographical references (p. [144]-152) and index. ISBN 0-7619-6194-1 (pbk.) ISBN 0-7619-6193-3
1. Psychoanalysis. 2. Psychoanalytic counseling. I. Title. II. Series.
BF173 .S569 2003

Smith, Edward E., 1940-.
Atkinson & Hilgard's introduction to psychology. 14th ed. Australia ; Belmont, CA : Wadworth/ Thomson Learning, c2003.
BF121 .I57 2003

Smith, Gordon, 1962- Spirit messenger : the remarkable story of a seventh son of a seventh son / Gordon Smith. Carlsbad, Calif. : Hay House, 2004. p. cm. Table of contents URL: http://www.loc.gov/catdir/toc/ecip042/2003007481.html CONTENTS: The awakening -- Natural gift -- Development -- Out on a limb -- Working medium -- Making the grade -- Funny moments -- Strange but true -- Unfinished business -- Life after death -- Prove it! -- Mediumship -- True spirituality -- Working abroad -- Of seances and sons -- Animals in the spirit world -- Trance, guides and teachings -- An attorney's account -- Mediumship and the media -- The Italian connection. ISBN 1401902693 (tradepaper) DDC 133.9/1/092
1. Smith, Gordon, - 1962- 2. Mediums - Scotland - Biography. I. Title.
BF1283.S616 A3 2004

SMITH, GORDON, 1962-.
Smith, Gordon, 1962- Spirit messenger. Carlsbad, Calif. : Hay House, 2004.
BF1283.S616 A3 2004

Smith, Huston. The way things are : conversations with Huston Smith on the spiritual life / edited and with a preface by Phil Cousineau. Berkeley : University of California Press, c2003. xxiv, 314 p. ; 24 cm. Includes bibliographical references (p. 281-284) and index. CONTENTS: The way things are -- The primordial tradition -- Winnowing the wisdom traditions -- This is it -- The soul of the community -- Encountering God -- The place of science -- The limits of the scientific worldview -- Science as the oracle of our age -- Science, faith, and infinity -- Toward a partnership between science and religion -- The battle for the human mind -- The new paradigm -- Countering scientism -- The striking parallels -- The sacred dimensions of everyday life -- Demystifying spiritual practice -- The varieties of religious explorations -- Cleansing the doors of perception -- Fathoming psychedelic mysticism -- The wisdom of faith --

Why religion matters now more than ever. ISBN 0-520-23816-8 (cloth : alk. paper) DDC 200/.92
1. Smith, Huston - Interviews. 2. Religion historians - United States - Interviews. 3. Religion. 4. Spiritual life. 5. Religion and science. I. Cousineau, Phil. II. Title. III. Title: Conversations with Huston Smith on the spiritual life
BL43.S64 A5 2003

SMITH, HUSTON - INTERVIEWS.
Smith, Huston. The way things are. Berkeley : University of California Press, c2003.
BL43.S64 A5 2003

Smith, Janna Malamud. A potent spell : mother love and the power of fear / Janna Malamud Smith. Boston : Houghton Mifflin, 2003. x, 289 p. ; 24 cm. Includes bibliographical references (p. [249]-276) and index. Publisher description URL: http://www.loc.gov/catdir/description/hm022/2002027632.html ISBN 0-618-06349-8 DDC 306.874/3
1. Motherhood - Psychological aspects. 2. Mothers - Psychology. 3. Mothers. 4. Mother and child. I. Title.
HQ759 .S618 2003

Smith, Jean, 1938- The beginner's guide to walking the Buddha's eightfold path / Jean Smith. New York : Bell Tower, 2002. xiii, 239 p. ; 21 cm. Includes bibliographical references (p. 215-220) and index. ISBN 0-609-80896-6 (trade paperback) DDC 294.3/444
1. Eightfold Path. 2. Spiritual life - Buddhism. 3. Buddhism - Doctrines. I. Title.
BQ4320 .S65 2002

SMITH, JOHN, 1580-1531.
Price, David, 1961- Love and hate in Jamestown. 1st ed. New York : Alfred A. Knopf : Distributed by Random House, 2003.
F234.J3 P68 2003

Smith, John Robert.
Ward, William Aidan. Trust and mistrust. Chichester, England ; Hoboken, NJ : John Wiley & Sons, c2003.
HD69.S8 W37 2003

Smith, Jonathan A.
Qualitative psychology. London ; Thousand Oaks, Calif. : SAGE Publications, 2003.
BF76.5 .Q3375 2003

Smith, Laura L.
Elliott, Charles H., 1948- Overcoming anxiety for dummies. New York : Wiley Pub., c2003.
BF575.A6 E46 2003

Smith, Maggie, ill.
Berry, Joy Wilt. Let's talk about feeling embarrassed. New York : Scholastic, c2002.
BF723.E44 B47 2002

Berry, Joy Wilt. Let's talk about feeling worried. New York : Scholastic Inc., c2002.
BF723.W67 B47 2002

Berry, Joy Wilt. Let's talk about getting hurt. New York : Scholastic, c2002.
BF723.W67 B475 2002

Berry, Joy Wilt. Saying no. New York : Scholastic, c2001.
BF723.R4 B37 2001

Smith, Maureen (Maureen J.), 1947- The ABCs of full tilt living : insights from A-Z / Maureen Smith. Boston, MA : Red Wheel/Weiser, 2003. p. cm. Table of contents URL: http://www.loc.gov/catdir/toc/ecip043/2003010536.html ISBN 1-59003-048-6 DDC 158.1
1. Conduct of life. I. Title.
BF637.C5 S5449 2003

Smith, Murray E. G. (Murray Edward George), 1950-.
Culture of prejudice. Peterborough, Ont. : Broadview Press, 2003.

Smith, Peter F. (Peter Frederick), 1930- Sustainability at the cutting edge : emerging technologies for low energy buildings / Peter F. Smith. Oxford ; Boston : Architectural Press, 2003. xiii, 178 p. : ill. ; 22 cm. Includes bibliographical references and index. CONTENTS: Introduction -- Solar thermal power -- Low energy techniques for cooling -- Geothermal energy -- Wind power -- Photovoltaic cells -- Fuel cells -- Biogas -- Micro-power -- Small-scale hydro -- Wave and tide -- Prospects for the energy infrastructure -- Materials -- The photonic revolution -- Building integrated renewable energy : case studies -- Sustainability on a knife edge. ISBN 0-7506-5678-6 DDC 720.47
1. Architecture and energy conservation. 2. Architecture - Environmental aspects. I. Title.
NA2542.3 .S65 2003

Smith, Quentin, 1952-.
Consciousness. Oxford : Clarendon Press ; New York : Oxford University Press, 2003.

B808.9 .C667 2003

Smith, R. Scott, 1957- Virtue ethics and moral knowledge : philosophy of language after MacIntyre and Hauerwas / R. Scott Smith. Aldershot, England ; Burlington, VT : Ashgate, c2003. ix, 230 p. ; 24 cm. (Ashgate new critical thinking in philosophy) Includes bibliographical references (p. 221-227) and index. ISBN 0-7546-0979-0 (alk. paper) DDC 170
1. MacIntyre, Alasdair C. 2. Hauerwas, Stanley, - 1940- 3. Wittgenstein, Ludwig, - 1889-1951. 4. Ethics. 5. Virtue. 6. Language and languages - Philosophy. I. Title. II. Series.
BJ1012 .S5195 2003

Smith, Roger, 1948-.
Essays for Colin Tapper. London : LexisNexis, 2003.

Smith, Rogers M., 1953- Stories of peoplehood : the politics and morals of political membership / Rogers M. Smith. Cambridge ; New York : Cambridge University Press, 2003. xii, 236 p. ; 24 cm. (Contemporary political theory) Includes bibliographical references (p. 213-225) and index. Table of contents URL: http://www.loc.gov/catdir/toc/cam031/2002041695.html Publisher description URL: http://www.loc.gov/catdir/description/cam031/2002041695.html ISBN 0-521-81303-4 ISBN 0-521-52003-7 (pb.) DDC 306.2
1. Political culture. 2. Political participation. 3. Political psychology. 4. Political sociology. I. Title. II. Series.
JA75.7 .S65 2003

Smith, Ronald Edward, 1940-.
Passer, Michael W. Psychology. 2nd ed. Boston, Mass. : McGraw-Hill, 2003.
BF121 .P348 2003

Smith, Shawn T., 1967- Surviving aggressive people : practical violence prevention skills for the workplace and the street / Shawn T. Smith. 1st Sentient Publications ed. Boulder, CO : Sentient Publications, 2003. xix, 235 p. : ill. ; 23 cm. (The culture tools series) Includes bibliographical references (p. [215]-225) and index. ISBN 1-59181-005-1 DDC 303.6/9
1. Aggressiveness - Prevention. 2. Violence - Prevention. I. Title. II. Series.
BF575.A3 S55 2003

Smith, Steve.
Marcum, Dave. BusinessThink. New York : Wiley, c2002.
HF5386 .M3087 2002

Smith, Terry (Terry L.), 1961- Haunted inns of America : go & know national directory of haunted hotels and bed & breakfast inns / Terry Smith and Mark Jean. Birmingham, Ala. : Crane Hill Publishers, c2003. p. cm. Table of contents URL: http://www.loc.gov/catdir/toc/ecip041/2003005399.html ISBN 1-57587-201-3 DDC 133.1/22
1. Haunted hotels - United States - Guidebooks. 2. Ghosts - United States. I. Jean, Mark, 1957- II. Title.
BF1474.5 .S65 2003

Smith, Timothy B.
Practicing multiculturalism. Boston, MA : Allyn and Bacon, c2004.
BF637.C6 P7 2004

Smith, Wes.
Pearlman, Lou. Bands, brands and billions. New York : London : McGraw-Hill, 2002.

SMITH, WILFRED TALBOT, 1885-1957.
Starr, Martin P., 1959- The unknown God. Bolingbrook, IL: Teitan Press, 2003.
BF1997.S73 2003

Smith, William A. (William Aloysius), 1929- Reflections on death, dying, and bereavement : a manual for clergy, counselors, and speakers / William A. Smith. Amityville, N.Y. : Baywood Pub., c2003. xi, 100 p. ; 24 cm. (Death, value, and meaning series) Includes bibliographical references (p. 89-93) and index. ISBN 0-89503-270-8 (alk. paper) DDC 128/.5
1. Death. 2. Bereavement. I. Title. II. Series.
BD444 .S57 2003

Smithson, Michael. Confidence intervals / Michael Smithson. Thousand Oaks, Calif. : Sage Publications, c2003. vi, 93 p. : ill. ; 22 cm. (Sage university papers. Quantitative applications in the social sciences ; no. 07/140) Includes bibliographical references (90-92). ISBN 0-7619-2499-X (pbk. : alk. paper) DDC 519.5/38
1. Social sciences - Statistical methods. 2. Confidence intervals. 3. Social sciences - Mathematics. I. Title. II. Series: Sage university papers series. Quantitative applications in the social sciences ; no. 07-140.
HA31.2 .S59 2003

SMOKE - MISCELLANEA.
Alexander, Jane. The smudging and blessings book. New York: Sterling Pub., 2001.

Smoking - Religious aspects - Judaism.

BF1999 .A6329 2001

SMOKING - RELIGIOUS ASPECTS - JUDAISM.
Koll, Shmuel, 1938- Sefer Ra'yonot u-mesarim. Yerushalayim : S. Kol, 761- [2001-

Smola, Alexander J.
Machine Learning Summer School 2002 (2002 : Canberra, N.C.T.) Advanced lectures on machine learning. Berlin ; New York : Springer, 2003.
Q325.5 .M344 2002

Smolik, Noemi.
Kupka, František, 1871-1957. [Création dans les arts plastiques. Czech. German] Die Schöpfung in der bildenden Kunst. Ostfildern-Ruit : Hatje Cantz, c2001.

The smudging and blessings book.
Alexander, Jane. New York: Sterling Pub., 2001.
BF1999 .A6329 2001

Smullyan, Raymond M. Who knows? : a study of religious consciousness / Raymond M. Smullyan. Bloomington : Indiana University Press, c2003. x, 142 p. ; 24 cm. Includes bibliographical references (p. [135]-136) and index. ISBN 0-253-34198-1 (alk. paper) ISBN 0-253-21574-9 (pbk. : alk. paper) DDC 210
1. Gardner, Martin, - 1914- - Whys of a philosophical scrivener. 2. Bucke, Richard Maurice, - 1837-1902. - Cosmic consciousness. 3. Religion. 4. Hell. 5. Future life. 6. God. 7. Christianity. I. Title.
BL50 .S59 2003

Smul'son, M. L. (Maryna Lazarivna) Psykholohiia rozvytku intelektu / M.L. Smul'son. Kyïv : Instytut psykholohiï im. H.S. Kostiuka APN Ukraïny, 2001. 272 p. ; 21 cm. Summary and table of contents in English. Includes bibliographical references (p. 243-270). ISBN 9666140306
1. Intellect. I. Instytut psykholohiï im. H.S. Kostiuka. II. Title.
BF431 .S68 2001

Smyser, W. R., 1931- How Germans negotiate : logical goals, practical solutions / W.R. Smyser. Washington, D.C. : U.S. Institute of Peace Press, 2003. xvii, 246 p. : 24 cm. Includes bibliographical references (p. 215-226) and index. CONTENTS: The foundation: geography, history, philosophy, and economics -- The principal elements of a negotiation with Germans -- The German negotiator: personality and tactics -- German business negotiations -- German official economic negotiations -- The future of German negotiating behavior -- How to negotiate with Germans. ISBN 1-929223-41-2 (alk. paper) ISBN 1-929223-40-4 (pbk. : alk. paper) DDC 302.3/0943
1. Negotiation. 2. National characteristics, German. I. Title.
BF637.N4 S59 2003

Snap out of it.
Segalove, Ilene, 1950- Boston, MA : Conari Press, 2004.
BF637.S4 S438 2004

Snelgar, Rosemary.
Brace, Nicola. SPSS for psychologists. 2nd ed. Mahwah, NJ : Lawrence Erlbaum Associates, 2003.
BF39 .K447 2003

Snell, Robert, 1951-.
Loewenthal, Del, 1947- Post-modernism for psychotherapists. Hove, East Sussex ; New York : Brunner-Routledge, 2003.
BF41 .L64 2003

Sny i videniia v narodnoĭ kul'ture / [sostavitel' O.B. Khristoforova]. Moskva : RGGU, 2002. 381 p. ; 20 cm. (Traditsiia, tekst, fol'klor. Tipologiia i semiotika) Includes bibliographical references. ISBN 5728103359
1. Dreams - Folklore. I. Khristoforova, O. B. (Ol'ga Borisovna) II. Series.
BF1078 .S563 2002

Snyder, Allan.
What makes a champion!. Camberwell, Vic., Australia ; New York : Penguin Books, 2002.
BF637.S8 W45 2002

Snyder, C. R. Handbook of hope : theory, measures & applications / editor, C.R. Snyder. San Diego, Calif. : Academic Press, c2000. xxv, 440 p. : ill. ; 24 cm. Includes bibliographical references and indexes. Table of contents URL: http://www.loc.gov/catdir/toc/els033/99068018.html Publisher description URL: http://www.loc.gov/catdir/description/els033/99068018.html ISBN 0-12-654050-0 (alk. paper) DDC 153.8
1. Hope. I. Snyder, C. R. II. Title.
BF575.H56 S69 2000

Snyder, C. R. Handbook of hope. San Diego, Calif. : Academic Press, c2000.
BF575.H56 S69 2000

Snyder, Christopher A. (Christopher Allen), 1966-
The Britons / Christopher A. Snyder. Malden, MA ; Oxford : Blackwell Pub., 2003. xvi, 331 p., [14] p. of plates : ill., maps ; 24 cm. (The peoples of Europe) Includes bibliographical references (p. [297]-317) and index. ISBN 0-631-22260-X (hbk. : alk. paper) ISBN 0-631-22262-6 (pbk. : alk. paper) DDC 941/.004916
1. Arthur, - King. 2. Britons. 3. Great Britain - Civilization - To 1066. 4. Great Britain - Antiquities, Celtic. 5. Great Britain - History - To 449. 6. Celts - Great Britain. 7. Druids and Druidism. I. Title. II. Series.
DA140 .S73 2003

Snyder, Graydon F. Irish Jesus, Roman Jesus : the formation of early Irish Christianity / Graydon F. Snyder. Harrisburg, Pa. : Trinity Press International, c2002. vii, 280 p. : ill. ; 23 cm. Includes bibliographical references (p. 261-270) and indexes. CONTENTS: The Celts -- Paul and the Galatians -- Intimations of culture in the Jesus tradition -- The Jesus tradition in Paul's writing -- Paul and Spain -- The Celts in Spain -- The insular Celts -- Early Christians in Ireland -- Early Christian art and architecture -- The Hebrew scriptures in sculptured art -- The New Testament in sculptured art -- The calendar and Irish Christian language -- Hagiography -- Gender and sexuality -- Commensality -- Theology -- Appendix : The Jesus tradition utilized by Paul. ISBN 1-56338-385-3 (pbk.) DDC 274.15
1. Celts - Religion. 2. Celtic Church - History. 3. Church history - Primitive and early church, ca. 30-600. I. Title.
BR737.C4 S69 2002

SOAP OPERAS - COLOMBIA - HISTORY AND CRITICISM.
Méndez, José Luis, 1941- El irresistible encanto de Betty la fea. San Juan, P.R. : Ediciones Milenio, 2001.

SOAP OPERAS - SOCIAL ASPECTS - COLOMBIA.
Méndez, José Luis, 1941- El irresistible encanto de Betty la fea. San Juan, P.R. : Ediciones Milenio, 2001.

Sobelman, David.
McLuhan's wake [videorecording]. [Montreal, Quebec] : Primitive Entertainment/National Film Board of Canada, c2002.

Sober, Harvey I.
Chuckrow, Robert. The tai chi book. Boston : YMAA Publication Center, c1998.
GV504 .C536 1998

Sobre las elites profesionales femeninas.
García de León, María Antonia. Herederas y heridas. 1a ed. [Madrid] : Ediciones Cátedra, Universitat de València, Instituto de la Mujer, 2002.
HD6054.2.S7 G37 2002

Sobre las identidades : lecciones Carlos Mendive (1998-1999) / Juan Manuel Iranzo Amatriaín, José Rubén Blanco Merlo (editores). Pamplona : Universidad Pública de Navarra, [2001] 180 p. : ill. ; 24 cm. (Colección Ciencias sociales / Universidad Pública de Navarra ; 11) Includes bibliographical references. ISBN 84-950757-4-1
1. Mendive, Carlos - (Mendive Arbeloa) 2. Identity (Philosophical concept) 3. Group identity. 4. Multiculturalism. I. Iranzo, Juan Manuel. II. Blanco Merlo, Rubén. III. Series: Colección Ciencias sociales (Universidad Pública de Navarra) ; 11.

SOCCER - PHILOSOPHY.
Goñi Zubieta, Carlos. Futbolsofía. Madrid : Ediciones del Laberinto, [2002]

SOCIAL ACCEPTANCE.
McClure, Joyce Kloc, 1955- Finite, contingent, and free. Lanham, Md. : Oxford : Rowman & Littlefield Publishers, c2003.
BJ1012 .M316 2003

Minsos, Susan Felicity, 1944- Culture clubs. Edmonton : Spotted Cow Press, c2002.

SOCIAL ACCOUNTING. *See* **QUALITY OF LIFE.**

SOCIAL ACTION.
Fernandes, Leela. Transforming feminist practice. 1st ed. San Francisco : Aunt Lute Books, 2003.
HQ1154 .F495 2003

SOCIAL ADJUSTMENT. *See also* **DEVIANT BEHAVIOR.**
Romm, M. V. (Mark Valerievich) Adaptatsiia lichnosti v sotsiume. Novosibirsk : "Nauka", 2002.
HM696 .R655 2002

Social aggression among girls.
Underwood, Marion K. New York ; London : Guilford Press, c2003.
BF723.A35 U53 2003

SOCIAL ANTHROPOLOGY. *See* **ETHNOLOGY.**

SOCIAL ARCHAEOLOGY.
Archaeologies of memory. Malden, MA ; Oxford : Blackwell, 2003.

CC72.4 .A733 2003

Theory and practice in late antique archaeology. Leiden ; Boston : Brill, 2003.
CC72.4 .T46 2003

SOCIAL BEHAVIOR. *See* **INTERPERSONAL RELATIONS.**

SOCIAL BEHAVIOR.
Kaluzniacky, Eugene. Managing psychological factors in information systems work. Hershey PA : Information Science Pub., c2004.
BF576 .K358 2004

SOCIAL BEHAVIOR - GREAT BRITAIN.
Hadikin, Ruth. The bullying culture. Oxford ; Boston : Books for Midwives, 2000.
BF637.B85 H33 2000

SOCIAL CASE WORK. *See also* **COUNSELING; INTERVIEWING.**
Constructing clienthood in social work and human services. London ; New York : Jessica Kingsley Publishers, c2003.
HV40 .C6615 2003

SOCIAL CHANGE. *See also* **SOCIAL EVOLUTION.**
Edgeworth, Brendan. Law, modernity, postmodernity. Aldershot, England ; Burlington, VT : Ashgate/Dartmouth, c2003.
K370 .E34 2003

Ernst, Waltraud, 1964- Diskurspiratinnen. Wien : Milena, c1999.
HQ1154 .E7 1999

Generationswechsel und historischer Wandel. München : Oldenbourg, 2003.

Lewis, Jane (Jane E.) Should we worry about family change? Toronto : University of Toronto Press, c2003.

Style, function, transmission. Salt Lake City : University of Utah Press, c2003.
CC173 .S79 2003

Tew, Jerry, 1955- Social theory, power and practice. Houndmills [England] ; New York : Palgrave, 2002.
HN49.P6 T49 2002

SOCIAL CHANGE - LATIN AMERICA.
Habitar la tierra. Buenos Aires : Grupo Editor Altamira, 2002.
CB358 .H32 2002

SOCIAL CHANGE - POLAND - CONGRESSES.
Psychologia w obliczu zachodzących przemian społeczno-kulturowych. Warszawa : Instytut Psychologii PAN, 2002.
BF20 .P79 2002

SOCIAL CHANGE - PSYCHOLOGICAL ASPECTS - CONGRESSES.
Psychologia w obliczu zachodzących przemian społeczno-kulturowych. Warszawa : Instytut Psychologii PAN, 2002.
BF20 .P79 2002

SOCIAL CHOICE.
Sen, Amartya Kumar. Rationality and freedom. Cambridge, Mass. : Belknap Press of Harvard University Press, 2002.
HB846.8 .S466 2002

SOCIAL CLASSES. *See* **ELITE (SOCIAL SCIENCES); INTELLECTUALS; POOR; WORKING CLASS.**

SOCIAL CLASSES AND LANGUAGE. *See* **SPEECH AND SOCIAL STATUS.**

SOCIAL CLASSES AND SPEECH. *See* **SPEECH AND SOCIAL STATUS.**

SOCIAL CLASSES - CZECH REPUBLIC - HISTORY - TO 1500.
Člověk českého středověku. Vyd. 1. Praha : Argo, 2002.

SOCIAL CLASSES IN LITERATURE.
Gerber, Nancy, 1956- Portrait of the mother-artist. Lanham, Md. : Lexington Books, c2003.
PS374.M547 G47 2003

Radulescu, Raluca, 1974- The gentry context for Malory's Morte Darthur. Cambridge [England] ; Rochester, NY : D.S. Brewer, 2003.
PR2047 .R33 2003

SOCIAL CLASSES - UNITED STATES - HISTORY - 20TH CENTURY.
Horowitz, David A. America's political class under fire. New York ; London : Routledge, 2003.
HN90.S6 H67 2003

SOCIAL COGNITION. *See also* **SOCIAL PERCEPTION.**
Bless, Herbert. Hove, East Sussex, UK ; New York : Psychology Press, 2003.
BF323.S63 B55 2003

Social cognition / edited by Marilynn Brewer and Miles Hewstone. Malden, MA : Blackwell Pub., 2003. p. cm. (Perspectives on social psychology) Includes bibliographical references and index. CONTENTS: Mental representations / Eliot R. Smith and Sarah Queller -- The social unconscious / Mahzarin R. Banaji, Kristi M. Lemm, and Siri J. carpenter -- How the mind moves : knowledge accessibility and the fine-tuning of the cognitive system / Leonard L. Martin, Fritz Strack, and Diederik A. Stapel -- Cognitive representations of attachment : the content and function of working models / Nancy L. Collins and Lisa M. Allard -- The root of all evil in intergroup relations? Unearthing the categorization process / Penelope Oates -- Stereotypes : content, structures, processes, and context / Don Operario and Susan T. Fiske -- Category dynamics and the modification of outgroup stereotypes / Myron Rothbart -- Attributions in close relationships : from Balkanization to integration / Frank D. Fincham -- Cognition and the development of close relationships / Benjamin R. Karney, James K. McNulty, and Thomas N. Nradbury -- Language and social cognition / Güen R. Semin -- Attitudes, norms, and social groups / Joel Cooper, Kimberly A. Kelly, and Kimberlee Weaver -- Shared cognition in small groups / R. Scott Tindale ... [et al.] -- Group processes and the construction of social representations / Fabio Lorenzi-Cioldi and Alain Clemence -- How language contributes to persistence of stereotypes as well as other, more general, intergroup issues / Klaus Fiedler and Jeannette Schmid. ISBN 1405110708 (pbk. : alk. paper) DDC 302/.1
1. Mental representation - Social aspects. 2. Social perception. I. Brewer, Marilynn B., 1942- II. Hewstone, Miles. III. Series.
BF316.6 .S65 2003

Social comprehension and judgment.
Wyer, Robert S. Mahwah, N.J. : L. Erlbaum Associates, Publishers, 2004.
BF323.S63 W94 2004

Social conceptions of time : structure and process in work and everyday life / edited by Graham Crow and Sue Heath. Houndmills, Basingstoke, Hampshire ; New York : Palgrave MacMillan, 2002. xvii, 266 p. : ill. 23 cm. (Explorations in sociology ; v.62) Includes bibliographical references (p. 247-263) and index. ISBN 0-333-98499-4 (alk. paper) DDC 304.2/3
1. Time - Social aspects. 2. Time - Psychological aspects. I. Crow, Graham. II. Heath, Sue. III. Series.
HM656 .S63 2002

SOCIAL CONDITIONS. *See* **SOCIAL HISTORY.**

SOCIAL CONFICT - COLOMBIA - HISTORY - 20TH CENTURY.
Idrobo Díaz, Hugo, 1954- La joda de la paz en Colombia. 1. ed. Cali, Colombia : [s.n., 2002?]

SOCIAL CONFLICT. *See also* **CONFLICT MANAGEMENT; CONFLICT OF GENERATIONS; INTERPERSONAL CONFLICT; SOCIAL CONTROL.**
Abrahamsson, Hans, 1949- Understanding world order and structural change. Basingstoke, Hampshire : New York : Palgrave Macmillan, 2003.
HF1359 .A24 2003

Ataöv, Türkkaya. Discrimination & conflict. Haarlem : SOTA, 2000.

Búfalo, Enzo del. Individuo, mercado y utopía. 1. ed. Caracas : Monte Ávila Editores Lationoamericana : Universidad Central de Venezuela, Centro de Investigaciones Post-Doctorales FACES, 1998.
BD222 .B86 1998

Creppell, Ingrid. Toleration and identity. New York ; London : Routledge, 2003.
HM1271 .C73 2003

Eidelberg, Paul. Clash of two decadent civilizations. Shaarei Tikva, Israel : ACPR Publications, 2002.
BM537 .E53 2002

Gould, Roger V. Collision of wills. Chicago : University of Chicago Press, 2003.
HM1121 .G68 2003

Granovskaia, R. M. (Rada Mikhaĭlovna) Konflikt i tvorchestvo v zerkale psikhologii. Moskva : Genezis, 2002.
BF637.I48 G72 2002

Liu, Peiping. She hui mao dun yu jin dai Zhongguo. Di 1 ban. Jinan Shi : Shandong jiao yu chu ban she, 2000.
HN733 .L569 2000

The meanings of violence. London ; New York : Routledge, 2003.

Monkeywrenching the new world order [sound recording]. Oakland, Calif : AK Press ; San Francisco, CA : Alternative Tentacles Records, 2001.

SOCIAL CONFLICT - CHINA - HISTORY - 20TH CENTURY.
Liu, Peiping. She hui mao dun yu jin dai Zhongguo. Di 1 ban. Jinan Shi : Shandong jiao yu chu ban she, 2000.
HN733 .L569 2000

SOCIAL CONFLICT - EGYPT - CAIRO.
El-Kholy, Heba Aziz. Defiance and compliance. New York : Berghahn Books, 2002.
HQ1793.Z9 C353 2002

SOCIAL CONFLICT - GOVERNMENT POLICY.
Evolutionary psychology and violence. Westport, Conn. : Praeger, 2003.
HM1116 .E96 2003

SOCIAL CONFLICT - PSYCHOLOGICAL ASPECTS.
Evolutionary psychology and violence. Westport, Conn. : Praeger, 2003.
HM1116 .E96 2003

Understanding terrorism. 1st ed. Washington, DC : American Psychological Association, 2004.
HV6431 .U35 2004

SOCIAL CONFLICT - UNITED STATES.
The fractious nation? Berkeley : University of California Press, c2003.
E169.12 .F69 2003

SOCIAL CONFORMITY. *See* **CONFORMITY.**

Social context and cognitive performance.
Monteil, Jean-Marc. Hove, East Sussex, UK : Psychology Press, c1999.
BF311 .M59 1999

SOCIAL CONTRACT. *See also* **CIVIL SOCIETY.**
Venne, Jean-François, 1972- Le lien social dans le modèle de l'individualisme privé. Paris : L'Harmattan, c2002.

SOCIAL CONTROL. *See also* **LIBERTY; SOCIAL ENGINEERING; SOCIAL NORMS.**
Bishop, Anne, 1950- Becoming an ally. 2nd ed. London ; New York : Zed Books ; Halifax, N.S. : Fernwood Pub. ; New York : Distributed in the USA exclusively by Palgrave, 2002.
HM1256 .B57 2002

Gould, Roger V. Collision of wills. Chicago : University of Chicago Press, 2003.
HM1121 .G68 2003

Limonov, Ėduard. Distsiplinarnyĭ sanatoriĭ. Sankt-Peterburg : Amfora, 2002.
CB428 .L556 2002

Violence and the body. Bloomington : Indiana University Press, c2003.
HM1116 .V557 2003

SOCIAL CONTROL - CONGRESSES.
21. Goldegger Dialoge. 1. Aufl. Goldegg : Kulturverein Schloss Goldegg, 2002.

SOCIAL CONTROL - DICTIONARIES.
Becker, Konrad. Tactical reality dictionary. Vienna : Edition Selene ; [s.l.] : Distribution Canada/UK/USA by Autonomedia, 2002.
BF637.P4 B33 2002

SOCIAL DARWINISM.
Historical materialism and social evolution. New York : Palgrave Macmillan, 2002.
HX523 .H565 2002

SOCIAL DEMOCRACY. *See* **SOCIALISM.**

SOCIAL DEVIANCE. *See* **DEVIANT BEHAVIOR.**

SOCIAL DISTANCE.
Papcke, Sven, 1939- Gesellschaft der Eliten. 1. Aufl. Münster : Westfälisches Dampfboot, 2001.
HM821 .P37 2001

SOCIAL ECOLOGY.
Kittredge, William. The nature of generosity. 1st Vintage Departures ed. New York : Vintage, 2001, c2000.
PS3561.I87 Z472 2001

Language acquisition and language socialization. London ; New York : Continuum, 2002.
P118 .L243 2002

SOCIAL ENGINEERING.
Approaches to peacebuilding. Houndmills, Basingstoke, Hampshire ; New York : Palgrave Macmillan, 2003.

JZ5538 .A675 2002

SOCIAL ENGINEERING - DICTIONARIES.
Becker, Konrad. Tactical reality dictionary. Vienna : Edition Selene ; [s.l.] : Distribution Canada/UK/USA by Autonomedia, 2002.
BF637.P4 B33 2002

Social epistemology : a philosophical study to the riddle of self-cognition of human society.
Ouyang, Kang, 1953- She hui ren shi lun. Di 1 ban. [Kunming] : Yunnan ren min chu ban she, 2002.
BF323.S63 O93 2002

SOCIAL ETHICS.
Burkhart, Dagmar. Ehre. Originalausg. München : Deutscher Taschenbuch Verlag, c2002.
BJ1533.H8 B87 2002

Collen, Lindsey. Natir imin. Port Louis, Mauritius : Ledikasyon pu travayer, [2000]

Karg, Hans Hartmut. Theoretische Ethik. Hamburg : Kovac, c1996-<c1999>
BJ1114 .K32 1997

Klosko, George. Jacobins and utopians. Notre Dame, Ind. : University of Notre Dame Press, c2003.
JC491 .K54 2003

Reemtsma, Jan Philipp. Wie hätte ich mich verhalten? München : Beck, c2001.
HM216 .R38 2001

SOCIAL EVOLUTION. *See also* **PRIMITIVE SOCIETIES; SOCIAL CHANGE.**
Beyond foraging and collecting. New York : Kluwer Academic/Plenum Publishers, c2002.
GN388 .B49 2002

Carneiro, Robert L. (Robert Leonard), 1927- Evolutionism in cultural anthropology. Boulder, Colo. : Westview Press, 2003.
GN360 .C37 2003

Culture and international history. New York : Berghahn Books, 2003.
JZ1251 .C84 2003

Kantor, Karl Moiseevich. Dvoĭnai͡a spiral' istorii. Moskva : I͡Azyk slavi͡anskoĭ kul'tury, 2002-
D16.8 .K224 2002

Longstaff, Bill, 1934- Confessions of a matriarchist. Calgary : Ballot Pub., 2003.

Michalon, Clair. Histoire de différences, différence d'histoires. Saint-Maur : Sépia, c2002.

Mithen, Steven J. After the ice. London : Weidenfeld & Nicolson, 2003.

Norton, Anne. Bloodrites of the post-structuralists. New York : Routledge, 2002.
HM626 .N6785 2002

Shlain, Leonard. Sex, time, and power. New York ; London : Viking, 2003.
HQ23 .S45 2003

Style, function, transmission. Salt Lake City : University of Utah Press, c2003.
CC173 .S79 2003

Washington, Johnny. Evolution, history and destiny. New York : Peter Lang, c2002.
E185.625 .W37 2002

SOCIAL EVOLUTION IN ANIMALS.
Trivers, Robert. Natural selection and social theory. New York : Oxford University Press, 2002.
GN365.9 .T76 2002

SOCIAL EVOLUTION - MISCELLANEA.
Argüelles, José, 1939- Time and the technosphere. Rochester, Vt. : Bear & Co., c2002.
BF1999 .A6398 2002

SOCIAL EXCHANGE.
Dolgin, Aleksandr. Pragmatika kul'tury. Moskva : Fond nauchnykh issledovaniĭ "Pragmatika kul'tury", 2002.

SOCIAL GROUPS. *See also* **DOMINANCE (PSYCHOLOGY); ELITE (SOCIAL SCIENCES); NEIGHBORHOOD; SMALL GROUPS; SOCIAL PSYCHOLOGY; SUBCULTURE.**
Chen, Xinhan. She hui ping jia lun. Di 1 ban. Shanghai : Shanghai she hui ke xue yuan chu ban she : Xin hua shu dian Shanghai fa xing suo fa xing, 1997.
HM131 .C7135 1997 <Asian China>

Gould, Roger V. Collision of wills. Chicago : University of Chicago Press, 2003.

HM1121 .G68 2003

Group cohesion, trust and solidarity. 1st ed. Amsterdam ; New York : JAI, 2002.

Lorenzi-Cioldi, Fabio, 1955- Les représentations des groupes dominants et dominés. Grenoble : Presses universitaires de Grenoble, c2002.
HM716 .L674 2002

McNiff, Shaun. Creating with others. 1st ed. Boston, Mass. : Shambhala Publications, 2003.
BF408 .M336 2003

Minsos, Susan Felicity, 1944- Culture clubs. Edmonton : Spotted Cow Press, c2002.

Pavlicevic, Mercedes. Groups in music. London ; New York : Jessica Kingsley Publishers, 2003.
ML3920 .P2279 2003

SOCIAL HIERARCHY (PSYCHOLOGY). See **DOMINANCE (PSYCHOLOGY).**

SOCIAL HISTORY. See also **QUALITY OF LIFE; SOCIAL CHANGE; SOCIAL MOVEMENTS; SOCIAL PROBLEMS; URBANIZATION.**
Udovik, S. L. (Sergeĭ Leonidovich) Globalizatsiia. [Moscow] : Refl-buk ; [Kiev] : Vakler, 2002.
CB430 .U36 2002

SOCIAL HISTORY - 1970-.
Limonov, Ėduard. Distsiplinarnyĭ sanatoriĭ. Sankt-Peterburg : Amfora, 2002.
CB428 .L556 2002

SOCIAL HISTORY - 20TH CENTURY.
Lal, Vinay. Empire of knowledge. London ; Sterling, Va. : Pluto Press, 2002.
HN16 .L35 2002

SOCIAL HISTORY - MEDIEVAL, 500-1500.
Cohen, Jeffrey Jerome. Medieval identity machines. Minneapolis : University of Minnesota Press, c2003.
CB353 .C64 2003

The construction of communities in the early Middle Ages. Leiden ; Boston : Brill, 2003.
HN11 .C66 2003

Duby, Georges. Qu'est-ce que la société féodale? Paris : Flammarion, c2002.

Gender and difference in the Middle Ages. Minneapolis : University of Minnesota Press, c2003.
HQ1143 .G44 2003

Gendering the master narrative. Ithaca : Cornell University Press, c2003.
HQ1143 .G46 2003

Nashim, zeḳenim ṿa-ṭaf. Yerushalayim : Merkaz Zalman Shazar le-toldot Yiśraʾel, [2001]

Negotiating the gift. Göttingen : Vandenhoeck & Ruprecht, c2003.

Pleij, Herman. [Dromen van Cocagne. English] Dreaming of Cockaigne. New York : Columbia University Press, c2001.
CB353 .P5413 2001

SOCIAL HISTORY - MODERN, 1500-. See **SOCIAL HISTORY.**

SOCIAL IDENTITY. See **GROUP IDENTITY.**

SOCIAL INFLUENCE. See **CONFORMITY; IMITATION.**

SOCIAL INFLUENCE - CONGRESSES.
21. Goldegger Dialoge. 1. Aufl. Goldegg : Kulturverein Schloss Goldegg, 2002.

Razvitie lichnosti v kul'turno-obrazovatel'nom prostranstve. Tambov : Tambovskiĭ gos. universitet im. G.R. Derzhavina, 2000.
BF698 .R342 2000

The social inheritance of the Holocaust.
Reading, Anna. Houndmills [England] ; New York : Palgrave Macmillan, 2002.
D804.3 .R42 2002

SOCIAL INSTITUTIONS. See **FAMILY.**

SOCIAL INSTITUTIONS - FRANCE - HISTORY.
Duby, Georges. Qu'est-ce que la société féodale? Paris : Flammarion, c2002.

SOCIAL INTELLIGENCE.
Earley, P. Christopher. Cultural intelligence. Stanford, Calif. : Stanford University Press, 2003.
HD57.7 .E237 2003

SOCIAL INTERACTION. See also **INTERGROUP RELATIONS.**
The afro-asian century. Durham, N.C. : Duke University Press, 2003.

Barash, David P. The survival game. 1st ed. New York : Times Books, 2003.
HM1111 .B37 2003

Boxer, Diana, 1948- Applying sociolinguistics. Amsterdam ; Philadelphia : J. Benjamins Pub., c2002.
P40 .B678 2002

Braun-Thürmann, Holger. Künstliche Interaktion. 1. Aufl. Wiesbaden : Westdeutscher Verlag, 2002.

Broth, Matthias, 1965- Agents secrets. Uppsala, Sweden : Uppsala Universitet, c2002.

Chazal, Gérard. Interfaces. Seyssel [France] : Champ Vallon, c2002.
HM1111 .C49 2002

Communication and cyberspace. 2nd ed. Creskill, N.J. : Hampton Press, c2003.
P96.D36 C66 2003

Constructing clienthood in social work and human services. London ; New York : Jessica Kingsley Publishers, c2003.
HV40 .C6615 2003

The development of the social self. 1st ed. London ; New York : Psychology Press, 2003.
BF723.S24 D48 2003

Earley, P. Christopher. Cultural intelligence. Stanford, Calif. : Stanford University Press, 2003.
HD57.7 .E237 2003

Emotions and sociology. Oxford ; Malden, MA : Blackwell Pub./Sociological Review, 2002.

Gendered landscapes. University Park, PA : Center for Studies in Landscape History, c2000.

Hardin, Russell, 1940- Indeterminacy and society. Princeton, N.J. : Princeton University Press, c2003.
HM1111 .H37 2003

Huls, Erica. Dilemma's in menselijke interactie. Utrecht : Lemma, 2001.

Patton, Bobby R., 1935- Decision-making group interaction. 4th ed. Boston : Allyn and Bacon, c2003.
HM736 .P37 2003

Studies in language and social interaction. Mahwah, N.J. : London : Lawrence Erlbaum, 2003.

Vazeilles, José Gabriel. Platonismo, marxismo y comunicación social. Buenos Aires : Editorial Biblos, c2002.

Woodward, Gary C. The idea of identification. Albany : State University of New York Press, c2003.
BF697.5.S65 W66 2003

SOCIAL INTERACTION IN CHILDREN.
Bierman, Karen L. Peer rejection. New York : Guilford Press, 2004.
BF723.R44 B54 2003

SOCIAL INTERACTION IN INFANTS.
Hobson, R. Peter. The cradle of thought. New York : Oxford University Press, 2004.
BF720.C63 H63 2004

Hobson, R. Peter. The cradle of thought. London : Macmillan, 2002.
BF720.C63 H63 2002

SOCIAL INTERACTION - NIGERIA.
Opata, Damian U. (Damian Ugwutikiri) Towards a genealogy of African time. Nsukka, Nigeria : AP Express Publishing Company Lt., 2001.
1. Black author.

SOCIAL ISOLATION. See **LONELINESS; MARGINALITY, SOCIAL.**

SOCIAL JUSTICE.
Fernandes, Leela. Transforming feminist practice. 1st ed. San Francisco : Aunt Lute Books, 2003.
HQ1154 .F495 2003

The politics of memory. London ; New York : Zed Books, c2000.
JC571 .P642 2000

Social justice, education, and identity / edited by Carol Vincent. London ; New York : RoutledgeFalmer, 2003. xi, 227 p. : ill. ; 24 cm. Includes bibliographical references and index. ISBN 0-415-29695-1 (hbk.) ISBN 0-415-29696-X (pbk.) DDC 370.11/5
1. Educational sociology. 2. Social justice - Study and teaching. 3. Identity (Philosophical concept) I. Vincent, Carol, 1963-
LC191 .S6564 2003

SOCIAL JUSTICE - STUDY AND TEACHING.
Social justice, education, and identity. London ; New York : RoutledgeFalmer, 2003.

LC191 .S6564 2003

The social life of emotions / edited by Larissa Z. Tiedens, Colin Wayne Leach. New York : Cambridge University Press, 2004. p. cm. (Studies in emotion and social interaction) Includes bibliographical references and index. ISBN 0-521-82811-2 (hb) ISBN 0-521-53529-8 (pbk.) DDC 152.4
1. Emotions - Social aspects - Textbooks. I. Tiedens, Larissa Z. II. Leach, Colin Wayne, 1967- III. Series.
BF531 .S634 2004

SOCIAL MARGINALITY. See **MARGINALITY, SOCIAL.**

Social marketing.
Kotler, Philip. 2nd ed. Thousand Oaks, Calif. ; London : Sage Publications, c2002.
HF5414 .K67 2002

SOCIAL MARKETING.
Kotler, Philip. Social marketing. 2nd ed. Thousand Oaks, Calif. ; London : Sage Publications, c2002.
HF5414 .K67 2002

SOCIAL MEDICINE. See **MEDICAL ETHICS.**

SOCIAL MEDICINE - UNITED STATES.
Elliott, Carl, 1961- Better than well. 1st ed. New York : W.W. Norton, c2003.
RA418.3.U6 E455 2003

SOCIAL MOBILITY.
Adkins, Lisa, 1966- Revisions. Buckingham [UK] ; Philadelphia : Open University Press, 2002.
HQ1075 .A24 2002

SOCIAL MOVEMENTS. See also **CIVIL RIGHTS MOVEMENTS; ENVIRONMENTALISM; NEW AGE MOVEMENT; WHITE SUPREMACY MOVEMENTS.**
Cantril, Hadley, 1906-1969. The psychology of social movements. New Brunswick, [N.J.] : Transaction Publishers, c2002.
HM881 .C36 2002

SOCIAL MOVEMENTS - UNITED STATES - HISTORY - 20TH CENTURY.
The achievement of American liberalism. New York : Columbia University Press, c2003.
E806 .M63 2003

Barber, Lucy G. (Lucy Grace), 1964- Marching on Washington. Berkeley : University of California Press, c2002.
E743 .B338 2002

SOCIAL NETWORKS.
Kilduff, Martin. Social networks and organizations. London : SAGE, 2003.

Social relations and the life course. Houndmills, Basingstoke New York : Palgrave Macmillan, 2003.
HM741 .S64 2003

Thompson, Grahame. Between hierarchies and markets. Oxford ; New York : Oxford University Press, 2003.
HD58.7 .T4786 2003

Social networks and organizations.
Kilduff, Martin. London : SAGE, 2003.

SOCIAL NORMS.
Nelson, Phillip J., 1929- Signaling goodness. Ann Arbor : University of Michigan Press, c2003.
HV31 .N45 2003

SOCIAL NORMS - CONGRESSES.
21. Goldegger Dialoge. 1. Aufl. Goldegg : Kulturverein Schloss Goldegg, 2002.

SOCIAL NORMS - PHILOSOPHY.
Pettit, Philip, 1945- Rules, reasons, and norms. Oxford : Oxford University Press ; New York : Clarendon Press, 2002.
B105.T54 P48 2002

Social origins of religion.
Bastide, Roger, 1898-1974. [Eléments de sociologie religieuse. English] Minneapolis : University of Minnesota Press, c2003.
BL60 .B313 2003

SOCIAL PARTICIPATION. See **POLITICAL PARTICIPATION.**

SOCIAL PERCEPTION. See also **AGEISM; SEXISM.**
Archer, Margaret Scotford. Structure, agency and the internal conversation. Cambridge, U.K. ; New York : Cambridge University Press, 2003.
HM708 .A73 2003

Bewes, Timothy. Reification, or, The anxiety of late capitalism. London ; New York : Verso, 2002.

HM449 .B49 2002

Bless, Herbert. Social cognition. Hove, East Sussex, UK ; New York : Psychology Press, 2003.
BF323.S63 B55 2003

El buscador de oro. [Madrid] : Lengua de Trapo Ediciones, c2002.

Foundations of social cognition. Mahwah, N.J. : L. Erlbaum, 2003.
BF323.S63 F68 2003

From girls in their elements to women in science. New York : P. Lang, 2003.
BF378.S65 F76 2003

Nelson, Phillip J., 1929- Signaling goodness. Ann Arbor : University of Michigan Press, c2003.
HV31 .N45 2003

Ouyang, Kang. 1953- She hui ren shi lun. Di 1 ban. [Kunming] : Yunnan ren min chu ban she, 2002.
BF323.S63 O93 2002

Social cognition. Malden, MA : Blackwell Pub., 2003.
BF316.6 .S65 2003

Wyer, Robert S. Social comprehension and judgment. Mahwah, N.J. : L. Erlbaum Associates, Publishers, 2004.
BF323.S63 W94 2004

Zeng, Jie. She hui si wei xue. Di 1 ban. Beijing : Ren min chu ban she : Xin hua shu dian jing xiao, 1996.
BF323.S63 T75 1996 <Asian China>

SOCIAL PERCEPTION - SEX DIFFERENCES - CONGRESSES.
Gender, vlast', kul'tura. Saratov : Saratovskiĭ gos. tekhn. universitet, 2000.
HQ1075 .G4667 2000

SOCIAL POLICY. See also **FAMILY POLICY; MEDICAL POLICY; MULTICULTURALISM.**
Kaplow, Louis. Fairness versus welfare. Cambridge, MA : Harvard University Press, 2002.
K247 .K37 2002

SOCIAL PREDICTION.
Kuz'menko, Volodymyr. Na porozi nadtsyvilizatsiï. L'viv : "Universum", 1998.
HM901 .K89 1998

Mason, Colin, 1926- The 2030 spike. London ; Sterling, VA : Earthscan Publications, 2003.
CB161 .M384 2003

Riding the next wave. Indianapolis, Ind. : Hudson Institute ; [Washington, DC : Distributed by the Brookings Institution Press], c2001.
HM901 .R43 2001

Some significant 21st century trends and issues. Islamabad : Pakistan Futuristics Foundation & Institute, 1998.
CB161 .S62 1998

Sterling, Bruce. Tomorrow now. 1st ed. New York : Random House, c2002.
HM901 .S74 2002

SOCIAL PRESSURE. See also **SOCIAL INFLUENCE.**
Hochschild, Arlie Russell, 1940- The commercialization of intimate life. Berkeley : University of California Press, 2003.
HM1106 .H63 2003

SOCIAL PROBLEMS. See **CHURCH AND SOCIAL PROBLEMS; CRIME; RACE RELATIONS.**

Social problems and social issues
Murphy, Elizabeth. Qualitative methods and health policy research. Hawthorne, N.Y. : Aldine de Gruyter, c2003.
RA394 .M87 2003

SOCIAL PROBLEMS AND THE CHURCH. See **CHURCH AND SOCIAL PROBLEMS.**

SOCIAL PROBLEMS - EGYPT.
Maḥfūẓ, Najlā'. Zawjī wa-al-ukhrá. al-Ṭab'ah 1. al-Qāhirah : al-Dār al-Miṣrīyah al-Lubnānīyah, 2003.
HQ1793 .M34 2003

SOCIAL PROBLEMS IN EDUCATION. See **EDUCATIONAL SOCIOLOGY.**

SOCIAL PROBLEMS IN LITERATURE.
Fichtelberg, Joseph. Critical fictions. Athens : University of Georgia Press, c2003.
PS366.S35 F53 2003

SOCIAL PROGRESS. See **PROGRESS.**

SOCIAL PSYCHOLOGY. See also **COOPERATIVENESS; INTERPERSONAL RELATIONS; INTERVIEWING; MORALE; OPPRESSION (PSYCHOLOGY); ORGANIZATIONAL BEHAVIOR; PUBLIC OPINION; SOCIAL CONFLICT; SOCIAL INFLUENCE; SOCIAL INTERACTION; SOCIAL MOVEMENTS; STEREOTYPE (PSYCHOLOGY); VIOLENCE.**
Carr, Stuart C. Milton, Qld. : John Wiley & Sons, 2003.

SOCIAL PSYCHOLOGY.
Amougou, Emmanuel. La construction de l'inconscient colonial en Alsace. Paris : L'Harmattan, 2002.
1. Black author.

Bishop, Anne, 1950- Becoming an ally. 2nd ed. London ; New York : Zed Books ; Halifax, N.S. : Fernwood Pub. ; New York : Distributed in the USA exclusively by Palgrave, 2002.
HM1256 .B57 2002

Cantril, Hadley, 1906-1969. The psychology of social movements. New Brunswick, [N.J.] : Transaction Publishers, c2002.
HM881 .C36 2002

Carr, Stuart C. Social psychology. Milton, Qld. : John Wiley & Sons, 2003.

Chen, Xinhan. She hui ping jia lun. Di 1 ban. Shanghai : Shanghai she hui ke xue yuan chu ban she : Xin hua shu dian Shanghai fa xing suo fa xing, 1997.
HM131 .C7135 1997 <Asian China>

Comfort, Kenneth Jerold. The ego and the social order. Cohoes, N.Y. : Public Administration Institute of New York State, 2000.
BF175.5.E35 C65 2000

Doise, Willem, 1935- Human rights as social representations. London ; New York : Routledge, 2002.
JC571 .D65 2002

Dolgin, Aleksandr. Pragmatika kul'tury. Moskva : Fond nauchnykh issledovaniĭ "Pragmatika kul'tury", 2002.

Donchenko, E. A. (Elena Andreevna) Arkhetypy sotsial'noho zhyttia i polityka. Kyiv : Lybid', 2001.
JA74.5 .D65 2001

Emotions and sociology. Oxford ; Malden, MA : Blackwell Pub./Socological Review, 2002.

Fromm, Erich, 1900- Escape from freedom. 1st Owl books ed. New York : H. Holt, 1994.
HM271 .F74 1994

The generative society. 1st ed. Washington, DC : American Psychological Association, c2003.
BF724.5 .G45 2003

The handbook of social psychology. 4th ed. Boston : McGraw-Hill ; New York : Distributed exclusively by Oxford University Press, c1998.
HM251 .H224 1998

Kaus, Rainer J. Psychoanalyse und Sozialpsychologie. Heidelberg : C. Winter, c1999.
BF109.F74 K38 1999

Kontexte und Kulturen des Erinnerns. Konstanz : UVK Verlagsgesellschaft, 2002.
BF378.S65 K65 2002

McLuhan, Marshall, 1911- The mechanical bride. Corte Madera, CA : Gingko Press, 2002.

Melman, Charles, 1931- L'homme sans gravité. Paris : Denoël, c2002.

Moessinger, Pierre Le jeu de l'identité. 1re éd. Paris : Presses universitaires de France, 2000.
BF697.5.S43 M634 2000

Morton, Adam. The importance of being understood. London ; New York : Routledge, 2003.
BF637.C45 M65 2003

Pataki, Ferenc, 1928- Élettörténet és identitás. Budapest : Osiris Kiadó, 2001.
BF697.5.S65 P38 2001

Psicologia social nos estudos culturais. Petrópolis : Editora Voces, c2003.
HM1033 .P75 2003

Romm, M. V. (Mark Valerievich) Adaptatsiia lichnosti v sotsiume. Novosibirsk : "Nauka", 2002.
HM696 .R655 2002

Stenzel, Lucia Marques. Obesidade. 1a ed. Porto Alegre : EDIPUCRS, 2002.

Toomela, Aaro. Cultural-historical psychology. Tartu : Tartu University Press, c2000.
BF109.V95 T66 2000

SOCIAL PSYCHOLOGY - BRAZIL - HISTORY.
Stubbe, Hannes, 1941- Kultur und Psychologie in Brasilien. Bonn : Holos, 2001.
BF108.B6 S783 2001

SOCIAL PSYCHOLOGY - CONGRESSES.
Psikhologiia otnosheniĭ. Vladimir : Vladimirskiĭ gos. pedagogicheskiĭ universitet, 2001.
BF637.C45 P74 2001

Razvitie lichnosti v kul'turno-obrazovatel'nom prostranstve. Tambov : Tambovskiĭ gos. universitet im. G.R. Derzhavina, 2000.
BF698 .R342 2000

Die Verortung von Gedächtnis. Wien : Passagen, c2001.

Social psychology (Philadelphia, Pa.)
Bless, Herbert. Social cognition. Hove, East Sussex, UK ; New York : Psychology Press, 2003.
BF323.S63 B55 2003

SOCIAL PSYCHOLOGY - RESEARCH.
Edgar, Iain R. Guide to imagework. London ; New York : Routledge, 2004.
BF367 .E34 2004

SOCIAL PSYCHOTECHNICS. See **PSYCHOLOGY, APPLIED.**

SOCIAL REFORM. See **SOCIAL PROBLEMS.**

SOCIAL REFORMERS. See also **FEMINISTS; WOMEN SOCIAL REFORMERS.**
Klosko, George. Jacobins and utopians. Notre Dame, Ind. : University of Notre Dame Press, c2003.
JC491 .K54 2003

SOCIAL REFORMERS - UNITED STATES - BIOGRAPHY.
Tonn, Joan C. Mary P. Follett. New Haven [Conn.] : Yale University Press, c2003.
HN57 .T695 2003

Social relations and the life course / edited by Graham Allan and Gill Jones. Houndmills, Basingstoke New York : Palgrave Macmillan, 2003. xii, 233 p. : ill. ; 23 cm. (Explorations in sociology ; 63) Includes bibliographical references (p. 214-227) and index. ISBN 0-333-98497-8 DDC 302.4
1. Social networks. 2. Interpersonal relations. 3. Family. 4. Life cycle, Human. I. Allan, Graham, 1948- II. Jones, Gill, 1942- III. Series: Explorations in sociology ; v. 63.
HM741 .S64 2003

SOCIAL RESPONSIBILITY OF BUSINESS.
Garten, Jeffrey E., 1946- The politics of fortune. Boston : Harvard Business School Press, c2002.
HD57.7 .G377 2002

Wenger, Andreas. Conflict prevention. Boulder, Colo. ; London : Lynne Rienner Publishers, 2003.
JZ5538 .W46 2003

SOCIAL ROLE. See also **SEX ROLE.**
Hoffmann, Arne. Sind Frauen bessere Menschen? Berlin : Schwarzkopf & Schwarzkopf, 2001.
HQ1075 .H64 2001

Miller, William Ian, 1946- Faking it. Cambridge ; New York : Cambridge University Press, 2003.
BF697 .M525 2003

Rishoi, Christy, 1958- From girl to woman. Albany : State University of New York Press, c2003.
HQ1186.A9 R57 2003

SOCIAL RULES. See **SOCIAL NORMS.**

SOCIAL SCIENCE. See **SOCIAL SCIENCES.**

SOCIAL SCIENCE LITERATURE - PUBLISHING - HANDBOOKS, MANUALS, ETC.
Publication manual of the American Psychological Association. 4th ed. Washington, DC : American Psychological Association, 1994.
BF76.7 .P82 1994

Publication manual of the American Psychological Association. 5th ed. Washington, DC : American Psychological Association, c2001.
BF76.7 .P83 2001

SOCIAL SCIENCE RESEARCH. See **SOCIAL SCIENCES - RESEARCH.**

SOCIAL SCIENCES. See also **CRIMINOLOGY; ECONOMICS; HUMAN BEHAVIOR; LIBERALISM; PLURALISM (SOCIAL SCIENCES); POLITICAL SCIENCE; POWER (SOCIAL SCIENCES); SOCIOLOGY.**

Verene, Donald Phillip, 1937- Knowledge of things human and divine. New Haven, Conn. : Yale University Press, c2003.
B3581.P73 V47 2003

SOCIAL SCIENCES AND PSYCHOANALYSIS.
Clark, Harold A. The age of intimacy. Laredo, TX : EBookcase.com, c2000.

Khanna, Ranjana, 1966- Dark continents. Durham, NC : Duke University Press, 2003.
BF175.4.S65 K43 2003

Psychoanalysis and management. Heidelberg : Physica-Verlag, c1994.
BF175.4.S65 P777 1994

SOCIAL SCIENCES AND PSYCHOANALYSIS - HISTORY.
Elliott, Anthony. Social theory since Freud. 1st ed. London ; New York : Routledge, 2004.
BF175.4.S65 E455 2004

SOCIAL SCIENCES AND PSYCHOANALYSIS - PERIODICALS.
[Pubblic/azione (Troina, Italy)] Pubblic/azione. Troina (Enna) : Oasi editrice, 2002-

SOCIAL SCIENCES - AUTHORSHIP.
Writing in the dark : phenomenological studies in interpretive inquiry. London, Ont. : Althouse Press, 2002.
B829.5 .W75 2002

SOCIAL SCIENCES - AUTHORSHIP - HANDBOOKS, MANUALS, ETC.
Publication manual of the American Psychological Association. 4th ed. Washington, DC : American Psychological Association, 1994.
BF76.7 .P82 1994

Publication manual of the American Psychological Association. 5th ed. Washington, DC : American Psychological Association, c2001.
BF76.7 .P83 2001

SOCIAL SCIENCES - BIBLIOGRAPHY. *See* SOCIAL SCIENCE LITERATURE.

SOCIAL SCIENCES - HISTORY.
Guillo, Dominique. Les figures de l'organisation. 1. éd. Paris : Presses universitaires de France, c2003.

SOCIAL SCIENCES - MATHEMATICS.
Smithson, Michael. Confidence intervals. Thousand Oaks, Calif. : Sage Publications, c2003.
HA31.2 .S59 2003

SOCIAL SCIENCES - METHODOLOGY.
Blaikie, Norman W. H., 1933- Analyzing quantitative data. London ; Thousand Oaks, CA : Sage Publications Ltd, 2003.
HA29 .B556 2003

Strategies of qualitative inquiry. 2nd ed. Thousand Oaks, CA : Sage, c2003.
H61 .S8823 2003

SOCIAL SCIENCES - PHILOSOPHY.
Gellner, Ernest. [Essays. Selections] Ernest Gellner. London ; New York : Routledge, 2003.
B1626.G441 G76 2003

Latour, Bruno. War of the worlds. Chicago : Prickly Paradigm Press, c2002.
H61.15 .L38 2002

Mićunović, Dragoljub. Filozofija minima. Beograd : "Filip Višnjić", 2001.
H61.15 .M5 2001

Tew, Jerry, 1955- Social theory, power and practice. Houndmills [England] ; New York : Palgrave, 2002.
HN49.P6 T49 2002

Vazeilles, José Gabriel. Platonismo, marxismo y comunicación social. Buenos Aires : Editorial Biblos, c2002.

SOCIAL SCIENCES - RESEARCH. *See* SOCIAL SURVEYS.

SOCIAL SCIENCES - RESEARCH - DATA PROCESSING.
Fraley, R. Chris. How to conduct behavioral research over the internet. New York : Guilford Press, 2005.
BF76.6.I57 F73 2005

SOCIAL SCIENCES - RESEARCH - METHODOLOGY.
Campbell, Marie L. (Marie Louise), 1936- Mapping social relations. Aurora, Ont. : Garamond Press, c2002.

Collecting and interpreting qualitative materials. 2nd ed. Thousand Oaks, Calif. : Sage, c2003.

H62 .C566 2003

Comparative historical analysis in the social sciences. Cambridge, U.K. ; New York : Cambridge University Press, 2003.
H61 .C524 2003

Cozby, Paul C. Methods in behavioral research. 8th ed. Boston : McGraw-Hill, c2004.
BF76.5 .C67 2004

Fiedler, Klaus, 1951- Stereotyping as inductive hypothesis testing. Hove (UK) ; New York : Psychology Press, c2003.
BF323.S63 F54 2003

Fraley, R. Chris. How to conduct behavioral research over the internet. New York : Guilford Press, 2005.
BF76.6.I57 F73 2005

Gravetter, Frederick J. Research methods for the behavioral sciences. Belmont, CA : Wadsworth, c2003.
BF76.5 .G73 2003

Gray, Ann, 1946- Research practice for cultural studies. London ; Thousand Oaks, Calif. : SAGE, 2003.
H62 .G73 2003

Janesick, Valerie J. "Stretching" exercises for qualitative researchers. 2nd ed. Thousand Oaks, Calif. : Sage Publications, c2004.
H62 .J346 2004

Morales Tomas, Marco Antonio. El que busca encuentra = Guatemala : ESEDIR : Editorial Saqil Tzij, 1999.

Morales Tomas, Marco Antonio. Una gráfica dice más que mil palabras = Guatemala : ESEDIR : Editorial Saqil Tzij, 1999.

Nardi, Peter M. Doing survey research. Boston ; London : Allyn and Bacon, c2003.
HN29 .N25 2003

Rossman, Gretchen B. Learning in the field. 2nd ed. Thousand Oaks, Calif. ; London : Sage Publications, c2003.
H62 .R667 2003

Strategies of qualitative inquiry. 2nd ed. Thousand Oaks, CA : Sage, c2003.
H61 .S8823 2003

Valle Bonilla, Otto René. Que no le cuenten cuentos = Guatemala : ESEDIR : Editorial Saqil Tzij, 1999.

Williams, Malcolm, 1953- Making sense of social research. London : SAGE, c2003.

Yin, Robert K. Case study research. 3rd ed. Thousand Oaks, Calif. : Sage Publications, c2003.
H62 .Y56 2003

SOCIAL SCIENCES - STATISTICAL METHODS.
The analysis and interpretation of multivariate data for social scientists. Boca Raton, Fla. : Chapman & Hall/CRC, c2002.
HA29 .A5824 2002

Blaikie, Norman W. H., 1933- Analyzing quantitative data. London ; Thousand Oaks, CA : Sage Publications Ltd, 2003.
HA29 .B556 2003

Cliff, Norman, 1930- Ordinal measurement in the behavioral sciences. Mahwah, N.J. : Lawrence Erlbaum Associates, 2003.
BF39 .C525 2003

Frankfort-Nachmias, Chava. Social statistics for a diverse society. 3rd ed. Thousand Oaks, Calif. : Pine Forge Press, c2002.
HA29 .N25 2002

Jaccard, James. Interaction effects in multiple regression. 2nd ed. Thousand Oaks, Calif. : Sage Publications, c2003.
HA31.3 .J33 2003

Meyer, Philip. Precision journalism. 4th ed. Lanham, Md. : Rowman & Littlefield Publishers, c2002.
PN4775 .M48 2002

Morales Tomas, Marco Antonio. Una gráfica dice más que mil palabras = Guatemala : ESEDIR : Editorial Saqil Tzij, 1999.

Smithson, Michael. Confidence intervals. Thousand Oaks, Calif. : Sage Publications, c2003.
HA31.2 .S59 2003

SOCIAL SECURITY. *See* FAMILY POLICY.

SOCIAL SERVICE.
Leading change. Bristol, UK : Policy Press, c2003.

Working with men in the human services. Crows Nest, N.S.W. : Allen & Unwin, c2001.

SOCIAL SERVICE AGENCIES. *See* SOCIAL SERVICE.

SOCIAL SERVICE - RELIGIOUS ASPECTS - HISTORY.
Religious organizations in community services. New York : Springer Pub., 2003.
HV530 .R25 2003

SOCIAL SERVICE - TEAMWORK.
Housley, William, 1970- Interaction in multidisciplinary teams. Aldershot, England ; Burlington, VT : Ashgate, c2003.
HV41 .H667 2003

SOCIAL SERVICE - UNITED STATES - RELIGIOUS ASPECTS.
Religious organizations in community services. New York : Springer Pub., 2003.
HV530 .R25 2003

SOCIAL SKILLS IN CHILDREN.
Shore, Hennie. The you & me scriptbook. [United States] : Childswork Childsplay, c2002.
BF723.S62 S46 2002

SOCIAL STABILITY. *See* PROGRESS.

Social statistics for a diverse society.
Frankfort-Nachmias, Chava. 3rd ed. Thousand Oaks, Calif. : Pine Forge Press, c2002.
HA29 .N25 2002

SOCIAL STATUS. *See* SOCIAL CLASSES; SPEECH AND SOCIAL STATUS.

SOCIAL STATUS AND LANGUAGE. *See* SPEECH AND SOCIAL STATUS.

SOCIAL STATUS AND SPEECH. *See* SPEECH AND SOCIAL STATUS.

SOCIAL STRATIFICATION. *See also* SOCIAL CLASSES.
Fuller, Robert W. Somebodies and nobodies. Gabriola Island, Canada : New Society Publishers, 2003.
HM821 .F84 2003

SOCIAL STRUCTURE. *See also* SOCIAL INSTITUTIONS.
Archer, Margaret Scotford. Structure, agency and the internal conversation. Cambridge, U.K. ; New York : Cambridge University Press, 2003.
HM708 .A73 2003

Emotions and sociology. Oxford ; Malden, MA : Blackwell Pub./Socological Review, 2002.

Tonn, Joan C. Mary P. Follett. New Haven [Conn.] : Yale University Press, c2003.
HN57 .T695 2003

SOCIAL STUDIES. *See* SOCIAL SCIENCES.

SOCIAL SURVEYS.
Nardi, Peter M. Doing survey research. Boston ; London : Allyn and Bacon, c2003.
HN29 .N25 2003

SOCIAL SURVEYS - CROATIA.
Mir u Hrvatskoj--rezultati istraživanja. Zagreb : Hrvatski Caritas ; Split : Franjevački in-t za kulturu mira, 2001.
HN638.A8 M57 2001

SOCIAL SYSTEMS. *See also* SOCIAL INSTITUTIONS.
Autopoietic organization theory. Oslo, Norway : Abstrakt forlag ; Malmö, Sweden : Liber Ekonomi ; Herndon, VA, USA : Copenhagen Business School Press, c2003.
HD31 .A825 2003

Van Gigch, John P. Metadecisions. New York : Kluwer Academic/Plenum Publishers, c2003.
HM701 .V36 2003

SOCIAL TENSIONS. *See* SOCIAL CONFLICT.

Social theory and religion.
Beckford, James A. Cambridge, U.K. ; New York : Cambridge University Press, 2003.
BL60 .B34 2003

Social theory and social practice.
Zetterberg, Hans Lennart, 1927- New Brunswick, NJ : Transaction Publishers, c2002.
HM511 .Z48 2002

Social theory, education & cultural change.
Chomsky, Noam. Chomsky on democracy & education. New York ; London : RoutledgeFalmer, 2003.
LB885.C5215 C46 2003

Social theory, power and practice.
Tew, Jerry, 1955- Houndmills [England] ; New York : Palgrave, 2002.
HN49.P6 T49 2002

Social theory, psychoanalysis, and racism.
Clarke, Simon, 1962- New York : Palgrave Macmillan, 2003.
BF175.4.R34 C58 2003

Social theory since Freud.
Elliott, Anthony. 1st ed. London ; New York : Routledge, 2004.
BF175.4.S65 E455 2004

SOCIAL VALUES.
Desarrollo de los valores en las instituciones educativas. Bilbao : Mensajero, 2001.

Riding the next wave. Indianapolis, Ind. : Hudson Institute ; [Washington, DC : Distributed by the Brookings Institution Press], c2001.
HM901.R43 2001

SOCIAL VALUES - UNITED STATES.
Madhubuti, Haki R., 1942- Tough notes. 1st ed. Chicago : Third World Press, c2002.
E185.86.T68 2002
1. Black author.

White, Curtis, 1951- The middle mind. 1st ed. [San Francisco] : HarperSanFrancisco, c2003.

SOCIAL VALUES - UNITED STATES - HISTORY - 18TH CENTURY.
Trees, Andrew S., 1968- The founding fathers and the politics of character. Princeton, N.J. : Princeton University Press, c2004.
E302.1.T74 2004

SOCIAL WELFARE. See SOCIAL PROBLEMS; SOCIAL SERVICE.

SOCIAL WORK. See SOCIAL SERVICE.

SOCIAL WORK ADMINISTRATION.
Constructing clienthood in social work and human services. London ; New York : Jessica Kingsley Publishers, c2003.
HV40.C6615 2003

Martin, Vivien, 1947- Leading change in health and social care. London ; New York : Routledge, 2003.
RA971.M365 2003

SOCIAL WORK WITH CHILDREN. See also CHILD WELFARE.
Dunlap, Linda L. What all children need. Lanham, Md. : University Press of America, c2002.
HQ778.5.D85 2002

SOCIAL WORK WITH CHILDREN - LATIN AMERICA.
Amar Amar, José Juan. Políticas sociales y modelos de atención integral a la infancia. Barranquilla, Colombia : Ediciones Uninorte, 2001.

SOCIAL WORK WITH MEN.
Working with men in the human services. Crows Nest, N.S.W. : Allen & Unwin, c2001.

SOCIAL WORK WITH YOUTH. See CHILD WELFARE.

SOCIAL WORKERS - RELIGIOUS LIFE - UNITED STATES.
Religious organizations in community services. New York : Springer Pub., 2003.
HV530.R25 2003

SOCIALISM. See also COMMUNISM; UTOPIAN SOCIALISM; UTOPIAS.
Canto-Sperber, Monique. Les règles de la liberté. [Paris] : Plon, c2003.

El-Ojeili, Chamsy. From left communism to post-modernism. Lanham, Md. : Oxford : University Press of America, c2003.
HX44.5.E46 2003

Milner, Andrew, 1950- Contemporary cultural theory. 3rd ed. Crows Nest, N.S.W. : Allen & Unwin, 2002.

SOCIALISM AND ART.
Postmodernism and the postsocialist condition. Berkeley : University of California Press, c2003.
N6494.P66 P684 2003

SOCIALISM AND CULTURE.
Freedman, Carl Howard. The incomplete projects. Middletown, Conn. : Wesleyan University Press, c2002.
HX523.F74 2002

SOCIALISM - HISTORY.
Wilson, Edmund, 1895-1972. To the Finland station. New York : New York Review of Books, 2003.

HX36.W5 2003

SOCIALISM, UTOPIAN. See UTOPIAN SOCIALISM.

SOCIALIST MOVEMENTS. See SOCIALISM.

SOCIALISTS - GERMANY. See NAZIS.

SOCIALIZATION. See also ASSIMILATION (SOCIOLOGY).
Bailey, Gordon, 1946- Ideology. Peterborough, Ont. : Broadview Press, 2003.

Children in the city. London : Routledge/Falmer, 2003.

From girls in their elements to women in science. New York : P. Lang, 2003.
BF378.S65 F76 2003

Hoffmann, Arne. Sind Frauen bessere Menschen? Berlin : Schwarzkopf & Schwarzkopf, 2001.
HQ1075.H64 2001

Language acquisition and language socialization. London ; New York : Continuum, 2002.
P118.L243 2002

Minsos, Susan Felicity, 1944- Culture clubs. Edmonton : Spotted Cow Press, c2002.

Rogoff, Barbara. The cultural nature of human development. Oxford ; New York : Oxford University Press, 2003.
HM686.R64 2003

Schwarte, Johannes. Der werdende Mensch. 1. Aufl. Wiesbaden : Westdeutscher Verlag, 2002.

Shore, Hennie. The you & me scriptbook. [United States] : Childswork Childsplay, c2002.
BF723.S62 S46 2002

SOCIALLY HANDICAPPED. See MARGINALITY, SOCIAL.

Sociedade mídia e violência.
Sodré, Muniz. Porto Alegre : Editora Sulina : EDIPUCRS, c2002.

Societas rationis : Festschrift für Burkhard Tuschling zum 65. Geburtstag / herausgegeben von Dieter Hüning, Gideon Stiening und Ulrich Vogel. Berlin : Duncker & Humblot, c2002. 400 p. : ill., port. ; 24 cm. (Philosophische Schriften, 0935-6053 ; Bd. 50) Includes bibliographical references. Contributions in German and English. ISBN 3-428-10428-5 (pbk.)
1. Philosophy. I. Vogel, Ulrich, 1963- II. Stiening, Gideon. III. Hüning, Dieter. IV. Tuschling, Burkhard. V. Series.
B29.S633 2002

Société d'études linguistiques et anthropologiques de France (Series)
(400.) Lexique et motivation. Paris ; Sterling, Va. : Peeters, c2002.
P326.L45 2002

SOCIETIES. See ASSOCIATIONS, INSTITUTIONS, ETC.; LEARNED INSTITUTIONS AND SOCIETIES.

Society and aging series
Invitation to the life course. Amityville, N.Y. : Baywood Pub. Co., c2003.
HQ1061.I584 2003

SOCIETY AND ARCHITECTURE. See ARCHITECTURE AND SOCIETY.

SOCIETY AND EDUCATION. See EDUCATIONAL SOCIOLOGY.

SOCIETY AND LITERATURE. See LITERATURE AND SOCIETY.

SOCIETY AND MEDICAL INNOVATIONS. See MEDICAL INNOVATIONS - SOCIAL ASPECTS.

SOCIETY AND RELIGION. See RELIGION AND SOCIOLOGY.

SOCIETY AND THE ARTS. See ARTS AND SOCIETY.

SOCIETY AND THEATER. See THEATER AND SOCIETY.

SOCIETY AND WAR. See WAR AND SOCIETY.

Society for Computer Simulation.
International Conference on Simulation in Engineering Education (2001 : Phoenix, Ariz.) Proceedings of the International Conference on Simulation and Multimedia in Engineering Education & Virtual Worlds and Simulation. San Diego, CA : Society for Computer Simulation International, c2001.

Society for Constructive Change.
Constructive change. Boise, Idaho : Center for Constructive Change, c1996-
BF698.9.P47 C66

Society for French Studies (Great Britain).
Britton, Celia. Race and the unconscious. Oxford : Legenda, 2002.

Society for the Promotion of Eriugenian Studies.
Internationales Eriugena-Colloquium (10th : Maynooth and Dublin : 2002) History and eschatology in John Scottus Eriugena and his time. Leuven : University Press, 2002.

SOCIETY, PRIMITIVE. See PRIMITIVE SOCIETIES.

SOCIOBIOLOGY.
Guillo, Dominique. Les figures de l'organisation. 1. éd. Paris : Presses universitaires de France, c2003.

Kessidi, F. Kh. Filosofskie i éticheskie problemy genetiki cheloveka. Moskva : Martis, 1994.
BF341.K45 1994

Sykes, Bryan. Adam's curse. London ; New York : Bantam, 2003.

Trivers, Robert. Natural selection and social theory. New York : Oxford University Press, 2002.
GN365.9.T76 2002

SOCIOLINGUISTICS. See also LITERATURE AND SOCIETY.
Boxer, Diana, 1948- Applying sociolinguistics. Amsterdam ; Philadelphia : J. Benjamins Pub., c2002.
P40.B678 2002

Broth, Matthias, 1965- Agents secrets. Uppsala, Sweden : Uppsala Universitet, c2002.

Discourse, the body, and identity. Basingstoke, Hampshire ; New York : Palgrave Macmillan, 2003.
HM636.D57 2003

Glinz, Hans, 1913- Languages and their use in our life as human beings. Münster : Nodus, c2002.
P107.G58 2002

Język w przestrzeni społecznej. Opole : Uniwersytet Opolski, 2002.
P40.J492 2002

Studies in language and social interaction. Mahwah, N.J. : London : Lawrence Erlbaum, 2003.

Us and others. Amsterdam ; Philadelphia : John Benjamins Pub., c2002.
HM753.U72 2002

Sociología de la identidad / Aquiles Chihu Amparán, coordinador. México : Miguel Angel Porrúa : Universidad Autónoma Metropolitana, Unidad Iztapalapa, 2002. 253, 10 p. ; 21 cm. (Las ciencias sociales) ISBN 9707012331 DDC 155.2
1. Identity (Psychologia). 2. Group identity. 3. National characteristics, Mexican. I. Chihu Amparán, Aquiles, coord. II. Series: Colección Las ciencias sociales.

SOCIOLOGICAL JURISPRUDENCE.
Edgeworth, Brendan. Law, modernity, postmodernity. Aldershot, England ; Burlington, VT : Ashgate/Dartmouth, c2003.
K370.E34 2003

Sociological review monograph.
Emotions and sociology. Oxford ; Malden, MA : Blackwell Pub./Sociological Review, 2002.

Sociologie d'aujourd'hui
Pulman, Bertrand. Anthropologie et psychanalyse. Paris : Presses universitaires de France, 2002.
GN502.P85 2002

Sociologies
Guillo, Dominique. Les figures de l'organisation. 1. éd. Paris : Presses universitaires de France, c2003.

Le sociologue
Moessinger, Pierre Le jeu de l'identité. 1re éd. Paris : Presses universitaires de France, 2000.
BF697.5.S43 M634 2000

SOCIOLOGY. See also COMMUNICATION; COMMUNITY; CONSERVATISM; DANCE - SOCIOLOGICAL ASPECTS; EDUCATIONAL SOCIOLOGY; INDIVIDUALISM; MARGINALITY, SOCIAL; POWER (SOCIAL SCIENCES); RACE RELATIONS; RELIGION AND SOCIOLOGY; SOCIAL CONFLICT; SOCIAL CONTROL; SOCIAL HISTORY; SOCIAL INSTITUTIONS; SOCIAL MEDICINE; SOCIAL PSYCHOLOGY; WAR AND SOCIETY.
Alexander, Jeffrey C. The meanings of social life. New York : Oxford University Press, 2003.

HM585 .A5 2003

Benítez Torres, Milton. Peregrinos y vagabundos. 1. ed. Quito, Ecuador : Ediciones Abya-Yala, 2002.

Rosental, Claude. La trame de l'évidence. 1 éd. Paris : Presses universitaires de France, c2003.

T͡Siolkovskiĭ, K. (Konstantin), 1857-1935. Geniĭ sredi li͡udeĭ. Moskva : Mysl', 2002.
TL781.85.T84 A25 2002

Unger, Roberto Mangabeira. False necessity--antinecessitarian social theory in the service of radical democracy. New ed. London ; New York : Verso, 2001.

SOCIOLOGY AND ARCHITECTURE. See **ARCHITECTURE AND SOCIETY.**

SOCIOLOGY AND LITERATURE. See **LITERATURE AND SOCIETY.**

SOCIOLOGY AND RELIGION. See **RELIGION AND SOCIOLOGY.**

SOCIOLOGY AND THE ARTS. See **ARTS AND SOCIETY.**

SOCIOLOGY, EDUCATIONAL. See **EDUCATIONAL SOCIOLOGY.**

SOCIOLOGY - METHODOLOGY.
Aux frontières des attitudes. Paris, France : Harmattan, c2002.

Cruickshank, Justin, 1969- Realism and sociology. London ; New York : Routledge, 2003.
HM511 .C78 2003

Zetterberg, Hans Lennart, 1927- Social theory and social practice. New Brunswick, NJ : Transaction Publishers, c2002.
HM511 .Z48 2002

SOCIOLOGY, MILITARY. See also **MORALE; PSYCHOLOGY, MILITARY; WAR AND SOCIETY.**
Military masculinities. Westport, Conn. : Praeger, 2003.
U21.5 .M4975 2003

Sociology of crime, law and deviance
(v. 4) Violent acts and violentization. Amsterdam ; Boston : JAI, 2003.

SOCIOLOGY OF CULTURE. See **CULTURE.**

SOCIOLOGY OF DANCE. See **DANCE - SOCIOLOGICAL ASPECTS.**

SOCIOLOGY OF RELIGION. See also **RELIGION AND SOCIOLOGY.**
Christiano, Kevin J. Walnut Creek, CA : AltaMira Press, c2002.
BL60 .C465 2002

SOCIOLOGY - PHILOSOPHY.
Caillois, Roger, 1913- The edge of surrealism. Durham : Duke University Press, 2003.
HM590 .C35 2003

Cruickshank, Justin, 1969- Realism and sociology. London ; New York : Routledge, 2003.
HM511 .C78 2003

Luhmann, Niklas. [Beobachtungen der Moderne. English] Observations on modernity. Stanford, CA : Stanford University Press, 1998.
HM24 .L88813 1998

Suspil'stvo na porozi XXI stolitti͡a. Kyïv : Ukraïns'kyĭ T͡Sentr dukhovnoï kul'tury, 1999.

Zetterberg, Hans Lennart, 1927- Social theory and social practice. New Brunswick, NJ : Transaction Publishers, c2002.
HM511 .Z48 2002

SOCIOLOGY, RELIGIOUS. See **RELIGION AND SOCIOLOGY.**

SOCIOLOGY - RESEARCH.
Aux frontières des attitudes. Paris, France : Harmattan, c2002.

SOCIOLOGY, RURAL. See **COMMUNITY; URBANIZATION.**

SOCIOLOGY, URBAN. See also **CITIES AND TOWNS; URBANIZATION.**
Identidades, sujetos y subjetividades. Buenos Aires : Prometeo Libros, c2002.

SOCRATES.
Plato. [Selections. Latvian] Platons dialogi un vēstules = [Rīga] : Zinātne, c1999.

Sode razaya.
Eleazar ben Judah, of Worms, 1176 (ca.)-1238. Sefer Sode razaya .... Bene-Beraḳ : Ḳorah, 759 [1998 or 1999]
BM525 .E432 1999

Sode razaya: ye-saviv lo Sodot shamayim.
Eleazar ben Judah, of Worms, 1176 (ca.)-1238. Sefer Sode razaya .... Bene-Beraḳ : Ḳorah, 759 [1998 or 1999]
BM525 .E432 1999

Śodhaprakāśana-granthamālā
(27) Lāla, Mukuta Bihārī. [Sāmyayogamīmāṃsā. Hindi & Sanskrit] Sāmyayogamīmāṃsā. 1. saṃskaraṇa. Vārāṇasī : Śaivabhāratī Śodhapratiṣṭhānam, 2001.
BL1237.32+

SODOMY IN LITERATURE.
Halpern, Richard, 1954- Shakespeare's perfume. Philadelphia : University of Pennsylvania Press, c2002.
PR2848 .H25 2002

Sodré, Muniz. Sociedade mídia e violência / Muniz Sodré. Porto Alegre : Editora Sulina : EDIPUCRS, c2002. 110 p. ; 21 cm. (Coleção Comunicação ; 22) Includes bibliographical references (p. 109-110). ISBN 85-205-0291-1
1. Violence. 2. Mass media - Social aspects. I. Title. II. Series.

Soeffner, Hans-Georg.
Schutz, Alfred, 1899-1959. Werkausgabe. Konstanz : UVK, Verlagsgesellschaft, 2003-
BD431 .S284916 2003

Sofer, Mikha'el Uri. Sefer 'Olamot shel ṭohar : otsar balum shel sipure emet, hanhagot ṿe-hashḳafat 'olam 'al nośeʼ e tseniʻut Bet Yaʻaḳov ... / neʻerakh ṿe-nilḳaṭ 'a. y. Mikha'el Uri Sofer. Mahad. 2. Bene Beraḳ : M.U. Sofer, 761 [2000 or 2001] 2 v. : ill. ; 25 cm. Cover title: 'Olamot shel ṭohar. Mostly vocalized.
1. Jewish women - Conduct of life. 2. Clothing and dress - Religious aspects - Judaism. 3. Modesty - Religious aspects - Judaism. 4. Sexual ethics. 5. Ethics, Jewish. I. Title. II. Title: 'Olamot shel ṭohar
BM726 .S633 2000

SOFER, MOSES, 1762-1839.
Shṭern, Shemuʼel Eliʻezer. Sefer Sene boʻer ba-esh. Bene Beraḳ : Mekhon "Mayim ḥayim", 762 [2002]

Sofferenza e senso.
Piazza, Giovanni. Torino : Camilliane, c2002.

SOFISM. See **SUFISM.**

Sofsky, Wolfgang. Violence : terrorism, genocide, war / Wolfgang Sofsky ; translated from the German by Anthea Bell. London : Granta, 2003, c2002. 273 p. ; 23 cm. Includes bibliographical references and index. Translated from the German. ISBN 1-86207-614-6 DDC 303.6
1. Violence. 2. Violence - Psychological aspects. 3. War. I. Title.

SOFT COMPUTING. See **EXPERT SYSTEMS (COMPUTER SCIENCE); NEURAL NETWORKS (COMPUTER SCIENCE).**

SOFTWARE AGENTS (COMPUTER SOFTWARE). See **INTELLIGENT AGENTS (COMPUTER SOFTWARE).**

SOFTWARE, COMPUTER. See **COMPUTER SOFTWARE.**

SOFTWARE ENGINEERING.
Schmid, U. (Ute) Inductive synthesis of functional programs. Berlin ; New York : Springer, c2003.
QA76.6 .S3855 2003

SOFTWARE PROTECTION - LAW AND LEGISLATION.
Matsuura, Jeffrey H., 1957- Managing intellectual assets in the digital age. Boston, MA : Artech House, c2003.
K1401 .M378 2003

Soggetto nomade.
Braidotti, Rosi. [Nomadic subjects. Italian] Roma : Donzelli, 1995.

I sogni della Bibbia.
Quaglia, Rocco. Roma : Borla, c2002.

La soif d'émotion : une recherche et un débat réalisés par Foreseen ; collaborent aux travaux Foreseen, Bertrand Cathelat ... [et al.]. Paris : Plon, c1999. 271 p. ; 21 cm. ISBN 2-259-19257-2
1. Emotions - Social aspects. I. Cathelat, Bernard. II. Foreseen (Observatory)
BF531 .S637 1999

Soi͡uz studentov Rossiĭskogo psikhologicheskogo obshchestva. Altaĭskie otdelenie.
Innovatsii v psikhologii. Biĭsk : Nauchno-izdatel'skiĭ tsentr Biĭskogo pedagog. gos. universiteta, 2001-
BF20 .I45 2001

Soko, Boston. Nchimi chikanga : the battle against witchcraft in Malawi / Boston Soko and Gerhard Kubik. Blantyre [Malawi] : Christian Literature Association in Malawi, 2002. 116 p. : ill., maps ; 21 cm. (Kachere text, 1025-0964 ; no. 10) Includes bibliographical references (p. 111) and index. ISBN 999081645X
1. Witchcraft - Malawi. 2. Magic - Malawi. 3. Magic - Religious aspects - Christianity. 4. Black author. I. Kubik, Gerhard, 1933- II. Title. III. Title: Battle against witchcraft in Malawi IV. Series.

Sokolewicz, Zofia.
Between tradition and postmodernity. Warsaw : Wydawnictwo DiG, 2003.

Sokolov, B. G. (Boris Georgievich) Gipertekst istorii / B.G. Sokolov. Sankt-Peterburg : Sankt-Peterburgskoe filosofskoe obshchestvo, 2001. 192 p. : ill. ; 21 cm. ISBN 5935970376
1. History - Philosophy. I. Title.
D16.9 .S65 2001

Soku, Leonard. From the coven of witchcraft to Christ / by Leonard Soku. Rev. ed. [Accra, Ghana? : s.n., c2000] 50 p. ; 20 cm. "Vol. 1." "A true life testimony of Rev. Leonard Soku." ISBN 9988752628
1. Soku, Leonard. 2. Witchcraft. 3. Christian converts - Ghana - Biography. 4. Christian biography. 5. Black author. I. Title.
BV4935 .S6 F76 2000

SOKU, LEONARD.
Soku, Leonard. From the coven of witchcraft to Christ. Rev. ed. [Accra, Ghana? : s.n., c2000]
BV4935 .S6 F76 2000
1. Black author.

Solar, Melanie B. The invisible bag / by Melanie B. Solar ; [illustrated by Holly Stone-Barker]. Greenwell Springs, LA : Solar Pub., 2000. 1 v. (unpaged) : col. ill. ; 27 cm. ISBN 0-9679326-0-2
1. Choice (Psychology) in children - Juvenile literature. I. Stone-Barker, Holly. II. Title.
BF723.C47 S65 2000

SOLAR SYSTEM. See **ASTEROIDS; COMETS; PLANETS.**

SOLDIERS - IRAQ - ATTITUDES.
Why they fight [electronic resource]. Carlisle, PA : Strategic Studies Institute, U.S. Army War College, [2003]
U22

SOLDIERS' LIFE. See **SOLDIERS.**

SOLDIERS - UNITED STATES - ATTITUDES.
Why they fight [electronic resource]. Carlisle, PA : Strategic Studies Institute, U.S. Army War College, [2003]
U22

Soler, Colette. L'inconscient à ciel ouvert de la psychose / Colette Soler. Toulouse : Presses universitaires du Mirail, c2002. 261 p. ; 22 cm. (Psychanalyse &) ISBN 2-85816-610-2 DDC 150
1. Subconsciousness. 2. Psychoses. 3. Mental illness. I. Title. II. Series. III. Series: Psychanalyse & (Toulouse, France)

Solère, J.-L. (Jean-Luc).
La servante et la consolatrice. Paris : Vrin, 2002.
B721 .S479 2002

Soleri, Paolo, 1919- What if? : collected writings 1986-2000 / Paolo Soleri. Berkeley, CA : Berkeley Hills Books, 2002. xxxvii, 370 p. : ill ; 30 cm. Includes index. ISBN 1-89316-344-X (alk. paper) DDC 720/.1/03
1. Architecture and society. 2. Architecture - Philosophy. 3. Architecture - Forecasting. I. Title.
NA2543.S6 S637 2002

SOLICITORS. See **LAWYERS.**

SOLIDARITY.
Group cohesion, trust and solidarity. 1st ed. Amsterdam ; New York : JAI, 2002.

SOLIDS. See **CRYSTALS.**

SOLIPSISM.
Symington, Neville. A pattern of madness. London ; New York : Karnac, 2002.

SOLITUDE. See **LONELINESS.**

Sollod, Robert N.
Monte, Christopher F. Beneath the mask. 7th ed. Hoboken, NJ : J. Wiley & Sons, c2003.
BF698 .M64 2003

SOLO CANTATAS.
Hann, Georg. Georg Hann [sound recording]. [Germany] : Preiser Records, p2001.

Malaniuk, Ira. Arien und Lieder [sound recording]. [Germany] : Preiser Records, p2000.

Solodin, A. I. Strategii͡a ontologicheskoĭ igry / A.I. Solodin. Sankt-Peterburg : Aleteĭi͡a, 2002. 239 p. ; 17 cm. ISBN 5893294939
1. Psychophysics. 2. Metaphysics. 3. Ontology. I. Title.
BF237 .S6 2002

Strategii͡a ontologicheskoĭ igry / A.I. Solodin. Sankt-Peterburg : Aleteĭi͡a, 2002. 239 p. : 18 cm. ISBN 5893294939
1. Self-actualization (Psychology) - Religious aspects. 2. Spiritual exercises. 3. Occultism. 4. Spiritual life. I. Title.

Solomon, Norman, 1951-.
Monkeywrenching the new world order [sound recording]. Oakland, Calif : AK Press ; San Francisco, CA : Alternative Tentacles Records, 2001.

Solomon, Sheldon.
Pyszczynski, Thomas A. In the wake of 9/11. Washington, DC : American Psychological Association, c2003.
HV6432 .P97 2003

Soloveichik, Ḥayyim, 1853-1918.
Otsrot rabotenu mi-Brisk. Bene Berak : Sh. L., molut u-mishar bi-sefarim, 762 [2001 or 2002]
BM602 .O+

Soloveichik, Isaac Ze'ev, ha-Levi, 1886-1960.
Otsrot rabotenu mi-Brisk. Bene Berak : Sh. L., molut u-mishar bi-sefarim, 762 [2001 or 2002]
BM602 .O+

Soloveichik, Joseph Baer, 1820-1892.
Otsrot rabotenu mi-Brisk. Bene Berak : Sh. L., molut u-mishar bi-sefarim, 762 [2001 or 2002]
BM602 .O+

SOLOVEITCHIK FAMILY.
Otsrot rabotenu mi-Brisk. Bene Berak : Sh. L., molut u-mishar bi-sefarim, 762 [2001 or 2002]
BM602 .O+

Solovyov, Vladimir Sergeyevich, 1853-1900. [Essays. English. Selections]
The heart of reality : essays on beauty, love, and ethics / by V.S. Soloviev ; edited and translated by Vladimir Wozniuk. Notre Dame, Ind. : University of Notre Dame Press, c2003. xviii, 244 p. ; 24 cm. Includes bibliographical references (p. 221-237) and indexes. CONTENTS: Three addresses in memory of Dostoevsky -- Beauty in nature -- The universal meaning of art -- The meaning of love -- A first step toward a positive aesthetic -- The fate of Pushkin -- Mickiewicz -- Lermontov. ISBN 0-268-03061-8 (acid-free paper) DDC 197
1. Aesthetics. 2. Ethics. 3. Aesthetics - Religious aspects - Orthodox Eastern Church. 4. Christian ethics - Orthodox Eastern authors. 5. Literature - Philosophy. I. Wozniuk, Vladimir. II. Title.
B4262.A5 W69 2003

Solso, Robert L., 1933- The psychology of art and the evolution of the conscious brain / Robert L. Solso. Cambridge, Mass. : MIT Press, 2003. p. cm. (MIT Press/Bradford Books series in cognitive psychology) Includes bibliographical references and index. ISBN 0-262-19484-8 (hc. : alk. paper) DDC 701/.15
1. Consciousness. 2. Cognition. 3. Brain - Evolution. 4. Visual perception. 5. Art - Psychology. I. Title. II. Series.
BF311 .S652 2003

Solutions for back pain [videorecording].
The Alexander technique [videorecording]. New York, N.Y. : Wellspring Media, c1999.

Solutions for back trouble [videorecording].
The Alexander technique [videorecording]. New York, N.Y. : Wellspring Media, c1999.

SOMATOLOGY. See **PHYSICAL ANTHROPOLOGY.**

SOMATOPSYCHICS. See **MIND AND BODY.**

Some significant 21st century trends and issues : poverty, population, peace, and sustainability / by Ikram Azam, ed. Islamabad : Pakistan Futuristics Foundation & Institute, 1998. ii, 355 p. : ill. ; 22 cm. Includes bibliographical references.
1. Twenty-first century - Forecasts. 2. Economic forecasting. 3. Population forecasting. 4. Social prediction. 5. Sustainable development. I. Ikram Azam, 1940- II. Title: Some significant twenty-first century trends and issues
CB161 .S62 1998

Some significant twenty-first century trends and issues.
Some significant 21st century trends and issues. Islamabad : Pakistan Futuristics Foundation & Institute, 1998.
CB161 .S62 1998

Somebodies and nobodies.
Fuller, Robert W. Gabriola Island, Canada : New Society Publishers, 2003.
HM821 .F84 2003

SOMESTHESIA. See **TOUCH.**

Something for nothing.
Lears, T. J. Jackson, 1947- New York : Viking, 2003.
HV6715 .L415 2003

Something worth leaving behind.
Beavers, Brett. Nashville, Tenn. : Rutledge Hill Press, c2002.
BF637.S8 B383 2002

Somknem ri͡ady, chtoby zhila Rossii͡a.
Shakhmagonov, N. (Nikolaĭ) Moskva : Ispo-Servis, 1999.

Sommer, Barbara W. The oral history manual / Barbara W. Sommer, Mary Kay Quinlan. Walnut Creek, CA ; Oxford : Altamira Press, c2002. vii, 129 p. : ill., facsims., forms ; 29 cm. (American Association for State and Local History book series) Includes bibliographical references (p. 123-125) and index. Includes web resources. ISBN 0-7591-0100-0 (hbk. : alk. paper) ISBN 0-7591-0101-9 (pbk. : alk. paper) DDC 907/.2
1. Oral history - Handbooks, manuals, etc. 2. Oral History - Methodology. 3. Interviewing - Handbooks, manuals, etc. 4. Historiography. I. Quinlan, Mary Kay. II. Title. III. Series.
D16.14 .S69 2002

Sommers-Flanagan, John, 1957- Counseling and psychotherapy : theory, strategy, and technique / John Sommers-Flanagan and Rita Sommers-Flanagan. Hoboken, NJ : John Wiley & Sons, 2004. p. cm. Includes bibliographical references and index. Publisher description URL: http://www.loc.gov/catdir/desc ription/wiley0310/2003053841.html Table of contents URL: http://www.loc.gov/catdir/toc/wiley032/2003053841.html ISBN 0-471-21105-2 (cloth) DDC 158/.3
1. Counseling. 2. Psychotherapy. I. Sommers-Flanagan, Rita, 1953- II. Title.
BF637.C6 S69 2004

Sommers-Flanagan, Rita, 1953-.
Sommers-Flanagan, John, 1957- Counseling and psychotherapy. Hoboken, NJ : John Wiley & Sons, 2004.
BF637.C6 S69 2004

Somogyi, Gábor. Libikóka : hogyan kellene szeretni egymást? / Somogyi Gábor. [Budapest?] : Honestus-Press, 2002. 199 p. ; 21 cm. ISBN 963-204-585-8
1. Love. 2. Interpersonal relations. I. Title.
BF575.L8 S623 2002

Sonawalla, Shamsah B., 1967-.
Women's health and psychiatry. Philadelphia, PA : Lippincott Williams & Wilkins, c2002.
RA564.85 .W6652 2002

Sonderforschungsbereich 541 - "Identitäten und Alteritäten".
Studien zu antiken Identitäten. Würzburg : Ergon Verlag, c2001.
DG78 .S78 2001

Song, Miri, 1964- Choosing ethnic identity / Miri Song. Cambridge, UK : Polity Press ; Oxford ; Malden, MA : Blackwell Publishing, 2003. 183 p. ; 24 cm. Includes bibliographical references (p. [161]-178) and index. CONTENTS: Ethnic identities : choices and constraints -- Comparing minorities' ethnic options -- Negotiating individual and group identities -- The growth of mixed race people -- The diversification of ethnic groups -- The second generation in a global context -- Debates about racial hierarchy -- The future of race and ethnic identity. ISBN 0-7456-2276-3 (hbk.) ISBN 0-7456-2277-1 (pbk.) DDC 305.8
1. Ethnicity. 2. Group identity. 3. Minorities - Race identity. 4. Racially mixed people - Ethnic identity. 5. Ethnic attitudes. 6. Race awareness. I. Title.
GN495.6 .S65 2003

Song of Brahm.
Hermes, Trismegistus. Divine Pymander. Rev. ed. Quakertown, PA : Philosophical Pub. Co., 2001.
BF1598.H5 E5 2001

Song of hope.
Lathan, Mark J., 1961- Emotional progression in sacred choral music. 2001.

Songe-Möller, Vigdis. Philosophy without women : the birth of sexism in Western thought / Vigdis Songe-Møller ; translated by Peter Cripps. London : Continuum, c2002. xvii, 178 p. ; 24 cm. (Athlone contemporary European thinkers) Includes bibliographical references and index. Translated from the Norwegian. ISBN 0-8264-5848-3 ISBN 0-8264-5849-1 (pbk.) DDC 180.82
1. Philosophy, Ancient. 2. Feminist theory. 3. Philosophy - History. I. Title. II. Series.

SONGS.
Hann, Georg. Georg Hann [sound recording]. [Germany] : Preiser Records, p2001.

Malaniuk, Ira. Arien und Lieder [sound recording]. [Germany] : Preiser Records, p2000.

Sanders, Mark D. I hope you dance!. Nashville, Tenn. : Rutledge Hill Press, 2003.
BF410 .S26 2003

SONGS (LOW VOICE) WITH ORCHESTRA.
Malaniuk, Ira. Arien und Lieder [sound recording]. [Germany] : Preiser Records, p2000.

SONGS (LOW VOICE) WITH PIANO.
Hann, Georg. Georg Hann [sound recording]. [Germany] : Preiser Records, p2001.

Malaniuk, Ira. Arien und Lieder [sound recording]. [Germany] : Preiser Records, p2000.

SONGS, POPULAR. See **POPULAR MUSIC.**

SONGS, UKRAINIAN.
Malaniuk, Ira. Arien und Lieder [sound recording]. [Germany] : Preiser Records, p2000.

SONGWRITERS. See **COMPOSERS.**

Sonnenberg, Petra.
[Pendelen van A tot Z. English]
The great pendulum book / Petra Sonnenberg. New York, NY : Sterling Pub. Co., 2003. p. cm. Includes index. Table of contents URL: http://www.loc.gov/catdir/toc/ecip046/2003015435.html ISBN 1402707223 DDC 133.3
1. Fortune-telling by pendulum. I. Title.
BF1779.P45 S6613 2003

SONNETS, ENGLISH - HISTORY AND CRITICISM - THEORY, ETC.
Halpern, Richard, 1954- Shakespeare's perfume. Philadelphia : University of Pennsylvania Press, c2002.
PR2848 .H25 2002

SONS. See **FATHERS AND SONS.**

SONS AND FATHERS. See **FATHERS AND SONS.**

SONS - PSYCHOLOGY.
Gottlieb, Andrew R. Sons talk about their gay fathers. New York : Harrington Park Press, c2003.
HQ76.13 .G67 2003

Sons talk about their gay fathers.
Gottlieb, Andrew R. New York : Harrington Park Press, c2003.
HQ76.13 .G67 2003

Sontag, Susan, 1933- Regarding the pain of others / Susan Sontag. 1st ed. New York : Farrar, Straus and Giroux, 2003. 131 p. ; 22 cm. Publisher description URL: http://www.loc.gov/catdir/description/hol031/2002192527.html ISBN 0-374-24858-3 (hbk. : alk. paper) DDC 303.6
1. War and society. 2. War photography - Social aspects. 3. War in art - Social aspects. 4. Photojournalism - Social aspects. 5. Atrocities. 6. Violence. I. Title.
HM554 .S65 2003

SOOTHSAYING. See **DIVINATION.**

Sophia, 1955- The little book of hot love spells / Sophia. Kansas City, Mo. : Andrews McMeel Pub., c2002. 145 p. : ill. ; 14 cm. ISBN 0-7407-2722-2 DDC 133.4/42
1. Magic. 2. Love - Miscellanea. 3. Charms. 4. Incantations. I. Title. II. Title: Hot love spells
BF1623.L6 S66 2002

The ultimate guide to goddess empowerment / Sophia. Kansas City : Andrews McMeel Pub., c2003. xviii, 283 p. : 18 cm. ISBN 0-7407-3496-2 DDC 291.2/114
1. Charms. 2. Magic. 3. Ritual. 4. Goddess religion. I. Title.
BF1621 .S67 2003

SOPHISMS (LOGIC). See **FALLACIES (LOGIC).**

SOPHISTRY (LOGIC). See **FALLACIES (LOGIC).**

SORCERERS. See **MAGICIANS.**

SORCERY. See **MAGIC; WITCHCRAFT.**

Les sorciers à l'assaut du village.
Taric Zumsteg, Fabienne. Lausanne : Editions du Zèbre, 2000.
BF1584.S9 T37 2000

Sören Kierkegaard.
Farago, France. 1. éd. Paris : Houdiard, c2002.

Sorenson, John, 1952-.
Culture of prejudice. Peterborough, Ont. : Broadview Press, 2003.

Sorenson, Randall Lehmann, 1954- Minding spirituality : perspectives from relational psychoanalysis / Randall Lehmann Sorenson. Hillsdale, NJ : Analytic Press, 2003. p. cm. (Relational perspectives book series ; v. 24) Includes bibliographical references and index. ISBN 0-88163-344-5 DDC 200/.1/9
1. Psychoanalysis and religion. 2. Spirituality - Psychology. I. Title. II. Series.
BF175.4.R44 S67 2003

Sornette, D. Why stock markets crash : critical events in complex financial systems / Didier Sornette. Princeton, N.J. : Princeton University Press, c2003. xx, 421 p. : ill. ; 25 cm. Includes bibliographical references (p. [397]-418) and index. ISBN 0-691-09630-9 (alk. paper) DDC 332.63/222
1. Financial crises - History. 2. Stocks - Prices - History. 3. Financial crises - United States - History. 4. Stock exchanges - United States - History. 5. Critical phenomena (Physics) 6. Complexity (Philosophy) I. Title.
HB3722 .S66 2003

Soroka, Petro, 1956-. Andrushkiv, Bohdan, 1947- Po toï bik bezodni, abo, Mertvi pro vartist' z̆hyttīa ne rozkaz̆hut'. Ternopil' : "Pidruchnyky & posibnyky", 1997.
HV6545 .A616 1997

SORROW. See **GRIEF.**

Sosa, Ernest.
Epistemology. Malden, Mass. : Blackwell Publishers, 2000.
BD161 .E615 2000

Soskin, Julie. Are you psychic? : dozens of techniques for boosting your innate powers / Julie Soskin. London : Carroll & Brown, 2002. 176 p. : col. ill. ; 22 cm. Includes index. ISBN 1-903258-20-0 (pbk.) DDC 133.8
1. Psychic ability. 2. Extrasensory perception. I. Title.
BF1031 .S674 2002

Sotsial'noe soglasie.
Efirov, S. A. (Svetozar Aleksandrovich) Moskva : Izd-vo In-ta sotsiologii RAN, 2002.

Sotsiokul'turnyĭ analiz mistifikat͡sii.
Svechnikov, Vladimir. Saratov : Saratovskiĭ gos. tekhn. universitet, 2000.
BF637.D42 S94 2000

Soucheray, Joe. Waterline : of fathers, sons, and boats / Joe Soucheray. Boston : D.R. Godine, 2002. vii, 205 p. ; 22 cm. (A nonpareil book) ISBN 1-56792-214-7 (pbk. : alk. paper) DDC 070.92
1. Soucheray, Joe. 2. Journalists - United States - Biography. 3. Fathers and sons. I. Title. II. Series.
PN4874.S576 A3 2002

SOUCHERAY, JOE.
Soucheray, Joe. Waterline. Boston : D.R. Godine, 2002.
PN4874.S576 A3 2002

Souchon, Gisèle. Nietzsche : généalogie de l'individu / Gisèle Souchon. Paris : Harmattan, c2003. 150 p. ; 22 cm. (Collection Commentaires philosophiques) Includes bibliographical references (p. 143-146). ISBN 2-7475-3886-9 DDC 193
1. Nietzsche, Friedrich Wilhelm, - 1844-1900. 2. Individualism. I. Title. II. Series: Collection Commentaires philosophiques.

Soukup, Johannes. Metaphysik der Zeit oder Wirklichkeit und Wissen : zur Grundlegung einer post-aufklärischen, nicht-individualistischen Ethik / Johannes Soukup ; mit einem Geleitwort von Günter Altner. Deutsche 1. Ausg. Wien : Passagen Verlag, c1998. 259 p. ; 24 cm. (Passagen Philosophie) ISBN 3-85165-307-6
1. Reality. 2. Metaphysics. 3. Knowledge, Theory of. I. Altner, Günther. II. Title. III. Series.

SOUL. See also **PERSONALITY; PSYCHOLOGY; REINCARNATION.**
Hinterhuber, H. (Hartmann) Die Seele. Wien ; New York : Springer, c2001.

Kather, Regine, 1955- Gotteshauch oder künstliche Seele. Stuttgart : Akademie der Diözese Rottenburg-Stuttgart, c2000.

Klatt, Norbert. Die Rivalin Gottes. Göttingen : N. Klatt, 2000.

Ma, Changyi. Zhongguo ling hun xin yang. Di 1 ban. Shanghai : Shanghai wen yi chu ban she, 1998.
BL290 .M28 1998

Moreau, Pierre-François, 1948- Lucrèce. 1. ed. Paris : Presses universitaires de France, 2002.

Novak, Peter, 1958- The lost secret of death. Charlottesville, VA : Hampton Roads Pub., 2003.

BF1999 .N73 2003

Das Rätsel von Leib und Seele. Herne : Heitkamp, c1997.
BF163 .R28 1997

Safty, Essam. La psyché humaine. Paris : Harmattan, c2003.
B528 .S34 2003

Saraydarian, Torkom. Dynamics of the soul. Cave Creek, Ariz. : T.S.G. Pub., c2001.
BF1999 .S3352 2001

Yhap, Jennifer. Plotinus on the soul. Selinsgrove : Susquehanna University Press ; London : Associated University Presses, c2003.
B693.Z7 Y43 2003

Soul & culture.
Gambini, Roberto, 1944- 1st ed. College Station : Texas A&M University Press, 2003.
BF698.9.C8 G35 2003

The soul aflame : a modern book of hours / edited and with an introduction by Phil Cousineau ; photographs by Eric Lawton. Berkeley, Calif. : Conari Press, 2000. 160 p. : col. ill. ; 18 cm. ISBN 1-57324-186-5 (trade paper) DDC 291.4/32
1. Meditations. I. Cousineau, Phil. II. Lawton, Eric.
BL624.2 .S675 2000

Soul and culture.
Gambini, Roberto, 1944- Soul & culture. 1st ed. College Station : Texas A&M University Press, 2003.
BF698.9.C8 G35 2003

The soul catcher.
Kava, Alex. Waterville, Me. : Thorndike Press, 2003, 2002.
PS3561.A8682 S6 2003

Soul coaching.
Linn, Denise. Carlsbad, CA : Hay House, 2003.
BF637.S4 L565 2003

SOUL - EARLY WORKS TO 1800.
Jean, de la Rochelle, d. 1245. Summa de anima. Paris : J. Vrin, 1995.
BD420 .J43 1995

SOUL - HISTORY OF DOCTRINES.
Hinterhuber, H. (Hartmann) Die Seele. Wien ; New York : Springer, c2001.

The soul in everyday life.
Chapelle, Daniel, 1951- Albany, NY : State University of New York Press, c2003.
BF175.4.P45 C48 2003

SOUL (JUDAISM).
Korah, Shelomoh ben Yahya. Netsah hayenu. Bene Berak : S. Korah, 762 [2001 or 2002]

SOUL - MISCELLANEA.
Kovalenko, A. P. Dusha. Moskva : Veteran otchizny : Megatron, 2000.
BF1999 .K685 2000

SOUL - PSYCHOLOGICAL ASPECTS.
Chapelle, Daniel, 1951- The soul in everyday life. Albany, NY : State University of New York Press, c2003.
BF175.4.P45 C48 2003

Plotkin, Bill, 1950- Soulcraft. Novato, Calif. : New World Library, c2003.
BF637.S4 P58 2003

Soul signs.
Todeschi, Kevin J. Virginia Beach, Va. : A.R.E. Press, c2003.
BF1045.S44 T63 2003

SOUL WORSHIP - CHINA.
Ma, Changyi. Zhongguo ling hun xin yang. Di 1 ban. Shanghai : Shanghai wen yi chu ban she, 1998.
BL290 .M28 1998

Soulcraft.
Plotkin, Bill, 1950- Novato, Calif. : New World Library, c2003.
BF637.S4 P58 2003

SOUND. See **NOISE; VASES, ACOUSTIC.**

SOUND DISCS. See **SOUND RECORDINGS.**

SOUND IN MASS MEDIA.
Sterne, Jonathan, 1970- The audible past. Durham : Duke University Press, 2003.
TK7881.4 .S733 2003

The sound of paper.
Cameron, Julia. New York : Jeremy P. Tarcher, 2004.
BF408 .C1758 2004

SOUND PERCEPTION. See **AUDITORY PERCEPTION.**

SOUND - PSYCHOLOGICAL ASPECTS - CONGRESSES.
Oldenburger Symposion zur Psychologischen Akustik (8th : 2000) Contributions to psychological acoustics. 1. ed. Oldenburg : BIS, Bibliotheks- und Informationssystem der Universität Oldenburg, 2000.
BF251 .O44 2000

SOUND RECORDING AND REPRODUCING. See **SOUND - RECORDING AND REPRODUCING.**

SOUND - RECORDING AND REPRODUCING - HISTORY.
Sterne, Jonathan, 1970- The audible past. Durham : Duke University Press, 2003.
TK7881.4 .S733 2003

SOUND RECORDING INDUSTRY - SOCIAL ASPECTS.
Sterne, Jonathan, 1970- The audible past. Durham : Duke University Press, 2003.
TK7881.4 .S733 2003

SOUND RECORDINGS. See **SOUND RECORDING INDUSTRY.**

SOUND RECORDINGS - SOCIAL ASPECTS.
Sterne, Jonathan, 1970- The audible past. Durham : Duke University Press, 2003.
TK7881.4 .S733 2003

SOUNDS - RECORDING AND REPRODUCING. See **SOUND - RECORDING AND REPRODUCING.**

The sourcebook of magic.
Hall, L. Michael. Wales, UK ; Williston, VT : Crown House Pub. Ltd., 2002.
BF637.N46 H36 2002

Sources and studies in world history
Racism. Armonk, N.Y. : M.E. Sharpe, c2003.
HT1521 .R323 2003

Sources of stress and relief for African American women.
Collins, Catherine Fisher. Westport, Conn. ; London : Praeger, 2003.
BF575.S75 C57 2003

Sousa, Joao M. C. Fuzzy decision making in modeling and control / Joao M.C. Sousa, Uzay Kaymak. Singapore ; River Edge, N.J. : World Scientific, 2002. xix, 335 p. : ill. ; 24 cm. (World Scientific series in robotics and intelligent systems ; vol. 27) Includes bibliographical references and index. ISBN 981-02-4877-6
1. Fuzzy decision making. 2. Decision making. 3. Control theory. I. Kaymak, Uzay. II. Title. III. Series.

SOUTH AFRICA. TRUTH AND RECONCILIATION COMMISSION.
Peace and conflict resolution. Part 2 [videorecording]. Derry, N.H. : Chip Taylor Communications, 1997.

Truth v. justice. Princeton, N.J. : Princeton University Press, c2000.
DT1945 .T78 2000

SOUTH ASIA.
South Asia, 2010. Delhi : Konark Publishers, 2002.

South Asia, 2010 : challenges and opportunities / edited by K.K. Bhargava, Sridhar K. Khatri. Delhi : Konark Publishers, 2002. 531 p. ; 22 cm. "Under the auspices of Friedrich-Ebert-Stiftung, New Delhi." SUMMARY: Contributed articles. Includes bibliographical references and index.
1. South Asia. 2. Twenty-first century - Forecasts. I. Bhargava, K. K. (Kant Kishore) II. Khatri, Srishar K. III. Friedrich-Ebert-Stiftung (India)

SOUTH ASIA - CIVILIZATION.
Antinomies of modernity. Durham : Duke University Press, 2003.
CB358 .A59 2003

South Asia Human Rights Documentation Centre.
Preventive detention and individual liberty. New Delhi : South Asia Human Rights Documentation Centre, 2000.
KNS4654 .P74 2000

SOUTH ASIA - POLITICS AND GOVERNMENT.
Searching for peace in Central and South Asia. Boulder, Colo. : Lynne Rienner Publishers, 2002.
JZ5597 .S43 2002

SOUTH EAST ASIA. See **ASIA, SOUTHEASTERN.**

SOUTH ENGLISH LEGENDARY.
Thompson, Anne Booth. Everyday saints and the art

of narrative in the South English legendary. Aldershot, England : Burlington, Vt. : Ashgate, c2003.
PR2143.S543 T48 2003

SOUTH WEST ASIA. *See* **MIDDLE EAST.**

Southall, R. H. (Richard H.), 1972-
[How to be a ghost hunter. Spanish]
Espíritus y fantasmas : cómo investigar evidencias paranormales / Richard Southall ; traducido al idioma español por Héctor Ramírez y Edgar Rojas. 1. ed. St. Paul, Minn. : Llewellyn Español, 2003. xxxix, 117 p. : ill. ; 21 cm. Includes bibliographical references (p. 107-108) and index. ISBN 0-7387-0382-6 DDC 133.1/07/2
1. Ghosts - Research - Methodology. I. Title.
BF1461 .S6618 2003

SOUTHEAST ASIA. *See* **ASIA, SOUTHEASTERN.**

SOUTHEASTERN ASIA. *See* **ASIA, SOUTHEASTERN.**

SOUTHERN ASIA. *See* **SOUTH ASIA.**

SOUTHERN STATES - HISTORY - CIVIL WAR, 1861-1865. *See* **UNITED STATES - HISTORY - CIVIL WAR, 1861-1865.**

SOUTHWEST ASIA. *See* **MIDDLE EAST.**

SOUTHWEST, NEW - DESCRIPTION AND TRAVEL.
Brosman, Catharine Savage, 1934- Finding higher ground. Reno : University of Nevada Press, c2003.
F787 .B76 2003

Souza, Eneida Maria de. Crítica cult / Eneida Maria de Souza. Belo Horizonte : Editora UFMG, 2002. 176 p. ; 23 cm. (Humanitas ; 79) Includes bibliographical references (p. [169]-176). CONTENTS: Algumas palavras -- Os livros de cabeceira da crítica -- Saudades de Lévi-Strauss -- O discurso crítico brasileiro -- A teoria em crise -- O não-lugar da literatura -- Nostalgias do cânone -- Notas sobre a crítica biográfica -- Madame Bovary somos nós -- Paisagens pós-utópicas -- Jeitos do Brasil -- Nem samba nem rumba. ISBN 85-7041-322-X
1. Criticism - History - 20th century. 2. Culture - Philosophy. 3. Literature - History and criticism - Theory, etc. I. Title. II. Series: Humanitas (Minas Gerais, Brazil) ; 79.
PN94 .S68 2002

Souza, Laura de Mello e.
[Diabo e a Terra de Santa Cruz. English]
The Devil and the land of the holy cross : witchcraft, slavery, and popular religion in colonial Brazil / Laura de Mello e Souza ; translated from the Portuguese by Diane Grosklaus Whitty. 1st ed. University of Texas Press : Teresa Lozano Long Institute of Latin American Studies, 2003. p. cm. (LLILAS Translations from Latin America series) Includes bibliographical references and index. ISBN 0-292-70228-0 (cloth : alk. paper) ISBN 0-292-70236-1 (pbk. : alk. paper) DDC 133.4/0981
1. Witchcraft - Brazil - History - 16th century. 2. Witchcraft - Brazil - History - 17th century. 3. Witchcraft - Brazil - History - 18th century. 4. Brazil - Religious life and customs. I. Title. II. Series.
BF1584.B7 S6813 2003

SOVEREIGNS. *See* **QUEENS.**

SOVEREIGNTY. *See also* **DECOLONIZATION; SELF-DETERMINATION, NATIONAL.**
Ryter, Jon Christian. Whatever happened to America? Tampa, FL : Hallberg Pub., 2001, c2000.
E743 .R98 2001

Sacerdoti, Gilberto, 1952- Sacrificio e sovranità. Torino : Einaudi, 2002.

SOVEREIGNTY - MORAL AND ETHICAL ASPECTS.
Luz, Ehud. [Ma'avak be-nahal Yabok. English] Wrestling with an angel. New Haven : Yale University Press, c2003.
DS143 .L8913 2003

Sovety psikhologa
Bodalev, A. A. Kak stanoviatsia velikimi ili vydaiushchimisia? Moskva : In-t psikhoterapii, 2003.
BF724.5 .B64 2003

SOVIET CENTRAL ASIA. *See* **ASIA, CENTRAL.**

SOVIET LITERATURE. *See* **RUSSIAN LITERATURE.**

SOVIET LITERATURE - POLITICAL ASPECTS.
Kul'tura i vlast' v usloviiakh kommunikatsionnoi revoliutsii XX veka. Moskva : "AIRO-XX", 2002.
HM621 .K858 2002

SOVIET UNION - INTELLECTUAL LIFE.
Kul'tura i vlast' v usloviiakh kommunikatsionnoi revoliutsii XX veka. Moskva : "AIRO-XX", 2002.
HM621 .K858 2002

SOVIET UNION - LITERATURES. *See* **SOVIET LITERATURE.**

SOVIET UNION - POLITICS AND GOVERNMENT.
Kul'tura i vlast' v usloviiakh kommunikatsionnoi revoliutsii XX veka. Moskva : "AIRO-XX", 2002.
HM621 .K858 2002

Sovremennaia psikhologiia motivatsii / pod redaktsieĭ D.A. Leont'eva. Moskva : Smysl, 2002. 342 p. ; 22 cm. (Psikhologicheskie issledovaniia) "Nauchnoe izdanie"-- Colophon. Includes bibliographical references. ISBN 5893571347
1. Motivation (Psychology) I. Leont'ev, D. A. II. Series.
BF503 .S68 2002

Sovremennaia psikhologiia : sostoianie i perspektivy issledovanii : materialy iubileinoi nauchnoi konferentsii IP RAN, 28-29 ianvaria 2002 g. / otvetstvenye redaktory A.V. Brushlinskiĭ, A.L. Zhuravlev. Moskva : In-t psikhologii RAN, 2002. 5 v. : ill. ; 21 cm. Includes bibliographical references. CONTENTS: ch. 1. Obshchaia psikhologiia, psikhologiia truda i inzhenernaia psikhologiia -- ch. 2. Obshchaia i sotsial'naia psikhologiia, psikhologiia lichnosti i psikhofiziologiia, ekonomicheskaia, organizatsionnaia i politicheskaia psikhologiia -- ch. 3. Sotsial'nye predstavleniia i myshlenie lichnosti -- ch. 4. Metodologichekie problemy istoriko-psikhologicheskogo issledovaniia -- ch. 5. Programmy i metodiki psikhologichekogo issledovaniia lichnosti i gruppy. ISBN 5927000207 (v. 1) ISBN 5927000231 (v. 2) ISBN 5927000347 (v. 3) ISBN 5927000207 (v. 4) ISBN 5927000363 (v. 5)
1. Psychology - Congresses. I. Brushlinskiĭ, A. V. (Andreĭ Vladimirovich) II. Zhuravlev, A. L.
BF20 .S64 2002

Sovremennoe obrazovanie
Kochetkov, V. V. (Vladimir Viktorovich) Psikhologiia mezhkul'turnykh razlichiĭ. Moskva : PER SE, 2002.
GN502 .K6 2002

Soy bueno para ayudar.
Day, Eileen. [I'm good at helping. Spanish] Chicago : Heinemann Library, 2003.
BF723.H45 D3918 2003

Sozidatel'naia psikhologiia.
Ponomarenko, V. A. (Vladimir Aleksandrovich) Moskva : Moskovskiĭ psikhologo-sotsial'nyĭ institut ; Voronezh : Izd-vo NPO "MODEK", 2000.
BF408 .P572 2000

Soznanie i poznanie 3. tysiacheletiia.
Raĭkov, V. L. (Vladimir Leonidovich), 1934- Soznanie i poznanie III tysiacheletiia. Moskva : [s.n.], 1999.
BF311 .R26 1999

Soznanie i poznanie III tysiacheletiia.
Raĭkov, V. L. (Vladimir Leonidovich), 1934- Moskva : [s.n.], 1999.
BF311 .R26 1999

Soznanie i poznanie tret'ego tysiacheletiia.
Raĭkov, V. L. (Vladimir Leonidovich), 1934- Soznanie i poznanie III tysiacheletiia. Moskva : [s.n.], 1999.
BF311 .R26 1999

SPACE AND ARCHITECTURAL MASS. *See* **SPACE (ARCHITECTURE).**

SPACE AND TIME. *See also* **RELATIVITY (PHYSICS); SPATIAL BEHAVIOR.**
Alackapally, Sebastian, 1961- Being and meaning. 1st ed. Delhi : Motilal Banarsidass Publishers, 2002.
PK541.B48 A43 2002

Castagnino, M. (Mario) Tempo e universo. Roma : Armando, c2000.
BD632 .C37 2000

Demuth, Volker. Topische Ästhetik. Würzburg : Königshausen & Neumann, c2002.

Gendered landscapes. University Park, PA : Center for Studies in Landscape History, c2000.

SPACE AND TIME - BENIN.
Vallier, Gilles-Félix. La logique de l'éternité. 1998.

SPACE AND TIME IN LANGUAGE.
Schmauks, Dagmar. Orientierung im Raum. Tübingen : Stauffenburg, c2002.
QP443 .S363 2002

SPACE AND TIME - MISCELLANEA.
Nicheva, Nina. Prez vremeto i prostranstvoto. [Bulgaria] : Gutoranov i sin, [1998?]
BF1999 .N46 1998

SPACE AND TIME - SOCIAL ASPECTS - BENIN.
Vallier, Gilles-Félix. La logique de l'éternité. 1998.

SPACE (ARCHITECTURE).
Palumbo, Maria Luisa. [Nuovi ventri. English] New wombs : electronic bodies and architectural disorders. Basel : Birkhäuser, 2000.
NA2765 .P35 2000

Saldarriaga Roa, Alberto. La Arquitectura como experiencia. 1. ed. Bogotá : Villegas Editores : Universidad Nacional de Colombia, Facultad de Artes, c2002.
NA2765 .S36 2002

SPACE (ART). *See also* **PERSPECTIVE.**
Ivinskaia, A. (Anna) Svet prelomlennogo vremeni v ikonnom prostranstve. Moskva : Khristianskiĭ Vostok, 2002.
N8189.G72 I95 2002

Summers, David, 1941- Real spaces. London : Phaidon, c2003.

SPACE BEHAVIOR. *See* **SPATIAL BEHAVIOR.**

Space clearing.
Clayton, Emily. San Diego, Calif. : Thunder Bay Press, c2003.
BF1779.F4 C58 2003

SPACE IN ARCHITECTURE. *See* **SPACE (ARCHITECTURE).**

SPACE PERCEPTION. *See also* **GEOGRAPHICAL PERCEPTION; PERSPECTIVE.**
The cognitive and neural bases of spatial neglect. Oxford ; New York : Oxford University Press, 2002.
RC394.N44 C64 2002

Kessler, Klaus. Raumkognition und Lokalisationsäusserungen. Wiesbaden : Deutscher Universitäts-Verlag, 2000.
BF469 .K47 2000

Schmauks, Dagmar. Orientierung im Raum. Tübingen : Stauffenburg, c2002.
QP443 .S363 2002

Spatial cognition III. Berlin ; New York : Springer, c2003.
Q387 .S73 2003

Unschaerferelationen. Wiesbaden : Nelte, c2002.
BF469 .U5 2002

SPACE PERCEPTION - CONGRESSES.
Human spatial memory. Mahwah, NJ : Lawrence Erlbaum Associates, 2003.
BF469 .H86 2003

SPACE PERCEPTION - EXAMINATIONS, QUESTIONS, ETC.
Wiesen, Joel P. (Joel Peter) How to prepare for mechanical aptitude & spatial relations tests. Hauppauge, NY : Barron's, 2003.
BF433.M4 W535 2003

SPACE PERCEPTION - PERIODICALS.
Spatial cognition and computation. [Dordrecht], The Netherlands : Kluwer Academic, c1999-
BF469 .S674

SPACE, SACRED. *See* **SACRED SPACE.**

SPACE SCIENCES. *See* **ASTRONOMY.**

Spaces of intercultural communication.
Lie, Rico. Creskill, N.J. : Hampton Press, c2003.
GN345.6 .L54 2003

SPAGIRIC MEDICINE. *See* **MEDICINE, MAGIC, MYSTIC, AND SPAGIRIC.**

SPAGYRIC MEDICINE. *See* **MEDICINE, MAGIC, MYSTIC, AND SPAGIRIC.**

SPAIN - ETHNIC RELATIONS.
Meyuhas Ginio, Alisa, 1937- Kerovim u-rehokim. Tel Aviv : Mif'alim Universitayim, 760 [1999]

SPAIN - HISTORY - 711-1492.
Meyuhas Ginio, Alisa, 1937- Kerovim u-rehokim. Tel Aviv : Mif'alim Universitayim, 760 [1999]

SPAIN - LITERATURES. *See* **SPANISH LITERATURE.**

Spain. Ministerio de Defensa.
Panorama estratégico, 2001-2002. [Madrid] : Ministerio de Defensa, 2002.

Spalding, John D. A pilgrim's digress : my perilous, fumbling quest for the celestial city / John D. Spalding. 1st ed. New York : Harmony Books, c2003. 222 p. ; 22 cm. ISBN 140004653X DDC 291.4
1. Religion. I. Title.

Spaniards - America - Historiography.

BL50 .S627 2003

SPANIARDS - AMERICA - HISTORIOGRAPHY.
Restall, Matthew, 1964- Seven myths of the Spanish conquest. Oxford ; New York : Oxford University Press, 2003.
F1230 .R47 2003

SPANISH AMERICA. *See* **LATIN AMERICA.**

SPANISH AMERICAN LITERATURE - 20TH CENTURY - HISTORY AND CRITICISM.
Latin America writes back. New York : Routledge, 2002.
PQ7081.A1 L336 2002

SPANISH LANGUAGE - ACQUISITION.
La Adquisición de la lengua materna. México : Universidad Nacional Autónoma de México : Centro de Investigaciones y Estudios Superiores en Antropología Social, 2001.
P118 .A227 2001

SPANISH LANGUAGE MATERIALS.
Day, Eileen. [I'm good at helping. Spanish] Soy bueno para ayudar. Chicago : Heinemann Library, 2003.
BF723.H45 D3918 2003

Johnston, Marianne. [Dealing with anger. Spanish] Como tratar la ira. New York : PowerKids Press, 2005.
BF575.A5 J6418 2005

Johnston, Marianne. [Dealing with bullying. Spanish] Como tratar a los bravucones. New York : PowerKids Press, 2005.
BF637.B85 J6418 2005

Johnston, Marianne. [Dealing with fighting. Spanish] Como tratar las peleas. New York : PowerKids Press, 2005.
BF637.I48 J6418 2005

Johnston, Marianne. [Dealing with insults. Spanish] Como tratar los insultos. New York : PowerKids Press, 2005.
BF637.V47 J6418 2005

Jordan, Denise. [We can listen. Spanish] Escuchamos. Chicago : Heinemann Library, c2004.
BF323.L5 J6718 2004

Jordan, Denise. [Your fair share. Spanish] A partes iguales. Chicago : Heinemann Library, c2004.
BF723.S428 J6718 2003

McLaughlin, Bob. [USA immigration & orientation. Spanish] USA inmigración y orientación. 1a. ed. en español. Satellite Beach, Fla. : Wellesworth Pub., c2001.

La palabra como cuerpo del delito. Santo Domingo, República Dominicana : Biblioteca Nacional "Dr. Pedro Henríquez Ureña", 2001.

Trevi, Gloria. Gloria. México, D.F. : Planeta, c2002.
ML420.T725 A3 2002

SPANISH LANGUAGE MATERIALS - BILINGUAL.
Johansen, Heidi Leigh. [What I look like when I am angry. Spanish & English] What I look like when I am angry = 1st ed. New York : Rosen PowerKids Press, 2004.
BF723.A4 J6318 2004

Johansen, Heidi Leigh. [What I look like when I am happy. Spanish & English] What I look like when I am happy = 1st ed. New York : Rosen Pub. Group's, 2004.
BF723.H37 J6418 2004

Randolph, Joanne. [What I look like when I am confused. Spanish & English] What I look like when I am confused = 1st ed. New York : Rosen Pub. Group's PowerKids Press, 2004.
BF723.I63 R3618 2004

Randolph, Joanne. [What I look like when I am sad. Spanish & English] What I look like when I am sad = 1st ed. New York : Rosen Pub. Group's PowerKids Press, 2004.
BF723.S15 R3618 2004

Shepherd, Joanne. [What I look like when I am scared. Spanish & English] What I look like when I am scared = 1st ed. New York : Rosen Pub. Group's PowerKids Press, 2004.
BF723.F4 S5418 2004

Shepherd, Joanne. [What I look like when I am surprised. Spanish & English] What I look like when I am surprised = 1st ed. New York : Rosen Pub. Group's PowerKids Press, 2004.

BF723.S87 S4418 2004

SPANISH LANGUAGE - RELATIVE CLAUSES.
Fernández, Eva M. Bilingual sentence processing. Amsterdam ; Philadelphia : J. Benjamins Pub., 2003.
P115.4 .F47 2003

SPANISH LITERATURE. *See* **SPANISH AMERICAN LITERATURE.**

SPANISH LITERATURE - 20TH CENTURY - HISTORY AND CRITICISM.
Marías, Julián, 1914- Entre dos siglos. Madrid : Alianza Editorial, c2002.
PQ6663.A72183 E68 2002

SPANISH LITERATURE - STUDY AND TEACHING - GREAT BRITAIN.
Read, Malcolm K. (Malcolm Kevin), 1945- Educating the educators. 1st American ed. Newark : University of Delaware Press ; Cranbury, NJ : Associated University Presses, 2003.
PC4064.R43 A3 2003

SPANISH PHILOSOPHY. *See* **PHILOSOPHY, SPANISH.**

Sparks, J. Gary (John Gary), 1948-.
Edinger, Edward F. Science of the soul. Toronto, Ont. : Inner City Books, c2002.
BF173 .E27 2002

Spasitel'
Sudakov, Vladimir Ivanovich. Moskva : TERRA-Sport, 2001.
BF1027.G73 S83 2001

Spata, Andrea. Research methods : science and diversity / Andrea Spata. New York : John Wiley & Sons, Inc., c2003. viii, 336 p. : ill. ; 24 cm. Includes bibliographical references (p. 323-328) and indexes. Publisher description URL: http://www.loc.gov/catdir/desc ription/wiley034/2003544775.html ISBN 0-471-36912-8 (alk. paper) DDC 150/.7/2
1. Psychology - Research - Methodology. 2. Psychometrics. I. Title.
BF76.5 .S63 2003

SPATIAL ABILITY - CONGRESSES.
Human spatial memory. Mahwah, NJ : Lawrence Erlbaum Associates, 2003.
BF469 .H86 2003

SPATIAL BEHAVIOR. *See also* **HUMAN TERRITORIALITY; SPACE PERCEPTION.**
Children in the city. London : Routledge/Falmer, 2003.

Gendered landscapes. University Park, PA : Center for Studies in Landscape History, c2000.

SPATIAL BEHAVIOR - CONGRESSES.
Human spatial memory. Mahwah, NJ : Lawrence Erlbaum Associates, 2003.
BF469 .H86 2003

Spatial cognition 3.
Spatial cognition III. Berlin ; New York : Springer, c2003.
Q387 .S73 2003

Spatial cognition and computation. [Dordrecht], The Netherlands : Kluwer Academic, c1999- v. : ill. ; 24 cm. Frequency: Quarterly. Vol. 1, no. 1 (1999)- . Title from cover. Published: Mahwah, N.J. : Lawrence Erlbaum Associates, vols. for 2003- Latest issue consulted: Vol. 3, no. 2 & 3 (2003). Some issues combined. Also available via World Wide Web; OCLC FirstSearch Electronic Collections Online: Subscription required for access to abstracts and full text. URL: http://firstsearch.oclc.org URL: http://firstsearch.oclc.org/jour nal=1387-5868;screen=info;ECOIP URL: http://www.erlbaum.com Available in other form: Spatial cognition and computation (Online) ISSN: 1542-7633 (DLC) 2002215607 (OCoLC)42897701. ISSN 1387-5868
1. Space perception - Periodicals. 2. Geographical perception - Periodicals. 3. Artificial intelligence - Periodicals. I. Title: Spatial cognition and computation (Online)
BF469 .S674

Spatial cognition and computation (Online).
Spatial cognition and computation. [Dordrecht], The Netherlands : Kluwer Academic, c1999-
BF469 .S674

Spatial cognition III : routes and navigation, human memory and learning, spatial representation and spatial learning / Christian Freksa ... [et al.], (eds.). Berlin ; New York : Springer, c2003. x, 414 p. : ill. ; 24 cm. (Lecture notes in computer science, 0302-9743 ; 2685. Lecture notes in artificial intelligence) Includes bibliographical references and index. ISBN 3-540-40430-9 (acid-free paper) DDC 006.3/32
1. Knowledge representation (Information theory) 2. Space perception. I. Freksa, C. II. Title: Spatial cognition 3 III. Title:

Spatial cognition three IV. Series: Lecture notes in computer science ; 2685. V. Series: Lecture notes in computer science. Lecture notes in artificial intelligence.
Q387 .S73 2003

Spatial cognition three.
Spatial cognition III. Berlin ; New York : Springer, c2003.
Q387 .S73 2003

SPATIAL PERCEPTION. *See* **SPACE PERCEPTION.**

SPATIALLY-ORIENTED BEHAVIOR. *See* **SPATIAL BEHAVIOR.**

Spätmittelalter und Reformation
(21.) Kuropka, Nicole. Philipp Melanchthon. Tübingen : Mohr Siebeck, c2002.
BR339 .K86 2002

(neue Reihe, 20.) Kleinöder-Strobel, Susanne, 1969- Die Verfolgung von Zauberei und Hexerei in den fränkischen Markgraftümern im 16. Jahrhundert. Tübingen : Mohr Siebeck, c2002.
BF1583 .K54 2002

Speak, Karl D., 1951-.
McNally, David, 1946- Be your own brand. 1st ed. San Francisco, CA : Berrett-Koehler, c2002.
BF697 .M385 2002

SPEAKING. *See* **RHETORIC; VOICE.**

Speaking from the heart.
Shields, Stephanie A. Cambridge, U.K. ; New York : Cambridge University Press, 2002.
BF531 .S55 2002

Speaking sex to power.
Califia-Rice, Patrick, 1954- 1st ed. San Francisco : Cleis Press, c2002.
HQ76.25 .C32 2002

Spears, Richard A. NTC's dictionary of everyday American English expressions : presented according to topic and situation / Richard A. Spears, Steven R. Kleinedler, Betty J. Birner. Lincolnwood, Ill. : National Textbook Co., c1994. xi, 415 p. ; 24 cm. (NTC language dictionaries) Includes index. ISBN 0-8442-5778-8 DDC 423/.1
1. English language - United States - Terms and phrases. 2. English language - Spoken English - United States. 3. English language - United States - Idioms. 4. Figures of speech. 5. Americanisms. I. Kleinedler, Steven Racek. II. Birner, Betty J. III. Title. IV. Series: National Textbook language dictionaries.
PE2839 .S65 1994

SPECIAL AGENTS (COMPUTER SOFTWARE). *See* **INTELLIGENT AGENTS (COMPUTER SOFTWARE).**

SPECIAL LIBRARIES. *See* **ART LIBRARIES.**

Special topics in tarot
Amberstone, Ruth Ann. Tarot tips. St. Paul, Minn. : Llewellyn, 2003.
BF1879.T2 A475 2003

Gillentine, Julie. Tarot & dream interpretation. 1st ed. St. Paul, Minn. : Llewellyn Publications 2003.
BF1879.T2 G585 2003

SPECIALISTS. *See* **INTELLECTUALS; SCHOLARS.**

SPECIALIZATION. *See* **EXPERTISE.**

SPECIE. *See* **MONEY.**

Species of origins.
Giberson, Karl. Lanham, Md. : Rowman & Littlefield, c2002.
BL240.3 .G53 2002

Species technica.
Hottois, Gilbert, 1946- Paris : Vrin, 2002.

SPECIMENS, ARCHAEOLOGICAL. *See* **ANTIQUITIES.**

Speck, Paul.
[Selections. English. 1999]
Understanding Byzantium : studies in Byzantine historical sources / Paul Speck ; edited by Sarolta Takács. Aldershot, Great Britain ; Burlington, Vt. : Ashgate/Variorum, c2003. xii, 301 p. ; 24 cm. (Variorum collected studies series ; CS631) Includes bibliographical references and index. ISBN 0-86078-691-9 (hc.) DDC 949.5/02
1. Byzantine Empire - Civilization - Study and teaching. 2. Byzantine literature - History and criticism. 3. Renaissance. 4. Byzantine Empire - History - Sources. I. Title. II. Series: Collected studies ; CS631.
DF503 .S742513 2003

SPECTERS. *See* **GHOSTS.**

Spector, Bertram I. (Bertram Irwin), 1949-.
Getting it done. Washington, D.C. : United States Institute of Peace Press, 2003.
KZ1321 .G48 2003

SPECTRES. *See* **GHOSTS.**

SPECULATION. *See* **STOCK EXCHANGES.**

Spee, Friedrich von, 1591-1635.
[Cautio criminalis. English]
Cautio criminalis, or, A book on witch trials / Friedrich Spee von Langenfeld ; translated by Marcus Hellyer. Charlottesville : University of Virginia Press, 2003. xxxvi, 233 p. : ill. ; 24 cm. (Studies in early modern German history) Includes bibliographical references and index. ISBN 0-8139-2181-3 (alk. paper) ISBN 0-8139-2182-1 (pbk. : alk. paper) DDC 133.4/3/0943
1. Witchcraft - Germany. 2. Trials (Witchcraft) - Germany. I. Hellyer, Marcus. II. Title. III. Title: Cautio criminalis IV. Title: Book on witch trials V. Series.
BF1583.A2 S6813 2003

SPEECH. *See* **SPEECH ACTS (LINGUISTICS); VOICE.**

SPEECH ACT THEORY (LINGUISTICS). *See* **SPEECH ACTS (LINGUISTICS).**

SPEECH ACTS (LINGUISTICS).
Sprache, Sinn und Situation. 1. Aufl. Wiesbaden : Deutscher Universitäts-Verlag, 2001.

SPEECH ACTS (LINGUISTICS) - RELIGIOUS ASPECTS.
Müller, Klaus E., 1935- Wortzauber. Frankfurt : Lembeck, c2001.
P35 .M945 2001

SPEECH AND SOCIAL CLASSES. *See* **SPEECH AND SOCIAL STATUS.**

SPEECH AND SOCIAL STATUS - ENGLAND.
Hoggart, Richard, 1918- Everyday language & everyday life. New Brunswick, N.J. ; London : Transaction Publishers, c2003.
PE1074.8 .H64 2003

SPEECH COMMUNICATION. *See* **ORAL COMMUNICATION.**

SPEECH EVENTS (LINGUISTICS). *See* **SPEECH ACTS (LINGUISTICS).**

SPEECH PERCEPTION.
Adeleye, Modupe, 1980- From our hearts. Rochester, N.Y. : Mo-Biz Publishing Co., 2003.
BF353 .A33 2003

Toda, Takako. Second language speech perception and production. Lanham, Md. ; Oxford : University Press of America, c2003.
PL541 .T63 2003

SPEECH PERCEPTION IN INFANTS.
Jusczyk, Peter W. The discovery of spoken language. 1st MIT Press pbk. ed. Cambridge, Mass. : MIT Press, 2000.
BF720.S67 J87 2000

SPEECH PERCEPTION IN NEWBORN INFANTS.
Jusczyk, Peter W. The discovery of spoken language. 1st MIT Press pbk. ed. Cambridge, Mass. : MIT Press, 2000.
BF720.S67 J87 2000

SPEECH - PHYSIOLOGICAL ASPECTS.
Sprache, Sinn und Situation. 1. Aufl. Wiesbaden : Deutscher Universitäts-Verlag, 2001.

SPEED PERCEPTION. *See* **MOTION PERCEPTION (VISION).**

Spekulation und Erfahrung. Abteilung I. Texte
(Bd. 5) Hotho, Heinrich Gustav, 1802-1873. Vorstudien für Leben und Kunst. Stuttgart : Frommann-Holzboog, 2002.

Spell success in your life.
Colwell, Peter G. Germantown, Md. : Dreams Unlimited Press, c2002.
BF637.S8 C57 2002

Spellbound.
Moorey, Teresa. Berkeley, CA : Ulysses Press : Distributed in the U.S.A. by Publishers Group West, 2002.
BF1571.5.T44 M66 2002

Spellcasters.
Bartel, Pauline C. Dallas : Taylor Trade Pub., c2000.
BF1566 .B27 2000

SPELLS. *See* **CHARMS; MAGIC.**

Spells dictionary.
Beattie, Antonia. San Diego, Calif. : Thunder Bay Press, 2003.
BF1611 .B43 2003

Spells for a perfect love life.
White, Lauren. Kansas City, Mo. : Andrews McMeel Pub., 2000.
BF1572.L6 .W45 2000

Spells for teenage witches.
Baker, Marina. Berkeley, Calif. : Seastone, c2000.
BF1571.5.T44 B34 2000

Spells for the solitary witch.
Holland, Eileen. Boston, MA : Weiser Books, 2004.
BF1566 .H643 2004

Spelman, Elizabeth V. Repair : the impulse to restore in a fragile world / Elizabeth V. Spelman. Boston : Beacon Press, c2002. 165 p. ; 22 cm. Includes bibliographical references (p. [140]-156) and index. ISBN 0-8070-2012-5 (alk. paper) DDC 128
1. Psychology, Applied. 2. Repairing - Psychological aspects. I. Title.
BF636 .S689 2002

Spence, Lewis, 1874-1955. An encyclopædia of occultism / Lewis Spence. Mineola, N.Y. : Dover Publications, 2003. 451 p. : ill. ; 28 cm. Originally published: London : G. Routledge & Sons, Ltd., 1920. Includes bibliographical references (p. [vii-viii]) and index. Publisher description URL: http://www.loc.gov/catdir/desc ription/dover031/2003041462.html ISBN 0-486-42613-0 (pbk.) DDC 133/.03
1. Occultism - Dictionaries. I. Title.
BF1025 .S7 2003

Spencer, Anne.
Spencer, John, 1954- Mysteries and magic. London : Orion, 2000.

Spencer, John, 1954- Mysteries and magic / John and Anne Spencer. London : Orion, 2000. 342 p. : ill. ; 18 cm. Originally published: 1999. Includes bibliographical references (p. 323-324) and index. ISBN 0-7528-3675-7 DDC 133
1. Cults. 2. Occultism. I. Spencer, Anne. II. Title. III. Series: Sci-Fi Channel true life encounters.

Spencer, Patricia Elizabeth.
Oxford handbook of deaf studies, language, and education. Oxford ; New York : Oxford University Press, c2003.
HV2380 .O88 2003

Spencer, Sabina A., 1951- Life changes : a guide to the seven stages of personal growth / Sabina A. Spencer, John D. Adams. New York : Paraview Special Editions, c2002. 192 p. : ill. ; 22 cm. Originally published: San Luis Obispo, Calif. : Impact, c1990. Includes bibliographical references (p. 181-186) and index. ISBN 1-931044-43-0 (pbk.) DDC 155.9
1. Life change events - Psychological aspects. 2. Life change events - Psychological aspects - Problems, exercises, etc. I. Adams, John D., 1942- II. Title.
BF637.L53 S64 2002

Sperry, Len. Becoming an effective health care manager : the essential skills of leadership / by Len Sperry. Baltimore, Md. : Health Professions Press, c2003. xiii, 289 p. ; 23 cm. Includes bibliographical references (p. 279-281) and index. ISBN 1-87881-286-6 DDC 362.1/068/3
1. Health services administrators. 2. Leadership. 3. Health facilities - Personnel management. 4. Health services administration. I. Title.
RA971 .S72 2003

Spezzano, Charles. Happiness is the best revenge : 30 days to letting go : a step by step guide to letting go of attachment and heartbreak / Chuck Spezzano ; illustrations by Brian Davis. Townsend, Wiltshire, England : Vision Products Limited, c1997. xi, 122 p. : ill. ; 21 cm. ISBN 0-9532366-0-9 DDC 158
1. Loss (Psychology) 2. Adjustment (Psychology) I. Title.
BF575.D35 S68 1997

Spiegel, Josef. Sexual abuse of males : the SAM model of theory and practice / Josef Spiegel. New York : Brunner-Routledge, 2003. xiii, 545 p. : ill. ; 24 cm. Includes bibliographical references (p. 461-519) and index. ISBN 1-56032-403-1 (Hardcover) DDC 618.9/285836/0081
1. Male sexual abuse victims - Mental health. 2. Adult child sexual abuse victims - Mental health. 3. Sexually abused children - Mental health. 4. Psychotherapy. I. Title.
RC569.5.A28 S65 2003

Spillmann, Kurt R.
Zeitgeschichtliche Hintergründe aktueller Konflikte V. Zürich : Forschungsstelle für Sicherheitspolitik und Konfliktanalyse, Eidgenössische Technische Hochschule, 1995.
JX1952 .Z45 1995

Spinath, Frank M.
Personality and temperament: genetics, evolution, and structure. Lengerich : Pabst Science Publishers, 2001.
BF698 .P3692 2001

SPINOZA, BENEDICTUS DE, 1632-1677. ETHICA PART 4.
Fortitude et servitude. Paris : Kimé, c2003.

SPINOZA, BENEDICTUS DE, 1632-1677.
Leibniz, Gottfried Wilhelm, Freiherr von, 1646-1716. Réfutation inédite de Spinoza. Arles [France] : Actes Sud ; [Montréal] : Leméac, 1999.

SPINSTERS. *See* **SINGLE WOMEN.**

Spiraldancer. Moon rites : ritual, myth & magic for the modern moon goddess / Spiraldancer. South Melbourne : [Great Britain] : Lothian, 2002. ix, 341 p. : ill. ; 24 cm. Includes bibliographical references and index. ISBN 0-7344-0366-6 DDC 155.333
1. Rites and ceremonies. 2. Menstruation - Mythology. 3. Women - Mythology. 4. Menopause. 5. Goddess religion. I. Title.

Spiridonov, V. F.
Issledovaniia obucheniia i razvitiia v kontekste kul'turno-istoricheskogo podkhoda. Moskva : Smysl, 2002.
BF712.5 .I88 2002

Mezhdunarodnaia psikhologicheskaia konferentsiia "Psikhicheskoe razvitie v ontogeneze-- zakonomernosti i vozmozhnye periodizatsii" (1999 : Moscow, Russia) Problemy psikhologii razvitiia. Moskva : RGGU, 2000.
BF712.5 .M49 2000

SPIRIT. *See also* **CONSCIOUSNESS; HOLY SPIRIT; SOUL.**
Hegel's Phenomenology of spirit. Amherst, N.Y. : Humanity Books, 2003.
B2929 .H349 2003

SPIRIT ART - EXHIBITIONS.
Art spirite, mediumnique, visionnaire. [Paris] : Hoëbeke, c1999.
BF1313 .A78 1999

SPIRIT CHANNELING. *See* **CHANNELING (SPIRITUALISM).**

SPIRIT GUIDES. *See* **GUIDES (SPIRITUALISM).**

SPIRIT, HOLY. *See* **HOLY SPIRIT.**

Spirit messenger.
Smith, Gordon, 1962- Carlsbad, Calif. : Hay House, 2004.
BF1283.S616 A3 2004

A spirit of inquiry.
Lichtenberg, Joseph D. Hillsdale, NJ : Analytic Press, 2002.
RC506 .L5238 2002

The spirit of terrorism and requiem for the Twin Towers.
Baudrillard, Jean. [Esprit du terrorisme. English] London : Verso, 2002.
HV6431 .B38 2002

Spirit of the witch.
Grimassi, Raven, 1951- 1st ed. St. Paul, Minn. : Llewellyn Publications, 2003.
BF1566 .G737 2003

The spirit of this age.
Aluko, Jonathan O. [[Akure, Nigeria : Christ Liberation Publications, c1996]]
BL480 .A494 1996

The spirit of yoga.
Rham, Cat de. London : Thorsons, 2001.

SPIRIT POSSESSION. *See also* **DEMONIAC POSSESSION.**
Chajes, Jeffrey Howard. Between worlds. Philadelphia : University of Pennsylvania Press, c2003.
BM729.D92 C53 2003

Hell, Bertrand. Le tourbillon des génies. Paris : Flammarion, c2002.

Klass, Morton, 1927- Mind over mind. Lanham, Md. ; Oxford : Rowman & Littlefield, c2003.
BF1555 .K58 2003

Lewis, I. M. Ecstatic religion. 3rd ed. London ; New York : Routledge, 2003.
BL626 .L48 2003

SPIRIT POSSESSION - INDIA - SAWAI MADHOPUR (DISTRICT).

Dwyer, Graham, 1959- The divine and the demonic. London ; New York : RoutledgeCurzon, 2003.
BL1226.82.E94 D89 2003

SPIRIT WRITINGS.
At-Hlan, Spirit. The voice of At-Hlan. Torquay : Pyramid Pub., c1996.

Dray, Maryvonne. Karine après la vie. Paris : Albin Michel, c2002.

Johnson, Deborah L., 1956- Letters from the Infinite. Aptos, CA : New Brighton Books, c2002-
BF1301 .J575 2002
1. Black author.

Santos, Robson Pinheiro, 1961- Tambores de Angola. Contagem [Brazil] : Casa dos Espíritos, 2002.
1. Black author.

Winter, Jean, 1909-1939 (Spirit) Dites-leur que la mort n'existe pas. Chambéry : Exergue, c1997, [1998]
BF1290 .W56 1997

SPIRITAL LIFE - HINDUISM.
Sivananda, Swami. Thought power. 13th ed. Uttaranchal, Himalayas, India : Divine Life Society, 2002.

SPIRITISM. See SPIRITUALISM.

SPIRITS. See also ANGELS; DEMONOLOGY; FAMILIARS (SPIRITS).
Egbunu, Fidelis Eleojo. Be not afraid, only believe. Enugu, Nigeria : Snaap Press, 2001.
1. Black author.

Rahbar'zādah, Ḥasan. Shinākht-i rūḥ. Chāp-i 1. Tihrān : Nashr-i Pārsā, 1380 [2001 04 2002]

Spirits, ghosts & guardians.
Andrews, Ted, 1952- 1st ed. Jackson, Tenn. : Dragonhawk Pub., c2002.
BF1461 .A53 2002

Spirits, ghosts, and guardians.
Andrews, Ted, 1952- Spirits, ghosts & guardians. 1st ed. Jackson, Tenn. : Dragonhawk Pub., c2002.
BF1461 .A53 2002

SPIRITS - JUVENILE LITERATURE.
Andrews, Ted, 1952- Spirits, ghosts & guardians. 1st ed. Jackson, Tenn. : Dragonhawk Pub., c2002.
BF1461 .A53 2002

SPIRITS - MISCELLANEA.
Cuevas Sosa, Andrés Alejandro, 1939- How do religious figures induce the establishment of sects? 2nd ed. Leicestershire : Upfront Pub., 2002.
BF1272 .C84 2002

Spirits of the Leonis adobe.
Wlodarski, Robert James. West Hills, Calif. : G-Host Pub., c2002.
BF1472.U6 W59 2002

The spiritual chicks question everything.
Coyne, Tami. York Beach, ME : Red Wheel/Weiser, 2002.
BL625.7 .C69 2002

Spiritual cleansing.
Mickaharic, Draja. York Beach, ME : Red Wheel/Weiser, 2003.
BF1040 .M53 2003

Spiritual discernment.
Goldsmith, Joel S., 1892-1964. Atlanta, Ga. : Acropolis Books, c2002.
BF639.G56886 2002

Spiritual doodles & mental leapfrogs.
Revoir, Katherine Q. Boston, MA : Red Wheel, 2002.
BF697.5.S427 R48 2002

Spiritual doodles and mental leapfrogs.
Revoir, Katherine Q. Spiritual doodles & mental leapfrogs. Boston, MA : Red Wheel, 2002.
BF697.5.S427 R48 2002

SPIRITUAL EXERCISES.
Revoir, Katherine Q. Spiritual doodles & mental leapfrogs. Boston, MA : Red Wheel, 2002.
BF697.5.S427 R48 2002

Solodin, A. I. Strategiia ontologicheskoĭ igry. Sankt-Peterburg : Aleteĭia, 2002.

Tubali, Shy. [Selections] Boker tov 'olam. Tel Aviv : Yedi'ot aḥaronot : Sifre ḥemed, c2003.

SPIRITUAL HEALERS. See HEALERS.

SPIRITUAL HEALING. See also HEALERS; MIRACLES.
Adekanmbi, Joseph. Disabilities. Ibadan [Nigeria] : Goalim Publishers, 2001.

Bennett, Robin Rose. Healing magic. New York : Sterling Pub., 2004.
BF1572.S65 B46 2004

Curcio, Kimberly Panisset. Man of light. 1st ed. New York : SelectBooks, c2002.
BF1045.M44 C87 2002

Frost, Gavin. A witch's guide to psychic healing. Boston, MA : Weiser Books, 2003.
BF1572.S65 F76 2003

Goldsmith, Joel S., 1892-1964. Spiritual discernment. Atlanta, Ga. : Acropolis Books, c2002.
BF639.G56886 2002

Kottler, Jeffrey A. American shaman. New York : Brunner-Routledge, 2004.
BF1598.K43 K68 2004

Ofoegbu, Mike. Exposing satanic manipulations. [Lagos, Nigeria : Holy Ghost Anointed Books Ministries, c1998]
1. Black author.

Sayers, Janet. Divine therapy. Oxford ; New York : Oxford University Press, 2003.
BF175.4.R44 S28 2003

Stein, Diane, 1948- Essential energy balancing II. Berkeley, Calif. : Crossing Press, c2003.
BF1045.K37 S735 2003

Strehlow, Wighard, 1937- Hildegard of Bingen's spiritual remedies. Rochester, Vt. : Healing Arts Press, c2002.
BT732.5 .S87 2002

Trasferetti, José Antônio. Deus a força que cura!. Campinas, SP : Editora Átomo, 2002.

Virtue, Doreen, 1958- Angel medicine. Carlsbad, Calif. : Hay House, 2004.
BF1999 .V585 2004

SPIRITUAL HEALING - EGYPT.
Sengers, Gerda. Vrouwen en demonen. Amsterdam : Het Spinhuis, 2000.
BF1275.F3 S46 2000

Sengers, Gerda. Women and demons. Leiden ; Boston : Brill, 2003.
BF1275.F3 S463 2003

SPIRITUAL HEALING - MISCELLANEA.
Scully, Nicki, 1943- Alchemical healing. Rochester, Vt. : Bear & Co., 2003.
BF1999 .S369 2003

SPIRITUAL LIFE. See also MEDITATION; MYSTICISM; SPIRITUALITY.
Aïvanhov, Omraam Mikhaël. L'amour plus grand que la foi. Fréjus : Prosveta, c2000.

Aïvanhov, Omraam Mikhaël. "Et il me montra un fleuve d'eau de la vie"-- Apocalypse de saint Jean 22:1. Fréjus : Prosveta, [2002]

Aïvanhov, Omraam Mikhaël. La foi qui transporte les montagnes. Fréjus : Prosveta, c1999.

Bernstein, Frances. Classical living. 1st ed. San Francisco : HarperSanFrancisco, 2000.
BL808 .B47 2000

Brossman, Sandra C. The power of oneness. Boston, MA : Red Wheel, 2003.
BF637.S4 B8 2003

Business, religion, & spirituality. Notre Dame, Ind. : University of Notre Dame Press, c2003.
HF5388 .B87 2003

Buxani, Shyam D. Salam. 1st ed. New York : SAU Salam Foundation, c2003.

Clarke, Robert B. The four gold keys. Charlottesville, VA : Hampton Roads Pub., c2002.
BF175.5.D74 C58 2002

Clow, Barbara Hand, 1943- Catastrophobia. Rochester, Vt. : Bear & Company, c2001.
BF1999 .C587 2001

Coyne, Tami. The spiritual chicks question everything. York Beach, ME : Red Wheel/Weiser, 2002.
BL625.7 .C69 2002

Cuin, Joao. A luz de um novo dia. Sao Paulo : DPL, c2001.

Curcio, Kimberly Panisset. Man of light. 1st ed. New York : SelectBooks, c2002.
BF1045.M44 C87 2002

Daniell, Beth, 1947- A communion of friendship. Carbondale : Southern Illinois University Press, c2003.
PE1405.U6 D36 2003

Del Moro, Franco. Il dubbio necessario. 1. ed. Murazzano (CN) : Ellin Selae, 2002.

Dobkin de Rios, Marlene. LSD, spirituality, and the creative process. Rochester, Vt. : Park Street Press, c2003.
BF209.L9 D57 2003

Dreller, Larry. Secrets of a medium. Boston, MA : Weiser Books, 2003.
BF1031 .D69 2003

Farcet, Gilles, 1959- Manuel de l'anti-sagesse. [Gordes] : Relié, c2002.

Glener, Doug. Wisdom's blossoms. Boston, Mass. : Shambhala, 2002.
BL2003 .G64 2002

Goldsmith, Joel S., 1892-1964. Spiritual discernment. Atlanta, Ga. : Acropolis Books, c2002.
BF639.G56886 2002

Goleman, Daniel. Destructive emotions. New York : Bantam Books, c2003.
BL65.E46 G65 2003

Grainger, Roger. Group spirituality. Hove, East Sussex ; New York : Brunner-Routledge, 2003.
BL628.4 .G73 2003

Grimassi, Raven, 1951- Spirit of the witch. 1st ed. St. Paul, Minn. : Llewellyn Publications, 2003.
BF1566 .G737 2003

Harvey, Andrew, 1952- A walk with four spiritual guides. Woodstock, VT : SkyLight Paths Pub., c2003.
BL624 .H3445 2003

Johnson, Deborah L., 1956- Letters from the Infinite. Aptos, CA : New Brighton Books, c2002-
BF1301 .J575 2002
1. Black author.

Kelly, Jill. Guardians of the Celtic way. Rochester, Vt. : Bear & Co., c2003.
BF1411 .K45 2003

Kelly, Kevin, 1966- Life. Ballintubber, Co. Roscommon : Inspiring Irish Publications, 2002.

Lattin, Don. Following our bliss. 1st ed. New York : HarperCollins, c2003.

Lowndes, Florin. [Belebung des Herzchakra. English] Enlivening the chakra of the heart. London : Sophia Books : Rudolf Steiner Press, c1998.
BF1442.C53 L6913 1998

Mallon, Brenda. A year of creativity. Kansas City, Mo. : Andrews McMeel Pub., c2003.
BF408 .M234 2003

Martinelli, Paolo, 1958- Vocazione e stati di vita del cristiano. Roma : Collegio San Lorenzo da Brindisi, 2001.

Moore, Thomas, 1940- Original self. 1st ed. New York : HarperCollins, c2000.
BL624 .M6643 2000

Ōkawa, Ryūhō, 1956- [Hito o aishi, hito o ikashi, hito o yuruse. English] Love, nurture, and forgive. New York : Lantern Books, c2002.
BP605.K55 O32413 2002

Ōkawa, Ryūhō, 1956- [Ōgon no hō. English] The golden laws. New York : Lantern Books, c2002.
BP605.K55 O33 2001

Osho, 1931-1990. Tantra, the supreme understanding. Delhi : Full Circle, 1999.
BP605.R34 T367 1999

Religious organizations in community services. New York : Springer Pub., 2003.
HV530 .R25 2003

Saraydarian, Torkom. Dynamics of the soul. Cave Creek, Ariz. : T.S.G. Pub., c2001.
BF1999 .S3352 2001

Slutskiĭ, O. I. (Oleg Isaakovich) Chto posle illiuzii? Moskva : Veche, 2002.
BV4509.R8 S58 2002

Smith, Huston. The way things are. Berkeley : University of California Press, c2003.
BL43.S64 A5 2003

Solodin, A. I. Strategiia ontologicheskoĭ igry. Sankt-Peterburg : Aleteĭia, 2002.

St. George, E. A. (Elizabeth Ann), 1937- Hathor, the cow goddess. London : Spook Enterprises, c2001.

Steiner, Rudolf, 1861-1925. Reverse ritual. Great Barrington, MA : Anthroposophic Press, c2001.

BP595.S894 R48 2001

Sylvan, Dianne, 1977- The circle within. 1st ed. St. Paul, MN : Llewellyn Publications, 2003.
BF1566 .S95 2003

Takahashi, Keiko, 1956- Kibō no genri = Tōkyō : Sanpō Shuppan, 1997.
BD216 .T35 1997

Telesco, Patricia, 1960- An enchanted life. Franklin Lakes, N.J. : New Page Books, c2002.
BF1621 .T42 2002

Toland, Diane. Inner pathways to the divine. Hygiene, CO : SunShine Press Publications, c2001.
BF1879.T2 .T65 2001

Vieira, Anselmo, 1923- Ser ou não ter. Lisboa : Roma Editora, [2002]-

Wood, Robert S. (Robert Snyder), 1930- Peaceful passing. Sedona, AZ : In Print Pub., c2000.
BF789.D4 W66 2000

SPIRITUAL LIFE - BUDDHISM.
Bstan-'dzin-rgya-mtsho, Dalai Lama XIV, 1935- Reflections from the journey of life. Berkeley, Calif. : North Atlantic Books, c2002.
BQ5670 .B76 2002

Encountering Buddhism. Albany : State University of New York Press, 2003.
BQ4570.P755 E62 2003

Nhất Hạnh, Thích. No death, no fear. New York : Riverhead Books, c2002.
BQ4302 .N43 2002

Smith, Jean, 1938- The beginner's guide to walking the Buddha's eightfold path. New York : Bell Tower, 2002.
BQ4320 .S65 2002

SPIRITUAL LIFE - GUIDEBOOKS.
Tubali, Shy. [Selections] Boker tov 'olam. Tel Aviv : Yedi'ot aharonot : Sifre hemed, c2003.

SPIRITUAL LIFE - HINDUISM.
Lāla, Mukuṭa Bihārī. [Sāṃyayogamīmāṃsā. Hindi & Sanskrit] Sāṃyayogamīmāṃsā. 1. saṃskaraṇa. Vārāṇasī : Śaivabhāratī Śodhapratiṣṭhānam, 2001.
BL1237.32+

Yoga. London ; New York : RoutledgeCurzon, 2003.
BL1238.52 .Y59 2003

SPIRITUAL LIFE - JUDAISM.
Chajes, Jeffrey Howard. Between worlds. Philadelphia : University of Pennsylvania Press, c2003.
BM729.D92 C53 2003

Chouchena, Emmanuel. L'homme, espoir de dieu. Paris : Trajectoire, 2001.

Eyal, Tsevi. Mi she-ta'am yayin Hungari. Tel Aviv : Yedi'ot aharonot : Sifre hemed, c2002.

Green, Arthur, 1941- Ehyeh. Woodstock, Vt. : Jewish Lights Publishing, c2003.
BM525 .G84 2003

Jarashow, Jonathan. The silent psalms of our son. Jerusalem, Israel : Feldheim Publishers, c2001.

Seidman, Richard. The oracle of Kabbalah. 1st ed. New York : St. Martin's Press, 2001.
PJ4589 .S42 2001

Tayir, Bracha Klein. ha-Manhig she-me'afsher le-elef perahim li-feroah. Tel Aviv : Yedi'ot aharonot : Sifre hemed, c2002.

Ziegler, Reuven. By his light. 2nd ed. Jersey City, NJ : KTAV Pub. House ; Alon Shevut, Israel : Yeshivat Har Etzion, 2003.
BM723 .Z54 2003

SPIRITUAL LIFE - MISCELLANEA.
Alexander, Jane. The smudging and blessings book. New York: Sterling Pub., 2001.
BF1999 .A6329 2001

Bongard, Jerry. The near birth experience. New York : Marlowe & Co. ; [Emeryville, CA?] : Distributed by Publishers Group West, c2000.
BF1156.R45 B66 2000

De Bergerac, Olivia. The dolphin within. East Roseville, NSW, Australia : Simon & Schuster, 1998.
BF1999 .D335 1998

Grabhorn, Lynn, 1931- Planet two. Charlottesville, VA : Hampton Roads Pub. Co., 2004.
BF1999 .G678 2004

Polich, Judith Bluestone, 1948- Return of the children of light. Santa Fe, N.M. : Linkage Publications, c1999.
BF1812.P4 P65 1999

Van Praagh, James. Looking beyond. New York : Simon & Schuster, c2003.
BF1272 .V36 2003

Voldeck, Joseph F., 1967- Immoral balance. Santa Fe, NM : Sunstone Press, 2003.
BF1999 .V63 2003

Walsch, Neale Donald. The new revelations. New York : Atria Books, c2002.
BF1999 .W2287 2002

Walsch, Neale Donald. Tomorrow's God. 1st ed. New York : Atria Books, 2004.
BF1999 .W2288 2004

Wills-Brandon, Carla, 1956- A glimpse of heaven. Avon, MA : Adams Media Corp., c2003.
BF1031 .W68 2003

SPIRITUAL LIFE - NEW AGE MOVEMENT.
McCulloch, Gillian. The deconstruction of dualism in theology. Carlisle : Paternoster Press, 2002.

Pinchbeck, Daniel. Breaking open the head. 1st ed. New York : Broadway Books, 2002.
BF1621 .P56 2002

SPIRITUAL LIFE - PROBLEMS, EXERCISES, ETC.
Linn, Denise. Soul coaching. Carlsbad, CA : Hay House, 2003.
BF637.S4 L565 2003

SPIRITUAL-MINDEDNESS. *See* **SPIRITUALITY.**

SPIRITUAL WARFARE. *See also* **DEMONOLOGY.**
Aransiola, Moses Olanrewaju. The roots and solutions to peculiar problems (dealing with bad luck, lost opportunities and failure). 1st ed.
1. Black author.

Koroma, Abu F. Exposing and destroying the dark satanic kingdom. [Freetown, Sierra Leone? : s.n.], c2000.
1. Black author.

Olorunfemi, Samuel Jimson. Breaking the evil blood covenant. Ibadan, Oyo State, Nigeria : Triumphant Faith Publications, 2001.
1. Black author.

SPIRITUALISM. *See also* **CHANNELING (SPIRITUALISM); GUIDES (SPIRITUALISM); LEVITATION; SPIRIT ART; WOMEN AND SPIRITUALISM.**
Aïvanhov, Omraam Mikhaël. "Et il me montra un fleuve d'eau de la vie"-- Apocalypse de saint Jean 22:1. Fréjus : Prosveta, [2002]

Anderson, Mary Beth, 1952- Good teachers carry on. St. Joseph, Mich. : Cosmic Concepts Press, c2003.
BF1261.2 .A45 2003

Braude, Stephen E., 1945- Immortal remains. Lanham, Md. : Oxford : Rowman & Littlefield, c2003.
BF1311.F8 B73 2003

Brooker, John L., 1923- If heaven is so wonderful-- why come here? Nevada City, CA : Blue Dolphin, 2004.
BF1261.2 .B76 2004

Brown, Robert, medium. We are eternal. New York : Warner Books, c2003.
BF1283.B717 A3 2003

Browne, Sylvia. Life on the other side. New York : Dutton, c2000.
BF1311.F8 B77 2000b

Buckland, Raymond. Buckland's book of spirit communications. 2nd ed., rev. and expanded. St. Paul, Minn. : Llewellyn, 2004.
BF1261.2 .B78 2004

Buckland, Raymond. Doors to other worlds. 1st ed. St. Paul, Minn. : Llewellyn, 2000.

Byrd, Da Juana. Ghosts talk. 1st ed. Cedar Hills, Tex. : Byrd Pub., c2002.
BF1031 .B97 2002

Cuevas Sosa, Andrés Alejandro, 1939- How do religious figures induce the establishment of sects? 2nd ed. Leicestershire : Upfront Pub., 2002.
BF1272 .C84 2002

Davis, Audrey Craft. Metaphysical techniques that really work. Nevada City, CA : Blue Dolphin Pub., 2004.

BF1411 .D38 2004

Dray, Maryvonne. Karine après la vie. Paris : Albin Michel, c2002.

Grant, Robert J. Universe of worlds. Virginia Beach, Va. : A.R.E. Press, 2005.
BF1261.2 .G73 2005

Greer, Jane, 1951- The afterlife connection. 1st ed. New York : St. Martin's Press, 2003.
BF1261.2 .G74 2003

Jordan, Kathie. The birth called death. 1st ed. Ashland, Or. : RiverWood Books, 2003.
BF1311.F8 B57 2003

Keller, Joyce (Joyce E.) Seven steps to heaven. New York : Simon & Schuster, 2003.
BF1261.2 .K45 2003

Konstantinos, 1972- Contact the other side. 1st ed. St. Paul, Minn. : Llewellyn Publications, 2001.
BF1275.D2 K66 2001

Magic and modernity. Stanford, Calif. : Stanford University Press, 2003.
GN475.3 .M34 2003

Mathews, Patrick, 1962- Never say goodbye. 1st ed. St. Paul, Minn. : Llewellyn Publications, 2003.
BF1283.M27 A3 2003

My proof of survival. 1st ed. St. Paul, Minn. : Llewellyn Publications, 2003.
BF1311.F8 M9 2003

Nwokogba, Isaac, 1957- Voices from beyond. Cranston, R.I. : Writers' Collective, 2003.
BF1261.2 .N96 2003

Obley, Carole J. Embracing the ties that bind. [Philadelphia] : Xlibris, c2003.
BF1275.S44 O25 2003

Occhino, MaryRose. Beyond these four walls. New York : Berkley Books, 2003.
BF1283.O27 A3 2003

Sant Baba Ishar Singh Ji. Hardwar : Nanak-Dar Sant Baba Nand Singh Sant Baba Ishar Singh Spiritual Mission, 2002.
BL2017.9.I84 S27 2002

Saraydarian, Torkom. Aura. Cave Creek, Ariz. : T.S.G. Pub. Foundation, 1999.
BF1389.A8 S35 1999

Scott, Christopher, 1946- Beyond death. Nevada City, CA : Blue Dolphin Pub., 2001.
BF1261 .S45 2001

Shine, Betty, 1929- A free spirit. London : HarperCollinsPublishers, 2001.

Silva, W. W. da Matta e (Woodrow Wilson da Matta e), 1917- Mistérios e práticas da lei de Umbanda. Sao Paulo : Icone Editora, c1999.

Van Praagh, James. Looking beyond. New York : Simon & Schuster, c2003.
BF1272 .V36 2003

Van Praagh, James. Meditations. New York : Simon & Schuster, 2003.
BF1272 .V355 2003

Vinokurov, Igor' Charodei ponevole. Moskva : AiF-Print, 2003.
BF1288 .V55 2003

SPIRITUALISM AND WOMEN. *See* **WOMEN AND SPIRITUALISM.**

SPIRITUALISM - BURMA.
'Arindamā, Cha rā krī". Pugguil' thū' myā" nhaṅ'' gambhīra lam''' mha phyac' rap' chan''' myā". Ran' kun' : Cin' Pan''' Mruiṅ' Cā pe : [Phran'' khyi re''], Cui' Cā pe, 2002-
BF1281 .A756 2002

SPIRITUALISM (CHANNELING).
Matheson, Richard. Mediums rare. 1st ed. Baltimore, Md. : Cemetery Dance Publications, 2000.

SPIRITUALISM - COMPARATIVE STUDIES.
Dermine, François-Marie, 1949- Mistici, veggenti e medium. Città del Vaticano : Libreria editrice vaticana, c2002.

SPIRITUALISM (PHILOSOPHY).
Medhananda, 1908-1994. [Au fil de l'eternité avec Medhananda. English. Selections] On the threshold of a new age with Medhananda. 1st ed. Pondicherry : Sri Mira Trust, 2000.
B841 .M4313 2000

SPIRITUALISM - UNITED STATES - HISTORY - 19TH CENTURY.
Cox, Robert S., 1958- Body and soul. Charlottesville : University of Virginia Press, 2003.
BF1242.U6 C69 2003

SPIRITUALISTS. *See* **MEDIUMS.**

SPIRITUALISTS - BURMA - BIOGRAPHY.
'Arindamā, Cha rā krī". Pugguil' thū" myā" nhaṅ'' gambhīra lam''' mha phyac' rap' chan''' myā". Ran' kun' : Cin' Pan''' Mruiṅ' Cā pe : [Phran'' khyi re"], Cui" Cā pe, 2002-
BF1281 .A756 2002

SPIRITUALISTS - UNITED STATES - BIOGRAPHY.
Ezell, Jessica. Reunion. Walpole, NH : Stillpoint Pub., c1996.
BF1283.E94 A3 1996

SPIRITUALITY. *See also* **SPIRITUAL LIFE.**
Boff, Leonardo. Espiritualidade. 2a ed. Rio de Janeiro : Sextante, c2001.

Farcet, Gilles, 1959- Manuel de l'anti-sagesse. [Gordes] : Relié, c2002.

Farrer, Frances, 1950- Sir George Trevelyan and the new spiritual awakening. Edinburgh : Floris, 2002.

Fernandes, Leela. Transforming feminist practice. 1st ed. San Francisco : Aunt Lute Books, 2003.
HQ1154 .F495 2003

Frame, Marsha Wiggins. Integrating religion and spirituality into counseling. Australia ; Pacific Grove, CA : Thomson/Brooks/Cole, c2003.
BF637.C6 F64 2003

Jannoud, Claude. La crise de l'esprit. Lausanne, Suisse : Age d'homme, c2001.

Jironet, Karin. The image of spiritual liberty in the western Sufi movement following Hazrat Inayat Khan. Leuven : Peeters, 2002.
BP189.2 .J57 2002

King, Ursula. Mysticism and contemporary society. [Lewisburg, Pa.] : American Teilhard Association, c2002.
B2430.T374 A18 no.44

Savchyn, Myroslav, 1950- Dukhovnyĭ potent͡sial li͡udyny. Ivano-Frankivs'k : Plaĭ, 2001.
BF698 .S288 2001

Spirituality, philosophy and education. London ; New York : RoutledgeFalmer, 2003.
BV4501.3 .S65 2003

Webster, Alison R. Wellbeing. London : SCM, c2002.

Spirituality and the occult.
Gibbons, B. J. London ; New York : Routledge, 2001.
BF1434.E85 G53 2001

SPIRITUALITY - HISTORY - 20TH CENTURY.
Galovic, Jelena. Los grupos místico-espirituales de la actualidad. México : Plaza y Valdés, 2002.
BL625 .G346 2002

SPIRITUALITY - MEDITERRANEAN REGION.
Ángeles, demonios y genios en el mundo Mediterráneo. Madrid : Ediciones Clásicas, 2000.

SPIRITUALITY - MISCELLANEA.
Miller, D. Patrick, 1953- News of a new human nature. 1st ed. Berkeley, Calif. : Fearless Books, 2002.
BF637.S4 M547 2002

Spirituality, philosophy and education / edited by David Carr and John Haldane. London ; New York : RoutledgeFalmer, 2003. ix, 229 p. ; 24 cm. Includes bibliographical references and index. ISBN 0-415-29669-2 DDC 370.114
1. Spirituality. 2. Religious education - Philosophy. I. Carr, David, 1944- II. Haldane, John.
BV4501.3 .S65 2003

SPIRITUALITY - PSYCHOLOGY.
Anderson, Walt, 1933- The next enlightenment. 1st ed. New York : St. Martin's Press, 2003.
BL476 .A53 2003

Fontana, David. Psychology, religion, and spirituality. Malden, MA : BPS Blackwell, 2003.
BL53 .F57 2003

Sorenson, Randall Lehmann, 1954- Minding spirituality. Hillsdale, NJ : Analytic Press, 2003.
BF175.4.R44 S67 2003

Spiritul civic.
Sporiș, Mihai, 1951- Râmnicu Vâlcea : Editura Adrianso, 1999-

Spiro business guides. Business skills
Clark, John, 1946- Stress. London ; Rollinsford, NH : Spiro Press, 2002.

Spitzenkandidaten und Wahlerfolg.
Brettschneider, Frank. 1. Aufl. Wiesbaden : Westdeutscher Verlag, 2002.

Spivak, M. L. Posmertnai͡a diagnostika genial'nosti : Ėduard Bagritskiĭ, Andreĭ Belyĭ, Vladimir Mai͡akovskiĭ v kollekt͡sii Instituta mozga : materialy iz arkhiva G.I. Poli͡akova / Monika Spivak. Moskva : Agraf, 2001. 493 p. : ill. ; 21 cm. (XX vek pli͡us) Includes bibliographical references. ISBN 5778401108
1. Bagritskiĭ, Ėduard, - 1895-1934. 2. Bely, Andrey, - 1880-1934. 3. Mayakovsky, Vladimir, - 1893-1930. 4. Gifted persons - Soviet Union - Biography. 5. Genius - Soviet Union - Case studies. 6. Gosudarstvennyĭ refleksologicheskiĭ institut po izuchenii͡u mozga (Russia) I. Poli͡akov, G. I. (Grigoriĭ Izrailevich) II. Title. III. Series.
BF416.A1 S68 2001

The Splendors of archaeology / [edited by Fabio Bourbon]. Cairo : American University in Cairo Press, 1998. 352 p. : ill. (chiefly col.) ; 37 cm. "Texts : Maria Ausilia Albanese [et al.]; editors: Fabio Bourbon, Valeria Manferto De Fabianis" "This edition published by arrangement with White Star S.r.l., Vercelli, Italy" Includes bibliographical references (p. 350-351) ISBN 977-424-493-1
1. Archaeology. I. Albanese, Maria Ausilia. II. Bourbon, Fabio. III. Manferto, Valeria.

Spoerri, Hubert M. Mensch und Kunst : kunstphilosophische Anthropologie / Hubert M. Spoerri. München : Scaneg, c2002. 503 p. ; 21 cm. (Punctum ; 16) Includes bibliographical references and index. ISBN 3-89235-116-3 (pbk.).
1. Philosophical anthropology. 2. Knowledge, Theory of. 3. Art - Philosophy. 4. Art - Social aspects. 5. Art - Psychology. I. Title. II. Series.

Spoglio dell'occidente
(17.) Sini, Carlo, 1933- La scrittura e il debito. Milano : Jaca book, 2002.

Spoglio dell'occidente. Saggi.
Sini, Carlo, 1933- La scrittura e il debito. Milano : Jaca book, 2002.

SPOKEN ENGLISH. *See* **ENGLISH LANGUAGE - SPOKEN ENGLISH.**

SPONTANEOUS DEMATERIALIZATION (PARAPSYCHOLOGY). *See* DISAPPEARANCES (PARAPSYCHOLOGY).

The spontaneous fulfillment of desire.
Chopra, Deepak. 1st ed. New York : Harmony Books, c2003.
BF1175 .C48 2003

Chopra, Deepak. New York : Random House Large Print, 2003.
BF1175 .C48 2003b

Sporiș, Mihai, 1951- Spiritul civic : stare de fapt și deziderat / Mihai Sporiș, Nicolae Sporiș. Râmnicu Vâlcea : Editura Adrianso, 1999- v. ; 21 cm. ISBN 9739914713 (v. 1) ISBN 9739914772 (v. 2)
1. Philosophy. I. Sporiș, Nicolae, 1932- II. Title.

Sporiș, Nicolae, 1932-.
Sporiș, Mihai, 1951- Spiritul civic. Râmnicu Vâlcea : Editura Adrianso, 1999-

SPORT FISHING. *See* **FISHING.**

SPORTS. *See* **GAMES.**

SPORTS FACILITIES. *See* **PLAYGROUNDS.**

SPORTS FOR CHILDREN.
Humphrey, James Harry, 1911- Child development through sports. Binghamton, N.Y. ; London : Haworth Press, c2003.
GV709.2 .H845 2003

SPORTS PERSONNEL. *See* **BASEBALL MANAGERS.**

SPORTS - PSYCHOLOGICAL ASPECTS.
Reichholf, Josef. Warum wir siegen wollen. München : Deutscher Taschenbuch, c2001.

Sposobnosti cheloveka.
Shadrikov, V. D. (Vladimir Dmitrievich) Moskva : In-t prakticheskoĭ psikhologii ; Voronezh : NPO "MODĖK", 1997.
BF431 .S46512 1997

Spotts, Dane. Super brain power : 28 minutes to a supercharged brain / Dane Spotts with Nancy Atkins. Seattle, Wash. : LifeQuest Pub. Group, c1998. 234 p. : ill. ; 23 cm. + 1 computer laser optical disc (4 3/4 in.). Includes bibliographical references (p. 231-234). ISBN 1-89280-500-6 DDC 153.4
1. Thought and thinking. 2. Altered states of consciousness. 3. Meditation. I. Atkins, Nancy. II. Title.
BF441 .S68 1998

SPOUSES. *See* **HUSBANDS; MARRIED PEOPLE.**

SPOUSES - DEATH - PSYCHOLOGICAL ASPECTS.
Isaacs, Diane R. Molly & Monet. Seattle, WA : Peanut Butter Pub., c1999.
BF575.G7 I86 1999

Die Sprache des Denkens.
Schröder, Jürgen. Würzburg : Königshausen & Neumann, c2001.

Sprache, Literatur und Geschichte
(Bd. 23) Roelcke, Thorsten. Kommunikative Effizienz. Heidelberg : Winter, c2002.

Sprache, Sinn und Situation : Festschrift für Gert Rickheit zum 60. Geburtstag / Lorenz Sichelschmidt, Hans Strohner (Hrsg.). 1. Aufl. Wiesbaden : Deutscher Universitäts-Verlag, 2001. 288 p. : ill. ; 21 cm. "DUV Sprachwissenschaft"--P. facing t.p. Includes bibliographical references. ISBN 3-8244-4448-8 (pbk.)
1. Speech acts (Linguistics) 2. Speech - Physiological aspects. 3. Psycholinguistics. I. Sichelschmidt, Lorenz. II. Strohner, Hans. III. Rickheit, Gert.

Spriggles.
Gottlieb, Jeff, 1954- Petoskey, Mich. : Mountain Watch Press, c2002.
BF723.M56 G68 2002

Spring, Janis Abrahms. How can I forgive you? : the courage to forgive, the freedom not to / Janis Abrahms Spring. 1st ed. New York : HarperCollins, 2004. p. cm. Includes bibliographical references and index. ISBN 0-06-000930-6 (alk paper) DDC 179/.9
1. Forgiveness. I. Title.
BF637.F67 S67 2004

Springer series in statistics
Santner, Thomas J., 1947- The design and analysis of computer experiments. New York : Springer, 2003.
QA279 .S235 2003

Spritual capital and the business of magic in modern Puerto Rico.
Romberg, Raquel. Witchcraft and welfare. 1st ed. Austin : University of Texas Press, c2003.
BF1584.P9 R66 2003

Sprott, Eric.
Beyond knowledge. Mahwah, N.J. : L. Erlbaum Associates, 2003.
BF412 .B44 2003

Sprott, Julien C. Chaos and time-series analysis / Julien Clinton Sprott. Oxford ; New York : Oxford University Press, 2003. xx, 507 p. : ill. ; 24 cm. Includes bibliographical references and index. ISBN 0-19-850839-5 ISBN 0-19-850840-9 (pbk.) DDC 003.857
1. Chaotic behavior in systems. 2. Time-series analysis. I. Title.

Spruch und Zahl.
Schilling, Dennis R. Aalen : Scientia, 1998.
BF1770.C5 S42 1998

Spruill, Connie.
Watson, Sylvia. Feng shui with what you have. Avon, MA : Adams Media, c2004.
BF1779.F4 W37 2004

Sprunger, David A.
Marvels, monsters, and miracles. Kalamazoo, Mich. : Medieval Institute Publications, 2002.
GR825 .M218 2002

SPSS (COMPUTER FILE).
SPSS explained. London ; New York : Routledge, 2004.
BF39 .S68 2004

SPSS explained / by Perry R. Hinton ... [et al.]. London ; New York : Routledge, 2004. p. cm. Includes bibliographical references. CONTENTS: Introduction -- Data entry -- Descriptive statistics -- Illustrative statistics -- Working with your dataset -- Introduction to statistical tests -- T tests -- Nonparametric two sample tests -- Introduction to analysis of variance (general linear model) -- One factor analysis of variance (ANOVA) -- Two factor analysis of variance (ANOVA) -- Introduction to multivariate analysis of variance (MANOVA) -- One factor anova for nonparametric data -- Crosstabulation and chi square -- Linear correlation and regression -- Introduction to multiple regression and multiple correlation -- Introduction to factor analysis -- Using SPSS to analyze questionnaires : reliability. ISBN 0-415-27409-5 (hbk) ISBN 0-415-27410-9 (pbk.) DDC 300/.285/536
1. SPSS (Computer file) 2. Psychology - Statistical methods - Computer programs. I. Hinton, Perry R. (Perry Roy), 1954-
BF39 .S68 2004

SPSS for psychologists.
Brace, Nicola. 2nd ed. Mahwah, NJ : Lawrence Erlbaum Associates, 2003.
BF39 .K447 2003

Spy, Terri.
Forgiveness and the healing process. Hove, East Sussex ; New York : Brunner-Routledge, c2003.
BF637.F67 F66 2003

SQL SERVER.
Shea, Linchi. Real world SQL server administration with Perl. [Berkeley, CA] : Apress ; New York : Distributed to the book trade in the U.S. by Springer-Verlag, c2003.
QA76.73.S67 S48 2003

SQL server administration with Perl.
Shea, Linchi. Real world SQL server administration with Perl. [Berkeley, CA] : Apress ; New York : Distributed to the book trade in the U.S. by Springer-Verlag, c2003.
QA76.73.S67 S48 2003

Squire, Charles. Celtic myth and legend : from Arthur and the round table to the Gaelic gods and the giants they battled-- the celebrated comprehensive treasury of Celtic mythology, legend, and poetry / Charles Squire ; introduction by Sirona Knight ; with illustrations after paintings by J.H.F. Bacon and other artists. Rev. ed. Franklin Lakes, NJ : New Page Books, c2001. xii, 450 p. : ill. ; 21 cm. Includes bibliographical references and index. ISBN 1-56414-534-4 DDC 299/.16
1. Mythology, Celtic. 2. Celts - Folklore. 3. Legends - Great Britain. 4. Legends - Ireland. I. Title.
BL900 .S6 2001

SQUIRES. See **GENTRY.**

Sreshti s Vangĭa.
Georgiev, Liuben, 1933- Sofii͡a : Knigo-TSvi͡at, 1996.
BF1283.V33 G46 1996

SRI LANKAN LITERATURE. See **TAMIL LITERATURE.**

Śrī Muhūrtarāja.
Gulābavijaya. Dvitīyāvrtti. Ji. Dhāra, Ma. Pra. : Rājendra Pravacana Kāryālaya, 1996.
BF1714.J28+

Śrī Vaidikasārvabhaumairviracitā Daśanirṇayī.
Veṅkaṭanāthārya. [Daśanirṇayī] Vaidikasārvabhaumanāmnā suprasiddhaih Veṅkaṭanāthāryaih Vaidikakarmānuṣṭhānasaukaryāya viracitā Daśanirṇayī. 1st ed. Mumbai : Śrīmadahobilamathena, 1998.
BL1226.72 .V36 1998

Śrīmadbhāgavata meṃ Sāṅkhyayoga ke tattva.
Karṇāṭaka, Vimalā. 1. saṃskaraṇa. Vārāṇasī : Sampūrṇānanda Saṃskrta Viśvavidyālaya, 2001.
BL1140.4.B437 K27 2001

Śrīmadbhāgavata meṅ Sāṅkhya-Yoga ke tattva.
Karṇāṭaka, Vimalā. Śrīmadbhāgavata meṃ Sāṅkhyayoga ke tattva. 1. saṃskaraṇa. Vārāṇasī : Sampūrṇānanda Saṃskrta Viśvavidyālaya, 2001.
BL1140.4.B437 K27 2001

Sriram, Chandra Lekha, 1971-.
From promise to practice. Boulder ; London : L. Rienner Publishers, 2003.
JZ6368 .S68 2003

Śṛṅgāra sarasī of Bhāva Miśra.
Bhāvamiśra, 19th cent. [Śṛṅgārasarasī. Hindi & Sanskrit] Śṛṅgārasarasī. Saṃskaraṇa 1. Vrndāvana : Vrndāvana Śodha Saṃsthāna, 2001.
PK2916+

Śṛṅgārasarasī.
Bhāvamiśra, 19th cent. [Śṛṅgārasarasī. Hindi & Sanskrit] Saṃskaraṇa 1. Vrndāvana : Vrndāvana Śodha Saṃsthāna, 2001.
PK2916+

Srpska književna zadruga (Series)
(kolo 93, knj. 617.) Jerotić, Vladeta. [Selections 2000] Izabrani ogledi. Beograd: Srpska književna zadruga, 2000.
BF109.J47 A25 2000

Srubar, Ilja.
Schutz, Alfred, 1899-1959. Werkausgabe. Konstanz : UVK, Verlagsgesellschaft, 2003-
BD431 .S284916 2003

St. Clair, Michael, 1940- Object relations and self psychology : an introduction / Michael St. Clair, with Jodie Wigren. 4th ed. Australia ; Belmont, CA : Thomson/Brooks/Cole, c2004. xv, 217 p. : ill. ; 24 cm. Includes bibliographical references (p. 199-205) and index. ISBN 0-534-53293-4
1. Object relations (Psychoanalysis) 2. Self psychology. 3. Personality disorders. I. Title.
BF175.5.O24 S7 2004

St. George, E. A. (Elizabeth Ann), 1937- Hathor, the cow goddess / by E.A. St. George. London : Spook Enterprises, c2001. 21 p. : 22 cm. DDC 299.31
1. Hathor (Egyptian deity) 2. Spiritual life. 3. Egypt - Religious life and customs. I. Title.

St. George's Hall.
Davenport, Anne Ashley. Pasadena : Mike Caveney's Magic Words, c2001.
BF1623 .D38 2001

ST. GEORGE'S HALL (LONDON, ENGLAND) - HISTORY.
Davenport, Anne Ashley. St. George's Hall. Pasadena : Mike Caveney's Magic Words, c2001.
BF1623 .D38 2001

Sta. Maria, Madelene A.
Forty years of Philippine psychology. Diliman, Quezon City, Philippines : Psychological Association of the Philippines, c2002.
BF108 .F67 2002

Stachel, Peter.
Die Verortung von Gedächtnis. Wien : Passagen, c2001.

Les stades du développement affectif selon Piaget.
Xypas, Constantin. Paris : Harmattan, c2001.

Stafford, Kim Robert. The muses among us : eloquent listening and other pleasures of the writer's craft / Kim Stafford. Athens : University of Georgia Press, c2003. xi, 138 p. ; 23 cm. ISBN 0-8203-2324-1 (hbk. : alk. paper) ISBN 0-8203-2496-5 (pbk. : alk. paper) DDC 808/.042
1. English language - Rhetoric. 2. Creative writing. 3. Report writing. 4. Authorship. I. Title.
PE1408 .S6667 2003

STAGE. See **DRAMA; THEATER.**

STAGE COSTUME. See **COSTUME.**

STAGE FRIGHT.
Mensch & Musik. Augsburg : Wissner, c2002.
ML3830 .M46 2002

Stage presence from head to toe.
Hagberg, Karen A., 1943- Lanham, Md. : Scarecrow Press, 2003.
ML3795 .H13 2003

Staging masculinities.
Mangan, Michael, 1953- Houndmills, Basingstoke, Hampshire ; New York : Palgrave Macmillan, 2003.
PN1650.M44 M36 2003

Stainton Rogers, Rex.
Stainton Rogers, Wendy. The psychology of gender and sexuality. Philadelphia : Open University Press, 2001.
BF692 .S72 2001

Stainton Rogers, Wendy. The psychology of gender and sexuality : an introduction / Wendy Stainton Rogers and Rex Stainton Rogers. Philadelphia : Open University Press, 2001. xii, 305 p. ; 24 cm. Includes bibliographical references (p. [273]-294) and index. ISBN 0-335-20224-1 (pbk.) ISBN 0-335-20225-X DDC 155.3
1. Sex (Psychology) 2. Sex. 3. Sex differences (Psychology) I. Stainton Rogers, Rex. II. Title.
BF692 .S72 2001

Stalcup, Brenda.
The 1000s. San Diego, Calif. : Greenhaven Press, c2001.
CB354.3 .A16 2001

Stalfelt, Pernilla.
[Döden boken. English]
The death book / Pernilla Stalfelt ; [translation by Maria Lundin]. Toronto, Ont. : Groundwood Books / Douglas & McIntyrenfrom ; Berkeley, CA : Distributed by Publishers Group West, c2002.
1 v. (unpaged) : col. ill. ; 24 cm. ISBN 0-88899-482-6
1. Children and death - Juvenile literature. 2. Death - Psychological aspects - Juvenile literature. I. Title.
BF723.D3 S7313 2002

Stalnaker, Robert. Ways a world might be : metaphysical and anti-metaphysical essays / Robert C. Stalnaker. Oxford : Clarendon ; New York : Oxford University Press, 2003. ix, 287 p. : 25 cm. Includes bibliographical references (p. [277]-281) and index. ISBN 0-19-925148-7 ISBN 0-19-925149-5 (PBK.) DDC 110
1. Metaphysics. 2. Possibility. 3. Supervenience (Philosophy) I. Title.
BD111 .S73 2003

Standard English and the politics of language.
Crowley, Tony. 2nd ed. New York : Palgrave Macmillan, c2003.
P368 .C76 2003

STANDARD LANGUAGE.
Crowley, Tony. Standard English and the politics of language. 2nd ed. New York : Palgrave Macmillan, c2003.
P368 .C76 2003

STANDARD OF VALUE. See **MONEY.**

STANDARDIZATION. See **QUALITY CONTROL.**

Standing on my head.
Prather, Hugh. Boston, MA : Conari Press, 2004.
BF637.C5 P82 2004

Stanford University. Computer Science Dept.
Washington, Richard. Abstraction planning in real time [microform]. Stanford, Calif. : Stanford University, Dept. of Computer Science, [1994] (Springfield, Va. : U.S. Dept. of Commerce, National Technical Information Service).

Stange, Mary Zeiss. Woman the hunter / Mary Zeiss Stange. Boston : Beacon Press, c1997. xi, 247 p. ; 24 cm. Includes bibliographical references (p. 231-242) and index. ISBN 0-8070-4638-8 DDC 306.3/64
1. Hunting - Philosophy. 2. Hunting - Moral and ethical aspects. 3. Women hunters. 4. Feminism. I. Title.
SK14 .S88 1997

Stangl, Wolfgang, 1949-.
Das äussere und innere Ausland. Wien : WUV, Universitätsverlag, c2000.
BF335 .A9 2000

STANISLAVSKY, KONSTANTIN, 1863-1938.
Tait, Peta, 1953- Performing emotions. Aldershot ; Burlington VT. : Ashgate, c2002.
PG3458.Z9 D774 2002

Stanislaw-Kemenah, Alexandra.
Komik der Renaissance, Renaissance der Komik. Frankfurt am Main ; New York : P. Lang, c2000.
BH301.C7 .K63 2000

Stanko, Elizabeth Anne, 1950-.
The meanings of violence. London ; New York : Routledge, 2003.
HM1116 .M436 2003

Stanley Collins.
Dawes, Edwin A. Washington, DC : Kaufman and Co., c2002.

Stanovich, Keith E., 1950- How to think straight about psychology / Keith E. Stanovich. 7th ed. Boston, MA : Allyn and Bacon, 2004. p. cm. Includes bibliographical references and index. ISBN 0-205-36093-9 (alk. paper) DDC 150/.7/2
1. Psychology - Research - Methodology. 2. Mass media - Psychological aspects. 3. Mass media - Objectivity. I. Title.
BF76.5 .S68 2004

Stanovlenie religioznogo kompleksa.
Romanova, A. P. (Anna Petrovna) Astrakhan : Izd-vo Astrakhanskogo pedagog. universiteta, 1999.
BF51 .R66 1999

Stansfield, Charles A.
Martinelli, Patricia A. Haunted New Jersey. Mechanicsburg, PA : Stackpole Books, 2005.
BF1472.U6 M38 2004

Star gazer.
Shaw, Maria, 1963- Maria Shaw's star gazer. 1st ed. St. Paul, Minn. : Llewellyn Publications, 2003.
BF1411 .S52 2003

Star guide to predictive astrology.
Parsai, K. B. [Predictive astrology] New Delhi : Rupa & Co., c2001.
BF1720.5 .P37 2001

Star power.
MacGregor, Rob. Franklin Lakes, NJ : New Page Books, c2003.
BF1571.5.T44 M23 2003

Starite khora.
Aleksandrova, Natalii͡a. 1. izd. Sofii͡a : Universitetsko izd-vo "Sv. Kliment Okhridski", 2001.
BF724.8 .A42 2001

Stark, Heinz. Plecher Kirchengeschichte im Mittelalter : zur kirchlichen Entwicklung im Nürnberger Umland / Heinz Stark. Simmelsdorf : Altnürnberger Landschaft, 2002. 52 p. : ill. ; 24 cm. (Mitteilungen. Sonderheft / Altnürnberger Landschaft ; 2002 (lfd. Nr. 49)) Includes bibliographical references. ISBN 3-927412-19-8
1. Catholic Church - Germany - Plech - History - To 1500. 2. Catholic Church - Germany - Nuremberg - History - To 1500. 3. Plech (Germany) - Church history - To 1500. 4. Nuremberg

Stark, Peter B.
Everyone negotiates.
Stark, Peter B. The only negotiating guide you'll ever need. 1st ed. New York : Broadway Books, 2003.
BF637.N4 S725 2003

Flaherty, Jane S. Lifetime leadership. San Diego : Bentley Press, c2001.
BF637.L4 F57 2001

The only negotiating guide you'll ever need : 101 ways to win every time in any situation / Peter B. Stark, Jane Flaherty. 1st ed. New York : Broadway Books, 2003. xiv, 223 p. ; 21 cm. Rev. ed. of: Everyone negotiates. 2002. Includes bibliographical references (p. 213) and index. ISBN 0-7679-1524-0 DDC 302.3
1. Negotiation. I. Flaherty, Jane S. II. Stark, Peter B. Everyone negotiates. III. Title.
BF637.N4 S725 2003

Stark, Rodney. For the glory of God : how monotheism led to reformations, science, witch-hunts, and the end of slavery / Rodney Stark. Princeton, N.J. : Princeton University Press, c2003. x, 488 p. : ill. ; 24 cm. Includes bibliographical references (p. 377-464) and index. Publisher description URL: http://www.loc.gov/catdir/desc ription/prin031/2002031746.html ISBN 0-691-11436-6 (alk. paper) DDC 291.1/4
1. Monotheism - History. 2. Reformation. 3. Religion and science - History. 4. Witchcraft - History. 5. Slavery - Religious aspects - History. I. Title.
BL221 .S747 2003

Starobinski, Jean. La relation critique / Jean Starobinski. Ed. rev. et augm. [Paris] : Gallimard, c2001. 408 p. ; 19 cm. (Collection Tel) (L'œil vivant ; 2) Includes bibliographical references (p. [404]-405). ISBN 2-07-076129-0 (pbk.).
1. Criticism. 2. Imagination. 3. Psychoanalysis and literature. I. Title. II. Series. III. Series: Starobinski, Jean. Œil vivant ; 2.
PN81 .S69 2001

Œil vivant
(2.) Starobinski, Jean. La relation critique. Ed. rev. et augm. [Paris] : Gallimard, c2001.
PN81 .S69 2001

Starr, Martin P., 1959- The unknown God : W.T. Smith and the Thelemites / Martin P. Starr. Bolingbrook, IL: Teitan Press, 2003. p. cm. Includes bibliographical references (p.   ) and index. ISBN 0-933429-07-X (alk. paper) DDC 130/.92
1. Smith, Wilfred Talbot, - 1885-1957. 2. Ordo Templi Orientis. 3. Occultism - United States. I. Title.
BF1997.S73 2003

STARS (IN RELIGION, FOLK-LORE, ETC.). See STARS - RELIGIOUS ASPECTS.

STARS - RELIGIOUS ASPECTS - HISTORY - CONGRESSES.
Prayer, magic, and the stars in the ancient and late antique world. University Park, Pa. : Pennsylvania State University Press, 2003.
BF1591 .P73 2003

Start something.
Woods, Earl, 1932- New York : Simon & Schuster, c2000.
BJ1631 .W726 2000

Starting out in the afternoon.
Frayne, Jill. Toronto : Random House Canada, c2002.

A starving madness.
Rabinor, Judith Ruskay, 1942- Carlsbad, CA : Gurze Books, c2002.
RC552.E18 R33 2001

Starwoman, Athena. Zodiac : Athena's sunsigns / [Athena Starwoman]. New York : Friedman/Fairfax : Distributed by Sterling Pub., c2000. 480 p. ; 24 cm. Publisher description URL: http://www.loc.gov/catdir/description/ste031/2003544938.html ISBN 1-58663-738-X
1. Astrology. I. Title. II. Title: Athena's sunsigns III. Title: Athena's sun signs
BF1708.1 .S695 2000

Staschen, Heidi. Hexen / Heidi Staschen, Thomas Hauschild. Originalausg. Krummwisch [Germany] : Königsfurt, 2001. 143 p. : ill., facsims. ; 23 cm. Includes bibliographical references (p. 140-143). ISBN 3-89875-001-5 (pbk.)
1. Witches - History. 2. Witchcraft - History. I. Hauschild, Thomas. II. Title.

Stasney, Sharon. Feng Shui living / Sharon Stasney. New York : Sterling Pub., c2003. p. cm. Publisher description URL: http://www.loc.gov/catdir/description/ste031/2003008827.html ISBN 1402703473 DDC 133.3/337
1. Feng shui. I. Title.
BF1779.F4 S792 2003

Feng shui your work spaces / Sharon Stasney. New York, NY : Sterling Pub. Co., c2004. p. cm. "A Sterling/Chapelle book." Includes index. ISBN 140270402X DDC 133.3/337
1. Feng shui. I. Title.
BF1779.F4 S796 2004

STATE AND ARCHITECTURE. See ARCHITECTURE AND STATE.

STATE AND FAMILY. See FAMILY POLICY.

STATE AND LANGUAGE. See LANGUAGE POLICY.

STATE AND MEDICINE. See MEDICAL POLICY.

STATE AND MUSIC. See MUSIC AND STATE.

STATE AND RELIGION. See RELIGION AND STATE.

STATE MEDICINE - GREAT BRITAIN.
Hadikin, Ruth. The bullying culture. Oxford ; Boston : Books for Midwives, 2000.
BF637.B85 H33 2000

STATE SUCCESSION. See SOVEREIGNTY.

STATE, THE. See also POLITICAL SCIENCE; RELIGION AND STATE.
Archard, David. Children, family, and the state. Aldershot, Hants, England ; Burlington, VT : Ashgate, 2003.
HQ789 .A695 2003

Brush, Lisa Diane. Gender and governance. Walnut Creek, CA ; Oxford : AltaMira Press, c2003.
JC330 .B75 2003

Foucault, cultural studies, and governmentality. Albany : State University of New York Press, c2003.
JC330 .F63 2003

Friedman, Milton, 1912- Capitalism and freedom. 40th anniversary ed. Chicago : University of Chicago Press, 2002.
HB501 .F7 2002

Pufendorf, Samuel, Freiherr von, 1632-1694. [De officio hominis et civis. English] The whole duty of man, according to the law of nature. Indianapolis, Ind. : Liberty Fund, c2003.
K457.P8 D4313 2003

STATE, THE - HISTORY OF THEORIES. See POLITICAL SCIENCE - HISTORY.

STATELESSNESS.
Migration, diasporas, and transnationalism. Cheltenham, UK ; Northampton, MA : Edward Elgar, 1999.
JV6032 .M54 1999

Stately bodies.
Cavarero, Adriana. [Corpo in figure. English] Ann Arbor : University of Michigan Press, c2002.
B105.B64 C3813 2002

STATES, IDEAL. See UTOPIAS.

STATESMEN. See LEGISLATORS.

STATESMEN - CHINA.
Shi, Sheng. Fan Zhongyan li shen xing shi jiu jiu fang lüe. Di 1 ban. Beijing : Zhongguo xi ju chu ban she, 2001.
DS751.6.F3 S5 2001

STATESMEN - CHINA - BIOGRAPHY.
Sima, Lieren. Tong jing. Di 1 ban. Beijing : Zhongguo hua qiao chu ban she, 2002.
DS758.23.T74 S575 2002

STATESMEN - ROME - BIOGRAPHY.
Radford, Robert T. Cicero. Amsterdam ; New York, NY : Rodopi, 2002.
DG260.C5 R33 2002

STATESMEN - UNITED STATES - HISTORY - 18TH CENTURY.
Trees, Andrew S., 1968- The founding fathers and the politics of character. Princeton, N.J. : Princeton University Press, c2004.
E302.1 .T74 2004

STATESWOMEN. See STATESMEN.

Statistical design and analysis of experiments.
John, Peter William Meredith. Philadelphia : Society for Industrial and Applied Mathematics, c1998.
QA279 .J65 1998

STATISTICAL MECHANICS. See OPEN SYSTEMS (PHYSICS).

STATISTICAL PHYSICS. See OPEN SYSTEMS (PHYSICS).

STATISTICS. See also SAMPLING (STATISTICS); SCALE ANALYSIS (PSYCHOLOGY).
Frankfort-Nachmias, Chava. Social statistics for a diverse society. 3rd ed. Thousand Oaks, Calif. : Pine Forge Press, c2002.
HA29 .N25 2002

Statistics explained.
Hinton, Perry R. (Perry Roy), 1954- 2nd ed. New York : Routledge, 2004.
BF39 .H54 2004

Statistics for the behavioural sciences.
Russo, Riccardo. 1st ed. Hove, East Sussex ; New York, N.Y. : Psychology Press, 2003.
BF39 .R82 2003

STATISTICS OF SAMPLING. See SAMPLING (STATISTICS).

Statnekov, Daniel K., 1943- Animated earth : a story of Peruvian whistles and transformation / by Daniel K. Statnekov. 2nd ed. Berkeley Calif. : North Atlantic Books, 2003. 202 p. : col. ill. ; 23 cm. Includes bibliographical references (p. 201-202). ISBN 1-55643-463-4 (pbk.) DDC 001.94
1. Vases, Acoustic - Miscellanea. 2. Chimu pottery. 3. Indian pottery - Peru. 4. Statnekov, Daniel K., - 1943- I. Title.
BF1999 .S719 2003

STATNEKOV, DANIEL K., 1943-.
Statnekov, Daniel K., 1943- Animated earth. 2nd ed. Berkeley Calif. : North Atlantic Books, 2003.
BF1999 .S719 2003

Statt, David A., 1942- A students dictionary of psychology / David A. Statt. 1st ed. Hove, UK ; New York : Psychology Press, 2003. p. cm. Table of contents URL: http://www.loc.gov/catdir/toc/ecip044/2003012043.html ISBN 1-84169-341-3 ISBN 1-84169-342-1 (pbk.) DDC 150/.3
1. Psychology - Dictionaries. I. Title.
BF31 .S64 2003

STATUES. See MONUMENTS.

Staume, David, 1961- The beginner's guide for the recently deceased : a comprehensive travel guide to the only inevitable destination / David Staume. 1st ed. St. Paul, Minn. : Llewellyn Publications, 2004. p. cm. ISBN 0-7387-0426-1 DDC 133.9/01/3
1. Future life. I. Title.
BF1311.F8 S78 2004

Stave, Maria Bushkin.
Chicken soup for the soul celebrates sisters. Deerfield Beach, Fla. : Health Communications, 2004.
BF723.S43 C43 2004

Staying on top and keeping the sand out of your pants.
Miller, Scott D. Deerfield Beach, Fla. : Health Communications, c2003.
BF637.S8 M565 2003

STD (DISEASES). See SEXUALLY TRANSMITTED DISEASES.

STDS (DISEASES). See SEXUALLY TRANSMITTED DISEASES.

Stearns, Rob, 1952- Winning smart after losing big : revitalizing people, reviving enterprises / Rob Stearns. 1st ed. San Francisco, CA : Encounter Books, 2003. p. cm. Includes bibliographical references. ISBN 1-89355-476-7 (alk. paper) DDC 155.9/3
1. Loss (Psychology) 2. Success - Psychological aspects. I. Title.
BF575.D35 S74 2003

Stecker, Robert, 1928- Interpretation and construction : art, speech, and the law / Robert Stecker. Malden, MA : Blackwell, 2003. x, 212 p. ; 24 cm. (New directions in aesthetics ; 1) Includes bibliographical references (p. [201]-207) and index. CONTENTS: Interpreting the everyday -- Art interpretation: the central issues -- A theory of art interpretation: substantive claims -- A theory of art interpretation: conceptual and ontological claims -- Radical constructivism -- Moderate and historical constructivism -- Interpretation and construction in the law -- Relativism v. pluralism. ISBN 1405101741 (alk. paper) ISBN 140510175X (pbk. : alk. paper) DDC 121/.68
1. Hermeneutics. 2. Constructivism (Philosophy) 3. Art - Philosophy. 4. Law - Interpretation and construction. I. Title. II. Series.
BD241 .S78 2003

Stedman, Stephen John.
Ending civil wars. Boulder, Colo. : Lynne Rienner, 2002.

JZ6368 .E53 2002

Steedman, Carolyn. Dust : the archive and cultural history / Carolyn Steedman. New Brunswick, N.J. : Rutgers University Press, 2002, c2001. xi, 195 p. ; 21 cm. (Encounters) Includes bibliographical references (p. 171-191) and index. ISBN 0-8135-3046-6 (alk. paper) ISBN 0-8135-3047-4 (pbk. : alk. paper) DDC 027
1. Archives. 2. History - Philosophy. 3. Memory (Philosophy) 4. Culture - History. I. Rutgers University Press. II. Title. III. Series: Encounters (Rutgers University Press)
CD947 .S73 2002

Steele, Bruce.
Lawrence, D. H. (David Herbert), 1885-1930. [Psychoanalysis and the unconscious] Psychoanalysis and the unconscious; New York : Cambridge, 2003.
BF173 .L28 2003

Steelsmith, Shari.
McManus, Martha Hansen, 1948- Understanding the angry child. Seattle, Wash. : Parenting Press, 2004.
BF723.A4 M38 2004

Steen, M. F.
Celebrity death certificates. Jefferson, N.C. : McFarland, c2003.

Steiger, Brad. The Gale encyclopedia of the unusual and unexplained / Brad Steiger and Sherry Hansen Steiger. Detroit : Thomson/Gale, c2003. 3 v. : ill. ; 29 cm. Includes bibliographical references and indexes. ISBN 0-7876-5382-9 (set : hardcover : alk. paper) ISBN 0-7876-5383-7 (v. 1 : alk. paper) ISBN 0-7876-5384-5 (v. 2 : alk. paper) ISBN 0-7876-5385-3 (v. 3 : alk. paper) DDC 130/.3
1. Parapsychology - Encyclopedias. 2. Occultism - Encyclopedias. 3. Supernatural - Encyclopedias. I. Steiger, Sherry Hansen. II. Title. III. Title: Encyclopedia of the unusual and unexplained
BF1025 .S79 2003

Steiger, Sherry Hansen.
Steiger, Brad. The Gale encyclopedia of the unusual and unexplained. Detroit : Thomson/Gale, c2003.
BF1025 .S79 2003

Stein, Diane, 1948- Essential energy balancing II : healing the goddess / Diane Stein. Berkeley, Calif. : Crossing Press, c2003. ix, 165 p. : ill. ; 23 cm. Includes index. Table of contents URL: http://www.loc.gov/catdir/toc/ecip044/2003011232.html ISBN 1-58091-154-4 (pbk.) DDC 291.2/2
1. Karma - Miscellanea. 2. Force and energy - Miscellanea. 3. Spiritual healing. I. Title. II. Title: Essential energy balancing two III. Title: Essential energy balancing 2
BF1045.K37 S735 2003

Stein, Michelle.
LeBeau, Kara R. Guan yin's chakra meditations. Boulder, Colo. : Mahasimhananda Press, c2001.
BF1442.C53 L43 2001

Stein, Stephan, 1963- Textgliederung : Einheitenbildung im geschriebenen und gesprochenen Deutsch : Theorie und Empirie / Stephan Stein. Berlin ; New York : Walter de Gruyter, 2003. 479 p. : ill. ; 24 cm. (Studia linguistica Germanica ; 69) Includes bibliographical references and index. ISBN 3-11-017672-6
1. German language - Idioms. 2. German language - Rhetoric. 3. German language - Style. 4. Communication. I. Title. II. Series.

Steinberg, Laurence D., 1952- Adolescence / Laurence Steinberg. 7th ed. Boston, Mass. : McGraw-Hill, 2005. p. cm. Includes bibliographical references and index. ISBN 0-07-291787-3 (alk. paper) DDC 305.235
1. Adolescent psychology - Textbooks. I. Title.
BF724 .S75 2005

Lerner, Richard M. Handbook of adolescent psychology. 2nd ed. Hoboken, N.J. : John Wiley & Sons, 2004.
BF724 .L367 2004

Steiner, Rudolf, 1861-1925.
[Lectures. English. Selections]
Sleep and dreams : a bridge to the spirit : selected talks, 1910-1924 / Rudolf Steiner ; translated, edited, and introduced by Michael Lipson. 1st ed. Great Barrington, MA : SteinerBooks, 2003. p. cm. Includes bibliographical references. CONTENTS: The secrets of sleep -- Sleep and the three-part soul -- Sleep and the world of the stars -- Understanding sleep through imagination, inspiration and intuition -- An active spirit : dreams and the spiritual researcher -- Our inner undercurrent : a continual dreaming -- Preparing for a new birth -- Dreaming and the etheric body -- Inspiration : bringing the unconscious to consciousness -- Confronting the totality of our lives through dreams -- The logic and illogic of dreams -- Dreams and human development -- Interpreting dream images. ISBN 0-88010-512-7 DDC 299/.935
1. Dreams. 2. Dreams - Religious aspects. 3. Dream interpretation. I. Title.
BF1091 .S715213 2003

Reverse ritual : spiritual knowledge is true communion / Rudolf Steiner, Friedrich Benesch ; with an introduction by Christopher Schaefer. Great Barrington, MA : Anthroposophic Press, c2001. xxi, 288 p. : ill. ; 22 cm. Includes bibliographical references (p. 287-288). ISBN 0-88010-487-2 DDC 299/.935
1. Anthroposophy. 2. Spiritual life. I. Benesch, Friedrich. II. Title.
BP595.S894 R48 2001

STEINER, RUDOLF, 1861-1925.
Majorek, Marek B. Objektivität, ein Erkenntnisideal auf dem Prüfstand. Tübingen : Francke, c2002.

Steinhauer, Kimberly Marie. The relationship among voice onset, voice quality and fundamental frequency : a dynamical perspective / by Kimberly Marie Steinhauer. 2000. xi, 142 p. : ill. Thesis (doctoral)-- University of Pittsburgh, 2000. Includes bibliographical references. Photocopy. Ann Arbor, Mich. : UMI Dissertation Services, 2002. 22 cm.
1. Voice. 2. Voice culture. 3. Singing. 4. Voice frequency. 5. Motor learning. I. Title.

Steininger, Christian.
Zeit in den Medien, Medien in der Zeit. München : Fink, c2002.

Steinlight, Steven.
The fractious nation? Berkeley : University of California Press, c2003.
E169.12 .F69 2003

Steinsaltz, Adin.
[Be'ur Tanya. English]
Opening the Tanya : discovering the moral and mystical teachings of a classic work of Kabbalah / Adin Steinsaltz ; Hebrew text edited by Meir Hanegbi ; translated by Yaacov Tauber. 1st ed. San Francisco : Jossey-Bass, c2003. xxiv, 360 p. ; 24 cm. "An Arthur Kurzweil book." Includes bibliographical references (p. 335-349) and index. Publisher description URL: http://www.loc.gov/catdir/desc ription/wiley039/2003001614.html Table of contents URL: http://www.loc.gov/catdir/toc/wiley032/2003001614.html ISBN 0-7879-6798-X (alk. paper) DDC 296.8/332
1. Shneur Zalman, -of Lyady, - 1745-1813. - Likute amarim. 2. Hasidism. 3. Cabala. I. Shneur Zalman, of Lyady, 1745-1813. Likute amarim. English. II. Hanegbi, Me'ir. III. Title.
BM198.2.S563 S7413 2003

Steinunn Eyjólfsdóttir, 1936- Undir verndarhendi Bjarni Kristjánssonar mi!ill / Steinunn Eyjólfsdóttir. Reykjavík : Skjaldborg, 1995. 163 p. : ill. ; 24 cm. Includes index. ISBN 9979572779
1. Bjarni Kristjánsson, - 1953- 2. Mediums - Iceland - Biography. I. Title.
BF1283.B58 S74 1995

The stellar man.
Baines, John. [Hombre estelar. English] 2nd ed. New York : John Baines Institute, Inc., 2002.
BF1621 .B3513 2002

Stellas, Constance. The astrology gift guide / Constance Stellas. New York : Signet, c2002. xiv, 290 p. ; 19 cm. ISBN 0-451-20726-2 (pbk.) DDC 133.5
1. Astrology. 2. Gifts - Miscellanea. I. Title.
BF1729.G53 S74 2002

Stengers, Isabelle. Penser avec Whitehead : une libre et sauvage création de concepts / Isabelle Stengers. Paris : Seuil, c2002. 581 p. ; 21 cm. (L'ordre philosophique) Includes bibliographical references (p. 573-[575]) and index. ISBN 2-02-053560-2
1. Whitehead, Alfred North, - 1861-1947. 2. Philosophy, Modern - 20th century. I. Title. II. Series: Ordre philosophique.

Stenning, Keith. Seeing reason : image and language in learning to think / Keith Stenning. Oxford ; New York : Oxford University Press, 2002. viii, 296 p. : ill. ; 24 cm. (Oxford cognitive science series) Includes bibliographical references (p. [279]-286) and index. ISBN 0-19-850773-9 (alk. paper) ISBN 0-19-850774-7 (pbk. : alk. paper) DDC 153.1
1. Thought and thinking. 2. Visual learning. 3. Reasoning. I. Title. II. Series.
BF441 .S775 2002

Stenson, Anna.
Stenson, Lila. Daddy, up and down. 1st ed. Snowmass Village, CO : Peaceful Village Pub., 2002.
BF723.G75 S74 2002

Stenson, Lila. Daddy, up and down : sisters grieve the loss of their daddy / by Lila Stenson and Anna Stenson as told to Melanie Friedersdorf Humphrey ; illustrations by Cheryl Biddix. 1st ed. Snowmass Village, CO : Peaceful Village Pub., 2002. 1 v. (unpaged) : col. ill. ; 23 x 27 cm. ISBN 0-9658061-1-1
1. Grief in children - Juvenile literature. 2. Bereavement in children - Juvenile literature. 3. Fathers - Death - Psychological aspects - Juvenile literature. 4. Loss (Psychology) in children - Juvenile literature. 5. Children and death - Juvenile literature. I. Stenson, Anna. II. Humphrey, Melanie Friedersdorf. III. Biddix, Cheryl. IV. Title.
BF723.G75 S74 2002

Stenzel, Lucia Marques. Obesidade : o peso da exclusão / Lucia Marques Stenzel. 1a ed. Porto Alegre : EDIPUCRS, 2002. 124 p. : ill. ; 21 cm. Includes bibliographical references (p. 121-124). ISBN 85-7430-249-X
1. Obesity - Social aspects. 2. Social psychology. 3. Teenage girls - Psychology. 4. Discrimination against overweight women. I. Title.

Step-by-step guide to creating effective policy reports.
Duitch, Suri. The big idea. New York : City Limits Community Information Service, c2002.

A step-by-step guide to starting an effective mentoring program.
Cohen, Norman H. Amherst, Mass. : HRC Press, c2000.
HF5385 .C64 2000

Stepanenko, Valeriĭ. Etyka v problemnykh i analitychnykh zadachakh : navchal'nyĭ posibnyk / Valeriĭ Stepanenko. Kyiv : Libra, 1998. 266 p. ; 20 cm. At head of title: Mizhnarodnyĭ fond "Vidrodzhennia". Prohrama "Transformatsiia humanitarnoï osvity v Ukraïni." Authorized for instructional purposes. Includes bibliographical references (p. 265-[267]). ISBN 9667035077
1. Ethics. I. International Renaissance Foundation (Ukraine). Transformation of the Humanities Program. II. Title.

Stepanov, S. IU. (Sergeĭ IUr'evich).
Rastiannikov, A. V. Refleksivnoe razvitie kompetentnosti v sovmestnom tvorchestve. Moskva : PER SE, 2002.
BF408 .R235 2002

Refleksivnaia praktika tvorcheskogo razvitiia cheloveka i organizatsiĭ / S.IU. Stepanov. Moskva : Nauka, 2000. 173 p. : ill. ; 21 cm. Includes bibliographical references (p. 165-[172]). ISBN 5020083461
1. Creation (Literary, artistic, etc.) - Psychological aspects. 2. Personality and creative ability. 3. Self-knowledge, Theory of. I. Title.
BF408 .S75 2000

Stepanov, S. S. (Sergeĭ Sergeevich) Psikhologiia v litsakh : tvorcheskie biografii zamechatel'nykh uchenykh, opredelivshikh napravleniia razvitiia sovremennoĭ psikhologii / Sergeĭ Stepanov. Moskva : EKSMO-Press, 2001. 380 p. : ill ; 21 cm. ISBN 5040066031
1. Psychologists - Biography. 2. Psychology - History. I. Title.
BF109.A1 S74 2001

Vek psikhologii : imena i sud'by / Sergeĭ Stepanov. Izd. 2., ispr. i dop. Moskva : EKSMO, 2002. 590 p. : ill. ; 21 cm. ISBN 5699009930
1. Psychologists - Biography. 2. Psychology - History. I. Title.
BF109.A1 S75 2002

Stepanova, Natal'ia (Natal'ia Ivanovna) Gadaniia sibirskoĭ tselitel'nitsy / N.I. Stepanova. Moskva : RIPOL klassik, 1999. 138 p. : ill. ; 21 cm. (IA vam pomogu) ISBN 5879072002
1. Fortune telling - Russia (Federation) - Siberia. I. Title. II. Series.
BF1866 .S73 1999

Stephan, Achim.
Ethik ohne Dogmen. Paderborn : Mentis, 2001.

Stephenson, Niamh.
International Society for Theoretical Psychology. Conference (9th : 2001 : Calgary, Alta.) Theoretical psychology. Concord, Ont. : Captus Press, c2003.

Stepin, V. S. (Viacheslav Semenovich).
Sub"ekt, poznanie, deiatel'nost'. Moskva : Kanon+, 2002.
BD166 .S84 2002

Stepping up.
Kazerounian, Nadine. London : McGraw-Hill, c2002.

STEPS, TWELVE (SELF-HELP). *See* **TWELVE-STEP PROGRAMS.**

Sterelny, Kim.
From mating to mentality. New York, NY : Psychology Press, 2003.
BF698.95 .F76 2003

Thought in a hostile world : the evolution of human cognition / Kim Sterelny. Malden, MA : Blackwell, 2003. p. cm. Includes bibliographical references and index.

ISBN 0-631-18886-X (alk. paper) ISBN 0-631-18887-8 (pbk. : alk. paper) DDC 155.7
1. Evolutionary psychology. 2. Cognition. 3. Brain - Evolution. 4. Cognition and culture. I. Title.
BF698.95 .S74 2003

STEREOTYPE (PSYCHOLOGY).
Bitches, bimbos, and ballbreakers. New York, N.Y. : Penguin Books, 2003.
HQ1206 .B444 2003

Brashears, Deya. Challenging biases-- facing our fears. Dubuque, Iowa : Kendall/Hunt Pub., c1999.
BF575.P9 B735 1999

Gender nonconformity, race, and sexuality. Madison : University of Wisconsin Press, [2002]
HQ1075 .G4645 2002

Schauer, Frederick F. Profiles, probabilities, and stereotypes. Cambridge, Mass. : Belknap Press of Harvard University Press, 2003.
HM1096 .S34 2003

Schneider, David J., 1940- The psychology of stereotyping. New York : Guilford Press, c2004.
BF323.S63 S36 2003

STEREOTYPE (PSYCHOLOGY) - RESEARCH - METHODOLOGY.
Fiedler, Klaus, 1951- Stereotyping as inductive hypothesis testing. Hove (UK) ; New York : Psychology Press, c2003.
BF323.S63 F54 2003

STEREOTYPED BEHAVIOR. See **STEREOTYPE (PSYCHOLOGY).**

Stereotyping as inductive hypothesis testing.
Fiedler, Klaus, 1951- Hove (UK) ; New York : Psychology Press, c2003.
BF323.S63 F54 2003

STERILIZATION (BIRTH CONTROL). See **STERILIZATION, EUGENIC.**

STERILIZATION, EUGENIC - GERMANY - HISTORY - 20TH CENTURY.
Simon, Jürgen, 1966- Kriminalbiologie und Zwangssterilisation. Münster ; New York : Waxmann, c2001.

STERILIZATION OF CRIMINALS AND DEFECTIVES. See **STERILIZATION, EUGENIC.**

Sterling, Bruce. Tomorrow now : envisioning the next fifty years / Bruce Sterling. 1st ed. New York : Random House, c2002. xxiv, 320 p. ; 20 cm. Includes index. ISBN 0-679-46322-4 (acid-free paper) DDC 303.49
1. Social prediction. 2. Twenty-first century - Forecasts. I. Title.
HM901 .S74 2002

Stern, Daniel N. The first relationship : infant and mother / Daniel N. Stern. Cambridge, Mass. : Harvard University Press, 2002, 1977. 178 p. : ill. ; 22 cm. Originally published: Cambridge : Harvard University Press, 1977. With new introd. Includes bibliographical references (p. 163-169) and index. ISBN 0-674-00783-2 (alk. paper) DDC 155.42/218
1. Mother and infant. 2. Mother and child. I. Title.
BF720.M68 S74 2002

STERN, WILLIAM, 1871-1938.
Lamiell, James T. Beyond individual and group differences. Thousand Oaks, Calif. : Sage Publications, c2003.
BF105 .L36 2003

Sternberg, Robert J.
Creativity. 1st ed. Washington, DC : American Psychological Association, c2004.
BF408 .C7548 2004

Culture and competence. Washington, DC : American Psychological Association, 2004.
BF311 .C845 2004

International handbook of intelligence. Cambridge ; New York : Cambridge University Press, 2003.
BF431 .I59 2003

Motivation, emotion, and cognition. Mahwah, N.J. : L. Erlbaum Associates, 2004.
BF431 .M72 2004

The nature of reasoning. Cambridge, U.K. ; New York : Cambridge University Press, 2003.
BF442 .N38 2003

The psychologist's companion : a guide to scientific writing for students and researchers / Robert J. Sternberg ; chapter 5 was contributed by Richard Sherman and Beth Dietz-Uhler ; chapter 7 and appendix B were contributed by Chris Leach. 4th ed. Cambridge, U.K. ; New York : Cambridge University Press, 2003. p. cm. Includes bibliographical references and index. Publisher description URL: http://www.loc.gov/catdir/description/cam032/2003043595.html Table of contents URL: http://www.loc.gov/catdir/toc/cam031/2003043595.html ISBN 0-521-82123-1 ISBN 0-521-52806-2 (pbk.) DDC 808/.06615
1. Report writing. 2. Psychological literature I. Dietz-Uhler, Beth. II. Leach, Chris. III. Title.
BF76.8 .S73 2003

Psychology 101 1/2 : the unspoken rules for success in academia / Robert J. Sternberg. Washington, DC : American Psychological Association, 2004. xiii, 241 p. ; 23 cm. Includes bibliographical references (p. 223-227) and index. ISBN 1-59147-029-3 (pbk. : alk. paper) DDC 150/.71/1
1. Psychology - Study and teaching (Higher) 2. Psychology - Study and teaching (Graduate) I. Title. II. Title: Psychology one hundred one and a half III. Title: Psychology one hundred and one and a half
BF77 .S68 2004

The psychology of gender. 2nd ed. New York : Guilford Press, 2004.
BF692.2 .P764 2004

Psychology / Robert J. Sternberg ; with contributions by Josephine F. Wilson. 4th ed. Belmont, CA : Thomson/Wadsworth, c2004. xxix, 666, A-1-A-163 p. : col. ill. ; 29 cm. + 2 CD-ROMs (4 3/4 in.). Includes bibliographical references (p. A-61-A-125) and indexes. System requirements for accompanying CD-ROMs: Windows 98, ME, 2000, XP (not NT) with Pentium II 233 MHz and 32 MB RAM (64 MB recommended); MacOs 8.6+ with PowerPC or later and 64 MB RAM. ISBN 0-534-61812-X (Student Ed.) ISBN 0-534-61820-0 (Instructor's Ed.) DDC 150
1. Psychology. I. Wilson, Josephine F. II. Title.
BF121 .S84 2004

Wisdom, intelligence, and creativity synthesized / Robert J. Sternberg. Cambridge, UK ; New York : Cambridge University Press, 2003. p. cm. Includes bibliographical references and index. Publisher description URL: http://www.loc.gov/catdir/description/cam032/2003043751.html Table of contents URL: http://www.loc.gov/catdir/toc/cam031/2003043751.html ISBN 0-521-80238-5 ISBN 0-521-00271-0 (pbk.) DDC 153.9
1. Intellect. 2. Creative ability. 3. Creative thinking. 4. Wisdom. I. Title.
BF431 .S7385 2003

Sterne, Jonathan, 1970- The audible past : cultural origins of sound reproduction / Jonathan Sterne. Durham : Duke University Press, 2003. xvi, 450 p. : ill. ; 25 cm. Includes bibliographical references (p. [415]-436) and index. ISBN 0-8223-3013-X ISBN 0-8223-3004-0 (cloth) DDC 621.389/3/09
1. Sound - Recording and reproducing - History. 2. Sound recording industry - Social aspects. 3. Sound in mass media. 4. Sound recordings - social aspects. 5. Popular culture. I. Title.
TK7881.4 .S733 2003

STERNHAGEN, FRANCES, 1930-.
Vint/age 2001 conference : [videorecording]. New York, c2001.

Sternhagen, Frances, 1930- panelist.
Vint/age 2001 conference : [videorecording]. New York, c2001.

Stetson, Brad. Living victims, stolen lives : parents of murdered children speak to America / Brad Stetson. Amityville, N.Y. : Baywood Pub., c2003. xi, 124 p. ; 24 cm. (Death, value, and meaning series) Includes bibliographical references (p. 115-116) and index. ISBN 0-89503-229-5 (cloth : alk. paper) ISBN 0-89503-230-9 (pbk. : alk. paper) DDC 362.88/085
1. Parents of murder victims - California - Interviews. 2. Murder - California - Case studies. 3. Children - Death - Psychological aspects - Case studies. 4. Bereavement - Case studies. I. Title. II. Series.
HV6533.C2 S73 2003

Stewardson, John (John E.) Success is the best revenge : gold medal career management / John Stewardson & Bob Evans. Toronto : Productive Publications, c1994. xii, 277, 25 p. ; 28 cm. "Your career repair kit: how to survive the nasty nineties". Last group of paging consists of publisher's ads. ISBN 0-920847-88-9 DDC 650.14
1. Career development. 2. Vocational guidance. 3. Success in business. I. Evans, Bob. II. Title.

Stewart, Frances, 1940-.
Group behaviour and development. Oxford ; New York : Oxford University Press, 2002.
HD58.7 .G76 2002

Stewart, Ian, 1940-.
Joines, Vann. Personality adaptations. Nottingham ; Chapel Hill, N.C. : Lifespace, 2002.
BF698.3 .J65 2002

Stich, Stephen P.
The Blackwell guide to philosophy of mind. Malden, MA ; Oxford : Blackwell Pub., 2003.
BD418.3 .B57 2003

Nichols, Shaun. Mindreading. Oxford : Clarendon Press ; New York : Oxford University Press, 2003.

Stieglitz, Nadia.
Your birthday sign through time. New York : Atria Books, c2002.
BF1728.A2 Y57 2002

Stiehler, Gottfried. Mensch und Geschichte : Studien zur Gesellschaftsdialektik / Gottfried Stiehler. Köln : PapyRossa, c2002. 162 p. ; 21 cm. (PapyRossa Hochschulschriften ; 39) Includes bibliographical references. ISBN 3-89438-252-X (pbk.)
1. History - Philosophy. I. Title. II. Series.
D16.8 .S75 2002

Stiening, Gideon.
Societas rationis. Berlin : Duncker & Humblot, c2002.
B29 .S633 2002

Stier, Oren Baruch, 1966- Committed to memory : cultural mediations of the Holocaust / Oren Baruch Stier. 1st ed. Amherst : University of Massachusetts Press, 2003. xvi, 277 p. : ill. ; 24 cm. Includes bibliographical references (p. 257-269) and index. ISBN 1-55849-408-1 (Cloth : alk. paper) DDC 940.53/18
1. Holocaust, Jewish (1939-1945) - Influence. 2. Memory. 3. Holocaust, Jewish (1939-1945) - Historiography. 4. Holocaust, Jewish (1939-1945), in literature. 5. Holocaust, Jewish (1939-1945), in motion pictures. 6. Holocaust memorials. I. Title.
D804.3 .S79 2003

Stikker, Allerd, 1928- Closing the gap : exploring the history of gender relations / Allerd Stikker. Amsterdam : Amsterdam University Press : Salomé, c2002. 287 p. : ill. ; 23 cm. Includes bibliographical references (p. 273-277) and index. ISBN 90-5356-574-4
1. Sex role - History. I. Title.

Still bored in a culture of entertainment.
Winter, Richard, 1945- Downers Grove, Ill. : InterVarsity Press, c2002.
BV4599.5.B67 W56 2002

Still true to type.
Jeffries, William C. Noblesville, IN : Buttermilk Ridge Pub. ; Zionsville, Ind. : Distributed by Executive Strategies International, c2002.
BF698.8.M94 J435 2002

Stimpson, Quenton.
Clinical counselling in voluntary and community settings. New York, NY : Brunner-Routledge, 2003.
BF637.C6 C456 2003

Stobbe, Heinz-Günther, 1948- Vom Geist der Übertretung und Vernichtung : der Ursprung der Gewalt im Denken des Marquis de Sade / Heinz-Günther Stobbe. Regensburg : Friedrich Pustet, c2002. 118 p. ; 22 cm. Includes bibliographical references (p. 114-118). ISBN 3-7917-1793-6 (pbk.)
1. Sade, - marquis de, - 1740-1814 - Criticism and interpretation - Biography. 2. Violence in literature. 3. Ethics. I. Title. II. Title: Der Ursprung der Gewalt im Denken des Marquis de Sade

STOCK AND STOCK-BREEDING. See **LIVESTOCK.**

STOCK (ANIMALS). See **LIVESTOCK.**

STOCK COMPANIES. See **CORPORATIONS.**

STOCK CORPORATIONS. See **CORPORATIONS.**

STOCK-EXCHANGE. See **STOCK EXCHANGES.**

STOCK EXCHANGE CRASHES. See **FINANCIAL CRISES.**

STOCK EXCHANGES - UNITED STATES - HISTORY.
Sornette, D. Why stock markets crash. Princeton, N.J. : Princeton University Press, c2003.
HB3722 .S66 2003

STOCK ISSUES. See **STOCKS.**

Stock, Karl F. Freud-Bibliographien : selbständige und versteckte Bibliographien und Nachschlagewerke zu Leben und Werk / Karl F. Stock, Rudolf Heilinger, Marylène Stock. Graz : Stock & Stock, 1998. iv, 90 p. ; 21 cm. (Bibliographieverzeichnisse grosser Österreicher in Einzelbänden) Includes index. ISBN 3-900818-23-1
1. Freud, Sigmund, - 1856-1939 - Bibliography. 2. Psychoanalysis - Bibliography. 3. Psychoanalytic counseling - Bibliography. 4. Psychoanalytic Theory - Bibliography. 5. Psychoanalytic Therapy - Bibliography. I. Heilinger, Rudolf. II. Stock, Marylène. III. Title. IV. Series.

BF109.F73 S76 1998

STOCK MARKET. *See* **STOCK EXCHANGES.**

STOCK MARKET PANICS. *See* **FINANCIAL CRISES.**

Stock, Marylène.
Stock, Karl F. Freud-Bibliographien. Graz : Stock & Stock, 1998.
BF109.F73 S76 1998

STOCK OFFERINGS. *See* **STOCKS.**

STOCK REPURCHASING. *See* **STOCKS.**

STOCK TRADING. *See* **STOCKS.**

STOCKHOLDERS. *See* **STOCKS.**

STOCKS. *See* **CORPORATIONS.**

STOCKS - PRICES - HISTORY.
Sornette, D. Why stock markets crash. Princeton, N.J. : Princeton University Press, c2003.
HB3722 .S66 2003

Stoddard, David A., 1953- The heart of mentoring : ten proven principles for developing people to their fullest potential / David A. Stoddard with Robert J. Tamasy. Colorado Springs, Colo. : NavPress, 2003. p. cm. Includes bibliographical references. Table of contents URL: http://www.loc.gov/catdir/toc/ecip041/2003005257.html CONTENTS: Introduction: a tale of two mentors -- It starts with the heart -- It's the journey that counts -- Into their world-through yours -- Addressing the desires of the heart -- Advancing through adversity -- Let your values filter be your guide -- The substance of mentoring -- The fuel that drives the engine -- The vision gap: focusing on the future. ISBN 1-57683-401-8 DDC 158/.3
1. Mentoring. I. Tamasy, Robert. II. Title.
BF637.C6 S773 2003

STOELTING BRIEF NONVERBAL INTELLIGENCE TEST.
Roid, Gale H. S-BIT, Stoelting Brief Nonverbal Intelligence Test. Wood Dale, IL : Stoelting Co., c1999.
BF432.5.S85 R65 1999

STOICS.
Protopapas-Marneli, Maria. La rhétorique des stoïciens. Paris : Harmattan, c2002.

Safty, Essam. La psyché humaine. Paris : Harmattan, c2003.
B528 .S34 2003

Stokes, Trevor, 1951-.
A small matter of proof. Reno, NV : Context Press, c2003.
BF121 .S545 2003

Stoller, Silvia.
Philosophie in Aktion. Wien : Turia + Kant, 2000.

Stöltzner, Michael.
Appraising Lakatos. Dordrecht ; Boston : Kluwer Academic, c2002.
Q175 .A685 2002

Stolz, Fritz. Weltbilder der Religionen : Kultur und Natur, Diesseits und Jenseits, Kontrollierbares und Unkontrollierbares / Fritz Stolz. Zürich : Pano Verlag, c2001. viii, 263 p. : ill. ; 21 cm. (Theophil ; 4. Bd) Includes bibliographical references (p. [253]-259) and index. ISBN 3-907576-35-7 (pbk.)
1. Psychology, Religious. 2. Art and religion. I. Title. II. Series.

Stone-Barker, Holly.
Solar, Melanie B. The invisible bag. Greenwell Springs, LA : Solar Pub., 2000.
BF723.C47 S65 2000

STONE CROSSES - FRANCE - HENDAYE - MISCELLANEA.
Weidner, Jay. The mysteries of the great cross of Hendaye. Rochester, Vt. : Destiny Books, 2003.
BF1999 .W435 2003

Stone, Jon R., 1959-.
Expecting Armageddon. New York : Routledge, 2000.
BL503 .E97 2000

Muller, F. Max (Friedrich Max), 1823-1900. The essential Max Muller. 1st ed. New York ; Houndmills, England : Palgrave Macmillan, 2002.
BL50 .M785 2002

STONE, LUCY (FICTITIOUS CHARACTER) - FICTION.
Meier, Leslie. Birthday party murder. Waterville, Me. : Thorndike Press, 2003.
PS3563.E3455 B57 2003

Stone-McCown, Karen.
Self-science. 2nd ed., rev. and updated. San Mateo, Calif. : Six Seconds, c1998.

BF697 .S84 1998

STONE, PHILOSOPHERS'. *See* **ALCHEMY.**

STONES, PRECIOUS. *See* **PRECIOUS STONES.**

Stonewall Jackson's book of maxims.
Jackson, Stonewall, 1824-1863. Nashville, Tenn. : Cumberland House, 2002.
E467.1.J15 J17 2002

Stopka, Katja.
Rauschen. Würzburg : Königshausen & Neumann, c2001.

Stoppino, Mario. Potere e teoria politica / Mario Stoppino. 3. ed. riv. e accresciuta. Milano : Giuffrè, 2001. 393 p. ; 24 cm. Includes bibliographical references. ISBN 88-14-08722-9 DDC 303
1. Power (Social sciences) 2. Political science. 3. Political sociology. I. Title.

Storey, John, 1950- Inventing popular culture : from folklore to globalization / John Storey. Malden, MA : Blackwell Pub., 2003. xii, 148 p. ; 23 cm. (Blackwell manifestos) Includes bibliographical references (p. [130]-139) and index. ISBN 0-631-23459-4 (hardcover : alk. paper) ISBN 0-631-23460-8 (pbk. : alk. paper) DDC 306
1. Popular culture. 2. Popular culture - Philosophy. 3. Culture - Philosophy. I. Title. II. Series.
CB19 .S7455 2003

Storia della lingua e antropologia nella locuzioni italiane ed europee.
Lurati, Ottavio. Per modo di dire--. Bologna : CLUEB, c2002.

Storia dell'Accademia dei Lincei. Studi
(3) Baldriga, Irene. L'occhio della lince. Roma : Accademia nazionale dei Lincei, 2002.

Storia delle idee e delle istituzioni politiche, Età contemporanea. Sezione Studi
(5.) Cospito, Giuseppe, 1966- Il "gran Vico". Genova : Name, c2002.

Storia e letteratura (Edizioni di storia e letteratura)
(215.) Hankins, James. Humanism and platonism in the Italian Renaissance. Roma : Edizioni di storia e letteratura, 2003-

Storia. Ricerche (Rome, Italy)
Zerbi, Piero. "Philosophi" e "logici". Roma : Istituto storico italiano per il Medio Evo ; Milano : Vita e pensiero, 2002.
B765.A24 Z473 2002

STORIES. *See* **FICTION.**

Stories of peoplehood.
Smith, Rogers M., 1953- Cambridge ; New York : Cambridge University Press, 2003.
JA75.7 .S65 2003

Storkey, Elaine, 1943- Created or constructed? : the great gender debate / Elaine Storkey. Carlisle [Eng.] : Paternoster Press, 2000. viii, 129 p. ; 22 cm. Includes bibliographical references [p. [120]-124) and indexes. ISBN 0-85364-983-9
1. Sex role - History. 2. Sex differences (Psychology) - History. 3. Women in Christianity. I. Title.

Storm clouds over Sun City : the urgent need to recast the Congolese peace process. Brussels ; Nairobi : International Crisis Group, 2002. ii, 29 p. : map ; 28 cm. (ICG Africa report ; no. 44) "14 March 2002." Includes bibliographical references. CONTENTS: I. Introduction -- II. "Place your bets!" : the dialogue at Sun City or Botswanan roulette -- III. "Game over"? : no new political order on the horizon for the Congo -- IV. Conclusion : moving beyond Lusaka while adhering to the principles.
1. Congo (Democratic Republic) - Politics and government - 1997- 2. Negotiation - Congo (Democratic Republic) 3. Peace. I. International Crisis Group. II. Series.

Story, Ronald. The encyclopedia of extraterrestrial encounters : a definitive illustrated A-Z guide to all things alien / compiled and edited by Ronald D. Story. New York : New American Library, c2001. xviii, 681 p. : ill. ; 24 cm. Includes bibliographical references and index. Library's copy signed by author. ISBN 0-451-20424-7 (alk. paper) DDC 001.942/03
1. Unidentified flying objects - Encyclopedias. 2. Human-alien encounters - Encyclopedias. I. Title.
TL789.16 .S76 2001

STORYTELLING. *See* **FOLKLORE.**

STORYTELLING ABILITY IN CHILDREN.
Revealing the inner worlds of young children. New York : Oxford University Press, 2003.
BF723.S74 A37 2003

Stout, Chris E.
Fairley, Stephen. Getting started in personal and executive coaching. Hoboken, N.J. : J. Wiley & Sons, 2003.
BF637.P36 F35 2003

The psychology of terrorism. Westport, CT : Praeger, 2002.
HV6431 .P798 2002

Stoynoff, Natasha.
Edward, John (John J.) After life. New York : Princeton Books, c2003.
BF1283.E34 A3 2003

Strack, Fritz, 1950-.
Bless, Herbert. Social cognition. Hove, East Sussex, UK ; New York : Psychology Press, 2003.
BF323.S63 B55 2003

Straight talk.
Murray, Karel, 1954- Portland, Or. : Arnica Pub., c2003.
BF637.C5 M87 2003

Strakh.
Buianov, M. I. (Mikhail Ivanovich), vrach. Moskva : Rossiĭskoe ob-vo medikov-literatorov, 2002.
BF575.F2 B85 2002

Stranac na rijeci.
Twitchell, Paul, 1908-1971. [Stranger by the river. Croation] Minneapolis, MN : ECKANKAR, c1994.

Strandberg, Åke. The Orphic voice : T.S. Eliot and the Mallarmean quest for meaning / Åke Strandberg. Uppsala : Acta Universitatis Upsaliensis, 2002. 188 p. ; 23 cm. (Acta Universitatis Upsaliensis. Studia Anglistica Upsaliensia, 0562-2719 ; 122) Originally presented as the author's thesis (doctoral)--Uppsala University, 2002. Includes bibliographical references (p. 178-183) and index. ISBN 91-554-5434-8 (pbk.)
1. Eliot, T. S. - (Thomas Stearns), - 1888-1965 - Criticism and interpretation. 2. Mallarmé, Stéphane, - 1842-1898 - Influence - Eliot. 3. Aesthetics. I. Title. II. Series.
PS3509.L43 Z87 2002

Strangers, Gods, and monsters.
Kearney, Richard. London ; New York : Routledge, 2003.
BD236 .K43 2003

Straś-Romanowska, Maria.
Szkice psychologiczne. Wrocław : Wydawn. Uniwersytetu Wrocławskiego, 2002.
BF76.5 .S97 2002

Strasser, Gerhard F. Emblematik und Mnemonik der frühen Neuzeit im Zusammenspiel Johannes Buno und Johann Justus Winckelmann / Gerhard F. Strasser. Wiesbaden : Harrassowitz Wolfenbüttel : Herzog August Bibliothek, c2000. 154 p. : ill. ; 28 cm. (Wolfenbütteler Arbeiten zur Barockforschung ; Bd. 36) Includes bibliographical references and index. ISBN 3-447-04405-5
1. Buno, Johannes, - 1617-1697. 2. Winckelmann, Johann Just, - 1620-1699. 3. Emblems - Germany - History - 17th century. 4. Memory. 5. Symbolism in art - Germany - History - 17th century. 6. Signs and symbols - Germany - History - 17th century. 7. Visual communication - Germany - History - 17th century. I. Herzog August Bibliothek. II. Title. III. Series.
PN6348.5 .S873 2000

Strate, Lance.
Communication and cyberspace. 2nd ed. Creskill, N.J. : Hampton Press, c2003.
P96.D36 C66 2003

STRATEGIC ALLIANCES (BUSINESS).
Huotari, Maija-Leena. Trust in knowledge management and systems in organizations. Hershey, PA ; London : Idea Group Publishing, c2004.
HD30.2 .H865 2004

Ward, William Aidan. Trust and mistrust. Chichester, England : Hoboken, NJ : John Wiley & Sons, c2003.
HD69.S8 W37 2003

STRATEGIC BUSINESS ALLIANCES. *See* **STRATEGIC ALLIANCES (BUSINESS).**

Strategic computing.
Roland, Alex, 1944- Cambridge, Mass. : MIT Press, c2002.
QA76.88 .R65 2002

STRATEGIC CORPORATE ALLIANCES. *See* **STRATEGIC ALLIANCES (BUSINESS).**

STRATEGIC MANAGEMENT. *See* **STRATEGIC PLANNING.**

STRATEGIC PARTNERSHIPS (BUSINESS). *See* **STRATEGIC ALLIANCES (BUSINESS).**

STRATEGIC PLANNING.
Cummings, Stephen. Recreating strategy. London ; Thousand Oaks : Sage Publications, 2002.

Strategic planning.

HD30.28 .C855 2002

Gilad, Benjamin. Early warning. New York, NY : American Management Association, c2003.
HD61 .G533 2003

Greve, Henrich R. Organizational learning from performance feedback. Cambridge : Cambridge University Press, 2003.

Hamel, Gary. Leading the revolution. Rev. and updated hardcover ed. [Boston, Mass.] : Harvard Business School Press, c2002.

Harmon, Paul, 1942- Business process change. Amsterdam ; Boston : Morgan Kaufmann, c2003.
HD58.8 .H37 2003

Kennedy, Kevin (Kevin John), 1955- Going the distance. Upper Saddle River, NJ : Prentice Hall/Financial Times, c2003.
HD57.7 .K465 2003

Lindgren, Mats, 1959- Scenario planning. Houndmills [England] ; New York : Palgrave Macmillan, 2002.
HD30.28 .L543 2002

McAfee, R. Preston. Competitive solutions. Princeton, N.J. : Princeton University Press, c2002.
HD30.28 .M3815 2002

STRATEGIC PLANNING - CASE STUDIES.
McAfee, R. Preston. Competitive solutions. Princeton, N.J. : Princeton University Press, c2002.
HD30.28 .M3815 2002

Strategies for theory : from Marx to Madonna / edited by R.L. Rutsky and Bradley J. Macdonald. Albany : State University of New York Press, c2003. xvi, 283 p. : ill. ; 23 cm. Includes bibliographical references and index. ISBN 0-7914-5730-3 (pbk : alk. paper) ISBN 0-7914-5729-X (alk. paper) DDC 306
1. Theory (Philosophy) 2. Popular culture. 3. Poststructuralism. 4. Marxist criticism. 5. Postmodernism. I. Rutsky, R. L. II. Macdonald, Bradley J.
B842 .S77 2003

Strategies of qualitative inquiry / editors, Norman K. Denzin, Yvonna S. Lincoln. 2nd ed. Thousand Oaks, CA : Sage, c2003. xi, 460 p. : ill. ; 23 cm. Includes bibliographical references and indexes. CONTENTS: The choreography of qualitative research design : minuets, improvisations, and crystallization / Valerie J. Janesick -- An untold story? : doing funded qualitative research / Julianne Cheek -- Performance ethnography : a brief history and some advice / Michal M. McCall -- Case studies / Robert E. Stake -- Ethnography and ethnographic representation / Barbara Tedlock -- Analyzing interpretive practice / Jaber F. Gubrium and James A. Holstein -- Grounded theory : objectivist and constructivist methods / Kathy Charmaz -- Undaunted courage : life history and the postmodern challenge / William G. Tierney -- Testimonio, subalternity, and narrative authority / John Beverley -- Participatory action research / Stephen Kemmis and Robin McTaggart -- Clinical research / William L. Miller and Benjamin F. Crabtree. ISBN 0-7619-2691-7 (Paper) DDC 300/.7/2
1. Social sciences - Methodology. 2. Social sciences - Research - Methodology. I. Denzin, Norman K. II. Lincoln, Yvonna S. III. Title: Handbook of qualitative research.
H61 .S8823 2003

Strategii sakral'nogo smysla.
Maler, Arkadiĭ. Moskva : Parad izdatel'skiĭ dom, 2003.

Strategii͡a ontologicheskoĭ igry.
Solodin, A. I. Sankt-Peterburg : Aleteĭi͡a, 2002.
BF237 .S6 2002

Solodin, A. I. Sankt-Peterburg : Aleteĭi͡a, 2002.

Strategy.
De Kluyver, Cornelis A. Upper Saddle River, N.J. : Prentice Hall, c2003.
HD38.2 .D425 2003

Strategy representation.
Gordon, Andrew S. Mahwah, NJ : L. Erlbaum, 2003.
BF316.6 .G67 2003

STRATIFICATION, SOCIAL. *See* **SOCIAL CLASSES.**

Straumann, Barbara.
Bronfen, Elisabeth. Die Diva. München : Schirmer/Mosel, c2002.
BJ1470.5 .B76 2002

Strauss, Johann, 1825-1899.
Zigeunerbaron Ja, das Schreiben und das Lesen. Hann, Georg. Georg Hann [sound recording]. [Germany] : Preiser Records, p2001.

Straw dogs.
Gray, John, 1948- London : Granta, 2002.

Strawbridge, Sheelagh.
Handbook of counselling psychology. 2nd ed. London ; Thousand Oaks, Calif. : SAGE Publications, 2003.
BF637.C6 H316 2003

Strčić, Petar.
Bošković, Hijacint. Filozofski izvori fašizma i nacionalnog socijalizma. 2. izd. Zagreb : Dom i svijet, 2000.
B804 .B66 2000

Strean, Herbert S. Psychotherapy with the unattached : resolving problems of single people / by Herbert S. Strean. Northvale, N.J. : Jason Aronson Inc., 1995. xviii, 223 p. ; 21 cm. Includes bibliographical references (p. 211-217) and index. ISBN 1-56821-539-8 (softcover : alk. paper) DDC 616.89/14/08652
1. Single people - Mental health. 2. Psychotherapy. I. Title.
RC451.4.S55 S77 1995

STREET ADDRESSES - DIRECTORIES.
Schlein, Alan M. Find it online. 3rd ed. Tempe, AZ : Facts on Demand Press, c2003.

STREET ART. *See* **GRAFFITI.**

STREET NUMBERS. *See* **STREET ADDRESSES.**

STREET PEOPLE. *See* **HOMELESS PERSONS.**

Streeter, Michael. Witchcraft : a secret history / Michael Streeter. Hauppauge, N.Y. : Barron's, c2002. 192 p. : ill. (chiefly col.) ; 28 cm. "A Quarto book." Includes bibliographical references (p. 192) and index. ISBN 0-7641-5465-6 DDC 133.4/3/09
1. Witchcraft - History. I. Title.
BF1566 .S79 2002

Strehlow, Wighard, 1937- Hildegard of Bingen's spiritual remedies / Wighard Strehlow. Rochester, Vt. : Healing Arts Press, c2002. xiii, 257 p. : ill. ; 26 cm. Includes bibliographical references (p. 252) and index. ISBN 0-89281-985-5 (pbk.) DDC 615.8
1. Hildegard, - Saint, - 1098-1179. 2. Spiritual healing. 3. Alternative medicine. I. Title.
BT732.5 .S87 2002

Strenger, Carlo. The quest for voice in contemporary psychoanalysis / Carlo Strenger. Madison, Conn. : International Universities Press, c2002. 276 p. ; 22 cm. Includes bibliographical references (p. 249-257) and indexes. ISBN 0-8236-5762-0 (pbk.) DDC 616.89/17
1. Psychoanalysis. 2. Psychoanalysis and philosophy. I. Title.
RC506 .S773 2002

Streri, Arlette.
Touching for knowing. Amsterdam ; Philadelphia : John Benjamins Pub., c2003.
BF275 .T69 2003

Stress.
Clark, John, 1946- London ; Rollinsford, NH : Spiro Press, 2002.

Stress : a bibliography with indexes / Clarke M. Ivanich, editor. New York : Nova Science Publishers, c2002. 162 p. ; 26 cm. Includes indexes. ISBN 1-59033-311-X
1. Stress (Psychology) - Bibliography. I. Ivanich, Clarke M.
BF575.S75

STRESS DISORDER, POST-TRAUMATIC. *See* **POST-TRAUMATIC STRESS DISORDER.**

STRESS IN ADOLESCENCE - STUDY AND TEACHING (SECONDARY) - ACTIVITY PROGRAMS.
De Anda, Diane. Stress management for adolescents. Champaign, Ill. : Research Press, 2002.
BF724.3.S86 D4 2002

STRESS IN CHILDREN.
Humphrey, James Harry, 1911- Childhood stress in contemporary society. New York : Haworth Press, 2004.
BF723.S75 H842 2004

Thomas, Patrice Olympius. The power of relaxation. 1st U.S. ed. St. Paul, MN : Redleaf Press, 2003.
BF723.S75 T48 2003

STRESS IN CHILDREN - JUVENILE LITERATURE.
Mundy, Michaelene. Getting out of a stress mess!. St. Meinrad, IN : One Caring Place, c2000.
BF723.S75 M86 2000

STRESS IN TEENAGERS. *See* **STRESS IN ADOLESCENCE.**

STRESS MANAGEMENT.
Childre, Doc Lew, 1945- Transforming anger. Oakland, Calif. : New Harbinger ; London : Hi Marketing, 2003.
BF575.A5 C45 2003

Clark, John, 1946- Stress. London ; Rollinsford, NH : Spiro Press, 2002.

Decker, Dru Scott, 1942- Stress that motivates. Rev. ed. Menlo Park, CA : Crisp Publications, c2002.
BF575.S75 D38 2002

Elliott, Charles H., 1948- Overcoming anxiety for dummies. New York : Wiley Pub., c2003.
BF575.A6 E46 2003

Frost, Peter J. Toxic emotions at work. Boston : Harvard Business School Press, c2003.
HD42 .F76 2003

Gallant, Mary J. Coming of age in the Holocaust. Lanham, Md. : University Press of America, c2002.
D804.3 .G353 2002

Greenberg, Jerrold S. Comprehensive stress management. 8th ed. Boston : McGraw-Hill, [2003?]
BF575.S75 G66 2003

McGhee, Paul E. Health, healing and the amuse system. 3rd ed. Dubuque, Iowa : Kendall/Hunt Pub., c1999.
BF575.L3 M38 1999

Mornell, Adina. Lampenfieber und Angst bei ausübenden Musikern. Frankfurt am Main : P. Lang, 2002.
ML3830 .M67 2002

Weiss, Brian L. (Brian Leslie), 1944- Eliminating stress, finding inner peace. Carlsbad, Calif. : Hay House, c2003.
BF575.S75 W44 2003

Wiseman, Carol. A patchwork of comforts. Boston, MA : Conari Press, 2004.
BF515 .W57 2004

Stress management for adolescents.
De Anda, Diane. Champaign, Ill. : Research Press, 2002.
BF724.3.S86 D4 2002

STRESS MANAGEMENT FOR CHILDREN.
Thomas, Patrice Olympius. The power of relaxation. 1st U.S. ed. St. Paul, MN : Redleaf Press, 2003.
BF723.S75 T48 2003

STRESS MANAGEMENT FOR CHILDREN - JUVENILE LITERATURE.
Mundy, Michaelene. Getting out of a stress mess!. St. Meinrad, IN : One Caring Place, c2000.
BF723.S75 M86 2000

STRESS MANAGEMENT FOR TEENAGERS - STUDY AND TEACHING (SECONDARY) - ACTIVITY PROGRAMS.
De Anda, Diane. Stress management for adolescents. Champaign, Ill. : Research Press, 2002.
BF724.3.S86 D4 2002

STRESS MANAGEMENT FOR WOMEN.
Collins, Catherine Fisher. Sources of stress and relief for African American women. Westport, Conn. ; London : Praeger, 2003.
BF575.S75 C57 2003

STRESS MANAGEMENT - HUMOR.
Shulman, Mark, 1962- The voodoo revenge book. New York : Main Street, c2002.
BF637.R48 S55 2002

STRESS (PHYSIOLOGY). *See also* **JOB STRESS.**
Greenberg, Jerrold S. Comprehensive stress management. 8th ed. Boston : McGraw-Hill, [2003?]
BF575.S75 G66 2003

STRESS (PHYSIOLOGY) IN ADOLESCENCE. *See* **STRESS IN ADOLESCENCE.**

STRESS (PHYSIOLOGY) IN CHILDREN. *See* **STRESS IN CHILDREN.**

STRESS (PSYCHOLOGY). *See also* **ANXIETY; BURN OUT (PSYCHOLOGY); JOB STRESS; LIFE CHANGE EVENTS; POST-TRAUMATIC STRESS DISORDER.**
Bowman, Marjorie A. Women in medicine. 3rd ed. New York : Berlin : Springer, c2002.
R692 .B69 2002

Collins, Catherine Fisher. Sources of stress and relief for African American women. Westport, Conn. ; London : Praeger, 2003.
BF575.S75 C57 2003

Decker, Dru Scott, 1942- Stress that motivates. Rev. ed. Menlo Park, CA : Crisp Publications, c2002.
BF575.S75 D38 2002

Elliott, Charles H., 1948- Overcoming anxiety for dummies. New York : Wiley Pub., c2003.

BF575.A6 E46 2003
Ėmotsii cheloveka v normal'nykh i stressornykh usloviiakh. Grodno : Grodnenskiĭ gos. universitet im. IAnki Kupaly, 2001.
BF531 .E54 2001

Greenberg, Jerrold S. Comprehensive stress management. 8th ed. Boston : McGraw-Hill, [2003?]
BF575.S75 G66 2003

Kitaev-Smyk, L. A. (Leonid Aleksandrovich) Stress voĭny. Moskva : Ministerstvo kul'tury RF : Rossiĭskiĭ in-t kul'turologii, 2001.

Weiss, Brian L. (Brian Leslie), 1944- Eliminating stress, finding inner peace. Carlsbad, Calif. : Hay House, c2003.
BF575.S75 W44 2003

Work-related mental stress injuries in the NYS workers' compensation system. [Albany, N.Y. : The Board, 1997]
HF5548.85 .W668 1997

Zautra, Alex. Emotions, stress, and health. Oxford ; New York : Oxford University Press, 2003.
R726.7 .Z38 2003

STRESS (PSYCHOLOGY) - BIBLIOGRAPHY.
Stress. New York : Nova Science Publishers, c2002.
BF575.S75

STRESS (PSYCHOLOGY) IN ADOLESCENCE. See **STRESS IN ADOLESCENCE.**

STRESS (PSYCHOLOGY) IN CHILDREN. See **STRESS IN CHILDREN.**

STRESS (PSYCHOLOGY) - PREVENTION.
Greenberg, Jerrold S. Comprehensive stress management. 8th ed. Boston : McGraw-Hill, [2003?]
BF575.S75 G66 2003

Machačová, Helena. [Behaviorální prevence stresu. English] Behavioural prevention of stress. 1st ed. Prague : Karolinum Press, 1999.
BF575.S75 M26513 1999

Mornell, Adina. Lampenfieber und Angst bei ausübenden Musikern. Frankfurt am Main : P. Lang, 2002.
ML3830 .M67 2002

STRESS (PSYCHOLOGY) - RELIGIOUS ASPECTS - CHRISTIANITY.
Johnson Cook, Suzan D. (Suzan Denise), 1957- Too blessed to be stressed. Nashville, Tenn. : T. Nelson, c1998.
BV4527 .J65 1998
1. Black author.

STRESS (PSYCHOLOGY) - RESEARCH - METHODOLOGY - HISTORY.
Cooper, Cary L. A brief history of stress. 1st ed. Oxford, U.K. ; Malden, MA : Blackwell Pub., 2004.
BF575.S75 C646 2004

Stress that motivates.
Decker, Dru Scott, 1942- Rev. ed. Menlo Park, CA : Crisp Publications, c2002.
BF575.S75 D38 2002

Stress voĭny.
Kitaev-Smyk, L. A. (Leonid Aleksandrovich) Moskva : Ministerstvo kul'tury RF : Rossiĭskiĭ in-t kul'turologii, 2001.

STRESSFUL EVENTS. See **LIFE CHANGE EVENTS.**

STRESSFUL LIFE EVENTS. See **LIFE CHANGE EVENTS.**

"Stretching" exercises for qualitative researchers.
Janesick, Valerie J. 2nd ed. Thousand Oaks, Calif. : Sage Publications, c2004.
H62 .J346 2004

Strickland, Albert Lee.
DeSpelder, Lynne Ann, 1944- The last dance. 7th ed. Boston : McGraw-Hill, 2005.
BF789.D4 D53 2005

Strickrodt, Sabine.
Komik der Renaissance, Renaissance der Komik. Frankfurt am Main ; New York : P. Lang, c2000.
BH301.C7 .K63 2000

Strien, P. J. van.
Driekwart eeuw psychotechniek in Nederland. Assen : Van Gorcum, 2001.
HF5548.8 .D73 2001

STROBOSCOPES - PHYSIOLOGICAL EFFECT.
Geiger, John, 1960- Chapel of extreme experience. 1st ed. Toronto, Ont. : Gutter Press, c2002.

QP495 .G45 2002

STROBOSCOPES - PSYCHOLOGICAL ASPECTS.
Geiger, John, 1960- Chapel of extreme experience. 1st ed. Toronto, Ont. : Gutter Press, c2002.
QP495 .G45 2002

Strock, Margaret. Medications [electronic resource]. [4th ed., rev. Apr. 2002, repr. Sept. 2002]. [Bethesda, Md.] : Dept. of Health and Human Services, Public Health Service, National Institutes of Health, National Institute of Mental Health, 2002. (NIH publication ; no. 02-3929) System requirements: Adobe Acrobat Reader. Mode of access: Internet from the NIMH/NIH web site. Address as of 4/23/03: http://www.nimh.nih.gov/publicat/medicate.pdf; current access is available via PURL. Title from title screen (viewed on Apr. 23, 2003). "Revised by Margaret Strock"--P. 36. URL: http://purl.access.gpo.gov/GPO/LPS30017 Available in other form: Strock, Margaret. Medicines 36 p. (OCoLC)51057264.
1. Mental illness - Treatment. 2. Medicine and psychology. I. National Institute of Mental Health (U.S.) II. Title. III. Title: Strock, Margaret. Medicines 36 p. IV. Series.

Strock, Margaret. Medicines 36 p.
Strock, Margaret. Medications [electronic resource]. [4th ed., rev. Apr. 2002, repr. Sept. 2002]. [Bethesda, Md.] : Dept. of Health and Human Services, Public Health Service, National Institutes of Health, National Institute of Mental Health, 2002.

Ströhmer, Michael, 1968- Von Hexen, Ratsherren und Juristen : die Rezeption der peinlichen Halsgerichtsordnung Kaiser Karls V. in den frühen Hexenprozessen der Hansestadt Lemgo, 1583-1621 / Michael Ströhmer. Paderborn : Bonifatius, c2002. 339 p. : ill. ; 25 cm. (Studien und Quellen zur westfälischen Geschichte ; Bd. 43) Originally presented as the author's thesis (doctoral)--Universität Paderborn, 2000/01, under the title: "Constitutio in praxi." Includes bibliographical references (p. 327-339). ISBN 3-89710-225-0
1. Trials (Witchcraft) - Germany - Lemgo - History. 2. Witchcraft - Germany - Lemgo - History. 3. Holy Roman Empire. - Constitutio Criminalis Carolina. 4. Lemgo (Germany) - History. I. Title. II. Series.
BF1583 .S77 2002

Strohner, Hans.
Sprache, Sinn und Situation. 1. Aufl. Wiesbaden : Deutscher Universitäts-Verlag, 2001.

Stróżewski, Władysław. Wokół piękna : szkice z estetyki / Władysław Stróżewski. Kraków : Universitas, c2002. 398 p. : ill. ; 21 cm. Includes bibliographical references and index. ISBN 83-7052-511-3
1. Philosophy, Modern - 20th century. 2. Culture. 3. Aesthetics. I. Title.

Strozier, Charles B. Heinz Kohut : the making of a psychoanalyst / by Charles Strozier. 1st pbk. ed. New York : Other Press, 2004. p. cm. Includes bibliographical references and index. ISBN 1-59051-102-6 (pbk. : alk. paper) DDC 150.19/5/092
1. Kohut, Heinz. 2. Psychoanalysts - United States - Biography. I. Title.
BF109.K6 S77 2004

STRUCTURAL LINGUISTICS. See **FUNCTIONALISM (LINGUISTICS).**

STRUCTURALISM.
Milner, Andrew, 1950- Contemporary cultural theory. 3rd ed. Crows Nest, N.S.W. : Allen & Unwin, 2002.

Structure, agency and the internal conversation.
Archer, Margaret Scotford. Cambridge, U.K. ; New York : Cambridge University Press, 2003.
HM708 .A73 2003

The structure of being in Aristotle's Metaphysics.
Yu, Jiyuan. Dordrecht, Boston : Kluwer Academic, c2003.
B434 .Y8 2003

The structure of thinking.
Weed, Laura E. Exeter : Imprint Academic, c2003.

STRUCTURE PSYCHOLOGY. See **WHOLE AND PARTS (PSYCHOLOGY).**

STRUCTURES. See **BUILDINGS.**

Struening, Karen, 1960- New family values : liberty, equality, diversity / Karen Struening. Lanham : Rowman & Littlefield Publishers, c2002. xxii, 215 p. ; 24 cm. Includes bibliographical references and index. ISBN 0-7425-1230-4 (alk. paper) ISBN 0-7425-1231-2 (pbk. : alk. paper) DDC 306.85/0973
1. Family - United States. 2. Liberty. I. Title.
HQ536 .S82 2002

STRUGGLE.
Olivetti, Alberto. Gara e bellezza. Fiesole, Firenze : Cadmo, c2002.

Die Struktur des Bewusstseins.
Roehle, Friedrich, 1916-1995. Frankfurt am Main ; New York : Peter Lang, c2001.

Strukturbildung und Lebensstil / herausgegeben von Ulrike Lehmkuhl ; mit Beiträgen von Heide Bade ... [et al.]. München : Ernst Reinhardt, c2002. 215 p. : ill. ; 24 cm. (Beiträge zur Individualpsychologie, 0722-8902 : Bd. 28) Papers from the Jahrestagung für Individualpsychologie, held spring 2001 in Mainz. Includes bibliographical references. ISBN 3-497-01617-9 (pbk.)
1. Developmental psychology - Congresses. I. Lehmkuhl, Ulrike. II. Bade, Heide. III. Series.

La struttura parentale nelle fiabe dei fratelli Grimm.
Bosco Coletsos, Sandra. Alessandria : Edizioni dell'Orso, 2001.

Stuart Hall.
Rojek, Chris. Cambridge, UK : Polity in association with Blackwell, 2003.
HM621 .R64 2003

STUART, JANE (FICTITIOUS CHARACTER) - FICTION.
Marshall, Evan, 1956- Icing Ivy. Waterville, Me. : Thorndike Press, 2003, c2002.
PS3563.A72236 I27 2003

Stubbe, Hannes, 1941- Kultur und Psychologie in Brasilien : eine ethnopsychologische und wissenschaftshistorische Studie / Hannes Stubbe. Bonn : Holos, 2002. 409 p. : ill. ; 21 cm. Includes bibliographical references (p. 363-388). ISBN 3-86097-184-0 (pbk.) DDC 150/.981
1. Psychology - Brazil - History. 2. Social psychology - Brazil - History. I. Title.
BF108.B6 S783 2001

Stubbs, Ron.
Hogan, Kevin. Can't get through. Gretna, La. : Pelican Pub. Co., c2003.
BF637.C45 H635 2003

STUDENT ACHIEVEMENT. See **ACADEMIC ACHIEVEMENT.**

STUDENT PROTESTERS.
Fahlenbrach, Kathrin. Protest-Inszenierungen. 1. Aufl. Wiesbaden : Westdeutscher Verlag, 2002.

STUDENT VIOLENCE. See **SCHOOL VIOLENCE.**

STUDENTS. See **COLLEGE STUDENTS; EDUCATION.**

STUDENTS - CRIMES AGAINST. See **SCHOOL VIOLENCE.**

A students dictionary of psychology.
Statt, David A., 1942- 1st ed. Hove, UK ; New York : Psychology Press, 2003.
BF31 .S64 2003

A student's guide to psychology.
Robinson, Daniel N., 1937- 1st ed. Wilmington, Del. : ISI Books, c2002.
BF121 .R598 2002

Studi (Accademia toscana di scienze e lettere La Colombaria)
(202.) Pagnini, Marcello. Letteratura ed ermeneutica. Firenze : L.S. Olschki, 2002.

Studi Bompiani. Filosofia
Berto, G. (Graziella) Freud, Heidegger. Milano : Bompiani, c1998.
BF175.4.P45 B46 1998

Studi di filosofia (Rome, Italy)
(22.) Castagnino, M. (Mario) Tempo e universo. Roma : Armando, c2000.
BD632 .C37 2000

Studi e ricerche (Istituto Giovanni Paolo II per studi su matrimonio e famiglia)
Noriega, José. "Guiados por el espíritu". Roma : Pontificia università lateranense ; [Milano] : Mursia, 2000.

Studi sulle società e le culture del Medioevo per Girolamo Arnaldi / a cura di Ludovico Gatto e Paola Supino Martini. [Firenze] : All'insegna del giglio, 2002. 2 v. (970 p.) : ill. ; 24 cm. Università degli studi di Roma La Sapienza. Includes bibliographical references and indexes. Italian, English, French, and German. ISBN 88-7814-204-2
1. Dante Alighieri, - 1265-1321. - Divina commedia. 2. Arnaldi, Girolamo. 3. Italy - Civilization - 476-1268. 4. Italian literature - To 1400 - History and criticism. 5. Civilization, Medieval. I. Arnaldi, Girolamo. II. Gatto, Ludovico. III. Supino Martini, Paola, 1942-
DG443 .S78 2002

Studi superiori (Carocci editore)
(416.) Trabattoni, Franco. La filosofia antica. 1a ed. Roma : Carocci, 2002.

Studi superiori (Carocci editore). Filosofia.
Trabattoni, Franco. La filosofia antica. 1a ed. Roma : Carocci, 2002.

Studi vichiani
(34) Sanna, Manuela. La "fantasia, che è l'occhio dell'ingegno". Napoli : A. Guida editore, c2001.
B3583 .S26 2001

Studia culturae Islamicae
(no. 62) Kūshyār, d. ca. 961. [Introduction to astrology] Kūšyār ibn Labbān's introduction to astrology. Tokyo : Institue for the Study of Languages and Cultures of Asia and Africa, 1997.
BF1714.I84 K87 1997

Studia Fennica. Ethnologica
(7) Making and breaking of borders. Helsinki : Finnish Literature Society, 2003.
JC323 .M35 2003

Studia humaniora
(Bd. 35) Botschaften aus dem Jenseits. [Düsseldorf] : Droste, c2002.

Studia in Veteris Testamenti pseudepigrapha
(v. 17) Buitenwerf, Rieuwerd. Book III of the Sibylline oracles and its social setting. Leiden ; Boston, MA : Brill, 2003.
BF1769 .B85 2003

Studia linguistica Germanica
(69) Stein, Stephan, 1963- Textgliederung. Berlin ; New York : Walter de Gryuter, 2003.

Studien und Materialien zur Geschichte der Philosophie
(Bd. 63) Greimann, Dirk. Freges Konzeption der Wahrheit. Hildesheim ; New York : Georg Olms, c2003.
B3318.T78 G74 2003

Studien und Quellen zur westfälischen Geschichte
(Bd. 43) Ströhmer, Michael, 1968- Von Hexen, Ratsherren und Juristen. Paderborn : Bonifatius, c2002.
BF1583 .S77 2002

Studien zu antiken Identitäten / herausgegeben von Stefan Faller. Würzburg : Ergon Verlag, c2001. 192 p. : ill., maps ; 23 cm. (Identitäten und Alteritäten ; Bd. 9. Altertumswissenschaftliche Reihe ; Bd. 2) "Diese Arbeit ist im Sonderforschungsbereich 541 "Identitäten und Alteritäten -- Die Funktion von Alterität für die Konstitution und Konstruktion von Identität" der Albert-Ludwigs-Universität Freiburg entstanden"--T.p. verso. Includes bibliographical references. Seven contributions in German, 1 in French, and 1 in Italian. ISBN 3-89913-215-7 (pbk.)
1. Rome - Civilization. 2. Latin drama (Tragedy) - History and criticism. 3. Rome - Religion. 4. Group identity - Rome. 5. Other (Philosophy) 6. Identity (Psychology) 7. Difference (Psychology) 8. Cross-cultural orientation. I. Faller, Stefan. II. Sonderforschungsbereich 541--"Identitäten und Alteritäten". III. Series: Identitäten und Alteritäten ; Bd. 9. IV. Series: Identitäten und Alteritäten. Altertumswissenschaftliche Reihe ; Bd. 2.
DG78 .S78 2001

Studien zur Geschichte des Alltags
(Bd. 19) Patzel-Mattern, Katja. Geschichte im Zeichen der Erinnerung. Stuttgart : Franz Steiner, 2002.

Studien zur Kognitionswissenschaft
Kessler, Klaus. Raumkognition und Lokalisationsäusserungen. Wiesbaden : Deutscher Universitäts-Verlag, 2000.
BF469 .K47 2000

Studien zur österreichischen Philosophie
(Bd. 34-35) Benussi, V. (Vittorio) [Selections. 2002] Psychologische Schriften. Amsterdam ; New York : Rodopi, 2002.

Studien zur Sozialwissenschaft (Westdeutscher Verlag)
Braun-Thürmann, Holger. Künstliche Interaktion. 1. Aufl. Wiesbaden : Westdeutscher Verlag, 2002.

Studies in African literature
Remembering Africa. Portsmouth, NH : Heinemann, c2002.
DT14 .R46 2002

Studies in art, culture, and communities
Art and essence. Westport, Conn. ; London : Praeger, 2003.
BH39 .A685 2003

Art and experience. Westport, Conn. ; London : Praeger, 2003.
BH39 .A686 2003

Studies in comparative philosophy and religion
Varieties of ethical reflection. Lanham, Md. ; Oxford : Lexington Books, c2002.
BJ1031 .V37 2002

Studies in comparative religion (Columbia, S.C.)
Berger, Helen A., 1949- Voices from the pagan census. Columbia, S.C. : University of South Carolina Press, c2003.
BF1573 .B48 2003

Studies in consciousness
Vasil'ev, Leonid Leonidovich. Experiments in mental suggestion. [Rev. ed.]. Charlottesville, VA : Hampton Roads Pub., c2002.
BF1156.S8 V313 2002

Wilkins, George H. (George Hubert), Sir, 1888-1958. Thoughts through space. Charlottesville, VA : Hampton Roads Pub. Co., 2004.
BF1171 .W49 2004

Studies in contemporary German social thought
Habermas, Jürgen. [Wahrheit und Rechtfertigung. English] Truth and justification. Cambridge, Mass. : MIT Press, c2003.
B3258.H323 W3413 2003

Studies in Continental thought
Race and racism in continental philosophy. Bloomington : Indiana University Press, c2003.
HT1523 .R2514 2003

Schürmann, Reiner, 1941- [Des hégémonies brisées. English] Broken hegemonies. Bloomington : Indiana University Press, c2003.
BD162 .S48 2003

Vallega-Neu, Daniela, 1966- Heidegger's contributions to philosophy. Bloomington, IN : Indiana University Press, c2003.
B3279.H48 B454 2003

Studies in curriculum theory
McKnight, Douglas. Schooling, the Puritan imperative, and the molding of an American national identity. Mahwah, N.J. ; London : L. Erlbaum Associates, 2003.
LC311 .M24 2003

Studies in early modern European history
Rowlands, Alison. Witchcraft narratives in Germany. Manchester, UK ; New York : Manchester University Press ; New York : Distributed exclusively in the USA by Palgrave, 2003.
BF1583 .R69 2003

Studies in early modern German history
Spee, Friedrich von, 1591-1635. [Cautio criminalis. English] Cautio criminalis, or, A book on witch trials. Charlottesville : University of Virginia Press, 2003.
BF1583.A2 S6813 2003

Studies in economic theory (Berlin, Germany)
(14.) Vind, Karl. Independence, additivity, uncertainty. Berlin ; New York : Springer, c2003.
HB135 .V56 2003

Studies in emotion and social interaction
Feelings and emotions. New York : Cambridge University Press, 2003.
BF531 .F445 2003

The social life of emotions. New York : Cambridge University Press, 2004.
BF531 .S634 2004

Studies in emotion and social interaction. Second series
Shields, Stephanie A. Speaking from the heart. Cambridge, U.K. ; New York : Cambridge University Press, 2002.
BF531 .S55 2002

Studies in German literature, linguistics, and culture
Berg, Henk de, 1963- Freud's theory and its use in literary and cultural studies. Rochester, NY : Camden House, 2003.
PN56.P92 B36 2003

Studies in German literature, linguistics, and culture (Unnumbered)
A companion to Gottfried von Strassburg's "Tristan". Rochester, NY : Camden House, 2003.
PT1526 .C66 2003

Recasting German identity. Rochester, NY : Camden House, 2002.
DD239 .R43 2002

Studies in imagination
Sardello, Robert J., 1942- Facing the world with soul. 2nd ed. Great Barrington, MA : Lindisfarne Books, c2003.
BF637.C5 S27 2003

Studies in Judaism
Neusner, Jacob, 1932- Analysis and argumentation in Rabbinic Judaism. Lanham, Md. : University Press of America, c2003.
BM496.5 .N4775 2003

Studies in Jungian psychology by Jungian analysts
Bond, D. Stephenson. The archetype of renewal. Toronto : Inner City Books, c2003.

Edinger, Edward F. Science of the soul. Toronto, Ont. : Inner City Books, c2002.
BF173 .E27 2002

Hollis, James, 1940- On this journey we call our life. Toronto, Ont. : Inner City Books, c2003.
BF697.5.S43 H65 2003

Hollis, James, 1940- On this journey we call our life. Toronto : Inner City Books, c2003.

(106) Harding, M. Esther (Mary Esther), 1888-1971. The parental image. 3rd ed. Toronto : Inner City Books, c2003.

Studies in language and social interaction : in honour of Robert Hopper / edited by Phillip J. Glenn, Curtis D. LeBaron, Jenny Mandelbaum. Mahwah, N.J. : London : Lawrence Erlbaum, 2003. xi, 625 p. : ill., ports. ; 24 cm. Includes bibliographical references and index. ISBN 0-8058-3732-9 DDC 306.44
1. Sociolinguistics. 2. Interpersonal communication. 3. Social interaction. 4. Conversation. I. Hopper, Robert, 1945- II. Glenn, Phillip J. III. LeBaron, Curtis D. IV. Mandelbaum, Jenny S.

Studies in law and economics
Epstein, Richard A. Skepticism and freedom. Chicago : University of Chicago Press, c2003.
K487.L5 E67 2003

Studies in literary criticism and theory
(v. 13.) Washington, Johnny. Evolution, history and destiny. New York : Peter Lang, c2002.
E185.625 .W37 2002

Studies in medieval and Reformation thought
(v. 91) Zika, Charles. Exorcising our demons. Leiden ; Boston : Brill, 2003.
BF1584.E85 Z55 2003

Studies in medieval culture
(42) Marvels, monsters, and miracles. Kalamazoo, Mich. : Medieval Institute Publications, 2002.
GR825 .M218 2002

Studies in military history and international affairs
York, Neil Longley. Turning the world upside down. Westport, Conn. : London : Praeger, 2003.
E210 .Y67 2003

Studies in neurophilosophy.
Churchland, Patricia Smith. Brain-wise. Cambridge, Mass. : MIT Press, c2002.
RC343 .C486 2002

Studies in political science (Lewiston, N.Y.)
(v. 6.) Moreno-Riaño, Gerson, 1971- Political tolerance, culture, and the individual. Lewiston, N.Y. : E. Mellen Press, c2002.
JA74.5 .M653 2002

Studies in public policy (Lanham, Md.)
Policymaking and peace. Lanham, Md. : Lexington Books, c2003.
JZ5538 .P65 2003

Studies in the evolution of language
(3) Language evolution. Oxford ; New York : Oxford University Press, 2003.
P140 .L256 2003

Studies in the history of religions
(95.) Modern societies & the science of religions. Leiden ; Boston : Brill, 2002.
BL48 .M542 2002

Studies in the theology and sociology of Yoruba indigenous religion / edited by E. O. Babalola. Lagos, Nigeria : Concept Publications (Nig.), 2002. vii, 105 p. ; 20 cm. Cover title: Theology and sociology of Yoruba indigenous religion. ISBN from stamp on t.p. verso. Includes bibliographical references. CONTENTS: Abiku phenomenon in Owo Yoruba Kingdom / by E.O. Babalola -- Ancestral phenomenon in traditional Africa / by E.O. Babalola -- In search of an identity : the Yoruba Christian woman in a socio-cultural context / by Bolaji O. Bateye -- Islamic values in interaction with political and socio-religion systems of the traditional Yoruba community / by M.O. Adeniyi -- Modern trends in the Islamized music of the traditional Yoruba / by Michael Olutayo Olatunji -- Changing roles of Satan : Christian and African Traditional religious perspectives / by Jide Gbadegesin -- Esu worship and praise

chants in Yorubaland / by Oyewole Arohunmolase -- Yoruba orature : a strategy for socio-religious harmony in Yorubaland / by J.B. Agbaje -- The effect of acculturation on traditional African music : Ifa music of the Yoruba as a case study / by 'Femi Adedeji -- Magical complexion in Africa Christian prayers / by S.I. Ogunsakin-Fabarebo -- Prayers in traditional religion and Islam among the Yoruba / by M.O. Adeniyi.
1. Yoruba (African people) - Religion. 2. Religion and sociology - Nigeria. 3. Nigeria - Religion. I. Babalola, E. O. II. Title: Theology and sociology of Yoruba indigenous religion

Studies in the understanding of the human condition
Bertelsen, Preben. Free will, consciousness, and the self. New York : Berghahn Books, 2003.
BF621 .B47 2003

Studies in theoretical psycholinguistics
(v. 29) Hamann, Cornelia, 1953- From syntax to discourse. Dordrecht, The Netherlands ; Boston : Kluwer Academic Publishers, c2002.
P118 .H327 2002

Studies in writing & rhetoric
Daniell, Beth, 1947- A communion of friendship. Carbondale : Southern Illinois University Press, c2003.
PE1405.U6 D36 2003

Studies in written language and literacy
(v. 11) Precursors of functional literacy. Amsterdam ; Philadelphia : J. Benjamins Pub., c2002.
P118.7 .P74 2002

Studies of action and organisation
(v. 6.) Kallinikos, Jannis. Technology and society. Munich : Accedo : Distributed in the U.S.A. by The Institute of Mind and Behavior, c1996.

Studies of nonlinear phenomena in life sciences
(v. 9) Orsucci, Franco. Changing mind. River Edge, NJ : World Scientific, c2002.
BF161 .O77 2002

Studies on femininity / edited by Alcira Mariam Alizade ; for the Committee on Women and Psychoanalysis of the International Psychoanalysis Association. London ; New York : Karnac, 2003. xi, 144 p. (Psychoanalysis & women series) Includes bibliographical references (p. 137-144) ISBN 1-85575-957-8 DDC 155.333
1. Femininity. 2. Sex (Psychology) I. Alizade, Alcira Mariam. II. International Psychoanalysis Association. Committee on Women and Psychoanalysis. III. Series.

Studies on language acquisition
(19) Kecskés, István. Situation-bound utterances in L1 and L2. Berlin ; New York : Mouton de Gruyter, 2002.
P95.45 .K4 2002

(21) Development of verb inflection in first language acquisition. Berlin ; New York : Mouton de Gruyter, 2003.
P118 .D465 2003

Study needed to assess the effects of recent divestitures on competition in retail markets.
United States. General Accounting Office. Federal Trade Commission [electronic resource]. [Washington, D.C.] : U.S. General Accounting Office, [2002]

Study of the moral foundations of Descartes' theory of knowledge.
Araujo, Marcelo de. Scepticism, freedom and autonomy. Berlin : De Gruyter, 2003.

Studying individual development in an interindividual context.
Bergman, Lars R. Mahwah, N.J. : L. Erlbaum Associates, 2003.
BF713 .B464 2003

Stumme Sprache der Bilder.
Rehm, Ulrich. München : Deutscher Kunstverlag, 2002.

STUPIDITY - ANECDOTES.
Fenster, Bob. Well, duh!. Kansas City, MO : Andrews McMeel Pub., 2004.
BF431 .F37 2004

Gregory, Leland. Hey idiot!. Kansas City, MO : Andrews McMeel Pub., 2003.
BF431 .G7825 2003

Scalzi, John, 1969- Uncle John's presents Book of the dumb. San Diego, CA : Portable Press, 2003.
BF431 .S273 2003

STUPIDITY - HISTORY.
Fenster, Bob. Well, duh!. Kansas City, MO : Andrews McMeel Pub., 2004.
BF431 .F37 2004

STUPIDITY - HUMOR.
Scalzi, John, 1969- Uncle John's presents Book of the dumb. San Diego, CA : Portable Press, 2003.
BF431 .S273 2003

STUPIDITY - UNITED STATES - ANECDOTES.
Unusually stupid Americans. 1st ed. New York : Villard, 2003.
BF431 .U65 2003

Sturge, Kate.
Nietzsche, Friedrich Wilhelm, 1844-1900. [Selections. English. 2003] Writings from the late notebooks. Cambridge, UK ; New York : Cambridge University Press, c2003.
B3312.E5 B58 2003

Sturm, Hermann, 1936- Dinge im Fluss, Fluss der Verzeichnungen / Hermann Sturm. Frankfurt a.M. : Anabas-Verlag, 2002. 240 p. : ill. : 23 cm. Includes bibliographical references. ISBN 3-87038-346-1 (pbk.)
1. Aesthetics. 2. Architecture. 3. Art. I. Title.

Stutley, Margaret, 1917- Shamanism : an introduction / Margaret Stutley. London ; New York : Routledge, 2003. vii, 134 p. ; 23 cm. Includes bibliographical references (p. [113]-126) and index. ISBN 0-415-27317-X (hbk.) ISBN 0-415-27318-8 (pbk.) DDC 291.1/44
1. Shamanism. I. Title.
BL2370.S5 S88 2003

Stutzer, Alois.
Frey, Bruno S. Happiness and economics. Princeton, N.J. : Princeton University Press, c2002.
BF575.H27 F75 2002

Styers, Randall. Making magic : religion, magic, and science in the modern world / Randall Styers. New York : Oxford University Press, 2003. p. cm. (Reflection and theory in the study of religion) Includes bibliographical references (p.   ) and index. ISBN 0-19-515107-0 (alk. paper) ISBN 0-19-516941-7 (pbk. : alk. paper) DDC 133.4/3/0903
1. Magic. 2. Magic - Religious aspects. 3. Magic - Social aspects. I. Title. II. Series.
BF1611 .S855 2003

Styhre, Alexander. Understanding knowledge management : critical and postmodern perspectives / Alexander Styhre. Malmö, Sweden : Liber ; Oslo, Norge : Abstrakt ; Herndon, VA : Copenhagen Business School Press, c2003. 187 p. ; 25 cm. Includes bibliographical references and index. ISBN 91-47-06575-3 (Sweden) ISBN 82-7935-055-1 (Norway) ISBN 87-630-0109-8 (rest of the world)
1. Knowledge management. 2. Knowledge management - Philosophy. 3. Knowledge, Theory of. I. Title.
HD30.2 .S84 2003

Style, function, transmission : evolutionary archaeological perspectives / edited by Michael J. O'Brien and R. Lee Lyman. Salt Lake City : University of Utah Press, c2003. viii, 358 p. : ill., maps ; 27 cm. (Foundations of archaeological inquiry) Includes bibliographical references (p. 295-348) and index. ISBN 0-87480-747-6 (alk. paper) ISBN 0-87480-748-4 (pbk. : alk. paper) DDC 930.1/01
1. Archaeology. 2. Social evolution. 3. Human evolution. 4. Social change. I. O'Brien, Michael J. (Michael John), 1950- II. Lyman, R. Lee. III. Series.
CC173 .S79 2003

STYLE IN DRESS. *See* **FASHION.**

STYLE, LITERARY. *See* **CRITICISM; LITERATURE - HISTORY AND CRITICISM; RHETORIC.**

Su zhi yu ming yun.
Xie, Sizhong. Di 1 ban. Beijing : Zuo jia chu ban she, 2002.
BD450 .X54 2002

SUB-SAHARA AFRICA. *See* **AFRICA, SUB-SAHARAN.**

SUB-SAHARAN AFRICA. *See* **AFRICA, SUB-SAHARAN.**

Sub-urbanism and the art of memory.
Marot, Sébastien, 1961- [Art de la mémoire, la territoire et l'architecture] London : Architectural Association, c2003.

SUBCEPTION. *See* **SUBLIMINAL PROJECTION.**

SUBCHAPTER C CORPORATIONS. *See* **CORPORATIONS.**

SUBCONSCIOUSNESS. *See also* **ARCHETYPE (PSYCHOLOGY); DREAMS; HALLUCINATIONS AND ILLUSIONS.**

Apollon, Willy. After Lacan. Albany : State University of New York Press, 2002.
RC506 .A65 2002

Birtchnell, John. The two of me. Hove, East Sussex [England] ; New York : Routledge, 2003.
BF311 .B533 2003

Broqueville, Paulette Renée. Unraveling your past to get into the present. Rev. ed. Costa Mesa, Calif. : Broqueville Pub., c2002-
BF315 .B76 2002

Gambini, Roberto, 1944- Soul & culture. 1st ed. College Station : Texas A&M University Press, 2003.
BF698.9.C8 G35 2003

Lawrence, D. H. (David Herbert), 1885-1930. [Psychoanalysis and the unconscious] Psychoanalysis and the unconscious; New York : Cambridge, 2003.
BF173 .L28 2003

MacIntyre, Alasdair C. The unconscious. Rev. ed. New York : Routledge, 2004.
BF315 .M23 2004

Miller, Jeffrey C., 1951- The transcendent function. Albany : State University of New York Press, c2003.
BF175.5.I53 M55 2003

Motycka, Alina. Nauka o nieświadomości. Wrocław : Leopoldinum, 1998.

The new unconscious. New York : Oxford University Press, 2004.
BF315 .N47 2004

Soler, Colette. L'inconscient à ciel ouvert de la psychose. Toulouse : Presses universitaires du Mirail, c2002.

SUBCONSCIOUSNESS - CONGRESSES.
L'inconscio antinomico. Milano : F. Angeli, c1999.
BF315 .I56 1999

SUBCULTURE - UNITED STATES.
Fletcher, John Wright. A hermeneutic study of generational music. 2002.

Sub"ekt, poznanie, dei͡atel'nost' : k 70-letiiu V.A. Lektorskogo / [redaktsionnai͡a kollegii͡a V.S. Stepin ... et al.]. Moskva : Kanon+, 2002. 718 p. ; 21 cm. Includes bibliographical references. ISBN 5883731562
1. Lektorskiĭ, V. A. 2. Knowledge, Theory of. 3. Cognition. 4. Act (Philosophy) 5. Rationalism. 6. Truth. 7. Science - Philosophy. I. Stepin, V. S. (Vi͡acheslav Semenovich) II. Lektorskiĭ, V. A.
BD166 .S84 2002

Sub"ekt v mire, Mir sub"ekta
Chelovek kak sub"ekt kul'tury. Moskva : Nauka, 2002.

SUBJECT DICTIONARIES. *See* **ENCYCLOPEDIAS AND DICTIONARIES.**

The subject of care : feminist perspectives on dependency / [edited by] Eva Feder Kittay and Ellen K. Feder. Lanham, Md. ; Oxford : Rowman & Littlefield Publishers, c2002. ix, 382 p. ; 24 cm. (Feminist constructions) Includes bibliographical references and index. ISBN 0-7425-1362-9 (hbk. : alk. paper) ISBN 0-7425-1363-7 (pbk. : alk. paper) DDC 305.42
1. Feminism. 2. Child welfare - United States. 3. Mother and child - United States. 4. Caregivers - Family relationships. 5. Family services - United States. I. Kittay, Eva Feder. II. Feder, Ellen K. III. Series.
HQ1206 .S9 2002

SUBJECT (PHILOSOPHY).
Chelovek kak sub"ekt kul'tury. Moskva : Nauka, 2002.

Zima, P. V. Theorie des Subjekts. Tübingen : A. Francke, c2000.
BD223 .Z56 2000

SUBJECTIVISM. *See* **SUBJECTIVITY.**

SUBJECTIVITY.
Baldus, Claus, 1947- Weg im Nicht. Stuttgart : Hatje, c1994.

Búfalo, Enzo del. Individuo, mercado y utopía. 1. ed. Caracas : Monte Ávila Editores Lationoamericana : Universidad Central de Venezuela, Centro de Investigaciones Post-Doctorales FACES, 1998.
BD222 .B86 1998

Ensaios. João Pessoa : Editora Universitária, 2001.

Read, Jason. The micro-politics of capital. Albany : State University of New York Press, c2003.
HB97.5 .R42 2003

Sequeri, Pier Angelo. L'umano alla prova. Milano : V & P Università, c2002.

Subjectivity.

BD222.S47 U6 2002

Zima, P. V. Theorie des Subjekts. Tübingen : A. Francke, c2000.
BD223 .Z56 2000

SUBJECTIVITY - CONGRESSES.
Der Grund, die Not und die Freude des Bewusstseins. Würzburg : Königshausen & Neumann, c2002.
B808.9 .G78 2002

[Nuevos paradigmas. English.] New paradigms, culture, and subjectivity. Cresskill, N.J. : Hampton Press, c2002.
BD161 .N8413 2002

Der Subjektbegriff bei Lacan und Althusser.
Hong, Joon-kee, 1962- Frankfurt am Main : New York : Peter Lang , c2000.
BF109.L28 H66 2000

SUBLANGUAGE. See **TERMS AND PHRASES.**

SUBLIMATION (PSYCHOLOGY).
Moyaert, Paul, 1952- Begeren en vereren. Amsterdam : SUN, c2002.
BF175.5.S92 M69 2002

SUBLIME, THE.
Lyotard. New York ; London : Routledge, 2002.

SUBLIME, THE, IN LITERATURE.
Halpern, Richard, 1954- Shakespeare's perfume. Philadelphia : University of Pennsylvania Press, c2002.
PR2848 .H25 2002

SUBLIMINAL PROJECTION - UNITED STATES.
Constantine, Alex. Virtual government. 1st ed. Venice, CA : Feral House, 1997.
BF633 .C67 1997

SUBORDINATION OF WOMEN. See **SEX ROLE.**

SUBSAHARA AFRICA. See **AFRICA, SUB-SAHARAN.**

SUBSAHARAN AFRICA. See **AFRICA, SUB-SAHARAN.**

SUBSCRIPTION TELEVISION. See **CABLE TELEVISION.**

SUBSTANCE ABUSE.
High culture. Albany : State University of New York Press, c2003.
HV4998 .H544 2003

The substance of style.
Postrel, Virginia I., 1960- 1st ed. New York : HarperCollins, c2003.
BH39 .P6692 2003

SUBSTANCE (PHILOSOPHY).
Caropreso, Paolo. Von der Dingfrage zur Frage nach Gott. Berlin ; New York : W. de Gruyter, 2003.

Jadacki, Jacek Juliusz. From the viewpoint of the Lvov-Warsaw school. Amsterdam ; New York, NY : Rodopi, 2003.

SUBTERFUGE. See **DECEPTION.**

Subtlety of emotions.
Ben-Ze'ev, Aharon. Be-sod ha-regashot. Lod : Zemorah-Bitan, 2001.

SUBURBS.
Marot, Sébastien, 1961- [Art de la mémoire, la territoire et l'architecture] Sub-urbanism and the art of memory. London : Architectural Association, c2003.

SUBVERSIVE ACTIVITIES. See **TERRORISM.**

SUCCESS. See also **ACADEMIC ACHIEVEMENT; FAILURE (PSYCHOLOGY); SELF-REALIZATION.**
Chiodi, Michael. The art of building people. 1st ed. St. Paul, Minn. : Chiberry Press, c2003.
BF637.S4 C497 2003

Clayton, Charles Walker, 1951- Connections!. Radcliffe, IA : Ide House Publishers, 2004.
BF637.C45 C54 2004

Daniels, Joni T. Power tools for women. 1st ed. New York : Three Rivers Press, c2002.
HQ1221 .D26 2002

Deniau, Jean-François, 1928- La gloire à vingt ans. [Paris] : XO editions, c2003.

Eckblad, John. If your life were a business, would you invest in it? New York : McGraw-Hill, c2003.
BF637.S4 E38 2003

Fang yuan bing fa. Di 1 ban. Beijing : Jin cheng chu ban she, 1998.

Farber, Barry J. Diamond in the rough. New York : Berkley Books, c1995.
BF637.S8 F34 1995

Farson, Richard Evans, 1926- Whoever makes the most mistakes wins. New York ; London : Free Press, c2002.
HD45 .F357 2002

Ferry, Luc. Qu'est-ce qu'une vie réussie? Paris : Grasset, c2002.
BJ1612 .F47 2002

Hall, Judy, 1943- The intuition handbook. London : Vega, 2003.
BF315.5 .H35 2003

Harry, Lou, 1963- The game of life. Philadelphia : Running Press, c2003.
BF637.S4 H357 2003

Holmes, Ernest, 1887-1960. [This thing called life] The art of life. New York : J.P. Tarcher/Penguin, c2004.
BF645 .H572 2004

Kaufman, Ronald A. Anatomy of success. Dubuque, Iowa : Kendall/Hunt Pub., c1999.
BF637.S8 .K379 1999

Lowry, Don. Keys to personal success. Riverside, Calif. : True Colors, Inc. ; c2001.
BF637.S8 .L77 2001

Monahan, Tom. The do-it-yourself lobotomy. New York : J. Wiley, c2002.
BF408 .M59 2002

The right words at the right time. New York : Atria Books, c2002.
BJ1611.2 .R52 2002

Silverman, Robin Landew. Reaching your goals. New York : F. Watts, 2003.
BF505.G6 S57 2003

Whalen, Charles E., Jr. The gift of renewal. 1st ed. Gainesville, GA : Warren Featherbone Foundation, c2003 (Gainesville, GA : Matthews Print.)
BF637.S4 W47 2003

Yazi. Qing hua Bei da xue bu dao. Di 1 ban. Beijing : Xin hua chu ban she, 2002.
BJ1618.C5 Y38 2002

Zeng, Guofan, 1811-1872. Fan jing. Di 1 ban. Beijing : Zhongguo Hua qiao chu ban she, 2001.
BJ1618.C5 H44 2001

SUCCESS - CASE STUDIES - JUVENILE LITERATURE.
Survivors. New York : Scholastic, c2002.
BF637.S8 S8317 2002

SUCCESS IN ADOLESCENCE.
Beyond coping. Oxford ; New York : Oxford University Press, 2002.
BF335 .B49 2002

Ladner, Joyce A. Launching our Black children for success. 1st ed. San Francisco : Jossey-Bass, c2003.
BF723.S77 L33 2003

SUCCESS IN ADOLESCENCE - JUVENILE LITERATURE.
Mawi Asgedom. The code. New York : Little, Brown, 2003.
BF724.3.S9 M34 2003

SUCCESS IN BUSINESS. See also **CREATIVE ABILITY IN BUSINESS.**
Allen, Robert G. Multiple streams of internet income. New York : Wiley, c2001.
HF5548.32 .A45 2001

Allenbaugh, Eric. Deliberate success. Franklin Lakes, NJ : Career Press, c2002.
HF5386 .A5434 2002

Capp, Ray, 1953- When you mean business about yourself. Nashville, Tenn. : Rutledge Hill Press, c2002.
BF637.S8 C37 2002

Christensen, Clayton M. The innovator's solution. Boston, Mass. : Harvard Business School Press, c2003.

Davenport, Thomas H. What's the big idea? Boston, Mass. : Harvard Business School Press, c2003.
HD53 .D38 2003

Eppler, Mark, 1946- The Wright way. New York : AMACOM, c2004.
TL540.W7 E64 2004

Farson, Richard Evans, 1926- Whoever makes the most mistakes wins. New York ; London : Free Press, c2002.
HD45 .F357 2002

Finkelstein, Sydney. Why smart executives fail and what you can learn from their mistakes. New York ; London : Portfolio, 2003.
HD38.2 .F56 2003

Gelb, Michael. More balls than hands. New York, NY : Prentice Hall, 2003.
BF637.S8 G39 2003

Hiam, Alexander. Making horses drink. [Irvine, Calif.] : Entrepreneur Press, c2002.
HD57.7 .H52 2002

Israel-Curley, Marcia. Defying the odds. 1st ed. Woodstock, N.Y. : Overlook Press, 2002.
HB615 .I75 2002

Kazerounian, Nadine. Stepping up. London : McGraw-Hill, c2002.

Kleiner, Art. Who really matters. 1st ed. New York ; London : Currency/Doubleday, 2003.
HD2741 .K478 2003

Kushell, Jennifer. Secrets of the young & successful. New York : Simon & Schuster, c2003.
BF637.S8 K875 2003

Lewis-Hall, Jennifer, 1964- Life's a journey--not a sprint. Carlsbad, Calif. : Hay House, c2003.
BF637.S8 L455 2003

Marcum, Dave. BusinessThink. New York : Wiley, c2002.
HF5386 .M3087 2002

McConnell, Carmel. Change activist. Cambridge, MA : Perseus Pub., c2001.
BF481 .M393 2001

McQuillar, Tayannah Lee, 1977- Rootwork. New York : Simon & Schuster, c2003.
BF1622.A34 M37 2003
1. Black author.

Neely, A. D. (Andy D.) The performance prism. London ; New York : Financial Times/Prentice Hall, 2002.
HF5549.5.P35 N44 2002

O'Loughlin, James. The real Warren Buffett. London ; Yarmouth, ME : Nicholas Brealey, 2003.

Pearlman, Lou. Bands, brands and billions. New York ; London : McGraw-Hill, 2002.

Salmon, William A. The mid-career tune-up. New York : Amacom, c2000.
HF5381 .S256 2000

Stewardson, John (John E.) Success is the best revenge. Toronto : Productive Publications, c1994.

Trainor, Norm, 1946- The eight best practices of high-performing salespeople. Toronto ; New York : Wiley, c2000.
HF5438.25 .T72 2000

Zeer, Darrin. Office Feng Shui. San Francisco : Chronicle Books, 2004.
BF1779.F4 Z44 2004

Zhongguo, shui zui fu. Di 1 ban. Beijing : Qi ye guan li chu ban she, 2001.
HC426.5.A2 Z457 2001

SUCCESS IN BUSINESS - PERIODICALS.
[Success (Kampala, Uganda)] Success. Kampala, Uganda : Success Magazine Ltd., [1998-
BF637.S8

SUCCESS IN BUSINESS - POLAND - WARSAW.
Firkowska-Mankiewicz, Anna. Intelligence and success in life. Warsaw : IFiS Publishers, 2002.
BF412 F57 2002

SUCCESS IN CHILDREN.
Ladner, Joyce A. Launching our Black children for success. 1st ed. San Francisco : Jossey-Bass, c2003.
BF723.S77 L33 2003

Success is the best revenge.
Stewardson, John (John E.) Toronto : Productive Publications, c1994.

[Success (Kampala, Uganda)] Success. Kampala, Uganda : Success Magazine Ltd., [1998- v. : ill. ; 30 cm. Frequency: Four no. a year. Vol. 1, no. 1 (1998)- . Other title: Success : the magazine for achievers. Title from cover. Some issues designated by vol., no., and year, e.g., v. 1, no. 1 (1998), v. 1, no. 3 (1998); some by vol. and no, e.g., v. 2, no. 1; some by date only, e.g., Apr./May 1999.
1. Success - Psychological aspects - Periodicals. 2. Success in

business - Periodicals. 3. Uganda - Periodicals. I. Title:
Success : the magazine for achievers
BF637.S8

SUCCESS - MISCELLANEA.
Hite, Sheilaa, 1958- Secrets of a psychic counselor.
Needham, Mass. : Moment Point Press ; [Oakland,
Calif.] : Distributed to the trade by Words Distributing
Co., c2003.
BF1045.R43 H58 2003

SUCCESS - PSYCHIC ASPECTS.
Miller, Larry, 1947- Exploring the "zone". Gretna,
La. : Pelican, 2001.
BF1045.S83 M55 2001

SUCCESS - PSYCHOLOGICAL ASPECTS.
Allenbaugh, Eric. Deliberate success. Franklin Lakes,
NJ : Career Press, c2002.
HF5386 .A5434 2002

Allyn, David (David Smith) I can't believe I just did
that. New York : Jeremy P. Tarcher/Penguin, 2004.
BF575.E53 A45 2004

Bain, Dwight, 1960- Destination success. Grand
Rapids, Mich. : F.H. Revell, c2003.
BF637.S8 B314 2003

Beavers, Brett. Something worth leaving behind.
Nashville, Tenn. : Rutledge Hill Press, c2002.
BF637.S8 B383 2002

Beyond coping. Oxford ; New York : Oxford
University Press, 2002.
BF335 .B49 2002

Binford, Virgie M. Avenues for success. Franklin,
Tenn. : Providence House Publishers, c2001.
BF637.S8 B477 2001

Bruce, Anne, 1952- Discover true north. New York :
McGraw-Hill, c2004.
BF637.S4 B82 2004

Capp, Ray, 1953- When you mean business about
yourself. Nashville, Tenn. : Rutledge Hill Press,
c2002.
BF637.S8 C37 2002

Carson, Richard David. Taming your gremlin. Rev.
ed. New York : Quill, 2003.
BF575.H27 C38 2003

Colwell, Peter G. Spell success in your life.
Germantown, Md. : Dreams Unlimited Press, c2002.
BF637.S8 C57 2002

Dahl, Bernhoff A., 1938- Optimize your life with the
one-page strategic planner. Bangor, Me. : Wind-
Breaker Press, c2003.
BF637.S8 D26 2003

Edwards, Jaroldeen. The daffodil principle. Salt Lake
City, Utah : Shadow Mountain, 2004.
BF637.S4 E4 2004

Farber, Barry J. Diamond power. Franklin Lakes, NJ :
Career Press, 2004.
BF637.S8 F342 2004

Fettke, Rich. Extreme success. New York : Fireside
Book, c2002.
BF637.S8 F46 2002

Fralix, Patti. How to thrive in spite of mess, stress and
less!. 1st ed. Raleigh, NC : Triunity Publishers, c2002.
BF637.S4 F72 2002

Gelb, Michael. More balls than hands. New York,
NY : Prentice Hall, 2003.
BF637.S8 G39 2003

A guide to getting it. 1st ed. Portland, Or. : Clarity of
Vision Pub., 2002.
BF637.S8 G84 2002

Hays, Kate F. You're on!. 1st ed. Washington, DC :
American Psychological Association, c2003.
BF637.C6 H366 2003

Henry, Dale. The proverbial Cracker Jack.
Hagerstown, Md. : Autumn House Pub., c2002.
BF637.S4 H857 2002

Ibay, Manny. Thank you, Tony Robbins. 1st Destini
Books ed. Santa Monica, Calif. : Destini Books, 2002.
BF637.S8 I23 2002

Jeff, Peter. Get a grip on your dream. [Grand Rapids,
MI] : Possibility Press, c2000.
BF637.S8 J45 2000

Johnston, Daniel H. Lessons for living. 1st ed. Macon,
Ga. : Dagali Press, c2001.
BF637.S4 J65 2001

Kushell, Jennifer. Secrets of the young & successful.
New York : Simon & Schuster, c2003.

BF637.S8 K875 2003
Kyriazi, Paul. The complete live the James Bond
lifestyle seminar. Los Angeles, CA : Ronin Books,
c2002.
BF637.S8 K97 2002

Levine, Leslie. Wish it, dream it, do it. New York :
Simon & Schuster, c2004.
BF637.S8 L449 2004

Lewis-Hall, Jennifer, 1964- Life's a journey--not a
sprint. Carlsbad, Calif. : Hay House, c2003.
BF637.S8 L455 2003

Llewellyn, Jack H. Coming in first. Atlanta :
Longstreet Press, c2000.
BF637.S8 L56 2000

Maxwell, John C., 1947- Today matters. New York :
Warner Books, 2004.
BF637.S8 M3423 2004

Miller, Scott D. Staying on top and keeping the sand
out of your pants. Deerfield Beach, Fla. : Health
Communications, c2003.
BF637.S8 M565 2003

Nogales, Ana, 1951- Latina power!. New York :
Simon & Schuster, c2003.
BF637.S8 N64 2003

North, Dia. The smart spot. Boston, MA : Red Wheel,
2003.
BF637.S8 N655 2003

Phillips, Nicola. The big difference. Cambridge, MA :
Perseus Pub., c2001.
BF619 .P48 2001

Scott, Steve, 1948- Mentored by a millionaire.
Hoboken, N.J. : J. Wiley & Sons, 2004.
BF637.S8 S388 2004

Secunda, Al. The 15-second principle. Franklin Lakes,
NJ : Career Press, 2004.
BF637.S4 S43 2004

Shabazz, David L. Discover your gold mind. Clinton,
S.C. : Awesome Records, c2001.
BF637.S8 S428 2001

Skiffington, Jeannie. Winning is contagious. 1st ed.
East Amherst, N.Y. : Winning Track Press, c2002.
BF637.S8 S548 2002

Stearns, Rob, 1952- Winning smart after losing big.
1st ed. San Francisco, CA : Encounter Books, 2003.
BF575.D35 S74 2003

Taylor, Scott L., 1964- The opportunity in every
problem. 1st ed. Salt Lake City : Gibbs Smith, c2003.
BF637.S8 T285 2003

Tips, Jack. Passion play. 1st ed. Austin, Tex. : Apple-
A-Day Press, c2002.
BF503 .T56 2002

Tracy, Brian. Change your thinking, change your life.
Hoboken, N.J. : J. Wiley & Sons, c2003.
BF637.S8 T634 2003

Waitley, Denis. Psychology of success. 4th ed.
Boston : McGraw-Hill Higher Education, c2004.
BF637.S8 W269 2004

What makes a champion!. Camberwell, Vic.,
Australia ; New York : Penguin Books, 2002.
BF637.S8 W45 2002

White, Howard, 1950- Believe to achieve. Hillsboro,
Or. : Beyond Words Pub., c2003.
BF637.S8 W453 2003

Wilde, Liz. Unlock your potential. New York : Ryland
Peters & Small, 2004.
BF637.S4 W488 2004

Williams, Redford B., 1940- The type E personality.
Emmaus, Pa. : Rodale, c2004.
BF576.3 .W55 2004

Williamson, James C. Roadways to success. 3rd ed.
Upper Saddle River, NJ : Pearson/ Prentice Hall,
2004.
BF637.S8 W5216 2004

Wowisms. 1st ed. New York : Newmarket Press,
c2003.
BF637.S8 W7 2003

Zoglio, Suzanne Willis. Recharge in minutes. 1st ed.
Doylestown, PA : Tower Hill Press, c2003.
BF632 .Z64 2003

**SUCCESS - PSYCHOLOGICAL ASPECTS -
PERIODICALS.**
[Success (Kampala, Uganda)] Success. Kampala,
Uganda : Success Magazine Ltd., [1998-

BF637.S8

**SUCCESS - PSYCHOLOGICAL ASPECTS -
QUOTATIONS, MAXIMS, ETC.**
Baggett, Byrd. The past doesn't have a future, but you
do. Nashville, Tenn. : Cumberland House Pub., c2003.
BF637.S8 B25 2003

SUCCESS - RELIGIOUS ASPECTS - JUDAISM.
Fridman, Aharon (Aharon ben Yehoshuʻa) [Gam atah
yakhol. Yiddish] Du ḳenst oykh!. Nyu Yorḳ : Lev
Yiśroel, 762, 2002.

Success : the magazine for achievers.
[Success (Kampala, Uganda)] Success. Kampala,
Uganda : Success Magazine Ltd., [1998-
BF637.S8

SUCCESSFUL PEOPLE - POLAND - WARSAW.
Firkowska-Mankiewicz, Anna. Intelligence and
success in life. Warsaw : IFiS Publishers, 2002.
BF412 F57 2002

**SUCCESSFUL PEOPLE - UNITED STATES -
BIOGRAPHY.**
Summer, Lauralee, 1976- Learning joy from dogs
without collars. New York ; London : Simon &
Schuster, c2003.
HV4505 .S86 2003

SUCCESSION, INTESTATE. *See* **INHERITANCE
AND SUCCESSION.**

SUCKLEY FAMILY.
Philip, Cynthia Owen. Wilderstein and the Suckleys.
Rhinebeck, N.Y. : Wilderstein Preservation, 2001.
F129.W747 P48 2001

Suckling, Nigel. Legends & lore / [Nigel Suckling ;
illustrated by Wayne Anderson]. New York :
Friedman/Fairfax Publishers : Distributed by Sterling
Pub., c2002. 95 p. : col. ill., col. map ; 25 cm. Spine title:
Year of the dragon. Originally published: London : Pavilion
Books, 2000. ISBN 1-58663-930-7 DDC 398/.469/0951
1. Astrology, Chinese. 2. Horoscopes. 3. Dragons - China -
Folklore. I. Title. II. Title: Legends and lore III. Title: Year of
the dragon
BF1714.C5 S93 2002

SUD-KIVO (CONGO) - ETHNIC RELATIONS.
Le dialogue intercongolais. Bruxelles ; Nairobi :
International Crisis Group, [2001]

Sudakov, Vladimir Ivanovich. Spasitel' : fenomen
tysi︠a︡cheletii︠a︡ Grigorii︠a︡ Grabovoĭ / Vladimir Sudakov.
Moskva : TERRA-Sport, 2001. 160 p. ; 20 cm. ISBN
593127104X
1. Grabovoĭ, Grigoriĭ. 2. Parapsychologists - Russia
(Federation) - Biography. I. Title.
BF1027.G73 S83 2001

Sudhākaradvivedī.
Works. 1987
(vol. 6.) Śukla, Kamalākānta, 1911-
Vāstusārasaṅgrahaḥ. 1. saṃskaraṇam. Vārāṇasī :
Sampūrṇānanda Saṃskṛta Viśvavidyālaye, 2002.
BF1729.A7+

Sueda, Masu.
Jido koen.
Edo-e kara shomotsu made. Tōkyō : Kyūzansha,
1997.
HQ792.J3 N54 1997 v.19

SUFFERING. *See also* **LONELINESS; PAIN.**
I concetti del male. Torino : Einaudi, c2002.

Croix, Laurence. La douleur en soi. Ramonville
Saint-Agne (France) : Erès, c2002.

Natoli, Salvatore. L'esperienza del dolore. 1. ed.
nell'"Universale economica"--Saggi. Milano :
Feltrinelli, 2002.

O'Hanlon, William Hudson. Thriving through crisis.
1st Perigee ed. New York : Perigee, 2004.
BF789.O35 2004

Tudor, Steven. Compassion and remorse. Leuven ;
Sterling, Va. : Peeters, 2001.
BJ1475 .T84 2001

SUFFERING - NEPAL.
Ḍiyara Kalyāṇa, mero kathā mero gīta. 1. saṃskaraṇa.
[Kathmandu] : Sañjanā Gautama, 2059- [2002-
BF789.S8+

SUFFERING - RELIGIOUS ASPECTS.
Siṃha, Kīrti Kumāra. Bhāratīya darśana meṃ duḥkha
aura mukti. 1. saṃskaraṇa. Ilāhābāda : Śekhara
Prakāśana, 2001.
B132.M64 S56 2001

**SUFFERING - RELIGIOUS ASPECTS -
CHRISTIANITY.**
Aransiola, Moses Olanrewaju. The roots and solutions

Sufism.
to peculiar problems (dealing with bad luck, lost opportunities and failure). 1st ed.
1. Black author.

Trasferetti, José Antônio. Deus a força que cura!. Campinas, SP : Editora Átomo, 2002.

SUFISM.
Jambet, Christian. L'acte d'être. [Paris] : Fayard, c2002.

Jironet, Karin. The image of spiritual liberty in the western Sufi movement following Hazrat Inayat Khan. Leuven : Peeters, 2002.
BP189.2 .J57 2002

SUFISM - NETHERLANDS.
Jironet, Karin. The image of spiritual liberty in the western Sufi movement following Hazrat Inayat Khan. Leuven : Peeters, 2002.
BP189.2 .J57 2002

SUFISM - RITUALS.
Hell, Bertrand. Le tourbillon des génies. Paris : Flammarion, c2002.

Sugarman, Jeff, 1955-.
Martin, Jack, 1950- Psychology and the question of agency. Albany : State University of New York Press, c2003.
BF575.A88 M37 2003

Sugrue, Thomas, 1907- There is a river : the story of Edgar Cayce / by Thomas Sugrue ; foreword by Raymond Moody. Virginia Beach, Va. : A.R.E. Press, c2003. p. cm. "Includes a Special Section: Auras / the only book written by Edgar Cayce Himself." Originally published: Virginia Beach, VA : A.R.E. Press, c1988. Includes bibliographical references and index. Table of contents URL: http://www.loc.gov/catdir/toc/ecip042/2003008180.html ISBN 0-87604-448-8 (trade pbk.) DDC 133.8/092
1. Cayce, Edgar, - 1877-1945. 2. Psychics - United States - Biography. 3. Association for Research and Enlightenment - Biography. I. Title.
BF1027.C3 S8 2003

Sugumaran, Vijayan, 1960-.
Intelligent support systems. Hershey, PA : IRM Press, c2002.
QA76.9.D3 I5495 2002

Suhamy, Ariel.
Fortitude et servitude. Paris : Kimé, c2003.

Suhrkamp Taschenbuch Wissenschaft
(1478) Wind, Edgar, 1900- Das Experiment und die Metaphysik. 1. Aufl. Frankfurt am Main : Suhrkamp, 2001.

(1513) Blumenberg, Hans. Ästhetische und metaphorologische Schriften. 1. Aufl. Frankfurt : Suhrkamp, 2001.

(1530) Rössler, Beate. Der Wert des Privaten. 1. Aufl. Frankfurt am Main : Suhrkamp, 2001.

(1533) Die Öffentlichkeit der Vernunft und die Vernunft der Öffentlichkeit. 1. Aufl. Frankfurt am Main : Suhrkamp, 2001.
B3258.H324 O34 2001

(1535) Tugendhat, Ernst. Aufsätze 1992-2000. 1. Aufl. Frankfurt : Suhrkamp, 2001.

(1549) Zons, Raimar. Die Zeit des Menschen. 1. Aufl., Originalausg. Frankfurt : Suhrkamp, c2001.

SUICIDE.
Andrushkiv, Bohdan, 1947- Po toï bik bezodni, abo, Mertvi pro vartist' zhyttía ne rozkazhut'. Ternopil' : "Pidruchnyky & posibnyky", 1997.
HV6545 .A616 1997

DiGaetani, John Louis, 1943- Wagner and suicide. Jefferson, N.C. : McFarland, c2003.
ML410.W13 D45 2003

Living with suicide [electronic resource]. [Alexandria, Va.] : PBS Online ; [New York, N.Y.] : Web Lab
BF789.D4

Suicide & risk-taking deaths of children & young people / NSW Commission for Children & Young People, NSW Child Death Review Team and the Centre for Mental Health ; [report written by Melissa Sankey; study conception and design by Ruth Lawrence]. Surry Hills, NSW : The Commission, c2003. xiii, 143 p. : ill. ; 30 cm. ISBN 0-7347-7113-4
1. Suicide victims - Australia - New South Wales. 2. Children - Suicidal behavior - Australia - New South Wales. 3. Teenagers - Suicidal behavior - Australia - New South Wales. 4. Risk-taking (Psychology) in children - Australia - New South Wales. 5. Risk-taking (Psychology) in adolescence - Australia - New South Wales. 6. Accidents - Psychological aspects. I. Sankey, Melissa. II. Lawrence, Ruth. III. NSW Commission for Children & Young People. IV. Child Death Review Team

(N.S.W.) V. New South Wales. Centre for Mental Health. VI. Title: Suicide and risk-taking deaths of children and young people

Suicide and risk-taking deaths of children and young people.
Suicide & risk-taking deaths of children & young people. Surry Hills, NSW : The Commission, c2003.

SUICIDE VICTIMS - AUSTRALIA - NEW SOUTH WALES.
Suicide & risk-taking deaths of children & young people. Surry Hills, NSW : The Commission, c2003.

SUICIDES. *See* **SUICIDE VICTIMS.**

O sujeito imaginário no discurso de auto-ajuda.
Chagas, Arnaldo Sousa das Chagas. Rio Grande do Sul : Editora UNIJUÍ, 2002.

Le sujet et la mort dans La mort Artu.
Greene, Virginie Elisabeth, 1959- Saint-Genouph : Nizet, 2002.

Sukla, Ananta Charana, 1942-.
Art and essence. Westport, Conn. ; London : Praeger, 2003.
BH39 .A685 2003

Art and experience. Westport, Conn. ; London : Praeger, 2003.
BH39 .A686 2003

Śukla, Kamalākānta, 1911- Vāstusārasaṅgrahaḥ : Hindīvyākhyayā samalaṅkṛtaḥ / lekhakaḥ sampādakaśca Kamalākāntaśuklaḥ ; Rājendramiśrasya prastāvanayā vibhūṣitah. 1. saṃskaraṇam. Vārāṇasī : Sampūrṇānanda Saṃskṛta Viśvavidyālaye, 2002. 23, 372 p. ; 22 cm. (Ma. Ma. Sudhākaradvivedi-granthamālā ; 6 puṣpam) Spine title: Vāstusārasaṅgraha. In Sanskrit; introduction in Hindi. SUMMARY: On Hindu domestic architecture and astrology. Includes index. ISBN 81-7270-096-2
1. Astrology and architecture. 2. Domestic architecture - India. I. Sampūrṇānanda Saṃskṛta Viśvavidyālaya. II. Title. III. Title: Vāstusārasaṅgraha IV. Series: Sudhākaradvivedī. Works. 1987 ; vol. 6.
BF1729.A7+

Sullivan, Karen. Finding the inner you : how well do you know yourself? / Karen Sullivan ; introduction John Church. 1st ed. Hauppauge, N.Y. : Barrons Educational Series, 2003. 192 p. : col. ill. ; 24 cm. Includes index. ISBN 0-7641-2270-3 DDC 158.1
1. Self-perception. 2. Self-knowledge, Theory of. 3. Self (Philosophy) I. Title.
BF697.5.S43 S95 2003

Sullivan, Kathleen, 1941- Recurring dream symbols : maps to healing your past / Kathleen Sullivan. New York : Paulist Press, c2004. p. cm. Includes bibliographical references (p.   ). ISBN 0-8091-4184-1 DDC 154.6/32
1. Dream interpretation. 2. Self-realization. I. Title.
BF1091 .S813 2004

Sullivan, Timothy, 1954-.
Creativity and music education. Edmonton, Canada : Canadian Music Educators' Association, c2002.

al-Sulūk al-siyāsī.
Sayyid, 'Azīzah Muḥammad. al-Ṭabʻah 1. [Cairo] : Dār al-Maʻārif, 1994.
JA74.5 .S29 1994

Summa de anima.
Jean, de la Rochelle, d. 1245. Paris : J. Vrin, 1995.
BD420 .J43 1995

Summer, Lauralee, 1976- Learning joy from dogs without collars : a memoir / Lauralee Summer. New York ; London : Simon & Schuster, c2003. x, 351 p. ; 22 cm. ISBN 0-7432-0102-7 DDC 305.23/092
1. Summer, Lauralee, - 1976- - Childhood and youth. 2. Homeless children - United States - Biography. 3. Homeless persons - United States - Psychology. 4. Parent and child - United States. 5. Self-actualization (Psychology) 6. Successful people - United States - Biography. I. Title.
HV4505 .S86 2003

SUMMER, LAURALEE, 1976- -CHILDHOOD AND YOUTH.
Summer, Lauralee, 1976- Learning joy from dogs without collars. New York ; London : Simon & Schuster, c2003.
HV4505 .S86 2003

Summer, Lori. The ghost hunter's handbook / by Lori Summers. New York : Price Stern Sloan, c2002. 83 p. : col. ill. ; 15 cm. Includes bibliographical references (p. 80-83). ISBN 0-8431-4916-7
1. Ghosts - Juvenile literature. I. Title.
BF1461 .S88 2002

Summers, David, 1941- Real spaces : world art history and the rise of Western modernism / David Summers. London : Phaidon, c2003. 687, [16] p. : ill. ; 25cm. CONTENTS: Facture--Places--The Appropriation of the Centre--Images--Planarity--Virtuality--The Conditions of Modernism ISBN 0-7148-4244-3 DDC 701.18
1. Art criticism. 2. Art - History. 3. Space (Art) I. Title.

Summers, Selena, 1945-
[Feng shui in 5 minutes. Spanish]
Feng shui : práctico y al instante / Selena Summers ; traducido al idioma español por Héctor Ramírez y Edgar Rojas. 1. ed. St. Paul, Minn. : Llewellyn Español, 2003. viii, 205 p. : ill. 21 cm. Includes index. ISBN 0-7387-0292-7 DDC 133.3/337
1. Feng shui. I. Title.
BF1779.F4 S84518 2003

Sun, Changwu. Zhongguo wen xue zhong di Weimo yu Guanyin / Sun Changwu zhu. Di 1 ban. Beijing : Gao deng jiao yu chu ban she : Xin hua shu dian zong dian Beijing fa xing suo fa xing, 1996. 2, 424 p. ; 21 cm. Includes bibliographical references (p. 407-420). Table of contents also in English, with title: Vimalakīrti and Avalokiteśvara in Chinese literarure. ISBN 7-04-005752-2
1. Chinese literature - History and criticism. 2. Buddhism and literature. 3. Vimalakīrti (Buddhist character) - In literature. 4. Avalokiteśvara (Buddhist deity) - In literature. I. Title.
PL2275.B8 S85 1996 <Orien China>

Sunbeck, Deborah. The complete Infinity walk / Deborah Sunbeck. Rochester, N.Y. : Leonardo Foundation Press, c2001- v. < 1 > : ill. ; 23 cm. Includes bibliographical references and index. SUMMARY: Infinity Walk training develops an intimate working relationship between the neural organ we call the brain and the person's desires and intentions. Mind, will and purpose discover their channel for manifesting themselves in the person's lilfe through natural, freed movements. PARTIAL CONTENTS: bk. 1. The physical self. ISBN 0-9705164-6-0 DDC 153.15
1. Learning, Psychology of. 2. Left and right (Psychology) 3. Perceptual-motor learning. I. Title.
BF318 .S86 2001

SUNBELT STATES. *See* **SOUTHWEST, NEW.**

Sunderland, Jane.
Gender identity and discourse analysis. Amsterdam ; Philadelphia : John Benjamins Pub., c2002.
HQ1075 .G428 2002

Sundial.
Bryden, Barbara E., 1954- Gainesville, FL : Center for Applications of Psychological Type, 2003.
BF698.3 .B79 2003

SUNKEN TREASURE. *See* **TREASURE-TROVE.**

SUNY series, alternatives in psychology
About psychology. Albany : State University of New York Press, c2003.
BF38 .A28 2003

Martin, Jack, 1950- Psychology and the question of agency. Albany : State University of New York Press, c2003.
BF575.A88 M37 2003

SUNY series, hot topics
High culture. Albany : State University of New York Press, c2003.
HV4998 .H544 2003

SUNY series in aesthetics and the philosophy of art
Thinking the limits of the body. Albany : State University of New York Press, c2003.
HM636 .T47 2003

SUNY series in ancient Greek philosophy
Couprie, Dirk, 1940- Anaximander in context. Albany : State University of New York Press, c2003.
B208.Z7 C68 2003

Schreiber, Scott G. (Scott Gregory), 1952- Aristotle on false reasoning. Albany : State University of New York Press, 2003.
B491.R4 S37 2003

SUNY series in Chinese philosophy and culture
Wagner, Rudolf G. Language, ontology, and political philosophy in China. Albany : State University of New York Press, c2003.
B126 .W284 2003

SUNY series in communication studies
Petronio, Sandra Sporbert. Boundaries of privacy. Albany : State University of New York Press, c2002.
BF697.5.S427 P48 2002

Woodward, Gary C. The idea of identification. Albany : State University of New York Press, c2003.
BF697.5.S65 W66 2003

SUNY series in contemporary continental philosophy
Heidegger, Martin, 1889-1976. [Essays. English. Selections] Supplements. Albany : State University of New York Press, c2002.
B3279.H47 E5 2002d

Russon, John Edward, 1960- Human experience. Albany : State University of New York Press, c2003.
BF204.5 .R87 2003

SUNY series in dream studies
Dreaming and the self. Albany : State University of New York Press, c2003.
BF1091 .D735 2003

SUNY series in feminist criticism and theory
Rishoi, Christy, 1958- From girl to woman. Albany : State University of New York Press, c2003.
HQ1186.A9 R57 2003

SUNY series in Israeli studies
Grosbard, Ofer, 1954- [Yiśra'el 'al ha-sapah. English] Israel on the couch. Albany : State University of New York Press, c2003.
DS126.5 .G694 2003

SUNY series in Latin American and Iberian thought and culture
Ferrater Mora, José, 1912- [Selections. English. 2003] Three Spanish philosophers. Albany : State University of New York Press, c2003.
B4568.U54 F3913 2003

SUNY series in philosophy
Rescher, Nicholas. Epistemology. Albany : State University of New York Press, c2003.
BD161 .R477 2003

SUNY series in postmodern culture
Rishoi, Christy, 1958- From girl to woman. Albany : State University of New York Press, c2003.
HQ1186.A9 R57 2003

SUNY series in psychoanalysis and culture
Apollon, Willy. After Lacan. Albany : State University of New York Press, 2002.
RC506 .A65 2002

McGowan, Todd. The end of dissatisfaction? Albany : State University of New York Press, c2004.
BF175.4.C84 M4 2004

Meissner, W. W. (William W.), 1931- The ethical dimension of psychoanalysis. Albany : State University of New York Press, c2003.
BF173 .M3592 2003

SUNY series in religious studies
Coward, Harold G. Yoga and psychology. Albany : State University of New York Press, 2002.
BF51 .C69 2002

SUNY series in transpersonal and humanistic psychology
Encountering Buddhism. Albany : State University of New York Press, 2003.
BQ4570.P755 E62 2003

Visser, Frank, 1958- [Ken Wilber. English] Ken Wilber. Albany, NY : State University of New York Press, c2003.
BF109.W54 V5713 2003

SUNY series in Western esoteric traditions
Szőnyi, György Endre. John Dee's occultism. Albany : State University of New York Press, 2004.
BF1598.D5 S98 2004

SUNY series, second thoughts
Gonick, Marnina. Between femininities. Albany : State University of New York Press, c2003.
HQ777 .G65 2003

Super brain power.
Spotts, Dane. Seattle, Wash. : LifeQuest Pub. Group, c1998.
BF441 .S68 1998

Super searchers on Madison Avenue.
Villamora, Grace Avellana. Medford, N.J. : CyberAge Books/Information Today, c2003.
HF5415.2 .V497 2003

Super tarot.
Fenton, Sasha. New York : Sterling Pub., 2003.
BF1879.T2 F465 2003

SUPEREGO. See **CONSCIENCE.**

SUPERHEROES. See **HEROES.**

SUPERNATURAL. See also **MIRACLES; OCCULTISM; SPIRITS.**
Holzer, Hans, 1920- Hans Holzer's the supernatural. Franklin Lakes, NJ : New Page Books, c2003.
BF1031 .H672 2003

SUPERNATURAL.
Brandon, Trent. The book of ghosts. Mineva, Ohio : Zerotime Pub., c2003.
BF1461 .B6949 2003

Brandon, Trent. The ghost hunter's Bible. Definitive ed. [Ohio?] : Zerotime Paranormal and Supernatural Research, 2002.
BF1461 .B695 2002

Demonio, religión y sociedad entre España y América. Madrid : Consejo Superior de Investigaciones Científicas, 2002.

Fleming, Maurice. Not of this world. Edinburgh : Mercat, 2002.

Holzer, Hans, 1920- Hans Holzer's the supernatural. Franklin Lakes, NJ : New Page Books, c2003.
BF1031 .H672 2003

Mason, Paul, 1967- Investigating the supernatural. Chicago, Ill. : Heinemann Library, 2004.
BF1029 .M37 2004

Miller, Larry, 1947- Exploring the "zone". Gretna, La. : Pelican, 2001.
BF1045.S83 M55 2001

Pandian, Jacob. Supernaturalism in human life. New Delhi : Vedams ebooks, [2002]
BF1031.A4-Z+

Werewolves, witches, and wandering spirits. Kirksville, MO : Truman State University Press, c2002.
GR135 .W47 2002

SUPERNATURAL - CASE STUDIES - JUVENILE LITERATURE.
Mason, Paul, 1967- Investigating the supernatural. Chicago, Ill. : Heinemann Library, 2004.
BF1029 .M37 2004

SUPERNATURAL DISAPPEARANCES. See **DISAPPEARANCES (PARAPSYCHOLOGY).**

SUPERNATURAL - ENCYCLOPEDIAS.
Steiger, Brad. The Gale encyclopedia of the unusual and unexplained. Detroit : Thomson/Gale, c2003.
BF1025 .S79 2003

SUPERNATURAL IN ART.
Duplessis, Yvonne, 1912- Surréalisme et paranormal. Agnières : JMG, 2002.
BF1023 .D87 2002

SUPERNATURAL IN LITERATURE.
Royle, Nicholas, 1963- The uncanny. Manchester (UK) ; New York : Manchester University Press, 2003.
PN49 .R75 2002

Supernaturalism in human life.
Pandian, Jacob. New Delhi : Vedams ebooks, [2002]
BF1031.A4-Z+

SUPERSTITION. See also **AMULETS; CHARMS; MEDICINE, MAGIC, MYSTIC, AND SPAGIRIC; OMENS; ORDEAL; TALISMANS; VAMPIRES; WEREWOLVES.**
Ellis, Bill, 1950- Lucifer ascending. Lexington : University Press of Kentucky, c2003.
BF1548 .E44 2003

Leland, Charles Godfrey, 1824-1903. [Etruscan roman remains in popular tradition] Etruscan Roman remains and the old religion. London ; New York : Kegan Paul ; New York : Distributed by Columbia University Press, 2002.
DG223 .L54 2002

SUPERSTITION - RELIGIOUS ASPECTS - CHRISTIANITY.
Emtcheu, André. Psychologie et révélation. Yaoundé, Cameroun : Editions SHERPA, c2001.
1. Black author.

SUPERSTITION - SOCIAL ASPECTS.
Lozito, Vito. Agiografia, magia, superstizione. Bari : Levante, [1999]
BF1775 .L69 1999

SUPERVENIENCE (PHILOSOPHY).
Stalnaker, Robert. Ways a world might be. Oxford : Clarendon ; New York : Oxford University Press, 2003.
BD111 .S73 2003

Supino Martini, Paola, 1942-.
Studi sulle società e le culture del Medioevo per Girolamo Arnaldi. [Firenze] : All'insegna del giglio, 2002.
DG443 .S78 2002

Supplements.
Heidegger, Martin, 1889-1976. [Essays. English. Selections] Albany : State University of New York Press, c2002.
B3279.H47 E5 2002d

SUPPLY AND DEMAND. See **COMPETITION; PRODUCTION (ECONOMIC THEORY).**

SUPPLY-SIDE ECONOMICS. See **PRODUCTION (ECONOMIC THEORY).**

Supporting early learning
Pound, Linda. Supporting musical development in the early years. Buckingham ; Philadelphia : Open University Press, 2003.
MT1 .P66 2003

Supporting musical development in the early years.
Pound, Linda. Buckingham ; Philadelphia : Open University Press, 2003.
MT1 .P66 2003

Suprynowicz, Vin. The ballad of Carl Drega : essays on the freedom movement, 1994-2001 / by Vin Suprynowicz. Reno, NV : Mountain Media, 2002. 696 p. ; 22 cm. Includes bibliographical references (p. 687-689). Library has copy signed by author. ISBN 0-9670259-2-3
1. Civil rights - United States. 2. Government, Resistance to - United States. 3. Liberty. I. Title.

Sur le peuple, l'église et la république.
Renouvier, Charles, 1815-1903. Paris : Harmattan, c2002.

Surendra Kumar. Legends of Indian cinema : pen portraits / Surendra Kumar. New Delhi : Har-Anand Publications, c2003. 224 p. ; 22 cm. SUMMARY: On Indian motion picture actors and directors; articles. Includes index. ISBN 81-241-0872-2
1. Motion pictures - India. 2. Motion picture actors and actresses - India. 3. Motion pictures - Production and direction - India. 4. Celebrities. I. Title.
PN1993.5.I4 S87 2003

SURGERY, AESTHETIC. See **SURGERY, PLASTIC.**

SURGERY, COSMETIC. See **SURGERY, PLASTIC.**

SURGERY, PLASTIC.
Vint/age 2001 conference : [videorecording]. New York, c2001.

SURGERY, PLASTIC - PSYCHOLOGICAL ASPECTS.
Western eyes [videorecording]. New York, NY : First Run/Icarus Films, 2000.

SURGERY, PRIMITIVE. See **TRADITIONAL MEDICINE.**

SURGERY, RECONSTRUCTIVE. See **SURGERY, PLASTIC.**

Surprenant, Aimée M.
Neath, Ian, 1965- Human memory. 2nd ed. Australia ; Belmont, CA : Thomson/Wadsworth, c2003.
BF371 .N43 2003

SURPRISE.
Shepherd, Joanne. What I look like when I am surprised. 1st ed. New York : Rosen Pub. Group's PowerStart Press, 2004.
BF723.S87 S44 2004

Shepherd, Joanne. [What I look like when I am surprised. Spanish & English] What I look like when I am surprised = 1st ed. New York : Rosen Pub. Group's PowerKids Press, 2004.
BF723.S87 S4418 2004

SURPRISE IN CHILDREN - JUVENILE LITERATURE.
Shepherd, Joanne. What I look like when I am surprised. 1st ed. New York : Rosen Pub. Group's PowerStart Press, 2004.
BF723.S87 S44 2004

Shepherd, Joanne. [What I look like when I am surprised. Spanish & English] What I look like when I am surprised = 1st ed. New York : Rosen Pub. Group's PowerKids Press, 2004.
BF723.S87 S4418 2004

The surreal lives.
Brandon, Ruth. London : Papermac, 2000, c1999.

SURREALISM.
Brandon, Ruth. The surreal lives. London : Papermac, 2000, c1999.

Clair, Jean, 1940- Du surréalisme considéré dans ses rapports au totalitarisme et aux tables tournantes. [Paris] : Mille et une nuits, 2003.

Surrealism.

Duplessis, Yvonne, 1912- Surréalisme et paranormal. Agnières : JMG, 2002.
BF1023 .D87 2002

Fotiade, Ramona. Conceptions of the absurd. Oxford : Legenda, 2001.

Meyer, Michel. Michel Meyer présente Manifestes du surréalisme d'André Breton. Paris : Gallimard, 2002.
NX600.S9 B735 2002

Okanoue, Toshiko. Drop of dreams. Tucson, AZ : Nazraeli Press, c2002.

Tythacott, Louise. Surrealism and the exotic. London ; New York : Routledge, 2003.
NX456.5.S8 T98 2003

Surrealism and the exotic.
Tythacott, Louise. London ; New York : Routledge, 2003.
NX456.5.S8 T98 2003

SURREALISM IN LITERATURE. See SURREALISM (LITERATURE).

SURREALISM (LITERATURE).
Clair, Jean, 1940- Du surréalisme considéré dans ses rapports au totalitarisme et aux tables tournantes. [Paris] : Mille et une nuits, 2003.

Surréalisme et paranormal.
Duplessis, Yvonne, 1912- Agnières : JMG, 2002.
BF1023 .D87 2002

Surrealists, 1917-1945.
Brandon, Ruth. The surreal lives. London : Papermac, 2000, c1999.

SURVEYING - UNITED STATES - HISTORY.
Linklater, Andro. Measuring America. New York : Walker & Co., 2002.
E161.3 .L46 2002

SURVEYORS - UNITED STATES - HISTORY.
Linklater, Andro. Measuring America. New York : Walker & Co., 2002.
E161.3 .L46 2002

SURVEYS. See SOCIAL SURVEYS.
SURVEYS, SOCIAL. See SOCIAL SURVEYS.
SURVIVAL.
Gott, Robert. One in a million. Littleton, Mass. : Sundance, c2001.
BF1175 .G68 2001

Philbrick, Nat. Revenge of the whale. New York : G.P. Putnam, 2002.
G530.E77 P454 2002

The survival game.
Barash, David P. 1st ed. New York : Times Books, 2003.
HM1111 .B37 2003

Surviving aggressive people.
Smith, Shawn T., 1967- 1st Sentient Publications ed. Boulder, CO : Sentient Publications, 2003.
BF575.A3 S55 2003

Surviving saturn's return.
Schostak, Sherene. 1st ed. New York : McGraw-Hill, 2004.
BF1724.2.S3 S36 2004

SURVIVORS, HOLOCAUST. See HOLOCAUST SURVIVORS.

Survivors : true stories about real kids / Elizabeth Murray ... [et al. ; compiled by Noelle Morris]. New York : Scholastic, 2003. 60 p. : ill. (some col.) ; 20 cm. (Read 180. Stage C) "Level 1"--P. [4] of cover.
1. Success - Case studies - Juvenile literature. 2. Heroes - Case studies - Juvenile literature. 3. Youth - Case studies - Juvenile literature. I. Murray, Elizabeth. II. Morris, Noelle. III. Series.
BF637.S8 S8317 2002

Survivre.
Mongeau, Pierre, 1954- Sainte-Foy : Presses de l'Université du Québec, 2002.
BF122 .M66 2002

SÜSKIND, PATRICK.
Małyszek, Tomasz, 1971- Ästhetik der Psychoanalyse. Wrocław : Wydawn. Uniwersytetu Wrocławskiego, 2000.

El suspendido vuelo del ángel creador.
Medina, Narciso. La Habana : Ediciones Alarcos, 2003.

Suspil'stvo na porozi 21-ho stolittīā.
Suspil'stvo na porozi XXI stolittīā. Kyïv : Ukraïns'kyĭ TSentr dukhovnoï kul'tury, 1999.

Suspil'stvo na porozi dvadtsīāt' pershoho stolittīā.
Suspil'stvo na porozi XXI stolittīā. Kyïv : Ukraïns'kyĭ TSentr dukhovnoï kul'tury, 1999.

Suspil'stvo na porozi XXI stolittīā : filosofs'ke osmyslennīā plynnoho svitu : [navchal'nyĭ posibnyk / vidpovidal'nyĭ redaktor: Pazenok V.S.]. Kyïv : Ukraïns'kyĭ TSentr dukhovnoï kul'tury, 1999. 265 p. ; 20 cm. At head of title: Kyïvs'kyĭ instytut filosofii im. H.S. Skovorody. Kyïvs'kyĭ instytut turyzmu, ekonomiky i prava. Authorized for instructional purposes. "Navchal'ne vydannīā"--Colophon. Includes bibliographical references. ISBN 9667276376
1. Sociology - Philosophy. 2. Philosophy, Modern - 20th century. I. Pazenok, V. S. (Viktor Sergeevich) II. Instytut filosofiï NAN Ukraïny im. H. Skovorody. III. Kyïvs'kyĭ instytut turyzmu, ekonomiky i prava. IV. Title: Suspil'stvo na porozi 21-ho stolittīā V. Title: Suspil'stvo na porozi dvadtsīāt' pershoho stolittīā

Sustainability at the cutting edge.
Smith, Peter F. (Peter Frederick), 1930- Oxford ; Boston : Architectural Press, 2003.
NA2542.3 .S65 2003

SUSTAINABLE ARCHITECTURE.
Environmentally sustainable buildings. Paris : Organisation for Economic Co-operation and Development, 2003.

SUSTAINABLE DEVELOPMENT.
Riding the next wave. Indianapolis, Ind. : Hudson Institute ; [Washington, DC : Distributed by the Brookings Institution Press], c2001.
HM901 .R43 2001

Saúde e ambiente sustentável. Rio de Janeiro, RJ : Editora Fiocruz : Abrasco, 2002.

Some significant 21st century trends and issues. Islamabad : Pakistan Futuristics Foundation & Institute, 1998.
CB161 .S62 1998

[Wohlstand entschleiern. English] Unveiling wealth. Dordrecht ; Boston : Kluwer, c2002.
HD75.6 .U58 2002

SUSTAINABLE DEVELOPMENT - ENVIRONMENTAL ASPECTS.
Leff, Enrique. Saber ambiental. 3a ed. correg. y aument. México : PNUMA ; Siglo Veintiuno, 2002.

SUSTAINABLE DEVELOPMENT - STUDY AND TEACHING.
Flores Bedregal, Teresa. Comunicación para el desarrollo sostenible. La Paz : Plural Editores : LIDEMA : Konrad-Adenauer-Stiftung, c2002.

SUSTAINABLE DEVELOPMENT - STUDY AND TEACHING (HIGHER) - BOLIVIA.
Flores Bedregal, Teresa. Comunicación para el desarrollo sostenible. La Paz : Plural Editores : LIDEMA : Konrad-Adenauer-Stiftung, c2002.

SUSTAINABLE ECONOMIC DEVELOPMENT. See SUSTAINABLE DEVELOPMENT.

Sustentabilidad, racionalidad, complejidad, poder.
Leff, Enrique. Saber ambiental. 3a ed. correg. y aument. México : PNUMA ; Siglo Veintiuno, 2002.

Suster, Gerald.
Dee, John, 1527-1608. [Selections. 2003] John Dee. Berkeley, Calif. : North Atlantic Books, c2003.
BF1598.D5 A25 2003

Sutcliffe, Adam. Judaism and Enlightenment / Adam Sutcliffe. Cambridge ; New York : Cambridge University Press, 2003. xv, 314 p. : ill. ; 24 cm. (Ideas in context ; 66) Includes bibliographical references (p. 262-306) and index. Publisher description URL: http://www.loc.gov/catdir/description/cam031/2002031069.html Table of contents URL: http://www.loc.gov/catdir/toc/cam031/2002031069.html ISBN 0-521-82015-4 DDC 296/.094/09032
1. Judaism - Europe - History. 2. Judaism - History - 17th century. 3. Judaism - History - 18th century. 4. Enlightenment. 5. Europe - Intellectual life - 17th century. 6. Europe - Intellectual life - 18th century. 7. Europe - Ethnic relations. I. Title. II. Series.
BM290 .S88 2003

Sutcliffe, Alistair, 1951- Multimedia and virtual reality : designing multisensory user interfaces / Alistair Sutcliffe. Mahwah, N.J. ; London : Lawrence Erlbaum, c2003. xvi, 333 p. : ill. ; 24 cm. Includes bibliographical references (p. 295-305) and indexes. ISBN 0-8058-3950-X (hc. : alk. paper) DDC 006.7
1. Interactive multimedia. 2. Virtual reality. 3. User interfaces (Computer systems) I. Title.
QA76.76.I59 S88 2003

Sutcliffe, Eileen, 1934- Eve returns Adam's rib : life stories to awaken today's woman to seek her full potential / by Eileen Sutcliffe and Lorna Rowsell ; illustrations by Judy McCloskey. Calgary : Loraleen Enterprises, c2002. xiii, 222 p. : ill. ; 22 cm. + 1 CD-ROM. CD-ROM in pocket on p. [3] of cover. Limited edition of 300 copies. Includes bibliographical references. ISBN 0-9689700-0-1 (pbk.) DDC 155.6/33
1. Self-help techniques. 2. Self-esteem in women. 3. Women - Psychology. I. Rowsell, Lorna V., 1933- II. Title.

Sutker, Catharine.
McKay, Matthew. The self-nourishment companion. Oakland, CA : New Harbinger Publications, c2001.
BF637.S4 M3925 2001

Sutton, Tina.
Whelan, Bride M. The complete color harmony. Gloucester, Mass. : Rockport Publishers, 2004.
BF789.C7 W47 20041

Svechnikov, Vladimir. Sotsiokul'turnyĭ analiz mistifikatsii / Vladimir Svechnikov. Saratov : Saratovskiĭ gos. tekhn. universitet, 2000. 135,[1] p. ; 21 cm. "Nauchnoe izdanie"--Colophon. Includes bibliographical references (p. 135-[136]). ISBN 5743306338
1. Deception - Psychological aspects. 2. Deception - Social aspects. I. Title.
BF637.D42 S94 2000

Svendsen, Lars Fr. H., 1970- Kunst : en begrepsavvikling / Lars Fr. H. Svendsen. Oslo : Universitetsforlaget, c2000. 154 p. : col. ill. ; 21 cm. Includes bibliographical references (p. 143-149) and index. ISBN 82-00-45430-4
1. Art, Modern - 20th century. 2. Aesthetics. I. Title.
N6490 .S88499 2000

Svet prelomlennogo vremeni v ikonnom prostranstve.
Ivinskaīā, A. (Anna) Moskva : Khristianskiĭ Vostok, 2002.
N8189.G72 I95 2002

Svetlina na misŭlta.
Dŭnov, Petŭr, 1864-1944. Sofiīā : Kulturna asotsiatsiīā Beīnsà Dunò, 1998.
BF641 .D79 1998

Svīāshchennye prarodiny slavīān.
Asov, A. I. (Aleksandr Igorevich) Moskva : Veche, 2002.
BL930 .A863 2002

Svoboda kak sotsial'nyĭ i dukhovno-psikhicheskiĭ fenomen.
Shubnīākov, B. P. IAroslavl' : DIA-press, 2000.

Svobodnye razmyshleniīā, 1917-1993.
Moiseev, N. N. (Nikita Nikolaevich) Kak daleko do zavtrashnego dnīā--. Moskva : Taĭdeks Ko, 2002.
DK49 .M64 2002

Svobodnyĭ vzglīād na literaturu : problemy sovremennoĭ filologii : sbornik stateĭ k 60-letīīu nauchnoĭ deīātel'nosti akademika N.I. Balashova / [redaktsionnaīā kollegiīā A.D.Mikhaĭlov (predsedatel') ... et al.]. Moskva : Nauka, 2002. 447 p. : ill., plates ; 22 cm. Added title page title: Vue libre sur la science littéraire : problèmes de la philologie contemporaine. "Nauchnoe izdanie"--T.p. verso. On page preceding t.p.: Rossiĭskaīā akademiīā nauk. Institut mirovoĭ literatury im. A.M. Gor'kogo. ISBN 5020118109
1. Balashov, N. I. - (Nikolaĭ Ivanovich) - 1919- 2. Literature, Comparative - 19th century. 3. Literature, Comparative - 20th century. 4. Philology. 5. Philosophy. 6. Art - Criticism and interpretation. I. Mikhaĭlov, A. D. (Andreĭ Dmitrievich) II. Balashov, N. I (Nikolaĭ Ivanovich), 1919- III. Title: Vue libre sur la science littéraire : problèmes de la philologie contemporaine

Swanton, Christine, 1947- Virtue ethics : a pluralistic view / Christine Swanton. Oxford ; New York : Oxford University Press, 2003. xi, 312 p. ; 23 cm. ISBN 0-19-925388-9 (hc.) DDC 179/.9
1. Virtue. 2. Ethics. I. Title.
BJ1531 .S93 2003

Swarowsky, Hans.
Malaniuk, Ira. Arien und Lieder [sound recording]. [Germany] : Preiser Records, p2000.

Swatos, William H.
Christiano, Kevin J. Sociology of religion. Walnut Creek, CA : AltaMira Press, c2002.
BL60 .C465 2002

Swearingen, James E., 1939-.
Extreme beauty. London ; New York : Continuum, 2002.
BH39 .E98 2002

Sweeney, Jennifer Foote.
Life as we know it. 1st Washington Square Press trade pbk. ed. New York : Washington Square Press, 2003.

Sweeney, Paul D., 1955- Organizational behavior : solutions for management / Paul D. Sweeney, Dean B. McFarlin. Boston : McGraw-Hill Irwin, c2002. xx, 476 p. : ill. ; 27 cm. Includes bibliographical references and index. Publisher description URL: http://www.loc.gov/catdir/description/mh021/2001030308.html Table of contents URL: http://www.loc.gov/catdir/toc/mh021/2001030308.html ISBN 0-07-365908-8 (alk. paper) DDC 658.3
1. Organizational behavior. 2. Personnel management. I. McFarlin, Dean B. II. Title.
HD58.7 .S953 2002

Sweetman, Caroline.
Gender, development and money. Oxford : Oxfam, 2001.

Świętorzecka, Kordula.
Salamucha, Jan. [Selections. English. 2003] Knowledge and faith. Amsterdam ; New York, NY : Rodopi, 2003.

Swiggers, Pierre.
Grammatical theory and philosophy of language in antiquity. Leuven ; Sterling, Va. : Peeters, 2002.
P63 .G73 2002

SWITZERLAND - ETHNIC RELATIONS.
Büchi, Christophe. "Röstigraben". 2. aufl. Zürich : NZZ, c2001.

Syddansk universitet. Dept. of Greek and Roman Studies.
Divination and portents in the Roman world. Odense : Odense University Press, c2000.
BF1768 .D57 2000

Sydney Omarr's astrology, love, sex, and you.
Omarr, Sydney. [Astrology, love, sex, and you] New York : Signet, c2002.
BF1729.S4 O58 2002

Sykes, Bryan. Adam's curse : a future without men / Bryan Sykes. London ; New York : Bantam, 2003. x, 310 p. : ill. ; 25 cm. Includes index. ISBN 0-593-05004-5 ISBN 0-593-05005-3 (TRADE PBK.) DDC 305.3101576
1. Y chromosome - Popular works. 2. Men. 3. Sociobiology. 4. Human genetics. I. Title.

Syktyvkarskiĭ gosudarstvennyĭ universitet.
Mezhregional'naia Rossiĭskaia nauchno-prakticheskaia konferentsiia "Psikhologicheskie osobennosti preodoleniia ėkstremal'nykh i ėmotsiogennykh situatsiĭ v podrostkovo-iunosheskom vozraste" (2002 : Syktyvkar, Russia) Psikhologicheskie osobennosti preodoleniia ėkstremal'nykh i ėmotsiogennykh situatsiĭ v podrostkovo-iunosheskom vozraste. Syktyvkar : Syktyvkarskiĭ gos. universitet, 2002.
BF724 .M48 2002

SYLLOGISM. *See* **LOGIC, SYMBOLIC AND MATHEMATICAL.**

Sylvan, Dianne, 1977- The circle within : creating a wiccan spiritual tradition / Dianne Sylvan. 1st ed. St. Paul, MN : Llewellyn Publications, 2003. xv, 189 p. ; 21 cm. Includes bibliographical references (p. 179-183) and index. ISBN 0-7387-0348-6 DDC 299
1. Witchcraft. 2. Spiritual life. I. Title.
BF1566 .S95 2003

Sylvest, Vernon M. The formula : who gets sick, who gets well, who is happy, who is unhappy, and why / Vernon M. Sylvest. Fairfield, Iowa : Sunstar Pub., c1996. 207 p. ; 24 cm. Includes bibliographical references (p. 199-207). ISBN 0-9647130-0-4 DDC 299/.93
1. Mind and body. 2. Healing. 3. Medicine and psychology. I. Title.
BF161 .S95 1996

Symbol and sacrament.
Chauvet, Louis Marie. [Symbole et sacrement. English] Collegeville, Minn. : Liturgical Press, c1995.
BV800 .C5213 1995

SYMBOLIC AND MATHEMATICAL LOGIC. *See* **LOGIC, SYMBOLIC AND MATHEMATICAL.**

SYMBOLIC ASPECTS OF ANIMALS. *See* **ANIMALS - SYMBOLIC ASPECTS.**

SYMBOLIC ASPECTS OF THE HUMAN BODY. *See* **BODY, HUMAN - SYMBOLIC ASPECTS.**

SYMBOLIC COLORS. *See* **SYMBOLISM OF COLORS.**

SYMBOLIC INTERACTION. *See* **SOCIAL INTERACTION.**

SYMBOLIC NUMBERS. *See* **SYMBOLISM OF NUMBERS.**

SYMBOLISM. *See also* **ANIMALS - SYMBOLIC ASPECTS; BODY, HUMAN - SYMBOLIC ASPECTS; EMBLEMS; SEMANTICS (PHILOSOPHY); SIGNS AND SYMBOLS.**
A che servono i simboli? Milano : FrancoAngeli, c2002.

Bonvecchio, Claudio. La maschera e l'uomo. Milano : F. Angeli, 2002.

Buckland, Raymond. Signs, symbols & omens. 1st ed. St. Paul, Minn. : Llewellyn Publications, 2003.
BF1623.S9 B83 2003

Chauvet, Louis Marie. [Symbole et sacrement. English] Symbol and sacrament. Collegeville, Minn. : Liturgical Press, c1995.
BV800 .C5213 1995

Hall, Adelaide S. (Adelaide Susan), b. 1857. [Glossary of important symbols in their Hebrew, pagan, and Christian forms] Important symbols in their Hebrew, pagan, and Christian forms. Berwick, Me. : Ibis Press, 2003.
BF1623.S9 H35 2003

Hall, Manly Palmer, 1901- The secret teachings of all ages. Reader's ed. New York : Jeremy P. Tarcher/Putnam, 2003.
BF1411 .H3 2003

Herrschaft des Symbolischen. Berlin : Vistas, c2002.

Kurganov, E. Anekdot, simvol, mif. Sankt-Peterburg : Izd-vo zhurnala "Zvezda", 2002.

Midgley, Mary, 1919- The myths we live by. London ; New York : Routledge, 2003.
BL304 .M53 2003

Monahan, Brian. From ground zero to ground hero. [Newark, Del.?] : Disaster Research Center, University of Delaware, 2001.

Signos de identidad histórica para Navarra. Pamplona : Caja de Ahorros de Navarra, 1996.
DP302.N267 S54 1996

Szőnyi, György Endre. John Dee's occultism. Albany : State University of New York Press, 2004.
BF1598.D5 S98 2004

Wunenburger, Jean-Jacques. La vie des images. [Nouvelle édition augmentée]. Grenoble : Presses universitaires de Grenoble, 2002.
BF367 .W85 2002

Zhongguo xiang zheng wen hua. Di 1 ban. Shanghai : Shanghai ren min chu ban she : Xin hua shu dian Shanghai fa xing suo jing xiao, 2001.
DS721 .Z4985 2001

SYMBOLISM IN ARCHITECTURE - INDIA.
Kollar, L. Peter (Laszlo Peter), 1926- Symbolism in Hindu architecture as revealed in the Shri Minakshi Sundareswar. New Delhi : Aryan Books International, 2001.
NA6002 .K65 2001

SYMBOLISM IN ARCHITECTURE - WASHINGTON (D.C.).
Ovason, David. [Secret zodiacs of Washington DC] The secret architecture of our nation's capital. 1st Perennial ed. New York, NY : Perennial, 2002.

SYMBOLISM IN ART.
Rehm, Ulrich. Stumme Sprache der Bilder. München : Deutscher Kunstverlag, 2002.

Romero, Pedro G., 1964- En el ojo de la batalla. Valencia : Universitat de València, 2002.

SYMBOLISM IN ART - GERMANY - HISTORY - 17TH CENTURY.
Strasser, Gerhard F. Emblematik und Mnemonik der frühen Neuzeit im Zusammenspiel Johannes Buno und Johann Justus Winckelmann. Wiesbaden : Harrassowitz Wolfenbüttel : Herzog August Bibliothek, c2000.
PN6348.5 .S873 2000

SYMBOLISM IN COMMUNICATION.
Rehm, Ulrich. Stumme Sprache der Bilder. München : Deutscher Kunstverlag, 2002.

Symbolism in Hindu architecture as revealed in the Shri Minakshi Sundareswar.
Kollar, L. Peter (Laszlo Peter), 1926- New Delhi : Aryan Books International, 2001.
NA6002 .K65 2001

SYMBOLISM IN POLITICS.
Baudrillard, Jean. [Esprit du terrorisme. English] The spirit of terrorism and requiem for the Twin Towers. London : Verso, 2002.
HV6431 .B38 2002

Bonvecchio, Claudio. La maschera e l'uomo. Milano : F. Angeli, 2002.

Rowland, Robert C., 1954- Shared land/conflicting identity. East lansing : Michigan State University Press, 2002.
DS119.7 .R685 2003

SYMBOLISM IN PSYCHOLOGY. *See* **SYMBOLISM (PSYCHOLOGY).**

SYMBOLISM OF ANIMALS. *See* **ANIMALS - FOLKLORE.**

SYMBOLISM OF COLORS - HISTORY.
Pastoureau, Michel, 1947- Bleu. [Paris] : Seuil, c2000.
BF789.C7 P36 2000

SYMBOLISM OF NUMBERS. *See also* **NUMEROLOGY.**
Drayer, Ruth. Numerology. 3rd ed. Mesilla, N.M. : Jewels of Light Pub., 2002.
BF1623.P9 D72 2002

Kellner, Herbert Anton. Musicalische Temperatur der Bachsöhne. Darmstadt : Herbert Anton Kellner, c2001.

King, Richard Andrew. The king's book of numerology. Aptos, Calif. : New Brighton Books, 2003-
BF1729.N85 K56 2003

Padma, N. K., 1956- Navam and the Karṇāṭak group kṛtis. New Delhi : Kanishka Publishers, Distributors, 2002.
ML338 .P197 2002

SYMBOLISM OF NUMBERS - DICTIONARIES.
Saṅkhyāparaka śabda kośa. 1. saṃskaraṇa. Ilāhābāda : Sāhitya Bhavana, 2002.
BF1623.P9+

SYMBOLISM (PSYCHOLOGY). *See also* **ARCHETYPE (PSYCHOLOGY).**
Abadie, M. J. (Marie-Jeanne) Teen dream power. Rochester, Vt. : Bindu Books, 2003.
BF1099 .T43 2003

Beskova, I. A. Ėvoliutsiia i soznanie. Moskva : "Indrik", 2002.
B808.9 .B476 2002x

Dolgin, Aleksandr. Pragmatika kul'tury. Moskva : Fond nauchnykh issledovaniĭ "Pragmatika kul'tury", 2002.

Hamilton-Parker, Craig. Fantasy dreaming. New York : Sterling Pub., c2002.
BF1091 .H347 2002

Matière à symbolisation. Lausanne : Delachaux et Niestlé, c1998.
BF458 .M38 1998

SYMBOLISM (PSYCHOLOGY) - DICTIONARIES.
Collier-Thompson, Kristi. The girls' guide to dreams. New York : Sterling Pub., c2003.
BF1099.C55 C65 2003

Dream dictionary San Diego, CA : Thunder Bay Press, 2003.
BF1091 .D69 2003

MacGregor, Rob. Dreams. Philadelphia, Pa. : Running Press, c2002.
BF1091 .M314 2002

Phillips, Sara. Dream symbols. Philadelphia, Pa. : Courage Books, c2002.
BF1091 .P46 2002

Shepherd, Rowena. 1000 symbols. New York : Thames & Hudson, 2002.
BF458 .S63 2002

SYMBOLISM (PSYCHOLOGY) - DICTIONARIES - JUVENILE LITERATURE.
Collier-Thompson, Kristi. The girls' guide to dreams. New York : Sterling Pub., c2003.
BF1099.C55 C65 2003

SYMBOLISM (PSYCHOLOGY) - ENCYCLOPEDIAS.
Caspari, Elizabeth, 1926- Animal life in nature, myth and dreams. Wilmette, Ill. : Chiron Publications, c2003.
BF458 .C37 2003

SYMBOLISM (PSYCHOLOGY) - MISCELLANEA.
Todeschi, Kevin J. Soul signs. Virginia Beach, Va. : A.R.E. Press, c2003.
BF1045 .S44 T63 2003

SYMBOLS. *See* **SIGNS AND SYMBOLS.**

Symbols of the craft.
Madigan, M. A., 1962- 1st ed. St. Paul, Minn. : Llewellyn Publications, 2003.
BF1773 .M29 2003

Symington, Neville. A pattern of madness / Neville Symington. London ; New York : Karnac, 2002. xii, 234 p. ; 23 cm. Includes bibliographical references (p. 219-223) and index. ISBN 1-85575-279-4
1. Psychoanalysis. 2. Psychology, Pathological. 3. Narcissism. 4. Solipsism. 5. Insanity. I. Title.

SYMMETRY. *See* **AESTHETICS.**

Symons, Frank James, 1967-.
Pellegrini, Anthony D. Observing children in their natural worlds. 2nd ed. Mahwah, N.J. : L. Erlbaum Associates, 2004.
BF722 .P45 2004

SYMPATHY.
Tudor, Steven. Compassion and remorse. Leuven ; Sterling, Va. : Peeters, 2001.
BJ1475 .T84 2001

SYMPATHY IN LITERATURE.
Fichtelberg, Joseph. Critical fictions. Athens : University of Georgia Press, c2003.
PS366.S35 F53 2003

SYMPTOMATOLOGY. *See* **PAIN.**

SYNARCHISM. *See* **FASCISM.**

Synchro-signs.
McNaughton, Mary. Charlottesville, VA : Hampton Roads Pub., 2003.
BF1773 .M38 2003

SYNCHRONICITY. *See* **COINCIDENCE.**

SYNCHRONISM. *See* **COINCIDENCE.**

Synconomy.
DiVanna, Joseph A. Houndmills [England] ; New York : Palgrave Macmillan, 2003.
HD64.2 .D575 2003

SYNCRETISM (CHRISTIANITY). *See* **CHRISTIANITY AND OTHER RELIGIONS.**

SYNDICALISM. *See* **SOCIALISM.**

SYNESTHESIA. *See* **PERCEPTION.**

SYNKELLOS, GEORGE. ECLOGA CHRONOGRAPHICA.
Geōrgios, Synkellos, fl. 800. [Ecloga chronographica English] The chronography of George Synkellos. Oxford ; New York : Oxford University Press, 2002.

SYNTACTICS. *See* **SEMANTICS (PHILOSOPHY).**

Synthese library
(v. 298) Esfeld, Michael. Holism in philosophy of mind and philosophy of physics. Dordrecht ; Boston : Kluwer Academic Publishers, c2001.
B818 .E74 2001

SYRIA - HISTORY - 750-1260. *See* **CRUSADES.**

Syrkin, A. I͡A. (Aleksandr I͡Akovlevich), 1930-.
Jagaddeva. [Svapnacintāmaṇi. Russian] Volshebnoe sokrovishche snovideniĭ. Moskva : Ladomir, 1996.
BF1088.S26 J34 1996

SYSTEM ANALYSIS.
Lempert, Robert J. Shaping the next one hundred years. Santa Monica, CA : RAND, 2003.
T57.6 .L46 2003

SYSTEM DESIGN.
Crabtree, Andy. Designing collaborative systems. London ; [New York] : Springer, c2003.
QA76.9.S88 C725 2003

SYSTEM THEORY. *See also* **CHAOTIC BEHAVIOR IN SYSTEMS.**
Foley, Duncan K. Unholy trinity. London ; New York : Routledge, 2003.
HB135 .F65 2003

Herdina, Philip. A dynamic model of multilingualism. Clevedon, England Buffalo, N.Y. : Multilingual Matters, 2002.
P115.4 .H47 2002

Rihani, Samir, 1938- Complex systems theory and development practice. London ; New York : Zed Books, 2002.
HB71 .R485 2002

SYSTEMATIC THEOLOGY. *See* **THEOLOGY, DOCTRINAL.**

Le système et le rêve / sous la direction de Jean-Marie Paul. Paris : Harmattan, c2002. 300 p. : ill. ; 22 cm. (Collection Ouverture philosophique) At head of title: Université d'Angers, U.F.R. Lettres, langues et sciences humaines, Centre d'études et de recherche sur imaginaire, écritures et cultures. Includes bibliographical references. ISBN 2-7475-2856-1 DDC 194
1. Dreams. 2. Philosophy. I. Paul, Jean-Marie. II. Université d'Angers. Centre d'études et de recherche sur imaginaire, écritures et cultures. III. Series: Collection L'ouverture philosophique.
BF1078 .S97 2002

SYSTEMS ENGINEERING.
Chaos control. Berlin ; New York : Springer, c2003.
QA402.3 .C48 2003

SYSTEMS, EXPERT (COMPUTER SCIENCE). *See* **EXPERT SYSTEMS (COMPUTER SCIENCE).**

SYSTEMS, OPEN (PHYSICS). *See* **OPEN SYSTEMS (PHYSICS).**

Szczygiel, Bonj.
Gendered landscapes. University Park, PA : Center for Studies in Landscape History, c2000.

Szkice psychologiczne : doniesienia z badań, aplikacje, refleksje / pod redakcją Marii Straś-Romanowskiej. Wrocław : Wydawn. Uniwersytetu Wrocławskiego, 2002. 274 p. : ill. ; 24 cm. (Acta Universitatis Wratislaviensis, 0239-6661 ; no 2420) (Prace psychologiczne ; 55) Includes bibliographical references. ISBN 83-229-2286-8
1. Psychology - Research. I. Straś-Romanowska, Maria. II. Series. III. Series: Prace psychologiczne ; 55
BF76.5 .S97 2002

Szőnyi, György Endre. John Dee's occultism : magical exaltation through powerful signs / György Endre Szőnyi. Albany : State University of New York Press, 2004. p. cm. (SUNY series in Western esoteric traditions) ISBN 0-7914-6223-4 (alk. paper) DDC 133/.092
1. Dee, John, - 1527-1608. 2. Symbolism. 3. Magic - History. 4. Occultism - History. 5. Renaissance. I. Title. II. Series.
BF1598.D5 S98 2004

T-JTA. *See* **TAYLOR-JOHNSON TEMPERAMENT ANALYSIS.**

T-JTA scoring program [electronic resource] : computer scoring software system. Windows version 2.0. Thousand Oaks, CA : Psychological Pub., c2002. 1 CD-ROM ; 4 3/4 in. + 1 user's guide. Title from user's guide: Taylor-Johnson Temperament Analysis. System requirements: Windows 95 or later; CD-ROM drive. Title from disc label. SUMMARY: Software designed to facilitate the scoring process of the Taylor-Johnson Tempermeent Analysis test. DDC 155.2
1. Taylor-Johnson Temperament Analysis - Software. I. Psychological Publications, Inc. II. Title: Taylor-Johnson Temperament Analysis
BF698.8.T35

Ta chuan.
Karcher, Stephen L. 1st ed. New York : St. Martin's Press, 2000.
BF1773.2.C5 K368 2000

Ta-Shma, Israel M. ha-Nigleh sheba-nistar : le-ḥeker shekiʻe ha-Halakah be-Sefer ha-Zohar / Yiśraʼel M. Ta-Shemaʻ. Nusaḥ murḥav. [Tel Aviv] : ha-Kibuts ha-meʼuḥad, c2001. 156 p. ; 21 cm. (Sifriyat "Helal Ben-Ḥayim") Title on verso of t.p. Nigle she-banistar : the Halachic residue in the Zohar. Includes bibliographical references (p. 105-149) and index.
1. Zohar - Sources. 2. Cabala. 3. Jewish law - Influence. I. Title. II. Title: Nigle she-banistar : the Halachic residue in the Zohar III. Title: Halachic residue in the Zohar IV. Series.

Tabatabai, Sayyid Muhammad Husayn. The elements of Islamic metaphysics (Bidāyat al-Ḥikmah) / Sayyid Muhammad Husayn Tabatabai ; translated and annotated by Sayyid ʼAlī Qūlī Qaraʼī. London : ICAS, 2003. xiv, 191 p. ; 21 cm. Includes index. ISBN 1-904063-06-3 DDC 181.07
1. Philosophy, Islamic. 2. Philosophy, Iranian. 3. Philosophy, Modern - 20th century. I. Title.

Tabensky, Pedro Alexis, 1964- Happiness : personhood, community, purpose / Pedro Alexis Tabensky. Aldershot, Hampshire, England ; Burlington, VT : Ashgate, c2003. ix, 226 p. ; 25 cm. Includes bibliographical references (p. 213-217) and index. ISBN 0-7546-0734-8 DDC 170
1. Happiness. 2. Conduct of life. I. Title.
BJ1481 .T25 2003

Taberner, Stuart.
Recasting German identity. Rochester, NY : Camden House, 2002.
DD239 .R43 2002

TABLE. *See* **DINNERS AND DINING; FOOD.**

Tabori, Lena.
The love almanac. New York : Welcome Books : Distributed to the trade in the U.S. and Canada by Andrews McMeel Distribution Service, 2003.
BF575.L8 L6675 2003

La tâche civilisatrice de la psychanalyse selon Freud.
Chebili, Saïd. Paris : L'Harmattan, c2002.

Tactical reality dictionary.
Becker, Konrad. Vienna : Edition Selene ; [s.l.] : Distribution Canada/UK/USA by Autonomedia, 2002.
BF637.P4 B33 2002

TACTILE PERCEPTION. *See* **TOUCH.**

TACTUAL PERCEPTION. *See* **TOUCH.**

Tadié, Jean-Yves, 1936- Le sens de la mémoire / Jean-Yves et Marc Tadié. Paris : Gallimard, c1999. 355 p. : ill. ; 21 cm. Includes bibliographical references (p. [347]-350). ISBN 2-07-075223-2
1. Memory. 2. Recollection (Psychology) I. Tadié, Marc. II. Title.
BF371 .T32 1999

Tadié, Marc.
Tadié, Jean-Yves, 1936- Le sens de la mémoire. Paris : Gallimard, c1999.
BF371 .T32 1999

Tadtaev, Kh. B. (Khristofor Bagratovich) Ėtnos, natsii͡a, rasa : natsionalʼno-kulʼturnye osobennosti determinat͡sii protsessa poznanii͡a / Kh.B. Tadtaev ; pod redakt͡sieĭ S.I. Zamogilʼnogo. Saratov : Saratovskiĭ gos. universitet, 2001. 241 p. ; 21 cm. Includes bibliographical references. ISBN 5292026034
1. Ethnology - Philosophy. 2. Nationalism - Philosophy. I. Zamogilʼnyĭ, S. I. II. Title.
GN345 .T33 2001

Tagle Frías de Cuenca, Matilde. Notas sobre historia del libro / Matilde Tagle de Cuenca. Córdoba, República Argentina : Ediciones del Copista, c1997. 201 p. : ill. ; 24 cm. (Biblioteca de historia) Includes bibliographical references (p. [195]-196). ISBN 9879192087
1. Books - History. 2. Writing - History. 3. Printing - History. I. Title. II. Series: Biblioteca de historia (Córdoba, Argentina)
Z4

Tagliasco, Vincenzo, 1941-.
Manzotti, Riccardo. Coscienza e realtà. Bologna : Società editrice il mulino, c2001.
BF311 .M35 2001

Tagore, Rabindranath, 1861-1941. [Sādhanā. Marathi]
Sādhanā : jīvanācā sākshātkāra / Ravīndranātha Thākūra ; [anuvādaka] Sāne Guruji. Kolhāpūra : Mahārāshṭra Grantha Bhāṇḍāra, 2000. 176 p. ; 23 cm. SUMMARY: Lectures delivered at Harvard University on Hindu philosophy and values in life. In Marathi.
1. Philosophy, Hindu. 2. Values. I. Title.
B131 .T28 2000

Tagträume, Anliegen und Motivation.
Langens, Thomas A. Göttingen ; Seattle : Hogrefe, c2002.

Ṭaḥḥān, Aḥmad. Tajāʼīd fī wajh al-zaman al-ʻArabī / Aḥmad Ṭaḥḥān. al-Ṭabʻah 1. Bayrūt : Dār al-Fārābī, 2001. 461 p. ; 22 cm. In Arabic. ISBN 9953411360
1. Civilization, Arab. 2. East and West. I. Title.

Tahon, Marie-Blanche.
Le deuxième sexe. Montréal : Éditions du Remue-ménage, 2001.

TAI CHI.
Chuckrow, Robert. The tai chi book. Boston : YMAA Publication Center, c1998.
GV504 .C536 1998

Chuckrow, Robert. Tai chi walking. Boston, Mass. : YMAA Publication Center, c2002.

The tai chi book.
Chuckrow, Robert. Boston : YMAA Publication Center, c1998.
GV504 .C536 1998

Tai chi walking.
Chuckrow, Robert. Boston, Mass. : YMAA Publication Center, c2002.

Tai ji wen hua. Xianggang : Zhongguo zhe xue wen hua xie jin hui, [2001- v. ; 21 cm. Frequency: Irregular. Di 1 ji (2001)- . (Shu shu cong shu)
1. Divination - China. I. Zhongguo zhe xue wen hua xie jin hui. II. Series: Shu shu cong shu (Zhongguo zhe xue wen hua xie jin hui)
BF1770.C5 T35

TAILORS. *See* **CLOTHING TRADE.**

Taĭny zemli russkoĭ.
Asov, A. I. (Aleksandr Igorevich) Svi͡ashchennye prarodiny slavi͡an. Moskva : Veche, 2002.
BL930 .A863 2002

Tait, Peta, 1953- Performing emotions : gender, bodies, spaces, in Chekhov's drama and Stanislavski's theatre / Peta Tait. Aldershot ; Burlington Vt. : Ashgate, c2002. viii, 199 p. ; 23 cm. Includes bibliographical references (p. 172-195) and index. ISBN 0-7546-0638-4 DDC 891.72/3
1. Chekhov, Anton Pavlovich, - 1860-1904 - Dramatic works. 2. Stanislavsky, Konstantin, - 1863-1938. 3. Emotions in literature. 4. Gender identity in literature. 5. Acting. I. Title.
PG3458.Z9 D774 2002

Tajā'id fī wajh al-zaman al-'Arabī.
Ṭaḥḥān, Aḥmad. al-Ṭab'ah 1. Bayrūt : Dār al-Fārābī, 2001.

Tajik Neelkanthi.
Nīlakaṇṭha, 16th cent. [Tājikanīlakaṇṭhī. English & Sanskrit] Tajik Nilkanthi = 1st ed. New Delhi : Ranjan Publications, 2001.
BF1714.H5 N4813 2001

Tajik Nilkanthi.
Nīlakaṇṭha, 16th cent. [Tājikanīlakaṇṭhī. English & Sanskrit] 1st ed. New Delhi : Ranjan Publications, 2001.
BF1714.H5 N4813 2001

Tājika Nīlakaṇthī.
Nīlakaṇṭha, 16th cent. [Tājikanīlakaṇṭhī. English & Sanskrit] Tajik Nilkanthi = 1st ed. New Delhi : Ranjan Publications, 2001.
BF1714.H5 N4813 2001

Takahashi, Keiko, 1956- Kibō no genri = The principle of hope / Takahashi Keiko. Tōkyō : Sanpō Shuppan, 1997. 323 p. : ill. ; 20 cm. Includes bibliographical references (p. 321). ISBN 4-87928-027-5
1. Hope. 2. Spiritual life. I. Title. II. Title: Principle of hope
BD216 .T35 1997

Take control of your life.
James, Jacqueline. London : Hodder & Stoughton, 1995, c1994.

Takeichi, Akihiro, 1933-.
Kuno Akira Kyōju kanreki kinen tetsugaku ronbunshū. Tōkyō : Ibunsha, 1995.
B29 .K826 1995 <Orien Japan>

TAKEOVERS, CORPORATE. *See* **CONSOLIDATION AND MERGER OF CORPORATIONS.**

Taking charge of anger.
Nay, W. Robert. New York : Guilford Press, c2003.
BF575.A5 N39 2003

Taking our places.
Fischer, Norman, 1946- 1st ed. San Francisco : HarperSanFrancisco, c2003.
BF710 .F57 2003

TAKING RISKS. *See* **RISK-TAKING (PSYCHOLOGY).**

Taleb, Mohammed.
Sciences et archétypes. Paris : Dervy, 2002.

TALENTED PERSONS. *See* **GIFTED PERSONS.**

TALES. *See* **FAIRY TALES; LEGENDS.**

TALES - EGYPT.
Contes de l'Egypte ancienne. Paris : Flammarion, c2002.

TALES, MEDIEVAL - HISTORY AND CRITICISM.
Matthews, Caitlin, 1952- King Arthur and the goddess of the land. 2nd ed. Rochester, Vt. : Inner Traditions, 2002.
PB2273.M33 M36 2002

Matthews, Caitlin, 1952- Mabon and the guardians of Celtic Britain. Rochester, Vt. : Inner Traditions, c2002.
PB2273.M33 M37 2002

TALES - THEMES, MOTIVES.
Caillois, Roger, 1913- The edge of surrealism. Durham : Duke University Press, 2003.
HM590 .C35 2003

TALES - WALES - HISTORY AND CRITICISM.
Matthews, Caitlin, 1952- King Arthur and the goddess of the land. 2nd ed. Rochester, Vt. : Inner Traditions, 2002.
PB2273.M33 M36 2002

Matthews, Caitlin, 1952- Mabon and the guardians of Celtic Britain. Rochester, Vt. : Inner Traditions, c2002.
PB2273.M33 M37 2002

TALISMANS. *See also* **AMULETS; CHARMS.**
McQuillar, Tayannah Lee, 1977- Rootwork. New York : Simon & Schuster, c2003.
BF1622.A34 M37 2003
1. Black author.

Webster, Richard, 1946- Amulets & talismans for beginners. St. Paul, Minn. : Llewellyn Publications, 2004.
BF1561 .W43 2004

TALISMANS - SLAVIC COUNTRIES.
Telúch, Peter. Amulety a talizmany. Bratislava : Print-Servis, 1998.

TALKING. *See* **CONVERSATION; SPEECH.**

Talking about sexual orientation and gender identity with high school students through drama.
Ressler, Paula. Dramatic changes. Portsmouth, NH : Heinemann, c2002.
PN3171 .R47 2002

Talking to extraterrestrials.
Larkins, Lisette. Charlottesville, VA : Hampton Roads Pub., c2002.
BF2050 .L37 2002

Tallis, Raymond. The hand : a philosophical enquiry into human being / Raymond Tallis. Edinburgh : Edinburgh University Press, c2003. ix, 364 p. : ill. ; 21 cm. Includes bibliographical references and index. ISBN 0-7486-1737-X ISBN 0-7486-1738-8 (PBK.) DDC 128.2
1. Hand. 2. Philosophy of mind. 3. Human-animal relationships. I. Title.
BF908 .T35 2003

Tallon, Robert, 1947- From awareness to action : emotional intelligence, the enneagram, and change : a guide to improving performance / by Robert Tallon and Mario Sikora. Scranton, Pa. : University of Scranton Press, 2003. p. cm. Includes bibliographical references and index. ISBN 1-58966-070-6 (pbk.) DDC 155.2/6
1. Enneagram. 2. Emotional intelligence. I. Sikora, Mario, 1963- II. Title.
BF698.35.E54 T35 2003

TALMUD - COMMENTARIES.
Shelomoh ben Ḥayim Haikel. Sefer Liḳuṭe u-ferushe niglot Leshem shevo ve-aḥlamah. Kiryat Sefer : Mosheh Vais, 762 [2002]
BM525 .H4332 2002

TALMUD - HERMENEUTICS.
Neusner, Jacob, 1932- Analysis and argumentation in Rabbinic Judaism. Lanham, Md. : University Press of America, c2003.
BM496.5 .N4775 2003

TALMUD TORAH (JUDAISM).
Kuntres Kevod ha-Torah. Bene Beraḳ : ha-Meḥaber, 761 [2000 or 2001]

Liḳuṭ le-'idud ve-ḥizuḳ. Yerushalayim : [ḥ. mo. l.], 756 [1995 or 1996]

Mitelman, Yiśra'el Yehudah. Ḳuntres Ḥazaḳ ve-nitḥazeḳ. Ashdod : T. T. di-ḥaside Belza, 762 [2002]

Mosheh ben Shelomoh El'azar. Sefer Yede Mosheh ve-Torah or. Bene Beraḳ : Sifre Or ha-ḥayim, [760 i.e. 2000]

Otsrot rabotenu mi-Brisḳ. Bene Beraḳ : Sh. L., molut u-mishar bi-sefarim, 762 [2001 or 2002]
BM602 .O+

Tamari, Meir. Maśa u-matan be-emunah : 'iyunim ba-yidui / Me'ir Tamari. Yerushalayim : Śimḥonim, [761, 2001] 160 p. ; 24 cm. (Sifriyat ha-Merkaz la-'arakhim ba-'asaḳim ve-aḥrayut ḥevratit)
1. Tamari, Meir. 2. Merkaz la-'arakhim ba-'asaḳim ve-aḥrayut ḥevratit. 3. Commercial law (Jewish law) 4. Economics - Religious aspects - Judaism. 5. Ethics, Jewish. 6. Confession (Prayer) - Judaism. 7. Repentance - Judaism. I. Merkaz la-'arakhim ba-'asaḳim ve-aḥrayut ḥevratit. II. Title.

Tamari, Meir. Maśa u-matan be-emunah. Yerushalayim : Śimḥonim, [761, 2001]

Tamasy, Robert.
Stoddard, David A., 1953- The heart of mentoring. Colorado Springs, Colo. : NavPress, 2003.
BF637.C6 S773 2003

Tambores de Angola.
Santos, Robson Pinheiro, 1961- Contagem [Brazil] : Casa dos Espíritos, 2002.

Tambovskiĭ gosudarstvennyĭ universitet imeni G.R. Derzhavina.
Razvitie lichnosti v kul'turno-obrazovatel'nom prostranstve. Tambov : Tambovskiĭ gos. universitet im. G.R. Derzhavina, 2000.
BF698 .R342 2000

Tambrun-Krasker, Brigitte.
Gemistus Plethon, George, 15th cent. [Magika logia tōn apo Zōroastrou magōn. French & Greek] Magika logia tōn apo Zōroastrou magōn. Athēnai : Akadēmia Athēnōn, 1995.
BF1762 .G45 1995

TAMIL LITERATURE. *See* **RELIGIOUS LITERATURE, TAMIL.**

TAMIL LITERATURE - 20TH CENTURY - HISTORY AND CRITICISM.
Cujātā, 1935- Kaṟṟatum peṟṟatum. 1. patippu. Ceṉṉai : Vicā Paplikēṣaṉs, 2000.
PL4758.9.S8758+

TAMIL NADU (INDIA) - POLITICS AND GOVERNMENT - 20TH CENTURY.
Cujātā, 1935- Kaṟṟatum peṟṟatum. 1. patippu. Ceṉṉai : Vicā Paplikēṣaṉs, 2000.
PL4758.9.S8758+

TAMIL RELIGIOUS LITERATURE. *See* **RELIGIOUS LITERATURE, TAMIL.**

Tamil wisdom.
Robinson, Edward Jewitt. New Delhi : Asian Educational Services, 2001.
BJ1571 .R63 2001

Tamiḻ tiraippaṭaṅkaḷil āṇ-peṇ pāl pēṭam.
Kōvintaṉ, Ka. 1. patippu. Ceṉṉai : Kumaraṉ Papḷiṣars, 2001.
BF692.2 .K68 2001

Tamiḻ tiraippaṭaṅkaḷil āṇ-peṇ pālpēṭam.
Kōvintaṉ, Ka. Tamiḻt tiraippaṭaṅkaḷil āṇ-peṇ pāl pēṭam. 1. patippu. Ceṉṉai : Kumaraṉ Papḷiṣars, 2001.
BF692.2 .K68 2001

Taming your gremlin.
Carson, Richard David. Rev. ed. New York : Quill, 2003.
BF575.H27 C38 2003

Tamiozzo Villa, Patrizia. L'astrologia e i miti del mondo antico : un viaggio affascinante nello zodiaco e nella mitologia greca e romana alla scoperta delle affascinanti connessioni che legano il destino dell'uomo alla vita dell'universo / Patrizia Tamiozzo Villa. 1. ed. Roma : Newton & Compton, 2001. 206 p. : ill. ; 23 cm. (I big Newton ; 65) Includes bibliographical references (p. [195]-196) and index. ISBN 88-8289-572-6 DDC 133.5
1. Astrology. 2. Mythology, Greek. 3. Mythology, Roman. I. Title. II. Series.
BF1729.M9 T35 2001

Tan, Allen L.
Forty years of Philippine psychology. Diliman, Quezon City, Philippines : Psychological Association of the Philippines, c2002.
BF108 .F67 2002

Tan, Amy The opposite of fate : a book of musings / Amy Tan. New York : Putnam c2003. 398 p. : ill. ; 22 cm. ISBN 0-399-15074-9 (alk. paper) DDC 813/.54
1. Tan, Amy. 2. Tan, Amy - Family. 3. Novelists, American - 20th century - Family relationships. 4. Novelists, American - 20th century - Biography. 5. Chinese Americans - Biography. 6. Free will and determinism. 7. Chinese American families. 8. Fiction - Authorship. 9. Fate and fatalism. I. Title.
PS3570.A48 Z47 2003

TAN, AMY.
Tan, Amy The opposite of fate. New York : Putnam c2003.
PS3570.A48 Z47 2003

TAN, AMY - FAMILY.
Tan, Amy The opposite of fate. New York : Putnam c2003.
PS3570.A48 Z47 2003

Tan xun yu sui.
Li, Zehou. Di 1 ban. Shanghai : Shanghai wen yi chu ban she, 2000.
B126 .L532 2000

Tandrup, Leo.
Haugen Sørensen, Arne, 1932- Samtaler på en bjergtop. 1. oplag. Højbjerg : Hovedland, c2002.

Tang, Jean.
Levitt, Susan. Taoist astrology. Rochester, Vt. : Destiny Books, c1997.
BF1714.T34 L48 1997

Tang soo do

TANG SOO DO. *See* **KARATE.**

TANG TAIZONG, EMPEROR OF CHINA, 597-649.
An, Lizhi. "Zhen guan zheng yao" yu ling dao yi shu. Di 1 ban. Shanghai : Shanghai gu ji chu ban she, 1999.
DS749.3.W813 A63 1999

Tang, Yijie. Xi bu zhi jin / Tang Yijie ; Qian Wenzhong bian. Di 1 ban. Shanghai : Shanghai wen yi chu ban she, 1999. 5, 2, 352 p., [2] p. of plates : ill., col. port. ; 21 cm. (Xue yuan ying hua) ISBN 7-5321-1829-0
1. Philosophy, Chinese. 2. Taoism. 3. China - Civilization. I. Qian, Wenzhong. II. Title. III. Series.
B126 .T1965 1999

Tang yin ge lun wen ji.
Huo, Songlin. [Shijiazhuang Shi] : Hebei jiao yu chu ban she, [2000?]
PL2866.O236 A6 2000 v.1

Tang yin ge sui bi ji.
Huo, Songlin. [Shijiazhuang Shi] : Hebei jiao yu chu ban she, [2000?]
PL2866.O236 A6 2000 v.4

Tang, Yongtong, 1893-1964. [Works. 2000]
Tang Yongtong quan ji. Di 1 ban. Shijiazhuang Shi : Hebei ren min chu ban she, 2000. 7 v. : ill. ; 21 cm. Includes bibliographical references. ISBN 7-202-02518-3 (set)
1. Buddhism - China - History. 2. Philosophy. 3. Philosophy, Chinese. 4. Philosophy, Indic. I. Title.
BQ626 .T37 2000

Tang Yongtong quan ji.
Tang, Yongtong, 1893-1964. [Works. 2000] Di 1 ban. Shijiazhuang Shi : Hebei ren min chu ban she, 2000.
BQ626 .T37 2000

Tankens pilgrimer.
Ambjörnsson, Ronny, 1936- Stockholm : Natur och Kultur, c2002.

Tantra.
Urban, Hugh B. Berkeley : University of California Press, c2003.
BL1283.84 .U73 2003

Tantra, the supreme understanding.
Osho, 1931-1990. Delhi : Full Circle, 1999.
BP605.R34 T367 1999

TANTRIC BUDDHISM.
[Aids to Sadhana series. Tibetan & Sanskrit. Selections.] Sādhanamālā, Avalokiteśvara section. Delhi : Adroit Publishers ; New Delhi : Distributors, Akhil Book Distributors, 2002.
BQ8915 .S23 2002

Urban, Hugh B. Tantra. Berkeley : University of California Press, c2003.
BL1283.84 .U73 2003

TANTRIC BUDDHISM - DOCTRINES.
Osho, 1931-1990. Tantra, the supreme understanding. Delhi : Full Circle, 1999.
BP605.R34 T367 1999

The Tantric Dakini oracle.
Douglas, Nik. Rochester, Vt. : Destiny Books, 2003.
BF1879.T2 D695 2003

TANTRISM.
Douglas, Nik. The Tantric Dakini oracle. Rochester, Vt. : Destiny Books, 2003.
BF1879.T2 D695 2003

Urban, Hugh B. Tantra. Berkeley : University of California Press, c2003.
BL1283.84 .U73 2003

TANTRISM, BUDDHIST. *See* **TANTRIC BUDDHISM.**

Tantrums.
Kennedy, Michelle. Hauppauge, N.Y. : Barron's, c2003.
BF723.A4 .K46 2003

Tanxin yusui.
Li, Zehou. Tan xun yu sui. Di 1 ban. Shanghai : Shanghai wen yi chu ban she, 2000.
B126 .L532 2000

Die tanzende Göttin.
Göttner-Abendroth, Heide. 6. vollst. überarb. Neuaufl. München : Frauenoffensive, 2001, c1982.

TAO.
Towler, Solala. Tao paths to love. Kansas City, Mo. : Andrews McMeel Pub., 2002.
BD436 .T65 2002

Tao, Jinsheng, 1933-.
Excursions in Chinese culture. Hong Kong : Chinese University Press, c2002.

The tao of integrity.
Lipinski, Barbara. San Buenaventura, CA : Pacific Meridian Publications, c2001.
BF75 .L655 2001

Tao paths to love.
Towler, Solala. Kansas City, Mo. : Andrews McMeel Pub., 2002.
BD436 .T65 2002

Taofen, 1895-1944. Taofen "Du zhe xin xiang" / Guan Dongsheng bian. Di 1 ban. Beijing : Zhongguo cheng shi chu ban she, 1998. 4, 7, 278 p. : ill. ; 20 cm. ISBN 7-5074-1010-2
1. Conduct of life. 2. Family - China. I. Guan, Dongsheng. II. Title.

Taofen "Du zhe xin xiang".
Taofen, 1895-1944. Di 1 ban. Beijing : Zhongguo cheng shi chu ban she, 1998.

Taoism.
Toropov, Brandon. The complete idiot's guide to Taoism. Indianapolis, IN : Alpha, c2002.
BL1920 .T67 2002

TAOISM.
Levitt, Susan. Teen feng shui. Rochester, Vt. : Bindu Books, c2003.
BF1779.F4 L465 2003

Miller, James, 1968- Daoism. Oxford : Oneworld, c2003.
BL1920 .M55 2003

Schipper, Kristofer Marinus. Dao zang suo yin. Di 1 ban. Shanghai : Shanghai shu dian chu ban she : Xin hua shu dian Shanghai fa xing suo fa xin, 1996.
BL1900.T387 S35 1996 <Orien China>

Tang, Yijie. Xi bu zhi jin. Di 1 ban. Shanghai : Shanghai wen yi chu ban she, 1999.
B126 .T1965 1999

Toropov, Brandon. The complete idiot's guide to Taoism. Indianapolis, IN : Alpha, c2002.
BL1920 .T67 2002

Willoughby, Leonard. Every day Tao. Boston, MA : Weiser Books, 2001.
BL1920 .W55 2001

Taoist astrology.
Levitt, Susan. Rochester, Vt. : Destiny Books, c1997.
BF1714.T34 L48 1997

Levitt, Susan. Taoist astrology. Rochester, Vt. : Destiny Books, c1997.
BF1714.T34 L48 1997

Tapergi, Fausto, 1909- La filosofia come scienza della vita / Fausto Tapergi. 1a ed. Milano : Spirali, 2001. 316 p. ; 22 cm. (L'alingua ; 176) (Università internazionale del secondo Rinascimento ; 8) Includes indexes. ISBN 88-7770-588-4 DDC 100
1. Philosophy. 2. Life. I. Title. II. Series. III. Series: Università internazionale del secondo Rinascimento ; 8 IV. Series: Università internazionale del secondo Rinascimento (Series) ; 8.

Tapper, Alan.
Kovesi, Julius. Values and evaluations. New York ; Bern : P. Lang, c1998.
BD232 .K68 1998

Tapper, Colin.
Essays for Colin Tapper. London : LexisNexis, 2003.

TAPS-R : Test of Auditory-Perceptual Skills-Revised : manual / Morrison F. Gardner. [Rev. ed.]. Hydesville, CA : Psychological and Educational Publications, c1996. 264 p. ; 28 cm. Spine title: Test of auditory-perceptual skills-revised. Includes bibliographical references (p. 46-47). ISBN 0-931421-97-7 DDC 152.1/5/0287
1. Test of Auditory-Perceptual Skills-Revised. I. Title: Test of auditory-perceptual skills-revised
BF251.5.T44 T36 1996

Tardieu, Michel.
Gemistus Plethon, George, 15th cent. [Magika logia tōn apo Zōroastrou magōn. French & Greek] Magika logia tōn apo Zōroastrou magōn. Athēnai : Akadēmia Athēnōn, 1995.
BF1762 .G45 1995

Targ, Russell. Limitless mind : a guide to remote viewing and transformation of consciousness / Russell Targ. Novato, Calif. : New World Library, c2004. p. cm. Includes bibliographical references and index. CONTENTS: Introduction: the unknowable end of science -- Our limitless mind : living in a nonlocal universe -- On a clear day we can see forever : what we know about remote viewing -- For your viewing pleasure : how you can practice remote viewing -- Precognition : there's no time like the future or the past -- Intuitive medical diagnosis : things to do before the doctor arrives -- Distant healing : is it my mind over my matter? -- Why bother with esp? : discovering that you are the love you seek -- Afterword : Elisabeth's story. ISBN 1-57731-413-1 (pbk. : alk. paper) DDC 133.8
1. Remote viewing (Parapsychology) 2. Extrasensory perception. I. Title.
BF1389.R45 T37 2004

Taric Zumsteg, Fabienne. Les sorciers à l'assaut du village : Gollion, 1615-1631 / Fabienne Taric Zumsteg. Lausanne : Editions du Zèbre, 2000. 363 p. : ill., maps ; 21 cm. (Etudes d'histoire moderne, 1422-7541 ; 2) Includes bibliographical references (p. [341]-360). ISBN 2970023520
1. Witchcraft - Switzerland - Vaud - History. 2. Trials (Witchcraft) - Switzerland - Vaud - History. 3. Vaud (Switzerland) - History. I. Title. II. Series.
BF1584.S9 T37 2000

TAROT. *See also* **MAJOR ARCANA (TAROT).**
HaloEyes. Bloomington : 1stBooks Library, c2002.
BF1879.T2 H3355 2002

Hederman, Mark Patrick. Dublin : Currach Press, 2003.

Tognetti, Arlene. The complete idiot's guide to tarot. 2nd ed. Indianapolis, IN : Alpha, c2003.
BF1879.T2 T64 2003

TAROT.
Akron, 1948- H.R. Giger tarot. Köln : Evergreen, c2000.

Alexander, Skye. 10-minute tarot. Gloucester, Mass. : Fair Winds Press, c2003.
BF1879.T2 A445 2003

Aoumiel. Tarot for the green witch. 1st ed,. St. Paul, Minn. : Llewellyn Publications, 2003.
BF1879.T2 A58 2003

Bunning, Joan. Learning tarot reversals. Boston, MA : Weiser Books, 2003.
BF1879.T2 .B834 2003

Daniels, Kooch. Tarot d'amour. Boston, MA : Weiser Books, 2003.
BF1879.T2 D35 2003

Douglas, Nik. The Tantric Dakini oracle. Rochester, Vt. : Destiny Books, 2003.
BF1879.T2 D695 2003

DuQuette, Lon Milo, 1948- Understanding Aleister Crowley's thoth tarot. Boston, MA : Weiser Books, 2003.
BF1879.T2 D873 2003

Fairchild, Dennis. The fortune telling handbook. 1st ed. Philadelphia, PA : Running Press, c2003.
BF1861 .F35 2003

Fenton, Sasha. Super tarot. New York : Sterling Pub., 2003.
BF1879.T2 F465 2003

Francis-Cheung, Theresa. Teen tarot. Avon, MA : Adams Media Corp., 2003.
BF1879.T2 F7 2003

Gilbert, Toni. Messages from the archetypes. Ashland, Or. : White Cloud Press, c2003.
BF1879.T2 G53 2003

Gillentine, Julie. Tarot & dream interpretation. 1st ed. St. Paul, Minn. : Llewellyn Publications 2003.
BF1879.T2 G585 2003

Greer, Mary K. (Mary Katherine) Understanding the tarot court. 1st ed. St. Paul, Minn. : Llewellyn Publications, 2004.
BF1879.T2 G75 2004

Guide to the Golden Dawn Enochian skrying tarot. St. Paul, Minn. : Llewellyn, 2004.
BF1623.E55 G65 2004

HaloEyes. Tarot. Bloomington : 1stBooks Library, c2002.
BF1879.T2 H3355 2002

Hazel, Elizabeth. Tarot decoded. Boston, MA : Weiser Books, 2004.
BF1879.T2 H339 2004

Hederman, Mark Patrick. Tarot. Dublin : Currach Press, 2003.

Hoeller, Stephan A. [Royal road] The fool's pilgrimage. 2nd Quest ed. Wheaton, Ill. : Quest Books/Theosophical Pub. House, 2004.
BF1879.T2 H6 2004

Jacobi, Eleonore. [Tarot für Liebe und Partnerschaft. English] Tarot for love & relationships. New York : Sterling Pub. Co., c2003.

BF1879.T2 J3413 2003
Jette, Christine, 1953- Professional tarot. 1st ed. St. Paul, Minn. : Llewellyn Publications, 2003.
BF1879.T2 J475 2003
Kelly, Dorothy, 1952 Aug. 6- Tarot card combinations. Boston, MA : York Beach, ME : Weiser Books, 2003, c1995.
BF1879.T2 K45 2003
Lerner, Isha, 1954- The triple goddess tarot. Rochester Vt. : Bear & Co., c2002.
BF1879.T2 L4365 2002
Llewellyn, A. Bronwyn (Anita Bronwyn) Shakespeare oracle. Gloucester, Mass. : Fair Winds Press, 2003.
BF1879.T2 L59 2003
Mangiapane, John. It's all in the cards. New York : Sterling Pub., c2004.
BF1879.T2 M332 2004
McCluskey, John William. Amazing mystic tarot. 1st ed. East Hampton, N.Y. : Arden Book Co., c2002.
BF1879.T2 M42 2004
McCormack, Kathleen. The tarot workbook. 1st ed. Hauppauge, NY : Barron's, c2002.
BF1879.T2 M33 2002
Moore, Barbara, 1963- What tarot can do for you. 1st ed. St. Paul, Minn. : Llewellyn Publications, 2004.
BF1879.T2 M653 2004
Osho, 1931-1990. Tarot in the spirit of Zen. 1st ed. New York : St. Martin's Griffin, 2003.
BF1879.T2 O85 2003
Place, Robert Michael. The Buddha tarot companion. St. Paul, Minn. : Llewellyn, 2004.
BF1879.T2 P547 2004
Place, Robert Michael. [Gnostic book of saints. Spanish] El mensaje de los santos. St. Paul, Minn. : Llewellyn Español, 2003.
BF1879.T2 P5518 2003
Ricklef, James, 1954- Tarot tells the tale. St. Paul, Minn. : Llewellyn Publications, 2003.
BF1879.T2 R53 2003
Samul, A. L. Wisdom in the cards. 1st ed. Stamford, CT : U.S. Games Systems, c2002.
BF1879.T2 S26 2002
Seidman, Richard. The oracle of Kabbalah. 1st ed. New York : St. Martin's Press, 2001.
PJ4589 .S42 2001
Sharman-Burke, Juliet. Beginner's guide to tarot. 1st St. Martin's Griffin ed. New York : St. Martin's Griffin, 2001.
BF1879.T2 S52 2001
Thomson, Sandra A. Pictures from the heart. 1st ed. New York : St. Martin's Press, c2003.
BF1879.T2 T52 2003
Tognetti, Arlene. The complete idiot's guide to tarot. 2nd ed. Indianapolis, IN : Alpha, c2003.
BF1879.T2 T64 2003
Toland, Diane. Inner pathways to the divine. Hygiene, CO : SunShine Press Publications, c2001.
BF1879.T2 .T65 2001

Tarot & dream interpretation.
Gillentine, Julie. 1st ed. St. Paul, Minn. : Llewellyn Publications 2003.
BF1879.T2 G585 2003

Tarot and dream interpretation.
Gillentine, Julie. Tarot & dream interpretation. 1st ed. St. Paul, Minn. : Llewellyn Publications 2003.
BF1879.T2 G585 2003

Tarot and other meditation decks.
Auger, Emily E. Jefferson, N.C. : McFarland & Co., c2004.
BF1879.T2 A94 2004

Tarot card combinations.
Kelly, Dorothy, 1952 Aug. 6- Boston, MA : York Beach, ME : Weiser Books, 2003, c1995.
BF1879.T2 K45 2003

TAROT CARDS.
Akron, 1948- H.R. Giger tarot. Köln : Evergreen, c2000.

Douglas, Nik. The Tantric Dakini oracle. Rochester, Vt. : Destiny Books, 2003.
BF1879.T2 D695 2003

HaloEyes. Tarot. Bloomington : 1stBooks Library, c2002.

BF1879.T2 H3355 2002
McElroy, Mark, 1964- Putting the tarot to work. 1st ed. St. Paul, Minn. : Llewellyn Publications, 2004.
BF1879.T2 M43 2004

Tarot d'amour.
Daniels, Kooch. Boston, MA : Weiser Books, 2003.
BF1879.T2 D35 2003

Tarot decoded.
Hazel, Elizabeth. Boston, MA : Weiser Books, 2004.
BF1879.T2 H339 2004

TAROT - DICTIONARIES.
Thomson, Sandra A. Pictures from the heart. 1st ed. New York : St. Martin's Press, c2003.
BF1879.T2 T52 2003

Tarot for love & relationships.
Jacobi, Eleonore. [Tarot für Liebe und Partnerschaft. English] New York : Sterling Pub. Co., c2003.
BF1879.T2 J3413 2003

Tarot for love and relationships.
Jacobi, Eleonore. [Tarot für Liebe und Partnerschaft. English] Tarot for love & relationships. New York : Sterling Pub. Co., c2003.
BF1879.T2 J3413 2003

Tarot for teens.
Abadie, M. J. (Marie-Jeanne) Rochester, Vt. : Bindu Books, c2002.
BF1879.T2 A28 2002

Tarot for the green witch.
Aoumiel. 1st ed,. St. Paul, Minn. : Llewellyn Publications, 2003.
BF1879.T2 A58 2003

TAROT - HISTORY - 20TH CENTURY.
Auger, Emily E. Tarot and other meditation decks. Jefferson, N.C. : McFarland & Co., c2004.
BF1879.T2 A94 2004

Tarot in the spirit of Zen.
Osho, 1931-1990. 1st ed. New York : St. Martin's Griffin, 2003.
BF1879.T2 O85 2003

TAROT - JUVENILE LITERATURE.
Abadie, M. J. (Marie-Jeanne) Tarot for teens. Rochester, Vt. : Bindu Books, c2002.
BF1879.T2 A28 2002

Francis-Cheung, Theresa. Teen tarot. Avon, MA : Adams Media Corp., 2003.
BF1879.T2 F7 2003

Olmstead, Kathleen. The girls' guide to tarot. New York : Sterling Pub., c2002.
BF1879.T2 O38 2002

TAROT - MISCELLANEA.
Amberstone, Ruth Ann. Tarot tips. St. Paul, Minn. : Llewellyn, 2003.
BF1879.T2 A475 2003

Tarot tells the tale.
Ricklef, James, 1954- St. Paul, Minn. : Llewellyn Publications, 2003.
BF1879.T2 R53 2003

Tarot tips.
Amberstone, Ruth Ann. St. Paul, Minn. : Llewellyn, 2003.
BF1879.T2 A475 2003

The tarot workbook.
McCormack, Kathleen. 1st ed. Hauppauge, NY : Barron's, c2002.
BF1879.T2 M33 2002

TARYAG MIẒWOT. *See* **COMMANDMENTS, SIX HUNDRED AND THIRTEEN.**

TASTE (AESTHETICS). *See* **AESTHETICS.**

Tate, Trudi.
Literature, science, psychoanalysis, 1830-1970. Oxford ; New York : Oxford University Press, 2003.
PN55 .L58 2003

O tato.
Jackson, Holbrook, 1874-1948. [Anatomy of bibliomania. Portuguese. Selections] São Paulo : Imprensa Oficial do Estado, 2002.
Z992 .J33 2002

La tautología darwinista.
Vallejo, Fernando. 1a. ed. México : Universidad Nacional Autónoma de México, 1998.

Taviani-Carozzi, Huguette.
Année mille An Mil. Aix-en-Provence : Publications de l'université de Provence, 2002.

Tavris, Carol.
Wade, Carole. Invitation to psychology. 3rd ed. Upper Saddle River, NJ : Pearson/Prentice Hall, 2004.
BF121 .W265 2004

TAY-SACHS DISEASE.
Jarashow, Jonathan. The silent psalms of our son. Jerusalem, Israel : Feldheim Publishers, c2001.

Ṭayeb, Eli.
Eyal, Tsevi. Mi she-taʻam yayin Hungari. Tel Aviv : Yediʻot aḥaronot : Sifre ḥemed, c2002.

Tayir, Bracha Klein. ha-Manhig she-meʼafsher le-elef peraḥim li-feroaḥ : manhigut ruḥanit matslihah shel ha-meʼah ha-21 / Berakhah Ḳlain Taʼir. Tel Aviv : Yediʻot aḥaronot : Sifre ḥemed, c2002. 208 p. : ill. ; 23 cm. Title on verso of t.p.: Leader who enables thousand flowers to blossom : successful spiritual leadership of the 21st century. Includes bibliographical references (p. 203-208). ISBN 9655111210
1. Personality change - Study and teaching. 2. Personality development - Study and teaching. 3. Religous leaders. 4. Leadership. 5. Spiritual life - Judaism. I. Title. II. Title: Leader who enables thousand flowers to blossom : successful spiritual leadership of the 21st century.

Taylor-Johnson Temperament Analysis.
T-JTA scoring program [electronic resource]. Windows version 2.0. Thousand Oaks, CA : Psychological Pub., c2002.
BF698.8.T35

TAYLOR-JOHNSON TEMPERAMENT ANALYSIS - SOFTWARE.
T-JTA scoring program [electronic resource]. Windows version 2.0. Thousand Oaks, CA : Psychological Pub., c2002.
BF698.8.T35

Taylor, Lawrence Douglas. El nuevo norteamericano : integración continental, cultura e identidad nacional / Lawrence Douglas Taylor Hansen. México : Universidad Nacional Autónoma de México, Coordinación de Humanidades : Centro de Investigaciones sobre América del Norte ; Tijuana, B.C. : El Colegio de la Frontera Norte, 2001. 309 p. ; 23 cm. Includes bibliographical references (p. 235-309). URL: http://www.colef.mx URL: http://www.cisan.unam.mx ISBN 968-36-9665-1 DDC 327.7308
1. North America - Civilization - 20th century. 2. North America - Economic integration. 3. National characteristics, American. 4. National characteristics, Canadian. 5. National characteristics, Mexican. I. Title.
E40 .T39 2001

Taylor, Marilyn M.
Learning toward an ecological consciousness. New York : Palgrave Macmillan, 2003.
BF353 .L42 2003

Taylor, Scott L., 1964- The opportunity in every problem / by Scott L. Taylor. 1st ed. Salt Lake City : Gibbs Smith, c2003. 127 p. ; 21 cm. CONTENTS: Meeting Mr. Lucky -- Beginning the journey -- What are problems? -- Looking beyond the solution -- What's holding you back? -- Resource masterminding. ISBN 1-58685-320-1 DDC 158.1
1. Success - Psychological aspects. 2. Problem solving. I. Title.
BF637.S8 T285 2003

T'BILISIS SAXELMCIP'O UNIVERSITETI - HISTORY.
Cherchi, Marcello. Disciplines and nations. Pittsburgh, Pa. : Center for Russian and East European Studies, University Center for International Studies, University of Pittsburgh, c2002.

TDKS. Sovremennye issledovaniia
Levkievskaia, E. E. (Elena Evgen'evna) Slavianskiĭ obereg. Moskva : Indrik, 2002.
BL480 .L38 2002

Tea leaf fortune cards.
Hepburn, Rae. 1st ed. Boston : Journey Editions, c2000.
BF1881 .H47 2000

TEACHER EFFECTIVENESS.
Meighan, Roland. John Holt. 2nd ed. Nottingham : Educational Heretics Press, 2002.
LB885.H64 M454 2002

Shilony, Tamar. Model mentali shel morim menusim ṿe-tironim be-miḳtsoʻot madaʻiyim ṿe-humaniyim le-gabe lemidah be-ḳerev yeladim. [Israel : h. mo. l., 1994?]

TEACHER-STUDENT RELATIONSHIP - RELIGIOUS ASPECTS - JUDAISM.
Adler, Yitshaḳ Eliyahu, ha-Kohen. Sefer Kibud ṿe-hidur. Ofakim : Y.E. ha-Kohen Adler, 754 [1994]

Teacher-student relationships.

TEACHER-STUDENT RELATIONSHIPS.
Schultz, Katherine. Listening. New York : Teachers College Press, c2003.
LB1027 .S36638 2003

TEACHERS. *See* **EDUCATORS; TEACHERS OF PROBLEM CHILDREN.**

TEACHERS OF PROBLEM CHILDREN - UNITED STATES.
Lampert, Khen. Compassionate education. Lanham, Md. : University Press of America, c2003.

TEACHING. *See* **EDUCATION.**

TEACHING - AIDS AND DEVICES. *See* **EDUCATIONAL TECHNOLOGY.**

Teaching, learning, and the meditative mind.
Wingerter, J. Richard. Lanham, Md. ; Oxford : University Press of America, c2003.
LB1025.3 .W55 2003

TEACHING - PHILOSOPHY.
Augustine, Saint, Bishop of Hippo. De magistro = Paderborn : F. Schöningh, 2002.
BR65.A5 G4 2002

Teaching youth media.
Goodman, Steven. New York : Teachers College Press, c2003.
LB1043 .G59 2003

TEAMS IN THE WORKPLACE.
Cohen, Allan R. The portable MBA in management. 2nd ed. New York : J. Wiley, c2002.
HD31 .C586 2002

The collaborative work systems fieldbook. San Francisco : Jossey-Bass/Pfeiffer, c2003.
HD66 .C547 2003

Gottlieb, Marvin R. Managing group process. Westport, Conn. ; London : Praeger, 2003.
HD66 .G6778 2003

Harris, Chris. Building innovative teams. Houndmills [England] ; New York : Palgrave Macmillan, 2003.
HD66 .H3744 2003

Heim, Pat. In the company of women. New York : J.P. Tarcher/Putnam, c2001.
HD6053 .H387 2001

Housley, William, 1970- Interaction in multidisciplinary teams. Aldershot, England ; Burlington, VT : Ashgate, c2003.
HV41 .H667 2003

Implementing collaboration technologies in industry. London ; New York : Springer, c2003.
HD30.2 .I38 2003

Keen, Thomas R. Creating effective & successful teams. West Lafayette, Ind. : Ichor Business Books, c2003.
HD66 .K396 2003

Kliem, Ralph L. The organizational engineering approach to project management. Boca Raton : St. Lucie Press, c2003.
HD66 .K585 2003

McNiff, Shaun. Creating with others. 1st ed. Boston, Mass. : Shambhala Publications, 2003.
BF408 .M336 2003

Virtual teams. Hershey, PA ; London : Idea Group Publishing, c2004.
HD66 .V56 2004

Teams that lead.
Kline, Theresa, 1960- Mahwah, N.J. : L. E. Associates, 2003
HD57.7 .K549 2003

TECHNICAL ASSISTANCE - ANTHROPOLOGICAL ASPECTS. *See* **INTERCULTURAL COMMUNICATION.**

TECHNICAL INNOVATIONS. *See* **TECHNOLOGICAL INNOVATIONS.**

Technical manual.
McGrew, Kevin S. Woodcock-Johnson III technical manual / Itasca, IL : Riverside Pub., c2001.
BF432.5.W66 M345 2001

TECHNOCRACY.
Toshchenko, Zhan Terent'evich. Tri osobennykh lika vlasti. Moskva : RGGU, 2002.
JC330 .T674 2002

TECHNOLOGICAL BREAKTHROUGHS. *See* **TECHNOLOGICAL INNOVATIONS.**

TECHNOLOGICAL CHANGE. *See* **TECHNOLOGICAL INNOVATIONS.**

TECHNOLOGICAL FORECASTING. *See also* **NEW PRODUCTS.**
A parliament of science. Albany : State University of New York Press, c2003.
Q158.5 .P38 2003

TECHNOLOGICAL INNOVATIONS. *See also* **MEDICAL INNOVATIONS.**
DiVanna, Joseph A. Synconomy. Houndmills [England] ; New York : Palgrave Macmillan, 2003.
HD64.2 .D575 2003

Farson, Richard Evans, 1926- Whoever makes the most mistakes wins. New York ; London : Free Press, c2002.
HD45 .F357 2002

Rantanen, Kalevi. Simplified TRIZ. Boca Raton : St. Lucie Press, c2002.
TA153 .R26 2002

Von Stamm, Bettina. Managing innovation, design and creativity. Chichester, England ; Hoboken, NJ : J. Wiley, c2003.
HD45 .V65 2003

TECHNOLOGICAL INNOVATIONS - ECONOMIC ASPECTS.
Mezias, Stephen J. Organizational dynamics of creative destruction. Houndmills [England] ; New York : Palgrave Macmillan, 2002.
HB615 .M49 2002

TECHNOLOGICAL INNOVATIONS - MANAGEMENT.
Burke, Dan, 1965- Business @ the speed of stupid. Cambridge, MA : Perseus Pub., c2001.
HD45 .B7995 2001

Harvard business essentials. Boston, Mass. : Harvard Business School Press, c2003.
HD45 .H3427 2003

Howkins, John, 1945- The creative economy. London : Allen Lane, 2001.

Kennedy, Kevin (Kevin John), 1955- Going the distance. Upper Saddle River, NJ : Prentice Hall/Financial Times, c2003.
HD57.7 .K465 2003

Management. Cambridge, Mass. : MIT Press, 2003.
HD31 .M2928 2003

Von Stamm, Bettina. Managing innovation, design and creativity. Chichester, England ; Hoboken, NJ : J. Wiley, c2003.
HD45 .V65 2003

TECHNOLOGICAL INNOVATIONS - SOCIAL ASPECTS.
Hirata, Helena Sumiko. [División sexual del trabajo. Portuguese] Nova divisão sexual do trabalho? 1a ed. São Paulo : Boitempo, 2002.
HD6060.6 .H5717 2002

Tenner, Edward. Our own devices. 1st ed. New York : Alfred A. Knopf, 2003.
T14.5 .T4588 2003

TECHNOLOGICAL LITERACY. *See* **MEDIA LITERACY.**

TECHNOLOGY. *See* **ENGINEERING; INFORMATION TECHNOLOGY.**

TECHNOLOGY - AESTHETICS.
Adrift in the technological matrix. Lewisburg, PA : Bucknell University Press ; London : Associated University Presses, c2003.

TECHNOLOGY AND CIVILIZATION.
Adrift in the technological matrix. Lewisburg, PA : Bucknell University Press ; London : Associated University Presses, c2003.

Arthurs, Jane. Crash cultures. Bristol, UK ; Portland, OR : Intellect, 2002.

Habitar la tierra. Buenos Aires : Grupo Editor Altamira, 2002.
CB358 .H32 2002

Technology and society.
Kallinikos, Jannis. Munich : Accedo : Distributed in the U.S.A. by The Institute of Mind and Behavior, c1996.

TECHNOLOGY, EDUCATIONAL. *See* **EDUCATIONAL TECHNOLOGY.**

TECHNOLOGY - ENGLAND - MANCHESTER - HISTORY - 19TH CENTURY.
Cardwell, D. S. L. (Donald Stephen Lowell) The development of science and technology in nineteenth-century Britain. Aldershot, Great Britain ; Burlington, VT : Ashgate/Variorum, c2003.

Q127.G4 C37 2003

TECHNOLOGY - GREAT BRITAIN - HISTORY - 19TH CENTURY.
Cardwell, D. S. L. (Donald Stephen Lowell) The development of science and technology in nineteenth-century Britain. Aldershot, Great Britain ; Burlington, VT : Ashgate/Variorum, c2003.
Q127.G4 C37 2003

Technology in counselling and psychotherapy : a practitioner's guide / edited by Stephen Goss and Kate Anthony. New York : Palgrave Macmillan, 2003. p. cm. Includes bibliographical references and index. ISBN 1403900604 (pbk.) DDC 158/.3/028
1. Counseling - Computer network resources. 2. Counseling - Computer programs. 3. Psychotherapy - Computer network resources. 4. Psychotherapy - Computer programs. I. Goss, Stephen, 1966- II. Anthony, Kate.
BF637.C6 T467 2003

TECHNOLOGY - PHILOSOPHY.
Arthurs, Jane. Crash cultures. Bristol, UK ; Portland, OR : Intellect, 2002.

TECHNOLOGY - SOCIAL ASPECTS.
Adrift in the technological matrix. Lewisburg, PA : Bucknell University Press ; London : Associated University Presses, c2003.

Clark, Andy, 1957- Natural-born cyborgs. Oxford ; New York : Oxford University Press, c2003.
T14.5 .C58 2003

The end of everything. Cambridge : Icon, 2003.

Tenner, Edward. Our own devices. 1st ed. New York : Alfred A. Knopf, 2003.
T14.5 .T4588 2003

TECHNOLOGY - SOCIAL ASPECTS - UNITED STATES - HISTORIOGRAPHY.
Nye, David E., 1946- America as second creation. Cambridge : MIT Press, c2003.
E179.5 .N94 2003

TECHNOLOGY - SOCIAL ASPECTS - UNITED STATES - HISTORY.
Nye, David E., 1946- America as second creation. Cambridge : MIT Press, c2003.
E179.5 .N94 2003

TECHNOLOGY TRANSFER. *See* **NEW PRODUCTS; TECHNOLOGICAL INNOVATIONS.**

Técnicas e instrumentos de investigación.
Valle Bonilla, Otto René. Que no le cuenten cuentos = Guatemala : ESEDIR : Editorial Saqil Tzij, 1999.

TEEN-AGE. *See* **ADOLESCENCE.**

TEEN-AGERS. *See* **TEENAGERS.**

Teen dream power.
Abadie, M. J. (Marie-Jeanne) Rochester, Vt. : Bindu Books, 2003.
BF1099 .T43 2003

Teen feng shui.
Levitt, Susan. Rochester, Vt. : Bindu Books, c2003.
BF1779.F4 L465 2003

Teen goddess.
Wishart, Catherine, 1965- 1st ed. St. Paul, Minn. : Llewellyn Publications, c2003.
BF1623.G63 W57 2003

TEEN SUICIDE. *See* **TEENAGERS - SUICIDAL BEHAVIOR.**

Teen tarot.
Francis-Cheung, Theresa. Avon, MA : Adams Media Corp., 2003.
BF1879.T2 F7 2003

TEENAGE GIRLS.
Wiseman, Rosalind, 1969- Queen bees & wannabes. 1st ed. New York : Crown Publishers, c2002.
HQ798 .W544 2002

TEENAGE GIRLS - MISCELLANEA.
Wishart, Catherine, 1965- Teen goddess. 1st ed. St. Paul, Minn. : Llewellyn Publications, c2003.
BF1623.G63 W57 2003

TEENAGE GIRLS - PSYCHOLOGY.
Dellasega, Cheryl. Girl wars. New York : Simon & Schuster, c2003.
BF637.B85 D45 2003

Stenzel, Lucia Marques. Obesidade. 1a ed. Porto Alegre : EDIPUCRS, 2002.

Wiseman, Rosalind, 1969- Queen bees & wannabes. 1st ed. New York : Crown Publishers, c2002.

HQ798 .W544 2002

TEENAGE GIRLS - RELIGIOUS LIFE.
Wishart, Catherine, 1965- Teen goddess. 1st ed. St. Paul, Minn. : Llewellyn Publications, c2003.
BF1623.G63 W57 2003

TEENAGE SUICIDE. See **TEENAGERS - SUICIDAL BEHAVIOR.**

TEENAGED GIRLS. See **TEENAGE GIRLS.**

TEENAGERS. See also **TEENAGE GIRLS.**
Levitt, Susan. Teen feng shui. Rochester, Vt. : Bindu Books, c2003.
BF1779.F4 L465 2003

TEENAGERS AND DEATH.
Liotta, Alfred J. When students grieve. Horsham, PA : LRP Publications, 2003.
BF724.3.D43 L56 2003

TEENAGERS - CONDUCT OF LIFE.
Dobson, James C., 1936- Life on the edge. Nashville : Word Pub., c2000.
BF637.L53 D63 2000

TEENAGERS - COUNSELING OF.
Buckley, Maureen A., 1964- Mentoring children and adolescents. Westport, Conn. : Praeger, 2003.
BF637.C6 B8 2003

Liotta, Alfred J. When students grieve. Horsham, PA : LRP Publications, 2003.
BF724.3.D43 L56 2003

Perschy, Mary Kelly, 1942- Helping teens work through grief. 2nd ed. New York : Brunner-Routledge, 2004.
BF724.3.G73 P47 2004

TEENAGERS - DEATH - PSYCHOLOGICAL ASPECTS.
Wilkins, David, 1944- United by tragedy. Nampa, Idaho : Pacific Press Pub. Association, c2003.
BF575.G7 W555 2003

TEENAGERS - DEVELOPMENT. See **ADOLESCENCE.**

TEENAGERS' DREAMS.
Abadie, M. J. (Marie-Jeanne) Teen dream power. Rochester, Vt. : Bindu Books, 2003.
BF1099 .T43 2003

TEENAGERS' DREAMS - PROBLEMS, EXERCISES, ETC.
Abadie, M. J. (Marie-Jeanne) Teen dream power. Rochester, Vt. : Bindu Books, 2003.
BF1099 .T43 2003

TEENAGERS - FAMILY RELATIONSHIPS.
Eiguer, Alberto. La famille de l'adolescent. Paris : In press, c2001.

TEENAGERS - HEALTH AND HYGIENE. See **STRESS MANAGEMENT FOR TEENAGERS.**

TEENAGERS IN LITERATURE.
Tremblay-Dupré, Thérèse. La mère absente. Monaco : Rocher, 2003.

TEENAGERS - JUVENILE LITERATURE.
Mawi Asgedom. The code. New York : Little, Brown, 2003.
BF724.3.S9 M34 2003

TEENAGERS - MISCELLANEA.
Baker, Marina. Spells for teenage witches. Berkeley, Calif. : Seastone, c2000.
BF1571.5.T44 B34 2000

Dugan, Ellen, 1963- Elements of witchcraft. 1st ed. St. Paul, Minn. : Llewellyn Publications, 2003.
BF1571.5.T44 D86 2003

Edut, Tali. Astrostyle. New York : Simon & Schuster, c2003.
BF1729.T44 E38 2003

MacGregor, Rob. Star power. Franklin Lakes, NJ : New Page Books, c2003.
BF1571.5.T44 M23 2003

TEENAGERS - MISCELLANEA - JUVENILE LITERATURE.
Moorey, Teresa. Spellbound. Berkeley, CA : Ulysses Press : Distributed in the U.S.A. by Publishers Group West, 2002.
BF1571.5.T44 M66 2002

TEENAGERS - PHYSIOLOGY. See **STRESS IN ADOLESCENCE.**

TEENAGERS - PSYCHOLOGICAL TESTING.
Gumbiner, Jann. Adolescent assessment. Hoboken, N.J. : J. Wiley & Sons, c2003.

BF724.25 .G86 2003

TEENAGERS - PSYCHOLOGY. See **ADOLESCENT PSYCHOLOGY.**

TEENAGERS - RELIGIOUS LIFE.
Dobson, James C., 1936- Life on the edge. Nashville : Word Pub., c2000.
BF637.L53 D63 2000

TEENAGERS - RELIGIOUS LIFE - MISCELLANEA.
Van Praagh, James. Looking beyond. New York : Simon & Schuster, c2003.
BF1272 .V36 2003

TEENAGERS - SEXUAL BEHAVIOR - CONGRESSES.
Sexual development in childhood. Bloomington : Indiana University Press, 2003.
BF723.S4 S47 2003

TEENAGERS - SUICIDAL BEHAVIOR - AUSTRALIA - NEW SOUTH WALES.
Suicide & risk-taking deaths of children & young people. Surry Hills, NSW : The Commission, c2003.

TEENS. See **TEENAGERS.**

A teen's guide to coping : when a loved one is sick and preparing to die / Fairview Hospice, Fairview Health Services. Minneapolis : Fairview Press, 2003. p. cm. Includes bibliographical references. Table of contents URL: http://www.loc.gov/catdir/toc/ecip048/2003019924.html ISBN 1-57749-140-8 (pbk. : alk. paper) DDC 155.9/37/0835 1. Death - Psychological aspects. 2. Grief. 3. Bereavement - Psychological aspects. I. Fairview Hospice. II. Fairview Health Services.
BF789.D4 T44 2003

Teerikorpi, Pekka, 1948-.
Baryshev, Yurij. Discovery of cosmic fractals. River Edge, N.J. : World Scientific, c2002.
QB981 .B285 2002

Teichman, Jenny. Philosophers' hobbies and other essays / by Jenny Teichman ; illustrated by Michael Jorgensen. Carlton, Vic. : Black Jack Press, 2003. 122 p. : ill. ; 21 cm. Includes bibliographical references. ISBN 0-9580785-0-5 (pbk.)
1. Ethics. 2. Philosophy. I. Title.

TEILHARD DE CHARDIN, PIERRE - CONTRIBUTIONS IN SPIRITUALITY.
King, Ursula. Mysticism and contemporary society. [Lewisburg, Pa.] : American Teilhard Association, c2002.
B2430.T374 A18 no.44

Teilhard studies
(no. 44) King, Ursula. Mysticism and contemporary society. [Lewisburg, Pa.] : American Teilhard Association, c2002.
B2430.T374 A18 no.44

TELECOMMUNICATION. See **COMPUTER NETWORKS; TELEVISION.**

TELECOMMUNICATION AND STATE. See **TELECOMMUNICATION POLICY.**

TELECOMMUNICATION - ECONOMIC ASPECTS - UNITED STATES.
United States. Congress. House. Committee on Energy and Commerce. Subcommittee on Telecommunications and the Internet. Health of the telecommunication sector. Washington : U.S. G.P.O. : For sale by the Supt. of Docs., U.S. G.P.O. [Congressional Sales Office], 2003.

United States. Congress. House. Committee on Energy and Commerce. Subcommittee on Telecommunications and the Internet. Health of the telecommunication sector. Washington : U.S. G.P.O. : For sale by the Supt. of Docs., U.S. G.P.O., [Congressional Sales Office], 2003.

TELECOMMUNICATION - GERMANY.
Die Politik der Massenmedien. Köln : Halem, 2001.

TELECOMMUNICATION - GOVERNMENT POLICY. See **TELECOMMUNICATION POLICY.**

TELECOMMUNICATION - HISTORY.
Deciphering cyberspace. Thousand Oaks, Calif. : Sage Publications, c2003.
TK5102.2 .D43 2003

TELECOMMUNICATION IN EDUCATION. See **DISTANCE EDUCATION.**

TELECOMMUNICATION INDUSTRY. See **TELECOMMUNICATION.**

TELECOMMUNICATION POLICY - UNITED STATES.
United States. Congress. House. Committee on Energy and Commerce. Subcommittee on Telecommunications and the Internet. Health of the telecommunication sector. Washington : U.S. G.P.O. : For sale by the Supt. of Docs., U.S. G.P.O. [Congressional Sales Office], 2003.

United States. Congress. House. Committee on Energy and Commerce. Subcommittee on Telecommunications and the Internet. Health of the telecommunication sector. Washington : U.S. G.P.O. : For sale by the Supt. of Docs., U.S. G.P.O., [Congressional Sales Office], 2003.

United States. General Accounting Office. Telecommunications [electronic resource]. Washington, D.C. : U.S. General Accounting Office, [2002]

TELECOMMUNICATIONS. See **TELECOMMUNICATION.**

Telecommunications [electronic resource].
United States. General Accounting Office. [Washington, D.C.] : U.S. General Accounting Office, [2003]

United States. General Accounting Office. Washington, D.C. : U.S. General Accounting Office, [2002]

Telecommunications : Federal Communications Commission should include call quality in its annual report on competition in mobile phone services.
United States. General Accounting Office. Telecommunications [electronic resource]. [Washington, D.C.] : U.S. General Accounting Office, [2003]

TELECOMMUTING. See **TELECOMMUNICATION.**

TELEJOURNALISTS. See **TELEVISION JOURNALISTS.**

TELEMATICS. See **INFORMATION TECHNOLOGY.**

TELEOLOGY. See also **CREATION.**
Redfield, James. God and the evolving universe. New York : Jeremy P. Tarcher/Putnam, c2002.
BD541 .R43 2002

TELEPATHY.
Brunke, Dawn Baumann. Animal voices. Rochester, Vt. : Bear & Co., c2002.
QL776 .B78 2002

Mandelberg, Robert. Mystifying mind reading tricks. New York : Sterling Pub., 2002.
GV1553 .M35 2002

Nichols, Shaun. Mindreading. Oxford : Clarendon Press ; New York : Oxford University Press, 2003.

Rauscher, William V. The mind readers. Woodbury, N.J. : Mystic Light Press, c2002.
BF1171 .R28 2002

Wilkins, George H. (George Hubert), Sir, 1888-1958. Thoughts through space. Charlottesville, VA : Hampton Roads Pub. Co., 2004.
BF1171 .W49 2004

TELEPATHY - HISTORY.
Luckhurst, Roger. The invention of telepathy, 1870-1901. Oxford ; New York : Oxford University Press, 2002.
BF1171 .L77 2002

TELEPATHY - LATVIA.
Rīgas gaišregis Eižens Finks. Jauns papildināts izdevums. [Rīga] : Jumava, c2002.
BF1283.F55 R66 2002

TELEPHONE. See **LOCAL TELEPHONE SERVICE.**

TELEPROCESSING NETWORKS. See **COMPUTER NETWORKS.**

Telesco, Patricia, 1960- Animal spirit : spells, sorcery, and symbols from the wild / Patricia Telesco and Rowan Hall. Franklin Lakes, NJ : New Page Books, c2002. 221 p. ; 21 cm. Includes bibliographical references (p. 213-214) and index. ISBN 1-56414-594-8 (pbk.) DDC 133.4/3 1. Animals - Miscellanea. 2. Magic. I. Hall, Rowan. II. Title.
BF1623.A55 T445 2002

Drew, A. J. God/goddess. Franklin Lakes, N.J. : New Page Books, 2003.

Telesco, Patricia, 1960

BF1571 .D73 2003

An enchanted life : an adept's guide to masterful magick / by Patricia Telesco. Franklin Lakes, N.J. : New Page Books, c2002. 224 p. : ill. ; 21 cm. Includes bibliographical references (p. 215-216) and index. ISBN 1-56414-566-2 DDC 133.4/3
1. Magic. 2. Spiritual life. I. Title.
BF1621 .T42 2002

Exploring candle magick : candle spells, charms, rituals, and divinations / Patricia Telesco. Franklin Lakes, NJ : New Page Books, c2001. 190 p. : ill. ; 21 cm. Includes bibliographical references (p. 179-181) and index. ISBN 1-56414-522-0 DDC 133.4/3
1. Candles and lights - Miscellanea. 2. Magic. I. Title.
BF1623.C26 T45 2001

Knight, Sirona, 1955- The cyber spellbook. Franklin Lakes, NJ : New Page Books, c2002.
BF1571 .T425 2002

A little book of mirror magick : meditations, myths, spells / Patricia Telesco. Berkeley, Calif. : Crossing Press, c2003. p. cm. Includes bibliographical references and index. Table of contents URL: http://www.loc.gov/catdir/toc/ecip045/2003014120.html ISBN 1-58091-144-7 (pbk.) DDC 133.4/3
1. Magic mirrors. I. Title.
BF1891.M28 T45 2003

A witch's beverages and brews : magick potions made easy / by Patricia Telesco. Franklin Lakes, NJ : New Page Books, c2001. 221 p. ; 21 cm. Includes bibliographical references (p. 211-216) and index. ISBN 1-56414-486-0 (pbk.) DDC 133.4/4
1. Witchcraft. 2. Beverages - Miscellanea. 3. Brewing - Miscellanea. I. Title.
BF1572.R4 T447 2001

TELEVISION. *See* **DANCE IN MOTION PICTURES, TELEVISION, ETC.**

TELEVISION ACTORS AND ACTRESSES - GREAT BRITAIN - BIOGRAPHY.
Driver, Betty, 1920- Betty. Large print ed. Long Preston : Magna, 2000.

TELEVISION ADVERTISING.
Bühler, Gerhard, 1959- Postmoderne auf dem Bildschirm, auf der Leinwand. Sankt Augustin : Gardez!, c2002.

TELEVISION ANCHORS. *See* **TELEVISION NEWS ANCHORS.**

TELEVISION AND WOMEN.
Warhol, Robyn R. Having a good cry. Columbus : Ohio State University Press, c2003.
PN56.5.W64 W375 2003

TELEVISION AND WOMEN - COLOMBIA.
Méndez, José Luis, 1941- El irresistible encanto de Betty la fea. San Juan, P.R. : Ediciones Milenio, 2001.

TELEVISION BROADCASTERS OF NEWS. *See* **TELEVISION JOURNALISTS.**

TELEVISION BROADCASTING. *See* **CABLE TELEVISION; DIRECT BROADCAST SATELLITE TELEVISION.**

TELEVISION BROADCASTING - EMPLOYEES. *See* **TELEVISION JOURNALISTS.**

TELEVISION, CABLE. *See* **CABLE TELEVISION.**

TELEVISION COMMENTATORS. *See* **TELEVISION JOURNALISTS.**

TELEVISION IN ART - HISTORY.
Wentscher, Herbert, 1951- Vor dem Schirm. 1. Aufl. [Freiburg im Breisgau] : Modo, 2002.

TELEVISION IN POLITICS.
Martín Salgado, Lourdes. Marketing político. Barcelona : Paidós, c2002.

TELEVISION JOURNALISTS. *See* **TELEVISION NEWS ANCHORS.**

TELEVISION JOURNALISTS - UNITED STATES - BIOGRAPHY.
Brokaw, Tom. A long way from home. 1st trade ed. New York : Random House, c2002.
PN4874.B717 A3 2002b

TELEVISION MUSIC. *See* **MUSIC VIDEOS.**

TELEVISION NEWS ANCHORS - UNITED STATES - BIOGRAPHY.
Brokaw, Tom. A long way from home. 1st trade ed. New York : Random House, c2002.
PN4874.B717 A3 2002b

TELEVISION PERSONALITIES. *See* **TELEVISION NEWS ANCHORS.**

TELEVISION PLAYS. *See* **SOAP OPERAS.**

TELEVISION PROGRAMS. *See* **MUSIC VIDEOS.**

TELEVISION RELAY SYSTEMS. *See* **CABLE TELEVISION.**

TELEVISION REPORTERS. *See* **TELEVISION JOURNALISTS.**

TELEVISION SERIALS. *See* **SOAP OPERAS.**

TELEVISION - SOCIAL ASPECTS.
Lie, Rico. Spaces of intercultural communication. Creskill, N.J. : Hampton Press, c2003.
GN345.6 .L54 2003

Tell me this isn't happening / collected by Robynn Clairday. New York : Scholastic, c1999. 107 p. ; 18 cm. ISBN 0-439-09502-6
1. Embarrassment in children - Juvenile literature. I. Clairday, Robynn.
BF723.E44 T45 1999

Telle fille, quel père?.
Liaudet, Jean-Claude. Paris : Archipel, c2002.

Téllez, Edgar. Diario íntimo de un fracaso : historia no contada del proceso de paz con las FARC / Edgar Téllez, Oscar Montes, Jorge Lesmes. 1. ed. Bogotá, D.C., Colombia : Planeta, 2002. 381 p. ; 22 cm. ISBN 958-42-0349-5
1. Fuerzas Armadas Revolucionarias de Colombia. 2. Colombia - Politics and government - 1974- 3. Guerrillas - Colombia. 4. Insurgency - Colombia. 5. Political violence - Colombia. 6. Negotiation - Colombia. 7. Peace. I. Montes, Oscar (Montes Padilla) II. Lesmes, Jorge. III. Title.

Telúch, Peter. Amulety a talizmany : ochranné predmety človeka v kultúre Slovanov a iných národov Bratislava : Print-Servis, 1998. 225 p : ill. (some col.) ; 21 cm. Includes bibliographical references (p. 225). ISBN 80-88755-64-6
1. Amulets - Slavic countries. 2. Talismans - Slavic countries. 3. Magic. I. Title.

Temi e testi
(44) Reinhold, Karl Leonhard, 1757-1823. [Ueber den Begriff der Philosophie. Italian] Concetto e fondamento della filosofia. Roma : Edizioni di storia e letteratura, 2002.

TEMPER. *See* **ANGER.**

TEMPER TANTRUMS IN CHILDREN.
Kennedy, Michelle. Tantrums. Hauppauge, N.Y. : Barron's, c2003.
BF723.A4 .K46 2003

TEMPERAMENT. *See also* **CHARACTER TESTS; PERSONALITY; TYPOLOGY (PSYCHOLOGY).**
Castillo, Heather. Personality disorder. London ; Philadelphia : J. Kingsley Pub., 2003.
RC554 .C37 2003

Giannini, John L., 1921- Compass of the soul. Gainesville, Fla. : Center for Applications of Psychological Type, 2003.
BF698.3 .G53 2003

TEMPERAMENT - TESTING. *See* **TAYLOR-JOHNSON TEMPERAMENT ANALYSIS.**

Tempest, Raven. Bewitching love potions & charms / Raven Tempest. London : Cassell Illustrated ; New York, NY : Distributed in the USA by Sterling Pub. Co., c2003. 139 p. : ill. (some col.) ; 18 cm. Includes index. ISBN 1-84403-072-5 DDC 133.4/42
1. Love - Miscellanea. 2. Magic - Miscellanea. 3. Witchcraft - Miscellanea. I. Title. II. Title: Love potions and charms
BF575.L8 .T45 2003

TEMPLE OF HATHOR (DANDARA, EGYPT).
Cauville, Sylvie. Le zodiaque d'Osiris. Leuven : Peeters, 1997.
BL2450.O7 C399 1997

Temple of Jagannātha.
Pathy, Dinanath. Art, regional traditions, the Temple of Jagannātha. New Delhi : Sundeep Prakashan, 2001.
NA6002 .P37 2001

TEMPLES, HINDU.
Kollar, L. Peter (Laszlo Peter), 1926- Symbolism in Hindu architecture as revealed in the Shri Minakshi Sundareswar. New Delhi : Aryan Books International, 2001.
NA6002 .K65 2001

TEMPLES, HINDU - INDIA - ORISSA.
Pathy, Dinanath. Art, regional traditions, the Temple of Jagannātha. New Delhi : Sundeep Prakashan, 2001.
NA6002 .P37 2001

Tempo e universo.
Castagnino, M. (Mario) Roma : Armando, c2000.
BD632 .C37 2000

Temporality in music.
Gavalchin, John. 2000.

The temporalization of time.
Sandbothe, Mike, 1961- [Verzeitlichung der Zeit. English] Lanham, MD : Rowman & Littlefield, c2001.
BD638 .S27 2001

Le temps d'une question
Ogien, Ruwen. La honte est-elle immorale? Paris : Bayard, c2002.

Temps et espaces.
Palais et pouvoir. Vincennes : Presses universitaires de Vincennes, c2003.

TEN COMMANDMENTS - PARENTS.
Yosef, Yitshak. [Yalkut Yosef (Kibud av va-em)] Sefer Yalkut Yosef. Yerushalayim : Mekhon "Hazon 'Ovadyah", 761 [2001]
BM523.5.R4 Y72 2001

Ten minute magic spells.
Alexander, Skye. 10-minute magic spells. Gloucester, Mass. : Fair Winds Press, 2003.
BF1611 .A43 2003

Ten-minute tarot.
Alexander, Skye. 10-minute tarot. Gloucester, Mass. : Fair Winds Press, c2003.
BF1879.T2 A445 2003

Ten sure signs a movie character is doomed, and other surprising movie lists.
Roeper, Richard, 1959- 10 sure signs a movie character is doomed, and other surprising movie lists. 1st ed. New York : Hyperion, c2003.
PN1998 .R568 2003

Ten thousand ways to say I love you.
Godek, Gregory J. P., 1955- 10,000 ways to say I love you. Naperville, Ill. : Casablanca Press, c1999.
BF575.L8 G63 1999

Tener, Lisa.
Middelton-Moz, Jane, 1947- Good and mad. Deerfield Beach, Fla. : Health Communications Inc., c2003.
BF575.A5 M519 2003

Tenner, Edward. Our own devices : the past and future of body technology / Edward Tenner. 1st ed. New York : Alfred A. Knopf, 2003. xviii, 314 p. : ill. ; 24 cm. Includes bibliographical references (p. [302]-304) and index. Table of contents URL: http://www.loc.gov/catdir/toc/fy041/2002040694.html ISBN 0-375-40722-7 DDC 303.48/3
1. Technology - Social aspects. 2. Technological innovations - Social aspects. 3. Human beings - Effect of technological innovations on. 4. Body, Human - Social aspects. 5. Body, Human (Philosophy) I. Title.
T14.5 .T4588 2003

TENOCHA INDIANS. *See* **AZTECS.**

TENSION (PHYSIOLOGY). *See* **STRESS (PHYSIOLOGY).**

TENSION (PSYCHOLOGY). *See* **STRESS (PSYCHOLOGY).**

TENTH CENTURY. *See* **ONE THOUSAND, A.D.**

TENURE OF LAND. *See* **LAND TENURE.**

Teodorani, Massimo.
Pinotti, Roberto, 1944- Oltre. Firenze : Olimpia, c2002.

Teoreticheskie osnovy psikhologii sub"ektogeneza.
Ognev, A. S. (Aleksandr Sergeevich) Voronezh : Izd-vo VF RAGS, 1997.
BF698 .O36 1997

Teoría y práctica del arte.
Malvido Arriaga, Adriana. Por la vereda digital. 1. ed. México : CONACULTA (Consejo Nacional para la Cultura y las Artes), 1999.
QA76.9.C66 M35 1999

Teoriia i praktika stanovleniia i razvitiia obraza IA doshkol'nika.
Korepanova, M. V. (Marina Vasil'evna) Volgograd : Peremena, 2001.
BF723.S28 K66 2001

Teoriia stadial'nogo razvitiia iskusstva i stat'i.
Klimov, R. B. Moskva : O.G.I., 2002.
N5300 .K55 2002

Teoriia tsivilizatsii.
Ionov, I. N. (Igor' Nikolaevich) Sankt-Peterburg : Aleteiia, 2002.
CB19 .I656 2002

Terceira idade.
Veras, Renato P. (Renato Peixoto) Rio de Janeiro : UNATI : Relume Dumará, 2002.

TERM PAPER WRITING. *See* **REPORT WRITING.**

TERMINAL CARE. *See also* **DEATH.**
Overall, Christine, 1949- Aging, death, and human longevity. Berkeley : University of California Press, c2003.
RA564.8 .O95 2003

TERMINAL CARE - UNITED STATES.
Burt, Robert, 1939- Death is that man taking names. Berkeley : University of California Press ; New York : Milbank Memorial Fund, c2002.
R726.8 .B875 2002

TERMINALLY ILL. *See* **DEATH; TERMINALLY ILL CHILDREN.**

TERMINALLY ILL - CARE AND TREATMENT. *See* **TERMINAL CARE.**

TERMINALLY ILL CHILDREN. *See* **CHILDREN - DEATH.**

TERMINALLY ILL CHILDREN - FAMILY RELATIONSHIPS - CASE STUDIES.
Polcz, Alaine. Gyermek a halál kapujában. Budapest : PONT, c2001.
BF723.D3 P65 2001

TERMINALLY ILL CHILDREN - PSYCHOLOGY - CASE STUDIES.
Polcz, Alaine. Gyermek a halál kapujában. Budapest : PONT, c2001.
BF723.D3 P65 2001

TERMINALLY ILL - MEDICAL CARE. *See* **TERMINAL CARE.**

TERMINALLY ILL PARENTS. *See* **PARENTS - DEATH.**

TERMINALLY ILL - PSYCHOLOGY.
Hedtke, Lorraine, 1957- Re-membering lives. Amityville, N.Y. : Baywood Pub. Co., 2004.
BF789.D4 H4 2004

TERMINOLOGY. *See* **TERMS AND PHRASES.**

TERMS AND PHRASES - EUROPE.
Lurati, Ottavio. Per modo di dire--. Bologna : CLUEB, c2002.

Terndrup, Anthony I.
Ritter, Kathleen. Handbook of affirmative psychotherapy with lesbians and gay men. New York : Guilford Press, c2002.
RC451.4.G39 R55 2002

Ternes, Bernd.
Was kostet den Kopf? Marburg : Tectum Verlag, 2001.

TERPENES. *See* **ESSENCES AND ESSENTIAL OILS.**

Terre (Rome, Italy). Scritture
(42.) Celli, Pier Luigi. Breviario di cinismo ben temperato. 1. ed. Roma : Fazi, 2002.

Terrel, Jean.
Foucault au Collège de France. Pessac : Presses universitaires de Bordeaux, c2003.
B2430.F724 F6855 2003

Terricabras, Josep-Maria, 1946-.
Ferrater Mora, José, 1912- [Selections. English. 2003] Three Spanish philosophers. Albany : State University of New York Press, c2003.
B4568.U54 F3913 2003

Terrin, Aldo N. (Aldo Natale) Mistiche dell'Occidente : new age, orientalismo, mondo pentecostale / Aldo Natale Terrin. 1. ed. Brescia : Morcelliana, 2001. 284 p. ; 23 cm. (Le scienze umane) Includes bibliographical references and index. ISBN 88-372-1840-0 DDC 299
1. New Age movement. 2. Pentecostalism. 3. Hinduism. I. Title. II. Title: New age, orientalismo, mondo pentecostale III. Series: Scienze umane (Brescia, Italy)
BP605.N48 T477 2001

Le territoire pensé : géographie des représentations territoriales / sous la direction de Frédéric Lasserre et Aline Lechaume ; préface de Luc Bureau, Sainte-Foy : Presses de l'Université du Québec, 2003. xvii, 328 p. : ill., maps ; 23 cm. (Géographie contemporaine) Includes bibliographical references and index. ISBN 276051224X DDC 304.2/3
1. Human territoriality. 2. Human geography. 3. Group identity. 4. Geopolitics. 5. Human territoriality - Québec (Province) I. Lasserre, Frédéric, 1967- II. Lechaume, Aline. III. Series.

TERRITORIAL BEHAVIOR. *See* **HUMAN TERRITORIALITY.**

The territorial management of ethnic conflict / editor, John Coakley. 2nd rev. and expanded ed. London ; Portland, OR : F. Cass, 2003. xiii, 330 p. : maps ; 24 cm. (The Cass series in regional and federal studies, 1363-5670) Includes bibliographical references and index. CONTENTS: Introduction : the challenge / John Coakley -- Canada : the case for ethnolinguistic federalism in a multilingual society / Jean Laponce -- Northern Ireland : religion, ethnic conflict and territoriality / Joseph Ruane and Jennifer Todd -- Belgium : from regionalism to federalism / Liesbet Hooghe -- South Africa : the failure of ethnoterritorial politics / Anthony Egan and Rupert Taylor -- Israel : ethnic conflict and political exchange / Alex Weingrod -- Pakistan : ethnic diversity and colonial legacy / Charles H. Kennedy -- Sri Lanka : ethnic strife and the politics of space / A. Jeyeratnam Wilson -- The dissolution of the Soviet Union : federation, commonwealth, secession / Ronald J. Hill -- The dissolution of Czechoslovakia : a case of failed state building? / Stanislav J. Kirschbaum -- The dissolution of Yugoslavia : secession by the centre? / Daniele Conversi -- Conclusion : towards a solution? / John Coakley. ISBN 0-7146-4988-0 (cloth) ISBN 0-7146-8051-6 (paper) DDC 305.8
1. Ethnic conflict. 2. Conflict management. 3. Human territoriality. 4. Jurisdiction, Territorial. I. Coakley, John. II. Series.
GN496 .T47 2003

TERRITORIALITY, HUMAN. *See* **HUMAN TERRITORIALITY.**

TERROR. *See also* **TERRORISM.**
Pyszczynski, Thomas A. In the wake of 9/11. Washington, DC : American Psychological Association, c2003.
HV6432 .P97 2003

Terror bombing.
Granot, Hayim. Tel Aviv : Dekel Pub. House, 2002.
HV6431 .G73 2002

Terror, counter-terror : women speak out / edited by Ammu Joseph & Kalpana Sharma. London ; New York : Zed Books ; New Delhi : Kali for Women ; New York : Distributed in the U.S. exclusively by Palgrave, 2003. xxiii, 283 p. ; 22 cm. Includes bibliographical references. ISBN 1-84277-352-6 (cased) ISBN 1-84277-353-4 (limp) DDC 303.6/082
1. Women and war. 2. Women and peace. 3. Terrorism. 4. Violence. I. Joseph, Ammu, 1953- II. Sharma, Kalpana, 1947-
HQ1236 .T47 2003

TERRORISM. *See also* **POLITICAL VIOLENCE.**
Baudrillard, Jean. [Esprit du terrorisme. English] The spirit of terrorism and requiem for the Twin Towers. London : Verso, 2002.
HV6431 .B38 2002

Braudy, Leo. From chivalry to terrorism. New York : Alfred A. Knopf : Distributed by Random House, 2003.
HQ1090 .B7 2003

Cornblit, Oscar. Violencia social, genocidio y terrorismo. 1. ed. México, D.F. : Fondo de Cultura Económica, 2002.
HM886 .C67 2002

Granot, Hayim. Terror bombing. Tel Aviv : Dekel Pub. House, 2002.
HV6431 .G73 2002

Medvedko, Leonid Ivanovich. Rossiia, Zapad, Islam. Zhukovskiĭ ; Moskva : Kuchkovo pole, 2003.
BP173.5 .M44 2003

Terror, counter-terror. London ; New York : Zed Books ; New Delhi : Kali for Women ; New York : Distributed in the U.S. exclusively by Palgrave, 2003.
HQ1236 .T47 2003

Vidal, Jordi. Résistance au chaos. Paris : Allia, 2002.

Terrorism and disaster : individual and community mental health interventions / edited by Robert J. Ursano, Carol S. Fullerton, Anne E. Norwood. Cambridge, UK ; New York : Cambridge University Press, 2003. xii, 349 p. : ill. ; 25 cm. + 1 CD-ROM (4 3/4 in.). Includes bibliographical references and index. System requirements for accompanying disk: Windows 98 or higher ; computer capable of playing MPEG-1 and MP3 files. CONTENTS: Introduction : trauma, terrorism and disaster / Carol S. Fullerton, Robert J. Ursano, Ann E. Norwood and Harry H. Holloway -- Terrorism: National and International: September 11, 2001, and its aftermath in New York City / John M. Oldham -- Leadership in the wake of disaster / Prudence Bushnell -- The children of Oklahoma City / Betty Pfefferbaum -- Individual and organizational interventions after terrorism: September 11th and the USS Cole / Thomas A. Grieger, Ralph E. Bally, John L. Lyszczarz, John S. Kennedy, Benjamin T. Griffeth and James J. Reeves -- Interventions in Disaster and Terrorism: Applications from previous disaster research to guide mental health interventions after September 11th / Carol S. North and Elizabeth T. Westerhaus -- A consultation-liaison psychiatry approach to disaster/terrorism victim assessment and management / James R. Rundell -- The role of screening in the prevention of psychological disorders arising after major traumas: pros and cons / Simon Wessely -- Early interventions and the debriefing debate / Beverley Raphael -- Clinical interventions for survivors of prolonged adversities / Arieh Y. Shalev et al -- Collaborative care for injured victims of individual and mass trauma: a health services research approach to developing early interventions / Douglas Zatzick -- The Intersection of Disasters and Terrorism: Effects of Contamination on Individuals: Responses of individuals and groups to consequences of technological disasters and radiation exposure / Lars Weisth and Arnfinn Tønnessen -- Psychological effects of contamination: radioactivity, industrial toxins and bioterrorism / Jacob D. Lindy, Mary C. Grace and Bonnie L. Green -- Relocation stress following catastrophic events / Ellen T. Gerrity and Peter Steinglass -- Population-based health care: a model for restoring community health and productivity following terrorist attack / Charles C. Engel, Ambereen Jaffer, Joyce Adkins, Vivian Sheliga, David Cowan and Wayne J. Katon -- Traumatic death in terrorism and disasters: the effects of posttraumatic stress and behavior / Robert J. Ursano, James E. McCarroll and Carol S. Fullerton -- Conclusion: terrorism and disasters: prevention, intervention and recovery / Robert J. Ursano, Carol S. Fullerton and Ann E. Norwood. ISBN 0-521-82606-3 (hbk.) ISBN 0-521-53345-7 (pbk.) DDC 155.9/35
1. Disasters - Psychological aspects. 2. Terrorism - Psychological aspects. 3. Victims of terrorism - Psychological aspects. 4. Post-traumatic stress disorder - Patients - Rehabilitation. 5. Psychic trauma - Treatment. 6. Emergency management. I. Ursano, Robert J., 1947- II. Fullerton, Carol S. III. Norwood, Ann E., 1953-
RC552.P67 T476 2003

TERRORISM IN ART.
The day our world changed. New York : Harry N. Abrams Inc., 2002.

TERRORISM - PHILOSOPHY.
Civilisation et barbarie. 1re éd. Paris : Presses universitaires de France, c2002.

TERRORISM - PREVENTION.
Potorti, David. September 11th Families for Peaceful Tomorrows. New York, NY : RDV Books, c2003.

The psychology of terrorism. Westport, CT : Praeger, 2002.
HV6431 .P798 2002

Understanding terrorism. 1st ed. Washington, DC : American Psychological Association, 2004.
HV6431 .U35 2004

TERRORISM - PSYCHOLOGICAL ASPECTS.
Baudrillard, Jean. [Esprit du terrorisme. English] The spirit of terrorism and requiem for the Twin Towers. London : Verso, 2002.
HV6431 .B38 2002

Children's fears of war and terrorism. Olney, MD : Association for Childhood Education International, c2003.
BF723.W3 C48 2003

Granot, Hayim. Terror bombing. Tel Aviv : Dekel Pub. House, 2002.
HV6431 .G73 2002

L'incubo globale. Bergamo : Moretti & Vitali, c2002.

The psychology of terrorism. Westport, CT : Praeger, 2002.
HV6431 .P798 2002

Pyszczynski, Thomas A. In the wake of 9/11. Washington, DC : American Psychological Association, c2003.
HV6432 .P97 2003

Rojas Marcos, Luis, 1943- Más allá del 11 de septiembre. [Madrid] : Espasa, c2002.
HV6432.7 .R64 2002

Terrorism and disaster. Cambridge, UK ; New York : Cambridge University Press, 2003.
RC552.P67 T476 2003

Understanding terrorism. 1st ed. Washington, DC : American Psychological Association, 2004.
HV6431 .U35 2004

Terrorism : psychosocial roots, consequences, and interventions.
Understanding terrorism. 1st ed. Washington, DC : American Psychological Association, 2004.
HV6431 .U35 2004

TERRORISM - RELIGIOUS ASPECTS.
Lincoln, Bruce. Holy terrors. Chicago : University of Chicago Press, 2003.
BL65.T47 L56 2003

TERRORISM - UNITED STATES.
Ruthven, Malise, 1942- A fury for God. London ; New York : Granta, 2002.
HV6432 .R87 2002

TERRORISM - UNITED STATES - PSYCHOLOGICAL ASPECTS.
Pyszczynski, Thomas A. In the wake of 9/11. Washington, DC : American Psychological Association, c2003.
HV6432 .P97 2003

TERRORISM VICTIMS. See **VICTIMS OF TERRORISM.**

TERRORIST ACTS. See **TERRORISM.**

TERRORISTS - PSYCHOLOGY.
The psychology of terrorism. Westport, CT : Praeger, 2002.
HV6431 .P798 2002

Understanding terrorism. 1st ed. Washington, DC : American Psychological Association, 2004.
HV6431 .U35 2004

Terry, Jack, 1952-.
Appel, Dee. Friend to friend. Sisters, Or. : Multnomah Publishers, c2002.
BF575.F66 A66 2002

Terry, Larry D. Leadership of public bureaucracies : the administrator as conservator / Larry D. Terry. 2nd ed. Armonk, N.Y. : M.E. Sharpe, c2003. xxiv, 196 p. ; 24 cm. Includes bibliographical references and index. ISBN 0-7656-0958-4 (alk. paper) DDC 352.3/9
1. Leadership. 2. Bureaucracy. 3. Public administration. I. Title.
JF1525.L4 .T47 2003

The Terry lectures
Singer, Peter, 1946- One world. New Haven, Conn. : London : Yale University Press, 2002.

Tersis, Nicole.
Lexique et motivation. Paris ; Sterling, Va. : Peeters, c2002.
P326 .L45 2002

Ṭeruf, seṭiyah yi-yetsirah.
Shoham, S. Giora, 1929- [Israel] : Miśrad ha-biṭahon, [2002]

Tesi (Firenze University Press)
(1.) Fabiani, Paolo, 1968- La filosofia dell'immaginazione in Vico e Malebranche. Firenze : Firenze University Press, 2002.
B3583.F25 F55 2002

TESLA, NIKOLA, 1856-1943.
Jonnes, Jill, 1952- Empires of light. 1st ed. New York : Random House, c2003.
TK18 .J66 2003

Test of auditory-perceptual skills-revised.
TAPS-R. [Rev. ed.]. Hydesville, CA : Psychological and Educational Publications, c1996.
BF251.5.T44 T36 1996

TEST OF AUDITORY-PERCEPTUAL SKILLS-REVISED.
TAPS-R. [Rev. ed.]. Hydesville, CA : Psychological and Educational Publications, c1996.
BF251.5.T44 T36 1996

Le testament de Maître Persin.
Diedler, Jean-Claude. [Metz] : Editions serpenoise, [2000]
BF1517.F5 D515 2000

Um testemunho de mãe.
Caniato, Benilde Justo. 2a. ed. São Paulo : Lato Senso, 2001.
HV901.B6 C36 2001

Testi e pretesti (Milan, Italy)
Di Ciaccia, Antonio. Jacques Lacan. Milano : B. Mondadori, 2000.
BF109.L28 D53 2000

Testi e saggi (Università degli studi di Lecce. Dipartimento di filologia classica e di scienze filosofiche)
(24.) Sava, Gabriella. La psicologia filosofica in Italia. Galatina (Lecce) : Congedo, 2000.
BF38 .S235 2000

Testi e studi per il "Corpus philosophorum Medii Aevi"
(16) Panti, Cecilia, 1964- Moti, virtù e motori celesti nella cosmologia di Roberto Grossatesta. Firenze : SISMEL : Edizioni del Galluzzo, 2001.
B765.G74 P36 2001

Testi (Terziaria (Firm : Milan, Italy))
(7.) Borromeo, Federico, 1564-1631. Manifestazioni demoniache. Milano : Terziaria : ASEFI, 2001.
BF1520 .B67 2001

TESTIMONY. See also **WITNESSES.**
(GAO-03-171 T) Hecker, JayEtta Z. Commercial aviation [electronic resource]. [Washington, D.C.] : U.S. General Accounting Office, [2002]

TESTING. See **PSYCHOLOGICAL TESTS.**

TESTS, CHARACTER. See **CHARACTER TESTS.**

Tests of cognitive abilities.
Woodcock, Richard W. Woodcock-Johnson III tests of cognitive abilities. Itasca, IL : Riverside Pub., c2001.
BF432.5.W66 W66 2001

TESTS, PSYCHOLOGICAL. See **PSYCHOLOGICAL TESTS.**

Tetens, Holm, 1948- Geist, Gehirn, Maschine : philosophische Versuche über ihren Zusammenhang / Holm Tetens. Stuttgart : Reclam, c1994. 174 p. ; 15 cm. (Universal-Bibliothek ; Nr. 8999) Includes bibliographical references (p. [170]-174). ISBN 3-15-008999-9
1. Mind and body - Philosophy. 2. Brain - Philosophy. 3. Artificial intelligence - Philosophy. I. Title. II. Series: Universal-Bibliothek (Stuttgart, Germany) ; Nr. 8999.
BF163 .T48 1994x

Tetsugaku ronbunshū.
Kuno Akira Kyōju kanreki kinen tetsugaku ronbunshū. Tōkyō : Ibunsha, 1995.
B29 .K826 1995 <Orien Japan>

TEUTONIC KNIGHTS. BALLEI BÖHMEN - HISTORY - TO 1500.
Sankt Georg und sein Bilderzyklus in Neuhaus/Böhmen (Jindřichuv Hradec). Marburg : N.G. Elwert, c2002.
BR1720.G4 S26 2002

Teutonic magick.
Thorsson, Edred. The truth about Teutonic magick. 2nd ed. Saint Paul, MN : Llewellyn Publications, 1994.
BF1622.G3 T488 1994

Tew, Jerry, 1955- Social theory, power and practice / Jerry Tew. Houndmills [England] ; New York : Palgrave, 2002. x, 233 p. ; 23 cm. Includes bibliographical references (p. 207-226) and index. ISBN 0-333-80306-X DDC 303.3
1. Power (Social sciences) 2. Social change. 3. Social sciences - Philosophy. I. Title.
HN49.P6 T49 2002

Tewksbury, Richard A.
Gendered sexualities. New York : JAI, 2002.
HQ1075.A27 vol. 6

Texas psychology : a history of the Psychology Department at the University of Texas at Austin / edited by George W. Holden & Louise K. Iscoe. Austin : The University of Texas at Austin, c2002. 112 p. : ill. (some col.) ; 28 cm. Icludes bibliographical references (p. 76-81).
1. University of Texas at Austin. - Dept. of Psychology - History. 2. Psychology - Study and teaching (Higher) - Texas - Austin - History. I. Holden, George W. II. Iscoe, Louise. III. Title: History of the Psychology Department at the University of Texas at Austin
BF80.7.U62 T48 2002

TEXAS, WEST - DESCRIPTION AND TRAVEL.
Brosman, Catharine Savage, 1934- Finding higher ground. Reno : University of Nevada Press, c2003.
F787 .B76 2003

TEXT GRAMMAR. See **DISCOURSE ANALYSIS.**

Text/work : representing organization and organizing representation / edited by Stephen Linstead. London ; New York : Routledge, 2003. viii, 292 p. ; 24 cm. (Management, organizations and society) Includes bibliographical references and index. ISBN 0-415-30473-3 DDC 302.35
1. Organizational behavior. 2. Communication in organizations. I. Linstead, Stephen. II. Series.

TEXTBOOKS. See **READERS.**

Texte et théâtralité : mélanges offerts à Jean Claude / édités par Raymonde Robert. Nancy : Presses universitaires de Nancy, 2000. 295 p. : ill. ; 24 cm. (Le texte et ses marges)
1. Drama - History and criticism. I. Robert, Raymonde. II. Claude, Jean.

Textes de base en psychologie
Qu'est-ce-donc qu'apprendre? Lausanne : Delachaux et Niestlé, 1999.
BF318 .Q84 1999

Textes et traditions
(3) La servante et la consolatrice. Paris : Vrin, 2002.
B721 .S479 2002

Textes philosophiques du Moyen Age
(19) Jean, de la Rochelle, d. 1245. Summa de anima. Paris : J. Vrin, 1995.
BD420 .J43 1995

Textgliederung.
Stein, Stephan, 1963- Berlin ; New York : Walter de Gruyter, 2003.

TEXTILE FABRICS.
Fiore, Ann Marie. Understanding aesthetics for the merchandising and design professional. New York : Fairchild, c1997.

Simard-Laflamme, Carole. Habit Habitat Habitus. Trois-Rivières, Québec, Canada : Editions d'art Le Sabord, [2002]
TT507 .S653 2002

TEXTILE INDUSTRY. See **CLOTHING TRADE.**

Texts and monographs in symbolic computation
Automated practical reasoning. Wien ; New York : Springer-Verlag, c1995.
QA76.9.A96 A9 1995

Texts in statistical science
The analysis and interpretation of multivariate data for social scientists. Boca Raton, Fla. : Chapman & Hall/CRC, c2002.
HA29 .A5824 2002

Textures (New York, N.Y.)
Between philosophy and poetry. New York : Continuum, 2002.
B66 .B48 2002

Extreme beauty. London ; New York : Continuum, 2002.
BH39 .E98 2002

Panorama. New York : Continuum, 2002.
BH39 .P2292 2002

T.H. Green and the development of ethical socialism.
Carter, Matt. Thorverton : Imprint Academic, 2003.
B1638.E8 C37 2003

Thame, Marisa.
Comstock, Kani. Journey into love. Ashland, OR : Willow Press, c2000.
BF575.L8 C647 2002

THANATOLOGY. See **DEATH.**

Thank you, Tony Robbins.
Ibay, Manny. 1st Destini Books ed. Santa Monica, Calif. : Destini Books, 2002.
BF637.S8 I23 2002

Tharp, Twyla. The creative habit : learn it and use it for life : a practical guide / Twyla Tharp, with Mark Reiter. New York : Simon & Schuster, c2003. vii, 243 p. : ill. ; 24 cm. ISBN 0-7432-3526-6 DDC 153.3/5
1. Creative ability. 2. Creative thinking. 3. Creation (Literary, artistic, etc.) I. Reiter, Mark. II. Title.
BF408 .T415 2003

Thartharat muʻallimāt.
Bulayhid, Muná bint Ṣāliḥ. al-Ṭabʻah 1. al-Riyāḍ : Maktabat al-ʻUbaykān, 2001.
BJ1291 .B85 2001

The key to understanding the I Ching and its place in your life.
Karcher, Stephen L. Ta chuan. 1st ed. New York : St. Martin's Press, 2000.
BF1773.2.C5 K368 2000

THE MALL (WASHINGTON, D.C.). See **MALL, THE (WASHINGTON, D.C.).**

The new Jews : reflections on the love of power and on the power of love.
Amodélé, Jons. The new Jews. Banjul, The Gambia : Vinasha Publishing, 2000.
1. Black author.

THEATER. See also **THEATER AND SOCIETY.**
Land/scape/theater. Ann Arbor : University of Michigan, c2002.
PN2020 .L32 2002

Ma, Wenqi. Shui yue jing hua. Di 1 ban. Beijing : Zhongguo she hui chu ban she, 1994.

PN2039 .M28 1994 <Orien China>
Rolland, Romain, 1866-1944. Le théâtre du peuple. Nouvelle éd. Bruxelles : Complexe, c2003.
PN1655 .R68 2003

Wang, Xiaoying, 1957- Xi ju yan chu zhong di jia ding xing. Di 1 ban. Beijing : Zhongguo xi ju chu ban she : Xin hua shu dian zong dian Beijing fa xing suo fa xing, 1995.
PN2039 .W35 1995 <Orien China>

THEATER AND SOCIETY.
Herrschaft des Symbolischen. Berlin : Vistas, c2002.

THEATER AND SOCIETY - HISTORY - 19TH CENTURY.
Goodall, Jane. Performance and evolution in the age of Darwin. London ; New York : Routledge, 2002.
NX180.S3 G66 2002

THEATER - COSTUME. See **COSTUME.**

THEATER - EUROPE - HISTORY.
West, William. Theatres and encyclopedias in early modern Europe. Cambridge : Cambridge University Press, 2002.

THEATER - GREAT BRITAIN - HISTORY.
West, William. Theatres and encyclopedias in early modern Europe. Cambridge : Cambridge University Press, 2002.

THEATER - HISTORY.
Kalisch, Eleonore. Konfigurationen der Renaissance. Berlin : Vistas, c2002.

THEATER, IMPROMPTU. See **IMPROVISATION (ACTING).**

THEATER - PHILOSOPHY.
Wahrnehmung und Medialität. Tübingen : Francke, c2001.
PN2039 .W347 2001

THEATER - PSYCHOLOGICAL ASPECTS.
Armstrong, Gordon Scott, 1937- Theatre and consciousness. New York ; Oxford : Peter Lang, c2003.
BH301.P78 A75 2003

THEATER - SOCIAL ASPECTS. See **THEATER AND SOCIETY.**

Theater--theory/text/performance
Land/scape/theater. Ann Arbor : University of Michigan, c2002.
PN2020 .L32 2002

Theatralität
(Bd. 3) Wahrnehmung und Medialität. Tübingen : Francke, c2001.
PN2039 .W347 2001

THEATRE. See **THEATER.**

Theatre and consciousness.
Armstrong, Gordon Scott, 1937- New York ; Oxford : Peter Lang, c2003.
BH301.P78 A75 2003

Le théâtre du peuple.
Rolland, Romain, 1866-1944. Nouvelle éd. Bruxelles : Complexe, c2003.
PN1655 .R68 2003

Le théâtre en question
Rolland, Romain, 1866-1944. Le théâtre du peuple. Nouvelle éd. Bruxelles : Complexe, c2003.
PN1655 .R68 2003

Théâtre National de la Colline.
Inédits et commentaires. Paris : L'Arche, 2002.

Theatres and encyclopedias in early modern Europe.
West, William. Cambridge : Cambridge University Press, 2002.

THEATRICAL AGENTS. See **LITERARY AGENTS.**

THEATRICAL COSTUME. See **COSTUME.**

THEISM. See **GOD; MONOTHEISM.**

Thélot, Claude. L'origine des génies / Claude Thélot. Paris : Seuil, c2003. 178 p. ; 22 cm. Includes bibliographical references. ISBN 2-02-057181-1 DDC 300
1. Genius. 2. Creation (Literary, artistic, etc.) I. Title.

Thematic cartography and visualization.
Slocum, Terry A. Upper Saddle River, N.J. : Prentice Hall, c1999.
GA108.7 .S58 1999

THEOCRACY.
Toshchenko, Zhan Terent'evich. Tri osobennykh lika vlasti. Moskva : RGGU, 2002.

JC330 .T674 2002

THEODICY.
I concetti del male. Torino : Einaudi, c2002.

THEOLOGIANS, MUSLIM.
Arnaldez, Roger. Fakhr al-Dîn al-Râzî. Paris : J. Vrin, 2002.

THEOLOGICAL EDUCATION. See **RELIGIOUS EDUCATION; THEOLOGY - STUDY AND TEACHING.**

THEOLOGICAL VIRTUES.
Cultivating citizens. Lanham : Lexington Books, c2002.
JK1759 .C85 2002

THEOLOGY. See also **RELIGION; THEOLOGY, DOCTRINAL.**
Kovesi, Julius. Values and evaluations. New York ; Bern : P. Lang, c1998.
BD232 .K68 1998

Schweitzer, Albert, 1875-1965. Vorträge, Vorlesungen, Aufsätze. München : C.H. Beck, c2003.

THEOLOGY - 19TH CENTURY. See **THEOLOGY.**

THEOLOGY - 20TH CENTURY. See **THEOLOGY.**

Theology and sociology of Yoruba indigenous religion.
Studies in the theology and sociology of Yoruba indigenous religion. Lagos, Nigeria : Concept Publications (Nig.), 2002.

Theology and the sciences
Peterson, Gregory R., 1966- Minding God. Minneapolis, MN : Fortress Press, c2003.
BL53 .P42 2003

THEOLOGY, ASCETICAL. See **ASCETICISM.**

THEOLOGY, CHRISTIAN. See **THEOLOGY.**

THEOLOGY, DOCTRINAL. See also **ESCHATOLOGY; HOLY SPIRIT; KNOWLEDGE, THEORY OF (RELIGION); MAN (CHRISTIAN THEOLOGY); PHILOSOPHICAL THEOLOGY; TRINITY.**
Cho, Hyeon-Kweon Stephan, 1962- Heiliger Geist als Lebenskraft in Kirche und Menschheit. Frankfurt am Main ; New York : Peter Lang, c2002.
BT121.3 .C56 2002

THEOLOGY, DOCTRINAL - HISTORY - 20TH CENTURY.
Martinelli, Paolo, 1958- Vocazione e stati di vita del cristiano. Roma : Collegio San Lorenzo da Brindisi, 2001.

THEOLOGY, DOCTRINAL - HISTORY - MIDDLE AGES, 600-1500.
La servante et la consolatrice. Paris : Vrin, 2002.
B721 .S479 2002

THEOLOGY, DOCTRINAL - HISTORY - MIDDLE AGES, 600-1500 - CONGRESSES.
Internationales Eriugena-Colloquium (10th : Maynooth and Dublin : 2002) History and eschatology in John Scottus Eriugena and his time. Leuven : University Press, 2002.

THEOLOGY, DOGMATIC. See **THEOLOGY, DOCTRINAL.**

THEOLOGY - EARLY WORKS TO 1800.
Vizantijska filozofija u srednjevekovnoj Srbiji. Beograd : Stubovi kulture, 2002.

THEOLOGY, ETHICAL. See **CHRISTIAN ETHICS.**

THEOLOGY - HISTORY - 16TH CENTURY.
Sacerdoti, Gilberto, 1952- Sacrificio e sovranità. Torino : Einaudi, 2002.

THEOLOGY - MISCELLANEA.
Walsch, Neale Donald. The new revelations. New York : Atria Books, c2002.
BF1999 .W2287 2002

THEOLOGY, MORAL. See **CHRISTIAN ETHICS.**

THEOLOGY, MYSTICAL. See **MYSTICISM.**

THEOLOGY, PHILOSOPHICAL. See **PHILOSOPHICAL THEOLOGY.**

THEOLOGY, PRACTICAL. See also **FASTS AND FEASTS.**
Ofori Onwona, Samuel. Shadows come to light. Achimota, Ghana : Africa Christian Press, 2000.
BV215 .O46 2000

THEOLOGY - STUDY AND TEACHING - FRANCE - PARIS - HISTORY.
Goglin, Jean-Marc. L'enseignement de la théologie dans les ordres mendiants à Paris au XIIIe siècle. Paris : Editions franciscaines, c2002.

THEOLOGY, SYSTEMATIC. See **THEOLOGY, DOCTRINAL.**

THEOMACHY. See **GODS.**

Theophil
(4. Bd) Stolz, Fritz. Weltbilder der Religionen. Zürich : Pano Verlag, c2001.

Theophrastean studies.
Fortenbaugh, William W. Stuttgart : Steiner, 2003.
B626.T34 F678 2003

THEOPHRASTUS - CRITICISM AND INTERPRETATION.
Fortenbaugh, William W. Theophrastean studies. Stuttgart : Steiner, 2003.
B626.T34 F678 2003

Theoretical models of counseling and psychotherapy.
Fall, Kevin A. New York : Brunner-Routledge, 2003.
BF637.C6 F324 2003

Theoretical psychology.
International Society for Theoretical Psychology. Conference (9th : 2001 : Calgary, Alta.) Concord, Ont. : Captus Press, c2003.

Theoretische Ethik.
Karg, Hans Hartmut. Hamburg : Kovac, c1996- <c1999>
BJ1114 .K32 1997

Theoretische Philosophiegeschichte.
Beelmann, Axel. Basel : Schwabe, c2001.

Theorie des Subjekts.
Zima, P. V. Tübingen : A. Francke, c2000.
BD223 .Z56 2000

Théorie générale de la schématisation.
Estivals, Robert. Paris : Harmattan, c2002-

Theorie und Methode. Sozialwissenschaften
Kontexte und Kulturen des Erinnerns. Konstanz : UVK Verlagsgesellschaft, 2002.
BF378.S65 K65 2002

Theories of contemporary culture
(v. 26) Representing animals. Bloomington : Indiana University Press, c2002.
QL85 .R46 2002

Theories of counseling and psychotherapy.
Murdock, Nancy L. Upper Saddle River, N.J. : Merrill/Prentice Hall, 2004.
BF637.C6 M846 2004

Theories of personality.
Cloninger, Susan C., 1945- 4th ed. Upper Saddle River, N.J. : Pearson/Prentice Hall, c2004.
BF698 .C543 2004

Ryckman, Richard M. 8th ed. Belmont, CA : Thomson/Wadsworth, c2004.
BF698 .R96 2004

Theorizing feminism
Kītā, Va. Gender. Calcutta : Stree, 2002.
HQ1075 .K576 2002

The theory and interpretation of narrative series
Warhol, Robyn R. Having a good cry. Columbus : Ohio State University Press, c2003.
PN56.5.W64 W375 2003

Theory and practice in late antique archaeology / edited by Luke Lavan and William Bowden. Leiden ; Boston : Brill, 2003. xvi, 428 p., [27] p. of plates : ill., maps ; 25 cm. (Late antique archaeology, 1570-6893 : v. 1) Includes bibliographical references and index. ISBN 90-04-12567-1 DDC 930.1
1. Social archaeology. 2. Civilization, Medieval. 3. Archaeology - Philosophy. 4. Archaeology - Methodology. 5. Archaeology - Field work. 6. Excavations (Archaeology) I. Lavan, Luke. II. Bowden, William. III. Series.
CC72.4 .T46 2003

Theory and practice of group counseling.
Corey, Gerald. 6th ed. Australia ; Belmont, CA : Thomson/Brooks/Cole, c2004.
BF637.C6 C576 2004

Theory, culture & society (Unnumbered)
Turner, Stephen P., 1951- Liberal democracy 3.0. London ; Thousand Oaks, Calif. : SAGE Publications, 2003.
JC423 .T87 2003

Theory in an uneven world.
Radhakrishnan, R. (Rajagopalan) Oxford ; Malden, MA : Blackwell, 2003.

The theory of everything.
Hawking, S. W. (Stephen W.). [Cambridge lectures] Beverly Hills, CA : New Millennium Press, c2002, 1996.
QB985 .H39 2002

THEORY OF FEMINISM. *See* **FEMINIST THEORY.**

A theory of immediate awareness.
Estep, Myrna. Dordrecht ; Boston : Kluwer Academic Publishers, 2003.
BF311 .E79 2003

THEORY OF MIND. *See* **PHILOSOPHY OF MIND.**

A theory of physical probability.
Johns, Richard, 1968- Toronto : University of Toronto Press, c2002.

The theory of reality.
Tolsdorf, Samuel, 1926- Vancouver, B.C. : Leumas Publications, [1998]
BF1999 .T62 1998

Theory out of bounds
(v. 23) Connolly, William E. Neuropolitics. Minneapolis, MN : University of Minnesota Press, c2002.

THEORY (PHILOSOPHY).
Del Bufalo, Erik. Deleuze et Laruelle. Paris : Kimé, 2003.

Radhakrishnan, R. (Rajagopalan) Theory in an uneven world. Oxford ; Malden, MA : Blackwell, 2003.

Strategies for theory. Albany : State University of New York Press, c2003.
B842 .S77 2003

THEOSOPHY. *See also* **REINCARNATION; YOGA.**
Ėzotericheskaia filosofiia. Rostov-na-Donu : Foliant, 2002.
BF1416 .E96 2002

Therapeutic action.
Lear, Jonathan. New York : Other Press, c2003.
BF175.4.C68 L43 2003

THERAPEUTIC COMMUNITIES.
Therapeutic communities for children and young people. London : Jessica Kingsley, 2003.

Therapeutic communities
(10) Therapeutic communities for children and young people. London : Jessica Kingsley, 2003.

Therapeutic communities for children and young people / edited by Adrian Ward ... [et al.] London : Jessica Kingsley, 2003. 336 p. ; 24 cm. (Therapeutic communities ; 10) Includes bibliographical references and index. ISBN 1-84310-096-7 DDC 362.732
1. Therapeutic communities. 2. Children - Institutional care. 3. Child psychotherapy. I. Ward, Adrian, 1953- II. Series.

Therapeutic monographs
Blumenthal, Mark. Popular herbs in the U.S. market. Austin : American Botanical Council, 1997.

THERAPEUTICS. *See also* **HEALING; PLACEBO (MEDICINE); PSYCHOTHERAPY.**
Pharmacum carthusiense. Salzburg, Austria : Institut für Anglistik und Amerikanistik, Universität Salzburg, 2002.
BX2435 .P43 2002

THERAPEUTICS, SUGGESTIVE.
Cherepanova, I. IU. (Irina IUr'evna) Dom koldun'i. Perer., dop. i ispravlennoe izd. Moskva : KSP+, 2001.
BF1156.S8 C53 2001

Therapies with women in transition : toward relational perspectives with today's women / [edited by] Jean Bovard Sanville, Ellen Bassin Ruderman. Madison, Conn. : International Universities Press, c2003. xxxiii, 328 p. : ill. ; 22 cm. Includes bibliographical references and indexes. ISBN 0-8236-6490-2 DDC 616.89/0082
1. Women - Mental health - United States. 2. Women and psychoanalysis. 3. Psychoanalysis and feminism.
RC451.4.W6 T46 2003

There is a river.
Sugrue, Thomas, 1907- Virginia Beach, Va. : A.R.E. Press, c2003.
BF1027.C3 S8 2003

There is only one you.
Danzig, Robert J., 1932- Washington, D.C. : Child and Family Press, c2003.
BF723.I56 D36 2003

THERMOCHROMISM. *See* **COLOR.**

Thèse. Anthropologie.
Vallier, Gilles-Félix. La logique de l'éternité. 1998.

These detestable slaves of the devill.
Hudson, Carson O. Haverford, PA : Infinity Pub., c2001.
BF1577.V8 H83 2001

Thewes, F. (Frans).
Topographies of power in the early Middle Ages. Leiden ; Boston : Brill, 2001.
D117 .T67 2001

Thick description and fine texture : studies in the history of psychology / edited by David B. Baker. 1st ed. Akron, Ohio : University of Akron Press, 2003. p. cm. Includes bibliographical references and index. ISBN 1-931968-02-0 (alk. paper) DDC 150/.7/22
1. Psychology - Historiography. I. Baker, David B.
BF81 .T47 2003

The thief of happiness.
Friedman, Bonnie, 1958- Boston, Mass. : Beacon Press, 2002.
RC464.F75 A3 2002

Thiel, Rainer.
Ammonius, Hermiae. Commentaria in quinque voces Porphyrii. Stuttgart : Frommann-Holzboog, 2002.

THINGS (LAW). *See* **PROPERTY.**

The things we mean.
Schiffer, Stephen R. Oxford ; New York : Clarendon, 2003.

Think love.
Hare, Jenny. London : Vega, 2002.
BF575.L8 H338 2002

THINKING. *See* **THOUGHT AND THINKING.**

Thinking about knowing.
Rosenberg, Jay F. Oxford : Clarendon Press ; New York : Oxford University Press, 2002.
BD161 .R65 2002

Thinking about the environment : our debt to the classical and medieval past / edited by Thomas M. Robinson and Laura Westra. Lanham, Md. : Lexington Books, c2002. xii, 228 p. ; 24 cm. Includes bibliographical references and index. Essays in English and Italian. ISBN 0-7391-0420-9 (cloth : alk. paper)
1. Environmentalism - History. 2. Philosophy, Ancient. 3. Philosophy, Medieval. 4. Nature in literature. I. Robinson, T. M. II. Westra, Laura.
GE50 .T48 2002

Thinking and seeing : visual metacognition in adults and children / edited by Daniel T. Levin. Cambridge, MA : Mit Press, 2004. p. cm. "A Bradford book." Includes bibliographical references and index. ISBN 0-262-12262-6 (hc. : alk. paper) ISBN 0-262-62181-9 (pbk. : alk. paper) DDC 152.14
1. Visual perception - Congresses. 2. Metacognition - Congresses. I. Levin, Daniel T.
BF241 .T48 2004

THINKING, ARTIFICIAL. *See* **ARTIFICIAL INTELLIGENCE.**

The thinking eye, the seeing brain.
Enns, James T. New York : W.W. Norton, 2004.
BF241 .E56 2004

Thinking in action
Salecl, Renata, 1962- On anxiety. 1st ed. London ; New York : Routledge, 2004.
BF575.A6 S25 2004

Thinking : psychological perspectives on reasoning, judgment, and decision making / edited by David Hardman and Laura Macchi. Hoboken, NJ : Wiley, c2003. p. cm. Includes bibliographical references and index. ISBN 0-471-49457-7 DDC 153.4
1. Thought and thinking. 2. Reasoning (Psychology) 3. Judgment. 4. Decision making. I. Hardman, David. II. Macchi, Laura, 1961-
BF441 .T466 2003

Thinking the limits of the body / edited by Jeffrey Jerome Cohen and Gail Weiss. Albany : State University of New York Press, c2003. vi, 203 p. : ill. ; 23 cm. (SUNY series in aesthetics and the philosophy of art) Includes bibliographical references and index. ISBN 0-7914-5599-8 (alk. paper) ISBN 0-7914-5600-5 (pbk. : alk. paper) DDC 306.4
1. Body, Human - Social aspects. 2. Body, Human (Philosophy) I. Cohen, Jeffrey Jerome. II. Weiss, Gail, 1959- III. Series.
HM636 .T47 2003

Thinking without words.
Bermudez, Jose Luis. Oxford ; New York : Oxford University Press, 2003.

BD418.3 .B47 2003

The third level of reality.
Seymour, Percy. [Paranormal] New York : Paraview Special Editions, c2003.
BF1045.S33 S48 2003

THIRD MILLENNIUM - FORECASTS.
Clark, Harold A. The age of intimacy. Laredo, TX : EBookcase.com, c2000.

THIRD PARTIES (LAW). *See* **DISPUTE RESOLUTION (LAW).**

THIRD WORLD. *See* **DEVELOPING COUNTRIES.**

This book is for all kids, but especially my sister Libby, Libby died.
Simon, Jack. Kansas City, Mo. : Andrews McMeel Pub., c2002.
BF723.D3 S59 2002

This book is no joke!.
Haviland, James J. [Philadelphia?] : Xlibris, c2001.
BF637.C45 H38 2001

Thoele, Sue Patton. Growing hope : sowing seeds of positive change in yourself and the world / Sue Patton Thoele. York Beach, ME : Conari Press, 2004. p. cm. Table of contents URL: http://www.loc.gov/catdir/toc/ecip047/2003018339.html CONTENTS: Growing hope -- Sowing hope -- Cultivating hope -- Harvesting hope -- Spreading hope -- Watering seeds of hope. ISBN 1-57324-911-4 DDC 170/.44
1. Hope. I. Title.
BF575.H56 T48 2004

THOMAS, AQUINAS, SAINT, 1225?-1274. DE ENTE ET ESSENTIA.
Balmès, Marc. Pour un plein accès à l'acte d'être avec Thomas d'Aquin et Aristote. Paris : Harmattan, c2003.

QUAESTIONES DISPUTATAE DE VERITATE.
González Ayesta, Cruz. Hombre y verdad. 1. ed. Pamplona : Universidad de Navarra, Ediciones, 2002.

THOMAS, AQUINAS, SAINT, 1225?-1274.
González, Angel Luis. Ser y participación. 3. ed. revisada y ampliada. Pamplona : Ediciones Universidad de Navarra, c2001.
BX4700.T6 G66 2001

Ledda, Antonio. La fenomelogia tra essenza ed esistenza. 1. ed. Roma : Carocci editore, 2002.

Luciani Rivero, Rafael Francisco. El misterio de la diferencia. Roma : Pontificia università gregoriana, 2001.

THOMAS, AQUINAS, SAINT, 1225?-1274 - CONTRIBUTIONS IN DOCTRINE OF THE HOLY SPIRIT.
Noriega, José. "Guiados por el espíritu". Roma : Pontificia università lateranense ; [Milano] : Mursia, 2000.

THOMAS, AQUINAS, SAINT, 1225?-1274 - CONTRIBUTIONS IN DOCTRINE OF THE TRINITY.
Noriega, José. "Guiados por el espíritu". Roma : Pontificia università lateranense ; [Milano] : Mursia, 2000.

THOMAS, AQUINAS, SAINT, 1225?-1274 - CRITICISM AND INTERPRETATION.
González Ayesta, Cruz. Hombre y verdad. 1. ed. Pamplona : Universidad de Navarra, Ediciones, 2002.

THOMAS, AQUINAS, SAINT, 1225?-1274 - ETHICS.
Rhonheimer, Martin, 1950- Die Perspektive der Moral. Berlin : Akademie Verlag, c2001.

Thomas, Marlo.
The right words at the right time. New York : Atria Books, c2002.
BJ1611.2 .R52 2002

Thomas, Pat, 1959-.
First look at ... book.
Thomas, Pat, 1959- My friends and me. 1st ed. Hauppauge, N.Y. : Barron's Educational Series, c2001.
BF723.F68 T48 2001

My friends and me : a first look at friendship / Pat Thomas ; illustrated by Lesley Harker. 1st ed. Hauppauge, N.Y. : Barron's Educational Series, c2001. 29 p. : col. ill. ; 22 cm. (A first look at .... book) Includes bibliographical references (p. 29). ISBN 0-7641-1763-7
1. Friendship in children - Juvenile literature. 2. Child rearing.

I. Harker, Lesley. II. Title. III. Series: Thomas, Pat, 1959- First look at ... book.
BF723.F68 T48 2001

Thomas, Patrice Olympius. The power of relaxation : using tai chi and visualization to reduce children's stress / Patrice Thomas. 1st U.S. ed. St. Paul, MN : Redleaf Press, 2003. p. cm. ISBN 1-929610-37-8 (pbk.) DDC 155.4/18
1. Stress in children. 2. Stress management for children. 3. Mind and body in children. 4. Mind and body in children - Problems, exercises, etc. I. Title.
BF723.S75 T48 2003

Thomashauer, Regena. Mama Gena's School of Womanly Arts : using the power of pleasure to have your way with the world / Regena Thomashauer. New York : Simon & Schuster, c2002. vi, 181 p. ; 21 cm. Publisher description URL: http://www.loc.gov/catdir/desc ription/simon032/2002017687.html ISBN 0-7432-2684-4 DDC 305.4
1. Women - Psychology. 2. Women - Conduct of life. 3. Pleasure. 4. Self-realization. I. Title.
HQ1206.T4673 2002

Thomasset, Claude Alexandre.
Dans l'eau, sous l'eau. [Paris] : Presses de l'Université de Paris-Sorbonne, 2002.
CB353.D27 2002

Thomist realism and the linguistic turn.
O'Callaghan, John (John P.) Notre Dame, Ind. : University of Notre Dame Press, c2003.
BD161.O3 2003

THOMISTS.
O'Callaghan, John (John P.) Thomist realism and the linguistic turn. Notre Dame, Ind. : University of Notre Dame Press, c2003.
BD161.O3 2003

Thompson, Anne Booth. Everyday saints and the art of narrative in the South English legendary / Anne B. Thompson. Aldershot, England ; Burlington, Vt. : Ashgate, c2003. x, 224 p. ; 23 cm. Includes bibliographical references (p. 219-212) and index. ISBN 0-7546-3293-8 (alk. paper) DDC 820.9/3823
1. South English legendary. 2. Christian literature, English (Middle) - History and criticism. 3. English language - Middle English, 1100-1500 - Rhetoric. 4. Christian saints - Legends - History and criticism. 5. Manners and customs in literature. 6. Narration (Rhetoric) 7. Rhetoric, Medieval. 8. Hagiography. I. Title.
PR2143.S543 T48 2003

Thompson, Bruce, 1951- Exploratory and confirmatory factor analysis : understanding concepts and applications / Bruce Thompson. 1st ed. Washington, DC : American Psychological Association, c2004. p. cm. Includes bibliographical references. ISBN 1-59147-093-5 DDC 150/.1/5195354
1. Factor analysis - Textbooks. I. Title.
BF39.2.F32 T48 2004

Thompson, Dennis F. (Dennis Frank), 1940-.
Truth v. justice. Princeton, N.J. : Princeton University Press, c2000.
DT1945.T78 2000

Thompson, Grahame. Between hierarchies and markets : the logic and limits of network forms of organization / Grahame F. Thompson. Oxford ; New York : Oxford University Press, 2003. x, 272 p. : ill. ; 23 cm. Other title: Between hierarchies & markets. Includes bibliographical references (p. [239]-261) and index. ISBN 0-19-877526-1 (hbk.) ISBN 0-19-877527-X (pbk.) DDC 302.3/5
1. Organizational behavior. 2. Business networks. 3. Social networks. I. Title. II. Title: Between hierarchies & markets
HD58.7.T4786 2003

Thompson, Janice, 1964-.
Martin, Jack, 1950- Psychology and the question of agency. Albany : State University of New York Press, c2003.
BF575.A88 M37 2003

Thompson, Patricia J.
Hestia trilogy
(bk. 2.) Thompson, Patricia J. In bed with Procrustes. New York : P. Lang, c2003.
HQ1190.T52 2002 bk. 2

In bed with Procrustes : feminism's flirtation with patriarchy / Patricia J. Thompson. New York : P. Lang, c2003. xx, 290 p. ; 24 cm. (The Hestia trilogy ; bk. 2) Includes bibliographical references (p. 249-278) and indexes. CONTENTS: Feminism : in bed with procrustes? -- Feminism and perspectivism -- A Hestian feminist systems perspective -- The Hestian and the Hermean : the double Helix of everyday life -- A Hestian feminist critique of "pure feminism" -- The classics : following "Ariadne's thread" -- Hestia, Heraclitus, and Heidegger -- His-story through a Hestian lens : the case of home economics -- Domestic science and political science : the "body domestic" and the "body politic" -- The Hestian family and the Hermean state : a sociological perspective -- The Hestian archetype -- The Hestian economy -- Hestian science and technology -- Ethics in the Hestian/Hermean systems. ISBN 0-8204-5783-3 (hb : alk. paper) DDC 305.42/01
1. Feminist theory. 2. Feminism. 3. Home economics - Philosophy. 4. Sex role - Philosophy. 5. Patriarchy. I. Title. II. Series: Thompson, Patricia J. Hestia trilogy ; bk. 2
HQ1190.T52 2002 bk. 2

Thomsen, Marie-Louise.
Cryer, Frederick H. Biblical and pagan societies. Philadelphia : University of Pennsylvania Press, 2001.
BF1567.C79 2001

Thomson, Emma.
Emma Thomson's Felicity wishes
Thomson, Emma. Little book of happiness. 1st ed. London : Hodder Children's, 2001.
BF575.H27.T56 2001

Little book of happiness / [written by Emma Thomson and Helen Bailey ; illustrated by Emma Thomson]. 1st ed. London : Hodder Children's, 2001. [20] p. : col. ill. ; 13 cm. (Emma Thomson's Felicity wishes) ISBN 0-340-84404-3 DDC 158.1
1. Happiness - Juvenile literature. I. Bailey, Helen. II. Title. III. Series: Thomson, Emma. Emma Thomson's Felicity wishes
BF575.H27.T56 2001

Thomson, Garrett. On the meaning of life / Garrett Thomson. Australia ; United States : Thomson/Wadsworth, c2003. 161 p. ; 22 cm. (Wadsworth philosophers series) Includes bibliographical references (p. 158-161). ISBN 0-534-59580-4
1. Life. I. Title. II. Series.
BD431.T296 2003

Thomson, Sandra A. Pictures from the heart : a tarot dictionary / Sandra A. Thomson. 1st ed. New York : St. Martin's Press, c2003. xii, 466 p. ; 21 cm. Includes bibliographical references (p. 459-466). ISBN 0-312-29128-0 DDC 133.3/2424
1. Tarot. 2. Tarot - Dictionaries. I. Title.
BF1879.T2 T52 2003

Thorndike Press large print senior lifestyles series
Meier, Leslie. Birthday party murder. Waterville, Me. : Thorndike Press, 2003.
PS3563.E3455 B57 2003

Thorne, Robert. Marihuana : the burning bush of Moses : mysticism & cannabis experience / by Robert Thorne. Portland, Or. : Clarus Books Pub., c1998 (1999 printing) v, 399 p. ; 23 cm. Includes bibliographical references (p. [377]-393) and index. ISBN 0-9671056-0-9 DDC 291.4/2
1. Marijuana - Psychological aspects. 2. Marijuana - History. 3. Mysticism. I. Title.
BF209.C3 T48 1998

THORNHILL, RANDY.
NATURAL HISTORY OF RAPE.
Evolution, gender, and rape. Cambridge, Mass. : MIT Press, c2003.
HV6558.E92 2003

Thornton, George C., 1940-.
Condon, Margaret E. Exercises in psychological testing. Boston : Allyn and Bacon, c2002.
BF176.T47 2002

Thorp, Rosemary.
Group behaviour and development. Oxford ; New York : Oxford University Press, 2002.
HD58.7.G76 2002

Thorpe, Richard, 1951-.
Management and language. London ; Thousand Oaks : SAGE, 2003.
HD30.3.H65 2003

Thorsson, Edred. The truth about Teutonic magick / by Edred Thorsson. 2nd ed. Saint Paul, MN : Llewellyn Publications, 1994. 55 p. : ill. ; 18 cm. (Llewellyn's vanguard series) ISBN 0-87542-779-0 DDC 133.4/3/0893
1. Magic, Germanic. 2. Runes - Miscellanea. I. Title. II. Title: Teutonic magick III. Series.
BF1622.G3 T488 1994

Þór#ur Ingi Gu#jónsson.
Jón Magnússon, 1610-1696. Píslarsaga séra Jóns Magnússonar. Reykjavík : Mál og menning, 2001.
BF1584.I2 J66 2001

THOUGHT AND THINKING. *See also* **CREATIVE THINKING; IDEOLOGY; INSIGHT; INTELLECT; LOGIC; MEMORY; PERCEPTION; REASONING; REASONING (PSYCHOLOGY); SELF; STEREOTYPE (PSYCHOLOGY).**

Bruce, William C. The dimensional thinker. 1st ed. Tyler, TX : Home Tree Media, 2000.
BF441.B799 2000

Burnett, Ron, 1947- How images think. Cambridge, Mass. : MIT Press, 2004.
BF241.B79 2004

Cabrera, Derek. Remedial genius. 1st ed. Loveland, Colo. : Project N Press, 2001.
BF441.C23 2001

Cimatti, Felice. La mente silenziosa. 1. ed. Roma : Editori riuniti, 2001.

Connolly, William E. Neuropolitics. Minneapolis, MN : University of Minnesota Press, c2002.

Conscious experience. Paderborn : Schöningh/Imprint Academic, 1995 (Lawrence, Kan. : Allen Press)
BF311.C6443 1995

Demmin, Herbert S., 1959- The ghosts of consciousness. St. Paul, Minn. : Paragon House, c2003.
BF441.D395 2003

Gelven, Michael. What happens to us when we think. Albany : State University of New York Press, c2003.
BD111.G45 2003

Goldin-Meadow, Susan. Hearing gesture. Cambridge, Mass. : Belknap Press of Harvard University Press, 2003.
P117.G65 2003

Gordon, Barry, M.D. Intelligent memory. New York : Viking, 2003.
BF371.G66 2003

Heidegger, Martin, 1889-1976. Was heisst Denken? Frankfurt am Main : Vittorio Klostermann, c2002.
B3279.H45 1976 Bd.8

Heuermann, Hartmut. Welt und Bewusstsein. Frankfurt am Main ; New York : Peter Lang, c2002.

Hobson, R. Peter. The cradle of thought. New York : Oxford University Press, 2004.
BF720.C63 H63 2004

Hobson, R. Peter. The cradle of thought. London : Macmillan, 2002.
BF720.C63 H63 2002

Hugl, Ulrike. Qualitative Inhaltsanalyse und Mind-Mapping. Wiesbaden : Gabler, 1995.

Humphrey, Nicholas. The inner eye. Oxford ; New York : Oxford University Press, c2002.
BF311.H778 2002

Korsström, Tuva. Kan kvinnor tänka? Stockholm/Stehag : Symposion, 2002.

Le leggi del pensiero tra logica, ontologia e psicologia. Milano : UNICOPLI, 2002.

El lenguaje y la mente humana. 1. ed. Barcelona : Ariel Editorial, 2002.

Lenk, Hans. Das Denken und sein Gehalt. München : Oldenbourg, 2001.
BF441.L455 2001

Lenk, Hans. Das Denken und sein Gehalt. München : Oldenbourg, 2001.

Li, Tianming, 1945- Li Tianming di si kao yi shu. Beijing di 1 ban. Beijing : Sheng huo, du shu, xin zhi san lian shu dian, 1996.

Mapes, James J., 1945- Quantum leap thinking. Naperville, Ill. : Sourcebooks, c2003.
BF441.M265 2003

Matiushkina, A. A. (Anna Alekseevna) Reshenie problemy kak poisk smyslov. Moskva : Izdatel'skiĭ tsentr GUU, 2003.
BF463.M4 M33 2003

Nichols, Shaun. Mindreading. Oxford : Clarendon Press ; New York : Oxford University Press, 2003.

Pearce, Joseph Chilton. The crack in the cosmic egg. Rochester, Vt. : Park Street Press, c2002.
BD331.P3915 2002

Perspectives on thinking and reasoning. Hove, UK ; Hillsdale : Lawrence Erlbaum Associates, c1995.
BF441.P48 1995

Pettit, Philip, 1945- Rules, reasons, and norms. Oxford : Oxford University Press ; New York : Clarendon Press, 2002.
B105.T54 P48 2002

Ruggiero, Vincent Ryan. The art of thinking. 7th ed. New York : Pearson/Longman, c2004.

BF441 .R84 2004

Schröder, Jürgen. Die Sprache des Denkens. Würzburg : Königshausen & Neumann, c2001.

Spotts, Dane. Super brain power. Seattle, Wash. : LifeQuest Pub. Group, c1998.
BF441 .S68 1998

Stenning, Keith. Seeing reason. Oxford ; New York : Oxford University Press, 2002.
BF441 .S775 2002

Thinking. Hoboken, NJ : Wiley, c2003.
BF441 .T466 2003

Toševski, Jovo. Nerazumna mreža. Novi Sad : Prometej ; [Kragujevac] : Jefimija, c2002.

Wingerter, J. Richard. Teaching, learning, and the meditative mind. Lanham, Md. ; Oxford : University Press of America, c2003.
LB1025.3 .W55 2003

THOUGHT AND THINKING - HISTORY - 17TH CENTURY.
Denkwelten um 1700. Köln : Böhlau, 2002.
BF441 .D46 2002

THOUGHT AND THINKING - HISTORY - 18TH CENTURY.
Denkwelten um 1700. Köln : Böhlau, 2002.
BF441 .D46 2002

THOUGHT AND THINKING - PROBLEMS, EXERCISES, ETC.
Gamon, David. Building mental muscle. Rev. and updated ed. New York : Walker & Co., 2003.
BF441 .G35 2003

Ruggiero, Vincent Ryan. The art of thinking. 7th ed. New York : Pearson/Longman, c2004.
BF441 .R84 2004

THOUGHT AND THINKING - SOCIAL ASPECTS.
Monteil, Jean-Marc. Social context and cognitive performance. Hove, East Sussex, UK : Psychology Press, c1999.
BF311 .M59 1999

THOUGHT AND THINKING - STUDY AND TEACHING - EUROPE - HISTORY.
Moss, Ann, 1938- Printed commonplace-books and the structuring of Renaissance thought. Oxford : Clarendon Press ; New York : Oxford University Press, 1996.
PA2047 .M67 1996

THOUGHT CONTROL. See BRAINWASHING.

Thought in a hostile world.
Sterelny, Kim. Malden, MA : Blackwell, 2003.
BF698.95 .S74 2003

Thought power.
Sivananda, Swami. 13th ed. Uttaranchal, Himalayas, India : Divine Life Society, 2003.

THOUGHT-TRANSFERENCE. See TELEPATHY.

Thoughts from the underworld.
Charlton-Davis, Mark K. Los Angeles, Calif. : Amen-Ra Theological Seminary Press, c2001 (Kearney, NE : Morris Pub.)
BF1999 .C5145 2001

Thoughts through space.
Wilkins, George H. (George Hubert), Sir, 1888-1958. Charlottesville, VA : Hampton Roads Pub. Co., 2004.
BF1171 .W49 2004

A thousand suns.
Johnsen, Linda, 1954- St. Paul, MN : Yes International Publishers, 2003.
BF1714.H5 J665 2003

THREAT (PSYCHOLOGY).
Jay, Timothy. Why we curse. Philadelphia : John Benjamins Publishing Company, c2000.
BF463.158 J38 2000

Three-dimensional user interfaces for immersive virtual reality [microform] : final report (April 1, 1996 to March 31, 1997) / principal investigator, Andries van Dam. Providence, RI : Brown University Computer Graphics Group, [1997] 29 p. : ill. ([NASA contractor report] ; NASA CR-204997) Shipping list no.: 98-0317-M. Microfiche. [Washington, D.C. : National Aeronautics and Space Administration, 1997] 1 microfiche. Includes bibliographical references (p. 27-29). NAG2-830.
1. User interfaces (Computer systems) 2. Virtual reality. I. Van Dam, Andries, 1938- II. United States. National Aeronautics and Space Administration. III. Series.

Three hundred sixty-five glorious nights of love and romance.

Darbo, Patrika. 365 glorious nights of love and romance. 1st ed. New York : ReganBooks, c2002.
HQ46 .D35 2002

Three philosophical dialogues.
Anselm, Saint, Archbishop of Canterbury, 1033-1109. [Dialogues. English. Selections] Indianapolis, IN : Hackett Pub., c2002.
B765.A81 .A2513 2002

Three Spanish philosophers.
Ferrater Mora, José, 1912- [Selections. English. 2003] Albany : State University of New York Press, c2003.
B4568.U54 F3913 2003

Thresholds of the mind.
Harris, Bill, 1950- Beaverton : Centerpointe Press, c2002.
BF637.B4 H36 2002

Thriving through crisis.
O'Hanlon, William Hudson. 1st Perigee ed. New York : Perigee, 2004.
BF789.S8 O35 2004

THROAT. See VOICE.

Thubten Chodron, 1950- Working with anger / by Thubten Chodron. Ithaca, NY : Snow Lion Publication, 2001. 169 p. ; 23 cm. Includes bibliographical references (p.[167]-169). ISBN 1-55939-163-4 (alk. paper) DDC 294.3/5698
1. Anger - Religious aspects - Buddhism. 2. Patience - Religious aspects - Buddhism. 3. Compassion - Religious aspects - Buddhism. 4. Religious life - Buddhism. 5. Buddhism - Doctrines. I. Title.
BQ4430.A53 T48 2001

Thüringen gestern & heute
(11) Füssel, Ronald. Hexen und Hexenverfolgung in Thüringen. Erfurt : Landeszentrale für Politische Bildung Thüringen, 2001.
BF1583 .F87 2001

THURINGIA (GERMANY) - HISTORY.
Füssel, Ronald. Hexen und Hexenverfolgung in Thüringen. Erfurt : Landeszentrale für Politische Bildung Thüringen, 2001.
BF1583 .F87 2001

Jonscher, Reinhard. Kleine thüringische Geschichte. 3., überarb. und erw. Aufl. Jena : Jenzig-Verlag Köhler, 2001.
DD801.T44 J658 2001

Westphal, Siegrid, 1963- Kaiserliche Rechtsprechung und herrschaftliche Stabilisierung. Köln : Böhlau, 2002.

THURINGIA (GERMANY) - POLITICS AND GOVERNMENT.
Westphal, Siegrid, 1963- Kaiserliche Rechtsprechung und herrschaftliche Stabilisierung. Köln : Böhlau, 2002.

Thürlemann, Felix.
Die Unvermeidlichkeit der Bilder. Tübingen : G. Narr, c2001.
N72.A56 U58 2001x

Thurnherr, Urs. Vernetzte Ethik : zur Moral und Ethik von Lebensformen / Urs Thurnherr. Freiburg : Alber, 2001. 288 p. ; 22 cm. (Alber-Reihe Praktische Philosophie ; Bd. 70) Originally presented as the author's habilitation (Basel) under the title: "Vernetzte Ethik. Entwurf einer 'Ethik der Typen' und vorbereitende Gedanken zu einer Prä-Ethik.". Includes bibliographical references and indexes. ISBN 3-495-48047-1
1. Conduct of life. 2. Ethics. I. Title. II. Series.

Thye, Shane R.
Group cohesion, trust and solidarity. 1st ed. Amsterdam ; New York : JAI, 2002.

Tiberghien, Gilles A., 1953- Amitier / Gilles A. Tiberghien. Paris : Desclée de Brouwer, c2002. 173 p. ; 21 cm. (Collection DDB) (Philosophie) Includes bibliographical references. ISBN 2-220-05017-3 DDC 194
1. Friendship. 2. Philosophy. I. Title. II. Series. III. Series: Philosophie (Desclée De Brouwer (Firm))

TIBET (CHINA) - MISCELLANEA.
Moon, Peter. The black sun. New York : Sky Books, c1997.
BF1434.U6 M66 1997

TIBETAN LITERATURE - HISTORY AND CRITICISM.
Bod Rgya rtsom rig gśib bsdur gyi dpyad brjod. Par theṅs 1. Pe-cin : Mi rigs dpe skrun khaṅ, 2001.
PL3705 (P-PZ22)+

The Tibetan oracle : ancient wisdom for everyday guidance / Roger Housden, Stephen Hodge. 1st ed. New York : Harmony Books, c1998. 109 p. : ill. ; 18 cm. Three traditional-style bar dice with velvet carrying pouch in box. ISBN 0-609-60164-4 (pbk.) DDC 133.3/09515
1. Divination - China - Tibet. I. Housden, Roger. II. Hodge, Stephen, 1947-
BF1773.2.C5 T43 1998

Tie bi jin zhen.
Lin, Shu, 1852-1924. Di 1 ban. Tianjin Shi : Bai hua wen yi chu ban she, 2002.
PL2718.I5 T54 2002

Tiedemann, Rolf.
Adorno, Theodor W., 1903-1969. [Ob nach Auschwitz noch sich leben lasse. English] Can one live after Auschwitz? Stanford, Calif. : Stanford University Press, 2003.
B3199.A33 O213 2003

Tiedens, Larissa Z.
The social life of emotions. New York : Cambridge University Press, 2004.
BF531 .S634 2004

Tiempo y verdad en la literatura.
Vergara, Gloria, 1964- 1a. ed. México, D.F. : Universidad Iberoamericana, 2001.

Tiere des klassischen Altertums in kulturgeschichtlicher Beziehung.
Keller, Otto, 1838-1920. [Thiere des klassischen Alterthums in kulturgeschichtlicher Beziehung] Hildesheim : Olms, c2001, 1887.

La tierra nueva : ensayos sobre una cultura de la paz y la no violencia / Abelardo Barra Ruatta, compilador. Río Cuarto, Argentina : Universidad Nacional de Río Cuarto, Facultad de Ciencias Humanas, Centro de Estudios y Actividades para una Cultura de la Paz, 2000. 170 p. ; 26 cm. Includes bibliographical references.
1. Peace. 2. Nonviolence. I. Barra Ruatta, Abelardo, 1953-

Tierrechte, Menschenpflichten
(Bd. 3) Brüder, Bestien, Automaten. 1. Aufl. Erlangen : H. Fischer, c2000.

Tietz, Udo. Ontologie und Dialektik : Heidegger und Adorno über das Sein, das Nichtidentische, die Synthesis und die Kopula / Udo Tietz. Wien : Passagen, c2003. 159 p. ; 21 cm. (Passagen Philosophie) Includes bibliographical references (p.151-159). ISBN 3-85165-542-7 DDC 111
1. Heidegger, Martin, - 1889-1976. 2. Adorno, Theodor W., - 1903-1969. 3. Ontology. 4. Dialectic. I. Title. II. Series.
B3279.H49 T54 2003

Tiger Woods Foundation.
Woods, Earl, 1932- Start something. New York : Simon & Schuster, c2000.
BJ1631 .W726 2000

Tijan Bangura, Abubakar. The truth can be discovered in the Qur'an / Abubakar Tijan Banura. [Freetown, Sierra Leone : s.n., 2002] 40 p. ; 19 cm. "Improved edition."
1. Islam - Relations - Christianity. 2. Islam - Africa. 3. Koran and philosophy. 4. Christianity and other religions. 5. Religion. 6. Truth. 7. Black author. I. Title.

Tikhomirov, Oleg Konstantinovich.
Tvorcheskoe nasledie A.V. Brushlinskogo i O.K. Tikhomirova i sovremennai͡a psikhologii͡a myshlenii͡a (k 70-letii͡u so dni͡a rozhdenii͡a). Moskva : In-t psikhologii RAN, 2003.
BF109.B86 T86 2003

TIKHOMIROV, OLEG KONSTANTINOVICH - CONGRESSES.
Tvorcheskoe nasledie A.V. Brushlinskogo i O.K. Tikhomirova i sovremennai͡a psikhologii͡a myshlenii͡a (k 70-letii͡u so dni͡a rozhdenii͡a). Moskva : In-t psikhologii RAN, 2003.
BF109.B86 T86 2003

TIKKUNEI ZOHAR - COMMENTARIES.
Alter, Judah Aryeh Leib, 1847-1905. [Śefat emet (Torah). Selections] Sefer Śefat emet. Yerushalayim : Mir, 762 [2001 or 2002]

Tiḳune ha-Zohar.
Alter, Judah Aryeh Leib, 1847-1905. [Śefat emet (Torah). Selections] Sefer Śefat emet. Yerushalayim : Mir, 762 [2001 or 2002]

Till, Geoffrey.
The challenges of high command. Houndmills, Basingstoke ; New York : Palgrave Macmillan, 2003.
UB210 .C477 2003

Tilley, Debbie.
Brian, Sarah Jane. The quiz book 2. Middleton, Wis. : Pleasant Co. , c2001.
BF831 .B75 2001

TILOPĀDA, 988-1069.
Osho, 1931-1990. Tantra, the supreme understanding. Delhi : Full Circle, 1999.
BP605.R34 T367 1999

Tilton, Hereward. The quest for the phoenix : spiritual alchemy and Rosicrucianism in the work of Count Michael Maier (1569-1622) / by Hereward Tilton. Berlin ; New York : Walter de Gruyter, 2003. 322 p. : ill. ; 24 cm. (Arbeiten zur Kirchengeschichte ; Bd. 88) Includes bibliographical references and index. ISBN 3-11-017637-8 (cl.)
1. Maier, Michael, - 1568?-1622. 2. Alchemy - History. 3. Rosicrucians - History. 4. Jungian psychology. I. Title. II. Series.
QD24.M3 T558 2003

TIMBER. *See* **TREES.**

Timbers, Sylvia, 1955-.
Redfield, James. God and the evolving universe. New York : Jeremy P. Tarcher/Putnam, c2002.
BD541.R43 2002

TIME. *See also* **NIGHT.**
Agacinski, Sylviane. [Passeur de temps. English] Time passing. New York : Columbia University Press, c2003.
BD638.A27713 2003

Aveni, Anthony F. Empires of time. Rev. ed. Boulder, Colo. : University Press of Colorado, c2002.
QB209.A94 2002

Galison, Peter Louis. Einstein's clocks, Poincaré's maps. 1st ed. New York : W.W. Norton, c2003.
QB209.G35 2003

Hägglund, Martin. Kronofobi. Stockholm : B. Östlings Bokförlag Symposion, 2002.

Orosz, László Wladimir. A jelen és az idő. Debrecen : Stalker Stúdió, 2001.
BF1999.O69 2000

Sandbothe, Mike, 1961- [Verzeitlichung der Zeit. English] The temporalization of time. Lanham, MD : Rowman & Littlefield, c2001.
BD638.S27 2001

Vergara, Gloria, 1964- Tiempo y verdad en la literatura. 1a. ed. México, D.F. : Universidad Iberoamericana, 2001.

Zeit in den Medien, Medien in der Zeit. München : Fink, c2002.

Zerubavel, Eviatar. Time maps. Chicago : University of Chicago Press, 2003.
BD638.Z48 2003

Time and information management that really works.
Allen, Kathleen R. Los Angeles, Calif : Affinity Pub., c1995.

Time and the technosphere.
Argüelles, José, 1939- Rochester, Vt. : Bear & Co., c2002.
BF1999.A6398 2002

Time capsules.
Jarvis, William E., 1945- Jefferson, N.C. : McFarland & Co., c2003.
CB151.J37 2003

TIME CAPSULES - HISTORY.
Jarvis, William E., 1945- Time capsules. Jefferson, N.C. : McFarland & Co., c2003.
CB151.J37 2003

TIME, COGNITION OF. *See* **TIME PERCEPTION.**

TIME ESTIMATION. *See* **TIME PERCEPTION.**

TIME IN LITERATURE.
Vergara, Gloria, 1964- Tiempo y verdad en la literatura. 1a. ed. México, D.F. : Universidad Iberoamericana, 2001.

TIME IN MUSIC.
Gavalchin, John. Temporality in music. 2000.

Time in psychoanalysis.
Green, André. London ; New York : Free Association Books, 2002.
BF468.G6713 2002

TIME MANAGEMENT.
Allen, David, 1945 Dec. 28- Ready for anything. New York : Viking, 2003.
BF637.T5 A46 2003

Allen, Kathleen R. Time and information management that really works. Los Angeles, Calif : Affinity Pub., c1995.

Making time. Oxford ; New York : Oxford University Press, 2002.
HD69.T54 M34 2002

Opata, Damian U. (Damian Ugwutikiri) Towards a genealogy of African time. Nsukka, Nigeria : AP Express Publishing Company Lt., 2001.
1. Black author.

Time maps.
Zerubavel, Eviatar. Chicago : University of Chicago Press, 2003.
BD638.Z48 2003

Time matters : global and local time in Asian societies / editors, Willem van Schendel and Henk Schulte Nordholt. Amsterdam : VU University Press, 2001. 140 p. : ill. ; 24 cm. (Comparative Asian studies ; 21) Includes bibliographical references (p. [131]-140). ISBN 90-5383-745-0 DDC 304.2/3
1. Time perception - Asia - Cross-cultural studies. 2. Time - Social aspects - Asia - Cross-cultural studies. 3. Asia - History - Chronology. I. Schendel, Willem van. II. Schulte Nordholt, Henk, 1953- III. Series.
BF468.T555 2001

Time passing.
Agacinski, Sylviane. [Passeur de temps. English] New York : Columbia University Press, c2003.
BD638.A27713 2003

TIME - PERCEPTION. *See* **TIME PERCEPTION.**

TIME PERCEPTION.
Berezina, T. N. Mnogomernaia psikhika. Moskva : PER SĖ, 2001.
BF468.B47 2001

Gavalchin, John. Temporality in music. 2000.

Green, André. Time in psychoanalysis. London ; New York : Free Association Books, 2002.
BF468.G6713 2002

Opata, Damian U. (Damian Ugwutikiri) Towards a genealogy of African time. Nsukka, Nigeria : AP Express Publishing Company Lt., 2001.
1. Black author.

TIME PERCEPTION - ASIA - CROSS-CULTURAL STUDIES.
Time matters. Amsterdam : VU University Press, 2001.
BF468.T555 2001

TIME PERCEPTION - CROSS-CULTURAL STUDIES.
Litvinović, Gorjana. Čovek izmedu istorijskog i ličnog vremena. Beograd : Institut za psihologiju, 2001.
BF697.L543 2001

TIME - PHILOSOPHY.
Opata, Damian U. (Damian Ugwutikiri) Towards a genealogy of African time. Nsukka, Nigeria : AP Express Publishing Company Lt., 2001.
1. Black author.

TIME - PSYCHOLOGICAL ASPECTS.
Berezina, T. N. Mnogomernaia psikhika. Moskva : PER SĖ, 2001.
BF468.B47 2001

Givhan, Walter D. The time value of military force in modern warfare [electronic resource]. Maxwell Air Force Base, Ala. : Air University Press, [1996]

Green, André. La diachronie en psychanalyse. Paris : Minuit, c2000.
BF468.G66 2000

Green, André. Time in psychoanalysis. London ; New York : Free Association Books, 2002.
BF468.G6713 2002

Social conceptions of time. Houndmills, Basingstoke, Hampshire ; New York : Palgrave MacMillan, 2002.
HM656.S63 2002

TIME - RELIGIOUS ASPECTS - HINDUISM.
Venkatanāthārya. [Daśanirnayī] Vaidikasārvabhaumanāmnā suprasiddhaih Venkatanāthāryaih Vaidikakarmānusthānasaukaryāya viracitā Daśanirnayī. 1st ed. Mumbai : Śrīmadahobilamathena, 1998.
BL1226.72.V36 1998

TIME-SERIES ANALYSIS.
Sprott, Julien C. Chaos and time-series analysis. Oxford ; New York : Oxford University Press, 2003.

TIME - SOCIAL ASPECTS.
Social conceptions of time. Houndmills, Basingstoke, Hampshire ; New York : Palgrave MacMillan, 2002.
HM656.S63 2002

TIME - SOCIAL ASPECTS - ASIA - CROSS-CULTURAL STUDIES.
Time matters. Amsterdam : VU University Press, 2001.
BF468.T555 2001

TIME - SOCIAL ASPECTS - NIGERIA.
Opata, Damian U. (Damian Ugwutikiri) Towards a genealogy of African time. Nsukka, Nigeria : AP Express Publishing Company Lt., 2001.
1. Black author.

TIME - SOCIOLOGICAL ASPECTS.
Opata, Damian U. (Damian Ugwutikiri) Towards a genealogy of African time. Nsukka, Nigeria : AP Express Publishing Company Lt., 2001.
1. Black author.

The time value of military force in modern warfare [electronic resource].
Givhan, Walter D. Maxwell Air Force Base, Ala. : Air University Press, [1996]

The Times book of IQ tests. Book 1.
Russell, Kenneth, 1928- London : Kogan Page, 2001.

The Times book of IQ tests. Book 2.
Russell, Kenneth, 1928- London ; Milford, CT : Kogan Page, 2002.

The Times book of IQ tests. Book 3.
Russell, Kenneth A. London ; Sterling, VA : Kogan Page Ltd., 2003.
BF431.3.R87 2003

Times Newspapers.
Russell, Kenneth, 1928- The Times book of IQ tests. Book 2. London ; Milford, CT : Kogan Page, 2002.

TIMIDITY. *See* **BASHFULNESS.**

The timing of events.
Behari, Bepin. 1st ed. Delhi : Motilal Banarsidass Publishers, 2002.
BF1720.5+

Timmers, Teun.
A parliament of science. Albany : State University of New York Press, c2003.
Q158.5.P38 2003

Timmons, Mark, 1951- Moral theory : an introduction / Mark Timmons. Lanham, Md. : Rowman & Littlefield Publishers, c2002. x, 291 p. : ill. ; 23 cm. (Elements of philosophy) Includes bibliographical references and index. CONTENTS: An introduction to moral theory -- Divine command theory -- Moral relativism -- Natural law theory -- Classical utilitarianism -- Contemporary utilitarianism -- Kant's moral theory -- Moral pluralism -- Virtue ethics -- Moral particularism -- Conclusion -- Appendix: Standards for evaluating moral theories. ISBN 0-8476-9768-1 (alk. paper) ISBN 0-8476-9769-X (pbk. : alk. paper) DDC 171
1. Ethics. I. Title. II. Series.
BJ1012.T56 2002

Tipiṭaka. Suttapiṭaka. Khuddakanikāya. Jātaka. Manikanthajataka.
The jewel of friendship. Berkeley, CA : Dharma Pub., 2002.
BQ1462.E5 J48 2002

Tipler, Paul Allen, 1933- Modern physics / Paul A. Tipler, Ralph A. Llewellyn. 4th ed. New York : W.H. Freeman, 2002 printing, c2003. 1 v. (various pagings) : ill. ; 27 cm. Includes index. ISBN 0-7167-4345-0 DDC 530
1. Physics. I. Llewellyn, Ralph A. II. Title.
QC21.3.T56 2003

TIPPETT, MICHAEL, 1905-. CHILD OF OUR TIME.
Lathan, Mark J., 1961- Emotional progression in sacred choral music. 2001.

Tipping, Colin C. Radical forgiveness : making room for the miracle / by Colin C. Tipping. Atlanta, GA : GOLDENeight Publishers, c1997. 281 p. : ill. ; 22 cm. ISBN 1-89041-203-1 DDC 158.2
1. Forgiveness. 2. Interpersonal relations. I. Title.
BF637.F67 T57 1997

Tips for protecting your personal information.
Privacy [electronic resource]. [Washington, D.C.] : Federal Trade Commission, Bureau of Consumer Protection, Office of Consumer and Business Education, [2002]

Tips, Jack. Passion play / by Jack Tips. 1st ed. Austin, Tex. : Apple-A-Day Press, c2002. 286 p. : ill. ; 23 cm. ISBN 0-929167-20-1 DDC 158
1. Achievement motivation. 2. Success - Psychological aspects. 3. Goal (Psychology) I. Title.
BF503.T56 2002

A tirania de Narciso.
Campos, Edemilson Antunes de. 1. ed. São Paulo, SP, Brasil : Annablume/FAPESP, 2001.

Tirrito, Terry, 1945-.
Religious organizations in community services. New York : Springer Pub., 2003.
HV530 .R25 2003

TISHRI.
Levin, Yitshak, 1938- Sefer Netivot Yitshak. [Bene Berak] : Y. Levin, [2000-

Titania's book of hours.
Hardie, Titania. London : Quadrille, 2002.

Titania's magical compendium.
Hardie, Titania. San Diego, Calif. : Thunder Bay Press, 2003.
BF1611 .H235 2003

TITLES OF HONOR AND NOBILITY. *See* **NOBILITY.**

Titmuss, Christopher.
The Buddha's book of daily meditations. 1st ed. New York : Three Rivers Press, c2001.
BQ5579 .B83 2001

Titurel.
Wolfram, von Eschenbach, 12th cent. Berlin ; New York : Walter de Gruyter, 2002.

Titurel : Text, Übersetzung, Kommentar, Materialien.
Wolfram, von Eschenbach, 12th cent. Titurel. Berlin ; New York : Walter de Gruyter, 2002.

Tivārī, Rājīva.
Asalī prācīna Vaidika vāstu śāstra. 1. saṃskaraṇa. Dillī : Manoja Pôkeṭa Buksa, [2002?]
BF1729.A7 A83 2002

Śarmā, Kisanalāla. Lāla kitāba. 1. saṃskaraṇa. Dillī : Manoja Pôkeṭa Buksa, [2000?]
BF1714.H5+

Tkach, Mykola. Volodymyrovi bohy : mifolohichnyĭ zmist ta systematyzatsiia holovnykh personazhiv iazychnyts'koho kul'tu / Mykola Tkach. Kyïv : Ukraïns'kyĭ tsentr dukhovnoï kul'tury, 2002. 187 p. : ill. ; 20 cm. ISBN 9666280523
1. Vladimir, - Grand Duke of Kiev, - ca. 956-1015 - Cult. 2. Mythology, Slavic. 3. Paganism - Kievan Rus. I. Title.
DK75 .T53 2002

TLAXCALAN CALENDAR.
Messenger, Charles M. Nine Wind Tonalamatl Tolteca-fate papers. [United States] : C.M. Messenger, c2002-
BF1861 .M47 2002

To the Finland station.
Wilson, Edmund, 1895-1972. New York : New York Review of Books, 2003.
HX36 .W5 2003

TOBACCO HABIT. *See* **SMOKING.**

TOBACCO SMOKING. *See* **SMOKING.**

Tobias, Michael.
A parliament of science. Albany : State University of New York Press, c2003.
Q158.5 .P38 2003

Den Tod denken.
Bahr, Hans-Dieter. München : Fink, 2002.

Tod und Alterität.
Han, Byung-Chul. München : Fink, c2002.
BD444 .H36 2002

Toda, Takako. Second language speech perception and production : acquisition of phonological contrasts in Japanese / Takako Toda. Lanham, Md. ; Oxford : University Press of America, c2003. 213 p. : ill. ; 23 cm. Includes bibliographical references (p. [179]-207) and index. ISBN 0-7618-2586-X (cloth : alk. paper) DDC 495.6/8
1. Japanese language - Phonology. 2. Speech perception. 3. Second language acquisition - Methodology. I. Title.
PL541 .T63 2003

Today matters.
Maxwell, John C., 1947- New York : Warner Books, 2004.
BF637.S8 M3423 2004

Todd, Peaco.
Middelton-Moz, Jane, 1947- Good and mad. Deerfield Beach, Fla. : Health Communications Inc., c2003.
BF575.A5 M519 2003

Todd, Zazie.
Mixing methods in psychology. New York : Psychology Press, 2004.

BF76.5 .M59 2004

Toddler.
Disney's Mickey Mouse toddler [electronic resource]. Burbank, CA : Disney Interactive, c2000.
BF719

Toddler with active leveling advantage.
Disney's Mickey Mouse toddler [electronic resource]. Burbank, CA : Disney Interactive, c2000.
BF719

TODDLERS - PSYCHOLOGY - JUVENILE SOFTWARE.
Disney's Mickey Mouse toddler [electronic resource]. Burbank, CA : Disney Interactive, c2000.
BF719

Todeschi, Kevin J. Soul signs : life seals, aura charts, and the revelation / by Kevin J. Todeschi. Virginia Beach, Va. : A.R.E. Press, c2003. xix, 210 p., 16 p. of plates : col. ill. ; 21 cm. Includes bibliographical references (p. 209-210). Table of contents URL: http://www.loc.gov/catdir/toc/ecip044/2003011321.html ISBN 0-87604-476-3 (pbk.) DDC 131
1. Self-actualization (Psychology) - Miscellanea. 2. Symbolism (Psychology) - Miscellanea. I. Title.
BF1045.S44 T63 2003

Together yet apart : Jews and Christians in the Medieval Iberian Peninsula.
Meyuhas Ginio, Alisa, 1937- Kerovim u-reḥokim. Tel Aviv : Mif'alim Universiṭayim, 760 [1999]

Tognetti, Arlene. The complete idiot's guide to tarot / by Arlene Tognetti and Lisa Lenard. 2nd ed. Indianapolis, IN : Alpha, c2003. xix, 363 p. : ill. ; 24 cm. Includes index. ISBN 1-59257-066-6 (pbk.) DDC 133.3/2424
1. Tarot. I. Lenard-Cook, Lisa. II. Title. III. Title: Tarot
BF1879.T2 T64 2003

TOILET (GROOMING). *See* **BEAUTY, PERSONAL.**

Tokar, David A. Hans Kayser's Lehrbuch der Harmonik : an annotated translation of the preface and introduction, together with a critical evaluation of Kayser's contribution and influence / by David A. Tokar. 2002. xii, 238 leaves : ill. "May, 2002." Thesis (doctoral)--Rutgers University, 2002. Includes vita. Includes bibliographical references. Photocopy. Ann Arbor, Mich. : UMI Dissertation Services, 2003. 22 cm.
1. Kayser, Hans, - 1891-1964. - Lehrbuch der Harmonik. 2. Harmonics (Music) 3. Music theory. 4. Music - Religious aspects. 5. Harmony of the spheres. 6. Music - Acoustics and physics. 7. Cosmology. 8. Pythagoras and Pythagorean school. I. Kayser, Hans, 1891-1964. Lehrbuch der Harmonik. English. Selections. 2002. II. Title.

Toland, Diane. Inner pathways to the divine : exploring your spiritual self through the tarot's major mentors / by Diane Toland. Hygiene, CO : SunShine Press Publications, c2001. 128 p. : ill. ; 22 cm. Includes bibliographical references (p. 126). ISBN 1-88860-417-4 (alk. paper)
1. Tarot. 2. Spiritual life. I. Title.
BF1879.T2 T65 2001

Tolchard, Guylaine. The H-factor : solving the hidden puzzles of feelings! / Guylaine Tolchard and James Tolchard. Cary, N.C. : Process Viewpoint Pub., c2002. 305 p. ; 22 cm. (The processology of human dynamics series) Includes bibliographical references (p. [299]-302). ISBN 0-9718906-0-9 DDC 152.4
1. Emotions. I. Tolchard, James. II. Title. III. Series: Tolchard, Guylaine. Processology of human dynamics series.
BF511 .T65 2002

Processology of human dynamics series.
Tolchard, Guylaine. The H-factor. Cary, N.C. : Process Viewpoint Pub., c2002.
BF511 .T65 2002

Tolchard, James.
Tolchard, Guylaine. The H-factor. Cary, N.C. : Process Viewpoint Pub., c2002.
BF511 .T65 2002

Ṭoledano, Avraham ben Shemu'el.
Abi-Ḥaṣira, Jacob ben Masoud, 1808-1880. [Abir Ya'akov. Selections. 2002] Sefer Penine Avir Ya'akov. Yerushalayim : Hotsa'at ha-Makhon le-hotsa'at sefarim she-'a. y. Yeshivat Ner Yitshak : Mekhon Avraham : Shim'on Abiḥatsira, 763 [2002]
BS1485.X33 A25 2002

TOLERANCE, RELIGIOUS. *See* **RELIGIOUS TOLERANCE.**

TOLERATION. *See also* **DISCRIMINATION; RELIGIOUS TOLERANCE.**
Creppell, Ingrid. Toleration and identity. New York ; London : Routledge, 2003.

HM1271 .C73 2003

Denisovskiĭ, G. M. Politicheskaia tolerantnost' v reformiruemom rossiĭskom obshchestve vtoroĭ poloviny 90-kh godov. Moskva : TSentr obshchechelovecheskikh tsennosteĭ, 2002.
JN6699.A15 D46 2002

Holt, W. V. America by trial. München : Tuduv, c2001.

Moreno-Riaño, Gerson, 1971- Political tolerance, culture, and the individual. Lewiston, N.Y. : E. Mellen Press, c2002.
JA74.5 .M653 2002

Peace and conflict resolution. Part 1 [videorecording]. Derry, N.H. : Chip Taylor Communications, 1996.

Peace and conflict resolution. Part 2 [videorecording]. Derry, N.H. : Chip Taylor Communications, 1997.

Toleration and identity.
Creppell, Ingrid. New York ; London : Routledge, 2003.
HM1271 .C73 2003

Tolsdorf, Samuel, 1926- The theory of reality / Samuel Tolsdorf. Vancouver, B.C. : Leumas Publications, [1998] 132 p. : ill. ; 20 cm. ISBN 0-9684725-0-8
1. Prophecies (Occultism) 2. Civilization - Forecasting. 3. Human beings - Forecasting. I. Title.
BF1999 .T62 1998

Tomás Ferré, Facundo. Formas artísticas y sociedad de masas : elementos para una genealogía del gusto : el entresiglos XIX-XX / Facundo Tomás. Madrid : Antonio Machado Libros, c2001. 273 p. ; 22 cm. (La balsa de la Medusa ; 121) Includes bibliographical references (p. 261-273). ISBN 84-7774-621-4
1. Art and literature. 2. Aesthetics. 3. Literature. 4. Mass society. I. Title. II. Series: Balsa de Medusa (Series) ; 121.

Tomasello, Michael. Constructing a language : a usage-based theory of language acquisition / Michael Tomasello. Cambridge, Mass. : Harvard University Press, 2003. viii, 388 p. : ill. ; 25 cm. Includes bibliographical references (p. [331]-371) and index. ISBN 0-674-01030-2 DDC 401/.93
1. Language acquisition. 2. Cognition in children. I. Title.
P118 .T558 2003

Tomorrow now.
Sterling, Bruce. 1st ed. New York : Random House, c2002.
HM901 .S74 2002

Tomorrow's God.
Walsch, Neale Donald. 1st ed. New York : Atria Books, 2004.
BF1999 .W2288 2004

TOMORROW'S LEADERS CONFERENCE (1995 : VENICE, ITALY).
Peace and conflict resolution. Part 1 [videorecording]. Derry, N.H. : Chip Taylor Communications, 1996.

Tompkins, Sue. Aspects in astrology : a comprehensive guide to interpretation / Sue Tompkins. London : Rider, 2001. xii, 298 p. : ill. ; 24 cm. Originally published: Shaftesbury : Element Books Ltd., 1989. Includes bibliographical references (p. [297]-298). ISBN 0-7126-1104-5 DDC 133.5/3044
1. Aspect (Astrology) I. Title.
BF1717.2 .T65 2001

Tomskiĭ gosudarstvennyĭ universitet.
Vserossiĭskaia konferentsiia "Mezhdistsiplinarnyĭ sintez v metodologii gumanitarnykh issledovaniĭ" (2002 : Tomsk, Russia) Lichnost' v paradigmakh i metaforakh. Tomsk : Tomskiĭ gos. universitet, 2002.
BF698 .V74 2002

Tonalamatl Tolteca.
Messenger, Charles M. Nine Wind Tonalamatl Tolteca-fate papers. [United States] : C.M. Messenger, c2002-
BF1861 .M47 2002

Tong jing.
Sima, Lieren. Di 1 ban. Beijing : Zhongguo hua qiao chu ban she, 2002.
DS758.23.T74 S575 2002

Tongeren, Paul van.
Searching for peace in Central and South Asia. Boulder, Colo. : Lynne Rienner Publishers, 2002.
JZ5597 .S43 2002

Tonn, Joan C. Mary P. Follett : creating democracy, transforming management / Joan C. Tonn. New Haven [Conn.] : Yale University Press, c2003. xiv, 623 p. : ill. ; 25 cm. Includes bibliographical references (p. 497-603) and index. CONTENTS: A childhood that was rarely happy -- "An eager, fearless mind" -- "What shall we do with

our girls?" -- "Very unusual privileges" -- "The great milepost and turning point" -- The speaker of the House of Representatives -- "To L.L.B." -- Self-realization and service -- Ward 17 -- Substitutes for the saloon, schools, and suffrage -- Private funds for public purposes -- "My beloved centres" -- The functions, financing, and control of community centers -- The war years -- The new state -- Not neighborhood groups but an integrative group process -- "Too good a joke for the world" -- Creative experience -- Professional transition, personal tragedy -- "You have been extraordinarily helpful to executives" -- "I am almost at the same moment happy and unhappy" -- "Prepared to go or stay with equal graciousness". ISBN 0-300-09621-6 (hc : alk. paper) DDC 303.48/4/092
1. Follett, Mary Parker, - 1868-1933. 2. Women social reformers - United States - Biography. 3. Social reformers - United States - Biography. 4. Social structure. 5. Democracy. 6. Management. 7. Psychology, Industrial. I. Title.
HN57 .T695 2003

Tonnac, Jean-Philippe de.
Droit, Roger-Pol. Fous comme des sages. Paris : Seuil, c2002.

Tonoiu, Vasile. Omul dialogal : un concept răspîntie. București : Editura Fundației Culturale Române, 1995. 369 p. ; 20 cm. Includes bibliographical references. ISBN 9739155464
1. Dialogue. 2. Interpersonal communication. 3. Interpersonal relations. I. Title.

Tonolo, Giorgio. Adolescenza e identità / Giorgio Tonolo. Bologna : Il mulino, c1999. 333 p. ; 22 cm. (Studi e ricerche ; 437) Empirical study on youth in Italy. Includes bibliographical references. ISBN 88-15-07147-4 DDC 305
1. Identity (Psychology) in youth. 2. Adolescence - Italy. I. Title.
BF724.3.I3 T65 1999

Too blessed to be stressed.
Johnson Cook, Suzan D. (Suzan Denise), 1957- Nashville, Tenn. : T. Nelson, c1998.
BV4527 .J65 1998

Too, Lillian. Discover yourself : understand your mind, know your body, nurture your spirit, realize your potential / Lillian Too. Carlsbad, Calif. : Hay House, c2002 (2003 printing) 224 p. : ill. (chiefly col.) ; 26 cm. Includes index. ISBN 1401901522 DDC 158.1
1. Self-perception. I. Title.
BF697.5.S43 T66 2002

TOOL USE IN ANIMALS.
Baber, Christopher, 1964- Cognition and tool use. London ; New York : Taylor & Francis, 2003.
BF311 .B228 2003

Tooley, James. The miseducation of women / James Tooley. London ; New York : Continuum, 2002. viii, 258, [6] p. ; 24 cm. Includes bibliographical references (p. 247-258) and index. ISBN 0-8264-5094-6 ISBN 0-8264-5095-4 (pbk.) DDC 305.42
1. Feminism - History - 20th century. 2. Feminism. 3. Feminism and education. 4. Sex differences in education. 5. Women - Education - Social aspects. I. Title.
HQ1154 .T64 2002

TOOLS.
Baber, Christopher, 1964- Cognition and tool use. London ; New York : Taylor & Francis, 2003.
BF311 .B228 2003

Toomela, Aaro. Cultural-historical psychology : three levels of analysis / Aaro Toomela. Tartu : Tartu University Press, c2000. 170 p. : ill. ; 26 cm. (Dissertationes psychologicae Universitatis Tartuensis, 1024-3291 ; 7) Text in English with some Russian; summary in Estonian. Includes bibliographical references. ISBN 9985564804 DDC 150
1. Vygotskiĭ, L. S. - (Lev Semenovich), - 1896-1934. 2. Psychology. 3. Social psychology. I. Title. II. Series.
BF109.V95 T66 2000

Top shuang xin jia ting.
Hobfoll, Stevan E. [Work won't love you back. Chinese] Chu ban. Taibei Shi : Ye qiang chu ban she, 1997.

Topchik, Gary S. The accidental manager : get the skills you need to excel in your new career / Gary S. Topchik. [1st ed.]. New York : AMACOM, c2004. ix, 180 p. : ill. ; 23 cm. Includes index. ISBN 0-8144-7180-3 DDC 658.4/09
1. Management. I. Title.
HD31 .T6368 2004

Topics in cognitive psychology / Serge P. Shohov, editor. New York : Nova Science Publishers, 2003. p. cm. Includes bibliographical references and index. Table of contents URL: http://www.loc.gov/catdir/toc/ecip047/2003017280.html ISBN 1-59033-836-7 DDC 153
1. Cognitive psychology. I. Shohov, Serge P.

BF201 .T67 2003

Topische Ästhetik.
Demuth, Volker. Würzburg : Königshausen & Neumann, c2002.

Topographies of power in the early Middle Ages / edited by Mayke de Jong and Francis Theuws with Carine van Rhijn. Leiden ; Boston : Brill, 2001. x, 609 p. : ill., maps ; 25 cm. (The transformation of the Roman world, 1386-4165 ; v. 6) ISBN 90-04-11734-2
1. Middle Ages - History. 2. Power (Social sciences) I. De Jong, Mayke. II. Thewes, F. (Frans) III. Rhijn, Carine van. IV. Series.
D117 .T67 2001

TOPOI (ASTROLOGY). See **HOUSES (ASTROLOGY).**

Topoi library
(v. 3) Bencivenga, Ermanno, 1950- Exercises in constructive imagination. Dordrecht ; Boston : Kluwer Academic Publishers, c2001.
B3613.B3853 E93 2001

Torah mi-tokh ha-deḥaḳ.
Ḳuntres Ḳevod ha-Torah. Bene Beraḳ : ha-Meḥaber, 761 [2000 or 2001]

Torapiah.
Lamdan, Elimelekh. Yerushalayim : Feldhaim, 762 [2002]

Torat Avigdor.
Miler, Avigdor Hakohen. Sefer Torat Avigdor. Bene Braḳ : [ḥ. mo. l], 762- [2001 or 2002-

Torat ha-ḥalom ba-Yahadut.
Sheḳalim, Rami. Tel Aviv : R. Sheḳalim, 762, 2002.

Torat ḥovat ha-levavot ha-mefo'ar.
Baḥya ben Joseph ibn Paḳuda, 11th cent. [Hidāyah ilá farā'iḍ al-qulūb] Nyu York : Y. Vais : Star Ḳompozishan : [Hotsa'at Ateret], 760 [2000]

Torat ḥovot ha-levavot ha-mefo'ar.
Baḥya ben Joseph ibn Paḳuda, 11th cent. [Hidāyah ilá farā'iḍ al-qulūb] Torat ḥovat ha-levavot ha-mefo'ar. Nyu York : Y. Vais : Star Ḳompozishan : [Hotsa'at Ateret], 760 [2000]

Torat Mosheh.
Alshekh, Moses, 16th cent. [Torat Mosheh. Selections] Sefer 'Orot ha-Alshekh. Yerushalayim : [ḥ. mo. l.], 763 [2002 or 2003]

Torat rabi Yiśra'el mi-Salanṭ.
Salanter, Israel, 1810-1883. Sefer Torat rabi Yiśra'el mi-Salanṭ. Yerushalayim : [ḥ. mo. l], 763 [2003]

Torgashev, G. A.
Beliaev, G. G. Dukhovnye korni russkogo naroda. Moskva : Bylina, 2002.
DK32 .B358 2002

Toronto Italian studies
Roush, Sherry. Hermes' lyre. Toronto : University of Toronto Press, c2002.

Toronto studies in philosophy
Johns, Richard, 1968- A theory of physical probability. Toronto : University of Toronto Press, c2002.

Toronto studies in semiotics and communication
Merrell, Floyd, 1937- Sensing corporeally. Toronto ; Buffalo : University of Toronto Press, c2003.
P99 .M477 2003

Toropov, Brandon. The complete idiot's guide to Taoism / by Brandon Toropov and Chad Hansen. Indianapolis, IN : Alpha, c2002. xx, 315 p. ; 23 cm. Includes bibliographical references (p. [273]-275) and index. ISBN 0-02-864262-7 DDC 299/.514
1. Taoism. I. Hansen, Chad, 1942- II. Title. III. Title: Taoism
BL1920 .T67 2002

Torre, Francisco Javier de la. Aproximación a las fuentes clásicas latinas de Hannah Arendt / Francisco Javier de la Torre. Málaga : Universidad de Málaga, 2002. 116 p. ; 24 cm. (Analecta malacitana. Anejos ; 44) Includes bibliographical references (p. 111-113). ISBN 84-950733-1-5
1. Arendt, Hannah. 2. Philosophy, Ancient. I. Title. II. Series: Anejos de Analecta malacitana ; 44.

Torres, Maruja.
Amores de película. 1. ed. [Madrid] : Aguilar, 2002.
PN1998.2 .A46 2002

TORTS. See **LIBEL AND SLANDER; SEDUCTION.**

Toševski, Jovo. Nerazumna mreža : emocionalna, merorija, polova / Jovo Toševski. Novi Sad : Prometej ; [Kragujevac] : Jefimija, c2002. 262 p. : ill. ; 20 cm. Includes bibliographical references (p. 248-256). ISBN

86-7639-639-6
1. Thought and thinking. 2. Psychology. 3. Memory. I. Title.

Toshchenko, Zhan Terent'evich. Tri osobennykh lika vlasti / Zh.T. Toshchenko. Moskva : RGGU, 2002. 121 p. ; 20 cm. Includes bibliographical references. ISBN 5728105696
1. Power (Social sciences) 2. Political science. 3. Ethnocentrism - Political aspects. 4. Theocracy. 5. Technocracy. 6. Self-determination, National. 7. Nationalism. I. Title.
JC330 .T674 2002

Total palmistry.
Anderson, Rafe. Boston : Red Wheel, 2003.
BF935.L67 A53 2003

Total performance scorecard.
Rampersad, Hubert K. Amsterdam ; Boston ; London : Butterworth-Heinemann, c2003.
HD62.15 .R3598 2003

TOTAL QUALITY MANAGEMENT.
Burke, Dan, 1965- Business @ the speed of stupid. Cambridge, MA : Perseus Pub., c2001.
HD45 .B7995 2001

Rampersad, Hubert K. Total performance scorecard. Amsterdam ; Boston ; London : Butterworth-Heinemann, c2003.
HD62.15 .R3598 2003

Sen, Asim, 1935- Democratic management. Lanham, Md. ; Oxford : University Press of America, c2003.
HD30.65 .S46 2003

TOTALITARIANISM. See also **COMMUNISM; FASCISM; NATIONAL SOCIALISM.**
Fromm, Erich, 1900- Escape from freedom. 1st Owl books ed. New York : H. Holt, 1994.
HM271 .F74 1994

Limonov, Eduard. Distsiplinarnyĭ sanatoriĭ. Sankt-Peterburg : Amfora, 2002.
CB428 .L556 2002

Valle, Alexandre del. Le totalitarisme islamiste à l'assaut des démocraties. Paris : Syrtes, c2002.

Le totalitarisme islamiste à l'assaut des démocraties.
Valle, Alexandre del. Paris : Syrtes, c2002.

Totaro, Francesco, 1941-.
La persona e i nomi dell'essere. Milano : V&P Università, c2002.
B29 .P414 2002

Tou shi Meiguo : jin nian lai Zhongguo de Meiguo yan jiu / Hu Gucheng zhu bian. Di 1 ban. Beijing : Zhongguo she hui ke xue chu ban she : Jing xiao Xin hua shu dian, 2002. 2, 411 p. ; 21 cm. Includes bibliographical references. ISBN 7-5004-3341-7
1. United States - Study and teaching. 2. United States - Politics and government - 20th century. I. Hu, Gucheng. II. Title: Jin nian lai Zhongguo de Meiguo yan jiu
E175.8 .T78 2002

TOUCH.
Linson, William. Kinoetics. [United States] : Kinoetics Publishing, c2002.
BF637.N66 L56 2002

Sensible flesh. Philadelphia, PA : University of Pennsylvania Press, 2003.
BF275 .S46 2003

TOUCH - PSYCHOLOGICAL ASPECTS.
Touching for knowing. Amsterdam ; Philadelphia : John Benjamins Pub., c2003.
BF275 .T69 2003

Touching for knowing : cognitive psychology of haptic manual perception / edited by Yvette Hatwell, Arlette Streri, Edouard Gentaz. Amsterdam ; Philadelphia : John Benjamins Pub., c2003. ix, 320 p. : ill. ; 23 cm. (Advances in consciousness research, 1381-589X ; v. 53) Includes bibliographical references and indexes. ISBN 90-272-5185-1 (Eur. : alk. paper) ISBN 1-58811-423-6 (US : alk. paper) ISBN 90-272-5186-X (Eur. : pbk. : alk. paper) ISBN 1-58811-424-4 (US : pbk. : alk. paper) DDC 152.1/82
1. Touch - Psychological aspects. 2. Visual perception. 3. Perceptual-motor processes. I. Hatwell, Yvette. II. Streri, Arlette. III. Gentaz, Edouard. IV. Series.
BF275 .T69 2003

Tough notes.
Madhubuti, Haki R., 1942- 1st ed. Chicago : Third World Press, c2002.
E185.86 .T68 2002

TOULOUSE, EDOUARD, B. 1865.
Huteau, Michel. Psychologie, psychiatrie et société sous la troisième république. Paris : Harmattan, c2002.

TOURAINE, ALAIN - POLITICAL AND SOCIAL VIEWS.
Benitez, Juan Carlos. El concepto de poder en Alain Touraine. Buenos Aires : Editorial de Belgrano, 2002.
HM479.T6 B455 2002

Le tourbillon des génies.
Hell, Bertrand. Paris : Flammarion, c2002.

TOURNAMENTS. *See* **KNIGHTS AND KNIGHTHOOD.**

Tournier, Michel.
Ecriture et maladie. Paris : Editions Imago, c2003.

Tovray, Sandy.
Barzach, Amy Jaffe. Accidental courage, boundless dreams. 1st ed. West Hartford, CT : Aurora Pub., c2001.
BF575.G7 B375 2001

Toward a phenomenology of sexual difference.
Heinamaa, Sara, 1960- Lanham, Md. ; Oxford : Rowman & Littlefield Publishers, c2003.
HQ1208 .B3523 2003

Toward an integrated perspective on behavior.
Rumbaugh, Duane M., 1929- Respondents, operants, and emergents [microform]. [Washington, D.C. : National Aeronautics and Space Administration, 1997]

Towards a genealogy of African time.
Opata, Damian U. (Damian Ugwutikiri) Nsukka, Nigeria : AP Express Publishing Company Lt., 2001.

Towards the semantic web : ontology-driven knowledge management / edited by John Davies, Dieter Fensel and Frank van Harmelen. Chichester, England ; Hoboken, N.J. : J. Wiley, c2003. xx, 288 p. : ill. ; 24 cm. Includes bibliographical references (p. [267]-279) and index. ISBN 0-470-84867-7 (alk. paper) DDC 006.3/3
1. Semantic web. 2. Ontology. 3. Knowledge acquisition (Expert systems) I. Davies, John. II. Fensel, Dieter. III. Van Harmelen, Frank.
TK5105.88815 .T68 2003

Towards the third millennium.
Ikram Azam, 1940- Islamabad : Pakistan Futuristics Foundation & Institute, c1999.
BF408 .I445 1999

Towler, Solala. Tao paths to love / [Solala Towler]. Kansas City, Mo. : Andrews McMeel Pub., 2002. 463 p. : col. ill. ; 12 cm. First published by MQ Publications in London, 2002. Includes bibliographical references (p. 460-462). ISBN 0-7407-2297-2 (pbk.) DDC 299/.5144
1. Love. 2. Tao. I. Title.
BD436 .T65 2002

TOWN PLANNING. *See* **CITY PLANNING.**

Townley, John, 1945- Lunar returns / John Townley. 1st ed. St. Paul, Minn. : Llewellyn Publications, 2003. ix, 244 p. ; 24 cm. ISBN 0-7387-0302-8 DDC 133.5/32
1. Astrology. 2. Moon - Miscellanea. 3. Human beings - Effect of the moon on. I. Title.
BF1723 .T69 2003

TOWNS. *See* **CITIES AND TOWNS.**

Townsend, John. Mysterious disappearances / John Townsend. Chicago, IL : Raintree, 2004. p. cm. (Out there) SUMMARY: Relates cases of people who have mysteriously disappeared, never to be found. Includes bibliographical references. Table of contents URL: http://www.loc.gov/catdir/toc/ecip043/2003010543.html CONTENTS: Whatever happened? -- Into thin air -- The Bermuda Triangle -- More devil's triangles -- Kidnap or murder? -- Accident or more -- Lost and found -- Fact or fiction. ISBN 1410905616 DDC 001.94
1. Disappearances (Parapsychology) - Juvenile literature. 2. Disappearances (Parapsychology) 3. Missing persons. 4. Curiosities and wonders. I. Title. II. Series.
BF1389.D57 T69 2004

Mysterious encounters / John Townsend. Chicago, IL : Raintree, 2004. p. cm. (Out there) SUMMARY: Explores reports of mysterious objects that have landed on earth, from "frozen water meteorites" to live pink frogs to UFOs, as well as what may still be heading this way. Includes bibliographical references and index. Table of contents URL: http://www.loc.gov/catdir/toc/ecip043/2003010731.html CONTENTS: Falling from the sky -- Encounters of the 1st kind -- Mysteries solved? -- Encounters of the 2nd kind -- Encounters of the 3rd and 4th kinds -- Crashing to earth -- Scanning the skies. ISBN 1410905632 DDC 001.94
1. Human-alien encounters - Juvenile literature. 2. Unidentified flying objects - Juvenile literature. 3. Curiosities and wonders - Juvenile literature. 4. Human-alien encounters. 5. Unidentified flying objects. 6. Science - Miscellanea. 7. Curiosities and wonders. I. Title. II. Series.
BF2050 .T69 2004

Townsend, John, 1955- Mysteries of body and mind / John Townsend. Chicago, IL : Raintree, 2004. v. cm. (Out there?) Includes bibliographical references and index. Table of contents URL: http://www.loc.gov/catdir/toc/ecip043/2003010541.html CONTENTS: Mysteries of the body -- Mysteries of the mind -- Mysteries of sleep -- Twilight world -- Mysteries of life and death -- The weird and wonderful. ISBN 1410905608 DDC 001.94
1. Parapsychology - Juvenile literature. 2. Curiosities and wonders - Juvenile literature. 3. Parapsychology. 4. Curiosities and wonders. I. Title. II. Series: Townsend, John, 1955- Out there?
BF1031 .T65 2004

Mysterious signs / John Townsend. Chicago, IL : Raintree, c2004. v. cm. (Out there?) Includes bibliographical references and index. Table of contents URL: http://www.loc.gov/catdir/toc/ecip045/2003012626.html CONTENTS: Mystery meetings -- Ghosts -- Sightings -- Making contact -- Ghostly places -- Ghostly people -- Ghost FAQs. ISBN 1410905667 DDC 133.1
1. Ghosts - Juvenile literature. 2. Ghosts. I. Title. II. Series: Townsend, John, 1955- Out there?
BF1461 .T69 2004

Out there?
Townsend, John, 1955- Mysteries of body and mind. Chicago, IL : Raintree, 2004.
BF1031 .T65 2004

Townsend, John, 1955- Mysterious signs. Chicago, IL : Raintree, c2004.
BF1461 .T69 2004

Toxic emotions at work.
Frost, Peter J. Boston : Harvard Business School Press, c2003.
HD42 .F76 2003

Tożsamość metamorficzna a komunikacja językowa.
Dobosz, Artur. Poznań : Wydawn. Naukowe Instytutu Filozofii Uniwersytetu im. Adama Mickiewicza w Poznaniu, 2002.

Tra IV e V secolo : studi sulla cultura latina tardoantica / a cura di Isabella Gualandri. Milano : Cisalpino, 2002. x, 331 p. ; 24 cm. (Quaderni di Acme ; 50) Includes bibliographical references and index. At head of title: Università degli studi di Milano. Facoltà di lettere e filosofia. Dipartimento di scienze dell'antichità. Sezione di filologia classica. ISBN 88-323-4612-5
1. Latin literature - History and criticism. 2. Rome - Civilization. I. Gualandri, Isabella. II. Università di Milano. Sezione di filologia classica. III. Title: Tra quarto e quinto secolo IV. Series.

Tra le immagini.
Cherchi, Gavina, 1957- Fiesole (Firenze) : Cadmo ; Siena : Centro Mario Rossi per gli studi filosofici, 2002.

Tra quarto e quinto secolo.
Tra IV e V secolo. Milano : Cisalpino, 2002.

Trabattoni, Franco. La filosofia antica : profilo critico-storico / Franco Trabattoni. 1a ed. Roma : Carocci, 2002. 321 p. ; 22 cm. (Studi superiori ; 416. Filosofia) Includes bibliographical references and index. ISBN 88-430-2421-3 DDC 180
1. Philosophy, Ancient. I. Title. II. Series: Studi superiori (Carocci editore) ; 416. III. Series: Studi superiori (Carocci editore). Filosofia.

Tractat de prenostication de la vida natural dels hòmens. English & Catalan.
Lucas, John Scott, 1970- Astrology and numerology in medieval and early modern Catalonia. Leiden ; Boston : Brill, 2003.
BF1685 .L83 2003

Tractatus absolutus.
Dornseiff, Johannes. 1. Aufl. Berlin : Frieling, 2000.

Tractatus logico-philosophicus.
Ludwig Wittgenstein, Tractatus logico-philosophicus. Berlin : Akademie Verlag, 2001.

Tracy, Brian. Change your thinking, change your life : how to unlock your full potential for success and achievement / Brian Tracy. Hoboken, N.J. : J. Wiley & Sons, c2003. xviii, 270 p. ; 24 cm. Includes bibliographical references (p. 256-259) and index. Publisher description URL: http://www.loc.gov/catdir/desc ription/wiley039/2003006625.html Table of contents URL: http://www.loc.gov/catdir/toc/wiley031/2003006625.html CONTENTS: Change your thinking -- Change your life -- Dream big dreams -- Decide to become rich -- Take charge of your life -- Commit to excellence -- Put people first -- Think like a genius -- Unleash your mental powers -- Supercharge your thinking -- Create your own future -- Live a great life. ISBN 0-471-44858-3 (alk. paper) DDC 158.1
1. Success - Psychological aspects. I. Title.
BF637.S8 T634 2003

TRADE. *See* **BUSINESS.**

TRADE, INTERNATIONAL. *See* **INTERNATIONAL TRADE.**

TRADE REGULATION. *See* **ANTITRUST LAW; FOREIGN TRADE REGULATION.**

TRADE REGULATION - MORAL AND ETHICAL ASPECTS.
Singer, Peter, 1946- One world. New Haven, Conn. : London : Yale University Press, 2002.

TRADE-UNIONS - MINORITY MEMBERSHIP. *See* **DISCRIMINATION IN EMPLOYMENT.**

TRADEMARKS. *See* **BRAND NAME PRODUCTS.**

TRADES. *See* **OCCUPATIONS.**

TRADING, STOCK. *See* **STOCKS.**

Tradiție și libertate.
Nemoianu, Virgil. București : Curtea Veche, 2001.
JC585 .N42 2001

TRADITION, ORAL. *See* **ORAL TRADITION.**

TRADITION (PHILOSOPHY).
Maler, Arkadiĭ. Strategii sakral'nogo smysla. Moskva : Parad izdatel'skiĭ dom, 2003.

TRADITIONAL BIRTH ATTENDANTS. *See* **MIDWIVES.**

Traditional Chinese feng shui.
Lum, Alan S.F. (Alan Sun Fai) The centuries old philosophy and practice of traditional Chinese feng shui and the more advanced Flying Star feng shui. Honolulu : Lum Pub., c2002.
BF1779.F4 L86 2002

TRADITIONAL HEALERS. *See* **HEALERS.**

TRADITIONAL MEDICINE - BRAZIL.
Carvalho, Angela Maria B., 1954- A magia das ervas e seu axé. São Paulo, SP : Madras, 2003.
1. Black author.

TRADITIONALISM (PHILOSOPHY). *See* **TRADITION (PHILOSOPHY).**

TRADITIONS. *See* **FOLKLORE; LEGENDS; RITES AND CEREMONIES; SUPERSTITION.**

Traditsiia, tekst, fol'klor. Tipologiia i semiotika
Sny i videniia v narodnoĭ kul'ture. Moskva : RGGU, 2002.
BF1078 .S563 2002

TRAFFIC. *See* **COMMUNICATION AND TRAFFIC.**

TRAFFIC ACCIDENTS.
Ludwig, Timothy D. Intervening to improve the safety of occupational driving. New York : Haworth Press, 2000.
HE5614 .I586 2000

TRAGIC, THE.
Sagnol, Marc, 1956- Tragique et tristesse. Paris : Cerf, 2003.

Tragique et tristesse.
Sagnol, Marc, 1956- Paris : Cerf, 2003.

TRAINING. *See* **EDUCATION; TEACHING.**

TRAINING OF CHILDREN. *See* **CHILD REARING.**

TRAINING OF EMPLOYEES. *See* **EMPLOYEES - TRAINING OF.**

TRAINING OF THE MEMORY. *See* **MNEMONICS.**

TRAINING WITHIN INDUSTRY. *See* **EMPLOYEES - TRAINING OF.**

Trainor, Norm, 1946- The eight best practices of high-performing salespeople / Norm Trainor with Donald Cowper and Andrew Haynes. Toronto ; New York : Wiley, c2000. 201 p. ; 23 cm. ISBN 0-471-64528-1 DDC 658.85
1. Selling. 2. Sales personnel. 3. Success in business. I. Cowper, Donald. II. Haynes, Andrew. III. Title. IV. Title: 8 best practices of high-performing salespeople
HF5438.25 .T72 2000

Traité de l'agitation ordinaire.
Tretiack, Philippe. Paris : B. Grasset, c1998.
BF575.A35 T74 1998

TRAITS, PERSONALITY. *See* **PERSONALITY.**

La trame de l'évidence.
Rosental, Claude. 1 éd. Paris : Presses universitaires de France, c2003.

Transcendence in philosophy and religion / edited by James E. Faulconer. Bloomington, IN : Indiana University Press, c2003. v, 151 p. ; 25 cm. (Indiana series in the philosophy of religion) Includes bibliographical references and index. CONTENTS: Hermeneutics and philosophical reflection -- Whose philosophy? Which religion? Reflections on reason as faith / Merold Westphal -- The question into meaning and the question of God : A hermeneutic approach / Ben Vedder -- The sense of symbols as the core of religion : A philosophical approach to a theological debate / Paul Moyaert -- Philosophy and transcendence : religion and the possibility of justice / James E. Faulconer -- Rethinking phenomenology from religion -- The event, the phenomenon, and the revealed / Jean-Luc Marion -- Phenomenality and transcendence / Marlène Zarader -- Transcendence and the hermeneutic circle : some thoughts on Marion and Heidegger / Bătrice Han. ISBN 0-253-34199-X (alk. paper) ISBN 0-253-21575-7 (pbk. : alk. paper) DDC 111/.6
1. Philosophy and religion. 2. Transcendence (Philosophy) 3. Hermeneutics. I. Faulconer, James E. II. Series.
B56 .T73 2003

TRANSCENDENCE (PHILOSOPHY).
Caropreso, Paolo. Von der Dingfrage zur Frage nach Gott. Berlin ; New York : W. de Gruyter, 2003.

Transcendence in philosophy and religion. Bloomington, IN : Indiana University Press, c2003.
B56 .T73 2003

The transcendent function.
Miller, Jeffrey C., 1951- Albany : State University of New York Press, c2003.
BF175.5.I53 M55 2003

TRANSCENDENTALISM.
Illies, Christian. The grounds of ethical judgement. Oxford : Clarendon, 2003.

TRANSCENDENTALISM - CONGRESSES.
Der Grund, die Not und die Freude des Bewusstseins. Würzburg : Königshausen & Neumann, c2002.
B808.9 .G78 2002

TRANSEXUALS. See TRANSSEXUALS.

Transformation of the psyche.
Henderson, Joseph L. (Joseph Lewis), 1903- New York : Brunner-Routledge, 2003.
BF173 .H4346 2003

The transformation of the Roman world
(v. 12) The construction of communities in the early Middle Ages. Leiden ; Boston : Brill, 2003.
HN11 .C66 2003

(v. 6) Topographies of power in the early Middle Ages. Leiden ; Boston : Brill, 2001.
D117 .T67 2001

Transformations
Campbell, Kirsten, 1969- Jacques Lacan and feminist epistemology. New York, NY : Routledge, 2004.
BF175.4.F45 .C37 2004

Transforming anger.
Childre, Doc Lew, 1945- Oakland, Calif. : New Harbinger ; London : Hi Marketing, 2003.
BF575.A5 C45 2003

Transforming feminist practice.
Fernandes, Leela. 1st ed. San Francisco : Aunt Lute Books, 2003.
HQ1154 .F495 2003

Transgressões / Carlos Alberto Plastino (organização). Rio de Janeiro, RJ : Espaço Brasileiro de Estudos Psicanalíticos : Contra Capa, 2002. 251 p. ; 23 cm. (Coleção Espaço Brasileiro de Estudos Psicanalíticos ; 2) Papers presented at a seminar organized by the Espaço Brasileiro de Estudos Psicanalíticos. Includes bibliographical references. ISBN 85-86011-52-5
1. Psychology - Congresses. 2. Deviant behavior - Congresses. 3. Psychoanalysis - Congresses. I. Plastino, Carlos Alberto. II. Espaço Brasileiro de Estudos Psicanalíticos. III. Series.

TRANSITIONAL OBJECTS (PSYCHOLOGY). See ATTACHMENT BEHAVIOR.

TRANSLATING AND INTERPRETING - SOCIAL ASPECTS.
Translation and power. Amherst : University of Massachusetts Press, 2002.
P306.97.S63 T7 2002

TRANSLATING AND INTERPRETING - STUDY AND TEACHING.
Kiraly, Donald C., 1953- Pathways to translation. Kent, Ohio : Kent State University Press, c1995.
P306.5 .K57 1995

Translation and power / edited by Maria Tymoczko and Edwin Gentzler. Amherst : University of Massachusetts Press, 2002. xxviii, 244 p. ; 24 cm. Includes bibliogrpahical references (p. [219]-235) and index. Table of contents URL: http://www.loc.gov/catdir/toc/fy033/2002008285.html CONTENTS: Translation and the establishment of liberal democracy in nineteenth-century England : constructing the political as an interpretive act / Alexandra Lianeri -- Translation of the Treaty of Waitangi : a case of disempowerment / Sabine Fenton and Paul Moon -- Empire talks back : orality, heteronomy, and the cultural turn in interpretation studies / Michael Cronin / Writing, interpreting, and the power struggle for the control of meaning : scenes from Kafka, Borges, and Kosztolányi / Rosemary Arrojo -- Translation as testimony : on official histories and subversive pedagogies in Cortázar / Adriana S. Pagano -- Translating woman : Victoria Ocampo and the empires of foreign fascination / Christopher Larkosh -- Germaine de Staël and Gayatri Spivak : culture brokers / Sherry Simon -- Spanish film translation and cultural patronage : the filtering and manipulation of imported material during Franco's dictatorship / Camino Gutiérrez Lanza -- Translation as a catalyst for social change in China / Lin Kenan -- Translation, dépaysement, and their figuration / Carol Maier -- Translation, poststructuralism, and power / Edwin Gentzler. ISBN 1-55849-358-1 (lib. cloth : alk. paper) ISBN 1-55849-359-X (pbk. : alk. paper) DDC 418/.02
1. Translating and interpreting - Social aspects. 2. Power (Social sciences) 3. Language and culture. I. Tymoczko, Maria. II. Gentzler, Edwin, 1951-
P306.97.S63 T7 2002

Translation studies
(3) Kiraly, Donald C., 1953- Pathways to translation. Kent, Ohio : Kent State University Press, c1995.
P306.5 .K57 1995

TRANSLATORS. See TRANSLATING AND INTERPRETING.

TRANSLITERATION. See ALPHABET.

TRANSMIGRATION. See also REINCARNATION.
Klatt, Norbert. Die Rivalin Gottes. Göttingen : N. Klatt, 2000.

The transmission of affect.
Brennan, Teresa, 1952- Ithaca : Cornell University Press, 2003.
BF531 .B74 2003

TRANSMUTATION OF METALS. See ALCHEMY.

TRANSNATIONAL CORPORATIONS. See INTERNATIONAL BUSINESS ENTERPRISES.

Transparency and conspiracy : ethnographies of suspicion in the new world order / edited by Harry G. West and Todd Sanders. Durham : Duke University Press, 2003. 316 p. ; 25 cm. Includes bibliographical references and index. CONTENTS: Gods, markets and the IMF in the Korean spirit world / Laurel Kendall -- "Diabolic realities" : narratives of conspiracy, transparency and "ritual murder" in the Nigerian popular print and electronic media / Misty Bastian -- "Who rules us now?" Identity tokens, sorcery and other metaphors in the 1994 Mozambican elections / Harry G. West -- Through a glass darkly : charity, conspiracy, and power in new order Indonesia / Albert Schrauwers -- Invisible hands and visible goods : revealed and concealed economies in millennial Tanzania / Todd Sanders -- Stalin and the blue elephant : paranoia and complicity in post-communist metahistories / Caroline Humphrey -- Paranoia, conspiracy, and hegemony in American politics / Daniel Hellinger -- Making wanga : reality constructions and the magical manipulation of power / Karen McCarthy Brown -- Anxieties of influence : conspiracy theory and therapeutic culture in millennial America / Susan Harding and Kathleen Stewart. ISBN 0-8223-3036-9 (cloth : alk. paper) ISBN 0-8223-3024-5 (pbk. : alk. paper) DDC 303.3
1. Power (Social sciences) 2. Conspiracy. I. West, Harry G. II. Sanders, Todd, 1965-
JC330 .T73 2003

TRANSPERSONAL PSYCHOLOGY.
Pint, A. A. (Aleksandr Aleksandrovich) Nas mnogo, no my odno. Moskva : Shkola kholisticheskoĭ psikhologii, 2003.
BF202 .P56 2003

Schaub, Bonney Gulino. Dante's path. New York, N.Y. : Gotham Books, 2003.
BF204.7 .S33 2003

Vrinte, Joseph, 1949- The perennial quest for a psychology with a soul. 1st ed. Delhi : Motilal Banarsidass Publishers, 2002.

BF311+
Washburn, Michael, 1943- Embodied spirituality in a sacred world. Albany : State University of New York Press, 2003.
BF204.7 .W372 2003

TRANSPLANTATION OF ORGANS, TISSUES, ETC. See SURGERY, PLASTIC.

TRANSPORTATION. See COMMUNICATION AND TRAFFIC.

TRANSPORTATION ACCIDENTS. See AIRCRAFT ACCIDENTS.

TRANSSEXUALISM.
Califia-Rice, Patrick, 1954- Speaking sex to power. 1st ed. San Francisco : Cleis Press, c2002.
HQ76.25 .C32 2002

Campos, Maria Consuelo Cunha. De Frankenstein ao transgênero. Rio de Janeiro : Editora Agora da Ilha, 2001.

Castel, Pierre-Henri. La métamorphose impensable. Paris : Gallimard, c2003.
HQ77.9 .C38 2003

Finding the real me. 1st ed. San Francisco, CA : Jossey-Bass, c2003.
HQ77.7 .F56 2003

Queer counselling and narrative practice. Adelaide : Dulwich Centre Publications, c2002.

TRANSSEXUALISM - PATIENTS. See TRANSSEXUALS.

TRANSSEXUALISM - PSYCHOLOGICAL ASPECTS.
Bailey, J. Michael. The man who would be queen. Washington, D.C. : Joseph Henry Press, c2003.
HQ76.2.U5 B35 2003

TRANSSEXUALITY. See TRANSSEXUALISM.

TRANSSEXUALS - BIOGRAPHY.
Finding the real me. 1st ed. San Francisco, CA : Jossey-Bass, c2003.
HQ77.7 .F56 2003

TRANSSEXUALS - COUNSELING OF.
Queer counselling and narrative practice. Adelaide : Dulwich Centre Publications, c2002.

TRANSSEXUALS - IDENTITY.
Finding the real me. 1st ed. San Francisco, CA : Jossey-Bass, c2003.
HQ77.7 .F56 2003

Gendered sexualities. New York : JAI, 2002.
HQ1075.A27 vol. 6

TRANSSEXUALS - UNITED STATES - PSYCHOLOGY - CASE STUDIES.
Bailey, J. Michael. The man who would be queen. Washington, D.C. : Joseph Henry Press, c2003.
HQ76.2.U5 B35 2003

Transversals
Adamson, Gregory Dale, 1966- Philosophy in the age of science and capital. London ; New York : Continuum, 2002.
B804 .A33 2002

TRAPPING. See HUNTING.

Trappl, Robert.
Emotions in humans and artifacts. Cambridge, Mass. : MIT Press, c2002.
BF531 .E517 2002

Trasferetti, José Antônio. Deus a força que cura! / José Trasferetti. Campinas, SP : Editora Átomo, 2002. 246 p. ; 21 cm. Includes bibliographical references. ISBN 85-87585-19-3
1. Spiritual healing. 2. God - Will. 3. Healing - Religious aspects - Christianity. 4. Suffering - Religious aspects - Christianity. I. Title.

Trask, Richard B. The devil hath been raised : a documentary history of the Salem Village witchcraft outbreak of March 1692 : together with a collection of newly located and gathered withcraft documents / Richard B. Trask. Rev. ed. Danvers, Mass. : Yeoman Press, c1997. xxiv, 168 p. : ill., map ; 23 cm. Includes bibliographical references and index. ISBN 0-9638595-1-X DDC 133.4/3/097445
1. Witchcraft - Massachusetts - Salem - History - Sources. I. Title.
BF1576 .T73 1997

Tratat de descompunere.
Cioran, E. M. (Emile M.), 1911- [Précis de décomposition. Romanian] București : Humanitas, 2002, c1996.

Trauma and the memory of politics.
Edkins, Jenny. Cambridge ; New York : Cambridge University Press, 2003.
BF175.5.P75 E35 2003

TRAUMA, EMOTIONAL. *See* **PSYCHIC TRAUMA.**

TRAUMA, PSYCHIC. *See* **PSYCHIC TRAUMA.**

TRAUMATIC NEUROSES. *See* **POST-TRAUMATIC STRESS DISORDER.**

TRAUMATIC STRESS SYNDROME. *See* **POST-TRAUMATIC STRESS DISORDER.**

Traumdeutung und Traumforschung.
Walde, Christine, 1960- Antike Traumdeutung und moderne Traumforschung. Düsseldorf : Artemis & Winkler, c2001.

Träume nach Freud.
Marinelli, Lydia. Wien : Turia + Kant, c2002.

Travailler pour être heureux?.
Baudelot, Christian. [Paris] : Fayard, c2003.

Travaux d'humanisme et Renaissance
(no 375) Cité des hommes, cité de Dieu. Genève : Droz, 2003.
PN723 .C584 2003

Travaux du Centre de recherche sur le Proche-Orient et la Grèce antiques
(15) Colloque de Strasbourg (14th : 1995) Oracles et prophéties dans l'Antiquité. Strasbourg : Publications de l'Université de Strasbourg II, 1997.
BF1761 .C65 1995

Traverso, Paola. "Psiche è una parola greca--" : forme e funzioni della cultura classica nell'opera di Freud / Paola Traverso. Genova, Italy : Compagnia dei librai, 2000. 300 p. ; 22 cm. (Pubblicazioni del D.AR.FI.CL.ET. ; nuova ser., n. 194) Includes bibliographical references (p. 277-298). ISBN 88-86620-77-2
1. Freud, Sigmund, - 1856-1939. 2. Civilization, Western - Classical influences. I. Title. II. Series: Pubblicazioni del D.AR.FI.CL.ET. ; nuova ser., 194.
BF109.F74 T73 2000

Travis, Cheryl Brown, 1944-.
Evolution, gender, and rape. Cambridge, Mass. : MIT Press, c2003.
HV6558 .E92 2003

Trawny, Peter, 1964-.
Die erscheinende Welt. Berlin : Duncker & Humblot, c2002.

Traynor, Pamela, 1941-.
Roads to recovery. St. Leonards, NSW : Allen & Unwin, 1997.
BF698.35.D48 R63 1997

TREASURE, NATIONAL. *See* **CULTURAL PROPERTY.**

TREASURE-TROVE - FRANCE - RENNES-LE-CHÂTEAU.
Douzet, André. Nouvelles lumières sur Rennes-le-Château. Chêne-Bourg (Suisse) : Acquarius, c1998-
BF1434.F8 D69 1998

Treasurer, Bill, 1962- Right risk : 10 powerful principles for taking giant leaps with your life / Bill Treasurer (a.k.a. Captain Inferno). San Francisco : Berrett-Koehler, c2003. viii, 200 p. ; 22 cm. Includes bibliographical references (p. 183-189) and index. ISBN 1-57675-246-1 (alk. paper) DDC 158.1
1. Risk-taking (Psychology) I. Title.
BF637.R57 T74 2003

TREATIES.
Getting it done. Washington, D.C. : United States Institute of Peace Press, 2003.
KZ1321 .G48 2003

TREE OF LIFE.
Morgan, Shemu'el. 'Ets ha-da'at. Pedu'el : Sh. Morgan, [1998?]

Sasson, Gahl. A wish can change your life. New York : Simon & Schuster, 2003.
BF1623.C2 S27 2003

TREES. *See* **HEDGES.**

Trees, Andrew S., 1968- The founding fathers and the politics of character / Andrew S. Trees. Princeton, N.J. : Princeton University Press, c2004. xvi, 208 p. : ill., ports. ; 25 cm. Includes bibliographical references (p. [147]-203) and index. ISBN 0-691-11552-4 (alk. paper) DDC 973.4
1. Statesmen - United States - History - 18th century. 2. United States - Politics and government - 1783-1809. 3. Character - Political aspects - United States - History - 18th century. 4. National characteristics, American. 5. United States - History - Revolution, 1775-1783 - Influence. 6. Social values - United States - History - 18th century. 7. Political culture - United States - History - 18th century. 8. Rhetoric - Political aspects - United States - History - 18th century. I. Title.
E302.1 .T74 2004

TREES - MISCELLANEA.
Vega, Phyllis. Celtic astrology. Franklin Lakes, NJ : New Page Books, c2002.
BF1714.C44 V44 2002

TREES - MYTHOLOGY.
Mountfort, Paul Rhys. Ogam, the Celtic oracle of the trees. Rochester, Vt. : Destiny Books, c2002.
PB1217 .M68 2002

Vinšćak, Tomo. Vjerovanja o drveću u hrvata. [Jastrebarsko] : Naklada Slap, c2002.

TREES - RELIGIOUS ASPECTS - JUDAISM.
Mantovani, Massimo. Meditazioni sull'albero della cabala. Milano : Xenia, 2002.

Treitel, Corinna. A science for the soul : occultism and the genesis of the German modern / Corinna Treitel. Baltimore : Johns Hopkins University Press, 2004. p. cm. Includes bibliographical references (p.   ) and index. Table of contents URL: http://www.loc.gov/catdir/toc/ecip043/2003010642.html ISBN 0-8018-7812-8 DDC 133/.0943
1. Occultism - Germany - History. I. Title.
BF1434.G5 T74 2004

Tremblay-Dupré, Thérèse. La mère absente / Thérèse Tremblais-Dupré ; préface de Jean Gillibert. Monaco : Rocher, 2003. 218 p. ; 20 cm. Includes bibliographical references. ISBN 2-268-04559-5 DDC 809
1. Youth in literature. 2. Adolescence in literature. 3. Teenagers in literature. 4. Adolescent psychology. 5. Values in adolescence. I. Title.

Tremblay, Jacques, 1952-.
Mongeau, Pierre, 1954- Survivre. Sainte-Foy : Presses de l'Université du Québec, 2002.
BF122 .M66 2002

Treml, Martin, 1959-.
Tyrannis und Verführung. Wien : Turia + Kant, 2000.
JC381 .T973 2000

Trends in cognitive psychology / Serge P. Shohov, editor. New York : Nova Science Publishers, c2002. vi, 266 p. : ill. ; 26 cm. Includes bibliographical references and index. ISBN 1-59033-665-8 DDC 153
1. Cognition. 2. Cognitive science. 3. Cognitive therapy. I. Shohov, Serge P.
BF311 .T723 2002

Trenholm, Sarah, 1944- Interpersonal communication / Sarah Trenholm, Arthur Jensen. 5th ed. New York : Oxford University Press, 2003. p. cm. Includes bibliographical references and index. ISBN 0-19-517074-1 (alk. paper) DDC 153.6
1. Interpersonal communication. I. Jensen, Arthur, 1954- II. Title.
BF637.C45 T72 2003

Trepp, Anne-Charlott.
Antike Weisheit und kulturelle Praxis. Göttingen : Vandenhoeck & Ruprecht, 2001.
BF1586 .A58 2001

Tresch, John.
Latour, Bruno. War of the worlds. Chicago : Prickly Paradigm Press, c2002.
H61.15 .L38 2002

Tretiack, Philippe. Traité de l'agitation ordinaire / Philippe Trétiack. Paris : B. Grasset, c1998. 246 p. ; 21 cm. Includes bibliographical references. ISBN 2-246-53291-4
1. Agitation (Psychology) I. Title.
BF575.A35 T74 1998

TREVELYAN, GEORGE.
Farrer, Frances, 1950- Sir George Trevelyan and the new spiritual awakening. Edinburgh : Floris, 2002.

Trevi, Gloria. Gloria / por Gloria Trevi. México, D.F. : Planeta, c2002. 267 p., [16] p. of plates : ill. ; 23 cm. ISBN 970690767X DDC 782.42164/092
1. Trevi, Gloria. 2. Trevi, Gloria. - bidex 3. Singers - Mexico - Biography. 4. Spanish language materials. I. Title.
ML420.T725 A3 2002

TREVI, GLORIA.
Trevi, Gloria. Gloria. México, D.F. : Planeta, c2002.
ML420.T725 A3 2002

TREVI, GLORIA. BIDEX.
Trevi, Gloria. Gloria. México, D.F. : Planeta, c2002.
ML420.T725 A3 2002

Tri osobennykh lika vlasti.
Toshchenko, Zhan Terent'evich. Moskva : RGGU, 2002.

JC330 .T674 2002

TRIADS (PHILOSOPHY). *See* **TRINITY.**

TRIAL BY ORDEAL. *See* **ORDEAL.**

TRIAL EVIDENCE. *See* **EVIDENCE (LAW).**

TRIAL PRACTICE. *See* **EVIDENCE (LAW).**

TRIAL PRACTICE - UNITED STATES - AUTOMATION.
Brenden, Ann E. Persuasive computer presentations. Chicago, Ill. : Law Practice Management Section, American Bar Association, c2001.
KF320.A9 B74 2001

TRIALS (WITCHCRAFT) - EUROPE - HISTORY.
Geschlecht, Magie und Hexenverfolgung. Bielefeld : Verlag für Regionalgeschichte, 2002.

TRIALS (WITCHCRAFT) - EUROPE - HISTORY - 17TH CENTURY.
Guillou, Jan, 1944- Häxornas försvarare. [Stockholm?] : Piratförlaget, c2002.
BF1584.S8 G85 2002

TRIALS (WITCHCRAFT) - EUROPE - HISTORY - ENCYCLOPEDIAS.
Burns, William E., 1959- Witch hunts in Europe and America. Westport, Conn. : Greenwood Press, 2003.
BF1584.E9 B87 2003

TRIALS (WITCHCRAFT) - GERMANY.
Spee, Friedrich von, 1591-1635. [Cautio criminalis. English] Cautio criminalis, or, A book on witch trials. Charlottesville : University of Virginia Press, 2003.
BF1583.A2 S6813 2003

TRIALS (WITCHCRAFT) - GERMANY - FRANCONIA - HISTORY - 16TH CENTURY.
Kleinöder-Strobel, Susanne, 1969- Die Verfolgung von Zauberei und Hexerei in den fränkischen Markgraftümern im 16. Jahrhundert. Tübingen : Mohr Siebeck, c2002.
BF1583 .K54 2002

TRIALS (WITCHCRAFT) - GERMANY - LEMGO - HISTORY.
Ströhmer, Michael, 1968- Von Hexen, Ratsherren und Juristen. Paderborn : Bonifatius, c2002.
BF1583 .S77 2002

TRIALS (WITCHCRAFT) - GERMANY - RAVENSBURG.
Frühe Hexenverfolgung in Ravensburg und am Bodensee. Konstanz : UVK Verlagsgesellschaft, c2001.
BF1583 .F784 2001

TRIALS (WITCHCRAFT) - GERMANY - THURINGIA.
Füssel, Ronald. Hexen und Hexenverfolgung in Thüringen. Erfurt : Landeszentrale für Politische Bildung Thüringen, 2001.
BF1583 .F87 2001

TRIALS (WITCHCRAFT) - ITALY - PISA - HISTORY.
Caterina e il diavolo. Pisa : ETS, c1999.
BF1584.I8 C38 1999

TRIALS (WITCHCRAFT) - MASSACHUSETTS - SALEM.
Roach, Marilynne K. The Salem witch trials. 1st Cooper Square Press ed. New York : Cooper Square Press ; Distributed by National Book Network, 2002.
BF1575 .R63 2002

TRIALS (WITCHCRAFT) - SWEDEN - HISTORY - 17TH CENTURY.
Guillou, Jan, 1944- Häxornas försvarare. [Stockholm?] : Piratförlaget, c2002.
BF1584.S8 G85 2002

TRIALS (WITCHCRAFT) - SWITZERLAND - VAUD - HISTORY.
Taric Zumsteg, Fabienne. Les sorciers à l'assaut du village. Lausanne : Editions du Zèbre, 2000.
BF1584.S9 T37 2000

TRIALS (WITCHCRAFT) - UNITED STATES - HISTORY - ENCYCLOPEDIAS.
Burns, William E., 1959- Witch hunts in Europe and America. Westport, Conn. : Greenwood Press, 2003.
BF1584.E9 B87 2003

Tríbades galantes, fanchonos militantes.
Filho, Amilcar Torrão. São Paulo : Edições GLS, 2000.

Tribbe, Frank C. The Holy Grail mystery solved : a fully illustrated research odyssey / Frank C. Tribbe. 1st ed. Lakeville, Minn. : Galde Press, 2003. xv, 199 p. : ill., maps ; 23 cm. Includes bibliographical references (p.

193-196). ISBN 1-88009-005-8 (pbk.) DDC 001.94
1. Grail. 2. Holy Shroud. I. Title.
BF1442.G73 T75 2003

Il tridente. Saggi
(15) Donfrancesco, Francesco. Una poetica dell'analisi. Bergamo : Moretti & Vitali, 2000.

(23) L'incubo globale. Bergamo : Moretti & Vitali, c2002.

TRINITIES. See **TRINITY**.

TRINITY. See also **GOD; HOLY SPIRIT; MONOTHEISM**.
Luciani Rivero, Rafael Francisco. El misterio de la diferencia. Roma : Pontificia università gregoriana, 2001.

TRINITY - HISTORY OF DOCTRINES - MIDDLE AGES, 600-1500.
Noriega, José. "Guiados por el espíritu". Roma : Pontificia università lateranense ; [Milano] : Mursia, 2000.

The triple goddess tarot.
Lerner, Isha, 1954- Rochester Vt. : Bear & Co., c2002.
BF1879.T2 L4365 2002

Tripol'skaia, T. A.
Problemy interpretatsionnoĭ lingvistiki. Novosibirsk : Novosibirskiĭ gos. pedagog. universitet, 2001.
P128.E95 P762 2001

TRISTAN. See **TRISTAN (LEGENDARY CHARACTER)**.

TRISTAN (LEGENDARY CHARACTER) - ROMANCES - HISTORY AND CRITICISM.
A companion to Gottfried von Strassburg's "Tristan". Rochester, NY : Camden House, 2003.
PT1526.C66 2003

TRISTITIA. See **SADNESS**.

TRISTRAM (LEGENDARY CHARACTER). See **TRISTAN (LEGENDARY CHARACTER)**.

Trivers, Robert. Natural selection and social theory : selected papers of Robert L. Trivers / Robert Trivers. New York : Oxford University Press, 2002. viii, 345 p. : ill. ; 25 cm. (Evolution and cognition) A collection of 10 papers, 5 published in scholarly journals between 1971-1976 and 5 between 1982-2000. Reciprocal altruism -- Parental investment and reproductive success -- The Trivers-Willard effect -- Parent-offspring conflict -- Haplodiploidy and the social insects -- Size and reproductive success in a lizard -- Selecting good genes for daughters -- Self-deception in service of deceit -- Genomic imprinting -- Fluctuating asymmmetry and 2nd:4th digit ratio in children. Includes bibliographical references and index. ISBN 0-19-513061-8 ISBN 0-19-513062-6 (pbk.) DDC 304.5
1. Sociobiology. 2. Evolution (Biology) 3. Social evolution in animals. I. Title. II. Series.
GN365.9.T76 2002

TRIVIA. See **CURIOSITIES AND WONDERS**.

Trobe, Kala, 1969- The witch's guide to life / Kala Trobe. 1st ed. St. Paul, Minn. : Llewellyn Publications, 2003. xviii, 459 p. : ill. ; 24 cm. Includes bibliographical references and index. ISBN 0-7387-0200-5 DDC 133.4/3
1. Witchcraft. 2. Magic. I. Title.
BF1566.T76 2003

Trois rêves freudiens.
Cifali, Mario. Paris : Eshel, c1999.
BF175.5.O33 C54 1999

Trojan, Elizabeth A.
Malott, Richard W. Principles of behavior. 5th ed. Upper Saddle River, N.J. : Pearson/Prentice Hall, 2003.
BF319.5.O6 M34 2003

Tromellini, Pina. Un corredo per la vita : dieci valori da donare a un figlio / Pina Tromellini. Milano : Salani editore, c2002. 144 p. ; 19 cm. SUMMARY: Suggests ten fundamental values that parents can impart to their children as they develop morally and spiritually. ISBN 88-8451-097-X DDC 177
1. Moral education. 2. Child rearing. 3. Personality development. I. Title.

TROOPS, COMMAND OF. See **COMMAND OF TROOPS**.

Trübsbach, Claudia.
Mensch & Musik. Augsburg : Wissner, c2002.
ML3830.M46 2002

Trudy fakul'teta politicheskikh nauk i sotsiologii (Evropeĭskiĭ universitet v Sankt-Peterburge)
(vyp. 5.) Kharkhordin, Oleg, 1964- Oblichat' i litsemerit'. Sankt-Peterburg : Evropeĭskiĭ universitet v Sankt-Peterburge ; Moskva : Letniĭ Sad, 2002.
B2430.F724 K43 2002

Trudy Laboratorii virtualistiki
(vyp. 12) Nosov, N. A. Ne-virtualistika. Moskva : Gumanitariĭ, 2001.
BF38.N67 2001

True devotion.
Louise, Kim. Washington D.C. : BET Publications, 2002.

True religion.
Ward, Graham. Malden, MA ; Oxford : Blackwell Pub., 2003.
BL48.W189 2003

Trufanov, A. A. (Andreĭ Andreevich) Osnovy teorii intelligentnosti / A.A. Trufanov. Kazan' : ZAO "Novoe znanie", 2002. 271 p. ; 20 cm. Includes bibliographical references (p. 263-270). ISBN 5893471458
1. Intellect - Social aspects. 2. National characteristics, Russian. 3. Philosophy, Russian. I. Title.
BF431.T78 2002

Trujillo García, Carlos Holmes.
Al oído de Uribe. 1a. ed. Bogotá, Colombia : Editorial Oveja Negra, 2002.

Trust.
Nooteboom, B. Cheltenham, UK ; Northampton, MA : E. Elgar Pub., c2002.
HD2758.5.N66 2002

TRUST.
Distrust. New York : Russell Sage Foundation, 2004.
BF575.T7 D57 2004

Galford, Robert M., 1952- The trusted leader. New York ; London : Free Press, c2002.
HD57.7.G33 2002

Golin, Al, 1929- Trust or consequences. New York : American Management Association, c2004.
HF5387.G65 2004

Group cohesion, trust and solidarity. 1st ed. Amsterdam ; New York : JAI, 2002.

Huotari, Maija-Leena. Trust in knowledge management and systems in organizations. Hershey, PA ; London : Idea Group Publishing, c2004.
HD30.2.H865 2004

Marlow, Mary Elizabeth, 1940- Jumping Mouse. Norfolk, VA : Hampton Roads Pub. Co., c1995.
BF575.T7 M37 1995

McLeod, Carolyn. Self-trust and reproductive autonomy. Cambridge, Mass. : MIT Press, c2002.
RG133.5.M39 2002

Nooteboom, B. Trust. Cheltenham, UK ; Northampton, MA : E. Elgar Pub., c2002.
HD2758.5.N66 2002

Potter, Nancy Nyquist, 1954- How can I be trusted? Lanham, Md. ; Oxford : Rowman & Littlefield, c2002.
BJ1500.T78 P68 2002

Ratnasingam, Pauline. Inter-organizational trust in business-to-business e-commerce. Hershey, PA : IRM Press, c2003.
HF5548.32.R378 2003

The trust process in organizations. Cheltenham, UK ; Northampton, MA : Edward Elgar, c2003.
HD58.7.T744 2003

Ward, William Aidan. Trust and mistrust. Chichester, England ; Hoboken, NJ : John Wiley & Sons, c2003.
HD69.S8 W37 2003

Trust and mistrust.
Ward, William Aidan. Chichester, England ; Hoboken, NJ : John Wiley & Sons, c2003.
HD69.S8 W37 2003

TRUST IN GOD - JUDAISM.
Blokh, Yosef Zalman. Igeret 'al ha-biṭaḥon. Monsi : [h. mo. l.], 5761 [2000 or 2001]
BM729.T7.B56 2000

Trust in knowledge management and systems in organizations.
Huotari, Maija-Leena. Hershey, PA ; London : Idea Group Publishing, c2004.
HD30.2.H865 2004

Trust or consequences.
Golin, Al, 1929- New York : American Management Association, c2004.
HF5387.G65 2004

The trust process in organizations : empirical studies of the determinants and the process of trust development / edited by Bart Nooteboom, Frederique Six. Cheltenham, UK ; Northampton, MA : Edward Elgar, c2003. xi, 243 p. : ill. ; 24 cm. Includes bibliographical references and index. ISBN 1-84376-078-9 DDC 302.3/5
1. Organizational behavior. 2. Corporate culture. 3. Psychology, Industrial. 4. Management. 5. Leadership. 6. Trust. I. Nooteboom, B. II. Six, Frederique, 1962-
HD58.7.T744 2003

TRUST (PSYCHOLOGY). See **TRUST**.

The trusted leader.
Galford, Robert M., 1952- New York ; London : Free Press, c2002.
HD57.7.G33 2002

Trusting yourself.
Ryan, M. J. (Mary Jane), 1952- New York : Broadway Books, 2004.
BF575.S39 R93 2004

TRUSTS AND TRUSTEES. See **EXECUTORS AND ADMINISTRATORS; INHERITANCE AND SUCCESSION**.

TRUSTS, INDUSTRIAL. See **ANTITRUST LAW; COMPETITION; CONSOLIDATION AND MERGER OF CORPORATIONS; CORPORATIONS**.

TRUSTS, INDUSTRIAL - LAW. See **ANTITRUST LAW**.

TRUSTS, INDUSTRIAL - LAW AND LEGISLATION. See **ANTITRUST LAW**.

TRUTH. See also **KNOWLEDGE, THEORY OF**.
Anselm, Saint, Archbishop of Canterbury, 1033-1109. [Dialogues. English. Selections] Three philosophical dialogues. Indianapolis, IN : Hackett Pub., c2002.
B765.A81.A2513 2002

Greimann, Dirk. Freges Konzeption der Wahrheit. Hildesheim ; New York : Georg Olms, c2003.
B3318.T78 G74 2003

Hegel's Phenomenology of spirit. Amherst, N.Y. : Humanity Books, 2003.
B2929.H349 2003

Jadacki, Jacek Juliusz. From the viewpoint of the Lvov-Warsaw school. Amsterdam ; New York, NY : Rodopi, 2003.

Sub"ekt, poznanie, deĭatel'nost'. Moskva : Kanon+, 2002.
BD166.S84 2002

Tijan Bangura, Abubakar. The truth can be discovered in the Qur'an. [Freetown, Sierra Leone : s.n., 2002]
1. Black author.

The truth about Teutonic magick.
Thorsson, Edred. 2nd ed. Saint Paul, MN : Llewellyn Publications, 1994.
BF1622.G3 T488 1994

Truth and justification.
Habermas, Jürgen. [Wahrheit und Rechtfertigung. English] Cambridge, Mass. : MIT Press, c2003.
B3258.H323 W3413 2003

Truth behind earth changes in the coming age of light.
Clow, Barbara Hand, 1943- Catastrophobia. Rochester, Vt. : Bear & Company, c2001.
BF1999.C587 2001

The truth can be discovered in the Qur'an.
Tijan Bangura, Abubakar. [Freetown, Sierra Leone : s.n., 2002]

TRUTH COMMISSIONS.
Truth v. justice. Princeton, N.J. : Princeton University Press, c2000.
DT1945.T78 2000

TRUTH - CONGRESSES.
Collège de France. Symposium annuel. La vérité dans les sciences. Paris : Jacob, c2003.

TRUTH - RELIGIOUS ASPECTS - BUDDHISM.
Hagen, Steve, 1945- Buddhism is not what you think. 1st ed. [San Francisco] : HarperSanFrancisco, c2003.
BQ4570.F7 H34 2003

TRUTH - RELIGIOUS ASPECTS - CHRISTIANITY.
González Ayesta, Cruz. Hombre y verdad. 1. ed. Pamplona : Universidad de Navarra, Ediciones, 2002.

Henry, Michel, 1922- [C'est moi la vérité. English] I am the truth. Stanford, Calif : Stanford University Press, 2003.

BR100 .H39813 2003

Truth v. justice : the morality of truth commissions / edited by Robert I. Rotberg and Dennis Thompson. Princeton, N.J. : Princeton University Press, c2000. vi, 309 p. ; 24 cm. (The University Center for Human Values series) Includes bibliographical references and index. CONTENTS: Truth commissions and the provision of truth, justice, and reconciliation / Robert I. Rotberg -- The moral foundations of truth commissions / Amy Gutmann and Dennis Thompson -- Restoring decency to barbaric societies / Rajeev Bhargava -- Moral ambition within and beyond political constraints: reflections on restorative justice / Elizabeth Kiss -- Truth commissions, transitional justice, and civil society / David A. Crocker -- The moral foundations of the South African TRC: truth as acknowledgment and justice as recognition / André du Toit -- Truth and reconciliation in South Africa: the third way / Alex Boraine -- The uses of truth commissions: lessons for the world / Dumisa B. Ntsebeza -- Amnesty, truth, and reconciliation: reflections on the South African amnesty process / Ronald C. Slye -- Amnesty's justice / Kent Greenawalt -- Trials, commissions, and investigating committees: the elusive search for norms of due process / Sanford Levinson -- The hope for healing: what can truth commissions do? / Martha Minow -- Doing history, doing justice: the narrative of the historian and of the truth commission / Charles S. Maier -- Constructing a report: writing up the "truth" / Charles Villa-Vicencio and Wilhelm Verwoerd. ISBN 0-691-05071-6 (alk. paper) ISBN 0-691-05072-4 (pbk. : alk. paper) DDC 323/.06
1. South Africa. - Truth and Reconciliation Commission. 2. Apartheid - South Africa. 3. Human rights - South Africa. 4. Amnesty - South Africa. 5. Truth commissions. 6. Human rights. 7. Amnesty. 8. Reconciliation. I. Rotberg, Robert I. II. Thompson, Dennis F. (Dennis Frank), 1940- III. Title: Truth versus justice IV. Title: Truth vs. justice V. Series.
DT1945 .T78 2000

Truth versus justice.
Truth v. justice. Princeton, N.J. : Princeton University Press, c2000.
DT1945 .T78 2000

Truth vs. justice.
Truth v. justice. Princeton, N.J. : Princeton University Press, c2000.
DT1945 .T78 2000

TRUTHFULNESS AND FALSEHOOD. *See* **DECEPTION.**

Tsai, Hui-Liang. Information technology and business process reengineering : new perspectives and strategies / Hui-Liang Tsai. Westport, Conn. : Praeger, 2003. xvii, 298 p. ; 24 cm. Includes bibliographical references (p. [263]-285) and index. ISBN 1-56720-632-8 (alk. paper) DDC 658.4/06
1. Reengineering (Management) 2. Organizational change - Management. 3. Organizational learning - Management. 4. Information technology - Management. 5. Business enterprises - Technological innovations. I. Title.
HD58.87 .T73 2003

Tsai, Wenpin.
Kilduff, Martin. Social networks and organizations. London : SAGE, 2003.

T͡Sennostnye orientat͡sii lichnosti kak dinamicheskai͡a sistema.
I͡Anit͡skiĭ, M. S. (Mikhail Sergeevich) Kemerovo : Kuzbassvuzizdat, 2000.
BF698 .I18 2000

T͡Serkov' i obrazovanie
(vyp. 7) Dimitrievich, Vladimir. V plenu germeticheskogo kruga. Perm' : Panagii͡a, 2001.
BF173.J85 D56 2001

Tsevi Hirsh, mi-Ḳalish, 18th cent.
Yoman.
Oron, Michal. Mi-'Ba'al shed' le-'Ba'al Shem'. Yerushalayim : Mosad Byaliḳ : Bet ha-sefer le-mada'e ha-Yahadut 'a. sh. Ḥayim Rozenberg, Universiṭat Tel-Aviv, c763 [2002]

Tshe-riṅ-rdo-rje, 'Broṅ-bu. Nub phyogs śer rtogs rig pa'i tshig bum / 'Broṅ-bu Tshe-riṅ-rdo-rjes rtsom sgyur byas. Par theṅs 1. Pe-cin : Mi rigs dpe skrun khaṅ, 1995. 15, 232 p. ; 21 cm. Chinese title on t.p. verso: Xi fang zhe xue ci dian. SUMMARY: Critical analysis on the western philosophy. In Tibetan; includes glossary in Tibetan, English, and Chinese. ISBN 7-105-02392-9
1. Philosophy. I. Title. II. Title: Xi fang zhe xue ci dian

Tsiakkas, Christophoros A. Mageia-satanismos : mia Orthodoxē Christianikē theōrēsē tou provlēmatos / Christophorou Tsiakka. 3 ekd. Leukōsia : Ekdosē Hieras Monēs Trooditissēs, 2001. 266 p. : ill. ; 20 cm. Includes bibliographical references (p. 262-263).
1. Satanism. 2. Occultism - Religious aspects - Orthodox Eastern Church. 3. Orthodox Eastern Church - Doctrines. I. Title.

BF1550 .T73 2001

T͡Sinichnoto.
Lichev, Valeri. T͡Sinichnoto, ili, Igrata na vlast i udovolstvie. Sofii͡a : EON-2000, 2000.
B809.5 .L53 2000

T͡Sinichnoto, ili, Igrata na vlast i udovolstvie.
Lichev, Valeri. Sofii͡a : EON-2000, 2000.
B809.5 .L53 2000

T͡Siolkovskiĭ, K. (Konstantin), 1857-1935. Geniĭ sredi li͡udeĭ / K.Ė. T͡Siolkovskiĭ. Moskva : Mysl', 2002. 542 p. : port. ; 22 cm. Collected papers on philosophy and sociology, including the title essay "Geniĭ sredi li͡udeĭ", with (auto)biographical writings. Includes bibliographical references. ISBN 5244008315
1. T͡Siolkovskiĭ, K. - (Konstantin), - 1857-1935. 2. Astronautics and civilization. 3. Cosmology. 4. Sociology. 5. Philosophy, Russian. 6. Rocketry - Biography. I. Title.
TL781.85.T84 A25 2002

T͡SIOLKOVSKIĬ, K. (KONSTANTIN), 1857-1935.
T͡Siolkovskiĭ, K. (Konstantin), 1857-1935. Geniĭ sredi li͡udeĭ. Moskva : Mysl', 2002.
TL781.85.T84 A25 2002

Tsuri'el, Mosheh Yeḥi'el. Otsrot ha-musar : leḳeṭ mi-divre Ḥazal, rishonim ṿa-aḥaronim be-'inyene tiḳun ha-midot ṿe-haśagat emunah ṭehorah ... ; ṿe-khen Sefer "Otsar 'avodat H." : be-'inyan ḳedushat ha-avarim u-mitsṿotehem lefi ... "Sefer Ḥaredim" ; ṿe-khen Ḳunṭres "Segulot" ... / ... nitḥabru ṿe-nilḳeṭu ... 'al yede Mosheh Tsuri'el. Yerushalayim : Yerid ha-sefarim, 763, 2002. 2 v. (1378 p.) ; 24 cm. Cover title: Sefer Otsrot ha-musar. Cover has subtitle: Leḳeṭ divre maḥashavah musar ṿe-yir'at shamayim Includes bibliographical references and indexes.
1. Ethics, Jewish. 2. Body, Human - Religious aspects - Judaism. I. Title. II. Title: Otsar 'avodat H. III. Title: Otsar 'avodat ha-Shem. IV. Title: Ḳunṭres Segulot. V. Title: Segulot. VI. Title: Sefer Otsrot ha-musar

Tu po mang dian.
Wang, Furen. Di 1 ban. Beijing Shi : Zhongguo wen lian chu ban she, 2001.
PL2754.S5 Z89 2001

Tu, Wei-ming.
[Selections. 2002]
Du Weiming wen ji / Guo Qiyong, Zheng Wenlong bian. Wuhan Shi : Wuhan chu ban she, 2002. 5 v. : ill. (some col.), ports. ; 22 cm. Includes bibliographical references. ISBN 7-5430-2562-0
1. Philosophy, Confucian. 2. Philosophy, Chinese. 3. Philosophy. 4. Civilization. I. Guo, Qiyong, 1947- II. Zheng, Wenlong. III. Title.
B5233.C6 T813 2002

Tubali, Shy.
[Selections]
Boḳer ṭov 'olam : 20 morim ruḥaniyim gedolim 'al ha-ḥayim ṿe-'al he'arah. Tel Aviv : Yedi'ot aḥaronot : Sifre ḥemed, c2003. 478 p. : ports. ; 23 cm. Title on verso of t.p.: Good morning world. Includes bibliographical references (p. 477-478). ISBN 9655114074
1. Spiritual life - Guidebooks. 2. Conduct of life. 3. Mental healing. 4. Spiritual exercises. 5. Meditation. I. Title. II. Title: Good morning world

Tucci, Antonio. Individualità e politica : le contraddizioni della teoria politica identitaria in epoca tardo moderna / Antonio Tucci. Napoli : Edizioni scientifiche italiane, 2002. 258 p. ; 24 cm. (Università degli studi di Salerno, Dipartimento di teoria e storia del diritto. Sezione di storia e filosofia giuridico-politica ; 2) Includes bibliographical references. ISBN 88-495-0398-9 DDC 320
1. Individualism. 2. Political science - Philosophy. I. Title.

Tucker, Kenneth. Shakespeare and Jungian typology : a reading of the plays / Kenneth Tucker. Jefferson, N.C. ; London : McFarland & Co., c2003. v, 169 p. ; 23 cm. Includes bibliographical references (p. 162-166) and index. CONTENTS: "Cry havoc!" : King John and darkling plain -- One man's meat is another man's poison : psychetypes and individual realities -- Thought and feeling in the comedies -- Antony and Cleopatra and Troilus and Cressida : lovers and other strangers -- "Stay, we must not lose our senses" : the emergence of the inferior function -- Hamlet in hell : psychetypological chaos -- Shakespeare's romances : the return to Eden and the return of the goblins. ISBN 0-7864-1647-5 (softcover : alk. paper) DDC 822.3/3
1. Shakespeare, William, - 1564-1616 - Knowledge - Psychology. 2. Shakespeare, William, - 1564-1616 - Characters. 3. Jung, C. G. - (Carl Gustav), - 1875-1961. 4. Typology (Psychology) in literature. 5. Drama - Psychological aspects. 6. Psychology in literature. 7. Typology (Psychology) I. Title.
PR3065 .T83 2003

Tuckwell, Gill, 1948- Racial identity, White counsellors and therapists / Gill Tuckwell. Buckingham ; Philadelphia : Open University Press, 2002. 188 p. : ill. ; 24 cm. Includes bibliographical references (p. [172]-183) and index. ISBN 0-335-21021-X ISBN 0-335-21020-1 (pbk.) DDC 158/.3/089034
1. Counseling. 2. Psychotherapy. 3. Race awareness. 4. Whites - Race identity. I. Title.
BF637.C6 T84 2002

Tudor, Steven. Compassion and remorse : acknowledging the suffering other / Steven Tudor. Leuven ; Sterling, Va. : Peeters, 2001. xi, 235 p. ; 24 cm. (Morality and the meaning of life ; 11) Includes bibliographical references (p. 219-229) and index. ISBN 90-429-0920-X DDC 177.7
1. Sympathy. 2. Caring. 3. Suffering. 4. Remorse. I. Title. II. Series.
BJ1475 .T84 2001

Tuffin, Paul.
Geōrgios, Synkellos, fl. 800. [Ecloga chronographica English] The chronography of George Synkellos. Oxford ; New York : Oxford University Press, 2002.

Tugendhat, Ernst. Aufsätze 1992-2000 / Ernst Tugendhat. 1. Aufl. Frankfurt : Suhrkamp, 2001. 262 p. ; 18 cm. (Suhrkamp Taschenbuch Wissenschaft ; 1535) Includes bibliographical references. ISBN 3-518-29135-1
1. Philosophy. I. Title. II. Series.

Tul'chinskiĭ, G. L. (Grigoriĭ L'vovich)
Postchelovecheskai͡a personologii͡a : novye perspektivy svobody i rat͡sional'nosti / G.L. Tul'chinskiĭ. Sankt-Peterburg : Aletei͡a, 2002. 677 p. ; 22 cm. (Serii͡a Tela mysli) Includes bibliographical references (p. 649]-667) and index. ISBN 5893295331
1. Personality. 2. Liberty. 3. Rationalism. I. Title. II. Series.
BD331 .T84 2002

Tuḷunāḍinalli Koraga taniya.
Marike, Navīn Kumār. Puttūru, Da. Ka. : Śrī Mahāśakti Saṅgha, 2000.
BF1517.I5 M37 2000

TULUNADU (INDIA) - RELIGION.
Marike, Navīn Kumār. Tuḷunāḍinalli Koraga taniya. Puttūru, Da. Ka. : Śrī Mahāśakti Saṅgha, 2000.
BF1517.I5 M37 2000

Tumusov, F. S. (Fedot Semenovich) Budushchee mira i Rossii : vzgli͡ad iz Sakha / F.S. Tumusov. Moskva : "Mysl'", 2000. 237 p. : col. ill. ; 21 cm. ISBN 5244009729
1. Sakha (Russia) - Economic conditions. 2. Russia (Federation) - Economic conditions. 3. Economic forecasting - Russia (Federation) 4. Twenty-first century - Forecasts. 5. Globalization. I. Title.
HC340.12.Z7 S2357 2000

Tuning the mind.
Katz, Ruth, 1927- New Brunswick, N.J. : Transaction Publishers, c2003.
ML3838 .K28 2003

Turchyn, Sandie.
Olmstead, Kathleen. The girls' guide to tarot. New York : Sterling Pub., c2002.
BF1879.T2 O38 2002

Turchyn, Sandie, ill.
Collier-Thompson, Kristi. The girls' guide to dreams. New York : Sterling Pub., c2003.
BF1099.C55 C65 2003

TURIN (ITALY) - BUILDINGS, STRUCTURES, ETC.
Scott, John Beldon, 1946- Architecture for the shroud. Chicago : University of Chicago Press, c2003.
NA5621.T823 S36 2003

TURKESTAN. *See* **ASIA, CENTRAL.**

TURKEY - ANTIQUITIES. *See* **ÇATAL MOUND (TURKEY).**

Turkington, Carol. Memory : a self-teaching guide / Carol Turkington. Hoboken, N.J. : J. Wiley and Sons, c2003. iii, 188 p. ; 24 cm. (Self-teaching guides) Includes bibliographical references (p. 171-184) and index. Publisher description URL: http://www.loc.gov/catdir/desc ription/ wiley035/2003269340.html Table of contents URL: http:// www.loc.gov/catdir/toc/wiley032/2003269340.html ISBN 0-471-39364-9 (alk. paper) DDC 153.14
1. Mnemonics. I. Title. II. Series: Wiley self-teaching guides.
BF385 .T88 2003

Turner, Stephen P., 1951- Liberal democracy 3.0 : civil society in an age of experts / Stephen P. Turner. London ; Thousand Oaks, Calif. : SAGE Publications, 2003. x, 154 p. ; 24 cm. (Theory, culture & society) Includes bibliographical references (p. [144]-150) and index. ISBN 0-7619-5468-6 ISBN 0-7619-5469-4 (pbk.) DDC 300.1
1. Democracy. 2. Expertise - Political aspects. 3. Science - Political aspects. 4. Knowledge, Sociology of. 5. Civil society.

I. Title. II. Title: Liberal democracy three point zero III. Series: Theory, culture & society (Unnumbered)
JC423 .T87 2003

Turning points in historiography : a cross-cultural perspective / edited by Q. Edward Wang, Georg G. Iggers. Rochester, NY : University of Rochester Press, 2002. viii, 362 p. ; 24 cm. (Rochester studies in historiography, 1533-7014) Includes bibliographical references and index. SUMMARY: Examining turning points in historical thought in a variety of cultures, the essays here deal with reorientations in historical thinking in the pre-modern period since antiquity, mainly in ancient Greece and China and in medieval Christian Europe. ISBN 1-58046-097-6 (alk. paper) DDC 907/.2
1. Historiography - History. 2. History - Philosophy. 3. Historiography - Europe - History. 4. Historiography - Asia - History. 5. History - Methodology. I. Wang, Q. Edward, 1958- II. Iggers, Georg G. III. Series.
D13 .T87 2002

Turning the world upside down.
York, Neil Longley. Westport, Conn. ; London : Praeger, 2003.
E210 .Y67 2003

Turovich, V. (Vasiliĭ) 1000 primet pogody / V. Turovich. Perm' : Izd-vo "Poligrafist", 1997. 158 p. : port. ; 15 cm. (Sekrety prirody) ISBN 5858810144
1. Omens - Russia (Federation) 2. Nature - Folklore. I. Title. II. Title: Tysi͡acha primet pogody III. Series.
BF1777 .T87 1997

Turrisi, Robert.
Jaccard, James. Interaction effects in multiple regression. 2nd ed. Thousand Oaks, Calif. : Sage Publications, c2003.
HA31.3 .J33 2003

Tusa, John. On creativity : interviews exploring the process / John Tusa. London : Methuen, 2003. 267 p. ; 22 cm. ISBN 0-413-77299-3 DDC 700.922
1. Artists - Interviews. 2. Creation (Literary, artistic, etc.) I. Tusa, John.

Tusa, John. On creativity. London : Methuen, 2003.

Tuschling, Burkhard.
Societas rationis. Berlin : Duncker & Humblot, c2002.
B29 .S633 2002

Tusquets, Oscar, 1941- Más que discutible : observaciones dispersas sobre el arte como disciplina útil / Oscar Tusquets Blanca. 1a. ed. en Fabula. Barcelona : Fabula Tusquets Editores, 2002. 201 p. : ill. ; 21 cm. (Fabula ; 182) Includes bibliographical references. ISBN 84-8310-797-X
1. Aesthetics. I. Title. II. Series: Fábula (Tusquets Editores) ; 182.

Tutu, Desmond.
Peace and conflict resolution. Part 2 [videorecording]. Derry, N.H. : Chip Taylor Communications, 1997.

TUTU, DESMOND - INTERVIEWS.
Peace and conflict resolution. Part 2 [videorecording]. Derry, N.H. : Chip Taylor Communications, 1997.

Ṭuv ha-peninim.
Yalḳuṭ Ṭuv ha-peninim. Yerushala[y]im : P. Y. Liberman, 762 [2001 or 2002]
BS1225.53 .Y35 2001

TV. *See* **TELEVISION.**

Tverskoĭ gosudarstvennyĭ universitet.
Aktual'nye voprosy obshcheĭ, vozrastnoĭ i sotsial'noĭ psikhologii. Tver' : Tverskoĭ gos. universitet, 2001.
BF20 .A46 2001

Tvorcheskoe nasledie A.V. Brushlinskogo i O.K. Tikhomirova i sovremennai͡a psikhologii͡a myshlenii͡a (k 70-letii͡u so dni͡a rozhdenii͡a) : tezisy dokladov nauchnoĭ konferentsii (Institut psikhologii RAN, 22-23 mai͡a 2003 g.) / [otvetstvennye redaktory: V.V. Znakov, T.V. Kornilova]. Moskva : In-t psikhologii RAN, 2003. 392 p. : ports. ; 21 cm. Includes index. ISBN 5927000444
1. Brushlinskiĭ, A. V. - (Andreĭ Vladimirovich) - Congresses. 2. Tikhomirov, Oleg Konstantinovich - Congresses. I. Znakov, V. V. (Viktor Vladimirovich) II. Kornilova, T. V. III. Brushlinskiĭ, A. V. (Andreĭ Vladimirovich) IV. Tikhomirov, Oleg Konstantinovich. V. Institut psikhologii (Rossiĭskai͡a akademii͡a nauk)
BF109.B86 T86 2003

Tvorchestvo kak fenomen sotsial'nykh kommunikatsiĭ.
Dubina, I. N. (Igor' Nikolaevich) Novosibirsk : Sibirskoe otd-nie RAN, 2000.
BF411 .D82 2000

Tvorogova, N. D. (Nadezhda Tvorogova) Obshchenie : diagnostika i upravlenie / N.D. Tvorogova. Moskva : Smysl, 2002. 246 p. : map ; 22 cm. (Psikhologicheskie issledovanii͡a) Includes bibliographical references (p. [224]-246). ISBN 5893571096
1. Communication - Psychological aspects. 2. Interpersonal communication. I. Title. II. Series.
BF637.C45 T88 2002

TWARDOWSKI, KAZIMIERZ, 1866-1938.
Rzepa, Teresa. O interpretowaniu psychologicznym w kręgu szkoły lwowsko-warszawskiej. Warszawa : Polskie Tow. Semiotyczne, 2002.
BF108.P7 R94 2002

TWELVE-STEP PROGRAMS.
Corley, M. Deborah. Embracing recovery from chemical dependency. Sottsdale, AZ : Gentle Path Press, c2003.
BF632 .C63 2003

TWELVE-STEP PROGRAMS - UNITED STATES.
Daniell, Beth, 1947- A communion of friendship. Carbondale : Southern Illinois University Press, c2003.
PE1405.U6 D36 2003

TWELVE STEPS (SELF-HELP). *See* **TWELVE-STEP PROGRAMS.**

TWENTIETH CENTURY.
Emmott, Bill. 20:21 vision. London : Allen Lane, 2003.

Twentieth-century muse.
Vezin, Annette. [Egéries dans l'ombre des créateurs. English] The 20th-century muse. New York : Harry N. Abrams, 2003.
N71 .V4913 2003

TWENTY-FIRST CENTURY.
Jannoud, Claude. La crise de l'esprit. Lausanne, Suisse : Age d'homme, c2001.

Reig, Ramón. El éxtasis cibernético. 1. ed. Madrid : Ediciones Libertarias, 2001.

TWENTY-FIRST CENTURY - FORECASTS.
Emmott, Bill. 20:21 vision. London : Allen Lane, 2003.

The future of marketing. Houndmills [England] ; New York : Palgrave Macmillan, 2003.
HF5415 .F945 2003

Global security concerns [electronic resource]. Maxwell Air Force Base, Ala. : Air University Press, [1996]

Growing global migration and its implications for the United States. [Washington, D.C.?] : The Board, 2001.

Growing global migration and its implications for the United States [electronic resource]. Electronic document. [Washington, D.C.? : National Intelligence Council, 2001]
CB161 .G768

Hogue, John. The essential Nostradamus. London : Vega, c2002.
BF1815.N8 H58 2002

Lemesurier, Peter, 1936- Nostradamus in the 21st century. Rev. ed. London : Piatkus, 2000 (2001 printing).

Mason, Colin, 1926- The 2030 spike. London ; Sterling, VA : Earthscan Publications, 2003.
CB161 .M384 2003

Millennium projects. 1st ed. New Delhi : Small Scale Industries, Ministry of Small Scale Industries, Agro & Rural Industries, Govt. of India, 2000-
HD2346.I5 M45 2000

Moiseev, N. N. (Nikita Nikolaevich) Kak daleko do zavtrashnego dni͡a--. Moskva : Taĭdeks Ko, 2002.
DK49 .M64 2002

A parliament of science. Albany : State University of New York Press, c2003.
Q158.5 .P38 2003

Parshev, A. P. (Andreĭ Petrovich) Pochemu Amerika nastupaet. Moskva : AST : Astrel', 2002.
HF1558.2.Z4 P37 2002

Riding the next wave. Indianapolis, Ind. : Hudson Institute ; [Washington, DC : Distributed by the Brookings Institution Press], c2001.
HM901 .R43 2001

Some significant 21st century trends and issues. Islamabad : Pakistan Futuristics Foundation & Institute, 1998.

CB161 .S62 1998

South Asia, 2010. Delhi : Konark Publishers, 2002.

Sterling, Bruce. Tomorrow now. 1st ed. New York : Random House, c2002.
HM901 .S74 2002

Tumusov, F. S. (Fedot Semenovich) Budushchee mira i Rossii. Moskva : "Mysl'", 2000.
HC340.12.Z7 S2357 2000

Twenty-first century's new chakra healing.
Nudel, Michael. 21st century's new chakra healing. Los Angeles, CA : Bio-Energy System Services, c2000.
BF1999 .N83 2000

Twenty five things to do when grandpa passes away, mom and dad get divorced, or the dog dies.
Kanyer, Laurie A., 1959- 25 things to do when grandpa passes away, mom and dad get divorced, or the dog dies. Seatte Wash., : Parenting Press, 2004.
BF723.G75 K36 2003

The twenty-four carat Buddha and other fables.
Harris, Maxine. Baltimore, Md. : Sidran Institute Press, 2003.
BF637.S4 H355 2003

Twenty-one ideas for managers.
Handy, Charles B. 21 ideas for managers. 1st ed. San Francisco : Jossey-Bass, c2000.
HD31 .H31259 2000

Twenty-thirty spike.
Mason, Colin, 1926- The 2030 spike. London ; Sterling, VA : Earthscan Publications, 2003.
CB161 .M384 2003

Twilight dwellers.
Martin, MaryJoy, 1955- 2nd ed. Boulder, Colo. : Pruett, 2003.
BF1472.U6 M37 2003

TWINS - PSYCHOLOGY.
Klein, Barbara Schave. Not all twins are alike. Westport, Conn. : Praeger, 2003.
BF723.T9 K57 2003

Twitchell, Paul, 1908-1971.
[Stranger by the river. Croation]
Stranac na rijeci / Paul Twitchell. Minneapolis, MN : ECKANKAR, c1994. viii leaves, 154 p. ; 18 cm. Translated from the English. A poetic book on the secret knowledge of God. ISBN 9539612608
1. Eckists. 2. Astral projection. 3. Parapsychology. I. Title.

TWO-CAREER COUPLES. *See* **DUAL-CAREER FAMILIES.**

Two discourses and a commentary.
Pufendorf, Samuel, Freiherr von, 1632-1694. [De officio hominis et civis. English] The whole duty of man, according to the law of nature. Indianapolis, Ind. : Liberty Fund, c2003.
K457.P8 D4313 2003

TWO-EARNER FAMILIES. *See* **DUAL-CAREER FAMILIES.**

The two majorities and the puzzle of modern American politics.
Shafer, Byron E. Lawrence, Kan. : University Press of Kansas, c2003.
JK2261 .S4298 2003

The two of me.
Birtchnell, John. Hove, East Sussex [England] ; New York : Routledge, 2003.
BF311 .B533 2003

Two thousand and thirty spike.
Mason, Colin, 1926- The 2030 spike. London ; Sterling, VA : Earthscan Publications, 2003.
CB161 .M384 2003

Two thousand thirty spike.
Mason, Colin, 1926- The 2030 spike. London ; Sterling, VA : Earthscan Publications, 2003.
CB161 .M384 2003

Two thousand years and beyond.
2000 years and beyond. London ; New York : Routledge, 2003.
BR53 .T86 2003

Twyman, James F. Emissary of light / James F. Twyman. Forres : Findhorn, 2002. 229 p. : map ; 22 cm. Originally published: [Santa Rosa, Calif.] : Aslan, 1996. ISBN 1-89917-189-4 DDC 299.93
1. Emissaries of Light. 2. Mysticism. 3. Religious communities. 4. Peace - Religious aspects. I. Title.

Tyler, Carole-Anne. Female impersonation / Carole-Anne Tyler. New York : Routledge, c2003. ix, 234 p. ; 24 cm. Includes bibliographical references and index. ISBN 0-

Tyler, J. Michael.
415-91687-9 ISBN 0-415-91688-7 (pbk.) DDC 305.42/01
1. Feminist theory. 2. Sex role. 3. Women. 4. Femininity. I. Title.
HQ1190 .T95 2003

Tyler, J. Michael. Using technology to improve counseling practice : a primer for the 21st century / J. Michael Tyler, Russell Sabella. Alexandria, VA : American Counseling Association, 2003. p. cm. Includes bibliographical references. Table of contents URL: http://www.loc.gov/catdir/toc/ecip046/2003014835.html ISBN 1-55620-227-X (alk. paper) DDC 158/.3/0285
1. Counseling - Computer network resources. 2. Counseling - Computer programs. 3. Psychotherapy - Computer network resources. 4. Psychotherapy - Computer programs. I. Sabella, Russell A., 1965- II. Title.
BF637.C6 T89 2003

Tyler-Wood, Irma.
Lum, Grande. Expand the pie. Seattle, WA : Castle Pacific Pub. ; Cambridge, MA : ThoughtBridge, c2003.
BF637.N4 L86 2003

Tymoczko, Maria.
Translation and power. Amherst : University of Massachusetts Press, 2002.
P306.97.S63 T7 2002

TYPE A BEHAVIOR. *See* **STRESS (PSYCHOLOGY).**

The type E personality.
Williams, Redford B., 1940- Emmaus, Pa. : Rodale, c2004.
BF576.3 .W55 2004

TYPE (PSYCHOLOGY). *See* **TYPOLOGY (PSYCHOLOGY).**

TYPES, MENTAL. *See* **TYPOLOGY (PSYCHOLOGY).**

TYPES, PSYCHOLOGICAL. *See* **TYPOLOGY (PSYCHOLOGY).**

Typisch amerikanisch.
Gelfert, Hans-Dieter, 1937- Originalausg. München : Beck, c2002.
E169.1 .G44 2002

TYPOGRAPHY. *See* **PRINTING.**

Typological studies in language
(v. 50) Prepositions in their syntactic, semantic, and pragmatic context. Amsterdam ; Philadelphia, PA : J. Benjamins Pub., c2002.
P285 .P74 2002

TYPOLOGY (PSYCHOLOGY). *See also* **ENNEAGRAM.**
Bryden, Barbara E., 1954- Sundial. Gainesville, FL : Center for Applications of Psychological Type, 2003.
BF698.3 .B79 2003

Crisand, Ekkehard. Psychologie der Persönlichkeit. 8., durchgesehene Aufl. Heidelberg : I.H. Sauer-Verlag, 2000.
BF698 .C715 2000

Giannini, John L., 1921- Compass of the soul. Gainesville, Fla. : Center for Applications of Psychological Type, 2003.
BF698.3 .G53 2003

Jeffries, William C. Profiles of the 16 personality types. Noblesville, IN : Buttermilk Ridge Pub. ; Zionsville, Ind. : Distributed by Executive Strategies International, c2002.
BF698.8.M94 J43 2002

Jeffries, William C. Still true to type. Noblesville, IN : Buttermilk Ridge Pub. ; Zionsville, Ind. : Distributed by Executive Strategies International, c2002.
BF698.8.M94 J435 2002

Moravia, Sergio, 1940- L'esistenza ferita. 1. ed. in "Campi del sapere.". Milano : Feltrinelli, 1999.
BF41 .M67 1999

Tucker, Kenneth. Shakespeare and Jungian typology. Jefferson, N.C. ; London : McFarland & Co., c2003.
PR3065 .T83 2003

VanSant, Sondra. Wired for conflict. Gainesville, Fla. : Center for Applications of Psychological Type, c2003.
BF698.3 .V36 2003

TYPOLOGY (PSYCHOLOGY) IN LITERATURE.
Tucker, Kenneth. Shakespeare and Jungian typology. Jefferson, N.C. ; London : McFarland & Co., c2003.
PR3065 .T83 2003

TYPOLOGY (PSYCHOLOGY) - MISCELLANEA.
Leslie, Mike, 1956- The magical personality. 1st ed. St. Paul, Minn. : Llewellyn, 2002.
BF1621 .L47 2002

Tyrannis und Verführung / Wolfgang Pircher, Martin Treml (Hg.). Wien : Turia + Kant, 2000. 281 p. ; 24 cm. ISBN 3-85132-247-9
1. Despotism. 2. Despotism in literature. 3. Philosophy, Ancient. I. Pircher, Wolfgang, 1946- II. Treml, Martin, 1959-
JC381 .T973 2000

The tyranny of choice.
Schwartz, Barry, 1946- 1st ed. New York : ECCO, 2004.
BF611 .S38 2004

Tysiacha primet pogody.
Turovich, V. (Vasiliĭ) 1000 primet pogody. Perm' : Izd-vo "Poligrafist", 1997.
BF1777 .T87 1997

Tyson, Donald, 1954- Familiar spirits : a practical guide for witches & magicians / Donald Tyson. 1st ed. St. Paul, Minn. : Llewellyn Publications, 2004. p. cm. Includes bibliographical references and index. ISBN 0-7387-0421-0 DDC 133.4/3
1. Familiars (Spirits) I. Title.
BF1557 .T97 2004

Tyson, Lawrence E.
Critical incidents in group counseling. Alexandria, VA : American Counseling Association, 2004.
BF637.C6 C72 2004

Tythacott, Louise. Surrealism and the exotic / Louise Tythacott. London ; New York : Routledge, 2003. xii, 260 p. : ill., map ; 25 cm. Includes bibliographical references (p. [242]-252) and index. ISBN 0-415-27637-3 DDC 709/.04/063
1. Surrealism. 2. Exoticism in art. I. Title.
NX456.5.S8 T98 2003

"Über dem Grabe geboren".
Mörgeli, Christoph. Bern : Benteli, 2002.

Udovik, S. L. (Sergeĭ Leonidovich) Globalizatsiia : semioticheskie podkhody / S.L. Udovik. [Moscow] : Refl-buk ; [Kiev] : Vakler, 2002. 461 p. : ill., map ; 21 cm. (Obrazovatel'naia biblioteka) ISBN 9665430483 ISBN 5879831108 ISBN 9665430742
1. Civilization - History. 2. Globalization - Social aspects. 3. Social history. I. Title. II. Series.
CB430 .U36 2002

UFO ENCOUNTER PHENOMENA. *See* **UNIDENTIFIED FLYING OBJECTS - SIGHTINGS AND ENCOUNTERS.**

UFO ENCOUNTERS. *See* **UNIDENTIFIED FLYING OBJECTS - SIGHTINGS AND ENCOUNTERS.**

UFO PHENOMENA. *See* **UNIDENTIFIED FLYING OBJECTS.**

UFO SIGHTINGS. *See* **UNIDENTIFIED FLYING OBJECTS - SIGHTINGS AND ENCOUNTERS.**

UFOLOGY. *See* **UNIDENTIFIED FLYING OBJECTS.**

UFOS. *See* **UNIDENTIFIED FLYING OBJECTS.**

Uganda book news.
Uganda book news. Kampala, Uganda : UPABA, 1996-
Z467.U337 U34

Uganda book news : a quarterly magazine of UPABA. Kampala, Uganda : UPABA, 1996- v. : ill. ; 30 cm. Frequency: Quarterly. Vol. 1, no. 1 (Jan./Mar. 1996)- . Title from cover.
1. Publishers and publishing - Uganda - Periodicals. 2. Booksellers and bookselling - Uganda - Periodicals. 3. Uganda - Periodicals. I. UPABA (Organization) II. Title: Uganda book news
Z467.U337 U34

Uganda Law Society. Directory / Uganda Law Society. Kampala : The Society, [1999- v. : ill. ; 21 cm. 1998/99- . Running title: ULS members directory. Cover title: Uganda Law Society directory. Title from cover.
1. Uganda Law Society - Periodicals. 2. Lawyers - Uganda - Directories. 3. Uganda - Periodicals. I. Title. II. Title: ULS members directory III. Title: Uganda Law Society directory
KTW3.3 .U345

Uganda Law Society directory.
Uganda Law Society. Directory. Kampala : The Society, [1999-
KTW3.3 .U345

UGANDA LAW SOCIETY - PERIODICALS.
Uganda Law Society. Directory. Kampala : The Society, [1999-
KTW3.3 .U345

UGANDA - PERIODICALS.
The scope magazine. Kampala, Uganda : LDC Publishers, [2001-
K23 .C665

[Success (Kampala, Uganda)] Success. Kampala, Uganda : Success Magazine Ltd., [1998-
BF637.S8

Uganda book news. Kampala, Uganda : UPABA, 1996-
Z467.U337 U34

Uganda Law Society. Directory. Kampala : The Society, [1999-
KTW3.3 .U345

UKIYOE.
Edo-e kara shomotsu made. Tōkyō : Kyūzansha, 1997.
HQ792.J3 N54 1997 v.19

UKRAINE - HISTORIOGRAPHY.
Istoriohrafichni ta dz︠h︡ereloznavchi problemy istoriï Ukraïny. Dnipropetrovs'k : Vyd-vo Dnipropetrovs'koho universytetu, 2000.
DK508.46 .I84 2000

UKRAINE - HISTORY - SOURCES.
Istoriohrafichni ta dz︠h︡ereloznavchi problemy istoriï Ukraïny. Dnipropetrovs'k : Vyd-vo Dnipropetrovs'koho universytetu, 2000.
DK508.46 .I84 2000

UKRAINE - SOCIAL CONDITIONS - 1991-.
Donchenko, E. A. (Elena Andreevna) Arkhetypy sotsial'noho zhyttia i polityka. Kyïv : Lybid', 2001.
JA74.5 .D65 2001

Úl bichigdmèlùùd.
Khurmetbek, Khalikiĭn. Ulaanbaatar : "Monsudar" Khèvlèliĭn Gazar, 2001.
QA465 .K48 2001

Ulanov, Barry.
Creative dissent. Westport, Conn. : Praeger Publishers, 2003.
BF173 .C794 2003

Uleman, James S.
The new unconscious. New York : Oxford University Press, 2004.
BF315 .N47 2004

Ulman, Shalom.
Luzzatto, Moshe Ḥayyim, 1707-1747. Kitsur 138 pithe hokhmah. Yerushalayim : Mekhon Hadrat Yerushalayim, 761 [2000 or 2001]

Ulmer, Jeffery T., 1966-.
Violent acts and violentization. Amsterdam ; Boston : JAI, 2003.

Ul'rikh, I. V. Zhizn' cheloveka : vvedenie v metaistoriiu / I.V. Ul'rikh. Moskva : Izd-vo "Litan", 1999. 493, [3] p. : ill. ; 25 cm. (Seriia "Kniga Sitarkhisa") Includes bibliographical references (p. 493-[494]). ISBN 5932230010
1. Cosmology. 2. History - Philosophy. I. Title. II. Series.

ULS members directory.
Uganda Law Society. Directory. Kampala : The Society, [1999-
KTW3.3 .U345

The ultimate astrologer.
Campion, Nicholas. Carlsbad, Calif. : Astro Room, c2002 (2003 printing)
BF1708.1 .C357 2002

The ultimate guide to goddess empowerment.
Sophia, 1955- Kansas City : Andrews McMeel Pub., c2003.
BF1621 .S67 2003

Ultimate things.
Engleman, Dennis Eugene, 1948- Ben Lomond, Calif. : Conciliar Press, c1995.
BT876 .E54 1995

Ulybina, E. V. Psikhologiia obydennogo soznaniia / E.V. Ulybina. Moskva : Smysl, 2001. 264 p. ; 22 cm. (Psikhologicheskie issledovaniia) Includes bibliographical references (p. [244]-263). ISBN 589357091X
1. Consciousness. I. Title. II. Series.
BF311 .U52 2001

L'umano alla prova.
Sequeri, Pier Angelo. Milano : V & P Università, c2002.
BD222.S47 U6 2002

UMBANDA (CULT).
Carvalho, Angela Maria B., 1954- A magia das ervas e seu axé. São Paulo, SP : Madras, 2003.
1. Black author.

Santos, Robson Pinheiro, 1961- Tambores de Angola. Contagem [Brazil] : Casa dos Espíritos, 2002.
1. Black author.

Silva, W. W. da Matta e (Woodrow Wilson da Matta e), 1917- Mistérios e práticas da lei de Umbanda. Sao Paulo : Icone Editora, c1999.

UMBANDA (CULTUS). *See* **UMBANDA (CULT).**

Umberson, Debra. Death of a parent : transition to a new adult identity / Debra Umberson. Cambridge ; New York : Cambridge University Press, 2003. viii, 255 p. ; 24 cm. Includes bibliographical references and index. CONTENTS: Ordinary loss, extraordinary change -- Unexpected crisis -- Symbolic loss -- Turning point in adulthood -- Intimate relationships -- The next generation -- The parent left behind -- My brother's keeper -- Rite of passage. ISBN 0-521-81338-7 DDC 155.9/37/0854
1. Parents - Death - Psychological aspects. 2. Loss (Psychology) 3. Adulthood - Psychological aspects. I. Title.
BF789.D4 U48 2003

UNAMUNO, MIGUEL DE, 1864-1936.
Ferrater Mora, José, 1912- [Selections. English. 2003] Three Spanish philosophers. Albany : State University of New York Press, c2003.
B4568.U54 F3913 2003

The unanswered question.
Leland, Kurt. Charlottesville, VA : Hampton Roads Pub., c2002.
BF1045.N4 L45 2002

Unaufrichtigkeit.
Dandyk, Alfred. Würzburg : Königshausen & Neumann, c2002.

The uncanny.
Freud, Sigmund, 1856-1939. [Essays. English. Selections] New York : Penguin Books, 2003.
BF109.F75 A25 2003

Royle, Nicholas, 1963- Manchester (UK) ; New York : Manchester University Press, 2003.
PN49 .R75 2002

Uncanny networks.
Lovink, Geert. Cambridge, Mass. : MIT Press, c2002.
HM851 .L688 2002

Uncertain science - uncertain world.
Pollack, H. N. Cambridge, U.K. ; New York : Cambridge University Press, 2003.
Q175 .P835 2003

UNCERTAINTY.
Beyond Keynes. Cheltenham ; Northampton, Mass. : Edward Elgar, c2002.

Füredi, Frank, 1947- Culture of fear. Rev. ed. London ; New York : Continuum, 2002.
BF575.F2 F86 2002

The philosophy of Keynes' economics. London ; New York : Routledge, 2003.
HB99.7 .P45 2003

Pollack, H. N. Uncertain science-- uncertain world. Cambridge, U.K. ; New York : Cambridge University Press, 2003.
Q175 .P835 2003

Vind, Karl. Independence, additivity, uncertainty. Berlin ; New York : Springer, c2003.
HB135 .V56 2003

Uncertainty principles : spatial experiments.
Unschaerferelationen. Wiesbaden : Nelte, c2002.
BF469 .U5 2002

Uncle John's presents Book of the dumb.
Scalzi, John, 1969- San Diego, CA : Portable Press, 2003.
BF431 .S273 2003

Uncle Sam.
Azoulay, Paul. Anglet : Atlantica, c2002.

Uncle Sam : mythes et légendes.
Azoulay, Paul. Uncle Sam. Anglet : Atlantica, c2002.

UNCLE SAM (SYMBOLIC CHARACTER).
Azoulay, Paul. Uncle Sam. Anglet : Atlantica, c2002.

The unconscious.
MacIntyre, Alasdair C. Rev. ed. New York : Routledge, 2004.
BF315 .M23 2004

UNCONSCIOUSNESS. *See* **SUBCONSCIOUSNESS.**

Under the sign of nature.
Marshall, Ian, 1954- Peak experiences. Charlottesville : University of Virginia Press, 2003.
PS163 .M37 2003

UNDERACHIEVEMENT - SOCIAL ASPECTS.
Meighan, Roland. John Holt. 2nd ed. Nottingham : Educational Heretics Press, 2002.
LB885.H64 M454 2002

UNDERDEVELOPED AREAS. *See* **DEVELOPING COUNTRIES.**

UNDERDEVELOPED COUNTRIES. *See* **DEVELOPING COUNTRIES.**

UNDERGRADUATES. *See* **COLLEGE STUDENTS.**

Understanding aesthetics for the merchandising and design professional.
Fiore, Ann Marie. New York : Fairchild, c1997.

Understanding Aleister Crowley's thoth tarot.
DuQuette, Lon Milo, 1948- Boston, MA : Weiser Books, 2003.
BF1879.T2 D873 2003

Understanding Byzantium.
Speck, Paul. [Selections. English. 1999] Aldershot, Great Britain ; Burlington, Vt. : Ashgate/Variorum, c2003.
DF503 .S742513 2003

Understanding children's play.
Hartley, Ruth E. (Ruth Edith), b.1909 London : Routledge, 2000.
BF717 .H3 2000

Understanding complex sentences.
Chipere, Ngoni, 1965- New York : Palgrave Macmillan, 2003.
P295 .C485 2003

Understanding constitutional principles
Separation of powers. Washington, D.C. : CQ Press, a division of Congressional Quarterly Inc., c2003.
JK305 .S465 2003

Understanding creativity.
Piirto, Jane, 1941- Scottsdale, Ar. : Great Potential Press ; 2004.
BF408 .P87 2004

Understanding education and policy
Givens, Gretchen Zita. Black women in the field. Cresskill, N.J. : Hampton Press, c2003.
LC2781.5 .G58 2003

Understanding experience : psychotherapy and postmodernism / edited by Roger Frie. London ; New York : Routledge, 2003. xii, 234 p. ; 22 cm. Includes bibliographical references and index. CONTENTS: Introduction : between modernism and postmodernism : rethinking psychological agency / Roger Frie -- Sartre's contribution to psychoanalysis / Betty Cannon -- Martin Buber and dialogical psychotherapy / Maurice Friedman -- Truth and freedom in psychoanalysis / William J. Richardson -- Beyond postmodernism : from concepts through experiencing / Eugene Gendlin -- A phenomenology of becoming : reflections on authenticity / Jon Mills -- Language and subjectivity : from Binswanger through Lacan / Roger Frie -- Psychoanalysis and subjectivity in the work of Erich Fromm / Daniel Burston -- The primacy of experience in R.D. Laing's approach to psychoanalysis / M. Guy Thompson -- The eclipse of the person in psychoanalysis / Jon Frederickson. ISBN 1-58391-299-1 (hbk.) ISBN 1-58391-900-7 (pbk.) DDC 150.19/5
1. Experience. 2. Psychotherapy - Philosophy. 3. Psychoanalysis and philosophy. 4. Postmodernism - Psychological aspects. I. Frie, Roger, 1965-
B105.E9 U53 2003

Understanding knowledge management.
Styhre, Alexander. Malmö, Sweden : Liber ; Oslo, Norge : Abstrakt ; Herndon, VA : Copenhagen Business School Press, c2003.
HD30.2 .S84 2003

Understanding new religious movements.
Saliba, John A. 2nd ed. Walnut Creek, CA ; Oxford : Altamira Press, c2003.
BP603 .S25 2003

Understanding Ogboni fraternity.
Kómọláfé, Kóláwọlé. African traditional religion. Lagos : Ifa-Òrúnmìlà Organisation, 1995.
BL2480.Y6 K65 1995

Understanding people.
Butt, Trevor, 1947- New York : Palgrave Macmillan, 2003.
BF698 .B89 2003

Understanding systems.
Von Foerster, Heinz, 1911- New York : Kluwer Academic/Plenum Publishers ; Heidelberg : Carl-Auer-Systeme Verlag, c2002.

Understanding terrorism : psychosocial roots, consequences, and interventions / edited by Fathali M. Moghaddam and Anthony J. Marsella. 1st ed. Washington, DC : American Psychological Association, 2004. xiii, 343 p. ; 26 cm. Includes bibliographical references (p. 283-314) and index. ISBN 1-59147-032-3 (alk. paper) DDC 303.6/25
1. Terrorism - Psychological aspects. 2. Terrorists - Psychology. 3. Social conflict - Psychological aspects. 4. Victims of terrorism - Psychology. 5. Psychic trauma. 6. Terrorism - Prevention. I. Moghaddam, Fathali M. II. Marsella, Anthony J. III. Title: Terrorism : psychosocial roots, consequences, and interventions
HV6431 .U35 2004

Understanding the angry child.
McManus, Martha Hansen, 1948- Seattle, Wash. : Parenting Press, 2004.
BF723.A4 M38 2004

Understanding the brain : towards a new learning science. Paris : Organisation for Economic Co-operation and Development, 2002. 115 p. : ill. ; 23 cm. Includes bibliographical references and index. SUMMARY: "The book focuses on the importance of adopting a trans-disciplinary approach, involving cognitive neuroscience, psychology, education, health and policy makers - when teachers, the medical profession and scientists work together, there is real hope for early diagnosis of, and appropriate intervention in, conditions such as dyslexia and Alzheimer's disease."--P. [4] of cover. Also available via the Internet to SourceOECD libraries, including UF. Full text licensed only for UF students, faculty, staff. URL: http://www.sourceoecd.org/conten t/templates/co/co%5Fmain.htm?comm=educatio ISBN 92-64-19734-6 DDC 370
1. Cognitive neuroscience. 2. Learning, Psychology of. 3. Learning - Physiological aspects. 4. Brain. I. Organisation for Economic Co-operation and Development.
QP360.5 .U54 2002

Understanding the tarot court.
Greer, Mary K. (Mary Katherine) 1st ed. St. Paul, Minn. : Llewellyn Publications, 2004.
BF1879.T2 G75 2004

Understanding world order and structural change.
Abrahamsson, Hans, 1949- Basingstoke, Hampshire : New York : Palgrave Macmillan, 2003.
HF1359 .A24 2003

UNDERTAKERS AND UNDERTAKING - FRANCE.
Hanus, Michel. La Mort aujourd'hui. Paris : Frison-Roche, c2000.

UNDERWATER EXPLORATION. *See* **TREASURE-TROVE.**

Underwood, Marion K. Social aggression among girls / Marion K. Underwood ; foreword by Eleanor Maccoby. New York ; London : Guilford Press, c2003. xix, 300 p. : ill. ; 24 cm. (The Guilford series on social and emotional development) Includes bibliographical references (p. 253-290) and index. CONTENTS: Anger and aggression : the bind between feeling angry and being nice -- Childhood aggression : sticks and stones and social exclusion -- Gender and peer relations : separate worlds? -- Girls' anger in infancy : early lessons that anger is unwelcome -- Girls' anger and aggression in preschool : "if you don't do what I say, I won't be your friend" -- Middle childhood : gossip, gossip, evil thing? -- Adolescence : girl talk, moral negotiation, and strategic interactions to inflict social harm -- Developmental and psychosocial consequences of girls' aggression -- Prevention and intervention : harnessing the power of sisterhood -- New models of social aggression : for its own sake. ISBN 1-57230-866-4 (hbk.) ISBN 1-57230-865-6 (pbk.) DDC 302.5/4/08342
1. Aggressiveness in children. 2. Aggressiveness in adolescence. 3. Girls - Psychology. I. Title. II. Series.
BF723.A35 U53 2003

Undir verndarhendi.
Steinunn Eyjólfsdóttir, 1936- Reykjavík : Skjaldborg, 1995.
BF1283.B58 S74 1995

Uneasy ethics.
Lee, Simon (Simon F.) London : Pimlico, 2003.

Unequal childhoods.
Lareau, Annette. Berkeley : University of California Press, c2003.
HQ767.9 .L37 2003

The unexplained
Martin, Michael, 1948- Ghosts. Mankato, Minn. : Edge Books, 2004.
BF1461 .M365 2004

Martin, Michael, 1948- Near-death experiences. Mankato, Minn. : Edge Books, 2004.

BF1045.N4 M375 2004

Unexplained (Lerner Publications)
Herbst, Judith. Aliens. Minneapolis : Lerner Publications, 2005.
BF2050 .H465 2005

Herbst, Judith. Vanished. Minneapolis : Lerner Publications Co., 2005.
BF1389.D57 H47 2005

Unger, Roberto Mangabeira. False necessity--anti-necessitarian social theory in the service of radical democracy : from Politics, a work in constructive social theory / Roberto Mangabeira Unger. New ed. London ; New York : Verso, 2001. cxxix, 661 p. ; 24 cm. (Politics, a work in constructive social theory ; [pt. 1]) Spine title: False necessity. Includes bibliographical references (p. 604-639) and indexes. ISBN 1-85984-655-6 (cloth)
1. Sociology. 2. Political science. 3. Philosophy. I. Title. II. Title: False necessity III. Series: Unger, Roberto Mangabeira. Politics, a work in constructive social theory ; pt. 1.

Politics, a work in constructive social theory
(pt. 1.) Unger, Roberto Mangabeira. False necessity--anti-necessitarian social theory in the service of radical democracy. New ed. London ; New York : Verso, 2001.

Unholy trinity.
Foley, Duncan K. London ; New York : Routledge, 2003.
HB135 .F65 2003

Uni-Taschenbücher
(2176.) Zima, P. V. Theorie des Subjekts. Tübingen : A. Francke, c2000.
BD223 .Z56 2000

El unico libro de astrologia que necesitara.
Woolfolk, Joanna Martine. [Only astrology book you'll ever need. Spanish] Lanham, Md. : Taylor Trade Pub, 2003.
BF1708.1 .W6818 2003

UNIDENTIFIED FLYING OBJECTS.
Evans, Hilary, 1929- From other worlds. Pleasantville, N.Y. : Reader's Digest, c1998.
BF2050 .E93 1998

Herbst, Judith. Aliens. Minneapolis : Lerner Publications, 2005.
BF2050 .H465 2005

Pinotti, Roberto, 1944- Oltre. Firenze : Olimpia, c2002.

Townsend, John. Mysterious encounters. Chicago, IL : Raintree, 2004.
BF2050 .T69 2004

UNIDENTIFIED FLYING OBJECTS - ENCYCLOPEDIAS.
Story, Ronald. The encyclopedia of extraterrestrial encounters. New York : New American Library, c2001.
TL789.16 .S76 2001

UNIDENTIFIED FLYING OBJECTS - JUVENILE LITERATURE.
Townsend, John. Mysterious encounters. Chicago, IL : Raintree, 2004.
BF2050 .T69 2004

UNIDENTIFIED FLYING OBJECTS - SIGHTINGS AND ENCOUNTERS. See also **HUMAN-ALIEN ENCOUNTERS.**
Mishlove, Jeffrey, 1946- The PK man. Charlottesville, VA : Hampton Roads, [c2000]
BF1027.O94 M57 2000

UNIDENTIFIED FLYING OBJECTS - SIGHTINGS AND ENCOUNTERS - NEW ENGLAND.
Imbrogno, Philip J. Celtic mysteries in New England. 1st ed. St. Paul, Minn. : Llewellyn Publications, 2000.
BF2050 I435 2000

UNIFIED SCIENCE. See **SEMANTICS (PHILOSOPHY).**

UNIFORMS. See **COSTUME.**

UNILATERAL NEGLECT (NEUROLOGY). See **NEGLECT (NEUROLOGY).**

United by tragedy.
Wilkins, David, 1944- Nampa, Idaho : Pacific Press Pub. Association, c2003.
BF575.G7 W555 2003

UNITED METHODIST CHURCH (U.S.) - HYMNS - HISTORY AND CRITICISM..
Hickman, Martha Whitmore, 1925- Wade in the water. Nashville, TN : Abingdon Press, 2003.
BV310 .H53 2003

UNITED NATIONS.
2001, año de las Naciones Unidas del diálogo entre civilizaciones. Guatemala : Fundación Casa de la Reconciliación : MINUGUA, 2001.
JX1952 .A233 2001

From promise to practice. Boulder ; London : L. Rienner Publishers, 2003.
JZ6368 .S68 2003

UNITED NATIONS - AFRICA.
Kyelem, Apollinaire. L'éventuel et le possible. [Ouagadougou : Presses universitaires de Ouagadougou, 2002]
1. Black author.

UNITED NATIONS - CONGO (DEMOCRATIC REPUBLIC).
Masangana Diamaka, Robin, 1962- Dialogue politique. Paris : Editoo.com, 2002.
1. Black author.

United Nations Environment Programme.
Leff, Enrique. Saber ambiental. 3a ed. correg. y aument. México : PNUMA ; Siglo Veintiuno, 2002.

UNITED STATES.
Questions and answers about disability and service retirement plans under the Americans with Disabilities Act (ADA) [electronic resource]. [Washington, D.C.] : U.S. Equal Employment Opportunity Commission, [1995]

Questions and answers [electronic resource]. [Washington, D.C.] : U.S. Equal Employment Opportunity Commission, [2000?]

United States. Administration on Aging.
Promising practies in the field of caregiving [electronic resource]. [Washington, D.C.] : U.S. Dept. of Health and Human Services, Administration on Aging, [2003?]

UNITED STATES. AIR FORCE - MANAGEMENT.
Bird, David F. Quality Air Force in an emergency [electronic resource]. Maxwell Air Force Base, Ala. : Air War College, Air University, [1996]

UNITED STATES - ARMED FORCES - UNIT COHESION.
Why they fight [electronic resource]. Carlisle, PA : Strategic Studies Institute, U.S. Army War College, [2003]
U22

UNITED STATES. ARMY - DRILL AND TACTICS.
Leed, Maren. Keeping the warfighting edge. Santa Monica, CA : RAND, 2002.
UB413 .L386 2002

UNITED STATES. ARMY - OFFICERS.
Leed, Maren. Keeping the warfighting edge. Santa Monica, CA : RAND, 2002.
UB413 .L386 2002

UNITED STATES. ARMY - OFFICERS - EDUCATION.
Leed, Maren. Keeping the warfighting edge. Santa Monica, CA : RAND, 2002.
UB413 .L386 2002

UNITED STATES - BIOGRAPHY.
My America. New York : Scribner, c2002.
E169.1 .M968 2002

United States. Bureau of the Census.
Velkoff, Victoria Averil. Gender and aging [electronic resource]. [Washington, D.C.] : U.S. Dept. of Commerce, Economics and Statistics Administration, Bureau of the Census, [1998]

United States. Central Intelligence Agency.
Growing global migration and its implications for the United States. [Washington, D.C.?] : The Board, 2001.

UNITED STATES. CENTRAL INTELLIGENCE AGENCY.
Constantine, Alex. Virtual government. 1st ed. Venice, CA : Feral House, 1997.
BF633 .C67 1997

UNITED STATES - CIVILIZATION.
Gutfeld, Arnon. American exceptionalism. Brighton [England] ; Portland, Or. : Sussex Academic Press, 2002.
E169.1 .G956 2002

Matthews, Christopher, 1945- American. New York : Free Press, c2002.
E169.1 .M429 2002

Pessanha, Rodolfo Gomes. O irracionalismo--, dos Estados Unidos da América à globalizaçāp. Niterói : Muiraquitā, c1998.

UNITED STATES - CIVILIZATION - 1918-1945.
Hirsch, Jerrold, 1948- Portrait of America. Chapel Hill : University of North Carolina Press, c2003.
E175.4.W9 H57 2003

UNITED STATES - CIVILIZATION - 1945-.
How we have changed. Gretna, La. : Pelican Pub. Co., 2003.
E169.12 .H677 2003

UNITED STATES - CIVILIZATION - EUROPEAN INFLUENCES.
Gutfeld, Arnon. American exceptionalism. Brighton [England] ; Portland, Or. : Sussex Academic Press, 2002.
E169.1 .G956 2002

UNITED STATES. COAST GUARD.
Phillips, Donald T. (Donald Thomas), 1952- Character in action. Annapolis, Md. : Naval Institute Press, c2003.
VG53 .P49 2003

UNITED STATES - COLONIZATION.
Nye, David E., 1946- America as second creation. Cambridge : MIT Press, c2003.
E179.5 .N94 2003

United States. Congress. House. Report
(108-286.) United States. Congress. House. Committee on the Judiciary. Federal Prison Industries Competition in Contracting Act of 2003. [Washington, D.C. : U.S. G.P.O., 2003]

United States. Congress. House. Committee on Energy and Commerce. Subcommittee on Health.
Examining issues related to competition in the pharmaceutical marketplace : a review of the FTC report, Generic drug entry prior to patent expiration : hearing before the Subcommittee on Health of the Committee on Energy and Commerce, House of Representatives, One Hundred Seventh Congress, second session, October 9, 2002. Washington : U.S. G.P.O. : For sale by the Supt. of Docs., U.S. G.P.O. [Congressional Sales Office], 2002. iii, 142 p. ; 24 cm. Generic drug entry prior to patent expiration. Distributed to some depository libraries in microfiche. Shipping list no.: 2003-0102-P. Includes bibliographical references. "Serial no. 107-140." ISBN 0-16-069477-9
1. United States. - Federal Trade Commission. - Generic drug entry prior to patent expiration. 2. Generic drugs - Government policy - United States. 3. Drugs - Patents - United States. 4. Competition - United States. 5. Pharmaceutical industry - United States. 6. Witnesses, FTC. I. Muris, Timothy J. II. Title. III. Title: Generic drug entry prior to patent expiration

United States. Congress. House. Committee on Energy and Commerce. Subcommittee on Telecommunications and the Internet. Health of the telecommunication sector : a perspective from investors and economists : hearing before the Subcommittee on Telecommunications and the Internet of the Committee on Energy and Commerce, House of Representatives, One Hundred Eighth Congress, first session, February 5, 2003. Washington : U.S. G.P.O. : For sale by the Supt. of Docs., U.S. G.P.O. [Congressional Sales Office], 2003. iii, 69 p. ; 24 cm. Distributed to some depository libraries in microfiche. Shipping list no.: 2003-0184-P. Includes bibliographical references. "Serial no. 108-3." ISBN 0-16-070086-8
1. Telecommunication - Economic aspects - United States. 2. Telecommunication policy - United States. 3. Investments - United States. 4. Competition - United States. I. Title.

Health of the telecommunication sector : a perspective from the commissioners of the Federal Communications Commission : hearing before the Subcommittee on Telecommunications and the Internet of the Committee on Energy and Commerce, House of Representatives, One Hundred Eighth Congress, first session, February 26, 2003. Washington : U.S. G.P.O. : For sale by the Supt. of Docs., U.S. G.P.O., [Congressional Sales Office], 2003. iii, 114 p. ; 24 cm. Distributed to some depository libraries in microfiche. Shipping list no.: 2003-0207-P. "Serial no. 108-6." Also available via Internet from the GPO Access web site. Addresses as of 6/16/03: http://frwebgate.access.gpo.gov/cgi- bin/ getdoc.cgi?dbname=108%5Fhouse%5Fhearings&docid=f:86047.wais (text version), http://frwebgate.access.gpo.gov/cgi- bin/ getdoc.cgi?dbname=108%5Fhouse%5Fhearings&docid=f:86047.pdf (PDF version); current access is available via PURLS. Text version: URL: http://purl.access.gpo.gov/GPO/LPS32009 PDF version: URL: http://purl.access.gpo.gov/GPO/LPS32010 ISBN 0-16-070205-4
1. Telecommunication - Economic aspects - United States. 2.

Telecommunication policy - United States. 3. Competition - United States. I. Title.

United States. Congress. House. Committee on the Judiciary. Direct broadcast satellite service in the multichannel video distribution market : hearing before the Committee on the Judiciary, House of Representatives, One Hundred Eighth Congress, first session, May 8, 2003. Washington : U.S. G.P.O. For sale by the Supt. of Docs., U.S. G.P.O. [Congressional Sales Office], 2003. iii, 83 p. : ill. : 24 cm. Distributed to some depository libraries in microfiche. Shipping list no.: 2003-0246-P. Includes bibliographical references. "Serial no. 22." Also available via Internet from the Committee web site. Address as of 8/14/03: http://www.house.gov/judiciary/86953.PDF; current access is available via PURL. URL: http://purl.access.gpo.gov/GPO/LPS35156 ISBN 0-16-070400-6
1. Direct broadcast satellite television - United States. 2. Cable television - United States. 3. Competition - United States. I. Title.

Federal Prison Industries Competition in Contracting Act of 2003 : report together with dissenting views (to accompany H.R. 1829) (including cost estimate of the Congressional Budget Office). [Washington, D.C. : U.S. G.P.O., 2003] 181 p. ; 24 cm. (Report / 108th Congress, 1st session, House of Representatives : 108-286) Caption title. Distributed to some depository libraries in microfiche. Shipping list no.: 2004-0009-P. "September 25, 2003." Also available via Internet from the GPO Access web site. Address as of 10/24/03: http://frwebgate.access.gpo.gov/cgi- bin/getdoc.cgi?dbname=108%5Fcong%5Freports&docid=f:hr286.108.pdf; current access is available via PURL. URL: http://purl.access.gpo.gov/GPO/LPS38932
1. Federal Prison Industries, inc. 2. Prison industries - Law and legislation - United States. 3. Government purchasing - United States. 4. Public contracts - United States. 5. Competition - United States. I. Title. II. Series: United States. Congress. House. Report ; 108-286.

United States. Congress. House. Committee on Transportation and Infrastructure. Subcommittee on Aviation. Competition in the U.S. aircraft manufacturing industry : hearing before the Subcommittee on Aviation of the Committee on Transportation and Infrastructure, House of Representatives, One Hundred Seventh Congress, first session, July 26, 2001. Washington : U.S. G.P.O. : For sale by the Supt. of Docs., U.S. G.P.O., [Congressional Sales Office], 2001. v, 118 p. : ill. ; 24 cm. Distributed to some depository libraries in microfiche. Shipping list no.: 2002-0304-P. "107-39." ISBN 0-16-068961-9
1. Aircraft industry - United States. 2. Aeronautics, Commercial - United States. 3. Competition - United States. I. Title. II. Title: Competition in the US aircraft manufacturing industry

The financial condition of the airline industry : hearing before the Subcommittee on Aviation of the Committee on Transportation and Infrastructure, House of Representatives, One Hundred Seventh Congress, second session, September 24, 2002. Washington : U.S. G.P.O. : For sale by the Supt. of Docs., U.S. G.P.O. [Congressional Sales Office], 2002. iii, 142 p. : ill. ; 24 cm. Distributed to some depository libraries in microfiche. Shipping list no.: 2003-0207-P. "107-98." ISBN 0-16-070267-4
1. Airlines - United States - Cost of operation. 2. Airlines - Security measures - United States - Finance. 3. Aeronautics, Commercial - Security measures - United States. 4. Competition - United States. I. Title.

UNITED STATES. CONGRESS. HOUSE - SPEAKERS - BIOGRAPHY.
Kenneally, James J. (James Joseph), 1929- A compassionate conservative. Lanham, Md. : Lexington Books, c2003.
E748.M375 K46 2003

United States. Congress. Senate.
S. hrg.
(106-1133.) United States. Congress. Senate. Committee on Commerce, Science, and Transportation. Antitrust issues in the airline industry. Washington : U.S. G.P.O. : For sale by the Supt. of Docs., U.S. G.P.O., 2003.

(107-873.) United States. Congress. Senate. Committee on the Judiciary. Subcommittee on Antitrust, Business Rights, and Competition. Dominance in the sky. [Washington] : U.S. G.P.O. : For sale by the Supt. of Docs., U.S. G.P.O. [Congressional Sales Office], 2003.

(107-893.) United States. Congress. Senate. Committee on the Judiciary. Subcommittee on Antitrust, Business Rights, and Competition. Dominance on the ground. Washington : U.S. G.P.O. : For sale by the Supt. of Docs., U.S. G.P.O. [Congressional Sales Office], 2003.

(107-903.) United States. Congress. Senate. Committee on Commerce, Science, and Transportation. Subcommittee on Consumer Affairs, Foreign Commerce, and Tourism. Customer choice in automotive repair shops. Washington : U.S. G.P.O. : For sale by the Supt. of Docs., U.S. G.P.O., [Congressional Sales Office], 2003.

United States. Congress. Senate. Committee on Commerce, Science, and Transportation. Antitrust issues in the airline industry : hearing before the Committee on Commerce, Science, and Transportation, United States Senate, One Hundred Sixth Congress, second session, July 27, 2000. Washington : U.S. G.P.O. : For sale by the Supt. of Docs., U.S. G.P.O., 2003. iii, 47 p. : ill. ; 24 cm. (S. hrg. ; 106-1133) "Printed for the use of the Committee on Commerce, Science, and Transportation." Distributed to some depository libraries in microfiche. Shipping list no.: 2004-0003-P. Also available via Internet from the GPO Access web site. Addresses as of 10/29/03: http://frwebgate.access.gpo.gov/cgi- bin/getdoc.cgi?dbname=106%5Fsenate%5Fhearings&docid=f:84450.wais (text version), http://frwebgate.access.gpo.gov/cgi- bin/getdoc.cgi?dbname=106%5Fsenate%5Fhearings&docid=f:84450.pdf (PDF version); current access available via PURLS. Text version: URL: http://purl.access.gpo.gov/GPO/LPS38955 PDF version: URL: http://purl.access.gpo.gov/GPO/LPS38956 ISBN 0-16-070693-9
1. Airlines - Deregulation - United States. 2. Antitrust law - United States. 3. Competition - United States. I. Title. II. Series: United States. Congress. Senate. S. hrg. ; 106-1133.

United States. Congress. Senate. Committee on Commerce, Science, and Transportation. Subcommittee on Consumer Affairs, Foreign Commerce, and Tourism. Customer choice in automotive repair shops : hearing before the Subcommittee on Consumer Affairs, Foreign Commerce and Tourism of the Committee on Commerce, Science, and Transportation, United States Senate, One Hundred Seventh Congress, second session, July 30, 2002. Washington : U.S. G.P.O. : For sale by the Supt. of Docs., U.S. G.P.O., [Congressional Sales Office], 2003. iii, 43 p. ; 24 cm. (S. hrg. ; 107-903) "Printed for the use of the Committee on Commerce, Science, and Transportation." Distributed to some depository libraries in microfiche. Shipping list no.: 2003-0181-P. Also available via Internet from the GPO Access web site. Addresses as of 5/28/03: http://frwebgate.access.gpo.gov/cgi- bin/getdoc.cgi?dbname=107%5Fsenate%5Fhearings&docid=f:84857.wais (text version), http://frwebgate.access.gpo.gov/cgi- bin/getdoc.cgi?dbname=107%5Fsenate%5Fhearings&docid=f:84857.pdf (PDF version); current access is available via PURLS. Text version: URL: http://purl.access.gpo.gov/GPO/LPS31280 PDF version: URL: http://purl.access.gpo.gov/GPO/LPS31281 ISBN 0-16-069853-7
1. Automobile repair shops - United States. 2. Automobile dealers - United States. 3. Competition - United States. 4. Consumer protection - United States. I. Title. II. Series: United States. Congress. Senate. S. hrg. ; 107-903.

United States. Congress. Senate. Committee on the Judiciary. Subcommittee on Antitrust, Business Rights, and Competition. Dominance in the sky : cable competition and the EchoStar-DIRECTV merger : hearing before the Subcommittee on Antitrust, Business Rights, and Competition of the Committee onthe Judiciary, United States Senate, One Hundred Seventh Congress, second session, March 6, 2002. [Washington] : U.S. G.P.O. : For sale by the Supt. of Docs., U.S. G.P.O. [Congressional Sales Office], 2003. iv, 155 p. : ill., maps : 24 cm. (S. hrg. ; 107-873) Distributed to some depository libraries in microfiche. Shipping list no.: 2003-0168-P. Includes bibliographical references. "Serial no. J-107-65." ISBN 0-16-069785-9
1. EchoStar (Firm) 2. DIRECTV (Firm) 3. Direct broadcast satellite television - United States. 4. Cable television - United States. 5. Consolidation and merger of corporations - United States. 6. Competition - United States. I. Title. II. Title: Cable competition and the EchoStar-DIRECTV merger III. Series: United States. Congress. Senate. S. hrg. ; 107-873.

Dominance on the ground : cable competition and the AT&T-Comcast merger : hearing before the Subcommittee on Antitrust, Business Rights, and Competition of the Committee on the Judiciary, United States Senate, One Hundred Seventh Congress, second session, April 23, 2002. Washington : U.S. G.P.O. : For sale by the Supt. of Docs., U.S. G.P.O. [Congressional Sales Office], 2003. iii, 96 p. : ill. ; 24 cm. (S. Hrg. ; 107-893) Distributed to some depository libraries in microfiche. Shipping list no.: 2003-0178-P. Includes bibliographical references. "Serial no. J-107-75." Also available via Internet from the GPO Access web site. Address as of 5/9/03: http://frwebgate.access.gpo.gov/cgi- bin/getdoc.cgi?dbname=107%5Fsenate%5Fhearings&docid=f:85889.pdf; current access is available via PURL. URL: http://purl.access.gpo.gov/GPO/LPS30981 ISBN 0-16-069822-7
1. American Telephone and Telegraph Company. 2. Comcast Corporation. 3. Cable television - Law and legislation - United States. 4. Consolidation and merger of corporations - United States. 5. Competition - United States. I. Title. II. Series: United States. Congress. Senate. S. hrg. ; 107-893.

United States. Dept. of Agriculture. Economic Research Service.
King, John L. Concentration and technology in agricultural input industries [electronic resource]. [Washington, D.C.] : U.S. Dept of Agriculture, [2001].

United States. Dept. of Health and Human Services.
Mental health and mass violence [electronic resource]. [Bethesda, MD : National Institute of Mental Health, 2002]

UNITED STATES. DEPT. OF HEALTH AND HUMAN SERVICES. NATIONAL INSTITUTES OF HEALTH. NATIONAL INSTITUTE OF MENTAL HEALTH.
Helping children and adolescents cope with violence and disasters [electronic resource]. Bethesda, MD : Office of Communications and Public Liaison, [2001]

UNITED STATES - DISCOVERY AND EXPLORATION.
Nye, David E., 1946- America as second creation. Cambridge : MIT Press, c2003.
E179.5 .N94 2003

UNITED STATES - ECONOMIC POLICY.
Friedman, Milton, 1912- Capitalism and freedom. 40th anniversary ed. Chicago : University of Chicago Press, 2002.
HB501 .F7 2002

UNITED STATES - ECONOMIC POLICY - 1993-2001.
Monkeywrenching the new world order [sound recording]. Oakland, Calif : AK Press ; San Francisco, CA : Alternative Tentacles Records, 2001.

UNITED STATES - ECONOMIC POLICY - 2001-.
Monkeywrenching the new world order [sound recording]. Oakland, Calif : AK Press ; San Francisco, CA : Alternative Tentacles Records, 2001.

UNITED STATES - EMIGRATION AND IMMIGRATION.
McLaughlin, Bob. [USA immigration & orientation. Spanish] USA inmigraciǿn y orientaciǿn. 1a. ed. en español. Satellite Beach, Fla. : Wellesworth Pub., c2001.

UNITED STATES - EMIGRATION AND IMMIGRATION LAW. *See* **EMIGRATION AND IMMIGRATION LAW - UNITED STATES.**

United States. Equal Employment Opportunity Commission.
Notice
(915.002.) Questions and answers about disability and service retirement plans under the Americans with Disabilities Act (ADA) [electronic resource]. [Washington, D.C.] : U.S. Equal Employment Opportunity Commission, [1995]

Questions and answers about disability and service retirement plans under the Americans with Disabilities Act (ADA) [electronic resource]. [Washington, D.C.] : U.S. Equal Employment Opportunity Commission, [1995]

Questions and answers [electronic resource]. [Washington, D.C.] : U.S. Equal Employment Opportunity Commission, [2000?]

UNITED STATES. EQUAL EMPLOYMENT OPPORTUNITY COMMISSION.
Questions and answers about disability and service retirement plans under the Americans with Disabilities Act (ADA) [electronic resource]. [Washington, D.C.] : U.S. Equal Employment Opportunity Commission, [1995]

Questions and answers [electronic resource]. [Washington, D.C.] : U.S. Equal Employment Opportunity Commission, [2000?]

United States. Federal Trade Commission.
United States. General Accounting Office. Federal Trade Commission [electronic resource]. [Washington, D.C.] : U.S. General Accounting Office, [2002]

BIBLIOGRAPHIC GUIDE

United States. Federal Trade Commission. Bureau of 568

United States. General Accounting Office. Federal Trade Commission [electronic resource]. [Washington, D.C.] : U.S. General Accounting Office, [2002]

UNITED STATES. FEDERAL TRADE COMMISSION. BUREAU OF CONSUMER PROTECTION.
Privacy [electronic resource]. [Washington, D.C.] : Federal Trade Commission, Bureau of Consumer Protection, Office of Consumer and Business Education, [2002]

Privacy [electronic resource]. [Washington, D.C.] : Federal Trade Commission, Bureau of Consumer Protection, Office of Consumer and Business Education, [2002]

UNITED STATES. FEDERAL TRADE COMMISSION. GENERIC DRUG ENTRY PRIOR TO PATENT EXPIRATION.
United States. Congress. House. Committee on Energy and Commerce. Subcommittee on Health. Examining issues related to competition in the pharmaceutical marketplace. Washington : U.S. G.P.O. : For sale by the Supt. of Docs., U.S. G.P.O. [Congressional Sales Office], 2002.

United States. Federal Trade Commission. Office of Consumer and Business Education.
Privacy [electronic resource]. [Washington, D.C.] : Federal Trade Commission, Bureau of Consumer Protection, Office of Consumer and Business Education, [2002]

Privacy [electronic resource]. [Washington, D.C.] : Federal Trade Commission, Bureau of Consumer Protection, Office of Consumer and Business Education, [2002]

Privacy [electronic resource]. [Washington, D.C.] : Federal Trade Commission, Bureau of Consumer Protection, Office of Consumer and Business Education, [2002]

UNITED STATES - FOREIGN ECONOMIC RELATIONS - RUSSIA (FEDERATION).
Parshev, A. P. (Andreĭ Petrovich) Pochemu Amerika nastupaet. Moskva : AST : Astrel', 2002.
HF1558.2.Z4 P37 2002

UNITED STATES - FOREIGN PUBLIC OPINION.
Crockatt, Richard. America embattled. London ; New York : Routledge, 2003.
E902 .C76 2003

UNITED STATES - FOREIGN RELATIONS - 1783-1865.
Kaplan, Amy. The anarchy of empire in the making of U.S. culture. Cambridge, Mass. : Harvard University Press, 2002.
E661.7 .K37 2002

UNITED STATES - FOREIGN RELATIONS - 1865-1921.
Hansen, Jonathan M. The lost promise of patriotism. Chicago : University of Chicago Press, c2003.
E661 .H316 2003

Kaplan, Amy. The anarchy of empire in the making of U.S. culture. Cambridge, Mass. : Harvard University Press, 2002.
E661.7 .K37 2002

UNITED STATES - FOREIGN RELATIONS - 1989-.
Crockatt, Richard. America embattled. London ; New York : Routledge, 2003.
E902 .C76 2003

Kritik der Gewalt. Wien : Promedia, c2002.
D860 .K75 2002

Monkeywrenching the new world order [sound recording]. Oakland, Calif : AK Press ; San Francisco, CA : Alternative Tentacles Records, 2001.

UNITED STATES - FOREIGN RELATIONS - 2001-.
Crockatt, Richard. America embattled. London ; New York : Routledge, 2003.
E902 .C76 2003

Hirsh, Michael, 1957- At war with ourselves. New York : Oxford University Press, 2003.
E895 .H57 2003

UNITED STATES - FOREIGN RELATIONS - 20TH CENTURY.
Kivimäki, Timo. US-Indonesian hegemonic bargaining. Aldershot ; Burlington, VT : Ashgate, 2003.

UNITED STATES - FOREIGN RELATIONS - FORECASTING.
Emmott, Bill. 20:21 vision. London : Allen Lane, 2003.

UNITED STATES - FOREIGN RELATIONS - INDONESIA.
Kivimäki, Timo. US-Indonesian hegemonic bargaining. Aldershot ; Burlington, VT : Ashgate, 2003.

UNITED STATES - FOREIGN RELATIONS - PHILIPPINES.
Vestiges of war. New York : New York University Press, 2000.
DS679 .V47 2000

UNITED STATES - FOREIGN RELATIONS - PHILOSOPHY.
Hirsh, Michael, 1957- At war with ourselves. New York : Oxford University Press, 2003.
E895 .H57 2003

Hughes, Richard T. (Richard Thomas), 1943- Myths America lives by. Urbana : University of Illinois Press, c2003.
E175.9 .H84 2003

United States. General Accounting Office.
Christoff, Joseph A. Issues in implementing international peace operations [electronic resource]. [Washington, D.C.] : U.S. General Accounting Office, [2002]

Federal Trade Commission [electronic resource] : study needed to assess the effects of recent divestitures on competition in retail markets. [Washington, D.C.] : U.S. General Accounting Office, [2002] System requirements: Adobe Acrobat Reader. Mode of access: Internet from GAO web site. Address as of 06/25/03: http://www.gao.gov/new.items/d02793.pdf; current access available via PURL. Title from title screen (viewed on June 25, 2003). "September 2002." Paper version available from: General Accounting Office, 441 G St., NW, Rm. LM, Washington, D.C. 20548. Includes bibliographical references. "GAO-02-793." URL: http://purl.access.gpo.gov/GPO/LPS32503 Available in other form: United States. General Accounting Office. Federal Trade Commission : study needed to assess the effects of recent divestitures on competition in retail markets iii, 131 p. (OCoLC)51518348.
1. United States. - Federal Trade Commission. 2. Competition - United States. 3. Retail trade - United States. I. United States. Federal Trade Commission. II. Title. III. Title: Study needed to assess the effects of recent divestitures on competition in retail markets IV. Title: United States. General Accounting Office. Federal Trade Commission : study needed to assess the effects of recent divestitures on competition in retail markets iii, 131 p.

Hecker, JayEtta Z. Commercial aviation [electronic resource]. [Washington, D.C.] : U.S. General Accounting Office, [2002]

Telecommunications [electronic resource] : FCC should include call quality in its annual report on competition in mobile phone services. [Washington, D.C.] : U.S. General Accounting Office, [2003] Running title: Mobile phone call quality. Mode of access: Internet from GAO web site. Address as of 11/15/03: http://www.gao.gov/new.items/d03501.pdf; current access available via PURL. Title from title screen (viewed on Nov. 15, 2003). "April 2003." Paper version available from: General Accounting Office, 441 G St., NW, Rm. LM, Washington, D.C. 20548. Includes bibliographical references. "GAO-03-501." URL: http://purl.access.gpo.gov/GPO/LPS36965 Available in other form: United States. General Accounting Office. Telecommunications : FCC should include call quality in its annual report on competition in mobile phone services ii, 59 p. (OCoLC)53305902.
1. Cellular telephones - United States. 2. Competition - United States. I. Title. II. Title: Telecommunications : Federal Communications Commission should include call quality in its annual report on competition in mobile phone services III. Title: FCC should include call quality in its annual report on competition in mobile phone services IV. Title: Mobile phone call quality V. Title: United States. General Accounting Office. Telecommunications : FCC should include call quality in its annual report on competition in mobile phone services ii, 59 p.

Telecommunications [electronic resource] : GSA action needed to realize benefits of metropolitan area acquisition program / United States General Accounting Office. Washington, D.C. : U.S. General Accounting Office, [2002] Mode of access: Internet from the GAO web site. Address as of 11/12/2003: http://www.gao.gov/new.items/d02325.pdf ; current access available via PURL. Title from title screen (viewed on Nov. 12, 2003). Paper version available from: U.S. General Accounting Office, 441 G st, NW, Rm. LM, Washington, D.C. 20548. "April 2002." "GAO-02-325." Includes bibliographical references. URL: http://purl.access.gpo.gov/GPO/LPS38306 Available in other form: United States. General Accounting Office. Telecommunications : GSA action needed to realize benefits of Metropolitan Area Acquisition program i, 26 p. : ill. ; 28 cm. (OCoLC)49742888.
1. Local telephone service - Rates - United States. 2. Telecommunication policy - United States. 3. Competition - United States. I. Title. II. Title: United States. General Accounting Office. Telecommunications : GSA action needed to realize benefits of Metropolitan Area Acquisition program i, 26 p. : ill. ; 28 cm.

World Trade Organization [electronic resource] : early decisions are vital to progress in ongoing negotiations. [Washington, D.C.] : U.S. General Accounting Office, [2002] Running title: World Trade Organization : the Doha development agenda. System requirements: Adobe Acrobat Reader. Mode of access: Internet from GAO web site. Address as of 06/30/03: http://www.gao.gov/new.items/d02879.pdf; current access available via PURL. Title from title screen (viewed on June 30, 2003). "September 2002." Paper version available from: General Accounting Office, 441 G St., NW, Rm. LM, Washington, D.C. 20548. Includes bibliographical references. "GAO-02-879." URL: http://purl.access.gpo.gov/GPO/LPS32440 Available in other form: United States. General Accounting Office. World Trade Organization : early decisions are vital to progress in ongoing negotiations ii, 55 p. (OCoLC)50929806.
1. World Trade Organization - Decision making. 2. Negotiation. 3. International trade. 4. International relations. I. World Trade Organization. II. Title. III. Title: Early decisions are vital to progress in ongoing negotiations IV. Title: World Trade Organization : the Doha development agenda V. Title: United States. General Accounting Office. World Trade Organization : early decisions are vital to progress in ongoing negotiations ii, 55 p.

United States. General Accounting Office. Federal Trade Commission : study needed to assess the effects of recent divestitures on competition in retail markets iii, 131 p.
United States. General Accounting Office. Federal Trade Commission [electronic resource]. [Washington, D.C.] : U.S. General Accounting Office, [2002]

United States. General Accounting Office. Telecommunications : FCC should include call quality in its annual report on competition in mobile phone services ii, 59 p.
United States. General Accounting Office. Telecommunications [electronic resource]. [Washington, D.C.] : U.S. General Accounting Office, [2003]

United States. General Accounting Office. Telecommunications : GSA action needed to realize benefits of Metropolitan Area Acquisition program i, 26 p. : ill. ; 28 cm.
United States. General Accounting Office. Telecommunications [electronic resource]. Washington, D.C. : U.S. General Accounting Office, [2002]

United States. General Accounting Office. World Trade Organization : early decisions are vital to progress in ongoing negotiations ii, 55 p.
United States. General Accounting Office. World Trade Organization [electronic resource]. [Washington, D.C.] : U.S. General Accounting Office, [2002]

UNITED STATES - GEOGRAPHY.
Linklater, Andro. Measuring America. New York : Walker & Co., 2002.
E161.3 .L46 2002

UNITED STATES - GOVERNMENT. *See* **UNITED STATES - POLITICS AND GOVERNMENT.**

UNITED STATES - HISTORICAL GEOGRAPHY.
Nye, David E., 1946- America as second creation. Cambridge : MIT Press, c2003.
E179.5 .N94 2003

UNITED STATES - HISTORIOGRAPHY.
Hirsch, Jerrold, 1948- Portrait of America. Chapel Hill : University of North Carolina Press, c2003.
E175.4.W9 H57 2003

Pfitzer, Gregory M. Picturing the past. Washington [D.C.] : Smithsonian Institution Press, c2002.
E175 .P477 2002

UNITED STATES - HISTORY - 1809-1817.
Skeen, Carl Edward. 1816. Lexington : University Press of Kentucky, c2003.
E341 .S57 2003

UNITED STATES - HISTORY - 1933-1945.
McGovern, James R. And a time for hope. Westport, Conn. : Praeger, 2000.

E806 .M45 2000

UNITED STATES - HISTORY - CIVIL WAR, 1861-1865 - MISCELLANEA.
Kent, James H., 1939- Past life memories as a Confederate soldier. Huntsville, AR : Ozark Mountain Publishers, c2003.
BF1156.R45 K45 2003

UNITED STATES - HISTORY - CIVIL WAR, 1861-1865 - SOCIAL ASPECTS.
Lawson, Melinda, 1954- Patriot fires. Lawrence : University Press of Kansas, c2002.
E468.9 .L39 2002

UNITED STATES - HISTORY, MILITARY.
Cannon, Carl M. The pursuit of happiness in times of war. Lanham, MD ; Oxford : Rowman & Littlefield ; [Lanham, Md.] : Distributed by National Book Network, c2004.
E183 .C25 2004

UNITED STATES - HISTORY, MILITARY - MISCELLANEA.
What ifs? of American history. New York : G.P. Putnam's, c2003.
E179 .W535 2003

UNITED STATES - HISTORY - MISCELLANEA.
Civilization under attack. 1st ed. St. Paul, Minn. : Llewellyn Publications, 2001.
BF1729.U5 C57 2001

Davis, Kenneth C. History. 1st ed. New York : HarperCollins, c2003.
E178.25 .D37 2003

What ifs? of American history. New York : G.P. Putnam's, c2003.
E179 .W535 2003

UNITED STATES - HISTORY - PHILOSOPHY.
Hughes, Richard T. (Richard Thomas), 1943- Myths America lives by. Urbana : University of Illinois Press, c2003.
E175.9 .H84 2003

UNITED STATES - HISTORY, POLITICAL. See **UNITED STATES - POLITICS AND GOVERNMENT.**

UNITED STATES - HISTORY - RELIGIOUS ASPECTS - CHRISTIANITY.
Hughes, Richard T. (Richard Thomas), 1943- Myths America lives by. Urbana : University of Illinois Press, c2003.
E175.9 .H84 2003

UNITED STATES - HISTORY - REVOLUTION, 1775-1783 - INFLUENCE.
Trees, Andrew S., 1968- The founding fathers and the politics of character. Princeton, N.J. : Princeton University Press, c2004.
E302.1 .T74 2004

York, Neil Longley. Turning the world upside down. Westport, Conn. ; London : Praeger, 2003.
E210 .Y67 2003

UNITED STATES - HISTORY - WAR OF 1812 - INFLUENCE.
Skeen, Carl Edward. 1816. Lexington : University Press of Kentucky, c2003.
E341 .S57 2003

UNITED STATES - INTELLECTUAL LIFE.
Hansen, Jonathan M. The lost promise of patriotism. Chicago : University of Chicago Press, c2003.
E661 .H316 2003

UNITED STATES - INTELLECTUAL LIFE - 20TH CENTURY.
Hirsch, Jerrold, 1948- Portrait of America. Chapel Hill : University of North Carolina Press, c2003.
E175.4.W9 H57 2003

Macdonald, Dwight. Interviews with Dwight Macdonald. Jackson : University Press of Mississippi, c2003.
E169.1 .M1363 2003

UNITED STATES - LITERATURES. See **AMERICAN LITERATURE.**

UNITED STATES - MORAL CONDITIONS.
The fractious nation? Berkeley : University of California Press, c2003.
E169.12 .F69 2003

Holt, W. V. America by trial. München : Tuduv, c2001.

White, Curtis, 1951- The middle mind. 1st ed. [San Francisco] : HarperSanFrancisco, c2003.

UNITED STATES - MORAL CONDITIONS - HISTORY.
Lears, T. J. Jackson, 1947- Something for nothing. New York : Viking, 2003.
HV6715 .L415 2003

United States. National Aeronautics and Space Administration.
Eaton, Robert C. The octavolateralis system and Mauthner cell interactions and questions [microform]. [Washington, D.C. : National Aeronautics and Space Administration, 1997]

Rumbaugh, Duane M., 1929- Respondents, operants, and emergents [microform]. [Washington, D.C. : National Aeronautics and Space Administration, 1997]

Three-dimensional user interfaces for immersive virtual reality [microform]. Providence, RI : Brown University Computer Graphics Group, [1997]

United States. National Aeronautics and Space ASdministration.
Levy, Alon Y. (Alon Yitzchak) Irrelevance reasoning in knowledge based systems [miroform]. [Washington, DC : National Aeronautics and Space Administration] ; Springfield, VA : Available from the National Technical Information Service, [1998]

United States. National Foreign Intelligence Board.
Growing global migration and its implications for the United States. [Washington, D.C.?] : The Board, 2001.

Growing global migration and its implications for the United States [electronic resource]. Electronic document. [Washington, D.C.? : National Intelligence Council, 2001]
CB161 .G768

United States. National Intelligence Council.
Growing global migration and its implications for the United States [electronic resource]. Electronic document. [Washington, D.C.? : National Intelligence Council, 2001]
CB161 .G768

UNITED STATES - NATIONAL SECURITY. See **NATIONAL SECURITY - UNITED STATES.**

UNITED STATES - NATURALIZATION. See **NATURALIZATION - UNITED STATES.**

UNITED STATES - POLITICS AND GOVERNMENT.
Cannon, Carl M. The pursuit of happiness in times of war. Lanham, MD ; Oxford : Rowman & Littlefield ; [Lanham, Md.] : Distributed by National Book Network, c2004.
E183 .C25 2004

UNITED STATES - POLITICS AND GOVERNMENT - 1775-1783 - PHILOSOPHY.
York, Neil Longley. Turning the world upside down. Westport, Conn. ; London : Praeger, 2003.
E210 .Y67 2003

UNITED STATES - POLITICS AND GOVERNMENT - 1783-1809.
Trees, Andrew S., 1968- The founding fathers and the politics of character. Princeton, N.J. : Princeton University Press, c2004.
E302.1 .T74 2004

UNITED STATES - POLITICS AND GOVERNMENT - 1809-1817.
Skeen, Carl Edward. 1816. Lexington : University Press of Kentucky, c2003.
E341 .S57 2003

UNITED STATES - POLITICS AND GOVERNMENT - 1861-1865.
Lawson, Melinda, 1954- Patriot fires. Lawrence : University Press of Kansas, c2002.
E468.9 .L39 2002

Winger, Stewart Lance. Lincoln, religion, and romantic cultural politics. DeKalb : Northern Illinois University Press, c2003.
E457.2 .W77 2003

UNITED STATES - POLITICS AND GOVERNMENT - 1865-1900.
Barber, Lucy G. (Lucy Grace), 1964- Marching on Washington. Berkeley : University of California Press, c2002.
E743 .B338 2002

UNITED STATES - POLITICS AND GOVERNMENT - 1865-1933.
Hansen, Jonathan M. The lost promise of patriotism. Chicago : University of Chicago Press, c2003.
E661 .H316 2003

UNITED STATES - POLITICS AND GOVERNMENT - 1897-1901.
Gould, Lewis L. The modern American presidency. Lawrence : University Press of Kansas, c2003.
E176.1 .G68 2003

UNITED STATES - POLITICS AND GOVERNMENT - 1933-1945.
The achievement of American liberalism. New York : Columbia University Press, c2003.
E806 .M63 2003

UNITED STATES - POLITICS AND GOVERNMENT - 1989-.
The fractious nation? Berkeley : University of California Press, c2003.
E169.12 .F69 2003

Kook, Rebecca B., 1959- The logic of democratic exclusion. Lanham, Md. : Lexington Books, c2002.
E185.615 .K59 2002

Monkeywrenching the new world order [sound recording]. Oakland, Calif : AK Press ; San Francisco, CA : Alternative Tentacles Records, 2001.

UNITED STATES - POLITICS AND GOVERNMENT - 2001-.
Noonan, Peggy, 1950- A heart, a cross & a flag. New York : Free Press, c2003.
E903 .N66 2003

UNITED STATES - POLITICS AND GOVERNMENT - 20TH CENTURY.
The achievement of American liberalism. New York : Columbia University Press, c2003.
E806 .M63 2003

Barber, Lucy G. (Lucy Grace), 1964- Marching on Washington. Berkeley : University of California Press, c2002.
E743 .B338 2002

Constantine, Alex. Virtual government. 1st ed. Venice, CA : Feral House, 1997.
BF633 .C67 1997

Elfenbein, Stefan W., 1964- Die veränderte Rolle der New York Times. Frankfurt am Main ; New York : P. Lang, c1996.
PN4899.N42 N375 1996

Gould, Lewis L. The modern American presidency. Lawrence : University Press of Kansas, c2003.
E176.1 .G68 2003

Horowitz, David A. America's political class under fire. New York ; London : Routledge, 2003.
HN90.S6 H67 2003

Kenneally, James J. (James Joseph), 1929- A compassionate conservative. Lanham, Md. : Lexington Books, c2003.
E748.M375 K46 2003

Macdonald, Dwight. Interviews with Dwight Macdonald. Jackson : University Press of Mississippi, c2003.
E169.1 .M1363 2003

Ryter, Jon Christian. Whatever happened to America? Tampa, FL : Hallberg Pub., 2001, c2000.
E743 .R98 2001

Separation of powers. Washington, D.C. : CQ Press, a division of Congressional Quarterly Inc., c2003.
JK305 .S465 2003

Shafer, Byron E. The two majorities and the puzzle of modern American politics. Lawrence, Kan. : University Press of Kansas, c2003.
JK2261 .S4298 2003

Tou shi Meiguo. Di 1 ban. Beijing : Zhongguo she hui ke xue chu ban she : Jing xiao Xin hua shu dian, 2002.
E175.8 .T78 2002

Vestiges of war. New York : New York University Press, 2000.
DS679 .V47 2000

UNITED STATES - POLITICS AND GOVERNMENT - PHILOSOPHY.
Cannon, Carl M. The pursuit of happiness in times of war. Lanham, MD ; Oxford : Rowman & Littlefield ; [Lanham, Md.] : Distributed by National Book Network, c2004.
E183 .C25 2004

UNITED STATES - POLITICS AND GOVERNMENT - REVOLUTION, 1775-1783. See **UNITED STATES - POLITICS AND GOVERNMENT - 1775-1783.**

UNITED STATES - POPULAR CULTURE. See **POPULAR CULTURE - UNITED STATES.**

UNITED STATES - PUBLIC LANDS. *See* **PUBLIC LANDS - UNITED STATES.**

UNITED STATES - RACE QUESTION. *See* **UNITED STATES - RACE RELATIONS.**

UNITED STATES - RACE RELATIONS.
The afro-asian century. Durham, N.C. : Duke University Press, 2003.

Wernitznig, Dagmar. Going native or going naive? Lanham, MD : University Press of America, c2003.
E98.P99 W47 2003

UNITED STATES - RACE RELATIONS - POLITICAL ASPECTS.
Kook, Rebecca B., 1959- The logic of democratic exclusion. Lanham, Md. : Lexington Books, c2002.
E185.615 .K59 2002

UNITED STATES - RACE RELATIONS - PSYCHOLOGICAL ASPECTS.
Longing to tell. 1st ed. New York : Farrar, Straus and Giroux, 2003.
E185.625 .L66 2003

UNITED STATES - RACE RELATIONS - UNITED STATES - HISTORY - 19TH CENTURY.
Cox, Robert S., 1958- Body and soul. Charlottesville : University of Virginia Press, 2003.
BF1242.U6 C69 2003

UNITED STATES - RELATIONS - EUROPE.
Kazaaam! splat! ploof!. Lanham, Md. ; Oxford : Rowman & Littlefield, c2003.
D1055 .K39 2003

UNITED STATES - SOCIAL CONDITIONS - 1933-1945.
McGovern, James R. And a time for hope. Westport, Conn. : Praeger, 2000.
E806 .M45 2000

UNITED STATES - SOCIAL CONDITIONS - 1945-.
How we have changed. Gretna, La. : Pelican Pub. Co., 2003.
E169.12 .H677 2003

Limonov, Ėduard. Distsiplinarnyĭ sanatoriĭ. Sankt-Peterburg : Amfora, 2002.
CB428 .L556 2002

UNITED STATES - SOCIAL CONDITIONS - 1980-.
The fractious nation? Berkeley : University of California Press, c2003.
E169.12 .F69 2003

Holt, W. V. America by trial. München : Tuduv, c2001.

Noonan, Peggy, 1950- A heart, a cross & a flag. New York : Free Press, c2003.
E903 .N66 2003

White, Curtis, 1951- The middle mind. 1st ed. [San Francisco] : HarperSanFrancisco, c2003.

UNITED STATES - SOCIAL CONDITIONS - 20TH CENTURY.
The achievement of American liberalism. New York : Columbia University Press, c2003.
E806 .M63 2003

Macdonald, Dwight. Interviews with Dwight Macdonald. Jackson : University Press of Mississippi, c2003.
E169.1 .M1363 2003

UNITED STATES - SOCIAL LIFE AND CUSTOMS.
Gelfert, Hans-Dieter, 1937- Typisch amerikanisch. Originalausg. München : Beck, c2002.
E169.1 .G44 2002

Life as we know it. 1st Washington Square Press trade pbk. ed. New York : Washington Square Press, 2003.

Wernitznig, Dagmar. Going native or going naive? Lanham, MD : University Press of America, c2003.
E98.P99 W47 2003

UNITED STATES - SOCIAL LIFE AND CUSTOMS - 1918-1945.
McGovern, James R. And a time for hope. Westport, Conn. : Praeger, 2000.
E806 .M45 2000

UNITED STATES - SOCIAL LIFE AND CUSTOMS - 20TH CENTURY.
Brokaw, Tom. A long way from home. 1st trade ed. New York : Random House, c2002.
PN4874.B717 A3 2002b

UNITED STATES - SOCIAL POLICY.
Brush, Lisa Diane. Gender and governance. Walnut Creek, CA ; Oxford : AltaMira Press, c2003.
JC330 .B75 2003

UNITED STATES - SOCIAL POLICY - 1993-.
Holt, W. V. America by trial. München : Tuduv, c2001.

UNITED STATES - SOCIAL POLICY - EVALUATION.
Zigler, Edward, 1930- The first three years & beyond. New Haven : Yale University Press, c2002.
HQ767.9 .Z543 2002

UNITED STATES - STUDY AND TEACHING.
Tou shi Meiguo. Di 1 ban. Beijing : Zhongguo she hui ke xue chu ban she : Jing xiao Xin hua shu dian, 2002.
E175.8 .T78 2002

UNITED STATES - SURVEYS - HISTORY.
Linklater, Andro. Measuring America. New York : Walker & Co., 2002.
E161.3 .L46 2002

UNITED STATES - TERRITORIAL EXPANSION.
Gutfeld, Arnon. American exceptionalism. Brighton [England] ; Portland, Or. : Sussex Academic Press, 2002.
E169.1 .G956 2002

Kaplan, Amy. The anarchy of empire in the making of U.S. culture. Cambridge, Mass. : Harvard University Press, 2002.
E661.7 .K37 2002

Linklater, Andro. Measuring America. New York : Walker & Co., 2002.
E161.3 .L46 2002

York, Neil Longley. Turning the world upside down. Westport, Conn. ; London : Praeger, 2003.
E210 .Y67 2003

The unity of consciousness : binding, integration, and dissociation / edited by Axel Cleeremans. Oxford ; New York : Oxford University Press, 2003. xiii, 314 p. : ill. ; 25 cm. Includes bibliographical references and index. ISBN 0-19-850857-3 DDC 153
1. Consciousness. I. Cleeremans, Axel.
BF311 .U55 2003

Univers historique
Ferrières, Madeleine. Histoire des peurs alimentaires. Paris : Editions du Seuil, c2002.

Universal-Bibliothek (Stuttgart, Germany)
(Nr. 17626.) Matt, Peter von. Literaturwissenschaft und Psychoanalyse. Stuttgart : Reclam, c2001.

(Nr. 18118.) Baumann, Günter, 1962- Meisterwerke der Architektur. Stuttgart : Reclam, c2001.
NA200 .B33 2001

(Nr. 18164.) Habermas, Jürgen. Kommunikatives Handeln und detranszendentalisierte Vernunft. Stuttgart : Reclam, c2001.
P91 .H33 2001

(Nr. 8999.) Tetens, Holm, 1948- Geist, Gehirn, Maschine. Stuttgart : Reclam, c1994.
BF163 .T48 1994x

UNIVERSAL DESIGN.
Inclusive design. London ; New York : Springer, c2003.
TA174 .I464 2003

UNIVERSAL HISTORY. *See* **WORLD HISTORY.**

UNIVERSAL SUCCESSION. *See* **INHERITANCE AND SUCCESSION.**

The universal traveler.
Koberg, Don, 1930- 4th ed. Menlo Park, Calif. : Crisp Learning, c2003.
BF441 .K55 2003

UNIVERSE. *See* **COSMOLOGY.**

Universe of worlds.
Grant, Robert J. Virginia Beach, Va. : A.R.E. Press, 2005.
BF1261.2 .G73 2005

Universidad de Palermo (Palermo, Buenos Aires, Argentina). Facultad de Humanidades y Ciencias Sociales.
Psicodebate. Buenos Aires, Argentina : Universidad de Palermo, Facultad de Humanidades y Ciencias Sociales, [2000]-
BF5 .P+

Universidad Nacional Autónoma de México. Facultad de Filosofía y Letras.
Construcción de conocimiento y educación virtual. 1. ed. Ciudad Universitaria, México, D.F. : Universidad Nacional Autónoma de México, 2000.

LB1060 .C658 2000

Universidad Nacional de Tucumán. Instituto de Estudios Antropológicos y Filosofiá de la Religión.
Antropología e interpretación. Tucumán, Argentina : Instituto de Estudios Antropológicos y Filosofía de la Religión, Facultad de Filosofía y Letras, Universidad Nacional de Tucumán, c2001.
BD450 .A564 2001

Universidade Potiguar.
Escrita psi. Natal/RN : Universidade Potiguar, 2002-
BF5 .E83

Università di Milano. Sezione di filologia classica.
Tra IV e V secolo. Milano : Cisalpino, 2002.

Università internazionale del secondo Rinascimento
(8) Tapergi, Fausto, 1909- La filosofia come scienza della vita. 1a ed. Milano : Spirali, 2001.

Università internazionale del secondo Rinascimento (Series)
(8.) Tapergi, Fausto, 1909- La filosofia come scienza della vita. 1a ed. Milano : Spirali, 2001.

Universitat Bielefeld. Forschungsgruppe Historische Sinnbildung.
Identities. New York ; Oxford : Berghahn Books, 2002.
HM716 .I34 2002

Universität Bielefeld. Forschungsgruppe Historische Sinnbildung.
Western historical thinking. New York : Berghahn Books, 2002.
D16.9 .W454 2002

Universität Frankfurt am Main.
Die Öffentlichkeit der Vernunft und die Vernunft der Öffentlichkeit. 1. Aufl. Frankfurt am Main : Suhrkamp, 2001.
B3258.H324 O34 2001

Universität Heidelberg. Psychiatrische Klinik.
Ekel. 1. Aufl. Hürtgenwald : G. Pressler, c2003.
BF575.A886 E34 2003

Universität Salzburg. Institut für Anglistik und Amerikanistik.
Pharmacum carthusiense. Salzburg, Austria : Institut für Anglistik und Amerikanistik, Universität Salzburg, 2002.
BX2435 .P43 2002

Universität Thubingen. Institut für Geschichtliche Landeskunde und Historische Hilfswissenschaften.
Geschlecht, Magie und Hexenverfolgung. Bielefeld : Verlag für Regionalgeschichte, 2002.

Université d'Angers. Centre d'études et de recherche sur imaginaire, écritures et cultures.
Le système et le rêve. Paris : Harmattan, c2002.
BF1078 .S97 2002

Université de Bordeaux III. Laboratoire pluridisciplinaire de recherches sur l'imagination littéraire.
La fin des temps. Talence : Université Michel de Montaigne, Bordeaux III, L.A.P.R.I.L., 2000-[2001]

Université de Paris IV: Paris-Sorbonne.
Cathelineau, Pierre-Christophe, 1961- Lacan, lecteur d'Aristote. 2. éd., rev. et corr. Paris : Éditions de l'Association freudienne internationale, c2001 (2002 printing)

Université de Provence.
Année mille An Mil. Aix-en-Provence : Publications de l'université de Provence, 2002.

Université du Havre. Centre d'études et de recherches inter-langues.
Des odyssées à travers le temps. Paris : Harmattan, c2002.

Université Michel de Montaigne.
La fin des temps. Talence : Université Michel de Montaigne, Bordeaux III, L.A.P.R.I.L., 2000-[2001]

Universitet Rossiĭskoĭ akademii obrazovaniĭa.
Petrovskiĭ, A. V. (Artur Vladimirovich) Zapiski psikhologa. Moskva : Izd-vo URAO, 2001.
BF145 .P48 2001

UNIVERSITIES AND COLLEGES - ENTRANCE EXAMINATIONS. *See* **ADVANCED PLACEMENT PROGRAMS (EDUCATION).**

UNIVERSITIES AND COLLEGES - GRADUATE WORK - EXAMINATIONS. *See* **GRADUATE RECORD EXAMINATION.**

UNIVERSITIES AND COLLEGES - LAW AND LEGISLATION.
Monotti, Ann Louise. Universities and intellectual

property. Oxford ; New York : Oxford University Press, 2003.
KF4225.U55 M66 2003

UNIVERSITIES AND COLLEGES - STUDENTS. See **COLLEGE STUDENTS.**

Universities and intellectual property.
Monotti, Ann Louise. Oxford ; New York : Oxford University Press, 2003.
KF4225.U55 M66 2003

The University Center for Human Values series
Truth v. justice. Princeton, N.J. : Princeton University Press, c2000.
DT1945.T78 2000

University of Leipzig papers on Africa. Politics and economics series
(no. 31) Drews, Annette. Guardians of the society. Leipzig, Germany : Institut für Afrikanistik, Universität Leipzig, 2000.
BF1584.Z33 D44 2000

University of Michigan Business School management series
Yates, J. Frank (Jacques Frank), 1945- Decision management. 1st ed. San Francisco : Jossey-Bass, c2003.
HD30.23.Y386 2003

University of North Texas. Counseling Program.
Engels, Dennis W. The professional counselor. 3d ed. / Dennis W. Engels and associates. Alexandria, VA : American Counseling Association, c2004.
BF637.C6 P78 2004

University of Oxford. European Humanities Research Centre.
Britton, Celia. Race and the unconscious. Oxford : Legenda, 2002.

UNIVERSITY OF TEXAS AT AUSTIN. DEPT. OF PSYCHOLOGY - HISTORY.
Texas psychology. Austin : The University of Texas at Austin, c2002.
BF80.7.U62 T48 2002

University of Wisconsin - Madison. Law School.
On interpretation. Madison, Wis. : University of Wisconsin Press for the University of Wisconsin Law School, c2002.

University seminars/Leonard Hastings Schoff memorial lectures.
Katznelson, Ira. Desolation and enlightenment. New York : Columbia University Press, c2003.
JA71.K35 2003

UNIVERSITY STUDENTS. See **COLLEGE STUDENTS.**

Universum sapiens.
Karpenko, M. (Maksim) Vselennaia razumnaia = 2. perer. izd. Moskva : MAIK Nauka/Interperiodika, 2001.
BF1036.K37 2001

Uniwersytet Opolski. Instytut Filologii Polskiej.
Język w przestrzeni społecznej. Opole : Uniwersytet Opolski, 2002.
P40.J492 2002

Uniwersytet Wrocławski. Katedra Kryminalistyki.
Document, various specification. Wrocław : University of Wrocław, Faculty of Law and Administration, Department of Criminalistics, 2000-
BF905.C7 D63

Wrocławskie Sympozjum Badań Pisma (9th : 2000 : Wrocław, Poland) Contemporary problems of proof from a document. Wrocław : University of Wrocław, Faculty of Law, Administration, and Economy, Department of Criminalistics, 2002.
BF891.W76 2000

<uniz, Petrônio R. G.
Gaulle, Charles de, 1890-1970. [Fil de l'épée. Portuguese] O fio da espada. Rio de Janeiro : Biblioteca do Exército Editora, 2001.

The unknown God.
Starr, Martin P., 1959- Bolingbrook, IL: Teitan Press, 2003.
BF1997.S73 2003

Unlock your potential.
Wilde, Liz. New York : Ryland Peters & Small, 2004.
BF637.S4 W488 2004

UNMARRIED MOTHERS.
Bowers, Keri. Single pregnancy - single parenting. Pleasant Hill, CA : Park Alexander Press, c1996.
HQ759.45.B68 1996

UNMARRIED PEOPLE. See **SINGLE PEOPLE.**
UNMARRIED PERSONS. See **SINGLE PEOPLE.**
UNMARRIED WOMEN. See **SINGLE WOMEN.**

Unmasking bullies & victims.
Blakely, Mary Louise. Tamarac, Fl. : Llumina Press, 2004.
BF637.B85 B56 2004

Unmasking bullies and victims.
Blakely, Mary Louise. Unmasking bullies & victims. Tamarac, Fl. : Llumina Press, 2004.
BF637.B85 B56 2004

UNOBSERVED MATTER (ASTRONOMY). See **DARK MATTER (ASTRONOMY).**

Unprincipled virtue.
Arpaly, Nomy. Oxford ; New York : Oxford University Press, 2003.
BJ45.A76 2003

Unraveling your past to get into the present.
Broqueville, Paulette Renée. Rev. ed. Costa Mesa, Calif. : Broqueville Pub., c2002-
BF315.B76 2002

Unschaerferelationen : Experiment Raum = Uncertainty principles : spatial experiments / editors: Karin Damrau, Anton Markus Pasing ; [Übers.: Annette Wiethüchter]. Wiesbaden : Nelte, c2002. ca. 200 p. : ill. (chiefly col.) ; 22 x 29 cm. German and English. ISBN 3-932509-09-9 (hd.)
1. Space perception. 2. Architecture - Philosophy. I. Damrau, Karin. II. Pasing, Anton Markus, 1962- III. Title: Uncertainty principles : spatial experiments
BF469.U5 2002

UNSEEN MATTER (ASTRONOMY). See **DARK MATTER (ASTRONOMY).**

Unsung heroes.
Durschmied, Erik. London : Hodder & Stoughton, 2003.

Unter Übermenschen.
Junker, Helmut, 1934- Tübingen : Edition Diskord, c1997.
BF109.F74 J85 1997

Eine Untersuchung der Grundlagen der Moral.
Hume, David, 1711-1776. [Enquiry concerning the principles of morals. German] Göttingen : Vandenhoeck & Ruprecht, c2002.

Untersuchungen zur deutschen Literaturgeschichte
(Bd. 113) Hermetik. Tübingen : M. Niemeyer Verlag, c2002.
BF1586.H47 2002

Unterthurner, Gerhard.
Philosophie in Aktion. Wien : Turia + Kant, 2000.

Until today!.
Vanzant, Iyanla. New York : Simon & Schuster, c2000.
BL625.2.V369 2000

Unusually stupid Americans : a compendium of all-American stupidity / [compiled by] Kathryn Petras and Ross Petras. 1st ed. New York : Villard, 2003. xii, 288 p. ; 19 cm. ISBN 0-8129-7082-9 DDC 081
1. Stupidity - United States - Anecdotes. I. Petras, Kathryn. II. Petras, Ross.
BF431.U65 2003

[Wohlstand entschleiern. English]
Unveiling wealth : on money, quality of life, and sustainability / edited by Peter Bartelmus. Dordrecht ; Boston : Kluwer, c2002. xiv, 225 p. : ill. ; 25 cm. "Unveiling wealth is the translation and expansion of Wohlstand entschleiern--a book based on the congress of the same name organised by the Wuppertal Institute for Climate, Environment and Energy (Wuppertal, 10 December 1999)"--Pref. Includes bibliographical references and index. Table of contents URL: http://www.loc.gov/catdir/toc/fy033/2002031640.html ISBN 1402008147 (alk. paper) DDC 338.9/27
1. Sustainable development. 2. Wealth. 3. Money. 4. Quality of life. I. Bartelmus, Peter. II. Title. III. Title: Wohlstand entschleiern.
HD75.6.U58 2002

Die Unvermeidlichkeit der Bilder / Gerhart von Graevenitz, Stefan Rieger, Felix Thürlemann (Hrsg.). Tübingen : G. Narr, c2001. 287, [16] p. of plates : ill. ; 23 cm. (Literatur und Anthropologie, 1436-4573 ; Bd. 7) Includes bibliographical references. ISBN 3-8233-5706-9
1. Art and anthropology. 2. Image (Philosophy) 3. Visual perception. 4. Visual anthropology. 5. Idols and images. 6. Pictures. I. Graevenitz, Gerhart von. II. Rieger, Stefan. III. Thürlemann, Felix. IV. Series.

N72.A56 U58 2001x

Uomini, diavoli, esorcismi.
Proja, Giovanni Battista. Roma : Città nuova, 2002.

Uomo-donna.
Scola, Angelo. 1. ed. italiana. Genova : Marietti, c2002.

UPABA (Organization).
Uganda book news. Kampala, Uganda : UPABA, 1996-
Z467.U337 U34

Upādhyāya, Govindaprasāda. Āyurvedīya mānasaroga cikitsā / Govinda Prasāda Upādhyāya. 1. saṃskaraṇa. Vārāṇasī : Caukhabā Surabhāratī Prakāśana ; Dillī : Anya Prāptisthāna Caukhambā Saṃskṛta Pratishṭhāna, 2000. 12, 230 [1] p. ; 22 cm. (Caukhambā Āyurvijñāna granthamālā ; 66) SUMMARY: Ayurvedic work on psychiatry. Includes bibliographical references (p. [231]). In Sanskrit; includes passages in Sanskrit.
1. Medicine, Ayurvedic. 2. Psychology, Pathological. 3. Neurophysiology. I. Title. II. Title: Mānasaroga cikitsā III. Series.
R605.U67 2000

Upbin, Shari.
Vint/age 2001 conference : [videorecording]. New York, c2001.

UPBIN, SHARI.
Vint/age 2001 conference : [videorecording]. New York, c2001.

UPPER CLASS. See **GENTRY; NOBILITY.**

UPPER CLASS WOMEN.
García de León, María Antonia. Herederas y heridas. 1a ed. [Madrid] : Ediciones Cátedra, Universitat de València, Instituto de la Mujer, 2002.
HD6054.2.S7 G37 2002

UPRIGHT WALKING. See **BIPEDALISM.**

Uranić, Igor.
Girardi Jurkić, Vesna. Egipatska religija i antička Istra = Pula : Arheološki Muzej Istre, 2001.

Urban achievement in early modern Europe : golden ages in Antwerp, Amsterdam, and London / edited by Patrick O'Brien ... [et al.]. Cambridge ; New York : Cambridge University Press, 2001. xiv, 361 p. : ill., maps ; 24 cm. Includes bibliographical references and index. Publisher description URL: http://www.loc.gov/catdir/description/cam021/00040346.html Table of contents URL: http://www.loc.gov/catdir/toc/cam021/00040346.html CONTENTS: Reflections and mediations on Antwerp, Amsterdam and London in their golden ages / Patrick O'Brien -- 'No town in the world provides more advantages': economies of agglomeration and the golden age of Antwerp / Michael Limberger -- Clusters of achievement: the economy of Amsterdam in its golden age / Clé Lesger -- The economy of London, 1660-1730 / Peter Earle -- Antwerp in its golden age: 'one of the largest cities in the Low Countries' and 'one of the best fortified in Europe' / Piet Lombaerde -- The glorious city: monumentalism and public space in seventeenth-century Amsterdam / Marjorlein 'T Hart -- Architecture and urban space in London / Judi Loach -- The fine and decorative arts in Antwerp's golden age / Hans Vlieghe -- The rise of Amsterdam as a cultural centre: the market for paintings, 1580-1680 / Marten Jan Bok -- Cultural production and import substitution: the fine and decorative arts in London, 1660-1730 / David Ormrod -- Antwerp: books, publishing and cultural production before 1585 / Werner Waterschoot -- Metropolis of print: the Amsterdam book trade in the seventeenth century / Paul Hoftijzer -- Printing, publishing and reading in London, 1660-1720 / Adrian Johns -- Science for sale: the metropolitan stimulus for scientific achievements in sixteenth-century Antwerp / Geert Vanpaemel -- Amsterdam as a centre of learning in the Dutch golden age, c. 1580-1700 / Karel Davids -- Philosophers in the counting-houses: commerce, coffee-houses and experiment in early modern London / Larry Stewart ISBN 0-521-59408-1 (hbk.) DDC 940.2/2/091732
1. Cities and towns - Europe - Growth - History. 2. Europe - Economic conditions - 16th century. 3. Europe - Economic conditions - 17th century. 4. Europe - Economic conditions - 18th century. 5. Europe - Intellectual life. 6. Europe - Intellectual life - 17th century. 7. Europe - Intellectual life - 18th century. I. O'Brien, Patrick Karl.
HT131.U688 2001

URBAN AREAS. See **CITIES AND TOWNS.**

URBAN CRIME. See **CRIME.**

URBAN DESIGN. See **CITY PLANNING.**

URBAN DEVELOPMENT. See **CITY PLANNING; URBANIZATION.**

Urban, Hugh B. Tantra : sex, secrecy, politics, and power in the study of religion / Hugh B. Urban. Berkeley : University of California Press, c2003. xvi, 372 p. : ill. ; 23 cm. Includes bibliographical references (p. 337-366) and index. ISBN 0-520-23062-0 (cloth : alk. paper) ISBN 0-520-23656-4 (pbk. : alk. paper) DDC 294.5/514
1. Tantrism. 2. Tantric Buddhism. I. Title.
BL1283.84 .U73 2003

URBAN LEGENDS. *See* **LEGENDS.**

URBAN PLANNING. *See* **CITY PLANNING.**

URBAN POLICY. *See* **CITY PLANNING; URBANIZATION.**

URBAN RENEWAL. *See* **CITY PLANNING.**

URBAN VIOLENCE.
Ilardi, Massimo. In nome della strada. Roma : Meltemi, c2002.

URBAN YOUTH.
Children in the city. London : Routledge/Falmer, 2003.

URBANISM. *See* **CITIES AND TOWNS.**

URBANIZATION.
The emerging monoculture. Westport, Conn. : Praeger, 2003.
HM843 .E44 2003

URBANIZATION - PHILOSOPHY.
Habitar la tierra. Buenos Aires : Grupo Editor Altamira, 2002.
CB358 .H32 2002

URDU LANGUAGE. *See* **HINDI LANGUAGE.**

URNINGISM. *See* **HOMOSEXUALITY, MALE.**

URNINGS. *See* **GAY MEN.**

Ursano, Robert J., 1947-.
Terrorism and disaster. Cambridge, UK ; New York : Cambridge University Press, 2003.
RC552.P67 T476 2003

Das Urteil.
Löffelmann, Markus. Würzburg : Königshausen & Neumann, c2002.
BC181 .L64 2002

Us and others : social identities across languages, discourses and cultures / edited by Anna Duszak. Amsterdam ; Philadelphia : John Benjamins Pub., c2002. vii, 517 p. : ill. ; 23 cm. (Pragmatics & beyond New Series ; v. 98) Includes bibliographical references and index. ISBN 1-58811-205-5 ISBN 90-272-5118-5 DDC 302.4
1. Group identity. 2. Group identity - Cross-cultural studies. 3. Sociolinguistics. 4. Language and culture. I. Duszak, Anna. II. Series: Pragmatics & beyond ; new ser. v. 98.
HM753 .U72 2002

US-Indonesian hegemonic bargaining.
Kivimäki, Timo. Aldershot ; Burlington, VT : Ashgate, 2003.

US Indonesian hegemonic bargaining.
Kivimäki, Timo. US-Indonesian hegemonic bargaining. Aldershot ; Burlington, VT : Ashgate, 2003.

U.S. Nuclear Regulatory Commission. Division of Systems Analysis and Regulatory Effectiveness.
Human factors engineering program review model [microform]. Rev. 1. Washington, DC : Division of System Analysis and Regulatory Effectiveness, Office of Nuclear Regulatory Research, U.S. Nuclear Regulatory Commission : Supt. of Docs., U.S. G.P.O. [distributor], 2002.

USA inmigración y orientación.
McLaughlin, Bob. [USA immigration & orientation. Spanish] 1a. ed. en español. Satellite Beach, Fla. : Wellesworth Pub., c2001.

Use it or lose it!.
Bragdon, Allen D. 2nd ed., updated and expanded. New York : Walker & Co., 2004.
BF724.85.C64 B73 2004

USE OF LAND. *See* **LAND USE.**

USEFUL ARTS. *See* **TECHNOLOGY.**

USER INTERFACES (COMPUTER SYSTEMS).
Fuller, Matthew. Behind the blip. Brooklyn, NY, USA : Autonomedia, c2003.
QA76.76.H85 F85 2003

Hayes-Roth, Frederick, 1947- Radical simplicity. Upper Saddle River, N.J. ; London : Prentice Hall PTR, 2003.

Schreck, Jorg. Security and privacy in user modeling. Dordrecht ; Boston ; London : Kluwer Academic Publishers, c2003.

QA76.9.A25 S353 2003
Sutcliffe, Alistair, 1951- Multimedia and virtual reality. Mahwah, N.J. ; London : Lawrence Erlbaum, c2003.
QA76.76.I59 S88 2003

Three-dimensional user interfaces for immersive virtual reality [microform]. Providence, RI : Brown University Computer Graphics Group, [1997]

Ushakov, D. V.
Rastîannikov, A. V. Refleksivnoe razvitie kompetentnosti v sovmestnom tvorchestve. Moskva : PER SĖ, 2002.
BF408 .R235 2002

Using qualitative research in advertising: strategies, techniques, and applications / Margaret A. Morrison ... [et al.]. Thousand Oaks, Calif. : Sage, c2002. xi, 139 p. : ill. ; 24 cm. Includes bibliographical references (p. 132-134) and index. ISBN 0-7619-2599-6 ISBN 0-7619-2383-7 (p) DDC 659.1/07/2
1. Advertising - Research. 2. Marketing research - Methodology. 3. Qualitative research. I. Morrison, Margaret A.
HF5814 .U78 2002

Using technology to improve counseling practice.
Tyler, J. Michael. Alexandria, VA : American Counseling Association, 2003.
BF637.C6 T89 2003

UTB für Wissenschaft.
(2194) Albert, Hans, 1921- Lesebuch. Tübingen : Mohr Siebeck, 2001.

UTILITARIANISM. *See also* **PLEASURE.**
Mill, John Stuart, 1806-1873. 2nd ed. Malden, MA : Blackwell Pub., 2003.
B1602 .A5 2003

UTILITARIANISM.
Ethik ohne Dogmen. Paderborn : Mentis, 2001.

Mill, John Stuart, 1806-1873. Utilitarianism ; 2nd ed. Malden, MA : Blackwell Pub., 2003.
B1602 .A5 2003

Milner, Andrew, 1950- Contemporary cultural theory. 3rd ed. Crows Nest, N.S.W. : Allen & Unwin, 2002.

Utilitarianism ; and, On liberty.
Mill, John Stuart, 1806-1873. Utilitarianism ; 2nd ed. Malden, MA : Blackwell Pub., 2003.
B1602 .A5 2003

UTILITY THEORY.
Vind, Karl. Independence, additivity, uncertainty. Berlin ; New York : Springer, c2003.
HB135 .V56 2003

UTILIZATION OF LAND. *See* **LAND USE.**

Utonchennye priemy skrytogo upravleniîa.
Menîaĭlov, Alekseĭ. Durilka. Moskva : "Kraft+", 2003.

UTOPIAN LITERATURE. *See* **UTOPIAS.**

UTOPIAN SOCIALISM - FRANCE.
Fourier, Charles, 1772-1837. Du libre arbitre. Bordeaux : Saints Calus, 2003.

UTOPIAS - HISTORY.
Cioran, E. M. (Emile M.), 1911- [Histoire et utopie. Romanian] Istorie şi utopie. Bucureşti : Humanitas, 2002.

UTOPIAS IN LITERATURE.
Arenas, Fernando, 1963- Utopias of otherness. Minneapolis : University of Minnesota Press, c2003.
DP681 .A74 2003

Utopias of otherness.
Arenas, Fernando, 1963- Minneapolis : University of Minnesota Press, c2003.
DP681 .A74 2003

Uttal, William R. Psychomythics : sources of artifacts and misconceptions in scientific psychology / William R. Uttal. Mahwah, N.J. : L. Erlbaum Associates, 2003. x, 208 p. : ill. ; 24 cm. Includes bibliographical references (p. 188-197) and indexes. ISBN 0-8058-4584-4 (alk. paper) DDC 150/.1
1. Psychology - Methodology. 2. Psychology - Philosophy. I. Title.
BF38.5 .U88 2003

Utváření a vývoj osobnosti : psychologické, sociální a pedagogické aspekty / Vladimír Smékal, Petr Macek, eds. Vyd. 1. V Brně : Barrister & Principal, 2002. 264 p. : ill. ; 24 cm. (Edice Psychologie) Includes bibliographical references. ISBN 80-85947-83-8
1. Personality in children - Research - Czech Republic. 2. Personality in adolescence - Research - Czech Republic. 3.

Family - Research - Czech Republic. 4. Family - Psychological aspects. I. Smékal, Vladimír. II. Macek, Petr, 1956- III. Series.
BF723.P4 U88 2002

Uusitalo, Eeva.
Making and breaking of borders. Helsinki : Finnish Literature Society, 2003.
JC323 .M35 2003

V plenu germeticheskogo kruga.
Dimitrievich, Vladimir. Perm' : Panagiîa, 2001.
BF173.J85 D56 2001

Va-yavo Yosef.
Vaʻeknin, Yosef ben Avraham. Sefer Ka-sheleg yalbinu. Yerushalayim : Y. Vaʻeknin, 763 [2002 or 2003]

Vācaspatimiśra, fl. 976-1000.
Yogatattvavaisaradi. English.
Patañjali. The Yoga-darshana. 2nd ed.--throughly rev. [Fremont, Calif.] : Asian Humanities Press, [2002], 1934.
B132.Y6 P265 2002

VACATIONS. *See* **HOLIDAYS.**

Vadillo, Alicia E. Santería y Vodú : sexualidad y homoerotismo : caminos que se cruzan sobre la narrativa cubana contemporánea / Alicia E. Vadillo. Madrid : Biblioteca Nueva, c2002. 206 p. ; 21 cm. (Ensayos) Includes bibliographical references (p. [201]-206). CONTENTS: Los sistemas religiosos de origen africano -- Los orishas yorubás como paradigmas referenciales en la narrativa cubana contemporánea -- Un viaje a la modernidad de la leyenda religiosa a la ficción literaria -- El modelo dual yorubá como metáfora del neobarroco literario -- La leyenda del güije en el corpus de la literatura homoerótica cubana -- Otra vez el mar: la literatura de la diáspora. ISBN 84-974209-3-4 DDC 860.9/9721
1. Cuban literature - 20th century - History and criticism. 2. Santeria in literature. 3. Voodooism in literature. 4. Yoruba (African people) - Religion. 5. Religion in literature. 6. Homosexuality in literature. I. Title. II. Series: Ensayos (Biblioteca Nueva (Firm))
PQ7372 .V33 2002

Vaʻeknin, Yosef ben Avraham. Sefer Ka-sheleg yalbinu : ʻim meḳorot u-veurim Va-yavo Yosef ... ʻetsah tushiyah, marpe ve-arukhah le-nefesh ha-ḥoleh, la-ʻayonot meḥilah ... / Yosef Vaʻeknin. Yerushalayim : Y. Vaʻeknin, 763 [2002 or 2003] 230 p. ; 25 cm. Running title: Ka-sheleg yalbinu.
1. Healing - Religious aspects - Judaism. 2. Forgiveness - Religious aspects - Judaism. 3. Ethics, Jewish. I. Title. II. Title: Va-yavo Yosef. III. Title: Ka-sheleg yalbinu

Vaidika vāstu śāstra.
Asalī prācīna Vaidika vāstu śāstra. 1. saṃskaraṇa. Dillī : Manoja Pôkeṭa Buksa, [2002?]
BF1729.A7 A83 2002

Vaidikasārvabhaumanāmnā suprasiddhaiḥ Veṅkaṭanāthāryaiḥ Vaidikakarmānuṣṭhānasaukaryāya viracitā Daśanirṇayī.
Veṅkaṭanāthārya. [Daśanirṇayī] 1st ed. Mumbai : Śrīmadahobilamathena, 1998.
BL1226.72 .V36 1998

Vaidyanāthadīkṣita, 15th cent.
[Jātakapārijāta]
Jātakapārijātaḥ : "Jaya"-Hindīvyākhyopetaḥ / Daivajñavaidyanāthaviracitaḥ ; vyākhyākāra Hariśaṅkara Pāṭhaka. 1. saṃskaraṇa. Vārāṇasī : Caukhambā Surabhāratī Prakāśana ; Dillī : Caukhambā Saṃskṛti Pratiṣṭhāna, 2001. 13, 715 p. : ill. ; 22 cm. (Caukhambā Surabhāratī granthamālā ; 330) SUMMARY: Work with Hindi commentary on Hindu astrology. Sanskrit and Hindi.
1. Hindu astrology - Early works to 1800. I. Pāṭhaka, Hariśaṅkara. Jayā. II. Title. III. Series.
BF1714.H5 V253 2001

Vaidyanathan, T. G.
Vishnu on Freud's desk. Delhi ; Oxford : Oxford University Press, 1999 (2002 [printing])

Vainfas, Ronaldo. Os protagonistas anônimos da história : micro-história / Ronaldo Vainfas. Rio de Janeiro : Editora Campus, 2002. 163 p. ; 22 cm. Includes bibliographical references (p. [153]-163) ISBN 85-352-0989-1
1. History - Methodology. 2. Historiography. I. Title.
D16 .V35 2002

Vainshtok, Bentsiyon Mosheh Yaʼir ben Mordekhai Dayid. Sefer Or ha-daʻat : peraḳim be-histaklut penimit be-takhlit ha-beriʼah u-veriʼat ha-adam la-daʻat ha-maʻaśeh asher yaʻaśeh ... / me-et Mosheh Yaʼir Vainshtok. Yerushalayim : ha-Makhon le-hotsaʼat sifre ha-g. R. M.Y. Vainshtok, 762 [2001 or 2002] 233 p. ; 25 cm. Running title: Or ha-daʻat.

1. Cabala. 2. Jewish sermons, Hebrew. I. Title. II. Title: Or ha-da'at

Vairāgya.
Caturvedī, Saccidānanda. Itanagar : Himālayana Pablīśarsa, 2000.
BL1239.5.A82 C28 2000

Vais, Menaḥem Mendel.
Alshekh, Moses, 16th cent. [Torat Mosheh. Selections] Sefer 'Orot ha-Alshekh. Yerushalayim : [ḥ. mo. l.], 763 [2002 or 2003]

Vaisfish, Tsevi ben Shemu'el A. L. Sefer Dibrot Tsevi : shi'ure petiḥah she-ne'emru ba-yeshivah... "Even Yiśra'el" ; śiḥot musar, ma'arekhet ha-Torah - ma'arekhet ha-mo'adim ... / Tsevi b[en] ... Shemu'el Vaisfish. Yerushalayim : Makhon le-hotsa'at sefarim 'a. sh. Rabi Nahum mi-Shadiḳ, 762- [2002- v. ; 24 cm. Running title: Dibrot Tsevi.
1. Ethics, Jewish. 2. Jewish sermons, Hebrew. I. Title. II. Title: Dibrot Tsevi

VAJRAYĀNA BUDDHISM. See TANTRIC BUDDHISM.

Vakhṭfoigel, Nathan. Sefer No'am ha-musar : divre ḥokhmah u-musar 'a. pi seder parashiyot ha-Torah veha-zemanim me-et Natan Me'ir Vakhtfoigel. Laiḳvud : [ḥ. mo. l.], 762 [2001 or 2002] 258 p. : ports., facsim. ; 25 cm. Spine title: No'am ha-musar : Torah, zemanim. "Nikhtav mi-pi ha-shemu'ah." Includes index.
1. Bible. - O.T. - Pentateuch - Sermons. 2. Ethics, Jewish. 3. Jewish sermons, Hebrew - New York (State) - Lakewood. I. Title. II. Title: No'am ha-musar : Torah, zemanim
BJ1285 .V35 2001

Vakilzadian, Hamid.
International Conference on Simulation in Engineering Education (2001 : Phoenix, Ariz.) Proceedings of the International Conference on Simulation and Multimedia in Engineering Education & Virtual Worlds and Simulation. San Diego, CA : Society for Computer Simulation International, c2001.

Vaknin, Samuel. Narcissism book of quotes [electronic resource] : a selection of quotes from the collective wisdom of over 12,000 individual discussions / edited by Samuel Vaknin]. [Vancouver, B.C.] : Suite 101, [2003?] Mode of access: World Wide Web. Title from home page (viewed on Aug. 21, 2003) SUMMARY: Quotations selected from individual discussions posted at the Suite 101 Narcissistic Personality Disorder Discussion site selected and edited by Sam Vaknin. URL: http://www.suite101.com/files/topics/6514/files/NPDQuotes.rtf ISBN 998992922X
1. Narcissism. I. Title.
BF575.N35

Valabrega, Jean-Paul. Les mythes, conteurs de l'inconscient : Questions d'origine et de fin / Jean-Paul Valabrega. Paris : Payot, 2001. 182 p. ; 23 cm. (Bibliothèque scientifique Payot) Includes bibliographical references. ISBN 2-228-89494-X DDC 150
1. Causation. 2. Death. 3. Mythology - Psychological aspects. I. Title.
BD542 .V353 2001

Valencia, León. Adiós a la política, bienvenido la guerra : secretos de un malogrado proceso de paz / León Valencia. [Bogotá, Colombia?] : Intermedio, c2002. 337 p. ; 22 cm. Includes bibliographical references. ISBN 958-28-1307-5
1. Pastrana Arango, Andrés. 2. Fuerzas Armadas Revolucionarias de Colombia. 3. Colombia - Politics and government - 1974- 4. Guerrillas - Colombia. 5. Peace. I. Title. II. Title: Secretos de un malogrado proceso de paz

Valente, Michaela, 1972- Bodin in Italia : la Démonomanie des sorciers e le vicende della sua traduzione / Michaela Valente ; con un saggio introduttivo di D. Quaglioni. Firenze : Centro editoriale toscano, c1999. 226 p. ; 24 cm. (Politeia ; 5) Includes bibliographical references (p. 197-217) and index. ISBN 88-7957-136-2
1. Bodin, Jean, - 1530-1596 - Censorship - Italy. 2. Bodin, Jean, - 1539-1596. - De la démonomanie des sorciers. - Italian. I. Title. II. Series: Politeia (Florence, Italy) ; 5.
BF1602.B633 V35 1999

Valenzuela Muñoz, Oscar.
Masonería. Quito : [O. Valenzuela Muñoz], 2001.

VALÉRY, PAUL, 1871-1945 - CRITICISM AND INTERPRETATION.
Anders, Martin. Präsenz zu denken--. St. Augustin : Gardez!, c2002.
B3303 .A53 2002

Vallar, Giuseppe.
The cognitive and neural bases of spatial neglect. Oxford ; New York : Oxford University Press, 2002.

RC394.N44 C64 2002

Valle, Alexandre del. Le totalitarisme islamiste à l'assaut des démocraties / Alexandre Del Valle ; préface de Rachid Kaci. Paris : Syrtes, c2002. 463 p. ; 23 cm. Includes bibliographical references and index. ISBN 2-8454-5058-3 DDC 320
1. Islam and politics. 2. Islam and terrorism. 3. Islamic fundamentalism. 4. Totalitarianism. 5. Political correctness. 6. East and West. I. Title.

Valle Bonilla, Otto René.
Morales Tomas, Marco Antonio. El que busca encuentra = Guatemala : ESEDIR : Editorial Saqil Tzij, 1999.

Morales Tomas, Marco Antonio. Una gráfica dice más que mil palabras = Guatemala : ESEDIR : Editorial Saqil Tzij, 1999.

Que no le cuenten cuentos = Man tikitzijoj tzijonem chawe (kaqchikel) : técnicas e instrumentos de investigación / [elaborado por Otto René Valle Bonilla, Marco Antonio Morales Tomas]. Guatemala : ESEDIR : Editorial Saqil Tzij, 1999. 31 p. : ill. ; 28 cm. (Investigación social y estadística aplicada ; módulo 2) Includes bibliographical references (p. 31). Text in Spanish only.
1. Social sciences - Research - Methodology. 2. Research - Methodology. 3. Science - Methodology. I. Morales Tomas, Marco Antonio. II. Title. III. Title: Man tikitzijoj tzijonem chawe IV. Title: Técnicas e instrumentos de investigación V. Series.

Vallega-Neu, Daniela, 1966- Heidegger's contributions to philosophy : an introduction / Daniela Vallega-Neu. Bloomington, IN : Indiana University Press, c2003. viii, 121 p. ; 22 cm. (Studies in Continental thought) Includes bibliographical references and index. ISBN 0-253-34234-1 (alk. paper) ISBN 0-253-21599-4 (pbk. : alk. paper) DDC 193
1. Heidegger, Martin, - 1889-1976. - Beiträge zur Philosophie. 2. Philosophy. I. Title. II. Series.
B3279.H48 B454 2003

Vallejo, Fernando. La tautología darwinista : y otros ensayos de biología / Fernando Vallejo. 1a. ed. México : Universidad Nacional Autónoma de México, 1998. 327 p. : ill. ; 21 cm. (DiVersa ; 4) CONTENTS: La tautología darwinista -- El origen de las especies por medio del aislamiento reproductivo seguido del incesto -- El concepto vacío de adaptación -- Especiación y evolución -- Clasificadores -- El huevo y la gallina -- El río que fluye en el espejo -- Dominancia y recesividad -- Convergencias y divergencias -- Vida y muerte -- La primera célula y sus inmediatos descendientes. ISBN 968-36-5856-3
1. Darwin, Charles, - 1809-1882. - On the origin of species. 2. Evolution (Biology) 3. Natural selection. 4. Biology - Philosophy. 5. Natural history - Philosophy - Popular works. I. Title. II. Series: DiVersa (Mexico City, Mexico) ; 4.

Valletti, Serge.
Inédits et commentaires. Paris : L'Arche, 2002.

VALLEYS - NEW JERSEY. See HUDSON RIVER VALLEY (N.Y. AND N.J.).

VALLEYS - NEW YORK (STATE). See HUDSON RIVER VALLEY (N.Y. AND N.J.).

VALLEYS - UNITED STATES. See OHIO RIVER VALLEY.

VALLEYS - VIRGINIA. See JAMES RIVER VALLEY (VA.).

Vallicella, William F. A paradigm theory of existence : onto-theology vindicated / by William F. Vallicella. Dordrecht ; Boston : Kluwer Academic, c2002. xii, 281 p. ; 25 cm. (Philosophical studies series ; v. 89) Includes bibliographical references (p. 273-278) and index. ISBN 1402008872 (alk. paper) DDC 111/.1
1. Ontology. 2. Metaphysics. 3. Contingency (Philosophy) I. Title. II. Series.
BD331 .V36 2002

Vallier, Gilles-Félix. La logique de l'éternité : dimensions rituelles des pouvoirs politiques Yorùbá (République du Bénin) / Gilles-Félix Vallier. 1998. 2 v. (ix, 694, xxviii, 135 f. de pl.) : ill. (certaines en coul.), cartes (certaines en coul.). Thèse (Ph. D.)--Université Laval, 1998. Includes bibliographical references and index. Photocopy. Ann Arbor, Mich. : UMI Dissertation Services, 2002. ix, 694 p., cxxv, xxviii : ill., maps ; 22 cm. ISBN 0-612-43124-X (microfiche)
1. Religion and state - Benin. 2. Yoruba (African people) - Religion. 3. Yoruba (African people) - Politics and government. 4. Power (Social sciences) - Benin. 5. Space and time - Social aspects - Benin. 6. Space and time - Benin. 7. Yoruba (African people) - Rites and ceremonies. 8. Benin - Religion. I. Title. II. Title: Thèse. Anthropologie.

Il "valore" del padre : il ruolo paterno nello sviluppo del bambino / a cura di Rocco Quaglia ; contributi di Claudio Longobardi, Simona Pagani. Torino : UTET libreria, 2001. xiii, 143 p. : ill. ; 21 cm. (Collana di psicologia) Includes bibliographical references (p. [137]-143). ISBN 88-7750-695-4 DDC 155
1. Fathers. 2. Father and child. 3. Child development. I. Quaglia, Rocco. II. Longobardi, Claudio. III. Pagani, Simona. IV. Series: Collana di psicologia (Turin, Italy)
BF723.P25 V35 2001

valores.
Vieira, Anselmo, 1923- Ser ou não ter. Lisboa : Roma Editora, [2002]-

Los valores y las virtudes.
Barylko, Jaime. Buenos Aires : Emecé Editoral, c2002.

Los valores y sus desafíos actuales.
Fabelo Corzo, José Ramón. Puebla : Universidad Autónoma de Puebla, 2001.

Valsiner, Jaan.
Handbook of developmental psychology. London : Thousand Oaks, Calif. : SAGE Publications, 2003.
BF713 .H364 2003

VALUE. See also MONEY.
DiVanna, Joseph A. Synconomy. Houndmills [England] ; New York : Palgrave Macmillan, 2003.
HD64.2 .D575 2003

Dolgin, Aleksandr. Pragmatika kul'tury. Moskva : Fond nauchnykh issledovaniĭ "Pragmatika kul'tury", 2003.

VALUE ANALYSIS (COST CONTROL).
Woodhead, Roy (Roy M.) Achieving results. London : Thomas Telford, 2002.

VALUE ENGINEERING. See VALUE ANALYSIS (COST CONTROL).

Value inquiry book series.
(v. 117) Radford, Robert T. Cicero. Amsterdam ; New York, NY : Rodopi, 2002.
DG260.C5 R33 2002

(v. 126) Hartman, Robert S., 1910-1973. [Conocimiento del bien. English] The knowledge of good. Amsterdam ; New York, NY : Rodopi, c2002.
BD232 .H324 2002

(v. 134) Krieglstein, Werner J., 1941- Compassion. Amsterdam ; New York : Rodopi, c2002.

Value inquiry book series. Hartman Institute axiology studies
Hartman, Robert S., 1910-1973. [Conocimiento del bien. English] The knowledge of good. Amsterdam ; New York, NY : Rodopi, c2002.
BD232 .H324 2002

Value inquiry book series. Studies in the history of western philosophy.
Radford, Robert T. Cicero. Amsterdam ; New York, NY : Rodopi, 2002.
DG260.C5 R33 2002

The value of knowledge and the pursuit of understanding.
Kvanvig, Jonathan L. Cambridge, U.K. ; New York : Cambridge University Press, 2003.
BD232 .K92 2003

Value wars.
McMurtry, John, 1939- London ; Sterling, Va. : Pluto Press, c2002.
HF1359 .M39 2002

VALUES. See also DIGNITY; ETHICS; SOCIAL VALUES.
Barylko, Jaime. Los valores y las virtudes. Buenos Aires : Emecé Editoral, c2002.

Crowther, Paul. Philosophy after postmodernism. London ; New York : Routledge, 2003.
B831.2 .C76 2003

Desarrollo de los valores en las instituciones educativas. Bilbao : Mensajero, 2001.

Fabelo Corzo, José Ramón. Los valores y sus desafíos actuales. Puebla : Universidad Autónoma de Puebla, 2001.

Government reformed. Aldershot, England ; Burlington, VT : Ashgate, c2003.
JF1525.O73 G686 2003

Hartman, Robert S., 1910-1973. [Conocimiento del bien. English] The knowledge of good. Amsterdam ; New York, NY : Rodopi, c2002.

BD232 .H324 2002

Ī︠A︡nit︠s︡kiĭ, M. S. (Mikhail Sergeevich) T︠S︡ennostnye orientat︠s︡ii lichnosti kak dinamicheskai︠a︡ sistema. Kemerovo : Kuzbassvuzizdat, 2000.
BF698 .I18 2000

Kovesi, Julius. Values and evaluations. New York ; Bern : P. Lang, c1998.
BD232 .K68 1998

Kvanvig, Jonathan L. The value of knowledge and the pursuit of understanding. Cambridge, U.K. ; New York : Cambridge University Press, 2003.
BD232 .K92 2003

Leibowitz, Yeshayahu, 1903- Ben mada' le-filosofyah. Yerushalayim : Akademon, 762 [2002]

Mazumdar, Krishna, 1949- Determinants of human well-being. New York : Nova Science Publishers, c2003.
HB171 .M462 2003

McMurtry, John, 1939- Value wars. London ; Sterling, Va. : Pluto Press, c2002.
HF1359 .M39 2002

El milagro y el valor de la vida. 1. ed. Buenos Aires : Patria Grande, 2000.

Przełęcki, Marian, 1923- O rozumności i dobroci. Warszawa : "Semper", 2002.
B833 .P79 2002

Putnam, Hilary. The collapse of the fact/value dichotomy and other essays. Cambridge, MA : Harvard University Press, 2002.
B945.P873 C65 2002

Raz, Joseph. The practice of value. Oxford ; New York : Oxford University Press, 2003.
BD232 .R255 2003

Shayegan, Darius. La lumière vient de l'Occident. [La Tour-d'Aigues] : Éditions de l'Aube, c2001.
CB 430

Tagore, Rabindranath, 1861-1941. [Sādhanā. Marathi] Sādhanā. Kolhāpūra : Mahārāshṭra Grantha Bhāṇḍāra, 2000.
B131 .T28 2000

Values and evaluations.
Kovesi, Julius. New York ; Bern : P. Lang, c1998.
BD232 .K68 1998

VALUES IN ADOLESCENCE.
Tremblay-Dupré, Thérèse. La mère absente. Monaco : Rocher, 2003.

VALUES - PSYCHOLOGICAL ASPECTS.
Chapelle, Daniel, 1951- The soul in everyday life. Albany, NY : State University of New York Press, c2003.
BF175.4.P45 C48 2003

Nelson, Noelle C. The power of appreciation. Hillsboro, Or. : Beyond Words Pub., c2003.
BF575.G68 N45 2003

Valuing health in practice.
McCulloch, Douglas, 1950- Aldershot, Hampshire, England ; Burlington, VT : Ashgate, c2003.
RA410.5 .M37 2002

Valverde, Mariana, 1955- Law's dream of a common knowledge / Mariana Valverde. Princeton, N.J. ; Woodstock, Oxfordshire : Princeton University Press, c2003. x, 247 p. ; 25 cm. (Cultural lives of law) Includes bibliographical references (p. [229]-240) and index. Publisher description URL: http://www.loc.gov/catdir/desc ription/prin031/2002030720.html ISBN 0-691-08698-2 (cloth : alk. paper) ISBN 0-691-08699-0 (pbk. : alk. paper) DDC 340/.11
1. Law - Social aspects. 2. Law - Psychological aspects. 3. Knowledge, Sociology of. I. Title. II. Series.
K380 .V35 2003

VAMPIRES - ENCYCLOPEDIAS.
Guiley, Rosemary. The encyclopedia of vampires, werewolves, and other monsters. New York, NY : Facts on File, 2004.
BF1556 .G86 2004

VAMPIRES - PSYCHOLOGY.
Slate, Joe H. Psychic vampires. 1st ed. St. Paul, Minn. : Llewellyn Publications, 2002.
BF1045.S46 S53 2002

Van Auken, John. The end times : prophecies of coming changes : includes prophecies and predictions from the Bible, Edgar Cayce, Nostradamus, the Holy Mother / John Van Auken. New York : Signet Book, c2001. [Updated ed.]. xii, 241 p. : ill. ; 18 cm. Includes bibliographical references (p. 239-241). ISBN 0-451-20665-7 (pbk.) DDC 133.3
1. Prophecies (Occultism) 2. End of the world. 3. Bible - Prophecies - End of the world. 4. Cayce, Edgar, - 1877-1945. 5. Nostradamus, - 1503-1566. 6. Mary, - Blessed Virgin, Saint - Apparitions and miracles. I. Title.
BF1791 .V36 2001

Little, Lora. Secrets of the ancient world. Virginia Beach, Va. : A.R.E. Press, c2003.
BF1045.A74 L58 2003

Van Buren, John, 1956-.
Heidegger, Martin, 1889-1976. [Essays. English. Selections] Supplements. Albany : State University of New York Press, c2002.
B3279.H47 E5 2002d

Van Dam, Andries, 1938-.
Three-dimensional user interfaces for immersive virtual reality [microform]. Providence, RI : Brown University Computer Graphics Group, [1997]

Van de Weyer, Robert. Islam and the West : a new political and religious order post September 11 / Robert Van de Weyer. Alresford, Hampshire : O Books, c2001. xiii, 105 p. ; 24 cm. ISBN 1-903816-14-9 DDC 909/.097/671
1. East and West. 2. Civilization, Islamic - Western influences. 3. Islam and politics - History. 4. Islam - 20th century. I. Title.
CB251 .V36 2001

The shared well : a concise guide to relations between Islam and the West / Robert Van de Weyer. 1st ed. Washington, D.C. : Brassey's, c2002. xi, 131 p. ; 23 cm. Includes bibliographical references (p. 121-122) and index. CONTENTS: "Why do they hate us?": Islam and the West in conflict -- The Arab Empire. -- The crusades. -- The Ottoman Empire. -- Western imperialism. -- Islamic militancy. -- Zionism. -- The legacy. -- "Is mutual love and respect possible?": Islam and the West in harmony -- Christian roots of Islam. -- Philosophy and theology. -- Science, mathematics, and medicine. -- Politics and law. -- Warfare. -- The legacy. -- "What can we do--politically?": the politics of peace -- The globalization of goods and capital. -- The globalization of people and expertise. -- Politics after September 11. -- Towards political freedom. -- "What can we do--religiously?": the religion of peace -- The globalization of creeds and sects. -- False assumptions. -- The globalization of wisdom and symbols. -- Religion after September 11. -- Towards religious freedom. -- Conclusion: Freedom to live in peace -- Appendix 1: Muhammad, Islam, Judaism and Christianity -- Appendix 2: A guide to further reading. ISBN 1-57488-564-2 (alk. paper) DDC 303.48/2176710821
1. Religion and politics. 2. East and West. 3. Islam - Relations - Christianity. 4. Christianity and other religions - Islam. 5. September 11 Terrorist Attacks, 2001. I. Title.
BL65.P7 V36 2002

Van Dyke, Ruth.
Archaeologies of memory. Malden, MA ; Oxford : Blackwell, 2003.
CC72.4 .A733 2003

Van Gigch, John P. Metadecisions : rehabilitating epistemology / by John P. van Gigch ; with a foreword by C. West Churchman. New York : Kluwer Academic/Plenum Publishers, c2003. xviii, 341 p. : ill. ; 24 cm. (Contemporary systems thinking) Includes bibliographical references (p. 319-335) and index. ISBN 0-306-47458-1 DDC 301
1. Social systems. 2. Decision making. I. Title. II. Series.
HM701 .V36 2003

Van Harmelen, Frank.
Towards the semantic web. Chichester, England ; Hoboken, N.J. : J. Wiley, c2003.
TK5105.88815 .T68 2003

Van karmijn, purper en blauw.
Pleij, Herman. Amsterdam : Prometheus, 2002.

Van Löben Sels, Robin E., 1938- A dream in the world : poetics of soul in two women, modern and medieval / Robin E. van Löben Sels. New York, NY : Brunner-Routledge, 2003. p. cm. Includes bibliographical references and index. Table of contents URL: http://www.loc.gov/catdir/toc/ecip042/2003007326.html ISBN 1-58391-918-X (alk. paper) ISBN 1-58391-919-8 (pbk. : alk. paper) DDC 154.6/3
1. Dream interpretation - Case studies. 2. Jungian psychology - Case studies. 3. Dreams - Religious aspects - Christianity - Case studies. 4. Jungian psychology - Religious aspects - Christianity - Case studies. 5. Dreams - Therapeutic use - Case studies. 6. Hadewijch, - 13th cent. I. Title.
BF175.5.D74 V36 2003

Van Manen, Max.
Writing in the dark : phenomenological studies in interpretive inquiry. London, Ont. : Althouse Press, 2002.
B829.5 .W75 2002

Van Praagh, James. Looking beyond : a teen's guide to the spiritual world / James Van Praagh. New York : Simon & Schuster, c2003. xii, 160 p. : col. ill. ; 24 cm. "A Fireside book." ISBN 0-7432-2942-8 (pbk.) DDC 133.9
1. Spiritualism. 2. Spiritual life - Miscellanea. 3. Teenagers - Religious life - Miscellanea. I. Title.
BF1272 .V36 2003

Meditations / with James Van Praagh New York : Simon & Schuster, 2003. p. cm. ISBN 0-7432-2943-6 (pbk.) DDC 158.1/2
1. Spiritualism. 2. Meditations. I. Title.
BF1261.2 .V355 2003

Van Wyhe, John, 1971- Phrenology and the origins of Victorian scientific naturalism / John van Wyhe. Burlington, VT : Ashgate, c2003. p. cm. (Science, technology, and culture, 1700-1945) Includes bibliographical references (p.   ). ISBN 0-7546-3408-6 (alk. paper) DDC 139/.09
1. Phrenology - Great Britain - History - 19th century. 2. Science - Great Britain - History - 19th century. 3. Combe, George, - 1788-1858. - Constitution of man. 4. Naturalism - History - 19th century. I. Title. II. Series.
BF879 .V36 2003

Vanbremeersch, Marie-Caroline, 1944-.
Itinéraires de l'imaginaire. Paris : L'Harmattan, c1999.
BF408 .I86 1999

Vanden Bossche, Chris.
Carlyle, Thomas, 1795-1881. Historical essays. Berkeley ; London : University of California Press, c2002.
D208 .C34 2002

The Vanderbilt library of American philosophy
Lekan, Todd, 1967- Making morality. 1st ed. Nashville, TN : Vanderbilt University Press, 2003.
BJ1031 .L45 2003

Vandevelde, Pol.
Rousselot, Pierre, 1878-1915. [Pour l'histoire du problème de l'amour au moyen âge. English] The problem of love in the Middle Ages. Milwaukee : Marquette University Press, [2001?]
B738.L68 R68 2001

VANGA, 1911-.
Georgiev, Li︠u︡ben, 1933- Sreshti s Vangi︠a︡. Sofii︠a︡ : Knigo-TSvi︠a︡t, 1996.
BF1283.V33 G46 1996

Vanished.
Herbst, Judith. Minneapolis : Lerner Publications Co., 2005.
BF1389.D57 H47 2005

VANISHINGS (PARAPSYCHOLOGY). *See* **DISAPPEARANCES (PARAPSYCHOLOGY).**

VanSant, Sondra. Wired for conflict : the role of personality in resolving differences / Sondra S. VanSant. Gainesville, Fla. : Center for Applications of Psychological Type, c2003. xvii, 105 p. ; 23 cm. Includes bibliographical references (p. 103-104). ISBN 0-935652-68-X DDC 155.2/64
1. Typology (Psychology) 2. Myers-Briggs Type Indicator. 3. Interpersonal conflict. 4. Conflict management. I. Title.
BF698.3 .V36 2003

Yanunu, Shim'on.
Berlin, Naphtali Zevi Judah, 1817-1893. [Selections. 2001] Otsrot ha-Netsiv. Yerushalayim : Ben Arzah, 762 [2001 or 2002]
BM755.B52 A25 2001

Vanzant, Iyanla. Until today! : daily devotions for spiritual growth and peace of mind / Iyanla Vanzant. New York : Simon & Schuster, c2000. 1 v. (unpaged) ; 19 cm. Includes index. ISBN 0-684-84137-1 DDC 291.4/32
1. African Americans - Prayer-books and devotions - English. 2. Devotional calendars. I. Title.
BL625.2 .V369 2000

Varāhamihira, 505-587. Bṛhatsaṃhitā / Varāhamihirācāryaviracitā, Bhaṭṭotpalavivṛtisahitā, Hindīvyākhyayopabṛmhitā ; Hindīvyākhyākāraḥ sampādakaśca, Ācāryanāgendrapāṇḍeyaḥ ; Rāmamūrtiśarmaṇaḥ prastāvanayā vibhūṣitā. 1. saṃskaraṇam. Vārāṇasī : Sampūrṇānanda Saṃskṛta Viśvavidyālaye, 2002- v. ; 25 cm. (Gaṅgānāthajhā-granthamālā ; 20) Added t.p. in English. Includes index. SUMMARY: Classical treatise on Hindu astrology; critical edition with commentaries. In Sanskrit; commentaries in Hindi and Sanskrit. ISBN 81-7270-076-8 (set) ISBN 81-7270-077-6 (v. 1)
1. Hindu astrology - Early works to 1800. I. Pāṇḍeya, Nāgendra. II. Bhaṭṭotpala, 12th cent. Vivṛti. III. Sampūrṇānanda Saṃskṛta Viśvavidyālaya. IV. Title. V. Series: Gaṅgānāthajhā-granthamālā ; 20.

BF1714.H5+

VARĀHAMIHIRA, 505-587.
Dvivedī, Bhojarāja. Ācārya Varāhamihira kā jyotisha meṃ yogadāna. 1. saṃskaraṇa. Naī Dillī : Rañjana Pablikeśansa, 2002.
BF1679.8.V37 D85 2002

Śāstrī, Girijā Śaṅkara. Ācārya Varāhamihira. 1. saṃskaraṇa. Ilāhābāda : Jyotisha, Karmakāṇḍa evaṃ Adhyātma Śodha Saṃsthāna, 2001.
BF1679.8.V37 S27 2001

Vardi, Yoav, 1944- Misbehavior in organizations : theory, research, and management / Yoav Vardi, Ely Weitz. Mahwah, NJ ; London : Lawrence Erlbaum, 2004. xxi, 337 p. : ill. ; 24 cm. (Series in applied psychology) Includes bibliographical references (p. 261-288) and indexes. ISBN 0-8058-4332-9 (hbk. : alk. paper) ISBN 0-8058-4333-7 (pbk. : alk. paper) DDC 302.3/5
1. Organizational behavior. 2. Corporate culture. 3. Business ethics. 4. Work ethic. I. Weitz, Ely. II. Title. III. Series.
HD58.7 .V367 2004

Varela, Francisco J., 1946-.
The view from within. Thorverton, UK ; Bowling Green, OH : Imprint Academic, 2000.
BF311 .V512 2000

Vargas, Lilia Esther.
Jáidar, Isabel. La psicología. 1. ed. México, D.F. : Universidad Autónoma Metropolitana, Unidad Xochimilco, División de Ciencias Sociales y Humanidades, 2002.

VARIATION (BIOLOGY). *See also* **ADAPTATION (BIOLOGY); GENETICS.**
Boncinelli, Edoardo. Io sono, tu sei. 1. ed. Milano : Mondadori, 2002.

Varieties of ethical reflection : new directions for ethics in a global context / edited by Michael Barnhart. Lanham, Md. ; Oxford : Lexington Books, c2002. vii, 347 p. ; 24 cm. (Studies in comparative philosophy and religion) Includes bibliographical references (p. 329-336) and index. ISBN 0-7391-0443-8 (alk. paper) DDC 170/.9
1. Ethics. 2. Globalization - Moral and ethical aspects. I. Barnhart, Michael, 1956- II. Series.
BJ1031 .V37 2002

Varner, Don. How to get a really great job! : a complete program if you hate your job and don't know how to go about changing it / Donald L. Varner. Toronto : Productive Publications, 1998. 240 p. ; 22 cm. Includes bibliographical references. ISBN 1-89621-090-2 (pbk.) DDC 650.14
1. Career changes. 2. Career development. 3. Vocational guidance. I. Title.

Varnum, Keith. Inner coach, outer power / Keith Varnum. Phoenix, Ariz. : New Dimensions Pub., c2002. 304 p. : ill. ; 22 cm. ISBN 1-89156-949-X DDC 158.1
1. Self-actualization (Psychology) - Miscellanea. I. Title. II. Title: Outer power
BF1999 .V36 2002

Varshney, D. C., 1933- Hindū vijñāna evaṃ vidhi / Ḍī. Sī. Vārshṇeya. 1. saṃskaraṇa. Lakhanaū : Nyū Rôyala Buka Kampanī, 2001. xi, 279 p. : ill. ; 23 cm. Includes bibliographical references. In Hindi; includes passages in Awadhi and in Sanskrit. ISBN 81-85936-17-X
1. Hinduism and science. 2. Mythology, Hindu. 3. Hindu symbolism. I. Title.
BL1215.S36 V27 2001

Vaserman, Asher ben Avraham Betsal'el. Sefer Mishnat avot : 'al masekhet 'avot : 'im be'urim ... / ne'erakh ve-nisdar 'al yede Asher Vaserman. Bene Beraḳ : A. Vaserman, 760- [2000- v. ; 25 cm. Cover title: Mishnat avot. Mishnah text vocalized. PARTIAL CONTENTS: v.1. peraḳim 1-2 -- v.2 pereḳ 3 -- v.3 pereḳ 4.
1. Mishnah. - Avot - Commentaries. 2. Ethics, Jewish. I. Title. II. Title: Mishnah. Avot. 2000. III. Title: Mishnat avot

VASES, ACOUSTIC - MISCELLANEA.
Statnekov, Daniel K., 1943- Animated earth. 2nd ed. Berkeley Calif. : North Atlantic Books, 2003.
BF1999 .S719 2003

Vasil'ev, Leonid Leonidovich. Experiments in mental suggestion / L.L. Vasiliev. [Rev. ed.]. Charlottesville, VA : Hampton Roads Pub., c2002. lvi, 191 p. : ill. ; 23 cm. (Studies in consciousness) "Russell Targ editions". Includes bibliographical references (p. [163]-178). ISBN 1-57174-274-3 (pbk. : alk. paper) DDC 133.8/2
1. Mental suggestion. I. Title. II. Series.
BF1156.S8 V313 2002

Vasilkivski, Viacheslav.
Antologiia. 1. izd. Veliko Tŭrnovo : Izd-vo PAN-VT, 2001.
BF108.B9 A58 2001

Vasishth, Shravan, 1964- Working memory in sentence comprehension : processing Hindi center embeddings / Shravan Vasishth. New York ; London : Routledge, 2003. xxvii, 262 p. : ill. ; 24 cm. (Outstanding dissertations in linguistics) Slightly rev. version of the author's dissertation (Ph. D.--Ohio State University, 2000). Includes bibliographical references (p. 247-262) and index. ISBN 0-415-96761-9 (alk. paper) DDC 491.4/35
1. Hindi language - Psychological aspects. 2. Hindi language - Sentences. 3. Grammar, Comparative and general - Sentences - Psychological aspects. 4. Psycholinguistics. I. Title. II. Series.
PK1933 .V28 2003

Vass, Zoltán.
Gerő, Zsuzsa. A gyermekrajzok esztétikuma. Budapest : Flaccus Kiadó, 2003.
BF723.D7 G47 2003

Vastu.
Bansal, Ashwinie Kumar. Hauppauge, NY : Barron's, 2002.
BF1779.V38 B36 2002

VĀSTU.
Bansal, Ashwinie Kumar. Vastu. Hauppauge, NY : Barron's, 2002.
BF1779.V38 B36 2002

Whelan, Bilkis. Vastu in 10 simple lessons. 1st ed. New York : Watson-Guptill Publications, 2002.
BF1779.V38 W48 2002

Vastu in 10 simple lessons.
Whelan, Bilkis. 1st ed. New York : Watson-Guptill Publications, 2002.
BF1779.V38 W48 2002

Vastu in ten simple lessons.
Whelan, Bilkis. Vastu in 10 simple lessons. 1st ed. New York : Watson-Guptill Publications, 2002.
BF1779.V38 W48 2002

Vāstu-śāstram.
[Śilpaśāstra. English & Sanskrit.] Calcutta : Sanskrit Pustak Bhandar, 2001.
NA7427 .M34 2001

Vāstusārasaṅgraha.
Śukla, Kamalākānta, 1911- Vāstusārasaṅgrahaḥ. 1. saṃskaraṇam. Vārāṇasī : Sampūrṇānanda Saṃskrta Viśvavidyālaye, 2002.
BF1729.A7+

Vāstusārasaṅgrahaḥ.
Śukla, Kamalākānta, 1911- 1. saṃskaraṇam. Vārāṇasī : Sampūrṇānanda Saṃskrta Viśvavidyālaye, 2002.
BF1729.A7+

Vater, Michael G., 1944-.
Hegel's Phenomenology of spirit. Amherst, N.Y. : Humanity Books, 2003.
B2929 .H349 2003

VĀTSYĀYANA. KĀMASŪTRA.
Pinkney, Andrea Marion. [Kāmasūtra. English.] The Kama Sutra illuminated. New York, N.Y. : Abrams, c2002.

Pinkney, Andrea Marion. [Kāmasūtra. English.] The Kama Sutra illuminated. New York, N.Y. : Abrams, c2002.

VAUD (SWITZERLAND) - HISTORY.
Taric Zumsteg, Fabienne. Les sorciers à l'assaut du village. Lausanne : Editions du Zèbre, 2000.
BF1584.S9 T37 2000

VAUGHAN WILLIAMS, RALPH, 1872-1958. DONA NOBIS PACEM.
Lathan, Mark J., 1961- Emotional progression in sacred choral music. 2001.

Vault of the heavens.
Wilhelm, E. (Ernst) 1st ed. [S.l.] : Käla Occult Publishers, 2001.
BF1714.H5 W55 2001

Vazeilles, José Gabriel. Platonismo, marxismo y comunicación social / José Gabriel Vazeilles. Buenos Aires : Editorial Biblos, c2002. 175 p. ; 23 cm. Includes bibliographical references. ISBN 950-786-313-3
1. Social sciences - Philosophy. 2. Platonists. 3. Communism. 4. Social interaction. I. Title.

VD (DISEASE). *See* **SEXUALLY TRANSMITTED DISEASES.**

Vecchiotti, Icilio. Introduzione alla filosofia di Giordano Bruno / Icilio Vecchiotti. Urbino : QuattroVenti, c2000. 307 p. ; 21 cm. (Filosofia e storia delle idee) Includes bibliographical references (p. 301-306). ISBN 88-392-0547-0 DDC 195
1. Bruno, Giordano, - 1548-1600. 2. Philosophy, Renaissance. I. Title. II. Series: Collana di filosofia e storia delle idee.
B783.Z7 V43 2000

VEDIC LANGUAGE. *See* **SANSKRIT LANGUAGE.**

VEDIC LITERATURE - HISTORY AND CRITICISM.
Caturvedī, Saccidānanda. Vairāgya. Itanagar : Himālayana Pabliśarsa, 2000.
BL1239.5.A82 C28 2000

Ved'my.
Ivanova, E. V. (Elena Vladimirovna) Ekaterinburg : Ural'skiĭ gos. universitet, 2002.
BF1584.R9 I85 2002

Veen, Hans van de.
Searching for peace in Central and South Asia. Boulder, Colo. : Lynne Rienner Publishers, 2002.
JZ5597 .S43 2002

Veenstra, Jan R., 1939-.
The metamorphosis of magic from late antiquity to the early modern period. Leuven ; Dudley, MA : Peeters, 2002.
BF1589 .M55 2002

Veerman, David. When your father dies : how a man deals with the loss of his father / Dave Veerman and Bruce Barton. Nashville, Tenn. : Thomas Nelson, c2003. xiv, 204 p. ; 22 cm. Includes bibliographical references (p. 199-200). Table of contents URL: http://www.loc.gov/catdir/toc/ecip046/2003015246.html CONTENTS: Reality check : acknowledging the truth -- The shock : sensing the surprisingly wide range and power of emotions -- Aftershocks : experiencing emotional waves -- The tallest tree : feeling alone and vulnerable -- Mortality exposed : realizing that life is short -- Loss of audience : missing the one who cheered us on -- Powershift : receiving the mantle -- Over the shoulder : charting our own course -- Sensing the legacy : knowing what we have received and what we can pass on -- Facing the future : preparing the next generation. ISBN 0-7852-6366-7 (hardcover) DDC 155.9/37/081
1. Grief. 2. Bereavement. 3. Fathers - Death - Psychological aspects. 4. Fathers and sons. I. Barton, Bruce B. II. Title.
BF575.G7 V44 2003

Vega, Amador. Ramon Llull y el secreto de la vida / Amador Vega. Madrid : Siruela, 2002. 311 p. : ill. ; 22 cm. (Arbol del Paraíso ; 26) Includes bibliographical references (p. 301-308). ISBN 84-7844-600-1
1. Llull, Ramon, - 1232?-1316. 2. Philosophers - Spain - Biography. 3. Philosophy, Medieval. I. Title. II. Series.

Vega, Phyllis. Celtic astrology : how the mystical power of the Druid Tree signs can transform your life / Phyllis Vega. Franklin Lakes, NJ : New Page Books, c2002. 255 p. : ill. ; 21 cm. Includes bibliographical references (p. 243-247) and index. Table of contents URL: http://www.loc.gov/catdir/toc/fy033/2002019589.html ISBN 1-56414-592-1 (pbk.) DDC 133.5/93916
1. Astrology, Celtic. 2. Calendar, Celtic. 3. Trees - Miscellanea. 4. Mythology, Celtic. I. Title.
BF1714.C44 V44 2002

VEGETABLE OILS. *See* **ESSENCES AND ESSENTIAL OILS.**

The veiled female core.
Reenkola, Elina M. New York : Other Press, c2002.
BF173 .R368 2002

Vek psikhologii.
Stepanov, S. S. (Sergeĭ Sergeevich) Izd. 2., ispr. i dop. Moskva : EKSMO, 2002.
BF109.A1 S75 2002

Velásquez, Andrés, fl. 1553-1615. Libro de la melancholía / Andrés Velásquez ; edizione critica, introduzione e note a cura di Felice Gambin. Viareggio (Lucca) : M. Baroni, [2002] 159 p. ; 22 cm. (Agua y peña ; 16) Includes bibliographical references (p. 151-159) and index. Includes the original Spanish text. ISBN 88-8209-237-2 DDC 863
1. Melancholy - Early works to 1800. I. Gambin, Felice. II. Title. III. Series.
BF575.M44 V453 2002

Veličková, Helena. Grafologie, cesta do hlubin duše : přehled dějin písma a rozbory rukopisů slavných osobností s využitím hlubinné psychologie / Helena Veličková. Vyd. 1. Praha : Academia, 2002. 288 p. : facsims. ; 22 cm. Includes bibliographical references (p. 288) ISBN 80-200-0931-0
1. Graphology. 2. Writing - History. 3. Psychoanalysis. 4. Celebrities. I. Title.
BF896 .V45 2002

Velikie protivostoĭanĭia
Parshev, A. P. (Andreĭ Petrovich) Pochemu Amerika nastupaet. Moskva : AST : Astrel', 2002.

Velkoff, Victoria Averil.
HF1558.2.Z4 P37 2002

Velkoff, Victoria Averil. Gender and aging [electronic resource] : caregiving / by Victoria A. Velkoff and Valerie A. Lawson. [Washington, D.C.] : U.S. Dept. of Commerce, Economics and Statistics Administration, Bureau of the Census, [1998] (International brief ; IB/98-3) System requirements: Adobe Acrobat Reader. Mode of access: Internet from the U.S. Census Bureau web site. Address as of 3/8/03: http://www.census.gov/ipc/prod/ib-9803.pdf; current access ia available via PURL. Title from caption title screen (viewed on March 8, 2003). "Issued December 1998." URL: http://purl.access.gpo.gov/GPO/LPS27826 Available in other form: Velkoff, Victoria Averil. Gender and aging, caregiving 7 p. (OCoLC)42017113.
1. Aged - Care. 2. Caregivers. I. Lawson, Valerie A. II. United States. Bureau of the Census. III. Title. IV. Title: Caregiving V. Title: Velkoff, Victoria Averil. Gender and aging, caregiving 7 p. VI. Series: International brief (United States. Bureau of the Census) ; IB/98-3.

Velkoff, Victoria Averil. Gender and aging, caregiving 7 p.
Velkoff, Victoria Averil. Gender and aging [electronic resource]. [Washington, D.C.] : U.S. Dept. of Commerce, Economics and Statistics Administration, Bureau of the Census, [1998]

VENERATION OF CHRISTIAN SAINTS. *See* **CHRISTIAN SAINTS - CULT.**

VENEREAL DISEASES. *See* **SEXUALLY TRANSMITTED DISEASES.**

Venerella, John.
Leonardo, da Vinci, 1452-1519. [Selections. English. 1999] The manuscripts of Leonardo da Vinci in the Institut de France. Milano : Ente raccolta vinciana, 1999-
Q113 .L3513 1999

VENEZUELAN ESSAYS.
Morales Villaroel, Oscar. Huellas y relatos. Caracas : [s.n.], 2001.

VENGEANCE. *See* **REVENGE.**

Venini, Lucia.
La comunicazione nei processi sociali e organizzativi. Nuova ed. aggiornata. Milano, Italy : FrancoAngeli, [2001?], c1997.

Veṅkaṭanāthārya.
[Daśanirṇayī]
Vaidikasārvabhaumanāmnā suprasiddhaiḥ Veṅkaṭanāthāryaiḥ Vaidikakarmānuṣṭhānasaukaryāya viracitā Daśanirṇayī / Pa. Ca. Gopālācāryeṇa pariśodhya, Rāmabhadrācāryeṇa pariskrtya prakāśitā. 1st ed. Mumbai : Śrīmadahobilamaṭhena, 1998. [12], 324 p. : [2] leaves of plates : col. ill. ; 22 cm. Added title page title: Dasanirmayee. Spine title: Daśanirṇayī. Added title page title: Śrī Vaidikasārvabhaumairviracitā Daśanirṇayī. In Sanskrit.
1. Hinduism - Rituals. 2. Time - Religious aspects - Hinduism. 3. Hindu astrology. I. Gopālācārya, Pa. Ca. II. Rāmabhadrācārya. III. Title. IV. Title: Dasanirnayee V. Title: Daśanirṇayī VI. Title: Śrī Vaidikasārvabhaumairviracitā Daśanirṇayī
BL1226.72 .V36 1998

Venne, Jean-François, 1972-.
De chair et d'os.
Venne, Jean-François, 1972- Le lien social dans le modèle de l'individualisme privé. Paris : L'Harmattan, c2002.

Le lien social dans le modèle de l'individualisme privé : de chair et d'os / Jean-François Venne. Paris : L'Harmattan, c2002. 186 p. ; 22 cm. (Collection Questions contemporaines) Originally presented by the author as thesis (M.A.--Université du Québec à Montréal), 2001 under the title: De chair et d'os. Includes bibliographical references (p. [177]-186). ISBN 2-7475-2839-1 DDC 302.5/4
1. Individualism. 2. Postmodernism. 3. Social contract. I. Venne, Jean-François, 1972- De chair et d'os. II. Title. III. Series.

Venner, Dominique. Histoire et tradition des Européens : 30000 ans d'identité / Dominique Venner. Monaco : Rocher, c2002. 273 p. ; 24 cm. Includes bibliographical references. ISBN 2-268-04162-X DDC 940
1. Europe - History. 2. Europe - Historiography. 3. History - Philosophy. 4. Civilization, Medieval. 5. Civilization, Modern. 6. Civilization, Ancient. I. Title.
D80 .V46 2002

Ventrella, Tony, 1944- Smile in the mirror : let your light shine / Tony Ventrella. 1st ed. Sammamish, WA : Positive Energy Productions, c2001. 116 p. : ill. ; 22 cm. ISBN 0-9714118-0-8

1. Self-actualization (Psychology) 2. Ventrella, Tony, - 1944- I. Title.
BF637.S4 V46 2001

VENTRELLA, TONY, 1944-.
Ventrella, Tony, 1944- Smile in the mirror. 1st ed. Sammamish, WA : Positive Energy Productions, c2001.
BF637.S4 V46 2001

Vera i kul'tura.
Florovsky, Georges, 1893-1979. [Selections. Russian. 2002] Sankt-Peterburg : Izd-vo Russkogo Khristianskogo gumanitarnogo instituta, 2002.
BX260 .F552 2002

Die veränderte Rolle der New York Times.
Elfenbein, Stefan W., 1964- Frankfurt am Main ; New York : P. Lang, c1996.
PN4899.N42 N375 1996

Verantwortung, nein danke!.
Kricheldorf, Beate, 1949- 2., unveränderte Aufl. Frankfurt/Main : R.G. Fischer, 2001, c1998.

Veras, Renato P. (Renato Peixoto) Terceira idade : gestão contemporânea em saúde / Renato Peixoto Veras. Rio de Janeiro : UNATI : Relume Dumará, 2002. 190 p. ; 21 cm. Includes bibliographical references. ISBN 85-7316-269-4
1. Aged - Health and hygiene - Brazil. 2. Aged - Medical care - Brazil. 3. Aged - Care. I. Title.

VERBAL ABUSE. *See* **INVECTIVE.**

VERBAL BEHAVIOR. *See also* **VERBAL SELF-DEFENSE.**
Jay, Timothy. Why we curse. Philadelphia : John Benjamins Publishing Company, c2000.
BF463.I58 J38 2000

VERBAL COMMUNICATION. *See* **ORAL COMMUNICATION.**

VERBAL SELF-DEFENSE. *See* **QUARRELING.**

VERBAL SELF-DEFENSE - JUVENILE LITERATURE.
Johnston, Marianne. [Dealing with insults. Spanish] Como tratar los insultos. New York : PowerKids Press, 2005.
BF637.V47 J6418 2005

Verbruggen, Martien. Graphics programming with Perl / Martien Verbruggen. Greenwich : Manning, c2002. xxii, 303 p. : ill. ; 24 cm. Includes bibliographical references and index. ISBN 1-930110-02-2 DDC 006.6/633
1. Computer graphics. 2. Perl (Computer program language) I. Title.
T385 .V465 2002

Verderber, Kathleen S., 1949- Inter-act : interpersonal communication concepts, skills, and contexts / Kathleen S. Verderber, Rudolph F. Verderber. 10th ed. New York : Oxford University Press, 2004. 443 p. : ill. (some col.) ; 26 cm. + 1 CD-ROM (4 3/4 in.). Includes bibliographical references (p. [422]-429) and index. ISBN 0-19-516847-X (acid-free paper) DDC 158.2
1. Interpersonal communication. 2. Interpersonal relations. I. Verderber, Rudolph F. II. Title. III. Title: Interact
BF637.C45 V47 2004

Verderber, Rudolph F.
Verderber, Kathleen S., 1949- Inter-act. 10th ed. New York : Oxford University Press, 2004.
BF637.C45 V47 2004

Verdi, Giuseppe, 1813-1901.
Falstaff. Onore! Ladri! German.
Hann, Georg. Georg Hann [sound recording]. [Germany] : Preiser Records, p2001.

Nabucco. Del futuro nel bujo discerno. German.
Hann, Georg. Georg Hann [sound recording]. [Germany] : Preiser Records, p2001.

Operas. Selections.
Malaniuk, Ira. Arien und Lieder [sound recording]. [Germany] : Preiser Records, p2000.

Verdicchio, Massimo, 1945-.
Between philosophy and poetry. New York : Continuum, 2002.
B66 .B48 2002

Verdon, Jean. Boire au moyen âge / Jean Verdon. [Paris] : Perrin, c2002. 313 p. ; 23 cm. (Pour l'histoire) Includes bibliographical references (p. [287]-310). ISBN 2-262-01778-6 DDC 944
1. Drinking customs - Europe - History - To 1500. 2. Beverages - Europe - History - To 1500. 3. Civilization, Medieval. I. Title. II. Series: Collection "Pour l'histoire"

[Nuit au Moyen Age. English]
Night in the Middle Ages / Jean Verdon ; translated by George Holoch. Notre Dame, Ind. : University of Notre Dame Press, c2002. ix, 235 p. ; 22 cm. Includes bibliographical references (p. 219-229) and index. ISBN 0-268-03655-1 (cloth : alk. paper) ISBN 0-268-03656-X (pbk. : alk. paper) DDC 304.2/3/0902
1. Night - Social aspects. 2. Night - History. 3. Sleeping customs - History. 4. Compline - History. 5. Civilization, Medieval. I. Title.
HM1033 .V4713 2002

Verene, Donald Phillip, 1937- Knowledge of things human and divine : Vico's New science and Finnegans wake / Donald Phillip Verene. New Haven, Conn. : Yale University Press, c2003. xiv, 264 p., [10] p. of plates : ill. ; 25 cm. Includes bibliographical references (p. 241-254) and index. ISBN 0-300-09958-4 (alk. paper) DDC 195
1. Vico, Giambattista, - 1668-1744. - Principi di una scienza nuova. 2. Myth. 3. Philosophy. 4. Social sciences. I. Title.
B3581.P73 V47 2003

Die Verfolgung von Zauberei und Hexerei in den fränkischen Markgraftümern im 16. Jahrhundert.
Kleinöder-Strobel, Susanne, 1969- Tübingen : Mohr Siebeck, c2002.
BF1583 .K54 2002

Verführung, Trauma, Missbrauch / Hertha Richter-Appelt (Hg.). [2. Aufl.]. Giessen : Psychosozial-Verlag, c2002. 261 p. : ill. ; 21 cm. (Beiträge zur Sexualforschung, 0067-5210 ; Sonderbd) Papers from a conference held 1996 in the Universitätskrankenhaus Hamburg-Eppendorf. Includes bibliographical references. ISBN 3-89806-192-2 (pbk.)
1. Sex crimes - Psychological aspects. 2. Sexual abuse victims - Psychology. 3. Psychotherapy. I. Richter-Appelt, Hertha. II. Series.

Vergara, Gloria, 1964- Tiempo y verdad en la literatura / Gloria Vergara. 1a. ed. México, D.F. : Universidad Iberoamericana, 2001. 111 p. ; 12 cm. Includes bibliography (p. 106-111). ISBN 968-859-424-5 DDC 809.33
1. Ingarden, Roman, - 1893- - Philosophy. 2. Time in literature. 3. Time. I. Title.

Verger, Pierre. Saída de Iaô : cinco ensaios sobre a religiao dos orixás / Pierre Verger, fotos de Piere Verger ; organização e tradução de Carlos Eugênio Marcondes de Moura ; prefácio de Luis Pellegrini, com fotos de Lamberto Scipioni ; introdução biográfico por Rita Amaral e Vagner Gonçalves da Silva. Sao Paulo : Fundação Pierre Verger : Axis Mundi Editora, 2002. 190 p. : ill. ; 24 cm. Errata slip inserted. Includes bibliographical references (p. 187-188). ISBN 85-85554-25-8
1. Verger, Pierre. 2. Brazil - Religion - African influences. 3. Orishas. 4. Afro-Brazilian cults. 5. Voodooism - Brazil. 6. Yoruba (African people) - Religion. I. Moura, Carlos Eugênio Marcondes de. II. Amaral, Rita. III. Silva, Vagner Gonçalves da. IV. Title. V. Title: Cinco ensaios sobre a religiao dos orixás

VERGER, PIERRE.
Verger, Pierre. Saída de Iaô. Sao Paulo : Fundação Pierre Verger : Axis Mundi Editora, 2002.

Vergès, Jacques. Dictionnaire amoureux de la justice / Jacques Vergès. Paris : Plon, c2002. 780 p. : ill. ; 21 cm. ISBN 2-259-19556-3 DDC 365
1. Justice, Administration of - Case studies. 2. Law and ethics - Case studies. 3. Love. I. Title.

Verhoeven, Ludo Th.
Precursors of functional literacy. Amsterdam : Philadelphia : J. Benjamins Pub., c2002.
P118.7 .P74 2002

La vérité dans les sciences.
Collège de France. Symposium annuel. Paris : Jacob, c2003.

Verna, Arturo. Letture filosofiche / Arturo Verna. Padova : Unipress, 2002. 232 p. ; 21 cm. (Saggi filosofici) Includes bibliographical references. ISBN 88-8098-162-5 DDC 121
1. Philosophy. I. Title. II. Series: Saggi filosofici (Padua, Italy)

Vernes, Jean-René. The existence of the external world : the Pascal-Hume principle / Jean-René Vernes ; [translation, Mary Baker]. Ottawa : University of Ottawa Press, c2000. xi, 101 p. ; 23 cm. (Collection Philosophica ; no. 54) Translation of: L'existence du monde extérieur et l'erreur du rationalisme. Includes bibliographical references and index. ISBN 0-7766-0519-4 DDC 121
1. Knowledge, Theory of. 2. Matter. 3. Reason. 4. Probabilities. I. Baker, Mary. II. Title. III. Series.

Vernetzte Ethik.
Thurnherr, Urs. Freiburg : Alber, 2001.

Veröffentlichungen des Max-Planck-Instituts für Geschichte

(171) Antike Weisheit und kulturelle Praxis. Göttingen : Vandenhoeck & Ruprecht, 2001.
BF1586 .A58 2001

(Bd. 188) Negotiating the gift. Göttingen : Vandenhoeck & Ruprecht, c2003.

Die Verortung von Gedächtnis / Moritz Csáky, Peter Stachel (Hg.). Wien : Passagen, c2001. 344 p. : ill. ; 24 cm. (Orte des Gedächtnisses) Includes bibliographical references. Papers from a conference held November 2000, by the Kommission für Kulturwissenschaften und Theatergeschichte an der Österreichischen Akademie der Wissenschaften. ISBN 3-85165-489-7 (pbk.)
1. Memory - Social aspects - Congresses. 2. Social psychology - Congresses. I. Csáky, Moritz. II. Stachel, Peter. III. Series: Passagen Orte des Gedächtnisses.

VERTEBRATES. *See* **FISHES.**

Vertovec, Steven.
Migration, diasporas, and transnationalism. Cheltenham, UK ; Northampton, MA : Edward Elgar, 1999.
JV6032 .M54 1999

Very short introductions
Butler, Christopher, 1940- Postmodernism. Oxford ; New York : Oxford University Press, 2002.
NX456.5.P66 B88 2002

Gosden, Chris, 1955- Prehistory. Oxford ; New York : Oxford University Press, 2003.

VESTIBULE SCHOOLS. *See* **EMPLOYEES - TRAINING OF.**

Vestiduras y paramentos masónicos.
Masonería. Quito : [O. Valenzuela Muñoz], 2001.

Vestiges of war : the Philippine-American War and the aftermath of an imperial dream, 1899-1999 / edited by Angel Velasco Shaw and Luis H. Francia. New York : New York University Press, 2000. xxviii, 468 p. : ill. (some col.) ; 28 cm. "A project of Asian/Pacific/American Studies, New York University." Includes bibliographical references and index. ISBN 0-8147-9790-3 (cloth) ISBN 0-8147-9791-1 (pbk.) DDC 959.9/031
1. Philippines - History - Philippine American War, 1899-1902. 2. Philippines - Foreign relations - United States. 3. United States - Foreign relations - Philippines. 4. United States - Politics and government - 20th century. I. Shaw, Angel Velasco. II. Francia, Luis, 1945-
DS679 .V47 2000

Vestigia (Fribourg, Switzerland)
(28.) Canning, Joseph. [History of medieval political thought, 300-1450. French] Histoire de la pensée politique médiévale (300-1450). Fribourg, Suisse : Editions universitaires : Paris : Cerf, [2003]

VETERANS - MENTAL HEALTH - UNITED STATES.
Shay, Jonathan. Odysseus in America. New York : Scribner, c2002.
RC550 .S533 2002

Vezin, Annette. Egéries dans l'ombre des créateurs / Annette et Luc Vezin. Paris : Martinière, 2002. 314 p. : ill. (some col.) ; 24cm. ISBN 2-7324-2827-2
1. Artists - Relations with women. 2. Artist couples. 3. Artists' models. 4. Art patronage. 5. Arts, Modern - 20th century. 6. Man-woman relationships. I. Vezin, Luc. II. Title.
NX165 .V49 2002

[Egéries dans l'ombre des créateurs. English]
The 20th-century muse / Annette and Luc Vezin ; translated from the French by Toula Ballas. New York : Harry N. Abrams, 2003. 314 p. : ill. (some col.) ; 25 cm. ISBN 0-8109-9154-3 (flexibind) DDC 700/.92/2
1. Artists - Psychology. 2. Couples - Psychology. 3. Creation (Literary, artistic, etc.) I. Vezin, Luc. II. Title. III. Title: Twentieth-century muse
N71 .V4913 2003

Vezin, Luc.
Vezin, Annette. Egéries dans l'ombre des créateurs. Paris : Martinière, 2002.
NX165 .V49 2002

Vezin, Annette. [Egéries dans l'ombre des créateurs. English] The 20th-century muse. New York : Harry N. Abrams, 2003.
N71 .V4913 2003

Viatkina, G. V. Razvitie individual'nosti lichnosti v sovremennykh usloviiakh / G.V. Viatkina. Moskva : In-t molodezhi, 1997. 115 p. ; 20 cm. Includes bibliographical references (p. 110-114).
1. Individuality. 2. Self - Social aspects. 3. Identity (Psychology) - Social aspects. I. Title.
BF697 .V52 1997

VICE.
Krasikov, V. I. (Vladimir Ivanovich) Sindrom sushchestvovaniia. Tomsk : [s.n.], 2002.

Vichnyĭ vohon'
Smereka, Vira, 1923- L'viv : Vyd-vo "Spolom", 2000.
PG3949.29.M4 V5 2000

VICO, GIAMBATTISTA, 1668-1744. PRINCIPI DI UNA SCIENZA NUOVA.
Luft, Sandra Rudnick, 1934- Vico's uncanny humanism. Ithaca, N.Y. : Cornell University Press, 2003.
B3581.P73 L84 2003

Verene, Donald Phillip, 1937- Knowledge of things human and divine. New Haven, Conn. : Yale University Press, c2003.
B3581.P73 V47 2003

VICO, GIAMBATTISTA, 1668-1744.
Fabiani, Paolo, 1968- La filosofia dell'immaginazione in Vico e Malebranche. Firenze : Firenze University Press, 2002.
B3583.F25 F55 2002

Sanna, Manuela. La "fantasia, che è l'occhio dell'ingegno". Napoli : A. Guida editore, c2001.
B3583 .S26 2001

VICO, GIAMBATTISTA, 1668-1744 - INFLUENCE.
Cospito, Giuseppe, 1966- Il "gran Vico". Genova : Name, c2002.

Vico's uncanny humanism.
Luft, Sandra Rudnick, 1934- Ithaca, N.Y. : Cornell University Press, 2003.
B3581.P73 L84 2003

VICTIMOLOGY. *See* **VICTIMS OF CRIMES.**

VICTIMS. *See* **DISASTER VICTIMS; HOLOCAUST SURVIVORS; VICTIMS OF CRIMES.**

VICTIMS OF CRIMES. *See* **REPARATION; SEXUAL ABUSE VICTIMS; SUICIDE VICTIMS; VICTIMS OF TERRORISM.**

VICTIMS OF CRIMES - PSYCHOLOGY.
Mental health and mass violence [electronic resource]. [Bethesda, MD : National Institute of Mental Health, 2002]

VICTIMS OF DISASTERS. *See* **DISASTER VICTIMS.**

VICTIMS OF SEX CRIMES. *See* **SEXUAL ABUSE VICTIMS.**

VICTIMS OF SUICIDE. *See* **SUICIDE VICTIMS.**

VICTIMS OF TERRORISM - PSYCHOLOGICAL ASPECTS.
Terrorism and disaster. Cambridge, UK ; New York : Cambridge University Press, 2003.
RC552.P67 T476 2003

VICTIMS OF TERRORISM - PSYCHOLOGY.
Mental health and mass violence [electronic resource]. [Bethesda, MD : National Institute of Mental Health, 2002]

Understanding terrorism. 1st ed. Washington, DC : American Psychological Association, 2004.
HV6431 .U35 2004

VICTORIAN LITERATURE. *See* **ENGLISH LITERATURE - 19TH CENTURY.**

VICTORIUS, AQUITAINE. CALCULUS.
Abbo of Fleury and Ramsay. Oxford ; New York : Oxford University Press, 2002.

Vid IAïtsia-raïtsia do ideï Spasyteliā.
Chmykhov, M. O. (Mykola Oleksandrovych) Kyïv : "Lybid'", 2001.
BD518.U38 C48 2001

Vida y costumbres de los viejos filósofos.
Burlaeus, Gualterus, 1275-1345? [De vita et moribus philosophorum. Spanish] Madrid : Iberoamericana ; Frankfurt : Vervuert, 2002.

Vidal, Jordi. Résistance au chaos : pour une critique du nouvel ordre féodal / Jordi Vidal. Paris : Allia, 2002. 91 p. ; 17 cm. ISBN 2-8448-5100-2 DDC 194
1. World politics - 21st century. 2. Terrorism. 3. Globalization. 4. Liberty. I. Title.

VIDEO.
Big Dance [videorecording]. Buffalo, N.Y. : Kineticvideo.com, c1998.

The peak performance series. Vol. [4] [videorecording]. Longwood, Fla. : Pamela Bolling Enterprises, c1999.

VIDEO GAMES AND CHILDREN.
Children in the digital age. Westport, Conn. : Praeger, 2002.
HQ784.M3 C455 2002

VIDEO RECORDINGS. *See* **MUSIC VIDEOS.**

VIDEO RECORDINGS FOR THE HEARING IMPAIRED.
McLuhan's wake [videorecording]. [Montreal, Quebec] : Primitive Entertainment/National Film Board of Canada, c2002.

VIDEOS, MUSIC. *See* **MUSIC VIDEOS.**

La vie au moyen âge.
Ducret, Alix. Courtaboeuf : Didro, c2002.

La vie des images.
Wunenburger, Jean-Jacques. [Nouvelle édition augmentée]. Grenoble : Presses universitaires de Grenoble, 2002.
BF367 .W85 2002

Vieira, Anselmo, 1923- Ser ou não ter : rosários da minha alma / Anselmo Vieira Lisboa : Roma Editora, [2002]- v. : ill. ; 22 cm. At head of title: valores. ISBN 972-849-019-4
1. Self-realization - Religious aspects. 2. Spiritual life. 3. Conduct of life. I. Title. II. Title: valores

Vienna Circle Institute library
(1) Appraising Lakatos. Dordrecht ; Boston : Kluwer Academic, c2002.
Q175 .A685 2002

The Vienna series in theoretical biology
Origination of organismal form. Cambridge, Mass. : MIT Press, c2003.
QH491 .O576 2003

Vies sociales
Lorenzi-Cioldi, Fabio, 1955- Les représentations des groupes dominants et dominés. Grenoble : Presses universitaires de Grenoble, c2002.
HM716 .L674 2002

VIETNAM CONFLICT, 1961-1975. *See* **VIETNAMESE CONFLICT, 1961-1975.**

VIETNAM - HISTORY - 1945-1975. *See* **VIETNAMESE CONFLICT, 1961-1975.**

VIETNAM WAR, 1961-1975. *See* **VIETNAMESE CONFLICT, 1961-1975.**

VIETNAMESE CONFLICT, 1961-1975 - PERSONAL NARRATIVES.
Edwards, Charlene. Voices from Vietnam. Bayside, NY : Bayside, c2002.

VIETNAMESE CONFLICT, 1961-1975 - PSYCHOLOGICAL ASPECTS.
Shay, Jonathan. Odysseus in America. New York : Scribner, c2002.
RC550 .S533 2002

VIETNAMESE CONFLICT, 1961-1975 - SOURCES.
Edwards, Charlene. Voices from Vietnam. Bayside, NY : Bayside, c2002.

VIETNAMESE CONFLICT, 1961-1975 - VETERANS - INTERVIEWS.
Kingston, Maxine Hong. The fifth book of peace. 1st ed. New York : Alfred A. Knopf, 2003.
PS3561.I52 F44 2003

VIETNAMESE CONFLICT, 1961-1975 - VETERANS - MENTAL HEALTH - UNITED STATES.
Shay, Jonathan. Odysseus in America. New York : Scribner, c2002.
RC550 .S533 2002

VIETNAMESE WAR, 1961-1975. *See* **VIETNAMESE CONFLICT, 1961-1975.**

The view from within : first-person approaches to the study of consciousness / edited by Francisco J. Varela and Jonathan Shear. Thorverton, UK ; Bowling Green, OH : Imprint Academic, 2000. 313 p. : ill. ; 27 cm. (Journal of consciousness studies, 1355-8250 ; 6, no. 2-3) Special issue of the Journal of consciousness studies. Includes bibliographical references and index. ISBN 0-907845-30-4 ISBN 0-907845-25-8 (pbk.) DDC 153
1. Consciousness. 2. Experience. I. Shear, J. (Jonathan) II. Varela, Francisco J., 1946- III. Series
BF311 .V512 2000

VIEWING, REMOTE (PARAPSYCHOLOGY). *See* **REMOTE VIEWING (PARAPSYCHOLOGY).**

Vigna, Carmelo, 1940-.
La persona e i nomi dell'essere. Milano : V&P Università, c2002.

B29 .P414 2002

VILLA PALAGONIA (BAGHERIA, ITALY).
Hachet, Pascal. Psychanalyse d'un choc esthétique. Paris, France : Harmattan, c2002.

VILLAGE COMMUNITIES. *See* **COMMUNISM.**

Villamora, Grace Avellana. Super searchers on Madison Avenue : top advertising and marketing professionals share their online research strategies / Grace Avellana Villamora ; edited by Reva Basch. Medford, N.J. : CyberAge Books/Information Today, c2003. xii, 236 p. : ports. ; 24 cm. Includes bibliographical references (p. 201-222) and index. CONTENTS: Velda Ruddock : visionary for intelligence -- Douglas Buffo : indefatigable enabler of end-users -- Jordie Garvin Thomson : multicultural information expert -- Kristine Larsen Spanier : from copywriting to librarianship -- Gerard Seifert : creative-side researcher -- Robin Feuerstein : major league coach for the information services team -- Leslie Cole : expert on the African-American and urban consumer markets -- Dan Carlton : "Digger Dan" the account planner -- Liz Aviles : trend spotting and integrated marketing pro -- Dee Magnoni : independent research consultant -- Carlos Santiago : chief realist strategist -- Gretchen Reed : virtual research provider -- Marsha Appel : 4As for excellence. ISBN 0-910965-63-3 DDC 658.8/3/02854678
1. Marketing research - Computer network resources. 2. Marketing - Databases. 3. Internet searching. 4. Electronic information resource searching. I. Basch, Reva. II. Title.
HF5415.2 .V497 2003

Villari, Rafael Andrés. Literatura e psicanálise : Ernesto Sábato e a melancolia / Rafael Andrés Villari. Florianópolis : Editora da UFSC, 2002. 161 p. ; 21 cm. Includes bibliographcial references (p. [157]-161). ISBN 85-328-0232-X
1. Sábato, Ernesto R. - Criticism and interpretation. 2. Psychoanalysis and literature. 3. Melancholy in literature. I. Title.

VILLAS. *See* **ARCHITECTURE, DOMESTIC.**

VIMALAKĪRTI (BUDDHIST CHARACTER) - IN LITERATURE.
Sun, Changwu. Zhongguo wen xue zhong di Weimo yu Guanyin. Di 1 ban. Beijing : Gao deng jiao yu chu ban she : Xin hua shu dian zong dian Beijing fa xing suo fa xing, 1996.
PL2275.B8 S85 1996 <Orien China>

Vincent, Carol, 1963-.
Social justice, education, and identity. London ; New York : RoutledgeFalmer, 2003.
LC191 .S6564 2003

Vind, Karl. Independence, additivity, uncertainty / Karl Vind ; with contributions by Birgit Grodal. Berlin ; New York : Springer, c2003. xii, 277 p. : ill. ; 24 cm. (Studies in economic theory ; 14) Includes bibliographical references (p. [253]-268) and index. ISBN 3-540-41683-8 (alk. paper) DDC 330/.01/51
1. Economics, Mathematical. 2. Probabilities. 3. Uncertainty. 4. Utility theory. I. Grodal, Birgit. II. Title. III. Series: Studies in economic theory (Berlin, Germany) ; 14.
HB135 .V56 2003

Vinet, Dominique. Romanesque britannique et psyché : étude du signifiant dans le roman anglais / Dominique Vinet. Paris : L'Harmattan, c2003. 256 p. ; 22 cm. (Collection L'œuvre et la psyché) Includes bibliographical references. ISBN 2-7475-4080-4 DDC 809
1. English fiction - 20th century - History and criticism. 2. Psychoanalysis and literature. I. Title. II. Series.

Vinokurov, Igor' Charodei ponevole / Igor' Vinokurov. Moskva : AiF-Print, 2003. 328 p. : ill. ; 22 cm. (Seriia "Grani nashego mira") Includes bibliographical references. ISBN 5947360276
1. Spiritualism. I. Title. II. Series.
BF1288 .V55 2003

Ne smotrite im v glaza! / Igor' Vinokurov. Moskva : AiF-Print, 2001. 397 p. : ill. ; 23 cm. (Grani nashego vremeni) ISBN 5932291044
1. Apparitions. 2. Haunted houses. 3. Poltergeists. I. Title. II. Series.
BF1466 .V56 2001

Vinšćak, Tomo. Vjerovanja o drveću u hrvata : u kontekstu slavističkih istraživanja / Tomo Vinšćak. [Jastrebarsko] : Naklada Slap, c2002. 181 p. : folded maps ; 21 cm. (Spektar ; 5. knj.) Includes bibliographical references and index. Summary in English. ISBN 9531911878
1. Mythology, Slavic. 2. Trees - Mythology. I. Title.

Vint/age 2001 conference : positive solutions to an age old problem [videorecording] / The New York Coalition of Professional Women in the Arts and Media presents ; executive producer, Shari Upbin ; producer, Sandi Durell ; associate producer, Stacey Mark ; conference directors, Sue Lawless, William Martin, Nancy Rhodes ; [video prod. company] Character Generators, Inc. New York, c2001. 4 videocassettes (VHS) (298 min.) : sd., col. SP ; 1/2 in. Speakers: Shari Upbin, Tina Howe, Valerie Harper, Elsa Rael. Panel moderators: Gretchen Cryer, Pia Lindstrom, Tisa Chang, Denise Richardson. Panelists: Tina Howe, Graciela Daniele, Richard Dubin, Micki Grant, Frances Sternhagen, Margery Simkin, Carol Hall, Judith Gerberg, Jane Powell, John Nielson, Daniel Wolf, Anne Basting, Eileen Fulton, Jeri Sedlar, Tovah Feldshuh, Marie Anne Chiment, Margaret Hoorneman, Wendy Lewis, Carol Harris-Mannes, Phyllis Newman, Mark Silver, Ruth Lax. Performers: Lainie Kazan, Lesley Gore, Stephanie Pope. Pianists: Bob Kaye, George Caldwell. Videotaped at the John Jay College Theater, New York, N.Y., Oct. 13, 2001. SUMMARY: This conference devoted to the role of older women in the arts consists of four separate panel discussions, several speakers, and three musical performances. The last discussion, which was originally intended to focus on the psychological aspects of aging, also examines the psychological impact of the terrorist attacks of September 11, 2001. CONTENTS: Panel topics: Who gets to say who is too old? -- What has formed the American obsession with youth? -- How do we support each other to deal with the realities that exist to affect change? -- Mind, body, spirit, vitality! Exploring the psychological issues of aging. CONTENTS: Songs (performer): Here's to life (Lainie Kazan) -- My declaration of independence (Lesley Gore) -- God bless America (Stephanie Pope).
1. Upbin, Shari. 2. Howe, Tina. 3. Rael, Elsa. 4. Cryer, Gretchen. 5. Daniele, Graciela, - 1939- 6. Dubin, Richard. 7. Grant, Micki. 8. Sternhagen, Frances, - 1930- 9. Simkin, Margery. 10. Hall, Carol, - 1936- 11. Lindstrom, Pia. 12. Gerberg, Judith. 13. Powell, Jane, - 1929- 14. Nielson, John. 15. Wolf, Daniel. 16. Harper, Valerie, - 1940- 17. Chang, Tisa. 18. Basting, Anne Davis, - 1965- 19. Fulton, Eileen. 20. Sedlar, Jeri. 21. Feldshuh, Tovah. 22. Chiment, Marie Anne. 23. Hoorneman, Margaret. 24. Richardson, Denise. 25. Lewis, Wendy, - 1959- 26. Harris-Mannes, Carol. 27. Newman, Phyllis, - 1935- 28. Silver, Mark. 29. Lax, Ruth F. 30. Kazan, Lainie. 31. Gore, Lesley, - 1946- 32. Pope, Stephanie. 33. Age discrimination in employment - United States. 34. Ageism - United States. 35. Aging - Psychological aspects. 36. Sexism - United States. 37. Surgery, Plastic. 38. Women in the performing arts. 39. Women - Health and hygene. 40. September 11 Terrorist Attacks, 2001. 41. September 11 Terrorist Attacks, 2001 - Psychological aspects. 42. Panel discussions. I. Upbin, Shari. II. Durell, Sandi. III. Mark, Stacey. IV. Lawless, Sue. V. Martin, William. VI. Rhodes, Nancy. VII. Cryer, Gretchen. VIII. Howe, Tina, panelist. IX. Rael, Elsa. X. Daniele, Graciela, 1939- panelist. XI. Dubin, Richard, panelist. XII. Grant, Micki, panelist. XIII. Sternhagen, Frances, 1930- panelist. XIV. Simkin, Margery, panelist. XV. Hall, Carol, 1936- panelist. XVI. Lindstrom, Pia. XVII. Gerberg, Judith, panelist. XVIII. Powell, Jane, 1929- panelist. XIX. Nielson, John, panelist. XX. Wolf, Daniel, panelist. XXI. Harper, Valerie, 1940- XXII. Kaye, Bob, pianist. XXIII. Chang, Tisa. XXIV. Basting, Anne Davis, 1965- panelist. XXV. Fulton, Eileen, panelist. XXVI. Sedlar, Jeri, panelist. XXVII. Feldshuh, Tovah, panelist. XXVIII. Chiment, Marie Anne, panelist. XXIX. Hoorneman, Margaret, panelist. XXX. Richardson, Denise. XXXI. Lewis, Wendy, 1959- panelist. XXXII. Harris-Mannes, Carol, panelist. XXXIII. Newman, Phyllis, 1935- panelist. XXXIV. Silver, Mark, panelist. XXXV. Lax, Ruth F., panelist. XXXVI. Kazan, Lainie. XXXVII. Gore, Lesley, 1946- XXXVIII. Pope, Stephanie. XXXIX. Caldwell, George, synthesizer player. XL. New York Coalition of Professional Women in the Arts and Media, Inc. 41. Character Generators/Video. 42. Title: Vintage 2001

Vintage 2001.
Vint/age 2001 conference : [videorecording]. New York, c2001.

VIOLENCE. *See also* **CHILDREN AND VIOLENCE; FIGHTING (PSYCHOLOGY); POLITICAL VIOLENCE; SCHOOL VIOLENCE.**
Sofsky, Wolfgang. London : Granta, 2003, c2002.

VIOLENCE.
Alexander, Jeffrey C. The meanings of social life. New York : Oxford University Press, 2003.
HM585 .A5 2003

Benítez Torres, Milton. Peregrinos y vagabundos. 1. ed. Quito, Ecuador : Ediciones Abya-Yala, 2002.

Cornblit, Oscar. Violencia social, genocidio y terrorismo. 1. ed. México, D.F. : Fondo de Cultura Económica, 2002.
HM886 .C67 2002

Estudios sobre la violencia. 1. ed. México, D.F. : CIESAS : M.A. Porrúa, 2002.
HN120.Z9 V538 2002

Gewalt-Verhältnisse. Frankfurt ; New York : Campus, c2002.

Gould, Roger V. Collision of wills. Chicago : University of Chicago Press, 2003.
HM1121 .G68 2003

Handbook of violence. New York : Wiley, c2002.
HM1116 .H36 2002

Iadicola, Peter. Violence, inequality, and human freedom. 2nd ed. Lanham, Md. ; Oxford : Rowman & Littlefield Publishers, Inc., c2003.
HM886 .I18 2003

Jay, Martin, 1944- Refractions of violence. New York ; London : Routledge, 2003.
HM1116 .J39 2003

Köhler, Manfred. Apokalypse oder Umkehr? Marburg : Tectum, 2000.

La Branche, Stéphane. Mondialisation et terrorisme identitaire, ou, Comment l'Occident tente de transformer le monde. Paris : Harmattan, c2003.
JC330 .L2 2003

The meanings of violence. London ; New York : Routledge, 2003.
HM1116 .M436 2003

Mental health and mass violence [electronic resource]. [Bethesda, MD : National Institute of Mental Health, 2002]

Mitchell, Juliet, 1940- Siblings. Cambridge, UK : Polity Press, c2003.
BF723.S43 M58 2003

Santoni, Ronald E. Sartre on violence--curiously ambivalent. University Park, Pa. : Pennsylvania State University Press, c2003.
B2430.S34 S315 2003

Sodré, Muniz. Sociedade mídia e violência. Porto Alegre : Editora Sulina : EDIPUCRS, c2002.

Sofsky, Wolfgang. Violence. London : Granta, 2003, c2002.

Sontag, Susan, 1933- Regarding the pain of others. 1st ed. New York : Farrar, Straus and Giroux, 2003.
HM554 .S65 2003

Terror, counter-terror. London ; New York : Zed Books ; New Delhi : Kali for Women ; New York : Distributed in the U.S. exclusively by Palgrave, 2003.
HQ1236 .T47 2003

Violence and the body. Bloomington : Indiana University Press, c2003.
HM1116 .V557 2003

Violent acts and violentization. Amsterdam ; Boston : JAI, 2003.

VIOLENCE AND CHILDREN. *See* **CHILDREN AND VIOLENCE.**

Violence and the body : race, gender, and the state / edited by Arturo J. Aldama ; foreword by Alfred Arteaga. Bloomington : Indiana University Press, c2003. viii, 452 p. : ill. ; 24 cm. Includes bibliographical references and index. CONTENTS: Violence, bodies, and the color of fear: an introduction / Arturo J. Aldama -- Borders, violence, and the struggle for Chicana and Chicano subjectivity / Arturo J. Aldama -- Hungarian poetic nationalism or national pornography?: Eastern Europe and feminism-with a difference / Anikó Imre -- Militarizing the feminine body: women's participation in the Tamil nationalist struggle / Yamuna Sangarasivam -- Blood and dirt: politics of women's protest in Armagh prison, Northern Ireland / Leila Neti -- Bodily metaphors, material exclusions: the sexual and racial politics of domestic partnership in France / Catherine Raissiguier -- Mattering national bodies and sexualities: corporeal contest in Marcos and Brocka / Rolando B. Tolentino -- The time of violence: deconstruction and value / Elizabeth Grosz -- Consuming cannibalism: the body in Australia's Pacific archive / Mike Hayes -- Global genocide and biocolonialism: on the effect of the human genome diversity project on targeted indigenous peoples/ecocultures as "isolates of historic interest" / M. A. Jaimes Guerrero -- Angola, convict leasing, and the annulment of freedom: the vectors of architectural and discursive violence in the U.S. "slavery of prison" / Dennis Childs -- Bernhard Goetz and the politics of fear / Jonathan Markovitz -- Pierced tongues: language and violence in Carmen Boullosa's Dystopia / Margarita Saona -- Constituting transgressive interiorities: nineteenth-century psychiatric readings of morally mad bodies / Heidi Rimke -- When electrolysis proxies for the existential: a somewhat sordid meditation on what might occur if Frantz Fanon, Rosario Castellanos, Jacques Derrida, Gayatri Chakravorty Spivak, and Sandra Cisneros asked Rita Hayworth her name / William Anthony Nericcio and Guillermo Nericcio García -- Double cross: transmasculinity and Asian American gendering in trappings of transhood / Sel J. Wahng -- Teumsae-eso: Korean American women between feminism and nationalism / Elaine H. Kim -- Mapuche shamanic bodies and

the Chilean state: polemic gendered representations and indigenous responses / Ana Mariella Bacigalupo -- Re/membering the body: Latina testimonies of social and family violence / Yvette Flores-Ortiz -- Sita's war and the body politic: violence and abuse in the lives of South Asian women / Sunita Peacock -- Arturo Ripstein's El lugar sin límites and the hell of heteronormativity / David William Foster -- Medicalizing human rights and domesticizing violence in postdictatorship market-states / Lessie Jo Frazier -- Las super madres de Latino America: transforming motherhood and houseskirts by challenging violence in Juárez, México, Argentina, and El Salvador / Cynthia L. Bejarano. ISBN 0-253-34171-X (alk. paper) ISBN 0-253-21559-5 (pbk. : alk. paper) DDC 303.6
1. Violence. 2. Social control. 3. Feminist theory. 4. Body, Human - Political aspects. 5. Body, Human - Social aspects. 6. Race relations - Political aspects. 7. Sexism. 8. Marginality, Social. I. Aldama, Arturo J., 1964-
HM1116 .V557 2003

VIOLENCE - CONGO (DEMOCRATIC REPUBLIC).
Le dialogue intercongolais. Bruxelles ; Nairobi : International Crisis Group, [2001]

Masangana Diamaka, Robin, 1962- Dialogue politique. Paris : Editoo.com, 2002.
1. Black author.

VIOLENCE - GOVERNMENT POLICY.
Evolutionary psychology and violence. Westport, Conn. : Praeger, 2003.
HM1116 .E96 2003

VIOLENCE IN ADOLESCENCE.
Wilkinson, Deanna Lyn, 1968- Guns, violence, and identity among African American and Latino youth. New York : LFB Scholarly Pub., 2003.
HQ799.2.V56 W55 2003

VIOLENCE IN CHILDREN. See CHILDREN AND VIOLENCE.

VIOLENCE IN LITERATURE.
Stobbe, Heinz-Günther, 1948- Vom Geist der Übertretung und Vernichtung. Regensburg : Friedrich Pustet, c2002.

VIOLENCE IN MASS MEDIA.
Contrera, Malena Segura. Mídia e pânico. 1. ed. São Paulo : Annablume : FAPESP, 2002.

VIOLENCE IN SCHOOLS. See SCHOOL VIOLENCE.

VIOLENCE IN THE WORKPLACE.
Hearn, Jeff. Gender, sexuality and violence in organizations. London ; Thousand Oaks : SAGE, 2001.

Violence, inequality, and human freedom. Iadicola, Peter. 2nd ed. Lanham, Md. ; Oxford : Rowman & Littlefield Publishers, Inc., c2003.
HM886 .I18 2003

VIOLENCE - MEXICO.
Estudios sobre la violencia. 1. ed. México, D.F. : CIESAS : M.A. Porrúa, 2002.
HN120.Z9 V538 2002

VIOLENCE - PHILOSOPHY.
Violent acts and violentization. Amsterdam ; Boston : JAI, 2003.

VIOLENCE - PRESS COVERAGE.
Ross, Gina, 1947- Beyond the trauma vortex. Berkeley, Calif. : North Atlantic Books, c2003.
PN4784.D57 R67 2003

VIOLENCE - PREVENTION.
Handbook of violence. New York : Wiley, c2002.
HM1116 .H36 2002

Peace and conflict resolution. Part 1 [videorecording]. Derry, N.H. : Chip Taylor Communications, 1996.

Peace and conflict resolution. Part 2 [videorecording]. Derry, N.H. : Chip Taylor Communications, 1997.

Smith, Shawn T., 1967- Surviving aggressive people. 1st Sentient Publications ed. Boulder, CO : Sentient Publications, 2003.
BF575.A3 S55 2003

VIOLENCE - PSYCHOLOGICAL ASPECTS.
Evolutionary psychology and violence. Westport, Conn. : Praeger, 2003.
HM1116 .E96 2003

Helping children and adolescents cope with violence and disasters [electronic resource]. Bethesda, MD : Office of Communications and Public Liaison, [2001]

Marin, Isabel da Silva Kahn, 1954- Violências. São Paulo : Editora Escuta : FAPESP, 2002.

Sofsky, Wolfgang. Violence. London : Granta, 2003, c2002.

VIOLENCE - RELIGIOUS ASPECTS.
Promise and peril. Notre Dame, Ind. : University of Notre Dame Press, c2003.
BL50 .P65 2003

VIOLENCE - SOCIAL ASPECTS.
Violent acts and violentization. Amsterdam ; Boston : JAI, 2003.

Violencia social, genocidio y terrorismo. Cornblit, Oscar. 1. ed. México, D.F. : Fondo de Cultura Económica, 2002.
HM886 .C67 2002

Violências.
Marin, Isabel da Silva Kahn, 1954- São Paulo : Editora Escuta : FAPESP, 2002.

Violent acts and violentization : assessing, applying, and developing Lonnie Athens' theories / edited by Lonnie Athens, Jeffrey T. Ulmer. Amsterdam ; Boston : JAI, 2003. xii, 187 p. : ill. ; 23 cm. (Sociology of crime, law and deviance ; v. 4) Includes bibliographical references. ISBN 0-7623-0905-9 DDC 364.15
1. Violence. 2. Violence - Social aspects. 3. Violence - Philosophy. I. Athens, Lonnie H. II. Ulmer, Jeffery T., 1966- III. Series.

VIOLENT DEATHS. See ACCIDENTS; MURDER.

VIPAŚYANĀ (BUDDHISM).
Glickman, Marshall. Beyond the breath. 1st ed. Boston : Journey Editions ; North Clarendon, VT : Distributed by Tuttle Pub., 2002.
BQ5630.V5 G54 2002

VIRGINIA - GENEALOGY.
Skidmore, Warren. Lord Dunmore's little war of 1774. Bowie, Md. : Heritage Books, 2002.

VIRGINIA - HISTORY - COLONIAL PERIOD, CA. 1600-1775.
Gallivan, Martin D., 1968- James River chiefdoms. Lincoln : University of Nebraska Press, c2003.
E99.P85 G35 2003

Hudson, Carson O. These detestable slaves of the devill. Haverford, PA : Infinity Pub., c2001.
BF1577.V8 H83 2001

Price, David, 1961- Love and hate in Jamestown. 1st ed. New York : Alfred A. Knopf : Distributed by Random House, 2003.
F234.J3 P68 2003

Skidmore, Warren. Lord Dunmore's little war of 1774. Bowie, Md. : Heritage Books, 2002.

VIRTUAL COMPUTER SYSTEMS - CONGRESSES.
International Conference on Simulation in Engineering Education (2001 : Phoenix, Ariz.) Proceedings of the International Conference on Simulation and Multimedia in Engineering Education & Virtual Worlds and Simulation. San Diego, CA : Society for Computer Simulation International, c2001.

Virtual government.
Constantine, Alex. 1st ed. Venice, CA : Feral House, 1997.
BF633 .C67 1997

Virtual lesions : examining cortical function with reversible deactivation / edited by Stephen G. Lomber, Ralf A.W. Galuske. Oxford ; New York : Oxford University Press, c2002. xiii, 357 p., [16] p. of plates : ill. (some col.) ; 25 cm. Includes bibliographical references and index. cat 20030224 psg ISBN 0-19-850893-X DDC 612.825
1. Brain stimulation. 2. Cognitive neuroscience. 3. Cerebral cortex. I. Lomber, Stephen G. II. Galuske, Ralf A. W.
RC350.B72 V57 2002

VIRTUAL MACHINE SYSTEMS. See VIRTUAL COMPUTER SYSTEMS.

VIRTUAL REALITY.
Communication and cyberspace. 2nd ed. Creskill, N.J. : Hampton Press, c2003.
P96.D36 C66 2003

Knight, Sirona, 1955- The cyber spellbook. Franklin Lakes, NJ : New Page Books, c2002.
BF1571 .T425 2002

Malvido Arriaga, Adriana. Por la vereda digital. 1. ed. México : CONACULTA (Consejo Nacional para la Cultura y las Artes), 1999.
QA76.9.C66 M35 1999

Production methods. London ; New York : Springer, c2003.

QA76.76.I59 P76 2003

Sutcliffe, Alistair, 1951- Multimedia and virtual reality. Mahwah, N.J. ; London : Lawrence Erlbaum, c2003.
QA76.76.I59 S88 2003

Three-dimensional user interfaces for immersive virtual reality [microform]. Providence, RI : Brown University Computer Graphics Group, [1997]

Virtual reality. Frankfurt am Main ; New York : P. Lang, c2001.
QA76.9.H85 V5815 2001

Virtual'naia real'nost' v psikhologii i iskusstvennom intellekte. Moskva : Rossiĭskaia Assotsiatsiia iskusstvennogo intellekta, 1998.
BF204.5 .V57 1998

Virtual reality : cognitive foundations, technological issues & philosophical implications / Alexander Riegler ... [et al.], (eds.). Frankfurt am Main ; New York : P. Lang, c2001. 262 p. : ill. ; 21 cm. (Organismus und System, 1438-6909 ; Bd. 3) Includes bibliographical references. ISBN 0-8204-5451-6 (U.S.) ISBN 3-631-38345-2 DDC 004/.01/9
1. Human-computer interaction. 2. Virtual reality. I. Riegler, Alexander. II. Series.
QA76.9.H85 V5815 2001

VIRTUAL REALITY - CONGRESSES.
International Conference on Simulation in Engineering Education (2001 : Phoenix, Ariz.) Proceedings of the International Conference on Simulation and Multimedia in Engineering Education & Virtual Worlds and Simulation. San Diego, CA : Society for Computer Simulation International, c2001.

Nosov, N. A. Ne-virtualistika. Moskva : Gumanitariĭ, 2001.
BF38 .N67 2001

VIRTUAL REALITY IN MEDICINE - CONGRESSES.
International Conference on Simulation in Engineering Education (2001 : Phoenix, Ariz.) Proceedings of the International Conference on Simulation and Multimedia in Engineering Education & Virtual Worlds and Simulation. San Diego, CA : Society for Computer Simulation International, c2001.

Virtual teams : projects, protocols and processes / [edited by] David J. Pauleen. Hershey, PA ; London : Idea Group Publishing, c2004. xvi, 352 p. : ill. ; 26 cm. Includes bibliographical references and index. ISBN 1-59140-166-6 (hbk.) ISBN 1-59140-225-5 (pbk.) DDC 658.4/022
1. Virtual work teams. 2. Teams in the workplace. I. Pauleen, David, 1957-
HD66 .V56 2004

VIRTUAL WORK TEAMS.
Virtual teams. Hershey, PA ; London : Idea Group Publishing, c2004.
HD66 .V56 2004

Virtual Worlds and Simulation.
International Conference on Simulation in Engineering Education (2001 : Phoenix, Ariz.) Proceedings of the International Conference on Simulation and Multimedia in Engineering Education & Virtual Worlds and Simulation. San Diego, CA : Society for Computer Simulation International, c2001.

Virtual Worlds and Simulation Conference (4th : 2001 : Phoenix, Ariz.).
International Conference on Simulation in Engineering Education (2001 : Phoenix, Ariz.) Proceedings of the International Conference on Simulation and Multimedia in Engineering Education & Virtual Worlds and Simulation. San Diego, CA : Society for Computer Simulation International, c2001.

Virtual'naia real'nost' v psikhologii i iskusstvennom intellekte / [sost. N.V. Chudova]. Moskva : Rossiĭskaia Assotsiatsiia iskusstvennogo intellekta, 1998. 315 p. : ill. ; 22 cm. Includes bibliographical references.
1. Virtual reality. 2. Cognitive psychology. 3. Language and languages. 4. Communication. I. Chudova, N. V.
BF204.5 .V57 1998

VIRTUE. See also VIRTUES.
Ackeren, Marcel van. Das Wissen vom Guten. Amsterdam : Philadelphia : B.R. Gruner, c2003.
B398.V57 A33 2003

Smith, R. Scott, 1957- Virtue ethics and moral knowledge. Aldershot, England ; Burlington, VT : Ashgate, c2003.

BJ1012 .S5195 2003

Swanton, Christine, 1947- Virtue ethics. Oxford ; New York : Oxford University Press, 2003.
BJ1531 .S93 2003

Virtue, Doreen, 1958- Angel medicine : how to heal the body and mind with the help of the angels / Doreen Virtue. Carlsbad, Calif. : Hay House, 2004. p. cm. Includes bibliographical references and index. ISBN 1401902340 (hard) ISBN 1401902359 (pbk.) DDC 615.8/528
1. Spiritual healing. 2. Angels - Miscellanea. I. Title.
BF1999 .V585 2004

The crystal children : a guide to the newest generation of psychic and sensitive children / Doreen Virtue. Carlsbad, Calif. : Hay House, c2003. 168 p. ; 16 cm. ISBN 1401902294 (tradepaper) DDC 133.8/083
1. Children - Psychic ability. I. Title.
BF1045.C45 V57 2003

Virtue ethics.
Swanton, Christine, 1947- Oxford ; New York : Oxford University Press, 2003.
BJ1531 .S93 2003

Virtue ethics and moral knowledge.
Smith, R. Scott, 1957- Aldershot, England ; Burlington, VT : Ashgate, c2003.
BJ1012 .S5195 2003

Virtue, vice, and personality : the complexity of behavior / edited by Edward C. Chang and Lawrence J. Sanna. 1st ed. Washington, D.C. : American Psychological Association, c2003. xxvi, 189 p. : ill. ; 27 cm. Includes bibliographical references and index. Table of contents URL: http://www.loc.gov/catdir/toc/ecip041/2003006516.html CONTENTS: Positive personalities : when virtue can become vice: High self-esteem : a differentiated perspective / Michael H. Kernis -- Optimism as virtue and vice / Christopher Peterson and Robert S. Vaidya -- Intelligence : can one have too much of a good thing? / Robert J. Sternberg -- The hazards of goal pursuit / Laura A. King and Chad M. Burton -- The virtues and vices of personal control / Michael J. Strube, J. Scott Hanson, and Laurel Newman -- Negative personalities : when vice can become virtue: Pessimism : accentuating the positive possibilities / Julie K. Norem -- Rumination, imagination, and personality : specters of the past and future in the present / Lawrence J. Sanna, Shevaun L. Stocker, and Jennifer A. Clarke -- On the perfectibility of the individual : going beyond the dialectic of good versus evil / Edward C. Chang -- Neuroticism : adaptive and maladaptive features / David Watson and Alex Casillas -- Further thoughts: Going beyond (while remaining connected to) personality as virtue and vice / Howard Tennen and Glenn Affleck -- Beyond virtue and vice in personality : some final thoughts / Lawrence J. Sanna and Edward C. Chang. ISBN 1-59147-013-7 (alk. paper) DDC 155.2
1. Personality. I. Chang, Edward C. (Edward Chin-Ho) II. Sanna, Lawrence J.
BF698 .V57 2003

VIRTUES.
Gomes, Peter J. The good life. 1st ed. San Francisco : HarperSanFrancisco, c2002.
BJ1581.2 .G575 2002

VIRTUES - HANDBOOKS, MANUALS, ETC.
Peterson, Christopher, 1950 Feb. 18- Character strengths and virtues. New York : Oxford University Press, 2004.
BF818 .P38 2004

VIRUS-INDUCED IMMUNOSUPPRESSION. See AIDS (DISEASE).

Vishnu on Freud's desk : a reader in psychoanalysis and Hinduism / edited by T.G. Vaidyanathan and Jaffrey J. Kripal. Delhi ; Oxford : Oxford University Press, 1999 (2002 [printing]) x, 482 p. : ill. ; 22 cm. (Oxford India paperbacks) Includes bibliographical references (p. [456]-470) and index. ISBN 0-19-565835-3 DDC 294.5175
1. Hinduism - Psychology. 2. Psychoanalysis and religion - India. 3. Psychoanalysis and culture - India. I. Vaidyanathan, T. G. II. Kripal, Jeffrey John, 1962-

Visible thoughts.
Beattie, Geoffrey. Hove, East Sussex ; New York, NY : Routledge, 2003.
BF637.N66 B43 2003

VISION. See EYE; MOTION PERCEPTION (VISION); VISUAL PERCEPTION.

Vision and art.
Livingstone, Margaret. New York, N.Y. : Harry N. Abrams, c2002.
N7430.5 .L54 2002

VISION - PSYCHOLOGICAL ASPECTS. See VISUAL PERCEPTION.

VISION QUESTS.
Plotkin, Bill, 1950- Soulcraft. Novato, Calif. : New World Library, c2003.
BF637.S4 P58 2003

VISIONS. See DREAMS; FANTASY.

Visions of the Virgin Mary.
Roberts, Courtney, 1957- St. Paul, Minn. : Llewellyn, 2004.
BF1729.R4 R63 2004

Visits from the afterlife.
Browne, Sylvia. New York : Dutton, c2003.
BF1461 .B77 2003

Visser, Frank, 1958-
[Ken Wilber. English]
Ken Wilber : thought as passion / Frank Visser. Albany, NY : State University of New York Press, c2003. xv, 330 p. : ill. ; 23 cm. (SUNY series in transpersonal and humanistic psychology) Includes bibliographical references (p. 287-310) and index. "Bibliography, books by Ken Wilber": p. 311-320. ISBN 0-7914-5815-6 (alk. paper) ISBN 0-7914-5816-4 (pbk. : alk. paper) DDC 191
1. Wilber, Ken. I. Title. II. Series.
BF109.W54 V5713 2003

VISUAL ANTHROPOLOGY.
Die Unvermeidlichkeit der Bilder. Tübingen : G. Narr, c2001.
N72.A56 U58 2001x

VISUAL ARTS. See ART.

Visual Basic for behavioral psychologists.
Dixon, Mark R., 1970- Reno, NV : Context Press, c2003.
BF76.5 .D59 2003

VISUAL COMMUNICATION. See also COMMERCIAL ART; GRAPHIC ARTS; SIGNS AND SIGNBOARDS; SIGNS AND SYMBOLS.
Elkins, James, 1955- Visual studies. New York : Routledge, 2003.
N72.S6 E45 2003

Fahlenbrach, Kathrin. Protest-Inszenierungen. 1. Aufl. Wiesbaden : Westdeutscher Verlag, 2002.

The feminism and visual culture reader. London ; New York : Routledge, 2003.
HQ1121 .F46 2003

Visuality before and beyond the Renaissance. Cambridge, U.K. ; New York, NY, USA : Cambridge University Press, 2000.
N7430.5 .V54 2000

VISUAL COMMUNICATION - GERMANY - HISTORY - 17TH CENTURY.
Strasser, Gerhard F. Emblematik und Mnemonik der frühen Neuzeit im Zusammenspiel Johannes Buno und Johann Justus Winckelmann. Wiesbaden : Harrassowitz Wolfenbüttel : Herzog August Bibliothek, c2000.
PN6348.5 .S873 2000

VISUAL COMMUNICATION - SOCIAL ASPECTS - UNITED STATES - HISTORY - 19TH CENTURY.
Pfitzer, Gregory M. Picturing the past. Washington [D.C.] : Smithsonian Institution Press, c2002.
E175 .P477 2002

VISUAL DISCRIMINATION. See VISUAL PERCEPTION.

VISUAL LEARNING.
Stenning, Keith. Seeing reason. Oxford ; New York : Oxford University Press, 2002.
BF441 .S775 2002

VISUAL LITERACY.
Elkins, James, 1955- Visual studies. New York : Routledge, 2003.
N72.S6 E45 2003

VISUAL PERCEPTION. See also GAZE; MOTION PERCEPTION (VISION); PICTURE PERCEPTION; VISUALIZATION.
Burnett, Ron, 1947- How images think. Cambridge, Mass. : MIT Press, 2004.
BF241 .B79 2004

Carter, Rita, 1949- Exploring consciousness. Berkeley : University of California Press, c2002.
BF311 .C289 2002

Les dons de l'image. Paris : Harmattan, 2003.

Elkins, James, 1955- Visual studies. New York : Routledge, 2003.
N72.S6 E45 2003

Enns, James T. The thinking eye, the seeing brain. New York : W.W. Norton, 2004.
BF241 .E56 2004

Findlay, John M. (John Malcolm), 1942- Active vision. Oxford ; New York : Oxford University Press, 2003.
BF241 .F56 2003

Heijden, A. H. C. van der. Attention in vision. 1st ed. New York : Psychology Press, 2003.
BF241 .H42 2003

Livingstone, Margaret. Vision and art. New York, N.Y. : Harry N. Abrams, c2002.
N7430.5 .L54 2002

McConeghey, Howard. Art and soul. 1st ed. Putnam, CT : Spring Publications, Inc. ; [New York] : Distributed by Continuum, c2003.

Meo, Oscar. Mondi possibili. Genova : Il melangolo, c2002.
N68.3 .M46 2002

Perception of faces, objects, and scenes. Oxford ; New York : Oxford University Press, 2003.
BF241 .P434 2003

Pérez-Jofre, Ignacio. Huellas y sombras. Sada, A Coruña : Ediciós do Castro, [2001]
ND195 .P368 2001

Pylyshyn, Zenon W., 1937- Seeing and visualizing. Cambridge, Mass. : MIT Press, 2003.
BF241 .P95 2003

Solso, Robert L., 1933- The psychology of art and the evolution of the conscious brain. Cambridge, Mass. : MIT Press, 2003.
BF311 .S652 2003

Touching for knowing. Amsterdam ; Philadelphia : John Benjamins Pub., c2003.
BF275 .T69 2003

Die Unvermeidlichkeit der Bilder. Tübingen : G. Narr, c2001.
N72.A56 U58 2001x

Visuality before and beyond the Renaissance. Cambridge, U.K. ; New York, NY, USA : Cambridge University Press, 2000.
N7430.5 .V54 2000

Weber, Jürgen, 1928- The judgement of the eye. Wien ; New York : Springer, c2002.
BF241 .W38 2002

VISUAL PERCEPTION - CONGRESSES.
Thinking and seeing. Cambridge, MA : Mit Press, 2004.
BF241 .T48 2004

VISUAL PERCEPTION - PHILOSOPHY.
Holt, Jason, 1971- Blindsight and the nature of consciousness. Peterborough, Ont. : Broadview Press, c2003.

Visual studies.
Elkins, James, 1955- New York : Routledge, 2003.
N72.S6 E45 2003

VISUAL SYSTEM. See EYE.

Visuality before and beyond the Renaissance : seeing as others saw / edited by Robert S. Nelson. Cambridge, U.K. ; New York, NY, USA : Cambridge University Press, 2000. xiv, 269 p. : ill. ; 27 cm. (Cambridge studies in new art history and criticism) Includes bibliographical references (p. 253-260) and index. CONTENTS: Introduction: Descartes's cow and other domestications of the visual / Robert S. Nelson -- The eyes have it: votive statuary, Gilgamesh's axe, and cathected viewing in the ancient Near East / Irene J. Winter -- Between mimesis and divine power: visuality in the Greco-Roman world / Ja's Elsner -- The philosopher as Narcissus: vision, sexuality, and self-knowledge in classical antiquity / Shadi Bartsch -- The pilgrim's gaze in the age before icons / Georgia Frank -- Watching the steps: peripatetic vision in medieval China / Eugene Y. Wang -- To say and to see: Ekphrasis and vision in Byzantium / Robert S. Nelson -- Visio Dei: changes in medieval visuality / Cynthia Hahn -- Before the gaze: the internal senses and late medieval practices of seeing / Michael Camille -- Displaying secrets: visual piety in Senegal / Allen F. Roberts and Mary Nooter Roberts. ISBN 0-521-65222-7 (hardback) DDC 701/.15
1. Visual perception. 2. Visual communication. 3. Art, Comparative. 4. Art and religion. I. Nelson, Robert S., 1947- II. Series.
N7430.5 .V54 2000

VISUALIZATION. *See also* **IMAGERY (PSYCHOLOGY).**
Gawain, Shakti, 1948- Creative visualization. [Rev. ed.]. Navato, Calif. : Nataraj Pub./New World Library, c2002.
BF367 .G34 2002

Pickover, Clifford A. Chaos in Wonderland. 1st ed. New York : St. Martin's Press, 1994.
Q172.5.C45 P53 1994

Pylyshyn, Zenon W., 1937- Seeing and visualizing. Cambridge, Mass. : MIT Press, 2003.
BF241 .P95 2003

Slocum, Terry A. Thematic cartography and visualization. Upper Saddle River, N.J. : Prentice Hall, c1999.
GA108.7 .S58 1999

Visualizing argumentation. London ; New York : Springer, 2003.
QA76.9.H85 V67 2003

Visualizing the semantic Web. London ; [New York] : Springer, c2003.
TK5105.888 .V55 2003

Zhou, Xiang Sean. Exploration of visual data. Boston ; London : Kluwer Academic Publishers, c2003.
T385 .Z55 2003

VISUALIZATION - PROBLEMS, EXERCISES, ETC.
Bagley, Michael T. Red square & green squigglies. Woodcliff Lake, NJ : Green Squiggliess Press, c1996.
BF408 .B327 1996

Visualizing argumentation : software tools for collaborative and educational sense-making / Paul A. Kirschner ... [et al.] (eds.). London ; New York : Springer, 2003. xxvi, 216 p. : ill. ; 23 cm. (Computer supported cooperative work, 1431-1496) Includes bibliographical references and index. ISBN 1-85233-664-1 (alk. paper) DDC 004/.01/9
1. Human-computer interaction. 2. Persuasion (Rhetoric) - Data processing. 3. Reasoning - Data processing. 4. Visualization. I. Kirschner, Paul Arthur, 1951- II. Series.
QA76.9.H85 V67 2003

Visualizing the semantic Web : XML-based Internet and information visualization / Vladimir Geroimenko and Chaomei Chen (eds.). London ; [New York] : Springer, c2003. ix, 202 p. : ill. (some col.) ; 24 cm. Includes bibliographical references and index. ISBN 1-85233-576-9 (alk. paper) DDC 005.2/76
1. Web site development. 2. Visualization. 3. XML (Document markup language) 4. Semantic Web. I. Geroimenko, Vladimir, 1955- II. Chen, Chaomei, 1960-
TK5105.888 .V55 2003

VISUOSPATIAL NEGLECT (NEUROLOGY). *See* **NEGLECT (NEUROLOGY).**

Viśvavidyālaya-rajatajayantī-granthamālā
(37) Karṇāṭaka, Vimalā. Śrīmadbhāgavata meṃ Sāṅkhyayoga ke tattva. 1. saṃskaraṇa. Vārāṇasī : Sampūrṇānanda Saṃskṛta Viśvavidyālaya, 2001.
BL1140.4.B437 K27 2001

VITAL FORCE.
Cho, Hyeon-Kweon Stephan, 1962- Heiliger Geist als Lebenskraft in Kirche und Menschheit. Frankfurt am Main ; New York : Peter Lang, c2002.
BT121.3 .C56 2002

Slate, Joe H. Psychic vampires. 1st ed. St. Paul, Minn. : Llewellyn Publications, 2002.
BF1045.S46 S53 2002

Vital, Ḥayyim ben Joseph, 1542 or 3-1620. 'Ets ha-da'at ṭov / ḥibro Ḥayim Viṭal. Yerushalayim : Hotsa'at Ahavat shalom, 761 [2000 or 2001] 2 v. ; 25 cm. (Sifre Mekhon "Ahavat Shalom" Yerushalayim ; 278) Cover title: 'Ets ha-da'at ṭov : ha-shalem. Title on original t.p.: Sefer 'Ets ha-da'at ṭov. Reprint (v.1). Originally published: Zolkiev, 631 [1870 or 1871] Reprint (v.2). Originally published: Yerushalayim, 666 [1906] Vol. 2 published individually in 1982 as number 54 of the publisher's series. CONTENTS: Ḥelek 1. Ḥidushim u-ve'urim 'al ha-Torah be-derekh pardes ; uve-rosho ḳuntres "Shenot Ḥayim" me-toldot ha-meḥaber / me-et Ya'aḳov Mosheh Hilel. -- Ḥeleḳ 2. Derushim nifla'im ve-ḥidushim nora'im 'al ha-ketuvim u-ma'amare razal be-derekh nigleh, u-ferush pesuḳe Nakh.
1. Viṭal, Ḥayyim ben Joseph, - 1542 or 3-1620. 2. Bible. - O.T. - Commentaries. 3. Bible. - O.T. - Pentateuch - Commentaries. 4. Cabala. 5. Jewish sermons, Hebrew. 6. Rabbis - Biography. I. Hilel, Ya'aḳov Mosheh. Shenot Ḥayim. II. Title. III. Title: Ḳuntres Shenot Ḥayim. IV. Title: Shenot Ḥayim. V. Title: 'Ets ha-da'at ṭov : ha-shalem VI. Title: Sefer 'Ets ha-da'at ṭov VII. Series.

Ets hayim.
Eliyahu, Saliman. Sefer Kerem Shelomoh. Yerushala[y]im : Ḥevrat Ahavat shalom, 762 [2001 or 2002]

'ETS ḤAYIM.
Eliyahu, Saliman. Sefer Kerem Shelomoh. Yerushala[y]im : Ḥevrat Ahavat shalom, 762 [2001 or 2002]

SHA'AR HA-TIḲUN.
Hilel, Ya'aḳov Mosheh. Sefer Shorshe ha-Yam. Yerushalayim : ha-Makhon le-hotsa'at sefarim "Ahavat shalom", 759- [1999-
BM525.V532 H5 1999

VITAL, ḤAYYIM BEN JOSEPH, 1542 OR 3-1620.
Vital, Ḥayyim ben Joseph, 1542 or 3-1620. 'Ets ha-da'at tov. Yerushalayim : Hotsa'at Ahavat shalom, 761 [2000 or 2001]

The vitality of objects : exploring the work of Christopher Bollas / edited by Joseph Scalia. 1st US ed. Middletown, Conn. : Wesleyan University Press, 2002. xvi, 228 p. ; 24 cm. (Disseminations) Includes bibliographical references and index. ISBN 0-8195-6535-0 (pbk.) ISBN 0-8195-6534-2 (cloth) DDC 150.19/5
1. Bollas, Christopher. 2. Psychoanalysis. 3. Object relations (Psychoanalysis) I. Scalia, Joseph. II. Title: Exploring the work of Christopher Bollas III. Series.
BF173 .V55 2002

Vitouch, Peter.
Psychologie des Internet. Wien : WUV, Universitätsverlag, 2001.
BF637.C45 P759 2001

VITUPERATION. *See* **INVECTIVE.**

V'i̇unov, İU. A. Slovo o russkikh / İU.A. V'i̇unov. Moskva : Izd-vo IKAR, c2002. 293 p. : ill. ; 20 cm. Includes bibliographical references (p. 291-293). ISBN 5797400383
1. National characteristics, Russian. 2. Nationalism - Russia (Federation) - History. 3. Russians - Ethnic identity. 4. Slavs - History. 5. Russia (Federation) - Civilization. I. Title.

Viveros, M. (Mara) De quebradores y cumplidores : sobre hombres, masculinidades y relaciones de género en Colombia / Mara Viveros Vigoya. 1a ed. [Colombia] : CES Universidad Nacional de Colombia : Fundación Ford : Profamilia Colombia, 2002. 378, [1] p. ; 22 cm. Includes bibliographical references.
1. Masculinity - Colombia - Quibdó - Case stuides. 2. Masculinity - Colombia - Armenia (Quindío) - Case studies. 3. Androcentrism - Colombia. 4. Men - Identity. I. Title.

Vizantijska filozofija u srednjevekovnoj Srbiji / priredio Boris Milosavljević ; preveli Atanasije Jevtić, Dimitrije Bogdanović, Artemije Radosavljević, S. Jakšić. Beograd : Stubovi kulture, 2002. 501 p. ; 20 cm. (Stubovi kulture ; knj. 3) Includes bibliographical references. In Serbian (Cyrillic); summaries in English, French, German and Russian. ISBN 86-7979-019-2
1. Philosophy, Medieval. 2. Christian literature, Early - Translations into Serbian. 3. Serbia - Civilization - Byzantine influences. 4. Theology - Early works to 1800. 5. Mysticism - Early works to 1800. I. Milosavljević, Boris. II. Pseudo-Dionysius, the Areopagite. De mystica theologia. Serbian. III. John, Climacus, Saint, 6th cent. Scala Paradisi. Serbian. IV. Maximus, Confessor, Saint, ca. 580-662. Centuriae quatuor de charitate. Serbian. V. John, of Damascus, Saint. Dialectica. Serbian. VI. Gregory Palamas, Saint, 1296-1359. VII. Series: Monografije (Stubovi kulture (Firm)) ; knj. 3.

Vjerovanja o drveću u hrvata.
Vinšćak, Tomo. [Jastrebarsko] : Naklada Slap, c2002.

VLADIMIR, GRAND DUKE OF KIEV, CA. 956-1015 - CULT.
Tkach, Mykola. Volodymyrovi bohy. Kyïv : Ukraïns'kyĭ tsentr dukhovnoï kul'tury, 2002.
DK75 .T53 2002

Vladimirskiĭ gosudarstvennyĭ pedagogicheskiĭ universitet.
Psikhologii̇a otnoshenii̇. Vladimir : Vladimirskiĭ gos. pedagogicheskiĭ universitet, 2001.
BF637.C45 P74 2001

Vlora, Nedim R., 1943- Le porte del cielo : l'eredità dei faraoni / Nedim R. Vlora. Bari : M. Adda, c2001. 255 p. : ill. ; 25 cm. (Collana di astronomia culturale) Includes bibliographical references (p. 251-254). ISBN 88-8082-434-1 DDC 932
1. Astrology, Egyptian. 2. Astronomy, Egyptian. 3. Mythology, Egyptian. 4. Cosmology, Egyptian. 5. Egypt - Religion. I. Title. II. Series.
BF1674 .V56 2001

Vo dvore i̇azychnikov.
Rozanov, V. V. (Vasiliĭ Vasil'evich), 1856-1919. Moskva : Izd-vo "Respublika", 1999.

BL96 .R69 1999

[Vocabulaire de sciences cognitives. English.]
Dictionary of cognitive science : neuroscience, psychology, artificial intelligence, linguistics, and philosophy / Olivier Houdé, editor, with Daniel Kayser ... [et al.] ; Vivian Waltz, translator ; Christian Cav, scientific advisor. New York : Psychology Press, 2003. p. cm. Includes bibliographical references and index. Table of contents URL: http://www.loc.gov/catdir/toc/ecip044/2003011554.html ISBN 1-57958-251-6 DDC 153/.03
1. Cognitive science - Dictionaries. I. Houdé, Olivier. II. Title.
BF311 .V56713 2003

VOCAL DUETS WITH ORCHESTRA.
Hann, Georg. Georg Hann [sound recording]. [Germany] : Preiser Records, p2001.

VOCAL MUSIC, POPULAR. *See* **POPULAR MUSIC.**

VOCAL QUINTETS WITH ORCHESTRA.
Hann, Georg. Georg Hann [sound recording]. [Germany] : Preiser Records, p2001.

VOCAL TRIOS WITH ORCHESTRA.
Hann, Georg. Georg Hann [sound recording]. [Germany] : Preiser Records, p2001.

VOCALISTS. *See* **SINGERS.**

VOCATIONAL GUIDANCE. *See also* **OCCUPATIONS; PROFESSIONS.**
Brinkerhoff, Shirley. Psychologist. Broomall, Pa. : Mason Crest Publishers, c2003.
BF76 .B75 2003

Brown, Duane. Career choice and development. 4th ed. San Francisco, CA : Jossey-Bass, c2002.
HF5381 .C265143 2002

Palonen, Kari, 1947- Eine Lobrede für Politiker. Opladen : Leske + Budrich, 2002.
JF2051.W43 J35 2002

Stewardson, John (John E.) Success is the best revenge. Toronto : Productive Publications, c1994.

Varner, Don. How to get a really great job!. Toronto : Productive Publications, 1998.

Vocazione e stati di vita del cristiano.
Martinelli, Paolo, 1958- Roma : Collegio San Lorenzo da Brindisi, 2001.

VODOU. *See* **VOODOOISM.**

VODUN. *See* **VOODOOISM.**

Vogel, Ulrich, 1963-.
Societas rationis. Berlin : Duncker & Humblot, c2002.
B29 .S633 2002

Vogler, Candace A. Reasonably vicious / Candace Vogler. Cambridge, Mass. : Harvard University Press, 2002. viii, 295 p. ; 25 cm. Includes bibliographical references (p. 285-289) and index. Table of contents URL: http://www.loc.gov/catdir/toc/fy035/2002027250.html ISBN 0-674-00741-7 DDC 170/.42
1. Ethics. 2. Practical reason. I. Title.
BJ1031 .V64 2002

Vohs, Kathleen D.
Handbook of self-regulation. New York : Guilford Press, 2004.
BF632 .H262 2004

VOICE. *See also* **SPEECH.**
Flem, Lydia. La voix des amants. [Paris] : Seuil, c2002.

Steinhauer, Kimberly Marie. The relationship among voice onset, voice quality and fundamental frequency. 2000.

VOICE CULTURE.
Steinhauer, Kimberly Marie. The relationship among voice onset, voice quality and fundamental frequency. 2000.

VOICE FREQUENCY.
Steinhauer, Kimberly Marie. The relationship among voice onset, voice quality and fundamental frequency. 2000.

VOICE - HISTORY - CONGRESSES.
Zwischen Rauschen und Offenbarung. Berlin : Akademie Verlag, c2002.
PN56.V55 Z89 2002

VOICE IN LITERATURE - CONGRESSES.
Zwischen Rauschen und Offenbarung. Berlin : Akademie Verlag, c2002.
PN56.V55 Z89 2002

The voice of At-Hlan.
At-Hlan, Spirit. Torquay : Pyramid Pub., c1996.

Voices from beyond.
Nwokogba, Isaac, 1957- Cranston, R.I. : Writers' Collective, 2003.
BF1261.2 .N96 2003

Voices from the pagan census.
Berger, Helen A., 1949- Columbia, S.C. : University of South Carolina Press, c2003.
BF1573 .B48 2003

Voices from Vietnam.
Edwards, Charlene. Bayside, NY : Bayside, c2002.

La voix des amants.
Flem, Lydia. [Paris] : Seuil, c2002.

Voix nouvelles en psychanalyse
Costes, Alain. Lacan, le fourvoiement linguistique. Paris : Presses universitaires de France, 2003.

La voix sans repos.
Goux, Jean-Paul. Monaco : Rocher, c2003.

Voland, Eckart, 1949-.
Evolutionary aesthetics. Berlin ; New York : Springer, c2003.
BH301.P78 E96 2003

VOLATILE OILS. See **ESSENCES AND ESSENTIAL OILS.**

Voldeck, Joseph F., 1967- Immoral balance : the quondam dream / Joseph F. Voldeck, II. Santa Fe, NM : Sunstone Press, 2003. p. cm. ISBN 0-86534-376-4 (pbk.) DDC 291.4
1. Spiritual life - Miscellanea. I. Title.
BF1999 .V63 2003

Volek, Emil.
Latin America writes back. New York : Routledge, 2002.
PQ7081.A1 L336 2002

Volgger, Ewald.
Sankt Georg und sein Bilderzyklus in Neuhaus/Böhmen (Jindřichuv Hradec). Marburg : N.G. Elwert, c2002.
BR1720.G4 S26 2002

Volgogradskiĭ gosudarstvennyĭ pedagogicheskiĭ universitet.
Alefirenko, M. F. Poėticheskai͡a ėnergii͡a slova. Moskva : Academia, 2002.
P35 .A544 2002

VOLITION. See **WILL.**

Volodymyrovi bohy.
Tkach, Mykola. Kyïv : Ukraïns'kyĭ t͡sentr dukhovnoï kul'tury, 2002.
DK75 .T53 2002

VOLOF (AFRICAN PEOPLE). See **WOLOF (AFRICAN PEOPLE).**

Volovikova, M.
Razvitie nat͡sional'noĭ, ėtnolingvisticheskoĭ i religioznoĭ identichnosti u deteĭ i podrostkov = Moskva : In-t psikhologii RAN, 2001.
BF723.C5 R39 2001

Volshebnoe sokrovishche snovideniĭ.
Jagaddeva. [Svapnacintāmaṇi. Russian] Moskva : Ladomir, 1996.
BF1088.S26 J34 1996

VOLTERRANI, CATERINA - TRIALS, LITIGATION, ETC.
Caterina e il diavolo. Pisa : ETS, c1999.
BF1584.I8 C38 1999

Volti della storia (Città nuova editrice)
(11.) Ruggiero, Fabio. La follia dei cristiani. Roma : Città nuova, c2002.
BR166 .R84 2002

Volume of Xu Fancheng.
Xu, Fancheng. Xu Fancheng ji. Di 1 ban. Beijing : Zhongguo she hui ke xue chu ban she, 2001.
PL2262.2 .X84 2001

VOLUNTARISM. See **ASSOCIATIONS, INSTITUTIONS, ETC.**

Voluntary action : brains, minds, and sociality / edited by Sabine Maasen, Wolfgang Prinz, and Gerhard Roth. Oxford ; New York : Oxford University Press, 2003. viii, 379 p. : ill. ; 24 cm. "Based on a conference ... held at the Hanse Institute for Advanced Study in Delmenhorst, German, from March 16 to 18, 2000"--Acknowledgements. Includes bibliographical references and indexes. ISBN 0-19-857228-X ISBN 0-19-852754-3 (pbk. : alk. paper) DDC 153.8
1. Intentionalism. 2. Intentionality (Philosophy) 3. Free will and determinism. I. Maasen, Sabine, 1960- II. Prinz, Wolfgang, 1942- III. Roth, Gerhard, 1942 Aug. 15-
BF621 .V658 2003

VOLUNTARY ASSOCIATIONS. See **ASSOCIATIONS, INSTITUTIONS, ETC.**

VOLUNTARY ORGANIZATIONS. See **ASSOCIATIONS, INSTITUTIONS, ETC.**

VOLUNTEERS. See **CAREGIVERS.**

Vom Abschied.
Lenger, Hans-Joachim. Bielefeld : Transcript, c2001.
B105.D5 L46 2001

Vom Geist der Übertretung und Vernichtung.
Stobbe, Heinz-Günther, 1948- Regensburg : Friedrich Pustet, c2002.

Vom homo sapiens zum homo spaciens.
Sandvoss, Ernst. Berlin : Logos, c2002.

Vom Parergon zum Labyrinth : Untersuchungen zur kritischen Theorie des Ornaments / herausgegeben von Gérard Raulet und Burghart Schmidt. Wien : Böhlau, c2001. 288 p. : ill. ; 24 cm. Includes bibliographical references. ISBN 3-205-99256-3
1. Decoration and ornament - Philosophy. 2. Art - Philosophy. 3. Aesthetics. I. Raulet, Gérard. II. Schmidt, Burghart, 1942-
NK1505 .V65 2001

Von der Dingfrage zur Frage nach Gott.
Caropreso, Paolo. Berlin ; New York : W. de Gruyter, 2003.

Von Foerster, Heinz, 1911- Understanding systems : conversations on epistemology and ethics / Heinz von Foerster, Bernhard Poerksen ; translation by Karen Leube. New York : Kluwer Academic/Plenum Publishers ; Heidelberg : Carl-Auer-Systeme Verlag, c2002. 161 p. : ill. ; 22 cm. (International Federation for Systems Research international series on systems science and engineering ; v. 17) ISBN 0-306-46752-6 (Kluwer Academic/Plenum) ISBN 3-89670-234-3 (Carl-Auer-Systeme Verlag)
1. Knowledge, Theory of. 2. Ethics. 3. Cybernetics. I. Poerksen, Bernhard. II. Title. III. Series: IFSR international series on systems science and engineering ; v. 17.

Von Hexen, Ratsherren und Juristen.
Ströhmer, Michael, 1968- Paderborn : Bonifatius, c2002.
BF1583 .S77 2002

Von Mises, Ludwig, 1881-1973. Between the two World Wars : monetary disorder, interventionism, socialism, and the Great Depression / edited and with an introduction by Richard M. Ebeling. Indianapolis, Ind. : Liberty Fund, c2002. liii, 400 p. ; 24 cm. (Selected writings of Ludwig von Mises ; 2) Includes bibliographical references and index. ISBN 0-86597-384-9 (hbk.) ISBN 0-86597-385-7 (pbk.) DDC 330.15/7 s; 330.15/7
1. Von Mises, Ludwig, - 1881-1973. 2. Economics. 3. Free enterprise. 4. Liberty. I. Ebeling, Richard M. II. Title. III. Series: Von Mises, Ludwig, 1881-1973. Selections. 2000 ; 2.
HB101.V66A25 2002

Selections. 2000
(2.) Von Mises, Ludwig, 1881-1973. Between the two World Wars. Indianapolis, Ind. : Liberty Fund, c2002.
HB101.V66A25 2002

VON MISES, LUDWIG, 1881-1973.
Von Mises, Ludwig, 1881-1973. Between the two World Wars. Indianapolis, Ind. : Liberty Fund, c2002.
HB101.V66A25 2002

Von Stamm, Bettina. The innovation wave : meeting the corporate challenge / Bettina Von Stamm. Chichester : John Wiley & Sons, c2003. vii, 216 p. ; 24 cm. Includes bibliographical references and index. ISBN 0-470-84742-5 DDC 658.5752
1. Creative ability in business. 2. Organizational change. I. Title.

Managing innovation, design and creativity / Bettina von Stamm. Chichester, England ; Hoboken, NJ : J. Wiley, c2003. xii, 429 p. : ill. ; 25 cm. Cover title: Managing innovation, design & creativity. Includes bibliographical references (p. [405]-419) and index. ISBN 0-470-84708-5 (pbk. : alk. paper) DDC 658.5/14
1. Technological innovations. 2. Creative ability in business. 3. Technological innovations - Management. 4. Creative ability in business - Case studies. I. Title. II. Title: Managing innovation, design & creativity
HD45 .V65 2003

Von Weichs, Marie-Caroline.
Carey, Dennis. How to run a company. 1st ed. New York : Crown Business, c2003.
HD38.2 .C374 2003

VOODOO (CULT). See **VOODOOISM.**

The voodoo revenge book.
Shulman, Mark, 1962- New York : Main Street, c2002.
BF637.R48 S55 2002

VOODOOISM.
Hurbon, Laënnec. Dieu dans le vaudou haïtien. Nouv. éd. Paris : Maisonneuve et Larose, 2002.
1. Black author.

McQuillar, Tayannah Lee, 1977- Rootwork. New York : Simon & Schuster, c2003.
BF1622.A34 M37 2003
1. Black author.

VOODOOISM - BRAZIL.
Verger, Pierre. Saída de Iaô. Sao Paulo : Fundação Pierre Verger : Axis Mundi Editora, 2002.

VOODOOISM - HAITI - RELATIONS - CATHOLIC CHURCH.
Hurbon, Laënnec. Dieu dans le vaudou haïtien. Nouv. éd. Paris : Maisonneuve et Larose, 2002.
1. Black author.

VOODOOISM - HUMOR.
Shulman, Mark, 1962- The voodoo revenge book. New York : Main Street, c2002.
BF637.R48 S55 2002

VOODOOISM IN LITERATURE.
Vadillo, Alicia E. Santería y Vodú. Madrid : Biblioteca Nueva, c2002.
PQ7372 .V33 2002

Voprosy teorii arkhitektury
Arkhitekturnoe soznanie XX-XXI vekov. Moskva : Ėditorial URSS, 2001.
NA712 .A87 2001

Voprosy vozrastnoĭ i pedagogicheskoĭ psikhologii v tvorchestve P.P. Blonskogo.
Artamonova, E. R. Vladimir : Vladimirskiĭ gos. pedagog. universitet, 2001.
BF109.B59 A78 2001

Vor dem Schirm.
Wentscher, Herbert, 1951- 1. Aufl. [Freiburg im Breisgau] : Modo, 2002.

Die Vorstellung vom Willen in der Morallehre Senecas.
Zöller, Rainer. Leipzig : K.G. Saur, 2003.
PA6686 .Z65 2003

Vorstudien für Leben und Kunst.
Hotho, Heinrich Gustav, 1802-1873. Stuttgart : Frommann-Holzboog, 2002.

Vorträge und Forschungen
(Bd. 56) Deutschland und der Westen Europas im Mittelalter. Stuttgart : Thorbecke, c2002.

Vorträge, Vorlesungen, Aufsätze.
Schweitzer, Albert, 1875-1965. München : C.H. Beck, c2003.

Vosburgh, Bob. LIFT : leadership that soars above and beyond / Bob Vosburgh. [United Ustates?] : 9g Enterprises, c2002. 208 p. : ill. ; 23 cm. ISBN 0-9720483-0-8 DDC 158/.4
1. Leadership. I. Title.
BF637.L4 V67 2002

Vospominanii͡a o N.N. Moiseeve.
Moiseev, N. N. (Nikita Nikolaevich) Kak daleko do zavtrashnego dni͡a--. Moskva : Taĭdeks Ko, 2002.
DK49 .M64 2002

Vossenkuhl, Wilhelm, 1945-.
Ludwig Wittgenstein, Tractatus logico-philosophicus. Berlin : Akademie Verlag, 2001.

VOUDOU. See **VOODOOISM.**

VOUDOUISM. See **VOODOOISM.**

VOYAGES AND TRAVELS. See **SHIPWRECKS.**

Les voyages de Cyrus.
Ramsay, Chevalier (Andrew Michael), 1686-1743. Paris : Champion, 2002.

VOYAGES, IMAGINARY. See also **UTOPIAS.**
Ramsay, Chevalier (Andrew Michael), 1686-1743. Les voyages de Cyrus. Paris : Champion, 2002.

Vozrozhdaŭshchii͡si͡a Egipet.
Rozanov, V. V. (Vasiliĭ Vasil'evich), 1856-1919. Moskva : Izd-vo "Respublika", 2002.

Vrinte, Joseph, 1949- The perennial quest for a psychology with a soul : an inquiry into the relevance of Sri Aurobindo's metaphysical Yoga psychology in the context of Ken Wilber's integral psychology / Joseph Vrinte. 1st ed. Delhi : Motilal Banarsidass Publishers, 2002. xx, 568 p. ; 22 cm. Includes bibliographical references (p. [555]-559) and index. ISBN 81-208-1932-2
1. Ghose, Aurobindo, - 1872-1950. 2. Wilber, Ken. 3.

Consciousness. 4. Transpersonal psychology. 5. Yoga - Psychological aspects. I. Title.
BF311+

Vrouwen en demonen.
Sengers, Gerda. Amsterdam : Het Spinhuis, 2000.
BF1275.F3 S46 2000

Vselennaia razumnaia.
Karpenko, M. (Maksim) 2. perer. izd. Moskva : MAIK Nauka/Interperiodika, 2001.
BF1036.K37 2001

Vserossiĭskaia konferentsiia "Mezhdistsiplinarnyĭ sintez v metodologii gumanitarnykh issledovaniĭ" (2002 : Tomsk, Russia) Lichnost' v paradigmakh i metaforakh : mental'nost'- kommunikatsiia-tolerantnost' : Vserossiĭskaia konferentsiia "Mezhdistsiplinarnyĭ sintez v metodologii gumanitarnykh issledovaniĭ" / pod redaktsieĭ V.I. Kabrina. Tomsk : Tomskiĭ gos. universitet, 2002. 258 p. : ill. ; 21 cm. Includes bibliographical references. ISBN 5751115449
1. Personality - Congresses. I. Kabrin, V. I. II. Tomskiĭ gosudarstvennyĭ universitet. III. Title.
BF698.V74 2002

Vue libre sur la science littéraire : problèmes de la philologie contemporaine.
Svobodnyĭ vzgliad na literaturu. Moskva : Nauka, 2002.

Vuleta, Bože.
Mir u Hrvatskoj--rezultati istraživanja. Zagreb : Hrvatski Caritas ; Split : Franjevački in-t za kulturu mira, 2001.
HN638.A8 M57 2001

Vulnerable subjects.
Couser, G. Thomas. Ithaca : Cornell University Press, 2004.
CT25.C698 2004

Vvedenie v psikhologiiu chelovecheskoĭ unikal'nosti.
Ageev, Valentin. Tomsk : Izd-vo "Peleng", 2002.
BF697.A353 2002

Vvedenie v russkuiu filosofiiu.
Gidirinskiĭ, V. I. (Viktor Il'ich) Moskva : Russkoe slovo, 2003.
B4201.G536 2003

Vyas-sutram.
Śāstrī, Umeśa. Vyāsasūtram. Jayapura : Yūnika Tredarsa, 2002.
BF1714.H5 S287 2002

Vyāsa.
Samkhyapravacanabhashya. English.
Patañjali. The Yoga-darshana. 2nd ed.--throughly rev. [Fremont, Calif.] : Asian Humanities Press, [2002], 1934.
B132.Y6 P265 2002

Vyāsasūtram.
Śāstrī, Umeśa. Jayapura : Yūnika Tredarsa, 2002.
BF1714.H5 S287 2002

Vygotskiĭ, L. S. (Lev Semenovich), 1896-1934.
Issledovaniia obucheniia i razvitiia v kontekste kul'turno-istoricheskogo podkhoda. Moskva : Smysl, 2002.
BF712.5.I88 2002

VYGOTSKIĬ, L. S. (LEV SEMENOVICH), 1896-1934.
Morozov, S. M. (Stanislav Mikhaĭlovich) Dialektika Vygotskogo. Moskva : Smysl, 2002.
BF109.V95 M67 2002

Toomela, Aaro. Cultural-historical psychology. Tartu : Tartu University Press, c2000.
BF109.V95 T66 2000

Vyshe kryshi.
Rysev, Sergeĭ. Sankt-Peterburg : Gelikon Plius, 2001.
B105.C473 R97 2001

Vystrecil, Henri. Nostradamus : les Centuries du sud / Henri Vystrecil. Portet-sur-Garonne : Loubatières, c2002. 130 p. : ill. ; 21 cm. (Petit précis ; 10) (Histoire) Includes bibliographical references (p. 129-[131]). ISBN 2-86266-369-7 DDC 944
1. Nostradamus, - 1503-1566. 2. Prophets - France - Biography. I. Nostradamus, 1503-1566. Prophéties. Selections. 2002. II. Title. III. Series.

W stronę Bogoczłowieczeństwa.
Przesmycki, Piotr, 1965- Łódź : "Ibidem", 2002.
B4238.B44 P79 2002

Wachtendorf, Tricia.
Kendra, James M. Elements of community resilience in the World Trade Center attack. [Newark, Del.?] : Disaster Research Center, University of Delaware, 2001.

Wachter, Johann Georg, 1673-1757.
Spinozismus im Judenthumb.
Leibniz, Gottfried Wilhelm, Freiherr von, 1646-1716. Réfutation inédite de Spinoza. Arles [France] : Actes Sud ; [Montréal] : Leméac, 1999.

Wade, Carole. Invitation to psychology / Carole Wade, Carol Tavris. 3rd ed. Upper Saddle River, NJ : Pearson/Prentice Hall, 2004. p. cm. Includes bibliographical references and indexes. ISBN 0-13-114624-6 DDC 150
1. Psychology - Textbooks. I. Tavris, Carol. II. Title.
BF121.W265 2004

Wade in the water.
Hickman, Martha Whitmore, 1925- Nashville, TN : Abingdon Press, 2003.
BV310.H53 2003

Wadsworth philosophers series
Thomson, Garrett. On the meaning of life. Australia ; United States : Thomson/Wadsworth, c2003.
BD431.T296 2003

WAGER OF BATTLE. *See* **COMBAT.**

WAGERS. *See* **GAMBLING.**

Wagman, Morton. Logical processes in humans and computers : theory and research in psychology and artificial intelligence / by Morton Wagman. Westport, Conn. : Praeger, 2003. p. cm. Includes bibliographical references and index. ISBN 0-275-97860-5 (alk. paper) DDC 153.4/3
1. Cognition. 2. Reasoning. 3. Cognitive science. 4. Artificial intelligence. I. Title.
BF311.W26566 2003

Wagner and suicide.
DiGaetani, John Louis, 1943- Jefferson, N.C. : McFarland, c2003.
ML410.W13 D45 2003

Wagner de Reyna, Alberto. El privilegio de ser latinoamericano : fe, dignidad en la pobreza y cultura / Alberto Wagner de Reyna. 1. ed. Córdoba, Argentina : Editorial Alejandro Korn, c2002. 164 p. : ill. ; 18 cm. (Colección Reflexiones) Includes bibliographical references. ISBN 950-33-0340-0
1. Latin America - Civilization. 2. Faith. 3. Poverty. 4. Culture. I. Title. II. Series.
F1408.3.W35 2002

WAGNER, RICHARD, 1813-1883. OPERAS.
DiGaetani, John Louis, 1943- Wagner and suicide. Jefferson, N.C. : McFarland, c2003.
ML410.W13 D45 2003

WAGNER, RICHARD, 1813-1883 - MENTAL HEALTH.
DiGaetani, John Louis, 1943- Wagner and suicide. Jefferson, N.C. : McFarland, c2003.
ML410.W13 D45 2003

Wagner, Rudolf G. Language, ontology, and political philosophy in China : Wang Bi's scholarly exploration of the dark (xuanxue) / Rudolf G. Wagner. Albany : State University of New York Press, c2003. viii, 261 p. ; 23 cm. (SUNY series in Chinese philosophy and culture) Includes bibliographical references (p. 243-254) and index. ISBN 0-7914-5331-6 (alk. paper) ISBN 0-7914-5332-4 (pbk. : alk. paper) DDC 181/.11
1. Wang, Bi, - 226-249. 2. Philosophy, Chinese - 221 B.C.-960 A.D. 3. Metaphysics. I. Title. II. Title: Wang Bi's scholarly exploration of the dark (xuanxue) III. Series.
B126.W284 2003

Wahrheit, Wissen, Erinnerung :
Zeugenverhörprotokolle als Quellen für soziale Wissensbestände in der Frühen Neuzeit / Ralf-Peter Fuchs, Winfried Schulze (Hg.). Münster : Lit, [2002] 402 p. ; 21 cm. (Wirklichkeit und Wahrnehmung in der Frühen Neuzeit ; Bd. 1) Includes bibliographical references. ISBN 3-8258-5942-8 (pbk.)
1. Memory - Social aspects - History. 2. Historiography. 3. Witnesses - History. I. Fuchs, Ralf-Peter. II. Schulze, Winfried. III. Series.

Wahrnehmung und Medialität / herausgegeben von Erika Fischer-Lichte ... [et al.]. Tübingen : Francke, c2001. 431 p., [16] p. of plates : ill., ports. ; 23 cm. (Theatralität ; Bd. 3) Includes bibliographical references and indexes. English and German. ISBN 3-7720-2943-4 (pbk.)
1. Theater - Philosophy. 2. Mass media - Philosophy. 3. Perception. I. Fischer-Lichte, Erika. II. Series.
PN2039.W347 2001

Wahsner, Roderich. Yoga : Lebensphilosophie und Erfahrungswissenschaft : Indiens Beitrag zur philosophia perennis und zur transpersonalen Psychologie / Roderich Wahsner. Frankfurt am Main ; Nwe York : Peter Lang, c2002. 166 p. ; 21 cm. (Schriften zur Meditation und Meditationsforschung, 1615-469X ; Bd. 4) Includes bibliographical references. Errata slip inserted. ISBN 3-631-39325-3 (pbk.)
1. Yoga. I. Title.

Waite, Arthur Edward, 1857-1942. Devil-worship in France with Diana Vaughan and the question of modern palladism / A.E. Waite ; with an introduction by R.A. Gilbert. Boston, MA : Weiser Books, 2003. p. cm. Includes bibliographical references and index. Table of contents URL : http://www.loc.gov/catdir/toc/ecip044/2003011390.html CONTENTS: Satanism in the nineteenth century -- The mask of masonry -- The first witnesses of Lucifer -- Ex ore leonis -- The discovery M. Ricoux -- Art sacerdotal -- The devil and the doctor -- Dealings with Diana -- How Lucifer is unmasked -- The vendetta of Signor Margiotta -- Female freemasonry -- The passing of Doctor Bataille -- Diana unveiled -- The radix of modern diabolism -- Diana Vaughan and the question of modern palladism -- The conspiracy in outline -- The railleries of Dr. Bataille -- The Margiotta embroilment -- The Trent Congress and Diana Vaughan -- The secret doctrine of Albert Pike -- Women and freemasonry -- Who is Diana Vaughan? -- Some consequences of the conspiracy. ISBN 1-57863-286-2 (alk. paper) DDC 133.4/22/0944
1. Satanism - France - History. 2. Occultism - France - History. I. Title.
BF1548.W2 2003

Waiting with Gabriel.
Kuebelbeck, Amy, 1964- Chicago, Ill. : Loyola Press, c2003.
BF575.G7 K83 2003

Waitley, Denis. Psychology of success : finding meaning in work and life / Denis Waitley. 4th ed. Boston : McGraw-Hill Higher Education, c2004. xii, 404 p. : ill. ; 26 cm. Accompanied by: Psychology of success instructor's resource manual. Includes bibliographical references (p. 391-392) and index. Table of contents URL: http://www.loc.gov/catdir/toc/ecip041/2003005093.html CONTENTS: Psychology and success -- Self-awareness -- Goals and obstacles -- Self-esteem -- Positive thinking -- Self-discipline -- Self-motivation -- Managing your resources -- Communication and relationships. ISBN 0-07-829976-4 (student ed.) ISBN 0-07-829977-2 (instructor's resource manual) DDC 158.1
1. Success - Psychological aspects. 2. Self-esteem. 3. Self-confidence. I. Title.
BF637.S8 W269 2004

Wakenshaw, Martha. Caring for your grieving child / Martha Wakenshaw. Oakland, Calif. : New Harbinger ; London : Hi Marketing, 2002. 176 p. ; 23 cm. ISBN 1-57224-306-6 DDC 155.93083
1. Grief in children. 2. Loss (Psychology) in children. 3. Bereavement in children. 4. Grief therapy - Popular works. I. Title.
BF723.G75 W35 2002

Walde, Christine, 1960- Antike Traumdeutung und moderne Traumforschung / Christine Walde. Düsseldorf : Artemis & Winkler, c2001. 239 p. : ill. ; 21 cm. Includes bibliographical references. ISBN 3-538-07117-9
1. Artemidorus, - Daldianus. 2. Aristides, Aelius. 3. Dream interpretation - History - To 1500. 4. Dreams - History - To 1500. 5. Philosophy, Ancient. 6. Civilization, Greco-Roman. I. Title. II. Title: Traumdeutung und Traumforschung

Waldman, Mark Robert.
Gilbert, Toni. Messages from the archetypes. Ashland, Or. : White Cloud Press, c2003.
BF1879.T2 G53 2003

A walk with four spiritual guides.
Harvey, Andrew, 1952- Woodstock, VT : SkyLight Paths Pub., c2003.
BL624.H3445 2003

Walker, Jamie. 101 ways black women can learn to love themselves : a gift for women of all ages / Jamie Walker. Washington, D.C. : J.D. Publishing, c2002. 574 p. ; 22 cm. Gift for women of all ages. ISBN 1401057349 (pbk) ISBN 1401057357 (hardcover)
1. Self-esteem in women. 2. Self-acceptance. 3. Self-actualization. 4. Inspiration. 5. African American women. 6. Black author. I. Title. II. Title: One hundred one ways black women can learn to love themselves III. Title: Gift for women of all ages

Walker, Joel Thomas, 1968-.
Prayer, magic, and the stars in the ancient and late antique world. University Park, Pa. : Pennsylvania State University Press, 2003.
BF1591.P73 2003

Walker, John Albert, 1938- Art and celebrity / John A. Walker. London : Sterling, Va. : Pluto Press, 2003. vi, 297 p. : ill. ; 23 cm. Includes bibliographical references (p.

283-286) and index. CONTENTS: Celebrities as art collectors and artists -- Artists depict celebrities -- Simulation and celebrities -- Alternative heroes -- Art stars. ISBN 0-7453-1850-9 (hardback) ISBN 0-7453-1849-5 (pbk.) DDC 306.4/7
1. Arts and society. 2. Celebrities - Psychology. 3. Artists - Psychology. 4. Popular culture. 5. Celebrities in art. 6. Arts, Modern - 20th century. 7. Arts, Modern - 21st century. I. Title.
NX180.S6 W35 2003

Walkerdine, Valerie.
[Critical psychology (Lawrence & Wishart)] Critical psychology. London : Lawrence & Wishart, c2001-
BF39.9 .C75

WALKING.
Chuckrow, Robert. Tai chi walking. Boston, Mass. : YMAA Publication Center, c2002.

WALKING, BIPEDAL. *See* **BIPEDALISM.**

Walking the tightrope of reason.
Fogelin, Robert J. Oxford ; New York : Oxford University Press, 2003.
BC177 .F64 2003

WALKING, UPRIGHT. *See* **BIPEDALISM.**

WALL DECORATION. *See* **MURAL PAINTING AND DECORATION.**

WALL-PAINTING. *See* **MURAL PAINTING AND DECORATION.**

A Wall Street journal book
Noonan, Peggy, 1950- A heart, a cross & a flag. New York : Free Press, c2003.
E903 .N66 2003

Wallace, David A.
Archives and the public good. Westport, Conn. ; London : Quorum Books, 2002.

Wallace, David Rains, 1945- The Klamath knot : explorations of myth and evolution / David Rains Wallace ; illustrations by Karin Wikström. 20th anniversary ed. Berkeley : University of California Press, [2003] 167 p. : ill., map ; 23 cm. Originally published: 1st ed. San Francisco : Sierra Club Books, c1983. Includes bibliographical references (p. [165]-167). ISBN 0-520-23659-9 DDC 508.795/2
1. Natural history - Klamath Mountains (Calif. and Or.) 2. Evolution (Biology) 3. Klamath Mountains (Calif. and Or.) I. Title.
QH105.C2 W344 2003

Wallace, R. Jay.
Raz, Joseph. The practice of value. Oxford ; New York : Oxford University Press, 2003.
BD232 .R255 2003

Wallat, Cynthia. Family-institution interaction : new refrains / Cynthia Wallat. New York : P. Lang, c2002. xii, 131 p. ; 23 cm. Includes bibliographical references (p. [111]-131). ISBN 0-8204-5830-9 (pbk. : alk. paper) DDC 306.874
1. Parent and child. 2. Communication in the family. 3. Family. 4. Child development. I. Title.
HQ755.85 .W35 2002

WALOF (AFRICAN PEOPLE). *See* **WOLOF (AFRICAN PEOPLE).**

Walsch, Neale Donald. The new revelations : a conversation with God / Neale Donald Walsch. New York : Atria Books, c2002. ix, 358 p. ; 22 cm. Includes index. Publisher description URL: http://www.loc.gov/catdir/description/simon034/2003268325.html ISBN 0-7434-5694-7 DDC 204/.2
1. God - Miscellanea. 2. Imaginary conversations. 3. Spiritual life - Miscellanea. 4. Theology - Miscellanea. I. Title.
BF1999 .W2287 2002

Tomorrow's God : our greatest spiritual challenge / by Neale Donald Walsch. 1st ed. New York : Atria Books, 2004. p. cm. ISBN 0-7434-5695-5 DDC 204
1. God - Miscellanea. 2. Spiritual life - Miscellanea. 3. Imaginary conversations. I. Title.
BF1999 .W2288 2004

Walsh, Darryll. Ghosts of Nova Scotia / Darryll Walsh. East Lawrencetown, N.S. : Pottersfield Press, c2000. 127 p. : ill. ; 23 cm. Includes bibliographical references (p. 123-126). ISBN 1-89590-031-X DDC 133.1/09716
1. Ghosts - Nova Scotia. 2. Haunted places - Nova Scotia. I. Title.
BF1472.C3 W35 2000

Walsh, Froma.
Living beyond loss. 2nd ed. New York : W.W. Norton, 2004.
BF575.D35 L54 2004

Walter, Carolyn Ambler. The loss of a life partner : narratives of the bereaved / Carolyn Amber Walter. New York : Columbia University Press, c2003. xvii, 281 p. ; 24 cm. Includes bibliographical references (p. [261]-268) and index. ISBN 0-231-11968-2 (alk. paper) ISBN 0-231-11969-0 (pbk. : alk. paper) DDC 155.9/37
1. Bereavement - Psychological aspects. 2. Death - Psychological aspects. 3. Loss (Psychology) 4. Grief. I. Title.
BF575.G7 W3435 2003

Walter, Sven, 1974-.
Physicalism and mental causation. Exeter, UK ; Charlottesville, VA : Imprint Academic, c2003.
B825 .P494 2003

Walters, J. Donald. Secrets of comfort and joy / J. Donald Walters. [Nevada City, CA] : Crystal Clarity, 2000. 1 v. (unpaged) : col. ill. ; 13 cm.
1. Joy. 2. Human comfort. 3. Devotional calendars. I. Title.
BF575.H27 W362 2000

Secrets of friendship / J. Donald Walters. Nevada City, CA : Crystal Clarity Publishers, c2001. 1 v. (unpaged) : col. ill. ; 13 cm. ISBN 1-56589-134-1 DDC 1777/.62
1. Friendship. I. Title.
BF575.F66 WW355 2001

Walther, Eva, 1964-.
Fiedler, Klaus, 1951- Stereotyping as inductive hypothesis testing. Hove (UK) ; New York : Psychology Press, c2003.
BF323.S63 F54 2003

Walton, Douglas N. Ethical argumentation / Douglas Walton. Lanham, Md. ; Oxford : Lexington Books, c2003. xviii, 311 p. ; 24 cm. Includes bibliographical references (p. 289-302) and index. ISBN 0-7391-0349-0 (cloth) DDC 170/.1
1. Ethics. I. Title.
BJ1012 .W357 2003

Walton, Mark S., 1950- Generating buy-in : mastering the language of leadership / Mark S. Walton ; foreword by William Ury. New York : American Management Association, c2004. xviii, 108 p. ; 24 cm. Includes bibliographical references and index. CONTENTS: Pt. 1. Understanding the language of buy-in. What triggers buy-in? Every leader tells a story. How strategic stories will get you twenty-first century buy-in -- Pt. 2. Speaking the language of buy-in. A framework for buy-in. Developing your strategic story. The rule of three. When the going gets tough, the smart get buy-in. The charisma quotient. The best evidence -- Pt. 3. Putting the language to work. Using the tools of buy-in. Now it's your turn. Questions executives ask. ISBN 0-8144-0788-9 DDC 658.4/5
1. Communication in management. 2. Leadership. 3. Persuasion (Psychology) I. Title.
HD30.3 .W35 2004

Wanderley, Lula. O dragão pousou no espaço : arte contemporânea, sofrimento psíquico e o objeto relacional de Lygia Clark / Lula Wanderley. Rio de Janerio : Rocco, 2002. A. 159 p. ; 21 cm. Includes bibliographical references. ISBN 85-325-1339-5
1. Clark, Lygia, - 1920- 2. Art and mental illness. 3. Art therapy. 4. Art - Psychology. I. Title.

WANG, BI, 226-249.
Wagner, Rudolf G. Language, ontology, and political philosophy in China. Albany : State University of New York Press, c2003.
B126 .W284 2003

Wang, Bin. Zhongguo wen xue guan nian yan jiu / Wang Bin zhu. Beijing : Zhongguo wen lian, 1997. 9, 215 p. ; 18cm. ISBN 7-5059-2565-2
1. Chinese literature - History and criticism.

Wang, Bingquan.
Cheng zhang de Zhongguo. Di 1 ban. Beijing : Ren min chu ban she, 2002.
HQ799.2.P6 C449 2002

Wang Bi's scholarly exploration of the dark (xuanxue).
Wagner, Rudolf G. Language, ontology, and political philosophy in China. Albany : State University of New York Press, c2003.
B126 .W284 2003

Wang, Dongming.
Automated practical reasoning. Wien ; New York : Springer-Verlag, c1995.
QA76.9.A96 A9 1995

Wang, Furen. Tu po mang dian : shi ji mo she hui si chao yu Lu Xun / Wang Furen, Zhao Zhuo zhu. Di 1 ban. Beijing Shi : Zhongguo wen lian chu ban she, 2001. 3, 327 p. ; 21 cm. (Wo kan Lu Xun wen cong) ISBN 7-5059-3922-X
1. Lu, Xun, - 1881-1936. 2. Chinese literature - History and criticism. I. Zhao, Zhuo. II. Title. III. Title: Shi ji mo she hui si chao yu Lu Xun IV. Series.
PL2754.S5 Z89 2001

Wang, Jie.
Chen, Wei, 1957- Dong fang mei xue dui xi fang de ying xiang = Di 1 ban. Shanghai : Xue lin chu ban she, 1999.
BH221.C6 C444 1999

Wang, Lili.
Zhu, Ziqing, 1898-1948. Zhu Ziqing xue shu wen hua sui bi. Beijing di 1 ban. Beijing : Zhongguo qing nian chu ban she, 2000.

Wang, Q. Edward, 1958-.
Turning points in historiography. Rochester, NY : University of Rochester Press, 2002.
D13 .T87 2002

Wang, Xiaoming.
Dan shen gao bai. Di 1 ban. Beijing : Beijing chu ban she, 2001.
HQ800.2 .D36 2001

Wang, Xiaoying, 1957- Xi ju yan chu zhong di jia ding xing / Wang Xiaoying zhu. Di 1 ban. Beijing : Zhongguo xi ju chu ban she : Xin hua shu dian zong dian Beijing fa xing suo fa xing, 1995. 2, 5, 234 p. ; 19 cm. Originally presented as the author's thesis (doctoral), 1995. Includes bibliographical references. ISBN 7-104-00709-1
1. Theater. 2. Aesthetics. I. Title.
PN2039 .W35 1995 <Orien China>

Wanis-St. John, Anthony.
Lum, Grande. Expand the pie. Seattle, WA : Castle Pacific Pub. : Cambridge, MA : ThoughtBridge, c2003.
BF637.N4 L86 2003

WAR. *See also* **AIR WARFARE; CIVIL WAR; PEACE; WAR AND SOCIETY.**
Durschmied, Erik. Unsung heroes. London : Hodder & Stoughton, 2003.

Gaulle, Charles de, 1890-1970. [Fil de l'épée. Portuguese] O fio da espada. Rio de Janeiro : Biblioteca do Exército Editora, 2001.

Sofsky, Wolfgang. Violence. London : Granta, 2003, c2002.

War and reconciliation.
Long, William J., 1956- Cambridge, Mass. : MIT Press, c2003.
JZ5597 .L66 2003

WAR AND RELIGION. *See* **WAR - RELIGIOUS ASPECTS.**

WAR AND SOCIETY.
Medvedko, Leonid Ivanovich. Rossiía, Zapad, Islam. Zhukovskiĭ ; Moskva : Kuchkovo pole, 2003.
BP173.5 .M44 2003

Sontag, Susan, 1933- Regarding the pain of others. 1st ed. New York : Farrar, Straus and Giroux, 2003.
HM554 .S65 2003

WAR AND SOCIETY - UNITED STATES.
Robertson, Linda R. (Linda Raine), 1946- The dream of civilized warfare. Minneapolis : University of Minnesota Press, c2003.
D606 .R63 2003

WAR BETWEEN THE STATES, 1861-1865. *See* **UNITED STATES - HISTORY - CIVIL WAR, 1861-1865.**

WAR - ECONOMIC ASPECTS. *See* **COMPETITION, INTERNATIONAL.**

WAR - FORECASTING.
Global security concerns [electronic resource]. Maxwell Air Force Base, Ala. : Air University Press, [1996]

WAR - HISTORY.
Braudy, Leo. From chivalry to terrorism. New York : Alfred A. Knopf : Distributed by Random House, 2003.
HQ1090 .B7 2003

Howard, Michael, 1922 Nov. 29- The invention of peace and the reinvention of war. Rev. and extended ed. London : Profile, 2002, c2001.

Michael, Pamela. Care and treatment of the mentally ill in North Wales, 1800-2000. Cardiff : University of Wales Press, 2003.

WAR IN ART - SOCIAL ASPECTS.
Sontag, Susan, 1933- Regarding the pain of others. 1st ed. New York : Farrar, Straus and Giroux, 2003.
HM554 .S65 2003

WAR (IN RELIGION, FOLK-LORE, ETC.). See
  WAR - RELIGIOUS ASPECTS.

WAR (INTERNATIONAL LAW). See also
  INTERVENTION (INTERNATIONAL LAW).
Long, William J., 1956- War and reconciliation.
  Cambridge, Mass. : MIT Press, c2003.
  JZ5597 .L66 2003

War Michel aus Lönneberga aufmerksamkeitsgestört?.
Köhler, Henning, 1951- 2. Aufl. Stuttgart : Freies
  Geistesleben, 2002.

WAR NEUROSES.
Kitaev-Smyk, L. A. (Leonid Aleksandrovich) Stress
  voĭny. Moskva : Ministerstvo kul'tury RF : Rossiĭskiĭ
  in-t kul'turologii, 2001.

Shay, Jonathan. Odysseus in America. New York :
  Scribner, c2002.
  RC550 .S533 2002

WAR OF 1812. See **UNITED STATES - HISTORY - WAR OF 1812.**

The war of art.
Pressfield, Steven. Warner Books ed. New York :
  Warner Books, c2002, (2003 printing).
  BF408 .P69 2003

WAR OF SECESSION, U.S., 1861-1865. See
  UNITED STATES - HISTORY - CIVIL WAR, 1861-1865.

WAR OF THE AMERICAN REVOLUTION. See
  UNITED STATES - HISTORY - REVOLUTION, 1775-1783.

War of the worlds.
Latour, Bruno. Chicago : Prickly Paradigm Press,
  c2002.
  H61.15 .L38 2002

WAR ON TERRORISM, 2001-.
Crockatt, Richard. America embattled. London ; New
  York : Routledge, 2003.
  E902 .C76 2003

L'incubo globale. Bergamo : Moretti & Vitali, c2002.

Kritik der Gewalt. Wien : Promedia, c2002.
  D860 .K75 2002

Noonan, Peggy, 1950- A heart, a cross & a flag. New
  York : Free Press, c2003.
  E903 .N66 2003

WAR (PHILOSOPHY).
Katznelson, Ira. Desolation and enlightenment. New
  York : Columbia University Press, c2003.
  JA71 .K35 2003

WAR PHOTOGRAPHY - SOCIAL ASPECTS.
Sontag, Susan, 1933- Regarding the pain of others. 1st
  ed. New York : Farrar, Straus and Giroux, 2003.
  HM554 .S65 2003

WAR - PRESS COVERAGE.
Ross, Gina, 1947- Beyond the trauma vortex.
  Berkeley, Calif. : North Atlantic Books, c2003.
  PN4784.D57 R67 2003

WAR - PSYCHOLOGICAL ASPECTS.
Braudy, Leo. From chivalry to terrorism. New York :
  Alfred A. Knopf : Distributed by Random House,
  2003.
  HQ1090 .B7 2003

Children's fears of war and terrorism. Olney, MD :
  Association for Childhood Education International,
  c2003.
  BF723.W3 C48 2003

Kitaev-Smyk, L. A. (Leonid Aleksandrovich) Stress
  voĭny. Moskva : Ministerstvo kul'tury RF : Rossiĭskiĭ
  in-t kul'turologii, 2001.

Shay, Jonathan. Odysseus in America. New York :
  Scribner, c2002.
  RC550 .S533 2002

WAR - RELIGIOUS ASPECTS - ISLAM.
Medvedko, Leonid Ivanovich. Rossii︠a︡, Zapad, Islam.
  Zhukovskiĭ ; Moskva : Kuchkovo pole, 2003.
  BP173.5 .M44 2003

WAR - SOCIAL ASPECTS. See **WAR AND SOCIETY.**

WAR VETERANS. See **VETERANS.**

Ward, Adrian, 1953-.
Therapeutic communities for children and young
  people. London : Jessica Kingsley, 2003.

Ward, Andrew. The leadership lifecycle : matching
  leaders to evolving organizations / Andrew Ward.
  Houndmills [England] ; New York : Palgrave
  Macmillan, 2003. xi, 178 p. : ill. ; 24 cm. Includes
  bibliographical references and index. ISBN 0-333-99362-4
  DDC 658.4/092
  1. Leadership. 2. Executives. 3. Organizational change - Management. I. Title.
  HD57.7 .W367 2003

Ward, Graham. True religion / Graham Ward. Malden,
  MA : Oxford : Blackwell Pub., 2003. ix, 168 p. ; 24 cm.
  (Blackwell manifestos) Includes bibliographical references and
  index. CONTENTS: Religion before and after secularism --
  True religion and temporal goods -- True religion and
  consumption -- True religion as special effect. ISBN
  0-631-22173-5 (hbk. : alk. paper) ISBN 0-631-22174-3 (pbk. :
  alk. paper) DDC 200
  1. Religion. I. Title. II. Series.
  BL48 .W189 2003

Ward, Lawrence M.
Coren, Stanley. Sensation and perception. 6th ed.
  Hoboken, NJ : J. Wiley & Sons, c2004.
  BF233 .C59 2004

Ward, William Aidan. Trust and mistrust : radical risk
  strategies in business relationships / Aidan Ward and
  John Smith. Chichester, England ; Hoboken, NJ : John
  Wiley & Sons, c2003. xvi, 251 p. : ill. ; 24 cm. Includes
  bibliographical references (p. [233]-246) and index. ISBN
  0-470-85318-2 (cloth : alk. paper) DDC 650/.01
  1. Strategic alliances (Business) 2. Trust. 3. Business ethics. 4.
  Organizational effectiveness. I. Smith, John Robert. II. Title.
  HD69.S8 W37 2003

Warfield, Ted A., 1969-.
The Blackwell guide to philosophy of mind. Malden,
  MA ; Oxford : Blackwell Pub., 2003.
  BD418.3 .B57 2003

Warhol, Robyn R. Having a good cry : effeminate
  feelings and pop-culture forms / Robyn R. Warhol.
  Columbus : Ohio State University Press, c2003. xx,
  148 p. ; 23 cm. (The theory and interpretation of narrative
  series) Includes bibliographical references (p. 135-142) and
  index. CONTENTS: Introduction: effeminacy, feelings, forms.
  Effeminacy: a third term for gender studies -- Feelings: how do
  you really feel? -- Forms: feminist narratology and close
  reading -- The cry: effeminate sentimentalism. Having a good
  cry -- Sentimentalism and sexism -- A narratology of good-cry
  techniques -- Crying over The color purple -- The cringe:
  marriage plots, effeminacy, and feminist ambivalence. Reading
  too closely for comfort -- Discomforts of reading Pretty
  woman -- The thrill and the yawn: antieffeminate structures of
  feeling in serial forms. Self-conscious serial forms -- Reading
  the (boring) Victorian serial -- Antieffeminate affect -- E-mail
  as an antieffeminate form -- Bending gender and the habits of
  affect -- The climax and the undertow: effeminate intensities in
  soap opera. Who is the "I" who watches soaps? -- Intensities
  and long-term viewing -- Effeminate feeling and soap form --
  Afterword: the reader's body from the inside out. ISBN
  0-8142-0928-9 (hardcover : alk. paper) ISBN 0-8142-5108-0
  (pbk. : alk. paper) ISBN 0-8142-9011-6 (CD-ROM) DDC
  809/.89287
  1. Women and literature. 2. Television and women. 3. Women -
  Psychology. 4. Emotions. I. Title. II. Series.
  PN56.5.W64 W375 2003

WARLOCKS. See **WITCHES.**

WARLOCKS - EUROPE - BIOGRAPHY.
Lacotte, Daniel. Danse avec le diable. [Paris] :
  Hachette, c2002.
  BF1584.E85 L33 2002

WARLOCKS - EUROPE - HISTORY.
Apps, Lara. Male witches in early modern Europe.
  Manchester ; New York : Manchester University
  Press ; New York : Distributed exclusively in the USA
  by Palgrave, 2003.
  BF1584.E85 A66 2003

Lacotte, Daniel. Danse avec le diable. [Paris] :
  Hachette, c2002.
  BF1584.E85 L33 2002

Warmuth, Manfred.
Conference on Computational Learning Theory
  (16th : 2003 : Washington, D.C.) Learning theory and
  Kernel machines. Berlin ; New York : Springer,
  c2003.
  Q325.5 .C654 2003

Warneken, Bernd Jürgen, 1945-.
Inspecting Germany. Münster : Lit, c2002.
  DD76 .I57 2002

Warnock, Mary.
Mill, John Stuart, 1806-1873. Utilitarianism / 2nd ed.
  Malden, MA : Blackwell Pub., 2003.
  B1602 .A5 2003

Warren Bennis signature series
Cloke, Ken, 1941- The art of waking people up. 1st
  ed. San Francisco : Jossey-Bass, c2003.
  HF5385 .C54 2003

Warren, Joshua P. How to hunt ghosts : a practical
  guide / Joshua P. Warren. New York : Simon &
  Schuster, c2003. p. cm. "A Fireside book." Includes
  bibliographical references (p.   ) and index. ISBN
  0-7432-3493-6 (pbk.) DDC 133.1
  1. Ghosts. I. Title.
  BF1471 .W37 2003

Warrior series
  (39.) Wisdom, Stephen. Gladiators 100 BC-AD
  200. Oxford : Osprey, 2001 (2002 printing)

WARS. See **WAR.**

Warum wir siegen wollen.
Reichholf, Josef. München : Deutscher Taschenbuch,
  c2001.

Warwick, Ben.
The handbook of risk. Hoboken, N.J. : Wiley, c2003.
  HB615 .H266 2003

Was für Arbeit braucht der Mensch?.
Ivanova, Anna (Anna N.) Kakŭv trud e nuzhen na
  choveka? Sofii︠a︡ : Akademichno izd-vo "Prof. Marin
  Drinov", 2000.
  BF481 .I82 2000

Was heisst Denken?.
Heidegger, Martin, 1889-1976. Frankfurt am Main :
  Vittorio Klostermann, c2002.
  B3279 .H45 1976 Bd.8

Was heisst, sich an Differenz statt an Identität orientieren?.
Clam, Jean. Konstanz : UVK Verlagsgesellschaft,
  c2002.

Was ist Leben?.
Kather, Regine, 1955- Darmstadt : Wissenschaftliche
  Buchgesellschaft, c2003.

Was ist schön?.
Paál, Gábor. Würzburg : Königshausen & Neumann,
  c2003.
  BH39 .P33 2003

Was kostet den Kopf? : ausgesetztes Denken der
  Aisthesis zwischen Abstraktion und Imagination :
  Dietmar Kamper zum 65. Geburtstag / herausgegeben
  von Herbert Neidhöfer & Bernd Ternes. Marburg :
  Tectum Verlag, 2001. 631 p. : ill. ; 21 cm. Includes
  bibliographical references (p. 555-608) and index. ISBN 3-
  8288-8251-X (pbk.)
  1. Kamper, Dietmar, - 1936- 2. Aesthetics. 3. Abstraction. 4.
  Perception (Philosophy) 5. Imagination (Philosophy) I.
  Kamper, Dietmar, 1936- II. Neidhöfer, Herbert. III. Ternes,
  Bernd.

Washburn, David A.
Rumbaugh, Duane M., 1929- Respondents, operants,
  and emergents [microform]. [Washington, D.C. :
  National Aeronautics and Space Administration,
  1997]

Washburn, David A., 1961-.
Rumbaugh, Duane M., 1929- Intelligence of apes and
  other rational beings. New Haven : Yale University
  Press, c2003.
  QL737.P96 R855 2003

Washburn, Michael, 1943- Embodied spirituality in a
  sacred world / Michael Washburn. Albany : State
  University of New York Press, 2003. p. cm. Includes
  bibliographical references and index. ISBN 0-7914-5847-4
  (alk. paper) ISBN 0-7914-5848-2 (pbk. : alk. paper) DDC
  150.19/8
  1. Transpersonal psychology. 2. Developmental psychology. 3.
  Psychology, Religious. I. Title.
  BF204.7 .W372 2003

WASHINGTON (D.C.) - BUILDINGS, STRUCTURES, ETC.
Ovason, David. [Secret zodiacs of Washington DC]
  The secret architecture of our nation's capital. 1st
  Perennial ed. New York, NY : Perennial, 2002.

WASHINGTON (D.C.) - FICTION.
Kava, Alex. The soul catcher. Waterville, Me. :
  Thorndike Press, 2003, 2002.
  PS3561.A8682 S6 2003

WASHINGTON (D.C.) - POLITICS AND GOVERNMENT - 1878-1967.
Barber, Lucy G. (Lucy Grace), 1964- Marching on
  Washington. Berkeley : University of California
  Press, c2002.
  E743 .B338 2002

WASHINGTON (D.C.) - POLITICS AND GOVERNMENT - 1967-1995.
Barber, Lucy G. (Lucy Grace), 1964- Marching on

Washington, Johnny. Washington. Berkeley : University of California Press, c2002.
E743 .B338 2002

Washington, Johnny. Evolution, history and destiny : letters to Alain Locke (1886-1954) and others / Johnny Washington. New York : Peter Lang, c2002. vii, 401 p. ; 24 cm. (Studies in literary criticism and theory ; vol. 13) Includes bibliographical references (p. [365]-377) and index. ISBN 0-8204-4970-9 (alk. paper) DDC 973.04/96073
1. African Americans - Ethnic identity. 2. African Americans - History. 3. African Americans - Social conditions. 4. African American intellectuals. 5. Social evolution. 6. Human evolution. 7. Fate and fatalism. 8. African American philosophy. I. Title. II. Series: Studies in literary criticism and theory ; v. 13.
E185.625 .W37 2002

Washington, Richard. Abstraction planning in real time [microform] / by Richard Washington. Stanford, Calif. : Stanford University, Dept. of Computer Science, [1994] (Springfield, Va. : U.S. Dept. of Commerce, National Technical Information Service). xii, 105 p. : ill. ; 28 cm. (Report / Stanford University. Dept. of Computer Science : STAN-CS-TR-94-1512) (NASA/TM ; 97-205922) Cover title. Shipping list no.: 98-0599-M. "March 1994." Thesis (Ph. D.)--Stanford University, 1994. Microfiche. [Washington, D.C. : National Aeronautics and Space Administration, 1997] 2 microfiches : negative. Includes bibliographical references. Supported in part by the Defense Advanced Research Projects Agency. NAG 2-581 ; NIH 5P41 RR-00785 Supported in part by Cimflex Teknowledge Corporation. 71715-1 Supported in part by ARPA. DAAA21-92-C-0028 "Also numbered KSL 94-21."
1. Artificial intelligence. I. Stanford University. Computer Science Dept. II. Title. III. Series: Report (Stanford University. Computer Science Dept.) ; STAN- CS-TR-94-1512. IV. Series: NASA technical memorandum ; 205922.

Wasilewski, Susan. Christesen, Mirka. Character kaleidoscope. Port Chester, N.Y. : Dude Pub., c2000.
BF818 .C55 2000

Wason, P. C. (Peter Cathcart). Perspectives on thinking and reasoning. Hove, UK ; Hillsdale : Lawrence Erlbaum Associates, c1995.
BF441 .P48 1995

Wasserman, Elhanan Bunim, 1875-1941. Ḳovets maʼamre ʻIḳvata de-Meshiḥa ... : meluḳaṭim mi-sifre "Ḳovets maʼamarim ye-ʼigrot" / Elḥanan Bunem Vaserman. Yerushalayim : Yeshivat Or Elḥanan, 762 [2001 or 2002] 7, 159 p. ; 23 cm. ʻIḳvata de-Meshiḥa.
1. Messianic era (Judaism) 2. Messiah - Judasim. 3. Faith (Judaism) 4. Ethics, Jewish. I. Title. II. Title: ʻIḳvata de-Meshiḥa

WATER AND CIVILIZATION.
Dans l'eau, sous l'eau. [Paris] : Presses de l'Université de Paris-Sorbonne, 2002.
CB353 .D27 2002

Water and the Word.
Keefe, Susan A. Notre Dame, Ind. : University of Notre Dame Press, c2002.
BR200 .K44 2002

WATER IN ART.
River of words. Berkeley, Calif. : Heyday Books, c2003.
PS595.W374 R58 2003

WATER - POETRY.
River of words. Berkeley, Calif. : Heyday Books, c2003.
PS595.W374 R58 2003

WATER - RELIGIOUS ASPECTS. *See* **BAPTISM.**

WATER RIGHTS.
Conflict prevention and resolution in water systems. Cheltenham, UK ; Northampton, MA, USA : E. Elgar Pub., c2002.
HD1691 .C664 2002

WATER RIGHTS (INTERNATIONAL LAW).
Conflict prevention and resolution in water systems. Cheltenham, UK ; Northampton, MA, USA : E. Elgar Pub., c2002.
HD1691 .C664 2002

Waterline.
Soucheray, Joe. Boston : D.R. Godine, 2002.
PN4874.S576 A3 2002

Watson, Sylvia. Feng shui with what you have / Sylvia Watson and Connie Spruill. Avon, MA : Adams Media, c2004. p. cm. CONTENTS: Section I. The ABCs of feng shui -- The power of feng shui -- The big three : Tao, Yin/yang, Chi -- The five elements -- Goals and intentions : taking charge of your life -- The bagua : whats life got to do with it -- Activating the stations of life -- Section II. How to evaluate what you have -- Get a good look at what you have -- Taking inventory -- Clearing clutter : keeping it simple is not as simple as it seems -- Section III. Feng shui room by room -- The room evaluators -- Transitional spaces : the mood-setting themes -- The gathering room -- The kitchen and eating spaces -- The to-do rooms/office/work areas -- The quiet rooms : the bedroom and the bathroom -- Special situations : feng shui for entertaining, feng shui for visitors, feng shui for childrens spaces -- Section IV. Learning by example -- A cure for whatever ails you -- Clients who used what they had. ISBN 1-59317-013-X DDC 133.3/337
1. Feng shui. I. Spruill, Connie. II. Title.
BF1779.F4 W37 2004

Watts, Richard E.
Adlerian, cognitive, and constructivist therapies. New York : Springer Pub., c2003.
BF637.C6 A335 2003

WAVE-MOTION, THEORY OF. *See* **SOUND.**

WAX-MODELING.
Bloom, Michelle E. Waxworks. Minneapolis : University of Minnesota Press, c2003.
GV1836 .B56 2003

Waxworks.
Bloom, Michelle E. Minneapolis : University of Minnesota Press, c2003.
GV1836 .B56 2003

Bloom, Michelle E. Waxworks. Minneapolis : University of Minnesota Press, c2003.
GV1836 .B56 2003

The way of a pilgrim : annotated & explained / translation & annotation by Gleb Pokrovsky. London : Darton Longman & Todd, 2003, c2001. xvi, 138 p. : ill., facsims., ports. ; 22 cm. First published in USA: 2001. Includes bibliographical references. ISBN 0-232-52475-0 DDC 248.32
1. Prayer - Orthodox Eastern Church. 2. Christian life. I. Pokrovsky, Gleb, 1954-

The way of love.
Irigaray, Luce. [Voie de l'amour. English] London ; New York : Continuum, 2002.
BF575.L8 I7513 2002

Irigaray, Luce. London ; New York : Continuum, 2002.

The way of transition.
Bridges, William, 1933- Cambridge, Mass. : Perseus Pub., c2001.
BF335 .B717 2001

The way things are.
Smith, Huston. Berkeley : University of California Press, c2003.
BL43.S64 A5 2003

Ways a world might be.
Stalnaker, Robert. Oxford : Clarendon ; New York : Oxford University Press, 2003.
BD111 .S73 2003

Ways of being.
Witt, Charlotte, 1951- Ithaca : Cornell University Press, 2003.
B434 .W59 2003

We are eternal.
Brown, Robert, medium. New York : Warner Books, c2003.
BF1283.B717 A3 2003

We can be friends.
Jordan, Denise. Chicago, Ill. : Heinemann Library, c2003.
BF723.F68 J67 2003

We can listen.
Jordan, Denise. Chicago, Ill. : Heinemann Library, 2003.
BF323.L5 J67 2003

We fish.
Daniel, Jack L. (Jack Lee), 1942- Pittsburgh, Pa. : University of Pittsburgh Press, c2003.

We shall not fail.
Sandys, Celia. New York : Portfolio ; London : Penguin Books, 2003.
DA566.9.C5 S266 2003

WEALTH. *See also* **MONEY; PROPERTY.**
[Wohlstand entschleiern. English] Unveiling wealth. Dordrecht ; Boston : Kluwer, c2002.
HD75.6 .U58 2002

WEAPONS. *See* **FIREARMS.**

Web Lab (Firm).
Living with suicide [electronic resource]. [Alexandria, Va.] : PBS Online ; [New York, N.Y.] : Web Lab
BF789.D4

Web of deception : misinformation on the Internet / edited by Anne P. Mintz. Medford, N.J : CyberAge Books, c2002. xxv, 275 p. : ill. ; 23 cm. Includes bibliographical references and index. CONTENTS: Web hoaxes, counterfeit sites, and other spurious information on the Internet / Paul S. Piper -- Charlatans, leeches, and old wives : medical misinformation / Susan M. Detwiler -- It's a dangerous world out there : misinformation in the corporate universe / Helene Kassler -- Internet users at risk : the identity/privacy target zone / Stephen E. Arnold -- Brother have you got a dime? Charity scams on the Web / Carol Ebbinghouse -- Welcome to the dark side : how e-commerce, online consumer, and e-mail fraud rely on misdirection and misinformation / Lysbeth B. Chuck -- Make sure you read the fine print : legal advice on the Internet / Carol Ebbinghouse -- How to evaluate a web site / LaJean Humphries -- This is what I asked for? The searching quagmire / Susan Feldman -- How a search engine works / Elizabeth D. Liddy -- Getting mad, getting even, getting money : remedies for intentional misinformation / Carol Ebbinghouse -- Endnote : What a tangled web we weave / Barbara Quint and Anne P. Mintz. ISBN 0-910965-60-9 (pbk.) DDC 025.04
1. Internet fraud. 2. Electronic information resource literacy. 3. Computer network resources - Evaluation. 4. Internet searching. I. Mintz, Anne P.
ZA4201 .W43 2002

WEB SITE DEVELOPMENT.
Visualizing the semantic Web. London ; [New York] : Springer, c2003.
TK5105.888 .V55 2003

WEB SITES - DIRECTORIES.
Schlein, Alan M. Find it online. 3rd ed. Tempe, AZ : Facts on Demand Press, c2003.

Webb, Diane.
Pleij, Herman. [Dromen van Cocagne. English] Dreaming of Cockaigne. New York : Columbia University Press, c2001.
CB353 .P5413 2001

WEBB, JAMES, 1946-.
The occult Webb. Toronto : Colombo & Co., c1999.
BF1408.2.W42 O33 1999

Webb, Wyatt. Five steps for overcoming fear and self-doubt : journey into present-moment time / Wyatt Webb. Carlsbad, Calif. : Hay House, 2004. p. cm. CONTENTS: The origins of fear and self-doubt -- Breaking out of a self-imposed prison -- Acknowledge the fear and self-doubt -- Quantify the fear and self-doubt -- Imagine the worst-case scenario -- Gather information and support, confront the perception, and dissipate the fear -- Celebrate! ISBN 140190257X (hardcover) ISBN 1401902588 (pbk.) DDC 158.1
1. Fear. 2. Self-doubt. 3. Self-confidence. I. Title.
BF575.F2 W42 2004

Weber, Bruce H.
Evolution and learning. Cambridge, Mass. : MIT Press, c2003.
BF698.95 .E95 2003

Weber, Jürgen, 1928- The judgement of the eye : the metamorphoses of geometry-- one of the sources of visual perception and consciousness : a further development of Gestalt psychology / Jürgen Weber. Wien ; New York : Springer, c2002. 200 p. : ill. (some col.) ; 30 cm. Includes bibliographical references (p. 115) and index. ISBN 3-211-83768-X (alk. paper)
1. Visual perception. 2. Composition (Art) 3. Color in art. I. Title.
BF241 .W38 2002

WEBER, MAX, 1864-1920.
POLITIK ALS BERUF.
Palonen, Kari, 1947- Eine Lobrede für Politiker. Opladen : Leske + Budrich, 2002.
JF2051.W43 J35 2002

WEBER, SAMUEL M.
Wortham, Simon. Samuel Weber. Aldershot, England ; Burlington, VT : Ashgate, c2003.
PN81 .W64 2003

Webster, Alison R. Wellbeing / Alison Webster. London : SCM, c2002. xiv, 158 p. ; 20 cm. (Society and church) Includes bibliographical references and index. ISBN 0-334-02889-2 DDC 234.13
1. Spirituality. 2. Health - Religious aspects - Christianity. I. Title.

Webster-Doyle, Terrence, 1940- One encounter, one chance : the essence of the art of karate / Terence Webster-Doyle. 1st Weatherhill ed. Trumbull, CT : Weatherhill, 2000. 221 p. : ill. ; 24 cm. ISBN 0-8348-0477-8 DDC 796.8153
1. Karate - Philosophy. 2. Self-knowledge, Theory of. 3. Self-defense - Psychological aspects. I. Title. II. Title: Essence of the art of karate

GV1114.3 .W43 2000

Webster, Richard, 1946- Amulets & talismans for beginners / by Richard Webster. St. Paul, Minn. : Llewellyn Publications, 2004. p. cm. Includes bibliographical references (p.   ) and index. ISBN 0-7387-0504-7 DDC 133.4/4
1. Amulets. 2. Talismans. I. Title. II. Title: Amulets and talismans for beginners
BF1561 .W43 2004

[Palm reading for beginners. Spanish]
Quiromancia para principiantes / Richard Webster ; traducido al idioma español por Héctor Ramírez y Edgar Rojas. 1. ed. St. Paul, Minn. : Llewellyn Español, 2003. xvii, 220 p. : ill. ; 21 cm. Includes bibliographical references (p. 213-216) and index. ISBN 0-7387-0396-6 DDC 133.6
1. Palmistry. I. Title.
BF921 .W418 2003

WECHSLER INTELLIGENCE SCALE FOR CHILDREN - CROSS-CULTURAL STUDIES.
Culture and children's intelligence. Amsterdam ; Boston : Academic Press, c2003.
BF432.5.W42 C85 2003

WECHSLER PRESCHOOL AND PRIMARY SCALE OF INTELLIGENCE.
Lichtenberger, Elizabeth O. Essentials of WPPSI-III assessment. Hoboken, N.J. : John Wiley & Sons, 2003.
BF432.5.W424 L53 2003

WEDLOCK. See **MARRIAGE.**

Weed, Laura E. The structure of thinking : a process-oriented account of mind / Laura E. Weed. Exeter : Imprint Academic, c2003. 248 p. ; 22 cm. Includes bibliographical references and index. ISBN 0-907845-27-4 DDC 128.2
1. Philosophy of mind. 2. Cognition. I. Title.

Weg im Nicht.
Baldus, Claus, 1947- Stuttgart : Hatje, c1994.

Baldus, Claus, 1947- Weg im Nicht. Stuttgart : Hatje, c1994.

Wei cao ji.
He, Zhaowu. Di 1 ban. Beijing : Sheng huo, du shu, xin zhi san lian shu dian, 1999.
D16.8 .H42 1999

Weiblichkeit im Neuen Zeitalter.
Haen, Renate. Du bist die Göttin ; 1. Auf. Bergish Gladbach : Bastei Lübbe, 1999.

Weidner, Jay. The mysteries of the great cross of Hendaye : alchemy and the end of time / by Jay Weidner and Vincent Bridges. Rochester, Vt. : Destiny Books, 2003. p. cm. Includes bibliographical references and index. Table of contents URL: http://www.loc.gov/catdir/toc/ecip042/2003007981.html ISBN 0-89281-084-X DDC 001.94
1. End of the world - Miscellanea. 2. Stone crosses - France - Hendaye - Miscellanea. 3. Prophecies (Occultism) - France - Hendaye - History - 17th century. 4. Fulcanelli, - pseud. - Mystère des cathédrales. 5. Alchemy. I. Bridges, Vincent. II. Title.
BF1999 .W435 2003

Weigle, Sara Cushing. Assessing writing / Sara Cushing Weigle. Cambridge ; New York, NY : Cambridge University Press, 2002. xiv, 268 p. : ill. ; 24 cm. (Cambridge language assessment series) Includes bibliographical references and index. ISBN 0-521-78027-6 ISBN 0-521-78446-8 (PBK.) DDC 418.0071
1. Writing - Ability testing. 2. Educational tests and measurements. 3. English language - Written English - Ability testing. I. Title. II. Series.
PE1065 .W35 2002

Weil, Simone, 1909-1943.
[Pesanteur et la grâce. English]
Gravity and grace / Simone Weil ; translated by Emma Crawford and Mario von der Ruhr. 1st complete English language ed. / with an introduction and postscript by Gustave Thibon. London ; New York : Routledge, 2002. xl, 183 p. ; 20 cm. ISBN 0-415-29000-7 (alk. paper) ISBN 0-415-29001-5 (pbk. : alk. paper) DDC 194
1. Meditations. I. Title.
B2430.W473 P413 2002

WEIL, SIMONE, 1909-1943.
Simone Weil, la passion de la raison. Paris : Harmattan, c2003.
B2430.W474 S55 2003

Weiler, Gerda, 1921- Der enteignete Mythos : eine feministische Revision der Archetypenlehre C.G. Jungs und Erich Neumanns / Gerda Weiler. Königstein : Helmer, [1996] 263 p. : ill. ; 21 cm. (Aktuelle Frauenforschung) Includes bibliographical references (p. 244-248) and index. ISBN 3-927164-02-X (pbk.)
1. Jung, C. G. - (Carl Gustav), - 1875-1961. 2. Neumann, Erich. 3. Psychoanalysis and feminism. 4. Archetype (Psychology) I. Title. II. Series.

Weinberg, George H. Why men won't commit : getting what you both want without playing games / George Weinberg. New York : Atria Books, c2002. x, 213 p. ; 24 cm. Publisher description URL: http://www.loc.gov/catdir/desc ription/simon034/2003266339.html ISBN 0-7434-4569-4 DDC 155.3/3
1. Commitment (Psychology) 2. Men - Psychology. 3. Man-woman relationships. I. Title.
BF619 .W45 2002

Weinberg, Norma Pasekoff, 1941- Henna from head to toe! / Norma Pasekoff Weinberg ; illustrations by Catherine Cartwright-Jones. Pownal, Vt. : Storey Books, c1999. 75 p. : ill. (some col.) ; 20 cm. Includes bibliographical references (p. 72). CONTENTS: Decorated life -- Extraordinary plant -- Coloring hair and conditioning nails -- Henna as natural medicine -- Creating henna designs -- Preparation application techniques -- Spot and belly-button designs -- Arm and wrist designs -- Hand designs -- Foot, leg, and ankle designs -- Chest, back and neck designs -- Henna wedding traditions -- Gallery of celebrities. ISBN 1-58017-097-8 (hc : alk. paper) DDC 391.6
1. Body painting. 2. Body marking. 3. Henna. 4. Beauty, Personal. I. Title. II. Title: Henna
GT2343 .W45 1999

Weiner, Andrew D.
On interpretation. Madison, Wis. : University of Wisconsin Press for the University of Wisconsin Law School, c2002.

Weiner, Irving B.
Handbook of psychology. Hoboken, N.J. : John Wiley, c2003.
BF121 .H1955 2003

Weinstein, Marion. Earth magic : a book of shadows for positive witches / by Marion Weinstein. Rev. ed. Franklin Lakes, NJ : New Page Books, c2003. 223 p. : ill. ; 21 cm. Includes bibliographical references (p. 213-215) and index. ISBN 1-56414-638-3 (pbk.) DDC 133.4/3
1. Witchcraft. 2. Magic. I. Title.
BF1566 .W46 2003

Positive magic : ancient metaphysical techniques for modern lives / by Marion Weinstein. Rev. ed. Franklin Lakes, NJ : New Page Books, c2002. 302 p. : ill. ; 23 cm. Includes bibliographical references (p. 289-295) and index. ISBN 1-56414-637-5 (pbk.) DDC 133.4/3
1. Occultism. 2. Magic. I. Title.
BF1411 .W393 2002

Weinstein, Matt. Dogs don't bite when a growl will do : what your dog can teach you about living a happy life / Matt Weinstein and Luke Barber. 1st ed. New York : Perigee, 2003. p. cm. ISBN 0-399-52916-0 DDC 170/.44
1. Conduct of life. 2. Dogs - Miscellanea. I. Barber, Luke. II. Title.
BF637.C5 W445 2003

Weinstein, Steve, 1960-.
Sasson, Gahl. A wish can change your life. New York : Simon & Schuster, 2003.
BF1623.C2 S27 2003

Weiss, Brian L. (Brian Leslie), 1944- Eliminating stress, finding inner peace / Brian L. Weiss. Carlsbad, Calif. : Hay House, c2003. p. cm. CONTENTS: The nature of stress -- Causes of stress -- Signs and symptoms of stress -- Stress and illness -- Post-traumatic stress disorder -- A few clinical cases -- Stress and worry -- Stress and spirituality -- A threefold approach to stress reduction -- How to use the CD. ISBN 1401902448 (Hardcover) DDC 155.9/042
1. Stress (Psychology) 2. Stress management. I. Title.
BF575.S75 W44 2003

Weiss, Gail, 1959-.
Thinking the limits of the body. Albany : State University of New York Press, c2003.
HM636 .T47 2003

Weiss, Stefanie Iris. Everything you need to know about dealing with losses / Stefanie Iris Weiss. Rev. ed. New York : Rosen Pub. Group, 2000. 64 p. : ill. ; 25 cm. (The need to know library) Includes bibliographical references (p. 61-62) and index. SUMMARY: Describes different kinds of losses, including the death of a loved one, the end of a love affair, and the loss of virginity, and suggests such coping mechanisms as the natural grieving process, the finding of a creative outlet, and getting help from others. ISBN 0-8239-3302-4 DDC 155.9/37
1. Loss (Psychology) in adolescence - Juvenile literature. 2. Grief in adolescence - Juvenile literature. 3. Loss (Psychology) 4. Grief. I. Title. II. Title: Dealing with losses III. Series.

BF724.3.L66 W45 2000
Schostak, Sherene. Surviving saturn's return. 1st ed. New York : McGraw-Hill, 2004.
BF1724.2.S3 S36 2004

Weissman, David, 1936- Lost souls : the philosophic origins of a cultural dilemma / David Weissman. Albany : State University of New York Press, c2003. xiii, 210 p. : ill. ; 23 cm. Includes bibliographical references (p. 173-197) and index. ISBN 0-7914-5755-9 (alk. paper) ISBN 0-7914-5756-7 (pbk. : alk. paper) DDC 128/.2
1. Mind and body. I. Title.
B105.M53 W45 2003

Weissman, Karen.
Coyne, Tami. The spiritual chicks question everything. York Beach, ME : Red Wheel/Weiser, 2002.
BL625.7 .C69 2002

Der weite Blick des Historikers : Einsichten in Kultur-, Landes- und Stadtgeschichte : Peter Johanek zum 65. Geburtstag / herausgegeben von Wilfried Ehbrecht ... [et al.] ; Redaktion, Institut für Vergleichende Städtegeschichte. Köln : Böhlau, c2002. xxxi, 840 p. : ill., maps ; 25 cm. Includes bibliographical references (p. [789]-808) and index. Festschrift published in honor of Peter Johanek's 65th birthday. Articles in German, with one in English. ISBN 3-412-07602-3
1. Europe x Historiography. 2. Germany - Historiography. 3. Europe - Intellectual life. 4. Germany - Intellectual life. 5. History - Philosophy. I. Johanek, Peter. II. Ehbrecht, Wilfried. III. Institut für Vergleichende Städtegeschichte.
D116 .W44 2002

Weiten, Wayne, 1950- Psychology : themes and variations / Wayne Weiten ; with critical thinking applications by Diane F. Halpern. 6th ed. Australia ; Belmont, CA : Thomson/Wadsworth, c2004. xlv, 687, [143] p. : ill. (chiefly col.) ; 29 cm. Includes bibliographical references (p. R-1-R-67) and index. ISBN 0-534-59769-6 DDC 150
1. Psychology. I. Halpern, Diane F. II. Title.
BF121 .W38 2004

Weitz, Ely.
Vardi, Yoav, 1944- Misbehavior in organizations. Mahwah, NJ ; London : Lawrence Erlbaum, 2004.
HD58.7 .V367 2004

WELCH, JACK, 1935-.
Krames, Jeffrey A. The Jack Welch lexicon of leadership. 1st ed. New York : McGraw-Hill, 2001, c2002.
HD57.7 .K726 2001

Welch, Olga M.
Hodges, Carolyn R., 1947- Making schools work. New York : P. Lang, c2003.
LC213.2 .H63 2003
1. Black author.

Welch, R. W., 1929- Comet of Nostradamus : August 2004-impact! / R.W. Welch. 1st ed. St. Paul, Minn. : Llewellyn Publications, 2000 (2001 printing) xv, 318 p. : ill., maps ; 23 cm. Includes bibliographical references (p. 303-304) and index. ISBN 1-56718-816-8 DDC 133.3
1. Nostradamus, - 1503-1566. - Prophéties. 2. Comets - Collisions with Earth - Miscellanea. 3. Mediterranean Region - Miscellanea. 4. Prophecies (Occultism) I. Title.
BF1815.N8 A269 2000

WELFARE ECONOMICS.
Putnam, Hilary. The collapse of the fact/value dichotomy and other essays. Cambridge, MA : Harvard University Press, 2002.
B945.P873 C65 2002

WELL-BEING.
Frey, Bruno S. Happiness and economics. Princeton, N.J. : Princeton University Press, c2002.
BF575.H27 F75 2002

Well, duh!.
Fenster, Bob. Kansas City, MO : Andrews McMeel Pub., 2004.
BF431 .F37 2004

WELL-KNOWN PEOPLE. See **CELEBRITIES.**

The well-read witch.
McColman, Carl. Franklin Lakes, NJ : New Page Books, c2002.
BF1611

Wellbeing.
Webster, Alison R. London : SCM, c2002.

Wellman, Jeff.
[Clavicula Salomonis. English.] Lemegeton. Jacksonville, FL : Metatron Books, 1999.

WELLNESS. *See* **HEALTH.**

Wells, Celia Townsend, 1932- Brood bitch : a mother's reflection / Celia Townsend Wells. West Lafayette, Ind. : Purdue University Press, c2003. 147 p. ; 24 cm. ISBN 1-55753-236-2 (cloth : alk. paper) DDC 636.7/082/092
1. Wells, Celia Townsend, - 1932- 2. Dog breeders - Biography. 3. Pembroke Welsh corgi. 4. Human-animal relationships. 5. Mothers and daughters. I. Title.
SF422.82.W44 A3 2003

WELLS, CELIA TOWNSEND, 1932-.
Wells, Celia Townsend, 1932- Brood bitch. West Lafayette, Ind. : Purdue University Press, c2003.
SF422.82.W44 A3 2003

Wellspring Media.
The Alexander technique [videorecording]. New York, N.Y. : Wellspring Media, c1999.

Der Welt-Automat von Malcolm McLaren.
Bonz, Jochen. Wien : Turia + Kant, [2002]

Welt, Thomas.
Imagination, Fiktion, Kreation. München : Saur, c2003.
BH301.I53 I534 2003

Welt und Bewusstsein.
Heuermann, Hartmut. Frankfurt am Main ; New York : Peter Lang, c2002.

Weltbild und Wirklichkeit.
Schindewolf, Dorrit. [S.l.] : Schindewolf, [1999]
CB88 .S35 1999

Weltbilder der Religionen.
Stolz, Fritz. Zürich : Pano Verlag, c2001.

Welterfahrung und ästhetische Neugierde in Mittelalter und früher Neuzeit.
Curiositas. Göttingen : Wallstein, c2002.
BF323.C8 C872 2002

Wen shi tan wei.
Huang, Yongnian. [Selections. 2000] Di 1 ban. Beijing : Zhonghua shu ju, 2000.
DS736 .H795 2000

Wen shi tong yi jiao zhu.
Ye, Ying, 1896-1950. Di 1 ban. Beijing : Zhonghua shu ju : Xin hua shu dian Beijing fa xing suo fa xing, 1994.
DS734.7.C433 Y43 1985 <Orien China>

Wen xue li lun xin ti xi. Gao xiao wen ke jiao cai.
Wen xue yin lun. Di 1 ban. Ha'erbin Shi : Heilongjiang jiao yu chu ban she, 1999.

Wen xue xin shang yu pi ping.
Zhou, Xiuping. Di 1 ban. Changsha : Zhong nan gong ye da xue chu ban she, 1998.
PL2262 .Z468 1998

"Wen xue yi chan" bian ji bu.
Shi ji zhi jiao de dui hua. Di 1 ban. Shanghai : Shanghai gu ji chu ban she : Xin hua shu dian Shanghai fa xing suo fa xing, 2000.

Wen xue yin lun / Xiao Junhe zhu bian. Di 1 ban. Ha'erbin Shi : Heilongjiang jiao yu chu ban she, 1999. 3, 10, 6, 456 p. ; 21 cm. (Wen xue li lun xin ti xi. Gao xiao wen ke jiao cai) Colophon title also in pinyin: Wenxue yinlun. ISBN 7-5316-3514-3
1. Chinese literature - History and criticism. 2. Literature - History and criticism. I. Xiao, Junhe. II. Title: Wenxue yinlun III. Series: Wen xue li lun xin ti xi. Gao xiao wen ke jiao cai.

Wen, Yiduo, 1899-1946. Wen Yiduo xue shu wen hua sui bi / Qiao Zhihang bian. Beijing di 1 ban. Beijing : Zhongguo qing nian chu ban she, 2001. vii, 4, 305 p. ; 21 cm. (Er shi shi ji Zhongguo xue shu wen hua sui bi da xi. Di 3 ji) ISBN 7-5006-4418-3
1. Chinese literature - History and criticism. I. Qiao, Zhihang. II. Title. III. Series.
PL2272.5 .W46 2001

Wen Yiduo xue shu wen hua sui bi.
Wen, Yiduo, 1899-1946. Beijing di 1 ban. Beijing : Zhongguo qing nian chu ban she, 2001.
PL2272.5 .W46 2001

Wenger, Andreas. Conflict prevention : the untapped potential of the business sector / Andreas Wenger, Daniel Möckli. Boulder, Colo. ; London : Lynne Rienner Publishers, 2003. viii, 233 p. ; 24 cm. Includes bibliographical references (p. 181-216) and index. ISBN 1-58826-136-0 (alk. paper) DDC 658.4/053
1. Conflict management. 2. Pacific settlement of international disputes. 3. Social responsibility of business. I. Möckli, Daniel. II. Title.
JZ5538 .W46 2003

Wenk, Shari Lesser.
Woods, Earl, 1932- Start something. New York : Simon & Schuster, c2000.

BJ1631 .W726 2000

Wentscher, Herbert, 1951- Vor dem Schirm / Herbert Wentscher. 1. Aufl. [Freiburg im Breisgau] : Modo, 2002. 101 p. : ill. ; 27 cm. Includes bibliographical references. ISBN 3-922675-28-X (pbk.)
1. Art - History. 2. Glass art - History. 3. Television in art - History. I. Title.

Wenxue yinlun.
Wen xue yin lun. Di 1 ban. Ha'erbin Shi : Heilongjiang jiao yu chu ban she, 1999.

Der werdende Mensch.
Schwarte, Johannes. 1. Aufl. Wiesbaden : Westdeutscher Verlag, 2002.

Werder, Lutz von. Lehrbuch der philosophischen Lebenskunst für das 21. Jahrhundert / Lutz von Werder. Berlin : Schibri-Verlag, c2000. 634 p. : ill. ; 21 cm. Includes bibliographical references (p. 599-602). ISBN 3-928878-88-3 (hd.bd.)
1. Philosophy. 2. Ethics. I. Title.

WEREWOLVES.
Lecouteux, Claude. [Fées, sorcières et loups-garous au Moyen Age. English] Witches, werewolves, and fairies. 1st U.S. ed. Rochester, Vt. : Inner Traditions, 2003.
BF1045.D67 L4313 2003

WEREWOLVES - ENCYCLOPEDIAS.
Guiley, Rosemary. The encyclopedia of vampires, werewolves, and other monsters. New York, NY : Facts on File, 2004.
BF1556 .G86 2004

Werewolves, witches, and wandering spirits : traditional belief and folklore in early modern Europe / edited by Kathryn A. Edwards. Kirksville, MO : Truman State University Press, c2002. xxii, 226 p. : ill. ; 24 cm. (Sixteenth century essays & studies ; v. 62) Includes bibliographical references and index. CONTENTS: Introduction : expanding the analysis of traditional belief / Kathryn A. Edwards. -- Dangerous spirits : shapeshifting, apparitions, and fantasy in Lorraine witchcraft trials / Robin Briggs -- Living with the dead : ghosts in early modern Bavaria / David Lederer -- Reformed or recycled? : possession and exorcism in the sacramental life of early modern France / Sarah Ferber -- Revisiting El Encubierto : navigating between visions of Heaven and Hell on Earth / Sara T. Nalle -- Worms and the Jews : Jews, magic, and community in seventeenth-century Worms / Dean Phillip Bell -- Asmodea : a nun-witch in eighteenth-century Tuscany / Anne Jacobson Schutte -- When witches became false : séducteurs and crédules confront the Paris police at the beginning of the eighteenth century / Ulrike Krampl -- God killed Saul / Heinrich Bullinger and Jacob Rueff on the power of the devil / Bruce Gordon -- Such an impure, cruel, and savage beast : images of the werewolf in demonological works / Nicole Jacques-Lefèvre -- Charcot, Freud, and the demons / H. C. Erik Midelfort. ISBN 1-931112-09-6 (casebound : alk. paper) ISBN 1-931112-08-8 (pbk. : alk. paper) DDC 398.4
1. Folklore - Europe. 2. Folk literature - Europe - History and criticism. 3. Supernatural. 4. Witchcraft - Europe. 5. Demonology - Europe. I. Edwards, Kathryn A., 1964- II. Series.
GR135 .W47 2002

Werkausgabe.
Schutz, Alfred, 1899-1959. Konstanz : UVK, Verlagsgesellschaft, 2003-
BD431 .S284916 2003

Werke. Supplementa.
Cohen, Hermann, 1842-1918. [Works. 1977. Supplementa] Hildesheim : G. Olms, 2000-

Wermester, Karin.
From promise to practice. Boulder ; London : L. Rienner Publishers, 2003.
JZ6368 .S68 2003

Wernitznig, Dagmar. Going native or going naive? : white shamanism and the neo-noble savage / Dagmar Wernitznig. Lanham, MD : University Press of America, c2003. xxxix, 103 p. ; 22 cm. Includes bibliographical references (p. [91]-99) and index. ISBN 0-7618-2495-2 (pbk. : alk. paper) DDC 305.897/073
1. Indians of North America - Public opinion. 2. Indians in popular culture. 3. Indian philosophy - United States. 4. Shamanism - United States. 5. New Age movement - United States. 6. Whites - United States - Race identity. 7. Whites - United States - Psychology. 8. Public opinion - United States. 9. United States - Race relations. 10. United States - Social life and customs. I. Title. II. Title: White shamanism and the neo-noble savage
E98.P99 W47 2003

Der Wert des Privaten.
Rössler, Beate. 1. Aufl. Frankfurt am Main : Suhrkamp, 2001.

Wertime, Kent. Building brands & believers : how to connect with consumers using archetypes / Kent Wertime. Chichester : Wiley, 2002. xvi, 267 p. ; 24 cm. Includes bibliographical references and index. ISBN 0-470-82067-5 DDC 658.80019
1. Brand choice. 2. Marketing - Psychological aspects. 3. Consumer behavior. 4. Archetype (Psychology) I. Title. II. Title: Building brands and believers

WERWOLVES. *See* **WEREWOLVES.**

Weseley, Allyson.
McEntarffer, Robert. Barron's how to prepare for the AP pscyhology advanced placement examination. Hauppauge, N.Y. : Barron's, c2004.
BF78 .M34 2004

WEST AND EAST. *See* **EAST AND WEST.**

West-Eberhard, Mary Jane. Developmental plasticity and evolution / Mary Jane West-Eberhard. Oxford ; New York : Oxford University Press, 2003. xx, 794 p. : ill. ; 26 cm. Includes bibliographical references (p. 639-743) and indexes. ISBN 0-19-512235-6 ISBN 0-19-512234-8 (pbk. : alk. paper) DDC 578.4
1. Adaptation (Biology) 2. Phenotype. 3. Evolution (Biology) 4. Developmental biology. I. Title.
QH546 .W45 2003

WEST EUROPE. *See* **EUROPE, WESTERN.**

West, Harry G.
Transparency and conspiracy. Durham : Duke University Press, 2003.
JC330 .T73 2003

WEST TEXAS. *See* **TEXAS, WEST.**

WEST TURKESTAN. *See* **ASIA, CENTRAL.**

West, William. Theatres and encyclopedias in early modern Europe / William West. Cambridge : Cambridge University Press, 2002. xv, 293 p. : ill. ; 23 cm. (Cambridge studies in Renaissance literature and culture ; 44) Includes index. ISBN 0-521-80914-2 DDC 792.09409031
1. Theater - Europe - History. 2. Theater - Great Britain - History. 3. English drama - Early modern, 1500-1700. 4. Encyclopedias and dictionaries - Europe - History. 5. Renaissance. I. Title. II. Series.

WESTERN AND COUNTRY MUSIC. *See* **COUNTRY MUSIC.**

WESTERN ART. *See* **ART.**

WESTERN CIVILIZATION. *See* **CIVILIZATION, WESTERN.**

Western esoteric masters series
Dee, John, 1527-1608. [Selections. 2003] John Dee . Berkeley, Calif. : North Atlantic Books, c2003.
BF1598.D5 A25 2003

WESTERN EUROPE. *See* **EUROPE, WESTERN.**

Western eyes [videorecording] / [presented by] the National Film Board of Canada. New York, NY : First Run/Icarus Films, 2000. 1 videocassette (40 min.) : sd., col. ; 1/2 in. VHS. Maria Estante, Sharon Kim. Producer, Gerry Flahive ; director, Ann Shin ; photography, Stanislaw Barua ; editor, Nick Hector. SUMMARY: Examines the search for beauty and self-acceptance through the experiences of a young Filipina and Korean woman living in Canada who both believe their appearance, specifically their eyes, affect the way they are perceived. Both feel unsettled in Western society and are contemplating cosmetic surgery on their eyes. Layering interviews with references to super models and other pop-culture icons of beauty, the filmmaker captures the pain that almost always lies behind the desire for plastic surgery.
1. Blepharoplasty. 2. Eyelids - Surgery - Psychological aspects. 3. Surgery, Plastic - Psychological aspects. 4. Asians - Canada - Ethnic identity. 5. Koreans - Canada - Ethnic identity. 6. Koreans - Canada - Cultural assimilation. 7. Filipinos - Canada - Ethnic identity. 8. Filipinos - Canada - Cultural assimilation. 9. Conflict of generations - Canada. 10. Self-perception. 11. Feminine beauty (Aesthetics) 12. Beauty, Personal - Psychological aspects. 13. Body image in women. 14. Body image - Social aspects. I. Flahive, Gerry. II. Shin, Ann. III. National Film Board of Canada. IV. First Run/Icarus Films.

Western historical thinking : an intercultural debate / edited by Jörn Rüsen. New York : Berghahn Books, 2002. xiii, 206 p. ; 24 cm. (Making sense of history) Chiefly written by members of the Forschungsgruppe Historische Sinnbildung, Universität Bielefeld. Based in part on Westliches Geschichtsdenken (1999). Includes bibliographical references and index. CONTENTS: Western historical thinking in a global perspective - 10 theses / Peter Burke -- Perspectives in historical anthropology / Klaus E. Müller -- Searching for common principles : a plea and some remarks on the Islamic tradition / Tarif Khalidi -- The coherence of the West / Aziz Al-Azmeh -- Toward an archaeology of historical thinking / François Hartog -- Trauma and suffering : a forgotten source of

western historical consciousness / Frank R. Ankersmit --
Western deep culture and western historical thinking / Johan
Galtung -- What is uniquely western about the historiography
of the west in contrast to that of China? / Georg G. Iggers --
The westernization of world history / Hayden White -- Western
historical thinking from an Arabian perspective / Sadik J. Al-
Azm -- Cognitive historiography and normative
historiography / Masayuki Sato -- Western uniqueness? Some
counterarguments from an African perspective / Godfrey
Muriuki -- Programs for historians : a western perspective /
Mamadou Diawara -- Reflections on Chinese historical
thinking / Ying-shih Yü -- Must history follow rational patterns
of interpretation? Critical questions from a Chinese
perspective / Thomas H.C. Lee -- Some reflections on early
Indian historical thinking / Romila Thapar. ISBN
1-57181-781-6 (alk. paper) ISBN 1-57181-454-X (pbk.) DDC
901
*1. History - Philosophy. 2. Civilization, Western. 3. Africa -
Civilization - Historiography. 4. Asia - Civilization -
Historiography. 5. History - Methodology. 6. Historiography.
I. Rüsen, Jörn. II. Universität Bielefeld. Forschungsgruppe
Historische Sinnbildung. III. Title: Westliches
Geschichtsdenken. IV. Series.*
D16.9 .W454 2002

WESTERN LITERATURE. See LITERATURE.

Western supremacy.
Bessis, Sophie, 1947- [Occident et les autres. English]
London ; New York : Zed Books, 2003.
CB245 .B4613 2003

WESTINGHOUSE, GEORGE, 1846-1914.
Jonnes, Jill, 1952- Empires of light. 1st ed. New
York : Random House, c2003.
TK18 .J66 2003

Westliches Geschichtsdenken.
Western historical thinking. New York : Berghahn
Books, 2002.
D16.9 .W454 2002

Westphal, Merold. Overcoming onto-theology : toward
a postmodern Christian faith / Merold Westphal. 1st
ed. New York : Fordham University Press, 2001. xxi,
306 p. ; 24 cm. (Perspectives in continental philosophy, 1089-
3938 ; no. 21) Includes bibliographical references and index.
ISBN 0-8232-2130-X ISBN 0-8232-2131-8 (pbk.) DDC 230/
.01
*1. Christianity - Philosophy. 2. Postmodernism - Religious
aspects - Christianity. 3. Metaphysics. I. Title. II. Series.*
BR100 .W47 2001

Westphal, Siegrid, 1963- Kaiserliche Rechtsprechung
und herrschaftliche Stabilisierung :
Reichsgerichtsbarkeit in den thüringischen
Territorialstaaten 1648-1806 / von Siegrid Westphal.
Köln : Böhlau, 2002. x, 526 p. : ill., map ; 24 cm. (Quellen
und Forschungen zur höchsten Gerichtsbarkeit im alten Reich ;
Bd. 43) Revised habilitation - Universität, Jena, 2001. Includes
bibliographical references (p. [445]-484) and index. ISBN
3-412-08802-1 (hd.bd.)
*1. Thuringia (Germany) - Politics and government. 2.
Thuringia (Germany) - History. I. Title. II. Series.*

Westra, Laura.
Thinking about the environment. Lanham, Md. :
Lexington Books, c2002.
GE50 .T48 2002

Westwick, D. T. (David T.) Identification of nonlinear
physiological systems / David T. Westwick, Robert
E. Kearney. Piscataway, NJ : IEEE Press ; Hoboken,
NJ : Wiley-Interscience, c2003. xii, 261 p. : ill. ; 26 cm.
(IEEE Press series in biomedical engineering) "IEEE
Engineering in Medicine and Biology Society, sponsor."
Includes bibliographical references (p. 251-257) and index.
Table of contents URL: http://www.loc.gov/catdir/toc/
wiley032/2003043255.html ISBN 0-471-27456-9 (cloth) DDC
612/.01/5118
*1. Physiology - Mathematical models. 2. Nonlinear systems. I.
Kearney, Robert E., 1947- II. IEEE Engineering in Medicine
and Biology Society. III. Title. IV. Series.*
QP33.6.M36 W475 2003

Wettstein, Howard K.
Renaissance and early modern philosophy. Malden,
MA ; Oxford : Blackwell Pub., c2002.
B775 .R46 2002

Wexler, Jayne.
Cowen, Lauren. Daughters & mothers. Philadelphia
[Penn.] : Courage Books, c1997.
HQ755.85 .C695 1997

Whalen, Charles E., Jr. The gift of renewal / by
Charles E. "Gus" Whalen, Jr., with Phillip Rob
Bellury ; foreword by Edward C. Emma. 1st ed.
Gainesville, GA : Warren Featherbone Foundation,
c2003 (Gainesville, GA : Matthews Print.) xi, 114 p. :
ill. ; 20 cm. ISBN 0-9655107-3-5 DDC 158
*1. Self-actualization (Psychology) 2. Interpersonal relations. 3.
Success. I. Bellury, Phillip Rob. II. Title.*
BF637.S4 W47 2003

WHALING.
Philbrick, Nat. Revenge of the whale. New York :
G.P. Putnam, 2002.
G530.E77 P454 2002

What about Uranus?.
McWilliam, Erica. Sydney, NSW, Australia : UNSW
Press, 2002.
BF637.S4 M397 2002

McWilliam, Erica. Sydney : UNSW Press, 2002.

What all children need.
Dunlap, Linda L. Lanham, Md. : University Press of
America, c2002.
HQ778.5 .D85 2002

What babies say before they can talk.
Holinger, Paul C. New York : Simon & Schuster,
c2003.
BF720.C65 H64 2003

What can happen when we pray : daily devotional /
foreword by Rev. Dr. Jeremiah A. Wright Jr. ; [editor,
Ronald S. Bonner]. Minneapolis : Augsburg Fortress,
c2001. 383 p. ; 23 cm. Includes index. ISBN 0-8066-3406-5
(pbk.)
*1. Prayer books and devotions. 2. Devotional calendars. 3.
African Americans - Religion. I. Bonner, Ronald S.*

What children need when they grieve.
Rathkey, Julia Wilcox. 1st ed. New York : Three
Rivers Press, 2004.
BF723.G75 R38 2004

What doesn't kill you makes you stronger.
Schnall, Maxine. Cambridge, MA : Perseus Pub.,
c2002.
BF575.D35 S36 2002

What Einstein told his cook.
Wolke, Robert L. 1st ed. New York : W.W. Norton &
Co., c2002.
TX652 .W643 2002

What evolution is.
Mayr, Ernst, 1904- New York : Basic Books, c2001.
QH366.2 .M3933 2001

What happens to us when we think.
Gelven, Michael. Albany : State University of New
York Press, c2003.
BD111 .G45 2003

What I look like when I am angry.
Johansen, Heidi Leigh. 1st ed. New York : PowerStart
Press, 2004.
BF723.A4 J63 2004

Johansen, Heidi Leigh. [What I look like when I am
angry. Spanish & English] 1st ed. New York : Rosen
PowerKids Press, 2004.
BF723.A4 J6318 2004

What I look like when I am confused.
Randolph, Joanne. 1st ed. New York : PowerStart
Press, 2004.
BF723.I63 R36 2004

Randolph, Joanne. [What I look like when I am
confused. Spanish & English] 1st ed. New York :
Rosen Pub. Group's PowerKids Press, 2004.
BF723.I63 R3618 2004

What I look like when I am happy.
Johansen, Heidi Leigh. 1st ed. New York : PowerStart
Press, 2004.
BF723.H37 J64 2004

Johansen, Heidi Leigh. [What I look like when I am
happy. Spanish & English] 1st ed. New York : Rosen
Pub. Group's, 2004.
BF723.H37 J6418 2004

What I look like when I am sad.
Randolph, Joanne. 1st ed. New York : PowerStart
Press, 2004.
BF723.S15 R36 2004

Randolph, Joanne. [What I look like when I am sad.
Spanish & English] 1st ed. New York : Rosen Pub.
Group's PowerKids Press, 2004.
BF723.S15 R3618 2004

What I look like when I am scared.
Shepherd, Joanne. New York : Rosen Pub. Group's
PowerStart Press, 2004.
BF723.F4 S54 2004

Shepherd, Joanne. [What I look like when I am
scared. Spanish & English] 1st ed. New York : Rosen
Pub. Group's PowerKids Press, 2004.

BF723.F4 S5418 2004

What I look like when I am surprised.
Shepherd, Joanne. 1st ed. New York : Rosen Pub.
Group's PowerStart Press, 2004.
BF723.S87 S44 2004

Shepherd, Joanne. [What I look like when I am
surprised. Spanish & English] 1st ed. New York :
Rosen Pub. Group's PowerKids Press, 2004.
BF723.S87 S4418 2004

What if?.
Soleri, Paolo, 1919- Berkeley, CA : Berkeley Hills
Books, 2002.
NA2543.S6 S637 2002

What ifs? of American history : eminent historians
imagine what might have been / edited by Robert
Cowley. New York : G.P. Putnam's, c2003. xvi, 298
p. : ill., maps ; 24 cm. ISBN 0-399-15091-9 DDC 973
*1. United States - History - Miscellanea. 2. United States -
History, Military - Miscellanea. 3. Imaginary histories. I.
Cowley, Robert.*
E179 .W535 2003

What is Feng-Shui?.
Eitel, Ernest John, 1838-1908. Mineola, N.Y. : Dover
Publications, 2003.
BF1779.F4 E4 2003

What is history now? / edited by David Cannadine.
Houndmills [England] ; New York : Palgrave
Macmillan, 2002. xiv, 172 p. ; 23 cm. Includes
bibliographical references and index. ISBN 0-333-98646-6
(hbk.) DDC 901
*1. History - Philosophy. 2. Historiography. I. Cannadine,
David, 1950-*
D16.8 .W5 2002

What is religion?.
Crawford, Robert G. (Robert George), 1927- London ;
New York : Routledge, 2002.
BL48 .C722 2002

What kind of goddess are you?.
De Grandis, Francesca. Naperville, Ill. : Sourcebooks,
Inc., 2004.
BF1623.G63 D4 2004

What makes a champion! : fifty extraordinary
individuals share their insights / edited by Allan
Snyder. Camberwell, Vic., Australia ; New York :
Penguin Books, 2002. 227 p., [8] p. of plates : ill. (some
col.) ; 20 cm. "A Penguin original"--P. 4 of cover. ISBN
0-14-026370-5 (pbk.) DDC 158.1
*1. Success - Psychological aspects. 2. Self-actualization
(Psychology) I. Snyder, Allan.*
BF637.S8 W45 2002

What makes us think?.
Changeux, Jean-Pierre. [Ce qui nous fait penser.
English] Princeton, N.J. : Princeton University Press,
c2000.
BJ45 .C4313 2000

What not to wear.
Constantine, Susannah. London : Weidenfeld &
Nicolson, 2002.

What should I do with my life?.
Bronson, Po, 1964- Waterville, Me. : Thorndike Press,
2003.
BF637.S4 B79 2003

What tarot can do for you.
Moore, Barbara, 1963- 1st ed. St. Paul, Minn. :
Llewellyn Publications, 2004.
BF1879.T2 M653 2004

What the kolanut is saying.
Adeosun, Kola A. [Oro ti obi n so. English] Ibadan,
Nigeria : Creative Books, 1999.
BF1779.K6 A33 1999

What you call time.
Ruthven, Suzanne. London : Ignotus Press, c1998.

Whatever happened to America?.
Ryter, Jon Christian. Tampa, FL : Hallberg Pub.,
2001, c2000.
E743 .R98 2001

Whatever happened to good and evil?.
Shafer-Landau, Russ. New York ; Oxford : Oxford
University Press, 2004.
BJ1401 .S46 2004

What's money got to do with it?.
Broussard, Cheryl D. Oakland, CA : MetaMedia Pub.,
[c2002]

What's the big idea?.
Davenport, Thomas H. Boston, Mass. : Harvard
Business School Press, c2003.

HD53 .D38 2003

What's the good of counselling & psychotherapy? : the benefits explained / edited by Colin Feltham. London : Thousand Oaks, Calif. : SAGE Publications, 2002. x, 285 p. ; 24 cm. Includes bibliographical references and index. ISBN 0-7619-6955-1 (pbk.) ISBN 0-7619-6954-3 DDC 158/.3
1. Counseling. 2. Psychotherapy. I. Feltham, Colin, 1950-
BF637.C6 W465 2002

What's your Wicca IQ?.
Wildman, Laura A. New York : Citadel Press, c2002.
BF1566 .W63 2002

Wheeler, Brannon M., 1965-.
Prayer, magic, and the stars in the ancient and late antique world. University Park, Pa. : Pennsylvania State University Press, 2003.
BF1591 .P73 2003

Wheeler large print book series
Cook, Thomas H. The interrogation. Rockland, MA : Wheeler Pub., 2002.
PS3553.O55465 I58 2002

Whelan, Bilkis. Vastu in 10 simple lessons / Bilkis Whelan. 1st ed. New York : Watson-Guptill Publications, 2002. 143 p. : col. ill. ; 22 cm. Includes bibliographical references (p. 140) and index. ISBN 0-8230-5591-4 DDC 133.3/33
1. Vāstu. 2. Hindu astrology. I. Title. II. Title: Vastu in ten simple lessons
BF1779.V38 W48 2002

Whelan, Bride M. The complete color harmony : expert color information for professional color results / Bride M. Whelan, Tina Sutton. Gloucester, Mass. : Rockport Publishers, 2004. p. cm. ISBN 1-59253-031-1 (flexibind) DDC 155.9/1145
1. Color - Psychological aspects. I. Sutton, Tina. II. Title.
BF789.C7 W47 20041

When anger hurts your relationship.
Paleg, Kim. Oakland, CA : New Harbinger Publications, c2001.
BF575.A5 P35 2001

When goliaths clash.
Guttman, Howard M. New York ; London : AMACOM, c2003.
HD42 .G88 2003

When helping you is hurting me.
Berry, Carmen Renee. Revised and updated ed. New York : Crossroad Pub. Co., c2003.
BF637.S42 B47 2003

When I feel afraid.
Meiners, Cheri J., 1957- Minneapolis, MN : Free Spirit Pub., 2003.
BF723.F4 M45 2003

When someone you love is Wiccan.
McColman, Carl. Franklin Lakes, NJ : New Page Books, 2003.
BF1566 .M36 2003

When students grieve.
Liotta, Alfred J. Horsham, PA : LRP Publications, 2003.
BF724.3.D43 L56 2003

When will I stop hurting?.
Myers, Edward, 1950- Lanham, Md. : Scarecrow Press, 2004.
BF724.3.G73 M94 2004

When you mean business about yourself.
Capp, Ray, 1953- Nashville, Tenn. : Rutledge Hill Press, c2002.
BF637.S8 C37 2002

When your father dies.
Veerman, David. Nashville, Tenn. : Thomas Nelson, c2003.
BF575.G7 V44 2003

Where do we fall when we fall in love?.
Young-Bruehl, Elisabeth. New York : Other Press, c2003.
BF173 .Y68 2003

Where I was from.
Didion, Joan. 1st ed. New York : Alfred A. Knopf : Distributed by Random House, 2003.
F861 .D53 2003

Where we belong.
Shepard, Paul, 1925- Athens : University of Georgia Press, c2003.
GF21 .S524 2003

Where writing begins.
Carter, Michael, 1950 Aug. 8- Carbondale : Southern Illinois University Press, c2003.
P301 .C29 2003

Where's Jess?.
Johnson, Marvin. Rev. Omaha, NE : Centering Corp. Resource, 2003.
BF723.G75 J645 2003

Whicher, Ian.
Yoga. London ; New York : RoutledgeCurzon, 2003.
BL1238.52 .Y59 2003

Whipp, Richard.
Making time. Oxford ; New York : Oxford University Press, 2002.
HD69.T54 M34 2002

Whipple, Charles M.
Oklahoma psychology in the twentieth century. [Oklahoma City, OK : Oklahoma Psychological Association, 2003?]
BF77 .O35 2003

White awareness.
Katz, Judy H., 1950- 2nd ed., rev. Norman : University of Oklahoma Press, c2003.
HT1523 .K37 2003

White, Cheryl.
Working with the stories of women's lives. Adelaide : Dulwich Centre Publications, 2001.
HQ1185 .W68 2001

White, Curtis, 1951- The middle mind : why Americans don't think for themselves / Curtis White. 1st ed. [San Francisco] : HarperSanFrancisco, c2003. 205 p. ; 24 cm. Includes bibliographical references (p. [203]-205) ISBN 0-06-052436-7
1. Social values - United States. 2. Critical thinking. 3. United States - Social conditions - 1980- 4. United States - Moral conditions. I. Title.

White, Hayden V., 1928-.
Historiografía y memoria colectiva. 1. ed. Madrid ; Buenos Aires : Miño y Dávila, 2002.

White, Howard, 1950- Believe to achieve : see the invisible, do the impossible / Howard "H" White ; with a foreword by Philip H. Knight. Hillsboro, Or. : Beyond Words Pub., c2003. p. cm. ISBN 1-58270-094-X DDC 158.1
1. Success - Psychological aspects. I. Title.
BF637.S8 W453 2003

White, Lauren. Spells for a perfect love life / Lauren White. Kansas City, Mo. : Andrews McMeel Pub., 2000. 1 v. (unpaged) : col. ill. ; 14 cm. ISBN 0-7407-0551-2 (hardcover) DDC 133.4/42
1. Witchcraft. 2. Charms. 3. Love - Miscellanea. I. Title.
BF1572.L6 .W45 2000

White men are not.
DiPiero, Thomas, 1956- White men aren't. Durham : Duke University Press, 2002.
HQ1090 .D567 2002

White men aren't.
DiPiero, Thomas, 1956- Durham : Duke University Press, 2002.
HQ1090 .D567 2002

WHITE MEN IN LITERATURE.
DiPiero, Thomas, 1956- White men aren't. Durham : Duke University Press, 2002.
HQ1090 .D567 2002

WHITE MEN - PSYCHOLOGY.
DiPiero, Thomas, 1956- White men aren't. Durham : Duke University Press, 2002.
HQ1090 .D567 2002

White, Morton Gabriel, 1917- A philosophy of culture : the scope of holistic pragmatism / Morton White. Princeton, N.J. : Princeton University Press, c2002. xv, 193 p. ; 25 cm. Includes bibliographical references and index. ISBN 0-691-09656-2 (cloth : alk. paper) DDC 144/.3
1. Pragmatism. 2. Culture - Philosophy. 3. Holism. I. Title.
B945.W453 P48 2002

WHITE PEOPLE. See **WHITES.**

WHITE PERSONS. See **WHITES.**

White shamanism and the neo-noble savage.
Wernitznig, Dagmar. Going native or going naive? Lanham, MD : University Press of America, c2003.
E98.P99 W47 2003

White, Sharon. Field notes : a geography of mourning / Sharon White. Center City, Minn. : Hazelden, 2002. 194 p. ; 19 cm. Includes bibliographical references (p. [193]-194). ISBN 1-56838-878-0 (pbk.) DDC 155.9/37/092
1. White, Sharon. 2. Bereavement - Psychological aspects. 3. Widows - Biography. I. Title.
BF575.G7 W485 2002

WHITE, SHARON.
White, Sharon. Field notes. Center City, Minn. : Hazelden, 2002.
BF575.G7 W485 2002

White, Sheldon Harold, 1928- Developmental psychology as a human enterprise / Sheldon H. White ; drawing by Leonard Baskin. Worcester, Mass. : Clark University Press, c2001. 50 p. ; 21 cm. (2001 Heinz Werner lecture series ; v. 24) Includes bibliographical references (p. 48-50). ISBN 0-914206-38-9 (pbk. : alk. paper) DDC 155
1. Developmental psychology. I. Title. II. Series: Heinz Werner lectures ; v. 24.
BF713 .W48 2001

WHITE SUPREMACIST MOVEMENTS. See **WHITE SUPREMACY MOVEMENTS.**

WHITE SUPREMACY MOVEMENTS - RELIGIOUS ASPECTS.
Gardell, Mattias. Gods of the blood. Durham : Duke University Press, 2003.
BL65.W48 G37 2003

WHITE SUPREMACY MOVEMENTS - UNITED STATES.
Gardell, Mattias. Gods of the blood. Durham : Duke University Press, 2003.
BL65.W48 G37 2003

White, Vernon. Identity / Vernon White. London : SCM, c2002. x, 176 p. ; 20 cm. (Society and church) Includes bibliographical references and index. ISBN 0-334-02890-6 DDC 261.51
1. Identity (Philosophical concept) 2. Identity (Philosophical concept) - Religious aspects - Christianity. I. Title.

Whited, Lana A., 1958-.
The ivory tower and Harry Potter. Columbia : University of Missouri Press, 2002.
PR6068.O93 Z734 2002

WHITEHEAD, ALFRED NORTH, 1861-1947.
Stengers, Isabelle. Penser avec Whitehead. Paris : Seuil, c2002.

WHITEHEAD, ALFRED NORTH, 1861-1947 - INFLUENCE.
Greene, Herb. Painting the mental continuum. Berkeley, Calif. : Berkeley Hills Books ; [Berkeley, Calif.] : Distributed by Publishers Group West, c2003.
N71 .G683 2003

Whitehead, Neil L.
In darkness and secrecy. Durham, NC : Duke University Press, 2004.
BF1566 .I5 2004

Whitehead, Willis F. The mystic thesaurus : occultism simplified / Willis F. Whitehead. Berwick, Me. : Ibis Press, 2003. p. cm. Originally published: Chicago : W.F. Whitehead, 1899. ISBN 0-89254-069-9 (pbk. : alk. paper) DDC 133
1. Occultism. I. Title.
BF1411 .W46 2003

Whiteman, Martha C.
Matthews, Gerald. Personality traits. 2nd ed. New York : Cambridge University Press, 2003.
BF698 .M3434 2003

WHITES. See **WHITE MEN.**

WHITES - RACE IDENTITY.
Tuckwell, Gill, 1948- Racial identity, White counsellors and therapists. Buckingham : Philadelphia : Open University Press, 2002.
BF637.C6 T84 2002

WHITES - UNITED STATES - PSYCHOLOGY.
Wernitznig, Dagmar. Going native or going naive? Lanham, MD : University Press of America, c2003.
E98.P99 W47 2003

WHITES - UNITED STATES - RACE IDENTITY.
Wernitznig, Dagmar. Going native or going naive? Lanham, MD : University Press of America, c2003.
E98.P99 W47 2003

Whitledge, Jim.
Critical incidents in group counseling. Alexandria, VA : American Counseling Association, 2004.
BF637.C6 C72 2004

Who knows?.
Smullyan, Raymond M. Bloomington : Indiana University Press, c2003.
BL50 .S59 2003

Who owns native culture?.
Brown, Michael F. (Michael Fobes), 1950- Cambridge, Mass. : Harvard University Press, 2003.
K1401 .B79 2003

Who really matters.
Kleiner, Art. 1st ed. New York ; London : Currency/Doubleday, 2003.
HD2741 .K478 2003

Whoever makes the most mistakes wins.
Farson, Richard Evans, 1926- New York ; London : Free Press, c2002.
HD45 .F357 2002

WHOLE AND PARTS (PSYCHOLOGY).
Perception of faces, objects, and scenes. Oxford ; New York : Oxford University Press, 2003.
BF241 .P434 2003

Pint, A. A. (Aleksandr Aleksandrovich) Nas mnogo, no my odno. Moskva : Shkola kholisticheskoĭ psikhologii, 2003.
BF202 .P56 2003

The whole duty of man, according to the law of nature.
Pufendorf, Samuel, Freiherr von, 1632-1694. [De officio hominis et civis. English] Indianapolis, Ind. : Liberty Fund, c2003.
K457.P8 D4313 2003

WHOLENESS. *See* **WHOLE AND PARTS (PSYCHOLOGY).**

WHOLESALE TRADE. *See* **RETAIL TRADE.**

Who's pulling your strings?.
Braiker, Harriet B., 1948- New York : McGraw-Hill, c2004.
BF632.5 .B69 2004

Why America is squandering its chance to build a better world.
Hirsh, Michael, 1957- At war with ourselves. New York : Oxford University Press, 2003.
E895 .H57 2003

Why do men barbecue?.
Shweder, Richard A. Cambridge, Mass. : Harvard University Press, 2003.
GN502 .S59 2003

Why do people bully?.
Hibbert, Adam, 1968- Chicago, Ill. : Raintree, 2004.
BF637.B85 H53 2004

Why I love black women.
Dyson, Michael Eric. New York : Basic Civitas Books, c2003.

Why men won't ask for directions.
Francis, Richard C., 1953- Princeton, N.J. : Princeton University Press, 2004.
BF698.95 .F73 2004

Why men won't commit.
Weinberg, George H. New York : Atria Books, c2002.
BF619 .W45 2002

Why motor skills matter.
Losquadro-Liddle, Tara. Chicago : Contemporary Books, c2004.
BF723.M6 L67 2004

Why smart executives fail and what you can learn from their mistakes.
Finkelstein, Sydney. New York ; London : Portfolio, 2003.
HD38.2 .F56 2003

Why stock markets crash.
Sornette, D. Princeton, N.J. : Princeton University Press, c2003.
HB3722 .S66 2003

Why stoics box.
Randolph, Jeanne, 1943- Toronto : YYZ Books, 2003.

Why they fight [electronic resource] : combat motivation in the Iraq War / Leonard Wong ... [et al.]. Carlisle, PA : Strategic Studies Institute, U.S. Army War College, [2003] Electronic text (PDF) System requirements: Adobe Acrobat Reader. Mode of access: Internet from the SSI web site. Address as of 8/21/03: http://carlisle-www.army.mil/ssi/pubs/2003/whyfight/whyfight.pdf; current access available via PURL. Title from title screen (viewed on Aug. xx, 2003). "July 2003." Includes bibliographical references. URL: http://purl.access.gpo.gov/GPO/LPS35591
1. Iraq War, 2003 - Psychological aspects. 2. United States - Armed Forces - Unit cohesion. 3. Iraq - Armed Forces - Unit cohesion. 4. Soldiers - United States - Attitudes. 5. Soldiers - Iraq - Attitudes. 6. Morale. 7. Combat - Psychological aspects. 8. Motivation (Psychology) 9. Electronic books. I. Wong, Leonard. II. Army War College (U.S.) Strategic Studies Institute.
U22

Why this century will be a golden age for workers, the environment, and developing countries.
Riding the next wave. Indianapolis, Ind. : Hudson Institute ; [Washington, DC : Distributed by the Brookings Institution Press], c2001.
HM901 .R43 2001

Why we curse.
Jay, Timothy. Philadelphia : John Benjamins Publishing Company, c2000.
BF463.I58 J38 2000

Why we love.
Fisher, Helen E. 1st ed. New York : Henry Holt and Company, 2004.
BF575.L8 F53 2004

Whyte, William Hollingsworth. The organization man / William H. Whyte ; foreword by Joseph Nocera. Philadelphia : University of Pennsylvania Press, c2002, 1956. xvi, 429 p. : ill. ; 21 cm. (Sociology business) Originally published: New York : Simon & Schuster, 1956. With new foreword. Includes bibliographical references and index. ISBN 0-8122-1819-1 (alk. paper) DDC 302.3/5
1. Individuality. 2. Loyalty. I. Title.
BF697 .W47 2002

WICA. *See* **WITCHCRAFT.**

WICCA. *See also* **WITCHCRAFT.**
Cunningham, Scott, 1956- [Wicca. Spanish] 1. ed. St. Paul, Minn. : Llewellyn Español, 2003.
BF1566 .C8618 2003

Wicca and witchcraft.
Zimmermann, Denise. The complete idiot's guide to wicca and witchcraft. 2nd ed. Indianapolis, IN : Alpha, c2003.
BF1566 .Z55 2003

Wicca for couples.
Drew, A. J. Franklin Lakes, NJ : New Page Books, c2002.
BF1572.L6 D74 2002

The Wicca handbook.
Morgan, Sheena. London : Vega, 2003.
BF1566 .M716 2003

The Wicca herbal.
Wood, Jamie. Berkeley, Calif. : Celestial Arts, c2003.
BF1572.P43 W66 2003

Wicca spellcraft for men.
Drew, A. J. Franklin Lakes, N.J. : New Page Books, c2001.
BF1571.5.M45 D75 2001

A Wiccan Bible.
Drew, A. J. Franklin Lakes, N.J. : New Page Books, c2003.
BF1571 .D74 2003

Wiccan meditations.
Wildman, Laura A. New York : Citadel Press, c2002.
BF1571 .W55 2002

WICCANS. *See* **WITCHES.**

WICKEDNESS. *See* **GOOD AND EVIL.**

Wickham-Crowley, Kelley M. Writing the future : Lazamon's prophetic history / Kelley M. Wickham-Crowley. Cardiff : University of Wales Press, 2002. viii, 182 p. ; 23 cm. Bibliography: p. 163-174. - Inludes index. ISBN 0-7083-1714-6 DDC 821.1
1. Arthurian romances - History and criticism. 2. Prophecy in literature. 3. Literature and history - Great Britain - History - To 1500. 4. Britons in literature. 5. Kings and rulers in literature. I. Title.

Wider die Eindeutigkeit.
Engel, Antke. Frankfurt/Main ; New York : Campus, c2002.

Widerker, David, 1963-.
Moral responsibility and alternative possibilities. Aldershot, England ; Burlington, VT : Ashgate, c2003.
BJ1451 .M6472 2003

Widmer, Ellen.
Writing and materiality in China. Cambridge, Mass. : Published by Harvard University Asia Center for Harvard-Yenching Institute : distributed by Harvard University Press, 2003.
PL2262 .W74 2003

WIDOWS - BIOGRAPHY.
White, Sharon. Field notes. Center City, Minn. : Hazelden, 2002.
BF575.G7 W485 2002

Wie hätte ich mich verhalten?.
Reemtsma, Jan Philipp. München : Beck, c2001.
HM216 .R38 2001

Wie unnütz ist Descartes?.
Wohlers, Christian. Würzburg : Königshausen & Neumann, c2002.

Wiedebach, Hartwig.
Cohen, Hermann, 1842-1918. [Works. 1977. Supplementa] Werke. Supplementa. Hildesheim : G. Olms, 2000-

Wiegers, Gerard Albert, 1959-.
Modern societies & the science of religions. Leiden ; Boston : Brill, 2002.
BL48 .M542 2002

Wieland, Georg, 1937-.
Prudentia und Contemplatio. Paderborn : Ferdinand Schöningh, 2002.

Wiener Reihe (R. Oldenbourg Verlag)
(Bd. 11.) Freiheit, Gleichheit und Autonomie. Wien : Oldenbourg ; Berlin : Akademie Verlag, 2003.
JC575 .F74 2003

Wiener Staatsoper. Orchester.
Malaniuk, Ira. Arien und Lieder [sound recording]. [Germany] : Preiser Records, p2000.

Wiesel, Elie, 1928-.
Peace and conflict resolution. Part 1 [videorecording]. Derry, N.H. : Chip Taylor Communications, 1996.

WIESEL, ELIE, 1928- - INTERVIEWS.
Peace and conflict resolution. Part 1 [videorecording]. Derry, N.H. : Chip Taylor Communications, 1996.

Wiesen, Joel P. (Joel Peter) How to prepare for mechanical aptitude & spatial relations tests / Joel Wiesen. Hauppauge, NY : Barron's, 2003. p. cm. ISBN 0-7641-2340-8 DDC 153.9/46
1. Mechanical ability - Examinations, questions, etc. 2. Space perception (Psychology) - Examinations, questions, etc. I. Title. II. Title: Mechanical aptitude & spatial relations test
BF433.M4 W535 2003

WIFE ABUSE.
Mills, Linda G. Insult to injury. Princeton, N.J. : Princeton University Press, c2003.
HV6626 .M55 2003

Wifework.
Maushart, Susan, 1958- 1st U.S. ed. New York : Bloomsbury : Distributed to the trade by Holtzbrinck Publishers, 2002.
HQ759 .M3944 2002

Wigand, Molly. Help is here for facing fear / written by Molly Wigand ; illustrated by R.W. Alley. St. Meinrad, IN : One Caring Place/Abbey Press, c2000.
1 v. (unpaged) : col. ill. ; 21 cm. (Elf-help books for kids) ISBN 0-87029-344-3 (pbk. : alk. paper)
1. Fear in children - Juvenile literature. I. Alley, R. W. (Robert W.) II. Title. III. Series.
BF723.F4 W54 2000

Wiggins, Jerry S. Paradigms of personality assessment / by Jerry S. Wiggins. New York : Guilford Press, 2003. p. cm. Includes bibliographical references and index. ISBN 1-57230-913-X DDC 155.2/8
1. Personality assessment. I. Title.
BF698.4 .W525 2003

WILBER, KEN.
Visser, Frank, 1958- [Ken Wilber. English] Ken Wilber. Albany, NY : State University of New York Press, c2003.
BF109.W54 V5713 2003

Vrinte, Joseph, 1949- The perennial quest for a psychology with a soul. 1st ed. Delhi : Motilal Banarsidass Publishers, 2002.
BF311+

Wilcock, David, 1973-.
Free, Wynn, 1946- The reincarnation of Edgar Cayce? Berkeley, Calif. : Frog, 2004.
BF1815.W49 F74 2004

Free, Wynn, 1946- The reincarnation of Edgar Cayce? Berkeley, Calif. : Frog, 2004.
BF1815.W49 F74 2004

WILCOCK, DAVID, 1973- -PRE-EXISTENCE.
Free, Wynn, 1946- The reincarnation of Edgar Cayce? Berkeley, Calif. : Frog, 2004.
BF1815.W49 F74 2004

Wilde, Liz. Unlock your potential : coach yourself to a life you love, and discover the secrets of success in career and relationships / Liz Wilde. New York : Ryland Peters & Small, 2004. p. cm. ISBN 1-84172-592-7 DDC 158.1
1. Self-actualization (Psychology) 2. Success - Psychological aspects. 3. Self-help techniques. 4. Self-talk. I. Title.
BF637.S4 W488 2004

WILDE, OSCAR, 1854-1900.
PORTRAIT OF MR W.H.
Halpern, Richard, 1954- Shakespeare's perfume. Philadelphia : University of Pennsylvania Press, c2002.
PR2848 .H25 2002

Wilderstein and the Suckleys.
Philip, Cynthia Owen. Rhinebeck, N.Y. : Wilderstein Preservation, 2001.
F129.W747 P48 2001

WILDERSTEIN (N.Y.).
Philip, Cynthia Owen. Wilderstein and the Suckleys. Rhinebeck, N.Y. : Wilderstein Preservation, 2001.
F129.W747 P48 2001

Wilderstein Preservation.
Philip, Cynthia Owen. Wilderstein and the Suckleys. Rhinebeck, N.Y. : Wilderstein Preservation, 2001.
F129.W747 P48 2001

Wildfang, Robin Lorsch.
Divination and portents in the Roman world. Odense : Odense University Press, c2000.
BF1768 .D57 2000

WILDLIFE. See **ANIMALS.**

WILDLIFE-RELATED RECREATION. See **FISHING; HUNTING.**

Wildman, Laura A. What's your Wicca IQ? / Laura A. Wildman. New York : Citadel Press, c2002. xvi, 279 p. ; 21 cm. Includes bibliographical references (p. 277-278). ISBN 0-8065-2347-6 (pbk.) DDC 133.4/3/076
1. Witchcraft. I. Title.
BF1566 .W63 2002

Wiccan meditations : the witch's way to personal transformation / Laura A. Wildman. New York : Citadel Press, c2002. ix, 302 p. ; 21 cm. Includes bibliographical references. ISBN 0-8065-2346-8 (pbk.) DDC 299/.94
1. Witchcraft. 2. Meditations. I. Title.
BF1571 .W55 2002

Wiley self-teaching guides.
Turkington, Carol. Memory. Hoboken, N.J. : J. Wiley and Sons, c2003.
BF385 .T88 2003

Wiley series in nonlinear science
Coping with chaos. New York : J. Wiley, c1994.
Q172.5.C45 C67 1994

Wilhelm, E. (Ernst) Vault of the heavens : treatise on Vedic astrology / by Ernst Wilhelm. 1st ed. [S.l.] : Kāla Occult Publishers, 2001. xii, 369 p. : ill. ; 23 cm. Includes index. ISBN 0-9709636-0-2
1. Hindu astrology. I. Title.
BF1714.H5 W55 2001

Wilhelm Reich.
Corrington, Robert S., 1950- 1st ed. New York : Farrar, Straus and Giroux, 2003.
BF109.R38 C67 2003

Wilkens, Sander. Die Konvertibilität des Bewusstseins / Sander W. Wilkens. 1. Aufl. Würzburg ; Boston : Deutscher Wissenschafts-Verlag (DWV), c2002. 299 p. : ill. ; 21 cm. Includes bibliographical references (p. 281-292) and index. ISBN 3-935176-17-1
1. Knowledge, Theory of. 2. Consciousness. 3. Philosophy of mind. I. Title.
BD163 .E45 2002

Wilkins, Burleigh Taylor.
Essays in honor of Burleigh Wilkins. New York : Peter Lang, c2001.
JA71 .E694 2001

WILKINS, BURLEIGH TAYLOR.
Essays in honor of Burleigh Wilkins. New York : Peter Lang, c2001.
JA71 .E694 2001

Wilkins, David, 1944- United by tragedy / David Wilkins with Cecil Murphey. Nampa, Idaho : Pacific Press Pub. Association, c2003. 171 p. : ill. ; 23 cm. Includes bibliographical references. ISBN 0-8163-1980-4 DDC 248.8/66/092
1. Grief. 2. Bereavement - Psychological aspects. 3. Teenagers - Death - Psychological aspects. 4. Aircraft accident victims' families - Psychology. I. Murphey, Cecil B. II. Title.
BF575.G7 W555 2003

Wilkins, George H. (George Hubert), Sir, 1888-1958. Thoughts through space : a remarkable adventure in the realm of mind / Sir Hubert Wilkins and Harold M. Sherman. Charlottesville, VA : Hampton Roads Pub. Co., 2004. p. cm. (Studies in consciousness) Originally published: Hollywood : House-Warven, 1951. With new introd. ISBN 1-57174-314-6 (6x9 TP : alk. paper) DDC 133.8/2

1. Telepathy. 2. Arctic regions. I. Sherman, Harold Morrow, 1898- II. Title. III. Series.
BF1171 .W49 2004

Wilkinson, Deanna Lyn, 1968- Guns, violence, and identity among African American and Latino youth / Deanna L. Wilkinson. New York : LFB Scholarly Pub., 2003. x, 299 p. ; 23 cm. (Criminal justice) Includes bibliographical references (p. 287-296) and index. ISBN 1-59332-009-4 (alk. paper) DDC 303.6/0835/097471
1. Youth and violence - New York - New York. 2. Youth with social disabilities - New York - New York - Psychology. 3. African American young men - New York - New York - Social conditions. 4. Hispanic American young men - New York - New York - Social conditions. 5. Violence in adolescence. 6. Neighborhood - Social aspects. 7. Identity (Psychology) in youth. 8. Firearms - Social aspects. I. Title. II. Series: Criminal justice (LFB Scholarly Publishing LLC)
HQ799.2.V56 W55 2003

Wilkinson, Richard H. The complete gods and goddesses of ancient Egypt / Richard H. Wilkinson. New York : Thames & Hudson, 2003. 256 p. : ill. (some col.), map ; 27 cm. Includes bibliographical references (p. 244-248) and index. CONTENTS: Rise and fall of the gods -- Nature of the gods -- Worship of the gods -- Kingship and the gods -- The catalogue of deities. ISBN 0-500-05120-8
1. Gods, Egyptian. 2. Goddesses, Egyptian. 3. Mythology, Egyptian. 4. Egypt - Religion. I. Title.

Wilkoszewska, Krystyna.
Estetyka czterech żywiołów. Kraków : Universitas, c2002.

Wilks, Peter, ill.
Leaney, Cindy. Long walk to school. Vero Beach, Fla. : Rourke Pub., 2003.
BF637.B85 L43 2003

WILL. See also **BRAINWASHING; CHARACTER TESTS; SELF.**
Enç, Berent. How we act. Oxford : Clarendon Press ; New York : Oxford University Press, 2003.
B105.A35 E63 2003

WILL - HISTORY - 20TH CENTURY.
Ivannikov, V. A. (Viacheslav Andreevich) Psikhologicheskie mekhanizmy volevoĭ reguliatsii. [2. izd.]. Moskva : Izd-vo URAO, 1998.
BF616 .I93 1998

WILL-TEMPERAMENT TESTS. See **CHARACTER TESTS.**

Will you dance?.
Childs-Oroz, Annette. Incline Village, NV : Wandering Feather Press, c2002.
BF637.L53 C45 2002

Willaschek, Marcus. Der mentale Zugang zur Welt : Realismus, Skeptizismus und Intentionalität / Marcus Willaschek. Frankfurt am Main : Klostermann, 2003. xi, 321 p. ; 24 cm. (Philosophische Abhandlungen ; Bd. 87) Originally presented as the author's thesis (doctoral)-- Westfälische Wilhelms-Universität, Münster, 1999/2000. Includes bibliographical references (p.[295]-309) and index. ISBN 3-465-03247-0 (pbk).
1. Realism. 2. Philosophy. 3. Common sense. I. Title. II. Series.
B835 .W55 2003

Der Wille zum Recht und das Streben nach Glück.
Hossenfelder, Malte. Originalausg. München : C.H. Beck, c2000.

Williams, Andrew N. How do you compare? : 12 simple tests to discover hidden truths about your personality and fascinating facts about everyone else! / by Andrew N. Williams. 1st Perigee ed. New York : Perigee Book, 2004. p. cm. Includes bibliographical references and index. ISBN 0-399-52951-9 DDC 155.2/8
1. Personality tests. 2. Self-evaluation. I. Title.
BF698.5 .W55 2004

Williams, Bernard Arthur Owen.
Raz, Joseph. The practice of value. Oxford ; New York : Oxford University Press, 2003.
BD232 .R255 2003

Williams, Brian J.
Santner, Thomas J., 1947- The design and analysis of computer experiments. New York : Springer, 2003.
QA279 .S235 2003

Williams, Carolyn L., 1951-.
Sherwood, Nancy E. The MMPI-A content component scales. Minneapolis : University of Minnesota Press, c1997.
BF698.8.M5 S54 1997

Williams, Jaime Andrés. El argumento de la apuesta de Blaise Pascal / Jaime Andrés Williams. 1. ed. Pamplona : Ediciones Universidad de Navarra, 2002. 361 p. ; 24 cm. (Colección Filosófica ; 173) Includes bibliographical references (p. 349-346). ISBN 84-313-2004-4

1. Pascal, Blaise, - 1623-1662. - Pensées. 2. God - Proof - History of doctrines - 17th century. 3. Philosophical theology - Methodology. 4. Risk-taking (Psychology) - Religious aspects - Christianity. 5. Faith. I. Title. II. Series: Colección filosófica (Universidad de Navarra. Facultad de Filosofía y Letras) ; 173.

Williams, Malcolm, 1953- Making sense of social research / Malcolm Williams. London : SAGE, c2003. 222 p. : ill. ; 25 cm. Includes bibliographical references and index. ISBN 0-7619-6421-5 ISBN 0-7619-6422-3 (pbk.) DDC 300.72
1. Social sciences - Research - Methodology. I. Title.

Williams-Nickelson, Carol.
Internships in psychology. Washington, D.C. : American Psychological Association, c2004.
BF77 .I67 2004

Williams, Oliver F.
Business, religion, & spirituality. Notre Dame, Ind. : University of Notre Dame Press, c2003.
HF5388 .B87 2003

Williams, Redford B., 1940- The type E personality : 10 steps to emotional excellence in love, work, and life / Redford Williams and Virginia Williams. Emmaus, Pa. : Rodale, c2004. p. cm. Includes bibliographical references and index. Table of contents URL: http://www.loc.gov/catdir/toc/ecip048/2003018860.html CONTENTS: Live longer and laugh more as a type E -- The scientific perspective : becoming type E keeps you healthier and could save your life -- Are you type E? : the type E quiz -- Becoming type E -- Step 1 : don't stuff it -- Step 2 : bring in the jury -- Step 3 : get over it -- Step 4 : deal with it -- Step 5 : go for it -- Step 6 : stay in balance -- Step 7 : get heard -- Step 8 : be really here -- Step 9 : read others -- Step 10 : get the happiness habit. ISBN 1-57954-675-7 (hardcover) DDC 158
1. Emotional intelligence. 2. Personality and emotions. 3. Success - Psychological aspects. I. Williams, Virginia Parrott, 1940- II. Title.
BF576.3 .W55 2004

Williams, Robert Chadwell, 1938- The historian's toolbox : a student's guide to the theory and craft of history / Robert C. Williams. Armonk, N.Y. : M.E. Sharpe, c2003. xv, 170 p. : ill. ; 24 cm. Includes bibliographical references (p. 163-166) and index. ISBN 0-7656-1092-2 (alk. paper) DDC 907/.2
1. History - Methodology. 2. History - Study and teaching. 3. Historiography. 4. History - Research. I. Title.
D16 .W62 2003

Williams, Thomas, 1967-.
Anselm, Saint, Archbishop of Canterbury, 1033-1109. [Dialogues. English. Selections] Three philosophical dialogues. Indianapolis, IN : Hackett Pub., c2002.
B765.A81 .A2513 2002

Williams, Virginia Parrott, 1940-.
Williams, Redford B., 1940- The type E personality. Emmaus, Pa. : Rodale, c2004.
BF576.3 .W55 2004

Williamson, James C. Roadways to success / James C. Williamson, Debra A. McCandrew, Charles T. Muse. 3rd ed. Upper Saddle River, NJ : Pearson/ Prentice Hall, 2004. xvi, 319 p. : ill. ; 28 cm. Includes bibliographical references (p. 314) and index. ISBN 0-13-111343-7 DDC 378.1/70281
1. Success - Psychological aspects. I. McCandrew, Debra A. II. Muse, Charles T. III. Title.
BF637.S8 W5216 2004

Willingham, Daniel T. Cognition : the thinking animal / Daniel T. Willingham. 2nd ed. Upper Saddle River, NJ : Pearson/Prentice Hall, c2004. xvii, 613 p. : ill. ; 25 cm. Includes bibliographical references (p. 557-588) and indexes. ISBN 0-13-182447-3 DDC 153
1. Cognitive psychology. I. Title.
BF201 .W56 2004

Willingham, Lee.
Creativity and music education. Edmonton, Canada : Canadian Music Educators' Association, c2002.

Williston, Byron, 1965-.
Passion and virtue in Descartes. Amherst, N.Y. : Humanity Books, 2003.
B1868.P37 P37 2003

Willoughby, Leonard. Every day Tao : self-help in the here & now / Leonard Willoughby. Boston, MA : Weiser Books, 2001. xix, 268 p. : ill. ; 18 cm. Includes bibliographical references (p. [267]-268). ISBN 1-57863-217-X (pbk. : alk. paper) DDC 299/.51444
1. Taoism. I. Title.
BL1920 .W55 2001

Wills-Brandon, Carla, 1956- A glimpse of heaven / Carla Wills-Brandon. Avon, MA : Adams Media Corp., c2003. p. cm. Includes bibliographical references

(p.   ). ISBN 1-58062-947-4 DDC 133.9
1. Parapsychology. 2. Spiritual life - Miscellanea. I. Title.

WILLS, ETHICAL.
Naphtali ben Isaac, ha-Kohen, 1649-1719. Sefer Bet Rahel. Yerushalayim : Ahavat Shalom, 761 [2001]
BM665 .N257 2001

Wilson, Bryan R.
New religious movements. London ; New York : Routledge in association with the Institute of Oriental Philosophy European Centre, 1999.
BL80.2 .N397 1999

Wilson, Colin, 1931-.
The occult Webb. Toronto : Colombo & Co., c1999.
BF1408.2.W42 O33 1999

Wilson, Don E.
Animal. 1st American ed. New York : DK ; [Washington, D.C.] : Smithsonian Institution, 2001.

Wilson, Edmund, 1895-1972. To the Finland station : a study in the writing and acting of history / Edmund Wilson ; foreword by Louis Menand. New York : New York Review Books, 2003. xxxi, 507 p. ; 21 cm. (New York Review Books classics) Includes index. CONTENTS: Introduction. Michelet discovers Vico -- Michelet and the Middle Ages -- Michelet and the revolution -- Michelet tries to live his history -- Michelet between nationalism and socialism -- Decline of the revolutionary tradition : Renan -- Decline of the revolutionary tradition : Taine -- Decline of the revolutionary tradition : Anatole France -- Origins of socialism : Babeuf's defense -- Origins of socialism : Saint-Simon's hierarchy -- Origins of socialism : the communities of Fourier and Owen -- Origins of socialism : Enfantin and the American socialists -- Karl Marx : Prometheus and Lucifer -- Karl Marx decides to change the world -- Friedrich Engels : the young man from Manchester -- The partnership of Marx and Engels -- Marx and Engels : grinding the lens -- Marx and Engels take a hand at making history -- The myth of the dialectic -- Marx and Engels go back to writing history -- Historical actors : Lassalle -- Historical actors : Bakunin -- Karl Marx : poet of commodities and dictator of the proletariat -- Karl Marx dies at his desk -- Lenin : the brothers Ulynov -- Lenin : the great headmaster -- Trotsky : the young eagle -- Trotsky identifies history with himself with Lenin -- Lenin identifies himself with history -- Lenin at the Finland station. ISBN 1-59017-033-4 DDC 335.4
1. Socialism - History. 2. Communism - History. 3. History - Philosophy. I. Title. II. Series.
HX36 .W5 2003

Wilson, H. James.
Davenport, Thomas H. What's the big idea? Boston, Mass. : Harvard Business School Press, c2003.
HD53 .D38 2003

Wilson, Ian, 1941- Nostradamus : the man behind the prophecies / Ian Wilson. 1st U.S. ed. New York : St. Martin's Press, 2003. p. cm. Includes bibliographical references and index. ISBN 0-312-31790-5 DDC 133.3/092
1. Nostradamus, - 1503-1566. 2. Prophets - France - Biography. 3. Prophecies (Occultism) I. Title.
BF1815.N8 W56 2003

Wilson, Josephine F.
Sternberg, Robert J. Psychology. 4th ed. Belmont, CA : Thomson/Wadsworth, c2004.
BF121 .S84 2004

Wilson, Norman J.
The European Renaissance and Reformation, 1350-1600. Detroit, MI : Gale Group, 2001.
CB359 .W67 2001

WIMMIN. See **WOMEN.**

WINCKELMANN, JOHANN JUST, 1620-1699.
Strasser, Gerhard F. Emblematik und Mnemonik der frühen Neuzeit im Zusammenspiel Johannes Buno und Johann Justus Winckelmann. Wiesbaden : Harrassowitz Wolfenbüttel : Herzog August Bibliothek, c2000.
PN6348.5 .S873 2000

Wind, Edgar, 1900- Das Experiment und die Metaphysik : zur Auflösung der kosmologischen Antinomien / Edgar Wind ; herausgegeben und mit einem Nachwort versehen von Bernhard Buschendorf ; eingeleitet von Brigitte Falkenburg. 1. Aufl. Frankfurt am Main : Suhrkamp, 2001. 344, [1] p. : ill. ; 18 cm. (Suhrkamp Taschenbuch Wissenschaft ; 1478) Includes bibliographical references (p. 327-[345]). ISBN 3-518-29078-9
1. Metaphysics. 2. Antinomy. 3. Cosmology. I. Buschendorf, Bernhard. II. Falkenburg, Brigitte, 1953- III. Title. IV. Series.

Windeatt, Terry.
International Workshop on Multiple Classifier Systems (4th : 2003 : Guildford, England) Multiple classifier systems. Berlin ; New York : Springer, c2003.
Q325.5 .I574 2003

Windling, Terri.
Froud, Brian. Good faeries/bad faeries. London : Pavilion, 2000.

Wingate, Ealan.
Kiefer, Anselm, 1945- Merkaba. New York : Gagosian Gallery, c2002.
N6888.K43 A4 2002

Winger, Stewart Lance. Lincoln, religion, and romantic cultural politics / Stewart Winger. DeKalb : Northern Illinois University Press, c2003. viii, 271 p. ; 24 cm. Includes bibliographical references and index. ISBN 0-87580-300-8 (alk. paper) DDC 973.7/092
1. Lincoln, Abraham, - 1809-1865 - Views on religion. 2. Lincoln, Abraham, - 1809-1865 - Political and social views. 3. Lincoln, Abraham, - 1809-1865 - Oratory. 4. United States - Politics and government - 1861-1865. 5. Political culture - United States - History - 19th century. 6. Romanticism - Political aspects - United States - History - 19th century. 7. Religion and politics - United States - History - 19th century. 8. National characteristics, American. I. Title.
E457.2 .W77 2003

Wingert, Lutz, 1958-.
Die Öffentlichkeit der Vernunft und die Vernunft der Öffentlichkeit. 1. Aufl. Frankfurt am Main : Suhrkamp, 2001.
B3258.H324 O34 2001

Wingerter, J. Richard. Teaching, learning, and the meditative mind / J. Richard Wingerter. Lanham, Md. ; Oxford : University Press of America, c2003. x, 124 p. ; 23 cm. Includes bibliographical references (p. [113]-122) and index. ISBN 0-7618-2548-7 (hbk. : alk. paper) ISBN 0-7618-2549-5 (pbk. : alk. paper) DDC 370/.1
1. Education - Philosophy. 2. Thought and thinking. 3. Meditation. I. Title.
LB1025.3 .W55 2003

WINKY (FICTITIOUS CHARACTER) - FICTION.
Marshall, Evan, 1956- Icing Ivy. Waterville, Me. : Thorndike Press, 2003, c2002.
PS3563.A72236 I27 2003

WINNICOTT, D. W. (DONALD WOODS), 1896-1971.
The elusive child. London ; New York : Karnac, c2002.

Winnicott studies monograph series
The elusive child. London ; New York : Karnac, c2002.

WINNIE-THE-POOH (FICTITIOUS CHARACTER).
Winnie-the-Pooh's little book of feng shui. London : Methuen Children's, 1999.

Winnie-the-Pooh's little book of feng shui / inspired by A.A. Milne ; illustrated by E.H. Shepard. London : Methuen Children's, 1999. 96 p. : ill. ; 11 cm. ISBN 0-416-19650-0 DDC 133.3337
1. Feng shui. 2. Feng shui - Humor. 3. Winnie-the-Pooh (Fictitious character) I. Milne, A. A. (Alan Alexander), 1882-1956. II. Shepard, Ernest H. (Ernest Howard), 1879-1976. III. Title: Little book of feng shui IV. Title: Feng shui

WINNIE-THER-POOH (FICTITIOUS CHARACTER). See **WINNIE-THE-POOH (FICTITIOUS CHARACTER).**

Winning behavior.
Bacon, Terry R. New York : AMACOM, c2003.
HD58.7 .B3423 2003

Winning is contagious.
Skiffington, Jeannie. 1st ed. East Amherst, N.Y. : Winning Track Press, c2002.
BF637.S8 S548 2002

Winning smart after losing big.
Stearns, Rob, 1952- 1st ed. San Francisco, CA : Encounter Books, 2003.
BF575.D35 S74 2003

Winslade, John.
Hedtke, Lorraine, 1957- Re-membering lives. Amityville, N.Y. : Baywood Pub. Co., 2004.
BF789.D4 H4 2004

Winston, Andrew S.
Defining difference. 1st ed. Washington, DC : American Psychological Association, c2004.
BF76.45 .D44 2004

Winter, Graham. High performance leadership : creating, leading and living in a high performance world / Graham Winter. Singapore ; New York : John Wiley & Sons (Asia), c2003. xvi, 407 p. : ill. ; 24 cm.
Includes index. ISBN 0-470-82081-0
1. Leadership. 2. Executive ability. I. Title.

Winter, Jean, 1909-1939 (Spirit) Dites-leur que la mort n'existe pas : messages de l'au-delà / par Jean Winter et Gérald de Dampierre ; présentés et commentés par François Brune. Chambéry : Exergue, c1997, [1998] 379 p. ; 24 cm. (Collection Deux mondes, 1271-8998) Includes bibliographical references. ISBN 2-911525-18-3
1. Spirit writings. I. Dampierre, Gérald de (Spirit) II. Brune, François III. Title. IV. Series.
BF1290 .W56 1997

Winter, Richard, 1945- Still bored in a culture of entertainment : rediscovering passion and wonder / Richard Winter. Downers Grove, Ill. : InterVarsity Press, c2002. 160 p. ; 21 cm. Includes bibliographical references (p. [143]-156) and indexes. CONTENTS: Three yawns for boredom! -- Basics of boredom : understimulation, repetition and disconnection -- Two types of boredom : the long and the short of it -- Entertained to excess : leisure, overstimulation and the entertainment industry -- Advertised to apathy : the stimulation and disappointment of desire -- Why some people are more likely to get bored : perception, personality and proneness -- Negated to numbness : anxiety, disappointment and emotional shutdown -- A trip back in time : medieval boredom, melancholy and grief -- From sin to self-fulfillment : religion, the right to happiness and lack of inner resources -- Haunted by hopelessness : postmodernism, indifference and the loss of meaning -- The bitter fruits of boredom : sexual addiction, aggression and risk taking -- Counteracting boredom : six easy steps to an exciting, never-bored-again life! -- Not so easy, not so fast : some foundational themes of life -- Why get up in the morning? : boredom and the battle. ISBN 0-8308-2308-5 (pbk. : alk. paper) DDC 241/.3
1. Boredom - Religious aspects - Christianity. 2. Christian life. I. Title.
BV4599.5.B67 W56 2002

Wir in unserer Welt
Das Rätsel von Leib und Seele. Herne : Heitkamp, c1997.
BF163 .R28 1997

Wired for conflict.
VanSant, Sondra. Gainesville, Fla. : Center for Applications of Psychological Type, c2003.
BF698.3 .V36 2003

Wirklichkeit und Wahrnehmung in der Frühen Neuzeit
(Bd. 1) Wahrheit, Wissen, Erinnerung. Münster : Lit, [2002]

Wirz, Heinz.
Šik, Miroslav. Altneue Gedanken. Luzern : Quart, c2002.

WISC (INTELLIGENCE TEST). See **WECHSLER INTELLIGENCE SCALE FOR CHILDREN.**

WISDOM.
Maritain, Jacques, 1882-1973. [Degrés du savoir. English] Distinguish to unite, or, The degrees of knowledge. Notre Dame, Ind. : University of Notre Dame Press, 1998, c1995.
BD162 .M273 1998

Sternberg, Robert J. Wisdom, intelligence, and creativity synthesized. Cambridge, UK ; New York : Cambridge University Press, 2003.
BF431 .S7385 2003

Wisdom in the cards.
Samul, A. L. 1st ed. Stamford, CT : U.S. Games Systems, c2002.
BF1879.T2 S26 2002

Wisdom, intelligence, and creativity synthesized.
Sternberg, Robert J. Cambridge, UK ; New York : Cambridge University Press, 2003.
BF431 .S7385 2003

The wisdom of listening / edited by Mark Brady. Somerville, MA : Wisdom Publications, c2003. p. cm. CONTENTS: Listening with presence, awareness, and love / Christine Longaker -- Listening through the holes / A.H. Almaas -- Feeding one another / Anne and Charles Simpkinson -- The healing power of being deeply heard / Margaret Truxaw Hopkins -- American willing to listen / Fran Peavey -- On therapeutic attention / Kathleen Riordan Speeth -- The listening mind / Ram Dass and Paul Gorman -- The craft of council / Joan Halifax -- The rules of the listening game / Michael P. Nichols -- Listening through the body / Nancy Mangano Rowe -- Strategic questions are tools for rebellion / Fran Peavey -- The gift of attention / Kathleen Dowling Singh -- Being a good listener / Karen Kissel Wegela -- Liberating ourselves through nonviolent communication / Marshall Rosenberg -- Finding a new way to listen / Toni Packer -- Listening to the land / Michael S. Hutton -- Listening from the heart / Rodney Smith -- Fierce listening / Cheri Huber -- What I've learned from listening / Mark Brady. ISBN

The wisdom of strategic learning

0-86171-355-9 (pbk. : alk. paper) DDC 153.6/8
1. Listening. I. Brady, Mark, 1946-
BF323.L5 W57 2003

The wisdom of strategic learning.
Cunningham, Ian, 1943- London ; New York : McGraw-Hill, c1994.
HD58.8 .C857 1994

The wisdom of tenderness.
Manning, Brennan. 1st ed. New York : HarperCollins, c2002.
BV4520 .M36 2002

Wisdom of the Maya.
Bonewitz, Ra. 1st St. Martin's ed. New York : St. Martin's Press, 2000.
BF1878 .B66 2000

WISDOM - RELIGIOUS ASPECTS - BUDDHISM.
See **VIPAŚYANĀ (BUDDHISM).**

Wisdom, Stephen. Gladiators 100 BC-AD 200 / Stephen Wisdom ; illustrated by Angus McBride ; [editor, Nikolai Bogdanovic] Oxford : Osprey, 2001 (2002 printing) 64 p. : ill. (some col.) ; 25 cm. (Warrior ; 39) Includes index. ISBN 1-84176-299-7
1. Gladiators - Rome. 2. Games - Rome. 3. Rome - Civilization. I. Bogdanovic, Nikolai. II. McBride, Angus. III. Title. IV. Series: Warrior series ; 39.

The wisdom within.
Shooter, Jonathan. Southfield, MI : Targum Press ; Nanuet, NY : Distributed by Feldheim Publishers, 2002.

Wisdom's blossoms.
Glener, Doug. Boston, Mass. : Shambhala, 2002.
BL2003 .G64 2002

Wisdom's Goldenrod, Ltd.
Damiani, Anthony, 1922-1984. Astronoesis. Burdett, N.Y. : Published for Wisdom's Goldenrod, Ltd. by Larson Publications, c2000.
BD418.3 .D347 2000

Wiseman, Carol. A patchwork of comforts / Carol Wiseman. Boston, MA : Conari Press, 2004. p. cm. ISBN 1-57324-904-1 DDC 646.7
1. Pleasure. 2. Stress management. I. Title.
BF515 .W57 2004

Wiseman, Rosalind, 1969- Queen bees & wannabes : helping your daughter survive cliques, gossip, boyfriends, and other realities of adolescence / Rosalind Wiseman. 1st ed. New York : Crown Publishers, c2002. ix, 336 p. ; 25 cm. Includes bibliographical references (p. [319]-327) and index. CONTENTS: 1. Cliques and popularity -- 2. Passport from planet parent to girl world : communication and reconnaissance -- 3. The beauty pageant : who wants to be Miss Congeniality -- 4. Nasty girls : teasing, gossip, and reputations -- 5. Power plays : group dynamics and rites of passage -- 6. Boy world : the judges and the judged -- 7. Girls meets boy : crushes, matchmaking, and the birth of fruit cup girl -- 8. Pleasing boys, betraying girls : when relationships get more serious -- 9. Parties : sex, drugs, and rock 'n' roll -- 10. Getting help. ISBN 0-609-60945-9 (hardcover) DDC 649/.125
1. Teenage girls. 2. Teenage girls - Psychology. 3. Parent and teenager. I. Title. II. Title: Queen bees and wannabes.
HQ798 .W544 2002

Wisenberg, S. L. (Sandi L.) Holocaust girls : history, memory & other obsessions / S.L. Wisenberg. Lincoln : University of Nebraska Press, c2002. xii, 139 p., [8] p. of plates : ill. ; 24 cm. Includes bibliographical references (p. [137]-139). CONTENTS: Holocaust girls/ lemon -- Shema, the first prayer you learn -- Kavka/40 -- Holocaust girls/closet -- Flying -- The language of Heimatlos -- Plain scared, or: there is no such thing as negative space, the art teacher said -- Chicago: loss of property -- At the Rose of Sharon Spiritual Church -- Mexico on $15 a day -- Vacation at Club Dead -- Yizkor (memorial service) -- The children of Theresienstadt -- Afterwards -- Getting to Yiddish -- Monica and Hannah -- Margot's diary -- Eating horse -- The ones you break bread with -- In the mother tongue -- Amalek -- Juggling: the new year. ISBN 0-8032-4801-6 (cl. : alk. paper) DDC 940.53/18
1. Wisenberg, S. L. - (Sandi L.) - Anecdotes. 2. Jews - Psychology. 3. Jews - Identity. 4. Holocaust, Jewish (1939-1945) - Influence. 5. Memory - Social aspects. I. Title.
DS143 .W645 2002

WISENBERG, S. L. (SANDI L.) - ANECDOTES.
Wisenberg, S. L. (Sandi L.) Holocaust girls. Lincoln : University of Nebraska Press, c2002.
DS143 .W645 2002

A wish can change your life.
Sasson, Gahl. New York : Simon & Schuster, 2003.
BF1623.C2 S27 2003

Wish it, dream it, do it.
Levine, Leslie. New York : Simon & Schuster, c2004.
BF637.S8 L449 2004

Wishart, Catherine, 1965- Teen goddess : how to look, love & live like a goddess / Catherine Wishart. 1st ed. St. Paul, Minn. : Llewellyn Publications, c2003. xiii, 392 p. ; 24 cm. Includes bibliographical references (p. 385-387) and index. ISBN 0-7387-0392-3 (pbk.) DDC 299
1. Magic. 2. Goddesses - Miscellanea. 3. Teenage girls - Miscellanea. 4. Beauty, Personal - Miscellanea. 5. Goddess religion. 6. Teenage girls - Religious life. I. Title.
BF1623.G63 W57 2003

Wissen Macht Geschlecht : Philosophie und die Zukunft der "condition féminine" = Knowledge power gender : philosophy and the future of the "condition féminine" / Birgit Christensen ... [et al.] (Hg.). Zürich : Chronos, c2002. 862 p. : ill. ; 24 cm. "IX. symposium of the International Association of Women Philosophers IAPh"--P. facing t.p. Includes bibliographical references. 51 English, 46 German, 2 French contributions. ISBN 3-03-400525-3 (hd.bd.)
1. Women - Social conditions - Congresses. 2. Women's rights - Congresses. 3. Sex role - Congresses. 4. Feminism - Congresses. 5. Feminist theory - Congresses. 6. Feminist ethics - Congresses. I. Christensen, Birgit, 1960- II. Internationale Assoziation von Philosophinnen. Symposion (9th : 2000 : Zurich, Switzerland) III. Title: Knowledge power gender : philosophy and the future of the "condition féminine"

Das Wissen vom Guten.
Ackeren, Marcel van. Amsterdam ; Philadelphia : B.R. Gruner, c2003.
B398.V57 A33 2003

Wissenschaftliche Beiträge aus Forschung, Lehre und Praxis zur Rehabilitation behinderter Kinder und Jugendlicher
(42) Grundlagen und Modelle für den Hörgerichteten Spracherwerb. Villingen-Schwenningen : Neckar, c1995.

Wissenschaftliche Paperbacks
(Bd. 2.) Gadamer, Hans Georg, 1900- Die Lektion des Jahrhunderts. Münster : Lit, [2002]

Wissenschaftliche Paperbacks. Philosophie.
Gadamer, Hans Georg, 1900- Die Lektion des Jahrhunderts. Münster : Lit, [2002]

Wissensliteratur im Mittelalter
(Bd. 40) Ikas, Wolfgang-Valentin. Martin von Troppau (Martinus Polonus), O.P. (1278) in England. Wiesbaden : Reichert, 2002.

WIT AND HUMOR. *See* **ANECDOTES; COMIC, THE; LAUGHTER.**

WIT AND HUMOR - HISTORY AND CRITICISM.
Oring, Elliott, 1945- Engaging humor. Urbana : University of Illinois Press, c2003.
PN6147 .O74 2003

WIT AND HUMOR, PRIMITIVE. *See* **WIT AND HUMOR.**

WIT AND HUMOR - PSYCHOLOGICAL ASPECTS.
Haviland, James J. This book is no joke!. [Philadelphia?] : Xlibris, c2001.
BF637.C45 H38 2001

Klein, Allen. The healing power of humor. Waterville, Me. : Thorndike Press, 2003.
BF575.L3 K56 2003

McGhee, Paul E. Health, healing and the amuse system. 3rd ed. Dubuque, Iowa : Kendall/Hunt Pub., c1999.
BF575.L3 M38 1999

WIT AND HUMOR - PSYCHOLOGY.
McGhee, Paul E. Health, healing and the amuse system. 3rd ed. Dubuque, Iowa : Kendall/Hunt Pub., c1999.
BF575.L3 M38 1999

WIT AND HUMOR - SOCIAL ASPECTS.
McGhee, Paul E. Health, healing and the amuse system. 3rd ed. Dubuque, Iowa : Kendall/Hunt Pub., c1999.
BF575.L3 M38 1999

Witch hunts in Europe and America.
Burns, William E., 1959- Westport, Conn. : Greenwood Press, 2003.
BF1584.E9 B87 2003

A witch like me.
Knight, Sirona, 1955- Franklin Lakes, NJ : New Page Books, c2002.
BF1408 .K55 2002

WITCHCRAFT. *See also* **AMULETS; CHARMS; GODDESS RELIGION; ORDEAL; TRIALS (WITCHCRAFT).**
De Angeles, Ly, 1951- 1st ed. St. Paul, Minn. : Llewellyn Publications, 2000 (2003 printing)
BF1566 .D38 2000

Streeter, Michael. Hauppauge, N.Y. : Barron's, c2002.
BF1566 .S79 2002

WITCHCRAFT.
Aoumiel. Grimoire for the green witch. 1st ed. St. Paul, Minn. : Llewellyn Publications, c2003.
BF1572.P43 A583 2003

Aoumiel. Tarot for the green witch. 1st ed,. St. Paul, Minn. : Llewellyn Publications, 2003.
BF1879.T2 A58 2003

Baker, Marina. Spells for teenage witches. Berkeley, Calif. : Seastone, c2000.
BF1571.5.T44 B34 2000

Bennett, Robin Rose. Healing magic. New York : Sterling Pub., 2004.
BF1572.S65 B46 2004

Buckland, Raymond. [Complete book of witchcraft] Buckland's complete book of witchcraft. 2nd ed., rev. & expanded. St. Paul, Minn. : Llewellyn Publications, 2002.
BF1566 .B76 2002

Buckland, Raymond. Gypsy witchcraft & magic. 1st ed. St. Paul, Minn. : Llewellyn Publications, 2001, c1998.

Buckland, Raymond. Witchcraft from the inside. Rev. and enl. 3rd ed. St. Paul, Minn., U.S.A. : Llewellyn Publications, 1995 (2001 printing)
BF1566 .B77 1995

Crowley, Vivianne. The magickal life. New York : Penguin Compass, 2003.
BF1611 .C77 2003

Cunningham, Scott, 1956- [Wicca. Spanish] Wicca. 1. ed. St. Paul, Minn. : Llewellyn Español, 2003.
BF1566 .C8618 2003

De Angeles, Ly, 1951- Witchcraft. 1st ed. St. Paul, Minn. : Llewellyn Publications, 2000 (2003 printing)
BF1566 .D38 2000

DiZerega, Gus. Pagans & Christians. 1st ed. St. Paul, Minn. : Llewellyn Publications, 2001.
BF1566 .D59 2001

Drew, A. J. God/goddess. Franklin Lakes, N.J. : New Page Books, 2003.
BF1571 .D73 2003

Drew, A. J. Wicca for couples. Franklin Lakes, NJ : New Page Books, c2002.
BF1572.L6 D74 2002

Drew, A. J. Wicca spellcraft for men. Franklin Lakes, N.J. : New Page Books, c2001.
BF1571.5.M45 D75 2001

Drew, A. J. A Wiccan Bible. Franklin Lakes, N.J. : New Page Books, c2003.
BF1571 .D74 2003

Dugan, Ellen, 1963- Elements of witchcraft. 1st ed. St. Paul, Minn. : Llewellyn Publications, 2003.
BF1571.5.T44 D86 2003

Dunwich, Gerina. Exploring spellcraft. Franklin Lakes, NJ : New Page Books, c2001.
BF1566 .D866 2001

Dunwich, Gerina. Herbal magick. Franklin Lakes, NJ : New Page Books, c2002.
BF1572.P43 D85 2002

Dunwich, Gerina. The pagan book of Halloween. New York : Penguin/Compass, 2000.
BF1566 .D867 2000

Dunwich, Gerina. A witch's guide to ghosts and the supernatural. Franklin Lakes, NJ : New Page Books, c2002.
BF1471 .D86 2002

Eason, Cassandra. A practical guide to witchcraft and magick spells. London ; New York : Quantum, c2001.

Farrar, Janet. Progressive witchcraft. Franklin Lakes, NJ : New Page Books, 2004.
BF1571 .F346 2004

Frost, Gavin. The magic power of white witchcraft. Paramus, NJ : Prentice Hall, c1999.
BF1561 .F76 1999

Frost, Gavin. A witch's guide to psychic healing. Boston, MA : Weiser Books, 2003.

BF1572.S65 F76 2003

Galenorn, Yasmine, 1961- Magical meditations. [New ed.]. Berkeley, Calif. : Crossing Press, c2003.
BF1561 .G35 2003

Gardner, Gerald Brosseau, 1884-1964. The meaning of witchcraft. Boston : Weiser Books, 2004.
BF1566 .G3 2004

Garrison, Cal. The old girls' book of dreams. Boston, MA : Red Wheel, 2003.
BF1729.W64 G37 2003

Gillotte, Galen, 1952- Sacred stones of the goddess. 1st ed. St. Paul, Minn. : Llewellyn Publications, 2003.
BF1611 .G55 2003

Grimassi, Raven, 1951- Spirit of the witch. 1st ed. St. Paul, Minn. : Llewellyn Publications, 2003.
BF1566 .G737 2003

Hardie, Titania. Titania's book of hours. London : Quadrille, 2002.

Hardie, Titania. Titania's magical compendium. San Diego, Calif. : Thunder Bay Press, 2003.
BF1611.H235 2003

Hawke, Elen, 1947- An alphabet of spells. St. Paul, MN : Llewellyn Publications, 2003.
BF1566 .H376 2003

Holland, Eileen. Spells for the solitary witch. Boston, MA : Weiser Books, 2004.
BF1566 .H643 2004

Holland, Eileen. A witch's book of answers. York Beach, ME : Weiser Books, 2003.
BF1566 .H647 2003

Knight, Sirona, 1955- The cyber spellbook. Franklin Lakes, NJ : New Page Books, c2002.
BF1571 .T425 2002

Knight, Sirona, 1955- Empowering your life with wicca. Indianapolis, IN : Alpha Books, c2003.
BF1571 .K56 2003

Knight, Sirona, 1955- A witch like me. Franklin Lakes, NJ : New Page Books, c2002.
BF1408 .K55 2002

Lady Sheba. The book of shadows. 1st ed. St. Paul, Minn. : Llewellyn Publications, 2002.

Lady Sheba. The grimoire of Lady Sheba. Llewellyn's centennial ed. St. Paul, Minn. : Llewellyn Publications, 2001.
BF1566 .L335 2001

Lipp, Deborah, 1961- The elements of ritual. 1st ed. St. Paul, Minn. : Llewellyn Publications, 2003.
BF1571 .L56 2003

MacGregor, Rob. Star power. Franklin Lakes, NJ : New Page Books, c2003.
BF1571.5.T44 M23 2003

Madigan, M. A., 1962- Symbols of the craft. 1st ed. St. Paul, Minn. : Llewellyn Publications, 2003.
BF1773 .M29 2003

Magic and modernity. Stanford, Calif. : Stanford University Press, 2003.
GN475.3 .M34 2003

McColman, Carl. When someone you love is Wiccan. Franklin Lakes, NJ : New Page Books, c2003.
BF1566 .M36 2003

McCoy, Edain, 1957- Advanced witchcraft. 1st ed. St. Paul, Minn. : Llewellyn, 2004.
BF1571 .M45 2004

McCoy, Edain, 1957- If you want to be a witch. 1st ed. St. Paul, Minn. : Llewellyn Publications, 2004.
BF1571 .M455 2004

McLelland, Lilith. Out of the shadows. New York : Citadel Press, c2002.
BF1571 .M46 2002

McQuillar, Tayannah Lee, 1977- Rootwork. New York : Simon & Schuster, c2003.
BF1622.A34 M37 2003
1. Black author.

Moorey, Teresa. Magic house. 1st US ed. New York, NY : Ryland Peters & Small, 2003.
BF1623.H67 M66 2003

Paige, Anthony. Rocking the goddess. New York : Citadel Press, c2002.
BF1571.5.C64 P35 2002

Penczak, Christopher. Gay witchcraft. Boston, MA : Weiser Books, 2003.

BF1571.5.G39 P46 2003

Richardson, S. Cheryl. Magicka formularia. [Miami, Fla.] : S.C. Richardson, c2001.
BF1611 .R53 2001

Ruthven, Suzanne. What you call time. London : Ignotus Press, c1998.

Sabrina, Lady. Exploring Wicca. Franklin Lakes, NJ : New Page Books, c2001.

Shanddaramon, 1959- Self-initiation for the solitary witch. Franklin Lakes, NJ : New Page Books, c2004.
BF1566 .S44 2004

Soku, Leonard. From the coven of witchcraft to Christ. Rev. ed. [Accra, Ghana? : s.n., c2000]
BV4935.S6 F76 2000
1. Black author.

Sylvan, Dianne, 1977- The circle within. 1st ed. St. Paul, MN : Llewellyn Publications, 2003.
BF1566 .S95 2003

Telesco, Patricia, 1960- A witch's beverages and brews. Franklin Lakes, NJ : New Page Books, c2001.
BF1572.R4 T447 2001

Trobe, Kala, 1969- The witch's guide to life. 1st ed. St. Paul, Minn. : Llewellyn Publications, 2003.
BF1566 .T76 2003

Weinstein, Marion. Earth magic. Rev. ed. Franklin Lakes, NJ : New Page Books, c2003.
BF1566 .W46 2003

White, Lauren. Spells for a perfect love life. Kansas City, Mo. : Andrews McMeel Pub., 2000.
BF1572.L6 .W45 2000

Wildman, Laura A. What's your Wicca IQ? New York : Citadel Press, c2002.
BF1566 .W63 2002

Wildman, Laura A. Wiccan meditations. New York : Citadel Press, c2002.
BF1571 .W55 2002

Wood, Jamie. The Wicca herbal. Berkeley, Calif. : Celestial Arts, c2003.
BF1572.P43 W66 2003

Zimmermann, Denise. The complete idiot's guide to wicca and witchcraft. 2nd ed. Indianapolis, IN : Alpha, c2003.
BF1566 .Z55 2003

WITCHCRAFT - AMAZON RIVER REGION.
In darkness and secrecy. Durham, NC : Duke University Press, 2004.
BF1566 .I5 2004

Witchcraft and magic in Europe
Cryer, Frederick H. Biblical and pagan societies. Philadelphia : University of Pennsylvania Press, 2001.
BF1567 .C79 2001

Jolly, Karen Louise. The Middle Ages. Philadelphia : University of Pennsylvania Press, 2002, 2001. 12 300   xiv, 280 p. ; 24 cm.
BF1593 .J65 2002

WITCHCRAFT AND SEX.
Galenorn, Yasmine, 1961- Sexual ecstasy & the divine. Berkeley, Calif. : Crossing Press, c2003.
BF1572.S4 G35 2003

Witchcraft and society in England and America, 1550-1750 / edited by Marion Gibson. Ithaca, NY : Cornell University Press, 2003. xiii, 270 p. ; 24 cm.
Includes bibliographical references (p. [251]-261) and index.
ISBN 0-8014-4224-9 (cloth) ISBN 0-8014-8874-5 (paper) DDC 133.4/3/0903
1. Witchcraft - England - History. 2. Witchcraft - United States - History. I. Gibson, Marion, 1970-
BF1581 .W56 2003

Witchcraft and welfare.
Romberg, Raquel. 1st ed. Austin : University of Texas Press, c2003.
BF1584.P9 R66 2003

WITCHCRAFT - BRAZIL - HISTORY - 16TH CENTURY.
Souza, Laura de Mello e. [Diabo e a Terra de Santa Cruz. English] The Devil and the land of the holy cross. 1st University of Texas Press ed. Austin : University of Texas Press : Teresa Lozano Long Institute of Latin American Studies, 2003.
BF1584.B7 S6813 2003

WITCHCRAFT - BRAZIL - HISTORY - 17TH CENTURY.
Souza, Laura de Mello e. [Diabo e a Terra de Santa Cruz. English] The Devil and the land of the holy cross. 1st University of Texas Press ed. Austin :

University of Texas Press : Teresa Lozano Long Institute of Latin American Studies, 2003.
BF1584.B7 S6813 2003

WITCHCRAFT - BRAZIL - HISTORY - 18TH CENTURY.
Souza, Laura de Mello e. [Diabo e a Terra de Santa Cruz. English] The Devil and the land of the holy cross. 1st University of Texas Press ed. Austin : University of Texas Press : Teresa Lozano Long Institute of Latin American Studies, 2003.
BF1584.B7 S6813 2003

WITCHCRAFT - CALENDARS.
Sabrina, Lady. Celebrating Wiccan spirituality. Franklin Lakes, NJ : New Page Books, 2003.
BF1572.F37 S23 2003

WITCHCRAFT - CHINA - HISTORY.
Gao, Guofan. Zhongguo wu shu shi. Di 1 ban. Shanghai Shi : Shanghai san lian shu dian, 1999.
BF1584.C5 G36 1999

WITCHCRAFT - ENGLAND - HISTORY.
Davies, Owen, 1969- Cunning-folk. London ; New York : Hambledon and London, 2003.
BF1622.G7 D385 2002

Witchcraft and society in England and America, 1550-1750. Ithaca, NY : Cornell University Press, 2003.
BF1581 .W56 2003

WITCHCRAFT - EUROPE.
Werewolves, witches, and wandering spirits. Kirksville, MO : Truman State University Press, c2002.
GR135 .W47 2002

WITCHCRAFT - EUROPE - HISTORY.
Apps, Lara. Male witches in early modern Europe. Manchester ; New York : Manchester University Press ; New York : Distributed exclusively in the USA by Palgrave, 2003.
BF1584.E85 A66 2003

Geschlecht, Magie und Hexenverfolgung. Bielefeld : Verlag für Regionalgeschichte, 2002.

Lacotte, Daniel. Danse avec le diable. [Paris] : Hachette, c2002.
BF1584.E85 L33 2002

Zika, Charles. Exorcising our demons. Leiden ; Boston : Brill, 2003.
BF1584.E85 Z55 2003

WITCHCRAFT - EUROPE - HISTORY - ENCYCLOPEDIAS.
Burns, William E., 1959- Witch hunts in Europe and America. Westport, Conn. : Greenwood Press, 2003.
BF1584.E9 B87 2003

WITCHCRAFT - EUROPE - HISTORY - TO 1500.
Jolly, Karen Louise. The Middle Ages. Philadelphia : University of Pennsylvania Press, 2002, 2001. 12 300   xiv, 280 p. ; 24 cm.
BF1593 .J65 2002

WITCHCRAFT - FRANCE - LORRAINE - HISTORY - 16TH CENTURY.
Diedler, Jean-Claude. Le testament de Maître Persin. [Metz] : Editions serpenoise, [2000]
BF1517.F5 D515 2000

WITCHCRAFT - FRANCE - LORRAINE - HISTORY - 17TH CENTURY.
Diedler, Jean-Claude. Le testament de Maître Persin. [Metz] : Editions serpenoise, [2000]
BF1517.F5 D515 2000

Witchcraft from the inside.
Buckland, Raymond. Rev. and enl. 3rd ed. St. Paul, Minn., U.S.A. : Llewellyn Publications, 1995 (2001 printing)
BF1566 .B77 1995

WITCHCRAFT - GERMANY.
Spee, Friedrich von, 1591-1635. [Cautio criminalis. English] Cautio criminalis, or, A book on witch trials. Charlottesville : University of Virginia Press, 2003.
BF1583.A2 S6813 2003

WITCHCRAFT - GERMANY - FRANCONIA - HISTORY - 16TH CENTURY.
Kleinöder-Strobel, Susanne, 1969- Die Verfolgung von Zauberei und Hexerei in den fränkischen Markgraftümern im 16. Jahrhundert. Tübingen : Mohr Siebeck, c2002.
BF1583 .K54 2002

WITCHCRAFT - GERMANY - LEMGO - HISTORY.
Ströhmer, Michael, 1968- Von Hexen, Ratsherren und Juristen. Paderborn : Bonifatius, c2002.

BF1583 .S77 2002

WITCHCRAFT - GERMANY - RAVENSBURG.
Frühe Hexenverfolgung in Ravensburg und am Bodensee. Konstanz : UVK Verlagsgesellschaft, c2001.
BF1583 .F784 2001

WITCHCRAFT - GERMANY - ROTHENBURG OB DER TAUBER - HISTORY - 16TH CENTURY.
Rowlands, Alison. Witchcraft narratives in Germany. Manchester, UK ; New York : Manchester University Press ; New York : Distributed exclusively in the USA by Palgrave, 2003.
BF1583 .R69 2003

WITCHCRAFT - GERMANY - ROTHENBURG OB DER TAUBER - HISTORY - 17TH CENTURY.
Rowlands, Alison. Witchcraft narratives in Germany. Manchester, UK ; New York : Manchester University Press ; New York : Distributed exclusively in the USA by Palgrave, 2003.
BF1583 .R69 2003

WITCHCRAFT - GERMANY - THURINGIA - HISTORY.
Füssel, Ronald. Hexen und Hexenverfolgung in Thüringen. Erfurt : Landeszentrale für Politische Bildung Thüringen, 2001.
BF1583 .F87 2001

WITCHCRAFT - HANDBOOKS, MANUALS, ETC.
Frost, Gavin. A witch's grimoire of ancient omens, portents, talismans, amulets, and charms. Rev. and updated ed. New York : Reward Books, c2002.
BF1566 .F83 2002

Morgan, Sheena. The Wicca handbook. London : Vega, 2003.
BF1566 .M716 2003

WITCHCRAFT - HISTORY.
Aoumiel. Origins of modern witchcraft. 1st ed. St. Paul, Minn. : Llewellyn Publications, 2000 (2002 printing)
BF1566 .A56 2000

Bartel, Pauline C. Spellcasters. Dallas : Taylor Trade Pub., c2000.
BF1566 .B27 2000

Buckland, Raymond. Witchcraft from the inside. Rev. and enl. 3rd ed. St. Paul, Minn., U.S.A. : Llewellyn Publications, 1995 (2001 printing)
BF1566 .B77 1995

Stark, Rodney. For the glory of God. Princeton, N.J. : Princeton University Press, c2003.
BL221 .S747 2003

Staschen, Heidi. Hexen. Originalausg. Krummwisch [Germany] : Königsfurt, 2001.

Streeter, Michael. Witchcraft. Hauppauge, N.Y. : Barron's, c2002.
BF1566 .S79 2002

WITCHCRAFT - HISTORY - DICTIONARIES.
Bailey, Michael David, 1971- Historical dictionary of witchcraft. 1st ed. Lanham, Md. : Scarecrow Press, 2003.
BF1566 .B25 2003

WITCHCRAFT - HISTORY - SOURCES.
Levack, Brian P. The witchcraft sourcebook. London ; New York : Routledge, 2003.
BF1566 .L475 2003

WITCHCRAFT - HISTORY - TO 1500.
Bailey, Michael David, 1971- Battling demons. University Park, Pa. : Pennsylvania State University Press, c2003.
BF1569 .B35 2003

WITCHCRAFT - ICELAND.
Jón Magnússon, 1610-1696. Píslarsaga séra Jóns Magnússonar. Reykjavík : Mál og menning, 2001.
BF1584.I2 J66 2001

WITCHCRAFT IN ART.
Zika, Charles. Exorcising our demons. Leiden ; Boston : Brill, 2003.
BF1584.E85 Z55 2003

WITCHCRAFT - INDIA - SINGHBHŪM - CASE STUDIES.
Mishra, Archana, 1962- Casting the evil eye. New Delhi : Namita Gokhale Editions, Roli Books, 2003.
BF1584.A-ZI.Z7 2003+

WITCHCRAFT - ITALY - CAPUA - HISTORY.
Ferraiuolo, Augusto. "Pro exoneratione sua propria coscientia". Milano : F. Angeli, c2000.

BF1584.I8 F44 2000

WITCHCRAFT - ITALY - PISA - HISTORY.
Caterina e il diavolo. Pisa : ETS, c1999.
BF1584.I8 C38 1999

WITCHCRAFT - ITALY - SIENA - HISTORY - SOURCES.
Maghi, streghe e alchimisti a Siena e nel suo territorio (1458-1571). Monteriggioni (Siena) : Il leccio, c1999.
BF1622.I8 M295 1999

WITCHCRAFT - JUVENILE LITERATURE.
Dickinson, Rachel. The witch's handbook. New York : Price Stern Sloan, c2002.
BF1571 .D53 2002

Moorey, Teresa. Spellbound. Berkeley, CA : Ulysses Press ; Distributed in the U.S.A. by Publishers Group West, 2002.
BF1571.5.T44 M66 2002

WITCHCRAFT - MALAWI.
Soko, Boston. Nchimi chikanga. Blantyre [Malawi] : Christian Literature Association in Malawi, 2002.
1. Black author.

WITCHCRAFT - MALTA - HISTORY - 16TH CENTURY.
Cassar, Carmel. Witchcraft, sorcery, and the Inquisition. Msida, Malta : Mireva Publications, 1996.
BF1584.M35 C37 1996

WITCHCRAFT - MASSACHUSETTS - SALEM - HISTORY - 17TH CENTURY.
Roach, Marilynne K. The Salem witch trials. 1st Cooper Square Press ed. New York : Cooper Square Press : Distributed by National Book Network, 2002.
BF1575 .R63 2002

WITCHCRAFT - MASSACHUSETTS - SALEM - HISTORY - SOURCES.
Trask, Richard B. The devil hath been raised. Rev. ed. Danvers, Mass. : Yeoman Press, c1997.
BF1576 .T73 1997

WITCHCRAFT - MIDDLE EAST. *See* **ZĀR.**

WITCHCRAFT - MIDDLE EAST - HISTORY.
Cryer, Frederick H. Biblical and pagan societies. Philadelphia : University of Pennsylvania Press, 2001.
BF1567 .C79 2001

WITCHCRAFT - MISCELLANEA.
Tempest, Raven. Bewitching love potions & charms. London : Cassell Illustrated ; New York, NY : Distributed in the USA by Sterling Pub. Co., c2003.
BF575.L8 .T45 2003

Witchcraft narratives in Germany.
Rowlands, Alison. Manchester, UK ; New York : Manchester University Press ; New York : Distributed exclusively in the USA by Palgrave, 2003.
BF1583 .R69 2003

WITCHCRAFT - NEAR EAST. *See* **WITCHCRAFT - MIDDLE EAST.**

WITCHCRAFT - NEW ZEALAND.
Roundtree, Kathryn. Embracing the witch and the goddess. London ; New York : Routledge, 2003.
BF1584.N45 R68 2003

WITCHCRAFT - NIGERIA.
Drews, Annette. Guardians of the society. Leipzig, Germany : Institut für Afrikanistik, Universität Leipzig, 2000.
BF1584.Z33 D44 2000

WITCHCRAFT - PUERTO RICO.
Romberg, Raquel. Witchcraft and welfare. 1st ed. Austin : University of Texas Press, c2003.
BF1584.P9 R66 2003

WITCHCRAFT - SCOTLAND - HISTORY - 16TH CENTURY.
Maxwell-Stuart, P. G. Satan's conspiracy. East Linton, Scotland : Tuckwell Press, 2001.
BF1622.S38 .M39 2001

Witchcraft, sorcery, and the Inquisition.
Cassar, Carmel. Msida, Malta : Mireva Publications, 1996.
BF1584.M35 C37 1996

The witchcraft sourcebook.
Levack, Brian P. London ; New York : Routledge, 2003.
BF1566 .L475 2003

WITCHCRAFT - SPAIN - GRANADA - HISTORY.
Ceballos Gómez, Diana Luz, 1962- Zauberei und Hexerei. Frankfurt am Main ; New York : Peter Lang, c2000.
BF1584.S7 C43 2000

WITCHCRAFT - SWITZERLAND - LAUSANNE - HISTORY - TO 1500.
Modestin, Georg. Le diable chez l'évêque. Lausanne : Université de Lausanne, Section d'histoire, Faculté des lettres, 1999.
BF1584.S9 M64 1999

WITCHCRAFT - SWITZERLAND - VAUD - HISTORY.
Taric Zumsteg, Fabienne. Les sorciers à l'assaut du village. Lausanne : Editions du Zèbre, 2000.
BF1584.S9 T37 2000

WITCHCRAFT - UNITED STATES.
Berger, Helen A., 1949- Voices from the pagan census. Columbia, S.C. : University of South Carolina Press, c2003.
BF1573 .B48 2003

WITCHCRAFT - UNITED STATES - HISTORY.
Witchcraft and society in England and America, 1550-1750. Ithaca, NY : Cornell University Press, 2003.
BF1581 .W56 2003

WITCHCRAFT - UNITED STATES - HISTORY - ENCYCLOPEDIAS.
Burns, William E., 1959- Witch hunts in Europe and America. Westport, Conn. : Greenwood Press, 2003.
BF1584.E9 B87 2003

WITCHCRAFT - VIRGINIA - HISTORY - COLONIAL PERIOD, CA. 1600-1775.
Hudson, Carson O. These detestable slaves of the devill. Haverford, PA : Infinity Pub., c2001.
BF1577.V8 H83 2001

WITCHCRAFT - ZAMBIA.
Drews, Annette. Guardians of the society. Leipzig, Germany : Institut für Afrikanistik, Universität Leipzig, 2000.
BF1584.Z33 D44 2000

WITCHES. *See* **WARLOCKS.**

WITCHES - ENGLAND - HISTORY.
Davies, Owen, 1969- Cunning-folk. London ; New York : Hambledon and London, 2003.
BF1622.G7 D385 2002

WITCHES - EUROPE - BIOGRAPHY.
Lacotte, Daniel. Danse avec le diable. [Paris] : Hachette, c2002.
BF1584.E85 L33 2002

WITCHES - EUROPE - HISTORY.
Lacotte, Daniel. Danse avec le diable. [Paris] : Hachette, c2002.
BF1584.E85 L33 2002

WITCHES - EUROPE - HISTORY - 17TH CENTURY.
Guillou, Jan, 1944- Häxornas försvarare. [Stockholm?] : Piratförlaget, c2002.
BF1584.S8 G85 2002

WITCHES - GERMANY - RAVENSBURG.
Frühe Hexenverfolgung in Ravensburg und am Bodensee. Konstanz : UVK Verlagsgesellschaft, c2001.
BF1583 .F784 2001

WITCHES - HISTORY.
Staschen, Heidi. Hexen. Originalausg. Krummwisch [Germany] : Königsfurt, 2001.

WITCHES - RUSSIA (FEDERATION) - HISTORY.
Ivanova, E. V. (Elena Vladimirovna) Ved'my. Ekaterinburg : Ural'skiĭ gos. universitet, 2002.
BF1584.R9 I85 2002

WITCHES - SWEDEN - HISTORY - 17TH CENTURY.
Guillou, Jan, 1944- Häxornas försvarare. [Stockholm?] : Piratförlaget, c2002.
BF1584.S8 G85 2002

WITCHES - UNITED STATES - BIOGRAPHY.
Knight, Sirona, 1955- A witch like me. Franklin Lakes, NJ : New Page Books, c2002.
BF1408 .K55 2002

Witches, werewolves, and fairies.
Lecouteux, Claude. [Fées, sorcières et loups-garous au Moyen Age. English] 1st U.S. ed. Rochester, Vt. : Inner Traditions, 2003.
BF1045.D67 L4313 2003

A witch's beverages and brews.
Telesco, Patricia, 1960- Franklin Lakes, NJ : New Page Books, c2001.
BF1572.R4 T447 2001

A witch's book of answers.
Holland, Eileen. York Beach, ME : Weiser Books, 2003.

BF1566 .H647 2003

The witch's familiar.
Grimassi, Raven, 1951- 1st ed. St. Paul, Minn. : Llewellyn Publications, 2003.
BF1557 .G75 2003

A witch's grimoire of ancient omens, portents, talismans, amulets, and charms.
Frost, Gavin. Rev. and updated ed. New York : Reward Books, c2002.
BF1566 .F83 2002

A witch's guide to ghosts and the supernatural.
Dunwich, Gerina. Franklin Lakes, NJ : New Page Books, c2002.
BF1471 .D86 2002

The witch's guide to life.
Trobe, Kala, 1969- 1st ed. St. Paul, Minn. : Llewellyn Publications, 2003.
BF1566 .T76 2003

A witch's guide to psychic healing.
Frost, Gavin. Boston, MA : Weiser Books, 2003.
BF1572.S65 F76 2003

The witch's handbook.
Dickinson, Rachel. New York : Price Stern Sloan, c2002.
BF1571 .D53 2002

With eyes open [electronic resource]. San Francisco : KQED ; [Alexandria, Va.] : PBS Began in 2000? Mode of access: World Wide Web. Title from home page (viewed on Aug. 13, 2003). SUMMARY: Companion Web site to a four-part PBS television series. Designed to assist in considering the inevitability of death with eyes wide open. Focuses on topics such as grief, medical decision making, and caregiving. Includes educational resources as well as links to general resources available on the Web. URL: http://www.pbs.org/witheyesopen/
1. Death - Psychological aspects. 2. Bereavement - Psychological aspects. 3. Aged - Care. I. KQED-TV (Television station : San Francisco, Calif.) II. Public Broadcasting Service (U.S.)
BF789.D4

With pleasure.
Abramson, Paul R., 1949- Rev. ed. Oxford ; New York : Oxford University Press, 2002.
HQ23 .A25 2002

Witherall, Arthur, 1966- The problem of existence / Arthur Witherall. Aldershot, England ; Brookfield, VT : Ashgate, c2002. 158 p. ; 24 cm. (Ashgate new critical thinking in philosophy) Includes bibliographical references and index. ISBN 0-7546-0858-1 DDC 111/.1
1. Ontology. I. Title. II. Series.
BD331 .W58 2002

WITKIEWICZ, STANISŁAW IGNACY, 1885-1939 - PHILOSOPHY.
Gawor, Leszek. Katastrofizm konsekwentny. Lublin : Wydawn. Uniwersytetu Marii Curie Skłodowskiej, 1998.
B4691.Z384 G38 1998

Witkin, Robert W. (Robert Winston) Adorno on popular culture / Robert W. Witkin. London ; New York : Routledge, 2003. viii, 200 p. ; 24 cm. (International library of sociology) Includes bibliographical references (p. 188-190) and index. ISBN 0-415-26824-9 (hbk.) ISBN 0-415-26825-7 (pbk.) DDC 306/.092
1. Adorno, Theodor W., - 1903-1969. 2. Popular culture. I. Title. II. Series.
B3199.A34 W58 2003

WITNESS BEARING (CHRISTIANITY).
Manning, Brennan. The wisdom of tenderness. 1st ed. New York : HarperCollins, c2002.
BV4520 .M36 2002

WITNESSES, FTC.
United States. Congress. House. Committee on Energy and Commerce. Subcommittee on Health. Examining issues related to competition in the pharmaceutical marketplace. Washington : U.S. G.P.O. : For sale by the Supt. of Docs., U.S. G.P.O. [Congressional Sales Office], 2002.

WITNESSES - HISTORY.
Wahrheit, Wissen, Erinnerung. Münster : Lit, [2002]

WITNESSING FOR CHRIST. *See* **WITNESS BEARING (CHRISTIANITY).**

Witt, Charlotte, 1951- Ways of being : potentiality and actuality in Aristotle's Metaphysics / Charlotte Witt. Ithaca : Cornell University Press, 2003. x, 161 p. ; 24 cm. Includes bibliographical references (p. [147]-151) and index. CONTENTS: Aristotle's defense of Dunamis -- Power and potentiality -- Rational and nonrational powers -- The priority of actuality -- Ontological hierarchy, normativity, and gender. ISBN 0-8014-4032-7 (alk. paper) DDC 110
1. Aristotle. - Metaphysics. 2. Metaphysics. 3. Ontology. I. Title.
B434 .W59 2003

WITTGENSTEIN, LUDWIG, 1889-1951. TRACTATUS LOGICO-PHILOSOPHICUS.
Ludwig Wittgenstein, Tractatus logico-philosophicus. Berlin : Akademie Verlag, 2001.

WITTGENSTEIN, LUDWIG, 1889-1951.
Smith, R. Scott, 1957- Virtue ethics and moral knowledge. Aldershot, England ; Burlington, VT : Ashgate, c2003.
BJ1012 .S5195 2003

WITWICKI, WŁADYSŁAW, 1878-1948.
Rzepa, Teresa. O interpretowaniu psychologicznym w kręgu szkoły lwowsko-warszawskiej. Warszawa : Polskie Tow. Semiotyczne, 2002.
BF108.P7 R94 2002

Witzig, James Starr. Jungian psychology : theory and practice / James Starr Witzig. [Philadelphia, Pa.?] : Xlibris, c2002. 451 p. ; 23 cm. Includes bibliographical references (p. [413]-421). ISBN 1401058124 (hardcover) DDC 150.19/54
1. Jungian psychology. 2. Jung, C. G. - (Carl Gustav), - 1875-1961. I. Title.
BF173.J85 W58 2002

WIVES. *See also* **MATE SELECTION.**
Maushart, Susan, 1958- Wifework. 1st U.S. ed. New York : Bloomsbury : Distributed to the trade by Holtzbrinck Publishers, 2002.
HQ759 .M3944 2002

WIZARDS. *See also* **MAGICIANS; WARLOCKS.**
Lecouteux, Claude. [Fées, sorcières et loups-garous au Moyen Age. English] Witches, werewolves, and fairies. 1st U.S. ed. Rochester, Vt. : Inner Traditions, 2003.
BF1045.D67 L4313 2003

Rumstuckle, Cornelius, 1940- The book of wizardry. 1st ed. St. Paul, Minn. : Llewellyn Publications, 2003.
BF1611 .R85 2003

Zell-Ravenheart, Oberon, 1942- Grimoire for the apprentice wizard. Franklin Lakes, NJ : New Page Books, 2004.
BF1611 .Z45 2004

WIZARDS IN LITERATURE.
Gupta, Suman, 1966- Re-reading Harry Potter. Houndmills, Basingstoke ; New York : Palgrave Macmillan, 2003.
PR6068.O93 Z68 2003

Harry Potter's world. New York ; London : RoutledgeFalmer, 2003.
PR6068.O93 Z73 2003

The ivory tower and Harry Potter. Columbia : University of Missouri Press, 2002.
PR6068.O93 Z734 2002

Reading Harry Potter. Westport, Conn. ; London : Praeger Publishers, 2003.
PR6068.O93 Z84 2003

WJ III technical manual.
McGrew, Kevin S. Woodcock-Johnson III technical manual/ Itasca, IL : Riverside Pub., c2001.
BF432.5.W66 M345 2001

WJ III tests of cognitive abilities examiner's manual.
Mather, Nancy. Woodcock-Johnson III tests of cognitive abilities examiner's manual. Itasca, IL : Riverside Pub., c2001.
BF432.5.W66 M33 2001

Wlodarski, Anne Powell.
Wlodarski, Robert James. Spirits of the Leonis adobe. West Hills, Calif. : G-Host Pub., c2002.
BF1472.U6 W59 2002

Wlodarski, Robert James. The haunted Whaley house, Old Town, San Diego, California : a history and guide to the most haunted house in America / written by Robert Wlodarski and Anne Wlodarski. 2nd ed. West Hills, Calif. : G-HOST Pub., 2004. p. cm. SUMMARY: Presents an account of paranormal events at the home where a twenty-two-year-old Whaley daughter killed herself with a pistol in 1885. Includes bibliographical references and index. ISBN 0-9649088-7-5 (alk. paper) DDC 133.1/29794985
1. Haunted houses - United States - Juvenile literature. 2. Haunted houses. I. Nathan-Wlodarski, Anne. II. Title.
BF1472.U6 W584

Spirits of the Leonis adobe : history and hauntings in Calabasas, California / written by Robert Wlodarski and Anne Powell Wlodarski. West Hills, Calif. : G-Host Pub., c2002. vii, 134 p. : ill. ; 22 cm. Includes bibliographical references (p. 103-120). ISBN 0-9649088-6-7
1. Haunted houses - California - Calabasas. 2. Ghosts - California - Calabasas. I. Wlodarski, Anne Powell. II. Title.
BF1472.U6 W59 2002

Wo kan Lu Xun wen cong
Wang, Furen. Tu po mang dian. Di 1 ban. Beijing Shi : Zhongguo wen lian chu ban she, 2001.
PL2754.S5 Z89 2001

Wo zai, wo si.
Li, Xiaobing. Di 1 ban. Beijing : Dong fang chu ban she : Xin hua shu dian jing xiao, 1996.
CB425 .L39 1996 <Orien China>

Wo zai, wosi.
Li, Xiaobing. Wo zai, wo si. Di 1 ban. Beijing : Dong fang chu ban she : Xin hua shu dian jing xiao, 1996.
CB425 .L39 1996 <Orien China>

Wodarski, John S.
Handbook of violence. New York : Wiley, c2002.
HM1116 .H36 2002

Wohlers, Christian. Wie unnütz ist Descartes? : zur Frage metaphysischer Wurzeln der Physik / Christian Wohlers. Würzburg : Königshausen & Neumann, c2002. 145 p. ; 24 cm. Includes bibliographical references. ISBN 3-8260-2161-4 (pbk.)
1. Descartes, René, - 1596-1650. 2. Metaphysics. I. Title.

Wohlstand entschleiern.
[Wohlstand entschleiern. English] Unveiling wealth. Dordrecht ; Boston : Kluwer, c2002.
HD75.6 .U58 2002

Wokół piękna.
Stróżewski, Władysław. Kraków : Universitas, c2002.

Wolf, Aaron T.
Conflict prevention and resolution in water systems. Cheltenham, UK ; Northampton, MA, USA : E. Elgar Pub., c2002.
HD1691 .C664 2002

Wolf, Anthony E. "Mom, Jason's breathing on me!" : the solution to sibling bickering / Anthony E. Wolf. 1st ed. New York : Ballantine Books, 2003. xiii, 204 p. ; 22 cm. ISBN 0-345-46092-8 DDC 649/.143
1. Sibling rivalry. 2. Child rearing. I. Title.
BF723.S43 W65 2003

WOLF, DANIEL.
Vint/age 2001 conference : [videorecording]. New York, c2001.

Wolf, Daniel, panelist.
Vint/age 2001 conference : [videorecording]. New York, c2001.

Wolf, Dennie.
Revealing the inner worlds of young children. New York : Oxford University Press, 2003.
BF723.S74 A37 2003

Wolf, Jean-Claude. Ethik und Politik ohne Gewissheiten / Jean-Claude Wolf. Freiburg, Schweiz : Universitätsverlag, c2002. 163 p. ; 23 cm. (Ethik und politische Philosophie, 1422-4496 ; 6) Includes bibliographical references. ISBN 3-7278-1383-0 (pbk.)
1. Ethics. 2. Egoism. 3. Pessimism. I. Title. II. Series.

Wolf, Maryanne.
Dyslexia, fluency, and the brain. Timonium, Md. : York Press, 2001.
RC394.W6 D958 2001

Wolf Messing.
Küppers, Topsy, 1931- München : Langen Müller, c2002.
BF1027.M47 K87 2002

Wolfenbütteler Arbeiten zur Barockforschung
(Bd. 36) Strasser, Gerhard F. Emblematik und Mnemonik der frühen Neuzeit im Zusammenspiel Johannes Buno und Johann Justus Winckelmann. Wiesbaden : Harrassowitz Wolfenbüttel : Herzog August Bibliothek, c2000.
PN6348.5 .S873 2000

WOLFF, CHRISTIAN, FREIHERR VON, 1679-1754.
Paź, Bogusław. Epistemologiczne założenia ontologii Christiana Wolffa. Wrocław : Wydawn. Uniwersytetu Wrocławskiego, 2002.

WOLFRAM, VON ESCHENBACH, 12TH CENT. TITUREL.
Wolfram, von Eschenbach, 12th cent. Titurel. Berlin ; New York : Walter de Gruyter, 2002.

Wolfram, von Eschenbach, 12th cent. Titurel / Wolfram von Eschenbach ; herausgegeben, übersetzt und mit einem Kommentar und Materialien versehen von Helmut Brackert und Stephan Fuchs-Jolie. Berlin ; New York : Walter de Gruyter, 2002. viii, 516 p. : ill. (1 folded) ; 25 cm. Cover title: Titurel ; Text,

Wolinsky, Stephen.
Übersetzung, Kommentar, Materialien. Includes bibliographical references and index. German and Middle High German. ISBN 3-11-015122-7 (cl.)
1. Wolfram, - von Eschenbach, - 12th cent. - Titurel. 2. Arthurian romances - History and criticism. I. Brackert, Helmut. II. Fuchs-Jolie, Stephan. III. Title. IV. Title: Titurel : Text, Übersetzung, Kommentar, Materialien

Wolinsky, Stephen. The beginner's guide to quantum psychology / Stephen H. Wolinsky. Capitola, Calif. : S.H. Wolinsky, c2000. x, 183 p. ; 22 cm. Includes bibliographical references (p. [177]-183). ISBN 0-9670362-3-2 DDC 150.19/8
1. Psychology - Philosophy. I. Title.
BF38 .W7677 2000

Wolke, Robert L. What Einstein told his cook : kitchen science explained / Robert L. Wolke ; with recipes by Marlene Parrish. 1st ed. New York : W.W. Norton & Co., c2002. xviii, 350 p. : ill. ; 24 cm. Includes index. ISBN 0-393-01183-6 (hardcover) DDC 641.5
1. Cookery. 2. Science - Miscellanea. I. Parrish, Marlene. II. Title.
TX652 .W643 2002

WOLLHEIM, GERT H., 1894-1974.
Hornig, Christian. Wollheims Traum. Gauting : Lynx, c2001.

Wollheims Traum.
Hornig, Christian. Gauting : Lynx, c2001.

WOLOF (AFRICAN PEOPLE) - ECONOMIC CONDITIONS.
Mustafa, Huda Nura. Practicing beauty. 1997.

WOLOFS. See **WOLOF (AFRICAN PEOPLE).**

WOLVES - FOLKLORE. See **WEREWOLVES.**

Womack, Lee Ann.
Beavers, Brett. Something worth leaving behind. Nashville, Tenn. : Rutledge Hill Press, c2002.
BF637.S8 B383 2002

WOMAN. See **WOMEN.**

WOMAN (CHRISTIAN THEOLOGY). See **WOMEN IN CHRISTIANITY.**

WOMAN-MAN RELATIONSHIPS. See **MAN-WOMAN RELATIONSHIPS.**

WOMAN (PHILOSOPHY).
Le Dœuff, Michèle. The philosophical imaginary. London : Continuum, 2002.

Woman power.
Field, Lynda. Shaftesbury, Dorset ; Boston : Element, 1999.
HQ1206 .F4623 1999

Woman the hunter.
Stange, Mary Zeiss. Boston : Beacon Press, c1997.
SK14 .S88 1997

A woman's way to wisdom.
Ball, Pamela, 1940- London ; New York : Quantum, 2002.

WOMEN. See also **AGED WOMEN; CHURCH WORK WITH WOMEN; INDIAN WOMEN; JEWISH WOMEN; LESBIANS; MOTHERS; OVERWEIGHT WOMEN; SINGLE WOMEN; SISTERS; TELEVISION AND WOMEN; WIDOWS; YOUNG WOMEN.**
Reading, Anna. The social inheritance of the Holocaust. Houndmills [England] ; New York : Palgrave Macmillan, 2002.
D804.3 .R42 2002

Tyler, Carole-Anne. Female impersonation. New York : Routledge, c2003.
HQ1190 .T95 2003

WOMEN - AFRICA - SOCIAL CONDITIONS.
African women and feminism. Trenton, NJ : Africa World Press, c2003.
HQ1787 .A372 2003

Oduyoye, Mercy Amba. Les colliers et les perles. Yaoundé : Editions CLE, c2002.
1. Black author.

WOMEN - ALASKA. See **INUIT WOMEN.**

Women and demons.
Sengers, Gerda. Leiden ; Boston : Brill, 2003.
BF1275.F3 S463 2003

WOMEN AND JOURNALISM.
Debras, Sylvie. Lectrices au quotidien. Paris : L'Harmattan, c2003.

WOMEN AND LITERATURE. See also **WOMEN AUTHORS.**
Warhol, Robyn R. Having a good cry. Columbus : Ohio State University Press, c2003.
PN56.5.W64 W375 2003

WOMEN AND LITERATURE - FRANCE - HISTORY - 20TH CENTURY.
Aller, Annelies van, 1946- Levenskunst van twee vrouwen. Budel : Damon, c2001.
PS3527.I865 Z536 2001

WOMEN AND LITERATURE - GREAT BRITAIN - HISTORY - 20TH CENTURY.
D'Cruz, Doreen, 1950- Loving subjects. New York : P. Lang, c2002.
PR888.W6 D39 2002

WOMEN AND LITERATURE - HISTORY - TO 1500.
Gendering the master narrative. Ithaca : Cornell University Press, c2003.
HQ1143 .G46 2003

WOMEN AND LITERATURE - UNITED STATES - HISTORY - 20TH CENTURY.
Aller, Annelies van, 1946- Levenskunst van twee vrouwen. Budel : Damon, c2001.
PS3527.I865 Z536 2001

D'Cruz, Doreen, 1950- Loving subjects. New York : P. Lang, c2002.
PR888.W6 D39 2002

WOMEN AND PEACE.
Terror, counter-terror. London ; New York : Zed Books ; New Delhi : Kali for Women ; New York : Distributed in the U.S. exclusively by Palgrave, 2003.
HQ1236 .T47 2003

WOMEN AND PSYCHOANALYSIS.
Reenkola, Elina M. The veiled female core. New York : Other Press, c2002.
BF173 .R368 2002

Therapies with women in transition. Madison, Conn. : International Universities Press, c2003.
RC451.4.W6 T46 2003

WOMEN AND PSYCHOANALYSIS - HISTORY.
Musachi, Graciela. Mujeres en movimiento. Argentina : Fondo de Cultura Económica / Argentina, 2001.

Women and psychology
Greene, Sheila, 1946- The psychological development of girls and women. London ; New York : Routledge, 2003.
HQ1206 .G767 2003

WOMEN AND RELIGION - AFRICA.
Her-stories. Pietermaritzburg, South Africa : Cluster, 2002.

WOMEN AND SPIRITUALISM - ENGLAND - HISTORY - 19TH CENTURY.
Owen, Alex, 1948- The darkened room. Chicago : University of Chicago, 2004.
BF1275.W65 O94 2004

WOMEN AND TELEVISION. See **TELEVISION AND WOMEN.**

WOMEN AND WAR.
Terror, counter-terror. London ; New York : Zed Books ; New Delhi : Kali for Women ; New York : Distributed in the U.S. exclusively by Palgrave, 2003.
HQ1236 .T47 2003

WOMEN ARTISTS IN LITERATURE.
Gerber, Nancy, 1956- Portrait of the mother-artist. Lanham, Md. : Lexington Books, c2003.
PS374.M547 G47 2003

WOMEN AS AUTHORS. See **WOMEN AUTHORS.**

WOMEN AS JOURNALISTS. See **WOMEN JOURNALISTS.**

WOMEN AUTHORS. See also **WOMEN JOURNALISTS.**
Korsström, Tuva. Kan kvinnor tänka? Stockholm/Stehag : Symposion, 2002.

WOMEN AUTHORS - BIOGRAPHY - HISTORY AND CRITICISM.
Ingram, Susan. Zarathustra's sisters. Toronto ; Buffalo : University of Toronto Press, c2003.
PN471 .I537 2003

WOMEN AUTHORS, FILIPINO - 20TH CENTURY - BIOGRAPHY.
Feminine voices. [Manila?] : NCCA, c2001-

WOMEN - BIOGRAPHY.
Martoccia, María, 1957- Cuerpos frágiles, mujeres prodigiosas. Buenos Aires : Editorial Sudamericana, c2002.

Müller, Arno, 1930- Berühmte Frauen. Wien : Braumüller, 2002.

WOMEN - BIOGRAPHY - TO 500.
Ancient queens. Walnut Creek, Calif. ; Oxford : AltaMira Press, 2003.
HQ1127 .A53 2003

WOMEN, BLACK.
Dyson, Michael Eric. Why I love black women. New York : Basic Civitas Books, c2003.

WOMEN - CANADA. See **INUIT WOMEN.**

WOMEN CAT OWNERS - FICTION.
Marshall, Evan, 1956- Icing Ivy. Waterville, Me. : Thorndike Press, 2003, c2002.
PS3563.A72236 I27 2003

WOMEN, CATHOLIC. See **CATHOLIC WOMEN.**

Women, children and the elderly : essays in honour of Shulamit Shahar.
Nashim, zeḳenim va-ṭaf. Yerushalayim : Merkaz Zalman Shazar le-toldot Yiśra'el, [2001]

WOMEN - CIVIL RIGHTS. See **WOMEN'S RIGHTS.**

WOMEN - CLOTHING. See **CLOTHING AND DRESS.**

WOMEN - COMMUNICATION.
Heim, Pat. In the company of women. New York : J.P. Tarcher/Putnam, c2001.
HD6053 .H387 2001

WOMEN - CONDUCT OF LIFE.
Aller, Annelies van, 1946- Levenskunst van twee vrouwen. Budel : Damon, c2001.
PS3527.I865 Z536 2001

Hateley, B. J. Gallagher (Barbara J. Gallagher), 1949- Everything I need to know I learned from other women. York Beach, ME : Conari Press, c2002.
HQ1206 .H345 2002

Linn, Denise. Secrets & mysteries. Carlsbad, Calif. : Hay House, c2002.
HQ1206 .L513 2002

Thomashauer, Regena. Mama Gena's School of Womanly Arts. New York : Simon & Schuster, c2002.
HQ1206 .T4673 2002

Zawadzki, Roman. Kobieta--. Warszawa : Wydawn. von borowiecky, 2002.
PN56.5.W64 Z28 2002

WOMEN - CONGRESSES.
Jornadas de Roles Sexuales y de Género (2nd : 1995 : Madrid, Spain) Mujer, ideología y población. 1. ed. Madrid : Ediciones Clásicas, 1998.
HQ1075 .J67 1995

WOMEN - CORRESPONDENCE.
Hell hath no fury. 1st Carroll & Graf ed. New York : Carroll & Graf Publishers, 2002.
HQ801 .H45 2002

WOMEN - COSTUME. See **COSTUME.**

WOMEN - COUNSELING OF.
Counseling diverse populations. 3rd ed. Boston, Mass. : McGraw-Hill, c2004.
BF637.C6 C6372 2004

Handbook of counseling women. Thousand Oaks, Calif. ; London : Sage Publications, c2003.
RC451.4.W6 H36 2003

Working with the stories of women's lives. Adelaide : Dulwich Centre Publications, 2001.
HQ1185 .W68 2001

WOMEN DETECTIVES - FICTION.
Kava, Alex. The soul catcher. Waterville, Me. : Thorndike Press, 2003, 2002.
PS3561.A8682 S6 2003

WOMEN DETECTIVES - MAINE - FICTION.
Meier, Leslie. Birthday party murder. Waterville, Me. : Thorndike Press, 2003.
PS3563.E3455 B57 2003

WOMEN - DEVELOPED COUNTRIES - SOCIAL CONDITIONS - CONGRESSES.
The silent revolution. Bad Homburg v.d. Höhe : Herbert Quandt Foundation, 2000.
HQ1075 .S55 2000

WOMEN - DISEASES. See **WOMEN - HEALTH AND HYGIENE.**

WOMEN - DISEASES - PSYCHOLOGICAL ASPECTS - BIOGRAPHY.
Martoccia, María, 1957- Cuerpos frágiles, mujeres prodigiosas. Buenos Aires : Editorial Sudamericana, c2002.

WOMEN - DRESS. *See* **CLOTHING AND DRESS.**

WOMEN - ECONOMIC CONDITIONS.
Gender, development and money. Oxford : Oxfam, 2001.

WOMEN - EDUCATION, MEDIEVAL.
Gendt, Anne-Marie Emma Alberta de, 1952- L'art d'éduquer les nobles damoiselles. Paris : Champion, 2003.

WOMEN - EDUCATION - SOCIAL ASPECTS.
Tooley, James. The miseducation of women. London ; New York : Continuum, 2002.
HQ1154 .T64 2002

WOMEN - EDUCATION - UNITED STATES.
Daniell, Beth, 1947- A communion of friendship. Carbondale : Southern Illinois University Press, c2003.
PE1405.U6 D36 2003

WOMEN - EGYPT - CAIRO - ECONOMIC CONDITIONS.
El-Kholy, Heba Aziz. Defiance and compliance. New York : Berghahn Books, 2002.
HQ1793.Z9 C353 2002

WOMEN - EGYPT - CAIRO - SOCIAL CONDITIONS.
El-Kholy, Heba Aziz. Defiance and compliance. New York : Berghahn Books, 2002.
HQ1793.Z9 C353 2002

Sengers, Gerda. Women and demons. Leiden ; Boston : Brill, 2003.
BF1275.F3 S463 2003

WOMEN - EGYPT - SOCIAL CONDITIONS.
Mahfūz, Najlā'. Zawjī wa-al-ukhrá. al-Tab'ah 1. al-Qāhirah : al-Dār al-Miṣrīyah al-Lubnānīyah, 2003.
HQ1793 .M34 2003

Sengers, Gerda. Vrouwen en demonen. Amsterdam : Het Spinhuis, 2000.
BF1275.F3 S46 2000

WOMEN - EMANCIPATION. *See* **WOMEN'S RIGHTS.**

WOMEN EMPLOYEES.
Heim, Pat. In the company of women. New York : J.P. Tarcher/Putnam, c2001.
HD6053 .H387 2001

WOMEN - EUROPE - HISTORY.
Geschlecht, Magie und Hexenverfolgung. Bielefeld : Verlag für Regionalgeschichte, 2002.

WOMEN - EUROPE - MIDDLE AGES, 500-1500.
Nashim, zeḳenim va-taf. Yerushalayim : Merkaz Zalman Shazar le-toldot Yiśra'el, [2001]

WOMEN EXECUTIVES.
Kazerounian, Nadine. Stepping up. London : McGraw-Hill, c2002.

WOMEN, GAY. *See* **LESBIANS.**

WOMEN - GREENLAND. *See* **INUIT WOMEN.**

WOMEN - HEALTH AND HYGENE.
Vint/age 2001 conference : [videorecording]. New York, c2001.

WOMEN - HEALTH AND HYGIENE. *See also* **BEAUTY, PERSONAL; WOMEN - DISEASES; WOMEN - MENTAL HEALTH.**
Linn, Denise. Secrets & mysteries. Carlsbad, Calif. : Hay House, c2002.
HQ1206 .L513 2002

Women's minds, women's bodies. Basingstoke ; New York : Palgrave Macmillan, 2003.
RA778 .P724 2003

WOMEN - HEALTH AND HYGIENE - MISCELLANEA.
McCoy, Edain, 1957- [Enchantments. Spanish] Magia y belleza. 1st ed. St. Paul, Minn. : Llewellyn Español, 2002.
BF1623.B43 E6418 2002

WOMEN - HEALTH AND HYGIENE - PSYCHOLOGICAL ASPECTS.
Women's health and psychiatry. Philadelphia, PA : Lippincott Williams & Wilkins, c2002.
RA564.85 .W6652 2002

Women's minds, women's bodies. Basingstoke ; New York : Palgrave Macmillan, 2003.
RA778 .P724 2003

WOMEN - HEALTH AND HYGIENE - SOCIOLOGICAL ASPECTS.
Women's minds, women's bodies. Basingstoke ; New York : Palgrave Macmillan, 2003.
RA778 .P724 2003

WOMEN, HISPANIC AMERICAN. *See* **HISPANIC AMERICAN WOMEN.**

WOMEN - HISTORY.
Addams, Jane, 1860-1935. The long road of woman's memory. Urbana : University of Illinois Press, 2002.
HQ1206 .A25 2002

French, Marilyn, 1929- From Eve to dawn. Toronto : McArthur, 2002-

WOMEN - HISTORY - MIDDLE AGES, 500-1500.
Gender and difference in the Middle Ages. Minneapolis : University of Minnesota Press, c2003.
HQ1143 .G44 2003

Gendering the master narrative. Ithaca : Cornell University Press, c2003.
HQ1143 .G46 2003

WOMEN - HISTORY - TO 500.
Ancient queens. Walnut Creek, Calif. ; Oxford : AltaMira Press, c2003.
HQ1127 .A53 2003

WOMEN HOMOSEXUALS. *See* **LESBIANS.**

WOMEN HUNTERS.
Stange, Mary Zeiss. Woman the hunter. Boston : Beacon Press, c1997.
SK14 .S88 1997

WOMEN - HYGIENE. *See* **WOMEN - HEALTH AND HYGIENE.**

WOMEN - IDENTITY.
Budgeon, Shelley, 1967- Choosing a self. Westport, Conn. : Praeger, 2003.
HQ1229 .B83 2003

Eiguer, Alberto. L'éveil de la conscience féminine. Paris : Bayard, c2002.

Gromkowska, Agnieszka. Kobiecość w kulturze globalnej. POznań : Wolumin, 2002.

Rishoi, Christy, 1958- From girl to woman. Albany : State University of New York Press, c2003.
HQ1186.A9 R57 2003

Serret, Estela. Identidad femenina y proyecto ético. 1. ed. México : UNAM, PUEG : Universidad Autónoma Metropolitana, Azcapotzalco : M.A. Porrúa, 2002.

WOMEN IN ART. *See* **FEMININE BEAUTY (AESTHETICS).**

WOMEN IN CHRISTIANITY.
Alberione, James, 1884-1971. La donna associata allo zelo sacerdotale. Cinisello Balsamo, Milano : San Paolo, c2001.

Her-stories. Pietermaritzburg, South Africa : Cluster, 2002.

Storkey, Elaine, 1943- Created or constructed? Carlisle [Eng.] : Paternoster Press, 2000.

WOMEN IN CHRISTIANITY - AFRICA.
Oduyoye, Mercy Amba. Les colliers et les perles. Yaoundé : Editions CLE, c2002.
1. Black author.

WOMEN IN DEVELOPMENT.
Gender, development and money. Oxford : Oxfam, 2001.

WOMEN IN JOURNALISM. *See* **WOMEN JOURNALISTS.**

WOMEN IN LITERATURE.
Gendering the master narrative. Ithaca : Cornell University Press, c2003.
HQ1143 .G46 2003

Zawadzki, Roman. Kobieta--. Warszawa : Wydawn. von borowiecky, 2002.
PN56.5.W64 Z28 2002

WOMEN IN MEDICINE. *See also* **WOMEN PHYSICIANS.**
Bowman, Marjorie A. 3rd ed. New York ; Berlin : Springer, c2002.
R692 .B69 2002

WOMEN IN POLITICS.
Allard Olmos, Briseida, 1951- Mujer y poder. [Panamá] : Instituto de la Mujer - Universidad de Panamá, 2002.
HQ1154 .A62 2002

Lister, Ruth, 1949- Citizenship. 2nd ed. Basingstoke, Hampshire ; New York : Palgrave Macmillan, 2003.
HQ1236 .L57 2003

WOMEN IN POLITICS - LATIN AMERICA.
Allard Olmos, Briseida, 1951- Mujer y poder. [Panamá] : Instituto de la Mujer - Universidad de Panamá, 2002.
HQ1154 .A62 2002

WOMEN IN RELIGION. *See* **WOMEN AND RELIGION.**

WOMEN IN SCIENCE. *See* **WOMEN SCIENTISTS.**

WOMEN IN THE CIVIL SERVICE. *See* **WOMEN IN POLITICS.**

WOMEN IN THE MASS MEDIA INDUSTRY. *See* **WOMEN JOURNALISTS.**

WOMEN IN THE PERFORMING ARTS.
Vint/age 2001 conference : [videorecording]. New York, c2001.

WOMEN IN THE PROFESSIONS.
García de León, María Antonia. Herederas y heridas. 1a ed. [Madrid] : Ediciones Cátedra, Universitat de València, Instituto de la Mujer, 2002.
HD6054.2.S7 G37 2002

WOMEN IN THE PROFESSIONS - SPAIN.
García de León, María Antonia. Herederas y heridas. 1a ed. [Madrid] : Ediciones Cátedra, Universitat de València, Instituto de la Mujer, 2002.
HD6054.2.S7 G37 2002

WOMEN - INDIA - SEXUAL BEHAVIOR.
Khushwant Singh, 1915- Khushwant Singh on women, love & lust. New Delhi : Books Today, c2002.
HQ29 .K48 2002

WOMEN, INDIAN. *See* **INDIAN WOMEN.**

WOMEN - INTERVIEWS.
Orenstein, Peggy. Women on work, love, children & life. London : Piatkus, 2000.

WOMEN, INUIT. *See* **INUIT WOMEN.**

WOMEN - ISRAEL.
Gender, place, and memory in the modern Jewish experience. London ; Portland, Or. : Vallentine Mitchell, 2003.
DS143 .G36 2003

WOMEN, JEWISH. *See* **JEWISH WOMEN.**

WOMEN JOURNALISTS - SPAIN.
García de León, María Antonia. Herederas y heridas. 1a ed. [Madrid] : Ediciones Cátedra, Universitat de València, Instituto de la Mujer, 2002.
HD6054.2.S7 G37 2002

WOMEN LANDOWNERS - FICTION.
Quindlen, Anna. Blessings. 1st large print ed. New York : Random House Large Print, c2002.
PS3567.U336 B59 2002b

WOMEN - LIFE SKILLS GUIDES.
Daniels, Joni T. Power tools for women. 1st ed. New York : Three Rivers Press, c2002.
HQ1221 .D26 2002

Women, love & lust.
Khushwant Singh, 1915- Khushwant Singh on women, love & lust. New Delhi : Books Today, c2002.
HQ29 .K48 2002

WOMEN - MAINE - FICTION.
Meier, Leslie. Birthday party murder. Waterville, Me. : Thorndike Press, 2003.
PS3563.E3455 B57 2003

WOMEN MEDIUMS - ENGLAND - HISTORY - 19TH CENTURY.
Owen, Alex, 1948- The darkened room. Chicago : University of Chicago, 2004.
BF1275.W65 O94 2004

WOMEN MEDIUMS - GREAT BRITAIN - BIOGRAPHY.
Shine, Betty, 1929- A free spirit. London : HarperCollinsPublishers, 2001.

WOMEN-MEN RELATIONSHIPS. *See* **MAN-WOMAN RELATIONSHIPS.**

WOMEN - MENTAL HEALTH.
Handbook of counseling women. Thousand Oaks, Calif. ; London : Sage Publications, c2003.
RC451.4.W6 H36 2003

Women's health and psychiatry. Philadelphia, PA : Lippincott Williams & Wilkins, c2002.
RA564.85 .W6652 2002

WOMEN - MENTAL HEALTH - SOCIAL ASPECTS.
The complete guide to mental health for women. 1st ed. Boston : Beacon Press, c2003.

RC451.4.W6 C65 2003

WOMEN - MENTAL HEALTH - UNITED STATES.
The complete guide to mental health for women. 1st ed. Boston : Beacon Press, c2003.
RC451.4.W6 C65 2003

Therapies with women in transition. Madison, Conn. : International Universities Press, c2003.
RC451.4.W6 T46 2003

WOMEN - MISCELLANEA.
Adams, Jessica. The new astrology for women. [New ed.]. Pymble, Sydney, N.S.W. : HarperCollins, 1998 (2002 printing)

Alvrez, Alicia. The ladies' room reader revisited. Berkeley, Calif. : Conari Press ; [Emeryville, Calif.] : Distributed by Publishers Group West, c2002.
HQ1233 .A68 2002

Alvrez, Alicia. The ladies' room reader. Berkeley, Calif. : Conari Press, c2000.
HQ1233 .A68 2000

Brondwin, C. C., 1945- Clan of the Goddess. Franklin Lakes, NJ : New Page Books, c2002.
BF1623.G63 B76 2002

De Grandis, Francesca. What kind of goddess are you? Naperville, Ill. : Sourcebooks, Inc., 2004.
BF1623.G63 D4 2004

Garrison, Cal. The old girls' book of dreams. Boston, MA : Red Wheel, 2003.
BF1729.W64 G37 2003

WOMEN MYSTICS.
Jantzen, Grace. Power, gender, and Christian mysticism. Cambridge ; New York : Cambridge University Press, 1995.
BV5083 .J36 1995

WOMEN - MYTHOLOGY.
Spiraldancer. Moon rites. South Melbourne : [Great Britain] : Lothian, 2002.

Women on power : leadership redefined / edited by Sue J.M. Freeman, Susan C. Bourque, Christine M. Shelton ; with a foreword by Jill Ker Conway. Boston : Northeastern University Press, c2001. xxiii, 328 p. : ill. ; 23 cm. (Women's studies) Includes bibliographical references and index. CONTENTS: Foreword: Amazons and warriors: the image of the powerful woman / Jill Ker Conway -- Introduction: Leadership and power: new conceptions / Sue J.M. Freeman and Susan C. Bourque -- pt. 1. Theoretical issues: Women at the top: "you've come a long way, baby" / Sue J.M. Freeman -- The problem of silence in feminist psychology / Maureen A. Mahoney -- Political leadership for women: redefining power and reassessing the political / Susan C. Bourque -- Leadership, sport, and gender / Mary Jo Kane -- pt. 2. Case studies: Knowledge is power: Our bodies, Ourselves and the Boston Women's Health Book Collective / Barbara A. Brehm -- From Beijing to Atlanta and beyond: the international challenge for women in sport / Christine M. Shelton -- pt. 3. Maternal politics: Marching along with mothers and children / Myron Peretz Glazer and Penina Migdal Glazer -- Mothers as leaders: the Madres Veracruzanas and the Mexican antinuclear movement / Velma Garcia-Gorena -- pt. 4. Professional enclaves: Women in veterinary medicine: past achievements and future challenges / Miriam Slater -- Intersections: women's sport leadership and feminist praxis / Carole A. Oglesby. ISBN 1-55553-478-3 (pbk. : alk. paper) ISBN 1-55553-479-1 (cloth : alk. paper) DDC 303.3/4/082
1. Leadership in women. 2. Leadership. I. Freeman, Sue Joan Mendelson, 1944- II. Bourque, Susan Carolyn, 1943- III. Shelton, Christine.
HQ1233 .W597 2001

Women on work, love, children & life.
Orenstein, Peggy. London : Piatkus, 2000.

WOMEN PHILOSOPHERS.
Broad, Jacqueline. Women philosophers of the seventeenth century. Cambridge, UK ; New York : Cambridge University Press, 2002.
B105.W6 B76 2002

Le Dœuff, Michèle. The philosophical imaginary. London : Continuum, 2002.

Women philosophers of the seventeenth century.
Broad, Jacqueline. Cambridge, UK ; New York : Cambridge University Press, 2002.
B105.W6 B76 2002

WOMEN PHYSICIANS - FICTION.
Cameron, Stella. Cold day in July. Waterville, Me. : Wheeler Pub. ; Bath, England : Chivers Press, 2002.
PS3553.A4345 C65 2002

WOMEN PHYSICIANS - MENTAL HEALTH.
Bowman, Marjorie A. Women in medicine. 3rd ed. New York ; Berlin : Springer, c2002.
R692 .B69 2002

WOMEN PHYSICIANS - PSYCHOLOGY.
Bowman, Marjorie A. Women in medicine. 3rd ed. New York ; Berlin : Springer, c2002.
R692 .B69 2002

WOMEN - POLITICAL ACTIVITY. *See* **WOMEN IN POLITICS.**

WOMEN - PRESS COVERAGE.
Debras, Sylvie. Lectrices au quotidien. Paris : L'Harmattan, c2003.

WOMEN - PSYCHOLOGY. *See also* **WOMEN - MENTAL HEALTH.**
Addams, Jane, 1860-1935. The long road of woman's memory. Urbana : University of Illinois Press, 2002.
HQ1206 .A25 2002

Alborch Bataller, Carmen. Malas. 3. ed. [Madrid] : Aguilar, 2002.

Ball, Pamela, 1940- A woman's way to wisdom. London ; New York : Quantum, 2002.

Bitches, bimbos, and ballbreakers. New York, N.Y. : Penguin Books, 2003.
HQ1206 .B444 2003

Borysenko, Joan. Inner peace for busy women. Carlsbad, Calif. : Hay House, 2003.
BF637.P3 B673 2003

Campbell, Sue, 1956- Relational remembering. Lanham, Md. : Oxford : Rowman & Littlefield, c2003.
BF378.A87 C36 2003

Carter, Jay. Nasty women. Chicago : Contemporary Books, c2003.
BF632.5 .C365 2003

Daniels, Joni T. Power tools for women. 1st ed. New York : Three Rivers Press, c2002.
HQ1221 .D26 2002

Eiguer, Alberto. L'éveil de la conscience féminine. Paris : Bayard, c2002.

Femenilidades. Rio de Janeiro : Espaço Brasileiro de Estudos Psicanalíticos : Contra Capa, c2002.

Freedman, Rita Jackaway. Bodylove. Updated ed. Carlsbad, CA : Gürze Books, c2002.
BF697.5.B63 F74 2002

Género, desarrollo psicosocial y trastornos de la imagen corporal. Madrid : Instituto de la Mujer, 2001.

Giuffrida, Angela, 1943- Il corpo pensa. Roma : Prospettiva, c2002.

Goodison, Lucy. The dreams of women. 1st American ed. New York : W.W. Norton, 1996.
BF1078 .G475 1996

Greene, Sheila, 1946- The psychological development of girls and women. London ; New York : Routledge, 2003.
HQ1206 .G767 2003

Haen, Renate. Du bist die Göttin ; 1. Auf. Bergish Gladbach : Bastei Lübbe, 1999.

Hateley, B. J. Gallagher (Barbara J. Gallagher), 1949- Everything I need to know I learned from other women. York Beach, ME : Conari Press, c2002.
HQ1206 .H345 2002

Heim, Pat. In the company of women. New York : J.P. Tarcher/Putnam, c2001.
HD6053 .H387 2001

Henehan, Mary Pat. Integrating spirit and psyche. New York ; London : Haworth Pastoral Press, c2003.
RC489.F45 H46 2003

Israel-Curley, Marcia. Defying the odds. 1st ed. Woodstock, N.Y. : Overlook Press, 2002.
HB615 .I75 2002

Lewis-Hall, Jennifer, 1964- Life's a journey--not a sprint. Carlsbad, Calif. : Hay House, c2003.
BF637.S8 L455 2003

Linn, Denise. Secrets & mysteries. Carlsbad, Calif. : Hay House, c2002.
HQ1206 .L513 2002

López, Carmen Adela, 1935- Madres e hijas. Caracas, Venezuela : Vadell Hermanos, 2002.

Louden, Jennifer. Comfort secrets for busy women. Naperville, Ill. : Sourcebooks, c2003.

BF637.C5 L676 2003

Margarit i Tayà, Remei. Acerca de la mujer. 1. ed. Barcelona : Plaza & Janés, 2002.

Marraccini, Eliane Michelini. Encontro de mulheres. São Paulo : Casa do Psicólogo, c2001.

Mauthner, Melanie L., 1964- Sistering. New York : Palgrave Macmillan, 2002.
BF723.S43 M385 2002

Nicolson, Paula. Having it all? Chichester, West Sussex, England ; Hoboken, NJ : J. Wiley, c2002.
HQ1206 .N645 2002

Reenkola, Elina M. The veiled female core. New York : Other Press, c2002.
BF173 .R368 2002

Rider, Elizabeth A. Our voices. Belmont, CA : Wadsworth, c2000.
HQ1206 .R54 2000

Serret, Estela. Identidad femenina y proyecto ético. 1. ed. México : UNAM, PUEG : Universidad Autónoma Metropolitana, Azcapotzalco : M.A. Porrúa, 2002.

Sutcliffe, Eileen, 1934- Eve returns Adam's rib. Calgary : Loraleen Enterprises, c2002.

Thomashauer, Regena. Mama Gena's School of Womanly Arts. New York : Simon & Schuster, c2002.
HQ1206 .T4673 2002

Warhol, Robyn R. Having a good cry. Columbus : Ohio State University Press, c2003.
PN56.5.W64 W375 2003

Women's health and psychiatry. Philadelphia, PA : Lippincott Williams & Wilkins, c2002.
RA564.85 .W6652 2002

Yuracko, Kimberly A., 1969- Perfectionism and contemporary feminist values. Bloomington : Indiana University Press, c2003.
HQ1206 .Y87 2003

Zawadzki, Roman. Kobieta--. Warszawa : Wydawn. von borowiecky, 2002.
PN56.5.W64 Z28 2002

WOMEN - RELATIONS WITH MEN. *See* **MAN-WOMAN RELATIONSHIPS.**

WOMEN - RELIGIOUS LIFE.
Alberione, James, 1884-1971. La donna associata allo zelo sacerdotale. Cinisello Balsamo, Milano : San Paolo, c2001.

Brondwin, C. C., 1945- Clan of the Goddess. Franklin Lakes, NJ : New Page Books, c2002.
BF1623.G63 B76 2002

Coyne, Tami. The spiritual chicks question everything. York Beach, ME : Red Wheel/Weiser, 2002.
BL625.7 .C69 2002

Her-stories. Pietermaritzburg, South Africa : Cluster, 2002.

Holl, Adolf, 1930- Brief an die gottlosen Frauen. Wien : Zsolnay, 2002.

Johnson Cook, Suzan D. (Suzan Denise), 1957- Too blessed to be stressed. Nashville, Tenn. : T. Nelson, c1998.
BV4527 .J65 1998
1. Black author.

Oduyoye, Mercy Amba. Les colliers et les perles. Yaoundé : Editions CLE, c2002.
1. Black author.

Rose, Sharron. Path of the priestess. Rochester, VT. : Inner Traditions, c2002.
BL625.7 .R67 2002

WOMEN - RIGHTS OF WOMEN. *See* **WOMEN'S RIGHTS.**

WOMEN - RUSSIA (FEDERATION) - HISTORY.
Ivanova, E. V. (Elena Vladimirovna) Ved'my. Ekaterinburg : Ural'skiĭ gos. universitet, 2002.
BF1584.R9 I85 2002

WOMEN - RUSSIA (FEDERATION) - PSYCHOLOGY.
Ivanova, E. V. (Elena Vladimirovna) Ved'my. Ekaterinburg : Ural'skiĭ gos. universitet, 2002.
BF1584.R9 I85 2002

WOMEN SCIENTISTS - PSYCHOLOGY.
From girls in their elements to women in science. New York : P. Lang, 2003.
BF378.S65 F76 2003

WOMEN - SEXUAL BEHAVIOR.
Femenilidades. Rio de Janeiro : Espaço Brasileiro de Estudos Psicanalíticos : Contra Capa, c2002.

Musachi, Graciela. Mujeres en movimiento. Argentina : Fondo de Cultura Económica / Argentina, 2001.

WOMEN - SOCIAL CONDITIONS.
Kricheldorf, Beate, 1949- Verantwortung, nein danke!. 2., unveränderte Aufl. Frankfurt/Main : R.G. Fischer, 2001, c1998.

Margarit i Tayà, Remei. Acerca de la mujer. 1. ed. Barcelona : Plaza & Janés, 2002.

Nicolson, Paula. Having it all? Chichester, West Sussex, England ; Hoboken, NJ : J. Wiley, c2002.
HQ1206 .N645 2002

Orenstein, Peggy. Women on work, love, children & life. London : Piatkus, 2000.

WOMEN - SOCIAL CONDITIONS - CONGRESSES.
The silent revolution. Bad Homburg v.d. Höhe : Herbert Quandt Foundation, 2000.
HQ1075 .S55 2000

Wissen Macht Geschlecht. Zürich : Chronos, c2002.

WOMEN - SOCIAL CONDITIONS - CROSS-CULTURAL STUDIES.
Feminist futures. London ; New York : Zed Books ; New York : Distributed in the USA exclusively by Palgrave, c2003.
HQ1161 .F455 2003

WOMEN - SOCIAL CONDITIONS - PSYCHOLOGICAL ASPECTS.
Rider, Elizabeth A. Our voices. Belmont, CA : Wadsworth, c2000.
HQ1206 .R54 2000

WOMEN SOCIAL REFORMERS - UNITED STATES - BIOGRAPHY.
Tonn, Joan C. Mary P. Follett. New Haven [Conn.] : Yale University Press, c2003.
HN57 .T695 2003

WOMEN - SOCIALIZATION.
Margarit i Tayà, Remei. Acerca de la mujer. 1. ed. Barcelona : Plaza & Janés, 2002.

WOMEN STUDIES. See **WOMEN'S STUDIES.**

WOMEN - STUDY AND TEACHING. See **WOMEN'S STUDIES.**

WOMEN - UNITED STATES. See **HISPANIC AMERICAN WOMEN.**

WOMEN - UNITED STATES - BIOGRAPHY.
Kuhn, Annette. Family secrets. New ed. London ; New York : Verso, 2002.
CT274 .K84 2002

WOMEN - VIOLENCE AGAINST.
Gewalt-Verhältnisse. Frankfurt ; New York : Campus, c2002.

Women who hear voices.
Callahan, Sidney Cornelia. New York : Paulist Press, 2003.
BV5091.R4 C35 2003

Women's best friendships.
Rind, Patricia. New York : Haworth Press, c2002.
BF575.F66 R56 2002

WOMEN'S CLOTHING. See **CLOTHING AND DRESS; COSTUME.**

WOMEN'S DREAMS - CASE STUDIES.
Burch, Wanda Easter, 1947- She who dreams. Novato, Calif. : New World Library, c2003.
BF1099.W65 B87 2003

WOMEN'S EDUCATION. See **WOMEN - EDUCATION.**

WOMEN'S FRIENDSHIP. See **FEMALE FRIENDSHIP.**

Women's health and psychiatry / editors, Kimberly H. Pearson, Shamsah B. Sonawalla, and Jerrold F. Rosenbaum. Philadelphia, PA : Lippincott Williams & Wilkins, c2002. xi, 166 p. : ill. ; 26 cm. Includes bibliographical references and index. ISBN 0-7817-3779-6 (print : alk. paper) DDC 616.89/0082
1. Women - Health and hygiene - Psychological aspects. 2. Women - Mental health. 3. Women - Psychology. 4. Clinical health psychology. I. Pearson, Kimberly H., 1970- II. Sonawalla, Shamsah B., 1967- III. Rosenbaum, J. F. (Jerrold F.)
RA564.85 .W6652 2002

WOMEN'S LAND ARMY - BIOGRAPHY.
Grimwood, Irene. Land girls at the old rectory. Large print ed. Oxford : ISIS, 2001.

WOMEN'S LIB. See **FEMINISM.**

WOMEN'S LIBERATION. See **WOMEN'S RIGHTS.**

WOMEN'S LIBERATION MOVEMENT. See **FEMINISM.**

Women's minds, women's bodies : interdisciplinary approaches to women's health / edited by Gwyneth Boswell and Fiona Poland. Basingstoke ; New York : Palgrave Macmillan, 2003. xv, 258 p. : ill. ; 23 cm. Includes bibliographical references (p. 221-246) and indexes. ISBN 0-333-91969-6 (cloth) DDC 613/.042
1. Women - Health and hygiene. 2. Women - Health and hygiene - Psychological aspects. 3. Women - Health and hygiene - Sociological aspects. 4. Mind and body. I. Boswell, Gwyneth. II. Poland, Fiona.
RA778 .P724 2003

WOMEN'S MOVEMENT. See **FEMINISM.**

WOMEN'S RIGHTS.
Goldrick-Jones, Amanda, 1956- Men who believe in feminism. Westport, Conn. ; London : Praeger, 2002.
HQ1236 .G57 2002

Women's rights. San Diego, Calif. : Greenhaven Press, c2002.
HQ1236 .W6526 2002

WOMEN'S RIGHTS - CONGRESSES.
Wissen Macht Geschlecht. Zürich : Chronos, c2002.

WOMEN'S RIGHTS - HISTORY - SOURCES.
Women's rights. San Diego, Calif. : Greenhaven Press, c2002.
HQ1236 .W6526 2002

Women's rights / Jennifer A. Hurley, book editor. San Diego, Calif. : Greenhaven Press, c2002. 240 p. ; 23 cm. (Great speeches in history series) Includes bibliographical references (p. 232-234) and index. CONTENTS: In defense of women's rights / Elizabeth Cady Stanton -- Discourse on woman / Lucretia Mott -- Remedying the wrongs done to women / Ernestine Potowski Rose -- Aren't I a woman? / Sojourner Truth -- On being arrested for voting / Susan B. Anthony -- Why women need the ballot / Frances D. Gage -- The solitude of self : an argument for women's suffrage / Elizabeth Cady Stanton -- Militant suffragists / Emmeline Pankhurst -- The fundamental principle of a Republic / Anna Howard Shaw -- A woman's civil right / Betty Friedan -- Funeral oration for the burial of traditional womanhood / Kathie Amatnick -- A strategy to strengthen women's political power / Bella S. Abzug -- For the Equal Rights Amendment / Shirley Chisholm -- Women's liberation is men's liberation / Gloria Steinem -- The argument that won Roe v. Wade / Sarah Weddington -- The women's movement is incompatible with family life / Phyllis Schlafly -- Promoting the human rights of women / Charlotte Bunch -- The status of women in Islamic nations / Benazir Bhutto -- Let women all rise together / Angela Y. Davis -- In support of Roe v. Wade / Kate Michelman -- The feminist case against abortion / Serrin M. Foster -- On the 150th anniversary of the first women's rights convention / Hillary Rodham Clinton. ISBN 0-7377-0773-9 (lib. : alk. paper) ISBN 0-7377-0772-0 (pbk. : alk. paper) DDC 305.42
1. Women's rights. 2. Women's rights - History - Sources. 3. Feminism. I. Hurley, Jennifer A., 1973- II. Series.
HQ1236 .W6526 2002

WOMEN'S STUDIES.
Alonso, Graciela. Hacia una pedagogía de las experiencias de las mujeres. 1. ed. Buenos Aires : Miño y Dávila, 2002.

WOMEN'S STUDIES - BIOGRAPHICAL METHODS.
Working with the stories of women's lives. Adelaide : Dulwich Centre Publications, 2001.
HQ1185 .W68 2001

WOMEN'S STUDIES - UNITED STATES - BIOGRAPHICAL METHODS.
Rishoi, Christy, 1958- From girl to woman. Albany : State University of New York Press, c2003.
HQ1186.A9 R57 2003

WOMON. See **WOMEN.**

WOMYN. See **WOMEN.**

WONDERS. See **CURIOSITIES AND WONDERS.**

Wong, Angi Ma. Feng shui dos & taboos for love / Angi Ma Wong. Carlsbad, Calif. : Hay House, c2002. 361 p. : ill. ; 11 x 11 cm. ISBN 1401900801 (pbk.) DDC 133.3/337
1. Feng shui. 2. Love - Miscellanea. I. Title. II. Title: Feng shui dos and taboos for love
BF1779.F4 W67 2002

Wong, Leonard.
Why they fight [electronic resource]. Carlisle, PA : Strategic Studies Institute, U.S. Army War College, [2003]
U22

Wood, Ellen R. Green.
Wood, Samuel E. Mastering the world of psychology. Boston : Pearson/Allyn and Bacon, c2004.
BF121 .W656 2004

Wood, Gaby. Edison's Eve : a magical history of the quest for mechanical life / Gaby Wood. 1st American ed. New York : A.A. Knopf, c2002. xxviii, 304 p., [8] p. of plates : ill. ; 20 cm. Includes bibliographical references (p. 271-289) and index. ISBN 0-679-45112-9 DDC 629.8/92
1. Robots - Design and construction - History. 2. Artificial intelligence. I. Title.
TJ211 .W65 2002

Wood, Jamie. The Wicca herbal : a guide to healing body and spirit with magickal herbs / Jamie Wood. Berkeley, Calif. : Celestial Arts, c2003. p. cm. "A Kirsty Melville book"--T.p. verso. Includes bibliographical references (p.   ) and index. ISBN 1-58761-169-4 (paper) DDC 133.4/3
1. Witchcraft. 2. Herbs - Miscellanea. 3. Magic. I. Title.
BF1572.P43 W66 2003

Wood, Michael, 1936- The road to Delphi : the life and afterlife of oracles / Michael Wood. 1st ed. New York : Farrar, Straus and Giroux, 2003. 271 p. ; 22 cm. Includes bibliographical references (p. 255) and index. Publisher description URL: http://www.loc.gov/catdir/description/hol032/2003048060.html ISBN 0-374-52610-9 (alk. paper) DDC 809/.9337
1. Oracles in literature. 2. Divination in literature. 3. Oracles. 4. Divination - History. I. Title.
PN56.O63 W66 2003

Wood, Robert S. (Robert Snyder), 1930- Peaceful passing : die when you choose with dignity and ease / Robert S. Wood. Sedona, AZ : In Print Pub., c2000. 240 p. : ill. ; 19 cm. Includes bibliographical references (p. 237-238) ISBN 1-88696-617-6 (pbk.).
1. Death - Psychological aspects. 2. Death - Social aspects. 3. Channeling (Spiritualism) 4. Spiritual life. I. Title. II. Title: Die when you choose with dignity and and ease
BF789.D4 W66 2000

Wood, Samuel E. Mastering the world of psychology / Samuel E. Wood, Ellen Green Wood, Denise Boyd. Boston : Pearson/Allyn and Bacon, c2004. xxix, 575 p. : ill. (some col.) ; 28 cm. Includes bibliographical references (p. 437-475) and indexes. ISBN 0-205-35868-3 (pbk.) DDC 150
1. Psychology. I. Wood, Ellen R. Green. II. Boyd, Denise Roberts. III. Title.
BF121 .W656 2004

Woodall, Trinny.
Constantine, Susannah. What not to wear. London : Weidenfeld & Nicolson, 2002.

Woodcock-Johnson 3 technical manual.
McGrew, Kevin S. Woodcock-Johnson III technical manual/ Itasca, IL : Riverside Pub., c2001.
BF432.5.W66 M345 2001

Woodcock-Johnson 3 tests of cognitive abilities examiner's manual.
Mather, Nancy. Woodcock-Johnson III tests of cognitive abilities examiner's manual. Itasca, IL : Riverside Pub., c2001.
BF432.5.W66 M33 2001

Woodcock-Johnson III technical manual/.
McGrew, Kevin S. Itasca, IL : Riverside Pub., c2001.
BF432.5.W66 M345 2001

Woodcock-Johnson III tests of cognitive abilities.
Woodcock, Richard W. Itasca, IL : Riverside Pub., c2001.
BF432.5.W66 W66 2001

Woodcock-Johnson III tests of cognitive abilities examiner's manual.
Mather, Nancy. Itasca, IL : Riverside Pub., c2001.
BF432.5.W66 M33 2001

WOODCOCK-JOHNSON TESTS OF COGNITIVE ABILITY.
Mather, Nancy. Woodcock-Johnson III tests of cognitive abilities examiner's manual. Itasca, IL : Riverside Pub., c2001.
BF432.5.W66 M33 2001

McGrew, Kevin S. Woodcock-Johnson III technical manual/ Itasca, IL : Riverside Pub., c2001.
BF432.5.W66 M345 2001

Woodcock, Richard W. Woodcock-Johnson III tests of cognitive abilities. Itasca, IL : Riverside Pub., c2001.

Woodcock-Johnson Tests of Cognitive Ability.
BF432.5.W66 W66 2001

Woodcock-Johnson three technical manual.
McGrew, Kevin S. Woodcock-Johnson III technical manual/ Itasca, IL : Riverside Pub., c2001.
BF432.5.W66 M345 2001

Woodcock-Johnson three tests of cognitive abilities examiner's manual.
Mather, Nancy. Woodcock-Johnson III tests of cognitive abilities examiner's manual. Itasca, IL : Riverside Pub., c2001.
BF432.5.W66 M33 2001

Woodcock, Richard W.
McGrew, Kevin S. Woodcock-Johnson III technical manual/ Itasca, IL : Riverside Pub., c2001.
BF432.5.W66 M345 2001

Woodcock-Johnson III tests of cognitive abilities / Richard W. Woodcock, Kevin S. McGrew, Nancy Mather. Itasca, IL : Riverside Pub., c2001. 2 v. : ill. (some col.) ; 20 X 27 cm. CONTENTS: Standard test book -- Extended test book. DDC 153.9/3
1. Woodcock-Johnson Tests of Cognitive Ability. I. McGrew, Kevin S. II. Mather, Nancy. III. Title. IV. Title: Tests of cognitive abilities
BF432.5.W66 W66 2001

Woodhead, Roy (Roy M.) Achieving results : how to create value / by Roy Woodhead and James McCuish. London : Thomas Telford, 2002. xi, 160 p. : ill. ; 24 cm. Includes bibliographical references and index. ISBN 0-7277-3184-X DDC 658.4
1. Value analysis (Cost control) 2. Leadership. 3. Management. I. McCuish, James (James D.) II. Title.

Woods, Earl, 1932- Start something : you can make a difference / Earl Woods and the Tiger Woods Foundation with Shari Lesser Wenk. New York : Simon & Schuster, c2000. 137 p. : ill. ; 19 cm. ISBN 0-7432-1096-4 DDC 158.1
1. Woods, Tiger. 2. Children - Conduct of life - Juvenile literature. 3. Conduct of life. 4. Self-esteem. I. Wenk, Shari Lesser. II. Tiger Woods Foundation. III. Title.
BJ1631 .W726 2000

WOODS, TIGER.
Woods, Earl, 1932- Start something. New York : Simon & Schuster, c2000.
BJ1631 .W726 2000

Woodward, Gary C. The idea of identification / Gary C. Woodward. Albany : State University of New York Press, c2003. xii, 176 p. : ill. ; 23 cm. (SUNY series in communication studies) Includes bibliographical references (p. 147-169) and index. ISBN 0-7914-5819-9 (alk. paper) ISBN 0-7914-5820-2 (pbk. : alk. paper) DDC 302/.1
1. Self - Social aspects. 2. Identification. 3. Identity (Philosophical concept) 4. Social interaction. I. Title. II. Series.
BF697.5.S65 W66 2003

WOODY PLANTS. See **TREES.**

WOOING. See **COURTSHIP.**

Woolcock, Stephen.
The new economic diplomacy. Aldershot, Hampshire, England ; Burlington, VT : Ashgate, c2003.
HF1359 .N4685 2003

Woolf, Virginia, 1882-1941. On being ill / by Virginia Woolf ; introduction by Hermione Lee. Ashfield, Mass. : Paris Press, 2002. xxxiv, 28 p. ; 22 cm. Originally published as an individual volume by The Hogarth Press, 1930. ISBN 1-930464-06-1 DDC 823/.912
1. Woolf, Virginia, - 1882-1941 - Health. 2. Sick - Psychology. I. Title.
PR6045.O72 O5 2002

WOOLF, VIRGINIA, 1882-1941 - HEALTH.
Woolf, Virginia, 1882-1941. On being ill. Ashfield, Mass. : Paris Press, 2002.
PR6045.O72 O5 2002

Woolfe, Lorin. The Bible on leadership : from Moses to Matthew : management lessons for contemporary leaders / Lorin Woolfe. New York : American Management Association, c2002. xiii, 240 p. ; 24 cm. Includes bibliographical references (p. 219-228) and index. ISBN 0-8144-0682-3 (hardcover) DDC 658.4/092
1. Leadership. 2. Executive ability. 3. Management. 4. Leadership in the Bible. I. Title.
HD57.7 .W666 2002

Woolfe, Ray.
Handbook of counselling psychology. 2nd ed. London ; Thousand Oaks, Calif. : SAGE Publications, 2003.
BF637.C6 H316 2003

Woolfolk, Joanna Martine.
[Only astrology book you'll ever need. Spanish]
El unico libro de astrologia que necesitara / Joanna Martine Woolfolk. Lanham, Md. : Taylor Trade Pub, 2003. p. cm. Includes bibliographical references and index. Table of contents URL: http://www.loc.gov/catdir/toc/ecip047/2003016916.html CONTENTS: Los signos solares -- Los signos solares en el amor -- Los decanatos y las cspides de los signos solares -- La astrologa y la salud -- Signos lunares -- Tu ascendente y su poder -- T y los planetas -- Su papel en tu destino -- Para comprender la astrologa -- Las casas de la astrologa -- Como preparar tu propio horscopo -- Los aspectos y la sinastra : examen mas profundo de tu carta natal -- La historia de la astrologma -- El zodaco : la leyenda originaria de cada signo -- La era de acuario. ISBN 0-87835-301-0 (pbk. : alk. paper) DDC 133.5
1. Astrology. I. Title.
BF1708.1 .W6818 2003

WORD DEAFNESS. See **AUDITORY PERCEPTION.**

Word order and scrambling / edited by Simin Karimi. Malden, MA : Blackwell Pub., 2003. xx, 385 p. : ill. ; 26 cm. (Explaining linguistics ; 4) Includes bibliographical references (p. [345]-367) and index. ISBN 0-631-23327-X ISBN 0-631-23328-8 (pbk.) DDC 415
1. Grammar, Comparative and general - Word order. 2. Language acquisition. 3. Psycholinguistics. I. Karimi, Simin. II. Series.
P295 .W65 2003

WORK. See **OCCUPATIONS; PERFORMANCE.**

WORK AND FAMILY. See also **DUAL-CAREER FAMILIES.**
Orenstein, Peggy. Women on work, love, children & life. London : Piatkus, 2000.

WORK AND FAMILY - UNITED STATES.
Job stress in a changing workforce. 1st ed. Washington, DC ; London : American Psychological Association, c1994.
HF5548.85 .J654 1994

WORK DESIGN.
Allcorn, Seth. The dynamic workplace. Westport, Conn. ; London : Praeger, 2003.
HF5547.2 .A43 2003

The new workplace. Chichester, UK ; Hoboken, NJ : Wiley, c2003.
HD6955 .N495 2003

WORK ENVIRONMENT. See also **BULLYING IN THE WORKPLACE.**
Allcorn, Seth. The dynamic workplace. Westport, Conn. ; London : Praeger, 2003.
HF5547.2 .A43 2003

The new workplace. Chichester, UK ; Hoboken, NJ : Wiley, c2003.
HD6955 .N495 2003

WORK ETHIC.
Vardi, Yoav, 1944- Misbehavior in organizations. Mahwah, NJ ; London : Lawrence Erlbaum, 2004.
HD58.7 .V367 2004

WORK, METHOD OF. See **WORK.**

WORK - PHYSIOLOGICAL ASPECTS. See **JOB STRESS.**

WORK - PSYCHOLOGICAL ASPECTS. See also **JOB STRESS.**
Baudelot, Christian. Travailler pour être heureux? [Paris] : Fayard, c2003.

Bstan-'dzin-rgya-mtsho, Dalai Lama XIV, 1935- The art of happiness at work. New York : Riverhead Books, 2003.
BF481 .B76 2003

Driekwart eeuw psychotechniek in Nederland. Assen : Van Gorcum, 2001.
HF5548.8 .D73 2001

Frost, Peter J. Toxic emotions at work. Boston : Harvard Business School Press, c2003.
HD42 .F76 2003

Hochschild, Arlie Russell, 1940- The managed heart. 20th anniversary ed. Berkeley, Calif. : University of California Press, 2003.
BF531 .H62 2003

Ivanova, Anna (Anna N.) Kakŭv trud e nuzhen na choveka? Sofiĭa : Akademichno izd-vo "Prof. Marin Drinov", 2000.
BF481 .I82 2000

Job stress in a changing workforce. 1st ed. Washington, DC ; London : American Psychological Association, c1994.
HF5548.85 .J654 1994

Marar, Ziyad. The happiness paradox. London : Reaktion, 2003.

McConnell, Carmel. Change activist. Cambridge, MA : Perseus Pub., c2001.
BF481 .M393 2001

Osty, Florence. Le désir de métier. Rennes [France] : Presses universitaires de Rennes, [2003]

Work related mental stress injuries in the NYS Workers' Compensation system.
Work-related mental stress injuries in the NYS workers' compensation system. [Albany, N.Y. : The Board, 1997]
HF5548.85 .W668 1997

Work-related mental stress injuries in the NYS workers' compensation system : a report / submitted by the New York State Workers' Compensation Board in accordance with chapter 635 of the Laws of 1996. [Albany, N.Y. : The Board, 1997] 68, xxix p. : ill. ; 28 cm. Report prepared by the Board's Mental Stress Injury Committee. "September 1997." Includes bibliographical references (p. i-iv).
1. Job stress - New York (State) 2. Workers' compensation claims - New York (State) 3. Stress (Psychology) I. New York (State). Workers' Compensation Board. II. New York (State). Workers' Compensation Board. Mental Stress Injury Committee. III. Title: Work related mental stress injuries in the NYS Workers' Compensation system
HF5548.85 .W668 1997

WORK - RELIGIOUS ASPECTS - BUDDHISM.
Bstan-'dzin-rgya-mtsho, Dalai Lama XIV, 1935- The art of happiness at work. New York : Riverhead Books, 2003.
BF481 .B76 2003

WORK - RELIGIOUS ASPECTS - JUDAISM.
Mark, Shelomoh Zalman ben Nehemyah. Sefer Ma'aśeh uman. Yerushalayim : Nahalat kolel "Bet ulpana de-rabenu Yoḥanan, 763 [2002 or 2003]

WORK STRESS. See **JOB STRESS.**

WORKERS. See **EMPLOYEES.**

WORKERS' COMPENSATION - ADJUSTMENT OF CLAIMS. See **WORKERS' COMPENSATION CLAIMS.**

WORKERS' COMPENSATION CLAIMS - NEW YORK (STATE).
Work-related mental stress injuries in the NYS workers' compensation system. [Albany, N.Y. : The Board, 1997]
HF5548.85 .W668 1997

WORKING CLASS. See **PEASANTRY.**

WORKING CLASS - EMPLOYMENT. See **WORKING CLASS.**

WORKING CLASS - ENGLAND - LANGUAGE.
Hoggart, Richard, 1918- Everyday language & everyday life. New Brunswick, N.J. ; London : Transaction Publishers, c2003.
PE1074.8 .H64 2003

WORKING CLASSES. See **WORKING CLASS.**

WORKING COUPLES. See **DUAL-CAREER FAMILIES.**

WORKING DRAWINGS (ART). See **ARTISTS' PREPARATORY STUDIES.**

WORKING MEMORY. See **SHORT-TERM MEMORY.**

Working memory in sentence comprehension.
Vasishth, Shravan, 1964- New York ; London : Routledge, 2003.
PK1933 .V28 2003

Working on working memory / [edited by] Erich Schröger, Axel Mecklinger & Angela D. Friederici. Leipzig : Leipziger Universitätsverlag, 2000. viii, 163 p. : ill. (some col.) ; 21 cm. (Leipzig series in cognitive sciences ; 1) Includes bibliographical references (p. 156-160) and index. ISBN 3-934565-49-2 DDC 153.1/3
1. Short-term memory - Congresses. I. Schröger, Erich. II. Mecklinger, Axel. III. Friederici, Angela D. IV. Series.
BF378.S54 W675 2000

Working paper (University of Nairobi. Institute for Development Studies)
(no. 530.) Frederiksen, Bodil Folke, 1943- Popular culture, family relations, and issues of everyday democracy. [Nairobi] : Institute for Development Studies, University of Nairobi, [2000]
HQ799.K42 N354 2000

Working with anger.
Thubten Chodron, 1950- Ithaca, NY : Snow Lion Publication, 2001.
BQ4430.A53 T48 2001

Working with culture.
Khademian, Anne M., 1961- Washington, D.C. : CQ Press, c2002.
JF1351 .K487 2002

Working with men in the human services / edited by Bob Pease and Peter Camilleri. Crows Nest, N.S.W. : Allen & Unwin, c2001. viii, 248 p. ; 22 cm. Includes bibliographical references (p. 219-241) and index. ISBN 1-86508-480-8 (pbk.)
 1. Social work with men. 2. Social service. 3. Men - Political aspects. 4. Masculinity. I. Pease, Bob. II. Camilleri, Peter James.

Working with the stories of women's lives. Adelaide : Dulwich Centre Publications, 2001. v, 272 p. ; 24 cm. "Introd. [by] Cheryl White, on behalf of the many people who worked on this book."--P. v. Includes bibliographical references. ISBN 0-9577929-3-X (pbk.) DDC 305.4889915
 1. Women's studies - Biographical methods. 2. Women - Counseling of. 3. Indigenous women. 4. Feminist therapy. I. White, Cheryl.
HQ1185 .W68 2001

Workman, Lance. Evolutionary psychology : an introduction / Lance Workman and Will Reader. New York : Cambridge University Press, 2004. p. cm. Includes bibliographical references (p.   ) and index. ISBN 0-521-80146-X ISBN 0-521-80532-5 (pb.) DDC 155.7
 1. Evolutionary psychology - Textbooks. I. Reader, Will. II. Title.
BF698.95 .W67 2004

WORKPLACE BULLYING. See **BULLYING IN THE WORKPLACE.**

WORKPLACE - PSYCHOLOGY - GREAT BRITAIN.
Hadikin, Ruth. The bullying culture. Oxford ; Boston : Books for Midwives, 2000.
BF637.B85 H33 2000

Workshop on achievement and task motivation.
International Conference on Motivation (8th : 2002 Moscow, Russia) 8th International Conference on Motivation. Moscow : Russian State University for Humanities, 2002.
BF501.5 .I58 2002

Workshop on Adaptive Behavior in Anticipatory Learning Systems (1st : 2002 : Edinburgh, Scotland) Anticipatory behavior in adaptive learning systems : foundations, theories, and systems / Martin V. Butz, Olivier Sigaud, Pierre Gérard, eds. Berlin ; New York : Springer, c2003. x, 301 p. : ill. ; 24 cm. (Lecture notes in computer science, 0302-9743 ; 2684. Lecture notes in artificial intelligence.) Includes bibliographical references and index. ISBN 3-540-40429-5 (pbk. : alk. paper) DDC 006.3/1
 1. Machine learning - Congresses. 2. Expectation (Philosophy) - Congresses. I. Butz, Martin V., 1975- II. Sigaud, Olivier. III. Gerard, Pierre. IV. International Conference on Simulation of Adaptive Behavior (7th : 2002 : University of Edinburgh) V. Title. VI. Series: Lecture notes in computer science ; 2684. VII. Series: Lecture notes in computer science.
Q325.5 .W65 2003

WORLD CITIZENSHIP.
Clark, Harold A. The age of intimacy. Laredo, TX : EBookcase.com, c2000.

WORLD DECADE FOR CULTURAL DEVELOPMENT, 1988-1997. See **CIVILIZATION.**

The world dream book.
Bluestone, Sarvananda. Rochester, Vt. : Destiny Books, c2002.
BF1091 .B616 2002

WORLD ECONOMICS. See **COMPETITION, INTERNATIONAL.**

WORLD, END OF THE. See **END OF THE WORLD.**

World eras
 (v. 1) The European Renaissance and Reformation, 1350-1600. Detroit, MI : Gale Group, 2001.
CB359 .W67 2001

 (v. 4) Medieval Europe, 814-1350. Detroit, MI : Gale Group, c2002.
D102 .M38 2001

WORLD HISTORY. See also **HISTORY, ANCIENT; HISTORY, MODERN; MIDDLE AGES; WORLD POLITICS.**

Brazier, Chris. The no-nonsense guide to world history. Oxford : New Internationalist Publications ; London : in association with Verso, c2001.
D21 .B78 2001

Nosovskiĭ, G. V. (Gleb Vladimirovich), 1958- Rekonstruktsii︠a︡ vseobshcheĭ istorii. Moskva : FID "Delovoĭ ėkspress", 2002.
DK38 .N68 2002

WORLD HISTORY, ANCIENT. See **HISTORY, ANCIENT.**

WORLD HISTORY - HISTORIOGRAPHY.
Alonso-Nuñez, José Miguel. The idea of universal history in Greece. Amsterdam : J.C. Gieben, 2002.
D13.5.G8 A46 2002

WORLD HISTORY, MODERN. See **HISTORY, MODERN.**

WORLD LITERATURE. See **LITERATURE.**

The world of Ripley's believe it or not!.
Mooney, Julie. New York : Black Dog & Leventhal, c1999.
AG243 .M653 1999

WORLD ORDER. See **INTERNATIONAL RELATIONS.**

WORLD POLITICS. See also **GEOPOLITICS; INTERNATIONAL RELATIONS; PEACEFUL CHANGE (INTERNATIONAL RELATIONS).**
Corm, Georges. Orient-Occident, la fracture imaginaire. Paris : Découverte, 2002.

Heiwagaku ga wakaru. Tōkyō : Asahi Shinbunsha, 2002.
JZ5534 .H44 2002

WORLD POLITICS - 1945-.
Zeitgeschichtliche Hintergründe aktueller Konflikte V. Zürich : Forschungsstelle für Sicherheitspolitik und Konfliktanalyse, Eidgenössische Technische Hochschule, 1995.
JX1952 .Z45 1995

WORLD POLITICS - 1945-1989.
Katznelson, Ira. Desolation and enlightenment. New York : Columbia University Press, c2003.
JA71 .K35 2003

WORLD POLITICS - 1989-.
Kritik der Gewalt. Wien : Promedia, c2002.
D860 .K75 2002

WORLD POLITICS - 20TH CENTURY.
Emmott, Bill. 20:21 vision. London : Allen Lane, 2003.

Lal, Vinay. Empire of knowledge. London ; Sterling, Va. : Pluto Press, 2002.
HN16 .L35 2002

Naumann, Klaus, 1939- Frieden, der noch nicht erfüllte Auftrag. Hamburg : Mittler & Sohn, c2002.
UA710 .N38 2002

WORLD POLITICS - 21ST CENTURY.
Naumann, Klaus, 1939- Frieden, der noch nicht erfüllte Auftrag. Hamburg : Mittler & Sohn, c2002.
UA710 .N38 2002

Vidal, Jordi. Résistance au chaos. Paris : Allia, 2002.

WORLD POLITICS - 21ST CENTURY - BIBLICAL TEACHING.
Glazerson, Matityahu. Migdele ha-te'omim be-diluge otiyot ba-Torah. Yerushalayim : Yerid ha-sefarim, 2002.

World Scientific series in 20th century physics
 (v. 30) Schrieffer, J. R. (John Robert), 1931- [Papers. Selections] Selected papers of J. Robert Schrieffer. River Edge, NJ : World Scientific, c2002.
QC21.3 .S37 2002

World Scientific series in robotics and intelligent systems
 (vol. 27) Sousa, Joao M. C. Fuzzy decision making in modeling and control. Singapore ; River Edge, N.J. : World Scientific, 2002.

World Scientific series on nonlinear science. Series A, Monographs and treatises
 (v.44) Zhusubaliyev, Zhanybai T. Bifurcations and chaos in piecewise-smooth dynamical systems. River Edge, New Jersey : World Scientific, c2003.

World social change
Gunn, Geoffrey C. First globalization. Lanham, Md. : Rowman & Littlefield, c2003.
CB251 .G87 2003

WORLD TRADE. See **INTERNATIONAL TRADE.**

WORLD TRADE CENTER (NEW YORK, N.Y.).
Glazerson, Matityahu. Migdele ha-te'omim be-diluge otiyot ba-Torah. Yerushalayim : Yerid ha-sefarim, 2002.

World Trade Organization.
United States. General Accounting Office. World Trade Organization [electronic resource]. [Washington, D.C.] : U.S. General Accounting Office, [2002]

WORLD TRADE ORGANIZATION - DECISION MAKING.
United States. General Accounting Office. World Trade Organization [electronic resource]. [Washington, D.C.] : U.S. General Accounting Office, [2002]

World Trade Organization [electronic resource].
United States. General Accounting Office. [Washington, D.C.] : U.S. General Accounting Office, [2002]

World Trade Organization : the Doha development agenda.
United States. General Accounting Office. World Trade Organization [electronic resource]. [Washington, D.C.] : U.S. General Accounting Office, [2002]

WORLD WAR, 1914-1918.
Frantzen, Allen J., 1947- Bloody good. Chicago : University of Chicago Press, 2004.
D523 .F722 2004

WORLD WAR, 1914-1918 - AERIAL OPERATIONS, AMERICAN.
Robertson, Linda R. (Linda Raine), 1946- The dream of civilized warfare. Minneapolis : University of Minnesota Press, c2003.
D606 .R63 2003

WORLD WAR, 1914-1918 - BATTLES, SIEGES, ETC. See **WORLD WAR, 1914-1918 - CAMPAIGNS.**

WORLD WAR, 1914-1918 - CAMPAIGNS - WESTERN FRONT.
Robertson, Linda R. (Linda Raine), 1946- The dream of civilized warfare. Minneapolis : University of Minnesota Press, c2003.
D606 .R63 2003

WORLD WAR, 1914-1918 - MILITARY OPERATIONS. See **WORLD WAR, 1914-1918 - CAMPAIGNS.**

WORLD WAR, 1914-1918 - SOCIAL ASPECTS - UNITED STATES.
Robertson, Linda R. (Linda Raine), 1946- The dream of civilized warfare. Minneapolis : University of Minnesota Press, c2003.
D606 .R63 2003

WORLD WAR, 1939-1945 - ATROCITIES. See **HOLOCAUST, JEWISH (1939-1945).**

WORLD WAR, 1939-1945 - CAUSES. See **NATIONAL SOCIALISM.**

WORLD WAR, 1939-1945 - INFLUENCE.
The achievement of American liberalism. New York : Columbia University Press, c2003.
E806 .M63 2003

WORLD WAR, 1939-1945 - JEWISH RESISTANCE. See **HOLOCAUST, JEWISH (1939-1945).**

WORLD WAR, 1939-1945 - JEWS. See **HOLOCAUST, JEWISH (1939-1945).**

WORLD WAR, 1939-1945 - OCCUPIED TERRITORIES.
Schaller, Helmut Wilhelm, 1940- Der Nationalsozialismus und die slawische Welt. Regensburg : Pustet, c2002.
DD256.5 .S259 2002

WORLD WAR, 1939-1945 - SOCIAL ASPECTS - GREAT BRITAIN.
Grimwood, Irene. Land girls at the old rectory. Large print ed. Oxford : ISIS, 2001.

WORLD WAR, 1939-1945 - SOCIAL ASPECTS - UNITED STATES.
The achievement of American liberalism. New York : Columbia University Press, c2003.
E806 .M63 2003

WORLD WAR, 1939-1945 - WOMEN - GREAT BRITAIN.
Grimwood, Irene. Land girls at the old rectory. Large print ed. Oxford : ISIS, 2001.

WORLD WAR I. *See* **WORLD WAR, 1914-1918.**

WORLD WAR II. *See* **WORLD WAR, 1939-1945.**

WORLD WIDE WEB.
Hayes-Roth, Frederick, 1947- Radical simplicity. Upper Saddle River, N.J. ; London : Prentice Hall PTR, 2003.
Knowledge-based information retrieval and filtering from the Web. Boston : Kluwer Academic Publishers, c2003.
TK5105.888 .K58 2003

World without design.
Rea, Michael C. (Michael Cannon), 1968- Oxford : Clarendon Press ; New York : Oxford University Press, 2002.
B828.2 .R43 2002

The world's children and their companion animals : developmental and educational significance of the child/pet bond / Mary Renck Jalongo, editor. Olney, MD : Association for Childhood Education International, 2004. p. cm. Includes bibliographical references. ISBN 0-87173-162-2 DDC 155.4/18
1. Children and animals. I. Jalongo, Mary Renck.
BF723.A45 W67 2004

The world's great philosophers / edited by Robert L. Arrington. Malden, MA : Blackwell Pub., 2003. xiii, 361 p. ; 24 cm. "Most of the essays contained in this book were originally published in A companion to the philosophers (Oxford: Blackwell, 1999). Several have been revised, and three ... are new"--Pref. Includes bibliographical references and index. ISBN 0-631-23145-5 (hardcover : alk. paper) ISBN 0-631-23146-3 (pbk. : alk. paper) DDC 109/.2
1. Philosophers. 2. Philosophy. I. Arrington, Robert L., 1938- II. Title: Companion to the philosophers.
B29 .W69 2003

The world's most mysterious objects.
Fanthorpe, R. Lionel. Toronto ; Tonawanda NY : Dundurn Press, 2002.

Worldwide directory of psychology departments and research institutes.
Psychology, IUPsyS global resource [electronic resource]. Hove, East Sussex, UK : published on behalf of the international Union of Psychological Science by Psychology Press Ltd., 2000-
BF76.5 .P79

The worried child.
Foxman, Paul. 1st ed. Alameda, CA : Hunter House, c2004.
BF723.A5 F69 2004

WORRY. *See* **ANXIETY.**

WORRY IN CHILDREN - JUVENILE LITERATURE.
Berry, Joy Wilt. Let's talk about feeling worried. New York : Scholastic Inc., c2002.
BF723.W67 B47 2002
Berry, Joy Wilt. Let's talk about getting hurt. New York : Scholastic, c2002.
BF723.W67 B475 2002

WORSHIP. *See* **DIVINATION; PRAYER; SOUL WORSHIP.**

WORSHIP (JUDAISM). *See also* **JUDAISM - LITURGY.**
Fridlander, Hayim ben Mosheh. Sefer Śifte ḥayim. Bene-Beraḳ : ha-Rabanit Fridlander, 763- [2002 or 2003-

WORSHIP OF CHRISTIAN SAINTS. *See* **CHRISTIAN SAINTS - CULT.**

WORSHIP OF SATAN. *See* **SATANISM.**

Wort und (Kon)text / Piroska Kocsány, Anna Molnár (Hrsg.). Frankfurt : Lang, 2001. 290 p. : ill. ; 21 cm. (Metal.inguistica, 0946-4174 ; Bd. 7) Wort und Kontext. Includes bibliographical references. English, French and German. CONTENTS: Interlingual lexical equivalence in machine translation / Elizaveta Kotorova, Nico Weber -- Konzeptuelle Fokussierung: Bemerkungen zur Behandlung der Polysemie in der Zwei-Ebenen-Semantik / Gergely Pethő -- On the development of the category 'modal': a cognitive view: how changes in image-schematic structure led to the emergence of the grounding predication / Péter Pelyvás -- Ein möglicher Weg der Grammatikalisierung der Modalpartikel 'wohl': eine Fallstudie / Anna Molnár -- Die kontextuellen Varianten des Konnektors 'doch': ein Ausdruck von Relationen zwischen Widerspruch und Begründung / Ursula Brausse -- A propos de l'anaphore conceptuelle / Franciska Skutta -- Syntagme nominal et représentation pronominale en français et en hongrois / Sándor Kiss -- Word finding processes: research on conversation analysis and its research methodological implications / Zsuzsanna Iványi -- Wort und Rhetorik: Enallage und Hypallage : eine besondere Art Bedeutungstransfer / Piroska Kocsány. ISBN 3-631-36790-2 (pbk.)
1. Context (Linguistics) 2. Discourse analysis. 3. Semantics. 4. Pragmatics. 5. Machine translating. 6. Modality (Linguistics) I. Kocsány, Piroska. II. Molnár, Anna. III. Title: Wort und Kontext IV. Series.
P325.5.C65 W678 2001

Wort und Kontext.
Wort und (Kon)text. Frankfurt : Lang, 2001.
P325.5.C65 W678 2001

WORTH. *See* **VALUES.**

Wortham, Simon. Samuel Weber : acts of reading / Simon Morgan Wortham. Aldershot, England ; Burlington, VT : Ashgate, c2003. xiii, 147 p. ; 24 cm. Includes bibliographical references (p. [141]-144) and index. ISBN 0-7546-3122-2 (alk. paper) DDC 801/.95/092
1. Weber, Samuel M. 2. Criticism. 3. Psychoanalysis and literature. 4. Mass media criticism. I. Title.
PN81 .W64 2003

Wortham, Stanton Emerson Fisher, 1963-.
Linguistic anthropology of education. Westport, Conn. ; London : Praeger, 2003.
P40.8 .L55 2003

Worthington, Everett L., 1946-.
Five steps to forgiveness.
Worthington, Everett L., 1946- Forgiving and reconciling. Rev. ed. Downers Grove, Ill. : InterVarsity Press, c2003.
BF637.F67 W67 2003

Forgiving and reconciling : bridges to wholeness and hope / Everett Worthington. Rev. ed. Downers Grove, Ill. : InterVarsity Press, c2003. 268 p. : ill. ; 23 cm. Rev. ed. of: Five steps to forgiveness. c2001. Includes bibliographical references and indexes. Table of contents URL: http://www.loc.gov/catdir/toc/ecip041/2003006825.html CONTENTS: Why forgive? -- Unforgiveness, justice and forgiveness -- The Christian foundation of forgiveness -- R: Recall the hurt -- E: Empathize -- A: Altruistic gift of forgiveness -- C: Commit publicly to forgive -- H: Hold onto forgiveness -- Decisions -- Discussion -- Detoxification -- Devotion. ISBN 0-8308-3244-0 (pbk.) DDC 158.2
1. Forgiveness. 2. Reconciliation. I. Worthington, Everett L., 1946- Five steps to forgiveness. II. Title.
BF637.F67 W67 2003

Wortzauber.
Müller, Klaus E., 1935- Frankfurt : Lembeck, c2001.
P35 .M945 2001

WOUNDS AND INJURIES IN CHILDREN. *See* **CHILDREN - WOUNDS AND INJURIES.**

Wounds not healed by time.
Schimmel, Solomon. Oxford ; New York : Oxford University Press, 2002.
BJ1476 .S34 2002

Wouters, Alfons.
Grammatical theory and philosophy of language in antiquity. Leuven ; Sterling, Va. : Peeters, 2002.
P63 .G73 2002

Wowisms : words of wisdom for dreamers and doers / [compiled by] Ron Rubin and Stuart Avery Gold. 1st ed. New York : Newmarket Press, c2003. p. cm. ISBN 1-55704-590-9 (alk. paper) DDC 158
1. Success - Psychological aspects. 2. Change (Psychology) 3. Risk-taking (Psychology) I. Rubin, Ron. II. Gold, Stuart Avery.
BF637.S8 W7 2003

Wozniuk, Vladimir.
Solovyov, Vladimir Sergeyevich, 1853-1900. [Essays. English. Selections] The heart of reality. Notre Dame, Ind. : University of Notre Dame Press, c2003.
B4262.A5 W69 2003

WRATH. *See* **ANGER.**

WRECKS. *See* **SHIPWRECKS.**

Wrestling with an angel.
Luz, Ehud. [Ma'avaḳ be-naḥal Yaboḳ. English] New Haven : Yale University Press, c2003.
DS143 .L8913 2003

Wreszin, Michael.
Macdonald, Dwight. Interviews with Dwight Macdonald. Jackson : University Press of Mississippi, c2003.
E169.1 .M1363 2003

Wright, Gill.
A parliament of science. Albany : State University of New York Press, c2003.
Q158.5 .P38 2003

Wright, Jeremiah A., Jr.
From one brother to another. Volume 2. Valley Forge, PA : Judson Press, c2003.

WRIGHT, ORVILLE, 1871-1948 - PHILOSOPHY.
Eppler, Mark, 1946- The Wright way. New York : AMACOM, c2004.
TL540.W7 E64 2004

Wright, Robin, 1950-.
In darkness and secrecy. Durham, NC : Duke University Press, 2004.
BF1566 .I5 2004

The Wright way.
Eppler, Mark, 1946- New York : AMACOM, c2004.
TL540.W7 E64 2004

WRIGHT, WILBUR, 1867-1912 - PHILOSOPHY.
Eppler, Mark, 1946- The Wright way. New York : AMACOM, c2004.
TL540.W7 E64 2004

Wrisberg, Craig A.
Schmidt, Richard A., 1941- Motor learning and performance. 3rd ed. Champaign, IL : Human Kinetics, 2004.
BF295 .S249 2004

WRITERS. *See* **AUTHORS.**

Writers and poets on sources of inspiration.
Me-ayin nahalti et shiri. Tel Aviv : Yedi'ot aḥaronot : Sifre ḥemed, c2002.

WRITING. *See* **GRAPHOLOGY.**

WRITING - ABILITY TESTING.
Weigle, Sara Cushing. Assessing writing. Cambridge ; New York, NY : Cambridge University Press, 2002.
PE1065 .W35 2002

Writing and materiality in China : essays in honor of Patrick Hanan / edited by Judith T. Zeitlin & Lydia H. Liu, with Ellen Widmer. Cambridge, Mass. : Published by Harvard University Asia Center for Harvard-Yenching Institute : distributed by Harvard University Press, 2003. xvii, 639 p. : ill. ; 24 cm. (Harvard-Yenching Institute monograph series ; 58) Includes bibliographical references and index. CONTENTS: Pt. 1. The circulation of writing. On rubbings: their materiality and historicity / Wu Hung ; Disappearing verses: writing on walls and anxieties of loss / Judith T. Zeitlin ; The literary consumption of actors in seventeenth-century China / Sophie Volpp -- Pt. 2. Print culture and networks of reading. Jin Ping Mei and late Ming print culture / Shang Wei ; Duplicating the strength of feeling: the circulation of Qingshu in the late Ming / Kathryn Lowry ; Considering a coincidence: the "female reading public" circa 1828 / Ellen Widmer -- Pt. 3. The late Qing periodical press: new images, new fiction. The new novel before the new novel: John Fryer's fiction contest / Anonymous ; The weird in the newspaper / Rania Huntington ; Creating the urban beauty: the Shanghai courtesan in late Qing illustrations / Catherine Vance Yeh -- Pt. 4. Ethnography, media, and ideology. Texts on the right and pictures on the left: reading the Qing record of frontier Taiwan / Emma J. Teng ; Tope and Topos: the Leifeng pagoda and the discourse of the demonic / Eugene Y. Wang ; A folksong immortal and official popular culture in twentieth-century China / Lydia H. Liu. ISBN 0-674-01098-1 (alk. paper) DDC 895.1/09
1. Chinese literature - History and criticism. 2. Mass media and culture. I. Hanan, Patrick. II. Zeitlin, Judith T., 1958- III. Liu, Lydia He. IV. Widmer, Ellen. V. Series.
PL2262 .W74 2003

WRITING (AUTHORSHIP). *See* **AUTHORSHIP; JOURNALISM.**

WRITING, FICTION. *See* **FICTION - TECHNIQUE.**

Writing for psychology.
Mitchell, Mark L. 1st ed. Australia ; Belmont, CA : Wadsworth/Thomson, 2004.
BF76.7 .M58 2004

WRITING - HISTORY.
Bichakjian, Bernard H. Language in a Darwinian perspective. Frankfurt am Main ; New York : Peter Lang, c2002.
P142 .B53 2002

Haarmann, Harald. Geschichte der Schrift. Originalausg. München : C.H. Beck, c2002.

Marchand, Valère-Marie. Les alphabets de l'oubli. Paris : Editions Alternatives, 2002.
P211 .M373 2002

Sini, Carlo, 1933- La scrittura e il debito. Milano : Jaca book, 2002.

Tagle Frías de Cuenca, Matilde. Notas sobre historia del libro. Córdoba, República Argentina : Ediciones del Copista, c1997.
Z4

Veličková, Helena. Grafologie, cesta do hlubin duše. Vyd. 1. Praha : Academia, 2002.

BF896 .V45 2002

Writing in the dark : phenomenological studies in interpretive inquiry / edited by Max van Manen. London, Ont. : Althouse Press, 2002. ii, 252 p. ; 23 cm. Includes bibliographical references. ISBN 0-920354-49-1 DDC 808/.0663
1. Readers - Social sciences. 2. Social sciences - Authorship. 3. Qualitative research. I. Van Manen, Max.
B829.5 .W75 2002

The writing of Orpheus.
Detienne, Marcel. [Ecriture d'Orphee. English] Baltimore : Johns Hopkins University Press, 2002, c2003.
BL783 .D4813 2003

The writing on the wall.
Hannas, Wm. C., 1946- Philadelphia : University of Pennsylvania Press, c2003.
P381.E18 H36 2003

WRITING - PHILOSOPHY.
Sini, Carlo, 1933- La scrittura e il debito. Milano : Jaca book, 2002.

WRITING - PSYCHOLOGICAL ASPECTS.
Florenskaīa, O. Psikhologiīa bytovogo shrifta. Sankt-Peterburg : Krasnyĭ matros, 2001.
BF896 .F66 2001

Writing science
Luhmann, Niklas. [Beobachtungen der Moderne. English] Observations on modernity. Stanford, CA : Stanford University Press, 1998.
HM24 .L88813 1998

Writing the future.
Wickham-Crowley, Kelley M. Cardiff : University of Wales Press, 2002.

Writings from the ancient world
(no. 12) Nissinen, Martti. Prophets and prophecy in the ancient Near East. Atlanta, GA : Society of Biblical Literature, c2003.
BF1762 .N58 2003b
(no. 12) Nissinen, Martti. Prophets and prophecy in the ancient Near East. Leiden ; Boston : Brill, 2003.
BF1762 .N58 2003

Writings from the late notebooks.
Nietzsche, Friedrich Wilhelm, 1844-1900. [Selections. English. 2003] Cambridge, UK ; New York : Cambridge University Press, c2003.
B3312.E5 B58 2003

Writings on art.
Marioni, Tom, 1937- San Francisco, Calif. : Crown Point Press, 2000.

Writings on art, Tom Marioni, 1969-1999.
Marioni, Tom, 1937- Writings on art. San Francisco, Calif. : Crown Point Press, 2000.

WRITTEN COMMUNICATION. See also **ENGLISH LANGUAGE - WRITTEN ENGLISH.**
Destinos das letras. Passo Fundo : Universidade de Passo Fundo, 2002.
P211 .D47 2002

Marcuschi, Luiz Antônio. Investigando a relação oral/escrito e as teorias do letramento. Campinas, SP : Mercado de Letras, 2001.

Roelcke, Thorsten. Kommunikative Effizienz. Heidelberg : Winter, c2002.

WRITTEN ENGLISH. See **ENGLISH LANGUAGE - WRITTEN ENGLISH.**

Wrocławskie Sympozjum Badań Pisma (9th : 2000 : Wrocław, Poland) Contemporary problems of proof from a document : proceedings of the IXth Wroclaw Symposium of Handwriting Research, Wroclaw, June 14-16, 2000 / edited by Zdzisław Kegel. Wroclaw : University of Wroclaw, Faculty of Law, Administration, and Economy, Department of Criminalistics, 2002. 393 p., [4] leaves of plates : ill. (some col.) ; 24 cm. ISBN 83-88955-30-6 DDC 363.25/65
1. Graphology - Congresses. I. Kegel, Zdzisław. II. Uniwersytet Wrocławski. Katedra Kryminalistyki. III. Title.
BF891 .W76 2000

Wruck, Wilfried, 1938- Zur Ruhe kommst du, Adrian Bruegge, nie : eine Lebensbeschreibung / Wilfried Wruck. 1. Aufl. Berlin : Frieling, 2000. 175 p. ; 19 cm. ISBN 3-8280-1193-4 (pbk.)
1. Wruck, Wilfried, - 1938- 2. Bereavement - Psychological aspects. I. Title.

WRUCK, WILFRIED, 1938-.
Wruck, Wilfried, 1938- Zur Ruhe kommst du, Adrian Bruegge, nie. 1. Aufl. Berlin : Frieling, 2000.

WU, JING, 670-749.
ZHENGUAN ZHENG YAO.
An, Lizhi. "Zhen guan zheng yao" yu ling dao yi shu. Di 1 ban. Shanghai : Shanghai gu ji chu ban she, 1999.
DS749.3.W813 A63 1999

Wu, Xinming.
Fang yuan bing fa. Di 1 ban. Beijing : Jin cheng chu ban she, 1998.

Wu zhong ban ben Dao zang tong jian.
Schipper, Kristofer Marinus. Dao zang suo yin. Di 1 ban. Shanghai : Shanghai shu dian chu ban she : Xin hua shu dian Shanghai fa xing suo fa xin, 1996.
BL1900.T387 S35 1996 <Orien China>

Wulf, Christoph, 1944-.
Logik und Leidenschaft. Berlin : D. Reimer Verlag, c2002.

Wulf, Volker.
Sharing expertise. Cambridge, Mass. : MIT Press, c2003.
HD30.2 .S53 2003

Wunderlich, Uli.
Mörgeli, Christoph. "Über dem Grabe geboren". Bern : Benteli, 2002.

Wunenburger, Jean-Jacques. La vie des images / Jean-Jacques Wunenburger. [Nouvelle édition augmentée]. Grenoble : Presses universitaires de Grenoble, 2002. 275 p. ; 21 cm. (La bibliothèque de l'imaginaire) Includes bibliographical references. ISBN 2-7061-1041-4
1. Imagery (Psychology) 2. Symbolism. 3. Myth. I. Title. II. Series.
BF367 .W85 2002

Wurzer, Wilhelm S.
Panorama. New York : Continuum, 2002.
BH39 .P2292 2002

Wyer, Robert S.
Foundations of social cognition. Mahwah, N.J. : L. Erlbaum, 2003.
BF323.S63 F68 2003

Social comprehension and judgment : the role of situation models, narratives, and implicit theories / Robert S. Wyer, Jr. Mahwah, N.J. : L. Erlbaum Associates, Publishers, 2004. xv, 421 p. : ill. ; 24 cm. Includes bibliographical references (p. 380-403) and indexes. DDC 153
1. Social perception. 2. Human information processing - Social aspects. 3. Judgement. 4. Memory. I. Title.
BF323.S63 W94 2004

XENOPHOBIA.
Fremderfahrung und Repräsentation. 1. Aufl. Weilerswist : Velbrück, 2002.

XHTML (DOCUMENT MARKUP LANGUAGE).
Musciano, Chuck. HTML and XHTML, the definitive guide. 5th ed. Beijing ; Sebastopol [Calif.] : O'Reilly, 2002.

Xi bu zhi jin.
Tang, Yijie. Di 1 ban. Shanghai : Shanghai wen yi chu ban she, 1999.
B126 .T1965 1999

Xi fang zhe xue ci dian.
Tshe-riṅ-rdo-rje, 'Broṅ-bu. Nub phyogs śer rtogs rig pa'i tshig bum. Par theṅs 1. Pe-cin : Mi rigs dpe skrun khaṅ, 1995.

Xi ju yan chu zhong di jia ding xing.
Wang, Xiaoying, 1957- Di 1 ban. Beijing : Zhongguo xi ju chu ban she : Xin hua shu dian zong dian Beijing fa xing suo fa xing, 1995.
PN2039 .W35 1995 <Orien China>

Xi zang fo jiao cai hui cai su yi shu.
Xizang fo jiao cai hui cai su yi shu. Di 1 ban. Beijing : Zhongguo Zang xue chu ban she : Xin hua shu dian Beijing fa xing suo fa xing, 1997.
ND1489 .X593 1997

Xian dai mi shu xi lie jiao cai.
Zhou, Xiuping. Wen xue xin shang yu pi ping. Di 1 ban. Changsha : Zhong nan gong ye da xue chu ban she, 1998.
PL2262 .Z468 1998

Xiao, Junhe.
Wen xue yin lun. Di 1 ban. Ha'erbin Shi : Heilongjiang jiao yu chu ban she, 1999.

Xiao, Ying. Xing xiang yu sheng cun : shen mei shi dai di wen hua li lun / Xiao Ying zhu. Beijing di 1 ban. Beijing : Zuo jia chu ban she : Jing xiao Xin hua shu dian Beijing fa xing suo, 1996. 3, 204 p. ; 21 cm. (Dang dai shen mei wen hua xi) "Guo jia 'ba wu' gui hua zhe xue she hui ke xue zhong dian ke ti." Includes bibliographical references. ISBN 7-5063-1051-1
1. Arts, Chinese - 20th century. 2. Aesthetics. I. Title. II. Title: Shen mei shi dai di wen hua li lun III. Series.
NX583.A1 H756 1996 <Asian China>

Xie jiao zhen xiang / zhu bian Chen Zhimin, Zhang Xianglin ; fu zhu bian Zhao Wenyao. Di 1 ban. Beijing : Dang dai shi jie chu ban she, 2001. 2 v. : ill. ; 21 cm. ISBN 7-80115-437-1 (set)
1. Heresy. 2. Cults. 3. Religion. I. Chen, Zhimin. II. Zhang, Xianglin. III. Zhao, Wenyao.
BT1315.2 .X54 2001

Xie, Sizhong. Su zhi yu ming yun / Xie Sizhong zhu. Di 1 ban. Beijing : Zuo jia chu ban she, 2002. 2, 3, 308 p. : facsims., ports. ; 21 cm. ISBN 7-5063-2293-5
1. Human beings. 2. Ethics. I. Title.
BD450 .X54 2002

Xin shi xun.
Feng, Youlan, 1895- Di 1 ban. Beijing : Beijing da xue chu ban she : Jing xiao zhe Xin hua shu dian, 1996.
BJ1588.C5 F42 1996 <Asian China>

Xin yu wen jian she shi hua.
Ling, Yuanzheng. Di 1 ban. Kaifeng Shi : Henan da xue chu ban she : Henan sheng Xin hua shu dian fa xing, 1995.
PL1175 .L55 1995 <Orien China>

Xing, Li. Guanyin : Shen sheng yu shi su / Xing Li zhu. Beijing di 2 ban. Beijing : Xue yuan chu ban she, 2001. 10, 5, 5, 400 p. : ill. ; 20 cm. (San zu wu wen cong) ISBN 7-5077-1095-5
1. Avalokiteśvara (Buddhist deity) 2. Gods, Buddhist. 3. Mythology, Chinese. I. Title. II. Series.
BQ4710.A8 X564 2001

Xing qing nan nü.
Xu, Kun. Beijing di 1 ban. Beijing : Zhong'guo qing nian chu ban she, 2001.

Xing xiang yu sheng cun.
Xiao, Ying. Beijing di 1 ban. Beijing : Zuo jia chu ban she : Jing xiao Xin hua shu dian Beijing fa xing suo, 1996.
NX583.A1 H756 1996 <Asian China>

Xizang fo jiao cai hui cai su yi shu : "Rulai fo shen liang ming xi bao lun", "Cai hui gong xu ming jian". Di 1 ban. Beijing : Zhongguo Zang xue chu ban she : Xin hua shu dian Beijing fa xing suo fa xing, 1997. 153 p. ; 19 cm. Cover title also in pinyin: Xi zang fo jiao cai hui cai su yi shu. Includes bibliographical references (p. 152). CONTENTS: Rulai fo shen liang ming xi bao lun / by Menladunzhu -- Cai hui gong xu ming jian / by Dumagexi Danzhenpengcuo. ISBN 7-80057-320-6
1. Color in art. 2. Painting, Tibetan. 3. Painting, Buddhist - China - Tibet. I. Sman-bla Don-grub, 15th cent. Rulai fo shen liang ming xi bao lun. II. Dri med śel gon dan śel phren, 1725- Cai hui gong xu ming jian. III. Title: Xi zang fo jiao cai hui cai su yi shu
ND1489 .X593 1997

Xizang shi dian cong shu
Cai, Zhichun. Huo fo zhuan shi. Di 1 ban. Beijing : Hua wen chu ban she : Xin hua shu dian jing xiao, 2000.
BL515 .C345 2000

XML (DOCUMENT MARKUP LANGUAGE).
Visualizing the semantic Web. London ; [New York] : Springer, c2003.
TK5105.888 .V55 2003

Xu, Fancheng. Xu Fancheng ji / Zhongguo she hui ke xue yuan ke yan ju zu zhi bian xuan. Di 1 ban. Beijing : Zhongguo she hui ke xue chu ban she, 2001. 5, 2, 413 p. : ill. ; 22 cm. (Zhongguo she hui ke xue yuan xue zhe wen xuan) English title (p. [4] of cover: Volume of Xu Fancheng. Includes bibliographical references. ISBN 7-5004-3208-9
1. Chinese literature - History and criticism. 2. Philosophy, Chinese. 3. Buddhism - China. I. Zhongguo she hui ke xue yuan. Ke yan ju. II. Title. III. Title: Volume of Xu Fancheng IV. Series.
PL2262.2 .X84 2001

Xu Fancheng ji.
Xu, Fancheng. Di 1 ban. Beijing : Zhongguo she hui ke xue chu ban she, 2001.
PL2262.2 .X84 2001

Xu, Fen. Zou xiang hou xian dai yu hou zhi min / Xu Fen zhu. Di 1 ban. Beijing : Zhongguo she hui ke xue chu ban she : Xin hua shu dian jing xiao, 1996. 2, 313 p. : ill. ; 21 cm. Includes bibliographical references. ISBN 7-5004-1912-0
1. Criticism. 2. Postmodernism (Literature) 3. Decolonization in literature. 4. Popular culture. I. Title.

Xu, Guiting.
PN81 .H76 1996 <Asian China>

Xu, Guiting.
Lin, Shu, 1852-1924. Tie bi jin zhen. Di 1 ban. Tianjin Shi : Bai hua wen yi chu ban she, 2002.
PL2718.I5 T54 2002

Xu, Kun. Xing qing nan nü / Xu Kun zhu. Beijing di 1 ban. Beijing : Zhong'guo qing nian chu ban she, 2001. 407 p. : ill. ; 21 cm. (Xu Kun zuo pin jing hua. San wen juan) ISBN 7-5006-4093-5
1. Love. I. Title. II. Series.

Xu Kun zuo pin jing hua. San wen juan
Xu, Kun. Xing qing nan nü. Beijing di 1 ban. Beijing : Zhong'guo qing nian chu ban she, 2001.

Xu, Wenjing, 1667-1756? Guan cheng shi ji / Xu Wenjing zhu ; Fan Xiangyong dian jiao. Di 1 ban. Beijing : Zhonghua shu ju : Xin hua shu dian Beijing fa xing suo fa xing, 1998. 2, 3, 2, 3, 576 p. ; 21 cm. (Xue shu bi ji cong kan) Includes bibliographical references. ISBN 7-101-01191-8
1. Chinese classics - History and criticism. 2. Chinese literature - History and criticism. I. Fan, Xiangyong. II. Title. III. Series.
PL2461.Z6 H77 1998

Xu wu piao miao de gui shen shi jie.
Zhao, Xi. Di 1 ban. Beijing : Zong jiao wen hua chu ban she, 2001.
BL1812.G63 Z436 2001

Xue lin chun qiu. Chu bian.
Xue lin chun qiu. Di 1 ban. Beijing : Chao hua chu ban she, 1999.
PL2272.5 .X846 1999

Xue lin chun qiu. Er bian.
Xue lin chun qiu. Di 1 ban. Beijing : Chao hua chu ban she, 1999.
PL2272.5 .X846 1999

Xue lin chun qiu. San bian.
Xue lin chun qiu. Di 1 ban. Beijing : Chao hua chu ban she, 1999.
PL2272.5 .X846 1999

Xue lin chun qiu / Zhang Shilin bian. Di 1 ban. Beijing : Chao hua chu ban she, 1999. 6 v. : ports. ; 22 cm. CONTENTS: [1]-[2] Chu bian -- [3]-[4] Er bian -- [5]-[6] San bian. ISBN 7-5054-0639-6
1. China - Study and teaching. 2. Chinese literature - History and criticism. 3. Philosophy, Chinese - China. 4. Chinese language - History. I. Zhang, Shilin. II. Title: Xue lin chun qiu. Chu bian. III. Title: Xue lin chun qiu. Er bian. IV. Title: Xue lin chun qiu. San bian.
PL2272.5 .X846 1999

Xue shu bi ji cong kan
Xu, Wenjing, 1667-1756? Guan cheng shi ji. Di 1 ban. Beijing : Zhonghua shu ju : Xin hua shu dian Beijing fa xing suo fa xing, 1998.
PL2461.Z6 H77 1998

Xue shu chuang xin
Zhongguo xiang zheng wen hua. Di 1 ban. Shanghai : Shanghai ren min chu ban she : Xin hua shu dian Shanghai fa xing suo jing xiao, 2001.
DS721 .Z4985 2001

Xue shu de nian lun.
Jiang, Yin. Di 1 ban. [Beijing] : Zhongguo wen lian chu ban she, 2000.
PL2262 .J536 2000

Xue shu jiu guo.
Huang, Minlan. Di 1 ban. Zhengzhou Shi : Henan ren min chu ban she, 1995.
D16.9 .H795 1995 <Asian China>

Xue yuan jing dian wen ku
Yan, Zhitui, 531-591. Yan shi jia xun zhu ping. Di 1 ban. Beijing Shi : Xue yuan chu ban she, 2000.
BJ117 .Y4 2000

Xue yuan ying hua
Li, Zehou. Tan xun yu sui. Di 1 ban. Shanghai : Shanghai wen yi chu ban she, 2000.
B126 .L532 2000

Liu, Shuxian, 1934- Li yi fen shu. Di 1 ban. Shanghai : Shanghai wen yi chu ban she, 2000.
B29 .L68 2000

Shi, Zhecun. Beishan si chuang. Di 1 ban. Shanghai : Shanghai wen yi chu ban she : Xin hua shu dian jing xiao, 2000.
PL2272.5 .S543 2000

Tang, Yijie. Xi bu zhi jin. Di 1 ban. Shanghai : Shanghai wen yi chu ban she, 1999.
B126 .T1965 1999

XX vek : metodologicheskie problemy istoricheskogo poznaniia : sbornik obzorov i referatov / [redkollegiia A.L. IAstrebitskaia... et al.]. Moskva : INION RAN, 2001- 2 v. ; 20 cm. (Seriia "Sotsial'nye i gumanitarnye nauki v XX veke") (Sotsial'nye i gumanitarnye nauki v XX veke) At head of title: Rossiĭskaia akademiia nauk. Institut nauchnoĭ informatsii po obshchestvennym naukam. Includes bibliographical references. CONTENTS: 1. Istoriia kak otrasl' znaniia. "Spor bez kontsa" : Istoriograficheskiĭ protsess v kontekste "Bol'shogo vremeni" samoraskrytiia evropeĭskoĭ intellektual'noĭ kul'tury : Istoricheskaia nauka 2000 -- ISBN 5248013763 (set) ISBN 5248013755 (v.1)
1. Historiography. I. IAstrebitskaia, Alla L'vovna. II. Institut nauchnoĭ informatsii po obshchestvennym naukam (Rossiĭskaia akademiia nauk) III. Title: 20. vek : metodologicheskie problemy istoricheskogo poznaniia IV. Title: Dvadtsatyĭ vek : metodologicheskie problemy istoricheskogo poznaniia V. Series. VI. Series: Seriia "Sotsial'nye i gumanitarnye nauki v XX veke"

XX vek plus
Spivak, M. L. Posmertnaia diagnostika genial'nosti. Moskva : Agraf, 2001.
BF416.A1 S68 2001

Xypas, Constantin. Les stades du développement affectif selon Piaget / Constantin Xypas. Paris : Harmattan, c2001. 169 p. ; 22 cm. (Psycho-logiques) Includes bibliographical references (p. 153-157). ISBN 2-7475-0648-7 DDC 150
1. Emotions in children. 2. Moral development. 3. Child psychology. I. Title. II. Series.

Y.
Jones, Steve, 1944- Boston : Houghton Mifflin, 2003.
GN281 .J62 2003

Y CHROMOSOME
Jones, Steve, 1944- Y. Boston : Houghton Mifflin, 2003.
GN281 .J62 2003

Y CHROMOSOME - POPULAR WORKS.
Sykes, Bryan. Adam's curse. London ; New York : Bantam, 2003.

Yahav, Avino'am Shemu'el. Kuntres E'eśeh lo 'ezer : 'etsot ve-hanhagot ... be-'inyene ḥaye ha-niśu'in .. / Avino'am Shemu'el Yahav. Betar 'Ilit : A. S. Yahav, 761, 2001. 104 p. ; 24 cm.
1. Marriage - Religious aspects - Judaism. 2. Jewish families - Religious life. 3. Ethics, Jewish. I. Title. II. Title: E'eśeh lo 'ezer

YAHVEH. See **GOD (JUDAISM) - NAME.**

YAHWEH. See **GOD (JUDAISM) - NAME.**

Yale Assessment of Thinking.
Mangieri, John N. San Francisco : Jossey-Bass, c2003.
BF442 .M34 2003

Yalḳuṭ Leḳaḥ ṭov.
Baifus, Ya'akov Yiśra'el, ha-Kohen. [Leḳaḥ ṭov (Ḥayim shel Torah)] Rekhasim : "Tashbar ha-Rav", 760- [1999 or 2000-

Yalḳuṭ Or ha-ḥayim ha-ḳadosh.
Lugasi, Ya'akov Yiśra'el. Yerushalayim : [ḥ. mo. l], 762 [2001 or 2002]

Yalḳuṭ Sefer ha-Ḥinukh.
Globerman, Daniyel Aharon. Modi'in 'Ilit : D. A. Globerman, Kolel "Libo ḥafets", 761 [2000 or 2001]
BM520.8.A32 G4 2001

Yalḳuṭ Ṭuv ha-peninim : 'al ha-Torah u-mo'adim : ve-hu osef perushim ... shel gedole ha-dorot ... be-derekh musar ya-'avodat H. ... / hekhin u-fa'al Pinḥas Yehudah Liberman. Yerushala[y]im : P. Y. Liberman, 762 [2001 or 2002] 2 v. (384, 400 p.) ; 25 cm. Running title: Ṭuv ha-peninim. T.p. partially vocalized. CONTENTS: ḥeleḳ 1. Be-reshit. Shemot -- ḥeleḳ 2. Va-yiḳra. Ba-midbar. Devarim.
1. Bible. - O.T. - Pentateuch - Commentaries. 2. Festival-day sermons, Jewish. 3. Jewish sermons, Hebrew. 4. Ethics, Jewish. I. Liberman, Pinḥas Yehudah. II. Title: Ṭuv ha-peninim
BS1225.53 .Y35 2001

Yalḳuṭ Yosef.
Yosef, Yitsḥaḳ. [Yalḳuṭ Yosef (Kibud av va-em)] Sefer Yalḳuṭ Yosef. Yerushalayim : Mekhon "Ḥazon 'Ovadyah", 761 [2001]
BM523.5.R4 Y72 2001

YALLOF (AFRICAN PEOPLE). See **WOLOF (AFRICAN PEOPLE).**

Yammarino, Francis J., 1954-.
Multi-level issues in organizational behavior and strategy. Amsterdam : London : JAI, 2003.

Yan shi jia xun yi zhu.
Zhuang, Huiming. Di 1 ban. Shanghai : Shanghai gu ji chu ban she : Xin hua shu dian Shanghai fa xing suo fa xing, 1999.

Yan shi jia xun zhu ping.
Yan, Zhitui, 531-591. Di 1 ban. Beijing Shi : Xue yuan chu ban she, 2000.
BJ117 .Y4 2000

Yan, Xianglin, 1960- Si wang mei xue / Yan Xianglin zhu. Di 1 ban. Shanghai : Xue lin chu ban she, 1998. 3, 2, 347 p. ; 21 cm. Includes bibliographical references. Summary in English. ISBN 7-80616-537-1
1. Death. 2. Aesthetics. 3. Death in literature. 4. Death in art. I. Title.

YAN, ZHITUI, 531-591.
YAN SHI JIA XUN.
Zhuang, Huiming. Yan shi jia xun yi zhu. Di 1 ban. Shanghai : Shanghai gu ji chu ban she : Xin hua shu dian Shanghai fa xing suo fa xing, 1999.

Yan shi jia xun. 1999.
Zhuang, Huiming. Yan shi jia xun yi zhu. Di 1 ban. Shanghai : Shanghai gu ji chu ban she : Xin hua shu dian Shanghai fa xing suo fa xing, 1999.

Yan shi jia xun zhu ping / Yan Zhitui zhuan ; Liu Yanjie, Liu Shi zhu ping. Di 1 ban. Beijing Shi : Xue yuan chu ban she, 2000. 4, 2, 313 p. ; 21 cm. (Xue yuan jing dian wen ku) ISBN 7-80060-974-X
1. Ethics - China. 2. Conduct of life. I. Liu, Yanjie. II. Liu, Shi, 1963- III. Title. IV. Series.
BJ117 .Y4 2000

Yanai, Me'ir. Orot ha-tamtsit / Me'ir Yanai. Yerushalayim : Nezer David - Ari'el, 761 [2000 or 2001] 1 v. (various pagings) ; 25 cm. CONTENTS: Tamtsit ha-ḥayim -- tamtsit ha-en veha-yesh -- tamtsit ha-adam -- tamtsit ha-tsatsit.
1. Ethics, Jewish. 2. Jew - Conduct of life. I. Title.

Yang, Chunshi, 1948-.
Li, Zehou. Tan xun yu sui. Di 1 ban. Shanghai : Shanghai wen yi chu ban she, 2000.
B126 .L532 2000

Liu, Zaifu, 1941- Shu yuan si xu. Xianggang : Tian di tu shu you xian gong si, 2002.
PL2879.T653 S58 2002

Yang gu wen cong
Huang, Shizhong. Hun bian, dao de yu wen xue. Di 1 ban. Beijing : Ren min wen xue chu ban she, 2000.

Yang, Kai. Design for Six Sigma : a roadmap for product development / Kai Yang, Basem El-Haik. New York ; London : McGraw-Hill, c2003. xvi, 624 p. : ill. ; 24 cm. Includes bibliographical references (p. 611-617) and index. ISBN 0-07-141208-5 DDC 658.5/62
1. Quality control - Statistical methods. 2. Experimental design. I. El-Haik, Basem. II. Title.
TS156 .Y33 2003

Yankelevich, Héctor, 1946- Du père à la lettre : dans la clinique, la littérature, la métapsychologie / Hector Yankelevich. Ramonville Saint-Agne : Erès, c2003. 284 p. : ill. ; 22 cm. (Point hors ligne) Includes bibliographical references. ISBN 2-7492-0117-9 DDC 150
1. Autism in children. 2. Psychoanalysis and literature. 3. Psychoanalysis. I. Title. II. Series.

Yano, Michio, 1944-.
Kūshyār, d. ca. 961. [Introduction to astrology] Kūšyār ibn Labbān's introduction to astrology. Tokyo : Institue for the Study of Languages and Cultures of Asia and Africa, 1997.
BF1714.I84 K87 1997

Yanow, Dvora. Constructing "race" and "ethnicity" in America : category-making in public policy and administration / Dvora Yanow. Armonk, N.Y. : M.E. Sharpe, c2003. viii, 252 p. : ill. ; 24 cm. Includes bibliographical references (p. 231-245) and index. CONTENTS: Part I. Laying the groundwork : giving a(n) (ac)count. 1. Constructing categories : naming, counting, science, and identity -- 2. Toward an American categorical "science" of race and ethnicity : OMB Directive No. 15 -- Part II. Making race-ethnicity through public policies. 3. Color, culture, country : race and ethnicity in the U.S. Census -- 4. Identity choices? : agency policies and individual resistance -- Part III. Making race-ethnicity through administrative practices. 5. Ethnogenesis by the numbers, ethnogenesis by "eyeballing" -- 6. Constructing race-ethnicity through social science research : managing workplace diversity -- Part IV. Telling identities : the contemporary legacy. 7. Public policies as identity stories : American race-ethnic discourse -- 8. Changing (ac)counting practices : meditation on a problem. ISBN 0-7656-0800-6 (hc : alk. paper) DDC 305.8/00973
1. Group identity - United States. 2. Race. 3. Ethnicity. I. Title.
HM753 .Y36 2003

YANTRAS.
Bühnemann, Gudrun. Mandalas and Yantras in the Hindu traditions. Leiden ; Boston : Brill, 2003.
BL2015.M3 B85 2003

YARIBA (AFRICAN PEOPLE). *See* **YORUBA (AFRICAN PEOPLE).**

Yasue, Kunio.
No matter, never mind. Amsterdam ; Philadelphia : John Benjamins Pub. Co., c2002.
QP411.N598 2002

Yates, J. Frank (Jacques Frank), 1945- Decision management : how to assure better decisions in your company / J. Frank Yates. 1st ed. San Francisco : Jossey-Bass, c2003. xx, 230 p. : ill. ; 24 cm. (University of Michigan Business School management series) Includes bibliographical references (p. 207-211) and index. CONTENTS: The art of decision management -- "What is a decision?" and other fundamentals -- Deciding to decide : the need issue -- Determining the means for deciding : the mode and investment issues -- Prospecting for solutions : the options issue -- Anticipating outcomes : the possibilities and judgment issues -- Accounting for taste : the value and tradeoffs issues -- Ensuring smooth sailing : the acceptability and implementation issues -- Starting and sustaining decision management improvement efforts. ISBN 0-7879-5626-0 (alk. paper) DDC 658.4/03
1. Decision making. I. Title. II. Series.
HD30.23.Y386 2003

Yazi. Qing hua Bei da xue bu dao / Yazi bian zhu. Di 1 ban. Beijing : Xin hua chu ban she, 2002. 5, 11, 337 p. ; 21 cm. (Cai zhi li lian xi lie) ISBN 7-5011-5684-0
1. Success. 2. Conduct of life. I. Title. II. Series.
BJ1618.C5 Y38 2002

Ye, Ying, 1896-1950. Wen shi tong yi jiao zhu / Zhang Xuecheng zhu ; Ye Ying jiao zhu. Di 1 ban. Beijing : Zhonghua shu ju : Xin hua shu dian Beijing fa xing suo fa xing, 1994. 2 v. (7, 6, 9, 1094 p.) ; 21 cm. Bibliography: v. 2, p. 1085-1094. ISBN 7-101-01186-1 DDC 951/.0072
1. Zhang, Xuecheng, - 1738-1801. - Wen shi tong yi. 2. China - Historiography. 3. Chinese literature - History and criticism. I. Zhang, Xuecheng, 1738-1801. Wen shi tong yi. 1994. II. Title.
DS734.7.C433 Y43 1985 *<Orien China>*

A year of creativity.
Mallon, Brenda. Kansas City, Mo. : Andrews McMeel Pub., c2003.
BF408.M234 2003

Year of the dragon.
Suckling, Nigel. Legends & lore. New York : Friedman/Fairfax Publishers : Distributed by Sterling Pub., c2002.
BF1714.C5 S93 2002

YEAR ONE THOUSAND, A.D. *See* **ONE THOUSAND, A.D.**

Yede Mosheh ye-Torah or.
Mosheh ben Shelomoh El'azar. Sefer Yede Mosheh ye-Torah or. Bene Berak : Sifre Or ha-hayim, [760 i.e. 2000]

YEHOVAH. *See* **GOD (JUDAISM) - NAME.**

Yerxa, Donald A., 1950-.
Giberson, Karl. Species of origins. Lanham, Md. : Rowman & Littlefield, c2002.
BL240.3.G53 2002

YESER HARA' (JUDAISM). *See* **YETZER HARA (JUDAISM).**

Yesh'ayahu, Yiśra'el.
Kafah, Yosef, 1917- Halikhot Teman. Mahad. 5, metukenet. Yerushalayim : Mekhon Ben-Tsevi le-heker kehilot Yiśra'el ba-Mizrah : Yad Yitshak ben-Tsevi : ha-Universitah ha-Ivrit bi-Yerushalayim, 2002.

Yeshivat Da'at u-tevunah (Ashdod, Israel).
Sihot musar Da'at u-tevunah. Ashdod : Sh. ben E. Bamnolker, 761 [2001]
BJ1280.B34 2001

YETSER HA-RA' (JUDAISM). *See* **YETZER HARA (JUDAISM).**

YETZER HARA (JUDAISM).
Cordovero, Moses ben Jacob, 1522-1570. Sefer Mesilot teshuvah. Bene Berak : Da'at kedoshim, 762 [2002]
BM645.R45 C67 2002

YEZER HA-RA (JUDAISM). *See* **YETZER HARA (JUDAISM).**

Yhap, Jennifer. Plotinus on the soul : a study in the metaphysics of knowledge / Jennifer Yhap. Selinsgrove : Susquehanna University Press ; London : Associated University Presses, c2003. 233 p. ; 25 cm. Includes bibliographical references (p. 217-224) and indexes. ISBN 1-57591-069-1 (alk. paper) DDC 128/.1/092
1. Plotinus - Contributions in concept of soul. 2. Soul. I. Title.
B693.Z7 Y43 2003

YHWH. *See* **GOD (JUDAISM) - NAME.**

Yi jing.
Zong, Baihua. Di 2 ban. Beijing : Beijing da xue chu ban she, 1998.
MLCSC 92/01825 (B)

Karcher, Stephen L. Ta chuan. 1st ed. New York : St. Martin's Press, 2000.
BF1773.2.C5 K368 2000

Nielsen, Bent. A companion to Yi jing numerology and cosmology. London ; New York : RoutledgeCurzon, 2003.

Schilling, Dennis R. Spruch und Zahl. Aalen : Scientia, 1998.
BF1770.C5 S42 1998

YI JING - TERMINOLOGY.
Nielsen, Bent. A companion to Yi jing numerology and cosmology. London ; New York : RoutledgeCurzon, 2003.

Yi shu mei xue cong shu
Chou, Laixiang. Gu wen de mei, jin dai de mei, xian dai de mei. Di 1 ban. Changchun Shi : Dongbei shi fan da xue chu ban she : Jilin sheng Xin hua shu dian fa xing, 1996.
BH39.C5455 1996 *<Orien China>*

The yin & yang of love.
Hsu, Shan-Tung, 1942- 1st ed. St. Paul, Minn. : Llewellyn Publications, 2003.
BF1779.F4 H763 2003

Yin and yang of love.
Hsu, Shan-Tung, 1942- The yin & yang of love. 1st ed. St. Paul, Minn. : Llewellyn Publications, 2003.
BF1779.F4 H763 2003

Yin, Robert K. Case study research : design and methods / Robert K. Yin. 3rd ed. Thousand Oaks, Calif. : Sage Publications, c2003. xvi, 181 p. : ill. ; 22 cm. (Applied social research methods series ; v. 5) Includes bibliographical references (p. 167-174) and index. ISBN 0-7619-2552-X (alk. paper) ISBN 0-7619-2553-8 (pbk. : alk. paper) DDC 300/.7/22
1. Social sciences - Research - Methodology. I. Title. II. Series.
H62.Y56 2003

Ying, Han.
Hong, Zicheng, fl. 1596. [Cai gen tan] Dao jie cai gen tan. Di 1 ban. Beijing Shi : Zong jiao wen hua chu ban she, 1996 (1997 printing)
BJ1558.C5 H85 1996 *<Asian China>*

Hong, Zicheng, fl. 1596. [Cai gen tan] Ru jie cai gen tan. Di 1 ban. Beijing Shi : Zong jiao wen hua chu ban she, 1996 (1997 printing)
BJ1558.C5 H85 1996b *<Asian China>*

Yingling, Julie. A lifetime of communication : transformation through relational dialogues / Julie Yingling. Mahwah, N.J. : Lawrence Erlbaum Associates, 2004. p. cm. (LEA's series on personal relationships) Includes bibliographical references and index. ISBN 0-8058-4092-3 (hard : alk. paper) ISBN 0-8058-4093-1 (pbk. : alk. paper) DDC 153.6
1. Interpersonal communication - Textbooks. 2. Developmental psychology - Textbooks. I. Title. II. Series.
BF637.C45 Y56 2004

Yiśra'el 'al ha-sapah.
Grosbard, Ofer, 1954- Tel-Aviv : Yedi'ot aharonot : Sifre hemed, c2000.

Yitshak ben Eli'ezer, 15th cent.
Sefer ha gan.
He lakhem hamishah sefari.. [Brooklyn, NY : Renaissance Hebraica, 2000?]

YO SOY BETTY LA FEA (TELEVISION PROGRAM).
Méndez, José Luis, 1941- El irresistible encanto de Betty la fea. San Juan, P.R. : Ediciones Milenio, 2001.

YOGA. *See also* **CHAKRAS; YOGIS.**
Wahsner, Roderich. Frankfurt am Main ; Nwe York : Peter Lang, c2002.

YOGA.
Ānanda, Aruṇā, 1957- Pātañjalayoga evaṃ Jainayoga kā tulanātmaka adhyayana. 1. saṃskaraṇa. Dillī : Motīlāla Banārasīdāsa Pabliśarsa aura Bhogīlāla Leharacanda Bhāratīya Saṃskṛti Saṃsthāna, 2002.
B132.Y6 A496 2002

Coward, Harold G. Yoga and psychology. Albany : State University of New York Press, 2002.
BF51.C69 2002

Feuerstein, Georg. The deeper dimension of Yoga. Boston : Shambhala, 2003.
B132.Y6 F4875 2003

Ghose, Aurobindo, 1872-1950. Records of Yoga. 1st ed. Pondicherry : Sri Aurobindo Ashram, 2001.
B132.Y6+

Grinshpon, Yohanan, 1948- Demamah ve-herut ba-yogah ha-Kelasit. [Tel Aviv] : Miśrad ha-bitahon, [2002]

Karṇāṭaka, Vimalā. Śrīmadbhāgavata meṃ Sāṅkhyayoga ke tattva. 1. saṃskaraṇa. Vārāṇasī : Sampūrṇānanda Saṃskṛta Viśvavidyālaya, 2001.
BL1140.4.B437 K27 2001

Medhananda, 1908-1994. [Au fil de l'eternitè avec Medhananda. English. Selections] On the threshold of a new age with Medhananda. 1st ed. Pondicherry : Sri Mira Trust, 2000.
B841.M4313 2000

The original Yoga. 2nd rev. ed. New Delhi : Munshiram Manoharlal Publishers, 1999.
B132.Y6 O74 1999

Patañjali. The Yoga-darshana. 2nd ed.--throughly rev. [Fremont, Calif.] : Asian Humanities Press, [2002], 1934.
B132.Y6 P265 2002

The peak performance series. Vol. [4] [videorecording]. Longwood, Fla. : Pamela Bolling Enterprises, c1999.

Rham, Cat de. The spirit of yoga. London : Thorsons, 2001.

Wahsner, Roderich. Yoga. Frankfurt am Main ; Nwe York : Peter Lang, c2002.

Yoga. London ; New York : RoutledgeCurzon, 2003.
BL1238.52.Y59 2003

Yoga and psychology.
Coward, Harold G. Albany : State University of New York Press, 2002.
BF51.C69 2002

The Yoga-darshana.
Patañjali. 2nd ed.--throughly rev. [Fremont, Calif.] : Asian Humanities Press, [2002], 1934.
B132.Y6 P265 2002

YOGA (JAINISM).
Ānanda, Aruṇā, 1957- Pātañjalayoga evaṃ Jainayoga kā tulanātmaka adhyayana. 1. saṃskaraṇa. Dillī : Motīlāla Banārasīdāsa Pabliśarsa aura Bhogīlāla Leharacanda Bhāratīya Saṃskṛti Saṃsthāna, 2002.
B132.Y6 A496 2002

YOGA - PSYCHOLOGICAL ASPECTS.
Vrinte, Joseph, 1949- The perennial quest for a psychology with a soul. 1st ed. Delhi : Motilal Banarsidass Publishers, 2002.
BF311+

Yoga Sādhana Āśrama.
Smārikā. Jayapura : Yoga Sādhanā Āśrama, 2001.
BL1175.A4955 S62 2001

Yoga : the Indian tradition / edited by Ian Whicher and David Carpenter. London ; New York : RoutledgeCurzon, 2003. xii, 206 p. ; 24 cm. Includes bibliographical references (p. 185-198) and index. ISBN 0-7007-1288-7 DDC 181/.45
1. Yoga. 2. Spiritual life - Hinduism. I. Whicher, Ian. II. Carpenter, David, 1949-
BL1238.52.Y59 2003

YOGA - THERAPEUTIC USE.
Ranchan, Som P., 1932- Aurotherapy. Delhi : Indian Publishers Distributors, 2001.
BF173.A25 R36 2001

Smārikā. Jayapura : Yoga Sādhanā Āśrama, 2001.
BL1175.A4955 S62 2001

YOGIS - INDIA - BIOGRAPHY.
Smārikā. Jayapura : Yoga Sādhanā Āśrama, 2001.
BL1175.A4955 S62 2001

YOOBA (AFRICAN PEOPLE). *See* **YORUBA (AFRICAN PEOPLE).**

York, Michael, 1939- Pagan theology : paganism as a world religion / Michael York. New York ; London : New York University Press, c2003. x, 239 p. ; 24 cm. Includes bibliographical references (p. 207-227) and index. ISBN 0-8147-9702-4 (alk. paper) DDC 299
1. Religions. 2. Paganism. I. Title.
BL85.Y67 2003

York, Neil Longley. Turning the world upside down : the War of American Independence and the problem of Empire / Neil Longley York. Westport, Conn. ; London : Praeger, 2003. xiii, 193 p. : 25 cm. (Studies in military history and international affairs) Includes bibliographical references (p. [185]-186) and index. ISBN 0-275-97693-9 DDC 973.3/11
1. United States - Politics and government - 1775-1783 - Philosophy. 2. United States - History - Revolution, 1775-1783 - Influence. 3. Imperialism - History - 18th century. 4. Balance of power - History - 18th century. 5. United States - Territorial expansion. 6. Messianism, Political - United States. 7. National characteristics, American. I. Title. II. Series.
E210 .Y67 2003

Yorke, James A.
Coping with chaos. New York : J. Wiley, c1994.
Q172.5.C45 C67 1994

Yorke, Laura.
Losquadro-Liddle, Tara. Why motor skills matter. Chicago : Contemporary Books, c2004.
BF723.M6 L67 2004

YORUBA (AFRICAN PEOPLE) - CUBA.
Oricha. 1. ed. Barcelona : Editorial Humanitas, 2003.

YORUBA (AFRICAN PEOPLE) - HISTORIOGRAPHY.
Adediran, A. A. The problem with the past. Ile-Ife, Nigeria : Obafemi Awolowo University Press, c2002.
1. Black author.

YORUBA (AFRICAN PEOPLE) - HISTORY.
Ká má baa gbàgbé. [Nigeria] : Jadeas Productions, [2003]

YORUBA (AFRICAN PEOPLE) - NIGERIA - RELIGION.
Drews, Annette. Guardians of the society. Leipzig, Germany : Institut für Afrikanistik, Universität Leipzig, 2000.
BF1584.Z33 D44 2000

YORUBA (AFRICAN PEOPLE) - POLITICS AND GOVERNMENT.
Vallier, Gilles-Félix. La logique de l'éternité. 1998.

YORUBA (AFRICAN PEOPLE) - RELIGION.
Adeniyi, M. O. Yoruba Muslim-Christian understanding. Majiyagbe, Ipaja, Nigeria : Eternal Communications, 2001.
1. Black author.

Adeosun, Kola A. [Oro ti obi n so. English] What the kolanut is saying. Ibadan, Nigeria : Creative Books, 1999.
BF1779.K6 A33 1999

Babalola, E. O. African cultural revolution of Islam and Christianity in Yoruba land. Ipaja-Lagos : Eternal Communications, 2002.
1. Black author.

Beniste, José. As águas de Oxalá = Rio de Janeiro, RJ, [Brazil] : Editora Bertrand Brasil, c2001 (2002 printing)
BL2592.C35 B46 2001

Ká má baa gbàgbé. [Nigeria] : Jadeas Productions, [2003]

Karade, Akinkugbe. Path to priesthood. Brooklyn, N.Y. : Kânda Mukûtu Books, c2001.
BL2523.I33 K37 2001
1. Black author.

Kómoláfé, Koláwolé. African traditional religion. Lagos : Ifa-Òrúnmìlà Organisation, 1995.
BL2480.Y6 K65 1995

Oricha. 1. ed. Barcelona : Editorial Humanitas, 2003.

Salles, Alexandre de. Esù ou Exu? Rio de Jaeiro : Ilú Aiye, 2001.
1. Black author.

Studies in the theology and sociology of Yoruba indigenous religion. Lagos, Nigeria : Concept Publications (Nig.), 2002.

Vadillo, Alicia E. Santería y Vodú. Madrid : Biblioteca Nueva, c2002.
PQ7372 .V33 2002

Vallier, Gilles-Félix. La logique de l'éternité. 1998.

Verger, Pierre. Saída de Iaô. Sao Paulo : Fundação Pierre Verger : Axis Mundi Editora, 2002.

YORUBA (AFRICAN PEOPLE) - RITES AND CEREMONIES.
Beniste, José. As águas de Oxalá = Rio de Janeiro, RJ, [Brazil] : Editora Bertrand Brasil, c2001 (2002 printing)
BL2592.C35 B46 2001

Oricha. 1. ed. Barcelona : Editorial Humanitas, 2003.

Vallier, Gilles-Félix. La logique de l'éternité. 1998.

YORUBA (AFRICAN PEOPLE) - SOCIAL LIFE AND CUSTOMS.
Ká má baa gbàgbé. [Nigeria] : Jadeas Productions, [2003]

YORUBA LANGUAGE.
Ká má baa gbàgbé. [Nigeria] : Jadeas Productions, [2003]

YORUBA LITERATURE.
Ká má baa gbàgbé. [Nigeria] : Jadeas Productions, [2003]

Yoruba Muslim-Christian understanding.
Adeniyi, M. O. Majiyagbe, Ipaja, Nigeria : Eternal Communications, 2001.

Yoruba Muslim-Christian understanding in Nigeria.
Adeniyi, M. O. Yoruba Muslim-Christian understanding. Majiyagbe, Ipaja, Nigeria : Eternal Communications, 2001.
1. Black author.

YORUBAS. See **YORUBA (AFRICAN PEOPLE).**

Yosef, Yitshak.
[Yalkut Yosef (Kibud av ya-em)]
Sefer Yalkut Yosef : hilkhot kibud av ya-em / me-et Yitshak Yosef. Yerushalayim : Mekhon "Hazon 'Ovadyah", 761 [2001] 2 v. ; 25 cm. Running title: Yalkut Yosef. Includes index. CONTENTS: kerekh 1. Ba-halakhah uve-agadah -- kerekh 2. [without special title]
1. Ten commandments - Parents. 2. Parent and child (Jewish law) 3. Ethics, Jewish. I. Title. II. Title: Yalkut Yosef
BM523.5.R4 Y72 2001

The you & me scriptbook.
Shore, Hennie. [United States] : Childswork Childsplay, c2002.
BF723.S62 S46 2002

You and me scriptbook.
Shore, Hennie. The you & me scriptbook. [United States] : Childswork Childsplay, c2002.
BF723.S62 S46 2002

You are not alone.
Gross, Esther. Jerusalem, Israel ; Nanuet, NY : Feldheim, 2002.

YOUNG ADULTS. See **YOUNG MEN; YOUNG WOMEN.**

YOUNG ADULTS - BIOGRAPHY.
Deniau, Jean-François, 1928- La gloire à vingt ans. [Paris] : XO editions, c2003.

YOUNG ADULTS - CONDUCT OF LIFE.
Dobson, James C., 1936- Life on the edge. Nashville : Word Pub., c2000.
BF637.L53 D63 2000

YOUNG ADULTS - RELIGIOUS LIFE.
Dobson, James C., 1936- Life on the edge. Nashville : Word Pub., c2000.
BF637.L53 D63 2000

Young-Bruehl, Elisabeth. Where do we fall when we fall in love? / Elisabeth Young-Bruehl. New York : Other Press, c2003. xvii, 339 p. ; 24 cm. Many of the essays in this book appeared previously in various journals between 1998 and 2002. Includes bibliographical references and index. CONTENTS: Where do we fall when we fall in love? -- Cherishment culture -- The hidden history of the ego instincts -- The wise baby as the voice of the true self -- The developmental matrix of the ego ideal -- A visit to the Budapest school -- Reflections on women and psychoanalysis -- Are all human beings "by nature" bisexual? -- Beyond "the female homosexual" -- The characters of violence -- Homophobia : a diagnostic and political manual -- Psychoanalysis and characterology -- Amae in ancient Greece. ISBN 1-59051-068-2 (alk. paper) DDC 150.19/5
1. Freud, Sigmund, - 1856-1939. 2. Psychoanalysis. I. Title.
BF173 .Y68 2003

Young Doctor Freud.
Young Dr. Freud [electronic resource]. [Alexandria, Va.?] : PBS, 2002.
BF109.F74

Young Dr. Freud [electronic resource] : a film by David Grubin. [Alexandria, Va.?] : PBS, 2002. Updates began and ceased in 2002? Mode of access: World Wide Web. SUMMARY: Describes and provides background information of the documentary film Young Dr. Freud by David Grubin, shown on PBS television stations. Includes theories, analysis, perspectives, family and epilogue. Includes bibliographical references. Title from html header (viewed on July 8, 2003). URL: http://www.pbs.org/youngdrfreud/index.htm
1. Freud, Sigmund, - 1856-1939. 2. Young Dr. Freud (Motion Picture) I. Grubin, David. II. Public Broadcasting Service (U.S.) III. Title: Young Dr. Freud (Motion Picture) IV. Title: Dr. Freud V. Title: Young Doctor Freud
BF109.F74

Young Dr. Freud (Motion Picture).
Young Dr. Freud [electronic resource]. [Alexandria, Va.?] : PBS, 2002.
BF109.F74

Young Dr. Freud [electronic resource]. [Alexandria, Va.?] : PBS, 2002.
BF109.F74

YOUNG MEN. See **BOYS.**

YOUNG MEN - EUROPE - HISTORY - TO 1500.
Karras, Ruth Mazo, 1957- From boys to men. Philadelphia : University of Pennsylvania Press, c2003.
HQ775 .K373 2003

YOUNG PEOPLE. See **YOUNG ADULTS; YOUTH.**

YOUNG PERSONS. See **YOUNG ADULTS; YOUTH.**

Young person's school of magic and mystery
(v. 1) Andrews, Ted, 1952- Magic of believing. 1st ed. Jackson, Tenn. : Dragonhawk Pub., c2000.
BF1611 .A53 2000

(v. 5) Andrews, Ted, 1952- Spirits, ghosts & guardians. 1st ed. Jackson, Tenn. : Dragonhawk Pub., c2002.
BF1461 .A53 2002

The young, the old, and the state : social care systems in five industrial nations / edited by Anneli Anttonen, John Baldock, Jorma Sipilä. Cheltenham, UK ; Northhampton, MA : E. Elgar Pub., c2003. x, 206 p. ; 24 cm. (Globalization and welfare) Includes bibliographical references and index. ISBN 1-84064-628-4 DDC 362.71/2
1. Child care. 2. Aged - Care. 3. Human services. I. Anttonen, Anneli. II. Baldock, John, 1948- III. Sipilä, Jorma. IV. Series.
HQ778.5 .Y69 2003

YOUNG WOMEN. See **GIRLS.**

YOUNG WOMEN - GERMANY - PSYCHOLOGY.
Liebe und Abhängigkeit. Weinheim : Juventa, 2001.

YOUNG WOMEN - PSYCHOLOGY.
Budgeon, Shelley, 1967- Choosing a self. Westport, Conn. : Praeger, 2003.
HQ1229 .B83 2003

Your angry child.
Davis, Daniel Leifeld. New York : Haworth Press, c2004.
BF723.A4 D38 2004

Your anxious child.
Shaw, Mary Ann. 2nd ed. Irving, Tex. : Tapestry Press, c2003.
BF723.A5 S43 2003

Your birthday sign through time : a chronicle of the forces that shape your destiny / Skye Alexander ... [et al.] ; editor-in-chief, Rochelle Gordon ; general editor, Nadia Stieglitz. New York : Atria Books, c2002. 864 p. : ill., map ; 29 cm. ISBN 0-7434-6261-0 DDC 133.5/4
1. Horoscopes. 2. Houses (Astrology) I. Alexander, Skye. II. Gordon, Rochelle. III. Stieglitz, Nadia.
BF1728.A2 Y57 2002

Your child's growing mind.
Healy, Jane M. 3rd ed. New York : Broadway Books, 2004.
BF318 .H4 2004

Your fair share.
Jordan, Denise. Chicago, Ill. : Heinemann Library, 2003.
BF723.S428 J67 2003

Your guardian angel and you.
Sargent, Denny, 1956- York Beach, ME : Red Wheel/Weiser, 2004.
BF1275.G85 S27 2004

Your healing journey through grief.
Cornils, Stanley P. San Francisco, CA : Robert D. Reed Publishers, c2003.
BF575.G7 C677 2003

Your life as art.
Fritz, Robert, 1943- 1st ed. Newfane, VT : Newfane Press, c2003.
BF637.S4 F753 2003

Your thoughts can change your life.
Curtis, Donald. New York : Warner Books, 1996.
BF639 .C885 1996

You're on!.
Hays, Kate F. 1st ed. Washington, DC : American Psychological Association, c2003.
BF637.C6 H366 2003

YOUTH. *See also* **TEENAGERS; YOUNG ADULTS.**
Helping children and adolescents cope with violence and disasters [electronic resource]. Bethesda, MD : Office of Communications and Public Liaison, [2001]

Youth cultures. Westport, Conn. : Praeger, 2003.
HQ796 .Y59273 2003

YOUTH AND VIOLENCE - NEW YORK - NEW YORK.
Wilkinson, Deanna Lyn, 1968- Guns, violence, and identity among African American and Latino youth. New York : LFB Scholarly Pub., 2003.
HQ799.2.V56 W55 2003

YOUTH AND VIOLENCE - PSYCHOLOGICAL ASPECTS.
Helping children and adolescents cope with violence and disasters [electronic resource]. Bethesda, MD : Office of Communications and Public Liaison, [2001]

YOUTH - ATTITUDES.
Peace and conflict resolution. Part 1 [videorecording]. Derry, N.H. : Chip Taylor Communications, 1996.

YOUTH - BIOGRAPHY.
Deniau, Jean-François, 1928- La gloire à vingt ans. [Paris] : XO éditions, c2003.

YOUTH - CASE STUDIES - JUVENILE LITERATURE.
Survivors. New York : Scholastic, c2002.
BF637.S8 S8317 2002

YOUTH - CRIMES AGAINST. *See* **SCHOOL VIOLENCE.**

Youth cultures : texts, images, and identities / edited by Kerry Mallan and Sharyn Pearce. Westport, Conn. : Praeger, 2003. xix, 203 p. : ill. ; 24 cm. Includes bibliographical references and index. ISBN 0-275-97409-X (alk. paper) DDC 305.235
1. Youth. 2. Popular culture. 3. Mass media and youth. 4. Motion pictures and youth. 5. Music and youth. 6. Youth in mass media. 7. Youth in motion pictures. 8. Youth in literature. I. Mallan, Kerry. II. Pearce, Sharyn.
HQ796 .Y59273 2003

YOUTH - EDUCATION. *See* **EDUCATION.**

YOUTH IN LITERATURE.
Tremblay-Dupré, Thérèse. La mère absente. Monaco : Rocher, 2003.

Youth cultures. Westport, Conn. : Praeger, 2003.
HQ796 .Y59273 2003

YOUTH IN MASS MEDIA.
Youth cultures. Westport, Conn. : Praeger, 2003.
HQ796 .Y59273 2003

YOUTH IN MOTION PICTURES.
Youth cultures. Westport, Conn. : Praeger, 2003.
HQ796 .Y59273 2003

YOUTH - ISRAEL - ATTITUDES.
Peace and conflict resolution. Part 2 [videorecording]. Derry, N.H. : Chip Taylor Communications, 1997.

YOUTH - KENYA - NAIROBI.
Frederiksen, Bodil Folke, 1943- Popular culture, family relations, and issues of everyday democracy. [Nairobi] : Institute for Development Studies, University of Nairobi, [2000]
HQ799.K42 N354 2000

YOUTH - NORTHERN IRELAND - ATTITUDES.
Peace and conflict resolution. Part 2 [videorecording]. Derry, N.H. : Chip Taylor Communications, 1997.

YOUTH - POLITICAL ASPECTS - CHINA.
Cheng zhang de Zhongguo. Di 1 ban. Beijing : Ren min chu ban she, 2002.
HQ799.2.P6 C449 2002

YOUTH - PSYCHOLOGICAL ASPECTS. *See* **YOUTH - PSYCHOLOGY.**

YOUTH - PSYCHOLOGY - CONGRESSES.
Mezhregional′naia Rossiĭskaia nauchno-prakticheskaia konferentsiia "Psikhologicheskie osobennosti preodoleniia ėkstremal′nykh i ėmotsiogennykh situatsiĭ v podrostkovo-iunosheskom vozraste" (2002 : Syktyvkar, Russia) Psikhologicheskie osobennosti preodoleniia ėkstremal′nykh i ėmotsiogennykh situatsiĭ v podrostkovo-iunosheskom vozraste. Syktyvkar : Syktyvkarskiĭ gos. universitet, 2002.
BF724 .M48 2002

YOUTH - RELIGIOUS LIFE.
Chiwlean, Eghishē. Patanineru hawatk′ē. Venetik ; Halēp : Mkhit′arean Hratarakut′iwn, S. Ghazar, 1998.

YOUTH WITH SOCIAL DISABILITIES - NEW YORK - NEW YORK - PSYCHOLOGY.
Wilkinson, Deanna Lyn, 1968- Guns, violence, and identity among African American and Latino youth. New York : LFB Scholarly Pub., 2003.
HQ799.2.V56 W55 2003

YOUTHS. *See* **YOUTH.**

YOUTHS' WRITINGS.
River of words. Berkeley, Calif. : Heyday Books, c2003.
PS595.W374 R58 2003

YOUTHS' WRITINGS, AMERICAN.
River of words. Berkeley, Calif. : Heyday Books, c2003.
PS595.W374 R58 2003

Yu, Jiyuan. The structure of being in Aristotle's Metaphysics / by Jiyuan Yu. Dordrecht, Boston : Kluwer Academic, c2003. xx, 238 p. ; 25 cm. (The new synthese historical library ; v. 52) Includes bibliographical references (p. 211-221) and indexes. ISBN 1402015372 DDC 111/.1
1. Aristotle. - Metaphysics. 2. Ontology. I. Title. II. Series.
B434 .Y8 2003

Yu, Tang.
Liang Qichao, Zhang Taiyan jie du Zhonghua wen hua jing dian. Di 1 ban. Shenyang Shi : Liao Hai chu ban she, 2003.
PL2262.2 .L54 2003

Yu, Xing Huo.
Chaos control. Berlin ; New York : Springer, c2003.
QA402.3 .C48 2003

Yudaiḳin, Shemu'el Yitshaḳ Gad, ha-Kohen.
Cordovero, Moses ben Jacob, 1522-1570. Sefer Mesilot teshuvah. Bene Beraḳ : Da'at ḳedoshim, 762 [2002]
BM645.R45 C67 2002

Yúdice, George.
La (indi)gestión cultural. 1. ed. Bs. As., Argentina : Ediciones Ciccus-La Crujía, 2002.
HM621 .I535 2002

YUGOSLAV LITERATURE. *See* **SERBIAN LITERATURE.**

YUGOSLAVS. *See* **SERBS.**

Yuracko, Kimberly A., 1969- Perfectionism and contemporary feminist values / Kimberly A. Yuracko. Bloomington : Indiana University Press, c2003. x, 169 p. ; 25 cm. Includes bibliographical references (p. [137]-164) and index. CONTENTS: Three hard choices -- An introduction to perfectionism -- Coercion critiques -- Socialization critiques -- Equality arguments -- Vulnerability-based choice critiques -- Four perfectionist principles. ISBN 0-253-34208-2 (hb : acid-free) ISBN 0-253-21580-3 (pk : acid-free) DDC 305.42
1. Feminism. 2. Women - Psychology. I. Title.
HQ1206 .Y87 2003

Yusty, Miguel. Negociar en medio de la guerra : una estrategia fracasada / Miguel Yusty. [Cali, Colombia] : Editorial Universidad Santiago de Cali, 2002. 266 p. ; 21 cm. (Colección Biblionova) ISBN 958-811-947-2 (pbk.)
1. Pastrana Arango, Andrés. 2. Fuerzas Armadas Revolucionarias de Colombia. 3. Colombia - Politics and government - 1974- 4. Guerrillas - Colombia. 5. Negotiation - Colombia - 20th century. 6. Peace. I. Title. II. Series.

Za psikhosemantichnata spetsifika na ezikovoto vŭzpriiatie.
Raĭnov, Vasil G. Sofiia : Akademichno izd-vo "Prof. Marin Drinov", 1998.
P37 .R27 1998

Zahariadis, Nikolaos, 1961- Ambiguity and choice in public policy : political decision making in modern democracies / Nikolaos Zahariadis. Washington, D.C. : Georgetown University Press, c2003. x, 198 p. : ill. ; 23 cm. (American governance and public policy series) Includes bibliographical references (p. 175-190) and index. CONTENTS: Multiple streams and public policy -- Privatization in Britain and France -- Ideas and policy change in Britain and Germany -- Windows of opportunity and the choice to sell British Rail -- Symbols, framing, and manipulation in Greek foreign policy -- Structure and performance in a multiple streams computer simulation -- Ambiguity and policy choice. ISBN 0-87840-135-0 (pbk. : alk. paper) DDC 320/.6/01156
1. Political planning. 2. Decision making. I. Title. II. Series: American governance and public policy.

H97 .Z34 2003

Zaĭtseva, L. I. Russkie providtsy o rossiĭskoĭ gosudarstvennosti : seredina XVI-nachalo XX vv. / L. Zaĭtseva. Moskva : In-t ėkonomiki RAN, 1998- v. ; 21 cm. Vol. 1- includes bibliographical references. PARTIAL CONTENTS: ch. 1. XVI v. ISBN 5201030173 (ch. 1)
1. Sil′vestr, - d. ca. 1566. 2. Peresvetov, Ivan Semenovich, - fl. 1530-1549. 3. Maximus, - the Greek, Saint, - 1480-1556. 4. Kurbskiĭ, Andreĭ Mikhaĭlovich, - kni͡az′, - d. 1583. 5. Russia - History - Prophecies. 6. Philosophy, Russian. 7. Prophets - Russia - Biography. 8. Philosophers - Russia - Biography. I. Title.
DK49 .Z35 1998

Zakai, Avihu. Jonathan Edwards's philosophy of history : the reenchantment of the world in the Age of Enlightenment / Avihu Zakai. Princeton, N.J. : Princeton University Press, c2003. xvii, 348 p. ; 24 cm. Includes bibliographical references and index. Publisher description URL: http://www.loc.gov/catdir/desc ription/prin031/2002031742.html ISBN 0-691-09654-6 (alk. paper) DDC 231.7/6/092
1. Edwards, Jonathan, - 1703-1758 - Contributions in history of philosophy. 2. History - Philosophy. 3. Enlightenment. I. Title. II. Title: Jonathan Edwards' philosophy of history
B873 .Z35 2003

Zakaria, Fareed. The future of freedom : illiberal democracy at home and abroad / Fareed Zakaria. 1st ed. New York : W.W. Norton, c2003. 286 p. ; 25 cm. Includes bibliographical references (p. 257-267) and index. CONTENTS: A brief history of human liberty -- The twisted path -- Illiberal democracy -- The Islamic exception -- Too much of a good thing -- The death of authority -- The way out. ISBN 0-393-04764-4 DDC 321.8
1. Democracy. 2. Liberty. 3. Political science - Philosophy. I. Title.
JC423 .Z35 2003

Zaltman, Gerald. How customers think : essential insights into the mind of the market / Gerald Zaltman. Boston, Mass. : Harvard Business School Press, c2003. xxii, 323 p. : ill. ; 25 cm. Includes bibliographical references (p. 291-310) and index. CONTENTS: A voyage from the familiar -- A voyage to new frontiers -- Illuminating the mind/brain. pt. a: Metaphor elicitation -- Interviewing the mind/brain, pt. b: Response latency and neuroimaging -- Come to think of it -- Reading the mind of the market : using consensus maps -- Memory's fragile power -- Memory, metaphors, and stories -- Stories and brands -- Crowbars for creative thinking -- Quality questions beget quality answers -- Launching a new mind-set. ISBN 1-57851-826-1 (alk. paper) DDC 658.8/342
1. Consumer behavior - Psychological aspects. 2. Consumers - Psychology. 3. Marketing - Psychological aspects. 4. Creative thinking. I. Title.
HF5415.32 .Z35 2003

Zamaleev, A. F. (Aleksandr Fazlaevich) Idei i napravleniia otechestvennogo liubomudriia : lektsii, stat′i, kritika / A.F. Zamaleev. Sankt-Peterburg : Izdatel′sko-torgovyĭ dom "Letniĭ sad", 2003. 208 p. : ill. ; 25 cm. Includes bibliographical references. ISBN 5897400717
1. Philosophy, Russian. I. Title.
B4201 .Z33 2003

Zambrano, María. De la aurora / María Zambrano. Córdoba, Argentina : Alción Editora, c1999. 128 p. ; 22 cm.
1. Philosophy. I. Title.

Zamogil′nyĭ, S. I.
Tadtaev, Kh. B. (Khristofor Bagratovich) Ėtnos, natsiia, rasa. Saratov : Saratovskiĭ gos. universitet, 2001.
GN345 .T33 2001

Zamosc, Israel ben Moses, Halevi, ca. 1700-1772. Tuv ha levanon.
Baḥya ben Joseph ibn Paḳuda, 11th cent. [Hidāyah ilá farā'id al-qulūb] Torat hovat ha-levavot ha-mefo'ar. Nyu York : Y. Vais : Star Ḳompozishan : [Hotsa'at Ateret], 760 [2000]

Zamysly.
Bibler, V. S. (Vladimir Solomonovich), 1918- Moskva : Rossiĭskiĭ gos. gumanitarnyĭ universitet, 2002.
B99.R9 B53 2002

Zan, Aizong.
Ai ni, dan bu xiang xin ni. Di 1 ban. Beijing : Zhongguo hua qiao chu ban she, 2000.
PL2608.L6 A5 2000

Zang Han wen xue ming zhu bi jiao yan jiu.
Bod Rgya rtsom rig gśib bsdur gyi dpyad brjod. Par theṅs 1. Pe-cin : Mi rigs dpe skrun khaṅ, 2001.

Zanvot ha-udim ha-'ashenim.
PL3705 (P-PZ22)+

Zanvot ha-udim ha-'ashenim.
Koll, Shmuel, 1938- Sefer Ra'yonot u-mesarim. Yerushalayim : S. Kol, 761- [2001-

Zapiski psikhologa.
Petrovskiĭ, A. V. (Artur Vladimirovich) Moskva : Izd-vo URAO, 2001.
BF145 .P477 2001

Petrovskiĭ, A. V. (Artur Vladimirovich) Moskva : Izd-vo URAO, 2001.
BF145 .P48 2001

Zapiski zi͡ati͡a glavravvina.
Meni͡aĭlov, Alekseĭ. Durilka. Moskva : "Kraft+", 2003.

ZĀR - EGYPT.
Sengers, Gerda. Vrouwen en demonen. Amsterdam : Het Spinhuis, 2000.
BF1275.F3 S46 2000

Sengers, Gerda. Women and demons. Leiden ; Boston : Brill, 2003.
BF1275.F3 S463 2003

Zarathustra's sisters.
Ingram, Susan. Toronto ; Buffalo : University of Toronto Press, c2003.
PN471 .I537 2003

Zaretsky, Eli. Secrets of the soul : psychoanalysis, modernity, and personal life / Eli Zaretsky. 1st ed. New York : A.A. Knopf, 2004. p. cm. Includes bibliographical references and index. ISBN 0-679-44654-0 (alk. paper) DDC 150.19/5/09
1. Psychoanalysis - History. 2. Psychoanalysis - Social aspects - History. I. Title.
BF173 .Z37 2004

Zartman, I. William.
Getting it done. Washington, D.C. : United States Institute of Peace Press, 2003.
KZ1321 .G48 2003

Zashchirinskai͡a, Oksana Vladimirovna.
Fundamental'nye problemy psikhologii. Sankt-Peterburg : Izd-vo S.-Peterburgskogo universiteta, 2002.
BF20 .F86 2002

Zauberei und Hexerei.
Ceballos Gómez, Diana Luz, 1962- Frankfurt am Main ; New York : Peter Lang, c2000.
BF1584.S7 C43 2000

Zautra, Alex. Emotions, stress, and health / Alex J. Zautra. Oxford ; New York : Oxford University Press, 2003. xvi, 310 p. : ill. ; 24 cm. Includes bibliographical references (p. [267]-299) and index. ISBN 0-19-513359-5 (cloth : alk. paper) DDC 616/.001/9
1. Clinical health psychology. 2. Stress (Psychology) 3. Emotions. I. Title.
R726.7 .Z38 2003

Zawadzki, Roman. Kobieta-- / Roman Zawadzki. Warszawa : Wydawn. von borowiecky, 2002. 180 p. ; 21 cm. ISBN 83-87689-45-9
1. Women in literature. 2. Women - Psychology. 3. Women - Conduct of life. I. Title.
PN56.5.W64 Z28 2002

Zawjī wa-al-ukhrá.
Maḥfūẓ, Najlā'. al-Ṭab'ah 1. al-Qāhirah : al-Dār al-Miṣrīyah al-Lubnānīyah, 2003.
HQ1793 .M34 2003

ZDZIECHOWSKI, MARJAN, 1861-1938 - PHILOSOPHY.
Gawor, Leszek. Katastrofizm konsekwentny. Lublin : Wydawn. Uniwersytetu Marii Curie Skłodowskiej, 1998.
B4691.Z384 G38 1998

Zec, Safet.
Biserje. 3., dop. izd. Sarajevo : Ljiljan, 1998.

Zeer, Darrin. Office Feng Shui : creating harmony in your work space / by Darrin Zeer. San Francisco : Chronicle Books, 2004. p. cm. Table of contents URL: http://www.loc.gov/catdir/toc/ecip042/2003007906.html CONTENTS: Five Feng shui tips for the workplace -- Feng shui demystified -- Feng shui for your desk -- Feng shui for stress relief -- Feng shui for prosperity -- Feng shui for the entire office -- Feng shui on the go. ISBN 0-8118-4215-0 DDC 133.3/337
1. Feng shui. 2. Success in business. 3. Environmental psychology. I. Title.
BF1779.F4 Z44 2004

Zeichen des Todes in der psychoanalytischen Erfahrung / Gerd Kimmerle (Hg.) ; [Beiträge von, Barbara Dehm-Gauwerky ... et al.]. Tübingen : Edition Diskord, c2000. 287 p. ; 21 cm. (Anschlüsse ; Bd. 4) Includes bibliographical references. ISBN 3-89295-687-1
1. Psychoanalytic interpretation. 2. Death. I. Kimmerle, Gerd, 1947- II. Dehm-Gauwerky, Barbara. III. Series.

Zeidner, Moshe.
Matthews, Gerald. Emotional intelligence. Cambridge, Mass. : MIT Press, c2002.
BF576 .M28 2002

Zeĭgarnik, B. V. (Bli͡uma Vul'fovna) Psikhologii͡a lichnosti : norma i patologii͡a : izbrannye psikhologicheskie trudy / B.V. Zeĭgarnik ; pod red. M.R. Ginzburga. Moskva : Moskovskiĭ psikhologo-sotsial'nyĭ in-t, 1998. 347 p. ; 21 cm. (Psikhologi otechestva: izbrannye psikhologicheskie trudy) Includes bibliographical references (p. 335-345). ISBN 5891120399
1. Personality. I. Moskovskiĭ psikhologo-sotsial'nyĭ institut. II. Title. III. Series: Psikhologi otechestva.
BF698 .Z43 1998

Die Zeit des Menschen.
Zons, Raimar. 1. Aufl., Originalausg. Frankfurt : Suhrkamp, c2001.

Zeit in den Medien, Medien in der Zeit / herausgegeben von Werner Faulstich und Christian Steininger. München : Fink, c2002. 155 p. : ill. ; 24 cm. Includes bibliographical references. ISBN 3-7705-3656-8 (pbk.)
1. Mass media. 2. Time. I. Faulstich, Werner. II. Steininger, Christian.

Zeiten des Endes.
Gäbler, Ulrich. Basel : Schwabe & Co., c2002.

Zeitgeschichtliche Hintergründe aktueller Konflikte V : Vorlesung für Hörer aller Abteilungen, Sommersemester 1995 / Kurt R. Spillmann (Hrsg.). Zürich : Forschungsstelle für Sicherheitspolitik und Konfliktanalyse, Eidgenössische Technische Hochschule, 1995. 161 p. ; 30 cm. (Zürcher Beiträge zur Sicherheitspolitik und Konfliktforschung ; Heft Nr. 37) Includes bibliographical references. ISBN 3-905641-44-5
1. Security, International. 2. Peace. 3. World politics - 1945- I. Spillmann, Kurt R. II. Series.
JX1952 .Z45 1995

Zeitlin, Judith T., 1958-.
Writing and materiality in China. Cambridge, Mass. : Published by Harvard University Asia Center for Harvard-Yenching Institute : distributed by Harvard University Press, 2003.
PL2262 .W74 2003

Zeitschrift für experimentelle Psychologie (Online).
[Experimental psychology (Online)] Experimental psychology [electronic resource]. Göttingen, Germany : Hogrefe & Huber, c2002-
BF3

Zell-Ravenheart, Oberon, 1942- Grimoire for the apprentice wizard / by Oberon Zell-Ravenheart. Franklin Lakes, NJ : New Page Books, 2004. p. cm. Includes bibliographical references and index. ISBN 1-56414-711-8 (pbk.) DDC 133.4/3
1. Magic. 2. Wizards. I. Title.
BF1611 .Z45 2004

Zemirot.
Naphtali ben Isaac, ha-Kohen, 1649-1719. Sefer Bet Raḥel. Yerushalayim : Ahavat Shalom, 761 [2001]
BM665 .N257 2001

Zeng, Changyong. Zeng Guofan ling dao fang lüe / yuan dian Zeng Guofan; jie du Zeng Changyong. Di 1 ban. Beijing Shi : Zhongguo hua qiao chu ban she, 2001. 539 p. ; 21 cm. Cover title: Zeng Guofan cheng jiu da shi de xue wen. ISBN 7-80120-474-3
1. Zeng, Guofan, - 1811-1872. 2. Leadership. I. Zeng, Guofan, 1811-1872. Selections. II. Title. III. Title: Zeng Guofan cheng jiu da shi de xue wen
DS758.23.T74 Z48 2001 East Asian

Zeng, Guofan, 1811-1872. Fan jing : Zeng Guofan fan bai wei sheng de ba da ce lüe / [Zeng Guofan yuan dian ; He Jun bian zhu] Di 1 ban. Beijing : Zhongguo Hua qiao chu ban she, 2001. 3, 508 p. : ill. ; 21 cm. (Ling dao zhe bi bei. Zeng Guofan cheng jiu da shi de xue wen ; 4) (Zeng Guofan cheng jiu da shi de xue wen ; zhi 3) At head of title: Zeng Guofan zhi hui shu xi : yong heng de ren sheng jing dian. ISBN 7-80120-475-1
1. Success. 2. Conduct of life. I. He, Jun. II. Title. III. Title: Zeng Guofan zhi hui shu xi : yong heng de ren sheng jing dian. IV. Title: Zeng Guofan fan bai wei sheng de ba da ce lüe V. Series. VI. Series: Zeng Guofan cheng jiu da shi de xue wen ; zhi 3
BJ1618.C5 H44 2001

Selections.
Zeng, Changyong. Zeng Guofan ling dao fang lüe. Di 1 ban. Beijing Shi : Zhongguo hua qiao chu ban she, 2001.
DS758.23.T74 Z48 2001 East Asian

Selections. 1999.
Shi, Lin. Zhi xin jing. Di 1 ban. Beijing : Zhongguo yan shi chu ban she, 1999.
DS758.23.T74 S522 1999

Sima, Lieren. Tong jing. Di 1 ban. Beijing : Zhongguo hua qiao chu ban she, 2002.
DS758.23.T74 S575 2002

ZENG, GUOFAN, 1811-1872.
Shi, Lin. Zhi xin jing. Di 1 ban. Beijing : Zhongguo yan shi chu ban she, 1999.
DS758.23.T74 S522 1999

Zeng, Changyong. Zeng Guofan ling dao fang lüe. Di 1 ban. Beijing Shi : Zhongguo hua qiao chu ban she, 2001.
DS758.23.T74 Z48 2001 East Asian

ZENG, GUOFAN, 1811-1872 - PHILOSOPHY.
Sima, Lieren. Tong jing. Di 1 ban. Beijing : Zhongguo hua qiao chu ban she, 2002.
DS758.23.T74 S575 2002

Zeng Guofan ba shi yi ge zhong gao.
Sima, Lieren. Tong jing. Di 1 ban. Beijing : Zhongguo hua qiao chu ban she, 2002.
DS758.23.T74 S575 2002

Zeng Guofan cheng jiu da shi de xue wen.
Zeng, Changyong. Zeng Guofan ling dao fang lüe. Di 1 ban. Beijing Shi : Zhongguo hua qiao chu ban she, 2001.
DS758.23.T74 Z48 2001 East Asian

(zhi 3) Zeng, Guofan, 1811-1872. Fan jing. Di 1 ban. Beijing : Zhongguo Hua qiao chu ban she, 2001.
BJ1618.C5 H44 2001

Zeng Guofan fan bai wei sheng de ba da ce lüe.
Zeng, Guofan, 1811-1872. Fan jing. Di 1 ban. Beijing : Zhongguo Hua qiao chu ban she, 2001.
BJ1618.C5 H44 2001

Zeng Guofan ling dao fang lüe.
Zeng, Changyong. Di 1 ban. Beijing Shi : Zhongguo hua qiao chu ban she, 2001.
DS758.23.T74 Z48 2001 East Asian

Zeng Guofan zhi hui shu xi : yong heng de ren sheng jing dian.
Zeng, Guofan, 1811-1872. Fan jing. Di 1 ban. Beijing : Zhongguo Hua qiao chu ban she, 2001.
BJ1618.C5 H44 2001

Zeng, Jie. She hui si wei xue / Zeng Jie, Zhang Shuxiang zhu. Di 1 ban. Beijing : Ren min chu ban she : Xin hua shu dian jing xiao, 1996. 4, 5, 280 p. : ill. ; 21 cm. Colophon title also in pinyin: Shehui siwei xue. Includes bibliographical references (p. 279). ISBN 7-01-002285-2
1. Social perception. I. Zhang, Shuxiang. II. Title. III. Title: Shehui siwei xue
BF323.S63 T75 1996 <Asian China>

Zenith, Richard.
Pessoa, Fernando, 1888-1935. [Erostratus. Portuguese & English] Heróstrato e a busca da imortalidade. Lisboa : Assírio e Alvim, c2000.

ZENJŌ, B. 1772.
Bolitho, Harold. Bereavement and consolation. New Haven : Yale University Press, c2003.
DS822.2 .B65 2003

Zenka, Lorraine.
Darbo, Patrika. 365 glorious nights of love and romance. 1st ed. New York : ReganBooks, c2002.
HQ46 .D35 2002

Zen'ko, I͡U. M. Psikhologii͡a i religii͡a / I͡U.M. Zen'ko. Sankt-Peterburg : Aletei͡a, 2002. 381 p. ; 22 cm. Includes bibliographical references. ISBN 5893294718
1. Psychology and religion. 2. Psychology, Religious. I. Title.
BF51 .Z46 2002

Zentner, John J., 1965- The art of wing leadership and aircrew morale in combat [electronic resource] / John J. Zentner. Maxwell Air Force Base, Ala. : Air University Press, [2001] (CADRE paper ; no. 11) System requirements: Adobe Acrobat Reader. Mode of access: Internet from the Air University Press web site. Address as of 10/7/03: http://aupress.au.af.mil/CADRE%5FPapers/PDF%5FBin/zentner.pdf; current access is available via PURL. Title from title screen (viewed on Oct. 7, 2003). "June 2001." Includes bibliographical references. URL: http://purl.access.gpo.gov/GPO/LPS38553 Available in other form: Zentner, John J., 1965- The art of wing leadership and aircrew morale in combat xi, 110 p. (OCoLC)46641566.
1. Air warfare - Case studies. 2. Flight crews - Case studies. 3. Leadership - Case studies. 4. Morale - Case studies. I. Air University (U.S.). Press. II. Title. III. Title: Zentner, John J.,

1965- The art of wing leadership and aircrew morale in combat xi, 110 p. IV. Series: CADRE paper ; 11.

Zentner, John J., 1965- The art of wing leadership and aircrew morale in combat xi, 110 p.
Zentner, John J., 1965- The art of wing leadership and aircrew morale in combat [electronic resource]. Maxwell Air Force Base, Ala. : Air University Press, [2001]

Zerbi, Piero. "Philosophi" e "logici" : un ventennio di incontri e scontri : Soissons, Sens, Cluny, 1121-1141 / Pietro Zerbi. Roma : Istituto storico italiano per il Medio Evo ; Milano : Vita e pensiero, 2002. xi, 196 p. ; 26 cm. (Nuovi studi storici ; 59) (Storia. Ricerche) Includes bibliographical references and index. DDC 270
1. Abelard, Peter, - 1079-1142. 2. Bernard, - of Clairvaux, Saint, - 1090 or 91-1153. 3. Philosophy, Medieval. I. Title. II. Series. III. Series: Storia. Ricerche (Rome, Italy)
B765.A24 Z473 2002

Zerubavel, Eviatar. Time maps : collective memory and the social shape of the past / Eviatar Zerubavel. Chicago : University of Chicago Press, 2003. xii, 180 p. : ill. ; 24 cm. Includes bibliographical references (p. 111-163) and indexes. CONTENTS: The social shape of the past -- Historical continuity -- Ancestry and descent -- Historical discontinuity -- In the beginnings. ISBN 0-226-98152-5 (hardcover : alk. paper) DDC 304.2/3
1. Time. 2. History - Philosophy. 3. Civilization - Philosophy. I. Title.
BD638 .Z48 2003

Zest for life.
Breslin, Dawn, 1969- Carlsbad, Calif. : Hay House, 2004.
BF637.S4 B735 2004

Zetterberg, Hans Lennart, 1927- Social theory and social practice / Hans L. Zetterberg ; with a new introduction by the author. New Brunswick, NJ : Transaction Publishers, c2002. xliii, 190 p. ; 23 cm. Includes bibliographical references. ISBN 0-7658-0906-0 (paper : alk. paper) DDC 301/.01
1. Sociology - Methodology. 2. Sociology - Philosophy. 3. Knowledge, Sociology of. I. Title.
HM511 .Z48 2002

Zevalkink, Dina Johanna, 1962- Attachment in Indonesia : the mother-child relationship in context / Dina Johanna Zevalkink. [Netherlands? : s.n.], c1997 (Ridderkerk : Ridderprint) 209 p. : ill., map ; 24 cm. Summary in Dutch. Thesis (doctoral)--Katholieke Universiteit Nijmegen, Oct., 1997. Includes bibliographical references (p. 164-173). ISBN 9090108297
1. Attachment behavior - Indonesia. 2. Mother and child - Indonesia. I. Title.
BF575.A86 Z48 1997

Zhang, Fan. Mei xue yu yan xue : jian lun han yu min zu xing ge / Zhang Fan zhu. Di 1 ban. Beijing : Shou du shi fan da xue chu ban she, 1998. 4, [1], 197 p. : ill. ; 21 cm. Includes bibliographical references. ISBN 7-81039-933-0
1. Linguistics. 2. Aesthetics. 3. Chinese language. I. Title. II. Title: Jian lun han yu min zu xing ge
P121 .Z465 1998

Zhang, Hong. Ai qing de di er zhang mian kong = Aiqing de di er zhang miankong / Zhang Hong zhu. Di 1 ban. Jinan : Shandong ren min chu ban she, 2001. 247 p. : ill. ; 21 cm. ISBN 7-209-02645-2
1. Love. I. Title. II. Title: Aiqing de di er zhang miankong

Zhang, Shilin.
Xue lin chun qiu. Di 1 ban. Beijing : Chao hua chu ban she, 1999.
PL2272.5 .X846 1999

Zhang, Shunhui. Zhang Shunhui xue shu wen hua sui bi / Zhou Guolin bian. Beijing di 1 ban. Beijing : Zhongguo qing nian chu ban she, 2001. vi, 7, 390 p. ; 21 cm. (Er shi shi ji zhongguo xue shu wen hua sui bi da xi. Di 3 ji) Includes author's chronology (p. 383-384) Includes author's work (p. 385-386) ISBN 7-5006-4352-7
1. Chinese literature - History and criticism. 2. Chinese classics - History and criticism. 3. China - Historiography. 4. Philosophy, Chinese. I. Zhou, Guolin. II. Title. III. Series.
PL2272.5 .Z427 2001

Zhang Shunhui xue shu wen hua sui bi.
Zhang, Shunhui. Beijing di 1 ban. Beijing : Zhongguo qing nian chu ban she, 2001.
PL2272.5 .Z427 2001

Zhang, Shuxiang.
Zeng, Xia. She hui si wei xue. Di 1 ban. Beijing : Ren min chu ban she : Xin hua shu dian jing xiao, 1996.
BF323.S63 T75 1996 <Asian China>

Zhang, Taiyan, 1868-1936.
Liang Qichao, Zhang Taiyan jie du Zhonghua wen hua jing dian. Di 1 ban. Shenyang Shi : Liao Hai chu ban she, 2003.
PL2262.2 .L54 2003

Zhang, Xianglin.
Xie jiao zhen xiang. Di 1 ban. Beijing : Dang dai shi jie chu ban she, 2001.
BT1315.2 .X54 2001

Zhang, Xiong, 1953- Jing ji zhe xue : cong li shi zhe xue xiang jing ji zhe xue de kua yue / Zhang Xiong zhu. Di 1 ban. [Kunming] : Yunnan ren min chu ban she, 2002. 2, 10, 328 p. ; 22 cm. (Zhe xue li lun chuang xin cong shu = Philosophy series : new ideas and innovations) Cover title also in English: Philosophy of economics : stepping forward from the philosophy of history to the philosophy of economics. Fu can kao wen xian. ISBN 7-222-03119-7
1. History - Philosophy. 2. Economics - Philosophy. I. Title. II. Title: Cong li shi zhe xue xiang jing ji zhe xue de kua yue III. Title: Philosophy of economics : stepping forward from the philosophy of history to the philosophy of economics IV. Series: Zhe xue li lun chuang xin cong shu.
D16.8 .Z536 2002

ZHANG, XUECHENG, 1738-1801. WEN SHI TONG YI.
Ye, Ying, 1896-1950. Wen shi tong yi jiao zhu. Di 1 ban. Beijing : Zhonghua shu ju : Xin hua shu dian Beijing fa xing suo fa xing, 1994.
DS734.7.C433 Y43 1985 <Orien China>

Wen shi tong yi. 1994.
Ye, Ying, 1896-1950. Wen shi tong yi jiao zhu. Di 1 ban. Beijing : Zhonghua shu ju : Xin hua shu dian Beijing fa xing suo fa xing, 1994.
DS734.7.C433 Y43 1985 <Orien China>

Zhang, Yi.
Luo, Zongqiang. Luo Zongqiang gu dai wen xue si xiang lun ji. Di 1 ban. Shantou Shi : Shantou da xue chu ban she, 1999.
PL2264 .L95 1999

Zhang, Yihe.
Zhuang, Huiming. Yan shi jia xun yi zhu. Di 1 ban. Shanghai : Shanghai gu ji chu ban she : Xin hua shu dian Shanghai fa xing suo fa xing, 1999.

Zhanna d'Ark, Samson i russkaia istoriia.
Nosovskii, G. V. (Gleb Vladimirovich), 1958- Rekonstruktsiia vseobshchei istorii. Moskva : FID "Delovoi ekspress", 2002.
DK38 .N68 2002

Zhao, Wenyao.
Xie jiao zhen xiang. Di 1 ban. Beijing : Dang dai shi jie chu ban she, 2001.
BT1315.2 .X54 2001

Zhao, Xi. Xu wu miao de gui shen shi jie / Zhao Xi zhu. Di 1 ban. Beijing : Zong jiao wen hua chu ban she, 2001. 16, 385 p. ; 21 cm. Fu can kao wen xian. ISBN 7-80123-309-3
1. Mythology. 2. Ghosts. 3. Legends - China. I. Title.
BL1812.G63 Z436 2001

Zhao, Yaotang. Gu dai zuo jia lun / Zhao Yaotang zhu. Di 1 ban. Jinan : Shandong you yi chu ban she, 1994. 2, 2, 340 p ; 21 cm. ISBN 7-80551-629-4
1. Authors, Chinese - Biography. 2. Chinese literature - History and criticism. I. Title.
PL2277 .C355 1994 <Asian China>

Zhao, Zhuo.
Wang, Furen. Tu po mang dian. Di 1 ban. Beijing Shi : Zhongguo wen lian chu ban she, 2001.
PL2754.S5 Z89 2001

Zhe xue li lun chuang xin cong shu.
Han, Zhen. Li shi zhe xue. Di 1 ban. Kunming : Yunnan ren min chu ban she, 2002.
D16.8 .H3597 2002

Ouyang, Kang, 1953- She hui ren shi lun. Di 1 ban. [Kunming] : Yunnan ren min chu ban she, 2002.
BF323.S63 O93 2002

Zhang, Xiong, 1953- Jing ji zhe xue. Di 1 ban. [Kunming] : Yunnan ren min chu ban she, 2002.
D16.8 .Z536 2002

"Zhen guan zheng yao" yu ling dao yi shu.
An, Lizhi. Di 1 ban. Shanghai : Shanghai gu ji chu ban she, 1999.
DS749.3.W813 A63 1999

An, Lizhi. "Zhen guan zheng yao" yu ling dao yi shu. Di 1 ban. Shanghai : Shanghai gu ji chu ban she, 1999.
DS749.3.W813 A63 1999

Zheng, Chengduo, 1898-1958. Zhongguo su wen xue shi / Zheng Zhenduo. Di 1 ban. Beijing : Dong fang chu ban she, 1996. 2, 1, 618 p. ; 20 cm. (Min guo xue shu jing dian wen ku) Colophon title: Zhongguo suwenxue shi. In Chinese. "Ben shu ju Shang wu yin shu guan 1938 nian ban bian jiao zai ban" --Colophon. ISBN 7-5060-0695-2
1. Folk literature, Chinese - History and criticism. 2. Chinese literature - History and criticism. I. Title. II. Title: Zhongguo suwenxue shi
PL2445 .C44 1996

Zheng, Manqing.
Chuckrow, Robert. The tai chi book. Boston : YMAA Publication Center, c1998.
GV504 .C536 1998

Zheng ti lun mei xue guan gang yao.
Chang, Zhiqi. Di 1 ban. Chengdu : Sichuan ren min chu ban she : Sichuan sheng Xin hua shu dian jing xiao, 1994.
BH39 .C435 1994 <Orien China>

Zheng, Wenlong.
Tu, Wei-ming. [Selections. 2002] Du Weiming wen ji. Wuhan Shi : Wuhan chu ban she, 2002.
B5233.C6 T813 2002

Zheng, Yanping.
Bu ping ze ming. Di 2 ban. Beijing : Zhongguo cheng shi chu ban she, 2001.

Zheng, Yuanzhe, 1964-.
Jiang, Kongyang. Jiang Kongyang xue shu wen hua sui bi. Beijing di 1 ban. Beijing : Zhongguo qing nian chu ban she, 2000.
BH39 .J435 2000

Zhi shi fen zi li shi guan yu Zhonggu zheng zhi.
Huang, Minlan. Xue shu jiu guo. Di 1 ban. Zhengzhou Shi : Henan ren min chu ban she, 1995.
D16.9 .H795 1995 <Asian China>

Zhi xin jing.
Shi, Lin. Di 1 ban. Beijing : Zhongguo yan shi chu ban she, 1999.
DS758.23.T74 S522 1999

Zhixinjing.
Shi, Lin. Zhi xin jing. Di 1 ban. Beijing : Zhongguo yan shi chu ban she, 1999.
DS758.23.T74 S522 1999

Zhizn' cheloveka.
Ul'rikh, I. V. Moskva : Izd-vo "Litan", 1999.

Zhong guo wen xue tong shi.
Chen, Yugang. Zhongguo wen xue tong shi. Di 1 ban. Beijing Shi : Xi yuan chu ban she : Xin hua shu dian jing xiao, 1996.
PL2264 .C442527 1996 <Orien China>

Zhong xi wen hua peng zhuang yu jin dai wen xue.
Guo, Yanli. Di 1 ban. Jinan Shi : Shandong jiao yu chu ban she, 1999.
PL2274 .G86 1999

Zhongguo jin dai si xiang zhe cong shu
Lin, Shu, 1852-1924. Tie bi ji zhen. Di 1 ban. Tianjin Shi : Bai hua wen yi chu ban she, 2002.
PL2718.I5 T54 2002

Zhongguo ling hun xin yang.
Ma, Changyi, Di 1 ban. Shanghai : Shanghai wen yi chu ban she, 1998.
BL290 .M28 1998

Zhongguo ren min da xue bo shi wen ku
Lin, Jian. Ren di zi you zhi zhe xue si suo. Di 1 ban. Beijing : Zhongguo ren min da xue chu ban she : Jing xiao xin hua shu dian, 1996.
B99.C52 L55 1996 <Orien China>

Zhongguo she hui ke xue yuan. Ke yan ju.
Xu, Fancheng. Xu Fancheng ji. Di 1 ban. Beijing : Zhongguo she hui ke xue chu ban she, 2001.
PL2262.2 .X84 2001

Zhongguo she hui ke xue yuan xue zhe wen xuan
Xu, Fancheng. Xu Fancheng ji. Di 1 ban. Beijing : Zhongguo she hui ke xue chu ban she, 2001.
PL2262.2 .X84 2001

Zhongguo, shui zui fu : "Fubusi" Zhongguo da lu 50 fu hao pai shui bang / Li Chunlin, Jin Dan zhu bian ; Wang Suying, Jiang Shaomin fu zhu bian. Di 1 ban. Beijing : Qi ye guan li chu ban she, 2001. 3, 13, 531 p. : port. ; 21 cm. ISBN 7-80147-455-4
1. Millionaires - China - Biography. 2. Businesspeople - China - Biography. 3. Success in business. I. Li, Chunlin. II. Forbes Inc. III. Title: "Fubusi" Zhongguo da lu 50 fu hao pai hang bang
HC426.5.A2 Z457 2001

Zhongguo su wen xue shi.
Zheng, Chengduo, 1898-1958. Di 1 ban. Beijing : Dong fang chu ban she, 1996.
PL2445 .C44 1996

Zhongguo suwenxue shi.
Zheng, Chengduo, 1898-1958. Zhongguo su wen xue shi. Di 1 ban. Beijing : Dong fang chu ban she, 1996.

Zhongguo wen xue tong shi.
Chen, Yugang. Di 1 ban. Beijing Shi : Xi yuan chu ban she : Xin hua shu dian jing xiao, 1996.
PL2264 .C442527 1996 <Orien China>

Zhongguo wen xue zhong di Weimo yu Guanyin.
Sun, Changwu. Di 1 ban. Beijing : Gao deng jiao yu chu ban she : Xin hua shu dian zong dian Beijing fa xing suo fa xing, 1996.
PL2275.B8 S85 1996 <Orien China>

Zhongguo wu shu shi.
Gao, Guofan. Di 1 ban. Shanghai Shi : Shanghai san lian shu dian, 1999.
BF1584.C5 G36 1999

Zhongguo xian dai wen xue yan jiu cong shu (Shanghai, China)
Zhuang, Zhongqing. Mao Dun de wen lun li cheng. Di 1 ban. Shanghai : Shanghai wen yi chu ban she : Xin hua shu dian jing xiao, 1996.
PL2801.N2 Z64 1996

Zhongguo xian dai xue shu jing dian. Tai Yuanpei juan.
Cai, Yuanpei, 1868-1940. [Selections. 1996] Cai Yuanpei juan. Di 1 ban. Shijiazhuang Shi : Hebei jiao yu chu ban she, 1996.
BJ117 .T74 1996 <Asian China>

Zhongguo xiang zheng wen hua / Ju Yueshi, Qu Ming'an zhu bian. Di 1 ban. Shanghai : Shanghai ren min chu ban she : Xin hua shu dian Shanghai fa xing suo jing xiao, 2001. 6, 759 p. : ill. ; 21 cm. (Xue shu chuang xin) Includes bibliographical references (p. [751]-756). ISBN 7-208-03676-4
1. China - Civilization. 2. Symbolism. I. Ju, Yueshi. II. Qu, Ming'an. III. Series.
DS721 .Z4985 2001

Zhongguo zhe xue wen hua xie jin hui.
Tai ji wen hua. Xianggang : Zhongguo zhe xue wen hua xie jin hui, [2001-
BF1770.C5 T35

Zhongguo zhi shi fen zi cong shu
Huang, Minlan. Xue shu jiu guo. Di 1 ban. Zhengzhou Shi : Henan ren min chu ban she, 1995.
D16.9 .H795 1995 <Asian China>

Zhonghua ben tu wen hua cong shu (Shanghai, China)
Gao, Guofan. Zhongguo wu shu shi. Di 1 ban. Shanghai Shi : Shanghai san lian shu dian, 1999.
BF1584.C5 G36 1999

Zhonghua gu ji yi zhu cong shu
Zhuang, Huiming. Yan shi jia xun yi zhu. Di 1 ban. Shanghai : Shanghai gu ji chu ban she : Xin hua shu dian Shanghai fa xing suo fa xing, 1999.

Zhou, Guolin.
Zhang, Shunhui. Zhang Shunhui xue shu wen hua sui bi. Beijing di 1 ban. Beijing : Zhongguo qing nian chu ban she, 2001.
PL2272.5 .Z427 2001

Zhou, Xiang Sean. Exploration of visual data / Xiang Sean Zhou, Yong Rui, Thomas S. Huang. Boston ; London : Kluwer Academic Publishers, c2003. xvi, 187 p. : ill. ; 24 cm. (The Kluwer international series in video computing) Includes bibliographical references (p. [167]-183) and index. ISBN 1402075693 (alk. paper) DDC 006.6
1. Computer graphics. 2. Visualization. 3. Computer vision. I. Rui, Yong. II. Huang, Thomas S., 1936- III. Title. IV. Series.
T385 .Z55 2003

Zhou, Xiuping. Wen xue xin shang yu pi ping / Zhou Xiuping bian zhu. Di 1 ban. Changsha : Zhong nan gong ye da xue chu ban she, 1998. 2, 225 p. ; 20 cm. (Xian dai mi shu xi lie jiao cai = Xiandai mishu xilie jiaocai). Includes bibliographical references (p.224). ISBN 7-81061-077-5
1. Chinese literature - History and criticism - Theory, etc. 2. Literature. 3. Chinese literature - History and criticism. 4. Literature - History and criticism. I. Title. II. Series: Xian dai mi shu xi lie jiao cai.
PL2262 .Z468 1998

Zhou, Xunchu.
[Selections. 2000]
Zhou Xunchu wen ji. Di 1 ban. Nanjing Shi : Jiangsu gu ji chu ban she, 2000. 7 v. : ill. (some col.) ; 21 cm. Includes bibliographical references. CONTENTS: 1. Jiu ge xin kao ; "Han Feizi" zha ji ; Han Fei -- 2. Zhang Zhi "Wen shi zhuan" ji ben ; "Wen xin diao long" jie xi (shi san pian) ; Zhongguo wen xue pi ping xiao shi -- 3. Wen shi tan wei ; Wen shi zhi xin -- 4. Gao Shi nian pu ; Shi xian Li Bai zhi mi ; Tang shi wen xian zong shu -- 5. Tang ren bi ji shuo kao suo ; Tang dai bi ji xiao shuo kao suo ; Tang dai bi ji xiao shuo xu lu -- 6. Dang dai xue shu yan jiu si bian ; Xi xue dong jian he Zhongguo gu dai wen xue yan jiu -- 7. Wu wei ji. ISBN 7-80643-402-X (set)
1. Chinese literature - History and criticism. 2. Chinese classics - History and criticism. I. Title.
PL2264 .Z485 2000

Zhou Xunchu wen ji.
Zhou, Xunchu. [Selections. 2000] Di 1 ban. Nanjing Shi : Jiangsu gu ji chu ban she, 2000.
PL2264 .Z485 2000

Zhu, Ziqing, 1898-1948. Zhu Ziqing xue shu wen hua sui bi / Wang Lili bian. Beijing di 1 ban. Beijing : Zhongguo qing nian chu ban she, 2000. vi, 4, 331 p. ; 21 cm. (Er shi shi ji Zhongguo xue shu wen hua sui bi da xi. Di 3 ji) Includes bibliographical references. ISBN 7-5006-3769-1
1. Chinese literature - History and criticism. I. Wang, Lili. II. Series.

Zhuang, Huiming. Yan shi jia xun yi zhu / Zhuang Huiming, Zhang Yihe zhuan. Di 1 ban. Shanghai : Shanghai gu ji chu ban she : Xin hua shu dian Shanghai fa xing suo fa xing, 1999. 9, 2, 365 p. ; 21 cm. (Zhonghua gu ji yi zhu cong shu) ISBN 7-5325-2558-9
1. Yan, Zhitui, - 531-591. - Yan shi jia xun. 2. Ethics - China. 3. Conduct of life. I. Zhang, Yihe. II. Yan, Zhitui, 531-591. Yan shi jia xun. 1999. III. Title. IV. Series.

Zhuang, Zhongqing. Mao Dun de wen lun li cheng / Zhuang Zhongqing zhu. Di 1 ban. Shanghai : Shanghai wen yi chu ban she : Xin hua shu dian jing xiao, 1996. 1, 241 p. ; 21 cm. (Zhongguo xian dai wen yan jiu cong shu) Includes bibliographical references. ISBN 7-5321-1446-5
1. Mao, Dun, - 1896- - Criticism and interpretation. 2. Chinese literature - History and criticism. I. Series: Zhongguo xian dai wen xue yan jiu cong shu (Shanghai, China)
PL2801.N2 Z64 1996

Zhuravlev, A. L.
Sovremennaia psikhologiia. Moskva : In-t psikhologii RAN, 2002.
BF20 .S64 2002

Zhuravlev, V. K. (Vladimir Konstantinovich) Russkii iazyk i russkii kharakter / V.K. Zhuravlev. Moskva : Moskovskii patriarkhat, 2002. 255 p. ; 20 cm.
1. Russian language. 2. National characteristics, Russian. I. Title.
PG2095 .Z48 2002

Zhusubaliyev, Zhanybai T. Bifurcations and chaos in piecewise-smooth dynamical systems / Zhanybai T. Zhusubaliyev, Erik Mosekilde. River Edge, New Jersey : World Scientific, c2003. 363 p. : ill. ; 27 cm. (World Scientific series on Nonlinear science. Series A ; v.44) Includes bibliographical references and index. ISBN 981-238-420-0
1. Bifurcation theory. 2. Chaotic behavior in systems. 3. Differentiable dynamical systems. I. Mosekilde, Erik. II. Title. III. Series: World Scientific series on nonlinear science. Series A, Monographs and treatises ; v.44.

Ziegelmüller, Martin, 1935- Der Maler auf seinem Drehstuhl : Bilder und Texte / Martin Ziegelmüller. [Frauenfeld] : Waldgut, c2001. 167 p. : ill. (some col.) ; 22 cm. Includes bibliographical references. ISBN 3-7294-0314-1 (hd. bd.)
1. Art. 2. Aesthetics. I. Title.

Ziegler, Gudrun.
Baur, Manfred, 1959- Die Odyssee des Menschen. München : Ullstein, c2001.

Ziegler, Reuven. By his light : character and values in the service of God / based on addresses by Aharon Lichtenstein ; adapted by Reuven Ziegler. 2nd ed. Jersey City, NJ : KTAV Pub. House ; Alon Shevut, Israel : Yeshivat Har Etzion, 2003. xv, 272 p. ; 24 cm. Includes bibliographical references and indexes. CONTENTS: To cultivate and to guard : the universal duties of mankind -- In all your ways, know him : two modes of serving God -- Mitzva : a life of command -- Make your Torah permanent : the centrality of Torah study -- Determining objectives in religious growth : spiritual specialization of spiritual breadth? -- Being frum and being good : on the relationship between religion and morality -- Bittachon : trust in God -- I am with him in distress : the challenges of the Holocaust -- If you remain silent at this time : concern for the Jewish people -- Teshuva : repentance and return A pure heart : refining character and balancing values -- Centrist Orthodoxy : a spiritual accounting. ISBN 0-88125-796-6 DDC 296.3/6
1. Spiritual life - Judaism. 2. Ethics, Jewish. 3. Jewish way of life. I. Lichtenstein, Aharon. II. Title.
BM723 .Z54 2003

Zig Ziglar's life lifters.
Ziglar, Zig. Nashville, Tenn. : Broadman & Holman, c2003.
BF637.C5 Z54 2003

Ziglar, Zig. Zig Ziglar's life lifters : moments of inspiration for living life better / Zig Ziglar. Nashville, Tenn. : Broadman & Holman, c2003. xvi, 220 p. ; 19 cm. ISBN 0-8054-2689-2 DDC 158
1. Conduct of life. I. Title. II. Title: Life lifters
BF637.C5 Z54 2003

Zigler, Edward, 1930- The first three years & beyond : brain development and social policy / Edward F. Zigler, Matia Finn-Stevenson, and Nancy W. Hall. New Haven : Yale University Press, c2002. viii, 263 p. ; 25 cm. (Current perspectives in psychology) Includes bibliographical references (p. 213-251) and index. CONTENTS: The more things change : politics and PET scans -- The science of brain research -- Family leave -- Early intervention and child care -- Home visitation and parent education -- Child abuse and the brain -- The Mozart effect : not learning from history -- The brain, prenatal development, and nutrition -- The brain campaign : brain development and the media -- Implications of the infant brain debate. ISBN 0-300-09364-0 (cloth : alk. paper) DDC 305.231
1. Child development. 2. Infants - Development. 3. Brain - Research - Social aspects. 4. Child welfare - United States. 5. Family policy - United States. 6. United States - Social policy - Evaluation. I. Finn-Stevenson, Matia. II. Hall, Nancy Wilson. III. Title. IV. Title: First three years and beyond V. Series.
HQ767.9 .Z543 2002

Zika, Anna.
Brock, Bazon, 1936- Der Barbar als Kulturheld. Köln : DuMont, 2002.

Zika, Charles. Exorcising our demons : magic, witchcraft, and visual culture in early modern Europe / by Charles Zika. Leiden ; Boston : Brill, 2003. xxi, 603 p. : ill. ; 25 cm. (Studies in medieval and Reformation thought, 0585-6914 ; v. 91) Includes bibliographical references and indexes. ISBN 90-04-12560-4 (hard cover) DDC 133.4/3/094
1. Witchcraft - Europe - History. 2. Magic - Europe - History. 3. Witchcraft in art. I. Title. II. Series.
BF1584.E85 Z55 2003

Zillmann, Dolf.
Communication and emotion. Mahwah, N.J. ; London : Lawrence Erlbaum, c2003.
BF637.C45 C6375 2003

Zima, P. V. Theorie des Subjekts : Subjektivität und Identität zwischen Moderne und Postmoderne / Peter V. Zima. Tübingen : A. Francke, c2000. xiv, 454 p. ; 19 cm. (UTB ; 2176) Includes bibliographical references (p. 431-444) and index. ISBN 3-8252-2176-8 (UTB-Bestellnummer) ISBN 3-7720-2970-1
1. Subject (Philosophy) 2. Philosophy, Modern. 3. Subjectivity. 4. Postmodernism. I. Title. II. Series: Uni-Taschenbücher ; 2176.
BD223 .Z56 2000

ZIMBABWE.
Peace-building. [Harare] : ACPD, 2002.

Zimmerman, Toni Schindler.
Integrating gender and culture in parenting. New York : Haworth Press, 2003.
BF723.P75 I57 2003

Zimmermann, Denise. The complete idiot's guide to wicca and witchcraft / by Denise Zimmermann and Katherine A. Gleason. 2nd ed. Indianapolis, IN : Alpha, c2003. xxiii, 359 p. : ill. ; 23 cm. Includes bibliographical references (p. [337]-340) and index. ISBN 1-59257-111-5 (pbk.)
1. Witchcraft. I. Gleason, Katherine. II. Title. III. Title: Wicca and witchcraft
BF1566 .Z55 2003

Zimmermann, Sandra Hundley, 1944-.
Buckley, Maureen A., 1964- Mentoring children and adolescents. Westport, Conn. : Praeger, 2003.
BF637.C6 B8 2003

Zinn, Howard, 1922-.
Monkeywrenching the new world order [sound recording]. Oakland, Calif : AK Press ; San Francisco, CA : Alternative Tentacles Records, 2001.

The power of nonviolence. Boston, Mass. : Beacon Press, c2002.
JZ5538 .P685 2002

Zins, Joseph E.
Elias, Maurice J. Bullying, peer harassment, and victimization in the schools. New York : Haworth Press, 2003.
BF637.B85 E45 2003

Ziolkowska, Aleksandra. Podróże z moją kotką : i inne opowieści o kotach, psach, papugach, oposach i króliku / Aleksandra Ziółkowska-Boehm. Wyd. 1. Warszawa : Wydawn. Nowy Świat, 2002. 255 p., [13] p. of plates : col. ill. ; 21 cm. The book entitled "Journeys with my cat" explains the author's observations on her cat named Suzy who comes from Texas, her relationships with Suzy, and

Suzy's personality, and other stories about cats, dogs, parrots, opossums and rabbits. ISBN 83-88576-90-9
1. Cats. 2. Cats - Behavior. 3. Animal behavior. 4. Human-animal relationships. I. Title.

ZIONISM. See **PROPAGANDA, ZIONIST.**

ZIONISM AND JUDAISM.
Luz, Ehud. [Ma'avak be-naḥal Yabok. English] Wrestling with an angel. New Haven : Yale University Press, c2003.
DS143 .L8913 2003

ZIONIST PROPAGANDA. See **PROPAGANDA, ZIONIST.**

Zirfas, Jörg.
Brenner, Andreas. Lexikon der Lebenskunst. Leipzig : Reclam-Verlag, 2002.

Žižek, Slavoj, 1949-
[Fragile absolute. Spanish]
El frágil absoluto, o, Por qué merece la pena luchar por el legado cristiano? / Slavoj Zizek ; traducción de Antonio Gimeno. 1. ed. Valencia : Pre-Textos, 2002. 215 p. ; 19 cm. (Pre-textos. Ensayo ; 579) Translation of: The fragile absolute, or, Why is the Christian legacy worth fighting for? ISBN 84-8191-467-3 DDC 230
1. Apologetics. 2. Communism. 3. Postmodernism. 4. Communism and Christianity. I. Gimeno, Antonio. II. Title. III. Title: Por qué merece la pena luchar por el legado cristiano? IV. Series.
BT1102 .Z58

Zlatanović, Ljubiša, 1958- Jung, jastvo i individuacija / Ljubiša Zlatanović. 1. izd. Niš : Studenski informativno-izdavački centar Niš, 2001. 173 p. ; 25 cm. In Serbian (Roman). Includes bibliographical references (p. 167-173). ISBN 86-7178-038-4
1. Jung, C. G. - (Carl Gustav), - 1875-1961. 2. Self. 3. Individuation (Psychology) I. Title.
BF109.J8 Z53 2001

Znakov, V. V. (Viktor Vladimirovich).
Tvorcheskoe nasledie A.V. Brushlinskogo i O.K. Tikhomirova i sovremennaia psikhologiia myshleniia (k 70-letiiu so dnia rozhdeniia). Moskva : In-t psikhologii RAN, 2003.
BF109.B86 T86 2003

Zobkov, V. A.
Psikhologiia otnoshenii. Vladimir : Vladimirskii gos. pedagogicheskii universitet, 2001.
BF637.C45 P74 2001

ZODIAC. See also **HOUSES (ASTROLOGY).**
Starwoman, Athena. New York : Friedman/Fairfax : Distributed by Sterling Pub., c2000.
BF1708.1 .S695 2000

ZODIAC.
Goldsmith, Martin. The zodiac by degrees. Boston, MA : Weiser Books, 2004.
BF1708.1 .G62 2004

Hodges, Jane. Cosmic grooves. San Francisco, Calif. : Chronicle Books, c2001.
BF1726 .H59 2001

Knight, Michele. Good fortune. Kansas City, Mo. : Andrews McMeel Pub., c2002.
BF1726 .K55 2002

The zodiac by degrees.
Goldsmith, Martin. Boston, MA : Weiser Books, 2004.
BF1708.1 .G62 2004

ZODIAC IN ART.
Ovason, David. [Secret zodiacs of Washington DC] The secret architecture of our nation's capital. 1st Perennial ed. New York, NY : Perennial, 2002.

ZODIAC - RELIGIOUS ASPECTS.
Cauville, Sylvie. Le zodiaque d'Osiris. Leuven : Peeters, 1997.
BL2450.O7 C399 1997

ZODIAC - RELIGIOUS ASPECTS - JUDAISM.
Erlanger, Gad. [Mazalot, ha-Yahadut va-ani. English] Signs of the times. Jerusalem ; New York : Feldheim Pub., 2000.
BF1714.J4 E74 2001

Le zodiaque d'Osiris.
Cauville, Sylvie. Leuven : Peeters, 1997.
BL2450.O7 C399 1997

Zoglauer, Thomas. Geist und Gehirn : das Leib-Seele-Problem in der aktuellen Diskussion / Thomas Zoglauer. Göttingen : Vandenhoeck & Ruprecht, 1998. 243 p. ; 19 cm. (Uni-Taschenbücher ; 2066) "UTB für Wissenschaft"--Cover. Includes bibliographical references (p. [230]-240) and index. ISBN 3-8252-2066-4 (UTB) ISBN 3-525-03322-2 (Vandenhoeck und Ruprecht)
1. Mind and body. 2. Philosophy of mind. I. Title.
BF163 .Z64 1998

Zoglio, Suzanne Willis. Create a life that tickles your soul : finding peace, passion, and purpose at midlife / Suzanne Willis Zoglio. Doylestown, Pa. : Tower Hill Press, c1999. 203 p. ; 22 cm. Includes bibliographical references: (p. 196-197). ISBN 0-941668-09-6
1. Self-actualization (Psychology) in middle age. 2. Middle aged persons - Psychology. I. Title.
BF724.65.S44 Z65 1999

Recharge in minutes : the quick-lift way to less stress, more success, and renewed energy! / Suzanne Willis Zoglio. 1st ed. Doylestown, PA : Tower Hill Press, c2003. p. cm. Includes bibliographical references and index. Table of contents URL: http://www.loc.gov/catdir/toc/ecip042/2003007683.html CONTENTS: I can't think straight! : finding focus -- Oh, for a week at the beach! : chilling out -- Nothing's wrong, I'm just stuck in a rut! : revving up -- Pass the antacid! : calming down -- I haven't got a clue! : inviting inspiration -- Is this all there is? : creating meaning -- It's lonely in here : building connections -- If I'm so smart, why don't I know it? : boosting confidence -- What if it doesn't work? : discovering courage -- Just my luck! : remembering abundance. ISBN 0-941668-14-2 (alk. paper) DDC 158.1
1. Self-help techniques. 2. Success - Psychological aspects. I. Title.
BF632 .Z64 2003

[Zohar ḥadash.] Sefer Zohar ḥadash / meha-tana Shim'on bar Yoḥai. Ve-'alav ḥoneh perush Matok mi-devash ha-shalem. Yerushalayim : Mekhon Da'at Yosef ; Brooklyn, N.Y. (225 Division Ave., Brooklyn 11211) : Le-haśig, B. Daskal, 760- [1999 or 2000- v. : facsims. ; 25 cm. Cover title: Sefer ha-kadosh Zohar ḥadash 'im perush Matok mo-devash. Running title: Zohar ḥadash. Commentary by Daniyel Frish. PARTIAL CONTENTS: ḥelek 1. Sefer Be-reshit, dape 3 'a. 1-37 'a. ḥelek 2. Sefer Shemot, Va-yikra, Ba-midbar, Devarim, dape 37b-74a
1. Bible. - O.T. - Pentateuch - Commentaries. 2. Zohar ḥadash. 3. Cabala. I. Simeon bar Yoḥai, 2nd cent. II. Frish, Daniyel. III. Title. IV. Title: Sefer ha-kadosh Zohar ḥadash 'im perush Matok mo-devash V. Title: Zohar ḥadash VI. Title: Matok mi-devash
BM525.A6 Z6+

Zohar ḥadash.
[Zohar ḥadash.] Sefer Zohar ḥadash. Yerushalayim : Mekhon Da'at Yosef ; Brooklyn, N.Y. (225 Division Ave., Brooklyn 11211) : Le-haśig, B. Daskal, 760- [1999 or 2000-
BM525.A6 Z6+

[Zohar ḥadash.] Sefer Zohar ḥadash. Yerushalayim : Mekhon Da'at Yosef ; Brooklyn, N.Y. (225 Division Ave., Brooklyn 11211) : Le-haśig, B. Daskal, 760- [1999 or 2000-
BM525.A6 Z6+

[Zohar ḥadash. Lamentations. 2000.] Zohar ḥadash Megilat Ekhah : 'im perush Matok mi-devash ... / ḥubar 'a. y. Daniyel Frish. "Hotsa'ah meyuhedet li-yeme ben ha-metsarim". Yerushalayim : Mekhon Da'at Yosef, 761 [2000 or 2001] 148, [4] p. ; 18 cm. Running title: Midrash Ekhah. Running title: Midrash Rut.
1. Bible. - O.T. - Lamentations - Commentaries. 2. Zohar ḥadash. - Lamentations - Commentaries. 3. Zohar ḥadash. - Ruth - Commentaries. 4. Bible. - O.T. - Ruth - Commentaries. 5. Jewish martyrs. 6. Cabala. I. Simeon bar Yoḥai, 2nd cent. II. Frish, Daniyel. Matok mi-devash. III. Mekhon Da'at Yosef (Jerusalem) IV. Title. V. Title: Midrash ha-ne'lam Lamentations. VI. Title: Midrash ha-ne'lam Ruth. VII. Title: Matok mi-devash. VIII. Title: Ma'amar 'Aśarah haruge malkhut. IX. Title: Midrash Ekhah X. Title: Midrash Rut
BM525.A6 Z6 2001

ZOHAR ḤADASH. LAMENTATIONS - COMMENTARIES.
[Zohar ḥadash. Lamentations. 2000.] Zohar ḥadash Megilat Ekhah. "Hotsa'ah meyuhedet li-yeme ben ha-metsarim". Yerushalayim : Mekhon Da'at Yosef, 761 [2000 or 2001]
BM525.A6 Z6 2001

Zohar ḥadash Megilat Ekhah.
[Zohar ḥadash. Lamentations. 2000.] "Hotsa'ah meyuhedet li-yeme ben ha-metsarim". Yerushalayim : Mekhon Da'at Yosef, 761 [2000 or 2001]
BM525.A6 Z6 2001

ZOHAR ḤADASH. RUTH - COMMENTARIES.
[Zohar ḥadash. Lamentations. 2000.] Zohar ḥadash Megilat Ekhah. "Hotsa'ah meyuhedet li-yeme ben ha-metsarim". Yerushalayim : Mekhon Da'at Yosef, 761 [2000 or 2001]
BM525.A6 Z6 2001

ZOHAR - SOURCES.
Ta-Shma, Israel M. ha-Nigleh sheba-nistar. Nusaḥ murḥav. [Tel Aviv] : ha-Ḳibuts ha-me'uḥad, c2001.

Zoja, Luigi.
L'incubo globale. Bergamo : Moretti & Vitali, c2002.

Żołądź, Dorota.
Dziecko w rodzinie i społeczeństwie. Bydgoszsz : Wydawnictwo Uczelniane Akademii Bydgoskiej, 2002.

Zolar. Zolar's encyclopedia and dictionary of dreams / Zolar. Fully rev. and updated for the 21st century. New York : Simon & Schuster, 2004. p. cm. "A Fireside book." ISBN 0-7432-2263-6 (pbk.) DDC 135/.3/03
1. Dreams - Encyclopedias. 2. Dreams - Dictionaries. I. Title. II. Title: Encyclopedia and dictionary of dreams
BF1091 .Z65 2004

Zolar's encyclopedia and dictionary of dreams.
Zolar. Fully rev. and updated for the 21st century. New York : Simon & Schuster, 2004.
BF1091 .Z65 2004

Zolla, Elémire. Catàbasi e anàstasi : discesa nell'ade e resurrezione. Alpignano, [Italy] : Tallone Editore, 2001. 109, [9] p. ; 30 cm. Includes bibliographical references. Bound in wrappers, in portfolio, in a slipcase. Edition limited to 250 copies in arabic numbering on Magnani di Pescia, 18 copies in roman numbering on Vergata Cinese. Library has copy no. 72. DDC 291
1. Future life. 2. Heaven. 3. Hell. 4. Eschatology. I. Title.

Zöller, Rainer. Die Vorstellung vom Willen in der Morallehre Senecas / von Rainer Zöller. Leipzig : K.G. Saur, 2003. 273 p. ; 24 cm. (Beiträge zur Altertumskunde ; Bd. 173) Revised version of the author's thesis (doctoral)--Universität Hamburg, 2001. Includes bibliographical references (p. 263-273) ISBN 3-598-77722-1
1. Seneca, Lucius Annaeus, - ca. 4 B.C.-65 A.D. - Criticism and interpretation. 2. Free will and determinism. I. Title. II. Series.
PA6686 .Z65 2003

Zong, Baihua. Yi jing / Zong Baihua zhu. Di 2 ban. Beijing : Beijing da xue chu ban she, 1998. 5, 461 p. : ill. ; 21 cm. (Bei da ming jia ming zhu wen cong) Includes bibliographical references. ISBN 7-301-00898-8
1. Aesthetics. 2. Literature - Aesthetics. 3. Aesthetics, Chinese. I. Title. II. Series.
MLCSC 92/01825 (B)

Zons, Raimar. Die Zeit des Menschen : zur Kritik des Posthumanismus / Raimar Zons. 1. Aufl., Originalausg. Frankfurt : Suhrkamp, c2001. 298 p. ; 18 cm. (Suhrkamp Taschenbuch Wissenschaft ; 1549) Collection of texts partly published previously. Includes bibliographical references (p. 261-293) and index. ISBN 3-518-29149-1 (pbk.)
1. Human beings. 2. Postmodernism. 3. Philosophy, Modern - 20th century. I. Title. II. Series.

ZOOLOGICAL MYTHOLOGY. See **ANIMALS, MYTHICAL.**

ZOOLOGY. See also **ANIMALS; PSYCHOLOGY, COMPARATIVE.**
Animal. 1st American ed. New York : DK ; [Washington, D.C.] : Smithsonian Institution, 2001.

ZOOLOGY, ECONOMIC. See **DOMESTIC ANIMALS.**

Zorić, Pavle, 1934-.
Jerotić, Vladeta. [Selections 2000] Izabrani ogledi. Beograd: Srpska književna zadruga, 2000.
BF109.J47 A25 2000

Zorin, A. L. (Andreĭ L.).
Filosofsko-metodologicheskie osnovy gumanitarnogo znaniia. Moskva : Rossiĭskiĭ gosudarstvennyĭ gumanitarnyĭ universitet, 2001.
BD166 .F489 2001

Zou xiang he chu.
Li, Yi. Di 1 ban. Beijing : Zhongguo she hui chu ban she : Xin hua shu dian Beijing fa xing suo jing xiao, 1994.
ND196.P66 L5 1994 <Orien China>

Zou xiang hou xian dai yu hou zhi min.
Xu, Fen. Di 1 ban. Beijing : Zhongguo she hui ke xue chu ban she : Xin hua shu dian jing xiao, 1996.
PN81 .H76 1996 <Asian China>

Zournazi, Mary. Hope : new philosophies for change / Mary Zournazi. Annandale, N.S.W. : Pluto Press, 2002. 288 p. ; 21 cm. Includes bibliographical references and index. ISBN 1-86403-140-9 (pbk.)
1. Political science - Philosophy. 2. Political culture. 3. Political alienation. 4. Hope. I. Title.

Źródła i monografie (Katolicki Uniwersytet Lubelski. Towarzystwo Naukowe)
(230.) Draw-a-family test in psychological

Zubiri, Xavier.
  research. Lublin : Towarzystwo Naukowe Katolickiego Uniwersytetu Lubelskiego, 2002.
  BF698.8.D68 D73 2002

Zubiri, Xavier.
  [Estructura dinámica de la realidad. English]
  Dynamic structure of reality / Xavier Zubiri ; translated from the Spanish and annotated by Nelson R. Orringer. Urbana : University of Illinois Press, c2003. xxi, 267 p. : 24 cm. (Hispanisms) Includes bibliographical references (p. [253]-259) and index. ISBN 0-252-02822-8 (alk. paper) DDC 111
  1. Ontology. 2. Becoming (Philosophy) I. Orringer, Nelson R. II. Title. III. Series.
  B4568.Z83 E7713 2003

Zuckerman, Michael, 1939-.
  Beyond the century of the child. Philadelphia : University of Pennsylvania Press, c2003.
  HQ767.87 .B49 2003

Zukav, Gary. The mind of the soul : responsible choice / Gary Zukav and Linda Francis. New York : Free Press, 2003. xvii, 215 p. : ill. : 23 cm. Includes index. ISBN 0-7432-3698-X DDC 153.8/3
  1. Choice (Psychology) - Miscellanea. 2. New Age movement. I. Francis, Linda. II. Title.
  BF611 .Z85 2003

Die Zukunft der Geschichte.
  Krockow, Christian, Graf von. München : List, c2002.
  D16.8 .K722 2002

ZUNDEL, MAURICE.
  Simonetta, Catherine. Renoncement et narcissisme chez Maurice Zundel. Saint-Maurice : Editions Saint-Augustin, c2002.

Žunjić, Slobodan, 1949-.
  Kriza i perspektive filozofije. 1. izd. Beograd : Tersit, 1995.
  B99.S462 K75 1995

Zupančič, Alenka. Esthétique du désir, éthique de la jouissance / Alenka Zupančič ; préface d'Alain Badiou. Lecques : Théétète, c2002. 188 p. : ill. ; 21 cm. ISBN 2-912860-22-9 DDC 100
  1. Desire. 2. Desire (Philosophy) 3. Pleasure. 4. Pleasure - Philosophy. I. Badiou, Alain. II. Title.

Zur Kritik ihrer geschichtlichen Verknüpfung.
  Genuss und Egoismus. Berlin : Akademie Verlag, c2002.

Zur Ruhe kommst du, Adrian Bruegge, nie.
  Wruck, Wilfried, 1938- 1. Aufl. Berlin : Frieling, 2000.

Zur Verwindung der Methaphysik / herausgegeben von Giorgio Guzzoni. Bonn : Bouvier, 2002. xlvii, 955 p. ; 24 cm. Includes bibliographical references and index. ISBN 3-416-03009-5 (hd.bd.)
  1. Metaphysics.

Zürcher Beiträge zur Sicherheitspolitik und Konfliktforschung
  (Heft Nr. 37) Zeitgeschichtliche Hintergründe aktueller Konflikte V. Zürich : Forschungsstelle für Sicherheitspolitik und Konfliktanalyse, Eidgenössische Technische Hochschule, 1995.
  JX1952 .Z45 1995

Zürcher, Johann, 1926-.
  Schweitzer, Albert, 1875-1965. Vorträge, Vorlesungen, Aufsätze. München : C.H. Beck, c2003.

Zvinorwadza.
  Dahlin, Olov, 1962- Frankfurt am Main ; New York : P. Lang, c2002.
  R726.5 .D34 2002

Zwang, Gérard. Aux origines de la sexualité humaine / Gérard Zwang. 1re éd. Paris : Presses universitaires de France, 2002. 347 p. : ill. ; 22 cm. Includes bibliographical references (p. [339]-342). ISBN 2-13-053085-0 DDC 300
  1. Sex. 2. Sex (Biology) I. Title.
  HQ21 .Z935 2002

Zweig, Connie. The holy longing : the hidden power of spiritual learning / Connie Zweig. New York : Jeremy P. Tarcher/Putnam, c2003. 238 p. ; 22 cm. Includes index. ISBN 1-58542-204-5 (alk. paper) DDC 291. 4/2
  1. Psychology, Religious. I. Title.
  BL53 .Z84 2003

Zwischen Rauschen und Offenbarung : zur Kultur- und Mediengeschichte der Stimme / herausgegeben von Friedrich Kittler, Thomas Macho und Sigrid Weigel. Berlin : Akademie Verlag, c2002. xii, 416 p. : ill. ; 24 cm. (Einstein Bücher) Includes bibliographical references (p. 377-395) and index. Proceedings from international conference held in Potsdam, February 1999. ISBN 3-05-003571-4
  1. Voice in literature - Congresses. 2. Voice - History - Congresses. 3. Expression - History. 4. Civilization - History. I. Series: Einstein Bücher.
  PN56.V55 Z89 2002

Zwischen Traum und Wirklichkeit
  (Bd. 3) Mörschel, Thomas. Die Historia vom heiligen Gral. Saarbrücken : Logos, 1994-

Zwölf Weltanschauungen.
  Grünewald, Lars. 1. Aufl. Borchen : Ch. Möllmann, 2001.

Życie i obyczajowość średniowiecznego duchowieństwa.
  Radzimiński, Andrzej. Warszawa : Wydawn. DiG, 2002.
  BX1565 .R32 2002

Żydek-Bednarczuk, Urszula.
  Język w przestrzeni społecznej. Opole : Uniwersytet Opolski, 2002.
  P40 .J492 2002

Zysk, Kenneth G.
  Nāgārjuna, Siddha. [Ratiśāstra. English & Sanskrit] Conjugal love in India. Leiden Boston, MA : Brill, 2002.
  HQ470.S3 N3413 2002

ISBN 0-7838-0481-4